ALABAMA · COLORADO · ARIZONA · MAINE · TEXAS · UTAH · ALASKA ·

· IOWA · LOUISIANA · WISCONSIN · TENNESSEE · IDAHO ·

1817 2004

The Official Catholic Directory

Anno Domini

2004

Published Annually by

P. J. Kenedy & Sons

GEORGIA · DELAWARE · ILLINOIS · KANSAS · NORTH CAROLINA · OREGON · NEBRASKA · KENTUCKY

NEW HAMPSHIRE · NEW JERSEY · NEW MEXICO · CONNECTICUT · FLORIDA · MASSACHUSETTS

· INDIANA · OKLAHOMA · RHODE ISLAND · MONTANA ·

· HAWAII · WASHINGTON · VIRGINIA · VERMONT · WYOMING · OHIO ·

CALIFORNIA · MICHIGAN · MINNESOTA · MISSISSIPPI · MISSOURI · WEST VIRGINIA · NEW YORK · NEVADA

NORTH DAKOTA · PENNSYLVANIA · SOUTH CAROLINA · SOUTH DAKOTA · MARYLAND · ARKANSAS

The Official Catholic Directory
P.J. Kenedy & Sons, Publishers

Jeanne Hanline
Publication Director

FOREWORD

We are proud to present the 2004 edition of The Official Catholic Directory commemorating the 25th Papal Anniversary of His Holiness Pope John Paul II. This year's publication is dedicated to the Pontiff's global accomplishments, His future endeavors and His dynamic impact on history. We wish to acknowledge the ecclesiastical authorities and diocesan officials involved in the production of the Directory and gratefully thank them for their cooperation, efforts and prayers.

Once again this year, we have expanded our coverage with new parishes and institutions. Under Pope John Paul II, the Catholic Church has grown throughout the World. This past year has seen many events around the World and it is the bond of the people of the Catholic Church that delivers the sign of hope and optimism during these troubled times.

As always we are proud to produce The Official Catholic Directory and we assure the Catholic community that our goal is to strive for excellence by continually improving this unique and valuable reference tool. We wish you peace and success in the coming year.

Sincerely,

Jeanne Hanline
Publication Director

121 Chanlon Road • New Providence, New Jersey 07974 • (908) 673-1000 • (800) 621-9669

In Celebration of the 25th Anniversary of the Pontificate.

John Paul's Quarter-Century

By John Thavis

Rome Bureau Chief of the Catholic News Service

As Pope John Paul II celebrates 25 years in office, the world is taking stock of a pontificate that has helped shape political events, set new directions for the Catholic Church and offered spiritual inspiration to millions of people around the globe.

BY ANY MEASURE, THIS IS A PAPACY FOR THE AGES. Since his election Oct. 16, 1978, Pope John Paul has delivered more speeches, met with more world leaders, canonized more saints and kissed more babies than any previous pontiff. Visiting 129 countries — from the steppes of Asia to the Rocky Mountains — he has implemented the church's own form of globalization. And in more than 50 major documents, on themes ranging from economics to the rosary, he has brought the Gospel and church teachings to bear on nearly every aspect of modern life.

Vatican officials are focusing on the accomplishments, but are going out of their way to make sure the anniversary celebration does not take on the tone of a retirement party. "The pope still has an important message to deliver, and people are listening — perhaps more than ever," Vatican spokesman Joaquin Navarro-Valls said in an interview with Catholic News Service.

Pope John Paul II kneeling in prayer after opening the Holy Door in St. Peter's Basilica in March 1983. (above)

Pope John Paul II prays during an evening service in 2003, in St. Peter's. (left)

"He is the only global leader who is worried about the spiritual well-being of today's men and women, as opposed to their material well-being. He asks, 'Who are you?' instead of 'What do you want to do?' or 'What do you want to buy?' And people understand this and respond to it," he said. At the start of the 21st century, a time of rapid changes in technology and biology, the pope has hewed closer to this dominant theme, Navarro-Valls said.

As the analyses and accolades rolled in ahead of the 25th anniversary celebration, the pope was busy keeping a low profile. He purposely upstaged himself by scheduling the beatification of Mother Teresa of Calcutta for Oct. 19 — a Sunday that falls between the anniversary of his election and his inaugural Mass. Whether for Mother Teresa or Pope John Paul, tens of thousands of Catholics are planning to converge on Rome and join in the festivities. The world's cardinals have been invited, too.

So far, the pope has avoided great retrospective speeches or documents on his first quarter-century. In fact, he has spoken more about Mary, to whom he's dedicated this year in a special way, than about his own accomplishments.

At 83, he is frail and hobbled by Parkinson's disease and other ailments. He no longer walks in public; instead, he sits and rides on a variety of newfangled mechanisms that allow him to keep celebrating liturgies and meeting with groups. But, thanks in part to a new regime of therapy, he has regained strength in his voice and seems to breathe easier than he did a year ago. Those improvements have encouraged aides and put an end to speculation over papal retirement — at least for now.

Many at the Vatican believe the pope's infirmities have added a new dimension to his message. "When the Mass is celebrated by someone in his condition, the sacrifice of

Clockwise from top, left:

Karol Wojtyia waves to waiting crowds in St. Peter's Square on October 16, 1978, when, after eight rounds of voting, he was elected the first non-Italian pope in 455 years.

Meeting with President Jimmy Carter, his wife, Rosalynn, and daughter, Amy, at the Vatican in June of 1980.

Pope John Paul II admires a pair of skis during one of his first audiences.

John Paul II greets enthusiastic crowds on the streets of Mexico City in January 1979 during his first trip as pontiff.

 Article and photographs printed with permission of the Catholic News Service

Christ becomes even more evident," Cardinal Jozef Tomko, a longtime friend and retired Vatican official, said.

THE FIRST NON-ITALIAN PONTIFF in 455 years, Pope John Paul II declared early on that the Second Vatican Council had set his agenda. In particular, his global ministry quickly focused on Vatican II's engagement of modern culture. As for teaching, the pope has penned three major encyclicals on economic and social justice issues and has addressed the rich-poor imbalance continent-by-continent in post-synodal documents.

Newly installed Pope John Paul II and Cardinal Stefan Wyszynski of Poland embrace at the Vatican in this 1978 photo. During an emotional moment, Cardinal Wyszynski knelt in front of the pontiff, and was joined by the pope, who also fell to his knees.

Over the last 10 years, he also has authored three other encyclicals that strongly challenge what he sees as a prevailing moral relativism in post-modern society. *Veritatis Splendor* (1993) spoke of the truth of the church's moral teachings, *Evangelium Vitae* (1995) defended the inviolability of human life against what the pope calls a "culture of death," and *Fides et Ratio* (1998) argued that human reason cannot be detached from faith in God.

Meanwhile, under his guidance, Vatican agencies have issued important instructions on such specific questions as foreign debt, in vitro fertilization, the arms industry, the role of the mass media and the impact of the Internet.

Through all these pronouncements runs a central theme: that human freedom becomes destructive when people forget they are created in God's image. Whether an unborn child, an impoverished African or an elderly shut-in, the pope says, every human being has a value that goes beyond earthly advantages and accomplishments.

While pushing Catholic teaching into virtually every area of modern life, the pope also has taken the measure of the church's past mistakes. At his insistence, the church acknowledged historical errors in condemning 16th-century astronomer Galileo Galilei, in participating in European religious wars, and even in its missionary approach in some New World territories.

Against considerable resistance within his own Vatican hierarchy, the pope commissioned critical studies on the church's role in the Inquisition and the Crusades and on the failings of Christians during the Holocaust.

In the area of interreligious relations, Pope John Paul has reached out in ways that were once considered impossible or even heretical. In 1986 he visited a Jewish synagogue in Rome, then in 2000 prayed at the Western Wall in Jerusalem — a gesture that won the hearts of many Jews worldwide. In Syria, he became the first pope to visit a mosque, and in Morocco he spoke to thousands of cheering Muslim youths. Twice he convened leaders of other religions and other churches for prayer meetings in Assisi, where participants denounced all acts of war and terrorism carried out in the name of religion.

Within the church, the pope has been no less dynamic. He has disciplined dissenting theologians and self-styled "traditionalists," promulgated a new Code of Canon Law, issued new directives calling for clearer Catholic identity in church universities, and defended, with the full weight of his authority, the church's all-male priesthood.

As a teacher of the faith, the pope has been exhaustive, demanding and authoritative. The "Catechism of the Catholic Church" is his longest document and will no doubt be seen as one of the great accomplishments of this pontificate; a shorter compendium of church teaching is also in the works.

The pope brooks no dissent among the faithful, and in a 1998 document he invoked penalties against Catholics who reject the church's wide range of "definitive" positions, including those on human sexuality. That has prompted criticism by some groups of laity and theologians, especially in Europe and the United States. Such groups say the pope has presided over an excessive centralization of church power and authority at the expense of local churches.

While supporting Vatican II's promotion of the laity in the church, the pope has warned against confusing the roles of lay Catholics and ordained priests. He has supported clerically managed lay organizations like Opus Dei, which has grown in influence.

As opposed to models of power-sharing in the church, Pope John Paul has proposed models of holiness to the world's 1.1 billion Catholics. He has canonized more than 470 people from dozens of countries and beatified more than 1,300 — including the first lay couple.

Thousands gather on the Washington Mall in 1979, attending an outdoor Mass celebrated by Pope John Paul II.

AT THE 25 YEAR MARK, the pope's record on ecumenism contains a long list of agreements, joint declarations and mutual gestures of good will, especially with some ancient Eastern churches.

But as common ground has been staked out among the churches, the remaining obstacles have stood in even higher relief. The Vatican's clear injunction against shared Eucharist with Protestant churches may seem arbitrary to critics, but the pope views it as a painful reminder of the distance yet to travel in ecumenical dialogue.

In recent years, relations with the Russian Orthodox Church have sharply deteriorated as a result of the pope's determination to rebuild Catholic communities in Russia and other parts of Eastern Europe. Surely one of the pope's biggest disappointments after 25 years has been the failure to visit Moscow, which he would undertake only with the Orthodox Church's blessing.

Pope John Paul's pontificate is the fourth-longest in history, and perhaps more than any of his predecessors he has shaped the hierarchy in his image. He has named more than three-fourths of the world's active bishops and 96 percent of the cardinals who will elect his successor.

During his papacy, the church has expanded greatly in Africa and made significant advances in Asia and Oceania. This distinctly Third World tilt has been spotlighted during the pope's more than

100 foreign trips, when he has used local customs in his liturgies, spoken the native language and praised indigenous writers and thinkers.

But the trips have enormous missionary objectives, as well. While respectful of the non-Catholic or non-Christian majorities along his itinerary, the pope has always presented the figure of Christ and the Gospel message to any and all of his listeners.

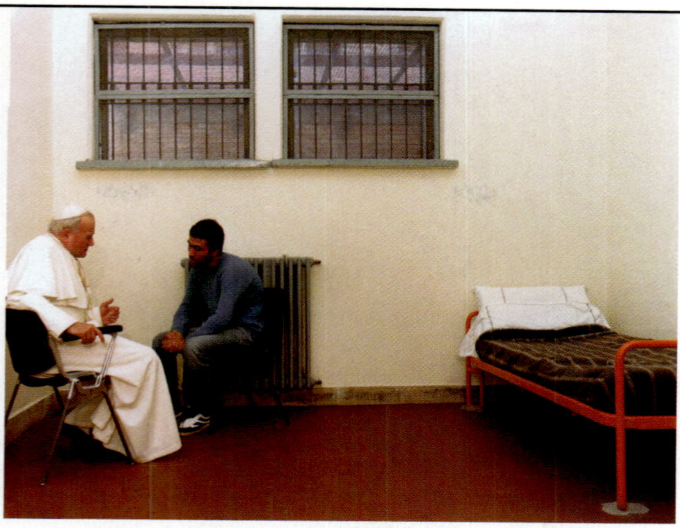

John Paul II talks with his would-be assasin, Mehmet Ali Agoa, in a Roman prison in 1983, two years following the attempt on the pontiff's life.

Visiting India in 1999, the pope delineated the church's approach on the Asian continent, where he predicted "a great harvest of faith" in the years to come. He praised his hosts' non-Christian spiritual traditions but also preached the Gospel, and said the best way for Christians to evangelize was by living the Gospel values.

That is in keeping with the pope's conviction that while all people can be saved, Christ is the unique savior for all people — a point made forcefully in the controversial document *Dominus Iesus*, which emphasized proclamation of Christ over dialogue.

As the pope has aged, his rapport with young people has remained consistently — and sometimes amazingly — fresh and energetic. World Youth Day celebrations, like the last one in Toronto in 2002, seem to bring out the pope's good humor and vigor. He jokes more easily

Clockwise from top, left:

Kenyans greet John Paul in Nairobi in September 1995.

Surrounded by students in Melbourne, Australia, during his visit to their classroom in November 1986.

Greeted by Rabbi Elio Toaff, chief rabbi of Rome, during the pope's landmark visit to the Grand Synagogue of Rome, 1986.

with the young, but there is a serious side to all this, too.

As the years of this pontificate roll by, the encyclicals and teaching documents have become fewer and the speeches shorter. Those close to him say the pope has clearly not run out of things to say, however — he is just saying them in different ways.

Rabbi Michael Melchior looks on as John Paul prays at the Western Wall in Jerusalem in March 2000.

"At the start of the 21st century, the pope continues to open people up to the transcendent, telling them that we're more than genetics, we're more than psychology, we're more than DNA," said Navarro-Valls. This is a message that is resonating with Catholics and non-Catholics around the world, he added.

The pope is also finding time for more reflective writing. Earlier this year, he published a small book of poetry, meditations that were inspired by the Sistine Chapel frescoes.

As his 25th anniversary approached, the pope was in the final phase of writing a book on his 20 years as a bishop in Poland. He authored a similar volume in 1996 on his life as a priest, an intensely personal review of the

Receiving ashes from Cardinal Josef Tomko at Rome's Basilica of Santa Sabina in 2002

The pope in his "popemobile" makes his way past the domes of an Orthodox monastary in Kiev in 2001.

spiritual path that eventually led to the papacy.

DURING THE PAST 25 YEARS, the face of the church has changed — in some aspects dramatically. Numbers tell part of the story.

At the broadest level, the number of Catholics in the world has jumped more than 40 percent, from 757 million to 1.06 billion at the end of 2001, the last year for which official church statistics have been published.

More significant under this pontificate are the geographical areas of growth, which indicate a Third World shift. Catholics in Africa have increased nearly 150 percent and in Asia more than 80 percent. In Europe the increase has been only 5 percent, and the number of Catholics has actually gone down in recent years. In the United States, the number of Catholics rose from 48 million to 64 million over the same period. That is an increase of about 33 percent, 4 percentage points higher than the growth of the general U.S. population.

When it comes to those who work in a ministerial or teaching capacity for the church, there's been an increase in most categories under Pope John Paul, but a decrease among members of religious orders.

Overall, the "workforce for the church's apostolate" has jumped from 1.6 million to 2.8 million. The number of bishops in the world increased from 3,600 to more than 4,600 — and more than 70 percent of them have been appointed by Pope John Paul.

After declining for several years, the number of diocesan priests was up to 266,500 at the end of 2001, about 8,000 more than when the pope took office. The number of religious priests has declined

Holding up the cross during the final station of the Way of the Cross in Rome's Colosseum in 2002

steadily, from about 158,000 to 139,000, and religious brothers are down from about 75,000 to 55,000. The sharpest drop has been in the number of women religious, which has gone from 985,000 to 792,000.

While the number of foreign missionary priests has declined in many parts of the world, the number of indigenous catechists has exploded. When Pope John Paul assumed the papacy, the church had 173,000 catechists; today there are more than 2.8 million. The number of lay missionaries — not even a category when the pope was elected — has now reached 139,000, most of them in South America.

Permanent deacons have emerged as a pastoral force during this pope's term. They numbered 5,500 in 1978 and are more than 28,000 today. Nearly half of them are in the United States.

Despite what the Vatican considers as hopeful trends in priestly vocations, there are far fewer priests per Catholic today than when the pope came to office. In 1978 the worldwide ratio was 1,800 Catholics for every priest; today it is more than 2,600 Catholics per priest.

But the church has bolstered its social and educational roles under Pope John Paul II. For example, there are more than 106,000 church-run health and welfare institutions today, compared to 64,000 in 1978. The figure includes clinics, homes for the elderly and disabled, orphanages and marriage counseling centers.

The number of church-run schools has gone way up, and enrollment has increased by 40 percent or more under Pope John Paul. At the university level, the increase is more dramatic. Enrollment at

Catholic higher institutes of learning has risen from about 2 million in 1978 to 4.6 million today.

At the Vatican, the pope has continued the internationalization of the Roman Curia. When he came to office, Italians controlled about half the Vatican's top 20 departments. Today, Italians hold only four of those top spots.

The pope also has made a direct and strong impact on the makeup of the College of Cardinals, the institution that will elect his successor. He expanded the total number of cardinals to a record 184 in 2001. Of the 109 cardinals under the age of 80 at the end of August and eligible to vote in a conclave, the pope has appointed all but five.

HOW WILL POPE JOHN PAUL II BE REMEMBERED in the history books? On an ecclesiastical level, for his energetic missionary ministry that took him around the globe and saw rapid church growth in the third world. Internationally, he will go down as the godfather of Communism's demise in Europe, and as a moral statesman whose pronouncements on poverty, human life and war often challenged conventional politics. But much of the world will remember him simply as a man of deep prayer, whose spiritual intensity impressed believers of every faith. ✞

Bowing his head during a weekly audience at St. Peter's, 2001.

Special thanks to John Thavis and the Catholic News Service for permission to reprint *John Paul's Quarter-Century* as well as the many photographs that accompany this article.

Photo of His Holiness The Pope courtesy of Arturo Mari, L'Osservatore Romano.

His Holiness the Pope John Paul II

The Seal of P.J. Kenedy & Sons
The Official Catholic Directory

SIGNIFICANCE:

The shield is the central part of a heraldic device, which is more commonly known as a coat of arms. If that shield is enclosed within a body of text, or other type of surrounding configuration, the device becomes know as a seal, yet it is the shield portion of the design that is the most important, and that which is described technically as the blazon. As the design is examined, it must be remembered that by heraldic tradition the design is described (blazoned) as if being done by the bearer with the shield being worn on the arm. Therefore, the terms dexter and sinister will be reversed as the design is viewed from the front.

The shield of the seal for The Official Catholic Directory has been designed to reflect the character and heritage of this publication of P.J. Kenedy & Sons.

The shield is in two major portions. The right half (sinister impalement) is composed of the blue field on which are seen a silver tree, two candles (in silver or white) in their candleholders (of gold or yellow) and an open book, edged in gold and with a red bookmark. These symbols have been used over the years as the sign of the P.J. Kenedy and Sons publishing organization. These are the traditional symbols of knowledge and learning, so appropriate to a publisher.

The other side of the shield (the dexter impalement) is composed of a silver (white) field on which is seen a red cross, throughout, and a gold eagle. These symbols, combined with the field of the sinister impalement, are represented in the color of the flag of the United States of America and the eagle, the symbol of the United States. The cross represents Christianity and all of this combines to signify that The Official Catholic Directory annually reports on the Catholic Church in the United States.

The shield is surrounded by a laurel wreath of excellence and is enclosed within the legend that states the name of the company, the name of the publication and date (1817) of its founding.

by: Paul J. Sullivan

THE J.T. VERDIN CO., CINCINNATI, OHIO

Timeless design, devoted craftsmanship, traditional
materials and friendly, trustworthy service.
These are the hallmarks of CM Almy,
outfitters to the church and clergy since 1892.
CM ALMY
Three American Lane PO Box 2644
Greenwich, CT 06836
800.225.2569 www.almy.com

"Lord, when did we see You hungry?"

Matthew 25:37b

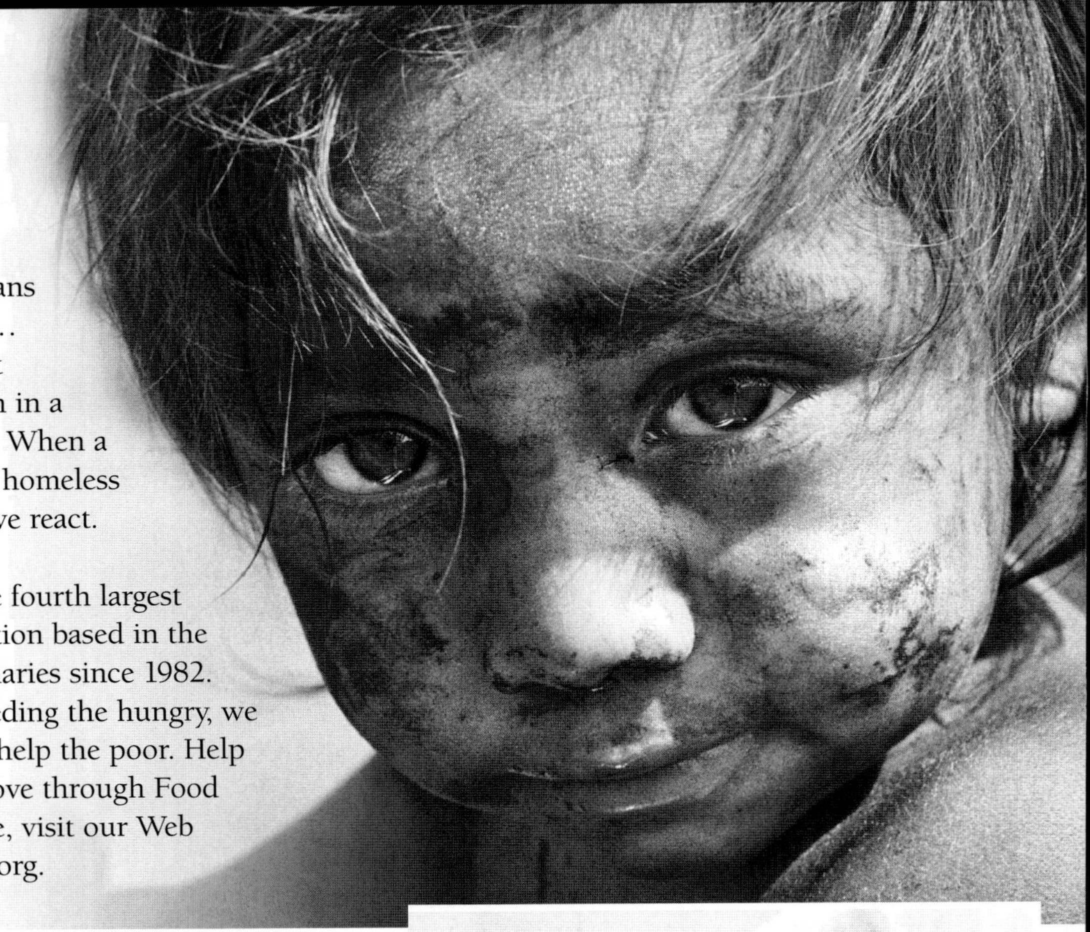

At Food For The Poor, we care for our poorest brothers and sisters by serving those who directly aid the hungry, sick and homeless… When a nun needs food for hungry orphans in El Salvador, we are there… When a missionary runs out of medicine for sick children in a Haitian slum, we respond… When a pastor pleads for houses for homeless parishioners in Nicaragua, we react.

Food For The Poor is the fourth largest international relief organization based in the US.* We have aided missionaries since 1982. From building houses to feeding the hungry, we ship whatever they need to help the poor. Help spread Christ's message of love through Food For The Poor. To learn more, visit our Web site at www.foodforthepoor.org.

* *Chronicle of Philanthropy*, Oct, 2003

"From providing food to the hungry to building homes for the dispossessed, Food For The Poor has answered Christ's call to serve the needy."

Most Reverend Paul M. Boyle, C.P., D.D., Bishop of Mandeville, Jamaica.

Sister Marta of the Jardin de Amor orphanage in El Salvador

FOOD FOR THE POOR, INC.

550 SW 12th Avenue • Deerfield Beach, FL 33442 • (954) 427-2222 • www.foodforthepoor.org

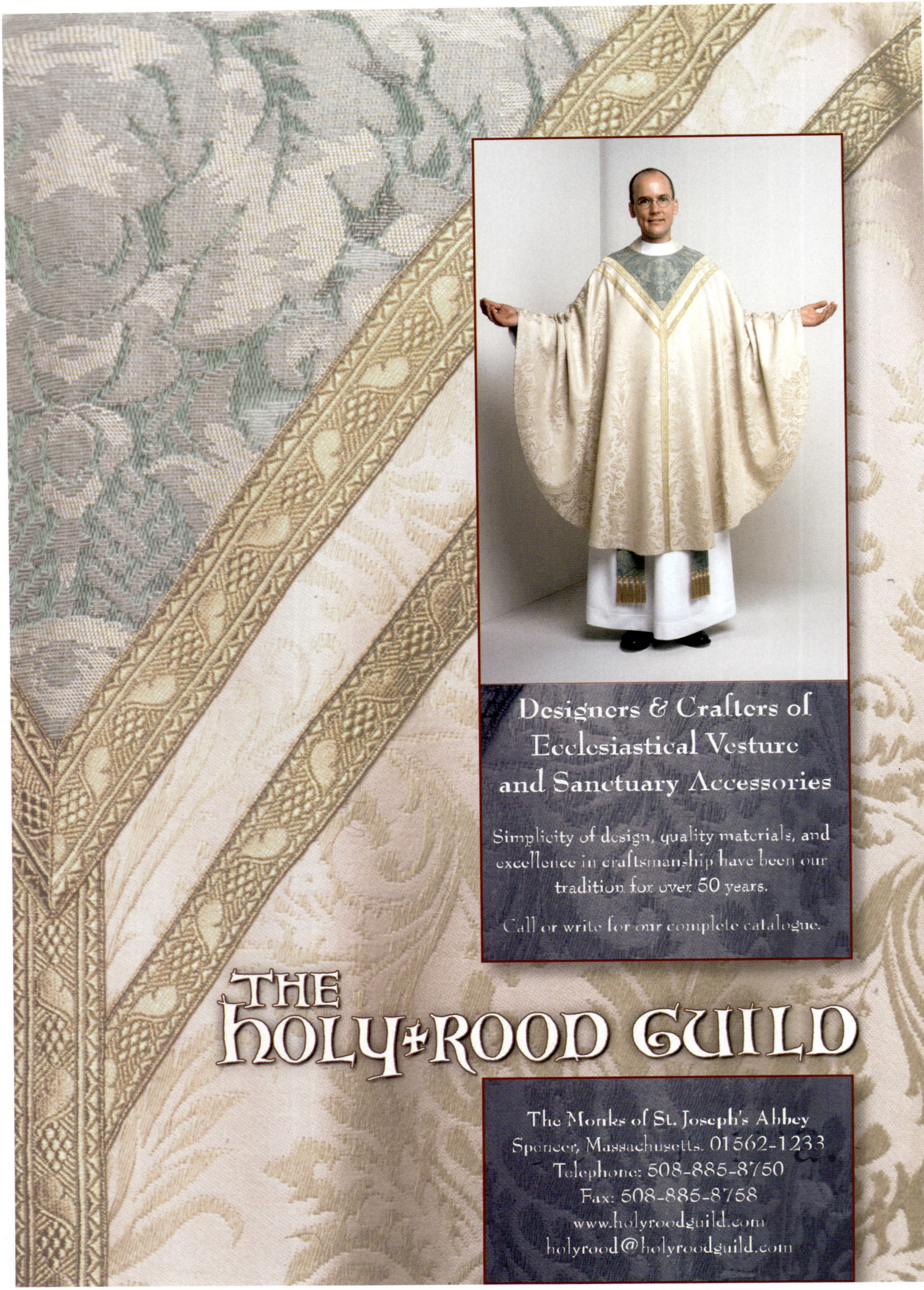
Designers & Crafters of
Ecclesiastical Vesture
and Sanctuary Accessories
Simplicity of design, quality materials, and excellence in craftsmanship have been our tradition for over 50 years.
Call or write for our complete catalogue.
THE
HOLY+ROOD GUILD
The Monks of St. Joseph's Abbey
Spencer, Massachusetts. 01562-1233
Telephone: 508-885-8750
Fax: 508-885-8758
www.holyroodguild.com
holyrood@holyroodguild.com

Giving Glory to God
through Art

King Richard's Religious Artifacts
Antique Marble, Plaster & Wood Altars
Antique Marble Shrines
King Richard's Religious Artifacts...
The nations largest buyer and seller of antique stained glass windows, altars, statuary and altarware.
Single & Complete Sets of Antique Stained Glass Windows
New & Antique Statuary
And Now...
The best web site in the world for marble and bronze statuary, unusual altarware, new traditional furniture, altars, stations, lighting, and the largest selection of antique stained glass windows.
Marble & Wood Altar Rails
New & Antique Tabernacles
Thousands of New & Antique Altarware Items
Yes... We are buying!
Over 500 candle stands to choose from
Church Lighting
email: info@kingrichards.com • www.kingrichards.com • toll free 877.248.3366

These gorgeous windows are for sale by us.
We buy and sell pre-owned stained glass windows.
Our windows come to you with a history of prior church service at substantial savings over comparable quality new windows. We offer the following services:
• We pay top dollar for stained glass windows no longer needed.
• Our used windows are top quality such as Munich, Oidtmann, Lamb, Rudy and Tiffany.
• We remove or install windows and can adjust window sizes to meet your needs.
• Complete restoration and preservation services.
• We will buy complete church interiors.
• Appraisals available.
• Inquiries invited from architects and dealers.
• Custom-made new windows.
PHILLIP A. GALLO
6318 Seventh St.
Alexandria, VA 22312
703-354-7445 toll free 888-742-8500
Visit our website: preownedchurchitems.com

St. Mary's Church
Renovation

St. Patrick St. Anthony Church
Restoration Renovation

St. Elizabeth Ann Seton
Renovation

St. Mary of Chestochowa
Renovation

St. Patrick Church
Restoration Renovation

Church of St. Ann
Restoration Renovation

Corpus Christi Church
Restoration Renovation

St. Rose of Lima Church
Restoration Renovation

St. Ann Church

St. Francis of Assisi

St. Joseph Church
Renovation

Majesty™

Jubilaeum™

Exsultet™

Imperat™

Jerusalem™

The Mark of Human Hands™

Individually made to order.
Fashioned entirely by hand with the finest of beeswax.
Each style available in 23 standard sizes.

A Marklin Paschal Candle,
hallmark of beauty, symbol of grace.™

Marklin Candle Design
www.marklincandle.com
603-746-2211

Splendor™

Dominion™

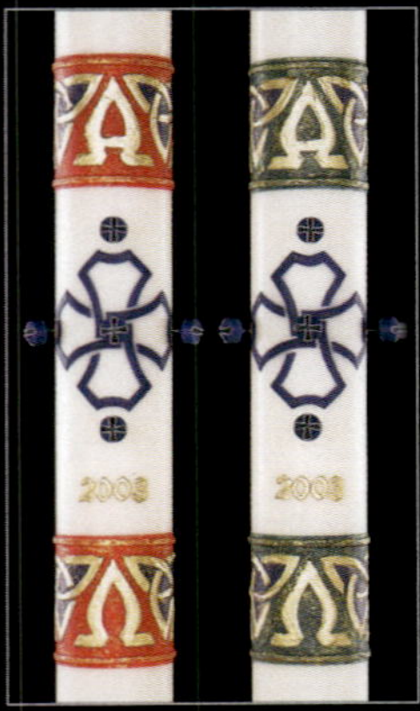
Trinitas™

Resurrexit™

Arise™

Laetare™

Morning Light™

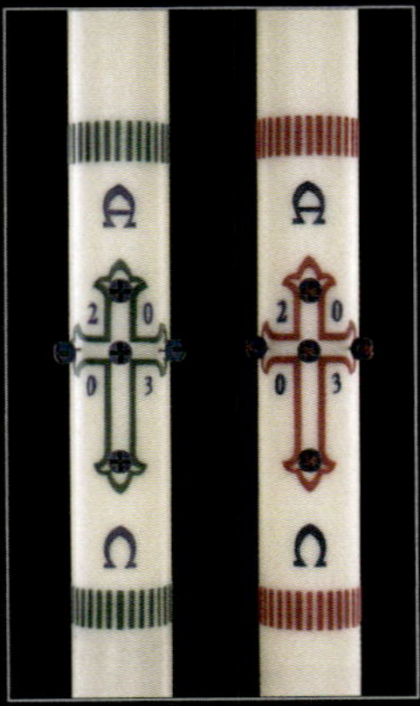
Restoring Grace™

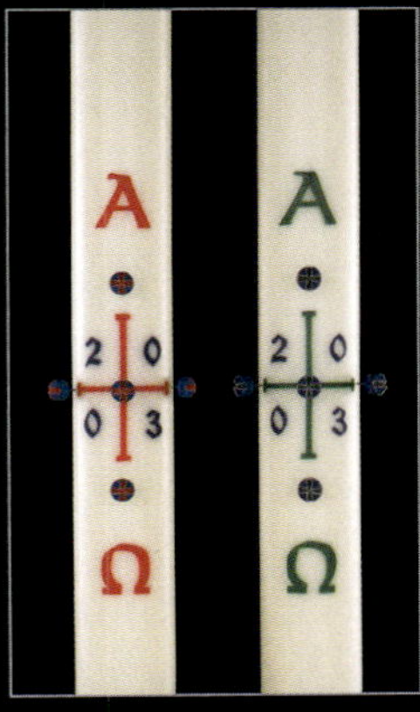
Evening Praise™

See also Los Angeles tab.

Interior Design Services, Decorating & Restoration
Ecclesiastical Consultants & Project Management
New & Antique Liturgical Products & Furnishings
Five Generations of Old World Craftsmanship
The Berlinger Company

The Jubilee Museum at Holy Family Church (Diocese of Columbus) is dedicated to the preservation of the Catholic mind and memory. In its many exhibit rooms this Catholic museum uniquely houses also a synagogue (a memorial to the Holocaust), relic chapel, Tridentine chapel, and on the first floor, a soup kitchen that serves over 600 hot meals each day.

Archbishop Francesco Marchisano, President of the Pontifical Commission for the Cultural Heritage of the Church, visited the Jubilee Museum at its opening in 1998 and again in 2002 when he conducted a seminar on diocesan museums. Archbishop Francesco Marchisano worked in our soup kitchen, where he commented, "You have treasures of art that teach the truths of Christ, and you feed the poor, the very treasures that reveal the face of Christ. A perfect blend of Christian art and Christian charity."

The Jubilee Museum contains thousands of items: Eucharistic vessels, Russian icons, relics, stained glass, vestments, religious habits, Latin altar missals (including rare 1607 and 1713 editions), paintings, carvings, four pipe organs, statuary, military chaplain kits, vestment fragments of the first American bishop, John Carroll, a first edition of the New Testament dated 1582 at Rheims, and much more

The Jubilee Museum

Tours, Seminars and Retreats

Tours of the museum are available by appointment for churches, organizations, schools, and individuals. The museum can also host retreats, religious symposiums and seminars.

Items For Sale

The Jubilee Museum is able to locate many items for churches, and works with companies and agents for hard-to-find items to complete older sets of candles, vessels, and statuary.

At Your Service

Our staff will conduct a seminar in your diocese to help establish your own diocesan museum. Such a museum is a great public relations asset, educational resource, and evangelization tool. Our seminar focuses on funding, volunteers, procurement and networking. We also consult on sacred art in churches considering restoration or renovation.

Donations

With its national focus, the Jubilee Museum welcomes gifts of sacred art (even in damaged condition) that tell the story of the Catholic Church. Monetary gifts enable us to continue to preserve our heritage and sustain our service to the poor.

For More Information On:

Tours, Seminars and Retreats - Linda Hamilton (Director), Bill Antoniak (Assistant Director) (614) 461-6204
Donations/Items for sale - Sheila Lutz (Director of Development) (614) 221-4323
Establishing your own Diocesan Museum - Father Kevin F. Lutz, Consulter to the Pontifical Commission for the Cultural Heritage of the Catholic Church, (614) 221-4323
584 West Broad Street • Columbus, Ohio 43215
Fax: (614) 461-1737
Email: jubileemuseum@columbus.rr.com Web Site: www.holyfamilycolumbus.org

A J Bellomo
STUDIOS
Gaze Into The Winter Sky
Maranatha
AN ADVENT WREATH
FOR CHURCH & HOME PRAYER
LORD
A
COME
JESUS
Ω
MARANATHA
Church
Home
For More Information Please Contact Us:
Phone: 586-954-4800
310 Euclid, Mt. Clemens, MI 48043 Email: blackfor@bignet.net Website: www.ajbellomostudios.com
We design & produce...
OUTDOOR
SIGNS
That Proclaim the Good News!
THE
BLACK FOREST
COMPANY

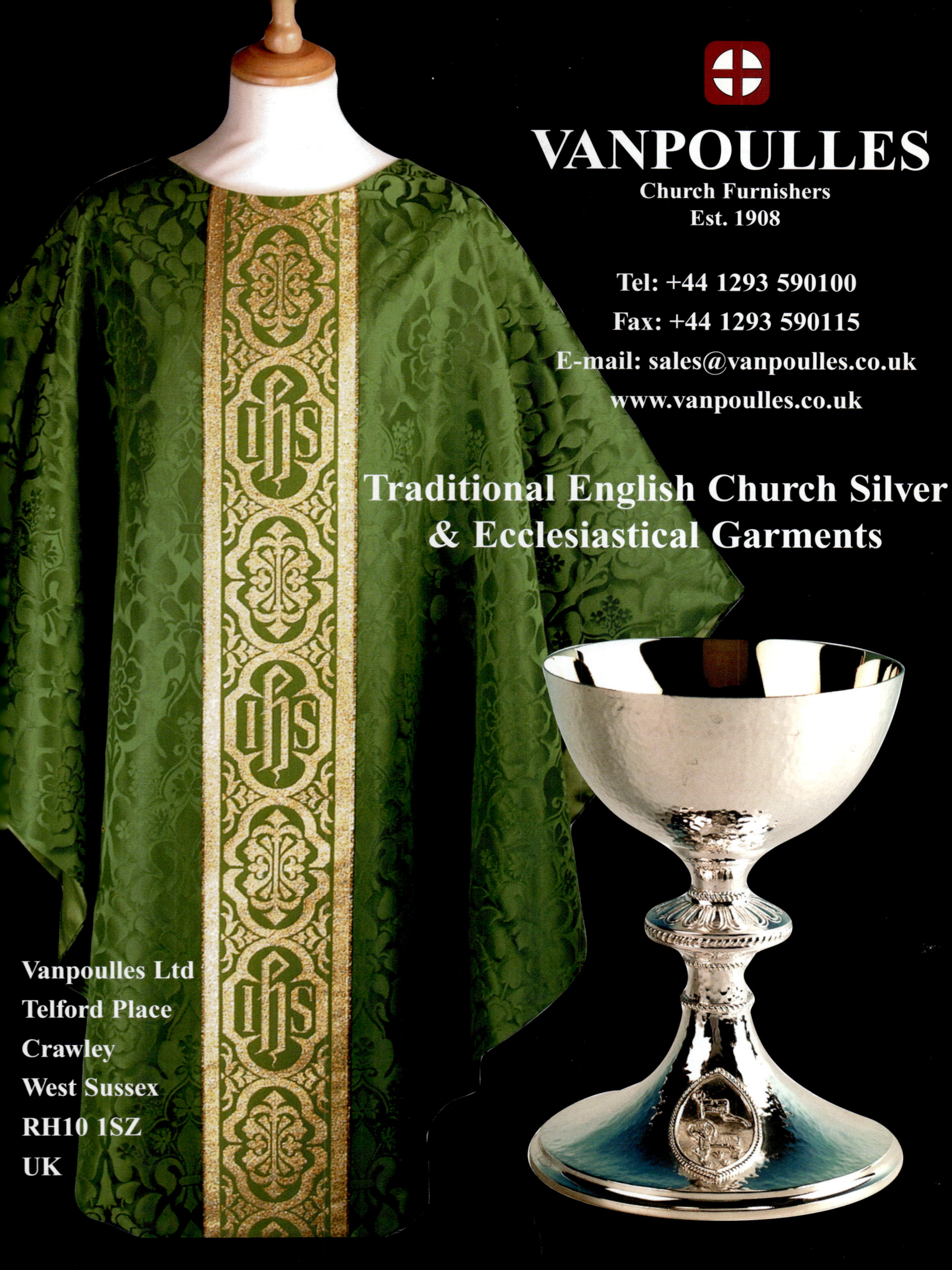
VANPOULLES
Church Furnishers
Est. 1908
Tel: +44 1293 590100
Fax: +44 1293 590115
E-mail: sales@vanpoulles.co.uk
www.vanpoulles.co.uk
Traditional English Church Silver
& Ecclesiastical Garments
Vanpoulles Ltd
Telford Place
Crawley
West Sussex
RH10 1SZ
UK

TABLE OF CONTENTS

TABLE OF CONTENTS

The Official Catholic Directory

for the Year of Our Lord

2004

GIVING STATUS OF THE CATHOLIC CHURCH AS OF JANUARY 1, 2004

Containing Ecclesiastical Statistics of

THE UNITED STATES, PUERTO RICO,
THE VIRGIN ISLANDS, AGANA, CAROLINE AND MARSHALL ISLANDS,
AND FOREIGN MISSIONARY ACTIVITIES.

The information contained in this Directory is derived from reports submitted to the publishers by the ecclesiastical authorities of the countries concerned, and neither the publishers nor the ecclesiastical authorities assume responsibility for any errors or omissions.

25th PAPAL ANNIVERSARY EDITION

P.J. KENEDY & SONS

Publishers of the Holy Apostolic See

For inquiries call: 908-673-1001, or write:
562 Central Avenue, New Providence, NJ 07974
To place an order call: 1-800-473-7020

The Official Catholic Directory

Published by P.J. Kenedy & Sons in association with National Register Publishing

Photo of His Holiness The Pope, courtesy of Arturo Mari, L'Osservatore Romano.

Printed and bound in the United States of America
International Standard Book Number: 0-87217-364-X
International Standard Serial Number: 0078-3854
Library of Congress Catalog Card Number: 81-30961

CONTENTS

ARCHDIOCESES AND DIOCESES

APOSTOLATE

PERSONAL PRELATURES

EASTERN CHURCHES

TERRITORIAL SEES

MISSION SECTION

RELIGIOUS INSTITUTION SECTION

GENERAL SUMMARY

THE ARCHDIOCESES AND DIOCESES OF THE UNITED STATES—BY STATES

A—Indicates Archdiocese. The Archdiocese of Washington includes the District of Columbia and five counties of Maryland. Dioceses traverse state license in the following instances only: Cheyenne includes all of Yellowstone National Park; South Norwich includes Fisher's Island; Wilmington includes the eastern shores of Maryland; and Gallup includes parts of Arizona and New Mexico.

A USER'S GUIDE TO *THE OFFICIAL CATHOLIC DIRECTORY*

Each year the editors of ***The Official Catholic Directory*** seek added ways of serving their subscribers. Although the book may never answer every question, this is the conscientious goal; its format, arrangement and editorial features are directed toward the convenience and needs of the public. Comments and suggestions are welcome. For the benefit of the subscriber and a more efficient use of ***The Official Catholic Directory*** and its cross references, a summary of the contents and their meaning follows:

***The Official Catholic Directory* Glossary**
A listing of some of the ecclesiastical terms and organizations found in the *Directory.*

The Governing Bodies in Vatican City
A chronological table of the **Supreme Roman Pontiffs**; the **Pope**, and an alphabetical list of the **College of Cardinals**; the duties of each of the agencies of the **Roman Curia**, and other commissions and institutions associated with the Holy See, along with their officers; a list of the **Seminaries** and **National Colleges** in Rome; the **Apostolic Nunciature** and the **Permanent Observer Mission to the United Nations**, with their staff. As foreign organizations, these entities are not included in the USCCB group tax exemption ruling ("Group Ruling").

The Catholic Church in the United States (Provinces)
The archdioceses and dioceses of the United States arranged under the provinces to which they belong, listed with their active archbishops and bishops.

Ecclesiastical forms of address recognized in the United States. Formal forms of address for correspondence with the clergy in the United States.

U.S. Cardinals, Archbishops, Bishops, Archabbots and Abbots
An alphabetical list of Cardinals, Archbishops, Bishops, Archabbots and Abbots, arranged within their specific title. Also listed is their address and status, followed by a hierarchical/chronological list by year.

United States Conference of Catholic Bishops
The United States Conference of Catholic Bishops is a permanent institute composed of Catholic bishops of the United States of America in and through which the bishops exercise in a communal or collegial manner the pastoral mission entrusted to them by the Lord Jesus of sanctification, teaching, and leadership, especially by devising forms and methods of the apostolate suitably adapted to the circumstances of the times. Such exercise is intended to offer appropriate assistance to each bishop in fulfilling his particular ministry in the local Church, to effect a commonality of ministry addressed to the people of the United States of America, and to foster and express communion with the Church in other nations within the Church universal, under the leadership of its chief pastor, the Pope.

Victims Assistance Coordinators pages.

Alphabetical Places List
The cities, towns, and villages where there is a church with a resident priest, or a Catholic institution, or both, together with the abbreviations of the archdiocese or diocese to which it belongs.

Dioceses and Archdioceses (in alphabetical sequence)
The most detailed information on the Catholic Church in the United States, including the Military Services, Eastern Churches, Personal Prelatures, and Apostolates to the Hungarians and Lithuanians. Listings are in alphabetical order according to the name of the diocese/archdiocese and include the diocesan curia and administrative offices; a parish-by-parish listing of clergy, churches, missions, and parochial schools; information on institutions, and the religious institutes of men and women located in the diocese/archdiocese; and a statistical profile for each diocese/archdiocese.

United States Territorial Sees
This section contains information on U.S. territories similar to that found in the preceding section.

American Foreign Missions
This section highlights the Religious working specifically in foreign countries. Each Province lists their U.S. members and the countries they serve in. For specific address requests, contact the mission office listed.

Missionary Activities
Organizations involved in missionary work in the U.S. and foreign countries.

United States Conference of Secular Institutes
An alphabetical list of secular organizations and their purposes.

U.S. Catholic Mission Association
An alphabetical list of countries served by the U.S. Catholic Mission Association, detailing the number and religious order or laity personnel working there.

Mission Churches
A list, by city, of mission churches in the U.S. and the parishes to which they are attached.

Religious Institutes of Men and Women
An alphabetical list of religious institutes of men and of women, using a P.J. Kenedy identification number. Each listing contains the general headquarters, provinces, provincialates, a summary of legal titles and holdings taken from the individual archdioceses and dioceses within the *Directory*, various forms of ministry and works, statistical data of personnel, and representation in the U.S. dioceses and archdioceses. Foreign religious institutes are not included in the USCCB Group Ruling.

Special Care Facilities
An alphabetical list of special care facilities by state and diocese.

Religious Order Initials for Men and **Religious Order Initials for Women**
Indexes of abbreviations relevant to the religious institute name and the applicable identification number.

Diocesan and Religious Priests
An alphabetical list of diocesan and religious priests denoting their year of ordination, the archdiocese or diocese they are assigned to or work in, and the church or institution with which they are affiliated.

Necrology of U.S. Cardinals, Archbishops, Bishops, Archabbots, Abbots, and Priests
An alphabetical list of the U.S. hierarchy and priests who have died since the last issue of the *Directory*, along with their date of death and last assignment.

The General Summary
A 40+ page general summary of statistics arranged alphabetically by state, listing the archdiocese first within each state, followed by the dioceses. This information, extracted from the Statistical Overview of each diocese/archdiocese, pertains to personnel, parishes, health and welfare, education, and specific sacramental figures, as well as Catholic and total population figures for each diocese/archdiocese. U.S. territories and Eastern Church statistics are also included.

Map of Catholic Diocesan and Province Boundaries in the United States
Map defining the diocesan, archdiocesan, provincial, and state boundaries.

Products & Services Guide
Includes a diverse array of products and services offered to the Catholic community.

The Official Catholic Directory
Provides a comprehensive listing of archdioceses and dioceses of the world. Also contains mid-year updates to the U.S. (arch)dioceses. More information on *The OfficialCatholic Directory Part II* can be obtained from the publisher.

SPECIAL NOTATIONS USED IN THE DIRECTORY

An asterisk (*) denotes a tax-exempt organization that has its own IRS exemption status and is not covered by the USCCB Group Ruling. The Group Ruling allows for the exemption from federal income tax of all Catholic institutions listed in *The Official Catholic Directory* for that year. The exemption was established in 1946 and has been extended every year since then.

[CEM] in a parish listing indicates that a cemetery is connected to the parish.

[JC] indicates a joint cemetery, which is a cemetery being utilized by more than one parish. A number following [CEM] or [JC] indicates the number of cemeteries owned by the parish or joint cemeteries shared with other parishes.

A dagger † next to a name in the Necrology denotes a deceased priest. A Maltese cross ✠ denotes a deceased member of the hierarchy.

THE GENERAL SUMMARY

Certain terms used in the General Summary may need additional explanation.

Extern Priests are priests who have not been incardinated into the diocese in which they are currently working and residing.

Health Care Centers include ancillary care systems, medical centers, sanitoriums, and hospices.

Specialized Homes refers to institutions which provide aid to abused children or adults, halfway homes, AIDS patients, ARC patients, ex-offenders, pregnant women, adjudicated delinquents, or runaway youths.

Special Centers for Social Services are institutions or services that provide assistance, such as hotline centers, food banks, homeless centers, legal aid services, or counseling services.

Residential Care of Children refers to orphanages, as opposed to day care centers.

Non-residential Schools for Handicapped are day schools which provide regular and religious education for physically and/or mentally handicapped students.

Received into Full Communion is used to describe people who have been baptized earlier in life and have now been received into full communion in the Catholic Church.

USER GUIDE

THE OFFICIAL CATHOLIC DIRECTORY GLOSSARY

Abbot

The superior of an autonomous community of men religious. He has general and sacramental jurisdiction over his community. The head of a prominent monastery or a congregation consisting of several monasteries is an *archabbot*.

Advocate

An ecclesiastical advocate is someone approved by Church authority to safeguard the rights of a party in a canonical process by arguments regarding the law and the facts of the case. [Cf. c. 1481 and CLSA Comm., p. 967]

Apostolate

Apostolate is the mission of Christ and participation in it. Its object is to bring Christ to others, its goal is the greater glory of God, its scope is universal. The work is carried out by every human agency by which the life of grace may be given or increased in the soul. A mandate from the Church is essential to the Catholic apostolate.

Archbishop

A bishop of a main or metropolitan diocese in an ecclesiastical province. The term is equivalent to *metropolitan* in the Western Church. It may also be granted to other ordinaries and non-residential bishops, and to the ordinary of a diocese outside a province.

Auditor

An official of a diocesan court, who gathers evidence and testimony and draws up a record of an ecclesiastical case.

Bishop

A bishop, by divine institution, carries on the work of the apostles. By reason of episcopal consecration, he shares in the triple apostolic function of teacher of doctrine, priest of sacred worship, and minister of church government. Bishops are responsible for the pastoral care of their dioceses. In addition, bishops have a responsibility to act in council to guide the Church. The term *eparch* is used in Eastern-rite churches.

The bishop to whom a particular or local church is entrusted is called a *diocesan bishop* or a *residential bishop.* Some other bishops receive *Titular Sees* over which they exercise no pastoral authority.

When the pastoral needs of a diocese or archdiocese warrant, an *auxiliary bishop* may be assigned to aid the residential bishop in governing his diocese. An auxiliary bishop is assigned when the residential bishop needs assistance in carrying out his duties because of ill health, advanced age, or amount of work. An auxiliary bishop does not have the right of succession within his diocese.

In special circumstances, such as the advanced age or ill health of a diocesan bishop, a *coadjutator bishop* may be appointed to assist the principal bishop of a diocese. Coadjutator bishops have the *right of succession* in the diocese of their appointment from the time the See becomes vacant upon the death or retirement of its bishop.

Brother

A man who is a member of a religious order, but is not ordained or studying for the priesthood.

Cana Conference

A Catholic family movement, originally designed to aid married couples and families in their spiritual and interpersonal relationships. The program is now divided into *Pre-Cana,* for couples engaged to be married, and *Cana Conferences,* programs for married people.

Catholic Fraternal Organizations

National Catholic fraternal organizations operating in the United States include the Knights of Columbus and the Knights of Peter Claver. These organizations are not included in the USCCB group tax exemption ruling.

Censor Librorum

A theologian empowered by a bishop to judge a book's soundness in regard to Church teaching before publication.

Chancellor

The office of the chancellor (or the *chancery*) evolved from the practice in the early Church of appointing an official to sign and preserve the letters of the bishop. The first function of the chancellor in the present day is gathering, arranging, and safeguarding the acts of the diocesan curia. Dispensations and other official documents also originate from the chancery. In many dioceses, the chancellor continues to exercise ordinary jurisdiction as delegated by the diocesan bishop. He or she may be assisted by a separate official, the *vice-chancellor.*

Chapter

The *general chapter* of a religious order is an assembly of elected or appointed members and provincials. General chapters are convened for the election of officers, amendments to the constitution, and discussion and legislation of matters of concern to members and the order as a whole.

A *provincial chapter* conducts elections and handles legislation on a provincial level. The assembly is comprised of superiors and representatives of the religious.

A *chapter of canons* is a group of diocesan priests, appointed by the bishop of a diocese, with assigned authority or responsibilities.

College of Cardinals

The College of Cardinals is made up of the cardinals of the Church, who advise the Pope, assist in the central administration of the Church, head the various curial offices and congregations, administer the Holy See during a vacancy, and elect a new Pope. There are three ranks in the College of Cardinals, corresponding to the historical origins of cardinals in the Roman Catholic Church. All cardinals are bishops, but their rank within the College of Cardinals is characterized by one of the hierarchical ranks of bishop, priest, or deacon. Cardinals are given honorary title to churches in the city of Rome. [CF. c. 350; CLSA Comm., pp. 288-289]

1. Cardinal Bishops

There are two types of Cardinal Bishops: 1) those appointed by the Pope as titular bishops to one of the six suburban dioceses of Rome, and 2) Eastern-rite Patriarchs who are heads of Sees with apostolic origins that have been assigned to the College of Cardinals.

2. Cardinal Priests

Heads of Sees outside the city of Rome are assigned a "titular church," one of the churches in Rome. They have no pastoral authority over their titular church.

3. Cardinal Deacons

Cardinals of diaconal rank are bishops without Sees who head the various departments, offices, congregations, committees, and the Secretariat of State of the Roman Curia.

Confraternity of Christian Doctrine [CCD]

A lay organization established for religious education throughout a person's entire life. The term is currently used to describe Catholic parish-based religious education of children from kindergarten through high school. At the diocesan level, the offices are now more commonly known as offices of *religious education* or *Christian formation.* Nationally, the confraternity's religious education component has been taken over by the USCCB's Department of Education. It still exists as a separate entity under the USCCB Administrative Board, with responsibility for licensing religious and spiritual literature.

Consolidated School

The term, as used in the *Directory,* may refer to a school that takes students from more than one parish, or a school that was formed by the consolidation of two or three other schools. In both cases, it is a means of keeping a Catholic school in a given area open by taking students from the surrounding areas, regardless of parish boundaries.

Convent

In common usage, the term refers to a house of women religious. Originally, it referred to a building where members of religious institutes lived, and was not restricted to communities of women.

Cursillo

The *cursillo de cristianidad*, or "little course in Christianity," is a three-day program for achieving spiritual renewal or spiritual awakening. It seeks to convey a new sense of individual and organized apostolic action. The program, conducted by priests and laypeople, consists of a three-day weekend focused on prayer, study, and Christian action, and a follow-up program known as the *post-cursillo.*

Deacons

The diaconate is the first order or grade in ordained ministry. Its origins are in early apostolic times, when deacons preached and baptized under the direction of the presbyters or bishops. Any man who is to be ordained to the priesthood must first be ordained as a *transitional deacon*. Deacons serve in the ministry of liturgy, of the word, and of charity.

In 1967, Pope Paul VI reinstituted the *Permanent Diaconate* for men who do not plan to become ordained priests. Although men ordained as permanent deacons are sometimes referred to as "married deacons," the permanent diaconate is open to both married and unmarried men, with the understanding that after ordination, they may not marry even after the death of a spouse. Under the authority of the diocesan bishop, they perform the same functions as the transitional deacons while, at the same time, retaining their roles in society as family and business men.

Dean/Vicar Forane

The title of a priest appointed by the bishop to aid him in administering the parishes in a certain vicinity, called a "deanery," or "vicariates forane." The function of a dean, or vicar forane, involves promotion, coordination, and supervision of the common pastoral activity within the deanery or vicariate.

Defender of the Bond

A member of a diocesan tribunal, either a cleric or a lay person, holding a graduate degree in canon law, who is appointed by the diocesan bishop for cases concerning the nullity of sacred ordination or the nullity or dissolution of the marriage bond. The defender of the bond is responsible for a review of the evidence, scrutiny of the briefs, examination of witnesses, and maintenance of proper procedures during the trial. The defender also deals with some situations concerning the content of the litigation rather than the legal procedures.

Diocesan Consultors

An advisory council of diocesan priests, as appointed by a diocesan bishop, that assists in the administrative affairs of the diocese.

Diocesan Curia

The personnel and offices assisting the diocesan bishop in directing the pastoral activity, administration, and the exercise of judicial power of his diocese. The curia includes among its officers laity and religious as well as clergy. Principal officers of a diocesan curia are the vicar general of the diocese, the chancellor, officials of the diocesan tribunal, examiners, consultors, auditors, the promoter of justice and the defender of the bond.

Diocese

The standard term for a territorial division of the Church, entrusted to a bishop who rules in his own name as local ordinary, and not as a delegate of another. The chief diocese of a province is an *archdiocese*. It is headed by an archbishop. A diocese is usually limited to a definite territory so that it comprises all the faithful who inhabit that territory. [Cf. cc. 369 and 372, #1] In Eastern-rite churches, the term eparchy is used.

Eastern-rite [Oriental] Church

The term used to describe the Catholic churches which developed in Eastern Europe, Asia, and Africa. The Eastern-rite churches have their own distinctive liturgical and organizational systems. Each is considered equal to the Latin rite within the Church.

Ecumenism/Ecumenical Movement

A movement for spiritual understanding and unity among Christians and their churches. The term is also extended to apply to efforts toward greater understanding and cooperation between Christians and members of other faiths.

Exarch/Exarchy

A church jurisdiction, similar to a diocese, established for Eastern-rite Catholics living outside their native land. The head of an exarchy, usually a bishop, is an *exarch*.

Hierarchy

In general, the term refers to the ordered body of clergy, divided into bishops, priests, and deacons. In Catholic practice, the term refers to the bishops of the world or of a particular region.

Holy Name Society

A lay organization which seeks to aid its members in living a genuinely Christian life. The society organizes retreats and other spiritual and devotional exercises.

Holy See

The term refers to the diocese of Rome. Used in reference to the governance of the Church, it refers to the Pontiff, the Roman Curia, and the Sacred College.

Legion of Mary

A lay organization established to assist the clergy in the sanctification of its members' souls, and the spread of the Christian faith and spiritual service to others. Members participate in almost every form of social service and Catholic action, including evangelization. The organization was founded in 1921.

Metropolitan

The archbishop of an archdiocese in a province. He has limited supervisory powers and influence over the other dioceses and bishops in the province.

Military Ordinariate [Archdiocese for the Military Services, U.S.A.]

A nonterritorial diocese for American Catholics and their dependents who are in the military or affiliated with the armed forces. Personnel employed by or engaged in diplomatic missions for the U.S. government in countries where U.S. military forces are stationed also belong to the Military Ordinariate.

Mission

A mission, or *quasi-parish,* is a parish which has not been established because it lacks one or more of the following qualifications: a resident pastor; necessary financial resources; territorial boundaries; or a natural grouping by way of rite, nationality, or language. Missions are attached to some parishes under the care of their pastors.

Moderator of the Curia

A bishop or priest, appointed by the diocesan bishop, who is concerned primarily with administrative matters and with supervising those working in the curia.

Monastery

An autonomous community house of a religious order, which may or may not be a monastic order. The term is used more specifically to refer to a community house of men religious or women religious in which they lead a contemplative life separate from the world.

Monsignor

An honorary ecclesiastical title granted by the Pope to some diocesan priests. In the United States, the title is given to the vicar general of a diocese. In Europe, the title is also given to bishops.

Newman Apostolate

An apostolate to the Catholic college and university community, now commonly known as "campus ministry."

Notary

An elected or appointed ecclesiastical official who acts as a secretary in formal church proceedings. The notary records the minutes, testimony, etc., of the proceedings.

Opus Dei

A personal prelature dedicated to spreading through society an awareness of the call to Christian virtue, awareness, and witness in one's life and work. The organization was founded in 1928 and in 1950, it received Vatican approval as a secular institution. In 1982, it was designated a personal prelature, the *Prelature of the Holy Cross and Opus Dei*. Members are not members of a religious order, do not take vows, and do not live in community.

Ordinary

Diocesan bishops, religious superiors, and certain other diocesan authorities with jurisdiction over the clergy in a specific geographical area, or the members of a religious order.

Ordination/Ordain

The sacramental rite by which a "sacred order" is conferred (diaconate, priesthood, episcopacy).

Papal Audience

Request for attendance at papal audiences and similar functions may be addressed to: Bishops' Office for United States Visitors to the Vatican. Postal address: North American College, Via dell 'Umilta 30, 00187 Rome, Italy. Tel.: 06-690-011; Fax: 011-39-06-679-1448. Rev. Msgr. Roger C. Roensch.

Papal Representatives

There are three types of representatives of the Roman Pontiff:
1) those who represent him to particular churches and civil government;
2) those who represent him to particular churches;
3) those who represent him in international organizations or at various conferences and meetings. [Cf. c. 363; CLSA Comm., p. 302]

1. Apostolic Nuncio

In the United States, the papal representative is sent by the Pope to both the local church and to the government. His title is Apostolic Nuncio.

2. Legate

An individual appointed by the Pope to be his personal representative to a nation, international conference, or local church. The legate may be chosen from the local clergy of a country.

3. Permanent Observer to the United Nations

The Apostolic See maintains permanent legates below the ambassadorial level to several world organizations. Since the papal representative does not enjoy the right to vote within the organization, his title at the United Nations is that of *Observer*.

Parish

A specific community of the Christian faithful within a diocese, which has its own church building, under the authority of a *pastor* who is responsible for providing them with ministerial service. Most parishes are formed on a geographic basis, but they may be formed along national or ethnic lines.

Parish Coordinator

A deacon, religious, or lay person who is responsible for the pastoral care of parish. The parish coordinator is in charge of the day-to-day life of the parish in the areas of worship, education, pastoral service and administration.

Pastor

A priest in charge of a parish or congregation. He is responsible for administering the sacraments, instructing the congregation in the doctrine of the Church, and other services to the people of the parish.

Pastoral Associate

A member of the laity who is part of a parish ministry team.

Pastoral Council

A consultative body which the pastor or bishop consults concerning the pastoral activity within the diocese. Its members include laity, religious, and clergy. The pastoral council's purpose is to study practical situations, difficulties and problems, and make concrete recommendations and proposals to the diocesan bishop. The pastoral council is always subject to the final authority of the pastor or bishop.

Patriarch

The Pope is the traditional "Patriarch of the West." All other bishops in the Latin Rite, even those with the honorary title of "Patriarch," are subject to him. Similarly, patriarchs within nations have only an honorary title unless special provisions are made otherwise. Eastern-rite Patriarchs are subject to the Pope while serving as heads of the faithful belonging to their rites throughout the world.

Personal Prelature

In addition to the territorial arrangement of the Church into particular or local churches or dioceses, canon law also provides for non-territorial areas of religious jurisdiction, incorporating secular clergy and deacons. Membership is also open to lay persons. These *prelatures* are established to meet specific pastoral or missionary needs at the regional, national, or international level without infringing on the rights of the local bishops. A prelature is presided over by a *personal prelate,* who is an ordinary with the right to establish seminaries and ordain priests as members of the prelature.

Canon law also allows for laity to be associated in the works of prelatures without being withdrawn from the jurisdiction of their own diocesan bishop.

Presbyteral Council

Also known as the *priests' council,* the presbyteral council is the principal consultative body mandated by the Code of Canon Law to advise the diocesan bishop in matters of pastoral governance. It consists of bishops and priests serving the diocese.

Propagation of the Faith

An organization, headquartered in Rome, which distributes aid to Catholic missions and organizes the work of missionaries all over the world. The organization has responsibility for fostering missionary vocations, assigning missionaries to field work, defining ecclesiastical boundaries and assigning clergy to them, and encouraging training and installation of native-born clergy.

Promoter of Justice

A cleric or lay person, holding a graduate degree in canon law, who is appointed by the diocesan bishop to serve in the role of a "prosecuting attorney" in trials of crimes against church law and of other judicial litigations in the diocese. A promoter of justice may be appointed for a specific case by the bishop.

Province

A defined geographic area containing an archdiocese, or *Metropolitan See,* and at least one diocese, or *Suffragen See.* The archbishop of the archdiocese has no direct powers over the Suffragen Sees, but does have limited advisory and appellate authority and obligations. The term also refers to a territorial grouping of particular churches or communities, or a territory of a religious order.

Provincial

The superior of the communities of a religious order that constitute a province.

Provincial Council

An assembly of the bishops of an ecclesiastical province, called by the metropolitan archbishop. The term is also used in reference to the provincial superior of a province, along with his or her chief advisors.

Receptions into the Church

Can take two forms: baptism of those not previously validly baptized, or "reception into full communion" with the Church for those who have already been baptized, in which case a profession of faith affects the reception.

Religious Priest/Diocesan Priest

Religious, or regular, priests are those who are professed members of a religious order or institute. Religious clergy live according to the rule of their respective orders. In pastoral ministry, they are under the jurisdiction of their local bishop, as well as the superiors of their order. Diocesan, or secular, priests are under the direction of their local bishop. They commit to serving their congregations and other institutions.

Retreat

A period of time spent in meditation and religious exercise. Retreats may take various forms, from traditional closed forms, to open retreats, which do not disengage the participants from day-to-day life. Both clergy and lay people of all ages participate in retreats. Houses and centers providing facilities for retreats are *retreat houses.*

Rite of Christian Initiation of Adults [RCIA]

The liturgical book containing the norms and rituals of the Catholic Church for people who wish to join the Church. Part of the book is intended for baptized Christians who wish to become Catholics. The term is used in a general sense to refer to the process of entering the Catholic Church.

Roman Curia

The official collective name for the administrative agencies and courts, and their officials, who assist the Pope in governing the Church. Members are appointed and granted authority by the Pope.

St. Vincent DePaul Society

Originally known as the *Conference of Charity,* this is an organization of lay people who serve the poor through spiritual and material works of mercy. The society operates stores, rehabilitation workshops, food centers, shelters, criminal justice and other programs.

Scholastic

A member of a religious order who has completed his novitiate, but has not yet been ordained.

Scholastic Teaching

Usually refers to Scholastic Philosophy, which is the basis for much Catholic Theology. It comes from the canonical "schools" of the 12th-13th centuries, St. Thomas Aquinas, St. Bonaventure, St. Albert the Great, etc., who developed "scholasticism" based mainly on Aristotle. It is the semi-official philosophy of the Church.

Secular Institute

Canonically erected institute of consecrated life for single laity and clerics who strive for the perfection of charity and work for the sanctification of the world while remaining in a lifestyle within the world.

See

The word is taken from the Latin word "sedes" ("seat"), and is used to denote a diocese or ecclesiastical district. The term *Holy See* is reserved to the diocese of Rome whose bishop is the Pope.

Seminary

An educational institution for men preparing for *Holy Orders*. The term originates from the time of St. Augustine, when those preparing for the priesthood were educated in the "cathedral school." During the Middle Ages, the clergy were educated in a university setting where faculties of philosophy, theology, and canon law existed. Eventually individual dioceses or provinces came to establish their own schools for educating their clerical students. Traditional seminaries date from the Council of Trent in the 16th century.

A school for the spiritual, academic, and pastoral education and formation of priesthood candidates is known as a *major seminary* in which the focus is on philosophical and theological education. To prepare for entrance into a major seminary, a period of study is set aside for the required courses in the humanities and the sciences in institutions called *minor seminaries*.

Serra Club

Local units of *Serra International,* an organization which promotes vocations to the priesthood and religious life, and offers instruction to lay leaders.

Sister

The term, in the strictest sense, refers to women religious who belong to institutes which have professed simple vows. However, in everyday usage, the term is used for any woman religious.

Sodality

A group of laity established for the promotion of Christian life and worship, or some other religious purpose.

Special Centers for Social Services

This would seem to overlap with Specialized Homes. Some of the categorization is fairly arbitrary. Catholic Charities might have its own proper distinctions for government or private funding purposes.

Specialized Homes

Includes such institutions as homes for handicapped (e.g., Misericordia Homes), youth homes (e.g., Maryville, Mercy Boys and Girls, Homes), homes for battered women, drug rehab centers, homes for unwed mothers, etc.

Superior

The head of a religious order or congregation. He or she may be the head of a province, or an individual house.

Synod

A gathering of designated officials and representatives of a church, that has legislative and policy-making powers.

1. Synod of Bishops

The Synod of Bishops is a consultative body, unless explicitly stated otherwise by His Holiness, expressing the communion of the hierarchy. A synod of bishops meets in general assembly, either in "Ordinary" or "Extraordinary" session, when the matter for treatment concerns the whole Church and in "Special Assembly" when the matter deals directly with a definite region or regions.

2. Synod of Oriental Churches

The synods of the Oriental Churches enjoy various prerogatives including the right to elect bishops, regulate discipline and exercise pastoral authority in their respective churches.

3. Diocesan Synod

A diocesan synod is an expression of the communion of the particular church. A diocesan synod enjoys the participation of priests, women and men religious and laypersons; the bishop is the sole legislator.

Theologate

An institution which provides the last four years of study for candidates for the priesthood.

Titular See

A former diocese which no longer physically or geographically exists. Titular Sees are given as an honorary title to certain bishop not serving as a chief pastor of a diocese, i.e., auxiliary bishops, papal representatives, and bishops of the Roman Curia.

Tribunal

A tribunal (court) is the name given to the person or persons who exercise the Church's judicial powers. By its very nature, this procedure involves the determination of a legal controversy. A major concern of tribunals is conducting the process leading to the dissolution or annulment of marriages. In ecclesiastical matters, definite procedural norms for conducting a trial are found in the Code of Canon Law to settle disputes. There are various grades of tribunals, including diocesan tribunals, the first court of trial for most cases; regional and metropolitan tribunals, located in an archdiocese, the appellate court for all cases tried within the province; and the tribunals of the Holy See, which act as the Church's central appellate court, try cases reserved to the Holy See, deal with questions of procedure and jurisdiction of the other courts, and act as the Church's supreme court.

United States Conference of Catholic Bishops

The United States Conference of Catholic Bishops is a permanent institute composed of Catholic bishops of the United States of America in and through which the bishops exercise in a communal or collegial manner the pastoral mission entrusted to them by the Lord Jesus of sanctification, teaching, and leadership, especially by devising forms and methods of the apostolate suitably adapted to the circumstances of the times. Such exercise is intended to offer appropriate assistance to each bishop in fulfilling his particular ministry in the local Church, to effect a commonality of ministry addressed to the people of the United States of America, and to foster and express communion with the Church in other nations within the Church universal, under the leadership of its chief pastor, The Pope.

Vicar

The appointment of a priest or a bishop as an *episcopal vicar* is an option given to a diocesan bishop when he needs a deputy for governing a specific territory within the diocese, a group of persons or a specific rite, or a type of apostolic work within the diocese.

By Church law, the diocesan bishop is the judge of all cases in the diocesan tribunal of first trial. He must appoint a priest with ordinary power to judge cases not reserved to the bishop himself. This priest must have a graduate degree in canon law. He is called the *judicial vicar,* and is sometimes referred to as the chief judge or officialis. He may be given another priest as an assistant with the title of *adjutant judicial vicar*.

A bishop or priest appointed to participate in the executive (administrative) governance of the diocese with executive jurisdiction as a deputy of the diocesan bishop is a *vicar general.* The appointment of a vicar general is mandatory for every diocese. This office is designed to facilitate and unify diocesan administration.

Vicar for Religious

A priest appointed by a bishop to act as his representative in dealing with the religious communities in his diocese.

Information for this glossary was taken from the *Catholic News Service's Stylebook on Religion,* the *Modern Catholic Dictionary,* published by Doubleday and Company, Inc., the *Concise Oxford Dictionary of the Christian Church,* published by Oxford University Press, and the *Encyclopedic Dictionary of Religion,* published by the Sisters of St. Joseph of Philadelphia. The publishers of the *Official Catholic Directory* also wish to thank the Vice Chancellors of the Archdiocese of Chicago for their work in the preparation of this glossary.

THE SUPREME ROMAN PONTIFFS

St. Peter of Bethsaida in Galilee, Prince of the Apostles, who received from Jesus Christ the Supreme Pontifical Power to be transmitted to his Successors, resided first at Antioch, then at Rome for twenty-five years where he was martyred in the year 64, or 67 of the common reckoning.

	END OF PONTIFICATE, A.D.
St. Linus	76
St. Anacletus or Cletus	88
St. Clement I	97
St. Evaristus	105
St. Alexander I	115
St. Sixtus I	125
St. Telesphorus	136
St. Hyginus	140
St. Pius I	155
St. Anicetus	166
St. Soterus	175
St. Eleuterius	189
St. Victor I	199
St. Zephyrinus	217
St. Callistus I	222
St. Urban I	230
St. Pontian	235
St. Anterus	236
St. Fabian	250
St. Cornelius	253
St. Lucius I	254
St. Stephen I	257
St. Sixtus II	258
St. Dionysius	268
St. Felix I	274
St. Eutychian	283
St. Caius	296
St. Marcellinus	304
St. Marcellus I	309
St. Eusebius	309
St. Melchiades	314
St. Sylvester I	335
St. Mark	336
St. Julius I	352
Liberius	366
St. Damasus I	384
St. Siricius	399
St. Anastasius I	401
St. Innocent I	417
St. Zozimus	418
St. Boniface I	422
St. Celestine I	432
St. Sixtus III	440
St. Leo I (the Great)	461
St. Hilary	468
St. Simplicius	483
St. Felix III or II	492
St. Gelasius I	496
Anastasius II	498
St. Symmacus	514
St. Hormisdas	523
St. John I	526
St. Felix IV or III	530
Boniface II	532
John II	535
St. Agapitus	536
St. Silverius	537
Vigilius	555
Pelagius I	561
John III	574
Benedict I	579
Pelagius II	590
St. Gregory I (the Great)	604
Sabinianus	606
Boniface III	607
St. Boniface IV	615
St. Deusdeditus or Adeodatus I	618
Boniface V	625
Honorius I	638
Severinus	640
John IV	642
Theodore I	649
St. Martin I	655
St. Eugene I	657
St. Vitalian	672
Adeodatus II	676
Donus I	678
St. Agathonus	681
St. Leo II	683
St. Benedict II	685
John V	686
Conon	687
St. Sergius I	701
John VI	705
John VII	707
Sisinnius	708
Constantine	715
St. Gregory II	731
St. Gregory III	741
St. Zachary	752
Stephen III	757
St. Paul I	767
Stephen IV	772
Adrian I	795
St. Leo III	816
Stephen V	817
St. Paschal I	824
Eugene II	827
Valentine	827
Gregory IV	844
Sergius II	847
St. Leo IV	855
Benedict III	858
St. Nicholas I (the Great)	867
Adrian II	872
John VIII	882
Marinus I	884
St. Adrian III	885
Stephen VI	891
Formosus	896
Boniface VI	896
Stephen VII	897
Romanus	897
Theodore II	897
John IX	900
Benedict IV	903
Leo V	903
Sergius III	911
Anastasius III	913
Landus	914
John X	928
Leo VI	928
Stephen VIII	931
John XI	935
Leo VII	939
Stephen IX	942
Marinus II	946
Agapitus II	955
John XII	964
Leo VIII	965
Benedict V	966
John XIII	972
Benedict VI	974
Benedict VII	983
John XIV	984
John XV	996
Gregory V	999
Sylvester II	1003
John XVII	1003
John XVIII	1009
Sergius IV	1012
Benedict VIII	1024
John XIX	1032
Benedict IX	1044
Benedict IX	1045
Sylvester III	1045
Gregory VI	1046
Clement II	1047
Benedict IX	1048
Damasus II	1048
St. Leo IX	1054
Victor II	1057
Stephen X	1058
Nicholas II	1061
Alexander II	1073
St. Gregory VII	1085
B. Victor III	1087
B. Urban II	1099
Paschal II	1118
Gelasius II	1119
Callistus II	1124
Honorius II	1130
Innocent II	1143
Celestine II	1144
Lucius II	1145
B. Eugene III	1153
Anastasius IV	1154
Adrian IV	1159
Alexander III	1181
Lucius III	1185
Urban III	1187
Gregory VIII	1187
Clement III	1191
Celestine III	1198
Innocent III	1216
Honorius III	1227
Gregory IX	1241
Celestine IV	1241
Innocent IV	1254
Alexander IV	1261
Urban IV	1264
Clement IV	1268
B. Gregory X	1276
B. Innocent V	1276
Adrian V	1276
John XXI	1277
Nicholas III	1280
Martin IV	1285
Honorius IV	1287
Nicholas IV	1292
St. Celestine V	1296
Boniface VIII	1303
B. Benedict XI	1304
Clement V	1314
John XXII	1334
Benedict XII	1342
Clement VI	1352
Innocent VI	1362
B. Urban V	1370
Gregory XI	1378
Urban VI	1389
Boniface IX	1404
Innocent VII	1406
Gregory XII	1415
Martin V	1431
Eugene IV	1447
Nicholas V	1455
Callistus III	1458
Pius II	1464
Paul II	1471
Sixtus IV	1484
Innocent VIII	1492
Alexander VI	1503
Pius III	1503
Julius II	1513
Leo X	1521
Adrian VI	1523
Clement VII	1534
Paul III	1549
Julius III	1555
Marcellus II	1555
Paul IV	1559
Pius IV	1565
St. Pius V	1572
Gregory XIII	1585
Sixtus V	1590
Urban VII	1590
Gregory XIV	1591
Innocent IX	1591
Clement VIII	1605
Leo XI	1605
Paul V	1621
Gregory XV	1623
Urban VIII	1644
Innocent X	1655
Alexander VII	1667
Clement IX	1669
Clement X	1676
B. Innocent XI	1689
Alexander VIII	1691
Innocent XII	1700
Clement XI	1721
Innocent XIII	1724
Benedict XIII	1730
Clement XII	1740
Benedict XIV	1758
Clement XIII	1769
Clement XIV	1774
Pius VI	1799
Pius VII	1823
Leo XII	1829
Pius VIII	1830
Gregory XVI	1846
Pius IX	1878
Leo XIII	1903
St. Pius X	1914
Benedict XV	1922
Pius XI	1939
Pius XII	1958
John XXIII	1963
Paul VI	1978
John Paul I	1978
John Paul II	now reigning.

PART I
Hierarchy of the Catholic Church

The Hierarchy, as the supreme governing body of the Catholic Church, consists of the Roman Pontiff, the successor of Peter, and the Bishops joined together with him and never without him (canons 330,331,336) in one apostolic college to provide for the common good of the Church. The Roman Pontiff in the exercise of his office is assisted by the College of Cardinals, and further by the departments also called "dicasteries" of the Roman Curia. The Bishops, of whom some bear the titles of Patriarch and Archbishop, are united with the Roman Pontiff in the governance of the whole Church; the Bishops, when assigned to particular Sees, are individually responsible for the teaching, sanctification and governance of their particular Church. Apostolic Vicars and Prefects together with certain Abbots and other Prelates are also joined in this work.

HIS HOLINESS THE POPE

Bishop of Rome and Vicar of Jesus Christ,
Successor of St. Peter, Prince of the Apostles,
Supreme Pontiff of the Universal Church.
Patriarch of the West
Primate of Italy.
Archbishop and Metropolitan of the Roman Province,
Servant of the Servants of God
Sovereign of Vatican City State.

JOHN PAUL II

KAROL WOJTYLA

The present successor of St. Peter was born in Wadowice, Diocese of Krakow, May 18, 1920; ordained Priest, November 1, 1946; appointed Titular Bishop of Ombi July 4, 1958; Promoted to Archbishop of Krakow, January 13, 1964; Proclaimed and created Cardinal June 26, 1967. Elected Pope, October 16, 1978; installed October 22, 1978.

VATICAN CITY

Vatican City is the smallest state in the world, occupying 108.7 acres, of which about one third is covered with buildings and is situated on the right side of the Tiber River. Vatican City has territory, population, and sovereignity. This territory, limited as it is, suffices to guarantee the spiritual and temporal independence needed for the exercise of the Holy See's spiritual mission. In 1870 the Kingdom of Italy seized all Vatican possessions which for several centuries had constituted the papal temporal domain. But even after 1870 the Holy See continued to regard itself as a separate entity in international law, and was recognized as such by numerous states with which it retained normal diplomatic relations. After long discussions the Holy See and the then Kingdom of Italy signed the Lateran Pacts on February 11, 1929, so that the complete and independent authority of the Vatican State was and is recognized by the Italian state.

The Sovereign of this small state is His Holiness, the Pope.

The government presently is administered by a Pontifical Commission of which His Eminence Edmund Casimir Cardinal Szoka is President.

THE COLLEGE OF CARDINALS

The Cardinals constitute a special college and they assist the Roman Pontiff collegially when they are called together to deal with questions of major importance; they do so individually when they assist the Pope especially in the daily care of the universal Church by means of the different offices which they perform (canons 349-350). The Cardinals who are under eighty years of age elect his successor.

The College of Cardinals is divided into three ranks: Cardinal-Bishops, Cardinal-Priests, and Cardinal-Deacons. The College of Cardinals, when complete formerly consisted of 70 members: 6 Cardinal Bishops, 50 Cardinal Priests and 14 Cardinal Deacons, but the late Pontiffs, Pope John XXIII and Pope Paul VI enlarged the College of Cardinals. At the moment the maximum number of Cardinal electors (those under 80 years of age) must not exceed 120.

The Cardinal Bishops (except the Patriarch-Cardinals of the Oriental Rites), have as Titular Sees the Suburban Sees of Rome, which are: Porto Santa Rufina, Albano, Palestrina, Sabina, Frascati, Velletri, Segni. The Cardinal Dean has united to his See the See of Ostia. The Cardinal Priests take their title from the Titular Churches to which they are appointed: the Cardinal Deacons are appointed to other Churches called Deaconries. The first Cardinal Bishop is Dean; the first Cardinal Priest is First Priest; and the first Cardinal Deacon is First Deacon of the Sacred College. The Dean has the right of ordaining the new Pope if he is not already a bishop; the First Deacon the right of proclaiming him and investing him with the sacred Pallium. On the death of the Pontiff, the Cardinal Camerlengo has the Administration of the affairs of the Holy See.

Sometimes the Roman Pontiff promotes a person to the dignity of Cardinal but does not make public his name and keeps it in pectore. Upon the publication of his name, this Cardinal enjoys his right of precedence from the day on which his name was reserved in pectore by the Pope (cfr. Can. 351¶ 3).

The Cardinals of the Holy Roman Church

(Listed in Alphabetical Order)

Agnelo, Geraldo Majella (Cardinal Priest), Titular of San Gregorio Magno alla Magliana Nuova, Archbishop of Sao Salvador da Bahia; born in Juiz de Fora, October 19, 1933. Created and proclaimed February 21, 2001. Address: Av. Cardenal da Silva 26, Casa 33-Federação, 40220-140 Salvador, BA, Brazil.

Agre, Bernard (Cardinal Priest), Titular of San Giovanni Crisostomo a Monte Sacro Alto, Archbishop of Abidjan; born in Monga, Archdiocese of Abidjan, March 2, 1926. Created and proclaimed February 21, 2001. Address: 01 B.P. 1287, Abidjan 01, Cote D'Ivoire.

Agustoni, Gilberto (Cardinal Deacon) Deacon of Ss. Urbano e Lorenzo a Primaporta, Prefect Emeritus of the Supreme Tribunal of the Apostolic Signatura; born in Schaffhausen, Switzerland, Diocese of Basel, July 26, 1922. Created and proclaimed November 26, 1994. Address: 00120 Vatican City State, Europe.

Alvarez Martinez, Francisco (Cardinal Priest), Titular of Santa Maria Regina Pacis a Monte Verde, Archbishop Emeritus of Toledo; born in Santa Eulalia de Ferrones Llanera, Archdiocese of Oviedo, July 14, 1925. Created and proclaimed February 21, 2001. Address: Calle Doctor Gómez Ulla 10, 3° drcha., 28028 Madrid, Spain.

Ambrozic, Aloysius Matthew (Cardinal Priest), Titular of Sts. Marcellinus and Peter, Archbishop of Toronto,

Canada; born in Gabrje, Archdiocese of Ljubljana, January 27, 1930. Created and proclaimed February 21, 1998. Address: Chancery Office, 1155 Yonge St., Toronto, M4T 1W2 Ontario, Canada.

Amigo Vallejo, Carlos, O.F.M., (Cardinal Priest), Titular of Santa Maria di Monserrato degli Spagnoli, Archbishop of Seville; born in Medina de Rioseco, Diocese of Valladolid, August 23, 1934. Created and proclaimed October 21, 2003. Address: Apartado 6, Plaza Virgen de los Reyes s/n, 41004 Sevilla, Spain.

Angelini, Fiorenzo (Cardinal Deacon), Deacon of S. Spirito in Sassia; President Emeritus of the Pontifical Council for Pastoral Assistance to Health Care Workers; born in Rome, Italy, August 1, 1916. Created and proclaimed June 28, 1991. Address: 00120 Vatican City State, Europe.

Antonelli, Ennio, (Cardinal Priest), Titular of Sant'Andrea delle Fratte, Archbishop of Florence; born in Todi, Diocese of Orvieto-Todi, November 18, 1936. Created and proclaimed October 21, 2003. Address: Arcivescovado, Piazza s. Giovanni 3, 50129 Firenze, Italy.

Antonetti, Lorenzo (Cardinal Deacon), Deacon of Saint Agnes in Agone; President Emeritus of the Administration of the Patrimony of the Apostolic See; born in Romagnano Sesia, diocese of Novara, July 31, 1922. Created and proclaimed February 21, 1998. Address: 00120 Vatican City State, Europe.

Aponte Martinez, Luis (Cardinal Priest), Titular of S. Maria Madre della Provvidenza a Monte Verde, Archbishop Emeritus of San Juan; born in Lajas, diocese of Mayaguez, August 4, 1922. Created and proclaimed March 5, 1973. Address: Urbanizacion San Ignacio, Calle San Alejandro 1763, San Juan, PR 00927-1967.

Aramburu, Juan Carlos (Cardinal Priest), Titular of San Giovanni Battista dei Fiorentini, Archbishop Emeritus of Buenos Aires; born in Reduccion, Diocese of Villa de la Concepcion del Rio Cuarto, February 11, 1912. Created and proclaimed May 24, 1976. Address: La Pampa 4022, C1430EXP Buenos Aires, Argentina.

Arinze, Francis (Cardinal Priest), Titular of San Giovanni della Pigna; Prefect of the Congregation for Divine Worship and the Discipline of the Sacraments; born in Eziowelle, Archdiocese of Onitsha, November 1, 1932. Created and proclaimed May 25, 1985. Address: Largo del Colonnato 3, 00193 Rome, Italy.

Arns, Paul Evaristo, o.f.m. (Cardinal Priest), Titular of S. Antonio da Padova in Via Tuscolana, Archbishop Emeritus of Sao Paulo; born in Forquilhinha, Diocese of Tubarao, September 14, 1921. Created and proclaimed March 5, 1973. Address: C.P. 916, Rua Antonietta Altenfelder 1000, 02717-170, Sao Paulo, SP, Brazil.

Backis, Audrys Juozas (Cardinal Priest), Titular of Nativita di Nostro Signore Gesu Cristo a Via Gallia, Archbishop of Vilnius; born in Kaunas February 1, 1937. Created and proclaimed February 21, 2001. Address: Sventaragio 4, 2001 Vilnius, Lithuania.

Bafile, Corrado (Cardinal Priest), Titular of Santa Maria in Portico; born in L'Aquila, July 4, 1903. Created and proclaimed May 24, 1976. Address: Via P. Pancrazio Pfeiffer 10, 00193 Rome, Italy.

Barbarin, Philippe Xavier Ignace, (Cardinal Priest), Titular of Santissima Trinita al Monte Pincio, Archbishop of Lyon; born in Rabat, Morocco, October 17, 1950. Created and proclaimed October 21, 2003. Address: Archeveche, 1 Place de Fourviere, 69321 Lyon, Cedex 05, France.

Baum, William Wakefield (Cardinal Priest), Titular of Santa Croce in Via Flaminia; Major Penitentiary Emeritus; born in Dallas, Texas, November 21, 1926. Created and proclaimed, May 24, 1976. Address: Via Rusticucci 13, 00193 Rome, Italy

Bergoglio, Jorge Mario, S.J. (Cardinal Priest), Titular of San Roberto Bellarmino, Archbishop of Buenos Aires; born in Buenos Aires, December 17, 1936. Created and proclaimed February 21, 2001. Address: Arzobispado, Av. Rivadavia 415, C1002AAC Buenos Aires, Argentina.

Bertone, Tarcisio, S.D.B., (Cardinal Priest), Titular of Santa Maria Ausiliatrice in via Tuscolana, Archbishop of Genova; born in Romano Canavese, Italy, December 2, 1934. Created and proclaimed October 21, 2003. Address: Piazza Matteotti 4, 16123 Genova, Italy.

Bevilacqua, Anthony J. (Cardinal Priest), Titular of SS. Redentore e S. Alfonso in Via Merulana, Archbishop Emeritus of Philadelphia; born in Brooklyn, New York, June 17, 1923. Created and proclaimed June 28, 1991. Address: 100 East Wynnewood Road, Wynnewood, PA 19096.

Biffi, Giacomo (Cardinal Priest), Titular of Ss. Giovanni Evangelista e Petronio, Archbishop Emeritus of Bologna; born in Milan, June 13, 1928. Created and proclaimed May 25, 1985. Address: Arcivescovado, Via Altabella 6, 40126 Bologna, Italy.

Bozanic, Josip, (Cardinal Priest), Titular of San Girolamo dei Croati, Archbishop of Zagreb; born in Rijeka, Croatia, March 20, 1949. Created and proclaimed October 21, 2003. Address: Nadbiskupski Duhovni Stol, Kaptol 21, p.p. 553, 10001 Zagreb, Croatia.

Cacciavillan, Agostino (Cardinal Deacon), Deacon of Santi Angeli Custodi a Citta Giardino, President Emeritus of Administration of the Patrimony of the Apostolic See; born in Novale, Diocese of Vincenza, August 14, 1926. Created and proclaimed February 21, 2001. Address: 00120 Vatican City State, Europe.

Canestri, Giovanni (Cardinal Priest), Titular of St. Andrea della Valle, Archbishop Emeritus of Genoa; born in Castelspina, Diocese of Alessandria, September 30 1918. Created and proclaimed June 28, 1988. Address: Via Cernaia 9, 00185 Rome, Italy.

Caprio, Giuseppe (Cardinal Priest), Titular of S. Maria della Vittoria; born in Lapio, Archdiocese of Benevento, November 15, 1914. Created and proclaimed June 30, 1979. Address: 00120 Vatican City State, Europe.

Carles Gordo, Ricardo Maria (Cardinal Priest), Titular of S. Maria Consolatrice al Tiburtino, Archbishop of Barcelona, Spain; born in Valencia, September 24, 1926. Created and proclaimed November 26, 1994, Address: Arzobispado, Carrer del Bisbe 5, 08002 Barcelona, Spain.

Cassidy, Edward I. (Cardinal Priest), Titular of S. Maria in Via Lata, President Emeritus of the Pontifical Council for Promoting Christian Unity; born in Sydney, Australia, July 5, 1924. Created and proclaimed June 28, 1991. Address: 16 Coachwood Dr., Warabrook, NSW 2304, Australia.

Castillo Lara, Rosalio Jose, s.d.b. (Cardinal Priest), Titular of Nostra Signora di Coromoto in S. Giovanni di Dio, President Emeritus of the Pontifical Commission for Vatican City State; born in San Casimiro, Diocese of Maracay, September 4, 1922. Created and proclaimed May 25, 1985. Address: San Casimiro, Edo. Aragua, Venezuela.

Castrillon Hoyos, Dario (Cardinal Deacon), Deacon of the Most Holy Name of Mary at Trajan's Forum, Prefect of the Congregation of Clergy & President of the Pontifical Commission Ecclesia Dei ; born in Medellin July 4, 1929. Created and proclaimed February 21, 1998. Address: 00120 Vatican City State, Europe.

Ce', Marco (Cardinal Priest), Titular of S. Marco, Patriarch Emeritus of Venice; born in Izano, Diocese of Crema, July 8, 1925. Created and proclaimed June 30, 1979. Address: Dorsoduro 2807, 30123 Venezia, Italy.

Cheli, Giovanni (Cardinal Deacon), Deacon of Ss. Cosmos and Damian at Via Sacra, President Emeritus of the Pontifical Council for the Pastoral Care of Migrants and Itinerant People; born in Torino, October 4 1918. Created and proclaimed February 21, 1998. Address: Piazza S. Calisto 16, 00153 Rome, Italy.

Cipriani Thorne, Juan Luis (Cardinal Priest), Titular of San Camillo di Lellis, Archbishop of Lima; born in Lima, December 28, 1943. Created and proclaimed February 21, 2001. Address: Calle Los Nogales 249, San Isidro, Lima 27, Peru.

Clancy, Edward Bede (Cardinal Priest), Titular of S. Maria in Vallicella, Archbishop Emeritus of Sydney; born in Lithgow, Diocese of Bathurst, December 13, 1923. Created and proclaimed June 28, 1988. Address: 54 Cranbrook Rd., Bellevue Hall, NSW 2023, Australia.

Connell, Desmond (Cardinal Priest), Titular of San Silvestro in Capite, Archbishop of Dublin; born in Dublin, March 24, 1926. Created and proclaimed February 21, 2001. Address: Archbishop's House, Drumcondra, Dublin 9, Ireland.

Corripio Ahumada, Ernesto (Cardinal Priest), Titular dell'Immacolata al Tiburtino, Archbishop Emeritus of Mexico City; born in Tampico, June 29, 1919. Address: Calle 5 n.54, Colonia Ampliacion Tepepan, 16029, Mexico D.F. Mexico.

Cottier, Georges Marie Martin, O.P., (Cardinal Deacon), Deacon of Santi Domenico e Sisto, Theologian of the Pontifical Household; born in Carouge, Diocese of Laussane, Geneve et Fribourg, April 25, 1922. Created and proclaimed October 21, 2003. Address: 00120 Vatican City State, Europe.

da Cruz Policarpo, José (Cardinal Priest), Titular of Sant'Antonio in Campo Marzio, Patriarch of Lisbon; born in Alvorninha, Patriarchate of Lisbon, February 26, 1936. Created and proclaimed February 21, 2001. Address: Casa Patriarcal, Quinta do Cabeço, Rua do Seminário, 1885 – 076 Moscavide, Portugal.

Daly, Cahal Brendan (Cardinal Priest), Titular of S. Patrizio, Archbishop Emeritus of Armagh; born in Loughguile, Diocese of Down and Connor, October 1, 1917. Created and proclaimed June 28, 1991. Address: Ard Mhacha, 23 Rosetta Avenue, Belfast BT7 3HG, Ireland.

Danneels, Godfried (Cardinal Priest), Titular of S. Anastasia, Archbishop of Malines-Bruxelles; born in Kanegem, Diocese of Brugge, June 4, 1933. Created and proclaimed February 2, 1983. Address: Aartsbisdom, Wollemarkt 15, B-2800 Mechelen, Belgium.

Daoud, Ignace Moussa I (Cardinal Bishop), Prefect of the Congregation for the Oriental Churches; born in Meskane, Archeparchy of Homs of the Syrians, September 18, 1930. Created and proclaimed February 21, 2001. Address: 00120 Vatican City State, Europe.

Darmaatmadja, Julius Riyadi, s.j. (Cardinal Priest), Titular of S. Cuore di Maria, Archbishop of Jakarta, Indonesia; born in Muntilan, Archdiocese of Semarang, December 20, 1934. Created and proclaimed November 26, 1994. Address: Keuskupan Agung, Jl. Katedral 7, Jakarta 10710, Indonesia.

De Giorgi, Salvatore (Cardinal Priest), Titular of S. Maria in Ara Coeli, Archbishop of Palermo; born in Vernole, Archdiocese of Lecce, September 6, 1930. Created and proclaimed February 21, 1998. Address: Via Matteo Bonello 2, 90134 Palermo, Italy.

Deskur, Andrzej Maria (Cardinal Priest), Titular of S. Cesareo in Palatio; born in Sancygniow, Diocese of Kielce, February 29, 1924. Created and proclaimed May 25, 1985. Address: 00120 Vatican City State, Europe.

Dias, Ivan (Cardinal Priest), Titular of Spirito Santo alla Ferratella, Archbishop of Bombay; born in Mumbai, April 14, 1936. Created and proclaimed February 21, 2001. Address: 21 Nathalal Parekh Marg, Mumbai-400001, India.

do Nascimento, Alexandre (Cardinal Priest), Titular of San Marco in Agro Laurentino, Archbishop Emeritus of Luanda; born in Malanje, Angola, March 1, 1925. Created and proclaimed February 2, 1983. Address: Arcebispado, C.P. 87, 1230-C. Luanda, Angola.

Dulles, Avery, S.J. (Cardinal Deacon), Deacon of Santissimi Nomi di Gesu e Maria in Via Lata; born in Auburn, Diocese of Rochester, August 24, 1918. Created and proclaimed February 21, 2001. Address: Fordham University, 441 E. Fordham Rd., Bronx, NY 10458.

Egan, Edward M. (Cardinal Priest), Titular of Santi Giovanni e Paolo, Archbishop of New York; born in Oak Park, Archdiocese of Chicago, February 4, 1932. Created and proclaimed February 21, 2001. Address: 1011 First Ave., New York, NY 10022.

Erdõ, Péter, (Cardinal Priest), Titular of Santa Balbina, Archbishop of Esztergom-Budapest; born in Budapest, June 25, 1952. Created and proclaimed October 21, 2003. Office: Primasi es Erseki Hivatal, Uri utca 62, H-1014 Budapest, Hungary.

Errázuriz Ossa, Francisco Javier (Cardinal Priest), Titular of Santa Maria della Pace, Archbishop of Santiago de Chile; born in Santiago de Chile, September 4, 1933. Created and proclaimed February 21, 2001. Address: Simon Bolivar 2845, Santiago, Chile.

Etchegaray, Roger (Cardinal Bishop), Titular of the suburbicarian church of Porto-Santa Rufina, President Emeritus of the Pontifical Council for Justice and Peace; born in Espelette, Diocese of Bayonne, September 25, 1922. Created and proclaimed June 30, 1979. Address: Piazza San Calisto 16, 00153 Rome, Italy.

Etsou-Nzabi-Bamungwabi, Frederic, C.I.C.M. (Cardinal Priest), Titular of S. Lucia a Piazza d'Armi, Archbishop of Kinshasa; born in Mazalonga, Diocese of Lisala, December 3, 1930. Created and proclaimed June 28, 1991. Address: Archeveche, B.P. 8431, Kinshasa 1, Democratic Republic of Congo.

Falcao, Jose Freire (Cardinal Priest), Titular of S. Luca a Via Prenestina, Archbishop Emeritus of Brasilia; born in Erere, Diocese of Limoeiro do Norte, October 23, 1925. Created and proclaimed June 28, 1988. Address: QL 12-Cj12, Lote 1, Lago Sul, 71630-325 Brasilia, D.F., Brazil.

Felici, Angelo (Cardinal Priest), Titular of Ss. Biagio e Carlo ai Catinari, President Emeritus of the Pontifical Commission Ecclesia Dei ; born in Segni, July 26, 1919. Created and proclaimed June 28, 1988. Address: Piazza della Citta Leonina 9, 00193 Rome, Italy.

Fernandes de Araujo, Serafim (Cardinal Priest), Titular of S. Luigi Maria Grignion de Montfort, Archbishop Emeritus of Belo Horizonte, Brazil; born in Minas Novas, Diocese of Aracuai, August 13, 1924. Created and proclaimed February 21, 1998. Address: Praça da Liberdade 263, Bairro Funcionários, 30140-010 Belo Horizonte, MG, Brazil.

Fresno Larrain, Juan Francisco (Cardinal Priest), Titular of S. Maria Immacolata di Lourdes a Boccea, Archbishop Emeritus of Santiago de Chile; born in Santiago de Chile on July 26, 1914. Created and proclaimed May 25, 1985. Address: Echaurren 4, Casilla 13520, Correo 21, Santiago, Chile.

Furno, Carlo (Cardinal Deacon), Deacon of S. Cuore di Cristo Re, Grand Master of the Equestrian Order of the Holy Sepulchre of Jerusalem, Archpriest of the Patriarchal Liberian Basilica of St. Mary Major; born in Bairo Canavese, Diocese of Ivrea, December 2, 1921. Created and proclaimed November 26, 1994. Address: Piazza della Citta Leonina 1, 00193 Rome, Italy.

Gagnon, Edouard, p.s.s. (Cardinal Priest), Titular of S. Marcello; President Emeritus of the Pontifical Committee for International Eucharistic Congresses; born in Port-Daniel, Diocese of Gaspe, January 15, 1918. Created and proclaimed May 25, 1985. Address: 116 Rue Notre - Dame Ouest, Montreal, Q.C. H2Y 1T2, Canada.

Gantin, Bernardin (Cardinal Bishop), Titular of the suburbicarian church of Palestrina, Prefect Emeritus of the Congregation for the Bishops and President Emeritus of the Pontifical Commission for Latin America; Dean Emeritus of the College of Cardinals; born in Toffo, Archdiocese of Cotonou, May 8, 1922. Created and proclaimed June 27, 1977. Address: 01 B.P. 752 – Recette Principale, Cotonou, Bénin.

George, Francis E., o.m.i. , (Cardinal Priest) Titular of S. Bartolomeo all'Isola, Archbishop of Chicago; born in Chicago, Illinois, U.S.A., January 16, 1937. Created and proclaimed February 21, 1998. Address: Post Office Box 1979, Chicago, IL 60690.

Ghattas, Stéphanos II, C.M. (Cardinal Bishop), Patriarch of Alexandria of the Copts; born in Cheikh Zeinel-Dine, Eparchy of Sohag, January 16, 1920. Created and proclaimed February 21, 2001. Address: Patriarcat Copte Catholique, B.P. 69, 34 Rue Ibn Sandar, Pont de Koubbeh, 11712 Le Caire, Egypt.

Giordano, Michele (Cardinal Priest), Titular of S. Gioacchino ai Prati di Castello, Archbishop of Naples; born in S. Arcangelo, Diocese of Tursi-Lagonegro, September 26, 1930. Created and proclaimed June 28, 1988. Address: Largo Donnaregina 23, 80138 Napoli, Italy.

Glemp, Jozef (Cardinal Priest), Titular of S. Maria in Trastevere, Archbishop of Warsaw; born in Inowroclaw, Archdiocese of Gniezno, December 18, 1929. Created and proclaimed February 2, 1983. Address: ul. Miodowa 17-19, 00-246 Warsaw, Poland.

Gonzalez Martin, Marcelo (Cardinal Priest), Titular of S. Agostino, Archbishop Emeritus of Toledo; born in Villanubla, Archdiocese of Valladolid, January 16, 1918. Created and proclaimed March 5, 1973. Address: Residencia Madre Genoveva, Avda. de Francia 6, 45005 Toledo, Spain.

González Zumárraga, Antonio José (Cardinal Priest), Titular of Santa Maria in Via, Archbishop Emeritus of Quito; born in Pujili, Diocese of Latacunga, March 18, 1925. Created and proclaimed February 21, 2001. Address: Apartado 17-01-00106, Calle Chile 1140, Quito, Ecuador.

Grocholewski, Zenon (Cardinal Deacon), Deacon of San Nicola in Carcere, Prefect of the Congregation for Catholic Education; born in Brodki, Archdiocese of Poznan, October 11, 1939. Created and proclaimed February 21, 2001. Address: 00120 Vatican City State, Europe.

Gulbinowicz, Henryk Roman (Cardinal Priest), Titular dell'Immacolata Concezione di Maria a Grottarossa, Archbishop of Wroclaw; born in Sukiskes, Archdiocese of Vilnius, October 17, 1928. Created and proclaimed May 25, 1985. Address: ul. Katedralna 11, 50-328 Wroclaw, Poland.

Hamao, Stephen Fumio, (Cardinal Deacon), Deacon of San Giovanni Bosco in via Tuscolana, President of the Pontifical Council for the Pastoral Care of Migrants and Itinerant Peoples; born in Tokyo, March 9, 1930. Created and proclaimed October 21, 2003. Address: 00120 Vatican City State, Europe.

Herranz Casado, Julian, (Cardinal Deacon), Deacon of Sant' Eugenio, President of the Pontifical Council for the Interpretation of Legislative Texts; born in Baena, Spain, March 31, 1930. Created and proclaimed October 21, 2003. Address: 00120 Vatican City State, Europe.

Hickey, James Aloysius (Cardinal Priest), Titular of Maria Madre del Redentore a Tor Bella Monaca, Archbishop Emeritus of Washington; born in Midland, Michigan, Diocese of Saginaw, October 11, 1920. Created and proclaimed June 28, 1988. Address: Archdiocesan Pastoral Center, 5001 Eastern Ave., P.O. Box 29260, Washington, DC 20017, U.S.A.

Honoré, Jean (Cardinal Priest), Titular of Santa Maria della Salute a Primavalle, Archbishop Emeritus of Tours; born in Saint-Brice-en-Cogles, Archdiocese of Rennes, August 13, 1920. Created and proclaimed February 21, 2001. Address: 1 Allee de la Rocaille, 37390 La Membrolle-sur-Choisille, France.

Hummes, Claudio, O.F.M. (Cardinal Priest), Titular of Sant' Antonio da Padova in Via a Merulana, Archbishop of Sao Paulo; born in Montenegro, Archdiocese of Porto Alegre, August 8, 1934. Created and proclaimed February 21, 2001. Address: Rua Alfredo Maia 195, Luz, 01106-010 Sao Paulo, SP, Brazil.

Husar, Lubomyr, M.S.U. (Cardinal Priest), Titular of Santa Sofia a Via Boccea, Major Archbishop of Lviv of the Ukrainians; born in Lviv, February 26, 1933. Created and proclaimed February 21, 2001. Address: Ploscha Sviatoho Jura 5, 79000 Lviv, Ukraine.

Innocenti, Antonio (Cardinal Priest), Titular of S. Maria in Aquiro, born in Poppi, Diocese of Fiesole, August 23, 1915. Created and proclaimed May 25, 1985. Address: Piazza della Citta Leonina 9, 00193 Rome, Italy.

Javierre Ortas, Antonio Maria, s.d.b. (Cardinal Priest), Titular of S. Maria Liberatrice a Monte Testaccio, Prefect Emeritus of Congregation for Divine Worship and the Discipline of the Sacraments; born at Sietamo, Diocese of Huesca, February 21, 1921. Created and proclaimed June 28, 1988. Address: Via Rusticucci 13, 00193 Rome, Italy.

Jaaworski, Marian, (Cardinal Priest), Titular of St. Sisto, Archbishop of Lviv of the Latins; born in Lviv August 21, 1026. Created and reserved in pectore February 21, 1998; proclaimed February 21, 2001. Address: Pl. Katedralny 1, 79008 Lviv, Ukraine.

Joos, Gustaaf, (Cardinal Deacon), Deacon of San Pier Damiani ai Monti di San Paolo; born in Sint-Niklaas, Diocese of Gent, July 5, 1923. Created and proclaimed October 21, 2003. Address: c/o Diocese of Gent, Bisdomplein 1, 9000 Gent, Belgium.

Kasper, Walter (Cardinal Deacon), Deacon of Ognissanti in Via Appia Nuova, President of the Pontifical Council for Promoting Christian Unity; born in Heidenheim/Brenz, Diocese of Rottenburg-Stuttgart, March 5, 1933. Created and proclaimed February 21, 2001. Address: 00120 Vatican City State, Europe.

Keeler, William Henry (Cardinal Priest), Titular of S. Maria degli Angeli, Archbishop of Baltimore; born in San Antonio, Texas, March 4, 1931. Created and proclaimed November 26, 1994. Address: 320 Cathedral Street, Baltimore, Maryland 21201. U.S.A.

Kim, Stephen Sou Hwan (Cardinal Priest), Titular of S. Felice da Cantalice a Centocelle, Archbishop Emeritus of Seoul; born in Tae Gu, May 8, 1922. Created and proclaimed April 28, 1969. Address: Episcopal Residence, Seoul Catholic University, 90-1 Hyehwadong, Chongro-Ku, Seoul 110-758, Korea.

Kitbunchu, Michael Michai (Cardinal Priest), Titular of S. Lorenzo in Panisperna, Archbishop of Bangkok; born in Samphran, Archdiocese of Bangkok, January 25, 1929. Created and proclaimed February 2, 1983. Address: Assumption Cathedral, 51 Oriental Ave., Bangkok 10500, Thailand.

Konig, Franz (Cardinal Priest), Titular of S. Eusebio, Archbishop Emeritus of Vienna; born in Rabenstein, Diocese of St. Poelten, August 3, 1905. Created and proclaimed December 15, 1958. Address: Wollzeile 2, A-1010 Wien, Austria.

Korec, Jan Chryzostom, s.j. , (Cardinal Priest), Titular of Ss. Fabiano e Venanzio a Villa Fiorelli, Bishop of Nitra; born in Bosany, Diocese of Nitra, January 22, 1924. Created and proclaimed June 28, 1991. Address: Biskupsky urad, post. schranka 46A, 950 50 Nitra, Slovakia.

Kozlowiecki, Adam, s.j. , (Cardinal Priest), Titular of S. Andrea al Quirinale; born in Huta Komorowska, Diocese of Sandomierz, April 1, 1911. Created and proclaimed February 21, 1998. Address: P.O. Box 80858, Kabwe, Zambia.

Laghi, Pio (Cardinal Priest), Titular of San Pietro in Vincoli; Prefect Emeritus of the Congregation for Catholic Education; born in Castiglione, Diocese of Forli-Bertinoro, May 21, 1922. Created and proclaimed June 28, 1991. Address: Piazza della Citta Leonina 1, 00193 Roma, Italy, Europe.

Law, Bernard Francis (Cardinal Priest), Titular of S. Susanna, Archbishop Emeritus of Boston; born in Torreon, November 4, 1931. Created and proclaimed May 25, 1985. Address: 2101 Commonwealth Ave., Brighton, MA 02135, U.S.A.

Lehmann, Karl (Cardinal Priest), Titular of San Leone I, Bishop of Mainz; born in Sigmaringen, Archdiocese of Freiburg im Breisgau, May 16, 1936. Created and proclaimed February 21, 2001. Address: Bischofsplatz 2A, D-55116 Mainz, Germany.

Lopez Rodriguez, Nicolas de Jesus (Cardinal Priest), Titular of S. Pio X alla Balduina, Archbishop of Santo Domingo; born in Barranca, Diocese of La Vega, October 31, 1936. Created and proclaimed June 28, 1991. Address: Calle Pellerano Alfau 1, Ciudad Colonial, Santo Domingo, Dominican Republic.

Lopez Trujillo, Alfonso (Cardinal Bishop), Titular of the Suburbicarian Church of Frascati, President of the Pontifical Council for the Family; born in Villahermosa, Diocese of Libano-Honda, November 8, 1935. Created and proclaimed February 2, 1983. Address: Piazza S. Calisto 16, 00153 Rome, Italy.

Lorscheider, Aloisio, o.f.m. (Cardinal Priest), Titular of San Pietro in Montorio, Archbishop Emeritus of Aparecida; born in Estrela, Archdiocese of Porto Alegre, October 8, 1924. Created and proclaimed May 24, 1976. Address: Curia Metropolitana, Rua Barao do Rio Branco 412, Centro, C.P. 82, 12570-970, Aparecida, S.P., Brazil.

Lourdusamy, D. Simon (Cardinal Priest), Titular of S. Maria delle Grazie alle Fornaci fuori Porta Cavalleggeri; born in Kalleri, Archdiocese of Pondicherry and Cuddalore, February 5, 1924. Created and proclaimed May 25, 1985. Address: Via dei Corridori 64, 00193 Rome, Italy.

Lozano Barragan, Javier, (Cardinal Deacon), Deacon of San Michele Arcangelo, President of the Pontifical Council for Pastoral Assistance to Health Care Workers; born in Toluca, Mexico, January 26, 1933. Created and proclaimed October 21, 2003. Address: 00120 Vatican City State, Europe.

Lustiger, Jean-Marie (Cardinal Priest), Titular of S. Luigi dei Francesi, Archbishop of Paris; born in Paris, September 17, 1926. Created and proclaimed February 2, 1983. Address: 32 Rue Barbet de Jouy, 75007 Paris Cedex, France.

Macharski, Franciszek (Cardinal Priest), Titular of S. Giovanni a Porta Latina, Archbishop of Krakow; born in Krakow, May 20, 1927. Created and proclaimed June 30, 1979. Address: ul. Franciszkanska 3, 31-004 Krakow, Poland.

Mahony, Roger M. (Cardinal Priest), Titular of Ss. Quattro Coronati, Archbishop of Los Angeles; born in Hollywood, California, Archdiocese of Los Angeles, February 27, 1936. Created and proclaimed June 28, 1991. Address: 3424 Wilshire Blvd,. Los Angeles, CA 90010-2241, U.S.A.

Maida, Adam Joseph (Cardinal Priest), Titular of Ss. Vitale, Valeria, Gervasio e Protasio, Archbishop of Detroit; born in East Vandergrift, Pennsylvania, Diocese of Greensburg, March 18, 1930. Created and proclaimed November 26, 1994. Address: 1234 Washington Blvd., Detroit, Michigan 48226, U.S.A.

Marchisano, Francesco, (Cardinal Deacon), Deacon of Santa Lucia del Gonfalone, Archpriest of the Vatican Basilica; born in Racconigi, Italy, June 25, 1929. Created and proclaimed October 21, 2003. Address: 00120 Vatican City State, Europe.

Margeot, Jean (Cardinal Priest), Titular of S. Gabriele Arcangelo all' Acqua Traversa, Bishop Emeritus of Port-Louis; born at Quatre-Bornes, Diocese of Port Louis, February 3, 1916. Created and proclaimed June 28, 1988. Address: Bonne-Terre, Vavoas, Ile Maurice.

Martinez Somalo, Eduardo (Cardinal Priest), Titular of SS. Nome di Gesu', Prefect Emeritus of the Congregation for Institutes of Consecrated Life and for Societies of Apostolic Life, Chamberlain of the Holy Roman Church; born at Banos de Rio Tobia, Diocese of Calahorra y La Calzada-Logrono, March 31, 1927. Created and proclaimed June 28, 1988. Address: 00120 Vatican City State, Europe.

Martini, Carlo Maria, s.j. (Cardinal Priest), Titular of S. Cecilia, Archbishop Emeritus of Milan; born in Turin, February 15, 1927. Created and proclaimed February 2, 1983. Address: Pontifical Biblical Institute, P.O. Box 497, 91006 Jerusalem, Israel.

Martino, Renato Raffaele, (Cardinal Deacon), Deacon of San Francesco di Paola ai Monti, President of the Pontifical Council for Justice and Peace; born in Salerno, Italy, November 23, 1932. Created and proclaimed October 21, 2003. Address: 00120 Vatican City State, Europe.

Mayer, Paul Augustin, o.s.b. (Cardinal Priest), Titular of S. Anselmo all' Aventino; born in Altotting, Diocese of Passau, May 23, 1911. Created and proclaimed May 25, 1985. Address: Via Rusticucci 13, 00193 Rome, Italy.

McCarrick, Theodore E. (Cardinal Priest), Titular of Santi Nereo e Achilleo, Archbishop of Washington; born in New York, July 7, 1930. Created and proclaimed February 21, 2001. Address: P.O. Box 29260, Washington, DC 20017.

Medina Estevez, Jorge Arturo (Cardinal Deacon), Deacon of St. Saba, Prefect Emeritus of the Congregation for Divine Worship and the Discipline of the Sacraments; born in Santiago de Chile, December 23, 1926. Created and proclaimed February 21, 1998. Address: 00120 Vatican City State, Europe.

Meisner, Joachim (Cardinal Priest), Titular of S. Pudenziana, Archbishop of Cologne; born in Breslau, December 25, 1933. Created and proclaimed February 2, 1983. Address: Kardinal-Frings-Strasse 10, D-50668 Koln 1, Germany.

Mejía, Jorge María (Cardinal Deacon), Deacon of San Girolamo della Carita, Librarian Emeritus and Archivist Emeritus of the Holy Roman Church; born in Buenos Aires, January 31, 1923. Created and proclaimed February 21, 2001. Address: 00120 Vatican City State, Europe.

Monduzzi, Dino (Cardinal Deacon), Deacon of S. Sebastiano al Palatino, Prefect Emeritus of the Papal Household; born in Brisighella, Diocese of Faenza-Modigliana, April 2, 1922. Created and proclaimed February 21, 1998. Address: 00120 Vatican City State, Europe.

Murphy-O'Connor, Cormac (Cardinal Priest), Titular of Santa Maria sopra Minerva, Archbishop of Westminster; born in Reading, Diocese of Portsmouth, August 24, 1932. Created and proclaimed February 21, 2001. Address: Ambrosden Avenue, Westminster, London SW1P 1QJ England.

Nagy, Stanislaw, S.C.I., (Cardinal Deacon), Deacon of Santa Maria della Scala; born in Bieru, Archdiocese of Katowice, September 30, 1921. Created and proclaimed October 21, 2003. Address: c/o University of Lublin, AL. Racawickie, 14, 20-950 Lublin, Poland.

Napier, Wilfrid Fox, O.F.M. (Cardinal Priest), Titular of San Francesco d'Assisi ad Acilia, Archbishop of Durban; born in Swartberg, Diocese of Kokstad, March 8, 1941. Created and proclaimed February 21, 2001. Address: 154 Gordon Rd., Durban 4001, Kwazulu-Natal, South Africa.

Nicora, Attilio, (Cardinal Deacon), Deacon of San Filippo Neri in Eurosia, President of the Administration of the Patrimony of the Apostolic See; born in Varese, Italy, March 16, 1937. Created and proclaimed October 21, 2003. Address: 00120 Vatican City State, Europe.

Noe', Virgilio (Cardinal Priest), Titular of Regina Apostolorum, Vicar General Emeritus of His Holiness for Vatican City State, Archpriest Emeritus of St. Peter Basilica; born in Zelata di Bereguardo, Diocese of Pavia, March 30, 1922. Created and proclaimed June 28, 1991. Address: 00120 Vatican City State, Europe.

Obando Bravo, Miguel, s.d.b. (Cardinal Priest), Titular of S. Giovanni Evangelista a Spinaceto, Archbishop of Managua; born in La Libertad, Diocese of Juigalpa, February 2, 1926. Created and proclaimed May 25, 1985. Address: Arzobispado, Apartado 2008, Managua, Nicaragua.

O'Brien, Keith Michael Patrick, (Cardinal Priest), Titular of Santi Gioacchino e Anna al Tuscolano, Archbishop of Saint Andrews and Edinburgh; born in Ballycastle, County Antrim, Northern Ireland, March 17, 1938. Created and proclaimed October 21, 2003. Address: Gills Centre, 113 Whitehouse Loan, Edinburgh EH9 1BB, Scotland, Great Britain.

Okogie, Anthony Olubunmi, (Cardinal Priest), Titular of Beata Vergine Maria del Monte Carmelo a Mostacciano, Archbishop of Lagos; born in Lagos, June 16, 1934. Created and proclaimed October 21, 2003. Address: P.O. Box 8, 19 Catholic Mission Street, Lagos, Nigeria.

Ortega y Alamino, Jaime Lucas (Cardinal Priest), Titular of Ss. Aquila e Priscilla, Archbishop of San Cristobal de La Habana, Cuba; born in Jaguey Grande, Diocese of Matanzas, October 18, 1936. Created and proclaimed November 26, 1994. Address: Calle Habana 152, Apartado 594, La Habana, 10100 Cuba.

Ouellet, Marc, P.S.S., (Cardinal Priest), Titular of Santa Maria in Traspontina, Archbishop of Quebec; born in Lamotte, Diocese of Amos, June 8, 1944. Created and proclaimed October 21, 2003. Address: Chancellerie, 1073 boul. Rene-Levesque Ouest, Sillery, Que. G1S 4R5, Canada.

Panafieu, Bernard Louis Auguste Paul, (Cardinal Priest), Titular of San Gregorio Barbarigo alle Tre Fontane, Archbishop of Marseille; born in Chatellerault, France, January 26, 1931. Created and proclaimed October 21, 2003. Address: 14 Place du Colonel-Edon, 13007 Marseille Cedex 07, France.

Pappalardo, Salvatore (Cardinal Priest), Titular of S. Maria Odigitria dei Siciliani, Archbishop Emeritus of Palermo; born in Villafranca Sicula, Archdiocese of Agrigento, September 23, 1918. Created and proclaimed March 5, 1973. Address: Casa Diocesana, Piazza Baida 1, 90136 Palermo, Italy.

Paskai, Laszlo, o.f.m. (Cardinal Priest), Titular of S. Teresa al Corso d'Italia, Archbishop Emeritus of Esztergom-Budapest; born at Szeged, May 8, 1927. Created and proclaimed June 28, 1988. Address: Dobozy Mihaly u. 12, H-2500 Esztergom, Hungary.

Pell, Georges Marie Martin, (Cardinal Priest), Titular of Santa Maria Domenica Mazzarello, Archbishop of Sydney; born in Ballarat, Australia, June 8, 1941. Created and proclaimed October 21, 2003. Address: Polding House, 13th Flr., 276 Pitt St., Sydney NSW 2000, Australia.

Pengo, Polycarp (Cardinal Priest), Titular of Nostra Signora de La Salette, Archbishop of Dar-es-Salaam, Tanzania; born in Mwazye, Diocese of Sumbawanga, August 5, 1944. Created and proclaimed February 21, 1998. Address: Archbishop's House, P.O Box 167, Dar-es-Salaam, Tanzania.

Pham Dinh Tung, Paul Joseph (Cardinal Priest), Titular of S. Maria Regina Pacis in Ostiamare, Archbishop of Ha Noi, Viet Nam; born in Binh Hoa, Diocese of Phat Diem, June 15, 1919. Created and proclaimed November 26, 1994. Address: Toa Tong Giam Muc, 40 Pho Nha Chung, Ha Noi, Viet Nam.

Pham Minh Man, Jean-Baptiste, (Cardinal Priest), Titular of San Giustino, Archbishop of Ho Chi Minh; born in Hoa Thanh, Ca Mau, Vietnam, in the year 1934. Created and proclaimed October 21, 2003. Address: Toa Tong Giam Muc, 189 Nguyen Dinh, Chieu, Q-3 Thanh-Pho Ho Chi Minh, Vietnam.

Pimenta, Simon Ignatius (Cardinal Priest), Titular of S. Maria Regina Mundi a Torre Spaccata, Archbishop Emeritus of Bombay; born in Marol, Archdiocese of Bombay, March 1, 1920. Created and proclaimed June 28, 1988. Address: Archbishop's House, 21 Nathalal Parekh Marg, Mumbai-400001, India.

Piovanelli, Silvano (Cardinal Priest), Titular of S. Maria delle Grazie a Via Trionfale, Archbishop Emeritus of Florence; born in Ronta di Mugello, Archdiocese of Florence, February 21, 1924. Created and proclaimed May 25, 1985. Address: Via Dante Da Castiglione 32, 50010 Trespiano, Italy.

Poggi, Luigi (Cardinal Deacon), Proto Deacon of S. Maria in Domnica, Librarian Emeritus and Archivist Emeritus of the Holy Roman Church; born in Piacenza, Italy, November 25, 1917. Created and proclaimed November 26, 1994. Address: 00120 Vatican City State, Europe.

Poletto, Severino (Cardinal Priest), Titular of San Giuseppe in Via Trionfale, Archbishop of Turin; born in Salgareda, Diocese of Treviso, March 18, 1933. Created and proclaimed February 21, 2001. Address: Via Arcivescovado 12, 10121 Turin, Italy.

Pompedda, Mario Francesco (Cardinal Deacon), Deacon of Annunciazione della B.V.M. a Via Ardeatina, Prefect of the Supreme Tribunal of the Apostolic Signatura; born in Ozieri, April 18, 1929. Created and proclaimed February 21, 2001. Address: 00120 Vatican City State, Europe.

Poupard, Paul (Cardinal Priest), Titular of S. Prassede, President of the Pontifical Council of Culture; born in Bouzille, Diocese of Angers, August 30, 1930. Created and proclaimed May 25, 1985. Address: Piazza San Calisto 16, 00153 Rome, Italy.

Primatesta, Raul Francisco (Cardinal Priest), Titular of Beata Maria Vergine Addolorata a Piazza Buenos Aires, Archbishop Emeritus of Cordoba; born in Capilla del Senor, Diocese of Zarate-Campana, April 14, 1919. Created and proclaimed March 5, 1973. Address: Caseros 160 2o Piso, X5000AHD Cordoba, Argentina.

Pujats, Janis (Cardinal Priest), Titular of Santa Silvia, Archbishop of Riga; born in Nautrani, Diocese of Rezekne-Aglona, November 14, 1930. Created and proclaimed February 21, 2001. Address: Metropolijas Kurija, Maza Pils iela 2/a, 1050 Riga, Latvia.

Puljic, Vinko (Cardinal Priest), Titular of S. Chiara a Vigna Clara, Archbishop of Vrhbosna, Bosnia-Hercegovina; born in Prijecani, Diocese of Banja Luka, September 8, 1945. Created and proclaimed November 26, 1994. Address: Nadbiskupski Ordinarijat, Kaptol 7, 71000 Sarajevo, Bosnia Hercegovina.

Quezada Toruño, Rodolfo, (Cardinal Priest), Titular of San Saturnino, Archbishop of Guatemala; born in Guatemala City, March 8, 1932. Created and proclaimed October 21, 2003. Address: Arzobispado, Apartado 723, 7a Avenida 6-21, Zona 1, 01001 Ciudad de Guatemala, Guatemala.

Ratzinger, Joseph (Cardinal Bishop), Titular of the suburbicarian church of Velletri-Segni, Prefect of the Congregation for the Doctrine of the Faith, President of the Pontifical Bible Commission and Dean of the College of Cardinals; born in Marktl am Inn, Diocese of Passau, April 16, 1927. Created and proclaimed June 27, 1977. Address: 00120 Vatican City State, Europe.

Razafindratandra, Armand Gaetan (Cardinal Priest), Titular of Ss. Silvestro e Martino ai Monti, Archbishop of Antananarivo, Madagascar; born in Ambohimalaza, Archdiocese of Antananarivo, August 7, 1925. Created and proclaimed November 26, 1994. Address: Archeveche, Andohalo, B.P. 3030 Antananarivo 101, Madagascar.

Re, Giovanni Battista (Cardinal Bishop), Titular of the suburbicanan Church of Sabina Poggio-Mirteto, Apostoli, Prefect of the Congregation for Bishops; born in Borno, Diocese of Brescia, January 30, 1934. Created and proclaimed February 21, 2001. Address: 00120 Vatican City State, Europe.

Rigali, Justin Francis, (Cardinal Priest), Titular of Santa Prisca, Archbishop of Philadelphia; born in Los Angeles, California, April 19, 1935. Created and proclaimed October 21, 2003. Address: 222 North 17th St., Philadelphia, PA 19103-1299.

Rivera Carrera, Norberto (Cardinal Priest), Titular of S. Francesco d' Assisi a Ripa Grande, Archbishop of Mexico City; born in Tepehuanes, Archdiocese of Durango, June 6, 1942. Created and proclaimed February 21, 1998. Address: Camelia 110, Col. Florida, 01030 Mexico D.F., Mexico.

Rodríguez Maradiaga, Oscar Andrés, S.D.B., (Cardinal Priest), Titular of Santa Maria della Speranza, Archbishop of Tegucigalpa; born in Tegucigalpa, December 29, 1942. Created and proclaimed February 21, 2001. Address: Apartado 106, 3 y 2 Av. 1113, Tegucigalpa, Honduras.

Rossi, Opilio (Cardinal Priest), Titular of S. Lorenzo in Lucina; born in New York, May 14, 1910. Created and proclaimed May 24, 1976. Address: Via della Scrofa, 70, 00186 Rome, Italy.

Rouco Varela, Antonio Maria (Cardinal Priest), Titular of S. Lorenzo in Damaso, Archbishop of Madrid, Spain; born in Villalba, Diocese of Mondonedo-Ferrol, August 24, 1936. Created and proclaimed February 21, 1998. Address: Calle San Justo 2, 28005 Madrid, Spain.

Rubiano Sáenz, Pedro (Cardinal Priest), Titular of Trasfigurazione di Nostro Signore Gesu Cristo, Archbishop of Bogotá; born in Cartago, September 13, 1932. Created and proclaimed February 21, 2001. Address: Carrera 7 N. 10-20, Santafe de Bogota, Colombia.

Ruini, Camillo (Cardinal Priest), Titular of S. Agnese Fuori le Mura, Vicar General of His Holiness for the Diocese of Rome, Archpriest of the Patriarchal Lateran Basilica, Grand Chancellor of the Pontifical Lateran University; born in Sassuolo, Diocese of Reggio Emilia-Guastalla, February 19, 1931. Created and proclaimed June 28, 1991. Address: Piazza San Giovanni in Laterano 4, 00184 Rome, Italy.

Saldarini, Giovanni (Cardinal Priest), Titular of S. Cuore di Gesu' a Castro Pretorio, Archbishop Emeritus of Torino; born in Cantu, Archdiocese of Milan, December 11, 1924. Created and proclaimed June 28, 1991. Address: Via Montenapoleone 22, 20121 Milano, Italy.

Sales, Eugenio de Araujo (Cardinal Priest), Titular of S. Gregorio VII, Archbishop Emeritus of Sao Sebastiao do Rio de Janeiro; born in Acari, Diocese of Caico, November 8, 1920. Created and proclaimed April 28, 1969. Address: Rua Visconte de Piraja 339, 22410-003 Rio de Janeiro, R.J., Brazil.

Sanchez, Jose T. (Cardinal Priest), Titular of St. Pio V, Prefect Emeritus of the Congregation for the Clergy; born in Pandan, Diocese of Virac, March 17, 1920. Created and proclaimed June 28, 1991. Address: 00120 Vatican City State, Europe.

Sandoval Iniguez, Juan (Cardinal Priest), Titular of Nostra Signora di Guadalupe e S. Filippo Martire in Via Aurelia, Archbishop of Guadalajara, Mexico; born in Yahualica, Diocese of San Juan de los Lagos, March 28, 1933. Created and proclaimed November 26, 1994. Address: Morelos 244, 45500 San Pedro Tlaquepaque, Jal., Mexico.

Santos, Alexandre Jose Maria dos, o.f.m. (Cardinal Priest), Titular of S. Frumenzio ai Prati Fiscali, Archbishop Emeritus of Maputo; born in Zavala, Diocese of Inhambane, March 18, 1924. Created and proclaimed June 28, 1988. Address: Av. Julius Nyerere 882, Maputo, Mozambique.

Saraiva, Martins, José, C.M.F. (Cardinal Deacon), Deacon of Nostra Signora del Sacro Cuore, Prefect of the Congregation for the Causes of Saints; born in Gagos, Diocese of Guarda, January 6, 1932. Created and proclaimed February 21, 2001. Address: 00102 Vatican City State, Europe.

Scheffczyk, Leo (Cardinal Deacon), Deacon of San Francesco Saverio alla Garbatella; born in Beuthen, Archdiocese of Wroclaw, February 21, 1920. Created and proclaimed February 21, 2001. Address: St. Michaelstr. 87, 81673 Munich, Germany.

Scheid, Eusebio Oscar, S.C.I., (Cardinal Priest), Titular of Santi Bonifacio e Alessio, Archbishop of Sao Sebastiao de Rio de Janeiro; born in Bom Retiro, Joacaba, Brazil, December 8, 1932. Created and proclaimed October 21, 2003. Address: Rua Benjamin Constant 23/502, Gloria, 20241-150 Rio de Janeiro, RJ, Brazil.

Schonborn, Christoph, o.p., (Cardinal Priest), Titular of Gesu' Divin Lavoratore, Archbishop of Vienna, Austria; born in Skalsko, Diocese of Litomerice, January 22, 1945. Created and proclaimed February 21, 1998. Address: Wollzeile 2, A-1010 Vienna, Austria.

Schotte, Jan P., c.i.c.m. (Cardinal Deacon), Deacon of S. Giuliano dei Fiamminghi, General Secretary Emeritus of the Synod of Bishops and President of the Office of Labor of the Apostolic See; born in Beveren-Leie, Diocese of Brugge, April 20, 1928. Created and proclaimed November 26, 1994. Address: Palazzo del Bramante, Via della Conciliazione, 34, 00193 Rome, Italy.

Schwery, Henri (Cardinal Priest), Titular of Ss. Protomartiri a Via Aurelia Antica, Bishop Emeritus of Sion; born in Saint Leonard, Diocese of Sion, June 14, 1932. Created and proclaimed June 28, 1991. Address: C.P. 2334, CH-1950 Sion 2, Switzerland.

Scola, Angelo, (Cardinal Priest), Titular of Santi XII Apostoli, Patriarch of Venice; born in Malgrate, Archdiocese of Milan, November 7, 1941. Created and proclaimed October 21, 2003. Address: Curia Patriarcale, S. Marco 320/a, 30124 Venice, Italy.

Sebastiani, Sergio (Cardinal Deacon), Deacon of Sant' Eustachio, President of the Prefecture for the Economic Affairs of the Holy See; born in Montemonaco, Diocese of San Benedetto del Tronto-Ripatransone-Montalto, April 11, 1931. Created and proclaimed February 21, 2001. Address: 00120 Vatican City State, Europe.

Sepe, Crescenzio (Cardinal Deacon), Deacon of Dio Padre Misericordioso, Prefect of the Congregation for the Evangelization of Peoples; born in Carinaro, Diocese of Aversa, June 2, 1943. Created and proclaimed February 21, 2001. Address: 00120 Vatican City State, Europe.

Sfeir, Nasrallah Pierre (Cardinal Bishop), Patriarch of Antioch of the Maronites, Lebanon; born in Reyfoun, Lebanon, Eparchy of Sarba of the Maronites, May 15, 1920. Created and proclaimed November 26, 1994. Address: Patriarcat Maronite, Bkerke, Lebanon.

Shan Kuo-hsi, Paul, s.j. , (Cardinal Priest), Titular of S. Crisogono, Bishop of Kaohsiung, Taiwan; born in Puyang, Diocese of Taming, December 3, 1923. Created and proclaimed February 21, 1998. Address: Bishop's House, 125 Szu-wei 3rd Rd., Kaohsiung 80203, Taiwan.

Shirayanagi, Peter Seiichi (Cardinal Priest), Titular of S. Emerenziana a Tor Fiorenza, Archbishop Emeritus of Tokyo, Japan; born in Hachioji, Archdiocese of Tokyo, June 17, 1928. Created and proclaimed November 26, 1994. Address: Cardinal's Residence, 301, 2-11. Shimoochiai, 3 Chome, Shinjuku-ku, Tokyo –Post 161-0033, Japan.

Silvestrini, Achille (Cardinal Priest), Titular of S. Benedetto fuori Porta S. Paolo, Prefect Emeritus of the Congregation for Oriental Churches; born in Brisighella, Diocese of Faenza-Modigliana, October 25, 1923. Created and proclaimed June 28, 1988. Address: Palazzina della Zecca, 00120 Vatican City State, Europe.

Simonis, Adrianus Johannes (Cardinal Priest), Titular of S. Clemente, Archbishop of Utrecht; born in Lisse, Diocese of Rotterdam, November 26, 1931. Created and proclaimed May 25, 1985. Address: Aartsbisdom, P.B. 14019, 3508 SB Utrecht, Netherlands.

Sin, Jaime L. (Cardinal Priest), Titular of Santa Maria ai Monti, Archbishop Emeritus of Manila; born in New Washington, Diocese of Kalibo, August 31, 1928. Created and proclaimed May 24, 1976. Address: P.O. Box 132, 1099 Manila, Philippines.

Sodano, Angelo, (Cardinal Bishop), Titular of the suburbicarian church of Albano, Secretary of State; Vice-Dean of the College of Cardinals; born in Isola d'Asti, Diocese of Asti, November 23, 1927. Created and proclaimed June 28, 1991. Address: 00120 Vatican City State, Europe.

Špidlik, Tomas, S.J., (Cardinal Deacon), Deacon of Sant' Agata de' Goti; born in Boskovice, Czech Republic, December 17, 1919. Created and proclaimed October 21, 2003. Address: Via Paolina, 25 –00184 Roma, Italy.

Stafford, James Francis (Cardinal Deacon), Deacon of Gesu' Buon Pastore alla Montagnola, Major Apostolic Penitentiary. Born in Baltimore, Maryland, U.S.A., July 26, 1932. Created and proclaimed February 21, 1998. Address: 00120 Vatican City State, Europe.

Sterzinsky, Georg M. (Cardinal Priest), Titular of S. Giuseppe all' Aurelio, Archbishop of Berlin; born in Warlack, Archdiocese of Warmia, February 9, 1936. Created and proclaimed June 28, 1991. Address: Wundstrasse 48-50, 14057 Berlin, Germany.

Stickler, Alfons Maria, s.d.b. (Cardinal Priest), Titular of S. Giorgio in Velabro; born in Neunkirchen, Archdiocese of Vienna, August 23, 1910. Created and proclaimed May 25, 1985. Address: Piazza del S. Uffizio 11, 00193 Rome, Italy.

Suarez Rivera, Adolfo Antonio (Cardinal Priest), Titular of Nostra Signora di Guadalupe a Monte Mario, Archbishop Emeritus of Monterrey in Mexico; born in San Cristobal de las Casas, January 9, 1927. Created and proclaimed November 26, 1994. Address: Apartado Postal 7, Loma Larga 2429 con Sierra Madre, 64040 Monterrey, N.L., Mexico.

Suquia Goicoechea, Angel (Cardinal Priest), Titular of Gran Madre di Dio, Archbishop Emeritus of Madrid; born in Zaldivia, Diocese of San Sebastian, October 2, 1916. Created and proclaimed May 25, 1985. Address: Javier Barcaiztegui 7-3, 20010 San Sebastian, Spain.

Swiatek, Kazimierz (Cardinal Priest), Titular of S. Gerardo Maiella, Archbishop of Minsk-Mohilev, Apostolic Administrator of Pinsk, Belarus; born in Walga, Ap. Adm. of Estonia, October 21, 1914. Created and proclaimed November 26, 1994. Address: pl. Swobody 9, 220030 Minsk, Belarus.

Szoka, Edmund Casimir (Cardinal Priest), Titular of Ss. Andrea e Gregorio al Monte Celio, President of the Pontifical Commission for Vatican City State; President of the Governaterate of Vatican City State. Born in Grand Rapids, Michigan, September 14, 1927. Created and proclaimed June 28, 1988. Address: 00120 Vatican City State, Europe.

Taofinu'u, Pio, s.m. (Cardinal Priest), Titular of S. Onofrio, Archbishop Emeritus of Samoa-Apia; born in Falealupo, Archdiocese of Samoa-Apia, December 8, 1923. Created and proclaimed March 5, 1973. Address: Archbishop's House, P.O. Box 532, Apia, Western Samoa, Oceania.

Tauran, Jean-Louis Pierre, (Cardinal Deacon), Deacon of Sant' Apollinare alle Terme Neroniane-Alessandrine; born in Bordeaux, April 5, 1943. Created and proclaimed October 21, 2003. Address: 00120 Vatican City State, Europe.

Terrazas Sandoval, Julio, C.S.S.R. (Cardinal Priest), Titular of San Giovanni Battista de' Rossi, Archbishop of Santa Cruz de la Sierra; born in Valle Grande, Archdiocese of Santa Cruz de la Sierra, March 7, 1936. Created and proclaimed February 21, 2001. Address: Calle Paquio Esquina Achachairu S/N, Santa Cruz, Bolivia.

Tettamanzi, Dionigi (Cardinal Priest), Titular of Ss. Ambrogio e Carlo, Archbishop of Milan, Italy; born in Renate, Archdiocese of Milan, March 14, 1934. Created and proclaimed February 21, 1998. Address: Palazzo Arcivescovile, Piazza Fontana 2, 20122 Milan, Italy.

Thiandoum, Hyacinthe (Cardinal Priest), Titular of Santa Maria del Popolo, Archbishop Emeritus of Dakar; born in Poponguine, Archdiocese of Dakar, February 2, 1921. Created and proclaimed May 24, 1976. Address: B.P. 5082, Villa Les Badamiers, Dakar-Fann, Senegal.

Tomko, Jozef (Cardinal Priest), Titular of S. Sabina, Prefect Emeritus of the Congregation for the Evangelization of Peoples; President for the Pontifical Committee for International Eucharistic Congresses; born in Udavske, Archdiocese of Kosice, March 11, 1924. Created and proclaimed May 25, 1985. Address: Via della Conciliazione 44, 00193 Rome, Italy.

Tonini, Ersilio (Cardinal Priest), Titular of Ss. Redentore a Val Melaina, Archbishop Emeritus of Ravenna-Cervia, Italy; born in Centovera di San Giorgio Piacentino, Diocese of Piacenza-Bobbio, July 20, 1914. Created and proclaimed November 26, 1994. Address: Via Santa Teresa 8, 48100 Ravenna, Italy.

Toppo, Telesphore Placidus, (Cardinal Priest), Titular of Sacro Cuore di Gesu agonizzante a Vitinia, Archbishop of Ranchi; born in Chainpur, India, October 15, 1939. Created and proclaimed October 21, 2003. Address: P.O. Box 5, Purulia Road, Ranchi-834001 Jharkhand, India.

Tucci, Roberto, S.J. (Cardinal Deacon), Deacon of Sant' Ignazio di Loyola a Campo Marzio; born in Naples, Italy, April 19, 1921. Created and proclaimed February 21, 2001. Address: Via Di Porta Pinciana 1, 00187 Rome, Italy.

Tumi, Christian Wiyghan (Cardinal Priest), Titular of Ss. Martiri dell' Uganda a Poggio Ameno, Archbishop of Douala; born in Kikaikelaki, Diocese of Kumbo, October 15, 1930. Created and proclaimed June 28, 1988. Address: Archeveche, B.P. 179, Douala, Cameroon.

Turcotte, Jean-Claude (Cardinal Priest), Titular of Nostra Signora del Ss. Sacramento e Santi Martiri Canadesi, Archbishop of Montreal, Canada; born in Montreal, June 26, 1936. Created and proclaimed November 26, 1994. Address: 1071 rue de la Cathedrale, Montreal, P.Q. H3B 2V4, Canada.

Turkson, Peter Kodwo Appiah, (Cardinal Priest), Titular of San Liborio, Archbishop of Cape Coast; born in Wassaw Nsuta, Archdiocese of Cape Coast, October 11, 1948. Created and proclaimed October 21, 2003. Address: P.O. Box 112, Cape Coast, Ghana.

Vachon, Louis-Albert (Cardinal Priest), Titular of S. Paolo della Croce a Corviale, Archbishop Emeritus of Quebec; born in Saint Frederic-de-Beauce, Archdiocese of Quebec, February 4, 1912. Created and proclaimed May 25, 1985. Address: 1 rue des Remparts, Quebec PQ, G1R 5L7, Canada.

Vidal, Ricardo J. (Cardinal Priest), Titular of Ss. Pietro e Paolo a Via Ostiense, Archbishop of Cebu; born in Mogpoc, Diocese of Boac, February 6, 1931. Created and proclaimed May 25, 1985. Address: 234 D. Jakosalem Str., P.O. Box 52, 6000 Cebu City, Philippines.

Vithayathil, Varkey, C.SS.R. (Cardinal Priest), Titular of San Bernardo alle Terme, Major Archbishop of Ernakulam-Angamaly of the Syro-Malabar; born in Parur, Archeparchy of Ernakulam-Angamaly of the Syro-Malabar, May 29, 1927. Created and proclaimed February 21, 2001. Address: Major Archbishop's House, P.O. Box 10, Thrikkakara P.O., Kochi-682021, India.

Vlk, Miloslav (Cardinal Priest), Titular of S. Croce in Gerusalemme, Archbishop of Prague, Czech Republic; born in Lisnice-Sepekov, Diocese of Ceske Budejovice, May 17, 1932. Created and proclaimed November 26, 1994. Address: Arcibiskupska Kurie, Hradcanske nam. 16, 119 02 Praha 1, Czech Republic.

Wako, Gabriel Zubeir, (Cardinal Priest), Titular of Sant' Atanasio a Via Tiburtina, Archbishop of Khartoum; born in Mboro, Sudan, February 27, 1941. Created and proclaimed October 21, 2003. Address: P.O. Box 49, Khartoum, Sudan.

Wamala, Emmanuel (Cardinal Priest), Titular of S. Ugo, Archbishop of Kampala, Uganda; born in Kamaggwa, Diocese of Masaka, December 15, 1926. Created and proclaimed November 26, 1994. Address: Archbishop's House, P.O. Box 14125, Mengo-Kampala, Uganda.

Wetter, Friedrich (Cardinal Priest), Titular of S. Stefano al Monte Celio, Archbishop of Munich und Freising; born in Landau, Diocese of Speyer, February 20, 1928. Created and proclaimed May 25, 1985. Address: Postfach 10051, Kardinal-Faulhaber Str., 7, D-80079 Munchen, Germany.

Willebrands, Johannes (Cardinal Priest), Titular of S. Sebastiano alle Catacombe; born in Bovenkarspel, Diocese of Haarlem, September 4, 1909. Created and proclaimed April 28, 1969. Address: Pontificio Collegio Olandese, Via Ercole Rosa 1, 00153 Rome, Italy.

Williams, Thomas Stafford (Cardinal Priest), Titular of Gesu' Divin Maestro alla Pineta Sacchetti, Archbishop of Wellington; born in Wellington, March 20, 1930. Created and proclaimed February 2, 1983. Address: Archbishop's House, P.O. Box 1937, 21 Eccleston Hill, Wellington 6015, New Zealand.

Patriarchs

Alexandria (Egypt), *Coptic Rite*— His Beatitude Stephanos II Cardinal Ghattas, C.M. born January 16, 1920 in Cheikh Zein-el-Dine; ordained March 25, 1944; elected to Luqsor of the Copts May 8, 1967; consecrated June 9, 1967; elected Patriarch June 9, 1986; elevated to the College of Cardinals February 21, 2001. Address: B.P. 69, 34 rue Ibn Sandar, Pont-de-Koubbeh, 11712 Le Caire, Egypt.

Antioch (Syria), *Syriac Rite*— His Beatitude Ignace Pierre VIII Abdel-Ahad; born in Alep June 28, 1930; elected Patriarch February 16, 2001. Address: Rue Damas, B.P. 1106-2010 Beyrouth, Lebanon.

Maronite Rite— His Beatitude Nasrallah Peter Cardinal Sfeir; born in Reyfoun, May 15, 1920; elected Patriarch April 19, 1986; elevated to the College of Cardinals November 26, 1994. Address: Patriarcat Maronite Bkerke, Lebanon.

Melkite Greek Catholic— His Beatitude Gregoire III Laham, B.S., born December 15, 1933 in Daraya; elected Patriarch November 29, 2000. Address: B.P. 22249, Avenue Az-Zeitoon 12, Bab Charki, Damascus, Syria.

Jerusalem (Israel)— His Beatitude Michel Sabbah, born in Nazareth, Israel, March 19, 1933; elected Patriarch of Jerusalem of the Latins December 11, 1987; consecrated January 6, 1988. Address: Patriarcat Latin, P.O. Box 14152, 91141 Jerusalem (Old City).

Babylon of the Chaldeans— His Beatitude Emmanuel III Delly, born in Telkaif, October 6, 1927; elected Patriarch December 3, 2003. Address: Patriarcat Chaldeen Catholique, P.O. Box 6112, Al-Mansour, Baghdad, Iraq.

Cilicia of the Armenians— His Beatitude Nerses Bedros XIX Tarmouni, born in LeCaire January 17, 1940; elected Patriarch October 7, 1999. Address: Patriarcat Armenien Catholique, Rue de L'Hopital Orthodoxe, Jeitaoui, 2078 5605 Beyrouth, Lebanon.

East Indies— Most Rev. Raul Nicholau Gonsalves; born in Bambolim, Archdiocese of Goa, June 15, 1927; promoted Archbishop January 30, 1978. Address: Paco Patriarcal P.O. Box 216, Panaji, Goa-403001, India.

Lisbon, (Portugal) — His Eminence Jose da Cruz Cardinal Policarpo, born in Alvorninha, Patriarchate of Lisbon, February 26, 1936; consecrated June 29, 1978; appointed Coadjutor Archbishop of the Patriarchate of Lisbon March 5, 1997; promoted Patriarch March 24, 1998; elevated to the College of Cardinals February 21, 2001. Address: Mosteiro de Sao Vicente De Fora, Campo de Santa Clara 1149-085 Lisbon, Portugal.

Venice, (Italy) — Most Reverend Angelo Scola, born in Malgrate, Italy November 7, 1941; ordained July 18, 1970; consecrated as Bishop September 21, 1991; elected Patriarch January 5, 2002. Address: Curia Patriarcale, S. Marco 320/a, 30124 Venice, Italy.

Synod of Bishops

Synodus Episcoporum President: The Holy Father. Secretary General: His Eminence Jan Pieter Cardinal Schotte, C.I.C.M. General Secretariat: Palazzo del Bramante, Via della Conciliazione, 34, 00193 Rome, Italy. Tel: 69.88.48.21 or 69.88.43.24. Fax: 69.88.33.92.

Office of Labor of the Apostolic See

Officium Laboris Apostolicae Sedia President: His Eminence Jan Cardinal Schotte, C.I.C.M. Vice President: Most Rev. Archbishop Giovanni De Andrea. Assessor of the Presidency: Prof. Matteo Dell'Olio. Assessor of the Presidency: Prof. Gian Carlo Perone. Office: Via della Conciliazione, 1, 00193 Rome, Italy. Tel: 69.88.44.49. Fax: 69.88.38.00.

The Roman Curia

The present norms regarding the Roman Curia were publicly announced June 28, 1988, in the Pastor Bonus - Constitutio Apostolica de Romana Curia, and published in A.A.S. LXXX/1988, Commentarium Officiale; pp. 841-934. The Supreme Pontiff usually conducts business of the universal Church by means of the Roman Curia, which fulfills its duty in his name and by his authority for the good and the service of the Churches; it consists of the Secretariat of State or the Papal Secretariat, congregations, tribunals and other institutions, whose structure and competency are defined in special law (can. 360). The Roman curia is the complex of departments and institutes which assist the Roman Pontiff in the exercise of his supreme pastoral function for the good and service of the universal Church and of the particular churches, by which the unity of faith and communion of the people of God is strengthened and the mission is promoted which is proper to the Church in the world.

I. THE SECRETARIAT OF STATE TO HIS HOLINESS

The Secretariat of State

The Secretariat of State is the dicastery of the Roman Curia which works most closely with the Supreme Pontiff in the exercise of his universal mission (*Pastor Bonus*, Art. 39). The Secretariat of State is presided over by a Cardinal who assumes the title of Secretary of State. As the Pope's first Collaborator in the governance of the universal Church, the Cardinal Secretary of State is the one primarily responsible for the diplomatic and political activity of the Holy See, in some circumstances representing the person of the Supreme Pontiff himself.

The Secretariat of State includes two sections, namely: the First Section that is headed by an Archbishop, the *Substitute for General Affairs*, assisted by a Prelate, the *Assessor for General Affairs*; and the Second Section of the Secretariat of State headed by an Archbishop, the *Secretary for Relations with States*, aided by a Prelate, the *Under-Secretary for Relations with States*, and assisted by Cardinals and Bishops.

Secretary of State: His Eminence Angelo Cardinal Sodano.

Office: Apostolic Palace, 00120 Vatican City State, Europe. Tel: 06-69.88.39.13; Fax: 06-69.88.52.55.

First Section: For General Affairs

In conformity with Arts. 41-44 of *Pastor Bonus*, the Section for General Affairs or the First Section is responsible for handling matters regarding the everyday service of the Supreme Pontiff, both in caring for the universal Church and in dealing with the dicasteries of the Roman Curia. It attends to the preparation of whatever documents the Holy Father entrusts to it. It enacts the provisions for appointments within the Roman Curia and keeps custody of the Lead Seal and the Fisherman's Ring. It regulates the duties and activity of the Holy See's Representatives, especially in relation to the local Churches. It attends to all that concerns the Embassies accredited to the Holy See. It supervises the Holy See's official communication agencies and is responsible for publishing the "Acta Apostolicae Sedis" and the "Annuario Pontificio".

Substitute: Most Rev. Archbishop Leonardo Sandri.

Assessor: Rev. Msgr. Gabriele Giordano Caccia.

Office: Apostolic Palace, 00120 Vatican City State, Europe. Tel: 06.69.88.34.38 Fax: 06.69.88.50.88.

Second Section: For Relations with States

On the basis of Arts. 45-47 of Pastor Bonus, the Section for Relations with States or Second Section has the specific duty of attending to matters which involve civil governments. It has responsibility for the Holy See's diplomatic relations with States, including the establishing of Concordats or similar agreements; for the Holy See's presence in international organizations and conferences; in special circumstances, by order of the Supreme Pontiff and in consultation with the competent dicasteries of the Curia, provides for appointments to particular Churches, and for their establishment or modification; in close collaboration with the Congregation for Bishops, it attends to the appointment of Bishops in countries which have entered into treaties or agreements with the Holy See in accordance with the norms of international law.

Secretary: Most Rev. Archbishop Giovanni Lajolo.

Under-Secretary: Rev. Monsignor Pietro Parolin.

Office: Apostolic Palace, 00120 Vatican City State, Europe. Tel: 06.69.88.30.14; Fax: 06.69.88.53.64.

II. THE CONGREGATIONS

By the name of department (dicasteria) is understood: the congregations, tribunals, councils and offices, namely the Apostolic Camera, the Administration of the Patrimony of the Apostolic See, and the Prefecture of Economic Affairs of the Holy See. The departments are juridically equal among themselves. Attached to the institutes of the Roman Curia are the Prefecture of the Papal Household and the Office of Liturgical Celebrations of the Supreme Pontiff.

The Congregation for the Doctrine of the Faith

The proper function of the Congregation on the Doctrine of the Faith is to promote and safeguard the doctrine of faith and morals in the whole Catholic world; therefore, those things belong to it which touch this matter in any way. Fulfilling the function of promoting doctrine, it fosters studies in order that the understanding of the faith might grow and that a response can be prepared under the light of faith for new questions arising from developments in science and human culture. It is a help to bishops, whether individually or gathered in assemblies, in the exercise of the function by which they are constituted authentic teachers and doctors of the faith as well as the office by which they are held to safeguard and promote the integrity of that faith. This Sacred Congregation reproves doctrines opposed to the principles of the faith after the interested Bishops of a region have been heard. It studies the books referred to it and, if necessary, reproves them after the author has been heard and has had an opportunity to defend himself and after the Ordinary has been forewarned. It also examines whatever concerns "the privilege of the faith" whether in law and in fact. It is competent to pass judgement on errors about the faith according to the norms of an ordinary process. It safeguards the dignity of the sacrament of Penance. The Congregation proceeds administratively or judicially according to the nature of the question to be treated.

Cardinal Prefect: His Eminence Joseph Cardinal Ratzinger.

Secretary: Most Rev. Archbishop Angelo Amato, S.D.B.

Office: Piazza del S. Uffizio 11, 00193 Rome, Italy. Tel: 69.88.33.57; 69.88.34.13; Fax: 69.88.34.09.

The Congregation for the Causes of Saints

The Congregation for the Causes of Saints is competent in all matters which in any way pertain to the Beatification of Servants of God or to the Canonization of the Blessed or to the Preservation of Relics.

This Congregation is divided into three offices.

Prefect: Most Rev. Archbishop Jose Saraiva Martins, C.M.F.

Secretary: Most Rev. Archbishop Edward Nowak.

Office: Piazza Pio XII 10, 00193 Rome, Italy. Tel: 011 39 06 69.88.42.47; Fax: 011 39 06 6988 1935.

The Congregation for the Oriental Churches

This Congregation considers those matters, whether regarding persons or things, which touch on the Eastern Catholic Churches. It treats all questions which pertain either to persons, or to discipline, or to the rites of the Oriental Churches, even if they are mixed in that by the nature of the thing or of persons they involve Latins. Territories in which a major part of the Christians belong to Oriental rites are subject only to this Congregation. Even in Latin territories it carefully supervises the faithful of Oriental rites and provides as much as possible for their spiritual needs even by the establishment of their own hierarchy if the number of faithful and circumstances require this.

Prefect: His Beatitude Ignace Moussa I Cardinal Daoud

Secretary: Most Rev. Archbishop Antonio Maria Vegliò, Titular Archbishop of Cadi.

Office: Via della Conciliazione 34, 00193 Rome, Italy. Tel: 69.88.42.82; Fax: 69.88.43.00.

The Congregation for Bishops

This congregation examines what pertains to the constitution and provision of particular churches as well as the exercise of the episcopal function in the Latin Church, except for the competence of the Congregation for the Evangelization of Peoples. It belongs to the Congregation for Bishops to propose to the Roman Pontiff, for approval, the constitution of new dioceses, provinces and regions; to divide, unite and realign them after consulting the interested Episcopal Conferences; it deals also with the erection of the military ordinariates and, after consulting the Episcopal Conference, prelacies for special pastoral ministries for various regions or social groups. This Congregation provides also for the naming of bishops, apostolic administrators, coadjutors and auxiliaries of bishops, military and other vicars and prelates enjoying personal jurisdiction.

It is competent for all things that have to do with bishops and publishes norms which, through the Episcopal Conference, provide for the more urgent needs of the faithful.

Prefect: His Eminence Giovanni Battista Cardinal Re

Secretary: Most Rev. Archbishop Francesco Monterisi.

Office: Piazza Pio XII 10, 00193 Rome, Italy. Tel: 69.88.42.17; Fax: 69.88.53.03.

Pontifical Commission for Latin America

(Directly responsible to Congregation for Bishops)

President: His Eminence Giovanni Battista Cardinal Re.

Vice President: Most Rev. Archbishop Luis Robles Diaz.

The Congregation for Divine Worship and the Discipline of the Sacraments

This congregation does those things which pertain to the Apostolic See as to the moderation and promotion of the sacred liturgy, especially the sacraments, with due regard for the competence of the Congregation on Doctrine of the Faith. It fosters and safeguards the discipline of the sacraments, especially what pertains to their valid and licit celebration; moreover, it concedes favors and dispensations for matters which are not contained in the facilities of diocesan bishops in this line. It alone examines the non-consummation of a marriage and the presence of causes for the granting of a dispensation and everything connected with them. It has competence with regard to the obligations connected with major orders and it examines questions about the validity of sacred ordination.

Prefect: His Eminence Francis Cardinal Arinze.

Secretary: Most Rev. Archbishop Domenico Sorrentino.

Office: Piazza Pio XII 10, 00193 Rome, Italy. Tel: 69.88.43.16; Fax: 69.88.34.99.

The Congregation for the Evangelization of Peoples or for the Propagation of the Faith

It belongs to this congregation to direct and coordinate throughout the world the work of the evangelization of peoples itself and missionary cooperation, while respecting the competence of the Congregation for Eastern Churches. It is competent for those things which pertain to all the missions established for the spread of the Kingdom of Christ throughout the world and therefore for whatever is connected with the assignment and transferral of the necessary ministers, for describing ecclesiastical boundaries and proposing those who will govern them. It encourages also the development of an indigenous clergy. The congregation sponsors missionary initiatives and promotes missionary vocations and spirituality. In the territories subject to it, the Congregation has charge of all that pertains to the holding of synods and councils, to the establishing of episcopal conferences and to the review of their statutes and decrees. The Congregation has a Supreme Council for the direction of Pontifical Missionary Works, on which depend the general Councils of the Missionary Union of the Clergy, the Society for the Propagation of the Faith, the Society of St. Peter the Apostole, and the Society of the Holy Childhood.

Cardinal Prefect: His Eminence Crescenzio Cardinal Sepe.

Secretary: Most Rev. Archbishop Robert Sarah.

Office: Palazzo di Propaganda Fide, Piazza di Spagna 48, 00187 Rome, Italy. Tel: 011 39 06 6987 9299; Fax: 011 39 06 6988 01 18.

The Congregation for Institutes of Consecrated Life and for Societies of Apostolic Life

The principal function of this congregation is to promote and supervise, in the whole Latin Church, the practices of the evangelical counsels as they are exercised in approved forms of consecrated life and at the same time the activities of societies of apostolic life. The Congregation takes care of Religious Institutes of Consecrated Life and Secular Institutes.

Religious Institutes: the Congregation is entrusted with the affairs of all religious institutes of the Latin Rite and their members. It is also competent in matters which pertain to societies of common life, whose members live like religious, or to Third Orders as such.

Secular Institutes: the Congregation is competent in the same way, all else being equal, for Apostolic Societies which, although not religious, make a true and complete profession of the evangelical counsels in the world.

Cardinal Prefect: Most Rev. Archbishop Franc Rode.

Secretary: Most Rev. Archbishop Piergiorgio Silvano Nesti, C.P.

Office: Piazza Pio XII 3, 00193 Rome, Italy. Tel: 69.88.41.28; Fax: 69.88.45.26.

The Congregation for the Clergy

With due regard for the rights of bishops and their conferences, this congregation examines those things which concern priests and deacons of the secular clergy with regard to their persons, pastoral ministry, matters which are in support of the exercise of these things, and in all this provides opportune assistance to the bishops. The Congregation has many functions: studies, proposes and urges the means and aids by which priests strive for sanctity. This office also has charge of everything which concerns the work and discipline of the diocesan clergy. Particularly it promotes the preaching of the Word of God and the works of the apostolate and organization of catechesis evaluates and approves pastoral and catechetical directories, fosters national and international Catechetical Congresses and indicates the opportune norms for religious instruction of children, young people and adults. The Congregation looks also to the preservation and administration of the temporal goods of the Church without prejudice to the other Congregations which have temporal goods committed to their vigilance.

Prefect: His Eminence Dario Cardinal Castrillon Hoyos.

Secretary: Most Rev. Archbishop Csaba Ternyak.

Office: Piazza Pio XII 3, 00193 Rome, Italy. Tel: 69.88.41.51; Fax: 69.88.48.45.

The Congregation for Catholic Education (of Seminaries and Institutes of Studies)

This Congregation expresses and exercises the Apostolic See's solicitude for the formation of those who are called to holy orders as well as for the promotion and organization of Catholic education. It is competent for all that pertains to the formation of clerics and the Catholic education both of clerics and of the laity.

The Congregation has many functions and is charged with the direction, discipline and temporal administration of seminaries and whatever touches the education of the diocesan clergy and the scientific formation of religious and secular institutes.

The Congregation oversees universities, faculties, athenaea and any institute of higher learning which has the name "Catholic" in so far as they depend on the authority of the Church, not excluding those directed by religious or the laity.

The Congregation cares for the establishment of parochial and diocesan schools; watches over all Catholic schools below the level of a university and faculty, as well as all institutes of instruction or education dependent on the authority of the Church.

Also within the Congregation is located the Pontifical Work for Vocations, which is charged with coordinating and promoting the work of fostering all ecclesiastical vocations.

Prefect: His Eminence Zenon Cardinal Grocholewski.

Secretary: Most Rev. Archbishop Michael Miller, C.S.B.

Office: Piazza Pio XII 3, 00193 Rome, Italy. Tel: 69 88 41 67; Fax: 69 88 41 72.

III. TRIBUNALS

Apostolic Penitentiary

The competence of this Tribunal is concerned with those matters which pertain to the internal forum, for both the sacramental and non-sacramental internal forum. It is competent in matters pertaining to the granting and use of indulgences.

Major Penitentiary: His Eminence J. Francis Cardinal Stafford.

Office: Piazza della Cancelleria 1, 00186 Rome, Italy. Tel: 011 39 06 6988 75 26; Fax: 011 39 06 6988 75 57.

Supreme Tribunal of the Apostolic Signatura

This department, in addition to the function which it exercises as Supreme Tribunal, consults that justice may be correctly administered in the Church.

With the many functions, the Apostolic Signatura judges the matters assigned to it in the Code of Canon Law; it prorogues the competence of tribunals; it extends the forum for strangers in Rome to cases of matrimonial nullity in extraordinary circumstances and for grave reasons; it supervises the proper administration of justice; it provides for the establishment of regional and interregional tribunals; it enjoys the rights assigned to it in concordats between the Holy See and the various nations.

The Tribunal settles questions about the exercise of administrative ecclesiastical power which are referred to it. It also passes on conflicts of competence among the departments of the Holy See; it examines administrative matters referred to it by the Congregations of the Roman Curia as well as questions committed to it by the Holy Father.

Prefect: His Eminence Mario Francesco Cardinal Pompedda.

Secretary: Most Rev. Bishop Velasio De Paolis, C.S.

Office: Piazza della Cancelleria 1, 00186 Rome, Italy. Tel: 69.88.75.20; Fax: 69.88.75.53.

Tribunal of the Roman Rota

This tribunal acts as a higher instance at the Apostolic See, usually in the grade of appeal, for safeguarding rights in the Church; it fosters the unity of jurisprudence and, through its own sentences, is a help to lower tribunals. It is also a court of first instance for cases specified in the law and for others committed to the Rota by the Roman Pontiff. The greater part of its decisions concern the nullity of marriage. In such cases its competence includes marriages between two Catholics, between a Catholic and non-Catholic, and between two non-Catholic parties whether one or both of the baptized parties belongs to a Latin or Oriental Rite.

Dean: His Excellency Monsignor Antoni Stankiewicz.

Office: Piazza della Cancelleria 1, 00186 Rome, Italy. Tel: 69.88.75.02; Fax: 69.88.75.54.

IV. PONTIFICAL COUNCILS

Pontifical Council for the Laity

This council is competent in those matters which pertain to the Apostolic See in promoting and coordinating the apostolate of the lay persons and, generally, in those things which look to the Christian life of lay persons as such. The norms were published in the apostolic letter, Catholicam Christi Ecclesiam of January 6, 1967 (A.A.S., LIX, pp. 25-28).

President: Most Rev. Archbishop Stanislaw Rylko.

Secretary: Most Rev. Bishop Josef Clemens.

Office: Piazza S. Calisto 16, 00153 Rome, Italy. Tel: 69.88.73.22; Fax: 69.88.72.14.

Pontifical Council for Promoting Christian Unity

The function of this Council is to concentrate in an appropriate way on initiatives and ecumenical activities for the restoration of unity among Christians. It has charge of relations with those of other communities; considers the correct interpretation and observance of the principles of ecumenism; promotes Catholic groups and coordinates the efforts at unity, both on the national and international levels; institutes colloquies on ecumenical questions and activities with Churches and ecclesial communities separated from the Holy See; deputes Catholic observers for Christian congresses; invites to Catholic gatherings observers of the separated brethren; orders into practice conciliar decrees on ecumenical matters. Furthermore, it is competent for all questions concerning religious relations with Judaism.

President: His Eminence Walter Cardinal Kasper.

Secretary: Most Rev. Bishop Brian Farrell, L.C.

Office: Via dell' Erba 1, 00193 Rome, Italy. Tel: 6988 3072; Fax: 6988 53 65.

Pontifical Council for the Family

This Council promotes the pastoral care of families and fosters their rights and dignity in the Church and in civil society, in order that they might ever more suitably fulfill their own functions.

President: His Eminence Alfonso Cardinal Lopez Trujillo.

Secretary: Most Rev. Bishop Karl Josef Romer.

Office: Piazza S. Calisto 16, 00153 Rome, Italy. Tel: 69.88.72.43; Fax: 69.88.72.72.

Pontifical Council for Justice and Peace

This Council looks to those things which will promote justice and peace in the world according to the Gospel and the social teaching of the Church.

President: His Eminence Renato Cardinal Martino.

Secretary: Most Rev. Bishop Giampaolo Crepaldi.

Office: Piazza S. Calisto 16, 00153 Rome, Italy. Tel: 6987.9911. Fax: 69.88.72.05.

Pontifical Council Cor Unum

This Council shows the solicitude of the Catholic Church toward the needy, in order that human fraternity might be fostered and the charity of Christ be made manifest.

President: Most. Rev. Archbishop Paul Josef Cordes.

Secretary: Rev. Msgr. Karel Kasteel.

Office: Piazza S. Calisto 16, 00153 Rome, Italy. Tel: 69.88.9411; Fax: 69.88.7311.

Pastoral Council for the Pastoral Care of Migrants and Itinerant People

This Council directs the pastoral concern of the Church toward the special needs of those who are forced to leave their own native land or who perhaps lack one; it also sees that there is appropriate study of the questions which touch on this matter.

President: His Eminence Stephen Fumio Cardinal Hamao.

Secretary: Most Rev. Archbishop Agostino Marchetto.

Office: Piazza S. Calisto 16, 00153 Rome, Italy. Tel: 69.88.71.93; Fax: 69.88.71.11.

Pontifical Council for the Pastoral Assistance to Health Care Workers

This Council shows the solicitude of the Church for the sick by aiding those who carry out a ministry toward the sick and suffering, in order that the apostolate of mercy, which they carry out, may ever more suitably respond to new needs.

President: His Eminence Javier Cardinal Lozano Barragan.

Secretary: Most Rev. Bishop Jose Luis Redrado Marchite, O.H.

Office: Via della Conciliazione, 00193 Rome, Italy. Tel: 69.88.31.38; Fax: 69.88.31.39.

Pontifical Council for the Intepretation of Legislative Texts

The function of this Council consists especially in interpreting the Church's laws.

President: His Eminence Julian Cardinal Herranz.

Secretary: Most Rev. Bishop Bruno Bertagna.

Office: Palazzo delle Congregazioni Piazza Pio XII 10, 00193 Rome, Italy. Tel: 69.88.40.08; Fax: 69.88.47.10.

Pontifical Council for Inter-Religious Dialogue

This Council fosters and moderates relations with members and bodies of religions which do not carry the name of Christian, as well as with those who in any way possess a religious spirit. It fosters studies and promotes relations with non-Christians to bring about an increase in mutual respect and seeks ways to establish a dialogue with them; it receives and carefully weighs the wishes of the Ordinaries; it provides for the formation of those who participate in dialogue.

President: Most Rev. Archbishop Michael Louis Fitzgerald.

Secretary: Most Rev. Archbishop Pier Luigi Celata Office: Via dell' Erba 1, 00193 Rome, Italy. Tel: 69.88.43.21; Fax: 69.88.44.94.

Pontifical Council for Culture

The Council embodies the Church's pastoral concern over the relationship between faith and cultures. Its tasks include: studying unbelief and religious indifference, as present in different cultures; supporting the Church's inculturation of the Gospel; promoting initiatives of dialogue between faith and culture, as well as dialogue with those who do not believe in God. Its activities include seminars, intercultural exchanges, and coordinating the activities of Pontifical Academies and the Pontifical Commission for the Cultural Patrimony of the Church. An important hope of the Council is to show faith as the inspiration of science, literature and the arts.

President: His Eminence Paul Cardinal Poupard.

Secretary: Very Rev. Bernard Ardura, O.Praem.

Office: Piazza S. Calisto 16, 00153 Rome, Italy. Tel: 6989.3811; Fax: 69.88.73.68.

Pontifical Council for Social Communications

This Council is involved in questions touching on the instruments of social communication so that the proclamation of salvation and human progress might be promoted even through them in order to foster civil culture.

President: Most Rev. Archbishop John Foley.

Secretary: Most Rev. Bishop Renato Boccardo.

Office: Palazzo S. Carlo, 00120 Vatican City State, Europe. Tel: 69.88.31.97; Fax: 69.88.53.73.

V. OFFICES

Apostolic Camera

The Apostolic Camera is presided over by the cardinal chamberlain of the Holy Roman Church, assisted by the vice-chamberlain together with certain prelates chamberlain. It chiefly exercises the function which is given to it in the special law on the vacancy of the Apostolic See.

Camerlengo: His Eminence Eduardo Cardinal Martinez Somalo.

Prefecture of the Papal Household

The Prefecture looks after the internal order of the pontifical household and supervises everything which pertains to discipline and service either by clergy or laity who constitute the pontifical chapel and family. It is in charge of the Apostolic Palace and is at the service of the Holy Father, both there and wherever he goes. It arranges audiences with His Holiness and supervises papal ceremonies other than the strictly liturgical.

Prefect: Most Reverend Archbishop James M. Harvey.
Adjunct Prefect: Most Reverend Archbishop Stanislaw Dziwisz.

Administration of the Patrimony of the Apostolic See

This Office is competent to administer the goods proper to the Holy See, the income from which is destined to support the expenditures necessary for the functions of the Roman Curia.

Extraordinary Section: Handles the duties committed to it by the Sovereign Pontiff.
President: His Eminence Attilio Cardinal Nicora.
Secretary: Most Rev. Archbishop Claudio Maria Celli.
Office: 00120 Vatican City State, Europe. Tel: 011 39 06 6989.3403; Fax: 011 39 06 6988 31 41.

Central Office of Statistics of the Church

This Office gathers and organizes the data which seems necessary or useful for a better understanding of the state of the Church and for assistance to its Bishops.

Director: Rev. Msgr. Vittorio Formenti.

Prefecture of the Economic Affairs of the Holy See

The Prefecture has the function of supervising and governing the administration of goods which belong to the Holy See or which it is in charge of, no matter what kind of autonomy they may perhaps enjoy. This is directed by a Commission of three Cardinals and coordinates and watches over the administration of the possessions of the Holy See. It receives the reports on the receipts and disbursements of the Church's goods and the various budgets.

President: His Eminence Sergio Cardinal Sebastiani.
Secretary: Most Rev. Bishop Franco Croci.
Office: Largo del Colonnato 3, 00193 Rome, Italy. Tel: 69.88.42.63; Fax: 69.88.50.11.

Office of the Liturgical Celebrations of the Supreme Pontiff

This Office prepares whatever is necessary for liturgical and other sacred celebrations which are carried out by the Supreme Pontiff or in his name and, in keeping with existing prescription of liturgical law, to supervise them.

Master of Ceremonies: Most Rev. Archbishop Piero Marini.

VI. COMMISSIONS AND COMMITTEES

Pontifical Commission for the Cultural Heritage of the Church

President: Most Rev. Bishop Mauro Piacenza.
Secretary: Rev. Carlo Chenis, S.D.B.

Pontifical Commission for Sacred Archeology

President: Most Rev. Bishop Mauro Piacenza.
Secretary: Prof. Fabrizio Bisconti.

Pontifical Commission "Ecclesia Dei"

President: His Eminence Dario Cardinal Castrillon Hoyos.

Council of Cardinals for the Study of Organizational and Economic Problems of the Apostolic See

American Members: His Eminence Roger M. Cardinal Mahony, His Eminence Edward M. Cardinal Egan and His Eminence Bernard F. Cardinal Law.

International Theological Commission

President: His Eminence Joseph Cardinal Ratzinger.
General Sec.: His Eminence Georges Cardinal Cottier, O.P.

Pontifical Biblical Commission

President: His Eminence Joseph Cardinal Ratzinger.
Secretary: Rev. Klemens Stock, S.J.

Pontifical Committee for the International Eucharistic Congresses

President: His Eminence Jozef Cardinal Tomko.

Pontifical Commission for the Vatican City State

President: His Eminence Edmund Casimir Cardinal Szoka.

Pontifical Committee for Historical Sciences

President: Rev. Msgr. Walter Brandmuller
Secretary: Rev. Cosimo Semeraro, S.D.B.

VII. INSTITUTIONS CONNECTED WITH THE HOLY SEE

Vatican Secret Archives

Archivist: His Eminence Jean Louis Cardinal Tauran.
Prefect: Rev. Sergio B. Pagano.

Vatican Apostolic Library

Librarian: His Eminence Jean Louis Cardinal Tauran.
Prefect: Very Rev. Raffaele Farina, S.D.B.

Pontifical Academy of Sciences

President: Prof. Nicola Cabibbo.

Pontifical Academy of Social Sciences

President: Prof. Edmond Malinvaud.

Pontifical Academy for Life

President: Prof. Juan de Dios Vial Correa.
Vice President: Most Rev. Bishop Elio Sgreccia.

Vatican Radio

Director General: Rev. Pasquale Borgomeo, S.J.

Vatican Television Centre

President of the Administrative Council: Dr. Emilio Rossi.
Director General: Rev. Federico Lombardi, S.J.

Fabric of St. Peter's

President: His Eminence Francesco Cardinal Marchisano.

Office of Papal Charities

Almoner: Most Rev. Archbishop Oscar Rizzato.

Vatican Polyglot Press

Director General: Rev. Elio Torrigiani, S.D.B.
Administrative Director: Rev. Mario Ercole, S.D.B.

Vatican Publishing House

President: Rev. Msgr. Giuseppe Scotti.
Director: Rev. Claudio Rossini, S.D.B.

Institute for Works of Religion

Director General: Dr. Lelio Scaletti.

L'Osservatore Romano

Director: Prof. Mario Agnes.
Secretary: Dr. Carlo DeLucia.
English Language Weekly - Contact Person: Rev. Paul S. Quinter.
Translations of English, French, Spanish, German, Portuguese, and Polish editions available.

Press Office of the Holy See

Director: Dr. Joaquin Navarro-Valls.

VIII. AMERICANS WORKING IN THE ROMAN CURIA

Secretariat of State I. Section for General Affairs: Rev. Msgr. James Green; Rev. Msgr. Peter Wells; Rev. Reginald Foster, O.C.D.; Rev. Msgr. William Millea; Rev. Msgr. Steven Zak; Sr. Yvonne Mary Loucks, R.S.M.; Sr. Ruth Aubrey, A.S.C.J.
II. Section for Relations with States: Rev. Msgr. Joseph Marino; Rev. Msgr. Michael Banach.
Congregation for the Doctrine of the Faith: Rev. Joseph DiNoia, O.P.; Rev. Msgr. Michael O. Jackels; Rev. Msgr. Charles Brown.
Congregation for Divine Worship and the Discipline of the Sacraments: Rev. Msgr. Thomas Fucinaro; Rev. Michael K. Magee.
Congregation for Causes of Saints: Rev. Msgr. Robert Sarno.
Congregation for Bishops: Rev. Msgr. David Thomas; Rev. Msgr. James D. Conley; Rev. Andrew Baker.
Congregation for the Clergy: Rev. Christopher Nalty.
Congregation for The Institutes of Consecrated Life and for Societies of Apostolic Life: Sr. Sharon Holland, I.H.M.; Rev. Msgr. Charles Mangan.
Congregation for Catholic Education: Rev. Albin Grous.
Apostolic Penitentiary: His Eminence J. Francis Cardinal Stafford.
Supreme Tribunal of the Apostolic Signatura: Rev. Msgr. Joseph Punderson.
Tribunal of the Roman Rota: Rev. Msgr. Kenneth Boccafola; Rev. Msgr. Robert Sable.
Pontifical Council For Promoting Christian Unity: Rev. Msgr. John Radano.
Pontifical Council for the Family: Ms. Joan E. Collemacine-Parenti, Ph.D.
Pontifical Council for Justice and Peace: Rev. Msgr. Frank Dewane.
Pontifical Council for the Interpretation of Legislative Texts: Rev. Msgr. Bernard Hebda.
Pontifical Council for Social Communications: Most Rev. John Foley.
Pontifical Council "Cor Unum": Rev. Michael Osborn.
Pontifical Council for Migration and Itinerant Peoples: Rev. Michael Blume, S.V.D.
Administration for the Patrimony of the Apostolic See: Sr. Judith Zoebelein, F.S.E.
Prefecture of the Papal Household: Prefect: Most Rev. James M. Harvey.
Pontifical Commission for Vatican City State: His Eminence Edmund Cardinal Szoka.
L'Osservatore Romano: Rev. Paul S. Quinter, Editor. For subscription information for North America please contact: The Cathedral Foundation, Inc., 320 Cathedral St., Baltimore, MD 21201. Tel: 410-547-5380; Fax: 410-385-0113.
Synod of Bishops: Rev. Msgr. John Abruzzese.
Pontifical Commission Ecclesia Dei: Rev. Msgr. Arthur Calkins.
Residence for American Diocesan Priests working in the Roman Curia: Villa Stritch, Via della Nocetta 63, 00164 Rome, Italy. Tel: 011 39 06 6616 2662; or 6616 2676; Fax: 011 39 06 6616 2700.

INSTITUTES OF GRADUATE STUDIES IN ROME

Pontifical Gregorian University (Associated with the Pontifical Biblical Institute and the Pontifical Oriental Institute. Constituted in 1552. *Address*: Piazza della Pilotta 4, 00187 Rome, Italy. His Eminence Zenon Cardinal Grocholewski, Grand Chancellor; Very Rev. Peter-Hans Kolvenbach, S.J., Vice Chancellor; Very Rev. Franco Imoda, S.J., Rector; Very Rev. Stephen F. Pisano, S.J., Rector of the Biblical Institute; Very Rev. Hector Vall, S.J., Rector of the Oriental Institute.

Pontifical Lateran University Founded in 1824. *Address*: Piazza S. Giovanni in Laterano 4, 00184 Rome, Italy. His Eminence Camillo Cardinal Ruini, Grand Chancellor; Most Rev. Bishop Salvatore Fisichella, Rector.

Patristic Institute Augustinianum at the Pontifical Lateran University Founded in 1969. *Address*: Via Paolo VI 25, 00193 Rome, Italy. Very Rev. Angelo Di Berardino, O.S.A., Pres.

Pontifical Urban University Founded in 1627. *Address*: Via Urbano VIII 16, 00165 Rome, Italy. His Eminence Crescenzio Cardinal Sepe, Grand Chancellor; Rev. Msgr. Giuseppe Cavallotto, Rector.

Pontifical University of St. Thomas Aquinas Founded in 1580. *Address*: Largo Angelicum 1, 00184 Rome, Italy. Very Rev. Carlos Alfonso Azpiroz Costa, Master General of the Order of Preachers and Grand Chancellor; Very Rev. Francesco Compagnoli, O.P., Rector.

Pontifical Atheneum of St. Anselm Founded in 1687. *Address*: Piazza Cavalieri di Malta 5, 00153 Rome, Italy. Tel: (06) 579.1279. Very Rev. Wolf D. Notker, O.S.B., Grand Chancellor and Abbot Primate; Very Rev. Albert Schmidt, O.S.B., Rector.

Pontifical Salesian University Founded in 1940. *Address*: Piazza Ateneo Salesiano 1, 00139 Rome, Italy. Very Rev. Pascual Chavez Villanueva, Grand Chancellor; Very Rev. Mano Toso, Rector.

Pontifical Atheneum Antonianum Founded in 1933. *Address*: Via Merulana 124, 00185 Rome, Italy. Very Rev. Giacomo Bini, O.F.M., Grand Chancellor and Minister General of the Order of Friars Minor; Very Rev. Marco Nobile, O.F.M., Rector.

Pontifical Institute of Sacred Music Founded in 1911. *Address*: Via di Torre Rossa 21, 00165, Rome, Italy. His Eminence Zenon Cardinal Grocholewski, Grand Chancellor; Rev. Msgr. Valentin Miserachs Grau, President.

Pontifical Institute of Christian Archeology Founded in 1925. *Address*: Via Napoleone III 1, 00185 Rome, Italy. His Eminence Zenon Cardinal Grocholewski, Grand Chancellor; Prof. Philippe Pergola, Rector.

Pontifical Theological Faculty of St. Bonaventure Erected in 1935. *Address*: Via del Serafico 1, 00142 Rome, Italy. Very Rev. Joachim Giermek, O.F.M.Conv., Grand Chancellor and Minister General of the Order of Friars Minor Conventual; Rev. Orlando Todisco, O.F.M.Conv., President.

Pontifical Theological Faculty Teresianum Founded in 1935. *Address*: Piazza S. Pancrazio 5-A, 00152 Rome, Italy. Very Rev. Camilo Maccise, O.C.D., Grand Chancellor and Prepositor General of the Discalced Carmelites; Very Rev. Virgilio Pasquetto, O.C.D., President.

Pontifical Theological Faculty Marianum Founded in 1955. *Address*: Viale 30 Aprile 6, 00153 Rome, Italy. Very Rev. Angel M. Ruiz, Grand Chancellor and Prior General of the Servites; Very Rev. Silvano M. Maggiani, President.

Pontifical University of the Holy Cross Erected on January 9, 1990. *Address*: Piazza S. Apollinare 49, 00186 Rome, Italy. Most Rev. Bishop Javier Echevarria Rodriguez, Grand Chancellor; Rev. Mariano Fazio, Rector.

SEMINARIES AND NATIONAL COLLEGES IN ROME

Pontifical Roman Major Seminary Founded in 1565 by Pius IV. Address: Piazza S. Giovanni in Laterano 4, 00184 Rome, Italy. Rev. Msgr. Giovanni Tani, Rector.

Pontifical Roman Minor Seminary Address: Viale Vaticano 42, 00165 Rome, Italy. Rev. Msgr. Paolo Selvadagi, Rector.

French Seminary (Pontifical) Founded on October 2, 1853. Address: Via di S. Chiara 42, 00186 Rome, Italy. Rev. Yves-Marie Fradet, Rector.

Lombard Seminary of SS. Ambrose and Charles (Pontifical) Founded in 1863. Address: Piazza S. Maria Maggiore 5, 00185 Rome, Italy. Rev. Tullio Citrini, Rector.

North American College (Pontifical) Corporate Title: The American College of the Roman Catholic Church of the United States. A Maryland Corporation. Founded in 1859 by Pope Pius IX. Postal Address: Via del Gianicolo 14, 00120 Vatican City State, Europe. Rev. Msgr. Kevin C. McCoy, Rector. (See AMERICAN COLLEGES ABROAD on the next page for further details.)

Armenian College (Pontifical) Founded on March 1, 1883. Address: Salita S. Nicola da Tolentino 17, 00187 Rome, Italy. Rev. Joseph Bezezian, Rector.

Beda College (Pontifical) Founded in 1852; separated from the English College in 1917. Address: Viale San Paolo 18, 00146 Rome, Italy. Rev. Charles R. Strange, Rector.

Belgian College (Pontifical) Founded in 1844. Rev. Address: Via G.B. Pagano 35, 00167 Rome, Italy. Rev. Johan Bonny, Rector.

Canadian College (Pontifical) Founded in 1888. Address: Via Crescenzio 75, 00193 Rome, Italy. Rev. Pierre-Jean Jolicoeur, P.S.S., Rector.

Capranica College (Almo) Founded in 1457 by Cardinal Capranica. Address: Piazza Capranica 98, 00186 Rome, Italy. Rev. Msgr. Alfredo Abbondi, Rector.

Ethiopian College (Pontifical) Founded on October 1, 1919. Address: 00120 Citta del Vaticano, Europe. Rev. P. Tekle Mekonnen, Rector.

German-Hungarian College (Pontifical) Founded on October 28, 1552. Address: Via S. Nicola da Tolentino 13, 00187 Rome, Italy. Rev. Gerwin Komma, S.J., Rector.

Greek College (Pontifical) Founded on January 13, 1577. Address: Via del Babuino 149, 00187 Rome, Italy. Very Rev. Manuel Nin, O.S.B., Rector.

English College (Venerabile) Founded on April 23, 1578. Address: Via Monserrato 45, 00186 Rome, Italy. Rev. Msgr. Patrick Michael Kilgarriff, Rector.

Irish College (Pontifical) Founded in 1628. Address: Via dei Ss. Quattro 1, 00184 Rome, Italy. Rev. Msgr. Liam Bergin, Rector.

Lithuanian College (Pontifical) Founded in 1946. Address: Via Casalmonferrato 20, 00182 Rome, Italy. Rev. Msgr. Antanas Algimantas Bartkus, Rector.

Maronite College Founded on June 17, 1584. Address: Via Porta Pinciana 18, 00187 Rome, Italy. Rev. Msgr. Hanna G. Alwan, Rector

Nepomucene College (Pontifical) Address: Via Concordia 1, 00183 Rome, Italy. Rev. Jan Mraz, Rector.

Philippine College (Pontifical) Founded on June 29, 1961. Address: Via Aurelia 490, 00165 Rome, Italy. Rev. Msgr. Ruperto C. Santos, Rector.

Dutch College (Pontifical) Founded on October 26, 1930. Address: Via Ercole Rosa 1, 00153 Rome, Italy. Rev. Johannes Heeffer, Rector.

Brazilian College (Pontifical) Founded in 1934 by Pius XI. Address: Via Aurelia 527, 00165 Rome, Italy. Very Rev. Geraldo A. Coelho de Almeida, S.J., Rector.

Latin American College (Pio Latino Americano) (Pontifical) Founded in 1858. Address: Via Aurelia Antica 408, 00165 Rome, Italy. Rev. Andres Swinnen, S.J., Rector.

Polish College (Pontifical) Founded on March 9, 1866. Address: Piazza Remuria 2-A, 00153 Rome, Italy. Rev. Msgr. Marek Stepien, Rector.

Portuguese College (Pontifical) Founded on October 28, 1900. Address: Via Nicolo V 3, 00165 Rome, Italy. Rev. Nuno Bras da Silva Martins, Rector.

Russian College of S. Theresa of the Child Jesus (Pontifical) Founded on August 15, 1929. Address: Via Carlo Cattaneo 2, 00185 Rome, Italy. Rev. Alojz Cvikl, S.J., Rector.

Ukrainian College of Saint Josephat (Pontifical) Founded in 1897. Address: Passeggiata del Gianicolo 7, 00165 Rome, Italy. Rev. Genesio Viomar, O.S.B.M., Rector.

College of St. Jerome of the Croatians (Pontifical) Founded on August 1, 1901. Address: Via Tomacelli 132, 00186 Rome, Italy. Rev. Msgr. Jure Bogdan.

St. Thomas Aquinas Founded in 1948. Address: Via degli Ibernesi 20, 00184 Rome, Italy. Very Rev. Luke Dempsey, O.P., Rector.

Scots College (Pontifical) Founded on December 5, 1600. Address: Via Cassia 481, 00189 Rome, Italy. Rev. Msgr. Christopher Joseph McElroy, Rector.

Spanish College (Pontifical) Founded on April 1, 1892. Address: Via Di Torrerrossa 2, 00165 Rome, Italy. Rev. Lope Rubio Parrado, Rector.

Teutonic College (S. Maria dell'Anima) Founded in 1859. Address: Via della Pace 20, 00186 Rome, Italy. Rev. Msgr. Richard Mathes, Rector.

Teutonic College (S. Maria in Camposanto), for the study of Sacred Archaeology and Ecclesiastical History Founded on November 21, 1876. Address: Via della Sagrestia 17, 00120 Citta del Vaticano, Europe. Rev. Msgr. Erwin Gatz, Rector.

Polish Ecclesiastical Institute (Pontifical) Founded in 1958. Address: Via Pietro Cavallini, 38, 00193 Rome, Italy. Rev. Grzegorz Kaszak, Rector.

American Church Santa Susanna Address: Via Venti Settembre 15, Postal Address: Via Antonio Salandra 6, 00187 Rome, Italy. Tel: 011 39 6 488.2748; Fax: 011 39 6 474.0236. Very Rev. Paul G. Robichaud, C.S.P., Rector; Rev. Gregory Apparcel, C.S.P., Vice Rector; Rev. Dennis W. Hickey, C.S.P., Vice Rector.

AMERICAN COLLEGES ABROAD

American College. Louvain, Belgium. Corporate title: The American College of the Immaculate Conception, Catholic University of Louvain, a corporation of the District of Columbia. Founded in 1857, the American College is the oldest national seminary operated under the auspices of a special committee of the United States Conference of Catholic Bishops. Most Rev. Edward Braxton, S.T.D., Ph.D., Chairman. Postal Address: Naamsestraat 100, B-3000 Leuven, Belgium. Tel: 32.16.32.00.11; Fax: 32.16.32.00.12.

Faculty and Staff: Very Rev. Kevin A. Codd, S.T.B., M.A., Rector; Rev. John A. DeSocio, Vice Rector-Formation & Dir.-Admissions; Rev. Aurelius Boberek, O.S.B., Dir.-Liturgical Formation; Rev. Philip Wallace Platt, C.S.B., Dir.-Spiritual Formation; Rev. Dr. David E. Windsor, C.M., Psy. D., Rector Emeritus and Dir.-Development; Mr. Stephen Zavesky, Vice Pres.-Finance.

The American College operates four major programs, all in the English language, in conjunction with the Institute of Philosophy, the Faculty of Theology and the Faculty of Canon Law of the Katholieke Universiteit te Leuven (K.U. Leuven) and of the Universite Catholique de Louvain (U.C.L.). These are The Seminary Program of Priestly Formation both on the level of Philosophy, Pre-theology and Theology; The Graduate Studies Programs in Canon Law, Theology and Philosophy; monthly and semester Sabbatical Programs and a summer session for ministerial renewal.

Office for Development and Recruitment for the American College of Louvain, Postal Address: The American College, USCCB, 3211 Fourth St., N.E., Washington, DC 20017-1194. Tel: 202-541-3108; Fax: 202-541-3133. E-mail: admissions@acl.be or szavesky@acl.be; alumni@acl.be. Quarterly newsletter of the American College, *Sodales*.

The American College founded and remains associated with the English-speaking Parish of Our Lady of Mercy in the Brussels area. Parish Postal Address: 64 Avenue Reine Astrid 1410, Waterloo, Belgium. Tel: 32.2.354.5343; Fax: 32.2.351.2314.

North American College, Rome, Italy.®MDNM (Pontifical) Corporate Title: The American College of the Roman Catholic Church of the United States. A Maryland Corporation. Operates under the auspices of a special committee of the United States Conference of Catholic Bishops. Chairman: Most Reverend Wilton D. Gregory Founded in 1859 by Pope Pius IX, the express purpose being to bring American seminarians and student priests into close association with the Holy See. Seminarians live and take their priestly formation at the College, while studying at the theological universities in Rome. Three major departments: Seminary, Graduate and Institute for Continuing Theological Education.

Postal Address: North American College, 00120 Vatican City State, Europe. Rev. Msgr. Kevin C. McCoy, Rector; Rev. Msgr. James F. Checchio, Vice Rector for Administration.

Seminary Department, Postal Address: North American College, 00120 Vatican City State, Europe. Tel: (011 39 06) 684-931; Fax: (011 39 06) 686-7561; E-mail: pnac@pnac.org.; Student Fax: (011 39 06) 686-9665. Rev. Msgr. Kevin C. McCoy, Rector; Rev. Msgr. James F. Checchio, Vice Rector for Administration; Rev. Peter M. McGuine, Vice Rector for Community Life; Rev. Msgr. Giuseppe Barbieri, Dir.-Studies & Admissions; Rev. Msgr. Ross A. Shecterle, Ph.D., Staff Psychologist; Rev. John D. Murphy, S.J., Spiritual Dir.; Rev. Msgr. William J. Lyons, Spiritual Dir.; Rev. Frederick L. Miller, Spiritual Dir.; Rev. Brendan G. Lally, S.J., Spiritual Dir.; Rev. G. Dennis Gill, Dir.-Liturgy & Music; Rev. Vincent Tobin, O.S.B., Dir.-Homiletics; Rev. Steven R. Biegler, Dir.-Pastoral & Apostolic Formation; Rev. Pierre Paul, O.M.V., Dir.-Liturgical Music; Sr. Susan Hooks, O.S.B., Comptroller; Sr. Rebecca Abel, O.S.B., Librarian; Sr. Norma Fultz, O.S.B., Archivist; Rev. Msgr. Daniel E. Thomas, in residence. Students 154, representing 78 Dioceses and Archdioceses.

Institute for Continuing Theological Education, Postal Address: North American College, 00120 Vatican City State, Europe. Tel: (011 39 06) 6849-3853; Fax: (011 39 06) 687-1529; E-mail: romeshabat @pnac.org. Rev. Msgr. Robert C. Evans, Dir. Fall & Spring 12-week sabbatical sessions for priests. Participants 38.

Graduate Department: Casa Santa Maria, *Postal Address*: Via dell'Umiltà 30, 00187 Rome, Italy. Tel: (011 39 06) 690-011; Fax: (011 39 06) 69-00-18-23. Residence of North American College for post-graduate priests. Rev. Msgr. Steven J. Raica, Superior.; Rev. Msgr. Richard Mahowald, P.A., Spiritual Dir.; Sr. Mary Carol Kinghorn, Librarian. Graduate priests 61, representing 50 Dioceses and Archdioceses.

Bishops' Office for United States Visitors to the Vatican, Postal Address: Via dell'Umiltà 30, 00187 Rome, Italy. Tel: (011 39 06) 690-011; Fax: (011 39 06) 679-1448. Request for attendance at Papal audiences and similar functions may be addressed to this office. Rev. Msgr. Roger C. Roensch, Dir.

Office for Development of the North American College, Postal Address: 3211 Fourth St., N.E., Washington, DC 20017-1194. Tel: 202-541-5403; Fax: 202-722-8804. E-mail: Nacrome@aol.com. Mrs. Tricia Morrin Lloyd, Dir.-Development.

The Apostolic Nunciature

Established As Apostolic Delegation January 24, 1893; Nunciature January 10, 1984.
Address: 3339 Massachusetts Ave., N.W., Washington, DC 20008-3687. Tel: 202-333-7121. Fax: 202-337-4036.

APOSTOLIC NUNCIO TO THE UNITED STATES

His Excellency
The Most Reverend

GABRIEL MONTALVO, J.C.D.
Titular Archbishop of Celene
Apostolic Nuncio

Born in Santafe de Bogota, Colombia, January 27, 1930; ordained a priest for the Archdiocese of Santafe de Bogota, January 18, 1953. Entered the diplomatic service of the Holy See in 1957; served in Bolivia, Argentina, and El Salvador; from 1964 through 1974 he served at the Secretariat of State, section for Eastern European Countries. On June 14, 1974, he was appointed Apostolic Nuncio to Nicaragua and to Honduras. Received the Episcopal Ordination by His Holiness Pope Paul VI on June 30, 1974. He was named in 1980 Apostolic Pro-Nuncio in Algeria and Tunisia and Apostolic Delegate in Libya. In 1982 he was chosen as a Member of the Papal Mediation Office for resolving the controversy between Argentina and Chile, and then to head the same Office. On June 12, 1986 he was appointed Apostolic Pro-Nuncio to Yugoslavia and remained in Belgrade until May 1996. In the meantime he was named as the first Apostolic Nuncio to Belarus on April 17, 1993. On March 20, 1993 he was appointed President of the Pontifical Ecclesiastical Academy. On December 7, 1998, Pope John Paul II appointed him Apostolic Nuncio to the United States and Permanent Observer of the Holy See to the Organization of American States.

Rev. Msgr. Lepoldo Girelli, S.T.D., J.C.L., *First Counselor*; Rev. Msgr. Peter G. Magee, J.C.D., S.T.L., *First Counselor;* Rev. Msgr. Cecilio Julian B. Rotor, J.C.D., M.A., *First Secretary*;

Rev. Msgr. Salvatore R. Matano, PA, S.T.L., J.C.D., *Secretary*; Rev. Msgr. John H. Maksymowicz, S.T.L., *Secretary*; Rev. Thomas F. Petrillo, M.A., Ed.D., *Secretary.*

Former Apostolic Delegates:

His Eminence Francesco Cardinal Satolli 1893-1896
His Eminence Sebastiano Cardinal Martinelli 1896-1902
His Eminence Diomede Cardinal Falconio 1902-1911
His Eminence Giovanni Cardinal Bonza 1911-1922
His Eminence Pietro Cardinal Fumasoni-Biondi 1922-1933
His Eminence Amleto G. Cardinal Cicognani 1933-1958
His Eminence Egidio Cardinal Vagnozzi 1958-1967
His Eminence Luigi Cardinal Raimondi 1967-1973
His Excellency Most Reverend Jean Jadot 1973-1980
His Eminence Pio Cardinal Laghi 1980-1984

Apostolic Pro-Nuncios:

His Eminence Pio Cardinal Laghi 1984-1990
His Eminence Agostino Cardinal Cacciavillan 1990-1998

Apostolic Nuncios:

His Excellency Most Reverend Gabriel Montalvo .... 1998—

The Permanent Observer Mission of the Holy See to the United Nations

Established January 26, 1964
Office Address: 25 E. 39th St., New York, NY 10016-0903. Tel.: 212-370-7885; Fax: 212-370-9622.
E-mail: holysee@un.int. Website: www.holyseemission.org.

PERMANENT OBSERVER OF THE HOLY SEE TO THE UNITED NATIONS

His Excellency
The Most Reverend

CELESTINO MIGLIORE
Titular Archbishop of Canosa
Apostolic Nuncio

Born in Cuneo, in the Piedmont region of Italy, on July 1, 1952. Ordained a priest on June 25, 1977. Obtained a master's degree in Theology at the Center of Theological Studies in Fossano; finished his Doctorate in Canon Law at the Pontifical Lateran University; joined the Holy See's diplomatic service in 1980. Served in Angola from 1980-1984; then in Washington, D.C., serving also as an Alternate Observer to the Organization of American States; Appointed for a year at the Apostolic Nunciature in Egypt in 1988; served in Warsaw, Poland, a post he held until his appointment on April 14, 1992 as Special Envoy with the role of Permanent Observer of the Holy See to the Council of Europe in Strasbourg, France. From December 1995-October 2002, serverd as Under-Secretary of the Section for Relations with States of the Vatican Secretariat of State while serving for six years at the Pontifical Lateran University in Rome as Visiting Professor, teaching Ecclesiastical Diplomacy.

Appointed Apostolic Nuncio and Permanent Observer of the Holy See to the United Nations on October 30, 2002.
Office Address: 25 East 39th St., New York, NY 10016-4196. Tel: 212-734-2900; Fax: 212-988-3633.

Rev. Msgr. Francis Chullikatt, Counselor; Rev. Msgr. Ruben M. Dimaculangan, Counselor; Rev. Fr. Vittorio Guerrera, Attache; Rev. Fr. Rober Araujo, S.J., Attache; Miss Olivetta Danese, Secretary; Miss Maria Ceruti, Secretary.

Former Permanent Observers:
Rev. Msgr. Alberto Giovannetti 1964-1973
His Eminence Giovanni Cardinal Cheli 1973-1986
His Eminence Renato Cardinal Martino 1986-2002

The Catholic Church in the United States

The organizational structure of the Catholic Church in the United States consists of 33 Provinces with as many Archdioceses (Metropolitan Sees); 149 Suffragan Sees (Dioceses); The Military Archdiocese; four Eastern-Rite jurisdictions immediately subject to the Holy See in Rome. The Eparchies of St. Maron (Maronites), Newton (Melkites), St. Thomas the Apostle of Detroit (Chaldeans) and St. George Martyr of Canton, Ohio (Romanians), St. Thomas of Chicago of the Syro-Malabarians. Each of these jurisdictions is under the direction of an Archbishop and Bishop called an Ordinary, who has apostolic responsibility and authority for the pastoral service of the people in his care.

The structure includes the territorial episcopal conference known as the United States Conference of Catholic Bishops. In and through this body, which is strictly ecclesiastical and has defined juridical authority, the Bishops exercise their collegiate pastorate over the Church in the entire country.

Related to the USCCB is the civil corporation and operational secretariat through which the Bishops, in cooperation with other members of the Church, act on a wider-than-ecclesiastical scale for the good of the Church and society in the United States.

The following is a list of the thirteen regions in the United States and provinces within those regions.

Region I: Includes the states of Maine, Vermont, New Hampshire, Massachusetts, Rhode Island, and Connecticut. Provinces of Boston and Hartford. Eparchy of Stamford and Eparchy for Melkites.

Region II: Includes the state of New York. Province of New York and Eparchy of St. Maron.

Region III: Includes the states of New Jersey and Pennsylvania. Provinces of Newark and Philadelphia; Archeparchy of Philadelphia, Ukrainian Archeparchy of Pittsburgh, Byzantine Eparchy of Passaic, and Apostolic Exarchate for Armenians.

Region IV: Includes the states of Delaware, District of Columbia, Florida, Georgia, Maryland, North Carolina, South Carolina, Virgin Islands, Virginia and West Virginia. Provinces of Atlanta, Baltimore, Miami, Washington, and the Military Archdiocese.

Region V: Includes the states of Alabama, Kentucky, Louisiana, Mississippi and Tennessee. Provinces of Louisville, Mobile and New Orleans.

Region VI: Includes the states of Michigan and Ohio. Provinces of Cincinnati, Detroit; Eparchy of Parma, Apostolic Exarchate for Chaldeans, and Apostolic Exarchate for Romanians.

Region VII: Includes the states of Illinois, Indiana and Wisconsin. Provinces of Chicago, Indianapolis, Milwaukee; Eparchy of St. Nicholas in Chicago-Ukrainian.

Region VIII: Includes the states of Minnesota, North Dakota and South Dakota. Provinces of St. Paul and Minneapolis.

Region IX: Includes the states of Kansas, Missouri and Nebraska. Provinces of Dubuque, Kansas City in Kansas, Omaha and St. Louis.

Region X: Includes the states of Arkansas, Oklahoma and Texas (excluding El Paso). Provinces of Oklahoma City and San Antonio.

Region XI: Includes the states of California, Hawaii and Nevada. Provinces of Los Angeles and San Francisco (excluding Salt Lake City); Eparchy of Van Nuys.

Region XII: Includes the states of Alaska, Idaho, Montana, Oregon and Washington. Provinces of Anchorage, Portland and Seattle.

Region XIII: Includes the states of Utah, Arizona, New Mexico, Colorado and Wyoming. Provinces of Denver, Santa Fe, part of San Francisco, Salt Lake City, and El Paso.

Please refer to individual Diocesan and Archdiocesan listing for complete and detailed information. The following list does not include the retired Archbishops or retired Bishops.

PROVINCE OF ANCHORAGE

Includes the State of Alaska.

Archdiocese of Anchorage, AK—Most. Rev. Roger L. Schwietz, O.M.I., Archbishop of Anchorage.

Diocese of Fairbanks, AK—Most Rev. Donald J. Kettler, Bishop of Fairbanks.

Diocese of Juneau, AK—Most Rev. Michael Warfel, Bishop of Juneau.

PROVINCE OF ATLANTA

Includes the States of Georgia, North Carolina and South Carolina.

Archdiocese of Atlanta, GA—Most Rev. John F. Donoghue, Archbishop of Atlanta.

Diocese of Charleston, SC—Most Rev. Robert J. Baker, Bishop of Charleston.

Diocese of Charlotte, NC—Most Rev. Peter J. Jugis, Bishop of Charlotte.

Diocese of Raleigh, NC—Most Rev. F. Joseph Gossman, Bishop of Raleigh.

Diocese of Savannah, GA—Most Rev. J. Kevin Boland, Bishop of Savannah.

PROVINCE OF BALTIMORE

Includes the States of Maryland (except Montgomery, Prince Charles, St. Mary's, Calvert and Charles Counties), Delaware, Virginia and West Virginia.

Archdiocese of Baltimore, MD—His Eminence William Cardinal Keeler, Archbishop of Baltimore. Most Rev. Gordon D. Bennett, S.J., Auxiliary Bishop. Most Rev. William F. Malooly, Auxiliary Bishop.

Diocese of Arlington, VA—Most Rev. Paul S. Loverde, Bishop of Arlington.

Diocese of Richmond, VA— Most Rev. Francis X. DiLorenzo, Bishop of Richmond.

Diocese of Wheeling-Charleston, WV—Most Rev. Bernard W. Schmitt, Bishop of Wheeling-Charleston.

Diocese of Wilmington, DE—Most Rev. Michael A. Saltarelli, Bishop of Wilmington.

PROVINCE OF BOSTON

Includes the States of Maine, New Hampshire, Vermont and Massachusetts.

Archdiocese of Boston, MA—Most Rev. Sean O'Malley, Archbishop of Boston. Most Rev. Richard G. Lennon, Auxiliary Bishop. Most Rev. John P. Boles, Auxiliary Bishop. Most Rev. Walter J. Edyvean, Auxiliary Bishop. Most Rev. Francis X. Irwin, Auxiliary Bishop. Most Rev. Emilio Allue, S.D.B., Auxiliary Bishop.

Diocese of Burlington, VT—Most Rev. Kenneth A. Angell, Bishop of Burlington.

Diocese of Fall River, MA—Most Rev. George W. Coleman, Bishop of Fall River.

Diocese of Manchester, NH—Most Rev. John B. McCormack, Bishop of Manchester. Most Rev. Francis J. Christian, Auxiliary Bishop.

Diocese of Portland, ME— Most Rev. Richard J. Malone, Bishop of Portland.

Diocese of Springfield, MA—Most Rev. Timothy A. McDonnell, Bishop of Springfield.

Diocese of Worcester, MA—Most Rev. Robert J. McManus, Bishop of Worcester. Most Rev. George Rueger, Auxiliary Bishop.

PROVINCE OF CHICAGO

Includes the State of Illinois.

Archdiocese of Chicago, IL—His Eminence Francis Cardinal George, O.M.I., Archbishop of Chicago. Most Rev. Edwin M. Conway, Auxiliary Bishop. Most Rev. John R. Manz, Auxiliary Bishop. Most Rev. Joseph N. Perry, Auxiliary Bishop. Most Rev. Jerome E. Listecki, Auxiliary Bishop. Most Rev. Francis J. Kane, Auxiliary Bishop. Most Rev. Thomas J. Paprocki, Auxiliary Bishop. Most Rev. Gustavo Garcia-Siller, M.Sp.S., Auxiliary Bishop.

Diocese of Belleville, IL—Most Rev. Wilton D. Gregory, Bishop of Belleville.

Diocese of Joliet, IL—Most Rev. Joseph L. Imesch, Bishop of Joliet.

Diocese of Peoria, IL— Most Rev. Daniel R. Jenky, C.S.C., Bishop of Peoria.

Diocese of Rockford, IL—Most Rev. Thomas G. Doran, Bishop of Rockford.

Diocese of Springfield, IL—Most Rev. George J. Lucas, Bishop of Springfield.

PROVINCE OF CINCINNATI

Includes the State of Ohio.

Archdiocese of Cincinnati, OH—Most Rev. Daniel E. Pilarczyk, Archbishop of Cincinnati. Most Rev. Carl K. Moeddel, Auxiliary Bishop.

Diocese of Cleveland, OH—Most Rev. Anthony M. Pilla, Bishop of Cleveland. Most Rev. Martin John Amos, Auxiliary Bishop. Most Rev. Roger W. Gries, O.S.B., Auxiliary Bishop. Most Rev. A. James Quinn, Auxiliary Bishop.

Diocese of Columbus, OH—Most Rev. James A. Griffin, Bishop of Columbus.

Diocese of Steubenville, OH—Most Rev. R. Daniel Conlon, Bishop of Steubenville.

Diocese of Toledo, Diocese of Toledo, OH—Most Rev. Leonard P. Blair, Bishop of Toledo. Most Rev. Robert W. Donnelly, Auxiliary Bishop.

Diocese of Youngstown, OH—Most Rev. Thomas J. Tobin, Bishop of Youngstown.

PROVINCE OF DENVER

Includes the States of Colorado and Wyoming.

Archdiocese of Denver, CO—Most Rev. Charles J. Chaput, O.F.M.Cap., Archbishop of Denver. Most Rev. Jose H. Gomez, Auxiliary Bishop.

Diocese of Cheyenne, WY—Most Rev. David L. Ricken, Bishop of Cheyenne.

Diocese of Colorado Springs, CO—Most Rev. Michael J. Sheridan, Bishop of Colorado Springs.

Diocese of Pueblo, CO—Most Rev Arthur N. Tafoya, Bishop of Pueblo.

PROVINCE OF DETROIT

Includes the State of Michigan.

Archdiocese of Detroit, MI—His Eminence Adam Cardinal Maida, Archbishop of Detroit. Most Rev. Thomas J. Gumbleton, Auxiliary Bishop. Most Rev. Earl A. Boyea, Auxiliary Bishop. Most Rev. Walter A. Hurley, Auxiliary Bishop. Most Rev. John M. Quinn, Auxiliary Bishop. Most Rev. Francis R. Reiss, Auxiliary Bishop.

Diocese of Gaylord, MI—Most Rev. Patrick R. Cooney, Bishop of Gaylord.

Diocese of Grand Rapids, MI—Most Rev. Kevin M. Britt, Bishop of Grand Rapids.

Diocese of Kalamazoo, MI—Most Rev. James A. Murray, Bishop of Kalamazoo.

Diocese of Lansing, MI—Most Rev. Carl F. Mengeling, Bishop of Lansing.

Diocese of Marquette, MI—Most Rev. James H. Garland, Bishop of Marquette.

Diocese of Saginaw, MI—Vacant See.

PROVINCE OF DUBUQUE

Includes the State of Iowa.

Archdiocese of Dubuque, IA—Most Rev. Jerome G. Hanus, O.S.B., Archbishop of Dubuque.

Diocese of Davenport, IA—Most Rev. William E. Franklin, Bishop of Davenport.

Diocese of Des Moines, IA—Most Rev. Joseph L. Charron, C.P.P.S., Bishop of Des Moines.

Diocese of Sioux City, IA—Vacant See.

PROVINCE OF HARTFORD

Includes the States of Connecticut and Rhode Island.

Archdiocese of Hartford, CT—Most Rev. Henry J. Mansell, Archbishop of Hartford. Most Rev. Peter A. Rosazza, Auxiliary Bishop. Most Rev. Christie A. Macaluso, Auxiliary Bishop.

Diocese of Bridgeport, CT—Most Rev. William E. Lori, Bishop of Bridgeport.

Diocese of Norwich, CT—Most Rev. Michael R. Cote, Bishop of Norwich.

Diocese of Providence, RI—Most Rev. Robert E. Mulvee, Bishop of Providence.

PROVINCE OF INDIANAPOLIS

Includes the State of Indiana.

Archdiocese of Indianapolis, IN—Most Rev. Daniel M. Buechlein, O.S.B., Archbishop of Indianapolis.

Diocese of Evansville, IN—Most Rev. Gerald A. Gettelfinger, Bishop of Evansville.

Diocese of Fort Wayne-South Bend, IN—Most Rev. John M. D'Arcy, Bishop of Fort Wayne-South Bend.

Diocese of Gary, IN—Most Rev. Dale J. Melczek, Bishop of Gary.

Diocese of Lafayette in Indiana, IN—Most Rev. William L. Higi, Bishop of Lafayette in Indiana.

PROVINCE OF KANSAS CITY, KANSAS

Includes the State of Kansas.

Archdiocese of Kansas City, KS—Most Rev. James P. Keleher, Archbishop of Kansas City. Most Rev. Joseph F. Naumann, Coadjutor Bishop of Kansas City.

Diocese of Dodge City, KS—Most Rev. Ronald M. Gilmore, Bishop of Dodge City.
Diocese of Salina, KS—Most Rev. George K. Fitzsimons, Bishop of Salina.
Diocese of Wichita, KS—Vacant See.

PROVINCE OF LOS ANGELES

Includes Southern California and Central California.
Archdiocese of Los Angeles, CA—His Eminence Roger Cardinal Mahony, Archbishop of Los Angeles. Most Rev. Thomas J. Curry, Auxiliary Bishop. Most Rev. Gabino Zavala, Auxiliary Bishop. Most Rev. Gerald E. Wilkerson, Auxiliary Bishop. Most Rev. Edward W. Clark, Auxiliary Bishop. Most Rev. Oscar Azarcon Solis, Auxiliary Bishop.
Diocese of Fresno, CA—Most Rev. John T. Steinbock, Bishop of Fresno.
Diocese of Monterey, CA—Most Rev. Sylvester D. Ryan, Bishop of Monterey.
Diocese of Orange, CA—Most Rev. Tod D. Brown, Bishop of Orange. Most Rev. Jaime Soto, Auxiliary Bishop. Most Rev. Dominic M. Luong, Auxiliary Bishop.
Diocese of San Bernardino, CA—Most Rev. Gerald R. Barnes, Bishop of San Bernardino.
Diocese of San Diego, CA—Most Rev. Robert H. Brom, Bishop of San Diego. Most Rev. Gilbert E. Chavez, Auxiliary Bishop. Most Rev. Salvatore J. Cordileone, Auxiliary Bishop.

PROVINCE OF LOUISVILLE

Includes the States of Kentucky and Tennessee.
Archdiocese of Louisville, KY—Most Rev. Thomas C. Kelly, O.P., Archbishop of Louisville.
Diocese of Covington, KY—Most Rev. Roger J. Foys, Bishop of Covington.
Diocese of Knoxville, TN—Most Rev. Joseph E. Kurtz, Bishop of Knoxville.
Diocese of Lexington, KY—Most Rev. Ronald W. Gainer, Bishop of Lexington.
Diocese of Memphis, TN—Most Rev. J. Terry Steib, S.V.D., Bishop of Memphis.
Diocese of Nashville, TN—Most Rev. Edward U. Kmiec, Bishop of Nashville.
Diocese of Owensboro, KY—Most Rev. John J. McRaith, Bishop of Owensboro.

PROVINCE OF MIAMI

Includes the State of Florida.
Archdiocese of Miami, FL—Most Rev. John C. Favalora, Archbishop of Miami. Most Rev. Felipe de Jesus Estevez, Auxiliary Bishop.
Diocese of Orlando, FL—Most Rev. Norbert Dorsey, C.P., Bishop of Orlando. Most Rev. Thomas G. Wenski, Coadjutor Bishop.
Diocese of Palm Beach, FL—Most Rev. Gerald M. Barbarito, Bishop of Palm Beach.
Diocese of Pensacola-Tallahassee, FL—Most Rev. John H. Ricard, S.S.J., Bishop of Pensacola-Tallahassee.
Diocese of St. Augustine, FL—Most Rev. Victor Galeone, Bishop of St. Augustine.
Diocese of St. Petersburg, FL—Most Rev. Robert N. Lynch, Bishop of St. Petersburg.
Diocese of Venice, FL—Most Rev. John J. Nevins, Bishop of Venice.

PROVINCE OF MILWAUKEE

Includes the State of Wisconsin.
Archdiocese of Milwaukee, WI—Most Rev. Timothy M. Dolan, Archbishop of Milwaukee. Most Rev. Richard J. Sklba, Auxiliary Bishop.
Diocese of Green Bay, WI—Most Rev. David A. Zubik, Bishop of Green Bay. Most Rev. Robert F. Morneau, Auxiliary Bishop.
Diocese of La Crosse, WI—Vacant See.
Diocese of Madison, WI—Most Rev. Robert C. Morlino, Bishop of Madison.
Diocese of Superior, WI—Most Rev. Raphael M. Fliss, Bishop of Superior.

PROVINCE OF MOBILE

Includes the states of Alabama and Mississippi.
Archdiocese of Mobile, AL—Most Rev. Oscar H. Lipscomb, Archbishop of Mobile.
Diocese of Birmingham, AL—Most Rev. David E. Foley, Bishop of Birmingham.
Diocese of Biloxi, MS—Most Rev. Thomas J. Rodi, Bishop of Biloxi.
Diocese of Jackson MS—Most Rev. Joseph N. Latino, Bishop of Jackson.

PROVINCE OF NEWARK

Includes the State of New Jersey.
Archdiocese of Newark, NJ—Most Rev. John J. Myers, Archbishop of Newark. Most Rev. David Arias, O.A.R., Auxiliary Bishop. Most Rev. Charles J. McDonnell, Auxiliary Bishop. Most Rev. Arthur J. Serratelli, Auxiliary Bishop. Most Rev. Edgar M. daCunha, S.V.D., Auxiliary Bishop.
Diocese of Camden, NJ—Most Rev. Joseph A. Galante, Bishop of Camden.
Diocese of Metuchen, NJ—Most Rev. Paul G. Bootkoski, Bishop of Metuchen.
Diocese of Paterson, NJ—Most Rev. Frank J. Rodimer, Bishop of Paterson.
Diocese of Trenton, NJ—Most Rev. John M. Smith, Bishop of Trenton.

PROVINCE OF NEW ORLEANS

Includes the State of Louisiana.
Archdiocese of New Orleans, LA—Most Rev. Alfred C. Hughes, Archbishop of New Orleans. Most Rev. Dominic Carmon, S.V.D., Auxiliary Bishop. Most Rev. Roger P. Morin, Auxiliary Bishop.
Diocese of Alexandria, LA—Vacant See.
Diocese of Baton Rouge, LA—Most Rev. Robert W. Muench, Bishop of Baton Rouge.
Diocese of Houma-Thibodaux, LA—Most Rev. Sam G. Jacobs, Bishop of Houma-Thibodaux.
Diocese of Lafayette, LA—Most Rev. Michael C. Jarrell, Bishop of Lafayette.
Diocese of Lake Charles, LA—Most Rev. Edward K. Braxton, Bishop of Lake Charles.
Diocese of Shreveport, LA —Most Rev. William B. Friend, Bishop of Shreveport.

PROVINCE OF NEW YORK

Includes the State of New York.
Archdiocese of New York, NY—His Eminence Edward Cardinal Egan, Archbishop of New York. Most Rev. Robert A. Brucato, Auxiliary Bishop. Most Rev. Robert J. Iriondo, Auxiliary Bishop. Most Rev. Dominick J. Lagonegro, Auxiliary Bishop.
Diocese of Albany, NY—Most Rev. Howard J. Hubbard, Bishop of Albany.
Diocese of Brooklyn, NY—Most Rev. Nicholas A. DiMarzio, Bishop of Brooklyn. Most Rev. Joseph M. Sullivan, Auxiliary Bishop. Most Rev. Rene A. Valero, Auxiliary Bishop. Most Rev. Ignatius Catanello, Auxiliary Bishop.
Diocese of Buffalo, NY—Vacant See. Most Rev. Edward M. Grosz, Auxiliary Bishop.
Diocese of Ogdensburg, NY—Most Rev. Robert J. Cunningham, Bishop of Ogdensburg.
Diocese of Rochester, NY—Most Rev. Matthew H. Clark, Bishop of Rochester.
Diocese of Rockville Centre, NY—Most Rev. William F. Murphy, Bishop of Rockville Centre. Most Rev. John C. Dunne, Auxiliary Bishop. Most Rev. Emil A. Wcela, Auxiliary Bishop. Most Rev. Paul H. Walsh, Auxiliary Bishop.
Diocese of Syracuse, NY—Most Rev. James M. Moynihan, Bishop of Syracuse.

PROVINCE OF OKLAHOMA CITY

Includes States of Arkansas and Oklahoma.
Archdiocese of Oklahoma City, OK—Most Rev. Eusebius J. Beltran, Archbishop of Oklahoma City.
Diocese of Little Rock, AR—Most Rev. James Peter Sartain, Bishop of Little Rock.
Diocese of Tulsa, OK—Most Rev. Edward J. Slattery, Bishop of Tulsa.

PROVINCE OF OMAHA

Includes the State of Nebraska.
Archdiocese of Omaha, NE—Most Rev. Elden F. Curtiss, Archbishop of Omaha.
Diocese of Grand Island, NE—Most Rev. Lawrence J. McNamara, Bishop of Grand Island.
Diocese of Lincoln, NE—Most Rev. Fabian W. Bruskewitz, Bishop of Lincoln.

PROVINCE OF PHILADELPHIA

Includes the State of Pennsylvania.
Archdiocese of Philadelphia, PA—His Eminence Justin Cardinal Rigali, Archbishop of Philadelphia. Most Rev. Robert P. Maginnis, Auxiliary Bishop. Most Rev. Michael F. Burbidge, Auxiliary Bishop.
Diocese of Allentown, PA—Most Rev. Edward P. Cullen, Bishop of Allentown.
Diocese of Altoona-Johnstown, PA—Most Rev. Joseph V. Adamec, Bishop of Altoona-Johnstown.
Diocese of Erie, PA—Most Rev. Donald W. Trautman, Bishop of Erie.
Diocese of Greensburg, PA—Most Rev. Lawrence E. Brandt, Bishop of Greensburg.
Diocese of Harrisburg, PA—Vacant See.
Diocese of Pittsburgh, PA—Most Rev. Donald W. Wuerl, Bishop of Pittsburgh. Most Rev. William J. Winter, Auxiliary Bishop.
Diocese of Scranton, PA—Most Rev. Joseph F. Martino, Bishop of Scranton. Most Rev. John M. Dougherty, Auxiliary Bishop.

PROVINCE OF PORTLAND IN OREGON

Includes the States of Oregon, Idaho and Montana.
Archdiocese of Portland, OR—Most Rev. John G. Vlazny, Archbishop of Portland in Oregon. Most Rev. Kenneth D. Steiner, Auxiliary Bishop.
Diocese of Baker, OR—Most Rev. Robert F. Vasa, Bishop of Baker.
Diocese of Boise, ID—Most Rev. Michael P. Driscoll, Bishop of Boise.
Diocese of Great Falls-Billings, MT—Most Rev. Anthony M. Milone, Bishop of Great Falls-Billings.
Diocese of Helena, MT— Most Rev. George L. Thomas, Bishop of Helena.

PROVINCE OF ST. LOUIS

Includes the State of Missouri.
Archdiocese of St. Louis, MO—Most Rev. Raymond L. Burke, Archbishop of St. Louis. Most Rev. Robert J. Hermann, Auxiliary Bishop.
Diocese of Jefferson City, MO—Most Rev. John R. Gaydos, Bishop of Jefferson City.
Diocese of Kansas City-St. Joseph, MO—Most Rev. Raymond J. Boland, Bishop of Kansas City-St. Joseph. Most Rev. Robert W. Finn, Coadjutor Bishop.
Diocese of Springfield-Cape Girardeau, MO—Most Rev. John J. Leibrecht, Bishop of Springfield-Cape Girardeau.

PROVINCE OF ST. PAUL AND MINNEAPOLIS

Includes the States of Minnesota, South Dakota and North Dakota.
Archdiocese of St. Paul and Minneapolis, MN—Most Rev. Harry J. Flynn, Archbishop of St. Paul and Minneapolis. Most Rev. Frederick F. Campbell, Auxiliary Bishop. Most Rev. Richard E. Pates, Auxiliary Bishop.
Diocese of Bismarck, ND—Most Rev. Paul A. Zipfel, Bishop of Bismarck.
Diocese of Crookston, MN—Most Rev. Victor H. Balke, Bishop of Crookston.
Diocese of Duluth, MN—Most Rev. Dennis M. Schnurr, Bishop of Duluth.
Diocese of Fargo, ND—Most Rev. Samuel J. Aquila, Bishop of Fargo.
Diocese of New Ulm, MN—Most Rev. John C. Nienstedt, Bishop of New Ulm.
Diocese of Rapid City, SD—Most Rev. Blase J. Cupich, Bishop of Rapid City.
Diocese of St. Cloud, MN—Most Rev. John F. Kinney, Bishop of St. Cloud.
Diocese of Sioux Falls, SD—Most Rev. Robert J. Carlson, Bishop of Sioux Falls.
Diocese of Winona, MN—Most Rev. Bernard J. Harrington, Bishop of Winona.

PROVINCE OF SAN ANTONIO

Includes the State of Texas.
Archdiocese of San Antonio, TX—Most Rev. Patrick F. Flores, Archbishop of San Antonio. Most Rev. Thomas J. Flanagan, Auxiliary Bishop. Most Rev. Patrick J. Zurek, Auxiliary Bishop.
Diocese of Amarillo, TX—Most Rev. John W. Yanta, Bishop of Amarillo.
Diocese of Austin, TX— Most Rev. Gregory M. Aymond, Bishop of Austin.
Diocese of Beaumont, TX—Most Rev. Curtis J. Guillory, S.V.D., Bishop of Beaumont.
Diocese of Brownsville, TX—Most Rev. Raymundo J. Peña, Bishop of Brownsville.
Diocese of Corpus Christi, TX—Most Rev. Edmond Carmody, Bishop of Corpus Christi.
Diocese of Dallas, TX—Most Rev. Charles V. Grahmann, Bishop of Dallas.
Diocese of El Paso, TX—Most Rev. Armando X. Ochoa, Bishop of El Paso.
Diocese of Fort Worth, TX—Most Rev. Joseph P. Delaney, Bishop of Fort Worth.
Diocese of Galveston-Houston, TX—Most Rev. Joseph A. Fiorenza, Bishop of Galveston-Houston. Most Rev. Daniel N. DiNardo, Coadjutor Bishop. Most Rev. Vincent M. Rizzotto, Auxiliary Bishop. Most Rev. Jose S. Vasquez, Auxiliary Bishop.
Diocese of Laredo, TX—Most Rev. James A. Tamayo, Bishop of Laredo.
Diocese of Lubbock, TX—Most Rev. Placido Rodriguez, C.M.F., Bishop of Lubbock.
Diocese of San Angelo, TX—Most Rev. Michael D. Pfeifer, O.M.I., Bishop of San Angelo.

Diocese of Tyler, TX— Most Rev. Alvaro Corrada del Rio, S.J., Bishop of Tyler.

Diocese of Victoria, TX—Most Rev. David E. Fellhauer, Bishop of Victoria.

PROVINCE OF SAN FRANCISCO

Includes Northern California and the States of Nevada, Utah and Hawaii.

Archdiocese of San Francisco, CA—Most Rev. William J. Levada, Archbishop of San Francisco. Most Rev. Ignatius Wang, Auxiliary Bishop. Most Rev. John Charles Wester, Auxiliary Bishop.

Diocese of Honolulu, HI—Vacant See.

Diocese of Las Vegas, NV—Most Rev. Joseph A. Pepe, Bishop of Las Vegas.

Diocese of Oakland, CA—Most Rev. Allen H. Vigneron, Bishop of Oakland.

Diocese of Reno, NV—Most Rev. Phillip F. Straling, Bishop of Reno.

Diocese of Sacramento, CA—Most Rev. William K. Weigand, Bishop of Sacramento. Most Rev. Richard J. Garcia, Auxiliary Bishop.

Diocese of Salt Lake City, UT—Most Rev. George H. Niederauer, Bishop of Salt Lake City.

Diocese of San Jose, CA—Most Rev. Patrick J. McGrath, Bishop of San Jose.

Diocese of Santa Rosa, CA— Most Rev. Daniel F. Walsh, Bishop of Santa Rosa.

Diocese of Stockton, CA—Most Rev. Stephen E. Blaire, Bishop of Stockton.

PROVINCE OF SANTA FE

Includes the States of New Mexico, and Arizona.

Archdiocese of Santa Fe, NM—Most Rev. Michael J. Sheehan, Archbishop of Santa Fe.

Diocese of Gallup, NM—Most Rev. Donald E. Pelotte, S.S.S., Bishop of Gallup.

Diocese of Las Cruces, NM—Most Rev. Ricardo Ramirez, C.S.B., Bishop of Las Cruces.

Diocese of Phoenix, AZ—Most Rev. Thomas J. Olmsted, Bishop of Phoenix.

Diocese of Tucson, AZ—Most Rev. Gerald F. Kicanas, Bishop of Tucson.

PROVINCE OF SEATTLE

Includes the State of Washington.

Archdiocese of Seattle, WA—Most Rev. Alexander J. Brunett, Archbishop of Seattle.

Diocese of Spokane, WA—Most Rev. William S. Skylstad, Bishop of Spokane.

Diocese of Yakima, WA—Most Rev. Carlos A. Sevilla, S.J., Bishop of Yakima.

PROVINCE OF WASHINGTON

Includes the District of Columbia, and Montgomery, Prince Georges, Charles, Calvert and St. Mary's Counties in Maryland, also Virgin Islands.

Archdiocese of Washington, DC—His Eminence Theodore Cardinal McCarrick, Archbishop of Washington. Most Rev. Leonard J. Olivier, S.V.D., Auxiliary Bishop. Most Rev. Kevin J. Farrell, Auxiliary Bishop. Most Rev. Francisco Gonzalez, S.F., Auxiliary Bishop.

Diocese of St. Thomas, V.I.—Most Rev. George V. Murry, S.J., Bishop of St. Thomas, V.I.

Archdiocese for the Military Services—Most Rev. Edwin F. O'Brien, Archbishop for the Military Services. Most Rev. Francis X. Roque, Auxiliary Bishop. Most Rev. Joseph J. Madera, M.Sp.S., Auxiliary Bishop. Most Rev. John J. Kaising, Auxiliary Bishop.

EASTERN CATHOLIC JURISDICTIONS
ANTIOCHENE TRADITION

Maronite Rite—

Eparchy of St. Maron of Brooklyn—Most Rev. Gregory John Mansour, Bishop St. Maron.

Eparchy of Our Lady of Lebanon of Los Angeles—Most Rev. Robert J. Shaheen, Bishop of Our Lady of Lebanon.

ARMENIAN TRADITION

Armenian Catholic Exarchate of U.S.A. and Canada—Most Rev. Manuel Batakian, Apostolic Exarch for the Armenians.

CHALDEAN TRADITION

Eparchy of St. Thomas the Apostle—Most Rev. Ibrahim Ibrahim, Eparch of St. Thomas the Apostle.

Eparchy of St. Peter the Apostle—Most Rev. Sarhad Y. Jammo, Eparch of St. Peter the Apostle.

CONSTANTINOPOLITAN TRADITION

Melkite - Greek Rite—

Diocese of Newton—Most Rev. John A. Elya, B.S.O., Bishop of Newton. Most Rev. Nicholas J. Samra, Auxiliary Bishop.

Romanian Rite—

Romanian Catholic Diocese of St. George's in Canton—Most Rev. John M. Botean, Bishop of St. George's in Canton.

Ruthenian Rite—

Metropolitan Archeparchy of Pittsburgh Byzantine—Most Rev. Basil M. Schott, O.F.M., Archbishop of Pittsburgh of the Byzantine.

Byzantine Eparchy of Parma—Most Rev. John M. Kudrick, Bishop of Parma

Byzantine Catholic Eparchy of Passaic—Most Rev. Andrew Pataki, Bishop of Passaic.

Byzantine Eparchy of Van Nuys—Most Rev. William C. Skurla, Bishop of Van Nuys.

Russian Rite—

Two parishes—

Ukrainian Rite—

Metropolitan Archdiocese of Philadelphia Ukrainian—Most Rev. Stephen Soroka, Archbishop of Philadelphia for Ukrainian Catholics.

Ukrainian Catholic Diocese of St. Josaphat in Parma—Most Rev. Robert M. Moskal, Bishop of St. Josaphat in Parma.

Diocese of St. Nicholas in Chicago for Ukrainians—Most Rev. Richard Stephen Seminack, Bishop of St. Nicholas of Chicago.

Ukrainian Catholic Diocese of Stamford—Most Rev. Basil H. Losten, Bishop of Stamford.

Syrian Rite—

Diocese of Our Lady of Deliverance—Most Rev. Joseph Younan, Bishop of Our Lady of Deliverance.

Syro-Malabar—

St. Thomas Syro-Malabar Catholic Diocese of Chicago—Most Rev. Jacob Angadiath, Bishop of St. Thomas of Chicago.

ECCLESIASTICAL FORMS OF ADDRESS RECOGNIZED IN THE UNITED STATES

These are the formal forms of address used in correspondence:

CARDINALS:

Address on envelope: His Eminence (Christian name) Cardinal (Surname)

Salutation: Your Eminence:

Concluding a letter: I have the honor to be, Your Eminence, *etc.*

ARCHBISHOPS:

Address on envelope: Most Reverend N_______ N_______

Salutation: Your Excellency:

Concluding a letter: I have the honor to be, Your Excellency, *etc.*

BISHOPS:

Address on envelope: Most Reverend N_______ N_______

Salutation: Your Excellency:

Concluding a letter: I have the honor to be, Your Excellency, *etc.*

ABBOTS:

Address on envelope: Right Reverend N_______ N_______ *(add religious order initials)*

Salutation: Right Reverend Abbot:

Concluding a letter: I have the honor to be, Right Reverend Abbot, *etc.*

PROTONOTARIES APOSTOLIC:

Address on envelope: Rev. Msgr. N_______ N_______

Salutation: Rev. Msgr.:

Concluding a letter: I am, Rev. Msgr., *etc.*

PRELATE OF HONOR OF HIS HOLINESS:

Address on envelope: Rev. Msgr. N_______ N_______

Salutation: Rev. Msgr.:

Concluding a letter: I am, Rev. Msgr., *etc.*

CHAPLAIN TO HIS HOLINESS:

Address on envelope: Rev. Msgr. N_______ N_______

Salutation: Rev. Msgr.:

Concluding a letter: I am, Rev. Msgr., *etc.*

SECULAR PRIESTS:

Address on envelope: Rev. N_______ N_______

Salutation: Dear Reverend Father:

Concluding a letter: I am, Reverend Father, *etc.*

RELIGIOUS ORDER PRIESTS:

Address on envelope: Rev. N_______ N_______ *(add religious order initials)*

Salutation: Dear Reverend Father:

Concluding a letter: I am, Reverend Father, *etc.*

DEACONS:

Address on envelope: Rev. Mr. N_______

Salutation: Dear Deacon N_______

Concluding a letter: I am, Respectfully yours, *etc.*

BROTHERS:

Address on envelope: Brother N_______

Salutation: Dear Brother N_______

Concluding a letter: I am, Respectfully yours, *etc.*

SISTERS:

Address on envelope: Sister N_______

Salutation: Dear Sister N_______

Concluding a letter: I am, Respectfully yours, *etc.*

AN ALPHABETICAL LIST OF THE

Cardinals, Archbishops, Bishops, Archabbots & Abbots of the United States

CARDINALS

His Eminence Luis Aponte Martinez, Retired Archbishop of San Juan, P.O. Box 9021967, San Juan, PR 00902-1967.
His Eminence William Baum, Prefect of Sacred Congregation for Catholic Education, Piazza Pio XII, Vatican City State, Europe 00120.
His Eminence Anthony Bevilacqua, Former Archbishop of Philadelphia, 100 E. Wynnewood R., Wynnewood, PA 19096.
His Eminence Avery Dulles, S.J., Fordham University, Spellman Hall, 441 East Fordham Rd., Bronx, NY 10458.
His Eminence Edward Egan, Archbishop of New York, 1011 First Ave., New York, NY 10022.
His Eminence Francis George, o.m.i., Archbishop of Chicago, 155 E. Superior St., Chicago, IL 60611.
His Eminence James Hickey, Retired Archbishop of Washington, DC, P.O. Box 29260, Washington, DC 20017.
His Eminence William Keeler, Archbishop of Baltimore, 320 Cathedral St., Baltimore, MD 21201.
His Eminence Bernard Law, Former Archbishop of Boston, 2121 Commonwealth Ave., Boston, MA 02135-3193.
His Eminence Roger Mahony, Archbishop of Los Angeles, 3424 Wilshire Blvd., Los Angeles, CA 90010-2241.
His Eminence Adam Maida, Archbishop of Detroit, 1234 Washington Blvd., Detroit, MI 48226.
His Eminence Theodore McCarrick, Archbishop of Washington, DC, P.O. Box 29260, Washington, DC 20017.
His Eminence Justin F. Rigali, Archbishop of Philadelphia, 222 N. 17th St., Philadelphia, PA 19103.
His Eminence Francis Stafford, President - Pontifical Council for the Laity, Piazza San Calisto 16, Vatican City State, Europe 00120.
His Eminence Edmund Szoka, President Pontifical Commission, Vatican City State, Europe. 00120.

ARCHBISHOPS

His Excellency,
The Most Reverend

Apuron, Anthony Sablan, o.f.m.cap., Archbishop of Agana, 196-B Cuesta San Ramon, Agana, Guam 96910.
Beltran, Eusebius J., Archbishop of Oklahoma City, P.O. Box 32180, Oklahoma City, OK 73123.
Borders, William D., Retired Archbishop of Baltimore, 320 Cathedral St., Baltimore, MD 21201.
Brunett, Alexander J., Archbishop of Seattle, 910 Marion St., Seattle, WA 98104.
Buechlein, Daniel M., o.s.b., Archbishop of Indianapolis, 1400 N. Meridian St., P.O. Box 1410, Indianapolis, IN 46206.
Burke, Raymond L., Archbishop of St. Louis, 4445 Lindell Blvd., St. Louis, MO 63108-2497.
Chaput, Charles J., o.f.m.cap., Archbishop of Denver, 1300 S. Steele St., Denver, CO 80210.
Cronin, Daniel A., Former Archbishop of Hartford, 469 Bloomfield Ave., Bloomfield, CT 06002.
Curtiss, Elden F., Archbishop of Omaha, 100 N. 62nd St., Omaha, NE 68132-2795.
Dimino, Joseph T., Retired Archbishop for the Military Services, P.O. Box 4469, Washington, DC 20017.
Dolan, Timothy M., Archbishop of Milwaukee, 3501 S. Lake Shore Dr., Milwaukee, WI 53235.
Donoghue, John F., Archbishop of Atlanta, 680 W. Peachtree St., N.W., Atlanta, GA 30308.
Favalora, John C., Archbishop of Miami, 9401 Biscayne Blvd., Miami Shore, FL 33138.
Flores, Patrick F., Archbishop of San Antonio, 2600 W. Woodlawn Ave., San Antonio, TX 78228.
Flynn, Harry J., Archbishop of St. Paul and Minneapolis, 226 Summit Ave., St. Paul, MN 55102.
Gerety, Peter Leo, Retired Archbishop of Newark, 60 Home Ave., Rutherford, NJ 07070.
Gonzalez, Roberto O., o.f.m., Archbishop of San Juan, P.O. Box 9021967, San Juan, PR 00902-1967.
Hannan, Philip M., Retired Archbishop of New Orleans, 106 Metairie Lawn Dr., Metairie, LA 70001.
Hanus, Jerome G., o.s.b., Archbishop of Dubuque, 1229 Mt. Loretto Ave., P.O. Box 479, Dubuque, IA 52004-0479.
Hughes, Alfred C., Archbishop of New Orleans, 7887 Walmsley Ave., New Orleans, LA 70125-3496.
Hunthausen, Raymond G., Retired Archbishop of Seattle, 910 Marion St., Seattle, WA 98104.
Hurley, Francis T., Archbishop Emeritus of Anchorage, P.O. Box 2239, Anchorage, AK 99510.
Keleher, James P., Archbishop of Kansas City in Kansas, 12615 Parallel Pkwy., Kansas City, KS 66109.
Kelly, Thomas C., o.p., Archbishop of Louisville, 212 E. College St., P.O. Box 1073, Louisville, KY 40201.
Kucera, Daniel W., o.s.b., Retired Archbishop of Dubuque, 13952 E. Marina Dr., #612, Aurora, CO 80014.
Levada, William J., Archbishop of San Francisco, One Peter Yorke Way, San Francisco, CA 94109.
Lipscomb, Oscar H., Archbishop of Mobile, 400 Government St., Mobile, AL 36633.
Mansell, Henry J., Archbishop of Hartford, 134 Farmington Ave., Hartford, CT 06105.
McCarthy, Edward A., Retired Archbishop of Miami, 9401 Biscayne Blvd., Miami Shores, FL 33138.
Myers, John Joseph, Archbishop of Newark, 171 Clifton Ave., Newark, NJ 07104-9500.
Naumann, Joseph F., Coadjutor Archbishop of Kansas City in Kansas, 12615 Parallel Pkwy., Kansas City, Kansas 66109.

His Excellency,
The Most Reverend

O'Brien, Edwin F., Archbishop for the Military Services USA, P.O. Box 4469, Washington, DC 20017.
O'Malley, Sean, o.f.m.cap., Archbishop of Boston, 2121 Commonwealth Ave., Boston, MA 02135-3101.
Pilarczyk, Daniel E., Archbishop of Cincinnati, 100 E. 8th St., Cincinnati, OH 45202.
Quinn, John R., Retired Archbishop of San Francisco, 322 Middlefield Rd., Menlo Park, CA 94025.
Sanchez, Robert F., Former Archbishop of Santa Fe, Catholic Center, St. Joseph's Pl., N.W., Albuquerque, NM 87120.
Schleck, Charles A., c.s.c., Titular Archbishop of Africa, Congregation for Evangelization, Palazzo di Propaganda Fide, Piazza di Spagna 48, Rome, Italy 00187.
Schott, Basil, o.f.m., Archbishop of Pittsburgh Byzantine, 66 Riverview Ave., Pittsburgh, PA 15214.
Schulte, Francis B., Former Archbishop of New Orleans, 7887 Walmsley Ave., New Orleans, LA 70125.
Schwietz, Roger L., o.m.i., Archbishop of Anchorage, 225 Cordova St., P.O. Box 2239, Anchorage, AK 99501-2409.
Sheehan, Michael J., Archbishop of Santa Fe, Catholic Center, 4000 Saint Joseph's Place, N.W., Albuquerque, NM 87120.
Soroka, Stefan, Archbishop of the Ukrainian Catholic Archeparchy of Philadelphia, 827 N. Franklin St., Philadelphia, PA 19123.
Sulyk, Stephen, Archbishop Emeritus of Ukrainian Catholic Archeparchy of Philadelphia, 827 N. Franklin St., Philadelphia, PA 19123.
Vlazny, John G., Archbishop of Portland in Oregon, 2838 E. Burnside St., Portland, OR 97214-1895.
Weakland, Rembert G., o.s.b. Retired Archbishop of Milwaukee, 3501 S. Lake Dr., St. Francis, WI 53235.
Zayek, Francis M., Retired Archbishop and Former Eparch (Bishop) of St. Maron of Brooklyn, 4010 Galt Ocean Dr., Apt. 1230, Fort Lauderdale, FL 33308.

BISHOPS

His Excellency,
The Most Reverend

Adamec, Joseph V., Bishop of Altoona-Johnstown, 126 Logan Blvd., Hollidaysburg, PA 16648.
Ahern, Patrick V., Retired Auxiliary Bishop of New York, St. Thomas More, 65 E. 89th St., New York, NY 10128.
Allue, Emilio, s.d.b., Auxiliary Bishop of Boston, 107 North Main St., Westford, MA 01886.
Amos, Martin John, Auxiliary Bishop of Cleveland, Akron Catholic Center, 795 Russell Ave., Akron, OH 44307-1115.
Anderson, Moses B., s.s.e., Retired Auxiliary Bishop of Detroit, 650 Waverly, Dearborn, MI 48128-1628.
Angadiath, Jacob, Bishop of St. Thomas Syro-Malabar Catholic Diocese of Chicago, 3009 S. 49th Ave., Cicero, IL 60804.
Angell, Kenneth A., Bishop of Burlington, 351 North Ave., P.O. Box 489, Burlington, VT 05402-0489.
Aquila, Samuel J., Bishop of Fargo, 5201 Bishops Blvd., Ste. A, Fargo, ND 58104-7605.
Arias, David, o.a.r., Auxiliary Bishop of Newark, St. Joseph of the Palisades Rectory, 6401 Palisade Ave., West New York, NJ 07093.

His Excellency,
The Most Reverend

Arzube, Juan, Retired Auxiliary Bishop of Los Angeles, Sacred He Nazareth Hse-3333 Manning Ave., Los Angeles, CA 90064-4804.
Aymond, Gregory M., Bishop of Austin, 1600 N. Congress Ave., P.O. Box 13327, Austin, TX 78711.
Baker, Robert J., Bishop of Charleston, 119 Broad St., Charleston, SC 29401.
Balke, Victor, Bishop of Crookston, 1200 Memorial Dr., Crookston, NY 56716.
Baltakis, Paul A., o.f.m., Retired Bishop for Lithuanian Catholics Outside Lithuania, 64-14 Clinton Ave., Maspeth, NY 11378-2418.
Banks, Robert J., Retired Bishop of Green Bay, 1910 S. Webster Ave., P.O. Box 23825, Green Bay, WI 54305-3825.
Barbarito, Gerald, Bishop of Palm Beach, 9995 N. Military Tr., Palm Beach Gardens, FL 33410.
Barnes, Gerald R., Bishop of San Bernardino, 1201 E. Highland Ave., San Bernardino, CA 92404.
Batakian, Manuel, Apostolic Exarch for Armenian Catholics in the U.S., 167 N. 6th St., Brooklyn NY 11211-3207.
Bennett, Gordon D., s.j., Auxiliary Bishop of Baltimore, 320 Cathedral St., Baltimore, MD 21201.
Blair, Leonard P., Bishop of Toledo, P.O. Box 985, Toledo, OH 43697-0985.
Blaire, Stephen E., Bishop of Stockton, 1105 N. Lincoln St., Stockton, CA 95203.
Boland, J. Kevin, Bishop of Savannah, 601 E. Liberty St., Savannah, GA 31401.
Boland, Raymond J., Bishop of Kansas City-St. Joseph, P.O. Box 419037, Kansas City, MO 64141.
Boles, John P., Auxiliary Bishop of Boston, 307 Bowdoin St., Boston, MA 02122.
Bootkoski, Paul G., Bishop of Metuchen, 10 Library Pl., Metuchen, NJ 08840.
Bosco, Anthony G., Retired Bishop of Greensburg, 723 E. Pittsburgh St., Greensburg, PA 15601.
Botean, John M., Bishop of St. George's in Canton, 1123 44th St., N.E., Canton, OH 44714-1297.
Boyea, Earl A., Auxiliary Bishop of Detroit, 8075 Ritter Ave., Centerline, MI 48015-1499.
Brandt, Lawrence E., Bishop of Greensburg, 723 E. Pittsburgh St., Greensburg, PA 15601.
Braxton, Edward K., Bishop of Lake Charles, 414 Iris St., Lake Charles, LA 70602.
Breitenbeck, Joseph M., Retired Bishop of Grand Rapids, 660 Burton St., S.E., Grand Rapids, MI 49507.
Britt, Kevin M., Bishop of Grand Rapids, 660 Burton St., S.E., Grand Rapids, MI 49507.
Broderick, Edwin B., Former Bishop of Albany, 900 Park Ave., New York, NY 10021.
Brom, Robert H., Bishop of San Diego, P.O. Box 85728, San Diego, CA 92186-5728.
Brown, Tod D., Bishop of Orange, Marywood Center, 2811 E. Villa Real Dr., Orange, CA 92867.
Brucato, Robert A., Auxiliary Bishop of New York, 1011 First Ave., New York, NY 10022.
Bruskewitz, Fabian W., Bishop of Lincoln, P.O. Box 80328, Lincoln, NE 68510-0328.
Bullock, William H., Retired Bishop of Madison, 702 S. High Point Rd., Madison, WI 53744-4983.
Burbidge, Michael F., Auxiliary Bishop of Philadelphia, 100 E. Wynnewood Rd., Wynnewood, PA 19096.

His Excellency,
The Most Reverend

Buswell, Charles A., Retired Bishop of Pueblo, Villa Pueblo Towers, 855 Hunter Dr., #810, Pueblo, CO 81001-1837.

Camacho, Tomas A., Bishop of Chalan Kanoa, Our Lady of Mt. Carmel, P.O. Box 745, Saipan, MP 96950.

Campbell, Frederick F., Auxiliary Bishop of St. Paul and Minneapolis, 226 Summit Ave., St. Paul, MN 55102.

Carlson, Robert J., Bishop of Sioux Falls, 523 N. Duluth Ave., Sioux Falls, SD 57104.

Carmody, Edmond, Bishop of Corpus Christi, 620 Lipan St., P.O. Box 2620, Corpus Christi, TX 78403.

Carmon, Dominic, s.v.d., Auxiliary Bishop of New Orleans, P.O. Box 641000, Kenner, LA 70064-1000.

Casiano-Vargas, Ulises, Bishop of Mayaguez, P.O. Box 2272, Mayaguez, PR 00709.

Catanello, Ignatius, Auxiliary Bishop of Brooklyn, 175-20 74th Ave., Flushing, NY 11366.

Charron, Joseph L., c.pp.s., Bishop of Des Moines, 601 Grand Ave., Des Moines, IA 50309.

Chavez, Gilbert E., Auxiliary Bishop of San Diego, 2020 Alaquinas Dr., San Ysidro, CA 92173-2107.

Chedid, John, Retired Bishop of Our Lady of Lebanon of Los Angeles, 333 S. San Vicente Blvd., Los Angeles, CA 90048.

Christian, Francis J., Auxiliary Bishop of Manchester, St. Joseph Cathedral, 145 Lowell St., Manchester, NH 03104.

Clark, Edward W., Auxiliary Bishop of Los Angeles, Our Lady of the Angels Pastoral Region, 2636 S. Mansfield Ave., Los Angeles, CA 90016-3512.

Clark, Matthew H., Bishop of Rochester, 1150 Buffalo Rd., Rochester, NY 14624.

Clinch, Harry A., Retired Bishop of Monterey, 3400 Paul Sweet Rd., #C-119, Santa Cruz, CA 95065.

Coleman, George W., Bishop of Fall River, 47 Underwood St., Fall River, MA 02722.

Conlon, R. Daniel, Bishop of Steubenville, 422 Washington St., Steubenville, OH 43952-5969.

Connolly, Thomas J., Former Bishop of Baker, P.O. Box 5999, Bend, OR 97708.

Conway, Edwin M., Auxiliary Bishop of Chicago, 1555 N. State Pkwy., Chicago, IL 60610.

Cooney, Patrick R., Bishop of Gaylord, 611 W. North St., Gaylord, MI 49735-8349.

Cordileone, Salvatore J., Auxiliary Bishop of San Diego, P.O. Box 85728, San Diego, CA 92186-5728

Corrada del Rio, Alvaro, s.j., Bishop of Tyler, 1015 E.S.E. Loop 323, Tyler, TX 75701-9663.

Costello, Thomas J., Retired Auxiliary Bishop of Syracuse, 1515 Midland Ave, P.O. Box 511, Syracuse, NY 13205.

Cote, Michael R., Bishop of Norwich, 201 Broadway, Norwich, CT 06360.

Cullen, Edward P., Bishop of Allentown, P.O. Box F., 4029 W. Tilghman St., Allentown, PA 18105.

Cummins, John S., Former Bishop of Oakland, 634 21st St., Oakland, CA 94612.

Cunningham, Joseph, Bishop of Ogdensburg, P.O. Box 369, Ogdensburg, NY 13669.

Cupich, Blase, Bishop of Rapid City, 606 Cathedral Dr., Rapid City, SD 57701.

Curlin, William G., Retired Bishop of Charlotte, 1521 Dilworth Rd., P.O. Box 36776, Charlotte, NC 28236.

Curry, Thomas J., Auxiliary Bishop of Los Angeles, Santa Barbara Pastoral Region, 3240 Calle Pinon, Santa Barbara, CA 93105.

da Cunha, Edgar M., s.d.v., Auxiliary Bishop of Newark, 171 Clifton Ave., Newark, NJ 07104-0500.

Daily, Thomas V., Retired Bishop of Brooklyn, 7200 Douglaston Pkwy., Douglaston, NY 11362.

Daly, James J., Retired Auxiliary Bishop of Rockville Centre, 25 Lanes Rd., Blue Point, NY 11715.

D'Antonio, Nicholas, o.f.m., Retired Vicar for Latin American Apostolate, Archdiocese of New Orleans, 2820 Burdette St., New Orleans, LA 70125-2541.

D'Arcy, John M., Bishop of Fort Wayne-South Bend, P.O. Box 390, Fort Wayne, IN 46801.

Delaney, Joseph P., Bishop of Fort Worth, 800 West Loop 820 S., Fort Worth, TX 76108.

DeSimone, Louis A., Former Auxiliary Bishop of Philadelphia, St. Monica Church, St. Justin Martyr Rectory, 1222 Hagysford Rd., Narberth PA 19072.

DiLorenzo, Francis X., Bishop of Richmond, 811 Cathedral Pl., Richmond, VA 23220-4801.

DiMarzio, Nicholas A., Bishop of Brooklyn, 75 Greene Ave., P.O. Box C, Brooklyn, NY 11202.

DiNardo, Daniel N., Coadjutor Bishop of Galveston-Houston, 1700 San Jacinto St., Houston, TX 77002.

Dinh Mai Luong, Dominic, Auxiliary Bishop of Orange, 2811 E. Villa Real Dr., Orange, CA 92613-1595.

Donnelly, Robert, Auxiliary Bishop of Toledo, 2544 Parkwood Ave., P.O. Box 985, Toledo, OH 43610.

Donovan, Paul V., Retired Bishop of Kalamazoo, 238 Falkirk Ct., Kalamazoo, MI 49006-4355.

His Excellency,
The Most Reverend

Doran, Thomas G., Bishop of Rockford, 555 Coleman Dr., Rockford, IL 61108.

Dorsey, Norbert L., c.p., Bishop of Orlando, 46 E. Robinston St., Orlando, FL 32801.

Doueihi, Hector, Retired Bishop of the Maronite Eparchy of St. Maron of Brooklyn, Our Lady of Lebanon Cathedral, 109 Remsen St., Brooklyn, NY 11201-4212.

Dougherty, John M., Auxiliary Bishop of Scranton, 300 Wyoming Ave., Scranton, PA 18503.

Driscoll, Michael P., Bishop of Boise, 303 Federal Way, Boise, ID 83705-5925.

Dudick, Michael J., Retired Bishop of Passaic, 445 Lackawanna Ave., West Paterson, NJ 07424.

Dudley, Paul V., Retired Bishop of Sioux Falls, Church of St. Dominic, 116 North Linden, Northfield, MN 55057-1435.

DuMaine, R. Pierre, Former Bishop of San Jose, 20 Willow Rd., Unit 43, Menlo Park, CA 94025.

Dunne, John C., Auxiliary Bishop of Rockville Centre, P.O. Box 39, Farmingdale, NY 11735-0039.

Dupre, Thomas L., Retired Bishop of Springfield, 68 Elliot St., P.O. Box 1730, Springfield, MA 01101.

Edyvean, Walter J., Auxiliary Bishop of Boston, St.Patrick, 44 East Central St., Natick, MA 01760.

Elya, John A., b.s.o., Eparch of Newton, 3 VFW Pkwy., Roslindale, MA 02131.

Estevez, Felipe J., Auxiliary Bishop of Miami, 5260 N.E. 7th Ave., Miami, FL 33137.

Farrell, Kevin J., Auxiliary Bishop of Washington, P.O. Box 29260, Washington, DC 20017.

Fellhauer, David E., Bishop of Victoria, P.O. Box 4070, Victoria, TX 77903.

Fernandez, Gilberto, Retired Auxiliary Bishop of Miami, 5260 N.E. 7th Ave., Miami, FL 33137.

Finn, Robert W., Coadjutor Bishop of Kansas City-St. Joseph, P.O. Box 419037, Kansas City, MO 64141.

Fiorenza, Joseph A., Bishop of Galveston-Houston, 1700 San Jacinto, Houston, TX 77002-8291.

Fitzpatrick, John J., Retired Bishop of Brownsville, P.O. Box 2279, Brownsville, TX 78522-2279.

Fitzsimons, George K., Bishop of Salina, 103 N. Ninth Ave., P.O. Box 980, Salina, KS 67402-0980.

Flanagan, Thomas J., Auxiliary Bishop of San Antonio, P.O. Box 28410, San Antonio, TX 78228-0410.

Fliss, Raphael M., Bishop of Superior, 1201 Hughitt Ave., P.O. Box 969, Superior, WI 54880.

Foley, David E., Bishop of Birmingham, 2121 Third Ave., N., Birmingham, AL 35203.

Forst, Marion F., Retired Auxiliary Bishop of Kansas City in Kansas, Villa St. Francis, 16600 W. 126th St., Olathe, KS 66062-1184.

Foys, Roger J., Bishop of Covington, P.O. Box 18548, Erlanger, KY 41018-0548.

Franklin, William E., Bishop of Davenport, 2761 Scott St., Davenport, IA 52803.

Franzetta, Benedict C., Retired Auxiliary Bishop of Youngstown, 144 W. Wood St., Youngstown, OH 44503.

Frey, Gerard L., Retired Bishop of Lafayette, 1408 Carmel Ave., P.O. Drawer 3387, Lafayette, LA 70501.

Friend, William B., Bishop of Shreveport & Apostolic Admin. of Alexandria, 3500 Fairfield Ave., Shreveport, LA 71104-4108.

Gainer, Ronald W., Bishop of Lexington, 1310 W. Main St., Lexington, KY 40508-2048.

Galante, Joseph A., Bishop of Camden, 631 Market St., P.O. Box 708, Camden, NJ 08101.

Galeone, Victor B., Bishop of St. Augustine, P.O. Box 24000, Jacksonville, FL 32241-4000.

Garcia, Richard J., Auxiliary Bishop of Sacramento, 2110 Broadway, Sacramento, CA 95818.

Garcia-Siller, Gustavo M.Sp.S., Auxiliary Bishop of Chicago, 2330 W. 118th St., Chicago, IL 60643.

Garland, James H., Bishop of Marquette, 300 Rock St., P.O. Box 550, Marquette, MI 49855.

Garmendia, Francisco, Retired Auxiliary Bishop of New York, St. Vincent de Paul, 900 Intervale Ave., Bronx, NY 10459.

Gaydos, John R., Bishop of Jefferson City, Bishop's House, P.O. Box 417, Jefferson City, MO 65102.

Gelineau, Louis E., Retired Bishop of Providence, One Cathedral Square, Providence, RI 02903.

Gendron, Odore J., Retired Bishop of Manchester, St. Joseph Cathedral Rectory, 145 Lowell St., Manchester, NH 03104-6135.

Gerber, Eugene J., Retired Bishop of Wichita, 505 Sandtrap Wichita, KS 67235.

Gerry, Joseph J., o.s.b., Retired Bishop of Portland in Maine, 510 Ocean Ave., P.O. Box 11559, Portland, ME 04104-7559.

Gettelfinger, Gerald A., Bishop of Evansville, 4200 N. Kentucky Ave., Evansville, IN 47711.

Gilmore, Ronald M., Bishop of Dodge City, 910 Central Ave., Box 137, Dodge City, KS 67801.

His Excellency,
The Most Reverend

Glynn, John J., Retired Auxiliary Bishop for the Military Services, 20 Cypress Rd., Milton, MA 02086.

Goedert, Raymond E., Retired Auxiliary Bishop of Chicago, 1555 N. State Pkwy., Chicago, IL 60610.

Gomez, Jose H., Auxiliary Bishop of Denver, 1300 Steele St., Denver, CO 80210.

Gonzalez, Francisco, s.f., Auxiliary Bishop of Washington, P.O. Box 29260, Washington, DC 20017.

Gorman, John R., Retired Auxiliary Bishop of Chicago, 10731 West 131st. St., Orland Park, IL 60462.

Gossman, F. Joseph, Bishop of Raleigh, 715 Nazareth, Raleigh, NC 27606.

Gracida, Rene H., Bishop Emeritus of Corpus Christi, 620 Lipan St., P.O. Box 2620, Corpus Christi, TX 78403.

Grahmann, Charles V., Bishop of Dallas, 3725 Blackburn, P.O. Box 190507, Dallas, TX 75219.

Gregory, Wilton D., Bishop of Belleville, 222 South Third St., Belleville, IL 62220.

Gries, Roger W., o.s.b., Auxiliary Bishop of Cleveland, 5135 Superior Ave., Cleveland, OH 44103.

Griffin, James A., Bishop of Columbus, 198 E. Broad St., Columbus, OH 43215.

Grosz, Edward M., Auxiliary Bishop of Buffalo, St. Stanislaus Parish, 123 Townsend St., Buffalo, NY 14212-1299.

Guillory, Curtis J., Bishop of Beaumont, 703 Archie St., P.O. Box 3948, Beaumont, TX 77704-3948.

Gumbleton, Thomas J., Auxiliary Bishop of Detroit, 1234 Washington Blvd., Detroit, MI 48226.

Hanifen, Richard C., Former Bishop of Colorado Springs, 228 N. Cascade Ave., Colorado Springs, CO 80903.

Harrington, Bernard J., Bishop of Winona, 55 W. Sanborn St., P.O. Box 588, Winona, MN 55987.

Harrison, Frank J., Retired Bishop of Syracuse, Dillon Hall, 714 E. Brighton Ave., Syracuse, NY 13205.

Hart, Daniel A., Retired Bishop of Norwich, 213 Broadway, Norwich, CT 06360.

Hart, Joseph H., Bishop Emeritus of Cheyenne, Box 1468, Cheyenne, WY 82003-1468.

Head, Edward D., Retired Bishop of Buffalo, 795 Main St., Buffalo, NY 14203-1250.

Hermann, Robert J., Auxiliary Bishop of St. Louis, 4445 Lindell Blvd., St. Louis, MO 63108.

Higi, William L., Bishop of Lafayette in Indiana, 610 Lingle Ave., Lafayette, IN 47902.

Hogan, James J., Retired Bishop of Altoona- Johnstown, 126 Logan Blvd., Hollidaysburg, PA 16648.

Houck, William R., Retired Bishop of Jackson, 150 S. Wacker Dr., 20th Floor, Chicago, IL 60606-4200.

Howze, Joseph L., Retired Bishop of Biloxi, P.O. Box 8152, Biloxi, MS 39535-8152.

Hubbard, Howard J., Bishop of Albany, 125 Eagle St., Albany, NY 12202.

Hughes, Edward T., Bishop Emeritus of Metuchen, 914 Milford-Warren Glen Rd., Milford NJ 08848-1619.

Hughes, William A., Retired Bishop of Covington, Cathedral Basilica of the Assumption, 1140 Madison Ave., Covington, KY 41011-3116.

Hurley, Walter A., Auxiliary Bishop of Detroit, 1234 Washington Blvd., Detroit, MI 48226.

Ibrahim, Ibrahim, Bishop-Eparch to St. Thomas the Apostle (Chaldean), 25603 Berg Rd., Southfield, MI 48034.

Imesch, Joseph L., Bishop of Joliet, 425 Summit St., Joliet, IL 60435.

Iriondo, Robert Josu, Auxiliary Bishop of New York, St. Anthony Padua Parish, 832 W. 166th St., Bronx, NY 10459.

Irwin, Francis X., Auxiliary Bishop of Boston, 99 Margin St., Peabody, MA 01960.

Jacobs, Sam, Bishop of Houma-Thibodaux, P.O. Box 505, Schriever, LA 70395.

Jakubowski, Thad J., Retired Auxiliary Bishop of Chicago, 6002 W. Berteau Ave., Chicago, IL 60634-1630.

Jammo, Sarhad Y., Bishop of St. Peter the Apostle (Chaldean), 1627 Jamacha Way, El Cajon, CA 92019.

Jarrell, Michael, Bishop of Lafayette, 1408 Carmel Ave., Lafayette, LA 70501.

Jenky, Daniel R., c.s.c., Bishop of Peoria, 412 N.E. Madison Ave., Peoria, IL 61603-3720.

Jugis, Peter J., Bishop of Charlotte, 1123 S. Church St., Charlotte, SC 28203.

Kaffer, Roger L., Retired Auxiliary Bishop of Joliet, 425 Summit St., Joliet, IL 60435.

Kaising, John J., Auxiliary Bishop of the Archdiocese for the Military Services, P.O. Box 4469, Washington, DC 20017.

Kane, Francis, Auxiliary Bishop of Chicago, 1651 W. Diversey, Chicago, IL 60614.

Kettler, Donald J., Bishop of Fairbanks, 1316 Peger Rd., Fairbanks, AK 99709.

Kicanas, Gerald F., Bishop of Tucson, P.O. Box 31, Tucson AZ 85702.

Kinney, John F., Bishop of St. Cloud, 214 Third Ave., S., Box 1248, St. Cloud, MN 56302-1248.

His Excellency,
The Most Reverend

Kmiec, Edward U., Bishop of Nashville, 2400 Twenty-First Ave., S., Nashville, TN 37212.
Kudrick, John M., Bishop of Parma, 1900 Carlton Rd., Parma, OH 44134.
Kurtz, Joseph E., Bishop of Knoxville, 805 Northshore Dr., S.W., P.O. Box 11127, Knoxville, TN 37939-1127.
Kuzma, George M., Retired Bishop of Van Nuys, Byzantine Eparchy of Van Nuys, 8105 North 16th St., Phoenix, AZ 85020-3999.
Lagonegro, Dominick J., Auxiliary Bishop of New York, St. Columba Parish, 301 Ann St., Newburgh, NY 12550-5467.
Larkin, W. Thomas, Retired Bishop of St. Petersburg, 908 S. Prospect Ave., Clearwater, FL 33756.
Latino, Joseph N., Bishop of Jackson, P.O. 2248, Jackson, MS 39225-2248.
Leibrecht, John J., Bishop of Springfield-Cape Girardeau, The Catholic Center, 601 S. Jefferson, Springfield, MO 65806-3143.
Lennon, Richard G., Auxiliary Bishop of Boston, 2121 Commonwealth Ave., Boston, MA 02135-3193.
Lessard, Raymond W., Retired Bishop of Savannah, St. Vincent de Paul Seminary, 10701 S. Military Tr., Boynton Beach, FL 33436-4899.
Listecki, Jerome E., Auxiliary Bishop of Chicago, St. Ignatius Parish, 200 N. Milwaukee Ave., Ste. 200, Libertyville, IL 60048-2250.
Lohmuller, Martin N., Retired Auxiliary Bishop of Philadelphia, Villa Maria House of Studies, 1140 King Rd., Immaculata, PA 19345.
Lori, William E., Bishop of Bridgeport, 238 Jewett Ave., Bridgeport, CT 06606-2892.
Losten, Basil, Bishop of Stamford, 14 Peveril Rd., Stamford, CT 06902-3019.
Lotocky, Innocent, o.s.b.m., Retired Bishop of St. Nicholas in Chicago, 2245 W. Rice St., Chicago, IL 60622.
Loverde, Paul S., Bishop of Arlington, 200 N. Glebe Rd., Arlington, VA 22203.
Lucas, George J., Bishop of Springfield in Illinois, 1615 W. Washington St., P.O. Box 3187, Springfield, IL 62708.
Lynch, Robert N., Bishop of St. Petersburg, P.O. Box 40200, St. Petersburg, FL 33743-0200.
Lyne, Timothy J., Retired Auxiliary Bishop of Chicago, Holy Name Cathedral, 730 N. Wabash, Chicago, IL 60611.
Macaluso, Christie A., Auxiliary Bishop of Hartford, 134 Farmington Ave., Hartford, CT 06105-3784.
Madera, Joseph J., m.sp.s., Auxiliary Bishop for the Military Services, P.O. Box 4469, Washington, DC 20017.
Maginnis, Robert P., Auxiliary Bishop of Philadelphia, St. Colman Rectory, 11 Simpson Rd., Ardmore, PA 19003-2812.
Maguire, Joseph F., Retired Bishop of Springfield, 68 Elliot St., Springfield, MA 01101.
Malone, Richard J., Bishop of Portland in Maine, 510 Ocean Ave., Portland, ME 04104-7559.
Maloney, Charles G., Retired Auxiliary Bishop of Louisville, 212 E. College St., P.O. Box 1073, Louisville, KY 40201.
Malooly, William Francis, Auxiliary Bishop of Baltimore, 320 Cathedral St., Baltimore, MD 21201.
Mansour, Gregory J., Bishop of the Eparchy of St. Maron of Brooklyn, 109 Remsen St., Brooklyn, NY 11201.
Manz, John R., Auxiliary Bishop of Chicago, 1820 S. Leavitt St., Chicago, IL 60608.
Marconi, Dominic A., Retired Auxiliary Bishop of Newark, 71 Washington Ave., Chatham, NJ 07928.
Martino, Joseph F., Bishop of Scranton, 300 Wyoming Ave., Scranton, PA 18503.
Matthiesen, Leroy T., Retired Bishop of Amarillo, P.O. Box 5644, Amarillo, TX 79117-5664.
McAuliffe, Michael F., Retired Bishop of Jefferson City, Bishop's House, P.O. Box 417, Jefferson City, MO 65102.
McCarthy, James F., Retired Auxiliary Bishop of New York, St. Elizabeth Ann Seton, 1377 N. Main St., Shrub Oak, NY 10588.
McCarthy, John E., Bishop Emeritus of Austin, P.O. Box 13327, Austin, TX 78711.
McCormack, John B., Bishop of Manchester, 153 Ash St., P.O. Box 310, Manchester, NH 03105.
McCormack, William J., Retired Auxiliary Bishop of New York, 142 E. 29th St., New York, NY 10016.
McDonald, Andrew J., Former Bishop of Little Rock St. Joseph's Home, 80 W. Northwest Hwy., Palatine, IL 60067.
McDonnell, Timothy A., Bishop of Springfield in Massachusetts, P.O. Box 1730, Springfield, MA 01101.
McDonnell, Charles J., Auxiliary Bishop of Newark, 34 Maple Ave., Hackensack, NJ 07601.
McDowell, John B., Former Auxiliary Bishop of Pittsburgh, 111 Blvd. of the Allies, Pittsburgh, PA 15222.
McFarland, Norman F., Retired Bishop of Orange, Marywood Center, 2811 E. Villa Real Dr., Orange, CA 92867.

His Excellency,
The Most Reverend

McGrath, Patrick J., Bishop of San Jose, 900 Lafayette St., Ste. 301, Santa Clara, CA 95050-4966.
McKinney, Joseph C., Retired Auxiliary Bishop of Grand Rapids, 1315 Walker Ave., Grand Rapids, MI 49504.
McLaughlin, Bernard J., Retired Auxiliary Bishop of Buffalo, 204 Knoche Rd., Tonawand, NY 14150.
McManus, Robert J., Bishop of Worcester, 49 Elm St., Worcester, MA 01609.
McNamara, Lawrence J., Bishop of Grand Island, P.O. Box 1531, Grand Island, NE 68802.
McRaith, John J., Bishop of Owensboro, 501 W. Fifth St., Owensboro, KY 42301.
Medina, Ruben Antonio Gonzalez, c.m.f., Bishop of Caguas, P.O. Box 8698, Caguas, PR 00726.
Melczek, Dale J., Bishop of Gary, 9292 Broadway, Merrillville, IN 46410.
Mengeling, Carl F., Bishop of Lansing, 300 West Ottawa St., Lansing, MI 48933.
Mestice, Anthony F., Retired Auxiliary Bishop of New York, Resurrection, 910 Boston Post Rd., Rye, NY 10580.
Michaels, James E., s.s.c., Resigned Auxiliary Bishop of Wheeling-Charleston, Benedictine Mr #21, 200 Janeway Dr., N.E., Cullman, AL 35055.
Mikloshazy, Attila, s.j., Bishop to Hungarians, St. Augustine's Seminary, 2661 Kingston Rd., Scarborough, Ontario, Canada, M1M 1M3.
Milone, Anthony M., Bishop of Great Falls-Billings, 121-23rd St., S., Great Falls, MT 59401-3939.
Moeddel, Carl K., Auxiliary Bishop of Cincinnati, 100 East 8th St., Cincinnati, OH 45202.
Montrose, Donald, Bishop of Stockton, 1105 N. Lincoln St., Stockton, CA 95204-0237.
Moreno, Manuel D., Retired Bishop of Tucson, 192 S. Stone Ave., Tucson, AZ 85702.
Morin, Roger P., Auxiliary Bishop of New Orleans, 7887 Walmsley Ave., New Orleans, LA 70125.
Morlino, Robert C., Bishop of Madison, 702 S. High Point Rd., Madison, WI 53744-4983.
Morneau, Robert F., Auxiliary Bishop of Green Bay, 1910 S. Webster, P.O. Box 23825, Green Bay, WI 54305-3825.
Moskal, Robert M., Bishop of St. Josaphat in Parma, 5720 State Rd., Parma, OH 44134.
Moynihan, James M., Bishop of Syracuse, 240 East Onondaga St., P.O. Box 511, Syracuse, NY 13201.
Muench, Robert W., Bishop of Baton Rouge, 1800 S. Acadian Thruway, P.O. Box 2028, Baton Rouge, LA 70821-2028.
Mulvee, Robert E., Bishop of Providence, One Cathedral Sq., Providence, RI 02903.
Murphy, Michael J., Retired Bishop of Erie, 130 E. Fourth St., Erie, PA 16507.
Murphy, William F., Bishop of Rockville Centre 50 N. Park Ave., Rockville Centre, NY 11570.
Murray, James A., Bishop of Kalamazoo, 215 N. Westnedge Ave., Kalamazoo, MI 49007-3760.
Murry, George V., s.j., Bishop of St. Thomas, Virgin Islands, P.O. Box 301825, Charlotte Amalie, VI 00803.
Nevins, John J., Bishop of Venice, P.O. Box 2006, Venice, FL 34284.
Newman, William C., Retired Auxiliary Bishop of Baltimore, 6536 Cherry Hill Rd., Baldwin, MD 21013-9300.
Neylon, Martin J., s.j., Retired Bishop of the Caroline Islands, St. Ignatius Loyola Res., 53 E. 83rd St., New York, NY 10028.
Niederauer, George H., Bishop of Salt Lake City 27 C St., Salt Lake City, UT 84103.
Niedergeses, James D., Retired Bishop of Nashville, 239 Cana Cir., Nashville, TN 37205.
Nienstedt, John C., Bishop of New Ulm, 1400 6th St., N., New Ulm, MN 56073-2099.
O'Brien, Thomas J., Retired Bishop of Phoenix, 48 E. Wagon Wheel Dr., Phoenix, AZ 85020.
O'Connell, Anthony J., Resigned Bishop of Palm Beach, P.O. Box 109650-9995 N. Military Tr., Palm Beach Gardens, FL 33410-9650.
O'Donnell, Edward J., Retired Bishop of Lafayette, 7500 Cromwell, Clayton, MO 63105.
O'Neill, Arthur J., Retired Bishop of Rockford, 14 Country Club Beach, Rockford, IL 61103.
Ochoa, Armando, Bishop of El Paso, 499 St. Matthews St., El Paso TX 79907.
Olivier, Leonard J., s.v.d., Auxiliary Bishop of Washington, 2657 Woodley Rd., N.W., Washington, DC 20008.
Olmsted, Thomas J. Bishop of Phoenix, 400 E. Monroe St., Phoenix, AZ 85004-2336.
Ottenweller, Albert H., Retired Bishop of Steubenville, 2544 Parkwood Ave., Toledo, OH 43610-1317.
Paprocki, Thomas J. Auxiliary Bishop of Chicago, 1400 S. Austin Ave., Chicago, IL 60804.
Paska, Walter, Retired Auxiliary Bishop of Philadelphia Ukraine, 827 N. Franklin St., Philadelphia, PA 19123.

His Excellency,
The Most Reverend

Pataki, Andrew, Bishop of Passaic of the Ruthenians, 445 Lackawanna Ave., West Paterson, NJ 07424.
Pates, Richard E., Auxiliary Bishop of St. Paul and Minneapolis, 226 Summit Ave., St. Paul, MN 55102.
Paul, John J., Retired Bishop of La Crosse, P.O. Box 69, La Crosse, WI 54601.
Pelotte, Donald, s.s.s., Bishop of Gallup, 711 S. Puerco Dr., Gallup, NM 87305.
Pena, Raymundo J., Bishop of Brownsville, 1910 E. Elizabeth St., Brownsville, TX 78522-2279.
Pepe, Joseph A., Bishop of Las Vegas, 336 Cathedral Way, Las Vegas, NV 89109.
Perry, Joseph N., Auxiliary Bishop of Chicago, P.O. Box 733, South Holland, IL 60473-0733.
Pevec, A. Edward, Retired Auxiliary Bishop of Cleveland, 28700 Euclid Ave., Wickliffe, OH 44092.
Pfeifer, Michael D., o.m.i., Bishop of San Angelo, P.O. Box 1829, San Angelo, TX 76902.
Pilla, Anthony M., Bishop of Cleveland, 1027 Superior Ave., Cleveland, OH 44114.
Popp, Bernard F., Retired Auxiliary Bishop of San Antonio, 8520 Cross Mountain Tr., San Antonio, TX 78255.
Puscas, Vasile Louis, Former Apostolic Eparch of St. George Martyr in Canton for Romanian-Byzantine Catholics, 111 W. Park Ave., Aurora, IL 60506.
Quinn, A. James, Auxiliary Bishop of Cleveland, 2500 Elyria Ave., Lorain, OH 44055.
Quinn, Francis A., Retired Bishop of Sacramento, 8840 E. 22nd St., Tucson, AZ 85710.
Quinn, John M., Auxiliary Bishop of Detroit, 9357 Westwood St., Detroit, MI 48228-1797.
Ramirez, Ricardo, c.s.b., Bishop of Las Cruces, 1280 Med Park Dr., Las Cruces, NM 88005.
Reilly, Daniel P., Retired Bishop of Worcester, 49 Elm St., Worcester, MA 01609.
Reiss, Francis R., Auxiliary Bishop of Detroit, 976 Pope John Paul II Ave., Wyandotte, MI 48192.
Reiss, John C., Retired Bishop of Trenton, Villa Vianney, 2301 Lawrenceville Rd. Trenton, NJ 08648.
Ricard, John H., s.s.j., Bishop of Pensacola-Tallahassee, 11 N. B St., Pensacola, FL 32501.
Ricken, David L., Bishop of Cheyenne, 2121 Capitol Ave., P.O. Box 1468, Cheyenne, WY 82003.
Rivera, Enrique Hernandez, Retired Bishop of Caguas, P.O. Box 8698, Caguas, PR 00726.
Rivera, Hector M., Auxiliary Bishop of San Juan, P.O. Box 9021967, San Juan, PR 00902-1967.
Rizzotto, Vincent M., Auxiliary Bishop of Galveston-Houston, P.O. Box 907, Houston, TX 77001-0907.
Rodi, Thomas J., Bishop of Biloxi, 1790 Popps Ferry Rd., Biloxi, MS 39532.
Rodimer, Frank J., Bishop of Paterson, 178 Derrom Ave., Paterson, NJ 07504.
Rodriguez, Placido, c.m.f., Bishop of Lubbock, P.O. Box 98700, Lubbock, TX 79499-8700.
Roman, Agustin A., Retired Auxiliary Bishop of Miami, 3605 S. Miami Ave., Miami, FL 33133.
Roque, Francis X., Auxiliary Bishop for the Military Services, P.O. Box 4469, Washington, DC 20017.
Rosazza, Peter A., Auxiliary Bishop of Hartford, 1450 Chapel St., New Haven, CT 06511.
Rose, Robert J., Retired Bishop of Grand Rapids, 1200 104th, Apt. 4, Byron Center, MI 49315.
Rueger, George E., Auxiliary Bishop of Worcester, 2 High Ridge Rd., Worcester, MA 01602.
Ryan, Daniel L., Former Bishop of Springfield in Illinois, 1400 Guemes Ct., Springfield, IL 62702.
Ryan, Sylvester D., Bishop of Monterey, 631 Abrego St., Monterey, CA 93940.
Saltarelli, Michael A., Bishop of Wilmington, P.O. Box 2030, Wilmington, DE 19899-2030.
Samo, Amando, Bishop of the Caroline Islands, P.O. Box 939, Chuuk, Caroline Islands, FM 96942.
Samra, Nicholas J., Auxiliary Bishop of Newton, 8525 Cole St., Warren, MI 48093.
Santana, Hermin Negron, Auxiliary Bishop of San Juan, Calle 6, D-9 Urb. Royal Town, Bayamon, PR 00956.
Sartain, J. Peter, Bishop of Little Rock, 2500 N. Tyler St., P.O. Box 7239, Little Rock, AR 72217.
Sartoris, Joseph M., Retired Auxiliary Bishop of Los Angeles, San Pedro Pastoral Region, 1988 Rolling Vista Dr., Unit 12, Lomita, CA 90717-3761.
Schlarman, Stanley G., Retired Bishop of Dodge City, Fiat House, 113 N. Ottawa, Joliet, IL 60432.
Schmitt, Bernard W., Bishop of Wheeling-Charleston, 1300 Byron St., Box 230, Wheeling, WV 26003.
Schmitt, Mark F., Retired Bishop of Marquette, HC01 Box 159, Marquette, MI 49855.
Schnurr, Dennis M., Bishop of Duluth, 2830 E. Fourth St., Duluth, MN 55812.
Schoenherr, Walter J., Retired Auxiliary Bishop of Detroit, 14465 Levan Rd., Apt. A, Livonia, MI 48154-5092.

His Excellency,
The Most Reverend

Seminack, Richard S., Bishop of St. Nicholas in Chicago for Ukrainians, 2245 W. Rice St., Chicago, IL 60622.
Serratelli, Arthur J., Auxiliary Bishop of Newark, Cathedral Basilica of the Sacred Heart, 89 Ridge St., Newark, NJ 07104.
Sevilla, Carlos, s.j., Bishop of Yakima, 5301-A Tieton Dr., Yakima, WA 98908.
Shaheen, Robert J., Bishop of Our Lady of Lebanon, 1021 S. 10th St., St. Louis, MO 63104.
Sheldon, Gilbert I., Retired Bishop of Steubenville, 609 N. Seventh St., Steubenville, OH 43952.
Sheridan, Michael J., Bishop of Colorado Springs, 228 North Cascade Ave., Colorado Springs, CO 80903.
Sheridan, Patrick J., Retired Auxiliary Bishop of New York, 5655 Arlington Ave., Bronx, NY 10471.
Sklba, Richard J., Auxiliary Bishop of Milwaukee, 2491 N. Murray Ave., Milwaukee, WI 53211.
Skurla, William, Bishop of Van Nuys, Byzantine Eparchy, 8105 N. 16th St., Phoenix, AZ 85020.
Skylstad, William S., Bishop of Spokane, W. 1023 Riverside Ave., Spokane, WA 99201.
Slattery, Edward J., Bishop of Tulsa, P.O. Box 690240, Tulsa, OK 74169.
Smith, John M., Bishop of Trenton, P.O. Box 5147, 701 Lawrenceville Rd., Trenton, NJ 08638-0147.
Snyder, John J., Retired Bishop of St. Augustine, 5 Casa San Pedro, 1714 State Rd. 13, Ste. 6, Jacksonville, FL 32259.
Soens, Lawrence D., Former Bishop of Sioux City, 1703 W. 25th, Apt. 208, Sioux City, IA 51103.
Solis, Oscar A., Auxiliary Bishop of Los Angeles, 3424 Wilshire Blvd., Los Angeles, LA 90010.
Soto, Jaime, Auxiliary Bishop of Orange, Office of Hispanic Ministry-Marywood Ctr., 2811 Villa Real Dr., Orange, CA 92867.
Speyrer, Jude, Bishop Emeritus of Lake Charles, 118 Marcus Dr., Carenco, LA 70502.
Steib, James Terry, s.v.d., Bishop of Memphis, The Catholic Center, P.O. Box 341669, Memphis, TN 38184-1669.
Steinbock, John T., Bishop of Fresno, 1550 N. Fresno St., Fresno, CA 93703-3788.
Steiner, Kenneth D., Auxiliary Bishop of Portland in Oregon, 2838 E. Burnside St., Portland, OR 97214.
Straling, Phillip F., Bishop of Reno, 290 S. Arlington Ave., Ste. 200, Reno, NV 89501.
Sullivan, James S., Retired Bishop of Fargo, Holy Spirit Parish, 1420 7th St., N., Fargo, ND 58102.
Sullivan, Joseph M., Auxiliary Bishop of Brooklyn, 378 Clermont Ave., Brooklyn, NY 11238.
Sullivan, Walter F., Bishop Emeritus of Richmond, 3203 Hawthorne Ave., Richmond, VA 23227.
Surinach-Carreras, Ricardo, Retired Bishop of Ponce, Obispado de Ponce, Bishop's House, P.O. Box 32205, Ponce, PR 00732-2205.
Symons, J. Keith, Former Bishop of Palm Beach, P.O. Box 7, Alma, MI 48801-0007.
Tafoya, Arthur N., Bishop of Pueblo, 1001 N. Grand Ave., Pueblo, CO 81003.
Tamayo, James A., Bishop of Laredo, Chancery, 1901 Corpus Christi St., Laredo, TX 78043.
Thomas, Elliot G., Former Bishop of St. Thomas, in the Virgin Islands, Natl. Shrine of Divine Mercy, 2 Prospect Hill Rd., Stockbridge, MA 01262.
Thomas, George, Bishop of Helena, 515 N. Ewing, P.O. Box 1729, Helena, MT 59624-1729.
Thompson, David B., Former Bishop of Charleston, 4479 Downing Pl., Mount Pleasant, SC 29466.
Timlin, James C., Retired Bishop of Scranton, 300 Wyoming Ave., Scranton, PA 18503.
Tobin, Thomas J., Bishop of Youngstown, 144 W. Wood St., Youngstown, OH 44503.
Torres Oliver, Fremiot, Bishop Emeritus of Ponce, Obispado de Ponce, Carretera Estatal 504 P.R., Glenview Gardens hacia Rio Chiquito, Ponce, PR 00731.
Trautman, Donald W., Bishop of Erie, 205 West 9th St., P.O. Box 10397, Erie, PA 16514.
Tschoepe, Thomas, Retired Bishop of Dallas, St. Joseph Res., 330 W. Pembroke, Dallas, TX 75208.
Txertudi, Inaki Mallona, c.p. Bishop of Arecibo, 206 Dr. Salas St., Box 616, Arecibo, PR 00613-0616.
Valero, Rene, Auxiliary Bishop of Brooklyn, 34-43 93rd St., Jackson Heights, NY 11372.
Vasa, Robert Francis, Bishop of Baker, P.O. Box 5999, Bend, OR 97708.
Vasquez, Joe S., Auxiliary Bishop of Galveston-Houston, 1700 San Jacinto, Houston, TX 77002-8291.
Vigneron, Allen H., Bishop of Oakland, 2900 Lakeshore Ave., Oakland, CA 94610-3697.
Walsh, Daniel F., Bishop of Santa Rosa, 320 Tenth St., Santa Rosa, CA 95401.
Walsh, Paul H., Auxiliary Bishop of Rockville Centre, Western Vicariate, P.O. Box 933, Roosevelt, NY 11575-6340.

His Excellency,
The Most Reverend

Wang, Ignatius, Auxiliary Bishop of San Francisco, One Peter Yorke Way, San Francisco, CA 94109.
Ward, John J., Former Auxiliary Bishop of Los Angeles, 3424 Wilshire Blvd., Los Angeles, CA 90010.
Warfel, Michael, Bishop of Juneau, 415 6th St., Suite 300, Juneau, AK 99801.
Watters, Loras J., Retired Bishop of Winona, 1455 W. Broadway, Winona, MN 55980.
Wcela, Emil A., Auxiliary Bishop of Rockville Centre, Eastern Vicariate, P.O. Box 780, Riverhead, NY 11901.
Weigand, William K., Bishop of Sacramento, Pastoral Center, 2110 Broadway, Sacramento CA 95818.
Weitzel, John Quinn, m.m., Bishop of Samoa-Pago Pago, Fatuoaiga, P.O. Box 596, Pago Pago, American Samoa 96799.
Welsh, Thomas J., Retired Bishop of Allentown, 1325 Prospect Ave., Bethlehem, PA 18018.
Wenski, Thomas G., Coadjutor Bishop of Orlando, P.O. Box 1800, Orlando, FL 32802.
Wester, John Charles, Auxiliary Bishop of San Francisco, One Peter Yorke Way, San Francisco, CA 94109.
Wilkerson, Gerald E., Auxiliary Bishop of Los Angeles, 15101 San Fernando Mission Blvd., Mission Hills, CA 91345-1109.
Williams, James K., Retired Bishop of Lexington, 1310 West Main St., Lexington, KY 40508.
Winter, William J., Auxiliary Bishop of Pittsburgh, Sacred Heart Church, 310 Shady Ave., Pittsburgh, PA 15206-4389.
Wirz, George O., Retired Auxiliary Bishop of Madison, 3577 S. High Point Rd., P.O. Box 44983, Madison WI 53714.
Wiwchar Michael, Bishop of Saskatoon (Ukrainian), 2245 W. Rice St., Chicago, IL 60622.
Wuerl, Donald W., Bishop of Pittsburgh, 111 Blvd. of the Allies, Pittsburgh, PA 15222-1618.
Wycislo, Aloysius J., Retired Bishop of Green Bay, 1825 Riverside Dr., Green Bay, WI 54301.
Yanta, John W., Bishop of Amarillo, 1800 N. Spring St., P.O. Box 5644, Amarillo, TX 79117-5644.
Younan, Joseph, Bishop of Our Lady of Deliverance of Newark, P.O. Box 8366, Union City, NJ 07087-8262.
Zavala, Gabino, Auxiliary Bishop of Los Angeles, San Gabriel Pastoral Region, 16009 E. Cypress Ave., Irwindale, CA 91706-2122.
Ziemann, G. Patrick, Former Bishop of Santa Rosa, 320 10th St., Santa Rosa, CA 95401.
Zipfel, Paul A., Bishop of Bismarck, 420 Raymond St., Bismarck, ND 58502-1575.
Zubik, David A., Bishop of Green Bay, 1910 Webster Ave, P.O. Box 23825, Green Bay, WI 54305.
Zurek, Patrick J., Auxiliary Bishop of San Antonio, P.O. Box 28410, San Antonio, TX 78228-0410.

U.S. HIERARCHY SERVING IN OTHER COUNTRIES

Adams, Edward J., Archbishop Apostolic Nuncio in Bangladesh, P.O. Box 6003, Dhaka, Bangladesh.
Boyle, Paul M., c.p., Apostolic Vicar of Mandeville, Jamaica, West Indies.
De Paoli, Ambrose, Apostolic Nuncio to Japan: 9-2 Sanban-cho, Chiyodku, Tokyo.
Dion, George E., o.m.i., Retired Bishop of Jolo, Oblates of Notre Dame Motherhouse, Sinsuat Ave., 9600 Cotabato City, Philippines.
Echevarria, Javier, Prelate of the Prelature of the Holy Cross and Opus Dei, Viale Bruno Buozzi 73, 00197, Rome, Italy.
Foley, John P., Archbishop, President of the Pontifical Council for Social Communications, 00120 Vatican City State, Europe.
Harvey, James M., Titular Bishop of Memfi, Archbishop/Prefect of the Papal Household, 00120 Vatican City State, Europe.
Marcinkus, Paul C., Working Outside Chicago Archdiocese, Vatican City State, Europe.
McGarry, Urban E., t.o.r., Bishop of Bhagalpur, Chancery Office: Nawab Colony, P.O. Box 61, Bhagalpur 812001, Bihar, India.
McNaughton, William J., m.m., Bishop of Inchon, 3 Tap Tong, P.O. Box 19, Chung Ku, Inchon 400-600, Korea.
Pelletier, Donald L., Bishop of Morondava Madagascar, Bishop's House, P.O. Box 132, Morondava 619, Madagascar.
Schmitz, Paul Evin, o.f.m.cap., Vicariate Apostolic of Bluefields, Apartado Postal 8, Bluefields, R.A.A.S., Nicaragua, C.A.
Smith, Philip Francis, m.m., Archbishop of Cotabato, Residence, P.O. Box 186, Sinsuat Ave., Cotabato City 9600, Philippines.

OTHER HIERARCHY RESIDING IN THE UNITED STATES

Boland, Ernest B., o.p., Former Bishop of Multan, St. Thomas Aquinas Priory, Providence College, Providence, RI 02918-0001.
Comber, John W., m.m., Former Superior & Bishop of Maryknoll, 141 E. 43rd St., New York, NY 10017-4007.
DePalma, Joseph A., s.c.j. Former Bishop of De Aar, South Africa, Sacred Heart Residence, 6701 82nd Ave., N., Pinellas Park, FL 34665.
Durning, Dennis V., c.s.sp., Bishop Emeritus of Arusha Tanzania, East Africa, Holy Ghost Provincialate, 6230 Brush Run Rd., Bethel Park, PA 15102.
Meeking, Basil, Retired Bishop from New Zealand, 4635 S.W. 148th Ave., Beaverton, OR 97007.
Nolker, Bernard J., c.ss.r., Retired Bishop of Paranagua Brazil, 600 S. Conkling St., Baltimore, MD 21224-4203.
Pearce, George H., s.m., Former Archbishop of Suva, 30 Fenner St., Providence, RI 02903.
Schmidt, Firmin, o.f.m.cap., Former Bishop of Papua, New Guinea, c/o Diocese of Salina, 103 N. Ninth, Salina, KS 67402-0980.
Sowada, Alphonse, o.s.c., Retired Bishop of Agats, Indonesia, 396 1st Ave., S., St. Cloud, MN 56301.
Veigle, Adriano J., t.o.r., Retired Bishop of Borba, Brazil, Mount Assisi Monastery, Loretto, PA 15940.

ARCHABBOTS

The Right Reverend

Knaebel, Bonaventure, o.s.b., (Resigned), St. Meinrad Archabbey, St. Meinrad, St. Meinrad, IN 47577.
Maher, Paul R., o.s.b., (Resigned) St. Vincent Archabbey, 300 Fraser Purchase Rd., Latrobe, PA 15650-2686.
Nowicki, Douglas R., o.s.b., St. Vincent Archabbey, 300 Fraser Purchase Rd., Latrobe, PA 15650-2686.
Reilly, Lambert, o.s.b., St. Meinrad Archabbey, St. Meinrad, St. Meinrad, IN 47577.

ABBOTS

Anderson, Hugh R., o.s.b., St. Procopius Abbey, 5601 College Rd., Lisle, IL 60532.
Augustine, Dom, o.c.s.o., Retired. Monastery of the Holy Spirit, Inc., 2625 Hwy. 212 S.W., Conyers, GA 30094-4044.
Balsavich, Marion E., o.s.b., Retired. St. Bede Abbey, Peru, IL 61354.
Bamberger, John E., o.c.s.o., Abbey of Genesee, Piffard, NY 14533.
Barnes, Robert, o.c.s.o., Abbey of Our Lady of the Holy Cross, 901 Cool Spring Ln., Berryville, VA 22611-2700.
Bataille, Vincent, o.s.b., Marmion Abbey, Butterfield Rd., Aurora, IL 60504.
Benedict, Francis, o.s.b., St. Andrew's Abbey, 31001 N. Valyermo Rd., Valyermo, CA 93563.
Benkert, Gerald, o.s.b., Resigned. Marmion Abbey, Butterfield Rd., Aurora, IL 60504.
Berndt, Alan, o.s.b., Retired. Blue Cloud Abbey, P.O. Box 98, Marvin, SD 57252.
Berning, Philip, o.s.b., Retired. St. Gregory Abbey, Shawnee, OK 74801.
Bock, David R., o.c.s.o., Retired. New Melleray Abbey, 6500 Melleray Circle, Peosta, IA 52068.
Boultwood, Alban, o.s.b., St. Anselm Abbey, 4501 S. Dakota Ave., N.E., Washington, DC 20017.
Boyle, Joseph, o.c.s.o., St. Benedict Monastery, 1012 Monastery Rd., Snowmass, CO 81654.
Burne, Martin J., o.s.b., Retired. St. Mary Abbey, Delbarton, Mendham Rd., Morristown, NJ 07960.
Burnett, Oscar, o.s.b., Retired. Belmont Abbey,100 Belmont-Mount Holly Rd., Belmont, NC 28012-1802.
Burns, Flavian, o.c.s.o., Abbey of Our Lady of the Holy Cross, Rte. 2, Box 3870, Berryville, VA 22611.
Campbell, Edward C., o.s.b., Retired. Glastonbury Abbey,16 Hull St., Hingham, MA 02043.
Carr, Christian Aidan, o.c.s.o., Retired. Serving as chaplain in Africa. Our Lady of Mepkin Abbey, HC 69, Box 800, Moncks Corner, SC 29461.
Cassell, Leonard G., o.s.b., Retired. St. Mary Abbey, Delbarton, Mendham Rd., Morristown, NJ 07960.
Chassagne, M. Anthony, o.c.s.o., Retired. Our Lady of Mepkin Abbey, HC 69, Box 800, Moncks Corner, SC 29461.
Clark, Victor J., o.s.b., St. Bernard Abbey, 1600 St. Bernard Dr., Cullman, AL 35055.
Clarke, Brian H., o.s.b., St. Mary Abbey, Delbarton, Mendham Rd., Morristown, NJ 07960.
Cole, Edwin J., o.s.b., St. Anselm Church, 530 S. Mason Rd., St. Louis, MO 63141.
Confroy, Thomas J., o.s.b., St. Mary's Abbey, Delbarton, Morristown, NJ 07960.
Connor, James, o.c.s.o., Retired. Assumption Abbey, Rte. 5, P.O. Box 1056, Ava, MO 65608.
Corpus, Roger, o.s.b., St. Bede Abbey, Peru, IL 61354.
Cyr, David J., o.s.b., Marmion Abbey, Butterfield Rd., Aurora, IL 60504.
Dagher, George, b.s.o., American Headquarters, 30 East St., Methuen, MA 01844.
Davis, Thomas X., o.c.s.o., Our Lady of New Clairvaux Abbey, P.O. Box 80, Vina, CA 96092.

De Wane, Thomas E., o.praem., St. Norbert Abbey, 1016 N. Broadway, De Pere, WI 54115-2697.
Denburger, John J., o.c.s.o., Abbey of the Genesee, Piffard, NY 14533.
Dimitrijevich, Nicholas, Our Lady of the Valley, P.O. Box 419, Gloverville, SC 29828.
Dosch, Leander, o.c.s.o., Abbey of the Holy Trinity, 1250 S. 9500 E., Huntsville, UT 84317.
Driscoll, William J., o.mar., Monastery of the Most Holy Trinity, 67 Dugway Rd., Petersham, MA 01366-9725.
Dzikowicz, Justin E., o.s.b., Retired. St. Paul Abbey, Newton, NJ 07860.
Eberle, Peter, o.s.b., Mount Angel Abbey, St. Benedict, OR 97373.
Ehringer, Claude, o.s.b., Prince of Peace Abbey, Oceanside, CA 92054.
Eidenschink, John, o.s.b., Chaplain. Mother of Mercy Nursing Home & Retirement Center, Albany, MN 56307.
Farkasfalvy, Denis, o.cist., Abbey of Our Lady of Dallas, 1 Cistercian Rd., Irving, TX 75039.
Flaherty, Malachy, o.c.s.o., Abbey of Our Lady of the Holy Trinity, 1250 S. 9500 E., Huntsville, UT 84317.
Freeman, Brendan J., o.c.s.o., Abbey of Our Lady of New Melleray, 6500 Melleray Circle, Peosta, IA 52068-9736.
Frerking, Thomas, o.s.b., Abbey of St. Mary and St. Louis, 500 S. Mason Rd., St. Louis, MO 63141.
Fuez, Blaise J. o.cist., Our Lady of Spring Bank Abbey, Rt. 3, Box 211, Sparta, WI 54656.
Garber, Andrew V., o.s.b., Resigned. St. Benedict Abbey, Benet Lake, WI 53102.
Geraets, David, o.s.b., Our Lady of Guadalupe Abbey, Pecos, NM 87552.
Gibbs, Gabriel, o.s.b., St. Benedict Abbey, 252 Still River Rd., P.O. Box 67, Still River, MA 01467-0067.
Hacker, Louis, o.s.b., Corpus Christi Abbey, HCR 2, Box 6300, Sandia, TX 78383.
Harrison, Cyprian, o.c.s.o., Assumption Abbey, Rte. 5, Box 1056, Ava, MO 65608.
Havlik, Thomas J., o.s.b., St. Procopius Abbey, 5601 College Rd., Lisle, IL 60532.
Hayes, Eugene, o.praem., St. Michael Abbey, 19292 El Toro Rd., Silverado, CA 92676-9710.
Heidgen, Warren J., o.s.b., Retired. Holy Cross Abbey, P.O. Box 1510, Canon City, CO 81215-1510.
Hein, Kenneth, o.s.b., Retired Abbot, Holy Cross Abbey, P.O. Box 1510, Canon City, CO 81215-1510.
Hillenbrand, Thomas, o.s.b., Blue Cloud Abbey, P.O. Box 98, Marvin, SD 57251.
Hinches, Augustine J., o.s.b., Resigned. St. Paul Abbey, Newton, NJ 07860.
Jones, James, o.s.b., Retired. Conception Abbey, Conception, MO 64433.
Keating, Thomas, o.c.s.o., St. Benedict Monastery, 1012 Monastery Rd., Snowmass, CO 81654.
Kelly, Timothy, o.s.b., Newark Abbey, 528 Dr. Martin Luther King Jr. Blvd., Newark, NJ 07102.
Kerndt, James J., o.c.s.o., Retired. New Melleray Abbey, 6500 Melleray Circle, Dubuque, IA 52068.
Kline, Francis, o.c.s.o., Our Lady of Mepkin Abbey, HC 69, Box 800, Moncks Corner, SC 29461.
Kodell, Jerome, o.s.b., New Subiaco Abbey, Subiaco, AR 72865.
Koehler, Ralph, o.s.b., Retired. St. Benedicts, Abbey, Atchison, KS 66002.
Lawrence, Philip, o.s.b., Monastery of Christ in the Desert, Abiquiu, NM 87510.
Leavy, Matthew K., o.s.b., St. Anselm Abbey, Manchester, NH 03102.
Liprie, James, o.s.b., Abbot of Our Lady of Guadalupe Abbey, Pecos NM 87552.
Logan, John M., o.praem., Daylesford Abbey, 220 S. Valley Rd., Paoli, PA 19301.
Lugo, Martin, o.s.b., St. Gregory's Abbey, Shawnee, OK 74804.
Luykx, Boniface Holy Transfiguration Monastery, 17001 Tomki Rd., Redwood Valley, CA 95470.
Mackin, Benjamin T., o.praem., Retired. St. Norbert Abbey, 1016 N. Broadway, De Pere, WI 54115-2610.
Macrae, Maurus, o.s.b., Westminster Abbey Mission, British Columbia, Canada V2V 4J2.
Macul, Joel P., o.s.b., St. Paul's Abbey, Newton, NJ 07860.
Massoth, Charles, o.s.b., Retired. St. Gregory Abbey, Shawnee, OK 74801.
Matter, Robert, o.c.s.o., Retired. Assumption Abbey, Rte. 5, Box 1056, Ava, MO 65608.
McCaffrey, Edmund F., Former Abbot-Ordinary Belmont Abbey, P.O. Box 70548, Myrtle Beach, SC 29572-0028.
McCarthy, Peter, o.c.s.o., The Cistercian (Trappist) Abbey of Our Lady of Guadalupe, Lafayette, OR 97127.
McCorkell, Edward, o.c.s.o., Retired. Abbey of Our Lady of the Holy Cross, Rte. 2, Box 3870, Berryville, VA 22611-9526.
McDermott, Benedict, o.s.b., Mary Mother of Church Abbey, 12829 River Rd., Richmond, VA 23221.
McGonigle, Kevin, o.s.b., Retired. Conception Abbey, Conception, MO 64433.
Meagher, Cletus D., o.s.b., St. Bernard Abbey, Cullman, AL 35055.
Moore, Augustine J. o.c.s.o., Retired. Monastery of the Holy Spirit, 2625 Hwy. 212 S.W., Conyers, GA 30094-4044.
Moore, Patrick, o.s.b., Assumption Abbey, P.O. Box A, Richardton, ND 58652.
Morcone, Nicholas J., o.s.b., Glastonbury Abbey, 16 Hull St., Hingham, MA 02043.
Neitzel, John E., o.praem., Retired. Daylesford Abbey, 220 S. Valley Rd., Paoli, PA 19301.
Neville, Gary, o.praem., Abbot St. Norbert Abbey, DePere, WI 54115-2610.
O'Connor, Philip J., o.c.s.o., Retired. New Melleray Abbey, 6500 Melleray Circle, Peosta, IA 52068.
Odenbrett, Stephen, o.s.b., Our Lady of Guadalupe Abbey, Pecos, NM 87552.
Parcher, Adrian, o.s.b., Retired. St. Martin's Abbey, 5300 Pacific Ave., S.E., Lacey, WA 98503.
Parker, Ladislaus K., o.praem., Retired, St. Michael Abbey, 19292 E. Toro Rd., Silverado, CA 92676.
Pennington, M. Basil, o.c.s.o., Monastery of the Holy Spirit, 2625 Hwy., 212 S.W., Conyers, GA 30094-4044.
Polan, Gregory, o.s.b., Abbot of Conception Abbey, Conception, MO 64433.
Purcell, Owen, o.s.b., Retired. St. Benedict's Abbey, Atchison, KS 66002.
Quinkert, Denis, o.s.b., Blue Cloud Abbey, P.O. Box 98, Marvin, SD 57251.
Rausch, Conrad, o.s.b., Retired. St. Martin's Abbey, 5300 Pacific Ave. S.E., Lacey, WA 98503.
Regan, Patrick, o.s.b., St. Joseph Abbey, St. Benedict, LA 70457.
Rigby, Luke, o.s.b., Abbey of St. Mary and St. Louis, 500 S. Mason Rd., St. Louis, MO 63141.
Roberts, Augustine, o.c.s.o., St. Joseph Abbey, Spencer, MA 01562.
Rodriguez-Santiago, Jose M., o.s.b., Abbey of San Antonio, Box 729, Humacao, PR 00661.
Rooney, Marcel, o.s.b., Conception Abbey, Conception, MO 64433.
Roth, Neal G., o.s.b., St. Martin's Abbey, 5300 Pacific Ave. S.E., Lacey, WA 98503.
Ryska, Leo M., o.s.b., St. Benedict's Abbey and Retreat Center, Benet Lake, WI 53102.
Schoofs, Robert, o.s.b., St. Benedict's Abbey, Benet Lake, WI 53102.
Senecal, Barnabas, o.s.b., St. Benedict's Abbey, Atchison, KS 66002.
Serna, Dom Mark, o.s.b., Abbey of St. Gregory, Cory's Ln., Portsmouth, RI 02871.
Shea, Aidan, o.s.b., St. Anselm Abbey, 4501 South Dakota Ave., N.E., Washington, DC 20017-2753.
Shelton, Patrick, o.s.b., St. Leo Abbey, St. Leo, FL 33574.
Solari, Placid D., o.s.b., Belmont Abbey, 100 Belmont-Mount Holly Rd., Belmont, NC 28012-1802.
Spillane, M. Emmanuel, o.c.s.o., Retired. Abbey of Our Lady of the Trinity, 1250 S. 9500 E. Huntsville, UT 84317.
Stark, Matthew, o.s.b., Abbey of St. Gregory the Great, Cory's Ln., Portsmouth, RI 02871.
Thompson, Damien, o.s.c.o., Abbey of Gethsemani, Trappist, KY 40051.
Tremel, Jerome G., o.praem., Admin., Daylesford Abbey Norbertine Canonry, 220 S. Valley Rd., Paoli, PA 19301-1900.
Valvano, Melvin J., o.s.b., Retired. Newark Abbey, 528 Dr. Martin Luther King Jr. Blvd., Newark, NJ 07102.
Veilleux, Armand J., o.s.c.o., Monastery of the Holy Spirit, 2625 Hwy. 212 S.W., Conyers, GA 30094-4044.
Vollmer, Edward J., o.s.b., Retired. Holy Cross Abbey, P.O. Box 1510, Canon City, CO 81215-1510.
Vorderlandwehr, Adrian R., o.s.b., Retired. St. Gregory Abbey, Shawnee, OK 74801.
Wagner, Lawrence, o.s.b., Retired. Assumption Abbey, P.O. Box A, Richardton, ND 58652.
Walsh, Raphael, o.s.b., Mt. Michael Abbey, Elkhorn, NE 68022.
Warles, o.s.b., Prince of Peace Abbey, 650 Benet Hill Rd., Oceanside, CA 92054.
Wechter, David L., o.s.c.o., Retired. New Melleray Abbey, 6500 Melleray Circle, Peosta, IA 52068.
West, Robert, o.s.b., Retired. Assumption Abbey, P.O. Box A, Richardton, ND 58652.
Wiseman, James, o.s.b., Resigned. St. Anselm Abbey, 4501 South Dakota Ave., N.E., Washington, DC 20017-2753.
Wolff, Theodore, o.s.b., Mount Michael Abbey, 22520 Mount Michael Rd., Elkhorn, NE 68022.
Wood, Joseph, o.s.b., Mt. Angel Abbey, St. Benedict, OR 97373.

A LIST OF CARDINALS IN THE UNITED STATES IN THE ORDER OF THEIR SENIORITY

CARDINALS

His Eminence Luis Cardinal Aponte Martinez, San Juan
His Eminence William Cardinal Baum, Vatican City State
His Eminence Bernard Cardinal Law, Boston
His Eminence James Cardinal Hickey, Washington
His Eminence Edmund Cardinal Szoka, Vatican City State
His Eminence Roger Cardinal Mahony, Los Angeles
His Eminence Anthony Cardinal Bevilacqua, Philadelphia
His Eminence William Cardinal Keeler, Baltimore
His Eminence Adam Cardinal Maida, Detroit
His Eminence Francis Cardinal Stafford, Vatican City State
His Eminence Francis Cardinal George, O.M.I., Chicago
His Eminence Avery Cardinal Dulles
His Eminence Edward Cardinal Egan, New York
His Eminence Theodore Cardinal McCarrick, Washington
His Eminence Justin Cardinal Rigali, Philadelphia

A CHRONOLOGICAL LIST OF CARDINAL, ARCHBISHOP & BISHOP ACTIVITY BY YEAR

1954

Bishop

Maloney, Charles G., Appointed Dec. 30. Ordained Dec. 8, 1937. Auxiliary Bishop of Louisville.

1956

Bishops

Clinch, Harry A., Appointed Dec. 5. Ordained June 6, 1936. Auxiliary Bishop of Monterey-Fresno.

Hannan, Philip M., Appointed June 16. Ordained Dec. 8, 1939. Auxiliary Bishop of Washington.

1959

Bishops

Buswell, Charles A., Appointed Aug. 8. Ordained July 9, 1939. Bishop of Pueblo.

Hogan, James J., Appointed Nov. 27. Ordained Dec. 8, 1937. Auxiliary Bishop of Trenton.

1960

Bishops

Aponte Martinez, Luis, Appointed July 23. Ordained April 10, 1950. Auxiliary of Ponce.

Forst, Marion F., Appointed Jan. 2. Ordained June 10, 1934. Bishop of Dodge City.

Wycislo, Aloysius J., Appointed Oct. 17. Ordained April 7, 1934. Auxiliary Bishop of Chicago.

1962

Bishops

Hunthausen, Raymond G., Appointed July 8. Ordained June 1, 1946. Bishop of Helena.

Zayek, Francis M., Appointed May 30. Ordained March 17, 1946. Titular Bishop of Callinicum.

1963

Bishops

Aponte Martinez, Luis, Appointed Nov. 18. Ordained April 16, 1950. Coadjutor Bishop of Ponce to Bishop of Ponce.

D'Antonio, Nicholas, Appointed Dec. 31. Ordained June 7, 1942. Bishop of Olancho, Honduras.

Ward, John J., Appointed Oct. 16. Ordained May 4, 1946. Auxiliary Bishop of Los Angeles

1964

Archbishop

Aponte Martinez, Luis, Appointed Nov. 11. Ordained April 10, 1950. Archbishop of San Juan.

Bishop

Torres, Juan Fremiot, Appointed Nov. 4. Ordained April 10, 1950. Bishop of Ponce.

1965

Archbishop

Hannan, Philip M., Appointed Sept. 29. Ordained Dec. 8, 1939. Archbishop of New Orleans.

Bishops

Breitenbeck, Joseph M., Appointed Oct. 18. Ordained May 30, 1942. Auxiliary Bishop of Detroit.

McCarthy, Edward A., Appointed April 21. Ordained May 29, 1943. Auxiliary Bishop of Cincinnati.

Watters, Loras J., Appointed June 23. Ordained June 7, 1941. Auxiliary Bishop of Dubuque.

1966

Bishops

Gerety, Peter Leo, Appointed March 4. Ordained June 29, 1939. Coadjutor Bishop of Portland (in Maine).

Hogan, James J., Appointed May 23. Ordained Dec. 8, 1937. Bishop of Altoona-Johnstown.

McDowell, John B., Appointed July 18. Ordained Nov. 4, 1945. Auxiliary Bishop of Pittsburgh.

Michaels, James, s.s.c., Appointed Feb. 15. Ordained Dec. 21, 1951. Auxiliary Bishop of Wheeling-Charleston.

Tschoepe, Thomas, Appointed Jan. 12. Ordained May 30, 1943. Bishop of San Angelo.

1967

Bishops

Broderick, Edwin B., Appointed March 4. Ordained May 30, 1942. Auxiliary Bishop of New York.

Clinch, Harry A., Appointed Dec. 14. Ordained June 6, 1936. Retired Bishop of Monterey.

Frey, Gerard L., Appointed May 31. Ordained April 2, 1938. Bishop of Savannah.

Gerety, Peter Leo, Appointed Feb. 18. Ordained June 29, 1939. Apostolic Administrator of Portland (in Maine).

Hickey, James A., Appointed April 14. Ordained June 15, 1946. Auxiliary Bishop of Saginaw.

Quinn, John R., Appointed Oct. 21. Ordained July 19, 1953. Auxiliary Bishop of San Diego.

Reiss, John C., Appointed Oct. 21. Ordained May 31, 1947. Auxiliary Bishop of Trenton.

1968

Bishops

Borders, William D., Appointed May 8. Ordained May 18, 1940. Bishop of Orlando.

Cronin, Daniel A., Appointed June 10. Ordained Dec. 20, 1952. Auxiliary Bishop of Boston.

Dudick, Michael J., Appointed Aug. 21. Ordained Nov. 13, 1945. Bishop of Passaic.

Fitzpatrick, John J., Appointed June 24. Ordained Dec. 13, 1942. Auxiliary Bishop of Miami.

Gossman, F. Joseph, Appointed July 15. Ordained Dec. 17, 1955. Auxiliary Bishop of Baltimore.

Gumbleton, Thomas J., Appointed March 8. Ordained June 2, 1956. Auxiliary Bishop of Detroit.

McKinney, Joseph C., Appointed July 24. Ordained Dec. 20, 1953. Auxiliary Bishop of Grand Rapids.

McLaughlin, Bernard J., Appointed Dec. 28. Ordained Dec. 21, 1935. Retired Auxiliary Bishop of Buffalo.

O'Neill, Arthur J., Appointed Aug. 19. Ordained March 27, 1943. Bishop of Rockford.

Schoenherr, Walter J., Appointed March 8. Ordained Oct. 27, 1945. Auxiliary Bishop of Detroit.

Shea, Robert L., s.j., Succeeded to See Nov. 30. Bishop of Fairbanks.

Wycislo, Aloysius J., Appointed March 8. Ordained April 7, 1934. Bishop of Green Bay.

1969

Bishops

Breitenbeck, Joseph, Appointed Oct. 15. Ordained May 30, 1942. Bishop of Grand Rapids.

Broderick, Edwin B., Appointed March 19. Ordained May 30, 1942. Bishop of Albany.

Gerety, Peter Leo, Succeeded to See Sept. 15. Bishop of Portland (in Maine).

McAuliffe, Michael F., Appointed July 2. Ordained May 31, 1945. Bishop of Jefferson City.

McCarthy, Edward A., Appointed Aug. 25. Ordained May 29, 1943. Bishop of Phoenix.

Neylon, Martin J., s.j., Appointed Oct. 2. Ordained June 18, 1950. Titular Bishop of Libertina.

Tshoepe, Thomas, Appointed Aug. 27. Ordained May 30, 1943. Bishop of Dallas.

Watters, Loras J., Appointed Jan. 8. Ordained June 7, 1941. Bishop of Winona.

1970

Bishops

Ahern, Patrick V., Appointed Feb. 3. Ordained Jan. 27, 1945. Auxiliary Bishop of New York.

Baum, William, Appointed Feb. 18. Ordained May 12, 1951. Bishop of Springfield-Cape Girardeau.

Bosco, Anthony G., Appointed May 14. Ordained June 7, 1952. Auxiliary Bishop of Pittsburgh.

Cronin, Daniel A., Appointed Oct. 30. Ordained Dec. 20, 1952. Bishop of Fall River.

Flores, Patrick F., Appointed March 18. Ordained May 26, 1956. Auxiliary Bishop of San Antonio.

Head, Edward D., Appointed Jan. 27. Ordained Jan. 27, 1945. Auxiliary Bishop of New York.

Hurley, Francis T., Appointed Feb. 4. Ordained June 16, 1951. Auxiliary Bishop of Juneau.

Lohmuller, Martin N., Appointed Feb. 11. Ordained June 3, 1944. Auxiliary Bishop of Philadelphia.

McFarland, Norman F., Appointed June 5. Ordained June 15, 1946. Auxiliary Bishop of San Francisco.

Schmitt, Mark F., Appointed May 5. Ordained May 22, 1948. Auxiliary Bishop of Green Bay.

Sullivan, Walter F., Appointed Oct. 20. Ordained May 9, 1953. Auxiliary Bishop of Richmond.

Welsh, Thomas J., Appointed Feb. 18. Ordained May 30, 1946. Auxiliary Bishop of Philadelphia.

1971

Bishops

Arzube, Juan, Appointed Feb. 9. Ordained May 5, 1954. Auxiliary Bishop of Los Angeles.

Connolly, Thomas J., Appointed May 4. Ordained April 8, 1947. Bishop of Baker.

Donovan, Paul V., Appointed June 15. Ordained May 20, 1950. Bishop of Kalamazoo.

Fitzpatrick, John J., Appointed April 21. Ordained Dec. 13, 1942. Bishop of Brownsville.

Gelineau, Louis E., Appointed Dec. 6. Ordained June 5, 1954. Bishop of Providence.

Gracida, Rene H., Appointed Dec. 6. Ordained May 23, 1959. Auxiliary Bishop of Miami.

Harrison, Frank J., Appointed March 1. Ordained June 4, 1937. Auxiliary Bishop of Syracuse.

Hurley, Francis T., Appointed July 20. Ordained June 16, 1951. Bishop of Juneau.

Losten, Basil, Appointed March 15. Ordained June 10, 1957. Auxiliary Bishop of Philadelphia Ukrainian.

Maguire, Joseph F., Appointed Dec. 1. Ordained June 29, 1945. Auxiliary Bishop of Boston.

Neylon, Martin J., s.j., Appointed Sept. 20. Ordained June 18, 1950. Vicar Apostolic of The Carolines-Marshalls.

Szoka, Edmund, Appointed June 15. Ordained June 5, 1954. Bishop of Gaylord.

Zayek, Francis M., Appointed Nov. 11. Ordained March 17, 1946. Eparch of St. Maron.

1972

Archbishop

Quinn, John R., Appointed Dec. 13. Ordained July 19, 1953. Archbishop of Oklahoma City.

Bishops

Frey, Gerard L., Appointed Bishop of Lafayette in Louisiana Nov. 7. Ordained April 2, 1938.

Howze, Joseph L., Appointed Nov. 8. Ordained May 7, 1959. Auxiliary Bishop of Jackson.

McDonald, Andrew J., Appointed July 4. Ordained May 8, 1948. Bishop of Little Rock.

Snyder, John J., Appointed Dec. 19. Ordained June 9, 1951. Auxiliary Bishop of Brooklyn.

Sullivan, James S., Appointed July 25. Ordained June 4, 1955. Auxiliary Bishop of Lansing.

1973

Cardinal

Aponte Martinez, Luis Cardinal, Created March 5. Archbishop of San Juan.

Archbishop

Baum, William, Appointed May 9. Ordained May 12, 1951. Archbishop of Washington.

Bishops

Head, Edward D., Appointed Jan. 17. Ordained Jan. 27, 1945. Bishop of Buffalo.

Imesch, Joseph L., Appointed Feb. 8. Ordained Dec. 16, 1956. Auxiliary Bishop of Detroit.

Law, Bernard, Appointed Oct. 22. Ordained May 21, 1961. Bishop of Springfield-Cape Girardeau.

Lessard, Raymond W., Appointed March 5. Ordained Dec. 16, 1956. Bishop of Savannah.

Mestice, Anthony F., Appointed March 5. Ordained June 4, 1949. Auxiliary Bishop of New York.

Sullivan, Walter F., Appointed April 30. Ordained May 9, 1953. Apostolic Administrator of Richmond.

1974

Archbishops

Borders, William D., Appointed March 25. Ordained May 18, 1940. Archbishop of Baltimore.

Gerety, Peter Leo, Appointed April 2. Ordained June 29, 1939. Archbishop of Newark.

Sanchez, Robert F., Appointed June 1. Ordained Dec. 20, 1959. Archbishop of Santa Fe.

Bishops

Angell, Kenneth A., Appointed Aug. 9. Ordained May 26, 1956. Auxiliary Bishop of Providence.

Chavez, Gilbert E., Appointed April 19. Ordained March 19, 1960. Auxiliary Bishop of San Diego.

Cummins, John S., Appointed Feb. 26. Ordained Jan. 24, 1953. Auxiliary Bishop of Sacramento.

Daily, Thomas V., Appointed Dec. 31. Ordained Jan. 10, 1952. Auxiliary Bishop of Boston.

D'Arcy, John M., Appointed Dec. 31. Ordained Feb. 2, 1957. Auxiliary Bishop of Boston.

Gendron, Odore J., Appointed Dec. 12. Ordained May 31, 1947. Retired Bishop of Manchester.

Hanifen, Richard C., Appointed July 6, 1974. Ordained June 6, 1959. Auxiliary Bishop of Denver.

Hickey, James A., Appointed June 4. Ordained June 15, 1946. Bishop of Cleveland.

Hughes, William A., Appointed July 23. Ordained April 6, 1946. Auxiliary Bishop of Youngstown.

McFarland, Norman F., Appointed Dec. 6. Ordained June 15, 1946. Apostolic Administrator of Reno-Las Vegas.

Ottenweller, Albert H., Appointed April 17. Ordained June 19, 1943. Auxiliary Bishop of Toledo.

Pilarczyk, Daniel E., Appointed Nov. 12. Ordained Dec. 20, 1959. Auxiliary Bishop of Cincinnati.

Sullivan, Walter F., Succeeded to See June 6. Bishop of Richmond.

Welsh, Thomas J., Appointed June 4. Bishop of Arlington.

1975

Archbishop

Hunthausen, Raymond G., Appointed Feb. 25. Ordained June 1, 1946. Archbishop of Seattle.

Bishops

Fitzsimons, George K., Appointed May 27. Ordained March 18, 1961. Auxiliary Bishop of Kansas City-St. Joseph.

Gossman, F. Joseph, Appointed April 8. Ordained Dec. 17, 1955. Bishop of Raleigh.

Gracida, Rene H., Appointed Oct.1. Ordained May 23, 1959. Bishop of Pensacola-Tallahassee.

Mahony, Roger M., Appointed Jan. 7. Ordained May 1, 1962. Auxiliary Bishop of Fresno.

Niedergeses, James D., Appointed April 8. Ordained May 20, 1944. Bishop of Nashville.

Reilly, Daniel P., Appointed June 17. Ordained May 30, 1953. Bishop of Norwich.

Surinach Carreras, Ricardo, Appointed May 26. Ordained April 13, 1957. Auxiliary Bishop of Ponce.

1976

Cardinal

Baum, William Cardinal, Created May 24. Prefect of Sacred Congregation for Catholic Education, Vatican

Archbishops

Hurley, Francis T., Appointed May 4. Ordained June 16, 1951. Archbishop of Anchorage.

McCarthy, Edward A., Appointed Sept. 17. Ordained May 29, 1943. Coadjutor Archbishop of Miami.

Bishops

Balke, Victor, Appointed July 7. Ordained May 24, 1958. Bishop of Crookston.

Broderick, Edwin B., Appointed June 3. Exec. Dir. Catholic Relief Services; resigned Bishop of Albany

Casiano-Vargas, Ulises, Appointed March 4. Ordained May 30, 1967. Bishop of Mayaguez.

Curtiss, Elden F., Appointed March 4. Ordained May 24, 1958. Bishop of Helena.

Dudley, Paul V., Appointed Nov. 16. Ordained June 2, 1951. Auxiliary Bishop of St. Paul-Minneapolis.

Forst, Marion E., Appointed Oct. 16. Ordained June 10, 1934. Auxiliary Bishop of Kansas City in Kansas.

Gerber, Eugene J., Appointed Oct. 16. Ordained May 19, 1959. Bishop of Dodge City.

Harrison, Frank J., Appointed Nov. 16. Ordained June 4, 1937. Bishop of Syracuse.

Hart, Daniel A., Appointed Aug. 30. Ordained Feb. 2, 1953. Auxiliary Bishop of Boston.

Hart, Joseph H., Appointed July 1. Ordained May 1, 1956. Bishop of Cheyenne.

Hughes, Edward T., Appointed June 14. Ordained May 31, 1947. Auxiliary Bishop of Philadelphia.

Kinney, John F., Appointed Nov. 16. Ordained Feb. 2, 1963. Auxiliary Bishop of St. Paul-Minneapolis.

Losten, Basil H., Appointed June 8. Ordained June 10, 1957. Apostolic Administrator Philadelphia Ukrainian.

Maguire, Joseph F., Appointed April 3. Ordained June 29, 1945. Coadjutor Bishop of Springfield.

Marconi, Dominic A., Appointed May 3. Ordained May 30, 1953. Auxiliary Bishop of Newark.

McFarland, Norman F., Appointed Feb. 10. Ordained June 15, 1946. Bishop of Reno-Las Vegas.

Moreno, Manuel D., Appointed Dec. 20. Ordained April 25, 1961. Auxiliary Bishop of Los Angeles.

Murphy, Michael J., Appointed April 20. Ordained Feb. 28, 1942. Auxiliary Bishop of Cleveland.

Pena, Raymundo, J., Appointed Oct. 16. Ordained May 25, 1957. Auxiliary Bishop of San Antonio.

Sheldon, Gilbert I., Appointed April 20. Ordained Feb. 28, 1953. Auxiliary Bishop of Cleveland.

Stafford, J. Francis, Appointed Jan. 27. Ordained Dec. 15, 1957. Auxiliary Bishop of Baltimore.

Timlin, James C., Appointed Aug. 3. Ordained July 16, 1951. Auxiliary Bishop of Scranton.

1977

Archbishops

McCarthy, Edward A., Succeeded to See July 26. Archbishop of Miami.

Quinn, John R., Appointed Feb. 22. Ordained July 19, 1953. Archbishop of San Francisco.

Weakland, Rembert, G., o.s.b., Appointed Sept. 20. Ordained June 24, 1951. Archbishop of Milwaukee.

Bishops

Cummins, John S., Appointed May 3. Ordained Jan. 24, 1953. Bishop of Oakland.

Daly, James J., Appointed Feb. 28. Ordained May 22, 1948. Auxiliary Bishop of Rockville Centre.

D'Antonio, Nicholas, o.f.m., Appointed Aug. 22. Vicar for Spanish-speaking, New Orleans.

Garmendia, Francisco, Appointed May. Auxiliary Bishop of New York.

Howze, Joseph L., Appointed March 1. Ordained May 7, 1959. Bishop of Biloxi from Auxiliary Bishop of Jackson.

Hubbard, Howard J., Appointed Feb. 1. Ordained Dec. 18, 1963. Bishop of Albany.

Kelly, Thomas C., o.p., Appointed July 12. Ordained June 5, 1958. Auxiliary Bishop of Washington

Kucera, Daniel W., o.s.b., Appointed June 6. Ordained May 26, 1949. Auxiliary Bishop of Joliet.

Losten, Basil H., Appointed Sept. 20. Ordained June 10, 1957. Bishop of Stamford.

Maguire, Joseph F., Succeeded to See Nov. 4. Bishop of Springfield.

McCarrick, Theodore E., Appointed May 24. Ordained May 31, 1958. Auxiliary Bishop of New York.

Mulvee, Robert E. Appointed Feb. 15. Ordained June 30, 1957. Auxiliary Bishop of Manchester.

Ottenweller, Albert H., Appointed Oct. 11. Ordained June 19, 1943. Bishop of Steubenville.

Paul, John J., Appointed May 17. Ordained Jan. 24, 1943. Auxiliary Bishop of La Crosse.

Rodimer, Frank J. Appointed Dec. 13. Ordained May 19, 1951. Bishop of Paterson.

Skylstad, William, Appointed Feb. 22. Ordained May 21, 1960. Bishop of Yakima.

Steiner, Kenneth, Appointed Dec. 6. Ordained May 19, 1962. Auxiliary Bishop of Portland in Oregon.

Wirz, George O., Appointed Dec. 20. Ordained May 31, 1952. Auxiliary Bishop of Madison.

1978

Bishops

Beltran, Eusebius J., Appointed Feb. 28. Ordained May 14, 1960. Bishop of Tulsa.

Costello, Thomas J., Appointed Jan. 10. Ordained June 5, 1954. Auxiliary Bishop of Syracuse.

Dudley, Paul V., Appointed Sept. 26. Ordained June 2,1951. Bishop of Sioux Falls.

DuMaine, R. Pierre, Appointed April 28. Ordained June 5, 1957. Auxiliary Bishop of San Francisco.

Flores, Patrick F., Appointed April 4. Ordained May 26, 1956. Bishop of El Paso.

McNamara, Lawrence J., Appointed Jan. 10. Ordained May 30, 1953. Bishop of Grand Island.

Morneau, Robert F., Appointed Dec. 19. Ordained May 28, 1966. Auxiliary Bishop of Green Bay.

Murphy, Michael J., Appointed Nov. 28. Ordained Feb. 28, 1942. Coadjutor Bishop of Erie.

Quinn, Francis A., Appointed April 28. Ordained June15, 1946. Auxiliary Bishop of San Francisco.

Rosazza, Peter A., Appointed Feb. 28. Ordained June 29, 1961. Auxiliary Bishop of Hartford.

Schmitt, Mark F., Appointed March 21. Ordained May 22, 1948. Bishop of Marquette.

Straling, Phillip F., Appointed July 18. Ordained March 19, 1959. Bishop of San Bernardino.

1979

Archbishop

Flores, Patrick F., Appointed Aug. 28. Ordained May 26, 1956. Archbishop of San Antonio.

Bishops

Buswell, Charles A., Retired Sept. Bishop of Pueblo.

Clark, Matthew H., Appointed May 2. Ordained Dec. 19, 1962. Bishop of Rochester.

Fiorenza, Joseph A., Appointed Sept. 4. Ordained May 29, 1954. Bishop of San Angelo.

Fliss, Raphael M., Appointed Nov. 6. Ordained May 26, 1956. Coadjutor Bishop of Superior.

Friend, William B., Appointed Aug. 31. Ordained May 7, 1959. Auxiliary Bishop of Alexandria-Shreveport.

Griffin, James A., Appointed June 30. Ordained May 28, 1960. Auxiliary Bishop of Cleveland.

Houck, William R., Appointed March 28. Ordained May 19, 1951. Auxiliary Bishop of Jackson.

Hughes, William A., Appointed April 13. Ordained April 6, 1946. Bishop of Covington.

Imesch, Joseph L., Appointed June 30. Ordained Dec. 16, 1956. Bishop of Joliet.

Keeler, William H., Appointed July 24. Ordained July 17, 1955. Auxiliary Bishop of Harrisburg.

Larkin, W. Thomas, Appointed April 24. Ordained May 15, 1947. Bishop of St. Petersburg.

Madera, Joseph J., m.sp.s., Appointed Dec. 18. Ordained June 15, 1957. Coadjutor Bishop of Fresno.

McCarthy, John E., Appointed Jan. 23. Ordained May 26, 1956. Auxiliary Bishop of Galveston-Houston.

Nevins, John J., Appointed Feb. 6. Ordained June 6, 1959. Auxiliary Bishop of Miami.

Neylon, Martin J., s.j., Appointed May 3. Ordained June 18, 1950. Bishop of The Carolines-Marshalls.

Pilla, Anthony M., Appointed June 30. Ordained May 23, 1959. Auxiliary Bishop of Cleveland.

Quinn, Francis A., Appointed Dec. 18. Ordained June 15, 1946. Bishop of Sacramento.

Rivera, Hector M., Appointed June 11. Ordained June 12, 1966. Auxiliary Bishop of San Juan.

Rivera, Enrique Hernandez, Appointed June 11. Ordained June 8, 1968. Auxiliary Bishop of San Juan.

Roman, Agustin A., Appointed Feb. 6. Ordained July 5, 1959. Auxiliary Bishop of Miami.

Schlarman, Stanley G., Appointed March 13. Ordained July 13, 1958. Auxiliary Bishop of Belleville.

Sklba, Richard J., Appointed Nov. 6. Ordained Dec. 20, 1959. Auxiliary Bishop of Milwaukee.

Snyder, John J., Appointed Oct. 2. Ordained June 9, 1951. Bishop of St. Augustine.

1980

Archbishops

Hickey, James A., Appointed June 17. Ordained June 15, 1946. Archbishop of Washington.

Lipscomb, Oscar H., Appointed July 29. Ordained July 15, 1956. Archbishop of Mobile.

Sulyk, Stephen, Appointed Dec. 29. Archbishop of Philadelphia Ukrainian.

Bishops

Bevilacqua, Anthony, Appointed Oct. 7. Ordained June 11, 1949. Auxiliary Bishop of Brooklyn.

Bullock, William H., Appointed June 3. Ordained June 7, 1952. Auxiliary Bishop of St. Paul-Minneapolis.
Chedid, John, Appointed Oct. 28. Ordained Dec. 21, 1951. Auxiliary Bishop of St. Maron.
Franzetta, Benedict C., Appointed July 29. Ordained April 29, 1950. Auxiliary Bishop of Youngstown.
Kucera, Daniel W., o.s.b., Appointed March 11. Ordained May 26, 1949. Bishop of Salina.
Madera, Joseph J., m.sp.s., Succeeded to See July 1. Bishop of Fresno.
Mahony, Roger M., Appointed Feb. 26. Ordained May 1, 1962. Bishop of Stockton.
Matthiesen, Leroy T., Appointed March 25. Ordained March 10, 1946. Bishop of Amarillo.
Pena, Raymundo J., Appointed April 29. Ordained May 25, 1957. Bishop of El Paso.
Pilla, Anthony M., Appointed Nov. 18. Ordained May 23, 1959. Bishop of Cleveland.
Reiss, John C., Appointed March 4. Ordained May 31, 1947. Bishop of Trenton.
Speyrer, Jude, Appointed Jan. 29. Ordained July 25, 1953. Bishop of Lake Charles.
Sullivan, Joseph M., Appointed Oct. 7. Ordained June 2, 1956. Auxiliary Bishop of Brooklyn.
Tafoya, Arthur N., Appointed July 1. Ordained May 12, 1962. Bishop of Pueblo.
Valero, Rene, Appointed Oct. 7. Ordained June 2, 1956. Auxiliary Bishop of Brooklyn.
Weigand, William K., Appointed Sept. 3. Ordained May 25, 1963. Bishop of Salt Lake City.

1981

Archbishops

Kelly, Thomas C., o.p., Appointed Dec. 29. Ordained June 5, 1958. Archbishop of Louisville.
Marcinkus, Paul C., Appointed Sept. 26. Ordained May 3, 1947. Titular Archbishop of Orta, Vatican City State.
Szoka, Edmund C., Appointed March 28. Ordained June 5, 1954. Archbishop of Detroit.

Bishops

Delaney, Joseph P., Appointed July 10. Ordained Dec. 18, 1960. Bishop of Fort Worth.
DeSimone, Louis A., Appointed June 27. Ordained May 10, 1952. Auxiliary Bishop of Philadelphia.
Dumaine, R., Pierre, Appointed Jan. 27. Ordained June 5, 1957. Bishop of San Jose.
Grahmann, Charles V., Appointed June 30. Ordained March 17, 1956. Auxiliary Bishop of San Antonio.
Hughes, Alfred C., Appointed July 21. Ordained Dec. 15, 1957. Auxiliary Bishop of Boston.
Lotocky, Innocent, o.s.b.m., Appointed Jan. 29. Ordained Nov. 24, 1940. Bishop of St. Nicholas Chicago.
McCarrick, Theodore E., Appointed Nov. 24. Bishop of Metuchen.
Milone, Anthony M., Appointed Nov. 10. Ordained Dec. 15, 1957. Auxiliary Bishop of Omaha.
Moskal, Robert M., Appointed Aug. 3. Ordained March 25, 1963. Auxiliary Bishop of the Archeparchy of Philadelphia.
O'Brien, Thomas J., Appointed Nov. 24. Ordained May 7, 1961. Bishop of Phoenix.
Ramirez, Ricardo, c.s.b., Appointed Oct. 27. Ordained Dec. 10, 1966. Auxiliary Bishop of San Antonio.
Rivera, Enrique Hernandez, Appointed Feb. 13. Ordained June 8, 1968. Bishop of Caguas.
Rose, Robert J., Appointed Oct. 13. Ordained Dec. 21, 1955. Bishop of Gaylord.
Ryan, Daniel L., Appointed Aug. 14. Ordained May 3, 1956. Auxiliary Bishop of Joliet.
Santana, Hermin Negron, Appointed June 30. Ordained May 30, 1969. Auxiliary Bishop of San Juan.
Schulte, Francis B., Appointed June 27. Ordained May 10, 1952. Auxiliary Bishop of Philadelphia.
Symons, J. Keith, Appointed Jan. 16. Ordained May 18, 1958. Auxiliary Bishop of St. Petersburg.
Walsh, Daniel F., Appointed June 30. Ordained March 30, 1963. Auxiliary Bishop of San Francisco.

1982

Archbishops

Pilarczyk, Daniel E., Appointed Nov. 2. Ordained Dec. 20, 1959. Archbishop of Cincinnati.
Zayek, Francis M., Appointed Dec. 22. Ordained March 17, 1946. Archbishop of St. Maron, Brooklyn.

Bishops

Anderson, Moses B., s.s.e., Appointed Dec. 3. Ordained May 30, 1958. Auxiliary Bishop of Detroit.
Cooney, Patrick, R., Appointed Dec. 7. Ordained Dec. 20, 1959. Auxiliary Bishop of Detroit.
Friend, William B., Appointed Nov. 23. Bishop of Alexandria-Shreveport.
Gerber, Eugene J., Appointed Nov. 23. Ordained May 19, 1959. Bishop of Wichita.
Grahmann, Charles V., Appointed April 14. Ordained March 17, 1956. Bishop of Victoria.
Kinney, John F., Appointed June 28. Ordained Feb. 2, 1963. Bishop of Bismarck.
Kmiec, Edward V., Appointed Aug. 26. Ordained Dec. 20, 1961. Auxiliary Bishop of Trenton.
McRaith, John J., Appointed Oct. 23. Ordained Feb. 21, 1960. Bishop of Owensboro.
Melczek, Dale J., Appointed Dec. 3. Ordained June 6, 1964. Auxiliary Bishop of Detroit.
Moreno, Manuel D., Appointed Jan. 12. Ordained April 25, 1961. Bishop of Tucson.
Murphy, Michael J., Succeeded to See July 16. Bishop of Erie.
Pevec, Edward A., Appointed April 13. Ordained April 29, 1950. Auxiliary Bishop of Cleveland.
Puscas, Louis, Appointed Dec. 4. Ordained May 14, 1942. Eparch of Romanian Diocese of Canton.
Ramirez, Ricardo, c.s.b., Appointed Aug. 31. Ordained Dec. 10, 1966. Bishop of Las Cruces.
Stafford, J. Francis, Appointed Nov. 16. Ordained Dec. 15, 1957. Bishop of Memphis.

1983

Archbishop

Kucera, Daniel, W., Appointed Dec. 20. Archbishop of Dubuque.

Bishops

Apuron, Anthony S., o.f.m.cap., Appointed Dec. 8. Auxiliary Bishop of Agana.
Arias, David, o.a.r., Appointed Jan. 25. Auxiliary Bishop of Newark.
Bevilacqua, Anthony, Appointed Oct. 7. Bishop of Pittsburgh.
Brom, Robert, Appointed March 25. Bishop of Duluth.
Carlson, Robert, J., Appointed Nov. 22. Auxiliary Bishop of St. Paul-Minneapolis.
Dimino, Joseph, Appointed March 29. Auxiliary Bishop of Military Services.
Gracida, Rene, Appointed May 19. Bishop of Corpus Christi.
Gregory, Wilton, Appointed Oct. 31. Auxiliary Bishop of Chicago.
Griffin, James, Appointed Feb. 7. Bishop of Columbus.
Hanifen, Richard, Appointed Nov. 10. Bishop of Colorado Springs.
Keeler, William, Appointed Nov. 10. Bishop of Harrisburg.
Levada, William, J., Appointed March 29. Auxiliary Bishop of Los Angeles.
Lyne, Timothy, Appointed Oct. 31. Auxiliary Bishop of Chicago.
Maida, Adam, Appointed Nov. 8. Bishop of Green Bay.
Montrose, Donald, Appointed March 25. Auxiliary Bishop of Los Angeles.
Moskal, Robert, Appointed Dec. 5. Bishop of St. Josaphat in Parma.
O'Donnell, Edward, Appointed Dec. 6. Auxiliary Bishop of St. Louis.
Pataki, Andrew, Appointed May 30. Auxiliary Bishop of Passaic.
Paul, John J., Appointed Oct. 18. Bishop of LaCrosse.
Popp, Bernard, Appointed June 7. Auxiliary Bishop of San Antonio.
Quinn, A. James, Appointed Oct. 14. Auxiliary Bishop of Cleveland.
Rodriquez, Placido, Appointed Oct. Auxiliary Bishop of Chicago.
Roque, Francis, Appointed March 29. Auxiliary Bishop of Military Services.
Ryan, Daniel, Appointed Nov. 22. Bishop of Springfield in Illinois.
Schlarmann, Stanley, Appointed March 1. Bishop of Dodge City.
Sheehan, Michael, J., Appointed March 29. Bishop of Lubbock.
Soens, Lawrence, Appointed June 15. Bishop of Sioux City.
Steib, James Terry, s.v.d., Appointed Dec. 6. Auxiliary Bishop of St. Louis.
Symons, J. Keith, Appointed Sept. 29. Bishop of Pensacola-Tallahassee.
Vlazny, John G., Appointed Oct. 31. Auxiliary Bishop of Chicago.
Welsh, Thomas, Appointed Feb. 8. Bishop of Allentown.
Wycislo, Aloysius, J., Retired May. Bishop of Green Bay.

1984

Archbishops

Foley, John, Appointed April 9. Archbishop to the Pontifical Commission for Social Communication.
Law, Bernard, Appointed Jan. 24. Archbishop of Boston.

Bishops

Baltakis, Paul, Appointed June 1. Bishop for the Lithuanian Apostolate.
Camacho, Tomas A., Appointed Nov. 8. Bishop of Chalan Kanoa.
Daily, Thomas, Appointed July 17. Bishop of Palm Beach.
Donnelly, Robert, Appointed March 20. Auxiliary Bishop of Toledo.
Donoghue, John, Appointed Nov. 6. Bishop of Charlotte.
Fiorenza, Joseph, A., Appointed Dec. 18. Bishop of Galveston-Houston.
Fitzsimons, George, Appointed March 22. Bishop of Salina.
Garland, James, H., Appointed June 25. Auxiliary Bishop of Cincinnati.
Higi, William, Appointed April 7. Bishop of Lafayette in Indiana.
Houck, William, Appointed April 24. Bishop of Jackson.
Keleher, James, Appointed Oct. 23. Bishop of Belleville.
Leibrecht, John, Appointed Oct. 23. Bishop of Springfield-Cape Girardeau.
Nevins, John, J., Appointed July 17. Bishop of Venice.
Newman, William, Appointed July 2. Auxiliary Bishop of Baltimore.
O'Malley, Sean, P., o.f.m.cap., Appointed May 30. Coadjutor Bishop of St. Thomas Virgin Islands.
Pataki, Andrew, Appointed June 19. Bishop of Parma.
Ricard, John, s.s.j., Appointed May 29. Auxiliary Bishop of Baltimore.
Steinbock, John T., Appointed May 29. Auxiliary Bishop of Orange.
Timlin, James, Appointed April 24. Bishop of Scranton.
Williams, J. Kendrick, Appointed April 15. Auxiliary Bishop of Covington.

1985

Cardinal

Law, Bernard Cardinal, Created May 25. Archbishop of Boston.

Archbishop

Mahony, Roger, Appointed July 16. Archbishop of Los Angeles.

Bishops

Apuron, Anthony S., o.f.m.cap., Appointed Oct. 27. Apostolic Administrator of Agana.
Banks, Robert J., Appointed June 26. Auxiliary Bishop of Boston.
Corrada del Rio, Alvaro, s.j., Appointed Aug. 4. Auxiliary Bishop of Washington.
D'Arcy, John M., Appointed Feb. 26. Bishop of Fort Wayne-South Bend.
Egan, Edward M., Appointed April 1. Auxiliary Bishop of New York.
Fliss, Raphael M., Succeeded to See June 27. Bishop of Superior.
Ibrahim, Ibrahim, Appointed Sept. 14. Eparch of St. Thomas the Apostle.
Kaffer, Roger L., Appointed April 25. Auxiliary Bishop of Joliet.
McCarthy, John E., Appointed Dec. 24. Bishop of Austin.
Montrose, Donald, Appointed Dec. 19. Bishop of Stockton.
Mulvee, Robert E., Appointed Feb. 16. Bishop of Wilmington.
O'Malley, Sean, P., o.f.m.cap., Succeeded to See Oct. 16. Bishop of St. Thomas Virgin Islands.
Pfeifer, Michael, o.m.i., Appointed July 26. Bishop of San Angelo.
Schulte, Francis B., Appointed June 4. Bishop of Wheeling-Charleston.
Sullivan, James S., Appointed April 2. Bishop of Fargo.
Trautman, Donald W., Appointed Feb. 27. Auxiliary Bishop of Buffalo.
Wuerl, Donald, Appointed Dec. 3. Auxiliary Bishop of Seattle.

1986

Archbishops

Apuron, Anthony S., o.f.m.cap., Succeeded to See May 11. Archbishop of Agana.
Gerety, Peter, Leo, Retired June. Archbishop of Newark.
Levada, William J., Appointed July 1. Archbishop of Portland in Oregon.
McCarrick, Theodore E., Appointed June 1. Archbishop of Newark.
Stafford, J. Francis, Appointed June 3. Archbishop of Denver.

Bishops

Dorsey, Norbert, c.p., Appointed Jan. 10. Auxiliary Bishop of Miami.
Elya, John A., b.s.o., Appointed April 2. Auxiliary Bishop of Newton.
Favalora, John C., Appointed June 16. Bishop of Alexandria.
Flynn, Harry, Appointed April 19. Coadjutor Bishop of Lafayette.
Foley, David, Appointed May 3. Auxiliary Bishop of Richmond.
Forst, Marion F., Retired Dec. Auxiliary Bishop of Kansas City in Kansas.
Friend, William B., Appointed June 1. Bishop of Shreveport.

Gerry, Joseph J., o.s.b., Appointed April 21. Auxiliary Bishop of Manchester.
Hogan, James J., Retired Oct. 17. Bishop of Altoona, Johnstown.
Hughes, Edward, Appointed Dec. 11. Bishop of Metuchen.
Kuzma, George M., Appointed Nov. 11. Auxiliary Bishop of Passaic.
McCormack, William J., Appointed Dec. 23. Auxiliary Bishop of New York.
McFarland, Norman F., Appointed Dec. 29. Bishop of Orange.
Ochoa, Armando, Appointed Dec. 29. Auxiliary Bishop of Los Angeles.
Pelotte, Donald E., s.s.s., Appointed Feb. 24. Coadjutor Bishop of Gallup.
Watters, Loras J., Appointed Oct. 14. Retired Bishop of Winona. Apostolic Administrator of Winona.
Weitzel, John Q., m.m., Appointed Oct. 29. Bishop of Samoa-Pago Pago.
Ziemann, G. Patrick, Appointed Dec. 29. Auxiliary Bishop of Los Angeles.

1987

Bishops
Adamec, Joseph V., Appointed March 12. Bishop of Altoona-Johnstown.
Bosco, Anthony G., Appointed April 14. Bishop of Greensburg.
Buechlein, Daniel, M., o.s.b., Appointed Jan. 20. Bishop of Memphis.
Bullock, William H., Appointed Feb. 10. Bishop of Des Moines.
Franklin, William, E., Appointed Jan. 29. Auxiliary Bishop of Dubuque.
Guillory, Curtis, Appointed Dec. 29. Auxiliary Bishop of Galveston-Houston.
Hanus, Jerome, G., o.s.b., Appointed July 6. Bishop of St. Cloud.
Harrison, Frank J., Retired June. Bishop of Syracuse.
Milone, Anthony M., Appointed Dec. 14. Bishop of Great Falls-Billings.
Michaels, James, Resigned Sept. Auxiliary Bishop of Wheeling-Charleston.
Myers, John J., Appointed July 14. Coadjutor Bishop of Peoria.
Rueger, George, Appointed Jan. 19. Auxiliary Bishop of Worcester.
Samo, Amando, Appointed May 10. Auxiliary Bishop of The Carolines-Marshalls.
Smith, John M., Appointed Dec. 1. Auxiliary Bishop of Newark.
Steinbock, John T., Appointed March 31. Bishop of Santa Rosa.
Vlazny, John G., Appointed May 19. Bishop of Winona
Walsh, Daniel F., Appointed June 9. Bishop of Reno-Las Vegas.

1988

Cardinals
Hickey, James Cardinal, Created June 29. Archbishop of Washington.
Szoka, Edmund Cardinal, Created June 29. Pres. Prefecture for Economic Affairs of the Holy See, Vatican.

Archbishops
Bevilacqua, Anthony J., Appointed Feb. 11. Archbishop of Philadelphia.
Schulte, Francis B., Appointed Dec. 13. Archbishop of New Orleans.

Bishops
Boland, Raymond J., Appointed Feb. 2. Bishop of Birmingham.
Brown, Tod D., Appointed Dec. 27. Bishop of Boise
Carmody, Edmond, Appointed Nov. 8. Auxiliary Bishop of San Antonio.
Chaput, Charles, o.f.m.cap., Appointed April 11. Bishop of Rapid City.
Curlin, William G., Appointed Dec. 20. Auxiliary Bishop of Washington.
DiLorenzo, Francis, Appointed Jan. 26. Auxiliary Bishop of Scranton.
Dunne, John C., Appointed Oct. 21. Auxiliary Bishop of Rockville Centre.
Egan, Edward, M., Appointed Nov. 8. Bishop of Bridgeport.
Gerry, Joseph, J., o.s.b., Appointed Dec. 27. Bishop of Portland (in Maine).
Gonzalez, Roberto O., o.f.m., Appointed July 19. Auxiliary Bishop of Boston.
Gorman, John R., Appointed Feb. 16. Auxiliary Bishop of Chicago.
Jakubowski, Thaddeus J., Appointed Feb. 16. Auxiliary Bishop of Chicago.
Larkin, Thomas W., Retired Nov. Bishop of St. Petersburg.
Loverde, Paul S., Appointed Feb. 3. Auxiliary Bishop of Hartford.
Maloney, Charles G., Retired Jan. Auxiliary Bishop of Louisville.
McGrath, Patrick, J., Appointed Dec. 6. Auxiliary Bishop of San Francisco.
O'Connell, Anthony J., Appointed June 7. Bishop of Knoxville.
Olivier, Leonard J., s.v.d., Appointed Dec. 20. Auxiliary Bishop of Washington.
Schmitt, Bernard W., Appointed May 31. Auxiliary Bishop of Wheeling-Charleston.
Sevilla, Carlos A. s.j., Appointed Dec. 6. Auxiliary Bishop of San Francisco.
Wcela, Emil A., Appointed Oct. 21. Auxiliary Bishop of Rockville Centre.
Williams, J. Kendrick, Appointed March 2. Bishop of Lexington.
Winter, William J., Appointed Dec. 27. Auxiliary Bishop of Pittsburgh.
Wuerl, Donald, Appointed Feb. 11. Bishop of Pittsburgh.

1989

Archbishops
Borders, William D., Retired April. Archbishop of Baltimore.
Hannan, Philip M., Retired Feb. Archbishop of New Orleans.
Keeler, William, Appointed April 6. Archbishop of Baltimore.

Bishops
Breitenbeck, Joseph M., Retired Aug. Bishop of Grand Rapids.
Brom, Robert, Appointed April 22. Coadjutor Bishop of San Diego.
Charron, Joseph L., c.pp.s., Appointed Nov. 6. Auxiliary Bishop of St. Paul-Minneapolis.
Cooney, Patrick, R., Appointed Nov. 21. Bishop of Gaylord.
Driscoll, Michael P., Appointed Dec. 19. Auxiliary Bishop of Orange.
Favalora, John, C, Appointed March 7. Bishop of St. Petersburg.
Flynn, Harry J., Succeeded to the See May 13. Bishop of Lafayette.
Frey, Gerard L., Retired May 13. Bishop of Lafayette.
Gettelfinger, Gerald A., Appointed March 11. Bishop of Evansville.
Grahmann, Charles V., Appointed Dec. 18. Coadjutor Bishop of Dallas.
Grosz, Edward, Appointed Nov. 22. Auxiliary Bishop of Buffalo.
Jacobs, Sam, Appointed July 1. Bishop of Alexandria.
Mikloshazy, Attila s.j., Appointed Aug. 12. Bishop for the Apostolate to the Hungarians.
Rose, Robert J., Appointed July 11. Bishop of Grand Rapids.
Samra, Nicholas J., Appointed June 29. Auxiliary Bishop of Newton.
Schmitt, Bernard W., Appointed March 30. Bishop of Wheeling-Charleston.
Schwietz, Roger L., o.m.i., Appointed Dec. 12. Bishop of Duluth.
Thompson, David B., Appointed May 9. Coadjutor Bishop of Charleston.
Zipfel, Paul A., Appointed May 16. Auxiliary Bishop of St. Louis.

1990

Archbishop
Maida, Adam J., Appointed June 11. Archbishop of Detroit.

Bishops
Banks, Robert J., Appointed Oct. 16. Bishop of Green Bay.
Blaire, Stephen E., Appointed Feb. 17. Auxiliary Bishop of Los Angeles.
Brom, Robert H., Succeeded to the See July 10. Bishop of San Diego.
Daily, Thomas V., Appointed Feb. 20. Bishop of Brooklyn.
Dorsey, Norbert M., c.p., Appointed March 20. Bishop of Orlando.
Dupre, Thomas L., Appointed April 19. Auxiliary Bishop of Springfield in Massachusetts.
Fellhauer, David E., Appointed April 19. Bishop of Victoria.
George, Francis E., o.m.i., Appointed July 10. Bishop of Yakima.
Grahmann, Charles V., Succeeded to See July 14. Bishop of Dallas.
Kuzma, George M., Appointed Oct. 23. Bishop of Van Nuys.
Muench, Robert W., Appointed May 8. Auxiliary Bishop of New Orleans.
Murphy, Michael J., Retired July. Bishop of Erie.
Myers, John J., Succeeded to See Jan. 23. Bishop of Peoria.
Pelotte, Donald E., s.s.s., Succeeded to See March 20. Bishop of Gallup.
Ryan, Sylvester D., Appointed Feb. 17. Auxiliary Bishop of Los Angeles.
Saltarelli, Michael A., Appointed June 12. Auxiliary Bishop of Newark.
Sheridan, Patrick J., Appointed Dec. 12. Auxiliary Bishop of New York.
Skylstad, William S., Appointed April 17. Bishop of Spokane.
Symons, J. Keith, Appointed June 2. Bishop of Palm Beach.
Thompson, David B., Succeeded to See Feb. 22. Bishop of Charleston.
Trautman, Donald W., Appointed July 16. Bishop of Erie.
Tschoepe, Thomas, Retired Bishop of Dallas.

1991

Cardinals
Bevilacqua, Anthony Cardinal, Created June 28. Archbishop of Philadelphia.
Mahony, Roger Cardinal, Created June 28. Archbishop of Los Angeles.

Archbishops
Cronin, Daniel A., Appointed Dec. 9. Archbishop of Hartford.
Dimino, Joseph T., Succeeded to the See June 21. Archbishop of the Military Services.
Hunthausen, Raymond G., Retired Aug. Archbishop of Seattle.

Bishops
D'Antonio, Nicholas, Retired July. Vicar for Spanish-speaking, New Orleans.
Fitzpatrick, John, Retired Nov. Bishop of Brownsville.
Glynn, John J., Appointed Dec. 10. Auxiliary Bishop of the Military Services.
Goedert, Raymond E., Appointed July 8. Auxiliary Bishop of Chicago.
Madera, Joseph J., m.sp.s., Appointed May 28. Auxiliary Bishop of the Military Services.
Maguire, Joseph F., Retired Dec. Bishop of Springfield.
Smith, John M., Appointed June 24. Bishop of Pensacola-Tallahassee.
Steinbock, John T., Appointed Oct. 15. Bishop of Fresno.
Txertudi, Inaki Mallona, c.p., Appointed Dec. 14. Bishop of Arecibo.

1992

Archbishops
Beltran, Eusebius J., Appointed Nov. 24. Archbishop of Oklahoma City, from Bishop of Tulsa.
Buechlein, Daniel M., o.s.b., Appointed July 14. Archbishop of Indianapolis, from Bishop of Memphis.

Bishops
Angell, Kenneth A., Appointed Oct. 10. Bishop of Burlington, from Auxiliary Bishop of Providence.
Barnes, Gerald R., Appointed Jan. 28. Auxiliary Bishop of San Bernardino.
Boles, John P., Appointed April 14. Auxiliary Bishop of Boston.
Bruskewitz, Fabian W., Appointed March 24. Bishop of Lincoln.
Carmody, Edmond, Appointed March 24. Bishop of Tyler, from Auxiliary Bishop of San Antonio.
Carmon, Dominic, s.v.d., Appointed Dec. 16. Auxiliary Bishop of New Orleans.
Galante, Joseph A., Appointed Oct. 13. Auxiliary Bishop of San Antonio.
Garland, James H., Appointed Oct. 10. Bishop of Marquette, from Auxiliary Bishop of Cincinnati.
Jarrell, Michael Charles, Appointed Dec. 29. Bishop of Houma-Thibodaux.
Kmiec, Edward Urban, Appointed Oct. 13. Bishop of Nashville, from Auxiliary Bishop of Trenton.
Mansell, Henry J., Appointed Nov. 24. Auxiliary Bishop of New York.
Niedergeses, James D., Retired Oct. Bishop of Nashville.
O'Malley, Sean P., o.f.m.cap., Appointed June 16. Bishop of Fall River from Bishop of St. Thomas, Virgin Islands.
Ottenweller, Albert H., Retired April. Bishop of Steubenville.
Paska, Walter, Appointed Jan. 26. Auxiliary Bishop of Philadelphia Ukrainian.
Ryan, Sylvester D., Appointed Jan. 21. Bishop of Monterey, from Auxiliary Bishop of Los Angeles.
Schmitt, Mark F., Retired Nov. Bishop of Marquette.
Sheldon, Gilbert I., Appointed Jan. 28. Bishop of Steubenville, from Auxiliary Bishop of Cleveland.
Tobin, Thomas J., Appointed Nov. 3. Auxiliary Bishop of Pittsburgh.
Ziemann, G. Patrick, Appointed July 14. Bishop of Santa Rosa, from Auxiliary Bishop of Los Angeles.

1993

Archbishops
Curtiss, Elden F., Appointed May 4. Archbishop of Omaha, from Bishop of Helena.

Donoghue, John F., Appointed June 22. Archbishop of Atlanta, from Bishop of Charlotte.
Keleher, James P., Transferred Sept. 8. Archbishop of Kansas City in Kansas, from Bishop of Belleville.
Sanchez, Robert F., Retired April. Archbishop of Santa Fe.
Sheehan, Michael J., Appointed April 6. Archbishop of Santa Fe.

Bishops

Arzube, Juan A., Retired June. Auxiliary Bishop of Los Angeles.
Boland, Raymond J., Appointed June 22. Bishop of Kansas City - St. Joseph, from Bishop of Birmingham, June.
Britt, Kevin M., Appointed Nov. 23. Auxiliary Bishop of Detroit.
Bullock, William H., Appointed April 13. Bishop of Madison, from Bishop of Des Moines.
Charron, Joseph L., c.pp.s. Appointed Nov. 12. Bishop of Des Moines, from Auxiliary Bishop of St. Paul and Minneapolis.
Elya, John A., b.s.o. Appointed Dec. 7. Bishop of Newton from Auxiliary Bishop of Newton.
Franklin, William E., Appointed Nov. 12. Bishop of Davenport, from Auxiliary Bishop of Dubuque.
Gregory, Wilton, Appointed Dec. 29. Bishop of Belleville from Auxiliary Bishop of Chicago.
Harrington, Bernard J., Appointed Nov. 23. Auxiliary Bishop of Detroit.
Hughes, Alfred C., Appointed Sept. 7. Bishop of Baton Rouge, from Auxiliary Bishop of Boston.
Lotocky, Innocent, Resigned July. Bishop of St. Nicholas of Chicago.
Loverde, Paul S., Appointed Nov. 11. Bishop of Ogdensburg, from Auxiliary Bishop of Hartford.
Moeddel, Carl K., Appointed June 15. Auxiliary Bishop of Cincinnati.
Popp, Bernard F., Retired March. Auxiliary Bishop of San Antonio.
Puscas, Louis, Retired Eparch of Romanian Diocese of Canton.
Quinn, Francis A., Retired Nov. Bishop of Sacramento.
Slattery, Edward J., Appointed Nov. 11. Bishop of Tulsa.
Steib, James Terry, s.v.d. Appointed March 23. Bishop of Memphis, from Auxiliary Bishop of St. Louis.
Tamayo, James A., Appointed Jan. 26. Auxiliary Bishop of Galveston-Houston.
Thomas, Elliot G., Appointed Oct. 10. Bishop of St. Thomas, Virgin Islands.
Weigand, William K., Appointed Nov. 3. Bishop of Sacramento from Bishop of Salt Lake City.
Wiwchar, Michael, c.ss.r. Appointed July 15. Bishop of St. Nicholas in Chicago for Ukrainians.

1994

Cardinals

Keeler, William Cardinal, Created Nov. 26. Archbishop of Baltimore.
Maida, Adam Cardinal, Created Nov. 26. Archbishop of Detroit.

Archbishops

Favalora, John C., Appointed Nov. 3. Archbishop of Miami.
Flynn, Harry J., Appointed Feb. 2. Coadjutor Archbishop of St. Paul-Minneapolis.
Hanus, Jerome, G., o.s.b. Appointed Aug. 23. Coadjutor Archbishop of Dubuque.
McCarthy, Edward A., Retired Nov. Archbishop of Miami.
Rigali, Justin F., Appointed Jan. 25. Archbishop of St. Louis.

Bishops

Ahern, Patrick V., Retired April. Auxiliary Bishop of New York.
Barbarito, Gerald, Appointed June 28. Auxiliary Bishop of Brooklyn.
Brunett, Alexander J., Appointed April 19. Bishop of Helena.
Burke, Raymond L., Appointed Dec. 10. Bishop of La Crosse.
Carlson, Robert J., Appointed Jan. 13. Coadjutor Bishop of Sioux Falls, from Auxiliary Bishop of St. Paul-Minneapolis.
Catanello, Ignatius, Appointed June 28. Auxiliary Bishop of Brooklyn.
Chedid, John G., Appointed March 1. First Bishop of Our Lady of Lebanon in Los Angeles, from Auxiliary Bishop of Saint Maron.
Cullen, Edward P., Appointed Feb. 8. Auxiliary Bishop of Philadelphia.
Curlin, William G., Appointed Feb. 22. Bishop of Charlotte, from Auxiliary Bishop of Washington.
Curry, Thomas J., Appointed Feb. 8. Auxiliary Bishop of Los Angeles.
DiLorenzo, Francis X., Appointed Oct. 4. Bishop of Honolulu.
Donovan, Paul V., Retired Nov. Bishop of Kalamazoo.
Doran, Thomas G., Appointed April 19. Bishop of Rockford.
Foley, David E., Appointed March 22. Bishop of Birmingham, from Auxiliary Bishop of Richmond.
Galante, Joseph A., Appointed April 5. Bishop of Beaumont, from Auxiliary Bishop of San Antonio.
Lohmuller, Martin N., Retired Oct. Auxiliary Bishop of Philadelphia.
McDonnell, Charles J., Appointed March 15. Auxiliary Bishop of Newark.
Niederauer, George H., Appointed Nov. 3. Bishop of Salt Lake City.
O'Donnell, Edward J., Appointed Nov. 8. Bishop of Lafayette (Louisiana).
O'Neill, Arthur J., Retired April. Bishop of Rockford.
Paul, John J., Retired Dec. Bishop of La Crosse.
Reilly, Daniel P., Appointed Oct. 27. Bishop of Worcester.
Rodriguez, Placido, c.m.f., Appointed April 5. Bishop of Lubbock, from Auxiliary Bishop of Chicago.
Samo, Amando, Appointed Feb. Coadjutor Bishop of the Caroline Islands.
Sartoris, Joseph M., Appointed Feb. 8. Auxiliary Bishop of Los Angeles.
Yanta, John W., Appointed Oct. 27. Auxiliary Bishop of San Antonio.
Zavala, Gabino, Appointed Feb. 8. Auxiliary Bishop of Los Angeles.

1995

Archbishops

Flynn, Harry J., Appointed Sept. 8. From Coadjutor to Archbishop of St. Paul-Minneapolis.
Hanus, Jerome G., o.s.b., Succeeding as Archbishop of Dubuque from status of Coadjutor.
Kucera, Daniel W., Retired Oct. Archbishop of Dubuque.
Quinn, John R., Retired Dec. Archbishop of San Francisco.
Levada, William J., Succeeding as Archbishop of San Francisco Dec. 1995.
Schleck, Charles A., c.s.c., Appointed Feb. 10.

Bishops

Barnes, Gerald R., Appointed Dec. 28, 1995. Bishop of San Bernardino, from Auxiliary of same Diocese.
Boland, J. Kevin, Appointed Feb. 7, 1995. Bishop of Savannah.
Braxton, Edward K., Appointed March 28. Auxiliary Bishop of St. Louis.
Carlson, Robert J., Succeeding as Bishop of Sioux Falls in March, from status of Coadjutor.
Conway, Edwin M., Appointed Jan. 24. Auxiliary Bishop of Chicago.
Cote, Michael R., Appointed May 9. Auxiliary Bishop of Portland in Maine.
Dougherty, John M., Appointed Feb. 7, 1995. Auxiliary Bishop of Scranton.
Dudick, Michael J., Retired Nov. Bishop of Passaic.
Dudley, Paul V., Retired March. Bishop of Sioux Falls.
Dupre, Thomas L., Appointed March 14. Bishop of Springfield, from Auxiliary Bishop of Springfield.
Gonzalez, Roberto O., o.f.m., Appointed May 16. Coadjutor Bishop of Corpus Christi, from Auxiliary Bishop of Boston.
Head, Edward D., Retired June. Bishop of Buffalo.
Hart, Daniel A., Appointed Sept. 12. Bishop of Norwich, from Auxiliary Bishop of Boston.
Hughes, William A., Retired July. Bishop of Covington.
Kicanas, Gerald F., Appointed Jan. 24. Auxiliary Bishop of Chicago.
Kinney, John F., Appointed May 8. Bishop of St. Cloud from Bishop of Bismarck.
Lessard, Raymond W., Retired Feb. Bishop of Savannah.
Lori, William E., Appointed Feb. 27. Auxiliary Bishop of Washington.
Lynch, Robert N., Appointed Bishop of St. Petersburg Dec. 4, 1995.
Mansell, Henry J., Appointed April 18. Bishop of Buffalo, from Auxiliary Bishop of New York.
McCormack, John B., Appointed Nov. Auxiliary Bishop of Boston.
Melczek, Dale J., Appointed Nov. 9. Coadjutor Bishop of Gary.
Mengeling, Carl F., Appointed Nov. Bishop of Lansing.
Moynihan, James M., Appointed April 29. Bishop of Syracuse.
Mulvee, Robert Edward, Appointed Feb. 7. Coadjutor Bishop of Providence from Bishop of Wilmington.
Murphy, William F., Appointed Nov. Auxiliary Bishop of Boston.
Murry, George V., s.j. Appointed Jan. 24. Auxiliary Bishop of Chicago.
Neylon, Martin J., Retired June. Bishop of The Caroline Islands.
Pataki, Andrew, Appointed Bishop of Passaic Nov., from Bishop of Parma.
Pena, Raymundo J., Appointed May 23. Bishop of Brownsville, from Bishop of El Paso.
Saltarelli, Michael A., Appointed Bishop of Wilmington, from Auxiliary of Newark.
Samo, Amando, Appointed March. Bishop of the Caroline Islands.
Schoenherr, Walter J., Retired March. Auxiliary Bishop of Detroit.
Smith, John M., Named Coadjutor of Trenton from Bishop of Pensacola-Tallahassee.
Straling, Phillip F., Appointed March 21. Bishop of Reno, from Bishop of San Bernadino.
Tobin, Thomas J., Appointed Bishop of Youngstown, from Auxiliary of Pittsburgh.
Walsh, Daniel F., Appointed Bishop of Las Vegas March 21.

1996

Archbishops

George, Francis, E. o.m.i., Appointed Archbishop of Portland in Oregon from Bishop of Yakima, April.
Zayek, Francis M., Retired Archbishop of St. Maron of Brooklyn, Nov.

Bishops

Allue, Emilio, s.d.b., Appointed Auxiliary Bishop of Boston, July 24.
Aymond, Gregory M., Appointed Auxiliary Bishop of New Orleans, Nov. 19.
Botean, John Michael, Appointed Bishop of Romanian Catholic Diocese of St. George in Canton.
Christian, Francis J., Appointed Auxiliary Bishop of Manchester, April 2.
Daly, James J., Retired Auxiliary Bishop of Rockville Centre, July.
DiMarzio, Nicholas A., Appointed Auxiliary Bishop of Newark, Sept.
Doueihi, Hector, Appointed Bishop of St. Maron of Brooklyn.
Franzetta, Benedict C., Retired Auxiliary Bishop of Youngstown, Sept.
Irwin, Francis X., Appointed Auxiliary Bishop of Boston, July 24.
Maginnis, Robert P., Appointed Auxiliary Bishop of Philadelphia, Jan. 23.
Manz, John R., Appointed Auxiliary Bishop of Chicago, Jan. 23.
Martino, Joseph F., Appointed Auxiliary Bishop of Philadelphia, Jan. 23.
McDowell, John B., Retired Auxiliary Bishop of Pittsburgh, Sept.
Melczek, Dale J., Succeeded to Bishop of Gary, June 1.
Muench, Robert W., Appointed Bishop of Covington from Auxiliary Bishop of New Orleans, Jan. 5.
Nienstedt, John C., Appointed Auxiliary Bishop of Detroit, June 11.
O'Brien, Edwin F., Appointed Auxiliary Bishop of New York.
Ochoa, Armando, Appointed Bishop of El Paso from Auxiliary Bishop of Los Angeles, April.
Schott, Basil, o.f.m. , Bishop of Parma (Ruthenians).
Sevilla, Carlos A., s.j. Appointed Bishop of Yakima from Auxiliary Bishop of San Francisco Dec. 31.
Vigneron, Allen H., Appointed Auxiliary Bishop of Detroit June 11.
Ward, John J., Retired Auxiliary Bishop of Los Angeles, July.
Warfel, Michael, Appointed Bishop of Juneau Nov. 19.
Younan, Joseph, Appointed Bishop of Our Lady of Deliverance of Newark.
Zipfel, Paul A., Appointed Bishop of Bismarck from Auxiliary Bishop of St. Louis Dec. 31.

1997

Archbishops

Brunett, Alexander J., Appointed Archbishop of Seattle, Oct.
Chaput, Charles J., o.f.m.cap., Appointed Archbishop of Denver Feb. 18, 1997, from Bishop of Rapid City.
Dimino, Joseph T., Retired Archbishop for the Military Services, Aug.
George, Francis, E. o.m.i., Appointed Archbishop of Chicago from Archbishop of Portland in Oregon from Bishop of Yakima, April.
O'Brien, Edwin F., Appointed Archbishop for the Military Services from Auxiliary Bishop of New York.
Vlazny, John G., Appointed Archbishop of Portland in Oregon, Oct.

Bishops

Bennett, Gordon D., Appointed Auxiliary Bishop of Baltimore, Dec. 23.
Bootkoski, Paul G., Appointed Auxiliary Bishop for the Archdiocese of Newark, July.
Brucato, Robert A., Appointed Auxiliary Bishop for the Archdiocese of New York, July.
Cullen, Edward P., Appointed Bishop of Allentown from Auxiliary Bishop of Philadelphia, Dec 16.
DeSimone, Louis A., Retired Auxiliary Bishop of Philadelphia, April.
Fernandez, Gilberto, Appointed Auxiliary Bishop for the Archdiocese of Miami, June 23.
Garcia, Richard J., Appointed Auxiliary Bishop of Sacramento, Nov.

Gaydos, John R., Appointed June 24. Bishop of Jefferson City.
Gelineau, Louis E., Retired Bishop of Providence, June.
Gonzalez, Roberto O., Appointed Bishop of Corpus Christi, March 31.
Gracida, Rene H., Retired Bishop of Corpus Christi, April.
Hughes, Edward T., Retired Bishop of Metuchen, Sept.
Jenky, Daniel R., c.s.c., Appointed Auxiliary Bishop of Fort Wayne-South Bend,
Macaluso, Christie A., Appointed Auxiliary Bishop of Hartford, March 18.
Matthiesen, Leroy T., Retired Bishop of Amarillo, Jan. 21.
McAuliffe, Michael F., Resigned Bishop of Jefferson City, June.
Mulvee, Robert E., Succeeds as Bishop of Providence from Coadjutor Bishop of Providence, June.
Murray, James A., Appointed Bishop of Kalamazoo, Nov.
Naumann, Joseph F., Appointed Bishop of St. Louis, July.
Reiss, John C., Retired Bishop of Trenton, July.
Ricard, John H., s.s.j., Appointed Bishop of Pensacola-Tallahassee Jan.
Sheridan, Michael J., Appointed Auxiliary Bishop of St. Louis, July.
Smith, John M., Succeeds as Bishop of Trenton from Coadjutor Bishop of Trenton, July.
Welsh, Thomas, Retired Bishop of Allentown, Dec. 16.
Wenski, Thomas G., Appointed Auxiliary Bishop for the Archdiocese of Miami, June 23.
Wilkerson, Gerald E., Appointed Auxiliary Bishop of Los Angeles, Nov. 5.
Yanta, John W., Appointed Bishop of Amarillo, from Auxiliary of San Antonio in Jan.
Zubik, David A., Appointed Auxiliary Bishop of Pittsburgh Feb. 18.

1998

Cardinals

George, Francis Cardinal, o.m.i., Created Feb. 21. Archbishop of Chicago.
Stafford, Francis Cardinal, Pres.-Pontifical Council for the Laity, Vatican.

Bishops

Brown, Tod D., Appointed Bishop of Orange from Bishop of Boise, June.
Cupich, Blase J., Appointed Bishop of Rapid City, July 6.
DiNardo, Daniel N., Appointed Bishop of Sioux City, Dec.
Flanagan, Thomas Joseph, Appointed Auxiliary Bishop of San Antonio, Jan. 5.
Gilmore, Ronald M., Appointed Bishop of Dodge City, May.
Harrington, Bernard J., Appointed Bishop of Winona, from Auxiliary Bishop of Detroit, Nov.
Harvey, James M., Bishop and Prefect of the Papal Household, March.
McCormack, John B., Appointed Bishop of Manchester from Auxiliary Bishop of Boston, July.
McFarland, Norman F., Retired Bishop of Orange, June.
McManus, Robert Joseph, Appointed Auxiliary Bishop of Providence, Dec. 1.
Murry, George V., s.j., Appointed Coadjutor to St. Thomas Virgin Islands, May.
Perry, Joseph N., Appointed Auxiliary Bishop of Chicago, May.
Rivera, Enrique Hernandez, Retired Bishop of Caguas, July.
Soens, Lawrence D., Retired Bishop of Sioux City. Nov.
Symons, Joseph K., Retired Bishop of Palm Beach, June.
Wester, John Charles, Appointed Auxiliary Bishop of San Francisco, June 30.
Zurek, Patrick J., Appointed Auxiliary Bishop of San Antonio, Jan. 5.

1999

Cardinal

Martinez, Luis Cardinal Aponte, Retired Archbishop of San Juan, March.

Bishops

Baker, Robert J. Appointed Bishop of Charleston July 12.
Barbarito, Gerald M., Appointed Bishop of Ogdensburg, from Auxiliary Bishop of Brooklyn.
Blair, Leonard P., Appointed Auxiliary Bishop of Detroit.
Blaire, Stephen E., Appointed Bishop of Stockton, from Auxiliary Bishop of Los Angeles, Sept.
Campbell, Frederick F., Appointed Auxiliary Bishop of St. Paul and Minneapolis, March.
DiMarzio, Nicholas A., Appointed Bishop of Camden.
Dumaine, Pierre, Retired Bishop of San Jose, Nov.
Driscoll, Michael P., Appointed Bishop of Boise, from Auxiliary Bishop of Orange, Jan.
Galante, Joseph A., Appointed Coadjutor Bishop of Dallas, from Bishop of Beaumont, Nov. 23.
Kurtz, Joseph E., Appointed Bishop of Knoxville, Dec.
Loverde, Paul S., Appointed Bishop of Arlington, from Bishop of Ogdensburg, Jan.
Lucas, George J., Appointed Bishop of Springfield, Illinois, Oct. 19.
McCarthy, James F., Auxiliary Bishop of New York, May.
McGrath Patrick J., Succeeded to Bishop of San Jose, from Coadjutor, Nov. 27.
Montrose, Donald W., Retired Bishop of Stockton, Jan.
Morlino, Robert C. Appointed Bishop of Helena July 6.
Murry, George V., s.j., Appointed Bishop to St Thomas Virgin Islands, June 30.
O'Connell, Anthony J., Resigned Bishop of Palm Beach, from Bishop of Knoxville.
Olmsted, Thomas J., Appointed Coadjutor Bishop of Wichita, Feb
Ricken, David L., Appointed Coadjutor Bishop of Cheyenne, Dec.
Ryan, Daniel C., Retired Bishop of Springfield in Illinois, Oct.
Sartain, J. Peter, Appointed Bishop of Little Rock, Dec.
Thomas, George Appointed Auxiliary Bishop of Seattle, Nov. 19.
Thomson, David B., Retired Bishop of Charleston, July.
Vasa, Robert F., Appointed Bishop of Baker, Nov. 19.

2000

Archbishops

Egan, Edward M., Appointed Archbishop of New York, from Bishop of Bridgeport, June.
Gonzalez, Roberto O., o.f.m., Archbishop of San Juan.
McCarrick, Theodore E., Appointed Archbishop of Washington from Archbishop of Newark, Dec.
Schwietz, Roger L., o.m.i., Appointed Coadjutor Archbishop of Anchorage from Bishop of Duluth, Jan.
Soroka, Stephen, Appointed Archbishop of the Ukrainian Archeparchy of Philadelphia.
Sulyk, Stephen, Retired Archbishop of Philadelphia Ukrainian, Nov.

Bishops

Aymond, Gregory M., Appointed Coadjutor Bishop of Austin, June.
Batakian, Manuel Appointed Exarch of Amenian Catholics in U.S.A. and Canada, Nov. 30.
Braxton, Edward K., Appointed Bishop of Lake Charles, Dec. 11.
Carmody, Edmond, Appointed Bishop of Corpus Christi, from Bishop of Tyler, Feb. 2.
Chedid, John G., Retired Bishop of Our Lady of Lebanon, Dec.
Connoly, Thomas J., Retired Bishop of Baker, Jan.
Corrada del Rio, Alvaro, s.j. from Auxiliary Bishop of Washington; Administrator of Caguas to Bishop of Tyler.
Guillory, Curtis J. Appointed Bishop of Beaumont from Auxiliary Bishop of Galveston-Houston, June
Kaising, John J., Appointed Auxiliary Bishop to the Archdiocese for the Military Services, Feb.
Kuzma, George M., Retired Bishop of Van Nuys Dec.
Listecki, Jerome E., Appointed Auxiliary Bishop of Chicago, Nov. 7.
Malone, Richard J., Appointed as Auxiliary Bishop of Boston, Feb.
Malooly, William Frances, Appointed Auxiliary Bishop of Baltimore, Dec. 11.
McCarthy, James F., Appointed Auxiliary Bishop for the Archdiocese of New York.
McDonald, Andrew J., Retired Bishop of Little Rock, Jan.
Paska, Walter, Retired Auxiliary Bishop of Philadelphia Ukrainian, Nov
Serratelli, Arthur J., Appointed Auxiliary Bishop of Newark, July 3
Shaheen, Robert J., Eparch of Our Lady of Lebanon, Dec. 4.
Snyder, John J., Retired Bishop of St. Augustine Dec.
Soto, Jaime, Appointed Auxiliary Bishop of Orange, March 23.
Speyrer, Jude, Resigned Bishop of Lake Charles, Dec.
Surinach-Carreras, Ricardo, Appointed Bishop of Ponce, from Auxiliary Bishop of Ponce, Nov.
Tamayo, James A. Appointed Bishop of Laredo, July 3.
Torres, Juan Fremiot, Retired Bishop of Ponce, Nov.
Walsh, Daniel F., Appointed Bishop of Santa Rosa, April 4.

2001

Cardinals

Egan, Edward Cardinal, M., Created Feb. 21, Archbishop of New York.
McCarrick, Theodore Cardinal, E., Created Feb., Archbishop of Washington.

Archbishops

Hughes, Alfred C., Coadjutor Archbishop of New Orleans from Bishop of Baton Rouge, Feb.
Hurley, Francis T., Retired Archbishop of Anchorage, March 3.
Myers, John J., Appointed Archbishop of Newark, July.
Schwietz, Roger L., o.m.i., Succeeded March 3, as Archbishop of Anchorage from Coadjutor Archbishop of Anchorage.

Bishops

Amos, Martin John, Appointed Auxiliary Bishop of Cleveland, April 3.
Aquila, Samuel J., Appointed Coadjutor Bishop of Fargo June 12.
Angadiath, Jacob, Appointed Bishop of St. Thomas Syro-Malabar Catholic Diocese of Chicago, March 12.
Aymond, Gregory M., Appointed Bishop of Austin from Coadjutor Bishop of Austin, Jan. 2.
Clark, Edward W., Appointed Auxiliary Bishop of Los Angeles, Jan. 16.
Dolan, Timothy, M., Appointed Auxiliary Bishop of St. Louis, June 19.
Edyvean, Walter, Appointed Auxiliary Bishop of Boston, June 29.
Farrell, Kevin, Appointed Auxiliary Bishop of Washington, D.C., Dec. 28.
Galeone, Victor, Appointed Bishop of St. Augustine, June 26.
Garmendia, Francisco, Retired Auxiliary Bishop of New York, Oct.
Gerber, Eugene J., Retired Bishop of Wichita, Oct.
Gomez, Jose H., Appointed Auxiliary Bishop of Denver, Jan. 22.
Gonzalez, Francisco, Appointed Auxiliary Bishop of Washington, Dec.
Gries, Roger W., o.s.b., Appointed Auxiliary Bishop of Cleveland, April 3.
Hart, Joseph H., Retired Bishop of Cheyenne, Sept. 26.
Howze, Joseph L., Retired Bishop of Biloxi, May 15.
Iriondo, Josu, Appointed Auxiliary Bishop of New York, Oct. 29.
Kicanas, Gerald F., Appointed Coadjutor Bishop of Tucson, from Auxiliary Bishop of Chicago, Oct. 30.
Lagonegro, Dominick J., Appointed Auxiliary Bishop of New York, Oct. 29.
Lennon, Richard, Appointed Auxiliary Bishop of Boston, June 29.
Lori, William E., Bishop of Bridgeport from Auxiliary Bishop of Washington, Jan. 16.
McCormack, William J., Retired Auxiliary Bishop of New York, Oct.
McDonnell, Timothy A., Appointed Auxiliary Bishop of New York, Oct. 29.
McKinney, Joseph C., Resigned Auxiliary Bishop of Grand Rapids, Oct.
Medina, Ruben Antonio Gonzalez, c.m.f., Bishop of Caguas.
Mestice, Anthony F., Retired Auxiliary Bishop of New York, Oct.
Muench, Robert W., Appointed Bishop of Baton Rouge, from Bishop of Covington, Dec. 14.
Murphy, William, Appointed Bishop of Rockville Centre from Auxiliary Bishop of Boston June 26.
Myers, John, J., Appointed Archbishop of Newark from Bishop of Peoria, July 24.
Nienstedt, John C., Appointed Bishop of New Ulm, from Auxiliary Bishop of Detroit.
Olmsted, Thomas J., Succeeds as Bishop of Wichita, from Coadjutor Bishop, Oct. 4.
Pates, Richard E., Appointed Auxiliary Bishop of St. Paul and Minneapolis.
Pepe, Joseph A., Appointed Bishop of Las Vegas, April 6.
Pevec, Edward A., Retired Auxiliary Bishop of Cleveland, April.
Ricken, David, Appointed Bishop of Cheyenne, Sept. 26.
Rizzotto, Vincent, Appointed Auxiliary Bishop of Galveston-Houston, June 22.
Rodi, Thomas, Appointed Bishop of Biloxi, May 15.
Schnurr, Dennis M., Appointed Bishop of Duluth, Jan. 18.
Sheridan, Michael, Appointed Coadjutor Bishop of Colorado Springs from Auxiliary Bishop of St. Louis Dec. 3.
Sheridan, Patrick, J., Retired Auxiliary Bishop of New York, Jan.
Vasquez, Jose S., Appointed Auxiliary Bishop of Galveston-Houston, Nov. 29.

2002

Cardinal

Law, Bernard, Retired Archbishop of Boston, Dec.

Archbishops

Dolan, Timothy, M., Appointed Archbishop of Milwaukee, June 25.
Hughes, Alfred C., Succeeds as Archbishop of New Orleans from Coadjutor, Jan. 3.
Schott, Basil M., o.f.m., Appointed Archbishop of Pittsburgh Byzantine May 3.
Schulte, Francis B., Retired Archbishop of New Orleans, Jan.
Weakland, Rembert G., o.s.b., Retired Archbishop of Milwaukee, May 24.

Bishops

Aquila, Samuel J., Succeeds as Bishop of Fargo March 18.
Bootkoski, Paul G., Appointed Bishop of Metuchen from Auxiliary Bishop of Newark, Jan. 4.
Boyea Earl A., Appointed Auxiliary Bishop July 22.

Britt, Kevin M., Appointed Coadjutor Bishop of Grand Rapids Dec. 9.
Burbidge, Michael F., Installed as Auxiliary Bishop of Philadelphia Sept. 5.
Conlon, R. Daniel, Appointed Bishop of Steubenville June.
Cordileone, Salvatore J., Appointed Auxiliary Bishop of San Diego, July.
Curlin, William G., Retired Bishop of Charlotte, Sept. 10.
Fernandez, Gilberto, Retired Auxiliary Bishop of Miami, Dec. 10.
Foys, Roger J., Appointed Bishop of Covington May 30,
Gainer, Ronald W., Appointed Bishop of Lexington Dec. 12.
Glynn, John J., Retired Auxiliary Bishop for the Military Services, August 12.
Hermann, Robert J., Appointed Auxiliary Bishop of St. Louis Oct. 16.
Jammo, Sarhad Y., Appointed Bishop of Eparchy of St. Peter the Apostle (Chaldean) May 4.
Jarrell, Michael C., Appointed Bishop of Lafayette in Louisiana Nov. 8.
Jenky, Daniel R., c.s.c., Appointed Bishop of Peoria, from Auxiliary Bishop of Fort Wayne-South Bend, Feb. 11.
Kaffer, Roger L., Retired Auxiliary Bishop of Joliet, Aug.
Kettler, Donald J., Appointed Bishop of Fairbanks June 6.
Kudrick, John M., Installed as Bishop of Parma July 10.
Lazaro, Felix, Appointed Coadjutor Bishop of Ponce, March.
Marconi, Dominic A., Retired Auxiliary Bishop of Newark, July.
McCarthy, James F., Retired Auxiliary Bishop of New York, June.
O'Connell, Anthony J., Resigned Bishop of Palm Beach, March.
O'Donnell, Edward J., Retired Bishop of Lafayette (Louisiana), Nov. 8.
O'Malley, Sean P., o.f.m.cap., Appointed as Bishop of Palm Beach Sept. 3.
Pevec, Edward A., Retired Sept. 1.
Sartoris, Joseph M., Retired Auxiliary Bishop of Los Angeles, Dec. 31.
Sheldon, Gilbert I., Retired as Bishop of Steubenville Aug. 6.
Skurla, William, Appointed Bishop of the Eparchy of Van Nuys, Feb. 19.
Sullivan, James S., Retired Bishop of Fargo, March 18.
Wang, Ignatius, Appointed Auxiliary Bishop of San Francisco Dec. 12.
Williams, J. Kendrick, Retired Bishop of Lexington, June 11.

2003

Cardinals
Bevilacqua, Anthony Retired Archbishop of Philadelphia July 21.
Rigali, Justin Cardinal, Created Oct. 21, Archbishop of Philadelphia.
Archbishops
Burke, Raymond L., Appointed Archbishop of St. Louis Dec. 2.
Cronin, Daniel A., Retired as Archbishop of Hartford Oct. 20.
Mansell, Henry J., Appointed as Archbishop of Hartford Oct. 20.
O'Malley, Sean P., o.f.m.cap., Appointed as Archbishop of Boston July 1.
Rigali, Justin F., Appointed as Archbishop of Philadelphia July 21.
Bishops
Anderson, Moses B., s.s.e., Retired Auxiliary Bishop of Detroit Oct. 24.
Baltakis, Paul A., Retired Bishop for the Lithuanian Apostolate July.
Banks, Robert J., Retired Bishop of Green Bay, Oct. 10.
Barbarito, Gerald M., Appointed Bishop of Palm Beach July 1.
Blair, Leonard P., Appointed Bishop of Toledo Dec. 4.
Britt, Kevin M., Succeeded as Bishop of Grand Rapids Oct. 13.
Bullock, William H., Retired Bishop of Madison, May 22.
Carreras, Ricardo Surinach, Retired Bishop of Ponce June.
Chanifen, Richard, Retired Bishop of Colorado Springs Jan.
Coleman, George W., Appointed Bishop of Fall River April 30.
Cote, Michael R., Appointed Bishop of Norwich March 10.
Cummins, John S., Retired Bishop of Oakland, Oct. 1.
da Cunha, Edgar M., s.d.v., Appointed Auxiliary Bishop of Newark June 27.
Daily, Thomas V., Retired Bishop of Brooklyn, August 1.
DiMarzio, Nicholas A., Appointed Bishop of Brooklyn Aug. 1.
Dinh Mai Luong, Dominic Appointed Auxiliary Bishop of Orange April 25.
Estevez, Felipe J., Appointed Auxiliary Bishop of Miami Nov. 21.
Garcia-Siller, Gustavo, m.sp.s., Appointed Auxiliary Bishop of Chicago Jan. 23.
Goedert, Raymond E., Retired Auxiliary Bishop of Chicago Jan. 23.
Gorman, John R., Retired Auxiliary Bishop of Chicago Jan. 23.
Hanifen, Richard C., Retired Bishop of Colorado Springs, Jan.
Hart, Daniel A., Retired Bishop of Norwich March 10.
Houck, William R., Retired Bishop of Jackson Jan. 3.
Hurley, Walter A., Appointed Auxiliary Bishop of Detroit July 7.
Jacobs, Sam G., Appointed Bishop of Houma-Thibodaux Aug. 1.
Jakubowski, Thaddeus J., Retired Auxiliary Bishop of Chicago Jan. 23.
Jugis Peter J., Appointed Bishop of Charlotte August 1.
Kane, Francis Appointed Auxiliary Bishop of Chicago Jan. 23.
Kicanas, Gerald F., Succeeded as Bishop of Tucson March 7.
Latino, Joseph N., Appointed Bishop of Jackson Jan. 3.
Lazaro, Felix, Succeeded as Bishop of Ponce, June.
Luong, Dominic Mai, Appointed Auxiliary Bishop of Orange in California April.
Martino, Joseph F., Appointed Bishop of Scranton July 25.
Moreno, Manuel D., Retired Bishop of Tucson March 7.
Morin, Roger P., Appointed Auxiliary Bishop of New Orleans Feb. 11.
Morlino, Robert C., Appointed Bishop of Madison May 22.
Newman, William C., Retired Auxiliary Bishop of Baltimore Aug. 28.
O'Brien, Thomas J., Resigned Bishop of Phoenix June 18.
Olmsted, Thomas J., Appointed Bishop of Phoenix Nov. 25.
Paprocki, Thomas J., Appointed Auxiliary Bishop of Chicago Jan. 23.
Quinn, John M., Appointed Auxiliary Bishop of Detroit July 7.
Reiss, Francis R., Appointed Auxiliary Bishop of Detroit July 7.
Roman, Agustin A., Retired Auxiliary Bishop of Miami June 6.
Rose, Robert J., Retired as Bishop of Grand Rapids Oct. 13.
Seminack, Richard S. Appointed Bishop of St. Nicholas in Chicago Ukrainian March 24.
Sheridan, Michael, J., Succeeded as Bishop of Colorado Springs Jan. 30.
Solis, Oscar A., Appointed Auxiliary Bishop of Los Angeles Dec. 11.
Sullivan, Walter F., Retired as Bishop of Richmond Sept. 16.
Timlin, James, C., Retired Bishop of Scranton July 25.
Vigneron, Allen H., Appointed Coadjutor Bishop of Oakland Jan. 9.
Vigneron, Allen H., Succeeded as Bishop of Oakland Oct. 1.
Walsh, Paul H., Appointed Auxiliary Bishop of Rockville Centre April 2.
Wenski, Thomas G., Named Coadjutor Bishop of Orlando June 30.
Zubik, David A., Appointed Bishop of Green Bay Oct. 10.

2004

Archbishop
Naumann, Joseph F., Named Coadjutor Archbishop of Kansas City in Kansas Jan. 7.
Bishops
Bosco, Anthony G., Retired Bishop of Greensburg Jan. 2.
Brandt, Lawrence E., Appointed Bishop of Greensburg Jan. 2.
Costello, Thomas J., Retired Auxiliary Bishop of Syracuse March 23.
DiLorenzo, Francis X., Appointed Bishop of Richmond March 31.
DiNardo, Daniel N., Named Coadjutor Bishop of Galveston-Houston Jan. 25.
Doueihi, Hector, Retired Bishop of St. Maron of Brooklyn Jan. 12.
Dupre, Thomas L., Retired Bishop of Springfield February 11.
Finn, Robert W., Named Coadjutor Bishop of Kansas City-St. Joseph March.
Galante, Joseph A., Appointed Bishop of Camden from Coadjutor Bishop of Dallas March 23.
Gerry, Joseph, J., o.s.b., Retired Bishop of Portland Feb. 10.
Malone, Richard J., Appointed Bishop of Portland in Maine Feb.
Mansour, Gregory J., Appointed Bishop of the Eparchy of St. Maron, Brooklyn Jan.
McDonnell, Timothy A., Appointed Bishop of Springfield in Massachusetts March.
McManus, Robert J., Appointed Bishop of Worcester March.
Reilly, Daniel P., Retired Bishop of Worcester March.
Thomas, George, Appointed Bishop of Helena from Auxiliary Bishop of Seattle March 23.
Wirz, George O., Retired Auxiliary Bishop of Madison Feb 10.

United States Conference of Catholic Bishops

Address—3211 Fourth St., N.E., Washington, DC 20017-1194. Tel: 202-541-3000. Website: www.usccb.org.

The United States Conference of Catholic Bishops is a permanent institute composed of Catholic bishops of the United States of America in and through which the bishops exercise in a communal or collegial manner the pastoral mission entrusted to them by the Lord Jesus of sanctification, teaching, and leadership, especially by devising forms and methods of the apostolate suitably adapted to the circumstances of the times. Such exercise is intended to offer appropriate assistance to each bishop in fulfilling his particular ministry in the local Church, to effect a commonality of ministry addressed to the people of the United States of America, and to foster and express communion with the Church in other nations within the Church universal, under the leadership of its chief pastor, the Pope.

USCCB GENERAL SECRETARIAT

General Secretary— Rev. Msgr. William P. Fay
Associate General Secretary— Mr. Bruce E. Egnew
Associate General Secretary— Rev. Msgr. David J. Malloy
Associate General Secretary— Sr. Lourdes Sheehan, R.S.M.
Deputy of the General Secretary— Sr. Andree Fries, C.P.P.S.

OFFICES

President— Bishop Wilton D. Gregory
Vice-President— Bishop William S. Skylstad
Treasurer— Archbishop James P. Keleher
Secretary— Bishop William B. Friend

STAFF OFFICES

Finance— Mr. Kenneth W. Korotky, Dir.
Accounting— Ms. Sharon Heinle, Dir.
General Counsel— Mr. Mark Chopko, Esq.
Associate General Counsel— Ms. Deirdre Dessingue
General Services— Mr. Keith Manley, Dir.
Government Liaison— Mr. Frank Monahan, Dir.
Human Resources— Ms. Linda Hunt, Dir.
Library Services— Ms. Anne LeVeque, Dir.
Management Information Systems— Mr. William Kissane, Dir.
Publishing— Mr. Paul Henderson, Dir.
Child & Youth Protection— Ms. Kathleen McChesney, Dir.
National Review Board— The Honorable Justice Anne M. Burke
Mr. Robert Bennett, Esq.
Mr. Michael Bland, Phy.D.,D.Min.
Mr. William R. Burleigh
Mr. Nicholas Cafardi
Mrs. Jane Chiles
Dr. Alice B. Hayes
Ms. Pamela D. Hayes, Esq.
Mr. Paul R. McHugh, M.D.
The Honorable Leon Panetta, Esq.
The Honorable Justice Petra Maes
Mr. Ray Siegfried

USCCB COMMITTEES
EXECUTIVE LEVEL
ADMINISTRATIVE COMMITTEE

Chairman—Bishop Wilton D. Gregory
Members — Anthony Cardinal Bevilacqua
Francis Cardinal George, O.M.I.
Theodore Cardinal McCarrick
Archbishop Daniel M. Buechlein, O.S.B.
Archbishop James P. Keleher
Archbishop Basil M. Schott, O.F.M.
Archbishop Michael J. Sheehan (Region XIII)
Bishop Gregory M. Aymond
Bishop Robert J. Baker (Region XIV)
Bishop Victor Balke (Region VIII)
Bishop Gordon D. Bennett, S.J.
Bishop Stephen E. Blaire
Coadjutor Bishop Kevin M. Britt
Bishop Edmond Carmody
Bishop Matthew H. Clark (Region II)
Bishop Edward P. Cullen
Bishop Nicholas C. Dattilo (Region III)
Bishop Francis X. DiLorenzo
Bishop Thomas G. Doran
Bishop William B. Friend
Coadjutor Bishop Joseph A. Galante
Bishop John R. Gaydos
Bishop Bernard J. Harrington
Bishop Joseph L. Imesch (Region VII)
Bishop Edward U. Kmiec (Region V)
Bishop Robert N. Lynch
Bishop John B. McCormack (Region I)
Bishop Dale J. Melczek
Bishop Robert C. Morlino
Bishop George V. Murry, S.J.
Bishop John C. Nienstedt
Bishop Thomas J. Olmsted (Region IX)
Bishop Sean P. O'Malley, O.F.M.Cap.
Bishop John H. Ricard, S.S.J.
Bishop Vincent M. Rizzotto (Region X)
Bishop Michael A. Saltarelli (Region IV)
Bishop Carlos A. Sevilla, S.J. (Region XII)
Bishop William S. Skylstad
Bishop Edward J. Slattery
Bishop James A. Tamayo
Bishop Thomas J. Tobin (Region VI)
Bishop Donald W. Trautman
Bishop Thomas G. Wenski
Bishop Gerald E. Wilkerson (Region XI)
Bishop Paul A. Zipfel
Alternate (Region I): Bishop Robert J. McManus
Alternate (Region II): Bishop James M. Moynihan
Alternate (Region III): Bishop Paul G. Bootkoski
Alternate (Region IV): Bishop Kevin J. Farrell
Alternate (Region V): (Vacant)
Alternate (Region VI): Bishop Patrick R. Cooney
Alternate (Region VII): Bishop Edwin M. Conway
Alternate (Region VIII): Bishop John F. Kinney
Alternate (Region IX): Bishop Joseph F. Naumann
Alternate (Region X): Bishop Michael D. Pfeifer, O.M.I.
Alternate (Region XI): Bishop John T. Steinbock
Alternate (Region XII) Bishop George L. Thomas
Alternate (Region XIII): Bishop Donald E. Pelotte, S.S.S.
Alternate (Region XIV) Bishop Victor B. Galeone

EXECUTIVE COMMITTEE

Chairman—Bishop Wilton D. Gregory
Vice President— Bishop William S. Skylstad
Treasurer— Archbishop James P. Keleher
Secretary— Bishop William B. Friend
Members— Bishop Robert N. Lynch
Staff— Rev. Msgr. William P. Fay

COMMITTEE ON BUDGET AND FINANCE

Chairman— Archbishop James P. Keleher
Members— Archbishop Daniel M. Buechlein, O.S.B.; Bishop J. Kevin Boland; Bishop Robert N. Lynch; Rev. Msgr. William P. Fay
Staff— Mr. Kenneth Korotky

COMMITTEE ON PERSONNEL

Chairman— Bishop William S. Skylstad
Members— Bishop Gregory M. Aymond; Coadjutor Bishop Kevin M. Britt; Rev. Msgr. William P. Fay
Staff— Mr. Bruce E. Egnew; Ms. Linda Hunt

COMMITTEE ON PRIORITIES AND PLANS

Chairman— Bishop Wilton D. Gregory
Vice President— Bishop William S. Skylstad
Treasurer— Archbishop James P. Keleher
Past President— Bishop Joseph A. Fiorenza
Members—Bishop Gregory M. Aymond; Bishop George V. Murry, S.J.; Rev. Msgr. William P. Fay
Staff— Sr. Lourdes Sheehan, R.S.M.

STANDING COMMITTEES
COMMITTEE ON AFRICAN AMERICAN CATHOLICS

Chairman— Bishop Gordon D. Bennett, S.J.
Members — Bishop Gerald R. Barnes; Bishop Francisco Gonzalez, S.F.; Bishop Christie A. Macaluso; Bishop John C. Nienstedt; Bishop Joseph N. Perry; Bishop John H. Ricard, S.S.J.
Consultants— Theodore Cardinal McCarrick; Archbishop John G. Vlazny; Bishop J. Terry Steib, S.V.D.
Staff— Ms. Beverly A. Carroll, Exec. Dir.; Mr. Ono Ekeh, Program Coord.

AMERICAN BISHOP'S OVERSEAS APPEAL

Chairman— Bishop Wilton D. Gregory
Members— Administrative Committee Members
Staff— Mr. Bruce E. Egnew

AMERICAN COLLEGE OF LOUVAIN

Chairman— Bishop Edward K. Braxton
Member Region I: Bishop Francis J. Christian
Member Region II: Bishop Matthew H. Clark
Member Region III: Bishop Nicholas A. DiMarzio
Member Region IV: Bishop John J. Kaising
Member Region V: Bishop Edward K. Braxton
Member Region VI: Bishop James A. Murray
Member Region VII: Bishop George J. Lucas
Member Region VIII: Bishop Samuel J. Aquila
Member Region IX: Bishop George K. Fitzsimons
Member Region X: Bishop James A. Tamayo
Member Region XI: Bishop Sylvester D. Ryan
Member Region XII: Archbishop Roger L. Schwietz, O.M.I.
Member Region XIII: Bishop David L. Ricken
Member Region XIV: Bishop Thomas G. Wenski
Consultants— Bishop Charles A. Buswell; Bishop Benedict C. Franzetta.
Staff— Rev. Kevin Codd, Rector; Rev. David Windsor, Rector Emeritus; Rev. Francis T. Maione, Exec. Dir.; Mr. Stephen C. Zavesky, Vice Pres.-Fin.

COMMITTEE ON CANONICAL AFFAIRS

Chairman— Past President Bishop Thomas G. Doran
Members — Archbishop John J. Myers; Bishop Salvatore Cordileone; Bishop Michael R. Cote; Bishop David E. Fellhauer; Coadjutor Bishop Joseph A. Galante; Bishop A. James Quinn; Bishop Gabino Zavala
Consultants— Sr. Sharon A. Euart, R.S.M.; Ms. Barbara Anne Cusack; Rev. Robert T. Kennedy; Rev. Msgr. John A. Renken; Rev. Lawrence G. Wrenn
Staff— Rev. Msgr. David J. Malloy

COMMITTEE ON CATECHESIS

Chairman— Bishop Donald W. Wuerl
Members — Bishop Gordon D. Bennett, S.J.; Bishop Daniel N. DiNardo; Bishop William E. Lori; Rev. John E. Hurley, C.S.P.; Rev. John Kachuba; Rev. Daniel J. Kutys; Mr. Robert Colbert; Sr. Eva Lumas, S.S.S.; Ms. Catherine Minkiewicz; Sr. Alice Molina, R.S.M.; Mr. Neil A. Parent; Rev. Kris Stubna; Ms. Terri Telepak; Dr. Cris Vallapando
Consultants— Sr. Catherine Dooley, O.P.
Staff— Sr. Glenn Anne McPhee, O.P., Sec.-Education; Sr. Maureen Shaughessy, S.C., Asst. Sec.-Catecheses & Leadership Formation; Mr. Daniel Mulhall, Asst. Sec.-Cathechesis & Inculturation

CATHOLIC CAMPAIGN FOR HUMAN DEVELOPMENT COMMITTEE

Chairman— Bishop George V. Murry, S.J.
Members — Bishop Howard J. Hubbard; Bishop Dale J. Melczek; Bishop Joseph A. Pepe; Bishop John H. Ricard, S.S.J.; Bishop J. Terry Steib, S.V.D.; Bishop George L. Thomas
Consultants— Bishop Nicholas A. DiMarzio; Rev. David E. Baldwin; Mr. Daniel E. Curtin; Sr. Annette McDermott; Ms. Kerry A. Robinson
Staff— Rev. Robert J. Vitillo, Exec. Dir.; Mr. Timothy Collins, Deputy Dir.; Mr. Douglas M. Lawson, Assoc. Dir.- Program; Ms. Barbara Stephenson, Assoc. Dir.- Communications

COMMITTEE ON THE CHURCH IN LATIN AMERICA

Chairman— Bishop Edmond Carmody
Chair-elect— Bishop John R. Manz
Members — Archbishop Eusebius J. Beltran; Archbishop John F. Donoghue; Archbishop James P. Keleher; Bishop Gerald R. Barnes; Bishop Thomas V. Daily; Bishop Thomas G. Wenski
Staff— Mr. Daniel Lizarraga, Asst. Dir.

COMMITTEE ON COMMUNICATIONS

Chairman— Coadjutor Bishop Joseph A. Galante
Chair-elect— Bishop Gerald F. Kicanas
Members — Archbishop Michael J. Sheehan; Bishop J. Kevin Boland; Bishop Thomas J. Costello; Bishop Blase J. Cupich; Bishop John R. Gaydos; Bishop John B. McCormack; Bishop George V. Murry, S.J.; Bishop George Niederauer; Ms. Annette Gonzales Taylor.
Consultants— William Cardinal Keeler; Mr. Clarence Gilyard; Mr. John Bookser Feister; Mr. Dennis M. Heaney; Ms. Gail McGrath; Mr. Frank Morock; Sr. Mary Parks, C.S.J.; Mr. Owen Phelps
Staff— Rev. Msgr. Francis J. Maniscalco, Dir. for Communications; Mr. David Early, Senior Communications Officer; Ms. Patricia R. Garcia, Dir.-Catholic Communication Campaign Distribution; Mr. Thomas N. Lorsung, Dir. & Editor-in-Chief Catholic News Service; Ms. Carol Mays, CCC. Distrb. Coord; Ms. Ellen McCloskey, Dir.-Catholic Communication Campaign Productions; Ms. Anne Navarro, Assoc. Dir.- Office of Film & Broadcasting; Ms. Gerri Pare, Dir.- Film and Broadcasting; Ms. Terry Raffelt, Communications Officer; Mr. Ramon E. Rodriguez, Dir.-Catho-

lic Communication Campaign Development; Mr. William Ryan, Deputy Dir.-Communications; Mr. Ken Stockard, CCC Prod. Coord.; Sr. Mary Ann Walsh, Deputy Dir.-Media Relations.

Catholic Communication Campaign Advisory Board
Bishop Thomas J. Costello

Subcommittee for Catholic News Service
Bishop George H. Niederauer

Subcommittee of Standards and Policy
Bishop John B. McCormack

COMMITTEE ON CONSECRATED LIFE

Chairman— Bishop Sean P. O'Malley, O.F.M.Cap.
Chair-elect— Archbishop Jerome G. Hanus, O.S.B.
Members— Bishop Raymond L. Burke; Bishop Alvaro Corrada del Rio, S.J.; Bishop George V. Murry, S.J.; Bishop Thomas J. Olmsted
Staff— Rev. Msgr. William P. Fay

COMMITTEE ON THE DIACONATE

Chairman— Bishop Robert C. Morlino
Members— Bishop Samuel J. Aquila; Bishop Howard J. Hubbard; Bishop Carl F. Mengeling; Bishop Michael W. Warfel
Staff— Deacon William T. Ditewig, Exec. Dir.

COMMITTEE ON DOCTRINE

Chairman— Bishop Donald W. Trautman
Chair-elect— Archbishop William J. Levada
Members— Bishop Edward K. Braxton; Bishop James A. Griffin; Bishop Gerald F. Kicanas; Bishop William E. Lori; Bishop Robert J. McManus; Bishop Emil A. Wcela
Consultants— Avery Cardinal Dulles, S.J.; William Cardinal Keeler; Bishop Francis X. DiLorenzo; Bishop Robert J. McManus; Bishop Emil A. Wcela
Staff— Rev. Msgr. John Strynkowski, Exec. Dir.; Mrs. Siobhan Verbeek, Assoc. Dir.; Dr. James LeGrys, Theological Advisor

COMMITTEE ON DOMESTIC POLICY

Chairman—Theodore Cardinal McCarrick
Members—Bishop Nicholas A. DiMarzio; Bishop Curtis J. Guillory, S.V.D.; Bishop Dennis M. Schnurr; Bishop Joseph M. Sullivan; Bishop Gabino Zavala
Consultants— Roger Cardinal Mahony; Archbishop John J. Myers; Bishop William E. Lori; Bishop George V. Murry, S.J.; Mr. W. Shepherdson Abell; Sr. Carol Keehan, D.C.; Dr. John Dilulio; Sr. Margaret John Kelly, D.C.; Mr. Juan Marinez; Mr. Alfonso Martinez-Fonts; Mr. John Sweeney
Observers— Bro. David Andrews, C.S.C.; Ms. Beverly Carroll; Mr. Ronaldo Cruz; Mr. Edward Dolejsi; Rev. Bryan Hehir; Ms. Susan Muskett; Rev. Michael Place; Rev. Robert Vitillo; Mr. George Horton
Staff— Mr. John Carr, Sec. for Social Development and World Peace; Ms. Nancy Wisdo, Dir. for Domestic Social Development; Mr. Daniel Misleh, Outreach Coordinator; Ms. Kathleen Curran, Policy Advisor-Health and Welfare Issues; Mr. Andrew Rivas, Policy Advisor, Agricultural Issues Environment & Nonviolence; Mr. Thomas Shellabarger, Policy Advisor-Urban and Economic Issues; Ms. Joan Rosenhauer, Coord.-Special Projects

COMMITTEE ON ECUMENICAL AND INTERRELIGIOUS AFFAIRS

Chairman— Bishop Stephen E. Blaire
Members— William Cardinal Keeler; Archbishop Alexander J. Brunett; Archbishop William J. Levada; Bishop Tod D. Brown; Bishop Donald E. Pelotte, S.S.S.; Bishop John H. Ricard, S.S.J.; Bishop Placido Rodriguez, C.M.F.; Bishop Nicholas J. Samra; Bishop Carlos A. Sevilla, S.J.
Consultants— Archbishop Oscar H. Lipscomb; Archbishop Daniel E. Pilarczyk; Bishop Gerald R. Barnes; Bishop Patrick R. Cooney; Bishop Howard J. Hubbard; Bishop Richard J. Sklba; Bishop James C. Timlin
Staff— Dr. John Borelli; Rev. Arthur Kennedy, Exec. Dir.; Dr. Eugene Fisher, Ph.D., Assoc. Dir.; Bro. Jeffrey Gros, F.S.C., Assoc. Dir.; Rev. Ronald G. Roberson, C.S.P., Assoc. Dir.

Subcommittee on Interreligious Dialogue
Bishop Tod D. Brown, Chairman

COMMITTEE ON EDUCATION

Chairman — Bishop Bernard J. Harrington
Members— Bishop Gregory M. Aymond; Bishop Daniel R. Jenky, C.S.C.; Bishop Robert J. McManus; Bishop Richard E. Pates; Bishop Joseph N. Perry; Bishop Michael J. Sheridan
Consultants—Dr. James Brennan; Dr. Dennis Golden; Sr. Jane Herb, I.H.M.; Rev. Joseph O'Connell, S.J.; Mr. Neil Parent; Sr. Dominica Rocchio, S.C.; Mrs. Mary Ellen Russell; Ms. Jan Slattery; Mr. Michael Guerra
Staff— Sr. Glenn Anne McPhee, O.P., Sec. for Education; Rev. William Davis, O.S.F.S., Deputy Sec. for Catholic School; Dr. Michael Galligan-Stierle, Asst. Sec. for Catholic Higher Education and Campus Ministry; Mrs. Marie Powell, Asst. Sec. For Catholic Schools Parental Advocacy.

Subcommittee on Bishops and Catholic College and University Presidents
Archbishop John G. Vlazny, Chairman

Subcommittee on Campus Ministry
Bishop Daniel R. Jenky, C.S.C., Chairman

Subcommittee on Public Policy and Catholic Schools
Bishop Bernard J. Harrington

Subcommittee on Sapientia Christiana
Bishop Michael F. Burbidge

COMMITTEE ON EVANGELIZATION

Chairman—Bishop Edward J. Slattery
Members—Adam Cardinal Maida; Bishop Edward K. Braxton; Bishop Robert W. Donnelly; Bishop Richard J. Malone; Bishop Joseph F. Naumann; Bishop Nicholas J. Samra.
Staff— Rev. John E. Hurley, C.S.P., Exec. Dir.

COMMITTEE ON HISPANIC AFFAIRS

Chairman—Bishop James A. Tamayo
Members—Archbishop John C. Favalora; Archbishop John J. Myers; Bishop Jose H. Gomez; Bishop Dennis P. O'Neil; Bishop Jose S. Vasquez
Consultants— Archbishop Patrick F. Flores; Bishop Emilio Allué, S.D.B.; Bishop David Arias, O.A.R.; Bishop Gerald R. Barnes; Bishop Gilbert E. Chávez; Bishop Alvaro Corrada del Rio, S.J.; Bishop Richard J. Garcia; Bishop Francisco Gonzalez, S.F.; Bishop Josu Iriondo; Bishop Joseph J. Madera, M.Sp.S.; Bishop Manuel D. Moreno; Bishop Armando X. Ochoa; Bishop Raymuñdo J. Pena; Bishop Ricardo Ramírez, C.S.B.; Bishop Placido Rodríguez, C.M.F.; Bishop Agustin A. Román; Bishop Carlos A. Sevilla, S.J.; Bishop Jaime Soto; Bishop Arthur N. Tafoya; Bishop René A. Valero; Bishop Gabino Zavala; Sr. Angela Erevia, M.C.D.P.; Sr. Leticia Salazar, S.C.M.
Staff— Mr. Ronaldo M. Cruz, Exec. Dir.; Mr. Alejandro Aguilera-Titus, Assoc. Dir.; Ms. Rosalva Castaneda, Program Specialist

COMMITTEE ON THE HOME MISSIONS

Chairman—Bishop Paul A. Zipfel
Chair-elect— Bishop J. Peter Sartain
Members—Bishop John A. Elya, B.S.O.; Bishop Bernard J. Harrington; Bishop Joseph F. Naumann; Bishop Joseph N. Perry; Bishop James A. Tamayo; Bishop Daniel F. Walsh
Consultant— Bishop Sam G. Jacobs
Staff— Dr. David M. Byers, Exec. Dir.; Dr. David J. Suley, Resource Development Coordinator.

COMMITTEE ON INTERNATIONAL POLICY

Chairman—Bishop John H. Ricard, S.S.J.
Members—Bernard Cardinal Law; Theodore Cardinal McCarrick; Archbishop Edwin F. O'Brien; Bishop William F. Murphy; Bishop Ricardo Ramirez, C.S.B.
Consultants— Adam Cardinal Maida; Bishop Robert N. Lynch; Bishop Thomas G. Wenski; Major Gen. William F. Burns; Dr. Mary Ann Glendon; Sr. Doris Gottemoeller, R.S.M.; Mr. Paul Michael Kennedy; Dr. Maryann Cusimano Love; Amb. Anthony C. E. Quainton; Mr. John Steinbruner; Mr. Thomas Trebat.
Staff— Mr. John Carr, Sec.-Social Devel. and World Peace; Mr. Gerard Powers, Dir. for International Justice and Peace; Mr. Daniel Misleh, Dir.-Diocesan Relations; Mr. Walt Grazer, Policy Advisor, Eastern Europe & Mgr. Environmental Justice; Ms. Kelly Hicks, Policy Advisor, International Economic Affairs; Rev. Michael Perry, O.F.M., Policy Advisor, African Affairs; Mr. Thomas Quigley, Policy Advisor, Latin American, Caribbean, and Asian Affairs; Ms. Joan Rosenhauer, Coord-Special Projects

COMMITTEE ON THE LAITY

Chairman—Bishop Dale J. Melczek
Members— Bishop Howard J. Hubbard; Bishop Gerald F. Kicanas; Bishop Joseph N. Perry; Bishop Michael A. Saltarelli; Bishop Dennis M. Schnurr; Bishop Arthur N. Tafoya
Staff— Dr. H. Richard McCord, Exec. Dir.; Ms. Ana Villamil, Assoc. Dir.; Ms. Barbara Anderson, Program Specialist

Subcommittee on Lay Ministry
Bishop Gerald F. Kicanas, Chairman

Subcommittee on Youth and Young Adults
Bishop Dennis M. Schnurr, Chairman

COMMITTEE ON THE LITURGY

Chairman—Francis Cardinal George, O.M.I.
Members— Archbishop Oscar H. Lipscomb; Archbishop Daniel E. Pilarczyk; Archbishop Justin F. Rigali; Bishop Blase J. Cupich; Bishop John M. Smith; Bishop Allen H. Vigneron
Consultants— Bernard Cardinal Law; Roger Cardinal Mahony; Bishop Daniel N. DiNardo; Bishop George V. Murry, S.J.; Bishop Carlos A. Sevilla, S.J.; Sr. Janet Baxendale; Rev. Msgr. M. Francis Mannion; Rev. Chrysoeonus Waddell, O.C.S.O.
Staff— Rev. Msgr. James P. Moroney, Exec. Dir.; Mr. Dennis D. McManus, Assoc. Dir.; Rev. Msgr. Anthony F. Sherman, Assoc. Dir.; Sr. Doris Turek, S.S.N.D., Staff Advisor

COMMITTEE ON MARRIAGE AND FAMILY LIFE

Chairman—Bishop J. Kevin Boland
Members — Bishop Michael P. Driscoll; Bishop Francisco Gonzalez, S.F.; Bishop Joseph E. Kurtz; Bishop Jerome Listecki; Bishop Joseph F. Naumann; Bishop Sean P. O'Malley, O.F.M.Cap.
Staff— Dr. H. Richard McCord, Exec. Dir.; Ms. Sheila Garcia, Asst. Dir.

COMMITTEE ON MIGRATION

Chairman—Bishop Thomas G. Wenski
Members— Bishop Nicholas A. DiMarzio; Bishop Richard J. Garcia; Bishop John F. Kinney; Bishop John R. Manz; Bishop William F. Murphy; Bishop Ricardo Ramirez, C.S.B.; Bishop John C. Wester.
Consultants— Adam Cardinal Maida; Theodore Cardinal McCarrick; Bishop Jacob Angadiath; Bishop Raymond J. Boland; Bishop Robert A. Brucato; Bishop Curtis J. Guillory, S.V.D.; Bishop Armando X. Ochoa; Bishop Peter A. Rosazza; Bishop Phillip F. Straling; Bishop James C. Timlin; Sr. Ray Monda DuVall, C.H.S.; Mr. Donald Kerwin; Mr. Robert Castagna; Mr. Kenneth F. Hackett
Staff— Mr. Mark Franken, Exec. Dir.; Rev. Anthony McGuire, Dir.-Pastoral Care for Migrants and Refugees; Mr. Kevin Appleby, Dir.- Policy; Ms. Anastasia Brown, Dir.-Refugee Programs

NORTH AMERICAN COLLEGE ROME

Chairman—Archbishop Edwin F. O'Brien
Members —
Region I: Bishop Walter J. Edyvean
Region II: Edward Cardinal Egan
Region III: Bishop Donald W. Wuerl
Region IV: Archbishop Edwin F. O'Brien
Region V: Bishop Edward U. Kmiec
Region VI: Bishop Leonard P. Blair
Region VII: Bishop Richard J. Sklba
Region VIII: Bishop Richard E. Pates
Region IX: Archbishop Justin F. Rigali
Region X: Bishop Patrick J. Zurek
Region XI: Archbishop William J. Levada
Region XII: Bishop Anthony M. Milone
Region XIII: Bishop Michael J. Sheridan
Region XIV Bishop Victor B. Galeone
Consultants— Mr. James Crowley; Mr. John Lloyd
Staff— Ms. Trish Morrin-Lloyd; Ms. Jennifer Hazelton

COMMITTEE ON PASTORAL PRACTICES

Chairman—Vacant
Members — Bishop Thomas L. Dupre; Bishop Jerome E. Listecki; Bishop Thomas J. O'Brien; Bishop Richard E. Pates; Bishop Rene A. Valero; Bishop John C. Wester
Consultant— Bishop Dominic A. Marconi
Staff— Rev. Msgr. John Strynkowski, Exec. Dir.; Mrs. Siobhan Verbeek, Assoc. Dir.

COMMITTEE ON PRIESTLY FORMATION

Chairman—Bishop John C. Nienstedt
Members— Bishop Gordon D. Bennett, S.J.; Bishop Michael F. Burbidge; Bishop Salvatore Cordileone; Bishop Jose H. Gomez; Bishop Carl F. Mengeling; Bishop John W. Yanta
Consultant— Archbishop Daniel M. Buechlein, O.S.B.; Bishop Thomas J. Olmsted; Bro. Bernard F. Stratman, S.M.; Rev. Ronald D. Witherup, S.S.
Staff— Rev. Edward J. Burns, Exec. Dir.

Subcommittee for the 5th Edition of the Program of Priestly Formation
Bishop John C. Nienstedt, Chairman

COMMITTEE ON PRIESTLY LIFE AND MINISTRY

Chairman—Bishop John R. Gaydos
Chair-elect— Archbishop Timothy M. Dolan
Members— Bishop Robert J. Baker; Bishop John F. Kinney; Bishop George J. Lucas; Bishop Daniel P. Reilly; Bishop Robert F. Vasa; Bishop David A. Zubik
Staff— Rev. Cletus Kiley, Exec. Dir.

COMMITTEE FOR PRO-LIFE ACTIVITIES

Chairman—Anthony Cardinal Bevilacqua
Members — Archbishop Charles J. Chaput, O.F.M.Cap.; Bishop Daniel N. DiNardo; Bishop Joseph E. Kurtz; Bishop William E. Lori; Bishop William F. Murphy; Bishop Joseph F. Naumann; Bishop Daniel F. Walsh
Consultants— Avery Cardinal Dulles, S.J.; Edward Cardinal Egan; Francis Cardinal George, O.M.I.; James

Cardinal Hickey; William Cardinal Keeler; Bernard Cardinal Law; Roger Cardinal Mahony; Adam Cardinal Maida; Theodore Cardinal McCarrick; Bishop Robert A. Brucato; Bishop Victor B. Galeone; Rev. Michael Place; Ms. Helen Alvare; Mr. Carl Anderson; Mr. John M. Haas; Mr. Juan Montoya
Staff— Ms. Gail Quinn, Exec. Dir.; Ms. Cathleen Cleaver, Dir. Information and Planning; Mr. Richard Doerflinger, Assoc. Dir. for Policy Devel.; Ms Susan Wills, Asst. Dir. for Programming; Ms. Theresa Notare, Special Asst. for Natural Family Planning

COMMITTEE ON THE RELATIONSHIP BETWEEN EASTERN AND LATIN CATHOLIC

Chairman-Elect— Archbishop Basil Schott, O.F.M.
Members— Theodore Cardinal McCarrick; Archbishop Justin F. Rigali; Archbishop Stefan Soroka; Bishop Anthony M. Pilla; Bishop Joseph Younan
Staff— Rev. Msgr. David J. Malloy

COMMITTEE ON SCIENCE AND HUMAN VALUES

Chairman—Bishop Francis X. DiLorenzo
Members— Bishop Francis J. Christian; Bishop John S. Cummins; Bishop John C. Dunne; Bishop William B. Friend; Bishop John C. Nienstedt; Bishop Joseph A. Pepe
Consultants— Bishop R. Pierre DuMaine; Bishop Sylvester D. Ryan; Dr. David M. Byers; Dr. Eric Fischer; Dr. John E. Haught; Rev. James Salmon, S.J.; Dr. Phillip Sloan; Dr. Robert J. White
Staff— Rev. Msgr. John Strynkowski

SELECTION OF BISHOPS

Chairman—Bishop Wilton D. Gregory
Members—
Region I: Bishop Christie A. Macaluso
Region II: Bishop Rene A. Valero
Region III: Bishop John M. Dougherty
Region IV: Bishop Gordon D. Bennett, S.J.
Region V: Archbishop Thomas C. Kelly, O.P.
Region VI: Bishop Kevin M. Britt
Region VII: Bishop Raymond E. Goedert
Region VIII: Bishop Samuel J. Aquila
Region IX: Bishop Raymond J. Boland
Region X: Bishop David E. Fellhauer
Region XI: Roger Cardinal Mahony
Region XII: Archbishop Alexander J. Brunett
Region XIII: Bishop George H. Niederauer
Staff— Rev. Msgr. William P. Fay

COMMITTEE ON VOCATIONS

Chairman—Bishop Kevin M. Britt
Members— Archbishop Roger L. Schwietz, O.M.I.; Bishop Moses B. Anderson, S.S.E.; Bishop Gregory M. Aymond; Bishop John Michael Botean; Bishop Sam G. Jacobs; Bishop John J. Kaising; Bishop Thomas J. O'Brien; Bishop Arthur N. Tafoya
Consultants— Bro. Paul Bednarczyk, C.S.C.; Mr. James DeNike; Ms. Dorothy Foss; Ms. Patricia Skarda
Staff— Rev. Edward J. Burns, Exec. Dir.

COMMITTEE ON WOMEN IN SOCIETY AND IN THE CHURCH

Chairman—Bishop Edward P. Cullen
Members— Bishop Leonard P. Blair; Bishop Richard J. Garcia; Bishop Richard E. Pates; Bishop Joseph A. Pepe; Bishop Thomas J. Rodi; Bishop Arthur J. Serratelli
Consultants— Sr. Carroll Juliano, S.H.C.J.; Ms. Sharon D'Agostino; Ms. Mar Munoz; Ms. Bernadette O'Connell; Dr. Claire Wolfterich
Staff— Dr. H. Richard McCord, Exec. Dir.; Ms. Sheila Garcia, Asst. Dir.; Sr. Amy Hoey, R.S.M., Project Coord.

COMMITTEE ON WORLD MISSION

Chairman—Bishop Gregory M. Aymond
Members— Theodore Cardinal McCarrick; Bishop Richard G. Lennon; Bishop Edmond Carmody; Bishop John M. Dougherty; Bishop Michael W. Warfel; Bishop John C. Wester
Consultants— Bishop Curtis J. Guillory, S.V.D.; Bishop William J. McCormack; Sr. Barbara Anne Gooding, R.S.M.; Rev. Ted Keating, S.M.; Rev. John Kozar; Rev. Dennis Cleary, M.M.; Sr. Judy Gomila, M.S.C.; Rev. Eugene LaVerdiere; Mr. James Lindsay; Sr. Mary Motte; Sr. Rosanne Rustemeyer, S.S.N.D.
Staff— Sr. Marie de la Trinite Siopongco, Asst. Sec.

AD HOC COMMITTEE ON AGRICULTURAL ISSUES

Chairman—Bishop Ronald M. Gilmore
Members— Bishop Nicholas A. DiMarzio; Bishop Richard J. Garcia; Bishop Charles V. Grahmann; Bishop J. Peter Sartain
Consultant— Bro. David Andrews

Staff— Mr. Mark Franken, Exec. Dir.-Migration and Refugee Services; Mr. John Carr, Sec. for Social Development and World Peace; Mr. Frank J. Monahan, Dir., Government Liaison

AD HOC COMMITTEE TO AID THE CATHOLIC CHURCH IN CENTRAL AND EASTERN EUROPE

Chairman—Adam Cardinal Maida
Members — Theodore Cardinal McCarrick; Archbishop John J. Myers; Archbishop Justin F. Rigali; Archbishop Francis B. Schulte; Archbishop Stefan Soroka.
Staff— Rev. Msgr. R. George Sarauskas, Exec. Dir.; Mr. Christian Kostko, Grants Coord.

AD HOC COMMITTEE ON BISHOPS' LIFE AND MINISTRY

Chairman—Bishop Robert H. Brom
Members — Archbishop John C. Favalora; Bishop Samuel J. Aquila; Bishop Richard C. Hanifen; Bishop Joseph N. Perry
Staff— Rev. Msgr. William P. Fay

AD HOC COMMITTEE ON CHARISMATIC RENEWAL

Chairman—Bishop Sam G. Jacobs
Members— Bishop Robert J. Carlson; Bishop Thomas J. Flanagan; Bishop Joseph C. McKinney; Bishop Agustin A. Roman
Staff— Rev. Msgr. David J. Malloy

AD HOC COMMITTEE ON CATHOLIC HEALTH CARE ISSUES AND THE CHURCH

Chairman—Bishop Robert C. Morlino
Members — Bishop Henry J. Mansell; Bishop William F. Murphy; Bishop John C. Nienstedt; Bishop Joseph M. Sullivan
Staff— Rev. Msgr. John Strynkowski

AD HOC COMMITTEE ON ECONOMIC CONCERNS OF THE HOLY SEE

Chairman—Archbishop John G. Vlazny
Members— Theodore Cardinal McCarrick; Archbishop James P. Keleher; Bishop Gregory M. Aymond Coadjutor Bishop Joseph A. Galante
Staff— Mr. Bruce E. Egnew

AD HOC COMMITTEE ON NATIVE AMERICAN CATHOLICS

Chairman—Bishop Donald E. Pelotte, S.S.
Members— Archbishop Alexander J. Brunett; Archbishop Charles J. Chaput, O.F.M.Cap.; Bishop Blase J. Cupich; Bishop Anthony M. Milone
Consultants— Rev. Raymond Bucko, S.J.; Rev John Hatcher, S.J.; Rev. Msgr. Paul Lenz; Sr. Kateri Mitchell
Staff— Sr. Lourdes Sheehan, R.S.M.; Mr. Daniel Mulhall

NOMINATION OF CONFERENCE OFFICES

Chairman—Archbishop Daniel E. Pilarczyk
Members—
Region I: Bishop Richard J. Malone
Region II: Bishop Gerald M. Barbarito
Region III: Bishop Michael A. Saltarelli
Region IV: Bishop John H. Ricard, S.S.J.
Region V: Bishop Edward K. Braxton
Region VI: Bishop John Michael Botean
Region VII: Bishop Joseph N. Perry
Region VIII: Bishop Dennis M. Schnurr
Region IX: Archbishop Justin F. Rigali
Region X: Bishop Joseph A. Fiorenza
Region XI: Bishop Robert H. Brom
Region XII: Bishop Donald J. Kettler
Region XIII: Bishop Jose H. Gomez
Region XIV: Bishop Robert N. Lynch
Staff— Rev. Msgr. William P. Fay

AD HOC COMMITTEE TO OVERSEE THE USE OF THE CATECHISM

Chairman—Archbishop Alfred C. Hughes
Members— Archbishop William J. Levada; Bishop Robert J. Banks; Bishop Leonard P. Blair; Bishop Daniel N. DiNardo; Bishop Donald W. Wuerl
Consultants— Archbishop Daniel M. Buechlein, O.S.B.; Rev. John Pollard
Staff— Rev. Daniel Kutys, Exec. Dir.; Mr. Brian Keane, Coord. of Assessment; Sr. Glenn Anne McPhee, Sec.-Education

PLENARY COUNCIL VARIUM

Chairman—Archbishop Daniel M. Buechlein, O.S.B.
Members— Avery Cardinal Dulles, S.J.; Archbishop Timothy M. Dolan; Archbishop John R. Quinn; Archbishop Justin F. Rigali; Bishop Armando X. Ochoa; Bishop Joseph N. Perry, Bishop Dennis M. Schnurr; Bishop Allen H. Vigneron
Staff— Rev. Msgr. David J. Malloy

AD HOC COMMITTEE FOR THE REVIEW OF SCRIPTURE TRANSLATIONS

Chairman—Bishop Arthur J. Serratelli
Members— Archbishop Justin F. Rigali; Bishop Blase J. Cupich; Bishop Richard J. Sklba; Bishop Emil A. Wcela
Staff— Rev. Msgr. John Strynkowski; Mrs. Siobhan M. Verbeek

AD HOC COMMITTEE ON SEXUAL ABUSE

Chairman—Archbishop Harry J. Flynn
Members — Archbishop Stefan Soroka; Bishop Robert J. Baker; Bishop Stephen E. Blaire; Bishop Blasé J. Cupich; Bishop Thomas G. Doran; Coadjutor Bishop Joseph A. Galante; Bishop John R. Gaydos; Bishop Howard J. Hubbard; Bishop William E. Lori; Bishop W. Francis Malooly; Bishop James A. Murray; Bishop George H. Niederauer; Bishop Thomas J. Rodi; Bishop Robert F. Vasa
Staff— Rev. J. Cletus Kiley; Rev. Msgr. Francis Maniscalco; Mr. Mark Chopko, Esq.

AD HOC COMMITTEE ON SHRINES

Chairman—Archbishop James P. Keleher
Members— Francis Cardinal George, O.M.I.; Archbishop Daniel M. Buechlein, O.S.B.; Archbishop Charles J. Chaput, O.F.M.Cap.; Archbishop John J. Myers; Archbishop John G. Vlazny; Bishop Sean P. O'Malley, O.F.M.Cap.
Staff— Rev. James P. Moroney

AD HOC COMMITTEE ON STEWARDSHIP

Chairman—Bishop Sylvester D. Ryan
Members— Archbishop James P. Keleher; Bishop Robert J. Baker; Bishop Ronald M. Gilmore; Bishop Joseph L. Imesch
Staff— Mr. Bruce E. Egnew

NATIONAL ADVISORY COUNCIL

Chairman—Mr. Brian Corbin
Chairman-Elect— Ms. Adriana Vlasic
Secretary— Mr. Juan Escobar
Members— Bishop Paul A. Zipfel; Bishop Gordon D. Bennett, S.J.; Bishop Kevin M. Britt; Bishop Thomas G. Wenski
Diocesan Priests— Rev. William D. Hammer; Rev. Stephen J. Knox; Rev. James F. Kuhns; Rev. Msgr. Arturo Meza; Rev. William P. Sheridan; Rev. Msgr. Richard Sniezyl; Rev. Steven Verhelst
Religious Men— Rev. Michael Higgins, C.P.; Rev. Arthur M. Johnson, S.A.
Religious Women— Sr. Joanne M. Hanrahan, S.S.N.D.; Sr. Julia Jamink, S.J.H.; Sr. Linda Werthman, R.S.M.
Regional Representatives—
Region I: Mr. Marcos Brizuela
Region II: Mr. Brian Evers; Ms. JoAnn Perou
Region III: Mr. Juan Escobar; Ms. Claudia Pastrana
Region IV: Vacant
Region V: Ms. Sandra L. Henry; Mr. Anh Quang Cao
Region VI: Mr. Brian Corbin; Ms. Adriana Vlasic
Region VII: Mrs. Anne Verbeke; Mr. William Weber
Region VIII: Mrs. Bernadette Dunn; Mr. Perri Schafer
Region IX: Ms. Beatrice E. Swoopes; Mr. David G. Mueckl
Region X: Ms. Charolette Davis
Region XI: Ms. Rosalina Domondon; Mr. George Takahashi
Region XII: Ms. Lita T. McBride; Mr. Eric P. Schiedermayer
Region XIII: Mr. Antonio Lujan; Ms. Brenda A. Moran-Hobbs
Region XIV: Vacant
Staff— Mr. Bruce E. Egnew; Mr. John A. Henderson

CATHOLIC LEGAL IMMIGRATION NETWORK, INC. (CLINIC)

CLINIC: BOARD OF DIRECTORS

Chairman—Bishop Nicholas A. DiMarzio
Vice President— Bishop James A. Tamayo
Treasurer— Bishop Armando X. Ochoa
Members — Bishop Robert J. Baker; Bishop Thomas J. Flanagan; Bishop Thomas J. Olmsted; Bishop Jaime Soto; Bishop Thomas G. Wenski; Bishop John C. Wester; Ms. Jane Golden Belford, Esq.; Sr. Ray Monda DuVall, C.H.S.; Ms. Margaret Hatton; Mr. Austin Fragomen; Ms. Lily Gutierrez
Staff— Mr. Donald Kerwin

RELATED ORGANIZATIONS

*** Catholic Legal Immigration Network, Inc. (CLINIC) Theological College,**
National Office, 401 Michigan Washington, DC 20017. Tel: 202-635-2556; Fax: 202-635-2649. Corporate Officers: Most Rev. Nicholas A. DiMarzio, Chm. & Pres.; Most Rev. James A. Tamayo, Vice Pres.; Most Rev. Armando X. Ochoa, Treas.; Mr. Donald Kerwin, Sec. & Exec. Dir.

Members—Most. Rev. Jaime Soto; Most Rev. Thomas J. Flanagan; Most Rev. Thomas J. Olmsted; Most Rev. Robert Baker; Most Rev. Thomas G. Wenski; Most Rev. John C. Wester; Sr. Lourdes Sheehan, RSM; Ms. Margaret Hatton; Ms. Lily Gutierrez; Mr. Mark Franken; Sr. RayMonda DuVall; Mr. Austin T. Fragomen; Ms. Jane Golden Belford, Esq. E-mail: national @cliniclegal.org; Web site: www.cliniclegal.org

The Catholic Legal Immigration Network, Inc. (CLINIC), a subsidiary of the United States Catholic Conference of Bishops (USCCB), operates a legal support agency for a rapidly growing national network of Catholic immigration programs. CLINIC advocates for transparent, fair and generous immigration policies, and expresses the Church's commitment to the full membership of migrants in U.S. society.

Catholic Relief Services—

CRS World Headquarters, 209 W. Fayette St., Baltimore, MD 21201. Tel: 410-625-2220; Fax: 410-234-2986. Mr. Kenneth F. Hackett, Exec. Dir. (Each diocese has a local CRS diocesan director listed in this book.)

Catholic Relief Services Board of Directors:

Chairman—Bishop Robert N. Lynch

Members—Theodore Cardinal McCarrick; Archbishop Harry J. Flynn; Archbishop Roger L. Schwietz, O.M.I.; Bishop Joseph L. Charron, C.PP.S.; Bishop Joseph L. Imesch; Bishop John B. McCormack; Bishop Dale J. Melczek; Bishop William C. Newman; Bishop Michael A. Saltarelli; Bishop J. Terry Steib, S.V.D.; Bishop John W. Yanta; Rev. Msgr. William P. Fay

Staff—Mr. Kenneth Hackett, Exec. Dir.; Mr. Al Brill, Deputy Exec. Dir.; Ms. Dorrett Byrd, Deputy Exec. Dir.; Mr-. Frank Carlin, Deputy Dir.; Fr. William Headley, Deputy Exec. Dir.; Ms. Joan F Neal, Deputy Exec. Dir.; Mr. David Piraino, Dir.-Human Resources; Mr. Mark Palmer, Chief Finance Officer; Sr. Marilyn Spellman, SUSC, Liaison to Board of Directors; Mrs. Peggy Trendler, Exec. Sec. Web Site: www.catholic relief.org

Catholic Relief Services-USCC The official overseas relief and development agency of U.S. Catholic community is a separately incorporated organization of the U.S. Catholic Conference of Catholic Bishops.

CRS was founded in 1943 by the bishops of the United States to assist the poor and disadvantaged outside this country. The fundamental motivating force in all activities of CRS is the Gospel of Jesus Christ as it pertains to the alleviation of human suffering, the development of people and the fostering of charity and justice in the world.

CRS reaches out to people in more than 80 countries and territories around the world with programs in emergency response, agriculture, health, HIV/AIDS, microfinance, peace building and safety net programming. The core of the agency's work is to honor the dignity of the human person, and to work for a world in which all flourish in accordance with that dignity.

Domestically, CRS works with local dioceses and parishes to engage Catholics in the United States and help them grow in solidarity with the poor overseas. CRS sponsors education programs (like Operation Rice Bowl and Food Fast), diocese-to-diocese partnership projects and trips for educators that allow them to witness the needs overseas and to see first-hand how CRS is helping the poorest of the poor.

In fiscal year 2001, CRS' programming had a total value of $344 million dollars.

RELATED ORGANIZATIONS

National Religious Retirement Office

3211 Fourth St., N.E., Washington, DC 20017-1194. Tel: 202-541-3215. Sr. Andrée Fries, C.P.P.S., Exec. Dir.

The USCCB Commission on Certification and Accreditation

3211 South Lake Drive, Ste 317, Saint Francis, WI 53235-3702. Tel: 414-486-0139; Fax: 414-489-0006. Maureen O'Brien, Ph.D., Board Chm.; Sr. Kay L. Sheskaitis, I.H.M., Exec. Dir.; Jean Marie Weber, Dir. -Certification

Established in 1982 by the Administrative Board of the United States Conference of Catholic Bishops, the USCCB Commission serves as an accrediting agency of the Catholic Bishops of the United States, establishes accreditation standards, policies, and procedures, and accredits quality ministry formation programs that prepare persons for ministry. The USCCB Commission also establishes and approves certification standards and procedures for the certification of specialized ecclesial ministers by (Arch)Dioceses and organizations of ecclesial ministers.

NATIONAL ORGANIZATIONS

Listing in this category is not related to classification under Canon Law as a public juridic person.

American Catholic Correctional Chaplains Association—

701 Lawrenceville Rd.- P.O. Box 5147, Trenton, NJ 08638. Tel: 609-406-7400 ext. 5655. Most Rev. Gabino Zavala, D.D., Episcopal Advisor; Rev. Robert R. Schulze, Pres.;Rev. Mark C. Schmieder,Vice Pres.; Rev. Thomas Houle, O.F.M.Cap., Treas.; Ms. Mary D'Ambrogi, Sec.

The Board of Directors include the Episcopal Advisor, Elected Officers, Regional Vice Presidents, and the immediate Past Presidents. Address all Communications to the President or Secretary.

A nonprofit organization for the purposes of unifying and implementing the Church's corrective and restorative efforts for the spiritual welfare of persons committed to the Catholic Chaplains' care, and to foster a Catholic approach issues of criminal justice in accord with the principles of Sacred Scripture and Catholic social justice teaching. Affiliated with the Social Development and World Peace Department, USCCB, the International Commission of Catholic Prison Pastoral Care, American Correctional Association, American Correctional Chaplains Association, National Council on Crime and Delinquency and The Catholic University of America, it was established with approval of the American Bishops in 1952. Grants USCCB-recognized certification to qualified members.

Publication: tri-annually, ACCCA News.

The American College of the Roman Catholic Church of the United States-North American College (1859)—

3211 Fourth St., N.E., Washington, DC 20017-1194. Tel: 202-541-5411; Fax: 202-722-8804. Most Rev. Edwin F. O'Brien, Chm; Rev. Msgr. Kevin C. McCoy, Rector, 00120, Vatican City, Europe. Ms. Tricia Morrin Lloyd, Dir. Office for Devel. & Public Rels.

The College is owned and operated by the Bishops of the United States and incorporated under the laws of the State of Maryland.

American Catholic Historical Association (1919)—

The Catholic University of America, Washington, DC 20064. Tel: 202-319-5079; Fax: 202-319-5079. Christopher J. Kauffman, Pres.; Rev. Msgr. Robert Trisco, Sec. & Treas. E-Mail: CUAchracha@CUA.edu; Web site: research.cua.edu/acha

A membership organization, founded to promote the study of church history understood in the broad sense and to assist American Catholics and other members in all fields of history.

Apostleship of the Sea in the United States of America (AOSUSA)—

1500 Jefferson Dr., Port Arthur, TX 77642-0646. Tel: 409-985-4545; Fax: 409-985-5945. Rev. John A. Jamnicky, National Dir.; Bishop Curtis J. Guillory, Bishop of Beaumont, Bishop Promoter; Rev. Sinclair K. Oubre, J.C.L., Pres.; Ms. Doreen M. Badeaux, Exec. Sec. E-Mail: aosusa@stellamaris.net

AOSUSA is a membership organization of Catholic maritime chaplains, seafarers, pastoral associates, and affiliates serving the people of the sea in ports throughout the USA, in collaboration with the Committee on Migration of the United States Conference of Catholic Bishops.

Monthly Publication: Catholic Maritime News.

Association of Catholic Diocesan Archivists—

Archdiocese of Chicago Archives & Record Ctr., 711 W. Monroe, Chicago, IL 60661. Tel: 312-831-0711. His Eminence Roger Cardinal Mahony, Episcopal Moderator; Tricia Pyne, Pres.; John J. (Jac) Treanor, Treas.; Audrey Newcomer, Sec.

The Association of Catholic diocesan archivists first met in 1979 and formally organized the Association of Catholic Diocesan Archivists in 1982. The organization promotes professionalism in the management of diocesan archives in the United States and Canada, and fosters cooperation between diocesan archivists and others on regional, national and international levels. Membership information is available through the above address and telephone number.

Catholic Association of Teachers of Homiletics (CATH)—

Our Lady of the Elm Motherhouse, 1230 W. Market St., Akron, OH 44313-7108.

Officers: Sr. Mary Ann Wiesemann-Mills, O.P., Pres.; Rev. Donald J. Heet, O.S.F.S., Vice- Pres.; Patricia Hughes Baumer, Sec./Treas.

Catholic Campus Ministry Association—

National Office, 1118 Pendleton St., Ste. 300, Cincinnati, OH 45202-8805. Tel: 513-842-0167; Fax: 513-842-0171. Edmund L. Franchi, Exec. Dir.

Founded in 1969 by campus ministers, the association promotes the mission of the Church in higher education and implements the 1985 Pastoral Letter on Campus Ministry through educational programs and services, leadership, the development of cooperative relationships with other organizations and development activities. Membership is open to individuals interested in campus ministry.

Publications: Crossroads, bi-monthly publication; The Catholic Campus Ministry Directory.

Catholic Charities USA—

1731 King St., Alexandria, VA 22314. Tel: 703-549-1390; Fax: 703-549-1656. Most Rev. Michael Driscoll, Episcopal Liaison; Rev. J. Bryan Hehir, S.J., Pres.

Catholic Charities USA is a national network of 1,640 local Catholic Charities agencies and institutions that provide help and create hope for more than seven million people a year regardless of their religious, social or economic backgrounds.

For more than 275 years, local Catholic Charities agencies have been providing a wide range of vital services in their communities ranging from daycare, adoption, and refugee resettlement to advocacy, counseling, and emergency food and housing. Today, the Catholic Charities network is made up of more than 51,000 staff and 168,000 volunteers. In addition, more than 7,000 individual serve as volunteer members of local boards.

The national service center – Catholic Charities USA – was founded in 1910 as the National Conference of Catholic Charities by Most Rev. Thomas J. Shahan and Rt. Rev. Msgr. William J. Kerby in cooperation with lay leaders of the Society of St. Vincent De Paul.

Catholic Charities USA provides its members a national voice, networking opportunities, training and technical assistance, program development, and financial support. Catholic Charities USA has been commissioned by the USCCB to represent the Catholic community in times of domestic disaster. Catholic Charities USA's president represents North America before Caritas International, maintaining contact with the Catholic Charities movement through out the world.

Publications: quarterly membership magazine, Charities USA; Annual Report; Annual Survey of Catholic Charities services nationwide; various books, pamphlets and studies.

The Catholic Communications Foundation (CCF)—

c/o 6363 St. Charles Ave., New Orleans, LA 70118. Dr. William H. Hummell, Board Member & Contact Person.

The Catholic Communications Foundation was established and is supported by Catholic Fraternal Benefit Societies. Its mission is to assist the communications apostolates of the Catholic Church in the United States, with particular emphasis at the diocesan level. The Foundation awards religious communications training scholarships.

The Catholic Health Association of the United States (1919)—

Headquarters, 4455 Woodson Rd., St. Louis, MO 63134. Tel: 314-427-2500; Fax: 314-427-0029. Rev. Michael D. Place, Pres. & CEO; Matthew J. Thibeau, S.V.P., Strategy-Organizational Effectiveness; Cal Smith, Vice-Pres. Chief Admin. Officer; Sr. Patricia A. Talone, R.S.M., Ph.D., Vice Pres.-Mission Services; Michael F. Rodgers, Vice Pres.; Public Policy & Advocacy; Rhonda Mueller, Chief Financial Officer; J. Fred Caesar, Sr., Dir. Public Affairs; Lisa J. Gilden, Vice Pres.-General Counsel. Web Site: www.chausa.org.

CHA represents the combined strength of its members, more than 2,000 Catholic healthcare sponsors, systems, facilities, and related organizations. Founded in 1915, CHA unites members to advance selected strategic directions. Presents annual awards recognizing contribution to the health ministry by organizations and individuals. Sponsors continuing education for healthcare personnel.

Service Areas: Planning and Policy Development, Public Policy and Advocacy, Communications, Sponsorship, Ethics and Mission Services. Annual Assembly: Annual assembly and membership meeting for Catholic healthcare leaders.

Publications: 6 times-year, Health Progress; bi-monthly Catholic Health World; booklets, books & audio-visual on healthcare, Church-related subjects.

Catholic Kolping Society of America (1849)—

9 East 8th St., Clifton, NJ 07011-1101. (Please direct all correspondence to the National Administrator.) Edward Farkas, Natl. Admin.

The Society was founded by Rev. Adolph Kolping in Cologne, Germany, and established in the United States in 1856. The Catholic Kolping Society of America is a part of the world-wide Kolping movement and belongs to the International Kolping Society. There are 12 branches in principal cities of the United States with a combined membership of approximately 2,500. The membership is open to men and women of all ages. The Society's mission statement reads: We, the members of the Catholic Kolping Society of America, extend the vision of our founder, Blessed Adolph Kolping, by promoting the development of the individual and family; we foster a sense of belonging and friendship through our program of spiritual, educational, charitable and social activities.

Catholic Network Of Volunteer Service—
6930 Carroll Ave., Ste. 506, Takoma Park, MD 20912-4423. Tel: 301-270-0900; 800-543-5046; Fax: 301-270-0901. Most Rev. John J. Snyder, Episcopal Advisor; James G. Lindsay, Exec. Dir. E-Mail: volunteer@cnvs.org; Web Site: www.cnvs.org
Catholic Network of Volunteer Service promotes, recruits and refers volunteers to missions in the United States and overseas. We represent more than 230 faith-based volunteer programs worldwide and work with the U.S. dioceses, religious communities and the private sector to determine their needs for help. Catholic Network of Volunteer Service (CNVS) is committed to the goal that every Catholic man and woman be invited to consider a period of service in the missions, as a vital and important manifestation of the baptismal call of all Catholic people. Currently, 9000 men and women are serving in CNVS member mission programs offering their gifts and abilities in full-time service to people in need and living their Catholic faith more fully than many had imagined possible. These volunteers are serving domestically for a summer, six months, a year or more, and they are serving internationally for two or more years at a time. They are single and married, recent college graduates and early retirees, doctors and teachers, parish ministers and social workers, community organizers, computer programmers, legal aides and more. Gatherings: Annual Conference; Formation Workshops, Training Seminars.
Publications: annual, Response: Directory of Volunteer Opportunities; monthly, How Can I Help?; quarterly, Lay Mission Handbook.
Awards: The Father George Mader Award, given annually to honor organizations and individuals who promote the value of lay mission service.

The Catholic Press Association of the United States and Canada, Inc.—
3555 Veterans Memorial Hwy. -Unit O, Ronkonkoma, NY 11779. Tel: 631-471-4730. Most Rev. Joseph A. Galante, Honorary Pres.; Mr. Dennis Heaney, Pres.; Mr. Owen McGovern, Exec. Dir. E-Mail: cathjourn@catholicpress.org; Web site: www.catholic press.org
The Catholic Press Association of the United States and Canada, Inc., is the trade and professional association of Catholic newspapers, magazines, and general publishers in the U.S. and Canada and their staff personnel. The CPA was established in 1911. It serves a professional Catholic press market of nearly 2,000 persons working in more than 600 publications with a wide promotion and representation of Catholic press interests in legal, postal, tax and professional matters.

The Catholic Theological Society of America—
John Carroll University, 20700 North Park Blvd., University Hgts., OH 44118. Tel: 216-397-1631; Fax: 216-397-1804. M. Shawn Copeland, Pres., Milwaukee, WI; Roberto Goizueta, Pres. Elect, Chestnut Hill, MA; Mary Catherine Hilkert, Vice-Pres., Notre Dame, IN; M. Therese Moser, Sec., San Francisco, CA; Robert E. McGrath, Treas. Somerdale, NJ; Jon Nilson, Past Pres., Chicago, IL. Board *Members:* Maria-Pilar Aquino, San Diego, CA; Dan Finn, Collegeville, MN; Mary Hines, Boston, MA; Leo Lefebure, Yonkers, NY; Dolores L. Christie, Exec. Dir., University Hgts, OH; Richard Sparks, Editor of Proceedings, Berkeley, CA.
An association of professional theologians. Its purpose is to promote studies and research in theology within the Roman Catholic tradition, to relate theological science to current problems, and to foster a more effective theological education by providing a forum for an exchange of views among theologians and with scholars in other disciplines.

CCD: BOARD OF TRUSTEES

Conference for Catholic Facility Management—
P.O. Box 177, Bowie, MD 20719-0177. Tel: 301-805-8847; Fax: 301-805-8847. Most Rev. Carl K. Moeddel, Episcopal Moderator; Doug Cissel, Exec. Dir. E-mail address: ccfm@comcast.net; Web Site: www.ccfm.net
Mindful of their special ministry in the Roman Catholic Church in facility and real estate matters, the members of the CCFM united to be of service to the Church in ministry of facility and real estate concerns. In particular, this organization promotes the spiritual growth of its membership; promotes facility and real estate knowledge and expertise in service to the local and national Church, facilitates the exchange of ideas and information through personal contacts, quarterly newsletters and annual meetings.

Conference of Diocesan Coordinators of Health Affairs—
1031 Superior Ave.-Rm. 327, Cleveland OH 44114. Tel: 216-429-8307; Fax: 216-429-8033. Rev. Frank Godic, Chm.
Membership in this Conference is by direct appointment and authority from the Ordinary of the appointee and gives members an opportunity of maintaining mutually helpful relationships with the Catholic Health Association, with one another, and with all religious, professional and governmental organizations in the health and hospital field.

The Conference of Major Superiors of Men's Institutes of the United States, Inc.—
8808 Cameron St., Silver Spring, MD 20910. Tel: 301-588-4030; Fax: 301-587-4575. Rev. Ronald D. Witherup, S.S.,Pres.; Rev. John L. Doctor, O.F.M., Vice-Pres.; Bro. Daniel F. Casey, F.S.C., Sec./Treas.; Rev. Ted Keating, S.M., Exec. Dir.
A canonical conference of the major superiors of religious communities and institutes of men for the purpose of promoting the spiritual and apostolic welfare of priests and brothers.

The Confraternity of Christian Doctrine, Inc.—
3211 Fourth St. N.E., Washington, DC 20017. Tel: 202-541-3098; Fax: 202-541-3089. Mary Elizabeth Sperry, Assoc. Dir.

CCD: BOARD OF TRUSTEES—
Members: Bishop William B. Friend; Bishop Wilton D. Gregory; Archbishop James Keleher; Bishop William S. Skylstad; Bishop Donald W. Trautman
The Confraternity is a distinct entity, separately incorporated and directed by a Board of Trustees from the United States Conference of Catholic Bishops. The purpose of the Corporation is to foster and promote the teachings of Christ as understood and handed down by the Roman Catholic Church. To this end it licenses use of the Lectionary for Mass and the New American Bible, translations made from the original languages.

Council of Major Superiors of Women Religious in the United States of America—
1211 Lawrence St., N.E.- P.O. Box 4467, Washington, DC 20017-0467. Tel: 202-832-2575; Fax: 202-832-6325. Sr. Mary McGreevy, R.S.M., Chm.
A canonically erected conference of Major Superiors of women's religious communities established in 1992 to promote mutual support among them and to foster coordination and cooperation with the Bishops' conference and individual Bishops.

Diocesan Fiscal Management Conference—
National Office, P.O. Box 199, Waterville, OH 43566-0199. Tel: 877-709-3362; 419-878-3146; Fax: 419-878-7265. Most Rev. Donald W. Trautman, S.T.D., S.S.L., Episcopal Moderator; Rev. Robert J Yeager, Ed.D., Exec Dir.; Richard L. Runde, Pres.; Rev. Daniel J. Maher, Vice-Pres.; Ernest W. Armstrong, Sec. & Treas.
Mindful of their special ministry in the Roman Catholic Church as the extension of the Diocesan Bishop in fiscal matters, the members of the DFMC unite to be of service to the Church in the ministry of fiscal management.
In particular, this organization promotes the spiritual growth of its members; promotes financial and administrative knowledge and expertise in service to the local and national Church; facilitates the free exchange of ideas and information, and serves as a liaison among the fiscal managers of the Dioceses and Archdioceses of the Church.

Federation of Diocesan Liturgical Commissions—
National Office, 415 Michigan Ave., N.E., Ste. 70, Washington, DC 20017. Tel: 202-635-6990; Fax: 202-529-2452. Ms. Lisa A Tarker, Exec. Dir.; Rev. John H. Burton, Chm.; Ms. Dolly Sokol, Vice Chm.; Mrs. Judy Bullock, Treas.; Rev. Robert E. Webster, Delegate-at-Large; Rev. Steven Dublinski, Delegate-at-Large. Web site: www.FDLC.org
The FDLC is a voluntary association of all diocesan liturgical commissions/offices from the United States. Two members of each diocesan liturgical commission/office serve as diocesan representatives to the FDLC. From this membership are elected 24 representatives (two from each of the 12 Episcopal regions) to serve as the National Board of Directors. The day-to-day activities of the FDLC are directed by the Executive Director. The FDLC relates closely to the Bishops because its membership consists of their appointees. The Federation serves the Bishops and local commissions in matters of ongoing liturgical renewal. It also serves through education and other coordinated services requested by individual commissions or through consultation and voting at national meetings. The FDLC is organized and operated exclusively for religious and educational purposes.

Instituto Nacional Hispana de Liturgia, Inc.—
P.O. Box 29387, Washington, DC 20017-0387. Tel: 202-319-6450; Fax: 202-319-6449. Rev. Juan J. Sosa, Pres.; Sr. Paulina Hurtado, O.P., Vice Pres.; Mrs. Mary Frances Reza, Sec.; Rev. John Brogan, Treas.; Rev. John F. Brogan, Treas.
The Instituto is a national organization committed to assist the bishops of the country in promoting the liturgical reforms mandated by the Second Vatican Council, while it studies, reflects and celebrates more authentically the Catholic faith from the various religious traditions of Hispanics who reside in the United States. Instituto members assist the Church at the national, diocesan and parish levels by providing lectures, translations, and other Spanish and bilingual resources that may meet the liturgical needs of Hispanics whenever they surface. Membership to the organization is open to all persons and institutions interested in liturgy. Board members meet twice a year, members meet annually. National Conference every 2 years and/or symposium on liturgical topics.

International Catholic Migration Commission (ICMC) & ICMC, Inc.—
c/o USCCB 3211 Fourth St., N.E. Washington, DC 20017-1194. Prof. Stefano Zamagni, Pres.; William A. Canny, Sec. Gen.
Provides technical assistance and coordination in area of service to migrants and refugees. Nonprofit New York Corporation.

Jesuit Conference, Inc.—
1616 P St., N.W., Ste. 300, Washington, DC 20036. Tel: 202-462-0400; Fax: 202-328-9212. Revs. Bradley M. Schaeffer, S.J., Pres.; Thomas P. Gaunt, S.J., Exec. Sec.

Ladies of Charity of the United States of America (LCUSA)—
National Center, P.O. Box 31697, St. Louis, MO 63131-0697. Tel: 314-344-1184 ext. 102; Fax: 314-344-2989. Margaret Hanson, Pres.; Most Rev. Howard J. Hubbard, Episcopal Chm.; Spiritual Advisors: Revs. J. Bryan Hehir.; Richard Gielow.
Ladies of Charity in the United States of America (LCUSA) is a national organization with local associations of Ladies of Charity as its members. The local Associations are dedicated to the service of the poor in their communities in the spirit of St. Vincent de Paul, St. Louise de Marillac and St. Elizabeth Ann Seton. Nationally about 17,000 members contribute volunteers hours and financial support to services that may include the operation of a thrift shop, food pantry, meal and transportation services. LCUSA participates in social co-responsibility as a member of the International Association of Charities. They are advocates for the disadvantaged and the poor and help to empower the poor to help themselves. National Assembly annually.
Publications; quarterly, Servicette.

Leadership Conference of Women Religious in the United States of America—
Office, 8808 Cameron St., Silver Spring, MD 20910. Tel: 301-588-4955; Fax: 301-587-4575. Sr. Constance Phelps, S.C.L., Pres.; Sr. Christine Vladimiroff, O.S.B., Vice Pres.; Sr. Mary Ann Zollmann, B.V.M., Past-Pres.; Sr. Rose Jochmann, O.S.F., Treas.; Sr. Anne Hennessy, C.S.J., Sec.; Sr. Carole Shinnick, S.S.N.D., Exec. Dir.
A conference of leaders of U.S. women religious congregations, founded in 1956, canonically approved in 1959 with a name change in 1972 and canonical approval of revised by-laws in 1972 and 1989, to promote a developing understanding and living of religious life, to assist members to carry out more collaboratively their service of leadership, to provide a vehicle for dialogue with the Bishops' Conference and other ecclesiastical authority, and to collaborate with other groups concerned with the needs of society in continuing the mission of Christ in the world today.

Legal Resource Center for Religious, Inc.—
8812 Cameron St., Silver Spring, MD 20910. Tel: 301-589-8143; Fax: 301-589-2897. Daniel J. Ward, O.S.B., Exec. Dir. E-mail: lrcr@lrcr.org; Web site: www.lrcr.org.

Lithuanian Roman Catholic Federation of America—
4545 W. 63rd St., Chicago, IL 60629. Tel: 312-585-9500. Most Rev. Paulius Baltakis, O.F.M., Episcopal Advisor; Saulius V. Kuprys, Pres., 150 S. Wacker Dr., Ste. 1050, Chicago, IL 60606. Tel: 312-346-5275; 708-243-0416; Fax: 312-346-5640; 708-243-0418.
A not-for-profit corporation founded in 1906 in Wilkes-Barre, PA, to promote and coordinate religious, educational and charitable activities among Lithuanian American Catholics, their organizations, institutions, religious communities, and parishes (for detailed information regarding religious institutions please refer to the Apostolate for Lithuanians).

Mariological Society of America (1949)—
Secretariat: Marian Library, University of Dayton, Day-

ton, OH 45469-1390. Tel: 937-229-4294; Fax: 937-229-4258. Rev. Thomas A. Thompson, S.M., Exec. Sec.

The objects and purposes of this organization are to promote interest and research in the theology of the Virgin Mary. Professional and associate membership. Proceedings of annual meeting published in Marian Studies. Annual convention in late May or early June.

The Mexican American Cultural Center (1972)—

3115 West Ashby Pl. San Antonio, TX 78228. Tel: 210-732-2156. Most Rev. Placido Rodriguez, C.M.F., Chm.; Sr. Maria Elena Gonzalez, R.S.M., Pres.

The Mexican American Cultural Center (MACC) is a National Catholic Institute for Pastoral Leadership and Language Studies. This multicultural institutes offers courses and workshops to prepare pastoral leaders for service in Hispanic and multicultural communities. Programs include: Hispanic Pastoral Ministry, a program that offers a creative response to the need for preparation for U.S. Hispanic ministry – a 4-month course preparing pastoral leaders for service in a Hispanic community; the Mini-Pastoral, a 3-week intensive introduction to Hispanic Ministry; Leadership for a Multicultural World, a series of 4 workshops developing leadership for multicultural communities; various workshops for leaders of Hispanic and multicultural communities; and intensive language studies preparing pastoral leaders for service in their second language of English or Spanish. Accredited by USCCB/CCA and working in cooperation with various U.S. based universities. By request, MACC faculty members offer workshops throughout the United States.

National Apostolate for Inclusion Ministry NAFIM (1997)—

Mailing Address, P.O. Box 218, Riverdale, MD 20738-0218. Tel: 800-736-1280; 301-699-9500; Fax: 240-220-8374. Most Rev. Robert W. Donnelly, Episcopal Moderator; Charles M. Luce, Pres.; Barbara J. Lampe, Exec. Dir. E-mail: executivedirector@nafim.org; Web Site: www.nafim.org

Established in 1968 to promote the full participation and inclusion of Catholics with mental retardation in the life of their church community. Formerly known as National Apostolate with Persons with Mental Retardation (NAPMR) 1992-1997, National Apostolate with Mentally Retarded Persons (NAMRP) 1974-1992 and National Apostolate for the Mentally Retarded (NAMR) 1968-1974.

Publication: quarterly journal; newsletter; pamphlets; training materials.

National Association for Treasurers of Religious Institutes, Inc. (NATRI) (1981)—

8824 Cameron St., Silver Spring, MD 20910. Tel: 301-587-7776; Fax: 301-589-2897. Sr. Laura Reicks, R.S.M., Exec. Dir.

Serving finance officers and staffs of religious institutes by assisting them in fulfilling their stewardship responsibilities. An annual national conference, seminar for new personnel in financial offices, and a consulting service are key program components. All Roman Catholic religious institutes are eligible for membership in NATRI and currently approximately 585 belong.

Publication: annual membership and service directories and other miscellaneous publications 5 times a year, Accounting and Financial Management.

National Association of African American Catholic Deacons, Inc.—

Office of the Pres., 1418 Glen View Rd., Yellow Springs, OH 45387. Tel: 937-767-2848 or 767-5381; Fax: 937-767-7465. Deacons Paul E. Richardson, Pres.; Ralph Cyrus, Vice Pres., Ft. Washington, MD; Marvin Threatt, Sec., Spring Valley, CA.; Jerry Lett, Treas., Lithonia, GA.

To establish an organization of Permanent deacons of African heritage ordained in the Roman Catholic Church. To promote unity among deacons of African descent by facilitating effective communication network on a national, regional, and diocesan level. To be a pro-active organization in promoting and contributing to the future of the African American family with emphasis on African American men. To promote justice, peace, equality; and end to racism, and the sharing of resources among all peoples in light of the social teachings of the Roman Catholic Church.

National Association of Catholic Chaplains—

National Office, P.O. Box 070473, Milwaukee, WI 53207-0473. Tel: 414-483-4898; Fax: 414-483-6712. Most Rev. Dale J. Melczek, Episcopal Liaison; Rev. Richard M. Leliaert, O.S.C., Chm. Board; Rev. Joseph J. Driscoll, Pres. & CEO. E-mail: info@nacc.org; Web Site: www.nacc.org

The NACC is a professional association for certified chaplains and CPE educators who participate in the healing mission of Jesus Christ. We provide standards, certification, education, advocacy, and professional development for our members in service to the church and society.

Publication: 10 times-year, journal-newsletter, Vision.

The National Association of Catholic Family Life Ministers—

300 College Park, Dayton, OH 45469-2512. Tel: 937-229-3324; Fax: 937-229-4902. David Abele, Exec. Dir.; Barbara MacDonald, Pres.; Steve Beirne, Pres.-Elect; Joe Schmitt, Treas.; Maureen Wood, Sec. E-mail: nacflm@udayton.edu

The National Association of Church Personnel Administrators (NACPA)—

Headquarters, 100 E. Eighth St., Cincinnati, OH 45202. Tel: 513-421-3134; Fax: 513-421-3085. Mr. Thomas P. Conklin, Pres.; Sr. Ellen Doyle, O.S.U., Exec. Dir.

The National Association of Church Personnel Administrators (NACPA) is a membership association of lay, religious and clergy Personnel Directors, Assistant Directors, and Personnel Board Members serving dioceses, religious congregations and other church-related institutions. The purpose of the Association is to identify skills and competencies for human resource managers, develop personnel systems which integrate management and pastoral values, and advocate standards of just treatment for Church Personnel.

National Association of Deacon Organizations—

11 Lincoln Ave., West Yarmouth, MA 02673. Tel: 508-862-6385. Deacon Ron Lesjak, Exec. Sec.; Deacon Michael Hickey, Pres. E-mail: mmhickey1@msn.com

National Association of Diaconate Directors (1977)—

National Office, 2136 12th St., Ste.105, Rockford, IL 61104. Tel: 815-965-2100. Deacon Gregory Urban, Exec. Dir.; Deacon Alfred Mitchell, Pres.; Deacon Tim McAuliffe, Pres.-Elect

Directors, vicars of deacons, and others responsible for the formation of candidates and the ongoing growth and development of deacons in the U.S. Promotes communication and facilitates the exchange of information and resources among members. Seeks to develop professional expertise among members through research, dialogue, formation and self-evaluation procedures. Proposes ways and means for effective implementation of solutions to national and regional issues relating to the diaconate. Maintains library on related issues.

National Association of Diocesan Directors of Campus Ministry—

305 Michigan Ave., Detroit, MI 48226. Tel: 313-237-5962. Ms. Krista Bajoka, Contact Person

National Association of Diocesan Ecumenical Officers (NADEO)—

8003 Mobud, Houston, TX 77036-6403. Tel: 713-774-0097; Fax: 713-774-0320. Ms. Garland Debner Pohl, Pres.; Rev. Joseph Witmer, Vice Pres.; Rev. John Ciurpita, Treas.; Rev. George Appleyard, Sec.

The purposes of NADEO are to stimulate an exchange of ideas, experiences and evaluations among the ecumenical officers of the (Arch)Dioceses in union with Rome; to promote programs which further the work of Christian unity and of interreligious cooperation; and to cooperate with the Bishops' Committee for Ecumenical and interreligious Affairs of the National Conference of Catholic Bishops, and with other ecumenical and interreligious agencies.

Publication: quarterly Newsletter; annual booklets on various ecumenical topics, Handbook for Catholic Ecumenical Officers.

National Association of Pastoral Musicians—

National Office, 962 Wayne Ave., Ste. 210, Silver Spring, MD 20910-4461. Tel: 240-247-3000; Fax: 240-247-3001. Dr. J. Michael McMahon, Pres. & CEO; Most Rev. Daniel N. DiNardo, Episcopal Moderator E-mail: npmsing@npm.org; Web Site: www.npm.org.

A national membership organization for the improvement of music within the parish, with special emphasis on liturgical music. Membership includes parish musicians and parish clergy simultaneously, with a unique interest in the practical issues facing the practicing musician and parish clergy.

Services: NPM Conventions—national and regional gatherings for clergy and musicians. Director of Music Ministries Division (DMMD)—division for members who are full-time, salaried music staff in a parish or diocese and have responsibility for managing the overall liturgical music program. NPM Mus.Ed—division for music educators working in Catholic schools. NPM Hotline assists musicians seeking positions, and parishes looking for musicians. Resources for Association members are issued under the name, NPM Council.

The Association has Sections for Liturgists, Clergy, Choir Directors, Organists, responsible for leadership in Music Ministry, Cantors, Ensemble Musicians, Pianists, Seminary Music Educators, Pastoral Military Musicians, Campus Ministers, Eastern Church Musicians, Young Musicians, Hispanic Musicians, Asian & Pacific Rim Musicians and Musicians serving African-American parishes. The NPM Council provides committee leadership in each of these areas. National Training programs: annually, for Choir Directors, Children's Choir Directors, Organists, Guitarists and Cantors with emphasis on developing musical skills, leadership abilities, and ministerial skills.

Publications: six times a year with membership, Pastoral Music; bi-monthly with membership, Pastoral Music Notebook.

National Black Catholic Clergy Caucus—

Office, 328 Congress St., P.O. Box 1088, Opelousas, LA 70571-1088. Tel: 318-942-2392; Fax: 318-942-9201. Rev. Albert J. McKnight, C.S.Sp., Exec. Dir.

National Catholic Cemetery Conference—

National Office, 710 North River Rd., Des Plaines, IL 60016. Tel: 847-824-8131. Mrs. Irene K. Pesce, Exec. Dir.; Most Rev. John G. Vlazny, D.D., Episcopal Moderator

The Conference is an organization of Diocesan Directors of Cemeteries and parish cemetery administrators from throughout the United States, Canada, Australia and Guam. Guided by the principle: "That burial of the dead is one of the Corporal Works of Mercy," the Conference promotes high standards of Catholic cemetery management, development, operation and maintenance consistent with Christian service to the Catholic community; and fosters and promotes the religious, charitable and educational interests of Catholic cemeteries and the people they serve.

Publications: monthly magazine, Catholic Cemetery; various booklets on cemetery management & evaluation services; funeral liturgy at the cemetery. Annual Convention; John Carroll University -Summer Seminar on Leadership.

National Catholic Committee on Scouting Executive Committee (1934)—

1325 W. Walnut Hill Lane, P.O. Box 152079, Irving, TX 75015-2079. Fax: 972-580-2535. Most Rev. Gerald A. Gettelfinger Bishop of Evansville, IN, Episcopal Liaison; Edward Gargiulo, Chm., (Wilmington, DE); Edward Martin, Vice-Chm., (Medina, OH); Gerard Scanlan, Vice Chr., (New York, NY); Thomas Nishikubo, Vice Chr. (Gardena, CA); Robert Oldowski, Past Chm., (Bloomington, MN); Rev. Dennis O'Rourke, PastNatl. Chap., (Chandler, AZ); John Ribar, Vice Chm., (Louisville, KY); John Hammerschmidt, Vice Chm., (O'Fallon, MO); Bray B. Barnes, Vice Chm., (Red Bank, NJ); Rev. Donald Hummel, National Chap., (Westfield, NJ); Rev. Roger LaChance, Assoc. Natl. Chap., (Coeur d'Alene, ID)

A voluntary organization of clergy and laymen, members include a chaplain and lay chairman from all of the dioceses in the United States Conferences. It serves as an advisory committee to the Boy Scouts of America. It has the responsibility of promoting and guiding cooperative contracts between the proper authorities of the Catholic Church in the United States and the Boy Scouts of America.

National Catholic Conference for Total Stewardship, (NCCTS)—

National Office: 300 Liguori Dr., Liguori, MO 63057-9998. Tel: 636-464-3666; Fax: 636-464-4717. Rev. Francis A. Novak, C.SS.R., Pres.; Mr. G. William Sefton, Chm.; Mrs.Debbie Lewis, Admin. Asst.

The mission of the National Catholic Conference for Total Stewardship (NCCTS) is to initiate in parishes and dioceses the concept of total stewardship through a pastoral process called Celebrating Life as a Catholic Christian (CLCC). The concept joins the components of the bible, Evangelization, Discipleship and Stewardship (Service), and presents then not as separate apostolates but as a single unit through the CLCC process providing formation in authentic catechetics and spirituality. Formation includes motivating the active Catholic to reach out to lapsed, non-regular church going Catholic by home visiting, evangelization, pursuit of holiness and inter-personal support and communion. The CLCC process prepares one for return to the Church and is available in book format available to parishes and dioceses.

National Catholic Council on Alcoholism and Related Drug Problems, Inc.—

Headquarters, 1550 Hendrickson St., Brooklyn, NY 11234-3514. Tel: 718-951-7177; Fax: 718-951-7233. Mr. Thomas A. Russell, Exec. Dir.; Rev. Thomas M. Haggerty, Pres.; Sr. M. Damien Adams, C.S.J., Vice Pres.; Rev. Msgr. Kieran Martin, Treas.; Sr. Janet Jeffers, I.H.M., Sec.; His Eminence Anthony Cardinal Bevilacqua, Episcopal Moderator. E-mail: Kieranncca@aol.com

N.C.C.A. is an agency of the Church, which is dedicated to the promotion of adequate treatment for all clergy, men and women religious, and laity who are suffering from alcoholism and other drug dependencies. N.C.C.A. also provides educational programs, especially through and an annual symposium and publication of the Blue Book, to reach all those engaged in pastoral ministry and (or) education concerning the problems associated with the use, misuse and abuse of alcohol and other drugs in our society.

National Catholic Development Conference, Inc. (1968)—
86 Front St., Hempstead, NY 11550. Tel: 516-481-6000. Sr. Georgette Lehmuth, O.S.F., Pres. & CEO; Rev. Joseph M. Hertel, O.F.M., Chm.; Sr. Kathleen Lunsmann, I.H.M., Vice Chm.; Ms. Sally Pietrofitta, Sec.; Mr. Richard Heist, CFRE., Treas.; Most Rev. Robert F. Morneau, D.D., Episcopal Advisor.

Members of one of the nation's largest association of religious fundraising organizations, include religious orders, colleges, high schools, hospitals, Catholic social service organizations and other institutions engaged in raising funds to support their activities. The function of the NCDC is to assist its members in developing effective, professional, ethical methods of raising funds. Members of the NCDC have subscribed to a code of ethics called Precepts of Stewardship. The national office serves as a center of information, issues special interest bulletins, conducts an annual conference and numerous seminars, workshops and regional meetings, maintains a library, follows and reports on legislative matters, conducts a special public information program, Giving is an Act of Faith, and maintains relations with a number of associations and organizations in related fields.

Publications: Dimensions, frequently issued; Monitor on postal, regulatory and tax issues, A Guide for Preparing a Statement of Accountability.

National Catholic Educational Association (1904)—
National Headquarters, 1077-30th St. N.W., Ste. 100, Washington, DC 20007. Tel: 202-337-6232; Fax: 202-333-6706. Most Rev. Gregory M. Aymond, D.D., Chm.; Mr. Michael J. Guerra, Pres.

The National Catholic Educational Association (NCEA) has been providing leadership and service to American Catholic educators since 1904. NCEA's institutional and individual memberships represent Catholic education at all levels and in a variety of settings: preschools, elementary and secondary schools, parish catechetical/religious education programs, diocesan offices, colleges, universities and seminaries. The Association advances the educational and catechetical mission of the Church; provides leadership and service to its members; articulates the contribution of Catholic education to the Church and society; proclaims the uniqueness of Catholic schools; advocates recognition of and support for Catholic education in parish, school, college and university communities; enhances and supports leadership among the members; and fosters local, national and international collaboration.

National Catholic Office for the Deaf (1971)—
NCOD Office, 7202 Buchanan St., Landover Hills, MD 20784-2236. Tel: 301-577-1684 (V); 577-4184 (TTY) Fax: 301-577-1690; Arvilla Rank, Exec. Dir. E-mail: ncod@erols.com; Web site: www.ncod.org

The NCOD, established by the Catholic pastoral workers of the deaf in 1971 at Trinity College, Washington, DC is devoted to coordinating the Church's pastoral ministry to deaf and hard-of-hearing persons at the national level; developing special liturgies, catechetical texts and materials; organizing workshops, leadership programs, cursillos and marriage encounters, and national and regional pastoral workers meetings; coordinating a training program for ministers with the deaf; and serving as an information and referral center for all those involved in this special ministry as well as members of the deaf community and their families. Policy is established by a board of directors elected by the members.

Publication: pastoral journal, Vision.

National Catholic Partnership on Disability_
415 Michigan Ave., N.E.-Suite 240, Washington, DC 20017-1557. Tel: 202-529-2933 (TTY 202-529-2934); Fax: 202-529-4678. Mary Jane Owen, Exec. Dir.; Kent A. Peters, Chm. Web site: www.ncpd.org.

Established to foster and facilitate the challenges of "Pastoral Statement of U.S. Catholic Bishops on People with Disabilities." Provides resources and enhances visibility of diocesan offices addressing access and inclusion; works with USCCB staff and other national Catholic organizations in advocating for disability involvement and concerns; collaborates with other ministries of the church to enhance meaningful participation; affirms the culture of life through promoting the giftedness of all people with assorted disabilities at all stages of the life cycle. Mission is promoted through appropriate media, consultation, lectures, workshops, and regional gatherings.

National Catholic Rural Life Conference—
National Headquarters, 4625 Beaver Ave., Des Moines, IA 50310-2145. Tel: 515-270-2634; Fax: 515-270-9447. Bro. David G. Andrews, Esq., C.S.C., Exec. Dir.; Most Rev. David L. Ricken, Bishop of Cheyenne, Pres. of the Bd. of Directors of the National Catholic Rural Life Conference. E-mail address: ncrlc@aol.com; Web site: www.ncrlc.com

The National Catholic Rural Life Conference is a membership organization grounded in a spiritual tradition which brings together the Church, care for creation and care for community. The NCRLC fosters programs of direct service and systemic change. As an educator in the faith, the NCRLC seeks to relate religion to the rural world; develops support services for rural pastoral ministers; serves as a prophetic voice and as a catalyst and convener for social justice.

National Catholic Stewardship Council, Inc. (NCSC)—
National Office: 1275 K St. N.W., Ste. 980, Washington, DC 20005. Tel: 202-289-1093; Fax: 202-682-9018; Most Rev. James P. Keleher, S.T.D.; Archbishop of Kansas City, KS, Episcopal Moderator; Mr. Matthew R. Paratore, Sec. Gen. E-mail: icsc@catholicsteward ship.org; Web site: www.catholicstewardship.org.

Through its Annual Conference, Stewardship and Development Institutes, events, publications and audio materials, the NCSC allows people committed to Christian stewardship to gather, share ideas, and learn from each other. At one with the universal church, NCSC fosters solidarity of stewardship as a way of life in parishes and dioceses all over the world. Membership in NCSC is extended to several categories of Christian stewards: (Arch)Dioceses, parishes, Catholic associations, religious congregations, Catholic colleges/universities and professional firms from the United States and around the world. Members receive a number of essential benefits to enable them to live stewardship and bring this way of life to others in their communities and organizations.

NCSC encourages the growing professionalism of diocesan development procedures and programs, as well as the development of parish-centered stewardship renewal aimed at increasing the time, talent and treasure contributed by parishioners. These principles of stewardship outlined outlined in the 1992 NCCB Pastoral Letter: Stewardship: A Disciple's Response.

Publication: newsletter, Nota Bene; journal, Resource; manual for pastoral leaders; Stewardship: Disciples Respond A Practical Guide to Pastoral Leaders; diocesan guidelines concerning the role of Diocesan Stewardship and Development Directors, Stewardship and Development: Guidelines for a Diocesan Office; inspirational prayer book for the Christian stewardship, available in English and Spanish, Pray Always and Never Lose Heart (Luke 18:1): A Treasury of Private Prayers for the Christian Steward, Ora Siempre y No Te Desanimes: San Lucas 18:1: Un Tesoro de Oraciones Privadas para el Administrador Cristiano de los Bienes de dios, Steward Saints for Every Day/Santos Administradores de los Bienes de Dios papa Todos los Dias and The Stewardship Rosary. For a complete listing of services and publications contact the NCSC Office or visit the NCSC web site at www.catholicsteward ship.org. Membership information is available upon request.

National Catholic Student Coalition (1988)—
c/o Brain Zanin, 344 N. Pearl St., Whitewater, WI 53190. Tel: 262-473-5555; Fax: 262-473-5855. Katherine Pierce, Natl. Chm.

The National Catholic Student Coalition (NCSC) is a national coalition of Catholic student communities in institutes of higher education. The coalition provides a platform for Catholic students to reflect, speak, and act on issues within the university, the Church and society. The NCSC promotes the development of campus ministry and Catholic lay and religious leaders for the Church and society. The NCSC is a member of the International Movement of Catholic Students. Membership is open to groups or individuals associated with Catholic student groups in higher education. The NCSC holds an annual leadership conference.

Publication: The Catholic Collegian.

The National Center for Urban Ethnic Affairs (1971)—
National Office, P.O. Box 20, Cardinal Station, Washington, DC 20064. Tel: 202-232-3600; 319-5128. Dr. John A. Kromkowski, Pres.; Rev. George F. McLean, Sec.; Rev. Msgr. Salvatore Polizzi, Chm.; Ruth Dee, Treas.

"The great task incumbent on all men of good will is to restore the relations of the human family in truth, in justice, in love, and in freedom." (Pope John XXIII, Peace on Earth.) The independent program of this nonprofit organization has evolved from the efforts initiated by the former Task Force on Urban Problems of the United States Catholic Conference. Its aims and purposes are to continue the expression of the Catholic Church's concern for the problems facing our urban society. NCUEA promotes the celebration of cultural pluralism in America and bridges the gaps between groups of various ethnic and cultural traditions. The Center disseminates information, conducts research, develops and supports programs concerned with ethnic Americans and urban society. The Center in association with various community and church groups develops workshops, conferences, and programs related to the quality of human life, national priorities and the development of an urban mission strategy. The Center is also associated with public and private agencies in developing urban economic, social, and intercultural programs, etc.

The National Conference for Catechetical Leadership (NCCL)—
3021 Fourth St. N.E., Washington, DC 20017-1102. Tel: 202-636-3826; Fax: 202-832-2712; Ms. Anne Comeaux, Pres.; Mr. Neil Parent, Exec. Dir. Web site: www.nccl.org.

A voluntary organization composed of diocesan and parish catechetical personnel, academics specializing in religious education, and various associate and affiliated members, including publishers of catechetical texts. The Conference operates on three levels: national, regional and provincial. The purpose of the Conference is to promote and develop professional competence within catechetical leadership and to assist its members in their roles as leaders in the Church's catechetical ministry through networking, resource development, research, training, consultation and advocacy. The Conference is committed to collaboration with other national groups concerned with catechesis/religious education as a means of expanding and coordinating a service to catechetical ministry.

National Conference of Catholic Airport Chaplains (NCCAC)—
Chicago O'Hare International Airport – P.O. Box 66353 Chicago, IL 60666-0353. Tel: 773-868-2636; Fax: 773-686-0130. Deacon James A. O'Malley, Pres., (Chicago O'Hare International Airport); Rev. John P. Fitzgerald, Vice-Pres. (Pittsburgh International Airport); Deacon Ben Wenning, Sec., (Charlotte Douglas International Airport); Rev. James T. Devine, Treas. (Kennedy International Airport); Francis Cardinal George, Archbishop of Chicago, Episcopal Liaison. E-mail: ohareairportchapel.org.

This Conference provides support and communication for all Catholics performing pastoral ministry to airport & airline workers, and travelers; in affiliation with the Bishop's Committee on Migration of the National Conference of Catholic Bishops.

National Council for Catholic Evangelization (1983)—
415 Michigan Ave., N.E., Ste. 90, Washington, DC 20017. Tel: 800-786-6223; Fax: 202-832-2610; Most Rev. Edward J. Slattery, Episcopal Liaison; Rev. Lawrence Esposito, Pres., Worcester, MA; Dr. Terry Jackson, Vice Pres., Raleigh, NC; Mrs. Stella Lopez, Sec., Houston, TX; Bro. Douglas Zlatis, C.F.C., Treas.,Phoenix, AZ; Sr. Priscilla Lemire, R.J.M., Exec. Dir., Washington, DC. Web site: www.catholic evangelization.org.

Established in 1983 by the Bishops' Committee on Evangelization, NCCE is an independent membership organization which seeks to bring together (Arch)Dioceses, organizations, religious congregations, parishes and individuals to promote evangelization as the primary and essential mission of the Church. NCCE sponsors an Annual Conference and Evangelization Training Workshops and Seminars.

Publications: NCCE Newsletter; Resources: Go and Make Disciples and Teams in the Making: A Catholic Parish Manual, Evangelization, and audio tapes. Memberships are available to (Arch)Dioceses, religious congregations, organizations, parishes and individuals.

National Council of Catholic Women—
200 N. Glebe Rd., Ste 703, Arlington, VA 22203. Tel: 703-224-0990; Fax: 703-224-0991. Margaret Gray, Pres.; Susan T. Muskett, Exec. Dir. E-mail: nccw01@winstarmail.com; Web site: www.nccw.org.

The NCCW consists of Catholic women's organizations in the United States, numbering 5,000+ local, diocesan and national organizations. It programs through its six commissions, Church, Family Concerns, Community Concerns, International Concerns, Legislation and Organization. The program of the Council is furthered through leadership training institutes and national conventions.

Publication: bi-monthly, Catholic Woman.

National Council of the Catholic Men—

5664 Midforest Ln., Cincinatti, OH 45233. Mr. Ferd Niehaus, Pres.The NCCM, a federation of Catholic organizations of men, has pioneered in promoting parish councils and diocesan renewal.

National Federation for Catholic Youth Ministry, Inc. (NFCYM)(1981)—

415 Michigan Ave., N.E. – Ste. 40, Washington, DC 20017-4502. Tel: 202-636-3825. Most Rev. Matthew H. Clark, Episcopal Liaison; Mr. Robert J. McCarty, Exec. Dir.; Sr. Jude Ruggeri, A.S.C.J., Chm.

A membership association of diocesan youth offices and collaborating organizations, founded after a reorganization of the USCC Department of Education and the National CYO Federation. The NFCYM fosters the development of youth ministry in the "United States to, with, by, and for youth. The NFYCM mission is "to serve those who serve the young church". Members of the Federation work through diocesan, regional and national structures to provide national leadership, resources and vision for adults and youth in youth ministry. Key services include the biennial National Conference on Catholic Youth Ministry (for adults working with youth); the biennial National Catholic Youth Conference (for teenagers and their adult chaperones); the development of resources for parish workers; religious recognitions for Catholic Girl Scouts/Camp Fire; position papers on current topics and issues in youth ministry; regional and diocesan consultations and programs for diocesan youth ministry leaders.

National Federation of Catholic Physicians' Guilds (1932)—

P.O. Box 757, Pewaukee, WI 53072. Tel: 262-523-6201; 877-CATHDOC; Fax: 262-523-6211. Officers1999-2000: Michael R. Aiello, M.D., Pres., Lake Placid, NY; Charles P. Prezzia, M.D., Pres. Elect, Pittsburgh, PA; Robert J. Saxer, M.D., Vice Pres., Ft. Walton Beach, FL; Dennis M. Doody, M.D., Sec., Columbus, OH; John D. Lane, M.D., Treas., Philadelphia, PA; Most. Rev. Edwin O'Brien, S.T.D. D.D., Episcopal Advisor, Yonkers, NY; Richard A. Watson, M.D., Past Pres., Mountainside, NJ; Robert H. Herzog, Exec. Dir. E-mail address: cathmed@cathmed.com; Web site: www.cathmed.com

Upholding the principles of the Catholic faith and morality as related to the science and practice of medicine.

Catholic Youth Foundation USA—

415 Michigan Ave., N.E., Ste. 40, Washington, DC 20017-4503. Tel: 202-636-3825. Fax: 202-526-7544. Mr. Robert J. McCarty, Exec. Dir.; Rev. Msgr. Michael Cherup, Pres. E-mail: info@cyfusa.org; Web site: www.cyfusa.org/foundation

National Office for Black Catholics (1972)—

The Paulist Center, 3025 Fourth St., N.E., Washington, DC 20017. Tel: 202-635-1778. Walter T. Hubbard, Exec. Dir.

The National Office for Black Catholics, organized in 1970, is a central agency with the general purpose of promoting active and full participation by Black Catholics in the Church and of making more effective the presence and ministry of the Church in the Black community. Its operations support the aspirations of Black Catholics for objectives that include: representation and voice among Bishops and other leaders of the Church; promotion of vocations to the priesthood and religious life; sponsorship of programs of evangelization, pastoral ministry, education and liturgy on national and regional levels; recognition of Black heritage in liturgy, community life, theology and education; and establishment of an Institute for Leadership

Training Formation and Development.

National Organization for Continuing Education of Roman Catholic Clergy, Inc. (NOCERCC)

1337 W. Ohio St., Chicago, IL 60622. Tel: 312-226-1890; Fax: 312-829-8915. Rev. Mark R. Hession, Pres.; James H. Alphen, Exec. Dir. E-mail: nocercc@nocercc.org; Web site: www.nocercc.org.

The National Organization for Continuing Education of Roman Catholic Clergy (NOCERCC) is a membership association of dioceses and religious communities committed to promoting and supporting continuing formation for priests. Founded in 1973, NOCERCC's current membership includes over 220 Roman Catholic dioceses and religious provinces in the United States as well as more than 90 other organizations and individuals around the world that are part of the continuing clergy formation community. Professional services offered to members include an annual convention, regional meetings, specialized workshops, bi-monthly newsletters, practical resources in diverse media and individual consultation. By keeping abreast of contemporary pastoral needs and by sponsoring research on concerns of the presbyteraten NOCERCC seeks to educate its constituencies, promote ongoing formation of the Roman Catholic clergy and foster more effective ministry in the Church.

Publications: NewsNotes, Sabbatical Programs, Handbook for Continuing Formation of Priests, other print and video resources.

National Pastoral Center for the Chinese Apostolate, Inc.—

60 Home Ave., Rutherford, NJ 07070. Tel: 201-935-3068; 933-5155; 889-9399. Fax: 201-935-3068. Rev. Msgr. Joseph Chiang, Dir. E-mail: msgrchiang@yahoo.com.

National Pastoral Life Center—

Headquarters, 18 Bleecker St., New York, NY 10012-2404. Tel: 212-431-7825; Fax: 212-274-9786. Catherine Patten, R.S.H.M., Acting Dir. & Coord.-Catholic Common Ground; Ms. Karen Sue Smith, Editorial Dir.; Donna Ciangio, O.P., Project Dir.; Initiative; Mr. Jeffry Korgen, Sec.-The Roundtable. E-mail: nplc@nplc.org; Web site: www.nplc.org.

The Center is an information, training, and consulting resource for diocesan and parish leaders. The Center conducts and staffs educational and training programs for pastors and others in ministry. It also sponsors pastoral ministry conventions, conducts pastoral research, and serves as a resource and referral center for parish and diocesan staffs.

Publications: magazine, Church Magazine; Center Papers and other publications.

North American Pastoral Center for Czech Catholics—

00 E. Taft Ave., Orange, CA 92865-4330. Tel: 714-998-0251; Fax: 714-637-0201. Most Rev. Peter Esterka, Pres.

The Papal Foundation—

Office, 222 North 17th St., Philadelphia, PA 19103. Tel: 215-587-2491 & 2492. Fax: 215-965-1712 Mr. James V. Coffey, Vice Pres.-Devel.; Mr. Glenn J. Masakowski, Chief Financial Officer. E-mail: PF1988@aol.com

Board of Trustees: Anthony Cardinal Bevilacqua, Chm.; Avery Cardinal Dulles; Edward Cardinal Egan; Francis Cardinal George, O.M.I.; James Cardinal Hickey; William Cardinal Keeler, Vice Chm.; Roger Cardinal Mahony; Adam Cardinal Maida; Theodore Cardinal McCarrick, Pres. Trustees: Most Rev. Harry J. Flynn; Most Rev. William J. Levada; Most Rev. Justin Rigali; Mr. Charles Drury; Mr. L.B. Eckelkamp; Mrs. Mary Ellen Fox; E.F. Hansen, Jr., Sec.; Robert C. Hawk; Mr. Warren Hayford; Most Rev. John J. Myers; Mr. Jeremiah O'Connor; Mr. Edward J. Piszek; Mr. Gerald A. Rauenhorst, Sec.; Mr. Antonio Rea; John V. Saeman, Jr.; Sir Daniel J. Donohue, Trustee Emeritus.

The Parish Evaluation Project—

3195 South Superior St., Milwaukee, WI 53207. Tel: 414-483-7370; Fax: 414-483-7380. Rev. Thomas P. Sweetser, S.J., Dir.; Sr. Peg Bishop, O.S.F., Assoc. Dir. pep@pitnet.net. Web site: www.pepparish.org

The Parish Evaluation Project is a nonprofit organization under the laws of Wisconsin, whose purpose is to provide religious and educational services to Catholic parishes in the United States in the areas of surveying, needs assessment, leadership skills, goal setting, evaluation techniques, staff development, pastoral council formation and other resources helpful in parish planning and renewal.

Pax Christi U.S.A., National Catholic Peace Movement—

532 W. 8th St., Erie, PA 16502-1343. Tel: 814-453-4955; Fax: 814-452-4784. Mr. Etienne de'Jonghe, Intl. Sec.; Most Rev. Gabino Zavala, Pres.; Eric LeCompte, Chm.; Beatrice Parwatikar, Vice Chm.; Barbara Baker, Treas.

Pax Christi has as its primary objective to develop alternatives to violence always witnessing to the peace of Christ. The movement of 14,000 members is rooted in a gospel vision of peace. It asks its members to ground their peacemaking in prayer, study and action. Pax Christi keeps as its priorities the Christian vision of spirituality, nonviolence and peacemaking, disarmament, demilitarization, reconciliation with justice, human rights and global restoration, and economic and interracial justice in the United States.

Publications: quarterly newspaper and peace education materials.

Religious Brothers Conference—

National Office, 5420 S. Cornell Ave., Chicago, IL 60615. Tel: 773-493-2306; Fax: 773-493-2356. Bros. Stephen Synan, F.M.S., Exec. Dir. & Past.; G. Timothy Smyth, C.F.C., Past Pres.; Leo Shea, F.M.S., Vice Pres.; David Turmel, C.S.C., Treas.; Tim Raible, M.M., Sec.; Stephen Pardy, S.V.D., Sec.

Publication: Brothers' Voice; Reflections.

Religious Formation Conference—

National Office, 8820 Cameron St., Silver Spring, MD 20910-4152. Tel: 301-588-4938; Fax: 301-585-7649. Sr. Janet Mock, C.S.J., Exec. Dir.; Sr. Phyllis Giroux, S.C., Assoc. Dir.; Co-Chm.: Sr. Rose Anna Marti, C.S.J.P.; Sr. Pauline Gilmore, F.M.M.

A national organization which assists Women and Men Religious who are engaged in the ministry of initial and on-going formation in their congregations.

Retreats International, Inc.—

National Office, Box 1067, Notre Dame, IN 46556. Tel: 219-631-5320; Fax: 219-631-6968. Anne M. Luther, Exec. Dir.; Most Rev. Robert Morneau, Bishop Advisor; Rev. Robert Aaron, O.M.I., Pres.; Sr. Barbara Schmitz, O.S.B., Vice Pres.; Robert Smith, Sec. & Treas. Trustees: Abigail Gessler, Richard Way, Jamie Jo Dunn-McInerey, Steve Hill, Dwayne Daehler

Created in 1928 under the guidance of the Archbishops and Bishops of the United States. The national headquarters for information and all phases of the retreat movement in the United States.

The Slovak Catholic Federation (1911)—

408 N. Main St., Taylor, PA 18517-1108. Tel: 570-562-1341; Fax: 570-562-2807. Rev. Philip A. Altavilla, Pres.; Most Rev. Joseph V. Adamec, Episcopal Advisor; Rev. Thomas A. Derzack, Spiritual Dir.; Dolores M. Evanko, Sec. & Treas.

Founded by Father Joseph Murgas at Wilkes-Barre, Pennsylvania as a nonprofit corporation to promote and coordinate religious activities among Slovak Catholic fraternal societies, religious communities, and Slovak ethnic parishes in their effort to address themselves to the pastoral needs of Slovak Catholics in the United States.

Catholic Academy for Communication Arts Professionals—

National Office: 901 Irving Ave., Dayton, OH 45409-2316. Tel: 937-229-2303; Fax: 937-229-2300. Mr. Frank Morock, Pres.; Jeanean Merkel, 1st Vice Pres.; Vicki Bedard, 2nd Vice Pres.; John E. Kearns, Jr., Treas.; Steve Schoen, Sec. E-mail: admin@catholicacademy.org; Web site: www.catholicacademy.org

The Catholic Academy for Communication Arts Professionals is the U.S. affiliate of SIGNIS, the international Vatican-approved organization for communication. The Catholic Academy grew out of the international merger of two other associations founded in the 1920's in Europe: UNDA for radio and television and OCIC the International Catholic Organization for Cinema. These groups joined to form the Catholic Academy in October 2002. The Catholic Academy is a national network of broadcasters, communications directors, public relations personnel, independent producers, syndicators, internet and other media professionals. This national network provides professional support and access to a broad base of experience and resources. Principal activities of the Catholic Academy: annual General Assembly for all members, annual Gabriel Awards for excellence in commercial and religious communications.

Publication: electronic newsletter, White Papers.

United States Catholic Mission Association—

3029 Fourth St. N.E., Washington, DC 20017. Tel: 202-832-3112; Fax: 202-832-3688. Sr. Christine Beckett, G.H.M.S., Pres; Sr. Rosanne Rustemeyer, S.S.N.D., Exec. Dir.

The USCMA was juridically established September 1, 1981. Its members include U.S. missioners, mission organizations, diocesan mission offices, and others concerned about the mission of the Church and global solidarity. The Association seeks to help missioners to stay up-to-date on mission and world trends, to promote greater global awareness, sensibility, and solidarity in the U.S., and periodically to be a voice for U.S. missioners speaking out in defense of the poor and oppressed throughout the world. USCMA activities include a national conference and regional seminars that highlight specific mission themes and issues, liaison and cooperation with missionary bodies of other Christian churches. The USCMA is responsible for gathering statistical data on the U.S. missionary personnel, which is published bi-annually.

Publications: quarterly newsletter, Mission Update; reports, U.S. Catholic Missionary Statistics, and education programs on mission and global awareness.

NATIONAL ORGANIZATIONS WITH INDIVIDUAL I.R.S. RULINGS

The Beginning Experience—

International Ministry Center, 1657 Commerce Dr., South Bend, IN 46628. Tel: 574-283-0279; 866-610-8877. Fax: 574-283-0287; Most Rev. A. Edward Pevec, Episcopal Moderator; Kathleen Murphy, Exec. Dir.; Dorothy Van Poppel-Ray, Pres.; Charlotte Wall, Vice Pres.; Eileen

Bennett, Sec. & Treas. E-mail: imc@beginningexperience.org; Web site: www.beginningexperience.org.

The Beginning Experience is a copyrighted weekend program to help divorced, separated and widowed persons, as well as their families, work through the trauma of the loss of their spouse and make a new beginning in life. The program was designed by and for Catholics and has its roots in sound Catholic tradition and the sacramental life of the Church. True to the ecumenical spirit in the Church since Vatican II, it has been open to persons of all faiths from the beginning. The BE Weekend was originated in 1974 by Sr. Josephine Stewart in Fort Worth, TX. It has spread throughout the United States as well as other countries. Trained teams make the Beginning Experience Weekend available on a regular basis. It also serves as an informational and materials resource for the establishment of support groups to minister to the needs of the divorced, separated and widowed and their families at various points in their growth process.

Canon Law Society of America—

Catholic University, Washington, DC 20064. Tel: 202-269-3491; Fax: 202-319-5719. Rev. Arthur J. Espelage, O.F.M., Exec. Coord.; Rev. Msgr. Mark L. Bartchak, Pres.; Sr. Sharon Euart, RSM, Vice-Pres.; Deacon Gerald Jorgensen, Sec.; Rev. William King, Treas.

A membership association of Bishops, Clergy, Religious and Laity for the purpose of promoting research and professional collaboration in the area of Canon Law.

Catholic Engaged Encounter, Inc.—

4239 Shirley Rd., Richmond, VA 23225. Tel: 1-800-339-9790. Jim & Sandy Dyk; Rev. Jay Biber

Catholic Library Association—

100 North Street, Ste. 224, Pittsfield, MA 01201-5109. Tel: 413-443-2252 (2CLA); Fax: 413-442-2252. Sr. Jean R. Bostley, S.S.J., Exec. Dir. E-mail: cla@cathla.org; Web Site: www.cathla.org

The Catholic Mutual Relief Society of America—

10843 Old Mill Rd., Ste. 300, Omaha, NE 68154-2600. Tel: 402-551-8765. Mr. Joseph T. Beveridge, Pres. & CEO; Mr. Michael A. Intrieri, Exec. Vice Pres. & Chief Oper. Officer

The Catholic Relief Insurance Company of America—

10843 Old Mill Rd., Ste. 300 Omaha, NE 68154-2600. Tel: 402-551-8765. Mr. Joseph T. Beveridge, Pres. & CEO; Mr. Michael A. Intrieri, Exec. Vice Pres. & Chief Oper. Officer

Conference for Pastoral Planning and Council Development—

12545 Olive Blvd. #175, St. Louis, MO 63141. Tel: 314-579-9577. William L. Pickett, Chm.; Maria Rodgers O'Rourke, Exec Dir. E-mail: info@cppcd.org; Web Site: www.cppcd.org

National Association for Lay Ministry (NALM)—

National Office, 6896 Laurel St., N.W., Washington, DC 20012. Tel: 202-291-4100; Fax: 202-291-8550. Christopher Anderson, Exec. Dir. E-mail: nalm@nalm.org; Web Site: www.nalm.org

The National Association for Lay Ministry is a professional organization which supports, educates and advocates for lay ministers and promotes the development of lay ministry in the Catholic Church. Rejoicing in our baptismal call to be disciples of Jesus Christ and claiming our vocation to minister in the Roman Catholic Church, we value: 1) the universal call to holiness; 2) sharing in the mission and ministry of Jesus; 3) faith that works for justice; 4) the dignity of each person and the richness that results from diversity; 5) the ongoing conversion of persons and structures; 6) collaboration in ministry and participative Church leadership, and; 7) the life experiences lay ministers bring to ministry from their unique relationships and responsibilities as family members, workers, and citizens.

Publications: quarterly, Lay Ministry; Competency-Based Certification Standards for Pastoral Ministers, Pastoral Associates and Parish Life Coordinators; Ministry Formation Self-Assessment Instrument; Moving Ministry Forward; Forging a Ministerial Identity; No Turning Back: A Lay Perspective on Ministry in the Catholic Church of the United States; More Than Manna; Research, Chapters, Affiliations, Networking.

National Catholic Conference for Interracial Justice (NCCIJ)(1959)—

Office, 1200 Varnum St., N.E., Washington, DC 20017-2796. Tel: 202-529-6480; Fax: 202-526-1262. Co-Chm., Most Rev. Charles J. Chaput, O.F.M.; Hon. Lindy Boggs; Deacon Joseph M. Conrad, Jr., Exec. Dir.

Established to implement the teaching of the Catholic Church on cultural and racial justice and to promote the church's vision of multicultural, multiracial understanding, mutual respect and collaboration.

The National Catholic Risk Retention Group, Inc.—

National Office, 801 Warrenville Rd. Ste. 175, Lisle, IL 60532-4334. Tel: 630-725-0986; 877-486-2774; Fax: 630-725-1374. Most Rev. Gregory M. Aymond, D.D., Episcopal Moderator; Mr. Michael J. Beni, Pres. & CEO; Rev. Edward J. Arsenault, Chm. Bd.; Bro. William Walz, F.S.C., Vice-Chm.; Rev. Jay C. Haskin, Sec.; Mr. John J. Maxwell, Treas.

The Company is wholly owned by 60 Catholic (Arch)Dioceses and one Catholic Risk Pooling Trust. It underwrites excess liability insurance for Dioceses and other Church organizations listed in the Official Catholic Directory. Coverage is always subject to a minimum self-insured retention or underlying coverage of $250,000. Maximum limits of coverage available are $9,750,000. The company has the capability to underwrite insurance in all states, Territories and Possessions of the U.S.

National Catholic Young Adult Ministry Association, Inc.—

National Office, P.O. Box 32253, Washington, DC 20007. Tel: 888-629-2621; 202-298-8178; Fax: 202 298-8374. Cindee Case, Pres.; Michelle Miller, Exec. Dir.; Paul Combest, Treas. Web site: www.ncyama.org

Founded in 1982, NCYAMA is an organization supporting those who minister to and with single and married people in their late teens, twenties or thirties. We develop and promote programs and resources while providing opportunities for networking and communication. We advocate for the full integration of young adults in the life of the Catholic faith community in order to connect them with Jesus, the Church, the mission of the Church and their peers.

Publication: quarterly, NCYAMA News.

National Conference of Diocesan Vocation Directors (1962)—

National Office: P.O. Box 1570, Little River, SC 29566. Tel: 843-280-7191. Revs. John Regan, Pres.; Leonard J.M. Plazewski, Vice Pres.; Mark Catalana, Sec./Treas.; David F. Hulshof, Past Pres.; Mrs. Dorothy Foss, Exec.

NCDVD is a professional organization that supports, educates and provides resources for diocesan vocation directors as they promote all Church vocations, but particularly diocesan priesthood. This organization serves all dioceses associated with the United States Conference of Catholic Bishops and dioceses in Canada, Ireland, England, and Australia.

Publications: four times a year, Newsletter annual, Vocation Journal; documents of interest & training institutes; Meetings annually for Regional Conferences and a National Convention.

The National Federation of Priests' Councils (1968)—

National Office, 1337 W. Ohio, Chicago, IL 60622-6490. Tel: 312-226-3334; Fax: 312-829-8915. Rev. Robert Silva, Pres.; Mr. Victor J. Doucette, Dir.-Programs & Publications; Mr. Frank M. Corrado, Dir.- Devel & Communications. E-mail: nfpc@nfpc.org; Web site: www.nfpc.org

The NFPC promotes priestly fraternity by facilitating communication among priests' councils, provides a forum for priests to discuss pastoral matters, enables priests' councils to speak with a common voice, promotes and collaborate on programs of pastoral research, furthers the spiritual renewal of priestly life, collaborates with national lay and religious groups in ways that promote renewal in the Church, collaborates with the USCCB in addressing the needs of the Church in the U.S.A., encourages priests' councils to promote justice in light of the social teachings of the Church, and participates in developing a national and universal perspective of church and ministry.

The NFPC represents over120 priests' councils, priests' associations and affiliates. Elected delegates of member councils meet annually to set policy, and a national executive board meets regularly to carry out the work of the NFPC, assisted by standing committees. Member councils represent approximately 26,000 priests.

Publications: quarterly newsletter, Touchstone; weekly; NFPC This week e-letter; books; occasional papers and studies concerned with various aspects of ministry, the ministerial priesthood and the spiritual renewal of priests.

National Institute for the Word of God—

Headquarters, 487 Michigan Ave. N.E., Washington, DC 20017. Tel: 202-529-0001; Episcopal Advisory Board: Most Rev. John R. Quinn; Most Rev. David E. Foley; Most Rev. Patrick R. Cooney; Most Rev. William G. Curlin; Staff: Rev. John Burke, O.P., Exec. Dir.; Mr. William H. Graham, Assoc. Dir.; Rev. George P. M. Schommer, O.P., Assoc. Dir.; Mary C. Graham, Sec.; Very Rev. Joseph P. Allen, O.P., Treas. Board of Advisors: Rev. Msgr. Raymond East; Revs. James Patrick Moroney; Rutilio J. del Riego; James Walsh; Martha Fernandez; Carol Graham Lehan; Mary Ann McGuire; Michael M. McGuire. E-mail: burkeop@aol.com; Web site: www.wordofgod institute.org.

The Institute is an unaffiliated nonprofit organization incorporated under the laws of the District of Columbia, whose purpose is to promote, support, conduct and assist in any way whatsoever educational, liturgical, and remedial programs and activities, public and private, through the use of any and all media, to further effective communication of the revealed word of God, as the primary pastoral work of the Church. Ongoing efforts include the dissemination of scriptural, theological and pastoral aids such as books, films and tape albums, and the conducting of parish missions, conferences and retreats for clergy and laity.

National Service Committee of the Catholic Charismatic Renewal of the United States Inc.—

P.O. Box 628, Locust Grove, VA 22508-0628. AggieNeck, Chm.; Mr. Walter Matthews, Exec. Dir.

Our focus is to foster baptism in the Holy Spirit in the life of the Church in the United States and throughout the world, to broaden and deepen the understanding that baptism in the Holy Spirit is the Christian inheritance of all, and to strengthen the Catholic Charismatic Renewal. The National Service Committee has established and supported numerous programs to help further our mission. Some of the activities and programs include the establishment of Chariscenter USA, which serves as the national headquarters for our committee and a national office for the Catholic Charismatic Renewal.

Publications: Magazine, "Pentecost Today"; Catholic Charismatic Renewal Directory and leadership training materials as well as an annual national conference, outreach to youth, and evangelization training. The NSC has supported the International Catholic Charismatic Renewal Office in Rome.

The North American Forum on the Catechumenate—

3033 Fourth St., N.E., Washington, DC 20017-1102. Tel: 202-529-9493; Fax: 202-529-9497. James M. Schellman, Exec. Dir.

The North American Forum on the Catechumenate is an international network committed to the implementation of the Rite of Christian Initiation of Adults. The work of FORUM is overseen by a Board of Directors of seven elected representatives. A variety of institutes are offered in co-sponsorship with a hosting diocese to serve the local Church. FORUM networks with other U.S., Canadian and international groups, promotes research into issues raised by Christian Initiation (including outreach to the inactive through a process of Re-Membering Church), and provides a newsletter which focuses on the impact of Christian Initiation on the Church as well as key issues related to its implementation.

Worldwide Marriage Encounter (1969)—

National Office, 2210 E. Highland Ave., Ste. 106, San Bernardino, CA 92404. Tel: 909-863-9963; Fax: 909-863-9986. Secretariat Team: Rev. Mark Willenbring; Bob Tabone; Huli Tabone

Organized to foster a program of Christian information to instruct married couples in the means to find God's plan and matrimony in their lives, for their own spiritual development and the betterment of all humankind; and to develop, foster and disseminate an adult catechesis supporting, furthering and building upon such instruction. Worldwide Marriage Encounter offers the marriage encounter weekend experience in 150 dioceses in the United States as well as in 88 foreign countries. In the United States over 1,500,000 couples and over 5,000 priests and bishops have experienced the Worldwide weekend.

Publication: quarterly; Matrimony - A Sign of Our Church.

MISCELLANEOUS

Catholic Committee for Refugees & Children—

3211 Fourth St. N.E., Washington, DC 20017-1194. Fax: 202-722-8755. Mr. Mark Franken, Pres.

In operation since January 4, 1937, and incorporated since 1954, the Catholic Committee for Refugees and Children was founded to counsel and cooperate with European refugees during and after World War II. Since that time its mission has been expanded to include service to refugees worldwide. It has a special mandate from the bishops concerning its work with children through international child welfare, child care or placement, and international adoption. The USCCB Committee on Migration serves as the Board of Directors for CCRC.

Victim Assistance Coordinators

Alabama

Archdiocese of Mobile—Rev. James J. Cink Dir., P.O. Box 230 Mobile, AL 36601. Tel: 251-432-2737; 800-856-4184. E-mail: childprotection@bellsouth.net.

Diocese of Birmingham—Al Manzella. Tel: 205-776-7130. E-mail: amanzella@bhmdiocese.org.

Alaska

Archdiocese of Anchorage—Sr. Barbara Scanlon, C.S.J. Tel: 907-276-3455. E-mail: scanlonba@juno.com.

Diocese of Fairbanks—Coleen Turner, Exec. Dir. Tel: 907-456-2866, Ext. 107; 800-969-7272. E-mail: cturner@rcpcfairbanks.org.

Diocese of Juneau—Roberta Izzard. Tel: 907-586-2227, Ext. 25. E-mail: robbiei@gci.net.

Arizona

Diocese of Phoenix—Jennifer O'Connor. Tel: 602-354-2396. E-mail: joconnor@diocesephoenix.org

Diocese of Tucson—Paul N. Duckro, Ph.D. Tel: 520-792-3410. E-mail: pauld@diocesetucson.org.

Byzantine Eparchy of Van Nuys—Rosemarie Ludwig, Ph.D. Tel: 602-997-1550. E-mail: rlstussy@hotmail.com. Helen Vogel. E-mail: cath7@sbcglobal.net.

Arkansas

Diocese of Little Rock—Dr. Carol Siemon. Tel: 501-664-0340. E-mail: csiemon@aristotle.net.

California

Archdiocese of Los Angeles—Sr. Sheila McNiff. Tel: 213-637-7650; 800-355-2545. E-mail: srsmcniff@la-archdiocese.org.

Archdiocese of San Francisco—Barbara Elordi. Tel: 415-614-5506; Fax: 415-614-5658. E-mail: belordi@ccasf.org.

Diocese of Fresno—Rev. Msgr. Myron J. Cotta, V.G. Tel: 559-488-7400. E-mail: msgrmyron@dioceseoffresno.org; Mr. Pat Gordon, Human Resource Dir. E-mail: pat@dioceseoffresno.org.

Diocese of Monterey—Martina O'Sullivan. Tel: 831-373-4345, Ext. 285. E-mail: MOSullivan@dioceseofmonterey.org.

Diocese of Oakland—Sr. Barbara Flannery, C.S.J. Tel: 510-267-8334. E-mail: bflannery@oakdiocese.org.

Diocese of Orange in California—Diane Gomez-Valenzuela. Tel: 714-293-9050. E-mail: dgomezval@cs.com.

Diocese of Sacramento—Nancy J. Milton. Tel: 916-733-0227. E-mail: nmilton@diocese-sacramento.org.

Diocese of San Bernardino—Sr. Rosaline O'Connor, R.S.M. Tel: 909-855-2296. E-mail: roconnor@sbdiocese.org.

Diocese of San Diego—Adlin De Cardi. Tel: 858-571-8317. E-mail: adecardi@yahoo.com.

Diocese of San Jose in California—Bernard Nojadera. Tel: 408-983-0113. E-mail: nojadera@dsj.org.

Diocese of Stockton—Sr. Barbara Thiella, S.N.Den. Tel: 209-466-0636. E-mail: bthiella@stocktondiocese.org.

Eparchy of St. Peter the Apostle (Chaldean)—Rt. Rev. Sabri A. Kejbo. Tel: 619-444-9911. E-mail: st.michaels@cox.net.

Colorado

Archdiocese of Denver—Nancy A. Walla. Tel: 303-715-3226. E-mail: nancy.walla@archden.org.

Diocese of Colorado Springs—Barbara Mahoney. Tel: 719-633-8182.

Diocese of Pueblo—Mrs. Jane Mazur, M.S., M.S.W. Tel: 719-544-4233. E-mail: jmazur@pueblocharities.org.

Connecticut

Diocese of Bridgeport—Ms. Linda Michaud, L.C.S.W., 238 Jewett Ave. Bridgeport, CT 06606. Tel: 203-650-3265. E-mail: lam472@cs.com.

Diocese of Norwich—Ms. Sheree Antoch. Tel: 800-844-5669.

Delaware

Diocese of Wilmington—Mary Elizabeth "Beth" Krieger. Tel: 302-655-9624. E-mail: bkrieger@ccwilm.org.

District of Columbia

Archdiocese of Washington—Marcia D. Zvara. Tel: 301-853-5328. E-mail: mzvara@adw.org.

Florida

Archdiocese of Miami—Vicki Kaufmann, M.A., M.P.S.T. Tel: 866-802-2873. E-mail: vkaufmann@catholiccharitiesadm.org.

Diocese of Orlando—Sr. Lucy Vazquez. Tel: 407-246-4826. E-mail: slvafj@aol.com.

Diocese of Palm Beach—Ms. Theresa Fretterd. Tel: 561-801-0999. E-mail: tfretterd@cardinalnewman.com.

Diocese of Pensacola-Tallahassee—Dr. James Gagnon, M.S.W., L.C.S.W. Tel: 850-877-0205. Ms. Danielle Malone, L.M.H.L. Tel: 850-438-3131, Ext. 17. E-mail: maloned@ptdiocese.org.

Diocese of St. Augustine—Judy Pinson. Tel: 904-262-3200. E-mail: jpinson@dosafl.com.

Diocese of St. Petersburg—Ms. Marti Zeitz, M.A., 1213 16th St. N., St. Petersburg, FL 33705. Tel: 866-407-4505. E-mail: mzeitz@ccdosp.org.

Diocese of Venice—Mrs. Beverly Zeiss, R.N., D.Min. Tel: 941-416-6114.

Georgia

Archdiocese of Atlanta—Ann Price. Tel: 404-885-7459. E-mail: aprice@archatl.com; Kathi Stearns, Vice Chancellor. Tel: 404-885-7445. E-mail: kstearns@archatl.com.

Diocese of Savannah—Rosemary Downing. Tel: 912-356-2112; 912-921-6121.

Idaho

Diocese of Boise—Bobbi K. Dominick, J.D., S.P.H.R. Tel: 208-342-1311, Ext. 137. E-mail: bdominick@rcdb.org.

Illinois

Archdiocese of Chicago—Ralph Bonaccorsi. Tel: 312-751-8267; Fax: 312-751-8307. E-mail: rbonaccorsi@archchicago.org.

Diocese of Belleville—Lynn Muscarello. Tel: 618-277-8181. E-mail: lmuscarello@diobelle.org.

Diocese of Joliet in Illinois—Sr. Mary Frances Seeley, O.S.F. Tel: 815-263-6467.

Diocese of Rockford—Mr. Dick Kunnert. Tel: 815-962-9347. E-mail: chancery99@aol.com.

Diocese of Springfield in Illinois—Ms. Patricia Kornfeld. Tel: 217-698-8500. E-mail: pkornfeld@dio.org.

St.Thomas Syro-Malabar Catholic Diocese of Chicago—Dr. Paul Cherian. Tel: 01144-158-2415517; 630-769-9603. E-mail: pcherian14@hotmail.com.

Indiana

Archdiocese of Indianapolis—Suzanne L. Yakimchick. Tel: 800-382-9836, Ext. 7325; 317-236-7325.

Diocese of Evansville—Martha Halterman. Tel: 812-423-5456. E-mail: mhalterman@evansville-diocese.org.

Diocese of Fort Wayne - South Bend—Rev. Robert C. Schulte, Vicar Gen. & Chancellor. Tel: 260-422-4611. E-mail: mraatz@fw.diocesefwsb.org.

Diocese of Gary—Marcella Walters, 6919 Indianapolis Blvd., Hammond, IN 46324. Tel: 219-844-4883. E-mail: kflanagan@catholiccharities.org.

Diocese of Lafayette in Indiana—David Wilson, M.S.W. Tel: 800-533-7018. E-mail: drwilson@iquest.net.

Iowa

Archdiocese of Dubuque—Dr. Thomas Anderegg. Tel: 563-556-1225; Joan Hoffmann. Tel: 866-319-4636; Maureen Oates. Tel: 800-803-6758.

Diocese of Davenport—Thomas Crowley, P.O. Box 232, Bettendorf, IA 52722-0004. Tel: 563-349-5002. E-mail: vacdav@attglobal.net.

Diocese of Des Moines—Jo Mulvihill. Tel: 515-286-2031. E-mail: advocate@dmdiocese.org.

Diocese of Sioux City—Angie Mack. Tel: 712-279-5610; 866-435-4397. E-mail: macka@mercyhealth.com.

Kansas

Archdiocese of Kansas City in Kansas—Mr. Dan W. Pope, Ed.D. Tel: 913-681-1863. E-mail: dm@sprintmail.com.

Diocese of Dodge City—Mrs. Donna Staab, M.S.N., R.N., B.C. Tel: 620-793-1960. E-mail: donna@cpcis.net.

Diocese of Salina—Anne Kresin. Tel: 785-827-5024. E-mail: reportabuse@salinadiocese.org.

Diocese of Wichita—Katherine J. Lambertz. Tel: 316-264-8344, Ext. 230. E-mail: klambertz@wkscatholiccharities.org.

Kentucky

Archdiocese of Louisville—Brenda Marshall, M.S.S.W., L.C.S.W., L.F.M.T.; Tom Robbins, Ph.D., L.F.M.T. Tel: 502-636-1044. E-mail: family@archlou.org; trobbins@archlou.org.

Diocese of Covington—Ms. Margaret M. Schack. Tel: 859-283-6215. E-mail: mschack@covingtondiocese.org

Diocese of Lexington—Sr. Frances E. Moore, O.P. Tel: 859-253-1993, Ext. 215. E-mail: fmoore@cdlex.org.

Diocese of Owensboro—Rita Heinz. Tel: 270-683-1545. E-mail: heinzr@pastoral.org.

Louisiana

Archdiocese of New Orleans—Sr. Carmelita Centanni, Ph.D., 7887 Walmsley Ave., New Orleans, LA 70125-3496. Tel: 504-861-6253; Fax: 504-866-2906. E-mail: srcarmelita@archdiocese-no.org.

Diocese of Alexandria—Ms. Mary Girard. Tel: 318-449-8571.

Diocese of Baton Rouge—Rev. David E. Allen. Tel: 225-242-0250. E-mail: dallen@diobr.org.

Diocese of Houma-Thibodaux—Sr. Miriam Mitchell, S.H.Sp. Tel: 985-850-3122. E-mail: mmitchell@htdiocese.org.

Diocese of Lafayette—Ms. Carmer Falgout, R.N., M.S.W., L.C.S.W., B.C.D, 100 Coulee Shore Dr., Lafayette, LA 70503. Tel: 337-235-5749.

Diocese of Shreveport—Ann Inabnet. Tel: 318-221-6121.

Maine

Diocese of Portland (In Maine)—Sr. Rita-Mae Bissonnette, J.C.L. Tel: 207-773-6471. E-mail: rbissonnette@portlanddiocese.net.

Maryland

Archdiocese of Baltimore—Judy Dobson, L.C.S.W. Tel: 410-547-5446. E-mail: jdobson@archbalt.org.

Massachusetts

Archdiocese of Boston—Barbara Thorp. Tel: 617-244-9603. E-mail: barbara_thorp@pastoralsupportandoutreach.com.

Diocese of Fall River—Arlene A. McNamee, L.C.S.W. Tel: 508-674-4681. E-mail: aam@cssdioc.org.

Diocese of Newton (Melkite-Greek Catholic)—Rt. Rev. Andre. Tel: 603-674-4049. E-mail: abounaandre@msn.com.

Diocese of Springfield in Massachusetts—Laura F. Reilly. Tel: 413-452-0624. E-mail: l.reilly@diospringfield.org.

Diocese of Worcester—Frances J. Nugent. Tel: 508-929-4363. E-mail: fnugent@worcesterdiocese.org.

Michigan

Archdiocese of Detroit—Sr. Beverly Hindson, I.H.M. Tel: 866-343-8055.

Diocese of Gaylord—Candace Neff. Tel: 989-732-5147. E-mail: cneff@dioceseofgaylord.org.

Diocese of Grand Rapids—Edgar R. Donatelli. Tel: 616-942-8396.

Diocese of Kalamazoo—Mr. T. Edward Carey, Jr. Tel: 269-349-8714, Ext. 116. E-mail: edcarey@dioceseofkalamazoo.org.

Diocese of Lansing—Rev. Msgr. Michael D. Murphy. Tel: 517-342-2450. E-mail: mmurph@dioceseoflansing.org; Rev. Msgr. Robert D. Lunsford. Tel: 517-342-2454. E-mail: rlunsf&dioceseoflansing.org.

Diocese of Marquette—Rosalyn Groves, Coord., 623 Ludington St., Ste. 200, Escanaba, MI 49829. Tel: 906-233-9306. E-mail: regroves@uplogon.com.

Diocese of Saginaw—Sr. Janet Fulgenzi. Tel: 989-797-6682. E-mail: janet@dioceseofsaginaw.org.

Minnesota

Archdiocese of St. Paul and Minneapolis—Phyllis A. Willerscheidt. Tel: 651-291-4497. E-mail: willerscheidtp@archspm.org.

Diocese of Crookston—Bernadette Dunn. Tel: 218-281-4533. E-mail: bdunn@crookston.org.

Diocese of Duluth—Esther Reagan. Tel: 218-820-9220.

Diocese of New Ulm—Christopher A. Loetscher. Tel: 507-359-2966, Ext. 338. E-mail: cloetscher@dnu.org.

Diocese of St. Cloud—Maxine Barnett. Tel: 320-253-6900. E-mail: maxine@annamaries.org.

Diocese of Winona—Mrs. P. J. Thompson. Tel: 507-454-4643, Ext. 223. E-mail: pjthompson@dow.org.

Mississippi

Diocese of Biloxi—Sr. Mary Riordan, R.S.M. Tel: 228-896-6302. E-mail: maryrb@worldnetatt.net.

Diocese of Jackson—Linda Raff. Tel: 601-355-8634. E-mail: linda.raff@catholiccharitiesjackson.org.

Missouri

Archdiocese of St. Louis—Nancy Brown, Ph.D. Tel: 314-633-2279. E-mail: nancybrown@archstl.org.

Diocese of Jefferson City—Sr. Ethel-Marie Biri, S.S.N.D. Tel: 573-635-9127, Ext. 201. E-mail: chancellor@diojeffcity.org.

Diocese of Kansas City-St. Joseph—Sr. Jeanne Christensen, R.S.M. Tel: 816-756-1850, Ext. 534. E-mail: christensen@diocesekcsj.org.

Diocese of Springfield-Cape Girardeau—Kathleen Griesemer, Psy.D. Tel: 417-848-4601. E-mail: kpoirotg@aol.com.

Eparchy of Our Lady of Lebanon—Deacon Philip R. Hengen. Tel: 636-391-6837. E-mail: harvath@kennrick.edu.

Montana

Diocese of Great Falls – Billings—Sr. Kathleen Kane, O.P. Tel: 406-378-2369. E-mail: kkop@ttc-cmc.net.

Diocese of Helena—Kevin Phelan. Tel: 406-442-5820. E-mail: kphelan@diocesehelena.org.

Nebraska

Archdiocese of Omaha—Tel: 402-558-3100.

Diocese of Grand Island—Aileen D. Gruendel, Ph.D. Tel: 308-382-2233. E-mail: gruendel@hamilton.net.

Diocese of Lincoln—Rev. Mark D. Huber, J.C.L. Tel: 402-488-0921.

Nevada

Diocese of Las Vegas—Joanne Garramone-Halt. Tel: 702-360-1027. E-mail: garramonehalt@aol.com.

Diocese of Reno—Patricia R. Williams. Tel: 775-851-4020. E-mail: wmsfamrno@earthlink.net.

New Hampshire

Diocese of Manchester—Joseph P. Naff, L.I.C.S.W. Tel: 603-668-0014. Tel: 800-475-5585. E-mail: jnaff@catholiccharitiesnh.org

New Jersey

Archdiocese of Newark—Ms. Sheri A. Rickert, Esq. Tel: 973-497-4009. E-mail: rickersh@rcan.org.

Diocese of Camden—Barbara Ann Gondek, L.C.S.W. Tel: 856-524-4552.

Diocese of Metuchen—Sr. Elizabeth O'Hara, R.S.M. Tel: 908-722-1881. E-mail: eohara@ccdom.org.

Diocese of Paterson—Ms. Peggy Zanello. Tel: 973-879-1489.

Diocese of Trenton—Rev. Msgr. Gregory D. Vaughan, V.G. Tel: 609-406-7400. E-mail: gvaugh@dioceseoftrenton.org.

New Mexico

Archdiocese of Santa Fe—Sr. Nancy Kazik, O.S.F. Tel: 505-831-8188. E-mail: nk@archdiocesesantafe.org.

Diocese of Gallup—Sr. Mary Thurllough. Tel: 505-722-4406.

Diocese of Las Cruces—Elizabeth A. Ennis. Tel: 505-523-7577. E-mail: eennis@dioceseoflascruces.org.

New York

Archdiocese of New York—Rev. Msgr. Desmond O'Connor. Tel: 212-371-1000, Ext. 2931. E-mail: victimsassistance@archny.org; Sr. Eileen Clifford. Tel: 212-371-1000, Ext. 2949.

Diocese of Albany—Ms. Terry Rodrigues. Tel: 518-453-6646. E-mail: RodriguT@rcda.org.

Diocese of Brooklyn—Sr. Ellen Patricia Finn, O.P. Tel: 718-722-6050. E-mail: srepfinn@ccbq.org.

Diocese of Buffalo—Kathryn Marsh. Tel: 716-895-3010. E-mail: kathy.march@ccwny.org.

Diocese of Rochester—Mrs. Barbara Pedeville. Tel: 585-328-3228, Ext. 1215. E-mail: pedeville@dor.org; Rev. Robert P. Ring. Tel: 315-730-0882. E-mail: ring@dor.org.

Diocese of Rockville Centre—Eileen Puglisi. Tel: 516-678-5800, Ext. 573. E-mail: epuglisi@drvc.org.

Diocese of Syracuse—Teresa Secreti, P.O. Box 511, Syracuse, NY 13201-0511. Tel: 315-470-1465; Fax: 315-478-4619. E-mail: tsecreti@broadviewnet.net.

Eparchy of St. Maron of Brooklyn—Rosanne Solomon. Tel: 781-828-5183. E-mail: rosannesolomon@hotmail.com.

North Carolina

Diocese of Charlotte—David W. Harold. Tel: 336-714-3202. E-mail: dwharold@charlottediocese.org; Michelle Sheppard. Tel: 828-255-0146. E-mail: mmsheppard@charlottediocese.org; Nancy M. Campbell. Tel: 704-370-3217.

Diocese of Raleigh—John Pendergrass, Dir. Program for Child & Youth Protection. Tel: 866-535-7233; 919-821-8157. E-mail: safe@raldioc.org; Kathleen Walsh, A.C.S.W. Tel: 919-821-9752. E-mail: walsh@raldioc.org.

North Dakota

Diocese of Bismarck—Deacon Joel Melarvie. Tel: 701-223-1347. E-mail: jmelarvie@bismarckdiocese.com.

Ohio

Archdiocese of Cincinnati—Rev. Joseph R. Binzer. Tel: 513-421-3131, Ext. 401. E-mail: jbinzer@catholiccincinnati.org.

Diocese of Cleveland—Sr. Laura Bouhall. Tel: 216-696-6525, Ext. 2060. E-mail: lbouhall@dioceseofcleveland.org.

Diocese of Columbus—Rev. Msgr. Stephan J. Moloney, M.A., M.Div., J.C.L. Tel: 614-224-2251. E-mail: smoloney@colsdioc.org.

Diocese of Steubenville—Dr. Theresa Peach, Ph.D., 407 Tonawanda Tr., Hartville, OH 44632. Tel: 330-877-2766; Dan Obertance, 500 Market St., Steubenville, OH 43952. Tel: 740-282-1300; Roseann Braniff, 827 N. Fourth St., Steubenville, OH 43952. Tel: 740-282-3631; Chad Sokolowski, 102 Park Dr., St. Clairsville, OH 43950. Tel: 740-695-3500 (work); Dr. Susan Apple, Ph.D., 3 W. Stimson Ave., Athens, OH 45701. Tel: 740-592-2103; Dr. Jim Hayes, Ph.D., 90 Hospital Dr., Athens, OH 45701. Tel: 740-592-3091; Elizabeth Brislen, 1041 Gomber Ave., Cambridge, OH. Tel: 740-282-3631; Jane Engott, 575 Harding Rd., Zanesville, OH 43701. Tel: 740-432-2611; Patty Johnson, 111 N. 7th St., Cambridge OH 43725. Tel: 740-439-4532; Angela Miracle, 108 Riley Dr., Apt. 5, Marietta, OH 45750. Tel: 740-376-6882; Dr. Elizabeth Evans, Ph.D., 160 Twp. Rd. 1273, Chesapeake, OH 45619-3565. Tel: 740-867-6123; Victoria Neighborgall, 912 S. Sixth St., Ironton, OH 45638. Tel: 740-532-1485.

Diocese of Toledo—Mr. Frank DiLallo, M.Ed., L.P.C. Tel: 419-243-2150. E-mail: fdilallo@toledodiocese.org.

Diocese of Youngstown—Nancy Yuhasz. Tel: 330-744-8451. E-mail: nyuhasz@youngstowndiocese.org.

Byzantine Eparchy of Parma—Sharon DiLauro, M.D. Tel: 330-659-3195. E-mail: jpetrus@adelphia.net.

Romanian Catholic Diocese of Saint George's in Canton—Carol Ann Gall. Tel: 216-444-4095. E-mail: gallc@ccf.org

Ukrainian Catholic Diocese of St. Josaphat in Parma—Kristin Ligus. Tel: 330-273-8244. E-mail: liguskrm@notes.udayton.edu.

Oklahoma

Archdiocese of Oklahoma City—Mrs. Caroline Linehan, P.O. Box 32180, Oklahoma City, OK 73123. Tel: 405-721-5651, Ext. 150. E-mail: clinehan@catharchdioceseokc.org.

Diocese of Tulsa—Mr. Quentin Henley. Tel: 918-585-8167.

Oregon

Archdiocese of Portland in Oregon—Cathy Shannon. Tel: 503-416-8810. E-mail: cshannon@archdpdx.org.

Diocese of Baker—Eve McFarland. Tel: 541-385-0557.

Pennsylvania

Archdiocese of Philadelphia—Martin R. Frick, L.S.W., M.P.A.; Karen Becker. Tel: 215-587-2485; 215-587-3590.

Diocese of Allentown—Mrs. Barbara W. Murphy, M.S.W. Tel: 610-791 3888; Fax: 610-791-1878. E-mail: bmurphy@allentowndiocese.org.

Diocese of Altoona-Johnstown—Sr. Marilyn Welch, C.C.W. Tel: 814-886-8250. E-mail: srmarilyn@dioceseaj.org.

Diocese of Erie—Dr. Robert Nelsen. Tel: 814-871-7723. E-mail: nelsen001@gannon.edu.

Diocese of Greensburg—Rev. Roger A. Statnick, V.G., S.T.L., Ph.D. Tel: 724-837-0901. E-mail: rstatnick@dioceseofgreensburg.org

Diocese of Harrisburg—Tom Thorpe. Tel: 717-657-4804. E-mail: tthorpe@hbgdiocese.org.

Diocese of Pittsburgh—Mrs. Rita E. Flaherty, M.S.W. Tel: 412-456-3060. E-mail: rflaherty@diopitt.org.

Diocese of Scranton—Joan L. Holmes. Tel: 570-344-5216. E-mail: jloueliz@aol.com.

Metropolitan Archdiocese of Philadelphia Ukrainian—Sr. Natalya Stoczanyn, S.S.M.I. Tel: 215-873-6162. E-mail: srnatalya@catholic.org.

Metropolitan Archeparchy of Pittsburgh, Byzantine—Sr. Seraphim, M.S.W. Tel: 412-322-8307. E-mail: sseraphim@aol.com.

Rhode Island

Diocese of Providence—Mr. Michael Hansen. Tel: 401-946-0728; Fax: 401-946-1587. E-mail: mhansen@dioceseofprovidence.org.

South Carolina

Diocese of Charleston—Deacon Alfred C. Payne. Tel: 843-853-2130. E-mail: al@catholic-doc.org.

South Dakota

Diocese of Rapid City—Maryann Tully. Tel: 605-209-3418. E-mail: fredoldford@cs.com.

Diocese of Sioux Falls—Sr. Mary Carole Curran, Ph.D. Tel: 605-988-3775. E-mail: mcurran@sfcatholic.org.

Tennessee

Diocese of Knoxville—Marla Lenihan. Tel: 865-482-1388.

Diocese of Memphis—Mr. Ron Ambuehl. Tel: 901-276-9002.

Diocese of Nashville—Deacon Hans M. Toecker, 2400 21st Ave., S. Nashville, TN 37212. Tel: 615-783-0765; Fax: 615-292-8411. E-mail: hans.toecker@dioceseofnashville.com.

Texas

Archdiocese of San Antonio—Judy Anderson Perillo, M.A., S.W.A., St. Paul Community Center, 1202 Donaldson, San Antonio, TX 78228. Tel: 210-734-7786. E-mail: jperillo@archdiosa.org.

Diocese of Amarillo—Belinda Taylor Gonzalez, P.O. Box 5644, Amarillo, TX 79107. Tel: 806-372-7960; 806-383-2243; Fax: 806-383-8452.

Diocese of Austin—Patricia Stankus. Tel: 512-476-4888. E-mail: pat-stankus@austindiocese.org.

Diocese of Beaumont—Bro. Bernard Palmeri, C.S.C., L.P. Tel: 409-347-1316. E-mail: bpalmeri@aol.com.

Diocese of Brownsville—Mr. Walter Lukaszek, L.M.S.W. Tel: 956-781-5323. E-mail: wlukaszek@cdob.org.

Diocese of Corpus Christi—Grace S. Rank, R.N., B.S.N. Tel: 361-882-6191, Ext. 388. E-mail: grank@diocesecc.org.

Diocese of Dallas—Mary E. Edlund. Tel: 214-528-2240. E-mail: medlund@cathdal.org.

Diocese of El Paso—Mrs. Susan Martinez. Tel: 915-872-8407. E-mail: susanm@elpasodiocese.org.

Diocese of Fort Worth—Ms. Judy Locke. Tel: 817-560-3300, Ext. 201. E-mail: jlocke@fwdioc.org.

Diocese of Galveston-Houston—Sr. Maureen O'Connell, O.P. Tel: 713-659-5461, Ext. 499. E-mail: moconnell@diogh.org.

Diocese of Laredo—Bro. John A. Allen, F.M.S. Tel: 956-727-2140. E-mail: chancellor@dioceseoflaredo.org.

Diocese of Lubbock—Mrs. Charlotte Amato. Tel: 806-792-6168. E-mail: camato@ctkcathedral.org.

Diocese of San Angelo—Mr. Michael Wyse. Tel: 325-651-7500.

Diocese of Tyler—Rev. Gavin N. Vaverek, J.C.L. Tel: 903-266-2159. E-mail: promoter@dioceseoftyler.org.

Diocese of Victoria in Texas—Rev. Gary Janak, J.C.L. Tel: 979-543-3770. E-mail: apostle@sephilipapostle.org.

Utah

Diocese of Salt Lake City—Monica Howa-Johnson. Tel: 801-328-8641, Ext. 344. E-mail: monica.howa-johnson@dioslc.org.

Vermont

Diocese of Burlington—Tel: 802-658-6110. Mary McNamara. E-mail: mmcnamara@vermontcatholic.org; Sr. Susan Fortier, R.S.M. E-mail: sfortier@vermontcatholic.org; Ellie Calabrese. E-mail: ecalabrese@vermontcatholic.org; Rev. Wendell Searles. E-mail: wsearles@vermontcatholic.org.

Virginia

Diocese of Arlington—Catherine M. Nolan, M.S.W., A.C.S.W., 200 N. Glebe Rd., Ste. 914, Arlington, VA 22203. Tel: 703-841-2530. E-mail: c.nolan@arlingtondiocese.org.

Diocese of Richmond—Rev. Pasquale J. Apuzzo. Tel: 804-359-5661. E-mail: papuzzo@richmonddiocese.org.

Washington

Archdiocese of Seattle—Jessie Clayton Dye, J.D. Tel: 800-446-7762. E-mail: hotline@seattlearch.org.

Diocese of Spokane—Mrs. Mary Butler. Tel: 509-353-0442. E-mail: mbutler@dioceseofspokane.org.

Diocese of Yakima—Linda Bernard. Tel: 509-965-7100. E-mail: lbernard@cfcsyakima.org; Susan M. Romzek. Tel: 509-965-7100. E-mail: sromzek@cfcsyakima.org.

West Virginia

Diocese of Wheeling-Charleston—Very Rev. John R. Gallagher, V.G. Tel: 304-233-0880. E-mail: jgallagher@dwc.org.

Wisconsin

Archdiocese of Milwaukee—Barbara Reinke, Ph.D. Tel: 414-769-3436. E-mail: reinkeb@archmil.org.

Diocese of Green Bay—Sr. Mary Bride Grubbs. Tel: 920-437-7531, Ext. 8174. E-mail: mgrubbs@gbdioc.org.

Diocese of La Crosse—Daniel Lynch. Tel: 715-832-6644.

Diocese of Superior—Barbara Dickenson, M.S.W. Tel: 715-398-7765. E-mail: tgd56@aol.com.

Wyoming

Diocese of Cheyenne—Deacon Rolland Raboin. Tel: 307-532-8296. E-mail: rraboin@ewc.wy.edu.

National Association of State Catholic Conference Directors

An Association of the Directors of the State Catholic Conferences, organized in 1968 to facilitate and encourage the exchange of information among its members pertaining to the activities, programs and organization of the Conferences. A State Catholic Conference is a Church agency composed of the dioceses within a state to provide for the coordination of the public policy concerns of the Church. Thus a Conference of the Church communicates with state government, other Church Agencies, non-Catholic churches and secular agencies. Bishops, priests, religious and lay persons are involved in the work of the State Conferences. National Association: NCCB-USCC, 3211 4th St., N.E., Washington, DC 20017-1194.

ALASKA

Alaska Catholic Conference, 225 Cordova, Anchorage, AK 99501. Tel: 907-297-7738; Fax: 907-297-3885.
Contact Person: Mr. Robert Flint

ARIZONA

Arizona Catholic Conference, 400 E. Monroe St., Phoenix, AZ 85004-2336. Tel: 602-354-2391; Fax: 602-354-2466.
Chairman: Bishop Gerald Kicanas
Executive Director: Ron Johnson

CALIFORNIA

California Catholic Conference, 1119 K St.-2nd Fl., Sacramento, CA 95814. Tel: 916-443-4851; Fax: 916-443-5629. E-mail: conference@ca catholic.org. Web site: cacatholic.org.
President: Bishop Sylvester D. Ryan
Vice President: Bishop William K. Weigand
Secretary-Treasurer: Bishop Stephen Blaire
Executive Director: Mr. Edward E. Dolejsi

COLORADO

Colorado Catholic Conference, 1535 Logan St., Denver, CO 80203. Tel: 303-894-8808; Fax: 303-894-7939. E-mail: ccc@cocatholicconference.org.

CONNECTICUT

Connecticut Catholic Conference, 134 Farmington Ave., Hartford, CT 06105. Tel: 860-524-7882; Fax: 860-525-0750. E-mail: ccc@ctcatholic.org.
President and Chairman of the Board: Archbishop Daniel A. Cronin
Secretary: Bishop Michael R. Cote
Executive Director: Dr. Marie T. Hilliard, Ph.D., R.N.

FLORIDA

Florida Catholic Conference, 313 S. Calhoun St., Tallahassee, FL 32301. Tel: 850-222-3803; Fax: 850-681-9548.
President: Archbishop John Clement Favalora
Executive Director: D. Michael McCarron, Ph.D.

GEORGIA

Georgia Catholic Conference, Office Building, 3200 Deans Bridge Rd., Augusta, GA 30906. Tel: 706-798-1719; Fax: 706-798-6037.
President: Mr. Cheatham E. Hodges, Jr.
Executive Director: Mr. Francis J. Mulcahy, Esq.

HAWAII

Hawaii Catholic Conference, 1184 Bishop St., Honolulu, HI 96813-2858. Tel: 808-585-3341; 800-530-1790, Ext 341. Fax: 808-521-8428. Email: wyoshimitsu@rcc hawaii.org.
Program Director: Deacon Walter Yoshimitsu

ILLINOIS

Catholic Conference of Illinois, 65 East Wacker Place, Suite 1620, Chicago, IL 60601. Tel: 312-368-1066 and 108 E. Cook St., Springfield, IL 62701. Tel: 217-528-9200.
Chairman: His Eminence Francis Cardinal George, O.M.I.
Executive Director: Mr. Robert F. Gilligan
Associate Director: Zachary Wichmann
Associate Director: Marilou Gervacio

INDIANA

Indiana Catholic Conference, 1400 N. Meridian St., P.O. Box 1410, Indianapolis, IN 46206. Tel: 317-236-1455; Fax: 317-236-1456.
General Chairman: Archbishop Daniel M. Buechlein, O.S.B., D.D.
Executive Chairman: Bishop William L. Higi, D.D.
Executive Director: Dr. M. Desmond Ryan, Ph.D.

IOWA

Iowa Catholic Conference, 505 5th Ave., Ste. 818, Des Moines, IA 50309-2393. Tel: 515-243-6256; Fax: 515-243-6257; E-mail: iacathconf@aol.com.
President: Archbishop Jerome Hanus, O.S.B.
Vice President: Bishop William E. Franklin
Secretary-Treasurer: Bishop Joseph Charron, C.PP.S.
Executive Director: Dr. Thomas Feld
Assistant Director: Sara Deeny

KANSAS

Kansas Catholic Conference, 6301 Antioch, Merriam, KS 66202. Tel: 913-722-6633. Web site: www.kscath conf.org.
Chairman: Archbishop James P. Keleher, S.T.D.
Executive Director: Mr. Michael P. Farmer
Associate Director: Ms. Beatrice E. Swoopes

KENTUCKY

Catholic Conference of Kentucky,1042 Burlington Ln., Frankfort, KY 40601. Tel: 502-875-4345; Fax: 502-875-2841.
Chairman: Archbishop Thomas C. Kelly, O.P.
Executive Director: Mrs. Jane J. Chiles

LOUISIANA

Louisiana Catholic Conference, 3423 Hundred Oaks Ave., Baton Rouge, LA 70808. Tel: 225-344-7120; Fax: 225-383-9591.
Chairman: Archbishop Alfred C. Hughes
Executive Director: Mr. Daniel J. Loar
Assistant Director for Administrative Services: Mrs. Barbara Bovard

MARYLAND

Maryland Catholic Conference, 188 Duke of Gloucester St., Annapolis, MD 21401-2515. Tel: 410-269-1155; Fax: 410-269-1790.
Chairman: His Eminence William Cardinal Keeler
Executive Director: Richard J. Dowling, Esq.

MASSACHUSETTS

Massachusetts Catholic Conference, 150 Staniford St.-W. End Pl., Ste. 5, Boston, MA 02114. Tel: 617-367-6060.
Executive Director: Mr. Gerald D. D'Avolio

MICHIGAN

Michigan Catholic Conference, 510 S. Capitol Ave., Lansing, MI 48933. Tel: 517-372-9310; Fax: 517-372-3940.
Chairman: His Eminence Adam Cardinal Maida
Vice Chairman: Bishop Robert J. Rose
President & CEO: Sr. Monica Kostielney, R.S.M.
Secretary-Treasurer: Bishop Patrick R. Cooney

MINNESOTA

Minnesota Catholic Conference, 475 University Ave., W., Ste. B, St. Paul, MN 55103-1959. Tel: 651-227-8777; Fax: 651-227-2675.
President: Archbishop Harry J. Flynn
Secretary / Treasurer: Bishop Frederick Campbell
Executive Director: Mr. Christopher Leifeld
Education Department Director: Dr. Peter Noll
Social Concerns Dept. Director: Ms. Kate Krisik

MISSOURI

Missouri Catholic Conference, 600 Clark Ave., P.O. Box 1022, Jefferson City, MO 65102. Tel: 573-635-7239; Fax: 573-635-7431.
General Chairman: Archbishop Raymond Burke
Executive Chairman: Bishop John R. Gaydos
General Counsel Executive Director: Deacon Lawrence A. Weber
Assistant Director: Mike Hoey
Administrative Assistant: Josetta M. Forck

MONTANA

Montana Catholic Conference, P.O. Box 1708, Helena, MT 59624. Tel: 406-442-5761; Fax: 406-442-9047. E-mail: mcc@mt.net. Web site: www.mt.net/~mcc.
President: Sr. Mary Jo McDonald, S.C.L.
Vice President: Mr. Kim Larsen
Treasurer: Sr. Lillian Maguire, S.C.L.
Executive Director: Lani Kobelia Candelora

NEBRASKA

Nebraska Catholic Conference, 215 Centennial Mall South, Ste. 410, Lincoln, NE 68508-1890. Tel: 402-477-7517.
President: Archbishop Elden Francis Curtiss
Director: Bishop Fabian W. Bruskewitz
Director: Bishop Lawrence J. McNamara
Executive Director: James R. Cunningham

NEVADA

Nevada Catholic Conference, 290 South Arlington Ave., Ste. 200, Reno, NV 89501-1713. Tel: 775-322-7412; Fax: 775-322-1838.
Executive Director: Judge Robert Payant

NEW JERSEY

New Jersey Catholic Conference, 211 N. Warren St., Trenton, NJ 08618. Tel: 609-599-2110.
President: Archbishop John J. Myers
Executive Director: William F. Bolan, Jr. , J.D.

NEW YORK

New York State Catholic Conference, 465 State St., Albany, NY 12203. Tel: 518-434-6195.
President: His Eminence Edward Cardinal Egan
Vice President: Vacant
Secretary- Treasurer: Bishop William F. Murphy
Chairman-Public Policy Committee: Bishop Howard J. Hubbard
Executive Director: Richard E. Barnes

NORTH DAKOTA

North Dakota Catholic Conference, 227 W. Broadway, Ste. 2, Bismarck, ND 58501. Tel: 701-223-2519; Fax: 701-223-6075.
President: Bishop Paul A. Zipfel
Vice-President: Bishop Samuel J. Aquila
Executive Director: Christopher T. Dodson

OHIO

Catholic Conference of Ohio, 9 East Long St., Suite 201, Columbus, OH 43215. Tel: 614-224-7147. E-mail: cco@cdeducation.org.
President: Archbishop Daniel E. Pilarczyk
Vice President: Bishop Anthony M. Pilla
Secretary-Treasurer: Bishop James A. Griffin
Executive Director: Timothy V. Luckhaupt

OREGON

Oregon Catholic Conference, 2838 E. Burnside St., Portland, OR 97214. Tel: 503-233-8387; Fax: 503-235-2630.
President: Archbishop John G. Vlazny
Vice President: Bishop Robert F. Vasa
Secretary-Treasurer: Rev. Dennis O'Donovan
General Counsel & Executive Director: Mr. Robert J. Castagna

PENNSYLVANIA

Pennsylvania Catholic Conference, 223 North St., P.O. Box 2835, Harrisburg, PA 17105. Tel: 717-238-9613; Fax: 717-238-1473.
Chairman: Archbishop Justin Rigali
President: Bishop Nicholas C. Dattilo
Vice President: Rev. Msgr. Joseph G. Quinn
Secretary: Bishop David A. Zubik
Executive Director: Dr. Robert J. O'Hara, Jr.
Treasurer: Rev. Msgr. Michael E. Servinsky

TEXAS

Texas Catholic Conference, 1625 Rutherford Ln., Bldg. D, Austin, TX 78754-5105. Tel: 512-339-9882.
Chairman: Archbishop Patrick F. Flores
Executive Director: Bro. Richard Daly, C.S.C.
Associate Director: Rev. Msgr. William L. Broussard
Associate Director for Education: Mr. George Solana
Director, Catholic Archives of Texas: Ms. Susan Eason.

WASHINGTON

Washington State Catholic Conference, 508 2nd Avenue West, Seattle, WA 98119. Tel: 206-301-0556; Fax: 206-301-0558.
President: Archbishop Alex J. Brunett, Ph.D.
Executive Director: Sr. Sharon Park, O.P.
Administrative Assistant: JoAnn St. Pierre

WEST VIRGINIA

West Virginia State Catholic Conference, 1300 Byron St., P.O. Box 230, Wheeling, WV 26003. Tel: 304-233-0880, Ext. 242; Fax: 304-233-4086.
Director: Very Rev. John R. Gallagher, V.G.

WISCONSIN

Wisconsin Catholic Conference, 131 W. Wilson St., Rm. 1105, Madison, WI 53703. Tel: 608-257-0004; Fax: 608-257-0376.
Chairman: Archbishop Timothy M. Dolan
Vice Chairman: Bishop Robert C. Morlino
Executive Director: John A. Huebscher
Associate Director Respect Life: Kathy M. Markeland
Associate Director Education: Barbara A. Sella

Alphabetical List of Places in the United States

This comprehensive list includes all cities and towns in the United States in which a Catholic Institution is located.

The abbreviations identify each city or town to the corresponding Diocese or Archdiocese.

Abbeville, LA	LAF
SC	CHR
Abbotsford, WI	LC
Abbott, TX	FWT
Abbottstown, PA	HBG
Aberdeen, ID	B
MD	BAL
MS	JKS
SD	SFS
WA	SEA
Abilene, KS	SAL
TX	SAN
Abingdon, IL	PEO
MD	BAL
VA	RIC
Abington, MA	BO
PA	PH
Abiquiu, NM	SFE
Abita Springs, LA	NO
Abrams, WI	GB
Absecon, NJ	CAM
Ackerman, MS	JKS
Ackley, IA	DUB
Acme, MI	GAY
Acoma, NM	GLP
Acosta, PA	ALT
Acton, MA	BO
Acushnet, MA	FR
Ada, MI	GR
MN	CR
OH	COL
OK	OKL
Adair, IA	DM
Adams, MA	SPR
MN	WIN
NY	OG
WI	LC
Adamstown, MD	BAL
Addison, IL	JOL
NY	ROC
Adel, IA	DM
Adelanto, CA	SB
Adell, WI	MIL
Adelphi, MD	WDC
Adena, OH	STU
Adjuntas, PR	PCE
Adona, AR	LR
Adrian, MI	LAN
MN	WIN
Advance, MO	SPC
Affton, MO	STL
Afton, IA	DM
MI	GAY
Agana, GU	AGN
Agana Heights, GU	AGN
Agat, GU	AGN
Agawam, MA	SPR
Agoura Hills, CA	LA
Agua Dulce, TX	CC
Aguada, PR	MGZ
Aguadilla, PR	MGZ
Aguas Buenas, PR	CGS
Aguilar, CO	PBL
Aguirre, PR	PCE
Ahmeek, MI	MAR
Ahoskie, NC	R
Aibonito, PR	CGS
Aiea, HI	HON
Aiken, SC	CHR
Ainsworth, NE	GI
Aitkin, MN	DUL
Ajo, AZ	TUC
Akeley, MN	CR
Akron, CO	DEN
IA	SC
NY	BUF
OH	CLV
OH	NTN
OH	PRM
OH	SJP
Alakanuk, AK	FBK
Alameda, CA	OAK
Alamo, TX	BWN
Alamogordo, NM	LSC
Alamosa, CO	PBL
Albany, GA	SAV
KY	L
LA	BR
MN	SCL
NY	ALB
OR	P
TX	FWT
WI	MAD
Albee, MI	SAG
Albemarle, NC	CHL
Albers, IL	BEL
Albert Lea, MN	WIN
Alberta, AL	MOB
Albertville, MN	STP
Albia, IA	DAV
Albion, IN	FTW
MI	KAL
NE	OM
NY	BUF
PA	E
Albuquerque, NM	SFE
NM	VNN
Alburg, VT	BUR
Alcoa, TN	KNX
Alden, NY	BUF
Alden Station, PA	PHU
Aledo, IL	PEO
TX	FWT
Aleppo, KS	WCH
Aleppo Township, PA	PIT
Alexander, IL	SFD
Alexander City, AL	BIR
Alexandria, IN	LFT
KY	COV
LA	ALX
MN	SCL
SD	SFS
VA	ARL
Alexandria Bay, NY	OG
Alexis, IL	PEO
Alfred, ME	PRT
NY	BUF
Algoma, WI	GB
Algona, IA	SC
Algonac, MI	DET
Algonquin, IL	RCK
Alhambra, CA	LA
Alhambra, Ponce, PR	PCE
Alice, ND	FAR
TX	CC
Aliquippa, PA	PBR
PA	PIT
PA	SJP
Aliso Viejo, CA	ORG
Allegan, MI	KAL
Allegany, NY	BUF
Allen, TX	DAL
Allen Park, MI	DET
MI	PRM
Allendale, NJ	NEW
Allenspark, CO	DEN
Allenstown, NH	MAN
Allenton, MI	DET
WI	MIL
Allentown, NJ	TR
PA	ALN
PA	PHU
PA	PSC
Alliance, NE	GI
OH	ROM
OH	Y
Allison, IA	DUB
Allison Park, PA	PIT
Alma, KS	KCK
MI	SAG
MN	CR
NE	LIN
WI	LC
Alma Center, WI	LC
Almena, WI	SUP
Almond, NY	BUF
WI	LC
Aloha, OR	P
Aloys, NE	OM
Alpena, MI	GAY
Alpha, MI	MAR
NJ	MET
Alpharetta, GA	ATL
Alpine, AZ	GLP
CA	SD
MI	GR
TX	ELP
Alsip, IL	CHI
Alta Loma, CA	SB
Alta Vista, IA	DUB
Altadena, CA	LA
Altamont, IL	SFD
NY	ALB
Altamonte Springs, FL	ORL
Altdorf, WI	LC
Alton, IA	SC
IL	SFD
NH	MAN
TX	BWN
Altona, NY	OG
Altoona, IA	DM
PA	ALT
PA	SJP
WI	LC
Altura, MN	WIN
Alturas, CA	SAC
Altus, AR	LR
OK	OKL
Alva, OK	OKL
Alvada, OH	TOL
Alverno, MI	GAY
WI	GB
Alvin, TX	GAL
Alviso, CA	SJ
Ama, LA	NO
Amargosa Valley, NV	LAV
Amarillo, TX	AMA
Amberg, WI	GB
Ambler, PA	PH
PA	SYM
Amboy, IL	RCK
Ambridge, PA	PBR
PA	PIT
PA	SJP
Amelia, LA	HT
OH	CIN
VA	RIC
Amenia, NY	NY
American Canyon, CA	SR
American Falls, ID	B
American Fork, UT	SLC
Americus, GA	SAV
Amery, WI	SUP
Ames, IA	DUB
TX	BEA
Amesbury, MA	BO
Amherst, MA	SPR
NY	BUF
NY	PSC
OH	CLV
VA	RIC
WI	LC
Amite, LA	BR
Amity, OR	P
Amityville, NY	BRK
NY	RVC
Ammannsville, TX	VIC
Amory, MS	JKS
Amsterdam, NY	ALB
NY	STF
OH	STU
Anaconda, MT	HEL
Anacortes, WA	SEA
Anacostia, Washington, DC	WDC
Anadarko, OK	OKL
Anaheim, CA	OLL
CA	ORG
CA	VNN
Anaheim Hills, CA	LA
Anahuac, TX	BEA
Anamoose, ND	FAR
Anamosa, IA	DUB
Anasco, PR	MGZ
Anchorage, AK	ANC
AK	VNN
Anchorville, MI	DET
Andale, KS	WCH
Andalusia, AL	MOB
IL	PEO
Anderson, CA	SAC
IN	LFT
SC	CHR
TX	GAL
Andice, TX	AUS
Andover, MA	BO
NJ	PAT
NY	BUF
OH	Y
SD	SFS
Andrew, IA	DUB
Andrews, NC	CHL
TX	SAN
Aneta, ND	FAR
Angelica, NY	BUF
Angels Camp, CA	STO
Angelus, KS	SAL
Angleton, TX	GAL
Angola, IN	FTW
NY	BUF
Aniak, AK	FBK
Anita, IA	DM
PA	E
Aniwa, WI	GB
Ankeny, IA	DM
Ann Arbor, MI	LAN
Anna, IL	BEL
Annandale, MN	STP
VA	ARL
VA	PSC
Annapolis, MD	BAL
Annawan, IL	PEO
Anniston, AL	BIR
Annville, PA	HBG
Anoka, MN	STP
Anselmo, NE	GI
Anson, TX	LUB
Ansonia, CT	HRT
CT	STF
Antelope, CA	SAC
Anthon, IA	SC
Anthony, KS	WCH
NM	LSC
Antigo, WI	GB
Antioch, CA	OAK
IL	CHI
TN	NSH
Antlers, OK	TLS
Anton Chico, NM	SFE
Antonino, KS	SAL
Antwerp, OH	TOL
Anza, CA	SB
Apache Junction, AZ	TUC
Apalachicola, FL	PT
Apalachin, NY	ROC
Apex, NC	R
Apollo, PA	GBG
Apopka, FL	ORL
FL	SJP
Apple Creek, MO	STL
Apple River, IL	RCK
Apple Valley, CA	SB
Applegate, CA	SAC
Appleton, MN	NU
WI	GB
Appomattox, VA	RIC
Aptos, CA	MRY
Aquadilla, PR	MGZ
Arabi, LA	NO
Aragon, NM	GLP
Aransas Pass, TX	CC
Arbor Vitae, WI	SUP
Arcade, NY	BUF

Arcadia, CA	LA
FL	VEN
IA	SC
PA	PBR
WI	LC
Arcata, CA	SR
Archbald, PA	SCR
Archbold, OH	TOL
Arco, ID	B
Arcola, IL	SFD
IN	FTW
Arden, NC	CHL
Ardmore, OK	OKL
PA	PH
Ardoch, ND	FAR
Ardon, IA	DAV
Ardsley, NY	NY
PA	PH
Arecibo, PR	ARE
Arenzville, IL	SFD
Argo, IL	CHI
Argonne, WI	GB
Argusville, ND	FAR
Argyle, MI	SAG
MN	CR
MO	JC
WI	MAD
Arkadelphia, AR	LR
Arkansas City, KS	WCH
Arkansaw, WI	LC
Arleta, CA	LA
Arlington, IL	PEO
MA	BO
MN	NU
OR	BAK
SD	SFS
TX	FWT
VA	ARL
VT	BUR
WA	SEA
Arlington Heights, IL	CHI
Arma, KS	WCH
Armada, MI	DET
Armonk, NY	NY
Armour, SD	SFS
Armstrong, IA	SC
WI	MIL
Armstrong Creek, WI	GB
Arnaudville, LA	LAF
Arnheim, OH	CIN
Arnold, MO	STL
PA	GBG
Aromas, CA	MRY
Arpin, WI	LC
Arroyo, PR	PCE
Arroyo Grande, CA	MRY
Arroyo Seco, NM	SFE
Artesia, CA	LA
NM	LSC
Artesian, SD	SFS
Arvada, CO	DEN
Arvin, CA	FRS
Asan, GU	AGN
Asbury, NJ	MET
Asbury Park, NJ	TR
Ashburn, VA	ARL
Ashburnham, MA	WOR
Asheboro, NC	CHL
Asherton, TX	LAR
Asheville, NC	CHL
Ashford, CT	NOR
WI	MIL
Ashkum, IL	JOL
Ashland, AL	BIR
IL	SFD
KS	DOD
KY	LEX
MA	BO
ME	PRT
MT	GF
NE	LIN
NH	MAN
OH	CLV
OR	P
PA	ALN
VA	RIC
WI	SUP
Ashland City, TN	NSH
Ashley, ND	FAR
PA	SCR
Ashtabula, OH	PBR
OH	Y
Ashton, IA	SC
WI	MAD
Ashville, PA	ALT
Askeaton, WI	GB
Aspen, CO	DEN
Aspinwall, PA	PIT
Assinins, MI	MAR
Assonet, MA	FR
Assumption, IL	SFD

OH	TOL
Aston, PA	PH
Astoria, NY	BRK
NY	ROM
OR	P
Atascadero, CA	MRY
Atchison, KS	KCK
Atco, NJ	CAM
Athens, AL	BIR
GA	ATL
IL	SFD
NY	ALB
OH	STU
PA	SCR
TN	KNX
TX	TYL
WI	LC
WV	WH
Atherton, CA	SFR
Athol, MA	WOR
SD	SFS
Athol Springs, NY	BUF
Atkins, AR	LR
Atkinson, IL	PEO
NE	OM
Atlanta, GA	ATL
GA	NTN
GA	SAM
MI	GAY
TX	TYL
Atlantic, IA	DM
Atlantic Beach, FL	STA
Atlantic City, NJ	CAM
Atlantic Highlands, NJ	TR
Atmore, AL	MOB
Attica, IN	LFT
NY	BUF
OH	TOL
Attleboro, MA	FR
Attleboro Falls, MA	FR
Atwater, CA	FRS
Atwood, KS	SAL
Au Sable Forks, NY	OG
Auburn, AL	MOB
CA	SAC
IA	SC
IL	SFD
IN	FTW
MA	WOR
ME	PRT
MI	SAG
NE	LIN
NH	MAN
NY	ROC
NY	STF
NY	SY
WA	SEA
WI	MIL
Auburn Hills, MI	DET
Auburndale, WI	LC
Audubon, IA	DM
NJ	CAM
PA	PH
AuGres, MI	SAG
Augusta, GA	NTN
GA	SAV
IA	DAV
KS	WCH
KY	COV
ME	PRT
MO	STL
WI	LC
Ault, CO	DEN
Auriesville, NY	ALB
Aurora, CO	DEN
IL	JOL
IL	RCK
IL	ROM
IN	IND
KS	SAL
KY	OWN
MN	DUL
MO	SPC
NE	LIN
NY	ROC
OH	Y
SD	SFS
WI	GB
Austin, MN	WIN
TX	AUS
TX	DUB
TX	OLL
Austintown, OH	SJP
OH	Y
Ava, IL	BEL
MO	SPC
Avalon, CA	LA
NJ	CAM
PA	PIT
Avella, PA	PBR
PA	PIT

Avenal, CA	FRS
Avenel, NJ	MET
Avenue, MD	WDC
Averill Park, NY	ALB
Avilla, IN	FTW
Aviston, IL	BEL
Avoca, IA	DM
PA	SCR
WI	MAD
Avon, CT	HRT
MA	BO
MN	SCL
NJ	TR
NY	ROC
OH	CLV
Avon Lake, OH	CLV
Avon Park, FL	VEN
Avondale, AZ	PHX
CO	PBL
LA	NO
Avonmore, PA	GBG
Awak, FM	CI
Awak, Pohnpei, FM	CI
Awendaw, SC	CHR
Axtel, KY	OWN
Axtell, KS	KCK
Ayer, MA	BO
Aztec, NM	GLP
Azusa, CA	LA
Babbitt, MN	DUL
Babcock, WI	LC
Babeldaob, FM	CI
Babylon, NY	RVC
Bad Axe, MI	SAG
Baden, MD	WDC
PA	PIT
Badger, MN	CR
Bagdad, AZ	PHX
Bagley, MN	CR
Bailey, CO	COS
Baileys Harbor, WI	GB
Baileyville, KS	KCK
ME	PRT
Bainbridge, GA	SAV
NY	SY
Bainbridge Island, WA	SEA
Bairdford, PA	PIT
Baker, LA	BR
MT	GF
OR	BAK
Baker City, OR	BAK
Bakersfield, CA	FRS
Bakerton, PA	ALT
Bakerville, WI	LC
Bal Harbour, FL	MIA
Bala Cynwyd, PA	PH
Baldwin, IA	DUB
KS	KCK
LA	LAF
MI	GR
NY	RVC
Baldwin Boro, PA	PIT
Baldwin Park, CA	LA
Baldwinsville, NY	SY
Baldwinville, MA	WOR
Balfour, ND	FAR
Ball Club, MN	DUL
Ballinger, TX	SAN
Ballouville, CT	NOR
Ballston Lake, NY	ALB
Ballston Spa, NY	ALB
Balltown, IA	DUB
Ballwin, MO	STL
Bally, PA	ALN
Balmorhea, TX	ELP
Balsam Lake, WI	SUP
Balta, ND	FAR
Baltic, CT	NOR
Baltimore, MD	BAL
MD	PHU
MD	PSC
MD	SYM
Bancroft, IA	SC
NE	OM
Bandera, TX	SAT
Bandon, OR	P
Bangall, NY	NY
Bangor, ME	PRT
MI	KAL
PA	ALN
WI	LC
Bankston, IA	DUB
Banning, CA	SB
Bannister, MI	SAG
Banquete, TX	CC
Bantam, CT	HRT
Bapchule, AZ	PHX
Baptistown, NJ	MET
Bar Harbor, ME	PRT
Baraboo, WI	MAD
Baraga, MI	MAR

Barbeau, MI	MAR
Barberton, OH	CLV
OH	PRM
Barbourville, KY	LEX
Barceloneta, PR	ARE
Barclay, IA	DUB
Bardonia, NY	NY
Bardstown, KY	L
Bardwell, KY	OWN
Barefoot Bay, FL	ORL
Barhamsville, VA	RIC
Baring, MO	JC
Bark River, MI	MAR
Barker, NY	BUF
Barling, AR	LR
Barnegat, NJ	TR
Barnesboro, PA	ALT
Barnesville, MD	WDC
MN	CR
OH	STU
PA	ALN
Barneveld, WI	MAD
Barnum, IA	SC
Barnwell, SC	CHR
Barrackville, WV	WH
Barranquitas, PR	CGS
Barre, MA	WOR
VT	BUR
Barrenspot, VI	STV
Barrett Station, TX	GAL
Barrigada, GU	AGN
Barrington, IL	CHI
NJ	CAM
RI	PRO
Barrio Bairoa, PR	CGS
Barrio Canaboncito, PR	CGS
Barrio Hormigas, PR	CGS
Barrio Rio Canas, PR	CGS
Barron, WI	SUP
Barrow, AK	FBK
Barry, IL	SFD
MN	NU
Barrytown, NY	NY
Barryville, NY	NY
Barstow, CA	SB
Bartelso, IL	BEL
Bartlesville, OK	TLS
Bartlett, IL	CHI
Barton, OH	STU
VT	BUR
Bartonville, IL	PEO
Bartow, FL	ORL
Basalt, CO	DEN
Bascom, OH	TOL
Basehor, KS	KCK
Basile, LA	LAF
Basking Ridge, NJ	MET
Bass Lake, CA	FRS
Bassfield, MS	BLX
Bastress, PA	SCR
Bastrop, LA	SHP
TX	AUS
Batavia, IL	RCK
NY	BUF
OH	CIN
Batchtown, IL	SFD
Batesburg, SC	CHR
Batesville, AR	LR
IN	IND
MS	JKS
Bath, ME	PRT
NY	ROC
NY	STF
PA	ALN
Bathgate, ND	FAR
Baton Rouge, LA	BR
LA	OLL
Battle Creek, MI	KAL
NE	OM
Battle Ground, WA	SEA
Battle Lake, MN	SCL
Battle Mountain, NV	RNO
Baudette, MN	CR
Bauer, IA	DAV
Baxter Springs, KS	WCH
Bay City, MI	PRM
MI	SAG
TX	VIC
Bay Head, NJ	TR
Bay Mills, MI	MAR
Bay Minette, AL	MOB
Bay Point, CA	OAK
Bay St. Louis, MS	BLX
Bay Settlement, WI	GB
Bay Shore, MI	GAY
NY	RVC
Bay Village, OH	CLV
Bayamon, PR	SJN
Bayard, IA	DM
NM	LSC
Bayfield, WI	SUP

Bayonne, NJ	NEW
NJ	PHU
NJ	PSC
Bayou Black, LA	HT
Bayou George, FL	PT
Bayou LaBatre, AL	MOB
Bayou Pigeon, LA	BR
Bayou Vista, LA	LAF
Bayport, MN	STP
Bayside, NY	BRK
Baytown, TX	GAL
Bayville, NJ	TR
NY	RVC
Beach, ND	BIS
Beachwood, OH	CLV
Beacon, NY	NY
Beacon Falls, CT	HRT
Beal City, MI	SAG
Beans Cove, PA	ALT
Bear, DE	WIL
Bear Creek, WI	GB
Bear Creek Township, PA	SCR
Bear Valley, WI	LC
Beardsley, KS	SAL
MN	NU
Beardstown, IL	SFD
Beasley, TX	GAL
Beatrice, NE	LIN
Beattie, KS	KCK
Beattyville, KY	LEX
Beaufort, SC	CHR
Beaulieu, MN	CR
Beaumont, CA	SB
TX	BEA
Beaver, KS	DOD
MI	SAG
PA	PBR
PA	PIT
Beaver Crossing, NE	LIN
Beaver Dam, KY	OWN
WI	MIL
Beaver Falls, PA	PIT
Beaver Island, MI	GAY
Beaver Meadows, PA	ALN
PA	PSC
Beaver Prairie, IL	BEL
Beavercreek, OH	CIN
Beaverdale, PA	ALT
PA	PBR
Beaverton, OR	P
Beaverville, IL	JOL
Bechyn, MN	NU
Bechyne, ND	FAR
Beckemeyer, IL	BEL
Becker, MN	SCL
Beckley, WV	WH
Bedford, IA	DM
IN	IND
MA	BO
NH	MAN
NY	NY
OH	CLV
OH	PRM
PA	ALT
TX	FWT
VA	RIC
Bedford Heights, OH	CLV
Beech Bottom, WV	WH
Beech Grove, IN	IND
Beemer, NE	OM
Beeville, TX	CC
Bejou, MN	CR
Bel Air, MD	BAL
Belchertown, MA	SPR
Belcourt, ND	FAR
Belding, MI	GR
Belen, NM	SFE
Belfast, ME	PRT
NY	BUF
Belfield, ND	BIS
ND	STN
Belgique, MO	STL
Belgium, WI	MIL
Belgrade, MN	NU
MN	SCL
Belington, WV	WH
Bell City, LA	LKC
Bell Gardens, CA	LA
Bella Vista, AR	LR
Bellaire, MI	GAY
OH	STU
Belle, MO	JC
WV	WH
Belle Chasse, LA	NO
Belle Creek, MN	STP
Belle Fontaine, AL	MOB
Belle Fourche, SD	RC
Belle Glade, FL	PMB
Belle Mead, NJ	MET
Belle Plaine, IA	DUB
MN	STP

Belle Prairie, MN	SCL
Belle River, MN	SCL
Belle Rose, LA	BR
Belle Valley, OH	STU
Belle Vernon, PA	GBG
Belleair Bluffs, FL	SP
Bellechester, MN	STP
Belledeau, LA	ALX
Bellefontaine, OH	CIN
Bellefontaine Neighbors, MO	STL
Bellefonte, DE	WIL
PA	ALT
Belleview, FL	ORL
IL	SFD
Belleville, IL	BEL
KS	SAL
MI	DET
NJ	NEW
WI	MAD
Bellevue, IA	DUB
KY	COV
MI	LAN
NE	OM
OH	TOL
PA	PIT
WA	SEA
Bellflower, CA	LA
Bellingham, MA	BO
WA	SEA
Bellmawr, NJ	CAM
Bellmore, NY	RVC
Bellows Falls, VT	BUR
Bellport, NY	RVC
Bellville, TX	GAL
Bellwood, IL	CHI
IL	SYM
NE	LIN
PA	ALT
Belmar, NJ	TR
Belmond, IA	DUB
Belmont, CA	SFR
MA	BO
MI	GR
NC	CHL
NH	MAN
NY	BUF
WI	MAD
Beloit, KS	SAL
WI	MAD
WI	MIL
Belpre, KS	DOD
OH	STU
Bel-Ridge, MO	STL
Belt, MT	GF
Belton, MO	KC
TX	AUS
Beltrees, IL	SFD
Beltsville, MD	PSC
MD	WDC
Belvidere, IL	RCK
NJ	MET
Belzoni, MS	JKS
Bement, IL	PEO
Bemidji, MN	CR
Bemus Point, NY	BUF
Ben Avon, PA	PIT
Bena, MN	DUL
Benavides, TX	CC
The Bend, OH	TOL
Bend, OR	BAK
Bendena, KS	KCK
Benedict, MD	WDC
Benedicta, ME	PRT
Benet Lake, WI	MIL
Benicia, CA	SAC
Benkelman, NE	LIN
Benld, IL	SFD
Bennington, NH	MAN
VT	BUR
Bennington Center, NY	BUF
Bensalem, PA	PH
Bensenville, IL	JOL
Benson, AZ	TUC
IL	PEO
MN	NU
VT	BUR
Bentley Creek, PA	SCR
Bentleyville, PA	PIT
Benton, AR	LR
IL	BEL
MO	SPC
WI	MAD
Benton City, WA	YAK
Benton Harbor, MI	KAL
Bentonville, AR	LR
Benwood, MN	CR
WV	WH
Berea, KY	LEX
OH	CLV
Beresford, SD	SFS
Bergen, NY	BUF

Bergenfield, NJ	NEW
Berger, MO	STL
Berkeley, CA	OAK
MO	STL
Berkeley Heights, NJ	NEW
Berkeley Springs, WV	WH
Berkley, MI	DET
Berlin, MA	WOR
NH	MAN
NJ	CAM
NY	ALB
WI	MAD
Berlinsville, PA	ALN
Bernalillo, NM	SFE
Bernardsville, NJ	MET
Beroun, MN	DUL
Berryville, AR	LR
VA	ARL
Bertha, MN	SCL
Bertram, TX	AUS
Berwick, LA	LAF
ME	PRT
PA	HBG
PA	PHU
Berwyn, IL	CHI
PA	PH
Besancon, IN	FTW
Bessemer, AL	BIR
MI	MAR
PA	PIT
Bethalto, IL	SFD
Bethany, IL	SFD
MO	KC
OK	OKL
WV	WH
Bethany Beach, DE	WIL
Bethel, AK	FBK
CT	BGP
OH	CIN
VT	BUR
Bethel Park, PA	PIT
Bethesda, MD	WDC
Bethlehem, CT	HRT
OH	TOL
PA	ALN
PA	PHU
PA	PSC
Bethpage, NY	RVC
Bettendorf, IA	DAV
Beulah, ND	BIS
Bevent, WI	LC
Beverly, MA	BO
NJ	TR
OH	STU
Beverly Hills, CA	LA
FL	SP
MI	DET
Beverly Shores, IN	GRY
Bicknell, IN	EVN
Biddeford, ME	PRT
Biehle, MO	STL
Big Bear Lake, CA	SB
Big Bend, SD	SFS
WI	MIL
Big Clifty, KY	OWN
Big Elbow Lake, MN	CR
Big Lake, LA	LKC
MN	SCL
TX	SAN
Big Long Lake, IN	FTW
Big Pine Key, FL	MIA
Big Rapids, MI	GR
Big River, WI	LC
Big Sandy, MT	GF
Big Spring, TX	SAN
Big Stone City, SD	SFS
Big Stone Gap, VA	RIC
Big Sur, CA	MRY
Big Timber, MT	GF
Bigelow, AR	LR
Bigfork, MN	DUL
MT	HEL
Billerica, MA	BO
Billings, MO	SPC
MT	GF
Biloxi, MS	BLX
Bingham, ME	PRT
Binghamton, NY	PSC
NY	SY
Birch Coolie, MN	NU
Birch Run, MI	SAG
Birchwood, WI	SUP
Bird City, KS	SAL
Bird Island, MN	NU
Birdsboro, PA	ALN
Birmingham, AL	BIR
AL	NTN
AL	OLL
MI	DET
Birnamwood, WI	GB
Bisbee, AZ	TUC

ND	FAR
Bishop, CA	FRS
TX	CC
Bishop Creek, IL	SFD
Bismarck, ND	BIS
Bismark, OH	TOL
Bison, OK	OKL
SD	RC
Bissell Hills, MO	STL
Biwabik, MN	DUL
Bixby, OK	TLS
Black Brook, NY	OG
Black Canyon City, AZ	PHX
Black Creek, WI	GB
Black Diamond, WA	SEA
Black Eagle, MT	GF
Black Jack, IL	SFD
Black River, MI	GAY
NY	OG
Black River Falls, WI	LC
Blackduck, MN	CR
Blackfoot, ID	B
Blacksburg, VA	RIC
Blackstone, IL	PEO
MA	WOR
VA	RIC
Blackwell, OK	OKL
Blackwood, NJ	CAM
Bladensburg, MD	WDC
Blaine, KS	KCK
MN	STP
OH	STU
Blair, NE	OM
WI	LC
Blairstown, IA	DUB
NJ	MET
Blairsville, GA	ATL
PA	GBG
Blakely, GA	SAV
Blakeslee, OH	TOL
PA	SCR
Blanchardville, WI	MAD
Blanchester, OH	CIN
Blanco, NM	GLP
TX	AUS
Blasdell, NY	BUF
Blauvelt, NY	NY
Blawnox, PA	PIT
Blenker, WI	LC
Blessing, IA	DUB
TX	VIC
Bliss, NY	BUF
Blissfield, MI	LAN
Bloomer, WI	LC
Bloomfield, CT	HRT
IA	DAV
IN	EVN
NE	OM
NJ	NEW
NM	GLP
Bloomfield Hills, MI	DET
Blooming Prairie, MN	WIN
Bloomingdale, IL	JOL
NY	OG
OH	STU
Bloomington, CA	SB
IL	PEO
IN	IND
MN	STP
TX	VIC
WI	MAD
Bloomsburg, PA	HBG
Bloomsbury, NJ	MET
Bloomsdale, MO	STL
Bloomville, WI	SUP
Blossburg, PA	SCR
Blossom, NY	BUF
Blountstown, FL	PT
Blue Anchor, NJ	CAM
Blue Creek, OH	CIN
Blue Earth, MN	WIN
Blue Grass, IA	DAV
Blue Island, IL	CHI
Blue Point, NY	RVC
Blue Rapids, KS	KCK
Blue Ridge, GA	ATL
Blue Ridge Summit, PA	HBG
Blue Springs, MO	KC
Bluefield, WV	WH
BlueGrass, MN	SCL
Bluffs, IL	SFD
Bluffton, IA	DUB
IN	FTW
MN	SCL
OH	TOL
SC	CHR
Blunt, SD	SFS
Blythe, CA	SB
Blytheville, AR	LR
Blythewood, SC	CHR

Boardman, OH	PBR
OH	Y
OR	BAK
Bobtown, PA	PIT
Boca Grande, FL	VEN
Boca Raton, FL	PMB
Bode, IA	SC
Boerne, TX	SAT
Bogalusa, LA	NO
Bogota, NJ	NEW
Bohemia, NY	RVC
Boise, ID	B
Bokeelia, FL	VEN
Bolingbrook, IL	JOL
Bolivar, MO	SPC
NY	BUF
TN	MEM
Boliver, PA	GBG
Bolton, CT	NOR
MA	WOR
Bolton Landing, NY	ALB
Bombay, NY	OG
Bondsville, MA	SPR
Bonesteel, SD	RC
Bonham, TX	DAL
Bonifay, FL	PT
Bonita, CA	LA
CA	SD
Bonita Springs, FL	VEN
Bonne Terre, MO	STL
Bonneauville, PA	HBG
Bonner, MT	HEL
Bonners Ferry, ID	B
Bonnots Mill, MO	JC
Bono, OH	TOL
Boone, IA	SC
NC	CHL
Booneville, AR	LR
MS	JKS
Boonton, NJ	PAT
Boonville, IN	EVN
MO	JC
NY	SY
Boothbay Harbor, ME	PRT
Boothwyn, PA	PH
Bordelonville, LA	ALX
Bordentown, NJ	TR
Borger, TX	AMA
Borrego Springs, CA	SD
Boscobel, WI	MAD
Bossier City, LA	SHP
Boston, IN	ROM
MA	ARM
MA	BO
MA	NTN
MA	STF
NY	BUF
Boswell, PA	ALT
Bothell, WA	SEA
Botkins, OH	CIN
Bottineau, ND	FAR
Boulder, CO	DEN
MT	HEL
Boulder City, NV	LAV
Boulder Creek, CA	MRY
Boulder Junction, WI	SUP
Boulevard, CA	SD
Bound Brook, NJ	MET
Bountiful, UT	SLC
Bourbon, MO	JC
Bourbonnais, IL	JOL
Bourg, LA	HT
Bovard, PA	GBG
Bovina, TX	AMA
Bow Valley, NE	OM
Bowbells, ND	BIS
Bowdle, SD	SFS
Bowie, MD	WDC
TX	FWT
Bowling Green, KY	OWN
OH	TOL
Bowlus, MN	SCL
Bowman, ND	BIS
Bowmansville, NY	BUF
Boyce, LA	ALX
Boyceville, WI	LC
Boyd, WI	LC
Boyers, PA	PIT
Boyertown, PA	ALN
Boyes Hot Springs, CA	SR
Boylston, MA	WOR
Boyne City, MI	GAY
Boyne Falls, MI	GAY
Boynton Beach, FL	PMB
Boys Town, NE	OM
Bozeman, MT	HEL
Brackett, WI	LC
Brackettville, TX	SAT
Braddock, PA	PBR
PA	PIT
Braddock Hills, PA	PIT
Bradenton, FL	VEN
Bradenville, PA	PBR
Bradford, IL	PEO
IN	IND
NY	ROC
OH	CIN
PA	E
VT	BUR
Bradley, IL	JOL
ME	PRT
Bradley Beach, NJ	TR
Bradshaw, MD	BAL
Brady, TX	SAN
Brady's Bend, PA	GBG
Braham, MN	SCL
Braidwood, IL	JOL
Brainard, NE	LIN
Brainerd, MN	DUL
Braintree, MA	BO
Branchdale, PA	ALN
Branchville, NJ	PAT
Brandamore, PA	PH
Brandenburg, KY	L
Brandon, FL	SP
MN	SCL
MS	JKS
SD	SFS
VT	BUR
WI	MIL
Brandy Camp, PA	E
Brandywood, DE	WIL
Branford, CT	HRT
FL	STA
Branson, MO	SPC
Brant, NY	BUF
Brant Beach, NJ	TR
Brasher Falls, NY	OG
Brattleboro, VT	BUR
Brawley, CA	SD
Brazil, IN	IND
Brazoria, TX	GAL
Brea, CA	ORG
Breaux Bridge, LA	LAF
Breckenridge, CO	DEN
MN	SCL
TX	FWT
Brecksville, OH	CLV
OH	PRM
Breda, IA	SC
Breese, IL	BEL
Bremen, IN	FTW
ND	FAR
OH	COL
Bremerton, WA	SEA
Bremond, TX	AUS
Brenham, TX	AUS
Brennyville, MN	SCL
Brentwood, CA	OAK
MO	STL
NY	BRK
NY	RVC
PA	PIT
TN	NSH
Brevard, NC	CHL
Brewer, ME	PRT
MO	STL
Brewerton, NY	SY
Brewster, MA	FR
MN	WIN
NY	NY
OH	Y
WA	SPK
Brewton, AL	MOB
Briarcliff Manor, NY	NY
Briarwood, NY	BRK
Brick, NJ	TR
Brick Town, NJ	TR
Bridal Veil, OR	P
Bridge City, LA	NO
TX	BEA
Bridgehampton, NY	RVC
Bridgeport, CT	BGP
CT	PSC
CT	STF
IL	BEL
MI	SAG
NE	GI
NY	SY
OH	STU
PA	PH
PA	PHU
TX	FWT
WA	YAK
WV	WH
Bridger, MT	GF
Bridgeton, MO	SFD
MO	STL
NJ	CAM
Bridgeview, IL	CHI
Bridgeville, PA	PIT
Bridgewater, MA	BO
NJ	MET
SD	SFS
Bridgman, MI	KAL
Bridgton, ME	PRT
Brigantine, NJ	CAM
Briggsville, WI	MAD
Brigham City, UT	SLC
Bright, IN	IND
Brighton, CO	DEN
IL	SFD
MA	BO
MI	LAN
WI	MIL
Brilliant, OH	STU
Brillion, WI	GB
Brimfield, IL	PEO
MA	SPR
Brimley, MI	MAR
Brinkley, AR	LR
Brinktown, MO	JC
Bristol, CT	HRT
IN	FTW
NH	MAN
PA	PH
PA	PHU
RI	PRO
SD	SFS
VA	RIC
VT	BUR
WI	MIL
WI	PRM
Bristow, VA	ARL
Britt, IA	DUB
Britton, SD	SFS
Broad Brook, CT	HRT
Broad Run, VA	ARL
Broadalbin, NY	ALB
Broadus, MT	GF
Broadview, IL	CHI
Broadview Heights, OH	CLV
Broadwater, NE	GI
Brocket, ND	FAR
Brockport, NY	ROC
Brockton, MA	BO
MA	LIT
MA	SAM
PA	ALN
PA	PSC
Brockway, PA	E
Brocton, IL	SFD
NY	BUF
Brodhead, WI	MAD
Brodheadsville, PA	SCR
Broken Arrow, OK	TLS
Broken Bow, NE	GI
Bronson, MI	KAL
Bronx, NY	NY
NY	STF
NY	SYM
Bronxville, NY	NY
Brook Park, OH	CLV
Brookeville, MD	WDC
Brookfield, CT	BGP
IL	CHI
MA	WOR
MO	JC
WI	MIL
Brookhaven, MS	JKS
PA	PH
Brookings, OR	P
SD	SFS
Brooklandville, MD	BAL
Brooklawn, NJ	CAM
Brookline, MA	BO
PA	PH
Brooklyn, CT	NOR
IA	DAV
MI	LAN
NY	ARM
NY	BRK
NY	LIT
NY	NTN
NY	PSC
NY	SAM
NY	STF
OH	CLV
OH	NTN
Brooklyn Center, MN	STP
Brooklyn Park, MN	STP
Brookneal, VA	RIC
Brooks, MN	CR
WI	LC
Brooksville, FL	SP
KY	COV
MS	JKS
Brookville, IN	IND
KS	SAL
NY	RVC
PA	E
Broomall, PA	PH
Broomfield, CO	DEN
Brooten, MN	SCL
Brouillette, LA	ALX
Broussard, LA	LAF
Browerville, MN	SCL
Brown Deer, WI	MIL
Brown's Valley, KY	OWN
MN	SCL
Brownfield, TX	LUB
Browning, MT	HEL
Browns Mills, NJ	TR
Browns Valley, MN	SCL
Brownsburg, IN	IND
Brownsdale, MN	WIN
Brownstown, IN	IND
Brownsville, MN	WIN
PA	GBG
PA	PBR
TN	MEM
TX	BWN
Brownville, NY	OG
Brownville Junction, ME	PRT
Brownwood, TX	SAN
Bruce, MS	JKS
WI	SUP
Bruno, MN	DUL
NE	LIN
Brunswick, GA	SAV
MD	BAL
ME	PRT
MI	GR
MO	JC
OH	CLV
OH	PRM
Brush, CO	DEN
Brushton, NY	OG
Brusly, LA	BR
Brussels, IL	SFD
WI	GB
Bryan, OH	TOL
TX	AUS
Bryant, IA	DAV
IN	LFT
SD	SFS
Bryantown, MD	WDC
Bryn Mawr, PA	PH
Bryson City, NC	CHL
Buchanan, MI	KAL
ND	FAR
NY	NY
Buchanan Valley, PA	HBG
Buchtel, OH	STU
Buckeye, AZ	PHX
Buckeye Lake, OH	COL
Buckeystown, MD	BAL
Buckhannon, WV	WH
Buckingham, PA	PH
VA	RIC
Buckley, WA	SEA
Bucklin, KS	DOD
Buckman, MN	SCL
Buckner, MO	KC
VA	RIC
Bucksport, ME	PRT
Bucyrus, OH	TOL
Buda, TX	AUS
Budd, IL	PEO
Budd Lake, NJ	PAT
Buena Borough, NJ	CAM
Buena Park, CA	ORG
Buena Vista, CO	COS
WI	LC
Buffalo, IA	DAV
IL	SFD
MN	STP
MO	SPC
ND	FAR
NY	BUF
NY	STF
SD	RC
TX	TYL
WI	MAD
WY	CHY
Buffalo Center, IA	DUB
Buffalo Grove, IL	CHI
Buford, GA	ATL
Buhl, ID	B
MN	DUL
Bulger, PA	PIT
Bullhead City, AZ	PHX
Buna, TX	BEA
Bunker Hill, IL	SFD
Bunkerville, NV	LAV
Bunkie, LA	ALX
Bunnell, FL	STA
Buras, LA	NO
Burbank, CA	LA
IL	CHI
Burdett, KS	DOD
Burgaw, NC	R
Burgettstown, PA	PIT

Burkburnett, TX	FWT
Burke, NY	OG
SD	RC
VA	ARL
Burkettsville, OH	CIN
Burkhart, OH	STU
Burleson, TX	FWT
Burley, ID	B
Burlingame, CA	SFR
Burlington, CA	SB
CO	COS
IA	DAV
KS	KCK
KY	COV
MA	BO
NC	R
ND	BIS
NJ	TR
VT	BUR
WA	SEA
WI	MIL
Burnet, TX	AUS
Burney, CA	SAC
Burnham, IL	CHI
Burns, KS	WCH
OR	BAK
Burnstad, ND	FAR
Burnsville, MN	STP
Burr Ridge, IL	JOL
Burrillville, RI	PRO
Burt Lake, MI	GAY
Burton, MI	LAN
OH	PRM
Burtonsville, MD	WDC
Burwell, NE	GI
Bushnell, FL	ORL
IL	PEO
Bushton, KS	WCH
Bushwood, MD	WDC
Butler, AL	MOB
MN	SCL
MO	KC
NJ	PAT
PA	PBR
PA	PIT
WI	MIL
Butner, NC	R
Butte, MT	HEL
NE	OM
Butternut, WI	SUP
Buttonwillow, CA	FRS
Buttonwood, PA	SCR
Buxton, NC	R
Buzzards Bay, MA	FR
Byers, CO	DEN
Byesville, OH	STU
Byron, CA	OAK
IL	RCK
MN	WIN
WI	MIL
Byron Center, MI	GR
MI	KAL
Cabery, IL	JOL
Cable, WI	SUP
Cabo Rojo, PR	MGZ
Cabot, PA	PIT
Cadet, MO	STL
Cadillac, MI	GAY
Cadiz, KY	OWN
OH	STU
Cadogan, PA	GBG
Cadott, WI	LC
Cadyville, NY	OG
Caguas, PR	CGS
Cahokia, IL	BEL
Cairo, IL	BEL
NY	ALB
Calais, ME	PRT
Calamine, WI	MAD
Caldwell, ID	B
KS	WCH
NJ	NEW
OH	STU
TX	AUS
Caledonia, MI	GR
MN	WIN
NY	ROC
WI	MIL
Calexico, CA	SD
Calhan, CO	COS
Calhoun, GA	ATL
KY	OWN
Caliente, NV	LAV
Califon, NJ	MET
California, KY	COV
MO	JC
PA	PIT
California City, CA	FRS
Calimesa, CA	SB
Calipatria, CA	SD
Calistoga, CA	SR

Callahan, FL	STA
Callaway, MN	CR
Callicoon, NY	NY
Calmar, IA	DUB
Calumet, MI	MAR
OK	OKL
PA	GBG
Calumet City, IL	CHI
Calumet Park, IL	CHI
Calvary, KY	L
Calvert, TX	AUS
Calvert City, KY	OWN
Calwell, ID	B
Camanche, IA	DAV
Camarillo, CA	LA
Camas, WA	SEA
Cambria, CA	MRY
Cambridge, MA	BO
MD	WIL
MN	SCL
NE	LIN
NY	ALB
OH	STU
VT	BUR
WI	MAD
Cambridge City, IN	IND
Cambridge Springs, PA	E
Camden, AL	MOB
AR	LR
ME	PRT
MS	JKS
NJ	CAM
NY	SY
OH	CIN
SC	CHR
TN	MEM
WV	WH
Camdenton, MO	JC
Cameron, LA	LKC
MO	KC
TX	AUS
WI	SUP
WV	WH
Camillus, NY	SY
Camp Douglas, WI	LC
Camp Grove, IL	PEO
Camp Hill, PA	HBG
Camp Point, IL	SFD
Camp Springs, KY	COV
MD	WDC
Camp Verde, AZ	PHX
Campbell, CA	SJ
NE	LIN
OH	PBR
OH	Y
Campbellsport, WI	MIL
Campbellsville, KY	L
Campti, LA	ALX
Campus, IL	PEO
Camuy, PR	ARE
Canaan, CT	HRT
VT	BUR
Canadensis, PA	PSC
PA	SCR
Canadian, TX	AMA
Canajoharie, NY	ALB
Canal Fulton, OH	Y
Canal Winchester, OH	COL
Canandaigua, NY	ROC
Canaseraga, NY	BUF
Canastota, NY	SY
Canby, MN	NU
OR	P
Candia, NH	MAN
Candler, FL	ORL
Cando, ND	FAR
Caney, KS	WCH
Canfield, OH	Y
Canisteo, NY	ROC
Cankton, LA	LAF
Cannelburg, IN	EVN
Cannelton, IN	IND
Cannon Falls, MN	STP
Canoga Park, CA	LA
Canon City, CO	PBL
Canonsburg, PA	PBR
PA	PIT
Canovanas, PR	SJN
Canterbury, CT	NOR
Canton, GA	ATL
IL	PEO
MA	BO
MI	DET
MN	WIN
MO	JC
MS	JKS
NY	OG
OH	ROM
OH	SJP
OH	Y
OK	OKL

PA	SCR
SD	SFS
TX	TYL
Cantonment, FL	PT
Canutillo, TX	ELP
Canyon, TX	AMA
Canyon Lake, TX	SAT
Capac, MI	DET
Capaldo, KS	WCH
Cape Charles, VA	RIC
Cape Coral, FL	VEN
Cape Elizabeth, ME	PRT
Cape Girardeau, MO	SPC
Cape May, NJ	CAM
Cape May Court House, NJ	CAM
Cape May Point, NJ	CAM
Cape Vincent, NY	OG
Capistrano Beach, CA	ORG
Capitola, CA	MRY
Capulin, CO	PBL
Carbondale, IL	BEL
PA	SCR
Cardale, PA	GBG
Cardington, OH	COL
Carefree, AZ	PHX
Carencro, LA	LAF
Carey, OH	TOL
Caribou, ME	PRT
Carle Place, NY	RVC
Carleton, MI	DET
Carlin, NV	RNO
Carlinville, IL	SFD
Carlisle, AR	LR
IA	DM
KY	LEX
MA	BO
OH	STU
PA	HBG
Carlsbad, CA	SD
NM	LSC
TX	SAN
Carlton, MN	DUL
Carlyle, IL	BEL
Carmel, CA	MRY
IN	LFT
NY	NY
Carmel Valley, CA	MRY
CA	SD
Carmi, IL	BEL
Carmichael, CA	SAC
Carmichaels, PA	PIT
Carnegie, PA	PIT
PA	SAM
PA	SJP
Carneys Point, NJ	CAM
Caro, MI	SAG
Carol Stream, IL	JOL
Carolina, PR	SJN
Caroline County, VA	RIC
Carpentersville, IL	RCK
Carpinteria, CA	LA
Carrington, ND	FAR
Carrizo Springs, TX	LAR
Carrizozo, NM	LSC
Carroll, IA	SC
Carroll Township IA	DUB
Carrollton, GA	ATL
IL	SFD
KY	COV
MI	SAG
MO	KC
OH	STU
TX	DAL
TX	FWT
Carrolltown, PA	ALT
Carson, CA	LA
ND	BIS
Carson City, MI	GR
NV	RNO
Carter Lake, IA	DM
Carteret, NJ	MET
NJ	PHU
NJ	PSC
Cartersville, GA	ATL
IA	DUB
Carterville, IL	BEL
Carthage, IL	PEO
MO	SPC
MS	JKS
NY	OG
TX	TYL
Carthagena, OH	CIN
Caruthersville, MO	SPC
Carver, MA	BO
MN	STP
Carverton, PA	SCR
Cary, IL	RCK
NC	PSC
NC	R
Casa Grande, AZ	TUC

Cascade, CO	COS
IA	DUB
NH	MAN
WI	MIL
Casco, ME	PRT
Casco/Slovan, WI	GB
Caseville, MI	SAG
Casey, IA	DM
IL	SFD
Caseyville, IL	BEL
Cashion, AZ	PHX
Cashmere, WA	YAK
Cashton, WI	LC
Casper, WY	CHY
Caspian, MI	MAR
Cass City, MI	SAG
Cass Lake, MN	DUL
Cassadaga, NY	BUF
Cassandra, PA	ALT
Cassel, WI	LC
Casselberry, FL	ORL
Cassella, OH	CIN
Casselton, ND	FAR
Cassopolis, MI	KAL
Cassville, MO	SPC
WI	MAD
Castaner, PR	PCE
Castine, ME	PRT
Castle Grove, IA	DUB
Castle Hayne, NC	R
Castle Rock, CO	COS
WA	SEA
WI	MAD
Castle Rock Lake, WI	LC
Castle Shannon, PA	PIT
Castleton, KS	WCH
NY	ALB
VT	BUR
Castleton-on-Hudson, NY	ALB
Castlewood, SD	SFS
Castro Valley, CA	OAK
Castroville, CA	MRY
TX	SAT
Catahoula, LA	LAF
Catano, PR	SJN
Catasauqua, PA	ALN
Catawba, WI	SUP
Catawissa, MO	STL
Catharine, KS	SAL
Cathedral City, CA	SB
Cato, NY	ROC
Catonsville, MD	BAL
Catskill, NY	ALB
Cattaraugus, NY	BUF
Cavalier, ND	FAR
Cavour, SD	SFS
Cawker City, KS	SAL
Cayey, PR	CGS
Cayucos, CA	MRY
Cayuga, ND	FAR
NY	ROC
Cazenovia, NY	SY
WI	LC
Cecil, OH	TOL
PA	PIT
WI	GB
Cecilia, KY	L
LA	LAF
Cedar, MI	GAY
MN	STP
Cedar City, UT	SLC
Cedar Falls, IA	DUB
Cedar Grove, IN	IND
NJ	NEW
WI	MIL
Cedar Knolls, NJ	PAT
Cedar Lake, IN	GRY
MN	STP
Cedar Park, TX	AUS
Cedar Rapids, IA	DUB
NE	OM
Cedar Vale, KS	WCH
Cedarburg, WI	MIL
Cedarhurst, NY	RVC
Cedartown, GA	ATL
Cedarville, NJ	CAM
Ceiba, PR	CGS
Celestine, IN	EVN
Celina, OH	CIN
Centennial, CO	DEN
Center, CO	PBL
ND	BIS
TX	TYL
Center Harbor, NH	MAN
Center Moriches, NY	RVC
Center Ossipee, NH	MAN
Center Ridge, AR	LR
Center Square, PA	PH
Center Township, PA	PIT
Center Valley, PA	ALN
Centereach, NY	RVC

Centerline, MI	DET
Centerport, NY	BRK
NY	RVC
Centerville, IA	DAV
LA	LAF
MA	FR
MN	STP
MO	STL
NY	NY
OH	CIN
SD	SFS
TN	NSH
Central City, IA	DUB
KY	OWN
NE	OM
PA	ALT
Central Falls, RI	PRO
Central Islip, NY	RVC
Central Point, OR	P
Central Square, NY	SY
Centralia, IL	BEL
MO	JC
PA	HBG
PA	PHU
WA	SEA
Centreville, IL	BEL
MD	WIL
Centuria, WI	SUP
Ceres, CA	STO
Cerrillos, NM	SFE
Cestohowa, TX	SAT
Chacahoula, LA	HT
Chackbay, LA	HT
Chadds Ford, PA	PH
Chadron, NE	GI
Chadwicks, NY	SY
Chaffee, MO	SPC
Chagrin Falls, OH	CLV
Chalan Kanoa Village, MP	CHK
Chalan Pago, GU	AGN
Chalfont, PA	PH
Chalmette, LA	NO
Chama, NM	SFE
Chamberino, NM	LSC
Chamberlain, SD	SFS
Chambers Island, WI	GB
Chambersburg, PA	HBG
Chamblee, GA	ATL
Chamois, MO	JC
Champaign, IL	PEO
Champion, MI	MAR
OH	Y
WI	GB
Champlain, NY	OG
Chandler, AZ	PHX
OK	OKL
Chandlerville, IL	SFD
Chanhassen, MN	STP
Channahon, IL	JOL
Channelview, TX	GAL
Channing, MI	MAR
TX	AMA
Chantilly, VA	ARL
Chanute, KS	WCH
Chaparral, NM	LSC
Chapel Hill, NC	R
Chapel Point, MD	WDC
Chapin, SC	CHR
Chapman, KS	SAL
Chappaqua, NY	NY
Chappell, NE	GI
Chappell Hill, TX	AUS
Chaptico, MD	WDC
Chardon, OH	CLV
Charenton, LA	LAF
Chariton, IA	DM
Charleroi, PA	PBR
PA	PIT
Charles City, IA	DUB
Charles Town, WV	WH
Charlesburg, WI	GB
Charleston, AR	LR
IL	SFD
MO	SPC
MS	JKS
SC	CHR
WV	WH
Charlestown, IN	IND
MA	BO
NH	MAN
RI	PRO
WI	GB
Charleton, MA	WOR
Charlevoix, MI	GAY
Charlotte, IA	DAV
MI	LAN
NC	CHL
TX	SAT
VT	BUR
Charlottesville, VA	RIC
Charlton City, MA	WOR
Charter Oak, IA	SC
Chase, KS	WCH
WI	GB
Chaska, MN	STP
Chasm Falls, NY	OG
Chassell, MI	MAR
Chastang, AL	MOB
Chataignier, LA	LAF
Chatawa, MS	JKS
Chateaugay, NY	OG
Chatfield, MN	WIN
Chatham, IL	SFD
MA	FR
NJ	PAT
NY	ALB
Chatham Township, NJ	PAT
Chatom, AL	MOB
Chatsworth, CA	LA
CA	SYM
IL	PEO
Chattahoochee, FL	PT
Chattanooga, TN	KNX
Chaumont, NY	OG
Chauncey, OH	STU
Chauvin, LA	HT
Chazy, NY	OG
Cheat Lake, WV	WH
Chebanse, IL	JOL
Cheboygan, MI	GAY
Cheek, TX	BEA
Cheektowaga, NY	BUF
Chefornak, AK	FBK
Chehalis, WA	SEA
Chelan, WA	YAK
Chelmsford, MA	BO
Chelsea, IA	DUB
MA	BO
MI	LAN
SD	SFS
WI	SUP
Cheltenham, PA	PH
Chenango Forks, NY	SY
Cheney, NE	LIN
WA	SPK
Cheneyville, LA	ALX
Chenoa, IL	PEO
Cheraw, SC	CHR
Cherokee, IA	SC
KS	WCH
OK	OKL
Cherokee Village, AR	LR
Cherry, IL	PEO
Cherry Creek, NY	BUF
Cherry Hill, NJ	CAM
NJ	PHU
Cherry Mound, IA	DUB
Cherry Valley, NY	ALB
Cherryvale, KS	WCH
Chesaning, MI	SAG
Chesapeake, OH	STU
VA	RIC
Chesapeake City, MD	PHU
Cheshire, CT	HRT
MA	SPR
Chest Springs, PA	ALT
Chester, CT	NOR
IA	DUB
IL	BEL
MT	GF
NJ	PAT
NY	NY
PA	PH
PA	PHU
SC	CHR
VT	BUR
WV	WH
Chester Heights, PA	PH
Chester, Kent Island, MD	WIL
Chesterfield, MO	STL
Chesterland, OH	CLV
OH	ROM
Chesterton, IN	GRY
Chestertown, MD	WIL
NY	ALB
Chestnut Hill, MA	BO
Chetek, WI	SUP
Chetopa, KS	WCH
Chevak, AK	FBK
Cheverly, MD	WDC
Chevy Chase, MD	WDC
Chewelah, WA	SPK
Cheyenne, WY	CHY
Cheyenne Wells, CO	COS
Chicago, IL	CHI
IL	EST
IL	LIT
IL	PRM
IL	ROM
IL	STN
IL	SYM
Chicago Heights, IL	CHI
Chicago Ridge, IL	CHI
Chichiltah, NM	GLP
Chickasaw, AL	MOB
OH	CIN
Chickasha, OK	OKL
Chico, CA	SAC
Chicopee, KS	WCH
MA	SPR
Chicora, PA	PIT
Chiefland, FL	STA
Childress, TX	AMA
Childs, MD	WIL
Chili, WI	LC
Chillicothe, IL	PEO
MO	KC
OH	COL
Chillum, MD	WDC
Chiloquin, OR	BAK
Chilton, WI	GB
Chimayo, NM	SFE
China, TX	BEA
China Spring, TX	AUS
Chincoteague, VA	RIC
Chinle, AZ	GLP
Chino, CA	SB
Chino Hills, CA	SB
Chinook, MT	GF
Chipley, FL	PT
Chippewa Falls, WI	LC
Chippewa Lake, OH	CLV
Chippewa Township, PA	PIT
Chisholm, MN	DUL
Chittenango, NY	SY
Chittenden, VT	BUR
Chokio, MN	SCL
Choteau, MT	HEL
Chowchilla, CA	FRS
Chrisney, IN	EVN
Christiansburg, VA	RIC
Christiansted, VI	STV
Christopher, IL	BEL
Christoval, TX	SAN
Chubbuck, ID	B
Chula Vista, CA	SD
Church Point, LA	LAF
Church Rock, NM	GLP
Churchill Borough, PA	PIT
Churchtown, OH	STU
Churchville, IA	DM
NY	ROC
Churdan, IA	SC
Churubusco, IN	FTW
NY	OG
Chuuk, FM	CI
Ciales, PR	ARE
Cibecue, AZ	GLP
Cicero, IL	CHI
IN	LFT
NY	SY
Cidra, PR	CGS
Cimarron, NM	SFE
Cincinnati, OH	CIN
OH	OLL
Cinnaminson, NJ	TR
Circle, MT	GF
Circleville, OH	COL
Cisco, TX	FWT
Cistern, TX	VIC
Citronelle, AL	MOB
Citrus Heights, CA	SAC
Citrus Springs, FL	SP
Claflin, KS	DOD
Clairton, PA	PBR
PA	PIT
Clam Lake, WI	SUP
Clara City, MN	NU
Clare, IA	SC
MI	SAG
Claremont, CA	LA
MN	WIN
NH	MAN
Claremore, OK	TLS
Clarence, MO	JC
NY	BUF
PA	ALT
PA	PBR
Clarence Center, NY	BUF
Clarendon, TX	AMA
Clarendon Hills, IL	JOL
Clarinda, IA	DM
Clarion, IA	DUB
PA	E
Clarissa, MN	SCL
Clark, NJ	NEW
SD	SFS
Clark Mills, NY	SY
Clarkesville, GA	ATL
Clarkfield, MN	NU
Clarklake, MI	LAN
Clarks, NE	OM
Clarks Green, PA	SCR
Clarks Mills, WI	GB
Clarks Summit, PA	PSC
PA	SCR
Clarksburg, CA	SAC
WV	WH
Clarksdale, MS	JKS
Clarkson, KY	OWN
NE	OM
Clarkston, MI	DET
WA	SPK
Clarksville, AR	LR
IN	IND
MD	BAL
PA	PIT
TN	NSH
TX	TYL
VA	RIC
Claudell, KS	SAL
Clawson, MI	DET
Claxton, GA	SAV
Clay Center, KS	SAL
Claymont, DE	WIL
Clayton, MO	STL
NC	R
NJ	CAM
NM	SFE
NY	OG
WA	SPK
Clayville, NY	SY
Cle Elum, WA	YAK
Clear Creek, IA	DAV
Clear Lake, IA	DUB
IN	FTW
MN	SCL
SD	SFS
WI	SUP
Clearfield, PA	E
SD	RC
Clearlake, CA	SR
Clearwater, FL	SP
MN	STP
Clearwater Beach, FL	SP
Cleburne, TX	FWT
Clements, MN	NU
Clementsville, KY	L
Clemmons, NC	CHL
Clemson, SC	CHR
Clermont, FL	ORL
IA	DUB
Clermont Harbor, MS	BLX
Cleveland, MN	STP
MS	JKS
NY	SY
OH	CLV
OH	OLL
OH	PRM
OH	ROM
OH	SJP
OK	TLS
TN	KNX
TX	BEA
WI	GB
Cleveland Heights, OH	CLV
Clewiston, FL	VEN
Cliffside Park, NJ	NEW
NJ	NTN
Clifton, AZ	TUC
IL	JOL
KS	SAL
NJ	PAT
TX	FWT
VA	ARL
Clifton Forge, VA	RIC
Clifton Heights, PA	PH
PA	PHU
Clifton Park, NY	ALB
Clifton Springs, NY	ROC
Clint, TX	ELP
Clinton, CT	NOR
IA	DAV
IL	PEO
IN	IND
KY	OWN
MA	WOR
MD	WDC
MI	LAN
MN	NU
MO	KC
MS	JKS
NC	R
NJ	MET
NY	SY
OH	CLV
OK	OKL
SC	CHR
TN	KNX
WI	MAD
Clinton Heights, NY	ALB
Clinton Township, MI	DET
Clinton Twp., MI	DET
Clintonville, WI	GB

Clintwood, VA	RIC
Clio, MI	LAN
Clonmel, KS	WCH
Clontarf, MN	NU
Cloquet, MN	DUL
Closter, NJ	NEW
Cloudcroft, NM	LSC
Cloutierville, LA	ALX
Clover Bottom, MO	STL
Cloverdale, CA	SR
OH	TOL
Cloverport, KY	OWN
Clovis, CA	FRS
NM	SFE
Clute, TX	GAL
Clutier, IA	DUB
Clyde, KS	SAL
MO	KC
NY	ROC
OH	TOL
WI	MAD
Clyman, WI	MIL
Clymer, PA	GBG
PA	PBR
Coachella, CA	SB
Coal City, IL	JOL
Coal Run, PA	PBR
Coal Township, PA	HBG
Coal Valley, IL	PEO
Coaldale, PA	ALN
Coalgate, OK	TLS
Coalinga, CA	FRS
Coalport, PA	E
Coalton, WV	WH
Coamo, PR	PCE
Coates, MN	STP
Coatesville, PA	PH
PA	PSC
Cobden, IL	BEL
Cobleskill, NY	ALB
Cockeysville, MD	BAL
Cocoa, FL	ORL
Cocoa Beach, FL	ORL
Coconut Creek, FL	MIA
FL	PSC
Coconut Grove, FL	MIA
Cody, WY	CHY
Coeur D'Alene, ID	B
Coffeen, IL	SFD
Coffeyville, KS	WCH
Coffman, MO	STL
Coggon, IA	DUB
Cogswell, ND	FAR
Cohasset, MA	BO
MN	DUL
Cohocton, NY	ROC
Cohoes, NY	ALB
NY	STF
Colbert, WA	SPK
Colby, KS	SAL
WI	LC
Colchester, CT	NOR
CT	STF
VT	BUR
Cold Spring, KY	COV
MN	SCL
Cold Spring-on-Hudson, NY	NY
Colden, NY	BUF
Coldwater, KS	DOD
MI	KAL
OH	CIN
Colebrook, NH	MAN
Coleman, MI	SAG
TX	SAN
WI	GB
Colerain, OH	STU
Coleraine, MN	DUL
Coleridge, NE	OM
Colesburg, IA	DUB
KY	L
Colesville, PA	ALN
Colfax, CA	SAC
IA	DAV
IL	PEO
LA	ALX
WA	SPK
Colgate, WI	MIL
College Park, MD	WDC
College Point, NY	BRK
College Station, TX	AUS
Collegeville, MN	SCL
PA	PH
Colleyville, TX	FWT
Collierville, TN	MEM
Collingdale, PA	PH
Collings Lakes, NJ	CAM
Collingswood, NJ	CAM
Collins Center, NY	BUF
Collinsville, CT	HRT
IL	SFD
OK	TLS

Collyer, KS	SAL
Colma, CA	SFR
Colman, SD	SFS
Colo, IA	DUB
Cologne, MN	STP
Colome, SD	RC
Colon, NE	LIN
Colona, IL	PEO
Colonia, NJ	MET
NJ	NEW
Colonia, Yap, FM	CI
Colonial Beach, VA	ARL
Colonial Heights, VA	RIC
Colonie, NY	ALB
The Colony, TX	FWT
TX	STN
Colorado City, TX	SAN
Colorado Springs, CO	COS
CO	VNN
Colstrip, MT	GF
Colton, CA	SB
NY	OG
WA	SPK
Colts Neck, NJ	TR
Columbia, CT	NOR
IL	BEL
MD	BAL
MO	JC
MO	OLL
MS	BLX
PA	HBG
SC	CHR
TN	NSH
VA	RIC
Columbia City, IN	FTW
Columbia Falls, MT	HEL
Columbia Heights, MN	STP
Columbia Station, OH	CLV
Columbiana, OH	Y
Columbus, GA	SAV
IN	IND
KS	WCH
MI	DET
MS	JKS
MT	GF
NE	OM
NJ	TR
OH	COL
OH	NTN
OH	OLL
OH	PRM
TX	VIC
WI	MAD
Columbus Grove, OH	TOL
Columbus Junction, IA	DAV
Colusa, CA	SAC
Colver, PA	ALT
Colville, WA	SPK
Colwich, KS	WCH
Comanche, TX	FWT
Combined Locks, WI	GB
Comerio, PR	CGS
Comfort, TX	SAT
Comfrey, MN	NU
Commack, NY	BRK
NY	RVC
Commerce, TX	DAL
Commerce City, CO	DEN
Compton, CA	LA
Conception, MO	KC
Conception Junction, MO	KC
Concho, AZ	GLP
Concord, CA	OAK
MA	BO
MI	LAN
NC	CHL
NH	MAN
Concord Hill, MO	STL
Concord Twp., OH	CLV
Concord Village, MO	STL
Concordia, KS	SAL
Conde, SD	SFS
Condon, OR	BAK
Conejos, CO	PBL
Conemaugh, PA	ALT
PA	PBR
Conewago Township, PA	HBG
Congers, NY	NY
Conifer, CO	DEN
Conklin, MI	GR
Conneaut, OH	Y
Conneaut Lake, PA	E
Conneautville, PA	E
Connell, WA	SPK
Connellsville, PA	GBG
Connersville, IN	IND
Conrad, MT	HEL
Conroe, TX	GAL
Conshohocken, PA	PH
Constable, NY	OG
Constableville, NY	OG

Constance, NE	OM
Continental, OH	TOL
Convent, LA	BR
Convent Station, NJ	PAT
Converse, TX	SAT
Conway, AR	LR
MI	GAY
MO	SPC
ND	FAR
PA	PIT
SC	CHR
Conway Springs, KS	WCH
Conyers, GA	ATL
GA	SJP
Conyngham, PA	SCR
Cook, MN	DUL
Cookeville, TN	NSH
Cooks, MI	MAR
Cooks Valley, WI	LC
Coolidge, AZ	TUC
Coon Rapids, IA	SC
MN	STP
Coon Valley, WI	LC
Cooper City, FL	MIA
Coopersburg, PA	ALN
Cooperstown, ND	FAR
NY	ALB
WI	GB
Coopersville, MI	GR
NY	OG
Coos Bay, OR	P
Copake Falls, NY	ALB
Copemish, MI	GAY
Copenhagen, NY	OG
Copiague, NY	RVC
Coplay, PA	ALN
Copley, OH	CLV
Coppell, TX	DAL
Copperas Cove, TX	AUS
Copperhill, TN	KNX
Copperopolis, CA	STO
Copperton, UT	SLC
Coquille, OR	P
Coral, PA	GBG
Coral Gables, FL	MIA
Coral Springs, FL	MIA
FL	PMB
Coram, NY	RVC
Coraopolis, PA	PIT
Corbin, KY	LEX
Corcoran, CA	FRS
MN	STP
Cordele, GA	SAV
Cordova, AK	ANC
TN	MEM
Corfu, NY	BUF
Corinth, MS	JKS
NY	ALB
Cornelius, OR	P
Cornell, WI	LC
Corning, CA	SAC
IA	DM
KS	KCK
NY	ROC
OH	COL
Cornucopia, WI	SUP
Cornwall, NY	NY
PA	HBG
Cornwall Bridge, CT	HRT
Cornwall-on-Hudson, NY	NY
Corona, CA	SB
Coronado, CA	SD
Corozal, PR	ARE
Corozal-Padilla, PR	ARE
Corozal-Palmarito, PR	ARE
Corozal-Palos Blancos, PR	ARE
Corpus Christi, (1969)	CC
TX	CC
Corrales, NM	SFE
Corralitos, CA	MRY
Corrigan, TX	BEA
Corry, PA	E
Corsicana, TX	DAL
Cortaro, AZ	TUC
Cortez, CO	PBL
Cortland, NE	LIN
NY	SY
OH	Y
Cortlandt Manor, NY	NY
Corvallis, OR	P
Corwith, IA	DUB
Corydon, IA	DM
IN	IND
Cosgrove, IA	DAV
Coshocton, OH	COL
Costa Mesa, CA	ORG
Cotati, CA	SR
Coteau, LA	LAF
Coteau Holmes, LA	LAF
Coto Laurel, PR	PCE

Cottage Grove, MN	STP
OR	P
WI	MAD
Cottleville, MO	STL
Cottonport, LA	ALX
Cottonwood, AZ	PHX
ID	B
MN	NU
Cotulla, TX	LAR
Coudersport, PA	E
Coulee Dam, WA	SPK
Coulterville, IL	BEL
Council, ID	B
Council Bluffs, IA	DM
Council Grove, KS	WCH
Country Club Hills, IL	CHI
Countryside, IL	CHI
Coupon, PA	ALT
Courtenay, ND	FAR
Coushatta, LA	SHP
Coventry, CT	NOR
RI	PRO
Covina, CA	LA
Covington, GA	ATL
IN	LFT
KY	COV
LA	NO
OH	CIN
TN	MEM
VA	RIC
WA	SEA
Cow Island, LA	LAF
Coweta, OK	TLS
Cowiche, WA	YAK
Coxsackie, NY	ALB
Coylesville, PA	PIT
Cozad, NE	GI
Crabtree, PA	GBG
Crafton, PA	PIT
Craig, AK	JUN
CO	DEN
Cranberry Prairie, OH	CIN
Cranberry Township, PA	PIT
Cranbury, NJ	MET
Crandon, WI	GB
Crane, TX	SAN
Cranford, NJ	NEW
Cranston, RI	PRO
Crary, ND	FAR
Crawford, NE	GI
Crawfordsville, IN	LFT
Creighton, NE	OM
PA	PIT
Creole, LA	LKC
Cresaptown, MD	BAL
Crescent, NY	ALB
OH	STU
Crescent City, CA	SR
FL	STA
Crescent Lake, WI	SUP
Crescent Springs, KY	COV
Cresco, IA	DUB
PA	SCR
Cresskill, NJ	NEW
Cresson, PA	ALT
Crested Butte, CO	PBL
Crestline, CA	SB
OH	TOL
Creston, IA	DM
Crestone, CO	PBL
Crestview, FL	PT
Crestwood, IL	CHI
KY	L
MO	STL
NY	NY
Crete, IL	JOL
NE	LIN
Creve Coeur, IL	PEO
MO	STL
Crewe, VA	RIC
Crittenden, NY	BUF
Crivitz, WI	GB
Crocker, MO	JC
Crockett, CA	OAK
TX	TYL
Crofton, MD	BAL
NE	OM
Croghan, NY	OG
Cromwell, CT	NOR
MN	DUL
Crookston, MN	CR
Crooksville, OH	COL
Crosby, MN	DUL
ND	BIS
TX	GAL
Cross Plains, WI	MAD
Cross Village, MI	GAY
Crossett, AR	LR
Crossingsville, PA	E
Crosslake, MN	DUL
Crossville, TN	KNX

Croswell, MI	SAG
Croton Falls, NY	NY
Croton-on-Hudson, NY	NY
Crow Agency, MT	GF
Crow Hill, ND	FAR
Crowell, TX	FWT
Crowley, LA	LAF
TX	FWT
Crown, PA	E
Crown Butte, ND	BIS
Crown Point, IN	GRY
LA	NO
NY	OG
Crownpoint, NM	GLP
Croydon, PA	PH
PA	SYM
Crozet, VA	RIC
Cruz Bay, VI	STV
Crystal, MN	STP
ND	FAR
Crystal City, MO	STL
TX	LAR
Crystal Falls, MI	MAR
Crystal Lake, IL	RCK
Crystal River, FL	SP
Crystal Springs, MS	JKS
Cuba, KS	SAL
MO	JC
NM	GLP
NY	BUF
OH	TOL
Cuba City, WI	MAD
Cudahy, CA	LA
WI	MIL
Cuero, TX	VIC
Culbertson, MT	GF
Culebra, PR	CGS
Cullman, AL	BIR
Cullom, IL	PEO
Culpeper, VA	ARL
Culver, IN	FTW
Culver City, CA	LA
Culvertown, KY	L
Cumberland, IA	DM
KY	LEX
MD	BAL
RI	PRO
WI	SUP
Cumbola, PA	ALN
Cumming, GA	ATL
IA	DM
Cunningham, KS	WCH
Cupertino, CA	SJ
Curdsville, KY	OWN
Curlew, WA	SPK
Currie, MN	WIN
Curtis, NE	LIN
Curtis Bay, MD	PHU
Curwensville, PA	E
Cushing, OK	TLS
Cusick, WA	SPK
Custar, OH	TOL
Custer, MI	GR
SD	RC
WI	LC
Cut Bank, MT	HEL
Cutchogue, NY	RVC
Cutler, CA	FRS
Cut-Off, LA	HT
Cuyahoga Falls, OH	CLV
Cuyahoga Heights, OH	CLV
Cyclone, TX	AUS
Cygnet, OH	TOL
Cynthiana, KY	COV
Cypress, CA	ORG
Czestochowa, WI	LC
D'Hanis, TX	SAT
Dacada, WI	MIL
Dade City, FL	SP
Daggett, MI	MAR
Dagsboro, DE	WIL
Daguscahonda, PA	E
Dahlgren, IL	BEL
Dahlonega, GA	ATL
Daigle, ME	PRT
Daingerfield, TX	TYL
Dakota, MN	WIN
Dakota Dunes, SD	SFS
Dale, IN	EVN
Dale City, VA	ARL
Dalhart, TX	AMA
Dallas, OR	P
PA	SCR
TX	DAL
Dallastown, PA	HBG
The Dalles, OR	BAK
Dalton, GA	ATL
MA	SPR
PA	SCR
Dalton City, IL	SFD
Daly City, CA	SFR

Dalzell, IL	PEO
Damar, KS	SAL
Damascus, MD	WDC
Damiansville, IL	BEL
Damon, TX	GAL
Dana Point, CA	ORG
Danbury, CT	BGP
CT	NTN
CT	PSC
CT	SAM
IA	SC
TX	GAL
WI	SUP
Dane, WI	MAD
Dania, FL	MIA
Danielson, CT	NOR
Dannemora, NY	OG
Dansville, NY	ROC
Dante, SD	SFS
Danvers, MA	BO
MN	NU
Danville, CA	OAK
IL	PEO
IN	IND
KS	WCH
KY	LEX
OH	COL
PA	HBG
VA	RIC
Daphne, AL	MOB
Darboy, WI	GB
Darby, PA	PH
Dardanelle, AR	LR
Dardenne, MO	STL
Darien, CT	BGP
IL	JOL
Darien Center, NY	BUF
Darlington, NJ	NEW
PA	PIT
WI	MAD
Darnestown, MD	WDC
Darrow, LA	BR
Darwin, MN	NU
Dauby, WI	SUP
Dauphin, PA	HBG
Dauphin Island, AL	MOB
Davenport, CA	MRY
IA	DAV
WA	SPK
Davey, NE	LIN
David City, NE	LIN
Davidsonville, MD	BAL
Davidsville, PA	ALT
Davie, FL	MIA
Davis, CA	SAC
Davis Park, NY	RVC
Davison, MI	LAN
Dawson, MN	NU
NE	LIN
Dawson Springs, KY	OWN
Dayton, IA	SC
KY	COV
MN	STP
NV	RNO
NY	BUF
OH	CIN
OH	OLL
OH	PRM
TN	KNX
TX	BEA
WA	SPK
WI	MAD
WY	CHY
Daytona Beach, FL	ORL
Dayville, CT	NOR
Dazey, ND	FAR
De Forest, WI	MAD
De Funiak Springs, FL	PT
De Graff, MN	NU
De Kalb Junction, NY	OG
De Land, FL	ORL
De Leon, TX	FWT
De Motte, IN	LFT
De Pere, WI	GB
De Queen, AR	LR
De Quincy, LA	LKC
De Ridder, LA	LKC
De Smet, SD	SFS
De Soto, MO	STL
WI	LC
De Witt, MI	LAN
Deadwood, SD	RC
Deal, NJ	TR
Dearborn, MI	DET
MI	ROM
MI	STN
Dearborn Heights, MI	DET
MI	STN
DeBary, FL	ORL
Decatur, AL	BIR
GA	ATL

IL	SFD
IN	FTW
MI	KAL
TX	FWT
Decherd, TN	NSH
Decorah, IA	DUB
Dededo, GU	AGN
Dedham, IA	SC
MA	BO
Deep River, CT	NOR
Deephaven, MN	STP
Deer Lodge, MT	HEL
Deer Park, NY	RVC
TX	GAL
WA	SPK
Deer River, MN	DUL
Deerbrook, WI	GB
Deerfield, IL	CHI
KS	DOD
MI	LAN
MN	WIN
Deerfield Beach, FL	MIA
Deerwood, MN	DUL
Deferiet, NY	OG
Defiance, IA	DM
OH	TOL
DeKalb, IL	RCK
Del Mar, CA	SD
Del Norte, CO	PBL
Del Rey, CA	FRS
Del Rio, TX	SAT
Delafield, WI	MIL
Delair, NJ	CAM
Delancey, PA	E
Delano, CA	FRS
MN	STP
Delanson, NY	ALB
Delavan, IL	PEO
MN	WIN
WI	MIL
Delaware, OH	COL
Delaware City, DE	WIL
Delcambre, LA	LAF
Delevan, NY	BUF
Delhi, IA	DUB
NY	ALB
Delia, KS	KCK
DeLisle, MS	BLX
Dell Rapids, SD	SFS
Delmar, IA	DAV
NY	ALB
Delmont, PA	GBG
Deloit Township, NE	OM
Delphi, IN	LFT
PA	PH
Delphos, KS	SAL
OH	TOL
Delran, NJ	TR
Delray Beach, FL	NTN
FL	PMB
Delta, CO	PBL
Delta Junction, AK	FBK
Delton, MI	KAL
Deltona, FL	ORL
Demarest, NJ	NEW
Deming, NM	LSC
Demopolis, AL	BIR
Denham Springs, LA	BR
Denison, IA	SC
TX	DAL
Denmark, WI	GB
Dennehotso, AZ	NSH
Dennison, OH	COL
Densmore, KS	SAL
Dent, MN	SCL
Denton, NE	LIN
TX	FWT
Denver, CO	DEN
CO	OLL
CO	STN
CO	VNN
NC	CHL
Denver City, TX	LUB
Denville, NJ	PAT
Depew, NY	BUF
Deposit, NY	SY
Deptford, NJ	CAM
Depue, IL	PEO
Derby, CT	HRT
KS	WCH
NY	BUF
Derby Line, VT	BUR
Derry, NH	MAN
PA	GBG
Derwood, MD	WDC
Des Allemands, LA	NO
Des Moines, IA	DM
WA	SEA
Des Peres, MO	STL
Des Plaines, IL	CHI
Descanso, CA	SD

Desert Hot Springs, CA	SB
Deshler, OH	TOL
DeSmet, ID	B
Destin, FL	PT
Destrehan, LA	NO
DeTour, MI	MAR
Detroit, MI	ARM
MI	DET
MI	EST
MI	OLL
MI	PRM
MI	ROM
MI	STN
Detroit Lakes, MN	CR
Deville, LA	ALX
Devils Lake, ND	FAR
Devine, TX	SAT
Devon, PA	PH
Dewey, OK	TLS
DeWitt, IA	DAV
Dewitt, NY	SY
Dexter, IA	DM
ME	PRT
MI	LAN
MO	SPC
NM	LSC
Diamond, LA	NO
Diamond Bar, CA	LA
Diboll, TX	TYL
Dickey, ND	FAR
Dickeyville, WI	MAD
Dickinson, ND	BIS
TX	GAL
Dickson, TN	NSH
Dickson City, PA	SCR
Dieterich, IL	SFD
Dighton, KS	DOD
MA	FR
Dike, IA	DUB
Dilley, TX	SAT
Dillingham, AK	ANC
Dillon, MT	HEL
SC	CHR
Dillonvale, OH	STU
Dilly, WI	LC
Dilworth, MN	CR
Dime Box, TX	AUS
Dimmitt, TX	AMA
Dimock, SD	SFS
Dimondale, MI	LAN
Dinuba, CA	FRS
Dittmer, MO	STL
Divernon, IL	SFD
Dix Hills, NY	RVC
Dixon, CA	SAC
IL	RCK
MO	JC
NM	SFE
Dobbs Ferry, NY	NY
Dobie, WI	SUP
Dodge, NE	OM
Dodge Center, MN	WIN
Dodge City, KS	DOD
Dodgeville, IA	DAV
WI	MAD
Dodson Prairie, TX	FWT
Doland, SD	SFS
Dolgeville, NY	ALB
Dominican Republic, VA	ARL
Dona Ana, NM	LSC
Donaldson, IN	FTW
Donaldsonville, LA	BR
Donegal, PA	GBG
Doniphan, KS	KCK
MO	SPC
NE	LIN
Donna, TX	BWN
Donnelly, MN	SCL
Donora, PA	PBR
PA	PIT
Dorado, PR	SJN
Doraville, GA	ATL
Dorchester, IA	DUB
WI	LC
Dorothy, MN	CR
Dorr, MI	KAL
Dorrance, KS	SAL
PA	SCR
Dos Palos, CA	FRS
Dothan, AL	MOB
Dotyville, WI	MIL
Dougherty, IA	DUB
Douglas, AZ	TUC
GA	SAV
MI	KAL
WY	CHY
Douglas Co., NE	OM
Douglaston, NY	BRK
Douglasville, GA	ATL
Dousman, WI	MIL

Dover, DE	WIL
IN	IND
MA	BO
NH	MAN
NH	SAM
NJ	PAT
OH	COL
TN	NSH
Dover Plains, NY	NY
Dover-Foxcroft, ME	PRT
Dow City, IA	SC
Dowagiac, MI	KAL
Downers Grove, IL	JOL
Downey, CA	LA
Downieville, CA	SAC
Downingtown, PA	PH
Downs, IL	PEO
KS	SAL
Doylesburg, PA	HBG
Doylestown, OH	CLV
PA	PH
WI	MAD
Dracut, MA	BO
Drake, ND	FAR
Draper, UT	SLC
Drayton, ND	FAR
Dresden, OH	COL
Drexel Hill, PA	PH
Drexil Hill, PA	PH
Dripping Springs, TX	AUS
Drummond, MT	HEL
Drums, PA	SCR
Dryden, MI	DET
NY	ROC
Drywood, WI	LC
Du Bois, PA	E
PA	PBR
Du Quoin, IL	BEL
Duarte, CA	LA
Dublin, CA	OAK
GA	SAV
OH	COL
TX	FWT
Dubois, IL	BEL
IN	EVN
Dubuque, IA	DUB
KS	DOD
Dudley, MA	WOR
PA	ALT
Due West, SC	CHR
Duelm, MN	SCL
Dufur, OR	BAK
Duluth, GA	ATL
MN	DUL
Dumas, AR	LR
TX	AMA
Dumont, IA	DUB
MN	SCL
NJ	NEW
Dunbar, PA	GBG
WV	WH
Duncan, IA	DUB
NE	OM
OK	OKL
SD	SFS
Duncan Mills, CA	SR
Duncansville, PA	ALT
Duncanville, TX	DAL
Duncombe, IA	SC
Dundee, IL	RCK
MI	DET
MN	WIN
Dunedin, FL	SP
Dunellen, NJ	MET
NJ	PSC
Dungannon, OH	Y
Dunkirk, IN	LFT
MD	BAL
MD	WDC
NY	BUF
Dunlap, IA	DM
IL	PEO
TN	KNX
Dunlo, PA	ALT
PA	PBR
Dunmore, PA	PSC
PA	SCR
Dunn, NC	R
Dunnellon, FL	ORL
Dunnington, IN	LFT
Dunseith, ND	FAR
Dunsmuir, CA	SAC
Dunwoody, GA	ATL
Dupo, IL	BEL
Dupont, LA	ALX
PA	SCR
Duquesne, PA	PBR
PA	PIT
Duralde, LA	LAF
Durand, IL	RCK
MI	LAN
WI	LC
Durango, CO	PBL
Durant, OK	TLS
Durham, CT	NOR
NC	R
NH	MAN
Durhamville, NY	SY
Durward's Glen, WI	MAD
Duryea, PA	SCR
Dushore, PA	SCR
Duson, LA	LAF
Dutton, MT	HEL
Dutzow, MO	STL
Duxbury, MA	BO
Dwight, IL	PEO
NE	LIN
Dyckesville, WI	GB
Dyer, IN	GRY
Dyersburg, TN	MEM
Dyersville, IA	DUB
Dysart, IA	DUB
Eagan, MN	STP
Eagle, CO	DEN
ID	B
WI	MIL
Eagle Butte, SD	RC
Eagle Center, IA	DUB
Eagle Grove, IA	DUB
Eagle Harbor, MI	STN
Eagle Lake, ME	PRT
TX	VIC
Eagle Pass, TX	LAR
Eagle River, AK	ANC
WI	SUP
Eagle Township, IL	PEO
Earl Park, IN	LFT
Earlimart, CA	FRS
Earling, IA	DM
Earlington, KY	OWN
Earlville, IA	DUB
IL	PEO
Early, IA	SC
Earth City, MO	STL
East Alton, IL	SFD
East Arcade, NY	BUF
East Aurora, NY	BUF
East Bay, NY	ROC
East Berlin, CT	HRT
East Bernard, TX	VIC
East Bethany, NY	BUF
East Bloomfield, NY	ROC
East Brady, PA	E
East Bridgewater, MA	BO
East Bristol, WI	MAD
East Brookfield, MA	WOR
East Brunswick, NJ	MET
NJ	PSC
East Carbon, UT	SLC
East Chain, MN	WIN
East Chicago, IN	GRY
IN	PRM
IN	ROM
East Cleveland, OH	CLV
East Dorset, VT	BUR
East Douglas, MA	WOR
East Dubuque, IL	RCK
East Eden, NY	BUF
East Elmhurst, NY	BRK
East Falmouth, MA	FR
East Freetown, MA	FR
East Gary, IN	GRY
East Goshen, PA	PH
East Grand Forks, MN	CR
East Greenbush, NY	ALB
East Greenwich, RI	PRO
East Hampton, CT	NOR
NY	RVC
East Hanover, NJ	NEW
NJ	PAT
East Hartford, CT	HRT
East Haven, CT	HRT
East Helena, MT	HEL
East Islip, NY	RVC
East Jordan, MI	GAY
East Kingston, NY	NY
East Lansdowne, PA	PH
East Lansing, MI	LAN
East Liverpool, OH	Y
East Longmeadow, MA	SPR
East Lyme, CT	NOR
East McKeesport, PA	PIT
East Meadow, NY	RVC
East Millinocket, ME	PRT
East Moline, IL	PEO
East Newark, NJ	NEW
East Northport, NY	RVC
East Orange, NJ	NEW
East Palestine, OH	Y
East Palo Alto, CA	SFR
East Patchogue, NY	RVC
East Pembroke, NY	BUF
East Peoria, IL	PEO
East Pittsburgh, PA	PBR
PA	PIT
East Pleasant Plain, IA	DAV
East Providence, RI	PRO
East Rochester, NY	ROC
East Rockaway, NY	RVC
East Rutherford, NJ	NEW
East St. Louis, IL	BEL
East Stroudsburg, PA	SCR
East Syracuse, NY	SY
East Taunton, MA	FR
East Tawas, MI	GAY
East Templeton, MA	WOR
East Troy, WI	MIL
East Vandergrift, PA	GBG
East Wenatchee, WA	YAK
East Windsor, CT	HRT
Eastgate, TX	BEA
Easthampton, MA	SPR
Eastlake, OH	CLV
Eastland, TX	FWT
Eastman, GA	SAV
WI	LC
Easton, CA	FRS
CT	BGP
KS	KCK
MA	FR
MD	WIL
MN	WIN
MO	KC
PA	ALN
PA	SAM
Eastpointe, MI	DET
Eastport, ME	PRT
NY	RVC
Eaton, OH	CIN
WI	GB
Eaton Rapids, MI	LAN
Eatontown, NJ	TR
Eau Claire, WI	LC
Eau Galle, WI	LC
Ebensburg, PA	ALT
Ebeye, MH	MI
Echo, LA	ALX
Ecorse, MI	DET
Edcouch, TX	BWN
Eddystone, PA	PH
Eddyville, IA	DAV
KY	OWN
Eden, NC	CHL
NY	BUF
SD	SFS
TX	SAN
WI	MIL
Eden Prairie, MN	STP
Eden Valley, MN	NU
MN	SCL
Edenton, NC	R
Edgar, WI	LC
Edgard, LA	NO
Edgartown, MA	FR
Edgefield, SC	CHR
Edgeley, ND	FAR
Edgerton, KS	KCK
OH	TOL
WI	MAD
Edgewater, MD	BAL
NJ	NEW
Edgewood, IA	DUB
IL	SFD
KY	COV
MD	BAL
Edina, MN	STP
MO	JC
Edinboro, PA	E
Edinburg, TX	BWN
Edinburgh, IN	IND
Edison, NJ	MET
NJ	PSC
Edisto Island, SC	CHR
Edmond, OK	OKL
Edmonds, WA	SEA
Edmonton, KY	L
Edmore, MI	GR
Edna, TX	VIC
Edson, WI	LC
Edwards, CO	DEN
NY	OG
Edwardsburg, MI	KAL
Edwardsville, IL	SFD
PA	PHU
PA	SCR
Effingham, IL	SFD
KS	KCK
Ege, IN	FTW
Egg Harbor, WI	GB
Egg Harbor City, NJ	CAM
Egg Harbor Township, NJ	CAM
Eggertsville, NY	BUF
Egypt, OH	CIN
Ehrenfeld, PA	ALT
El Cajon, CA	SD
CA	SPA
El Campo, TX	VIC
El Centro, CA	SD
El Cerrito, CA	OAK
El Dorado, AR	LR
KS	WCH
El Dorado Hills, CA	SAC
El Dorado Springs, MO	SPC
El Mirage, AZ	PHX
El Monte, CA	LA
El Paso, IL	PEO
TX	ELP
TX	OLL
El Reno, OK	OKL
El Rito, NM	SFE
El Segundo, CA	LA
CA	NTN
El Sobrante, CA	OAK
El Toro, CA	ORG
Eland, WI	GB
Elba, MN	WIN
NY	BUF
WI	MIL
Elberon, NJ	TR
Elberta, AL	MOB
Elbow Lake, MN	SCL
Elburn, IL	RCK
Elcho, WI	GB
Eldon, IA	DAV
MO	JC
Eldora, IA	DUB
Eldorado, IL	BEL
TX	SAN
WI	MIL
Eldred, PA	E
Eldridge, IA	DAV
Electra, TX	FWT
Elgin, IL	RCK
NE	OM
OK	OKL
OR	BAK
TX	AUS
Elizabeth, CO	COS
IL	RCK
MN	SCL
NJ	NEW
NJ	PHU
NJ	PSC
PA	PIT
Elizabeth City, NC	R
Elizabethton, TN	KNX
Elizabethtown, IL	BEL
KY	L
NY	OG
PA	HBG
Elk, TX	AUS
Elk City, OK	OKL
Elk Grove, CA	SAC
WI	MAD
Elk Grove Village, IL	CHI
Elk Mound, WI	LC
Elk Point, SD	SFS
Elk Rapids, MI	GAY
Elk River, MN	SCL
Elkader, IA	DUB
Elkhart, IA	DM
IL	PEO
IN	FTW
KS	DOD
Elkhart Lake, WI	MIL
Elkhorn, NE	OM
WI	MIL
Elkins, WV	WH
Elkins Park, PA	PH
Elkland, PA	SCR
Elko, NV	RNO
Elkton, FL	STA
KY	OWN
MD	WIL
SD	SFS
VA	RIC
Elkview, WV	WH
Ellenburg, NY	OG
Ellenburg Center, NY	OG
Ellendale, MN	WIN
ND	FAR
Ellensburg, WA	YAK
Ellenville, NY	NY
Ellicott City, MD	BAL
Ellicottville, NY	BUF
Ellington, CT	NOR
MO	SPC
Ellinwood, KS	DOD
Ellis, KS	SAL
Ellis Grove, IL	BEL
Ellisville, MO	STL

Ellsworth, KS	SAL
ME	PRT
MN	WIN
PA	PIT
WI	LC
Ellwood City, PA	PIT
Elm Creek, NE	GI
Elm Grove, WI	MIL
Elma, IA	DUB
NY	BUF
WA	SEA
Elmdale, MN	SCL
Elmendorf, TX	SAT
Elmer, NJ	CAM
Elmhurst, IL	JOL
NY	BRK
PA	LIT
PA	SCR
Elmira, MI	GAY
NY	ROC
Elmira Heights, NY	ROC
NY	STF
Elmo, KS	SAL
Elmont, NY	RVC
NY	SYM
Elmora, PA	ALT
Elmsford, NY	NY
Elmwood, IL	PEO
WI	LC
Elmwood Park, IL	CHI
NJ	NEW
Elon, NC	R
Eloy, AZ	TUC
Elrama, PA	PIT
Elrosa, MN	SCL
Elroy, WI	LC
Elsa, TX	BWN
Elsberry, MO	STL
Elsmere, DE	WIL
KY	COV
Elton, LA	LKC
Eltopia, WA	SPK
Elverson, PA	PH
Elwood, IN	LFT
Ely, MN	DUL
NV	LAV
Elyria, NE	GI
OH	CLV
Elyria Township, OH	CLV
Elysburg, PA	HBG
Elysian, MN	STP
Emeigh, PA	ALT
Emerald, KS	KCK
Emerson, NE	OM
NJ	NEW
Emery, SD	SFS
Emeryville, CA	OAK
Emily, MN	DUL
Emlenton, PA	E
Emmaus, PA	ALN
Emmetsburg, IA	SC
Emmett, ID	B
KS	KCK
MI	DET
Emmitsburg, MD	BAL
Emmonak, AK	FBK
Empire, MI	GAY
Emporia, KS	KCK
VA	RIC
Emporium, PA	E
Emsworth, PA	PIT
Encinal, TX	LAR
Encinitas, CA	SD
Encino, CA	LA
Enderlin, ND	FAR
Enders Island, CT	NOR
Endicott, NY	PSC
NY	SY
Endwell, NY	SY
Enfield, CT	HRT
IL	BEL
NH	MAN
Engadine, MI	MAR
Engelberg, AR	LR
Englewood, CO	DEN
FL	VEN
NJ	NEW
OH	CIN
Englewood Cliffs, NJ	NEW
Englishtown, NJ	TR
Enhaut, PA	HBG
Enid, OK	OKL
Ennis, TX	DAL
Enochsburg, IN	IND
Enola, PA	HBG
Enosburg Falls, VT	BUR
Ensenada, PR	PCE
Enterprise, AL	MOB
OR	BAK
Enumclaw, WA	SEA
Ephraim, UT	SLC
Ephrata, PA	HBG
WA	YAK
Epiphany, SD	SFS
Epping, NH	MAN
Epworth, IA	DUB
Equality, IL	BEL
Erath, LA	LAF
Erie, CO	DEN
KS	WCH
MI	DET
PA	E
PA	PBR
Erin, WI	SUP
Erlanger, KY	COV
Ernest, PA	GBG
PA	PBR
Esbon, KS	SAL
Escalon, CA	STO
Escanaba, MI	MAR
Escobares, TX	BWN
Escondido, CA	SD
Eskridge, KS	KCK
Esmond, ND	FAR
Esopus, NY	NY
Espanola, NM	SFE
Essex, CT	NOR
MA	BO
NY	OG
Essex Center, VT	BUR
Essex Junction, VT	BUR
Essexville, MI	SAG
Essington, PA	PH
Estacada, OR	P
Estate Elizabeth, VI	STV
Estate Tutu, VI	STV
Estelline, SD	SFS
Estes Park, CO	DEN
Estherville, IA	SC
Ethan, SD	SFS
Etna, PA	PIT
Ettrick, WI	LC
Euclid, MN	CR
OH	CLV
OH	PRM
Eudora, KS	KCK
Eufaula, AL	MOB
Eugene, OR	P
Eunice, LA	LAF
Eureka, CA	SR
IL	PEO
KS	WCH
MO	STL
MT	HEL
NV	RNO
SD	SFS
UT	SLC
Eureka Springs, AR	LR
Europa, MS	JKS
Eustis, FL	ORL
Eutaw, AL	BIR
Evangeline, LA	LAF
Evans City, PA	PIT
Evans Mills, NY	OG
Evansdale, IA	DUB
Evanston, IL	CHI
WY	CHY
Evansville, IL	BEL
IN	EVN
WI	MAD
Evart, MI	GR
Eveleth, MN	DUL
Everett, MA	BO
PA	ALT
WA	SEA
Evergreen, CO	DEN
LA	ALX
Evergreen Park, IL	CHI
Everson, PA	GBG
Evesham Township, NJ	TR
Ewa, HI	HON
Ewa Beach, HI	HON
Ewen, MI	MAR
Ewing, MO	JC
NE	OM
Excelsior, MN	STP
Excelsior Springs, MO	KC
Exeter, CA	FRS
NE	LIN
NH	MAN
PA	SCR
RI	PRO
Exira, IA	DM
Export, PA	GBG
Exton, PA	PH
Eynon, PA	SCR
Eyota, MN	WIN
Fabens, TX	ELP
Fair Haven, NJ	TR
VT	BUR
Fair Lawn, NJ	NEW
Fair Oaks, CA	SAC
Fairbank, IA	DUB
Fairbanks, AK	FBK
Fairborn, OH	CIN
Fairburn, GA	ATL
Fairbury, IL	PEO
NE	LIN
Fairchance, PA	GBG
Fairchild, WI	LC
Fairfax, CA	SFR
DE	WIL
IA	DUB
MN	NU
OK	TLS
SD	RC
VA	ARL
VT	BUR
Fairfax Station, VA	ARL
Fairfield, AL	BIR
CA	SAC
CT	BGP
IA	DAV
IL	BEL
KY	L
ME	PRT
MT	HEL
ND	STN
NJ	NEW
OH	CIN
PA	HBG
TX	TYL
VT	BUR
Fairfield Bay, AR	LR
Fairfield Glade, TN	KNX
Fairhaven, MA	FR
Fairhope, AL	MOB
Fairlawn, OH	CLV
OH	OLL
Fairless Hills, PA	PH
Fairmont, MN	WIN
WV	WH
Fairmont City, IL	BEL
Fairmount, ND	FAR
NY	SY
Fairmount Springs, PA	SCR
Fairpoint, OH	STU
Fairport, NY	ROC
Fairport Harbor, OH	CLV
OH	PRM
Fairview, NJ	NEW
PA	E
TN	NSH
WI	LC
Fairview Heights, IL	BEL
Fairview Park, OH	CLV
OH	PRM
Faith, SD	RC
Fajardo, PR	CGS
Falconer, NY	BUF
Falfurrias, TX	CC
Fall Creek, WI	LC
Fall River, MA	FR
MA	SAM
MA	STF
Fallbrook, CA	SD
Fallentimber, PA	ALT
Fallon, NV	RNO
Falls Church, VA	ARL
Falls City, NE	LIN
TX	SAT
Falls Creek, PA	E
Fallsington, PA	PH
Fallston, MD	BAL
Falmouth, KY	COV
MA	FR
ME	PRT
Falun, MN	CR
Fancher, WI	LC
Fancy Farm, KY	OWN
Fannett, TX	BEA
Far Hills, NJ	MET
Fargo, ND	FAR
Faribault, MN	STP
Farley, IA	DUB
Farmer, SD	SFS
Farmer City, IL	PEO
Farmersville, CA	FRS
IL	SFD
Farming, MN	SCL
Farmingdale, NJ	TR
NY	BRK
NY	RVC
Farmington, CT	HRT
IA	DAV
IL	PEO
ME	PRT
MI	DET
MN	STP
MO	STL
NH	MAN
NM	GLP
PA	GBG
WI	MIL
WI	SUP
WV	WH
Farmington Hills, MI	DET
MI	OLD
Farmingville, NY	RVC
Farmville, NC	R
VA	RIC
Farnham, NY	BUF
Farrell, PA	E
Farwell, NE	GI
Faulkner, MD	WDC
Faulkton, SD	SFS
Faxon Township, MN	NU
Fayette, AL	BIR
IA	DUB
MO	JC
MS	JKS
OH	TOL
Fayette City, PA	GBG
Fayetteville, AR	LR
GA	ATL
IL	BEL
NC	R
NC	SAM
NY	SY
OH	CIN
TN	NSH
TX	AUS
Feasterville, PA	PH
Federal Dam, MN	DUL
Federal Way, WA	SEA
Feeding Hills, MA	SPR
Fefan, FM	CI
Felicity, OH	CIN
Fellsmere, FL	PMB
Felton, CA	MRY
MN	CR
Fennimore, WI	MAD
Fenton, LA	LKC
MI	LAN
MO	STL
Ferdinand, ID	B
IN	EVN
Fergus Falls, MN	SCL
Ferguson, MO	STL
Fernandina Beach, FL	STA
Ferndale, CA	SR
MI	DET
WA	SEA
Fernley, NV	RNO
Ferriday, LA	ALX
Ferris, TX	DAL
Fertile, MN	CR
Fessenden, ND	FAR
Festina, IA	DUB
Festus, MO	STL
Fidelity, KS	KCK
Fieldon, IL	SFD
Fife, WA	SEA
Fife Lake, MI	GAY
Fifield, WI	SUP
Fifth Ward, LA	ALX
Fillmore, CA	LA
IA	DUB
NY	BUF
Fincastle, VA	RIC
Findlay, OH	TOL
Fingal, ND	FAR
Finlayson, MN	DUL
Finley, KY	L
ND	FAR
Finleyville, PA	PIT
Firebaugh, CA	FRS
Fish Creek, WI	GB
Fish Lake, IN	GRY
Fisher, MN	CR
Fishers, IN	LFT
Fishers Island, NY	NOR
Fisherville, MI	SAG
Fishkill, NY	NY
Fiskdale, MA	WOR
Fitchburg, MA	WOR
Flagler Beach, FL	STA
Flagstaff, AZ	PHX
Flaherty, KY	L
Flambeau, WI	SUP
Flanders, NJ	PAT
NJ	PSC
Flandreau, SD	SFS
Flasher, ND	BIS
Flat Rock, MI	DET
Flatonia, TX	VIC
Fleming, NY	ROC
Flemingsburg, KY	COV
Flemington, NJ	MET
Flensburg, MN	SCL
Flint, MI	LAN
MI	OLL
MI	STN
Flint Hill, MO	STL

Flintville, WI GB
Floodwood, MN DUL
Flora, IL BEL
Flora Vista, NM GLP
Floral Park, NJ SYM
NY RVC
NY SYM
Florence, AL BIR
AZ TUC
CO PBL
KS WCH
KY COV
NJ TR
NY SY
OR P
SC CHR
SD SFS
WI GB
Floresville, TX SAT
Florham Park, NJ PAT
Florian, MN CR
Florida, NY NY
PR ARE
Florissant, LA NO
MO STL
Flossmoor, IL CHI
Flourtown, PA PH
Floydada, TX LUB
Flush, KS KCK
Flushing, MI LAN
MI PRM
NY BRK
OH STU
Foley, AL MOB
MN SCL
Folk, MO JC
Follansbee, WV WH
Folly Beach, SC CHR
Folsom, CA SAC
LA NO
Fond du Lac, WI MIL
Fonda, IA SC
NY ALB
Fontana, CA SB
CA VNN
WI MIL
Footedale, PA GBG
Footville, WI MAD
Forbes Road, PA GBG
Force, PA E
Ford, WA SPK
Ford City, PA GBG
PA SJP
Fords, NJ MET
Fordsville, KY OWN
Fordyce, AR LR
NE OM
Forest, MS JKS
Forest City, IA DUB
MN NU
NC CHL
PA PSC
PA SCR
Forest Grove, OR P
Forest Hill, LA ALX
Forest Hills, NY BRK
PA PIT
Forest Lake, MN STP
Forest Park, IL CHI
Forestburgh, NY NY
Foreston, MN SCL
Forestport, NY SY
Forestville, CT HRT
MD WDC
NY BUF
Forked River, NJ TR
Forks, WA SEA
Forman, ND FAR
Forney, TX DAL
Forrest City, AR LR
Forsyth, MO SPC
MT GF
Fort Ann, NY ALB
Fort Ashby, WV WH
Fort Atkinson, IA DUB
WI MAD
Fort Bend Co., TX GAL
Fort Benton, MT GF
Fort Bragg, CA SR
Fort Branch, IN EVN
Fort Calhoun, NE OM
Fort Collins, CO DEN
Fort Covington, NY OG
Fort Davis, TX ELP
Fort Defiance, AZ GLP
Fort Dodge, IA SC
Fort Edward, NY ALB
Fort Fairfield, ME PRT
Fort Hancock, TX ELP
Fort Jennings, OH TOL
Fort Jones, CA SAC
Fort Kent, ME PRT
Fort Lauderdale, FL MIA
Fort Leavenworth, KS KCK
Fort Lee, NJ NEW
Fort Loramie, OH CIN
Fort Lupton, CO DEN
Fort Madison, IA DAV
Fort McClellan, AL BIR
Fort Mill, SC CHR
Fort Mitchell, KY COV
Fort Monroe, VA RIC
Fort Morgan, CO DEN
Fort Myers, FL VEN
Fort Myers Beach, FL VEN
Fort Oglethorpe, GA ATL
Fort Payne, AL BIR
Fort Pierce, FL PMB
FL PSC
Fort Pierre, SD RC
Fort Plain, NY ALB
Fort Recovery, OH CIN
Fort Riley, KS SAL
Fort Ripley, MN DUL
Fort Scott, KS WCH
Fort Shaw, MT GF
Fort Smith, AR LR
Fort Stockton, TX SAN
Fort Sumner, NM SFE
Fort Thomas, KY COV
Fort Thompson, SD SFS
Fort Totten, ND FAR
Fort Totten Reservation, ND FAR
Fort Walton Beach, FL PT
Fort Washington, MD WDC
PA PH
Fort Wayne, IN FTW
Fort Wingate, NM GLP
Fort Worth, TX FWT
Fort Yates, ND BIS
Fortuna, CA SR
Fortville, IN IND
Forty Fort, PA SCR
Fosston, MN CR
Foster, RI PRO
Foster City, CA SFR
Fostoria, OH TOL
Fountain, CO COS
FL PT
MN WIN
Fountain City, WI LC
Fountain Hill, PA ALN
Fountain Hills, AZ PHX
Fountain Valley, CA ORG
Four Corners, LA LAF
Fowler, CA FRS
IN LFT
KS DOD
MI LAN
Fowlerville, MI LAN
Fox Chase Manor, PA PH
PA PHU
Fox Lake, IL CHI
WI MIL
Fox Point, WI MIL
Foxborough, MA BO
Foxholm, ND BIS
Foxhome, MN SCL
Frackville, PA ALN
PA PHU
Framingham, MA BO
Francesville, IN LFT
Francis Creek, WI GB
Frankenmuth, MI SAG
Frankenstein, MO JC
Frankfort, IL JOL
IN LFT
KS KCK
KY LEX
MI GAY
NY ALB
SD SFS
Franklin, IL SFD
IN IND
KY OWN
LA LAF
MA BO
MN NU
NC CHL
NH MAN
NJ PAT
OH CIN
PA E
TN NSH
TX AUS
VA RIC
WI MIL
WV WH
Franklin Furnace, OH STU
Franklin Lakes, NJ NEW
Franklin Park, IL CHI
Franklin Park Borough, PA PIT
Franklin Square, NY RVC
Franklinton, LA NO
Franklinville, NJ CAM
NY BUF
Fraser, MI DET
Frazee, MN CR
Frazier Park, CA FRS
Frederic, WI SUP
Frederick, CO DEN
MD BAL
OK OKL
Fredericksburg, TX SAT
VA ARL
Fredericktown, MO SPC
PA PIT
Frederiksted, VI STV
Fredonia, KS WCH
NY BUF
WI MIL
Free Soil, MI GR
Freeburg, IL BEL
MO JC
Freedom, PA PIT
WI GB
Freehold, NJ TR
Freeland, MI SAG
PA PSC
PA SCR
Freeport, FL PT
IL RCK
MN SCL
NY RVC
OH STU
PA GBG
TX GAL
Freer, TX CC
Frelsburg, TX VIC
Fremont, CA OAK
CA SYM
MI GR
NE OM
OH TOL
Fremont Center, IL CHI
French Creek, NY BUF
French Lick, IN IND
French Settlement, LA BR
Frenchburg, KY LEX
Frenchtown, IN IND
MT HEL
OH CIN
OH TOL
PA E
Frenchville, ME PRT
PA E
Frenstat, TX AUS
Fresh Meadows, NY BRK
NY STF
Fresno, CA FRS
CA VNN
Frewsburg, NY BUF
Friday Harbor, WA SEA
Fridley, MN STP
Fried, ND FAR
Friend, NE LIN
Friendship, NY BUF
Friendsville, PA SCR
Friendswood, TX GAL
Friona, TX AMA
Frisco, TX DAL
Front Royal, VA ARL
Frontenac, KS WCH
MN STP
MO STL
Frostburg, MD BAL
Fruita, CO PBL
Fruitland, ID B
Fryburg, OH CIN
PA E
Frydek, TX GAL
Fulda, IN IND
MN WIN
ND FAR
OH STU
Fullerton, CA ORG
ND FAR
NE OM
Fulton, IL RCK
KS WCH
KY OWN
MD BAL
MO JC
NY SY
Fuquay-Varina, NC R
NC SAM
Gackle, ND FAR
Gadsden, AL BIR
Gaffney, SC CHR
Gagetown, MI SAG
Gagil-Tomil, FM CI
Gahanna, OH COL
Gaines, MI LAN
Gainesville, FL STA
GA ATL
TX FWT
Gaithersburg, MD WDC
Galena, AK FBK
IL RCK
KS WCH
MD WIL
Galena Park, TX GAL
Gales Ferry, CT NOR
Galesburg, IL PEO
Galesville, WI LC
Galeton, PA E
Galion, OH TOL
Gallatin, TN NSH
Galliano, LA HT
Gallipolis, OH STU
Gallitzin, PA ALT
Galloway, WI LC
Gallup, NM GLP
Galt, CA SAC
Galva, IL PEO
Galveston, TX GAL
Gambrills, MD BAL
Ganado, AZ GLP
TX VIC
Garapan Village, District 11, MP CHK
Garber, IA DUB
Garberville, CA SR
Garden, MI MAR
Garden City, KS DOD
MI DET
NY RVC
SC CHR
Garden Grove, CA ORG
Garden Plain, KS WCH
Garden Valley, ID B
Gardena, CA LA
Gardendale, AL BIR
Gardenville, MO STL
Gardiner, ME PRT
NY NY
Gardner, CO PBL
KS KCK
MA WOR
Gardnerville, NV RNO
Garfield, NJ NEW
NM LSC
Garfield Heights, OH CLV
Garfield Park, DE WIL
Garland, TX DAL
TX SYM
Garnavillo, IA DUB
Garner, IA DUB
NC R
Garnerville, NY NY
Garnett, KS KCK
Garretson, SD SFS
Garrett, IN FTW
Garrett Park, MD WDC
Garrettsville, OH Y
Garrison, MN DUL
ND BIS
NY NY
Garryowen, IA DUB
SD SFS
Garwin, IA DUB
Garwood, NJ NEW
Gary, IN GRY
SD SFS
WV WH
Gary-New Duluth, MN DUL
Garyville, LA NO
Gas City, IN LFT
Gasport, NY BUF
Gassaway, WV WH
Gastonia, NC CHL
Gate City, VA RIC
Gates Mills, OH CLV
Gatesville, TX AUS
Gatlinburg, TN KNX
Gautier, MS BLX
Gaylord, MI GAY
MN NU
Gays Mills, WI LC
Geddes, SD SFS
Genesee, ID B
Genesee Depot, WI MIL
Geneseo, IL PEO
ND FAR
NY ROC
Geneva, IA DUB
IL RCK
IN FTW
MN WIN
NE LIN
NY ROC
OH Y

Genoa, IL	RCK
NE	OM
OH	TOL
WI	LC
Gentilly, MN	CR
George West, TX	CC
Georgetown, CA	SAC
CT	BGP
DE	WIL
IA	DAV
IL	PEO
IN	IND
KY	LEX
MA	BO
MN	CR
OH	CIN
SC	CHR
TX	AUS
WI	SUP
Gering, NE	GI
Germantown, IL	BEL
MD	WDC
NY	ALB
OH	CIN
TN	MEM
WI	MIL
Gervais, OR	P
Gettysburg, PA	HBG
SD	SFS
Getzville, NY	BUF
Gheens, LA	HT
Ghent, MN	NU
Gibbon, MN	NU
Gibbsboro, NJ	CAM
Gibbstown, NJ	CAM
Gibraltar, MI	DET
Gibson, LA	HT
Gibson City, IL	JOL
Gibsonburg, OH	TOL
Gibsonia, PA	PBR
Giddings, TX	AUS
Gig Harbor, WA	SEA
Gila Bend, AZ	PHX
Gilberg, SC	CHR
Gilbert, AZ	PHX
AZ	VNN
IA	DUB
MN	DUL
Gilbertville, IA	DUB
MA	WOR
Gilcrest, CO	DEN
Gildehaus, MO	STL
Gilford, NH	MAN
Gillespie, IL	SFD
Gillett, WI	GB
Gillette, WY	CHY
Gills Pier, MI	GAY
Gilman, IL	JOL
MN	SCL
WI	SUP
Gilmanton Iron Works, NH	MAN
Gilmer, TX	TYL
Gilmore City, IA	SC
Gilroy, CA	SJ
Girard, IL	SFD
KS	WCH
OH	Y
PA	E
PA	PBR
Girardville, PA	ALN
Glade Mills, PA	PIT
Gladstone, MI	MAR
MO	KC
NJ	PAT
Gladwin, MI	SAG
Gladwyne, PA	PH
Glandorf, OH	TOL
Glasco, KS	SAL
NY	NY
Glasgow, DE	WIL
KY	L
MO	JC
MT	GF
Glasgow Village, MO	STL
Glassboro, NJ	CAM
Glassport, PA	PIT
Glastonbury, CT	HRT
CT	STF
Glen Allen, VA	SAM
Glen Burnie, MD	BAL
Glen Campbell, PA	GBG
Glen Carbon, IL	SFD
Glen Cove, NY	BRK
NY	RVC
NY	STF
Glen Dale, WV	WH
Glen Ellyn, IL	JOL
Glen Falls, NY	ALB
Glen Haven, WI	MAD
Glen Head, NY	RVC
Glen Lyon, PA	PHU
PA	PSC
PA	SCR
Glen Owen, MO	STL
Glen Rock, NJ	NEW
Glen Rose, TX	FWT
Glen Spey, NY	STF
Glen Ullin, ND	BIS
Glenbeulah, WI	MIL
Glenburn, ND	BIS
Glencoe, MN	NU
MO	STL
Glendale, AZ	PHX
CA	ARM
CA	LA
NY	BRK
Glendale Heights, IL	JOL
Glendive, MT	GF
Glendora, CA	LA
MS	JKS
Glenfield, NY	OG
Glenmora, LA	ALX
Glenmore, WI	GB
Glenmore/Stark, WI	GB
Glennallen, AK	ANC
Glennie, MI	GAY
Glennonville, MO	SPC
Glenns Ferry, ID	B
Glenolden, PA	PH
Glenrock, WY	CHY
Glens Falls, NY	ALB
Glenshaw, PA	PIT
Glenside, PA	PH
Glenview, IL	CHI
Glenville, NY	ALB
WV	WH
Glenwood, IA	DM
IL	CHI
MN	SCL
Glenwood City, WI	SUP
Glenwood Springs, CO	DEN
Glidden, WI	SUP
Globe, AZ	TUC
Glocester, RI	PRO
Gloucester, MA	BO
NJ	CAM
VA	RIC
Glouster, OH	STU
Gloversville, NY	ALB
Gloverville, SC	CHR
Glyndon, MD	BAL
Glynwood, OH	CIN
GMF, GU	AGN
Gnesen, MN	DUL
Gobles, MI	KAL
Goddard, KS	WCH
Godfrey, IL	SFD
Goetzville, MI	MAR
Goffstown, NH	MAN
Gold Hill, OR	P
Golden, CO	DEN
Golden Gate, FL	VEN
Golden Meadow, LA	HT
Golden Valley, MN	STP
Goldendale, WA	YAK
Goldsboro, NC	R
Goldthwaite, TX	AUS
Goleta, CA	LA
Goliad, TX	VIC
Gonic, NH	MAN
Gonzales, CA	MRY
LA	BR
TX	SAT
Good Hart, MI	GAY
Good Thunder, MN	WIN
Gooding, ID	B
Goodland, IN	LFT
KS	SAL
Goodman, MS	JKS
WI	GB
Goodrich, IL	JOL
MI	LAN
Goodridge, MN	CR
Goodyear, AZ	PHX
Goose Creek, SC	CHR
Gordon, NE	GI
PA	ALN
WI	SUP
Gordonsville, VA	ARL
Gorham, KS	SAL
ME	PRT
NH	MAN
Goshen, CA	FRS
CT	HRT
IN	FTW
KY	L
MA	SPR
NY	NY
Gouldsboro, PA	SCR
Gouverneur, NY	OG
Gowanda, NY	BUF
Graceville, MN	NU
Graettinger, IA	SC
Graford, TX	FWT
Grafton, IL	SFD
MA	WOR
ND	FAR
NE	LIN
NY	ALB
OH	CLV
WI	MIL
WV	WH
Graham, TX	FWT
Grainfield, KS	SAL
Grambling, LA	SHP
Gramercy, LA	BR
Grampian, PA	E
Granada Hills, CA	LA
Granbury, TX	FWT
Granby, CT	HRT
MA	SPR
Grand Bay, AL	MOB
Grand Blanc, MI	LAN
Grand Caillou, LA	HT
Grand Canyon, AZ	PHX
Grand Chain, IL	BEL
Grand Chenier, LA	LKC
Grand Coteau, LA	LAF
Grand Coulee, WA	YAK
Grand Forks, ND	FAR
Grand Haven, MI	GR
Grand Island, NE	GI
NY	BUF
Grand Isle, LA	HT
ME	PRT
Grand Junction, CO	PBL
IA	SC
Grand Lake, CO	DEN
Grand Ledge, MI	LAN
Grand Marais, MI	MAR
MN	DUL
Grand Meadow, MN	WIN
Grand Mound, IA	DAV
Grand Portage, MN	DUL
Grand Prairie, LA	LAF
TX	DAL
Grand Rapids, MI	GR
MI	STN
MN	DUL
Grand River, IA	DM
Grand Rivers, KY	OWN
Grand Ronde, OR	P
Grand Terrace, CA	SB
Grandview, ID	B
MO	KC
WA	YAK
Grandville, MI	GR
Granger, IA	DM
IN	FTW
TX	AUS
WA	YAK
Grangeville, ID	B
Granite City, IL	SFD
Granite Falls, MN	NU
Graniteville, VT	BUR
Grant, NE	LIN
Grant Town, WV	WH
Grantfork, IL	SFD
Grants, NM	GLP
Grants Pass, OR	P
Grantsburg, WI	SUP
Grants-Milan, NM	GLP
Grantsville, MD	BAL
Grantwood, MO	STL
Granville, IA	SC
IL	PEO
ND	FAR
NY	ALB
NY	PSC
OH	COL
Grapevine, TX	FWT
Grass Lake, MI	LAN
Grass Valley, CA	SAC
Gratiot, WI	MAD
Gray, ME	PRT
Grayling, MI	GAY
Graymoor, NY	NY
Grayslake, IL	CHI
Grayson, KY	LEX
Grayson Springs, KY	OWN
Great Barrington, MA	SPR
Great Bend, KS	DOD
PA	SCR
Great Falls, MT	GF
VA	ARL
Great Meadows, NJ	MET
NJ	PHU
Great Mills, MD	WDC
Great Neck, NY	RVC
Greater Cincinnati, OH	CIN
Greeley, CO	DEN
IA	DUB
KS	KCK
NE	GI
Green Bay, WI	GB
Green Cove Springs, FL	STA
Green Creek, IL	SFD
Green Island, IA	DUB
NY	ALB
Green Isle, MN	NU
Green Lake, WI	MAD
Green Pond, NJ	PAT
Green River, WY	CHY
Green Springs, OH	TOL
Green Tree, PA	PIT
Green Valley, AZ	TUC
MN	NU
Greenacres, FL	PMB
Greenbelt, MD	WDC
Greenbrae, CA	SFR
Greenburgh, NY	NY
Greenbush, KS	WCH
MN	CR
Greencastle, IN	IND
PA	HBG
Greencreek, ID	B
Greendale, WI	MIL
Greene, IA	DUB
NY	SY
Greeneville, TN	KNX
Greenfield, CA	MRY
IA	DM
IL	SFD
IN	IND
MA	SPR
OH	CIN
WI	MIL
Greenfield Center, NY	ALB
Greenlawn, NY	RVC
Greenleaf, KS	SAL
MN	NU
WI	GB
Greenport, NY	RVC
Greensboro, GA	ATL
NC	CHL
Greensburg, IN	IND
KS	DOD
KY	L
PA	GBG
PA	PBR
Greenup, IL	SFD
Greenville, AL	MOB
DE	WIL
IL	SFD
ME	PRT
MI	GR
MS	JKS
NC	R
NH	MAN
NY	ALB
OH	CIN
PA	E
RI	PRO
SC	CHR
TX	DAL
WI	GB
Greenwald, MN	SCL
Greenwell Springs, LA	BR
Greenwich, CT	BGP
NY	ALB
Greenwood, IN	IND
MS	JKS
SC	CHR
WI	LC
Greenwood Lake, NY	NY
Greer, SC	CHR
Gregory, SD	RC
TX	CC
Grenada, MS	JKS
Grenora, ND	BIS
Grenville, SD	SFS
Gresham, OR	P
WI	GB
Gretna, LA	NO
NE	OM
Grey Eagle, MN	SCL
Greybull, WY	CHY
Gridley, CA	SAC
Griffin, GA	ATL
Griffith, IN	GRY
Griggsville, IL	SFD
Grindstone, PA	GBG
Grinnell, IA	DAV
KS	SAL
Griswold, CT	NOR
IA	DM
Groom, TX	AMA
Grosse Ile, MI	DET
Grosse Pointe, MI	DET
Grosse Pointe Farms, MI	DET
Grosse Pointe Park, MI	DET
Grosse Tete, LA	BR

Groton, CT	NOR
MA	BO
NY	ROC
SD	SFS
Grove, OK	TLS
Grove City, FL	VEN
OH	COL
PA	E
Grove Hill, AL	MOB
Groveland, MA	BO
Groveport, OH	COL
Grover, SD	SFS
Groves, TX	BEA
Groveton, NH	MAN
Grulla, TX	BWN
Grundy Center, IA	DUB
Gruver, TX	AMA
Grygla, MN	CR
Guadalupe, AZ	PHX
CA	LA
Guanica, PR	PCE
Guasti, CA	SB
Guayama, PR	PCE
Guayanilla, PR	PCE
Guaynabo, PR	SJN
Guckeen, MN	WIN
Guerneville, CA	SR
Guernsey, WY	CHY
Gueydan, LA	LAF
Guilderland, NY	ALB
Guilford, CT	HRT
Gulf Breeze, FL	PT
Gulf Shores, AL	MOB
Gulfport, FL	SP
MS	BLX
Gull Lake, MI	KAL
Gun Barrel City, TX	TYL
Gunnison, CO	PBL
Guntersville, AL	BIR
Gurabo, PR	CGS
Gurnee, IL	CHI
IL	JOL
Gustine, CA	FRS
Guthrie, KY	OWN
OK	OKL
Guthrie Center, IA	DM
Guttenberg, IA	DUB
NJ	NEW
Guymon, OK	OKL
Gwinn, MI	MAR
Gwinner, ND	FAR
Gwynedd Valley, PA	PH
Gypsum, KS	SAL
Hacienda Heights, CA	LA
Hackberry, LA	LKC
Hackensack, MN	DUL
NJ	NEW
Hackettstown, NJ	MET
Haddon Heights, NJ	CAM
Haddon Township, NJ	CAM
Haddonfield, NJ	CAM
Hadley, MA	SPR
Hagaman, IL	SFD
NY	ALB
Hagatna, GU	AGN
Hagerman, ID	B
Hagerstown, MD	BAL
Hague, ND	BIS
NY	ALB
Hahnville, LA	NO
Haiku, HI	HON
Hailey, ID	B
Haines, AK	JUN
Haines City, FL	ORL
Haines Falls, NY	ALB
Hainesport, NJ	CAM
NJ	TR
Hainesville, NJ	PAT
Halbur, IA	SC
Halder, WI	LC
Hale, MI	GAY
Hale Center, TX	LUB
Haledon, NJ	PAT
Hales Corners, WI	MIL
Half Moon Bay, CA	SFR
Halifax, MA	BO
Hallandale, FL	MIA
Hallettsville, TX	VIC
Halliday, ND	BIS
Hallock, MN	CR
Hallowell, ME	PRT
Halstad, MN	CR
Halstead, KS	WCH
Ham Lake, MN	STP
Hamburg, AR	LR
IA	DM
IN	IND
MI	LAN
NJ	PAT
NY	BUF
PA	ALN
Hamden, CT	HRT
Hamel, MN	STP
Hamilton, AL	BIR
GA	SAV
KS	WCH
MA	BO
MO	KC
MT	HEL
NJ	TR
NY	SY
OH	CIN
TX	AUS
VA	ARL
Hamler, OH	TOL
Hamlet, IN	GRY
NC	CHL
Hamlin, ME	PRT
NY	ROC
Hammond, IN	GRY
IN	NTN
LA	BR
MN	WIN
NY	OG
WI	SUP
Hammondsport, NY	ROC
Hammondsville, OH	STU
Hammonton, NJ	CAM
Hampden, MA	SPR
ME	PRT
Hampshire, IL	RCK
Hampstead, MD	BAL
NC	R
NH	MAN
Hampton, IA	DUB
MN	STP
NH	MAN
NJ	MET
VA	RIC
Hampton Bays, NY	RVC
Hampton Beach, NH	MAN
Hamptonburgh, NY	STF
Hamptonville, NC	CHL
Hamtramck, MI	DET
MI	STN
Hana, HI	HON
Hanceville, AL	BIR
Hancock, MD	BAL
MI	MAR
NY	ALB
Hancock Township, MN	STP
Hanford, CA	FRS
Hankinson, ND	FAR
Hannah, MI	GAY
Hannastown, PA	PBR
Hannibal, MO	JC
NY	SY
Hanover, IA	DUB
IL	RCK
KS	SAL
MA	BO
NH	MAN
PA	HBG
Hanover Park, IL	CHI
Hansboro, ND	FAR
Hanson, MA	BO
Hanston, KS	DOD
Hapeville, GA	ATL
Happy, TX	AMA
Harahan, LA	NO
Harbor Beach, MI	SAG
Harbor Springs, MI	GAY
Harborcreek, PA	E
Hardin, IL	SFD
MT	GF
Harding, MN	SCL
PA	SCR
Hardinsburg, KY	OWN
Hardwick, VT	BUR
Harker Heights, TX	AUS
Harlan, IA	DM
KY	LEX
Harleigh, PA	SCR
Harlingen, TX	BWN
Harlowton, MT	HEL
Harmarville, PA	PIT
Harmon, IL	RCK
Harmony, MN	WIN
Harper, IA	DAV
KS	WCH
TX	SAT
Harper Woods, MI	DET
Harpers Ferry, IA	DUB
WV	WH
Harrah, OK	OKL
Harrietta, MI	GAY
Harriettsville, OH	STU
Harriman, NY	NY
TN	KNX
Harrington, WA	SPK
Harrington Park, NJ	NEW
Harris Hill, NY	BUF
Harrisburg, IL	BEL
PA	HBG
PA	PSC
Harrison, AR	LR
MI	SAG
NJ	NEW
NY	NY
WI	SUP
Harrison City, PA	GBG
Harrison Twp., MI	DET
Harrisonburg, VA	RIC
Harrisonville, MO	KC
Harrisville, MI	DET
MI	GAY
NH	MAN
NY	OG
WV	WH
Harrodsburg, KY	LEX
Harrold, SD	SFS
Harsens Island, MI	DET
Hart, MI	GR
Hartford, AR	LR
CT	HRT
CT	STF
CT	SYM
KS	KCK
KY	OWN
MI	KAL
SD	SFS
WI	MIL
Hartford City, IN	LFT
Hartington, NE	OM
Hartland, IL	RCK
MI	LAN
WI	MIL
Hartline, WA	YAK
Hartsdale, NY	NY
Hartshorne, OK	TLS
Hartsville, SC	CHR
Hartwell, GA	ATL
Harvard, IL	RCK
MA	WOR
NE	LIN
Harvey, IL	CHI
LA	NO
ND	FAR
Harvey Cedars, NJ	TR
Harveys Lake, PA	SCR
Harwichport, MA	FR
Harwick, PA	PIT
Harwinton, CT	HRT
Harwood Heights, IL	CHI
Hasbrouck Heights, NJ	NEW
Haskell, NJ	PAT
Hassan Township, MN	STP
Hastings, MI	KAL
MN	STP
NE	LIN
PA	ALT
Hastings-on-Hudson, NY	NY
Hatboro, PA	PH
Hatch, NM	LSC
Hatfield, MA	SPR
PA	PH
Hathaway Manor, MO	STL
Hatillo, PR	ARE
Hatley, WI	LC
Hato Rey, PR	SJN
Hattiesburg, MS	BLX
Haubstadt, IN	EVN
Haugen, WI	SUP
Hauppauge, NY	RVC
Havana, IL	PEO
Havelock, NC	R
Haverford, PA	PH
Haverhill, IA	DUB
MA	BO
Haverstraw, NY	NY
Havertown, PA	PH
Havre, MT	GF
Havre de Grace, MD	BAL
Hawaiian Gardens, CA	LA
Hawarden, IA	SC
Hawesville, KY	OWN
Hawi, HI	HON
Hawk Point, MO	STL
Hawk Run, PA	PBR
Hawkeye, IA	DUB
Hawkins, WI	SUP
Hawley, MN	CR
PA	SCR
Haworth, NJ	NEW
Hawthorne, CA	LA
NJ	PAT
NV	RNO
NY	NY
Hayden, AZ	TUC
Haydenville, MA	SPR
Hayfield, MN	WIN
Hayneville, AL	MOB
Hays, KS	SAL
MT	GF
Haysville, KS	WCH
Hayward, CA	OAK
WI	SUP
Hazard, KY	LEX
Hazel Crest, IL	CHI
Hazel Green, WI	MAD
Hazel Park, MI	DET
Hazelton, ND	BIS
Hazelwood, MN	STP
MO	STL
Hazen, ND	BIS
Hazlehurst, GA	SAV
Hazleton, IA	DUB
PA	PHU
PA	PSC
PA	SCR
Healdsburg, CA	SR
Healy, AK	FBK
Hearne, TX	AUS
Heart Butte, MT	HEL
Heath, OH	COL
Hebbronville, TX	CC
TX	LAR
Hebron, CT	NOR
IN	GRY
ND	BIS
NE	LIN
Hecker, IL	BEL
Heckscherville, PA	ALN
Hecla, SD	SFS
Hector, MN	NU
Heffron, WI	LC
Hegbert, MN	NU
Heidelberg, MN	STP
Heilwood, PA	GBG
Helena, AR	LR
MI	SAG
MT	HEL
Helenwood, TN	KNX
Hellertown, PA	ALN
Helmetta, NJ	MET
Helmville, MT	HEL
Helotes, TX	SAT
Helper, UT	SLC
Hemet, CA	SB
Hemingford, NE	GI
Hemlock, MI	SAG
Hemphill, TX	TYL
Hempstead, NY	RVC
NY	STF
TX	GAL
Henderson, KY	OWN
LA	LAF
MN	NU
NC	R
NV	LAV
TX	TYL
Hendersonville, NC	CHL
TN	NSH
Hennepin, IL	PEO
Hennessey, OK	OKL
Henniker, NH	MAN
Henning, MN	SCL
Henrietta, NY	ROC
TX	FWT
Henry, IL	PEO
LA	LAF
SD	SFS
Henryetta, OK	TLS
Henryville, IN	IND
Henshaw, KY	OWN
Heppner, OR	BAK
Herculaneum, MO	STL
Hercules, CA	OAK
Hereford, AZ	TUC
TX	AMA
Herington, KS	SAL
Herkimer, NY	ALB
Herman, MN	SCL
PA	PIT
Hermann, MO	JC
Hermansville, MI	MAR
Herminie, PA	GBG
PA	PBR
Hermiston, OR	BAK
Hermitage, MO	JC
PA	E
PA	PBR
Hermosa, SD	RC
Hermosa Beach, CA	LA
Hernando, MS	JKS
Herndon, KS	SAL
VA	ARL
Heron Bay, AL	MOB
Heron Lake, MN	WIN
Herreid, SD	SFS
Herrin, IL	BEL
Herron, MI	GAY
Herscher, IL	JOL
Hershey, PA	HBG

Hesperia, CA	SB
Hessmer, LA	ALX
Hettinger, ND	BIS
Heun, NE	OM
Heuvelton, NY	OG
Hewitt, NJ	PAT
TX	FWT
WI	LC
Hewlett, NY	RVC
Hialeah, FL	MIA
Hialeah Gardens, FL	MIA
Hiawatha, IA	DUB
KS	KCK
Hibbing, MN	DUL
Hickman, KY	OWN
Hickory, MD	BAL
NC	CHL
Hickory Hills, IL	CHI
Hicksville, NY	RVC
OH	TOL
Hidalgo, TX	BWN
Higganum, CT	NOR
Higgins Lake, MI	GAY
Higginsville, MO	KC
High Bridge, NJ	MET
High Hill, TX	VIC
High Point, NC	CHL
High Ridge, MO	STL
High Springs, FL	STA
Highbridge, WI	SUP
Highgate Center, VT	BUR
Highland, CA	SB
IL	SFD
IN	GRY
MI	DET
NY	NY
WI	MAD
Highland Beach, FL	PMB
Highland Falls, NY	NY
Highland Heights, KY	COV
OH	CLV
Highland Lakes, NJ	PAT
Highland Mills, NY	NY
Highland Park, IL	CHI
MI	DET
NJ	MET
PA	PH
Highland Springs, VA	RIC
Highlands, NJ	TR
TX	GAL
Highlands Ranch, CO	COS
Highmore, SD	SFS
Hightstown, NJ	TR
Highwood, IL	CHI
Higley, AZ	PHX
Hilbert, WI	GB
Hill City, KS	SAL
MN	DUL
SD	RC
Hillcrest Heights, MD	WDC
Hilliard, OH	COL
Hillje, TX	VIC
Hillman, MI	GAY
MN	DUL
MN	SCL
Hills, IA	DAV
Hillsboro, IL	SFD
MO	STL
ND	FAR
NH	MAN
OH	CIN
OR	P
TX	FWT
WI	LC
Hillsborough, NC	R
NJ	MET
Hillsborough Township, NJ	PSC
Hillsdale, MI	LAN
NJ	NEW
Hillside, IL	CHI
IL	OLL
NJ	NEW
NJ	PHU
Hillsville, PA	PIT
Hilltop, MD	WDC
Hilltown, PA	PH
PA	PSC
Hilmar, CA	FRS
Hilo, HI	HON
Hilton, NY	ROC
Hilton Head Island, SC	CHR
Hinckley, MN	DUL
NY	SY
OH	CLV
Hinesburg, VT	BUR
Hinesville, GA	SAV
Hingham, MA	BO
Hinsdale, IL	JOL
MA	SPR
NH	MAN
NY	BUF
Hinton, WV	WH
Hirlingen, MO	KC
Hitchcock, OK	OKL
TX	GAL
Hobart, IN	GRY
OK	OKL
Hobbs, NM	LSC
Hobe Sound, FL	PMB
Hoboken, NJ	NEW
Hobson, TX	SAT
Hockessin, DE	WIL
Hodge, LA	SHP
Hodgenville, KY	L
Hofa Park, WI	GB
Hoffman Estates, IL	CHI
Hogansburg, NY	OG
Hohenwald, TN	NSH
Hohokus, NJ	NEW
Hoisington, KS	DOD
Hokah, MN	WIN
Holbrook, AZ	GLP
IA	DAV
MA	BO
NY	RVC
Holden, MO	KC
WV	WH
Holdenville, OK	TLS
Holdingford, MN	SCL
Holdrege, NE	LIN
Holgate, OH	TOL
Holiday, FL	SP
Holiday Park, PA	PIT
Holland, MI	GR
NY	BUF
PA	LIT
PA	PH
Holland Patent, NY	SY
Hollandale, WI	MAD
Hollandtown, WI	GB
Holley, NY	BUF
Hollidaysburg, PA	ALT
Hollis Hills, NY	BRK
Hollister, CA	MRY
Holliston, MA	BO
Holloway, MN	NU
Holly, CO	PBL
MI	DET
Holly Hill, SC	CHR
Holly Springs, MS	JKS
Hollywood, FL	MIA
MD	WDC
Holmdel, NJ	TR
Holmen, WI	LC
Holmes Beach, FL	VEN
Holstein, IA	SC
Holton, KS	KCK
Holts Summit, MO	JC
Holtville, CA	SD
Holy Cross, AK	FBK
IA	DUB
KY	L
WI	MIL
Holy Hill, WI	MIL
Holy Trinity, AL	MOB
Holyoke, CO	DEN
MA	SPR
Holyrood, KS	SAL
Homedale, ID	B
Homer, AK	ANC
NY	SY
Homer City, PA	PBR
Homer Glen, IL	JOL
Homestead, FL	MIA
PA	PIT
Hometown, IL	CHI
Homewood, IL	CHI
Hominy, OK	TLS
Homosassa, FL	SP
Honaunau, HI	HON
Hondo, TX	SAT
Honeoye, NY	ROC
Honeoye Falls, NY	ROC
Honesdale, PA	SCR
Honey Brook, PA	PH
Honokaa, HI	HON
Honolulu, HI	HON
HI	STN
Hood River, OR	BAK
Hooksett, NH	MAN
Hoonah, AK	JUN
Hoopa, CA	SR
Hooper, NE	OM
Hooper Bay, AK	FBK
Hoopeston, IL	PEO
Hooppole, IL	PEO
Hoosick Falls, NY	ALB
Hooversville, PA	ALT
Hopatcong, NJ	PAT
Hope, AR	LR
KS	SAL
ND	FAR
Hope Mills, NC	R
Hopedale, MA	WOR
OH	STU
Hopewell, NJ	TR
VA	RIC
Hopewell Junction, NY	NY
Hopewell Township, PA	PIT
Hopkins, MN	STP
Hopkins Park, IL	JOL
Hopkinsville, KY	OWN
Hopkinton, IA	DUB
MA	BO
NY	OG
RI	PRO
Hoquiam, WA	SEA
Horicon, WI	MIL
Horizon City, TX	ELP
Hormigueros, PR	MGZ
Hornell, NY	ROC
Hornick, IA	SC
Horseheads, NY	ROC
Horseshoe Bay, TX	AUS
Horseshoe Bend, AR	LR
ID	B
Horsham, PA	PH
Horton, KS	KCK
Hortonville, WI	GB
Hoschton, GA	ATL
Hosmer, SD	SFS
Hospers, IA	SC
Hostyn, TX	VIC
Hostyn Hill, TX	AUS
Hot Springs, AR	LR
NC	CHL
SD	RC
VA	RIC
Hot Springs National Park, AR	LR
Hot Springs Village, AR	LR
Houck, AZ	GLP
Houghton, IA	DAV
MI	MAR
Houghton Lake, MI	GAY
Houlton, ME	PRT
Houma, LA	HT
Housatonic, MA	SPR
House Springs, MO	STL
Houseville, NY	OG
Houston, MN	WIN
MO	SPC
TX	GAL
TX	OLL
TX	PBR
TX	STN
TX	SYM
Houtzdale, PA	E
Hoven, SD	SFS
Howard, SD	SFS
WI	GB
Howard City, MI	GR
Howardstown, KY	L
Howell, MI	LAN
Howell Township, NJ	TR
Howells, NE	OM
Howes, SD	RC
Howland, ME	PRT
Hoxie, KS	SAL
Hoyt Lakes, MN	DUL
Hubbard, OH	Y
Hubbardston, MI	GR
Hubbell, MI	MAR
Hubertus, WI	MIL
Hudson, FL	SP
MA	BO
MI	LAN
NH	MAN
NY	ALB
NY	STF
OH	CLV
PA	SCR
WI	SUP
Hudson Falls, NY	ALB
Huffman, TX	GAL
Hughestown, PA	SCR
Hughson, CA	STO
Hugo, MN	STP
OK	TLS
Hugoton, KS	DOD
Hulbert, OK	TLS
Hull, MA	BO
Humacao, PR	CGS
Humacao Playa, PR	CGS
Humble, TX	GAL
Humboldt, IA	SC
KS	WCH
SD	SFS
TN	MEM
WI	GB
Humbolt, WI	GB
Hume, IL	SFD
Humphrey, NE	OM
NY	BUF
Hungerford, TX	VIC
Hunt Valley, MD	BAL
Hunter, ND	FAR
NY	STF
Huntersville, NC	CHL
Huntimer, SD	SFS
Huntingburg, IN	EVN
Huntingdon, PA	ALT
TN	MEM
Huntingdon Valley, PA	PH
Huntington, IN	FTW
MA	SPR
NY	RVC
WV	WH
Huntington Beach, CA	ORG
Huntington Park, CA	LA
Huntington Station, NY	RVC
Huntingtown, MD	WDC
Huntley, IL	RCK
Huntsville, AL	BIR
AR	LR
OH	CIN
TX	GAL
UT	SLC
Hurdsfield, ND	FAR
Hurley, NM	LSC
NY	NY
WI	SUP
Huron, CA	FRS
OH	TOL
SD	SFS
Hurricane, WV	WH
Hurt, VA	RIC
Hurtsboro, AL	MOB
Hutchinson, KS	WCH
MN	NU
Huttonsville, WV	WH
Hyannis, MA	FR
Hyattsville, MD	WDC
Hyde Park, NY	NY
Hydes, MD	BAL
Iamsville, MD	BAL
Ida, MI	DET
Ida Grove, IA	SC
Idabel, OK	TLS
Idaho City, ID	B
Idaho Falls, ID	B
Idaho Springs, CO	DEN
Idalou, TX	LUB
Idyllwild, CA	SB
Idylwilde, SD	SFS
Ignacio, CO	PBL
Ilasco, MO	JC
Iliff, CO	DEN
Ilion, NY	ALB
Illiopolis, IL	SFD
Imlay City, MI	DET
Immaculata, PA	PH
Immokalee, FL	VEN
Imogene, IA	DM
Imperial, CA	SD
MO	STL
NE	LIN
PA	PIT
Imperial Beach, CA	SD
Inarajan, GU	AGN
Inchelium, WA	SPK
Incline Village, NV	RNO
Independence, IA	DUB
KS	WCH
KY	COV
LA	BR
MO	KC
OH	CLV
OR	P
WI	LC
Indialantic, FL	ORL
Indian Creek, IL	CHI
MO	JC
WI	LC
Indian Grove, MO	JC
Indian Head, MD	WDC
Indian Island, ME	PRT
Indian Lake, NY	OG
Indian Orchard, MA	SPR
Indian River, MI	GAY
Indian Rocks Beach, FL	SP
Indian Township, ME	PRT
Indiana, PA	GBG
Indiana Harbor Co., IN	PRM
Indianapolis, IN	IND
IN	PRM
Indianola, IA	DM
MS	JKS
NE	LIN
Indiantown, FL	PMB
Indio, CA	SB
Industry, PA	PIT
Inez, TX	VIC
Ingalls, KS	DOD

Ingleside, IL	CHI
TX	CC
Inglewood, CA	LA
Ingram, PA	PIT
Inkerman, PA	SCR
Inkster, MI	DET
Inlet, NY	OG
Ino, WI	SUP
Institute, WI	GB
Interlachen, FL	STA
Interlaken, NY	ROC
International Falls, MN	DUL
Inver Grove Heights, MN	STP
Inverness, FL	SP
IL	CHI
Inwood, NY	RVC
WV	WH
Iola, KS	WCH
Iona, MN	WIN
Ione, CA	SAC
OR	BAK
WA	SPK
Ionia, IA	DUB
MI	GR
Iota, LA	LAF
Ioueldoab, FM	CI
Iowa, LA	LKC
Iowa City, IA	DAV
Iowa Falls, IA	DUB
Iowa Park, TX	FWT
Ipswich, MA	BO
SD	SFS
Ipwutek, FM	CI
Ireland, IN	EVN
Irene, SD	SFS
Irish Settlement, IA	DM
Iron Mountain, MI	MAR
Iron River, MI	MAR
WI	SUP
Irons, MI	GR
Ironton, MO	SPC
OH	STU
Ironwood, MI	MAR
Iroquois, SD	SFS
Irvine, CA	ORG
KY	LEX
Irving, TX	DAL
TX	PBR
Irvington, KY	OWN
NJ	NEW
Irvington-on-the-Hudson, NY	NY
Irwin, IL	JOL
PA	GBG
Irwindale, CA	LA
Isaar, WI	GB
Isabela, PR	ARE
Isanti, MN	SCL
Iselin, NJ	MET
PA	GBG
Ishpeming, MI	MAR
Island Falls, ME	PRT
Island Grove, IL	SFD
Island Park, NY	RVC
Island Pond, VT	BUR
Isle Brevelle, LA	ALX
Isle La Motte, VT	BUR
Isleta, NM	SFE
Isleton, CA	SAC
Islip, NY	RVC
Islip Terrace, NY	RVC
Issaquah, WA	SEA
Issue, MD	WDC
Itasca, IL	JOL
Ithaca, MI	SAG
NY	ROC
Ivanhoe, MN	NU
Ivesdale, IL	PEO
Jackman, ME	PRT
Jacksboro, TX	FWT
Jackson, CA	SAC
KY	LEX
MI	LAN
MN	WIN
MO	SPC
MS	JKS
NE	OM
NJ	MET
NJ	TR
OH	COL
PA	SCR
TN	MEM
WY	CHY
Jacksonport, WI	GB
Jacksonville, AL	BIR
AR	LR
FL	OLD
FL	PSC
FL	SAM
FL	STA
IL	SFD
NC	R

TX	TYL
Jacksonville Beach, FL	STA
Jacob's Prairie, MN	SCL
Jacumba, CA	SD
Jaffrey, NH	MAN
Jal, NM	LSC
Jamaica, IA	DM
NY	BRK
NY	NY
Jamaica Estates, NY	BRK
NY	NY
Jamaica Plain, MA	SAM
Jamaica Plains, MA	BO
Jamesburg, NJ	MET
Jamestown, KS	SAL
KY	L
ND	FAR
NY	BUF
OH	CIN
RI	PRO
Jamesville, NY	SY
Jamison, PA	PH
Jamul, CA	SD
Janesville, MN	WIN
WI	MAD
Jarrell, TX	AUS
Jasonville, IN	EVN
Jasper, AL	BIR
IN	EVN
MN	WIN
TX	BEA
Java Center, NY	BUF
Jay, ME	PRT
Jayuya, PR	PCE
Jeanerette, LA	LAF
Jeannette, PA	GBG
PA	SJP
Jeffers, MN	WIN
Jefferson, IA	SC
LA	NO
MA	WOR
NC	CHL
OH	Y
SD	SFS
TX	TYL
WI	MAD
Jefferson Boro, PA	PIT
Jefferson City, MO	JC
TN	KNX
Jeffersonville, IN	IND
NY	NY
Jellico, KY	LEX
Jemez Pueblo, NM	SFE
Jemez Springs, NM	SFE
Jena, LA	ALX
Jenison, MI	GR
Jenkins, KY	LEX
Jenkintown, PA	PH
PA	PHU
Jennings, LA	LKC
MO	STL
Jensen Beach, FL	PMB
Jericho, WI	GB
Jermyn, PA	SCR
Jerome, AZ	PHX
ID	B
PA	PBR
Jersey City, NJ	NEW
NJ	PHU
NJ	PSC
NJ	SYM
Jersey Shore, PA	SCR
Jerseyville, IL	SFD
Jessenland, MN	NU
Jessie, ND	FAR
Jessup, MD	BAL
PA	PSC
PA	SCR
Jesup, GA	SAV
IA	DUB
Jetmore, KS	DOD
Jewell, IA	DUB
Jewett, OH	STU
Jewett City, CT	NOR
Jim Falls, WI	LC
Jim Thorpe, PA	ALN
Joanna, SC	CHR
Joelton, TN	NSH
Johannesburg, MI	GAY
John Day, OR	BAK
Johns Island, SC	CHR
Johnsburg, IL	RCK
MN	WIN
WI	MIL
Johnson, KS	DOD
Johnson City, NY	STF
NY	SY
TN	KNX
Johnson Creek, WI	MAD
Johnsonburg, PA	E
Johnsonville, NY	ALB

Johnston, IA	DM
RI	PRO
Johnston City, IL	BEL
Johnstown, CO	DEN
NY	ALB
OH	COL
PA	ALT
PA	PBR
PA	SJP
Joliet, IL	JOL
IL	PRM
Jolon, CA	MRY
Jones, OK	OKL
Jonesboro, AR	LR
GA	ATL
Jonesburg, MO	JC
Jonestown, MS	JKS
TX	AUS
Jonesville, VA	RIC
Joplin, MO	SPC
Joppa, MD	BAL
Jordan, MN	STP
NY	SY
OR	P
Jordan Valley, OR	BAK
Josephville, MO	STL
Joshua Tree, CA	SB
Jourdanton, TX	SAT
Juana Diaz, PR	PCE
Juarez, Mexico	CIN
Judice, LA	LAF
Julesburg, CO	DEN
Julian, CA	SD
Jump River, WI	SUP
Juncos, PR	CGS
Junction, OH	TOL
TX	SAN
Junction City, KS	SAL
OH	COL
OR	P
WI	LC
Juneau, AK	JUN
WI	MIL
Juno Beach, FL	PMB
Jupiter, FL	PMB
Justice, IL	CHI
Kadoka, SD	RC
Kagman Village, MP	CHK
Kahoka, MO	JC
Kahuku, HI	HON
Kahului, HI	HON
Kailua, HI	HON
Kailua-Kona, HI	HON
Kalaheo, HI	HON
Kalamazoo, MI	KAL
Kalaupapa, HI	HON
Kalida, OH	TOL
Kalispell, MT	HEL
Kalkaska, MI	GAY
Kaltag, AK	FBK
Kamiah, ID	B
Kampsville, IL	SFD
Kamuela, HI	HON
Kanab, UT	SLC
Kandiyohi, MN	NU
Kane, PA	E
Kaneohe, HI	HON
Kankakee, IL	JOL
Kanopolis, KS	SAL
Kansas, OH	TOL
Kansas City, KS	KCK
MO	KC
Kansas City North, MO	KC
Kansasville, WI	MIL
Kapaa, HI	HON
Kaplan, LA	LAF
Karlsruhe, ND	FAR
Karlstad, MN	CR
Karnes City, TX	SAT
Kaskaskia, IL	BEL
Kasson, MN	WIN
Katonah, NY	NY
Katy, TX	GAL
Kaufman, TX	DAL
Kaukauna, WI	GB
Kaunakakai, HI	HON
Kawkawlin, MI	SAG
Kayenta, AZ	GLP
Keams Canyon, AZ	GLP
Keansburg, NJ	TR
Kearney, MO	KC
NE	GI
Kearneysville, WV	WH
Kearns, UT	SLC
Kearny, AZ	TUC
NJ	NEW
Keaukaha, Hilo, HI	HON
Keene, NH	MAN
NY	OG
Keeseville, NY	OG
Keewatin, MN	DUL

Keizer, OR	P
Kekaha, HI	HON
Kelayres, PA	ALN
Keller, TX	FWT
WA	SPK
Kelley's Island, OH	TOL
Kelliher, MN	CR
Kellnersville, WI	GB
Kellogg, ID	B
MN	WIN
Kelly, KS	KCK
Kelso, MO	SPC
WA	SEA
Kemmerer, WY	CHY
Kenai, AK	ANC
Kendall, NY	BUF
WI	LC
Kendall Park, NJ	MET
Kendallville, IN	FTW
Kenedy, TX	SAT
Kenel, SD	RC
Kenesaw, NE	LIN
Kenilworth, NJ	NEW
Kenmare, ND	BIS
Kenmore, NY	BUF
NY	STF
WA	SEA
Kennebec, SD	RC
Kennebunk, ME	PRT
Kennebunkport, ME	PRT
Kennedy Township, PA	PIT
Kenner, LA	NO
Kennesaw, GA	ATL
Kennett, MO	SPC
Kennett Square, PA	PH
PA	WIL
Kennewick, WA	YAK
Kenosha, WI	MIL
WI	PRM
Kensal, ND	FAR
Kensington, CA	OAK
CT	HRT
MD	WDC
MN	SCL
Kent, CT	HRT
MN	SCL
OH	Y
PA	GBG
WA	SEA
Kentfield, CA	SFR
Kentland, IN	LFT
Kenton, KY	COV
OH	COL
Kenton Hills, KY	COV
Kenyon, MN	STP
Keokuk, IA	DAV
Keota, IA	DAV
Kerhonkson, NY	STF
Kerman, CA	FRS
Kermit, TX	ELP
WV	WH
Kernersville, NC	CHL
Kerrville, TX	SAT
Kersey, PA	E
Keshena, WI	GB
Keswick, IA	DAV
Ketchikan, AK	JUN
Kettle Falls, WA	SPK
Keuterville, ID	B
Kewanee, IL	PEO
Kewanna, IN	LFT
Kewaskum, WI	MIL
Kewaunee, WI	GB
Key Biscayne, FL	MIA
Key Largo, FL	MIA
Key West, FL	MIA
IA	DUB
Keyesville, WI	LC
Keyport, NJ	TR
Keyser, WV	WH
Keystone Heights, FL	STA
Kickapoo, IL	PEO
Kiel, WI	GB
Kieler, WI	MAD
Kihei, HI	HON
Kilgore, TX	TYL
Kilkenny, MN	STP
Killdeer, ND	BIS
Killeen, TX	AUS
Killingworth, CT	NOR
Kilmarnock, VA	ARL
Kiln, MS	BLX
Kimball, MN	SCL
NE	GI
SD	SFS
Kimberling City, MO	SPC
Kimberly, WI	GB
Kimberton, PA	PH
Kimeo, KS	SAL
Kincaid, IL	SFD
Kinde, MI	SAG

Kinder, LA	LKC
Kindred, ND	FAR
King, WI	GB
King City, CA	MRY
King Ferry, NY	ROC
King of Prussia, PA	PH
Kingfisher, OK	OKL
Kingman, AZ	PHX
KS	WCH
Kings Park, NY	RVC
Kingsburg, CA	FRS
Kingsford, MI	MAR
Kingsford Heights, IN	GRY
Kingsland, TX	AUS
Kingsley, IA	SC
Kingsport, TN	KNX
Kingston, MA	BO
NY	NY
PA	PSC
PA	SCR
WI	MAD
Kingstree, SC	CHR
Kingsville, OH	Y
TX	CC
Kingwood, TX	GAL
WV	WH
Kinloch, MO	STL
Kinmundy, IL	BEL
Kinnelon, NJ	PAT
Kinross, IA	DAV
Kinsley, KS	DOD
Kinsman, IL	JOL
OH	Y
Kinston, NC	R
Kintyre, ND	FAR
Kiowa, KS	DOD
Kirby, OH	TOL
TX	SAT
Kirbyville, TX	BEA
Kirkland, WA	SEA
Kirksville, MO	JC
Kirkwood, MO	STL
NY	SY
Kirtland, OH	CLV
Kissimmee, FL	ORL
Kittanning, PA	GBG
Kittery, ME	PRT
Kitty Hawk, NC	R
Klacking Creek, MI	GAY
Klamath Falls, OR	BAK
Klondike, WI	GB
Kloten, WI	GB
Knapp Creek, NY	BUF
Knights Landing, CA	SAC
Knightstown, IN	IND
Knottsville, KY	OWN
Knowlton, WI	LC
Knox, IN	GRY
ND	FAR
Knox City, TX	FWT
Knoxville, IA	DAV
TN	KNX
Kodiak, AK	ANC
Koerth, TX	VIC
Kohler, WI	MIL
Kokomo, IN	LFT
Koloa, HI	HON
Kolonia, FM	CI
Kolonia, Pohnpei, FM	CI
Konawa, OK	OKL
Koppel, PA	PIT
Korona, FL	STA
Koror, FM	CI
Koror, Palau, PW	CI
Kosciusko, MS	JKS
Kosciuszko, TX	SAT
Kossuth, WI	GB
Kotlik, AK	FBK
Kotzebue, AK	FBK
Kountze, TX	BEA
Kouts, IN	GRY
Kovar, TX	AUS
Koyukuk, AK	FBK
Kraemer, LA	HT
Krakow, MO	STL
NE	OM
WI	GB
Kranzburg, SD	SFS
Krebs, OK	TLS
Kremmling, CO	DEN
Krok, WI	GB
Krotz Springs, LA	LAF
Kula, HI	HON
Kulpmont, PA	HBG
Kutztown, PA	ALN
Kwajalein, MH	MI
Kyle, SD	RC
TX	AUS
L'Anse, MI	MAR
La Canada Flintridge, CA	LA
La Conner, WA	SEA

La Crescent, MN	WIN
La Crescenta, CA	LA
La Crosse, WI	LC
La Feria, TX	BWN
La Grande, OR	BAK
La Grange, IL	CHI
TX	AUS
La Grange Park, IL	CHI
La Habra, CA	ORG
La Jolla, CA	SD
La Joya, NM	SFE
TX	BWN
La Junta, CO	PBL
La Marque, TX	GAL
La Mesa, CA	NTN
CA	SD
NM	LSC
La Mirada, CA	LA
La Motte, IA	DUB
La Moure, ND	FAR
La Pine, OR	BAK
La Place, LA	NO
La Plata, MD	WDC
La Porte, IN	GRY
TX	GAL
La Porte City, IA	DUB
La Pryor, TX	LAR
La Puente, CA	LA
La Quinta, CA	SB
La Rue, OH	COL
La Salle, IL	PEO
La Valle, WI	MAD
La Verne, CA	LA
La Vernia, TX	SAT
Labadieville, LA	BR
LaBelle, FL	VEN
Lac du Flambeau, WI	SUP
LaCenter, KY	OWN
Lacey, WA	SEA
Laceyville, PA	SCR
Lackawanna, NY	BUF
NY	STF
Lacombe, LA	NO
Lacon, IL	PEO
Lacona, IA	DM
NY	SY
Laconia, NH	MAN
LaConner, WA	SEA
LaCoste, TX	SAT
LaCrosse, KS	DOD
Lacrosse, WA	SPK
LaCygne, KS	KCK
Ladd, IL	PEO
Ladue, MO	STL
Lady Lake, FL	ORL
Ladysmith, WI	SUP
Lafargeville, NY	OG
Lafayette, CA	OAK
CO	DEN
IN	LFT
LA	LAF
LA	OLL
MN	NU
NJ	PAT
NY	SY
OR	P
TN	NSH
Lafayette Hill, PA	PH
Lafferty, OH	STU
Lafitte, LA	NO
Laflin, PA	SCR
LaFollette, TN	KNX
Lago Vista, TX	AUS
LaGrange, GA	ATL
IN	FTW
KY	L
TX	AUS
LaGrange Park, IL	CHI
Lagro, IN	FTW
Laguna, NM	GLP
Laguna Beach, CA	ORG
Laguna Hills, CA	ORG
Laguna Niguel, CA	ORG
Lagunitas, CA	SFR
Lahaina, HI	HON
Laingsburg, MI	LAN
Lajas, PR	MGZ
Lake Andes, SD	SFS
Lake Ariel, PA	SCR
Lake Arrowhead, CA	SB
Lake Arthur, LA	LKC
Lake Benton, MN	NU
Lake Charles, LA	LKC
LA	OLL
Lake Charles Shores, FL	PMB
Lake City, FL	STA
IA	SC
MI	GAY
MN	WIN
SC	CHR
SD	SFS

Lake Clear, NY	OG
Lake Crystal, MN	WIN
Lake Dallas, TX	FWT
Lake Elmo, MN	STP
Lake Elsinore, CA	SB
Lake Eunice Township, MN	CR
Lake Five, WI	MIL
Lake Forest, CA	ORG
IL	CHI
Lake Gaston, VA	RIC
Lake Geneva, WI	MIL
Lake George, NY	ALB
Lake Harmony, PA	ALN
Lake Havasu City, AZ	PHX
Lake Henry, MN	SCL
Lake Hopatcong, NJ	PAT
Lake Itasca, MN	CR
Lake Jackson, TX	GAL
Lake Katrine, NY	NY
Lake Leelanau, MI	GAY
Lake Lillian, MN	NU
Lake Linden, MI	MAR
Lake Luzerne, NY	ALB
Lake Mills, IA	DUB
WI	MAD
Lake Milton, OH	Y
Lake Nebagamon, WI	SUP
Lake Odessa, MI	GR
Lake Orion, MI	DET
Lake Oswego, OR	P
Lake Ozark, MO	JC
Lake Park, MN	CR
Lake Placid, FL	VEN
NY	OG
Lake Pleasant, NY	OG
Lake Providence, LA	SHP
Lake Reno, MN	SCL
Lake Ridge, VA	ARL
Lake Ronkonkoma, NY	RVC
Lake St. Croix Beach, MN	STP
Lake St. Louis, MO	STL
Lake San Marcos, CA	SD
Lake Silkworth, PA	SCR
Lake Station, IN	GRY
Lake Tamarisk, CA	SB
Lake Tomahawk, WI	SUP
Lake View, NY	BUF
Lake Villa, IL	CHI
Lake Village, AR	LR
IN	LFT
Lake Wales, FL	ORL
Lake Williams, ND	FAR
Lake Wilson, MN	WIN
Lake Winola, PA	SCR
Lake Worth, FL	PMB
FL	PSC
Lake Zurich, IL	CHI
Lakefield, MN	WIN
Lakehurst, NJ	TR
Lakeland, FL	ORL
GA	SAV
LA	BR
NY	SY
Lakeport, CA	SR
MI	DET
NH	MAN
Lakeside, CA	SD
Lakeview, MI	GR
OR	BAK
Lakeville, CT	HRT
IN	FTW
MA	BO
MN	STP
Lakeway, TX	AUS
Lakewood, CA	LA
CO	DEN
NJ	TR
NY	BUF
OH	CLV
OH	PRM
WA	SEA
WI	GB
Lakewood Club, MI	GR
Lakin, KS	DOD
Lakota, ND	FAR
Lamar, CO	PBL
CO	SYM
MO	SPC
Lamberton, MN	NU
Lambertville, NJ	MET
Lame Deer, MT	GF
Lamesa, TX	LUB
Lamoille, MN	WIN
Lamont, CA	FRS
IA	DUB
Lampasas, TX	AUS
Lanai City, HI	HON
Lanark, WI	LC
Lanark Village, FL	PT
Lancaster, CA	LA
KY	LEX

MA	WOR
MN	CR
NH	MAN
NY	BUF
NY	STF
OH	COL
PA	HBG
SC	CHR
TX	DAL
WI	MAD
Lancing, TN	KNX
Land O'Lakes, FL	SP
Landeck, OH	TOL
Lander, WY	CHY
Landisville, NJ	CAM
Land-O'-Lakes, WI	SUP
Landover Hills, MD	WDC
Lanesboro, MA	SPR
MN	WIN
Lanesville, IN	IND
Lanett, AL	BIR
Langdon, ND	FAR
Langford, NY	BUF
Langhorne, PA	PH
PA	PHU
Langlade, WI	GB
Langley, OK	TLS
WA	SEA
Lanham, MD	WDC
Lanham-Seabrook, MD	WDC
Lankin, ND	FAR
Lansdale, PA	PH
PA	PHU
Lansdowne, PA	PH
Lansford, PA	ALN
PA	PSC
Lansing, IA	DUB
IL	CHI
KS	KCK
MI	LAN
MI	NTN
NY	ROC
Lantana, FL	PMB
Laona, WI	GB
Lapeer, KS	KCK
MI	DET
LaPointe, WI	SUP
Laporte, MN	CR
Lapwai, ID	B
Laramie, WY	CHY
Larchmont, NY	NY
Larchwood, IA	SC
Laredo, TX	LAR
Lares, PR	ARE
Largo, FL	SP
MD	WDC
Larimore, ND	FAR
Larks Lake, MI	GAY
Larkspur, CA	SFR
Larksville, PA	SCR
Larned, KS	DOD
Larose, LA	HT
Las Animas, CO	PBL
Las Cruces, NM	LSC
NM	VNN
Las Marias, PR	MGZ
Las Piedras, PR	CGS
Las Vegas, NM	SFE
NV	LAV
NV	OLL
NV	VNN
LaSalle, IL	PEO
Lastrup, MN	SCL
Latham, NY	ALB
Latium, TX	AUS
Laton, CA	FRS
Latrobe, PA	GBG
PA	SJP
Lattimer Mines, PA	SCR
Lattnerville, IA	DUB
Laughlin, NV	LAV
LaUnion, NM	LSC
Laurel, MD	BAL
MD	WDC
MS	BLX
MT	GF
NE	OM
Laurence Harbor, NJ	MET
Laurens, IA	SC
Laurie, MO	JC
Laurinburg, NC	R
Lavallette, NJ	TR
Laveen, AZ	PHX
Laverock, PA	PH
Lawler, IA	DUB
Lawrence, KS	KCK
MA	BO
MA	NTN
MA	SAM
NE	LIN
PA	PIT

Lawrenceburg, IN	IND
KY	LEX
TN	NSH
Lawrenceton, MO	STL
Lawrenceville, GA	ATL
GA	SYM
IL	BEL
NJ	TR
Lawtell, LA	LAF
Lawton, OK	OKL
Layton, UT	SLC
Le Center, MN	STP
Le Claire-Princeton, IA	DAV
Le Mars, IA	SC
Le Roy, MN	WIN
NY	BUF
WI	MIL
Le Sueur, MN	STP
Lead, SD	RC
Leadore, ID	B
Leadville, CO	COS
League City, TX	GAL
Leander, TX	AUS
Leavenworth, KS	KCK
MN	NU
WA	YAK
Leawood, KS	KCK
Lebanon, CT	NOR
IL	BEL
IN	LFT
KY	L
MO	SPC
NH	MAN
OH	CIN
OR	P
PA	HBG
TN	NSH
VA	RIC
Lebanon Junction, KY	L
Lebanon Township, WI	GB
Lebeau, LA	LAF
Lecanto, FL	SP
Leckrone, PA	GBG
Lecompte, LA	ALX
Ledyard, IA	SC
Lee, IL	RCK
MA	SPR
Lee Center, NY	SY
Lee's Summit, MO	KC
Leechburg, PA	GBG
Leeds, AL	BIR
MA	SPR
ND	FAR
Leesburg, FL	ORL
VA	ARL
Leesville, LA	ALX
Leetonia, OH	Y
Lefor, ND	BIS
Leggett, CA	SR
Lehigh Acres, FL	VEN
Lehighton, PA	ALN
Leicester, MA	WOR
NY	ROC
Leigh, NE	OM
Leipsic, OH	TOL
Leisenring, PA	GBG
PA	PBR
Leisure City, FL	MIA
Leitchfield, KY	OWN
Leland, MS	JKS
LeMars, IA	SC
Lemay, MO	STL
Lemhi, ID	B
Lemmon, SD	RC
Lemon Grove, CA	SD
Lemont, IL	CHI
IL	LIT
Lemoore, CA	FRS
Lena, IL	RCK
WI	GB
Lena/Spruce, WI	GB
Lenexa, KS	KCK
Lenni, PA	PH
Lennox, SD	SFS
Lenoir, NC	CHL
Lenoir City, TN	KNX
Lenox, IA	DM
MA	SPR
Lenox Dale, MA	SPR
Leo, MN	CR
Leola, SD	SFS
Leominster, MA	WOR
Leon, IA	DM
Leon Springs, TX	SAT
Leonardtown, MD	WDC
Leone, AS	SPP
Leonia, NJ	NEW
Leonore, IL	PEO
Leonville, LA	LAF
Leopold, IN	IND
MO	SPC

Leopolis, WI	GB
Leoti, KS	DOD
Leoville, KS	SAL
Lepua, AS	SPP
Lepuapua, AS	SPP
Leroy, LA	LAF
ND	FAR
LeRoy, NY	BUF
Leslie, MI	LAN
Lester Prairie, MN	NU
Lesterville, SD	SFS
Letcher, SD	SFS
Levelland, TX	LUB
Levittown, NY	RVC
PA	PH
PA	PSC
Lewes, DE	WIL
Lewis Center, OH	COL
Lewis Run, PA	E
Lewisburg, PA	HBG
TN	NSH
Lewisport, KY	OWN
Lewiston, ID	B
ME	PRT
MI	GAY
MN	WIN
NY	BUF
Lewistown, IL	PEO
MT	GF
PA	HBG
Lewisville, TX	FWT
TX	OLL
Lexington, KY	LEX
MA	ARM
MA	BO
MI	SAG
MN	STP
MO	KC
MS	JKS
NC	CHL
NE	GI
OH	TOL
OK	OKL
SC	CHR
TN	MEM
TX	AUS
VA	RIC
Lexington Park, MD	WDC
Libby, MT	HEL
Liberal, KS	DOD
Liberty, IL	SFD
IN	IND
KS	WCH
MO	KC
NY	NY
OH	TOL
TN	NSH
TX	BEA
Liberty Boro, PA	PIT
Liberty Township, OH	CIN
Libertytown, MD	BAL
Libertyville, IL	CHI
Lidderdale, IA	SC
Lidgerwood, ND	FAR
Liebenthal, KS	DOD
Liftwood, DE	WIL
Lighthouse Point, FL	MIA
Ligonier, IN	FTW
PA	GBG
Liguori, MO	STL
Lihue, HI	HON
Lilburn, GA	ATL
Lillian, AL	MOB
Lillis, KS	KCK
Lilly, PA	ALT
Lillyville, IL	SFD
Lily, SD	SFS
Lima, NY	ROC
OH	TOL
WI	LC
WI	MIL
Lime Ridge, WI	MAD
Lime Rock, NY	BUF
Limeport, PA	ALN
Limerick, ME	PRT
Limestone, ME	PRT
NY	BUF
Limon, CO	COS
Lincoln, CA	SAC
IL	PEO
KS	SAL
MA	BO
ME	PRT
NE	LIN
NE	STN
NH	MAN
NH	NTN
RI	PRO
WI	GB
Lincoln City, OR	P
Lincoln Park, MI	DET

NJ	PAT
Lincolndale, NY	NY
Lincolnton, NC	CHL
Lincroft, NJ	TR
Lind, WA	SPK
Lindale, TX	TYL
Linden, CA	STO
NJ	NEW
NJ	PSC
Lindenhurst, NY	RVC
Lindenwold, NJ	CAM
NJ	SYM
Lindsay, CA	FRS
NE	OM
TX	FWT
Lindsborg, KS	WCH
Lindstrom, MN	STP
Linesville, PA	E
Linfield, PA	PH
Linn, MO	JC
Lino Lakes, MN	STP
Linthicum, MD	BAL
Linthicum Heights, MD	BAL
Linton, IN	EVN
ND	BIS
Linwood, MA	WOR
MI	SAG
NJ	CAM
PA	PH
Lisbon, ME	PRT
ND	FAR
NH	MAN
NY	OG
OH	Y
Lisbon Falls, ME	PRT
Lisle, IL	JOL
Lismore, MN	WIN
Litchfield, CT	HRT
IL	SFD
MN	NU
OH	CLV
Litchfield Park, AZ	PHX
Lithia Springs, GA	ATL
Lithonia, GA	ATL
Lititz, PA	HBG
Litomysl, MN	WIN
Little Canada, MN	STP
Little Chute, WI	GB
Little Compton, RI	PRO
Little Falls, MN	SCL
NJ	PAT
NY	ALB
NY	STF
Little Ferry, NJ	NEW
Little Hocking, OH	STU
Little Kohler, WI	MIL
Little Meadows, PA	SCR
Little River, KS	WCH
Little Rock, AR	LR
Little Suamico, WI	GB
Little Turkey, IA	DUB
Little Valley, NY	BUF
Little York, NJ	MET
Littlefield, TX	LUB
Littlefork, MN	DUL
Littleport, IA	DUB
Littlestown, PA	HBG
Littleton, CO	DEN
MA	BO
NH	MAN
Live Oak, FL	STA
Lively Grove, IL	BEL
Livermore, CA	OAK
IA	SC
KY	OWN
Liverpool, NY	SY
Livingston, AL	BIR
CA	FRS
IL	SFD
MT	GF
NJ	NEW
TX	BEA
Livingston Manor, NY	NY
Livonia, LA	BR
MI	DET
MI	PRM
NY	ROC
Livonia Center, NY	ROC
Llano, TX	AUS
Lock Haven, PA	ALT
Lockbourne, OH	COL
Lockeford, CA	STO
Lockhart, TX	AUS
Lockport, IL	JOL
IL	PRM
LA	HT
NY	BUF
Lockport South, IL	JOL
Locust Gap, PA	HBG
Locustdale, PA	HBG
Lodge Grass, MT	GF

Lodi, CA	STO
NJ	NEW
OH	CLV
WI	MAD
Logan, IA	DM
KS	SAL
OH	COL
UT	SLC
WV	WH
Logansport, IN	LFT
Lohrville, IA	SC
Loiza, PR	SJN
Loma, NE	LIN
Loma Linda, CA	SB
Lombard, IL	JOL
Lometa, TX	AUS
Lomice, ND	FAR
Lomira, WI	MIL
Lomita, CA	LA
Lompoc, CA	LA
Lonaconing, MD	BAL
London, KY	LEX
OH	COL
Londonderry, NH	MAN
Lone Pine, CA	FRS
Lone Rock, WI	LC
Lone Tree, IA	DAV
Lonedell, MO	STL
Long Beach, CA	LA
MS	BLX
NY	RVC
Long Branch, NJ	TR
Long Grove, IA	DAV
Long Island City, NY	BRK
NY	NY
NY	STF
Long Lake, MN	STP
NY	OG
WI	GB
Long Praire, MN	SCL
Long Prairie, MN	SCL
Long Valley, NJ	PAT
Longboat Key, FL	VEN
Longmeadow, MA	SPR
Longmont, CO	DEN
Longport, NJ	CAM
Longview, TX	TYL
WA	SEA
Longville, MN	DUL
Longwood, FL	ORL
Lonsdale, AR	LR
MN	STP
Loogootee, IN	EVN
Lookout Mountain, GA	ATL
Loomis, CA	SAC
Loose Creek, MO	JC
Lopez, PA	PSC
Lorain, OH	CLV
OH	PRM
OH	ROM
OH	SJP
Lords Valley, PA	SCR
Lordsburg, NM	LSC
Lore City, OH	STU
Loreauville, LA	LAF
Loreto, WI	MAD
Loretto, IL	PEO
KS	DOD
KY	L
MN	STP
PA	ALT
TN	NSH
Los Alamitos, CA	ORG
Los Alamos, NM	SFE
Los Altos, CA	SFR
CA	SJ
Los Altos Hills, CA	SJ
Los Angeles, CA	ARM
CA	LA
CA	OLD
CA	OLL
CA	ROM
CA	STN
CA	SYM
Los Banos, CA	FRS
Los Fresnos, TX	BWN
Los Gatos, CA	MRY
CA	SJ
CA	VNN
Los Lunas, NM	SFE
Los Nietos, CA	LA
Los Ojos, NM	SFE
Los Osos, CA	MRY
Losoya, TX	SAT
Lost Creek, PA	ALN
Lost Lake, WI	MIL
Lost Nation, IA	DAV
Lostant, IL	PEO
Lott, TX	AUS
Loudonville, NY	ALB
OH	CLV

Louisa, KY	LEX
LA	LAF
Louisburg, KS	KCK
NC	R
Louisiana, MO	JC
Louisville, CO	DEN
KY	L
KY	OLL
MS	JKS
NY	OG
OH	Y
Loup City, NE	GI
Lourdes, IA	DUB
Loveland, CO	DEN
OH	CIN
Lovell, WY	CHY
Lovelock, NV	RNO
Loves Park, IL	RCK
Lovilia, IA	DAV
Loving, NM	LSC
Lovingston, VA	RIC
Lovington, IL	SFD
NM	LSC
Lowell, IN	GRY
MA	BO
MI	GR
OH	STU
Lowellville, OH	Y
Lower Brule, SD	RC
Lower Burrell, PA	GBG
Lower Makefield, PA	PH
Lowville, NY	OG
Loyal, OK	OKL
WI	LC
Lubbock, TX	LUB
Lubec, ME	PRT
Lubeck, WV	WH
Lublin, WI	SUP
Lucan, MN	NU
Lucerne, IN	LFT
Lucerne Valley, CA	SB
Lucernemines, PA	GBG
Lucinda, PA	E
Ludington, MI	GR
Ludlow, KY	COV
MA	SPR
MA	STF
VT	BUR
Luebbering, MO	STL
Lufkin, TX	TYL
Lukachukai, AZ	GLP
Luling, LA	NO
TX	AUS
Lumberton, MS	BLX
NC	R
NM	GLP
TX	BEA
Lunenburg, MA	WOR
Luquillo, PR	SJN
Luray, VA	ARL
Lusk, WY	CHY
Lutherville, MD	BAL
Luverne, MN	WIN
Luxemburg, IA	DUB
MN	SCL
WI	GB
Luzerne, PA	SCR
Lycurgus, IA	DUB
Lydia, LA	LAF
Lyford, TX	BWN
Lykens, PA	HBG
Lyle, MN	WIN
Lyman, ME	PRT
Lynbrook, NY	RVC
Lynch, KY	LEX
NE	OM
Lynchburg, VA	RIC
Lynden, WA	SEA
Lyndhurst, NJ	NEW
OH	CLV
Lyndon Station, WI	LC
Lyndonville, NY	BUF
VT	BUR
Lyndora, PA	PBR
PA	PIT
PA	SJP
Lynn, MA	BO
Lynnfield, MA	BO
Lynnwood, WA	SEA
Lynwood, CA	LA
Lyon Mountain, NY	OG
Lyons, IL	CHI
KS	WCH
NE	OM
NY	ROC
OH	TOL
WI	MIL
Lyons Point, LA	LAF
Lytle, TX	SAT
Mabel, MN	WIN
Mableton, GA	ATL
Mabton, WA	YAK
Macclenny, FL	STA
Macdona, TX	SAT
Macedon, NY	ROC
Macedonia, OH	CLV
Machias, ME	PRT
NY	BUF
Mackinac Island, MI	MAR
Mackinaw City, MI	GAY
Mackville, WI	GB
Macomb, IL	PEO
MI	DET
Macon, GA	SAV
IL	SFD
MO	JC
Madawaska, ME	PRT
Maddock, ND	FAR
Madelia, MN	WIN
Madera, CA	FRS
Madison, AL	BIR
CT	HRT
FL	PT
IL	SFD
IL	STN
IN	IND
KS	WCH
ME	PRT
MN	NU
MS	JKS
MT	HEL
NE	OM
NJ	PAT
OH	CLV
SD	SFS
TN	NSH
TX	TYL
VA	ARL
WI	MAD
WV	WH
Madison Heights, MI	DET
Madison Lake, MN	WIN
Madisonville, KY	OWN
LA	NO
TN	KNX
TX	TYL
Madonnaville, IL	BEL
Madras, OR	BAK
Madrid, IA	SC
NY	OG
Magee, MS	JKS
Maggie Valley, NC	CHL
Magna, UT	SLC
Magnolia, AR	LR
DE	WIL
NJ	CAM
TX	GAL
Magnolia Springs, AL	MOB
Mahanoy City, PA	ALN
PA	PHU
PA	PSC
Mahanoy Plane, PA	ALN
Mahnomen, MN	CR
Mahomet, IL	PEO
Mahopac, NY	NY
Mahtomedi, MN	STP
Mahwah, NJ	NEW
NJ	PSC
Maina, GU	AGN
Maine, MN	SCL
NY	SY
Maizeville, PA	ALN
PA	PHU
Majuro, MH	MI
Makakilo, HI	HON
Makawao, HI	HON
Malaga, NJ	CAM
Malden, MA	BO
MO	SPC
Malibu, CA	LA
Mallard, IA	SC
Mallet, LA	LAF
Malojlo, GU	AGN
Malone, NY	OG
Maloy, IA	DM
Malta, MT	GF
Malvern, AR	LR
OH	STU
PA	PH
Malverne, NY	RVC
Mamaroneck, NY	NY
Mammoth, AZ	TUC
Mammoth Lakes, CA	STO
Mamou, LA	LAF
Man, WV	WH
Manahawkin, NJ	TR
Manalapan, NJ	TR
Manannah, MN	NU
Manasquan, NJ	TR
Manassas, VA	ARL
VA	PHU
Manati, PR	ARE
Manawa, WI	GB
Mancelona, MI	GAY
Manchaug, MA	WOR
Manchester, CT	HRT
IA	DUB
KY	LEX
MD	BAL
MI	LAN
MI	LIT
MO	STL
NH	MAN
NH	NTN
NH	STF
OH	CIN
PA	PIT
TN	NSH
Manchester by the Sea, MA	BO
Manchester Center, VT	BUR
Mancos, CO	PBL
Mandan, ND	BIS
Mandaree, ND	BIS
Manderson, SD	RC
Mandeville, LA	NO
Mangilao, GU	AGN
Mangum, OK	OKL
Manhasset, NY	RVC
Manhattan, IL	JOL
KS	SAL
NY	NY
Manhattan Beach, CA	LA
Manheim, PA	HBG
Manilla, IA	SC
Manistee, MI	GAY
Manistique, MI	MAR
Manitou Beach, MI	LAN
Manitowish Waters, WI	SUP
Manitowoc, WI	GB
WI	MIL
Mankato, KS	SAL
MN	WIN
Manley, NE	LIN
Manlius, NY	SY
Manly, IA	DUB
Manning, IA	SC
Mannington, WV	WH
Manoa, PA	PH
Manor, TX	AUS
Manorhaven, NY	RVC
Manorville, NY	RVC
Mansfield, LA	SHP
MA	FR
MO	SPC
OH	TOL
PA	SCR
TX	FWT
Manson, IA	SC
Mansura, LA	ALX
Mantador, ND	FAR
Manteca, CA	STO
Manteno, IL	JOL
Manton, MI	GAY
Mantua, NJ	CAM
OH	Y
Manvel, ND	FAR
TX	GAL
Manville, NJ	MET
NJ	PHU
RI	PRO
Many, LA	SHP
Maple City, MI	GAY
Maple Glen, PA	PH
Maple Grove, MI	SAG
MN	STP
WI	GB
Maple Heights, OH	CLV
Maple Hill, KS	KCK
Maple Lake, MN	STP
Maple Mount, KY	OWN
Maple Park, IL	RCK
Maple River, IA	SC
Maple Shade, NJ	TR
Mapleton, IA	SC
MI	GAY
MN	WIN
WI	MIL
Maplewood, MN	STP
MO	STL
NJ	NEW
WI	GB
Maquoketa, IA	DUB
Marak, TX	AUS
Marana, AZ	TUC
Marathon, FL	MIA
NY	SY
Marathon City, WI	LC
Marble, MN	DUL
Marble Falls, TX	AUS
Marblehead, MA	BO
OH	PRM
OH	TOL
Marbury, AL	MOB
Marceline, MO	JC
Marcellus, NY	SY
Marchand, WI	GB
Marco Island, FL	VEN
Marcus, IA	SC
Marcus Hook, PA	PH
Marengo, IA	DAV
IL	RCK
Marfa, TX	ELP
Margaretville, NY	ALB
Margate, FL	MIA
NJ	CAM
Marguerite, PA	GBG
Maria Stein, OH	CIN
Mariah Hill, IN	EVN
Marianna, AR	LR
FL	PT
Maricao, PR	MGZ
Marienthal, KS	DOD
Marietta, GA	ATL
OH	STU
PA	HBG
Marina, CA	MRY
Marina Del Rey, CA	LA
Marine, IL	SFD
Marine City, MI	DET
Marine on St. Croix, MN	STP
Marinette, WI	GB
Maringouin, LA	BR
Marion, IA	DUB
IL	BEL
IN	LFT
KS	WCH
KY	OWN
MA	FR
MI	GR
ND	FAR
NY	ROC
OH	COL
SD	SFS
VA	RIC
WI	GB
Marion Heights, PA	HBG
PA	PHU
Marionville, MO	SPC
Mariposa, CA	FRS
Marked Tree, AR	LR
Markesan, WI	MAD
Markham, IL	CHI
Marks, MS	JKS
Marksville, LA	ALX
Marlboro, NJ	PHU
NJ	TR
NY	NY
Marlborough, CT	HRT
MA	BO
NH	MAN
Marlette, MI	SAG
Marlin, TX	AUS
Marlinton, WV	WH
Marlton, NJ	TR
Marmora, NJ	CAM
Marne, MI	GR
Marquette, MI	MAR
Marrero, LA	NO
Marriottsville, MD	BAL
Mars, PA	PIT
Mars Hill, ME	PRT
NC	CHL
Marseilles, IL	PEO
Marshall, AK	FBK
IL	SFD
MI	KAL
MN	NU
MO	JC
TX	TYL
WI	MAD
Marshalltown, IA	DUB
Marshfield, MA	BO
MO	SPC
WI	LC
Martin, KY	LEX
SD	RC
TN	MEM
Martindale, TX	AUS
Martinez, CA	OAK
TX	SAT
Martins Creek, PA	ALN
Martins Ferry, OH	STU
Martinsburg, MO	JC
WV	WH
Martinsville, IN	IND
NJ	MET
VA	RIC
WI	MAD
Martinton, IL	JOL
Marty, SD	SFS
Marvin, SD	SFS
Mary Esther, FL	PT
Mary's Home, MO	JC
Marydale, IL	BEL

Marydel, MD	WIL
Marygrove, OH	TOL
Maryhill, IA	SC
Maryknoll, NY	NY
Maryland Heights, MO	STL
Marylhurst, OR	P
Marysburg, MN	STP
Marysdale, OH	TOL
Marystown, MN	STP
Marysville, CA	SAC
KS	KCK
MI	DET
OH	COL
PA	HBG
WA	SEA
Marytown, WI	MIL
Maryville, IL	SFD
MO	KC
ND	FAR
Marywood, OH	TOL
Masaryktown, FL	SP
Mascoutah, IL	BEL
Mashpee, MA	FR
Mason, MI	LAN
OH	CIN
TX	AUS
Mason City, IA	DUB
Masontown, PA	GBG
WV	WH
Masonville, IA	DUB
Massapequa, NY	RVC
Massapequa Park, NY	RVC
Massena, IA	DM
NY	OG
Massillon, OH	Y
Mastic Beach, NY	RVC
Masury, OH	Y
Matamoras, PA	SCR
Matawan, NJ	PSC
NJ	TR
Matherville, IL	PEO
Mathews, VA	RIC
Mathis, TX	CC
Mattapoisett, MA	FR
Mattawa, WA	YAK
Mattawan, MI	KAL
Mattese, MO	STL
Matteson, IL	CHI
Mattoon, IL	SFD
WI	GB
Mattydale, NY	SY
Mauldin, SC	CHR
Maumee, OH	TOL
Maunabo, PR	CGS
Maurice, LA	LAF
Mauriceville, TX	BEA
Mauston, WI	LC
Maximo, OH	Y
Maxwell, CA	SAC
PA	GBG
May's Lick, KY	COV
Mayaguez, PR	MGZ
Mayaquez, Mayaguez	MGZ
PR	MGZ
Maybee, MI	DET
Maybrook, NY	NY
Mayetta, KS	KCK
Mayfield, KY	OWN
PA	SCR
SD	SFS
Mayhew Lake, MN	SCL
Maynard, MA	BO
OH	STU
Mays Landing, NJ	CAM
Maysel, WV	WH
Maysville, KY	COV
Maytown, IL	RCK
Mayville, MI	SAG
ND	FAR
NY	BUF
WI	MIL
Maywood, CA	LA
IL	CHI
NJ	NEW
Mazeppa, MN	WIN
Mazomanie, WI	MAD
McAdoo, PA	ALN
PA	PHU
PA	PSC
McAfee, NJ	PAT
McAlester, OK	TLS
McAllen, TX	BWN
McBain, MI	GAY
McCall, ID	B
McCamey, TX	SAN
McCartyville, OH	CIN
McCloud, CA	SAC
McClusky, ND	FAR
McComb, MS	JKS
McConchie, MD	WDC
McConnellsburg, PA	ALT
McConnelsville, OH	STU
McCook, NE	LIN
TX	BWN
McCool Junction, NE	LIN
McCracken, KS	DOD
McDonald, OH	Y
PA	PIT
McDonough, GA	ATL
McDowell, KS	SAL
McEwen, TN	NSH
McFarland, CA	FRS
WI	MAD
McGehee, AR	LR
McGrath, AK	FBK
MN	DUL
McGregor, IA	DUB
MN	DUL
MN	STP
TX	AUS
McHenry, IL	RCK
ND	FAR
McIntire, IA	DUB
McIntosh, SD	RC
McKean, PA	E
McKees Rocks, PA	PBR
PA	PIT
PA	SJP
McKeesport, PA	PBR
PA	PIT
PA	ROM
PA	SJP
McKenzie Bridge, OR	P
McKinleyville, CA	SR
McKinney, TX	DAL
McLaughlin, SD	RC
McLean, VA	ARL
VA	NTN
VA	WDC
McLeansboro, IL	BEL
McLoud, OK	OKL
McMechen, WV	WH
McMinnville, OR	P
TN	NSH
McNair, TX	GAL
McNary, AZ	GLP
McPherson, KS	WCH
McQuady, KY	OWN
McRae, GA	SAV
McSherrystown, PA	HBG
Mead, NE	LIN
Meade, KS	DOD
Meadowbrook, PA	PH
Meadowlands, MN	DUL
PA	PIT
Meadville, PA	E
Mecca, CA	SB
Mechanic Falls, ME	PRT
Mechanicsburg, OH	CIN
PA	HBG
Mechanicsville, IA	DAV
MD	WDC
VA	RIC
Mechanicville, NY	ALB
Medart, FL	PT
Medaryville, IN	LFT
Medfield, MA	BO
Medford, MA	BO
MN	WIN
NJ	TR
NY	RVC
OK	OKL
OR	P
WI	SUP
Media, PA	PH
Mediania Alta, Loiza, PR	SJN
Medical Lake, WA	SPK
Medicine Lodge, KS	DOD
Medina, ND	FAR
NY	BUF
OH	CLV
Medley's Neck, MD	WDC
Medora, IL	SFD
Medway, MA	BO
Meeker, CO	DEN
Megargel, TX	FWT
Mehlville, MO	STL
Meire Grove, MN	SCL
Melbourne, FL	ORL
KY	COV
Melbourne Beach, FL	ORL
Melcher, IA	DAV
Mellen, WI	SUP
Mellette, SD	SFS
Melrose, IA	DAV
MA	BO
MN	SCL
WI	LC
Melrose Park, IL	CHI
Melville, LA	LAF
NY	RVC
Melvindale, MI	DET
Memphis, MI	DET
MO	JC
TN	MEM
TX	AMA
Mena, AR	LR
Menahga, MN	SCL
Menands, NY	ALB
Menard, TX	SAN
Menasha, WI	GB
Mendham, NJ	PAT
Mendocino, CA	SR
Mendon, IL	SFD
MA	WOR
MI	KAL
NY	ROC
Mendota, CA	FRS
IL	PEO
MN	STP
Mendota Heights, MN	STP
Menlo Park, CA	SFR
CA	SJ
Menoken, ND	BIS
Menominee, IL	RCK
MI	MAR
NE	OM
Menomonee Falls, WI	MIL
Menomonie, WI	LC
Mentor, MN	CR
OH	CLV
Mentor-on-the-Lake, OH	PRM
Mentz, TX	VIC
Meppen, IL	SFD
Mequon, WI	MIL
Meraux, LA	NO
Merced, CA	FRS
Mercedes, TX	BWN
Mercer, PA	E
WI	SUP
Mercer Island, WA	SEA
Merchantville, NJ	CAM
Meredith, KS	SAL
NH	MAN
Meriden, CT	HRT
CT	PSC
KS	KCK
Meridian, ID	B
MS	JKS
PA	PIT
Merion, PA	PH
Merion Station, PA	PH
Merizo, GU	AGN
Mermentau, LA	LAF
Merna, NE	GI
Merrick, NY	RVC
Merrill, IA	SC
MI	SAG
OR	BAK
WI	SUP
Merrillville, IN	GRY
IN	PRM
Merrimac, MA	BO
WI	MAD
Merrimack, NH	MAN
Merriman, NE	GI
Merritt Island, FL	ORL
Mesa, AZ	PHX
ID	B
Mescalero, NM	LSC
Meshoppen, PA	SCR
Mesilla, NM	LSC
Mesilla Park, NM	LSC
Mesquite, TX	DAL
Meta, MO	JC
Metairie, LA	NO
Metaline Falls, WA	SPK
Metamora, IL	PEO
Methuen, MA	BO
MA	NTN
Metropolis, IL	BEL
Metuchen, NJ	MET
Metz, MI	GAY
Mexia, TX	AUS
Mexico, ME	PRT
MO	JC
NY	SY
Mexico Beach, FL	PT
Meyer, IA	DUB
Meyersdale, PA	ALT
Meyersville, TX	VIC
Miami, AZ	TUC
FL	MIA
FL	NTN
FL	PSC
FL	SAM
FL	SJP
OK	TLS
Miami Beach, FL	MIA
Miami Lakes, FL	MIA
Miami Shores, FL	MIA
Miami Springs, FL	MIA
Miamisburg, OH	CIN
Michael, IL	SFD
Michigan, ND	FAR
Michigan Center, MI	LAN
Michigan City, IN	GRY
Middle Lake, MN	NU
Middle Ridge, WI	LC
Middle River, MN	CR
Middle Village, NY	BRK
Middleborough, MA	BO
Middlebranch, OH	Y
Middleburg, FL	STA
VA	ARL
Middleburg Heights, OH	CLV
Middleburgh, NY	ALB
Middlebury, CT	HRT
VT	BUR
Middlefield, CT	NOR
OH	CLV
Middleport, NY	BUF
PA	PHU
Middlesboro, KY	LEX
Middlesex, NJ	MET
Middlesex County, VA	RIC
Middleton, MA	BO
WI	MAD
Middletown, CA	SR
CT	NOR
DE	WIL
MD	BAL
NJ	TR
NY	NY
NY	STF
OH	CIN
PA	HBG
RI	PRO
Middletown Springs, VT	BUR
Midland, MD	BAL
MI	SAG
PA	PIT
SD	RC
TX	SAN
Midland Park, NJ	NEW
Midlothian, IL	CHI
Midvale, UT	SLC
Midway City, CA	ORG
Miesville, MN	STP
Mifflintown, PA	HBG
Mikado, MI	GAY
Milaca, MN	SCL
Milan, IL	PEO
IN	IND
MI	LAN
MO	JC
NM	GLP
OH	TOL
TN	MEM
WI	LC
Milbank, SD	SFS
Mildred, PA	SCR
Miles, TX	SAN
Miles City, MT	GF
Milford, CT	HRT
DE	WIL
IA	SC
IN	FTW
MA	WOR
MI	DET
NH	MAN
NJ	MET
OH	CIN
PA	SCR
UT	SLC
Mililani Town, HI	HON
Mill Creek, WI	LC
WI	MAD
Mill Valley, CA	SFR
Milladore, WI	LC
Millbrae, CA	OLL
CA	SFR
Millbrook, AL	MOB
NY	NY
Millbury, MA	WOR
Milledgeville, GA	ATL
Millen, GA	SAV
Miller, SD	SFS
Miller City, OH	TOL
Miller Heights, PA	ALN
Millers Falls, MA	SPR
Millersburg, OH	COL
PA	HBG
Millersville, MD	BAL
OH	TOL
PA	HBG
Millerville, MN	SCL
Millhousen, IN	IND
Millinocket, ME	PRT
Millis, MA	BO
Millstadt, IL	BEL
Milltown, NJ	MET
NJ	SYM
Millvale, PA	PIT

Millville, MA	WOR
NJ	CAM
NJ	PHU
OH	CIN
Millwood, MO	STL
Milmont Park, PA	PH
Milnor, ND	FAR
Milpitas, CA	SJ
Milroy, MN	NU
Milton, FL	PT
LA	LAF
MA	BO
ND	FAR
NY	NY
PA	HBG
VT	BUR
WI	MAD
Milton Freewater, OR	BAK
Miltonsburg, OH	STU
Miltonvale, KS	SAL
Milwaukee, WI	MIL
WI	NTN
WI	STN
Milwaukie, OR	P
Mims, FL	ORL
Minatare, NE	GI
Minden, LA	SHP
NE	LIN
Mineola, NY	RVC
TX	TYL
Mineral, VA	RIC
Mineral City, OH	COL
Mineral Point, WI	MAD
Mineral Ridge, OH	Y
Mineral Wells, TX	FWT
Minersville, PA	ALN
PA	PHU
PA	PSC
Minerva, OH	STU
Minetto, NY	SY
Mineville, NY	OG
Mingo Junction, OH	PBR
OH	STU
Minneapolis, KS	SAL
MN	OLL
MN	PRM
MN	STN
MN	STP
Minneiska, MN	WIN
Minneota, MN	NU
Minnesota City, MN	WIN
Minnesota Lake, MN	WIN
Minnetonka, MN	STP
Minnewaukan, ND	FAR
Minoa, NY	SY
Minocqua, WI	SUP
Minong, WI	SUP
Minonk, IL	PEO
Minooka, IL	JOL
Minot, ND	BIS
Minotola, NJ	CAM
Minster, OH	CIN
Minto, ND	FAR
Minturn, CO	DEN
Mio, MI	GAY
Miramar, FL	MIA
Mire, LA	LAF
Miriam, MI	GR
Mishawaka, IN	FTW
IN	STN
Mishicot, WI	GB
Mission, KS	KCK
SD	RC
TX	BWN
Mission Hills, CA	LA
Mission San Jose, CA	OAK
Mission Viejo, CA	ORG
Missoula, MT	HEL
Missouri City, TX	GAL
Missouri Valley, IA	DM
Mitchell, IN	IND
NE	GI
SD	SFS
WI	MIL
Mitchellville, MD	WDC
Moab, UT	SLC
Moberly, MO	JC
Mobile, AL	MOB
Mobridge, SD	SFS
Moca, PR	MGZ
Mocanaqua, PA	SCR
Mocksville, NC	CHL
Modesto, CA	STO
Modoc, IL	BEL
Mohall, ND	BIS
Mohawk, NY	ALB
Mohnton, PA	ALN
Mokane, MO	JC
Mokena, IL	JOL
Molalla, OR	P
Moline, IL	PEO

KS	WCH
Momence, IL	JOL
Mon Luis Island, AL	MOB
Monaca, PA	PIT
Monahans, TX	ELP
Monarch, MT	GF
Monches, WI	MIL
Moncks Corner, SC	CHR
Mondamin, IA	DM
Mondovi, WI	LC
Monee, IL	JOL
Monessen, PA	GBG
PA	PBR
Moneta, VA	RIC
Monett, MO	SPC
Mongmong, GU	AGN
Monmouth, IL	PEO
Monmouth Beach, NJ	TR
Monmouth Junction, NJ	MET
Monona, IA	DUB
Monongah, WV	WH
Monongahela, PA	PBR
PA	PIT
Monroe, CT	BGP
GA	ATL
LA	SHP
MI	DET
NC	CHL
NY	NY
OH	CIN
OR	P
UT	SLC
WA	SEA
WI	MAD
Monroe City, MO	JC
Monroeville, AL	MOB
IN	FTW
OH	TOL
PA	PBR
PA	PIT
Monrovia, CA	LA
Monsey, NY	NY
Monson, MA	SPR
Mont Belvieu, TX	BEA
Mont Clare, PA	PSC
Montague, MI	GR
NJ	PAT
TX	FWT
Montauk, NY	RVC
Montclair, CA	SB
NJ	NEW
Montdale, PA	SCR
Monte Rio, CA	SR
Monte Vista, CO	PBL
Montebello, CA	LA
Montecito, CA	LA
Montegut, LA	HT
Montello, WI	MAD
Monterey, CA	MRY
IN	LFT
NE	OM
Monterey Park, CA	LA
Montevallo, AL	BIR
Montevideo, MN	NU
Montezuma, IN	IND
NY	ROC
OH	CIN
Montfort, WI	MAD
Montgomery, AL	MOB
IN	EVN
MN	STP
NY	NY
WV	WH
Montgomery City, MO	JC
Monti, IA	DUB
Monticello, AR	LR
FL	PT
IA	DUB
IL	PEO
IN	LFT
KY	LEX
MN	STP
NY	NY
UT	SLC
Montoursville, PA	SCR
Montpelier, IN	LFT
OH	TOL
VA	RIC
VT	BUR
WI	GB
Montreal, WI	SUP
Montrose, CA	ARM
CA	LA
CO	PBL
IA	DAV
IL	SFD
MI	LAN
MO	KC
NY	NY
PA	SCR
SD	SFS

Montvale, NJ	NEW
Montville, CT	NOR
NJ	PAT
Monument, CO	COS
Moodus, CT	NOR
Moody, TX	AUS
Mooers, NY	OG
Mooers Forks, NY	OG
Moon Township, PA	PIT
Moonachie, NJ	NEW
Mooney Creek, KS	KCK
Moore, OK	OKL
Moore Haven, FL	VEN
Moorefield, WV	WH
Moorestown, NJ	TR
Mooresville, IN	IND
NC	CHL
Mooreton, ND	FAR
Moorhead, MN	CR
Moorland, IA	SC
Moorpark, CA	LA
Moose Lake, MN	DUL
Moosup, CT	NOR
Moquah, WI	SUP
Mora, MN	SCL
NM	SFE
Moraga, CA	OAK
Moran, MI	MAR
MN	SCL
Moravia, NY	ROC
Moreauville, LA	ALX
Morehead, KY	LEX
Morehead City, NC	R
Morenci, AZ	TUC
Moreno Valley, CA	SB
Morgan, MN	NU
TX	FWT
Morgan City, LA	HT
Morgan Hill, CA	SJ
Morganfield, KY	OWN
Morganton, NC	CHL
Morgantown, KY	OWN
WV	PBR
WV	WH
Morganza, LA	BR
MD	WDC
Morges, OH	STU
Moriarty, NM	SFE
Morovis, PR	ARE
Morrice, MI	LAN
Morrill, MN	SCL
Morrilton, AR	LR
Morris, IL	JOL
IN	IND
MN	SCL
NY	ALB
Morris Plains, NJ	PAT
Morrisdale, PA	E
Morrison, IL	RCK
MO	JC
Morrison Bluff, AR	LR
Morrisonville, IL	SFD
NY	OG
Morristown, NJ	PAT
NY	OG
SD	RC
TN	KNX
Morrisville, NY	SY
PA	PH
VT	BUR
Morro Bay, CA	MRY
Morrow, LA	LAF
OH	CIN
Morrowville, KS	SAL
Morse, LA	LAF
Morse Bluff, NE	LIN
Mortlock Islands, FM	CI
Morton, IL	PEO
MN	NU
PA	PH
TX	LUB
WA	SEA
Morton Grove, IL	CHI
Moscow, ID	B
PA	PHU
PA	SCR
TN	MEM
Moselle, MO	STL
Moses Lake, WA	YAK
Mosinee, WI	LC
Moss Beach, CA	SFR
Moss Bluff, LA	LKC
Moss Point, MS	BLX
Motley, MN	SCL
Mott, ND	BIS
Moulton, AL	BIR
TX	VIC
Moultrie, GA	SAV
Mound, MN	STP
Mound Bayou, MS	JKS
Mound City, IL	BEL

KS	KCK
Moundsville, WV	WH
Mount Airy, NC	CHL
Mt. Angel, OR	P
Mount Arlington, NJ	PAT
Mt. Ayr, IA	DM
Mount Calvary, WI	MIL
Mount Carbon, PA	ALN
Mount Carmel, IA	SC
IL	BEL
ND	FAR
OH	CIN
PA	HBG
PA	PHU
Mount Carroll, IL	RCK
Mount Clemens, MI	DET
Mount Dora, FL	ORL
Mount Ephraim, NJ	CAM
Mount Holly, NJ	TR
Mount Hope, NJ	PAT
WI	MAD
Mount Horeb, WI	MAD
Mount Jewett, PA	E
Mount Joy, PA	HBG
Mt. Kisco, NY	NY
Mount Laurel, NJ	TR
Mt. Lebanon, PA	PIT
Mount Morris, MI	LAN
NY	ROC
Mount Olive, IL	SFD
NC	R
Mount Orab, OH	CIN
Mount Pleasant, IA	DAV
MI	SAG
PA	GBG
TX	TYL
Mt. Pleasant, VI	STV
Mount Pocono, PA	SCR
Mt. Prospect, IL	CHI
Mount Rainier, MD	WDC
Mount Repose, OH	CIN
Mount Saint Francis, IN	IND
Mount Savage, MD	BAL
Mount Shasta, CA	SAC
Mount Sinai, NY	RVC
Mount Sterling, IL	SFD
Mt. Sterling, KY	LEX
Mount Union, PA	ALT
Mt. Upton, NY	SY
Mount Vernon, AL	MOB
IA	DUB
IL	BEL
IN	EVN
KS	WCH
Mt. Vernon, KY	LEX
Mount Vernon, MO	SPC
Mt. Vernon, NY	NY
OH	COL
Mount Vernon, SD	SFS
TX	TYL
WA	SEA
Mount Washington, KY	L
Mt. Zion, IL	SFD
Mountain City, TN	KNX
Mountain Grove, MO	SPC
Mountain Home, AR	LR
ID	B
TX	SAT
Mountain Home Air Force Base, ID	B
Mountain Iron, MN	DUL
Mountain Lakes, NJ	PAT
Mountain View, CA	SJ
HI	HON
MO	SPC
Mountain Village, AK	FBK
Mountainair, NM	SFE
Mountainside, NJ	NEW
Mountaintop, PA	SCR
Mountlake Terrace, WA	SEA
Moville, IA	SC
Mowata, LA	LAF
Moweaqua, IL	SFD
Moxee City, WA	YAK
Muenster, TX	FWT
Mukwonago, WI	MIL
Mulberry, KS	WCH
Muleshoe, TX	LUB
Mullen, NE	GI
Mullens, WV	WH
Mullica Hill, NJ	CAM
Mulvane, KS	WCH
Muncie, IN	LFT
Muncy, PA	SCR
Mundelein, IL	CHI
Munden, KS	SAL
Mundys Corner, PA	ALT
Munger, MI	SAG
Munhall, PA	PBR
PA	PIT
Munich, ND	FAR
Munising, MI	MAR

Munjor, KS	SAL
Munnsville, NY	SY
Munster, IN	GRY
IN	PRM
IN	STN
Murdo, SD	RC
Murdock, FL	VEN
MN	NU
Murfreesboro, TN	NSH
Murphy, NC	CHL
Murphy Village, SC	CHR
Murphysboro, IL	BEL
Murray, KY	OWN
UT	OLL
UT	SLC
Murray City, OH	COL
Murrayville, IL	SFD
Murrieta, CA	SB
Murrysville, PA	GBG
Muscatine, IA	DAV
Muscoda, WI	MAD
Muse, PA	PIT
Muskego, WI	MIL
Muskegon, MI	GR
Muskegon Heights, MI	GR
Muskogee, OK	TLS
Mustang, OK	OKL
Myerstown, PA	HBG
Myrtle Beach, SC	CHR
Myrtle Creek, OR	P
Mystic, CT	NOR
IA	DAV
Naalehu, HI	HON
Nabob, WI	MIL
Naches, WA	YAK
Nacogdoches, TX	TYL
Nada, TX	VIC
Nadeau, MI	MAR
Naguabo, PR	CGS
Nahant, MA	BO
Nahma, MI	MAR
Nampa, ID	B
Namur, WI	GB
Nanakuli, HI	HON
Nanticoke, PA	PHU
PA	PSC
PA	SCR
Nantucket, MA	FR
Nanty-Glo, PA	ALT
PA	PBR
Nanuet, NY	NY
NY	SYM
Napa, CA	SR
Napanee, IN	FTW
Naperville, IL	JOL
Naples, FL	VEN
NY	ROC
Napoleon, IN	IND
ND	FAR
OH	TOL
Napoleonville, LA	BR
Naranja, FL	MIA
Naranjito, PR	CGS
Narberth, PA	PH
Narragansett, RI	PRO
Narrowsburg, NY	NY
Nashua, IA	DUB
NH	MAN
Nashville, IL	BEL
IN	IND
TN	NSH
Nashwauk, MN	DUL
Nassau, MN	NU
NY	ALB
Nassau Bay, TX	GAL
Natchez, MS	JKS
Natchitoches, LA	ALX
Natick, MA	BO
National City, CA	SD
National Park, NJ	CAM
Natrona, PA	PIT
Natrona Heights, PA	PIT
Naugatuck, CT	HRT
Nauvoo, IL	PEO
Navajo, NM	GLP
Navarino, WI	GB
Navarre, FL	PT
OH	Y
Navasota, TX	GAL
Navilleton, IN	IND
Naytahwaush, MN	CR
Nazareth, KY	L
MI	KAL
PA	ALN
TX	AMA
Nebish, MN	CR
Nebraska City, NE	LIN
Necedah, WI	LC
Neche, ND	FAR
Nederland, TX	BEA
Needham, MA	BO
Needles, CA	SB
Needville, TX	GAL
Neenah, WI	GB
Neenah/Menasha, WI	GB
Neepwukos, FM	CI
Neepwukos, Chuuk, FM	CI
Neffs, OH	STU
Negaunee, MI	MAR
Neier, MO	STL
Neillsville, WI	LC
Nekoma, ND	FAR
Nekoosa, WI	LC
Neligh, NE	OM
Nelsonville, OH	STU
Nemacolin, PA	PIT
Nemar, FM	CI
Nenana, AK	FBK
Nenno, WI	MIL
Neodesha, KS	WCH
Neoga, IL	SFD
Neola, IA	DM
Neopit, WI	GB
Neosho, MO	SPC
WI	MIL
Neptune, IA	SC
NJ	TR
Nerinx, KY	L
Nesbit, MS	JKS
Nesconset, NY	RVC
Neshannock, PA	PIT
Neshkoro, WI	MAD
Nespelem, WA	SPK
Nesquehoning, PA	ALN
PA	PSC
Ness City, KS	DOD
Netcong, NJ	PAT
Neva, WI	GB
Nevada, IA	DUB
MO	KC
Nevada City, CA	SAC
Nevis, MN	CR
New Albany, IN	IND
MS	JKS
OH	COL
New Albin, IA	DUB
New Alexandria, PA	GBG
PA	SJP
New Almelo, KS	SAL
New Alsace, IN	IND
New Athens, IL	BEL
New Auburn, WI	LC
New Baden, IL	BEL
New Baltimore, MI	DET
PA	ALT
New Bavaria, OH	TOL
New Bedford, MA	FR
MA	SAM
PA	PIT
New Berlin, IL	SFD
NY	SY
WI	MIL
New Bern, NC	R
New Bethlehem, PA	E
New Bloomfield, PA	HBG
New Boston, IN	EVN
MI	DET
OH	COL
TX	TYL
New Braunfels, TX	SAT
New Bremen, OH	CIN
New Brighton, MN	STP
PA	PIT
New Britain, CT	HRT
CT	PSC
CT	STF
New Brunswick, NJ	MET
NJ	PHU
NJ	PSC
New Buffalo, MI	KAL
New Canaan, CT	BGP
New Caney, TX	GAL
New Carlisle, IN	FTW
OH	CIN
New Castle, DE	WIL
IN	IND
PA	PIT
PA	SAM
New Chicago, IN	GRY
New City, NY	NY
New Cleveland, OH	TOL
New Cumberland, PA	HBG
WV	WH
New Cuyama, CA	LA
New Denmark, WI	GB
New Derry, PA	GBG
New Douglas, IL	SFD
New Effington, SD	SFS
New Egypt, NJ	TR
New England, ND	BIS
New Fairfield, CT	BGP
New Franken, WI	GB
New Freedom, PA	BAL
PA	HBG
New Garden Township, PA	PH
New Hamburg, MO	SPC
New Hampton, IA	DUB
New Harmony, IN	EVN
New Hartford, CT	HRT
IA	DUB
NY	SY
New Haven, CT	HRT
CT	STF
IA	DUB
IN	FTW
KY	L
MO	STL
New Holland, PA	HBG
New Holstein, WI	GB
New Hope, KY	L
MN	STP
PA	PH
New Hyde Park, NY	RVC
New Iberia, LA	LAF
New Ipswich, NH	MAN
New Kensington, PA	GBG
PA	SJP
New Lebanon, NY	ALB
New Lenox, IL	JOL
New Lexington, OH	COL
New Lisbon, WI	LC
New London, CT	NOR
NH	MAN
NY	SY
OH	TOL
WI	GB
New Madrid, MO	SPC
New Marion, IN	IND
New Market, MN	STP
New Martinsville, WV	WH
New Melle, MO	STL
New Melleray, IA	DUB
New Miami, OH	CIN
New Middletown, IN	IND
OH	Y
New Milford, CT	HRT
NJ	NEW
NJ	SYM
New Monmouth, NJ	TR
New Munich, MN	SCL
New Munster, WI	MIL
New Orleans, LA	NO
LA	OLL
LA	PBR
New Oxford, PA	HBG
New Paltz, NY	NY
New Paris, OH	CIN
New Philadelphia, OH	COL
PA	ALN
New Plymouth, ID	B
New Port Richey, FL	PSC
FL	SP
New Post, WI	SUP
New Prague, MN	STP
New Providence, NJ	NEW
New Richland, MN	WIN
New Richmond, OH	CIN
WI	SUP
New Riegel, OH	TOL
New Ringgold, PA	ALN
New Roads, LA	BR
New Rochelle, NY	NY
New Rockford, ND	FAR
New Salem, ND	BIS
PA	GBG
PA	PBR
New Shoreham, RI	PRO
New Smyrna Beach, FL	ORL
New Taiton, TX	VIC
New Town, ND	BIS
New Trier, MN	STP
New Ulm, MN	NU
New Underwood, SD	RC
New Vernon, NJ	PAT
New Vienna, IA	DUB
OH	CIN
New Washington, OH	TOL
New Waverly, TX	GAL
New Windsor, NY	NY
New York, NY	ARM
NY	BUF
NY	NY
NY	PSC
NY	STF
New York Mills, NY	SY
Newald, WI	GB
Newark, CA	OAK
DE	WIL
NJ	NEW
NJ	PHU
NJ	PSC
NY	ROC
OH	COL
Newark Valley, NY	ROC
Newaygo, MI	GR
Newberg, OR	P
Newberry, MI	MAR
SC	CHR
Newberry Springs, CA	SB
CA	VNN
Newburg, WI	MIL
Newburgh, IN	EVN
NY	NY
Newbury, OH	CLV
Newbury Park, CA	LA
Newburyport, MA	BO
Newcastle, ME	PRT
NE	OM
WY	CHY
Newcomb, NY	OG
Newcomerstown, OH	COL
Newell, SD	RC
Newfane, NY	BUF
Newfield, NJ	CAM
Newhall, IA	DUB
Newington, CT	HRT
Newkirk, OK	OKL
Newman, CA	STO
Newmarket, NH	MAN
Newnan, GA	ATL
Newport, AR	LR
IA	DAV
KY	COV
MD	WDC
MI	DET
NH	MAN
NY	ALB
OH	CIN
OR	P
RI	PRO
TN	KNX
VT	BUR
WA	SPK
Newport Beach, CA	ORG
Newport News, VA	RIC
Newry, PA	ALT
Newtok, AK	FBK
Newton, IA	DAV
IL	SFD
KS	WCH
MA	BO
NC	CHL
NH	MAN
NJ	PAT
WI	GB
Newton Falls, OH	PBR
OH	Y
Newton Grove, NC	R
Newtown, CT	BGP
PA	ALN
PA	PH
Newtown Square, PA	PH
PA	SAM
Newtowne, MD	WDC
Nezperce, ID	B
Niagara, WI	GB
Niagara Falls, NY	BUF
NY	STF
Niagara University, NY	BUF
Niantic, CT	NOR
IL	SFD
Niceville, FL	PT
Nicholasville, KY	LEX
Nichols, IA	DAV
Nicholson, PA	SCR
Nicktown, PA	ALT
Nicollet, MN	NU
Nicoma Park, OK	OKL
Nightmute, AK	FBK
Niland, CA	SD
Niles, IL	CHI
KS	SAL
MI	KAL
OH	Y
Nine Mile, MI	SAG
Nipomo, CA	MRY
Niskayuna, NY	ALB
Nisswa, MN	DUL
Nitro, WV	WH
Nix Settlement, IN	FTW
Nixon, TX	SAT
Noble, LA	SHP
Noblesville, IN	LFT
Nocona, TX	FWT
Nogales, AZ	TUC
Nokomis, FL	VEN
IL	SFD
Nolan Settlement, IA	DAV
Nome, AK	FBK
Norbeck, MD	WDC
Norco, CA	SB
LA	NO
Norcross, GA	ATL
Norfolk, CT	HRT

MA	BO
NE	OM
NY	OG
VA	RIC
Norge, VA	RIC
Normal, IL	PEO
Norman, OK	OKL
WI	GB
Normandy, MO	STL
Normandy Beach, NJ	TR
Norridge, IL	CHI
Norris, SD	RC
TN	KNX
Norristown, PA	PH
North Adams, MA	SPR
North Andover, MA	BO
North Arlington, NJ	NEW
North Arm, IL	SFD
North Attleboro, MA	FR
North Auburn, OH	TOL
North Augusta, SC	CHR
North Aurora, IL	RCK
North Baltimore, OH	TOL
North Bangor, NY	OG
North Bay, NY	SY
North Beach, MD	WDC
North Bend, NE	OM
OR	P
North Bennington, VT	BUR
North Bergen, NJ	NEW
North Bethesda, MD	WDC
North Branch, MI	DET
MN	STP
North Branford, CT	HRT
North Brookfield, MA	SAM
MA	WOR
North Brunswick, NJ	MET
North Buena Vista, IA	DUB
North Caldwell, NJ	NEW
North Canton, OH	Y
North Cape May, NJ	CAM
North Chicago, IL	CHI
North Chili, NY	ROC
North Collins, NY	BUF
North Conway, NH	MAN
North Creek, NY	ALB
OH	TOL
WI	LC
North Dartmouth, MA	FR
North Dighton, MA	FR
North East, PA	E
North Easton, MA	FR
North Ellinwood, KS	DOD
North English, IA	DAV
North Evans, NY	BUF
North Falmouth, MA	FR
North Fond du Lac, WI	MIL
North Fort Myers, FL	PSC
North Grafton, MA	WOR
North Greenbush, NY	ALB
North Grosvenordale, CT	NOR
North Guilford, CT	HRT
North Haledon, NJ	PAT
North Haven, CT	HRT
North Highlands, CA	SAC
North Hollywood, CA	LA
CA	NTN
CA	SPA
North Huntingdon, PA	GBG
PA	PBR
North Jackson, OH	Y
North Java, NY	BUF
North Judson, IN	GRY
North Kingstown, RI	PRO
North Kinsley, KS	DOD
North Lake, WI	MIL
North Las Vegas, NV	LAV
North Lauderdale, FL	MIA
North Lawrence, NY	OG
North Lewisburg, OH	CIN
North Lima, OH	Y
North Little Rock, AR	LR
North Manchester, IN	FTW
North Mankato, MN	NU
North Merrick, NY	RVC
North Miami, FL	MIA
North Miami Beach, FL	MIA
North Muskegon, MI	GR
North Myrtle Beach, SC	CHR
North Oakland, PA	PIT
North Olmsted, OH	CLV
North Oxford, MA	WOR
North Palm Beach, FL	PMB
North Plainfield, NJ	MET
North Plains, OR	P
North Platte, NE	GI
NE	LIN
North Pole, AK	FBK
North Port, FL	SJP
FL	VEN
North Prairie, MN	SCL
North Providence, RI	PRO
North Reading, MA	BO
North Ridgeville, OH	CLV
North Riverside, IL	CHI
North Rochester, PA	PIT
North Royalton, OH	CLV
OH	PRM
North St. Paul, MN	STP
North Smithfield, RI	PRO
North Star, OH	CIN
North Stonington, CT	NOR
North Stratford, NH	MAN
North Syracuse, NY	SY
North Tarrytown, NY	NY
North Tonawanda, NY	BUF
North Topsail Beach, NC	R
North Troy, VT	BUR
North Vassalboro, ME	PRT
North Vernon, IN	IND
North Wales, PA	PH
North Walpole, NH	MAN
North Washington, IA	DUB
North Wildwood, NJ	CAM
North Wilkesboro, NC	CHL
Northampton, MA	SPR
PA	ALN
PA	PHU
Northboro, MA	WOR
Northbridge, MA	WOR
Northbrook, IL	CHI
Northeast Harbor, ME	PRT
Northeim, WI	GB
Northern Cambria, PA	ALT
PA	PBR
PA	SJP
Northfield, IL	CHI
MA	SPR
MN	STP
NJ	CAM
OH	CLV
VT	BUR
Northford, CT	HRT
Northglenn, CO	DEN
Northlake, IL	CHI
IL	NTN
Northome, MN	DUL
Northport, MI	GAY
NY	RVC
WA	SPK
Northridge, CA	LA
Northumberland, PA	HBG
Northvale, NJ	NEW
Northville, MI	DET
NY	ALB
Northwood, OH	PRM
Norton, KS	SAL
MA	FR
OH	CLV
VA	RIC
Nortonville, KS	KCK
ND	FAR
Norwalk, CA	LA
CT	BGP
OH	TOL
WI	LC
Norway, IA	DUB
ME	PRT
MI	MAR
Norwell, MA	BO
Norwich, CT	NOR
NY	SY
Norwood, MA	BO
MN	STP
NJ	NEW
NY	OG
PA	PH
Notre Dame, IN	FTW
Novato, CA	SFR
Novi, MI	DET
Nulato, AK	FBK
Nunda, NY	ROC
Nutley, NJ	NEW
NJ	SYM
Nyack, NY	NY
Nyssa, OR	BAK
O'Donnell, TX	LUB
O'Fallon, IL	BEL
MO	STL
O'Hara Township, PA	PIT
O'Neill, NE	OM
Oak Bluffs, MA	FR
Oak Brook, IL	JOL
Oak Creek, CO	DEN
WI	MIL
Oak Forest, IL	CHI
IN	IND
Oak Grove, KY	OWN
LA	SHP
Oak Harbor, OH	TOL
WA	SEA
Oak Hill, WV	WH
Oak Lawn, IL	CHI
Oak Park, IL	CHI
MI	DET
MI	EST
Oak Ridge, MN	WIN
NJ	PAT
TN	KNX
Oak Ridge-Milton, NJ	PAT
Oakbrook Terrace, IL	JOL
Oakdale, CA	STO
CT	NOR
LA	LKC
MN	STP
NE	OM
NY	RVC
PA	PIT
Oakes, ND	FAR
Oakesdale, WA	SPK
Oakfield, NY	BUF
WI	MIL
Oakland, CA	NTN
CA	OAK
MD	BAL
ME	PRT
NJ	NEW
Oakland City, IN	EVN
Oakley, CA	OAK
KS	SAL
MI	SAG
Oaklyn, NJ	CAM
Oakmont, PA	PIT
Oakridge, OR	P
Oakville, CA	SR
CT	HRT
MO	STL
Oakwood, ND	FAR
Oberlin, KS	SAL
LA	LKC
OH	CLV
Obernburg, NY	NY
Oblong, IL	SFD
Ocala, FL	ORL
Occidental, CA	SR
Occum, CT	NOR
Ocean Beach, NY	RVC
Ocean City, MD	WIL
NJ	CAM
Ocean Grove, NJ	TR
Ocean Shores, WA	SEA
Ocean Springs, MS	BLX
Oceanside, CA	OLD
CA	SD
NY	RVC
Oconee, IL	SFD
Oconomowoc, WI	MIL
Oconto, WI	GB
Oconto Falls, WI	GB
Odanah, WI	SUP
Odebolt, IA	SC
Odell, IL	PEO
Odem, TX	CC
Odenton, MD	BAL
Odessa, MO	KC
NY	ROC
TX	SAN
WA	SPK
Odin, KS	DOD
Oelwein, IA	DUB
Offerle, KS	DOD
Ogallala, NE	GI
Ogden, IA	SC
KS	SAL
UT	SLC
Ogdensburg, NJ	PAT
NY	OG
Ogema, MN	CR
Ogilvie, MN	SCL
Oglala, SD	RC
Oglesby, IL	PEO
Ogletown, DE	WIL
Ohio, IL	PEO
Oil City, PA	E
Oildale, CA	FRS
Ojai, CA	LA
Okanogan-Omak, WA	SPK
Okarche, OK	OKL
Okawville, IL	BEL
Okeechobee, FL	PMB
Okeene, OK	OKL
Okemos, MI	LAN
Oklahoma City, OK	OKL
OK	PBR
Oklee, MN	CR
Okmulgee, OK	TLS
Olathe, KS	KCK
Olcott, NY	BUF
Old Bridge, NJ	MET
Old Fields, WV	WH
Old Forge, NY	OG
PA	PSC
PA	SCR
Old Hickory, TN	NSH
Old Lyme, CT	NOR
Old Mines, MO	STL
Old Monroe, MO	STL
Old Orchard Beach, ME	PRT
Old Saybrook, CT	NOR
Old Tappan, NJ	NEW
Old Town, ME	PRT
Old Washington-on-the-Brazos, TX	AUS
Old Westbury, NY	RVC
Oldenburg, IN	IND
Oldham, SD	SFS
Oldsmar, FL	SP
Olean, NE	OM
NY	BUF
NY	PSC
NY	SAM
Olema, CA	SFR
Olfen, TX	SAN
Olga, ND	FAR
Olive Branch, MS	JKS
Olive Hill, KY	LEX
Olivia, MN	NU
Olmitz, KS	DOD
Olmsted Falls, OH	CLV
Olmstedville, NY	OG
Olney, IL	BEL
MD	WDC
TX	FWT
Olpe, KS	KCK
Olympia, WA	SEA
WA	VNN
Olympia Fields, IL	CHI
Olyphant, PA	PHU
PA	SCR
Omaha, NE	OM
NE	STN
Omak, WA	SPK
Omer, MI	PRM
Omro, WI	GB
Ona, WV	WH
Onaga, KS	KCK
Onaka, SD	SFS
Onalaska, WI	LC
Onamia, MN	SCL
Onawa, IA	SC
Onaway, MI	GAY
Oneida, NY	SY
WI	GB
Oneida Township, WI	GB
Onekama, MI	GAY
Oneonta, AL	BIR
NY	ALB
Onida, SD	SFS
Onley, VA	RIC
Onondaga Hill, NY	SY
Onset, MA	FR
Onsted, MI	DET
Ontario, CA	SB
NY	ROC
OR	BAK
Ontonagon, MI	MAR
Opa Locka, FL	MIA
Opelika, AL	MOB
Opelousas, LA	LAF
Opole, MN	SCL
Oquossoc, ME	PRT
Oradell, NJ	NEW
Oran, MO	SPC
Orange, CA	ORG
CT	HRT
MA	SPR
NJ	NEW
TX	BEA
VA	ARL
Orange Beach, AL	MOB
Orange Cove, CA	FRS
Orange Grove, TX	CC
Orange Park, FL	STA
Orange Village, OH	CLV
Orangeburg, NY	NY
SC	CHR
Orangefield, TX	BEA
Orangevale, CA	SAC
Orchard Lake, MI	DET
Orchard Park, NY	BUF
Ord, NE	GI
Ordot, GU	AGN
Oreana, ID	B
Orefield, PA	ALN
Oregon, IL	RCK
OH	TOL
WI	MAD
Oregon City, OR	P
Oreland, PA	PH
Orient, IA	DM
SD	SFS
Oriental, NC	R
Orinda, CA	OAK
Orion, IL	PEO

Orion Township, MI	DET
Oriska, ND	FAR
Oriskany, NY	SY
Oriskany Falls, NY	SY
Orland, CA	SAC
Orland Hills, IL	CHI
Orland Park, IL	CHI
Orlando, FL	ORL
FL	PSC
FL	SAM
Orleans, MA	FR
NE	LIN
VT	BUR
Ormond Beach, FL	ORL
FL	PSC
Orocovis, PR	ARE
Orofino, ID	B
Orono, ME	PRT
Oroville, CA	SAC
WA	SPK
Orr, MN	DUL
Orrin, ND	FAR
Orrville, AL	MOB
OH	CLV
Ortonville, MI	DET
MN	NU
Orwell, OH	Y
VT	BUR
Orwigsburg, PA	ALN
Osage, IA	DUB
Osage Bend, MO	JC
Osage City, KS	KCK
Osakis, MN	SCL
Osawatomie, KS	KCK
Osborne, KS	SAL
Osceola, AR	LR
IA	DM
NE	LIN
WI	SUP
Oscoda, MI	GAY
Osgood, IN	IND
OH	CIN
Oshkosh, WI	GB
Oskaloosa, IA	DAV
Oslo, MN	CR
Osman, WI	GB
Osmond, NE	OM
Osnabrock, ND	FAR
Osprey, FL	VEN
Osseo, MN	STP
Ossian, IA	DUB
Ossineke, MI	GAY
Ossining, NY	NY
Ost, KS	WCH
Osterville, MA	FR
Oswego, IL	JOL
KS	WCH
NY	SY
Othello, WA	SPK
Otis, IN	GRY
Otis Orchards, WA	SPK
Otisville, MI	LAN
NY	NY
Otsego, MI	KAL
Ottawa, IL	PEO
KS	KCK
OH	TOL
Ottenheim, KY	LEX
Otter Creek, IA	DUB
Otter River, MA	WOR
Otterbein, IN	LFT
Ottoville, OH	TOL
Ottsville, PA	PH
Ottumwa, IA	DAV
Otway, OH	COL
Ouray, CO	PBL
Overbrook, PA	PH
PA	PIT
Overgaard, AZ	GLP
Overland, MO	STL
Overland Park, KS	KCK
Overton, NV	LAV
Ovid, MI	LAN
NY	ROC
Owasso, OK	TLS
Owatonna, MN	WIN
Owego, NY	ROC
Owen, WI	LC
Owensboro, KY	OWN
Owensville, MO	JC
OH	CIN
Owingsville, KY	LEX
Owosso, MI	LAN
Oxford, CT	HRT
IA	DAV
IN	LFT
KS	WCH
MA	WOR
MI	DET
MS	JKS
NJ	MET
NY	SY
OH	CIN
PA	PH
Oxford Junction, IA	DUB
Oxnard, CA	LA
Oxon Hill, MD	WDC
Oyens, IA	SC
Oyster Bay, NY	RVC
Ozark, AL	MOB
AR	LR
MO	SPC
Ozona, TX	SAN
Ozone Park, NY	BRK
NY	STF
Ozora, MO	STL
Pacific, MO	STL
Pacific City, OR	P
Pacific Grove, CA	MRY
Pacific Palisades, CA	LA
Pacifica, CA	SFR
Pacoima, CA	LA
Paden City, WV	WH
Paderborn, IL	BEL
Padua, MN	SCL
Paducah, KY	OWN
Page, AZ	GLP
ND	FAR
Pagedale, MO	STL
Pago Pago, AS	SPP
Pagosa Springs, CO	PBL
Pahala, HI	HON
Pahoa, HI	HON
Pahokee, FL	PMB
Pahrump, NV	LAV
Paia, HI	HON
Paincourtville, LA	BR
Painesville, OH	CLV
Painted Post, NY	ROC
Paintsville, KY	LEX
Pala, CA	SD
Pala Indian Missions, CA	SD
Palacios, TX	VIC
Palatine, IL	CHI
IL	STN
Palatka, FL	STA
Palau, PW	CI
Palenville, NY	ALB
Palestine, TX	TYL
Palikir, FM	CI
Palisades Park, NJ	NEW
Palm Bay, FL	ORL
Palm Beach, FL	PMB
Palm Beach Gardens, FL	PMB
Palm City, FL	PMB
Palm Coast, FL	STA
Palm Desert, CA	SB
Palm Harbor, FL	SP
Palm Springs, CA	SB
CA	VNN
FL	PMB
Palmdale, CA	LA
Palmer, AK	ANC
MA	SPR
PA	GBG
Palmerton, PA	ALN
PA	PHU
PA	PSC
Palmerton-Slatington, PA	ALN
Palmetto, FL	VEN
Palms, MI	SAG
Palmyra, IL	SFD
MO	JC
NE	LIN
NY	ROC
PA	HBG
VA	RIC
WI	MAD
Palo Alto, CA	SJ
Palo Cedro, CA	SAC
Palos Heights, IL	CHI
Palos Hills, IL	CHI
Palos Park, IL	CHI
IL	STN
Pampa, TX	AMA
Pana, IL	SFD
Panama, IA	DM
IL	SFD
NY	BUF
Panama City, FL	PT
Panama City Beach, FL	PT
Panhandle, TX	AMA
Panna Maria, TX	SAT
Panora, IA	DM
Panorama City, CA	LA
Paola, KS	KCK
Paoli, IN	IND
PA	PH
WI	MAD
Paonia, CO	PBL
Papaaloa, HI	HON
Papaikou, HI	HON
Papillion, NE	OM
Paradis, LA	NO
Paradise, CA	SAC
MI	DET
Paradox, NY	ALB
Paragould, AR	LR
Paramount, CA	LA
Paramus, NJ	NEW
NJ	SYM
Parchment, MI	KAL
Pardeesville, PA	SCR
Pardeeville, WI	MAD
Paris, AR	LR
IL	SFD
KY	LEX
TN	MEM
TX	TYL
WI	MIL
Parish, NY	SY
Parisville, MI	SAG
Park, KS	SAL
Park City, UT	SLC
Park Falls, WI	SUP
Park Forest, IL	CHI
IL	JOL
Park Hills, MO	STL
Park Rapids, MN	CR
Park Ridge, IL	CHI
NJ	NEW
Park River, ND	FAR
Parker, AZ	TUC
CO	COS
PA	GBG
SD	SFS
Parkers Prairie, MN	SCL
Parkersburg, IA	DUB
WV	WH
Parkesburg, PA	PH
Parkland, FL	MIA
Parkman, OH	CLV
Parks, LA	LAF
Parkston, SD	SFS
Parkton, MD	BAL
Parlier, CA	FRS
Parlin, NJ	MET
Parma, ID	B
OH	CLV
OH	PRM
OH	SJP
Parma Heights, OH	CLV
Parmelee, SD	RC
Parnell, IA	DAV
MI	GR
MO	KC
Parrish, FL	VEN
Parshall, ND	BIS
Parsippany, NJ	PAT
Parsons, KS	WCH
Pasadena, CA	LA
MD	BAL
TX	GAL
Pasadina, CA	LA
Pascagoula, MS	BLX
Pasco, WA	SPK
Pascoag, RI	PRO
Paso Robles, CA	MRY
Pass Christian, MS	BLX
Passaic, NJ	PAT
NJ	PHU
NJ	PSC
Patagonia, AZ	TUC
Pataskala, OH	COL
Patch Grove, WI	MAD
Patchogue, NY	RVC
Paterson, NJ	ARM
NJ	PAT
Patillas, PR	PCE
Patterson, CA	STO
LA	LAF
NY	NY
Pattison/Brookshire, TX	GAL
Patton, PA	ALT
PA	PBR
Paul, NE	LIN
Paulding, MS	JKS
OH	TOL
Paulina, LA	BR
Pauls Valley, OK	OKL
Paulsboro, NJ	CAM
Pavilion, NY	BUF
Paw Paw, MI	KAL
Pawcatuck, CT	NOR
Pawhuska, OK	TLS
Pawleys Island, SC	CHR
Pawling, NY	NY
Pawnee, IL	SFD
OK	TLS
Pawnee Rock, KS	DOD
Pawtucket, RI	PRO
RI	SAM
Paxico, KS	KCK
Paxton, IL	JOL
MA	WOR
Payette, ID	B
Payne, OH	TOL
Paynesville, MN	SCL
Payneville, KY	L
Payson, AZ	TUC
UT	SLC
Pe Ell, WA	SEA
Peabody, MA	BO
Peachtree City, GA	ATL
Peaks Island, ME	PRT
Peapack, NJ	MET
Pearisburg, VA	RIC
Pearl, MI	KAL
MS	JKS
Pearl City, HI	HON
Pearl Lake, MN	SCL
Pearl River, LA	NO
NY	NY
Pearland, TX	GAL
Pearlington, MS	BLX
Pearsall, TX	SAT
Pecatonica, IL	RCK
Peckville, PA	SCR
Pecos, NM	SFE
TX	ELP
Peebles, OH	CIN
Peekskill, NY	NY
NY	PSC
Peetz, CO	DEN
Pekin, IL	PEO
Pelham, NH	MAN
NY	NY
Pelham Manor, NY	NY
Pelican Lake, WI	SUP
Pelican Rapids, MN	SCL
Pell City, AL	BIR
Pell Lake, WI	MIL
Pella, IA	DAV
Pellston, MI	GAY
Pembina, ND	FAR
Pembine, WI	GB
Pembroke, MA	BO
Pembroke Pines, FL	MIA
Pen Argyl, PA	ALN
Pena Blanca, NM	SFE
Penacook, NH	MAN
Penasco, NM	SFE
Pence, WI	SUP
Pender, NE	OM
Pendleton, NY	BUF
OR	BAK
Penelope, TX	FWT
Penfield, IL	PEO
NY	ROC
Pengilly, MN	DUL
Peninsula, OH	CLV
Penn, ND	FAR
PA	GBG
Penn Hills, PA	PIT
Penn Valley, PA	PH
Penn Yan, NY	ROC
Penndel, PA	PH
Penngrove, CA	SR
Pennington, MN	CR
NJ	TR
Penns Grove, NJ	CAM
Penns Valley, PA	ALT
Pennsauken, NJ	CAM
Pennsburg, PA	PH
Pennsville, NJ	CAM
Pensacola, FL	PT
Pensacola Beach, FL	PT
Penuelas, PR	PCE
Peonia, KY	OWN
Peoria, AZ	PHX
IL	OLL
IL	PEO
Peoria Heights, IL	PEO
Peosta, IA	DUB
Peotone, IL	JOL
Peplin, WI	LC
Pepper Pike, OH	CLV
Pepperell, MA	BO
Pequannock, NJ	PAT
Pequot Lakes, MN	DUL
Peralta, NM	SFE
Perezville-Tamuning, GU	AGN
Perham, MN	SCL
Perkins, MI	MAR
Perkinsville, NY	ROC
Perris, CA	SB
Perronville, MI	MAR
Perry, FL	PT
GA	SAV
IA	DM
KS	KCK
ME	PRT
MO	JC
NY	BUF

OH	CLV
OK	OKL
WI	MAD
Perryopolis, PA	GBG
PA	PBR
Perrysburg, NY	BUF
OH	TOL
Perrysville, PA	PIT
Perryton, TX	AMA
Perryville, MD	WIL
MO	STL
Perth Amboy, NJ	MET
NJ	PHU
NJ	PSC
Peru, IL	PEO
IN	LFT
NY	OG
OH	TOL
Peshabestown, MI	GAY
Peshtigo, WI	GB
Pesotum, IL	PEO
Petal, MS	BLX
Petaluma, CA	SFR
CA	SR
Peterborough, NH	MAN
Peters Township, PA	PIT
Petersburg, AK	JUN
IA	DUB
IL	SFD
IN	EVN
NE	OM
TX	LUB
VA	RIC
WV	WH
Petersham, MA	SAM
MA	WOR
Peterstown, IL	PEO
Petersville, IA	DAV
Petoskey, MI	GAY
Pevely, MO	STL
Pewamo, MI	GR
Pewaukee, WI	MIL
Pewee Valley, KY	L
Pfeifer, KS	SAL
Pflugerville, TX	AUS
Pharr, TX	BWN
Phelan, CA	SB
Phelps, NY	ROC
WI	SUP
Phenix City, AL	MOB
Philadelphia, MS	JKS
PA	ARM
PA	HBG
PA	PH
PA	PHU
PA	PSC
PA	SAM
Philip, SD	RC
Philippi, WV	WH
Philipsburg, MT	HEL
PA	ALT
Phillips, WI	SUP
Phillipsburg, KS	SAL
NJ	MET
NJ	PSC
Philmont, NY	ALB
Philo, IL	PEO
Philothea, OH	CIN
Philpot, KY	OWN
Phlox, WI	GB
Phoenicia, NY	NY
Phoenix, AZ	NTN
AZ	OLL
AZ	PHX
AZ	STN
AZ	VNN
NY	SY
Phoenixville, PA	PH
PA	PHU
Picayune, MS	BLX
Pickens, SC	CHR
Pickerel, WI	GB
Pickerington, OH	COL
Pico Rivera, CA	LA
Piedmont, CA	OAK
MO	SPC
OK	OKL
SD	RC
Piedmont-Black Hawk, SD	RC
Pierce, NE	OM
Pierce City, MO	SPC
Pierceton, IN	FTW
Piermont, NY	NY
Pierre, SD	SFS
Pierre Part, LA	BR
Pierron, IL	SFD
Pier-Willow, WI	SUP
Pierz, MN	SCL
Piffard, NY	ROC
Pigeon, MI	SAG
Pigeon Forge, TN	KNX
Pikeville, KY	LEX
Pilot Grove, MO	JC
Pilot Knob, MO	SPC
Pilot Point, TX	FWT
Pilot Rock, OR	BAK
Pilot Station, AK	FBK
Pilsen, KS	WCH
Pin Oak, TX	AUS
Pinckney, MI	LAN
Pinckneyville, IL	BEL
Pinconning, MI	SAG
Pine Apple, AL	MOB
Pine Beach, MN	DUL
Pine Bluff, AR	LR
WI	MAD
Pine Bluffs, WY	CHY
Pine Bush, NY	NY
Pine City, MN	DUL
NY	ROC
Pine Creek, WI	LC
Pine Grove, OH	STU
PA	SCR
WI	GB
Pine Hill, NJ	CAM
Pine Island, MN	STP
NY	NY
Pine Lawn, MO	STL
Pine Plains, NY	NY
Pine Prairie, LA	LAF
Pine Ridge, SD	RC
Pine River, MN	DUL
Pinedale, WY	CHY
Pinehaven, NM	GLP
Pinehurst, NC	R
Pinellas Park, FL	SP
Pinetop, AZ	GLP
Pineville, LA	ALX
MS	BLX
WV	WH
Piney Fork, OH	STU
Pingree, ND	FAR
Pinhook, IA	DUB
Pinnebog, MI	SAG
Pinole, CA	OAK
Pinon, AZ	GLP
Piopolis, IL	BEL
Piper City, IL	JOL
Pipestone, MN	WIN
Piqua, KS	WCH
OH	CIN
Pirtleville, AZ	TUC
Piscataway, MD	WDC
NJ	MET
Pisek, ND	FAR
Pismo Beach, CA	MRY
Pitcairn, PA	PIT
Piti, GU	AGN
Pitman, NJ	CAM
Pittsboro, NC	R
Pittsburg, CA	OAK
KS	WCH
TX	TYL
Pittsburgh, PA	PBR
PA	PIT
PA	SJP
Pittsfield, IL	SFD
MA	SPR
MA	STF
ME	PRT
NH	MAN
Pittsford, NY	ROC
VT	BUR
Pittsgrove, NJ	CAM
Pittston, PA	PSC
PA	SCR
Pittstown, NJ	MET
NY	ALB
Pittsville, WI	LC
Placentia, CA	NTN
CA	ORG
Placerville, CA	SAC
Placid, IA	DUB
Plain, WI	MAD
Plain City, OH	COL
Plainfield, CT	NOR
IL	JOL
IN	IND
NJ	NEW
WI	GB
Plains, KS	DOD
MT	HEL
PA	SCR
Plainsboro, NJ	MET
Plainview, MN	WIN
NE	OM
NY	RVC
TX	LUB
Plainville, CT	HRT
KS	SAL
MA	BO
Plaisance, LA	LAF
Plaistow, NH	MAN
Planada, CA	FRS
Plankinton, SD	SFS
Plano, IL	JOL
TX	DAL
Plant City, FL	SP
Plantation, FL	MIA
Plantersville, TX	GAL
Plantsville, CT	HRT
Plaquemine, LA	BR
Plateau, AL	MOB
Platte, SD	SFS
Platte Center, NE	OM
Plattekill, NY	NY
Plattenville, LA	BR
Platteville, CO	DEN
WI	MAD
Plattsburg, MO	KC
Plattsburgh, NY	OG
Plattsmouth, NE	LIN
Plaucheville, LA	ALX
Playa De Ponce, PR	PCE
Playa del Rey, CA	LA
Playa Ponce, PR	PCE
Pleasant City, OH	PBR
Pleasant Hill, CA	OAK
Pleasant Hills, PA	PIT
Pleasant Mount, PA	SCR
Pleasant Point, ME	PRT
Pleasant Prairie, WI	MIL
Pleasant Valley, NY	NY
Pleasanton, CA	OAK
NE	GI
TX	SAT
Pleasantville, NJ	CAM
NY	NY
Pleasure Ridge Park, KY	L
Plentywood, MT	GF
Plover, WI	LC
Plum, PA	PIT
TX	VIC
Plum City, WI	LC
Plummer, MN	CR
Plymouth, IA	DUB
IN	FTW
MA	BO
MI	DET
MI	LAN
MI	NTN
MN	STP
NC	R
NH	MAN
OH	TOL
PA	PHU
PA	SCR
WI	MIL
Plymouth Meeting, PA	PH
Plymouth Rock, IA	DUB
Pocahontas, AR	LR
IA	SC
IL	SFD
VA	RIC
Pocasset, MA	FR
Pocatello, ID	B
Pocomoke City, MD	WIL
Pocono Pines, PA	SCR
Pocono Summit, PA	PSC
Pohnpei, FM	CI
Poinciana, FL	ORL
Point Arena, CA	SR
Point Lookout, NY	RVC
Point Marion, PA	GBG
Point Pleasant, NJ	TR
WV	WH
Point Pleasant Beach, NJ	TR
Point Richmond, CA	OAK
Pointe a la Hache, LA	NO
Pointe-Aux-Chenes, LA	HT
Pojoaque, NM	SFE
Poland, OH	Y
Polo, IL	RCK
SD	SFS
Polonia, WI	LC
Polson, MT	HEL
Pomeroy, IA	SC
OH	STU
WA	SPK
Pomfret, CT	NOR
MD	WDC
Pomona, CA	LA
NJ	CAM
Pompano Beach, FL	MIA
FL	SYM
Pompey, NY	SY
Pompton Lakes, NJ	PAT
Pompton Plains, NJ	PAT
Ponca, NE	OM
Ponca City, OK	OKL
Ponce, PR	PCE
Ponchatoula, LA	BR
LA	NO
Pond Settlement, IL	BEL
Poniatowski, WI	LC
Ponsford, MN	CR
Ponte Vedra Beach, FL	STA
Pontiac, IL	PEO
MI	DET
Poolesville, MD	WDC
Poplar, MT	GF
Poplar Bluff, MO	SPC
Poplar Springs, MD	BAL
Poquonock, CT	HRT
Porcupine, SD	RC
Porrassapw, FM	CI
Port Allegany, PA	E
Port Allen, LA	BR
Port Angeles, WA	SEA
Port Aransas, TX	CC
Port Arthur, TX	BEA
Port Austin, MI	SAG
Port Barre, LA	LAF
Port Bolivar, TX	GAL
Port Carbon, PA	ALN
Port Charlotte, FL	VEN
Port Chester, NY	NY
Port Clinton, OH	TOL
Port Edwards, WI	LC
Port Ewen, NY	NY
Port Gibson, MS	JKS
Port Henry, NY	OG
Port Hudson, MO	STL
Port Huron, MI	DET
Port Isabel, TX	BWN
Port Jefferson, NY	RVC
Port Jefferson Station, NY	RVC
Port Jervis, NY	NY
Port Lavaca, TX	VIC
Port Leyden, NY	OG
Port Murray, NJ	MET
Port Neches, TX	BEA
Port Orange, FL	ORL
Port Orchard, WA	SEA
Port Reading, NJ	MET
Port Richey, FL	SP
Port St. Joe, FL	PT
Port St. Lucie, FL	PMB
Port Sanilac, MI	SAG
Port Sulphur, LA	NO
Port Tobacco, MD	WDC
Port Townsend, WA	SEA
Port Vue, PA	PIT
Port Washington, NY	RVC
WI	MIL
Port Wentworth, GA	SAV
Portage, IN	GRY
MI	KAL
PA	ALT
PA	PBR
WI	MAD
Portage Des Sioux, MO	STL
Portageville, MO	SPC
NY	BUF
Portales, NM	SFE
Porterville, CA	FRS
Portland, CT	NOR
IN	LFT
ME	PRT
MI	GR
OR	OLL
OR	P
OR	VNN
TX	CC
Portola, CA	SAC
Portola Valley, CA	SFR
Portsmouth, IA	DM
NH	MAN
OH	COL
RI	PRO
VA	RIC
Portville, NY	BUF
Posen, IL	BEL
IL	CHI
MI	GAY
Poseyville, IN	EVN
Post, TX	LUB
Post Falls, ID	B
Postville, IA	DUB
Poteau, OK	TLS
Poteet, TX	SAT
Poth, TX	SAT
Potlatch, ID	B
Potomac, MD	WDC
Potomac Falls, VA	ARL
Potosi, MO	STL
Potsdam, NY	OG
Pottstown, PA	PH
PA	PHU
PA	PSC
Pottsville, PA	ALN
Poughkeepsie, NY	NY
Poulsbo, WA	SEA
Poultney, VT	BUR

Poway, CA	SD
Powell, OH	COL
WY	CHY
Powhatan, LA	ALX
VA	RIC
WV	WH
Powhatan Point, OH	STU
Poy Sippi, WI	GB
Poynette, WI	MAD
Praga, MI	GAY
Prague, NE	LIN
OK	OKL
Praha, TX	VIC
Prairie, IA	DUB
Prairie du Chien, WI	LC
Prairie du Rocher, IL	BEL
Prairie du Sac, WI	MAD
Prairie View, TX	GAL
Prairie Village, KS	KCK
Prairieburg, IA	DUB
Prairieville, LA	BR
Pratt, KS	DOD
Prattville, AL	MOB
Premont, TX	CC
Prentice, WI	SUP
Prescott, AZ	PHX
MI	GAY
WI	LC
Prescott Valley, AZ	PHX
Presho, SD	RC
Presidio, TX	ELP
Presque Isle, ME	PRT
WI	SUP
Preston, CT	NOR
IA	DUB
MN	WIN
Prestonsburg, KY	LEX
Price, UT	SLC
Prichard, AL	MOB
Priest River, ID	B
Primos, PA	PH
Prince Frederick, MD	WDC
Prince George County, VA	RIC
Princess Anne, MD	WIL
Princeton, IL	PEO
IN	EVN
KY	OWN
MA	WOR
MN	SCL
NJ	MET
NJ	TR
WI	MAD
WV	WH
Princeville, IL	PEO
Prineville, OR	BAK
Prior Lake, MN	STP
Proctor, MN	DUL
VT	BUR
Progreso, TX	BWN
Prophetstown, IL	RCK
Prospect, CT	HRT
PA	PIT
Prospect Heights, IL	CHI
Prospect Park, NJ	PAT
Prosser, WA	YAK
Protivin, IA	DUB
Providence, KY	OWN
OH	TOL
RI	OLD
RI	PRO
Provincetown, MA	FR
Provo, UT	SLC
Prudenville, MI	GAY
Pryor, MT	GF
OK	TLS
Pueblo, CO	PBL
Puerta De Tierra, PR	SJN
Puerto Nuevo, PR	SJN
Pukwana, SD	SFS
Pulaski, NY	SY
TN	NSH
WI	GB
Pulaskifield, MO	SPC
Pullman, WA	SPK
Punta Gorda, FL	VEN
Punxsutawney, PA	E
PA	PBR
Purcell, KS	KCK
OK	OKL
Purcellville, VA	ARL
Purchase, NY	NY
Put-In-Bay, OH	TOL
Putnam, CT	LIT
CT	NOR
IL	LIT
Putney, VT	BUR
Puyallup, WA	SEA
Pylesville, MD	BAL
Quaker Hill, CT	NOR
Quakertown, PA	PH
Quanah, TX	FWT
Quarryville, PA	HBG
Quebradillas, PR	ARE
Queens, NY	BRK
Queens Village, NY	BRK
Queensbury, NY	ALB
Quemado, NM	GLP
Questa, NM	SFE
Quincy, CA	SAC
FL	PT
IL	SFD
MA	BO
WA	YAK
Quinebaug, CT	NOR
Quinnesec, MI	MAR
Quinque, VA	RIC
Quinton, VA	RIC
Raceland, LA	HT
Racine, WI	MIL
Radcliff, KY	L
Raddle, IL	BEL
Radford, VA	RIC
Radisson, WI	SUP
Radnor, PA	ARM
PA	PH
Radom, IL	BEL
Raeford, NC	R
Raeville, NE	OM
Rahway, NJ	NEW
NJ	PSC
Rainelle, WV	WH
Rainier, OR	P
Raleigh, NC	R
ND	BIS
Ralls, TX	LUB
Ralston, NE	OM
Rambin, LA	SHP
Ramey, PA	E
PA	SJP
Ramona, CA	SD
CA	VNN
SD	SFS
Ramsay, MI	MAR
Ramsey, IL	SFD
NJ	NEW
NJ	PHU
Ranchito, TX	BWN
Rancho Cordova, CA	SAC
Rancho Cucamonga, CA	SB
Rancho Dominguez, CA	LA
Rancho Murieta, CA	SAC
Rancho Palos Verdes, CA	LA
CA	ORG
Rancho Santa Fe, CA	SD
Rancho Santa Margarita, CA	ORG
Ranchos De Taos, NM	SFE
Randall, MN	SCL
Randallstown, MD	BAL
Randolph, MA	BO
NE	OM
NJ	PAT
NY	BUF
VT	BUR
WI	MIL
Randolph Township, OH	Y
Random Lake, WI	MIL
Rangely, CO	DEN
Ranger, TX	FWT
Rankin, PA	PBR
PA	PIT
Ranshaw, PA	HBG
Ransom, IL	PEO
KS	DOD
Ransomville, NY	BUF
Rantoul, IL	PEO
Rapid City, SD	RC
Rapid River, MI	MAR
Rapids City, IL	PEO
Rapson, MI	SAG
Raquette Lake, NY	OG
Raritan, IL	PEO
NJ	MET
Ratcliff, AR	LR
Rathbun, IA	DAV
Rathdrum, ID	B
Raton, NM	SFE
Ravena, NY	ALB
Ravenna, KY	LEX
MI	GR
NE	GI
OH	Y
Ravenswood, WV	WH
Rawlins, WY	CHY
Ray Township, MI	DET
Raymond, IA	DUB
IL	SFD
LA	LKC
MN	NU
MS	JKS
WA	SEA
Raymondville, NY	OG
TX	BWN
Rayne, LA	LAF
Raynham, MA	FR
Raytown, MO	KC
Rayville, LA	SHP
Raywick, KY	L
Raywood, TX	BEA
Reading, KS	KCK
MA	BO
PA	ALN
PA	PHU
Readsboro, VT	BUR
Reardan, WA	SPK
Red Bank, NJ	TR
Red Bluff, CA	SAC
Red Brush, IN	EVN
Red Bud, IL	BEL
Red Cliff, WI	SUP
Red Cloud, NE	LIN
Red Creek, NY	ROC
Red Feathers Lakes, CO	DEN
Red Hook, NY	NY
Red Lake, MN	CR
Red Lake Falls, MN	CR
Red Lodge, MT	GF
Red Oak, IA	DM
Red Wing, MN	STP
Redding, CA	SAC
CT	BGP
Redfield, SD	SFS
Redford, MI	DET
NY	OG
Redford Township, MI	DET
Redgranite, WI	GB
Redland, OR	P
Redlands, CA	SB
CA	VNN
Redmond, OR	BAK
WA	SEA
Redondo Beach, CA	LA
Redwood, NY	OG
Redwood City, CA	ROC
CA	SFR
CA	SJ
Redwood Falls, MN	NU
Redwood Valley, CA	STN
Reed, KY	OWN
OH	TOL
Reed City, MI	GR
Reedley, CA	FRS
Reedsburg, WI	MAD
Reedsport, OR	P
Reedsville, WI	GB
Reese, MI	SAG
Reeseville, WI	MIL
Refugio, TX	CC
Regal, MN	NU
Regent, ND	BIS
Rego Park, NY	BRK
Rehoboth, DE	WIL
Reidsville, NC	CHL
Reilly Settlement, IA	DUB
Reinbeck, IA	DUB
Reliance, SD	RC
Remer, MN	DUL
Remington, IN	LFT
Remsen, IA	SC
Remus, MI	GR
Renault, IL	BEL
Renner, SD	SFS
Reno, NV	RNO
Renovo, PA	ALT
Rensselaer, IN	LFT
NY	ALB
Renton, WA	SEA
Renville, MN	NU
Republic, MI	MAR
MO	SPC
OH	TOL
PA	GBG
WA	SPK
Reseda, CA	LA
Reserve, LA	NO
WI	SUP
Reserve Township, PA	PIT
Reston, VA	ARL
Revere, MA	BO
Revillo, SD	SFS
Revloc, PA	ALT
PA	SJP
Rexmere, LA	ALX
Rexville, NY	ROC
Reynolds, IN	LFT
ND	FAR
Reynoldsburg, OH	COL
Reynoldsville, PA	E
Rhine, OH	CIN
Rhinebeck, NY	NY
Rhineland, MO	JC
TX	FWT
Rhinelander, WI	SUP
Rhodelia, KY	L
Rhodell, WV	WH
Rhodes, IA	DUB
Rialto, CA	SB
Rib Lake, WI	SUP
Ribera, NM	SFE
Rice, MN	SCL
Rice Lake, WI	SUP
Riceville, IA	DUB
Rich Fountain, MO	JC
Richard, LA	LAF
Richardson, TX	DAL
Richardton, ND	BIS
Richboro, PA	PH
Richeyville, PA	PIT
Richfield, MN	STP
OH	CLV
WI	MIL
Richfield Center, OH	TOL
Richfield Springs, NY	ALB
Richford, VT	BUR
Richland, IA	DAV
MO	JC
NJ	CAM
NY	SY
OR	BAK
WA	YAK
Richland Center, WI	LC
Richland Township, PA	PIT
Richlands, VA	RIC
Richmond, CA	OAK
IA	DAV
IL	RCK
IN	IND
KS	KCK
KY	LEX
ME	PRT
MI	DET
MN	SCL
MO	KC
OH	STU
TX	GAL
VA	PHU
VA	RIC
VT	BUR
Richmond Heights, MO	STL
Richmond Hill, GA	SAV
Richwood, TX	GAL
WV	WH
Richwoods, MO	STL
Rickardsville, IA	DUB
Ridge, MD	WDC
Ridge Manor, FL	SP
Ridgecrest, CA	FRS
Ridgefield, CT	BGP
NJ	NEW
Ridgefield Park, NJ	NEW
Ridgeland, SC	CHR
Ridgeley, WV	WH
Ridgely, MD	WIL
Ridgeway, WI	MAD
Ridgewood, NJ	NEW
NY	BRK
Ridgway, IL	BEL
PA	E
Ridley Park, PA	PH
Riegelsville, PA	PH
Riegelwood, NC	R
Rifle, CO	DEN
Riggsville, MI	GAY
Rincon, PR	MGZ
Rindge, NH	MAN
Ringtown, PA	ALN
Ringwood, NJ	PAT
Rio, WI	MAD
Rio Bravo, TX	LAR
Rio Grande, OH	STU
PR	SJN
Rio Grande City, TX	BWN
Rio Hondo, TX	BWN
Rio Piedras, PR	SJN
Rio Rancho, NM	SFE
Rio Rico, AZ	TUC
Rio Vista, CA	SAC
Ripley, MS	JKS
NY	BUF
OH	CIN
Ripon, CA	STO
WI	MIL
Rising Sun, WI	LC
Rittman, OH	CLV
Ritzville, WA	SPK
River Aux Vases, MO	STL
River Edge, NJ	NEW
River Falls, WI	SUP
River Forest, IL	CHI
River Grove, IL	CHI
River Ridge, LA	NO
River Rouge, MI	DET
River Vale, NJ	NEW
Riverbank, CA	STO
Riverdale, CA	FRS

GA	ATL
IL	CHI
MD	WDC
NY	NY
Riverdale Park, MD	WDC
Riverhead, NY	RVC
NY	STF
Riverside, CA	NTN
CA	SB
CT	BGP
IA	DAV
IL	CHI
NJ	TR
Riverton, IL	SFD
NJ	TR
WY	CHY
Riverview, FL	SP
MI	DET
Riverview Gardens, MO	STL
Rivesville, WV	WH
Riviera Beach, FL	PMB
Roanoke, IL	PEO
IN	FTW
VA	RIC
VA	SAM
Roanoke Rapids, NC	R
Roaring Creek, PA	HBG
Roaring Spring, PA	ALT
Robbinsdale, MN	STP
Robert's Cove, LA	LAF
Robertsdale, AL	MOB
Robesonia, PA	ALN
Robinson, IL	SFD
Robinson Township, PA	PIT
Robstown, TX	CC
Rochdale, MA	WOR
Rochelle, IL	RCK
Rochelle Park, NJ	NEW
Rochester, IL	SFD
IN	LFT
MA	BO
MI	DET
MN	WIN
NH	MAN
NY	NTN
NY	ROC
NY	STF
PA	PIT
Rochester Hills, MI	DET
Rock Creek, OH	Y
Rock Falls, IL	RCK
WI	LC
Rock Hill, SC	CHR
Rock Island, IL	PEO
Rock Lake, ND	FAR
PA	SCR
Rock Rapids, IA	SC
Rock Springs, WY	CHY
Rock Valley, IA	SC
Rockaway, NJ	PAT
NY	BRK
OR	P
Rockaway Park, NY	BRK
Rockdale, IL	JOL
TX	AUS
Rockford, IA	DUB
IL	RCK
MI	GR
OH	CIN
WA	SPK
Rockland, MA	BO
ME	PRT
MI	MAR
Rockledge, FL	ORL
Rocklin, CA	SAC
Rockne, TX	AUS
Rockport, IN	EVN
MA	BO
TX	CC
Rocksprings, TX	SAT
Rockville, CT	NOR
IN	IND
MD	WDC
MN	SCL
VA	RIC
Rockville Centre, NY	RVC
Rockwall, TX	DAL
Rockway, NJ	PAT
Rockwell, IA	DUB
Rockwell City, IA	SC
Rockwood, MI	DET
Rocky Ford, CO	PBL
Rocky Hill, CT	HRT
Rocky Mount, NC	R
VA	RIC
Rocky Point, NY	RVC
Rocky River, OH	CLV
Rodeo, CA	OAK
Roebling, NJ	PSC
NJ	ROM
NJ	TR
Roeland Park, KS	KCK
Rogers, AR	LR
CT	NOR
MN	STP
TX	AUS
Rogers City, MI	GAY
Rogersville, TN	KNX
Roggen, CO	DEN
Rohnert Park, CA	SR
Rohrerstown, PA	HBG
Rolesville, NC	R
Rolette, ND	FAR
Rolfe, IA	SC
Rolla, MO	JC
ND	FAR
Rolling Ground, WI	LC
Rolling Meadows, IL	CHI
Rolling Prairie, IN	GRY
Rollingstone, MN	WIN
Rollinsford, NH	MAN
Roma, TX	BWN
Rome, GA	ATL
KY	OWN
NY	STF
NY	SY
Rome City, IN	FTW
Romeo, MI	DET
Romeoville, IL	JOL
Romney, WV	WH
Romulus, MI	DET
Ronan, MT	HEL
Ronceverte, WV	WH
Ronkonkoma, NY	RVC
Roosevelt, NY	RVC
UT	SLC
Rootstown, OH	Y
Rosalia, WA	SPK
Rosamond, CA	FRS
Rosario, PR	MGZ
Rosaryville, MD	WDC
Rosati, MO	JC
Roscoe, MN	SCL
PA	PIT
SD	SFS
Roscommon, MI	GAY
Rose Creek, MN	WIN
Roseau, MN	CR
Rosebud, SD	RC
TX	AUS
Roseburg, OR	P
Rosebush, MI	SAG
Rosedale, MS	JKS
Roseland, NE	LIN
NJ	NEW
Roselle, IA	SC
IL	JOL
NJ	NEW
Roselle Park, NJ	NEW
Rosemead, CA	LA
Rosemont, PA	PH
Rosemont-Des Plaines, IL	CHI
Rosemount, MN	STP
Rosen, MN	NU
Rosenberg, TX	GAL
Rosencrans, IL	CHI
Rosendale, NY	NY
Rosenhayn, NJ	CAM
Roseto, PA	ALN
Roseville, CA	SAC
IA	DUB
MI	DET
MI	SYM
MN	STP
Rosholt, SD	SFS
WI	LC
Rosiere, NY	OG
WI	GB
Rosiere/Lincoln, WI	GB
Roslindale, MA	NTN
Roslyn, NY	RVC
PA	PH
WA	YAK
Rosman, NC	CHL
Ross Township, PA	PIT
Rossford, OH	SJP
OH	TOL
Rossiter, PA	GBG
Rossville, KS	KCK
Rostraver, PA	GBG
Roswell, GA	ATL
GA	PSC
NM	LSC
OH	COL
Rota, MP	CHK
Rotan, TX	LUB
Rothbury, MI	GR
Rothschild, WI	LC
Rotterdam, NY	ALB
Rotterdam Junction, NY	ALB
Roulette, PA	E
Round Lake, IL	CHI
Round Rock, TX	AUS
Roundup, MT	GF
Rouses Point, NY	OG
Rouseville, PA	E
Rowena, TX	SAN
Rowland Heights, CA	LA
Rowlett, TX	DAL
Rowley, IA	DUB
MA	BO
Roxboro, NC	R
Roxbury, WI	MAD
Roy, NM	SFE
OR	P
Royal, IA	SC
PA	SCR
Royal City, WA	YAK
Royal Oak, MI	DET
Royal Palm Beach, FL	PMB
Royalton, MN	SCL
Royalton-Zeigler, IL	BEL
Royersford, PA	PH
Rozellville, WI	LC
Rubicon, WI	MIL
Ruby, AK	FBK
Rudolph, WI	LC
Rudyard, MI	MAR
Rugby, ND	FAR
Ruidoso, NM	LSC
Rulo, NE	LIN
Ruma, IL	BEL
Rumford, ME	PRT
Rumson, NJ	TR
Runge, TX	SAT
Runnemede, NJ	CAM
Running Springs, CA	SB
Rupert, ID	B
Rush, NY	ROC
Rush City, MN	STP
Rush Lake, MN	SCL
Rushford, MN	WIN
NY	BUF
Rushville, IL	PEO
IN	IND
Ruskin, FL	SP
Russell, KS	SAL
MA	SPR
Russells Point, OH	CIN
Russellton, PA	PIT
Russellville, AL	BIR
AR	LR
KY	OWN
MO	JC
Russia, OH	CIN
Ruston, LA	SHP
Ruth, MI	SAG
Rutherford, NJ	NEW
NJ	PHU
Ruthven, IA	SC
Rutland, IL	PEO
MA	WOR
VT	BUR
Ryan, IA	DUB
MI	SAG
Rydal, PA	PH
Rye, CO	PBL
NY	NY
Rye Beach, NH	MAN
Rynella, LA	LAF
Sabana Grande, PR	MGZ
Sabattus, ME	PRT
Sabetha, KS	KCK
Sabin, MN	CR
Sabinal, TX	SAT
Sabine Pass, TX	BEA
Sabula, IA	DUB
Sac City, IA	SC
Sackets Harbor, NY	OG
Saco, ME	PRT
Sacramento, CA	NTN
CA	SAC
CA	STN
CA	VNN
Saddle Brook, NJ	NEW
Saddle River, NJ	NEW
Saddle River Borough, NJ	NEW
Safety Harbor, FL	SP
Safford, AZ	TUC
Sag Harbor, NY	RVC
Sagamore, PA	GBG
PA	PBR
Saginaw, MI	SAG
MN	DUL
St. Agatha, ME	PRT
St. Albans, ME	PRT
VT	BUR
WV	WH
St. Albans Bay, VT	BUR
St. Amant, LA	BR
St. Ann, MO	STL
St. Anna, MN	SCL
WI	GB
St. Anne, IL	JOL
IN	IND
St. Ansgar, IA	DUB
St. Anthony, IA	DUB
ID	B
IN	EVN
MN	SCL
MO	JC
OH	CIN
St. Augusta, MN	SCL
St. Augustine, FL	STA
IL	PEO
PA	ALT
St. Augustine Shores, FL	STA
St. Benedict, IA	SC
KS	KCK
LA	NO
MN	STP
OR	P
St. Bernard, LA	NO
St. Bonaventure, NY	BUF
St. Boniface, PA	ALT
St. Bonifacius, MN	STP
St. Catharine, KY	L
St. Catherine, IA	DUB
St. Cecilia, IA	DUB
St. Charles, IL	RCK
MI	SAG
MN	WIN
MO	STL
NE	OM
St. Clair, MI	DET
MN	WIN
MO	STL
Saint Clair, PA	ALN
St. Clair, PA	PHU
PA	PSC
St. Clair Shores, MI	DET
St. Clairsville, OH	STU
St. Clement, MO	JC
St. Cloud, FL	ORL
MN	SCL
WI	MIL
St. Columbans, NE	OM
St. Croix, IN	IND
VI	STV
St. David, AZ	TUC
St. Denis, IN	IND
St. Donatus, IA	DUB
St. Edward, NE	OM
St. Elizabeth, MO	JC
St. Elmo, IL	SFD
St. Francis, KS	SAL
KY	L
ME	PRT
MN	SCL
SD	RC
WI	MIL
St. Francisville, IL	BEL
LA	BR
St. Gabriel, LA	BR
St. George, IL	JOL
UT	SLC
WI	MIL
St. Hedwig, TX	SAT
St. Helen, MI	GAY
Saint Helena, CA	SR
St. Helena, NE	OM
St. Helena Island, SC	CHR
St. Helens, OR	P
St. Henry, MN	STP
OH	CIN
St. Ignace, MI	MAR
St. Ignatius, MT	HEL
St. Inigoes, MD	WDC
St. Jacob, IL	SFD
St. James, LA	BR
MN	WIN
MO	JC
NE	OM
NY	RVC
St. Joe, WI	MIL
Saint John, IN	GRY
St. John, KS	DOD
KY	L
ME	PRT
ND	FAR
TX	VIC
WA	SPK
WI	GB
St. Johns, AZ	GLP
MI	LAN
St. Johnsbury, VT	BUR
St. Johnsville, NY	ALB
St. Joseph, FL	SP
IN	EVN
IN	IND
KS	SAL
KY	L

KY	OWN
LA	ALX
MI	KAL
MN	SCL
MO	KC
MO	STN
OH	CIN
Saint Joseph, TN	NSH
St. Joseph Hill, IN	IND
Saint Joseph Ridge, WI	LC
St. Joseph Settlement, WV	WH
St. Kilian, MN	WIN
WI	MIL
St. Lawrence, PA	ALT
TX	SAN
WI	MIL
Saint Leo, FL	SP
St. Leo, KS	WCH
MN	NU
St. Leon, IN	IND
St. Libory, IL	BEL
NE	GI
St. Louis, KS	KCK
MI	SAG
MO	JC
MO	OLL
MO	PRM
MO	STL
MO	STN
OR	P
St. Louis County, MO	STL
St. Louis Park, MN	STP
St. Lucas, IA	DUB
Saint Maries, ID	B
St. Mark, IN	IND
St. Mark's, KS	WCH
St. Martin, MN	SCL
Saint Martin, OH	CIN
St. Martin, WI	MIL
St. Martins, MO	JC
St. Martinville, LA	LAF
St. Mary, KS	DOD
KY	L
MO	STL
St. Mary's City, MD	WDC
Saint Mary's Ridge, WI	LC
St. Mary-of-the-Knobs, IN	IND
St. Mary-of-the-Rock, IN	IND
St. Mary-of-the-Woods, IN	IND
St. Marys, AK	FBK
GA	SAV
IA	DM
KS	KCK
OH	CIN
PA	E
WV	WH
St. Mathias, MN	DUL
St. Maurice, IN	IND
St. Meinrad, IN	EVN
IN	IND
St. Michael, AK	FBK
MN	STP
ND	BIS
ND	FAR
PA	ALT
WI	MIL
St. Michael's Ridge, OH	TOL
St. Michaels, AZ	GLP
St. Nazianz, WI	GB
St. Nicholas, IN	IND
MN	SCL
St. Paris, OH	CIN
St. Patrick, KS	KCK
MO	JC
OH	CIN
St. Paul, IA	DAV
KS	WCH
KY	OWN
MN	OLL
MN	STN
MN	STP
MN	SYM
MO	STL
NE	GI
OR	P
VA	RIC
St. Paul Park, MN	STP
St. Pete Beach, FL	SP
St. Peter, IN	IND
KS	SAL
MN	NU
WI	MIL
St. Peters, MO	STL
St. Petersburg, FL	PSC
FL	SJP
FL	SP
St. Pius, IN	IND
Saint Regis Falls, NY	OG
St. Robert, MO	JC
St. Rosa, MN	SCL
St. Rose, IL	BEL

OH	CIN
St. Sebastian, IL	BEL
OH	CIN
St. Simons Island, GA	SAV
St. Stephen, MN	SCL
OH	TOL
St. Stephens, WY	CHY
St. Theresa, IA	DUB
St. Thomas, KY	L
MN	STP
MO	JC
ND	FAR
VI	STV
St. Vincent, AR	LR
St. Vincent de Paul, IN	IND
St. Wendel, MN	SCL
St. Wendelin, OH	CIN
St. Xavier, MT	GF
Saipan, MP	CHK
Salado, TX	AUS
Salamanca, NY	BUF
Salem, IL	BEL
IN	IND
MA	BO
MA	STF
MO	SPC
NH	MAN
NJ	CAM
NY	ALB
OH	Y
OR	P
SD	SFS
VA	RIC
WV	WH
Salem Twp., OH	TOL
Salida, CO	COS
Salina, KS	SAL
Salinas, CA	MRY
PR	PCE
Saline, MI	LAN
Salineville, OH	Y
Salisbury, MA	BO
MD	WIL
MO	JC
NC	CHL
Salix, IA	SC
Sallisaw, OK	TLS
Salmon, ID	B
Salt Lake City, UT	SLC
UT	VNN
Saltaire, NY	RVC
Saltsburg, PA	GBG
Salyersville, KY	LEX
Sam Rayburn, TX	BEA
Sammamish, WA	SEA
Samuels, KY	L
San Andreas, CA	STO
San Angelo, TX	SAN
San Anselmo, CA	SFR
San Antonio, FL	SP
TX	OLL
TX	SAT
San Antonio Village, District 6, MP	CHK
San Benito, TX	BWN
San Bernardino, CA	NTN
CA	SB
San Bruno, CA	SFR
San Carlos, AZ	TUC
CA	SFR
TX	BWN
San Clemente, CA	ORG
San Diego, CA	OLD
CA	OLL
CA	SD
CA	STN
CA	VNN
TX	CC
San Dimas, CA	LA
San Elizario, TX	ELP
San Fernando, CA	LA
San Fidel, NM	GLP
San Francisco, CA	SFR
CA	STN
San Gabriel, CA	LA
San German, PR	MGZ
San Isidro, TX	BWN
San Jacinto, CA	SB
San Jose, CA	NTN
CA	SJ
CA	SPA
CA	SYM
San Jose Village, MP	CHK
San Jose Village, District 7, MP	CHK
San Juan, P.R.	SJN
PR	SJN
TX	BWN
San Juan Bautista, CA	MRY
San Juan Capistrano, CA	ORG
San Juan Pueblo, NM	SFE
San Leandro, CA	OAK

CA	SFR
San Lorenzo, CA	OAK
PR	CGS
San Luis, AZ	TUC
CO	PBL
San Luis Obispo, CA	MRY
CA	VNN
San Luis Rey, CA	SD
San Manuel, AZ	TUC
San Marcos, CA	SD
TX	AUS
San Marino, CA	LA
San Mateo, CA	SFR
CA	VNN
NM	GLP
San Miguel, CA	MRY
NM	LSC
San Pablo, CA	OAK
San Patricio, NM	LSC
San Pedro, CA	LA
San Pierre, IN	GRY
San Rafael, CA	SFR
NM	GLP
San Ramon, CA	OAK
San Roque Village, District 9, MP	CHK
San Saba, TX	AUS
San Sebastian, PR	MGZ
San Vicente Village, District 10, MP	CHK
San Ysidro, CA	SD
Sanborn, IA	SC
MN	NU
ND	FAR
NY	BUF
WI	SUP
Sanbornville, NH	MAN
Sand Lake, MI	GR
Sand Springs, IA	DUB
OK	TLS
Sanderson, TX	SAN
Sandia, TX	CC
Sandoval, IL	BEL
Sandpoint, ID	B
Sandstone, MN	DUL
Sandusky, MI	SAG
OH	TOL
Sandwich, IL	RCK
MA	FR
Sandy, OR	P
UT	SLC
Sandy Hook, KY	LEX
Sanford, FL	ORL
ME	PRT
MI	SAG
NC	R
Sanger, CA	FRS
Sanibel, FL	VEN
Sanitaria Springs, NY	SY
Santa Ana, CA	LA
CA	ORG
CA	SPA
Santa Barbara, CA	LA
Santa Clara, CA	SJ
CA	STN
NM	LSC
Santa Clarita, CA	LA
Santa Claus, IN	EVN
Santa Cruz, CA	MRY
NM	SFE
Santa Fe, NM	SFE
Santa Fe Springs, CA	LA
Santa Isabel, PR	PCE
Santa Margarita, CA	MRY
Santa Maria, CA	LA
Santa Monica, CA	LA
Santa Paula, CA	LA
Santa Rita, GU	AGN
Santa Rosa, CA	SR
NM	SFE
TX	BWN
Santa Rosa Beach, FL	PT
Santa Ynez, CA	LA
Santa Ysabel, CA	SD
Santa Ysabel Indian Missions, CA	SD
Sante Fe, NM	SFE
Santee, CA	SD
Santuce, PR	SJN
Santurce, PR	SJN
Sappington, MO	STL
Sapulpa, OK	TLS
Saranac, MI	GR
Saranac Lake, NY	OG
Sarasota, FL	VEN
Saratoga, CA	SJ
NY	ALB
WY	CHY
Saratoga Springs, NY	ALB
Sarcoxie, MO	SPC
Sardinia, NY	BUF
OH	CIN
Sardis, OH	STU

Sarita, TX	CC
Sarona, WI	SUP
Sarpy Co., NE	OM
Sartell, MN	SCL
Satanta, KS	DOD
Satin, TX	AUS
Saugerties, NY	NY
Saugus, MA	BO
Sauk Centre, MN	SCL
Sauk City, WI	MAD
Sauk Rapids, MN	SCL
Sauk Village, IL	CHI
Saukville, WI	MIL
Sault Sainte Marie, MI	MAR
Sausalito, CA	SFR
Savage, MN	STP
Savanna, IL	RCK
Savannah, GA	SAV
MO	KC
TN	MEM
Sawyer, MN	DUL
Saxon, WI	SUP
Saxonville, MA	BO
Sayner, WI	SUP
Sayre, PA	PHU
PA	SCR
Sayreville, NJ	MET
Sayville, NY	RVC
Scales Mound, IL	RCK
Scammon, KS	WCH
Scammon Bay, AK	FBK
Scappoose, OR	P
Scarborough, ME	PRT
NY	NY
Scarsdale, NY	NY
Schaffer, MI	MAR
Schaghticoke, NY	ALB
Schaller, IA	SC
Schaumburg, IL	CHI
Scheller, IL	BEL
Schenectady, NY	ALB
Schererville, IN	GRY
Schertz, TX	SAT
Schiller Park, IL	CHI
Schley, IA	DUB
Schnellville, IN	EVN
Schoenchen, KS	SAL
Schoharie, NY	ALB
School Hill, WI	GB
Schooley's Mountain, NJ	PAT
Schriever, LA	HT
Schroon Lake, NY	OG
Schulenburg, TX	VIC
Schulte, KS	WCH
Schuyler, NE	OM
Schuylerville, NY	ALB
Schuylkill Haven, PA	ALN
Scio, NY	BUF
OR	P
Sciota, NY	OG
Scipio, KS	KCK
Scipio Center, NY	ROC
Scituate, MA	BO
RI	PRO
Scobey, MT	GF
Scotch Plains, NJ	NEW
NJ	SYM
Scotia, CA	SR
NY	ALB
Scotland, SD	SFS
TX	FWT
Scott, LA	LAF
Scott AFB, IL	BEL
Scott City, KS	DOD
MO	SPC
Scott Township, PA	PIT
Scottdale, PA	GBG
PA	PBR
Scotts Valley, CA	MRY
Scottsbluff, NE	GI
Scottsboro, AL	BIR
Scottsburg, IN	IND
Scottsdale, AZ	PHX
AZ	SPA
Scottsville, KY	OWN
NY	ROC
VA	RIC
Scottville, MI	GR
Scranton, AR	LR
IA	SC
KS	KCK
PA	NTN
PA	PHU
PA	PSC
PA	SAM
PA	SCR
Sea Cliff, NY	RVC
Sea Girt, NJ	TR
Sea Isle City, NJ	CAM
Seabrook, NH	MAN
Seaford, DE	WIL

NY	RVC
Seaforth, MN	NU
Seahurst, WA	SEA
Seal Beach, CA	ORG
Sealy, TX	GAL
Searcy, AR	LR
Searles, MN	NU
Seaside, CA	MRY
OR	P
Seaside Heights, NJ	TR
Seaside Park, NJ	TR
Seat Pleasant, MD	WDC
Seattle, WA	SEA
WA	VNN
Seaview, WA	SEA
Sebastian, FL	PMB
Sebastopol, CA	SR
Sebewaing, MI	SAG
Seboyeta, NM	GLP
Sebree, KY	OWN
Sebring, FL	VEN
OH	Y
Secane, PA	PH
Secaucus, NJ	NEW
Secretary, MD	WIL
Security, CO	COS
Sedalia, CO	COS
MO	JC
Sedan, KS	WCH
MN	SCL
Sedona, AZ	PHX
Sedro Woolley, WA	SEA
Seekonk, MA	FR
Seelyville, IN	IND
Seffner, FL	SP
Seguin, KS	SAL
TX	SAT
Seinwar, FM	CI
Selah, WA	YAK
Selby, SD	SFS
Selden, KS	SAL
NY	RVC
Selfridge, ND	BIS
Seligman, AZ	PHX
Selinsgrove, PA	HBG
Sellersburg, IN	IND
Sellersville, PA	PH
Selma, AL	MOB
CA	FRS
TX	SAT
Selmer, TN	MEM
Selz, ND	FAR
Seminole, FL	SP
OK	OKL
TX	LUB
Semmes, AL	MOB
Senatobia, MS	JKS
Seneca, IL	PEO
KS	KCK
MO	SPC
SD	SFS
WI	LC
Seneca Falls, NY	ROC
Sentinel Butte, ND	BIS
Sepulveda, CA	LA
Sequim, WA	SEA
Sereno, MO	STL
Sesser, IL	BEL
Setauket, NY	RVC
Seven Hills, OH	CLV
Severn, MD	BAL
Severna Park, MD	BAL
Seville-Creston, OH	CLV
Seward, AK	ANC
KS	DOD
NE	LIN
PA	GBG
Sewickley, PA	PIT
Seymour, CT	HRT
IL	PEO
IN	IND
TN	KNX
TX	FWT
WI	GB
WI	MAD
Shade Gap, PA	ALT
Shady Cove, OR	P
Shadyside, OH	STU
Shafter, CA	FRS
Shaker Heights, OH	CLV
Shakopee, MN	STP
Shallotte, NC	R
Shallowater, TX	LUB
Shamokin, PA	HBG
PA	PHU
Shandon, OH	CIN
Shannon, IL	RCK
Sharon, CT	HRT
KS	DOD
MA	BO
PA	E
PA	ROM
WI	MIL
Sharon Hill, PA	PH
Sharon Springs, KS	SAL
Sharpsburg, OH	CIN
PA	PIT
Sharpsville, PA	E
Shavertown, PA	SCR
Shaw, MS	JKS
OR	P
Shaw Island, WA	SEA
Shawano, WI	GB
Shawnee, KS	KCK
OH	COL
OK	OKL
Shawneetown, IL	BEL
Sheboygan, WI	MIL
Sheboygan Falls, WI	MIL
Sheffield, IL	PEO
MA	SPR
OH	CLV
PA	E
PA	PBR
Sheffield Lake, OH	CLV
Shelbina, MO	JC
Shelburne, VT	BUR
VT	SAM
Shelburne Falls, MA	SPR
Shelby, IN	GRY
MI	GR
MS	JKS
MT	HEL
NC	CHL
NE	LIN
OH	TOL
Shelby Twp., MI	DET
Shelbyville, IL	SFD
IN	IND
KY	L
TN	NSH
Sheldon, IA	SC
ND	FAR
NY	BUF
WI	SUP
Sheldon Springs, VT	BUR
Shell Knob, MO	SPC
Shell Lake, WI	SUP
Shell Rock, IA	DUB
Shelter Island, NY	RVC
Shelter Island Heights, NY	RVC
Shelton, CT	BGP
WA	SEA
Shenandoah, IA	DM
PA	ALN
PA	PHU
Shepherd, MI	SAG
Shepherdstown, WV	WH
Shepherdsville, KY	L
Sheppton, PA	ALN
PA	PSC
Sherborn, MA	BO
Sherburn, MN	WIN
Sherburne, NY	SY
Sheridan, AR	LR
NY	BUF
OR	P
WY	CHY
Sherman, CT	BGP
IL	SFD
NY	BUF
TX	DAL
Sherman Oaks, CA	LA
Sherrill, IA	DUB
NY	SY
Sherwood, AR	LR
OR	P
WI	GB
Sherwood Park, DE	WIL
Shevlin, MN	CR
Shields, MI	SAG
Shieldsville, MN	STP
Shillington, PA	ALN
Shiloh, IL	BEL
Shiner, TX	VIC
Shinglehouse, PA	E
Shinnston, WV	WH
Shiocton, WI	GB
Shipman, IL	SFD
Shippensburg, PA	HBG
Shiprock, NM	GLP
Shirley, MA	BO
Shoal Creek, AR	LR
Shoals, IN	EVN
Shohola, PA	SCR
Shoreham, NY	RVC
Shoreview, MN	STP
Shorewood, IL	JOL
Short Hills, NJ	NEW
Shortsville, NY	ROC
Shoshone, ID	B
Show Low, AZ	GLP
Shreveport, LA	SHP
Shrewsbury, MA	WOR
MO	STL
Shrub Oak, NY	NY
Shullsburg, WI	MAD
Shumway, IL	SFD
Siberia, IN	IND
Sibley, IA	SC
Sicklerville, NJ	CAM
Sidney, MT	GF
NE	GI
NY	ALB
OH	CIN
Sierra Blanca, TX	ELP
Sierra Madre, CA	LA
Sierra Vista, AZ	TUC
Sigel, IL	SFD
SD	SFS
WI	LC
Signal Mountain, TN	KNX
Sigourney, IA	DAV
Sikeston, MO	SPC
Siler City, NC	R
Siloam Springs, AR	LR
Silsbee, TX	BEA
Silver Bay, MN	DUL
Silver City, NM	LSC
Silver Creek, MI	KAL
NE	OM
NY	BUF
Silver Lake, MN	NU
MO	STL
Silver Spring, MD	PHU
MD	WDC
Silver Springs, NY	BUF
Silverado, CA	ORG
Silverton, CO	PBL
OR	P
Silvis, IL	PEO
Simi, CA	LA
Simi Valley, CA	LA
Simmesport, LA	ALX
Simpson, PA	PHU
PA	SCR
Simpsonville, SC	CHR
Simsbury, CT	HRT
Sinajana, GU	AGN
Sinclair, ME	PRT
Sinclairville, NY	BUF
Sinking Spring, PA	ALN
Sinsinawa, WI	MAD
Sinton, TX	CC
Sioux City, IA	SC
Sioux Falls, SD	SFS
Sioux Rapids, IA	SC
Sisseton, SD	SFS
Sister Bay, WI	GB
Sisters, OR	BAK
Sistersville, WV	WH
Sitka, AK	JUN
Skagway, AK	JUN
Skaneateles, NY	SY
Skiatook, OK	TLS
Skidmore, TX	CC
Skidway Lake, MI	GAY
Skillman, NJ	MET
Skokie, IL	CHI
Skowhegan, ME	PRT
Slater, MO	JC
Slatington, PA	ALN
Slaton, TX	LUB
Slayton, MN	WIN
Sleepy Eye, MN	NU
Sleepy Hollow, NY	NY
Slickville, PA	GBG
Slidell, LA	NO
Slinger, WI	MIL
Slingerlands, NY	ALB
Slippery Rock, PA	PIT
Sloan, NY	BUF
Sloatsburg, NY	NY
NY	STF
Slovak, AR	LR
Slovan, WI	GB
Smethport, PA	E
Smiley, TX	SAT
Smith Center, KS	SAL
Smithfield, NC	R
OH	STU
RI	PRO
VA	RIC
Smithton, IL	BEL
PA	GBG
Smithtown, NY	PSC
NY	RVC
Smithville, MO	KC
TN	NSH
TX	AUS
Smock, PA	GBG
Smyrna, DE	WIL
GA	ATL
TN	NSH
Sneedville, TN	KNX
Snellville, GA	ATL
Snohomish, WA	SEA
Snoqualmie, WA	SEA
Snow Shoe, PA	ALT
Snowflake, AZ	GLP
Snowmass, CO	DEN
Snyder, NE	OM
NY	BUF
TX	LUB
Sobieski, MN	SCL
WI	GB
Soboba Indian Reservation, CA	SB
Socorro, NM	SFE
Soda Springs, ID	B
Soddy Daisy, TN	KNX
Sodus, NY	ROC
Sokehs, FM	CI
Solana Beach, CA	SD
Soldotna, AK	ANC
Soledad, CA	MRY
Solomon, AZ	TUC
KS	SAL
Solomons, MD	WDC
Solon, IA	DAV
OH	CLV
OH	PRM
OH	SJP
Solon Springs, WI	SUP
Solvang, CA	LA
Solvay, NY	SY
Somerdale, NJ	CAM
Somers, NY	NY
Somers Point, NJ	CAM
Somerset, KY	LEX
MA	FR
NJ	MET
NJ	PSC
NJ	SAM
OH	COL
PA	ALT
TX	SAT
WI	SUP
Somersville, CT	NOR
Somersworth, NH	MAN
Somerton, AZ	TUC
Somerville, MA	BO
NJ	MET
TN	MEM
TX	AUS
Somonauk, IL	RCK
Songsong Village, MP	CHK
Sonoita, AZ	TUC
Sonoma, CA	SR
Sonora, CA	STO
TX	SAN
Soquel, CA	MRY
Sorgho, KY	OWN
Sorrento, LA	BR
Sound Beach, NY	RVC
Sour Lake, TX	BEA
South Amboy, NJ	MET
South Amherst, OH	CLV
South Ashburnham, MA	WOR
South Barre, MA	WOR
South Beloit, IL	RCK
South Bend, IN	FTW
IN	NTN
South Berwick, ME	PRT
South Boston, VA	RIC
South Bound Brook, NJ	MET
South Branch, WI	GB
South Burlington, VT	BUR
South Byron, NY	BUF
South Charleston, OH	CIN
WV	WH
South Coventry, PA	PH
South Dartmouth, MA	FR
South Dayton, NY	BUF
South Deerfield, MA	SPR
MA	STF
South Easton, MA	FR
South El Monte, CA	LA
South Euclid, OH	CLV
South Fork, PA	ALT
PA	PBR
South Garryowen, IA	DUB
South Gate, CA	LA
South Glastonbury, CT	HRT
South Glens Falls, NY	ALB
South Grafton, MA	WOR
South Hadley, MA	PSC
MA	SPR
South Haven, MI	KAL
South Heart, ND	BIS
South Hero, VT	BUR
South Hill, VA	RIC
South Holland, IL	CHI
South Houston, TX	GAL
South Huntington, NY	RVC

South Kingstown, RI	PRO
South Kortright, NY	ALB
South Lake Tahoe, CA	SAC
South Lyon, MI	DET
South Mantoloking, NJ	TR
South Meriden, CT	HRT
South Milwaukee, WI	MIL
South Mountain, PA	HBG
South Onondaga, NY	SY
South Orange, NJ	NEW
South Ozone Park, NY	BRK
South Park, PA	PIT
South Pasadena, CA	LA
South Pittsburg, TN	KNX
South Plainfield, NJ	MET
South Portland, ME	PRT
South Range, MI	MAR
South River, NJ	MET
South St. Paul, MN	STP
South San Francisco, CA	SFR
South Sioux City, NE	OM
South Tucson, AZ	TUC
South Union, KY	OWN
South Waverly, PA	SCR
South Wayne, WI	MAD
South Williamsport, PA	SCR
South Wilmington, IL	JOL
South Windsor, CT	HRT
South Yarmouth, MA	FR
Southampton, NY	RVC
PA	PH
Southaven, MS	JKS
Southborough, MA	WOR
Southbridge, MA	WOR
Southbury, CT	HRT
Southeastern Portage County, WI	LC
Southern Pines, NC	R
Southfield, MI	DET
MI	EST
Southgate, KY	COV
MI	DET
Southhaven, MS	JKS
Southington, CT	HRT
Southold, NY	RVC
Southport, NC	R
Southwick, MA	SPR
Spalding, MI	MAR
NE	GI
Spanaway, WA	SEA
Spangler, PA	ALT
Spanish Lake, MO	STL
Sparkill, NY	NY
Sparks, MD	BAL
NV	RNO
Sparta, IL	BEL
MI	GR
NJ	PAT
TN	NSH
WI	LC
Spartanburg, SC	CHR
SC	SAM
Spaulding-City Point, WI	LC
Spearfish, SD	RC
Spearman, TX	AMA
Spearville, KS	DOD
Speigletown, NY	ALB
Spencer, IA	SC
IN	IND
MA	WOR
NE	OM
OH	CLV
SD	SFS
WI	LC
WV	WH
Spencer-Farmer, SD	SFS
Spencerport, NY	ROC
Spencerville, OH	TOL
Spicer, MN	NU
Spillville, IA	DUB
Spirit Lake, IA	SC
Splendora, TX	GAL
Spokane, WA	SPK
WA	VNN
Spooner, WI	SUP
Spotswood, NJ	MET
Spotsylvania, VA	ARL
Sprague, WA	SPK
Spreckels, CA	MRY
Spring, TX	GAL
Spring Branch, TX	SAT
Spring City, PA	PH
Spring Green, WI	MAD
Spring Grove, IL	RCK
PA	HBG
Spring Hill, FL	SJP
FL	SP
MN	SCL
Spring House, PA	PH
Spring Lake, MI	GR
NJ	TR
Spring Valley, CA	SD
IL	PEO
MN	WIN
NY	NY
NY	STF
WI	LC
Springbrook, IA	DUB
NY	BUF
Springdale, AR	LR
PA	PIT
WA	SPK
Springer, NM	SFE
Springerville, AZ	GLP
Springfield, CO	PBL
IL	SFD
KY	L
MA	SAM
MA	SPR
MN	NU
MO	SPC
NE	OM
NJ	NEW
OH	CIN
OR	P
OR	STN
PA	PH
SD	SFS
TN	NSH
VA	ARL
VT	BUR
WI	LC
Springfield Gardens, NY	BRK
Springvale, ME	PRT
WI	MIL
Springville, IA	DUB
NY	BUF
Spruce, WI	GB
Spruce Creek, IA	DUB
Spruce Pine, NC	CHL
Spur, TX	LUB
Squaw Lake, MN	DUL
Stacyville, IA	DUB
Stafford, VA	ARL
Stafford Springs, CT	NOR
Stamford, CT	BGP
CT	STF
NY	ALB
TX	LUB
Stamps, AR	LR
Stanberry, MO	KC
Standing Rock, SD	RC
Standish, ME	PRT
MI	SAG
Stanford, CA	SJ
MT	GF
Stangelville, WI	GB
Stanley, KY	OWN
ND	BIS
NY	ROC
WI	LC
Stanton, CA	ORG
CA	SYM
KY	LEX
MI	GR
NE	OM
TX	SAN
WI	SUP
Stanwood, WA	SEA
Staples, MN	SCL
Stapleton, NE	GI
Star, ID	B
Star City, AR	LR
IN	LFT
WV	WH
Star Lake, NY	OG
Starford, PA	GBG
Starke, FL	STA
Starkville, MS	JKS
Starkweather, ND	FAR
Starlight, IN	IND
Starrucca, PA	SCR
State Center, IA	DUB
State College, PA	ALT
Staten Island, NY	BRK
NY	NY
NY	STF
NY	SYM
Statesboro, GA	SAV
Statesville, NC	CHL
Staunton, IL	SFD
VA	RIC
Stayton, OR	P
Ste. Genevieve, MO	STL
Ste. Marie, IL	SFD
Stead, NV	RNO
Steamboat Springs, CO	DEN
Stebbins, AK	FBK
Steele, ND	FAR
Steelton, PA	HBG
Steelville, MO	JC
Steger, IL	CHI
IL	JOL
Steinauer, NE	LIN
Stella Niagara, NY	BUF
Stephan, SD	SFS
Stephen, MN	CR
Stephenson, MI	MAR
Stephensville, WI	GB
Stephenville, TX	FWT
Sterling, CO	DEN
IL	RCK
MA	WOR
VA	ARL
Sterling Heights, MI	DET
MI	PRM
Stetsonville, WI	SUP
Steubenville, OH	STU
Stevens Point, WI	LC
Stevenson, MD	BAL
Stevensville, MT	HEL
Stewart, MN	NU
Stewartsville, NJ	MET
Stewartville, MN	WIN
Stickney, IL	CHI
SD	SFS
Stiles, WI	GB
Still River, MA	WOR
Stillwater, MN	STP
NY	ALB
OK	TLS
Stirling, NJ	PAT
Stirum, ND	FAR
Stockbridge, MA	SPR
WI	GB
Stockdale, TX	SAT
Stockholm, ME	PRT
NJ	PAT
Stockton, CA	STO
CA	VNN
IL	RCK
KS	SAL
Stone Bank, WI	MIL
Stone City, IA	DUB
Stone Harbor, NJ	CAM
Stone Lake, WI	SUP
Stone Mountain, GA	ATL
Stoneboro, PA	E
Stonefort, IL	BEL
Stoneham, CO	DEN
MA	BO
Stonelick, OH	CIN
Stonewall, TX	SAT
Stonewood, WV	WH
Stonington, CT	NOR
IL	SFD
ME	PRT
Stony Point, NY	NY
TX	AUS
Storm Lake, IA	SC
Storrs, CT	NOR
Stottville, NY	ALB
Stoughton, MA	BO
WI	MAD
Stow, MA	BO
OH	CLV
Stowe, PA	PH
VT	BUR
Strafford, PA	PH
Strasburg, ND	BIS
OH	COL
VA	ARL
Stratford, CT	BGP
NJ	CAM
TX	AMA
WI	LC
Stratton, CO	COS
Strawberry Point, IA	DUB
Strawn, TX	FWT
Streamwood, IL	CHI
Streator, IL	PEO
Streetsboro, OH	Y
Strickland, WI	SUP
String Prairie, IA	DAV
TX	AUS
Stringtown, IL	BEL
Strong City, KS	WCH
Strongsville, OH	CLV
Stroudsburg, PA	SCR
Struble, IA	SC
Struthers, OH	Y
Stryker, OH	TOL
Strykersville, NY	BUF
Stuart, FL	PMB
IA	DM
NE	OM
Studio City, CA	LA
Sturgeon Bay, WI	GB
Sturgeon Lake, MN	DUL
Sturgis, KY	OWN
MI	KAL
SD	RC
Sturtevant, WI	MIL
Stuttgart, AR	LR
Stuyvesant, NY	ALB
Stuyvesant Falls, NY	ALB
Suamico, WI	GB
Subiaco, AR	LR
Sublette, IL	RCK
Sublimity, OR	P
Succasunna, NJ	PAT
Sudbury, MA	BO
Suffern, NY	NY
Suffield, CT	HRT
Suffolk, VA	RIC
Sugar Camp, WI	SUP
Sugar Creek, IA	DAV
MO	KC
MO	PRM
Sugar Grove, OH	COL
Sugar Island, MI	MAR
Sugar Land, TX	GAL
TX	SYM
Sugar Notch, PA	SCR
Sugarloaf, PA	PSC
Suitland, MD	WDC
Sulligent, AL	BIR
Sullivan, IL	SFD
IN	EVN
MO	STL
WI	MAD
Sulphur, LA	LKC
OK	OKL
Sulphur Springs, TX	TYL
Summerfield, KS	KCK
Summerhill, PA	ALT
Summersville, WV	WH
Summerton, SC	CHR
Summerville, SC	CHR
Summit, IL	CHI
NJ	NEW
NY	ALB
WI	LC
Summit Hill, PA	ALN
Summitville, OH	Y
Sumner, IA	DUB
WA	SEA
Sumter, SC	CHR
Sun City, AZ	PHX
CA	SB
Sun City Center, FL	SP
Sun City West, AZ	PHX
Sun Lakes, AZ	PHX
Sun Prairie, WI	MAD
Sun Valley, CA	LA
ID	B
NV	RNO
Sunbury, OH	COL
PA	HBG
Suncook, NH	MAN
Sunfish, KY	OWN
Sunland, CA	LA
Sunland Park, NM	LSC
Sunny Hills, FL	PT
Sunnyside, WA	YAK
Sunnyvale, CA	SJ
Sunrise, FL	MIA
Sunset, LA	LAF
Sunset Hills, MO	STL
Sunsites, AZ	TUC
Superior, AZ	TUC
NE	LIN
WI	SUP
Surf City, NC	R
Suring, WI	GB
Surprise, AZ	PHX
Susanville, CA	SAC
Susquehanna, PA	SCR
Sussex, NJ	PAT
Sutersville, PA	GBG
Sutherland, IA	SC
NE	GI
Sutherlin, OR	P
Sutter Creek, CA	SAC
Sutton, MA	WOR
NE	LIN
Suttons Bay, MI	GAY
Swainsboro, GA	SAV
Swainton, NJ	CAM
NJ	TR
Swaledale, IA	DUB
Swampscott, MA	BO
Swan Lake, MN	NU
MT	HEL
Swan Valley, MT	HEL
Swannanoa, NC	CHL
Swansboro, NC	R
Swansea, MA	FR
Swanton, OH	TOL
VT	BUR
Swanville, MN	SCL
Swanzey, NH	MAN
Swarthmore, PA	PH
Swartswood, NJ	PAT
Swartz Creek, MI	LAN

Swedesboro, NJ	CAM
Swedesburg, PA	PH
Sweeny, TX	GAL
Sweet Home, OR	P
TX	VIC
Sweetwater, FL	MIA
TX	SAN
Swissvale, PA	PIT
Switzerland, FL	STA
Swormville, NY	BUF
Swoyersville, PA	PSC
PA	SCR
Sybertsville, PA	PSC
Sycamore, IL	RCK
OH	TOL
Sykeston, ND	FAR
Sykesville, MD	BAL
PA	E
PA	PBR
Sylacauga, AL	BIR
Sylmar, CA	LA
Sylva, NC	CHL
Sylvania, GA	SAV
OH	TOL
Sylvia, IA	DUB
Syosset, NY	BRK
NY	RVC
Syracuse, IN	FTW
KS	DOD
NE	LIN
NY	STF
NY	SY
Tabb, VA	RIC
Taberg, NY	SY
Tabernacle, NJ	TR
Tabor, MN	CR
SD	SFS
Tacoma, WA	SEA
Taconite, MN	DUL
Taft, CA	FRS
TX	CC
Taftville, CT	NOR
Tahlequah, OK	TLS
Tahoe City, CA	SAC
Tai, GU	AGN
Takoma Park, MD	WDC
Talkeetna, AK	ANC
Talladega, AL	BIR
Tallahassee, FL	MIA
FL	PT
Tallassee, AL	MOB
Tallmadge, OH	CLV
Tallulah, LA	ALX
Talofofo, GU	AGN
Tamaqua, PA	ALN
Tamarac, FL	MIA
Tamaroa, IL	BEL
Tama-Toledo, IA	DUB
Tamoroi, FM	CI
Tampa, FL	SP
KS	WCH
Tampico, IL	RCK
Tamuning, GU	AGN
Tanana, AK	FBK
Tanapag Village, District 8, MP	CHK
Taneytown, MD	BAL
Tannersville, PA	SCR
Taos, MO	JC
NM	SFE
Tappahannock, VA	RIC
Tappan, NY	NY
Tappan Lake, OH	STU
Tappen, ND	FAR
Tarboro, NC	R
Tarentum, PA	PBR
PA	PIT
Tariffville, CT	HRT
Tarkio, MO	KC
Tarnov, NE	OM
Tarpon Springs, FL	SP
Tarrytown, NY	NY
Taunton, MA	FR
MN	NU
Tavernier, FL	MIA
Tawas City, MI	GAY
Taycheedah, WI	MIL
Taylor, MI	DET
MI	PRM
PA	PSC
PA	SCR
TX	AUS
Taylor Mill, KY	COV
Taylors, SC	CHR
Taylors Falls, MN	STP
Taylorsville, UT	SLC
Taylorville, IL	SFD
Tazewell, TN	KNX
VA	RIC
Tea, SD	SFS
Teaneck, NJ	NEW
Techny, IL	CHI
IL	OLD
Tecumseh, MI	LAN
NE	LIN
Tehachapi, CA	FRS
Tekamah, NE	OM
Tekoa, WA	SPK
Tell City, IN	IND
Teller, AK	FBK
Telluride, CO	PBL
Temecula, CA	SB
Tempe, AZ	PHX
Temperance, MI	DET
Temperanceville, OH	STU
Temple, TX	AUS
Temple City, CA	LA
Temple Hill, IA	DUB
Temple Terrace, FL	SP
Templeton, IA	SC
Tenafly, NJ	NEW
Tennessee Ridge, TN	NSH
Tennyson-Potosi, WI	MAD
Tequesta, FL	PMB
Terre Haute, IN	IND
Terrebonne, MN	CR
Terrell, TX	DAL
Terrytown, LA	NO
Terryville, CT	HRT
CT	STF
Teutopolis, IL	SFD
Tewksbury, MA	BO
Texarkana, AR	LR
TX	TYL
Texas City, TX	GAL
Theilman, MN	WIN
Theresa, WI	MIL
Theriot, LA	HT
Thermal, CA	SB
Thermopolis, WY	CHY
Thibodaux, LA	HT
Thief River Falls, MN	CR
Thiensville, WI	MIL
Thiry Daems, WI	GB
Thomas, WV	WH
Thomasboro, IL	PEO
Thomaston, CT	HRT
Thomasville, GA	SAV
NC	CHL
Thompson, CT	LIT
CT	NOR
ND	FAR
OH	CLV
WI	MIL
Thompson Falls, MT	HEL
Thomson, GA	ATL
Thoreau, NM	GLP
Thorndike, MA	SPR
ME	PRT
Thornwood, NY	NY
Thorp, WI	LC
Thousand Oaks, CA	LA
Thousand Palms, CA	SB
Three Bridges, NJ	MET
Three Forks, MT	HEL
Three Lakes, WI	SUP
Three Oaks, MI	KAL
Three Rivers, CA	FRS
MA	SPR
MI	KAL
TX	CC
Throckmorton, TX	FWT
Throop, PA	SCR
Thunderbolt, GA	SAV
Thurmont, MD	BAL
Tiburon, CA	SFR
Tickfaw, LA	BR
Ticonderoga, NY	OG
Tidioute, PA	E
Tierra Amarilla, NM	SFE
Tiff, MO	STL
Tiffin, OH	TOL
Tifton, GA	SAV
Tigard, OR	P
Tiger Point, FL	PT
Tigerton, WI	GB
Tijeras, NM	SFE
Tilden, NE	OM
WI	LC
Tillamook, OR	P
Tillman's Corner, AL	MOB
Tilton, NH	MAN
Tiltonsville, OH	STU
Timber Lake, SD	RC
Timken, KS	DOD
Timonium, MD	BAL
Tinaja, NM	GLP
Tinley Park, IL	CHI
Tintah, MN	SCL
Tioga, LA	ALX
ND	BIS
Tipp City, OH	CIN
Tipton, CA	FRS
IA	DAV
IL	BEL
IN	LFT
KS	SAL
MO	JC
Tisch Mills, WI	GB
Tiskilwa, IL	PEO
Titusville, FL	ORL
PA	E
Tiverton, RI	PRO
Tivoli, NY	NY
TX	CC
Toa Alta, PR	SJN
Toa Baja, PR	SJN
Tobyhanna, PA	SCR
Toccoa, GA	ATL
Todd's Mill, IL	BEL
Tohatchi, NM	GLP
Tok, AK	FBK
Tokio, ND	FAR
Toksook Bay, AK	FBK
Tol, FM	CI
Tol, Chuuk, FM	CI
Toledo, OH	OLL
OH	TOL
WA	SEA
Tolland, CT	NOR
Tolleson, AZ	PHX
Tolna, ND	FAR
Tolono, IL	PEO
Tolowas, FM	CI
Toluca, IL	PEO
Tomah, WI	LC
Tomahawk, WI	SUP
Tomales, CA	SFR
Tomball, TX	GAL
Tombstone, AZ	TUC
Tome, NM	SFE
Toms River, NJ	PHU
NJ	PSC
NJ	TR
Tonasket, WA	SPK
Tonawanda, NY	BUF
Tonet, WI	GB
Tonganoxie, KS	KCK
Tonkawa, OK	OKL
Tonopah, NV	LAV
Tontitown, AR	LR
Tony, WI	SUP
Tooele, UT	SLC
Topawa, AZ	TUC
Topeka, KS	KCK
Toppenish, WA	YAK
Topsfield, MA	BO
Toronto, IA	DAV
OH	PBR
OH	STU
Torrance, CA	LA
Torrington, CT	HRT
CT	SAM
WY	CHY
Torun, WI	LC
Toto, GU	AGN
Totowa, NJ	PAT
Totowa Borough, NJ	PAT
Tours, TX	AUS
Towanda, PA	SCR
Tower, MN	DUL
Tower City, PA	ALN
Town and Country, MO	STL
Town of Gates, NY	SY
Towner, ND	FAR
Townsend, MA	BO
MT	HEL
TN	KNX
Towson, MD	BAL
Tracy, CA	STO
MN	NU
Traer, IA	DUB
Trafford, PA	GBG
Tranquillity, CA	FRS
Trappist, KY	L
Trauger, PA	GBG
PA	PBR
Traverse City, MI	GAY
Treasure Island, FL	SP
Tremont, PA	ALN
Trempealeau, WI	LC
Trenary, MI	MAR
Trenton, IL	BEL
MI	DET
MO	KC
NE	LIN
NJ	PHU
NJ	PSC
NJ	ROM
NJ	TR
OH	CIN
Tres Pinos, CA	MRY
Tresckow, PA	ALN
Trevorton, PA	HBG
Triangle, VA	ARL
Tribes Hill, NY	ALB
Tribune, KS	DOD
Trimont, MN	WIN
Trinidad, CO	PBL
Trinity, TX	TYL
Tripp, SD	SFS
Trona, CA	SB
Trooper, PA	PH
Trout River, NY	OG
Troutville, VA	RIC
Troy, AL	MOB
IL	SFD
IN	IND
KS	KCK
MI	DET
MI	EST
MO	STL
NH	MAN
NY	ALB
NY	SAM
NY	STF
OH	CIN
VT	BUR
Truckee, CA	SAC
Trujillo Alto, PR	SJN
Truman, MN	WIN
WI	MAD
Trumansburg, NY	ROC
Trumbull, CT	BGP
CT	PSC
Truro, MA	FR
Trussville, AL	BIR
Truth or Consequences, NM	LSC
Truxton, NY	SY
Tryon, NC	CHL
Tualatin, OR	P
Tuba City, AZ	GLP
Tubac, AZ	TUC
Tuckahoe, NY	NY
Tucker, GA	ATL
Tuckerton, NJ	TR
Tucson, AZ	STN
AZ	TUC
AZ	VNN
Tucumcari, NM	SFE
Tujunga, CA	ARM
CA	LA
Tukwila, WA	SEA
Tulare, CA	FRS
Tularosa, NM	LSC
Tulelake, CA	SAC
Tulia, TX	AMA
Tullahoma, TN	NSH
Tully, NY	SY
Tulsa, OK	TLS
Tum Tum, WA	SPK
Tumon Bay, GU	AGN
Tumwater, WA	SEA
Tunkhannock, PA	SCR
Tunnuk, FM	CI
Tunnuk, Chuuk, FM	CI
Tununak, AK	FBK
Tupelo, MS	JKS
Tupper Lake, NY	OG
Tupper Plains, OH	STU
Turlock, CA	SPA
CA	STO
Turners Falls, MA	SPR
Turtle Creek, PA	PIT
Turtle Lake, WI	SUP
Turtle Mountain Reservation, ND	FAR
Turton, SD	SFS
Tuscaloosa, AL	BIR
Tuscarora, PA	ALN
Tuscola, IL	SFD
Tuscumbia, AL	BIR
Tuskegee Institute, AL	MOB
Tustin, CA	ORG
CA	SB
Tutwiler, MS	JKS
Tuxedo, NY	NY
Twain Harte, CA	STO
Twenty Mile Stand, OH	CIN
Twentynine Palms, CA	SB
Twin Falls, ID	B
Twin Lakes, MN	WIN
WI	MIL
Twin Rocks, PA	ALT
Twin Valley, MN	CR
Twinsburg, OH	CLV
Twisp, WA	SPK
Two Harbors, MN	DUL
Two Inlets, MN	CR
Two Rivers, WI	GB
Tybee Island, GA	SAV
Tyler, MN	NU
TX	TYL
Tyndall, SD	SFS
Tyngsborough, MA	BO
Tyringham, MA	SPR

Tyrone, GA	ATL
PA	ALT
Ubly, MI	SAG
Udot, FM	CI
Uhland, TX	AUS
Ukiah, CA	SR
CA	STN
Ulithi and Neighboring Islands, FM	CI
Ullin, IL	BEL
Ulysses, KS	DOD
NE	LIN
Uman, FM	CI
Umatac, GU	AGN
Umbarger, TX	AMA
Unadilla, NY	ALB
Unalakleet, AK	FBK
Uncasville, CT	NOR
Underhill Center, VT	BUR
Underwood, ND	BIS
Union, KY	COV
MO	STL
NJ	NEW
OR	BAK
SC	CHR
Union Beach, NJ	TR
Union Center, WI	LC
Union City, CA	OAK
CT	HRT
IN	LFT
NJ	NEW
NJ	OLD
OK	OKL
PA	E
TN	MEM
Union Gap, WA	YAK
Union Grove, WI	MIL
Union Grove-Gladewater, TX	TYL
Union Hill, MN	STP
Union Springs, NY	ROC
Uniondale, NY	RVC
Uniontown, KY	OWN
OH	CLV
OH	Y
PA	GBG
PA	PBR
PA	SAM
WA	SPK
Unionville, CT	HRT
United, PA	GBG
Unity, PA	PIT
Universal, IN	IND
University City, MO	STL
University Heights, OH	CLV
University Park, MD	WDC
PA	ALT
University Place, WA	SEA
Upland, CA	SB
Upper Darby, PA	PH
Upper Gwynedd, PA	PH
Upper Marlboro, MD	WDC
Upper Montclair, NJ	NEW
Upper Saddle River, NJ	NEW
Upper St. Clair, PA	PBR
PA	PIT
Upper Sandusky, OH	TOL
Upper Uwchlan, PA	PH
Upsala, MN	SCL
Upton, MA	WOR
Urbana, IA	DUB
IL	PEO
OH	CIN
Urbandale, IA	DM
Urbank, MN	SCL
Ushers, NY	ALB
Usk, WA	SPK
Utica, IL	PEO
MI	DET
NY	NTN
NY	SAM
NY	STF
NY	SY
OH	COL
Utuado, PR	ARE
Uvalde, TX	SAT
Uxbridge, MA	WOR
Vacaville, CA	SAC
Vacherie, LA	BR
Vail, AZ	TUC
CO	DEN
IA	SC
Valatie, NY	ALB
Valdez, AK	ANC
Valdosta, GA	SAV
Vale, NC	CHL
OR	BAK
Valentine, NE	GI
Valeria, IA	DAV
Valhalla, NY	NY
Valier, MT	HEL
Valinda, CA	LA
Vallejo, CA	SAC

Valley, NE	OM
WA	SPK
Valley Center, CA	SD
Valley City, ND	FAR
OH	CLV
Valley Falls, KS	KCK
Valley Forge, PA	PH
Valley Lee, MD	WDC
Valley Park, MO	STL
Valley Stream, NY	RVC
Valley View, TX	FWT
Valmeyer, IL	BEL
Valparaiso, IN	GRY
NE	LIN
Valrico, FL	SP
Valyermo, CA	LA
Van Buren, AR	LR
ME	PRT
Van Etten, NY	ROC
Van Horn, TX	ELP
Van Horne, IA	DUB
Van Nuys, CA	LA
CA	VNN
Van Wert, OH	TOL
Vanceburg, KY	COV
Vancleave, MS	BLX
Vancouver, WA	SEA
Vandalia, IL	SFD
MO	JC
NY	BUF
OH	CIN
Vanderbilt, MI	GAY
TX	VIC
Vandergrift, PA	GBG
Varina, IA	SC
Varysburg, NY	BUF
Vashon, WA	SEA
Vassar, MI	SAG
Vattman, TX	CC
Vaughn, NM	SFE
Veblen, SD	SFS
Vega, TX	AMA
Vega-Alta, PR	ARE
Vega-Baja, PR	ARE
Velva, ND	FAR
Veneta, OR	P
Venice, CA	LA
FL	VEN
IL	SFD
Ventnor, NJ	CAM
PA	PH
Ventura, CA	LA
Vera Cruz, OH	CIN
Verboort, OR	P
Verdigre, NE	OM
Verga, NJ	CAM
Vergennes, VT	BUR
Vermilion, OH	TOL
Vermillion, MN	STP
SD	SFS
Vernal, UT	SLC
Verndale, MN	SCL
Vernon, CA	LA
CT	NOR
NY	SY
TX	FWT
Vernon Center, MN	WIN
Vernonia, OR	P
Vero Beach, FL	PMB
Verona, MO	SPC
ND	FAR
NJ	NEW
NY	SY
PA	PIT
WI	MAD
Verplanck, NY	NY
Versailles, KY	LEX
OH	CIN
PA	PIT
Veseleyville, ND	FAR
Veseli, MN	STP
Vesper, WI	LC
Vesta, MN	NU
Vestaburg, MI	GR
Vestal, NY	SY
Vevay, IN	IND
Vicksburg, MI	KAL
MS	JKS
Victor, IA	DAV
NY	ROC
Victoria, KS	SAL
MN	STP
TX	VIC
Victorville, CA	SB
Vidalia, GA	SAV
LA	ALX
Vidor, TX	BEA
Vienna, IL	BEL
MO	JC
OH	Y
VA	ARL

WV	WH
Vieques, PR	CGS
Viera, FL	ORL
Villa Grove, IL	SFD
Villa Hills, KY	COV
Villa Maria, PA	PIT
Villa Nova, IA	DAV
Villa Park, IL	JOL
Villa Ridge, IL	BEL
Villalba, PR	PCE
Villanova, PA	PH
Villanueva, NM	SFE
Villard, MN	SCL
Villas, NJ	CAM
Ville Platte, LA	LAF
Villisca, IA	DM
Vina, CA	SAC
Vincennes, IN	EVN
Vincent, KS	SAL
OH	STU
Vine Grove, KY	L
Vineland, CO	PBL
MN	SCL
NJ	CAM
Vineyard Haven, MA	FR
Vining, IA	DUB
Vinita, OK	TLS
Vinita Park, MO	STL
Vinton, IA	DUB
LA	LKC
Violet, LA	NO
TX	CC
Virden, IL	SFD
Virgil, IL	RCK
Virginia, IL	SFD
MN	DUL
Virginia Beach, VA	RIC
Virginia City, NV	RNO
Virginia Dale, CO	DEN
Viroqua, WI	LC
Visalia, CA	FRS
Vista, CA	ORG
CA	SD
Vivian, LA	SHP
Vodnany, SD	SFS
Volga, IA	DUB
Volo, IL	CHI
Voluntown, CT	NOR
Von Ormy, TX	SAT
Voorheesville, NY	ALB
Vredenburgh, AL	MOB
Vulcan, MI	MAR
Wabash, IN	FTW
Wabasha, MN	WIN
Wabasso, MN	NU
Wabeno, WI	GB
Waco, TX	AUS
Waconia, MN	STP
Waddington, NY	OG
Wadena, IA	DUB
MN	SCL
Wading River, NY	RVC
Wadsworth, IL	CHI
OH	CLV
Waggaman, LA	NO
Wagner, SD	SFS
WI	GB
Wagon Mound, NM	SFE
Wagoner, OK	TLS
Wahiawa, HI	HON
Wahington, MO	STL
Wahkon, MN	SCL
Wahoo, NE	LIN
Wahpeton, ND	FAR
Waialua, HI	HON
Waialua, Oahu, HI	HON
Waianae, HI	HON
HI	STN
Waihee, HI	HON
Waikane, HI	HON
Wailuku, HI	HON
Waimanalo, HI	HON
Wainwright, OH	COL
Waipahu, HI	HON
Waipio, HI	HON
Waite Park, MN	SCL
Waitsburg, WA	SPK
Waitsfield, VT	BUR
Wake Forest, NC	R
WaKeeney, KS	SAL
Wakefield, MA	BO
MI	MAR
Wakeman, OH	TOL
Wakonda, SD	SFS
Walbridge, OH	TOL
Walden, CO	DEN
NY	NY
Waldorf, MD	WDC
MN	WIN
Waldport, OR	P
Waldron, AR	LR

Wales, ND	FAR
Walford, IA	DUB
Walhain, WI	GB
Walhalla, ND	FAR
Walker, IA	DUB
KS	SAL
MN	DUL
Walkersville, MD	BAL
Walkerton, IN	FTW
Walkerville, MT	HEL
Wall, PA	PBR
SD	RC
TX	SAN
Wall Lake, IA	SC
Walla Walla, WA	SPK
WA	VNN
Wallace, ID	B
KS	SAL
NE	LIN
Wallagrass, ME	PRT
Walled Lake, MI	DET
Wallingford, CT	HRT
PA	PH
VT	BUR
Wallington, NJ	NEW
Wallis, TX	GAL
Walls, MS	JKS
Walnut, CA	LA
IA	DM
IL	PEO
KS	WCH
Walnut Creek, CA	OAK
Walnut Grove, CA	SAC
MN	NU
Walnut Ridge, AR	LR
Walpole, MA	BO
Walsenburg, CO	PBL
Walsh, IL	BEL
WI	GB
Walston, PA	E
Walterboro, SC	CHR
Waltham, MA	BO
Walthill, NE	OM
Walton, IL	RCK
KY	COV
NY	ALB
Wamego, KS	KCK
Wampum, PA	PIT
Wanatah, IN	GRY
Wanblee, SD	RC
Wanda, MN	NU
Wantagh, NY	RVC
Wapakoneta, OH	CIN
Wapato, WA	YAK
Wapella, IL	PEO
Wapello, IA	DAV
Wappingers Falls, NY	NY
War, WV	WH
Warba, MN	DUL
Ward, SC	CHR
Ward Springs, MN	SCL
Warden, WA	YAK
Wardsville, MO	JC
Ware, MA	SPR
Wareham, MA	FR
Warminster, PA	PH
Warner, NH	MAN
Warner Robins, GA	SAV
Warners, NY	SY
Warren, IL	RCK
MA	WOR
MI	DET
MI	NTN
MI	OLL
MI	STN
MN	CR
NJ	MET
OH	PBR
OH	Y
PA	E
RI	PRO
Warrens, WI	LC
Warrensburg, MO	KC
NY	ALB
Warrensville Heights, OH	CLV
Warrenton, MO	STL
NC	R
VA	ARL
Warrenville, IL	JOL
Warrington, PA	PH
PA	PHU
Warroad, MN	CR
Warsaw, IL	PEO
IN	FTW
KY	COV
MO	JC
ND	FAR
NY	BUF
Warson Woods, MO	STL
Warwick, NY	NY
RI	PRO

Wasco, CA	FRS
OR	BAK
Waseca, MN	WIN
Washburn, IL	PEO
TN	KNX
WI	SUP
Washington, DC	CIN
DC	PHU
DC	SAM
DC	WDC
GA	ATL
IA	DAV
IL	PEO
IN	EVN
KS	SAL
LA	LAF
MI	DET
MO	STL
NC	R
NJ	MET
PA	PIT
Washington Court House, OH	COL
Washington Crossing, NJ	TR
Washington Depot, CT	HRT
Washington Park, IL	BEL
Washington Township, NJ	CAM
NJ	NEW
Washingtonville, NY	NY
Washtunca, WA	SPK
Wasilla, AK	ANC
Watauga, SD	RC
Watchung, NJ	MET
Water Mill, NY	RVC
Waterbury, CT	HRT
CT	SAM
VT	BUR
Waterflow, NM	GLP
Waterford, CT	NOR
CT	NTN
MI	DET
NJ	CAM
NY	ALB
PA	E
WI	MIL
Waterloo, IA	DUB
IL	BEL
IN	FTW
KS	WCH
NY	ROC
WI	MAD
Watersmeet, MI	MAR
Watertown, CT	HRT
MA	BO
MN	STP
NY	OG
SD	SFS
WI	MAD
Waterville, KS	KCK
ME	PRT
ME	SAM
MN	BIS
MN	STP
NY	SY
OH	TOL
WA	YAK
Watervliet, MI	KAL
NY	ALB
NY	STF
Watford City, ND	BIS
Wathena, KS	KCK
Watkins, IA	DUB
MN	NU
Watkins Glen, NY	ROC
Watseka, IL	JOL
Watsonville, CA	MRY
Wattenberg, CO	DEN
Waubay, SD	SFS
Waubun, MN	CR
Wauchula, FL	VEN
Waucoma, IA	DUB
Wauconda, IL	CHI
Waukee, IA	DM
Waukegan, IL	CHI
Waukesha, WI	MIL
Waukon, IA	DUB
Waumandee, WI	LC
Waunakee, WI	MAD
Waupaca, WI	GB
Waupun, WI	MIL
Wauregan, CT	NOR
Wausau, WI	LC
Wausaukee, WI	GB
Wauseon, OH	TOL
Wautoma, WI	GB
Wauwatosa, WI	MIL
Wauzeka, WI	LC
Waveland, MS	BLX
Waverly, IA	DUB
IL	SFD
KS	KCK
KY	OWN

MN	STP
NE	LIN
NY	ROC
OH	COL
SD	SFS
WI	MIL
Wax, KY	OWN
Waxahachie, TX	DAL
Waycross, GA	SAV
Wayland, MA	BO
MI	KAL
NY	ROC
Waymart, PA	SCR
Wayne, IL	JOL
MI	DET
NE	OM
NJ	PAT
PA	PH
WI	MIL
WV	WH
Waynesboro, GA	SAV
MS	BLX
PA	HBG
TN	NSH
VA	RIC
Waynesburg, OH	Y
PA	PIT
Waynesville, NC	CHL
OH	CIN
Wayside, NJ	TR
Wayzata, MN	STP
Wea, KS	KCK
Weare Twp., MI	GR
Weatherford, OK	OKL
TX	FWT
Weatherly, PA	ALN
Weaverville, CA	SAC
Webb City, MO	SPC
Webster, MA	WOR
NY	ROC
SD	SFS
WI	SUP
Webster City, IA	DUB
Webster Groves, MO	STL
Webster Springs, WV	WH
Wedron, IL	PEO
Weed, CA	SAC
Weedsport, NY	ROC
Weehawken, NJ	NEW
Weimar, TX	VIC
Weiner, AR	LR
Weingarten, MO	STL
Weir, KS	WCH
Weirton, WV	PBR
WV	WH
Weiser, ID	B
Welch, WV	WH
Weldona, CO	DEN
Weller, IA	DAV
Wellesley, MA	BO
Wellesley Hills, MA	BO
Wellfleet, MA	FR
Wellington, FL	PMB
KS	WCH
OH	CLV
SD	SFS
TX	AMA
Wellman, IA	DAV
Wellpinit, WA	SPK
Wells, ME	PRT
MI	MAR
MN	WIN
NY	OG
Wellsboro, PA	SCR
Wellsburg, WV	WH
Wellston, MO	STL
OH	COL
Wellsville, MO	JC
NY	BUF
OH	Y
Welsh, LA	LKC
Welton, IA	DAV
Wenatchee, WA	YAK
Wendelin, IL	BEL
Wendell, ID	B
NC	R
Wendover, UT	SLC
Wenham, MA	BO
Weno, Chuuk, FM	CI
Wenona, IL	PEO
Wentzville, MO	STL
Wernersville, PA	ALN
Weslaco, TX	BWN
TX	L
Wesley, IA	SC
Wesley Hills, NY	NY
Wessington, SD	SFS
Wessington Springs, SD	SFS
West, TX	AUS
West Albany, MN	WIN
West Aliquippa, PA	PIT
West Allis, WI	MIL

West Babylon, NY	RVC
West Bangor, PA	ALN
West Barnstable, MA	FR
West Bend, IA	SC
WI	MIL
West Bethesda, MD	WDC
West Bloomfield, MI	DET
MI	EST
West Boylston, MA	WOR
West Branch, IA	DAV
MI	GAY
West Brandywine Twp., PA	PH
West Brattleboro, VT	LIT
West Bridgewater, MA	BO
West Brookfield, MA	WOR
West Brooklyn, IL	RCK
West Burke, VT	STF
West Burlington, IA	DAV
West Chazy, NY	OG
West Chester, OH	CIN
PA	PH
West Chicago, IL	JOL
West Clarksville, NY	BUF
West Collingswood, NJ	CAM
West Concord, MN	WIN
West Conshohocken, PA	PH
West Covina, CA	LA
West Des Moines, IA	DM
West Duluth, MN	DUL
West Easton, PA	PHU
West Falls, NY	BUF
West Fargo, ND	FAR
West Frankfort, IL	BEL
West Greenwich, RI	PRO
West Grove, PA	PH
West Hartford, CT	HRT
West Harwich, MA	FR
West Haven, CT	HRT
West Hazleton, PA	SCR
West Hempstead, NY	NY
NY	RVC
West Hollywood, CA	LA
FL	MIA
West Hurley-Woodstock, NY	NY
West Hyattsville, MD	WDC
West Islip, NY	RVC
NY	STF
West Jefferson, OH	COL
West Jordan, UT	SLC
West Kewaunee, WI	GB
West Lafayette, IN	LFT
West Lake, OH	CLV
West Lake Forest, IL	CHI
West Lawn, PA	ALN
West Lebanon, NH	MAN
West Leechburg, PA	SJP
West Leyden, NY	OG
West Liberty, IA	DAV
KY	LEX
WV	WH
West Long Branch, NJ	TR
West Memphis, AR	LR
West Middlesex, PA	E
West Mifflin, PA	PIT
West Milford Township, NJ	PAT
West Milton, OH	CIN
West Mineral, KS	WCH
West Monroe, LA	SHP
West New York, NJ	NEW
West Newbury, MA	BO
West Newton, PA	GBG
West Newton Township, MN	NU
West Nyack, NY	NY
West Orange, NJ	NEW
West Overland, MO	STL
West Palm Beach, FL	PMB
FL	SAM
West Park, NY	NY
West Paterson, NJ	NTN
NJ	PAT
West Peoria, IL	PEO
West Pittsburg, PA	PIT
West Pittston, PA	SCR
West Plains, MO	SPC
West Point, IA	DAV
MS	JKS
NE	OM
NY	NY
VA	RIC
West Portsmouth, OH	COL
West Reading, PA	ALN
West Redding, CT	BGP
West Ridge, IA	DUB
West River, MD	BAL
West Rutland, VT	BUR
West Sacramento, CA	SAC
West St. Paul, MN	STP
West Salem, OH	CLV
WI	LC
West Salisbury, PA	ALT
West Seneca, NY	BUF

West Simsbury, CT	HRT
West Springfield, MA	SPR
West Stewartstown, NH	MAN
West Stockbridge, MA	SPR
West Sunbury, PA	PIT
West Swanzey, NH	MAN
West Taghkanic, NY	ALB
West Terre Haute, IN	IND
West Union, IA	DUB
MN	SCL
OH	CIN
WV	WH
West Valley, NY	BUF
West Valley City, UT	SLC
West View, PA	PIT
West Warren, MA	WOR
West Warwick, RI	PRO
West Willington, CT	NOR
West Windsor, NJ	TR
West Winfield, NY	ALB
West Wyoming, PA	SCR
West Yellowstone, MT	HEL
Westboro, WI	SUP
Westborough, MA	WOR
Westbrook, CT	NOR
ME	PRT
MN	WIN
Westbury, NY	PSC
NY	RVC
Westchester, IL	CHI
Westcliffe, CO	PBL
Westend, WA	SPK
Westerly, RI	PRO
Western Springs, IL	CHI
Westernport, MD	BAL
Westerville, OH	COL
Westfield, IN	LFT
MA	SPR
NJ	NEW
NY	BUF
VT	BUR
WI	MAD
Westford, MA	BO
Westhampton Beach, NY	RVC
Westhope, ND	FAR
Westlake, LA	LKC
OH	CLV
Westlake Village, CA	LA
CA	OLL
Westland, MI	DET
Westminster, CA	ORG
CO	DEN
MA	WOR
MD	BAL
Westmont, IL	JOL
NJ	CAM
Westmorland, CA	SD
Weston, CT	BGP
FL	MIA
IA	DM
MA	BO
MO	KC
NE	LIN
PA	SCR
VT	BUR
WI	LC
WV	WH
Westover, WV	WH
Westphalia, IA	DM
KS	KCK
MI	LAN
MO	JC
TX	AUS
Westport, CT	BGP
MA	FR
NY	OG
SD	SFS
WI	MAD
Westtown, PA	PH
Westville, IL	PEO
NJ	CAM
Westville Grove, NJ	CAM
Westwego, LA	NO
Westwood, CA	SAC
MA	BO
NJ	NEW
Wethersfield, CT	HRT
Wetmore, KS	KCK
Wever, IA	DAV
Wewahitchka, FL	PT
Wexford, IA	DUB
PA	PIT
Weyauwega, WI	GB
Weyerhaeuser, WI	SUP
Weymouth, MA	BO
Wharton, TX	VIC
What Cheer, IA	DAV
Wheat Ridge, CO	DEN
Wheatfield, IN	LFT
Wheatland, IA	DAV
WY	CHY

Wheaton, IL	JOL
IL	RCK
KS	KCK
MD	WDC
MN	SCL
Wheatville, NY	BUF
Wheelersburg, OH	COL
Wheeling, IL	CHI
WV	OLL
WV	SJP
WV	WH
Whippany, NJ	PAT
NJ	PHU
Whistler, AL	MOB
White, SD	SFS
White Bear Lake, MN	STP
White Castle, LA	BR
White Cloud, MI	GR
White Cypress, MS	BLX
White Deer, TX	AMA
White Earth, MN	CR
White Hall, IL	SFD
White Haven, PA	SCR
White Lake, MI	DET
SD	SFS
WI	GB
White Mills, KY	L
PA	SCR
White Oak Boro, PA	PIT
White Pigeon, MI	KAL
White Pine, MI	MAR
White Plains, NY	NY
NY	PSC
White Post, VA	ARL
White River, SD	RC
White River Junction, VT	BUR
White Salmon, WA	YAK
White Sulphur Springs, MT	HEL
WV	WH
White Swan, WA	YAK
Whitefield, ME	PRT
NH	MAN
Whitefish, MT	HEL
Whitefish Bay, WI	MIL
Whitehall, LA	BR
MT	HEL
NY	ALB
PA	ALN
PA	PIT
WI	LC
Whitehouse, OH	TOL
TX	TYL
Whitehouse Station, NJ	MET
Whitelaw, WI	GB
Whiteriver, AZ	GLP
Whitesboro, NY	SY
Whitestone, NY	BRK
Whitesville, KY	OWN
NY	BUF
WV	WH
Whitethorn, CA	SR
Whiteville, NC	R
Whitewater, CO	PBL
WI	MIL
Whiting, IN	GRY
IN	PRM
NJ	TR
Whitinsville, MA	WOR
Whitley City, KY	LEX
Whitman, MA	BO
Whitney, PA	GBG
Whitney Point, NY	SY
Whittemore, IA	SC
MI	GAY
Whittier, CA	LA
Whittlesey, WI	SUP
Wichita, KS	WCH
Wichita Falls, TX	FWT
Wickatunk, NJ	TR
Wickenburg, AZ	PHX
Wickliffe, OH	CLV
Wien, MO	JC
Wiggins, CO	DEN
MS	BLX
Wilber, NE	LIN
Wilbraham, MA	SPR
Wilbur, WA	SPK
Wilcox, PA	E
Wild Rice, ND	FAR
Wilder, KY	COV
Wildwood, MO	STL
NJ	CAM
PA	PIT
Wildwood Crest, NJ	CAM
Wilkes-Barre, PA	PHU
PA	PSC
PA	SAM
PA	SCR
Wilkinsburg, PA	PIT
Willacoochee, GA	SAV
Willard, OH	TOL
WI	LC
Willcox, AZ	TUC
Willey, IA	SC
Williams, AZ	PHX
IA	DUB
MN	CR
Williamsburg, IA	DAV
KY	LEX
OH	CIN
PA	ALT
VA	PSC
VA	RIC
Williamson, WV	WH
Williamsport, IN	LFT
MD	BAL
PA	SCR
Williamston, MI	LAN
NC	R
Williamstown, KY	COV
MA	SPR
NJ	CAM
NJ	PHU
PA	HBG
PA	PSC
Williamsville, NY	BUF
NY	SAM
Willimantic, CT	NOR
CT	STF
Willingboro, NJ	TR
Williston, FL	STA
ND	BIS
VT	BUR
Williston Park, NY	RVC
Willisville, IL	BEL
Willits, CA	SR
Willmar, MN	NU
Willoughby, OH	CLV
Willoughby Hills, OH	CLV
Willow City, ND	FAR
Willow Grove, PA	PH
Willow Lake, SD	SFS
Willow River, MN	DUL
Willow Springs, IL	CHI
MO	SPC
Willowdale, KS	WCH
Willowick, OH	CLV
Willows, CA	SAC
Wills Creek, OH	COL
Willsboro, NY	OG
Wilmerding, PA	PIT
PA	SJP
Wilmette, IL	CHI
Wilmington, CA	LA
DE	PHU
DE	WIL
IL	JOL
MA	BO
NC	R
OH	CIN
VT	BUR
Wilmington Manor, DE	WIL
Wilmont, MN	WIN
Wilmore, PA	ALT
Wilmot, MI	SAG
SD	SFS
WI	MIL
Wilno, MN	NU
Wilson, KS	SAL
MN	WIN
NC	R
NY	BUF
WI	LC
WI	SUP
Wilsonville, IL	SFD
OR	P
Wilton, CT	BGP
IA	DAV
ME	PRT
MN	CR
ND	BIS
ND	STN
NH	MAN
WI	LC
Wilton Center, IL	JOL
Wimberley, TX	AUS
Wimbledon, ND	FAR
Winamac, IN	LFT
Winburne, PA	E
Winchendon, MA	WOR
Winchester, IL	SFD
IN	LFT
KY	LEX
MA	BO
NH	MAN
VA	ARL
Winchester Center, CT	HRT
Wind Lake, WI	MIL
Windber, PA	ALT
PA	PBR
Winder, GA	ATL
Windham, CT	NOR
ME	PRT
NH	MAN
NY	ALB
OH	Y
Windom, MN	WIN
Windsor, CA	SR
CO	DEN
CT	HRT
ND	FAR
NY	SY
VT	BUR
Windsor Locks, CT	HRT
Windthorst, KS	DOD
TX	FWT
Winfield, AL	BIR
IL	JOL
KS	WCH
Winfield Township, IN	GRY
Winlock, WA	SEA
Winnebago, IL	RCK
MN	WIN
NE	OM
Winneconne, WI	GB
Winnemucca, NV	RNO
Winner, SD	RC
Winnetka, CA	LA
IL	CHI
Winnfield, LA	ALX
Winnie, TX	BEA
Winnsboro, LA	ALX
Winona, MN	WIN
Winooski, VT	BUR
Winslow, AR	LR
AZ	GLP
ME	PRT
Winsted, CT	HRT
MN	NU
Winston-Salem, NC	CHL
Winter, WI	SUP
Winter Garden, FL	ORL
Winter Haven, FL	ORL
Winter Park, CO	DEN
FL	ORL
Winter Springs, FL	ORL
Winterhaven, CA	SD
Winterport, ME	PRT
Winters, CA	SAC
TX	SAN
Winterset, IA	DM
Wintersville, OH	STU
Winthrop, IA	DUB
MA	BO
ME	PRT
MN	NU
Wireton, PA	PIT
Wisconsin Dells, WI	MAD
Wisconsin Rapids, WI	LC
Wishek, ND	FAR
Wisner, NE	OM
Withamsville, OH	CIN
Witherbee, NY	OG
Witt, IL	SFD
Wittenberg, WI	GB
Wittenberg/Eland, WI	GB
Wittensville, KY	LEX
Woburn, MA	BO
Woden, IA	DUB
Wofford Heights, CA	FRS
Wolcott, CT	HRT
NY	ROC
Woleai and Neighboring Islands, FM	CI
Wolf Point, MT	GF
Wolfeboro, NH	MAN
Wolfforth, TX	LUB
Wonder Lake, IL	RCK
Wonewoc, WI	LC
Wood Dale, IL	JOL
Wood River, IL	SFD
NE	GI
Woodbine, IA	DM
NJ	CAM
NJ	PHU
Woodbourne, NY	NY
Woodbridge, CT	HRT
NJ	MET
VA	ARL
Woodburn, OR	P
Woodbury, CT	HRT
MN	STP
NJ	CAM
NY	RVC
Woodbury Heights, NJ	CAM
Woodcliff Lake, NJ	NEW
Woodcrest, DE	WIL
Woodhaven, MI	DET
Woodhull, IL	PEO
WI	MIL
Woodlake, CA	FRS
Woodland, CA	SAC
WA	SEA
WI	MIL
Woodland Hills, CA	LA
Woodland Park, CO	COS
The Woodlands, TX	GAL
Woodlawn, NY	BUF
VA	RIC
Woodlynne, NJ	CAM
Woodmont, CT	HRT
Woodridge, IL	JOL
Wood-Ridge, NJ	NEW
Woodrow, TX	LUB
Woodruff, WI	SUP
Woods Hole, MA	FR
Woodsboro, TX	CC
Woodsfield, OH	STU
Woodside, CA	SFR
Woodson Terrace, MO	STL
Woodstock, GA	ATL
IL	RCK
MD	BAL
MN	WIN
VA	ARL
VT	BUR
Woodstown, NJ	CAM
Woodsville, NH	MAN
Woodville, FL	PT
MS	JKS
TX	BEA
Woodward, IA	DM
IA	SC
OK	OKL
Woonsocket, RI	NTN
RI	PRO
RI	STF
SD	SFS
Wooster, OH	CLV
Worcester, MA	NTN
MA	SAM
MA	WOR
NY	ALB
Worland, WY	CHY
Worth, IL	CHI
Worthing, SD	SFS
Worthington, IA	DUB
MN	WIN
Wrangell, AK	JUN
Wray, CO	DEN
Wrentham, MA	BO
Wright, KS	DOD
Wright Township, MI	GR
Wrightstown, WI	GB
Wrightsville Beach, NC	R
Wrightwood, CA	SB
Wuerzburg, WI	LC
Wurtsboro, NY	NY
Wyalusing, PA	SCR
Wyandanch, NY	RVC
Wyandotte, MI	DET
Wyckoff, NJ	NEW
Wykoff, MN	WIN
Wylie, TX	DAL
Wymore, NE	LIN
Wynantskill, NY	ALB
Wyncote, PA	PH
Wyndmere, ND	FAR
Wyndmoor, PA	PH
Wynne, AR	LR
Wynnewood, PA	PH
Wynot, NE	OM
Wyoming, IL	PEO
MI	GR
PA	SCR
Wytheville, VA	RIC
Xenia, OH	CIN
Yabucoa, PR	CGS
Yakima, WA	YAK
Yakutat, AK	JUN
Yale, MI	DET
Yalesville, CT	HRT
Yamhill, OR	P
Yankton, SD	SFS
Yardley, PA	PH
Yarmouth, ME	PRT
Yates Center, KS	WCH
Yatesboro, PA	GBG
Yauco, PR	PCE
Yazoo City, MS	JKS
Yeadon, PA	PH
Yellow Springs, OH	CIN
Yellowstone, WI	MAD
Yelm, WA	SEA
Yerington, NV	RNO
Yigo, GU	AGN
Yoakum, TX	VIC
Yoder, IN	FTW
Yona, GU	AGN
Yonges Island, SC	CHR
Yonkers, NY	NTN
NY	NY
NY	PSC
NY	STF
NY	SYM

Yorba Linda, CA	ORG
York, NE	LIN
PA	HBG
SC	CHR
York Harbor, ME	PRT
York Haven, PA	HBG
Yorktown, TX	VIC
VA	RIC
Yorktown Heights, NY	NY
Yorkville, IL	JOL
IN	IND
NY	SY
OH	STU
Yosemite National Park, CA	FRS
Youngstown, NY	BUF
OH	OLL
OH	PBR
OH	ROM
OH	SJP
OH	Y
PA	GBG
Youngsville, LA	LAF
NY	NY
PA	E
Youngwood, PA	GBG
Yountville, CA	SR
Ypsilanti, MI	ALB
MI	LAN
Yreka, CA	SAC
Yuba, WI	LC
Yuba City, CA	SAC
Yucaipa, CA	SB
Yucca Valley, CA	SB
Yukon, OK	OKL
PA	GBG
Yulan, NY	NY
Yuma, AZ	TUC
CO	DEN
Zachary, LA	BR
Zaleski, OH	COL
Zanesville, OH	COL
OH	NTN
Zapata, TX	LAR
Zearing, IA	DUB
Zeba, MI	MAR
Zeeland, ND	FAR
Zeigler, IL	BEL
Zelienople, PA	PIT
Zell, MO	STL
SD	SFS
Zenda, KS	WCH
Zephyr Cove, NV	RNO
Zephyrhills, FL	SP
Zillah, WA	YAK
Zilwaukee, MI	SAG
Zimmerman, MN	SCL
Zion-Beach Park, IL	CHI
Zionsville, IN	LFT
Zoar, OH	COL
Zumbrota, MN	STP
Zuni, NM	GLP
Zurich, KS	SAL
Zwolle, LA	SHP

Diocesan Abbreviations

ARCHDIOCESES AND DIOCESES

(ALB)	Albany (New York)
(ALN)	Allentown (Pennsylvania)
(ALT)	Altoona-Johnstown (Pennsylvania)
(ALX)	Alexandria (Louisiana)
(AGN)	Agana (Guam)
(AMA)	Amarillo (Texas)
(ANC)	Anchorage (Alaska)
(ARE)	Arecibo (Puerto Rico)
(ARL)	Arlington (Virginia)
(ARM)	Armenian Catholic Exarchate (Pennsylvania)
(ATH)	Apostolate To Hungarians (Washington, DC)
(ATL)	Atlanta (Georgia)
(AUS)	Austin (Texas)
(B)	Boise (Idaho)
(BAK)	Baker (Oregon)
(BAL)	Baltimore (Maryland)
(BEA)	Beaumont (Texas)
(BEL)	Belleville (Illinois)
(BGP)	Bridgeport (Connecticut)
(BIR)	Birmingham (Alabama)
(BIS)	Bismarck (North Dakota)
(BLX)	Biloxi (Mississippi)
(BO)	Boston (Massachusetts)
(BR)	Baton Rouge (Louisiana)
(BRK)	Brooklyn (New York)
(BUF)	Buffalo (New York)
(BUR)	Burlington (Vermont)
(BWN)	Brownsville (Texas)
(CAM)	Camden (New Jersey)
(CC)	Corpus Christi (Texas)
(CGS)	Caguas (Puerto Rico)
(CHI)	Chicago (Illinois)
(CHK)	Chalan Kanoa
(CHL)	Charlotte (North Carolina)
(CHR)	Charleston (South Carolina)
(CHY)	Cheyenne (Wyoming)
(CI)	Caroline Islands
(CIN)	Cincinnati (Ohio)
(CLV)	Cleveland (Ohio)
(COL)	Columbus (Ohio)
(COS)	Colorado Springs (Colorado)
(COV)	Covington (Kentucky)
(CR)	Crookston (Minnesota)
(DAL)	Dallas (Texas)
(DAV)	Davenport (Iowa)
(DEN)	Denver (Colorado)
(DET)	Detroit (Michigan)
(DM)	Des Moines (Iowa)
(DOD)	Dodge City (Kansas)
(DUB)	Dubuque (Iowa)
(DUL)	Duluth (Minnesota)
(E)	Erie (Pennsylvania)
(ELP)	El Paso (Texas)
(EST)	Eparchy of Saint Thomas the Apostle (Chaldean) (Michigan)
(EVN)	Evansville (Indiana)
(FAR)	Fargo (North Dakota)
(FBK)	Fairbanks (Alaska)
(FgM)	Foreign Mission Section
(FR)	Fall River (Massachusetts)
(FRS)	Fresno (California)
(FTW)	Fort Wayne-South Bend (Indiana)
(FWT)	Fort Worth (Texas)
(GAL)	Galveston-Houston (Texas)
(GAY)	Gaylord (Michigan)
(GB)	Green Bay (Wisconsin)
(GBG)	Greensburg (Pennsylvania)
(GF)	Great Falls-Billings (Montana)
(GI)	Grand Island (Nebraska)
(GLP)	Gallup (New Mexico)
(GR)	Grand Rapids (Michigan)
(GRY)	Gary (Indiana)
(HBG)	Harrisburg (Pennsylvania)
(HEL)	Helena (Montana)
(HON)	Honolulu (Hawaii)
(HRT)	Hartford (Connecticut)
(HT)	Houma-Thibodaux (Louisiana)
(IND)	Indianapolis (Indiana)
(JC)	Jefferson City (Missouri)
(JKS)	Jackson (Mississippi)
(JOL)	Joliet in Illinois
(JUN)	Juneau (Alaska)
(KAL)	Kalamazoo (Michigan)
(KC)	Kansas City-St. Joseph (Missouri)
(KCK)	Kansas City in Kansas
(KNX)	Knoxville (Tennessee)
(L)	Louisville (Kentucky)
(LA)	Los Angeles (California)
(LAF)	Lafayette (Louisiana)
(LAN)	Lansing (Michigan)
(LAR)	Laredo (Texas)
(LC)	La Crosse (Wisconsin)
(LEX)	Lexington (Kentucky)
(LFT)	Lafayette in Indiana
(LIN)	Lincoln (Nebraska)
(LIT)	Apostolate for Lithuanian Catholics
(LKC)	Lake Charles (Louisiana)
(LR)	Little Rock (Arkansas)
(LSC)	Las Cruces (New Mexico)
(LUB)	Lubbock (Texas)
(LAV)	Las Vegas (Nevada)
(MAD)	Madison (Wisconsin)
(MAN)	Manchester (New Hampshire)
(MAR)	Marquette (Michigan)
(MEM)	Memphis (Tennessee)
(MET)	Metuchen (New Jersey)
(MGZ)	Mayaguez (Puerto Rico)
(MI)	Marshall Islands
(MIA)	Miami (Florida)
(MIL)	Milwaukee (Wisconsin)
(MO)	Military Services (Maryland)
(MOB)	Mobile (Alabama)
(MRY)	Monterey in California
(NEW)	Newark (New Jersey)
(NO)	New Orleans (Louisiana)
(NOR)	Norwich (Connecticut)
(NSH)	Nashville (Tennessee)
(NTN)	Newton (Melkite, United States)
(NU)	New Ulm (Minnesota)
(NY)	New York (New York)
(OAK)	Oakland (California)
(OG)	Ogdensburg (New York)
(OKL)	Oklahoma City (Oklahoma)
(OLD)	Our Lady of Deliverance Syriac (Union City, New Jersey)
(OLL)	Our Lady of Lebanon of Los Angeles (California)
(OM)	Omaha (Nebraska)
(ORG)	Orange in California
(ORL)	Orlando (Florida)
(OWN)	Owensboro (Kentucky)
(P)	Portland in Oregon
(PAT)	Paterson (New Jersey)
(PBL)	Pueblo (Colorado)
(PBR)	Pittsburgh Byzantine (Pennsylvania)
(PCE)	Ponce (Puerto Rico)
(PEO)	Peoria (Illinois)
(PH)	Philadelphia (Pennsylvania)
(PHU)	Philadelphia Ukrainian (Pennsylvania)
(PHX)	Phoenix (Arizona)
(PIT)	Pittsburgh (Pennsylvania)
(PMB)	Palm Beach (Florida)
(PP)	Personal Prelatures
(PRM)	Parma Byzantine (Ohio)
(PRO)	Providence (Rhode Island)
(PRT)	Portland (Maine)
(PSC)	Passaic Byzantine (New Jersey)
(PT)	Pensacola-Tallahassee (Florida)
(R)	Raleigh (North Carolina)
(RC)	Rapid City (South Dakota)
(RCK)	Rockford (Illinois)
(RIC)	Richmond (Virginia)
(RNO)	Reno (Nevada)
(ROC)	Rochester (New York)
(ROM)	Romanian (Byzantine) (Ohio)
(RVC)	Rockville Centre (New York)
(SAC)	Sacramento (California)
(SAG)	Saginaw (Michigan)
(SAL)	Salina (Kansas)
(SAM)	St. Maron of Brooklyn (U.S.A.)
(SAN)	San Angelo (Texas)
(SAT)	San Antonio (Texas)
(SAV)	Savannah (Georgia)
(SB)	San Bernadino (California)
(SC)	Sioux City (Iowa)
(SCL)	St. Cloud (Minnesota)
(SCR)	Scranton (Pennsylvania)
(SD)	San Diego (California)
(SEA)	Seattle (Washington)
(SFD)	Springfield in Illinois
(SFE)	Santa Fe (New Mexico)
(SFR)	San Francisco (California)
(SFS)	Sioux Falls (South Dakota)
(SHP)	Shreveport (Louisiana)
(SJ)	San Jose in California
(SJN)	San Juan (Puerto Rico)
(SJP)	St. Josaphat in Parma (Ohio)
(SLC)	Salt Lake City (Utah)
(SP)	St. Petersburg (Florida)
(SPA)	Eparchy of St. Peter the Apostle (Chaldean)
(SPC)	Springfield-Cape Girardeau (Missouri)
(SPK)	Spokane (Washington)
(SPP)	Samoa-Pago Pago
(SPR)	Springfield in Massachusetts
(SR)	Santa Rosa in California
(STA)	St. Augustine (Florida)
(STF)	Stamford Ukrainian (Connecticut)
(STL)	St. Louis (Missouri)
(STN)	St. Nicholas in Chicago Ukrainian
(STO)	Stockton (California)
(STP)	St. Paul and Minneapolis (Minnesota)
(STU)	Steubenville (Ohio)
(STV)	St. Thomas, Virgin Islands
(SUP)	Superior (Wisconsin)
(SY)	Syracuse (New York)
(SYM)	St. Thomas Syro-Malabar (Illinois)
(TLS)	Tulsa (Oklahoma)
(TOL)	Toledo (Ohio)
(TR)	Trenton (New Jersey)
(TUC)	Tucson (Arizona)
(TYL)	Tyler (Texas)
(VEN)	Venice (Florida)
(VIC)	Victoria in Texas
(VNN)	Van Nuys Byzantine (California)
(WCH)	Wichita (Kansas)
(WDC)	Washington (District of Columbia)
(WH)	Wheeling-Charleston (West Virginia)
(WIL)	Wilmington (Delaware)
(WIN)	Winona (Minnesota)
(WOR)	Worcester (Massachusetts)
(Y)	Youngstown (Ohio)
(YAK)	Yakima (Washington)

Diocese of Albany

(Dioecesis Albanensis)

Most Reverend

HOWARD J. HUBBARD, D.D.

Bishop of Albany; ordained December 18, 1963; appointed February 1, 1977; ordained and installed March 27, 1977. *Res.: 125 Eagle St., Albany, NY 12202.* Tel: 518-462-3804.

Chancery Office: Pastoral Center, 40 N. Main Ave., Albany, NY 12203. Tel: 518-453-6600; Fax: 518-453-6793.

Web: www.rcda.org

Email: chancery@rcda.org

ESTABLISHED APRIL 23, 1847.

Square Miles 10,419.

(Incorporated by a special act of the Legislature of the State of New York, April 12, 1941, with the title "The Roman Catholic Diocese of Albany, New York.").

Comprises the entire Counties of Albany, Columbia, Delaware, Fulton, Green, Montgomery, Otsego, Rensselaer, Saratoga, Schenectady, Schoharie, Warren and Washington and that part of Herkimer and Hamilton Counties, south of the northern line of the townships of Ohio and Russia, as existing in 1872 in the State of New York.

For legal titles of parishes and diocesan institutions, consult the Chancery Office.

STATISTICAL OVERVIEW

Personnel	
Bishop	1
Priests: Diocesan Active in Diocese	156
Priests: Diocesan Active Outside Diocese	10
Priests: Retired, Sick or Absent	72
Number of Diocesan Priests	238
Religious Priests in Diocese	108
Total Priests in Diocese	346
Extern Priests in Diocese	10
Ordinations:	
Diocesan Priests	1
Religious Priests	2
Transitional Deacons	1
Permanent Deacons	6
Permanent Deacons in Diocese	101
Total Brothers	88
Total Sisters	886
Parishes	
Parishes	177
With Resident Pastor:	
Resident Diocesan Priests	141
Resident Religious Priests	15
Without Resident Pastor:	
Administered by Priests	1
Administered by Religious Women	14
Administered by Lay People	6
Missions	29
Closed Parishes	4
Professional Ministry Personnel:	
Sisters	14
Lay Ministers	6
Welfare	
Catholic Hospitals	4
Total Assisted	730,500
Health Care Centers	15
Total Assisted	58,000
Homes for the Aged	10
Total Assisted	1,400
Residential Care of Children	4
Total Assisted	938
Day Care Centers	7
Total Assisted	635
Specialized Homes	12
Total Assisted	1,509
Special Centers for Social Services	25
Total Assisted	260,000
Residential Care of Disabled	11
Total Assisted	357
Other Institutions	9
Total Assisted	906
Educational	
Diocesan Students in Other Seminaries	9
Total Seminarians	9
Colleges and Universities	4
Total Students	5,000
High Schools, Diocesan and Parish	4
Total Students	1,494
High Schools, Private	3
Total Students	1,474
Elementary Schools, Diocesan and Parish	34
Total Students	7,384
Elementary Schools, Private	2
Total Students	412
Catechesis/Religious Education:	
High School Students	9,529
Elementary Students	30,337
Total Students under Catholic Instruction	55,639
Teachers in the Diocese:	
Priests	1
Brothers	10
Sisters	37
Lay Teachers	716
Vital Statistics	
Receptions into the Church:	
Infant Baptism Totals	4,258
Adult Baptism Totals	762
First Communions	5,100
Confirmations	3,900
Marriages:	
Catholic	1,000
Interfaith	454
Total Marriages	1,454
Deaths	4,800
Total Catholic Population	400,000
Total Population	1,340,448

Former Bishops—His Eminence JOHN CARDINAL MCCLOSKEY, D.D., appt. Bishop of Axiere and Coadjutor to the Bishop of New York, Nov. 21, 1843;; consecrated March 10, 1844; transferred to Albany, May 21, 1847; promoted to New York, May 6, 1864; created Cardinal Priest of the Holy Roman Church, March 15, 1875, under the title Sanctae Mariae supra Minervam; died Oct. 10, 1885; Rt. Revs. JOHN J. CONROY, appt. Bishop July 7, 1865; consecrated Oct. 15, 1865; resigned Oct. 16, 1877; transferred to the See of Curium, March 22, 1878; died Nov. 20, 1895; FRANCIS MCNEIRNY, D.D., appt. Bishop of Rhesina and Coadjutor to the Bishop of Albany, Dec. 22, 1871; consecrated April 21, 1872; appt. Administrator of the Diocese of Albany, Jan. 18, 1874; Bishop of Albany, by right of succession, Oct. 16, 1877; died Jan. 2, 1894; THOMAS M. A. BURKE D.D., preconized May 18, 1894; consecrated July 1, 1894; died Jan 20, 1915; THOMAS F. CUSACK, D.D., consecrated Titular Bishop of Themiscyra and Auxiliary to the Archbishop of New York, April 25, 1904; transferred to Albany, July 5, 1915; died July 12, 1918; Most Revs. EDMUND F. GIBBONS, D.D., appt. Bishop, Feb. 1, 1919; consecrated March 25, 1919; resigned Nov. 10, 1954; transferred to See of Verbe; died June 19, 1964; WILLIAM A. SCULLY, D.D., appt. Coadjutor Bishop "cum jure successionis," Aug. 21, 1945; consecrated Oct. 24, 1945; succeeded to See, Nov. 10, 1954; died Jan. 5, 1969; EDWIN B. BRODERICK, D.D. (Retired), appt. Titular Bishop of Tizica and Auxiliary of New York, March 8, 1967; consecrated April 21, 1967; transferred to Albany, March 19, 1969; resigned June 2, 1976; appt. Exec. Dir. Catholic Relief Services, June 3, 1976; retired September, 1985.

Pastoral Center—Pastoral Center, 40 N. Main Ave., Albany, 12203. Tel: 518-453-6600; Fax: 518-453-6793. Office Hours: Mon.-Fri. 8:30-4:30

Vicar General—Rev. LEO P. O'BRIEN, 900 Madison Ave., Albany, 12208. Tel: 518-489-5408.

Chancellors—Pastoral Center, 40 N. Main Ave., Albany, 12203. Rev. KENNETH DOYLE, Chancellor Public Information. Tel: 518-453-6612; Sr. KATHLEEN TURLEY, R.S.M., Chancellor, Planning & Pastoral Svcs. Tel: 518-453-6612.

Chief Financial Officer—RICHARD FARRELL, 40 N. Main Ave., Albany, 12203. Tel: 518-453-6640.

Insurance Office—KATHLEEN WILLIAMS, Insurance Dir., 40 N. Main Ave., Albany, 12203. Tel: 518-453-6790; ROBIN OLSZEWSKI, Admin. Asst. Tel: 518-453-6790; DONALD WATERS, Insurance Inspector. Tel: 518-453-6789.

Office of Human Resources—Sr. MARILYN K. MURRAY, R.S.M., Dir. 40 N. Main Ave., Albany, 12203. Tel: 518-453-6635; MARY JO HELNARSKI, Personnel Asst. Tel: 518-453-6635.

Pastoral Planning—Sr. KATHLEEN TURLEY, R.S.M., Dir.; JOHN MANNING, Assoc. Dir., 40 N. Main Ave., Albany, 12203. Tel: 518-453-6612.

Archivist—Sr. NOLA BRUNNER, C.S.J., 40 N. Main Ave., Albany 12203. Tel: 518-453-6633.

Office of Canonical Services—40 N. Main Ave., Albany, 12203. Tel: 518-453-6620; Fax: 518-453-6778. Office Hours: 8:30-4:30 (By appointment only)

Vicar Judicial—Rev. JAMES I. DONLON, J.C.D.

Adjutant Vicar Judicial—Rev. PETER J. SULLIVAN III, J.C.L.

Judges—Revs. DAVID BERBERIAN, J.C.L.; JAMES I. DONLON, J.C.D.; PETER J. SULLIVAN III, J.C.L.

Defender of the Marriage Bond in First Instance—Sr. MARY ANN HAYES, C.S.J., J.C.L.

Promoter of Justice—Rev. ALMERICO F. DICERBO, J.C.D.

Advocates—Revs. THOMAS KRUPA; THOMAS BERARDI; JAMES LEFEBVRE; JOSEPH O'BRIEN; JOHN MOYNA; ARTHUR BECKER; FRANK GILCHRIST; MEG BERGH; MARY MORIARITY; Deacon CHARLES TAYLOR.

Bishop's Delegate for Marriage Dispensations—Revs. JAMES I. DONLON, J.C.D.; PETER J. SULLIVAN III, J.C.L.; DAVID V. BERBERIAN, J.C.L.

Notaries—JOANNNE MONAHAN; MARTHA MCEWAN.

Inter Diocesan Tribunal for the Province of NY—(Second Instance Appeal Court), Rev. Msgr. WALTER F. KENNY, Vicar Judicial; Sr. AILEEN KELLY, Admin. & Chief Exec. Sec., 201 Seminary Ave., Yonkers, 10704-1852. Tel: 914-968-4301; 800-293-6598; Fax: 914-968-4466.

Presbyteral Council—Most Rev. HOWARD J. HUBBARD, D.D., Pres.; Revs. JOHN MOLYN, Chm.; GEORGE FLEMING, Vice Chm.; JAMES BELOGI, Sec.; JOSEPH BUSCH; THOMAS CHEVALIER; JOHN YANAS; JAMES MCDEVITT, V.F.; JAMES LEFEBVRE; THOMAS KRUPA; JOHN M. MEDWID; JAMES SPENARD, O.S.A.; ROBERT LONGOBUCCO; KENNETH DOYLE; JAMES I. DONLON, J.C.D.; RICHARD FARRELL; LEO P. O'BRIEN; Sr. KATHLEEN TURLEY.

Diocesan Board of Consultors—Revs. JOSEPH BUSH; JOHN YANAS; THOMAS CHEVALIER; JAMES MCDEVITT, V.F.; GEORGE FLEMING; THOMAS KRUPA; JAMES LEFEBVRE; JOHN MOLYN; JOHN M. MEDWID; JAMES SPENARD, O.S.A.; JAMES BELOGI; ROBERT LONGOBUCCO; JAMES I. DONLON, J.C.D., Canonical Consultant to the Board.

Deans—Revs. JOHN BRADLEY, Albany Co.-City; LAWRENCE MCTAVEY, V.F., Northern; VACANT, Suburban; Revs. GARY GELFENBEIN, V.F., Colombia; JAMES MCDEVITT, V.F., Delaware; DONALD CZELUSNIAK, V.F., Fulton; JEREMIAH NUNAN, Greene; JOSEPH BENINTENDE, Herkimer; JAMES GULLEY, Montgomery; JOHN BURNS, Otsego; RANDALL P. PATTERSON, Rensselaer Co.-Northern; THOMAS KRUPA, Southern; THOMAS CONNERY, Saratoga; LEO MARKERT, Schenectady Co.; THOMAS BERARDI, Schoharie; JOSEPH ANSELMENT, Warren; BARRY LONERGAN, Washington.

Diocesan Offices and Directors

Unless otherwise indicated all Diocesan Offices and Directors are located at: *The Pastoral Center, 40 N. Main Ave., Albany, 12203.* Tel: 518-453-6600; Fax: 518-453-6793.

Office of Real Property—NOEL A. OLSEN, Dir. Tel: 518-453-6623.

Administrative Review Board (Due Process)—Rev. DAVID BERBERIAN, J.C.L., Chm. Tel: 518-453-6620.

Apostleship of Prayer—Rev. JOHN J. PARET, S.J., Auriesville, 12016. Tel: 518-853-3153.

Korean Catholic Apostolate—Rev. PAUL YOUNG HOON JUNG, 10 Lodge St., Albany, 12207. Tel: 518-427-6514.

Bishop's Appeal—JOHN MANNING, Dir.; ROSANNE VAN HEERTUM, Assoc. Dir. Tel: 518-453-6680.

Black Apostolate—Rev. KOFI NTSIFUL-AMISSAH, Admin., St. George's Church, 50 Thornton St., Albany, 12206. Tel: 518-462-9604.

Campus Ministry—Rev. THOMAS BERARDI, Diocesan Dir., 1 Washington Heights, Cobleskill, 12043. Tel: 518-489-8573.

Catholic Deaf Ministry—Rev. JAMES E. CLARK, Chap., St. Jude the Apostle Parish, 42 Dana Ave., P.O. Box 347, Wynantskill, 12198-0347. Tel: 518-283-1162; Fax: 518-286-2808 (TDD). Email: deafrcda@nycap.rr.com.

Cemeteries—RICHARD TOUCHETTE, Dir.. Email: rick.touchette@rcda.org; Albany Diocesan Cemeteries, 48 Cemetery Ave., Menands, Albany, 12204. Tel: 518-432-4953. Web: www.rcdacemeteries.org.

Censor Librorum—Rev. JOHN R. ROOS, J.C.D.

Catholic Office for Motion Pictures—Rev. ANTHONY D. GULLEY, Diocesan Dir. Tel: 518-842-4500.

Architecture and Building Commission—Rev. RANDALL P. PATTERSON, Chm.; CAROL FITZGERALD, Coord. Tel: 518-453-6622.

Public Information—Rev. KENNETH DOYLE, Chancellor. Tel: 518-453-6612; KENNETH GOLDFARB, Dir. Communications. Tel: 518-453-6618.

Cursillo in Christianity—Rev. VINCENT CIOTOLI, St. Patrick's Church, 21 Main St., Ravena, 12143. Tel: 518-756-3145; Deacon MICHAEL MELANSON, 27 Kyle Dr., Scotia, 12302. Tel: 518-399-1425.

Diocesan Service Committee for Charismatic Renewal—Liaisons: Deacon JERRY GRIGAITIS; MARIE GRIGAITIS, 7 Granada Dr., Clifton Park, 12065. Tel: 518-371-7911. Email: dcnjmgrigaitis@aol.com.

Diocesan Stewardship Office—JOHN MANNING, Dir.; ROSANNE VAN HEERTUM, Dir. Devel. Tel: 518-453-6680.

Department of Information Technology—GERALYN A. FOX, Dir. Tel: 518-453-6685; Fax: 518-453-6779.

Catholic Charities of Diocese of Albany, Inc.; St. Vincent's Child Care Society, Inc.—Sr. MAUREEN JOYCE, R.S.M., CEO & Sec. to the Bishop for Health & Social Svcs. Sec., St. Vincent's Child Care Society, IncTel: 518-453-6650; Fax: 518-453-6792; VACANT, CFO; JOSEPH POFIT, Developer Long Term Care Campus/Sr. Housing.

Catholic Charities Agencies—LINDA BONESTEEL, Dir., Catholic Charities of Albany & Rensselaer Counties, 100 Slingerland St., Albany, 12202. Tel: 518-426-3511; ALBERT TURO, Dir., Catholic Charities of Montgomery County, One Kimball St., Amsterdam, 12010. Tel: 518-842-4202; AGNES DONLON, Dir., Catholic Charities of Columbia & Greene Counties, 431 E. Allen St., Hudson, 12534. Tel: 518-828-8660; JOHN NASSO, Dir., Catholic Charities of Fulton County, 4 Nicholas St., Johnstown, 12095. Tel: 518-762-8313; TERRY LEONARD, Dir., Catholic Charities of Herkimer County, 61 West St., Ilion, 13357. Tel: 315-894-9917; KATHIE GREENBLATT, Dir., Catholic Charities of Delaware & Otsego Counties, 15 S. Main St., Oneonta, 13820. Tel: 607-432-0061; Sr. CHARLA COMMINS, C.S.J., Dir., Catholic Charities of Saratoga, Warren & Washington Counties, 142 Regent St., Saratoga, 12866. Tel: 518-587-5000; JOHN D. STEELE, Dir., Catholic Charities of Schenectady County, 818 Union St., Schenectady, 12308. Tel: 518-372-5667; THOMAS MAYER, Dir., Catholic Charities of Schoharie County, 489 W. Main St., Cobleskill, 12043. Tel: 518-234-3581.

Diocesan-wide Agencies and Commissions—JOSEPH POFIT, Dir., Commission on Aging. Tel: 518-453-6650; KAREN DEHAIS, Commission on Restorative Justice, 75 Wimmer Rd., Hopewell Junction, 12533-5426. Tel: 845-223-4990; BARBARA DITOMMASO, Dir., Commission on Peace & Justice. Tel: 518-453-6650; JOSIE HERRICK, Dir., Caregivers Respite Program of Catholic Charities, 100 Slingerland St., Albany, 12202. Tel: 518-449-2001; Sr. MARY ANN LOGIUDICE, R.S.M., Dir., Community Maternity Svcs., 27 N. Main Ave., Albany, 12203. Tel: 518-482-8836; GARY SIEGEL, Dir., Catholic Charities Disabilities Svcs., 15 Avis Dr., Latham, 12210. Tel: 518-783-1111; DEBORAH DAMM O'BRIEN, Dir., Diocesan Housing and Property Management Services, 41 N. Main Ave., Albany, 12203. Tel: 518-459-0183; Sisters CLAUDETTE HARRIS, C.S.J., Dir., Sunnyside Center, P.O. Box 1410, Troy, 12180. Tel: 518-274-5986; ANNE TRANELLI, C.S.J., Dir., Hispanic Outreach Svcs., 40 N. Main Ave., Albany, 12203. Tel: 518-453-6655; JOSEPH KERWIN, Catholic Charities Diocesan AIDS Svcs., 100 Slingerland St., Albany, 12202. Tel: 518-449-3581; TRACIE KILLAR, Dir., New Day Art Institute, 70 Second Ave., Albany, 12202. Tel: 518-462-7914; JAMES J. MCCORMACK, Ph.D., Health Care Coord., Diocesan Community Health Alliance, 40 N. Main Ave., Albany, 12203. Tel: 518-453-6650; Bro. LARRY BACKUS, C.S.C., Dir. Diocesan Jail Ministry, St. Joseph's Center, 49 Maple Ave., Valatie, 12184. Tel: 518-784-9481.

Catholic Campaign for Human Development—MARY COPPOLA, Catholic Charities of Diocese of Albany, 40 N. Main Ave., Albany, 12203. Tel: 518-453-6650.

Catholic Charities of the Diocese of Albany—Tel: 518-453-6650. MARY COPPOLA, 40 N. Main Ave., Albany, 12203. Tel: 518-453-6650.

Catholic Relief Services— Catholic Charities of the Diocese of Albany. Tel: 518-453-6650. MARY COPPOLA, Catholic Charities of Diocese of Albany, 40 N. Main Ave., Albany, 12203. Tel: 518-453-6650.

Disaster Relief Services— Catholic Charities of the Diocese of Albany. Tel: 518-453-6650. Sr. KATE CRISPO, C.S.J., Center for Community Collaboration, 326 Clinton Ave., Albany, 12206. Tel: 518-462-6829; DAVID MEYERS, Immigration Svcs., Catholic Charities of the Diocese of Albany, 40 N. Main Ave., Albany, 12203. Tel: 518-453-6650.

Health and Hospitals Office—Sr. MAUREEN JOYCE, R.S.M., Bishop's Rep. Tel: 518-453-6650.

Catholic Women's Service League—MAUREEN TOOHEY, Pres.; Bro. VINCENT REESE, F.S.C., Moderator; Rev. ROBERT HOHENSTEIN, Spiritual Advisor, c/o LaSalle School, 391 Western Ave., Albany, 12203. Tel: 518-242-4731.

Ladies of Charity—JACKIE DESANTI, Pres., 2 Joy Dr., Loudonville, 12211. Tel: 518-459-4519.

Spiritual Director—Rev. PATRICK BUTLER, Christ the King Church, 20 Sumpter Ave., Albany, 12203.

Society of St. Vincent de Paul—EDWARD NARE, Diocesan Central Council Pres., 202 S. Ballston Ave., Scotia, 12302. Tel: 518-374-2548; EMMET J. LYNCH, Pres. Emeritus; Rev. RICHARD DOWNS, Spiritual Dir., 12 Rosemont St., Albany, 12203. Tel: 518-489-8197.

Consultation Center of the Diocese of Albany— A nonprofit Mental Health Center which provides quality professional psychological counseling services and educational programs in the area of mental health to individuals and groups.

Office—Rev. ANTHONY J. CHIARAMONTE, Ph.D., Dir.; Sr. MARY FRANCES BECK, S.N.J.M., Admin. Dir.; Rev. JOHN J. MALECKI, Ph.D., Psychologist; KATHLEEN STIFFEN, Sec., 790 Lancaster St., Albany, 12203. Tel: 518-489-4431; Fax: 518-489-5189. Email: consultation.center@rcda.org.

Psychological Counseling— Provides individual therapy, marriage and couples counseling, psychological testing and consultative services to individuals and groups in matters calling for psychological expertise.

Group Therapy— Provides a variety of different kinds of therapy groups.

Educational Programs— Offers lectures and workshops in the area of mental health and personal growth. The Center also offers specialized workshops and training programs to meet the needs of various groups.

Spiritual Direction— Provides a program of individual spiritual direction for any person interested in developing a deeper relationship with God.

Counseling for Laity—Sr. ANNE BRYAN SMOLLIN, C.S.J., Ph.D., Exec. Dir.. Email: anne.smollin@rcda.org; ETTA JONES, Admin. Asst. Tel: 518-453-6625; Fax: 518-453-6793 Provides individual, family, marital and group psychological counseling-therapy by certified trained therapists. The staff provides services for the Young Married program and assessments for second marriages. Consultation and training programs are offered upon request. Workshops and lectures offered on select topics.

Diocesan Pastoral Care Association—Sr. HELEN MARIE LECLERC, C.S.J., Contact Person, Glens Falls Hospital, 100 Park St., Glens Falls, 12801. Tel: 518-926-3532.

Diocesan Pastoral Council—PATRICIA MOUSAW, Staff; RICHARD BERGERON, Chm.; JANE MOORE, Vice Chm.; DEBORAH HART, Sec.; ARTHUR PETERSON, At-Large; JOHN O'CONNELL, At-Large. Tel: 518-453-6661.

Prevention Services - Catholic Schools Office—CATHY GOLAS, Prog. Dir. Tel: 518-453-6771; Fax: 518-453-6667 Services students, faculty and parents of Catholic schools in the diocese.

Ecumenical and Interreligious Affairs of the Roman Catholic Diocese of Albany, Commission for—Mrs. AUDREY HUGHES; Deacons WILLIAM GAFFNEY; RAYMOND SULLIVAN; Mr. DAVID AMICO; JOAN HOLMAN; JOAN LIPSCOMB; Rev. THOMAS PHELAN (Retired); Ms. PATRICIA RAUP; Mrs. JOAN DUNHAM; Bro. JASON LODY, O.F.M.Conv.; Mr. FRANK M. PELL; Rev. JAMES BELOGI; Mr. WILLIAM PRZYLUCKI; Revs. MAURICE DROWN; JAMES KANE, Dir.; DAVID MICKIEWICZ; Mrs. MARGARET SEDLMEIR; Ms. ANNE SNYDER; Mrs. ELLEN SERVISS; Mrs. CHRISTINE MURPHY, Sec. Tel: 518-453-6660.

"The Evangelist"—JAMES P. BREIG, Editor. Tel: 518-453-6688; Fax: 518-453-8448. Diocesan Newspaper Albany Catholic Press Assoc., Inc.,

Family Life Office—MEG BERGH, Dir.; MARY MORIARTY, Assoc. Dir.; KAREN FONTANELLI, Admin. Asst. Tel: 518-453-6677 Bereavement Ministry; Catholic Singles; Family Perspective; Gay/Lesbian Family Ministry; Hispanic Ministry; Marriage & Remarriage Preparation; Marriage & Family Enrichment; Natural Family Planning; Parenting; Respect Life; Separated, Divorced & Widowed.

Education Sites for Natural Family Planning—HELENE WALLINGFORD, St. Peter's Hospital, 315 S. Manning Blvd., Albany, 12208. Tel: 518-525-1388; KITTY OLSIEWSKI, St. Mary's Hospital, 1300 Massachusetts Ave., Troy, 12180. Tel: 518-268-5628.

Holy Name Societies—Rev. WILLIAM W. CRANDALL, Dir., St. Joseph Rectory, 181 Main St., Worcester, 12197. Tel: 607-397-9373.

Initial & Ongoing Formation Cluster—Tel: 518-453-6670. C. ELIZABETH ROWE, Dir. Office of Ministry Formation. Tel: 518-453-6670; Rev. JOSEPH COTUGNO, Dir. Formation for Diaconate. Tel: 518-453-6670.

Formation for Priesthood / Vocation Awareness—Sr. KATHERINE HANLEY, C.S.J.; Revs. THOMAS KONOPKA; JAMES WALSH. Tel: 518-453-6670.

Legion of Mary—Deacon WILLIAM J. BRETT, 197 Woods Edge Ct., Voorheesville, 12186. Tel: 518-765-4654.

Office of Evangelization and Catechesis—JEANNE SCHREMPF, Diocesan Dir.; Sr. PATRICIA CONRON, C.S.J., Assoc. Dir., Catechist Formation; PATRICIA TAAFFE, Coord. Video and Resource Center; DAVID G. AMICO, Assoc. Dir., Adult Catechesis & Persons with Disabilities; Deacon WILLIAM GAFFNEY, Deacon Assoc. - Evangelization; MARY HARRISON, Assoc. Dir., Youth Ministry; JOYCE SOLIMINI, Assoc. Dir., Sacramental and Intergenerational Catechesis; Rev. ROBERT LONGOBUCCO, Clergy Assoc.

Permanent Diaconate Office—Deacon J. NEIL HOOK, Asst. Dir. Tel: 518-869-0602. Co-Directors: Deacons FRANK LUKOVITS. Tel: 518-766-5135; TIMOTHY MCAULIFFE. Tel: 518-869-0454.

Catholic Foundation—Most Rev. HOWARD J. HUBBARD, D.D., Pres.; JOHN MANNING, Exec. Dir.; ROSANNE VAN HEERTUM, Assoc. Exec. Dir. Tel: 518-453-6680.

Office of Prayer & Worship—ELIZABETH SIMCOE, Dir.; WILLIAM GLENN OSBORNE, Dir., Cathedral Music; VICTORIA TUCKER, Sec., 40 N. Main Ave., Albany, 12203. Tel: 518-453-6645; Fax: 518-453-6793. Email: prayerandworship@rcda.org.

Administrative Advocate for Priests—Rev. L. EDWARD DEIMEKE. Tel: 518-453-6643.

Priests Placement Committee—Revs. L. EDWARD DEIMEKE, Chm.; JOHN BRADLEY; GEORGE W. BRUCKER; LEO MARKERT; JAMES WALSH.

Priestly Life and Ministry Council—Revs. DOMINIC INGEMIE, Chm.; ERWIN SCHWEIGARDT; JOHN D.

KIRWIN; DOMINIC ISOPO; JOSEPH BENINTEDE; ROBERT HOHENSTEIN; BRIAN RAICHE; L. EDWARD DEIMEKE, Admin. Advocate.

Ministry to Priests—Revs. THOMAS CONNERY; THOMAS BERARDI; MICHAEL A. FARANO; FRANCIS J. GILCHRIST (Retired).

Ongoing Formation and Continuing Education for Priests—Revs. CHRISTOPHER DEGIOVINE, Co-Chm.; DAVID LEFORT, Co-Chm. Tel: 518-453-6643. Members: Revs. MARK CUNNINGHAM; L. EDWARD DEIMEKE, Advisor; JAMES FITZMAURICE; DOMINIC INGEMIE; ANTHONY KALL, O.F.M.Conv.; THOMAS KRUPA; RONALD MENTY; PETER RUSSO; CARL URBAN.

Priests Retirement Board—Revs. L. EDWARD DEIMEKE, Interim Chm. Tel: 518-453-6640; JOSEPH E. ANSELMENT; JOSEPH BARKER; WINSTON L. BATH; J. THOMAS CONNERY; PAUL COX; JOSEPH DWORAK; JAMES LEFEBVRE; JOHN T. PROVOST; ERWIN SCHWEIGART; RICHARD FARRELL, Ex Officio. Tel: 518-453-6612.

Priests' Retirement Plan Board—VACANT. Tel: 518-453-6640.

Propagation of the Faith-Pontifical Society—Revs. MICHAEL A. FARANO, Dir.; JAMES MACKEY, Assoc. Dir. Tel: 518-453-6675.

Schools: Diocesan School Board—DAN CUNNINGHAM, Chm. Tel: 518-436-1626.

Diocesan School Office—Sr. MARY JANE HERB, I.H.M., Ph.D., Supt. of Schools. Tel: 518-453-6602; THOMAS FITZGERALD, Ph.D., Asst. Supt., Admin. Svcs. Tel: 518-453-6666; EDITH TOOHEY, Asst. Supt. for Instructional Svcs. Tel: 518-453-6666; CATHY GOLAS, Preventative Svcs Program. Tel: 518-453-6771; CURTIS A. MCEWAN, Business Mgr. Tel: 518-453-6604; SAL CARBONE, Safety Coord. Tel: 518-853-4001; DARLENE CARDILLO, Dir. Educational Technology. Tel: 518-453-6666.

Scouting—Deacon WILLIAM H. GAUL JR., Diocesan Chap., 12 Woodlake Dr., Gansevoort, 12831-1817. Tel: 518-587-4631.

St. Bernard's School of Theology and Ministry—JOSEPH R. PICCOLINO, Ed.D., Dir. Tel: 518-453-6760; Fax: 518-453-6793. Email: joseph.piccolino@rcda.org.

Vicar for Religious—Sr. NOLA BRUNNER, C.S.J. Tel: 518-453-6662.

Victim and Survivor Assistance Coordinator—THERESA F. RODRIGUES. Tel: 518-453-6646. Email: rodrigut@rcda.org.

Vocations and Vocation Awareness Program—Sr. KATHERINE HANLEY, C.S.J.; Revs. THOMAS KONOPKA; JAMES WALSH. Tel: 518-453-6670.

CLERGY, PARISHES, MISSIONS AND PAROCHIAL SCHOOLS

CITY OF ALBANY
(ALBANY COUNTY)

1—CATHEDRAL OF THE IMMACULATE CONCEPTION, Rev. William H. Pape, Rector; Deacon Raymond J. Sullivan, Ph.D. In Res., Most Rev. Howard J. Hubbard.
Rectory Office—125 Eagle St., 12202. Tel: 518-463-4447; Fax: 518-436-5177. Email: ecathedr@nycap.com. Web: www.cathedralic.com.
Religious Education Office—Tel: 518-436-7918.
Cathedral Social Services—Tel: 518-463-2279.
Catechesis/Religious Program— Sr. Maria Mercurio, D.R.E. Students 50.
Convent—93 Park Ave., 12202. Tel: 518-436-7697. Email: ecathedr@nycap.com. Web: www.cathedralic.com. Sisters 15.

2—BLESSED SACRAMENT, Revs. John J. Bradley; G. Anthony Childs; Sr. Mary Coons, R.S.M., Pastoral Assoc.; Deacon William Fitzgerald. In Res., Rev. George St. John.
Res.: 607 Central Ave., 12206. Tel: 518-482-3375; Fax: 518-482-3376.
School—605 Central Ave., 12206. Tel: 518-438-5854; Fax: 518-438-1532. Sr. Patricia Lynch, R.S.M., Prin. Sisters of Mercy 2; Lay Teachers 16; Students 250.
Catechesis/Religious Program—Tel: 516-446-0997. Rosemarie Reed, D.R.E.; Cathy Fredette, D.R.E. Clustered with St. Mary Students 202.

3—ST. CASIMIR, , Clustered with Our Lady of Angels, Albany & St. Patrick, Albany. Revs. Paul Lininger, O.F.M.Conv.; Anthony Kall, O.F.M.Conv.; Joseph Angelini, O.F.M.Conv.; Alvin Somerville, O.F.M-.Conv.; Sr. Margaret Walker, D.C., Parish Life Dir.
Res.: 324 Sheridan Ave., 12206. Tel: 518-463-7147; Fax: 518-463-7147.

4—ST. CATHERINE OF SIENA, Rev. Kennth Doyle; Deacon Gerald Ladouceur; Sr. Margery Halpin, R.S.M., Pastoral Assoc. In Res., Revs. Robert Longobucco; John Tallman.
Res.: 40 Collins Pl., 12208. Tel: 518-489-3204; Fax: 518-482-3721.
School—35 Hurst Ave., 12208. Tel: 518-489-3111; Fax: 518-482-3721. Theresa L. Ewell, Prin. Lay Teachers 23; Students 268.
Catechesis/Religious Program—Bernadette McSparron, D.R.E. Students 269.

5—CHURCH OF THE HOLY CROSS, Rev. Daniel J. Maher; Sr. Helen Charles, Spiritual Growth Coord.
Res.: 12 Rosemont St., 12203. Tel: 518-489-8197; Fax: 518-435-0709.
School—Rosement St., 12203. Tel: 518-438-0066; Fax: 518-438-0066. Sr. Mary Ellen Owens, Prin. Sisters 1; Lay Teachers 16; Students 291.

6—ST. GEORGE, (African American), Rev. Kofi Ntsiful Amissah, Admin. & Dir. Black Apostolate.
Res.: 50 Thornton St., 12206. Tel: 518-462-9604.

7—ST. JAMES, Revs. Dominic Ingemie; Cabell B. Marbury; Deacons Gerald DeMauro; William A. Gorman, D.Min., Ph.D.; Sisters Mary Ellen Holohan, S.N.J.M., Pastoral Assoc.; Patricia Houlihan, C.S.J., Pastoral Assoc.; Phyllis Cardona, Pastoral Assoc. In Res., Revs. Joseph Cotugno; Anthony Sidoti, Pastor Emeritus.
Res.: 391 Delaware Ave., 12209. Tel: 518-434-4028; Fax: 518-434-1097.
School—50 Summit Ave., 12209. Tel: 518-465-1973; Fax: 518-465-3879. Bro. Jason Lody, O.F.M.Conv., Prin. Lay Teachers 16; Students 179.
Catechesis/Religious Program—Tel: 518-465-2876. Phyllis Cardona, D.R.E. Students 109.
Convent—58 Summit Ave., 12209. Tel: 518-449-7993.

8—ST. JOHN-ST. ANN, Revs. John Kirwin; Christopher DeGiovine.
Office—157 Franklin St., 12202. Tel: 518-472-9091; Fax: 518-427-5983.
Catechesis/Religious Program—Tel: 518-472-9091, Ext. 18. Roberta Grieco, D.R.E. Students 67.

9—ST. JOSEPH, , Records are kept at Sacred Heart of Jesus, Albany.
Parish Office—33 Walter St., 12204. Tel 518-463-3286; Fax: 518-462-0506.

10—ST. MARGARET MARY, Rev. Thomas H. Chevalier; Deacon J. Neil Hook. In Res., Rev. David Berberian.
Parish Office—1168 Western Ave., 12203. Tel: 518-482-4497; Fax: 518-482-4719.

11—ST. MARY, Rev. James Lefebvre; Deacon George Witko; Rev. Lloyd Rebeyro.
Res.: 10 Lodge St., 12207. Tel: 518-462-4254; Fax: 518-462-4255.
Catechesis/Religious Program— Clustered with Blessed Sacrament
Chapel— 111 Washington Ave., 12203.

12—OUR LADY HELP OF CHRISTIANS, (German), Closed., For inquiries for parish records please see Cathedral of the Immaculate Conception.

13—OUR LADY OF ANGELS, [CEM], Clustered with St. Casimir, Albany & St. Patrick, Albany. Revs. Paul Lininger, O.F.M.Conv.; Joseph Angelini O.F.M-.Conv.; Alvin Somerville, O.F.M.Conv.; Anthony Kall, O.F.M.Conv.; Gregory Spuhler, O.F.M.Cap.; Bro. Jason Lody, O.F.M.Conv.; Sr. Margaret Walker, D.C., Parish Life Dir.
Friary—20 Willet St., 12210. Tel: 518-432-0114.
Parish Office—183 Central Ave., 12206. Tel: 518-463-3262; Fax: 518-463-3264.

14—ST. PATRICK, , Clustered with St Casimir, Albany & Our Lacy of Angels, Albany. Sr. Margaret Walker, D.C., Parish Life Dir.
Office—283 Central Ave., 12206. Tel: 518-435-3685; Fax: 518-462-5487.
Catechesis/Religious Program— Claudia Ruiz-Peralta, D.R.E. Students 80.

15—SACRED HEART OF JESUS, Rev. Kofi Ntsiful Amissah. In Res., Rev. Martin Tran Vanban, C.M.C, Vietnamese Apostolate.
Res.: 33 Walter St., 12204. Tel: 518-463-3236; Fax: 518-462-0506.

16—ST. TERESA OF AVILA, Rev. Thomas M. Powers. In Res., Rev. Msgr. John L. Jones (Retired).
Res.: 435 New Scotland Ave., 12208. Tel: 518-438-7851; Fax: 518-489-6401.
School—(Grades PreK-4), 433 New Scotland Ave., 12208. Tel: 518-438-5268.
School—(Grades 5-8), 8 Hollywood Ave., 12208. Tel: 518-482-3736; Fax: 518-482-3745. Sr. Patricia Houlihan, R.S.M., Prin. Sisters of Mercy 4; Lay Teachers 15; Students 175.
Catechesis/Religious Program—Tel: 518-433-7436. Mr. Charles Miller, D.R.E. (K-6); Mary Ellen Stofilano, D.R.E. (7-12). Students 100.
Convent—401 New Scotland Ave., 12208. Tel: 518-482-8901
Mission—*Albany Medical Center*, Albany Co.

17—ST. VINCENT DE PAUL, Rev. Leo P. O'Brien; Deacon William Gaffney.
Parish Office—900 Madison Ave., 12208. Tel: 518-489-5408; Fax: 518-489-5474.
Res.: 35 Colonial Ave., 12203. Tel: 518-489-0563.

OUTSIDE THE CITY OF ALBANY

ALTAMONT, ALBANY CO., ST. LUCY, Rev. Paul Smith; Sr. Mary Lou Liptak, R.S.M., Parish Life Dir.
Parish House—109 Grand St., 12009 Tel: 518-861-8770.
Catechesis/Religious Program—Tel: 518-861-5810. Krista Gallup, D.R.E. Students 135.
Mission—*St. Bernadette* 1763 Helderberg Trail, Berne, Albany Co. 12023. Tel: 518-872-1131.

AMSTERDAM, MONTGOMERY CO.

1—ST. CASIMIR, (Lithuanian), [CEM] Rev. Stanislaus J. Swierzowski; Sr. Roberta O'Rourke, C.S.T., Pastoral Assoc.
Res.: 260 E. Main St., 12010. Tel: 518-842 5481; Fax: 518-842-5481.

2—ST. JOHN THE BAPTIST, (Polish), [CEM] Rev. Stanislaus J. Swierzowski.
Res.: 40 Van Derveer St., 12010. Tel: 518-842-6851.
Catechesis/Religious Program—Fax: 518-842-0913. Alice Larson, D.R.E. Students 77.

3—ST. JOSEPH, , Canonically merged in 1980 into St. Joseph-St. Michael-Our Lady of Mount Carmel. All inquiries should be directed to the listed address, 39 St. John St. & 58 Grove St., Amsterdam, NY 12010.

4—ST. JOSEPH-ST. MICHAEL-OUR LADY OF MOUNT CARMEL, , Canonically merged parishes in 1980. Rev. Lawrence J. Decker.
Mailing Address: P.O. Box 699, 12010.
Office—39 St. John St. & 58 Grove St., 12010. Tel: 518-843-3250; Fax: 518-843-4070.
Res.: 39 St. John St., 12010.
Catechesis/Religious Program— Mary A. Califano, D.R.E.; Ann Marie D'Addio, D.R.E. Students 118.

5—ST. MARY, [CEM] Rev. James Gulley. In Res., Revs. Victor Polito; Anthony Gulley.
Res.: 156 E. Main St., 12010. Tel: 518-842-4500; Fax: 518-842-4529.
School—*St. Mary Institute*, Upper Church St., 12010. Tel: 518-842-4100; Fax: 518-842-0217. Sr. Elizabeth Costanzo, C.S.J., Prin. Sisters 2; Lay Teachers 26; Students 273.

6—ST. MICHAEL THE ARCHANGEL, , Canonically merged in 1980 into St. Joseph-St. Michael-Our Lady of Mount Carmel. All inquiries should be directed to the listed address, 39 St. John St. & 58 Grove St., Amsterdam, NY 12010.

7—OUR LADY OF MT. CARMEL, (Italian),, Canonically merged in 1980 into St. Joseph-St. Michael-Our Lady of Mount Carmel. All inquiries should be directed to the listed address, 39 St. John St. & 58 Grove St., Amsterdam, NY 12010.

8—ST. STANISLAUS, (Polish), [CEM] Rev. David Mickiewicz.
Res.: 73 Reid St., 12010. Tel: 518-842-2771; Fax: 518-842-2771.
School—42-44 Cornell St., 12010. Tel: 518-842-6710; Fax: 518-842-3339. Sr. M. Bernice, C.S.S.F., Prin. Felician Sisters 2; Lay Teachers 14; Students 127.
Convent—46 Cornell St., 12010. Tel: 518-842-2621.

ATHENS, GREENE CO., ST. PATRICK,
Res.: 19 N. Franklin St., 12015. Tel: 518-945-1656.

AVERILL PARK, RENSSELAER CO., ST. HENRY, [CEM 2] Rev. Brian Raiche; Deacons Frank Lukovits; John W. Novak; Robert Pasquarelli.
Res.: Crystal Lake Rd., P.O. Box 550, 12018. Tel: 518-674-3818; Fax: 518-674-1043.

BALLSTON LAKE, SARATOGA CO., OUR LADY OF GRACE, Rev. Anthony C. Diacetis. In Res., Rev. John N. Varno.
Res.: 73 Midline Rd., 12019. Tel: 518-399-5713; Fax: 518-399-5713.
Catechesis/Religious Program—Tel: 518-384-0109. Mary Salm, D.R.E. Students 646.

BALLSTON SPA, SARATOGA CO., ST. MARY, [CEM] Rev. Thomas J. Kelly; Deacon Martin Beckman.
Res.: 167 Milton Ave., 12020. Tel: 518-885-7411; Fax: 518-885-6863.
School—40 Thompson St., 12020. Tel: 518-885-7300; Fax: 518-855-7378. Sr. Ranah Phelan, C.S.J., Prin. Sisters 1; Lay Teachers 14; Students 213.

BERLIN, RENSSELAER CO., SACRED HEART, Rev. Kenneth Gregory; Sr. Kenan McGowan, R.S.M., Parish Life Dir.
Res.: P.O. Box 243, 12022. Tel: 518-658-2780 (Office); Fax: 518-279-3055.
Catechesis/Religious Program—Students 8.

BOLTON LANDING, WARREN CO., BLESSED SACRAMENT, [CEM] Rev. Peter G. Young.
Res.: Goodman Ave., P.O. Box 266, 12814. Tel: 518-644-3861.

BROADALBIN, FULTON CO., ST. JOSEPH, Rev. Timothy Mangan, S.S.S.
Res.: 7 North St., P.O. Box 538, 12025. Tel: 518-883-3774; Fax: 518-883-3774.
Mission—*St. Mary* [CEM] Galway, Saratoga Co.

CAIRO, GREENE CO., SACRED HEART, Rev. Jeremiah Nunan.

Mailing Address: P.O. Box 778, 12413.
Res.: 35 Church St., 12413. Tel: 518-622-3319; Fax: 518-622-0131.
Mission—Our Lady of Knock Shrine P.O. Box 223, East Durham, Greene Co. 12423. Tel: 518-634-7448.
Mission—St. Mary East Durham, Greene Co.

CAMBRIDGE, WASHINGTON CO., ST. PATRICK, [CEM] Rev. Liam Condon; Dorothy A. Bunal, Parish Life Dir.
Res.: 17 S. Park St., 12816-1248. Tel: 518-677-2757; Fax: 518-677-2810.
Catechesis/Religious Program—Students 90.

CANAJOHARIE, MONTGOMERY CO., ST. PETER'S AND PAUL'S, [CEM] Rev. William J. Gaffigan.
Res.: 100 Cliff St., 13317-1199. Tel: 518-673-3333.

CASTLETON-ON-HUDSON, RENSSELAER CO., SACRED HEART, [CEM 2] Rev. Thomas J. Krupa.
Res.: 3 Catholic Way, 12033-1543. Tel: 518-732-2155; Fax: 518-732-4906.
Catechesis/Religious Program—Tel: 518-732-1106; Fax: 518-732-4960. Jane Forget, D.R.E. Students 367.

CATSKILL, GREENE CO., ST. PATRICK, Rev. John J. Murphy. In Res., Rev. Richard Jacobs.
Res.: 157 Bridge St., 12414. Tel: 518-943-3150.
School—80 Woodland Ave., 12414. Tel: 518-943-2952. Mary Ellen Hernandez, Prin. Franciscan Sisters of Allegany 1; Lay Teachers 10; Students 188.
Convent—82 Woodland Ave., 12414. Tel: 518-943-5341.
Mission—St. Bridget Leeds, Greene Co.

CHATHAM, COLUMBIA CO., ST. JAMES, Rev. Gary Paul Gelfenbien; Deacon Peter Trawinski.
Res.: 129 Hudson Ave., 12037. Tel: 518-392-4991; Fax: 518-392-9205.

CHERRY VALLEY, OTSEGO CO., ST. THOMAS THE APOSTLE, Rev. John Roos; Elizabeth M. Mahoney, Parish Life Dir.
Res.: 24 Maple Ave., 13320. Tel: 607-264-3779.
Catechesis/Religious Program—Maureen Blanchard, D.R.E. Students 43.
Mission—Blessed Sacrament Springfield Center, Otsego Co.

CHESTERTOWN, WARREN CO., ST. JOHN THE BAPTIST, Rev. George Fleming; Sr. Francesca Husselbeck, R.S.M., Parish Life Dir.
Res.: Riverside Dr., P.O. Box 471, 12817. Tel: 518-494-2617; Fax: 518-494-5663.
Catechesis/Religious Program—Tel: 518-494-5229. Millie Shutta, D.R.E.; Sara Juliano, D.R.E. Students 69.

CLIFTON PARK, SARATOGA CO., ST. EDWARD THE CONFESSOR, Revs. John L. Cairns; John R. Lanese; Deacons Jerry Grigaitis; Walter MacKinnon; Charles Taylor.
Office—Tel: 518-371-7372; Fax: 518-371-1206.
Church: 569 Clifton Park Center Rd., 12065-4838.
Priests' Residence: 21 Hemlock Dr., 12065-4845. Tel: 518-371-9595; Fax: 518-371-1206.
Catechesis/Religious Program— Richard Amico, D.R.E. Students 1,402.

CLINTON HEIGHTS, RENSSELAER CO., ST. MARY, Rev. Jerome R. Gingras.
Res.: 163 Columbia Tpke., East Greenbush, 12144-3521. Tel: 518-449-2232; Fax: 518-449-2234.
School—Tel: 518-449-2498; Fax: 518-465-1850. Sr. Katherine Arsenau, C.S.J., Prin. Lay Teachers 11; Students 150.

COBLESKILL, SCHOHARIE CO., ST. VINCENT DE PAUL, [CEM] Rev. Thomas F. Berardi; Deacon Gary Surman.
Res.: 138 Washington Ave., 12043. Tel: 518-234-2892.
Mission—St. Mary Sharon Springs, Schoharie Co.

COHOES, ALBANY CO.
1—ST. AGNES-ST. PATRICK, Merged, with St. Marie, Cohoes to form Holy Trinity, Cohoes.
2—ST. BERNARD, Revs. Lawrence G. McTavey; Marc L. Touchette; Sr. Margaret Totten, C.S.J., Pastoral Assoc. In Res., Rev. William F. Jillisky.
Res.: 107 Canvass St., P.O. Box 137, 12047. Tel: 518-237-2721; Fax: 518-237-7980.
3—HOLY TRINITY, Rev. Arthur Becker; Deacons Albert Schrempf; Gerard Matthews; Denise Miller, Youth Min.
Res.: 122 Vliet Blvd., 12047-1842. Tel: 518-237-2373; Fax: 518-238-9427.
School—Cohoes Consolidated Schools See separate listing.
Catechesis/Religious Program—Karen T. Beattie, D.R.E. Students 167.
4—ST. JOSEPH, (French), [CEM] Rev. Michael Cournoyer; Lorraine DeCuyper, Parish Life Dir.
Res.: 65 Congress St., 12047. Tel: 518-237-4241.
School—Cohoes Consolidated Catholic Schools See separate listing.
Catechesis/Religious Program—Tel: 518-237-6856. Kathy Burns, D.R.E. Tel: 518-237-0370. Students 81.
5—ST. MARIE, Merged, with St. Agnes-St. Patrick, Cohoes to form Holy Trinity, Cohoes.
6—ST. MICHAEL, (Polish), [CEM] Rev. Richard W. Dybas.
Res.: 36 Page Ave., 12047. Tel: 518-237-5151; Fax: 518-233-9381.
7—ST. RITA-SACRED HEART, Rev. John Facci, S.A.C.
Res.: 50 St. Rita Ln., 12047. Tel: 518-237-4444; Fax: 518-238-2546.
Catechesis/Religious Program—Tel: 518-237-6856. Katherine Burns, D.R.E. Consolidation of four parishes Students 333.
Mission—Sacred Heart of Jesus, Albany Co.

COLONIE, ALBANY CO.
1—ST. CLARE, Rev. Ronald A. Menty; Deacon George Nahm. In Res., Rev. L. Edward Deimeke.
Res.: 1947 Central Ave., 12205-4299. Tel: 518-456-3112; Fax: 518-456-1072.
Catechesis/Religious Program—Tel: 518-456-3113. Mr. Charles Miller, D.R.E. Students 590.
2—OUR LADY OF MERCY, Rev. John F. Waldron.
Res.: 424 Shaker Run, 12205. Tel: 518-456-8269.
Parish Center—26 Wilson Ave., 12205. Tel: 518-459-1272; Fax: 518-459-1285.

COOPERSTOWN, OTSEGO CO., ST. MARY, [CEM 2] Rev. John P. Rosson.
Res.: 31 Elm St., 13326. Tel: 607-547-2213; Fax: 607-547-5742.

COPAKE FALLS, COLUMBIA CO., ST. BRIDGET, [CEM] Rev. Joseph Falletta; Deacon Martin Stosiek.
Res.: 8074 State Rte. 22, 12517. Tel: 518-329-4711; 518-329-4240.

CORINTH, SARATOGA CO., IMMACULATE CONCEPTION, [CEM] Rev. Charles A. Gaffigan.
Res.: 409 Palmer Ave., 12822. Tel: 518-654-2113.
Catechesis/Religious Program—Tel: 518-654-2087. Margaret Watkins, D.R.E. Students 80.

COXSACKIE, GREENE CO., ST. MARY, [CEM] Rev. John L. Moyna.
Res.: 80 Mansion St., 12051. Tel: 518-731-8800; Fax: 518-731-8505.

CRESCENT, SARATOGA CO., ST. MARY, Rev. Thomas J. Hayes.
Parish Center—86 Church Hill Rd., Waterford, 12188. Tel: 518-371-9632; Fax: 518-371-7235.

DELANSON, SCHENECTADY CO., OUR LADY OF FATIMA, Unassigned.
Res.: 1735 Alexander Rd., P.O. Box 219, 12053-0219. Tel: 518-895-2788; Fax: 518-895-2991.
Catechesis/Religious Program—Tel: 518-895-2991. Angela Caraher, D.R.E. Students 204.

DELHI, DELAWARE CO., ST. PETER, Rev. Michael Flannery.
Res.: 8 Franklin St., 13753. Tel: 607-746-2503.
Catechesis/Religious Program—Sharon Gruver, D.R.E. Students 49.

DELMAR, ALBANY CO., ST. THOMAS THE APOSTLE, Revs. John T. Provost; James D. Daley, Pastor Emeritus (Retired); Richard J. Leskovar; Deacon Alfred Manzella.
Res.: 35 Adams Pl., 12054. Tel: 518-439-4951; Fax: 518-439-0108.
School—42 Adams Pl., 12054. Tel: 518-439-5573; Fax: 518-478-9773. Mr. Thomas Kane, Prin. Lay Teachers 21; Students 215.
Catechesis/Religious Program—Tel: 518-439-3945. Joseph Catalano, D.R.E. Students 1,110.

DOLGEVILLE, HERKIMER CO., ST. JOSEPH, [CEM 2] Rev. Leo F. Potvin; Deacon Peter Manno.
Res.: 31 N. Helmer Ave., 13329. Tel: 315-429-8338.
Catechesis/Religious Program—Students 52.

EAST GREENBUSH, RENSSELAER CO., HOLY SPIRIT, Rev. Joseph O'Brien; Deacon William Dringus. In Res., Rev. Joseph M. Siniskey (Retired).
Res.: 667 Columbia Tpke., 12061. Tel: 518-477-7925; Fax: 518-477-7926.
School—Highland Dr., 12061. Tel: 518-477-5739; Fax: 518-477-5743. Sr. Maureen Moffitt, C.S.J., Prin. Sisters 1; Lay Teachers 23; Students 322.
Catechesis/Religious Program—Tel: 518-477-8108. Sr. Carmella Ann Pfohl, C.S.T., D.R.E. Students 370.

FONDA, MONTGOMERY CO., ST. CECILIA, [CEM] Revs. Patrick Gallagher, O.F.M.Conv.; Kevin Kenny, O.F.M-.Conv.; Leon Dicks, O.F.M.Conv. In Res., Bro. James Amrhein, O.F.M.Conv.
Res.: 26 Broadway, P.O. Box 837, 12068. Tel: 518-853-4195.

FORT ANN, WASHINGTON CO., ST. ANN, Rev. David R. LeFort.
Res.: 85 George St., P.O. Box 226, 12827. Tel: 518-639-5218; Fax: 518-639-4073.
Catechesis/Religious Program—Diane Langlois, D.R.E.; Mark Miller, D.R.E. Combined with St. Philip Mission. Students 72.
Mission—St. Philip South Hartford, Washington Co.

FORT EDWARD, WASHINGTON CO., ST. JOSEPH, [CEM] Rev. Joseph Dworak. In Res., Rev. Frank Gilchrist.
Res.: 164 Broadway, 12828. Tel: 518-747-5117; Fax: 518-747-3444.
Catechesis/Religious Program— Carmela Porto, D.R.E. Students 120.

FORT PLAIN, MONTGOMERY CO., ST. JAMES, Rev. Kenneth J. Swain.
Parish Office—Tel: 518-993-3822.
Res.: 119 Reid St., P.O. Box 287, 13339-0287. Tel: 518-993-5523; Fax: 518-993-2105.

FRANKFORT, HERKIMER CO.
1—ST. MARY, Merged, with SS. Peter & Paul, Frankfort, to form Our Lady Queen of Apostles, Frankfort, Jan. 8, 1995.
2—OUR LADY QUEEN OF APOSTLES (1995), [CEM] Rev. John Yanas.
Res.: 414 Frankfort St., 13340. Tel: 315-894-2025; 315-894-2360; Fax: 315-894-2025.
Catechesis/Religious Program—Phyllis Luczka, D.R.E. Students 262.
3—SS. PETER & PAUL, Merged, with St. Mary, Frankfort, to form Our Lady Queen of Apostles, Frankfort, Jan. 8, 1995.

GERMANTOWN, COLUMBIA CO., RESURRECTION, [CEM] Rev. Theodore Gerken.
Res.: 9 Church Ave., P.O. Box 96, 12526. Tel: 518-537-6136; Fax: 518-537-3621.
Mission—Nativity of Our Lord Linlithgo, Columbia Co.

GLENS FALLS, WARREN CO.
1—ST. ALPHONSUS, [CEM] Deacon William F. Bazinet; George S. Forshey, Parish Life Dir.
Res.: 4 Crandall St., 12801. Tel: 518-792-1574; Fax: 518-792-6049.
School— Merged with St. Mary's Academy to form St Mary's/St. Alphonsus Regional School.
2—ST. MARY, Revs. James Mackey; Xavier Arockiasamy; Deacon F. David Powers. In Res., Rev. Edward Leroux.
Res.: 62 Warren St., 12801. Tel: 518-792-0989; Fax: 518-792-0251.
School—St. Mary's/St. Alphonsus Regional School, Tel: 518-792-3178; Fax: 518-792-6056. Mrs. Kathryn Mahoney Fowler, Prin.
Catechesis/Religious Program—Tel: 518-792-0989, Ext. 15. Jo Kaczmarek, Pastoral Assoc. Students 600.

GLENVILLE, SCHENECTADY CO., IMMACULATE CONCEPTION, Revs. J. Thomas Connery; R. Mansfield Starks, Pastor Emeritus (Retired); Laurenti Magesa Cornelli; Deacon Michael Melanson.
Res.: 400 Saratoga Rd., 12302. Tel: 518-399-9168; Fax: 518-384-3278.
Catechesis/Religious Program—Tel: 518-399-9210. Madeline Fretto, Pastoral Assoc.; Jeannette Leveillee, Pastoral Assoc. Students 828.

GLOVERSVILLE, FULTON CO.
1—ST. MARY, , Canonically merged with Our Lady of Mount Carmel in 1990. See St. Mary of Mount Carmel.
2—ST. MARY OF MT. CARMEL, [CEM] Consolidated Rev. Donald Czelusniak. from Our Lady of Mount Carmel and St. Mary in 1990.
Res.: 149 S. Main St., 12078. Tel: 518-725-3143; Fax: 518-725-7245.
Catechesis/Religious Program—Tel: 518-725-1213. Virginia Trippodo, D.R.E. Students 140.
3—SACRED HEART, Rev. David L. Tressic.
Res.: 189 Kingsboro Ave., 12078. Tel: 518-725-9375; Fax: 518-773-3341.
Catechesis/Religious Program—Tel: 518-773-8590. Karen Hoose, D.R.E. Students 315.

GRAFTON, RENSSELAER CO., ST. JOHN FRANCIS REGIS, Sr. Mary Kenan McGowan, R.S.M., Parish Life Dir.; Rev. Kenneth Gregory, Sacramental Min.
Mailing Address: P.O. Box 234, 12082. Tel: 518-279-4943; Fax: 518-279-3055.

GRANVILLE, WASHINGTON CO.
1—ST. MARY, Closed. For inquiries for parish records contact the chancery.
2—ROMAN CATHOLIC COMMUNITY OF GRANVILLE, Consolidated Rev. Thomas Zelker. St. Mary's, All Saints, and Our Lady of Mount Carmel.
Res.: 23 Bulkley Ave., 12832. Tel: 518-642-1262.
Parish Center—All Saints House, Morrison Ave., 12832.
Catechesis/Religious Program—Mary King, D.R.E. Students 207.

GREEN ISLAND, ALBANY CO., ST. JOSEPH, Rev. Donald Kelly.
Res.: 131 George St., 12183. Tel: 518-273-3552.
Catechesis/Religious Program—Students 40.

GREENFIELD CENTER, SARATOGA CO., ST. JOSEPH, Rev. Martin DeRose; Sr. Diane Schoff, Parish Life Dir.
Res.: 3159 Rte. 9N, P.O. Box 168, 12833. Tel: 518-893-7680; Fax: 518-893-0472.
Mission—St. Paul P.O. Box 136, Rock City Falls, Saratoga Co. 12863. Tel: 518-885-4877.

GREENVILLE, GREENE CO., ST. JOHN THE BAPTIST, Rev. William M. Bauer; Deacon Peter Sedlmeir.
Mailing Address: P.O. Box 340, 12083.
Office—4982 Rte. 81, 12083. Tel: 518-966-8317; Fax: 518-966-4652.
Catechesis/Religious Program—Tel: 518-966-4651. Connie Parente, D.R.E. Students 127.

GREENWICH, WASHINGTON CO., ST. JOSEPH, Rev. Christopher Welch; Deacon Herbert Howley.
Res.: 36 Bleecker St., 12834. Tel: 518-692-2159; Fax: 518-692-8706.

GUILDERLAND, ALBANY CO.
1—CHRIST THE KING, Rev. Patrick J. Butler; Deacon Joseph Markham.
Res.: 20 Sumpter Ave., 12203. Tel: 518-456-1644; Fax: 518-456-4696.
School—Tel: 518-456-5400. Mary Anne Panariello, Prin. Lay Teachers 19; Students 258.
2—ST. MADELEINE SOPHIE, Rev. James Belogi; Deacons Earle Flatt; Mark Leonard.
Res.: 3500 Carman Rd., Schenectady, 12303. Tel: 518-355-0421; Fax: 518-355-0412.
School—3510 Carman Rd., Schenectady, 12303. Tel: 518-355-3080; Fax: 518-355-3106. Miss Teresa Kovarovic, Prin. Lay Teachers 17; Students 211.
Convent—3514 Carman Rd., Schenectady, 12303. Tel: 518-355-8052.

HAGAMAN, MONTGOMERY CO., ST. STEPHEN, [CEM] Rev. Ronald Matulewicz.
Res.: 51 Pawling, 12086. Tel: 518-843-2951.

HAGUE, WARREN CO., BLESSED SACRAMENT, Rev. George Fleming, Admin.
Res.: Hague Rd., P.O. Box 529, 12836. Tel: 518-543-8828.
Catechesis/Religious Program—Fax: 518-494-5663. Sr. Francesca Husselbeck, R.S.M., D.R.E. Students 3.
Mission—St. Teresa of Avila Brant Lake, Warren Co.

HAINES FALLS, GREENE CO., IMMACULATE CONCEPTION, [CEM] Rev. Anthony Motta.
Res.: Mountain House Rd., 12436. Tel: 518-589-5577.
Mission—St. Francis de Sales Elka Park, Greene Co.
Mission—Wayside Shrine, Greene Co.

HANCOCK, DELAWARE CO., ST. PAUL THE APOSTLE, [CEM 2] Rev. Stephen P. Morris; Robert W. Carpenter, Admin.
Res.: 346 W. Main St., 13783. Tel: 607-637-2571; Fax: 607-637-3203.

HERKIMER, HERKIMER CO.
1—ST. ANTHONY-ST. JOSEPH, Rev. Robert Shinos; Deacon Dennis Jones, Pastoral Assoc. & Parish Operations; Ms. Christine Jones, Pastoral Assoc. & Liturgy.
Res.: 228 S. Main St., 13350. Tel: 315-866-2892; 315-866-6373 (Parish Office); Fax: 315-867-6186.
Catechesis/Religious Program—Carole Powers, D.R.E., (Grades K-6). Tel: 315-866-6821; Celia Grande, D.R.E., (Grades 7-12). Tel: 315-866-6755.
2—ST. FRANCIS DE SALES, [CEM] Rev. Mark Cunningham.
Parish Center—219 N. Bellinger St., 13350. Tel: 315-866-4282; Fax: 315-866-9043.
Res.: 25 Park Pl. S., 13350. Tel: 315-866-7301.
School—220 Henry St., 13350. Tel: 315-866-4831. Sr. Rosalie Kelly, C.S.J., Prin. Sisters of St. Joseph of Carondolet 3; Lay Teachers 10; Students 190.
Catechesis/Religious Program—Carole Powers, D.R.E., (Elementary); Celia Grande, D.R.E., (High School); Diane O'Donnell, D.R.E., (High School). Students 250.
Convent—One Park Pl., 13350. Tel: 315-866-4492.

HOOSICK FALLS, RENSSELAER CO., IMMACULATE CONCEPTION, [CEM] Rev. Joseph Manerowski.
Res.: 67 Main St., Box 269, 12090. Tel: 518-686-5064; Fax: 518-686-1625.
School—St. Mary Academy, 4 Parsons Ave., 12090. Tel: 518-686-4314; Fax: 518-686-5957. Mrs. Carol Geddes, Prin. Lay Teachers 16; Students 158

HUDSON FALLS, WASHINGTON CO.
1—CHURCH OF ST. MARY'S/ST. PAUL'S (Sandy Hill), [CEM 2], The Roman Catholic Community of Hudson Falls/Kingsbury. Rev. James B. Lonergan, V.F. In Res., Rev. Victor Owan.
Res.: 11 Wall St., 12839. Tel: 518-747-4823; Fax: 518-747-2265.
2—IMMACULATE HEART OF MARY (Sandy Hill), (French),, Canonically merged with St. Paul, Hudson Falls. Now called Church of St. Mary's/St. Paul's, Roman Catholic Community of Hudson Falls/Kingsbury.
3—ST. PAUL (Sandy Hill), (French),, Canonically merged with Immaculate Heart of Mary parish, Hudson Falls. Now called Church of St. Mary's/St. Paul's, Roman Catholic Community of Hudson Falls/Kingsbury.

HUDSON, COLUMBIA CO.
1—CHURCH OF ST. MARY, , Canonically merged with Our Lady of Mount Carmel and Our Lady of Perpetual Help-Sacred Heart in 1991. Rev. Winston L. Bath; Deacon Charles O'Neill.
Mailing Address: P.O. Box 323, 12534. In Res., Rev. Edward F. Cantwell.
Res.: 429 E. Allen St., 12534. Tel: 518-828-1334.
2—OUR LADY OF MT. CARMEL, , Canonically merged with Church of St. Mary in 1991. All inquiries should be directed to P.O. Box 323, Hudson, NY 12534. Tel: 518-828-1334.
3—OUR LADY OF PERPETUAL HELP-SACRED HEART, (Polish),, Canonically merged with Church of St. Mary in 1991. All inquiries should be directed to P.O. Box 323, Hudson, NY 12534. Tel: 518-828-1334.

ILION, HERKIMER CO., ANNUNCIATION, [CEM] Rev. Joseph Benintende.
Res.: 109 West St., 13357. Tel: 315-894-3766; Fax: 315-894-1550.

JOHNSONVILLE, RENSSELAER CO., ST. MONICA'S CHURCH, Merged, with St. John the Baptist, Schaghticoke to form Church of the Holy Trinity, Schaghticoke.

JOHNSTOWN, FULTON CO.
1—ST. ANTHONY, (Slovak), [CEM] Consolidated, with Immaculate Conception, Johnstown and St. Patrick, Johnstown to form Holy Trinity, Johnstown.
2—HOLY TRINITY, Rev. James T. Fitzmaurice.
Mailing Address: P.O. Box 930, 12095. Tel: 518-762-2636; Fax: 518-762-2690.
3—IMMACULATE CONCEPTION, (Italian), [CEM] Consolidated, with St. Anthony, Johnstown and St. Patrick, Johnstown to form Holy Trinity, Johnstown.
4—ST. PATRICK, [CEM] Consolidated, with Immaculate Conception, Johnstown and St Anthony, Johnstown to form Holy Trinity Parish, Johnstown.

LAKE GEORGE, WARREN CO., SACRED HEART, Revs. Joseph O'Brien; James I. Donlon, J.C.D.
Res.: 50 Mohican St., 12845. Tel: 518-668-2046; Fax: 518-668-4377.
Catechesis/Religious Program—Irene Filippelli, D.R.E.; Torie Wattendorf, D.R.E. Students 270.
Mission—Our Lady of the Assumption Ridge Rd., Queensbury, Warren Co. 12804. Tel: 518-668-2046.

LAKE LUZERNE, WARREN CO., HOLY INFANCY, [JC] Rev. Charles A. Gaffigan.
Res.: 323 Lake Ave., P.O. Box 470, 12846. Tel: 518-696-2625; Fax: 518-696-7274.

LATHAM, ALBANY CO.
1—ST. AMBROSE, Revs. Francis J. DuBois; Peter Tkocz; Deacon Helmut Neurohr. In Res., Rev. George Phillips.
Res.: 347 Old Loudon Rd., 12110. Tel: 518-785-1351; Fax: 518-785-8370.
School—Tel: 518-785-6453. Sr. James Marie, P.B.V.M., Prin. Sisters 4; Lay Teachers 12; Students 258.
Catechesis/Religious Program—Mary Kay Frederick, D.R.E. Students 393.
2—OUR LADY OF THE ASSUMPTION, Rev. Geoffrey D. Burke.
Res.: 498 Watervliet-Shaker Rd., 12110. Tel: 518-785-0234; Fax: 518-785-0420.
Catechesis/Religious Program—Tel: 518-785-1605. Linda Berkery, D.R.E. Students 552.

LITTLE FALLS, HERKIMER CO.
1—HOLY FAMILY, [CEM] Rev. Charles R. Celeste; Sr. Marilyn Hayes, C.S.J., Pastoral Assoc.; Deacon Michael Carbone.
Office—763 E. Main St., P.O. Box 247, 13365-0247. Tel: 315-823-2410; Fax: 315-823-2701.
Catechesis/Religious Program—Lori Casullo, D.R.E.; Lisa LaCoppolla, D.R.E. Students 192.
2—ST. JOSEPH, Consolidated, with St. Mary and Sacred Heart to form Holy Family Parish, Little Falls.
3—ST. MARY, Consolidated, with St. Joseph and Sacred Heart to form Holy Family Parish, Little Falls.
4—SACRED HEART, (Polish), Consolidated, with St. Joseph and St. Mary to form Holy Family Parish, Little Falls.

LOUDONVILLE, ALBANY CO.
1—ST. FRANCIS DE SALES (1972), Rev. David E. Noone.
Church & Offices: One Maria Dr., 12211. Tel: 518-489-8386; Fax: 518-489-6910.
Res.: 15 Exchange St., 12205. Tel: 518-489-8386.
Old Church—15 Exchange St., 12205.
2—ST. PIUS X, Revs. Michael A. Farano; James J. Walsh.
Mailing Address: 2 Fairview Rd., 12211.
School—Upper Loudon Rd., 12211. Tel: 518-465-4539. Dennis Mullahy, Prin. Students 617.
Convent—Tel: 518-449-1658.

MARGARETVILLE, DELAWARE CO., SACRED HEART, Rev. William Gorman.
Res.: Academy St., 12455. Tel: 845-586-2665.
Catechesis/Religious Program—Students 122.
Mission—St. Ann Andes, Delaware Co.
Mission—Our Lady of Good Counsel Roxbury, Delaware Co.

MECHANICVILLE, SARATOGA CO., ASSUMPTION-ST. PAUL, Revs. William A. Recchuti, O.S.A.; Edward J. Dixey, O.S.A. In Res., Rev. Joseph Getz, O.S.A.; Deacon Gregory Mansfield.
Res.: 52 William St., P.O. Box 308, 12118 Tel: 518-664-6196; Fax: 518-664-6782.
Convent—Sisters of St. Joseph, 77 Viall Ave., 12118. Tel: 518-664-4053.

MENANDS, ALBANY CO., ST. JOAN OF ARC, Rev. Kofi Ntsiful Amissah; Deacon Andy Cohen.
Parish Office & Res.: 76 Menand Rd., 12204. Tel: 518-463-0378; 518-462-2496; Fax: 518-463-0489.
Catechesis/Religious Program—Students 97.

MIDDLEBURGH, SCHOHARIE CO., ST. CATHERINE, Rev. Thomas Holmes, Admin.
Res.: 111 Wells Ave., 12122. Tel: 518-827-5132.
Catechesis/Religious Program—Tel: 518-827-5802. Vicki Hoerz, D.R.E. Students 61.

MOHAWK, HERKIMER CO., BLESSED SACRAMENT, Sr. Mary Jo Tallman, Parish Life Dir.
Res.: 54 E. Main St., 13407. Tel: 315-866-1752.

MORRIS, OTSEGO CO., HOLY CROSS, Rev. John Burns.
Res.: 43 W. Main St., P.O. Box 118, 13808. Tel: 607-263-5143.
Mission—Nativity of B.V.M. Edmeston, Otsego Co.

NASSAU, RENSSELAER CO., ST. MARY, [CEM] Rev. Antone Kandrac, O.F.M.Conv.; Deacon John Skelly.
Res.: 26 Church St., P.O. Box 435, 12123. Tel: 518-766-2701; Fax: 518-766-7535.

NEW LEBANON, COLUMBIA CO., IMMACULATE CONCEPTION, [CEM] Rev. John Close; Deacon Peter Quinn.
Church and Shrine of Our Lady of Lourdes: U.S. Rte. 20, 12125. Tel: 518-794-7651; 518-766-5651.
Mission—St. Joseph's Stephentown, Rensselaer Co.

NEWPORT, HERKIMER CO., ST. JOHN THE BAPTIST, Rev. Leo F. Potvin.
Res.: Main St., Box 475, 13416. Tel: 315-845-8017.
Mission—St. Mary of the Assumption [CEM] Middleville, Herkimer Co.

NORTH CREEK, WARREN CO., ST. JAMES, [CEM] Rev. George Fleming; Sr. M. Francesca Husselbeck, R.S.M., Parish Life Dir.
Res.: Main St., P.O. Box 23, 12853. Tel: 518-251-2518; Fax: 518-494-5663.
Catechesis/Religious Program— Karen Smith, D.R.E.; Joyce Parker, D.R.E. Students 37.

NORTHVILLE, FULTON CO., ST. FRANCIS OF ASSISI, Rev. Robert Powhida.
Mailing Address: P.O. Box 126, 12134.
Res.: 501 Bridge St., 12134. Tel: 518-863-4736; Fax: 518-863-4128.

ONEONTA, OTSEGO CO., ST. MARY, [CEM] Revs. Paul A. Roman; Thomas Babiuch; Mrs. Barbara Dugan Lilly, Pastoral Assoc.; Susan Nesbitt, Campus Ministry.
Res.: 39 Walnut St., 13820. Tel: 607-432-3920; Fax: 607-432-6437.
School—5588 State Hwy. 7, 13820. Tel: 607-432-1450; Fax: 607-433-1656. Sr. Mary Christopher Comproski, C.R., Prin. Religious 3; Lay Teachers 15; Students 224.
Catechesis/Religious Program—Tel: 607-431-9320. Susan Nesbit, D.R.E. Students 375.
Convent—10 Irving Pl., 13820. Tel: 607-433-2220.

PALENVILLE, GREENE CO., SACRED HEART, Revs. Albert F. McMahon, O.F.M. (HRT); Giles M. Barreda, O.F.M. (TR).
Mailing Address: Rte. 32 A, Box 40, 12463. Tel: 518-678-9937.

PHILMONT, COLUMBIA CO., SACRED HEART, [CEM] Rev. Raymond Ethier.
Res.: 141 Main St., 12565. Tel: 518-672-4655; Fax: 518-672-4778.
Mission—Pine Haven Home, Columbia Co.

PITTSTOWN, RENSSELAER CO., ST. GEORGE, Rev. John F. Riley.
Res.: 134 Factory Hollow Rd., Valley Falls, 12185-2904. Tel: 518-663-8378.
Catechesis/Religious Program—Marcy Smith, D.R.E., (Elementary); Michael Bromm, D.R.E., (Secondary). Students 89.

QUEENSBURY, WARREN CO., OUR LADY OF THE ANNUNCIATION, Rev. Joseph Anselment.
Res.: 448 Aviation Rd., 12804. Tel: 518-793-9677; Fax: 518-793-9678.
Catechesis/Religious Program—Tel: 518-798-1335. Catherine Vesterby, D.R.E. Students 915.

RAVENA, ALBANY CO., ST. PATRICK, [CEM] Rev. Vincent J. Ciotoli.
Res.: 21 Main St., 12143. Tel: 518-756-3145; Fax: 518-756-3145.
Catechesis/Religious Program—Tel: 518-756-8411. Sr. Carol Anne Porter, C.S.J., D.R.E. Students 285.

RENSSELAER, RENSSELAER CO.
1—ST. JOHN THE EVANGELIST, [CEM] Rev. R. Adam Forno; Sr. M. Andre, R.S.M., Pastoral Assoc.
Res.: 20 Lawrence St., 12144. Tel: 518-465-2209; Fax: 518-449-7088.
Parish Office—P.O. Box 256, 12144. Tel: 518-465-0482.
Catechesis/Religious Program—Linda Remington, D.R.E. Combined program with St. Joseph Students 202.
Convent—20 Lawrence St., 12144. Tel: 518-465-1514. Sr. Mary Agatha Smith, R.S.M., Coord. Sisters 15.
2—ST. JOSEPH (1915), Rev. R. Adam Forno.
Office—1620 Third St., 12144. Tel: 518-463-4401;

Fax: 518-463-3194.
School—St. Joseph-St. John, 1641 Third St., 12144. Tel: 518-465-1151. Frederick J. Talarico, Prin. Lay Teachers 12; Students 131.
Catechesis/Religious Program—Tel: 518-465-0482; Fax: 518-449-7088. Linda Remington, D.R.E. Combined program with St. John

RICHFIELD SPRINGS, OTSEGO CO., ST. JOSEPH, [CEM] Rev. Terence Healy; Sr. Patricia Woolheater, C.S.J., Parish Life Dir.
Res.: 35 Canadarago St., 13439-0791. Tel: 315-858-1682.
Catechesis/Religious Program—Sr. Patricia Woolheater, D.R.E. Students 31.

ROTTERDAM JUNCTION, SCHENECTADY CO., ST. MARGARET OF CORTONA, Rev. Dennis Murphy, Admin.
Res.: 2 Putnam St., 12150. Tel: 518-887-5288; Fax: 518-887-5288.
Catechesis/Religious Program—Tel: 518-399-1888. Katherine Skelly, D.R.E. Students 44.

ROTTERDAM, SCHENECTADY CO., ST. GABRIEL THE ARCHANGEL, Rev. Leo F. Markert; Deacon Kenneth Baechel.
Res.: 3040 Hamburg St., Schenectady, 12303. Tel: 518-355-6600; Fax: 518-355-6604.
Catechesis/Religious Program—Tel: 518-355-4193. Joan M. Forster, D.R.E. Students 505.

ST. JOHNSVILLE, MONTGOMERY CO., ST. PATRICK, Sr. Dolores Stevens, Parish Life Dir.
Res.: 30 Center St., 13452. Tel: 518-568-7418; Fax: 518-568-7656.

SALEM, WASHINGTON CO., HOLY CROSS, [CEM] Rev. Liam Condon.
Res.: 247 Main St., 12865. Tel: 518-854-7626.

SARATOGA SPRINGS, SARATOGA CO.
1—ST. CLEMENT, Revs. Joseph Tizio, C.SS.R.; Francis E. Sullivan, C.SS.R.; Arthur Tuttle, C.SS.R.; Deacons Larry Willette, Pastoral Assoc.; Arthur Turcotte, Pastoral Assoc.; Lee Hanson, Pastoral Assoc.
Res.: 231 Lake Ave., 12866. Tel: 518-584-6122; Fax: 518-584-2644.
School—Lake Ave., 12866. Tel: 518-584-7350; Fax: 518-587-2623. Dr. Thaddeus Obloy, Prin. Lay Teachers 23; Students 401.
Catechesis/Religious Program—Tel: 518-587-3611. Betty Smykowski, Pastoral Assoc.; Eileen Davenport, Pastoral Assoc.; Nicole Alonzo, D.R.E. Students 1,124.
Chapel—Gansevoort, St. Therese, Tel: 518-587-3180. Deacon Danny Boyd.
2—ST. PETER, [CEM] Rev. Robert J. LeFevre. Tel: 518-584-6113.
Res.: 241 S. Broadway, 12866. Tel: 518-584-2375; Fax: 518-584-5471.
Catechesis/Religious Program— Rita Usher. Tel: 518-587-4487. Students 375.

SCHAGHTICOKE, RENSSELAER CO.
1—CHURCH OF THE HOLY TRINITY, [CEM] Rev. Peter Pagones; Deacon Walter Rehder.
Mailing Address: P.O. Box 300, 12154. Tel: 518-753-4554; Fax: 518-273-0310.
Res.: 55 N. Lake Ave., Troy, 12180. Tel: 518-273-7609.
Catechesis/Religious Program—Tel: 518-753-6228; Fax: 518-753-6228. Cheri Foster, D.R.E. Students 210.
2—ST. JOHN THE BAPTIST, Merged, with St. Monica, Johnsonville to form Church of the Holy Trinity, Schaghticoke.

SCHENECTADY, SCHENECTADY CO.
1—ST. ANTHONY, (Italian), Revs. John M. Medwid; Anthony DeFranco, Pastor Emeritus; Sr. Maria Rose Querini, M.P.V., Pastoral Assoc.
Parish Office—331 Seward Pl., 12305. Tel: 518-374-4591; Fax: 518-377-5245.
School—1840 Van Vranken Ave., 12305. Tel: 518-372-5961; Fax: 518-372-7337. Mr. Richard Santelli, Prin. Venerini Sisters 2; Lay Teachers 10; Students 110.
Catechesis/Religious Program—Tel: 518-371-6552. Mrs. Clementine Carlin, D.R.E.; Paul Abate, D.R.E. Students 94.
Convent—1834 Van Vranken Ave., 12305. Tel: 518-346-2060.
2—CHURCH OF ST. ADALBERT, (Polish), [CEM] Rev. Carl A. Urban; Sr. Bernadette Filter, C.R., Pastoral Assoc. for Elderly.
Res.: 550 Lansing St., 12303-1195. Tel: 518-346-4204; Fax: 518-346-0348.
Catechesis/Religious Program—Tel: 518-372-8372. Jacqueline Burgoyne, D.R.E. Students 103.
3—SS. CYRIL AND METHODIUS, Closed., For inquiries for parish records contact Our Lady of Mount Carmel, Schenectady.
4—ST. HELEN, Rev. James J. Kane.
Res.: 1803 Union St., 12309. Tel: 518-346-6137; Fax: 518-346-5390.
School—1801 Union St., 12309. Tel: 518-382-8225; Fax: 518-382-2226. Sr. Anne Marie, P.B.V.M., Prin. Sisters of Presentation 4; Lay Teachers 11; Students 170.
Catechesis/Religious Program—Tel: 518-377-3119.
Convent—40 Ray St., 12309. Tel: 518-374-7055.
5—HOLY CROSS, Revs. Richard A. Carlino; Anthony Curran; Deacon Frank Schickel.
Mailing Address and Res.: 19 N. College St., 12305. Tel: 518-372-3381; Fax: 518-372-0992.
Catechesis/Religious Program—Tel: 518-372-3381, Ext. 110. Combined with St. John the Evangelist and St. Mary (See St. John the Evangelist)
6—IMMACULATE CONCEPTION, Rev. O. Robert De Martinis.
Res.: 523 Thompson St., 12306. Tel: 518-382-0451; Fax: 518-382-3243.
Office—520 Hegeman St., 12306.
Catechesis/Religious Program—Deborah Ploetz, D.R.E. Students 116.
7—ST. JOHN THE BAPTIST, [CEM] Revs. Michael Hogan; Ken Tunney. In Res., Rev. Bernard Turner.
Res.: 427 Franklin St., 12305. Tel: 518-374-9148; Fax: 518-374-9149.
8—ST. JOHN THE EVANGELIST, Revs. Richard A. Carlino; Anthony Curran; Deacon Frank Schickel. In Res., Rev. Anthony DeFranco.
Res.: 802 Union St., 12308. Fax: 518-372-0992.
Office—816 Union St., 12308. Tel: 518-372-3381; Fax: 518-372-0992.
School—806 Union St., 12308. Tel: 518-393-5331; Fax: 518-374-4663. Marie Keenan, Prin. Lay Teachers 171; Students 231.
Catechesis/Religious Program—Tel: 518-372-3381, Ext. 110; Fax: 518-372-0962. Jeanne Marie Hawkey, D.R.E. Combined with St. Mary and Holy Cross Students 650.
9—ST. JOSEPH, (German), [CEM 2] Rev. Michael Hogan.
Res.: 225 Lafayette St., 12305. Tel: 518-374-4466; Fax: 518-374-4466.
10—ST. LUKE, Rev. Dominic Isopo.
Res.: 1241 State St., 12304. Tel: 518-346-3405; Fax: 518-346-3406.
School—1252 Albany St., 12304. Tel: 518-377-7330; Fax: 518-377-7330. Sr. Ann Christi Brink, C.S.J., Prin. Sisters of St. Joseph of Carondelet 7; Lay Teachers 19; Students 250.
Convent—1252 Albany St., 12304. Tel: 518-372-2182.
Mission—St. Teresa Carmelite Monastery 428 Duane Ave., Schenectady Co. 12304.
11—ST. MARY, (Polish), [CEM] Revs. Richard Carlino; Michael W. Zakens, Pastor Emeritus (Retired); Anthony Curran; Deacon Frank Schickel.
Parish Office—828 Eastern Ave., 12308. Tel: 518-374-2423.
Catechesis/Religious Program—Tel: 518-372-3381, Ext. 110. Combined with St. John the Evangelist and Holy Cross (See St. John the Evangelist)
12—OUR LADY OF FATIMA, Unassigned.
Res.: 2216 Rosa Rd., 12309. Tel: 518-370-3136; Fax: 518-370-3137.
Catechesis/Religious Program—Tel: 518-370-0027. Patricia Policastro, D.R.E.; Catherine Rivera, D.R.E. Students 234.
13—OUR LADY OF MT. CARMEL, (Italian), Rev. Robert J. Hohenstein.
Res.: 1255 Pleasant St., 12303. Tel: 518-393-4109; Fax: 518-393-4100.
Our Lady of Mt. Carmel Center—1274 Pleasant St., 12303. Tel: 518-372-0336.
Catechesis/Religious Program—Tel: 518-372-8372. Jacquline Burgoyne, D.R.E. Students 82.
14—OUR LADY OF THE ASSUMPTION, Rev. Joseph Cebula; Deacon Frederick Scarletto.
Res.: 3034 Ford Ave., 12306. Tel: 518-346-4926; Fax: 518-374-5670.
15—ST. PAUL THE APOSTLE, Revs. George W. Brucker; Peter Pagones; Michael T. Schmitt; Deacon Owen South. In Res., Revs. Kenneth J. Tunny; Brian Cronin (Retired).
Res.: 2777 Albany St., 12304. Tel: 518-377-8886; Fax: 518-377-8887.
School—16 Van Zandt St., 12304. Tel: 518-377-0506. Mr. Mark Reilly, Prin. Lay Teachers 15; Students 130.
16—SACRED HEART-ST. COLUMBA, Rev. Michael Hogan; Deacon Ramon Tapia; Mr. George Vielkind, Admin.; Sisters Rosemary Endres, C.S.J., Pastoral Assoc.; Norina Mastro, M.P.V., Pastoral Assoc.; M. Therese Van de Mosselaer, I.C.M., Parish Visitor; Judy Fitzner-Atchinson, Artist-in-Residence.
Res.: 801 Stanley St., 12307. Tel: 518-377-8559; 518-346-0261; Fax: 518-393-9265.
17—ST. THOMAS THE APOSTLE, Closed., For inquires for parish records please see Our Lady of Mt. Carmel, Schenectady.

SCHOHARIE, SCHOHARIE CO., ST. JOSEPH, Rev. Thomas Holmes; Sr. Joan Curley, C.S.J., Parish Life Dir.
Res.: P.O. Box 514, 12157. Tel: 518-295-8923.

SCHUYLERVILLE, SARATOGA CO.
1—NOTRE DAME-VISITATION, [CEM 2] Rev. Christopher J. Welch.
Parish House—18 Pearl St., 12871. Tel: 518-695-3391; Fax: 518-695-4651.
Catechesis/Religious Program—Tel: 518-695-3318; Fax: 518-695-4854. Sisters Rene Drolet, D.R.E.; Rose Marita Lake, D.R.E. Students 130.
Convent—P.O.Box 55, 12871. Tel: 518-695-3318.
2—VISITATION OF THE BLESSED VIRGIN MARY, Closed., For inquiries for parish records contact Notre Dame de Lourdes Parish, Schuylerville.

SCOTIA, SCHENECTADY CO., ST. JOSEPH, Rev. Peter Russo; Deacon John P. Crane.
Res.: 231 Second St.., 12302. Tel: 518-346-4960.
Parish Center—45 MacArthur Dr., 12302. Tel: 518-346-2316; Fax: 518-374-3383.
Catechesis/Religious Program—Tel: 518-374-3382. Patricia A. Walsh, D.R.E. Students 480.

SIDNEY, DELAWARE CO., SACRED HEART, Rev. Gordon Polenz; Deacons Thomas E. Luby; Michael R. Donnell.
Res.: 15 Liberty St., 13838. Tel: 607-563-1591; Fax: 607-563-7066.
Catechesis/Religious Program—Fax: 607-563-7066. Paula Ciborowski, D.R.E.; Barbara Shafer, D.R.E. Students 161.
Mission—St. Ambrose Unadilla, Otsego Co. (Closed)
Mission—St. Paul Franklin, Delaware Co. (Closed)

SOUTH GLENS FALLS, SARATOGA CO., ST. MICHAEL THE ARCHANGEL, Rev. Robert Nugent.
Res.: 80 Saratoga Ave., 12803. Tel: 518-792-5859; Fax: 518-792-5850.
Catechesis/Religious Program—Tel: 518-793-6584. Carol O'Connor, D.R.E. Students 500.

SOUTH KORTRIGHT, DELAWARE CO., CHURCH OF THE MOST PRECIOUS BLOOD OF JESUS, Merged, with Sacred Heart, Stamford.

SPEIGLETOWN, RENSSELAER CO., ST. BONAVENTURE, Rev. Salvatore A. Rodino.
Res.: Hillview Dr., Troy, 12182. Tel: 518-235-0337; Fax: 518-235-8726.
Catechesis/Religious Program—Tel: 518-235-0337, Ext. 4. Barbara Colangione, D.R.E. Students 183.

STAMFORD, DELAWARE CO., SACRED HEART, [CEM] Rev. Anthony F. Ligato; Louise Evans, Pastoral Assoc.
Res.: 27 Harper St., P.O. Box 38, 12167. Tel: 607-652-7170; Fax: 607-652-9250.
Catechesis/Religious Program—Louise Evans, D.R.E. Combined with St. Philip Neri Mission Students 100.
Mission—St. Philip Neri Grand Gorge, Delaware Co.

STILLWATER, SARATOGA CO., ST. PETER THE APOSTLE, [CEM] Rev. William Turnbull.
Res.: 271 N. Hudson Ave., 12170. Tel: 518-664-3354; Fax: 518-664-3891.
Mission—St. Isaac Jogues Saratoga Lake, Saratoga Co. (Summer)

STOTTVILLE, COLUMBIA CO., HOLY FAMILY, Rev. Frank O'Connor.
Res.: 2824 Atlantic Ave., 12172. Tel: 518-828-1889; Fax: 518-822-9238.
Catechesis/Religious Program— Beth Carlin, D.R.E. Students 130.

STUYVESANT FALLS, COLUMBIA CO., ST. MARY/NATIVITY, [CEM] Rev. Frank O'Connor, Admin.
Church: 1820 Rte. 9, 12173. Tel: 518-799-5411; Fax: 518-799-3144.

STUYVESANT, COLUMBIA CO., NATIVITY OF THE BLESSED VIRGIN MARY, Unassigned., 1820 Rte. 9, 12173.

SUMMIT, SCHOHARIE CO., ST. ANNA, Rev. Edward Golding, Admin.
Res.: Main St., P.O. Box 124, 12175. Tel: 518-287-1553; Fax: 607-397-7732.
Mission—N.Y.S. Correctional Facility Camp Summit, Schoharie Co.
Mission—S.U.N.Y. Cobleskill College Camp Summit, Schoharie Co.

TRIBES HILL, MONTGOMERY CO., SACRED HEART, Rev. Patrick Gallagher, O.F.M.Conv.
Res.: 111 Third Ave., P.O. Box 264, 12177. Tel: 518-829-7301.
Catechesis/Religious Program—Tel: 518-922-6836. Marian Sarchet, D.R.E. Students 87.

TROY, RENSSELAER CO.
1—ST. ANTHONY OF PADUA (SHRINE CHURCH), (Italian), Revs. Bonaventure Bionda, O.F.M.; Marcellinus Borg, O.F.M.; Deacon Moises Gutierrez.
Friary: 28 State St., 12180-3916. Tel: 518-273-8622; Fax: 518-273-2731.
Catechesis/Religious Program—Tel: 518-283-5760. Mrs. Bernadette Curran, D.R.E. Students 7.
2—ST. AUGUSTINE, Revs. James Spenard, O.S.A.; Joseph D. Keffer, O.S.A.; Thomas Casey, O.S.A.; Michael Stanley, O.S.A.
Res.: 25 115th St., 12182. Tel: 518-235-3861; Fax: 518-233-0284.
School—525 Fourth Ave., 12182. Tel: 518-235-7287; Fax: 518-237-7943. James R. Clement, Prin. Lay Teachers 12; Students 140.
3—ST. FRANCIS DE SALES, Rev. Donald J. Ophals.
Res.: 316 Congress St., 12180. Tel: 518-274-4232.
Catechesis/Religious Program—Tel: 518-274-0224. Sr. Charla Whimple, C.S.J., D.R.E.; Mary Ackerson, D.R.E. Students 122.

4—Holy Trinity, (Polish), Rev. Romaeus Cooney, O.Carm., Admin.
Mailing Address: *St. Joseph's Priory*, 416 Third St., 12180. Tel: 518-274-6720; Fax: 518-272-6503.
5—St. Joseph, [CEM] Revs. Romaeus Cooney, O.Carm.; Albert Pavlik, O.Carm.
Res.: 416 Third St., 12180. Tel: 518-274-6720; Fax: 518-272-6503.
Catechesis/Religious Program—Mary Lou Kane, D.R.E. Students 56.
6—St. Lawrence, Closed., For inquiries for parish records contact St. Joseph Parish, Troy.
7—St. Mary, Unassigned.
Res.: 196 Third St., 12180. Tel: 518-272-5820.
Catechesis/Religious Program—Sam Marro, D.R.E. Students 144.
8—St. Michael the Archangel, Rev. Thomas E. Konopka; Deacons Frank Yankowski; Dan Ackerson.
Res.: 1424 Hampton Place Blvd., 12180. Tel: 518-286-1575.
Church: 175 Williams Rd., 12180. Tel: 518-283-6110; Fax: 518-283-3938.
Catechesis/Religious Program—Deacon Francis Yankowski, D.R.E. Tel: 518-283-6110, Ext. 12. Students 323.
Mission—Van Rensselaer Manor, County Welfare Home North Greenbush, Rensselaer Co.
Mission—Hallmark Nursing Home, Rensselaer Co.
9—Our Lady of Victory, Rev. Randall P. Patterson; Deacon John Maclutsky.
Res.: 55 N. Lake Ave., 12180. Tel: 518-273-7609; 518-273-7602 (Office); Fax: 518-273-0310.
School—451 Marshland Ct., 12180. Tel: 518-274-6202; Fax: 518-271-8680. Ms. Karen Snyder, Prin. Lay Teachers 14; Students 154.
10—St. Patrick, Revs. Thomas J. Kelly; Cyril F. Pereira (Retired).
Res.: 3027 Sixth Ave., 12180. Tel: 518-272-4666; Fax: 518-272-4666.
11—St. Paul the Apostle, Rev. James McNerney. In Res., Rev. Joseph Halloran.
Res.: 2238 Twelfth St., 12180. Tel: 518-274-4083; Fax: 518-274-4289.
12—St. Peter, [CEM] Rev. James McNerney.
Res.: 2310 Fifth Ave., 12180. Tel: 518-272-2750; Fax: 518-272-2751.
Catechesis/Religious Program—Students 15.
13—Sacred Heart, Revs. Gary Mercure; James Vaughan, Pastor Emeritus.
Res.: 310 Spring Ave., 12180. Tel: 518-274-1363; Fax: 518-274-8720.
School—308 Spring Ave., 12180. Tel: 518-274-3655; Fax: 518-274-8270. Susan Holland, Prin. Lay Teachers 18; Students 249.
14—St. Williams, Rev. Gary Mercure; Sr. Rita Duggan, C.S.J., Admin.
Parish Office—310 Spring Ave., 12180. Tel: 518-273-1680.
Ushers, Saratoga Co., Corpus Christi, Rev. Martin J. Fisher; Deacons Michael Sheppeck; John Tierney; Frank Herlihy.
Mailing Address: P.O. Box 628, Round Lake, 12151-0628.
Res.: 10 Southwood Dr., Ballston Lake, 12019-1302. Tel: 518-877-8506 (Office); Fax: 518-877-5620 (Office).
Catechesis/Religious Program—Tel: 518-877-8506, Ext. 302. Susan Sweeney, D.R.E. Students 900.
Valatie, Columbia Co., St. John the Baptist, [CEM] Rev. John Molyn.
Res.: 1025 Kinderhook St., 12184. Tel: 518-758-9401; Fax: 518-758-9409.
Catechesis/Religious Program—Tel: 518-758-1828. Connie Smith, D.R.E. Students 521.
Voorheesville, Albany Co., St. Matthew, Rev. Arthur A. Toole.
Res.: 25 Mountain View St., 12186. Tel: 518-765-2805; Fax: 518-765-3701.
Walton, Delaware Co., St. John the Baptist, Rev. Michael Flannery; Deacon Thomas O'Connell.
Mailing Address: 25 Benton Ave., 13856-0315.
Res.: 15 Benton Ave., 13856-0315. Tel: 607-865-7394.
Catechesis/Religious Program—Rev. Michael Flannery, D.R.E. Students 61.
Mission—Holy Family Downsville, Delaware Co.
Warrensburg, Warren Co., St. Cecilia, [CEM] Sr. Linda Hogan, C.S.J., Parish Life Dir.
Res.: 3802 Main St., 12885-1629. Tel: 518-623-3021.
Waterford, Saratoga Co.
1—St. Anne, Closed., For inquiries for parish records, contact St. Mary of the Assumption, Waterford.
2—St. Mary of the Assumption, [CEM] Revs. David Kelley, O.S.A.; Daniel J. Menihane, O.S.A. In Res., Rev. J. Riley Havener, O.S.A.
Res.: 119 Broad St., 12188-2397. Tel: 518-237-3131; Fax: 518-237-9625.
School—St. Mary's Catholic School, 12 Sixth St., 12188. Tel: 518-237-0652; Fax: 518-233-0898. Mr. John E. Houlihan, Prin. Lay Teachers 22; Students 365.
Catechesis/Religious Program—Paul Ruggeri, D.R.E. Faith Formation Program is located at St. Mary of the Assumption Students 32.
Watervliet, Albany Co.
1—St. Brigid, Rev. Joseph Busch.
Res.: 695 Fifth Ave., 12189. Tel: 518-273-2913.
School—700 Fifth Ave., 12189. Tel: 518-273-3321; Fax: 518-273-9355. Patricia Eldridge, Prin. (Regional) Sisters 3; Lay Teachers 18; Students 215.
2—Immaculate Conception, (Polish), [CEM] Carol Pickel, Parish Life Dir.; Rev. Paul J. Antos (Retired). In Res., Rev. Boleslaus M. Watroba, Pastor Emeritus (Retired).
Res.: 2420 Seventh Ave., 12189. Tel: 518-273-3173.
Convent—2425 Seventh Ave., 12189. Tel: 518-273-4423.
3—Our Lady of Mt. Carmel, (Italian), Rev. Emery Parillo, O.F.M.
Res.: 410 23rd St., 12189. Tel: 518-273-2932.
Catechesis/Religious Program—Mary Sorell, D.R.E. Students 113.
4—St. Patrick, Rev. Erwin H. Schweigardt.
Res.: 515 19th St., Box 388, 12189. Tel: 518-273-2971; Fax: 518-273-2972.
5—Sacred Heart of Mary, Rev. John J. Rooney.
Res.: 1511 Sixth Ave., 12189. Tel: 518-273-6252.
West Taghkanic, Columbia Co., Holy Cross, Rev. Raymond Ethier, Admin.
Res.: 880 Rte. 82, Elizaville, 12523. Tel: 518-851-7577.
Catechesis/Religious Program—Jo Ann Hayes, D.R.E. Students 60.
West Winfield, Herkimer Co., St. Joseph, [CEM] Rev. Terence P. Healy; Deacons Richard Brown; Michael Carbone.
Res.: 305 W. Main St., 13491-0360. Tel: 315-822-3191.
Whitehall, Washington Co.
1—Notre Dame des Victoires, Merged, with Our Lady of Angels, Whitehall to form Our Lady of Hope, Whitehall.
2—Our Lady of Angels, Merged, with Notre Dame des Victoires, Whitehall to form Our Lady of Hope, Whitehall
3—Our Lady of Hope, Rev. David R. LeFort.
Res.: 9 Wheeler Ave., 12887. Tel: 518-499-1656.
Catechesis/Religious Program—Tel: 518-499-1650; Fax: 518-499-2489. Bernie Perkins, D.R.E. Combined with Chapel of the Assumption Students 150.
Chapel—Assumption, Huletts Landing
Windham, Greene Co., St. Theresa of Child Jesus, Rev. James Schiffer, C.P.
Res.: Main St., 12496. Tel: 518-734-3352
Catechesis/Religious Program—Tel: 518-734-9685; Fax: 518-734-3352. Margaret Reinold Gulino, D.R.E. Students 128.
Mission—St. Joseph's Chapel Ashland, Greene Co.
Worcester, Otsego Co., St. Joseph, Rev. Edward Golding.
Res.: 181 Main St., 12197. Tel: 607-397-8373.
Mission—St. Mary [CEM] Schenevus, Otsego Co.
Wynantskill, Rensselaer Co., St. Jude the Apostle, Rev. James E. Clark.
Res.: 6 Schuyler Ct., P.O. Box 347, 12198. Tel: 518-283-1162; Fax: 518-286-2808.
School—Brookside Ave., 12198. Tel: 518 283-0333; Fax: 518-283-0475. Cathleen Carney, Admin. Lay Teachers 16; Students 170.

Chaplains of Public Institutions

Albany. *Albany County Jail*. Rev. Richard Broderick.
Albany County Nursing Home. Deacon Gerard O'Connor.
Albany Medical Center Hospital. Revs. Peter Tkocz, Kenneth Gregory, Robert E. de Leon, C.S.C.
Capital District Psychiatric Center. Rev. Joseph Cotugno, Deacon Charles Hall.
Columbia County Jail. Rev. Theodore Gerken.
Memorial Hospital. Rev. John T. Kelly.
New York State Department of Corrections. Rev. James Hayes, Chief of Chaplains.
St. Peter's Hospital. Rev. John Tallman, Chap., Bruce Swingle, Chap., Valerie Seyffert, Chap., David Dietsche, Chap., Sisters Joyce Houle, S.N.J.M., Chap., Patricia Mills, S.N.J.M., Chap., Mr. Younas Azad, Chap., Ms. Sally Conklin, Chap.
University Heights Nursing Home. Sr. Jane Carr, R.S.M., Chap.
Veterans' Administration Hospital. Rev. John Minkler.
Comstock. *Great Meadows Correctional Institution*. Ann Narcisso, Chap., Bros. Julian A. Davies, O.F.M., Sacramental Min., Dennis E. Tamburello, O.F.M., Sacramental Min.
Coxsackie. *Coxsackie Correctional Facility*. Rev. Richard Shaw, Sacramental Min., Deacon Angel Garcia, Chap.
Greene Correctional Facility. Rev. Richard Shaw.
Regional Medical Unit. Rev. John L. Moyna.
Glens Falls. *Glens Falls Hospital*. (Vacant)
Hudson Correctional Facility. Rev. Edward F. Cantwell, Chap.
Schenectady. *Ellis Hospital*. Rev. John N. Varno, Chap.
Hallmark Nursing Home. Deacon Earle Flatt, Chap.
Schenectady County Nursing Home. Sr. Clare Pelkey, C.S.J., Chap.
Troy. *Samaritan Hospital*. Rev. Michael Cournoyer, Deacon Frank Lukovits.
Seton Health. Rev. Michael Cournoyer, Deacon Albert Schrempf.
Van Rensselaer Manor. Rev. Thomas E. Konopka, Sacramental Min., Deacon Dana Ackerson, Chap.
Wilton. *Mount McGregor Correctional Facility*. Rev. Matthew T. Conlon, O.F.M., Sacramental Min., Lois Lippincott-Pino, Chap.

Special Assignment:
Rev.—
Gorman, William, c/o 2121 Fifteenth St., Troy, 12180.
Most Rev.—
Broderick, Edwin B., D.D. (Retired), 900 Park Ave., New York, 10021.
Revs.—
Berberian, David, Tribunal, 40 N. Main Ave., 12203.
Broderick, Richard J., Prison Chap., 330 Brownell Rd., Cambridge, 12816.
Cantwell, Edward F., Chap., Brookwood and Hudson Correctional Facility, 429 E. Allen St., Hudson, 12534.
Chiaramonte, Anthony, 790 Lancaster St., 12203. Consultation Center
Cotugno, Joseph, 40 N. Main Ave., 12203. Dir. Diaconate
DeGiovine, Christopher, 432 Western Ave., 12203. College of St. Rose
DeRose, Martin, 110 Evelyn Ave., Amsterdam, 12010.
Deimeke, L. Edward, Admin. Advocate for Priests, 40 N. Main Ave., 12203.
Donlon, James I., J.C.D., 40 N. Main Ave., 12203. Judicial Vicar, Tribunal, Pastoral Center
Falletta, Joseph, Hispanic/Latino Apostolate, One William St., P.O. Box 512, Kinderhook, 12106.
Farano, Michael A., Dir. Society of the Propagation of Faith, 2 Fairview Rd., Loudonville, 12211.
Gregory, Kenneth, Chap., Albany Medical Center, 12208.
Gulley, Anthony D., Prof. College of St. Rose, St. Mary's Rectory, 156 E. Main St., Amsterdam, 12010.
Hayes, James, Chief of Chaplains NYS Dept. of Corrections, St. Madeline Sophie, 3500 Carmen Rd., Schenectady, 12303.
Joslin, James R., Heritage Arms, 2 Tryon Ave., Apt. 237, Schenectady, 12302.
Kacerguis, Edward S., Slavin House, 2008 19th St., Troy, 12180.
Kane, James J., Dir., 40 N. Main Ave., 12203. Pastoral Center, Ecumenical & Interreligious Affairs
Kelly, John T., Chap. Memorial Hospital, 600 N. Blvd., 12010.
Konopka, Thomas E., Vocations Office, 40 N. Main Ave., 12203.
Longobucco, Robert, Chap., SUNY Albany, Chapel House, 12222.
Malecki, John, Chap., Teresian House, 200 Washington Ave. Extension, 12203-5394.
Marbury, Cabell B., Vice Prin. Bishop Maginn High School, 99 Slingerland St., 12202.
McCloskey, Francis, Charismatic Ministry, P.O. Box 223, East Durham, 12423.
Minkler, John, Chap. Veterans Administration Hospital, 113 Holland Ave., 12208.
Ntsiful-Amissah, Kofi, 50 Thornton St., 12206. Black Apostolate
O'Brien, Leo P., Vicar Gen., 900 Madison Ave., 12208.
Severson, Richard, Chap., Mt. McGregor Correctional Facility, P.O. Box 2264, 12866.
Shaw, Richard, Chap. Green Correctional Facility, St. Helen's Rectory, 1803 Union St., Schenectady, 12309.
Smith, Paul, 37 Parkwood St. E., 12203. Sacramental Min., St. Lucy's, Altamount
Son, Ignatius, Korean Apostolate, 10 Lodge St., 12207-2196.
Sullivan, Peter J., III, J.C.L., 40 N. Main Ave., 12203. Adjutant Vicar Judicial Tribunal, Pastoral Center
Tallman, John, Chap. St. Peter's Hospital, St. Catherine of Siena, 40 Collins Pl., 12208.
Testa, Richard (Retired), 512 Third Ave., Troy, 12182.
Tunny, Kenneth J., St. Paul's Rectory, 277 Albany St., Schenectady, 12304.

Vanban, Martin Tran, C.M.C, Vietnamese Apostolate, 10 Lodge St., 12207.
Varno, John N., Chap. Ellis Hospital, 1011 Nott St., Schenectady, 12308.
Vosko, Richard, Liturgical Design Consultant, 4611 Foxwood Dr., P.O. Box 2217, Clifton Park, 12605.
Walsh, James J., Vocation Office, 40 Main Ave., 12203.

On Duty Outside the Diocese:
Revs.—
Allie, Stanley J., Sacred Heart Church, 728 Peck St., Wasilla, AK 99654-6523.
Casey, Liam C., St. Francis Hospital, 114 Woodland St., Hartford, CT 06105.
Fragomeni, Richard, Chicago Theological Institute, 5401 S. Cornell Ave., Chicago, IL 60615-5698.
Hurst, Thomas R., S.S., Theological College, 401 Michigan Ave., N.E., Washington, DC 20017.
Nusbaum, Daniel C., Ph.D. (Retired), St. Elizabeth's Parish, 138 Goodell St., Wyandotte, MI 48192.
O'Grady, John F., S.S.D., S.T.D., 11300 N.E. Second Ave., Miami, FL 33161. Barry University
Polewczak, Michael J., Holy Trinity Parish, 2161 Griffith Dr., Orangeburg, SC 29118.
Redmond, Paul V., Mt. St. Mary College, P.O. Box 458, Emmitsburg, MD 21727.

Military Chaplains:
Revs.—
Estabrook, Joseph, Fleet Chap., Commander-in-Chief, Capt. CHC, USN, 2047 Nuuanu Ave., Unit 1304, Honolulu, HI 96817.
O'Keeffe, L. Joseph, 501 1st Division Rd., Fort Benning, GA 31905.
Rutherford, Donald L., 2 Alexander St., Fort Bragg, NC 28310.

Office of Administrative Advocate:
Revs.—
Bentley, David, 40 N. Main Ave., 12203.
McKay, Joseph, 40 N. Main Ave., 12203.

Leave of Absence:
Revs.—
Allman, Mark
Cioppa, Philip
Douglas, Louis
Harrison, Timothy
Jupin, Alan D.
Maione, Anthony
Opals, Donald
Rossi, Desmond
Tressic, David L.

Retired:
Rev. Msgr.—
Jones, John L., St. Teresa's Rectory, 435 New Scotland Ave., 12208-2397.
Revs.—
Ahern, Bernard, 4418 Poppy Tree Ln., Jacksonville, FL 32258.
Amato, Joseph, 5320 53rd St. E. V-16 Windmill Manor, Bradenton, FL 34203.
Antos, Paul J., 2420 Seventh Ave., Watervliet, 12189.
Baniak, Walter, 540 Second St., Troy, 12180.
Barker, Joseph, 316 Congress St., Troy, 12180.
Bondi, Paul, 167 Milton Ave., Ballston Spa, 12020.
Buckley, Robert, Our Lady of Mercy Life Center, 2 Mercy Ln., Guilderland, 12084.
Caldara, John N., 3028 Myrtle Ave., Schenectady, 12306.
Campagnone, Nicholas, Wesley Health Care Center, 131 Lawrence St., Hathorn Residence, Room 117, Saratoga Springs, 12866.
Ciani, Francis P., 856 Warner Rd., Valley Stream, 11580.
Clemente, Michael, 4906 Brittany Dr. S., Apt. #613, St. Petersburg, FL 33715.
Cox, Paul, P.O. Box 134, Kattskill Bay, 12844.
Crandall, William, 9 King St., Waterford, 12188.
Cronin, Brian, St. Paul the Apostle Rectory, 2777 Albany St., Schenectady, 12304.
Cyvas, Matthew, 555 68th Ave., St. Petersburg Beach, FL 33706.
D'Agostino, Joseph, 6 Bircher Ave., Poughkeepsie, 12601.
Daley, James D., 69 Murray Ave., Delmar, 12054.
De Franco, Anthony, 802 Union St., Schenectady, 12308.
De Pascale, Daniel, CDR, 2750 Blarrita Ct., Ponte Vedra Beach, FL 32802.
Delos, Bernard M., 11463 Waterview Cluster, Reston, VA 20190.
Di Cerbo, Almerico F., Teresian House, 200 Washington Ave. Ext., 12203.
DiMaggio, Joseph, Palatine Nursing Home, 154 Lafayette St., Palatine Bridge, 13428.
Donnelly, Robert, 103 Acorn Dr., Scotia, 12302.
Douglas, Louis, 1880 Superfine Ln., #8, Wilmington, DE 19802.
Downs, Richard J., 77 Crescent Dr., 12208.
Doyle, Donald, 178 E. Sanford St., Glens Falls, 12801.
Dunbar, Francis, 20 1/2 Williams St., Whitehall, 12887.
Esmond, William, Ledgewood Village, Rte. 149, 17 Ledgewood Dr., Lake George, 12845.
Fitzpatrick, Edward, 35 Joseph St., Saratoga Springs, 12866.
French, John F., 15 Priorslee Ln., Williamsburg, VA 23185.
Gilchrist, Francis J., 164 Broadway, Fort Edward, 12828.
Girzone, Joseph, 8 Leesome Ln., Altamont, 12209.
Grabys, Joseph, Matularitis Nursing Home, 10 Thurber Rd., Putnam, CT 06260.
Halloran, Joseph, St. Paul the Apostle Rectory, 138 12th St., Troy, 12180.
Ianotti, Pascal, 15 Steadwell Ave., Amsterdam, 12010.
Keyrouze, Joseph, Moran Nursing Home, 321 W. Sand Lake Rd., Rte. 150, Wynantskill, 12198.
Lamanna, Alfred, The Prospect Inn, 20 N. Prospect St., Apt. J, Herkimer, 13350.
Lemoyne, William, 29 Burgoyne St., Schuylerville, 12871.
Lynch, Patrick J., P.O. Box 68, Lansingburgh Sta., Troy, 12182.
Malecki, John, Teresian House, 200 Washington Avenue Ext., 12203.
Morrill, Giles, P.O. Box 6566, Delray Beach, FL 33482-6566.
Mulcahy, Howard J., Teresian House, 200 Washington Ave., Room #234, 12203.
Nabozny, Peter, 9 Morley Dr., Apt. F, Ballston Spa, 12020.
Nusbaum, Daniel C., Ph.D., St. Elizabeth's Parish, 138 Goodell St., Wyandotte, MI 48192.
O'Neill, James, 38 Middletown Rd., P.O. Box 421, Waterford, 12188.
Pereira, Cyril F., 3027 Sixth Ave., Troy, 12180.
Phelan, Thomas, 5 Whitman Ct., Troy, 12180.
Phillips, George, 347 Old Loudon Rd., Latham, 12110.
Piechocki, Raymond S., Mt. Loretto Rest Home, 301 Swart Hill Rd., Amsterdam, 12010.
Purcell, Robert, P.O. Box 169, Margaretville, 12455.
Roos, John, 203 Elm St., Apt. 7, Cobleskill, 12043.
Ryan, Edward J., P.O. Box 277, Stamford, 12167.
Shanley, Owen F., Broadalbin, 12025.
Sidoti, Anthony, 496 Delaware Ave., 12209.
Siniskey, Joseph M., 667 Columbia Tpke., East Greenbush, 12061.
Sipperly, Edward, c/o 1041 Loudon Rd., Cohoes, 12047.
St. John, George G., 608 Central Ave., 12206.
Starks, R. Mansfield, 400 Saratoga Rd., Scotia, 12302.
Tartaglia, Paul, 465 State St., 12203. (June-Nov.)
Testa, Richard, St. Joseph's Apartments, 2 Jeanne Jugan Ln., #5145, Latham, 12110.
Titta, Santino, 19 Juniper Pl., Grant City, 10306.
Tremblay, Nellis, P.O. Box 134, Kattskill Bay, 12844.
Vail, Thomas, 76 Moreland St., Little Falls, 13365.
Vaughan, James, 310 Spring Ave., Troy, 12180.
Watroba, Boleslaus M., 2420 Seventh Ave., Watervliet, 12189.
Zakens, Michael W., 28 Maplewood St., 12208.

Permanent Deacons:
Ackerson, Dana J., Van Rensselaer Manor Nursing Facility; St. Francis de Sales, Troy
Baechel, Kenneth, St. Gabriel, Rotterdam & Office of Prayer and Worship
Bazinet, William, St. Alphonsus, Glens Falls
Beck, Gary, St. Madeleine Sophie, Schenectady
Beckman, Martin L., St. Mary's, Ballston Spa
Boyd, Danny S., St. Therese Mission, Gansevoort
Brady, Robert, St. Joseph, Scotia; Glendale Nursing Home
Brett, William, Chap., Our Lady of Mercy Life Center, Guilderland
Brown, Richard Dr., St. Joseph, West Winfield
Canary, Arthur, (Retired)
Carbone, Michael S., Holy Family, Little Falls
Cechnicki, Joseph
Christiano, Gerald, St. Anthony, Troy
Cioppa, Richard, On Leave of Absence
Cohen, Andrew, St. Joan of Arc, Menands
Crane, John, Conifer Park, Scotia; St. Joseph's, Scotia
DeLorenzo, Joseph, Holy Family, Little Falls
DeMauro, Gerald, Family Life Office; St. James, Albany
Desormeaux, David, On Leave of Absence
Donnell, Michael, Sacred Heart, Sidney
Dringus, William, Holy Spirit Church, East Greenbush
Fitzgerald, William, Blessed Sacrament, Albany
Flatt, Earle, St. Madeleine Sophie & Hallmark Nursing Home Rotterdam
Gaffney, William, St. Vincent de Paul, Albany
Gallipeo, Paul, On Leave of Absence
Garcia, Angel, St. Patrick's Hispanic Community; Coxsackie Correctional
Gaul, William H., Jr., St. John Newman Residence, Saratoga Springs; Scouting
Gil, Joseph, (Retired)
Glennon, Dr. John E., Great Meadow Correctional Facility
Gorman, William A., D.Min., Ph.D., St. James, Albany
Grigaitis, Jerry, Liaison for Catholic Charimatic Renewal; St. Edward the Confessor, Cliffon Park
Gutierrez, Moises, St. Anthony's, Troy
Hall, Charles H., Capitol District Psychiatric Center, Albany
Hanson, Lee, Saratoga Hospital Nursing Home; St. Celement, Saratoga
Herlihy, Frank, Corpus Christi, Ushers; Sacred Heart, Lake George
Hewitt, William, St. Peter's, Saratoga; Crammer House, Saratoga
Hook, J. Neil, St. Margaret Mary, Albany
Jones, Dennis, St. Anthony and St. Joseph, Herkimer
Kratz, Russell J., On Leave of Absence
Ladouceur, Gerald J., St. Catherine of Siena, Albany
Leonard, Mark J., St. Madeleine Sophie, Schenectady
Luby, Thomas T., Rural Ministry, Sacred Heart, Sidney
Lukovits, Frank, St. Henry, Averill Park & Dir. Deacon Personnel
MacKinnon, Walter, St. Edward, Clifton Park
Maclutsky, John, Our Lady of Victory, Troy
Manno, Peter, St. Joseph's, Dolgeville
Mansfield, E. Gregory, Assumption-St. Paul's, Mechanicville
Manzella, Alfred R., St. Thomas, Delmar
Markham, Joseph, Christ the King, Albany; Family Life Office
Matthews, Gerard, Holy Trinity, Cohoes
McAuliffe, Timothy, Holy Cross, Albany; Dir. Deacon Administration
McDonald, Michael, Sacred Heart, Cairo; Diocesan Office of Pastoral Planning
McGarry, Frank, On Leave of Absence
Melanson, Michael, Immaculate Conception, Glenville
Monscko, Walter G., (Retired)
Nahm, George H., St. Clare's, Colonie
Neurohr, Helmut N., St. Ambrose, Latham
Novak, John W., (Retired)
O'Connell, Thomas
O'Connor, Gerard, Albany Co. Nursing Home
O'Neill, Charles, St. Mary's, Hudson
Pagano, Joseph, St. Francis, Northville; Youth Ministry
Pasquarelli, Robert, St. Henry's, Averill Park
Picher, Gary, Holy Infancy, Lake Luzerne
Powers, David F., St. Mary's, Glen Falls
Pudney, E. Jack, On Leave of Absence
Quinn, Peter, Immaculate Conception, New Lebanon
Raup, Konrad, Our Lady of Mercy, Colonie
Rehder, Walter, (Retired)
Roemer, Paul W., St. Patrick's, Catskill
Rucinski, Robert T., (Retired)
Santana, Richard, St. Joseph's, Greenfield Center
Scarletto, Frederick C., Our Lady of the Assumption, Schenectady; Youth Ministry
Schickel, Frank, Holy Cross, St. Mary and St. John the Evangelist, Schenectady
Schrempf, Albert G., Holy Trinity, Cohoes; Seton Health, Troy
Sedlmeir, Peter, St. John the Baptist, Greenville
Sharrow, Thomas, New York State Dept. of Corrections
Sheehan, George D., St. Peter, Delhi
Sheppeck, Michael, Corpus Christi, Ushers
Skelly, John, St. Mary's, Nassau; Our Lady of Mercy Life Center
Solar, Richard, (Retired)
South, Owen D., St. Paul the Apostle, Schenectady
Stosiek, Martin, St. Bridget's, Copake Falls; Diocesan Rural Affairs Coord.
Sullivan, Raymond, Cathedral of the Immaculate Conception, Albany
Surman, Dr. Gary, St. Vincent, Cobleskill
Szarejko, Walter, St. John the Baptist, Newport; Catholic Charities Aging Services
Tapia, Raymon, Sacred Heart, Schenectady
Taylor, Charles A., St. Edward the Confessor, Clifton Park; Diocesan Office of Canonical Services

Thiesen, Richard, Our Lady of Fatima, Delanson; Glendale Nursing Home
Tierney, John, Corpus Christi, Ushers
Trawinski, Peter, St. James, Chatham
Turcotte, Arthur W., (Retired)
VanPatten, August, (Retired)
Willette, Lawrence, St. Clement, Saratoga Springs
Wilson, Gerald, Unassigned
Witko, George, St. Mary, Albany
Wubbenhorst, Robert, Blessed Sacrament, Bolton Landing; Glens Falls Hospital
Yankowski, Frank, St. Michael, Troy; Eden Park, Troy
Zoltowski, Gregory, Our Lady of Grace, Ballston Lake

INSTITUTIONS LOCATED IN THE DIOCESE

[A] SEMINARIES, RELIGIOUS OR SCHOLASTICATES

CATSKILL. *St. Anthony Friary*, 24 Harrison St., P.O. Box 487, 12414. Tel: 518-943-3451; Fax: 518-943-1573. Revs. Michael Dominic W. Ledoux, O.F.M., Vicar; Owen Angeloni, O.F.M.; Frederick Fusco, O.F.M.; Valerian Faugno, O.F.M.; Albin Fusco, O.F.M.; Salvatore DeBenedictis, O.F.M.; James Tuxbury, O.F.M.; Alban V. Montella, O.F.M.; Bros. Fidelis DeBernardis, O.F.M.; Joseph Messina, O.F.M.; Lawrence Stumpo, O.F.M.; Vincent de Paul Ciaravino, O.F.M., Guardian, Dir. of Health Care. Order of Friars Minor

RENSSELAER. *Conventual Franciscan Friars Immaculate Conception Province*, Provincialate, Office of the Treasurer, P.O. Box 629, 12144. Tel: 518-472-1016; Fax: 518-472-1013. Email: PLininger@aol.com. Web: www.franaciscanseast.org. 517 Washington Ave., 12144. Order Friars Minor Conventual Priests 8; Brothers 2. In Res. Revs. Canice Connors, O.F.M.Conv., Min. Prov.; Briant Cullinane, O.F.M.Conv., Guardian; Firmin Finn, O.F.M.Conv., Chap.; Andre Lamont, O.F.M.Conv.; Rufino Maloney, O.F.M.Conv.; Duane Mastangelo, O.F.M.Conv., Chap.; Simon Mohr, O.F.M.Conv., Chap.; Germain Williams, O.F.M.Conv.; Bros. Stephen Merrigan, O.F.M.Conv., Archivist, Elder Care Dir.; Andre Picotte, O.F.M.Conv.

[B] COLLEGES AND UNIVERSITIES

ALBANY. *St. Bernard's School of Theology and Ministry at Albany*, Formerly St. Bernard's Institute at Albany Extension Program of St. Bernard's School of Theology and Ministry, Rochester, NY. , 40 N. Main Ave., 12203. Tel: 518-453-6760; Fax: 518-453-6793. Email: stbernardsinstitute@rcda.org. Dr. Joseph Piccolino, Dir. Graduate School of Theology & Ministry Studies.

The College of Saint Rose (Corporate Name) , 432 Western Ave., 12203. Tel: 518-454-5111; 800-637-8556; Fax: 518-458-5447. Web: www.strose.edu. Dr. Mark Sullivan, Pres.; Dr. William Lowe, Acting Vice Pres. Academic Affairs; Kathleen M. Sinel, Vice Pres. Fin. & Admin.; Kevin Carr, Vice Pres. Inst.Advancement; Charles E. Greene Jr., Assoc. Vice Pres. Admin.; Judith A. Kelly, Registrar; Dennis McDonald, Vice Pres. Student Svcs.; Mary Grondahl, Vice Pres. Enrollment Planning & Undergraduate Admissions; Revs. Christopher DeGiovine, Chap. & Dean Spiritual Life; Anthony D. Gulley, Non-Resident Priest. Founded by the Sisters of St. Joseph of Carondelet in 1920. Priests 2; Sisters 7; Lay Teachers 159; Students 4,441.

Maria College, 700 New Scotland Ave., 12208. Tel: 518-438-3111; Fax: 518-438-7170. Web: MariaCollege.edu. Sr. Laureen Fitzgerald, Pres.; Dr. Margie Byrd, Dean for Academic Affairs; Ms. Laurie Gilmore, Dir. Admissions; Ms. Deborah Corrigan, Dean Students; Mrs. Frances Bernard, Dir. Business Affairs; Revs. Paul R. Smith; Thomas F. Berardi. Two Year College Sisters of Mercy 7; Sisters of St. Joseph 1; Sisters of Notre Dame 1; Lay Teachers 32; Students 1,077.

LOUDONVILLE. *Siena College* 12211. Tel: 518-783-2300; Fax: 518-783-4293. Web: www.siena.edu. Revs. Kevin E. Mackin, O.F.M., Pres.; James Toal, O.F.M., Vice Pres.; Dr. Linda Richardson, Vice Pres. Academic Affairs; Paul Stec, Vice Pres. Fin. & Admin.; Dr. Gregory Stahl, Vice Pres. Inst. Advancement; Noel Hogan, Vice Pres. Enrollment & Planning; Ned Jones, Asst. Vice Pres. Admissions; Dr. Mary Ellen Gilroy, Vice Pres. Student Affairs; Suzanne Allegretti, Dir. Continuing & Professional Educ.; Rev. William Beaudin, O.F.M., Chap.; Mary Lawyer, Dir. Fin. Aid; William Kelley, Dir. of Physical Plant; James A. Serbalik, Registrar; Gary B. Thompson, Dir. of Library; Thomas Denham, Dir. of Career Center.

Legal Title: *Siena College*, Founded in 1937 by the Franciscan Friars, Order of Friars Minor, Province of the Most Holy Name of Jesus. Students 3,365.

The Friary: Revs. Callistus Bamberg, O.F.M.; William Beaudin, O.F.M.; Matthew T. Conlon, O.F.M.; James Czerwinski, O.F.M., Dir. St. Francis Chapel, Vicar; Julian A. Davies, O.F.M.; Daniel P. Dwyer, O.F.M.; Peter A. Fiore, O.F.M.; Capistran Hanlon, O.F.M.; Gerard Lee, O.F.M.; Kevin E. Mackin, O.F.M.; Henry L. Madden, O.F.M.; Daniel C. Nelson, O.F.M.; Sean O'Brien, O.F.M.; Kenneth Paulli, O.F.M.; Laurence P. Rainville, O.F.M.; Reginald J. Reddy, O.F.M.; Blaise R. Reinhart, O.F.M.; Sennen C San Fratello, O.F.M.; Dennis Tamburello, O.F.M.; James Toal, O.F.M.; John E. Van Hook, O.F.M.; Bros. Brian Belanger, O.F.M.; Romuald Chinetsky, O.F.M.; Thomas E. Conway, Vicar; Michael Harlan, O.F.M.; Gary Maciag, O.F.M.; Gerald Paciello, O.F.M.

[C] HIGH SCHOOLS, DIOCESAN

ALBANY. *Bishop Maginn High School*, 99 Slingerland St., 12202. Tel: 518-463-2247; Fax: 518-463-9880. Email: maginn@capital.net. Web: www.capital.net/~Maginn. Mr. Joseph Grasso, Prin.; Rev. Cabell B. Marbury, Vice Prin. Priests 1; Sisters 2; Lay Teachers 27; Students 360.

AMSTERDAM. *Bishop Scully High School*, Upper Church St., 12010. Tel: 518-842-4100.

GLENS FALLS. *St. Mary-St. Alphonsus Regional Catholic School*, 10-12 Church St., 12801. Tel: 518-792-3178; Fax: 518-792-6056. Email: albsmsa@rcdaschools.org. Rev. Philip Cioppa, Pastor. Lay Teachers 26; Students 315.

SARATOGA SPRINGS. *Saratoga Central Catholic High School*, (Grades 7-12), 247 Broadway, 12866. Tel: 518-587-7070; Fax: 518-587-0678. Email: scc@saratogacatholichigh.org. Web: www.saratogacatholichigh.org. Mr. Edwin Hammond Jr., Prin.; Rev. Christopher Welch. Lay Teachers 24; Students 240.

SCHENECTADY. *Notre Dame-Bishop Gibbons School*, (Grades 6-12) , (Coed) , 2600 Albany St., 12304. Tel: 518-393-3131; Fax: 518-370-3817 Email: info@ndbg.org. Richard A. Bahan, Prin. Conducted by the Congregation of Christian Brothers. Brothers 2; Sisters 1; Lay Teachers 38; Students 397.

TROY. *Catholic Central High School*, (Grades 7-12), 625 Seventh Ave., 12182. Tel: 518-235-7100; Fax: 518-237-1796. Email: cchsprincipal@yahoo.com. Web: www.cchstroy.org. Michael Piatek Jr., Prin. Sisters 3; Lay Teachers 40; Students 550.

[D] HIGH SCHOOLS, PRIVATE

ALBANY. *Academy of the Holy Names Upper, Middle and Lower Schools*, 1073 New Scotland Rd., 12208. Tel: 518-438-7895; Fax: 518-438-7368. Email: sccasey@ahns.org. Sr. Constance Casey, S.N.J.M., Pres. (PreK-12); Ms. Mary Anne Vigliante, Prin. (Grades 9-12); Dr. Lauretta McGuirk, Prin. (Grades PreK-8). Sisters 10; Lay Teachers 72; Students 560.

The Christian Brothers' Academy of Albany, 12 Airline Dr., 12205. Tel: 518-452-9809; Fax: 518-452-9804. Email: mcguired@cba-albany.org. Web: www.cba-albany.org. Mr. David McGuire, Prin. Brothers of the Christian Schools, JROTC College Prep. Program. Brothers 7; Lay Teachers 38; Students 51[illegible].

The Doane Stuart School, (Grades N-12) , Ecumenical Day School. Coed. , 12202. Tel: 518-465-5222; Fax: 518-465-5230. Web: www.doanestuart.org. Religious of the Sacred Heart and the Episcopal Diocese of Albany Faculty 31; Students 276.

Mercy High, Private School for Girls, c/o 40 N. Main Ave., 12203.

LOUDONVILLE. *Saint Gregory's School*, 121 Old Niskayuna Rd., 12211. Tel: 518-785-6621; Fax: 518-782-1364. Email: marrao@saintgregorysschool.org. Francis X. Foley Jr., Headmaster.

TROY. *LaSalle Institute*, 174 Williams Rd., 12180. Tel: 518-283-2500; Fax: 518-283-6265. Email: info@lasalleinstitute.org. Web: www.lasalleinstitute.org. Bro. Christopher Belleman, F.S.C., Prin. Brothers of the Christian Schools Priests 1; Brothers 3; Sisters 1; Lay Teachers 54; Students 657.

[E] ELEMENTARY SCHOOLS, PRIVATE

LOUDONVILLE. *Saint Gregory's School*, 121 Old Niskayuna Rd., 12211-1399. Tel: 518-785-6621; Fax: 518-782-1364. Email: marrao@saintgregorysschool.org. Web: www.saintgregoryschool.org. Francis X. Foley Jr., Headmaster. An independent Catholic day school for boys staffed by laity (Nursery-8). Girls admitted in Nursery through Kindergarten classes. Lay Teachers 24; Students 176.

[F] CONSOLIDATED ELEMENTARY SCHOOLS

ALBANY. *Cathedral Academy*, 75 Park Ave., 12202. Tel: 518-449-5232.

COHOES. *Cohoes Catholic School*, One St. Marie's Ln., 12047. Tel: 518-235-5202; Fax: 518-235-8568. Email: albccs@rcdaschools.org. Web: www.cohoescatholic.org. Mrs. Jane Kromm, Prin. Lay Teachers 12; Students 73.

GLEN FALLS. *St. Mary's/St. Alphonsus Regional Catholic School*, 12 Brookwood Dr., Queensbury, 12804. Tel: 518-792-3178; Fax: 518-792-6056. Email: albsmsa@rcdaschools.org. Mr. Roger Marcy, Prin.

WATERFORD. *St. Mary's School*, (Grades PreK-8), 12 Sixth St., 12188. Tel: 518-237-0652; Fax: 518-233-0898. Email: stmarys1@nycap.rr.com. Web: www.smswaterford.org. Jack Houlihan, Prin. Lay Teachers 20; Students 318.

[G] RESIDENTIAL INSTITUTIONS FOR CHILDREN & ADOLESCENTS

ALBANY. *Saint Anne Institute*, 160 N. Main Ave., 12206. Tel: 518-437-6500; Fax: 518-437-6555. Email: rriccio@s-a-i.org. Web: www.stanneinstitute.org. Richard C. Riccio, Exec. Dir. Residential and Community-based Preventive Service Center. Regents accredited and certified junior and senior H.S. for the emotionally handicapped and Preschool program for 3-4 year olds who are speech impaired and emotionally disturbed. Residential care and Day Treatment for young women ages 12-18. Family Services, Vocational Training, Sex Abuse Prevention and Juvenile Sex Offender Programs for male and female adolescents in crisis and their families. Residential 129; Day Treatment 40; Juvenile Sex Offender & Sex Abuse Prevention Families 90.

Saint Catherine's Center for Children, 40 N. Main Ave., 12203. Tel: 518-453-6700; Fax: 518-453-6712. Web: www.st-cath.org. Ms. Helen Hayes, Exec. Dir. Residential and day treatment, group homes and foster family programs for children with special needs. Community based prevention programs; Parent aides; Parent Training; Transitional Program for Homeless Families. Individuals assisted 1,250.

The Foundation for St. Catherine's Center for Children Albany, NY 12203.

LaSalle School, Inc., 391 Western Ave., 12203. Tel: 518-242-4731; Fax: 518-242-4747. Email: information@lasalle-school.org. Web: www.lasalle-school.org. Mr. William Wolff, Exec. Dir. Residential and day programs, independent living program, sexual victim/offender program, licensed substance abuse treatment program, and preventative services for boys (ages 12-18) and their families in New York State. Registered New York State Junior and Senior High School and certified School of Special Education. Brothers of the Christian Schools 8; Prevention Families 64; Resident Students 83; Day Students 44; Community Connections 21.

The La Salle School Foundation of Albany Tel: 518-242-4731; Fax: 518-242-4744.

WATERVLIET. *St. Colman's Home* 12189. Tel: 518-273-4911; Fax: 518-273-3312. Sr. Mary Regina, Dir.; Rev. Kenneth Gregory, Chap. Sisters of the Presentation of the B.V.M. Children 45.

[H] GENERAL HOSPITALS

ALBANY. *St. Peter's Health Care Services*, 315 S. Manning Blvd., 12208. Tel: 518-525-1550; Fax: 518-525-1520. Email: sboyle@stpetershealthcare.org. Web: www.stpetershealthcare.org. Mr. Steven P. Boyle, Pres. & CEO; Rev. John Tallman, Chap. Bed Capacity 437; Patients Assisted Annually 193,077.

The Community Hospice, 295 Valley View Blvd., Rensselaer, 12144. Tel: 518-285-8100; 800-678-0711. Sr. Jean Roche, R.S.M., Contact Person.

Our Lady of Mercy Life Center, 2240 Western Ave., Guilderland, 12084. Tel: 518-464-8100. Wesley I. Hale, Exec. Dir.

St. Peter's Addiction Recovery Center, 8 Mercycare Ln., Guilderland, 12084. Tel: 518-452-6700.

Villa Mary Immaculate, 301 Hackett Blvd., 12208. Tel: 518-525-7600. Renee P. Cassano, Exec. Dir.

AMSTERDAM. *St. Mary's Hospital*, 427 Guy Park Ave., 12010. Tel: 518-842-1900; Fax: 518-842-0107. Email: capobiancop@SMHA.org. Mr. Peter E. Capobianco, Pres. & CEO; Revs. Joseph J. Dworak, Chap.; Gregory Weider. Sisters of St. Joseph of Carondelet 14; Bed Capacity 143; Patients Assisted Annually 191,673.

SCHENECTADY. *St. Clare's Holding Company, Inc.*, 600

McClellan St., 12304. Tel: 518-347-5660; Fax: 518-347-5409. Email: jowens@stclares.org. Web: www.stclares.org.

St. Clare's Hospital, 600 McClellan St., 12304. Tel: 518-382-2000; Fax: 518-347-5522. Email: jowens@stclares.org. Web: stclares.org. Paul Chodkowski, Pres. & CEO; Rt. Rev. Richard J. Leskovar, Chap., Dir. Pastoral Care; Sisters Mary Elizabeth, S.N.J.M.; Theresa Hansen, S.S.N.D.; Miriam Natale, O.S.F. Bed Capacity 200; Patients Assisted Annually 166,165.

TROY. *Seton Health System, Inc.*, 1300 Massachusetts Ave., 12180. Tel: 518-268-5000; Fax: 518-268-5257. Email: info@setonhealth.org. Web: www.setonhealth.org. Mr. Gino J. Pazzaglini, FACHE - Pres. & CEO; Kathleen L. Sousa, Dir. Spiritual Care; Sr. De Chantal LaRow, D.C., Chm. Bd. of Directors.

Legal Title: *Seton Health System, Inc.* Daughters of Charity of St. Vincent de Paul Sisters 11; Bed Capacity 201; Patients Assisted Annually 315,000.

[I] SERVICES FOR ELDERLY

ALBANY. *St. Peter's Licensed Home Care Agency*, 310 S. Manning, 12208. Tel: 518-525-5858; Fax: 518-525-6002. Email: bsmith@stpetershealthcareservices.org. Sr. Jean McGinty, R.S.M.

GERMANTOWN. *Carmelite System for the Aged and Infirm, Inc.*, 646 Woods Rd., 12526-5617. Tel: 518-537-7500; Fax: 518-537-7501. Email: xsusansan@carmelitesystem.org. Web: Carmelitesystem.org. Reverend Mother Mary Suzanne Sapa, O.Carm., Chair.

[J] NURSING AND AGED HOMES

ALBANY. *McAuley Living Services*, 310 S. Manning Blvd., 12208. Tel: 518-437-8400; Fax: 518-437-8418. Email: mhulihan@stpetershealthcare.org. Sr. Maria Hulihan, R.N.M.S., Exec. Dir. Sisters of Mercy of the Americas - Albany Regional Community.

Teresian House (1974), 200 Washington Ave. Ext., 12203. Tel: 518-456-2000; Fax: 518-456-1142. Email: info@teresianhouse.com. Web: www.teresianhouse.com. Sisters Pauline Brecanier, O.Carm., Admin.; Joan Lewis, O.Carm., Coord. Pastoral Care; Rev. John Malecki, Chap. Carmelite Sisters for the Aged and Infirm, Corporate Title: Teresian House Nursing Home Co., Inc. Bed Capacity 300; Respit Beds 2.

Teresian House Foundation

Villa Mary Immaculate, 301 Hackett Blvd., 12208. Tel: 518-525-7600; Fax: 518-525-7673. Email: rcassano@stpetershealthcare.org. Web: www.stpetershealthcare.org. Renee Cassano Lampila, Exec. Dir.; Sisters Barbara Dudley, R.S.M.; Mary Bruce, C.S.J. S.N.F. and long term skilled care nursing home. Sponsored St. Peter's Health Care Services. Member of Catholic Health East. Sisters 2; Bed Capacity 160; Patients Assisted Annually 300.

AMSTERDAM. *Mt. Loretto Nursing Home*, 302 Swart Hill Rd., 12010. Tel: 518-842-6790; Fax: 518-843-5993. Email: mtloretto@superior.net. Web: www.MountLoretto.com. Sisters Patricia Anne Corbett, C.R., Admin.; Mary Lucille Borowski, C.R., Supr. & Chap.; Rev. Raymond S. Piechocki, Priest In Res. (Retired). Health Care Facility, 24 Hour Skilled Nursing Care, Hospice, IV Therapy & Rehab.; Conducted by the Sisters of the Holy Family of Nazareth and the Sisters of the Resurrection. Capacity 120.

CASTLETON. *Resurrection Nursing Home* 12033. Tel: 518-732-7617; Fax: 518-732-4211. Email: rnh@ix.netcom.com. Web: www.resnursinghome.org. Conducted by the Sisters of the Holy Family of Nazareth and the Sisters of Resurrection., Nursing Home (Established 1962).; Corporate Name: Resurrection Nursing Home, Inc. Bed Capacity 80.

CATSKILL. *St. Joseph's Villa Senior Living Services*, Formerly St. Joseph's Villa, 38 Prospect Ave., 12414. Tel: 518-943-5701; Fax: 518-943-5033. Email: carlasjv@mhcable.com. Web: www.sjvadulthome.org. Carla Erhartic, Admin. Franciscan Sisters of Allegany, NY, An Adult Care Facility for Men and Women, Adult Day Care Program, Respite.

GERMANTOWN. *Avila Institute of Gerontology, Inc.*, 600 Woods Rd., 12526. Tel: 518-537-5000; Fax: 518-537-4579. Email: avila@valstar.net. Sisters Teresa Stephen, O.Carm., Pres.; M. Peter Lillian, O. Carm., Dir. Carmelite Sisters for the Aged and Infirm

LATHAM. *Our Lady of Hope Residence*, Little Sisters of the Poor, Jeanne Jugan Ln., 12110. Tel: 518-785-4551; Fax: 518-785-3331. Email: lmmslsp@attglobal.net. Rev. Firmin Finn, O.F.M.Conv. Nursing Facility 35; Apartments for the Elderly 48.

[K] APARTMENTS FOR ELDERLY

ALBANY. *Bishop Broderick Apartments Housing Development Fund Co., Inc.* dba Bishop Broderick Apts. , 50 Prescott St., 12205. Tel: 518-869-7441; Fax: 518-869-0443. Email: mrjbba@aol.com. Web: www.depaulhousing.com. Mona Johnson, Bldg. Dir. Senior Citizen and Handicapped Housing.

C.S.C. Housing Development Fund Co., Inc. dba Sanderson Court Senior Apts. , 6 Carondelet Dr., Watervliet, 12189. Tel: 518-782-1123; Fax: 518-782-1125. Email: mkscsa@aol.com. Web: www.depaulhousing.com. Michele Kramm, Dir.

Cusack Community Service Corporation, 40 N. Main Ave., 12203. Tel: 518-459-0183; Fax: 518-459-0202. Email: Deborah.DammOBrien@rcda.org.

DePaul Housing Management Corp., 41 N. Main Ave., 12203. Tel: 518-459-0183; Fax: 518-459-0202. Email: Deborah.DammOBrien@rcda.org. Web: www.depaulhousing.com. Deborah Damm O'Brien, Exec. Dir.; Jill McLellan Phelps, Dir. Operations. Managing diocesan sponsored housing for persons who are elderly or mobility impaired.

Rotterdam Housing Development Fund Co., Inc., c/o 41 N. Main Ave., 12203. Tel: 518-459-0183. E. Byrl Moore, Admin.; Deborah Damm-O'Brien, Admin.

St. Vincent Apartments Housing Development Fund Co., Inc. dba St. Vincent's Apts. , 475 Yates St., 12208. Tel: 518-482-8915; Fax: 518-489-1220. Email: ldcmrmsva@aol.com. Web: www.depaulhousing.com. Lorraine Caroccia, Bldg. Dir. Senior Citizen and Handicapped Housing. Total Apartments 59; Total Staff 4.

CLIFTON PARK. *Halfmoon Housing Development Fund Co., Inc.* dba Bishop Hubbard Senior Apartments , 54 Katherine Dr., 12065. Tel: 518-383-2705; Fax: 518-383-6350. Email: jmsbhsa@aol.com. Web: www.depaulhousing.com. Total Apartments 49; Total Staff 2.

LATHAM. *LSOP Housing, Inc.*, One Jeanne Jugan Ln., 12110. Tel: 518-785-4551; Fax: 518-785-4551. Email: lmmsl@attglobal.net. Sr. Maureen Weiss, L.S.P., Pres.

NORTH GREENBUSH. *S.J. Housing Development Fund Company, Inc.* dba St. Jude's Apartments , 50 Dana Ave., Wynantskill, 12198. Tel: 518-283-5690; Fax: 518-283-5893. Web: www.depaulhousing.com. Nonprofit housing facility for elderly and handicapped persons of very low income. Apartments 49.

RENSSELAER. *East Greenbush Housing Development Fund Co., Inc.* dba Branson Manor Senior Apartment , 3 Grandview Dr., 12144. Tel: 518-283-8280; Fax: 518-283-8292. Web: www.depaulhousing.com.

SCHENECTADY. *LCS Housing Development Fund Company, Inc.* dba The Lawrence Commons , 2660 Albany St., 12304. Tel: 518-346-2686; 518-393-2412; Fax: 518-346-2686. Email: mrjbba@aol.com. Web: www.depaulhousing.com. Mona Johnson, Bldg. Dir. Apartments 12; Staff 4.

SLINGERLANDS. *Marie-Rose Manor HDFCI* dba Marie Rose Manor , 100 Marquis Dr., 12159. Tel: 518-459-0204; Fax: 518-459-0527. Email: ldcmrmsva@aol.com. Web: www.depaulhouseing.com. Lorraine Caroccia, Bldg. Dir. Senior Citizen and Handicapped Housing. Total Apartments 49; Total Staff 4.

WATERVLIET. *Delatour Housing Development Fund Company, Inc.* dba Carondelet Commons Senior Apartments , 2 Carondelet Dr., 12189. Tel: 518-783-0444; Fax: 518-783-0456. Web: www.depaulhousing.com. Sharie Gregware, Bldg. Dir.

Fontbonne Manor Housing Development Fund Company, Inc. dba Fontbonne Manor Senior Apts. , 10 Carodelet Dr., 12189. Tel: 518-782-2780; Fax: 518-782-2778. Email: mkscsa@aol.com. Web: www.depaulhousing.com. Michele Kramm, Bldg. Dir.

Italian-American Housing Development Fund Co., Inc. dba Cabrini Acers Senior Apts. , 4 Carondelet Dr., 12189. Tel: 518-785-0050; Fax: 518-785-0110. Web: www.depaulhousing.com. Sharie Gregware, Bldg. Dir.

[L] MONASTERIES AND RESIDENCES OF PRIESTS AND BROTHERS

ALBANY. *Vincentian Fathers Residence*, 110 Menands Rd., 12204-1499. Tel: 518-433-1003. Email: svinz@nycap.rr.com. Rev. Stephen J. India, C.M., Supr. Priests 1.

LAKE GEORGE. *St. Mary of the Lake*, P.O. Box 31, 12845. Tel: 518-668-5594. c/o 40 N. Main Ave., 12203. Rev. Ken McGuire, Dir. Summer retreat of the Paulist Fathers.

RENSSELAER. *Franciscan Mission House*, Washington Ave., 12144. Tel: 518-465-0062; Fax: 518-465-3673. Email: frhenryfma@att.net. Web: www.thefma.org. Most Rev. Henry Madigan, O.F.M.Conv., Guardian; Revs. Antone Kandrac, O.F.M.Conv.; Angelus Netzer, O.F.M.Conv.; Giles Van Wormer, O.F.M.Conv.; Bro. Leo Merriman, O.F.M.Conv. Promotion Center for Order's Missions.

Provincialate, Immaculate Conception Friary - Order of Friars Minor Conventual (1872), (Immaculate Conception Province) , P.O. Box 629, 12144. Tel: 518-472-1000; Fax: 518-472-1013. Email: caniceofmc@aol.com. Web: www.franciscanseast.org. Revs. Canice Connors, O.F.M.Conv., Min. Prov.; Briant Cullinane, O.F.M.Conv., Guardian; Rufino Maloney, O.F.M.Conv.; Firman Finn, O.F.M.Conv., Chap.; Germain Williams, O.F.M.Conv.; Simon Mohr, O.F.M.Conv.; Duane Mastangelo, O.F.M.Conv., Archivist; Andre Lambert, O.F.M.Conv.; Bros. Stephen Merrigan, O.F.M.Conv., Elder Care Dir.; Andre Picotte, O.F.M.Conv. (Corporate Name: Order Minor Conventuals, Inc.)

SARATOGA SPRINGS. *St. John Neumann Residence*, 233 Lake Ave., 12866-2729. Tel: 518-584-7500; Fax: 518-581-8421. Very Rev. Arthur P. Gildea, C.SS.R., Rector; Revs. George H. Bridge, C.SS.R.; Robert Gaugler, C.SS.R.; Thomas F. O'Toole, C.SS.R.; Richard Knappik, C.SS.R.; Vincent J. Kelly, C.SS.R. (BO); Andrew Skeabeck, C.SS.R. (TR); Edward Dunne, C.SS.R. (BRK); Joseph Oppitz, C.SS.R.; John Salamon, C.SS.R.; Charles Fehrenbach; James Ferris, C.SS.R.; Edward Tardiff, C.SS.R.; Donald Bolton, C.SS.R. (ORL); Francis Freel, C.SS.R.; George Deimel, C.SS.R.; William Heanue, C.SS.R.; John O'Toole, C.SS.R. (PH); William Biffar, C.SS.R.; Charles Gildea, C.SS.R.; Joseph Buono, C.SS.R.; George Drew, C.SS.R.; John Graham, C.SS.R.; John Drum, C.SS.R.; Bros. Barnabas Hipkins, C.SS.R.; Francis Alfone, C.SS.R.; John Bosco Hammond, C.SS.R.; David Skarda, C.SS.R.; Gilbert Hunter, C.SS.R. Redemptorist Priests and Brothers of the Baltimore Province

VALATIE. *St. Joseph Center* Residence for retired Holy Cross Brothers and Priests. , 495 Maple Ln., 12184. Tel: 518-784-9481; Fax: 518-784-9494. Email: regilroy@yahoo.com. Rev. Robert E. deLeon, C.S.C., Pastoral Care Albany Medical Center & Chap.; Bros. Robert Gilroy, C.S.C., Supr.; Peter A. Martin, C.S.C., Admin. In Res. Rev. James P. Madden, C.S.C.

[M] CONVENTS AND RESIDENCES FOR SISTERS

ALBANY. *Franciscan House, Mill Hill Sisters* Regional House , 1006 Madison Ave., 12208-2600. Tel: 518-482-1991; Fax: 518-482-8320. Sr. Joan Kerley, F.M.S.J., Regl. Sisters 5.

Religious of the Sacred Heart, Kenwood Convent of the Sacred Heart, 799 S. Pearl St., 12202. Tel: 518-465-3341; Fax: 518-465-3663. Email: mcanty@rscj.org. Web: www.rscj.org. Rev. James Donlon, Chap.; Sisters Margaret Mary Canty, R.S.C.J., Campus Admin.; Marie Buonato, R.S.C.J., Area Dir.; Martha Curry, R.S.C.J., Dir. Community; Karen O'Rourke, Dir. Nursing. Corporate Name: Female Academy of the Sacred Heart Sisters 82.

Sisters of Mercy of the Americas Albany Regional Community, 310 S. Manning Blvd., 12208. Tel: 518-437-3000; Fax: 518-437-3030. Email: bhines@mercyalbany.org. Web: www.mercyalbany.org. Sisters Katherine Graber, R.S.M., Pres.; Helen Dillon, R.S.M., Councilor; Jane Somerville, R.S.M., Councilor. Administrative Offices of Sisters of Mercy. Sisters 143.

Sisters of the Holy Names of Jesus and Mary, Province Center, 1061 New Scotland Ave., 12208-1198. Tel: 518-489-5469; Fax: 518-489-5804. Email: khughes@snjmny.org. Web: www.snjmny.org. Sr. Barbara Pavlic, S.N.J.M., Province Dir. (Corporate Name: Sisters of the Holy Names of Jesus and Mary of the New York Province, Inc.)

Academy of the Holy Names of New York, 1075 New Scotland Ave., 12208. Tel: 518-438-7895; Fax: 518-438-7368.

CASTLETON-ON-HUDSON. *Provincial House, Juniorate and Novitiate of the Sisters of Resurrection*, 35 Boltwood Ave., 12033-1097. Tel: 518-732-2226; Fax: 518-732-2898. Email: crsister@resurrectionsisters.org. Web: www.resurrectionsisters.org. Sisters Cecilia Mary Berdar, C.R., Prov. Supr.; Mary Lucille Borowski, C.R., Local Supr.; Dolores Palermo, C.R., Dir. Novices. Sisters 24.

Chaplain's Residence, 34 Boltwood Ave., 12033.

Retreat and Vacation Home, 325 Madonna Lake Rd., Cropseyville, 12052-1819. Tel: 518-279-1673.

GERMANTOWN. *St. Teresa's Motherhouse*, Avila on the Hudson, 600 Woods Rd., 12526-5639. Tel: 518-537-5000; Fax: 518-537-5226. Sr. M. Suzanne Sapa, O.Carm., Supr. Gen.; Rev. Joseph E. Finch, Chap. Carmelite Sisters for the Aged and Infirm,

Motherhouse and Novitiate. Sisters 28; Novices 1.

Postulation Office Tel: 518-537-5000; Fax: 518-537-5226. Sr. M. Angeline Teresa, O.Carm., Servant of God; Rev. Mario Esposito, O.Carm.; Sr. M. Gabriel, O.Carm., Coord. of the Cause.

LATHAM. *Provincial House of the Sisters of St. Joseph of Carondelet (Albany Province)* 12110-4799. Tel: 518-783-3500; Fax: 518-783-5209. Web: www.csjalbany.org. Rev. Geoffrey D. Burke, Chap.; Sisters Lauren Vandermark, C.S.J., Province Leadership Team; Danielle Bonetti, C.S.J., Province Leadership Team; Laura Anne Bufano, C.S.J., Province Leadership Team; Christine Partisano, C.S.J., Province Leadership Team; Mary Catherine Ryan, C.S.J., Province Leadership Team; Miriam Dorothy Ukeritis, C.S.J., Province Leadership Team. Sisters 507.

MENANDS. *De Paul Provincial House* (Corporate Name: Daughters of Charity of St. Vincent de Paul, N.E. Prov.) , 96 Menand Rd., 12204. Tel: 518-462-5593; Fax: 518-462-5024. Email dcinfo@dc-northeast.org. Web: www.dc-northeast.org. Sr. Mary Francis Martin, Prov. Supr.; Rev. Thomas Casella, C.M., Prov. Dir.

SCHENECTADY. *Monastery of St. Teresa of Jesus of Discalced Carmelites*, 428 Duane Ave., 12304. Tel: 518-346-4752. Sr. Mary St. John of the Cross, O.C.D., Prioress. Professed Sisters 12.

WATERVLIET. *St. Colman's Convent* 12189. Tel: 518-273-4911; Fax: 518-273-3312. Sr. M. Carmel, P.B.V.M., Mother Gen.; Rev. Kenneth Gregory, Chap. Motherhouse and Novitiate of Sisters of the Presentation of the B.V.M.

[N] HOUSES OF PRAYER AND RETREAT HOUSES

ALBANY. *Abba House of Prayer* A nonprofit corporation. , 647 Western Ave., 12203. Tel: 518-438-8320. Email: abba.house@verizon.net.

AURIESVILLE. *Jesuit Retreat House at Auriesville* Tel: 518-853-3033; Fax: 518-853-3051. Email: info@martyrshrine.org. Web: www.martyrshrine.org. *Shrine of Our Lady of Martyrs*, c/o Rev. John G. Marzolf, S.J., 12016.

Shrine of Our Lady of Martyrs 12016. Tel: 518-853-3033; Fax: 518-853-3051. Email: info@martyrshrine.org. Web: www.martyrshrine.org. Revs. John G. Marzolf, S.J., Supr. & Dir.; John J. Paret, S.J., Asst. Dir. & Vice Postulator Cause of Kateri Tekakwitha; Peter J. Murray, S.J. National Shrine of the Jesuit Martyrs of North America. Priests 3.

CHESTERTOWN. *The Priory of St. Benedict, Inc.*, Formerly The Priory, 135 Priory Rd., P.O. Box 336, 12817-0336. Tel: 518-494-3733; Fax: 518-494-3733. Email: prioryretreat@aol.com. Web: www.prioryretreathouse.com. Sisters Constance M. Messitt, C.S.J., Dir.; Francis Anne Gilchrist, C.S.J., Co-Dir.

FONDA. *Blessed Kateri Guest House*, Rte. 5, P.O. Box 627, 12068. Tel: 518-853-3646; Fax: 518-853-3371. Email: katerishrine@nycap.rr.com. Web: www.katerishrine.com. Rev. Kevin Kenny, O.F.M.Conv., Dir.

GLEN FALLS. *Wellsprings*, 93 Maple St., P.O. Box 406, Glens Falls, 12801. Tel: 518-745-8714; Fax: 518-792-3184. Email: info@wsprings.org. Web: www.wsprings.org. Sr. Margaret Picha, S.S.N.D., Dir.; Michael Laratonda, F.M.S., Assoc. Dir. A Program for Christian Members.; Holistic Sabbatical/Renewal/Retreat Center

MIDDLEBURGH. *Bethany Ministries*, 176 Mill Ln., P.O. Box 420, 12212. Tel: 518-827-4699. Email: bethmin@midtel.net. Web: www.midtel.net/~bethmin.

PARADOX. *Pyramid Life Center* Corporation name: Albany Catholic Youth Association, Inc. , 12858. Tel: 518-585-7545; Fax: 518-585-7545. Email: monicaplc@aol.com. Web: www.pyramidlife.com. Summer, fall and winter retreat house, located at Pyramid Lake.

SCHENECTADY. *Dominican Retreat and Conference Center*, Formerly Dominican Spiritual Life Center, 1945 Union St., 12309. Tel: 518-393-4169; Fax: 518-393-4525. Email: dslcny@nycap.rr.com. Web: www.dslcny.org. Jeanne Qualters, Exec. Dir. Residence Facilities for 45; Non-resident Facilities for 90 to 100.

STILLWATER. *Still Point Interfaith Retreat House*, Rte. 423, Box 53, 12170. Tel: 518-587-4967; Fax: 518-587-4967. Email: stillpt423@aol.com. Web: www.stillpointretreatcenter.org. Sr. Lillian Needham, S.S.J., Dir.

UNADILLA. *Gilead, Inc.*, 1011 State Hwy. 7, 13849. Tel: 607-563-3713. Email: tngilead@aol.com. Web: www.gilead.org. Eucharistic Community

VALATIE. *St. Joseph Center*, Formerly St. Joseph Spiritual Life Center, 495 Maple Ln., 12184. Tel: 518-784-9481; Fax: 518-784-9494. Email: bcmcsc@berk.com. Bros. Francis Feeley, Dir.; Peter Martin, C.S.C., Admin.; Renatus Foldenauer, C.S.C., Dir. Retreats.

[O] YOUTH TREATMENT FACILITIES

ALBANY. *Hospitality House Therapeutic Community Inc.*, 271 Central Ave., 12206. Tel: 518-434-6468; Fax: 518-434-6302. Email: lbecker@hospitalityhouse.info. A private, not-for-profit, residential treatment program for young people, 16 years or older, with a history of drug and/or substance abuse.

ALTAMONT. *Bernard and Caroline Cobb Memorial School*, 100-300 Mt. Presentation Way., 12009. Tel: 518-861-6446; Fax: 518-861-5228. Email: cobbschool@msn.com. Web: www.timesunion/communities/cobbschool. 12 month special education program for students 5-21 years.

[P] SHRINES

ALTAMONT. *La Salette Shrine* Leesome Ln., P.O. Box 680, 12009-0680. Tel: 518-861-8159; Fax 518-861-7052. Email: shrine.admin@lasalette.com. Web: www.lasalette.com. Rev. Jeffrey L'Arche, M.S., Dir.; Bro. Anthony Casso, M.S., Asst. Dir. Corporate Titles: Missionaries of Our Lady of La Salette Inc., Altamont, NY; La Salette Seminary, Altamont, NY.

FONDA. *The National Shrine of Blessed Kateri Tekakwitha and Friary* P.O. Box 627, 12068. Tel: 518-853-3646; Fax: 518-853-3371. Email: katerishrine@nycap.rr.com. Web: www.katerishrine.com. Bros. Kevin Kenny, O.F.M.Conv., Shrine Dir. & Guardian; James Amrhein, O.F.M.Conv., Assoc. Dir.; Patrick Gallagher, O.F.M.Conv., Local Pastor In Res. Bro. Leon Dicks, O.F.M.Conv., Assoc. Pastor.

[Q] CAMPUS MINISTRY

ALBANY. *New York State University at Albany* , (Albany Collegiate Interfaith Center, Inc.) with offices at Albany-Chapel House. , 1400 Washington Ave., 12222. Tel: 518-489-8573; Fax: 518-489-8573. Email: moleary@uamail.alb.edu. Sr. Maureen O'Leary, F.S.P., Chap.

COBLESKILL. *State University of New York College of Agricultural & Technology at Cobleskill* Main St., P.O. Box 124, 12175. Tel: 518-234-2892. Rev. Thomas F. Berardi.

DELHI. *State University of New York College of Agricultural & Technology at Delhi* St. Peter Rectory, 8 Franklin St., 13753. Tel: 607-746-2503. Rev. Joseph Manerowski.

GLENS FALLS. *Adirondack Community College* c/o 40 N. Main Ave., 12203. Tel: 518-793-9677.

HUDSON. *Columbia-Greene Community College* P.O. Box 1000, 12534. Tel: 518-828-4181.

LOUDONVILLE. *Siena College* 12211. Tel: 518-783-2332; Fax: 518-783-4293. Email: ministry@siena.edu. Web: www.siena.edu. Rev. William Beaudin, O.F.M., Chap.; Marjorie Voyko, Dir. Music; Ms. Judy Dougherty, Sec.; Margaret Motto, Assoc. Campus Min.

ONEONTA. *New York State University at Oneonta and Hartwick College* Newman House, 77 Spruce St., 13820. Tel: 607-432-4400. Email: newman@dmcom.net. Web: www.dmcom.net/newmanhouse/. Susan Nesbitt, Campus Min. Tel: 607-432-4400; Maureen DeBonis, Pres. of Foundation, Bd. of Dir.; Susan Johnson, Admin. & Sec. Corporate Title: Oneonta Newman Foundation.

SARATOGA. *Skidmore College* 815 N. Broadway, 12866. Tel: 518-580-5682; Fax: 518-580-5555. Email: cminnery@skidmore.edu. Catherine W. Minnery, Coord. Catholic Student Life.

SCHENECTADY. *Union College, Catholic Campus Ministry* 12308. Tel: 518-388-6087. Email: forsheyg@union.edu. Web: www.union.edu/CampusLife/Religious_Service/ccm/. George S. Forshey, Chap. Religious Programs Office of Union College, Silliman Hall

TROY. *Hudson Valley Community College* 80 Vandenburgh Ave., 12180. Tel: 518-629-7168. Email: cuneoros@hvcc.edu. Sr. Rosemary Ann Cuneo, C.R., Campus Min.

Rensselaer Polytechnic Institute Office of the Resident Catholic Chaplain, Rm. 3514 Rensselaer Union, 12180. Tel: 518-276-6518; Fax: 518-274-5945. Email: fred@rpi.edu Web: www.rpi.edu/web/c+cc. Rev. Edward Kacerguis, Chap.; Margaret Leathem, Chap.

The Rensselaer Newman Foundation Rm. 3514 Rensselaer Union, 12180. Tel: 518-276-6518; Fax: 518-274-5945. James Ljunglin, Pres.

University Parish of Christ Sun of Justice Tel: 518-274-7793; Fax: 518-274-5945. Rev. Edward S. Kacergius.

Chapel & Cultural Center 2125 Burdett Ave., 12180. Tel: 518-274-7793; Fax: 518-274-5945. 10 Phelan Pl., 12180.

Russell Sage College Campus Ministry Office, Rm. #304 Student Center, 12180. Tel: 518-244-4507. Email: cuneor@sage.edu. Sr. Rosemary Ann Cuneo, C.R.

[R] MISCELLANEOUS LISTINGS

ALBANY. *Birthright of Albany*, 586 Central Ave., 12206. Tel: 518-438-2978; Fax: 518-438-2978.

Burke Community Service Corp., Inc., 40 N. Main Ave., 12203. Tel: 518-453-6623; Fax: 518-453-6792. Email: noel.olsen@rcda.org.

The Cathedral Restoration Corp., 40 N. Main Ave., 12203. Tel: 518-463-4447; Fax: 518-436-5177. Email: ecathedra@nycap.rr.com. Rev. William H. Pape, Sec. & Treas.

Diocesan HIV/AIDS Services, 100 Slingerlands St., 12202. Tel: 518-449-3581; Fax: 518-426-3662. Email: joek@ccalbany.org.

Emmaus House Albany Catholic Worker Community , 35 N. Main Ave., 12203.

Family Rosary Albany Office, 16 Cornell Ave., 12203. Tel: 518-452-3082; Fax: 518-452-3956. Email: lrhatigan@hcfm.org. Web: www.hcfm.org. Laetitia Rhatigan, Albany Mission Dir. Sponsored by Congregation of Holy Cross (Eastern Prov.).

Crusade for Family Prayer, Inc., North Easton, MA. Tel: 508-238-4095; Fax: 508-238-3953. Rev. John P. Phalen, C.S.C., Pres. Sponsored by Congregation of Holy Cross (Eastern Prov.)

The Foundation of the Roman Catholic Diocese of Albany, New York, Inc., 40 N. Main Ave., 12203. Tel: 518-453-6680; Fax: 518-453-8440. Mr. Jack Manning, Exec. Dir.; Ms. Rosanne Heertum, Assoc. Exec. Dir.

St. Francis Chapel, Wolf Road Shoppers Park, 145A Wolf Rd., 12205. Tel: 518-459-2854; Fax: 518-783-4195. Web: www.TimesUnion/communities/StFrancischapel. Revs. James Czerwinski, O.F.M., Dir.; Callistus Bamberg, O.F.M.; Gerard Lee, O.F.M.; Henry L. Madden, O.F.M.; Reginald J. Reddy, O.F.M. Order of Friars Minor Province of the Most Holy Name of Jesus

Kenwood Braille Association, Inc., Kenwood Convent of the Sacred Heart, 799 S. Pearl St., 12202. Tel: 518-465-3341; Fax: 518-465-3663. Sr. Priscilla Meier, R.S.C.J., Dir.

LaSalle Albany, Inc., De La Salle Rd., 12208. Bros. Michael Corry, F.S.C., Chm.; Stephen McCabe, F.S.C., Vice Chm.; E. James Stolz, F.S.C., Sec.

The Marillac-N.E. Charitable Trust, 96 Menands Rd., 12204-1499. Tel: 518-462-5596; Fax: 518-462-5192. Email: patbouza@yahoo.com.

McCloskey Community Service Corporation, 41 N. Main Ave., 12203. Tel: 518-459-0183; Fax: 518-459-0202. Email: Diocesan.Housing@rcda.org. Deborah Damm O'Brien, Exec. Dir.

New York State Catholic Conference, 465 State St., 12203. Tel: 518-434-6195; Fax: 518-434-9796. Email: info@nyscatholic.org. Web: www.nyscatholic.org. Richard E. Barnes, Exec. Dir.

Noonan Community Service Corporation, 40 N. Main Ave., 12203-1422. Tel: 518-453-6641; Fax: 518-453-8454. Rev. Paul Roman, Contact Person.

Sisters of the Holy Names of Jesus & Mary of the New York Province, Inc. Continuing Support Charitable Trust to provide for the needs of the Tutwiler Clinic, Tutwiler, Mississippi. , 1061 New Scotland Ave., 12208-1198. Tel: 601-345-8334; Fax: 518-489-5804. Email: khughes@snjmny.org.

Sisters of the Holy Names of Jesus and Mary Community Support Charitable Trust. , 1061 New Scotland Ave., 12208-1198. Tel: 518-489-5469; Fax: 518-489-5804. Email: khughes@snjmny.org.

Support Fund Trust of the Province of St. Thomas of Villanova, c/o 40 N. Main Ave., 12203.

CASTLETON-ON-HUDSON. *Cooperative Christian Ministries of Schodack, Inc.*, Formerly C.C.M. of Schodack, Inc.92 S. Main St., 12033.

COHOES. *Apostolate for the Suffering*, c/o St. Rita Rectory, 50 St. Rita Pl., 12047. Tel: 518-237-4444. Rev. Mario Pacini, S.A.C.

GERMANTOWN. *Oneness in Peace Center, Inc.*, 49 Main St., 12526. Tel: 518-537-5678. Email: ajl4269@valstar.net. Web: fad.cc/onenessinpeace. Sr. Vergilia Jim, O.S.F., Co-Dir.; Claire Langie, Co-Dir.

LATHAM. *The Sister M. Athanasia Gurry Trust Fund of the Sisters of St. Joseph*, 385 Watervliet-Shaker Rd., 12110-4799. Tel: 518-783-3538; Fax: 518-783-1123.

NISKAYUNA. *Villa Fusco Child Day Care Center*, 955 Balltown Rd., 12309. Tel: 518-377-1613; Fax: 518-377-1613. Email: dcPBchalouxl@aol.com. Sr. Maria Goretti Chaloux, Supr. Daughters of Charity of the Most Precious Blood Capacity 14.

NORTH CREEK. *North Country Ministry*, Leaven House, P.O. Box 111, 12853. Tel: 518-251-4425; Fax: 518-251-5483. Bro. James Posluszny, C.S.C., Dir.

RENSSELAER. *Circles of Mercy, Inc.*, 11 Washington St., Ste. A, 12144. Tel: 518-462-0899; Fax: 518-462-2892. Email: circlesofmercy@yahoo.com. Web: www.circlesofmercy.org. Sr. Kathleen Pritty, R.S.M., Dir.

Franciscorps, Inc., 517 Washington Ave., 12144. Tel: 518-472-1000; Fax: 518-472-1013. Email: FranCorps@aol.com. Web: www.Franciscanseast.org.

Order of Friars Minor Conventual Immaculate Conception Province Charitable Trust (Established 1990) , P.O. Box 629, 12144. Tel: 518-472-1000; Fax: 518-472-1013. Email: plininger@aol.com. Web: conventualfranciscanfriars.com; www.Franciscanseast.org. Rev. Paul Lininger, O.F.M.Conv., Trustee.

SCHENECTADY. *St. Luke's Guild*, c/o St. Clare Hospital, 600 McClellan St., 12304. Tel: 518-347-5760. Email: brissonP@ash.shine.org.

Secular Order of Discalced Carmelites, 428 Duane Ave., 12304-2691. Tel: 518-374-1110. Email: avila@localnet.com phelanphel@aol.com. David W. Phelan, Pres.

TROY. *Catholic School Administrators' Association of New York State*, 406 Fulton St., Ste. 512, 12180. Tel: 518-273-1205; Fax: 518-273-1206. Email: office@csaanys.org. Web: www.csaanys.org. Stephen Partisano, Ed.D., Exec. Dir.

[S] SUMMER CAMPS

ALBANY. *Camp Scully*, 100 Slingerland St., 12202. Tel: 518-426-3511; 518-283-1617 (Snyders Lake); Fax: 518-426-3662. Email: campscully@ccalbany.org. Web: www.campscully.bunk1.com. *Summer Address*, 24 Camp Scully Way, Wynantskill, 12198. Fax: 518-286-1943. A program of Catholic Charities of Albany and Rensselaer Counties; Summer Residential Camp for children 7-14. Under direction of Catholic Charities of the Diocese of Albany. Financed by local Youth Bureaus, the Albany Catholic Diocese, USDA Summer Program and by contributions. Capacity 110.

TROY. *Troy CYO Day Camp*, Box 867, 237 Fourth St., 12180. Tel: 518-274-2630. Raymond R. Piscitelli, Exec. Dir.; Mara A. Wager, Prog. Dir.; Jeanne Mailloux, Exec. Sec. Sponsored by Troy Youth Organization, Inc. for Boys and Girls, ages 5-12 yrs.

RELIGIOUS INSTITUTES OF MEN REPRESENTED IN THE DIOCESE

For further details refer to the corresponding bracketed number in the Religious Institutes of Men or Women section.

[0140]—*The Augustinians*—O.S.A.
[0330]—*Brothers of the Christian Schools* (New York Prov.)—F.S.C.
[0600]—*Brothers of the Congregation of Holy Cross* (Eastern Prov.)—C.S.C.
[0270]—*Carmelite Fathers & Brothers*—O.Carm.
[0310]—*Congregation of Christian Brothers* (Eastern US)—C.F.C.
[0220]—*Congregation of the Blessed Sacrament*—S.S.S.
[1330]—*Congregation of the Mission* (Eastern Prov.)—C.M.
[0480]—*Conventual Franciscans* (Prov. of Immaculate Conception)—O.F.M.Conv
[0520]—*Franciscan Friars* (Most Holy Name Prov.)—O.F.M.
[0690]—*Jesuit Fathers and Brothers* (New York Prov.)—S.J.
[0720]—*The Missionaries of Our Lady of La Salette* (Prov. of Our Lady of Seven Dolors)—M.S.
[0990]—*Pallotine Father (Italian Province)*—S.A.C.
[1030]—*Paulist Fathers* (New York)—C.S.P.
[0610]—*Priests of the Congregation of Holy Cross* (Eastern Prov.)—C.S.C.
[1070]—*Redemptorist Fathers* (Baltimore Prov.)—C.SS.R.
[0990]—*Society of the Catholic Apostolate*—S.A.C.

RELIGIOUS INSTITUTES OF WOMEN REPRESENTED IN THE DIOCESE

[0330]—*Carmelite Sisters for the Aged and Infirm*—O.Carm.
[2980]—*Congregation of Notre Dame*—C.N.D.
[0760]—*Daughters of Charity of St. Vincent de Paul*—D.C.
[0740]—*Daughters of Charity of the Most Precious Blood*—D.C.P.B.
[0420]—*Discalced Carmelite Nuns*—O.C.D.
[1070-17]—*Dominican Sisters - Congregation of St. Catherine de Ricci*—O.P.
[1105]—*Dominican Sisters of Hope*—O.P.
[1170]—*Felician Sisters*—C.S.S.F.
[1180]—*Franciscan Sisters of Allegany, New York*—O.S.F.
[1425]—*Franciscan Sisters of Peace*—F.S.P.
[1190]—*Franciscan Sisters of the Atonement*—S.A.
[2340]—*Little Sisters of the Poor*—L.S.P.
[1410]—*Mill Hill Sisters (Franciscan Missionaries of St. Joseph)*—F.M.S.J.
[2750]—*Missionary Sisters of the Immaculate Heart*
[1830]—*Religious of the Good Shepherd - RGS of Mary*—I.C.M.
[2070]—*Religious of the Holy Union of the Sacred Hearts*—S.U.S.C.
[2970]—*School Sisters of Notre Dame*—S.S.N.D.
[2575]—*Sisters of Mercy of the Americas* (Albany)—R.S.M.
[2990]—*Sisters of Notre Dame*—S.N.D.
[1660]—*Sisters of St. Francis of the Providence of God*—O.S.F.
[3840]—*Sisters of St. Joseph of Carondelet*—C.S.J.
[0150]—*Sisters of the Assumption*—S.A.S.V.
[2980]—*Sisters of the Congregation de Notre Dame*—C.N.D.
[1990]—*Sisters of the Holy Names of Jesus and Mary*—S.N.J.M.
[3320]—*Sisters of the Presentation of the B.V.M.*—P.B.V.M.
[3480]—*Sisters of the Resurrection*—C.R.
[1490]—*Sisters of the Third Franciscan Order*—O.S.F.
[4070]—*Society of the Sacred Heart*—R.S.C.J.

DIOCESAN CEMETERIES

COHOES. *St. Agnes Cemetery*, St. Agnes Hwy., 12047. Tel: 518-463-0134.

GLENVILLE. *St. Anthony Cemetery*, Glenridge Rd., 12325. Tel: 518-374-5319.

MENANDS. *St. Agnes Cemetery*, 48 Cemetery Ave.. Tel: 518-463-0134.

ROTTERDAM. *Holy Cross Cemetery*, Tel: 518-374-5319.

SCHENECTADY. *St. Cyril & St. Methodius Cemetery*, Tel: 518-374-5319.

Most Holy Redeemer Cemetery, 2501 Troy Rd..

TROY. *St. Jean Baptiste Cemetery*, 968 Spring Ave., 12180. Tel: 518-272-0931.

St. John Cemetery, Tel: 518-272-0931.

St. Mary's Cemetery of Troy, Inc., Brunswick Rd., 12180. Tel: 518-272-0931.

WATERVLIET. *St. Patrick Cemetery*, Troy Rd., 12189. Tel: 518-463-0134.

NECROLOGY

† Clune, Gerald, (Retired)—Died Oct. 25, 2002
† DeCaprio, John (Retired)—Died May 29, 2003
† Donaghy, Harry Troy, NY St. Mary's—Died Aug. 25, 2003
† Doyle, Richard J. Athens, NY St. Patrick's—Died July 10, 2003
† Gagnon, Rev. George Glens Falls, NY St. Alphonsus
† Husselbeck, Francis E. (Retired)—Died May 15, 2003
† Jonaitis, Peter (Retired)—Died Oct. 21, 2002
† Kampfer, Gerald D. (Retired)—Died Jan. 6, 2003
† Klementowicz, Chester, (Retired)—Died Dec. 22, 2002
† Konisky, Edward (Retired)—Died Feb. 21, 2003
† Lysogorski, Rev. John Special Assignment, AIDS Ministry
† Manny, Howard F., (Retired)—Died Oct. 8, 2002
† Roos, Robert E., (Retired)—Died Oct. 1, 2003
† Steuer, James A., Mohawk, NY Blessed Sacrament—Died May 13, 2003
† Whalen, William F., (Retired)—Died March 2, 2003

Diocese of Alexandria

(Dioecesis Alexandrina in Louisiana)

Most Reverend

WILLIAM B. FRIEND, D.D.

Apostolic Administrator of Alexandria; Bishop of Shreveport; ordained May 7, 1959; appointed Titular Bishop of Pomaria and Auxiliary Bishop of Alexandria-Shreveport August 31, 1979; ordained Bishop October 30, 1979; appointed Bishop of Alexandria-Shreveport November 23, 1982; installed January 11, 1983; appointed Bishop of Shreveport June 16, 1986; Secondarily Appointed Apostolic Administrator of Alexandria October 10, 2003.

(VACANT SEE)

Chancery Office: 4400 Coliseum Blvd., P.O. Box 7417, Alexandria, LA 71306. Tel: 318-445-2401; Fax: 318-448-6121.

Web: www.diocesealex.org

ERECTED AS DIOCESE OF NATCHITOCHES JULY 29, 1853.

Square Miles 22,212.

Transferred to Alexandria August 6, 1910 and became Diocese of Alexandria.

Redesignated Diocese of Alexandria-Shreveport on January 12, 1977; split, forming two Dioceses, the Diocese of Alexandria and the Diocese of Shreveport as of June 16, 1986.

Comprises the counties (parishes) of Rapides, Avoyelles, Concordia, Catahoula, LaSalle, Grant, Natchitoches, Vernon, Tensas, Caldwell, Winn, Franklin and Madison.

Legal Title: For legal titles of parishes and diocesan institutions, consult the Chancery Office.

STATISTICAL OVERVIEW

Personnel	
Priests: Diocesan Active in Diocese	38
Priests: Diocesan Active Outside Diocese	4
Priests: Retired, Sick or Absent	18
Number of Diocesan Priests	60
Religious Priests in Diocese	14
Total Priests in Diocese	74
Extern Priests in Diocese	12
Ordinations:	
Diocesan Priests	4
Permanent Deacons in Diocese	5
Total Brothers	4
Total Sisters	39
Parishes	
Parishes	48
With Resident Pastor:	
Resident Diocesan Priests	34
Resident Religious Priests	11
Without Resident Pastor:	
Administered by Priests	2
Administered by Religious Women	1
Missions	24
Pastoral Centers	1
Professional Ministry Personnel:	
Sisters	4
Lay Ministers	12
Welfare	
Catholic Hospitals	2
Total Assisted	121,249
Homes for the Aged	2
Total Assisted	164
Special Centers for Social Services	18
Total Assisted	89,861
Residential Care of Disabled	2
Total Assisted	172
Educational	
Diocesan Students in Other Seminaries	11
Total Seminarians	11
High Schools, Diocesan and Parish	3
Total Students	652
Elementary Schools, Diocesan and Parish	8
Total Students	2,330
Catechesis/Religious Education:	
High School Students	1,274
Elementary Students	2,484
Total Students under Catholic Instruction	6,751
Teachers in the Diocese:	
Brothers	4
Sisters	14
Lay Teachers	201
Vital Statistics	
Receptions into the Church:	
Infant Baptism Totals	671
Adult Baptism Totals	59
Received into Full Communion	148
First Communions	684
Confirmations	593
Marriages:	
Catholic	121
Interfaith	80
Total Marriages	201
Deaths	656
Total Catholic Population	48,050
Total Population	392,639

Former Bishops—Rt. Revs. AUGUSTUS M. MARTIN, consecrated Nov. 30, 1853; died Sept. 29, 1875; FRANCIS XAVIER LERAY, consecrated Bishop of Natchitoches, April 22, 1877; named Bishop of Janopolis, Coadjutor of New Orleans, and Administrator of Natchitoches, Oct. 23, 1879; promoted to the See of New Orleans, Dec. 1883; died Sept. 23, 1887; ANTHONY DURIER, D.D., consecrated March 19, 1885; died Feb. 28, 1904; Most Revs. CORNELIUS VAN DE VEN, consecrated Nov. 30, 1904;; made assistant at the Pontifical Throne, Nov. 12, 1929;; died May 8, 1932; DANIEL FRANCIS DESMOND, D.D., consecrated Bishop of Alexandria Jan. 5, 1933; died Sept. 11, 1945; CHARLES P. GRECO, D.D. (Retired), consecrated Feb. 25, 1946; retired May 22, 1973; died Jan. 20, 1987; LAWRENCE P. GRAVES, D.D., J.C.L. (Retired), consecrated April 25, 1969; installed Bishop of Alexandria, Sept. 18, 1973; retired July 14, 1982; died Jan. 15, 1994; WILLIAM B. FRIEND, D.D., ord. Oct. 30, 1979; installed Bishop of Alexandria-Shreveport Jan. 11, 1983; then after Diocese of Alexandria-Shreveport was split into two dioceses June 16, 1986;; installed Bishop of Shreveport July 30, 1986; JOHN C. FAVALORA, D.D., ord. Dec. 20, 1961; appt. Bishop of Alexandria June 16, 1986; ord. and installed July 29, 1986; installed Bishop of St. Petersburg May 16, 1989; installed Archbishop of Miami Dec. 20, 1994; SAM G. JACOBS, D.D., ord. June 6, 1964; appt. Bishop of Alexandria July 1, 1989; ord. and installed Aug. 24, 1989; appt. Bishop of Houma-Thibodaux Aug. 1, 2003; installed Oct. 10, 2003.

Vicar General—Rev. Msgr. RONALD C. HOPPE, V.G., P.O. Box 7417, Alexandria, 71306. Tel: 318-445-2401.

Chancery Office—4400 Coliseum Blvd., Alexandria, 71303. Mailing Address, P.O. Box 7417, Alexandria, 71306. Tel: 318-445-2401; Fax: 318-448-6121. Office Hours: Mon.-Fri. 8-12 & 1-4:30

Moderator of the Curia—Rev. Msgr. RONALD C. HOPPE, V.G.

Chancellor—Rev. Msgr. JOSEPH M. SUSI (Retired).

Ecclesiastical Notaries—Rev. Msgr. JOSEPH M. SUSI, Chancellor (Retired); Ms. DEBORAH DEROSAN; Mrs. PATRICIA LACAZE; Ms. MARY ANN MANUEL; Mrs. PATRICIA THOMAS.

Diocesan Tribunal—P.O. Box 7417, Alexandria, 71306. Tel: 318-445-2401.

Judicial Vicar—Rev. BRUCE MILLER, J.C.L.

Presiding Judge—Rev. BRUCE MILLER, J.C.L.

Defender of the Bond—Rev. JAMES A. FERGUSON, J.C.L.

Promoters of Justice—Revs. JAMES A. FERGUSON, J.C.L.; STEPHEN SCOTT CHEMINO, J.C.L. (Cand.).

Advocates—Rev. DANIEL P. O'CONNOR, V.F.; Mrs. PATRICIA THOMAS; Mrs. YVETTE HEBERT.

College of Consultors—Rev. Msgrs. RONALD C. HOPPE, V.G.; JOSEPH M. SUSI, Chancellor (Retired); STEVE J. TESTA, V.F.; Revs. KENNETH J. ROY, V.F.; H. GERALD BORDELON, V.F.; DANIEL P. O'CONNOR, V.F.; RUSSELL J. LEMOINE; GERARD M. FOLEY, V.F.; VINCENT MANUEL.

Finance Council—Mr. SHERMAN COOK; Mr. DARRELL DUBROC; Mr. WILLIE OBEY; Mr. NORMAN OLSON; Mrs. DOROTHY PUGH; Mr. GREGORY WALKER; Rev. Msgrs. RONALD C. HOPPE, V.G.; JOSEPH M. SUSI, Chancellor (Retired); STEVE J. TESTA, V.F.

Building Review Committee—Mr. GEORGE C. ADAMS; Mr. C. KEITH CAPDEPON; Mr. DONALD A. MANSOUR; Mr. G. LYNN MCCAIN; Mr. BO NEELY; Mr. FINLEY L. PONTHIE; Mr. REX L. PONTHIE; Mr. WILLIE PUGH JR.; Mr. WILLIAM O. ROLLINS; Mr. JOSEPH T. SIMMS JR.; Mr. WILLIAM J. THEVENOTE.

Priests Council—Revs. BRUCE MILLER, J.C.L., Chm.; M. CRAIG SCOTT, Vice Chm.; DANIEL P. O'CONNOR, V.F., Sec.; Rev. Msgrs. RONALD C. HOPPE, V.G.; JOSEPH M. SUSI, Chancellor (Retired); STEVE J. TESTA, V.F.; Revs. GERARD M. FOLEY, V.F.; H. GERALD BORDELON, V.F.; ANGELO MESSINA; RUSSELL J. LEMOINE; VINCENT MANUEL; ANTHONY DHARMARAJ, M.S.F.S.; KENNETH J. ROY, V.F.; KENNETH J. MICHIELS; STEPHEN SCOTT CHEMINO, J.C.L. (Cand.); PATRICK X. BRAQUET; JAMES A. FOSTER.

Administrator and Assessor—Rev. STEPHEN SCOTT CHEMINO, J.C.L. (Cand.), P.O. Box 13, Natchitoches, 71458-0013. Tel: 318-352-3422.

Retirement Board—Rev. Msgrs. FREDERICK J. LYONS (Retired); JOHN TIMMERMANS (Retired); Rev. GERARD M. FOLEY, V.F.; Dr. VINCENT VINCENT.

Rural Deans—Rev. Msgr. STEVE J. TESTA, V.F.; Revs. H. GERALD BORDELON, V.F.; DANIEL P. O'CONNOR, V.F.; KENNETH J. ROY, V.F.

Vicar for Clergy—Rev. M. CRAIG SCOTT, P.O. Box 7056, Alexandria, 71306-0056. Tel: 318-445-7120.

The Catholic Foundation of North-Central Louisiana, Inc.—P.O. Box 8021, Alexandria, 71306. Tel: 318-487-9222. JOSEPH L. HEBERT, Pres.-Treas.; Mrs. BETTY CHOP, Corp. Sec.

Diocesan Offices and Directors

Archivist—Rev. Msgr. JOSEPH M. SUSI, Chancellor (Retired), P.O. Box 7417, Alexandria, 71306-0417. Tel: 318-445-2401.

Black Affairs—VACANT.

Business Affairs—Mr. DAVID BROOK, Dir., P.O. Box 7417, Alexandria, 71306-0417. Tel: 318-445-2401.

Campaign for Human Development—Sr. MARY BORDELON, C.D.P., Dir., P.O. Box 7417, Alexandria,

71306-0417. Tel: 318-445-2401.

Campus Ministry—Rev. JASON E. GOOTEE, Dir., LSU-A, 8100 Hwy. 71-S, Alexandria, 71302-9633. Tel: 318-473-6494.

Catholic Community Services—Sr. MARY BORDELON, C.D.P., Dir., P.O. Box 7417, Alexandria, 71306-0417. Tel: 318-445-2401.

Catholic Relief Services—Sr. MARY BORDELON, C.D.P., Dir., P.O. Box 7417, Alexandria, 71306-0417. Tel: 318-445-2401.

Cemeteries—Rev. Msgr. JOHN TIMMERMANS, Coord. (Retired), 238 Mon Borde St., Moreauville, 71355. Tel: 318-985-1774.

Charismatic Movement—Rev. H. GERALD BORDELON, V.F., Diocesan Liaison, P.O. Box 40, Cloutierville, 71416-0040. Tel: 318-379-2231.

Church Financial Development—Mrs. ANN MASDEN, Dir., P.O. Box 7417, Alexandria, 71301. Tel: 318-445-2401.

Vocation Discernment Committee—Revs. PATRICK X. BRAQUET; JOSE A. ROBLES-SANCHEZ; Sr. JULIANA B. GAPASIN, D.L.J.C.; MARK SAMPSON; ALFREDA SAMPSON; ERIC KUEHLER; JULIE KUEHLER.

Clergy and Religious—VACANT.

Communications—MARK ADAMS, Print Media; Mrs. ANN MASDEN, Electronic Media, P.O. Box 7417, Alexandria, 71306-0417. Tel: 318-445-2401.

Continuing Formation of the Clergy—Rev. RUSTY P. RABALAIS, 1315 Eggbend Rd., Marksville, 71351-4223. Tel: 318-253-9936.

Ecumenical—Rev. STEPHEN SCOTT CHEMINO, J.C.L. (Cand.), Liaison, P.O. Box 13, Natchitoches, 71458-0013. Tel: 318-352-3422.

Eucharistic League, Priests—Rev. Msgr. JOSEPH M. SUSI, Dir. & Chancellor (Retired), P.O. Drawer 7417, Alexandria, 71306-0417. Tel: 318-445-2401.

Evangelization—Rev. CRAIG SCOTT, Chm., P.O. Box 7056, Alexandria, 71306-0056. Tel: 318-445-7120.

Family Life Ministry—Sr. MARY BORDELON, C.D.P., Dir., P.O. Box 7417, Alexandria, 71306-0417. Tel: 318-445-2401.

Fiscal Management—Mr. DAVID BROOK, Dir. Business Affairs, P.O. Box 7417, Alexandria, 71306-0417. Tel: 318-445-2401.

Hispanic Apostolate—Rev. PEDRO J. SIERRA-POSADA, P.O. Box 7417, Alexandria, 71306-0417. Tel: 318-445-2401.

Holy Childhood Association—Rev. Msgr. STEVE J. TESTA, V.F., Dir., P.O. Box 7417, Alexandria, 71306-0417. Tel: 318-445-2401.

Liturgy Committee—Rev. JOSE A. ROBLES-SANCHEZ, 2211 E. Texas Ave., Alexandria, 71301-4207. Tel: 318-445-4588.

Maryhill Renewal Center—Mr. TODD J. MARYE, M.P.S., Dir., 600 Maryhill Rd., Pineville, 71360. Tel: 318-640-1378.

Newspaper "The Church Today"—MARK ADAMS, Editor, P.O. Box 7417, Alexandria, 71306-0417. Tel: 318-445-2401.

Permanent Deacons—Rev. Msgr. RONALD C. HOPPE, V.G., P.O. Box 7417, Alexandria, 71306-0417. Tel: 318-445-2401.

Personnel/Property Management—Mr. SAM BROCATO, Dir., P.O. Box 7417, Alexandria, 71306-0417. Tel: 318-445-2401.

Print Media— ("The Church Today" and "Digest of the News")-- MARK ADAMS, Dir. & Editor, P.O. Box 7417, Alexandria, 71306-0417. Tel: 318-445-2401.

Propagation of the Faith and Foreign Mission Education—Rev. Msgr. STEVE J. TESTA, V.F., Dir., P.O. Box 7417, Alexandria, 71306-0417. Tel: 318-445-2401.

Public Affairs—Mrs. ANN MASDEN, Dir., P.O. Box 7417, Alexandria, 71306-0417. Tel: 318-445-0417.

Religious, Coordinator for—Bro. ANDRE M. LUCIA, F.S.E., P.O. Box 25, Plaucheville, 71362. Tel: 318-922-3630.

Religious Education—Sr. MARY ELLEN THERIOT, S.S.N.D., Dir., P.O. Box 7417, Alexandria, 71306-0417. Tel: 318-445-2401.

Renew—Mr. TOM WEBB, Dir., P.O. Box 7417, Alexandria, 71306-0417. Tel: 318-445-2401.

Rural Life Ministry—VACANT, Coord.

Schools—Sr. MARICE ELVEKROG, S.S.N.D., Supt., P.O. Box 7417, Alexandria, 71306-0417. Tel: 318-445-2401.

Scouting—Revs. CHARLES J. MORGAN, Region 5 Chap., P.O. Box 130, Mansura, 71350-0130. Tel: 318-964-2921; STEPHEN J. BRANDOW, Diocesan & Ouachita Valley Council Chap., P.O. Box 39, Tioga, 71477. Tel: 318-473-0010.

Seminarians—Rev. JASON E. GOOTEE, Dir., P.O. Box 7417, Alexandria, 71306-0417. Tel: 318-445-7120.

Social Ministry—Sr. MARY BORDELON, C.D.P., Admin., P.O. Box 7417, Alexandria, 71306-0417. Tel: 318-445-2401.

School Food Service—Ms. GWEN TYSON, Food and Nutrition Supvr., P.O. Box 7417, Alexandria, 71306-0417. Tel: 318-445-2485.

Steubenville South Catholic Youth Conference—Mrs. SALLY DUBROC, Coord., P.O. Box 7417, Alexandria, 71306-0417. Tel: 318-473-0539.

The Beginning Experience—Rev. BRUCE MILLER, J.C.L., P.O. Box 7417, Alexandria, 71306-0417. Tel: 318-445-2401.

Victim Assistance Coordinator—Ms. MARY GIRARD. Tel: 318-449-8571.

Vocations Recruitment—Rev. JASON E. GOOTEE, Dir., P.O. Box 7417, Alexandria, 71306-0417. Tel: 318-445-7120.

Youth Ministry—Miss CHRISTINA THERIOT, Dir., P.O. Box 7417, Alexandria, 71306-0417. Tel: 318-445-2401.

CLERGY, PARISHES, MISSIONS AND PAROCHIAL SCHOOLS

CITY OF ALEXANDRIA
(RAPIDES PARISH)

1—ST. FRANCIS XAVIER CATHEDRAL (1834), Revs. Edwin Rodriguez, Rector; D. Wade DeCoste. In Res., Rev. Pedro J. Sierra-Posada (Colombia).
Res.: 626 Fourth St., 71301-8424. Tel: 318-445-1451; Fax: 318-445-1433.
Catechesis/Religious Program—Sr. Mary Bordelon, C.D.P., D.R.E. Students 32.

2—ST. FRANCES XAVIER CABRINI (1947), Revs. Jose A. Robles-Sanchez; John K. Brocato. In Res., Rev. John Gabriel (India).
Office—2211 E. Texas Ave., 71301-4207. Tel: 318-445-4588; Fax: 318-443-7156.
Res.: 2012 Wedgewood Ave., 71301. Tel: 318-487-4443; Fax: 318-443-7156.
School—Tel: 318-448-3333; Fax: 318-448-3343. Sisters of Charity of the Incarnate Word 2; Lay Teachers 18; Students 234.
Catechesis/Religious Program—Students 108.

3—ST. JAMES MEMORIAL (1911), Rev. Kenneth J. Michie.
Church: 705 Winn St., 71301. Tel: 318-487-9512; Fax: 318-487-9511.

4—ST. JULIANA (1959), Rev. Vincent Manuel (India).
Res.: 900 Daspit St., 71302-5343. Tel: 318-445-6700; Fax: 318-445-9826.

5—OUR LADY OF PROMPT SUCCOR (1947), Revs. Daniel P. O'Connor, V.F.; Jack H. Michalchuk. In Res., Rev. David J. Braquet.
Res.: 401 21st St., 71301-7022. Tel: 318-445-3693; Fax: 318-445-8471.
School—Tel: 318-487-1862; Fax: 318-473-9321. Sisters of Divine Providence 1; Lay Teachers 31; Students 499.
Catechesis/Religious Program—Jennifer W. Pearce, D.R.E. Students 159.

6—ST. RITA (1940), Revs. Michael Craig Scott; Chad A. Partain.
Mailing Address: P.O. Box 7056, 71306.
Office—2386 Vandenburg Dr., 71303. Tel: 318-445-7120; Fax: 318-448-0704.
Res.: 214 N. 17th St., 71301. Tel: 318-445-5031.
Church: 4401 Bayou Rapides Rd., 71303.
Child Development Center—1005 Seip Dr., 71303. Tel: 318-448-9999; Fax: 318-445-3003.
School—Tel: 318-473-0538; Fax: 318-473-0403. Lay Teachers 19; Students 282.
Catechesis/Religious Program—Tel: 318-445-7141, Ext. 15. Sr. Nell Murray, M.S.C., D.R.E. Students 182.

OUTSIDE THE CITY OF ALEXANDRIA

BELLEDEAU, AVOYELLES PARISH, ST. MARTIN OF TOURS (1950), [CEM] Rev. Russell J. Lemoine.
Res.: 1981 Hwy. 114, Hessmer, 71341-4234. Tel: 318-563-4533; Fax: 318-563-4385.
Catechesis/Religious Program—Tel: 318-563-4336. Amos P. Lacombe, D.R.E. Students 38.

BORDELONVILLE, AVOYELLES PARISH, ST. PETER (1903), [CEM] Rev. Terry E. Allen.
Res.: P.O. Box 31, 71320-0031. Tel: 318-997-2151; Fax: 318-997-2159.
Catechesis/Religious Program—Tel: 318-997-2502. Gary L. Bordelen, D.R.E. Students 80.

BOYCE, RAPIDES PARISH, ST. MARGARET (1936), Rev. Thomas Chandy, C.M.I. (India).
Res.: 402 Ryan St., 71409. Tel: 318-793-8811; Fax: 318-793-8815.
Mission—St. Cyril Flatwoods, Rapides Parish.
Mission—St. Margaret Mary Gorum, Natchitoches Parish.

BROUILLETTE, AVOYELLES PARISH, ST. GENEVIEVE (1953), [CEM] Rev. Thomas M. Jezak.
Res.: 4052 Hwy. 452, Marksville, 71351-3530. Tel: 318-253-9237; Fax: 318-253-0703.
Catechesis/Religious Program—Cindy Dupuy, D.R.E. Students 34.

BUNKIE, AVOYELLES PARISH, ST. ANTHONY OF PADUA (1904), [CEM] Rev. Patrick X. Braquet.
Res.: 409 St. John St., P.O. Box 719, 71322-0719. Tel: 318-346-7274; Fax: 318-346-7475.
School—Tel: 318-346-2739; Fax: 318-346-9191. Lay Teachers 14; Students 217.
Catechesis/Religious Program—Sandra West, D.R.E.; Denise Richie, D.R.E. Students 117.

CAMPTI, NATCHITOCHES PARISH, NATIVITY OF THE BLESSED VIRGIN MARY (1831), [CEM 3] Rev. Paul Thomas, O.C.D. (India).
Res.: 119 Tally St., P.O. Box 439, 71411-0439. Tel: 318-476-2116; Fax: 318-476-2815.
Mission—St. Joseph Trichel, Natchitoches Parish.
Mission—Our Lady of the Holy Rosary Black Lake, Natchitoches Parish.

CHENEYVILLE, RAPIDES PARISH, ST. JOSEPH (1966), [CEM] Rev. Msgr. Julius G. Walle (Retired).
Res.: P.O. Box 446, 71325-0446. Tel: 318-279-2394; Fax: 318-279-2394.

CLOUTIERVILLE, NATCHITOCHES PARISH, ST. JOHN THE BAPTIST (1816), [CEM] Rev. H. Gerald Bordelon, V.F.
Res.: P.O. Box 40, 71416-0040. Tel: 318-379-2231; Fax: 318-379-2236.
Catechesis/Religious Program—Students 54.
Mission—Holy Rosary Emmanuel, Natchitoches Parish.
Mission—Holy Family Monet Ferry, Natchitoches Parish.

COLFAX, GRANT PARISH, ST. JOSEPH (1897), Rev. James A. Foster.
Res.: 801 Third St., P.O. Box 243, 71417-0243. Tel: 318-627-5442; Fax: 318-627-3011.
Mission—St. Patrick P.O. Box 243, Montgomery, Grant Parish 71417.

COTTONPORT, AVOYELLES PARISH, ST. MARY ASSUMPTION (1889), [CEM 3] Rev. Anthony Dharmaraj, M.S.F.S.
Res.: P.O. Box 1123, 71327-1123. Tel: 318-876-3681; Fax: 318-876-2816.
School—Tel: 318-876-3651; Fax: 318-876-3651. Sisters 1; Lay Teachers 10; Students 209.

DEVILLE, RAPIDES PARISH, ST. JOHN THE BAPTIST (1942), [CEM 2] Rev. Rickey J. Gremillion.
Res.: P.O. Box 7, 71328-0007. Tel: 318-466-5587; Fax: 318-466-5265.
Mission—Sts. Francis and Anne Kolin, Rapides Parish.
Mission—St. Winifred Effie, Avoyelles Parish.

DUPONT, AVOYELLES PARISH, IMMACULATE CONCEPTION (1945), [CEM] Rev. Kurian Zachariah (India).
Res.: P.O. Box 385, 71329-0385. Tel: 318-922-3243; Fax: 318-922-3807.
Catechesis/Religious Program—Tel: 318-922-3707. Angie Dixon, D.R.E. Students 48.

ECHO, RAPIDES PARISH, ST. FRANCIS DE SALES (1894), [CEM] Rev. Louis E. Sklar.
Res.: P.O. Box 37, 71330-0037. Tel: 318-563-4530; Fax: 318-563-4530.

EVERGREEN, AVOYELLES PARISH, LITTLE FLOWER (1928), [CEM 2] Rev. James Nellikunnell, C.M.I. (India).
Res.: P.O. Box 20, 71333-0020. Tel: 318-346-2840; Fax: 318-346-4989.
Mission—St. Charles Goudeau, Avoyelles Parish.

FERRIDAY, CONCORDIA PARISH, ST. PATRICK (1952), [JC] Rev. Jamie Medina-Cruz, S.T.L.
Res.: P.O. Box 369, 71334. Tel: 318-757-3834.
Mission—St. Gerard P.O. Box 863, Jonesville, Catahoula Parish 71343. Tel: 318-339-6143.

FIFTH WARD, AVOYELLES PARISH, OUR LADY OF LOURDES (1948), [CEM 4] Rev. Rusty P. Rabalais.
Res.: 1315 Eggbend Rd., 71351-4223. Tel: 318-253-9936; Fax: 318-253-6300.
Mission—St. John the Baptist Moncla, Avoyelles Parish.

GLENMORA, RAPIDES PARISH, ST. LOUIS (1941), [CEM] Rev. Msgr. Ronald C. Hoppe, V.G.; Revs. David J. Braquet; Pedro J. Sierra-Posada (Colombia). In Res., Sr. Marie T. Brogan, S.S.N.D., Parish Life Coord.
Res.: 826 8th St., P.O. Box 636, 71433-0636. Tel: 318-748-8324; Fax: 318-748-8324.
Mission—St. Peter Elmer, Rapides Parish.
Mission—St. Jude Sieper, Rapides Parish.

HESSMER, AVOYELLES PARISH, ST. ALPHONSUS (1898), [CEM] Rev. Michael Manase, O.C.D. (India).
Res.: P.O. Box 66, 71341-0066. Tel: 318-563-4550; Fax: 318-563-8395.
Catechesis/Religious Program—Tel: 318-563-4965. Lindia Guillory, D.R.E. Students 140.

ISLE BREVELLE, NATCHITOCHES PARISH, ST. AUGUSTINE'S (1856), [CEM] Rev. Marc A. Noel.
Res.: 2262 Hwy. 484, Natchez, 71456-3622. Tel: 318-379-2521; Fax: 318-379-6085.
Catechesis/Religious Program—Theresa Fuller, D.R.E. Students 90.
Mission—St. Charles Bermuda, Natchitoches Parish.
Mission—St. Anne Old River, Natchitoches Parish.

JENA, LASALLE PARISH, ST. MARY (1949), Rev. George

Pookkattu, C.M.I. (India).
Mailing Address: P.O. Box 2240, 71342. Tel: 318-765-3798; Fax: 318-765-2530.
Mission—St. Edward Fishville, Grant Parish.

LECOMPTE, RAPIDES PARISH, ST. MARTIN (1860), Rev. Bruce Miller, J.C.L., Judicial Vicar.
Res.: P.O. Box 459, 71346-0459. Tel: 318-776-9480; Fax: 318-776-9921.
Catechesis / Religious Program—Tel: 318-748-7389; Fax: 318-748-7389. Kim Litton, D.R.E. Students 22.
Mission—Mary, Mother of Jesus 9323 Hwy. 1655, Woodworth, Rapides Parish 71485. Tel: 318-487-9894; Fax: 318-487-9894.
Catechesis / Religious Program—Tel: 318-448-1068. Minnie Rougeau, D.R.E. Students 14.

LEESVILLE, VERNON PARISH, ST. MICHAEL (1946), Rev. Angelo Messina.
Res.: 604 S. Fifth St., P.O. Box 240, 71496-0240. Tel: 337-239-2656; Fax: 337-239-2657.
Catechesis / Religious Program—Tel: 337-238-4941. Tammy Cecil, D.R.E. Students 153.

MANSURA, AVOYELLES PARISH
1—OUR LADY OF PROMPT SUCCOR (1937), Rev. Micle Poovathumkudy (India).
Res.: Escude St., P.O. Box 67, 71350-0067. Tel: 318-964-2654; Fax: 318-964-5469.
2—ST. PAUL THE APOSTLE (1796), [CEM] Rev. Charles J. Morgan.
Res.: P.O. Box 130, 71350-0130. Tel: 318-964-2921; Fax: 318-964-2921.

MARKSVILLE, AVOYELLES PARISH
1—HOLY GHOST (1919), [CEM 2] Revs. Silverino Kwebuza, A.J. (Uganda); William Okot, A.J. (Uganda).
Res.: 121 S. Preston St., 71351-3034. Tel: 318-253-7131; Fax: 318-253-7131.
Mission—St. Richard Hickory Hill, Avoyelles Parish.
2—ST. JOSEPH'S (1869), [CEM 2] Rev. Msgr. Steve J. Testa, V.F.; Rev. Keith E. Ishmael.
Res.: 141 S. Washington, 71351-3025. Tel: 318-253-5610; 318-253-7561 (Office); Fax: 318-253-8871.

MOREAUVILLE, AVOYELLES PARISH
1—OUR LADY OF SORROWS (1944), [CEM] Rev. Timothy R. Marceau, O.S.B.
Res.: P.O. Box 247, 71355-0247. Tel: 318-985-2968.
2—SACRED HEART (1860), [CEM] Rev. George Krosfield (India).
Res.: 9986 Bayou Des Glaises St., 71355-9702. Tel: 318-985-2774; Fax: 318-985-2397.
School—Tel: 318-985-2772; Fax: 318-985-2164. Sisters of Our Lady of Sorrows 4; Lay Teachers 12; Students 216.
Catechesis / Religious Program—Students 128.

NATCHITOCHES, NATCHITOCHES PARISH
1—ST. ANTHONY (1935), [JC] Rev. Gregory Downs.
Res.: 911 Fifth St., P.O. Box 432, Nachitoches, 71458-0432. Tel: 318-352-2559; Fax: 318-352-5170.
2—HOLY CROSS (1968), Rev. A. Cook.
Res.: 129 Second St., P.O. Box 211, Nachitoches, 71458-0211. Tel: 318-352-2615; Fax: 318-352-8989.
3—IMMACULATE CONCEPTION (1728), [CEM] Rev. Stephen Scott Chemino, J.C.L. (Cand.).
Res.: 145 Church St., P.O. Box 13, Nachitoches, 71458-0013. Tel: 318-352-3422; Fax: 318-352-3822.
School—St. Mary, (Grades PreK-8), 1101 E. Fifth St., P.O. Box 2070, 71458-2070. Tel: 318-352-8394; Fax: 318-352-5798. Lay Teachers 18; Students 226.
High School—Lay Teachers 21; Students 181.

PINEVILLE, RAPIDES PARISH, SACRED HEART (1933), Rev. Kenneth J. Roy, V.F.
Res.: 600 Lakeview, P.O. Drawer 3009, 71361-3009. Tel: 318-445-2496; Fax: 318-443-0808.

PLAUCHEVILLE, AVOYELLES PARISH, MATER DOLOROSA (1879), [CEM] Rev. James A. Ferguson, J.C.L.
Res.: P.O. Box 9, 71362-0009. Tel: 318 922-3131; Fax: 318-922-3545.
School—Tel: 318-922-3401; Fax: 318-922-3776. Brothers of the Holy Eucharist 2; Marianites of the Holy Cross 2; Lay Teachers 13; Students 251.
High School—Brothers of the Holy Eucharist 2; Sisters 4; Lay Teachers 4; Students 79.
Catechesis / Religious Program—Bro. Paul Casey, F.S.E., D.R.E. Students 334.

POWHATAN, NATCHITOCHES PARISH, ST. FRANCIS OF ASSISI (1952), Rev. Antony Aelavanthara (India).
Res.: P.O. Box 82, 71066-0082. Tel: 318-352-8819; Fax: 318-352-8008.
Mission—St. Anne [CEM] Spanish Lake, Natchitoches Parish.

REXMERE, AVOYELLES PARISH, ST. MICHAEL (1964), [CEM] Rev. Terry E. Allen.
Res.: P.O. Box 31, Bordelonville, 71320-0031. Tel: 318-997-2151; Fax: 318-997-2159.

ST. JOSEPH, TENSAS PARISH, ST. JOSEPH (1940), [CEM] Rev. Jacob Thomas (India).
Res.: P.O. Box 198, 71366-0198. Tel: 318-766-3565; Fax: 318-766-3560.
Mission—St. Francis of Assisi Waterproof, Tensas Parish.

SIMMESPORT, AVOYELLES PARISH, CHRIST THE KING (1935), [CEM] Rev. Daniel Corkery (Ireland).
Res.: P.O. Box 186, 71369-0186. Tel: 318-941-2381.
Catechesis / Religious Program—Fax: 318-941-2381. Janie Deshotels, D.R.E.; Lisa Jones, D.R.E. Students 153.

TALLULAH, MADISON PARISH, ST. EDWARD (1936), Rev. Ferreolus D'Cruz (India).
Res.: 204 Hwy. 80 E., P.O. Box 1308, 71282-1308. Tel: 318-574-1677; Fax: 318-574-1677.
Catechesis / Religious Program—Tel: 318-574-2916; Fax: 318-574-2916. Ann Keene, D.R.E. Students 18.

TIOGA, RAPIDES PARISH, IMMACULATE HEART OF MARY (1971), Rev. Gerard M. Foley, V.F.
P.O. Box 687, 71477-0687. Tel: 318-640-5314; 318-640-9445 (Office); Fax: 318-640-3864.
Res.: 1220 Tioga Rd., Pineville, 71360.
Catechesis / Religious Program—Helen Craig, D.R.E. Students 144.

VIDALIA, CONCORDIA PARISH, OUR LADY OF LOURDES (1887), [JC] Rev. Paul Kunnumpuram, M.S.F.S. (India).
Res.: 503 Texas St., P.O. Box 460, 71373. Tel: 318-336-5450; Fax: 318-336-9770.
Catechesis / Religious Program—Tel: 601-446-5757. Christine Roberts, D.R.E. Students 33.

WINNFIELD, WINN PARISH, OUR LADY OF LOURDES (1988), Rev. John O'Brien (Newfoundland).
Res.: P.O. Box 1412, 71483-1412. Tel: 318-628-2561; Fax: 318-648-2288.
Mission—St. William Olla, La Salle Parish.

WINNSBORO, FRANKLIN PARISH, ST. MARY (1945), Rev. Dwight De Jesus (Philippines).
Res.: 1712 West St., 71295-3240. Tel: 318-435-5658; Fax: 318-435-2002.
Catechesis / Religious Program—Cindy Futch, D.R.E. Students 39.
Mission—St. John 7900 Hwy. 165, Columbia, Caldwell Parish 71295.

Chaplains of Public Institutions

PINEVILLE. *Central Louisiana State Hospital*, W. Shamrock Ave., P.O. Box 5031, 71361. Tel: 318-484-6357; 318-484-6352. Rev. J. Ronald Mathews.
Veterans Administration Medical Center, Shreveport Hwy., 71360. Tel: 318-473-0010. Rev. Stephen J. Brandow.

Special Assignment:
Rev. Msgr.—
Susi, Joseph M., Chancellor (Retired)

On Duty Outside the Diocese:
Rev. Msgr.—
Bordelon, Roland, USCC Relief Services, New York, NY
Revs.—
Hasieber, Joseph S., St. Joseph, Coatesville, PA
Viviano, Nino, St. Michael Church, Clearwater, FL

Military Chaplains:
Rev.—
Fey, Thomas J., U.S.A.F.

Absent on Leave:
Revs.—
Deevy, Edward
Vead, Victor P.

Retired:
Rev. Msgrs.—
Anderson, Marcel
Early, Thomas C.
Lyons, Frederick J.
Murphy, Patrick J. (Ireland)
Susi, Joseph M.
Timmermans, John
Walle, Julius G.
Revs.—
Cunningham, John H.
Gagnard, Louis
Montalbano, Joseph E.
Roy, James
Ryan, John
Thompson, August L.
Van-Hoorn, Leo
Voorhies, Louis
Zagst, Bernard L.

Permanent Deacons:
Daigrepont, William, Avoyelles Prison Ministry
Foster, John, (Retired)
Giaco, Vincent, Chap., Christus St. Frances Cabrini Hospital
Gremillion, Norman, Immaculate Conception, Dupont
Peltier, Joseph, St. Augustine, Isle Brevelle

INSTITUTIONS LOCATED IN THE DIOCESE

[A] HIGH SCHOOLS, DIOCESAN

ALEXANDRIA. *Holy Savior Menard Central*, 4603 Coliseum Blvd., 71303. Tel: 318-445-8233; Fax: 318-448-8170. Email: hsmenard@centuryinter.net. Mr. Dale Skinner, Prin.; Rev. John K. Brocato, Chap. Junior & High School. Sisters 1; Lay Teachers 43; Students 590.

[B] GENERAL HOSPITALS

ALEXANDRIA. *Christus Health Central Louisiana* dba St. Frances Cabrini Hospital , 3330 Masonic Dr., 71301. Tel: 318-487-1122; Fax: 318-448-6754. Web: www.cabrini.org. Mr. Stephen Wright, CEO; Revs. Christudas Nayak (India), Dir. Pastoral Care; John Gabriel (India), Chap. Sisters of Charity of the Incarnate Word 6; Bed Capacity 260; Total Staff 1,460; Patients Assisted Annually 120,902.
Christus St. Frances Cabrini Hospital Foundation of Alexandria, Inc., 3330 Masonic Dr., 71301. Tel: 318-448-6849; Fax: 318-443-3072.
The Dubuis Hospital of Alexandria, 3330 Masonic Dr., 71301. Tel: 318-448-4938; Fax: 318-483-4033. Email: ray.owens@sfc.christushealth.org. Web: www.dubuis.org. Mr. Ray Owens, Admin. Bed Capacity 33; Total Staff 112; Patients Assisted Annually 347.

[C] PROTECTIVE INSTITUTIONS

ALEXANDRIA. *St. Mary's Residential Training School, Inc.*, P.O. Box Drawer 7768, 71306. Tel: 318-445-6443; Fax: 318-449-8520. Email: srmarysmtf@hotmail.com. Web: www.stmarys-rts.com. Sr. Mary Coleman, O.L.S., Admin. Congregation of the Sisters of Our Lady of Sorrows of the U.S.A., Inc. Sisters 5; Lay Staff 270; Bed Capacity 152; Students 152.
Our Lady of Sorrows Community Homes, 347 Browns Bend Rd., 71303. Tel: 318-487-8897; Fax: 318-487-9987. Congregation of the Sisters of Our Lady of Sorrows of the U.S.A., Inc. Sisters 3; Lay Staff 17; Bed Capacity 20; Residents 20.

[D] HOMES FOR AGED

ALEXANDRIA. *Our Lady's Manor, Inc.*, 402 Monroe St., 71301. Tel: 318-473-2560; Fax: 318-443-2449. Ms. Barbara Robbins, Admin. Apartments 114.

MOREAUVILLE. *St. John's Village*, 116 Beridon St., 71355-3004. Tel: 318-985-2948. Rev. Msgr. John Timmermans Admin. (Retired). Apartments 50.

[E] RESIDENCES OF PRIESTS AND BROTHERS

PLAUCHEVILLE. *Brothers of the Holy Eucharist*, P.O. Box 25, 71362. Tel: 318-922-3630. Bro. Andre M. Lucia, F.S.E., Supr. Brothers 4.

[F] CONVENTS AND RESIDENCES FOR SISTERS

ALEXANDRIA. *Congregation of the Marianites of Holy Cross*, St. Rita Convent, 1717 Ashley Ave.., 71301. Tel: 318-448-8001. Sisters 2.
Congregation of the Sisters of Charity of the Incarnate Word, St. Frances Cabrini Convent, 3330 Prescott Rd., 71301-3915. Tel: 318-448-3187; Fax: 318-448-8143. Email: sisterperpetua@cox-internet.com. Sisters 2.
Congregation of the Sisters of Charity of the Incarnate Word, Nazareth Community, 340 Park Pl., 71301-3942. Tel: 318-443-5520. Sisters 3.
Disciples of the Lord Jesus Christ, 4609 Coliseum Blvd., 71303. Tel: 318-443-4495; Fax: 318-443-4495. Email: dljcalex@juno.com. Sisters 3.
Sisters of Our Lady of Sorrows, St. Mary's Convent, P.O. Box 7768, 71306. Tel: 318-445-6461; Fax: 318-445-7124. Email: corianousa@aol.com. Sisters 5.
Sisters of Our Lady of Sorrows, St. Joseph Convent, 440 Browns Bend Rd., 71303. Tel: 318-443-4688; Fax: 318-443-0994. Email: stjoe97@aol.com. Sisters 5.

GLENMORA. *School Sisters of Notre Dame*, Miryam House, P.O. Box 636, 71433. Tel: 318-748-8324. Email: sisters@juno.com. Sisters 2.

MOREAUVILLE. *Sisters of Our Lady of Sorrows*, Sacred Heart Convent, P.O. Box 179, 71355. Tel: 318-985-2772. Sisters 4.

[G] RETREAT HOUSES

PINEVILLE. *Maryhill Renewal Center*, 600 Maryhill Rd., 71360. Tel: 318-640-1378; Fax: 318-640-8604. Email: maryhill@maryhill.org. Web: www.maryhill.org. Rev. Harold Imamshah, Spiritual Dir. & Chap.; Mr. Todd J. Marye, M.P.S., Exec. Dir.; Mr. Leland G. McCullough III, D.Min.

[H] CATHOLIC COMMUNITY SERVICES

ALEXANDRIA. *Catholic Community Services*, 4400 Coliseum Blvd., P.O. Box 7417, 71306. Tel: 318-445-2401; Fax: 318-448-6121. Email: mbordelon@diocesealex.org. Web: www.diocesealex.org. Sr. Mary Bordelon, C.D.P., Dir.

[I] NEWMAN CENTERS

ALEXANDRIA. *Louisiana State University at Alexandria* Catholic Student Center, 8100 Hwy. 71-S, 71302-9633. Tel: 318-473-6494. Rev. Jason E. Gootee, Dir.

NATCHITOCHES. *Northwestern State University* Catholic Student Center, 129 Second St., P.O. Box 211, 71458. Tel: 318-352-2615; Fax: 318-352-8989. Email: holycross@cp.tel.net. Rev. Daniel A. Cook, Chap.

[J] PIOUS ASSOCIATION

PINEVILLE. *Daughters of St. Joseph*, 600 Maryhill Rd., 71360. Deborah McCullough, Contact Person. Daughters 5.

[K] MISCELLANEOUS

ALEXANDRIA. *Catholic Charitable Endowment of Alexandria*, 4400 Coliseum Blvd., 71303. Tel: 318-445-2401; Fax: 318-448-6121. Rev. Msgr. Ronald C. Hoppe, V.G., Pres. & Contact Person.

Kuumba Center, 1407 Eighth St., 71301. Tel: 318-442-0494 (Center); Fax: 318-487-9511. Sr. Linda Anne Ranard, A.S.C., Dir. Center for Creative Formation.

FOREST HILL. *Our Lady of Guadelupe Mission*, 10 Butter Cemetary Rd., 71430. Tel: 318-445-2401; Fax: 318-448-6121. Email: frpsierra@diocesealex.org. Web: www.diocesealex.org. 4400 Coliseum Blvd., 71303. Franciscan Religious of Our Lady of Refuge 4.

HESSMER. *Magnificat - Central Louisiana Chapter of the Diocese of Alexandria*, P.O. Box 37, 71341. Tel: 318-563-8213; Fax: 318-253-8247. Email: msgd@kricket.net. M. Sue Dauzat, Coord.

RELIGIOUS INSTITUTES OF MEN REPRESENTED IN THE DIOCESE

For further details refer to the corresponding bracketed number in the Religious Institutes of Men or Women section.

[]—*Apostles of Jesus (Uganda)*—A.J.

[0200]—*Benedictine Monks* (Lisle, IL)—O.S.B.

[0620]—*Brothers of the Holy Eucharist*—F.S.E.

[0275]—*Carmelites of Mary Immaculate*—C.M.I.

[0260]—*Discalced Carmelite Friars*—O.C.D.

[]—*Missionaries of St. Francis de Sales (of India)*—M.S.F.S.

[0990]—*Society of the Catholic Apostolate*—S.A.C.

RELIGIOUS INSTITUTES OF WOMEN REPRESENTED IN THE DIOCESE

[]—*Congregation of the Franciscan Religious of Our Lady of Refuge* (Guadalajara, Mexico)—R.F.R.

[2410]—*Congregation of the Marianites of Holy Cross* (Louisiana Prov.)—M.S.C.

[0470]—*Congregation of the Sisters of Charity of the Incarnate Word*—C.C.V.I.

[0965]—*Disciples of the Lord Jesus Christ*—D.L.J.C.

[2970]—*School Sisters of Notre Dame*—S.S.N.D.

[1010]—*Sisters of Divine Providence of San Antonio, Texas*—C.D.P.

[3120]—*Sisters of Our Lady of Sorrows*—O.L.S.

[4070]—*Society of the Sacred Heart*—R.S.C.J.

DIOCESAN CEMETERIES

LECOMPTE. *Lecompte Cemetery*

PINEVILLE. *Maryhill Cemetery for Clergy*

NECROLOGY

(No Deaths)

Diocese of Allentown

(Dioecesis Alanopolitana)

Most Reverend

EDWARD P. CULLEN, D.D.

Bishop of Allentown; appointed Auxiliary Bishop of Philadelphia and Titular Bishop of Paria in Proconsilare February 8, 1994; consecrated April 14, 1994; appointed Bishop of Allentown December 16, 1997; installed Third Bishop of Allentown February 9, 1998 *Office: 4029 W. Tilghman St., Allentown, PA 18104. Mailing Address: Bishop's Office,* P.O. Box F, Allentown, PA 18105.

Most Reverend

THOMAS J. WELSH

Retired Bishop of Allentown; ordained May 30, 1946; appointed Titular Bishop of Scattery Island and Auxiliary Bishop of Philadelphia on February 18, 1970; consecrated April 2, 1970; appointed as First Bishop of Arlington on June 4, 1974; installed on August 13, 1974; appointed Bishop of Allentown February 8, 1983; installed Second Bishop of Allentown on March 21, 1983; resigned December 16, 1997 *Mailing Address: 1325 Prospect Ave., Bethlehem, PA 18018.*

Chancery Office: 4029 W. Tilghman St., Allentown, PA 18104. Mailing Address: P.O. Box F, Allentown, PA 18105-1538. Tel: 610-437-0755; Fax: 610-433-7822.

ESTABLISHED JANUARY 28, 1961.

Square Miles 2,773.

Comprises the Counties of Berks, Carbon, Lehigh, Northampton and Schuylkill in the State of Pennsylvania.

STATISTICAL OVERVIEW

Personnel	
Bishop	1
Retired Bishops	1
Priests: Diocesan Active in Diocese	163
Priests: Diocesan Active Outside Diocese	12
Priests: Diocesan in Foreign Missions	2
Priests: Retired, Sick or Absent	53
Number of Diocesan Priests	230
Religious Priests in Diocese	74
Total Priests in Diocese	304
Extern Priests in Diocese	1
Ordinations:	
Diocesan Priests	2
Transitional Deacons	6
Permanent Deacons in Diocese	97
Total Sisters	409
Parishes	
Parishes	153
With Resident Pastor:	
Resident Diocesan Priests	112
Resident Religious Priests	4
Without Resident Pastor:	
Administered by Priests	34
Missions	7
Welfare	
Catholic Hospitals	3
Total Assisted	565,109
Health Care Centers	1
Total Assisted	44,496
Homes for the Aged	10
Total Assisted	598
Day Care Centers	40
Total Assisted	1,683
Specialized Homes	2
Total Assisted	4,182
Special Centers for Social Services	16
Total Assisted	79,730
Residential Care of Disabled	16
Total Assisted	114
Educational	
Diocesan Students in Other Seminaries	22
Total Seminarians	22
Colleges and Universities	2
Total Students	5,249
High Schools, Diocesan and Parish	9
Total Students	3,987
Elementary Schools, Diocesan and Parish	52
Total Students	12,248
Non-residential Schools for the Disabled	3
Total Students	123
Catechesis/Religious Education:	
Elementary Students	17,397
Total Students under Catholic Instruction	39,026
Teachers in the Diocese:	
Priests	10
Sisters	58
Lay Teachers	1,040
Vital Statistics	
Receptions into the Church:	
Infant Baptism Totals	3,622
Adult Baptism Totals	278
First Communions	3,649
Confirmations	3,683
Marriages:	
Catholic	764
Interfaith	472
Total Marriages	1,236
Deaths	3,202
Total Catholic Population	273,599
Total Population	1,161,932

Former Bishops—Most Revs. JOSEPH MCSHEA, D.D. (Retired), appt. Titular Bishop of Mina and Auxiliary Bishop of Philadelphia Feb. 8, 1952; consecrated March 19, 1952; appt. Bishop of Allentown Feb. 15, 1961; installed April 11, 1961; retired Feb. 8, 1983; died Nov. 28, 1991; THOMAS J. WELSH, D.D., J.C.D. (Retired), appt. Titular Bishop of Scattery Island and Auxiliary Bishop of Philadelphia, Feb. 18, 1970; consecrated April 2, 1970; appt. First Bishop of Arlington, June 4, 1974; installed Aug. 13, 1974; appt. Bishop of Allentown, Feb. 8, 1983; installed Second Bishop of Allentown, March 21, 1983; resigned Dec. 16, 1997.

Vicar General—Rev. Msgr. ALFRED A. SCHLERT, V.G., J.C.L., 4029 W. Tilghman St., Allentown, 18105-1538. P.O. Box F, Allentown, 18105-1538. Tel: 610-437-0755; Fax: 610-433-7822.

Chancellor—Rev. Msgr. GERALD E. GOBITAS, Th.M., 4029 W. Tilghman St., Allentown, 18105-1538. P.O. Box F, Allentown, 18105-1538. Tel: 610-437-0755; Fax: 610-433-7822.

Secretary to the Bishop—Rev. Msgr. GERALD E. GOBITAS, Th.M., 4029 W. Tilghman St., Allentown, 18105. P.O. Box F, Allentown, 18105-1538. Tel: 610-437-0755; Fax: 610-433-7822.

Victim Assistance Coordinator—Mrs. BARBARA W. MURPHY, M.S.W. Tel: 610-791-3888; Fax: 610-791-1878. Email: bmurphy@allentowndiocese.org.

Censor of Books—Rev. Msgr. JAMES J. MULLIGAN.

Diocesan Tribunal—Very Rev. JOHN J. PAUL, M.S.C., V.J., S.T.L. J.C.D., Judicial Vicar, 202 N. 17th St., Allentown, 18104. Tel: 610-434-3200; Fax: 610-433-3104.

Judges—Rev. Msgrs. DAVID J. MORRISON Retired); NEVIN J. KLINGER, M.A., J.C.L.; Revs. VICTOR F. FINELLI, J.C.L., M.Div.; JAMES J. WARD; Very Rev. THOMAS P. KOONS, V.R., J.C.L., M.A., M.Div.

Promoter of Justice—Rev. VICTOR F. FINELLI, J.C.L., M.Div.

Defenders of the Bond—Rev. DAVID J. KOZAK; Rev. Msgr. ALFRED A. SCHLERT, V.G., J.C.L.

Secretary—Deacon EUGENE J. WYRWA.

Advocates—Rev. DAVID L. JAMES; Deacon EUGENE J. WYRWA.

Notaries—Mrs. JUDITH CHUSS; Mrs. PATRICIA ECHTERNACH; Mrs. DIANE SELDOMRIDGE; Mrs. COLETTE SNYDER.

Vicar for Religious—Very Rev. THOMAS P. KOONS, V.R., J.C.L., M.A., M.Div., St. Thomas More Rectory, 1040 Flexer Ave., Allentown, 18103-5520. Tel: 610-433-7413; Fax: 610-433-2308.

Vicars Forane—Rev. Msgr. JOHN G. CHIZMAR, V.F., M.Div., Carbon Deanery; Very Revs. ALBERT J. BYRNE, V.F., M.Div., Lehigh Deanery; DENNIS T. HARTGEN, V.F., Berks Deanery; Rev. Msgr. MICHAEL J. CHABACK, S.T.D., Northampton Deanery; Very Revs. EDWARD S. ZEMANIK, North Schuylkill Deanery; EDWARD J. O'CONNOR, M.Th., M.S.W., V.F., South Schuylkill Deanery.

Secretariat for Clergy—Rev. Msgr. GERALD E. GOBITAS, Th.M., Sec., P.O. Box F, Allentown, 18105-1538. Tel: 610-437-0755; Fax: 610-433-7822.

Priest Personnel Office—Rev. Msgr. GERALD E. GOBITAS, Th.M., Dir., P.O. Box F, Allentown, 18105-1538. Tel: 610-437-0755; Fax: 610-433-7822.

Holy Family Villa for Priests—Rev. RICHARD W. CAMPO, Rector, 1325 Prospect Ave., Bethlehem, 18018-4916. Tel: 610-694-0395; Fax: 610-694-9990.

Permanent Diaconate Office—Rev. Msgr. JAMES J. MULLIGAN, Dir., 2145 Madison Ave. at Dewberry Ave., Bethlehem, 18018. Tel: 610-866-0581; Fax: 610-867-8702. P.O. Box 20607, Lehigh Valley, 18002-0607.

Vocations Office—Rev. FRANCIS A. NAVE, M.Div., Dir., 4029 W. Tilghman St., Allentown, 18105-1538. Tel: 610-437-0755; Fax: 610-433-7822.

Priestly Life and Ministry Office—Rev. Msgr. JAMES J. MULLIGAN, Dir., Mary Immaculate Center, 300 Cherryville Rd., Northampton, 18067-9548. Tel: 610-262-1885; Fax: 610-262-6766.

Secretariat for Catholic Life and Evangelization—Very Rev. E. MICHAEL CAMILLI, M.S.C., H.E.L., S.T.L., Sec., 900 S. Woodward St., Allentown, 18103-4179. Tel: 610-289-8900; Fax: 610-289-7917.

Ecumenical and Interreligious Affairs Office—Rev. RICHARD J. FORD, Dir., 510 Union St., Allentown, 18101-2307. Tel: 610-439-0111; Fax: 610-439-6048.

Office of Worship—Rev. Msgr. EDWARD J. COYLE, Dir.; Mrs. CAROLE C. CHUK, M.A., Asst. Dir., 900 S. Woodward St., Allentown, 18103-4179. Tel: 610-289-8900; Fax: 610-289-7917. Email: ecoyle@allentowndiocese.org.

Catechumenate Office—Mrs. CAROLE C. CHUK, M.A., Dir., 900 S. Woodward St., Allentown, 18103-4179. Tel: 610-289-8900; Fax: 610-289-7917. Email: cchuk@allentowndiocese.org.

Office of Hispanic Affairs—VACANT, Dir., 900 S. Woodward St., Allentown, 18103-4179. Tel: 610-289-8900; Fax: 610-289-7917.

Office of Communications—MATTHEW T. KERR, Dir., P.O. Box F, Allentown, 18105-1538. Tel: 610-871-5200, Ext. 265; Fax: 610-439-7694.

Office of Family Life Ministries—Dr. WILLIAM F. URBINE, 900 S. Woodward St., Allentown, 18103-4179. Tel: 610-289-8900; Fax: 610-289-7917. Email: wurbine@allentowndiocese.org. Lehigh-Northampton County: Mrs. SUZIE LEE, 530 Union Blvd., Allentown, 18109-3230. Tel: 610-435-1541. Berks-Schuylkill-Carbon County: Mrs. PATRICIA HARTMAN, 900 W. Market St., Orwigsburg, 17961. Tel: 570-366-1405.

The A.D. Times—Mrs. JILL M. CARAVAN, Editor, 1101 W. Hamilton St., Allentown, 18105-1538. Tel: 610-871-5200, Ext. 264; Fax: 610-439-7694. Email: adtimes@allentowndiocese.org; P.O. Box F, Allentown, 18105-1538.

Campus Ministry Office—Rev. JOHN A. KRIVAK, M.Div., Th.M., M.Ed., Ed.D., Dir., The Newman Center, 2339 Liberty St., Allentown, 18104. Tel: 484-664-3122; Fax: 484-664-3123.

Office of Youth Ministry and Young Adult Ministry—Mrs. MARY ELLEN JOHNS, B.A., Dir., St. Francis Center, 900 W. Market St., Orwigsburg, 17961-1006. Tel: 570-366-1405; Fax: 570-366-1426.

Social Action Bureau—Mrs. MARY ANN HAMMER, Dir., 900 S. Woodward St., Allentown, 18103-4179. Tel: 610-289-8900; Fax: 610-289-7917.

Office of Pro-Life Activities—Mrs. MARYANN W. DUNN, Dir., 900 S. Woodward St., Allentown, 18103-4179. Tel: 610-289-8900; Fax: 610-289-7917.

Office of Adult Formation—JEANINE BREAULT, Dir., 900 S. Woodward St., Allentown, 18103-4179. Tel: 610-289-8900; Fax: 610-289-7917.

Secretariat for Temporal Affairs—Mr. FRED A. WILLIAMS, Sec. & CFO, 1101 W. Hamilton St., P.O. Box F, Allentown, 18105-1538. Tel: 610-871-5200; Fax: 610-871-5211.

Financial Administration—Mr. RONALD J. JACOBS, SPHR, Dir.

Accounting Services—Mrs. DARLENE F. HERTZOG, Dir.

Parish Support—Mr. CHRISTOPHER E. DOMYAN, Dir.

School Support Services—Mr. CHRISTOPHER E. DOMYAN, Dir.

Information Systems—Mrs. NANCY A. TORO, Dir.

Cemeteries—Rev. Msgr. WILLIAM F. BAVER, Th.M., M.Div., Dir., 1101 W. Hamilton St., P.O. Box F, Allentown, 18105-1538. Tel: 610-871-5200, Ext. 234; Fax: 610-871-5211.

Human Resources—Mr. RONALD J. JACOBS, SPHR, Dir., 1101 W. Hamilton St., P.O. Box F, Allentown, 18105-1538. Tel: 610-871-5200, Ext. 204; Fax: 610-871-5211.

Diocesan Benefit Programs—Mrs. CAROLE A. SARMIR, Dir.

Insurance and Real Estate—Ms. KELLY C. BRUCE, A.R.M., Dir.

Development Office—Mr. MICHAEL J. PRINCIPATO, Dir., 1101 W. Hamilton St., P.O. Box F, Allentown, 18105-1538. Tel: 610-871-5200; Fax: 610-871-5211.

School Development and Government Affairs—1101 W. Hamilton St., P.O. Box F, Allentown, 18105-1538. Tel: 610-871-5200; Fax: 610-871-5211.

Secretariat for Catholic Education—Mr. PHILIP J. FROMUTH, M.Ed., Sec., 2145 Madison Ave., Bethlehem, 18017. Tel: 610-866-0581; Fax: 610-867-8702.

Elementary School Religious Education—Ms. BARBARA AMABILE, Asst. Supt.

Religious Education—Ms. BARBARA AMABILE, Asst. Supt.

Curriculum, Supervision and Professional Development (Elementary/Secondary Schools)—Sr. ANITA PATRICK GALLAGHER, I.H.M., Asst. Supt.

Personnel (Elementary and Secondary)—Sr. ROBERTA PETERS, I.H.M., Asst. Supt.

Early Childhood Education—Sr. ANITA PATRICK GALLAGHER, I.H.M., Asst. Supt.

Secondary Schools—Ms. KATHLEEN HANLON, Asst. Supt.

Government Programs and Instructional Technology—Sr. ANN MONICA BUBSER, I.H.M., Asst. Supt.

Media Library—Mrs. SUZANNE M. MELLO, Librarian.

Board of Education—Very Rev. ALBERT J. BYRNE, V.F., M.Div., Pres. Tel: 610-433-6461.

Secretariat for Catholic Human Services—Mrs. BARBARA W. MURPHY, M.S.W., Sec., 2141 Downyflake Ln., Allentown, 18103-4774. Tel: 610-791-3888; Fax: 610-791-1878.

Catholic Social Agency—Mrs. BARBARA W. MURPHY, M.S.W., Exec. Dir., 2141 Downyflake Ln., Allentown, 18103-4774. Tel: 610-791-3888; Fax: 610-791-1878.

Ministry with Persons with Disabilities—Sr. JANICE MARIE JOHNSON, R.S.M., 2141 Downyflake Ln., Allentown, 18103-4774. Tel: 610-791-3888; Fax: 610-791-1878.

Holy Family Manor, Inc.—1200 Spring St., Bethlehem, 18018. Tel: 610-865-5595; Fax: 610-997-8454.

Residential Services, Inc.—Mr. R. JAMES POLASKI, Dir., 1318 Spring St., Bethlehem, 18018. Tel: 610-865-5595; Fax: 610-997-8454.

Collaborative Residential and Home Care Services—MARY ANN CHAKLOS, Admin., Seton Manor Nursing Home, 1000 Seton Dr., Orwigsburg, 17961. Tel: 570-366-0400; Fax: 570-366-1970. Covenant Home Care, 1510 Hwy. 61 S., Pottsville, 17901-8409. Tel: 570-385-5522; 800-726-8781; Fax: 570-385-5287; HALYNA I. STEGURA, R.N., M.S.N., Dir., 2615 Perkiomen Ave., Reading, 19606. Tel: 610-779-6432; 800-300-3007; Fax: 610-779-5002.

Diocesan Medical Ethicist—Rev. Msgr. JAMES J. MULLIGAN, Dir., Mary Immaculate Center, 300 Cherryville Rd., Northampton, 18067-0027. Tel: 610-262-1885; Fax: 610-262-6766.

Council of Priests/Diocesan Consultors—4029 W. Tilghman St., P.O. Box F, Allentown, 18105. Tel: 610-437-0755; Fax: 610-433-7822.

College of Consultors—Rev. Msgrs. ALFRED A. SCHLERT, V.G., J.C.L.; JOHN B. MCCANN; Rev. JOSEPH A. DESANTIS, V.F., M.Div.; Rev. Msgr. JOHN P. MURPHY; Rev. JOHN M. GIBBONS; Rev. Msgr. GERALD E. GOBITAS, Th.M.; Rev. STEPHEN J. RADOCHA; Rev. Msgrs. JAMES J. REICHERT; EDWARD R. SACKS; JOSEPH P.T. SMITH.

Ex Officio Members—Rev. Msgrs. ALFRED A. SCHLERT, V.G., J.C.L.; GERALD E. GOBITAS, Th.M.

Elected Members—Rev. Msgr. JOSEPH P.T. SMITH; Rev. JAMES J. WARD; Rev. Msgr. JOSEPH R. SOBIESIAK; Revs. STEPHEN J. RADOCHA; WILLIAM T. CAMPION; STANLEY M. MOCZYDLOWSKI; THOMAS J. ORSULAK; FRANS J. BERKHOUT; JOSEPH T. WHALEN, M.Div.; MICHAEL J. BRIGGMAN (Retired).

Appointed Members—Rev. Msgrs. JAMES J. REICHERT; JOHN P. MURPHY; Rev. RONALD V. JANKAITIS.

Finance Council—Most Rev. EDWARD P. CULLEN, D.D.; Rev. Msgr. ALFRED A. SCHLERT, V.G., J.C.L., 4029 W. Tilghman St., P.O. Box F, Allentown, 18105-1538. Tel: 610-437-0755; Fax: 610-433-7822; Ms. ROSE MARIE L. BUKICS; Mr. P. MICHAEL EHLERMAN; Mr. JOHN F. HORRIGAN JR.; Mr. HERMAN L. RIJ; Mr. FRANK J. RYAN; Mr. JAMES A. TIEFENBRUNN; THOMAS F. TRAUD ESQ.

Affiliated Organizations

American Catholic Overseas Aid Fund—Rev. RICHARD J. FORD, Diocesan Dir., 510 Union St., Allentown, 18101-2307. Tel: 610-439-0111; Fax: 610-439-6408.

Apostleship of Prayer—VACANT, Dir., 55 Rothermel St., Reading, 19605. Tel: 610-929-2025; Fax: 610-929-4397.

Beginning Experience—Office of Family Life Ministries, 900 S. Woodward St., Allentown, 18103-4179. Tel: 610-289-8900.

Blue Army of Our Lady of Fatima—Rev. DOMINIC THAO PHAM, M.Div., Spiritual Dir., Sacred Heart Rectory, 210 E. Northampton St., Bath, 18014-1625. Tel: 610-837-7874; Fax: 610-837-4570.

Catholic Daughters of the Americas—Rev. FLOYD CAESAR JR., Diocese Committee Chap.

Charismatic Renewal—Rev. LARRY J. HESS, M.A., Bishop's Liaison, Our Lady of Good Counsel Rectory, 436 S. 2nd St., Bangor, 18013-2514. Tel: 610-588-5445; Fax: 610-599-6997.

Courage—P.O. Box F, Allentown, 18105-1538. Tel: 610-670-3674.

Cursillo Movement—Rev. MARTIN F. KERN, Spiritual Dir., 1046 W. Cedar St., Allentown, 18102-1304. Tel: 610-433-6102.

Father Walter Ciszek Prayer League, Inc. (The)—Most Rev. THOMAS J. WELSH, D.D., J.C.D., Pres. (Retired), The Ciszek Center, 231 N. Jardin St., Shenandoah, 17976-1642. Tel: 570-462-2270; Fax: 570-462-2274.

Holy Childhood Association—Rev. Msgr. JOHN P. MURPHY, Dir., 1040 Flexer Ave., Allentown, 18103-5520. Tel: 610-433-7413; Fax: 610-433-2308.

Holy Name Societies—Deacon STEPHEN ANDRUSISIAN, Dir., 516 N. Front St., Minersville, 17954-1421. Tel: 570-544-5339.

Knights of Columbus—

St. Peter the Fisherman Council #10772, Lake Harmony—ANTHONY CARANGELO, Grand Knight, P.O. Box 1257, Albrightsville, 18210-3012. Tel: 570-722-1576.

St. Joseph the Worker Council #10921, Orefield—JOHN CAVALLI, Grand Knight, 115 Wolf Dr., Allentown, 18104. Tel: 610-398-7413.

St. Paul Council #10922, Allentown—JOHN M. LEVCHAK, Grand Knight, 2437 S. 5th St., Allentown, 18103. Tel: 610-791-4876.

Calvary Council #528, Allentown—JOSEPH E. MEDL, Grand Knight; Rev. FRANCIS A. NAVE, M.Div., Chap., 1013 N. 17th St., Allentown, 18104. Tel: 610-435-9058; 484-951-4473.

Sarto Council #1322, Ashland—THOMAS P. COLIHAN, Grand Knight, 75 S. Hoffman Blvd., Ashland, 17921-1951. Tel: 570-875-2091.

Father DeNisco Council #3862, Bangor—RONALD CESARE, Grand Knight, 1646 Alpine Dr., Pen Argyl, 18072. Tel: 610-863-4053; 610-863-6205.

Trinity Council #313, Bethlehem—JAMES HOGG III, Grand Knight, 1604 Jill St., Bethlehem, 18017-6213.

Holy Cross Council #4754, Bethlehem—ROBERT J. NAVIN, Grand Knight, 1713 Budd Ave., Bethlehem, 18018-4601. Tel: 610-865-1639.

Union Council #345, Easton—FRANK S. GUALANO, Grand Knight, 328 Ellwood St., Easton, 18045-3719. Tel: 610-253-6933.

St. Ann Council #12886, Emmaus—THOMAS MULKERN, 415 S. 6th St., Emmaus, 18049-2908. Tel: 610-965-2426.

Rev. James A. Hogan Council #2580, Frackville—SAMUEL A. BENDER, Grand Knight, 156 N. Center St., Frackville, 17931-1226. Tel: 570-874-1438.

Father Sheridan Council #748, Girardville—WADE RICHARDS, Grand Knight, 223 W. Main St., Girardville, 17935. Tel: 570-278-1014.

Damien Council #598, Jim Thorpe— (Serving Jim Thorpe, Lehighton, Nesquehoning and the surrounding areas). CHRISTOPHER A. HEERY, Grand Knight, 383 S. Third St., Lehighton, 18235. Tel: 610-379-0406.

Archbishop Ryan Council #1552, Lansford—FRANK SERINA, Grand Knight, 107 W. Bertsch St., Lansford, 18232-1908. Tel: 570-645-5221.

Mahanoy City Council #549, Mahanoy City—GEORGE J. GAYDOSH, Grand Knight, 407 W. Pine St., Mahanoy City, 17948-2515. Tel: 570-773-2844.

Our Lady of the Sacred Heart Council #4282, Nazareth—WILLIAM J. TANZOSH, Grand Knight, 615 Hill Ave., Nazareth, 18064-9507. Tel: 610-759-3161; Fax: 610-746-7069.

Queenship of Mary Council #4050, Northampton—BRUCE WERMANN, Grand Knight, P.O. Box 422, Laurys Station, 18059-0422. Tel: 610-262-8381.

Lafayette Council #2522, Palmerton—GEORGE KATTNER, Grand Knight, 203 Howard Ave., Palmerton, 18071-1222. Tel: 610-823-6336.

Schuylkill Council #431, Pottsville—Dr. LUIS R. VISOT, Grand Knight, 1323 Mahantongo St., Pottsville, 17901. Tel: 570-621-9500.

Reading Council #793, Reading—RODNEY SHAPPELL, Grand Knight, 950 Weiser St., Reading, 19601. Tel: 610-376-5734.

Holy Eucharist Council #4198, Reading—EDWARD W. KOSAK, Grand Knight, 210 Fairway Dr., Reading, 19606-3667. Tel: 610-370-0739.

Francis Cardinal Brennan Council #618, Shenandoah—DWAYNE M. HIXSON, Grand Knight, 228 Indiana Ave., Shenandoah, 17976. Tel: 570-462-3580.

Holy Name Council #7179, Shillington—JOSEPH D. GILES, Grand Knight, 825 Old Fritztown Rd., Sinking Spring, 19608-9151. Tel: 610-777-7276.

Light of Christ Council #8726, Sinking Spring—JOHN J. KUZIO, Grand Knight, 1738 York Rd., Wyomissing Hills, 19610.

Father Henry Baker Council #2711, Tamaqua—WILLIAM SOMMERS, Grand Knight, RR 1, Box 329, Tamaqua, 18252-9474.

Father Henry Baker Council #12105, Weatherly—JOSEPH THOMAS, Grand Knight, 435 Carbon St., Weatherly, 18255-4137. Tel: 570-427-8474.

Legion of Mary, Reading Curia—Mrs. AIDA TORRES, Pres., 1226 Perkiomen Ave., Reading, 19602. Tel: 610-478-1346.

Marriage Encounter—Rev. ROBERT A. DRESSLER, Dir. (Retired), St. Ursula Rectory, 1300 Broadway, Bethlehem, 18018-4099. Tel: 610-867-5122; Fax: 610-867-6569.

National Shut-In Visitation Society—Rev. Msgr. FELIX A. LOSITO, Natl. Dir., 237 Franklin St., Reading, 19602-1099. Tel: 610-373-5579.

Operation Rice Bowl—Rev. Msgr. JOHN P. MURPHY, Dir., 1040 Flexer Ave., Allentown, 18103-5520. Tel: 610-433-7413; Fax: 610-433-2308.

Our Lady's Missionaries of the Eucharist—Most Rev. THOMAS J. WELSH, D.D., J.C.D. (Retired) A Public Association of Christ's Faithful. Magnificat House, 4530 Vera Cruz Rd., Center Valley, 18034-9740. Tel: 610-797-1950; Fax: 610-797-1715. Email: olme@olme.org. Web: www.olme.org.

Pontifical Society for the Propagation of the Faith—Rev. Msgr. JOHN P. MURPHY, Dir., 1040 Flexer Ave., Allentown, 18103-5520. Tel: 610-433-7413; Fax: 610-433-2308.

Saint Vincent De Paul Society—Rev. FRANCIS P. STRAKA, Spiritual Advisor; Mr. EDWARD BUTLER, Pres. Diocesan Council, 529 Lytle St., Minersville, 17954. Tel: 570-544-2739.

Secular Franciscan Order—St. Francis Retreat House, 3918 Chipman Rd., Easton, 18045-3014. Tel: 610-258-3053; Fax: 610-258-2412. Mr. WILLIAM SHEETS, 1525 Mine Lane Rd., Easton, 18045. Tel: 610-559-0995.

Serra Clubs—

Serra Club of Bethlehem—Rev. ANTHONY P. MONGIELLO, Chap.; VIOLET ULIANA, Pres., 1710 Stokes Park Rd., Bethlehem, 18017-2239. Tel: 610-865-3054.

Forks of the Delaware Serra—Rev. PATRICK H. LAMB, Chap.; PATRICIA SMITH, Pres., 820 Spring Garden St., Easton, 18042. Tel: 610-252-2381.

Serra Club of Allentown—Rev. FRANS J. BERKHOUT, Chap.; JOSEPH BECHTEL, Pres., 314 Second St., Slatington, 18080-1814. Tel: 610-767-6283.

Reading Serra—Rev. ROBERT T. FINLAN, Chap.; JOSEPHINE HOZZA, Pres., 404 Windsor St., Reading, 19606. Tel: 610-375-7911.

Third Order Dominican Chapter & Expectation of Blessed Virgin Mother Chapter—Dr. FELICIDAD QUILO, Moderator, 4290 Vassar Ave., Bethlehem, 18017. Tel: 610-691-6761.

Miscellaneous Affiliated Organizations

Catholic Men of Good News (CMOGN)—Rev. LARRY J. HESS, M.A., Our Lady of Good Counsel, 436 S. 2nd St., Bangor, 18013-2514. Tel: 610-588-5445; Fax: 610-599-6997.

Dayspring Homes, Inc.—Sr. FRANCIS BISLAND, C.P.S., C.E.O. & Dir., P.O. Box 172, Reading, 19607-0172. Tel: 610-376-5648; Fax: 610-374-9086 Email: dayspringhomes@dayspringhomes.org.

Mary's Shelter—Sr. M. EILEEN KANTZ M.S.C., Program Dir.; CHRISTINE FOLK, Admin., 325 S. 12th St., Reading, 19602-2021. Tel: 610 376-1973; Fax: 610-376-5391. Mary's Home, 733 Upland Ave., Reading, 19607. Tel: 610-603-8010; Fax: 610-603-8012.

U.S. Province Director's Offices—460 St. Bernardine St., Reading, 19607-1737. Tel: 610-777-4174; Fax: 610-777-3973. Email: bfprovoff@talon.net. Web: www.franciscan.org.

Office of Communication—Sr. ROSE JAMESON, Dir. Tel: 610-777-4174; Fax: 610-777-3973. Email: srose@talon.net srose50@aol.com.

Office of Development—Sr. DOLORICE DOMIN, Dir. Tel: 610-796-8970; Fax: 610-777-3973. Email: sdolorice@talon.net.

Office of Finance—Sisters ANTOINETTE KEISER, Dir.; MARIE JANEEN OBARA, Sec.; VACANT, Bookkeeper. Tel: 610-777-2967; 800-777-1894; Fax: 610-777-3973. Email: antoin13@aol.com.

Health Benefits Office—Sr. JANET TAPHORN, O.S.F. Tel: 800-777-1894; 610-777-2967.

Office of Formation—Sr. CLAUDE MARIE JABLONSKI, Dir., Initial Formation and Vocations/Assocs. Tel: 610-796-7713. Email: sclaude@talon.net.

Office of Justice, Peace, Earthcare—Sr. ROSE MACDERMOTT, O.S.F., Dir., 2627 W. Ninth St., Chester, 19013-2115. Tel: 610-497-3641; Fax: 610-497-3434. Email: jperose@aol.com.

Office of Personnel—Sr. KATERI PEAKE, Dir. Tel: 610-796-8972. Email: skateri@talon.net.

Office of Retirement—VACANT.

Office of Vocations/Associates—JENNIFER GLASS, Asst. Vocations/Assoc. Dir. Tel: 610-796-8971. Email: jglass@talon.net.

CLERGY, PARISHES, MISSIONS AND PAROCHIAL SCHOOLS

CITY OF ALLENTOWN
(LEHIGH COUNTY)

1—CATHEDRAL OF ST. CATHARINE OF SIENA (1919), (Indian), Very Rev. Albert J. Byrne, V.F., M.Div.; Revs. David L. James; Keith R. Laskowski, M.Div.; Deacon William Hassler. In Res., Rev. Msgrs. Alfred A. Schlert, V.G., J.C.L.; Alfred R. Ott, V.F., M.Div., Pastor Emeritus (Retired).
Res.: 1825 W. Turner St., 18104. Tel: 610-433-6461; Fax: 610-433-5452.
School—(Grades PreK-8), 210 N. 18th St., 18104. Tel: 610-435-8981; Fax: 610-437-7951. Mrs. H. Jacqueline Greco, Prin. Lay Teachers 30; Students 500.
Catechesis/Religious Program—Tel: 610-432-7655. Sr. Laura Berryman, S.C.C., D.R.E. Students 185.

2—ST. FRANCIS OF ASSISI (1928), Rev. Msgr. Thomas J. Benestad, M.Div.; Rev. Martin F. Kern; Deacon Eugene M. Flanley Jr.
Res.: 801 N. 11th St., 18102-1304. Fax: 610-434-6972.
Business Office—1046 W. Cedar St.. Tel: 610-433-6102.
School—(Grades PreK-8), 1035 Washington St., 18102. Tel: 610-435-0364; Fax: 610-435-2666. Sisters of St. Francis of Philadelphia 1; Lay Teachers 12; Students 209.
Parish Center—1046 W. Cedar St., 18102.
Catechesis/Religious Program—Tel: 610-434-8299. Students 246.

3—IMMACULATE CONCEPTION (1857), [CEM], (Declared National Shrine of Our Lady of Guadalupe, Mother of the Americas 1974). Rev. Harold F. Dagle; Deacons Brian J. Monahan; Richard L. Benkovic.
Res.: 501 Ridge Ave., 18102. Tel: 610-433-4404; Fax: 610-433-8401.
School—Holy Spirit Regional Catholic Elementary School, Allentown, Tel: 610-434-4044; Fax: 610-434-5458. See separate listing.
Catechesis/Religious Program— Located at Holy Spirit Elementary School, Allentown. Students 143.

4—ST. JOHN THE BAPTIST, (Slovak), [CEM] Rev. Msgr. Robert F. Kozel.
Res.: 924 N. Front St., 18102-1999. Tel: 610-432-0034; Fax: 610-432-2776.
School—Holy Spirit Regional Catholic Elementary School, Allentown See separate listing.
Convent—920 N. Front St., 18102. Tel: 610-434-1471.

5—OUR LADY HELP OF CHRISTIANS (1927), Rev. Bernard A. Flanagan; Deacon Charles A. Coyle. In Res., Rev. Msgr. Robert M. Forst (Retired).
Res.: 444 N. Jasper St., 18109. Tel: 610-432-9384; Fax: 610-782-9297.
School—934 Hanover Ave., 18109. Tel: 610-433-1592. Sisters of Christian Charity 2; Lay Teachers 9; Students 153.
Catechesis/Religious Program—Students 60.
Convent—922 Hanover Ave., 18109. Tel: 610-433-4915.

6—OUR LADY OF MT. CARMEL (1911), (Italian), [CEM] Rev. John J. Grabish; Deacon Dominick F. Amedeo.
Res.: 336 N. 4th St., 18102-3008. Tel: 610-434-5171; Fax: 610-434-2441.
School—Sacred Heart Regional Catholic Elementary School, Allentown, Tel: 610-437-3031; Fax: 610-437-1310. See separate listing.
Catechesis/Religious Program—Tel: 610-434-5171, Ext. 21. Located at Sacred Heart, Allentown.

7—ST. PAUL (1928), Rev. Msgr. Joseph R. Sobiesiak; Rev. Victor F. Finelli, J.C.L., M.Div.; Deacons Daniel A. Thomson; Gary Granato.
Res.: 920 S. Second St., 18103. Tel: 610-797-9733; Fax: 610-797-9537.
Church: Second St. & Susquehanna St., 18103.
School—(Grades K-8), 219 W. Susquehanna St., 18103. Tel 610-797-5321; Fax: 610-797-0200. Janet Brogan, Prin. Lay Teachers 12; Students 210.
Catechesis/Religious Program—Students 315.

8—SS. PETER AND PAUL (1912), (Polish), Rev. Ladislaus J. Dudek.
Res.: 1065 Fullerton Ave., 18102. Tel: 610-432-2252; Fax: 610-432-0247.
School—Holy Spirit Regional Catholic Elementary School, Allentown See separate listing.
Catechesis/Religious Program—Students 4.

9—SACRED HEART OF JESUS (1869), (German—Spanish), [CEM] Revs. John J. Grabish; Andrew N. Gehringer; Deacons Saul Hernandez; Alfonso Solis; Dominic Amadeo.
Res.: 336 N. Fourth St., 18102. Tel: 610-434-5171; Fax: 610-434-2441.
School—(Grades PreK-8), 325 N. Fourth St., 18102. Tel: 610-437-3031; Fax: 610-437-1310. James Krupka, Prin. Lay Teachers 10; Students 199.
High School—Tel: 610-437-4601; Fax: 610-437-6760. Rev. Frans J. Berkhout, Prin.
Catechesis/Religious Program—Parish Center, 317 N. 4th St., 18102. Mrs. Nilsa Noelia Fernandez, D.R.E. Students 405.

10—ST. STEPHEN OF HUNGARY (1915), (Hungarian), Rev. Richard J. Ford.
Res.: 510 Union St., 18101-2307. Tel: 610 439-0111; Fax: 610-439-6048.
School—Sacred Heart Regional Catholic Elementary School, Allentown See separate listing.

11—ST. THOMAS MORE (1966), Rev. Msgr. John P. Murphy; Rev. Stanley M. Moczydlowski; Deacons James R. Duncan; Thomas J. Mullins; Ralph J. Jaccodine. In Res., Very Rev. Thomas P. Koons, V.R., J.C.L., M.A., M.Div.
Res.: 1040 Flexer Ave., 18103-5520. Tel: 610-433-7413; Fax: 610-433-2308.
School—Tel: 610-432-0396; Fax: 610-432-1395. Bernardine Sisters 1; Lay Teachers 41; Students 651.
Catechesis/Religious Program—Tel: 610-437-3491; Fax: 610-437-4935. Kevin Damitz, D.R.E Students 473.
Convent—992 Flexer Ave., 18103-3664. Tel: 610-437-9520; Fax: 610-432-9359.

OUTSIDE CITY OF ALLENTOWN

ASHLAND, SCHUYLKILL CO.

1—ST. JOSEPH (1856), [CEM] Rev. John A. Frink, M.Div.; Deacon Robert McManus.
Res.: 802 Pine St., 17921. Tel: 570-875-1521; Fax: 570-875-2635.
Office—1115 Walnut St., 17921.
School—Immaculate Heart Regional Catholic Elementary School, Girardville, Tel: 570-276-6568. See separate listing.
Catechesis/Religious Program—Students 65.
Convent—1123 Walnut St., 17921. Tel: 570-875-3553.

2—ST. MAURITIUS (1856), (German), [CEM] Rev. John A. Frink, M.Div.; Deacon Robert McManus.
Res.: 802 Pine St., 17921. Tel: 570-875-2990; Fax: 570-875-2635.
School—Immaculate Heart Regional Catholic Elementary School, Girardville, Tel: 570-276-6568. See separate listing.
Catechesis/Religious Program—Tel: 570-875-1521. Students 32.
Mission—St. Elizabeth Main St., Lavelle, Schuylkill Co. 17943.

BALLY, BERKS CO., MOST BLESSED SACRAMENT (1741), [CEM] Rev. Msgr. Edward J. Coyle; Revs. Michael J. Briggman, Pastor Emeritus (Retired); Robert Freed; Deacon Thomas J. Murphy.
Res.: 610 Pine St., Box C, 19503. Tel: 610-845-2460; Fax: 610-845-2660.
School—St. Francis Academy, Bally, Tel: 610-845-7364; Fax: 610-845-2223. See separate listing.
Catechesis/Religious Program—Students 220.

BANGOR, NORTHAMPTON CO., OUR LADY OF GOOD COUNSEL (1915), [CEM] Rev. Larry J. Hess, M.A.
Res.: 436 S. Second St., 18013-2514. Tel: 610-588-5445; Fax: 610-599-6997.
School—Our Lady of Mt. Carmel Regional Catholic Elementary School, Roseto, Tel: 610-588-2629; Fax: 610-588-3423. See separate listing.
Catechesis/Religious Program—Tel: 570-897-6941; Fax: 610-588-8811. Elizabeth Thompson, D.R.E. Students 105.
Mission—St. Vincent de Paul Church St., Portland, Northampton Co. 18351.

BARNESVILLE, SCHUYLKILL CO., ST. RICHARD OF CHICHESTER (1950), Rev. Stephen J. Halabura.
Res.: 799 Barnesville Dr., 18214-9747. Tel: 570-467-2315; Fax: 570-467-2462.
Catechesis/Religious Program—Students 9.

BATH, NORTHAMPTON CO., SACRED HEART (1920), [CEM] Revs. Daniel J. Yenushosky; Dominic Thao Pham, M.Div.; Deacon John A. Hanni.
Res.: 210 E. Northampton St., 18014-1524. Tel: 610-837-7874; Fax: 610-837-4570.
School—(Grades PreK-8), 115 Washington St., 18014. Tel: 610-837-6391; Fax: 610-837-2469. Louise Glass, Prin. Lay Teachers 9; Students 228.
Catechesis/Religious Program—Mrs. Helen M. Browne, D.R.E. Students 231.

BEAVER MEADOWS, CARBON CO., ST. MARY (1841), [CEM] Rev. John J. Duminiak.
Res.: 121 Berwick St., P.O. Box 235, 18216. Tel: 570-455-2613; Fax: 570-455-3125.
Catechesis/Religious Program—Fax: 570-455-2613. Students 53.

BERLINSVILLE, NORTHAMPTON CO., ST. NICHOLAS (1974), [CEM] Rev. Francis P. Schoenauer.
Res.: 1152 Oak Rd., Walnutport, 18088-9728. Tel: 610-767-3107; Fax: 610-760-6241.
School—St. John Neumann Regional Catholic Elementary School, Palmerton-Slatington, Tel: 610-826-2354; Fax: 610-826-6444. See separate listing
Catechesis/Religious Program—Students 126.

BETHLEHEM, LEHIGH CO.

1—NOTRE DAME OF BETHLEHEM (1954), Rev. Msgrs. William E. Handges; John A. Auchter; Rev. Edward J. Essig; Deacon Richard T. Sewald. In Res., Rev. Bernard J. Ezaki.
Res.: 1861 Catasauqua Rd., 18018-1298. Tel: 610-866-4371; Fax: 610-866-9065.

School—(Grades K-8), 1835 Catasauqua Rd., 18018. Tel: 610-866-2231; Fax: 610-866-4374. Sr. Patricia A. Cullen, S.S.J., Prin. Sisters of St. Joseph 1; Lay Teachers 24; Students 434.
Catechesis/Religious Program—Tel: 610-866-1418. Mrs. Stephanie Kalavoda, D.R.E. Students 360.
Convent—1823 Catasauqua Rd., 18018. Tel: 610-866-4310.

2—SS. SIMON AND JUDE (1917), Revs. Robert J. Reed; James L. Maranki. In Res., Rev. John J.L. Little, M.Div.
Res.: 730 W. Broad St., 18018. Tel: 610-866-5582; Fax: 610-866-2992.
School—(Grades K-8), 6th Ave. & North St., 18018. Tel: 610-867-9530. Sr. Mary Sue Carwile, I.H.M., Prin. Sisters of the Immaculate Heart of Mary 2; Lay Teachers 12; Students 175.
Catechesis/Religious Program—Tel: 610-861-7507. Students 181.
Convent—714 W. Broad St., 18018. Tel: 610-867-9546.

BETHLEHEM, NORTHAMPTON CO.

1—ST. ANNE (1929), Revs. Anthony P. Mongiello; Thomas J. Orsulak; Deacons Francis Cosgrove; Richard G. Scrak.
Res.: 450 E. Washington Ave., 18017-5944. Tel: 610-867-5039; Fax: 610-882-4094.
School—(Grades PreK-8), 375 Hickory St., 18017-5944. Tel: 610-868-4182; Fax: 610-868-8709. Mrs. Norma Romberger, Prin. Lay Teachers 20; Students 415.
Catechesis/Religious Program—Tel: 610-868-7514. Mrs. Monica Emrock, D.R.E. Students 527.

2—SS. CYRIL AND METHODIUS (1891), (Slovak), [CEM] Rev. Msgr. Michael J. Chaback, S.T.D.; Deacons Frank J. Danyi Jr.; Jeffrey R. Trexler.
Res.: 617 Pierce St., 18015. Tel: 610-866-3391; Fax: 610-866-6490.
School—(Grades K-8), 551 Thomas St. & Pierce St., 18015. Tel: 610-866-0042; Fax: 610-866-4914. Mrs. Joan M. West, Prin. Lay Teachers 9; Students 105.
Catechesis/Religious Program—Students 55.
Convent—520 Buchanan St., 18015. Tel: 610-866-0275.

3—HOLY GHOST (1871), (German), [CEM] Rev. Francis P. Straka; Deacon Franklin J. Chiles.
Res.: 417 Carlton Ave., 18015. Tel: 610-867-9382; Fax: 610-867-6839.
School—Holy Child Regional Catholic Elementary School, Bethlehem, Tel: 610-865-0861; Fax: 610-997-0180. See separate listing.
Catechesis/Religious Program—Students 26.

4—HOLY INFANCY (1861), [CEM] Rev. Msgr. Robert J. Biszek; Rev. David J. Kozak; Deacons Nicasio Rodriguez; Roberto DeJesus; Victor M. Quiles; Manuel Ramirez. In Res., Rev. Robson Luis Weber, Portugese Apostolate.
Res.: 312 E. Fourth St., 18015-1706. Tel: 610-866-1121; Fax: 610-866-7094.
School—(Grades PreK-8), 4th & Webster Sts., 18015. Tel: 610-868-2621; Fax: 610-868-5402. Sr. Joyce Valese, Prin. Sisters of St. Joseph 2; Sisters of St. Francis 1; Lay Teachers 12; Students 172.
Catechesis/Religious Program—Tel: 610-866-5302; Fax: 610-866-9530. Stephanie Rivera, D.R.E. Students 159.
Convent—Sisters of St. Joseph of Chestnut Hill, Philadelphia, 202 E. 4th St., 18015. Tel: 610-867-7384.
Convent—Poor Sisters of St. Joseph, Argentina, Casa Belen, 305 E. Fourth St., 18015. Tel: 610-867-4030.

5—ST. JOHN CAPISTRANO (1903), (Hungarian), Rev. Edward C. Bolez.
Res.: 910 E. Fourth St., 18015-1904. Tel: 610-866-2714; Fax: 610-317-8026.
School—SS. Cyril and Methodius Regional Catholic Elementary School, Bethlehem, Tel: 610-866-0042; Fax: 610-866-4914. See separate listing.
Catechesis/Religious Program—Students 8.

6—ST. JOSEPH (1913), (Slovenian—Croatian), Rev. Joseph N. Galic, O.F.M.
Res.: 416 E. Fifth St., 18015-1893. Tel: 610-866-4102; Fax: 610-866-4258.
School—SS. Cyril and Methodius Regional Catholic Elementary School, Bethlehem, Tel: 610-866-0042. See separate listing.
Catechesis/Religious Program—Tel: 610-868-2567. Students 13.

7—OUR LADY OF PERPETUAL HELP (1963), Rev. Msgr. Edward R. Sacks; Rev. Cletus S. Onyegbule; Deacon George C. Kelly Jr. In Res., Rev. Msgr. David J. Morrison (Retired).
Res.: 3219 Santee Rd., 18020. Tel: 610-867-8409; Fax: 610-867-4870.
School—3221 Santee Rd., 18020. Tel: 610-868-6570; Fax: 610-868-7941. Lay Teachers 14; Students 295.
Catechesis/Religious Program—Students 564.

8—OUR LADY OF POMPEII (1902), (Italian), Rev. Msgr. Paul B. della Picca.
Res.: 826 E. Fourth St., 18015. Tel: 610-691-0719; Fax: 610-691-0719.
School—SS. Cyril and Methodius Regional Catholic Elementary School, Bethlehem, Tel: 610-866-0042; Fax: 610-866-6490. See separate listing.
Catechesis/Religious Program— Located at SS. Cyril and Methodius School, Bethlehem.

9—ST. STANISLAUS (1906), (Polish), Rev. Francis J. Opps, Admin.
Res.: 429 Hayes St., 18015. Tel: 610-867-9323.
School—SS. Cyril and Methodius Regional Catholic Elementary School, Bethlehem See separate listing.
Catechesis/Religious Program—Students 19.

BIRDSBORO, BERKS CO., IMMACULATE CONCEPTION (1916), [CEM 2] Rev. Msgr. Nevin J. Klinger, M.A., J.C.L.; Deacons Gerard E. End Jr.; Jose N. Rodriguez-Trejo.
903 Chestnut St., Douglassville, 19518. In Res., Rev. Msgr. Richard J. Loeper, M.A. (Retired); Rev. Joseph A. Barnes, Pastor Emeritus (Retired).
Res.: 640 E. Main St., 19508. Tel: 610-582-2411; Fax: 610-404-2609.
School—Immaculate Conception Academy, (Grades K-7) Tel: 610-404-8645; Fax: 610-404-4890. Mrs. Christine Foley, Prin. See separate listing. Total Enrollment 148.
Catechesis/Religious Program—Tel: 610-582-3880; Fax: 610-404-2609. Antoinette Kaucher, D.R.E. Students 350.

BOYERTOWN, BERKS CO., ST. COLUMBKILL (1921), Rev. Robert C. Quinn; Deacons Michael Woodall; Joseph L. Paschall Jr.
Res.: 200 Indian Spring Rd., 19512. Tel: 610-367-2371; Fax: 610-369-0242.
School—St. Francis Academy, Bally, Tel: 610-845-7364; Fax: 610-845-2223. See separate listing.
Catechesis/Religious Program—Tel: 610-367-5975. Sr. Nancy Kramer, S.S.J., D.R.E.; Constance Boyer, D.R.E. Students 875.

BRANCHDALE, SCHUYLKILL CO., ST. MARY STAR OF THE SEA (1886), [CEM] Rev. Leo J. Maletz.
Res.: State Rd., P.O. Box 385, 17923. Tel: 570-544-2592; Fax: 570-544-5742.
School—Good Shepherd Regional Catholic Elementary School, Minersville, Tel: 570-544-3766; Fax: 570-544-4870. See separate listing.
Catechesis/Religious Program—301 Heffner St., Minersville, 17954. Tel: 570-544-6288; Fax: 570-544-3317. Students 12.

BROCKTON, SCHUYLKILL CO., ST. BARTHOLOMEW (1846), [CEM] Rev. Edward W. Coleman.
Res.: 214 Green St., Box 292, 17925. Tel: 570-668-1500; Fax: 570-668-5487.
School—St. Jerome Regional Catholic Elementary, Tamaqua, Tel: 570-668-2757. See separate listing.
Catechesis/Religious Program—Tel: 570-668-4416. Located at St. Jerome Regional, Tamaqua. Students 13.

CATASAUQUA, LEHIGH CO., ANNUNCIATION B.V.M. - ST. MARY'S (1857), (German), [CEM] Rev. Edward R. Domin; Deacon Joseph H. Bogusky.
Res.: 122 Union St., 18032-1923. Tel: 610-264-0332; Fax: 610-264-5271.
Catechesis/Religious Program—Tel: 610-264-9383. Mrs. Marjorie Kovacs, D.R.E. Students 110.

CATASAUQUA, NORTHAMPTON CO.

1—ST. ANDREW (1902), (Slovak), [CEM] Rev. William T. Baker.
Mailing Address: 1001 2nd St., 18032. Tel: 610-264-1972; Fax: 610-264-2105.
Church: Third St. & Cypress St., North Catasauqua, 18032.
School—Our Lady of Hungary Regional Catholic Elementary School, Northampton, Tel: 610-262-9171; Fax: 610-262-2202. See separate listing.
Catechesis/Religious Program—Tel: 610-264-1972. Located at St Lawrence, Catasauqua Students 15.

2—ST. LAWRENCE (Lehigh Co.) (1858), [CEM 2] Rev. William T. Baker.
Res.: 1001 Second St., 18032. Tel: 610-264-1972; Fax: 610-264-2105.
School— Please see separate listing under Regional Catholic Elementary Schools, Diocesan in the Institutions section.
Catechesis/Religious Program—Students 94.

COALDALE, SCHUYLKILL CO.

1—SS. CYRIL AND METHODIUS (1920), (Slovak), [CEM] Rev. John J. Pavlosky.
Res.: 41 E. Ruddle St., 18218-1206. Tel: 570-645-4647; Fax: 570-645-4849.
School—Our Lady of the Angels Academy, Lansford, Tel: 570-645-7170. See separate listing.
Catechesis/Religious Program—Students 6.

2—ST. JOHN THE BAPTIST (1914), (Lithuanian), [JC] Rev. John J. Pavlosky.
Res.: 41 E. Ruddle St., 18218-1206. Tel: 570-645-4647; Fax: 570-645-4849.
School—Our Lady of the Angels Academy, Lansford, Tel: 570-645-7170. See separate listing.
Catechesis/Religious Program—Students 4.

3—ST. MARY OF THE ASSUMPTION (1892), (Irish), Rev. John J. Pavlosky.
Res.: 41 E. Ruddle St., 18218-1206. Tel: 570-645-4647; Fax: 570-645-4849.
School—Our Lady of the Angels Academy, Lansford, Tel: 570-645-7170; Fax: 570-645-5278. See separate listing.
Catechesis/Religious Program—Students 7.
Convent—231 Second St., 18218. Tel: 570-645-2310.

COLESVILLE, LEHIGH CO., ASSUMPTION B.V.M. (1927), Rev. Msgr. John J. Martin; Rev. James P. Finnegan, O.S.F.S.; Patricia Herbst, Pastoral Min.; Deacons Bernard M. Wisser; Richard Thoden.
Res.: 4101 Old Bethlehem Pike, Bethlehem, 18015. Tel: 610-867-7424; Fax: 610-867-8301.
School—St. Michael the Archangel Regional Catholic Elementary School, Colesville-Limeport See separate listing.
Catechesis/Religious Program—Tel: 610-814-0712. Christina Bigatel Durback, D.R.E. Students 256.

COPLAY, LEHIGH CO., ST. PETER (1927), (Austrian—Hungarian), [CEM] Rev. Msgr. William F. Baver, Th.M., M.Div.; Rev. Paul L. Bader, Pastor Emeritus (Retired); Deacon Stephen F. Nemeth. In Res., Rev. Francis J. Opps.
Res.: 4 S. Fifth St., 18037. Tel: 610-262-2417; Fax: 610-262-2652.
School—Christ the King Regional Catholic Elementary School, Coplay, Whitehall, Tel: 610-262-5822; Fax: 610-262-5632. See separate listing.
Catechesis/Religious Program—Tel: 610-261-2975. Deacon Stephen F. Nemeth, D.R.E. Students 104.

CUMBOLA, SCHUYLKILL CO., ST. ANTHONY OF PADUA (1907), (Polish), [CEM] Rev. Joseph J. Kweder, M.Div.
Market St., 17930. Tel: 570-277-0064.
Parish Office—99 Valley St., New Philadelphia, 17959-1120. Tel: 570-277-6815; Fax: 570-277-0528.
Catechesis/Religious Program—Students 2.

EASTON, NORTHAMPTON CO.

1—ST. ANTHONY OF PADUA (1909), (Italian), [CEM] Revs. Floyd Caesar Jr.; Luigi Palmieri; Deacon Charles A. DeBellis. In Res., Rev. Joseph A. Sheehan.
Res.: 900 Washington St., 18042-4342. Tel: 610-253-7188; Fax: 610-253-6184.
School—, Formerly Easton Catholic School, Easton For details, refer to Easton Catholic School, Easton located in Regional Catholic Elementary Schools, Diocesan in the Institutions section.
Catechesis/Religious Program—Mrs. Karen Donato, D.R.E. Students 170.
Convent—770 Washington St., 18042. Tel: 610-258-7792; Fax: 610-258-7792.
Chapel—South Easton, St. Mary's

2—ST. BERNARD (1829), [CEM] [JC] Rev. Msgr. John S. Campbell; Deacons Henry Fleck Jr.; Thomas C. Reichard; Rodoberto Matos.
Res. and Parish Center: 132 S. Fifth St., 18042. Tel: 610-252-7381; Fax: 610-252-6757.
School—Easton Catholic School, Easton, Tel: 610-252-1393; Fax: 610-253-6184. See separate listing.
Catechesis/Religious Program—Karen Corpora, D.R.E. Students 213.

3—ST. JANE FRANCES DE CHANTAL (1920), [JC] Revs. Stephen Radocha; Scott Ardinger; Robert Fagan; Deacons Robert W. Rodgers; William C. Vanzino.
Res.: 123 S. Nulton, 18045. Tel: 610-253-3553; Fax: 610-253-5711.
School—(Grades PreK-8), 1946 Washington Blvd., 18042. Tel: 610-253-8442; Fax: 610-253-2427. Lay Teachers 23; Students 516.
Catechesis/Religious Program—Tel: 610-253-7794. Students 463.

4—ST. JOSEPH (1852), (German), [CEM 2] Revs. Joseph A. Sheehan, Pastor Emeritus; William N. Seifert.
Res.: 129 Davis St., 18042-6295. Tel: 610-252-0242; Fax: 610-253-7558.
School—Easton Catholic School, Easton See separate listing.
Catechesis/Religious Program—Students 105.

5—ST. MICHAEL (1915), (Lithuanian), [CEM] Rev. Msgr. John S. Campbell; Deacons Thomas C. Reichard; Henry Fleck Jr.
Res.: 132 S. Fifth, 18042. Tel: 610-252-7381; Fax: 610-252-6757.
School—Easton Catholic School, Easton, Tel: 610-252-1393; Fax: 610-253-6184. See separate listing.
Catechesis/Religious Program—Students 9.

ELLENGOWAN, SCHUYLKILL CO., ST. AIDAN, Closed., Parish from November 1919 to July 9, 1948. Records at the Annunciation B.V.M. Church, Shenandoah.

EMMAUS, LEHIGH CO., ST. ANN (1931), [CEM] Rev. Msgr. Thomas E. Hoban; Rev. Paul A. DaDamio; Deacons Richard B. Close; Gerald R. Schmidt.
Res.: 415 S. Sixth St., 18049. Tel: 610-965-2426; Fax: 610-967-1099.
School—(Grades PreK-8), 570 Wood St., 18049. Tel:

610-965-9220. Loretta Chapin, Prin. Sisters 2; Lay Teachers 16; Students 382.
Catechesis/Religious Program—Tel: 610-965-6888. Angela Faidley, D.R.E. Students 540.
Convent—526 Fairview St., 18049. Tel: 610-965-6818.

FOUNTAIN HILL, LEHIGH CO., ST. URSULA (Bethlehem P.O.) (1919), Rev. Vincent P. York; Deacon Joseph G. Buragino. In Res., Revs. Frederick F. Sattler; Robert A. Dressler (Retired).
Res.: 1300 Broadway, 18015. Tel: 610-867-5122; Fax: 610-867-6569.
School—Holy Child Regional Catholic Elementary School, Bethlehem, Tel: 610-865-0861; Fax: 610-997-0180. See separate listing.
Catechesis/Religious Program—Students 65.

FRACKVILLE, SCHUYLKILL CO.
1—ST. ANN (1924), (Polish), Rev. Dominik P. Kalata, M.Ed.; Deacon John A. Setlock.
Res.: 7 S. Broad Mountain Ave., 17931. Tel: 570-874-0842; Fax: 570-874-2265.
School—Holy Family Regional Catholic Elementary School, Frackville, Tel: 570-874-0285. See separate listing.
Catechesis/Religious Program—Tel: 570-874-0610. Located at St. Joseph, Frackville.
2—ANNUNCIATION B.V.M. (1917), (Lithuanian), [CEM] Rev. Dominik P. Kalata, M.Ed.; Deacon John A. Setlock.
Res.: 7 S. Broad Mountain Ave., 17931. Tel: 570-874-0842; Fax: 570-874-2265.
School—Holy Family Regional Catholic Elementary School, Frackville, Tel: 570-874-0285. See separate listing.
Catechesis/Religious Program—Tel: 570-874-0610. Located at St. Joseph, Frackville.
Convent—25 S. Broad Mountain Ave., 17931. Tel: 570-874-0351.
3—ST. JOSEPH (1909), [CEM] Rev. David W. Karns; Deacon Joseph Burda.
Res.: 14 N. Nice St., 17931-1310. Tel: 570-874-0610; Fax: 570-874-0969.
School—Holy Family Regional Catholic Elementary School, Frackville, Tel: 717-874-0285. See separate listing.
Catechesis/Religious Program— Clustered with St. Ann and Annunciation BVM, Frackville. Students 110.

GIRARDVILLE, SCHUYLKILL CO.
1—ST. JOSEPH (1870), [CEM] Rev. Gregory R. Karpyn, B.A., M.A., M.Div.
Res.: 211 W. Main St., 17935. Tel: 570-276-6239; Fax: 570-276-1444.
School—Immaculate Heart Regional Catholic Elementary School, Girardville, Tel: 570-276-6568; Fax: 570-276-6568. See separate listing.
Catechesis/Religious Program—Students 86.
2—ST. VINCENT DE PAUL (1907), (Lithuanian), [CEM] Rev. David M. Liebner.
Res.: 260 N. Second St., 17935. Tel: 570-276-6033.
School—Immaculate Heart Regional Catholic Elementary School, Girardville, Tel: 570-276-6568. See separate listing.
Catechesis/Religious Program—Students 10.

GORDON, SCHUYLKILL CO., OUR LADY OF GOOD COUNSEL (1922), Revs. Gregory R. Karpyn, B.A., M.A., M.Div.; Thomas A. Horan, Pastor Emeritus (Retired).
Res.: 220 W. Biddle St., 17936-9999. Tel: 570-875-0774; Fax: 570-875-2443.
School—Immaculate Heart Regional Catholic Elementary School, Girardville, Tel: 570-276-6568. See separate listing.
Catechesis/Religious Program—Students 32.

HAMBURG, BERKS CO., ST. MARY (1854), [CEM] Rev. Donald W. Cieniewicz; Deacon Henry G. Gordon.
Res.: 94 Walnut Rd., P.O. Box 189, 19526. Tel: 610-562-4251; Fax: 610-562-0379.
Catechesis/Religious Program—Parish Hall, 501 State St., 19526. Tel: 610-562-8110. Miss Elizabeth Kimmel, D.R.E. Students 185.
Station—Hamburg State School and Hospital, Tel: 610-562-6063.

HECKSCHERVILLE, SCHUYLKILL CO., ST. KIERAN (1857), [CEM] Rev. Walter J. Hall.
Res.: 225 Church Rd., Pottsville, 17901-9171. Tel: 570-544-4857; Fax: 570-544-4854.
School—, Formerly Good Shepherd Regional Catholic School, Minersville For details, refer to Good Shepherd Regional Catholic School, Minersville located in Regional Catholic Elementary Schools, Diocesan in the Institutions section.
Catechesis/Religious Program—Tel: 570-544-2811; Fax: 570-544-4742. Located at St. Vincent de Paul, Minersville.

HELLERTOWN, NORTHAMPTON CO., ST. THERESA OF THE CHILD JESUS (1925), Rev. Msgr. Raymond F. Merman; Rev. William J. Nahn.
Res.: 1408 Easton Rd., 18055. Tel: 610-838-7045; Fax: 610-838-0932.
School—(Grades PreK-8), 300 Leonard St., 18055. Tel: 610-838-8161; Fax: 610-838-1915. Mrs. Isabel Conlin, Prin. Lay Teachers 9; Students 156.
Catechesis/Religious Program—Tel: 610-838-7645. Sister Servants of the Immaculate Heart of Mary Students 141.
Convent—255 Wilson Ave., 18055.

JIM THORPE, CARBON CO.
1—IMMACULATE CONCEPTION (1848), [CEM] Rev. Msgr. John G. Chizmar, V.F., M.Div.
Res.: 180 W. Broadway, 18229. Tel: 570-325-2791; Fax: 570-325-2427.
School—St. Joseph Regional Academy, Jim Thorpe, Tel: 570-325-3186. See separate listing.
2—ST. JOSEPH (1871), [CEM] Rev. Francis J. Baransky.
Res.: 526 North St., 18229. Tel: 570-325-3731; Fax: 570-325-2523.
School—St. Joseph Regional Academy, Jim Thorpe, Tel: 570-325-3186; Fax: 570-325-9451. See separate listing.
Catechesis/Religious Program—Susan Strubinger, D.R.E. Students 60.
Convent—27 W. Sixth St., 18229. Tel: 570-325-2212.

KELAYRES, SCHUYLKILL CO., IMMACULATE CONCEPTION (1899), (Italian), [CEM] Very Rev. Edward S. Zemanik; Rev. Robert A. Dressler, Pastor Emeritus (Retired).
17 N. Cleveland St., McAdoo, 18237-1915. Tel: 570-929-1073; Fax: 570-929-1073.
School—McAdoo Regional Catholic Elementary School, McAdoo, Tel: 570-929-1442; Fax 570-929-3016. See separate listing.
Catechesis/Religious Program—Students 53.

KUTZTOWN, BERKS CO., ST. MARY (1919), Rev. Msgr. Walter T. Scheaffer; Deacon Michael Flanagan.
Res.: 14833 Kutztown Rd., 19530. Tel: 610-683-7443; 610-683-7466 (Church); Fax: 610-683-7625.
Catechesis/Religious Program—Tel: 610-683-6454. Students 221.

LAKE HARMONY, CARBON CO., ST. PETER THE FISHERMAN (1982), Rev. Anthony M. Drouncheck; Rev. Msgr. John A. Auchter, Pastor Emeritus; Deacon John F. Thompson.
Res.: Lake Dr., P.O. Box 237, 18624-0237. Tel: 570-722-2034; Fax: 570-722-1348.
Catechesis/Religious Program—Students 155.

LANSFORD, CARBON CO.
1—ST. ANN, Rev. Thomas A. Derzack.
Res.: 8 E. Bertsch St., 18232-2001. Tel 570-645-2575; Fax: 570-645-3723.
School—Our Lady of the Regional Catholic Elementary Angels Academy, Lansford. See separate listing.
2—ST. MICHAEL (1891), (Slovak), [CEM] Rev. Thomas A. Derzack.
Res.: 124 E. Abbott St., P.O. Box 177, 18232-2012. Tel: 570-645-2282; Fax: 570-645-2754.
School—Our Lady of the Angels Academy, Lansford, Tel: 570-645-7101; 570-645-7170; Fax: 570-645-5278. See separate listing.
3—SS. PETER AND PAUL (1907), (Polish), [CEM] Rev. Thomas A. Derzack.
Mailing Address: 217 E. Abbott St., 18232-2001. Church: 213 E. Abbott St., 18232-2001. Tel: 570-645-2575; Fax: 570-645-3723.
School—, Formerly St. Michael Regional Catholic Elementary School, Lansford For details, refer to Our Lady of the Angels Academy, Lansford located in Regional Catholic Elementary Schools Diocesan in the Institutions section.

LEHIGHTON, CARBON CO., SS. PETER AND PAUL (1885), (German), [CEM] Rev. James C. Bechtel; Deacon William J. Wagner.
Res.: 260 N. Third St., 18235-1595. Tel 610-377-3690; Fax: 610-377-0721.
School—307 Coal St., 18235. Tel: 610 377-4466; Fax: 610-377-8881. Mrs. Jeanne V. Garvey, Prin. Lay Teachers 6; Students 135.
Catechesis/Religious Program—Students 105.

LIMEPORT, LEHIGH CO., ST. JOSEPH (1923), [CEM] Rev. Thomas R. Buckley; Deacon James F. Giltrap III.
Res.: 5050 St. Joseph's Rd., P.O. Box 178, 18060-0178. Tel: 610-965-2877; Fax: 610 965-8317.
School—St. Michael the Archangel Regional Catholic Elementary School, Colesville-Limeport, Tel: 610-965-4441; Fax: 610-965-1030. See separate listing.
Catechesis/Religious Program—Tel: 610-965-0590. Students 285.

LOST CREEK, SCHUYLKILL CO., ST. MARY MAGDALEN (1879), [JC] Rev. Richard C. Brensinger. In Res., Rev. Charles J. Dene.
Res.: 218 W. Cherry St., Shenandoah, 17976. Tel: 570-462-1916; Fax: 570-462-1245.
School—Father Walter J. Ciszek Elementary School, Shenandoah, Tel: 570-462-9666. See separate listing.
Catechesis/Religious Program—Students 3.

MAHANOY CITY, SCHUYLKILL CO.
1—ASSUMPTION B.V.M. (1892), (Slovak), [CEM] Revs. Lawrence J. Bukaty; William J. Maslar, Pastor Emeritus (Retired).
Res.: 728 W. Centre St., 17948. Tel: 570-773-1990; Fax: 570-773-1990.
School—Mahanoy City Regional Catholic Elementary School, Mahanoy City See separate listing.
2—ST. CANICUS (1862), (Irish), [CEM] Rev. William F. Glosser.
Res.: 22 S. Catawissa St., 17948. Tel: 570-773-0550; Fax: 570-775-0668.
School—Academy of the Blessed Virgin Mary, Mahanoy City, Tel: 570-773-2668; Fax: 570-773-2015. See separate listing.
Catechesis/Religious Program—Students 145.
3—ST. CASIMIR (1893), (Polish), [CEM] Rev. Lawrence J. Bukaty.
Res.: 113 S. Catawissa St., 17948. Tel: 570-773-2461; Fax: 570-773-0610.
School—Academy of the Blessed Virgin Mary, Mahanoy City, Tel: 717-773-2668. See separate listing.
4—ST. FIDELIS (1863), (German), [CEM] Rev. William F. Glosser.
Res.: 22 S. Catawissa St., 17948. Tel: 570-773-2850; Fax: 570-773-0668.
School—Academy of the Blessed Virgin Mary, Mahanoy City, Tel: 570-773-2668; Fax: 570-773-2015. See separate listing.
Catechesis/Religious Program— Clustered with St. Canicus, Mahanoy. Students 20.
5—ST. JOSEPH (1888), (Lithuanian), [CEM] Rev. Msgr. Anthony F. Wassel.
Res.: 614 W. Mahanoy Ave., 17948-2416. Tel: 570-773-2771; Fax: 570-773-1937.
School—Mahanoy City Regional Catholic Elementary School, Mahanoy City See separate listing.
6—SACRED HEART (1907), (Italian), [CEM] Rev. Msgr. Anthony F. Wassel.
Res.: 614 W. Mahanoy Ave., 17948. Tel: 570-773-2771; Fax: 570-773-1937.
School—Mahanoy City Regional Catholic Elementary School, Mahanoy City See separate listing.

MAHANOY PLANE, SCHUYLKILL CO., HOLY ROSARY, Closed., 1988. Parish records at St. Joseph's, Girardville.

MAIZEVILLE, SCHUYLKILL CO., OUR LADY OF SILUVA (Gilberton P.O.) (1907), (Lithuanian), [CEM], (Formerly St. Louis) Administered by St. Joseph, Frackville. Rev. David W. Karns; Deacon Joseph Costa.
Res.: 14 N. Nice St., Frackville, 17931-1310. Tel: 570-874-0610; Fax: 570-874-0969.
School— For details, refer to Academy of the Blessed Virgin Mary, Mahonoy City located in Regional Catholic Elementary Schools, Diocesan in the Institutions section.
Catechesis/Religious Program—Tel: 570-773-1990; Fax: 570-773-1990. Clustered with Assumption B.V.M., Mahanoy City.

MARTINS CREEK, NORTHAMPTON CO., ST. ROCCO (1937), Rev. Msgr. James J. Reichert.
Res.: 6658 School St., Box 421, 18063-0010. Tel: 610-258-9059; Fax: 610-258-4780.
School—Immaculate Conception Regional Catholic Elementary School, Pen-Argyl, Tel: 610-863-4816; Fax: 610-863-8158. See separate listing.
Catechesis/Religious Program—Students 143.

MCADOO, SCHUYLKILL CO.
1—ST. KUNEGUNDA (1893), (Polish), [CEM] Very Rev. Edward S. Zemanik.
Mailing Address: 17 N. Cleveland St., 18237-1915.
Res.: Washington & Cleveland Sts., 18237. Tel: 570-929-2341; Fax: 570-929-1073.
School—McAdoo Regional Catholic Elementary School, McAdoo, Tel: 570-929-1442. See separate listing.
2—ST. MARY (1893), (Slovak), [CEM] Very Rev. Edward S. Zemanik.
Res.: 101 E. Grant St., 18237-1905. Tel: 570-929-2341; Fax: 570-929-1073.
School—McAdoo Regional Catholic Elementary School, McAdoo See separate listing.
3—ST. PATRICK (1869), (Irish), [CEM] Very Rev. Edward S. Zemanik. In Res., Rev. George R. Winne.
Res.: 17 N. Cleveland St., 18237-1915. Tel: 570-929-1073.
School—McAdoo Regional Catholic Elementary School, McAdoo, Tel: 570-929-1442; Fax: 570-929-3016. See separate listing.
4—ST. STEPHEN OF HUNGARY, (Hungarian), Attended by, St. Kunegunda, McAdoo, 36 E. Washington St., 18237 Tel: 570-929-2341.

MILLER HEIGHTS, NORTHAMPTON CO., SACRED HEART OF JESUS (1936), Rev. Thomas J. King; Deacon Hugh E. McShane. In Res., Rev. Robert J. George, M.Div.
Res.: 1817 First St., Bethlehem, 18020. Tel: 610-865-5042; Fax: 610-865-1912.
School—(Grades K-8) Tel: 610-867-0221; Fax: 610-867-8351. John Schulte, Prin. Lay Teachers 11; Students 195.
Catechesis/Religious Program—Students 202.

MINERSVILLE, SCHUYLKILL CO.
1—ST. BARBARA (1913), (Italian), [CEM] Rev. David C. Liebner.
Res.: 320 Spruce St., 17954-1529. Tel: 570-544-2234; Fax: 570-544-5043.
School—Good Shepherd Regional Catholic Elementary School, Minersville, Tel: 570-544-4360 (Grades PreK-3); 570-544-3766 (Grades 4-8); Fax: 570-544-4870 (Grades PreK-8). See separate listing under Regional Catholic Elementary Schools, Diocesan.
Catechesis/Religious Program—Students 20.
2—ST. FRANCIS OF ASSISI (1895), (Lithuanian), [CEM] Rev. David C. Liebner; Deacon James P. Henninger.
320 Spruce St., 17954-1529. Tel: 717-544-3766.
Res.: 320 Spruce St., 17954-1529. Tel: 570-544-2234; Fax: 570-544-5043.
School—Good Shepherd Regional School, (Grades PreK-3), 538 Sunbury St., 17954. Tel: 570-544-4360; Fax: 570-544-4870. Ms. Rosalie Novack, Prin. No longer Holy Redeemer Regional Catholic Elementary School. Merged to form Good Shepherd Regional School, Minersville.
School—(Grades 4-8), 301 St. Francis St., 17954. Tel: 570-544-3766.
Catechesis/Religious Program—Tel: 570-544-6288. Mary Sacarage. Students 65.
3—OUR LADY OF MOUNT CARMEL (1855), (German), [CEM] Rev. Eric J. Gruber, M.Div.
301 St. Francis St., 17954. Tel: 570-544-3766.
Res.: 519 School St., 17954-1331. Tel: 570-544-2031; Fax: 570-544-4978.
School—Good Shepherd Regional School Ms. Rosalie Novack, Prin. For details, refer to Good Shepherd Regional School located in Regional Catholic Elementary Schools, Diocesan in the Institutions section.
Catechesis/Religious Program—Tel: 570-544-2016. Students 27.
4—ST. STANISLAUS KOSTKA (1905), (Polish), [CEM 2] Rev. Leo J. Maletz.
301 Heffner St., 17954. Tel: 570-544-3766; Fax: 570-544-4870.
Res.: 139 Spruce St., 17954-1642. Tel: 570-544-2211; Fax: 570-544-2317.
School—Good Shepherd Regional School, (Grades PreK-3), 538 Sunbury St., 17954. Tel: 570-544-4360. Ms. Rosalie Novack, Prin.
Catechesis/Religious Program—Tel: 570-544-6288; Fax: 570-628-3317. Students 29.
5—ST. VINCENT DE PAUL (1842), [CEM 2] Rev. Eric J. Gruber, M.Div.
Res.: 539 Sunbury St., 17954. Tel: 570-544-4741; Fax: 570-544-4742.
School—Good Shepherd Regional Catholic School, Minersville See separate listing under Regional Catholic Elementary Schools, Diocesan.
Catechesis/Religious Program—Tel: 570-544-4360. Sr. Catherine T. Brennan, S.S.J., D.R.E. Students 136.
Convent—Sisters of St. Joseph, 534 Sunbury St., 17954. Tel: 570-544-2016.
MOHNTON, BERKS CO., ST. BENEDICT'S (1955), Rev. Philip F. Rodgers.
Res.: 2020 Chesnut Hill Rd., 19540-8243. Tel: 610-856-1006; Fax: 610-856-1035.
School—LaSalle Academy, Shillington, Tel: 610-777-7392; Fax: 610-777-1280. See separate listing.
Catechesis/Religious Program—Tel: 610-370-0199; 610-856-5146. Ms. Valerie Christo, D.R.E. Students 74.
MOUNT CARBON, SCHUYLKILL CO., ST. FRANCIS DE SALES (Pottsville P.O.) (1922), Rev. Edward B. Connolly.
Res.: 49 Main St., Pottsville, 17901-4098. Tel: 570-622-8270.
School—All Saints Regional Catholic Elementary School, Pottsville See separate listing.
NAZARETH, NORTHAMPTON CO., HOLY FAMILY (1908), [CEM 2] Revs. John P. Kavcak, M.S.C.; Anthony Ripp, M.S.C.; Jacob Welle, M.S.C.; Deacon Michael P. McGouldrick.
Res.: 23 Forest Dr., 18064-1326. Tel: 610-759-0870; Fax: 610-746-2026.
School—(Grades PreK-8), 17 Convent Ave., 18064. Tel: 610-759-5642; Fax: 610-759-0386. Mr. Eugene Lennon, Prin. Lay Teachers 22; Students 375.
Catechesis/Religious Program—Tel: 610-759-7467. Mrs. Laurel Wenson, D.R.E., (Grade 6) & Admin.; Marisa Snyder, D.R.E., (Grades 1-5); Mrs. Judeth Klotz, D.R.E., (Grades 7-8). Students 900.
NESQUEHONING, CARBON CO.
1—IMMACULATE CONCEPTION OF B.V.M. (1914), (Slovak), Rev. Msgr. John B. McCann.
Mailing Address: 140 W. Mill St., 18240. Tel: 570-669-6321; Fax: 570-669-9440.
Res.: 15 E. Garibaldi Ave., 18240. Tel: 570-669-6321; Fax: 570-669-9440.
School—, Formerly Our Lady of the Angels Academy, Lansford For details, refer to Our Lady of the Angels Academy, Lansford located in Regional Catholic Elementary Schools, Diocesan in the Institutions section.
Catechesis/Religious Program—Tel: 570-669-9135; 570-669-9964. Students 9.
2—OUR LADY OF MOUNT CARMEL (1913), (Italian), [CEM] Rev. Msgr. John B. McCann.
Res.: 15 E. Garibaldi Ave., 18240. Tel: 570-669-6321; Fax: 570-669-9440.
School—Our Lady of the Angels Academy, Lansford, Tel: 570-645-7101; 570-645-7170; Fax: 570-645-5278. See separate listing.
Catechesis/Religious Program—140 W. Mill St., 18240. Tel: 570-669-9135; 570-669-9964. Students 26.
3—SACRED HEART (1839), [CEM 2] Rev. Msgr. John B. McCann.
Res.: 15 E. Garibaldi Ave., 18240. Tel: 570-669-6321; Fax: 570-669-9440.
School—Our Lady of the Angels Academy, Lansford, Tel: 717-645-4700; Fax: 570-645-5278. See separate listing
Catechesis/Religious Program—Tel: 570-669-9135; 570-669-9964. Students 37.
Mission—Sacred Heart Chapel Lake Hauto, Carbon Co.
NEW PHILADELPHIA, SCHUYLKILL CO.
1—HOLY FAMILY (1866), (Irish), Rev. Joseph J. Kweder, M.Div.
101 Valley St., 17959.
Parish Office—99 Valley St., 17959-1120. Tel: 570-277-6800; Fax: 570-277-0528.
Catechesis/Religious Program—Holy Cross, Tel: 570-277-6815.
2—SACRED HEART (1895), (Lithuanian), [CEM] Rev. Joseph J. Kweder, M.Div.
Parish Office—99 Valley St., 17959-1120.
Res.: 41 Clay St., 17959. Tel: 570-277-6815; Fax: 570-277-0528.
Catechesis/Religious Program—Holy Cross
Mission—Immaculate Heart of Mary Chapel Washington St., Middleport, Schuylkill Co. 17953.
NEWTOWN, SCHUYLKILL CO., SACRED HEART (1896), (German), [CEM] Rev. David J. Loeper.
301 St. Francis St., Minersville, 17954. Tel: 570-544-3766.
Res.: 519 School St., Minersville, 17954. Tel: 570-544-2592; Fax: 570-544-5742.
School—Good Shepherd Regional School, (Grades PreK-3), 538 Sunbury St., Minersville, 17954. Tel: 570-544-2031. Ms. Rosalie Novack, Prin.
Catechesis/Religious Program—Students 8.
NORTHAMPTON, NORTHAMPTON CO.
1—ASSUMPTION OF THE BLESSED VIRGIN MARY (1922), (Slovak), [CEM] Rev. John S. Mraz; Deacon Gregory J. Bankos Sr.
Res.: 2174 Lincoln Ave., 18067. Tel: 610-262-2559; Fax: 610-262-1613.
School—Our Lady of Hungary Regional Catholic Elementary School, Northampton, Tel: 610-262-9171; Fax: 610-262-2202. See separate listing.
Catechesis/Religious Program—22nd & Washington Ave., 18067. Tel: 610-262-7343. Mrs. Linda Santucci, D.R.E. Students 110.
2—ST. MICHAEL (1914), (Polish), [JC] Revs. Edwin V. Schwartz; Paul L. Rothermel.
Res.: 829 Main St., 18067-1838. Tel: 610-262-2472; Fax: 610-261-4736.
School—Our Lady of Hungary Regional Catholic Elementary School, Northampton See separate listing.
Catechesis/Religious Program—Students 12.
3—OUR LADY OF HUNGARY (1907), [CEM] Revs. Edwin V. Schwartz; Paul L. Rothermel; Deacon Joseph F. Godiska. In Res., Rev. Patrick H. Lamb.
Res.: 1324 Newport Ave., 18067-1442. Tel: 610-262-2227; Fax: 610-262-4192.
School—Our Lady of Hungary Regional Catholic Elementary School, Northampton See separate listing.
Convent—1314 Newport Ave., 18067. Tel: 610-262-2427.
OREFIELD, LEHIGH CO., ST. JOSEPH THE WORKER (1948), Rev. Msgrs. Robert J. Wargo; Gerald E. Gobitas, Th.M.; Rev. Ronald J. Minner; Deacons Anthony T. Campanell; Daniel F. Metzker.
Res.: 1879 Applewood Dr., 18069-9507. Tel: 610-395-2876; Fax: 610-395-2616.
School—Preschool, Tel: 610-395-4010. Mrs. Theresa M. Heintzelman, Dir. Program for 3 & 4 year old children. Students 93.
School—(Grades K-8), 1858 Applewood Dr., 18069. Tel: 610-395-7221; Fax: 610-395-7904. Mrs. Patricia L. Johnson, Prin. Students 430.
Catechesis/Religious Program—Tel: 610-395-4920. Mrs. Charlane Faught, D.R.E. Students 860.
PALMERTON, CARBON CO., SACRED HEART (1908), [CEM] Rev. James J. Ward; Deacon William P. Pitts.
Res.: 243 Lafayette Ave., 18071-1511. Tel: 610-826-2335; Fax: 610-826-5360.
School—, Formerly St. John Neumann Regional Catholic Elementary School, Palmerton-Slatington For details, refer to St. John Neumann Regional Catholic Elementary School, Palmerton-Slatington located in Regional Catholic Elementary Schools, Diocesan in the Institutions section.
Catechesis/Religious Program—252 Lafayette Ave., 18071. Tel: 610-826-2849. Students 108.
PEN ARGYL, NORTHAMPTON CO., ST. ELIZABETH OF HUNGARY (1929), [CEM] Rev. Richard A. Schware. In Res., Rev. Donald J. Schaible.
Res.: 300 W. Babbitt Ave., P.O. Box 126, 18072-0126. Tel: 610-863-4777; Fax: 610-863-7449.
School—Immaculate Conception Regional Catholic Elementary School, Pen Argyl, Tel: 610-863-4816. See separate listing.
Catechesis/Religious Program—Students 120.
Convent—111-115 Lobb Ave., 18072. Tel: 610-863-9214.
PORT CARBON, SCHUYLKILL CO., ST. STEPHEN (1847), [CEM] Rev. John J. McNamara.
Res.: 218 Valley St., 17965. Tel: 570-622-6600; Fax: 570-622-3689. Cemetery office 570-622-9817
School— For details, refer to St. Stephen Elementary School, Port Carbon located in Regional Catholic Elementary Schools, Diocesan in the Institutions section.
Catechesis/Religious Program—Tel: 570-622-1461. Students 195.
Convent—Tel: 570-622-1461.
POTTSVILLE, SCHUYLKILL CO.
1—ST. JOHN THE BAPTIST (1841), (German), [CEM 3] Rev. David J. Loeper; Sr. Barbara J. Wojnicki, C.S.N.F., Pastoral Assoc.; Deacon Luis R. Visot.
Res.: 913 Mahantongo St., 17901. Tel: 570-622-5470; Fax: 570-622-4589.
School—All Saints Regional Catholic Elementary School, Pottsville, Tel: 570-622-0106. See separate listing.
Catechesis/Religious Program—Tel: 570-628-3002. Lucilla Kochol, D.R.E. Students 125.
2—ST. JOSEPH (1905), (Italian), [CEM] Rev. Edward B. Connolly.
Res.: 321 W. Howard Ave., 17901-3413. Tel: 570-622-3081; Fax: 570-622-3084.
School—All Saints Regional Catholic Elementary School, Pottsville See separate listing.
3—MARY QUEEN OF PEACE (1920), Rev. John W. Bambrick; Deacon Stephen Andrusisian.
Res.: 728 N. Centre St., 17901. Tel: 570-622-7004; Fax: 570-622-4287.
School—All Saints Regional Catholic Elementary School, Pottsville, Tel: 570-622-0106; Fax: 570-627-4737. See separate listing.
Catechesis/Religious Program—Peterine Wojcik, D.R.E. Students 45.
4—ST. PATRICK (1827), [CEM 3] Very Rev. Edward J. O'Connor, M.Th., M.S.W., V.F.; Rev. Jerome A. Tauber; Deacon John E. Quirk. In Res., Rev. Joseph T. Whalen, M.Div.
Res.: 319 Mahantongo St., 17901. Tel: 570-622-1802; Fax: 570-622-2593.
Catechesis/Religious Program—Students 190.
School— For details, refer to All Saints Elementary School, Pottsville located in Regional Catholic Elementary Schools, Diocesan in the Institutions section.
Convent—825 Mahantongo St., 17901. Tel: 570-622-0203; Fax: 570-622-0262. Sr. Marie Farrant, S.S.J., Supr.
Chapel—St. John Neumann 2051 W. Norwegian St., 17901.
READING, BERKS CO.
1—ST. ANTHONY (1913), (Lithuanian), Attended by, Priests of St. Peter. Rev. Christopher L. Wakefield.
322 S. 5th St., 19602-2395. Tel: 610-372-9652.
2—ST. ANTHONY OF PADUA (1914), (Polish), Rev. Richard E. Nachajski; Sr. Mary Joy Wasnesky, O.S.F., Pastoral Assoc.
Res.: 501 Summit Ave., 19611-1964. Tel: 610-374-1539; Fax: 610-374-0263.
School—LaSalle Academy & Early Childhood Center, Shillington, Tel: 610-777-7392; Fax: 610-777-1280. See separate listing.
Catechesis/Religious Program—Students 84.
Convent—234 Grace St., 19611-1946. Tel: 610-372-8578.
3—ST. CATHARINE OF SIENA (1925), Rev. Msgr. Joseph P.T. Smith; Revs. Ronald P. Bowman; James J. Chalangady, O.C.D.; Deacons George J. Faller; Richard A. Horst; Craig A. Fry. In Res., Rev. Adam C. Sedar.
Res.: 2427 Perkiomen Ave., 19606. Tel: 610-779-4005; Fax: 610-779-0859.
Church: 4975 Boyertown Pike, 19606. Tel: 610-779-4090.
School—St. Catharine of Siena Regional Catholic Elementary School, 2330 Perkiomen Ave., 19606. Tel: 610-779-5810; Fax: 610-779-6888. See separate listing. Students 472.
Catechesis/Religious Program—Tel: 610-779-8535. Constance Fry, D.R.E., (K-5); Lorraine Gajewski,

D.R.E., (6-8). Students 550.
Convent—2328 Perkiomen Ave., 19606. Tel: 610-779-5583.

4—SS. CYRIL AND METHODIUS (1895), (Slovak), Rev. Charles S. Sperlak; Deacon John J. Allison.
Res.: 449 S. Sixth St., 19602-2410. Tel: 610-373-0627; Fax: 610-371-9532.
Catechesis/Religious Program—Sr. Miriam Patrice Hausman, O.S.F., D.R.E. Students 58.
Convent—502 S. Sixth St., 19602. Tel: 610-375-8001.

5—HOLY GUARDIAN ANGELS (1929), Very Rev. Dennis T. Hartgen, V.F.; Rev. John S. Pendzick. In Res., Rev. Robert T. Finlan.
Res.: 3121 Kutztown Rd., 19605-2693. Tel: 610-921-2729; Fax: 610-921-8886.
School—Holy Guardian Angels Regional School, Reading, Tel: 610-929-4124; Fax: 610-929-1623. See separate listing.
Catechesis/Religious Program—Tel: 610-929-1416. Mrs. Rose Quaglia, D.R.E. Students 316.
Mission—St. Anthony 8th & Columbia, Temple, Berks Co. 19560.

6—HOLY ROSARY (1904), (Italian), Rev. Msgr. Felix A. Losito; Deacon Lawrence A. Dudeck. In Res., Rev. John P. Conte.
Res.: 237 Franklin St., 19602. Tel: 610-373-5579; Fax: 610-372-0130.
School—Cabrini Academy, (Grades PreK-8), 240 Franklin St., 19602. Tel: 610-374-8483; Fax: 610-374-0369. Sisters 4; Lay Teachers 8; Students 156.
Catechesis/Religious Program—Students 191.
Convent—234 Franklin St., 19602. Tel: 610-375-9072; Fax: 610-375-4895.
Mission—Holy Rosary Chapel Schuylkill Ave., Berks Co. 19601. Tel: 610-376-4383.

7—ST. JOSEPH (1891), Rev. Richard Clement; Deacons Peter M. LaFata; Jose Rodriguez-Trejo.
Res.: 1018 N. Eighth St., 19604-2210. Tel: 610-376-2976; Fax: 610-376-2825.
School—, Formerly Holy Guardian Angels Regional School, Reading For details, refer to Holy Guardian Angels Regional School, Reading located in Regional Catholic Elementary Schools, Diocesan in the Institutions section.
Catechesis/Religious Program—Students 96.

8—ST. MARGARET (1920), Rev. John M. Gibbons; Deacon John P. Konopelski.
Res.: 925 Centre Ave., 19601. Tel: 610-376-2919; Fax: 610-376-2462.
School—(Grades PreK-8) Tel: 610-375-1882. Sr. Diane Licordare, Prin. Servants of Immaculate Heart of Mary 2; Lay Teachers 12.
Catechesis/Religious Program—Tel: 610-376-2919. William Davis, D.R.E. Students 75.
Convent—233 Spring St., 19601. Tel: 610-372-1302.

9—ST. MARY (1888), (Polish), [CEM] Rev. Leo S. Stajkowski.
250 S. 12th St., 19602-2046. Tel: 610-376-6321; Fax: 610-376-1378.
Catechesis/Religious Program—Students 15.

10—ST. PAUL (1860), (German), [CEM] Revs. Andrew A. Ulincy; Aram Berard, S.J.
Res.: 151 N. 9th St., 19601. Tel: 610-372-1531; Fax: 610-372-7478.
Catechesis/Religious Program—Students 86.

11—ST. PETER (1752), (Spanish), [CEM] Revs. Christopher L. Wakefield; Luis Angel Bonilla; Angel L. Garcia Almodovar; Deacons Jesus Centeno; Mariano Torres; Julio Colon; Fernando L. Torres; Leopoldo Alvarado; Francisco Najera; Frank Colon.
Res.: 322 S. Fifth St., 19602. Tel: 610-372-9652; Fax: 610-374-3351.
School—218 S. Fifth St., 19602. Tel: 610-374-2447; Fax: 610-374-3415. Sisters of the Immaculate Heart of Mary 6; Lay Teachers 7; Students 210.
Catechesis/Religious Program—Tel: 610-378-1947. Students 266.
Convent—Tel: 610-373-6185.

RINGTOWN, SCHUYLKILL CO., ST. MARY (1923), [CEM] Rev. Richard C. Brensinger.
Mailing Address: 82 N. Center St., 17967. Tel: 570-889-3850; Fax: 570-889-5005.
Res.: 84 N. Center St., 17967. Tel: 570-839-3850.
School—Father Walter J. Ciszek Elementary School, Shenandoah, Tel: 570-462-3927; Fax: 570-462-4603. See separate listing.
Catechesis/Religious Program—Students 67.

ROBESONIA, BERKS CO., ST. FRANCIS DE SALES (1982), Rev. David J. Devlin, O.S.F.S.; Sr. Mary Heffron, I.H.M., Pastoral Assoc.
Res.: 321 N. Church St., 19551. Tel: 610-693-5851; Fax: 610-693-5852.
Catechesis/Religious Program—Students 205.

ROSETO, NORTHAMPTON CO., OUR LADY OF MT. CARMEL (1897), (Italian), [CEM 2] Revs. Thomas W. Prior, C.M.; James G. Prior, C.M.
Res.: P.O. Box 422, 18013. Tel: 610-588-2183; Fax: 610-588-6973.
School—Our Lady of Mt. Carmel Regional Catholic Elementary School, Roseto, Tel: 610-588-2629; Fax: 610-588-3423. See separate listing.
Catechesis/Religious Program—Students 216.

SAINT CLAIR, SCHUYLKILL CO.

1—ST. BONIFACE (1854), (German), [CEM] Rev. Kevin P. Gallagher.
Parish Office—Tel: 570-429-0370; Fax: 570-429-0630.
Res.: 250 E. Hancock St., St. Clair, 17970. Tel: 570-429-0701; Fax: 570-429-0630.
School—St. Stephen Regional Catholic School, Port Carbon, Tel: 570-622-3063; Fax: 570-622-3689. See separate listing.
Catechesis/Religious Program—Tel: 570 429-1621. Located at St. Mary's, St. Clair.

2—ST. CASIMIR (1912), (Lithuanian), [CEM] Rev. Ronald V. Jankaitis.
Res.: 441 S. Nichols St., St. Clair, 17970-9998. Tel: 570-429-2400.
School—, Formerly Saint Clair Regional Catholic Elementary School, Saint Clair For details, refer to St. Stephen Regional Catholic Elementary School, Port Carbon located in Regional Catholic Elementary Schools, Diocesan in the Institutions section.

3—IMMACULATE CONCEPTION (1905), (Slovak), [CEM] Rev. Paul E. Masiar.
1 East Carolina Ave., St. Clair, 17970-1301.
Res.: Caroline Ave., Diener's Hill, St. Clair, 17970-1361. Tel: 570-429-1315; Fax: 570-429-0369.
School— For details, refer to St. Stephen Regional Catholic Elementary School, Port Carbon located in Regional Catholic Elementary Schools, Diocesan in the Institutions section.
Catechesis/Religious Program—Tel: 717-429-0370; Fax: 717-429-0630. Located at St. Mary's Hall, St. Clair. Students 35.

4—ST. MARY (1864), [CEM 2] Rev. Kevin P. Gallagher; Deacon John F. Pogash.
Parish Office—Tel: 570-429-0370; Fax: 570-429-0630.
Res.: 250 E. Hancock St., St. Clair, 17970. Tel: 570-429-0701; Fax: 570-429-0630.
School—St. Stephen Regional Catholic School, Port Carbon, Tel: 570-622-3063; Fax: 570-622-3689. See separate listing.

5—SS. PETER AND PAUL (1918), (Polish), [CEM] Rev. Kevin P. Gallagher; Deacon John F. Pogash.
Res.: 250 E. Hancock St., St. Clair, 17970. Tel: 570-429-0701 (Res.); 570-429-0370 (Parish Office); Fax: 570-429-0630.
School—, Formerly St. Stephen Regional Catholic School, Port Carbon For details, refer to St. Stephen Regional Catholic School, Port Carbon located in Regional Catholic Elementary Schools, Diocesan in the Institutions section.

SCHUYLKILL HAVEN, SCHUYLKILL CO., ST. AMBROSE (1851), [CEM] Revs. Michael J. Stone; Ronald J. Yarrosh; Deacon Richard K. Braun.
Res.: 201 Randel St., 17972. Tel: 570-385-1031; Fax: 570-385-1035.
School—(Grades PreK-8), 302 Randel St., 17972. Tel: 570-385-2377; Fax: 570-385-2387 Anne B. Curry, Prin. Lay Teachers 14; Students 232.
Catechesis/Religious Program—Tel: 570-385-2472. Sr. Dolorita, C.S.F.N., D.R.E. Students 260.
Station—Schuylkill County Hospital and Home for Aged

SHENANDOAH, SCHUYLKILL CO.

1—ANNUNCIATION (1870), [CEM] Revs. Richard C. Brensinger; Stephen L. Maco.
Res.: 218 W. Cherry St., 17976-2209. Tel: 570-462-1916; Fax: 570-462-1245.
School—, Formerly Father Walter J. Ciszek Elementary School, Shenandoah For details, refer to Father Walter J. Ciszek Elementary School, Shenandoah located in Regional Catholic Elementary Schools, Diocesan in the Institutions section.
Convent—229 W. Cherry St., 17976. Tel: 570-462-1024.
Catechesis/Religious Program—Students 27.

2—ST. CASIMIR (1872), (Polish), [CEM] Rev. Msgr. Ronald C. Bocian.
Res.: 108 W. Cherry St., 17976-2207. Tel: 570-462-1968; Fax: 570-462-1388.
School—Father Walter J. Ciszek School, Shenandoah, Tel: 570-462-3927; Fax: 570-462-4603. See separate listing.
Catechesis/Religious Program—Tel: 570-773-1142. Students 14.
Convent—233 N. Jardin St., 17976. Tel: 570-462-0877; Fax: 570-462-9318.

3—ST. GEORGE (1891), (Lithuanian), [CEM 5] Revs. Robert J. Potts; Deogratias Rwegasira, A.J.
Res.: 129 S. Jardin St., 17976. Tel: 570-462-1989; Fax: 570-462-1980.
School—Father Walter J. Ciszek Elementary School, Shenandoah See separate listing.

4—HOLY FAMILY (1870-1934), Closed., Records kept at Annunciation, Shenandoah.

5—OUR LADY OF MT. CARMEL (1914), (Italian), [CEM] Revs. Robert J. Potts; Deogratias Rwegasira, A.J.
Res.: 129 S. Jardin St., 17976. Tel: 570-462-1989; Fax: 570-462-1980.
School—Father Walter J. Ciszek Elementary School, Shenandoah See separate listing.

6—ST. STANISLAUS (1898), (Polish), [CEM] Rev. Msgr. Ronald C. Bocian.
Res.: 108 W. Cherry St., 17976. Tel: 570-462-1968; Fax: 570-462-1388.
School—Father Walter J. Ciszek Elementary School, Shenandoah, Tel: 570-462-3927; Fax: 570-462-4603. See separate listing.
Catechesis/Religious Program—Tel: 570-773-1142. Students 9.

7—ST. STEPHEN (1899), (Slovak), [CEM] Rev. Robert J. Potts.
Church: 18 E. Oak St., 17976. Tel: 570-462-0331 (Office); Fax: 570-462-1747 (Office).
Res.: 129 S. Jardin St., 17976. Tel: 717-462-1989; Fax: 717-462-1980.
School—, Formerly Father Walter J. Ciszek Elementary School, Shenandoah For details, refer to Father Walter J. Ciszek Elementary School, Shenandoah located in Regional Catholic Elementary Schools, Diocesan in the Institutions section.
Catechesis/Religious Program— Located at Fr. Ciszek School, Shenandoah. Students 6.

SHEPPTON, SCHUYLKILL CO., ST. JOSEPH (1894), [CEM] [JC] Rev. Raymond P. Slezak.
Res.: 14 E. Oak St., P.O. Box 118, 18248-0118. Tel: 570-384-0157.
Catechesis/Religious Program—Students 9.
Mission—St. John the Baptist P.O. Box 118, Oneida, Schuykill Co. 18248.

SHILLINGTON, BERKS CO., ST. JOHN BAPTIST DE LA SALLE (1948), Rev. Msgr. Thomas J. Birch, Pastor Emeritus (Retired); Rev. David C. Gillis; Deacon Sylvester F. Simchick.
Res.: 420 Holland St., 19607. Tel: 610-777-1697; Fax: 610-777-4468.
School—LaSalle Academy, Shillington, Tel: 610-777-7392; Fax: 610-777-1280. See separate listing.
Catechesis/Religious Program—Bernadette H. Yohn, D.R.E. Students 310.

SINKING SPRING, BERKS CO., ST. IGNATIUS LOYOLA (1965), Rev. Msgr. James A. Treston, V.F.; Revs. Abraham Ha, M.Div.; Christopher M. Zelonis; Deacons John A. Coffin; John W. Murphy Jr.
Res.: 2810 St. Alban's Dr., 19608-1028. Tel: 610-678-3767; Fax: 610-678-4483.
School—(Grades PreK-8) Tel: 610-678-0111; Fax: 610-670-5795. Mrs. Janice Bayerle, Prin. Sisters of the Third Order of St. Francis 2; Lay Teachers 37; Students 541.
Catechesis/Religious Program—2710 St. Alban's Dr., Reading, 19609. Tel: 610-678-0676; Fax: 610-678-4274. Students 658.
Convent—2601 St. Alban's Dr., West Lawn, 19609. Tel: 610-678-2769.

SLATINGTON, LEHIGH CO., ASSUMPTION B.V.M. (1883), [CEM] Rev. Joseph L. Grembocki, M.Div.
Res.: 633 W. Washington St., 18080. Tel: 610-767-2214; Fax: 610-767-2702.
School—St. John Neumann Regional Catholic Elementary School, Palmerton-Slatington, Tel: 610-767-2935; Fax: 610-767-2948. See separate listing.
Catechesis/Religious Program—Students 165.

SUMMIT HILL, CARBON CO.

1—ST. JOSEPH (1850), [CEM 3] Rev. James M. Torpey.
Res.: 118 N. Market St., 18250. Tel: 570-645-2664; Fax: 570-645-5655.
School—Our Lady of the Angels Academy, Lansford, Tel: 570-645-7101. See separate listing.
Catechesis/Religious Program—Students 49.

2—ST. STANISLAUS (1924), (Polish), Rev. James M. Torpey.
Res.: 118 N. Market St., 18250. Tel: 717-645-3037; Fax: 717-645-5655.
School—Our Lady of the Angels Academy, Lansford, Tel: 570-645-7101. See separate listing.
Catechesis/Religious Program—Students 3.

TAMAQUA, SCHUYLKILL CO.

1—ST. JEROME (1833), Revs. William T. Campion; Henry E. Strassner (Retired).
Res.: 266 W. Broad St., 18252-1819. Tel: 570-668-2301; Fax: 570-668-4406.
School—250 W. Broad St., 18252-1819. Tel: 570-668-2757; Fax: 570-668-6101. Sr. Donna Ariente, I.H.M. Sisters of the Immaculate Heart of Mary 2; Lay Teachers 8; Students 180.
Catechesis/Religious Program—Tel: 570-668-4416. Sr. Mary Ellen Diehl, I.H.M., D.R.E. Students 215.
Convent—250 W. Broad St.. Tel: 570-668-2730. Sr. Anita M. Dixon, I.H.M., Supr.
Mission—St. Patrick (Seek) [CEM] [JC 2] Miner St., Coaldale, Schuylkill Co. 18218.

2—SS. PETER AND PAUL (1911), (Lithuanian), [CEM] [JC] Rev. William J. Linkchorst.
Res.: 307 Pine St., 18252. Tel: 570-668-1150; Fax: 570-668-6933.
Catechesis/Religious Program—Tel: 570-668-4416. Students 51.

TOWER CITY, SCHUYLKILL CO., SS. PETER AND PAUL (1896), [CEM] Rev. Michael E. Ahrensfield, M.Div.

Res.: 113 Cherry St., Tremont, 17981. Tel: 570-695-3648; Fax: 570-695-2275.
Church: 825 E. Grand Ave., 17980-1217. Tel: 570-695-3648; Fax: 570-695-2275.
School—, Formerly Good Shepherd Regional, Minersville For details, refer to Good Shepherd Regional, Minersville located in Regional Catholic Elementary Schools, Diocesan in the Institutions section.
Catechesis/Religious Program—Students 60.

TREMONT, SCHUYLKILL CO., IMMACULATE CONCEPTION (1853), (German—Irish), [CEM] Revs. James R. Brady, Pastor Emeritus; Michael E. Ahrensfield, M.Div.
301 St. Francis St., Minersville, 17954. Tel: 570-544-3766; Fax: 570-544-4870.
Res.: 113 Cherry St., P.O. Box 35, 17981. Tel: 570-695-3648; Fax: 570-695-2275.
School—Good Shepherd Regional School Ms. Rosalie Novack, Prin. For details, refer to Good Shepherd Regional School, Minersville located in Regional Catholic Elementary Schools, Diocesan in the Institutions section.
Catechesis/Religious Program—Students 60.

TRESCKOW, CARBON CO.
1—ST. BARTHOLOMEW (1917), (Italian), Rev. Thomas G. Shanfelt.
Res.: 25 E. Maple St., P.O. Box 238, 18254-0238. Tel: 570-455-0922; Fax: 570-454-1765.
School—McAdoo Regional Catholic Elementary School, McAdoo, Tel: 570-929-3016; Fax: 570-929-3016. See separate listing.
Catechesis/Religious Program—Students 17.
2—ST. MICHAEL (1908), (Slovak), [CEM] Rev. Thomas Shanfelt.
Res.: 14 S. Chestnut St., 18254-0236. Tel: 570-454-2802; Fax: 570-454-1765.
School—McAdoo Regional Catholic Elementary School, McAdoo, Tel: 570-929-1442; Fax: 570-929-3016. See separate listing.
Catechesis/Religious Program—Students 15.

TUSCARORA, SCHUYLKILL CO., ST. BERTHA (1922), [CEM] Rev. Edward W. Coleman.
Res.: 214 Green St., Brockton, 17925. Tel: 570-668-1500; Fax: 570-668-5487.
Church: 710 Broad St., 17982.
School—St. Jerome Regional Catholic Elementary School, Tamaqua, Tel: 570-668-2757. See separate listing.
Catechesis/Religious Program—Tel: 570-668-4416. Located at St. Jerome Regional, Tamaqua. Students 8.

WEATHERLY, CARBON CO., ST. NICHOLAS (1874), [CEM 2] [JC] Rev. James J. Burdess, Th.M.; Deacon Raymond W. Wilkinson.
Res.: 318 Plane St., 18255. Tel: 570-427-4123; Fax: 570-427-4615.
School—McAdoo Regional Catholic Elementary School, McAdoo, Tel: 717-929-1442; Fax: 717-929-3016. See separate listing.
Catechesis/Religious Program—Students 66.
Station—Carbon County District Home Weatherwood. Tel: 717-427-8683; Fax: 717-427-4988.

WEST BANGOR, NORTHAMPTON CO., ST. ROCH (1937), [CEM] Rev. Msgr. Charles T. Moss.
Res.: 1141 Verona Dr., Pen Argyl, 18072. Tel: 610-863-9055; Fax: 610-863-5971.
School—Immaculate Conception Regional Catholic Elementary School, Pen Argyl See separate listing.
Catechesis/Religious Program—Tel: 610-863-4816. Located at Immaculate Conception, Pen Argyl. Students 12.

WEST READING, BERKS CO., SACRED HEART (1917), (German), Rev. Joseph A. DeSantis, V.F., M.Div.; E. Jerry Yoder, Business Admin.; Deacon William R. Kase; Marianne McQuillen, Coord. Parish Ministries. In Res., Rev. David J. Fick.
Res.: Lakeview Dr. and Cherry St., P.O. Box 6217, Reading, 19610. Tel: 610-372-4010; Fax: 610-372-4926.
School—701 Franklin St., 19611. Tel: 610-373-3316. Anne Florian, Prin. Lay Teachers 12; Students 189.
Catechesis/Religious Program—Tel: 610-374-5430. Valerie Christo, D.R.E. Students 187.

WHITEHALL, LEHIGH CO.
1—ST. ELIZABETH (1941), Rev. Msgr. Anthony D. Muntone, S.T.L., P.A.; Rev. Eric R. Arnout; Deacon Alexander L. Maggitti Sr.
Res.: 618 Fullerton Ave., 18052. Tel: 610-266-0695; Fax: 610-266-1548.
School—(Grades PreK-8), 431 Pershing Blvd., 18052. Tel: 610-264-0143; Fax: 610-264-1563. Sr. Bonita Smith, R.S.M., Prin. Sisters of Mercy 1; Lay Teachers 15; Students 233.
Catechesis/Religious Program—Mrs. Carol O'Connor, D.R.E. Students 195.
2—HOLY TRINITY (1928), Rev. Thomas D. Baddick, M.Th.; Deacons Eugene J. Wyrwa; Michael J. Laroche. In Res., Rev. Frans J. Berkhout.
Res.: 4102 S. Church St., 18052-2415. Tel: 610-262-9315; Fax: 610-261-3576.
School—Christ the King Regional Catholic Elementary School, Coplay, Whitehall, Tel: 610-262-4177; Fax: 610-262-5632. See separate listing.
Catechesis/Religious Program—Mrs. Barbara Majkowski, D.R.E. Students 335.
3—ST. JOHN THE BAPTIST (1927), [CEM] Rev. Joseph J. Campion, M.Div.
Res.: 3024 S. Ruch St., 18052. Tel: 610-262-2260; Fax: 610-262-1935.
School—Christ the King Regional Catholic Elementary School, Coplay, Whitehall See separate listing.
Catechesis/Religious Program—Tel: 610-262-4177. Sr. Mary Dolora, D.R.E. Students 59.

Chaplains of Public Institutions

ALLENTOWN. *Allentown Manor.* (Sacred Heart)
Country Meadows. (St. Catherine of Siena)
Devon House Personal Care Home. (St. Thomas More)
Good Shepherd Home and Rehabilitation Hospital. Deacon Daniel A. Thomson. (St. Paul)
Lehigh County Prison. (Sacred Heart)
Lehigh Valley Hospital at 17th St.. (St. Catharine of Siena)
Lehigh Valley Hospital at Cedar Crest. Rev. Joseph P. Becker, O.S.F.S., Deacon Richard B. Close. (St. Thomas More)
Liberty Nursing Center. (St. Catharine of Siena)
St. Luke's Hospital, Allentown Campus. (St. Catharine of Siena)
Luthercrest. (St. Joseph, Orefield)
Manor Care Nursing Home (St. Thomas More)
New Seasons Personal Care Home (St. Thomas More)
Phoebe Devitt Home. (St. Catharine of Siena)
State Hospital. (Our Lady Help of Christians)
Westminster Village. (Our Lady Help of Christians)

ASHLAND. *Ashland Regional Medical Center.* Administered by St. Mauritius, Ashland; St. Joseph, Ashland; St. Joseph, Girardville; St. Vincent de Paul, Girardville; Our Lady of Good Counsel, Gordon.

BETHLEHEM. *Atria.* (Notre Dame of Bethlehem)
Lehigh Valley Muhlenberg Medical Center. (Notre Dame of Bethlehem)
Lehigh Valley Muhlenberg Rehab Center. (Notre Dame of Bethlehem)
Lutheran Manor of the Lehigh Valley, Inc.. (Notre Dame of Bethlehem)
Manor Care Nursing and Rehabilitation Centers I and II. (Notre Dame of Bethlehem)

COALDALE. *Miners Memorial Medical Center.* Administered by SS. Cyril & Methodius, St. John the Baptist, St. Mary of the Assumption, Coaldale; St. Michael, Lansford; St. Stanislaus, St. Joseph, Summit Hill; SS. Peter and Paul, Lansford.

EASTON. *Easton Home.* (St. Bernard)
Easton Hospital. (Priests of Easton Area)
Easton Nursing Center. (St. Bernard)
Northampton County Prison. (St. Bernard)
Praxis. (St. Bernard)

FOUNTAIN HILL. *Cedarbrook.* (Lehigh County Home) St. Ursula.
St. Luke's Hospital. (St. Ursula)

FRACKVILLE. *SCI-Mahoney.* Rev. John T. Whalen.

HAMBURG. *Hamburg Center.* (St. Mary)
Laurel Nursing Center. (St. Mary)

LEHIGHTON. *Gnaden Huetten Memorial Hospital.* (SS. Peter and Paul)
Gnaden Huetten Nursing Home. (SS. Peter & Paul)
Mahoning Valley Nursing Home. (SS. Peter & Paul)

MACUNGIE. *Lehigh Center Nursing Home.* (St. Thomas More, Allentown)
Lehigh Commons Personal Care Home. (St. Thomas More, Allentown)

MINERSVILLE. *FCI-Schuylkill, Federal Correctional Institute.* Rev. Charles J. Dene.

NAZARETH. *Gracedale.* Deacon Michael P. McGouldrick. (Northampton County Home) Holy Family.

NEW TRIPOLI. *Zimmerman Country Homestead.* (St. Joseph the Worker, Orefield)

ORWIGSBURG. *Holy Family Residence.* (St. Ambrose, Schuylkill Haven)
Orwigsburg Center, Formerly Orwigsburg Manor. (St. Ambrose, Schuylkill Haven)
Pinebrook Personal Care Center. (St. Ambrose, Schuylkill Haven)

PALMERTON. *Palmerton Hospital.* (Sacred Heart)

POTTSVILLE. *Luther Ridge.* (St. Patrick)
Manor Care. (Mary, Queen of Peace)
Pottsville Hospital and Warne Clinic. Sr. Marjorie Sweeney, S.S.J., Chap.
Providence Place. (St. Patrick)
Schuylkill County Prison. (Mary, Queen of Peace, Pottsville)
Schuylkill Manor. (St. Patrick)
York Terrace Nursing Home. St. John

READING. *Reading Hospital and Medical Center*, Formerly Reading Hospital. Rev. David J. Fick, Chap., Deacon John P. Konopelski, Chap. (Sacred Heart)

SCHUYLKILL HAVEN. *Rest Haven County Home.* (St. Ambrose)

TREXLERTOWN. *Mosser Nursing Home.* (St. Joseph the Worker, Orefield)

WEATHERWOOD. *Carbon County District Home.* (St. Nicholas, Weatherly)
Heritage Hill (Personal Care). (St. Nicholas, Weatherly)

WERNERSVILLE. *Berks County Prison.* (St. Ignatius Loyola, Sinking Spring; St. Peter, Reading)
Berks-Heim. (Berks County Home; St. Ignatius Loyola, Sinking Spring)
State Hospital. Deacon Richard A. Horst.

WESCOSVILLE. *Lehigh County Home.* (Cedarbrook) St. Catharine of Siena, Allentown.

On Duty Outside the Diocese:
Rev. Msgrs.—
Bartkus, Algimantas A., Pontificio Collegio Lituano, Via Casal Monferrato, 20, Rome 00182 Italy.
Callaghan, Aloysius R., Vicar Gen., Archdiocese for the Military Services, P.O. Box 4469, Washington, DC 20017-0469.
Revs.—
Baker, Andrew R., Congregation for Bishops, Piazza Pio XII, 10 00193 Vatican City State.
Beers, John Michael, Ph.D., Ave Maria University, 1025 Commons Cir., Naples, FL 34119.
Kuzmann, Robert J. (SP), Light Of Christ Rectory, 2176 Marilyn St., Clearwater, FL 33765.
McConaghy, Robert J., Greenbelt Chapel, Ayala Center, Makati, Philippines.

Military Chaplains:
Revs.—
Connolly, James M.T., Lt., CHC, USNR Waterfront Support Unit, 9170 Second St., Suite 120, Norfolk, VA 23511-2393.
Czartorynski, David F., Chap. Major USAF, PSC 80 Box 13377 APO AP 96367, Tyndall Afb, FL 32403.
Medve, Kenneth A., Chap. Lt., CHC, USNR, 2nd Marine Division, 15th MEU Chaplain Section UIC 39728, Fpo, AP 96609-9728.
Thomas, James J., Chap. Lt. Col. USAF, PSC 1, Unit 604, Scott AFB, IL 62225-5608.

Unassigned:
Revs.—
Brennan, Edmund J.
Czaus, Joseph C.
Donahue, Edward J.
Gaffney, James F.
Onushco, William J.
Schaible, Donald J.

Retired:
Rev. Msgrs.—
Barrett, Francis X., Saw Creek Estates, #89, Bushkill, 18324-9403.
Bender, Thomas J., P.O. Box F, 18105.
Birch, Thomas J., 1315 Penn Forest Streams, Jim Thorpe, 18229-9404.
Coll, Robert J., P.O. Box 363, Marco, FL 34146.
Dooley, Joseph P., St. Joseph Rectory, 1879 Applewood Dr., Orefield, 18069.
Forst, Robert M., Our Lady Help of Christians Rectory, 444 N. Jasper St., 18109-2699.
Jones, William E., P.O. Box F, 18105.
Loeper, Richard J., M.A., Immaculate Conception Rectory, 640 E. Main St., Birdsboro, 19508-2002.
Morrison, David J., Our Lady of Perpetual Help Parish Center, 3219 Santee Rd., Bethlehem, 18020-2833.
Ott, Alfred R., V.F., M.Div., 11718 Brandon Rd., Philadelphia, 19154.
Rigney, Dennis A., 611 Wynonah Dr., Auburn, 17922.
Revs.—
Bader, Paul L., Holy Family Villa, 1325 Prospect Ave., Bethlehem, 18018.
Barnes, Joseph A., Holy Family Villa, 1325 Prospect Ave., Bethlehem, 18018-4998.
Brady, James J., Holy Family Villa, 1325 Prospect Ave., Bethlehem, 18018.
Briggman, Michael J., Holy Family Villa, 1325 Prospect Ave., Bethlehem, 18018-4998.
Cervella, Albert T., Holy Family Villa, 1325 Prospect Ave., Bethlehem, 18018-4998.
Dressler, Robert A., St. Ursula Rectory, 1300 Broadway - Fountain Hill, Bethlehem, 18015.
Flynn, Stephen F.X., Holy Family Villa, 1325 Prospect Ave., Bethlehem, 18018.
Fromholzer, Francis J., P.O. Box F, 18105.
Gillespie, Francis T., Holy Family Villa, 1325 Prospect Ave., Bethlehem, 18018.
Grundowski, Francis M., P.O. Box 13553, Reading, 19612.

Hulko, Joseph D., Holy Family Villa, 1325 Prospect Ave., Bethlehem, 18018.
Jones, William P., P.O. Box F, 18105.
Kean, Joseph H., P.O. Box F, 18105.
Kerestus, Thomas J., Holy Family Villa, 1325 Prospect Ave., Bethlehem, 18018-4998.
Lawrence, Michael S., P.O. Box F, 18105.
Lofton, James J., 132 Rolling View Dr., Schuylkill Haven, 17972.
Martinkovic, Joseph (Slovakia), c/o A. Vojacek, Legionarska 19, Trnava 91701 Slovakia.
Maslar, William J., P.O. Box F, 18105.
McElduff, Edward W., 2586 Mountain Rd., Slatington, 18080.
McGarr, Joseph M., Holy Family Villa, 1325 Prospect Ave., 18102.
McKenna, F. Charles, Holy Family Villa, 1325 Prospect Ave., Bethlehem, 18018-4998.
McNelis, Francis J., P.O. Box F, 18105.
Mihalak, James J., P.O. Box F, 18105.
O'Donnell, William J., Holy Family Villa, 1325 Prospect Ave., Bethlehem, 18018-4998.
Ondic, John L., Holy Family Villa, 1325 Prospect Ave., Bethlehem, 18018-4998.
Oranczak, Ronald J., Holy Family Villa, 1325 Prospect Ave., Bethlehem, 18018-4998.
Paskowicz, Marian, 611 Caroline Dr., Norristown, 19401.
Puza, Paul G., P.O. Box F, 18105.
Rock, Joseph A., Holy Family Villa, 1325 Prospect Ave., Bethlehem, 18018-4998.
Strassner, Henry E., Immaculate Conception Rectory, 501 Ridge Ave., 18102.
Tucci, Bruno M., P.O. Box F, Allentown 18105.

Permanent Deacons:
Allison, John J., SS. Cyril and Methodius, Reading
Alvarado, Leopoldo, Spanish Apostolate, Berks County & St. Peter, Reading
Amedeo, Dominick F., Jr., Sacred Heart & Our Lady of Mt. Carmel, Allentown
Andrusisian, Stephen, Mary, Queen of Peace, Pottsville
Autrey, William L., SS. Simon and Jude, Bethlehem
Bankos, Gregory J., Sr., Assumption B.V.M., Northampton
Benkovic, Richard L., Immaculate Conception, Allentown
Bogusky, Joseph H., Annunciation B.V.M., Catasauqua
Braun, Richard K., St. Ambrose, Schuylkill Haven
Buragino, Joseph G., St. Ursula, Bethlehem
Burda, Joseph R., St. Joseph, Frackville
Campanell, Anthony T., St. Joseph the Worker, Orefield
Centeno, Jesus, Hispanic Apostolate, Berks Co. & St. Peter, Reading
Chiles, Franklin J., Holy Ghost, Bethlehem
Chin-Fatt, Arthur L., (On Duty Outside the Diocese)
Close, Richard B., Lehigh Valley Hospital Center, Allentown & St. Ann, Emmaus
Coffin, John A., St. Ignatius Loyola, Sinking Spring
Colon, Francisco De La Gracia, St. Peter, Reading
Colon, Julio, Hispanic Apostolate, Berks Co. & St. Peter, Reading
Cosgrove, Francis J., Office of the Permanent Diaconate & St. Anne, Bethlehem
Costa, Joseph J., Our Lady of Siluva, Maizeville
Coyle, Charles A., Our Lady Help of Christians, Allentown
Cummings, John D., (On Duty Outside the Diocese)
Danyi, Frank J., Jr., SS. Cyril and Methodius, Bethlehem
De Bellis, Charles A., St. Anthony of Padua, Easton
De Jesus, Jaime
De Jesus, Roberto, Hispanic Apostolate, Northampton County & Holy Infancy, Bethlehem
Dudeck, Lawrence A., Holy Rosary, Reading
Duncan, James R., St. Thomas More, Allentown
End, Gerard Edward, Jr., Immaculate Conception, Birdsboro
Faller, George J., St. Catharine of Siena, Mt. Penn, Reading
Flanagan, Michael D., St. Mary, Kutztown
Flanley, Eugene M., Jr., St. Francis of Assisi, Allentown
Fleck, Henry, Jr., St. Bernard, Easton
Fry, Craig A., St. Catharine of Siena, Reading
Giltrap, James F., III, St. Joseph, Limeport
Godiska, Joseph F., Our Lady of Hungary, Northampton
Gonzalez, Jose
Gordon, Henry G., St. Mary, Hamburg
Granato, Gary J., St. Paul, Allentown
Hanni, John A., Sacred Heart, Bath
Hassler, William R., Cathedral of St. Catharine of Siena, Allentown
Henninger, James P., St. Francis of Assisi, Minersville
Hernandez, Saul, Hispanic Apostolate Lehigh County and Sacred Heart, Allentown
Horst, Richard A., St. Catharine of Siena, Reading & Wernersville State Hospital, Wernersville
Hunkele, Thomas H.
Jaccodine, Ralph J., St. Thomas More, Allentown
Kase, William R., Sacred Heart, West Reading
Kelly, George C., Jr., Our Lady of Perpetual Help, Bethlehem
Konopelski, John P., Reading Hospital and Medical Center & St. Margaret, Reading
Koval, Edward P.
Lafata, Peter M., St. Joseph, Reading
Laroche, Michael J., Holy Trinity, Whitehall
Maggitti, Alexander L., Sr., St. Elizabeth, Whitehall
Matos, Rodoberto, Hispanic Apostolate, Northampton Co. and St. Bernard, Easton
McGouldrick, Michael P., Gracedale County Home & Holy Family, Nazareth
McManus, Robert J., St. Mauritius & St Joseph, Ashland
McShane, Hugh E., Sacred Heart, Miller Heights, Bethlehem
Metzker, Daniel F., Phobe Devitt Home, Cathedral of Catharine of Siena, Allentown; St. Joseph the Worker, Orefield
Mihalik, Andrew J., Jr., Sacred Heart, Palmerton
Monahan, Brian J., Immaculate Conception, Allentown
Morales, Edison
Mullins, Thomas J., St. Thomas More, Allentown
Murphy, John W., Jr., St. Ignatius Loyola, Sinking Spring
Murphy, Thomas J., Most Blessed Sacrament & St. Francis Academy, Bally
Najera-Ramirez, Francisco, Hispanic Apostolate, Berks County and St. Peter, Reading
Nemeth, Stephen F., St. Peter, Coplay
Paschall, Joseph L., Jr., St. Columbkill, Boyertown
Pitts, William P., Sacred Heart, Palmerton
Pogash, John F., SS. Peter and Paul & St. Mary, St. Clair
Quiles, Victor M., Hispanic Apostolate, Northampton Co. & Holy Infancy, Bethlehem
Quirk, John E., St. Patrick, Pottsville
Ramirez, Manuel L., Holy Infancy, Bethlehem
Reichard, Thomas C., St. Bernard & St. Michael, Easton
Rodgers, Robert W., St. Jane Frances de Chantal, Easton
Rodriguez, Nicasio, Hispanic Apostolate, Northampton Co. & Holy Infancy, Bethlehem
Schmidt, Gerald R., St. Ann, Emmaus
Scrak, Richard G., Catholic Social Agency, Ecumenical Soup Kitchen, Allentown & St. Anne, Bethlehem
Setlock, John A., Annunciation & St. Ann, Frackville
Sewald, Richard T., Notre Dame of Bethlehem, Bethlehem
Simchick, Sylvester F., St. John Baptist de la Salle, Shillington
Solis, Alfonso D., Hispanic Apostolate, Lehigh Co. & Sacred Heart, Allentown
Thoden, Richard M., Jr., Assumption B.V.M., Bethlehem
Thompson, John F., St. Peter the Fisherman, Lake Harmony
Thomson, Daniel A., Good Shepherd Home and Rehabilitation Hospital & St. Paul, Allentown
Torres, Fernando L., Hispanic Apostolate, Berks Co. & St. Peter, Reading
Torres, Mariano, Hispanic Apostolate, Berks Co. & St. Peter, Reading
Trejo, Jose N. Rodriguez, Immaculate Conception, Birdsboro; St. Joseph, Reading
Trexler, Jeffrey R., SS. Cyril and Methodius, Bethlehem
Tyson, Robert J.
Vanzino, William C., St. Jane Frances de Chantal, Easton
Visot, Luis R., St. John the Baptist, Pottsville
Wagner, William J., S.S. Peter and Paul, Lehighton
Wilkinson, Raymond, St. Nicholas, Weatherly
Wisser, Bernard M., Assumption B.V.M., Bethlehem
Woodall, Michael V., St. Columbkill, Boyertown
Wyrwa, Eugene J., Holy Trinity, Whitehall; Diocesan Tribunal, Allentown

INSTITUTIONS LOCATED IN THE DIOCESE

[A] SEMINARIES, RELIGIOUS OR SCHOLASTICATES

CENTER VALLEY. *Sacred Heart Villa, Missionaries of the Sacred Heart*, 3300 Station Ave., 18034-9563. Tel: 610-282-1415; Fax: 610-282-0610. Email: mscvilla@aol.com. Web: www.misacor-usa.org. Very Rev. E. Michael Camilli, M.S.C., H.E.L., S.T.L.; Revs. Thomas Cain, M.S.C.; Robert Cell, M.S.C., M.A.; Raymond Costello, M.S.C.; Walter Downs, M.S.C.; Joseph Gaspar, M.S.C., S.T.D.; David DeLuca, M.S.C., M.A. (Y); William Gies, M.S.C.; Jacob Welle, M.S.C.; Philip Yandrisevits, M.S.C.; Bros. Edward Baker, M.S.C.; Richard Kuhl, M.S.C.; John Peralta, M.S.C.; Robert Murphy, M.S.C.; Alois Schirmers, M.S.C.; Wilfred Miller, M.S.C. Priests 10; Brothers 6; Total Staff 16.

NORTHAMPTON. *Mary Immaculate Center*, 300 Cherryville Rd., 18067-9548. Tel: 610-262-7866; Fax: 610-262-6766. Email: maryimmaculatecenter@adphila.org. Web: www.maryimmaculatecenter.org. Conducted by the Archdiocese of Philadelphia as a seminary for the Spirituality Year Program for seminarians and for the ongoing formation of priests, and as a house of prayer and retreat for priests, religious, and laity.

Spirituality Year Program Tel: 610-262-9674. Mr. William Kefer, M.S.W., Admin.

WERNERSVILLE. *Jesuit Center*, P.O. Box 223, 19565-0223. 501 N. Church Rd., 19565-0223. Tel: 610-678-8085; Fax: 610-678-8747. Email: jescntsec@talon.net. Web: www.jesuitcenter.webjump.com. Revs. Joseph A. Panuska, S.J., Rector; James A. Borbely, S.J., Admin. & Treas.; Lucien F. Longtin, S.J (WDC), Dir. Spiritual Center. Priests 25; Brothers 3; Lay Staff 24; Total Staff 30. In Res. Revs. Michael L. Barber, S.J.; John P. Barron, S.J.; James A. Borbely, S.J.; Robert B. Cullen, S.J.; Robert J. Dullahan, S.J.; Henry J. Erhart, S.J.; Henry B. Haske, S.J. (WDC); Joseph Henry, S.J.; Harold J. Hocking, S.J.; John J. Keenan, S.J.; Joseph A. Kemme, S.J.; Thomas J. Kuller, S.J.; Daniel F. Lawler, S.J.; Clarence A. Martin, S.J.; John T. McCaslin, S.J.; Richard W. Norman, S.J.; Bernard C. O'Leary, S.J.; Joseph A. Panuska, S.J.; Eugene J. Power, S.J.; Edwin J. Sanders, S.J.; Joseph P. Sanders; William E. Schaffner; William J. Sneck, S.J.; D. Gilbert Sweeney, S.J.; George S. Williams, S.J.; Bros. John T. Gibbons, S.J.; Robert A. Larouere, S.J.; William J. Sudzina, S.J.

[B] COLLEGES AND UNIVERSITIES

CENTER VALLEY. *DeSales University*, 2755 Station Ave., 18034-9568. Tel: 610-282-1100; Fax: 610-282-2255. Email: admiss@desales.edu. Web: www.DeSales.edu. Very Rev. Bernard F. O'Connor, O.S.F.S., Ph.D., Pres.; Rev. Alexander T. Pocetto, O.S.F.S., Ph.D., Senior Vice Pres.; Dr. Tim Fitzgerald, Dean Students; Mr. Gerard Joyce, Dean Enrollment Mgmt.; Mr. Thomas Mantoni, Registrar; Mr. Willard Cressman, Vice Pres. Admin. & Fin.; Mr. Tom Campbell, Vice Pres. Devel.; Dr. Mohamed A.S. Latib, Vice Pres. Prog. & Strategic Devel.; Dr. Karen Doyle Walton, Vice Pres. Academic Affairs & Provost; Rev. John A. Hanley, O.S.F.S., M.Div., Dir. Campus Min.; Robert Snyder, Assoc. Vice Pres. Finance & Treas.; Revs. Joseph P. Becker, O.S.F.S.; Douglas C. Burns, O.S.F.S., M.Div.; Thomas F. Dailey, O.S.F.S.; Joseph F. DiMauro, O.S.F.S., M.A.; Bernard F. Donahue, O.S.F.S., Ph.D.; James P. Finnegan, O.S.F.S.; Daniel G. Gambet, O.S.F.S., Ph.D.; John A. Hanley, O.S.F.S., M.Div.; John F. Harvey, O.S.F.S. (NY); Christopher J. Hudgin, O.S.F.S., M.A.; Very Rev. Peter J. Leonard, O.S.F.S., Ph.D.; Revs. A. Robert McGilvray, O.S.F.S., Ph.D.; Robert G. Mulligan, O.S.F.S., M.A.; Very Rev. Bernard F. O'Connor, O.S.F.S., Ph.D.; Revs. Alexander T. Pocetto, O.S.F.S., Ph.D.; Gerard H. Schubert, O.S.F.S., Ph.D.; Bro. Daniel P. Wisniowski, M.A. Coeducational liberal arts college conducted by the Oblates of St. Francis de Sales (1965); Accredited. Priests on Faculty 8; Brothers 1; Lay Teachers 129; Students 2,914.

READING. *Alvernia College* 19607. Tel: 610-796-8200; Fax: 610-796-8324. Email: larry.mazzeno@alvernia.edu. Web: www.alvernia.edu. Laurence W. Mazzeno, Ph.D., Pres. Bernardine Sisters of the Third Order of St. Francis Priests 2; Sisters 5; Lay Teachers 72; Students 2,335.

[C] HIGH SCHOOLS, DIOCESAN

ALLENTOWN. *Allentown Central Catholic High School*, 301 N. Fourth St., 18102-3098. Tel: 610-437-4601; Fax: 610-437-6760. Email: altlcchs@ptd.net. Web: www.acchs.info. Rev. Frans J. Berkhout, Prin.; Mr. William F. Tielman, Vice Prin.; Rev. Msgr. Francis C. Revak. Priests 2; Sisters 2; Lay Teachers 50; Students 940.

ASHLAND. *Cardinal Brennan Jr./Sr. High School*, 130 Academy Ln., 17921. Tel: 570-874-3921; Fax: 570-874-2239. Email: altscbhs@ptd.net. Web:

www.pottsville.com/cardinalbrennan/. Rev. Stephen L. Maco, Prin.; Mr. Paul Brutto, Dir. Studies. Lay Teachers 19; Students 272.

BANGOR. *Pius X High School*, 580 Third Ave., 18013-1399. Tel: 610-588-3291; Fax: 610-599-3048. Email: altnpxhs@ptd.net. Web: www.piusxhs.com. Mr. Thomas Klepeisz, Prin.; Rev. Patrick H. Lamb, Pres. Priests 1; Lay Teachers 18; Students 177.

BETHLEHEM. *Bethlehem Catholic High School*, 2133 Madison Ave., 18017-4699. Tel: 610-866-0791; Fax: 610-866-9892. Email: altnbchs@ptd.net. Web: www.BethlehemCatholichs.org. Mr. Richard B. Culver, M.Ed., Prin.; Sr. Marjorie Keenan, S.S.J., Vice Prin.; Mr. Richard F. Mazza, Dir. Admissions; Rev. Bernard J. Ezaki, Dir. Spiritual Activities; Very Rev. Peter J. Hosak, M.S. (PSC), Guidance Counselor. Founded as two-year commercial high school, 1897.; Founded as four-year comprehensive high school, 1925. Sisters of St. Joseph 4; Lay Teachers 37; Students 740; Bernardine Sisters 1.

EASTON. *Notre Dame High School*, 3417 Church Rd., 18045-2999. Tel: 610-868-1431; Fax: 610-868-6710. Email: altnndhs@ptd.net. Web: www.notredamehseastonpa.org. Mr. Joseph R. Kramer Jr., Prin.; Mr. James E. Steiner, Vice Prin.; Rev. Robert J. George, M.Div., Dir. of Spiritual Activities; Mrs. Jan Spinato, Dir. of Devel. Priests 1; Sisters 2; Lay Teachers 33; Students 570.

POTTSVILLE. *Nativity B.V.M. High School*, One Lawtons Hill, 17901. Tel: 570-622-8110; Fax: 570-622-0454. Email: altsnhs@ptd.net. Web: www.pottsville.com/nativity/index.htm. Rev. Ronald V. Jankaitis, Prin.; Mr. J. William Norton, Asst. Prin.; Mrs. Jennifer Daubert, Dir. Devel. Sisters 3; Lay Teachers 16; Students 215.

READING. *Central Catholic High School of Berks County*, 1400 Hill Rd., 19602-1499. Tel: 610-373-4178; Fax: 610-375-4898. Email: admins@rcchsbc.pvt.k12.pa.us. Web: www.cchsbc.pvt.k12.pa.us. Thomas P. Mirabella, M.Ed., Prin.; Sr. Jonathan Moyles, S.C.C., Asst. Prin. Sisters 5; Lay Teachers 22; Administrators 2; Students 367.

Holy Name High School, 955 E. Wyomissing Blvd., 19611-1799. Tel: 610-374-8361; Fax: 610-374-4309. Email: altbhnhs@impresso.com. Web: www.holynamehighschool.com. Keith Laser, Prin.; William Hess, Vice Prin.; Rev. Robert T. Finlan, Dir. of Spiritual Activities. Priests 1; Sisters 2; Lay Teachers 38; Students 524.

TAMAQUA. *Marian Catholic High School*, 166 Marian Ave., 18252. Tel: 570-467-3335; Fax: 570-467-0186. Email: altsmhs@ptd.net. Web: www.mariancatholics.org. Sr. Bernard Agnes, I.H.M., Prin.; Mr. Paul Coombe, Vice Prin.; Rev. George R. Winne. Priests 1; Servants of the Immaculate Heart of Mary 5; Lay Teachers 24; Students 308.

[D] REGIONAL CATHOLIC ELEMENTARY SCHOOLS, DIOCESAN

ALLENTOWN. *Holy Spirit School*, (Grades PreK-8), 920 N. Front St., 18102. Tel: 610-434-4044; Fax: 610-434-5458. Email: altlhs@ptd.net. Serving St. John the Baptist, Immaculate Conception, SS. Peter & Paul, Allentown.

Primary School (Grades PreK-3), 920 N. Front St., 18102. Tel: 610-820-0220.

Middle School (Grades 4-8), 510 Ridge Ave., 18102. Tel: 610-434-4044; Fax: 610-434-5458. Sr. Catherine Bones, S.S.J., Prin. Tel: 610-434-4044; Fax: 610-434-5458. Total Enrollment 180.

Sacred Heart School, 325 N. Fourth St., 18102. Tel: 610-437-3031; Fax: 610-437-1310. Email: altlsh@ptd.net. Mr. James Krupka, Prin. Serving Sacred Heart, Our Lady of Mt. Carmel, St. Stephen, Allentown. Lay Teachers 10; Students 199.

BALLY. *St. Francis Academy*, 668 Pine St., 19503. Tel: 610-845-7364; Fax: 610-845-2223. Email: altbsfa@impresso.com. Deacon Thomas J. Murphy, Prin. Serving Most Blessed Sacrament, Bally, St. Columbkill, Boyertown, and St. Mary, Kutztown. Lay Teachers 10; Students 261.

BETHLEHEM. *SS. Cyril and Methodius Regional Catholic Elementary School*, 551 Thomas St., 18015. Tel: 610-866-0042; Fax: 610-866-4914. Email: altnsscm@ptd.net. Mrs. Joan M. West, Prin. Serving SS. Cyril and Methodius, St. Joseph, St. John Capistrano, Our Lady of Pompeii, St. Stanislaus. Lay Teachers 12; Students 105.

Holy Child School, (Grades K-8), 1301 Sioux St., 18015-4400. Tel: 610-865-0861; Fax: 610-997-0180. Email: altlhc@ptd.net. Mrs. Annette Filler, Prin. Serving Holy Ghost, St. Ursula, Bethlehem. Lay Teachers 10; Students 146.

St. Michael the Archangel School Serving Assumption B.V.M., Colesville; St. Joseph, Limeport.

Primary Bldg. (Grades K-4), 5040 St. Joseph's Rd., Limeport, 18060. Tel: 610-965-4441; Fax: 610-965-1030.

Middle School (Grades 5-8) , Main Office. , 4121 Old Bethlehem Pike, 18015. Tel: 610-867-8422; Fax: 610-865-2098. Carol Sonon, Prin. Priests 2; Lay Teachers 25; Students 374.

EASTON. *Easton Catholic School*, (Grades K-3), Primary Bldg., 283 W. St. Joseph St., 18042. Tel: 610-253-0651; Fax: 610-250-0700. Email: altnec@ptd.net. Web: www.eastoncatholic.com. Serving St. Anthony, St. Joseph, St. Michael, St. Bernard.

Middle Bldg. (Grades 4-8), 841 Washington St., 18042. Tel: 610-252-1393; Fax: 610-250-0606. Heidi Fritts, Prin. Lay Teachers 10; Students 160.

FRACKVILLE. *Holy Family School*, (Grades PreK-6), 29 S. Broad Mountain Ave., 17931. Tel: 570-874-0285; Fax: 570-874-3193. Email: altshf@ptd.net. Mrs. Dolores Bartashus, Prin. Serving Annunciation, B.V.M., St. Joseph, St. Ann. Sisters 1; Lay Teachers 6; Students K-6 90; Students Pre-K 21.

GIRARDVILLE. *Immaculate Heart Elementary School*, (Grades PreK-6), 20 S. Richard St., 17935-1823. Tel: 570-276-6610; Fax: 570-276-6610. Email: altsih@ptd.com. Sr. Stephen Anne, I.H.M., Prin. Serving St. Joseph, St. Mauritius, Ashland; St. Joseph, St. Vincent, Girardville; Our Lady of Good Counsel, Gordon. Religious 2; Lay Teachers 10; Students 158.

JIM THORPE. *St. Joseph Regional Academy*, (Grades K-8), 25 W. 6th St., 18229-2120. Tel: 570-325-3186; Fax: 570-325-9451. Email: altcsjra@ptd.net. Sr. Donna Brady, S.C.C., Prin. Serving St. Joseph, Immaculate Conception, Jim Thorpe, St. Peter the Fisherman, and Lake Harmony. Sisters 2; Lay Teachers 8; Students 149.

LANSFORD. *Our Lady of the Angels Academy*, (Grades K-8), 123 E. Water St., 18232-2001. Tel: 570-645-7170; Fax: 570-645-5278. Email: altcola@ptd.net. Sr. Regina Elinich, I.H.M., Prin. Serving St. Joseph, St. Stanislaus, Summit Hill; St. Ann, St. Michael, SS. Peter & Paul, Lansford; Immaculate Conception, Our Lady of Mt. Carmel, Sacred Heart, Nesquehoning; St. John the Baptist, St. Mary, SS. Cyril & Methodius, Coaldale. Sisters 1; Lay Teachers 9; Students 204.

MAHANOY CITY. *Academy of the Blessed Virgin Mary*, (Grades K-8), 29 S. Catawissa, 17948-2563. Tel: 570-773-2668; Fax: 570-773-2015. Email: altsobvm@ptd.net. Ms. Barbara Purcell, Prin. Serving St. Canicus, St. Casimir, St. Joseph, Assumption B.V.M., Sacred Heart, St. Fidelis, Mahanoy City; St. Richard, Barnesville; Our Lady of Silva, Maizeville. Lay Teachers 10; Students 89.

MCADOO. *McAdoo Catholic Elementary School*, (Grades PreK-8), 35 N. Cleveland St., 18237. Tel: 570-929-1442; Fax: 570-929-3016. Email: altsmacc@ptd.net. Sr. Anita M. Dixon, I.H.M., Prin. Serving St. Patrick, St. Kunegunda, St. Mary, McAdoo; St. Bartholomew, St. Michael, Tresckow; Immaculate Conception, Kelayres; St. Nicholas, Weatherly; St. Mary, Beaver Meadows. Sisters 1; Lay Teachers 9; Students 122.

MINERSVILLE. *Good Shepherd Regional School*, (Grades PreK-3), 538 Sunbury St., 17954. Tel: 570-544-4360. Email: altsgsr@ptd.net. Web: www.pottsville.com/goodshep/. Serving St. Kieran, Heckscherville; St. Mary, Star of the Sea, Branchdale; Sacred Heart, Newtown; Immaculate Conception, Tremont; SS. Peter and Paul, Tower City; St. Barbara, St. Francis of Assisi, St. Stanislaus Kostka, St. Vincent de Paul, Our Lady of Mt. Carmel, Minersville.

(Grades 4-8), 301 Heffner St., 17954. Tel: 570-544-3766; Fax: 570-544-4870. Ms. Rosalie Novack, Prin. Lay Teachers 11; Students 138.

NORTHAMPTON. *Our Lady of Hungary Regional School*, 1300 Newport Ave., 18067. Tel: 610-262-9171; Fax: 610-262-2202. Email: altnolh@ptd.net. Mrs. Elizabeth J. Smith, Prin. Serving Our Lady of Hungary, Assumption B.V.M., St. Michael, Northampton; St. Lawrence and St. Andrew, Catasauqua. Sisters 1; Lay Teachers 16; Students 288.

PALMERTON-SLATINGTON. *St. John Neumann Regional School* Tel: 610-826-2354; Fax: 610-826-6444. Email: altcsjn@impresso.com. Serving St. Nicholas, Berlinsville; Sacred Heart, Palmerton; Assumption B.V.M., Slatington.

(Grades K-3), 641-645 W. Washington St., Slatington, 18080. Tel: 610-767-2935; Fax: 610-767-2948.

(Grades 4-8), 259 Lafayette Ave., 18071. Tel: 610-826-2354; Fax: 610-826-6444. Mrs. Mary Ellen Chuss-Mirro, M.Ed., Prin. Lay Teachers 9; Students 170.

PEN ARGYL. *Immaculate Conception School*, (Grades K-6), Babbitt Ave. & Heller Ave., 18072. Tel: 610-863-4816; Fax: 610-863-8158. Email: altnics@ptd.net. Web: www.immaculateconceptionschool.net. Sr. Maria Luz, O.P., Prin. Serving St. Elizabeth, Pen Argyl; St. Rocco, Martins Creek; St. Roch, West Bangor. Sisters 6; Lay Teachers 2; Students 115.

PORT CARBON. *St. Stephen Regional School*, (Grades PreK-8), 214 Valley St., 17965. Tel: 570-622-3063; Fax: 570-622-3689. Email: altsss@ptd.net. Web: www.pottsville.com/st_stephen. Mrs. Mildred T. Scarbinsky, Prin. Serving the following parishes: St. Stephen, Port Carbon; St. Mary, Immaculate Conception & St. Casimir, Ss. Peter & Paul & St. Boniface, St. Clair; Sacred Heart, Holy Family, New Philadelphia; St. Anthony, Cumbola. Sisters 1; Lay Teachers 10; Students 185.

POTTSVILLE. *All Saints Elementary School*, (Grades K-8), 112 S. Seventh St., 17901-3079. Tel: 570-622-0106; 570-622-1765; Fax: 570-622-4737. Email: altsase@ptd.net. Web: www.all-saintscatholicschool.net. Mrs. Mary Franko, M.Ed., Prin. Serving St. Patrick, St. John the Baptist, Mary, Queen of Peace, St. Joseph, Pottsville and St. Francis de Sales, Mt. Carbon. Lay Teachers 15; Students 250.

Little Saints Preschool, 2051 W. Norwegian St., 17901. Tel: 570-622-1073. Sr. M. Leonore Bauer, S.S.J., Dir. Serving the Pottsville area. Sisters 1; Lay Teachers 2; Students 58.

READING. *St. Catharine of Siena School* Serving St. Catharine of Siena, Reading. , 2330 Perkiomen Ave., 19606-2048. Tel: 610-779-5810; Fax: 610-779-6888. Email: altbscs@ptd.net. Sr. Monica Therese Sicilia, I.H.M., Prin. Sisters 4; Lay Teachers 23; Students 470.

Holy Guardian Angels Regional School, Reading, (Grades PreK-8), 3125 Kutztown Rd., 19605. Tel: 610-929-4124; Fax: 610-929-1623. Email: altbhga@ptd.net. Web: www.hgaparish.com. Mrs. Maureen Wallin, Prin. Serving Holy Guardian Angels and St. Joseph, Reading. Lay Teachers 23; Students 468.

ROSETO. *Our Lady of Mt. Carmel School*, 80 Ridge St., 18013--139. Tel: 610-588-2629; Fax: 610-588-3423. Email: altnolmc@impresso.com. Mr. Joseph Yannuzzi, Prin. Serving Our Lady of Mt. Carmel, Roseto, and Our Lady of Good Counsel, Bangor. Lay Teachers 7; Students 150.

SHENANDOAH. *Father Walter J. Ciszek Elementary School*, (Grades PreK-6), 233 W. Cherry St., 17976. Tel: 570-462-3927; Fax: 570-462-4603. Email: altsfwc@ptd.net. Web: www.ces-msa.org/registry.html. Sr. Catherine Danielle LeTourneau, I.H.M., Prin. Serving Annunciation, St. Casimir, St. George, Our Lady of Mt. Carmel, St. Stanislaus, St. Stephen, Shenandoah; St. Mary Magdalen, Lost Creek; St. Mary, Ringtown. Religious 5; Lay Teachers 13; Students 194.

SHILLINGTON. *La Salle Academy and Early Childhood Center*, (Grades PreK-8), 440 Holland St., 19607. Tel: 610-777-7392; Fax: 610-777-1280. Email: altblsa@ptd.net. Web: www.lsabear.org. Mrs. Patti Fisher, M.Ed., M.A., Prin. Serving St. John Baptist de La Salle, Shillington; St. Benedict, Plowville; St. Anthony, Millmont. Lay Teachers 25; Students 385.

SINKING SPRING. *St. Ignatius Loyola School*, (Grades PreK-8), 2700 St. Alban's Dr., 19609. Tel: 610-678-0111; Fax: 610-670-5795. Email: altbsil@ptd.net. Web: www.stignatiusreading.org/. Mrs. Janice E. Bayerle, Prin. Serving St. Ignatius Loyola, Sinking Spring; St. Francis de Sales, Robesonia. Sisters 21; Lay Teachers 34; Students 541.

TAMAQUA. *St. Jerome Regional School*, 250 W. Broad St., 18252. Tel: 570-668-2757; Fax: 570-668-6101. Email: altssj@ptd.net. Web: www.sjrs.net. Sr. Donna Ariente, I.H.M., Prin. Serving St. Jerome, SS. Peter and Paul, Tamaqua; St. Bartholomew, Brockton; St. Bertha, Tuscarora. Sisters 1; Lay Teachers 8; Students 166.

WHITEHALL. *Christ the King School*, Primary Bldg., 3008 Ruch St., 18052. Tel: 610-262-4177; Fax: 610-262-5632. Email: altlck@ptd.net. Web: www.ctk-wc.org. Serving St. Peter, Coplay; St. John the Baptist, Whitehall; Holy Trinity, Egypt.

Middle Bldg., 22 S. Fifth St., Coplay, 18037. Tel: 610-262-5822. Ms. Irene M. Quigley, Prin. Lay Teachers 13; Students 295.

Preschool, 40 S. Fifth St., Coplay, 18037. Tel: 610-262-4064.

St. Elizabeth Regional School, 433 Pershing Blvd., 18052. Tel: 610-264-0143; Fax: 610-264-1563. Email: altlse@ptd.net. Web: www.sercc.org/school.htm. Sr. Bonita Smith, R.S.M., Prin. Serving St. Elizabeth, Whitehall; Annunciation, Catasauqua. Religious 1; Lay Teachers 9; Students 202.

[E] SPECIAL SCHOOLS

ALLENTOWN. *Mercy Special Learning Center*, 830 S. Woodward St., 18103-3440. Tel: 610-797-8242; Fax: 610-797-9092. Email: altlmslc@pdt.net.

Ages: Newborn to 21. Lay Teachers 8; Students 95.

BETHLEHEM. *The Aquinas Program*, SS. Cyril & Methodius School, 551 Thomas St., 18015. Tel: 610-866-0042; Fax: 610-866-6490. Email: altnsscm@ptd.net. Mrs. Joan West, Prin.; Sr. Janice Marie Johnson, R.S.M., Supvr., Learning Disabilities. Lay Teachers 3; Students 34.

The Aquinas Program St. Margaret School, 233 Spring St., Reading, 19601-2121. Tel: 610-375-1882; Fax: 610-376-2291. Email: altbsmg@ptd.net. Sisters Diane Licordare, Prin.; Janice Marie Johnson, R.S.M., Supvr.

The Aquinas Program - Secondary Level Notre Dame High School, 3417 Church St., Easton, 18045-2999. Tel: 610-868-1431; Fax: 610-868-6710. Email: altnndhs@ptd.net. Mr. Joseph R. Kramer Jr., Prin.; Sr. Janice Marie Johnson, R.S.M., Supvr.

POTTSVILLE. *St. Joseph Center*, 2075 W. Norwegian St., 17901-1907. Tel: 570-622-4638; Fax: 570-622-3420. Email: altssjc@ptd.net. Julia Leskin, M.S., Prin. Lay Teachers 3; Students 15.

READING. *Alvernia Montessori School at Sacred Heart School*, Formerly Alvernia Montessori School, (Grades N-K), 701 Franklin St., West Reading, 19611. Tel: 610-396-0882. Sr. Ann Marie Coll, Dir. Sisters 3; Lay Teachers 1; Students 65.

SHILLINGTON. *John Paul II Center for Special Learning*, 1092 Welsh Rd., 19607. Tel: 610-777-0605; Fax: 610-777-0682. Email: jp2center@comcast.net. Web: www.jp2center.org. Lay Teachers 4; Students 30.

[F] CATHOLIC CHARITIES AND SOCIAL AGENCIES

ALLENTOWN. *Catholic Social Agency-Catholic Charities Administrative Office*, 2141 Downyflake Ln., 18103-4774. Tel: 610-791-3888; Fax: 610-791-1878. Email: bmurphy@allentowndiocese.org Mrs. Barbara W. Murphy, M.S.W., Exec. Dir. of Catholic Social Agency. Parish-based Counseling Centers: St. Fidelis, Mahanoy City; St. Columbkill, Boyertown; Easton Area Neighborhood Center, Easton; St. Joseph, Jim Thorpe; St. Mary's, Kutztown.

Branch Offices:

Branch Office, 530 Union Blvd., 18109-3230. Tel: 610-435-1541; Fax: 610-435-4367.

1720 W. Market St., Pottsville, 17901. Tel: 570-628-0466; Fax: 570-628-3343.

Berks County Branch Office, The Madison Building, 400 Washington St., Ste. 100, Reading, 19601-3966. Tel: 610-376-7144; Fax: 610-376-7145.

Adult Outreach Center, Formerly Senior Outreach 218 W. Cherry St., Shenandoah, 17976-2209. Tel: 570-462-1154.

Adult Outreach Center, 310 E. Mahanoy Ave., Mahanoy City, 17948. Tel: 570-773-2010.

Pregnancy Crisis Center Tel: 800-841-2353. (24-Hour Hotline)

Bangor, PA Tel: 610-599-8858.

Easton. Tel: 610-899-2020.

Pen Argyl, PA Tel: 610-863-8231.

Pen Argyl, 18072. Tel: 610-863-8231.

[G] GENERAL HOSPITALS

ALLENTOWN. *Sacred Heart Hospital*, 421 Chew St., 18102-3490. Tel: 610-776-4500; Fax: 610-776-5154. Web: shh.org. James M. Seitzinger, Pres. & CEO; Rev. John G. Hilferty, Chap. & Dir. Pastoral Care. Sisters 5; Bed Capacity 243; Skilled Nursing Beds 22; Total Staff 1,617; Patients Assisted Annually 166,439.

POTTSVILLE. *Good Samaritan Regional Medical Center*, 700 E. Norwegian St., 17901. Tel: 570-621-4000; Fax: 570-622-7950. Web: www.gsrmc.com. Mr. Peter U. Bergmann, Pres.& C.E.O.; Rev. James Morgan, Chap. Daughters of Charity 8; Total Staff 653; Bed Capacity 174; Patients Assisted Annually 127,075.

Good Samaritan Foundation, Inc., 700 E. Norwegian St., 17901. Tel: 570-621-4252; Fax: 570-621-4480.

Seton Medical Group, Inc., 700 E. Norwegian St., 17901. Tel: 570-621-4003; Fax: 570-622-7950.

READING. *Bornemann Health Corporation*, c/o Saint Joseph Hospital, 12th St. & Walnut St., P.O. Box 316, 19603-0316. Tel: 610-378-2729; Fax: 610-208-8875. Web: www.sjmcberks.org. Mr. John Morahan, Pres. & CEO. Total Staff 93; Bed Capacity 92; Total Assisted 44,496.

Community Campus of St. Joseph Medical Center, 215 N. 12th St., Box 316, 19603. Tel: 610-358-4215. Mr. Patrick F. Roche, Pres.

Saint Joseph Medical Center, 215 N. 12th St., P.O. Box 316, 19603-0316. Tel: 610-378-2000; Fax: 610-378-2798. Email: bridgetmcnamara@chi-east.org. John R. Morahan, Pres. & CEO; Sr. Bridget McNamara, O.S.F., Vice Pres., Mission & Ministry Healthy Communities. Opened Aug. 26, 1873. Sisters 10; Total Staff 1,498; Bed Capacity 279; Bassinets 16; Patients Assisted Annually 271,595.

[H] SKILLED NURSING FACILITIES

BETHLEHEM. *Holy Family Manor*, 1200 Spring St., 18018. Tel: 610-865-5595; Fax: 610-865-5866. Email: jpolaski@HFManor.com. Web: www.hfmanor.com. Judee Bavaria, Pres.; Mr. R. James Polaski, Admin.; Rev. John J.L. Little, M.Div., Chap. Skilled and intermediate nursing care facility for the aged, chronically ill, or invalid. Total Capacity 208; Total Assisted 321; Total Staff 315.

POTTSVILLE. *Covenant Home Care*, Schuylkill County Branch Office and Admin. Office, 1510 Hwy. 61 S., 17901-8409. Tel: 570-385-5522; 800-726-8761; Fax: 570-385-5287. Email: holyfmly@ptd.net. Total Staff 48; Patients Assisted Annually 1,010.

[I] HOMES AND SERVICES FOR THE ELDERLY AND CONVALESCENT

BETHLEHEM. *Grace Mansion Assisted Living Residence of Holy Family Manor*, 1200 Spring St., 18018. Tel: 610-865-6748; Fax: 610-997-8444. Email: kabruzzese@HRManor.com. Web: www.hfmanor.com. Judee Bavaria, Pres.; Karen Abruzzese, Admin. & Coord. Residential Svcs.; Mr. Jim Polaski, Dir. Residential Svcs. Personal care/assisted living facility for 25 elderly. Total in Residence 23; Total Staff 12; Total Assisted 36.

Holy Family Apartments, 330-338 13th Ave., 18018. Tel: 610-866-4603; Fax: 610-866-1622. Email: hfabeth@rnni.com. Melissa Kohler, Mgr. Catholic housing for the elderly. Total Staff 2; Apartments 50; Residents 50.

Trexler Pavilion, Assisted Living Residence of Holy Family Manor, 1220 Prospect Ave., 18018. Tel: 610-868-7776; Fax: 610-865-7775. Email: kabruzzese@HFManor.com. Web: www.hfmanor.com. Judee Bavaria, Pres. Mary Jo Kuebler, Admin.; Mr. James Polaski, Dir. Residential Svcs.; Karen Abruzzese, Coord. Residential Svcs. Personal care/assisted living facility for 23 elderly. Total in Residence 20; Total Staff 15; Total Assisted 27.

EASTON. *Antonian Towers*, 2405 Hillside Ave., 18042. Tel: 610-258-2033; Fax: 610-258-6541. Email: antonian@rnni.com. Rev. Floyd Cesare Jr., Pres.; Mrs. Judith Kern, Mgr. Catholic housing for the elderly. Apartments 50; Total in Residence 51; Total Staff 2.

NEW PHILADELPHIA. *Holy Family Apartments*, c/o Neumann Apartments, 25 N. Nichols St., St. Clair, 17970. Tel: 570-429-0699; Fax: 570-429-2368. Email: neumann@voicenet.com. Apartments 11; Total Staff 2.

ORWIGSBURG. *Holy Family Adult Day Care at St. Francis Center*, 900 W. Market St., 17961. Tel: 570-366-2924; Fax: 570-366-2301. Mrs. Linda Herb, Dir. Day care for the elderly. Total Staff 8; Clients 30.

Holy Family Assisted Living Residence 900 W. Market St., 17961. Tel: 570-366-2912; Fax: 570-366-7781. Web: www.hfmanor.com. Judee Bavaria, Pres.; Patricia Miske, Admin.; Mr. James Polaski, Dir. Residential Svcs.; Karen Abruzzese, Asst. Dir. Residential Svcs. Personal care/assisted living facility for 59 elderly of Holy Family Manor. Total in Residence 59; Total Staff 21; Total Assisted 76.

POTTSVILLE. *Queen of Peace Apartments*, 777 Water St., 17901 Tel: 570-628-4504; Fax: 570-628-4712. Email: qpeace@voicenet.com. Rev. Bernard A. Flanagan, Pres.; Mrs. Diane Hess, Mgr Catholic housing for the elderly. Apartments 48; Total in Residence 48; Total Staff 4.

READING. *Queen of Angels Apartment*, 22 Rothermel St., Hyde Park, 19605. Tel: 610-921-3115; Fax: 610-921-8576. Email: qangels@voicenet.com. Very Rev. Dennis T. Hartgen, V.F., Pres.; Hazel C. Black, Mgr. Catholic housing for the elderly. Apartments 45; Total in Residence 48; Total Staff 4.

Sacred Heart Villa - Assisted Living Community, 51 Seminary Ave., 19605. Tel: 610-929-5751; Fax: 610-929-0762. Sr. Mary Anne Bigos, M.S.C., Exec. Dir.

SAINT CLAIR. *Neumann Apartments*, 25 N. Nichols St., St. Clair, 17970. Tel: 570-429-0699; Fax: 570-429-2368. Rev. Ronald V. Jankaitis, Pres.; Mr. John T Stiles, Mgr. Catholic housing for the elderly. Apartments 24; Total in Residence 24; Total Staff 2; Total in Residence 24; Total Staff 2.

[J] HOMES FOR PRIESTS

BETHLEHEM. *Holy Family Villa*, 1325 Prospect Ave., 18018. Tel: 610-694-0395; Fax: 610-694-9990. Rev. Richard V. Campo, Rector In Res. Most Rev. Thomas J. Welsh, D.D., J.C.D., Retired Bishop (Retired); Rev. Msgr. John Rusek; Revs. Paul L. Bader (Retired); Joseph A. Barnes (Retired); James J. Brady (Retired); Michael J. Briggman (Retired); Albert T. Cervella (Retired); Stephen Flynn; Francis T. Gillespie (Retired); William P. Jones (Retired); Thomas J. Kerestus (Retired); Michael S. Lawrence (Retired); Joseph M. McGarr (Retired); F. Charles McKenna (Retired); Francis J. McNelis (Retired); William J. O'Donnell (Retired); John Ondic; Ronald Oranczak; Francis C. Revak; Joseph A. Rock, Chap. (Retired); Francis J. Schuster, K.H.S.

[K] MONASTERIES AND RESIDENCES OF PRIESTS AND BROTHERS

BETHLEHEM. *The Barnabite Fathers Barnabite Spiritual Center*, 4301 Hecktown Rd., 18020. Tel: 610-691-8648; Fax: 610-691-8649. Email: gp00@desales.edu. Web: www.catholic-church.org/barnabites. Revs. Anthony M. Bianco, C.R.S.P., M.A., Vicar, House Sec.; Richard M. Delzingaro, C.R.S.P., M.A., Supr., Mod. of Spiritual Center, Coord. of Activities, Prefect of Sacristy, Prov. Counselor & NACC Chap.; Gabriel M. Patil, C.R.S.P., M.A., S.T.L., S.S.L., Theology College Professor, House Treas., & Scheduler of Masses.

CENTER VALLEY. *Oblates of St. Francis de Sales*, Wills Hall, 2755 Station Ave., 18034-9568. Tel: 610-282-3300; Fax: 610-282-2254. Email: peter.leonard@desales.edu. Web: www.desales.edu. Total in Residence 18. In Res. Revs. Joseph P. Becker, O.S.F.S.; Douglas C. Burns, O.S.F.S., M.Div.; Thomas F. Dailey, O.S.F.S.; Joseph A. DiMauro, O.S.F.S., M.A.; Bernard F. Donahue, O.S.F.S., Ph.D.; James P. Finnegan, O.S.F.S.; Daniel G. Gambet, O.S.F.S., Ph.D.; John A. Hanley, O.S.F.S., M.Div.; John F. Harvey, O.S.F.S. (NY); Very Rev. Peter J. Leonard, O.S.F.S., Ph.D., Supr.; Revs. A. Robert McGilvray, O.S.F.S., Ph.D.; Robert G. Mulligan, O.S.F.S., M.A.; Very Rev. Bernard F. O'Connor, O.S.F.S., Ph.D., Pres.; Revs. Alexander T. Pocetto, O.S.F.S., Ph.D.; Gerard H. Schubert, O.S.F.S., Ph.D.; Bro. Daniel P. Wishniewski, M.A.

EASTON. *St. Francis Friary*, 3908 Chipman Rd., 18045. Tel: 610-515-0867; Fax: 610-515-0902. Email: bire@v35.com. Web: www.catholic-church.org/stfran-retreat. Revs. William Reisteter, O.F.M.; Charles Smiech, O.F.M., Guardian; Carl Hawver, O.F.M.; Mike Pfalzer, O.F.M.; Marian Douglas, O.F.M.; Bros. Marcel Groth, O.F.M.; Edward Skutka, O.F.M.; Edward Demyanovich, O.F.M. Franciscan Province of St. John the Baptist Brothers 13; Total in Residence 9.

NEW RINGGOLD. *Cistercian Monastery, St. Mary's Priory*, 70 Schuylkill Rd., 17960-9703. Tel: 570-943-2645; Fax: 570-943-3035. Very Rev. Luke Anderson, S.O.Cist., Th.M., Ph.D., Prior; Revs. Hugh Montague, S.O.Cist., M.A., Th.M.; Alphonsus Lachapelle, S.O.Cist., M.A., Th.M. Fathers 3.

READING. *Missionaries of the Sacred Heart*, 55 Rothermel St., 19605-2680. Tel: 610-929-2025; Fax: 610-929-4397. Email: genomsc@aol.com. Very Rev. John J. Paul, M.S.C., V.J., S.T.L., J.C.D., Supr.; Revs. Eugene Jung, M.S.C.; Robert Tobolski, M.S.C.; Philip DeRea, M.S.C.; Bro. Lawrence Viele, M.S.C.

1400 Michigan Ave., N.E., Washington, DC 20017. Tel: 202-635-3444, Ext. 202; Fax: 202-526-0830.

[L] CONVENTS AND RESIDENCES OF SISTERS

BETHLEHEM. *Casa Belen*, 305 E. Fourth St., 18015. Tel: 610-867-4030. Sr. Irma N. Candelaria, P.S.S.J., Supr. Residence of the Poor Sisters of St. Joseph who minister to the Spanish speaking people of the area. Sisters 3.

SS. Cyril & Methodius Convent, 520 Buchanan St., 18015-3449. Tel: 610-866-0275. Email: garganta@enter.net. Sisters 5.

St. Joseph Convent, 2133 Madison Ave., 18017-4642. Tel: 610-865-4691; Fax: 610-866-9892. Email: ssj2133@aol.com. Sisters of St. Joseph 13; Immaculate Heart Sisters (Scranton) 1.

Monocacy Manor, 395 Bridle Path Rd., 18017. Tel: 610-866-2597; Fax: 610-861-7478. Email: stfrancis395@rcn.com. Web: www.catholic-church.org/stfrancis-cfn. Sr. M. Rosaria Shina, O.S.F., Prov. Supr. Provincialate and Novitiate of the School Sisters of the Third Order Regular of St. Francis (Bethlehem Prov.). Professed Sisters 26; Retreat Center Total Staff 3.

COOPERSBURG. *Carmelite Monastery* St. Therese of the Child Jesus and St. Mary Magdalen de Pazzi, St. Therese's Valley. , 3551 Lanark Rd., 18036-9324. Tel: 610-797-3721. Sr. Marie Charlette, O.Carm., Prioress; Very Rev. Thomas P. Koons, V.R., J.C.L., M.A., M.Div., Chap. Carmelite Nuns of the Ancient Observance (Calced) O.Carm. Professed Nuns 9.

EMMAUS. *Transfiguration Monastery* (1998), 526 Fairview St., 18049-3837. Tel: 610-965-6818. Email: monasteryosb@enter.net. Web: www.emmausosb.org. Sr. Martina Revak, O.S.B.,

Supr. Corporate Title: Benedictine Sisters, Ministries in the fields of education, pastoral ministry, hospitality and spirituality. Charter Members 3; Affiliate 1.

MAHANOY CITY. *St. Joseph Convent*, 536 W. South St., 17948-2422. Tel: 570-773-1420. Missionaries of Charity Sisters 4.

NESQUEHONING. *Our Lady of Perpetual Help House of Prayer*, 140 W. Mill St., 18240-1225. Tel: 570-669-9858. Email: hopnesq@pt2.net. Sr. Claire Holzenthaler, I.H.M., Supr. Sister Servants of the Immaculate Heart of Mary Sisters 4.

PEN ARGYL. *Dominican Daughters of the Immaculate Mother*, 115 Lobb Ave., 18072. Tel: 610-863-9214; Fax: 610-863-9214. Email: ddimpa@yahoo.com. Sr. Marie Luz, O.P., Supr. Sisters 6.

POTTSVILLE. *Sisters House*, 700 E. Norwegian St., 17901. Tel: 570-621-4000; Fax: 570-622-7950. Email: ccorreia@gsrmc.com. Sr. Clarisse Correia, D.C., Supr. Res. of the Daughters of Charity of St. Vincent de Paul, Northeast Province, who staff Good Samaritan Regional Medical Center, and Nativity High Schools. Sisters 8.

READING. *Bethany Convent*, 1214 N. 14th St., 19604. Tel: 610-372-1753. Sr. Sheila Tague, M.S.C., Coord. Sisters 3.

Chevalier House, 43 Seminary Ave., 19605. Tel: 610-929-8348. Sr. Theresa Lepera, M.S.C., Coord. Sisters 3.

St. Clare Convent, 465 St. Bernardine St., 19607-1736. Tel: 610-777-4590; Fax: 610-777-3973. Email: stclares@talon.net. Web: www.bfranciscan.org. Sr. Paul Nowak, O.S.F., Contact Person. Bernardine Franciscan Sisters Sisters 4.

Daughters of Divine Zeal, F.D.Z., 1526 Hill Rd., 19602-1410. Tel: 610-375-1738; 610-375-9072; Fax: 610-375-2188. Email: srdivinezeal@aol.com. Sisters 4.

House of Nazareth (Casa Nazaret), 532 Spruce St., 19602. Tel: 610-378-1947; Fax: 610-374-3351. Sr. Maria Gonzalez, Supr. Residence of the Poor Sisters of St. Joseph who work in Spanish Apostolate of Berks County. Sisters 3.

Saint Ignatius Convent, 2601 St. Alban Dr., 19602. Tel: 610-678-2769. Sisters 2.

St. Joseph Villa, 464 Bernardine St., 19607. Tel: 610-777-5556; Fax: 610-777-5545. Email: jeananthony44@aol.com. Web: www.bfrancisan.org. Sisters Jean Anthony Rodgers, O.S.F., Admin.; Josandra Ciucci, O.S.F., Sisters Care Coord.; Rev. Robert Reece, O.S.F.S., Chap. Home of the Retired Bernardine Sisters of the Third Order of St. Francis. Sisters 91.

St. Michael Convent, 51 Seminary Ave, 19605-2621. Tel: 610-929-5751; Fax: 610-929-0762. Web: www.hometown.aol.com/mscvocdir/usa.html. Sisters Marie Raymond Gazo, M.S.C., Local Supr.; Marie Clark, M.S.C., Prov. Supvr. Missionary Sisters of the Sacred Heart of Jesus, Attended by Chaplain: Missionary Fathers of the Sacred Heart. Professed Sisters 56.

MSC Province Center, 2811 Moyers Ln., 19605. Tel: 610-929-5944; Fax: 610-929-3634. Email: mscsisters@aol.com. Web: www.hometown.aol.com/mscvocdir/usa.html. Sr. Marie Clark, M.S.C., Prov. Provincial offices of Missionary Sisters of the Sacred Heart of Jesus. Sisters 3.

Our Lady of the Sacred Heart Convent, 2811 Moyers Ln., 19605. Tel: 601-929-5944; Fax: 610-929-3634. Sisters 4.

Bethany Convent, 1214 N. 14th St., 19604. Tel: 610-372-1753. Sisters 3.

Neumann Convent Sisters of St. Francis of Philadelphia (Glen Riddle), 1235 Elm St., 19604. Tel: 610-374-4974. Email: sistersofs@cs.com. Sisters 6.

Our Lady of the Angels Convent - Alvernia College, 400 St. Bernardine St., 19607-1799. Tel: 610-796-8333. Email: pacelsr@alvernia.edu. Web: www.alvernia.edu. Residence for Bernardine Sisters on college faculty. Total in Residence 4.

Our Lady of the Assumption Convent, 1500 Eckert Ave., 19602. Tel: 610-373-8203. Faculty House of Sisters of Christian Charity, teaching in Central Catholic High School. Sisters 4.

Precious Blood Convent, 1094 Welsh Rd.P.O. Box 97, 19607-0097. Tel: 610-777-1624; Fax: 610-777-3359. Email: missioncps@aol.com. Web: members.aol.com/cpspa/index.html. Sisters Eva Janning, C.P.S., Prov. Supr.; Rosa Hoflacher, C.P.S., Local Supr. Residence for Missionary Sisters of the Precious Blood and Novitiate. Sisters 29.

House of Formation Tel: 610-777-1624; Fax: 610-777-3359. Email: cpspa@aol.com. Sisters Eva Janning, C.P.S., Prov. Supr.; Rosa Hoflacher, C.P.S., Local Supr.

Sacred Heart Convent, 460 St. Bernardine St., 19607-1798. Tel: 610-777-6111; Fax: 610-777-6029. Email: shconvent@aol.com. Web: www.bfranciscan.org. Sr. Mary Maxine, O.S.F., Admin. Tel: 610-777-7221; Rev. Msgr. Edward W. Sarzynski, Chap. Residence for Bernardine Sisters of Third Order of St. Francis.; U.S. Province Offices. Professed Sisters 40; Total Staff 10.

Sisters of St. Francis Residence, 502 S. Sixth St., 19602. Tel: 610-375-8001. Email: frances@enter.net. Convent of the Sisters of St. Francis of Philadelphia who are on the staffs at Central Catholic High School and SS. Cyril and Methodius Parish. Sisters 2.

WHITEHALL. *Sisters for Christian Community/Poor Servants*, Two Maryland Cir.-120, 18052. Tel: 610-437-4463; Fax: 610-437-8843. Email: learnclub@aol.com. Web: www.learningclub.org. Sisters 2.

[M] RETREAT HOUSES

BETHLEHEM. *St. Francis Center for Renewal (Monocacy Manor)*, 395 Bridle Path Rd., 18017. Tel: 610-867-8890; Fax: 610-861-7478. Email: peaceosf@rcn.com. Web: www.catholic-church.org/stfrancis-cfn. Sr. M. Anita Kuchera, O.S.F., Dir. School Sisters of St. Francis, Weekend retreats (68) and days of recollection (70); retreats for men and women, marriage encounter; engaged encounters; parish retreats; workshops; youth groups; weekends; privately directed retreats; private retreats, spiritual direction. Total Staff 3.

EASTON. *St. Francis Friary and Retreat House*, 3918 Chipman Rd., 18045-3014. Tel: 610-258-3053; Fax: 610-258-2412. Email: stfranrh@localnet.com. Rev. Charles William Smiech, O.F.M., Dir. of Retreat; Mr. James W. McElrone, Exec. Dir.; Ritanne Pursel, Retreat Prog. Dir. Retreatants 80; Houses of Religious Men: Total in Residence 6; Total Staff 8; Retreat Centers: Total in Residence 6; Total Staff 10.

NORTHAMPTON. *Mary Immaculate Center*, 300 Cherryville Rd., 18067-9548. Tel: 610-262-7866; Fax: 610-262-6766. Email: maryimmaculatecenter@adphila.org. Web: www.maryimmaculatecenter.org. Mr. William Kefer, M.S.W., Admin.; Revs. William J. O'Donnell (Retired); James Olson.

ORWIGSBURG. *St. Francis Center*, 900 W. Market St., 17961-1006. Tel: 570-366-1016; Fax: 570-366-1017. Diocesan Agencies with Facilities in the St. Francis Center:

Office for Youth & Young Adult Ministry Tel: 570-366-1405; Fax: 570-366-1426. Overnight retreats, day retreats, weekend retreats and workshops.

Adult & Youth Retreats Tel: 570-366-1405; Fax: 570-366-1426. Email: oyyak@ptbprolog.net. Mrs. Mary Ellen Johns, B.A., Dir. Total Staff 6.

Holy Family Adult Day Care Tel: 570-366-2924; Fax: 570-366-2301. Mrs. Linda Herb, Dir. Total Assisted Average 25; Total Staff 5.

Holy Family Assisted Living Tel: 570-366-2912. Patricia Miske, Admin.

READING. *Mariawald Renewal Center*, 1094 Welsh Rd., P.O. Box 97, 19607-0097. Tel: 610-777-0135; Fax: 610-777-3359. Email: mariawald@aol.com. Web: www.hometown.aol.com/mariawald. Sisters Rosa Hoflacher, C.P.S., Supr.; Magdelena Vogt, C.P.S., Admin. For women, men and mixed groups. Total Staff 5; Total in Residence 2.

[N] CENTERS FOR SPIRITUAL GROWTH

WERNERSVILLE. *Jesuit Center for Spiritual Growth* 19565. Tel: 610-678-8085; Fax: 610-678-8747. Email: jescntsec@talon.net. Web: www.jesuitspiritualcenter.org. Revs. Lucien F. Longtin, S.J. (WDC); John P. Barron, S.J.; William J. Sneck, S.J.; George S. Williams, S.J.; Susan Bowers; Sr. Bernadette Duross, R.S.M.; Kathryn M. Fitzgerald, D.Min.; Sisters Maria McCoy, S.S.J.; Marie Ann Ellmer, R.S.M.; Susan Dentz, O.S.F. Directed retreats, programs in prayer, discernment, psychology and spirituality.

[O] NEWMAN CENTERS

ALLENTOWN. *The Newman Center* 2339 Liberty St., 18104. Tel: 484-664-3122; Fax: 484-664-3123. Rev. John A. Krivak, M.Div., Th.M., M.Ed., Ed.D., Diocesan Dir., Campus Ministry.

Albright College (Reading), Christopher House, 15207 Kutztown Rd., Kutztown, 19530-9218. Tel: 610-683-8330; Fax: 610-683-8467. Email: frcebjr@ptdprolog.net christopherhouse@@kutztown.edu. Rev. Clifton E. Bishop, Campus Ministry.

DeSales University (Center Valley), 2755 Station Ave., Center Valley, 18034-9568. Tel: 610-282-1100, Ext. 1898; Fax: 610-282-3798. Rev. John A. Hanley, O.S.F.S., M.Div.

Alvernia College, Office of Campus Ministry, 400 St. Bernardine St., Reading, 19607. Tel: 610-796-8300; Fax: 610-796-8378.

Cedar Crest College (Allentown), Catholic Chaplaincy Center, 2400 Chew St., 18104-5586. Tel: 610-821-3122; Fax: 610-821-3123. Rev. John A. Krivak, M.Div., Th.M., M.Ed., Ed.D.

Kutztown University (Kutztown), Christopher House, 15207 Kutztown Rd., Kutztown, 19530-9218. Tel: 610-683-8380; Fax: 610-683-8467. Email: christopherhouse@kutztown.edu. Rev. Clifton E. Bishop.

Lafayette College (Easton), 119 McCartney St., Easton, 18042-7647. Tel: 610-253-5044; Fax: 610-253-1391. Email: normanc@lafayette.edu. Rev. Charles Norman, O.S.F.S.

Lehigh University (Bethlehem), Newman Center at Lehigh University, Bldg. 41661 Taylor St., Bethlehem, 18015-3127. Tel: 610-758-4148; Fax: 610-758-6392. Email: wek4@lehigh.edu. Rev. Wayne E. Killian.

Moravian College (Bethlehem), Koinonia House, 1309 Main St., Bethlehem, 18018-6650. Tel: 610-625-7922; Fax: 610-625-7885. Email: normac@moravian.edu. Rev. Wayne E. Killian.

Muhlenberg College (Allentown), Newman Center, 2339 Liberty St., 18104-5586. Tel: 484-664-3122; Fax: 464-664-3123. Rev. John A. Krivak, M.Div., Th.M., M.Ed., Ed.D.

Penn State University (Schuylkill Haven Center, Schuylkill Haven), St. Ambrose Rectory, 201 Randel St., Schuylkill Haven, 17972. Tel: 570-385-1031; Fax: 570-385-1035. Rev. Cletus S. Onyegbule.

[P] MISCELLANEOUS

ALLENTOWN. *Eastern Pennsylvania Scholarship Foundation*, P.O. Box F, 18105-1538. Tel: 610-871-5200, Ext. 240; Fax: 610-871-5211. Web: www.allentowndiocese.org/epst.html. Mr. Fred A. Williams, CFO & Sec. Temporal Affairs.

BATH. *Blue Army of Our Lady of Fatima*, 2483 Community Dr., 18014. Tel: 610-614-1218. Email: thesixfamily@enter.net. Rev. Dominic Thao Pham, M.Div., Spiritual Dir.

BETHLEHEM. *Third Order Dominican Expectation of the Blessed Mother Chapter*, 4290 Vassar Ave., 18017. Tel: 610-691-6761. Dr. Felicidad Quilo, Moderator.

CENTER VALLEY. *DeSales Service Works*, 2755 Station Ave., 18034. Tel: 610-282-1100, Ext. 2018. Email: lukefour18@hotmail.com. Web: www.oblates.org. Rev. Richard Wojnecki, O.S.F.S. (VEN), Dir. Volunteer Svc. Prog. Membership are men and women at least 21 years of age, serving the urban poor in a selected placement for one year while living in a house community.

EASTON. *Secular Franciscan Fraternity, Secular Franciscan Order*, c/o St. Francis Retreat House, 3918 Chipman Rd., 18045-3014. Tel: 610-258-3053; Fax: 610-258-2412. Web: www.catholic-church.org/stfran-retreat.

NORTHAMPTON. *Apostles of Jesus*, 829 Main St., 18067-1838. Tel: 610-502-1732; Fax: 610-502-1733. Email: apostlesofjesus@verizon.net. Rev. Paul O. Gaggawala, A.J., Supr.

ORWIGSBURG. *Seton Manor, Inc.*, 1000 Seton Dr., 17961. Tel: 570-366-0400; Fax: 570-366-1970. Email: machaklos@hpmanor.com. Raymond Dee, Chm.; Mary Ann Chaklos, Admin. Total Staff 172; Bed Capacity 120.

Board of Directors: Rev. Michael J. Stone; Judith M. Bavaria, N.H.A., R.H.P.F.; Mr. Peter U. Bergmann, FACHE, C.E.O.; Raymond Dee, Chairperson; Diane Kimmel, Recording Sec.; Daniel Kochie, C.P.A., Treas.; Mrs. Barbara W. Murphy, M.S.W.; Mr. Fred A. Williams, Sec.

READING. *Mary's Home*, 736 Upland Ave., 19607. Tel: 610-603-8010; Fax: 610-603-8012. Christine Folk, Admin. Transitional home for mothers and babies after leaving Mary's Shelter

Mary's Shelter, 325 S. 12th St., 19602. Tel: 610-376-1973; Fax: 610-376-5391. Email: mshelter@juno.com. Christine Folk, Admin.; Sr. M. Eileen Kantz, M.S.C., Prog. Dir. A residence for mothers and babies. Please see Mary's Home for transitional housing.

SHENANDOAH. *Apostles of Jesus*, 129 S. Jardin St., P.O. Box 215, 17976-0215. Tel: 570-462-2104; Fax: 570-462-2321. Email: worldaj@email.com. Rev. Paul O. Gaggawala, A.J., Supr.

RELIGIOUS INSTITUTES OF MEN REPRESENTED IN THE DIOCESE

For further details refer to the corresponding bracketed number in the Religious Institutes of Men or Women section.

[]—*Apostles of Jesus*—A.J.

[]—*Cistercian Monks of the Strict Observance*—O.Cist.

[0160]—*Clerics Regular of St. Paul* (Bernabite Fathers)—C.R.S.P.

[1330]—*Congregation of the Mission (Vincentian Fathers)* (Eastern Prov.)—C.M.

[]—*Discalced Carmelite Fathers*—O.C.D.

[0520]—*Franciscan Fathers* (Holy Family; St. John

the Baptist Province) Custody—O.F.M.
[0690]—*Jesuit Fathers* (Maryland Prov.)—S.J.
[]—*Missionaries of the Queen of the Angels*—M.I.S.R.A.
[1110]—*Missionaries of the Sacred Heart* (American Prov.)—M.S.C.
[0920]—*Oblates of St. Francis de Sales*—O.S.F.S.

RELIGIOUS INSTITUTES OF WOMEN REPRESENTED IN THE DIOCESE

[0120]—*Angelic Sisters of St. Paul*—A.S.S.P.
[1810]—*Bernardine Sisters of the Third Order of St. Francis*—O.S.F.
[0320]—*Carmelite Nuns of the Ancient Observance*—O.Carm.
[]—*Congregation of Sisters of Holy Family Nazareth*—C.S.F.N.
[0760]—*Daughters of Charity of St. Vincent de Paul*—D.C.
[0795]—*Daughters of Divine Zeal*—F.D.Z.
[1065]—*Dominican Daughters of the Immaculate Mother*—C.P.
[2710]—*Missionaries of Charity*—M.C.
[]—*Missionary Sisters of the Most Sacred Heart of Jesus*—M.S.C.
[2850]—*Missionary Sisters of the Precious Blood*—C.P.S.
[3250]—*Poor Sisters of St. Joseph*—P.S.S.J.
[1700]—*School Sisters of the Third Order of St. Francis* (Bethlehem Prov.)—O.S.F.
[0660]—*Sisters of Christian Charity*—S.C.C.
[]—*Sisters of Mercy* (Merion)—R.S.M.
[3780]—*Sisters of Saints Cyril and Methodius*—SS.C.M.
[3700]—*Sisters of St. Benedict*—O.S.B.
[]—*Sisters of St. Francis of Philadelphia* (Glen Riddle)—O.S.F.
[3740]—*Sisters of St. Francis of Philadelphia*—O.S.F.
[3830]—*Sisters of St. Joseph*—S.S.J.
[2170]—*Sisters, Servants of the Immaculate Heart of Mary*—I.H.M.

DIOCESAN CEMETERIES

ALLENTOWN. *Resurrection*, 547 N. Krocks Rd., 18106-9732. Tel: 610-395-3819; Fax: 610-366-3713.
BETHLEHEM. *Holy Saviour*, 2575 Linden St., 18017-3842. Tel: 610-866-2372; Fax: 610-866-9277.

NECROLOGY

† Messaros, Rev. Msgr. Michael F., (Retired)—Died Feb. 26, 2003
† Iacono, Leonardo, (Retired)—Died March 18, 2003
† Marciano, Charles A., (Retired)—Died June 11, 2003
† McNulty, Charles L., Pottsville, PA St. Mary Queen of Peace—Died March 6, 2003
† Vandergeest, Peter J., (Retired)—Died July 16, 2003
† Welkie, Paul P.—Died March 27, 2003

Diocese of Altoona-Johnstown

(Dioecesis Altunensis-Johnstoniensis)

Most Reverend

JOSEPH V. ADAMEC, D.D., S.T.L.

Bishop of Altoona-Johnstown; ordained July 3, 1960; appointed Bishop of Altoona-Johnstown March 17, 1987; ordained and installed May 20, 1987. *Mailing Address: Chancery Office*, 126 Logan Blvd., Hollidaysburg, PA 16648.

The Chancery: 126 Logan Blvd., Hollidaysburg, PA 16648. Tel: 814-695-5579; Fax: 814-695-8894.

Web: www.diocesealtjtn.org

Email: dajreply@diocese.org

Most Reverend

JAMES J. HOGAN, D.D.

Retired Bishop of Altoona-Johnstown; ordained December 8, 1937; appointed Titular Bishop of Philomelium and Auxiliary of Trenton November 27, 1959; consecrated February 25, 1960; appointed to the See of Altoona-Johnstown May 23, 1966; installed July 6, 1966; retired October 17, 1986. *Office: 126 Logan Blvd., Hollidaysburg, PA 16648.*

ESTABLISHED DIOCESE OF ALTOONA, MAY 27, 1901.

Square Miles 6,674.

Redesignated Diocese of Altoona-Johnstown, October 9, 1957.

Comprises the Counties of Bedford, Blair, Cambria, Centre, Clinton, Fulton, Huntingdon and Somerset in the State of Pennsylvania.

Legal Title: For legal titles of parishes and diocesan institutions, consult the Chancery Office.

STATISTICAL OVERVIEW

Personnel	
Bishop	1
Retired Bishops	1
Priests: Diocesan Active in Diocese	94
Priests: Diocesan Active Outside Diocese	9
Priests: Retired, Sick or Absent	44
Number of Diocesan Priests	147
Religious Priests in Diocese	53
Total Priests in Diocese	200
Ordinations:	
Diocesan Priests	1
Permanent Deacons	2
Permanent Deacons in Diocese	32
Total Brothers	10
Total Sisters	90
Parishes	
Parishes	99
With Resident Pastor:	
Resident Diocesan Priests	75
Resident Religious Priests	13
Without Resident Pastor:	
Administered by Priests	9
Administered by Deacons	2
Missions	5
Welfare	
Catholic Hospitals	1
Total Assisted	138,245
Health Care Centers	1
Total Assisted	225
Homes for the Aged	3
Total Assisted	317
Special Centers for Social Services	2
Total Assisted	32,192
Educational	
Diocesan Students in Other Seminaries	13
Total Seminarians	13
Colleges and Universities	2
Total Students	4,012
High Schools, Diocesan and Parish	3
Total Students	1,214
Elementary Schools, Diocesan and Parish	24
Total Students	3,965
Catechesis/Religious Education:	
High School Students	3,714
Elementary Students	8,100
Total Students under Catholic Instruction	21,018
Teachers in the Diocese:	
Priests	8
Sisters	25
Lay Teachers	467
Vital Statistics	
Receptions into the Church:	
Infant Baptism Totals	1,444
Adult Baptism Totals	111
Received into Full Communion	138
First Communions	1,454
Confirmations	1,714
Marriages:	
Catholic	370
Interfaith	226
Total Marriages	596
Deaths	1,680
Total Catholic Population	108,202
Total Population	645,268

Former Bishops—Rt. Rev. EUGENE A. GARVEY, D.D., ord. Sept. 22, 1869; consecrated Sept. 8, 1901; died Oct. 22, 1920; Most Revs. JOHN JOSEPH MCCORT, D.D., ord. Oct. 14, 1883; consecrated Titular Bishop of Azotus and Auxiliary to the Archbishop of Philadelphia, Sept. 17, 1912; appt. Coadjutor cum jure successionis to the Bishop of Altoona, Jan. 27, 1920; appt. Bishop of Altoona, Oct. 22, 1920; appt. Assistant at the Pontifical Throne, Oct. 5, 1933; died April 21, 1936; RICHARD T. GUILFOYLE, D.D., ord. June 2, 1917; appt. Aug. 8, 1936; consecrated Nov. 30, 1936; died June 10, 1957; HOWARD J. CARROLL, D.D., ord. April 2, 1927; appt. Dec. 5, 1957; consecrated Jan. 2, 1958; died March 21, 1960; J. CARROLL MCCORMICK, D.D. (Retired), ord. July 10, 1932; consecrated April 20, 1947; appt. June 25, 1960; transferred to See of Scranton March 4, 1966; retired Feb. 15, 1983; died Nov. 2, 1996; JAMES J. HOGAN, D.D. (Retired), ord. Dec. 8, 1937; appt. Titular Bishop of Philomelium and Auxiliary of Trenton, Nov. 27, 1959; consecrated Feb. 25, 1960; appt. to the See of Altoona-Johnstown May 23, 1966; retired Oct. 17, 1986.

Diocesan Officials

Bishop—Most Rev. JOSEPH V. ADAMEC, D.D., S.T.L., 126 Logan Blvd., Hollidaysburg, 16648. Tel: 814-695-5579; Fax: 814-695-8894.

Secretary to the Bishop—Rev. LUBOMIR J. STRECOK, 126 Logan Blvd., Hollidaysburg, 16648. Tel: 814-695-5579; Fax: 814-695-8894. Email: lubomir@dioceseaj.org.

Retired Bishop—Most Rev. JAMES J. HOGAN, D.D., J.C.D., 126 Logan Blvd., Hollidaysburg, 16648. Tel: 814-695-5571.

Chancellor—Rev. Msgr. DENNIS R. BOGGS, 126 Logan Blvd., Hollidaysburg, 16648. Tel: 814-695-5579; Fax: 814-695-8894.

Vicars General—Rev. Msgrs. STANLEY B. CARSON, V.G., Admin. (Secretariats), 126 Logan Blvd., Hollidaysburg, 16648. Tel: 814-695-5579; 814-943-8553 (Res.); Fax: 814-695-8894; GEORGE B. FLINN, V.G., Pastoral Life and Ministry, 126 Logan Blvd., Hollidaysburg, 16648. Tel: 814-695-5579; 814-536-0117 (Res.); Fax: 814-695-8894.

Judicial Vicar—Rev. Msgr. MICHAEL E. SERVINSKY, 126 Logan Blvd., Hollidaysburg, 16648. Tel: 814-693-9485; 814-943-8464 (Res.); Fax: 814-695-8894.

Bishop's Vicar for Religious—Most Rev. BONAVENTURE MIDILI, T.O.R., St. Anthony of Padua Rectory, 2201 Graham Ave., Windber, 15901. Tel: 814-467-7292.

Secretary for Communications—Sr. MARY PARKS, C.S.J., 126 Logan Blvd., Hollidaysburg, 16648. Tel: 814-695-5579; Fax: 814-695-8894. Email: srmary@dioceseaj.org.

Vicars Forane

Allegheny Deanery—Rev. Msgr. JOHN R. SASWAY, Our Lady of the Allegheniès, 608 Main St., Lilly, 15938. Tel: 814-886-2504.

Altoona Deanery—Very Rev. CARL A. SPISHAK, St. Rose of Lima Rectory, 5514 Roselawn Ave., Altoona, 16602. Tel: 814-944-8509.

Cambria Deanery—Very Rev. LEONARD E. VOYTEK, V.F., St. Elizabeth Ann Rectory, 605 Graham Ave., Windber, 15963. Tel: 814-467-7191.

Johnstown Deanery—Very Rev. PAUL E. TURNBULL, V.F., Our Mother of Sorrows Rectory, 407 Tioga St., Johnstown, 15905. Tel: 814-535-7646.

Juniata Deanery—Very Rev. CLEMENT G. GARDNER, V.F., St. Michael Parish, 301 Spruce St., Hollidaysburg, 16648. Tel: 814-695-0912.

Northern Deanery—VACANT.

Prince Gallitzin Deanery—Very Rev. Msgr. TIMOTHY J. SWOPE, V.F., St. Michael the Archangel Parish, 321 St. Mary's St., P.O. Box 144, Loretto, 15940. Tel: 814-472-8551 Minor Basilica.

Southern Deanery—Rev. Msgr. SAMUEL J. TOMASELLI, St. Peter Parish, 433 W. Church St., Somerset, 15501. Tel: 814-443-6574.

Diocesan Offices

Adult Formation & Lay Ministry—CONNIE RAE STOWE, M.Div., S.T.L., Ph.D., Dir. Tel: 814-693-9605; Fax: 814-695-8894. Email: crstowe@dioceseaj.org.

Building Commission—Mr. JERRY MCMULLEN. Tel: 814-472-0603.

Campus Ministry— (For further details regarding Campus Ministries please refer to Institutions Located in the Diocese).

Catholic Social Service—Rev. Msgr. ROBERT J. SALY, Dir.. Email: cssaltpa@dioceseaj.org.

Altoona Offices—1300 12th Ave., P.O. Box 1349, Altoona, 16603. Tel: 814-944-9388; Fax: 814-941-2677.

Johnstown Offices—741 Railroad St., Johnstown, 15901. Tel: 814-535-6538; Fax: 814-535-2235. Email: cssjtown@dioceseaj.org.

State College Offices—276 W. Hamilton Ave., P.O. Box 680, State College, 16801. Tel: 814-238-4937; Fax: 814-238-4207. Email: cyoung@dioceseaj.org.

"The Catholic Register"—Rev. TIMOTHY P. STEIN, Editor, P.O. Box 413, Hollidaysburg, 16648. Tel: 814-695-7563; Fax: 814-695-7517. Email: frtimdio@aol.com.

Communications—Sr. MARY PARKS, C.S.J., 126 Logan Blvd., Hollidaysburg, 16648. Tel: 814-695-5579; Fax: 814-695-8894. Email: srmary@dioceseaj.org.

Cemetery Commission—Rev. DAVID H. ROESCH, St. Joseph Rectory, 623 E. Third St., Bellwood, 16617. Tel: 814-742-7075. Email: sanjoe@nb.net.

Chancery—Rev. Msgr. DENNIS R. BOGGS, Chancellor, 126 Logan Blvd., Hollidaysburg, 16648. Tel: 814-695-5579; Fax: 814-695-8894. Email: drboggs@stbenedictchurch.org.

Christian Initiation—Mrs. JEANNE THOMPSON, 126A Logan Blvd., Hollidaysburg, 16648. Tel: 814-695-5579; Fax: 814-695-8894. Email: jtchrin@dioceseaj.org.

Computer Systems—RONALD MULDOON, Dir. Email: rmuldoon@dioceseaj.org; Mr. DON LAYO, Asst. Dir.. Email: dlayo@dioceseaj.org; 126 Logan Blvd., Hollidaysburg, 16648. Tel: 814-695-5579; Fax: 814-695-8894.

Development & Stewardship Office—Mr. JOSEPH M. SCIALABBA, Dir.. Email: scialaj@dioceseaj.org; Mr. CHRIS RINGKAMP, Asst. Dir.. Email: ringkamp@dioceseaj.org; Mrs. LORI HARTNETT, H.S. Devel. Dir.. Email: lhartnet@dioceseaj.org; 124 Logan Blvd., Hollidaysburg, 16648. Tel: 814-695-5577; Fax: 814-696-9516.

Diaconal Formation—Deacon GENE NERAL, 124 Logan Blvd., Hollidaysburg, 16648. Tel: 814-693-9870; Fax: 814-695-8894.

Diocesan Shrines—Rev. JOHN BYRNES, J.C.L., Prince Gallitzin Chapel House, P.O. Box 99, Loretto, 15940. Tel: 814-472-5441; Fax: 814-472-5446. Email: jbyrnes@dioceseaj.org.

Education—CHARLES J. KOREN, Ed.D., Dir., 126A Logan Blvd., Hollidaysburg, 16648. Tel: 814-695-5579; Fax: 814-695-8894. Email: ckoren@dioceseaj.org. Assistant Directors: CHARLEEN BLUM, Religious Ed.. Email: charleen@dioceseaj.org; Sr. MARK PLESCHER C.S.A., Elementary. Email: srmark@dioceseaj.org; Mr. THOMAS J MCCONNELL, Campus/Youth Ministry. Email: tmcconn@dioceseaj.org.

Ecumenical Minister—Rev. HAROLD N. BILLER, 609 Park Ave., Johnstown, 15902. Tel: 814-539-2186.

Family Life Office—Mrs. SUSAN STITH, Dir.; Sr. ROSELLA LACOVITCH, C.S.J., Asst. Dir., 5379 Portage St., Lilly, 15938. Tel: 814-886-8551; Fax: 814-886-7697. Email: familylife@dioceseaj.org. Divorced/Separated & Bereaved Ministries; Parent & Marriage Preparation Ministries. Programs: Persons with Disabilities Ministry; Natural Family Planning; Respect Life.

Finance Office—LARRY R. SUTTON, Dir., 126 Logan Blvd., Hollidaysburg, 16648. Tel: 814-695-5579; Fax: 814-695-8894. Email: sutton@dioceseaj.org; MATTHEW REILLY, Comptroller. Email: mreilly@dioceseaj.org; JEANNE BRYAN, Accounting Asst.. Email: jbryan@dioceseaj.org.

Holy Childhood Association—Rev. ROBERT J. KELLY, Dir.; Sr. PATTI ROSSI, C.S.J., Assoc. Dir., 124 Logan Blvd., Hollidaysburg, 16648. Tel 814-695-5579; Fax: 814-695-8894.

Liturgical Commission—Rev. D. TIMOTHY GRIMME, Dir., St. Therese of the Child Jesus, 2301 Fifth St., Altoona, 16601. Tel: 814-942-4479. Email: stcath@vicon.net.

Liturgy & Worship—Rev. ROBERT C. MAZUR, 124 Logan Blvd., Hollidaysburg, 16648. Tel 814-695-5579; Fax: 814-695-8894.

Fulton County Catholic Mission—110 S. Third St., McConnellsburg, 17233. Tel: 717-485-5917; Fax: 717-485-3856. Email: fccm@cvn.net.

Ongoing Formation Clergy—Very Rev. Msgr. TIMOTHY J. SWOPE, V.F., Prince Gallitzin Chapel House, P.O. Box 99, Loretto, 15940-0099. Tel: 814-472-5441; Fax: 814-472-5446.

Permanent Deacon—Deacon GENE NERAL, 124 Logan Blvd., Hollidaysburg, 16648. Tel: 814-695-5579; Fax: 814-695-8894.

Presbyteral Council—Rev. JOHN J. PALKO, Chm., P.O. Box 317, 312 Clark St., Hollidaysburg, 16648-0317. Tel: 814-695-0622; Fax: 814-696-9609. Email: stmaryhol@aol.com.

Priests' Personnel Board—Rev. Msgr. GEORGE B. FLINN, V.G., 126 Logan Blvd., Hollidaysburg, 16648. Tel: 814-695-5579; Fax: 814-695-8894.

Priests' Residence - Dmitri Manor—Rev. Msgr. ROBERT J. SALY, 126 Logan Blvd., Hollidaysburg, 16648. Tel: 814-695-5579.

Retreat & Conference Center—St. John the Baptist Retreat Center, P.O. Box 10, New Baltimore, 15553. Tel: 814-733-2210; Fax: 814-733-2966.

Scouting—Rev. JOSEPH ORR, 406 W. 11th St., Tyrone, 16686. Tel: 814-684-1480. Email: saintmat@nb.net.

Self Insurance Program—JOSEPH WATT, Gallagher Bassett Insurance, 540 Pellis Rd., Ste. 3000, Greensburg, 15601. Tel: 800-831-3247; Fax: 412-836-8684.

Society for the Propagation of the Faith—Rev. ROBERT J. KELLY, Dir.. Email: bkelly@dioceseaj.org; Sr. PATTI ROSSI, C.S.J., Assoc. Dir.. Email: srpatti@dioceseaj.org; 124 Logan Blvd., Hollidaysburg, 16648. Tel: 814-695-5579; Fax: 814-695-8894.

St. Vincent de Paul Society—Deacon JOHN E. SROKA, Exec. Dir., 566 Vine St., Johnstown, 15901. Tel: 814-535-4357; Fax: 814-536-6690. Email: jesroka@aol.com.

Tribunal Office—Rev. Msgr. MICHAEL E. SERVINSKY; Rev. JOHN BYRNES, J.C.L., 126 Logan Blvd., Hollidaysburg, 16648. Tel: 814-693-9485; Fax: 814-695-8894.

Victim Assistance Coordinator—Sr. MARILYN WELCH, C.C.W. Tel: 814-886-8250. Email: srmarilyn@dioceseaj.org.

Vocation Office—Rev. JOHN BYRNES, J.C.L., Prince Gallitzin Chapel House, P.O. Box 99, Loretto, 15940. Tel: 814-472-5441; Fax: 814-472-5446. Email: jbyrnes@dioceseaj.org.

CLERGY, PARISHES, MISSIONS AND PAROCHIAL SCHOOLS

CITY OF ALTOONA
(BLAIR COUNTY)

1—CATHEDRAL OF THE BLESSED SACRAMENT (1851), Rev. Msgr. Robert C. Mazur, Rector; Rev. Brian R. Saylor; Rev. Msgr. Roy F. Kline, Senior Priest; Deacons James F. Leap; John R. Rys.
Church: One Cathedral Square, Altoona, 16601-3315. Tel: 814-944-4603; Fax: 814-942-4337.
School—1300 13th St., Altoona, 16601. Tel: 814-943-7423; Fax: 814-943-7609. Sr. Kevin Breen, O.S.F., Prin. Tel: 814-944-6517. (Altoona Central Catholic School) For detailed information see Elementary Diocesan Schools under Institutions Located in the Diocese. Students 84; Lay Teachers 5.
Business Office—Tel: 814-943-4371; Fax: 814-943-4376.
Catechesis / Religious Program—Tel: 814-949-4794. Jeanne H. Thompson, D.R.E. & Dir. Christian Initiation. Students 138.

2—HOLY ROSARY (1901), Rev. William A. Rosensteel.
Res.: 900 N. Fourth St., Altoona, 16601. Tel: 814-944-6676; Fax: 814-946-9207.
Catechesis / Religious Program—Tel: 814-944-4611. Mrs. Margaret M. McCulloch, D.R.E. Students 93.

3—IMMACULATE CONCEPTION (1860), [CEM], (St. Mary's) Rev. Robert G. Neugebauer.
Res.: 1405 Fifth Ave., Altoona, 16602. Tel: 814-942-2416.
School—Immaculate Conception, 1400 Fourth Ave., Altoona, 16602. Tel: 814-944-1250. (Altoona Central Catholic School) See Elementary Diocesan Schools under Institutions Located in the Diocese. Lay Teachers 8; Students 130.
Catechesis / Religious Program—Tel: 814-944-1250. Mrs. Sheridan Luke, D.R.E. Students 152.

4—ST. JOHN THE EVANGELIST (1921), Rev. Mark S. Begly; Deacon Gene Neral.
Res.: 309 Lotz Ave., Lakemont, Altoona, 16602. Tel: 814-942-5503.
School—Tel: 814-943-4966; Fax: 814-943-8332. Gary Evangelisto, Prin. Lay Teachers 9; Students 109.
Catechesis / Religious Program—Tel: 814-943-4966. Ms. Joan Price, D.R.E. Students 191.

5—ST. LEO THE GREAT (1911), Merged, with SS. Peter & Paul to form Our Lady of Fatima, Altoona.

6—ST. MARK'S (1889), Rev. James B. Coveney. In Res., Rev. John J. Neugebauer.
Res.: 416 Sixth Ave., Altoona, 16602. Tel: 814-942-0364; Fax: 814-942-1127.
Catechesis / Religious Program—Tel: 814-942-2488. Students 102.
Chapel—Valley View Home for the Aged, Tel: 814-944-0845.
Chapel—Bellemeade Manor, Tel: 814-942-2423.

7—OUR LADY OF FATIMA (1995), (Irish—Polish), [CEM] Rev. Leo A. Lynch.
Res.: 2010 12th Ave., Altoona, 16601. Tel: 814-942-0371.
School—Altoona Central Catholic School See Elementary Diocesan Schools under Institutions Located in the Diocese.
Catechesis / Religious Program—1304 13th Ave., Altoona, 16603. Tel: 814-943-7423. Students 28.

8—OUR LADY OF LOURDES (1923), Revs. Dennis M. Kurdziel; Edward L. Eckenrod.
Res.: 2716 Broad Ave., Altoona, 16601. Tel: 814-943-6185; Fax: 814-943-1968.
Catechesis / Religious Program—Tel: 814 943-1685. Colleen Sheehan, D.R.E. Students 66.

9—OUR LADY OF MT. CARMEL (1905), (Italian), Revs. Frank Scornaienchi, T.O.R.; William Santre, T.O.R.; Christopher Panagoplos, T.O.R. In Res., Revs. Bradley Baldwin, T.O.R., Chap. Bon Secours Hospital; Louis J. Secondo, T.O.R.
Res.: 806 11th St., Altoona, 16602. Tel 814-942-8501; Fax: 814-944-2208.
School—Our Lady of Mount Carmel, 1012 8th Ave., Altoona, 16602. Tel: 814-943-5931; Fax 814-943-1837. Sr. Mary Kevin Breen, O.S.F., Prin. (Altoona Central Catholic School) Franciscan Sisters of the Immaculate Conception 2; Lay Teachers 8; Students 134.
Catechesis / Religious Program—Tel: 814 941-4960. Mr. Ronald Petak, D.R.E. Students 151.
Convent—Tel: 814-942-8964.
Mission—Our Lady of the Assumption (1925), 15 1/2 Hileman St., Pleasant Valley, Blair Co. 16602.

10—SS. PETER AND PAUL (1911), (Polish), Merged, with St. Leo the Great to form Our Lady of Fatima, Altoona.

11—ST. ROSE OF LIMA (1924), Rev. James F. Crookston; Very Rev. Carl A. Spishak.
Res.: 5514 Roselawn Ave., Altoona, 16602. Tel: 814-944-8509; Fax: 814-942-8345 (Call first).
School—5519 Sixth Ave., Altoona, 16602. Tel: 814-942-7835; Fax: 814-942-1095. Patricia Ronan, Prin. Lay Teachers 15; Students 257.
Catechesis / Religious Program—Students 162.

12—SACRED HEART (1890), Rev. Msgr. Stanley B. Carson, V.G.
Res.: 511 20th St., Altoona, 16602. Tel: 814-943-8553; Fax 814-943-1556.
Formation Center—2009 Sixth Ave., Altoona, 16602. Tel: 814-944-3922.
Catechesis / Religious Program—Students 184.

13—ST. THERESE OF THE CHILD JESUS (1927), Rev. D. Timothy Grimme.
Res.: 2301 5th St., Altoona, 16601. Tel: 814-942-4479; Fax: 814-942-1873.
School—Altoona Central Catholic Schools See Elementary Diocesan Schools under Institutions Located in the Diocese.
Catechesis / Religious Program—Andrew Callaghan, D.R.E. Students 161.

CITY OF JOHNSTOWN
(CAMBRIA COUNTY)

1—ST. ANDREW'S (1956), Rev. Barry J. Baroni; Deacon Samuel M. Cammarata. In Res., Rev. Sylvester J. Bendzella.
Res.: 1621 Ferndale Ave., Johnstown, 15905. Tel: 814-288-4324; Fax: 814-288-6750.
School—(Grades PreK-8), 1629 Ferndale Ave., Johnstown, 15905. Tel: 814-288-1854. Lay Teachers 11; Students 180.
Catechesis / Religious Program—Students 106.

2—ST. ANTHONY'S (1905), (Italian), Merged, with SS. Peter & Paul, Johnstown to form St. Clare of Assisi, Johnstown.

3—ST. BARNABAS (1954), (Slovenian), Merged, with St. Gregory, Johnstown to form SS. Gregory & Barnabas, Johnstown.

4—ST. BENEDICT'S (1930), Rev. Msgr. Dennis R. Boggs, Chancellor; Revs. Robert P. Reese; Jozef Kovacik.
Res.: 2310 Bedford St., Johnstown, 15904. Tel: 814-266-9718; Fax: 814-269-4220.
School—2306 Bedford St., Johnstown, 15904. Tel: 814-266-3837; Fax: 814-266-7718. Sr. Carol Ann Ziecina, C.S.J., Prin. Lay Teachers 24; Students 359.
Catechesis / Religious Program—Tel: 814-266-9718, Ext. 304 (Elem); (High School). Sr. Cindy Burns, D.R.E. (High School); Mrs. Michelle Robatin, D.R.E. (Elem). Students 376.

5—SS. CASIMIR & EMERICH (1997), (Polish—Hungarian), [CEM 2] Revs. Romulus Rosolowski, O.F.M.Conv.; Marcel Sokalski, O.F.M.Conv.
Res.: 501 Power St., Johnstown, 15906. Tel: 814-535-2139; Fax: 814-539-1942.
School—West End Catholic, Tel: 814-536-4722. See Elementary Diocesan Schools under Institutions Located in the Diocese.
Catechesis / Religious Program—Students 27.

6—ST. CLARE OF ASSISI (2000), (Italian—Polish), [CEM 2] Revs. Edward S. Sabo, T.O.R.; Fabian

Sheganosky, T.O.R.; Eugene Kubina, T.O.R.
Office—218 Maple Ave., Johnstown, 15901. Tel: 814-535-1133.
Res.: 124 Maple Ave., Johnstown, 15901. Tel: 814-535-4228; Fax: 814-535-1664.
School—Central Catholic Elementary, Tel: 814-536-1532. See Elementary Diocesan Schools under Institutions Located in the Diocese.
Catechesis/Religious Program—Tel: 814-535-2360. Students 37.

7—ST. CLEMENT'S (1956), Rev. William E. Rosenbaum; Very Rev. Robert Radasky.
Res.: 114 Lindberg Ave., Johnstown, 15905. Tel: 814-255-4422; Fax: 814-255-2623.
School—110 Lindberg Ave., Johnstown, 15905. Tel: 814-255-1964. A. Ernest Papinchak, Prin. Lay Teachers 10; Students 190.
Catechesis/Religious Program—Ms. Mary Drager, D.R.E. Students 153.

8—ST. COLUMBA'S (1888), [CEM] Rev. Romulus Rosolowski, O.F.M.Conv.
Res.: 916 Broad St., Johnstown, 15906. Tel: 814-535-1627; Fax: 814-534-0031.
School—West End Catholic, Tel: 814-536-4722. See Elementary Diocesan Schools under Institutions Located in the Diocese.
Catechesis/Religious Program—Tel: 814-255-9599. Students 35.

9—ST. EMERICH'S (1905), (Hungarian), Merged, with St. Casimir's, Johnstown to form Saints Casimir & Emerich's, Johnstown.

10—ST. FRANCIS OF ASSISI (1922), (Slovak), [CEM] Rev. Martin A. Cingle.
Res.: 120 Barron Ave., Johnstown, 15906. Tel: 814-539-1632; Fax: 814-539-1632.
School—West End Catholic, Tel: 814-536-4722. See Elementary Diocesan Schools under Institutions Located in the Diocese.
Catechesis/Religious Program—Students 114.

11—SS. GREGORY & BARNABAS (2001), Rev. Robert L. Ruston; Deacon Thomas M. Papinchak.
Res.: 120 Boltz St., Johnstown, 15902. Tel: 814-536-6818; Fax: 814-534-0651.
Catechesis/Religious Program—Students 126.

12—ST. GREGORY'S (1919), Merged, with St. Barnabas, Johnstown to form SS. Gregory & Barnabas, Johnstown.

13—IMMACULATE CONCEPTION (1859), (German), [CEM] Rev. Francis P. Balestino.
Res.: 308 Broad St., Johnstown, 15906. Tel: 814-535-4407.
School—West End Catholic, Tel: 814-536-4722. See Elementary Diocesan Schools under Institutions Located in the Diocese.
Catechesis/Religious Program—Students 10.

14—ST. JOHN GUALBERT CATHEDRAL (1835), [CEM 2] Rev. Msgr. George B. Flinn, V.G., Rector; Revs. John F. Brezovec; Clarence S. Bridges; Deacons John J. Concannon; Thomas M. Buige.
Res.: 117 Clinton St., P.O. Box 807, Johnstown, 15907. Tel: 814-536-0117; Fax: 814-535-6771.
School—Central Catholic Elementary, Tel: 814-536-1532; Fax: 814-536-0493. See Elementary Diocesan Schools under Institutions Located in the Diocese.
Catechesis/Religious Program—124 Maple Ave., Johnstown, 15901. Tel: 814-535-4228. Students 44.

15—ST. JOSEPH'S (1852), (German), Merged, with Our Lady of Mercy to form St. John Gualbert Cathedral, Johnstown.
School—Central Catholic Elementary, Tel: 814-536-1532. See Elementary Diocesan Schools under Institutions Located in the Diocese.

16—ST. MICHAEL'S (1910), (German), Very Rev. Paul E. Turnbull, V.F.
Res.: 180 Gilbert St., Johnstown, 15906. Tel: 814-535-6277.
Catechesis/Religious Program—Tel: 814-535-5409. Students 44.

17—OUR LADY OF MERCY (1921), Merged, with St. Joseph to form St. John Gualbert Cathedral, Johnstown.

18—OUR MOTHER OF SORROWS (1920), Very Rev. Paul E. Turnbull, V.F.; Rev. David R. Rizzo.
Res.: 407 Tioga St., Johnstown, 15905. Tel: 814-535-7646; Fax: 814-536-7850.
School—430 Tioga St., Johnstown, 15905. Tel: 814-539-5315; Fax: 814-539-5315. Mrs. Pamela Seidel, Prin. Lay Teachers 21; Students 295.
Catechesis/Religious Program—Tel: 814-255-1264. Mrs. Karen Fink, D.R.E. Students 150.

19—ST. PATRICK'S (1904), Rev. Msgr. Harold N. Biller.
Res.: 609 Park Ave., Johnstown, 15902. Tel: 814-539-2186; Fax: 814-539-2410.
School—617 Park Ave., Johnstown, 15902. Tel: 814-535-2926. Ms. Margaret Sindleri, Prin. Lay Teachers 11; Students 157.
Catechesis/Religious Program—Students 42.

20—SS. PETER AND PAUL'S (1918), Merged, with St. Anthony, Johnstown to form St. Clare of Assisi, Johnstown.

21—ST. ROCHUS (1900), (Croatian), [CEM] Rev. Charles M. Amershek Jr., V.F.; Sr. Nancy Spence, C.C.W., Pastoral Min.
Res.: 314 Eighth Ave., Johnstown, 15906. Tel: 814-539-1520; Fax: 814-539-8845.
School—West End Catholic, Tel: 814-536-4722. See Elementary Diocesan Schools under Institutions Located in the Diocese.
Catechesis/Religious Program—Tel: 814-535-5409. Students 206.

22—ST. STEPHEN, FIRST KING OF HUNGARY (1891), (Slovak), [CEM] Rev. Andrew C. Stanko.
Res.: 414 Fourth Ave., Johnstown, 15906. Tel: 814-539-6334; Fax: 814-539-6334.
School—West End Catholic, Tel: 814-536-4722; Fax: 814-539-9343. See Elementary Diocesan Schools under Institutions Located in the Diocese.
Catechesis/Religious Program—Tel: 814-539-6334; Fax: 814-539-5114. Students 67.

23—ST. THERESE OF THE CHILD JESUS (1929), (Slovenian), [CEM] Rev. Bernard Karmanocky, O.F.M.
Res.: 536 Decker Ave., Johnstown, 15906. Tel: 814-539-7633; Fax: 814-539-7633.
School—West End Catholic, Tel: 814-536-4722. See Elementary Diocesan Schools under Institutions Located in the Diocese.
Mission—St. Anne's (1935), 533 Woodland Ave., Moxham, Cambria Co. 15902. Tel: 814-539-7633.
Catechesis/Religious Program—Tel: 814-536-2287. Students 52.

24—VISITATION OF THE B.V.M. (1927), Rev. Richard D. Clark; Deacon John E. Sroka. In Res., Rev. Msgr. David A. Lockard.
Res.: 1127 McKinley Ave., Johnstown, 15905. Tel: 814-536-6110; Fax: 814-536-3709.
Catechesis/Religious Program—Tel: 814-536-7003. Students 40.

OUTSIDE THE CITIES OF ALTOONA AND JOHNSTOWN

ACOSTA, SOMERSET CO., ST. JOHN THE BAPTIST'S (1912), Merged, with St. Joseph, Boswell, and St. Stanislaus, Boswell, to form All Saints Church, Boswell.

ASHVILLE, CAMBRIA CO., ST. THOMAS AQUINAS (1889), [CEM] Rev. George M. Gulash.
Mailing Address: 692 Glendale Valley Blvd., Fallentimber, 16639. Tel: 814-943-5437.
Catechesis/Religious Program—Tel: 814-736-3774. Mrs. Jean Vasilko, D.R.E. Students 77.

BAKERTON, CAMBRIA CO., SACRED HEART (1904), Merged, with St. Patrick, Spangler, to form St. Jude, Elmora.

BARNESBORO, CAMBRIA CO.

1—CHRIST THE KING (1993), Merged, with St. Stanislaus Kostka, Barnesboro; St. John the Baptist, Northern Cambria; Our Lady of Mt. Carmel, Northern Cambria; Holy Cross, Northern Cambria to form Prince of Peace, Northern Cambria.

2—ST. STANISLAUS KOSTKA (1906), (Polish), Merged, with Christ the King, Barnesboro; St. John the Baptist, Northern Cambria; Our Lady of Mt. Carmel, Northern Cambria; Holy Cross, Northern Cambria to form Prince of Peace, Northern Cambria.

BEANS COVE, BEDFORD CO., SEVEN DOLORS B.V.M. (1878), [CEM] Rev. Donald W. Dusza, Admin.
Mailing Address: 2174 Beans Cove Rd., Clearville, 15535-7901. Tel: 814-767-9522; Fax: 814-767-8158.
Res.: 215 E. Penn St., Bedford, 15522. Tel: 814-623-5526; Fax: 814-623-1741.
Catechesis/Religious Program—Students 6.

BEAVERDALE, CAMBRIA CO.

1—ST. AGNES (1909), Merged, with St. Joseph, Beaverdale, and Corpus Christi, Dunlo, to form Holy Spirit Church, Beaverdale.

2—HOLY SPIRIT (1995), [CEM 2] Rev. Anthony J. Legarski.
Mailing Address: 802 Cameron Ave., P.O. Box 616, 15921. Tel: 814-487-5633; 814-487-5653 (Office); Fax: 814-487-5773.
Catechesis/Religious Program—Students 101.

3—ST. JOSEPH'S (1904), (Slovak), Merged, with St. Agnes, Beaverdale, and Corpus Christi, Dunlo, to form Holy Spirit Church, Beaverdale.

BEDFORD, BEDFORD CO., ST. THOMAS (1816), [CEM 2] Rev. Donald W. Dusza.
Res.: 215 E. Penn St., 15522. Tel: 814-623-5526; Fax: 814-623-1741.
School—129 W. Penn St., 15522. Tel: 814-623-8873; Fax: 814-623-1208. Joyce Wityk, Prin. Lay Teachers 8; Students 69.
Catechesis/Religious Program—Tel: 814-623-9525. Mrs. Debbie Will, D.R.E. Students 167.

BELLEFONTE, CENTRE CO., ST. JOHN THE EVANGELIST'S (1828), [CEM 2] Revs. Neil R. Dadey; Richard Tomkosky; Deacon Joseph F. Mazurkiewicz Sr.
Res.: 134 E. Bishop St., 16823. Tel: 814-355-3134; Fax: 814-355-4820.
School—(Grades PreK-5), 116 E. Bishop St., 16823. Tel: 814-355-7859; Fax: 814-355-2939. Mrs. Pamela Vaiana, Prin. Lay Teachers 9; Students 133.
Catechesis/Religious Program—Tel: 814-355-3135. Students 296.

BELLWOOD, BLAIR CO., ST. JOSEPH'S (1890), Rev. David H. Roesch.
Res.: 623 E. Third St., 16617. Tel: 814-742-7075.
Catechesis/Religious Program—Tel: 814-742-7894. Students 119.

BOSWELL, SOMERSET CO.

1—ALL SAINTS (1995), [CEM 3] Rev. Justin A. Ratajczak, O.F.M.Conv.
Res.: 325 Quemahoning St., 15531. Tel: 814-629-5551; Fax: 814-629-5677.
Catechesis/Religious Program—Students 91.

2—ST. STANISLAUS (1901), (Polish), Merged, with St. John the Baptist, Acosta to form All Saints Church, Boswell.

CARROLLTOWN, CAMBRIA CO., ST. BENEDICT'S (1846), [CEM 3] Rev. Vincent E. Zidek, O.S.B.
Res.: 100 Main St., P.O. Box 447, 15722. Tel: 814-344-6548; Fax: 814-344-8656.
School—119 S. Church St., 15722. Tel: 814-344-6512; Fax: 814-344-8530. Sister 1; Lay Teachers 12; Students 200.
Catechesis/Religious Program—Peggy J. Bowser, D.R.E. Students 203.

CASSANDRA, CAMBRIA CO., ST. AGNES (1909), Rev. Charles F. Bodziak.
Res.: P.O. Box 56, 15925. Tel: 814-736-8314; Fax: 814-736-8339.
Catechesis/Religious Program—Tel: 814-495-5360. Students 16.

CENTRAL CITY, SOMERSET CO.

1—ST. JOHN THE BAPTIST (1917), (Slovak), Merged, with Sacred Heart of Jesus, Central City to form Our Lady Queen of Angels, Central City.

2—OUR LADY QUEEN OF ANGELS (1999), [CEM 2] Rev. Joseph D. Maurizio Jr.
Res.: 738 Sunshine Ave., 15926-1233. Tel: 814-754-5224; Fax: 814-754-5224 (8:30-4:00).
Catechesis/Religious Program—Students 94.

3—SACRED HEART OF JESUS (1914), (Polish), Merged, with St. John the Baptist, Central City to form Our Lady Queen of Angels, Central City.

CHEST SPRINGS, CAMBRIA CO., ST. MONICA'S (1859), [CEM] Rev. Msgr. Timothy P. Stein.
Res.: 3037 Colonel Drake Hwy., 16624. Tel: 814-674-3712.
Catechesis/Religious Program—Tel: 814-674-5064. Students 33.

CLARENCE, CENTRE CO., ST. MICHAEL'S (1900), (Slovak), [CEM] Rev. Peter J. Kuligowski.
Res.: 102 Church St., 16829. Tel: 814-387-6762.
Catechesis/Religious Program—Tel: 814-387-6762. Students 57.

COLVER, CAMBRIA CO., HOLY FAMILY (1912), (Polish), [CEM] Rev. Bernard F. Grega.
Res.: 562 Fifth St., 15927. Tel: 814-748-7054; Fax: 814-748-7254.
Catechesis/Religious Program—Sr. Anna Marie, S.A., D.R.E. Students 70.

CONEMAUGH, CAMBRIA CO.

1—ASSUMPTION OF B.V.M. (1910), (Polish), [CEM] Rev. Robert C. Hall.
Res.: 340 Second St., 15909. Tel: 814-535-6432; Fax: 814-536-9770.
Catechesis/Religious Program—219 Oak St., 15909. Tel: 814-535-2250, Ext. 203. Students 43.

2—SACRED HEART (1902), [CEM] Rev. Robert C. Hall.
Res.: 340 Second St., 15909. Tel: 814-535-6432.
Catechesis/Religious Program—Tel: 814-535-2250; Fax: 814-536-9770. Students 52.

COUPON, CAMBRIA CO., ST. JOSEPH'S (1855), [CEM 2] Rev. Msgr. Michael E. Servinsky; Deacon Steve A. Luke.
Res.: P.O. Box 91, 16629. Tel: 814-943-8464.
Catechesis/Religious Program—Students 60.

CRESSON, CAMBRIA CO.

1—ST. ALOYSIUS (1838), [CEM] Rev. Msgr. John J. Little.
Res.: 7911 Admiral Peary Hwy., 16630. Tel: 814-886-2235.
School—All Saints Catholic, Tel: 814-886-7942; Fax: 814-886-7942. See Elementary Diocesan Schools under Institutions Located in the Diocese.
Catechesis/Religious Program—Tel: 814-886-2669. Marcia E. Hammond, D.R.E. Students 144.

2—ST. FRANCIS XAVIER (1908), [CEM] Rev. Angelo J. Patti.
Res.: 211 Powell Ave., 16630. Tel: 814-886-2374; Fax: 814-886-2498.
School—All Saints Catholic, Tel: 814-886-7942; Fax: 814-886-7942. See Elementary Diocesan Schools under Institutions Located in the Diocese.
Catechesis/Religious Program—Tel: 814-886-2374. Mrs. Laura Steffke, D.R.E. Students 123.

DAVIDSVILLE, SOMERSET CO., ST. ANNE (1911), [CEM 2] Rev. Michael Lewandowski, O.F.M.Conv.
Mailing Address: 205 Woodstown Hwy., P.O. Box 500, 15928. Tel: 814-479-2664; Fax: 814-479-7702. In Res., Revs. Karl Kolodziejski, O.F.M.Conv.;

Justin A. Ratajczak, O.F.M.Conv.
Catechesis / Religious Program—Students 68.

DUDLEY, HUNTINGDON CO., IMMACULATE CONCEPTION (1856), [CEM] Rev. Patrick R. Leahey.
Res.: P.O. Box 188, 16634. Tel: 814-635-2919.
Catechesis / Religious Program—Students 42.

DUNCANSVILLE, BLAIR CO., ST. CATHERINE OF SIENA (1963), Rev. Msgr. Robert J. Saly.
Res.: 49 Woodland Terr., 16635. Tel: 814-695-2337; Fax: 814-693-7518.
Catechesis / Religious Program—P.O. Box 88, 16635. Tel: 814-696-0616. Debra Terchanik, D.R.E. Students 88.

DUNLO, CAMBRIA CO., CORPUS CHRISTI (1903), Merged, with St. Agnes and St. Joseph, Beaverdale to form Holy Spirit Church, Beaverdale.

EBENSBURG, CAMBRIA CO., HOLY NAME (1816), [CEM] Rev. Msgr. Arnold L. Gaus; Rev. Matthew A. Reese.
Res.: 500 N. Julian St., 15931. Tel: 814-472-7244; Fax: 814-472-7249.
School—Tel: 814-472-8817; Fax: 814-471-0500. Ms. Joan Meintel, Prin. Lay Teachers 21; Students 249.
Catechesis / Religious Program—Students 524.

EHRENFELD, CAMBRIA CO., OUR LADY OF MT. CARMEL (1892), Merged, with St. James and St. Anthony's, South Fork to form Most Holy Trinity, South Fork.

ELMORA, CAMBRIA CO., ST. JUDE (1995), Closed. For inquiries for parish records contact the chancery.

EMEIGH, CAMBRIA CO., MOST PRECIOUS BLOOD, , See Christ the King, Barnesboro.

EVERETT, BEDFORD CO., ST. JOHN THE EVANGELIST (1971), Rev. Norman P. Imgrund.
Res.: 161 E. First Ave., 15537. Tel: 814-652-5854. Church: 163 E. First Ave., 15537.
Catechesis / Religious Program—Students 33.

FALLENTIMBER, CAMBRIA CO.

1—ST. JOAN OF ARC (1995), Rev. George M. Gulash.
Res.: 692 Glendale Valley Blvd., 16639. Tel: 814-943-5437.
Catechesis / Religious Program—Tel: 814-672-5123. Mrs. Nancy Francisco, D.R.E. Students 43.

2—ST. MARY MAGDALEN'S (1889), Closed. Rev. James F. Bunn (Retired). Merged with St. Richard's Mission, Blandburg to form St. Joan of Arc Church, Fallentimber.
Res.: 692 Glendale Valley Blvd., 16639. Tel: 814-943-5437.
Catechesis / Religious Program—Students 57.

GALLITZIN, CAMBRIA CO.

1—ST. DEMETRIUS (2000), [CEM 2] Rev. Msgr. Bernard A. Przybocki.
Res.: 811 Church St., 16641. Tel: 814-886-7941; Fax: 814-886-9374.
Catechesis / Religious Program—Tel: 814-886-9374. Students 161.

2—OUR LADY OF CZESTOCHOWA (1903), (Polish), Merged, with St. Patrick, Gallitzin to form St. Demetrius, Gallitzin.

3—ST. PATRICK'S (1850), Merged, with Our Lady of Czestochowa, Gallitzin to form St. Demetrius, Gallitzin.

HASTINGS, CAMBRIA CO., ST. BERNARD (1890), [CEM 2] Rev. Chad R. Ficorilli, O.S.B.
Res.: Beaver St., P.O. Box 497, 16646. Tel: 814-247-6558; Fax: 814-247-8522.
Catechesis / Religious Program—Tel: 814-674-5841. Mrs. Aileen Ropp, D.R.E. Students 155.
Mission—St. Boniface Chapel 1278 Main St., St. Boniface, Cambria Co. 16675.

HOLLIDAYSBURG, BLAIR CO.

1—ST. MARY'S (1841), [CEM 2] Rev. John J. Palko; Deacon John A. Tiernan.
Res.: 312 Clark St., P.O. Box 317, 16648. Tel: 814-695-0622; Fax: 814-696-9609.
School—Hollidaysburg Consolidated Catholic Elementary, Tel: 814-695-6112; Fax: 814-696-8960. See Elementary Diocesan Schools under Institutions Located in the Diocese.
Catechesis / Religious Program—Tel: 814-695-5678. Mrs. Connie Curfman, D.R.E. Students 276.

2—ST. MICHAEL'S (1862), (German), [CEM] Rev. Clement Gardner.
Res.: 301 Spruce St., 16648. Tel: 814-695-0912; Fax: 814-693-9820.
School—Hollidaysburg Consolidated Catholic Elementary, Tel: 814-695-6112; Fax: 814-695-1215. See Elementary Diocesan Schools under Institutions Located in the Diocese.
Catechesis / Religious Program—Tel: 814-695-9735. Susan M. Teske, D.R.E. Students 303.

HOOVERSVILLE, SOMERSET CO., HOLY FAMILY (1911), [CEM] Rev. Karl Kolodziejski, O.F.M.Conv.
Res.: 321 Sugar St., P.O. Box 187, 15936. Tel: 814-798-2933; Fax: 814-798-8601.
Catechesis / Religious Program—Students 59.

HUNTINGDON, HUNTINGDON CO., MOST HOLY TRINITY (1826), [CEM] Rev. David J. Arseneault.
Res.: 524 Mifflin St., 16652. Tel: 814-643-0160; Fax: 814-643-0160.
Catechesis / Religious Program—Students 195.

LILLY, CAMBRIA CO.

1—ST. BRIGID'S (1883), Merged, with Our Lady of Mount Carmel, Lilly to form Our Lady of the Alleghenies, Lilly.

2—OUR LADY OF MT. CARMEL (1910), (Polish), Merged, with St. Brigid, Lilly to form Our Lady of the Alleghenies, Lilly.

3—OUR LADY OF THE ALLEGHENIES (1995), [CEM 2] Rev. Msgr. John R. Sasway.
Res.: 608 Main St., 15938. Tel: 814-886-2504; Fax: 814-884-4952.
Catechesis / Religious Program—Tel: 814-886-2161. Sr. Theresa M. Kukla, S.S.C.J., D.R.E. Students 134.

LOCK HAVEN, CLINTON CO.

1—ST. AGNES (1873), [CEM] Rev. Sean K. Code.
Res.: 3 E Walnut St., 17745. Tel: 570-748-4594; Fax: 570-893-8229.
School—Lock Haven Catholic School, Tel: 717-742-7252. See Immaculate Conception for details.
Catechesis / Religious Program—Tel: 570-748-4828. Students 104.

2—IMMACULATE CONCEPTION (1852), [CEM] Rev. Daniel J. O'Neill; Deacon R. Kenneth Priew.
Res.: 310 W. Water St., 17745. Tel: 570-748-4535; Fax: 570-748-1674.
School—Lock Haven Catholic School, Tel: 570-748-7252. Sr. Mary Joan Gibson, O.P., Prin. Sisters of Sinsinawa Dominicans 2; Lay Teachers 17; Students 170.
Catechesis / Religious Program—Tel: 570-748-4828; Fax: 570-893-8229. Students 99.

LORETTO, CAMBRIA CO., BASILICA OF ST. MICHAEL THE ARCHANGEL (1799), [CEM] Very Rev. Msgr. Timothy J. Swope, V.F.; Deacon Michael Conder Jr. Tel: 814-886-4948. In Res., Rev. John D. Byrnes.
Res.: 321 St. Mary, P.O. Box 10, 15940. Tel: 814-472-8551; Fax: 814-471-4959.
School—Tel: 814-472-9117; Fax: 814-472-9117. Judy M. Noel, Prin. Lay Teachers 8; Students 138.
Catechesis / Religious Program—Tel: 814-471-4890. Maggie Biter, D.R.E. (Elementary & High School). Students 147.

MCCONNELLSBURG, FULTON CO., ST. STEPHEN'S (1962), Rev. Alan E. Thomas, Admin.
Res.: 303 Lincoln Way E., 17233. Tel: 717-485-3723; Fax: 717-485-3855.
Catechesis / Religious Program—Tel: 717-485-0661. Students 17.

MEYERSDALE, SOMERSET CO., SS. PHILIP AND JAMES (1850), [CEM 2] Rev. James M. Dugan.
Res.: 247 High St., 15552. Tel: 814-634-8150; Fax: 814-634-0983.
Catechesis / Religious Program—Students 111.
Mission—St. Gregory (1907), 247 High St., MacDonaldton, Somerset Co. 15552. Tel: 814-634-8150.

MOUNT UNION, HUNTINGDON CO., ST. CATHERINE'S (1912), [CEM] Rev. Leo Arnone.
Res.: 205 W. Market St., 17066. Tel: 814-542-4582; Fax: 814-542-4582.
Catechesis / Religious Program—Students 43.

MUNDYS CORNER, CAMBRIA CO., ST. JOHN VIANNEY'S (1950), Rev. Paul M. Robine.
Res.: 3513 William Penn Ave., Johnstown, 15909. Tel: 814-322-4789; Fax: 814-322-3799.
Catechesis / Religious Program—Tel: 814-322-1149. Yvonne Allbaugh. Students 166.

NANTY-GLO, CAMBRIA CO., ST. MARY'S (1902), [CEM] Rev. David S. Peles.
Res.: 1020 Caroline St., 15943. Tel: 814-749-9103; Fax: 814-749-5463.
School—1005 Caroline St., 15943. Tel: 814-749-9031; Fax: 814-749-0167. Mrs. Rosemary Conzo, Prin. Sisters of St. Agnes 2; Lay Teachers 9; Students 78.
Catechesis / Religious Program—Mrs Patricia LaMantia, D.R.E. Students 59.

NEW BALTIMORE, SOMERSET CO., ST. JOHN THE BAPTIST (1829), [CEM] Rev. Allen P. Zeth.
Res.: 101 Findley St., P.O. Box 10, 15553. Tel: 814-733-2210; Fax: 814-733-2966.
Catechesis / Religious Program—Dennis Hay, D.R.E.; Sharon Hay, D.R.E. Students 95.

NEWRY, BLAIR CO.

1—ST. PATRICK'S (1816), [CEM 2] Rev. Msgr. Anthony B. Little.
Res.: P.O Box 398, 16665. Tel: 814-695 3413; Fax: 814-948-8191.
School—Tel: 814-695-3819; Fax: 814-695-5274. Sr. Pauline Kawtoski, C.C.W., Prin. Sisters 2; Lay Teachers 9; Students 132.
Catechesis / Religious Program—Mrs. Linda Guiffre, D.R.E. Students 104.

NICKTOWN, CAMBRIA CO., ST. NICHOLAS (1861), [CEM] Rev. Job Foote, O.S.B.
Res.: 1169 Alverda Rd., P.O. Box 37, 15762. Tel: 814-948-9614; Fax: 814-948-8191.
School—Northern Cambria Catholic, Tel: 814-948-8900; Fax: 814-948-8720. See Elementary Diocesan Schools under Institutions Located in the Diocese.
Catechesis / Religious Program—Tel: 814-948-8794. Mrs. Julie Horuath, D.R.E. Students 187.

NORTHERN CAMBRIA, CAMBRIA CO.

1—HOLY CROSS (1893), Merged, with St. Stanislaus Kostka, Barnesboro; Christ the King, Barnesboro; St. John the Baptist, Northern Cambria; Our Lady of Mt. Carmel, Northern Cambria to form Prince of Peace, Northern Cambria.

2—ST. JOHN THE BAPTIST (1896), (Slovak), Merged, with St. Stanislaus Kostka, Barnesboro; Christ the King, Barnesboro; Holy Cross, Northern Cambria; Our Lady of Mt. Carmel, Northern Cambria to form Prince of Peace, Northern Cambria.

3—OUR LADY OF MT. CARMEL (1908), (Italian), Merged, with St. Stanislaus Kostka, Barnesboro; Christ the King, Barnesboro; Holy Cross, Northern Cambria; St. John the Baptist to form Prince of Peace, Northern Cambria.

4—PRINCE OF PEACE (2000), [CEM 5] Revs. John K. Nesbella; Lawrence L. Lacovic.
Res.: 811 Chestnut Ave., 15714. Tel: 814-948-6842; Fax: 814-948-6585.
School—Tel: 814-948-8900. See Elementary Diocesan Schools under Institutions Located in the Diocese.
Catechesis / Religious Program—Tel: 814-948-6622. Students 252.

PATTON, CAMBRIA CO.

1—ST. GEORGE (1907), (Slovak), Merged, with Our Lady of Perpetual Help, Patton and St. Lawrence to form Queen of Peace, Patton.

2—OUR LADY OF PERPETUAL HELP (1892), Merged, with St. George, Patton, and St. Lawrence to form Queen of Peace, Patton.

3—QUEEN OF PEACE (1995), [CEM] Revs. Ananias Buccicone, O.S.B.; Robert Roche, O.S.B.
Res.: 907 Sixth Ave., 16668. Tel: 814-674-8983; Fax: 814-674-8805.
Catechesis / Religious Program—Tel: 814-674-5591. Joanne VanOrmer, D.R.E. Students 217.

PENNS VALLEY, CENTRE CO., BLESSED KATERI TEKAKWITHA (1986), [JC] Rev. Neil R. Dadey, Admin.
Res.: 3503 Penns Vly Rd., P.O. Box 159, Spring Mills, 16875. Tel: 814-422-8983.
Catechesis / Religious Program—Students 83.

PHILIPSBURG, CENTRE CO., SS. PETER AND PAUL (1868), [CEM] [JC] Rev. Robert J. Kelly.
Res.: 400 S. Fourth St., 16866. Tel: 814-342-1700; Fax: 814-342-5480.
Catechesis / Religious Program—William J. Slother Jr., D.R.E. Students 201.

PORTAGE, CAMBRIA CO.

1—ASSUMPTION B.V.M. (1907), (Slovak), Merged, with Sacred Heart of Jesus to form Our Lady of the Sacred Heart, Portage

2—ST. JOHN THE BAPTIST (1923), (Hungarian), [CEM] Rev. Ronald B. Yogus.
Res.: 900 Johnson Ave., 15946. Tel: 814-736-9747.
Catechesis / Religious Program—812 Orchard St., 15946. Tel: 814-736-3588. Students 38.

3—ST. JOSEPH'S (1898), Rev. Walter J. Moll Jr.
Res.: 509 Caldwell Ave., 15946. Tel: 814-736-4279; Fax: 814-736-4764.
Catechesis / Religious Program—Tel: 814-736-9214. Mary E. Heinrich, D.R.E. Students 175.

4—OUR LADY OF THE SACRED HEART (1999), (Polish—Slovak), [CEM 2] Rev. Ronald V. Osinski.
Res.: 601 Mountain Ave., 15946. Tel: 814-736-4239; Fax: 814-736-9285.
School—(Grades PreK-K), 812 Orchard St., 15946. Tel: 814-736-3588. Sr. Theresa Marie, S.S.C.J., Prin. Students 26.
Catechesis / Religious Program—Students 145.
Convent—803 Orchard St., 15946. Tel: 814-736-3875.

5—SACRED HEART OF JESUS (1909), (Polish), Merged, with Assumption of the Blessed Virgin Mary, Portage to form Our Lady of the Sacred Heart, Portage.

RENOVO, CLINTON CO., ST. JOSEPH'S (1869), [CEM 2] Rev. Donald E. Boslett.
Res.: 925 Huron Ave., 17764. Tel: 570-923-0172.
Catechesis / Religious Program—Judy M. Kurutz, D.R.E. Students 94.

REVLOC, CAMBRIA CO., MOST HOLY REDEEMER (1920), Closed. For inquiries for parish records contact the chancery.

ROARING SPRING, BLAIR CO., ST. THOMAS MORE (1969), Rev. Msgr. William E. Shultz.
Res.: 825 Williams St., 16673. Tel: 814-224-4522; Fax: 814-224-4522.
Catechesis / Religious Program—Students 70.

ST. AUGUSTINE, CAMBRIA CO., ST. AUGUSTINE (1847), [CEM] Rev. Joseph W. Fleming.
Res.: 803 St. Augustine Rd., Dysart, 16636. Tel: 814-674-8550.
Catechesis / Religious Program—Students 87.

ST. BONIFACE, CAMBRIA CO., ST. BONIFACE CHAPEL (1859), Merged, to form St. Bernard, Hastings.

ST. LAWRENCE, CAMBRIA CO., ST. LAWRENCE'S (1853), Merged, with Our Lady of Perpetual Help and St. George Patton, to form Queen of Peace, Patton.
ST. MICHAEL, CAMBRIA CO., ST. MICHAEL'S (1913), [CEM] Rev. Msgr. George J. Valko.
Res.: 751 Locust St., Box 103, 15951. Tel: 814-495-9640; Fax: 814-495-9424.
Catechesis/Religious Program—Students 170.
SHADE GAP, HUNTINGDON CO., ST. MARY'S (1840), [CEM 2] Rev. George D. Koharchik.
Res.: Shade Gap, H.C. 62, Box 696, 17255. Tel: 814-447-3172; Fax: 814-447-9030.
Catechesis/Religious Program—Students 33.
SNOW SHOE, CENTRE CO., ST. MARY'S (1865), (Irish), [CEM] Rev. Peter J. Kuligowski.
Church: 102 Church St., Clarence, 16829. Tel: 814-387-6762.
Catechesis/Religious Program—Students 38.
SOMERSET, SOMERSET CO.
1—ST. PETER IN CHAINS (1995),, Mailing Address: *S.C.I.-Somerset*, 1590 Walters Mill Rd., 15501-0001. Tel: 814-443-8100.
2—ST. PETER'S (1920), [CEM] Rev. Msgr. Samuel J. Tomaselli; Deacon Frederick F. Weaver.
Res.: 433 W. Church St., 15501. Tel: 814-443-6574; Fax: 814-445-7766.
School—Tel: 814-445-6662. Mrs. Karen Ferry, Prin. Lay Teachers 7; Students 116.
Catechesis/Religious Program—Students 301.
SOUTH FORK, CAMBRIA CO.
1—ST. ANTHONY'S (1905), (Polish), Merged, with St. James, South Fork and Our Lady of Mt. Carmel, Ehrenfeld to form Most Holy Trinity, South Fork.
2—ST. JAMES (1906), Merged, with St. Anthony, South Fork and Our Lady of Mt. Carmel, Ehrenfeld to form Most Holy Trinity, South Fork.
3—MOST HOLY TRINITY (1995), [CEM 2] Rev. Louis J. Mulvehill.
Res.: 550 Main St., 15956. Tel: 814-495-4419; Fax: 814-495-4419.
Catechesis/Religious Program—Tel: 814-495-4028. Mrs. Betty Rosmus, D.R.E. Students 63.
SPANGLER, CAMBRIA CO., ST. PATRICK'S (1902), Merged, with Sacred Heart, Bakerton to form St. Jude, Elmora.
STATE COLLEGE, CENTRE CO.
1—GOOD SHEPHERD (1989), Rev. Philip M. Bender; Deacons Robert A. Killoren Jr. Tel: 814-867-5657; Michael A. Ondik. Tel: 814-237-1857.
Res.: 835 Gray's Woods Blvd., P.O. Box 8186, 16803. Tel: 814-238-7463.
Church: Tel: 814-238-2110; Fax: 814-238-3484.
Catechesis/Religious Program—Tel: 814-238-0649. Dorothy Kardohely, D.R.E. Students 534.
2—OUR LADY OF VICTORY (1908), Rev. Msgr. David A. Lockard, Admin.; Revs. Joseph Christopher Nale; James D. Zatalava; Deacons David C. Lapinski; Garth J. Gillan.
Res.: 820 Westerly Pkwy., 16801. Tel: 814-237-7832; Fax: 814-237-6709.
School—Preschool, Tel: 814-238-6616. Lay Teachers 5; Students 68.
School—800 Westerly Pkwy., 16801. Tel: 814-238-1592; Fax: 814-238-4553. Kathleen Bechdel, Prin.; Charles Loviscky, Asst. Prin. Lay Teachers 20; Students 339.
Catechesis/Religious Program—Tel: 814-234-3315. Shannon Jones, D.R.E. Students 443.
SUMMERHILL, CAMBRIA CO., ST. JOHN (1903), [CEM] Rev. Alfred Patterson, O.S.B.
Res.: 538 Main St., P.O. Box 248, 15958. Tel: 814-495-5241; Fax: 814-495-9522.
Mission—Immaculate Conception (1855), 1640 New Germany Rd., P.O. Box 248, New Germany, Cambria Co. 15958.
Catechesis/Religious Program—Madeline Wirfel, D.R.E. Students 218.
TWIN ROCKS, CAMBRIA CO.
1—ST. CHARLES (1917), Merged, with Immaculate Conception Mission, Vintondale to form SS. Timothy & Mark Church, Twin Rocks & SS. Timothy & Mark Chapel, Vintondale.
2—SS. TIMOTHY & MARK (1995), [CEM], Mailing Address: P.O. Box 275, 15960. Tel: 814-749-9331; Fax: 814-749-8000.
Catechesis/Religious Program—Students 57.
Mission—SS. Timothy & Mark Chapel 314 4th St., Vintondale, Cambria Co. 15961.
TYRONE, BLAIR CO., ST. MATTHEW'S (1853), [CEM 2] Rev. Joseph T. Orr.
Res.: 406 W. 11th St., 16686. Tel: 814-684-1480; Fax: 814-684-7969. Cemeteries: Oak Grove & St Luke's.
School—1107 Cameron Ave., 16686. Tel: 814-684-3510; Fax: 814-684-7833. Mrs. Jamie DiDomenico, Prin. Lay Teachers 6; Students 70.
Catechesis/Religious Program—Tel: 814-684-4808. Mark Raffetto, D.R.E. Students 108.
WEST SALISBURY, SOMERSET CO., ST. MICHAEL'S (1887), [CEM 2] Rev. Albert J. Anselmi.
Res.: 1316 St. Paul Rd., 15565. Tel: 814-662-2958.
Mission—St. Mary's (1906), P.O. Box 31, Pocahontas, Somerset Co. 15565. Tel: 814-662-2958.
Catechesis/Religious Program—Tel: 301-689-9189. Students 44.
WILLIAMSBURG, BLAIR CO., ST. JOSEPH (1861), [CEM 2] Rev. Bernard L. White.
Res.: 628 W. First St., 16693. Tel: 814-832-2137; Fax: 814-832-1025.
Catechesis/Religious Program—Students 46.
WILMORE, CAMBRIA CO., ST. BARTHOLOMEW'S (1840), [CEM] Rev. Charles F. Bodziak.
Res.: P.O. Box 96, 15962. Tel: 814-495-5360; 814-736-8314; Fax: 814-736-8339.
Catechesis/Religious Program—Students 59.
WINDBER, SOMERSET CO.
1—ST. ANTHONY OF PADUA (1908), (Italian), [CEM] Very Rev. Bonaventure N. Midili, T.O.R.; Revs. Blase R. Romano, T.O.R.; Adrian Tirpak, T.O.R.; Mark Reifel, T.O.R.
Res.: 2201 Graham Ave., 15963. Tel: 814-467-7292; Fax: 814-467-9182.
School—St. Benedict School, Tel: 814-266-3837; Fax: 814-266-7718. Students 7.
School—St. Andrew School, Tel: 814-288-2811; Fax: 814-288-6750. Students 1.
School—St. Clement School, Tel: 814-255-1964; Fax: 814-255-2623.
Catechesis/Religious Program—Tel: 814-467-9670. Sr. Evangelista, R.S.M., D.R.E.; Roxann Newcomer, D.R.E. Students 165.
2—SS. CYRIL AND METHODIUS (1906), (Slovak), [CEM 2] Rev. Matthew Misurda.
Res.: 604 Graham Ave., 15963. Tel: 814-467-7042; Fax: 814-467-0183.
Catechesis/Religious Program—600 Graham Ave., 15963. Tel: 814-467-9670. Students 47.
3—ST. ELIZABETH ANN SETON (2000), [CEM 2] Very Rev. Leonard E. Voytek, V.F.; Deacon Thaddeus J. Janisko.
Res.: 605 Graham Ave., 15963. Tel: 814-467-7191; Fax: 814-467-1621.
Catechesis/Religious Program—Tel: 814-467-9670. Sr. Evangelista Strohmier, D.R.E., (Elementary). Students 188.
4—HOLY CHILD JESUS (1921), (Irish), Closed., For inquiries for sacramental records, please contact SS. Cyril & Methodius
5—ST. JOHN CANTIUS (1898), (Polish), Merged, with St. Mary's, Windber to form St. Elizabeth Ann Seton, Windber
6—ST. MARY'S (1914), (Hungarian), Merged, with St. John Cantius, Windber to form St. Elizabeth Ann Seton, Windber

Chaplains of Public Institutions

ALTOONA. *Altoona Hospital*, Howard Ave. & Seventh St., 16601. Tel: 814-946-2011. Revs. Edward L. Eckenrod, Chap. Tel: 814-943-6185, Bradley Baldwin, T.O.R., Chap., David R. Becker, Chap. (Retired).
Veterans Medical Center, 2907 Pleasant Valley Blvd., 16602. Tel: 814-943-8164. Rev. David R. Becker (Retired).
JOHNSTOWN. *Conemaugh Memorial Medical Center*, 1083 Franklin St., 15905. Tel: 814-534-9250. Rev. Sylvester J. Bendzella, Dir. Pastoral Care Dept.
UPMC Lee Hospital, 320 Main St., 15901. Tel: 814-533-0123. (Vacant)
BELLEFONTE. *State Correctional Institution*, Our Lady of the Mount, Box A, 16823. Tel: 814-355-4874. Deacon Anthony E. Wagner.
CRESSON. *State Correctional Institution*, P.O. Box A, 16630. Tel: 814-886-8181; 814-736-9747 (Res.). Rev. Ronald B. Yogus, Chap.
EBENSBURG. *Laurel Crest Rehabilitation & Special Care Center*, 429 Manor Dr., 15931. Tel: 814-472-8100, Ext. 3119. Deacon Jim Marchu.
HUNTINGDON. *State Correctional Institution*, St. Dismas, 1100 Pike St., 16652. Tel: 814-643-2400, Ext. 213. Revs. George D. Koharchik, Bernard L. White.
LAURAL HIGHLANDS. *State Correctional Institution*, 5706 Glades Pike Rd., P.O. Box 631. Tel: 814-445-6501. Deacon Pasquale Valerio, Chap.
LORETTO. *Federal Correctional Institution*, P.O. Box 1000, 15940. Tel: 814-472-4140, Ext. 155. Sr. Mary Ann Palko, C.C.W., Chap.
SMITHFIELD. *State Correctional Institution*, 1120 Pike St., Huntingdon, 16652. Tel: 814-643-6520; 814-832-2137 (Res.). Rev. Bernard L. White.
SOMERSET. *State Correctional Institution*, St. Peter in Chains, 1590 Walters Mill Rd., 15510. Tel: 814-443-8100. Deacon Pasquale Valerio, Chap.

On Duty Outside the Diocese:
Rev. Msgr.—
Lenz, Paul A., 2021 H St., N.W., Washington, DC 20006. Tel: 202-331-8542
Revs.—
Hlubik, Joseph G., Our Lady of Good Counsel Rectory, 42 W. Main St., Moorestown, NJ 08057.
Ledoux, Albert H., St. Mary's Seminary, Emmittsburg, MD. Tel: 301-447-5809

On Special or Other Diocesan Assignment:
Rev.—
Strecok, Lubomir J., Diocese of Altoona-Johnstown, 126 Logan Blvd., 16648.

Military Chaplains:
Revs.—
Gergel, Stephen J., U.S. Navy
Gomulka, Eugene T., U.S. Navy
Halka, Frantisek A., U.S. Army

Absent on Leave:
Rev. Msgr.—
Becker, Michael
Revs.—
Norcavage, Albert R.
Petracca, Anthony

Retired:
Rev. Msgrs.—
Fleming, Joseph H., 14408 Gallagher Rd., Delray Beach, FL 33445. Tel: 561-498-7646
Fleming, Patrick V., Delray Beach, FL 33445. Tel: 561-498-7646
Kiniry, Joseph R., 106 Marilyn Way, Johnstown, 15904. Tel: 814-262-0135
Kline, Roy, Blessed Sacrament Cathedral, One Cathedral Sq., P.O. Box 33, Altoona, 16601. Tel: 814-944-1909
Lafferty, John J., 20 N. 12th St., Lemoyne, 17043. Tel: 717-612-9728
Mabon, Thomas K., 703 Lincoln-Lee Manor, 231 Walnut St., Johnstown, 15904. Tel: 814-535-2991
Madden, Thomas E., Garvey Manor, 128 Logan Blvd., 16648.
McCaa, Francis B., 311 Lincoln Dr., Martinsburg, WV 25401.
O'Toole, Anthony J., Garvey Manor Nursing Home, 128 Logan Blvd., 16648.
Panza, Paul D., P.A., Dmitri Manor, 1 St. Mary's Ln., 16648.
Pier, Joseph, 1776 Clapboard Run Rd., Johnstown, 15904.
Saylor, Philip, Mid Town Square, 310 S. Allen St., State College, 16801.
Wadas, Ignatius C., 221 Luray Ave., Johnstown, 15904. Tel: 814-266-8415
Walsh, Richard J., 1254 Lincoln Ave., P.O. Box 197, Tyrone, 16686. Tel: 814-684-2505
Revs.—
Becker, David R., 503 - 43 St., Altoona, 16602.
Boyle, John J., P.O. Box 159, Mill Hall, 17751.
Bunn, James F., 210 Ridge Ave., Apt. 8, Altoona, 16601. Tel: 814-949-5902
Cronauer, David, 1072 Carroll Rd., Patton, 16668.
Crosser, Raymond G., 100 Beckman Dr., 6F, Altoona, 16602.
Crouse, William S., R.R. 1 Box 24, Shirleysburg, 17260.
Dykas, Benjamin, 32 Knox St., Johnstown, 15906.
Ellias, John J., 118 Mechanic St., Everett, 15537.
George, J. Clark, Dmitri Manor, 2 St. Mary's Ln., 16648.
Greiner, Kenneth A., REAR 319 Cherry Ave., Altoona, 16601.
Joly, Henry L., P.O. Box 705, 16648.
Karr, Raymond E., 667 Murray Ave., Apt.113, Patton, 16668.
Knapik, Andrew G., P.O. Box 111, Bellefonte, 16823.
Kovach, William J., 1004 Holiday Hill Dr., Apt.1, 16648.
Leonardis, Charles F., 307 Seventh St., Winber, 15963.
Marshall, John J., Dmitri Manor, 6 St. Mary's Lane, 16648.
Michaels, Emmett T., Box 94, Accomac, VA 23301.
Myers, Regis F., Dmitri Manor, 10 St. Mary's Ln., 16648.
Orlando, John V., Garvey Manor Nursing Home, 128 Logan Blvd., 16648.
Pollack, Anthony, 513 - 27th Ave., Altoona, 16601.
Ream, Gerard J., P.O. Box 5002, Johnstown, 15906.
Stange, Henry A., P.O. Box 1133, Altoona, 16603.
Strittmatter, J. Joseph, Dmitri Manor, 8 St. Mary's Ln., 16648.

Permanent Deacons:
Beavers, Thomas T., Our Lady Queen of Angels, Central City
Buige, Thomas M., St. John Gualbert Cathedral, Johnstown
Cammarata, Samuel M., St. Andrew, Johnstown
Concannon, John J., Johnstown
Condor, Michael, Jr., Basilica of St. Michael, Loretto

Dalla Valle, Joseph R., (On Leave)
Gibson, Philip, St. Agnes, Lock Haven
Gillan, Garth J., Our Lady of Victory, State College
Ivantis, Laszlo P., Penn State Catholic Community
Janisko, Thaddeus J., St. Mary, Nanty Glo
Janosik, James, St. Elizabeth Ann Seton, Winber
Killoran, Bernard J., Good Shepherd, State College
Lapinski, David C., Our Lady of Victory, State College
Leap, James F., Blessed Sacrament Cathedral, Altoona
Luke, Steve A., St. Joseph, Coupon
Lux, Herman J., Holy Spirit, Beaverdale
Marchu, James F., SS. Timothy & Mark, Twin Rocks
Mazurkiewicz, Joseph F., Sr., St. John Evangelist, Bellefonte
Neral, Gene, St. John the Evangelist, Lakemont
Ondik, Michael A., Good Shepherd, State College
Papinchak, Thomas M., St. Gregory/St. Barnabas, Johnstown
Prien, R. Kenneth, Immaculate Conception, Lock Haven
Pyle, Jay A., All Saints, Boswell
Rys, John R., Cathedral of the Blessed Sacrament, Altoona
Schuette, Carl F., St. Thomas Apostle, Bedford
Sroka, John E., Visitation, Johnstown
Tiernan, John A., St. Mary, Holidaysburg
Underhill, William R., SS. Philip & James, Meyersdale; St. Gregory, MacDonaldton
Valerio, Pat N., St. Peter in Chains, SCI, Somerset
Wagner, Anthony E., Our Lady of the Mount, SCI, Rockview; Our Lady of Victory, State College
Weaver, Frederick F., St. Peter, Somerset
Zernick, Bernard J., Prince of Peace, Northern Cambria

INSTITUTIONS LOCATED IN THE DIOCESE

[A] COLLEGES AND UNIVERSITIES (NON-DIOCESAN)

CRESSON

Mount Aloysius College, 7373 Admiral Peary Hwy., 16630. Tel: 814-886-4131; Fax: 814-886-2978. Email: cmiller@mtaloy.edu. Web: www.mtaloy.edu. Sisters Mary Ann Dillon, R.S.M., Pres.; Virginia Bertschi, Asst. to the Pres. for Administrative Svcs.; Mr. Frank Crouse, Dean Enrollment Mgmt.; Dr. Ron Cromwell, Academic Dean; Dr. Dane R. Foust, Dean of Students; Rev. John J. Slovikovski, Chap. Sisters of Mercy Priests 1; Sisters 9; Lay Teachers 54; Total Staff 163; Students 2,000.

LORETTO

St. Francis University, P.O. Box 600, 15940-0600. Tel: 814-472-3001; Fax: 814-472-3003 Email: vsoyka@francis.edu. Web: www.francis.edu. Rev. Christian R. Oravec, T.O.R., Pres.; Dr. Richard Crawford, Asst. to the Pres.; Rev. Anthony J. De Conciliis, C.S.C., Vice Pres. Academic Affairs; Dr. F. Dennis Riegelnegg, Vice Pres. Student Devel.; Mr. Evan Lipp, Dean Enrollment Mgmt.; Mr. Kevin O'Flaherty, Vice Pres. Finance; Mr. Raymond Ponchione, Dir. Devel.; Mr. Randy Frye, Dir. M.B.A. Prog.; Dr. William Duryea, Dir. M.M.S. Prog.; Ms. Glenda Griffith, Dir. Residence Life; Ms. Patricia Serotkin, Dir. Library; Ms. Julie Barris, Dir. Career Devel.; Mr. George Pyo, Dir. Computer Svcs.; Dr. Philip Benham, Dir. Graduate School Human Resource Mgmt. & Industrial Rels.; Mr. Dominick Peruso, Dir. Student Activities; Ms. Denise Kovach, Dir. Learning Resource Center; Mr. Jeffrey Eisen, Dir. Athletics; Mr. David Wilson, Dir. Counseling; Revs. Kevin Queally, T.C.R.; John Mark Klaus, T.O.R.; Bradley LePage, T.O.R.; Daniel Sinisi, T.O.R.; Patrick Donahoe, T.O.R.; Bros. Gabriele Mary Amato, T.O.R.; Nathan Malavolti, T.O.R.; Malachi Van Tassell, T.O.R. Priests 6; Lay Professors 65; Students 2,012.

[B] HIGH SCHOOLS, DIOCESAN

JOHNSTOWN. *Bishop McCort High School*, 25 Osborne St., 15905. Tel: 814-536-8991; Fax: 814-535-4118. Email: mccort@nb.net. Web: www.mccort.org. Sr. Donna Marie Leiden, S.C., Prin. & Contact Person. Sisters 1; Lay Teachers 34; Students 516.

ALTOONA. *Bishop Guilfoyle High School*, 2400 Pleasant Valley Blvd., 16602. Tel: 814-944-4014; Fax: 814-944-8695. Email: llynch@dioceseaj.org. Web: www.bishopguilfoyle.org/index.html Rev. Leo A. Lynch, Prin.; Sr. Beverly Hmel, I.H.M., Asst. Prin. Priests 1; Sisters 1; Lay Teachers 27; Total Staff 49; Students 405.

EBENSBURG. *Bishop Carroll High School* 15931. Tel: 814-472-7500; Fax: 814-472-8020. Email: Bishopcarroll@USA.net. Web: diocesealtjtn.org. Mrs. Deborah L. Meckey, Prin. Sisters 1; Lay Teachers 24; Students 293.

[C] ELEMENTARY DIOCESAN SCHOOLS

JOHNSTOWN. *Central Catholic Elementary School*, (Grades PreK-8), 751 Railroad St., 15901. Tel: 814-536-1532; Fax: 814-536-0493. Email: centralcatholic@wpia.net. Mrs. Rosemary Batzel, Prin. & Contact Person. Consolidation of the following parishes: St. Clare of Assisi and St. John Gualbert. Lay Teachers 8; Students 100.

West End Catholic School, (Grades K-8), 317 Power St., 15906. Tel: 814-536-4722; Fax: 814-539-9343. Email: dstahl@dioceseaj.org. Mrs. Dee Ambrose-Stahl, Prin. Consolidation of the following parishes: St. Columba; St. Francis of Assisi; Immaculate Conception; St. Rochus; St. Stephen; St. Therese; Sts. Casimir and Emerich. Lay Teachers 9; Students 109.

ALTOONA. *Altoona Central Catholic School*, (Grades PreK-8), 1400 4th Ave., 16602. Tel: 814-944-1250; Fax: 814-944-1452. Email: altoonaccs@aol.com. Web: altoonacentralcatholic.org. Sisters 2; Lay Teachers 21; Students 347.

1300 13th St., 16601. Tel: 814-943-7423; Fax: 814-743-7609. Email: accs13st@aasdcat.com.

1012 8th Ave., 16602. Tel: 814-943-5931; Fax: 814-943-1837. Email: accs8ave@aasdcat.com.

1400 4th Ave., 16602. Tel: 814-944-1250; Fax: 814-944-1452. Email: altoonaccs@aol.com.

CRESSON. *All Saints Catholic School*, (Grades K-8), 220 Powell Ave., 16630. Tel: 814-886-7942; Fax: 814-886-7942. Email: allsaints@dioceseaj.org. Mrs. Susan Glass, Prin. Consolidation of the following parishes: St. Francis Xavier; St. Aloysius; St. Agnes; Our Lady of the Alleghenies; St. Thomas Aquinas; St. John the Baptist; St. Demetrius. Sisters 1; Lay Teachers 8; Students 140.

HOLLIDAYSBURG. *Hollidaysburg Consolidated Catholic Elementary School*, (Grades PreK-8), Spruce & Wayne Sts., P.O. Box 599, 16648. Tel: 814-695-6112; Fax 814-696-8960. Email: sab416@aol.com. Web: www.nb.net/~hcs/. Mr. Edward DiSabato, Prin. Consolidation of the following parishes: St. Michael's; St. Mary's. Lay Teachers 10; Students 225.

NICKTOWN. *Northern Cambria Catholic School*, 3278 Blue Goose Rd., P.O. Box 249, 15762. Tel: 814-948-8900; Fax: 814-948-8720. Email: nccs@northerncambria.org. Sr. Mary Lee Przybylski, C.S.S.F., Prin. Consolidation of the following parishes: St. Nicholas & Prince of Peace. Sisters 1; Lay Teachers 10; Students 133.

[D] GENERAL HOSPITALS (NON-DIOCESAN)

JOHNSTOWN

Good Samaritan Medical Center, 1020 Franklin St., 15905. Tel: 814-533-1000; Fax: 814-539-0264. Email: stucker@conemaugh.org. Sr. Rose Vogel, Staff Chap.; Mr. Steven E. Tucker, Pres. Skilled Nursing Care Center Beds 73; Patients Assisted Annually 225; Total Staff 56.

ALTOONA

Bon Secours - Holy Family Regional Health System, 2500 Seventh Ave., 16602. Tel: 814-944-1681; Fax: 814-949-5380. Email: david_cuzzolina@bshsi.com. Web: www.bonsecoursholyfamily.org. Daniel S. Duggan, CEO. Patients Assisted Annually 115,851; Total Assisted 138,245; Total Staff 743; Bed Capacity 182.

[E] HOMES FOR AGED (NON-DIOCESAN)

HOLLIDAYSBURG

Garvey Manor, 128 Logan Blvd., 16648. Tel: 814-695-5571; Fax: 814-695-8516. Web: www.garveymanor.org. Sr. M. Joachim Anne Ferenchak O.Carm., Admin. Carmelite Sisters for the Aged and Infirm 8; Aged Residents 150; Patients Assisted Annually 275; Total Staff 220.

St. Leonard's Home, Inc., 601 N. Montgomery St., 16648. Tel: 814-695-9581; Fax: 814-695-2606. Sr. Thea Krause, C.S.F.N., Exec. Dir.

Legal Title: *St. Leonard's Home, Inc.* Sisters of the Holy Family of Nazareth 2; Aged Residents 35; Total Staff 16; Total Assisted 35.

(DIOCESAN)

HOLLIDAYSBURG

Dmitri Manor Priests' Residence, St. Mary's Ln., 16648. Tel: 814-696-4698. Rev. Msgr. Robert J. Saly. Aged Residents 7; Staff 1.

[F] MONASTERIES AND RESIDENCES OF PRIESTS AND BROTHERS (NON-DIOCESAN)

HOLLIDAYSBURG

St. Joseph Friary, 501-503 Walnut St., 16648. Tel: 814-695-5802. Bros. Stephen P. Baker, T.O.R.; Bernard Dougherty, T.O.R., Supr.; Very Rev Canon Aloysius Hankinson, T.O.R.; Very Rev. Adalbert Wolski, T.O.R.

LORETTO

St. Bonaventure Friary, P.O. Box 155, 15940-0155. Tel: 814-472-9422; Fax: 814-472-3878. Revs. Laurence R. Uhlman, T.O.R., Dir. Novices; Richard L. Davis, T.O.R., Dir. Vocations. Priests 2; Novices 1; Postulants 2.

Mount Assisi Friary, P.O. Box 40, 15940. Tel: 814-472 5324; Fax: 814-471-1766. Email: edtor2@juno.com. Web: www.franciscansfor.org. Rev. Nicholas Polichnowski, T.O.R., Loretto Local Min. Tel: 814-472-5324, Ext. 302; Bro. Mark McBride, T.O.R., Vicar & Prov. Econome (APYC); Revs. Augustine Belinda, T.O.R.; Ronald Bodenschatz, T.O.R.; Patrick Donahoe, T.O.R.; Simon Mary Engler, T.O.R.; Kenneth Flaherty, T.O.R.; Bede Hines, T.O.R.; Bradley LePage, T.O.R.; John Mark Klaus, T.O.R.; Francis Moyher, T.O.R.; Daniel J. Mulkern, T.O.R.; Vincent Negherbon, T.O.R.; Christian R. Oravec, T.O.R., Pres. St. Francis Univ. Tel: 814-472-3001; Emil Resconich, T.O.R.; Daniel Sinisi, T.O.R.; Kevin Queally, T.O.R.; Andre Strittmatter, T.O.R.; John Wilger, T.O.R.; Bros. Gabriele Mary Amato, T.O.R.; Richard Gates, T.O.R.; Callistus Gerardi, T.O.R.; Damien Koehler, T.O.R.; Nathan Malavolti, T.O.R. Priests 18; Brothers 6.

NEWRY

St. Bernardine Monastery, P.O. Box 208, 16665. Tel: 814-695-3992; 814-695-8991; Fax: 814-695-1611. Email: gerard_tor@yahoo.com. Web: www.franciscanfriarstor.com. Revs. Gerard M. Connolly, T.O.R., Local Min. & Regl. Coord.; Camillus Angle, T.O.R.; Kenneth La Pan, T.O.R.; Alan Polimine, T.O.R.; Leonard Blostic, T.O.R.; Bro. Alexis Nagle, T.O.R. Priests 6.

Franciscan Development Office, P.O. Box 139, 16648. Tel: 814-695-3802; Fax: 814-695-1611. Email: broalexis@charter.net. Bro. Alexis Nagle, T.O.R., Dir. Devel. & Mass Association.

Province Econome's Office, P.O. Box 117, 16648. Tel: 814-696-3321; Fax: 814-695-1611. Rev. Gerard M. Connolly, T.O.R., Province Econome.

[G] CONVENTS AND RESIDENCES FOR SISTERS (NON-DIOCESAN)

ALTOONA

Our Lady of Perpetual Help Convent, 445 Baynton Ave., #A, 16602. Tel: 814-942-3819. Sisters, Servants of the Immaculate Heart of Mary Total in Residence 2; Total Staff 2.

St. John of the Cross Convent, 35 Seneca Ave., 16602. Tel: 814-942-5747; Fax: 814-942-8052. Email: lindalccw@cs.com. Carmelite Community of the Word Total in Residence 4.

JOHNSTOWN

St. Rochus Convent, 719 Chestnut St., 15901. Tel: 814-535-7118; Fax: 814-535-7145. Carmelite Community of the Word Total in Residence 4.

CRESSON

McAuley Hall, 4 College Dr., 16630-1900. Tel: 814-886-4159. Sr. M. Colman Krise, R.S.M., Coord. Institute of the Sisters of Mercy of the Americas (Silver Spring, MD) Total in Residence 20; Total Staff 10.

Sisters Servants of the Sacred Heart, Provincial House, 866 Cambria St., 16630-1713. Tel: 814-886-4223; Fax: 814-886-4735. Email: sscjusa@nb.net. Web: www.nb.net/~sscjusa. Sr. Clare Marie, S.S.C.J., Prov. Supr.

Personal Care Home Tel: 814-536-4546. Total in Residence 18; Total Staff 7.

EBENSBURG

Carmelite Community of the Word, St. Therese Convent, 218 W. Lloyd St., 15931. Tel: 814-472-9457; Fax: 814-472-5105. Email: ebensburgccw@aol.com. Total in Residence 2.

Mount St. Ann Retreat House and Novitiate, 1120 N. Center St., P.O. Box 328, 15931. Tel: 814-472-9354; Fax: 814-472-9354. Email: stann@cambrianews.com. Sr. Melany Pereira, S.S.A., Supr. Sisters of St. Ann Total in Residence 4.

GALLITZIN

Carmelite Community of the Word Administration Center, 394 Bem Rd., 16641. Tel: 814-886-4098; Fax: 814-886-5551. Email: incarnationctr@msn.com. Web: ccwsisters.org. Sr. Marilyn Welch, C.C.W., Admin. Gen. Total in Residence 2.

Little Sisters of Jesus, 347 Tunnel Hill St., 16641. Tel: 814-886-4679. Sr. Anne-Marie Boucher, Supr. Total in Residence 3.

LILLY

Family Life Office, 5379 Portage St., 15938. Tel: 814-886-5551; Fax: 814-886-7697. Email: famlifaj@aol.com. Web: www.diocesealtjtn.org. Mrs. Susan Stith, Family Life Dir. Total Staff 5; Total Assisted 13,200.

LORETTO

Carmel of St. Therese of Lisieux Monastery, P.O. Box 57, 15940. Tel: 814-472-8620. Sr. Teresa of Jesus, O.C.D., Prioress. Discalced Carmelite Nuns Nuns with Solemn Vows 9; Extern Professed 1; Nuns with Simple Vows 2; Candidates 1.

Our Lady of Loretto, 139 St. Ann St., P.O. Box 36, 15940. Tel: 814-472-2332. Sisters of Mercy Total in Residence 2.

MCCONNELLSBURG

Carmelite Community of the Word, Fulton County Mission, 110 S. Third St., 17223. Tel: 717-485-5917; 717-485-0661; Fax: 717-485-3855. Email: fccm@cun.net. Total in Residence 2.

PORTAGE

Sisters Servants of the Sacred Heart Novitiate, Sacred Heart Novitiate, 1872 Munster Rd., 15946. Tel: 814-886-7785. Sr. Jacinta Miryam, S.S.C.J., Novice Mistress. Sisters 6.

[H] CAMPUS MINISTRY

HOLLIDAYSBURG. *Campus Ministry* Altoona-Johnstown Diocese, 126A Logan Blvd., 16648. Tel: 814-693-1401; Fax: 814-695-8894. Email: tmcconn@dioceseaj.org. Mr. Thomas J. McConnell, Dir.

Juniata College, 17th & Moore St., Huntington, 16652. Tel: 814-641-3362 (Office); Fax: 814-641-3317. Rev. David J. Arseneault, Chap.

Lock Haven University (Lock Haven), Newman Center, 445 W. Main St., Lock Haven, 17745. Tel: 717-748-8592; Fax: 570-748-8592. Rev. Daniel J. O'Neill.

Mount Aloysius College (Cresson), 7373 Admiral Peary Hwy., Cresson, 16630. Tel: 814-886-6498; Fax: 814-886-2978. Sr. Benedict Joseph Watters, R.S.M., M.S., Dir.; Rev. John J. Slovikovski, Chap.

Penn State University, 205 Eisenhower Chapel, University Park, 16802. Tel: 814-865-4282; Fax: 814-863-7251. Email: shr13@psu.edu. Revs. Stephen R. Honeygosky, O.S.B., Chap.; David R. Griffin, O.S.B.

St. Francis College (Loretto), Loretto, 15940. Tel: 814-472-7000; Fax: 814-472-2776. Revs. John Mark Klaus, T.O.R., Campus Min. Tel: 814-472-3336; Bradley LePage, T.O.R. Tel: 814-472-3391; Kevin Queally, T.O.R. Tel: 814-472-3367; Daniel Sinisi, T.O.R., Campus Min. Tel: 814-472-2750.

University of Pittsburgh at Johnstown, 450 Schoolhouse Rd., Johnstown, 15904. Tel: 814-269-2007; Fax: 814-269-2014. Rev. David R. Rizzo, Chap.; Sr. Corinne Kirsch, C.S.J., Campus Min.

[I] NEWMAN CENTERS
(NON-DIOCESAN)

UNIVERSITY PARK

Penn State Catholic Community, 205 Pasquerilla Spiritual Center, 16802. Tel: 814-865-4281; Fax: 814-865-2972. Email: lcatholic@psu.edu. Web: www.psu.edu/catholic. Revs. Stephen R. Honeygosky, O.S.B., Dir.; David R. Griffin, O.S.B., Campus Min.; Deacon Laszlo P. Ivantis, Campus Min.; Rina Simpas, Campus Min. Catholic Students attending Penn State University 12,000; Total in Residence 3; Total Staff 10.

[J] MISCELLANEOUS LISTINGS
(NON-DIOCESAN)

ALTOONA

Second Century Scholarship Fund, Diocese of Altoona-Johnstown, 124 Logan Blvd., 16648. Tel: 814-695-5579; Fax: 814-695-8894. Email: lhartnet@dioceseaj.org. Web: www.secondcentury-fund.org. Mrs. Lori Hartnett, High School Devel. Dir.

BEDFORD

St. Mary's House of Greater Solitude, Passionist Community, 2970 Imlertown Rd., 15522-8101. Tel: 814-623-1796; Fax: 814-623-2457. Revs. Silvan Rouse, C.P., Supr.; Malachy McGill, C.P.; Howard Chirdon, C.P.; Albert Cabrera, C.P.

HOLLIDAYSBURG

Conference of Slovak Clergy, 126 Logan Blvd., 16648. Tel: 814-695-5579; Fax: 814-695-8894. Email: lubomir@dioceseaj.org. Most Rev. Joseph V. Adamec, Chm.; Rev. Msgr. Michael J. Chaback, Vice Chm.; Rev. Lubomir J. Strecok, Sec. The Conference was founded April 22, 1985, and incorporated on June 14, 2000. It associates priests and deacons of Slovak ancestry in the United States for the purposes of mutual pastoral support and financial assistance to those preparing themselves for ordained ministry of the churches in union with Rome, particularly those of Slovak ancestry.

LORETTO

American Parish Youth Center, Inc., P.O. Box 40, 15940. Tel: 814-472-9632; Fax: 814-472-5089. Email: framarco@aol.com.

Prince Gallitzin Chapel House (Diocesan) Tel: 814-472-5441; Fax: 814-472-5446. Email: mbecker253@aol.com. P.O. Box 99, 15940. Tel: 814-472-5441.

Office of Vocations

Office of Ongoing Formation of Clergy

NEW BALTIMORE

St. John The Baptist Retreat Center, P.O. Box 10, 15553. Tel: 814-733-2210; Fax: 814-733-2966. Total in Residence 1; Total Staff 7.

RELIGIOUS INSTITUTES OF MEN REPRESENTED IN THE DIOCESE

For further details refer to the corresponding bracketed number in the Religious Institutes of Men or Women section.

[0200]—*Benedictine Monks*—O.S.B.

[0470]—*The Capuchin Friars*—O.F.M.Cap.

[1000]—*Congregation of the Passion*—C.P.

[0480]—*Conventual Franciscans* (St. Anthony of Padua Prov.)—O.F.M.Conv

[0520]—*Franciscan Friars*—O.F.M.

[0560]—*Third Order Regular of Saint Francis* (Provs. of Sacred Heart, Immaculate Conception)—T.O.R.

RELIGIOUS INSTITUTES OF WOMEN REPRESENTED IN THE DIOCESE

[0100]—*Adorers of the Blood of Christ*—A.S.C.

[0315]—*Carmelite Community of the Word*—C.C.W.

[0330]—*Carmelite Sisters for the Aged and Infirm*—O.Carm.

[3710]—*Congregation of the Sisters of Saint Agnes*—C.S.A.

[0420]—*Discalced Carmelite Nuns*—O.C.D.

[1070-03]—*Dominican Sisters*—O.P.

[1170]—*Felician Sisters*—C.S.S.F.

[2330]—*Little Sisters of Jesus*—L.S.J.

[3630]—*Servants of the Most Sacred Heart of Jesus*—S.S.C.J.

[0570]—*Sisters of Charity of Seton Hill, Greensburg, Pennsylvania*—S.C.

[2575]—*Sisters of Mercy of the Americas* (Dallas Regional Community)—R.S.M.

[1620]—*Sisters of Saint Francis of Millvale, Pennsylvania*—O.S.F.

[3780]—*Sisters of Ss. Cyril and Methodius*—SS.C.M.

[3718]—*Sisters of St. Ann* (Italy)—S.S.A.

[3830]—*Sisters of St. Joseph*—C.S.J.

[1970]—*Sisters of the Holy Family of Nazareth*—C.S.F.N.

[3260]—*Sisters of the Precious Blood (Ohio)*—C.PP.S.

[2160]—*Sisters, Servants of the Immaculate Heart of Mary* (Scranton, PA)—I.H.M.

[4160]—*Vincentian Sisters of Charity*—V.S.C.

NECROLOGY

† Mattiello, Lucian C., (Retired)—Died May 6, 2003

† Mullen, Willian E., Central City, PA Our Lady Queen of Angels—Died May 14, 2003

† Vago, Giancarlo "John", Bedford, PA St. Thomas the Apostle—Died Dec. 14, 2002

Diocese of Amarillo

(Dioecesis Amarillensis)

Most Reverend

JOHN W. YANTA, D.D.

Bishop of Amarillo; ordained March 17, 1956; appointed Titular Bishop of Naratcata and Auxiliary Bishop of San Antonio October 27, 1994; consecrated December 30, 1994; appointed Bishop of Amarillo January 21, 1997; installed March 17, 1997.

Diocesan Pastoral Center: 1800 N. Spring St., P.O. Box 5644, Amarillo, TX 79117-5644. Tel: 806-383-2243; Fax: 806-383-8452.

Web: www.amarillodiocese.org

Most Reverend

LEROY T. MATTHIESEN, D.D., M.A., LITT.D.

Retired Bishop of Amarillo; ordained March 10, 1946; appointed March 25, 1980; ordained May 30, 1980; retired January 21, 1997. *Mailing Address: P.O. Box 5644, Amarillo, TX 79117-5664.*

ERECTED A DIOCESE BY POPE PIUS XI, AUGUST 25, 1926.

Square Miles 25,800.

Comprises that part of the State of Texas known as the Panhandle, and extending thence southward; bounded on the east by Oklahoma, and by the eastern county line of Childress and by the southern lines Childress, Hall, Briscoe, Swisher, Castro and Parmer Counties; the western boundary is the New Mexico state line from the southern line of Parmer County, Texas, northward to the northwestern corner of the Panhandle of Texas. There are 26 counties.

For legal titles of parishes and diocesan institutions, consult the Chancery Office.

STATISTICAL OVERVIEW

Personnel	
Bishop	1
Retired Bishops	1
Priests: Diocesan Active in Diocese	25
Priests: Diocesan Active Outside Diocese	5
Priests: Retired, Sick or Absent	15
Number of Diocesan Priests	45
Religious Priests in Diocese	10
Total Priests in Diocese	55
Extern Priests in Diocese	2
Ordinations:	
Transitional Deacons	1
Permanent Deacons in Diocese	51
Total Brothers	1
Total Sisters	106
Parishes	
Parishes	35
With Resident Pastor:	
Resident Diocesan Priests	19
Resident Religious Priests	6
Without Resident Pastor:	
Administered by Priests	9
Administered by Deacons	1
Missions	13
Professional Ministry Personnel:	
Brothers	1
Sisters	3
Lay Ministers	14
Welfare	
Homes for the Aged	1
Total Assisted	56
Day Care Centers	1
Total Assisted	127
Special Centers for Social Services	1
Total Assisted	35,000
Other Institutions	1
Total Assisted	4
Educational	
Diocesan Students in Other Seminaries	5
Total Seminarians	5
High Schools, Diocesan and Parish	1
Total Students	118
Elementary Schools, Diocesan and Parish	6
Total Students	675
Catechesis/Religious Education:	
High School Students	1,666
Elementary Students	4,102
Total Students under Catholic Instruction	6,566
Teachers in the Diocese:	
Sisters	12
Lay Teachers	126
Vital Statistics	
Receptions into the Church:	
Infant Baptism Totals	1,237
Adult Baptism Totals	122
Received into Full Communion	249
First Communions	1,351
Confirmations	1,304
Marriages:	
Catholic	179
Interfaith	44
Total Marriages	223
Deaths	331
Total Catholic Population	43,651
Total Population	432,190

Former Bishops—Most Revs. RUDOLPH ALOYSIUS GERKEN, D.D., ord. June 10, 1917; consecrated April 26, 1927; installed Bishop of Amarillo, April 28, 1927; elevated to the Metropolitan See of Santa Fe, NM, June 2, 1933; died March 2, 1943; ROBERT E. LUCEY, ord. May 14, 1916; consecrated May 1, 1934; installed May 16, 1934; elevated to the Metropolitan See of San Antonio, Jan. 22, 1941; LAURENCE J. FITZSIMON, D.D., ord. May 17, 1921; consecrated Oct. 22, 1941; installed Nov. 5, 1941; died July 2, 1958; JOHN L. MORKOVSKY, appt. Auxiliary of Amarillo, Dec. 22, 1955; named Bishop of Amarillo, Aug. 18, 1958; transferred to as Coadjutor Bishop of Galveston-Houston "cum jure successionis," April 16, 1963; LAWRENCE M. DEFALCO, D.D. (Retired), ord. June 11, 1942; appt. April 16, 1963; consecrated May 30, 1963; installed June 13, 1963; retired Aug. 28, 1979; died Sept. 22, 1979; LEROY T. MATTHIESEN, D.D., M.A., LITT.D (Retired), ord. March 10, 1946; appt. March 25, 1980; ord. Bishop, May 30, 1980; retired Jan. 21, 1997.

Diocesan Officials

Diocesan Pastoral Center—1800 N. Spring St., Amarillo, 79107. Tel: 806-383-2243; Fax: 806-383-8452. Web: www.amarillodiocese.org. *P.O. Box 5644, Amarillo, 79117-5644.*

Vicar General—Very Rev. MICHAEL P. COLWELL.

Moderator of the Curia—Rev. Msgr. HAROLD L. WALDOW.

Vicar of Clergy—Rev. Msgr. HAROLD L. WALDOW.

Vicars Forane—VACANT, South Deanery Rev. Msgr. HAROLD L. WALDOW, Central Deanery; Rev. JOHN VALDEZ, East Deanery; Rev. Msgr. HAROLD L. WALDOW, North Deanery.

Diocesan Tribunal—

Judicial Vicar—Rev. PHU T. PHAN.

Defender of the Bond—Rev. Msgr. JAMES C. GURZYNSKI (Retired).

Advocates—Rev. Msgrs. JOSEPH T. TASH; HAROLD L. WALDOW.

Notaries—Ms. CAROL SANFORD; Ms. SUSAN GARNER; Deacon FLOYD ASHELY.

Chancellor—Very Rev. MICHAEL P. COLWELL.

Vice Chancellor and Archivist—VACANT.

Executive Assistant to the Bishop—Deacon FLOYD ASHELY.

Diocesan Advisory Councils

Presbyteral Council—Rev. Msgr. JOSEPH T. TASH, Chm.; Revs. SCOTT RAEF, Vice Chm.; ROBERT BUSCH; Rev. Msgr. REX NICHOLL; Revs. FRANCISCO PEREZ; PHU PHAN, J.C.L.; HECTOR MADRIGAL. Bishop's Appointee: Rev. GABRIEL CARDIEL, O.F.M., Religious Rep. Ex Officio: Very Rev. MICHAEL P. COLWELL; Rev. Msgr. HAROLD L. WALDOW; Rev. JOHN VALDEZ.

College of Consultors—Rev. Msgrs. HAROLD L. WALDOW; JOHN MEYERS, V.F.; Rev. JOHN VALDEZ; Very Rev. MICHAEL P. COLWELL; Rev. PHU PHAN, J.C.L.

Diocesan Pastoral Council—Rev. Msgr. HAROLD L. WALDOW, Liaison.

Priests' Pension Plan Retirement Committee—Rev. Msgr. JOSEPH T. TASH; Revs. EDWARD SWEENEY; HECTOR MADRIGAL; ROBERT BUSCH.

Bishop's Appointee—Rev. Msgr. RAYMOND CROSIER.

Vocation Development Team—Very Rev. MICHAEL P. COLWELL, Dir.; Revs. JOHN VALDEZ; FRANCISCO PEREZ; SCOTT RAEF.

Deacon Director—Deacon BLAINE WESTLAKE.

Hispanic Diaconate Office—Rev. ADALBERTO RAMIREZ, O.F.M., Dir.

Diocesan Departments

Director of Youth—OSCAR GUZMAN.

Office for the Catholic Schools—BERNICE NOGGLER, Supt.

Christian Formation Commission—BERNICE NOGGLER, Dir.

Department of Communications—CATHY LEXA, Dir. Information & Editor ""The West Texas Catholic"; GENE BERING, Asst. Editor.

Department of Finances and Ecclesiastical Properties—

Fiscal Manager—PHIL WHITSON, Acting CFO.

Director of Administrative Services—PATSY GRAHAM.

Office of Development and Stewardship—NANCY KOONS, Dir., P.O. Box 1011, Canyon, 79015. Tel: 806-655-2556.

United Catholic Appeal—NANCY KOONS.

General Auxiliary Pastoral Services

Diocesan Attorney—FREDERICK J. GRIFFIN, 504 S. Polk, Amarillo, 79101.

Charter Board—

Promoter of Justice—Very Rev. MICHAEL P.

COLWELL. Email: mcolwell@amarillodiocese.org.
Victim Assistance Coordinator—BELINDA TAYLOR GONZALEZ, P.O. Box 5644, Amarillo, 79107. Tel: 806-372-7960; 806-383-2243; Fax: 806-383-8452.
Charter Review Board—LOUISE ROSS, Chm.; BELINDA TAYLOR GONZALEZ; FRANK JONES; DOROTHY GUGGEMOS; JIM ROGERS; ZEKE CASTRO. *Ex Officio*, Very Rev. MICHAEL P. COLWELL; Rev. Msgr. HAROLD L. WALDOW; FREDERICK J. GRIFFIN.
Coalition for Catholic Social Services - CCSS—VACANT.
Catholic Historical Society—EDITH DANILE, Pres.; MARGARET FERENCE, Museum Cur.
Rural Life Director—DALE ARTHO.
Holy Childhood Association—BERNICE NOGGLER.
Propagation of the Faith—Rev. MIECZYSLAW PRZEPIORA, O.Cist.
Rite of Christian Initiation of Adults Commission—BERNICE NOGGLER; Rev. Msgr. HAROLD L. WALDOW.

Auxiliary Pastoral Services for Laity

Diocesan Council of Catholic Women—Rev. Msgr. FRANCIS SMYER, Moderator (Retired); LINDA DOERFLER, 1200 S. Washington, Amarillo, 79102.
Director of Prison Ministry—Deacon MARK SEIDLITZ.
Engaged Encounter—Directors: Deacon BLAINE WESTLAKE; LOUISE WESTLAKE. Contact Couple: JENNY BALLARD; AGNES BALLARD. Tel: 806-353-0907.
Catholic Student Center at West Texas A & M University—Rev. SCOTT RAEF, Dir.-Chap., 2614 Fourth Ave., Canyon, 79015. Tel: 806-655-4345.
Scouting—Deacon ROBERT SMITH.
Serra Club—GERALD DILLER, Pres.
Natural Family Planning—SHELLEY SAMPLE, B.S., F.C.P., Coord. Tel: 806-379-9224.
Cursillo Movement—Rev. Msgr. HAROLD L. WALDOW, Spiritual Dir. Lay Directors: VICTORIA ROCHA; ROBERTO CASTRO.
A.C.T.S. Movement—Rev. Msgr. HAROLD L. WALDOW, Spiritual Dir.; Sr. M. THERESA ROZGA, S.C.S.J.A., Bishop DeFalco Retreat Center, 2100 N. Spring, Amarillo, 79107. Tel: 806-383-1811.
Family Life Commission—RITA DILLER.
Vicar for Religious—Sr. BERNADETTE BLACK, S.S.S.F., Sancta Maria Convent, P.O. Box 906, Pampa, 79068-0906. Tel: 806-537-3182.
Office for the Permanent Diaconate—Deacon BLAINE WESTLAKE, Coord.
Hispanic Diaconate Office—Rev. ADALBERTO RAMIREZ, O.F.M.
Continuing Education of Clergy—Rev. Msgr. HAROLD L. WALDOW.
Priests' Retirement—PATSY GRAHAM.

CLERGY, PARISHES, MISSIONS AND PAROCHIAL SCHOOLS

CITY OF AMARILLO
(POTTER COUNTY)

1—SACRED HEART CATHEDRAL, Closed., This parish ceased to exist 1/19/75. For inquiries contact the Diocese of Amarillo: P.O. Box 5644, Amarillo, TX 79117-5644. Tel: 806-383-2243.

2—BLESSED SACRAMENT, Rev. Francisco Perez; Deacons Mark Seidlitz; Willy Montano.
Res.: 4112 S.E. 25th St., 79103. Tel: 806-374-1132; Fax: 806-372-3631.
Catechesis/Religious Program—Bernice Noggler, D.R.E. Students 89.

3—ST. FRANCIS, Rev. John Dalton; Deacon James R. Ambs.
Res.: 5005 Klinke Rd., 79108-9628. Tel: 806-335-1872.
Catechesis/Religious Program—Evelyn Detten, D.R.E.; Judy Tomlinson, D.R.E. Students 54.

4—ST. HYACINTH'S, Rev. Patrick Carathers.
Res.: 4500 W. Hills Tr., 79106. Tel: 806-358-1351; Fax: 806-467-1708.
Catechesis/Religious Program—Sr. Pauline Brorman, O.S.F., D.R.E. Students 68.

5—ST. JOSEPH'S, Rev. Msgr. Raymond Crosier; Deacon Wilbur Mason.
Res.: 4122 Bonham St., 79110. Tel: 806-355-5621; Fax: 806-355-5622.
School— See Elementary Schools, City Wide under Institutions Located in the Diocese.
School—St. Joseph Day Care Center, 4108 Bonham, 79110. Tel: 806-359-1604. Students 102.
Catechesis/Religious Program—Sr. Mary Paul, S.S.S.F., D.R.E.; Sr. Colette Fiore, S.S.S.F., D.R.E. Students 190.

6—ST. LAURENCE CATHEDRAL, Revs. Gabriel Cardiel, O.F.M.; Federico Hernandez, O.F.M.; Adalberto Ramirez, O.F.M.; Bro. Joel Rodriguez Vivar, O.F.M.; Deacons Leo Ramos; Pete Valdez.
Res.: 2300 N. Spring St., 79107. Tel: 806-383-2261; Fax: 806-383-2266.
Catechesis/Religious Program—Students 273.

7—ST. MARTIN DE PORRES MISSION, Rt. Rev. Abbott Lewis Hacker, O.S.B.
Res.: P.O. Box 3381, 79116. Tel: 806-376-8871.

8—ST. MARY'S, Rev. Msgr. Harold L. Waldow; Deacons Floyd Ashely; Robert Smith. In Res., Rev. Msgr. Francis Smyer, Pastor Emeritus (Retired); Rev. Jose Gomez.
Res.: 1200 Washington St., 79102. Tel: 806-376-7204; Fax: 806-376-7972.
School— See Elementary Schools, City Wide under Institutions Located in the Diocese.
Catechesis/Religious Program—Kim Hoelscher, D.R.E. Students 325.

9—OUR LADY OF GUADALUPE, Rev. Msgr. Rex Nichol; Deacon Hector Gallegos. In Res., Rev. Moses Kallarackal, C.M.I.
Res.: 1210 E. 11th Ave., 79102. Tel: 806-372-1128; Fax: 806-372-2225.
School— See Elementary Schools, City Wide under Institutions Located in the Diocese.
Catechesis/Religious Program—Martha Loza, D.R.E. Students 640.

10—OUR LADY OF VIETNAM, Rev. Joseph M. Phan Nam.
Res.: 2001 N. Grand, 79107. Tel: 806-383-0467; Fax: 806-383-0467.
Catechesis/Religious Program—Students 90.

11—ST. THOMAS THE APOSTLE, Rev. Msgr. Joseph T. Tash; Deacons Terry Pevehouse; Timothy Reid; Blaine Westlake; Bill Hastings.
Res.: 4100 Coulter Dr., 79109. Tel: 806-358-2461; Fax: 806-358-2529.
Catechesis/Religious Program—Eileen Dolan, D.R.E. Students 530.

OUTSIDE THE CITY OF AMARILLO

BORGER, HUTCHINSON CO., ST. JOHN THE EVANGELIST, Rev. Msgr. Norbert Kuehler; Rev. Jose Gomez, Sacramental Min.; Deacon Zeferino Jimenez.
Res.: 201 St. John's Rd., 79007. Tel: 806-274-7064.
Catechesis/Religious Program—Patty Ann Knapp, D.R.E. Students 191.
Mission—St. Ann's Stinnett, Hutchinson Co.

BOVINA, PARMER CO., ST. ANN'S, Rev. Juan Carlos Barragan; Deacon Jose Luis Velo.
Res.: Box 657, 79009. Tel: 806-238-1511.
Catechesis/Religious Program—Nancy Schwertner, D.R.E. Students 176.

CANADIAN, HEMPHILL CO., SACRED HEART, Revs. John Valdez; David Contreras; Deacon Jose Jesus Gutierrez.
Res.: 801 W. 23rd, Pampa, 79065. Tel: 806-665-2840; Fax: 806-323-9643.
Church: 721 Main, P.O. Box 786, 79014. Tel: 806-323-9705.
Catechesis/Religious Program—Students 51.
Mission—St. Mary Wheeler, Collingsworth Co.

CANYON, RANDALL CO., ST. ANN'S, Rev. Phu T. Phan; Deacons August Hesse III; Mauro Hernandez; Gabriel Rivas.
Mailing Address: P.O. Box 59, 79015.
Res.: 605 38th St., 79015. Tel: 806-655-3302; Fax: 806-655-3384.
Catechesis/Religious Program—Ms. Carol Sanford, D.R.E. Students 192.

CHILDRESS, CHILDRESS CO., HOLY ANGELS, Rev. Hector Madrigal.
Res.: 308 Ave. B, S.W., P.O. Box 608, 79201. Tel: 940-937-3946; Fax: 940-937-3946.
Catechesis/Religious Program—Students 75.

CLARENDON, DONLEY CO., ST. MARY'S, Rev. Jose Palathara, C.M.I.; Deacon John Nino, Parish Life Coord.
Res.: 815 McClelland St., P.O. Drawer C, 79226. Tel: 806-874-3910.

DALHART, HARTLEY CO., ST. ANTHONY'S, Rev. Robert Busch, Parochial Admin.; Deacon Ronald Hein.
Res.: 411 Texas Blvd., Box 1029, 79022. Tel: 806-244-4128; Fax: 806-244-7128.
School—1302 Oak St., 79022. Tel: 806-244-4811; Fax: 806-244-4811. Sr. Mary Clare Jones, Prin. School Sisters of the Third Order of St. Francis 3; Lay Teachers 4; Students 48.
Mission—St. Mary's Texline, Dallum Co.

DIMMITT, CASTRO CO., IMMACULATE CONCEPTION, Revs. Fern Couture, S.P.; Ken Keller; Deacon Joseph Ortega.
Res.: 710 W. Halsell St., 79027. Tel: 806-647-4219 (Church); 806-647-0105 (Office).
Catechesis/Religious Program—Mary Helen Flores, D.R.E. Students 220.
Mission—St. John's Hart, Castro Co. Revs. Scott Raef; Guadalupe Mayorga; Deacon Robert Gonzalez.

DUMAS, MOORE CO., SS. PETER AND PAUL, Revs. Bernardo Gonzalez, O.F.M.; Rafael Garcia, O.F.M.; Deacon Joseph A. Schwertner.
Res.: Box 503, 79029. Tel: 806-935-5002; Fax: 806-934-3382.
Catechesis/Religious Program—Eva Gresham, D.R.E. Students 300.
Mission—Christ the King P.O. Box 681, Sunray, Moore Co. 79086. Deacon Wayne Norrell.

FRIONA, PARMER CO., ST. TERESA OF JESUS, Rev. Edward Sweeney.
Res.: HCR 2, Box 1B, 79035-9601. Tel: 806-250-2871; Fax: 806-250-3549.
Catechesis/Religious Program—Lourdes Benavides, D.R.E.; Alma Rivera, D.R.E.; Maria Loya, D.R.E. Students 244.

GROOM, CARSON CO., IMMACULATE HEART OF MARY, [CEM] Rev. Jose Palathara, C.M.I.
Res.: 411 Ware Ave., P.O. Box 130, 79039. Tel: 806-248-7584.
Catechesis/Religious Program—Students 57.

GRUVER, HANSFORD CO., CRISTO REDENTOR, Rev. Guillermo Morales.
Res.: 603 Main St., P.O. Box 238, 79040. Tel: 806-733-5236.
Catechesis/Religious Program—Elena Salazar, D.R.E. Students 50.

HAPPY, SWISHER CO., HOLY NAME OF JESUS, [CEM] Rev. Msgr. Mario Stortz.
Res.: 317 W. Main, P.O. Box 128, 79042. Tel: 806-558-2871.
Catechesis/Religious Program—Students 20.

HEREFORD, DEAF SMITH CO.

1—ST. ANTHONY'S, Unassigned.
Business Office—114 Sunset Dr.. Tel: 806-364-6150; Fax: 806-364-0969.
Res.: 115 N. 25 Mile Ave., 79045. Tel: 806-364-2793; Fax: 806-364-0969.
School—120 W. Park Ave., 79045. Tel: 806-364-1952. Ann Lueb, Prin. Franciscan Sisters of Mary Immaculate 2; Lay Teachers 12; Students 132.
Catechesis/Religious Program—Students 225.
Convent—114 Sunset, 79045. Tel: 806-364-3344.

2—SAN JOSE, Rev. Msgr. John Meyers, V.F. (DAL); Deacons Emilio Fuentes; Vicente H. Garcia.
Res.: 735 Brevard, 79045. Tel: 806-364-5053; Fax: 806-364-2880.
Catechesis/Religious Program—Tel: 806-364-5053. Students 190.

MEMPHIS, HALL CO., SACRED HEART, Rev. Hector Madrigal; Deacon John Nino, Parish Life Coord.
Mailing Address: 213 N. Third St., P.O. Box 239, 79245. Tel: 806-259-2178.
Catechesis/Religious Program—Mrs. Juanita Garza, D.R.E. Students 45.

NAZARETH, CASTRO CO., HOLY FAMILY, Rev. John Hickey; Deacons Jerome Brockman; Alfonse A. Maurer.
Res.: 210 St. Joseph, P.O. Box 100, 79063. Tel: 806-945-2616; Fax: 806-945-2564.
Catechesis/Religious Program—Gladys Fortenberry, D.R.E. Students 130.

PAMPA, GRAY CO., ST. VINCENT DE PAUL, Rev. John Valdez. In Res., Rev. David Contreras.
Res.: 810 W. 23rd St., 79065. Tel: 806-665-8933; Fax: 806-665-2840.
School—2300 N. Hobart, 79065. Tel: 806-665-5665. Students 40.
Catechesis/Religious Program—Students 155.

PANHANDLE, CARSON CO., ST. THERESA, Rev. John Hickey.
Res.: P.O. Box 366, 79068. Tel: 806-537-3677.
Catechesis/Religious Program—Karen Berry, D.R.E. Students 82.

PERRYTON, OCHILTREE CO., IMMACULATE CONCEPTION, Rev. Msgr. Joseph Bixenman, Parish Admin.
Res.: 1000 S.W. 15th Ave., 79070. Tel: 806-435-3802; Fax: 806-648-1490.
Catechesis/Religious Program—Amber Harges, D.R.E. Students 251.
Mission—St. Peter Booker, Lipscomb Co.

SPEARMAN, HANSFORD CO., SACRED HEART, Rev. Guillermo Morales; Deacon Jim Brown.
Res.: 901 S. Roland, P.O. Box 127, 79081. Tel: 806-659-2166; Fax: 806-659-1042.
Catechesis/Religious Program—Davin Winger, D.R.E. Students 100.
Mission—Cristo Redentor P.O. Box 238, Gruver, Hansford Co. 79040.

STRATFORD, SHERMAN CO., ST. JOSEPH'S, Rev. Darryl Birkenfeld; Deacon Willie F. Artho.
Mailing Address: Box 28, 79084. Tel: 806-366-5687.
Catechesis/Religious Program—Johnny Garza, D.R.E. Students 115.
Mission—Our Lady of Guadalupe Box 28, Cactus, Sherman Co. 79084. Tel: 806-396-5687. Deacon Vacilio Anaya.

TULIA, SWISHER CO., CHURCH OF THE HOLY SPIRIT, Revs. Scott Raef; Guadalupe Mayorga.
Res.: 513 S. Austin, P.O. Box 25, 79088. Tel: 806-995-3191; Fax: 806-995-3286.
Catechesis/Religious Program—Martha Rocha, D.R.E. Students 215.
Mission—Our Lady of Loreto P.O. Box 47, Silverton, Briscoe Co. 79257. Rev. Jose Gomez, Sacramental

Min.; Deacon Joseph Frausto, Parish Life coord.
Mission—St. Paul the Apostle P.O. Box 231, Kress, Swisher Co. 79052. Tel: 806-823-2548. Rev. Guadalupe Mayorga.
Station—Quitaque, Tel: 806-823-2548. Lupe Reyes, Pastoral Asst.

UMBARGER, RANDALL CO., ST. MARY'S, [CEM] Rev. Mieczyslaw Przepiora, O.Cist.
Res.: P.O. Box 105, 79091. Tel: 806-499-3531.
Catechesis/Religious Program—Students 68.

VEGA, OLDHAM CO., IMMACULATE CONCEPTION, Rev. Mieczyslaw Przepiora, O.Cist., Parish Life Coord.
Res.: P.O. Box 250, 79092. Tel: 806-267-0154.
Catechesis/Religious Program—Michelle Baca, D.R.E. Students 57.

WELLINGTON, COLLINGSWORTH CO., OUR MOTHER OF MERCY, Rev. Cal Stalter; Deacon Pedro Juarez.
Church: 1108 Floydada, P.O. Box 686, 79095. Tel: 806-256-5358; Fax: 806-256-2829.
Mission—St. Patrick Shamrock, Wheeler Co. Rev. Cal Stalter, Admin.

WHITE DEER, CARSON CO., SACRED HEART, Rev. Moses Kallarackal, C.M.I. In Res., Rev. Msgr. Kevin Hand, Pastor Emeritus (Retired).
Res.: Box 427, 79097. Tel: 806-883-4781.
Catechesis/Religious Program—Margie Bichsel, D.R.E. Students 67.

Absent on Leave:
Revs.—
Birkenfeld, Darryl
Castillo, Domingo
Guidry, Dale
Lindley, Philip

On Duty Outside the Diocese:
Revs.—
Afunugo, Emmanuel, D.D.
Busch, Robert
Greka, David
Jaramillo, Peter
Rosolen, Emil
Xavier, Alverez

Retired:
Rev. Msgrs.—
Corcoran, Clifton J., P.O. Box 1179, Panhandle, 79068.
Erpen, B.A., 318 S.E. Fifth, Tulia, 79088.
Gurzynski, James C., 2229 Loucust, 79109.
Hand, Kevin
Malnar, Matthew
Matthiesen, Monroe J.
Smyer, Francis, St. Mary's, 1400 S. Washington, 79102.
Revs.—
Burke, Terry
Chen, Raphael, 9170 Graham, Cypress, CA 90630.
Choong, Norbert, 5906 Aspen Ave., N.E., Albuquerque, NM 87110.
Kieferle, Norbert
Kieran, Edward, Ireland
Pawlak, Ed, 5431 Denise Ave., Orlando, FL 32810-3609.
Sherry, Brendan, Ireland
Stein, Jerry, P.O. Box 159, Nazareth, 79063.

Permanent Deacons:
Ambs, James R., Prison Ministry - St. Francis, Amarillo
Anaya, Vasilio, Sts. Peter and Paul Church, Dumas; Our Lady of Guadalupe, Cactus
Artho, Kenneth, (Inactive)
Artho, Willie F., St. Joseph's Church, Stratford
Ashely, Floyd, St. Mary's Church, Amarillo
Blunt, Orvel Ray, (On Leave of Absence)
Brock, Kenneth, Church of the Holy Spirit, Tulia
Brockman, Jerome, Holy Family, Nazareth
Brown, Jim, Sacred Heart Church, Spearman
Campos, Tony, (On Leave of Absence)
Castillo, Esteban, (On Leave of Absence)
Cloud, Jonny E., St. Anthony Church, Hereford
Correa, Jose, St. Teresa's Church, Friona
Dollins, Belvin G., (Retired)
Dorsey, Bill, St. Ann's, Canyon; St. Mary's, Umbarger
Frausto, Joseph, Our Lady of Lorreto, Silverton
Fuentes, Emilio, Sr., San Jose Church, Hereford
Gallegos, Hector, Our Lady of Guadalupe Church, Amarillo
Garcia, Vicente H., San Jose Church, Hereford
Gonzales, Roberto, St. John, Hart
Grossman, Jerry, (On Leave of Absence)
Guerrero, Jesse, (Admin. Leave)
Gutierrez, Jose Jesus, Sacred Heart Church, Canadian
Gutierrez, Robert, (Retired)
Hastings, Bill, (On Duty Outside the Diocese)
Hein, Ronald, St. Anthony's Church, Dalhart
Hernandez, Mauro, St. Ann's Church, Canyon
Hesse, August, III, St. Ann's Church, Canyon
Jimenez, Zeferino, St. John's Church, Borger
Jordan, Bill, (On Duty Outside the Diocese)
Keller, Robert C., Diocese of Galveston-Houston
Mason, Wilbur, St. Joseph's Church, Amarillo
Maurer, Alfonse A., Holy Family Nazareth
Montano, Willy, Blessed Sacrament Church, Amarillo
Nino, John, Sacred Heart, Memphis
Norrell, Wayne, Christ the King Church, Sunray
Ortega, Joseph, (Retired)
Perez, Amadeo, (Retired)
Pevehouse, Terry, St. Thomas the Apostle Church, Amarillo
Ramos, Leo, St. Laurence Cathedral, Amarillo
Reid, Timothy, St. Thomas Church, Amarillo
Riley, Richard D., (Retired)
Rivas, Gabriel, St. Ann's Church, Canyon
Rose, Daniel, Diocese of Tyler
Ruiz, Jesse P., Diocese of Fort Worth
Schwertner, Joseph A., SS. Peter & Paul Church, Dumas
Seidlitz, Mark, Blessed Sacrament Church, Amarillo
Smith, Robert, St. Mary's Church, Amarillo
Valdez, Pete, St. Laurence Cathedral, Amarillo
Velo, Joe, St. Ann's Church, Bovina; Immaculate Conception Church, Dimmitt
Westlake, Blaine, St. Thomas Church, Amarillo

INSTITUTIONS LOCATED IN THE DIOCESE

[A] HIGH SCHOOLS, CITY-WIDE

AMARILLO. *Holy Cross Catholic Academy* (Coed) , 4114 S. Bonham, 79110-1113. Tel: 806-355-9637; Fax: 806-353-9520. Email: hcca124@swbell.net. Web: www.holycrosscatholicacademy.org. Rev. Moses Kallarackal, C.M.I. Lay Teachers 14; Students 68; Lay Teachers 14; Students 50.

[B] ELEMENTARY SCHOOLS, CITY-WIDE

AMARILLO. *St. Joseph's School*, 4118 Bonham St., 79110. Tel: 806-359-1604; Fax: 806-355-5622. Email: stjosephelem@catholicexchange.com. Web: www.rc.net/amarillo/stjosephschool. Sr. Mary Paul Friemel, O.S.F., Prin. Priests 1; Sisters 2; Lay Teachers 8; Students 130.

St. Laurence Cathedral School (Temporarily Suspended) , 2300-B N. Spring St., 79107. Tel: 806-383-7155; Fax: 806-383-2266. Thomas Salzar, Prin. Lay Teachers 3; Students 32.

St. Mary School and St. Mary's Montessori Preschool, 1200 S. Washington, 79102. Tel: 806-376-9112; Fax: 806-376-9112. Email: 1reynolds@stmarysamarillocom. Lea Reynolds, Prin. Sisters 1; Lay Teachers 18; Students 255.

Our Lady of Guadalupe School, 1108 S. Houston, 79102. Tel: 806-372-2629; Fax: 806-372-2225. Simon Camarillo II, Prin. Lay Teachers 6; Students 86.

[C] HOMES FOR THE AGED

PANHANDLE. *St. Ann's Nursing Home*, P.O. Box 1179, 79068. Tel: 806-537-3194; Fax: 806-537-3003. Email: stannsnh@amaonline.com. Jimmie sue Chisum, Admin.

St. Joseph's Home for Retired Priests, P.O. Box 1179, 79068. Rev. Msgrs. Clifton J. Corcoran, Pastor Emeritus (Retired); Monroe J. Matthiesen, Dir. & Pastor Emeritus (Retired); Rev. Patrick Hoffman.

[D] COALITION OF CATHOLIC SOCIAL SERVICES

AMARILLO. **Catholic Family Service, Inc.*, 200 S. Tyler, 79101. Tel: 806-376-4571; Fax: 806-345-7911. Email: cfs@arn.net. Web: www.catholicfamilyservice.org. Box 15127, 79105-5127. Al Bednorz, Exec. Dir.

**Another Chance Houses, Inc.*, 209 S. Jackson, 79101. Tel: 806-372-3344. Dale Botts, Dir.

Downtown Women's Center, Inc., 409 S. Monroe, 79101. Tel: 806-373-6879. Email: dwcenter@arn.net. Diane Gilmore, Exec. Dir.

[E] CATHOLIC CHILDREN'S DEVELOPMENT CENTERS

AMARILLO. *Amarillo Catholic Children's Development Centers*

St. Joseph Campus, 4108 Bonham St., P.O. Box 19726, 79114. Tel: 806-383-4411. Theresa Pigott, Dir. Teachers 5; Caregivers 11; Students 102.

[F] RETREAT HOUSE

AMARILLO. *Bishop DeFalco Retreat Center*, 2100 N. Spring St., 79107. Tel: 806-383-1811; Fax: 806-383-6919. Email: bdrc@ls.net. Web: www.bdrc.org. Sisters M. Theresa Rozga, S.C.S.J.A., Dir.; Mary Cecilia Tagliavia; Deacon Robert Smith, Asst. Dir. & Business Mgr.

Bishop DeFalco Retreat Center Foundation

CHANNING. *Prayer Town Emmanuel Retreat House*, P.O. Box 17, 79018-0017. Tel: 806-534-2312; Fax: 806-534-2223. Web: www.amamatrix.com/dljc. Sr. Joan Rodriguez, Coord. The Disciples of the Lord Jesus Christ

[G] CONVENTS AND RESIDENCES FOR SISTERS

AMARILLO. *St. Francis Convent, Novitiate and U.S. Provincial House*, 4301 N.E. 18th, 79107 Tel: 806-383-5769; Fax: 806-383-6545. Email: francpro@worldnet.att.net. Web: www.members.cox.net/franciscansistersofmaryimmaculate. Sr. Rosa Gonzalez, F.M.I., Prov. Supr. Franciscan Sisters of Mary Immaculate of the Third Order of St. Francis Sisters 36.

St. Francis Mission Community, O.S.F., LaVerna Convent, 203 S. Avondale, 79106. Tel: 806-352-2981; Fax: 806-863-4906. Email: franciscan@door.net. Sr. Mary Jane Alaniz, O.S.F., Prov., Lubbock House. Sisters 4.

Madres Clarisas Capuchinas, Capuchin Nuns of St. Clare, 4201 N.E. 18th Ave., 79107. Tel: 806-383-9877. Sr. Theresa Cortes, O.S.C., Abbess. Convent of the Blessed Sacrament and Our Lady of Guadalupe. Professed Nuns 14; Apostulants 3.

CANYON. *St. Benedict's Monastery*, 17825 S. Western, 79015. Tel: 806-655-9317; Fax: 806-655-9736. Email: nuns@osbcanyontx.org. Web: www.osbcanyontx.org. Sr. Mary Hawkins, O.S.B., Supr. Sisters 6.

CHANNING. *Disciples of the Lord Jesus Christ*, P.O. Box 17, 79018-0017. Tel: 806-534-2312; Fax: 806-534-2223. Email: sisters@dljc.org. Web: www.dljc.org. Sr. Lucy Lukasiewicz, Supr. Gen.

DALHART. *St. Anthony's Convent*, 1301 Oak Ave., 79022. Tel: 806-244-2390; Fax: 806 244-4811. Email: stanthon@xit.net. School Sisters of St. Francis Sisters 3.

HEREFORD. *St. Anthony's Convent*, 114 Sunset Dr., 79045. Tel: 806-364-3344. Franciscan Sisters of Mary Immaculate Sisters 2.

PANHANDLE. *Sancta Maria Convent (North American Region and Novitiate)*, P.O. Box 906, 79068-0906. Tel: 806-537-3182; Fax: 806-537-3479. Email: schsrs@amaonline.com. Web: www.members.amaonline.com/schsrspanhandle. Sr. Bernadette Black, S.S.S.F., Regl. Supr. School Sisters of the Third Order of St. Francis Sisters 24.

[H] CAMPUS MINISTRY

CANYON. *Catholic Student Center at West Texas A & M University* 2610 Fourth Ave., 79015. Tel: 806-655-4345; Fax: 806-655-0534. Email: cscwtamu@arn.net. Web: www.wtcsc.org. Rev. Scott Raef, Chap. & Dir.; Amy Reid, Prog. Dir.

[I] MISCELLANEOUS LISTINGS

AMARILLO. *Amarillo Catholic School System*, 1800 N. Spring St., 79109. Tel: 806-383-2243, Ext. 110; Fax: 806-383-8452. Email: bnoggler@amarillodiocese.org.

Amarillo Scholarship Endowment and Assistance Fund, 1800 N. Spring St., 79107. Tel: 806-383-2243; Fax: 806-383-8452.

Engaged Encounter, 3600 Torre, 79109. Tel: 806-352-2607. Deacon Blaine Westlake, Dir.; Louise Westlake, Dir.; Jenny Ballard, Contact. Tel: 806-353-0907; Agnes Ballard, Contact.

Holy Family Parish of Nazareth, Texas Endowment Foundation, Diocese of Amarillo, 1800 N. Spring St., 79107. Tel: 806-383-2243; Fax: 806-383-8452. Email: pwhitson@amarillodiocese.org. Phil Whitson, Acting CFO; Most Rev. John W. Yanta, Bd.

Marriage Encounter, 1800 N. Spring, 79107. Email: pvkrat@msn.com. Very Rev. Michael P. Colwell; Patrick Kratochvil, Ecclesiastical Team; Virginia Kratochvil, Ecclesiastical Team.

Monsignor B.A. Erpen Trust Fund (1985), Diocese of Amarillo, 1800 N. Spring, 79107. Tel: 806-383-2243; Fax: 806-383-8452. Email: joelo2046@dellnet.com. Joe Ingraham, CFO; Rev. Msgr. B.A. Erpen, Trustee Chm. (Retired); Most Rev. John W. Yanta, Trustee; Rev. Msgrs. Kevin Hand, Trustee (Retired); Harold L. Waldow, Trustee.

Project Solidarity (1999), Diocese of Amarillo, 1800 N. Spring, 79107. Tel: 806-383-2243; Fax: 806-383-8452. Email: mcolwell@amarillodiocese.org. Very Rev. Michael P. Colwell, Chancellor.

Roman Catholic Diocese of Amarillo Deposit and

Loan Fund, P.O. Box 5644, 79117. Tel: 806-383-2243; Fax: 806-383-8452. Email: pwwhitson@amarillodiocese.org. Phil Whitson, Acting CFO; Most Rev. John W. Yanta; Very Rev. Joseph E. Bixenman.

Texas Panhandle Catholic Endowment Foundation (1985), 1800 N. Spring, 79107. Tel: 806-383-2243; Fax: 806-383-8452. Email: jingraham@amarillodiocese.org. Most Rev. John W. Yanta, D.D., Trustee; Robert Neslage, Trustee; Ed Wieck, Trustee; Frank Walsh, Trustee; Ed Lewis, Trustee; Daniel Martinez, Trustee; Dr. Anh My Do, Trustee.

RELIGIOUS INSTITUTES OF MEN REPRESENTED IN THE DIOCESE

For further details refer to the corresponding bracketed number in the Religious Institutes of Men or Women section.

[0275]—*Carmelite of Mary Immaculate*—C.M.I.
[0340]—*Cistercian Fathers*—O.Cist.
[0450]—*Congregacion De Jesus Y Maria*—C.J.M.
[]—*Congregation of Mother Coredemptrix*—C.M.C.
[1040]—*Piarist Fathers*—SCH.P.
[]—*Provincia de los SS. Francisco and Santiago* (Mexico)—A.R.

RELIGIOUS INSTITUTES OF WOMEN REPRESENTED IN THE DIOCESE

[0230]—*Benedictine Sisters of Pontifical Jurisdiction* (Little Rock, AR)—O.S.B.
[0460]—*Congregation of the Sisters of Charity of the Incarnate Word*—C.C.V.I.
[0965]—*Disciples of the Lord Jesus Christ*—D.L.J.C.
[1500]—*Franciscan Sisters of Mary Immaculate of the Third Order of St. Francis of Assisi*—F.M.I.
[]—*Franciscan Sisters of Perpetual Adoration*—F.F.P.A.
[]—*Missionary Catechist Sisters of St. Joseph* (Mexico)—O.F.M.
[1695]—*School Sisters of the Third Order of St. Francis, (Panhandle, Texas)*—O.S.F.
[0600]—*Sisters of Charity of St. Joan Antida*—S.C.S.J.A.
[1705]—*Sisters of the Third Order of St. Francis of Assisi*—O.S.F.
[]—*St. Clare Capuchin Sisters*—C.P.C.

NECROLOGY

† Couture, Fernand E., Silverton, TX Our Lady of Loretto—Died Sept. 9, 2003
† Graff, Ed, Silverton, TX Our Lady of Loretto—Died Nov. 25, 2002

Archdiocese of Anchorage

(Archidioecesis Ancoragiensis)

Most Reverend

ROGER L. SCHWIETZ, O.M.I., D.D.

Archbishop of Anchorage; ordained December 20, 1967; appointed Bishop of Duluth December 12, 1989; consecrated and installed Bishop of Duluth February 2, 1990; appointed Coadjutor Archbishop of Anchorage January 18, 2000; succeeded to the See March 3, 2001.

Chancery Office: 225 Cordova St., Anchorage AK 99501. Tel: 907-297-7700; Fax: 907-279-3885.

Web: www.archdioceseofanchorage.org

Email: archdiocesegeneraldelivery@caa-ak.org

Most Reverend

FRANCIS T. HURLEY

Archbishop Emeritus of Anchorage; ordained June 16, 1951; appointed Titular Bishop of Daimlaig and Auxiliary of Juneau February 4, 1970; consecrated March 19, 1970; appointed Bishop of Juneau July 20, 1971; installed September 8, 1971; appointed Archbishop of Anchorage May 4, 1976; installed July 8, 1976; retired March 3, 2001.

ESTABLISHED FEBRUARY 9, 1966.

Square Miles 138,985.

Comprises the Third Judicial Division of Alaska.

For legal titles of parishes and archdiocesan institutions, consult the Chancery Office.

STATISTICAL OVERVIEW

Personnel	
Archbishops	1
Retired Archbishops	1
Priests: Diocesan Active in Diocese	10
Priests: Diocesan in Foreign Missions	1
Priests: Retired, Sick or Absent	7
Number of Diocesan Priests	18
Religious Priests in Diocese	9
Total Priests in Diocese	27
Extern Priests in Diocese	12
Permanent Deacons in Diocese	19
Total Brothers	3
Total Sisters	41
Parishes	
Parishes	20
With Resident Pastor:	
Resident Diocesan Priests	10
Resident Religious Priests	5
Without Resident Pastor:	
Administered by Religious Women	2
Administered by Lay People	3
Missions	9
Professional Ministry Personnel:	
Brothers	1
Sisters	10
Lay Ministers	22
Welfare	
Catholic Hospitals	3
Total Assisted	427,079
Health Care Centers	2
Total Assisted	314
Homes for the Aged	1
Total Assisted	82
Specialized Homes	6
Total Assisted	3,105
Special Centers for Social Services	5
Total Assisted	26,000
Educational	
Diocesan Students in Other Seminaries	2
Total Seminarians	2
High Schools, Diocesan and Parish	1
Total Students	74
High Schools, Private	1
Total Students	48
Elementary Schools, Diocesan and Parish	2
Total Students	280
Elementary Schools, Private	1
Total Students	69
Catechesis/Religious Education:	
High School Students	974
Elementary Students	2,479
Total Students under Catholic Instruction	3,926
Teachers in the Diocese:	
Sisters	2
Lay Teachers	53
Vital Statistics	
Receptions into the Church:	
Infant Baptism Totals	547
Adult Baptism Totals	66
Received into Full Communion	74
First Communions	499
Confirmations	356
Marriages:	
Catholic	68
Interfaith	50
Total Marriages	118
Deaths	102
Total Catholic Population	29,693
Total Population	345,975

Former Bishop—Most Revs. JOSEPH T. RYAN, D.D., Archbishop of Anchorage; ord. June 3, 1939; consecrated March 25, 1966; installed April 14, 1966; transferred to as Coadjutor Military Vicar of U.S. Armed Forces Dec. 13, 1975; appt. First Archbishop of the Archdiocese for the Military Services, U.S.A., March 16, 1985; died Oct. 9, 2000; FRANCIS T. HURLEY, D.D. (Retired), Archbishop of Anchorage; ord. June 16, 1951; appt. Titular Bishop of Daimlaig and Auxiliary of Juneau, Feb. 4, 1970; consecrated March 19, 1970; appt. Bishop of Juneau, July 20, 1971; installed Sept. 8, 1971; appt. Archbishop of Anchorage, May 4, 1976; installed July 8, 1976; retired March 3, 2001.

Vicar General—Rev. DONALD BRAMBLE, O.P.

Pastoral Center—Sr. CHARLOTTE DAVENPORT, C.S.J.P., Chancellor, 225 Cordova St., Anchorage, 99501. Tel: 907-297-7700; Fax: 907-279-3885.

Secretary to Archbishop Emeritus—FRANCIS T. HURLEY; Ms. JOANN WHITE.

Secretary to Archbishop Roger L. Schwietz—Mrs. DELORES MALZAHN.

Office of Stewardship/Development—Mr. JAMES CALDAROLA.

Tribunal—225 Cordova St., Box 102239, Anchorage, 99510-2239. Tel: 907-297-7728.

Judicial Vicar—VACANT.

Defenders of the Bond—Deacon WILLIAM FINNEGAN; MIRIAM DONOHUE.

Case Manager and Data Entry—Sr. JOAN OBERLE, C.PP.S.

Notaries—MIRIAM DONOHUE; EILEEN T. KRAMER.

Diocesan Consultors—Revs. ALFRED W. GIEBEL; DONALD BRAMBLE, O.P.; RICHARD D. TERO; PAUL MACKE, S.J.; LEO WALSH; STEVEN C. MOORE; FRED BUGARIN; DANIEL J. HEBERT.

Archdiocesan Offices and Directors

Apostleship of the Sea— Port Chaplain: SALLY BOSTWICK, Anchorage.

Archdiocesan Newspaper—Mr. JOHN ROSCOE, Editor, c/o Chancery Office. Tel: 907-297-7708. "Catholic Anchor"

Russian Desk—Mr. BRIAN KUZEL, Dir., c/o Pastoral Center. Tel: 907-297-7756.

Campaign for Human Development—Ms. ANNETTE JOHNSON; Mrs. ANGELA LISTON, c/o Pastoral Center.

Catholic Social Services—Mrs. YVONNE CHASE, Exec. Dir.; VACANT, Deputy Dir.; Ms. MARY BETH BRAGIEL, Dir Human Resources, 225 Cordova St., Anchorage, 99501. Tel: 907-297-7742; Fax: 907-272-7370.

Board Members—DAVID GOTTSTEIN; JAMES PALMER; JOE MAFUSHACK; ROGER CHAN; DON ARGETSINGER; AL BOLEA; KATE SLYKER; RICH OWENS; ANGELA DIRKS; Mr. JOE MORAN; AL LEVY; BARBARA DONATELLI; Rev. LEO WALSH; PENNY WELLS; JIM CLOUD.

Communications—Bro. CHARLES MCBRIDE, C.S.C., c/o Pastoral Center.

Hispanic Ministry—VACANT.

Korean Ministry—Rev. IN YONG SHIN; Sisters MAGDELENA YU, S.P.C.; DORTHEA HAM, S.P.C., St. Anthony's Parish, 825 S. Klevin St., Anchorage, 99508. Tel: 907-337-5307.

Ministry—VACANT, Catechetical Formation: c/o Pastoral Center.

Native Ministry—Rev. GERALD BRUNET, O.M.I.; Sr. DONNA KRAMER, D.C., Dir., c/o Pastoral Center.

Office of Finance—Sr. CHARLOTTE DAVENPORT, C.S.J.P., C.F.O.; Mr. THOMAS RODDA, Finance Dir., c/o Pastoral Center.

Permanent Diaconate—Deacon FELIX MAGUIRE, c/o Pastoral Center.

Propagation of the Faith—JAMES CALDAROLA, Dir., Stewardship and Development, c/o Pastoral Center.

Retreats—Rev. PAUL MACKE, S.J., Dir., Holy Spirit Center, 10980 Hillside Dr., Anchorage, 99507. Tel: 907-346-2343.

Acting Superintendent of Schools—Mr. ROBERT FLINT, c/o Pastoral Center. Tel: 907-297-7738.

Catholic School Development—Mrs. BARBARA WEIL, Dir.

Victim Assistance Coordinator—Sr. BARBARA SCANLON,

C.S.J. Tel: 907-276-3455. Email: scanlonba@juno.com.

Vocations—Bro. CRAIG BONHAM, O.M.I., Dir., c/o Pastoral Center.

CLERGY, PARISHES, MISSIONS AND PAROCHIAL SCHOOLS

CITY OF ANCHORAGE

1—HOLY FAMILY CATHEDRAL, [JC] Revs. Donald Bramble, O.P.; Gary Cappleman, O.P.; Bro. John Thomas Mellein, O.P.; Sr. Barbara Scanlon, C.S.J., Pastoral Assoc.; Deacon Gerald Grewe, Pastoral Assoc.
Mailing Address: 811 W. 6th Ave., 99501-2093. Tel: 907-276-3455; Fax: 907-258-9785.
Catechesis/Religious Program—Mrs. Theresa Lutes, D.R.E. Students 274.

2—ST. ANTHONY, Revs. Fred Bugarin; Nelson Marilag; Deacon Theodore W. Greene, Pastoral Assoc. In Res., Revs. Gerald Brunet, O.M.I.; In Yong Shin.
Res.: 825 S. Klevin St., 99508-2698. Tel: 907-333-5544; Fax: 907-338-3864.
Catechesis/Religious Program—Students 160.

3—ST. BENEDICT, Rev. Alfred W. Giebel.
Res.: 8110 Jewel Lake Rd., 99502. Tel: 907-243-2195; Fax: 907-243-0088.
Catechesis/Religious Program—Students 450.

4—ST. ELIZABETH ANN SETON, Revs. Craig J. Loecker (OM); Balaswamy Gangarapu; Deacon Kenneth Donohue.
Res.: 2901 E. Huffman Rd., 99516. Tel: 907-345-4466; Fax: 907-345-6361.
Catechesis/Religious Program—Students 625.
Mission—Our Lady of Snows Girdwood, Anchorage Co.

5—HOLY CROSS, Rev. Daniel J. Herbert; Sr. Loretta Luecke, C.PP.S., Parish Admin.; Deacon William Finnegan.
Res.: 2627 Lore Rd., 99507. Tel: 907-349-3910; Fax: 907-349-3910.
Catechesis/Religious Program—Mrs. Janine Redding, D.R.E. Students 234.

6—OUR LADY OF GUADALUPE, Rev. Vincent Blanco.
Res.: 3900 Wisconsin St., 99517. Tel: 907-248-2000; Fax: 907-245-1600.
Catechesis/Religious Program—Students 145.

7—ST. PATRICK, Revs. Scott Medlock; Thomas C. Lilly. In Res., Very Rev. Steven Moore.
Res.: 2111 Muldoon Rd., 99504-3699. Tel: 907-337-1538; Fax: 907-337-5460.
Catechesis/Religious Program—Martha Rogers, D.R.E. Students 337.

8—ST. PAUL MIKI, Closed., For inquiries for parish records contact St. Elizabeth Ann Seton Parish, Anchorage.

OUTSIDE THE CITY OF ANCHORAGE

CORDOVA, VALDEZ-CORDOVA CO., ST. JOSEPH, Rev. Thomas Killeen, O.M.I.
Res.: 220 Adams Ave., P.O. Box 79, 99574. Tel: 907-424-3637; Fax: 907-424-3823.
Catechesis/Religious Program—Patricia Murphy, D.R.E. Students 35.

DILLINGHAM, DILLINGHAM CO., HOLY ROSARY, Brenda Moscarella, Pastoral Admin.
Res.: P.O. Box 810, 99576. Tel: 907-842-5581; Fax: 907-842-5581.
Catechesis/Religious Program—Students 21.
Mission—St. Theresa P.O. Box 73, Naknek, Bristol Bay Borough 99633. Tel: 907-246-6652.
Mission—St. Christopher By the Sea P.O. Box 405, Unalaska, Aleutian Islands Census Area 99685. Tel: 907-581-4022; Fax: 801-382-1060. Rev. Paul Scanlon, O.P.

EAGLE RIVER, ANCHORAGE BOROUGH, ST. ANDREW, Revs. Leo Walsh; Scott Garrett; Sr. Camilla Menting, S.S.S.F., Pastoral Assoc.; Deacons James Hostman; Jim Lee.
Res.: 16601 Artillery Rd., 99577. Tel: 907-694-2170; Fax: 907-694-1385.
Catechesis/Religious Program—Mr. Gerald Finkler, Pastoral Assoc. Students 406.

GLENNALLEN, VALDEZ-CORDOVA CO., HOLY FAMILY, Rev. Gerald Brunet, O.M.I.
Mailing Address: P.O. Box 126, 99588. Tel: 907-822-3442; Fax: 907-822-4208.

HOMER, KENAI PENINSULA BOROUGH, ST. JOHN THE BAPTIST, Annemiek Brunklaus, Pastoral Admin.
Res.: 255 Ohlson Ln., 99603. Tel: 907-235-5519; Fax: 907-235-5251.
Mission—St. James the Apostle Seldovia, Kenai Peninsula Borough. Tel: 907-235-5519.
Mission—St. Peter Box 39290, Ninilchik, Kenai Peninsula Borough 99639. Tel: 907-567-3490.
Catechesis/Religious Program—Ms. Maria Walli, D.R.E. Students 70.

KENAI, KENAI PENINSULA BOROUGH, OUR LADY OF THE ANGELS, Sisters Joyce Ross, R.S.M., Admin.; Joan Barina, M.M.S., Pastoral Assoc.
Res.: 225 S. Spruce Rd., 99611. Tel: 907-283-4555; Fax: 907-283-4555.
Catechesis/Religious Program—Ms. Margaret Menting, D.R.E. Students 95.

KODIAK, KODIAK ISLAND BOROUGH, ST. MARY'S OF KODIAK AND THE ISLANDS, Rev. Robert Bester.
Res.: 2934 Mill Bay Rd., 99615. Tel: 907-486-5411; Fax: 928-359-6049.
School—Tel: 907-486-3513. Sr. Diane Bardol, G.N.S.H., Prin. & D.R.E. Sisters 2; Lay Teachers 9; Students 151.
Catechesis/Religious Program—Students 93.

PALMER, MATANUSKA-SUSITNA BOROUGH, ST. MICHAEL, Rev. Leo Desso.
Res.: 432 E. Fireweed Ave., 99645. Tel: 907-745-3229; Fax: 907-746-7040.
Catechesis/Religious Program—Mrs. Joanne Rousculp, D.R.E. Students 205.

SEWARD, KENAI PENINSULA BOROUGH, SACRED HEART, Rev. Richard Tero; Deacon Walter Corrigan.
Res.: 409 Fifth Ave., P.O. Box 207, 99664. Tel: 907-224-5414; Fax: 907-224-5093.
Catechesis/Religious Program—Mrs. Kim Reierson, D.R.E.
Mission—St. John Neumann Church P.O. Box 737, Cooper Landing, Kenai Peninsula Borough 99572. Tel: 907-595-1300.

SOLDOTNA, KENAI PENINSULA BOROUGH, OUR LADY OF PERPETUAL HELP, Rev. Frank J. Reitter, S.M.
Res.: 222 Redoubt Ave., 99669. Tel: 907-262-4749; Fax: 907-262-5542.
Catechesis/Religious Program—Marlys Verba, D.R.E. Students 164.

TALKEETNA, MATANUSKA-SUSITNA BOROUGH, ST. BERNARD, Unassigned.
Res.: P.O. Box 510, 99676. Tel: 907-733-2442.
Catechesis/Religious Program—Students 12.
Mission—St. Philip Benizi P.O. Box 13475, Trapper Creek, Matanuska-Susitna Borough 99683.
Mission—St. Christopher P.O. Box 412, Willow, Matanuska-Susitna Borough 99688.

VALDEZ, VALDEZ-CORDOVA CO., ST. FRANCIS XAVIER, Sr. Marie Ann Brent, S.H.F., Pastoral Admin.
Res.: 341 Pioneer Dr., P.O. Box 908, 99686. Tel: 907-835-4556; Fax: 907-835-3583.
Catechesis/Religious Program—Carla Oster, D.R.E. Students 72.

WASILLA, MATANUSKA-SUSITNA BOROUGH, SACRED HEART, [CEM] Rev. Kasparaj Mallavarapu.
Res.: 1201 Bogard Rd., 99654-6523. Tel: 907-376-5087; Fax: 907-373-1156.
Catechesis/Religious Program—Students 155.
Mission—Our Lady of the Lake P.O. Box 520769, Big Lake, Matanuska-Susitna Borough 99652-0769. Tel: 907-892-6492; Fax: 907-892-6497. Kathy Bishop, Admin.

On Duty Outside Archdiocese:
Revs.—
Means, David A. (STL), Magadan, Russia
Shields, Michael, Magadan, Russia

On Sabbatical:
Very Rev.—
Moore, Steven
Rev.—
Paskey, Robert, S.J.

Retired:
Rev. Msgr.—
Murphy, Francis A., P.O. Box 1625, Cuba, NM 87013.
Revs.—
Abele, Alan Carl, 340 N. Worthy, Marblehead, OH 43440.
Daley, Neil, 100 4th Ave., Shalimar, FL 32579.
Houck, Peter, 4611 Kupreanof St., 99507.

Permanent Deacons:
Albert, Merle, Milan, NH
Allor, Raymond W., Albany, OR
Cable, Jay, Wasilla
Corrigan, Walter, Seward
Donohue, Kenneth
Finnegan, William
Foreman, Dennis, Anchorage
Frost, William, Cordova
Gnerich, Otto, Anchorage
Greene, Theodore, St. Anthony Church Anchorage
Grewe, Gerald, Holy Family Cathedral, Anchorage
Hoffman, Louis, Big Lake
Hostman, James, St. Andrew, Eagle River
Larroque, Robert, Portland, OR
Lee, Jim, St. Andrew, Eagle River
Maguire, Felix M., Anchorage
Martinez, Dez, Anchorage
Parsons, Bill, Anchorage
Schutt, David E., Wasilla

INSTITUTIONS LOCATED IN THE ARCHDIOCESE

[A] GRADE SCHOOLS, PAROCHIAL

ANCHORAGE. *St. Elizabeth Ann Seton School*, 2901 E. Huffman Rd., 99516. Tel: 907-345-3712; Fax: 907-345-2910. Email: admin@akseas.com. Web: www.akseas.com. Mr. Michael Murray, Prin. Lay Teachers 16; Students 137.
Lumen Christi Jr./Sr. High School, 8110 Jewel Lake Rd., 99502. Tel: 907-245-9231; Fax: 907-245-9232. Mr. James Yeargan, Prin. Students 74; Staff 11.

KODIAK. *St. Mary's*, 2932 Mill Bay Rd., 99615. Tel: 907-486-3513. Email: dbardol@kodiak.alaska.edu. Sr. Diane Bardol, G.N.S.H., Prin. Sisters 2; Lay Teachers 10; Students 143.

[B] PRIVATE SCHOOLS

ANCHORAGE. *Holy Rosary Academy*, (Grades K-12), 1010 W. Fireweed Ln., 99503. Tel: 907-276-5822; Fax: 907-258-1055. Email: ewassell@gci.net. Web: www.holyrosaryacademy.net. Mr. Edward Wassell, Exec. Dir.; Mrs. Barbara Dorner, Prin. Lay Teachers 16; Students 117.

[C] GENERAL HOSPITALS

ANCHORAGE. *Providence Alaska Medical Center*, 3200 Providence Dr., P.O. Box 196604, 99519. Tel: 907-562-2211; Fax: 907-261-3041. Mr. Gene O'Hara, Admin.; Ms. Monica Anderson, Mission Integration Svcs. Properties, entities, and divisions owned or operated: Providence Health System--Washington; Providence Alaska Medical Center, Anchorage, AK, Providence Extended Care Center, Anchorage, AK, Providence Health System Housing* dba- Providence Horizon House, Anchorage, AK, Mary Conrad Center, Anchorage, AK. Bed Capacity 345; Patients Assisted Annually 427,079; Staff 3,342.

KODIAK. *Province Kodiak Island Medical Center*, 1915 E. Rezanof Dr., 99615. Tel: 907-486-3281; Fax: 907-486-2336.

SEWARD. *Province Seward Medical Center*, 417 First Ave., 99664. Tel: 907-224-5205; Fax: 907-224-7248.

[D] NURSING HOMES

ANCHORAGE. *Providence Extended Care Center*, 4900 Eagle St., 99503. Tel: 907-562-2281; Fax: 907-762-0280. Ronald Bergstrom, Admin.; Sr. Patricia Collins, R.S.M., Mission Integration.
Legal Title: *Sisters of Providence in Washington.* Bed Capacity 224; Patients Assisted Annually 372; Staff 340.

[E] HOMES FOR AGED

ANCHORAGE. **Mary Conrad Center*, 9100 Centennial Dr., 99504. Tel: 907-269-3201; Fax: 907-338-6789. Email: kgarber@provak.org. Jody Howorth, Dir.; Sr. Maria Bouleris, C.S.J., Spiritual Care Coord. A long term care facility for the elderly, owned by Cook Inlet Housing Development Corporation and managed by Sisters of Providence in Washington. Patients Assisted Annually 90; Staff 143.

[F] CATHOLIC SOCIAL SERVICES

ANCHORAGE. *Brother Francis Shelter*, 1021 E. Third Ave., 99501. Tel: 907-277-1731. Mr. Dewayne Harris. Overnight shelter for homeless men and women.
Brother Francis Shelter, 411 Cedar St., P.O. Box 3421, Kodiak, 99615. Tel: 907-486-5610. Monte Hawver, Dir.
Catholic Social Services Center, Administrative Office, 225 Cordova St., 99501. Tel: 907-297-7742.
Catholic Social Services Center, 3710 E. 20th Ave., 99508. Tel: 907-276-5590. Mrs. Yvonne Chase, Exec. Dir.; Ms. Robin Bronen, Dir., Immigration & Refugee Svcs.; Ms. Marilyn Moreno, Pregnancy Support & Adoption Dir.; Ms. Stephanie Wheeler, Dir., Beyond Shelter Prog., St. Francis House; Gladys Langlon, Dir., Special Needs Svcs.; Mrs. Jackie Snyder, Program Manager, Healthy Families.
Charlie Elder House, 1513 Wintergreen, 99508. Tel: 907-277-8622; Fax: 907-277-8624. Linda McDevitt, Dir.
Clare House, 420 W. 54th Ave., 99518. Tel: 907-563-4545. Kjersti Langnes, Dir. Temporary shelter for homeless women and women with children.

McAuley Manor, 3015 Yale Dr., 99508. Ms. Linda McDivitt, Dir. Residence for homeless teenage girls.

KODIAK. *The Marian Center, Inc.*, 2934 Mill Bay Rd., 99615. Tel: 907-486-3820; Fax: 907-486-2605. Email: mariancenter@alaska.com. Sr. Barbara Harrington, O.P., Dir.

[G] MONASTERIES AND RESIDENCES OF PRIESTS AND BROTHERS

ANCHORAGE. *Anchorage Jesuit Community*, 1500 Birchwood, 99508. Tel: 907-279-4389 Revs. Joseph Schad, S.J.; Paul B. Macke, S.J., Supr.; Vincent Beuzer, S.J. Oregon Province of Society of Jesus

[H] CONVENTS AND RESIDENCES FOR SISTERS

ANCHORAGE. *Convent of Mercy*, 2627 Redwood St., 99508. Tel: 907-258-7802. Email: smercy@gci.net. Sisters 3.

Convent of the Daughters of Charity, 3424 E. 15th Ave., 99508. Tel: 907-258-3424; Fax: 907-272-7370. Email: docanchorage@aol.com. Sisters 3.

Marian House / Guadalupe Arms Apartments, 3005-7 W. 34th Ave., 99517. Priests 2; Sisters 2; Brothers 1.

Sisters of Perpetual Adoration, 2645 E. 72nd Ave., 99507. Tel: 907-344-3330; Fax: 907-522-2945. Sr. Maria de las Victorias Amezcua, A.P., Supr. Sisters 7.

Sisters of St. Paul de Chartres, 825 S. Klevin St., 99508. Tel: 907-258-3273. Sisters 2.

KENAI. *Kenai Convent*, 1122 Walnut St., 99611. Tel: 907-283-6466. Sisters 2.

KODIAK. *St. Mary's Convent*, 2932 Mill Bay Rd., 99615. Tel: 907-486-5214; Fax: 561-679-7666. Email: carolbartolgnsh@peaceaction.org. Web: www.greynuns.org. Sisters 4.

[I] RETREAT HOUSES

ANCHORAGE. *Holy Spirit Center*, 10980 Hillside Dr., 99507. Tel: 907-346-2343; Fax: 907-346-2140. Email: hsrh@alaska.com. Web: www.home.gci.net/~hsrh. Rev. Paul Macke, S.J., Dir.
Legal Title: *Catholic Retreat House Ministries, Inc.*

[J] MISCELLANEOUS

ANCHORAGE. *Alaska Catholic Conference*, 225 Cordova, 99501. Tel: 907-297-7738; Fax: 907-279-3885. Email: robert.flint@caa-ak.org. Mr. Robert Flint, Dir.

Archdiocese of Anchorage Priests Pension Trust, 225 Cordova St., 99501.

Catholic Foundation of Alaska, 225 Cordova St., 99501.

Catholic Retreat House Ministries, Inc., 225 Cordova St., 99501.

Covenant House Alaska, 609 F St., 99501. Tel: 907-272-1255. Ms. Deirdre Phayer, Exec. Dir. Crisis center for homeless and runaway youth.

Providence Alaska Foundation, Anchorage, Alaska, 3200 Providence Dr., P.O. Box 196604, 99519-6604 Tel: 907-261-3600; Fax: 907-261-3048. Email: jsix@provak.org. Elaine Christian, Pres.; Janice Six, Exec. Sec.; Peter Brennan, Devel. Mgr.; Catherine Albrant, Financial Analyst; Suzanne Rudolph, Children's Miracle Network Coord.

Providence Health System Housing, dba Providence Horizon House, 4140 Folker Ave., 99508. Tel: 907-261-4140; Fax: 907-261-4160. Email: ssamet@provak.org. Sue Samet, Prog. Dir. Guests 60.

Providence Home Health Care, Anchorage, Alaska, 4175 Tudor Centre Dr., Ste. 101, 99508. Tel: 907-563-0130; Fax: 907-563-0135. Email: klum@provak.org. Kathy Lum, Prog. Dir.

RELIGIOUS INSTITUTES OF MEN REPRESENTED IN THE ARCHDIOCESE

For further details refer to the corresponding bracketed number in the Religious Institutes of Men or Women section.

[0600]—*Brothers of the Congregation of Holy Cross*—C.S.C.

[0690]—*Jesuit Fathers and Brothers* (Oregon Prov.)—S.J.

[0910]—*Oblates of Mary Immaculate*—O.M.I.

[0430]—*Order of Preachers-Dominicans* (Oakland Prov.)—O.P.

[0610]—*Priests of the Congregation of Holy Cross*—C.S.C.

RELIGIOUS INSTITUTES OF WOMEN REPRESENTED IN THE ARCHDIOCESE

[0760]—*Daughters of Charity of St. Vincent DePaul*—D.C.

[1070-03]—*Dominican Sisters*—O.P.

[1840]—*Grey Nuns of the Sacred Heart*—G.N.S.H.

[2575]—*Institute of the Sisters of Mercy of the Americas* (Albany, NY; Merion, PA; Providence, RI)—R.S.M.

[2330]—*Little Sisters of Jesus*—L.S.J.

[2490]—*Medical Mission Sisters*—M.M.S.

[3190]—*Nuns of Perpetual Adoration of the Blessed Sacrament* (Mexico)—A.P.

[1680]—*School Sisters of St. Francis*—O.S.F.

[3350]—*Sisters of Providence*—S.P.

[3830-01]—*Sisters of St. Joseph* (Boston, MA)—C.S.J.

[3840]—*Sisters of St. Joseph of Charondelet*—C.S.J.

[3893]—*Sisters of St. Joseph of Chestnut Hill, Philadelphia*—S.S.J.

[3890]—*Sisters of St. Joseph of Peace* (Bellevue)—C.S.J.P.

[3980]—*Sisters of St. Paul de Chartres*—S.P.C.

[1960]—*Sisters of the Holy Family*—S.H.F.

[3270]—*Sisters of the Most Precious Blood* (O'Fallon, MO)—C.PP.S.

[4110]—*Ursuline Nuns*—O.S.U.

NECROLOGY

(No Deaths)

Diocese of Arlington

(Dioecesis Arlingtonensis)

Most Reverend

PAUL S. LOVERDE, D.D., S.T.L., J.C.L.

Bishop of Arlington; ordained December 18, 1965; appointed Titular Bishop of Ottabia and Auxiliary Bishop of Hartford February 3, 1988; consecrated April 12, 1988; appointed Bishop of Ogdensburg November 11, 1993; installed as Eleventh Bishop of Ogdensburg January 17, 1994; appointed Bishop of Arlington January 25, 1999; installed as Third Bishop of Arlington March 25, 1999.

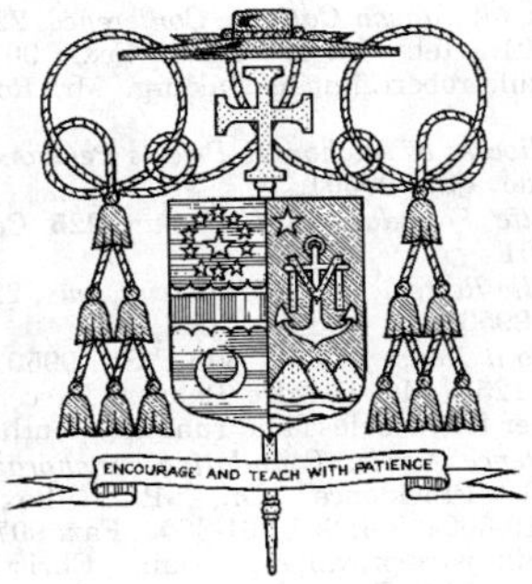

The Chancery: 200 N. Glebe Rd., Ste. 914, Arlington, VA 22203. Tel: 703-841-2500; Fax: 703-524-5028.

ESTABLISHED AUGUST 13, 1974.

Square Miles 6,541.

Comprises the following 21 Counties in Northern Virginia: Arlington, Clarke, Culpeper, Fairfax, Fauquier, Frederick, King George, Lancaster, Loudoun, Madison, Northumberland, Orange, Page, Prince William, Rappahannock, Richmond, Shenandoah, Spotsylvania, Stafford, Warren and Westmoreland and the 7 independent cities of Alexandria, Fairfax City, Falls Church, Fredericksburg, Manassas, Manassas Park and Winchester.

For legal titles of parishes and diocesan institutions, consult the Chancery Office.

STATISTICAL OVERVIEW

Personnel	
Bishop	1
Abbots	1
Retired Abbots	3
Priests: Diocesan Active in Diocese	128
Priests: Diocesan Active Outside Diocese	7
Priests: Diocesan in Foreign Missions	2
Priests: Retired, Sick or Absent	20
Number of Diocesan Priests	157
Religious Priests in Diocese	72
Total Priests in Diocese	229
Extern Priests in Diocese	20
Ordinations:	
Diocesan Priests	3
Permanent Deacons in Diocese	46
Total Brothers	19
Total Sisters	150
Parishes	
Parishes	66
With Resident Pastor:	
Resident Diocesan Priests	55
Resident Religious Priests	11
Missions	6
Professional Ministry Personnel:	
Sisters	13
Lay Ministers	98
Welfare	
Special Centers for Social Services	7
Total Assisted	30,183
Educational	
Diocesan Students in Other Seminaries	23
Total Seminarians	23
Colleges and Universities	4
Total Students	5,552
High Schools, Diocesan and Parish	3
Total Students	3,367
High Schools, Private	3
Total Students	799
Elementary Schools, Diocesan and Parish	35
Total Students	13,555
Elementary Schools, Private	1
Total Students	186
Non-residential Schools for the Disabled	1
Total Students	155
Catechesis/Religious Education:	
High School Students	3,227
Elementary Students	31,074
Total Students under Catholic Instruction	57,938
Teachers in the Diocese:	
Priests	10
Brothers	1
Sisters	45
Lay Teachers	1,089
Vital Statistics	
Receptions into the Church:	
Infant Baptism Totals	7,165
Adult Baptism Totals	795
Received into Full Communion	1,016
First Communions	7,538
Confirmations	5,905
Marriages:	
Catholic	1,017
Interfaith	615
Total Marriages	1,632
Deaths	1,557
Total Catholic Population	391,001
Total Population	2,423,982

Former Bishops—Most Revs. THOMAS J. WELSH, D.D., J.C.D. (Retired), appt. Titular Bishop of Scattery Island and Auxiliary Bishop of Philadelphia on Feb. 18, 1970; consecrated April 2, 1970; appt. as 1st Bishop of Arlington on June 4, 1974; installed on Aug. 13, 1974; transferred to the See of Allentown, Feb. 8, 1983; resigned Dec. 16, 1997; appt. Diocesan Administrator; retired Feb. 9, 1998; JOHN R. KEATING, D.D., J.C.D., ord. Dec. 20, 1958; appt. Second Bishop of Arlington on June 7, 1983; consecrated and installed on Aug. 4, 1983; died March 22, 1998.

The Chancery

The Chancery—200 N. Glebe Rd., Ste. 914, Arlington, 22203. Tel: 703-841-2500; Fax: 703-524-5028. Office Hours: Mon.-Fri. 8:30-4:30.; Address all official business to this office.

Bishop—Most Rev. PAUL S. LOVERDE, D.D., S.T.L., J.C.L., 200 N. Glebe Rd., Ste. 914, Arlington, 22203. Tel: 703-841-2511.

Vicar General—Rev. Msgr. R. ROY COSBY, V.G. (Retired), 5121 Woodland Way, Annandale, 22003-4165. Tel: 571-643-2008.

Secretary to the Bishop—Bro. DAVID S. EDDY, C.F.X., 200 N. Glebe Rd., Ste. 914, Arlington, 22203. Tel: 703-841-2511; Fax: 703-524-5028.

Moderator of the Curia & Episcopal Vicar for Pastoral Services—Rev. MARK S. MEALEY, O.S.F.S., J.C.D., Ph.D., 200 N. Glebe Rd., Ste. 914, Arlington, 22203. Tel: 703-841-2563; Fax: 703-524-5028.

Chancellor—Rev. ROBERT J. RIPPY, J.C.L., V.F., The Chancery, 200 N. Glebe Rd., Ste. 914, Arlington, 22203. Tel: 703-841-2508; Fax: 703-524-5028.

Episcopal Vicar for Parish Development—VACANT. Tel: 703-525-2500.

Bishop's Delegate for Clergy—Rev. ROBERT E. AVELLA, 200 N. Glebe Rd., Ste. 914, Arlington, 22203. Tel: 703-841-3809; Fax: 703-524-5028.

Episcopal Vicar for Finance—Rev. DANIEL J. MAHER, 200 N. Glebe Rd., Ste. 914, Arlington, 22203. Tel: 703-841-2577; Fax: 703-524-5028.

Diocesan Fiscal Manager—Mrs. SUSAN D. HANDLON, C.P.A., Fiscal Mgr., 200 N. Glebe Rd., Ste. 914, Arlington, 22203. Tel: 703-841-2577; Fax: 703-524-5028.

Director of Diocesan Charities—Rev. CHARLES C. MCCOART, 8710 Mount Vernon Hwy., Alexandria, 22309. Tel: 703-780-4055; Fax: 703-360-5385.

Deans—Revs. ROBERT J. RIPPY, J.C.L., V.F.; JOHN C. CREGAN, V.F.; WILLIAM F. RUEHL, V.F.; WILLIAM P. SAUNDERS, Ed.D., V.F.; ROBERT C. CILINSKI; DONALD C. GREENHALGH.

Vicar for Religious—Rev. MARK S. MEALEY, O.S.F.S., J.C.D., Ph.D. Tel: 703-841-2563; Fax: 703-524-5028.

The Tribunal

The Tribunal—200 N. Glebe Rd., Ste. 524, Arlington, 22203. Tel: 703-841-2555; Fax: 703-841-0693.

Judicial Vicar—Rev. MARK S. MEALEY, O.S.F.S., J.C.D., Ph.D. Tel: 703-841-2555; Fax: 703-841-0693.

Adjutant Judicial Vicar—Revs. DAVID A. WHITESTONE, J.C.L.; LEE R. ROOS. Tel: 703-841-2555; Fax: 703-841-0693.

Diocesan Judges—Revs. ROBERT C. BROOKS; JOHN C. CREGAN, V.F.; PAUL F. DELADURANTAYE, S.T.D.; HORACE H. GRINNELL; PATRICK HOLROYD; Mrs. TARA A. MCINTOSH, J.C.L.; Revs. MARK S. MEALEY, O.S.F.S., J.C.D., Ph.D.; LEE R. ROOS; DAVID A. WHITESTONE, J.C.L.; LEO J. ZONNEVELD, C.I.C.M.

Defenders of the Bond—Rev. ROBERT E. AVELLA; Rev. Msgr. R. ROY COSBY, V.G. (Retired); Deacons CHARLES A. COUTU; WILLIAM J. DONOVAN; Revs. PAUL M. EVERSOLE; THOMAS P. FERGUSON; DANIEL E. HAMILTON; THOMAS J. LEHNING; DANIEL L. MODE; RICHARD A. MULLINS; MATTHEW H. ZUBERBUELER.

Promoter of Justice—Rev. ROBERT J. RIPPY, J.C.L., V.F.

Auditors—Revs. RICHARD J. LEY; GERONIMO A. MAGAT; KEITH M. O'HARE.

Advocates—Revs. ALEXANDER R. DRUMMOND; RONALD S. ESCALANTE; RONALD J. GRIPSHOVER JR.; DANIEL J. MAHER; JOHN P. MOSIMANN; JAMES A. TUCKER.

Notaries—Revs. BRIAN G. BASHISTA; BRIAN W. BELLI; KEVIN J. BERES; RICHARD T. CARR; MARK F. CARRIER; TERRY A. CRAMER; MICHAEL J. DOBBINS; FREDERICK H. EDLEFSEN; PAUL M. GRANKAUSKAS; JOHN F. HEISLER; STEPHEN HOLMES; EDWARD R. HORKAN; JOSEPH R. KENNA; STEPHEN F. MCGRAW; JOHN M. O'DONOHUE; EDWIN E. PEREZ; JAMES M. POUMADE; MICHAEL D. WESTON.

Diocesan Offices

Diocesan Offices— Unless otherwise noted, all offices are located at: *200 N. Glebe Rd., Arlington, 22203.*

Accounting Office—CLARE M. FARISS, Accounting Dir., Ste. 600. Tel: 703-841-2582.

Archives—80 N. Glebe Rd., Arlington, 22203. Tel: 703-841-2508.

Arlington Catholic Herald, Inc.—MICHAEL F. FLACH, Editor & Gen. Mgr.; ANN AUGHERTON, Mng. Editor, Ste. 600. Tel: 703-841-2590; Fax: 703-524-2782. Web: www.catholicherald.com.

Bishop's Lenten Appeal—JUANITA PADGETT, Coord., Ste. 811. Tel: 703-841-2570; Fax: 703-528-3057.

Campaign for Human Development—Rev. CHARLES C. MCCOART, Diocesan Dir., Ste. 506. Tel: 703-780-4055.

Campus Ministry—Rev. JOHN P. PETERSON, Bishop's Liaison, 1600 Carlin Lane, McLean, 22201. Tel: 703-556-0914.

*Catholic Charities of the Diocese of Arlington—Ste. 506*Web: www.ccda.net. STEPHEN LUTERAN, M.S.W., L.C.S.W., Exec. Dir. Tel: 703-841-3835; Fax: 703-841-3840; MICHAEL J. O'ROURKE, Assoc. Dir. Finance & Admin. Tel: 703-841-2542; ELIANA V. TURINA, Assoc. Dir. Community Svcs., 200 N. Glebe Rd., Ste. 506, Arlington, 22203. Tel: 703-841-3838; HELEN P. MUDD, A.C.S.W., Assoc. Dir. Social Svcs., Ste. 506. Tel: 703-841-3837.

Catholic Charities Fredericksburg Office—PAMELA STASZAK, L.M.F.T., Program Dir., 305 Hanson

Ave., Ste. 180, Fredericksburg, 22401. Tel: 540-371-1124.
Catholic Charities Loudon Office—At Christ the Redeemer Parish, 46833 Harry Byrd Hwy., Sterling, 20164. Tel: 703-421-2317.
Children's Services—LINDA CULLEN, M.S.W., A.C.S.W., Prog. Dir., 5294 Lyngate Ct., Burke, 22015. Tel: 703-425-0100.
Christ House—VACANT, Prog. Dir., 131 S. West St., Alexandria, 22314. Tel: 703-549-8644.
Communications—JEANNE SPAETH, Coord. Tel: 703-841-3833.
Elderly Services—CAROL AUGUSTINE, M.A., Prog. Dir., St. Martin de Porres Senior Center, 4650 Taney Ave., Alexandria, 22304. Tel: 703-751-2766.
Emergency Assistance—VACANT, Prog. Dir., 131 S. West St., Alexandria, 22314. Tel: 703-548-4227.
Family Services—DAVID CAVANAUGH, M.S.W., L.C.S.W., Prog. Dir., 3838 N. Cathedral Ln., Arlington, 22203. Tel: 703-841-2531.
Hogar Hispano-Assistance to Immigrants—NANCY JANE SHESTACK, Esq., Prog. Dir., 6201 Leesburg Pike, Ste. 307, Falls Church, 22044. Tel: 703-534-9805.
Parish Social Ministry—ANNE MURPHY, Prog. Dir. Tel: 703-841-3831.
Prison Ministry—Sr. CONSTANCIA V. PARCASIO, S.N.D.S., Prog. Dir. Tel: 703-841-3832.
Services for Disabled Persons—HARRY BURKE, Prog. Dir., 3838 N. Cathedral Ln., Arlington, 22203. Tel: 703-841-2531. Western Regional Office: Tel: 540-667-7940.
Catholic Education, Office of Catechetics—Rev. PAUL F. DELADURANTAYE, S.T.D., Sec. for Religious Education and Sacred Liturgy, Ste. 503. Tel: 703-841-2554; Fax: 703-524-8670; Mrs. PROVIE RYDSTROM, Coord. Pastoral Ministry for the Hearing Impaired. Tel: 703-978-7997 (V-TTD); Mrs. NADINE HALLUMS, Dir., Special Religious Education (SPRED). Tel: 703-569-2428.
Office of Catholic Schools—TIMOTHY J. MCNIFF, Ed.D., Supt. of Schools., Ste. 503. Tel: 703-841-2519; Fax: 703-524-8670; VACANT, Asst. Supt. for Secondary Education & Director of Teacher Personnel. Tel: 703-841-2519; Sr. KARL ANN HOMBERG, S.S.J., Asst. Supt. for Elementary Education. Tel: 703-841-2519; DIANE ELLIOTT, Special Needs Coord. Tel: 703-841-2519.
Catholic Relief Services—Rev. CHARLES C. MCCOART, Dir., Ste. 506. Tel: 703-780-4055.
Central Purchasing—JIM FORNERIS, Purchasing Coord., Ste. 600. Tel: 703-841-2571.
Communications Office—SOREN JOHNSON, Dir., Ste. 914. Tel: 703-841-2767; Fax: 703-524-5028. Email: communications@arlingtondiocese.org.
Development Office—ROBERT P. MUELLER, Dir., Ste. 811. Tel: 703-841-2545; Fax: 703-528-3057.
Management Information Systems—WILFREDO MALDONADO, Dir.; Rev. LEE R. ROOS, Supvr., Ste. 600. Tel: 703-841-2567; Fax: 703-841-4786.
Construction Management, Office of—Ste. 600. Tel: 703-841-2572; Fax: 703-276-9486. Construction Supervisors: PETER B. FISHER; PAUL E. MAY; MOON C. KIM.
Ecumenical and Interreligious Affairs Commission—Rev. THOMAS P. FERGUSON, Chm. Tel: 703-841-2555.
Employee Benefits—LINDA HENNESSEY, C.E.B.S., Mgr., Ste. 600. Tel: 703-841-2588.
Family Life Office—Mr. ROBERT E. LAIRD, Dir., Ste. 523. Tel: 703-841-2550; Fax: 703-807-2032. Email: familylife@arlingtondiocese.org; ANDREA ALBANESE, Asst. Dir.
Gabriel Project-Arlington—CELESTE MCCLOSKEY, Coord., Ste. 814. Tel: 703-841-3810.
Marriage Preparation & Enrichment—JOHN L. O'BRIEN, Program Dir. Tel: 703-841-2550; Tel: 703-841-2550 Conferences for the Engaged.
Natural Family Planning—Tel: 703-841-2550.
Project Rachel Post-Abortion Counseling—GERRI LAIRD, Dir., 814. Tel: 703-276-0373; 888-456-4673 (24 hrs.). Email: projectrachel@arlingtondiocese.org.
Respect Life/Pro-Life Activities—ANDREA ALBANESE, Prog. Dir. Tel: 703-841-2550.
Young Adult Ministry—PAMELA ALBANESE, Dir. Tel: 703-841-2580. Email: yam@arlingtondiocese.org.
Liturgy, Office of Sacred—Rev. PAUL F. DELADURANTAYE, S.T.D., Sec. for the Liturgy, Ste. 503. Tel: 703-841-2554; RICHARD GIBALA, Diocesan Music Coord. Tel: 703-524-2815.
Permanent Diaconate—Rev. ROBERT E. AVELLA, Ste. 914. Tel: 703-841-3809; Fax: 703-524-5028.
Propagation of the Faith—Rev. BRIAN G. BASHISTA, Dir., Ste. 600. Tel: 703-841-2762; Fax: 703-841-4786.
Publications/List Maintenance—VERONICA M. DOHERTY, Coord., Ste. 811. Tel: 703-841-2513; Fax: 703-528-3057
Spanish Apostolate—Rev. OVIDIO PECHARROMAN, Dir.; BEATRIZ PACHON, Program Coord., 80 N. Glebe Rd., Arlington, 22203. Tel: 703-524-2122. Fax: 703-524-4261.
Office of Resettlement—SEYOUM BERHE, Dir., 80 N. Glebe Rd., Arlington, 22203. Tel: 703-524-2154; Fax: 703-524-2741.
Risk Management, Office of—RANDY JOUBEN, Dir., Ste. 600. Tel: 703-841-2503; Fax: 703-841-4786.
Stewardship and Development, Office of—ROBERT P. MUELLER, Dir., Ste. 811. Tel: 703-841-2545; Fax: 703-528-3057; SUZIE CULKIN, Assoc. Dir. Tel: 703-841-3813.
Vocations, Office of—Revs. BRIAN G. BASHISTA, Dir. & Promoter of Vocations; OVIDIO PECHARROMAN, Coord. Spanish Speaking Vocations, Ste. 600. Tel: 703-841-2514; Fax: 703-841-4786.
Youth Ministry, Office of—Mr. KEVIN BOHLI; Rev. MICHAEL G. TAYLOR, Spiritual Dir., Ste. 519. Tel: 703-841-2559; Fax: 703-807-2032.
Scouting & Camp Fire, Diocesan Committee on—PAT BERNEY, Chm., 1701 Gelding Lane, Vienna, 22182. Tel: 730-255-2445. Email: pmberney@juno.com.

Consultative Bodies

Clergy Personnel Board—Rev. ROBERT E. AVELLA, Chm., St. Mary, Alexandria, 22314. Tel: 703-836-4100.
Diaconal Council—Deacons SAMUEL M. TAUB, Chm. Tel: 703-256-3324; THOMAS M. BELLO, Vice Chm. Tel: 703-448-9677.
Diocesan Consultors—Rev. ROBERT C. CILINSKI; Rev. Msgr. R. ROY COSBY, V.G. (Retired); Revs. MARK S. MEALEY, O.S.F.S., J.C.D., Ph.D.; FRANK J. READY, V.F.; ROBERT J. RIPPY, J.C.L., V.F.; WILLIAM P. SAUNDERS, Ed.D., V.F.; MICHAEL G. TAYLOR.
Diocesan Finance Committee—Most Rev. PAUL S. LOVERDE, D.D., S.T.L., J.C.L., Chm. Tel: 703-841-2511; Rev. DANIEL J. MAHER, Episcopal Vicar for Finance. Tel: 703-841-2577.
Diocesan School Board—SAMUEL J. GERDANO, Chm. Tel: 703-739-0800.
Presbyteral Council—Most Rev. PAUL S. LOVERDE, D.D., S.T.L., J.C.L., Pres.; Rev. THOMAS P. FERGUSON, Recording Sec.
Sisters' Council—Sisters CECILIA DWYER, O.S.B., Pres. Tel: 703-361-0106; MARGARET KERR, S.N.D., Vice Pres. Tel: 703-527-3276. 1033 Riva Ridge Dr., Great Falls, 22066-1615.
Victim Assistance Coordinator—CATHERINE M. NOLAN, M.S.W., A.C.S.W., 200 N. Glebe Rd., Ste. 914, Arlington, 22203. Tel: 703-841-2530. Email: c.nolan@arlingtondiocese.org.

CLERGY, PARISHES, MISSIONS AND PAROCHIAL SCHOOLS

COUNTY OF ARLINGTON

1—CATHEDRAL OF ST. THOMAS MORE (1938), Revs. Robert E. Avella; Matthew H. Zuberbueler; Deacon Claudio F. Benedi. In Res., Rev. Paul F. deLadurantaye, S.T.D.
Res.: 3901 Cathedral Ln., 22203. Tel: 703-525-1300; 703-525-0450; Fax: 703-528-5760.
School—105 N. Thomas St., 22203. Tel: 703-528-6781; 703-528-1547; Fax: 703-528-5048. Mrs. Kathleen H. Swinehart, Prin. Lay Teachers 23; Students 363.
Catechesis/Religious Program—Tel: 703-528-7104. Sr. Maria Angelica McGovern, I.H.M., D.R.E. Students 254.

2—ST. AGNES (1936), Revs. Lee R. Roos; Christopher J. Pollard; Deacon William J. Donovan. In Res., Rev. Msgr. John T. Cilinski (Retired); Rev. Richard J. Ley.
Res.: 1914 N. Randolph St., 22207. Tel: 703-525-1166; Fax: 703-243-2840.
Office—2000 N. Randolph St., 22207.
School—2024 N. Randolph St., 22207. Tel: 703-527-5423; Fax: 703-527-6325. Mrs. Vivian Uthe, Prin. Sisters 1; Lay Teachers 29; Students 330.
Catechesis/Religious Program—Tel: 703-522-7045. Students 436.
Convent—Sisters of Notre Dame, Tel: 703-527-3276.
Convent—Maryknoll Sisters of St. Dominic, Fax: 703-527-3284.

3—ST. ANN (1947), Revs. William B. Schardt; Charles W. Merkle III; Deacon Eduardo Ramirez.
Res.: 5312 10th St. N., 22205. Tel: 703-528-6276; Fax: 703-522-4758.
School—980 N. Frederick St., 22205. Tel: 703-525-7599; Fax: 703-525-2687. Mrs. Sally Berra, Prin. Lay Teachers 19; Students 210.
Catechesis/Religious Program—Tel: 703-524-8377. Mr. Ryan Bolster, D.R.E. Students 263.

4—ST. CHARLES BORROMEO (1909), Revs. Gerard Creedon; Francisco Mendez de Dios; Deacon John B. Mallon.
Res.: 3304 N. Washington Blvd., 22201. Tel: 703-527-5500; Fax: 703-527-5505. In Res., Rev. David A. Whitestone, J.C.L.
School—Tel: 703-527-0608; Fax: 703-526-0262. Sr. Benedict Kesock, O.S.B., Prin. Sisters of St. Benedict 1; Lay Teachers 14; Students 188.
Catechesis/Religious Program—Tel: 703-527-5500, Ext. 19. Mrs. Anne Marie Kauffman, M.R.E., D.R.E. Students 207.
Convent—Benedictine Sisters of Virginia, 3299 N. Fairfax Dr., 22201.

5—HOLY MARTYRS OF VIETNAM (1979), (Vietnamese), Revs. John Baptist Vuong Duc Nguyen, O.P. John Baptist Minh Binh Doan, O.P.; Deacon Michael Kien Minh Pham, D.R.E.
Res.: 915 S. Wakefield St., 22204. Tel: 703-553-0370; Fax: 703-553-0371.
Catechesis/Religious Program—Tel: 703-471-0137. Students 357.

6—OUR LADY OF LOURDES (1946), Revs. Robert J. Rippy, J.C.L., V.F.; John M. O'Donohue; Deacon James F. Ambury. In Res., Revs. Brian G. Bashista; Joseph J. Loftus (Retired).
Res.: 830 S. 23rd St., 22202. Tel: 703-684-8261; 703-684-9211; Fax: 703-684-6342.
Catechesis/Religious Program—Students 156.

7—OUR LADY, QUEEN OF PEACE (1945), Rev. Leonard Tuozzolo, C.S.Sp.; Deacon Eugene D. Betit.
Res.: 2700 S. 19th St., 22204. Tel: 703-979-5580; Fax: 703-979-5590.
Catechesis/Religious Program—Adolphe Gervais, D.R.E. Students 170.

OUTSIDE THE COUNTY OF ARLINGTON

ALEXANDRIA, ALEXANDRIA CO.

1—BLESSED SACRAMENT (1946), Revs. John C. Cregan, V.F.; Bryan W. Belli; Joel D. Jaffe.
Church: 1427 W. Braddock Rd., 22302. Tel: 703-998-6100; Fax: 703-671-3219.
Res.: 1407 W. Braddock Rd., 22302.
School—1417 W. Braddock Rd., 22302. Tel: 703-998-4170; Fax: 703-998-5033. Mrs. Valerie Garcia, Prin. Lay Teachers 40; Students 355.
Catechesis/Religious Program— Colette Ellis, D.R.E. Students 387.

2—GOOD SHEPHERD (1965), Revs. Charles C. McCoart; Sean K. Rousseau; Deacon Thomas G. White. In Res., Rev. Jesus Navarrette (Spain).
Church & Mailing Address: 8710 Mount Vernon Hwy., 22309. Tel: 703-780-4055; Fax: 703-360-5385.
Res.: 3510 Surry Dr., 22309.
Catechesis/Religious Program—Diane Blair, D.R.E. Students 996.

3—ST. JOSEPH'S (1915), Rev. Francis M. Hull, S.S.J.
Res.: 711 N. Columbus St., 22314. Tel: 703-836-3725; Fax: 703-837-9066.
Catechesis/Religious Program—Tel: 301-839-3095. Mrs. Wilma Anderson, D.R.E. Students 50.

4—ST. LAWRENCE (Franconia) (1967), Rev. Christopher J. Mould. In Res., Rev. Ben M. Opara (Nigeria).
Res.: 6222 Franconia Rd., 22310. Tel: 703-971-4378; Fax: 703-971-0331.
Catechesis/Religious Program—Tel: 703-971-8541. James H. Drennan, D.R.E. Students 203.

5—ST. LOUIS (1949), Revs. John J. Riley; Ronald J. Gripshover Jr.; Francis M. deRosa; Deacon Paul J. Plaisance Jr.
Res.: 2907 Popkins Ln., 22306. Tel: 703-765-4421; Fax: 703-765-1750.
School—2901 Popkins Ln., 22306. Tel: 703-768-7732; Fax: 703-768-3836. Mrs. Noreen M. Gilmour, Prin. Lay Teachers 23; Students 437.
Catechesis/Religious Program—Tel: 703-765-6600. Students 260.

6—ST. MARY'S (1795), [CEM] Revs. Dennis W. Kleinmann; James M. Poumade; John H. Melmer. In Res., Rev. J. Bryan Hehir.
Res.: 310 Duke St., 22314. Tel: 703-549-3603; 703-836-4100; Fax: 703-549-3605.
School—400 Green St., 22314. Tel: 703-549-1646; Fax: 703-519-0840. Mrs. Kathleen Dolan, Prin. Lay Teachers 36; Students 700.
Catechesis/Religious Program—Tel: 703-836-5450. Students 195.

7—QUEEN OF APOSTLES (1963), Revs. Daniel L. Mode; Keith M. O'Hare. In Res., Revs. Reginald La Fleur; Charles F. Siewert (WCH); Deacons Richard C. Caporiccio; Julio T. Perez.
Res.: 4329 Sano St., 22312. Tel: 703-354-8711; Fax: 703-354-0766.
School—4409 Sano St., 22312. Tel: 703-354-0714; Fax: 703-354-1820. Mary L. West, Prin. Lay Teachers 16; Students 269.

Catechesis/Religious Program—Tel: 703-354-4360. James K. Ward, D.R.E. Students 247.

8—ST. RITA'S (1914), Revs. Denis M. Donahue; Richard A. Mullins. In Res., Rev. Daniel J. Maher.
Res.: 3815 Russell Rd., 22305. Tel: 703-836-1640; Fax: 703-836-7825.
School—3801 Russell Rd., 22305. Tel: 703-548-1888. Mrs. Mary Pat Schlickenmaier, Prin. Sisters of St. Joseph 1; Lay Teachers 12; Students 214.
Catechesis/Religious Program—Tel: 703-836-1356. Students 190.
Convent—Sisters of St. Joseph, 231 W. Glebe Rd., 22305. Tel: 703-683-1929.

ANNANDALE, FAIRFAX CO.

1—ST. AMBROSE (1966), Revs. Dominic P. Irace; John A. Ziegler. In Res., Rev. Daniel S. Spychala.
Church and Office Mailing Address: 3901 Woodburn Rd., 22003.
Res.: 3825 Woodburn Rd., 22003. Tel: 703-280-4400; Fax: 703-280-1123.
School—3827 Woodburn Rd., 22003. Tel: 703-698-7171; Fax: 703-698-7170. Mrs. Virginia Connell, Prin. Lay Teachers 15; Students 212.
Catechesis/Religious Program—Tel: 703-280-1122. Mr. John Mallory, D.R.E. Students 190.

2—HOLY SPIRIT (1964), Revs. Frank J. Ready, V.F.; Edward R. Horkan. In Res., Rev. Msgr. R. Roy Cosby, V.G. (Retired).
Res.: 5121 Woodland Way, 22003. Tel: 703-978-8074; Fax: 703-978-9671.
School—8800 Braddock Rd., 22003. Tel: 703-978-7117; Fax: 703-978-7438. Mrs. Deborah Mohney, Prin. Lay Teachers 28; Students 476.
Catechesis/Religious Program—Tel: 703-978-8925. Mrs. Margaret Whitehead, D.R.E. Students 838.

3—ST. MICHAEL'S (1953), Revs. Jerome R. Daly; John C. De Celles; Edwin E. Perez; Deacons David S. McCaffrey; Roger T. Ostrom.
Res.: 7401 St. Michael's Ln., 22003. Tel: 703-256-7822; Fax: 703-256-0446.
School—Tel: 703-256-1222; Fax: 703-941-9403. Sr. Dorothy Mayer, I.H.M., Prin. Servants of the Immaculate Heart of Mary 6; Lay Teachers 24; Students 385.
Catechesis/Religious Program—Tel: 703-941-9403. Mr. William Duffy, D.R.E. Students 285.
Convent—Sisters, Servants of the Immaculate Heart of Mary, 7421 St. Michael's Ln., 22003. Tel: 703-256-2130.

ASHBURN, LOUDOUN CO., ST. THERESA (1991), Revs. Richard M. Guest; Mark Mullaney.
Mailing Address: P.O. Box 526, 20146-0526. Tel: 703-729-2287; Fax: 703-729-9036 (Call First).
Rectory—43313 Dovetail Pl., 20147. Tel: 703-729-8655.
Church: 21370 St. Theresa Ln., 20147.
School—Tel: 703-729-3577; Fax: 703-729-8068. Mrs. Jacqueline MacKenzie, Prin. Lay Teachers 25; Students 503.
Catechesis/Religious Program—Tel: 703-729-3714. Mrs. Carol Anne Jones, D.R.E. Students 1,407.

BRISTOW, PRINCE WILLIAM CO., HOLY TRINITY (2001), Rev. Francis J. Peffley.
Res.: 13260 McCartney Ct., 20136. Tel: 703-753-6700; Fax: 703-753-6286.
Catechesis/Religious Program—Tel: 540-347-1152. Students 440.

BURKE, FAIRFAX CO., CHURCH OF THE NATIVITY (W. Springfield) (1973), Revs. Richard B. Martin; Kevin O'Keefe; Deacon Wilson I. Korpi.
Mailing Address: 6400 Nativity Ln., 22015. Tel: 703-455-2400; Fax: 703-455-6832.
Res.: 9523 Lyra Ct., 22015. Tel: 703-913-2306.
School—6398 Nativity Ln., 22015. Tel: 703-455-2300; Fax: 703-569-8109. Miss Maria E. Kelly, Prin. Lay Teachers 16; Students 256.
Catechesis/Religious Program—Tel: 703-455-0372. Sisters Donatella Merulla, A.R., M.R.E., D.R.E.; Mary Attilia Todaro, A.R., M.R.E., D.R.E. Students 1,600.
Convent—Handmaids of Reparation of the Sacred Heart of Jesus, 6300 Capella Ave., 22015. Tel: 703-455-4180.

CHANTILLY, FAIRFAX CO., ST. TIMOTHY (1969), Revs. Gerald Weymes; J. Edwin Thayer Tewes; Carroll L. Oubre; Deacons David E. Conroy; William J. Pyrek.
Res.: 13807 Poplar Tree Rd., 20151. Tel: 703-378-7461; 703-378-7646; Fax: 703-378-7552.
School—13809 Poplar Tree Rd., 20151. Tel: 703-378-6932; Fax: 703-378-1273. Mrs. Marilyn Valatka, Prin. Lay Teachers 32; Students 635.
Catechesis/Religious Program—Tel: 703-814-7981; Fax: 703-378-7552. Maria Ho, D.R.E. Students 1,322.

CLIFTON, FAIRFAX CO.

1—ST. ANDREW THE APOSTLE (1989), Revs. Jerome W. Fasano; Lawrence M. Violette; Joseph J. Clark.
Res.: 6720 Union Mill Rd., 20124. Tel: 703-817-1770; Fax: 703-817-0928.
School—Tel: 703-817-1774; Fax: 703-817-1721. Mrs. Phyllis Hammang, Prin. Lay Teachers 15; Students 290.
Catechesis/Religious Program—Tel: 703-817-1773. Mrs. Delores Nelson, D.R.E. Students 1,400.

2—ST. CLARE OF ASSISI (1981), Rev. Paul L. Dudzinski.
Mailing Address: 7616 Maple Branch Rd., 20124. Tel: 703-266-1310; Fax: 703-266-7011.
Church: 12409 Henderson Rd., 20124.
Catechesis/Religious Program—Peggy Mattie, D.R.E. Students 132.

COLONIAL BEACH, WESTMORELAND CO., ST. ELIZABETH (1906), [JC] Revs. Thomas P. Vander Woude; Geronimo A. Magat; Deacon Edward C. Cleary.
Res.: 21 Irving Ave. S., P.O. Box 275, 22443. Tel: 804-224-7221; Fax: 804-224-7221.
Catechesis/Religious Program—Students 102.
Mission—St. Anthony's [CEM] P.O. Box 275, King George, King George Co. 22443.

CULPEPER, CULPEPER CO., PRECIOUS BLOOD (1880), [CEM] Rev. Leo J. Zonneveld, C.I.C.M.
Res.: 114 E. Edmondson St., 22701. Tel: 540-825-8945; Fax: 540-825-8987.
Catechesis/Religious Program—Tel: 540-825-1339. Ms. Patricia Reed, D.R.E. Students 259.
Mission—St. Peter P.O. Box 27, Washington, Rappahannock Co. 22747. Tel: 540-675-3432; Fax: 540-675-1053. Rev. Robert J. DeMartino; Deacon Charles A. Coutu.

DALE CITY, PRINCE WILLIAM CO., HOLY FAMILY (1970), Revs. Jose Eugenio Hoyos; Mark F. Carrier; Tran Dinh Nhi; Donald J. Planty; Deacons Gerald J. Moore; Vincent Einsmann; Frederick J. Romanski.
Res.: 14160 Ferndale Rd., 22193. Tel: 703-670-8161; Fax: 703-670-8323.
School—Tel: 703-670-8161, Ext. 224. Barbara Mertens, Prin.; Pat Bihner, Dir. (PreK-4). Lay Teachers 16; Students 165.
Catechesis/Religious Program—Tel: 703-670-8161, Ext. 232. Students 1,000.

FAIRFAX STATION, ARLINGTON CO., ST. RAYMOND OF PENAFORT (1997), Rev. James R. Gould. In Res., Revs. Joseph G. Knapp, S.J.; Joseph O. Adhunga, A.J.
Res.: 8900 Triple Ridge Rd., 22039. Tel: 703-690-6650; Fax: 703-690-7399.
Catechesis/Religious Program—Bob Ward, D.R.E.; Beverly Ward, D.R.E. Students 309.

FAIRFAX, FAIRFAX CO.

1—ST. LEO'S (1957), Revs. John D. Kelly; Terry A. Cramer; Jerry A. Wooton; Deacon Nicholas LaDuca. In Res., Rev. Terry W. Specht.
Res.: 3700 Old Lee Hwy., 22030. Tel: 703-273-5369; Fax: 703-273-2371.
School—3704 Old Lee Hwy., 22030. Tel: 703-273-1211; Fax: 703-273-6913. Mrs. Diane Drews, Prin. Lay Teachers 25; Students 562.
Catechesis/Religious Program—Tel: 703-273-4868. Students 625.
Station—Fairfax Nursing Home, Tel: 703-273-7705.

2—ST. MARY OF SORROWS (1858), [CEM] Revs. Donald C. Greenhalgh; Paul M. Grankauskas; Michael D. Weston; Deacon John M. Ligon.
Mailing & Parish Center Address: 5222 Sideburn Rd., 22032-2640. Tel: 703-978-4141; Fax: 703-978-2568.
Historic Church—5612 Ox Rd., Fairfax Station, 22039.
Res.: 11112 Fairfax Station Rd., Fairfax Station, 22039.
School—Preschool, Tel: 703-978-9656. Elena Quartuccio, Dir.
Catechesis/Religious Program—Tel: 703-978-4283. Margaret Telesca, D.R.E., (PreK-8); William Gavin, D.R.E., (9-12). Students 1,266.

3—ST. PAUL CHUNG (1996), (Korean), Revs. Thaddaues Yong Song Kim (Wonju); Thomas Woo Sick Shin (Wonju); Deacon Paul Lee.
Res.: 4708 Rippling Pond Dr., 22033. Tel: 703-818-9707; Fax: 703-968-3013.
Church and Mailing Address: 4712 Rippling Pond Dr., 22033-5077. Tel: 703-968-3010.
Catechesis/Religious Program—Moon C. Kim, D.R.E. Tel: 703-841-2572. Students 480.

FALLS CHURCH, FAIRFAX CO.

1—ST. ANTHONY'S (1952), Revs. Horace H. Grinnell; Stephen F. McGraw; Deacon Mario Mendoza. In Res., Rev. Tarsicio Buitrago (Colombia).
Res.: 3305 Glen Carlyn Rd., 22041. Tel: 703-820-7111; Fax: 703-379-9195.
Catechesis/Religious Program—Tel: 703-820-2158. Mary Lou Miller, D.R.E. Students 1,299.

2—ST. JAMES (1892), [CEM] Rev. Cornelius O'Brien; Rev. Msgr. Frank E. Mahler; Rev. Frederick H. Edlefsen; Deacons James A. Fishenden; Thomas M. Bello. In Res., Rev. Michael G. Taylor.
Res.: 905 Park Ave., 22046. Tel: 703-532-8815; Fax: 703-533-7644.
School—830 W. Broad St., 22046. Tel: 703-533-1182, Ext. 100; Fax: 703-532-8316. Sr. Teresa Ballisty, I.H.M., Prin. Servants of the Immaculate Heart of Mary 7; Lay Teachers 25; Students 740.
Catechesis/Religious Program—Tel: 703-533-1182, Ext. 103. Michael Sirotniak, D.R.E. Students 338.
Convent—Sisters, Servants of the Immaculate Heart of Mary, 101 N. Spring St., 22046. Tel: 703-532-2388.

3—ST. PHILIP (1963), Revs. Kevin B. Walsh; Michael J. Dobbins; Deacon Noel Vivaldi.
Res.: 7500 St. Philip's Ct., 22042. Tel: 703-573-3808; Fax: 703-560-2832.
Catechesis/Religious Program—Tel: 703-573-1899; Fax: 703-573-6832. Students 177.

FREDERICKSBURG, FREDERICKSBURG CO.

1—ST. MARY (1858), Revs. Donald J. Rooney; Joseph R. Kenna; Stefan P. Starzynski.
Res.: 1009 Stafford Ave., 22401-5418. Tel: 540-373-6491; 540-373-6663; Fax: 540-371-0251.
Catechesis/Religious Program—Tel: 540-373-7770. Diane K. McFall, D.R.E. Students 1,021.
Convent—Oblate Sisters of St. Francis de Sales, St. Mary Convent, 1104 Augustine Ave., 22401. Tel: 540-371-1652; Fax: 540-371-1672.
Mission—St. Jude 5610 Southpoint Centre Blvd. Ste. 105, Spotsylvania Co. 22408. Tel: 540-891-7350; Fax: 540-891-1810. Rev. David L. Martin.

2—ST. PATRICK'S (1983), Revs. Philip S. Majka; Paul D. Scalia; Deacons David Conroy; David J. Geary; William D. Pivarnik.
Church & Res.: 9149 Elys Ford Rd., 22407. Tel: 540-785-5299; Fax: 540-785-5692.
School—9151 Ely's Ford Rd., 22407. Tel: 540-786-2277; Fax: 540-785-2213. Mr. George Elliott, Prin. Lay Teachers 11; Students 240.
Catechesis/Religious Program—Tel: 540-785-7857; Fax: 540-785-5758. Philip Camill, D.R.E. Students 450.

FRONT ROYAL, WARREN CO., ST. JOHN THE BAPTIST (1884), Revs. William F. Ruehl, V.F.; Vincent P. Bork; Deacon Richard Demers.
Res.: 123 W. Main St., 22630. Tel: 540-635-3780; Fax: 540-635-2683.
Catechesis/Religious Program—Tel: 540-635-9493. Sr. Eleanor Kelly, D.R.E. Students 211.

GORDONSVILLE, ORANGE CO., ST. MARK'S (1972), Merged, with St. John's, Orange to form St. Isidore the Farmer, Orange.

GREAT FALLS, FAIRFAX CO., ST. CATHERINE OF SIENA (1979), Revs. Franklyn M. McAfee; Alexander R. Drummond; M. Paul Richardson; James G. Mercer; Deacon Joseph G. Benin.
Mailing Address: 1020 Springvale Rd., 22066. Tel: 703-759-4350; Fax: 703-759-3753.
Catechesis/Religious Program—Tel: 703-759-3530; Fax: 703-759-7941. Brian Radzik, D.R.E. Students 550.

HERNDON, FAIRFAX CO.

1—ST. JOSEPH (1950), Revs. David C. Bonarrigo, T.O.R.; Christopher Dobson, T.O.R.; James Angert, T.O.R.
Res.: 750 Peachtree St., 20170. Tel: 703-437-3737; Fax: 703-437-8745.
School—Tel: 703-437-3014. Mrs. Joan Cargill, Prin. Lay Teachers 24; Students 596.
Catechesis/Religious Program—Students 836.

2—ST. VERONICA (1999), Rev. Marcus A. Pollard.
3300 Dairy Lou Dr., 20171. Tel: 703-689-4409; Fax: 703-689-4410. In Res., Most Rev. Christopher M. Buckner.
Catechesis/Religious Program—Carol Krieger, D.R.E. Students 380.

KILMARNOCK, LANCASTER CO., ST. FRANCIS DE SALES (1966), [CEM 2] Rev. James C. Bruse; Deacon Thomas D. Battaglia.
Res.: 151 E. Church St., P.O. Box 759, 22482-0759. Tel: 804-435-1511; Fax: 804-436-9614.
Catechesis/Religious Program—Fax: 804-436-9614. Anna Marie Rundall, D.R.E. Students 67.
Mission—St. Paul Hague, Westmoreland Co. 22469.

LAKE RIDGE, PRINCE WILLIAM CO., ST. ELIZABETH ANN SETON (1976), Revs. James S. Barkett; Mark E. Moretti; Deacons Emil P. Myskowski; Alvin R. McDaniel.
Mailing Address: 12805 Valleywood Dr., 22192. Tel: 703-494-4008; Fax: 703-494-1995.
Catechesis/Religious Program—Tel: 703-494-3966; Fax: 703-494-8005. Jackie Ezersky, D.R.E. Students 1,003.

LEESBURG, LOUDOUN CO., ST. JOHN THE APOSTLE (1926), [CEM] Revs. Robert C. Brooks; Stephen F. Leva.
Mailing Address: 101 Oakcrest Manor Dr., N.E., 20176-2221. Tel: 703-777-1317; Fax: 703-771-9016.
Res.: 302 N. King St., N.E., 20176.
Catechesis/Religious Program—Tel: 703-777-3891. Mrs. Kathleen A. Fridley, D.R.E. Students 826.

LURAY, PAGE CO., OUR LADY OF THE VALLEY (1954), Rev. Christopher Lemme, T.O.R.
Mailing Address: 200 Collins Ave., 22835. Tel: 540-743-4919; Fax: 540-743-2490.
Catechesis/Religious Program—Mrs. Irene Sommers, D.R.E. Students 55.

MADISON, MADISON CO., OUR LADY OF THE BLUE RIDGE (1977), Rev. Michael T. Orlowsky.
Res.: 692 Lonnie Burke Rd., 22727. Tel: 540-948-4144; Fax: 540-948-3325.
Catechesis/Religious Program—Students 100.

MANASSAS, PRINCE WILLIAM CO.
1—ALL SAINTS (1929), Revs. Robert C. Cilinski; Stephen Holmes; John P. Mosimann; James C. Hudgins; Deacons John W. Eberlein; Richard O'Connell.
Res.: 9300 Stonewall Rd., 20110. Tel: 703-368-4500; Fax: 703-257-9299.
School—9294 Stonewall Rd., 20110. Tel: 703-368-4400; Fax: 703-393-2157. Mr. David E. Conroy Jr., Prin.; Mrs. Judy Fisher, Asst. Prin. Lay Teachers 32; Students 550.
Catechesis/Religious Program—Tel: 703-393-2142. Joanna Catabui, D.R.E., (Elementary); Rob Tessier, D.R.E., (Junior-Senior Education); Maris Mattingly, RCIA Coord. Students 1,230.
2—SACRED HEART (1984), [CEM] Rev. Thomas J. Lehning; Deacon Thomas W. Wolter.
Mailing Address: 12975 Purcell Rd., 20112-3217. Tel: 703-590-0030; Fax: 703-590-0141. In Res., Rev. Peter C. Akpoghiran (Nigeria).
Res.: 6258 Terrapin Dr., 20112. Tel: 703-791-5131.
Catechesis/Religious Program—Tel: 703-590-0256. Students 632.

MCLEAN, FAIRFAX CO.
1—ST. JOHN'S (1913), Revs. Edward C. Hathaway; Wilhelm J. Ettner. In Res., Rev. Augustine Hoa Trung Tran (ATL).
Res.: 6420 Linway Ter., 22101. Tel: 703-356-7916; Fax: 703-356-4517.
School—6422 Linway Ter., 22101. Tel: 703-356-7554; Fax: 703-448-3811. Mrs. Christine Wells, Prin. Lay Teachers 18; Students 235.
Catechesis/Religious Program—Tel: 703-356-5275. Ms. Laura Pennefather, D.R.E. Students 326.
2—ST. LUKE'S (1961), Revs. Martin F. McGuill; Terrence R. Staples.
Res.: 7001 Georgetown Pike, 22101. Tel: 703-356-1255; Fax: 703-442-0848.
School—7005 Georgetown Pike, 22101. Tel: 703-356-1508; Fax: 703-356-1141. David DePippa, Prin. Lay Teachers 20; Students 243.
Catechesis/Religious Program—Tel: 703-356-8419; Fax: 703-356-3543. Carol Mournighan, D.R.E. Students 693.

MIDDLEBURG, LOUDOUN CO., ST. STEPHEN THE MARTYR (1975), Rev. Joseph P. Biniek.
Mailing Address: P.O. Box 474, 20118-0474. Tel: 540-687-6433; Fax: 540-687-5170.
Res.: 23309 Sam Fred Rd., 20117. Tel: 540-729-0696.
Church: Intersection Rte. 50 & Sam Fred Rd., 20117.
Catechesis/Religious Program—Students 374.

ORANGE, ORANGE CO.
1—ST. ISIDORE THE FARMER (2002),
Res.: 14405 St. Isidore Way, 22960. Tel: 540-672-4933; Fax: 540-661-4204. Rev. David L. Martin.
Catechesis/Religious Program—Mollie McMahon, D.R.E. Students 56.
2—ST. JOHN'S (1946), Merged, with St. Mark's, Gordonsville to form St. Isidore the Farmer, Orange.

POTOMAC FALLS, LOUDOUN CO., OUR LADY OF HOPE (2000), Rev. William P. Saunders, Ed.D., V.F.; Deacon William P. Emley.
Res.: 20648 Belwood Ct., 20165. Tel: 703-430-5702; Fax: 703-430-5727.
Catechesis/Religious Program—Sally Girardi, D.R.E.; Phil Girardi, D.R.E. Students 684.

PURCELLVILLE, LOUDOUN CO., ST. FRANCIS DE SALES (1967), Rev. Msgr. Thomas J. Cassidy (Retired); Rev. Patrick L. Posey.
Res.: 37730 St. Francis Ct., 20132. Tel: 540-338-6381; Fax: 540-338-6431.
Catechesis/Religious Program— Rebecca Sparks-LaPointe, D.R.E.; Janice Rees, D.R.E. Students 720.

RESTON, FAIRFAX CO.
1—ST. JOHN NEUMANN (1979), Revs. Robert A. Brown, O.S.F.S.; Charles M. Chamberlain, O.S.F.S.; William N. Dougherty, O.S.F.S.
Res.: 11900 Lawyers Rd., 20191-4299. Tel: 703-860-8510; Fax: 703-860-2136.
Catechesis/Religious Program—Tel: 703-860-8641. Cheryl Orwig Whapham, D.R.E. Students 1,487.
2—ST. THOMAS A BECKET (1970), Rev. Kevin J. Larsen.
Res.: 1421 Wiehle Ave., 20190. Tel: 703-437-7113; Fax: 703-689-3814.
Catechesis/Religious Program—Tel: 703-689-3816. Clem Gross, D.R.E. Students 569.

SPOTSYLVANIA, SPOTSYLVANIA CO., ST. MATTHEW (1999), Revs. David P. Meng; Ronald S. Escalante; Deacons Edward Whelan; John Hubbarth.
8200 Robert E. Lee Dr., 22553. Tel: 540-582-5575; Fax: 540-582-8639.
Catechesis/Religious Program—Tel: 540-582-8469. Ric Garrett, D.R.E. Students 302.

SPRINGFIELD, FAIRFAX CO., ST. BERNADETTE'S (1959), Revs. Thomas P. Ferguson; John F. Heisler; Kevin J. Beres; John T.B. Trong.
Res.: 7600 Old Keene Mill Rd., 22152-2022. Tel: 703-451-8576; Fax: 703-451-6893.
School—7602 Old Keene Mill Rd., 22152-2099. Tel: 703-451-8696; Fax: 703-451-8221. Sr. Maureen Vellon, R.S.H.M., Prin. Priests 2; Lay Teachers 24; Students 483.
Catechesis/Religious Program—Tel: 703-569-0512; Fax: 703-569-9728. Karen Murphy, D.R.E.; Claudia Fiebig, D.R.E. Students 867.
Convent—Daughters of Wisdom, 7676 Tiverton Dr., 22152.

STAFFORD, STAFFORD CO., ST. WILLIAM OF YORK (1971), Revs. Michael R. Duesterhaus; Paul M. Eversole; Deacon Richard P. Smith. In Res., Revs. Anthony J. Pinizzotto, O.S.F.S.; Joseph C. Howard.
Res. & Mailing Address: 3130 Jefferson Davis Hwy., 22554. Tel: 540-659-1102; Fax: 540-659-5637.
School—(Grades PreK-8) Tel: 540-659-5207. Mrs. Claire Dougherty, Prin. Franciscan Missionary Sisters of the Infant Jesus 3; Lay Teachers 13; Students 284.
Catechesis/Religious Program—Tel: 540-659-5705; 540-288-0201. Sr. Michele DeGregorio, F.M.I.J. Students 800.
Convent—Franciscan Missionary Sisters of the Infant Jesus, 14 Emerson Ct., 22554. Tel: 540-288-0201.

STERLING, LOUDOUN CO., CHRIST THE REDEEMER (1972), Revs. C. Donald Howard, S.A.; William F. Schmidt, S.A.; Timothy I. MacDonald; Deacons Joseph R. Singer; Lawrence V. Hammel.
Res.: 12494 Cliff Edge Dr., Herndon, 20170. Tel: 703-430-1686.
Church: 46833 Harry Byrd Hwy., 20164. Tel: 703-430-0811; Fax: 703-430-1590.
Catechesis/Religious Program—Tel: 703-430-0813. Mrs. Maureen Roan, D.R.E. Students 865.

TRIANGLE, PRINCE WILLIAM CO., ST. FRANCIS OF ASSISI (1957), Revs. John J. Marino, O.F.M.; Robert Menard, O.F.M.; Gene B. Pistacchio, O.F.M.
Res.: 18825 Fuller Heights Rd., 22172. Tel: 703-221-4575.
Church: Tel: 703-221-4044; Fax: 703-221-3246.
School—Tel: 703-221-3868; Fax: 703-221-0700. Dr. Tricia Barber, Prin. Lay Teachers 16; Students 343.
Catechesis/Religious Program—Tel: 703-221-4978. Mrs. Margaret Bruni, D.R.E. Students 1,000.

VIENNA, FAIRFAX CO.
1—ST. MARK (1965), [CEM] Rev. Patrick Holroyd. In Res., Rev. Msgr. Thomas J. Cassidy.
Res.: 9970 Vale Rd., 22181. Tel: 703-281-9100; Fax: 703-281-0675.
Catechesis/Religious Program—Tel: 703-938-1948. Sr. Anne Jordan, O.S.F., D.R.E.; Patricia Wheatley, D.R.E. Students 925.
2—OUR LADY OF GOOD COUNSEL (1956), Revs. John M. O'Neill, O.S.F.S.; Francis J. Rinaldi, O.S.F.S.; William J. Metzger, O.S.F.S. In Res., Revs. Mark S. Mealey, O.S.F.S.; Francis W. Danella, O.S.F.S., D.Min. (WDC).
Office & Mailing Address: P.O. Box 97, 22183. Tel: 703-938-2828; Fax: 703-938-2828.
Res.: 8601 Wolftrap Rd., 22182.
School—Tel: 703-938-3600; Fax: 703-255-1543. Mr. Austin Poole, Prin. Lay Teachers 30; Students 500.
Catechesis/Religious Program—Tel: 703-938-2553, Ext. 19. Ms. Patricia Jones, D.R.E. Students 519.

WARRENTON, FAUQUIER CO., ST. JOHN THE EVANGELIST (1874), Revs. Michael J. Bazan; Christopher D. Murphy; Deacon W. Bernard Ragan.
Res.: 271 Winchester St., 22186. Tel: 540-347-2922; Fax: 540-347-1274.
School—111 King St., 22186. Tel: 540-347-2458; Fax: 540-349-8007. Elizabeth Roach, Prin. Lay Teachers 9; Students 385.
Catechesis/Religious Program—Teresa Paccassi, D.R.E. Students 940.

WINCHESTER, FREDERICK CO., SACRED HEART OF JESUS (1870), [CEM] Revs. Stanley J. Krempa; Michael C. Kelly; Deacon Edward L. Christianson.
Res.: 130 Keating Dr., 22601-2806. Tel: 540-662-5858; Fax: 540-667-6156.
School—110 Keating Dr., 22601-2806. Tel: 540-662-7177. Mrs. Bonnie McGann. School Sisters of Notre Dame 1; Lay Teachers 15; Students 180.
Catechesis/Religious Program—Tel: 540-665-1975. Chester L. Lewandowski, M.A., D.R.E. Students 407.
Convent—School Sisters of Notre Dame, 140 Keating Dr., 22601 Tel: 540-662-6687.
Mission—St. Bridget of Ireland 22638. 130 Keating Dr., Berryville, Clarke Co. 22601.

WOODBRIDGE, PRINCE WILLIAM CO., OUR LADY OF ANGELS (1959), Revs. Robert A. Lange; James A. Tucker; Richard T. Carr; Deacons Danny E. Johnson; Jose I. Pardo.
Res.: 13752 Mary's Way, 22191. Tel: 703-494-2444; 703-494-5015; Fax: 703-494-0005.
Catechesis/Religious Program—Tel: 703-494-3696; Fax: 703-494-3605. Students 729.

WOODSTOCK, SHENANDOAH CO., ST. JOHN BOSCO (1888), Rev. William M. Aitcheson; Deacon Robert E. deLadurantaye.
Res.: 315 N. Main St., 22664. Tel: 540-459-4448; Fax: 540-459-4406.
Catechesis/Religious Program—Tel: 540-459-8334. Hugh Owen, D.R.E. Students 119.
Mission—Our Lady of the Shenandoah 240 Fretzel Way, P.O. Box 654, Basye, Shenandoah Co. 22810. Tel: 540-856-2411. Rev. Joseph A. Salazar, M.S.A.

DIOCESAN MISSION PARISH

DOMINICAN REPUBLIC
1—SAN FRANCISCO DE ASIS, BANICA, Revs. Daniel N. Gee; John T. O'Hara.
Mailing Address: BM #7038, 6911 N.W. 87 Ave., Miami, FL 33178-1625.
2—SAN JOSE, PEDRO SANTANA, Revs. Daniel N. Gee; John T. O'Hara.
Mailing Address: BM #7038, 6911 N.W. 87 Ave., Miami, FL 33178-1625.

On Duty Outside the Diocese:
Revs.—
Albertson, Eric J., Chap. Maj., Fort Leavenworth, KS
Carr, Matthew, Augustiner Chorherrenstift, Austria
Connelly, Christian T., Chap. 1st Lt., Fayetteville, NC
Fisher, Andrew J., Basilica of the National Shrine of the Immaculate Conception, Washington, D.C.
Gee, Daniel N., St. Joseph, Pedro Santana and Banica, Dominican Republic
Gross, Lee W., M.Div., Mount St. Mary Seminary, Emmitsburg, MD
O'Hara, John T., St. Joseph Parish, Pedro Santana and Banica, Dominican Republic
Pilon, Mark A., S.T.D., Mount St. Mary Seminary, Emmitsburg, MD
Pokorsky, Jerry L., Lincoln, NE

Military Chaplains:
Revs.—
Albertson, Eric J., Major, Fort Leavenworth, KS
Connelly, Christian T., Chap. 1st Lt., Fayetteville, NC

On Leave of Absence:
Revs.—
Berghout, Paul A.
Erbacher, William J.
Haley, James R.
Hamilton, Daniel E.
Mercer, James G.
Rahn, David C.

Retired:
Rev. Msgrs.—
Cassidy, Thomas J., St. Mark, Vienna
Cilinski, John T., St. Agnes, Arlington
Cosby, R. Roy, V.G., Holy Spirit, Annandale
Hendrick, Frank J., Boynton Beach, FL
Scannell, Thomas P., Falls Church
Revs.—
Cilinski, Julius J., Fairfax
Ciullo, Salvator L.
Dair, Richard J., Fairfax
Gerloff, Charles W., Virginia Beach
Hughes, John J., McLean
Loftus, Joseph J., Our Lady of Lourdes, Arlington
Slivonik, Stanley, Lovettsville
Trinkle, Clarence M., Fort Valley
Watkins, Clarence N., Falls Church

Permanent Deacons:
Ambury, James F., Our Lady of Lourdes, Arlington
Arquette, Lester K., St. Gerard, Detroit, MI; Immaculate Heart of Mary, Detroit, MI
Bayne, James L., Leave of Absence
Bello, Thomas M., St. James, Falls Church
Benedi, Claudio F., Cathedral of St. Thomas More, Arlington
Benin, Joseph G., St. Catherine, Great Falls
Betit, Eugene D., Our Lady Queen of Peace, Arlington
Braun, Richard L., Leave of Absence
Burrell, Richard L., Leave of Absence
Canonica, Donald A., St. Mary, Opelika, AL
Christianson, Edward L., Sacred Heart, Winchester
Conroy, David E., St. Timothy, Chantilly; St. Patrick, Fredericksburg
Coutu, Charles A., St. Peter Mission, Washington
deLadurantaye, Robert E., St. John Bosco, Woodstock

Demers, Richard L., St. John the Baptist, Front Royal
Donovan, William J., St. Agnes, Arlington
Eberlein, John W., All Saints, Manassas
Einsmann, W. Vincent, Holy Family, Dale City
Fishenden, James A., St. James, Falls Church
Frank, John L., Leave of Absence
Galvez, Rene A., Annunciation, West Hollywood, FL
George, Paul J., Leave of Absence
Henry, Lawrence B., Base Chapel, Peterson AFB, CO
Johnson, Danny E., Our Lady of Angels, Woodbridge
Kenski, Frank G., (Retired)
Korpi, Wilson I., Nativity, Burke
LaDuca, Nicholas J., St. Leo the Great, Fairfax
Lee, Paul, St. Paul Chung, Fairfax
Ligon, Jack M., St. Mary of Sorrows, Fairfax
Malinowski, Leonard P., (Retired)
Mallon, John B., St. Charles Borromeo, Arlington
Melvin, Gerald A., Leave of Absence
Mendoza, Mario L., St. Anthony, Falls Church
Moore, Gerald J., Holy Family, Dale City
Myskowski, Emil P., St. Elizabeth Ann Seton, Lake Ridge
Nickle, Dennis E., Leave of Absence
O'Connell, Richard T., All Saints, Manassas
Ostrom, Roger T., St. Michael, Annandale
Pardo, Jose I., Our Lady of Angels, Woodbridge
Pham, Kien Minh, Holy Martyrs of Vietnam, Arlington
Pivarnik, William D., St. Patrick, Fredericksburg
Prien, Richard K., Immaculate Conception, Lock Haven, PA
Pyrek, William J., St. Timothy, Chantilly
Ragan, W. Bernard, St. John the Evangelist, Warrenton
Ramirez, Eduardo A., St. Ann, Arlington
Rees, Paul J., Leave of Absence
Resendes, Daniel F., (Retired)
Singer, Joseph R., Christ the Redeemer, Sterling
Smith, Richard P., St. William of York, Stafford
Soutuyo, Francisco R., Leave of Absence
Taub, Samuel M., (Retired)
Vivaldi, Noel, St. Philip, Falls Church
Ward, Albert P., (Retired)
White, Thomas G., Good Shepherd, Alexandria
Wolter, Thomas W., Sacred Heart, Manassas

INSTITUTIONS LOCATED IN THE DIOCESE

[A] COLLEGES AND UNIVERSITIES

ARLINGTON. *Marymount University*, 2807 N. Glebe Rd., 22207. Tel: 703-522-5600; Fax: 703-522-0349. Email: admissions@marymount.edu. Web: www.marymount.edu. Dr. James E. Bundschuh, Pres.; Rev. John P. Peterson, Campus Min. Religious of the Sacred Heart of Mary, Resident and Non-resident coed students. Sisters 7; Lay Faculty & Staff 605; Students 3,825.

FRONT ROYAL. *Christendom College*, 134 Christendom Dr., 22630. Tel: 540-636-2900; Fax: 540-636-1655. Web: www.christendom.edu. Timothy T. O'Donnell, S.T.D., Pres. Resident and Non-resident students. Sisters 1; Lay Teachers 24; Students 477. In Res. Revs. Anthony J. Mastroeni (Vatican City State); James P. O'Kielty (PAT) (Retired); Robert L. Ruskamp.

[B] GRADUATE SCHOOLS

ARLINGTON. **The Institute for the Psychological Sciences, Inc.*, 2001 Jefferson Davis Hwy.,Ste. 511, 22202. Tel: 703-416-1441; Fax: 703-416-8588. Email: info@ipsciences.edu. Web: www.ipsciences.edu. Gladys Sweeney, Ph.D., Dean. Dedicated to the development and promotion of approaches to psychology founded in the Catholic vision of the human person. Master of Science (M.S.) and Doctor of Psychology (Psy.D.) degrees in Clinical Psychology.

ALEXANDRIA. *Notre Dame Graduate School of Christendom College*, 4407 Sano St., 22312. Tel: 703-658-4304; Fax: 703-658-2318. Email: ndgscc@yahoo.com. Web: www.christendom.edu. Kristin P. Burns, Ph.D., Dean; Luther P. Niehoff, Admin. Dir. Priests 4; Sisters 1; Lay Teachers 6; Total Staff 14; Total Enrollment 250.

[C] DISTANCE UNIVERSITY

HAMILTON. *The Catholic Distance University*, 120 E. Colonial Hwy., 20158-9012. Tel: 540-338-2700; Fax: 540-338-4788. Email: cdu@cdu.edu. Web: www.cdu.edu. Most Revs. Paul S. Loverde, D.D., S.T.L., J.C.L., Bd. Chm., Pres.; Christopher M. Buckner, Undergraduate Dean; Robert Royal, Graduate Dean; Marianne Evans Mount, Exec. Vice Pres. Accredited Catechetical Institute for Adults; Catechetical Diploma; Continuing Education; and Undergraduate College credit, Masters (M.A.) in Religious Studies. All programs through education. Priests 1; Adjunct Faculty 23; Staff 17; Total Staff 37; Total Students 700.

[D] HIGH SCHOOLS, DIOCESAN

ARLINGTON. *Bishop Denis J. O'Connell High School*, 6600 Little Falls Rd., 22213. Tel: 703-237-1400; Fax: 703-237-1465. Email: avburch@bishopoconnell.org. Web: www.pluto.ee.cua.edu/~oconnell/. Mr. Alward V. Burch, Prin.; Mr. John J. Gutter, Asst. Prin.; Mr. Richard J. Martin, Asst. Prin.; Sr. Regina Joseph Ryan, I.H.M., Asst. Prin.; Rev. Michael G. Taylor, Spiritual Dir.; Mr. Thomas McNichol, Guidance Dir. Priests 2; Sisters 11; Teachers 116; Total Staff 150; Sisters Servants of the Immaculate Heart of Mary 1; Lay Teachers 93; Students 1,418.

ALEXANDRIA. *Bishop Ireton High School*, 201 Cambridge Rd., 22314. Tel: 703-751-7606; Fax: 703-212-8173. Email: info@bishopireton.org. Web: www.bishopireton.org. Revs. Kevin M. Nadolski, O.S.F.S., Prin.; Matthew J. Hillyard, O.S.F.S., Prin.; Joseph T. Brennan, O.S.F.S., Chap. (See separate listing for Oblates of St. Francis de Sales Residence) Oblates of St. Francis de Sales 4; Brothers 1; Sisters 2; Lay Teachers 56; Students 815.

FAIRFAX. *Paul VI Catholic High School*, 10675 Lee Hwy., 22030. Tel: 703-352-0925; Fax: 703-273-9845. Email: website@paulvi.net. Web: www.paulvi.net. Philip V. Robey, Prin.; Mr. Patrick McGroarty, Asst. Prin.; Mrs. Margaret Latessa, Asst. Prin.; Mrs. Virginia Colwell, Asst. Prin.; Rev. Terry W. Specht, Chap. Lay Teachers 87; Students 1,134.

[E] HIGH SCHOOLS, PRIVATE

MIDDLEBURG. **Notre Dame Academy Inc.*, 35321 Notre Dame Ln., 20117. Tel: 540-687-5581; Fax: 540-687-3552. Web: www.notredameva.org. Sr. Cecilia Liberatore, S.N.D., Head of School. Sisters of Notre Dame 1; Lay Teachers 33; Students 281.

[F] ELEMENTARY SCHOOLS, PRIVATE

BRISTOW. *Linton Hall*, 9535 Linton Hall Rd., 20136. Tel: 703-368-3157; Fax: 703-368-3036. Email: lintonhall@aol.com. Web: www.lintonhall.com. Mr. Robert Manning, Prin. Benedictine Sisters of Virginia 7; Lay Teachers 14; Students 186.

[G] INTERPAROCHIAL SCHOOLS

CULPEPER. *Epiphany School*, (Grades PreK-5), Precious Blood, 114 E. Edmondson St., 22701. Tel: 540-825-9017; Fax: 540-825-8987. Email: pbcc@erols.com. Web: www.epiphanycatholicschool.org. Mrs. Barbara Terry, Prin. Sponsoring parishes: Precious Blood, Culpeper; Our Lady of the Blue Ridge, Madison; St. Isidore, Orange and St. Peter Mission, Washington, VA. Lay Teachers 14; Students 152.

FALLS CHURCH. *Corpus Christi School*, (Grades 1-8), 3301 Glen Carlyn Rd., 22041. Tel: 703-820-7450; Fax: 703-820-9635. Email: corpusc@mnsinc.com. Web: www.corpuschristischool.org. Mr. George Chiplock, Prin. Sponsoring parishes: St. Anthony and St. Philip. Lay Teachers 25; Students 648.

FREDERICKSBURG. *Holy Cross Academy*, (Grades PreK-8), 250 Stafford Lakes Pkwy., 22406. Tel: 540-286-1600; Fax: 540-286-1625. Email: holycrossacademy@erols.com. Web: www.rc.net/arlington/hca. Sr. Susan Louise Eder, O.S.F.S. Sponsoring parish: St. Mary, Fredericksburg. Oblate Sisters of St. Francis de Sales 3; Lay Teachers 28; Total Staff 42; Students 543.

WOODBRIDGE. *Aquinas School*, (Grades PreK-8), 13750 Mary's Way, 22191. Tel: 703-491-4447; Fax: 703-492-8828. Web: www.aquinasschool.org. Sr. Dominic Mary, O.P., Prin. Sponsoring parishes: Our Lady of Angels, Woodbridge; St. Elizabeth Ann Seton, Lake Ridge; and Sacred Heart, Manassas. Dominican Sisters, Congregation of St. Cecilia 4; Lay Teachers 24; Total Staff 46; Students 546.

[H] DAY CARE AND CHILD LEARNING CENTERS

ARLINGTON. *Holy Martyrs of Vietnam Child Enrichment Day Care Center* (Children 2 1/2-5 years) , 915 S. Wakefield St., 22204. Tel: 703-920-1049; Fax: 703-553-0371. Email: tamila915@cs.com. Tamila Mostamandy, Dir. Lay Teachers 2; Students 50.

ALEXANDRIA. *Blessed Sacrament Grade School and Early Childhood Center*, (Grades PreK-8), 1417 W. Braddock Rd., 22302. Tel: 703-998-4170; Fax: 703-671-3219. Email: vgarcia@blessedsacrament.org. Web: www.BlessedSacramentcc.org. Mrs. Valerie Garcia, Prin. Lay Teachers 40; Students 363.

St. Gabriel's (Children 2-5 years) , 4319 Sano St., 22312. Tel: 703-354-0395; Fax: 703-354-0395. Sr. Marta Munoz, P.S.S.J., Local Supr. Poor Sisters of St. Joseph (Buenos Aires) Sisters 5; Students 90.

FALLS CHURCH. *Corpus Christi Early Childhood Center* (Children 3-5 years) , 7506 St. Philip's Ct., 22042. Tel: 703-573-4570. Mr. George Chiplock, Prin.; Mrs. Allis Hanley, Dir. Sponsoring Parishes: St. Anthony and St. Philip. Lay Teachers 8; Students 150.

St. Joseph's Day Nursery & Kindergarten (Children 2-6 years) , 203 N. Spring St., 22046. Tel: 703-533-8441. Sr. Jacinta Salazar, S.S.J., Dir. Servants of St. Joseph (Salamanca, Spain) Sisters 3; Lay Teachers 7; Students 80.

[I] SCHOOLS FOR EXCEPTIONAL CHILDREN

ALEXANDRIA. **Saint Coletta of Greater Washington Inc.*, 207 S. Peyton St., 22314. Tel: 703-683-3686; Fax: 703-683-9888. Web: www.stcoletta.org. Ms. Sharon Raimo, Prin. Private, Non-residential School providing education and vocational training for students and young adults with mental retardation, autism and secondary disabilities ages 4 through 22. Medicaid waivered day program for adults, age 22 and up. Religious 1; Teachers 14; Teacher Aides 48; Speech Pathologists 5; Physical Therapists 3; Occupational Therapists 3; Music Teachers 1; Adaptive Physical Education Instructors 1; LCSW 1; Adult Program Instructors 3; Students 155.

[J] MONASTERIES AND RESIDENCES OF PRIESTS AND BROTHERS

ARLINGTON. *Missionary Servants of the Most Holy Trinity, S.T.*, 1215 N. Scott St., 22209-3097. Tel: 703-276-8646; Fax: 703-522-2656. Email: stgeneral@aol.com. Web: www.mssst.org. Revs. Austin Walsh, S.T., Gen. Custodian; Gary Banks, S.T., Gen. Councilor; Bro. Steven Vesely, S.T., Sec. Gen. & Gen. Councilor.
Legal Title: *Missionary Servants Charitable Trust*
Legal Title: *Father Judge Charitable Trust*, Generalate of the Missionary Servants of the Most Holy Trinity.

Missionhurst, C.I.C.M.-Central House and Provincialate, 4651 N. 25th St., 22207. Tel: 703-528-3800; Fax: 703-528-5355. Email: provincial@missionhurst.org. Web: www.missionhurst.org. Revs. William G. Quigley, C.I.C.M., Prov. Supr.; Joseph Giordano, C.I.C.M., Provincial Treas. & Dir. Promotion; Michael Hann, C.I.C.M., Rector; William Wyndaele, C.I.C.M., Dir. Mission Center; His Eminence Jan Cardinal Schotte, C.I.C.M.; Revs. Howard Picard, C.I.C.M.; Roger Van Cauwenbergh, C.I.C.M.; Joseph Dewaele, C.I.C.M.; Jerome Meersman, C.I.C.M.; Charles Denys, C.I.C.M.; John Morel, C.I.C.M.; Paul DeWolf, C.I.C.M.
Legal Title: *American I.H.M. Province, Inc.*
Legal Title: *Immaculate Heart Missions, Inc.*
Legal Title: *Missionhurst, Inc.*, Congregation of the Immaculate Heart of Mary foreign and home missions.

ALEXANDRIA. *Oblates of St. Francis de Sales Residence*, 708 Grandview Ave., 22305. Tel: 703-299-8330. Revs. Joseph T. Brennan, O.S.F.S.; Matthew J. Hillyard, O.S.F.S.; Edward J. Roszko, O.S.F.S., B.A. (WIL); Patrick J. Kifolo, O.S.F.S. (See separate listing for Bishop Ireton High School regarding staff.)

Third Order Regular of St. Francis of Penance, St. Jerome Friary, 4860 Eisenhower Ave., #180, 22304. Tel: 703-751-7442. Email: Wilson@ireton.org. Bro. Richard S. Wilson, T.O.R.

BERRYVILLE. *Cistercian Abbey of Our Lady of the Holy Cross*, 901 Cool Spring Ln., 22611-2700. Tel: 540-955-1425; Fax: 540-955-1356. Email: HolyCross@shentel.net. Web: www.holycrossabbeyberryvlle.org. Rt. Revs. Robert T. Barnes, O.C.S.O., Abbot; Flavian Burns, O.C.S.O., Retired Abbot & Chap. (Retired), Our Lady of the Angels, Crozet; Edward McCorkell, O.C.S.O., Retired Abbot (Retired); Mark Delery, O.C.S.O., Retreat House & Retired Abbot (Retired); Revs. Edmund Flynn, O.C.S.O., Prior & Treas.; Paschal Balkan, O.C.S.O.; Andrew Gries, O.C.S.O.; Vincent Collins, O.C.S.O.; Maurice Flood, O.C.S.O.; Joseph Wittstock, O.C.S.O.; James Orthmann, O.C.S.O., Novice Master & Vocation Dir.; Malachy Marrion, O.C.S.O.; Bros. Stephen Maguire, O.C.S.O., Guest Master; Michael Desilets, O.C.S.O., Cellarer; Barnabas Brownsey, O.C.S.O.; Gerald Giblin, O.C.S.O.; Christopher Harmon, O.C.S.O.; Edward McLean, O.C.S.O.; Luke Scheuerell, O.C.S.O.; Benedict Simmonds, O.C.S.O., Sec.; James Sommers, O.C.S.O.; Martin Statz, O.C.S.O.; Joseph Vantu, O.C.S.O. Order of Cistercians of the Strict Observance (Trappist) Community 25; Residents

23; Priests 12; Solemnly Professed Non-priest Monks 11.

WHITE POST, FREDERICK CO.. *Sacred Heart Friary*, P.O. Drawer B, 22663. Tel: 540-869-1599; Fax: 540-869-0106. Email: aidantor@aol.com. Revs. Aidan Mullaney, T.O.R., Local Min.; Marion Deck, T.O.R.; Francis McKinney, T.O.R.; Christopher Petrosky, T.O.R.; James Cleary, T.O.R.; Jude Ventiquattro, T.O.R.; Damian Noel, T.O.R.; Theodore Midile, T.O.R.; Peter Bush, T.O.R.; John Grinnen, T.O.R.; Marianus Lieb, T.O.R.; William Weider, T.O.R.; Earl Jennings, T.O.R. (BAL); Bros. Bernard Nicolosi, T.O.R., Vicar; Stephen Liebal, T.O.R.; Norman McNelis, T.O.R.; John Carosella, T.O.R.; Stanlislaus J. Prenatt, T.O.R. Third Order Regular of St. Francis Professed Brothers 4.

[K] CONVENTS AND RESIDENCES FOR SISTERS

ARLINGTON. *Religious of the Sacred Heart of Mary*, 2807 N. Glebe Rd., 22207-4299. Tel: 703-284-1495; Fax: 703-908-7526. Email: sister.cody@marymount.edu. Web: www.rshm.org. Sr. Jacqueline Murphy, R.S.H.M., Coord. Sisters 6.

Sisters Servants of the Immaculate Heart of Mary, 6600 Little Falls Rd., 22213. Tel: 703-237-1410; Fax: 703-237-1465. Email: ihmdjo@yahoo.com. Web: www.ihmimmaculata.org. Sr. Christine Virginia O'Donnell, I.H.M., Supr. Sisters 12.

ALEXANDRIA. *St. Gabriel Convent*, 4319 Sano St., 22312. Tel: 703-354-0395; Fax: 703-354-0395. Sr. Marta Munoz, P.S.S.J., Local Supr. Poor Sisters of St. Joseph's Buenos Aires Regional House and Novitiate 5.

Poor Clare Monastery of Mary, Mother of the Church, 2505 Stonehedge Dr., 22306. Tel: 703-768-4918; Fax: 703-765-2985. Observing the Primitive Rule of St. Clare. Solemnly Professed 13; Junior Professed 1; Postulants 1; Novices 1.

Sisters of the Holy Cross, 5582 First Statesman Ln., 22312. Tel: 703-658-9519.
Legal Title: *Sisters of the Holy Cross, Inc.* Sisters 2.

BRISTOW. *St. Benedict Monastery*, Benedictine Sisters of Virginia, 9535 Linton Hall Rd., 20136-1217. Tel: 703-361-0106; Fax: 703-361-0254. Email: osbva@erols.com. Web: www.osbva.org. Sr. Cecilia Dwyer, O.S.B., Prioress. Tel: 703-368-4848. B.E.A.C.O.N.: Benedictine Educational Assistance Community Outreach to Neighbors, Benedictine Pastoral Center, Linton Hall School, Benedictine Counseling Center Professed Sisters 34; Sisters Resident at Motherhouse 30.

FAIRFAX. *Adorers of the Holy Cross*, 10917 Marilta Ct., 22030. Tel: 703-591-0862; Fax: 703-591-0862. Email: tuvienmtgva@hotmail.com. Sr. Mary Nguyen Thi Trinh, M.T.G., Supr. Sisters 6.

Sisters of Our Lady of La Salette (Grenoble, France), 10600 Cedar Ave., 22030. Tel: 703-691-4294; Fax: 703-691-1767. Email: lasalettesisters@starpower.net. Web: lasaletteva.starpower.net. Sr. Maria Josephine S. Valenton, S.N.D.S., Supr.

FALLS CHURCH. *Holy Family House Convent, S.S.J.*, 3438 Charles St., 22041. Tel: 703-820-9785. Sr. Celia del Cano, S.S.J., Supr. Sisters 3.

Servants of St. Joseph Convent, 203 N. Spring St., 22046. Tel: 703-534-9549; Fax: 703-538-5168. Sisters 5.

FRONT ROYAL. *Pax Christi Institute*, 118 Jamestown Rd., 22630. Tel: 540-635-7690; Fax: 540-635-9139. Email: pax@rma.edu. Sr. Maria Guadalupe Licea, P.C.I., Supr. Sisters 8.

STRASBURG. *Sisters of Mercy of the Americas*, 112 N. Funk St., 22657-2402. Tel: 540-465-9368; Fax: 540-465-9368. Email: mwharton@su.edu. Web: www.sistersofmercy.org. Sr. Margaret Mary Wharton, R.S.M., Contact Person.

Sisters of Notre Dame de Namur, 112 N. Funk St., 22657-2402. Tel: 540-465-9368; Fax: 540-465-9368. Email: carolsnd@aol.com. Web: www.sndden.org. Sr. Carol A. Symons, S.N.D.deN., Contact Person.

WOODBRIDGE. *Dominican Sisters Convent* (Congregation of St. Cecilia) , 2655 Falmouth Ct., 22192. Tel: 703-494-4488; Fax: 703-491-8805. Email: aquinasconvent@starpower.net. Sr. Ignatius Connolly, O.P., Supr. Dominican Sisters Sisters 4.

[L] RETREAT HOUSES

BERRYVILLE. *Retreat House, Holy Cross Abbey*, 901 Cool Spring Ln., 22611-2700. Tel: 540-955-1425; Fax: 540-955-1356. Web: www.holycrossabbeyberryvlle.org. Rt. Rev. Mark Delery, O.C.S.O., Retreat House Counselor; Bro. Stephen Maguire, O.C.S.O., Guest Master.

MCLEAN. *Dominican Retreat House* Accommodations for 41 persons. , 7103 Old Dominion Dr., 22101-2799. Tel: 703-356-4243; Fax: 703-893-4502. Email: Dominicaninfo@aol.com. Web: www.dominicanretreat.org. Dominican Sisters of St. Catherine De Ricci. Sisters 4.

[M] CAMPUS MINISTRY

ARLINGTON. *Marymount University* , Campus Ministry , 2807 N. Glebe Rd., 22207. Tel: 703-284-1607; Fax: 703-284-3850. Email: father.jack@marymount.edu. Web: www.marymount.edu. Rev. John P. Peterson, Chap. & Dir. Campus Ministry.

FAIRFAX. *George Mason University, Catholic Campus Ministry House* 4521 Roberts Rd., 22032. Tel: 703-425-0022; Fax: 703-425-0753. Email: pnassett@gmu.edu. Web: www.gmu.edu/org/ccm. Rev. Peter W. Nassetta, Chap. & Dir. Campus Ministry; Mrs. Claire Wittenburg, Asst. Campus Min.

St. Robert Bellarmine Chapel George Mason University, 4515 Roberts Rd., 22032. Tel: 703-425-0022; Fax: 703-425-0753. Rev. Peter W. Nassetta; Mrs. Claire Wittenburg, Asst. Campus Min. Catholic Campus Ministry.

FREDERICKSBURG. *Mary-Washington College* Catholic Student Association, 1614 College Ave., 22401. Tel: 540-373-6746; Fax: 540-373-4875. Email: magicpadre@aol.com. Rev. Ronald S. Escalante, Chap.; Mrs Aimee Celio, Asst. Campus Min.

[N] MISCELLANEOUS

ARLINGTON. *Rooted in Faith-Forward in Hope, Inc.*, 200 N. Glebe Rd., Ste. 914, 22203. Tel: 703-841-2500; Fax: 703-841-5028. Rev. Daniel J Maher, Treas.

The Women's Apostolate to Youth, 5600 N. 16th St., 22205. Tel: 703-534-5821. Email: robinmaas@aol.com. Web: www.rcnet/arlington/way. Dr. Robin Maas, Dir.

Youth Apostles Institute, An Association of Christian Faithful, 1600 Carlin Ln., McLean, 22101-4100. Tel: 703-556-0914; Fax: 703-556-9455. Email: yas_admin@cox.net. Web: www.youthapostles.org. Rev. David M. Sharland.

ALEXANDRIA. *Pauline Book and Media (Daughters of St. Paul)*, 1025 King St., 22314. Tel: 703-549-3806; 703-683-1741 (Convent); Fax: 703-683-2568. Email: alexandria@pauline.org. Web: www.pauline.org. Sr. Elizabeth M. DeDomenico, F.S.P. An international congregation of women religious who serve the church with the communications media.

BROAD RUN. *National Association of Catholic Home Educators (NACHE)*, 6102 Saints Hill Ln., 20137. Tel: 540-349-4314; Fax: 540-347-7345. Email: lpayne@cts.com. Web: www.nache.org. Tim Hill, Co-Pres.; Michelle Hill, Co-Pres.

FRONT ROYAL. *Human Life International*, 4 Family Way, 22630. Tel: 540-635-7834; Fax: 540-636-7363. Email: hli@hli.org. Rev. Thomas J. Euteneur, Pres.

Seton Home Study School, 1350 Progress Dr., 22630. Tel: 540-636-9990; Fax: 540-636-1602. Email: info@setonhome.org. Web: www.setonhome.org. Dr. Mary K. Clark, Dir.

MANASSAS. *Cardinal Newman Society*, 10562 Associates Ct., 20109. Tel: 703-367-0333; Fax: 703-396-8663. Email: info@cardinalnewmansociety.org. Web: www.cardinalnewmansociety.org. Patrick J. Reilly, Pres.

McLean
Crusaders of St. Mary, 2001 Great Falls Rd., Mc Lean, 22101. Tel: 703-536-3546. Email: aperezalca@aol.com. Antonio Perez-Alcala, Dir.

SPOTSYLVANIA. *St. Francis Catholic Worker West*, 9631 Peppertree Rd., 22553. Tel: 540-972-3213. Web: www.catholicworker.org. Mr. John Mahoney. Total in Residence 2.

STAFFORD. *American Life League, Inc.*, P.O. Box 1350, 22555. Tel: 540-659-4171; Fax: 540-659-2586. Email: jbrown@all.org. Web: www.all.org. Mrs. Judie Brown, Pres.

VIENNA. *Alpha Omega Clinic and Consultation Services*, 2218B Gallows Rd., 22182. Tel: 703-242-3849; Fax: 703-847-1511. Email: abennett@arcol.org. Web: www.aoccs.org. Art Bennett, Dir.

Mount Tabor Society, Inc., 2363 Hunter Mill Rd., 22181. Tel: 703-938-2564. Rev. Paul G. Wynants, C.I.C.M., Dir. A House of Prayer and Christian Community.

WOODBRIDGE. *Apostolate for Family Consecration*, St. Damien Center, 1410 Harrison St., 22191-2215. Tel: 703-491-6544. Web: www.familyland.org. Jerome F. Coniker, Exec. Dir.

RELIGIOUS INSTITUTES OF MEN REPRESENTED IN THE DIOCESE

For further details refer to the corresponding bracketed number in the Religious Institutes of Men or Women section.

[]—*Apostles of Jesus*—A.J.
[1350]—*Brothers of St. Francis Xavier*—C.F.X.
[0350]—*Cistercians Order of the Strict Observance* (Trappists)—O.C.S.O.
[0650]—*Congregation of the Holy Spirit*—C.S.Sp.
[0520]—*Franciscan Friars* (Holy Name Prov.)—O.F.M.
[0530]—*Franciscan Friars of the Atonement*—S.A.
[0690]—*Jesuit Fathers and Brothers*—S.J.
[0840]—*Missionary Servants of the Most Holy Trinity*—S.T.
[0860]—*Missionhurst Congregation of the Immaculate Heart of Mary*—C.I.C.M.
[0920]—*Oblates of St. Francis de Sales* (Wilmington-Philadelphia Prov.)—O.S.F.S.
[0590]—*Society of the Missionaries of the Holy Apostles*—M.S.A.
[0700]—*St. Joseph's Society of the Sacred Heart* (Baltimore, MD)—S.S.J.
[0560]—*Third Order Regular of Saint Francis* (Sacred Heart Prov.)—T.O.R.
[]—*Vietnamese Dominican Fathers* (Calgary, Alberta, Canada)—O.P.

RELIGIOUS INSTITUTES OF WOMEN REPRESENTED IN THE DIOCESE

[4155]—*Adorers of the Holy Cross*—M.T.G.
[0230]—*Benedictine Sisters of Virginia*—O.S.B.
[1920]—*Congregation of the Sisters of the Holy Cross*—C.S.C.
[0960]—*Daughters of Wisdom*—D.W.
[1070-17]—*Dominican Sisters Congregation of St. Catherine deRicci*—O.P.
[1070-07]—*Dominican Sisters Congregation of St. Cecilia*—O.P.
[1105]—*Dominican Sisters of Hope*—O.P.
[1365]—*Franciscan Missionary Sisters of the Infant Jesus*—F.M.I.J.
[1310]—*Franciscan Sisters of Little Falls, Minnesota*—O.S.F.
[1880]—*Handmaidens of Reparation of the Sacred Heart of Jesus*—A.R.
[2470]—*Maryknoll Sisters of St. Dominic*—M.M.
[3060]—*Oblate Sisters of St. Francis de Sales*—O.S.F.S.
[3760]—*Order of St. Clare (Cloistered)*—P.C.C.
[]—*Pax Christi Institute* (Corpus Christi, TX)—P.C.I.
[0950]—*Pious Society of Daughters of St. Paul*—F.S.P.
[3250]—*Poor Sisters of St. Joseph*—P.S.S.J.
[3465]—*Religious of the Sacred Heart of Mary* (Eastern North Amer. Prov.)—R.S.H.M.
[2970]—*School Sisters of Notre Dame*—S.S.N.D.
[3595]—*Servants of St. Joseph* (Salamanca, Spain)—S.S.J.
[2575]—*Sisters of Mercy of the Americas*—R.S.M.
[2990]—*Sisters of Notre Dame*—S.N.D.
[3000]—*Sisters of Notre Dame de Namur*—S.N.D.deN.
[]—*Sisters of Our Lady of La Salette* (Grenoble, France)—S.N.D.S.
[1650]—*Sisters of St. Francis of Philadelphia*—O.S.F.
[3893]—*Sisters of St. Joseph of Chestnut Hill* (Philadelphia)—S.S.J.
[2170]—*Sisters, Servants of the Immaculate Heart of Mary*—I.H.M.

NECROLOGY

† Bradican, Rev. Msgr. Francis L., Annandale, VA Holy Spirit—Died March 31, 2003
† McMurtrie, Rev. Msgr. James W., Arlington, VA St. Agnes.

Archdiocese of Atlanta

(Archidioecesis Atlantensis)

Most Reverend

JOHN FRANCIS DONOGHUE, D.D.

Archbishop of Atlanta; ordained June 4, 1955; appointed Bishop of Charlotte November 6, 1984; appointed Archbishop of Atlanta June 22, 1993; installed August 18, 1993

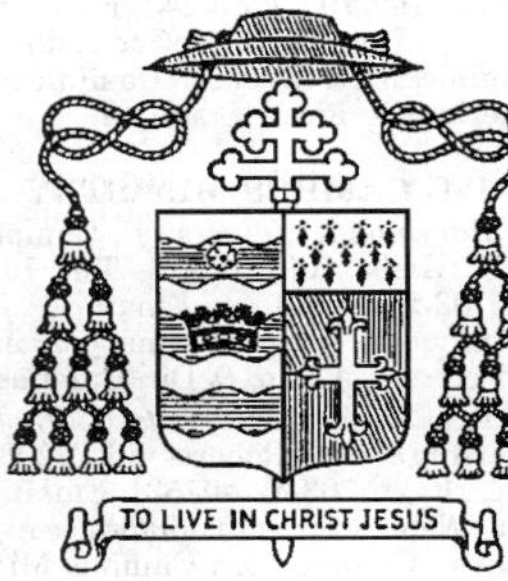

Catholic Center Archdiocese of Atlanta: 680 W. Peachtree St., N.W., Atlanta, GA 30308. Tel: 404-888-7802; Fax: 404-885-7494.

Web: www.archatl.com

ESTABLISHED JULY 2, 1956.

Square Miles 21,445.

Canonically Erected November 8, 1956; created an Archdiocese February 21, 1962.

Comprises the 69 Counties in the northern part of the State of Georgia, north of and including the following counties: Lincoln, McDuffie, Warren, Hancock, Baldwin, Putnam, Jasper, Monroe, Upson, Meriwether and Troup.

Patrons of the Archdiocese: I. Our Blessed Lady under the title of the Immaculate Heart of Mary; II. Saint Pius X.

Legal Title: For legal titles of parishes and archdiocesan institutions, consult the Archbishop's office.

STATISTICAL OVERVIEW

Personnel	
Archbishops	1
Priests: Diocesan Active in Diocese	134
Priests: Diocesan Active Outside Diocese	12
Priests: Retired, Sick or Absent	21
Number of Diocesan Priests	167
Religious Priests in Diocese	69
Total Priests in Diocese	236
Extern Priests in Diocese	18
Ordinations:	
Diocesan Priests	3
Transitional Deacons	4
Permanent Deacons	14
Permanent Deacons in Diocese	161
Total Sisters	102
Parishes	
Parishes	79
With Resident Pastor:	
Resident Diocesan Priests	68
Resident Religious Priests	11
Missions	16
Pastoral Centers	1
Professional Ministry Personnel:	
Brothers	1
Sisters	22
Lay Ministers	183
Welfare	
Catholic Hospitals	2
Total Assisted	295,030
Health Care Centers	1
Total Assisted	150
Homes for the Aged	4
Total Assisted	124
Specialized Homes	1
Total Assisted	23
Special Centers for Social Services	47
Total Assisted	9,800
Educational	
Diocesan Students in Other Seminaries	48
Seminaries, Religious	9
Total Seminarians	48
High Schools, Diocesan and Parish	3
Total Students	2,088
High Schools, Private	1
Total Students	894
Elementary Schools, Diocesan and Parish	15
Total Students	6,001
Elementary Schools, Private	4
Total Students	1,345
Catechesis/Religious Education:	
High School Students	5,259
Elementary Students	31,516
Total Students under Catholic Instruction	47,151
Teachers in the Diocese:	
Priests	6
Sisters	6
Lay Teachers	929
Vital Statistics	
Receptions into the Church:	
Infant Baptism Totals	9,391
Adult Baptism Totals	719
Received into Full Communion	1,425
First Communions	6,507
Confirmations	2,329
Marriages:	
Catholic	874
Interfaith	549
Total Marriages	1,423
Deaths	1,033
Total Catholic Population	371,139
Total Population	5,904,600

Former Bishops—Most Revs. FRANCIS E. HYLAND, D.D., J.C.D., appt. Titular Bishop of Gomphi and Auxiliary Bishop of Savannah-Atlanta, Oct. 15, 1949; consecrated Dec. 21, 1949; First Bishop of Atlanta, July 17, 1956; installed on Nov. 8, 1956; resigned and appointed Titular Bishop of Bisica, Oct. 11, 1961; died Jan. 31, 1968; PAUL J. HALLINAN, D.D., appt. Bishop of Charleston, Sept. 9, 1958; consecrated Oct. 28, 1958; elevated to the Archiepiscopal dignity, Feb. 21, 1962; installed First Archbishop of Atlanta, March 29, 1962; died March 27, 1968; JOSEPH L. BERNARDIN, D.D., appt. Auxiliary of Atlanta, March 9, 1966; consecrated April 26, 1966; appt. Gen. Sec. U.S.C.C., April 5, 1968; died Nov. 14, 1996.; THOMAS A. DONNELLAN, appt. Bishop of Ogdensburg, March 4, 1964; consecrated April 9, 1964; appt. to Atlanta, May 29, 1968; installed July 16, 1968; died Oct. 15, 1987; EUGENE A. MARINO, S.S.J., D.D., appt. Auxiliary of Washington, July 15, 1974; appt. Archbishop of Atlanta, March 14, 1988; installed May 5, 1988; resigned July 10, 1990; died Nov. 12, 2000; JAMES P. LYKE, O.F.M., Ph.D., appt. Auxiliary Bishop of Cleveland and Titular Bishop of Fornos Maggiore, June 30, 1979; consecrated Aug. 1, 1979; appt. Apostolic Administrator Archdiocese of Atlanta, July 10, 1990; appt. Archbishop of Archdiocese of Atlanta, April 30, 1991; installed June 24, 1991; Palium conferred June 29, 1991;; died Dec. 27, 1992.

Vicar for Clergy—Rev. FRANCIS G. MCNAMEE, V.F.

Associate Vicars for Clergy—Revs. LUKE BALLMAN; JOSE DUVAN GONZALEZ-FLOREZ.

Moderator of Religious—Sr. MARY-BETH BERES, O.P., 44 Coldstream Ct., N.W., Atlanta, 30328. Mailing Address, P.O. Box 76475, Atlanta, 30358.

Archdiocesan Offices and Directors

Catholic Center Archdiocese of Atlanta—680 W. Peachtree St., N.W., Atlanta, 30308.

Catholic Information—Tel: 404-885-7445.

Archbishop's Office—Tel: 404-888-7804; Fax: 404-885-7230.

Vicars General—Rev. Msgrs. R. DONALD KIERNAN, P.A., V.G., D.P.A., Ph.D., LL.D., Pastoral Ministries; PAUL H. REYNOLDS, Curia. Tel: 404-888-7805; Fax: 404-885-7230.

Chancellor—Rev. Msgr. PAUL H. REYNOLDS. Tel: 404-888-7805; Fax: 404-885-7230.

Vice Chancellor - Operations Officer—KATHI STEARNS. Tel: 404-885-7445; Fax: 404-978-2770.

Director of Priest Personnel—Rev. FRANK MCNAMEE, V.F. Tel: 404-888-7804; Fax: 404-885-7230.

Chief Financial Officer—GARY W. MEADER, Sec. Finance & Admin. Tel: 404-885-7408; Fax: 404-885-7223.

Secretary for Education—JUDITH MUCHEK, Supt. Schools; VACANT, Dir. Tel: 404-888-7833; Fax: 404-885-7430.

Continuing Education in Ministry—Rev. JAMES A. SCHILLINGER. Tel: 404-636-1418.

Secretariat for Catholic Charities—Dr. JAMES E. KANTNER, Ph.D. Tel: 404-885-7212; Fax: 404-885-7200 See separate listing for detailed information.

Catholic Construction Services—GEORGE BARRIE, Pres. & C.E.O. Tel: 404-885-7294; Fax: 404-885-7299.

Office for Black Catholic Ministry—Tel: 404-888-7848; Fax: 404-978-2778. CHARLES PREJEAN, Dir. Supervised by Chancellor.

Secretary for Communications—Media Rels.. Tel: 404-885-7445; Fax: 404-978-2770. KATHI STEARNS.

"The Georgia Bulletin"—Rev. Msgr. PAUL H. REYNOLDS, Assoc. Publisher. Tel: 404-888-7805; Fax: 404-888-7804; MARY ANN CASTRANIO, Exec. Editor. Tel: 404-877-5500; Fax: 404-877-5505.

Office for Ministry with Persons with Disabilities—Mr. ED MCCOY, Dir. Supervised by Chancellor. Tel: 404-888-7809.

Office for Information Technology—THOMAS MCHALE, MIS Dir. Supervised by Vice Chancellor. Tel: 404-885-7432.

Catholic Foundation of North Georgia—Rev. Msgr. EDWARD J. DILLON. Tel: 404-252-4513.

Court of Appeals—

Court of Appeals-Province of Atlanta—Tel: 404-888-7813; Fax: 404-888-7845.

Judicial Vicar—Very Rev. PAUL J. HACHEY, S.M., J.C.L., M.C.L., M.Div.

Defenders of the Bond—Rev. Msgr. PETER A. DORA; Revs. DANIEL J. MCCORMICK, B.A.; LUIS ZARAMA; Ms. ROBERTA I. SIEGWALD.

Judges—Revs. STEPHEN T. CHURCHWELL, J.C.D.; JOHN C. DRUDING; GREGORY D. GOOLSBY, M.Div., J.D.; ALBERT W. JOWDY, M.Div.; Rev. Msgr. R. DONALD KIERNAN, P.A., V.G., D.P.A., Ph.D., LL.D.; Very Rev. JAMES A. MICELI, V.F.; Rev. RICHARD B. MORROW (Retired); Rev. Msgr. PAUL H. REYNOLDS; Rev. JAMES A. SCHILLINGER.

Advocates—Rev. JAMES D. DUFFY, S.M.; Mrs. MARY CANDEE ELROD, M.R.E.; Revs. VICTOR A. GALIER; VICTOR J. REYES, M.Div.; Mrs. DOROTHY WESSELMANN, M.S.Ed.

Notaries—MARIANNE FRONEK; MARGUERITE V. FORTINO, B.M.

Promoter of Justice—Rev. DANIEL J. MCCORMICK, B.A.

Tribunal—

Metropolitan Tribunal—Tel: 404-888-7815; Fax: 404-888-7814.

Judicial Vicar—Rev. DUNG V. NGUYEN, J.C.L.

Director—KIM M. DANIEL, B.A.

Court Administrator—Deacon WHITNEY F. ROBICHAUX JR., B.S., M.A., M.P.S.

Auditors—Rev. ROBERT J. KAMPINE, J.C.L., S.T.B.,

B.A.; Sr. FRANCES WHITMAN, G.N.S.H., M.A.; Deacon AL MCHUGH, B.S.
Archdiocesan Judges—Rev. Msgrs. EDWARD J. DILLON; DAVID P. TALLEY; Revs. TIMOTHY A. GADZIALA, M.A., M.Div., J.C.L.; RICHARD A. ZIVIC; DUNG NGUYEN, J.C.L.; MICHAEL ONYEKURU, J.C.L.; AUGUSTINE TRAN, J.C.L. (Cand.); PAUL BURKE, J.C.L. (Cand.).
Defenders of the Bond—Mrs. KIM DANIEL, B.A.; Mrs. ELYN MACEK, J.D.; Rev. ROBERT J. KAMPINE, J.C.L., S.T.B., B.A.; ROBERT G. WESSELMANN, J.C.L., S.T.L.
Notaries—WENDY A. ABRAHAM; ANDREW L. HOECKELE, B.S., M.A.; JEAN M. SMITH; SARAN J. ENGE.
Catholic Social Services—
HIV/AIDS Ministry—IRENE MIRANDA, HIV/AIDS Coord. Supervised by Catholic Charities. Tel: 404-885-7207.
Catholic Housing Initiatives—Dr. JAMES E. KANTNER, Ph.D., Dir. Catholic Charities. Tel: 404-885-7212.
Catholic Personal Care Homes—Mrs. REGINA HARRIS, Dir. Catholic Social Svcs. Supervised by Secretary for Catholic Charities. Tel: 404-766-7121.
Village of St. Joseph—Dr. J. PAUL GALLANT, Ph.D., Dir. Catholic Social Svcs. Supervised by Secretary for Catholic Social Svcs. Tel: 404-321-2900.
Office of Child and Youth Protection—Dr. ANN PRICE, Dir. Supervised by Vice Chancellor. Tel: 404-885-7459.
Office of Vocations—Rev. BRIAN J. HIGGINS. Tel: 404-888-7844; Fax: 404-888-7849.
Office for Permanent Diaconate—Deacons ALFRED MITCHELL, Dir. Tel: 404-885-7407; Fax: 404-978-2778; LORIS SINANIAN, Dir. of Formation Supervised by Vicar GeneralTel: 404-885-7434; Fax: 404-978-2778; Rev. Msgr. PAUL H. REYNOLDS. Tel: 404-885-7805; Fax: 404-885-7230.
Office for Pro-Life—Mrs. MARY BOYERT, Dir., Supervised by Secretary for Catholic Charities. Tel: 404-888-7821; Fax: 404-978-2778.
Office of Family Concerns—Tel: 404-888-7819. MARY ELLEN HUGHES, Dir., Supervised by Secretary for Catholic Charities.
Office of Hispanic Apostolate—Rev. JOSE DUVAN GONZALEZ-FLOREZ, Dir. Supervised by Vicar General. Tel: 404-885-7289; Fax: 404-885-7430.
Development Office—
Director—VACANT, Dir., Supervised by Vice Chancellor. Tel: 404-885-7201; Fax: 404-885-7494.
Archdiocesan Annual Appeal and Stewardship—VACANT, Dir. Supervised by Vice Chancellor.
Archives—JOHN J. HANLEY, (Chancery), Supervised by Vicar General. Tel: 404-885-7253; Fax: 404-885-7230; CATHY A. HOOD, Secretariat for Human Resources, Supervised by Vice Chancellor. Tel: 404-978-2775; Fax: 404-885-7497.
Department of Religious Education & Faith Formation—
Senior Administrator and Director of Lay Formation & Initiation—Deacon LLOYD SUTTER, Supervised by Vice Chancellor. Tel: 404-885-7835; Fax: 404-885-7479.
Children and Youth Ministry—BARBARA GARVIN, Sr. Dir. Tel: 404-885-7491; Fax: 404-885-7479.
Young Adult and Adult Ministry—KERSTI PAYTON O'FARRELL Sr. Dir. Tel: 404-885-7290; Fax: 404-885-7479.
Children's Ministry and Initiation—SORANGEL GOVIN, Dir. Tel: 404-885-7221; Fax: 404-885-7479.
Hispanic Ministry—BERTHA O'MARA, Coord. Tel: 404-885-7447; Fax: 404-885-7479.

Other Archdiocesan Offices

AACCW—CELESTE GANEY, 1630 Elm Ridge Way, Stone Mountain, 30083. Tel: 770-808-0106; Rev. PAUL W. BERNY, Spiritual Moderator. Tel: 478-452-0892.
Apostleship of Prayer—VACANT, Ignatius House, 6700 Riverside Dr., N.W., Atlanta, 30328. Tel: 404-255-0503.
Girl and Boy Scouts—Rev. MICHAEL G. KINGERY, St. Clements Catholic Church, 875 Hwy. 53, W., Calhoun, 30701.
Cana Conferences—MARY ELLEN HUGHES, 680 W. Peachtree St., N.W., Atlanta, 30308. Tel: 404-888-7819.
Consultors—Rev. Msgrs. R. DONALD KIERNAN, P.A., V.G., D.P.A., Ph.D., LL.D.; PAUL H. REYNOLDS, Very Rev. Deans and Vicar for Clergy, Presbyteral Council Pres & Chancellor.
Cursillo—Sr. MARGARET MCANOY, I.H.M., Dir., 3731 Embry Cir., Atlanta, 30341. Tel: 770-455-1500.
Deans—Rev. Msgr. PAUL FOGARTY, Northeast Metro; Rev. FRANCIS G. MCNAMEE, V.F., Northwest Metro; Very Revs. KEVIN PEEK, V.F., South Metro; JOHN T. HOWREN, Northeast; Very Rev. Msgrs. WILLIAM G. HOFFMAN, V.F., Northwest; TERRY YOUNG, V.F., South.
Georgia Catholic Conference—FRANK MULCAHY, Exec. Sec., c/o Tinsley, Bacon & Tinsley, L.L.C., 3600 Mansell Rd., Ste. 300, Alpharetta, 30022. Tel: 770-521-8799.
Campus Ministry—Deacon LLOYD SUTTER.
Council of Priests—Rev. RICHARD TIBBETTS, Pres., Saint Theresa Catholic Church, 4401 Priestly Mill Rd., Douglasville, 30135.
Atlanta Conference of Sisters—Sr. MARY-BETH BERES, O.P., Pres., P.O. Box 76475, Atlanta, 30358. Tel: 404-294-8685.
Finance Council Adviser—GARY MEADER, 680 W. Peachtree St., N.W., Atlanta, 30308. Tel: 404-885-7408.
Project Review Board—GEORGE BARRIE, 680 W. Peachtree St., N.W., Atlanta, 30308. Tel: 404-885-7294.
Benefits Committee—CATHY HOOD, 680 W. Peachtree St., N.W., Atlanta, 30308. Tel: 404-885-7227.
Investment Committee—GARY MEADER, 680 W. Peachtree St., N.W., Atlanta, 30308. Tel: 404-885-7408.
Elementary and Secondary Catholic Schools Council—JUDITH MUCHECK, 615 Peachtree St., Atlanta, 30308. Tel: 404-885-7428.
Lay Review Board on Sexual Abuse—Most Rev. JOHN F. DONOGHUE; KATHI STEARNS, 680 W. Peachtree St., N.W., Atlanta, 30308. Tel: 404-885-7445.
Victim Assistance Coordinators—KATHI STEARNS, Vice Chancellor. Tel: 404-885-7445. Email: kstearns@archatl.com; ANN PRICE. Tel: 404-885-7459. Email: aprice@archatl.com.

Archdiocesan Councils, Boards, Commissions, and Committees

Boards—
Catholic Charities—Dr. JAMES E. KANTNER, Ph.D., Sec., 680 W. Peachtree St., N.W., Atlanta, 30308. Tel: 404-881-6571.
Clergy Retirement—Rev. Msgr. STEPHEN T. CHURCHWELL, J.C.D., St. Luke the Evangelist Catholic Church, 75 Park St. N.,, Dahlonega, 30533. Tel: 706-864-4779.
Commissions—
Liturgical—CLAUD SHIRLEY, 680 W. Peachtree St., N.W., Atlanta, 30308. Tel: 404-888-7804.

CLERGY, PARISHES, MISSIONS AND PAROCHIAL SCHOOLS

CITY OF ATLANTA
(FULTON COUNTY)

1—CATHEDRAL OF CHRIST THE KING (1936), Rev. Msgr. Thomas Kenny, Rector; Revs. Richard B. Morrow (Retired); Pedro Poloche Rodriguez; Vincent P. Sullivan; John M. Matejek; Deacons Whitney Robichaux; Scott J.N. McNabb. In Res., Revs. Michael Onyekuru, J.C.L.; Kevin J. Hargaden.
Res.: 2699 Peachtree Rd., N.E., 30305. Tel: 404-233-2145; Fax: 404-233-9711.
School—46 Peachtree Way, 30305. Tel: 404-233-0383; Fax: 404-266-0704. Mrs. Peggy Warner, Prin. Please refer to Elementary Schools, Archdiocese located in the Institutions Located in the Archdiocese for details. Lay Teachers 44; Students 541.
Catechesis/Religious Program—Tel: 404-267-3694; Fax: 404-233-4984. Students 822.

2—ST. ANTHONY OF PADUA (1903), (African American), Rev. Anthony T. Curran; Deacon Joseph Barker. In Res., Rev. Richard A. Zivic.
Res.: 928 Ralph David Abernathy Blvd., S.W., 30310. Tel: 404-758-8861; Fax: 404-755-6755.
Catechesis/Religious Program—Tel: 404-753-0787; Fax: 404-755-6755. Students 195.

3—HOLY CROSS (1964), Revs. Patrick Kingery; John B. Ugobueze (Nigeria); Peter Duc Vu; John Paul Ezeonyido; Deacons Lou Hettel; Sam Mure; Cece Reimer; Dick Suever; Tom Silvestri; James Weiss; Enrique Galvis.
Res.: 3175 Hathaway Ct., 30341. Tel: 770-939-3501; Fax: 770-723-7013.
Catechesis/Religious Program—Tel: 770-934-5757. Sr. Pilar Dalmau, D.R.E. Students 265.

4—HOLY SPIRIT (1964), Rev. Msgr. Edward J. Dillon; Rev. Luke Ballman; Deacons Thomas B. Shuler; William F. McCarthy; Joseph Ruberte. In Res. Rev. John C.K. Fallon.
Church & Res.: 4465 Northside Dr., N.W., 30327. Tel: 404-252-4513; Fax: 404-252-1162.
Catechesis/Religious Program—Students 395.

5—IMMACULATE HEART OF MARY (1958), Revs. James A. Schillinger; James H. Sexstone; Deacon James Stewart. In Res., Rev. Msgr. Richard Lopez; Revs. Guyma Noel; Juan Carlos Arce.
Res.: 2855 Briarcliff Rd., N.E., 30329. Tel: 404-636-1418; Fax: 404-636-4394.
School—Tel: 404-636-4488; Fax: 404-636-1853. Tricia DeWitt, Prin. Please refer to Elementary Schools, Archdiocesan located in the Institutions Located in the Archdiocese for details. Lay Teachers 28; Students 491.
Catechesis/Religious Program—Tel: 404-321-3175; Fax: 404-321-0071. Students 229.
Mission—Our Lady of the Americas 5913 New Peachtree Rd., Doraville, Dekalb Co. 30340. Tel: 770-454-8437 Fax: 770-454-4885. Rev. Fabio Sotelo.

6—ST. JUDE (1960), Rev. Msgr. James J. Fennessy; Revs. Sebastian Andrade (Brazil); Andrew Schoenfield.
Res.: 7171 Glenridge Dr. N.E., 30328. Tel: 770-394-3896; Fax: 770-399-7866.
School—Tel: 770-394-2880; Fax: 770-804-9248. Patty Childs, Prin. Please refer to Elementary Schools, Archdiocese located in the Institutions Located in the Archdiocese for details. Lay Teachers 30; Students 502.
Catechesis/Religious Program—Tel: 770-394-4588; Fax: 770-804-2733. Students 150.

7—MOST BLESSED SACRAMENT (1960), Rev. Bruce W. Wilkinson.
Church and Mailing Address: 2971 Butner Rd., S.W., 30331. Tel: 404-349-0176; Fax: 404-349-0178.
Res.: 1926 Austin Rd., 30331. Tel: 404-349-1106.
Catechesis/Religious Program—Tel: 404-629-1287. Students 56.

8—OUR LADY OF LOURDES (1912), Rev. John S. Adamski.
Res.: 25 Boulevard, N.E., 30312. Tel: 404-522-6776; Fax: 404-222-0202.
Catechesis/Religious Program—Students 80

9—OUR LADY OF THE ASSUMPTION (1951), Revs. James F. McGoldrick, S.M.; James D. Duffy, S.M.; Bro. Ernest Moraschi, S.M.; Deacons Bill Bevacqua; Robert Gresher; Michael O'Brien; Harold W. Gourgues Jr.; William Garrett; Chris Thompson; Terry Biglow.
Office—1350 Hearst Dr., N.E., 30319. Tel: 404-261-7181; Fax: 404-364-1913.
Res.: 1350 Hearst Dr., N.E., 30319. Tel: 404-365-0508; 404-365-0510.
School—1320 Hearst Dr., N.E., 30319. Tel: 404-364-1902; Fax: 404-364-1914. Dr. Joan Tiernan, Prin. Please refer to Elementary Schools, Archdiocese located in the Institutions Located in the Archdiocese for details. Lay Teachers 36; Students 490.
Catechesis/Religious Program—Students 140.
Chapel—Marist School, Tel: 404-457-7201; Fax: 404-457-8402.
Chapel—St. Joseph's Hospital, Tel: 404-851-7001; Fax: 404-851-5901.
Chapel—Sisters of Mercy Convent at St. Joseph's Hospital, Tel: 404-255-6427.

10—ST. PAUL OF THE CROSS (1954), (African American), Rev. Melvin Shorter, C.P.; Deacons Joseph P. Goolsby; Hilliard M. Lee Jr.
Res.: 551 Harwell Rd., N.W., 30318. Tel: 404-696-6704; Fax: 404-696-4735.
Catechesis/Religious Program—Students 55.

11—SACRED HEART OF JESUS (1880), Rev. Msgr. Frank J. Giusta; Rev. Thony R. Jean; Deacon Wayne D. Smith. In Res., Rev. Msgr. Walter J. Donovan (Retired).
Res.: 353 Peachtree St., N.E., 30308. Tel: 404-522-6800; Fax: 404-524-5440.
Catechesis/Religious Program—Students 160.
Mission—San Felipe de Jesus 925 Conley Rd., Forest Park, Clayton Co. 30297. Tel: 404-627-0821.

12—SHRINE OF THE IMMACULATE CONCEPTION (1848), Rev. Msgr. Henry C. Gracz; Rev. T. J. Meenan; Deacons William Payne; Bart DeSandre.
Res.: 48 Martin Luther King, Jr. Dr., S.W., 30303-3599. Tel: 404-521-1866; Fax: 404-524-2297.
Catechesis/Religious Program—Students 27.

OUTSIDE CITY OF ATLANTA

ALPHARETTA, FULTON CO.
1—ST. BRIGID (1998), [CEM] Revs. W. Joseph Corbett; Robert Frederick; Deacon William Lange.
3400 Old Alabama Rd., 30022. Tel: 678-393-0060; Fax: 678-393-0071. Email: office@saintbrigid.org. Web: www.saintbrigid.org.
Catechesis/Religious Program—Students 894.

2—ST. THOMAS AQUINAS (1972), [CEM] Rev. Msgr. David Talley; Revs. Douglas S. Medlin; Jesus D. Trujillo-Luna; Deacons William W. Keeling; Edmund LaHouse; John Strachan; Kevin F. Tracy.
Res.: 535 Rucker Rd., 30004. Tel: 770-475-4501; Fax: 770-772-0355.
Catechesis/Religious Program—Tel: 770-475-4508. Students 1,442.

ATHENS, CLARKE CO., ST. JOSEPH'S (1873), Rev. Dayro Rico (Colombia); Deacons Morry Chapple; Bill

Lakin; Jim Gaudin.
Res.: 134 Prince Ave., 30601. Tel: 706-548-6332; Fax: 706-354-1783.
School—Tel: 706-543-1621; Fax: 706-543-0149. Sr. Mary Glackin, I.H.M., Prin. Please refer to Elementary Schools, Archdiocesan located in the Institutions Located in the Archdiocese for details. Sisters 5; Lay Teachers 21; Students 369.
Catechesis / Religious Program—Tel: 706-548-5487; Fax: 706-548-5487. Students 478.
Chapel—St. Mary's Hospital, Tel: 706-548-7581; Fax: 706-355-7274. Email: tfitz@stmarysathens.org. Web: www.stmarysathens.org. Nurses 342; Total Staff 1,000.
Chapel—Catholic Student Center at The University of Georgia, Tel: 706-543-2293; Fax: 706-543-2541. Rev. John McDowell, O.F.M.

BLAIRSVILLE, UNION CO., ST. FRANCIS OF ASSISI (1966), [CEM] Rev. Richard P. Wise; Deacons Lawrence Casey; William Diehl.
Res.: 2839 Young Harris Hwy., 30512. Tel: 706-745-6400; Fax: 706-745-1468.
Catechesis / Religious Program—Tel: 706-745-7865. Students 73.
Mission—St. Paul the Apostle 1397 Helen Hwy., Cleveland, White Co. 30528. Tel: 706-865-4474; Fax: 706-219-3009. Rev. Thad B. Rudd.

BLUE RIDGE, FANNIN CO., ST. ANTHONY'S (1976), [CEM] Rev. Christopher Williamson; Deacon Loris Sinanian.
Res.: 967 E. Main St., P.O. Box 1448, 30513. Tel: 706-632-5970; Fax: 706-632-2120.
Catechesis / Religious Program—Students 35.
Mission—Good Samaritan (1982), 55 Church St., Ellijay, Gilmer Co. 30540. Tel: 706-636-2772.

BUFORD, GWINNETT CO., PRINCE OF PEACE (1978), Revs. Fred W. Wendel; Eric Hill; Sergio M. Anaya; Michael Campbell; Deacons Michael R. Jones; William Speed.
Mailing Address: 4300 S. Lee St., 30518. Tel: 770-945-2244 (Office); Fax: 770-945-4599.
Res.: 4300 S. Lee St., 30518. Tel: 770-945-0200.
Catechesis / Religious Program—Students 859.

CALHOUN, GORDON CO., ST. CLEMENTS (1958), (Spanish), Rev. Michael G. Kingery.
Mailing Address: 875 Hwy. 53 W., 30701. Tel: 706-629-2345; Fax: 706-625-5219.
Catechesis / Religious Program—Students 135.

CANTON, CHEROKEE CO., OUR LADY OF LASALETTE (1984), Revs. Neil G. Jones, M.S.; Denis Kolumber, M.S.
Mailing Address: P.O. Box 5046, 30114.
Res.: 2942 Sam Nelson Rd., P.O. Box 5046, 30114. Tel: 770-479-8923; Fax: 770-479-8923.
Catechesis / Religious Program—Students 167.
Mission—Our Lady of the Mountains Hwy. 108 & Refuge Rd., Jasper, Pickens Co. 30143. Tel: 706-692-3078. P.O. Box 5046, 30114.

CARROLLTON, CARROLL CO., CHURCH OF OUR LADY OF PERPETUAL HELP (1962), [CEM] Rev. Paul D. Williams Jr.; Deacon David Higgins.
Res.: 210 Old Center Point Rd., 30117. Tel: 770-832-8977; Fax: 770-832-1666.
Newman Center West Georgia College— Vacant.
Catechesis / Religious Program—Students 216.

CARTERSVILLE, BARTOW CO., ST. FRANCIS OF ASSISI (1969), [JC] Rev. Daniel Stack.
Res.: 850 Douthit Ferry Rd., 30120. Tel: 770-386-7811; Fax: 770-382-4506.
Catechesis / Religious Program—Ms. Rosa Rodriguez, D.R.E. Students 325.

CEDARTOWN, POLK CO., ST. BERNADETTE'S (1941), [JC] Rev. Rafael Castano.
Res.: 101 S. College St., 30125. Tel: 770-748-1517; Fax: 770-748-1568.
Catechesis / Religious Program—Fax: 770-748-1517. Students 95.

CLARKESVILLE, HABERSHAM CO., ST. MARK (1964), (Hispanic), Rev. Luis Zarama; Deacons John F. Thompson; Richard Marinchak; Lee J. Tollett.
Mailing Address: 5410 Hwy. 197 S., 30523. Tel: 706-754-4518; Fax: 706-754-9751.
Res.: 151 Salome Dr., 30523. Tel: 706-754-6504.
Church: 5410 Hwy. 197 S., 30523-9542.
Catechesis / Religious Program—Students 170.
Mission—St. Helena P.O. Box 534, Clayton, Rabun Co. 30525. Tel: 706-782-5152; Fax: 706-782-5152.

CONYERS, ROCKDALE CO., ST. PIUS X CATHOLIC (1974), Revs. John C. Kieran; Charles J. Kerscher (Retired); Norberto Mateus; Deacons John C. Jansen; Brian Kilkelly; Fred Johns.
Res.: 2621 Hwy. 20, S.E., 30013-2424. Tel: 770-483-3660; Fax: 770-483-7006.
Catechesis / Religious Program—Tel: 770-929-1017. Students 670.

COVINGTON, NEWTON CO., ST. AUGUSTINE CHURCH (1977), Very Rev. John T. Howren; Deacon Richard A. Mickle.
Res.: 11524 Hwy. 278 E., 30014. Tel: 770-787-1064; Fax: 770-787-0871.
Catechesis / Religious Program—Tel: 770-787-9052. Students 129.
Mission—St. James 562 Vine St., Madison, Morgan Co. 30650. Tel: 706-342-9661; Fax: 706-342-2860. Rev. Msgr. Peter A. Dora, Admin.; Deacon Herbert C. Berding.

CUMMING, FORSYTH CO.
1—ST. BRENDAN (2000), Rev. William M. Hickey; Deacons Roger A. Fraser; William J. Monahan.
4633 Shiloh Rd., 30040. Tel: 770-205-7969; Fax: 770-205-5040.
Catechesis / Religious Program—Students 1,700.
2—GOOD SHEPHERD (1975), Revs. Peter J. Rau; Liam Coyne.
Church: 3740 Holtzclaw Rd., 30041. Tel: 770-887-9861; Fax: 770-887-2241.
Catechesis / Religious Program—Tel: 770-887-9861, Ext. 16. Students 640.

DAHLONEGA, LUMPKIN CO., ST. LUKE CATHOLIC (1960), Rev. Stephen T. Churchwell, J.C.D.; Deacon Kenneth Williams.
Catholic Center—75 Park St. N., 30533. Tel: 706-864-4779; Fax: 706-864-2568.
Res.: 75 Park St. N., 30533.
Catechesis / Religious Program—Tel: 706-864-2331. Students 145.
Mission—Christ Redeemer P.O. Box 506, Dawsonville, Dawson Co. 30534. Tel: 706-265-1361.
Station—North Georgia College (Newman Club)

DALLAS, PAULDING CO., ST. VINCENT DE PAUL, , 680 W. Memorial Dr., 30132.

DALTON, WHITFIELD CO., ST. JOSEPH'S (1941), [JC] Revs. William G. Hoffman; Jose Refugio Onate Melendez; Deacon Rafael Carballo.
Res.: 1775 Haig Mill Rd., 30720. Tel: 706-278-3107; Fax: 706-278-6902.
Catechesis / Religious Program—Students 894.

DECATUR, DEKALB CO.
1—STS. PETER AND PAUL (1959), (African American), [JC] Deacons Jerry Lett; Alfred Mitchell; Adrun Wetherington, Pastoral Assoc. In Res., Very Rev. Kevin Peek, V.F.
Res.: 2372 Collier Dr., 30032. Tel: 404-241-5862; Fax: 404-241-5839.
School—St. Peter Claver Regional, 2560 Tilson Rd., 30032. Tel: 404-241-3063; Fax: 404-241-4382. Catherine Spencer, Prin. Please refer to Elementary Schools, Archdiocesan located in the Institutions Located in the Archdiocese for details. Daughters of Mary Mother of Mercy 1; Lay Teachers 23; Students 125.
Catechesis / Religious Program—Tel: 404-243-8333; Fax: 404-241-5839. Sr. Gloria George Patrick, D.R.E. Students 140.
2—ST. THOMAS MORE (1949), Rev. Msgr. Paul Fogarty; Rev. Pavol Brenkus.
Res.: 624 W. Ponce de Leon Ave., 30030. Tel: 404-378-4588; Fax: 404-378-0506.
School—Tel: 404-373-8456; Fax: 404-377-8554. Mrs. Gail M. Mszane, Prin. Please refer to Elementary Schools, Archdiocese located in the Institutions Located in the Archdiocese for details. Lay Teachers 30; Students 487.
Catechesis / Religious Program—Students 184.

DOUGLASVILLE, DOUGLAS CO., ST. THERESA (1985), Revs. Richard Tibbetts; Dennis R. Juan; Deacons Paul Dietz; Ronald A. St. Michel; Terry M. Holmer; Mrs. Pam Cates, Parish Sec.
Res.: Tel: 770-489-7671.
Church: 4401 Prestley Mill Rd., 30135. Tel: 770-489-7115; Fax: 770-489-4873.
Catechesis / Religious Program—Tel: 770-942-9765. Students 426.

DULUTH, FULTON CO., ST. BENEDICT (1987), (Hispanic), Rev. Msgr. Hugh M. Marren; Revs. Randall Mattox; Casmir Maduakor; Guillermo Cordoba; Deacon John Stroop.
Office & Mailing Address: 11045 Parsons Rd., 30097. Tel: 770-442-5903; Fax: 770-442-0744.
Res.: 11085 Parsons Rd., 30097.
Catechesis / Religious Program—Students 1,720.

DULUTH, GWINNETT CO., CATHOLIC CHURCH OF ST. MONICA (1994), Revs. Gregory Goolsby; Mansueto P. Palang (BR) (Retired); Deacons John Koppenaal; Alfred Samoranski.
Res.: 1700 Buford Hwy., 30097. Tel: 678-584-9947; Fax: 678-584-9760.
Catechesis / Religious Program—Tel: 678-584-9947. Students 1,100.

DUNWOODY, DEKALB CO., ALL SAINTS CATHOLIC (1977), Rev. Msgr. R. Donald Kiernan, P.A., V.G., D.P.A., Ph.D., LL.D.; Revs. Daniel J. McCormick, B.A.; David M. Dye; Brian Small; Deacon Raymond F. Egan.
Res.: 2443 Mount Vernon Rd., 30338-3099. Tel: 770-393-3255; Fax: 770-913-0140.
Catechesis / Religious Program—Students 662.
Mission—Mary, Our Queen 6260 The Corners Pkwy., Norcross, Gwinnett Co. 30092. Tel: 770-416-0002; Fax: 770-416-1846.

FAYETTEVILLE, FAYETTE CO., ST. GABRIEL (1993), Rev. James P. Adams; Deacons Al C. McHugh; I. Carl McBride; T.C. Meuninck; Tom Zaworski.
Office:—135 Antioch Rd., 30215-5702. Tel: 770-461-0492; Fax: 770-461-0374.
Catechesis / Religious Program—Tel: 770-461-0493. Students 343.

FORT OGLETHORPE, CATOOSA CO., ST. GERARD MAJELLA (1952), Rev. Michael J. Redden.
Res.: 3049 LaFayette Rd., 30742. Tel: 706-861-9410; Fax: 706-866-0574.
Catechesis / Religious Program—Tel: 706-861-0563. Students 70.

GAINESVILLE, HALL CO., ST. MICHAEL'S (1945), Revs. Victor Reyes; Francisco Estrado Sandoval; Joseph Liem Nguyen; Deacons Michael Kennedy; Gary Roche.
Office—1440 Pearce Cir., N.E., 30501-2457. Tel: 770-534-3338; Fax: 770-535-2440.
Catechesis / Religious Program—Students 1,114.

GREENSBORO, GREENE CO., CHRIST OUR KING AND SAVIOR (1992),, Consolidation of Christ Our Savior, Eatonton, and Christ Our King, Greensboro. Rev. Fernando Molina-Restrepo; Bro. Curt Kedley.
Office, Res. & Church Address: 6341 Lake Oconee Pkwy., 30642. Tel: 706-453-7292; 706-453-7035; Fax: 706-453-7095.
Catechesis / Religious Program—Students 50.

GRIFFIN, SPALDING CO., SACRED HEART (1941), Revs. G. Philip Ryan; Karl Duggan; Deacons James Hedderman, (Retired); Felix Marrero.
Res.: 1323 MacArthur Dr., 30224. Tel: 770-227-2378; Fax: 770-227-6440.
Catechesis / Religious Program—Tel: 770-227-2898. Students 143.
Mission—St. John the Baptist 2969 McCorkle's Curve Rd., Thomaston, Upson Co. 30286. Tel: 706-648-2599; Fax: 706-648-4040.
Mission—St. Ann Redbud Rd. & Hwy. 341, Barnesville, Lamar Co. 30204. Tel: 706-358-0635.

HAPEVILLE, DEKALB CO., ST. JOHN THE EVANGELIST (1950), Rev. Glenn Parker, C.Ss.R.; Most Rev. Thomas Burke, C.SsR.; Very Rev. Jerome Chavarria, C.Ss.R. (ORL); Rev. Charles Donovan, C.Ss.R.; Deacons Richard Beckman; Henry Akers.
Mailing Address: 230 Arnold St., 30354-1530. Tel: 404-768-5647 (Church); Fax: 404-767-6416.
Res.: 3370 Sunset Ave., 30354.
School—240 Arnold St., 30354. Tel: 404-767-4312; Fax: 404-767-0359. Karen Vogtner, Prin. Please refer to Elementary Schools, Archdiocesan located in the Institutions section for details. Lay Teachers 20; Students 288.
Catechesis / Religious Program—Tel: 404-767-5877; Fax: 404-767-6416. Mrs. Daphny Keel, D.R.E. Students 100.

HARTWELL, HART CO., SACRED HEART OF JESUS (1977), [CEM] Rev. Terence Kane; Deacon Jerry Korte.
Res.: 1009 Benson St., 30643. Tel: 706-376-4112; Fax: 706-376-1695.
Catechesis / Religious Program—Tel: 706-376-6207. Students 70.

JONESBORO, CLAYTON CO., ST. PHILIP BENIZI (1965), Revs. Gregory J. Hartmayer, O.F.M.Conv.; Pedro de Oliveira, O.F.M.Conv.; Vincent Gluc, O.F.M.Conv.; Deacons Joseph C. Anzalone; Peter B. Swan Sr.; Matias A. Casal; Richard P. Tolcher.
Res.: 591 Flint River Rd., 30238-3452. Tel: 770-478-0178; Fax: 770-471-2079.
Catechesis / Religious Program—Mary M. Mauldin, D.R.E. Students 585.

KENNESAW, COBB CO., ST. CATHERINE OF SIENA (1981), Revs. James Harrison; Theodore Book, Collegio Sant' Anselmo, Piazza Cavalieri di Malta 5, Rome 00153 Italy; Maxis St. Fleur; Deacons Pat O'Connor; Richard Conti; Stephen J. Bele.
Res.: 1620 Overlook Ct., 30144. Tel: 770-419-9112.
Church: 1618 Ben King Rd., N.W., 30144. Tel: 770-428-7139; Fax: 770-428-0131.
School—Tel: 770-419-8601; Fax: 678-626-0000. Robyn Planchard, Prin. Please refer to Elementary Schools, Archdiocese located in the Institutions Located in the Archdiocese for details.
Catechesis / Religious Program—Tel: 770-428-7440. Rita Bek, D.R.E.; Catherine Hackney; Ruth Gizinski; Jacqueline Reid; Deb Frost. Students 1,325.

LAGRANGE, TROUP CO., ST. PETER'S (1936), Rev. Balappa Selvaraj.
Res.: 200 LaFayette Pkwy., 30241. Tel: 706-884-0887 (Rectory); 706-884-4224 (Church); Fax: 706-884-1624.
Catechesis / Religious Program—Students 224.
Mission—St. Elizabeth Seton P.O. Box 638, Warm Springs, Meriwether Co. 31830. Tel: 706-846-5223.

LAWRENCEVILLE, GWINNETT CO.
1—ST. LAWRENCE (1971), Revs. Albert W. Jowdy, M.Div.; Nathan Calhoun; Joseph Mullakkara, M.S.F.S.; Deacons A.B. King III; Walter T. Bedard Sr. In Res., Rev. Joseph Fahy, C.P.
Res.: 319 Grayson Hwy., 30045. Tel: 770-963-8992; Fax: 770-963-1710.
Catechesis / Religious Program—Tel: 770-962-2765. Students 782.

2—St. Marguerite D'Youville (1994), Revs. Brendan Doyle; Stanislaw Drzal; Joseph Mendes, M.S.F.S.; Deacon George D. Angelich.
Res.: 85 Gloster Rd., 30044. Tel: 770-381-7337; Fax: 770-381-6568.
Catechesis/Religious Program—Tel: 770-381-6982. Students 335.

Lilburn, Gwinnett Co.
1—St. John Neumann (1977), Revs. Stewart A. Wilber; John C. Druding; William M. Williams; Hernan Queuedo; Deacons Raymond E. Brown; Gary Womack.
Church: 801 Tom Smith Rd., 30047-2299. Tel: 770-923-6633; Fax: 770-381-7856.
School—James Anderson, Prin. Please refer to Elementary Schools, Regional located in the Institutions Located in the Archdiocese for details.
Catechesis/Religious Program—Students 1,219.
2—St. Stephen the Martyr (1999), Rev. Patrick H.M. Donaghey; Deacons Evelio Garcia-Carreras; Michael K. Mobley Sr.
Res.: 382 Rockbridge Rd., 30047. Tel: 770-381-7488; Fax: 770-923-8061.
Church: 5373 Wydella Rd., 30047.
Catechesis/Religious Program—Students 220.

Lithia Springs, Douglas Co., St. John Vianney (1958), Revs. Carl Zdancewicz, O.F.M.Conv.; Mark-Thomas Booth, O.F.M.Conv.; Deacon William Lyday.
Mailing Address: 1920 Skyview Dr., 30122. Tel: 770-941-2807; Fax: 770-941-5821. In Res., Revs. Linus DeSantis, O.F.M.Conv.; Linus DeSantis, O.F.M.Conv.
Catechesis/Religious Program—Students 415.

Lithonia, DeKalb Co., Christ Our Hope (1984), Rev. John F. Durkin Jr.
Res.: 1786 Wellborn Rd., 30058. Tel: 770-482-5017; Fax: 770-482-9476.
Catechesis/Religious Program—Students 138.

Lookout Mountain, Walker Co., Our Lady of the Mount (1947), [JC] Rev. Msgr. Leo P. Herbert.
Res.: 1227 Scenic Hwy., P.O. Box 214, 30750. Tel: 706-820-0680; Fax: 706-820-2797. (Memorial Garden For Ashes)
Catechesis/Religious Program—Students 103.

Mableton, Cobb Co., St. Francis De Sales (1999), Revs. Robert Fromageot, F.S.S.P. (PAT); Laurent Demets, F.S.S.P.; Deacons Douglas Anderson; Rigoberto A. Santiago.
587 Landers Dr., 30126. Fax: 770-948-6888
Res.: 584 Landers Dr., 30126. Tel: 770-948-6888.
Catechesis/Religious Program—Students 90.

Marietta, Cobb Co.
1—Church of St. Ann (1978), Revs. Thomas A. Reilly, M.S.; Leo B. Cummings, M.S.; Jaroslaw Topolewski; Deacons Edmund M. Grabowy; J. Nicholas Morning. In Res., Revs. Joseph J. Nolan, M.S.; Gerald M. Baril, M.S.
Res.: 4905 Roswell Rd., N.E., 30062. Tel: 770-552-6400; Fax: 770-552-6420.
Catechesis/Religious Program—Tel: 770-552-6400, Ext. 6044; Fax: 770-552-6421. Students 2,300.
2—Church of the Transfiguration (1977), Rev. Msgr. Patrick A. Bishop; Revs. Roberto Orellana; Bryan Horn; Francis Tran; Deacon Bruce Publicover; Sisters Celeste Schoppy, I.H.M., Pastoral Assoc.; Lucy N. Ezeobi, D.M.M.M., Pastoral Assoc.; Immaculata Adide, D.M.M.M., Pastoral Assoc.
Res.: 1815 Blackwell Rd., N.E., 30066-2911. Tel: 770-977-1442; Fax: 770-578-1415.
Catechesis/Religious Program—Joyce Guris, D.R.E. Students 2,035.
3—Holy Family (1973), Revs. Edward Their; Juan de la Cruz; Samuel Porras; Deacons Ronald A. Comeau; Prudencio Rivera; Al Gallagher.
Res.: 3401 Lower Roswell Rd., 30068. Tel: 770-973-0038; Fax: 770-578-0475.
Catechesis/Religious Program—Tel: 770-973-7400. Students 385.
4—St. Joseph (1952), Revs. Paul W. Berny; Alvaro Avendano; Joseph Morris; Ricardo Bailey; Ricardo Bailey; Deacons Thomas Shaver; Joseph C. Eustace; Wayland Moncrief.
Res.: 87 Lacy St., N.W., 30060. Tel: 770-422-5633; Fax: 770-422-1148.
School—Tel: 770-428-3328; Fax: 770-424-2960. Mr. Charles A. Kraft, Prin. Please refer to Elementary Schools, Archdiocese located in the Institutions Located in the Archdiocese for details. Lay Teachers 30; Students 450.
Catechesis/Religious Program—Tel: 770-428-1833; Fax: 770-422-1472. Linda Hughey, D.R.E. Students 700.

McDonough, Henry Co., St. James The Apostle (1979), Rev. Msgr. Terry W. Young, V.F.; Revs. Michael S. Sherliza; John Murphy; Deacons Robert Rich; Robert Readdy.
Res.: 1000 Decatur Rd., 30252. Tel: 770-957-5441; Fax: 770-957-0383.
Catechesis/Religious Program—Fax: 770-898-5441. Students 701.
Mission—St. Mary's P.O. Box 901, Jackson, Butts Co. 30233. Tel: 770-775-4162; Fax: 770-775-4174.

Milledgeville, Baldwin Co., Sacred Heart of Jesus (1874), Rev. Michael L. McWhorter; Deacon John W. Shoemaker.
Res.: 110 N. Jefferson St., P.O. Box 754, 31061. Tel: 478-452-2421; Fax: 478-454-1110.
Catechesis/Religious Program—Students 139.
Chapel—Milledgeville, Central State Hospital

Monroe, Walton Co., St. Anna's (1951), [JC] Rev. Daniel R. Toof; Deacon Jerry F. Connell.
Res.: 836 E. Spring St., 30655. Tel: 770-267-7637; Fax: 770-267-0465.
Catechesis/Religious Program—Tel: 770-267-0420. Students 138.

Newnan, Coweta Co., St. George's (1952), [JC] Rev. Austin Fogarty; Deacons James R. Bishop; John Myers; Steve Beers.
Res.: 771 Roscoe Rd., 30263. Tel: 770-253-0512; Fax: 770-251-2053.
Catechesis/Religious Program—Tel: 770-254-9933. Students 295.

Norcross, Gwinnett Co., Saint Patrick's (1968), Revs. Thomas J. Hennessy; Abel Guerrero; Daniel Rogaczewski; Deacons Jose Narvaez; Edwin Martinez; Charles T. Borsavage.
Res.: 2140 Beaver Ruin Rd., 30071. Tel: 770-446-2041.
Church: Beaver Ruin Rd., 30071. Tel: 770-448-2028; Fax: 770-448-7046.
Catechesis/Religious Program—Tel: 770-448-6386. Students 636.

Peachtree City, Fayette Co., Holy Trinity Catholic (1973), (Hispanic), Revs. John P. Walsh; David McGuiness; Deacons Anthony F. Cuomo; Ben Gross. In Res., Revs. Paul Burke, J.C.L. (Cand.); Joseph Shaute.
Res.: 101 Walt Banks Rd., P.O. Box 2121, 30269. Tel: 770-487-7672; Fax: 770-486-9152.
Catechesis/Religious Program—Tel: 770-487-0175. Pamela Villacres, D.R.E. Students 1,305.

Riverdale, Clayton Co., Our Lady of Vietnam (1989), (Vietnamese), [JC] Rev. Msgr. Francis Pham Van Phuong; Rev. Joseph Hieu Minh Ha; Deacon Peter Hung Viet Huynh.
Res.: 91 Valley Hill Rd., 30274. Tel: 770-471-8453; Fax: 770-473-5211.
Catechesis/Religious Program—Students 220.

Rome, Floyd Co., St. Mary's (1930), Very Rev. James A. Miceli, V.F.; Deacon Philippe Russell.
Res.: 911 N. Broad St., 30161. Tel: 706-290-9000; Fax: 706-295-1717.
School—401 E. 7th St., 30161. Tel: 404-234-4953; Fax: 706-234-3030. Mrs. Angela Ritchie, Prin. Please refer to Elementary Schools, Archdiocese located in the Institutions Located in the Archdiocese for details. Lay Teachers 30; Students 360.
Catechesis/Religious Program—Students 185.

Roswell, Fulton Co.
1—St. Andrew (1981), Revs. Frank Richardson; Adam Z. Ozimek; Deacons William Keen; Robert Smith; Lloyd Sutter.
Mailing Address: 675 Riverside Rd., 30075
Res.: 115 River Lake Ct., 30075. Tel: 770-552-0485; Fax: 770-641-9750; Fax: 770-641-8584 (Office).
Catechesis/Religious Program—Tel: 770-641-0261; Fax: 770-641-8584. Students 415.
2—St. Peter Chanel (1998), Revs. Francis G. McNamee, V.F.; John Shramko; Deacons Michael K. Balfour; Keith M. Kolodziej; Martin J. Lampe.
11330 Woodstock Rd., 30075. Tel: 678-277-9424; Fax: 678-277-9423. In Res., Rev. Brian J. Higgins.
Catechesis/Religious Program—Tel: 678-832-1230. Students 734.

Sharpsburg, Coweta Co., St. Mary Magdalene, , 4046 Lower Fayetteville Rd., 30277. Tel: 770-253-1888.

Smyrna, Cobb Co., St. Thomas the Apostle (1966), Revs. James Caffery, M.S., V.F.; Eugene Barrette, M.S.; Jaime Molina Juarez, M.N.M.; Brian Schloth, M.S.; John A. Welch, M.S.; Deacon Albert G. Weber.
Res.: 4300 King Springs Rd., 30082. Tel: 770-432-8579; Fax: 770-432-8570.
Catechesis/Religious Program—Tel: 770-432-5296; Fax: 770-432-5296. Students 820.

Snellville, Gwinnett Co., St. Oliver Plunkett (1978), (Hispanic), Revs. James A. Henault, M.S.; Peter Jandaczek, M.S.; Deacons William Jindrich; Rafael Cintron.
Church & Mailing Address: 3200 Brooks Dr., 30078. Tel: 770-979-2500; Fax: 770-985-6590.
Res.: 1318 Summit Chase Dr., 30078. Tel: 770-979-3827; Fax: 770-985-6590.
Catechesis/Religious Program—Tel: 770-973-6751. Students 1,084.

Stone Mountain, DeKalb Co., Corpus Christi (1971), [JC] Revs. Gregory D. Kenny, C.M.F.; Milton Alvarez, C.M.F.; Severino Lopez, C.M.F.; James Curran, C.M.F.; Jose Kochuparampil C.M.F.; Deacon John J. McManus.
Res.: 600 Mountain View Dr., 30083. Tel: 770-469-0395; Fax: 770-469-6822.
Catechesis/Religious Program—Tel: 770-469-0597; Fax: 770-469-0568. Students 295.

Thomson, McDuffie Co., Queen of Angels (1955), Rev. Edward O'Connor.
Res.: 1326 Washington Rd., 30824. Tel: 706-595-2913; Fax: 706-595-2913.
Catechesis/Religious Program—Students 80.

Toccoa, Stephens Co., St. Mary's (1956), [JC] Rev. Darragh Griffith.
Res.: 6388 Rothell Rd. Ext., 30577. Tel: 706-886-2819; Fax: 706-886-8770.
Catechesis/Religious Program—Students 84.
Mission—St. Catherine Laboure 708 State St., Commerce, Jackson Co. 30529. Tel: 706-335-2622.

Tyrone, Fulton Co., St. Matthew's (1979), Rev. Victor A. Galier; Deacons William Hampton; Jean R. Moenk; Jim G. Weeks.
Church: 215 Kirkley Rd., P.O. Box 970, 30290. Tel: 770-964-5804; Fax: 770-964-1228.
Catechesis/Religious Program—Students 247.

Washington, Wilkes Co., St. Joseph's (1840), [CEM] [JC 2] Rev. John T. Conway.
Res.: P.O. Box 632, U.S. Hwy. 78, 30673. Tel: 706-678-2110; Fax: 706-678-3353.
Catechesis/Religious Program—Students 45.
Mission—St. Mary's Forest Ave., Elberton, Elbert Co. 30635.
Mission—Purification Hwy. 47, Sharon, Talifero Co. 30631.

Winder, Barrow Co., St. Matthew (1999), Rev. Jaime Barona; Deacon Timothy K. Kirksey.
25 Wilkins Rd., S.W., 30680-1009. Tel: 770-867-4876; Fax: 770-867-6034.
Rectory—450 Winston Manor Dr., 30680. Tel: 770-867-0605.
Catechesis/Religious Program—Students 170.

Woodstock, Cherokee Co., St. Michael the Archangel (1995), Revs. Paul Flood; Terence Crone, P.V.; Mario Pino; Deacons James M. Easterwood; William H. Heinsch; Charles E. Carignan.
Res.: 490 Arnold Mill Rd., 30188. Tel: 770-516-0009; Fax: 770-516-4664.
Catechesis/Religious Program—Tel: 770-516-9699; Fax: 770-516-4664. Students 1,050.

Chaplains of Public Institutions

Atlanta. *Atlanta Veterans Administration Hospital.* (Vacant)
Cobb County Jail.
Dobbins Air Force Base. Vacant.
94 AW/HC, 1311 Patrol Rd., Dobbins Air Force Base, 30069-5003. Tel: 404-919-4955; 404-919-4956.
Fort McPherson.
Office of the Garrison Chaplain, Bldg. 51, Fort McPherson, 30330-5000. Tel: 404-752-2616. Rev. Paul Bolton.
Office of the FORSCOM Chap., 1777 Hardee Ave., S.W., Fort McPherson, 30330. Tel: 404-464-6030. Vacant
Hartsfield International Airport. Deacon Donald A. Kelsey.
Prison Apostolate. Rev. John C. Fallon, Chap.
U.S. Penitentiary.

Jackson. *Georgia Diagnostic & Classification Center.* Deacon Thomas O. Silvestri, Chap.

Special or Other (Arch)Diocesan Assignment:
Rev. Msgrs.—
Kiernan, Donald R., Vicar Gen. for Pastoral Min.
Reynolds, Paul H., Vicar Gen. in Curia & Chancellor
Very Rev.—
Hachey, Paul J., S.M., J.C.L., M.C.L., M.Div., Judicial Vicar, Court of Appeals
Revs.—
Higgins, Brian J., Dir. Vocations
Ngyen, Dung, Judicial Vicar, Metropolitan Tribunal

Released from Archdiocesan Assignment:
Revs.—
Anderson, John
Calle-Perez, Sergio
Christancho, Jorge H., On Leave
Farrelly, John P.
Lacey, Mark W., Leave of Absence
Neary, Noel, Leave of Absence
Sidler, Gordon L., Leave of Absence
Ward, Serge E., Leave of Absence

On Duty Outside the Archdiocese:
Revs.—
Atkins, James P., Monastery of Our Savior, 711 North St., Steubenville, OH 43952.
Byrd, Charles A., Jr., 300 Fraser Purchase Rd., Latrobe, PA 15650. St. Vincent Seminary
David, Craig

Kinast, Robert L., Center for Theological Reflection, P.O. Box 726, Indian Rocks Beach, FL 34635.
Linus, Stephen (Ireland)
McBrearity, Gerald D., S.S., Assumption Seminary, 2600 W. Woodlawn Ave., San Antonio, TX 78226-5196.
McCormick, Patrick J.
Patterson, David L., Diocese of Savannah, GA
Sanches, Joseph A., Diocese of Nashville, TN
Scherer, James F., Diocese of Charlotte, NC
Tran, Augustine Hoa Trung, Catholic University of America
Woods, Michael A., Diocese of Knoxville, TN
Young, Richard K.

Military Chaplains:
Revs.—
Bolton, Paul, 1259 Haney Plaza, SW, 30332. Garrison Chaplain's Office
Heninger, Michael B., 450 AL Henderson Blvd. Apt. 1106, Savannah, 31419.
McCormick, Patrick J., PSC 561, P.O. Box 73, FPO, AP 96310-0011. Tel: 011-81-6116-53-5218

On Sick Leave:
Revs.—
Kieran, Richard A.
Mulhern, Patrick J.
Peek, Joseph

Retired:
Rev. Msgrs.—
Donovan, Walter J., Sacred Heart Church, 353 Peachtree St., 30308.
O'Connor, Daniel
Revs.—
Danneker, Edward A.J.
Dillman, Alan M., 3957 Woodridge Way, Tucker, 30084.
Drohan, Joseph W., 224 Park Ave., Worcester, MA 01602.
Dullea, Denis, P.O. Box 31, Farmington, NH 03835.
Foley, Walter W., 561 Raindrop Circle, Hartwell, 30643.
Kerscher, Charles J., 2621 Highway 20, SE, Conyers, 30013-2424. St. Pius X Church
Morrow, Richard B., 2699 Peachtree Rd., 30305. Cathedral of Christ the King
Ware, Joseph F., St. Francis Cabrini, 11500 Middleground Rd., Savannah, 31419.

Permanent Deacons:
Akers, Henry, St. John the Evangelist, Hapeville
Anderson, Douglas J., St. Francis De Sales, Mableton
Angelich, George D., St. Marguerite D'Youville, Lawrenceville
Anzalone, Joseph S., On Duty Outside the Diocese
Anzalone, Joseph C., St. Philip Benizi, Jonesboro
Balfour, Michael K., St. Peter Chanel Mission, Roswell
Barker, Joseph J., St. Anthony, Atlanta
Bathea, Val, On Duty Outside the Diocese
Beckman, Richard F., St. John the Evangelist, Hapeville
Bedard, Walter T., Sr., St. Lawrence, Lawrenceville
Beers, Steven (Steve), St. George, Newnan
Bek, Stephen J., St. Catherine, Kennesaw
Berding, Herbert C., (Retired), St. James, Madison
Bevacqua, Bill J., Our Lady of the Assumption, Atlanta
Biglow, Ernest, Our Lady of the Assumption, Atlanta
Bishop, James R., St. George's, Newnan
Borsavage, Charles T., St. Patrick's, Norcross
Bradach, Daniel D., (Retired)
Briesch, Forrest R., On Duty Outside the Diocese
Brown, Raymond E., St. John Neumann, Lilburn
Capozza, Michael A., St. Oliver Plunkett, Snellville
Carballo, Rafael, St. Joseph, Dalton
Carignan, Charles E., St. Michael the Archangel, Woodstock
Casal, Matias A., St. Philip Benizi, Jonesboro
Casey, Lawrence B., St. Francis of Assisi, Blairsville
Chapple, Maurice P., St. Joseph's, Athens
Cintron, Rafael, St. Oliver, Plunkett, Snellville
Comeau, Ronald A., Holy Family, Marietta
Connell, Jerry F., St. Anna's, Monroe
Conti, Richard J., St. Catherine of Siena, Kennesaw
Coughlin, Frank F., Unassigned
Cuomo, Anthony F., Holy Trinity, Peachtree City
DeSandre, Bart R., Shrine of the Immaculate Conception, Atlanta
Diehl, William P., St. Francis of Assisi, Blairsville
Dietz, Paul E., St. Theresa, Douglasville
Easterwood, James M., St. Michael the Archangel, Woodstock
Egan, Raymond F., All Saints, Dunwoody
Eustace, Joseph C., St. Joseph, Marietta
Fraser, Roger A., St. Brendan, Cumming
Gallagher, Alexander S., Holy Family, Marietta
Galvis, Enrique L., Sacred Heart, Atlanta
Garcia-Carreras, Evelio, St. Stephen the Martyr, Lilburn
Garrett, William, Our Lady of the Assumption, Atlanta
Gaudin, James M., Jr., St. Joseph's, Athens
Gillespie, Patrick (Pat) J., (On duty outside of the diocese)
Goolsby, Joseph B., St. Paul of the Cross, Atlanta
Gourgues, Harold W., Jr., Our Lady of Assumption, Atlanta
Grabowy, Edmund M., St. Ann's, Marietta
Gresher, Robert C., Our Lady of the Assumption, Atlanta
Griffin, Chester, Our Lady of Lourdes, Atlanta
Gross, Benedict, (Retired)
Hampton, William (Bill) L., St. Matthew's, Tyrone
Hedderman, James J., Sr., (Retired)
Heinsch, William H., St. Michael the Archangel, Woodstock
Henrich, Robert A., (On duty outside of the diocese)
Hettel, Louis A., Leave of Absence
Higgins, David J., Our Lady of Perpetual Help, Carrollton
Holmer, Terry M., St. Theresa, Douglasville
Huynh, Hung Viet (Vic), Our Lady of Vietnam, Riverdale
Jansen, John C., St. Pius X, Conyers
Jimenez, Arturo P., On Leave of Absence
Jindrich, William L., St. Oliver Plunkett, Snellville
Johns, Fred, St. Pius X, Conyers
Jones, Frederick T., Holy Family, Marietta
Jones, Michael R., Prince of Peace, Buford
Keeling, William W., St. Thomas Aquinas, Alpharetta
Keen, William, St. Andrew's, Roswell
Kelsey, Donald A., Holy Trinity, Peachtree City
Kennedy, Michael L., St. Michael's, Gainesville
Kilkelly, Brian, St. Pius X
King, A.B., III, St. Lawrence, Lawrenceville
Kirksey, Timothy K., St. Matthew's Mission, Winder
Kolodziej, Keith M., St. Peter Chanel Mission, Roswell
Koppenaal, John A., St. Monica, Duluth
Korte, Jerry R., Sacred Heart of Jesus, Hartwell
LaHouse, Edmund J., St. Thomas Aquinas, Alpharetta
Lakin, William P., St. Joseph's, Athens
Lampe, Martin J., St. Peter Chanel Mission, Roswell
Lange, William G., St. Brigid Mission, Alpharetta
Lee, Hilliard M., Jr., St. Paul of the Cross, Atlanta
Lett, Jerry M., Sts. Peter & Paul, Decatur
Lyday, William E., St. John Vianney, Lithia Springs
Mac Donald, Will, (Retired)
Mackin, Thomas F., (Retired)
Marchildren, Donald W., (Retired)
Marinchak, Richard J., St. Mark's, Clarkesville
Marrero, Felix, Sacred Heart, Griffin
Martinez, Edwin N., St. Patrick's, Norcross
Martorell, Gerardo G., (Retired)
Mc Carthy, Kevin J., On Duty Outside the Diocese
McBride, Carl I., St. Gabriel's, Fayetteville
McCarthy, William F., Holy Spirit, Atlanta
McGrane, Thomas J., (On duty outside the Diocese)
McHugh, Al C., St. Gabriel's, Fayetteville
McKenzie, William, Christ our Hope, Lithonia
McManus, John J., Corpus Christi, Stone Mountain
McNabb, Scott J.N., Christ the King, Atlanta
Meuninck, Tilton C., St. Gabriel's, Fayetteville
Mickle, Richard (Rich) A., St. Augustine, Covington
Miller, Paul M., (Retired)
Mitchell, Alfred, Sts. Peter & Paul, Decatur
Mobley, Michael K., Sr., St. Stephen the Martyr, Lilburn
Moenk, Jean R., Deacon Emeritus, St. Matthew, Tyrone
Monahan, William J., St. Brendan Mission, Cumming
Moncrief, Wayland, St. Joseph's, Marietta
Morning, J. Nicholas, St. Ann, Marietta
Mulligan, M. Robert, (Retired)
Mure, Samuel M., Holy Cross, Atlanta
Myers, John W., St. George's, Newnan
Nadeau, Donald N., Good Shepard, Cumming
Narey, Richard D., (Retired)
Narvaez, Jose A., St. Patrick's, Norcross
O'Brien, Michael J., Our Lady of the Assumption, Atlanta
O'Connor, D. Patrick, St. Catherine of Siena, Kennesaw
O'Neill, Robert A., (Retired)
Payne, William E., Jr., Shrine of the Immaculate Conception, Atlanta
Pond, Billy, St. Monica, Duluth
Prawdzik, Stanley T., Unassigned
Publicover, Bruce C., Archdiocesan Scout Chap., Transfiguration, Marietta
Readdy, Robert G., Mission Church of St. Mary's, Jackson
Reimer, Cecil R., Holy Cross, Atlanta
Rich, Robert M., St. James the Apostle, McDonough
Rivera, Prudencio I., Shrine of the Immaculate Conception, Atlanta
Robichaux, Whitney F., Jr., B.S., M.A., M.P.S., Cathedral of Christ the King, Atlanta
Roche, Gary J., St. Michael's, Gainesville
Ruberte, Joseph, Holy Spirit, Atlanta
Rusmisel, William O., Immaculate Heart of Mary, Atlanta
Russell, Philippe, St. Mary's, Rome
Sambrone, Fred J., Jr., Lyke House Catholic Center, Atlanta
Samovanski, Alfred T., St. Monica, Duluth
Santiago, Rigoberto A.
Shaver, Thomas R., St. Joseph's, Marietta
Shell, John B., (Retired)
Shoemaker, John W., Sacred Heart, Milledgeville
Shuler, Thomas B., Holy Spirit, Atlanta
Silvestri, Thomas D., Holy Cross, Atlanta; Chap., Georgia Diagnostic and Correctional Center, Jackson
Sinanian, Loris R., Dir. Diaconate Formation, St. Anthony's, Blue Ridge
Smith, Robert B., St. Andrew's, Roswell
Smith, Wayne D., Sacred Heart, Atlanta
Speed, William (Bill) E., Prince of Peace, Buford
St. Michel, Ronald A., St. Theresa, Douglasville
Stagg, James A., Holy Family Canett, Alabama
Stewart, James M., Immaculate Heart of Mary, Atlanta
Stives, Edward C., Our Lady of Lourdes, Melbourne, Fl.
Stone, James E., Mary Our Queen, Norcross
Strachan, John S., St. Thomas Aquinas, Alpharetta
Stroop, John, St. Benedict's, Duluth
Suever, Richard M., Holy Cross, Atlanta
Sutter, Edward L., St. Andrew's, Roswell
Swan, Peter B., Sr., St. Philip Benizi, Jonesboro
Thompson, John F., St. Mark's, Clarkesville
Timme, William G., (Retired)
Tipton, Robert F., St. Patrick's, Norcross
Tolcher, Richard P., St. Philip Benizi, Jonesboro
Tollett, Lee J., St. Mark's, Clarkesville
Tracy, Kevin F., St. Thomas Aquinas, Alpharetta
Weber, Albert G., St. Thomas the Apostle, Smyma
Weeks, Jim G., St. Matthew's, Tyrone
Weiss, Dr. James (Jim), Holy Cross, Atlanta
West, James, St. Peter's, La Grange
Williams, Kenneth, St. Luke, Dahlonega
Womack, Gary D., St. John Neumann, Lilburn
Zaworski, Thomas E., St. Gabriel's, Fayetteville

INSTITUTIONS LOCATED IN THE ARCHDIOCESE

[A] SEMINARIES, RELIGIOUS OR SCHOLASTICATES

ATLANTA. *Aquinas Center of Theology at Emory University*, 1703 Clifton Rd., F-5, 30322. Tel: 404-727-8860; Fax: 404-727-8862. Email: aqinasc@emory.edu. Web: www.aquinas.emory.edu. David A. Balunas, Chair; Jan Sebacher, Prog. Coord. Total Staff 5.

[B] HIGH SCHOOLS, ARCHDIOCESAN

ATLANTA. *St. Pius X Catholic High School* (Coed), 2674 Johnson Rd., N.E., 30345. Tel: 404-636-3023; Fax: 404-633-8387. Email: spellman@spx.org. Web: spx.org. Mr. Stephen Spellman, Prin.; Revs. Scott Reily, L.C.; Dan Rogaczewski; Rev. Msgr. Richard Lopez. Priests 3; Lay Teachers 80; Students 1,005.

ATHENS. *Monsignor Donovan Catholic High School*, 590 Lavender Rd., 30603. Tel: 706-433-0223; Fax: 706-433-0229. Email: sfleming@MDCHS.org. Dr. Scott Fleming, Contact Person.

FAIRBURN. *Our Lady of Mercy Catholic High School*, 861 Hwy. 279, 30213. Tel: 770-461-2202; Fax: 770-461-9353. Email: jcobis@olmbobcats.org. Web: www.olmbobcats.org. John Cobis, Prin.; Rev. Paul Burke, Chap. Priests 1; Lay Teachers 22; Total Staff 23; Total Enrollment 242.

ROSWELL. *Blessed Trinity Catholic High School*, 11320 Woodstock Rd., 30075. Tel: 678-277-9083; Fax: 678-277-9756. Email: fmoore@bttitans.org. Web: www.bttitans.org. Frank Moore, Prin.; Rev. Kevin J. Hargaden, Chap. Priests 1; Lay Teachers 72; Total Staff 96; Total Enrollment 842.

[C] HIGH SCHOOLS, PRIVATE

ATLANTA. *Marist School,* (Grades 7-12), 3790 Ashford-Dunwoody, N.E., 30319-1899. Tel: 770-457-7201; 770-451-1316 (Res.); Fax: 770-457-8402. Email: marist@marist.com. Web: www.marist.com. Revs. Joel M. Konzen, S.M., Prin.; Richmond J. Egan, S.M., Pres.; Paul Cabrita, S.M.; Francis J. Kissel, S.M.; Ralph F. Olek, S.M., Supr.; David D. Musso, S.M., Chap. A Private Catholic School.; College Preparatory Day School conducted by The Marist Fathers and Brothers. Corporate Title: Marist School, Inc. Priests 6; Lay Faculty 97; Total Staff 143; Students 1,032. In Res. Rev. Charles A. Girard, S.M., Prov. Archivist; Very Rev. Paul J. Hachey, S.M., J.C.L., M.C.L., M.Div., Court of Appeals; Revs. James L. Hartnett, S.M. (Retired); Thomas D. O'Donnell, S.M. (Retired); Lawrence R. Schmuhl, S.M. (Retired).

[D] ELEMENTARY SCHOOLS, ARCHDIOCESAN

ATLANTA. *Cathedral of Christ the King Catholic School,* 46 Peachtree Way, 30305. Tel: 404-233-0383; Fax: 404-266-0704. Mrs. Peggy Warner, Prin. Lay Teachers 44; Students 541.

Christ the King Catholic School (1937), 46 Peachtree Way, N.E., 30305. Tel: 404-233-0383; Fax: 404-266-0704. Mrs. Peggy Warner, Prin. Lay Teachers 45; Students 541.

Immaculate Heart of Mary Catholic School (1958), 2855 Briarcliff Rd., N.E., 30305. Tel: 404-636-4488; Fax: 404-636-1853. Tricia DeWitt, Prin. Lay Teachers 33; Students 493.

St. Jude the Apostle Catholic School (1962), 7171 Glenridge Dr., N.E., 30328. Tel: 770-394-2880; Fax: 770-804-9248. Patty Childs, Prin. Lay Teachers 33; Students 494.

Our Lady of the Assumption Catholic School (1952), 1320 Hearst Dr., N.E., 30319. Tel: 404-364-1902; Fax: 404-364-1914. Dr. Joan Tiernan, Prin. Lay Teachers 40; Students 490.

ATHENS. *St. Joseph Catholic School* (1949), 134 Prince Ave., 30612. Tel: 706-543-1621; Fax: 706-543-0149. Sr. Mary Glackin, I.H.M., Prin. Lay Teachers 21; Students 369.

DECATUR. *St. Peter Claver Regional Catholic School,* 2560 Tilson Rd., 30032. Tel: 404-241-3063; Fax: 404-241-4382. Catherine Spencer, Prin. Daughters of Mary Mother of Mercy 1; Lay Teachers 23; Students 125.

St. Thomas More Catholic School (1950), 630 W. Ponce De Leon Ave., 30030. Tel: 404-373-8456; Fax: 404-377-8554. Mrs. Gail M. Mszane, Prin. Lay Teachers 33; Students 449.

HAPEVILLE. *St. John the Evangelist Catholic School* (1954), 240 Arnold St., 30354. Tel: 404-767-4312; Fax: 404-767-0359. Karen Vogtner, Prin. Lay Teachers 22; Students 286.

KENNESAW. *St. Catherine of Siena Catholic School* (2002), 1618 Ben King Rd., 30144. Tel: 770-419-8601; Fax: 678-626-0000. Robyn Planchard, Prin.

MARIETTA. *St. Joseph Catholic School* (1953), 81 Lacey St., 30060. Tel: 770-428-3328; Fax: 770-424-2960. Mr. Charles A. Kraft, Prin. Lay Teachers 37; Students 423.

ROME. *St. Mary Catholic School* (1945), 401 E. Seventh St., 30161. Tel: 706-234-4953; Fax: 706-234-3030. Mrs. Angela Ritchie, Prin. Lay Teachers 31; Students 361.

[E] ELEMENTARY SCHOOLS, PRIVATE

ATLANTA. **The Solidarity School, Inc.,* 512 Means St., Ste. 305, 30318. Tel: 404-221-0203; Fax: 404-221-1006. Web: www.solidarityschool.org. Lay Teachers 5; Total Staff 5; Students 42.

CUMMING. *Pinecrest Academy,* 955 Peachtree Pkwy., 30041. Tel: 770-888-4477; Fax: 770-838-0404. Email: info@pinecrestacademy.org. Web: www.pinecrestacademy.org. William Guilfoil, Exec. Dir. Priests 1; Male Consecrated 1; Female Consecrated 2; Lay Teachers 70; Students 800.

[F] REGIONAL CATHOLIC ELEMENTARY SCHOOLS

ALPHARETTA. *Holy Redeemer,* 3380 Old Alabama Rd., 30022. Tel: 770-410-4056; Fax: 770-410-1454. Email: mreiling@hr.cathsch.org. Web: catholicacademics.org/holyredeemer. Mary Reiling, Prin. Lay Teachers 33; Students 519.

LILBURN. *St. John Neumann,* (Grades K-8) , (Regional) , 791 Tom Smith Rd., 30047. Tel: 770-381-0557; Fax: 770-381-0276. James Anderson, Prin. Lay Teachers 34; Students 580.

ROSWELL. *Queen of Angels,* 11340 Woodstock Rd., 30075. Tel: 770-518-1804; Fax: 770-518-0945. Email: kwood@qaschool.org. Web: www.qaschool.org. Kathy Wood, Prin.; Cindy Sabula, Asst. Principal; Catherine Anderson, Dir. Student Svcs. Lay Teachers 27; Students 502; Total Staff 62.

TYRONE. *Our Lady of Victory,* 211 Kirkley Rd., 30290. Tel: 770-306-9026; Fax: 770-306-0323. Web: www.catholicedga.org/olv. Craig Mousseau, Prin. Lay Teachers 20; Total Staff 33; Total Enrollment 269; Admin/Facilities Staff 13.

[G] RESIDENTIAL TREATMENT CENTER

ATLANTA. *Village of St. Joseph Counseling Services Program,* 1961 N. Druid Hills Rd., Ste. 205-B, 30329. Tel: 404-321-2900; Fax: 404-321-2911. Web: www.cssatlanta.com. Dr. J. Paul Gallant, Ph.D. A program of Catholic Social Services, Inc.

[H] CATHOLIC CHARITIES

Departmental Agencies

ATLANTA

Catholic Charities, 680 W. Peachtree St., N.W., 30308-1984. Tel: 404-885-7476; Fax: 404-885-7200. Email: jkantner@archatl.com. Dr. James E. Kantner, Ph.D., Dir.

Catholic Personal Care Homes, Inc., 3409 Washington Rd., East Point, 30344. Tel: 404-766-7121; Fax: 404-766-4344. Mrs. Regina Harris, Dir.

St. Thomas Manor, 3409 Washington Rd., East Point, 30344. Tel: 404-669-0143; Fax: 404-669-0458.

St. Teresa Manor, 227 Medical Way, Riverdale, 30244. Tel: 770-996-8707; Fax: 770-996-1586.

Catholic Housing Initiatives, Inc., Good Shepherd Place, 198 N. Corners Pkwy., Cumming, 30040. Tel: 404-766-7121; Fax: 404-766-4344. Mrs. Regina Harris, Dir.

Catholic Retirement Facilities, Inc., 3409 Washington Rd., East Point, 30344. Tel: 404-766-7121; Fax: 404-766-4344. Mrs. Regina Harris, Dir.

Catholic Social Services, Inc., 680 W. Peachtree St., N.W., 30308-1984. Tel: 404-881-6571; Fax 404-888-7816. Sandra Hollett, Exec. Dir. Counseling Services, Pregnancy, Parenting & Adoption, Immigration Services, Multicultural Services & Parish Social Ministry, Branch Offices outside the city of Atlanta:

Parish Social Ministry/Community Connections Tel: 404-881-6571; Fax: 404-888-7816. Simone Blanchard, Program Dir.

Pregnancy, Parenting & Adoption Services Tel: 404-885-7467; Fax: 404-888-7816. Sheila Reynolds, Program Dir.

Immigration Services Tel: 404-885-7454; Fax: 404-885-7210. Sue Colussy Esq., Prog. Dir.

Migration & Refugee Services Tel: 404-885-7465; Fax: 404-885-7281. Tanya Zeiliger, Dir.

Regional Offices, 680 W. Peachtree St., 30308-1984. Tel: 404-885-7268; Fax: 404-888-7816. Carmen Quezada, Prog. Dir.

CSS Doraville, 5238 Peachtree Rd., Chamblee, 30341. Tel: 770-454-6068; Fax: 770-454-1458. Meaghan Williams, Prog. Dir.

CSS/Athens, R.O., 160 Winston Dr., Ste. 1, Athens, 30607. Tel: 706-583-9637; Fax: 706-548-3897. Stella Sailors, Prog. Dir.

CSS/Cobb, R.O., 87 Lacy St., N.W., Marietta, 30060. Tel: 770-429-2369; Fax: 770-792-8002. Maria Teresa Bordon, Prog. Dir.

CSS/Gainesville, R.O., 1440 Pearce Cir., Gainesville, 30501. Tel: 770-534-3337; Fax: 770-534-3532. Lana Krummen, Prog. Dir.

Office of Family Concerns, 680 W. Peachtree St., N.W., 30308. Tel: 404-888-7819; Fax: 404-885-7494. Mary Ellen Hughes, Dir.

Village of St. Joseph, Child and Adolescent Counseling, 1961 N. Druid Hills, N.E., Ste. 204B, 30319. Tel: 404-349-2400; Fax: 404-321-2911. Dr. J. Paul Gallant, Ph.D., Program Dir.

[I] GENERAL HOSPITALS

ATLANTA. *Saint Joseph's Hospital of Atlanta, Inc.,* 5665 Peachtree Dunwoody Rd., N.E., 30342. Tel: 404-851-7001; Fax: 404-851-7339. Email: sjgerety@sjha.org. Web: www.st.josephsatlanta.org. Bonnie Phipps, CEO; Rev. Steven L. Yander, Resident Chap. Sisters of Mercy of Americas, Baltimore Regional Community. Sisters 11; Total Staff 2,382; Bed Capacity 346; In Patients 18,430; Patients Assisted Annually 140,000.

ATHENS. *St. Mary's Health Care System,* 1230 Baxter St., 30606-3791. Tel: 706-354-3033; Fax: 706-354-3197. Email: tfitz@stmarysathens.org. Web: www.stmarysathens.org. Mr. Thomas E. Fitz Jr., Pres. & CEO; Sr. M. Marguerite, M.S.C., Community Care Coord. Sisters of Mercy, Regional Community of Baltimore Nursing Sisters 3; Other Sister Personnel 3; Nurses 342; Bed Capacity 196; Patients Assisted Annually 106,776.

[J] SPECIAL HOSPITALS

ATLANTA. *Saint Joseph's Mercy Care Services,* 424 Decatur St., 30312-1848. Tel: 404-880-3550; Fax: 404-880-3551. Email: aebberwein@sjha.org. Division of Saint Joseph's Health System. Operates Saint Joseph's Mercy Care Services (Atlanta, Georgia). Operates Mercy Senior Care (Rome, Georgia). Total Staff 160; Sisters 1; Total Assisted 22,000.

Our Lady of Perpetual Help Home, 760 Pollard Blvd., S.W., 30315. Tel: 404-688-9515; Fax: 404-588-9568. Sr. Miriam Smith, O.P., Supr.; Rev. Dung V. Nguyen, J.C.L., Resident Chap.
Legal Title: *Servants of Relief for Incurable Cancer* Sisters of St. Dominic, Nursing Home for Free Care of Cancer Patients. Sisters 7; Total Staff 32; Patients Assisted Annually 130; Bed Capacity 40.

ROME. *Mercy Senior Care, Inc.,* 212 W. Third St., 30165. Tel: 706-291-0100; Fax: 706-295-5953. Email: rlawler@sjha.org. Sr. Angela Marie Ebberwein, R.S.M., Vice Pres.; Rita Lawler, Dir. Total Staff 35; Total Assisted 300.

[K] MONASTERIES AND RESIDENCES OF PRIESTS

ATLANTA. *Legionaries of Christ,* 2595 Spalding Ln., 30350. Tel: 770-394-2158; Fax: 770-393-3688; Fax: 770-393-0934. Email: atlanta@legionaries.org. Revs. Paul Moreau, L.C. (WDC), Vice Rector & Retreat Work; Scott Reily, L.C., Supr.; Patrick Murphy, L.C., Promotion, Retreats; Peter Devereux, Chap. at the Donnellan School and Promotion; James Larson, L.C., Chap. at the Donnellan School; Jeffrey Bowker, L.C., Retreat and Promotion Work; Eamon Shelly, Chap. at Pinecrest Academy; Bros. Peter Nowicki, L.C.; Hung Bui, L.C.; Donald Kaufman, L.C.; Ignatio Ortigas, L.C. Total In Residence 8.

Marist Provincial Office, Society of Mary - Atlanta Province, P.O. Box 81144, 30366-1144. Tel: 770-458-1435; Fax: 770-458-1044. Email: provincialoffice@marist.com djsteik@aol.com steikd@marist.com. Web: maristsociety.org.
Res.: 1485 Ashford Pl., 30319. Very Rev. Dennis J. Steik, S.M., Prov.

CONYERS. *The Monastery of the Holy Spirit,* 2625 Hwy. 212 S.W., 30094. Tel: 770-483-8705; Fax: 770-760-0989. Email: monastery@trappist.net. Web: www.trappist.net. Revs. Francis Michael Stiteler, O.C.S.O., Supr.; Richard Donarski, O.C.S.O., Prior; Bro. Chaminade Crabtree, O.C.S.O., Subprior; Rev. Methodius Telnack, O.C.S.O., Procurator; Bro. Elias Marachal, O.C.S.O., Novice Master; Revs. Clarence J. Biggers, O.C.S.O.; Edmund H. Brand, O.C.S.O.; Malachy Corley, O.C.S.O.; Philip R. Dehner, O.C.S.O.; Anthony Delisi, O.C.S.O.; Gerard Gross, O.C.S.O.; Jerome J. Hickey, O.C.S.O.; Francis X. Kavanagh, O.C.S.O.; Luke C. Kot, O.C.S.O.; Ed Morley, O.C.S.O.; John M. O'Brien, O.C.S.O.; Robert L. Pearson, O.C.S.O.; Eduardo Rodriguez, O.C.S.O.; Thomas F. Smith, O.C.S.O.; Lawrence Swartz, O.C.S.O.; Matt G. Torpey, O.C.S.O.; Damian C. Turk, O.C.S.O.; Joseph F. Tynan, O.C.S.O.; Charles Felix Zell, O.C.S.O.; Bernard Joseph Valoret, Oblate; Miami Archdiocese (Retired). Priests 23; Professed Brothers 20; Novices 6.
Located Elsewhere: Revs. George J. Evans, O.C.S.O. (SAT) (Retired), San Antonio, TX; Steven Scherrer, M.M., Oblate in Venezuela.

LAWRENCEVILLE. *The Missionaries of St. Francis De Sales,* Villa Luyet, 109 Johnson Rd., 30045-5521. Tel: 770-963-3774; Fax: 770-963-3774. Email: msfsjcd@mycidco.com. Web: www.msfs@mindspring.com. Revs. Martin Kopchik, M.S.F.S., Mission Supr.; John F. Tiernan III, M.S.F.S.; C. John DeVore, M.S.F.S.; Jose Mullakkara, M.S.F.S.; Kurian Karickal, M.S.F.S.; Abraham Mullenkuzhy, M.S.F.S.; Augustine Tharappel, M.S.F.S.
Priests of This Province Serving Elsewhere: Revs. Thomas Anchanickal, M.S.F.S., Demopolis, AL; Davis Chackalackel, M.S.F.S., Dover, TN; Anthony Dharamaraj, M.S.F.S., Ferriday, LA; Lukose Kalarickal, M.S.F.S., Chandler, TX; Raphael Karekatt, M.S.F.S., Echo, LA; Paul Kunnumpuram, M.S.F.S., Vidalia, LA; Ananda Prasad Maddineni, M.S.F. (India), Jacksonville, FL; Jose Maliekal, M.S.F.S., Demopolis, AL; Joseph Mendes, M.S.F.S., Lawrenceville, GA; Fredericks Montero, M.S.F.S., Akron, OH; Jose Mudavankunnel, M.S.F.S., Mobile, AL; Joseph Charles Pednekar, M.S.F.S., Cleveland, OH; Arokiam Santhiyagu, M.S.F.S., Jackson, MI; Matthew Thottiyil, M.S.F.S., Sugar Land, TX; Abraham Vettuvelil, M.S.F.S., Arlington Heights, IL.

[L] CONVENTS AND RESIDENCES OF SISTERS

ATLANTA. *Missionaries of Charity,* 995 St. Charles Ave., N.E., 30306-4211. Tel: 404-892-5111. Sisters 4; Total Assisted 145.

CHAMBLEE. *Missionary Sisters of the Sacred Heart "Ad Gentes",* 3152 Terramar Dr., 30341. Tel: 770-934-8939; Fax: 770-934-8939. Email: atlantamag@

aol.com. Sisters Gudelia Ramos Tapia, M.A.G., Supr. & Regl. Coord., of M.A.G. Sisters in U.S.A.; Pilar Hinojosa; Ricarda Taneco; Veronica F. Ramos; Xenia Gonzalez; Esther Ordonez; Esperanza Rivera; Ana Maria Lopez. To serve the Hispanic community. Sisters 8.

SNELLVILLE. *Monastery of the Visitation* (Maryfield) , 2055 Ridgedale Dr., 30278. Tel: 770-972-1060. Sr. Mary Jozefa Kowalewski, V.H.M., Supr. Maryfield. Strictly cloistered contemplative Office of First Federation. Private retreats for women, no more than 3 at a time. U.S. Professed Sisters 2; Novices 1.

[M] RETREAT HOUSES

ATLANTA. *Ignatius House*, 6700 Riverside Dr., N.W., 30328-2710. Tel: 404-255-0503; Fax: 404-256-0776. Email: ijesuit@bellsouth.net. Web: www.ignatiushouse.org. Revs. Niel J. Jarreau, Assoc. Dir.; Clyde H. LeBlanc, Assoc. Dir.; J. R. Fitzgerald, Lay Dir. Total In Residence 2; Total Staff 8.

Maisha House of Prayer, Inc., 520 Parkway Dr., N.E., 30308. Tel: 404-872-0096; Fax: 404-872-7925. Email: maishahouse@earthlink.net. Sr. Loretta McCarthy, Pres. Total in Residence 2; Total Staff 2.

GAINESVILLE. *Cedar Hill Enrichment Center, Inc.*, 5735 Dawsonville Hwy., 30506. Tel: 770-887-0051; Fax: 770-844-1371. Email: cedarhil@wans.net. Web: www.cedarhillenrichment.org. Sr. Carol Patron, C.S.J., Exec. Dir. Total Staff 5; Total In Residence 3.

HOSCHTON. *Sisters of the Cenacle*, 5913 Jackson Trail Rd., 30548. Tel: 706-654-3460; Fax: 706-654-1459. Sisters Susan Arcaro, R.C.; Barbara Young, R.C. Congregation of Our Lady of the Retreat in the Cenacle, Retreat Ministry, Spiritual Development Programs, Spiritual Direction, and Other Forms of Spiritual Ministry. Sisters 2.

[N] CAMPUS MINISTRY CENTERS

ATLANTA. *Campus Ministry* 680 W. Peachtree St., N.W., 30308. Tel: 404-888-7804.

The Catholic Center at Atlanta University Complex, 809 Beckwith St., S.W., 30314-3720. Tel: 404-755-2646; Fax: 404-755-3460. Rev. Edward B. Branch.

Berry College
3487 Frey Lake Rd., Kennesaw, 30144. Tel: 770-423-9909; Fax: 770-423-9605. Rev. Linus De Santis, O.F.M.Conv.

Emory University, Agnes Scott College, 1753 N. Decatur Rd., N.E., 30307. Tel: 404-636-7237; Fax: 404-636-6099. Rev. Timothy M. Hepburn.

Georgia Institute of Technology, 172 4th St., N.W., 30313. Tel: 404-892-6759; Fax: 404-829-6759. Rev. Mario Di Lella, O.F.M.

Oglethorpe University, 4484 Peachtree Rd., N.E., 30319. Tel: 404-261-1441.
Our Lady of the Assumption Catholic Church: 1350 Hearst Dr., N.E., 30319. Tel: 404-261-7181; Fax: 404-364-1913. Rev. James F. McGoldrick, S.M.

Catholic Student Center - University of Georgia, 1344 S. Lumpkin St., Athens, 30605. Tel: 706-543-2293; Fax: 706-543-2541. Rev. John McDowell, O.F.M., Dir. (Athens)

West Georgia College, Church of Our Lady of Perpetual Help, Center Point Rd., Rte. 5, P.O. Box 100, Carrollton, 30117. Tel: 706-832-8977; Fax: 770-832-1666. Rev. Paul Williams. (Carrollton)

North Georgia College (Dahlonega)
St. Luke the Evangelist Church: 301 Hawkins St., Dahlonega, 30533. Tel: 706-864-2568; Fax: 706-864-4294. Rev. Msgr. Stephen T. Churchwell, J.C.D.

Dalton Junior College (Dalton)
Church of St. Joseph: 1775 Old Haigmill Rd., Dalton, 30720. Tel: 706-278-3107; Fax: 706-278-6902. Rev. William Hoffman.

Brenau College, St. Michael's Catholic Church - 1440 Pearce Cir., N.E., Gainesville, 30501-2457. Tel: 706-534-3338; Fax: 706-535-2440. Rev. Victor Reyes. (Gainesville)

Kennesaw State University, 3487 Frey Lake Rd., Kennesaw, 30144. Tel: 770-423-9909; Fax: 770-423-9605. Rev. Linus DeSantis, O.F.M.Conv. (Kennesaw)

LaGrange Jr. College, 200 LaFayette Pkwy., LaGrange, 30240. Tel: 706-884-4224; Fax: 706-884-1624. Rev. Balapa Selvaraj. (LaGrange)

Georgia College (Milledgeville)
Sacred Heart Church: 110 N. Jefferson St., Milledgeville, 31061. Tel: 912-452-2421; Fax: 478-454-1110. Rev. Michael L. McWhorter.

Shorter College (Rome)
St. Mary's Church: 911 N. Broad St., Rome, 30161. Tel: 706-295-7014; Fax: 706-295-1717. Very Rev. James A. Miceli, V.F.

Dekalb Community College (Stone Mountain)
Corpus Christi Church: 600 Mountain View Dr., Stone Mountain, 30083. Tel: 770-469-0395; Fax: 770-469-6822. Rev. Gregory D. Kenny, C.M.F.

[O] MISCELLANEOUS LISTINGS

ATLANTA. *The Catholic Charismatic Renewal in Atlanta*, 1753 N. Decatur Rd., N.E., 30307.

Blessed Trinity High School, 11320 Woodstock Rd., Roswell, 30075. Tel: 404-636-7237. Email: thepbur@emory.edu. Rev. Timothy M. Hepburn, Liaison.

Catholic Construction Services, Inc., 688 W. Peachtree St., N.W., 30308-1984. Tel: 404-888-7838; Fax: 404-885-7299. Email: gbarrie@archatl.com. George Barrie, Pres. & CEO; Donna L. Worley, Office Mgr., Real Estate Acquisitions; Dick Jansen, Field Representaive, Quality Control; Rob McKinnon, Field Representaive, Quality Control; Rachel White, Admin. Asst.; Craig Nevels, Project Mgr.; Dennis W. Kelly, Project Mgr.; Steve Larkin, Project Mgr.; Joe Truitt, Facilities Asst.; Arthur Glover, Facilities Asst.

Catholic Education of North Georgia, Inc., 680 W. Peachtree St., N.W., 30308. Tel: 404-888-7833; Fax: 404-885-7479. Email: jmucheck@archatl.com. Web: www.archatl.com. Judith Mucheck, Supt. of Schools.

Catholic Foundation of North Georgia, Inc., 127 Peachtree St., Ste. 425, 30303. Tel: 404-588-0033; Fax: 404-588-0023. Email: cfnorthgeorgia@bellsouth.net. Rev. Msgr. Edward J. Dillon.

Good Shepherd Services of Atlanta, Inc. (Incorporated as Good Shepherd Corporation) Tel: 770-986-8279; Fax: 770-451-0156. Email: christinemyhanh@yahoo.com.

Main Office, 2430 Shallowford Terr., Chamblee, 30341. Tel: 770-455-9379; Fax: 770-451-0156. Email: shepherdatlanta@wmconnect.com. Sr. Christine Truong, Exec. Dir. Tel: 770-455-9379; 770-986-8279.

Good Shepherd Outreach Center, 2426 Shallowford Ter., Chamblee, 30341. Tel: 770-455-9379; Fax: 770-455-4776. Sr. Barbara Beasley, Pres. Sisters 2.

Greater Northeast Atlanta Serra Club #875, Dist. #169, 680 W. Peachtree St., N.W., 30308Web: serraatlanta.org. Pedro Villacorta, Pres. Tel: 678-230-9803; Joseph J. Krygiel, Region 14 Dir. Tel: 770-565-7792.

Home and Family, Inc., 8200 Roberts Dr., Ste. 201, 30350-4151. Tel: 770-396-2363. Email: atlanta@legionaries.org. Revs. Scott Reilly, L.C., Supr.; James Larson; Eamon Shelly; Bro. Peter Nowicki, L.C.

Saint Joseph's Health System, Inc., 5665 Peachtree Dunwoody Rd., N.E., 30342. Tel: 404-851-7120; Fax: 404-851-7339. Email: sjgerety@sjha.org. Web: www.stjosephsatlanta.org. Bonnie Phipps, CEO; Sr. Jane Gerety, R.S.M., Senior Vice Pres. for Sponsorship. Sponsorship. Holding Company Sponsored by Sisters of Mercy of Americas, Baltimore Regional Community, which operates: Saint Joseph's Hospital of Atlanta, Inc.; Saint Joseph's Mercy Foundation, Inc.; Saint Joseph's Mercy Care Services, Inc.; Saint Joseph's Care Management Corporation and Saint Joseph's Service Corporation.

Saint Joseph's Mercy Foundation, 5673 Peachtree Dunwoody Rd., Ste. 650, 30342-1746. Tel: 404-851-5710; Fax: 404-851-4986. Email: pmazzara@sjha.org. Web: www.stjosephsatlanta.org. Philip Mazzara, Pres.

St. Joseph's Research Institute, Inc., 5665 Peachtree - Dunwoody Rd., N.E., 30342. Tel: 404-851-5749. Email: pjustice@sjha.org. Paul G. Justice, Esq., Vice Pres. & General Counsel.

Mercy Housing Pembroke, Inc., 615 Peachtree St., N.E., Ste. 1105, 30308. Tel: 404-873-3887; Fax: 404-873-3889. Email: KBrownlee@MercyHousing.org. Kathleen Brownlee, Pres.

National Catholic Association of Diocesan Directors for Hispanic Ministry, Inc., 680 W. Peachtree St., N.W., 30308. Tel: 804-359-5661; Fax: 804-358-9159. Elisa Montalvo, Pres. Total Staff 13; Total Assisted 6,500.

National Christ Child Society of Atlanta, Georgia Inc., P.O. Box 88646, 30356. Tel: 770-379-0924; Fax: 770-379-0924. Email: christchildatl@bellsouth.net. Julie Moyers, Contact Person.

Patrons of the Arts in the Vatican Museums, Inc., 245 Perimeter Center Pkwy.m Ste. 600, 30346. Tel: 404-221-0203; Fax: 404-221-1006. Email: gngenner@isc-erh.com. Gareth N. Genner, Dir. & Sec.

Renovacion Carismatica Catolica Hispana De Atlanta, 305 Avalon Forest Dr., Lawrenceville, 30044. Tel: 770-921-8022.

Serra Club #120, Dist. 169 Metro Atlanta , 680 W. Peachtree St., N.W., 30308Web: serraatlanta.org. William B. Hare, Pres. Tel: 770-432-4333; Joseph J. Krygiel, Region 14 Dir. Tel: 770-565-7792.

Serra Club #684, Dist. 169 North Metro Atlanta , 680 W. Peachtree St., N.W., 30308Web: serraatlanta.org. Joseph J. Krygiel. Tel: 770-565-7792.

The Solidarity Association, 245 Perimeter Center Pkwy., Ste. 600, 30346. Tel: 678-259-8146; Fax: 770-454-0032. Gareth N. Genner, Trustee & Sec.

CHAMBLEE. *Atlanta Particular Council, St. Vincent de Paul Society, Inc.*, 2050 Chamblee - Tucker Rd., Ste. C, 30341. Tel: 770-457-2920; 770-458-5415; Fax: 770-457-3021. Email: sbissonnette@svdpatl.org. Web: www.svdpatl.org. Ms. Sheila Bissonnette, Exec. Dir. Total Assisted 68,000; Total Staff 20; Thrift Stores 9; Temporary Housing Programs 4; Conferences 67.

DORAVILLE. *Korean Martyrs Pastoral Center*, 6003 Buford Hwy., N.E., 30340. Tel: 770-455-1380; Fax: 770-455-4262. Email: office@kmccga.org. Web: www.kmccga.org. Rev. Msgr. Donald R. Kiernan; Rev. Gabriel Byong-Young Je, S.J., Chap.

LAWRENCEVILLE. *Catholic Home Educators of Georgia, Inc.*, 922 Chadwick Park Dr., 30045. Tel: 770-979-6424. Email: mcdonaldcrew@msn.com. Tammy Rowland, Co-Dir.; Kim McDonald, Co-Dir.; Liz Nelson, Newsletter; Kris Barnum, Membership & Treas.

LILBURN. *Magnificat - Joyful Visitation Chapter, Inc.*, 4405 Sirrocco Ln., 30047. Tel: 770-923-4277. Email: sgoose@bellsouth.net. Susie Goodrow, Coord.

TUCKER. *Faith Enrichment Institute, Inc.*, 3758 Lavista Rd., Ste. 100, 30084. Tel: 404-329-125-; Fax: 404-248-9335. Email: dennismackin@comcast.net. Mr. Dennis S. Mackin, Contact Person.

RELIGIOUS INSTITUTES OF MEN REPRESENTED IN THE ARCHDIOCESE

For further details refer to the corresponding bracketed number in the Religious Institutes of Men or Women section.

[0350]—*Cistercians Order of the Strict Observance-Trappists*—O.C.S.O.
[0360]—*Claretian Missionaries* (Eastern Province)—C.M.F.
[1000]—*Congregation of the Passion* (Prov. of St. Paul of the Cross)—C.P.
[0480]—*Conventual Franciscans* (Prov. of St. Anthony of Padua, Baltimore)—O.F.M.Conv
[0520]—*Franciscan Friars* (Prov. of the Most Holy Name of Jesus)—O.F.M.
[0690]—*Jesuit Fathers and Brothers* (New Orleans Prov.)—S.J.
[0730]—*Legionaries of Christ*—L.C.
[0780]—*Marist Fathers* (San Francisco-Washington Prov.)—S.M.
[0720]—*The Missionaries of Our Lady of La Salette*—M.S.
[]—*Missionaries of St. Francis de Sales* (Annecy, France)—M.S.F.S.
[1065]—*The Priestly Fraternity of St. Peter*—F.S.S.P.
[1070]—*Redemptorist Fathers* (Baltimore Prov.)—C.SS.R.

RELIGIOUS INSTITUTES OF WOMEN REPRESENTED IN THE ARCHDIOCESE

[3110]—*Congregation of Our Lady of the Retreat in the Cenacle*—R.C.
[]—*Daughters of Mary, Mother of Mercy*—D.M.M.M.
[1070-13]—*Dominican Sisters (Adrian, MI)*—O.P.
[1070-23]—*Dominican Sisters of St. Rose of Lima (Hawthorne, NY)*—O.P.
[1070-03]—*Dominican Sisters (Sinsinawa, WI)*—O.P.
[]—*Franciscan Sisters of Our Lady of Refuge*—R.F.R.
[1840]—*Grey Nuns of the Sacred Heart (Yardley, PA)*—G.N.S.H.
[1870]—*Handmaids of the Sacred Heart of Jesus (Philadelphia, PA)*—A.C.J.
[2575]—*Institute of the Sisters of Mercy of the Americas* (Merion, PA; Rochester, NY; Baltimore, MD)—R.S.M.
[2710]—*Missionaries of Charity*—M.C.
[2800]—*Missionary Sisters of the Most Sacred Heart of Jesus of Hiltrup*—M.S.C.
[]—*Missionary Sisters of the Sacred Heart* (Mexico)—M.A.G.
[]—*Sisters for Christian Community*—S.F.C.C.
[0650]—*Sisters of Charity of St. Vincent de Paul* (New York)—S.C.
[0430]—*Sisters of Charity of the Blessed Virgin Mary*—B.V.M.
[1570]—*Sisters of St. Francis of the Holy Family (Dubuque, IA)*—O.S.F.
[1580]—*Sisters of St. Francis (Sylvania, OH)*—O.S.F.
[3830-01]—*Sisters of St. Joseph (Boston, MA)*—C.S.J.
[3840]—*Sisters of St. Joseph of Carondelet (St. Louis, MO)*—C.S.J.
[3830-15]—*Sisters of St. Joseph of Concordia (Concordia, KS)*—C.S.J.
[0260]—*Sisters of the Blessed Sacrament*—S.B.S.

[1830]—*The Sisters of the Good Shepherd (Silver Spring, MD)*—R.G.S.

[1990]—*Sisters of the Holy Names of Jesus and Mary (Albany, NY*—S.N.J.M.

[4190]—*Sisters of the Visitation*—V.H.M.

[2170]—*Sisters, Servants of the Immaculate Heart of Mary (Immaculata, PA)*—I.H.M.

[2150]—*Sisters, Servants of the Immaculate Heart of Mary (Monroe, MI)*—I.H.M.

ARCHDIOCESAN CEMETERIES

ATLANTA. *Locust Grove*

NECROLOGY

† Henley, John R. (Retired)—Died 2003

Diocese of Austin

(Dioecesis Austiniensis)

Most Reverend

GREGORY M. AYMOND, D.D.

Bishop of Austin; ordained May 10, 1975; appointed Titular Bishop of Acolla and Auxiliary Bishop of New Orleans November 19, 1996; ordained January 10, 1997; appointed Coadjutor Bishop of Austin June 1, 2000; installed August 3, 2000; succeeded to the See of Austin January 2, 2001 *Office: P.O. Box 13327, Austin, TX 78711.*

Most Reverend

JOHN E. McCARTHY, D.D.

Retired Bishop of Austin; ordained May 26, 1976; appointed Titular Bishop of Pedena and Auxiliary Bishop of Galveston-Houston January 15, 1979; appointed Bishop of Austin December 19, 1985; retired January 2, 2001

Erected 1948.

Square Miles 19,511.

Comprises the Counties of Mills, Hamilton, San Saba, Lampasas, Coryell, McLennan, Limestone, Bell, Falls, Robertson, Mason, Llano, Burnet, Williamson, Milam, Brazos, Blanco, Travis, Bastrop, Lee, Burleson, Washington, Hays, Caldwell and the part of Fayette County north of the Colorado River in the State of Texas.

For legal titles of parishes and diocesan institutions, consult the Chancery Office.

Chancery Office: 1600 N. Congress Ave., P.O. Box 13327, Austin, TX 78711. Tel: 512-476-4888; Fax: 512-469-9537.

Web: www.austindiocese.org

Email: info@austindiocese.org

STATISTICAL OVERVIEW

Personnel	
Bishop	1
Retired Bishops	1
Priests: Diocesan Active in Diocese	127
Priests: Diocesan Active Outside Diocese	6
Priests: Retired, Sick or Absent	18
Number of Diocesan Priests	151
Religious Priests in Diocese	48
Total Priests in Diocese	199
Extern Priests in Diocese	12
Ordinations:	
Diocesan Priests	2
Permanent Deacons	18
Permanent Deacons in Diocese	191
Total Brothers	46
Total Sisters	97
Parishes	
Parishes	101
With Resident Pastor:	
Resident Diocesan Priests	84
Resident Religious Priests	17
Without Resident Pastor:	
Administered by Priests	25
Missions	25
Pastoral Centers	1
Closed Parishes	1
Professional Ministry Personnel:	
Brothers	3
Sisters	21
Lay Ministers	103
Welfare	
Catholic Hospitals	4
Total Assisted	713,482
Health Care Centers	4
Total Assisted	91,780
Homes for the Aged	2
Total Assisted	860
Day Care Centers	4
Total Assisted	185
Specialized Homes	1
Total Assisted	380
Special Centers for Social Services	1
Total Assisted	300
Residential Care of Disabled	1
Total Assisted	3,800
Educational	
Diocesan Students in Other Seminaries	31
Students Religious	2
Total Seminarians	33
Colleges and Universities	1
Total Students	4,443
High Schools, Diocesan and Parish	3
Total Students	493
High Schools, Private	2
Total Students	520
Elementary Schools, Diocesan and Parish	14
Total Students	3,190
Elementary Schools, Private	2
Total Students	763
Catechesis/Religious Education:	
High School Students	7,432
Elementary Students	27,000
Total Students under Catholic Instruction	43,874
Teachers in the Diocese:	
Priests	4
Sisters	9
Lay Teachers	566
Vital Statistics	
Receptions into the Church:	
Infant Baptism Totals	8,400
Adult Baptism Totals	700
Received into Full Communion	1,100
First Communions	6,500
Confirmations	4,100
Marriages:	
Catholic	825
Interfaith	400
Total Marriages	1,225
Deaths	1,556
Total Catholic Population	401,842
Total Population	2,300,863

Former Bishops—Most Revs. Louis J. Reicher, D.D., ord. Dec. 6, 1918; appt. first Bishop of Austin Nov. 29, 1947; consecrated April 14, 1948; died Feb. 23, 1984; Vincent M. Harris, D.D. (Retired), ord. March 19, 1938; appt. Bishop of Beaumont July 4, 1966; consecrated Sept. 28, 1966; transferred to Austin April 21, 1971; succeeded to the See Nov. 16, 1971; retired Feb. 25, 1986; died March 31, 1988; John E. McCarthy, D.D. (Retired), Bishop of Austin; ord. May 26, 1956; appt. Titular Bishop of Padena and Auxiliary Bishop of Galveston-Houston, Jan. 23, 1979; consecrated March 14, 1979; appt. Bishop of Austin, Dec. 24, 1985; installed Feb. 25, 1986; retired Jan. 2, 2001.

Vicar General—Rev. Msgr. Edward C. Matocha, P.A.

Moderator of the Curia—Rev. Chris Ferrer, M.F.

Chancery Office—1600 N. Congress Ave., P.O. Box 13327, Austin, 78711. Tel: 512-476-4888; Fax: 512-469-9537. Rev. Fred Chalupa, J.C.L., Chancellor, Chancery Office, P.O. Box 13327, Austin, 78711. Tel: 512-476-4888, Ext. 202; Fax: 512-478-5962. Office Hours: Mon.-Fri. 8:30-5

Notaries—Mrs. Linda Miller; Martina Davila.

Deans—Rev. Msgr. Lonnie Reyes, Central Austin; Revs. Samuel Hose, North Austin; John Korcsmar, C.S.C., South Austin; Dimitrij Colankin, Brazos Valley; Edward Dokupil, Southern; Louis Pavlicek, Temple; Isidore Rozycki, Northern; Rev. Msgr. Harry Mazurkiewicz, Eastern; Revs. Michael Mulvey, Central; James Harnan, M.S.C., Western.

Presbyteral Council—Most Rev. Gregory M. Aymond, D.D.; Rev. Msgr. Edward Matocha; Rev. Fred Chalupa, J.C.L.; Rev. Msgrs. Fred Bomar; Edward Jordan; Elmer Holtman; Lonnie Urban; Thomas Frank; Victor Goertz; Revs. Daniel Garcia; Kirby Garner; John Korcsmar, C.S.C.; Dean Wilhelm; Michael Mulvey; Joel McNeil; Richard O'Rourke, M.S.C.; Albert Ruiz; David Leibham; James McDonough, O.P.

Consultors—Rev. Msgrs. Fred Bomar; Lonnie Reyes; Mark Deering; Harry Mazurkiewicz; Revs. Kirby Garner; Albert Ruiz.

Diocesan Tribunal—1625 Rutherford Ln., Austin, 78754. Tel: 512-832-0313; Fax: 512-832-0316; 512-832-0016. Direct all inquiries concerning marriage nullity, dispensation and permissions to this address.

Judicial Vicar—Rev. Matthew Iwuji, J.C.D.

Adjutant Judicial Vicar—Rev. Christopher Ferrer, M.F., J.C.L.

Diocesan Judges—Revs. Robert L. Kincl, J.C.L.; Christopher Ferrer, M.F., J.C.L.; Deacons Frank Monroe, J.D.; Peter Schwab, Ph.D.; Ms. Tammy Edgerly, J.C.L.

Defenders of the Bond—Revs. Kirby Garner; Ronny E. Jenkins, M.A., S.T.L., J.C.D.; Jim O'Connor, J.C.L.; Robert Moriarty; Ms. Linda McDonald Budney.

Administrator—Miss Kim Thompson.

Notaries—Ms. Peggy Leazer; Ms. Kim Thompson.

Advocates—Ms. Myrtle Wilhelm; Sisters Agnes Murray, I.H.M.; Nancy Pewterbaugh, C.S.C.; Ms. Carolyn Ruffino; Ms. Jamie Creech, Including also priests or deacons exercising their ministry in the diocese.

Assessors—Deacons W. J. Ham; Larry Hansen; Rev. David Williams, S.T.B., J.D.

Finance Office—Mary Beth Koenig, Finance Officer, P.O. Box 13327, Austin, 78711. Tel: 512-476-4888; Fax: 512-469-9537.

Finance Council—Don E. Cox; Switzer Deason;

CAMPBELL MCGINNIS; DUTCH KELLERMAN; Rev. STEVEN NESRSTA; KARL KUYKENDALL; JIM SMOLIK; MARY BETH KOENIG.

Catholic Archives—SUSAN EASON, Archivist; ERIC J. HARTMANN, Archives Asst., P.O. Box 13124, Austin, 78711-3124. Tel: 512-476-6296; Fax: 512-476-3715.

Black Ministry—Mr. JOHNNY DORSEY, Dir., P.O. Box 13327, Austin, 78711. Tel: 512-388-1320; 512-472-3741.

Director of Facility Planning—Mr. CHARLES MULLER, P.O. Box 13327, Austin, 78711. Tel: 512-476-4888; Fax: 512-469-9537.

Catholic Campaign for Human Development—BARBARA BUDDE, Diocesan Pastoral Center, 1625 Rutherford Land, Bldg. D, Austin, 78754. Tel: 512-836-1213.

Campus Ministry—Rev. LEON STRIEDER, Dir., 9845 Memorial Dr., Houston, 77024. Tel: 713-682-4629.

Catholic Charities of Central Texas—Sr. MARY LOU STUBBS, Exec. Dir., 1625 Rutherford Lane, Bldg. D, Austin, 78754. Tel: 512-836-1213.

Immigration Department Director—LEO ANCHONDO, Catholic Charities of Central Texas, 1605 E. 7th St., Austin, 78702. Tel: 512-494-0148; Fax: 512-494-0246.

Catholic Schools Office—MARGARET MCGETTRICK, Supt., 1625 Rutherford Ln., Austin, 78754. Tel: 512-873-7771; Fax: 512-873-8338.

Stewardship and Development—SCOTT WHITAKER, Dir. Rels., P.O. Box 13327, Austin, 78711. Tel: 512-476-4888; Fax: 512-476-5341.

Planning and Research—ERIC SEDILLOS, Dir. Devel., P.O. Box 13327, Austin, 78711. Tel: 512-476-4888; Fax: 512-476-5341.

"Catholic Spirit"—HELEN OSMAN, Editor, P.O. Box 13327, Austin, 78711. Tel: 512-476-4888; Fax: 512-476-5341.

Office of Youth Ministry—MATTHEW ROBASZKIEWICZ, Dir., 1625 Rutherford Ln., Austin, 78754. Tel: 512-873-7771; Fax: 512-873-8338.

Young Adult Ministry—MATTHEW ROBASZKIEWICZ, Contact, 1625 Rutherford Lane, Austin, 78754. Tel: 512-873-7771; Fax: 512-873-8338.

Cemeteries—Rev. Msgr. JOHN MALINOWSKI (Retired), P.O. Box 3931, Bryan, 77805-3931. Tel: 409-776-3777, Ext. 2010.

Charismatic Renewal—JESSE MARTINEZ, Dir., 1104 Turtle Creek, Austin, 78745. Tel: 512-447-8977.

Communications—HELEN OSMAN, Dir., P.O. Box 13327, Austin, 78711. Tel: 512-476-4888.

Human Resource for Diocese of Austin—ERIC SEDILLOS, Dir., P.O. Box 13327, Austin, 78711. Tel: 512-476-4888, Ext. 242.

Priestly Life and Formation Committee—Rev. MICHAEL MULVEY, 2700 E. University Ave., Georgetown, 78626. Tel: 512-863-3041.

Council of Catholic Women—DOROTHY MAGGARD, Pres., 1713 Berkshire Dr., Waco, 78605. Tel: 254-799-4893.

Cursillo—Our Lady of Guadalupe Cursillo Center, Jarrell, 76537. Tel: 512-746-2041. LOUIS RUIZ, Center Dir., 3201 Shady Hill, Temple, 76502. Tel: 254-773-5905. Spanish:: ART SIERRA, Dir., 1418 W. Hopkins, San Marcos, 78666. Tel: 512-353-0691. English:: ADOLFO ALVAREZ, Pres., P.O. Box 142486, Austin, 78714-2486. Tel: 512-784-7964. Young Adults:: Deacon WILLIE CORTEZ, 1816 E Sixth St., Austin, 78762. Tel: 512-322-0632.

Deaf Ministry—Sr. DENISE MARIE HACKETT, C.S.C., Dir., St. Ignatius Church, 2309 Euclid St., Austin, 78704. Tel: 512-443-5330.

Diaconate—Deacon JEROME KLEMENT, Dir., St. Luke's, 2807 Oakdale, Temple, 76502. Tel: 254-773-1561.

Diocesan Pastoral Center—Sr. LOIS PAHA, O.P., Dir., 1625 Rutherford Ln., Austin, 78754. Tel: 512-873-7771; Fax: 512-873-8338.

Ecumenism—Rev. CHARLES L. COVINGTON Dir., St. Louis Church, 7601 Burnet Rd., Austin, 78757. Tel: 512-454-0384.

Mission/Evangelization—Dr. GERI TELEPAK, Acting Dir., 1625 Rutherford Ln., Austin, 78754. Tel: 512-873-7771; Fax: 512-873-8338.

Family Life Office—Dr. GERI TELEPAK, Dir. Diocesan Pastoral Center, 1625 Rutherford Ln., Austin, 78754. Tel: 512-873-7771; Fax: 512-873-8338.

Catholic Health Association of Texas—CYNTHIA COLBERT, Exec. Dir., 6225 U.S. Hwy. 290 E., P.O. Box 15364, Austin, 78761-5364. Tel: 512-465-1521; Fax: 512-453-4925.

Holy Childhood—Rev. Msgr. EDWARD MATOCHA, P.O. Box 13327, Austin, 78711-3327. Tel: 512-476-4888.

Criminal Justice Ministry—Deacon E. GENERES (DOOTS) DUFOUR, Dir., 1625 Rutherford Lane, Austin, 78754. Tel: 512-873-7771.

Catholic Adult Formation Office—CHARLENE O'CONNELL, Dir., 1625 Rutherford Ln., Austin, 78754. Tel: 512-873-7771; Fax: 512-873-8338.

Mission Council—Dr. GERI TELEPAK, Contact, 1625 Rutherford Lane, Austin, 78754. Tel: 512-873-7771; Fax: 512-873-8338; Rev. LOUIS PAVLICEK, Chm., St. Luke's, 2807 Oakdale, Temple, 76502. Tel: 254-773-4541; Fax: 254-774-7044.

Office of Hispanic Ministry—GIL LEIJA, Dir.; Rev. ALBERT RUIZ, Vicar, 1625 Rutherford Lane, Austin, 78754. Tel: 512-873-7771; Fax 512-873-8338. Email: gil-leija@austindiocese.org.

Parish Social Ministries—BARBARA BUDDE, Dir., 1625 Rutherford Lane, Bldg. D, Austin, 78754. Tel: 512-836-1213.

Propagation of the Faith—Rev. Msgr. EDWARD MATOCHA, P.O. Box 13327, Austin, 78711-3327. Tel: 512-476-4888.

Catechetical Office—CHARLENE O'CONNELL, Dir., 1625 Rutherford Ln., Austin, 78754. Tel: 512-873-7771; Fax: 512-873-8338.

Respect Life—ANN BIERSCHENK, 590 Young Ranch Rd., Georgetown, 78628. Tel: 512-931-2663; Fax: 512-868-5591.

Rural Life—Rev. JACK MADDUX JR., P.O. Box 57, Fayetteville, 78940. Tel: 979-378-2277.

Serra Club - Austin—Rev. WALTER CARR, Chap.-Austin; PAUL MYERS, Pres. Tel: 512-928-3841. Email: marg7301@aol.com.

Serra Club - Waco—MARTIN J. GINNANE, Pres., 4801 Lake Arrowhead, Waco, 76710. Tel: 254-772-5513.

Special Collections—SCOTT WHITAKER, Dir., P.O. Box 13327, Austin, 78711. Tel: 512-476-4888; Fax: 512-476-5341.

Vicar for Religious—Sr. MARIE ANDRE WALSH, I.H.M.; Bro. JOEL GIALANZA, C.S.C., Assoc. Vicar, 1600 N. Congress Ave., P.O. Box 13327, Austin, 78711. Tel: 512-476-4888, Ext. 203.

Victim Assistance Coordinator—PATRICIA STANKUS. Tel: 512-476-4888. Email: pat-stankus@austindiocese.org.

Vocations—Rev. DAVID KONDERLA, Vocation Dir., P.O. Box 13327, Austin, 78711-3327. Tel: 572-476-4888. Associates: Revs. DANIEL GARCIA, St. Vincent de Paul, 9500 Neenah Dr., Austin, 78717. Tel: 512-255-1389; EDWARD KARASEK, Church of the Assumption, P.O. Box 276, West, 76691. Tel: 254-826-3705; DEAN WILHELM, St. Thomas Aquinas, 2541 Earl Rudder Freeway, S., College Station, 77845. Tel: 979-693-6994; CELINA GALVAN, Admin. Asst. Tel: 512-476-4888, Ext. 230.

Worship Office & Liturgical Commission—Sr. LOIS PAHA, O.P., Dir., 1625 Rutherford Ln., Austin, 78754. Tel: 512-873-7771; Fax: 512-873-8338.

Foundations, Endowments and Trusts

Charitable Trusts—

Father Bernard C. Goertz Scholarship Trust Fund—Sacred Heart Church, 4045 FM 535, Bastrop, 78602.

John J. Kearns Memorial Charitable Trust Fund—P.O. Box 5040, Waco, 78708.

Clerical Endowment Fund—Rev. Msgr. HARRY MAZURKIEWICZ, Sacred Heart Church, P.O. Box 548, LaGrange, 78945. Tel: 409-968-3430.

Sts. Cyril & Methodius School Endowment—Rev. ISIDORE NDAGIZIMANA, Sts. Cyril & Methodius, P.O. Box 201, Granger, 76530.

Clergy Medical and Retirement Trust of the Diocese of Austin— the Diocese of Austin Pension Plan Committee Most Rev. GREGORY AYMOND, D.D., Chm., Diocesan Presbyteral Council.

Seton Fund of the Daughters of Charity of St. Vincent De Paul—GENE ATTAL, Pres., 1201 W. 38th St., Austin, 78705. Tel: 512-324-1990.

St. Joseph's Foundation of Bryan—MILTON L. DARE, Exec., 2801 Franciscan Dr., Bryan, 77802. Tel: 409-774-4087.

St. Jude Foundation, Inc.—1306 N. Park, Brenham, 77833.

St. Joseph's School Memorial Endowment Fund—Rev. JOHN A. MCCAFFREY, St. Joseph, 600 E. 26th St., Bryan, 77803.

CLERGY, PARISHES, MISSIONS AND PAROCHIAL SCHOOLS

CITY OF AUSTIN
(TRAVIS COUNTY)

1—ST. MARY'S CATHEDRAL (1852), Revs. Glynn (Bud) Roland Jr., Rector; Albert Laforet Jr., Assoc. In Res., Rev. Msgr. Edward C. Matocha, P.A., Rector Emeritus; Rev. Richard Tijerina; Deacons Willie Cortez; Ron Walker.
Res.: 203 E. 10th St., 78701. Tel: 512-476-6182; Fax: 512-476-8799.
School—Tel: 512-476-1480; Fax: 512-476-9922. Misty Poe, Prin. Lay Teachers 25; Students 210.
Catechesis/Religious Program—Tel: 512-476-4801; Fax: 512-476-8799. Amy Blount, D.R.E. Students 180.

2—ST. ALBERT THE GREAT (1987), [CEM] Rev. William C. Brooks.
Res.: 12041 Bittern Hollow, 78758. Tel: 512-837-7825; Fax: 512-834-2377.
Rectory—1800 Montana Sky, 78727. Tel: 512-251-3355.
Catechesis/Religious Program—Students 495.

3—ST. AUSTIN (1908), Revs. Patrick A. Johnson, C.S.P.; Ivan O. Tou, C.S.P.; Robert L. Pinkston, C.S.P. In Res., Revs. Ruben M. Patino, C.S.P.; Robert P. Michele, C.S.P.; Robert T. Scott, C.S.P.; Frank P. Sabatte, C.S.P.
Res.: 2026 Guadalupe St., 78705. Tel: 512-477-9471; Fax: 512-477-9430.
School—1911 San Antonio St., 78705. Tel: 512-477-3751; Fax: 512-477-3079. John Steven Cisneros, Prin. Lay Teachers 19; Students 220.
Catechesis/Religious Program—Tel: 512-477-9471, Ext. 302. Students 158.

4—ST. CATHERINE OF SIENA (1979), Rev. Msgr. Oliver F. Johnson; Deacons W. J. Ham; Jim Berg; Larry Terrell.
Church: 4800 Convict Hill Rd., 78749. Tel: 512-892-2420; Fax: 512-892-0488.
Res.: 4916 Flaming Oak, 78749. Tel: 512-892-1799.
Catechesis/Religious Program—Tel: 512-892-2426; Fax: 512-892-0488. Students 1,100.

5—CRISTO REY (1950), (Hispanic), Revs. Lawrence Mattingly, O.F.M.Conv.; Jayme Mathias, O.F.M.Conv.; Deacons Agapito Lopez; Juan Lopez.
Res.: 2110 E. 2nd St., 78702. Tel: 512-474-6376; Fax: 512-474-8417.
Catechesis/Religious Program—Tel: 512-477-1099; Fax: 512-479-7105. Sr. Martina Ponce, F.M.A., D.R.E. Students 1,148.

6—EMMAUS CATHOLIC CHURCH (1963), [CEM] [JC] Rev. Msgr. Richard McCabe; Deacons Boyce Foreman; John Hill; Jesse Martinez.
Mailing Address & Res.: 1718 Lohman's Crossing, Lakeway, 78734. Tel: 512-261-8500; Fax: 512-261-8200.
Catechesis/Religious Program—Students 643.
Mission—*Queen of Angels* 500 Alva Dr., Briarcliff, Travis Co. 78669. Tel: 512-264-1480.

7—HOLY CROSS (1936), (African American), Rev. Cletus Udoh, M.S.P. (Nigeria).
Res.: 1610 E. 11th St., 78702. Tel: 512-472-3741; Fax: 512-472-3783.
Catechesis/Religious Program—Tel: 512-244-3642. Debbie Juilke, D.R.E. Students 93.

8—HOLY VIETNAMESE MARTYRS (1990), (Vietnamese), Rev. Joe Van Anh Nguyen.
Res.: 1107 E. Yager Ln., 78753. Tel: 512-834-8483; Fax: 512-821-1155.
Catechesis/Religious Program—Students 360.

9—ST. IGNATIUS MARTYR (1937), Revs. Harold G. Zink, C.S.C.; Harold W. Essling, C.S.C.; Joseph A. Tomei, C.S.C.; Rick Wilkinson, C.S.C; Deacon Patrick Murray; Joe Juranek, Parish Admin.
Res.: 2309 Euclid Ave., 78704. Tel: 512-442-3602; Fax: 512-373-4631.
School—Tel: 512-442-8547; Fax: 512-442-8685. Sr. Alice Condon, C.S.C., Prin. Lay Teachers 14; Students 257.
Catechesis/Religious Program—Tel: 512-442-8586. Sisters M. Adelaide Cannon, C.S.C., D.R.E.; Denise Hackett, C.S.C., D.R.E.; Agnes Murray, I.H.M., D.R.E. Students 455.

10—ST. JOHN NEUMANN (1984), Rev. Msgr. Edward Jordan; Rev. Joseph F. Geniesse, C.S.C.; Deacons D. Mark Hamlet; Mike Gesch.
Res.: 5455 Beecave Rd., 78746. Tel: 512-328-3220; Fax: 512-328-3226.
Rectory—Tel: 512-415-0700.
Catechesis/Religious Program—Students 670.

11—ST. JULIA (1957), (Hispanic), Rev. Msgr. Lonnie C. Reyes; Deacons Ralph Arevalo Jr.; Kevin Nissen.
Res.: 3010 Lyons Rd., 78702. Tel: 512-926-4186; Fax: 512-926-7414.
Catechesis/Religious Program—Tel: 512-928-3381. Students 110.

12—ST. LOUIS (1952), Revs. Larry Covington; Victor Mayorga, M.P. (Colombia); Alirio Fernandez-Bueno (Colombia); Deacons Rob Embry; Donald Turner; Richard Bigelow; Tony Pynes.
Res.: 7601 Burnet Rd., 78757. Tel: 512-454-0384; Fax: 512-454-2010.
School—Tel: 512-454-0384, Ext. 242; Fax: 512-454-7252. Carolyn O'Connell, Prin. Lay Teachers 27; Students 380.
Catechesis/Religious Program—Tel: 512-454-0384, Ext. 225. Betty Danner, D.R.E., Childhood Ministries; Annette Phinney, D.R.E., Middle School; Eric Garza, D.R.E., Youth Ministries; Charles Balsam,

D.R.E., Adult Ministries. Students 786.
13—ST. MARGARET OF SCOTLAND (1984), Closed. For inquiries for parish records contact the chancery.
14—NUESTRA SENORA DE DOLORES (1952), (Hispanic), Revs. John S. Korcsmar, C.S.C.; Edwin J. Kadzielawski, C.S.C.; Paul Pudussery, C.S.C.; Deacon Hector Rosales.
Res.: 1111 Montopolis Dr., 78741. Tel: 512-385-4333; Fax: 512-385-6116.
Catechesis/Religious Program—Tel: 512-385-4333. Sr. Rose Moreno, F.H.M., D.R.E. Students 440.
Convent—Hijas De La Misericordia, Tel: 512-385-5090; Fax: 512-389-0692. Sisters 6.
15—OUR LADY OF GUADALUPE (1907), (Hispanic), Revs. Richard Hall, O.M.I. (LAR); J. C. Cain, O.M.I.; Deacon Mario Renteria.
Res.: 1206 E. 9th St., 78702. Tel: 512-478-7955; Fax: 512-478-8377.
Catechesis/Religious Program—Students 325.
16—ST. PATRICK (2000), Rev. Andrew Gunn; Deacon Joe Trujllo.
Mailing Address: P.O. Box 2539, Pflugerville, 78691-2539. Tel: 512-670-3400; Fax: 512-670-3403.
Catechesis/Religious Program—Students 26.
17—ST. PAUL'S (1989), (Hispanic), Rev. Paul F. McCallum; Deacon John Pickwell.
Res.: 10000 David Moore Rd., 78748. Tel: 512-280-4460; Fax: 512-280-7219.
Catechesis/Religious Program—Tel: 512-280-5777; Fax: 512-280-7219. Mary Armatta, D.R.E. Students 735.
18—ST. PETER THE APOSTLE (1962), Rev. Msgr. Fred Bomar.
Res.: P.O. Box 17575, 4600 E. Ben White Blvd., 78760. Tel: 512-442-0655.
Catechesis/Religious Program—Tel: 512-444-7477. Students 128.
19—SACRED HEART (1958), Rev. Robert Becker; Deacons Jesse M. Garza; Robert Martinez; William Vela; Michael Wright. In Res., Rev. Robert Bradley, S.J.
Res.: 5909 Reicher Dr., 78723. Tel: 512-926-2552; Fax: 512-926-5138.
Catechesis/Religious Program—Tel: 512-926-2116; Fax: 512-926-2983. Angelica Mishoe, D.R.E. Students 776.
20—SAN FRANCISCO (1941), (Hispanic), Rev. Gonzalo Ferrer, T.O.R., Admin.; Deacon Johnny Ojeda.
Res.: 9110 Hwy. 183 S., 78747. Tel: 512-243-1404; Fax: 512-243-2995.
Catechesis/Religious Program—Fax: 512-243-2995. Sisters Jacinta Amengual, F.H.M., D.R.E.; Martha Cupido, F.H.M. Students 458.
21—SAN JOSE (1939), (Hispanic), Revs. Tom Frank; Kevin Rai; Juan Lopez Carlos; Deacons Joe Gutierrez; John Rivera; Nathan Brewster; Romeo Sanchez; Richard Botello; Alfred Benavides.
Res.: 2435 Oak Crest, 78704. Tel: 512-444-7587; Fax: 512-443-1212.
Catechesis/Religious Program—Tel: 512-444-4664. Students 1,003.
22—SANTA BARBARA (1991), (Hispanic), Rev. Bernard C. Goertz; Mr. Joe Arellano, Admin.; Deacon Cruz Banda Jr.
Mailing Address: 13713 FM 969, 78724. Tel: 512-276-7718.
Catechesis/Religious Program—Students 120.
23—ST. THERESA (1968), Revs. Gregory A. Romanski; Larry Stehling; Deacons Ray James; John O'Neill; Ray Sanders; George Zacek.
Res.: 4311 Small Dr., 78731. Tel: 512-451-5121; Fax: 512-453-6824.
School—(Grades PreK-8) Tel: 512-451-7105; Fax: 512-451-8808. Lay Teachers 39; Students 360.
Catechesis/Religious Program—Tel: 512-451-2940; Fax: 512-453-6824. Dee Dee Schoenberger, D.R.E. Students 640.
24—ST. THOMAS MORE (1978), Revs. Elmer E. Holtman; Joseph F. Geleney Jr.; Deacons Peter Schwab; Thomas Mallinger; Edward Holicky; Thomas Johnson; Daniel Wright.
Office—10205 Ranch Rd., 620 N., 78726. Tel: 512-258-1161; Fax: 512-258-8812.
Catechesis/Religious Program—Tel: 512-258-1944; Fax: 512-331-9248. Cynthia Klaer, D.R.E. Students 1,702.
25—ST. THOMAS MORE CHAPEL (1958), Closed., For inquiries for Parish records please see St Mary's Cathedral, (512-476-6182).
26—ST. VINCENT DE PAUL (1995), Rev. Daniel E. Garcia; Deacon Allen Desorcie, Buisness Admin.
Mailing Address: 9500 Neenah Ave., 78717. Tel: 512-255-1389; Fax: 512-246-2373.
Rectory—13007 Partridge Bend, 78729. Tel: 512-249-1549.
Catechesis/Religious Program—Fax: 512-246-2373. Students 321.

OUTSIDE CITY OF AUSTIN

ANDICE, WILLIAMSON CO., SANTA ROSA (1937), [CEM] Rev. Walter F. Carr; Deacons Roger Collins; Ray Mooore.
Mailing Address: P.O. Box 20176, 78628. Tel: 254-863-3041; Fax: 512-863-8558.
Catechesis/Religious Program—Tel: 512-869-1544; 254-793-2047 (Church); Fax: 254-793-3247. Students 168.
BASTROP, BASTROP CO., ASCENSION (1911), Rev. Msgr. Edward J. Dokupil.
Res.: P.O. Drawer W, 78602. Tel: 512-321-2452; Fax: 512-303-6539.
Catechesis/Religious Program—Tel: 512-321-5511. Laura Geer, D.R.E. Students 387.
BELTON, BELL CO., CHRIST THE KING (1969), Rev. Richard Hudson; Deacons Armando Aguirre; Jose Jimenez; William Shoemake; Ronnie Lastovica.
Res.: 310 E. 24th Ave., 76513. Tel: 254-939-0806; 254-939-6109 (Rectory); Fax: 254-939-0811.
Catechesis/Religious Program—Tel: 254-939-0811. Students 255.
BERTRAM, BURNET CO., HOLY CROSS (1941), (Hispanic), Attended by, Our Mother of Sorrows, Burnet. Rev. Joseph DeVliegher, C.S.C.; Deacons Joe Ruiz; Michael Aaronson.
Mailing Address: P.O. Box 94, 78605. Tel: 512-355-2972.
Catechesis/Religious Program—Tel: 512-259-0314. Hope Ruiz, D.R.E. Students 113.
BLANCO, BLANCO CO., ST. FERDINAND'S (1940), [CEM] Rev. Nichodemus Ejimabo.
Res.: 25 Main St., 78606. Tel: 830-833-5227; Fax: 830-833-9978.
Catechesis/Religious Program—Tel: 830-833-0444. Students 183.
Mission—Good Shepherd P.O. Box 528, Johnson City, Blanco Co. 78636. Tel: 830-868-0370.
Mission—Our Lady Help of Christians CR 473, Twin Sisters, Blanco Co. 78606.
BREMOND, ROBERTSON CO., ST. MARY'S (1879), [CEM] Rev. Celso A. Yu, M.F. (Philippines).
Res.: 715 N. Main St., 76629. Tel: 254-746-7789; Fax: 254-746-7280.
Catechesis/Religious Program—Tel: 254-746-7789; Fax: 254-746-7280. Students 127.
BRENHAM, WASHINGTON CO., ST. MARY OF THE IMMACULATE CONCEPTION (1870), [CEM] Rev. David J. Ivey (LA); Deacon Bill Januszewski.
Res.: 701 Church St., 77833. Tel: 979-836-4441; Fax: 979-836-9383.
Catechesis/Religious Program—Tel: 979-830-8331. Students 524.
BRYAN, BRAZOS CO.
1—ST. ANTHONY'S (1896), (Italian), [JC] Rev. Kirby D. Garner.
Mailing Address: 401 S. Parker, 77803.
Res.: 306 S. Parker, 77803. Tel: 979-823-8145; Fax: 979-823-6001.
Catechesis/Religious Program—Tel: 979-822-3700. Students 400.
Mission—San Salvador, Brazos Co. 77803.
2—ST. JOSEPH'S (1873), [CEM 2] Rev. Msgr. John A. McCaffrey; Deacon Gary Nelson.
Res.: 600 E. 26th St., 77803. Tel: 979-822-2721; Fax: 979-779-3120.
School—Tel: 979-822-6641; Fax: 979-779-2810. Mr. Tim Luza, Prin.; Mr. Tom Deming, Asst. Prin. Lay Teachers 37; Students 441.
Catechesis/Religious Program—Tel: 979-823-5568; Fax: 979-779-3120. Becky Luza, D.R.E.; Lisa Storemski, D.R.E. Students 560.
3—SANTA TERESA'S (1940), (Hispanic), Rev. Albert Capello Ruiz.
Res.: 1212 Lucky, 77803. Tel: 979-822-2932; Fax: 979-822-6957.
Catechesis/Religious Program—Tel: 979-822-5557. Janie Duran, D.R.E. Students 499.
BUDA, HAYS CO., SANTA CRUZ (1941), (Hispanic), Rev. Joseph Deane; Deacons Rodolfo Gonzalez; Nelson Fahlund; Rey Garza; John Riojas; Joe Syring.
Res.: P.O. Box 187, 78610. Tel: 512-312-2520; Fax: 512-295-2034.
Catechesis/Religious Program— Rose M. Luera, D.R.E. Students 400.
BURNET, BURNET CO., OUR MOTHER OF SORROWS (1941), Rev. Joseph DeVliegher, C.S.C.; Deacon Eugene Montag.
Res.: 507 Buchanan Dr., 78611-2304. Tel: 512-756-4410; Fax: 512-756-1573.
Catechesis/Religious Program—Tel: 512-756-2323. Betty Buratti, D.R.E.; Hope Ruiz, D.R.E., Holy Cross. Students 270.
Mission—Holy Cross P.O. Box 94, Bertram, Burnet Co. 78605. Tel: 512-355-2972. Deacons Jose Ruiz; Michael Aaronson.
CALDWELL, BURLESON CO., ST. MARY'S (1895), (Hispanic), [CEM] Rev. Dimitrij Colankin; Deacon John Young.
Res.: 509 N. Thomas, 77836. Tel: 979-567-3667; Fax: 979-567-3667.
Catechesis/Religious Program—Fax: 979-567-3667. Students 323.
Mission—Holy Rosary [CEM] 509 N. Thomas, Burleson Co. 77836. Fax: 979-567-3667.
CALVERT, ROBERTSON CO., ST. MARY (1876), (Hispanic), [CEM] Attended by, St. Mary's Church, Hearne. Rev. Scott Mikkelson.
Mailing Address: 402 W. First St., Hearne, 77859.
Res.: 505 Logan St., 77837. Tel: 979-279-2233; Fax: 979-279-9606.
CAMERON, MILAM CO., ST. MONICA'S (1883), [CEM] Rev. Thomas J. Hanus; Deacons Juan Garza; Donald Sims.
Mailing Address: P.O. Box 673, 76520. Tel: 254-697-2107; Fax: 254-697-3334.
Church: 306 S. Nolan, 76520.
Catechesis/Religious Program—Tel: 254-697-4544. Elva Vargas, D.R.E. Students 285.
CEDAR PARK, WILLIAMSON CO., ST. MARGARET MARY (1942), Rev. Le-Minh Pham.
Mailing Address: P.O. Box 2410, 78630-2410. Tel: 512-259-3126; Fax: 512-259-9658.
Res.: 12451 RR 2243 W., Leander, 78641. Tel: 512-259-4233.
Catechesis/Religious Program—Tel: 512-260-0162; Fax: 512-259-9658. Robin Anthony, D.R.E. Students 575.
CHAPPELL HILL, WASHINGTON CO., ST. STANISLAUS (1889), (Polish), [CEM] [JC 2] Rev. Eugene Sheppard.
Mailing Address: 9175 FM 1371, 77426. Tel: 979-836-3030; Fax: 979-836-7170.
Res.: 9175 FM 1371, 77426. Tel: 979-836-8545.
Catechesis/Religious Program—Students 85.
CHINA SPRING, MCLENNAN CO., ST. PHILIP (1996), Rev. Hilario Guajardo, Pastoral Admin.
Mailing Address: P.O. Box 430, 76633. Tel: 254-836-4425; Fax: 254-840-0174.
Res.: 1581 Bend of the Bosque, P.O. Box 327, 76633. Tel: 254-840-3174.
Catechesis/Religious Program—Tel: 254-836-1969; Fax: 254-836-0600. Students 11.
COLLEGE STATION, BRAZOS CO.
1—ST. MARY'S (1926), Revs. Michael J. Sis; Keith Koehl; Deacons Bill Scott Jr.; David Reed.
Res.: 603 Church Ave., 77840. Tel: 979-846-5717; Fax: 979-846-4493.
2—ST. THOMAS AQUINAS (1982), Rev. Dean E. Wilhelm; Deacon Theodore Baker.
Res.: 2541 Earl Rudder Fwy S., 77845. Tel: 979-696-3284; 979-693-6994 (Office); Fax: 979-260-4502.
Catechesis/Religious Program—Tel: 979-693-7551. Josh Simmons, D.R.E. Students 581.
COPPERAS COVE, CORYELL CO., HOLY FAMILY (1963), Rev. Barry Cabell, C.S.C.; Deacons Weldon Bowling; David M. Cardona; John Consentino.
Res.: 1001 Georgetown Rd., 76522. Tel: 254-547-3735; Fax: 254-547-3735.
Catechesis/Religious Program—Tel: 254-542-7626. Leslie Noel, D.R.E. Students 385.
CYCLONE, BELL CO., ST. JOSEPH'S (1902), (Czech—German), [CEM] Rev. Walter J. Matus.
Mailing Address: 20120 FM 485, Burlington, 76519. Tel: 254-985-2280.
Res.: Farm Rd. 485. Tel: 254-985-2280.
Catechesis/Religious Program—1201 S. St. Joseph Rd. #400, Burlington, 76519. Tel: 817-985-2257. Students 94.
Mission—Ss. Cyril & Methodius Burlington. FM 485, Marak, Milam Co. 76519. Tel: 254-985-2280.
DIME BOX, LEE CO., ST. JOSEPH'S (1902), [CEM] Rev. Msgr. Emilian Foltyn.
Res.: 8282 FM 141, 77853. Tel: 979-884-3100.
Church: Farm-Market Rd. 141, 77853.
Catechesis/Religious Program—Students 35.
Mission—Holy Family (1990), P.O. Box 541, Lexington, Lee Co. 78947. Tel: 949-773-2244.
DRIPPING SPRINGS, HAYS CO., ST. MARTIN DE PORRES (1974), Rev. James L. Evans; Deacons Edward Rositas; Gene Davis; Paul Lavallee; Sr. Yvonne Feeney, O.P.
Mailing Address: P.O. Box 1062, 78620. Tel: 512-858-5667; Fax: 512-858-1467.
Res.: County Rd. 360, off Ranch Rd. 12, 78620. Tel: 512-306-8698.
Catechesis/Religious Program— Mary Carder, D.R.E. Students 250.
ELGIN, BASTROP CO., SACRED HEART (1908), (Hispanic), [JC] Rev. Juan Maravilla; Deacons Larry Dunne; Sam Santa Ana; John Franklin.
Res.: 302 W. 11th St., 78621. Tel: 512-281-3536; Fax: 512-281-2527.
Catechesis/Religious Program—Tel: 512-281-3536, Ext. 205. Students 126.
ELK, MCLENNON CO., ST. JOSEPH'S (1925), [CEM] Attended by, St. Martin, Tours.
Res.: 301 St. Martins Church Rd., West, 76691. Tel: 254-822-1145; Fax: 254-822-0171.
Catechesis/Religious Program—Tel: 254-863-5919; Fax: 254-822-0171. Mary Mann, D.R.E. Students 63.
FAYETTEVILLE, FAYETTE CO., ST. JOHN'S (1872), (Czech), [CEM] Rev. Jack Maddux Jr.
Mailing Address: P.O. Box 57, 78940. Tel: 979-378-2277; Fax: 979-378-4407.

Res.: 205 E. Bell St., 78940. Tel: 979-378-2003.
Catechesis/Religious Program—Tel: 979-378-2244. Janice Kasmiersky, D.R.E. Students 115.
Mission—St. Mary's Hostyn Hill, Fayette Co. 78940.
Mission—St. Martin's Warrenton, Fayette Co. 78940.

FRANKLIN, ROBERTSON CO., ST. FRANCIS OF ASSISI (1997), Rev. Joseph Frazer; Deacon Luis Dariocourt, Pastoral Admin.
Mailing Address: P.O. Box 543, 77856. Tel: 979-828-3719 (Rectory); 979-828-1269 (Office); Fax: 979-828-1269.
Catechesis/Religious Program—Students 78.

FRENSTAT, BURLESON CO., HOLY ROSARY (1888), (Czech), [CEM 2] Attended by, St. Mary's, Caldwell Rev. Dimitrij Colankin.
Mailing Address: 6978 SH 36 S., Caldwell, 77836-5462. Tel: 979-567-4994.
Church: 8610 FM 2774, Caldwell, 77836. Tel: 979-535-7704.
Rectory—509 N. Thomas, Caldwell, 77836. Tel: 979-567-3667; Fax: 979-567-3667.
Catechesis/Religious Program—Tel: 979-272-8136. Students 24.

GATESVILLE, CORYELL CO., OUR LADY OF LOURDES (1946), Rev. Robert Herald; Deacon James Gallagher.
Res.: 1108 W. Main St., 76528-1123. Tel 254-865-6710; Fax: 254-865-6710.
Catechesis/Religious Program— Deborah Grmela, D.R.E. Students 86.

GEORGETOWN, WILLIAMSON CO., ST. HELEN'S (1932), Revs. Wm. Michael Mulvey; Brian L. McMaster; Deacons Frank Monroe, J.D.; Joe Ruiz; Vern Dawson; Bill Davis, Parish Business Admin.
Res.: 2700 E. University Ave., 78626-7300. Tel: 512-863-3041; Fax: 512-863-8558.
School—Tel: 512-868-0744. Michael Miller, Prin.
Catechesis/Religious Program—Tel: 512-863-0799. Richard Phillips, D.R.E. Students 781.

GIDDINGS, LEE CO., ST. MARGARET (1944), (German—Hispanic), [JC] Rev. Albert Capello Ruiz.
Res.: 526 S. Grimes St., 78942. Tel: 979-542-3380; Fax: 979-542-4186.
Catechesis/Religious Program—Tel: 979-542-2017. Students 300.
Mission—St. Mary's in Pin Oak Smithville. 732 FM 2104, Pin Oak, Bastrop Co. 78957.

GOLDTHWAITE, MILLS CO., ST. PETER'S (1885), [JC] Rev. Gregory Mchaughlin; Deacon Richard Menchaca, Pastoral Admin.
Res.: P.O. Box 352, 76844. Tel: 325-648-3732; Fax: 325-648-3732.
Catechesis/Religious Program—Tel: 325-938-5441. Tani Menchaca, D.R.E. Students 70.

GRANGER, WILLIAMSON CO., SS. CYRIL AND METHODIUS (1891), (Czech), [CEM 2] [JC] Rev. Isidore Ndagizimana (Uganda). In Res., Rev. Msgr. John D. Frizelle (Retired).
Res.: 300 W. Davilla, P.O. Box 608, 76530. Tel: 512-859-2223; Fax: 512-859-2030.
School—Tel: 512-859-2927; Fax: 512-859-2649. Dr. Norlene Kunkel, Prin. Sisters 1; Lay Teachers 10; Students 68.
Catechesis/Religious Program—Tel: 512-359-2634. Cara Finn, D.R.E.; Virginia Loza-Lee, D.R.E. Students 170.

HAMILTON, HAMILTON CO., ST. THOMAS (1965), [JC] Rev. Hilario Guajardo; Deacon Victor Beltran, Pastoral Admin.
Res.: 707 N. Nicholson Ave., 76531. Tel: 254-386-5513.
Catechesis/Religious Program—Students 26.

HARKER HEIGHTS, BELL CO., ST. PAUL CHONG HASANG (1986), Rev. Richard O'Rourke, M.S.C.; Deacons Peter Kim; Klaus Adam; Ms. Margaret Hunt, Pastoral Assoc.
Mailing Address: P.O. Box 2414, 76548.
Res.: 1000 E. FM 2410, 76548. Tel: 254-698-4110; 254-698-4338; Fax: 254-698-4608.
Catechesis/Religious Program—Tel: 254-699-6855. Ms. Olga Touchet, D.R.E. Students 325.

HEARNE, ROBERTSON CO., ST. MARY'S (1872), (Italian—Mexican-American), [CEM] Rev. Scott Mikkelson.
Res.: 402 W. First St., 77859. Tel: 979-279-2233; Fax: 979-279-9606.
Catechesis/Religious Program—Tel: 979-279-2259. Judy Rekieta, D.R.E. Students 202.
Mission—St. Mary 505 Logan St., Calvert, Robertson Co. 77837. Tel: 979-279-2222.

HORSESHOE BAY, BURNET CO, ST. PAUL THE APOSTLE (1982), Rev. William J. Dougherty, C.S.P.
Mailing Address: P.O. Box 8019, 78657. Tel: 830-598-8342; Fax: 830-598-6350.
Res.: 201 Dalton Cir., 78657.
Catechesis/Religious Program—Students 34.

HOSTYN HILL, FAYETTE CO., ST. MARY'S (1855), (Czech), [CEM] Attended by, St. John's, Fayetteville. Rev. Jack Maddux Jr.
Mailing Address: P.O. Box 57, Fayetteville, 78940. Tel: 979-378-2277; Fax: 979-378-4407.
Catechesis/Religious Program—209 E. Bell St., Fayetteville, 78940. Tel: 979-378-2244 Fax: 979-378-2244 Students 38.

JARRELL, WILLIAMSON CO., HOLY TRINITY (1889), (Czech—German), [CEM] Rev. Msgr. Arthur Michalka.
Res.: 8625 FM 1105, 76537. Tel: 512-863-0401.
Catechesis/Religious Program—Tel: 512-863-3020. Betty Ann Vrabel, D.R.E. Students 109.

KILLEEN, BELL CO., ST. JOSEPH (1954), Revs. Raphael Clancy; Sang Yil Lee; Deacon Eugene Morse.
Res.: 2903 E. Rancier Ave., 76543. Tel: 254-634-7878; 254-634-7844; Fax: 254-634-1508.
School—(Grades PreK-5) Tel: 254-634-7272; Fax: 254-634-1224. Lay Teachers 10; Students 130.
Catechesis/Religious Program—Tel: 254-634-7878, Ext. 107; Fax: 254-634-1508. Students 369.

KINGSLAND, LLANO CO., ST. CHARLES BORROMEO (1965), Rev. Joseph Mitrano, C.S.B.; Deacons Larry Crochet; Dr. George Lillard.
Mailing Address: P.O. Box 1748, 78639.
Church: 205 Trinity Dr., 78639.
Rectory—1927 Hwy. 1431, 78639. Tel: 915-388-3742; Fax: 915-388-2567.
Catechesis/Religious Program—Students 70.
Mission—Our Lady of the Lake 233 Deer Dr., Sunrise Beach, Burnet Co. 78643. Tel: 512-598-8342.

KOVAR, BASTROP CO., STS. PETER AND PAUL (1909), (Czech), Closed., Now a mission of St. Paul the Apostle, Smithville.

KYLE, HAYS CO., ST. ANTHONY MARIE DE CLARET (1909), (Hispanic), Revs. Howard Goertz; John Boiko; Deacons John Peca; John Lawrence; Joe Flores.
Res.: 801 N. Burleson St., P.O. Box 268, 78640. Tel: 512-268-5312; 512-268-5311 (Office); Fax: 512-268-0144.
Catechesis/Religious Program—Tel: 512 268-5311. Students 300.
Mission—Blessed Juan Diego 200 Janzet Dr., Stoney Point, Travis Co. 78640. Tel: 512-312-0357. Deacon Richard Duecker.

LA GRANGE, FAYETTE CO., SACRED HEART OF JESUS (1886), [JC] Rev. Msgr. Harry C. Mazurkiewicz; Deacon Mike Meismer.
Res.: Box 548, 78945. Tel: 979-968-3430; Fax: 979-968-5740.
School—Tel: 979-968-3223. Elmer Faykus, Prin. Lay Teachers 19; Students 210.
Catechesis/Religious Program—Tel: 979-966-0107. Sr. Carmen Leal, M.C.D.P., D.R.E. Students 226.

LAGO VISTA, TRAVIS CO., ST. MARY, OUR LADY OF THE LAKE (1970), Rev. Msgr. Joseph J. Schmitt.
Mailing Address: 6100 Lohman Ford Rd., 78645. Tel: 512-237-2644; Fax: 512-267-2649.
Rectory—6502 Avenida Ann, 78645. Tel: 512-267-1336.
Catechesis/Religious Program—Tel: 512-267-2644. Students 91.

LAMPASAS, LAMPASAS CO., ST. MARY'S (1885), Rev. James Harnan, M.S.C.; Deacon Carlos Jasso.
Mailing Address: 701 N. Key Ave., 76550-0866. Tel: 512-556-5544; Fax: 512-556-6967.
Church: 701 N. Key Ave., Lampassas, 76550.
Catechesis/Religious Program—Chole Mendias, D.R.E. Students 170.
Mission—Good Shepherd Catholic Church (1927), 500 W. Main St., Lometa, Lampasas Co. 76853.

LATIUM, WASHINGTON CO., SACRED HEART (1872), (Polish—Czech), [CEM] Attended by, St. Mary's, Brenham. , 701 Church St., Brenham, 77833. Tel: 979-836-4441.

LEANDER, WILLIAMSON CO., ST. ANDREW KIM TAEGON KOREAN CATHOLIC CHURCH (1995), (Korean), Rev. Francis Chung, S.J.
Mailing Address: 12113 Metric, #1311, 73758.
Church: 311 S. Hwy. 183, 78646. Tel: 512-448-1705.
Catechesis/Religious Program—Students 21.

LEXINGTON, LEE CO., HOLY FAMILY (1990), [JC], Mission of St. Joseph, Dime Box. Rev. Msgr. Emilian Foltyn.
Mailing Address: 8282 FM 141, Dime Box, 77853. Tel: 979-884-3100.
Res.: FM 696 East of Hwy. 77, 78947.
Catechesis/Religious Program—Students 38.

LLANO, LLANO CO., HOLY TRINITY (1890), Rev. Pual Clogan; Deacon Richard Larner.
Mailing Address: P.O. Box 698, 78643. Tel: 325-247-4481; Fax 325-248-0691.
Catechesis/Religious Program—Students 66.
Mission—St. Joseph Box 1572, Mason, Mason Co. 76856.

LOCKHART, CALDWELL CO., ST. MARY'S (1887), [CEM 2] Rev. Adam Martinez; Deacons Guadalupe Aguilar; William Long; William Haywood; Patrick Venglar.
Res.: 205 W. Pecan, 78644. Tel: 512-398-4649; 512-376-3634; Fax: 512-398-2285.
Catechesis/Religious Program—Tel: 512-398-3506; Fax: 512-398-2205. Eva Mendez, D.R.E Students 581.

LOMETA, LAMPASAS CO., GOOD SHEPHERD (1927), Attended by, St. Mary's, Lampasas. Rev. James Harnan, M.S.C.; Deacon Carlos Jasso.
Mailing Address: 701 N. Key Ave., Lampasas, 76550-0866. Tel: 512-556-5544; Fax: 512-556-6967.
Church: 500 W. Main St., 76853.
Catechesis/Religious Program—Chole Mendias, D.R.E. Students 50.

LOTT, FALLS CO., SACRED HEART (1905), (Italian—German), [CEM] Attended by, St. Joseph's, Marlin. Rev. Christopher Ferrer, M.F., J.C.L.
Mailing Address: P.O. Box 371, Marlin, 76661. Tel: 254-803-8888; Fax: 254-883-2099.
Res.: 213 N. 6th St., 76656.
Catechesis/Religious Program— Clustered with St. Joseph, Marlin

LULING, CALDWELL CO., ST. JOHN THE EVANGELIST (1879), [CEM] Rev. Jesse Euresti; Deacon Wilfred Dub Hargraves.
Res.: 500 E. Travis St., 78648. Tel: 830-875-5354; Fax: 830-875-3533.
Catechesis/Religious Program—Tel: 830-875-3901. Sr. Mary Frances Bartsch, O.L.V.M., D.R.E. Students 270.

MANOR, TRAVIS CO., ST. JOSEPH'S (1876), (Hispanic), [JC] Rev. Thai Trinh; Deacons Roy Barkley; Alfredo Varguez.
Mailing Address: P.O. Box 389, 78653. Tel: 512-272-4004 (Rectory); Fax: 512-272-9272.
Catechesis/Religious Program—Tel: 512-272-5466. Students 150.

MARAK, MILAM CO., SS. CYRIL AND METHODIUS (1903), (Czech), [CEM] [JC 2], Attended from St. Joseph's, Cyclone. , 20120 FM 485, Burlington, 76519. Tel: 254-985-2280.
Catechesis/Religious Program—Tel: 254-697-4861. Students 74.

MARBLE FALLS, BURNET CO., ST. JOHN THE EVANGELIST (1961), Rev. Jairo Lopez; Deacon Eraclio Solarzano.
Church: 105 Hwy. 1431 E., 78654. Tel: 830-693-5134; Fax: 830-798-9574.
Catechesis/Religious Program—Tel: 830-693-3279. Students 107.

MARLIN, FALLS CO., ST. JOSEPH'S (1872), (Italian—Polish), Rev. Christopher Ferrer, M.F., J.C.L.; Deacon Julian Tyboroski.
Mailing Address: Box 371, 76661. Tel: 254-803-8888; Fax: 254-883-2099.
Church: 311 Oakes St., 76661.
Catechesis/Religious Program— Mr. Eddie Roberts, D.R.E. Students 105.
Mission—Sacred Heart [CEM] 6th & Hackberry, Lott, Falls Co. 76656.

MARTINDALE, CALDWELL CO., IMMACULATE HEART OF MARY (1908), (Hispanic), Rev. John Kelley III; Rebecca Oliva, Admin.
Mailing Address: P.O. Box 117, 78655. Tel: 512-357-6573; Fax: 512-357-2667.
Church: 87 Lockhart St., 78655.
Catechesis/Religious Program—Tel: 512-357-9076; Fax: 512-357-2754. Gloria Gonzales, D.R.E. Students 150.

MASON, MASON CO., ST. JOSEPH'S (1873), Attended by, Holy Trinity, Llano. Rev. Paul M. Clogan; Deacons Joe Rabke. Tel: 915-347-5105; George Keller. Tel: 915-347-5678.
Mailing Address: P.O. Box 698, Llano, 78643. Tel: 915-247-4481; Fax: 915-248-0691.
Church: 216 Ave. B, 76856. Tel: 915-247-4481.
Catechesis/Religious Program—Tel: 915-347-5327. Gladys Garner, D.R.E. Tel: 915-347-5327. Students 90.

MCGREGOR, MCLENNAN CO., ST. EUGENE (1958), (Hispanic), [JC] Rev. Hilario Guajardo; Deacon David Morales.
Res.: 207 N. Johnson Dr., 76657. Tel: 254-840-3174; Fax: 254-840-0174.
Catechesis/Religious Program—Students 120.
Mission—Our Lady of San Juan 207 N. Johnson Dr., Moody, McLennan Co. 76657. Tel: 254-853-9011.

MEXIA, LIMESTONE CO., ST. MARY'S (1886), [JC] Rev. Carlo Benjamin Magnaye, M.F.; Deacons Daniel Ramirez; Dwight Mahoney.
Mailing Address: 506 E. Sumpter, 76667. Fax: 254-562-6377.
Res.: 606 N. Bonham, 76667. Tel: 254-562-3619.
Catechesis/Religious Program—Students 191.

MOODY, MCLENNAN CO., OUR LADY OF SAN JUAN (1991), (Hispanic), Attended by, Mission of St. Eugene, McGregor. Rev. Hilario Guajardo.
Mailing Address: 207 N. Johnson Dr., McGregor, 76657. Tel: 254-840-3174.
Church: 2nd & Ave. A, 76557. Tel: 254-853-9011.
Catechesis/Religious Program—Tel: 254-853-9011. Students 40.

OLD WASHINGTON-ON-THE-BRAZOS, WASHINGTON CO., BLESSED VIRGIN MARY (1849), (African American), Attended by, St. Ann's, Somerville. Rev. Pedro Garcia; Deacon Limas Sweed Sr.

Mailing Address: P.O. Box 485, Washington, 77880.
Catechesis/Religious Program—Students 28.

PFLUGERVILLE, TRAVIS CO., ST. ELIZABETH (1932), Rev. George Joseph; Deacons Marc Washburne; Channing Fell; Alejandro Lara.
Mailing Address: 1520 Railroad Ave., 78660. Tel: 512-251-9838; Fax: 512-251-9868.
Res.: 304 S. 8th St.. Tel: 512-251-9866.
Catechesis/Religious Program—Tel: 512-251-9842. Students 1,100.

PIN OAK, BASTROP CO., ST. MARY'S (1866), (German), [CEM] Attended by, St. Margaret's, Giddings. Rev. James Robert Olnhausen.
Mailing Address: c/o St. Margaret's Catholic Church, 526 S. Grimes St., Giddings, 78942. Tel: 979-542-3380; Fax: 979-542-4186.
Church: 732 FM 2104, Smithville, 78957.

ROCKDALE, MILAM CO., ST. JOSEPH'S (1880), Rev. Edwin Kagoo; Deacon Gus Coelho.
Mailing Address: P.O. Box 548, 76567. Tel: 512-446-2049; Fax: 512-446-0411.
Rectory—521 E. Davilla St., 76567. Tel: 512-446-2196.
Church: 234 San Gabriel St., 76567.
Catechesis/Religious Program—Bonnie Holub, D.R.E. Students 246.

ROCKNE, BASTROP CO., SACRED HEART (1876), (German), [CEM] Rev. Krzysztof Bugno, S.D.S. (Poland); Deacon Roger Muehr.
Mailing Address: 4045 FM 535, Bastrop, 78602. Tel: 512-321-7991; Fax: 512-303-2723.
Church: Farm-Market Rd., 78602.
Catechesis/Religious Program—Tel: 512-303-3311. Carol Kadura, D.R.E. Students 201.
Mission—Assumption of the Blessed Virgin Mary [CEM] String Prairie, Bastrop Co. Tel: 830-839-4580.

ROGERS, BELL CO., ST. MATTHEW (1991), Attended by, St. Luke's, Temple. Rev. Louis Pavlicek; Deacon Willie Luna.
Mailing Address: P.O. Box 366, 76569.
Church: Tel: 254-773-1561.
Catechesis/Religious Program—Students 40.

ROSEBUD, FALLS CO., ST. ANN'S (1915), [CEM] Rev. Walter Dhanwar, I.M.S.
Mailing Address: P.O. Drawer 85, Burlington, 76519. Tel: 254-869-2525.
Church: Stalworth St. & Rowena St., Burlington, 76519.
Catechesis/Religious Program—Tel: 254-583-4624. Students 117.
Mission—St. Michael's (1879), P.O. Box 85, Burlington, Milam Co. 76519.

ROUND ROCK, WILLIAMSON CO.

1—ST. JOHN VIANNEY (1997), Rev. Samuel Hose; Deacon Don Burleson.
Res.: 3201 Sunrise, 78664. Tel: 512-218-1183; Fax: 512-218-8272.
Catechesis/Religious Program—Tel: 512-671-6519; Fax: 512-218-8272. Students 361.

2—ST. WILLIAM'S (1956), Revs. Joel D. McNeil; Pedro Alfonso Castillo Aguillon; Deacons Concho Castillo; Juan Gonzalez Jr.; Richard Kotrola; Willie Colon; Dennis Egan; Beverly Collin, Pastoral Assoc.
Mailing Address & Office: 1000 McNeil Rd., 78681. Tel: 512-255-4473; Fax: 512-255-8126.
Rectory—1700 St. William's St., 78681. Tel: 512-255-3825.
Catechesis/Religious Program—Tel: 512-255-9118. Students 1,526.

SALADO, BELL CO., ST. STEPHEN (1989), Most Rev. Charles Davis.
Mailing Address: P.O. Box 662, 76571. Tel: 254-947-8037; Fax: 254-947-8091.
Rectory—601 FM 2268, 76751. Tel: 254-947-5582.
Church: FM 2268 (Holland Rd.), 76751.
Catechesis/Religious Program—Tel: 254-947-0382. Laura Snyder, D.R.E. Students 43.

SAN MARCOS, HAYS CO., ST. JOHN THE EVANGELIST (1883), Revs. Kevin Manion; Ernesto Elizondo; Rafael Padilla Valdes; Deacons Lalo Duran; Domingo Vargas; Louis Endris; Jesse Mojica; Rodolfo Gonzalez; Jorge Guerrero; Luis F. Silguero.
Res.: 624 E. Hopkins, 78666. Tel: 512-353-8969; Fax: 512-396-7522.
Catechesis/Religious Program—Tel: 512-353-5065. Sisters Adelina Esquivel, M.C.M., D.R.E.; Roseann Castilleja, M.C.M., D.R.E.; Virginia Hernandez, M.C.M., D.R.E. Students 697.
Convent—964 Field St., 78666. Tel: 512-396-5333.
Mission—Guadalupe Chapel Corner of Roosevelt & Churchill, Hays Co. 78666.

SAN SABA, SAN SABA CO., ST. MARY'S (1967), (Hispanic), [JC] Rev. Greg McLaughlin; Deacon Richard Menchaca.
Mailing Address: P.O. Box 415, 76877. Tel: 325-372-3679; Fax: 325-372-6569.
Church: 504 W. Wallace, 76877.
Catechesis/Religious Program—Tani Menchaca, D.R.E., (Goldthwaite). Students 90.

SATIN, SATIN FALLS CO., SANTA RITA SHRINE (1921), (Hispanic), Attended by, St. Francis, Waco. , Mailing Address: 301 Jefferson Ave., Waco, 76701. Tel: 254-752-8434; Fax: 254-752-2415.

SMITHVILLE, BASTROP CO., ST. PAUL THE APOSTLE (1896), Rev. Karel Fink.
Res.: 204 Mills St., 78957.
Catechesis/Religious Program—Tel: 512-237-3299. Students 111.
Mission—Sts. Peter and Paul Kovar, Bastrop Co.

SOMERVILLE, BURLESON CO., ST. ANN'S (1913), Rev. Pedro Garcia-Ramirez.
Mailing Address: P.O. Box 99, 77879. Tel: 979-596-1966; Fax: 979-596-2857.
Church: Thornberry Rd., 77879.
Catechesis/Religious Program—Sr. Mary John Della Morte, D.R.E. Students 50.
Mission—Blessed Virgin Mary Chapel (1849), [JC] Washington. 17370 Sweed Rd., Old Washington, Washington Co. 77880. Tel: 936-878-2659.

STONY POINT, TRAVIS CO., BLESSED JUAN DIEGO (1987), (Mexican), Attended by, St. Dolores, Austin. Rev. John Korcsmar, C.S.C.; Deacons Rudy Rios; Jose Chavez.
Mailing Address: 200 Janzet Dr., Kyle, 78640.
Church: No. 22 & 43 Stoney Point Dr., Del Valle, 78617. Tel: 512-247-2476; 512-312-0357 (Parish Hall).
Catechesis/Religious Program—Students 90.

STRING PRAIRIE, BASTROP CO., ST. MARY'S OF THE ASSUMPTION (1876), (German), [CEM] Attended by, Sacred Heart, Rockne. Rev. Krzystof Bugno (Poland) (GRY).
Mailing Address: 4045 FM 535, Bastrop, 78602. Tel: 830-839-4580; Fax: 512-303-2723. 405 St. Mary's Rd., Bastrop, 78602. Tel: 830-839-4381.
Catechesis/Religious Program—Tel: 830-540-4089. Sharon Evans, D.R.E. Students 40.

TAYLOR, WILLIAMSON CO.

1—ST. MARY'S (1877), [CEM] Rev. Lonnie A. Urban; Deacon Dan Ozuna.
Res.: 408 Washburn St., 76574. Tel: 512-352-2175; Fax: 512-365-5313.
School—Tel: 512-352-2313. Harold Bludau, Prin. Sisters 2; Lay Teachers 16; Students 146.
Catechesis/Religious Program—Tel: 512-352-2133. Frances Albert, D.R.E. Students 268.
Convent—317 E. 4th St., 76574. Tel: 512-352-2144.

2—OUR LADY OF GUADALUPE (1914), (Hispanic), [CEM] Rev. Richard Aguilar; Deacons Alfredo Torres; Gumisindo Gonzales.
Res.: 113 Dickey St., 76574. Tel: 512-365-2380; Fax: 512-365-1733.
Catechesis/Religious Program—Students 334.

TEMPLE, BELL CO.

1—ST. LUKE'S (1969), [JC] Revs. Louis Pavlicek; Larry Heimsoth; Deacons Jerome J. Klement; James Madsen; Switzer Deason; Robert George.
Res.: 2807 Oakdale, 76502. Tel: 254-773-1561; Fax: 254-773-4623.
Catechesis/Religious Program—Tel: 254-773-2330; Fax: 254-773-2643. Students 390.
Mission—St. Matthew Hwy. 190, Rogers, Bell Co. 76569. Tel: 254-642-3450.

2—ST. MARY'S (1883), [JC] Revs. Sales T. (Ranjan) Cletus, I.M.S. (India) (TYL); Anselm A. Anukam (Nigeria); Deacons John Petter; Bonfacio (Barney) Rodriguez; Jesse Gonzales.
Res.: 1018 S. 7th St., 76504. Tel: 254-773-4541; Fax: 254-774-7044.
Rectory—1004 S. 7th St., 76504. Tel: 254-773-3238.
School—Tel: 254-778-8141; Fax: 254-778-1396. David Peterson, Ph.D., Prin. Lay Teachers 30; Students 295.
Catechesis/Religious Program—Tel: 254-773-1980. Loris Edwards, D.R.E. Students 256.

3—OUR LADY OF GUADALUPE (1952), (Hispanic), Rev. Tom Chamberlain; Deacons J. Margarito Alvarado; Jose Cruz Perez; Joseph Vela.
Res.: 707 S. 6th St., 76504. Tel: 254-773-6779; Fax: 254-773-5469.
Catechesis/Religious Program—Students 235.

TOURS, MCLENNAN CO., ST. MARTIN (1870), (German—Czech), [CEM] Rev. Isidore Rozycki.
Res.: 301 St. Martin's Church Rd., West, 76691-2135. Tel: 254-822-1145; Fax: 254-822-0171.
Catechesis/Religious Program—Tel: 254-822-1026. Dorothy Middleton, D.R.E. Students 102.
Mission—St. Joseph Elk, McLennon Co. 76691.

UHLAND, HAYS CO., ST. MICHAEL'S (1924), (Hispanic), [CEM] [JC] Rev. John Kelley; Deacon Lalo Duran.
Church and Mailing: 80 S. Old Spanish Tr., 78640. Tel: 512-398-7475.
Catechesis/Religious Program—Tel: 512-398-5720. Ofelia Cervantez, D.R.E. Students 70.

WACO, MCLENNAN CO.

1—ST. FRANCIS ON THE BRAZOS (1924), (Hispanic), [JC] Revs. Sergio Lopez, T.O.R.; Fernando Hernandez, T.O.R. (Mexico); Deacons Antonio Arocha; Jessie C. Garza.
Res.: 301 Jefferson Ave., 76701. Tel: 254-752-8434; Fax: 254-752-2415.
School—Nursery & Kindergarten, 612 N. 3rd St., 76701. Tel: 254-753-5565; Fax: 254-757-0537. Sr. Barbara Herrera, F.H.M., Prin. Sisters 3; Lay Teachers 6; Students 131.
Catechesis/Religious Program—Tel: 254-752-1159. Students 510.
Convent—612 N. 3rd St., 76701. Tel: 254-753-5565.
Mission—Santa Rita Satin, Satin Falls Co.

2—ST. JEROME (1982), Rev. Don Loftin; Deacons Jordan Pfuntner; Joseph Potter; Rae Carter; Greg George; Douglas F. Wuenschel.
Res.: 9820 Chapel Rd., 76712. Tel: 254-666-7722; Fax: 254-666-4848.
Catechesis/Religious Program—Tel: 254-666-3555. Lisa Sanders, D.R.E. Students 405.

3—ST. JOHN THE BAPTIST (1953), (African American), Attended by, St. Mary's, Waco. Deacon Alton Hithe, Pastoral Admin.
Mailing Address: P.O. Box 585, 76704-0585.
Res.: 1312 Dallas St., 76704-0585. Tel: 254-753-6742.
Catechesis/Religious Program—Students 950.
Mission—, McLennan Co.

4—ST. JOSEPH (1950), Rev. Timothy V. Vaverek.
Res.: 1011 Boston St., 76705. Tel: 254-799-2531.
Catechesis/Religious Program—Tel: 254-799-6646. Brenda Fetsch, D.R.E. Students 160.

5—ST. LOUIS (1964), Rev. David Leibham. In Res., Rev. Melvin Dornak.
Res.: 2001 N. 25th St., P.O. Box 5040, 76708. Tel: 254-754-1221; Fax: 254-754-4019.
School—Tel: 254-754-2041; Fax: 254-754-2091. Louis Gonzales, Prin. Lay Teachers 37; Students 360.
Catechesis/Religious Program—Tel: 254-754-2041. Sally Rue, D.R.E. Students 122.

6—ST. MARY OF THE ASSUMPTION (1870), Rev. Angelo Bertini; Deacons Frank Jasek; David Morales; Sidney Prewitt.
Mailing Address: 1401 Washington Ave., 76701. Tel: 254-753-0146; Fax: 254-753-5100.
Church: 205 N. 14th St., 76701.
Catechesis/Religious Program—Tel: 254-754-1622. Terri Bukowski, D.R.E. Students 78.
Mission—St. John the Baptist 1312 Dallas St., McLennan Co. 76704. Tel: 254-753-6742.

7—SACRED HEART (1957), (Spanish), Rev. Lawrence Soler, T.O.R.; Deacon Lorenzo Garcia.
Res.: 2621 Bagby Ave., 76711. Tel: 254-756-2656; Fax: 254-756-6302.
Catechesis/Religious Program—Tel: 254-756-2390. Students 288.

WEST, MCLENNAN CO., ASSUMPTION (1892), (Czech), [CEM] Rev. Edward Karasek; Deacon Buddy Shieldes.
Mailing Address: P.O. Box 276, 76691. Tel: 254-826-3705; Fax: 254-826-5497.
Church: 303 S. Harrison.
School—Tel: 254-826-5991; Fax: 254-826-7047. Joe Gough, Prin. Lay Teachers 15; Students 202.
Catechesis/Religious Program—Mrs. Charlotte Klaus, D.R.E.; Mrs. Edwina Deiterman, D.R.E. Students 388.

WESTPHALIA, FALLS CO., VISITATION (1883), (German), [CEM] Rev. Reinhold Schmitt, C.M.M.; Deacons Bill Smetana; Charlie Wright.
Res.: 144 County Rd. 3000, Lott, 76656-3827. Tel: 254-584-4983; Fax: 254-584-7063.
Catechesis/Religious Program—Tel: 254-584-4407. Marilyn Rudleff, D.R.E. Students 138.

WIMBERLEY, HAYS CO., ST. MARY (1956), [CEM] Rev. Everett Trebtoske.
Res.: 14711 Ranch Rd. 12, 78676. Tel: 512-847-9181 (Church); Fax: 512-847-5573.
Catechesis/Religious Program—Tel: 512-847-1662. Minerva Martinez, D.R.E. Students 126.

Chaplains of Public Institutions

AUSTIN. *St. David's Hospital*, 2010 Guadalupe, 78705. Tel: 512-477-9471. Rev. Robert Michele, C.S.P.
School for the Blind, 7601 Burnet Rd., 78757. Tel: 512-454-0384. Rev. Larry Covington.
School for the Deaf, 2309 Euclid St., 78704. Tel: 512-442-3602. Served by St. Ignatius Catholic Church.
Seton/Brackenridge Hospital, Tel: 512-324-7480; 512-324-7106. Rev. Matthew C. Iwuji.
State Hospital, 4110 Guadalupe, 78751. Tel: 512-451-5121. Rev. Lawrence J. Stehling.
State School, 2010 Guadalupe, 78705. Tel: 512-477-9471. Rev. Patrick A. Johnson, C.S.P.

BASTROP. *Federal Correctional Institute*. Sr. Thomasette Pittari, S.S.N.D., 2426 W. Cardinal Loop, Apt. A-102, Del Valle, TX 78617.

GATESVILLE. *Texas Department of Criminal Justice*, P.O. Box 665, 76528. Deacon James Gallagher, Chap.

GIDDINGS. *State School*. Attended by St. Margaret, Giddings. Tel: 409-542-3380.

MARLIN. *V.A. Hospital*. Attended by St. Joseph, Marlin, 254-803-8888. , P.O. Box 371, 76661.

MEXIA. *State School*, 606 N. Bonham, 76667. Tel: 254-562-3619. Rev. Carlo Benjamin Magnaye, M.F.

TEMPLE. *V.A. Hospital*, 1901 S. First St., 76501. Tel: 254-778-4811, Ext. 4879. Rev. Richard Beyer.

WACO. *V.A. Hospital*, 4800 Memorial Dr., 76711. Tel: 254-752-6581. Revs. Thomas J. Niemira, Richard Beyer.

Special Assignments:
Rev. Msgrs.—
Goertz, Victor, Cedarbrake Renewal Center, P.O. Box 58, Belton, 76513.
Matocha, Edward C., P.A., Vicar General
Rev.—
Goertz, Bernard C., Rte. 2, Box 129, Cedar Creek, 78612.

On Duty Outside the Diocese:
Rev. Msgr.—
Elmer, Charles, St. Mary Seminary, 9845 Memorial Dr., Houston, 77024.
Revs.—
Jenkins, Ron, Catholic University of America, Dept. of Canon Law, Washington, DC 20064.
Mahoney, Bernard, 1722 Chippendale, Houston, 77108.
McCabe, Peter, Regional Juvenile Center, 1304 Quamasia Ave., McAllen, 78504.
Moss, Donald G., Navy Base Ventura County, 1000 23rd Ave./Chapel, 93043. Naval Chaplain's School
Strieder, Leon, St. Mary's Seminary, 9845 Memorial Dr., Houston, 77024. Code 8E0000, 1 Administration Circle, China Lake, CA 93555.

Retired:
Rev. Msgrs.—
Brennan, Ralph, 921 St. Edward's Dr., 78704. Tel: 512-493-0130
Deering, Mark, 4700 Westchester, 76710. Tel: 254-772-5263
Frizelle, John D., 312 Granger St., Granger, 76530. Tel: 512-859-2223
Fuchs, Sylvester, Lost Prairie Villa, 9901 FM Rd. 2086, Temple, 76501-3528.
Malinowski, John, P.O. Box 3931, Bryan, 77805.
Mazurkiewicz, Ben, 2836 Ehlinger-Becker Rd., Fayetteville, 78940.
Miller, Frank, 434 FM1242, Abbott, 76621.
Royal, Peter, P.O. Box 1515, Moody, 76557.
Stram, Gideon, 400 Austin Ave., 76703. Tel: 512-746-2028; 512-746-2028
Tydlacka, George, 874 Burleson-Manor Rd., Manor, 78653.
Wozniak, Louis, 2212 Rifle Bend Dr., Georgetown, 78626. Tel: 512-864-1907
Revs.—
Collins, Robert, 3513 Seahorn Cir., San Diego, CA 92130.
Droll, Louis, 132 Retama Rd., Georgetown, 78626. Tel: 254-754-7788
Leddy, Leonard, Western Hill Village, 3000 W. Adams Ave. #301, Temple, 76504.
Maddox, Edward, 7902 Avellano, San Antonio, 78250. Tel: 210-523-8995
Palermo, Albert, 1104 Huntridge Cir., 78758.
Smith, Gerald, 4800 Convict Hill, 78749. Tel: 512-464-8874
Tzanakas, George M., 815 Slaughter Lane, #106, 78748. Tel: 572-291-1509

Permanent Deacons:
Aaronson, Michael, Holy Cross, Bertram
Abraham, Ellis, St. Anthony's, Bryan
Adam, Klaus, St. Paul Chong Hasnag, Harker Heights
Aguilar, Guadalupe, St. Mary's, Lockhart
Aguirre, Armando, Christ the King, Belton
Alvarado, J. Margarito, Our Lady of Guadalupe, Temple
Arellano, Joe, Santa Barbara, Hornsby Bend
Arevalo, Ralph, St. Julia's, Austin
Arocha, Antonio, St. Francis, Waco
Baker, Ted, St. Thomas Aquinas, College Station
Banda, Cruz, Jr., Santa Barbara, Hornsby Bend
Barkley, Roy, St. Joseph's, Manor
Beltran, Victor, St. Thomas, Hamilton
Benavides, Alfred, San Jose, Austin
Berg, James R., St. Catherine of Siena, Austin
Bigelow, Richard, Santa Cruz, Buda
Boren, David, St. Vincent de Paul, Austin
Botello, Richard, San Jose, Austin
Bowling, Weldon, Holy Family, Copperas Cove
Burleson, Don, St. John Vianney, Round Rock
Cardona, David
Carter, Ree, St. Jerome's, Waco
Castillo, Concepcion, St. Williams, Round Rock
Chavez, Jose, San Juan Diego, Stoney Point
Cochran, Lee, St. Anthony's, Bryan
Coelho, Gus, St. Joseph, Rockdale
Collins, Roger, (Retired)
Colon, Willie, St. William, Round Rock
Consentino, John, Holy Family, Copperas Cove
Cortez, Willie, St. Mary's Cathedral
Crochet, Larry, St. Charles Borromeo, Kingsland
Crowley, Joe, Our Lady's Maronite, Austin
Cruz, Cleo, Immaculate Heart of Mary, Martindale
Davis, Gene, St. Martin de Porres, Dripping Springs
Dawson, Vern, St. Helen's, Georgetown
Deason, Switzer, St. Luke's, Temple
Desorcie, Allen, St. Vincent de Paul, Austin
Doriocourt, Luis
Duecker, Richard, St. Anthony's, Kyle
Dufour, Generes "Doots", Diocesan Prison Ministry
Dunne, Larry, Sacred Heart, Elgin
Duran, Everardo "Lalo", St. Michael's, Uhland
Egan, Dennis, St. William's, Round Rock
Embry, Rob, St. Louis, Austin
Endris, Lou, St. John the Evangelist, San Marcos
Fahlund, Nelson, Santa Cruz, Buda
Fell, Channing, St. Elizabeth, Pflugerville
Flores, Joe, St. Anthony's, Kyle
Foreman, Boyce A., Emmaus, Lakeway
Franklin, John, Sacred Heart, Elgin
Fuller, James
Gallagher, James, Our Lady of Lourdes, Gatesville
Garcia, Lorenzo, Sacred Heart, Waco
Garza, De la, University of Texas Catholic Center
Garza, Jesse M., Sacred Heart, Austin
Garza, Jessie C., St. Francis, Waco
Garza, Juan, Rogers, TX
Garza, Ray, Santa Cruz, Buda
George, Gregory, St. Jerome's, Waco
George, Robert, St. John, Temple
Gesch, Michael, St. John Neumann, Austin
Gonzales, Gumisindo, Our Lady of Guadalupe, Taylor
Gonzales, Jesse, St. Mary's, Temple
Gonzalez, John, St. William, Round Rock
Gonzalez, Rodolfo, St. John's, San Marcos
Guerrero, Jorge, St. John's, San Marcos
Gutierrez, Joe, San Jose, Austin
Ham, W. J., St. Catherine's, Austin
Hamlet, Mark, St. John Neumann, Austin
Hansen, Clarence
Hargraves, Wilfred (Dub), St. John, Luling
Haywood, Daryl, St. Mary's, Lockhart
Hill, John, Jr., Emmaus, Lakeway
Hipskind, Gregory, St. Thomas More, Austin
Hithe, Alton, St. John's, Waco
Hoefling, Ed, (Retired)
Holicky, Edward, Jr., St. Thomas More, Austin
James, Ray, St. Theresa's, Austin
Januszewski, Bill, St. Mary's, Brenham
Jasek, Frank, St. Mary of Assumption, Waco
Jasso, Carlos, St. Mary's, Lampasas
Jenkins, Glen, St. John Neuman, Austin
Jimenez, Jose, Christ the King, Belton
Johnson, Tom, St. Thomas More, Austin
Jones, Fred, Catholic Community, Fork Hood
Keller, George, St. Joseph's, Mason
Kennedy, Pat, St. John's, Marble Falls
Kim, Peter, St. Paul Chong Hasang, Harker Heights
Klement, Jerry, St. Luke's, Temple; Dir. of Diaconal Ministry
Kotrola, Richard, St. William's, Round Rock
Krotzer, Philip, St. Martin de Porres, Dripping Springs
Lara, Alejandro, St. Elizabeth, Pflugerville
Larner, Richard, Holy Trinity, Llano
Lastovia, Ronnie, Christ the King, Belton
Lavallee, Paul, St. Martin de Porres, Dripping Springs
Lawrence, John, (Retired)
Lilliard, George, St. Charles, Kingsland
Long, Bill, St. Mary's, Lockhart
Lopez, Agapito, Cristo Rey, Austin
Lopez, Juan, Cristo Rey, Austin
Luna, Conception, St. Mary's, Hearne
Luna, Willie, St. Matthew's, Rogers
Madsen, James, St. Luke's, Temple
Mahoney, Dwight, St. Mary's, Mexia
Mallinger, Thomas, St. Thomas More, Austin
Martin, Terry, St. Mary's Lago Vista
Martinez, Jesse, Emmaus, Lakeway; Evangelization
Martinez, Roberto, Sacred Heart, Austin
Meismer, Mike, Sacred Heart, La Grange
Menchaca, Richard, St. Mary's, San Saba
Milton, Glen, St. Anthony's, Bryan
Moat, Jim
Mojica, Jessie, St. John's, San Marcos
Monroe, Frank, J.D., St. Helen, Georgetown
Montag, Eugene J., Our Mother of Sorrows, Burnet
Moore, Ray, Santa Rosa, Andice
Morales, David, St. Mary of Assumption, Waco
Moran, Elias, Immaculate Heart of Mary, Martindale
Morse, Eugene, St. Joseph, Killeen
Muehr, Roger, Sacred Heart, Rockne
Murray, Patrick, St. Ignatius, Austin
Murrell, Jack, Good Shepherd, Johnson City
Nelson, Gary, St. Joseph's, Bryan
Nissen, Kevin, St. Julia, Austin
Nowak, Dan, St. Stanislaus, Chappell Hill
O'Neill, John, St. Theresa's, Austin
Ojeda, Johnny, San Francisco Javier, Creedmoor
Orton, Dick, St. Edward's University, Austin
Ozuna, Dan, St. Mary's, Taylor
Parks, Kent, St. Paul's, Austin
Peca, John M., St. Anthony's, Kyle
Perez, Jose Cruz, Our Lady of Guadalupe, Temple
Petter, John, St. Mary's, Temple
Pfuntner, Jordan, St. Jerome's, Hewitt
Pickwell, John, St. Paul, Austin
Potter, Joseph, St. Jerome's, Hewitt
Prewitt, Sidney, St. Mary's, Waco
Pynes, Tony, St. Louis, Austin
Rabke, Joseph, St. Joseph's, Mason
Ramirez, Daniel, St. Mary's, Mexia
Reed, David, St. Mary's, College Station
Renteria, Mario, Our Lady of Guadalupe, Austin
Riojas, John, Santa Cruz, Buda
Rios, Rudy, San Juan Diego, Stoney Point
Rivera, John, San Jose, Austin
Rodriguez, Bonifacio, St. Mary, Temple
Rodriguez, J. Paul, St. Margaret Mary, Cedar Park
Rosales, Hector, Dolores, Austin
Rositas, Edward, St. Martin de Porres, Dripping Springs
Ruiz, Joe, St. Helen's, Georgetown
Ruiz, Joe, Holy Cross, Bertram
Sanchez, Romeo, San Jose, Austin
Sanders, Raymond, Jr., St. Theresa's, Austin
Santa Ana, Sam, Sacred Heart, Elgin
Scarmardo, Bill, St. Anthony's, Bryan
Schwab, Peter, St. Thomas More, Austin
Scott, Bill, St. Mary's, College Station
Shieldes, George, Church of the Visitation, West, TX
Shoemake, William, Christ the King, Belton
Silguero, Luis F., St. John's, San Marcos
Sims, Donald, St. Monica, Cameron
Sis, Ray, St. Joseph's, Bryan
Smerke, Tony, (Retired)
Smetana, Bill, Visitation, Westphalia
Solarzano, Eraclio, St. John the Evangelist, Marble Falls
Sweed, Limas, Blessed Virgin Mary, Washington
Syring, Joe, Santa Cruz, Buda
Terrell, John Larry, St. Catherine of Sienna, Austin
Thornton, Johnnie, Sts. Cyril & Methodius, Granger
Torres, Alfredo, Our Lady of Guadalupe, Taylor
Trujillo, Jose, St. Patrick's, Austin
Turner, Donald, St. Louis, Austin
Tyboroski, Julian, St. Joseph's, Marlin
Vargas, Domingo, St. John's, San Marcos
Vasquez, Alfredo, St. Joseph's, Manor
Vela, Joe, Our Lady of Guadalupe, Temple
Vela, William, Sacred Heart, Austin
Venglar, Patrick, St. Mary's, Lockhart
Walker, Ron, St. Mary's Cathedral, Austin
Washburne, Marc, St. Elizabeth, Pflugerville
Wearden, Glen, St. Joseph's, Dime Box
Wehrer, Robert, Sacred Heart, Waco
Weilert, Otto, Diocesan Pastoral Center
Weynand, Joe, St. Philip's, China Spring
Wright, Charlie, Visitation, Westphalia
Wright, Dan, St. Thomas More, Austin
Wright, Michael, Sacred Heart, Austin
Wuenchel, Douglas, St. Jerome's, Waco
Young, John, St. Mary's, Caldwell
Zacek, George, St. Theresa's, Austin

INSTITUTIONS LOCATED IN THE DIOCESE

[A] COLLEGES AND UNIVERSITIES

AUSTIN. *St. Edward's University* Established in 1878 by the Congregation of Holy Cross and chartered by the state in 1885. , 3001 S. Congress Ave., 78704-6489. Tel: 512-448-8400; Fax: 512-448-8492. Email: seu.admit@admin.stedwards.edu. Web: www.stedwards.edu. Priests 2; Holy Cross Brothers 11; Sisters 1; Lay Professors 329; Total Staff 738; Students 4,267.

Officers: Revs. Louis Brusatti, C.M., Dean School of Humanities; Rick Wilkinson, C.S.C., Dir. Campus Ministry; Sr. Donna M. Jurick, S.N.D., Exec. Vice Pres.; Bros. Romard Barthel, C.S.C.; Thomas Chady, C.S.C.; Louis Coe, C.S.C.; Richard Daly, C.S.C.; George Klawitter, C.S.C.; Victor Monette, C.S.C.; Gerald Muller, C.S.C.; John Paige, C.S.C.; John Paige, C.S.C., Dean School of Education; John Perron, C.S.C.; Edwin Reggio, C.S.C.; Donald

Steffers, C.S.C.; Paige Booth, Vice Pres. Asst. Mktg.; William Cahill, Vice Pres. Information Technology; David A. Dickson Jr., Vice Pres. Financial Affairs; H. Ramsey Fowler, Dean of New College; Dr. Lance Hayes, Registrar; Beth Henderson, Pres. Asst. for Special Events; Dr. Marianne F. Hopper, Dean Behavioral Social Science; Dr. John Houghton, Vice Pres. College of Professional & Graduate Studies; Patty Huffiness, Vice Pres. for Univ. Relations; Dr. James A. Johnson, Interim Dean MAHS Prog.; Ms. Marsha C. Kelliher, Dean Graduate School of Mgmt.; Dick Kinsey, Pres. Asst.; Dr. Frank Krafka, Dean Business Admin.; Dr. J. D. Lewis, Vice Pres. Undergraduate College; Dr. George E. Martin, Pres.; Molly Minus, Dean Academic Studies; Dr. Sandra L. Pacheco, Assoc. Vice Pres. Student Affairs; Dr. Scarborough Phillips, Librarian; Dr. Roger You, Interim Dean School of Natural Sciences.

[B] HIGH SCHOOL, DIOCESAN

AUSTIN. *Juan Diego Catholic High School*, 800 Herndon Ln., 78704. Tel: 512-804-1935; Fax: 512-804-1937. Email: edoherty@juandiegoprep.org. Web: http://juandiegoprep.org. Ed Doherty, Prin. Priests 1; Brothers 2; Sisters 2; Lay Teachers 5; Total Staff 15; Total Enrollment 100.

WACO. *Reicher Catholic High School*, 2102 N. 23rd St., 76708. Tel: 254-752-8349; Fax: 254-752-8408. Email: kcaspersen@reicher.org. Web: www.reicher.org. Dr. Kevin H. Caspersen, Ph.D., Pres./Prin. Deacons 1; Sisters 3; Lay Teachers 21; Students 205.

[C] HIGH SCHOOL, PRIVATE

AUSTIN. *St. Michaels's Catholic Academy*, 3000 Barton Creek Blvd., 78735. Tel: 512-328-2323; Fax: 512-328-2327. Email: awallace@stmichaelsacademy.org. Web: www.stmichaelsacademy.org. Dr. Avis Wallace, Head of School. Priests 2; Sisters 1; Lay Teachers 41; Students 448.

TEMPLE. *Holy Trinity Catholic High School*, 418 N. 11th, 76501. Tel: 254-771-0787; Fax: 254-771-2285. Email: holytrin@sbcglobal.net holytrinity@hot.rr.com. Web: www. holytrinitychs.org. Susan Terry, Prin. Priests 1; Lay Teachers 15; Total Enrolment 71; Total Staff 29.

[D] ELEMENTARY SCHOOL, PRIVATE

AUSTIN. *St. Gabriel's Catholic School* (Legal name: Southwest Austin Catholic School Inc.), 2500 Wimberly Ln., 78735. Tel: 512-327-7755; Fax: 512-327-4334. Email: judyknotts@sgs-austin.org. Web: sgs-austin.org. Dr. Judith Knotts, School Head. Lay Teachers 31; Total Enrollment 432.

Holy Family Catholic School, 9400 Neenah Ave., 78717. Tel: 512-246-4455; Fax: 512-246-4454. Email: holyfamilycs@holyfamilycs.org. Web: www.holyfamilycs.org. Falba F. Turner, Prin. Lay Teachers 20; Total Staff 35; Students 333; Sisters 1.

[E] GENERAL HOSPITALS

AUSTIN. *Daughters of Charity Health Services of Austin*, 1201 W. 38th St., 78750. Tel: 512-324-1000; Fax: 512-459-5629. Web: seton.net. Charles J. Barnet, Pres. & CEO. A member of Ascension Health.; Daughters of Charity of St. Vincent de Paul. Total Bed Capacity 752; Total Patients Assisted Annually 214,499.

SETON Cedar Park, 801 E. Whitestone Blvd., Cedar Park, 78613. Tel: 512-324-5300; Fax: 512-324-5330. Maria Talamo, Admin.

SETON Lakeway, 1602 Lohmans Crossing, 78734. Tel: 512-261-1758; Fax: 512-261-1736. Mary Faria, Admin.

SETON Medical Center, 1201 W. 38th St., 78750. Tel: 512-324-1000; Fax: 512-459-5629. Charlotte Shrasher, Hospital Admin.; Rev. Oliver Weerakkody, Interim Dir. of Chap. Svcs.; Barbara Halloway, Chap.; Jim Mahan, Chap.; Enid Ross, Chap.

SETON McCarthy Community Health Center, 2811 E. Second St., 78702. Tel: 512-324-4930; Fax: 512-324-4929. Jim Thomas, Dir. Operations.

SETON Northwest Hospital, 11113 Research Blvd., 78759. Tel: 512-324-6000; Fax: 512-324-6924. Email: cdurant@seton.org. Web: www.goodhealth.com. Charles E. Durant Jr., Hospital Admin.; Revs. Ed Banarsi, Chap.; Oliver Weerakkody, Chap.

SETON Pflugerville, 200 N. Heatherwilde Blvd., Pflugerville, 78660. Tel: 512-324-5350; Fax: 512-324-5351. Maria Talamo, Admin. Dir.

SETON Shoal Creek, 3501 Mills Ave., 78731. Tel: 512-324-2000; Fax: 512-324-2003. Armin Steegy, Admin.; Lee Colwell, Chap.

SETON South Community Health Center, 3706 S. First St., 78704. Tel: 512-324-4940; Fax: 512-324-4949. Sandra Gonzaley, Admin. Dir.

SETON Southwest Health Center, 7900 FM 1826, 78737. Tel: 512-324-9000; Fax: 512-324-9002. Mary Faria, Hospital Admin.; Sr. Jean Wesselman, Chap.

SETON Topfer Community Health Center, 8913 Collinfield Dr., 78758. Tel: 512-324-6850; Fax: 512-324-6851. Al Perz, Admin. Supvr.

SETON Lockhart Center for Healthcare, 300 S. Colorado, Ste. A, Lockhart, 78644. Tel: 512-376-9690; Fax: 512-398-3755. Neal Kelley, Admin.

SETON Lockhart Speciality Clinic, 1505 Main St., Lockhart, 78644. Tel: 512-376-3377; Fax: 512-398-1942. Neal Kelley, Admin.

BRENHAM. *Trinity Community Medical Center of Brenham*, 700 Medical Pkwy., 77833. Tel: 979-836-6173; Fax: 979-830-2277. Email: jsimms@mail.st-joseph.org. Web: trinitymed.org. John Simms, Admin.; Sr. Geraldine Paluszak, O.S.F., Dir. Pastoral Care & Mission. Sisters of St. Francis of Sylvania, OH 2; Bed Capacity 60; Patients Assisted Annually 30,000; Staff 275.

Trinity Care Center, 400 Sayles, 77833. Tel: 979-836-9770; Fax: 979-836-6100. Florence Julian, Exec. Dir.; Sr. Patricia Zielinski, O.S.F., Dir. Pastoral Care. Sisters of St. Francis of Sylvania, OH 1; Bed Capacity 120.

BRYAN. *Burleson St. Joseph Health Center of Caldwell, Texas*, 2801 Franciscan Dr., 77802. Tel: 979-776-2599; Fax: 409-774-4590. Email: info@mail.st-joseph.org. Web: www.st-joseph.org. Jim Crust, Chair-person. Patients Assisted Annually 31,996; Total Staff 86; Bed Capacity 25.

St. Joseph Regional Health Center, 2801 Franciscan Dr., 77802. Tel: 979-776-3777; Fax: 979-774-4590. Email: dbuch@mail.st-joseph.org. Web: www.st-joseph.org. Daniel L. Buche, CEO; Rev. Msgr. John C. Malinowski, Chap.; Dr. James W. Stegall, Bd. Chm. Sisters of St. Francis of Sylvania, OH 6; Bed Capacity 313; Patients Assisted Annually 247,000; Total Staff 1,535.

St. Joseph Services Corp., 2801 Franciscan Dr., 77802. Tel: 979-776-3777; Fax: 979-774-4590. Email: info@mail.st-joseph.org. Web: www.st-joseph.org. Sr. Gretchen Kunz, O.S.F., CEO; Dr. Bill H. Magee, Bd. Chm. Sisters of St. Francis of Sylvania, OH 8; Bed Capacity 356; LTC Beds 208; Patients Assisted Annually 317,400; LTC Staff 186; Total Staff 1,982.

BURNET. *SETON Highland Lakes*, Hwy. 281 S., 78611. Tel: 512-756-6000; Fax: 512-756-6405. Web: seton.net. Patricia A. Hayes, Ph.D., Interim Pres. & CEO; Janna Maturo, Hospital Admin.

Legal Title: *Daughters of Charity Health System of Austin.* Bed Capacity 42; Patients Assisted Annually 13,113.

SETON Highlands Lake Clinic Burnet, 300 County Rd., 340-A, Ste. 3, 78611. Tel: 512-715-0669; Fax: 512-715-0678. Janna Maturo, Admin.

Legal Title: *Daughters of Charity*

LULING. *SETON Edgar B. Davis Hospital*, 130 Hays St., 78648. Tel: 830-875-5643; Fax: 830-875-2100. Web: seton.net. Patricia A. Hayes, Ph.D., Interim Pres. & CEO; Neal Kelley, Admin.

Legal Title: *Daughters of Charity Health System of Austin.* Bed Capacity 30; Patients Assisted Annually 9,959.

WACO. *Providence Healthcare Network*, 6901 Medical Pkwy., P.O. Box 2589, 76702-2589. Tel: 254-751-4000; Fax: 254-751-4769. Email: kkeahey@phn-waco.org. Web: providence-waco.org. Kent A. Keahey, Pres.; Sr. Cecile Matushek, D.C., Vice Pres. Mission. Medical/Surgical/OB/Pediatrics acute care; DePaul Center - Psychiatric care; St. Catherine's Center - Long Term care; Providence Clinics; Providence Home Health; Providence Health Alliance. Daughters of Charity of St. Vincent de Paul 6; Bed Capacity 427; Patients Assisted Annually 173,681; Total Staff 1,343.

[F] SPECIAL HOSPITAL

WACO. *DePaul Center*, 301 Londonderry Dr., 76712. Tel: 254-776-5970; 800-777-5043. Sr. Rosemary Burke, C.C.V.I., Dir. Pastoral Care; Dr. Keith M. Hankins, Ed.D., Admin. Vice Pres. Psychiatric Hospital Daughters of Charity 1; Bed Capacity 48; Patients Assisted Annually 1,900.

[G] MONASTERIES AND RESIDENCES OF PRIESTS AND BROTHERS

AUSTIN. *Mackay St. Barbara*, St. Edward University, 3001 S. Congress Ave., 78704. Tel: 512-442-4534; Fax: 512-442-0589. Email: nosopher@aol.com. Web: www.stedwards.edu/holycross/. Bro. Patrick Sopher, C.S.C., Supr. Total in Residence 23; Brothers 23. In Res. Rev. Joseph E. Ekweariri.

Brother Andre House, 2113 Brackenridge St., 78704. Tel: 512-462-3540; Fax: 512-416-1216. Email: brotgk@southerncsc.org. Web: www.southerncsc.org. Bros. Thomas G. Krieter, C.S.C.; Matthew McKenna, C.S.C.; Revs. Richard S. Teall, C.S.C.; Paul C. Pudussery, C.S.C.

Brothers of the Congregation of Holy Cross Tel: 512-442-7856; Fax: 512-444-3133. Email: rbcritz@attglobal.net. Web: holycrossbrothers.org.

Brother John Baptist Province Center, 1101 St. Edward's Dr., 78704-6512. Tel: 512-442-7856; Fax: 512-444-3133. Email: jmclaug@acad.stedwards.edu. Web: www.stedwards.edu/holycross/home.htm. Bros. Richard Critz, C.S.C., Prov. Supr.; Stephen Walsh, C.S.C., Asst. Provinicial; Michael Brickman, C.S.C., Councilor; Johnny Juno, C.S.C., Asst. Steward; Carl Smith, C.S.C., Receptionist; Joel Giallanza, C.S.C., Sec. Total in Province 105.

Brother Vincent Pieau Residence, 921 St. Edward Dr., 78704. Tel: 512-493-0121; Fax: 512-493-0158. Bro. Matthew Lyons, Dir.

Congregation of Holy Cross - Southern Province, Provincial House, 2111 Brackenridge St., 78704. Tel: 512-443-3886; Fax: 512-416-1216. Email: brotgk@southerncsc.org. Web: www.southerncsc.org. Revs. John R. Birkmeyer, C.S.C. (Retired); Leon J. Boarman, C.S.C. (Retired); L. Peter Logsdon, C.S.C, Missionary; Daniel A. Panchot, C.S.C., Missionary; Robert G. Gilmour, C.S.C., Missionary; Leonard J. Collins, C.S.C., Missionary; John S. Korcsmar, C.S.C., Prov.; Paul B. Rankin, C.S.C. (Retired); Joseph W. Rehage, C.S.C. (Retired); Jeffrey Allison, Advanced Studies; Bros. Thomas G. Krieter, C.S.C., Asst. Prov., Prov. Steward; Matthew McKenna, C.S.C., Assoc. Vocation Dir.

Congregation of the Mission, C.M. (Earth City, MO), *St. Edward's University*, 3001 S. Congress Ave., 78704. Tel: 512-448-8643; Fax: 512-233-1695. Email: louisb@admin.stedwards.edu. Web: www.stedwards.edu. Rev. Louis Brusatti, C.M., Dean, Humanities.

Dominican Friars of Austin, 2502 Comburg Castle Way, 78748-5258. Tel: 512-282-3908; Fax: 512-280-9011. Email: chiefop@austin.rr.com. Revs. James A. McDonough, O.P., Supr.; Gerardo Guerra-Mayaudon, O.P. Tel: 512-292-3381; Bro. Angel Del Rio, O.P.

6008 Club Terrace, 78741. Tel: 512-385-1719. Rev. Ralph Rogawski, O.P.

Missionary of St. Paul, MSP, 1610 E. 11th St., 78702. Tel: 512-472-3741. Rev. Cletus Udoh, M.S.P. (Nigeria).

Moreau House, St. Edward University #1069, 3001 S. Congress, 78704. Tel: 512-448-8595; Fax: 512-442-0589. Email: rjlegros.aol.com. Web: www. holycross-sw.org. Bros. Robert LeGros, C.S.C., Dir.; John Perron.

Oratory of Saint Gregory the Great, 907 Lydia, 78702. Tel: 512-236-1101. Very Rev. James R.P. O'Connor, S.T.L., J.C.L., Mag. Theol.; Rev. David Williams, S.T.B., J.D.

Society of Our Lady of the Most Holy Trinity, S.O.L.T., Brackenridge Hospital, 601 E. 15th St., 78701. Tel: 512-448-3820. Rev. Robert Rank, S.O.L.T.

Steiner Lodge, 3117 Westlake Dr., 78746. Tel: 512-328-0459. Web: www.southerncsc.org. Revs. Harold W. Essling, C.S.C.; Edwin J. Kadzielawski, C.S.C.

BLANCO. *Missionaries of the Sacred Heart, M.S.C.* (Irish Providence), Rte. 1, Box 1, 78606. Tel: 830-833-5227; Fax: 830-833-2235. Email: stferd@moment.net. Revs. Richard O'Rourke, M.S.C.; Sean Horgan, M.S.C.

BREMOND. *Clerical Congregation Missionaries of Faith*, 715 N. Main St., 76629-5173. Tel: 254-746-7789; Fax: 254-746-7280. Email: jyucmf@hotmail.com. Web: www.mftexas.catholicweb.com. Rev. Celso A. Yu, M.F. (Philippines), Supr.

Missionaries of Faith, M.F. (U.S Region), 715 N. Main St., 76629. Tel: 254-746-7789. Rev. Celso A. Yu, M.F. (Philippines).

BRENHAM. *Order of Friars Minor*, St. Francis Friary, 9539 FM 2193, 77833-0139. Tel: 409-830-1554; Fax: 409-836-9652. Rev. Curt C. Lanzrath, O.F.M. Total in Residence 1.

JONESTOWN. *Hermitage*, 17818 Sandy Ln., 78645-3134. Tel: 512-267-1443. Rev. Francis Chruma.

[H] CONVENTS AND RESIDENCES FOR SISTERS

AUSTIN. *Adrian Dominican Sisters*, 1943 Dapplegrey Ln., 78727-4590. Tel: 512-834-9620; Fax: 512-873-8338. Email: loispaha@juno.com.

Congregation of Marianites of the Holy Cross, M.S.C., 802 Huntingdon Pl., 78745. Sr. Stephanie Brignac, M.S.C., Contact Person.

Daughters of Charity of St. Vincent De Paul, 1018 W. 31st St., 78705-2002. Tel: 512-453-9655; Fax: 512-459-5629. Email: DC31st@aol.com pelder@seton.org. Web: www.daughters-of-charity.org.index.php. Sisters 7.

Other Addresses:

5803 Fairlane Dr., 78757-4414. Tel: 512-452-8980; Fax: 512-459-5629. Email: DCFairlane@aol.com. Sisters 6.

11402 Pencewood Dr., 78750-2555. Tel: 512-336-2986; Fax: 512-324-7051. Email: daughtersoc@email.msn.com. Sisters 3.

Daughters of Mary Help of Christians (Salesian Sisters of St. John Bosco), St. Mary Mazzarello Convent, 2509 E. Cesar Chavez St., 78702. Tel: 512-474-2312; Fax: 512-474-2314. Email: fmasuoau@ix.netcom.com. Sisters 3.

Dominican Sisters of Houston Sisters 2.
3810 Valley View Rd. #111, 78704-6770. Tel: 512-383-8954.
317 E. Fourth St., Taylor, 76574-3624. Tel: 512-352-2144.

Franciscan Sisters Daughters of Mercy (Hermanas Franciscanas Hijas de la Misericordia), House of Formation, 1207 Montopolis Dr., 78741. Tel: 512-385-4333; 512-385-5090; Fax: 512-389-0692. Email: sr.rose@doloreschurch.org. Sr. Rose Moreno, F.H.M., Regl. Supr. Sisters 4.

St. Francis Convent, 612 N. 3rd St., Waco, 76701. Tel: 254-753-6816; Fax: 254-757-0537. Sisters 3.

Missionary Cathechists of Divine Providence, 1943 Dapplegrey Ln., 78727. Tel: 512-837-7562; 512-873-7771; Fax: 512-873-8338. Email: sr_celia_ann_cavazos@austindiocese.org.

Missionary Sisters of the Immaculate Conception of the Mother of God, 4211-B Shoalwood, 78756. Tel: 512-451-2890. Email: jriesch@prodigy.net.

Secular Institute of Schoenstatt Sisters of Mary, 225 Addie Roy Rd., 78746. Tel: 512-330-0602. Total in Residence 2.

Sinsinawa Dominican Sisters, 6008 Club Terr., 78741. Tel: 512-385-1719. Sisters 2.

Sisters of Divine Providence, 2600 Cockburn Dr., 78745. Tel: 572-707-8199. Sisters 7.

Sisters of Mercy of New Jersey, R.S.M. (Watchung, NJ) , 2600 Cockburn Dr., 78745. Tel: 512-707-8199. Email: lchebro@ev1.net. Sr. Linda Chebro, Contact Person.

Sisters of the Holy Cross, La Casa Convent, 2213 Euclid Ave., 78704. Tel: 512-441-6693.

Sisters of the Holy Cross, Our Lady of Victory Convent, 2215 Euclid Ave., 78704-5214. Tel: 512-441-2927. Sisters 3.

Sisters of the Holy Cross, Loretto Convent, 2301 E. Side Dr., 78704-5214. Tel: 512-441-3850; Fax: 512-441-3850. Email: alicecondon@aol.com. Sisters 3.

Sisters, Servants of the Immaculate Heart of Mary, 921 St. Edward's Dr., A104, 78704. Tel: 512-493-0125; Fax: 512-469-9537. Email: sr_marie_andre_walsh@austindiocese.org. Web: www.austindiocese.org. Sr. Marie Andre Walsh, I.H.M., Contact Person. Sisters 6.

BRENHAM. *Monastery of St. Clare*, 9300 Hwy. 105, 77833. Tel: 979-836-2444. Email: poorclaresisters@netscape.net. Web: www.franciscanpoorclares.org. Rev. Curt C. Lanzrath, O.F.M., Chap.; Sr. Clara Gomez, O.S.C., Abbess. Sisters 5.

Sisters of St. Francis of Our Lady of Lourdes (O.S.F.), 605 Church St. A. Tel: 979-836-9481; Fax: 979-830-2277. Sisters 5.

BRYAN. *Sisters of St. Francis of Our Lady of Lourdes*, 2801 Franciscan Dr., 77802. Tel: 979-776-3777; Fax: 409-774-4590. Email: info@mail.st-joseph.org. Web: www.st-joseph.org. Sisters 10.

BURNET. *Sisters of the Holy Cross/Council Creek Village*, Star Route, 78611. Tel: 512-756-2997. Sr. Mary Elizabeth, C.S.C., Contact Person.

ELGIN. *Sisters for Christian Community, S.F.C.C., Anawim Convent*, 150 S. Red Bud Tr., 78621. Tel: 512-308-1942; Fax: 512-258-8812. Sr. Carol Wagner, S.F.C.C., Contact Person.

LULING. *Our Lady of Victory Missionary Sisters*, 400 S. Pecan, 78648. Tel: 830-875-9484; Fax: 830-875-3533. Email: stjohn_luling@bcsnet.net.

SAN MARCOS. *Cordi-Marian Sisters*, 964 Field St., St. Anthony Claret Mission House, 78666. Tel: 512-396-5333. Email: addie_219@yahoo.com. Sisters 4.

SOMERVILLE. *Missionary Ecumenical*, P.O. Box 367, 77879. Tel: 979-595-1494; Fax: 979-596-1494.

TAYLOR. *Sisters of St. John Bosco*, St. John's Convent, 1101 Symes, 76574. Tel: 512-352-2802.

WACO. *Congregation of the Sisters of the Incarnate Word, C.C.V.I.*, 6901 Medical Pkwy., 76702. Tel: 817-751-4000.

Daughters of Charity of St. Vincent De Paul, 2416 Colcord, 76707. Tel: 254-753-3817. Email: dcswaco@email.com. Sisters 3.
213 Bonham Dr., 76643. Tel: 254-666-0611. Email: hewittdc@aol.com. Sisters 2.

Franciscan Sisters Daughters of Mercy (Franciscanas Hijas de la Misericordia) , 612 N. Third St., 76701. Tel: 817-753-5565. Sisters 8.
1111 Montopolis Dr., 78741.

Sisters of Charity of the Incarnate Word, 717 Cardinal, 76712. Tel: 254-776-2707; Fax: 254-754-0133.

Sisters of the Holy Cross

[I] HOMES FOR THE AGED & HANDICAPPED

BRENHAM. *Trinity Care Center*, 400 E. Sayles, 77833. Tel: 979-836-9770; Fax: 979-836-6100. Web: www.trinitymed.org. Florence Julian, Exec. Dir.; Sr. Patricia Zielinski, O.S.F., Dir. of Pastoral Care. Bed Capacity 120; Total Assisted 117; Total Staff 110.

BRYAN. *St. Joseph Manor*, 2801 Franciscan Dr., 77802. Tel: 979-821-7590; Fax: 979-821-7301. Email: jrouse@mail.st-joseph.org. Jane Rouse, Admin. Total Assisted 112; Total Staff 89.

CALDWELL. *Burleson St. Joseph Manor*, 1022 Presidential Corridor, Hwy. 21E, 77836 Tel: 979-821-7590; Fax: 979-567-4811. Email jrouse@mail.st-joseph.org. Jane Rouse, Admin. Bed Capacity 112; Sisters 1; Staff 89.

WACO. *CHRISTUS, The Regis Retirement Home & St. Elizabeth Nursing Home*, 400 Austin Ave., P.O. Box 1909, 76703. Tel: 254-756-5441; Fax 254-754-0133. Email: doug35@aol.com. Web: www.members.aol.com/regisst. Douglas F. Wuenschel, CEO & Pres. Christus Health (Dallas) 1; Residents 245; Total Assisted 432; Total Staff 230.

[J] MISSION CENTERS

SOMERVILLE. *St. Ann Mission Center*, P.O. Box 367, 77879. Tel 979-596-1696; Fax: 979-596-1496. Sr. M. John DellaMorte, M.E., Supr. Missionary Ecumenical. Kindergarten Students 20; Total Staff 1.

WACO. *St. Francis Mission Center*, 612 N. Third St., 76701. Tel: 254-753-5565; Fax: 254-757-0537. Email: barbarajhtexas@hotmail.com. Sisters Catherine Vallespir, F.H.M., Catechetical, Kindergarten & Nursery; Barbara Herrera, F.H.M., Supr. Franciscan Sisters Daughters of Mercy Sisters 3; Total Staff 11.

[K] RENEWAL CENTERS

BELTON. *Cedarbrake Renewal Center*, P.O. Box 58, 76513-0058 Tel: 254-780-2436; Fax: 254-780-2684. Email: sr_jean_burbo@austindiocese.org. Total in Residence 3; Total Staff 11.

[L] NEWMAN APOSTOLATE

AUSTIN. *University Catholic Center* 2010 University Ave., 78705. Tel: 512-476-7351; Fax: 512-476-7377. Email: terry@utcatholic.org. Web: http://www.utexas.edu/students/univcath. Revs. Ruben Patino, C.S.P., Dir.; Frank Sabatte, C.S.P., Assoc. Dir.; Richard Tijerina; Michelle Goodwin, Campus Min.; Terry M. Martin, Campus Min. & Admin. Serving the Catholic community at the University of Texas.

BRENHAM. *Blinn College Catholic Student Union* Blinn College, 902 College Ave., 77833. Tel: 979-830-4429. Deacon William Januszewski, Campus Min. Tel: 979-836-9329. For Catholic students attending Blinn Jr. College.

COLLEGE STATION. *St. Mary's Catholic Center* 603 Church Ave. 77840. Tel: 979-846-5717; Fax: 979-846-4493. Email: info@aggiecatholic.org Web: www.aggiecatholic.org. Revs. Michael J. Sis; Keith Koehl; Deacons Bill Scott Jr.; David Reed. Campus ministry at Texas A & M University and Blinn College. Total in Residence 2; Total Staff 30.

SAN MARCOS. *H.L. Grant Catholic Student Center at Southwest Texas State University* 100 Concho St., 78666. Tel: 512-392-5925; Fax: 512-392-5922. Email: catholic-studentcenter@swt.edu. Web: www.geocities.com/swtcsc. Rev. Bill Benish, Chap.; Melinda Habingreither, Assoc. Dir. Catholic Students attending Southwest Texas State University.

WACO. *St. Peter Catholic Student Center at Baylor University* 1415 S. 9th St., P.O. Box 6060, 76706-6060. Tel: 254-757-0636; Fax: 254-714-0639. Email: cstudentcenter@hot.rr.com. Web: www.baylorcatholic.org. Rev. James Deaconson, Chap./Dir.; Jerry Opperman, Admin. For Catholic students attending Baylor University, Texas State Technical College, and McLennan Community College.

[M] FOUNDATIONS, ENDOWMENTS & TRUSTS

AUSTIN. *Holy Family Catholic School Foundation*, 9400 Neenah Ave., 78717. Tel: 512-246-4455; Fax: 512-246-4454 Email: holyfamilycs@holyfamilycs.org. Web: www.holyfamilycs.org. Falba F. Turner, Contact Person.

The Reardon Foundation, c/o Seton Healthcare Network, 1201 W. 38th St., 78705. Tel: 512-324-3205; Fax: 512-324-1989. Email: brubio@seton.org. Charles J. Barnet, Senior Vice Pres.; Bryan Rubio, Exec. Dir.

Vincare Services of Austin Foundation, 2026 Guadalupe St., 78705. Tel: 512-302-0027 Fax: 512-454-0235. Email: vincare@vincare.org. Web: vincare.org. Sharon Bieser, Exec. Dir.

BRYAN. *St. Joseph Memorial Endowment Fund*, St. Joseph's, 600 E. 26th, 77803. Tel: 979-822-2721; Fax: 979-779-3120. Email: frjohn@stjosephbcs.org. Web: www.stjosephbcs.org. Rev. Msgr. John A. McCaffrey.

[N] MISCELLANEOUS

AUSTIN. P.O. Box 6067, 78762. Tel: 512-731-8434; Fax: 512-441-0928. Email: jdms2003@yahoo.com. Elias and Christina Limon, Dir.

Blue Ladies Minerals, Inc., 1206 W. 38th St., Ste. 4200, 78705-1056. Tel: 512-324-1990. Gene Attal, Contact Person.

Brothers of Holy Cross, South-West Province, Charitable Trust, 3001 S. Congress Ave., #1046, 78704. Tel: 512-442-7856; Fax: 512-444-3133. Bros. Richard Critz, C.S.C., Pres.; Stephen Walsh, C.S.C., Vice Pres.; Joel Giallanza, C.S.C., Sec.; Harold Ehlinger, C.S.C., Treas.; Michael Brickman, C.S.C., Trustee; Richard Daly, C.S.C., Trustee; William Nick, C.S.C., Trustee.

Catholic Archives of Texas, N. Congress & W. 16th St., P.O. Box 13124, 78711-3124. Tel: 512-476-6296; Fax: 512-476-3715. Email: cat@onr.com. Web: www.onr.com/usercat. Susan Eason, Archive Dir.; Eric J. Hartmann, Archives Asst. Historical collection of the Church in the Southwest and Texas from 1519.

Catholic Family Fraternal of Texas. KJZT, P.O. Box 1884, 78767-1844. Tel: 512-444-9586; Fax: 512-373-7013. Mrs. Geraldine Nekuza, Pres.; Loretta Stahl, Vice Pres.

Catholic Health Association of Texas, P.O. Box 15364, 78761-5364. Tel: 512-465-1521; Fax: 512-453-4925. Email: cha@tha.org. Web: www.chatexas.org. Cynthia N. Colbert, Pres.

Catholic Southwest, 1625 Rutherford Ln., Bldg. D, 78754-5105. Tel: 512-339-9882; Fax: 512-339-8670. Patrick Foley, Ph.D., Editor; Jesus F. de la Teja, Ph.D., Mng. Editor.

Children's Hospital Foundation of Austin, 1201 W. 38th St., 78705. Tel: 512-324-3820; Fax: 512-324-3835. Email: chf@seton.org. Web: www.childrensaustin.org. Mrs. Maureen H. Wood, M.R.E., Exec. Dir.

Juan Diego Work/Study Program, Inc., 800 Herndon Ln., 78704. Tel: 512-804-1935; Fax: 512-804-1937. Email: edoherty@juandiegoprep.org. Web: www.juandiegoprep.org. Ed Doherty, Pres.

Ladies of Charity of Austin, TX, 510 W. 26th St., 78705. Tel: 512-472-9251; Fax: 512-335-5713. Email: nickymer@wt.net. Web: www.main.ort/locaustin/index.html. Ida Smith, Pres.

North Central Catholic School Corporation, 9400 Neenah Ave., 78717. Tel: 512-246-4455; Fax: 512-246-4454. Email: holyfamilycs@holyfamilycs.org. Web: www.holyfamilycs.org.

Our Lady's Family Center, 1817 E. Sixth St., 78702. Tel: 512-322-0632; Fax: 512-322-0418. Email: ourlady78723@yahoo.com. Deacon Willie J. Cortez, Dir. Patients Assisted 300; Total Staff 4.

The Seton Cove - A Spirituality Center, 3708 Crawford St., 78731. Tel: 512-451-0272; Fax: 512-451-0284. Email: setoncove@seton.org. Web: seton.net. Total Staff 8.

Society of St. Katharine Drexel, 3308 River Rd., 78703. Tel: 512-459-5548; Fax: 512-459-2163. Mariene Glade, Pres.

Society of St. Vincent de Paul, P.O. Box 9070, 78766. Tel: 512-251-6995; Fax: 512-252-1117. Email: svdpaustin@sbeglobal.net. Rev. James McDonough, O.P., Spiritual Advisor; Randall Delgado, Pres.; Frederick L. Gale, Vice Pres.; Raymond DuPont, Co-Treas.; Jeannine DuPont, Co-Treas.; Melissa Delgado, Sec.; Melinda Rodriguez, Exec. Dir.

Texas Catholic Conference, 1625 Rutherford Ln., Bldg. D, 78754-5105. Tel: 512-339-9882; Fax: 512-339-8670. Email: txcclisa@aol.com. Web: www.txcatholic.org. Bro. Richard Daly, C.S.C., Exec. Dir.

Texas Catholic Historical Society, c/o Texas Catholic Conference, 1625 Rutherford Ln., Bldg. D, 78704-5105. Tel: 512-339-9882; Fax: 512-339-8670. Dr. Thomas W. Jodziewicz, Pres.

BASTROP. *Ladies of Charity of Bastrop, TX*, P.O. Drawer W, 78602. Tel: 512-321-9819; Fax: 512-321-1647. Email: locb@ev1.net. Putzie Martin, Pres.

LAGRANGE. *Catholic Union of Texas, The K.J.T.*, P.O. Box 297, 78945-0297. Tel: 979-968-5877; Fax: 979-968-5823. Email: kjt@cvtv.net. Web: www.kjtnet.org. Elo J. Goerig, Pres. KJT NEWS (official publication).

LAKEWAY. *Ladies of Charity*, P.O. Box 340026, 78734. Tel: 512-261-4241; Fax: 512-261-4247. Email: mail@erincurley.com. Erin Curley, Treas.

ROUND ROCK. *Christ the Child Society of Texas, Capital Area*, P.O. Box 5953, 78683. Tel: 512-864-9729. Email: JBHuels@aol.com. Janet Huelskamp, Treas.

WACO. *CHRISTUS Health Waco*, 106 S. 5th St., 76701-2105. Tel: 254-756-5441; Fax: 254-754-0133.
Ladies of Charity of Waco, TX, 622 N. 36th St., 76710-5429. Tel: 254-753-5059; Fax: 254-753-5059. Email: Lbb622@aol.com. Lorraine Brooks, Pres.

RELIGIOUS INSTITUTES OF MEN REPRESENTED IN THE DIOCESE

For further details refer to the corresponding bracketed number in the Religious Institutes of Men or Women section.

[0170]—*Basilian Fathers* (Galveston-Houston, TX)—C.S.B.
[0600]—*Brothers of the Congregation of Holy Cross* (Southwest Province)—C.S.C.
[0750]—*Congregation of Marian Hill Missionaries* (Dearborn Heights, MI)—C.M.M.
[1330]—*Congregation of the Mission* (Earth City, MO)—C.M.
[0480]—*Conventual Franciscans* (Mt. Francis, IN)—O.F.M.Conv
[0520]—*Franciscan Friars* (Cincinnati Prov.)—O.F.M.
[0690]—*Jesuit Fathers and Brothers* (New Orleans Province, LA)—S.J.
[]—*Missionaries of Faith* (U.S. Region, Bremond, TX)—M.F.
[]—*Missionaries of St. Paul* (Houston, TX)—M.S.P.
[1110]—*Missionaries of the Sacred Heart* (San Antonio, TX)—M.S.C.
[0910]—*Oblates of Mary Immaculate* (U.S. Province, Washington, D.C.)—O.M.I.
[0430]—*Order of Preachers-Dominicans* (New Orleans, LA)—O.P.
[1030]—*Paulist Fathers* (Jamaica Estates, NY)—C.S.P.
[0610]—*Priests of the Congregation of Holy Cross* (Southern Prov.; Austin, TX)—C.S.C.
[0975]—*Society of Our Lady of the Most Holy Trinity* (Robstown TX)—S.O.L.T.
[1200]—*Society of the Divine Savior* (Milwaukee, WI)—S.D.S.
[0560]—*Third Order Regular of Saint Francis of Waco, TX* (Vice-Province of Santa Maria de Guadalupe, Mexico)—T.O.R.

RELIGIOUS INSTITUTES OF WOMEN REPRESENTED IN THE DIOCESE

[2410]—*Congregation of Marianites of the Holy Cross* (New Orleans, LA)—M.S.C.
[0470]—*Congregation of the Sisters of Charity of the Incarnate Word* (Houston, Texas)—C.C.V.I.
[1920]—*Congregation of the Sisters of the Holy Cross* (Notre Dame, IN)—C.S.C.
[]—*Cordi-Marian Sisters* (San Antonio, TX)—M.C.M.
[0760]—*Daughters of Charity of St. Vincent de Paul* (St. Louis, MO)—D.C.
[0850]—*Daughters of Mary Help of Christian* (San Antonio, TX)—F.M.A.
[]—*Daughters of St. Theresa of the Child Jesus* (Uganda)—D.S.T.
[1070-13]—*Dominican Sisters* (Adrian, MI)—O.P.
[1070-19]—*Dominican Sisters* (Houston, TX)—O.P.
[1070-03]—*Dominican Sisters* (Sinsinawa, WI)—O.P.
[1235]—*Franciscan Sisters Daughters of Mercy (Franciscanas Hijas de la Misericordia)* (U.S. delegation: Waco, TX)—F.H.M.
[1430]—*Franciscan Sisters of Our Lady of Perpetual Help* (St. Louis, MO)—O.S.F.
[2690]—*Missionary Catechists of Divine Providence* (San Antonio, TX)—M.C.D.P.
[]—*Missionary Ecumenical* (Rome, Italy)—M.E.
[2760]—*Missionary Sisters of the Immaculate Conception of the Mother of God* (Paterson, NJ)—S.M.I.C.
[3760]—*Order of St. Clare* (Brenham, TX)—O.S.C.
[3130]—*Our Lady of Victory Missionary Sisters* (Huntington, IN)—O.L.V.M.
[2970]—*School Sisters of Notre Dame* (St. Louis, MO; Dallas, TX)—S.S.N.D.
[]—*Secular Institute of Schoenstatt Sisters of Mary* (Southern Prov., Rockport, TX)—I.S.S.M.
[]—*Sisters for Christian Community* (San Antonio, TX)—S.F.C.C.
[1010]—*Sisters of Divine Providence* (San Antonio, TX)—C.D.P.
[2575]—*Sisters of Mercy of New Jersey* (Watchung, NJ)—R.S.M.
[3000]—*Sisters of Notre Dame de Namur* (Cincinnati, OH)—S.N.D.deN.
[1530]—*Sisters of St. Francis of the Congregation of Our Lady of Lourdes* (Sylvania, OH)—O.S.F.
[]—*Sisters of St. John Bosco* (Taylor, TX)—S.J.B.
[2150]—*Sisters, Servants of the Immaculate Heart of Mary* (Monroe, MI)—I.H.M.

NECROLOGY

(No Deaths)

Diocese of Baker

(Dioecesis Bakeriensis)

Most Reverend

ROBERT FRANCIS VASA

Bishop of Baker; ordained May 22, 1976; appointed November 19, 1999; consecrated and installed January 26, 2000.

Diocesan Pastoral Office: P.O. Box 5999, Bend, OR 97708. Tel: 541-388-4004; Fax: 541-388-2566.

Email: chancellor@dioceseofbaker.org

Most Reverend

THOMAS J. CONNOLLY, D.D., J.C.D.

Retired Bishop of Baker; ordained April 8, 1947; appointed May 4, 1971; consecrated June 30, 1971; retired January 2000. *Res.: P.O. Box 5999, Bend, OR 97708.*

ESTABLISHED JUNE 19, 1903.

Square Miles 66,826.

Comprises the counties of Baker, Crook, Deschutes, Gilliam, Grant, Harney, Hood River, Jefferson, Klamath, Lake, Malheur, Morrow, Sherman, Umatilla, Union, Wallowa, Wasco and Wheeler in the State of Oregon.

Legal Title: For legal titles of parishes and diocesan institutions, consult the Chancery Office.

STATISTICAL OVERVIEW

Personnel	
Bishop	1
Retired Bishops	1
Priests: Diocesan Active in Diocese	21
Priests: Diocesan Active Outside Diocese	1
Priests: Diocesan in Foreign Missions	1
Priests: Retired, Sick or Absent	15
Number of Diocesan Priests	38
Religious Priests in Diocese	4
Total Priests in Diocese	42
Extern Priests in Diocese	11
Permanent Deacons in Diocese	13
Total Brothers	1
Total Sisters	20
Parishes	
Parishes	36
With Resident Pastor:	
Resident Diocesan Priests	26
Resident Religious Priests	2
Without Resident Pastor:	
Administered by Priests	7
Administered by Religious Women	1
Missions	27
Professional Ministry Personnel:	
Sisters	6
Lay Ministers	15
Welfare	
Catholic Hospitals	5
Total Assisted	347,162
Homes for the Aged	4
Total Assisted	200
Day Care Centers	5
Total Assisted	260
Special Centers for Social Services	5
Total Assisted	36,500
Educational	
Diocesan Students in Other Seminaries	4
Total Seminarians	4
Elementary Schools, Diocesan and Parish	3
Total Students	654
Catechesis/Religious Education:	
High School Students	1,259
Elementary Students	2,203
Total Students under Catholic Instruction	4,120
Teachers in the Diocese:	
Lay Teachers	45
Vital Statistics	
Receptions into the Church:	
Infant Baptism Totals	927
Adult Baptism Totals	210
Received into Full Communion	99
First Communions	956
Confirmations	1,102
Marriages:	
Catholic	134
Interfaith	81
Total Marriages	215
Deaths	306
Total Catholic Population	36,420
Total Population	439,500

Former Bishops—Most Revs. CHARLES J. O'REILLY, D.D., ord. June 29, 1890; appt. June 24, 1903; consecrated Bishop of Baker City, Aug. 25, 1903; transferred to the See of Lincoln March 20, 1918; died Feb. 4, 1923; LEO F. FAHEY, D.D., ord. May 29, 1926; appt. Titular Bishop of Ipsus and Coadjutor "cum jure successionis" March 13, 1948; consecrated May 26, 1948; died March 31, 1950; JOSEPH F. MCGRATH, D.D., appt. assistant at the Pontifical Throne, Bishop of Baker City; ord. Dec. 21, 1895; appt. Dec. 21, 1918; consecrated March 25, 1919; died April 12, 1950; FRANCIS P. LEIPZIG, D.D. (Retired), ord. April 14, 1920; appt. Bishop of Baker July 18, 1950; consecrated Sept. 12, 1950; retired May 4, 1971; died Jan. 17, 1981; THOMAS J. CONNOLLY, D.D., J.C.D. (Retired), ord. April 8, 1947; appt. May 4, 1971; consecrated June 30, 1971; retired Nov. 19, 1999.

Vicar General—Rev. Msgr. MATTHEW M. CROTTY.

Vicar of Canonical Affairs—Rev. JAMES P. LOGAN.

Chancellor—Rev. JAMES P. LOGAN.

Diocesan Pastoral Office—P.O. Box 5999, Bend, 97708. Tel: 541-388-4004; Fax: 541-388-2566. *911 S.E. Armour, Bend, 97702.*

Receptionist and Secretary—VIRGINIA MOHR.

Diocesan Tribunal—Tel: 541-388-4010.

Judicial Vicar and Chief Judge—Rev. JAMES P. LOGAN.

Judge—Rev. Msgr. MATTHEW M. CROTTY.

Defender of the Bond and Promoter of Justice—Rev. LEO F. WECKERLE.

Coordinator and Notary—DOLORES FRIBERG.

Council of Priests and Diocesan Consultors—Most Rev. ROBERT F. VASA, Pres. Ex Officio; Revs. TODD UNGER, Chm.; CHARLES V. DREISBACH; JAMES A. RADLOFF; RICHARD O. FISCHER; RAYMOND HOPP; JAMES P. LOGAN; RONALD E. MAAG; Rev. Msgr. MATTHEW M. CROTTY.

Priestly Life and Ministry—Revs. RICHARD O. FISCHER; CHARLES U. DREISBACH; RAYMOND HOPP; JAMES P. LOGAN.

Deans—Central: Rev. LEO F. WECKERLE. Eastern: Rev. RAYMOND JARBOE. Northern: Rev. JOSEPH REINIG. Southern: Rev. CHARLES V. DREISBACH. Western: Rev. TODD UNGER.

Diocesan Offices and Directors

Board of Education—Most Rev. ROBERT F. VASA; Sr. MARY CATHERINE PERKINS, O.P., Supt.; Revs. TODD UNGER; MARTIN HAGGINS, O.F.M.Cap.; W. RAYMOND JARBOE, Principals of Schools and Representatives from each Parish School Board.

Building Committee—Rev. Msgr. MATTHEW M. CROTTY; Rev. RONALD E. MAAG.

Campus Ministry Apostolate—Rev. W. RAYMOND JARBOE, 829 S.W. Second Ave., Ontario, 97914. Tel: 541-889-8469.

Catholic Services—JEAN WHITMORE, 67016 End Rd., Summerville, 97876.

Church Property, Administration of—Most Rev. ROBERT F. VASA, Pres.; Rev. Msgr. MATTHEW M. CROTTY, Sec.; JOSEPH LA CASSE, Realtor.

DeSales Program of Adult Education—Direct Inquiries to: . Tel: 800-488-0488. *Direct Orders to: St. Anthony Messenger Press, 1615 Republic St., Cincinnati, OH 45210.* Fax: 513-241-1197.

Diocesan Attorney—Mr. GREGORY LYNCH.

Diocesan Development Office—JOHN SCHIEMER, P.O. Box 5999, Bend, 97708. Tel: 541-388-4004.

Diocesan Finance Minister—HOPE BURKE.

Diocesan Financial Board—Most Rev. ROBERT F. VASA; Rev. CHARLES V. DREISBACH; HOPE BURKE; JOHN SCHIEMER; RICHARD GRALL; JOSEPH LA CASSE; CRAIG MINNIS.

Diocesan Superintendent of Schools—Sr. MARY CATHERINE PERKINS, O.P., P.O. Box 5999, Bend, 97708. Tel: 541-385-1865.

Director of Campaign for Human Development—Rev. RONALD E. MAAG, St. Mary Church, P.O. Box 693, Hood River, 97031. Tel: 541-386-3373.

Director of Catholic Hospitals—Rev. TODD UNGER, St. Peter Church, P.O. Box 41, The Dalles, 97058. Tel: 541-296-2026.

Friends of the Catholic University of America—Rev. JAMES P. LOGAN, P.O. Box 5999, Bend, 97708. Tel: 541-388-4004.

Health and Retirement Board—Most Rev. ROBERT F. VASA, Pres.; Revs. TODD UNGER, Sec. & Treas.; CHARLES V. DREISBACH, Chm.; LEO F. WECKERLE; JAMES P. LOGAN; Deacon P. KENNETH MORTON.

Office of Worship and Spirituality—Rev. JAMES P. LOGAN, Pastoral Office, P.O. Box 5999, Bend, 97708. Tel: 541-388-4004.

Natural Family Planning—Mr. CARL ROSSETTI, Pro-Life Dir., P.O. Box 5999, Bend, 97708. Tel: 541-388-4004.

Director of Youth Ministry—Mr. NICHOLAS WAVERS, P.O. Box 5999, Bend, 97708. Tel: 541-388-3991.

Director of Religious Education—GARY GANDREAU, P.O. Box 5999, Bend, 97708. Tel: 541-388-3991; Sr. PEGGY GLYNN, O.P., P.O. Box J, Vale, 97918. Tel: 541-473-3906.

Director of Hispanic Ministry and Adult Faith Development—Deacon GUSTANO RUIZ, P.O. Box 5999, Bend, 97708. Tel: 541-388-4004.

Priests' Continuing Education Committee—Most Rev.

ROBERT F. VASA; Rev. RONALD E. MAAG.
R.C.I.A. Office—VACANT.
Diocesan Scout Director—TED YAROSH, 5160 S. Etna St., Klamath Falls, 97603. Tel: 541-882-4611.
Victim Assistance Coordinator—EVE MCFARLAND. Tel: 541-385-0557.
Vocations—Rev. RICHARD O. FISCHER, Holy Family Church, 685 N. Fairview, Burns, 97720. Tel: 541-573-2613.

CLERGY, PARISHES, MISSIONS AND PAROCHIAL SCHOOLS

BAKER CITY
(COUNTY OF BAKER)

CATHEDRAL OF ST. FRANCIS DE SALES (1871), [CEM] Rev. Robert C. Irwin, Rector.
Res.: 2235 First St., Baker, 97814. Tel: 541-523-4521; Fax: 541-523-8362.
Catechesis/Religious Program—Tamara Skidmore, D.R.E. Students 150.
Mission—St. Therese Halfway, Baker Co.
Mission—St. Joseph's Unity, Baker Co.
Mission—St. Anthony North Powder, Union Co.

OUTSIDE BAKER CITY

ARLINGTON, GILLIAM CO., ST. FRANCIS (1931), Rev. Desmond Chilagorom, Admin.
Mailing Address: P.O. Box 485, Condon, 97823. Tel: 541-384-5271; Fax: 541-384-5271.

BEND, DESCHUTES CO., ST. FRANCIS OF ASSISI (1904), Revs. Martin Haggins, O.F.M.Cap.; Michael Walsh, O.F.M.Cap.; Brian McKenna, O.F.M.Cap.; Sr. Patricia Rayburn, O.S.F., Pastoral Assoc.; Deacon Bob Walling.
Office—2450 N.E. 27th St., 97701. Tel: 541-382-3631; Fax: 541-385-8879.
School—(Grades PreK-8) Tel: 541-382-4701; Fax: 541-312-9111. Todd Jeffrey, Prin. Lay Teachers 25; Students 349.
School—Day Care, Tel: 541-389-3906. Students 40.
Catechesis/Religious Program—Duke Johnson, D.R.E. Students 525.
Diocese of Baker - El Programa de Ayuda—Tel: 541-382-4366.

BOARDMAN, MORROW CO., OUR LADY OF GUADALUPE, Rev. Rogation Urassa.
Mailing Address: P.O. Box 1277, 97818. Tel: 541-481-2024.

BURNS, HARNEY CO., HOLY FAMILY (1899), Rev. Stanislaus Strzyz.
Res.: 685 N. Fairview Ave., 97720. Tel: 541-573-2613.
Catechesis/Religious Program—620 N. Egan Ave., 97720. Mary Lemos, D.R.E. Students 85.
Mission—Our Lady of Loretto Drewsey, Harney Co.
Mission—St. Thomas Crane, Harney Co.
Mission—St. Charles Juntura, Malheur Co.

CHILOQUIN, KLAMATH CO., OUR LADY OF MT. CARMEL (1927), Rev. Richard O. Fischer.
Res.: 503 W. Chocktoot, P.O. Box 396, 97624. Tel: 541-783-2411.
Catechesis/Religious Program—Students 7.
Mission—St. James the Apostle Bly, Klamath Co.

CONDON, GILLIAM CO., ST. JOHN'S (1925), Rev. Desmond Chilagorom, Admin.
Res.: P.O. Box 485, 97823. Tel: 541-384-5271; Fax: 541-384-5271.
Mission—St. Catherine Fossil, Wheeler Co.

DUFUR, WASCO CO., ST. ALPHONSUS (1911), Rev. Joseph A. Kelbel, Admin.
Res.: P.O. Box 395, 97021. Tel: 541-467-2580.
Catechesis/Religious Program—Students 28.
Mission—St. Mary's Maupin, Wasco Co.

ELGIN, UNION CO., ST. MARY (1966), Attended by, Our Lady of the Valley, La Grande. Deacon Joseph Garlitz.
Res.: P.O. Box 97, 97827. Tel: 541-437-8101.
Catechesis/Religious Program—Vicki Correll, D.R.E. Students 13.

ENTERPRISE, WALLOWA CO., ST. KATHERINE'S (1923), Rev. Peter Fernando, Admin.
Res.: 301 E. Garfield St., P.O. Box 370, 97828. Tel: 541-426-3043.
Parish Office—Tel: 541-426-4008.
Catechesis/Religious Program—Students 35.
Mission—St. Pius X South Pine St., Wallowa, Wallowa Co. 97885. Tel: 541-886-3165.

HEPPNER, MORROW CO., ST. PATRICK'S (1887), Rev. Gerald W. Condon.
Res.: 525 Gale St., P.O. Box 633, 97836. Tel: 541-676-9462.
Catechesis/Religious Program—Mike Armato, D.R.E.; Kim Armato, D.R.E. Students 43.

HERMISTON, UMATILLA CO., OUR LADY OF ANGELS (1910), Revs. Joseph Reinig; Andrew Colvin; Deacon Jesus Esparaza; Kay Edwards, Parish Mgr.
Res.: 565 Hermiston Ave., 97838. Tel: 541-567-5812; Fax: 541-564-0933.
Catechesis/Religious Program—Tel: 541-567-3825. Dorothy Cooney, D.R.E.; Raquel Rodriguez, D.R.E. Students 259.

HOOD RIVER, HOOD RIVER CO., IMMACULATE CONCEPTION (1906), [CEM] Rev. Ronald E. Maaq; Deacons Lou DeSitter, Pastoral Assoc.; David Raj, Pastoral Assoc.
Res.: 1501 Belmont Ave., P.O. Box 693, 97031. Tel: 541-386-3373; Fax: 541-386-1451.
Catechesis/Religious Program—Tel: 541-387-6797. Maria Ramirez, D.R.E., (Spanish); Sharon Foss, D.R.E., (English). Students 290.

IONE, MORROW CO., ST. WILLIAM, Rev. Gerald W. Condon.
Mailing Address: P.O. Box 633, Heppner, 97836. Tel: 541-676-9462.
Church: 110 Main St., 97843.
Catechesis/Religious Program—Jeri Mc Elligott, D.R.E. Students 26.

JOHN DAY, GRANT CO., ST. ELIZABETH'S (1939), Rev. Julian Cassar (Malta).
Res.: 111 S.W. 2nd St., P.O. Box 189, 97845. Tel: 541-575-1459; Fax: 541-575-5548.
Catechesis/Religious Program—Tel: 541-575-0415. Mary Ann Vidourek, D.R.E. Students 57.
Mission—St. Anne Monument, Grant Co.
Mission—St. Charles Seneca, Grant Co.
Mission—St. Katherine Long Creek, Grant Co.

JORDAN VALLEY, MALHEUR CO., ST. BERNARD'S (1915), Rev. Cajetan Onwujiariri.
Res.: P.O. Box 186, 97910. Tel: 541-586-2266; Fax: 541-586-2448.
Catechesis/Religious Program—Lily Garrard, D.R.E. Students 8.
Mission—Holy Family Arock Rd., Arock, Malheur Co. 97902.

KLAMATH FALLS, KLAMATH CO.
1—ST. PIUS X (1957), [CEM] Revs. Richard O. Fischer; Pirmin Ngolle, O.S.B.; James Roy (ALX) (Retired).
Res.: 4880 Bristol Ave., 97603. Tel: 541-884-4242; Fax: 541-885-8724.
Catechesis/Religious Program—Tel: 541-882-7593; Fax: 541-882-7593. Rev. James Roy (ALX), D.R.E. (Retired). Students 141.
2—SACRED HEART (1904), Revs. Charles V. Dreisbach; Saul Alba Infante; Deacon P. Kenneth Morton, Pastoral Assoc.
Res.: 815 High St., 97601. Tel: 541-884-4566; Fax: 541-882-0472.
Catechesis/Religious Program—Tel: 541-882-4864. Vicki Bauer, D.R.E. Students 176.

LA GRANDE, UNION CO., OUR LADY OF THE VALLEY (1914),, (Under the title of the Immaculate Conception) Rev. Louis Henry Albrecht.
Parish Office—1002 L Ave., 97850. Tel: 541-963-7341; Fax: 541-963-7341.
Res.: 1101 4th St., 97850. Tel: 541-963-0006.
Catechesis/Religious Program—Tel: 541-963-0861; Fax: 541-963-0861. Charlene Storoe, D.R.E. Students 115.

LA PINE, DESCHUTES CO., HOLY REDEEMER (1983), Revs. James A. Radloff; Remigius Nwabichie.
Res.: 16137 Burgess Rd., P.O. Box 299, 97739. Tel: 541-536-3571; Fax: 541-536-5647.
Catechesis/Religious Program—Tel: 541-536-9213. Debbie Garrett, D.R.E. Students 20.
Mission—Our Lady of the Snows Gilchrist, Klamath Co.
Mission—Holy Family Christmas Valley, Lake Co.
Mission—Holy Trinity 18143 Cottonwood, Sun River, Deschutes Co. 97707.

LAKEVIEW, LAKE CO., ST. PATRICK'S (1912), Rev. Raymond Hopp.
Res.: 12 G St. N., P.O. Drawer 29, 97630. Tel: 541-947-2741; Fax: 541-947-2756.
Catechesis/Religious Program—185 S. G St.. Tel: 541-947-3875. Students 107.
Mission—St. Richard Adel, Lake Co.
Mission—St. Thomas Plush, Lake Co.
Mission—St. John the Apostle Paisley, Lake Co.

MADRAS, JEFFERSON CO., ST. PATRICK'S (1955), Rev. James Stephens.
Res.: 341 S.W. J St., P.O. Box 786, 97741. Tel: 541-475-2936; Fax: 541-475-2444.
Catechesis/Religious Program—Tel: 541-475-2444. Elouise Kirsch, D.R.E. Students 159.
Mission—Blessed Kateri Tekakwitha P.O. Box 764, Warm Springs, Jefferson Co. 97761. Tel: 541-553-1235. Sr. Pauline Igoe, O.P., Dir. Native American Affairs. (Indian Reservation)

MERRILL, KLAMATH CO., ST. AUGUSTINE (1939), Rev. Richard O. Fischer. In Res., Rev. Robert Van Sickler.
Res.: 905 E. Front St., P.O. Box 340, 97633. Tel: 541-798-5823.
Catechesis/Religious Program—Tel: 541-891-6907. Tammera Burt, D.R.E. Students 58.
Mission—St. Frances Cabrini Bonanza, Klamath Co. Tel: 541-545-6002.
Catechesis/Religious Program—Students 24.

MILTON FREEWATER, UMATILLA CO., ST. FRANCIS OF ASSISI (1940), Rev. William A. Kalin.
Res.: 925 Vining, 97862. Tel: 541-938-5436.
Catechesis/Religious Program—Students 210.
Mission—Sacred Heart 5th St. & College St., Athena, Umatilla Co. 97813.

NYSSA, MALHEUR CO., ST. BRIDGET OF KILDARE (1951), Rev. John Jasper.
Res.: 504 Locust, 97913-3235. Tel: 541-372-3133.
Catechesis/Religious Program—Students 98.
Mission—Our Lady of Guadalupe 2nd St. & Owyhee St., Adrian, Malheur Co.

ONTARIO, MALHEUR CO., BLESSED SACRAMENT (1911), Rev. W. Raymond Jarboe; Mrs. Frances A. Schaffer, Pastoral Assoc.
Res.: 829 S.W. Second Ave., 97914-2695. Tel: 541-889-8469; Fax: 541-889-8483.
School—Saint Peter, (Grades K-8), 98 S.W. Ninth St., 97914. Tel: 541-889-7363; Fax: 541-889-2852. Sr. Carol Higgins, S.N.J.M., Prin. Lay Teachers 7; Students 110.
Catechesis/Religious Program—Tel: 541-889-8404. Tim Cables, D.R.E. Students 74.

PENDLETON, UMATILLA CO.
1—ST. ANDREW'S INDIAN MISSION (1847), [CEM] Rev. Michael J. Fitzpatrick, S.J.
Res.: 48022 St. Andrews Rd., 97801. Tel: 541-276-6155; Fax: 541-276-0767.
Catechesis/Religious Program—Tel: 541-276-0767. Lillian Moses, D.R.E. Students 28.
2—ST. MARY'S (1902), [CEM] Rev. Gregory Okorobia (Nigeria); Deacons Martin Omar Tores; Daniel Martinez.
Res.: 800 S.E. Court Ave., 97801. Tel: 541-276-3615; Fax: 541-276-7484.
Catechesis/Religious Program—Tel: 541-276-6163. Mrs. Darlene Ledbetter, D.R.E. Students 225.

PILOT ROCK, UMATILLA CO., ST. HELEN (1930), Attended by, St. Mary's, Pendleton.
Res.: 740 S.W. Birch, P.O. Box V, 97868. Tel: 541-443-3151; 541-276-3615.
Catechesis/Religious Program—Students 27.

PRINEVILLE, CROOK CO., ST. JOSEPH'S (1943), Rev. Robert Greiner.
Res.: 150 E. First, P.O. Box 1315, 97754. Tel: 541-447-6475; Fax: 541-416-9141.
Catechesis/Religious Program—200 E. First St., P.O. Box 721, 97754. Tel: 541-447-1227; 541-389-0888. Jennie Bachman, D.R.E. Students 70.

REDMOND, DESCHUTES CO., ST. THOMAS (1941), Rev. Leo F. Weckerle.
Res.: 526 S. 12th, P.O. Box 247, 97756. Tel: 541-923-3390; Fax: 541-548-6630.
Catechesis/Religious Program—535 S. 11th St., 97756. Tel: 541-923-0597. Mary Lehnertz, D.R.E. Students 210.

SISTERS, DESCHUTES CO., ST. EDWARD (1984), Rev. James P. Logan.
Res.: 123 Trinity Way, P.O. Box 489, 97759-0489. Tel: 541-549-0751 (Rectory); 541-549-9391 (Office); Fax: 541-549-1057.
Catechesis/Religious Program—Marcia Rietmann, D.R.E. Students 49.

THE DALLES, WASCO CO., ST. PETER'S (1848), [CEM] Rev. Todd Unger. In Res., Rev. Joseph A. Kelbel.
Res.: 1222 W. 10th St., P.O. Box 41, 97058. Tel: 541-296-2026; Fax: 541-296-5835.
School—St. Mary, (Grades PreK-8), 1112 Cherry Heights Rd.. Tel: 541-296-6004; Fax: 541-296-7858. Roger Richmond, Prin. Lay Teachers 13; Students 195.
Catechesis/Religious Program—1111 W. 10th, P.O. Box 41, 97058. Students 50.

UNION, UNION CO., SACRED HEART (1905), Attended by, Our Lady of the Valley, La Grande.
Church: 340 S. 10th St., P.O. Box 473, 97883. Tel: 541-562-6285.
Catechesis/Religious Program—Tel: 541-562-5486. Susan Sheehy, D.R.E. Students 29.

VALE, MALHEUR CO., ST. PATRICK'S (1946), Sr. Peggy Glynn, O.P., Parish Coord.
Res.: P.O. Box J, 97918. Tel: 541-473-3906; Fax: 541-473-2687.
Catechesis/Religious Program—Tel: 541-473-3848. Susan Seals, D.R.E. Students 76.

WASCO, SHERMAN CO., ST. MARY'S (1954), Rev. Joseph A. Kelbel, Admin.
Res.: 807 Barnett St., P.O. Box 14, 97065. Tel: 541-442-5496.
Catechesis/Religious Program—Molly Belshe, D.R.E. Students 33.
Mission—St. Mary's Antelope, Wasco Co.
Mission—St. John the Baptist Grass Valley, Sherman Co.

Special Assignment:
Rev. Msgr.—
Crotty, Matthew M., Vicar Gen., 1011 S.E. 15th, #31, 97702.

On Duty Outside the Diocese:
Revs.—
Hickie, J. Noel, Sacred Heart General Hospital, 1305 Willagillespie Rd., Eugene, 97401.
Kiely, Cornelius, Iglesia La Immaculada Concepcion, Puerto Lopez, Manabi, Ecuador.

Retired:
Rev. Msgrs.—
Beard, Raymond, P.O. Box 57, Athena, 97813.
Keating, Bernard A., P.O. Box 861, Redmond, 97756.
Revs.—
Bower, Lawrence C., 215 Woodward Blvd., Summerville, SC 29483. Tel: 843-815-1285
Collins, Timothy, Pendleton House, Avondale House, Kilrush Rd., Ennis, Co. Clare Ireland.
Conway, Richard J., 950 Pomona, #166, The Dalles, 97058.
Cribbin, Austin J., 220 Newcastle Rd., Klamath Falls, 97601.
Fisher, A. J., 1200 W. Dimond #14105, Anchorage, AK 99515.
Gillen, C. H., Milton-Freewater.
Homes, Dennis, Rainbow Retirement Home, 20-3rd St. N., Great Falls, MT 59401. Tel: 406-452-1994
Quigley, Martin J., 3564 E. 2nd, Sp. 72, The Dalles, 97058.
Reeves, Joseph, 15612 N.W. Clubhouse Dr., Portland, 97729. Tel: 503-690-3643
Scanlan, Thomas R., 11055 S.W. Summerfield Dr., #7, Tigard, 97224.

INSTITUTIONS LOCATED IN THE DIOCESE

[A] GENERAL HOSPITALS

BAKER CITY. *St. Elizabeth Health Services, Inc.*, 3325 Pocahontas Rd., 97814. Tel: 541-523-6461 (Hospital); 541-523-4452 (Nursing Care); Fax: 541-523-8151. Email: georgewinn@chiwest.com. George Winn, CEO. Bed Capacity 36; Nursing Home Beds 120; Patients Assisted Annually 26,027; Nursing Home 169.

BEND. *St. Charles Medical Center*, 2500 N.E. Neff Rd., 97701. Tel: 541-382-4321; Fax: 541-388-7723. Web: www.scmc.org. Mr. Jim Lussier, Pres , CEO; Karon Hack, D.Min., Pastoral Care Mgr. Bed Capacity 181; Total Staff 1,800; Patients Assisted Annually 160,500.

HOOD RIVER. *Providence Hood River Memorial Hospital*, 811 13th St., 97031. Tel: 541-386-3911; Fax: 541-387-6462. Email: gyoung@providence.org. Web: www.providence.org. Larry Bowe, CEO. Total Staff 388; Bed Capacity 32; Patients Assisted Annually 69,901.

ONTARIO. *Holy Rosary Medical Center*, 351 S.W. Ninth St., 97914. Tel: 541-881-7000; Fax: 541-881-7184. Web: holyrosary-ontario.org. Mr. Mark Dalley, Pres. & CEO; Mr. J. Michael Hamnigan, Bd. Chm.; Mr. Luke Larson, Vice Pres. Mission & Pastoral Care. Bed Capacity 74; Total Staff 515; Patients Assisted Annually 69,580.

PENDLETON. *St. Anthony Hospital*, 1601 S.E. Court Ave., 97801. Tel: 541-276-5121; Fax: 541-278-3227. Email: vonnismonton@chiwest.com. Web: www.sahpendleton.org. Jeffrey Drop, Pres. Sisters of St. Francis of Philadelphia 4; Bed Capacity 49; Patients Assisted Annually 26,431.

[B] MONASTERIES AND RESIDENCES FOR PRIESTS AND BROTHERS

LA PINE. *Monastery of Annunciation Hermitage*, 146640 Hwy. 97, 97739-9127. Tel: 541-433-2903; Fax: 928-441-2051. Email: hermit@copper.net. Bro. Monk Arsenius.

[C] MISCELLANEOUS

BEND. *Saint Vincent de Paul Society - District Council of Central Oregon*, P.O. Box 1011, 97709. Tel: 541-389-5117; Fax: 541-389-5093. Email: stvincent@coinet.com. George Neal, Pres. Bd. of Directors.
Bend Social Services Conference, 950 S.E. 3rd St.. Tel: 541-389-6643; Fax: 541-389-5093.
Thrift Store, 401 N.E. 2nd, 97701. Tel: 541-330-5023; Fax: 541-389-1455.
Thrift Store 950 S.E. 3rd St., 97702. Tel: 541-389-9547.

HERMISTON. *Hermiston Our Lady of Angels Conference of St. Vincent de Paul*, 565 W. Hermiston Ave., 97838. Tel: 541-567-5812; Fax: 541-564-0933.

HOOD RIVER. *Dethman Manor*, 1205 Moncello St., 97031. Tel: 541-386-5111; Fax: 541-387-6356.
Providence Brookside Manor, 1550 Brookside Dr., 97031. Tel: 541-387-6370; Fax: 541-387-8272.
Providence Down Manor, 1950 Sterling Pl., 97031. Tel: 541-386-5115; Fax: 541-386-2456.
Providence Hood River Memorial Hospital Foundation, 13th & May St., P.O. Box 149, 97031. Tel: 541-387-6474; Fax: 541-387-6462.

LA PINE. *Central Oregon Senior Living Communities, Inc. (The Redeemer Lodge)*, P.O. Box 1829, 97739. Tel: 541-536-8702; Fax: 541-536-1745. Web: www.centraloregonseniorliving.org. Rev. James A. Radloff, Board Pres. & Contact Person.
La Pine Conference, P.O. Box 1008, 97739. Tel: 541-536-1956; Fax: 541-536-6135. Email: lsvdp@uci.net. Arlene Mura, Pres.

PRINEVILLE. *Saint Vincent de Paul Society - Prineville Conference*, 150 E. 1st St., 97754. Tel: 541-447-6475. John Solitz, Pres.

REDMOND. *Saint Vincent de Paul Society - Redmond Conference*, 1114 S.W. Evergreen, 97756. Tel: 541-923-5264. Robert Haack, Pres.
Thrift Store, 2014 S. Hwy. 97, 97756. Tel: 541-548-3055.

RICHLAND. **North American Conference of Separated & Divorced Catholics*, P.O. Box 360, 97870. Tel: 541-893-6089; Fax: 541-893-6089. Email: nacsdc@pinetel.com. Web: www.NACSDC.org. Krista Dennis, Office Mgr., Contact for future mailings.

THE DALLES. *Saint Vincent de Paul Society - The Dalles Conference*, 505 W. 9th St., 97058. Tel: 541-298-7837; Fax: 541-298-7940. Email: svdptd@gorge.net. Deacon David Luther, Chm.

RELIGIOUS INSTITUTES OF MEN REPRESENTED IN THE DIOCESE

For further details refer to the corresponding bracketed number in the Religious Institutes of Men or Women section.

[0470]—*The Capuchin Friars*—O.F.M.Cap.
[0690]—*Jesuit Fathers and Brothers* (California, Oregon Provs.)—S.J.

RELIGIOUS INSTITUTES OF WOMEN REPRESENTED IN THE DIOCESE

[1070-25]—*Dominican Sisters of Kenosha, WI*—O.P.
[1070-03]—*Dominican Sisters of Sinsinawa, WI*—O.P.
[1070-20]—*Dominican Sisters of St. Thomas Aquinas*—O.P.
[2470]—*Maryknoll Sisters of St. Dominic*—M.M.
[1630]—*Sisters of St. Francis of Penance and Christian Charity*—O.S.F.
[1650]—*Sisters of St. Francis of Philadelphia*—O.S.F.
[3960]—*Sisters of St. Mary of Oregon*—S.S.M.O.
[1990]—*Sisters of the Holy Names of Jesus and Mary*—S.N.J.M.
[4060]—*Society of the Holy Child Jesus*—S.H.C.J.

NECROLOGY

(No Deaths)

Archdiocese of Baltimore

(Archidioecesis Baltimorensis)

His Eminence

WILLIAM CARDINAL KEELER, D.D., J.C.D.

Archbishop of Baltimore; ordained July 17, 1955; appointed Titular Bishop of Ulcinium and Auxiliary Bishop of Harrisburg July 24, 1979; ordained Bishop September 21, 1979; appointed Bishop of Harrisburg November 10, 1983; installed January 4, 1984; appointed Archbishop of Baltimore April 6, 1989; installed as Fourteenth Archbishop of Baltimore May 23, 1989; created Cardinal Priest November 26, 1994. *Office: 320 Cathedral St., Baltimore, MD 21201.* Tel: 410-547-5437.

Most Reverend

WILLIAM DONALD BORDERS, D.D.

Retired Archbishop of Baltimore; ordained May 18, 1940; appointed Bishop of Orlando May 2, 1968; consecrated June 14, 1968; appointed Archbishop of Baltimore March 25, 1974; installed June 26, 1974; retired April 6, 1989. *Office: 320 Cathedral St., Baltimore, MD 21201.* Tel: 410-547-5439.

Most Reverend

WILLIAM C. NEWMAN, D.D., V.G.

Retired Auxiliary Bishop of Baltimore; ordained May 29, 1954; appointed Auxiliary Bishop of Baltimore and Titular Bishop of Numluli May 25, 1984; installed Bishop July 2, 1984; retired August 28, 2003. *Office: 320 Cathedral St., Baltimore, MD 21201.* Tel: 410-547-5438. *Res.: 5300 N. Charles St., Baltimore, MD 21201.*

Chancery Office: 320 Cathedral St., Baltimore, MD 21201. Tel: 410-547-5446; Fax: 410-727-8234.

Web: www.archbalt.org

Email: chancery@archbalt.org

Most Reverend

GORDON D. BENNETT, S.J., D.D., V.G.

Auxiliary Bishop of Baltimore; ordained June 14, 1975; appointed Auxiliary Bishop of Baltimore and Titular Bishop of Nesqually December 23, 1997; ordained Bishop March 3, 1998. *Office: 320 Cathedral St., Baltimore, MD 21201.* Tel: 410-547-5453.

Most Reverend

WILLIAM FRANCIS MALOOLY

Auxiliary Bishop of Baltimore; ordained May 7, 1970; appointed Auxiliary Bishop of Baltimore and Titular Bishop of Flumenzer December 12, 2000; installed March 1, 2001.

Square Miles 4,801.

Established a Diocese November 6, 1789; Established an Archdiocese April 8, 1808.

Comprises the City of Baltimore and Allegany, Anne Arundel, Baltimore, Carroll, Frederick, Garrett, Harford, Howard and Washington Counties.

By a Decree of the Sacred Congregation of the Propaganda, July 19, 1858, approved by His Holiness, Pius IX, July 25, 1858, "Prerogative of Place" was conferred on the Archdiocese of Baltimore. By the explicit words of said decree of the Holy See, the Archbishop of Baltimore takes precedence over all Archbishops of the United States (not Cardinals) in Councils, gatherings and meetings of whatever kind of the Hierarchy (in concillis, coetibus et comitiis quibuscumque) regardless of the seniority of other Archbishops in promotion or ordination. Decree signed by Cardinal Barnabo, August 15, 1858.

Legal Title: For legal titles of parishes and archdiocesan institutions, consult the Chancery Office.

STATISTICAL OVERVIEW

Personnel	
Cardinals	1
Retired Archbishops	1
Auxiliary Bishops	2
Retired Bishops	1
Priests: Diocesan Active in Diocese	207
Priests: Diocesan Active Outside Diocese	15
Priests: Diocesan in Foreign Missions	1
Priests: Retired, Sick or Absent	56
Number of Diocesan Priests	279
Religious Priests in Diocese	265
Total Priests in Diocese	544
Extern Priests in Diocese	49
Ordinations:	
Diocesan Priests	7
Religious Priests	3
Transitional Deacons	3
Permanent Deacons	18
Permanent Deacons in Diocese	183
Total Brothers	40
Total Sisters	1,088
Parishes	
Parishes	153
With Resident Pastor:	
Resident Diocesan Priests	102
Resident Religious Priests	26
Without Resident Pastor:	
Administered by Priests	16
Administered by Deacons	3
Administered by Religious Women	3
Administered by Lay People	3
Administered by Pastoral Teams, etc.	1
Missions	8
Closed Parishes	1
Professional Ministry Personnel:	
Brothers	5
Sisters	57
Lay Ministers	250
Welfare	
Catholic Hospitals	6
Total Assisted	1,189,696
Health Care Centers	4
Total Assisted	6,121
Homes for the Aged	23
Total Assisted	1,781
Residential Care of Children	7
Total Assisted	849
Day Care Centers	7
Total Assisted	1,872
Specialized Homes	6
Total Assisted	209
Special Centers for Social Services	32
Total Assisted	822,315
Residential Care of Disabled	1
Total Assisted	220
Educational	
Seminaries, Diocesan	2
Students from This Diocese	23
Students from Other Diocese	192
Diocesan Students in Other Seminaries	4
Total Seminarians	27
Colleges and Universities	4
Total Students	11,382
High Schools, Diocesan and Parish	9
Total Students	4,221
High Schools, Private	13
Total Students	7,272
Elementary Schools, Diocesan and Parish	65
Total Students	23,227
Elementary Schools, Private	7
Total Students	2,252
Non-residential Schools for the Disabled	1
Total Students	103
Catechesis/Religious Education:	
High School Students	4,298
Elementary Students	31,454
Total Students under Catholic Instruction	84,236
Teachers in the Diocese:	
Priests	40
Brothers	12
Sisters	74
Lay Teachers	3,005
Vital Statistics	
Receptions into the Church:	
Infant Baptism Totals	6,826
Adult Baptism Totals	524
Received into Full Communion	894
First Communions	6,703
Confirmations	5,419
Marriages:	
Catholic	1,888
Interfaith	719
Total Marriages	2,607
Deaths	4,804
Total Catholic Population	506,587
Total Population	3,006,607

Former Bishops—Most Revs. JOHN CARROLL, D.D., cons. Aug. 15, 1790; Archbishop, April 8, 1808; died Dec. 3, 1815; LEONARD NEALE, D.D., consecrated Coadjutor, Dec. 7, 1800; acceded to the Dec. 3, 1815; died June 18, 1817; AMBROSE MARECHAL, S.S., D.D., consecrated Dec. 14, 1817; died Jan. 29, 1828; JAMES WHITFIELD, D.D., consecrated May 25, 1828; died Oct. 19, 1834; SAMUEL ECCLESTON, S.S., D.D., consecrated Sept. 14, 1834; died April 22, 1851; FRANCIS PATRICK KENRICK, D.D., consecrated June 6, 1830; Coadjutor Bishop of Philadelphia; promoted to Aug. 19, 1851;; died July 8, 1863; MARTIN JOHN SPALDING, D.D., consecrated Sept. 10, 1848; Coadjutor Bishop of Louisville; promoted to May 6, 1864;; died Feb. 7, 1872; JAMES ROOSEVELT BAYLEY, D.D., consecrated Oct. 30, 1853; Bishop of Newark; promoted to July 30, 1872; died Oct. 3, 1877; His Eminence JAMES CARDINAL GIBBONS, consecrated Vicar Apostolic of North Carolina, Aug. 16, 1868; transferred to See of Richmond, July 30, 1872; promoted to See of Baltimore, Oct. 3, 1877;; created Cardinal Priest of S. Maria in Trastevere, June 7, 1886; died March 24, 1921; Most Revs. MICHAEL J. CURLEY, D.D., consecrated Bishop of St. Augustine, June 30, 1914; promoted to Aug. 10, 1921; died May 16, 1947; FRANCIS P. KEOUGH, D.D., consecrated Bishop of Providence, May 22, 1934; promoted to Nov. 29, 1947;; died Dec. 8, 1961; His Eminence LAWRENCE CARDINAL SHEHAN (Retired), consecrated Auxiliary Bishop of Baltimore, Dec. 12, 1945; transferred to Diocese of Bridgeport, Aug. 25, 1953; appt. Coadjutor Archbishop of Baltimore, July 10, 1961; acceded to the Dec. 8, 1961; created Cardinal Priest of S. Clemente, Feb. 22, 1965; retired March 25, 1974; died Aug. 26, 1984; Most Rev. WILLIAM DONALD BORDERS, D.D. (Retired), appt. Bishop of Orlando, May 2, 1968; consecrated June 14, 1968; promoted to March 25, 1974; installed June 26, 1974; retired April 6, 1989.

Vicars General—Most Revs. WILLIAM C. NEWMAN, D.D., V.G. (Retired); GORDON D. BENNETT, S.J., D.D., V.G.; WILLIAM FRANCIS MALOOLY, V.G.

Office of the Former Archbishop—Most Rev. WILLIAM

D. BORDERS, 320 Cathedral St., Baltimore, 21201. Tel: 410-547-5439.

Chancery Office—320 Cathedral St., Baltimore, 21201. Tel: 410-547-5446; Fax: 410-727-8234. Office Hours: Mon.-Fri. 9-5; Closed holidays

Chancellor—Rev. Msgr. RICHARD W. WOY. Tel: 410-547-5435.

Vice Chancellor—Rev. Msgr. JEREMIAH F. KENNEY.

Canonical Adviser, Office of—Rev. JAMES J. CONN, S.J., Canonical & Theological Consultant to the Archbishop. Tel: 410-547-5435.

Consultors—Most Revs. WILLIAM C. NEWMAN, D.D., V.G. (Retired); GORDON D. BENNETT, S.J., D.D., V.G.; WILLIAM FRANCIS MALOOLY, V.G.; Rev. Msgrs. PAUL G. COOK; ROBERT ARMSTRONG; JAMES O. MCGOVERN; GEORGE MOELLER; G. MICHAEL SCHLEUPNER; ARTHUR VALENZANO; RICHARD WOY; Revs. PAUL A. BYRNES; RICHARD E. CRAMBLITT; JOHN DIETZENBACH; MITCHELL T. ROZANSKI.

Eastern Vicar, Office of the—VACANT, Vicar; Sr. CONSTANCE GILDER, S.S.J., Asst. to Eastern Vicar; Deacon PAUL MANN, Coord. Planning & Council Svcs., 320 Cathedral St., Baltimore, 21201. Tel: 410-547-5438; Fax: 410-727-5432. Email: evicar@archbalt.org.

Interdiocesan Tribunal of Appeals of the Province of Baltimore—320 Cathedral St., Baltimore, 21201. Tel: 410-547-5534.

Judicial Vicar—Rev. Msgr. JEREMIAH F. KENNEY.

Interdiocesan Judges—Rev. Msgrs. JOHN O. BARRES; JOHN P. HANNAN; CHARLES A. KELLY; JOSEPH REBMAN; THOMAS F. SHREVE, V.G., J.C.L.; Revs. FREDERICK P. ANNIE; FREDERICK J. FEUSAHRENS; GEORGE J. GRIFFIN; CHRISTIAN J. HAYDINGER; MARK R. LANE; JOHN S. LEDFORD; MARTIN MCGUILL; CHRISTOPHER P. MOORE; WILLIAM J. NOLTE JR.; EUGENE S. OSTROWSKI; RICHARD A. REISSMANN; JOHN E. RIDGELL; WILLIAM SCHARDT; RICHARD W. SHODA; EUGENE J. WEBER; Deacon ROBERT GRAHAM.

Defenders of the Bond—Rt. Rev. BENEDICT MCDERMOTT, O.S.B.; Revs. CHARLES DILLINGHAM; JAMES F. KAUFFMAN; RICHARD T. MOONEY; GILBERT J. SEITZ; GERALD T. WEYMES.

Notaries—Mrs. RENA BOWMAN; Revs. EDWARD C. HATHAWAY; MICHAEL G. TAYLOR; Ms. JOANNE D'SURNEY; JOANN KUBASKO; BARBARA A. LEE; BERTHA GOODMAN.

Metropolitan Tribunal—320 Cathedral St., Baltimore, 21201. Tel: 410-547-5533.

Judicial Vicar—Rev. Msgr. G. MICHAEL SCHLEUPNER.

Adjutant Judicial Vicar—Rev. WILLIAM A. COLLINS.

Judges—Revs. JAMES H. BRENNAN, S.S.; MICHAEL J. CARRION; JOHN B. WARD, J.C.L., J.D.; Deacon RAY BRITT.

Defenders of the Bond—Rev. Msgr. ROBERT A. ARMSTRONG; Rev. ALBAN HARMON, C.P., F.N.

Promoter of Justice—Rev. JAMES CONN, S.J.

Advocates and Procurators—Rev. Msgr. RICHARD W. WOY; Revs. BERNARD BAK; MICHAEL J. CALLAGHAN; PATRICK M. CARRION; E. JOSEPH COTE; RICHARD E. CRAMBLITT; JOHN A. ECKARD; MARTIN E. FEILD; WILLIAM FOLEY; JAMES HANNON; ROBERT HARTNETT; C. LOU MARTIN; EDWARD MILLER; KEVIN MUELLER; G. EUGENE NICKOL; MITCHELL ROZANSKI; C. DOUG KENNEY; Deacons JOHN ABELL; KEVIN BAGLEY; ALPHONSE C. BANKARD; ALBERT COSLA; NICHOLAS FEURER; GARY FULMER; HERMAN GRABENSTEIN; JOHN MCKENNA; ROBERT LEHR; DONALD MACKNEW; JOHN MANLEY; HUGH H. MILLS JR.; DONALD MURRAY; WILLIAM NAIRN; STANLEY G. PIET; GERALD RAIBLE; FRANK RONGIONE; WALTER SHIPLEY; EDWARD SULLIVAN; FREDDY WENDT; Sisters KATHERINE BELL, R.S.M.; REGINA BURGAN, S.S.N.D.; JUDITH CIANFROGNA S.S.J.; AGNESINE CONNORS, S.S.N.D.; MARIETTA CULHANE, O.S.F.; CAROL CZYZEWSKI, F.S.S.J.; ANGELA DEFONTES, O.S.F.; FRANCES DEMARCO, R.S.M.; JOAN BASTRESS, I.H.M.; SUSAN ENGEL, M.H.S.H.; JOYCE HOLDEN, M.H.S.H.; ELIZABETH KANE, O.S.F.; PATRICIA MCALPIN, O.S.F.; MARTINA MARIE WAGNER, S.S.N.D.; JOAN MINELLA, S.S.N.D.; Ms. PATRICIA BARBERNITZ; Mr. ANDREW BAUER; Mr. STEPHEN R. BEARD; Ms. JACQUELYN BENEDICT; Mrs. ANNE BUENING; Ms. MARY JOYCE BLESSING; Mr. LOUIS CASHIOLA; Mr. JOHN W. FISHER; Mr. JAMES MCSHERRY; Mr. ROBERT NICHOLSON; Mr. GERARD NOVAK; Mr. JOHN SAUER; Mr. JOHN KUTZ.

Notaries—Mrs. SUSAN NIVENS; Mrs. PATRICIA WALLS; Mrs. CLARA JULIAO.

Urban Vicar, Office of the—Most Rev. GORDON D. BENNETT, S.J., D.D., V.G.; Deacon PAUL WEBER, Asst. to Urban Vicar. Tel: 410-547-5486; KATHERINE SWANSON, Coord. Planning & Council Svcs., 320 Cathedral St., Baltimore, 21201. Tel: 410-547-5452; Fax: 410-727-5432.

Cardinal's Delegate for Canonical Affairs—Rev. Msgr. JEREMIAH F. KENNEY. Tel: 410-547-5551; Fax: 410-576-6932.

Western Vicar, Office of the—Most Rev. WILLIAM FRANCIS MALOOLY, V.G., 320 Cathedral St., Baltimore, 21201. Tel: 410-547-5447; Fax: 410-727-5432; Deacon CHARLES H. HIEBLER JR., Coord. Planning & Council Svcs. Tel: 410-547-5456.

Archdiocesan Offices and Directors

African American Ministries, Archdiocesan Office of—THERESE WILSON FAVORS, Dir., 320 Cathedral St., Baltimore, 21201. Tel: 410-625-8472; Fax: 410-727-5432.

Apostleship of Prayer—Rev. JAMES A. CASCIOTTI, S.J., Dir., 5704 Roland Ave., Baltimore, 21210-1399. Tel: 410-322-1412. Email: mdsjs@charm.net.

Archdiocesan Directory—PATTI MEDINGER Project Mgr., 320 Cathedral St., Baltimore, 21201. Tel: 410-547-5224 Official directory of the Archdiocese of Baltimore. Published annually by The Catholic Review. $35 per copy.

Archdiocesan Pastoral Council— (See Pastoral Council Archdiocesan)

Archives-Archivist—TRICIA PYNE, 5400 Roland Ave., Baltimore, 21210. Tel: 410-864-4074 (By appointment). Email: tpyne@stmarys.edu.

Boy Scouts— (See Catholic Youth Activities)

Campaign For Human Development, Archdiocese of Baltimore, Inc.—Rev. Msgr. WILLIAM F. BURKE, Dir., 320 Cathedral St., Baltimore, 21201. Tel: 410-235-5136; 410-547-5446.

Campus Ministry (Newman Apostolate)—Rev. ROBERT E. ALBRIGHT, Dir., 7909 York Rd., Baltimore, 21204. Tel: 410-828-0622; Fax: 410-828-4325.

The Cathedral Foundation, Inc.—His Eminence WILLIAM H. KEELER, D.D., J.C.D., Pres.; JAMES CURRAN, Chm. & Vice Pres., P.O. Box 777, Baltimore, 21203. Tel: 443-524-3150 Publishers of The Catholic Review, Official Archdiocesan Directory, Catholic International and Cathedral Foundation Press.

Catholic Center Operations, Div. of—NOLAN MCCOY, Facilities Mgr., 320 Cathedral St., Baltimore, 21201. Tel: 410-547-5312; Fax: 410-783-5993.

Catholic Charities Fund, Inc.—320 Cathedral St., Baltimore, 21201.

Catholic Education Ministries, Department of—Dr. RONALD J. VALENTI, Exec. Dir., 320 Cathedral St., Baltimore, 21201. Tel: 410-547-5383; Fax: 410-547-5566. Email: gurie@archbalt.org.

Catholic Relief Services—MARY D'AMBROGI, Archdiocesan Dir., 320 Cathedral St., Baltimore, 21201. Tel: 410-547-5548.

"The Catholic Review"—His Eminence WILLIAM H. KEELER, D.D., J.C.D., Publisher; DANIEL L. MEDINGER, Assoc. Publisher & Editor JOSEPH KIRK RYAN Mng. Editor, P.O. Box 777, Baltimore, 21203. Tel: 443-524-3150 Newspaper of the Archdiocese of Baltimore. Established 1913. Published every Thursday by the Cathedral Foundation, Inc.

Catholic Schools, Division of—Dr. RONALD J. VALENTI, Supt., Catholic Center, 320 Cathedral St., Baltimore, 21201. Tel: 410-547-5391; Fax: 410-547-5566. Email: schools@archbalt.org.

Catholic Students Mission Crusade— See Propagation of the Faith

New Cathedral Cemetery—4300 Old Frederick Rd., Baltimore, 21229. Tel: 410-566-7770; Fax: 410-566-0709.

Censor Librorum—VACANT, 363 Homeland Southway, Apt. 1-A, Baltimore, 21212. Tel: 410-433-6517.

Clergy Personnel, Division of—Revs. PATRICK M. CARRION, Div. Dir. Tel: 410-547-5428 Email: pcarrion@archbalt.org; JAY F. O'CONNOR, Assoc. Dir. Tel: 410-547-5558. Email: joconnor@archbalt.org; Mrs. CAROL PURWIN, Admin. Asst. Tel: 410-547-5427. Email: cpurwin@archbalt.org; 320 Cathedral St., Rm. 620, Baltimore, 21201.

Commission for Ecumenical and Inter-Religious Affairs—Rev. CHARLES J. TILLEY, S.J., Chm., 10431 Twin Rivers Rd., Columbia, 21044. Tel: 410-964-1425; Fax: 410-730-9253.

Deacon Personnel Board—Deacons JOHN LANGMEAD, Chm.; JOSEPH KRYSIAK, Vice Chm.; JOHN ABELL; JOHN BOSCOE; WILLIAM ALBAUGH; LAWRENCE TEIXEIRA; JOHN COSTER; JOHN GRAMLING; RUSS MATTHEWS; RON THOMPSON; Mrs. KAY FEE; Mrs. CAROL PETROSINO. Email: deacons@archbalt.org.

Facilities Management, Division of—LOUIS F. BAIRD, Dir. Facilities Planning; NOLAN MCCOY, Div. Dir. & Dir. Facilities Management; MATTHEW REGAN, Project Mgr.; DOUG JOHNSON, Project Mgr.; MYRTLE BUCHANAN, Office Mgr.; ROBERT CLANCY, Facilities Specialist III, 320 Cathedral St., Baltimore, 21201. Tel: 410-547-5366; Fax: 410-837-2932; NELSON PALMER, Facilities Specialist III.

Financial Administration, Board of—His Eminence WILLIAM CARDINAL KEELER, D.D., J.C.D., Chm.; MICHAEL BATZA, Vice Chm.; JOSEPH A. SPADARO, C.P.A., 320 Cathedral St., Baltimore, 21201.

Fiscal Services, Division of—JOHN M. MATERA, C.P.A., Controller, 320 Cathedral St., Baltimore, 21201. Tel: 410-547-5300; Fax: 410-332-8233. Email: fiscal@archbalt.org.

Fund Development, Department of—THOMAS J. SONNI, Exec. Dir. Devel.; GEORGE LEITNER, Dir. Devel. - Western Vicariate; JAMES EDWARDS, Dir. Devel. - Eastern Vicariate; ROBERT BROWN, Dir. Devel. - Urban Vicariate; JENNIFER HAMMOND, Dir. Major Gifts; PATRICIA RILEY, Mktg. & Communications Specialist; MATTHEW ANTHONY, Devel. Assoc. Partners In Excellence; ISABELLE GERBER, Exec. Asst.; ROSE NEWMAN, Devel. Asst.; ANDREA LUCHINI, Research & Data Specialist, 320 Cathedral St., Baltimore, 21201. Tel: 410-547-5356; Fax: 410-625-8485. Email: develop@archbalt.org.

Gay and Lesbian Ministries, Office of—Deacon PAUL WEBER, Dir., 320 Cathedral St., Baltimore, 21201. Tel: 410-547-5486.

Hispanic Ministries, Office of—MARIA T.P. JOHNSON, Dir., 320 Cathedral St., Baltimore, 21201. Tel: 410-547-5363.

Holy Childhood Association—Dr. RODRIGUE MORTEL, Dir., 320 Cathedral St., Baltimore, 21201.

Human Resources Committee—LEONARD STROM, Chm.

Human Resource Services, Division of—MICHELLY B. MERRICK, SPHR, Dir., 320 Cathedral St., Baltimore, 21201. Tel: 410-547-5448; Fax: 410-234-2953. Email: mmerrick@archbalt.org.

Information Technology, Division of—WILLIAM A. GLOVER, Dir., 320 Cathedral St., Baltimore, 21201. Tel: 410-547-5539; Fax: 410-332-8233. Email: iT@archbalt.org.

Technology Advisory Committee—JOHN MCFADDEN, Chm.

Senior Priests' Retirement Board—Rev. Msgr. JAMES O. MCGOVERN, Chm.; PETRA PHELPS, Sec.

Building Commission—ROBERT MINUTOLI, Chm.

Insurance, Division of—PETRA PHELPS, Dir., 320 Cathedral St., Baltimore, 21201. Tel: 410-547-5317; Fax: 410-783-5993. Email: pphelps@archbalt.org.

Insurance Committee—WILLIAM FRANEY, Chm.; PETRA PHELPS, Sec., 320 Cathedral St., Baltimore, 21201. Tel: 410-547-5317; Fax: 410-783-5993. Email: pphelps@archbalt.org.

Lay Employees Retirement Board—JAYNE MCGEEHAN, Chm.; PETRA PHELPS, Sec., 320 Cathedral St., Baltimore, 21201. Tel: 410-547-5317; Fax: 410-783-5993. Email: pphelps@archbalt.org.

League of the Little Flower—Rev. Msgr. PAUL G. COOK, Dir., 320 Cathedral St., Baltimore, 21201. Tel: 410-547-5361.

Ministry Formation and Development—RUTH A. PULS, Dir.. Email: rpuls@archbalt.org; M. BARBARA CLAGETT, Coord. Church Leadership Institute. Email: bclagett@archbalt.org; 320 Cathedral St., Baltimore, 21201. Tel: 410-547-5470; Fax: 410-234-2953.

Management Services, Department of—JOSEPH A. SPADARO, C.P.A., Exec. Dir. & C.F.O., 320 Cathedral St., Baltimore, 21201. Tel: 410-547-5322; Fax: 410-332-8233. Email: mgmtserv@archbalt.org.

Maryland Catholic Conference—RICHARD J. DOWLING ESQ., Exec. Dir., 188 Duke of Gloucester St., Annapolis, 21401. Tel: 410-269-1155 (Bal.); 301-261-1979 (Wash.); Fax: 410-269-1790. Email: mdcca@aol.com.

Office of Diaconate—Revs. PATRICK M. CARRION, Dir. Tel: 410-547-5428; JAY F. O'CONNOR, Assoc. Dir. Tel: 410-547-5558; Mrs. CAROL PURWIN, Admin. Asst., 320 Cathedral St., Rm. 620, Baltimore, 21201. Tel: 410-547-5427.

Office of Pastoral Service for Senior and Retired Clergy—Rev. JEFFREY W. CARLSEN, Dir., 320 Cathedral St., Baltimore, 21201. Tel: 410-547-5427; 410-671-7816, Ext. 286.

Clergy Personnel, Division of—Revs. PATRICK M. CARRION, Dir.; JAY F. O'CONNOR, Assoc. Dir.; Mrs. CAROL PURWIN, Admin. Asst., 320 Cathedral St., Baltimore, 21201. Tel: 410-547-5427; Fax: 410-234-2953. Email: clgypers@archbalt.org.

Pastoral Council, Archdiocesan—320 Cathedral St., Baltimore, 21201. Tel: 410-547-5435.

Permanent Deacon Formation Program—Rev. PATRICK M. CARRION, Dir., 320 Cathedral St., Baltimore, 21201. Tel: 410-547-5428. Email: pcarrion@archbalt.org.

Priests' Council—Revs. JAMES BARKER, Vice Chm.; JOSEPH F. BARR; Rev. Msgrs. ARTHUR BASTRESS; THOMAS BEVAN; Revs. JOHN DIETZENBACH; JAMES FARMER; WILLIAM P. FOLEY; RAYMOND L. HARRIS JR.; LAWRENCE M. JOHNSON; JOSEPH LACEY, S.J.; RICHARD T. LAWRENCE; Rev. Msgr. EDWARD J. LYNCH (Retired); Revs. C. LOUIS MARTIN; THOMAS

PHILLIPS; RICHARD SMITH, Sec.; Rev. Msgr. DENNIS TINDER, 320 Cathedral St., Baltimore, 21201. Tel: 410-547-5455.

Ex Officio—His Eminence WILLIAM CARDINAL KEELER, D.D., J.C.D.; Most Revs. GORDON D. BENNETT, S.J., D.D., V.G.; WILLIAM FRANCIS MALOOLY, V.G.; WILLIAM C. NEWMAN, D.D., V.G. (Retired); Rev. Msgr. RICHARD W. WOY, Chancellor. Consultors: Rev. Msgrs. ROBERT ARMSTRONG; PAUL G. COOK; JAMES O. MCGOVERN; GEORGE B. MOELLER; G. MICHAEL SCHLEUPNER; ARTHUR VALENZANO; Revs. RICHARD E. CRAMBLITT; MITCHELL T. ROZANSKI; PAUL A. BYRNES; JOHN DIETZENBACH.

Priest Personnel Board—Revs. ERIK J. ARNOLD; CARL CUMMINGS, Vice Chm.; JEFFREY DAUSES; Rev. Msgr. WILLIAM F. BURKE; Revs. JOHN JICHA; WILLIAM A. AU; MARTIN E. FEILD; RICHARD SMITH; JOHN WARD, O.M.I.; ALPHONSE ROSE; RICHARD TILLMAN.

Propagation of the Faith, Home and Foreign Mission Society—His Eminence WILLIAM CARDINAL KEELER, D.D., J.C.D., Gen. Dir.; Deacon RODRIGUE MORTEL, Dir., 320 Cathedral St., Baltimore, 21201. Tel: 410-547-5498; Fax: 410-625-8485.

Communications Office—VACANT, Dir. Communications, 320 Cathedral St., Baltimore, 21201. Tel: 410-547-5379; Fax: 410-625-8480. Email: communic@archbalt.org.

Evangelization and Catechesis, Division of—CAROL A. AUGUSTINE, Dir., 320 Cathedral St., Baltimore, 21201. Tel: 410-547-5403; Fax: 410-347-7896. Email: reled@archbalt.org.

Senior Priests Retirement Board—Rev. Msgr. JAMES O. MCGOVERN, Chm.; PETRA PHELPS, Sec., 320 Cathedral St., Baltimore, 21201. Tel: 410-547-5317; Fax: 410-783-5993. Email: pphelps@archbalt.org.

St. Vincent de Paul Society— Baltimore Council: His Eminence WILLIAM CARDINAL KEELER, D.D., J.C.D., Honorary Pres.; Rev. Msgr. JEREMIAH F. KENNEY, Spiritual Advisor; BARBARA H. MEDCALF, Pres.; JOHN J. SCHIAVONE, Exec. Dir., 320 Cathedral St., Baltimore, 21201. Tel: 410-547-5377. Web: www.vincentbaltimore.org.

Victim Assistance Coordinator—JUDY DOBSON, L.C.S.W. Tel: 410-547-5446. Email: jdobson@archbalt.org.

Vocation Office—Revs. GERARD FRANCIK, Dir. Tel: 410-547-5426; Fax: 410-234-2953. Email: vocations@archbalt.org; J. KEVIN FARMER, Assoc. Dir. Tel: 410-547-5426; Fax: 410-234-2953.

Youth and Young Adult Ministry, Division of—MARK PACIONE, Dir., 320 Cathedral St., Baltimore, 21201. Tel: 410-547-5372; Fax: 410-625-8481.

Associated Catholic Charities, Inc.

Catholic Charities— Associated Catholic Charities, Inc. (Catholic Charities) is Maryland's leading private provider of human services. The agency welcomes and serves people in need, regardless of faith, race or other circumstances. Through more than 80 programs, Catholic Charities improves the lives of children and families, seniors, the disadvantaged, and people with developmental disabilities. Headquartered in Baltimore, the agency operates in the city and nine Maryland counties under the auspices of the Roman Catholic Archdiocese of Baltimore *Catholic Charities, 2305 N. Charles St., Baltimore, 21218.* Tel: 410-261-5800. Email: info@catholiccharities-md.org. Web: www.catholiccharities-md.org. For detailed information on specific Catholic Charities and its programs, please refer to the Institution Section.

Executive Director—HAROLD A. SMITH, Catholic Charities, 320 Cathedral St., 3rd Fl., Baltimore, 21201-4493. Tel: 410-547-5495; Fax: 410-752-2873.

CLERGY, PARISHES, MISSIONS AND PAROCHIAL SCHOOLS

METROPOLITAN BALTIMORE

(BALTIMORE CITY AND BALTIMORE COUNTY)

1—CATHEDRAL OF MARY OUR QUEEN (1954), [CEM] Rev. Msgr. Robert A. Armstrong, Rector; Revs. John A. Williamson; Lawrence Adamczyk; Deacon Charles Hiebler. In Res., Revs. Joseph F. Breighner; J. Kevin Farmer; Gerard C. Francik; Robert Jaskot.
Res.: 5200 N. Charles St., 21210-2023. Tel: 410-464-4000; Fax: 410-464-4060.
School—111 Amberly Way, 21210. Tel: 410-464-4100; Fax: 410-464-4137. Sr. Eileen Weisman, S.S.N.D., Prin. Lay Teachers 27; Students 432.
Catechesis/Religious Program—5200 N. Charles St., 21210. Tel: 410-464-4010. Sr. Geraldine Majerowicz, D.R.E. Students 275.
Parish & Family Ministry—Tel: 410-464-4009. Mrs. Judith Ann Hvisc, Dir.
Youth Ministry—Tel: 410-464-4012. Mrs. Christine Goldberg, Dir.
Office of Music Ministry—Tel: 410-464-4020. Daniel Sansone.

2—ST. AGNES (Catonsville) (1852), [CEM] Revs. Carl F. Cummings; Larry G. Rock. In Res., Rev. Jamie Noel Deslate (Philippines).
Res.: 5422 Old Frederick Rd., 21229. Tel: 410-744-2900; Fax: 410-744-8304.
School—603 St. Agnes Ln., 21229. Tel: 410-747-4070; Fax: 410-747-0138. Mr. John McCaul, I.H.M., Prin. Lay Teachers 22; Religious 4; Students 453.
Catechesis/Religious Program—Tel: 410-747-9073. Students 185.

3—ST. ALPHONSUS, SHRINE OF (1842), (Lithuanian), Rev. Msgr. Arthur W. Bastress. In Res., Rev. William F. Spacek; Deacon Hugh H. Mills Jr.
Res.: 114 W. Saratoga St., 21201. Tel: 410-685-6090; Fax: 410-244-1670.

4—ST. AMBROSE (1907), Rev. John Pfannenstiel, O.F.M.Cap., Pastoral Ministry.
Res.: 4502 Park Heights Ave., 21215. Tel: 410-367-9918; Fax: 410-542-6056.
School—4506 Park Heights Ave., 21215. Tel: 410-664-2373; Fax: 410-664-0857. Pamela Sanders, Prin. Lay Teachers 24; Students 310.
Catechesis/Religious Program—Norma Townsend, D.R.E. Students 95.
Outreach Center—3445 Park Heights Ave., 21215. Tel: 410-225-0870. Sr. Charmaine Krohe, S.S.N.D., Dir.

5—ST. ANDREW, Closed., 1974. Parish records available at the Chancery. Tel: 410-547-5446.

6—ST. ANN (1873), (African American),, Twinned with St. Wenceslaus, Baltimore. Rev. Peter A. Lyons, T.O.R.; Deacon James E. Bee; Sr. Jeanne Barasha, S.S.N.D., Pastoral Admin.
Res.: 528 E. 22nd St., 21218. Tel: 410-235-8169; Fax: 410-235-8253.
Catechesis/Religious Program—Students 37.

7—ANNUNCIATION (1968), Rev. William P. Foley; Sr. Susan Engel, M.H.S.H., Pastoral Assoc. In Res., Rev. Salvatore J. Livigni.
Res.: 5212 McCormick Ave., 21206. Tel: 410-866-4020; Fax: 410-866-2754.
Catechesis/Religious Program—Tel: 410-866-4706. Mrs. Kathleen Brotzman, D.R.E. Students 90.

8—ST. ANTHONY OF PADUA (1884),, Twinned with Most Precious Blood. Revs. C. Lou Martin; Charles Phiri, M.S.C. (South Africa); Deacons Joseph C. Krysiak; Joseph Schultz; Dr. Gloria R. Carpeneto, Pastoral Assoc. In Res., Most Rev. Gordon D. Bennett, S.J., D.D., V.G.; Rev. Ronald J. Zoubek (Retired).
Res.: 4414 Frankford Ave., 21206. Tel: 410-488-0400; Fax: 410-488-0032.
School—4410 Frankford Ave., 21206. Tel: 410-488-4848; Fax: 410-325-4003. Mrs. Peggy Radziminski, Prin. Lay Teachers 21; Students 221.
Catechesis/Religious Program—Tel: 410-488-0400; Fax: 410-488-0032. Students 22.

9—ASCENSION (Halethorpe) (1913), Revs. Manuel R. Roman; E. Gerard Huesman, Pastor Emeritus (Retired); Conan H. Timoney, C.P.; Sr. Mary Catherine Lewandowski, O.S.F., Pastoral Assoc.
Res.: 4603 Poplar Ave., 21227. Tel: 410-242-2292; Fax: 410-242-6807.
School—(Grades PreK-8) Tel: 410-242-2020; Fax: 410-242-2384. Ms. Rita Ann Swift, M.S., Prin. Lay Teachers 17; Students 235.
Catechesis/Religious Program—Mrs. Marie Murphy, D.R.E. Students 160.

10—ST. ATHANASIUS (1891), Rev. Robert A. DiMattei Jr.; Deacon Ronald Thompson.
Res.: 4708 Prudence St., Curtis Bay, 21226. Tel: 410-355-5740; Fax: 410-355-8122.
Catechesis/Religious Program—Tel: 410-355-2540. Mary Beth Barnes, D.R.E. Students 70.

11—ST. AUGUSTINE (Elkridge) (1844), [CEM] Rev. Gerard J. Bowen.
Res.: 5976 Old Washington Rd., Elkridge, 21075. Tel: 410-796-1520; Fax: 410-796-8172.
School—5990 Old Washington Rd., Elkridge, 21075. Tel: 410-796-3040; Fax: 410-579-1165. Mrs. Patricia Schratz, Prin. School Sisters of Notre Dame 3; Lay Teachers 8; Students 321.
Catechesis/Religious Program—Tel: 410-796-8150. Mary Elizabeth Yoncha, D.R.E.; Mary Jane Thomas, D.R.E. Students 430.

12—ST. BARNABAS, , Closed 1931. Parish records available at St. Pius V Church. Tel: 410-523-1930.

13—BASILICA OF THE NATIONAL SHRINE OF THE ASSUMPTION OF THE BLESSED VIRGIN MARY (1795),, Co-Cathedral). Corporate Title: The Trustees of the Catholic Cathedral Church of Baltimore (The Basilica); Basilica of the Assumption Historic Trust, Inc. Established for the Preservation of the Basilica as a National Landmark of American Architecture. Cathedral & Mulberry St. Rev. Msgr. James V. Hobbs, Rector.
The Cardinal's Residence—408 N. Charles St., 21201. Tel: 410-727-3564; Fax: 410-539-0407. His Eminence William H. Keeler, D.D., J.C.D.
Parish Office—Tel: 410-727-3565.

14—ST. BENEDICT (1893), Rev. Paschal A. Morlino, O.S.B.; Sisters Beatrice Wise, D.C., Pastoral Assoc.; Jane Marie Otterson, D.C. In Res., Rev. George Kallampally, C.M.F.
Res.: 2612 Wilkens Ave., 21223. Tel: 410-947-4988; Fax: 410-947-6009.
Catechesis/Religious Program—Sr. Corinne Manzi, S.N.D., D.R.E.; Mary E. Salchunas, D.R.E. Students 38.

15—ST. BERNARD, (Korean), Closed., For parish records prior to 1989 contact the chancery office. For parish records past 1989 contact Holy Korean Martyrs, Baltimore.

16—ST. BERNARDINE (1928), (African American), Revs. Edward M. Miller; John A. Delclos; Deacons Phillip W. Harcum, (Retired); Wardell Barksdale Jr.
Res.: 3812 Edmondson Ave., 21229. Tel: 410-362-8664; Fax: 410-945-0459.
School—3601 Old Frederick Rd., 21229. Tel: 410-624-5088; Fax: 410-947-5439. Dr. Antoinette Lyles, Prin. Lay Teachers 18; Students 232.
Catechesis/Religious Program—Tel: 410-362-8978. Beverly White, D.R.E. Students 258.

17—BLESSED SACRAMENT CHURCH (1911), Rev. P. Edward Kenny Jr.; Sr. Marie Mack, S.S.N.D., Pastoral Admin.
Res.: 4103 Old York Rd., 21218. Tel: 410-323-0424; Fax: 410-323-4478.
Catechesis/Religious Program—Sr. Marie Mack, S.S.N.D., D.R.E. Students 14.

18—ST. BRIGID (1854), Rev. Joseph G. Bochenek; Bette Brocato, Pastoral Assoc.
Res.: 900 S. East Ave., 21224. Tel: 410-563-1717; Fax: 410-563-1776.
School—Bishop John Newman, Tel: 410-615-6271. See separate listing.
Catechesis/Religious Program—Tel: 410-558-3125. Karen M. Norcross, D.R.E. Students 50.

19—ST. CASIMIR (1902), Rev. Ross Syracuse, O.F.M.Conv. In Res., Rev. Timothy Kulbicki, O.F.M-.Conv.; Bro. Momuld Meogrossi, O.F.M.Conv.
Res.: 2736 O'Donnell St., 21224. Tel: 410-276-1981; Fax: 410-732-7436.
School—Father Kolbe School, Tel: 410-342-2681; Fax: 410-342-5715. See separate listing.

20—ST. CECILIA (1902),, (Twinned with Immaculate Conception, Baltimore.) Rev. Sylvester Peterka, C.M.; Bros. William Stover, C.M., Pastoral Assoc.; Frank W. Richardson.
Res.: 3300 Clifton Ave., 21216. Tel: 410-624-3600; Fax: 410-945-0157.
Catechesis/Religious Program—Irene Mallory, D.R.E. Students 39.

21—ST. CHARLES BORROMEO (Pikesville) (1848), [CEM] Sr. Constance Baker, S.S.N.D., Pastoral Assoc.; Rev. Raymond Chase; Sr. Joan Bastress, I.H.M., Pastoral Assoc. In Res., Rev. Patrick Carrion.
Res.: 101 Church Ln., 21208. Tel: 410-486-5400; Fax: 410-486-5421. Email: charlesst@comcast.net.
Catechesis/Religious Program—Sr. Joan Bastress, I.H.M., D.R.E. Tel: 410-653-9337. Students 87.

22—CHRIST THE KING (Dundalk) (1957), Closed., For inquiries for parish records please see St. Rita, Baltimore

23—CHURCH OF THE IMMACULATE CONCEPTION, Formerly Immaculate Conception (Towson) (1883), [CEM] Rev. Msgrs. F. Dennis Tinder; Edward J. Lynch, Pastor Emeritus (Retired); Rev. Paul Sparklin. In Res., Rev. Msgr. Jeremiah F. Kenney; Deacon John C. Gramling.
Res.: 200 Ware Ave., Towson, 21204. Tel: 410-427-4700; Fax: 410-427-4700.
School—(Grades PreK-8), 112 Ware Ave., Towson, 21204. Tel: 410-427-4800; Fax: 410-427-4895. Mrs. Jean Wimmer, Prin.
High School—Towson Catholic, 114 Ware Ave., 21204. Tel: 410-427-4900; Fax: 410-427-4717. Mr. Michael Lynch, Acting Prin.
Catechesis/Religious Program—School of Religion Ms. Lisa E. Padian, Dir. Students 903.

24—ST. CLARE (Essex) (1956), Deacon Kevin Bagley.
Res.: 714 Myrth Ave., 21221-4898. Tel: 410-687-6011; Fax: 410-687-3054.
School—Tel: 410-687-7787; Fax: 410-687-2715. Mrs. Dorothy Williams, Prin. Sisters 1; Lay Teachers 19; Students 305.
Catechesis/Religious Program—Tel: 410-686-7693; Fax: 410-687-2518. Sr. Bridget Mary Lyrs, R.S.H.M., D.R.E. Students 120.

25—ST. CLEMENT (Lansdowne) (1891), Mrs. Anne Buening, Pastoral Life Dir.; Rev. Tom Malia; Deacons John I. McKenna; Thomas J. Yannuzzi.
Parish Office Address: 1212 Chesaco Ave., Rosedale, 21237. Email: parishoffice@stclementhm.org.

Res.: 2700 Washington Ave., 21227. Tel: 410-242-1025; Fax: 410-536-0636.
Catechesis/Religious Program—Tel: 410-242-2230. Janet Yannuzzi, D.R.E. Students 108.

26—ST. CLEMENT MARY HOFBAUER (Rosedale) (1925), Revs. Richard Florek, O.F.M.Conv.; Victor Maksimowicz, O.F.M.Conv.; Albert Scherer, O.F.M.Conv.; Deacons Nicholas Feurer; Francis Zeiler.
Res.: 1220 Chesaco Ave., 21237. Tel: 410-686-6188; Fax: 410-686-6198. Email: parishoffice@stclementhm.org.
Parish Office Address: 1212 Chesaco Ave., Rosedale, 21237.
School—1216 Chesaco Ave., 21237. Tel: 410-686-3316. Angela Rebbert, Prin. Lay Teachers 24; Students 428.
Catechesis/Religious Program—Tel: 410-391-5028. Mrs. Patricia Wagner, D.R.E. Students 126.

27—CORPUS CHRISTI (1881), Rev. Richard J. Bozzelli; Deacon Frank Hodges; Dr. Patricia Fosarelli, Pastoral Assoc.
Res.: 110 W. Lafayette Ave., 21217. Tel: 410-523-4161; Fax: 410-523-5745.
Catechesis/Religious Program—Students 49.

28—ST. DOMINIC (1906), Rev. James P. Kiesel.
Res.: 5310 Harford Rd., 21214. Tel: 410-426-0360; Fax: 410-444-6963.
School—5304 Harford Rd., 21214. Tel: 410-426-0797; Fax: 410-426-3190. Valentina Hampson, Prin. Lay Teachers 15; Students 233.
Catechesis/Religious Program—Tel: 410-426-0360. Ms. Margaret Williams, D.R.E. Students 30.

29—ST. EDWARD (1880), Rev. Samuel Lupico; Sr. Anita B. Smith, O.S.F.; Deacon Joseph Neale.
Res.: 901 Poplar Grove St., 21216. Tel: 410-362-2000; Fax: 410-945-7113.
Catechesis/Religious Program—Dr. Cre Saundra Sills, D.R.E. Students 70.

30—ST. ELIZABETH OF HUNGARY (1895), Rev. Raymond Nedimyer, T.O.R.; Bro. Finbar Gallagher, T.O.R.; Deacon Richard Morris. In Res., Rev. Robert Sisk, T.O.R.
Mailing & Office Address: 2 N. Belnord Ave., 21224. Tel: 410-675-8260; Fax: 410-675-2530.
Res.: 2638 E. Baltimore St., 21224. Tel: 410-675-7771; Fax: 410-675-7772.
Catechesis/Religious Program—Students 20.

31—FOURTEEN HOLY MARTYRS, , Closed 1964. Parish records available at St. Martin Church. Tel: 410-947-1242.

32—ST. FRANCIS OF ASSISI (1927), Rev. Msgr. William F. Burke; Rev. Joseph J. Bonadio, S.S.; Sr. Katherine Bell, R.S.M., Pastoral Assoc.
Res.: 3615 Harford Rd., 21218. Tel: 410-235-5136; Fax: 410-467-9503. Email: sfabalt@archbalt.org.
School—3617 Harford Rd., 21218. Tel: 410-467-1683; Fax: 410-467-9449. J. Kevin Frye, Prin. Lay Teachers 19; Students 304.
Catechesis/Religious Program—Sr. Katherine M. Bell, D.R.E. Students 50.

33—ST. FRANCIS XAVIER (1793), Rev. James E. McLinden, S.S.J.; Deacons Russell Matthews; Charles Mercer; Walton Smith.
Res.: 1501 E. Oliver St., 21213. Tel: 410-727-3103; 410-727-3104; Fax: 410-625-9587. Email: j1mclinden@aol.com.
Catechesis/Religious Program—Tel: 410-837-0556. Sr. Magdala Marie Gilbert, O.S.P., D.R.E. Students 122.

34—ST. GABRIEL (1997),, Formerly St. Lawrence and Our Lady of Perpetual Help, Woodlawn. Rev. Thomas L. Phillips; Deacon John J. Codd; Sr. Joan Bunty, O.S.F., Pastoral Assoc.
Parish Office: 6950 Dogwood Rd., 21244. Tel: 410-298-8888; Fax: 410-944-7409.
School—John Paul Regional School See separate listing.

35—ST. GREGORY THE GREAT (1883), (African American), Rev. Damien Nalepa.
Res. & Church: 1542 N. Gilmor St., 21217. Tel: 410-523-0061; 410-523-0063; Fax: 410-669-1385.
Catechesis/Religious Program—Louise G. Tildon, D.R.E. Students 51.

36—HOLY CROSS (1858), (German), [CEM] Revs. Raymond Martin; Paul Maillet; Stephen Hook. In Res., Rev. Msgr. John L. Reinsfelder (Retired).
Res.: 110 E. West St., 21230. Tel: 410-752-8498; Fax: 410-752-2703.
School—Catholic Community School of South Baltimore, Tel: 410-685-6155; Fax: 410-685-0692. See separate listing.
Catechesis/Religious Program—Tel: 410-752-0205. Students 100.

37—HOLY KOREAN MARTYRS (1972), (Korean), [CEM] Rev. Joseph Y. Kim.
Res.: 5801 Security Blvd., 21207. Tel: 410-265-8885; Fax: 410-265-1655. Email: kmartyrs@archbalt.org.
Catechesis/Religious Program—Fax: 410-265-1055. Sr. Lee Nicopemo, D.R.E. Students 160

38—HOLY ROSARY (1887), (Polish), [CEM] Rev. Msgr. Chester J. Mieczkowski, Pastoral Emeritus (Retired); Rev. Janusz Zych, S.Ch. In Res., Rev. Francis Ckroy, S.Ch.
Res.: 408 S. Chester St., 21231. Tel: 410-732-3960; Fax: 410-375-4917.
Catechesis/Religious Program—Rev. Janusz Zych, S.Ch., D.R.E. Students 40.

39—ST. IGNATIUS (1856), Revs. William J. Watters, S.J.; Francis M. O'Connor, S.J.; Francis H. McGauley S.J.; Edward O'Donnell, S.J.
Church: 740 N. Calvert St., 21202. Tel: 410-727-3848; Fax: 410-727-1573. Web: www.st-ignatius.net.
Jesuit Community of St. Ignatius Parish: 102 E. Madison St., 21202. Tel: 410-727-8729.
School—St. Ignatius Loyola Academy, Tel: 410-539-8268; Fax: 410-539-4821. Mr. Jeffrey Sindler, Prin.
Catechesis/Religious Program—Students 30.

40—IMMACULATE CONCEPTION (1850), (African American), (Twinned with St. Cecilia, Baltimore.) Rev. Sylvester Peterka, C.M.; Bro. William Stover, C.M., Pastoral Assoc.
Mailing Address: P.O. Box 16570, 21217.
Res.: 1512 Druid Hill Ave., 21217. Tel: 410-523-0809; Fax: 410-945-0157.
Catechesis/Religious Program—Karen Sullivan, D.R.E. Students 26.

41—IMMACULATE HEART OF MARY (Baynesville) (1948), Revs. Michael W. Carrion; Joseph L. McManus, Pastor Emeritus (Retired); Edgar B. Graham, S.J.; James Risacher; Kevin W. Brooksbank; Deacons Jack Martin; Ken Pivec.
Res.: 8501 Loch Raven Blvd., 21286. Tel: 410-668-7935; Fax: 410-661-6560.
School—Tel: 410-668-8466; Fax: 410-668-6171. Mrs. Wilma Short, Prin. Sisters of Mercy 1; Lay Teachers 27; Students 606.
Catechesis/Religious Program—Tel: 410-661-3820; Fax: 410-661-3838. Sr. Regina De Angelis, D.R.E.; Dorothy Mitchell, D.R.E. Students 188.

42—ST. ISAAC JOGUES (1968), Rev. H. Martin Hammond; Rev. Msgr. James J. Cronin, Pastor Emeritus (Retired); Deacons Jack Kent, (Retired); Al Rose; Arthur L. Micozzi; James Westwater; Sr. Patricia Tryon, S.N.D., Pastoral Assoc.
Church Office: 9215 Old Harford Rd., 21234. Tel: 410-661-4888; Fax: 410-882-1484.
Res.: 9400 Old Harford Rd., 21234. Tel: 410-661-4883; Fax: 410-882-1484.
Catechesis/Religious Program—Tel: 410-665-2561; 410-668-3686 Youth Ministry Office. Sr. John Francis Kearney, S.S.N.D. Students 481.

43—ST. JAMES AND ST. JOHN, , Closed 1986. Parish records available at the Chancery. Tel: 410-547-5446.
School—Queen of Peace Elementary Cluster See separate listing.

44—ST. JEROME (1887), Rev. John D. Harvey, O.F.M.Cap.; Deacon Gerald Anthony Roberts; Sisters Margaret Brogden, M.H.S.H., Pastoral Assoc.; Suzanne Baumgartner, D.C., Pastoral Assoc. Tel: 410-947-1243.
Res.: 848 Hollins St., 21201.
Catechesis/Religious Program—Tel: 410-685-5044; Fax: 410-625-2406. Students 34.
Headstart & Social Hall—765 W. Hamburg St., 21230. Tel: 410-539-2429.

45—ST. JOHN GERMAN CATHOLIC CHURCH, , Closed 1841. Original records, stored at The Catholic Center, are available to researchers on microfilm at the Maryland State Archives in Annapolis.

46—ST. JOHN THE EVANGELIST, , Closed 1966. Parish records available at the Chancery. Tel: 410-547-5446.

47—ST. JOSEPH, , Closed 1962. Parish records available at Holy Cross Rectory. Tel: 410-752-8498.

48—ST. JOSEPH (Fullerton) (1850), (German), [CEM] Rev. Msgr. George B. Moeller; Rev. John A. Eckard; Deacons William J. DeAngelis; Charles A. Baynes; William S. Albaugh. In Res., Rev. Msgr. James J. Cronin (Retired).
Res.: 8420 Belair Rd., 21236. Tel: 410-256-1630; Fax: 410-529-2990.
School—Tel: 410-256-8026; Fax: 410-529-7234. Mrs. Joyce Thaler, Prin. Lay Teachers 29; Students 490.
Catechesis/Religious Program—Tel: 410-256-8235. Students 602.

49—ST. JOSEPH PASSIONIST MONASTERY PARISH (1868), Rev. William Murphy, C.P.; Frank J. McGlain, Pastoral Assoc.
Res.: 251 S. Morley St., 21229. Tel: 410-566-0877; Fax: 410-233-4974.
Catechesis/Religious Program—Gloria Rink, D.R.E. Students 48.

50—ST. JUDE SHRINE (1873), (Italian), Rev. Frank S. Donio, S.A.C. In Res., Rev. John G. Biermann, S.A.C.
Res.: 308 N. Paca St., P.O. Box 1455, 21203. Tel: 410-685-6026; 410-685-3497; Fax: 410-244-5728.
St. Jude Shrine Corp.—Tel: 410-685-6026.

51—ST. KATHARINE OF SIENNA, , Closed 1986. Parish records available at St. Wenceslaus Church. Tel: 410-675-7304.

52—ST. LAWRENCE (1962), Merged, with The Shrine of Our Lady of Perpetual Help, Baltimore, to form St. Gabriel Parish, Baltimore. Records available at St. Gabriel Parish.

53—ST. LEO (1881), (Italian), Rev. Michael Salerno, S.A.C.
Res.: 227 S. Exeter St., 21202. Tel: 410-675-7275; Fax: 410-675-8292.
School—Father Kolbe Interparochial, Tel: 410-685-8505. See separate listing.

54—LITTLE FLOWER, SHRINE OF (1926), Revs. Michael J. Orchik; James Miles. In Res., Deacon Henry L. Siarkowski.
Res.: 2854 Brendan Ave., 21213. Tel: 410-483-1700; Fax: 410-488-6482.
School—(Grades PreK-8), 2800 Brendan Ave., 21213. Tel: 410-488-1483; Fax: 410-488-0929. Mr. Richard G. Gatto, Prin. Lay Teachers 17; Students 208.
Catechesis/Religious Program—Students 15.

55—ST. LUKE (Edgemere) (1888), Rev. Joseph S. Lizor Jr.
Res.: 7517 Northpoint Rd., 21219-1499. Tel: 410-477-5200; Fax: 410-477-5996.
School—Our Lady of Hope/St. Luke's School, Tel: 410-288-2793.
Catechesis/Religious Program—Tel: 410-477-5201. Doris Lundin, D.R.E. Students 87.

56—ST. MARK (Catonsville) (1888), Revs. Christopher Whatley; John W. Bowen, S.S.; Ross A. Laporta, Pastor Emeritus. In Res., Rev. William Dawson, S.J., Senior Priest; Deacon Seigfried Presberry.
Res.: 27 Melvin Ave., 21228. Tel: 410-744-6560; Fax: 410-747-3182.
School—26 Melvin Ave., 21228. Fax: 410-747-3188. Mrs. Shirley T. Wise, Prin.
Catechesis/Religious Program—Students 903.

57—ST. MARTIN (1865), (African American), Rev. John D. Harvey, O.F.M.Cap.; Deacon Tony Roberts; Sr. Suzanne Baumgartner, D.C., Pastoral Assoc.
Res.: 818 Hollins St., 21201. Fax: 410-625-2406. Frances Murray, Business Mgr.
Catechesis/Religious Program—Tel: 410-685-5044. Sr. Margaret Brogden, M.H.S.H., D.R.E. Students 25.

58—ST. MARY OF THE ASSUMPTION (1849), [CEM] Rev. P. Edward Kenny Jr.; Deacons Miguel Sainz; Richard Bolgiano; Ms. Patricia Hartnett, Admin. & Pastoral Assoc. In Res., Rev. Rochus Vu Dinh Hoat.
Res.: 5502 York Rd., 21212. Tel: 410-435-5900; Fax: 410-435-4879.
School—Tel: 410-435-5850; Fax: 410-435-1256. Mrs. Elaine Reed, Prin. Lay Teachers 16; Students 158.
Catechesis/Religious Program—Miss Lisa O'Reily, D.R.E. Students 46.

59—ST. MARY, STAR OF THE SEA (1868), Revs. Raymond Martin; Stephen Hook. In Res., Rev. Msgr. John L. Reinsfelder (Retired).
Res.: 110 E. West St., 21230. Tel: 410-685-2255; Fax: 410-752-2703.
School—Catholic Community School of South Baltimore, Tel: 410-685-6155; Fax: 410-685-0692. See separate listing.
Catechesis/Religious Program—Tel: 410-752-0205; Fax: 410-576-0929. Students 43.
Convent—Sisters of St. Joseph, 1410 Riverside Ave., 21230. Tel: 410-752-4344; Fax: 410-685-0692.

60—ST. MATTHEW (1949), Rev. Joseph L. Muth.
Res.: 5401 Loch Raven Blvd., 21239. Tel: 410-433-2300; Fax: 410-433-5263. Email: stmattre@verizon.net.
School—Cardinal Shehan School, Tel: 410-433-2775; Fax: 410-323-6131. See separate listing.
Catechesis/Religious Program—Students 41.
Convent—Combonie Missionary Sisters, 5405 Loch Raven Blvd., 21239. Tel: 410-323-1469.

61—ST. MICHAEL (Broadway) (1852), (Hispanic), Merged Revs. James-Santiago W. Gilmour, C.SS.R.; Andrew Carr, C.SS.R.; Deacons Rafael Villagaray; Pablo Osorio; Richard Novak; Edison Morales; Michael Flamini; Sr. Sonia-Marie Fernandez, M.H.S.H., Pastoral Assoc. with St. Patrick 1995.
Res.: 7 S. Wolfe St., 21231-1913. Tel: 410-276-1646; Fax: 410-522-0789.
Catechesis/Religious Program—Tel: 410-563-0064; Fax: 410-563-0310. Olga Diaz, D.R.E. Students 145.

62—ST. MICHAEL (Overlea) (1913), Revs. James D. Proffitt; J. James Purvey. In Res., Revs. Jay F. O'Connor; Kennard Muller (Retired); Deacon Henry Davis, Pastoral Assoc.
Res.: 2 Willow Ave., 21206. Tel: 410-665-1054; Fax: 410-665-4024.
School—10 Willow Ave., 21206. Tel: 410-668-8797; Fax: 410-668-8797. Mrs. Patricia Rohde Kelly, Prin. Lay Teachers 38; Students 415.
Catechesis/Religious Program—Tel: 410-882-8120; Fax: 410-668-2738. Students 166.

63—ST. MILDRED CHURCH, , Closed 1967. Parish records available at Our Lady of Hope Rectory. Tel: 410-284-6600.

64—ST. MONICA, , Closed 1959. Parish records

available at the Chancery. Tel: 410-547-5446.

65—MOST PRECIOUS BLOOD (1948),, (Twinned with St. Anthony of Padua, Baltimore.) Rev. C. Lou Martin; Dr. Gloria R. Carpeneto, Pastoral Assoc.; Deacons Joseph C. Krysiak; Joseph Schultz. In Res., Most Rev. Gordon D. Bennett, S.J., D.D., V.G.; Rev. Ronald J. Zoubek (Retired).
Office—4414 Frankford Ave., 21206. Tel: 410-488-0400; Fax: 410-488-0032.
Church: 5010 Bowleys Ln., 21206.
Catechesis/Religious Program— Twinned with St. Anthony of Padua, Baltimore.

66—THE NEW ALL SAINTS (1912), (African American), Rev. Donald A. Sterling; Deacons Paul D. Shelton; Malcolm Thompson.
Res.: 4408 Liberty Heights Ave., 21207. Tel: 410-542-0445; Fax: 410-542-8852.
School—(Grades 4-8), 3510 Eldorado Ave., 21207. Tel: 410-664-9433; Fax: 410-664-9434. Mr. Henry Fortier, Prin. Lay Teachers 10.
Catechesis/Religious Program—Students 35.

67—OUR LADY OF FATIMA (1951), Revs. Michael D. Sergi, C.SS.R.; Francis A. Poux, C.SS.R.; Richard K. Poetzel, C.SS.R.; Stephen Haynes, C.SS.R.; Gerard Chylko, C.SS.R.; Bro. DeSales Zimpfer, C.SS.R., Pastoral Assoc.; Sr. Julianne Hau, M.H.S.H., Pastoral Assoc.; Deacon Alphonse Bankard III. In Res., Revs. Edwin Foley; Gerard Chylko, C.SS.R., Missionary.
Res.: 6420 E. Pratt St., 21224. Tel: 410-633-9393; Fax: 410-631-7239.
School—6400 E. Pratt St., 21224. Tel: 410-633-5882; Fax: 410-633-5268. Lay Teachers 15; Students 217.
Catechesis/Religious Program—Tel: 410-633-6256. Students 73.

68—OUR LADY OF GOOD COUNSEL (1889), Revs. Raymond D. Martin; Stephen Hook; Sr. Katherine Cress, Pastoral Assoc.
Office—1532 E. Fort Ave., 21230. Tel: 410-752-0205; Fax: 410-576-0929.
School—Catholic Community School of South Baltimore, Tel: 410-685-6155. See separate listing.
Catechesis/Religious Program—Patricia Hoffa, D.R.E.; Sr. Marylida Fria, D.R.E. Students 43.

69—OUR LADY OF HOPE (1967), Rev. John B. Ward, J.C.L., J.D.; Deacon Herman Wilkins.
Res.: 1727 Lynch Rd., 21222. Tel: 410-284-6600; Fax: 410-282-9361.
School—(Grades PreK-8), 8003 N. Boundary Rd., 21222. Tel: 410-288-2793; Fax: 410-288-2850. School Sisters of Notre Dame 1; Lay Teachers 23; Students 318.
Catechesis/Religious Program—8003 N. Boundary Rd.. Tel: 410-282-3120; Fax: 410-282-9361. Students 180.

70—OUR LADY OF LOURDES, , Closed 1995. Parish records available at The New All Saints Church. Tel: 410-542-0445.

71—OUR LADY OF MOUNT CARMEL (Middle River) (1887), Revs. Robert L. Hartnett; Jason Worley.
Res.: 1704 Old Eastern Ave., 21221. Tel: 410-686-4972; Fax: 410-574-8785. Web: olmcmd.org.
School—1702 Old Eastern Ave., 21221. Tel: 410-686-0859; Fax: 410-686-4916. Ms. Lisa Shipley, Prin. Sisters of St. Francis of Philadelphia 2; Lay Teachers 28; Students 532.
High School—1706 Old Eastern Ave., 21221. Tel: 410-686-1023; Fax: 140-686-2361. Mrs. Kathleen Sipes, Prin. Lay Teachers 22; Students 270.
Catechesis/Religious Program—Tel: 410-686-9016; Fax: 410-574-8785. Helen Scimeca, D.R.E. Students 241.

72—OUR LADY OF PERPETUAL HELP (1936), Merged, with St. Lawrence, Baltimore, to form St. Gabriel Parish, Baltimore. Records available at St. Gabriel.

73—OUR LADY OF POMPEI (1924), Revs. Luigi Esposito; Gilberto Leboroni-Pierozzi; Deacon Thom Kuhl.
Res.: 3600 Claremont St., 21224. Tel: 410-675-7790; Fax: 410-563-9067. Email: pompeich1@aol.com.
School—Archbishop Borders School, 201 S. Conkling St., 21224. Tel: 410-276-6534; Fax: 410-276-6915. Ms. M.C. Marshal, Prin. Lay Teachers 10; Students 193.

74—OUR LADY OF SORROWS, , Closed 1935. Parish records available at Holy Cross Rectory. Tel: 410-752-8498.

75—OUR LADY OF THE ANGELS CATHOLIC COMMUNITY (Catonsville) (1993), Rev. Leo J. Larrivee, S.S. (SEA); Sisters Victoria Kessler, S.S.N.D., Pastoral Assoc.; Eileen McFadden, S.S.N.D., Pastoral Assoc. Mailing Address: 711 Maiden Choice Ln., Catonsville, 21228. Tel: 410-247-4779; Fax: 410-737-8826. Email: llarrivee@eritsonmail.com. Service senior citizens w/in community.

76—OUR LADY OF VICTORY (Arbutus) (1952), Rev. Timothy Klunk; Deacon William Jauquet.
Res.: 4414 Wilkens Ave., 21229. Tel: 410-242-0131; 410-242-0180; Fax: 410-242-6963.
School—4416 Wilkens Ave., 21229. Tel: 410-242-3688; Fax: 410-242-8867. Thomas E. Riddle, Prin.; Deborah Reese, Asst. Prin. Lay Teachers 21; Students 516.
Catechesis/Religious Program—Tel: 410-242-9533. Students 60.

77—OUR LADY, QUEEN OF PEACE (1953), Rev. Brian Zielinski, O.Praem.; Deacons George Jenkins; Robert Hacker.
Res.: 10003 Bird River Rd., 21220. Tel: 410-686-3085; Fax: 410-687-1916.
School—10001 Bird River Rd., 21220. Tel: 410-687-8513; Fax: 410-687-7388. Ms. Cynthia Stewart, Prin. Lay Teachers 20; Students 238.
Catechesis/Religious Program—Tel: 410-868-3085; Fax: 410-687-1916. Kathy Shadrach, D.R.E.; Debbie Boblitz, D.R.E. Students 105.

78—ST. PATRICK (Broadway) (1792), (Hispanic), Revs. James W. Gilmour, C.SS.R.; Hernan Juarez; Andrew Carr, C.SS.R.; Sr. Sonia Marie Fernandez, M.H.S.H., Pastoral Assoc.; Deacons Richard Novak; Pablo Osorio; Rafael Villagary; Edison Morales; Michael Flamini. Twinned with St. Michael (Wolfe St.) 1995.
Res.: 7 S. Wolfe St., 21231. Tel: 410-276-1646; Fax: 410-522-0789. Email: snikepat@juno.com.
Catechesis/Religious Program—Tel: 410-563-0064; Fax: 410-563-0310. Students 145.

79—ST. PAUL'S (1888), Closed., Parish records available at St. Francis Xavier. Tel: 410-727-3103.

80—ST. PETER CLAVER (1888), (African American), Revs. Joseph Del Vecchio, S.S.J.; Henry Harper, S.S.J.; Deacon John Briscoe.
Res.: 1546 N. Fremont Ave., 21217. Tel: 410-669-0512; Fax: 410-383-8227.
School—Father Charles A. Hall Lower School, (Grades PreK-5), 1546 N. Fremont Ave., 21217. Tel: 410-225-7555; Fax: 410-225-7721. M. Kathleen Filippelli, Prin. Lay Teachers 11; Students 154.
Catechesis/Religious Program—Students 54.
Convent—1526 N. Fremont Ave., 21217. Tel: 410-383-1288.

81—ST. PETER THE APOSTLE (1842), Rev. John D. Harvey, O.F.M.Cap.; Sisters Kenneth McGuire, R.S.M., Parish Mgr.; Suzanne Baumgartner, D.C., Pastoral Assoc.; Deacon Tony Roberts, Pastoral Assoc.; Frances Murray, Business Mgr.
Res.: 848 Hollins St., 21201. Tel: 410-685-5044; Fax: 410-625-2406.
Catechesis/Religious Program—Tel: 410-497-1243. Sr. Margaret Brogden, M.H.S.H., D.R.E. Students 49.

82—SS. PHILIP AND JAMES (1897), Rev. William A. Au; Deacon D. Vincent Provenza.
Res.: 2801 N. Charles St., 21218. Tel: 410-235-2294; Fax: 410-243-5262.

83—ST. PIUS V (1878), (African American), [JC] Rev. Joseph Del Vecchio, S.S.J.
Res.: 521 N. Schroeder St., 21223. Tel: 410-523-1930; Fax: 410-523-8164.
Catechesis/Religious Program—Students 16.

84—ST. PIUS X (1957), Carol J. Pacione, Dir.; Rev. E. Joseph Cote; Ms. Pat Howlett, Parish Admin.
Res.: 6428 York Rd., 21212. Tel: 410-377-7440; Fax: 410-377-2651. Web: stpius10.org.
School—6432 York Rd., 21212. Tel: 410-377-9738; Fax: 410-372-0552. Mrs. Geri Morrison, Prin. Lay Teachers 23; Students 442.
Catechesis/Religious Program—Tel: 410-377-0722. Mrs. Pinky Howard, D.R.E. Students 277.

85—ST. RITA (1922), Loyes Spayd, Dir.; Deacons George T. Evans, Admin.; Paul T. Mann.
Res.: 2907 Dunleer Rd., 21222. Tel: 410-284-0388; Fax: 410-284-3998.
School—2905 Dunleer Rd., 21222. Tel: 410-284-3580; Fax: 410-284-1971. Sr. Mary Mark Carnes, I.H.M., Prin. Lay Teachers 19; Students 185.
Catechesis/Religious Program—Tel: 410-284-7355. Deacon David Nagel, D.R.E.; Bonnie Nagel, D.R.E. Students 120.

86—ST. ROSE OF LIMA (1914), Rev. Joseph M. O'Meara; Marianne Cromwell, Assoc. Admin.
Res.: 3803 4th St., 21225. Tel: 410-355-8515; 410-355-8516; Fax: 410-354-3392.
School—410 Jeffrey St., 21225. Tel: 410-355-1050; Fax: 410-355-2408. Madeleine Hobik, Prin. Lay Teachers 15; Students 206.
Catechesis/Religious Program—Tel: 410-354-3542. Madeleine Hobik, D.R.E. Students 32.

87—SACRED HEART OF JESUS (1873), Very Rev. Gerard J. Szymkowiak, C.SS.R.; Revs. John F. Murray, C.SS.R.; J. Scott Bailey, C.SS.R. In Res., Rev. Gerard Kurek, C.SS.R.
Res.: 600 S. Conkling St., 21224-4294. Tel: 410-342-4336; Fax: 410-522-2022.
School—Bishop John Neumann School, Tel: 410-675-6271; Fax: 410-327-1543. See separate listing.
Catechesis/Religious Program—Joan Turowski, D.R.E. Students 52.

88—SACRED HEART OF MARY (1925), [CEM] Rev. Msgr. Richard E. Parks; Rev. Edward S. Szymanski; Bro. William Ciganek, C.F.X., Pastoral Assoc.
Res.: 6736 Youngstown Ave., 21222-1097. Tel: 410-633-2828; Fax: 410-633-0349.
School—6726 Youngstown Ave., 21222-1098. Tel: 410-633-7040; Fax: 410-633-7644. Mrs. Helen Roby, Prin. Lay Teachers 18; Students 261.
Catechesis/Religious Program—Michael Demski, D.R.E. Students 123.

89—SHRINE OF THE SACRED HEART (Mt. Washington) (1867), Rev. Richard E. Cramblitt; Sr. Joan Donahue, R.S.M., Pastoral Assoc.; Deacon Mark Soloski.
Res.: 1701 Regent Rd., 21209. Tel: 410-466-6884; 410-466-6885; Fax: 410-664-0523.
School—5800 Smith Ave., 21209. Tel: 410-542-7406; Fax: 410-664-1463. Martha Pierorazio, Prin. Lay Teachers 14; Students 200.
Catechesis/Religious Program—Tel: 410-466-6884, Ext. 14. Students 174.

90—ST. STANISLAUS KOSTKA (1880), (Polish), Closed., For inquiries for parish records please contact St. Casimir, Baltimore. Tel: 410-276-1981; 732-7436 (fax).

91—ST. THOMAS AQUINAS (1867), Rev. James Farmer; Sr. Alice Catherine Rohe, O.S.F., Pastoral Assoc. In Res., Rev. George Restrepo, S.J.; Deacon Richard W. Montalto, (2).
Res.: 1008 W. 37th St., 21211. Tel: 410-366-4488; Fax: 410-366-8352.
School—(Grades PreK-8), 3710 Roland Ave., 21211. Tel: 410-889-4618; Fax: 410-889-1956. School Sisters of Notre Dame 2; Lay Teachers 15; Students 206.
Catechesis/Religious Program— Susan Sousa, D.R.E. Students 35.

92—ST. THOMAS MORE (1960), Rev. John P. Cunningham; Deacon Michael P. McCoy. In Res., Most Rev. Francis W. Malooly.
Parish Center & Mailing Address: 6806 McClean Blvd., 21234. Tel: 410-444-6500; Fax: 410-444-6502.
School—Cardinal Shehan School, Tel: 410-433-2775; Fax: 410-323-6131. See separate listing.
Catechesis/Religious Program—Tel: 410-444-4563. Sr. Susan Keating, S.S.G., D.R.E. Students 39.

93—ST. URSULA (Parkville) (1934), Rev. Msgrs. A. Thomas Baumgartner; Myles McGowan, Pastor Emeritus; Revs. Gerald Hynes, C.P.; Paul Holthaus; John W. Robbins; Deacons Robert Keenan; Frank Rongione Sr.
Res.: 8801 Harford Rd., 21234. Tel: 410-665-2111; Fax: 410-665-0758.
School—8900 Harford Rd., 21234. Tel: 410-665-3533; Fax: 410-661-1620. Sr. Joan Kelly, S.N.D., Prin.
Catechesis/Religious Program—Tel: 410-655-4106. Students 1,075.

94—ST. VERONICA (1945), (African American), Rev. Ausustine Inwang; Deacons Jhan Harris; Williard Pinkney Jr.
Res.: 806 Cherry Hill Rd., 21225. Tel: 410-355-7466; Fax: 410-355-7741.
Catechesis/Religious Program—Students 108.

95—ST. VINCENT DE PAUL (1840), [CEM] Revs. Richard T. Lawrence; Charles Canterna, MD State Dept. of Correction Chaplain; Ray Heil, Pres. Parish Council.
Res.: 120 N. Front St., 21202. Tel: 410-962-5078; Fax: 410-962-8427.
St. Vincent de Paul Church Historic Trust, Inc.—Tel: 410-962-5078.
Jonestown Planning Council, Inc.—Tel: 410-962-5078.
Catechesis/Religious Program—Students 55.

96—ST. WENCESLAUS (1872), Rev. Peter A. Lyons, T.O.R.; Arthur Lyons, Pres. Parish Council.
Res.: 2111 Ashland Ave., 21205. Tel: 410-675-7304; Fax: 410-675-5746.
School—Queen of Peace Elementary Cluster See separate listing.
Catechesis/Religious Program—Students 43.

97—ST. WILLIAM OF YORK (1914), Rev. Martin H. Demek; Deacons Donald Miller; John Langmead.
Res.: 600 Cooks Ln., 21229. Tel: 410-566-2140; Fax: 410-362-5475.
School—Tel: 410-945-1442; Fax: 410-945-4036. Lay Teachers 22; Students 208.
Catechesis/Religious Program—Tel: 410-566-6152. Students 69.

OUTSIDE METROPOLITAN BALTIMORE

ABERDEEN, HARFORD CO., ST. JOAN OF ARC (1920), Rev. Samuel V. Young; Deacons Daniel Kopczyk; Paul R. Ciesla.
Office: 222 S. Law St., 21001. Tel: 410-272-4535; 410-575-6909; Fax: 410-272-9025.
Res.: 257 S. Law St., 21001.
School—230 S. Law St., 21001. Tel: 410-272-1387; Fax: 410-272-1959. Dr. Jane Towery, Prin. Lay Teachers 16; Students 230.
Catechesis/Religious Program—Tel: 410-272-6944. Rosemarie Homberg, D.R.E. Students 152.

ABINGDON, HARFORD CO., ST. FRANCIS DE SALES (1866), [CEM] Rev. Msgr. G. Michael Schleupner; Deacons Richard Stine; James Sullivan; Alex

Rodriguez.
Res.: 1450 Abingdon Rd., 21009. Tel: 410-676-5119; 410-679-4555; Fax: 410-676-7520.
Catechesis/Religious Program—Tel: 410-676-3354. Doris McKibbon, D.R.E.(Preschool); Elizabeth Taneyhill, D.R.E. (K-8); Betty Burlin, Coord. (6-12); Patrick Perkins, Coord. (6-12). Students 701.

ANNAPOLIS, ANNE ARUNDEL CO.

1—ST. ANDREW BY THE BAY (Cape St. Claire) (1981), Rev. Stephen D. Gosnell; Deacons R. Paul Woofter; James C. Monaghan Jr.; John E. Connor; John L. Wilson.
Parish Center—701 College Pkwy., 21401. Tel: 410-974-4366; Fax: 410-974-4339.
Catechesis/Religious Program—Sr. Mary Teresa Day, S.N.D., D.R.E.; Veronica Weidenhammer, D.R.E. Students 619.

2—ST. MARY (1853), [CEM] Revs. Denis J. Sweeney, C.SS.R.; John G. Tizio, C.SS.R.; Alphonsus Olive, C.SS.R.; John Lavin, C.SS.R.; Theodore Heyburn, C.SS.R.; Patrick Flynn, C.SS.R.; Arthur Mahoney, C.SS.R.; James McDonald, C.SS.R.; Andrew Costello, C.SS.R.; Deacons Leroy S. Moore; Anthony F. Norcio. In Res., Rev. Bernard Baumgartner, C.SS.R.
Res.: 109 Duke of Gloucester St., 21401. Tel: 410-263-2396; 410-269-6092; Fax: 410-263-3027. Email: frdenis@stmaryschurch.org.
School—111 Duke of Gloucester St., 21401. Tel: 410-263-2869; Fax: 410-269-6513. Mrs. Margaret Dammeyer, Prin. Lay Teachers 37; Students 924.
High School—113 Duke of Gloucester St. 21401. Tel: 410-263-3294; Fax: 410-269-7843. Dr. Charles Reiter, Prin. School Sisters of Notre Dame 2; Lay Teachers 36; Students 574.
Catechesis/Religious Program—Tel: 410-268-5834; Fax: 410-263-7381. Joseph Goggin, D.R.E.; Stephen Beard, D.R.E. Students 1,498.
Convent—4 Shipwright St., 21401. Tel: 410-269-0568. School Sisters of Notre Dame 2.
Mission—St. John Neuman 620 N. Bestgate Rd., Anne Arundel Co. 21401. Tel: 410-266-2499; Fax: 410-266-2497.

BEL AIR, HARFORD CO., ST. MARGARET (1905), Rev. Francis X. Callahan; Karen Saccenti, Pastoral Assoc.; Deacons Patrick Goles; J. Donald MacKnew; Victor Petrosino. In Res., Rev. Msgr. Martin Stempack.
Res.: 141 Hickory Ave., 21014. Tel: 410-838-6969; Fax: 410-879-2518.
School—205 Hickory Ave., 21013. Tel: 410-879-1113. Mrs. Jane Dean, Prin. Lay Teachers 29; Students 599.
Catechesis/Religious Program—Tel: 410-838-4224. Mrs. Marge Troilo, D.R.E. Preschool & Elementary; Mrs. Karen Clemens, D.R.E. Middle & High School. Students 1,600.
Mission—St. Mary Magdalen 1716 Churchville Rd., Harford Co. 21015.

BRADSHAW, BALTIMORE CO., ST. STEPHEN (1863), [CEM] Revs. Lawrence F. Kolson; Paul Breczinski; Deacons Gilbert Hartlieb; Robert Schott; Frank R. Laws. In Res., Rev. Rony Kusnadi.
Res.: 8030 Bradshaw Rd., 21087. Tel: 410-592-7071; Fax: 410-592-6803.
School—8028 Bradshaw Rd., 21087. Tel: 410-592-7617; Fax: 410-592-7330. Mrs. Mary M. Patrick, Prin.
Catechesis/Religious Program—Tel: 410-592-8666. Sr. Angela DeFontes, O.S.F., D.R.E. Students 402.

BRUNSWICK, FREDERICK CO., ST. FRANCIS OF ASSISI (1893), [JC] Rev. Lawrence Gesy; Deacon Lawrence Teixeira, Dir.
Res.: 113 First Ave., 21716. Tel: 301-834-9185; Fax: 301-834-4162.
Catechesis/Religious Program—Tel: 301-834-8179. Mrs. Patricia Sigler, D.R.E. Students 108.
Mission—St. Mary's Petersville, Frederick Co.

BUCKEYSTOWN, FREDERICK CO., ST. JOSEPH-ON-CARROLLTON MANOR (1811), [CEM] Revs. Lawrence K. Frazier; Paul J. Iaia, Pastor Emeritus.
Mailing Address: P.O. Box 33, 21717. Tel: 301-663-0907; Fax: 301-874-0247.
Res.: 5843 Manor Woods Rd., Frederick, 21703.
Catechesis/Religious Program—Tel: 301-663-0907, Ext. 12. Miss Marian Cochran, D.R.E. Students 315.

CLARKSVILLE, HOWARD CO., ST. LOUIS (1855), [CEM] Rev. Msgr. Joseph L. Luca; Revs. Martin J. Burnham; Erik J. Arnold; Deacons Edward Kernan; Fred Mauser; Mr. Lyle K. Weiss, Pastoral Assoc.
Res.: 12500 Clarksville Pike, 21029. Tel: 410-531-6040; Fax: 410-531-6191.
School—Tel: 410-531-6664; Fax: 410-531-6690. Mrs. Mary Theresa Weiss, Prin. Lay Teachers 29; Students 518.
Catechesis/Religious Program—Tel: 410-531-6688; Fax: 410-531-6689. Vistoria Yozwiak, D.R.E.; Patrick Sprankle. Students 1,165.

COCKEYSVILLE, BALTIMORE CO., ST. JOSEPH (1852), [CEM] Rev. Msgr. Paul G. Cook; Revs. Charles Wible; J. Collin Poston; Sr. Rose Lindner, S.S.N.D., Pastoral Assoc.; Deacons Edward Sulivan; Martin Nocchi; Ann LaRocque, Pastoral Assoc.
Res.: 101 Church Ln., 21030. Tel: 410-683-0600; Fax: 410-628-2956.
School—105 Church Ln., 21030. Fax: 410-628-6814. Sr. Anne O'Donnell, R.S.M., Prin. Lay Teachers 25; Students 455.
Catechesis/Religious Program—Tel: 410-666-8840. Marie Lybelt, D.R.E. Students 454.

COLUMBIA, HOWARD CO., ST. JOHN THE EVANGELIST (1967), Revs. Charles J. Tilley, S.J. (MRY); Antonio Velez; Stephen Richardson; Deacons George Martin; James J. Benjamin, M.D.
5885 Robert Oliver Pl., 21045. Tel: 410-964-1434; Fax: 410-740-9323.
Interfaith Centers—10431 Twin Rivers Rd., 21044. Tel: 410-964-1425; Fax: 410-730-9253. (Wilde Lake)
Catechesis/Religious Program—Tel: 410-964-1440. Kathleen Armstrong, D.R.E. Students 513.

CRESAPTOWN, ALLEGANY CO., ST. AMBROSE (1887), [CEM] Rev. James Kurtz, O.F.M.Cap.; Ms. Margaret Gaughan, Pastoral Assoc. & D.R.E.
Res.: P.O. Box 5130, 21505-5130. Tel: 301-729-2790; Fax: 301-729-2436.
Catechesis/Religious Program—Students 136.

CROFTON, ANNE ARUNDEL CO., ST. ELIZABETH ANN SETON (1976), Rev. Edward C. Connelly; Sr. Katherine O'Donnell, R.S.M., Pastoral Assoc.; Deacon Frederick Seibold.
Office—1800 Seton Dr., 21114. Tel: 410-721-5770; Fax: 410-721-5508.
School—School of the Incarnation (See separate listing.)
Catechesis/Religious Program—Tel: 410-721-5774. Sr. Helen Milano, S.S.F., D.R.E. Students 638.

CUMBERLAND, ALLEGANY CO.

1—ST. MARY (1900), (Italian), [CEM] Rev. Milton A. Hipsley; Deacon David A. Conley.
Res.: 300 E. Oldtown Rd., 21502. Tel: 301-777-2990; Fax: 301-777-1108.
School—Bishop Walsh School
Catechesis/Religious Program—Tel: 301-722-3445. Yuette Leith, D.R.E. Students 80.

2—ST. PATRICK (1790), (Irish), [CEM] Rev. Thomas R. Bevan; Deacons Paul Dignan; Loren Mooney; Francis L. Werner Jr.; Teresa Files, Admin. Asst.
Res.: 201 N. Centre St., 21502. Tel: 301-777-1750; Fax: 301-777-2669. Email: spcumber@archbalt.org.
Catechesis/Religious Program—Loren L. Mooney, D.R.E. Students 107.

3—SS. PETER AND PAUL (1848), (German) [CEM] Revs. James Kurtz, O.F.M.Cap.; Vernon Busch, O.F.M.Cap. In Res., Revs. Bernard Finerty O.F.M.Cap.; Victor Kirley.
Res.: 109 N. Smallwood St., 21502-2992. Tel: 301-777-3131; Fax: 301-759-3568.
Catechesis/Religious Program—Students 111.

DAVIDSONVILLE, ANNE ARUNDEL CO., HOLY FAMILY (1929), Rev. Joseph F. Barr.
Res.: 826 W. Central Ave., P.O. Box 130, 21035-0130. Tel: 410-269-0586; 301-261-7399; Fax: 410-798-5315. Email: holyfamilychurch_davidsonville_md@juno.com.
Catechesis/Religious Program—Tel: 410-798-5680. Sharon Graham, D.R.E. Students 675.

EDGEWATER, ANNE ARUNDEL CO., OUR LADY OF PERPETUAL HELP (1976), Rev. Frank J. Brauer; Deacon Stephen Cooney.
Res.: 515 Loch Haven Rd., 21037. Tel: 410-956-2883; Fax: 410-798-0076.
Catechesis/Religious Program—Tel: 410-798-5161. Mary Ellen Fisher, D.R.E. Students 269.

EDGEWOOD, HARFORD CO., PRINCE OF PEACE (1975), Sr. Joan Minella, S.S.N.D., Pastoral Life Dir.
Office Address—2600 Willoughby Beach Rd. 21040. Tel: 410-679-5912; Fax: 410-679-6715.
Catechesis/Religious Program—Joanne Haney, D.R.E. Students 115.

ELLICOTT CITY, HOWARD CO.

1—OUR LADY OF PERPETUAL HELP (1893), [CEM] Revs. Richard E. Smith; Isaac Karoor; Sr. Mary Ann Pierson, S.N.D., Pastoral Assoc.
Res.: 4795 Ilchester Rd., 21043. Tel: 410-747-4334; Fax: 410-747-4339.
School—4801 Ilchester Rd., Elliott City, 21043. Tel: 410-744-4251; Fax: 410-788-5210. Lay Teachers 23; Students 259.
Catechesis/Religious Program—Tel: 410-747-0131; Fax: 410-788-3905. Mrs. Judy Gruel, D.R.E. Students 927.

2—ST. PAUL (1838), [CEM] Rev. Michael Jendrek.
Res.: 3755 St. Paul St., 21043. Tel: 410-465-1670; Fax: 410-313-8551.
Catechesis/Religious Program—Tel: 410-465-0622. Sr. Dorothy Franz, O.S.F. Students 237.

3—RESURRECTION (1974), Revs. James O. McGovern; Timothy J. Fell; John Dobranski; Deacons Ray Britt; John Comegna.
Office—3175 Paulskirk Dr., 21042. Tel: 410-461-9111; Fax: 410-203-9419.
School—Resurrection/St. Paul, Tel: 410-465-8746; Fax: 410-461-8621. Sr. Joan Elias, G.N.S.H., Prin. Grey Nuns of the Sacred Heart 2; Lay Teachers 22; Students 376.
Catechesis/Religious Program—Tel: 410-461-9111, Ext. 221. Linda Keedy, D.R.E. Students 983.

EMMITSBURG, FREDERICK CO.

1—ST. ANTHONY SHRINE (1805), [CEM] Revs. James Hannon; Edward T. Sargus, Pastor Emeritus (Retired); Sisters Carol C. Czyzewski, F.S.S.J., Pastoral Assoc. Tel: 301-271-4099; M. Valenta Rusin, F.S.S.J., Pastoral Min. Tel: 301-271-7300.
Res. & Office Address: 16150 St. Anthony Rd., 21727. Tel: 301-447-2367 (Office); Fax: 301-447-3618 (Office).
Catechesis/Religious Program—Tel: 301-271-4099; Fax: 301-271-7127. Sr. M. Valenta Rusin, F.S.S.J., D.R.E. & Pastoral Min. Students 32.

2—ST. JOSEPH (1793), [CEM 2] Revs. William J. O'Brien, C.M.; Stephen P. Trzecieski, C.M. In Res., Revs. William Goff, C.M.; Michael J. Kennedy, C.M.
Res.: 47 DePaul St., 21727. Tel: 301-447-2326; Fax: 301-447-3579. Email: stjosephparish@adelphia.net.
Catechesis/Religious Program—Students 110.

FALLSTON, HARFORD CO., ST. MARK (1887), Rev. Edward B. Hemler; Deacons T. Russell Gibson; Charles Hicks; Marty Perry; Mrs. Charlotte Henderson, Pastoral Assoc.
Res.: 812 Reckord Rd., 21047. Tel: 410-879-9110; 410-877-9750; Fax: 410-877-0576.
Catechesis/Religious Program—Tel: 410-879-1706; 410-877-1692; Fax: 410-877-3502. Mrs. Barbara S. Cupp, D.R.E. Students 565.

FREDERICK, FREDERICK CO.

1—ST. JOHN THE EVANGELIST (1763), [CEM] Revs. Wayne G. Funk; Rafael Murillo; Leo Tittler, Senior Priest; George I. Jakopac; Deacons John L. Manley; Daniel C. Roff; J. Michael Zusi.
Res.: 112 E. Second St., 21701. Tel: 301-662-8288; Fax: 301-698-1832.
School—St. John Regional Catholic School, Tel: 301-662-6722; Fax: 301-695-7024. See separate listing.
Catechesis/Religious Program—Tel: 301-662-8495; Fax: 301-695-7024. April Dietrich, D.R.E.; Stacey Ford. Students 827.
Mission—St. Katharine 2037 William Franklin Dr., Drexel, Frederick Co. 21702. Tel: 301-360-9581; Fax: 301-369-9582.

2—ST. KATHARINE DREXEL ROMAN CATHOLIC CONGREGATION, INC. (2003), Rev. Keith W. Boisvert.
2037 William Franklin Dr., 21702. Tel: 301-360-9581.

3—ST. KATHERINE DREXEL MISSION, , 2037 William Frankin Dr., 21702.

FROSTBURG, ALLEGANY CO., ST. MICHAEL (1850), [CEM] Revs. Paul A. Byrnes; Adam Parker; Douglas Kenney; Deacon Bertrand O. Michael.
Res.: 44 E. Main St., P.O. Box 402, 21532. Tel: 301-689-6767; Fax: 301-689-6411.
School—56 E. Main St., 21532. Tel: 301-689-2155. Mrs. Kathy Black, Prin. Lay Teachers 12; Students 147.
Catechesis/Religious Program—Tel: 301-689-2898. Camilla Rawe, D.R.E. Students 151.

FULTON, HOWARD CO., ST. FRANCIS OF ASSISI (1988), Rev. Dennis P. Diehl; Deacon Joseph McKenna.
Office: 8300 Old Columbia Rd., 20759. Tel: 410-792-0470; Fax: 410-792-0472. Email: stfran047@aol.com.
Res.: 10681 Glen Hannah Dr., Laurel, 20723. Tel: 410-880-3068.
Catechesis/Religious Program—Tel: 410-880-1285. Kathy Airel. Students 550.

GAMBRILLS, ANNE ARUNDEL CO., CHURCH OF THE HOLY APOSTLES (1999), Rev. Michael J. Callaghan.
Res.: 2601 Symphony Ln., 21054. Tel: 410-451-8285; Fax: 410-451-8285.
School—School of the Incarnation, Inc., Tel: 410-519-2285; Fax: 410-519-2286. Dr. Barbara Edmonson, Prin. See separate listing.
Church of the Holy Apostles Roman Catholic Congregation, Inc.—Tel: 410-793-0270; Fax: 410-793-0270.
Catechesis/Religious Program—Students 500.

GLEN BURNIE, ANNE ARUNDEL CO.

1—CHURCH OF THE GOOD SHEPHERD (1972), Revs. John L. Kelly; Joseph V. Messer (Retired).
Res.: 1451 Furnace Ave., 21060. Tel: 410-761-4607; Fax: 410-761-6019.
School—Arthur Slade Regional Catholic School, Tel: 410-766-7130; Fax: 410-787-0594. See separate listing.
Catechesis/Religious Program—Students 14.

2—CRUCIFIXION, CHURCH OF THE (1972), Rev. Dale Picarella.
Rectory—100 Scott Ave., 21060. Tel: 410-768-4880; Fax: 410-768-5025.
Catechesis/Religious Program—Sandy Klohr, D.R.E. Students 47.

3—HOLY TRINITY (1919), Revs. J. Bruce Jarboe; Brandon Carr; Sydney Griffith; Camilo Aristu;

Deacons John Boscoe; Leroy Beimel; Robert Herzog. In Res., Revs. Joseph McDonough; William Headley.
Res.: 7436 Baltimore-Annapolis Blvd., 21061. Tel: 410-766-1213.
Parish Center—126 Dorsey Rd., 21061. Tel: 410-766-5070; Fax: 410-760-6738.
School—Arthur Slade Regional Catholic School, Tel: 410-766-7130; Fax: 410-787-0594. See separate listing.
Catechesis/Religious Program—Tel: 410-768-3890; Fax: 410-760-6738. Pat Stanley, D.R.E. (PreK-5); Joy Wiburt, D.R.E. (6-8); Diana Healy, D.R.E. (9-12). Students 500.

GLYNDON, BALTIMORE CO., SACRED HEART (1873), Rev. Msgr. Lloyd E. Aiken; Sr. Judith Cianfrogna, S.S.J., Pastoral Assoc.; Deacon James A. Ryan.
Res.: 65 Sacred Heart Ln., 21071. Tel: 410-833-1696; Fax: 410-833-2676.
School—Tel: 410-833-0857; Fax: 410-833-0914. Anne H. Price, Prin.; Jeanne Cossentino, Asst. Prin. Sisters 2; Lay Teachers 39; Students 820.
Catechesis/Religious Program—Tel: 410-833-8515. Sr. Loretta Marchetti, S.S.J., D.R.E. Students 668.

GRANTSVILLE, NORTHERN GARRETT CO., ST. ANN (1976), Rev. Douglas Kenney.
Res.: 12814 New Germany Rd., 21536. Tel: 301-895-5877; Fax: 301-895-4353. Email: sagrants@archbalt.org.
Catechesis/Religious Program—Camilla Rawe, D.R.E. Students 54.

HAGERSTOWN, WASHINGTON CO.

1—ST. ANN (1966), Revs. Thomas Polk; Jon Kightlinger; Deacons William Nairn; Richard Kunkel.
Res.: 1010 Oak Hill Ave., 21742. Tel: 301-791-2727. Church: 1525 Oak Hill Ave., 21742. Tel: 301-733-0410; Fax: 301-733-6218.
School—Saint Maria Goretti High School, Tel: 301-739-4266; Fax: 301-739-4261. See Separate Listing.
Catechesis/Religious Program—Tel: 301-733-0411. Patricia Rogers, D.R.E. Students 392.

2—ST. JOSEPH (1951), Rev. Christopher P. Moore.
Res.: 17630 Virginia Ave., 21740. Tel: 301-797-9445; Fax: 301-797-2490.
Catechesis/Religious Program—Tel: 301-790-1610. Denise Kuhna, D.R.E. Students 134.

3—ST. MARY (1790), Rev. George A. Limmer; Rev. Msgr. Robert S. Passarelli, Pastor Emeritus (Retired); Rev. Robert Morey.
Res.: 224 W. Washington St., 21740. Tel: 301-739-0390; Fax: 301-739-7082.
School—218 Washington St., Hagertown, 21740. Tel: 301-733-1184; Fax: 301-745-4997. School Sisters of Notre Dame 3; Lay Teachers 25; Students 301.
Catechesis/Religious Program—Tel: 301-790-2444. Jan McCarter, D.R.E. Students 296.
Mission—St. Michels, Formerly St. James 224 Washington St., Clear Spring, Washington Co. 21722. Tel: 410-432-2887; Fax: 301-842-3253.

HANCOCK, WASHINGTON CO., ST. PETER'S (1834), [CEM] Rev. Joseph J. Cosgrove.
Res. & Mailing Address: 16 E. High St., 21750. Tel: 301-678-6339; Fax: 301-678-7578. Email: stpeters@nfif.com.
Mission—St. Patrick's (1860), [CEM] 12517 St. Patrick Rd., S.E., Little Orleans, Allegany Co. 21766.
Catechesis/Religious Program—Terri Staley, D.R.E.

HAVRE DE GRACE, HARFORD CO., ST. PATRICK'S (1847), [CEM] Rev. William J. O'Brien III; Sr. Frances Schiminsky, O.S.F., Pastoral Assoc.
Res.: 615 Congress Ave., 21078. Tel: 410-939-2525; 410-575-6741; Fax: 410-575-6490.
Catechesis/Religious Program—Tel: 410-939-2547. Coleen Branigan, D.R.E. Students 178.

HICKORY, HARFORD CO., ST. IGNATIUS (1792), [CEM] Revs. James Barker; Christopher Carney, Senior Priest; Stephen Sutton; Deacons Robert Lehr, Business Mgr.; Ralph Trautwein, Pastoral Assoc.; Deborah Czawlytko, Pastoral Assoc.
Res.: 533 E. Jarrettsville Rd., Forest Hill, 21050. Tel: 410-879-1926; Fax: 410-879-1352.
Catechesis/Religious Program—Tel: 410-879-9390. Mary Lou Hare, D.R.E.; Doris Wheeler, D.R.E. Students 1,217.

HUNT VALLEY, BALTIMORE CO., CATHOLIC COMMUNITY OF ST. FRANCIS XAVIER (1988), Rev. Jeffrey S. Dauses; Rev. Msgr. Thomas J. Donellan, Pastor Emeritus.
13717 Cuba Rd., P.O. Box 407, 21030. Tel: 410-785-0356; Fax: 410-785-1628.
Res.: 19 Rainflower Path #204, Sparks, 21152. Tel: 410-472-4836. Email: info@ccsfx.net.
Catechesis/Religious Program—Patricia Allshouse, D.R.E. Students 168.

HYDES, BALTIMORE CO., ST. JOHN THE EVANGELIST (1822), [CEM] Rev. William F. Franken; Rev. Msgrs. John C. Collopy (Retired); Charles F. Meisel (Retired); Deacons J. Donald Murray; Frederick X. Schoennagel.
Res.: 13305 Long Green Pike, 21082. Tel: 410-592-6206; Fax: 410-817-4432.
School—13311 Long Green Pike, 21082. Tel: 410-592-9585, Ext. 120; Fax: 410-817-4548. Mrs. Genevieve Delcher, Prin. Lay Teachers 30; Students 355.
Catechesis/Religious Program—M. Theresa Konitzer, D.R.E. Students 631.

IAMSVILLE, FREDERICK CO., ST. IGNATIUS LOYOLA (1879), Rev. John J. Jicha, Temp. Admin.
Office—4103 Prices Distillery Rd., 21754. Tel: 301-695-8845; Fax: 301-695-0259. Email: jjcha@frederickmd.com.
Res.: 4914 Bush Creek Dr., Monrovia, 21770.
School—St. John Regional School, Tel: 301-662-6722. See separate listing.
Catechesis/Religious Program—Theresa Ivanism, D.R.E. Students 434.

JESSUP, ANNE ARUNDEL CO., ST. LAWRENCE (1866), [CEM] Revs. John Dorn, O.SS.T.; Juan Vacquez, O.SS.T. In Res., Rev. Stanley W. DeBoe, O.SS.T.
Res.: 7669 Clark Rd., Hanover, 21076. Tel: 410-799-1970; Fax: 410-799-4425.
School—Arthur Slade Regional Catholic School, Tel: 410-766-7130; Fax: 410-787-0584. See separate listing.
Catechesis/Religious Program—St. Lawrence School of Religion, P.O. Box 1188, 20794. Tel: 410-799-7790; Fax: 410-799-6151. Students 118.

JOPPA, HARFORD CO., CHURCH OF THE HOLY SPIRIT (1963), Rev. Joseph C. Simmons.
Res.: 540 Joppa Farm Rd., 21085. Tel: 410-679-2191.
Office—Tel: 410-679-0377; Fax: 410-679-2874.
Catechesis/Religious Program—Sr. Joan Mikulski, M.H.S.H., D.R.E. Students 138.

LAUREL, ANNE ARUNDEL CO., RESURRECTION OF OUR LORD (1963), Revs. John T. Wielebski; Aristu Camilo, Hispanic Min.; Joseph F. Kitko, Pastor Emeritus (Retired). In Res., Rev. Francis R. Spencer.
Res.: 8400 Brock Bridge Rd., 20724. Tel: 410-792-7982; Fax: 410-792-8337.
Office Address: 8402 Brock Bridge Rd., 20724.
Catechesis/Religious Program—Tel: 301-498-9803. Sr. Eileen Dolak, S.S.J., D.R.E. & Pastoral Assoc. Students 195.

LIBERTYTOWN, FREDERICK CO., ST. PETER (1823), [CEM] Rev. John A. Dietzenbach; Deacon Michael Misulia.
P.O. Box 278, 21762.
Res.: 9201 A Church St., 21762. Tel: 301-898-5111 (Office); 301-898-9069 (Rectory); Fax: 301-898-0465.
Catechesis/Religious Program—Anne Mason, D.R.E.; Caroline Nolan, D.R.E.; Dawn Miller. Students 755.

LINTHICUM HEIGHTS, ANNE ARUNDEL CO., ST. PHILIP NERI (1964), Rev. Msgr. Francis X. Zorbach (Retired); Deacon Robert Keeley. In Res., Rev. John L. Lippold (Retired).
Parish Center—6405 S. Orchard Rd., 21090-2628. Tel: 410-859-0571; Fax: 410-859-5047.
School—6401 Orchard Rd., 21090. Tel: 410-859-1212; Fax: 410-859-5840. Teresa Baker, Prin. Lay Teachers 28; Students 570.
Catechesis/Religious Program—Tel: 410-859-0571, Ext. 22. Anne Nelson, D.R.E. Students 369.

LONACONING, ALLEGANY CO., ST. MARY OF THE ANNUNCIATION (1865), [CEM] Rev. Gerald LaPorta, Pastor Emeritus; Sr. Marietta Culhane, O.S.F., Pastoral Life Dir.
Res.: 16102 St. Mary Church Ter., 21539. Tel: 301-463-2514; Fax: 301-463-6729.
Catechesis/Religious Program—Students 42.

MANCHESTER, CARROLL CO., ST. BARTHOLOMEW (1865), Rev. Michael J. Roach.
Mailing Address & Parish Center: 3071 Park Ave., P.O. Box 448, 21102. Tel: 410-239-8881.
Res.: 2940 Park Ave., P.O. Box 448, 21102-0448. Tel: 410-239-8207; Fax: 410-239-3216.
Catechesis/Religious Program—Tom Abbott, D.R.E.; Lynn Szymanski. Students 473.

MIDDLETOWN, FREDERICK CO., HOLY FAMILY CATHOLIC COMMUNITY (1986), Rev. John Charles Moore; Deacon P. Gregory Rausch.
Mailing Address: 7321 Burkittsville Rd., 21769. Tel: 301-473-4800; Fax: 301-371-6810.
Res.: 3240 Old National Pike, 21769. Tel: 301-371-3239.
Church: 7321 Burkittsville Rd., 21769. Tel: 301-473-4800; Fax: 301-371-6810.
Catechesis/Religious Program—Students 476.

MIDLAND, ALLEGANY CO., ST. JOSEPH (1891), (Irish), [CEM] Sr. Joan Maenner, Pastoral Life Dir.
Mailing Address: 19925 Church St., P.O. Box 1, 21542. Tel: 301-777-7060; Fax: 301-463-6729.
Catechesis/Religious Program—Students 52.

MILLERSVILLE, ANNE ARUNDEL CO., OUR LADY OF THE FIELDS (1903), [CEM] Revs. Eugene Nickol; Andrew Aaron; Deacons Nick Pitocco; Anthony Grillo; Edward Stoops; Albert Kosla.
Res.: 1070 Cecil Ave. S., 21108. Tel: 410-987-1551; Fax: 410-987-9723.
School—School of the Incarnation, Tel: 410-519-2285. (See separate listing.)
Catechesis/Religious Program—Tel: 410-923-2195. Donna Fischer, D.R.E.; Margaret Adams, D.R.E.; Sue Dobryzkowski, D.R.E. Students 900.
Mission—Church of Holy Apostles, Anne Arundel Co.

MOUNT SAVAGE, ALLEGANY CO., ST. PATRICK (1863), [CEM] Rev. Douglas Kenney; Sisters Joan Minella, S.S.N.D., Pastoral Life Dir.; Eileen Carney, O.S.U., Pastoral Assoc.
Mailing Address: 15706 St. Patrick Church Rd., NW, 21545. Tel: 301-264-3521; Fax: 301-264-3603.
Catechesis/Religious Program—Students 55.

OAKLAND, GARRETT CO., ST. PETER THE APOSTLE (1851), [CEM] Rev. Donald J. Parson; Deacon James L. Comfort Sr.
Res.: 208 S. Fourth St., 21550. Tel: 301-334-2202; Fax: 301-334-9006.
Catechesis/Religious Program—Betty Eaton, D.R.E. Students 88.
Mission—Immaculate Conception 208 S. 4th St., Kitzmiller, Garrett Co. 21550. See separate listing under St. Peter the Apostle.
Mission—St. Peter of the Lake Deep Creek Lake, Garrett Co.

ODENTON, ANNE ARUNDEL CO., ST. JOSEPH (1924), Rev. William L. Viola; Deacon Richard C. Swann.
Mailing Address & Church: 1283 Odenton Rd., 21113. Tel: 410-551-9238; Fax: 410-674-4761. Web: www.geocities.com/st_joseph_odenton.
School—School of the Incarnation, Tel: 410-766-7130; Fax: 410-787-0594. (See separate listing.)
Catechesis/Religious Program—Deacon Patricia Dieterich, D.R.E. Students 448.

PARKTON, BALTIMORE CO., OUR LADY OF GRACE (1974), Rev. Msgr. Nicholas P. Amato.
Res.: 425 Everett Rd., P.O. Box 517, Monkton, 21111. Tel: 410-329-2102.
Parish Center—18310 Middletown Rd., P.O. Box 360, 21120. Tel: 410-329-6826; Fax: 410-329-6830.
Catechesis/Religious Program—Students 472.

PASADENA, ANNE ARUNDEL CO.

1—ST. JANE FRANCES DE CHANTAL (Riviera Beach) (1946), Rev. Msgr. Thomas J. Fannon, Pastor Emeritus (Retired); Revs. Kevin T. Schenning; Gregory Ferri; Deacon John Rafter.
Res.: 8499 Virginia Ave., 21122. Tel: 410-255-4646; Fax: 410-437-5191.
School—8513 Saint Jane Dr., 21122. Tel: 410-255-4750; Fax: 410-360-6720. Ronald Burinsky, Prin. Lay Teachers 27; Students 605.
Catechesis/Religious Program—Tel: 410-437-4727. Mary Beth Barnes, D.R.E. Students 481.

2—OUR LADY OF THE CHESAPEAKE (1979), Revs. Brian M. Rafferty; Walter J. Paulits, Ph.D., Pastor Emeritus (Retired); Donald Latrick, Pastoral Assoc.
Church: 8325 Ventnor Rd., 21122. Tel: 410-255-3677; Fax: 410-437-7527.
School—Tel: 410-766-7130; Fax: 410-787-0594. See separate listing
Catechesis/Religious Program—Fax: 410-437-7527. Timothy Janiszewski, D.R.E. Students 352.

POPLAR SPRINGS, HOWARD CO., ST. MICHAEL (1879), [CEM] Rev. Michael J. Ruane; Deacon Gary L. Fulmer.
Res.: 1200 St. Michael's Rd., Mount Airy, 21771-3299. Tel: 410-489-4211; 410-442-2845; Fax: 410-442-5939.
Parish Center—Tel: 410-489-7667; 410-442-1717; Fax: 410-442-1486.
Catechesis/Religious Program—Tel: 410-488-7667; Fax: 410-442-1486. Ms. Amy Sorensen, D.R.E. Students 715.

PYLESVILLE, HARFORD CO., ST. MARY (1853), [CEM] Rev. A. Henry Kunkel III; Deacons Simon Driesen; John R. Simpson Jr.; Gary Dumer Jr.
Res.: 1021 St. Mary's Rd., 21132. Tel: 410-838-7471; 410-879-4015; Fax: 410-452-8493.
Catechesis/Religious Program— Veronica Lux, D.R.E. Students 390.

RANDALLSTOWN, BALTIMORE CO., HOLY FAMILY (1876), [CEM] Revs. Andrew S. Mohl; Walter J. McGovern, Senior Priest (Retired); Dennis W. Kast, Business Mgr. In Res., Rev. William A. Collins.
Res.: 9535 Liberty Rd., 21133. Tel: 410-521-3883; Fax: 410-922-3804.
Office—Tel: 410-922-3800.
School—9535 Liberty Rd., 21133. Tel: 410-922-3677; Fax: 410-521-9764. Susan Nitsch, Prin. Lay Teachers 17; Students 195.
Catechesis/Religious Program—9531 Liberty Rd., 21133. Tel: 410-922-2805. David Brennan, D.R.E. Students 123.

SEVERN, ANNE ARUNDEL CO., ST. BERNADETTE (1969), Rev. Domenic L. Cieri; Ann McDonald, Pastoral Assoc. Tel: 410-969-2785.
Res.: 801 Stevenson Rd., 21144. Tel: 410-969-2783; Fax: 410-969-2789.
School—Arthur Slade Regional Catholic School, Tel: 410-766-7130; Fax: 410-787-0594. See separate listing.
Catechesis/Religious Program—Tel: 410-969-2786.

Theresa Platania, D.R.E. Students 228.

SEVERNA PARK, ANNE ARUNDEL CO., ST. JOHN THE EVANGELIST (1959), Revs. Mitchell T. Rozanski; George J. Gannon; Deacons John Naughton, (Retired); Dean Lopata. In Res., Rev. Msgr. John J. Aver.
Res.: 689 Ritchie Hwy., S.E., 21146. Tel: 410-647-4884; Fax: 410-544-3047.
School—669 Ritchie Hwy., 21146. Tel: 410-647-2283; Fax: 410-431-5438. Sr. Linda Larsen, S.S.J., Prin. Sisters of St. Joseph, Chestnut Hill 5; Lay Teachers 29; Students 596.
Catechesis/Religious Program—Tel: 410-647-4892; Fax: 410-431-8912. Maryann Lutz, D.R.E.; John Poland, D.R.E. Students 732.
Convent—Tel: 410-647-2041.

SYKESVILLE, CARROLL CO., ST. JOSEPH (1868), [CEM] Revs. Patrick J. Tonry, S.M.; Paul A. Reich, S.M.; Deacon Mark Ripper.
Office—915 Liberty Rd., Eldersburg, 21784. Tel: 410-795-7838; Fax: 410-795-7516.
Res.: 7620 Mellor Ave., P.O. Box 384, 21784. Tel: 410-795-2722.
Catechesis/Religious Program—Tel: 410-552-5402. Students 1,127.

TANEYTOWN, CARROLL CO., ST. JOSEPH (1797), [CEM] Revs. Martin Eugene Feild; Paul F. Dolan, Pastor Emeritus (Retired); Deacons Darrell W. Smith; Stanley Wise.
Res.: 44 Frederick St., 21787. Tel: 410-756-2500; Fax: 410-756-1260.
Catechesis/Religious Program—Tel: 410-876-8108. Terry Smith, D.R.E. Students 161.

THURMONT, FREDERICK CO., OUR LADY OF MOUNT CARMEL (1856), [CEM] Rev. James Hannon; Sisters Carol C. Czyzewski, F.S.S.J., Pastoral Assoc.; M. Valenta Rusin, F.S.S.J., Pastoral Min.
Office—16150 St. Anthony Rd., Emmitsburg, 21727. Tel: 301-447-6294; Fax: 301-447-3618.
Church: Church St., 21788.
Catechesis/Religious Program—Tel: 301-271-4099; Fax: 301-271-7127. Sr. M. Valenta Rusin, F.S.S.J., Pastoral Min. & D.R.E. Tel: 301-271-7300. Students 96.

TIMONIUM, BALTIMORE CO., CHURCH OF THE NATIVITY (1968), Rev. Michael J. White.
Office—20 E. Ridgely Rd., 21093. Tel: 410-252-6080; Fax: 410-252-2657. Web: www.churchnativity.org.
Res.: Tel: 410-252-0345.
Catechesis/Religious Program—Kristin Rupprecht, D.R.E. Students 562.

WALKERSVILLE, FREDERICK CO., ST. TIMOTHY (1985), Rev. Richard J. Murphy.
Res.: 200 Glade Blvd., 21793. Tel: 301-845-8028; Fax: 301-845-0332.
8651 Biggs Rd., 21793.
Catechesis/Religious Program—Tel: 301-845-8025; Fax: 301-845-8027. Sandra Maxey, D.R.E. Students 252.

WEST RIVER, ANNE ARUNDEL CO., OUR LADY OF SORROWS (1866), [CEM] Rev. Mark Logue; Deacon John H. Abell Jr.
Res.: 101 Owensville Rd., 20778. Tel: 410-867-2059; 410-269-6803; Fax: 410-867-8276. Email: frmark.logne@oloswestriver.org. Web: www.oloswestriver.org.
Catechesis/Religious Program—Tel: 410-867-1941. Joyce McMillan, D.R.E. Students 309.

WESTERNPORT, ALLEGANY CO., ST. PETER (1854), [CEM] Revs. Paul Byrnes; Adam Parker.
Res.: 127 Church St., 21562. Tel: 301-359-3055; Fax: 301-359-0657.
Catechesis/Religious Program—Tel: 301-359-9832. Kathleen Broadwater, D.R.E. Students 80.
Mission—St. Gabriel

WESTMINSTER, CARROLL CO., ST. JOHN (1852), [CEM] Rev. Msgr. Arthur F. Valenzano; Revs. Leo E. Patalinghug; Gerard Steffenes; Brian P. Nolan, Pastoral Assoc.; Deacons John Coster; Robert Malinowski.
Res.: 43 Monroe St., 21157. Tel: 410-848-4744; 410-876-2248; Fax: 410-857-1519.
School—45 Monroe St., 21157. Tel: 410-848-7455; Fax: 410-848-2822. Lay Teachers 30; Students 590.
Catechesis/Religious Program—Tel: 410-848-8443. Paul D. Gallagher, D.R.E. Students 1,050.

WILLIAMSPORT, WASHINGTON CO., ST. AUGUSTINE (1854), Rev. John P. Carter; Deacon Andrew Komarinski, (Retired).
Res.: 32 E. Potomac St., 21795. Tel: 301-223-7959; Fax: 301-223-9506.
Catechesis/Religious Program—Students 35.
Mission—St. James 127 N. Main St., Boonsboro, Washington Co. 21713.

WOODSTOCK, BALTIMORE CO., ST. ALPHONSUS RODRIGUEZ (1869), [CEM] Rev. Joseph P. Lacey, S.J.; Dee Papania, Pastoral Assoc.; Deacon William Fallon. In Res., Rev. Richard P. McHugh, S.J.
Res.: 10800 Old Court Rd., 21163. Tel: 410-461-5267; Fax: 410-750-7286.
Catechesis/Religious Program—Students 204.

SHRINES

NATIONAL SHRINE OF ST. ELIZABETH ANN SETON, Sr. Mary Clare Hughes, D.C., Admin.
333 S. Seton Ave., Emmitsburg, 21727. Tel: 301-447-6606; Fax: 301-447-6061.

Chaplains of Public Institutions

BALTIMORE. *Baltimore City Correctional Center, Baltimore Pre-Release Unit.* Rev. Chuck Canterna.
Baltimore City Jail. Rev. Damien Nalepa, Chap.
Baltimore City Jail, Women's Detention Center. Sr. Patricia Ash, Chap.
Carroll County Detention Center. St. John Westminister, Lay Coord., Debbie Loveland, Lay Coord. Tel 410-876-9249.
Charles H. Hickey School. Deacon Russell Matthews, Chap.
Dismas House. (Vacant)
Francis Scott Key Medical Center. Staffed by Our Lady of Fatima Parish.
Franklin Square Hospital. Deacons Nicholas F. Feurer, Daniel R. Kopczyk, Walter Shipley. Covered on rotating basis by Annunciation, St. Clement Mary Hoffbauer, Our Lady Queen of Peace, Our Lady of Mt. Carmel, St. Clare, Our Lady of Hope, St. Joseph-Fullerton, St. Anthony of Padua, St. Michael the Archangel-Overlea.
Greater Baltimore Medical Center. Immaculate Conception, Towson
Harbor Hospital. Rev. Charles Klein. Covered on rotating basis by Holy Cross, St. Mary Star of the Sea, Our Lady of Good Counsel, St. Veronica, St. Rose and St. Athanasius parish staff.
MD House of Correction. Rev. James Sanders.

Special Assignment:
Rev. Msgrs.—
Fitzgerald, John L., Apostleship of the Sea Chaplaincy for Port of Baltimore & Airport Chap. at BWI
Kenney, Jeremiah F., Tribunal, 320 Cathedral St., 21201.
Madden, Denis J. Nearest Welfare
Woy, Richard, Chancellor
Revs.—
Abrahams, John J., Special Ministry
Albright, Robert E., Campus Ministry, Towson, 21204.
Breighner, Joseph F., Special Ministry
Byrne, Glenn, St. Anthony Church, Allston, MA 02134.
Canterna, Charles J., Chap.
Carlsen, Jeffrey, Dir. Senior & Retired Priests
Carrion, Patrick M., Dir. Division of Clergy Personnel
Chase, Raymond
Collins, William A., Tribunal, 320 Cathedral St., 21201.
Cote, Joseph, Special Ministry, Chap.
Farmer, J. Kevin, Assoc. Dir. Vocations
Francik, Gerard, Dir. of Vocations, 320 Cathedral St., 21201.
Harris, Raymond L., Jr., Chap., Mt. St. Mary's College, Emmitsburg.
Hendricks, Edward S., Campus Min., Frostburg.
Henry, Paul, Spiritual Dir., VA Hospital, Perryville, 21903.
Janaites, Stanley, Chap.
Johnson, Lawrence M., Chap.
Lesnick, John F., Chap., St. Martins Home for the Aged.
Livigni, Salvatore J., Chap.
Lobert, Richard C., Educator
Martin, Joseph C., S.S. (Retired), 103 Foxridge Dr., Havre de Grace, 21078.
Mueller, Kevin A., Assoc. Dir., Msgr. O'Dwyer Retreat House, Sparks, 21152.
Murphy, Michael A., Chap. & Teacher
O'Brien, John E., Leave of Absence
Reusing, James M., Chap., Good Samaritan Hospital.
Ryan, Thomas, Chap., John Hopkins Univ, Newman Apostolate.
Seitz, Gilbert J., Archdiocesan Tribunal, 320 Cathederal St., 21201.
Spacek, William F., Chap.

On Duty Outside the Archdiocese:
Revs.—
Mahon, Matthew Shawn
Maillet, Paul
Obrimski, Paul G.
Warman, William C.
Wible, Charles

Graduate Studies:
Revs.—
Buening, Matthew, North American College, Rome, Italy.
Hilgartner, Richard
Murphy, T. Austin, Jr., North American College, Rome, Italy.

Military Chaplains:
Revs.—
Gills, Thomas, U.S.A.F.
Kruse, David B., U.S.A.F.
Spencer, F. Richard, Pentagon, Washington, DC 09832. U.S. Army
Zeller, Leonard H., Wright Patterson AFB, Patterson, OH 45843. U.S.A.F.

On Sabbatical:
Rev.—
Michael, Thornsberry

Absent on Leave:
Revs.—
Blackwell, Maurice J.
Bonderenko, Thomas S.
Cox, Brian
Dowdy, James H.
Kucharczyk, John J.
Le Fevre, Francis J.
Mannion, William
Messina, John
O'Brien, John
Pietropaoli, David
Rice, Charles
Rydzewski, Thomas
Smith, David G.
Waudby, Lawrence

Retired:
Most Rev.—
Borders, William Donald, 13th Archbishop of Baltimore, 320 Cathederal St., 21201.
Rev. Msgrs.—
Bozel, Robert A., St. Elizabeth Hall M-201, 2300 Dulaney Valley Rd., Timonium, 21093.
Collopy, John C., St. John Hall, Long Crandon, 2300 Dulaney Valley Rd., Timonium, 21093.
Cronin, James J., St. Joseph, 8420 Belair Rd., Fullerton, 21236.
Donellen, Thomas J., Hampton House, 204 E. Joppa Rd., 21204.
Fannon, Thomas J., St. Elizabeth Hall F 210, 2300 Dulaney Valley Rd., Timonium, 21093.
Lynch, Edward J., Long Crandon, 2300 Dulaney Valley Rd., Timonium, 21093.
McGowan, Myles, Long Crandon, 2300 Dulaney Valley Rd., Timonium, 21093.
Meisel, Charles F., Mercy Ridge, S614-2525 Pot Spring Rd., Timonium, 21093.
Mieczkowski, Chester J., 3215 Fleet St., 21224.
Passarelli, Robert S., 27 First St., Frostburg, 21532.
Phillips, Hugh J., Carroll Manor, Washington, DC.
Reinsfelder, John L., Holy Cross Rectory, 110 E. West St., 21230.
Schwalenberg, Martin
Strempeck, Martin R., St. Margaret, 141 Hickory Ave., Bel Air, 21014.
Tewes, Thomas, 5905 Walther Ave., 21206.
Zerhuson, Henry F., Long Crandon, 2300 Dulaney Valley Rd., Timonium, 21093.
Zorbach, Francis X.
Revs.—
Auer, John J.
Bak, Bernard, 1857 Portship Rd., 21222.
Barbernitz, John P., St. Martin's Home for the Aged.
Bayer, Edward J.
Buettner, George, 600 Light St., Apt. 351, 21230.
Buttner, Michael T.
Carey, David
Carney, John
Dolan, Paul F., Mercy Ridge, 2300 Dulaney Valley Rd., Timonium, 21093.
Donaghy, Thomas J., Wallingford, PA.
Fullen, John N., Fairfax, VA.
Gallagher, Joseph J., 3838 Roland Ave., #1302, 21211.
Gesy, Lawrence J., West Virginia
Gies, Norman J., 2453 Brazilia Dr., Apt. 21, Clearwater, FL 21163.
Girard, Stephen P.
Hill, Edward T., 4614 Eugene Ave., 21206. U.S.N.
Hopkins, Robert F.
Huesman, E. Gerard, Timonium.
Hughes, Joseph B., 2034 Park Ave., 21217.
Iaia, Paul P., 967 A. Tortoise St., Bethany Beach, DE 19930.
Kelmartin, John J., 9050 Waltham Woods Rd., Apt. C, 21234.
Kitko, Joseph F., Our Lady of Mt. Carmel, 1706 Old Eastern Ave., 21221.
Klein, Charles R., Harbor Hospital Center, 3001 S. Hanover St., 21225.
Krach, Joseph W.

La Porta, Gerald, 4136 Fairway Dr., Little River, SC 29566.
La Porta, Ross A.
Lafferty, Charles L., Long Crandon, 2300 Dulaney Valley Rd., Timonium, 21093.
Lentz, Robert F., Baltimore
Lippold, John L., St. Philip Neri
Loskarn, George, Baltimore
McGovern, Walter J., Holy Family Parish, Randallstown.
McManus, Joseph L., 6443 N.W. Fontana St., Port St. Lucie, FL 34986.
Messer, Joseph V., Good Shepherd Rectory, 1451 Furnace Ave., Glen Burnie, 21061.
Moody, William, 86 Mt. Pleasant St., Frostburg, 21532.
Muller, Kennard, 7 Joppawood Ct. A-1, 21236.
Muller, Myles, St. John Hall, Long Cramdon, 2300 Dulaney Valley Rd., Timonium, 21093.
Paulits, Walter J., Ph.D., 513 Sylview Dr., Pasadena, 21222.
Peterson, Casimir M.
Riepe, Charles K.
Rose, Alphonse G., 5510 Woodlawn Rd., 21210.
Sargus, Edward T., Lawn Acres, 420 S. 57 St., Hollywood, FL 33023.
Shaum, David W., Ph.D., Mount St. Mary's College, 16300 Old Emmitsburg Rd., Emmitsburg, 21727.
Simms, William
Smith, Alfred E., Hagerstown, 21742.
Snouffer, Philip T., 8820 Walther Blvd., Apt. 1401, 21234.
Spillane, Michael
Thomas, Paul K.
Vu, Hoat Dinh, St. Mary Rectory, 5502 York Rd., 21212.
Warczynski, Leon, 3316 Beverly Rd., 21214.
Wenderoth, Joseph R.
West, Gerald, Franciscan Sisters of Baltimore Generalate, 3725 Ellerslie Ave., 21218.
Wilson, Stuart T., 5269 North Spring Pointe Pl., Tucson, AZ 85749.
Witthauer, Paul G., Briarwood Estates, 719 Gregwood Ct., 21222.
Wojciechowski, Richard P., Lady of Mt. Carmel.
Zoubek, Ronald J.

Permanent Deacons:
Abell, John H., Jr., Our Lady of Sorrows, Owensville
Albaugh, William S., St. Joseph, Fullerton
Ames, John, St. Agnes
Anderson, Carl A., St. Edward, Baltimore
Antczak, George, St. Thomas Aquinas, Baltimore
Awalt, James L., (Retired)
Bagley, Kevin, St. Clare, Essex
Bankard, Alphonse, Our Lady of Fatima, Baltimore
Barksdale, Wardell, Jr., St. Bernardine
Baynes, Charles A., Our Lady of Mt. Carmel, Middle River
Bee, James E., St. Ann, Baltimore
Beimel, Leroy W., Holy Trinity, Glen Burnie
Benjamin, James, St. John the Evangelist, Columbia
Bolgiano, Richard, St. Mary of the Assumption & Blessed Sacrament
Boscoe, John, Holy Trinity, Glen Burnie
Briscoe, John, St. Peter Claver
Britt, Ray, (Retired)
Carpenter, Harry G., (Retired)
Chesnavage, Albert W., (Retired)
Ciesla, Paul R., St. Margaret, Bel Air
Codd, John J., St. Gabriel, Woodlawn
Comegna, John, Church of the Resurrection
Comfort, James L., Sr., St. Peter the Apostle, Oakland
Concordia, Louis, St. Michael, Frostburg
Conley, David, St. Mary, Cumberland
Cook, Charles E., (Retired)
Cooley, Stephen, Our Lady of Perpetual Help, Edgewater (Diocese of Joliet)
Coster, John E., St. John, Westminster
Crawford, Raymond C., Our Lady of Perpetual Help, Ellicott City
Davis, Henry, St. Michael the Archangel, Overlea
DeAngelis, William J., St. Joseph, Fullerton
DeCapite, James, St. Patrick, Havre de Grace
Derouaux, Bert, (Retired)
Dignan, Paul H., St. Patrick, Cumberland
Driesen, Simon, St. Mary, Pylesville
Dumer, Gary, Jr., St. Mary, Pylesville
Evans, George T., St. Rita, Baltimore
Fallon, William L., Prison Ministry and St. Alphonsus Rodriguez
Feurer, Nicholas E., St. Clement and Franklin Square Hospital, Rosedale
Fitzpatrick, T. Kelly, (Out of Diocese)
Flamini, Michael, St. Michael and St. Patrick Catholic Community
Fulmer, Gary Lee, St. Michael, Poplar Springs
Fulton, Watson, Jr., St. Ambrose, Baltimore
Gardner, Edward L., Sr., Holy Trinity, Glen Burnie
Gibson, T. Russell, (Retired)
Goles, Patrick J., St. Margaret, Bel Air
Grabenstein, Herman J., (Retired)
Graham, Robert L., Spencer, TN
Gramling, John C., Immaculate Conception, Towson
Grillo, Anthony, Our Lady of the Fields, Millersville
Gross, Theodore C., (Retired)
Hacker, Robert, Hospital Ministry, Baltimore
Harcum, Philip W., (Retired)
Harris, Jhan M., St. Veronica, Baltimore
Hartlieb, Gilbert J., (Retired)
Hawkins, John, Our Lady of Mt. Carmel, Thurmont; St. Anthony Shrine, Emmitsburg
Herzog, Robert, Holy Trinity, Glenburnie
Hicks, Charles, St. Mark, Fallston
Hiebler, Charles H., Jr., Cathedral of Mary Our Queen, Baltimore
Hodges, Frank P., Corpus Christi, Baltimore
Jauquet, William, Our Lady of Victory, Baltimore
Jenkins, George, Our Lady Queen of Peace, Baltimore
Jensen, Joseph E., Education Ministry
Johe, Richard, (Retired)
Keeley, Robert L., St. Philip Neri, Linthicum Heights
Keenan, Robert G., St. Clave, Baltimore
Kempf, William J., Jr., Unassigned
Kent, James R., Sr., (Retired)
Kernan, Edward, St. Louis
Knight, Charles, St. Bernardine, Baltimore
Komarinski, Andrew, (Retired)
Kopczyk, Daniel R., St. Joan of Arc, Aberdeen
Kosla, Albert F., Our Lady of the Fields, Millersville
Krysiak, Joseph C., St. Anthony Padua and Most Precious Blood, Baltimore
Kuhl, Thomas, Our Lady of Pompei, Baltimore
Kunkel, Richard, (Retired)
Langbehn, Eugene
Langmead, John T., St. William of York, Baltimore
Latrick, Donald P., Holy Family Ukrainian Catholic Church
Laws, Francis R., St. Stephen, Bradshaw
Lehr, Robert I., St. Ignatius, Hickory
Lopata, Dean M., St. John, Severna Park
Lynne, Robert O., SS. Philip and James, Baltimore
MacKnew, J. Donald, St. Margaret, Bel Air
Malinowski, Robert, St. John, Westminster
Manley, John L., St. Timothy, Walkersville
Mann, James L., Sr., St. Firancis Xavier, Hunt Valley
Mann, Paul T., St. Gabriel, Woodlawn
Martin, George W., St. John, Columbia
Martin, John, Immaculate Heart of Mary, Baltimore
Matthews, Russell, St. Francis Xavier and Maryland Training School for Boys, Baltimore
Matthews, Wayne
Mauser, Fred, St. Louis
McAndrews, George F., (Out of Diocese)
McCoy, Michael, St. Thomas More, Baltimore
McKenna, John I., St. Clement I, Lansdowne
McKenna, Joseph, St. Francis of Assisi, Fulton
Mercer, Charles S., St. Francis Xavier, Baltimore
Michael, Bertrand O., St. Michael, Frostburg
Micozzi, Arthur L., St. Isaac Jogues, Baltimore
Miller, Donald, St. William of York, Baltimore
Miller, Eugene, Jr., St. Mark, Fallston
Miller, Ferdinand G., (Retired)
Mills, Hugh H., Jr., St. Alphonsus, Baltimore
Misulia, Michael, (Retired)
Monaghan, James, St. Andrew by the Bay, Annapolis
Montalto, Richard W., Holy Family, Randallstown
Mooney, Loren, St. Patrick, Cumberland
Moore, LeRoy S., St. Mary, Annapolis
Moreau, Ray, Holy Family, Davidsonville
Moritz, Francis X., (Retired)
Morris, Richard F., St. Elizabeth of Hungary, Baltimore
Murray, Donald, St. John the Evangelist, Hydes
Nairn, William P., St. Ann, Hagerstown
Naughton, John F., (Retired)
Neale, Joseph L., St. Edward, Baltimore
Norcio, Anthony F., St. Mary, Annapolis
Novak, Richard D., St. Michael & St. Patrick, Baltimore
O'Neill, Harry St. A., (Retired)
Oliver, Robert W.
Osorio-Carmona, Pablo E., Spanish Ministry
Page, David A., St. Joseph, Odenton
Parrish, John N., Resurrection of Our Lord, Laurel
Perry, Martin, St. Mark, Fallston
Petrosino, Victor R., St. Margaret, Bel Air
Piet, Stanley G., (Retired)
Pinkney, Willard A., Jr., (Retired)
Pitocco, Nickolas, Our Lady of the Fields
Pivec, J. Kenneth, Immaculate Heart of Mary, Baltimore
Presberry, Seigfried, St. Mark, Cantonsville
Provenza, Vincent, (Retired)
Rafter, John J., Jr., St. Jane Frances de Chantal, Pasadena
Raible, Gerald A., St. Patrick, Cumberland
Rapisarda, Gregory A., St. Margaret
Rausch, Paul G., Holy Family, Middletown
Reinsfelder, Edward, On Duty Outside the Diocese
Resh, Michael K., Leave of Absence
Ripper, Mark
Roberts, Gerald A., Univ. of Maryland Hospital & St. Jerome, Baltimore
Rodriguez, Alex, Hispanic Ministry, St. Francis de Sales
Roff, Daniel, St. John the Evangelist, Frederick
Rongione, Frank, St. Ursula, Baltimore
Rose, Alan, Prison Ministry and St. Isaac Jogues, Baltimore
Roy, Americus M., (Retired)
Ryan, James A., Sacred Heart,Glyndon
Sainz, Miguel E., St. Mary Govans and Spanish Apostolate
Schoennagel, Frederick, Annunciation, Baltimore
Schott, Robert G., St. Stephen, Bradshaw
Schultz, Joseph L., St. Anthony of Padua/Most Precious Blood, Baltimore
Sedlevicius, John, St. Lawrence Martyr
Seibold, Frederick, St. Elizabeth Ann Seton, Crofton
Shelton, Paul D., All Saints, Baltimore
Shipley, Walter R., Jr., (Retired)
Siarkowski, Henry L., Shrine of the Little Flower, Baltimore
Simpson, John R., Jr., St. Mary, Pylesville
Smith, Darrell, St. Joseph, Taneytown
Smith, Earl A., (Retired)
Smith, Walton, St. Francis Xavier, Baltimore
Soloski, Mark, Shrine of the Sacred Heart
Stine, Richard J., St. Francis de Sales, Abingdon
Stoops, Edward, Our Lady of the Fields, Millersville
Stretmater, Daniel, Jr., (Retired)
Sullivan, Edward C., St. Joseph, Cockeysville
Sullivan, James, St. Francis de Sales
Swann, C. Richard, (Retired)
Teixeira, Lawrence, St. Louis, Clarksville
Thompson, Malcolm, All Saints, Baltimore
Thompson, Ronald, St. Athanasius, Curtis Bay
Trautwein, Ralph, St. Ignatius, Hickory
Vassie, Frederick, On Duty Outside the Diocese
Villagaray, Rafael F., Hispanic Ministry
Wachter, George C., Springfield Hospital Center, Sykesville
Walker, George W., Jr., (Out of Diocese)
Weber, Paul, St. Ignatius, Baltimore
Wendt, Fred, Pastoral Care, North Arundel Hospital,
Werner, Francis L., Jr., St. Patrick, Cumberland
Westwater, James, St. Isaac Jogues, Baltimore
Wiedel, Verdaw P., (Retired)
Wilkins, Herman, Church of Annunciation, Baltimore
Wilson, Larry L., Resurrection of Our Lord, Laurel
Wise, Stanley L., (Retired)
Woofter, R. Paul, St. Andrew by the Bay, Cape St. Claire
Wright, James, Leave of Absence
Yannuzzi, Thomas J., St. Clement I, Lansdowne
Yorkshire, Thomas X., St. Gregory, Baltimore
Zeiler, Francis, St. Clement, Rosedale
Zusi, Michael, St. John the Evangelist, Frederick

INSTITUTIONS LOCATED IN THE ARCHDIOCESE

[A] SEMINARIES, ARCHDIOCESAN

BALTIMORE. *St. Mary's Seminary and University*, 5400 Roland Ave., 21210. Tel: 410-864-4000; Fax: 410-864-4278. Email: pgrega@stmarys.edu. Web: stmarys.edu. His Eminence William Cardinal Keeler, Archbishop of Baltimore, Chancellor, Chm. Board of Trustees.
Legal Title: *St. Mary's Seminary and University*
Diocesan Seminarians 65; Diocesan Seminarians on Pastoral Leave 8; Studying 9; Priests 13; Lay Teachers 14.
Officers of the Administration: Revs. Robert F. Leavitt, S.S., S.T.D., Pres. Rector; Timothy Kulbicki, O.F.M.Conv., S.T.B., H.E.D., Dean, School of Theology; John W. Bowen, S.S., Alumni News Editor; Richard G. Childs, M.B.A., Vice Pres. for Admin. & Finance; Michael J. Gorman, Dean, Ecumenical Institute of Theology; Lawrence M. Lenoir, Ph.D.,

Dir. Field Education; Christa R. Klein, Ph.D., Dean, Center for Continuing Formation; Mrs. Kathleen P. Mignini, Dir. Institutional Svcs.; Mrs. Patricia Grega, M.A., Univ. Registrar and Dir. of Information Svcs.; Joyce Williams, M.S., Financial Aid Officer; Ms. Katie McGowan, M.L.S., Acting Dir., Library Svcs.; Mrs. Elizabeth L. Visconage, B.S., Vice Pres. Institutional Advancement.

Faculty: Revs. Michael L. Barre, S.S., S.T.L., Ph.D.; Phillip J. Brown, J.D., J.C.D.; Thomas J. Burke, O.SS.T., S.T.M., S.T.D.; John J. Donahue, S.J., S.T.L., Ph.D.; Corbin Eddy, S.T.L., M.A.; Tenley Newcomb, M.S.; Haydee Rodrigaez, B.A.; Michael J. Gorman, M.Div., Ph.D.; Daniel P. Haggerty, M.A., Ph.D., Candidate; Patricia A. Lamoureux, Ph.D.; Lawrence M. Lenoir, Ph.D.; Edward McCormack, Ph.D.; Revs. Philip S. Keane, S.S., S.T.D.; Timothy Kalbicki, O.F.M.Conv., S.T.B., H.E.D.; Robert F. Leavitt, S.S., S.T.D.; James Mazzone, M.Div.; Anthony R. Perez, S.S. M.Div., S.T.D.; Judith M. Ryan, Ph.D.; Rev. Gladstone H. Stevens, Ph.D.; Sr. Honora Werner, O.P., D.Min.; Rev. Paul Zilonka, C.P., M.A., S.S.L., S.T.D.

Adjunct Academic Faculty: Mr. Martin Becker; Sr. Therese Marie Dougherty, S.S.N.D., Ph.D.; Mr. Christopher Dreisbach, Ph.D.; Mary M. Reisinge; Tricia T. Pyne, Ph.D.; Rev. Thomas R. Ulshafer, S.S., S.T.L., Ph.D.; Mr. Lyle K. Weiss.

Ecumenical Institute of Theology, 5400 Roland Ave., 21210. Tel: 410-864-4200; Fax: 410-864-4205. Michael J. Gorman, M.Div., Ph.D. Students 239.

EMMITSBURG. *Mount St. Mary's Seminary* 21727-7797. Tel: 301-447-5295; Fax: 301-447-5895. Email: semweb@msmary.edu. Web: www.msmary.edu/seminary.

Legal Title: *An integral part of the corporation known as Mount St. Mary's College and Seminary.* Priests 14; Sisters 4; Lay Teachers 9; Lay Administrators 4; Support Staff 4; Total Staff 35; Diocesan Seminaries 196; Religious Seminarians 11; Others 1; Total Enrollment 208; Total Staff 35.

Administration: His Eminence William Cardinal Keeler (RIC), Chancellor & Chm. of Seminary Committee; Dr. Thomas H. Powell, Pres.; Sr. Paula Marie Buley, I.H.M., M.B.A., Ed.D., Treas.; Very Rev. Kevin C. Rhoades, S.T.L., J.C.L. (HBG), Rector; Revs. J. Wilfrid Parent, S.T.L., S.T.D., Vice Rector & Dir. of Formation Advising Prog.; Lee W. Gross, M.Div. (ARL), Dean of Students; J. Daniel Mindling, O.F.M.Cap., S.T.D., Academic Dean; John Dietrich, M.A., Dir. Spiritual Formation; Salvatore R. Lamendola, M.Div. (GBG), Dir. Pastoral Field Education; Sr. Ann Miriam Gallagher, R.S.M, Ph.D., Dir. Seminary Research & Planning; Mrs. Sherry Trocino, B.A., M.B.A., Dir. Seminary Devel. & Summer Prog.; Dr. D. Stephen Rockwood, Ph.D., M.L.S., Dir. Library; Mrs. Amelia Y. Rodriguez, Seminary Registrar & Asst. to the Academic Dean; Mrs. Rosemary S. Mick, Admin. Asst. to Rector, (Admissions, Finance, Formation).

Full Time Faculty: Revs. Albert H. Ledoux, M.Div., M.A., Ph.D. (Cand.) (ALT); Mark A. Pilon, S.T.D. (ARL); Peter F. Ryan, S.J., S.T.L., S.T.D.; Robert V. Zylla, O.S.C., S.T.L.; Sr. Joan Gormley, Ph.D.; William A. Bales, Ph.D.; Stephen A. Hipp, Ph.D.; Charles J. Merrill, Ph.D.; Robert D. Miller II, S.F.O., Ph.D.; Sherry L. Steeley, B.A., M.A.

Part Time Faculty: Revs. Ronald S. Gillis, S.T.L., J.C.D. (WDC); Raymon L. Harris; Michael J. Roach; John B. Ward, J.C.L., J.D.; Sr. Elizabeth McDonough, O.P., J.C.D., S.T.L.; Theresa H. Farnan, Ph.D.; Dr. Carol L. Houghton, S.T.D., J.C.D.; Dr. Germain Grisez, Ph.D.; Andrew B. Rosenfeld, D.M.A.

[B] COLLEGES AND UNIVERSITIES

BALTIMORE. *College of Notre Dame of Maryland*, 4701 N. Charles St., 21210. Tel: 410-435-0100; Fax: 410-532-5791. Web: www.ndm.edu. Sr. Jane Burke, S.S.N.D., Chm. Bd. of Trustees; Dr. Mary Pat Seurkamp, Ph.D., Pres.; Dr. Suzanne Shipley, Ph.D., Vice Pres. Academic Affairs; Dr. Jennifer Blair, Ph.D., Vice Pres. Enrollment Mgmt.; Richard Staisleff, Vice Pres. Financial & Admin.; Dina Vakiaros, Registrar; Dr. Jeanne Ortiz, Vice Pres. Student Devel.; Patricia Bosse, Vice Pres. Institutional Advancement; Sr. Eileen O'Dea, Vice Pres. Mission; Marellen Mayers, Campus Min. School Sisters of Notre Dame Sisters 25; Lay Professors 70; Students 2,850; Residents 315; Total Staff 244.

**Loyola College in Maryland*, 4501 N. Charles St., 21210. Tel: 410-617-2000, Ext. 5012 (Undergraduate Admissions); Fax: 410-617-2176. Web: www.loyola.edu. Priests 24; Lay Teachers 451; Total Staff 1,124; Total Enrollment 6,083.

Loyola Graduate Center-Columbia Campus 7135 Minstrel Way, Columbia, 21045-5245. Tel: 410-617-7600; Fax: 410-617-7643.

Loyola Graduate Center -Timonium Campus, 2034 Greenspring Dr., Timonium, 21093. Tel: 410-617-1500; Fax: 410-617-1518. Rev. Harold E. Ridley, S.J., Pres.; Dr. David Haddad, Vice Pres. Academic Affairs; Dr. James Buckley, Dean College of Arts and Sciences; Dr. Lee D. Dahringer, Dean Sellinger School of Business & Mgmt.; Dr. Susan Donovan, Vice Pres. & Dean Students; John Palmucci, Vice Pres. Admin & Finance & Treas.; Michael Goff, Vice Pres. Devel. & College Rels.; Ellen Hoadley, Ph.D., Assoc. Vice Pres. Academic Affairs; Anne Young, Ph.D., Assoc. Vice Pres. Academic Affairs; William Bossemeyer, Dean Admissions; Ilona McGuiness, Ph.D., Dean Freshmen; Revs. Ronald J. Anton, S.J. (Retired); Jeffrey P. Baerwald, S.J.; Charles Borges, S.J.; Michael L. Braden, S.J.; Keith A. Brehob, S.J.; James L. Connor, S.J.; John R. Donahue, S.J.; Jose Emoile, S.J.; Kurt M. Denk, S.J.; C. Kevin Gillespie, S.J.; Teodulo P. Gonzalez, S.J.; Edgar B. Graham, S.J.; Frank R. Haig, S.J.; Gregory C. Hartley, S.J.; Hank Hilton, S.J.; Bro. John B. Hollywood, S.J.; Revs. Dominic W. Maruca, S.J.; William K. McGroarty, S.J.; Francis G. McManamin, S.J.; Francis J. Nash, S.J.; Rigobert Nsibu Tona, S.J.; Harold E. Ridley, S.J.; Joseph S. Rossi, S.J.; Daniel M. Ruff, S.J.; James F. Salmon, S.J.; Joseph M. Kennedy, S.J.; Chde-uk Johan Lee, S.J.; Rony Kusnad, S.J.; Bro. Claude L. Dry, S.J.

Legal Title: *Loyola College in Maryland, Inc.*, Other locations at which courses are offered: Anne Arundel County, Bel Air, Prince George's County, Eastern Shore.; For additional information call Graduate Admissions: Tel: 410-617-2000, Ext. 5064; College Established 1852. Combined with Mt. St. Agnes College 1971. Students 6,144; Undergrad Division 3,488; Graduate Division 2,656; Priests 29; Total Faculty 480.

Jesuit Community of Loyola College, Inc. Tel: 410-617-2318; Fax: 410-617-2125. Rev. Eugene M. Geinzer, S.J., Rector; Bro. Claude Ory, S.J., Asst. to the Rector; Rev. Edgar B. Graham, S.J., Treas.

Mount St. Agnes College Sr. Margaret Beatty, R.S.M., Pres. Sisters of Mercy Baltimore Region. Sisters of Mercy of the Americas, (Merged with Loyola College.)

EMMITSBURG. *Mount Saint Mary's College* (1808), 21727. Tel: 301-447-6122; Fax: 301-447-5634. Email: communications@msmary.edu. Web: www.msmary.edu. Dr. Thomas Powell, Pres.; Dr. Stephen Rockwood, Librarian; Sr. Paula Marie Buley, I.H.M., M.B.A., Ed.D., Vice Pres. Finance & Admin.; Mr. David C. Reeder, Dir. Financial Aid; Dr. Carol L. Hinds, Provost; Dr. Stanley J. Werne, Dean of Academic Svcs.; Mr. Stephen P. Neitz, Dir. Admissions; Mr. John C. Gill, Registrar; Meg McKeon, Dean of Student Devel.; Very Rev. Kevin C. Rhoades S.T.L., J.C.L. (HBG), Rector of the Seminary; Revs. John Lombardi, Chap of the Grotto Shrine & Pres. Emeritus; Raymond L. Harris Jr., Chap.; Paul V. Redmond (ALE); David W. Shaum, Ph.D. (Retired); Carl J. Fives (SCR); James Donohue, C.R. Priests 1; Sisters 1; Lay Teachers 87 Total Enrollment 1,939.

[C] HIGH SCHOOLS, ARCHDIOCESAN

BALTIMORE. *Archbishop Curley High School*, 3701 Sinclair Ln., 21213. Tel: 410-485-5000; Fax: 410-483-2545. Email: mmartin@archbishopcurley.org. Web: www.archbishopcurley.org. Revs. Michael Heine, O.F.M.Conv.; Thomas E. Walsh, O.F.M.Conv. Michael Martin, O.F.M.Conv., Pres. & Guardian. Administered by Order of Friars Minor Conventual, St. Anthony of Padua Province (USA). Priests 4; Brothers 1; Lay Teachers 45; Students 562; Total Staff 61.

The Seton Keough High School, 1201 Caton Ave., 21227-1092. Tel: 410-646-4444; Fax: 443-573-0107. Email: info@setonkeough.com. Web: setonkeough.com. Sr. Kathleen Collins, S.F.C.C., Pres.; Dr. B. Curtis Turner, Ed.D., Prin.; Sr. Marcia Hall, O.S.P., Vice Prin. Sisters 9; Lay Teachers 42; Students 500.

SEVERN. *Archbishop Spalding High School*, 8080 New Cut Rd., 21144. Tel: 410-969-9105; Fax: 410-969-1026. Email: info@archbishopspalding.org. Web: www.archbishopspalding.org. Lay Teachers 75; Students 975.

[D] HIGH SCHOOLS, PRIVATE

BALTIMORE. *Calvert Hall*, 8102 La Salle Rd., 21286. Tel: 410-825-4266; Fax: 410-825-6826. Email: chc@calverthall.com. Web: www.calverthall.com. Bro. Kevin Stanton, F.S.C., Pres.; Mr. Joseph Baker, Asst. Prin. Academic Affairs; Mr. Charles Stembler, Asst. Prin. Student Affairs; Mr. Louis Heidrick, Prin. Conducted by the Brothers of the Christian Schools (F.S.C.). Brothers 9; Lay Teachers 84; Students 1,135.

The Catholic High School of Baltimore, 2800 Edison Hwy., 21213. Tel: 410-732-6200; Fax: 410-732-7639. Email: chsb@tchs.loyola.edu. Web: www.tchs.loyola.edu. Sisters of St. Francis of Philadelphia Sisters 4; Lay Teachers 28; Students 319; Total Staff 50.

St. Frances Academy (Coed), 501 E. Chase St., 21202. Tel: 410-539-5794; Fax: 410-685-2650. Email: sfa@sfacademy.org. Web: www.sfacademy.org; www.goodeyedesign.com/sfa/. Sr. John Francis Schilling, O.S.P., Pres. & Prin.; Ms. Mary Missouri, Asst. Prin.; Mr. Doral Palley, Asst. Prin.; Mrs. Stephanie Tragakis, Dir. Guidance. Oblate Sisters of Providence Brothers 2; Sisters 5; Lay Teachers 23; Students 350.

Institute of Notre Dame (1847), 901 Aisquith St., 21202. Tel: 410-522-7800; Fax: 410-522-7810. Email: indofmd@indofmd.org. Web: indofmd.org. Mary Fitzgerald, S.S.N.D., Pres.; Ann Seeley, Prin.

Legal Title: *Institute of Notre Dame, Inc.* Sisters 5; Lay Teachers 30; Lay Employees 24; Counselors 3; Students 432.

Loyola Blakefield, P.O. Box 6819, 21285-6819. Tel: 410-823-0601; Fax: 410-823-5277. Email: admindoc@blakefield.loyola.edu. Web: www.blakefield.loyola.edu. Revs. John M. Dennis, S.J., M.Ed., Pres.; F. Joseph Michini, S.J., Chap.; Jerome M. Hall, S.J.; William H. Millerd, S.J.; Mark C. Aita, S.J.; James Bradley, S.J.; Lloyd George, S.J. Priests 3; Brothers 1; Lay Teachers 100; Students 972.

Mercy High School, 1300 E. Northern Pkwy., 21239. Tel: 410-433-8880; Fax: 410-323-8816. Email: mhischo@archbalt.org. Web: www.mercyhighschool.com. Sr. Carol E. Wheeler, R.S.M., Prin. Sisters of Mercy of the Americas Sisters 5; Lay Teachers 52; Students 478; Total Staff 86.

Mount de Sales Academy, 700 Academy Rd., 21228. Tel: 410-744-8498; Fax: 410-747-5105. Email: htranquill@mountdesales.org. Web: www.mountdesales.org. Sr. Mary Reginald, O.P., Headmistress. Priests 1; Sisters 6; Lay Teachers 46; Students 462.

Mt. St. Joseph College High School, 4403 Frederick Ave., 21229. Tel: 410-644-3300; Fax: 410-646-6220. Email: barry@admin.msjnet.edu. Web: www.msjnet.edu. Bro. James M. Kelly, C.F.X., Pres.; Mr. Barry J. Fitzpatrick, Prin. Xaverian Brothers Priests 1; Brothers 3; Lay Teachers 87; Students 1,165; Total Staff 148.

BEL AIR. *The John Carroll School*, 703 Churchville Rd., 21014. Tel: 410-879-2480; Fax: 410-836-8514. Email: jcs@techcord.loyola.edu. Web: techcord.loyola.edu. Mr. Paul G. Barker, Prin.; Mrs. Patti Murphy, Campus Min. Priests 1; Sisters 3; Lay Teachers 63; Students 818; Total Staff 64.

CUMBERLAND. *Bishop Walsh School*, Formerly Bishop Walsh Middle-High School, (Grades K-12), 700 Bishop Walsh Rd., 21502. Tel: 301-724-5360; Fax: 301-722-0555. Email: bwalsh@pharmacarelink.net. Web: www.bishopwalsh.org. Sisters Phyllis McNally, S.S.N.D., Prin.; Kathleen Jancuk, S.S.N.I., Elementary School Dir.; Francita Hobbs, S.S.N.D., Middle School Dir.; Mr. Samuel Torres, High School Dir. Brothers of the Christian Schools, School Sisters of Notre Dame. Brothers 3; Sisters 3; Lay Teachers 39; Students 545.

FREDERICK. *St. John's Literary Institution at Prospect Hall* (1841), (Coed), 889 Butterfly Ln., 21703. Tel: 301-662-4210; Fax: 301-662-5166. Email: sjph@stjph.org. Web: www.asd.com. Mr. Richard E. Fairley, Headmaster; Mr. Robert Boyer, Academic Dean. Lay Teachers 37; Students 325; Total Staff 68.

HAGERSTOWN. *St. Maria Goretti High School* (Coed), 1535 Oak Hill Ave., 21742. Tel: 301-739-4266; Fax: 301-739-4261. Email: goretti@goretti.org. Web: www.goretti.org. Mr. Christopher Siedor, Prin. Lay Teachers 23; Students 242; Total Staff 42.

[E] MIDDLE/HIGH SCHOOLS, ARCHDIOCESAN

BALTIMORE. *Cardinal Gibbons School for Boys* (1962), (Grades 6-12), 3225 Wilkens Ave., 21229-4286. Tel: 410-644-1770; Fax: 410-525-3757. Email: cgschool@archbalt.org. Web: www.cardinalgibbons.com. Philip J. Forte, Prin. Lay Teachers 28; Students 377.

[F] MIDDLE/HIGH SCHOOLS, PRIVATE

BROOKLANDVILLE. *Maryvale Preparatory School*, (Grades 6-12), (Girls), 11300 Falls Rd., 21022-1490. Tel: 410-252-3366; Fax: 410-561-1826. Email: info@maryvale.com. Web: www.maryvale.com. Sr. Shawn Marie Maguire, S.N.D., Prin. Sisters of Notre Dame de Namur 1; Lay Teachers 40; Students 366; Total Staff 62.

TOWSON. *Notre Dame Preparatory School*, (Grades 6-12), 815 Hampton Ln., 21286. Tel: 410-825-6202; Fax: 410-832-2625. Web: www.notredameprep.com. Sr. Christine Mulcahy, S.S.N.D., Headmistress.

Legal Title: *Notre Dame Preparatory School, Inc.*

Sisters 7; Lay Teachers 73; Students 692; Total Staff 121.

[G] ELEMENTARY/MIDDLE SCHOOLS, PRIVATE

BALTIMORE. *John Paul Regional Catholic School, Inc.*, (Grades PreK-8), 6946 Dogwood Rd., 21244. Tel: 410-944-0367; Fax: 410-265-5316. Email: office@jprcs.org. Ms. Theresa Brooks, Prin. Early Childhood Program. Lay Teachers 20; Students 260.

COOKSVILLE. *Woodmont Academy*, 2000 Woodmont Dr., 21723. Tel: 410-203-0619; Fax: 410-465-9162. Email: admissions@woodmontacademy.org. Web: woodmontacademy.org. Miss Michele Blum, Prin. Lay Teachers 20; Students 273.

[H] ELEMENTARY/MIDDLE SCHOOLS, REGIONAL AND COMMUNITY

BALTIMORE. *Catholic Community School of South Baltimore*, (Grades PreK-8), 300 E. Gittings St., 21230. Tel: 410-685-6155; Fax: 410-685-0692. Email: vstaub@catholiccom.org. Web: www.archnet.edu. Sr. Vicki Staub, S.S.J., Prin. Consolidation of the following parishes: Holy Cross; Our Lady of Good Counsel; St. Mary, Star of the Sea. Sisters 1; Lay Teachers 19; Students 197.

Sisters of St. Joseph: 1410 Riverside Ave., 21230-4695. Tel: 410-752-4344.

[I] ELEMENTARY SCHOOLS, PRIVATE

BALTIMORE. *Mother Seton Academy*, 724 S. Ann St., 21231. Tel: 410-563-2833; Fax: 410-563-7353. Email: mbader@archbalt.org. Web: www.mothersetonacademy.org. Innovative Middle School for Inner City Youth. Sisters 6; Lay Teachers 5; Lay Volunteers 3; Students 68.

ELLICOTT CITY. *Trinity School*, 4985 Ilchester Rd., P.O. Box 299, 21041. Tel: 410-744-1524; Fax: 410-744-1225. Email: flewis@trinitynews.org. Web: trinitynews.org. Sr. Catherine Phelps, Pres.; Frangiska Lewis, Prin. Sisters of Notre Dame de Namur 2; Lay Teachers 26; Students 388.

EMMITSBURG. *Mother Seton School*, 100 Creamery Rd., 21727. Tel: 301-447-3161; Fax: 301-447-3914. Email: office@mothersetonschool.org. Web: www.mothersetonschool.org. Sr. Mary Catherine Conway, Prin. Daughters of Charity of St. Vincent de Paul 1; Lay Teachers 20; Students 385.

FREDERICK. *Academy of the Visitation*, 200 E. 2nd St., 21701. Tel: 301-662-3322; 301-662-2814; Fax: 301-695-8549. Email: info@frederickvisitation.com. Web: www.frederickvisitation.com. Dr. Bernadette Emerson, Prin. Sisters of the Visitation 5; Lay Teachers 25; Students 246.

[J] ELEMENTARY SCHOOLS, REGIONAL AND COMMUNITY

BALTIMORE. *Bishop John Neumann School*, (Grades PreK-8), 3500 Foster Ave., 21224. Tel: 410-675-6271; Fax: 410-327-1543. Email: bjn@sebca.org. Web: www.bjnschool.com. Mrs. Phyllis Karko, Prin. Lay Teachers 16; Students 184; Total Staff 22.

Cardinal Shehan School, 5407 Loch Raven Blvd., 21239-2996. Tel: 410-433-2775; Fax: 410-323-6131. Web: cardinalshehanschool.org. Paula Redman, Prin. Serving St. Matthew and St. Thomas More Parishes. Lay Teachers 29; Sisters 2; Total Staff 39; Students 425.

Holy Spirit School, 932 Gorsuch Ave., 21218. Tel: 410-889-0679; Fax: 410-889-4687. Email: holyspiritschool@archbalt.org. Pauline Tobias-Jones, Prin. Lay Teachers 13; Students 185.

St. Ignatius Loyola Academy, 740 N. Calvert St., 21202. Tel: 410-539-8268; Fax: 410-539-4821. Email: jsindler@saintignatius.org. Rev. William J. Watters, S.J., Pres.; Jeffrey Sindler, Headmaster. Middle School for boys from low income families. Lay Teachers 11; Students 76.

Queen of Peace Elementary Cluster, St. James and St. John School, (Grades PreK-5), 1012 Somerset St., 21202. Tel: 410-342-3222; Fax: 410-732-1323. Mrs. LaUanah King-Cassell, Prin. Sisters 2; Lay Teachers 14; Students 351.

St. Katherine of Sienna School, 1201 N. Rose St., 21213. Tel: 410-327-4738. Mr. Kirk Gaddy, Prin. Lay Teachers 10; Students 272.

Southeast Baltimore Catholic Alliance (SEBCA) - Father Kolbe Campus, 1035 S. Kenwood Ave., 21224. Tel: 410-342-2681; Fax: 410-342-5715. Email: kolbe@sebca.org. Web: fatherkolbe.org. Mrs. Elizabeth F. Phelan, Prin. Serving the parishes of St. Casimir and St. Leo. Lay Teachers 12; Students 161.

Southeast Baltimore Catholic Alliance, Inc. (SEBCA), Formerly Southeast Baltimore Catholic Academy, Inc. (SEBCA) Main Office, 320 Cathedral St., 21201. Tel: 410-547-5316; Fax: 410-332-8233. Email: tdowner@archbalt.org. Theresa Downer, Contact Person. Includes five elementary and one high school campus located in the Patterson Park Area of Southeast Baltimore. SEBCA Total Enrollment 809; Total Laystaff 111.

Elementary/Middle School Campuses:

Archbishop Borders, 201 S. Conkling St., 21224. Tel: 410-276-6534; Fax: 410-276-6915. Cathy Marshall, Prin. Students 186; Total Laystaff 20.

Our Lady of Fatima E.S., 6400 E. Pratt St., 21224. Tel: 410-633-5882; Fax: 410-633-5268. Sr. Rita Dorn, Prin. Students 171; Total Laystaff 24.

Fr. Kolbe E.S., 1035 S. Kenwood Ave., 21224. Tel: 410-342-2681; Fax: 410-342-5715. Ms. Elizabeth F. Phelan. Students 160; Total Laystaff 20.

Bishop John Neumann E.S., 3500 Foster Ave., 21224. Tel: 410-675-6271; Fax: 410-327-1543. Mrs. Phyllis Karko, Prin. Students 165; Total Laystaff 24.

High School Campus:

Our Lady of the Rosary High School, 420 S. Chester St., 21231. Tel: 410-327-0600; Fax: 410-327-1965. Mary Jo Warthen, Prin. Students 127; Total Laystaff 23.

BRADSHAW. *St. Stephen School*, 8028 Bradshaw Rd., 21087-1807. Tel: 410-592-7617; Fax: 410-592-7330. Email: sssch@archbalt.org. Web: www.ststephenbradshaw.org.

CUMBERLAND. *Bishop Walsh School*, (Grades K-5), 700 Bishop Walsh Rd., 21502. Tel: 301-724-4055; Fax: 301-724-4827. Email: SJNsch@archbalt.org. Sr. Kathleen F. Jancuk, S.S.N.D., Prin. Bishop Walsh Middle-High School. (See listing under High Schools, Private). Sisters 1; Lay Teachers 18; Students 271.

FREDERICK. *St. John Regional Catholic School*, (Grades K-8), 114 E. Second St., 21701. Tel: 301-662-6722; Fax: 301-695-7024. Email: webmaster@sjrcs.org. Web: www.sjrcs.org. Ms. Joyce Connelly, Prin. Lay Teachers 27; Students 496.

GAMBRILLS, ANNE ARUNDEL. *School of the Incarnation, Inc.* (1999), 2601 Symphony Ln., 21054. Tel: 410-519-2285; Fax: 410-519-2286. Email: bedmondson@schoolsoftheincarnation.org. Web: www.schooloftheincarnation.org. Dr. Barbara Edmonson, Prin. An interparish school of the Archdiocese of Baltimore established 1999 Parishes: Church of the Holy Apostles, Gambrills; Our Lady of the Fields, Millersville; St. Joseph, Odenton; Our Lady of Perpetual Help, Edgewater; Holy Family, Davidsonville; and St. Elizabeth Ann Seton, Crofton. Lay Staff 16; Lay Teachers 22; Students 396.

GLEN BURNIE. *Arthur Slade Regional Catholic School*, 120 Dorsey Rd., 21061. Tel: 410-766-7130; Fax: 410-787-0594. Email: asrcs@aol.com. Web: www.arthurslade.org. Patricia J. Hoffman, Prin. Serving Glen Burnie, Millersville, Pasadena, Odenton, Hanover and Severn Parishes. Lay Teachers 41; Students 890.

[K] SPECIAL EDUCATION

BALTIMORE. *St. Elizabeth School, Inc.*, 801 Argonne Dr., 21218-1998. Tel: 410-889-5054; Fax: 410-889-2356. Email: inforeg@stelizabeth-school.org. Web: www.stelizabeth-school.org. Christine Manlove, Ed.D., Exec. Dir. & Prin. Sisters of St. Francis of Assisi 4; Lay Teachers 23; Other Lay Staff 49; Aides 44; Children 121.

St. Peter's Adult Learning Center, 13 S. Poppleton St., 21201. Tel: 410-685-7340; Fax: 410-625-4696. Email: pcockrsml@juno.com. Chip Woods, Dir. Program for developmentally disabled adults(day vocational/supported employment). Sisters 1; Lay Teachers 8; Students 46.

TIMONIUM. *Villa Maria School* (Main Campus) , 2300 Dulaney Valley Rd., 21093. Tel: 410-252-6343; Fax: 410-560-1347. Revanette Gilmore, Dir. Education. Non-public (Level V and VI) special education for children with emotional disabilities, ages 3-14. Lay Teachers 22; Teacher Aides 20; Children 112.

Villa Maria School at St. Vincent's, 2600 Pot Spring Rd., 21093. Tel: 410-252-3725; Fax: 410-561-8109. Lay Teachers 7; Teacher Aides 9; Children 40.

Villa Maria School at Seton Keough, 1201 S. Caton Ave., 21227. Tel: 410-644-3792; Fax: 410-644-3796. Lay Teachers 6; Teacher Aides 4; Children 35.

Villa Maria- Children in Need of Services Program, 1301 Continental Dr., Ste. 101, Abingdon, 21009-2338. Tel: 410-676-1220; Fax: 410-538-3376.

Villa Maria- Landsowne Therapeutic After School Program, 500 3rd Ave., 21227-3218. Tel: 410-536-1205; Fax: 410-536-1831.

[L] CHILD CARE CENTERS

BALTIMORE. *Bon Secours Community Support Center*, 26 N. Fulton Ave., 21223. Tel: 410-362-3906; 410-362-3629; Fax: 410-362-3649. Harriet Bachman, Dir.

Legal Title: *Bon Secour of Maryland Foundation, Inc.* Total Staff 14; Total Assisted 200.

St. Frances Outreach Center, 1026 Brentwood Ave., 21202. Tel: 410-685-1975; Fax: 410-332-1299. Sr. Brenda Motte, O.S.P., Dir. Total Assisted 30; Total Staff 3.

Good Shepherd Center, 4100 Maple Ave., 21227. Tel: 410-247-2770; Fax: 410-247-3242. Email: info@goodshepherdcenter.org. Web: www.goodshepherdcenter.org. Sisters Mary Rosaria Baxter, R.G.S., Admin.; Kathleen Moore, R.G.S., Supr.

Legal Title: *House of the Good Shepherd*

Legal Title: *Sisters of the Good Shepherd, A Corporation*, Residential psychiatric treatment for adolescent girls with emotional and behavioral problems. Sisters 12; Capacity 105; Residents 81; Total Assisted 185; Total Staff 301.

Mount Providence Child Development Center, 701 Gun Rd., 21227. Tel: 410-247-0449; Fax: 410-242-4963. Web: www.sistersofdaycare.com. Sr. Mary Concetta Melton, O.S.P., Dir. Oblate Sisters of Providence Sisters 3; Students 80; Total Staff 14.

Sisters Servants of Mary Immaculate Day Nursery & Convent, 100-104 S. Patterson Park Ave., 21231. Tel: 410-276-2630. Sr. Lydia Eugenia Ziecina, Supr. Total Assisted 50.

St. Veronica's Headstart Center, 2920 Joseph Ave., Brooklyn, 21225-1139. Tel: 410-354-0220; Fax: 410-354-4785. For additional information please see the Associated Catholic Charities section.

TIMONIUM. *Francis X. Gallagher Services*, 2520 Pot Spring Rd., 21093. Tel: 410-252-4005; Fax: 410-560-3495. Email: jhillman@cc-md.org. Web: www.catholiccharities-md.org/programs/gallagher. Mark J. Schulz, Admin. Residential, day habilitation and medical day programs for the developmentally disabled. Residential Capacity 225; Day Capacity 245; Total Assisted 344; Total Staff 300.

Villa Maria Treatment Center, 2300 Dulaney Valley Rd., 21093. Tel: 410-252-4700; Fax: 410-252-3040. Email: jhackbar@catholiccharities-md.org. Web: www.catholiccharities-md.org. Mark Greenberg, Admin.; Rev. Raymond Chase, Chap. We operate a full continuum of 13 different mental health and special education programs for children and their families. Children 2,900; Total Staff 550.

St. Vincent's Center For additional information please see the Associated Catholic Charities section.

[M] GENERAL HOSPITALS

BALTIMORE. *St. Agnes HealthCare, Inc.*, 900 Caton Ave., 21229-5299. Tel: 410-368-6000; Fax: 410-368-2109. Email: info@stagnes.org. Web: www.stagnes.org. Sr. Elizabeth Ann Ling, Dir. Pastoral Care; Kenneth H. Bancroft, Pres. & CEO; Revs. Simon Raj, Chap.; Paul Tsau, Chap.; Simonraj Savarimathu; George Kallampally, C.M.F. Ascension Health Sisters 13; Bed Capacity 287; Patients Assisted Annually 258,611; Total Staff 3,012.

St. Agnes Foundation, Inc. Tel: 410-368-3155; Fax: 410-368-3533. (Subsidiary of St. Agnes Health-Care, Inc.)

Bon Secours Baltimore Health Corporation, Inc., 2000 W. Baltimore St., 21223. Tel: 410-362-3000; Fax: 410-362-3126. Email: phyllis_reese@bshsi.com. Web: www.bonsecours.org. Percy Allen II, CEO; Sisters Alice Talone, C.B.S., CBS, Pres.; Mary Skopal, S.S.J., Dir. of Pastoral Care; Arnold Williams, C.P.A., Chm. Sisters of Bon Secours Sisters 7; Bed Capacity 154; Patients Assisted Annually 180,000; Total Staff 1,259.

Bon Secours Hospital Baltimore, Inc. Tel: 410-362-3000; Fax: 410-362-3450.

Bon Secours Community Health Services, Inc. Tel: 410-362-3123; Fax: 410-362-3126.

Bon Secours Facilities, Inc. Tel: 410-362-3000; Fax: 410-362-3450.

Bon Secours of Maryland Foundation, Inc. Tel: 410-362-3185; Fax: 410-362-3443.

Primary Care:

Bon Secours Family Care Center Tel: 410-362-3079; Fax: 410-362-3321.

Imani Center Tel: 410-383-4030; Fax: 410-383-4498.

Bon Secours Park Circle Health Center Tel: 410-225-9696; Fax: 410-383-4471.

Bon Secours Washington Village Community Medical Center Tel: 410-539-3360; Fax: 410-539-5302.

Community Health Services:

Bon Secours Renal Dialysis Center (Baltimore) Tel: 410-362-3094; Fax: 410-362-3408.

Bon Secours Renal Dialysis Center (Glen Burnie) Tel: 410-760-7100; Fax: 410-787-9217.

Bon Secours Renal Dialysis Center (Charing Cross) Tel: 410-747-9356; Fax: 410-747-0603.

Bon Secours Renal Dialysis Center (Ravenwood) Tel: 410-837-2011; Fax: 410-837-2018.

Bon Secours Dialysis at North Charles Tel: 410-467-8236; Fax: 410-467-8385.

Community Institute of Behavorial Services (CIBS) Tel: 410-383-4900; Fax: 410-669-0450.
New Hope Treatment Center Tel: 410-945-7706; Fax: 410-945-8767.
New Phases Tel: 410-523-4400; Fax: 410-225-7056.
Next Passage Tel: 410-728-8901; Fax: 410-728-7817.
Community Outreach:
Bon Secours Apartments Tel: 410-566-2701; Fax: 410-566-7813.
Bon Secours Hollins Terrace (Apts. for the Elderly) Tel: 410-566-2701; Fax: 410-566-7813.
Bon Secours Benet House (Apts. for the Elderly) Tel: 410-566-0701; Fax: 410-566-1275.
Bon Secours Senior Apartments at Liberty Village Tel: 410-523-1113; Fax: 410-523-4494.
Bon Secours Community Support Center Tel: 410-362-3629; Fax: 410-362-3649.
Bon Secours Women's Resource Center Tel: 410-362-3547; Fax: 410-362-3637; 410-362-3389.
Urban Medical Institute (UMI) Tel: 410-383-4550; Fax: 410-383-4285.
Good Samaritan Hospital of Maryland Inc., 5601 Loch Raven Blvd., 21239.
Mercy Health Services Inc., 301 St. Paul Pl., 21202. Tel: 410-332-9000; Fax: 410-962-1303. Email: rrice@mercymed.com. Web: www.mercymed.com. Thomas Mullen, Pres. & CEO; Revs. Theodore E.A. Brady, S.J., Chap.; Bernard A. Suppe, S.J., Chap.; Thomas R. Malia, Chap.; Lawrence M. Johnson; Sr. Mary Harper, R.S.M., Chap. Institute of the Sisters of Mercy of the Americas. Subsidiaries: Mercy Medical Center Inc.; St. Paul Place Specialists, Inc.; Healthcare for the Homeless; Maryland Family Care; Mercy Transitional Care; Stella Maris Hospice at Mercy; Stella Maris, Inc.; Cardinal Shehan Center, Inc.; Mercy Health Foundation, Inc.; Mercy Ridge. Sisters 18; Employees 3,136; Patients Assisted Annually 441,680; Bed Capacity 214; Patients Assisted Annually 441,680; Total Staff 3,163.

CUMBERLAND. *Sacred Heart Hospital of the Western Maryland Health System*, 900 Seton Dr., 21502. Tel: 301-723-4200; Fax: 301-723-5583. Email: webmaster@wmhs.com. Web: www.wmhs.com. Francis A. Pommett Jr., Exec. Dir.; Rev. Victor Kriley, O.F.M.Cap., Chap. Daughters of Charity of St. Vincent de Paul Bed Capacity 148; Sisters 8; Nurses 219; Patients Assisted Annually 91,787; Total Staff 1,042.

TOWSON. *St. Joseph Medical Center, Inc.*, 7601 Osler Dr., 21204. Tel: 410-337-1000; Fax: 410-337-1024. Email: nancyconner@chi-east.org. Web: www.sjmcmd.org. John Tolmie, Pres. & CEO; Sr. Anne Patrice Hefner, O.S.F., Vice Pres. Mission & Ministry; Nancy Conner, Dir. Spiritual Care. Sisters of St. Francis of Philadelphia Sisters 14; Nurses 727; Beds 339; Patients Assisted Annually 210,847; Total Staff 2,310.
Chaplains: Revs. Joseph Lerch, S.J.; Gilberto Liboroni-Pierozzi; Bogdan Palka, S.D.S.; Sr. Evelyn Jane Grudza, O.S.F.; Joan Manning; Maureen O'Brien; Susan Anderson; Janette Silva; Kathy Edelmann; Jane Mayrer.

[N] NURSING HOMES (SKILLED) AND REHABILITATION CENTERS

BALTIMORE. *Dismas House West*, 105 S. Mount St., 21223-0435. Tel: 410-566-9400; Fax: 410-233-1622. Charles R. Muskauski, Exec. Dir., P.O. Box 4435, 21223-0435. Charles R. Muskauski, Exec Dir. Non-Sectarian-Use Diocesan Property Rehabilitation center under contract to the Maryland Division of Corrections to provide inmate services. Total Staff 27; Total in Residence 45.
St. Elizabeth Rehabilitation and Nursing Center, 3320 Benson Ave., 21227-1035. Tel: 410-644-7100; Fax: 410-646-6589. Email: info@catholiccharities-md.org. Web: www.catholiccharities-md.org. Ms. Christine Mour, Admin.
Legal Title: *The Jenkins Memorial Nursing Home, Inc.*, Sponsored by Associated Catholic Charities. Sisters 3; Bed Capacity 162; Total Assisted 375; Total Staff 220.
Good Samaritan Nursing Center Inc., 1601 E. Belvedere Ave., 21239. Tel: 410-532-5600; Fax: 410-532-8141.

EMMITSBURG. *Villa St. Catherine, Inc.*, 331 S. Seton Ave., 21727. Tel: 301-447-7000; Fax: 301-447-7015. Email: info@stcatherinesnursingcenter.org. Web: stcatherinesnursingcenter.org. Mr. Joseph P. Lydon, Admin. & CEO. Sponsored by Ascension Health. Bed Capacity 69; Total Staff 80.

[O] HOMES FOR AGED

BALTIMORE. *St. Charles Villa*, 603 Maiden Choice Ln., 21228. Tel: 410-747-1211; Fax: 410-747-2460. Email: jfatherjoe@aol.com. Revs. Lawrence A. Bender, S.S.; Joseph J. Bonadio, S.S.; John W. Bowen, S.S.; James H. Brennan, S.S.; Charles P. Dillon, S.S.; Claude H. Dukehart, S.S.; James J. Healy, S.S.; William J. Lee, S.S.; John F. Mattingly, S.S., Assoc. Dir.; Vincent deP. McMurry, S.S.; William S. Morris, S.S. John H. Olivier, S.S.; Robert L. Turner, S.S.; John A. Ward, S.S. Total in Residence 16; Total Staff 10.
St. Joseph's Nursing Home, 1222 Tugwell Dr., 21228. Tel: 410-747-0026; Fax: 410-747-0386. Email: st.josephs@erols.com. Rev. Gregory Kwapisz, O.F.M.; Sr. Krystyna Mroczek, Admin.
Legal Title: *Sisters Servants of Mary Immaculate, Inc.* Sisters 10; Residents 40; Total Assisted 40; Total Staff 51.
St. Martin's Home for Aged, Little Sisters of the Poor, 601 Maiden Choice Ln., 21228. Tel: 410-744-9367; Fax: 410-747-0835. Email: msbaltlsp@mindspring.com. Rev. John F. Lesnick, Chap. Sisters 19; Intermediate Care Beds 62; Assisted Living 22 Apartments 18; Aged Residents 101; Total Staff 125; Total Assisted 101.

TIMONIUM. *Stella Maris*, 2300 Dulaney Valley Rd., 21093. Tel: 410-252-4500 (office); Fax: 410-560-9675. Email: srabb@stellamorisinc.com. Web: www.stellamarisinc.com. Sr. Karen McNally, R.S.M., Chief Admin. Officer; Rev. Lawrence M. Johnson, Dir. of Pastoral Care. The management corporation for all programs of Stella Maris. Long-term care; subacute care; home health; rehabilitative services; hospice services; hospice inpatient; home/hospice care; outreach ministries program; independent living; group home; and counseling/bereavement services for adults and children. All applications for the facilities of the Center are processed directly through the Admissions Office at Stella Maris. Lay Personnel 680; Sisters 11; Residents 380.
Saint John Hall-Long Crandon Tel: 410-252-4500, Ext. 251; Fax: 410-560-0754. Rev. Msgrs. Edward J. Lynch (Retired); Myles McGowan; John C. Collopy (Retired); Revs. Charles L. Laferty (Retired); Myles Muller (Retired).
Stella Maris Tel: 410-252-4500; Fax: 410-560-9675. Rev. Conrad Miller, O.F.M.Conv.
St. Elizabeth Hall Tel: 410-252-4500; Fax: 410-560-9663. Rev. Msgrs. Robert A. Bozel (Retired); Thomas J. Fannon (Retired); Rev. James Brady.
Cardinal Shehan Center, Inc.

[P] SOCIAL SERVICES

BALTIMORE. *Franciscan Center*, 101 W. 23rd St., 21218. Tel: 410-467-5340; Fax: 410-467-4569. Email: adowell@franciscancenterbaltimore.org. Web: www.franciscancenterbaltimore.org. Rev. Aaron M Dowell, O.SS.T., Dir. Sisters of St. Francis of Assisi Total Assisted 188,000; Total Staff 25.
House of Mercy, Inc., 901 Hollins St., 21223. Tel: 410-244-6220; Fax: 410-244-6237. Email: houseofmercy@hotmail.com. Ms. Frances Lorenzi, Exec. Dir.
Mount Providence Reading Center, 701 Gun Rd., 21227. Tel: 410-247-0448. Sr. M. Constance Fenwick, O.S.P., Dir. Oblate Sisters of Providence Students 200; Total Assisted 200; Total Staff 10.
Trinitarian Counseling Services, Inc., 8400 Park Heights Ave. P.O. Box 5719, 21282. Tel: 410-486-5764; Fax: 410-486-0614. Email: tburke@stmarys.edu. Rev. Thomas J. Burke, O.SS.T., S.T.M., S.T.D., Pres. Total Assisted 183; Total Staff 2.

EMMITSBURG. *Seton Center, Inc.*, 16840 S. Seton Ave., 21727. Tel: 301-447-6102; Fax: 301-447-1748. Email: setoncenterinc@faithlink.net. Sr. Gloria Gilman, D.C. Daughters of Charity, Social Service; Outreach Thrift Shop. Total Assisted 22,500; Total Staff 8.

PASADENA. *Mary's Center*, P.O. Box 1804, 21123-1804. Tel: 410-224-0504. Anne Fitzsimmons, Dir. Pregnancy Support Services. Total Assisted 811; Total Staff 28.

[Q] ASSOCIATED CATHOLIC CHARITIES

BALTIMORE. *Associated Catholic Charities, Inc. (Catholic Charities)*
For more information on Catholic Charities and its programs please contact:
Catholic Charities, 320 Cathedral St., 3rd Floor, 21201-4421. Tel: 410-261-5800. Email: info@catholiccharities-md.org. Web: www.catholiccharities-md.org.
Management Team:
Associated Catholic Charities Inc., 320 Cathedral St., 3rd Floor, 21201-4421. Tel: 410-547-5497; Fax: 410-752-7260. Harold A. Smith, Exec. Dir.; Angelo Boer, Dir., Community Svcs. Div.
Associated Catholic Charities Inc., 320 Cathedral St., 3rd Floor, 21201-4421. Tel: 410-547-5459; 410-547-5495; Fax: 410-752-7260. James Gabriel, Assoc. Dir. & CFO.
Associated Catholic Charities Inc., 320 Cathedral St., 21201-4421. Tel: 410-547-5481; Fax: 410-576-2179. Stevenson W. Close Jr., Dir., Devel. and Communications Div.
Associated Catholic Charities Inc., 3320 Benson Ave., 21227-1035. Tel: 410-646-6501; Fax: 410-646-0500. Ann Rasenberger, Dir., Senior Life Svcs. Div.
Associated Catholic Charities Inc., 320 Cathedral St., 21201-4421. Tel: 410-547-5544; Fax: 410-576-0987. Dale R. McArdle, Dir., Housing Svcs. Div.
Associated Catholic Charities Inc., 2305 N. Charles St., 21218-5128. Tel: 410-261-5839; Fax: 410-889-9243. Kathleen H. Mills, Dir., Human Resources Div.
Associated Catholic Charities Inc., 2300 Dulaney Valley Rd., Timonium, 21093-2739. Tel: 410-252-4700, Ext. 101; Fax: 410-252-3040. John D. Rusinko, Children's Svcs. Div.
Children's Services Division:
2300 Dulaney Valley Rd., Timonium. Tel: 410-252-3040; Fax: 410-252-3040. John D. Rusinko, Dir.
Services For Children and Families:
Auburne Center, 5500 Old Frederick Rd., 21229-2302. Tel: 410-744-8961; 800-492-5530 (Hotline).
Catholic Charities Early Head Start, Harford County, 34 N. Philadelphia Blvd., Aberdeen, 21001. Tel: 410-538-3388; Fax: 410-538-3376.
Catholic Charities Head Start, Carroll County, 125 Airport Dr., Westminster, 21157. Tel: 410-871-2450; Fax: 410-871-2452.
Center for Family Services/Domestic and International Adoption Services, 1 E. Mount Royal Ave., 21201. Tel: 410-659-4050; Fax: 410-659-4060.
Center for Family Services/Family Strengthening Services, 1 E. Mount Royal Ave., 21201-5005. Tel: 410-659-4050; Fax: 410-659-4060.
Center for Family Services/Resource Parents Project, 11 E. Mount Royal Ave., 21202-2714. Tel: 410-385-0967; Fax: 410-685-2364.
Center for Family Services/Treatment Foster Care, 11 E. Mount Royal Ave., 21202. Tel: 410-685-2363; Fax: 410-685-2364.
1301 Continental Dr., Suite 101, Abingdon, 21009. Tel: 410-538-3388; Fax: 410-538-3376.
Herring Run Head Start, 5010 Bowleys Ln., 21206-6744. Tel: 410-485-1010; Fax: 410-485-1009.
St. Jerome's Head Start, 915 Sterrett St., 21230-2502. Tel: 410-685-1700; Fax: 410-659-3921.
St. Veronica's Head Start, 2920 Joseph Ave., Brooklyn, 21225-1139. Tel: 410-354-0220; Fax: 410-354-4785.
St. Vincent's Center, 2600 Pot Spring Rd., Timonium, 21093-2732. Tel: 410-252-4000, Ext. 1601; Fax: 410-561-8109.
St. Vincent Center - Chara House, 4203 Belview Ave., 21215-4812. Tel: 410-367-1191; Fax: 410-367-3039.
St. Vincent's Child Abuse Prevention Project, 2600 Pot Spring Rd., Timonium, 21093. Tel: 410-252-4000; Fax: 410-561-8109.
Upcounty Family Center, 303 W. Lincoln Ave., Emmitsburg, 21727. Tel: 301-447-2810; Fax: 301-447-6325.
Villa Maria- Baltimore Children and Adolescent Response System (B-CARS), 1118 S. Light St., 21230. Tel: 410-558-2212; Fax: 410-558-2240.
Villa Maria Behavioral Health Clinic-Outreach Program, 2300 Dulaney Valley Rd., Timonium, 21093. Tel: 410-252-4700, Ext. 245; Fax: 410-252-3040.
Villa Maria - Behavioral Health Clinics: (6 locations)
Villa Maria Treatment Foster Services, 11 E. Mt. Royal Ave., 21202. Tel: 410-685-2363.
Villa Maria Harford County, 1301 Continental Dr., Suite 103, Abingdon, 21009. Tel: 410-676-4002.
Villa Maria Carroll County, Winchester Exchange, 15 W. Main St., Ste. 221B, Westminster, 21157. Tel: 410-848-2037.
Frederick County Counseling Services, 112 2nd St., Frederick, 21701. Tel: 301-694-6654; Fax: 301-694-8221.
Washington County Counseling Services, 229 N. Potomac St., Hagerstown, 21740-3812. Tel: 301-733-5858.
Western Maryland Counseling Services, P.O. Box 1916, Cumberland, 21502-1916. Tel: 301-777-8685.
Villa Maria - Bridge to Success, 1301 Continental Dr., Ste. 103, Abingdon, 21009-2338. Tel: 410-676-4002; Fax: 410-676-7365.
Villa Maria - Bridges to Success, 1301 Continental Dr., Abingdon, 21009-2338. Tel: 410-676-4002; Fax: 410-676-7365.
Villa Maria Home-Based Respite Program, 2300 Dulaney Rd., Timonium, 21093. Tel: 410-252-4700, Ext. 276; Fax: 410-252-3040.
Villa Maria- In-Home Intervention Program, 1118 S. Light St., 21230. Tel: 410-230-0536; Fax: 410-558-2240.
Villa Maria- Project PrePARE, 1301 Continental Dr., Ste. 101, Abingdon, 21009-2338. Tel: 410-676-4002; Fax: 410-676-7365.
Villa Maria - Residential Treatment Center (Villa Maria, Inc.) (Friends of Villa Maria, Inc.), 2300 Dulaney Valley Rd., Timonium, 21093-2739. Tel: 410-252-4700; Fax: 410-252-3040.

Villa Maria- Retum and Diversion Services, 455 Bow St., Elkton, 21921-5476. Tel: 410-620-9849; Fax: 410-620-9849.

Villa Maria - Safe Schools-Healthy Students, 1118 S. Light St., 21230. Tel: 410-252-4700; Fax: 410-558-2240.

Villa Maria- Safe Start, 1301 Contineneta1 Dr., Abingdon, 21009-2338. Tel: 410-676-4002; Fax: 410-676-7365.

Villa Maria School, 2300 Dulaney Valley Rd., Timonium, 21093-2739. Tel: 410-252-6343; Fax: 410-560-1347.

Villa Maria School at St. Vincent's, 2600 Pot Spring Rd., Timonium, 21093-2732. Tel: 410-252-3725; Fax: 410-453-9712.

Villa Maria School at Seton Keough, 1201 S. Caton Ave., 21227-1092. Tel: 410-644-3792; Fax: 410-644-3796.

Villa Maria School Consultation Program, 1118 S. Light St., 21230. Tel: 410-252-4700; 410-230-0536; Fax: 410-558-2240.

Villa Maria Therapeutic Group Home, 1422 Gibsonwood Rd., Catonsville, 21228-2523. Tel: 410-788-9440; Fax: 410-788-9440.

Villa Maria - Therapeutic After School Program, 500 3rd Ave., 21227-3218. Tel: 410-536-1205; Fax: 410-536-1831.

2300 Dulaney Valley Rd., Timonium, 21093-2739. Tel: 410-252-4700; Fax: 410-252-3040.

Community Services:

Anna's House, P.O. Box 88, Bel Air, 21014-0088. Tel: 410-638-1479; Fax: 410-638-1753.

Apostolado Hispano/Hispanic Apostolate, 430 S. Broadway, 21231-2410. Tel: 410-522-2668; Fax: 410-675-1451.

Catholic Charities Workforce Development, 2305 N. Charles St., 21218-5128. Tel: 410-261-5800; Fax: 410-889-0203.

**Cherry Hill Town Center (Cherry Hill Town Center, Inc.)*, 2305 N. Charles St., 3rd Floor, 21218-5128. Tel: 410-261-6760; Fax: 410-889-0203.

Christopher Place Employment Academy, 709 E. Eager St., 21202-4234. Tel: 410-576-0066; Fax: 410-576-0914.

Damascus Career Center, 806 Cherry Hill Rd., Brookland, 21225. Tel: 410-354-7507; Fax: 410-354-0271.

Herring Run Career Center, 5010 Bowleys Ln., 21206. Tel: 410-485-1010; Fax: 410-485-1009.

Holden Hall, 761 W. Hamburg St., 21230. Tel: 410-347-9830; Fax: 410-347-9831.

Immigration Legal Services, 430 S. Broadway, 21231-2410. Tel: 410-534-8015; Fax: 410-675-1451.

Legislative Education Group (LEG), 2305 N. Charles St., 3rd Floor, 21218. Tel: 410-261-6781; Fax: 410-889-0203.

My Sister's Place, 123 W. Mulberry St., 21201-3619. Tel: 410-727-3523; Fax: 410-727-1611.

My Sister's Place Lodge, 111 W. Mulberry St., 21201-3619. Tel: 410-528-9002; Fax: 410-528-9004.

Our Daily Bread, 411 Cathedral St., 21201-4449. Tel: 410-659-4022; Fax: 410-659-4014.

Parish Social Ministry, 2305 N. Charles St., 21218-5128. Tel: 410-261-6782; Fax: 410-261-6781.

Project FRESH Start (Family Relocation, Empowerment, and Self-Help), 2305 N. Charles St., 21218-5128. Tel: 410-261-6777; Fax: 410-889-0203.

Project SERVE (Service and Education through Residential Volunteer Experience), 2305 N. Charles St., 21218-5128. Tel: 410-261-6776; Fax: 410-889-0203.

St. Jude Employment Center, 19 W. Franklin St., 21201. Tel: 410-659-4023; Fax: 410-659-4049.

Samaritan Center, 19 W. Franklin St., 21201. Tel: 410-659-4020; Fax: 410-659-4059.

Sarah's House, 2015 20th St., Fort Meade, 20755-1301. Tel: 410-551-7722; Fax: 410-551-7279.

Social Concerns, 2305 N. Charles St., 21218-5128. Tel: 410-261-5800; Fax: 410-889-0203.

Services for Seniors:

Answers for the Aging, 3320 Benson Ave., 21227-1035. Tel: 410-646-0100; 888-502-7587; Fax: 410-646-0500.

Caritas House Assisted Living, 3308 Benson Ave., 21227. Tel: 410-646-0100; Fax: 410-646-0500.

Catholic Charities Senior Housing at Arundel Woods (Glen Burnie Senior Housing, Inc.), 403 W. Ordinance Rd., Odenton, 21061. Tel: 410-424-3535; Fax: 410-424-4485.

Catholic Charities Senior Housing at Basilica Place (The Cathoic Charities Housing, Inc.), 124 W. Franklin Street, 21201-4576. Tel: 410-539-0418; Fax: 410-752-6207.

Catholic Charities Senior Housing at Coursey Station (Coursey Station Apartments, Inc.), 200 First Ave., Halethorpe, 21227-3031. Tel: 410-242-6167; Fax: 410-242-3459.

Catholic Charities Senior Housing at DePaul House (DePaul House, Inc.), 3300 Benson Ave., 21227-1030. Tel: 410-644-8484; Fax: 410-644-1334.

Catholic Charities Senior Housing at Everall Gardens, 6100 Everall Ave., 21206-1946. Tel: 410-444-5850; Fax: 410-444-0190.

Catholic Charities Senior Housing at Friendship Station (Odenton Senior Housing, Inc.), 1212 Odenton Rd., Odenton, 21113-1629. Tel: 410-519-6085; Fax: 410-519-6092.

Catholic Charities Senior Housing at Kessler Park, 4230 Hollins Ferry Rd., 21227-3440. Tel: 410-247-9244; Fax: 410-247-9245.

Catholic Charities Senior Housing at Reister's Clearing, 304 Cantata Ct., Reisterstown, 21136. Tel: 410-547-5483; 410-517-4994; Fax: 410-517-4995.

Catholic Charities Senior Housing at Reister's View, 306 Cantata Ct., Reisterstown, 21136. Tel: 410-517-4994; Fax: 410-517-4995.

Catholic Charities Senior Housing at St. Charles House (St. Charles House, Inc.), 11 Church Ln., Pikesville, 21208-6607. Tel: 410-484-6125; Fax: 410-242-3459.

Catholic Charities Senior Housing at St. Joachim House (St. Joachim House, Inc.), 3310 Benson Ave., 21227-1075. Tel: 410-644-8269; Fax: 410-525-9227.

Catholic Charities Senior Housing at St. Luke's (St. Luke's Apartments, Inc.), 2825 Lodge Farm Rd., Sparrows Point, 21219-1347. Tel: 410-477-3661; Fax: 410-477-0199.

Catholic Charities Senior Housing at St. Mark's Apartments, 19 Winters Lane, Catonsville, 21228-4499. Tel: 410-788-0972; Fax: 410-247-9245.

Catholic Charities Senior Housing at Starner Hill Apartments (Backbone Housing, Inc.), 25 N. Pennsylvania Ave., Grantsville, 21536-0489. Tel: 301-895-5842; Fax: 301-895-3762.

Catholic Charities Senior Housing at Trinity House Apartments (Trinity House Apartments, Inc.), 409 Virginia Ave., Towson, 21286-5372. Tel: 410-825-5288; Fax: 410-825-5592.

Cherry Hill SeniorLife Center, 606 Cherry Hill Rd., Suite 201, 21225-1229. Tel: 410-354-5101; Fax: 410-354-5103.

Congregate Housing Services Program, 320 Cathedral St., 21201. Tel: 410-625-8470; Fax: 410-576-0987.

Joseph SeniorLife Center, 430 S. Broadway, 21231-2409. Tel: 410-732-5000; Fax: 410-675-1451.

St. Ann Adult Day Services, 3320 Benson Ave., 21227-1001. Tel: 410-646-0320; Fax: 410-644-0840.

St. Elizabeth Rehabilitation and Nursing Center (Jenkins Memorial Nursing Home, Inc.), 3320 Benson Ave., 21227-1035. Tel: 410-644-7100; Fax: 410-644-2154.

Senior Center Plus at the Joseph SeniorLife Center, 430 S. Broadway, 21231-2409. Tel: 410-732-5000; Fax: 410-675-1451.

Services for People with Developmental Disabilities:

Gallagher Services (Gallagher Services Auxillary, Inc.), 2520 Pot Spring Rd., Timonium, 21093-2795. Tel: 410-252-4005; Fax: 410-560-3495. (The Father Raymond W. Gribbin Activity Center, Inc.)

The Bethany Community, Inc. Tel: 410-625-8470; Fax: 410-576-0987.

Group homes constructed and operated under the U.S. Dept. of Housing and Urban Development's Section 202-8 Porgram:

3731 Ellerslie Ave., 21218. Tel: 410-366-5002.
2421 Pot Spring Rd., 21093. Tel: 410-561-5733.
2292 Dulaney Valley Rd., 21093. Tel: 410-252-7875.
18314 Middletown Rd., 21120. Tel: 410-343-2536.
3400 Benson Ave., 21227. Tel: 410-368-3890.
8240 Jumpers Hole Rd., 21108. Tel: 410-544-0838.
4607 Mountain Rd., 21122. Tel: 410-360-5125.
2560 Pot Spring Rd., 21093. Tel: 410-561-5744.
501 Belfast Rd., 21152. Tel: 410-472-3066.
4605 Mountain Rd., 21122. Tel: 410-360-5126.
751 Argonne Dr., 21218. Tel: 410-467-7540.
47 Church Rd., 21012. Tel: 410-974-4356.
1925 Rockhaven Ave., 21228. Tel: 410-719-0681.

Special Programs:

Project AWARE, 320 Cathedral St., 21201-4421. Tel: 410-547-5521; Fax: 410-576-2179.

Other Associated Catholic Charities, Inc. Corporations:

661 Corporation, 320 Cathedral St., 21201. Tel: 410-547-5469.

The Children's Fund, Inc., 320 Cathedral St., 21201. Tel: 410-547-5469.

[R] RETREAT HOUSES FOR MEN, WOMEN AND YOUTH

BALTIMORE. *Holy Trinity Spiritual Center*, 8400 Park Heights Ave., P.O. Box 5719, 21282. Tel: 410-486-5171; Fax: 410-486-0614. Email: trinity@trinitarians.org. Web: trinitarians.org. Rev. Thomas Morris, O.SS.T., Dir. Spirituality Center. Total Assisted 1,113; Total Staff 7; Total in Residence 7.

St. Mary's Spiritual Center, 600 N. Paca St., 21201-1995. Tel: 410-728-6464; Fax: 410-669-8140. Email: SMSCBalto@aol.com. Web: www.stmarysspiritualcenter@catholic.org. Rev. John E. McMurry, S.S., Dir. Adjunct Staff 14; Auxiliary Staff 3.

ADAMSTOWN. *Christian Brothers Spiritual Center*, 2535 Buckeystown Pike, P.O. Box 29, 21710. Tel: 301-874-5180; Fax: 301-874-3757. Email: cbsc@crosslink.net. Web: www.crosslink.net/cbsc. Bro. Richard W. Breese, F.S.C., Admin. Brothers 2.

CATONSVILLE. *Our Lady of Guadalupe Renewal Center*, 1903 Norhurst Way N., 21228. Tel: 410-788-8821. Katherine Feddor, Dir.; Sr. Anne Colette Potthast, S.N.D., Dir. Emeritus. Spiritual Life and Renewal Programs for Religious and Laity. Total in Residence 2; Total Staff 2; Pastoral Team 13.

EMMITSBURG. *Seton Retreat Center*, 333 S. Seton Ave., 21727. Tel: 301-447-6021; Fax: 301-447-7095. Email: srvincen@doc.org. Sr. Vincentia Goeb, D.C., Dir.; Joan Little, Retreat Coord.; Jeanne Meister, Youth Coord. Daughters of Charity

SPARKS. *Msgr. Clare J. O'Dwyer Retreat House*, 15523 York Rd., 21152. Tel: 410-666-2400; Fax: 410-472-3281. Email: odwyer@archbalt.org. Rev. Kevin A. Mueller, Dir. Total Staff 16.

[S] MONASTERIES AND RESIDENCES OF PRIESTS AND BROTHERS

BALTIMORE. *St. Ambrose Friary*, 4502 Park Heights Ave., 21215. Tel: 410-367-0334; Fax: 410-542-6056. Email: jharvey@archbalt.org. Web: www.tri-parish.org. Revs. Michael Joyce, O.F.M.Cap., Pastor St. Ambrose Parish; John Harvey, O.F.M.Cap., Guardian & Pastor of Tri Parish Community; Dennis Klemash, O.F.M.Cap.; Roman Kozachesan, O.F.M.Cap., Pastoral Min. Good Shepherd Hospital; Bro. Clifford Ledger, O.F.M.

Blessed Alberto Hurtado, S.J. Jesuit Community, 317 S. Broadway, 21231. Tel: 410-522-0253. In Res. Revs. Mark C. Aita, S.J.. Email: maita@aol.com; Brendan Hurley, S.J., (E-mail: bhurley@mdsj.org); Joel Mascarenhas, S.J.. Email: jomascy@hotmail.com; Robert W. McChesney, S.J. (LA), Supr. & Treas.. Email: treasurercmcches@jesuits.net; Lawry Trinidade, S.J.. Email: ltrinidade@yahoo.co.uk.

Ferdinand Wheeler Jesuit Community, 3048 Guilford Ave., 21218. Tel: 410-338-1296. Email: kgillespie@loyola.edu. Revs. Charles Agbessi; Theodore E.A. Brady, S.J.; Kevin Gillespie, S.J.; Joachim Nthawie, S.J.; William Walsh, S.J.; Larry Yevenes; Bros. James Horan, S.J.; Ainsworth Walker, S.J. Priests 6; Brothers 2.

Holy Trinity Monastery, Prov. Admin. P.O. Box 5719, 21282-0719. Tel: 410-486-5171; Fax: 410-486-0614. Email: treasurer@trinitarians.org. Web: trinitarians.org. Priests 5; Brothers 3.

Office, 8400 Park Heights Ave., P.O. Box 5719, 21282-0719. Tel: 410-486-5764; Fax: 410-486-0614.

Priests 5; Brothers 3. In Res. Revs. Aaron M. Dowdell, O.SS.T. (NY); Joseph J. Gross, O.SS.T, Historian; Kurt J. Klismet, O.SS.T., Vocation Dir. & Prov. Treas.; Joseph K. Mitko, O.SS.T.; Thomas A. Morris, O.SS.T., Min. Conventual, Dir. Spiritual Center; Timothy Murphy, O.SS.T.; Bro. Daniel Montemarano, O.SS.T.

Assigned But Serving Elsewhere:

Holy Trinity Ashram, P.O. Aranattukara, Kerala State, Trichur, India. Tel: 011-91--0-48; Fax: 011-91--0-48. Rev. Matthew Maniamkerry, O.SS.T.

489 Jersey Avenue, Jersey City, NJ 07302-3457. Tel: 201-260-2262. Rev. Joseph C. Gidaro, O.SS.T.

P.O. Box 5719, 21282. Tel: 410-486-5171. Rev. Aaron M. Dowdell, O.SS.T. (NY).

Via Massimi, 114/C, Rome 00136 Italy. Tel: 011-39-063-542-0529; Fax: 001-39-063-534-1673. Rev. Jose T. Narlaly, O.SS.T.

Trinity House, 1511 E. Commercial, Victoria, TX 77901-7021. Tel: 361-573-7059. Rev. Damon Geiger, O.SS.T.; Bro. Richard J. Micka.

St. Clare Church: 321 Calumet St., Dallas, TX 75211. Tel: 214-337-3936; Fax: 214-333-9148. Rev. David Colella, O.SS.T.

17620 Virginia Ave., Hagerstown, 21740-7829. Tel: 301-745-4041. Rev. Weston J. Lamb, O.SS.T.

St. John's Seminary, 5012 Seminary Rd., Camarillo, CA 93012-2598. Tel: 805-482-2755; Fax: 805-484-4074. Rev. J. Edward Owens, O.SS.T.

1258 Lacey Oaks Loop, Round Rock, TX 78681. Tel: 803-865-5091. Rev. Carl Pfeiffer, O.SS.T.

St. Ann Church: 357 Dorrance St., P.O. Box 1175, Bristol, PA 19007-1175. Tel: 215-788-2128; Fax: 215-781-9782. Rev. Claude Gravel, O.SS.T.

, Formerly Assumption Seminary 208 W. River St., P.O. Box 2548, Victoria, TX 77901-2548. Tel: 210-732-6752; Fax: 210-734-2324. Rev. Thomas Dymcwski, O.SS.T.

408 W. 23rd St., 21211. Tel: 410-889-7281. Rev. Edward Wagner, O.SS.T., Chap.

St. Lawrence Rectory, 7669 Clark Rd., Hanover, 21076-1205. Tel: 410-799-1330; Fax: 410-799-4425. Rev. John Dorn, O.SS.T.

Meredith Memorial Home, 16 Illinois St., #604,

Belleville, IL 62220-2107. Tel: 618-277-2139. Bro. Eric Beardsley, O.SS.T.

The Trinitarian Community, 8636 Trail View Dr., Ellicott City, 21043. Tel: 410-203-3135; Fax: 410-203-2117. In Res. Revs. Thomas J. Burke, O.SS.T., S.T.M., S.T.D.; William J. Moorman, O.SS.T.; Bro. Adelson S. Moreira, O.SS.T.

The Trinitarian Community, 8612 Laverne Dr., Adelphi, 20783. Tel: 301-422-0155; Fax: 301-422-0070. In Res. Revs. Lawrence C. Hernandez, O.SS.T.; William Sullivan, O.SS.T.

The Trinitarians at Holy Rosary, 440 S. Chester St., 21231. Tel: 410-732-5425. Rev. Charles J. Flood, O.SS.T.; Bros. David Nash, O.SS.T.; Patrick G. Wildgen, O.SS.T.; Alfonso Serna, O.SS.T.; Maciej Sworek, O.SS.T.; Carl M. Frisch, O.SS.T.; Peter J. Ireton, O.SS.T.; Edward J. Donnelly, O.SS.T.; James Mark Adame, O.SS.T.; Revs. John Di Matteo, O.SS.T.; Daniel Giorgi, P.O. Box 49, Goliad, TX 77963-3095.

St. John Neumann Nursing Home, 10400 Roosevelt Blvd., Rm. 712, Philadelphia, PA 19116. Tel: 215-698-5600; Fax: 215-698-5755. Rev. William J. Axe, O.SS.T.

Ave Maria Retreat House, 8089 Barataria Blvd., Crown Point, LA 70072. Tel: 504-689-3839; Fax: 504-689-2785. Rev. Juam J. Molina, O.SS.T.

St. Brigid Parish, 119 Avenue B, New York, NY 10009-5003.

Immaculate Heart of Mary Friary, 4220 Erdman Ave., 21213. Tel: 410-485-5511; Fax: 410-483-2545. Email: mmartin@archbishopcurley.org. Revs. Joseph Grzybowski, O.F.M.Conv.; Michael Martin, O.F.M.Conv., Pres. & Guardian; Michael Heine, O.F.M.Conv.; Thomas E. Walsh, O.F.M.Conv.; Michael Miller, O.F.M.Conv.; Bro. Michael Buffy, O.F.M.Conv., Vicar. Residence of Franciscan Friars, O.F.M.Conv., conducting Archbishop Curley High School. Priests 5; Brothers 1; Total Staff 6.

Jesuit Community of Loyola College, Inc., Loyola College, 4603 Millbrook Rd., 21212-4721. Tel: 410-617-2318; Fax: 410-617-2125. Email: claudeory@hotmail.com. Revs. Eugene M. Geinzer, S.J., Rector; Ronald J. Anton, S.J. (Retired); Jeffrey P. Baerwald, S.J.; Charles Bonges, S.J.; Michael L. Braden, S.J.; Keith A. Brehob, S.J.; James L. Connor; Edwin H. Convey, S.J.; John R. Donahue, S.J.; Kurt M. Denk, S.J.; Edgar Graham, S.J.; Frank R. Haig, S.J.; Gregory C. Hartley, S.J.; Francis G. Hilton, S.J.; Bro. John B. Hollywood, S.J.; Revs. Joseph M. Kennedy, S.J.; Chae-uk Jonan Lee, S.J.; Dominic W. Maruca, S.J.; William K. McGroarty, S.J.; Francis G. McManamin, S.J.; Francis J. Nash, S.J.; Rigobert Nsibu Tona, S.J.; Harold E. Ridley, S.J.; Joseph S. Rossi, S.J.; Daniel M. Ruff, S.J.; Peter F. Ryan, S.J., S.T.L., S.T.D.; James F. Salmon, S.J.; Nathanael Miti, S.J.; Bro. Claude L. Ory, S.J. Total in Residence 29.

Jesuit Fathers and Brothers Maryland Provincial Curia, 5704 Roland Ave., 21210. Tel: 410-435-1833; Fax: 410-532-1419. Web: www.marprovincejesuits.org. Very Rev. Timothy B. Brown, S.J.; Revs. Michael D. French, S.J., Supr. & Min.; Charles P. Costello, S.J.; Walter J. Burghardt, S.J.; William A. Dawson, S.J.; James M. English, S.J.; Francis P. Ernst, S.J.; Joseph M. Hamernick, S.J.; Hugh A. Kennedy, S.J., Asst. Sec.; Liborio J. LaMartina, S.J., Resident Archivist; William F. Lamm, S.J., Asst. Treas. & Asst. Sec.; Joseph R. Lerch, S.J.; Thomas P. Martin, S.J., Asst. Treas.; Anthony I. McHale, S.J.; Francis X. Metzbower, S.J.; William P. Ryan, S.J., Treas.; John W. Swope, S.J.; John B. Woodward, S.J.

Legal Title: *Corporation of the Roman Catholic Clergymen, Maryland*

Military Chaplains: Revs. Paul J. Shaughnessy, S.J. Tel: 619-556-4718 USS Belleau Wood (LHA3), FPO, AP 46623-1610; Christopher S. Fronk, S.J., CHC, USNR, Office of the Chaplain, USS IWO JIMA (LHD7), FPO, AE 09574-1664.

Priests of the Province Serving Abroad:

Rezidence TJ, Kosi 8, 602 00 Brno, Czech Republic. Tel: 011-42-05-0-737-650970; Fax: 011-42-5-4221-6695. Rev. David G. Allen, S.J.

Pont. Univ. Greg., Piazza della Pilotta 4, Rome 00187 Italy. Tel: 011-39-06-6701-5467; Fax: 011-39-06-6701-5413. Rev. James J. Conn., S.J.

Curia SJ, CP 6139, Rome Prati 00195 Italy. Tel: 011-39-06-689-77455; Fax: 011-39-06-686-8214. Rev. James A. Casciotti, S.J.

Pont. Ist Orientale, Piazza S. Maria Maggiore 7, Rome 00185 Italy. Tel: 011-39-06-44741-7154; Fax: 011-39-06-446-5576. Rev. Michael J. Kuchera, S.J.

North American College, 00120 Vatican City State, Italy. Tel: 011-39-06-684-931. Rev. Brendan G. Lally, S.J.

Pont. Univ. Greg., Piazza della Pilotta 4, Rome 00187 Italy. Tel: 011-39-06-6701-5353; Fax: 011-39-06-6701-5413. Rev. Philip J. Rosato, S.J

15 St. Mary St., Toronto ON M4Y 2R5 Canada. Tel: 416-922-5474; Fax: 416-922-2898. Rev J. Allan Loftus, S.J.

Parroq. San Jose Obrero, Juan Larrea 1161, Barrio San Jose, Salta 4400 Argentina. Tel: 011-54-387-423-5519. Rev. Vincent J. Capuano, S.J.

Fu Jen University Theologate, P.O. Box 1-107, Taiwan 242. Tel: 011-886-2-29017270; Fax: 011-886-2-29080835. Rev. Jeffrey G.L. Chang, S.J.

Collegio S. Roberto Bellarmino, Via del Seminario 120, Rome 00186 Italy. Tel: 011-39-06-69527-6638. Rev. John J. O'Donnell, S.J.

Kolleg St. Georgen, Offenbacher Landstrasse 224, Frankfurt D-60599 Germany. Tel: 011-49-69-6061-391; Fax: 011-49-69-6061-330. Rev. John T. Kelly, S.J.

Jesuit Historical Institute, C.P. 6139, Rome Prati 00195 Italy. Tel: 011-39-06-689-77695; Fax: 011-39-06-686-8214. Rev. Thomas M. McCoog, S.J.

Curia SJ, CP 6139, Rome Prati 00195 Italy. Tel: 011-39-06-689-77-292; 011-39-06-689-77-294; Fax: 011-39-06-687-9283. Rev. Thomas E. Roach, S.J.

Comunidad Arnoldo Gutierrez, Calle Venezuela 68, Casilla 227, Potosi, Bolivia. Tel: 011-591-62-42737; Fax: 011-591-62-42737. Rev. Robert D. Wiesenbaugh, S.J.

Resid. S. Pedro Claver, Casilla 452, Arica, Chile. Tel: 011-56-58-22-9402; Fax: 011-56-58-22-9402. Rev. Eugene J. Barber, S.J.

SJ House Kioicho 7-1, Chiyoda-ku, Tokyo (102-8571), Japan. Tel: 011-81-3-3238-5182; Fax: 011-81-3-3238-5056. Rev. William J. Currie, S.J.

P.O. Box 341, Surulere, Lagos, Nigeria. Tel: 011-234-1-4526517. Rev. Edgar J. Debany, S.J.

P.O. Box "Inigo", 630051 Novosibirsk, Russia. Tel: 011-7-3832-77-2013; Fax: 011-7-3832-77-1413. Rev. James M. Desjardins, S.J.

Jesuit House of Studies, 4 Baron Rd., POB 409, Merrivale 3291 South Africa. Tel: 011-27-33-330-6274; Fax: 011-27-33-330-7929. Rev. Edward C.A. Dougherty, S.J.

DWSC, Post Box 47, Dhanbad, Bihar 326-001 India. Tel: 011-91-326-204552; Fax: 011-91-326-203214. Rev. John F. Guidera, S.J.

Loyola Bhavan, 58 Forest Park, Orissa 75100 India. Tel: 011-91-0674-2531212. Rev. George A. Hess, S.J.

SJ House, Kioicho 7-1, Chiyoda-ku, Tokyo (102-8571), Japan. Tel: 011-81-3-3238-5196; Fax: 011-81-3-3238-5056. Rev. F. Scott Howell, S.J.

SJ House, Kioicho 7-1, Chiyoda-ku, Tokyo (102-8571), Japan. Tel: 011-81-3-3238-5027; Fax: 011-81-3-3238-5056. Rev. Gerard S. Barry, S.J.

Loyola House, P.O. Box 21399, Nairobi, Kenya. Tel: 011-254-2-570436; Fax: 011-254-2-566873. Rev. Edward J. Brady, S.J.

Apartado A-90, Managua 11, Nicaragua. Tel: 011-505-278-4108. Rev. Robert F. Currie, S.J.

Loyola House, Box 21399, Nairobi, Kenya. Tel: 011-254-2-716829; Fax: 011-254-2-718711. Rev. Angelo D'Agostino, S.J.

St. Xavier's High School, PB 10, Lupungutu, Chaibasa Jharkhand 833 201 India. Tel: 011-91-06582-256513. Rev. John J. Deeney, S.J.

Jesu Bhavan, Old Purulia Rd., Mango, Jamshedpur, 831 012 Bihar, India. Tel: 011-91-0657-2460340. Rev. Carl L. Dincher, S.J.

Casa Ejercicios, Casilla 1, Padre Hurtado, Chile. Tel: 011-56-2-811-4171; Fax: 011-56-2-811-1123. Rev. Thomas M. Gavin, S.J.

P.O. Box 854, Benin City, Edo State, Nigeria. Tel: 011-234 52-258610. Rev. Robert E. Hamm, S.J.

Resid. S. Pedro Claver, Casilla 452, Arica, Chile. Tel: 011-56-58-22-9402; Fax: 011-56-58-22-9402. Rev. John F. Henry, S.J.

Loyola Hall, PB 153, Jamshedpur, Bihar 831 001, India. Tel: 011-91-0657-2222933. Rev Richard A. Kenna, S.J.

Loyola House, 91/1 Mu 6, Nakorn Pathom 73110 Thailand. Tel: 011-662-429-0100; Fax: 011-662-812-5628. Rev. Sigmund J. Laschenski, S.J.

St. Xavier's High School, P B 10, Lupungutu, Chaibasa 833 201, India. Tel: 011-91-06582-256513 Rev. Edward H. Nash, S.J.

P.O. Box 854, Benin City, Edo State, Nigeria. Tel: 011-234-52-253926; Fax: 011-234-52-253926. Rev. George W. Quickley, S.J.

San Ignacio, Casilla 597, Santiago, Chile. Tel: 011-56-2-695-5014; Fax: 011-56-2-672-2117. Rev. Eugene M. Rooney, S.J.

P.O. Box 854, Benin City, Edo State, Nigeria. Tel: 011-234-52-258610. Rev. Dominic J. Totaro, S.J.

P.O. Box 172 Novaliches, 1147 Quezon City. Tel: 011-63--939; Fax: 011-63--939. Rev. Charles E. Wolf, S.J.

Human Life Centre, 2 Unit 9, Bhuneswar 751 022 India. Tel: 011-91-0674-2404395. Rev. Edward H. McGrath, S.J.

S J House, Kioicho 7-1, Tokyo 102-8571 Japan. Tel: 011-81 3-3238-5062; Fax: 011-81-3-3238-5050. Rev. John J. Nissel, S.J.

XLRI, Post Box 222, Jamshedpur, Bihar 831 001, India. Tel: 011-91-657-228916; Fax: 011-91-657-227814. Rev. Eugene A. Welch, S.J.

Priests of the Province Serving Elsewhere:

12859 Oakfield Way, Poway, CA 92064-1520. Tel: 858-705-1145. Rev. Paul A. Donovan, S.J.

Catholic Campus Ministry at Stockton P.O. Box 1003, Pomona, NJ 08240. Tel: 609-652-0230. Rev. C. Jeffries Burton, S.J.

Campion Hall, Oxford OX1 1QS England. Tel: 44-1865-2861000; Fax: 44-1865-286148. Revs. John H. Duggan, S.J. (SCR); Brendan R. Horan, S.J.

801 Dominican Dr., Nashville, TN 37228. Tel: 615-255-5863. Rev. John J. Rock, S.J.

302-A Sea Oats Dr., Juno Beach, FL 33408. Tel: 407-775-3810; Fax: 407-622-6471. Rev. Bernard J. Dooley, S.J.

9784 Guisante Ter., San Diego, CA 92124. Tel: 858-278-1027. Rev. Bernard G. Filmyer, S.J.

Chancellor Park, 150 N. 20th St., Apt. 218, Philadelphia, PA 19103. Rev. Willy DeCraemer, S.J.

St. Lucy Church: 3510 S. Ocean Blvd., Highland Beach, FL 33487-3326. Tel: 561-272-4409; Fax: 561-278-8509. Rev. James N. Gelson, S.J.

St. Mary's Hospital, 2900 First Ave., Huntington, WV 25702. Tel: 304-526-1342. Rev. Leigh A. Fuller, S.J.

St. Joseph's Hospital, 1600 W. Girard Ave., Philadelphia, PA 19130-1615. Tel: 215-787-9013. Rev. Joseph F. Monaghan, S.J.

St. Mary's, 9845 Memorial Dr., Houston, TX 77024-3498. Tel: 713-686-6844, Ext. 262; Fax: 713-681-7550. Rev. A. Richard Sotelo, S.J.

P.O. Box 972141, El Paso, TX 79997-2141. Tel: 915-845-3899; Fax: 915-298-5325. Rev. Robert J. McTeigue, S.J.

P.O. Box 434648, San Ysidro, CA 92143-4648. Tel: 664-680-1825; Fax: 664-630-1591. Rev. David L. Ungerleider, S.J.

On Leave: Revs. Mark J. Connelly, S.J.; Daniel C. Doherty, S.J.

St. Joseph Society of the Sacred Heart House of Central Administration, 1130 N. Calvert St., 21202. Tel: 410-727-3386; Fax: 410-727-1006. Email: josephite1@aol.com. Web: www.josephite.com. Very Revs. Edward J. Chiffriller, S.S.J., Supr. Gen.; Rodger J. Caesar, S.S.J., Vicar Gen.; John G. Harfmann, S.S.J., Consultor Gen.; Nelson A. Moreira, S.S.J., Treas. & Rector; Revs. Charles P. Moffatt, S.S.J., Vocation Dir.; Peter E. Hogan, S.S.J., Archivist; Peter J. Kenney, S.S.J., Historian and Asst. Rector; Joseph L. Waters, S.S.J., Historian; Eugene P. McManus, S.S.J., Dir. Public Rels.; Joseph C. Verrett, S.S.J., The Josephite Harvest & Dir. Mission Office; Armand J. Manuel, S.S.J., Asst. to Admin.; Mrs. Bernice Jones, Asst. Archivist; Revs. John F. Byrne, S.S.J. (Retired); N. Wilfrid DesRosiers, S.S.J. (Retired); James A. Hayes, S.S.J. (Retired); Ralph R. Ransom, S.S.J. (Retired); William A. Richardson, S.S.J. (Retired); Joseph J. Rimshaw, S.S.J. (Retired); W. Dayton Salisbury, S.S.J. (Retired); Louis R. Saporito, S.S.J. (Retired); James P. Schappert, S.S.J. (Retired). Priests 12.

St. Joseph's Manor (Josephite Fathers and Brothers), 911 W. Lake Ave., 21210-1022. Tel: 410-323-3829; Fax: 410-435-1853. Very Revs. Edward J. Mullowney, S.S.J., Rector; Matthew J. O'Rourke, S.S.J., Vice Rector; Revs. Joseph Calamari, S.S.J.; John E. Hardman, S.S.J.; John C. Crotty, S.S.J.; Paul E. Kluthe, S.S.J.; Edward J. Lawlor, S.S.J.; Paul A. Ostner, S.S.J.; Francis J. Schroeder, S.S.J.; Eugene J. McKenna, S.S.J.; William J. Mckenna, S.S.J.; Eugene P. McManus, S.S.J.; Eugene J. Moynihan, S.S.J.; Robert J. O'Connell, S.S.J.; John J. Rawlins, S.S.J.; Philip J. Tarallo, S.S.J.; Bros. Andrew Hogya, S.S.J.; Charles Douglas, S.S.J.; Ricardo Gourrier. Priests 15; Brothers 3.

St. Joseph's Passionist Community, 251 S. Morley St., 21229. Tel: 410-566-3750; Fax: 410-233-4974. Email: stjomona@earthlink.net. Revs. Jerome Vereb, C.P.; Robert Carbonneau, C.P.; Alban Harmon, C.P., F.N.; Eustace McDonald, C.P.; William Murphy, C.P. Congregation of the Most Holy Cross and Passion of Our Lord Jesus Christ Priests 3.

Pallottine Center for Apostolic Causes, 512 W. Saratoga St., 21201. Tel: 410-685-3063; Fax: 410-234-1459. Rev. Peter T. Sticco, S.A.C. (NEW), Dir.

Legal Title: *St. Jude Shrine-Pallottine Missions; Pallottine Center for Apostolic Causes, Inc.*, Promotional Center for St. Jude Shrine.

Society of Mary (Marianists), Marianist Community, 4301 Roland Ave., 21210-2793. Tel: 410-366-1300; Fax: 410-889-5743. Rev. John Maniyatt, S.V.D.; Bros. Howard L. Hughes, S.M., Dir.; Frank O'Donnell, S.M. Priests 2; Brothers 4. In Res. Rev.

Inna Edara, S.V.D.; Bro. Victor Kamara, C.F.C.

Sulpician Provincial House (Associated Sulpicians of the United States) , 5408 Roland Ave., 21210. Tel: 410-323-5070; Fax: 410-433-6524. Email: RWitherup@sulpicians.org. Web: sulpicians.org. Very Rev. Ronald D. Witherup, S.S., U.S. Prov. of the Society of St. Sulpice; Revs. Thomas R. Ulshafer, S.S., S.T.L., Ph.D., Prov. Sec. & Dir. Discernment & Admissions; Gerald D. McBrearity, S.S., Dir. Formation; Mr. Joseph M. Reynolds, Exec. Asst. to Prov.; Laura Tester, Finance Dir. & Business Mgr. Priest Candidates 3.

Members and Candidates on Individual Assignments: Rev. Patrick Simutowe, S.S., Student Priest, St. Mary's Seminary and University, Baltimore.

Emmaus Spirituality Center, P.O. Box 320084 Woodlands, Lusaka 157101 Zambia. Tel: 011-260-126-3354; Fax: 011-260-126-3404. Revs. Cornelius Hankomoone, S.S.; Francis Musonda.

Catholic University of America, c/o Theological College, 401 Michigan Ave, N.E., Washington, DC 20064. Tel: 202-756-4923; Fax: 202-756-4909. Rev. Daniel J. Doherty, S.S.

634 E. St., N.E., Washington, DC 20002. Tel: 202-543-1075; Fax: 202-543-1670. Rev. William E. Hartgen, S.S. (Retired).

4006 York Dr., Havre De Grace, 21078-2100. Tel: 410-273-6600; Fax: 410-272-5617. Rev. Joseph C. Martin, S.S. (Retired).

7 Kirkland Rd., Cambridge, MA 02138-3012. Tel: 617-492-1960. Rev. John J. Kselman, S.S.

24 Killian Ave., Trumbull, CT 06611-4118. Tel: 203-268-3610. Rev. Addison G. Wright, S.S. (Retired).

1248 Brentwood Pointe, Brentwood, TN 37027-2945. Tel: 615-377-3009. Rev. Thomas Doyle, S.S. (Retired).

St. Augustine's Major Seminary, P.O. Box 81011, Kabwe 157101 Zambia. Tel: 011-260-97-791-229. Rev. Cale J. Crowley, S.S., Rector.

Emmaus Spirituality Center, P.O. Box 32-0084, Woodlands, Lusaka 157101 Zambia. Tel: 011-260-126-3354; Fax: 011-260-126-3404. Rev. John L. Bitterman, S.S., Rector.

Emmaus Spirituality Center, P.O. Box 32-0084, Woodlands, Lusaka 15710 Zambia. Tel: 410-323-5070; Fax: 410-433-6525. Rev. Gerald V. Lardner, S.S.

Casa de Nuestre Senore Dolorosa, Calle 31, no. 78 (Apdo.#712), Chuburna de Hidalgo, Merida, Yucantan 97200 Mexico. Rev. Louis M. Reitz, S.S. (Retired).

4210 N. Charles St., Apt. #2, 21218-1041. Tel: 410-243-9536. Rev. Robert L. Russell, S.S.

College Saint Paul, Rue du Discobole 2/23, 1348 Louivain-la-neuve, Belgium. Tel: 011-010-4597. Rev. Nam J. Kim, S.S.

Xaverian Brothers Generalate, 4409 Frederick Ave., 21229. Tel: 410-644-0034; Fax: 410-644-2762. Email: acaliman@xaverianbrothers.org. Web: xaverianbrothers.org. Bros. Arthur Caliman, C.F.X., Supr. Gen.; Edward Driscoll, C.F.X., Vicar Gen.; Lawrence Harvey, C.F.X., Dir. Xaverian Sponsored Schools; Richard Mazza, C.F.X., Dir. Pastoral Care; Michael McCarthy, C.F.X., Personnel; Michael Naccarato, CFO. Legal Titles and Schools Sponsored: Xaverian Brothers USA, Inc.;(f/k/a The American Central Province of the Xaverian Brothers Inc., The American Northeast Province of the Xaverian Brother, Inc., and the Working Boys Home, Inc.); St. Mary's-Ryken High School, Inc.; Our Lady of Good Counsel High School, Inc.; St. Xavier High School, Inc.; Xaverian High School, Inc.; Holy Family High School, Inc.; Mt. St. Joseph High School, Inc.; Xaverian Brothers Auxiliary; St. Michael's High School Alumni Association; Nazareth Regional High School, Inc.; St. John's Preparatory School, Inc.; St. John's High School, Inc.; Xaverian Brothers High School, Inc.; Malden Catholic High School, Inc.; Xavier High School, Inc.; Isidore Charitable Trust. Brothers 248.

ADAMSTOWN. *Christian Brothers Provincialate*, P.O. Box 29, 21710. Tel: 301-874-5188; Fax: 301-847-5674. Email: fscbaltimore.org. Web: fscbaltimore.org. Bros. Robert Schieler, F.S.C., Prov.; Timothy J. Froehlich, F.S.C., Dir. Finance; James L. Butler, F.S.C., Asst. Prov.

Legal Title: *Christian Brothers of Frederick, Inc.* Brothers of the Christians Schools, Baltimore Province Brothers 3; Total 182; Total Staff 4.

ANNAPOLIS. *Saint Mary Rectory*, 109 Duke of Gloucester St., 21401. Tel: 410-269-6092; Fax: 410-263-3027. Web: www.stmaryschurch.org. Revs. Denis J. Sweeney, C.SS.R.; Theodore Heyburn, C.SS.R.; John Lavin, C.SS.R.; Andrew Costello, C.SS.R.; James McDonald, C.SS.R.; John G. Tizio, C.SS.R.; Patrick Flynn, C.SS.R.; Alphonse Olive, C.SS.R.; Deacons Leroy Moore; Anthony F. Norcio. Residence of the Redemptorist Fathers and Brothers. Total in Residence 11. In Res. Revs. Bernard Baumgartner, C.SS.R.; Arthur Mahoney, C.SS.R.

CUMBERLAND. *SS. Peter and Paul Friary*, 109 N. Smallwood St., 21502. Tel: 301-777-3131; 301-777-3137; Fax: 301-759-3568. Email: ppaul@archbalt.org. Revs. James Kurtz, O.F.M.Cap., Vicar and Pastor, Ss. Peter and Paul (Cumberland); Pastor, St. Ambrose (Cresaptown); Vernon Busch, O.F.M.Cap., Guardian & Assoc. Pastor; Bernard Finerty, O.F.M.Cap.; Victor Kriley, O.F.M.Cap, Chap., Western Maryland Health System.

Legal Title: *Province of St. Augustine of the Capuchin Order* Priests 4.

ELLICOTT CITY. *Friary of St. Joseph Cupertino*, 12290 Folly Quarter Rd., 21042-1425. Tel: 410-531-2800; Fax: 410-531-2801. Revs. James McCurry, O.F.M.Conv., Guardian; Mark L. Curesky, O.F.M.Conv.; Bart Karwacki, O.F.M.Conv.; Eugene Kole, O.F.M.Conv.; Jude Winkler, O.F.M.Conv.; Bro. Gerry Seipp, O.F.M.Conv. Conventual Franciscan Friars., Corporate Title: Franciscan Fathers Minor Conventuals of MD, Inc.

Friars Minor Conventual

Sanctuary of St. Anthony Tel: 410-531-2800; Fax: 410-531-2801.

Companions of St. Anthony, 12290 Folly Quarter Rd., 21042. Tel: 410-531-2800; Fax: 410-531-2801.

Companions Evangelization & Mail Order Office Tel: 410-988-9833; Fax: 410-988-9705.

Order of Friars Minor Conventual, 12300 Folly Quarter Rd., 21042-1419. Tel: 410-531-1400; Fax: 410-531-4881. Email: vicar@saprov.org. Web: www.stanthonyprovince.org. Very Revs. Michael Kolodziej, O.F.M.Conv., Min. Prov.; Donald Grzymski, O.F.M.Conv., Vicar Prov.; Revs. Maurice Piszczatowski, O.F.M.Conv.; Martin Kobos, O.F.M.Conv., Dev. Dir.; Robert Twele, O.F.M.Conv., Treas.; Bro. Brian Newbigging, O.F.M.Conv. Legal Title: Order of Friars Minor Conventual, St. Anthony of Padua Province, U.S.A., Inc.; Franciscan Minor Conventuals of Maryland, Inc. of Ellicott City, MD.; The Franciscan Fathers, Minor Conventuals, of St. Stanislaus Church of Baltimore City, Inc.; Franciscan Friars, St. Anthony of Padua Province, Education Fund, Inc.; Franciscan Friars, St. Anthony of Padua Province, Fund for the Aged and Infirm Friars, Inc.; St. Francis of Assisi Community, Inc., Companions of St. Anthony; St. Stanislaus Cemetery, Inc., Anthony Corps, Inc. Total in Residence 180.

On Assignment Outside the U.S.A.:

Via di S. Teodoro - 26, Rome 00186 Italy. Tel: 011-39-06-679-4974; Fax: 011-39-06-233-245-688. Rev. Daniel Pietrzak, O.F.M.Conv.

Curia Generale dei Frati Minori Conventualli, Piazza Ss. Apostoli 51, Rome 00187 Italy. Tel: 011-39-06-699-571; Fax: 011-39-06-699-57321. Most Rev. Joachin Giermek, O.F.M.Conv., Min. General; Rev. Matteo Luo, O.F.M.Conv.

Convento S. Antonio, 56, Viale Guido Baccelli, 56, Rome 00153 Italy. Tel: 011-39-06-572-993-11; Fax: 011-39-06-572-993-42. Rev. Donald Kos, O.F.M-.Conv.

P.O. Box 24177, Nairobi, Kenya. Tel: 011-254-2-884488; Fax: 011-254-2-88420. Rev. David Blowey, O.F.M.Conv.

Asato Catholic Church: 3-7-2 Asato, Naha, Okinawa 902-0067 Japan. Tel: 011-81-98-863-2020; Fax: 011-81-98-863-8474. Rev. Vincent Lachendro, O.F.M.Conv. Metro Manila

St. Francis of Assisi Friary, P.O. Box 238, Saltpond, Ghana. Tel: 011-233-42-34555; Fax: 011-233-27-5403-76. Revs. Dominic Slemba, O.F.M.Conv.; Giles Zakowicz, O.F.M.Conv.

Individual Assignment Within the U.S.A.:

Pope John Paul II Center, 33 Lincoln Ave., Danbury, CT 06810. Tel: 203-790-9071. Rev. Thomas Gwozdz, O.F.M.Conv. (Retired).

Sts. Mary and Joseph Home, 4291 Richmond Rd. - #102, Cleveland, OH 44122-6103. Tel: 216-464-1222, Ext. 138. Rev. Paul Duzinski, O.F.M.Conv. (Retired).

Sacred Heart Home, 4520 Ransom Rd., Clarence, NY 14031. Rev. Patrick Rolak, O.F.M.Conv. (Retired).

Chaplain's Office, 5286 South Park Ave., Hamburg, NY 14075-1596. Tel: 716-649-1205; Fax: 716-646-0971. Rev. Ronald Sermak, O.F.M.Conv.

Stella Maris, Formerly Stella Manis 2300 Dulaney Valley Rd., Timonium, 21093. Revs. Conrad Miller, O.F.M.Conv.; Callistus Juras, O.F.M.Conv. (Retired); Bro. Thaddeus Grzankowski, O.F.M.Conv.

St. Joseph Nursing Home, 1222 Tugwell Dr., 21228. Tel: 410-747-0026; Fax: 410-747-0386. Rev. Gregory Kwapisz, O.F.M.Conv.

Sisters of Providence Infirmary, 1233 Main St., Holyoke, MA 01040-5399. Rev. Jeremy Chodacki, O.F.M.Conv. (Retired).

EMMITSBURG. *Vincentian House*, P.O. Box 376, 21727. Tel: 301-447-2326; Fax: 301-447-3579. Email: stjosephparish@adelphia.net. Revs. William J. O'Brien, C.M., Pastor, Supr.; Michael J. Kennedy, C.M., Chap.; William P. Goff, C.M., Asst.; Walter J. Menig, C.M., Chap.; Stephen P. Trzecieski, C.M., Assoc. Pastor, Asst. Supr. Priests 5.

[T] CONVENTS AND RESIDENCES FOR SISTERS

BALTIMORE. *Carmelite Communities Assoc.*, 1318 Dulaney Valley Rd., 21286-1399. Tel: 410-823-7415. Web: www.geocities/renewed_carmel.

Carmelite Sisters of Baltimore (1790), 1318 Dulaney Valley Rd., 21286-1399. Tel: 410-823-7415; Fax: 410-823-7418. Email: info@baltimorecarmel.org. Web: www.baltimorecarmel.org. Sr. Constance FitzGerald, Prioress. Discalced Carmelite Nuns Professed Sisters 14; Novices 2; Postulants 1.

Chesapeake Province of the Sisters of Notre Dame de Namur, Provincial Offices, 305 Cable St., 21210-2511. Tel: 410-243-1993; Fax: 410-243-2279. Email: chesprv@aol.com. Web: www.sndden.org.

Legal Title: *Chesapeake Province of the Sisters of Notre Dame de Namur, Inc.* Sisters in Province 76; Sisters in Baltimore Diocese 36.

Administrative Team: Sisters Mary Donohue, S.N.D-.deN.; Edithann Kane, S.N.D.deN.

Contemplative Sisters of the Good Shepherd (CGS), 4140 Maple Ave., Halethorpe, 21227-4099Web: goodshepherdsistes.org. Sisters 7.

Daughters of Charity, 900 Caton Ave., 21229. Tel: 410-368-2885; Fax: 410-368-3509. Email: stagneshouse@stagnes.org. Sr. Jo Ann Knight, Sister Servant. Total in Residence 15.

Little Sisters of Jesus-Regional Residence, 400 N. Streeper St., 21224-1230. Tel: 410-327-7863. Web: www.rc.net/org/littlesisters. Sr. Anne-Marie Boucher, Rgnl. Supr. Sisters 4.

Little Sisters of the Poor-Provincial Residence, 601 Maiden Choice Ln., 21228-3698. Tel: 410-744-9367; Fax: 410-747-0601. Sisters Mary Bernard Du St. Esprit, L.S.P., Prov.; Maria Christine Lynch, L.S.P., Supr. Sisters 20; Total Assisted 107; Total Staff 133.

Maria Health Care Center, Inc., 6401 N. Charles St., 21212. Tel: 410-377-3011; Fax: 410-377-6042. Email: gsciamanna@ssndba.org. Sr. Grace Sciamanna, S.S.N.D., Admin. Health Center for School Sisters of Notre Dame and other Religious Congregations.

Mission Helper Center, 1001 W. Joppa Rd., 21204-3787. Tel: 410-823-8585; Fax: 410-825-6355. Email: csbmhsh@aol.com. Web: www.missionhelpers.org. Sisters M. Judith Waldt, Pres.; Victoria Van Den Burs, Treas.; Natalie DeLuca, Asst.; Mary Louise Zaworski, Mgr. Sisters 31; Sisters in Diocese 49; Total Staff 7.

Missionaries of Charity, Gift of Hope Convent, 818 N. Collington Ave., 21205. Tel: 410-732-6056. Sr. M. Pietra, M.C., Supr. Sisters 6; Total Assisted Annually 370; Total Staff 9.

Our Lady of Mt. Providence Convent-Motherhouse, 701 Gun Rd., 21227. Tel: 410-242-8500; Fax: 410-242-4963. Email: aproctor@aol.com. Sisters Mary Crescentia, Proctor, Motherhouse; Rita Michelle, Proctor, Convent. Oblate Sisters of Providence, Attended by Sulpician Fathers and Josephite Fathers. Sisters in the Motherhouse 69; Sisters in the Diocese 78; Total in Residence 96; Total Assisted 60; Total Staff 39.

The School Sisters of Notre Dame in the City of Baltimore (Baltimore Prov.), 6401 N. Charles St., 21212. Tel: 410-377-7774; Fax: 410-377-5363. Email: jamohan@aol.com. Web: www.ssnd.org. Sr. Jane Burke, S.S.N.D., Prov. Leader; Rev. E. Joseph Cote, Chap. Sisters 83; Sisters in Province 347; Sisters in Diocese 256.

Sisters of Mercy, Mercy Center, 1322 E. Northern Pkwy., 21239-1919. Tel: 410-435-4400; Fax: 410-433-8868. Email: som@qis.net. Web: www.mercybaltimore.org. Sr. Barbara Wheeley, R.S.M., Pres.; Kathy Reich, Treas. Sisters of Mercy of the Americas, Baltimore Regional Community Sisters in Community 197; Sisters in Diocese 103.

Sisters of St. Francis of Assisi - Baltimore House, 3725 Ellerslie Ave., 21218. Tel: 410-235-0139; Fax: 410-243-2569. Email: fransrbalt@aol.com. Sisters of St. Francsi of Assisi Sisters 368.

Administrative Team: Sisters Maria Lunz, O.S.F.; Rose Sevenich, O.S.F.; Charlotte Roost, O.S.F.; Mary Therese White, O.S.F., Gen. Supr.; Rev. Gerald West, Chap. (Retired).

Sisters of St. Francis of Philadelphia Convents in the Diocese:

Congregational Office - Our Lady of Angels Convent, 609 S. Convent Rd., Aston, PA 19014. Tel: 610-459-4125; Fax: 610-459-0195. Web: www.osfphila.org.

Shrine of the Little Flower Convent, 2851 Kentucky Ave., 21213. Tel: 410-483-3484.

Our Lady of Mt. Carmel Convent, 37 Seaford Ave., 21221. Tel: 410-687-5335.

St. Clement Convent, 1212 Chesaco Ave., 21237. Tel: 410-687-4433.
St. Joseph Medical Center Convent, 7601 Osler Dr., Towson, 21204. Tel: 410-337-1100.
St. Stephen Convent, 8020 Bradshaw Rd., P.O. Box 62, Bradshaw, 21087. Tel: 410-592-9433.
Immaculate Conception Convent, 112 Ware Ave., Towson, 21204. Tel: 410-823-3470.
St. Joseph Convent, Box 1, Midland, 21542. Tel: 301-463-2248.
Franciscan Residence, 18 Treeway Ct., 4-A, Towson, 21286. Tel: 410-825-4189.
St. Anthony Convent, 4500 Frankford Ave., 21206. Tel: 410-488-0054.
Sisters of St. Francis, 34 Acorn Cir. #202, 21286. Tel: 410-832-1858.
Sisters of St. Francis, 806D Cinnamon Ridge Pl., Cockeysville, 21030. Tel: 410-683-1427.
Sisters of St. Francis, 3020-D Autumn Branch Ln., Ellicott City, 21043. Tel: 410-418-8823.
Sisters of St. Francis, 11 Peroba Ct., 21234. Tel: 410-882-3212.
Sisters of St. Francis, 303 Commerce St., Apt. 2, Havre de Grace, 21078. Tel: 410-942-0841.
Genesis House, 9 Skidmore Ct., Towson, 21204. Tel: 410-296-8071. Total in Residence 68.
Sisters of the Good Shepherd, 4100 Maple Ave., 21227-4099. Tel: 410-247-2770; Fax: 410-242-5890. Email: kmoore@goodshepherdcenter.org. Sr. Kathleen Moore, R.G.S., Supr. Sisters 14; Total Staff 2.
Sisters of the Good Shepherd-St. Joseph Residence, 4130 Maple Ave., 21227-4007. Tel: 410-247-3898; 410-247-2770; Fax: 410-242-5890. Email: rgseileen@hotmail.com. Infirmary and Retirement Center for Washington Province. Sisters 20; Total Staff 35.
Sisters Servants of Mary Immaculate, Inc. Convent and Novitiate. , 1220 Tugwell Dr., 21228. Tel: 410-747-1353; Fax: 410-747-0386. Sr. Bernadetta Kozyra, Prov. Sisters 19.
St. Clare of Assisi, Inc., 3725 Ellerslie Ave., 21218. Tel: 410-235-9277. Email: etcarr@msn.com. Sr. Ellen Carr, O.S.F., Contact Person.
The Villa, 6806 Bellona Ave., 21212-1299. Tel: 410-377-2450; Fax: 410-377-2501. Suzanne L. Carson, Admin.
Legal Title: *Joint Retirement Convent, Inc.-The Villa*, Convent for Retired Sisters of Mercy and Mission Helpers of the Sacred Heart. Sisters 70; Total Staff 70.

EMMITSBURG. *Daughters of Charity of St. Vincent de Paul, Emmitsburg Province* 21727. Tel: 301-447-3121; Fax: 301-447-6038. Web: www.daughtersofcharity-emmitsburg.org. Sr. Elyse Staab, D.C., Prov.
Legal Title: *Sisters of Charity of St. Joseph's, Emmitsburg, MD*, (St. Joseph's Provincial House) Sisters at Provincial House 22; Sisters in Diocese 141; Sisters in Province 212.
Villa St. Michael-St. Joseph's Provincial House, 333 S. Seton Ave., 21727-9299. Tel: 301-447-3121; Fax: 301-447-7082. Web: www.daughtersofcharity-emmitsburg.org. Martha Coleman, Admin. Retirement Home of Daughters of Charity of St. Vincent de Paul Daughters of the Charity 79; Sisters of Notre Dame 23; Visitation Sisters 3.

FREDERICK. *Contemplative Sisters of the Good Shepherd (CGS)*, 4140 Maple Ave., Halethorpe, 21227-4099Web: goodshepherdsisters.org. Sisters 7.
Visitation Monastery of Frederick, MD, 200 E. Second St., 21701. Tel: 301-662-3322; Fax: 301-695-8549. Email: srft@frederickvisitation.com. Web: frederickvisitation.com. Sr. Marguerite Therese Leary, V.H.M., Supr. Cloistered Community with Apostolate of Teaching (Grades PreK-8). Sisters 7.

LUTHERVILLE. *Emmanuel Monastery*, 2229 W. Joppa Rd., 21093-4601. Tel: 410-821-5792; Fax: 410-296-9560. Email: bensrs@emmanuelosb.org. Web: www.emmanuelosb.org. Benedictine Sisters of Baltimore, Ministering in Education, Pastoral Ministry and Counseling, Retreats and Spiritual Direction, Social Services, Justice Ministry, Hospital Ministry, and Business Admin. Sisters 15.

MARRIOTTSVILLE. *Sisters of Bon Secours, C.B.S., Provincial House* 21104. Tel: 410-442-1333; Fax: 410-442-1394. Web: www.bonsecours.org. Sr. Alice Talone, C.B.S., Pres. Retired Sisters 5; Total in Residence 38; Total Staff 63.

STEVENSON. *Maryland Province Center*, 1531 Greenspring Valley Rd., 21153. Tel: 410-486-5599; Fax: 410-486-5466. Email: sndmd@aol.com. Web: www.sndden.org. Sisters Marian Schaechtel, Prov. Moderator; Rosemary Donohue, Prov. Leadership; Joan Kerrigan, Prov. Leadership; Patricia Loome, Prov. Leadership.
Legal Title: *Baltimore Province of the Sisters of Notre Dame de Namur, Inc.*
Legal Title: *Maryvale Preparatory School, Inc.*
Legal Title: *Academy of Notre Dame de Namur, Inc.*
Legal Title: *Sisters of Notre Dame de Namur, Maryland Province, Charitable Trust* Maryland Province of the Sisters of Notre Dame de Namur, Additional Projects Sponsored: Maryland Province Center of Stevenson, MD; Villa Julie Stevenson, MD; Notre Dame Educ. Center, Washington, DC., Trinity School, Ellicott City, MD.; Additional Projects Co-Sponsored: The Development Office, a joint project of the Maryland, Chesapeake & Notre Dame Base Communities Provinces; Director: Mrs. Paula Henderson. Sisters in Province 120; Sisters in Diocese 58; Total Staff 11.
Villa Julie Residence, 1531 Greenspring Valley Rd., 21153. Tel: 410-486-6946; Fax: 410-484-6930. Email: sndvilla@aol.com. Web: www.sndden.org. Assisted Living Home for Sisters of Notre Dame and Staff Residence. Sisters 18.
St. Vincent Care Center, 333 S. Seton Ave., Emmitsburg, 21727-9200. Tel: 301-447-3121. Sisters of Notre Dame 11.
St. Julie Hall, 333 S. Seton Ave., Emmitsburg, 21727-9200. Tel: 301-447-5935. Sisters of Notre Dame 9.
Stella Maris, 2300 Dulaney Valley Rd., 21204. Tel: 410-252-4500. Sisters of Notre Dame 1

TIMONIUM. *Sisters of the Visitation-Stella Maris Hospice*, 2300 Dulaney Valley Rd., 21093. Tel: 410-252-4501; Fax: 410-560-9675. Web: stellamarisinc.com.
Legal Title: *Visitation Monasteries, Inc.*

[U] NEWMAN CENTERS

BALTIMORE. *Archdiocesan Office-Newman Center* 7909 York Rd., 21204. Tel: 410-828-0622; Fax: 410-828-4825. Email: albright@towson.edu. Web: ralbright@towson.edu. Rev. Robert E. Albright, Archdiocesan Dir. Total in Residence 2; Total Staff 4.
Johns Hopkins University, Newman House, 2941 N. Charles St., 21218. Tel: 410-243-7066; Fax: 410-877-2841. Rev. Thomas Ryan.
Morgan State University, St. Matthew Church, 5401 Loch Raven Blvd., 21239. Tel: 410-433-2300.
Towson University, Newman Center, 7909 York Rd., 21204. Tel: 410-828-0622; Fax: 410-828-4825. Rev. Robert E. Albright, Dir.
University of Maryland-Baltimore County, 5401 Wilkens Ave., 21228. Tel: 410-828-0622; Fax: 410-828-4825.
Hood College, St. John Church, Rosemont Ave., Frederick, 21701. Tel: 301-662-8288 410-828-0622; Fax: 410-828-4825.
Frostburg State University, Osborne Center, 130 S. Broadway, Frostburg, 21532. Tel: 301-689-5041; Fax: 301-689-8910. Rev. Edward S. Hendricks.
Western Maryland College, 2 College Hill, 21157. Tel: 410-876-2248; Fax: 410-857-2411. Contact St. John Church, Westminster, 21157. Tel: 410-848-4744.

[V] FOUNDATIONS, FUNDS AND TRUSTS

BALTIMORE. *Archbishop Curley High School Endowment Trust*, 3701 Sinclair Ln., 21213. Tel: 410-485-5000; Fax: 410-483-2545. Rev. Michael Martin, O.F.M.Conv.
Archdiocesan Priests Post-Retirement Benefits Plan Trust Fund, 320 Cathedral St., 21201. Tel: 410-547-5317; Fax: 410-783-5993. Email: pphelps@archbalt.org. Petra R. Phelps, Contact Person.
Bon Secours Baltimore Health Corp., Inc., 2000 W. Baltimore St., 21223. Tel: 410-362-3000.
Bon Secours Facilities, Inc.
Bon Secours of Maryland Foundation, Inc.
The Urban Medical Institute Foundation, Inc.
The Catholic Family Foundation of the Archdiocese of Baltimore, Inc., 320 Cathedral St., 21201. Tel: 410-547-8497; Fax: 410-625-8435. Email: jedwards@archbalt.org. Web: www.archbalt.org. Jim Edwards, Contact Person.
Chancery Office For further information and additional listings, please see Associated Catholic Charities Section. , 320 Cathedral St., 21201. Tel: 410-547-5444; Fax: 410-727-8234.
Archbishop of Baltimore Annual Appeal Trust Tel: 410-547-5439; Fax: 410-727-8234.
Archdiocesan Health Plan Trust Fund Agreement Tel: 410-547-5317; Fax: 410-783-5993.
Archdiocesan General Insurance Program Trust Tel: 410-547-5317; Fax: 410-783-5993.
Basilica of the Assumption Historic Trust, Inc. Tel: 410-727-3564; Fax: 410-539-0407.
Cemetery Continuing Care Trust St. Patrick's Havre de Grace, Cemetery Continuing Care Trust; Holy Cross Cemetery Continuing Care Trust; St. Joseph, Fullerton, Cemetery-Continuing Care Trust Agreement; St. Mary of the Assumption, Govans, Cemetery Continuing Care Trust; St. Mary's, Pylesville Cemetery, Continuing Care Trust
Christian Brothers Community Support Charitable Trust Tel: 410-539-3321.
Corpus Christi Jenkins Memorial Trust, Inc. Tel: 410-523-4161; Fax: 410-523-5745.
Dart, Inc.
The Dr. Charles J. Foley Sr. and Mildred H. Foley Memorial Endowment Trust Tel: 410-547-5322; Fax: 410-332-8233.
Franciscan Sisters of Baltimore, Inc., Trust Tel: 410-235-2496; Fax: 410-243-2569.
The Gallagher Family Fund, 320 Cathedral St., 21201. Tel: 410-547-5322; Fax: 410-332-8233.
**G S Housing, Inc.*
**G S Properties, Inc.*
John Carroll Foundation of the Roman Catholic Archdiocese of Baltimore Tel: 410-547-5300; Fax: 410-332-8233.
John Paul II Regional School, Inc. Tel: 410-944-0367; Fax: 410-265-5316.
St. Joseph's Texas, School Endowment Trust Tel: 410-666-0393; Fax: 410-628-6814.
Marian House, Inc. Tel: 410-467-4121.
The Marion Burk Knott Scholarship Fund, Educational Trust Tel: 301-603-9501.
Marianist Charitable Trust Tel: 410-366-1300; Fax: 410-889-5743.
Maryvale Educational Fund, Inc. Tel: 410-252-3366; Fax: 410-561-1826.
Mercy Primary Care Group, Inc. Tel: 410-332-9000; Fax: 410-962-1303.
The National Black Catholic Congress, Inc. Tel: 410-547-8496; Fax: 410-752-3958.
Neumann Early Childhood Center, Inc. Tel: 410-547-5495.
Our Lady of Good Counsel Historic Trust, Inc. Tel: 410-752-0205; Fax: 410-576-0929.
Pallottine Charitable, Educational and Apostolic Ministry Trust Tel: 301-422-3777.
Plan of Self-Insurance Trust Tel: 410-547-5317; Fax: 410-783-5993.
The Priests Continuing Education and Formation Endowment Trust Tel: 410-547-5317; Fax: 410-783-5993.
Prime E.A.P., Inc. Tel: 410-547-5317; Fax: 410-783-5993.
St. Agnes Clinical Practice Group, Inc. Tel: 410-368-6000.
St. Gregory the Great Housing Committee, Inc. Tel: 410-523-0061; Fax: 410-669-1385.
St. Agnes Hospital Foundation, Inc. Tel: 410-368-3155; Fax: 410-368-3533.
St. Augustine School Education Endowment Trust Tel: 301-796-3040; Fax: 410-579-1165.
St. Jane Frances Educational Endowment Trust Tel: 410-255-4750; Fax: 410-350-6720.
St. Jerome Housing Corporation, Inc. Tel: 410-547-5527.
St. John Neumann Regional School, Inc. Tel: 301-724-4055; Fax: 301-724-4827.
St. John the Evangelist School Endowment Trust, 689 Ritchie Hwy., Severna Park, 21146. Tel: 410-647-2283. Email: mrozanski@stjohnsp.org. Rev. Mitchell T. Rozanski, Contact Person.
St. Joseph, Texas, 101 Church Ln., Cockeysville, 21030. Tel: 410-683-0600. Email: pcook@stjostex.com. Rev. Msgr. Paul G. Cook, Contact Person.
St. Jude Shrine Corporation Tel: 410-685-6026; Fax: 410-244-5728.
St. Luke Parish Endowment Trust Tel: 410-477-5200; Fax: 410-477-5996.
St. Mark's Parish School Endowment Trust Tel: 410-747-6613; Fax: 410-747-3188.
St. Peter's Cemetery Restoration Fund, Inc. Tel: 410-547-5300; Fax: 410-332-8233.
St. Peter's, Westernport, School Endowment Trust Tel: 301-359-0892; Fax: 301-359-0657.
St. Pius V Housing Committee, Inc. Tel: 410-523-1930; Fax: 410-523-8164.
St. Thomas Aquinas School Foundation Trust, 3710 Roland Ave., 21211. Tel: 410-889-4618. Email: aquinas2@erols.com. William J. Frank, Contact Person.
St. Stephen School Endowment Trust Tel: 410-592-7617; Fax: 410-592-7330.
St. Vincent De Paul Historic Trust, Inc. Tel: 410-547-5377; Fax: 410-625-8483.
Sacred Heart Community Health Services, Inc. Tel: 301-723-5222.
Sacred Heart Foundation, Inc. Tel: 301-723-5222.
Sacred Heart Hospital of the Sisters of Charity, Inc. Tel: 410-723-5222.
The SS. Peter & Paul Parish Endowment Trust Tel: 301-777-3131; Fax: 301-759-3568.
School Sisters of Notre Dame in the City of Baltimore Charitable Trust, Inc. Tel: 410-377-7774; Fax: 410-377-5363.
The Seton Keough High School Endowment Trust Tel: 410-646-4444; Fax: 410-368-1591.
Sisters of Notre Dame de Namur Charitable Trusts Tel: 410-255-1577.

Sisters of Notre Dame de Namur, Maryland Province, Charitable Trust Tel: 410-486-5382; Fax: 410-486-5466.

**The Thomas O'Neill Catholic Health Care Fund, Inc.*

Women's Auxiliary Board

**St. Elizabeth School Foundation, Inc.*, 801 Argonne Dr., 21218-1998. Tel: 410-433-9244; Fax: 410-889-2356. Email: erniejg@bellatlantic.net. Web: www.stelizabeth-school.org. Ernie Glinka, Contact Person.

The Immaculate Heart of Mary School Endowment Trust, 8501 Loch Raven Blvd., 21286. Tel: 410-668-7935; Fax: 410-661-6560. Rev. Michael W. Carrion.

St. Joseph Manor Foundation, Inc., 1130 N. Calvert St., 21202. Tel: 410-727-3386. Email: chiffriller@josephite.com. Very Rev. Edward J. Chiffriller, S.S.J., Contact Person.

St. Luke Parish Education Endowment Trust, 7517 N. Point Rd., 21219. Tel: 410-477-5200; Fax: 410-477-5996. Email: stlukromcath@aol.com. Web: stlukes.freehomepage.com. Purpose: to support the youth of the parish who attend catholic schools. Total Assisted 61; Total Staff 1.

St. Matthew's Parish Endowment Trust, 5401 Loch Raven Blvd.. Tel: 410-433-2300. Email: Smatbalt@archbalt.org. Rev. Joseph L. Muth, Contact Person.

Mercy Health Foundation, Inc., 301 St. Paul Pl., 21201. Tel: 410-332-9874; Fax: 410-685-7464. Email: nkoas@mercymed.com. Web: mdmercy.com. Thomas R. Mullen, Pres.

The Seton Keough High School Endowment Trust, 1201 Caton Ave., 21227. Tel: 410-646-4444; Fax: 443-573-0107. Email: indo@setonkeough.com. Web: setonkeough.com.

St. Josephite Seminarian Education Trust, 1130 N. Calvert St., 21202. Tel: 410-727-3386. Email: chiffriller@josephite.org. Rev. Edward J. Chiffriller, S.S.J., Contact Person.

The Josephite Retirement and Disability Benefits Trusts, 1130 N. Calvert St., 21202. Tel: 410-727-3386. Email: chiffriller@josephite.org. Very Rev. Edward J. Chiffriller, S.S.J., Contact Person.

ANNAPOLIS. *St. Andrew by the Bay Endowment Trust*, 701 College Pkwy., 21401. Tel: 410-974-4366; Fax: 410-974-4339. Email: sabbanna@archbalt.org. Web: standrewbythebay.org. Rev. Stephen D. Gosnell, Contact Person.

COCKEYSVILLE. *St. Joseph, Texas*, 101 Church Ln., 21030. Tel: 410-683-0600. Email: pcook@stjostex.com. Rev. Msgr. Paul G. Cook, Contact Person.

CUMBERLAND. *The SS. Peter & Paul Parish Endowment Trust*, 109 N. Smallwood St., 21502-2992. Tel: 301-777-3131; Fax: 301-759-3568. Email: ppaul@archbalt.org.

ELLICOTT CITY. *The St. Paul's Parish Endowment Trust*, 3755 St. Paul St., 21043. Tel: 410-465-1670; Fax: 410-313-8550. Email: stpaulrc@aol.com. Rev. Michael J. Jewdrek.

FROSTBURG. *St. Michael School Endowment Trust*, 44 E. Main St., P.O. Box 402, 21532. Tel: 301-689-6767; Fax: 301-687-0738. Email: smfrosch@archbalt.org. Rev. Paul A. Byrnes.

GLEN BURNIE. *The Church of the Good Shepherd Parish Endowment Trust*, 1451 Furnace Ave., 21060. Tel: 410-761-4607; Fax: 410-761-6019. Email: pasture1@juno.com. Rev. John L. Kelly.

MARRIOTTSVILLE. *Bon Secours Health System, Inc.*, 1505 Marriottsville Rd., 21104. Tel: 410-442-5511; Fax: 410-442-6147. Web: www.bshsi.com. Sr. Patricia A. Eck, C.B.S., Chm. & Bd. of Directors; Christopher M. Carney, CEO & Pres.

Bon Secours Baltimore Health Corporation Tel: 410-362-3000; Fax: 410-362-3450.

Bon Secours, Inc., 1525 Marriottsville Rd., 21104. Tel: 410-442-1333; Fax: 410-442-1394. Web: www.bonsecours.org.

MIDLAND. *St. Joseph Midland Parish Endowment Trust*, 19925 Church St., 21542. Tel: 301-777-7060. Email: joanmacnner@msn.com. Sr. Joan Maenner, Contact Person.

St. Joseph, Mildland Cemetery Continuing Care Trust, 19925 Church St., 21542. Tel: 301-777-7060. Email: joanmaenner@msn.com. Sr. Joan Maenner, Contact Person.

PASADENA. *St. Jane Frances Educational Endowment Trust*, 8499 Virginia Ave., 21122. Tel: 410-255-4646; Fax: 410-437-5191. Email: postmaster@stjane.org. Web: stjane.org.

SYKESVILLE. *St. Joseph Catholic Community Endowment Trust*, 915 Liberty Rd., 21784. Tel: 410-795-7838; Fax: 410-795-7516. Email: sjcc@qis.net. Web: www.stjosephelderburg.org. Rev. Patrick J. Tonry, S.M., Contact Person.

TOWSON. *The Immaculate Conception Elementary School Endowment Trust*, 200 Ware Ave., 21204. Tel: 410-427-4700; Fax: 410-427-4795. Email: info@theimmaculate.org. Web: immaculateconception.net. Rev. Msgr. F. Dennis Tinder, Contact Person.

Towson Catholic High School Endowment Trust, 200 Ware Ave., 21204. Tel: 410-427-4700. Email: churchoftheimmaculateconception@archbalt.org. Vicki Farlow, Contact Person.

[W] MISCELLANEOUS

BALTIMORE. *St. Agnes Clinical Practice Group, Inc.* (inactive at this time) , 900 S. Caton Ave., 21229. Tel: 410-368-6000; Fax: 410-368-3594. Email: info@stagnes.org. Web: www.stagnes.org. Robert W. Adams, Pres. & CEO.

Alhambra, International Order of, Supreme Headquarters, 4200 Leeds Ave., 21229. Tel: 410-242-0660; Fax: 410-536-5729. Email: salaamone@att.net. Web: www.OrderAlhambra.org. Nonprofit organization dedicated to assisting the developmentally disabled.

**Cardijn Associates, Inc.*, 1806 Lancaster St., 21231. Tel: 410-563-3190. Ms. Nancy Lee Conrad, Pres.

Caroline Center, 900 Somerset St., 21202. Tel: 410-563-1303; Fax: 410-563-1302. Email: carolinecenter@covadad.net. Web: Caroline-Center.org. Sr. Patricia McLaughlin, S.S.N.D., Exec. Dir.

Legal Title: *The Caroline Freiss Center, Inc.*, Employment training and counseling center for women. Total Assisted Annually 150; Total Staff 15.

Cathedral Library, 5200 N. Charles St., 21210. Tel: 410-464-4041. Laura Perry, Dir. Staffed by the Catholic Evidence League. Total Staff 17.

Catholic Alumni Club, P.O. Box 22305, 21203-2305. Tel: 410-580-1250. Email: cac-skipjack@yahoo.com. Web: www.clark.net/cac/baltimore.html.

Catholic Community at Relay, 5025 Cedar Ave., 21227. Tel: 410-247-4033; Fax: 410-247-2557. Email: catholic.relay@verizon.net. Rev. Timothy Kulbicki, O.F.M.Conv. Total Staff 2.

Catholic Evidence League, 5200 N. Charles St., 21210. Tel: 410-426-6159; Fax: 410-468-0096. Email: eclombardi@aol.com.

Catholic Fraternity Incorporated 1910. , 951 Rosedale Ave., 21237. Tel: 410-687-8787; Fax: 410-780-0319. Email: jfesons@aol.com.

Catholic Relief Services, U.S.C.C.B. World Headquarters, 209 W. Fayette St., 21201. Tel: 410-625-2220; Fax: 410-234-2986. Email: srussell@catholicrelief.org. Web: www.catholicrelief.org. Kenneth Hackett, Pres. For a more detailed explanation of this organization, please consult the A-pages located in the front of the Directory.

Catholic Single Again Council of Baltimore, The Villa, 5537 Todd Ave., 21206. Tel: 410-485-8313; Fax: 410-617-5741. Email: singleagaincouncil@yahoo.com. Web: www.singleagain.itgo.com. Mary Ann Leard, Pres.

Catholic War Veterans, Inc., 5256 Millfield Rd., 21237. Tel: 410-933-0766. Rev. Conan H. Timoney, C.P., State Chap.; John A. Jarosinski, Commander; Lorraine Sutterfield, Auxiliary Pres.

Christ Child Society of Baltimore, 2525 Pot Spring Rd., Lutherville Timonium, 21093. Betty Bese, Contact Person.

Christian Life Community Regional Information Center, 719 Kent Ave., 21228. Tel: 410-788-3292. Email: cazieba@yahoo.com. Web: www.clc-usa.org. Carol A. Zieba, Chm..

Division of Ministry Formation and Development, 320 Cathedral St., 21201. Tel: 410-547-5470; Fax: 410-234-2953. Email: rpuls@archbalt.org. Web: www.archbalt.org/minform.

Efharisto Studio, Inc., 5130 N. Franklintown Rd., 21207-6598. Tel: 410-448-1711; Fax: 410-448-3259. Email: fharisto@charm.net. Web: www.efharistostudio.org. Sr. Stephana Toomey, O.P., Pres. Services to advance the Roman Catholic religion by charitable, religious, and educational efforts in pursuing a nonprofit ministry of preaching by developing colorful worship areas and art forms to communicate visual meditations and services for the liturgy.

Food for Thought, Inc., 1625 E. Baltimore, 21231. Tel: 410-563-0081; Fax: 410-327-1345. Email: srmaryannh@aol.com. Sr. Mary Ann Hartnett, S.S.N.D., Dir. Tutorial program for children & adult literacy.

**Franciscan Youth Center, Inc.*, 2209 Greenmount Ave., 21218-5421. Tel: 410-235-3577; Fax: 410-243-8191. Email: fycmcfadden@starpower.net. Sandi McFadden, Contact Person.

Holy Name Society (Union), P.O. Box 12032, 21281. Tel: 410-342-8018. Rev. Msgr. Jeremiah F. Kenney, Archdiocesan Dir.

Ignatian Lay Volunteer Corps, 801 St. Paul St., 21202. Tel: 410-752-4686; Fax: 410-752-8480. Email: sgeaney@ILVC.org. Web: www.ilvc.org. Ms. Suzanne Geaney, Exec. Dir.; Revs. Charles P. Costello, S.J., Founder; James R. Conroy, S.J., Founder; Eileen Capshaw, Dir. Devel. & Communications.

Jesuit Educational Association of Maryland, Inc., 5704 Roland Ave., 21210. Tel: 410-532-1400; Fax: 410-532-1419. Email: dsauter@sprep.org. Web: www.marprovincejesuits.org. Rev. David A. Sauter, S.J. Tel: 301-214-1265.

Jesuit Jamshedpur Mission Society, Inc., 5704 Roland Ave., 21210-1399.

Jesuit Mission Bureau, Maryland Province, Inc., 5704 Roland Ave., 21210-1399.

Jesuit Seminary Guild, Maryland Province, Inc., 5704 Roland Ave., 21210-1399.

Johns Hopkins Hospital Apostolate, Chaplain's Office, Johns Hopkins Medical Center, 600 N. Wolfe St., 21287-4170. Tel: 410-955-5842; Fax: 410-550-6765. Email: caoffice@jhmi.edu. Rev. Salvatore J. Livigni. Total Staff 20.

Ladies of Charity, 19 Maple Ave., 21206. Tel: 410-665-8876; Fax: 410-529-2042. Rev. Casimir M. Peterson, Spiritual Dir. (Retired); Sr. Claire Debes, D.C., Moderator & Vincentian Collaboration Coord.; Charlotte Casserly, Pres.

Legion of Mary, 3229 Birchmede Dr., Ellicott City, 21042. Tel: 410-465-1355. Email: jamessaboejimbo@aol.com. Rev. Msgr. John Reinsfelder, Spiritual Dir.; Mrs. Marilyn Saboe, Pres. Baltimore Comitium, governing body for the Legion of Mary in the Baltimore Archdiocese.

Maryland Family Care, Inc., 301 St. Paul Pl., 21202. Tel: 410-951-1705; Fax: 410-951-1752. Email: hleek@mercymed.com. Helen Leek, Contact Person.

Mission Helper Productions, Inc. (non-profit full-service video production studio) , 1001 W. Joppa Rd., 21204-3787. Tel: 410-823-8585, Ext. 240; Fax: 410-296-4050. Email: missionhelperoductions@missionhelpers.org. Web: www.missionhelpers.org. Sr. Anne Guinan, M.H.S.H., Contact Person.

Mother Seton House on Paca Street, Inc., 600 N. Paca St., 21201. Tel: 410-523-3443.

The Mount Saint Agnes Theological Center for Women, Inc., P.O. Box 10484, 21209. Tel: 410-435-7500; Fax: 410-435-9522. Email: msawomen@aol.com. Web: msawomen.org. Sr. Mary Aquin O'Neill, R.S.M., Dir. Total Staff 5.

Parish Social Ministry Outreach, 1512 Druid Hill Ave., 21217. Tel: 410-523-3256. Sr. Genevieve Noonan, D.C., Staff. Immaculate Conception Parish, Baltimore.

Radio Mass of Baltimore, Inc., St. Ignatius Church, 740 N. Calvert St., 21202. Tel: 410-539-7812; Fax: 410-727-1573. Rev. William J. Watters, S.J., Dir. Mass is broadcast every Sunday morning from St. Ignatius Church at 9:30 A.M., WBAL, 1090 AM Radio Dial. Contact Radio Broadcast 10-10:30.

Reparation Society of the Immaculate Heart of Mary, Inc., Fatima House, 7920 Beverly Ave., 21234. Tel: 410-665-1199. Rev. Casimir M. Peterson, Dir. (Retired). Volunteers 4; Total in Residence 1.

Serra Club Vocation Office, 320 Cathedral St., 21201. Tel: 410-547-5426; Fax: 410-234-2953. Email: gfrancik@archbalt.org. Web: www.grchbalt.org/vocations. Rev. Gerard C. Francik, Chap.

Stella Maris Maritime Center, Formerly Apostleship of the Sea (Baltimore)3048 Guilford Ave., 21218-3925. Tel: 410-338-1296; Fax: 410-532-1419. Bro. Jim Horan, S.J., Dir. & Pastoral Worker. Member of Apostleship of the Sea (USA).; Christian hospitality services in the Catholic tradition with spiritual, temporal, and emotional support for seafarers and their families. Also, transportation to and from ships for their crew members to the local Stella Maris Maritime Center and the city.

Vietnamese Catholic Community at Baltimore (VCCAB), 1314 Old Eastern Ave., 21221. Tel: 410-238-7870.

ANNAPOLIS. *Christ Child Society of Annapolis*, P.O. Box 561, Severna Park, 21146. Tel: 410-263-8742. E.V. Von Schwarz, Contact Person.

CATONSVILLE. *St. Thomas More Society of Maryland Inc.* The local branch of the St. Thomas More Society of Maryland Inc. , 3410 White Ave., 21214. Tel: 410-426-3000; Fax: 410-426-0001. Email: fraab@mrllaw.com.

CUMBERLAND. *Catholic Education Ministries of Western Maryland*, 300 E. Oldtown Rd., 21502. Tel: 301-777-9082; Fax: 301-722-6114. Email: catholicwmd@mindspring.com. Web: www.mindspring.com/~catholicwmd/cem. Margaret Meyers, Dir.

DUNKIRK. *Family of the Americas Foundation, Inc.*, P.O. Box 1170, 20754-1170. Tel: 301-627-3346; 800-443-3395; Fax: 301-627-0847. Email: family@upbeat.com. Web: familyplanning.net.

ELLICOTT CITY. *Advisory Committee on Deaf Ministry*, Formerly Catholic Deaf of Baltimore4747 Ilkley

Moor Ln., 21043. Tel: 410-750-2428; Fax: 410-750-1482. Email: deafmin@aol.com. Web: www.archbalt.org/content.asp?id=477. Chris Duck, Chm.; Eileen Colarusso, Coord. Deaf Min

Anthony Corps, Inc., 12300 Folly Quarter Rd., 21042. Tel: 410-531-1400. Email: duffym@ix.netcom.com. Bro. Michael Duffy, O.F.M.Conv., Contact Person.

Christlife, Inc., 12290-A Folly Quarter Rd., 21042. Tel: 410-531-7701; Fax: 410-531-7702. Email: info@christlife.org. Web: www.christlife.org. Mr. Dave Nodar, Dir.

**Faith Journeys Foundation, Inc*, P.O. Box 1222, 21041. Tel: 410-744-4910; Fax: 410-744-4910. Email: fjourneys@aol.com. Web: www.faithjourneys.org. Ms. Lynn A. Cassella, Contact Person.

HAMPSTEAD. *Knights of Columbus, MD State Council*, 6243 Gilston Park Rd., 21228. Tel: 410-521-6200. Rev. Msgr. Chester J. Mieczkowski, State Chap. (Retired); Richard L. Sherbert Jr., State Deputy; H. F. Behrens, Exec. Sec.

LINTHICUM. *Catholic Daughters of the Americas*, 4822 S. Haven Dr., Ellicott City, 21043. Tel: 410-465-1924. Rev. Alphonse G. Rose, State Chap. (Retired); Most Rev. William Newman, Clergy Consultant.

MILLERSVILLE. *Disciples Now Ministries Inc* , P.O. Box 1063, 21108. Tel: 410-729-1501; Fax 410-729-1502. Email: info@disciplesnow.com. Web: www.disciplesnow.com. Paul Raspa, Chm.

NEW FREEDOM. *International Federation of Catholic Alumnae, Maryland Chapter*, 2307 Bailey Ave., PA 17349. Tel: 410-235-0406; Fax: 717-227-9963. Email: rerug@juno.com. Marian Birck, Governor. Benefits & other fund raising activities are held to accumulate funds which are rewarded to members catholic schools in the archdiocese, for scholarships & financial assistance to students. Total Staff 79.

RELIGIOUS INSTITUTES OF MEN REPRESENTED IN THE ARCHDIOCESE

For further details refer to the corresponding bracketed number in the Religious Institutes of Men or Women section.

[0200]—*Benedictine Monks (Latrobe, PA)*—O.S.B.
[1350]—*Brothers of St. Francis Xavier*—C.F.X.
[0330]—*Brothers of the Christian Schools* (Baltimore Prov.)—F.S.C.
[0470]—*The Capuchin Friars* (Prov. of St. Augustine)—O.F.M.Cap.
[1330]—*Congregation of the Mission* (Eastern Prov.)—C.M.
[1000]—*Congregation of the Passion* (Prov. of St. Paul of the Cross)—C.P.
[0480]—*Conventual Franciscans* (Ellicott City, MD)—O.F.M.Conv
[0400]—*Crosier Fathers*—O.S.C.
[0520]—*Franciscan Friars (Most Holy Name* —O.F.M.
[0690]—*Jesuit Fathers and Brothers* Maryland Prov.)—S.J.
[0730]—*Legionaries of Christ*—L.C.
[0854]—*Missionary Society of St. Paul of Nigeria*
[]—*Norbertine Fathers* (Immaculate Conception Priory, DE)—O.Praem.
[1310]—*Order of the Most Holy Trinity, Immaculate Heart of Mary Province*—O.SS.T.
[1070]—*Redemptorist Fathers* (Baltimore Prov.)—C.SS.R.
[1260]—*Society of Christ*—S.Ch.
[0760]—*Society of Mary*—S.M.
[0990]—*Society of the Catholic Apostolate* (Immaculate Conception Prov.)—S.A.C.
[1200]—*Society of the Divine Saviour*—S.D.S.
[]—*Society of the Missionaries of the Sacred Heart*
[1290]—*Society of the Priests of St. Sulpice*—S.S.
[0700]—*St. Joseph's Society of the Sacred Heart*—S.S.J.
[]—*Sulpicians*—S.S.
[0560]—*Third Order Regular of St. Francis*—T.O.R.

RELIGIOUS INSTITUTES OF WOMEN REPRESENTED IN THE ARCHDIOCESE

[0230]—*Benedictine Sisters of Pontifical Jurisdiction* (Baltimore)—O.S.B.
[0270]—*Congregation of Bon Secours*—C.B.S.
[0760]—*Daughters of Charity of St. Vincent de Paul*—D.C.
[0420]—*Discalced Carmelite Nuns*—O.C.D
[1070-03]—*Dominican Sisters*—O.P.
[1070-13]—*Dominican Sisters*—O.P.
[1070-07]—*Dominican Sisters*—O.P.
[1470]—*Franciscan Sisters of St. Joseph*—F.S.S.J.
[1840]—*Grey Nuns of the Sacred Heart* (Pennsylvania)—G.N.S.H.
[2575]—*Institute of the Sisters of the Mercy of the Americas* (Baltimore, Merion)—R.S.M
[2330]—*Little Sisters of Jesus*
[2340]—*Little Sisters of the Poor*—L.S.P.
[2470]—*Maryknoll Sisters* (New York)—M.M.
[2490]—*Medical Missionary Sisters* (Pennsylvania)—M.M.S.
[2720]—*Mission Helpers of the Sacred Heart*—M.H.S.H.
[2710]—*Missionaries of Charity* (New York)—M.C.
[3040]—*Oblate Sisters of Providence*—O.S.P.
[]—*Oblates of St. Martha*
[2070]—*Religious of the Holy Union of the Sacred Hearts*—S.U.S.C.
[3465]—*Religious of the Sacred Heart of Mary* (New York)—R.S.H.M.
[2970]—*School Sisters of Notre Dame*—S.S.N.D.
[]—*Sisters for Christian Community*—C.F.C.C.
[0640]—*Sisters of Charity* (Halifax)—S.C.
[3000]—*Sisters of Notre Dame de Namur*—S.N.D.deN.
[4080]—*Sisters of Social Service*
[1705]—*Sisters of St. Francis of Assisi*—O.S.F.
[1650]—*Sisters of St. Francis of Philadelphia*—O.S.F.
[]—*Sisters of St. Francis of Rochester* (Minnesota)—O.S.F.
[3893]—*Sisters of St. Joseph*—S.S.J.
[3890]—*Sisters of St. Joseph of Peace*
[1030]—*Sisters of the Divine Savior*—S.D.S.
[1830]—*Sisters of the Good Shepherd* (Mid North American Prov.)—R.G.S.
[1920]—*Sisters of the Holy Cross*
[1990]—*Sisters of the Holy Names of Jesus and Mary*
[3610]—*Sisters Servants of Mary Immaculate*—S.S.M.I.
[2160]—*Sisters, Servants of the Immaculate Heart of Mary*—I.H.M.
[4120]—*Ursuline Nuns, of the Congregation of Kentucky*—O.S.U.
[4190]—*Visitation Nuns*—V.H.M.

ARCHDIOCESAN CEMETERIES

BALTIMORE. *New Cathedral*

NECROLOGY

† Karwel, Rev. Msgr. Henry, Ware, MA St. Mary's Parish—Died 2003
† Satterfield, Rev. Msgr. Carroll E., (Retired)—Died July 26, 2003
† Altmann, George, (Retired)—Died Jan. 14, 2003
† Bambol, John, (Retired)—Died 2003
† Bauernfeind, Thomas J., (Retired)—Died Jan. 1, 2003
† Hisky, William G., (Retired)—Died April 15, 2003
† Kaiser, Joseph A., (Retired)—Died July 10, 2003
† Lukaszewski, Jerome, Okinawa, Japan Asato Catholic Church—Died 2003
† Pytel, Ronald, Holy Rosery, Baltimore—Died Nov. 13, 2003
† Raum, Blair, (Special Assignment)—Died May 31, 2003
† Wegierski, Blase, Beaufort, SC USML Base at Parris Island—Died 2003
† Zientek, Timothy, (Retired)—Died 2003

Diocese of Baton Rouge

(Dioecesis Rubribaculensis)

Most Reverend

ROBERT WILLIAM MUENCH, D.D.

Bishop of Baton Rouge; ordained May 18, 1968; appointed Titular Bishop of Mactaris and Auxiliary Bishop of New Orleans May 8, 1990; consecrated June 29, 1990; appointed Bishop of Covington January 5, 1996; installed March 19, 1996; appointed Fifth Bishop of Baton Rouge December 15, 2001; installed March 14, 2002 *Office: Bishop's Office*, P.O. Box 2028, Baton Rouge, LA 70821-2028. Tel: 225-242-0247; Fax: 225-336-8768. Email: Bishop@diobr.org.

Chancery Office: Catholic Life Center, 1800 S. Acadian Thruway, P.O. Box 2028, Baton Rouge, LA 70821-2028. Tel: 225-387-0561; Fax: 225-336-8789.

Web: www.diobr.org

Email: chancery@diobr.org

ESTABLISHED JULY 20, 1961.

Square Miles 5,513.

Comprises the civil parishes (counties) of Ascension, Assumption, East Baton Rouge, West Baton Rouge, Iberville, Pointe Coupee, East Feliciana, West Feliciana, St. Helena, Tangipahoa, Livingston and St. James in the State of Louisiana.

Legal Title: For legal titles of parishes and diocesan institutions, consult the Chancery Office.

STATISTICAL OVERVIEW

Personnel	
Bishop	1
Priests: Diocesan Active in Diocese	60
Priests: Retired, Sick or Absent	18
Number of Diocesan Priests	78
Religious Priests in Diocese	37
Total Priests in Diocese	115
Extern Priests in Diocese	2
Ordinations:	
Diocesan Priests	2
Permanent Deacons in Diocese	40
Total Brothers	10
Total Sisters	103
Parishes	
Parishes	68
With Resident Pastor:	
Resident Diocesan Priests	51
Resident Religious Priests	8
Without Resident Pastor:	
Administered by Priests	8
Administered by Lay People	1
Closed Parishes	2
Professional Ministry Personnel:	
Brothers	1
Sisters	15
Lay Ministers	93
Welfare	
Catholic Hospitals	3
Total Assisted	311,882
Homes for the Aged	7
Total Assisted	645
Specialized Homes	5
Total Assisted	313
Special Centers for Social Services	8
Total Assisted	128,135
Educational	
Diocesan Students in Other Seminaries	16
Total Seminarians	16
Colleges and Universities	1
Total Students	1,550
High Schools, Diocesan and Parish	6
Total Students	2,772
High Schools, Private	2
Total Students	1,689
Elementary Schools, Diocesan and Parish	24
Total Students	12,107
Catechesis/Religious Education:	
High School Students	4,599
Elementary Students	9,569
Total Students under Catholic Instruction	32,302
Teachers in the Diocese:	
Priests	1
Brothers	3
Sisters	16
Lay Teachers	949
Vital Statistics	
Receptions into the Church:	
Infant Baptism Totals	2,527
Adult Baptism Totals	210
Received into Full Communion	404
First Communions	2,687
Confirmations	2,311
Marriages:	
Catholic	638
Interfaith	257
Total Marriages	895
Deaths	1,737
Total Catholic Population	210,464
Total Population	863,976

Former Bishops—Most Revs. ROBERT E. TRACY, D.D., LL.D. (Retired), appt. Titular Bishop of Sergentza and Auxiliary of Lafayette March 18, 1959; consecrated May 19, 1959; appt. First Bishop of Baton Rouge Aug. 10, 1961; retired March 21, 1974; died April 4, 1980; JOSEPH V. SULLIVAN, S.T.D., appt. Titular Bishop of Tagamuta and Auxiliary of Kansas City-St. Joseph March 3, 1967; consecrated April 3, 1967; appt. Second Bishop of Baton Rouge August 5, 1974; died September 4, 1982; STANLEY JOSEPH OTT, S.T.D., appt. Titular Bishop of Nicives and Auxiliary of New Orleans May 24, 1976; consecrated June 29, 1976; appt. Third Bishop of Baton Rouge January 18, 1983; died November 28, 1992; ALFRED C. HUGHES, S.T.D., ord. Dec. 15, 1957; appt. Auxiliary of Boston and Titular Bishop of Massimiana in Bizacena, July 21, 1981; ord. Bishop Sept. 14, 1981; appointed to Baton Rouge Sept. 7, 1993; installed Fourth Bishop of Baton Rouge, Nov. 4, 1993; appt. Coadjutor Archbishop of New Orleans, Feb. 16, 2001; installed May 2, 2001.

Vicar General/Moderator of the Curia—Very Rev. JOHN CARVILLE, S.T.D., V.G.

Chancery Office—Catholic Life Center, 1800 S. Acadian Thruway, P.O. Box 2028, Baton Rouge, 70821-2028. Tel: 225-387-0561; Fax: 225-336-8789. Email: chancery@diobr.org. Office Hours: Mon.-Fri. 8:30-4:30

Chancellor—Rev. Msgr. ROBERT H. BERGGREEN.

Vice-Chancellor—Very Rev. PAUL D. COUNCE, J.C.L., M.C.L.

Assistance Chancellor—Sr. DIANNE HEINRICH, C.D.P. Tel: 225-242-0257; Fax: 225-336-8789.

Diocesan Tribunal—Catholic Life Center, 1800 S. Acadian Thruway, P.O. Box 1087, Baton Rouge, 70821-1087. Tel: 225-336-8755; Fax: 225-242-0229. Email: tribunal@diobr.org.

Judicial Vicar—Very Rev. PAUL D. COUNCE, J.C.L., M.C.L.. Email: judicialvicar@diobr.org.

Promoter of Justice—Very Rev. VINCENT J. DUFRESNE, S.T.L., V.F., J.C.L.

Judges—Rev. Msgrs. WILLIAM L. GREENE (Retired); GERALD M. LEFEBVRE (Retired); Revs. FRANK M. UTER; MICHAEL J. MORONEY.

Defenders of the Bond—Very Rev. VINCENT J. DUFRESNE, S.T.L., V.F., J.C.L.; Revs. GARLAND T. BELSOME; THAN N. VU, S.T.L.; SHELTON J. FABRE; GERARD R. MARTIN.

Notaries—Mrs. JOSIE C. ZGANJAR; Mrs. PATRICIA F. SONIAT.

College of Consultors—Very Rev. JOHN CARVILLE, S.T.D., V.G.; Rev. Msgr. ROBERT H. BERGGREEN; Revs. THAN N. VU, S.T.L.; GERARD F. YOUNG; Very Rev. MICHAEL J. SCHATZLE, V.F.; Rev. SHELTON J. FABRE.

Diocesan Pro-Vicar—

Pro-Vicar for Religious Men and Women—Sr. LUCY SILVIO, C.S.J.

Diocesan Corporation (The Roman Catholic Church of the Diocese of Baton Rouge)—Most Rev. ROBERT WILLIAM MUENCH, D.D., Pres.; Very Rev. JOHN CARVILLE, S.T.D., V.G., Vice Pres.; Rev. Msgr. ROBERT H. BERGGREEN, Sec.; Mr. JOSEPH E. INGRAHAM, Treas.

Diocesan Offices and Directors

Apostolate to the Deaf—Mr. WILLIAM G. DUGAS, Dir., 2585 Brightside Ln., Baton Rouge, 70820-3504. Tel: 225-766-9320; 225-769-0223; Fax: 225-766-9320.

Archives—Mrs. LEE LEUMAS, P.O. Box 2028, Baton Rouge, 70821-2028. Tel: 225-242-0224; Fax: 225-242-0299. Email: archives@diobr.org.

Black Catholics—Rev. SHELTON J. FABRE, P.O. Box 8, Grosse Tete, 70740-0008. Tel: 225-648-2420. Email: bcatholics@diobr.org.

Campus Ministry—Rev. THAN N. VU, S.T.L., P.O. Box 25131, Baton Rouge, 70894-5131. Tel: 225-383-1574; Fax: 225-344-1920. Email: tvu@diobr.org.

Catholic Charismatic Renewal—Rev. HENRY W. GAUTREAU, Ph.D. (Retired), 421 D Longwood Ct., Baton Rouge, 70806-4048. Tel: 225-346-8873. Email: hgautreau@diobr.org.

Catholic Community Services—Ms. DEBORAH A. ROE, M.S.W., Exec. Dir., Office, 1900 S. Acadian Thruway, P.O. Box 1668, Baton Rouge, 70821-1668. Tel: 225-336-8770; Fax: 225-336-8745. Email: ccsgen@ccsbr.org. Web: www.ccsbr.org.

Catholic Social Services Dept.—Ms. JANICE ALLEN, M.S.W., 1900 S. Acadian Thruway, P.O. Box 1668, Baton Rouge, 70821-1668. Tel: 225-336-8770; Fax: 225-336-8745. Email: adopt@ccsbr.org. Web: www.adoptbatonrouge.com.

Social Responsibility Dept.—Ms. PEGGY STUART. Email: pstuart@ccsbr.org.

Family Life Dept.—Mr. WARREN DAZZIO, Dir., Office, 1900 S. Acadian Thruway, P.O. Box 1668, Baton Rouge, 70821-1668. Tel: 225-336-8770; Fax: 225-336-8745. Email: wdazzio@ccsbr.org.

Cemeteries—Rev. FRANK M. UTER, P.O. Drawer 1501, Gramercy, 70052-1501. Tel: 225-869-5324; Fax: 225-869-5325. Email: futer@diobr.org.

Clergy Personnel—Rev. THAN N. VU, S.T.L., Dir., P.O. Box 25131, LSU, Baton Rouge, 70894-5131. Tel: 225-344-8595; Fax: 225-344-8521. Email: personnel@diobr.org.

Board Members—Rev. FRED A. YOUNGS; Very Rev.

PHILIP F. SPANO, V.F.; Revs. SHELTON J. FABRE; GARLAND T. BELSOME.

Ecumenical Affairs—Rev. MICHAEL J. MORONEY, 11441 Goodwood Blvd., Baton Rouge, 70815-6299. Tel: 225-275-3940; Fax: 225-275-1407. Email: ecumenism@diobr.org.

Evangelization Office—Sr. PRISCILLA LEMIRE, R.J.M., Dir., P.O. Box 2028, Baton Rouge, 70821-2028. Tel: 225-242-0137; Fax: 225-242-0245. Email: plemire@diobr.org.

Communications—Deacon ROBERT FURLOW, Catholic Life Channel 15, P.O. Box 2028, Baton Rouge, 70821-2028. Tel: 225-242-0215; Fax: 225-242-0134. Email: television@diobr.org.

Continuing Formation for the Clergy—Rev. PATRICK J. MASCARELLA, Dir., P.O. Box 1501, Gramercy, 70052-1501. Tel: 225-869-5324; Fax: 225-869-5325. Email: clergyformation@diobr.org.

Stewardship Office—Mr. MARK J. BLANCHARD, Dir., P.O. Box 2028, Baton Rouge, 70821-2028. Tel: 225-336-8790; Fax: 225-336-8710. Email: development@diobr.org.

Finance—Mr. JOSEPH E. INGRAHAM, Fiscal Officer (Oeconomus), P.O. Box 2028, Baton Rouge, 70821-2028. Tel: 225-387-0561; Fax: 225-336-8789. Email: jingraham@diobr.org.

Christian Formation—CHARLES JUMONVILLE, M.R.E., P.O. Box 2028, Baton Rouge, 70821-2028. Tel: 225-336-8760; Fax: 225-336-8765. Email: formation@diobr.org.

Hispanic Apostolate—Rev. RAPHAEL JUANTORENA, S.T.L., Ph.D., Dir., 5850 Florida Blvd., Ste. B, Baton Rouge, 70806-4247. Tel: 225-927-8700; Fax: 225-927-8757. Email: apostolado2@juno.com.

Newspaper "The Catholic Commentator"—Mrs. LAURA G. DEAVERS, Exec. Editor & Gen. Mgr., Office, 1800 S. Acadian Thruway, Baton Rouge, 70821-1668. Email: tcc@diobr.org; Mailing Address, P.O. Drawer 14746, Baton Rouge, 70898-4746. Tel: 225-387-0983; Fax: 225-336-8710.

Permanent Diaconate Office—Deacon THOMAS E. LABAT, Dir., 619 S. Pleasant Ave., Gonzales, 70737-3425. Tel: 225-644-3314. Email: diaconate@diobr.org.

Presbyteral Council—Rev. Msgr. ROBERT H. BERGGREEN; Very Revs. JOHN CARVILLE, S.T.D., V.G.; PAUL D. COUNCE, J.C.L., M.C.L.; Rev. CHARLES R. LANDRY; Very Rev. PAUL A. McDUFFIE, V.F.; Revs. ROBERT F. STINE; SHELTON J. FABRE; MATTHEW C. DUPRE; MATTHEW P. LORRAIN; SAMUEL C. MARANTO, C.SS.R.; THOMAS C. RANZINO; LOUIS T. OUBRE; ROBERT U. PERRY, O.P.; Very Rev. MICHAEL J. SCHATZLE, V.F.

Propagation of the Faith and Association of Holy Childhood—Rev. N. JOHN NUTTER, Dir.; Mrs. BETTY LOU STOKES, Office Mgr., P.O. Box 2028, Baton Rouge, 70821-2028. Tel: 225-242-0115; Fax: 225-242-0243. Email: missions@diobr.org.

Religious Education—Ms. CAROLE OBROKTA, P.O. Box 2028, Baton Rouge, 70821-2028. Tel: 225-336-8730; Fax: 225-336-8731. Email: ore@diobr.org.

Catholic Schools—Sr. MARY MICHAELINE GREEN, O.P., Supt.; Dr. JACQUELINE C. LEWIS, Ed.D., Asst. Supt.; Mr. JOSEPH M. SCIMECA, Asst. Supt., P.O. Box 2028, Baton Rouge, 70821-2028. Tel: 225-336-8735; Fax: 225-336-8711. Email: secretary@csobr.org.

Separated and Divorced—Rev. FRED A. YOUNGS, Dir., 5657 Thomas Rd., Baton Rouge, 70811-7356. Tel: 225-775-8850; Fax: 225-775-7072. Email: fyoungs@diobr.org.

Serra Clubs—Rev. M. JEFFREY BAYHI, Spiritual Advisor, P.O. Box 2028, Baton Rouge, 70821-2028. Tel: 225-336-8778; Fax: 225-336-8710. Email: jbayhi@diobr.org.

Society of St. Vincent De Paul—Mr. MICHAEL J. ACALDO, CEO. Email: macaldo@svdpbr.com; Rev. MICHAEL A. MICELI, Spiritual Advisor, P.O. Box 127, Baton Rouge, 70821-0127. Tel: 225-383-7837.

Victim Assistance Coordinator—Rev. DAVID E. ALLEN. Tel: 225-242-0250. Email: dallen@diobr.org.

Vietnamese Apostolate—Rev. HUNG VIET NGUYEN, I.C.M., Dir., 2580 Tecumseh St., Baton Rouge, 70805-7999. Tel: 225-357-4787; Fax: 225-355-9794.

Vocations—Rev. M. JEFFREY BAYHI, Dir.; Sr. DIANNE HEINRICH, C.D.P., Assoc. Dir., P.O. Box 2028, Baton Rouge, 70821-2028. Tel: 225-336-8778; Fax: 225-336-8710. Email: vocations@diobr.org.

Worship, Office of—Rev. THOMAS C. RANZINO, Dir., P.O. Box 2028, Baton Rouge, 70821-2028. Tel: 225-387-0561; Fax: 225-336-8789. Email: worship@diobr.org.

Youth Ministry—Mr. COOPER RAY, Dir., P.O. Box 2028, Baton Rouge, 70821-2028. Tel: 225-336-8751; Fax: 225-336-8765. Email: youth@diobr.org.

CLERGY, PARISHES, MISSIONS AND PAROCHIAL SCHOOLS

CITY OF BATON ROUGE

(EAST BATON ROUGE PARISH)

1—ST. JOSEPH CATHEDRAL (1792), Rev. Gerard F. Young; Deacon Thomas Traylor.
Res.: 412 North St., 70802-5496. Tel: 225-387-5928; Fax: 225-387-5929.
Catechesis/Religious Program—Verna Clouatre, D.R.E. Students 37.

2—ST. AGNES (1917), Rev. Msgr. Robert H. Berggreen. In Res., Rev. M. Jeffrey Bayhi.
Res.: 749 East Blvd., 70802-6398. Tel: 225-383-4127; Fax: 225-383-4154.
Catechesis/Religious Program—Tel: 225-338-1511. Margaret Granger, D.R.E. Students 126.

3—ST. ALOYSIUS (1955), Revs. Gerald H. Burns; Arun John Injacka Pappu (India).
Mailing Address: 2025 Stuart Ave., 70808-3998. Tel: 225-343-6657; Fax: 225-344-6847.
School—Tel: 225-383-3871; Fax: 225-383-4500. Mr. John L. Bennett, Prin. Lay Teachers 58 Students 967.
Catechesis/Religious Program—Patricia Greely, D.R.E.; Sheryl Zeis, D.R.E. Students 95.

4—ST. ANTHONY OF PADUA (1920), Rev. Hung Viet Nguyen, I.C.M. (Vietnam).
Res.: 2580 Tecumseh St., 70805-7999. Tel: 225-357-4800; Fax: 225-354-0611.

5—ST. CHARLES BORROMEO (1964), Closed., For inquiries for parish records contact St. Gerard Majella, Baton Rouge.

6—CHRIST THE KING (1980), Rev. Than N. Vu, S.T.L.; Very Rev. John Carville, S.T.D., V.G.
Mailing Address: P.O. Box 25131, 70894-5131. Email: tru@ctk-lsu.org. Web: www.ctk-lsu.org.
Res.: 11 Fraternity Ln., 70803. Tel: 225-344-8595; 225-383-1574; Fax: 225-344-1920.
Catechesis/Religious Program—Rebecca East, D.R.E. Students 38.

7—ST. FRANCIS DE SALES PARISH (1979),, (Center for Hearing Impaired) Mr. William G. Dugas, Exec. Dir.
Res.: 2585 Brightside Dr., 70820-3504. Tel: 225-766-9320; 225-769-0223 (Voice/TDD). Email: hearingimpaired@diobr.org.
Catechesis/Religious Program—Fax: 225-766-6615. Mr. William G. Dugas, D.R.E. Students 40.

8—ST. FRANCIS XAVIER (1918), Rev. Michael K. Saah-Buckman, S.S.J.
Res.: 1143 S. 11th St., 70802-4997. Tel: 225-383-3479; Fax: 225-343-4259.
School—(Grades PreK-8) Tel: 225-387-6639; Fax: 225-383-1215. Dr. Alvin F. DeCuir Sr., Prin. Lay Teachers 18; Students 232.

9—ST. GEORGE (1908), [CEM] Revs. Thomas C. Ranzino; Joey F. Angeles; Deacons Albert R. Ellis; Guy E. Decker; Thomas Malinoski.
Office—7808 St. George Dr., 70809-4699. Tel: 225-293-2212; Fax: 225-291-8063. Web: www.st-george.org.
School—7880 St. George Dr., 70809-4699. Tel: 225-293-1298. Mrs. Ann Bertsch, Prin. Lay Teachers 70; Students 884.
Catechesis/Religious Program—Cherry Riggs, D.R.E.; Karen Fawley, D.R.E. Students 140.

10—ST. GERARD MAJELLA (1944), Rev. Samuel Maranto, C.SS.R.
Res.: 3808 Gerard St., 70805-2834. Tel: 225-355-2553; Fax: 225-356-7472. Email: stgmc@worldnet.att.net.
School—3655 St. Gerard Ave., 70805-2898. Tel: 225-355-1437; Fax: 225-355-1879. Joanie Hudson, Prin. Lay Teachers 15; Students 194.

11—IMMACULATE CONCEPTION (1953), Rev. Hilton L. Rivet, S.J. In Res., Rev. John L. Vessels, S.J. (FWT).
Res.: 1565 Curtis St., 70807-4906. Tel: 225-775-7067; Fax: 225-775-0775. Email: hlrsj@earthlink.net.

12—ST. JEAN VIANNEY (1975), Revs. Matthew P. Lorrain; Alexander J. Sheldon; Deacon Brent Duplessis.
Res.: 16166 S. Harrell's Ferry Rd., 70816-3199. Tel: 225-753-7950; Fax: 225-753-7965. Web: www.stjeanvianney.org.
School—(Grades K-8), 16266 S. Harrell's Ferry Rd., 70816-3103. Tel: 225-751-1831; Fax: 225-752-8774. Miss Christina Babin, Prin. Lay Teachers 34; Students 534.
School—Preschool, Tel: 225-752-5356. Mrs. Amie Williams Dir. Lay Teachers 16; Students 138.

13—ST. JUDE THE APOSTLE (1966), Rev. David E. Allen; Deacon Frank E. Bains.
Res.: 9150 Highland Rd., 70810-4096. Tel: 225-766-2431; Fax: 225-766-0722. Email: stjude@stjudecatholic.org. Web: stjudecatholic.org.
School—Grades PreK-8) Tel: 225-769-2344; Fax: 225-769-0671. Mrs. Karen Jackuback Prin. Lay Teachers 33; Students 621.

14—ST. LOUIS, KING OF FRANCE (1966), Revs. Maynard E. Hurst Jr., M.S.W., M.Ed.; Minh Hai Nguyen, I.C.M. (NEW).
Res.: 2121 N. Sherwood Forest Dr., 70815-1998. Tel: 225-275-7280; Fax: 225-275-5845.
School—(Grades PreK-8), 2311 N. Sherwood Forest Dr., 70815-1997. Tel: 225-273-3932; Fax: 225-273-3978. Mrs. Mary Clare Polito, Prin. Lay Teachers 24; Students 372.
School—Early Learning Center, Tel: 225-272-6438; Fax: 225-275-5845. Diane Blouin, Dir. Lay Teachers 20; Students 53.

15—MOST BLESSED SACRAMENT (1979), Rev. Michael J. Collins.
Res.: 7853 Broker Ave., 70817-6002. Tel: 225-752-6230; Fax: 225-756-5014. Email: www.mbsparish.org.
School—(Grades K-8) Tel: 225-751-0273; Fax: 225-753-7259. Lay Teachers 26; Students 553.
Catechesis/Religious Program—Tel: 225-751-5867; Fax: 225-751-6738. David Planche, D.R.E. Students 271.

16—OUR LADY OF MERCY (1947), Revs. Miles D. Walsh, S.T.D.; Victor G. Messina; Deacon James E. Wax.
Office—445 Marquette Ave., 70806-4497. Tel: 225-926-1883; Fax: 225-923-0448.
Res.: 450 Marquette Ave., 70806-4497. Tel: 225-927-7106. Email: admin@olomchurch.com
School—400 Marquette Ave., 70806-4498. Tel: 225-924-1054; Fax: 225-923-2201. Mrs. Carolyn Guidry, Prin. Lay Teachers 50; Students 836.
Catechesis/Religious Program—Kathy Screen, D.R.E. Students 64.

17—ST. PATRICK (1974), Rev. Gerard R. Martin; Deacon J. Peter Walsh.
Res.: 12424 Brogdon Ln., 70816-4801. Tel: 225-753-5750; Fax: 225-756-9636. Email: stpatrickbr@aol.com.
Catechesis/Religious Program—Lisa Trahan, D.R.E. Students 160.

18—ST. PAUL THE APOSTLE (1960), Rev. Jaison G. Mangalath, S.V.D.
Res.: 3912 Gus Young Ave., 70802-1727. Tel: 225-383-2537; Fax: 225-383-3702.
Catechesis/Religious Program—Karen Boyd, D.R.E. Students 51.

19—ST. PIUS X (1963), Rev. Jon C. Koehler.
Res.: 6380 Hooper Rd., 70811-2499. Tel: 225-357-5935; Fax: 225-357-6005. Email: stpiusx@bellsouth.net. Web: www.stpiusx.faithweb.com.

20—SACRED HEART OF JESUS (1928), Very Rev. Donald V. Blanchard, V.F. In Res., Revs. Francis V. Ferrier, S.J.; Michael Jung, O.S.B.
Res.: 2250 Main St., 70802-3198. Tel: 225-387-6671; Fax: 225-387-6674. Email: info@sacredheartbr.com. Web: www.sacredheartbr.com.
School—Tel: 225-383-7481; Fax: 225-383-1810. Sr. Patricia Sullivan, C.S.J., Prin. Sisters of St. Joseph 5; Lay Teachers 32; Students 512.
Catechesis/Religious Program—Vicki Nacol, D.R.E. Students 38.

21—ST. THOMAS MORE (1959), Revs. Michael J. Moroney; Frank B. Bass; Deacon Clayton Hollier, Ph.D., Pastoral Assoc.
Office—11441 Goodwood Blvd., 70815-6299. Tel: 225-275-3940; Fax: 225-275-1407. Email: info@stmchurch.org.
School—Tel: 225-275-2820; Fax: 225-275-0376. Mr. Steve Ketcham, Prin. Lay Teachers 55; Students 1,049.
School—Preschool, Tel: 225-272-3477; Fax: 225-272-0468. Ms. Angie Ducote, Dir. Lay Teachers 13; Students 135.

OUTSIDE THE CITY OF BATON ROUGE

ALBANY, LIVINGSTON PARISH, ST. MARGARET QUEEN OF SCOTLAND (1910), [CEM] Rev. Msgr. Leo Guillot, V.F.; Deacon Warren Fortenberry, Ed.D.
Res.: P.O. Box 100, 70711-0100. Tel: 225-567-3573; Fax: 225-567-2031.
Catechesis/Religious Program—Jacqui Courtney, D.R.E. Tel: 225-294-9471. Students 150.
Chapel—Springfield, St. Thomas

AMITE, TANGIPAHOA PARISH, ST. HELENA (1868), Rev. N. John Nutter; Deacon Michael A. Agnello.
Res.: P.O. Box 685, 70422-0685. Tel: 985-748-9057; Fax: 985-748-9094.
Catechesis/Religious Program—Mrs. Georgette Cristina, D.R.E. Students 192.
Chapel—Greensburg, St. Jude; Kentwood, St. Elizabeth

BAKER, EAST BATON ROUGE PARISH, ST. ISIDORE THE FARMER (1958), Rev. Fred Youngs; Deacons Bruno Rizzo; Willie Berthelot.
Res.: 5657 Thomas Rd., 70811-7356. Tel: 225-775-8850 (Office); Fax: 225-775-7072. Email:

parishoffice@stisidorecommunity.org. Web: www.stisidorecommunity.org.
School—Tel: 225-775-3336; Fax: 225-775-3351. Lay Teachers 23; Students 251.
Catechesis/Religious Program—Fax: 225-775-7972. Marlene Ortego, D.R.E. Students 62.

BAYOU PIGEON, IBERVILLE PARISH, ST. JOAN OF ARC (1965), Rev. Joseph M. Camilleri.
Res.: 39315 Hwy. 75, Plaquemine, 70764-9629. Tel: 225-545-8213; Fax: 225-545-8213.
Chapel—Bayou Sorrel, St. Catherine Laboure

BELLE ROSE, ASSUMPTION PARISH, ST. JULES (1912), [CEM 2] Rev. Garland T. Belsome.
Res.: P.O. Box 38, 70341-0038. Tel: 225-473-8569; Fax: 225-473-2950. Email: stjuleschurch@charter.net.
Chapel—Brusly/St. Martin, St. Martin

BRUSLY, WEST BATON ROUGE PARISH, ST. JOHN THE BAPTIST (1835), Rev. Matthew C. Dupre.
Res.: P.O. Box 248, 70719-0248. Tel: 225-749-2189; 225-687-8363; Fax: 225-749-1921.
Catechesis/Religious Program—Lucy Landry, D.R.E.; Susie Prejean, D.R.E. Students 455.

CONVENT, ST. JAMES PARISH, ST. MICHAEL THE ARCHANGEL (1812), [CEM 2] Revs. Frank M. Uter; Patrick J. Mascarella; Edward F. Fuss, S.M.; Deacon Alfred Adams Sr.
Res.: P.O. Box 65, 70723-0065. Tel: 225-562-3211; Fax: 225-562-3213. Email: stmichaelparish@riverroad-catholic.org. Web: www.riverroadcatholicparishes.org. In Res., Rev. Louis Poche, S.J.

DARROW, ASCENSION PARISH, ST. ANTHONY OF PADUA (1962), Rev. Kenneth A. Smith.
Mailing Address: P.O. Box 9, Sorrento, 70778. Tel: 225-675-8126; Fax: 225-675-6150.
Catechesis/Religious Program—Tel: 225-675-6528. Sr. Ann Ross, D.R.E. Combined with St. Anne, Sorrento

DENHAM SPRINGS, LIVINGSTON PARISH, IMMACULATE CONCEPTION (1960), Very Rev. Vincent J. Dufresne, S.T.L., V.F., J.C.L.; Rev. Christopher J. Roussell; Deacon Peter Schlette.
Mailing Address: P.O. Box 1609, 70727-1609.
Res.: 865 Hatchell Ln., 70726. Tel: 225-665-5359; Fax: 225-665-4422.
Catechesis/Religious Program—Tel: 225-665-5926. Dianne Fontenot, D.R.E. Students 1,230.
Chapel—Livingston, Sacred Heart of Jesus, Tel: 225-686-7322.

DONALDSONVILLE, ASCENSION PARISH
1—ASCENSION OF OUR LORD JESUS CHRIST (1772), [CEM] Rev. Randy M. Cuevas, S.T.L.; Deacon Peter J. Burns. In Res., Rev. Joseph U. Goss, O.P.; Deacon Peter J. Burns.
Res.: P.O. Box 508, 70346-0508. Tel: 225-473-3176; Fax: 225-473-3256.
2—ST. CATHERINE OF SIENA (1924), Rev. George W. Burden, S.S.J.
Res.: P.O. Box 428, 70346-0428. Tel: 225-473-8350; Fax: 225-473-9978.
Catechesis/Religious Program—Mrs. Ivory Joseph, D.R.E. Students 130.
3—ST. FRANCIS OF ASSISI (1884), [CEM] Rev. Michael A. Galea.
Res.: 818 W. Tenth St., 70346-9501. Tel: 225-473-8302; Fax: 225-474-0348.

FRENCH SETTLEMENT, LIVINGSTON PARISH, ST. JOSEPH (1849), [CEM] Rev. Rubin Reynolds; Deacon James A. Little.
Res.: 15710 Louisiana Hwy. 16, 70733-9802. Tel: 225-698-3110; Fax: 225-698-1512.
Catechesis/Religious Program—Tel: 225-698-6318. Barbara Bethelot, D.R.E. Students 174.
Chapel—Port Vincent, St. William

GONZALES, ASCENSION PARISH
1—ST. MARK (1973), Rev. J. Joel LaBauve.
Res.: 42021 Hwy. 621, 70737-9354. Tel: 225-647-8461; Fax: 225-647-5125. Email: stmarkoff@eatel.net.
Catechesis/Religious Program—Bonnie Bourgeois, D.R.E. Students 755.
2—ST. THERESA OF AVILA (1918), Very Rev. Philip F. Spano, V.F.; Deacons Thomas E. Labat; William Blair.
Res.: 1022 N. Burnside Ave., 70737-2551. Tel: 225-647-6588; Fax: 225-647-2223. Email: sttheresa@eatel.net.
School—212 E. New River St., 70737-2499. Tel: 225-647-2803; Fax: 225-647-7814. Mr. Jay L. Sullivan, Prin. Sisters 5; Lay Teachers 28; Students 640.
Catechesis/Religious Program—Alice Blair, D.R.E. Students 383.

GRAMERCY, ST. JAMES PARISH, MOST SACRED HEART OF JESUS (1961), Revs. Frank M. Uter; Patrick J. Mascarella; Edward F. Fuss, S.M. In Res., Rev. Louis A. Poche, S.J.
Res.: P.O. Box 1501, 70052-1501. Tel: 225-869-5324; Fax: 225-869-5325. Email: sacredheartparish@riverroad.catholic.org. Web: www.riverroadcatholicparishes.org.
Catechesis/Religious Program—Rose Vitrano, D.R.E. (Elementary); Milissa Laurent, D.R.E. (High School). Students 267.

GREENWELL SPRINGS, EAST BATON ROUGE PARISH, ST. ALPHONSUS LIGUORI (1962), Rev. Thomas P. Duhe; Deacon J. Phillip BeJeaux.
Res.: 14040 Greenwell Springs Rd., 70739-3302. Tel: 225-261-4650; Fax: 225-261-5650.
School—Tel: 225-261-5299; Fax: 225-261-2795. Sr. Mary Esther Hulin, C.S.J., Prin. Lay Teachers 35; Students 646.
Catechesis/Religious Program—Audrey Gipson, D.R.E. Students 199.

GROSSE TETE, IBERVILLE PARISH, ST. JOSEPH (1904), [CEM] Rev. Shelton J. Fabre.
Res.: P.O. Box 8, 70740-0008. Tel: 225-648-2420; Fax: 225-648-2506. Email: sfabre@diobr.org.
Catechesis/Religious Program—Tel: 225-625-2485; Fax: 225-625-3513. Mrs. Kendra Vallet, D.R.E. Students 46.

HAMMOND, TANGIPAHOA PARISH, HOLY GHOST (1902), Revs. Robert U. Perry, O.P.; Jaime A. Diaz, O.P.; Marcos R. Ramos, O.P.; Deacon Wallace L. Gainey Jr.; Rev. John G. Restrepo, O.P.
Res.: 601 North Oak St., 70401-2529. Tel: 985-345-3360; Fax: 985-542-4191. Email: holyghostchurch@I-55.com. Web: www.i-55.com/holyghost.
Catechesis/Religious Program—Tel: 985-542-0243. Mary Brouillette, D.R.E. Students 220.
School—506 N. Magnolia St., 70401-2598. Tel: 985-345-0977; Fax: 985-542-6545. Mrs. Cathy LeBlanc, Prin. Lay Teachers 45; Students 722.

INDEPENDENCE, TANGIPAHOA PARISH, MATER DOLOROSA (1908), Very Rev. Paul A. McDuffie, V.F.; Deacon Alfred P. Zeringue.
Res.: P.O. Box 349, 70443-0349. Tel: 985-878-9639; Fax: 985-878-6260.
School—P.O. Box 380, 70443-0380. Tel: 985-878-4295; Fax: 985-878-4888. Mr. Alfred Donaldson, Prin. Lay Teachers 11; Students 140.
Catechesis/Religious Program—Tel: 985-878-2852. Carol A. Young, D.R.E. Students 233.
Chapel—Husser, St. Dominic

LABADIEVILLE, ASSUMPTION PARISH, ST. PHILOMENA (1847), [CEM] Rev. Keun-Soo Lee, Ph.D.
Res.: P.O. Box 99, 70372-0099. Tel: 985-526-4247; Fax: 985-526-4128.
School—120 Convent St., 70732-9760. Tel: 985-526-8508; Fax: 985-526-8431. Ms. Toni P. Hare, Prin. Lay Teachers 12; Students 137.

LAKELAND, POINTE COUPEE PARISH, IMMACULATE CONCEPTION (1859), [CEM 2] Rev. Gregory J. Daigle.
Res.: P.O. Box 158, 70752-0158. Tel: 225-627-5124; Fax: 225-627-5125.

LIVONIA, POINTE COUPEE PARISH, ST. FRANCES XAVIER CABRINI (1955), [CEM] Revs. Joseph Thai-Doan Nguyen; Joseph Arogyasami, I.M.S. (India); Deacon Sammy Collura.
Res.: P.O. Box 128, 70755-0128. Tel: 225-637-2396; Fax: 225-637-2390. Email: stfrances@spillwaycable.com.
Catechesis/Religious Program—Paul Ransome Jr., D.R.E. Tel: 225-637-2081. Students 208.
Chapel—Fordoche, St. Catherine of Siena

MARINGOUIN, IBERVILLE PARISH, IMMACULATE HEART OF MARY (1964), [CEM] Rev. Shelton J. Fabre.
Res.: 11140 Hwy. 77, 70757-9703. Tel: 225-625-2438; Fax: 225-625-3513. Email: sfabre@diobr.org.
Catechesis/Religious Program—Tel: 225-625-2485. Mrs. Kendra Vallet, D.R.E. Students 45.

MAUREPAS, LIVINGSTON PARISH, ST. STEPHEN THE MARTYR (1964), Rev. Rubin R. Reynolds.
Res.: 22494 Hwy. 22, 70449-3404. Tel: 225-695-6310; Fax: 225-695-6039. Email: saintstephen@eatel.net.
Catechesis/Religious Program—Tel: 225-695-3117. Kimberly Bourgeois, D.R.E. Students 72.

MORGANZA, POINTE COUPEE PARISH, ST. ANN (1872), [CEM 3] Rev. Howard B. Hall.
Email: stanncc@eatel.net.
Res.: P.O. Box 128, 70759-0128. Tel: 225-694-3781; Fax: 225-694-3711. Email: stanncc@eatel.net.
Catechesis/Religious Program—Tel: 225-694-2132. Mrs. Sharon LeCoq, D.R.E. Students 76.
Chapel—Innis, St. Vincent De Paul

NAPOLEONVILLE, ASSUMPTION PARISH
1—ST. ANNE (1874), [CEM 2] Very Rev. Caye A. Nelson, V.F.
Res.: P.O. Box 99, 70390-0090. Tel: 985-369-6656; Fax: 985-369-9718. Email: stanne@charter.net.
Catechesis/Religious Program—Tel: 985-369-2130. Kathy Landry, D.R.E. Students 328.
2—ST. BENEDICT THE MOOR (1911), [CEM 2] Rev. Frederick Isek, M.S.P.
Res.: P.O. Box 220, 70390-0220. Tel: 985-369-7225; Fax: 985-369-2772.
Catechesis/Religious Program— twinned with St. Augustine. Patricia Brooks, D.R.E. Tel: 985-369-7188; Catherine Moore, D.R.E. Tel: 225-473-4322. Students 72.
Chapel—Klotzville, St. Augustine, Tel: 225-473-9670.

NEW ROADS, POINTE COUPEE PARISH
1—ST. AUGUSTINE (1923), Rev. John J. McBrearty, S.S.J.; Deacon Norman Christophe.
Res.: P.O. Box 548, 70760-0548. Tel: 225-638-7553; Fax: 225-638-2947.
2—ST. MARY OF FALSE RIVER (1865), [CEM 2] Very Rev. Michael J. Schatzle, V.F.; Deacons Norman Christophe; Thomas M. Robinson.
Res.: 348 W. Main St., 70760-3587. Tel: 225-638-9665; Fax: 225-638-6346. Email: stmaryfr@bellsouth.net.
Catechesis/Religious Program—Tel: 225-638-6508. Mrs. Patrice Robinson, D.R.E. Students 121.
Chapel—Pointe Coupee, St. Francis

PAINCOURTVILLE, ASSUMPTION PARISH, ST. ELIZABETH (1840), [CEM] Rev. Garland T. Belsome.
Mailing Address: P.O. Box 1, 70391-0001.
Res.: 6057 St. Elizabeth St., 70391. Tel: 985-369-7398; Fax: 985-369-9892. Email: stelizabeth@charter.net.

PAULINA, ST. JAMES PARISH, ST. JOSEPH (1900), [CEM] Revs. Frank M. Uter; Patrick J. Mascarella; Edward F. Fuss, S.M.
Res.: P.O. Box 129, 70763-0129. Tel: 225-869-5751; Fax: 225-869-4166. Email: stjosephparish@riverroad-catholic.org. Web: www.riverroadcatholicparishes.org. In Res., Rev. Louis Poche, S.J.
Catechesis/Religious Program—Tel: 225-869-5324 (High School); 958-- (Elementary); Fax: 225-869-5325. Melissa Laurent, D.R.E. (High School); Donna Waguespack, D.R.E. (Elementary). Students 456.
Chapel—Lutcher, Our Lady of Prompt Succor

PIERRE PART, ASSUMPTION PARISH, ST. JOSEPH THE WORKER (1858), [CEM 2] Rev. Clarence J. Waguespack.
Res.: P.O. Box 190, 70339-0190. Tel: 985-252-6008; Fax: 985-252-8011. Email: office@sjworker.org.
Catechesis/Religious Program—Tel: 985-252-6633. Georgiana C. Cox, D.R.E. Students 458.

PLAQUEMINE, IBERVILLE PARISH
1—ST. CLEMENT OF ROME (1964), Closed., For inquiries for parish records contact St. John the Evangelist, Plaquemine.
2—ST. JOHN THE EVANGELIST (1850), [CEM] Rev. Cleo J. Milano, S.T.L.
Office:—57805 Main St., 70764-2531.
Res.: 57810 Plaquemine St., 70764-2538. Tel: 225-687-2402; Fax: 225-687-1587.

PLATTENVILLE, ASSUMPTION PARISH, ASSUMPTION OF THE BLESSED VIRGIN MARY (1793), [CEM] Very Rev. Caye A. Nelson, V.F.
Mailing Address: P.O. Box 99, Napoleonville, 70390-0099. Tel: 985-369-6656; Fax: 985-369-9718. Email: stanne@charter.net.
Church: L.A. Hwy. 308.

PONCHATOULA, TANGIPAHOA PARISH, ST. JOSEPH (1875), [CEM] Rev. Justin R. Kauchak, O.P.; Deacon Larry Melancon; Rev. Harvey Blaschko, O.P. (Croatia).
Res.: P.O. Box 368, 70454-0368. Tel: 985-386-3749; Fax: 985-386-4188. Email: Kauchak@i-55.com.
School—(Grades PreK-8), 175 N. Eighth St., 70454-3306. Tel: 985-386-6421; Fax: 985-386-0560. Mrs. Shirley Bougere, Prin. Lay Teachers 24; Students 356.
Catechesis/Religious Program—Daphne Griffin, D.R.E. Students 660.

PORT ALLEN, WEST BATON ROUGE PARISH, HOLY FAMILY (1920), Rev. Henry C. Vavasseur; Deacon Angelo S. Nola.
Res.: P.O. Box 290, 70767-0290. Tel: 225-383-1838; Fax: 225-383-1839. Email: holyfamilych@aol.com.
School—(Grades K-8), 335 N. Jefferson Ave., 70767-2798. Tel: 225-344-4100; Fax: 225-344-1928. Sr. Joel Miller, M.S.C., Prin. Marianites of Holy Cross 1; Lay Teachers 24; Students 495.
School—Preschool, 415 N. Jefferson Ave., 70767-2727. Tel: 225-343-6541; Fax: 225-344-4100. Mrs. Diane Harkins, Dir. Lay Teachers 4; Students 58.
Catechesis/Religious Program—Tel: 225-336-4463. Greta LaFleur, D.R.E. Students 96.

PRAIRIEVILLE, ASCENSION PARISH, ST. JOHN THE EVANGELIST (1919), Rev. Martin A. Hernandez, J.C.L.; Eric V. Gyan; Rev. Jason M. Labbe; Deacon Randy Clement.
Res.: 15208 Hwy. 73, 70769-3507. Tel: 225-673-8307; Fax: 225-673-8680. Email: stjohnchurch@eatel.net.
Catechesis/Religious Program—Tel: 225-673-8402. Ms. Norma Houseal, D.R.E.; Mr. Jeff Young. Students 930.

ST. AMANT, ASCENSION PARISH, HOLY ROSARY (1905), [CEM 2] Revs. Robert F. Stine; Vicente C. Panaligan (Philippines); Sr. Mary John Hotard, C.S.J., Pastoral Assoc.; Deacon John Ferguson.
Res.: 44450 Hwy. 429, 70774-4597. Tel: 225-647-5321; Fax: 225-647-5322. Email: holyrosary@eatel.net.
Chapel—Lake, Sacred Heart

ST. FRANCISVILLE, WEST FELICIANA PARISH, OUR LADY OF MOUNT CARMEL (1874), Rev. Charles R. Landry.
Res.: P.O. Box 67, 70775-0067. Tel: 225-635-3630; Fax: 225-383-5219. Email: olmcphchurch@aol.com.
Chapel—Jackson, Our Lady of Perpetual Help, Tel: 225-634-5331.
Chapel—St. Augustine, Angola State Penitentiary [CEM]Tel: 225-655-4411, Ext. 2028; Fax: 225-634-5331.

ST. GABRIEL, IBERVILLE PARISH, ST. GABRIEL (1769), [CEM] Rev. Anthony J. Russo; Deacon Vernon J. Melancon.
Res.: 3625 Hwy. 75, 70776-9411. Tel: 225-642-8441; Fax: 225-642-8491. Email: sgabcatchchurch@aol.com.

ST. JAMES, ST. JAMES PARISH, ST. JAMES (1757), [CEM] Rev. Louis T. Oubre; Deacon Henry Zeringue.
Res.: 6613 Hwy. 18, 70086-9054. Tel: 225-265-4210; Fax: 225-265-4225.
Catechesis/Religious Program—Tel: 225-265-9549. Pamela Folse, D.R.E. Students 155.

SORRENTO, ASCENSION PARISH, ST. ANNE (1963), Rev. Kenneth A. Smith; Deacon Jerry Braud.
Res.: P.O. Box 9, 70778-0009. Tel: 225-375-8126; Fax: 225-675-6150.
Catechesis/Religious Program—Tel: 225-675-6528. Sr. Ann Ross, D.R.E. Attended by St. Anthony of Padua, Darrow Students 110.

TICKFAW, TANGIPAHOA PARISH, OUR LADY OF POMPEII (1973), Rev. Robert U. Perry, O.P.; Ms. Carole McCollester, Parish Life Coord.
Res.: P.O. Box 276, 70466-0276. Tel: 985-345-8957; Fax: 985-542-8490.

VACHERIE, ST. JAMES PARISH
1—OUR LADY OF PEACE (1864), [CEM] Rev. Michael A. Miceli.
Res.: 13281 Hwy. 644, 70090-3102. Tel: 225-265-3953; Fax: 225-265-2507. Email: olop@eatel.net.
Catechesis/Religious Program—Geralyn S. Millet, D.R.E. Students 348.
2—ST. PHILIP (1873), [CEM] Rev. David M. Chauvin; Deacon Francis Waguespack.
Res.: 1175 Hwy. 18, 70090-9527. Tel: 225-265-4085; Fax: 225-265-9348. Email: dmchauvin@eatel.net.
Catechesis/Religious Program—Tel: 225-265-4855; Fax: 225-265-4855. Pamela Felse, D.R.E. Students 128.

WHITE CASTLE, IBERVILLE PARISH, OUR LADY OF PROMPT SUCCOR (1899), [CEM 2] Rev. Jules A. Brunet.
Mailing Address: P.O. Box 249, 70788-0249. Tel: 225-545-3635; Fax: 225-545-8615. Email: olpschurch@cox.net.
Chapel—Bayou Goula, St. Paul

ZACHARY, EAST BATON ROUGE PARISH, ST. JOHN THE BAPTIST (1964), Rev. Kenneth W. Laird; Deacon Ronald D. Legrange.
Res.: 4727 McHugh Dr., 70791-3935. Tel: 225-654-5778; Fax: 225-654-5294.
Catechesis/Religious Program—Tel: 225-654-5885; Fax: 225-654-5885. Kathy Bellard, D.R.E.; Mima Mathews, D.R.E. Students 299.
Chapel—Clinton, Our Lady of the Assumption, Tel: 225-683-8836; Fax: 225-683-8559.

Chaplains of Public Institutions

BATON ROUGE. *Baton Rouge General Medical Center*, P.O. Box 3611, 70821-3611. Tel: 225-387-7000. Rev. Michael Jung, O.S.B., Chap.
Dixon Correctional Institute, Mailing Address:, 18367 Ednie Ln, Greenwell Springs, 70739. Tel: 225-261-4650 (Office); 225-261-5906. Deacon J. Phillip BeJeaux, Chap.
Jetson Correctional Institution For Youth Mailing Address:, 12424 Brogdon Ln., 70816-4801. Tel: 225-753-5750. Deacon J. Peter Walsh, Chap.

ANGOLA. *Louisiana State Penitentiary*, P.O. Box 428, 70712-0428. Tel: 225-655-4411, Ext. 2028; 225-655-3243. Rev. Charles R. Landry, Deacon Angelo S. Nola. St. Augustine Chapel

CARVILLE. *National Hansen's Disease Center*, Gillis Long Memorial Hospital.
5445 Point Clair Rd., 70721-9607. Tel: 225-642-5533. Rev. Anthony J. Russo, Chap.

ST. GABRIEL. *Hunt Correctional Institute.*
Mailing Address: P.O. Box 174, 70776-0174. Tel: 225-642-3306. Deacon Joseph Mamou, Chap.
LA Correctional Institute For Women, Mailing Address:, P.O. Box 26, 70726-0026. Tel: 225-642-5529, Ext. 240. Deacon Joseph Mamou, Chap.

Special Assignment:
Very Rev.—
Counce, Paul D., J.C.L., M.C.L., Diocesan Tribunal, P.O. Box 1087, 70821-1087. Tel: 225-387-0561
Revs.—
Ferrier, Francis V., S.J., 2250 Main St., 70802-3198. Tel: 225-387-6671 Nursing homes not under Catholic auspices.
Seynaeve, Jaak, M.Afr., S.T.D., 2187 Olive St., 70806-6621. Tel: 225-336-9867

On Leave:
Revs.—
Hernandez, Martin A., J.C.L.
Kearney, Myles J.

Retired:
Rev. Msgrs.—
Frey, Andrew F., P.O. Box 2458, Bay St. Louis, MS 39521-2458. Tel: 228-467-4382
Greene, William L., 3111 Kleinert Ave., 70806-6833. Tel: 225-336-0903
Lefebvre, Gerald M., P.O. Box 84126, 70884-4126. Tel: 225-925-8241
Revs.—
Caballero, Lloyd C., Ollie Steele Burden Manor, 4200 Essen Ln., 70809.
Crifasi, Peter D., Ollie Steele Burden Manor, 4200 Essen Ln., 70809.
Dugas, Jerome A., 4604 Perkins Rd., Apt. I-1, 70808-3037. Tel: 225-924-6367
Faschar, Matthew, Oakwood Village, 4400 McHugh Rd., Zachary, 70791. Tel: 225-654-2133
Gautreau, Henry W., Ph.D., 421 D Longwood Ct., 70806. Tel: 225-346-8873
Hewson, William J., 24546 Louand Dr., Lacombe, 70445-9801. Tel: 504-626-7765
Ibanez, Rodolfo, Domingo Sautu, 15, Murguia, Alava 01130 Spain.
Kinkead, James A., 318 E. Jeff St., Gonzales, 70737-3542. Tel: 225-644-1253
Marcel, Robert G., P.O. Box 80783, 70898-0783. Tel: 225-346-8258
McDonald, A. John, 333 Lee Dr., #134, 70808-4974. Tel: 225-767-8237
Palang, Mansueto P., 757 Rivermist Dr., Jonesboro, GA 30238. Tel: 770-719-1210
Rocheleau, Raymond, Carestone at River Center, 6665 E. River Rd., Tucson, AZ 85747-2043. Tel: 520-615-1448
Rodriguez, Aloysius M., 6802 Bluefield Ct., Springfield, VA 22152-3327. Tel: 703-866-2236

Permanent Deacons:
Adams, Alfred P., St. Michael the Archangel, Convent
Agnello, Michael A., St. Helena, Amite
Bains, Frank E., St. Jude the Apostle, Baton Rouge
BeJeaux, J. Phillip, St. Alphonsus Liguori, Greenwell Springs; Dixon Correctional Institute, Baton Rouge
Berthelot, Willie M., St. Isidore the farmer, Baker
Blair, William B., St. Theresa of Avila, Gonzales
Brady, Eugene F., Nursing Homes Coord.
Braud, Jerry W., St. Anne Church, Sorrento
Burns, Peter J., Ascension of Our Lord, Donaldsville; Chap., St. Elizabeth Hospital, Gonzales
Christophe, Norman, St. Mary of False River and St. Augustine, New Roads
Clement, Randall A., St. John the Evangelist, Prairieville
Collura, Samuel C., St. Joseph, Grosse Tete; Immaculate Heart of Mary, Maringouin; St. Francis Xavier Cabrini, Livonia
Decker, Guy E., St. George Parish, Baton Rouge
Duplessis, W. Brent, Immaculate Conception, Denham Springs
Ellis, Albert R., St. George, Baton Rouge
Ferguson, H. John, III, Holy Rosary, St. Amant
Fortenberry, Warren D., St. Margaret, Albany
Furlow, Robert E., Jr., Diocesan Communications Office
Gainey, Wallace L., Jr., Holy Ghost, Hammond
Hollier, Clayton A., St. Thomas More Church, Baton Rouge
Labat, Thomas E., St. Theresa of Avila, Gonzales
LeGrange, Ronald D., St. John the Baptist, Zachary
Little, James A., St. Joseph Church, French Settlement
Malinoski, Thomas J., St. George, Baton Rouge
Mamou, Joseph, Chap., LA Correctional Institute For Women, St. Gabriel
Melancon, Larry, St. Joseph, Ponchatoula
Melancon, Vernon J., St. Gabriel the Archangel, St. Gabriel
Nola, Angelo S., Holy Family, Port Allen; LA State Penitentiary, Angola
Ricard, Alfred J., II, St. John & St. Clement, Plaquemine
Rizzo, Bruno, St. Isidore the Farmer Church, Baker
Robinson, Thomas H., St. Jean Vianney, Baton Rouge
Salinas, Eliazar, Jr., Christ the King, Baton Rouge
Schanzbach, Dr. Milton, St. Joseph, Ponchatoula
Schlette, Peter, Immaculate Conception, Denham Springs
Traylor, John T., St. Joseph Cathedral, Baton Rouge
Waguespack, Francis, Jr., St. Philip Church, Vacherie
Walsh, J. Peter, St. Patrick and Jetson Correctional Institution For Youth, Baton Rouge
Wax, James E., Our Lady of Mercy, Baton Rouge
Zeringue, Alfred P., Mater Dolorosa, Independence
Zeringue, Henry J., St. James, St. James

INSTITUTIONS LOCATED IN THE DIOCESE

[A] COLLEGES AND UNIVERSITIES

BATON ROUGE. *Our Lady of the Lake College*, 5345 Brittany Dr., 70808-4398. Tel: 225-768-1710; Fax: 225-768-1726. Email: msmith@ololcollege.edu. Web: www.ololcollege.edu. Dr. Michael Smith, Pres. Lay Teachers 109; Students 1,421.

[B] DIOCESAN HIGH SCHOOLS, INTERPAROCHIAL

BATON ROUGE. *Bishop Joseph V. Sullivan Diocesan Regional Catholic High School*, 17521 Monitor Ave., 70817-2640. Tel: 225-753-9782; Fax: 225-753-0605. P.O. Box 86110, 70879-6110. Email: jwray@BSHSbr.org. Web: www.bshs-br.org. Mr. Joseph A. Wray, Prin. Sisters 1; Lay Teachers 52; Students 773.
Redemptorist High School, 4000 St. Gerard Ave., 70805-2999. Tel: 225-357-0936; Fax: 225-357-4555. Email: redempths@aol.com. Web: www.rhsbr.com. Mr. John C. Fabre, Prin. Serving parishes in Baton Rouge, Baker, Brusly, Denham Springs, Greenwell Springs, Lakeland, New Roads, Gonzales, Port Allen, St. Gabriel, Zachary, Plaquemine, Maringouin, Prairieville and Clinton. Lay Teachers 64; Students 880.

DONALDSONVILLE. *Ascension Catholic Interparochial High School*, 311 St. Vincent St., 70346-2697. Tel: 225-473-9227; Fax: 225-473-9235. Email: dawn@ascensioncatholic.org. Gene Harrell, Prin. Serving parishes in Donaldsonville, St. James, Belle Rose, Vacherie, White Castle, Darrow, Gonzales, Convent, Paincourtville and Plattenville. Lay Teachers 16; Students 231.

HAMMOND. *St. Thomas Aquinas Regional Catholic High School*, 14520 Voss Dr., 70401-9801. Tel: 985-542-7662; Fax: 985-542-4010. Email: stthomas@i-55.com. Web: www.i-55.com/falcon. Sr. Judith Anne Haase, O.P., Prin. Dominican Sisters, Springfield, IL Sisters 3; Lay Teachers 27; Students 326.

NEW ROADS. *Catholic High School of Pointe Coupee*, 504 Fourth St., 70760-3499. Tel: 225-638-3469; Fax: 225-638-6471. Email: catholichighpc@csobr.org. Web: www.catholicpc.com. Mrs. Marsha M. Langlois, Prin. Serving parishes in Lakeland, Livonia, Morganza, New Roads and Maringouin. Lay Teachers 22; Students 319.

PLAQUEMINE. *St. John Interparochial High School*, 24250 Regina St., 70764-3598. Tel: 225-687-3056; Fax: 225-687-3530. Email: info@stjohnschool.org. Web: www.stjohnschool.org. Mr. Lester Bourg, Admin.; Mrs. Mary T. Moran, Prin. Serving parishes in Plaquemine, Brusly, Port Allen, Grosse Tete and White Castle. Lay Teachers 16; Students 201.

[C] HIGH SCHOOLS, PRIVATE

BATON ROUGE. *Catholic High School*, 855 Hearthstone Dr., 70806-5599. Tel: 225-383-0397; Fax: 225-383-0381. Email: gbrandao@catholichigh.org. Web: www.catholichigh.org. Bro. Francis David, S.C., Pres.; Dr. Gregory Brandao, Prin. Brothers of the Sacred Heart 4; Lay Teachers 70; Boys 910.
St. Joseph's Academy, 3015 Broussard St., 70808-1198. Tel: 225-383-7207; Fax: 225-344-5714. Email: brunj@sjabr.org. Web: www.sjabr.org. Sr. Judith Brun, C.S.J., Prin. Sisters of St. Joseph 3; Lay Teachers 65; Girls 779.

[D] DIOCESAN ELEMENTARY SCHOOLS, INTERPAROCHIAL

DONALDSONVILLE. *Ascension Catholic Interparochial School*, 311 St. Vincent St., 70346-3499. Tel: 225-473-8559; Fax: 225-473-8559. Email: dawn@ascensioncatholic.org. Mrs. Janice M. Burns, Prin. Serving parishes in Donaldsonville, St. James, Belle Rose, Vacherie, White Castle, Darrow, Gonzales, Convent, Paulina, Paincourtville, and Plattenville. Lay Teachers 22; Students 402.

NEW ROADS. *Catholic Elementary School of Pointe Coupee*, 304 Napoleon St., 70760-3527. Tel: 225-638-9313; Fax: 225-638-9953. Email: catholicelemofpc@csobr.org. Web: www.catholicpc.com. Carrie S. Maillet, Prin.

Serving parishes in Lakeland, Livonia, Morganza, New Roads and Maringouin. Lay Teachers 18; Students 373.

PAINCOURTVILLE. *St. Elizabeth Interparochial,* (Grades PreK-8), P.O. Drawer M, 70391-0420. Tel: 985-369-7402; Fax: 985-369-1527. Email: St.Elizabeth@csobr.org. Mr. Paul E. Doucet, Prin. Serving parishes in Belle Rose, Bertrandville, Napoleonville, Paincourtville, Pierre Part and Plattenville. Lay Teachers 10; Students 263.

PAULINA. *St. Peter Chanel Interparochial School,* 2590 LA Hwy. 44, 70763. Tel: 225-869-5778; Fax: 225-869-8131. Email: StPeterChanel@csobr.org. Web: www.stpchanel.org. Mrs. Joanna Foltz, Prin. Serving parishes in Paulina, Gramercy, Convent, Vacherie, St. James and Grand Point. Lay Teachers 21; Students 325.

PLAQUEMINE. *St. John Interparochial Elementary/ Middle School,* 58645 St. Clement Ave., 70764-3599. Tel: 225-687-6616; Fax: 225-687-6280. Email: info@stjohnschool.org. Web: www.stjohnschool.org. Ms. Janette Haydell, Prin. Serving parishes in Plaquemine, Brusly, Grosse Tete, White Castle, Baton Rouge, St. Gabriel, Maringouin, Bayou Pigeon, and Donaldsonville. Lay Teachers 28; Students 555.

[E] SCHOOL, EXCEPTIONAL CHILDREN

BATON ROUGE. *Department of Special Education* Guardian Angels Center (7-14 yrs.) and Redemptorist Center (15-21 yrs.). , P.O. Box 2028, 70821-2028. Tel: 225-383-3066; Fax: 225-242-0344. Email: deptspecialed@csobr.org. Web: www.csobr.org. Mrs. Gail Campo, Admin. Housed on St. Gerard Elementary Campus and at Redemptorist High School. Teachers 5; Speech Therapist 1; Students 51.

[F] GENERAL HOSPITALS

BATON ROUGE. *Our Lady of the Lake Regional Medical Center,* 5000 Hennessy Blvd., 70808-4398. Tel: 225-765-6565; Fax: 225-766-5645. Web: www.ololrmc.com. Sr. Barbara Arceneaux, O.S.F., Supr.; Mr. Robert C. Davidge, CEO; Rev. Timothy J. Kerner, C.Ss.R., Chap. Franciscan Missionaries of Our Lady (North American Province) Bed Capacity 806; Sisters 12; Patients Assisted Annually 245,882.

Tau Center, 8080 Margaret Ann Dr., 70809-3444. Tel: 225-767-1320; Fax: 225-767-1327.

GONZALES. *St. Elizabeth Hospital,* 1125 W. Hwy. 30, 70737-5000. Tel: 225-647-5071; Fax: 225-647-6066. Email: swester@ololrmc.com. Mr. K. Scott Wester, Pres. & CEO. Bed Capacity 95; Total Staff 331; Patients Assisted Annually 45,000.

NAPOLEONVILLE. *Our Lady of the Lake Assumption Community Hospital, Inc.,* 135 Highway 402, 70390-2217. Tel: 225-765-6565; 985-369-3600; Fax: 985-369-4271. Mr. K. Scott Wester, Pres. & CEO.

[G] HOMES AND SPECIAL CARE FACILITIES

BATON ROUGE. *Elderly Housing of Our Lady of the Lake Medical Center,* 5000 Hennessy Blvd., 70808-4398. Tel: 225-765-6565. Mr. Robert C. Davidge, CEO.

Chateau Louise, 7555 Bishop Ott Dr., 70806. Tel: 225-926-5918. Patricia Pourciau, Exec. Dir. Housing for elderly and handicapped persons.

Assisi Village, Inc., of Our Lady of the Lake Medical Center, 7585 Bishop Ott Dr., 70806-8922. Tel: 225-927-5070; Fax: 225-927-1742. Housing facilities for elderly persons.

Calais House, Inc., of Our Lady of the Lake Medical Center, 7545 Bishop Ott Dr., 70806-8900. Tel: 225-927-1889; Fax: 225-927-1742. Housing facilities for elderly persons.

Villa St. Francis, Inc., of Our Lady of the Lake Medical Center, 7575 Bishop Ott Dr., 70806-8906. Tel: 225-927-0070; Fax: 225-927-1742. Housing facilities for elderly and handicapped persons.

Ollie Steele Burden Manor, 4250 Essen Ln., 70809-2196. Tel: 225-926-0091; Fax: 225-926-4937. Susan Folse, M.S., N.F.A., Admin. Our Lady of the Lake Regional Medical Center, Our Lady of the Lake Pastoral Care. Staff 170; Bed Capacity 184.

[H] MONASTERIES AND RESIDENCES OF PRIESTS OR BROTHERS

BATON ROUGE. *Brothers of the Sacred Heart,* 855 Hearthstone Dr., 70806-5599. Tel: 225-383-7117. Bro. Barry Landry, S.C., Supr. Brothers 8.

Incarnatio Consecratio Mission (Vietnamese Institute) , 2305 Choctaw Dr., 70805-7999. Tel: 225-357-1204; Fax: 225-354-0611. Email: nvhung@bellsouth.net. Revs. Hung Viet Nguyen, I.C.M. (Vietnam), Dir.; Martin Thanh Nguyen, I.C.M.; Thomas Tranh Dinh, I.C.M.; Minh Hai Nguyen, I.C.M. (NEW); Tam Viet Nguyen, I.C.M.

The Redemptorist Education and Formation Foundation, P.O. Box 53900, 70892-3900. Tel: 225-355-2600; Fax: 225-355-6200. Web: www.novp.org. Very Rev. Thomas Picton, C.Ss.R.

Redemptorist Vice Province, P.O. Box 53900, 70892-3900. Tel: 225-355-2600; Fax: 225-355-6200. Web: www.novp.org. Very Rev. Thomas D. Picton, C.Ss.R., Vice Prov.; Bro. Steven E. Fruge, C.Ss.R., Vice Pres. & Sec. Priests 6; Brothers 2. In Res. Revs. Eugene J. Staub, C.Ss.R.; Joseph Steffes, C.SS.R.; Bro. Clement J. Furno, C.SS.R.

Priests of Vice Province in Residences not listed elsewhere: Rev. John C. Vargas, C.Ss.R., J.C.L., Redemptorist Generalate, Rome.

[I] CONVENTS AND RESIDENCES FOR SISTERS

BATON ROUGE. *St. Joseph Convent,* 3080 Kleinert Ave., 70806-6899. Tel: 225-344-1517; Fax: 225-343-0261. Email: stjosephsbr@juno.com. Sr. Ursula Harelson, C.S.J., Local Coord. Sisters of St. Joseph 9.

Maryville Novitiate and Provincial House, 4200 Essen Lane, 70809-2196. Email: barcenea@ololrmc.com. Web: www.fmolsisters.com.

North American Province, 4200 Essen Ln., 70809-2196. Tel: 225-927-7481; 225-926-1627; Fax: 225-925-5268. Sr. Barbara Arceneaux, O.S.F., Prov. Supr. Final Vows 24.

TICKFAW. *Our Lady Queen Contemplative Monastery,* 50352 Antioch Rd., 70466-9747. Tel: 985-345-2630; Fax: 985-345-2630. Email: OLQMTLA70@aol.com. Very Sr. Mary Herbert Walsh, O.S.B., Prioress; Revs. Francis Sander, O.S.B. (NO), Chap.; Marion C. Walsh, O.S.B. (IND) (Retired). Benedictine Nuns Nuns 6.

[J] RETREAT HOUSES

BATON ROUGE. *Bishop Robert E. Tracy Center,* P.O. Box 2028, 70821-2028. Tel: 225-336-8750; Fax: 225-336-8765. Email: formation@diobr.org. 1800 S. Acadian Thruway, P.O. Box 2028, 70821-2028. Charles Jumonville, M.R.E., Admin.

CONVENT. *Manresa House of Retreats,* Office, P.O. Box 89, 70723-0089. Tel: 225-562-3596; 800-782-9431; Fax: 225-562-3147. Email: manresa@stargazer.net. Revs. Anthony H. Ostini, S.J., Dir.; Thomas J. Cronin, S.J., Assoc. Dir.; Hacker J. Fagot, S.J., Assoc. Dir.; Edward J. Romagosa, S.J., Assoc. Dir.; W. Peter Bayhi, S.J. (LAF), Assoc. Dir.

PONCHATOULA. *Rosaryville/Spirit Life Center,* 39003 Rosaryville Rd., 70454-9580. Tel: 225-294-0244; 800-742-0570; Fax: 225-294-3510. Email: dsslc@I-55.com. Web: www.rosaryville.org. Sr. M. Edmund Gibson, O.P., Dir.; Rev. William J. Aldridge, O.P., Chap. Dominican Sisters 2.

[K] CAMPUS MINISTRY

BATON ROUGE. *Christ the King Parish and Catholic Student Center* Louisiana State University, P.O. Box 25131, 70894-5131. Tel: 225-344-8595; 225-383-1574; Fax: 225-344-1920. Email: ctk-lsu.org. Rev. Than N. Vu, S.T.L.; Very Rev. John Carville, S.T.D., V.G.

11 Fraternity Ln., 70803. Total Catholic Students 16,000.

Martin Luther King, Jr. Student Center St. Joseph Chapel, Southern University, 586 Harding Blvd., 70807-5301. Tel: 225-775-8691; 225-775-1301; Fax: 225-775-7067. Email: jlvsj@juno.com. Rev. John L. Vessels, S.J. (FWT), Chap. & Dir. Total Catholic Students 3,000.

HAMMOND. *St. Albert the Great Catholic Student Center* 409 W. Dakota St., 70401-2517. Tel: 985-345-7206; Fax: 985-345-7223. Email: st_albert@bellsouth.net. Rev. Sean O. Sheehy, Ed.D., Dir. Serving Southeastern Louisiana University. Total Students 15,100.

[L] MISCELLANEOUS

BATON ROUGE. *Bishop Stanley J. Ott Shelter Program,* P.O. Box 127, 70821-0127. Tel: 225-383-7343; Fax: 225-383-6623. Email: macaldo@svdpbr.com. Mr. Michael Acaldo, CEO.

Catholic Community Services, 1900 S. Acadian Thruway, 70808-1688. Tel: 225-336-8770; Fax: 225-336-8745. Email: droe@ccsbr.org. Web: www.ccsbr.org. P.O. Box 1668, 70821-1668. Ms. Deborah Roe, M.S.W., Exec. Dir.

Catholic-Presbyterian Apts., Inc., 655 North St., 70802-5420. Tel: 225-383-5551; Fax: 225-383-0050. Email: diane2@intersurf.com. Web: www.catholicpresbyterianapartments.com. Diane F. Perkins, Exec. Dir.

Counseling, Maternity & Adoption, 1900 S. Acadian Thruway, 70808. Tel: 225-336-8708; Fax: 225-336-8703. Email: adopt@ccsbr.org. Web: www.adoptbatonrouge.com. Mailing Address: P.O. Box 4785, 70821-4785. Janice Allen, Dir.

FMOL Health Systems, Inc., 4200 Essen Ln., 70809-2196. Tel: 225-923-2701; Fax: 225-926-4846. Email: jfinan@ololrmc.com. Mr. John J. Finan Jr., Pres. & CEO.

Haiti Project, Inc., 4200 Essen Ln., 70809-2196. Tel: 225-926-1627; Fax: 225-925-5268. Email: barcenea@ololrmc.com. Sr. Barbara Arceneaux, O.S.F., Pres. Organized and under the supervision of the Franciscan Missionaries of Our Lady, North American Province.

MAGNIFICAT-Baton Rouge Chapter, 16047 Hickory Knoll, 70810-9515. Tel: 225-752-5678. Mrs. Mary Kestler, Coord. A Ministry to Catholic Women.

St. Michael's Home (Vietnamese) , 2305 Choctaw Dr., 70805-7999. Tel: 225-357-1204; Fax: 225-354-0611. Email: nvhung@bellsouth.net. Rev. Hung Viet Nguyen, I.C.M. (Vietnam), Dir. Tel: 225-355-9794.

Missionaries of Charity Queen of Peace Home and Soup Kitchen, 737 East Blvd., 70802-6399. Tel: 225-383-4127; 225-383-8367. Missionaries of Charity.

Myriam's House, Inc., 3027 Nicholson Dr., 70802-8432. Tel: 225-344-0662; Fax: 225-334-0663. Ms. Valerie Maurice, Pres.; Ms. Yolanda P. Perrilloux, Exec. Dir. (Sponsored in part by Sisters of St. Joseph); Facility for homeless women, providing temporary housing, assistance with job placement and other needed services.

Sisters of St. Joseph - St. Paul Center, 3920 Gus Young Ave., 70802-1727. Tel: 225-344-8590; Fax: 225-387-5169. Email: spalc@juno.com. David Jones, Dir.; Sr. Kathleen Bahlinger, C.S.J., Asst. Dir.

St. Vincent DePaul Community Pharmacy, Inc., Mailing Address: P.O. Box 127, 70821-0127. Tel: 225-383-7450; Fax: 225-383-6623. Email: macaldo@svdpbr.com. Mr. Michael J. Acaldo, CEO.

St. Vincent DePaul Dining Room, Mailing Address: P.O. Box 127, 70821-0127. Tel: 225-383-7837; 225-383-7439; Fax: 225-383-6623. Email: macaldo@svdpbr.com. Mr. Michael J. Acaldo, CEO.

St. Vincent DePaul Stores, Mailing Address: P.O. Box 127, 70821-0127. Tel: 225-356-5158; Fax: 225-383-6623. Email: macaldo@svdpbr.com. Mr. Michael J. Acaldo, CEO. Tel: 225-383-7837.

[M] FOUNDATIONS, FUNDS AND TRUSTS

BATON ROUGE. *Baton Rouge Chancery Office,* Mailing Address: P.O. Box 2028, 70821-2028. 1800 S. Acadian Thruway, 70808-1698. Tel: 225-387-0561; Fax: 225-336-8789. Email: chancery@diobr.org.

Ascension Catholic Interparochial School Endowment Fund, Donaldsonville.

Bishop Stanley J. Ott Works of Mercy Trust

Diocese of Baton Rouge Clergy Retirement Plan

Diocese of Baton Rouge Lay Retirement Plan

Diocese of Baton Rouge Trust Fund

Nim Pecquet Holy Family School Foundation

Our Lady of Perpetual Help Trust

Pamphile and Mabyn Donaldson Trust for St. Louis King of France Church

Pointe Coupee Catholic Interparochial School Endowment Fund, New Roads.

Sacred Heart Parish Endowment Fund

St. Aloysius School Endowment Fund

St. Joseph Cathedral Cemetery Fund

St. Joseph Cathedral Trust

St. Theresa of Avila Catholic School Educational Foundation, Gonzales.

St. Thomas More School Endowment Trust

Sherri Lyn Shaffer Trust for St. Thomas More Church

Veritas Foundation, Hammond.

CHS Foundation, 855 Hearthstone Dr., 70806-5599. Tel: 225-389-0978; Fax: 225-389-0983. Bro. Aquin Gauthier, S.C., Pres.

Our Lady of the Lake Foundation, 5000 Hennessy Blvd., 70808-9907. Tel: 225-765-5000.

CONVENT. *Hynes Fund,* 5858 Hwy. 44, 70723-0089. Tel: 800-782-9431; Fax: 225-562-3147. Mailing Address: P.O. Box 89, 70723-0089. Bro. Lawrence J. Lundin, S.J., Treas.

Legal Title: *The Administrators of the Rev. John W. Hynes, S.J., Manresa Memorial Endowment Fund, Inc.*

RELIGIOUS INSTITUTES OF MEN REPRESENTED IN THE DIOCESE

For further details refer to the corresponding bracketed number in the Religious Institutes of Men or Women section.

[0200]—*Benedictine Monks* (St. Meinrad Archabbey)—O.S.B.

[0200]—*Benedictine Monks* (St. Joseph Abbey, St. Benedict, LA)—O.S.B.

[1100]—*Brothers of the Sacred Heart* (New Orleans Prov.)—S.C.

[0470]—*The Capuchin Friars*—O.F.M.Cap.

[1070]—*Congregation of the Most Holy Redeemer-Redemptorists* (New Orleans Vice Prov.)—C.Ss.R.

[]—*Incarnatio Consecratio Missionaries*—I.C.M.
[]—*Indian Missionary Society*—I.M.S.
[]—*Missionaries of St. Paul*—M.S.P.
[0430]—*Order of Preachers-Dominicans* (Prov. of St. Martin de Porres)—O.P.
[0690]—*Society of Jesus* (New Orleans Prov.)—S.J.
[0760]—*Society of Mary-Marists* (American Prov.)—S.M.
[0420]—*Society of the Divine Word* (Southern Prov.)—S.V.D.
[0700]—*St. Joseph's Society of the Sacred Heart-Josephites*—S.S.J.

RELIGIOUS INSTITUTES OF WOMEN REPRESENTED IN THE DIOCESE

[0233]—*Benedictine Nuns*—O.S.B.
[0760]—*Daughters of Charity of St. Vincent de Paul* (West Central Prov.)—D.C.
[1070-08]—*Dominican Sisters*—O.P.
[1070-10]—*Dominican Sisters*—O.P.
[1380]—*Franciscan Missionaries of Our Lady*—O.S.F.
[]—*Incarnatio Consecratio Missio*—I.C.M.
[2410]—*Marianites of Holy Cross*—M.S.C.
[2590]—*Mercedarian Sisters of the Blessed Sacrament*—H.M.S.S.
[2710]—*Missionaries of Charity*—M.C.
[3450]—*Religious of Jesus and Mary*—R.J.M.
[2970]—*School Sisters of Notre Dame*—S.S.N.D.
[]—*Sisters for Christian Community*—S.F.C.C.
[0500]—*Sisters of Charity of Nazareth* (Southern Region)—S.C.N.
[0990]—*Sisters of Divine Providence*—C.D.P.
[2570]—*Sisters of Mercy of Philadelphia*—R.S.M.
[2630]—*Sisters of Mercy of the Holy Cross*—S.C.S.C.
[3880]—*Sisters of St. Joseph of Medaille*—C.S.J.
[3830-16]—*Sisters of St. Joseph of Springfield, Mont Marie*—S.S.J.
[0260]—*Sisters of the Blessed Sacrament for Indians and Colored People*—S.B.S.
[2940]—*Sisters of the Most Holy Sacrament*—M.H.S.
[4070]—*Society of the Sacred Heart*—R.S.C.J.

NECROLOGY

† Landry, Clyde B.—Died Aug. 19, 2003

Diocese of Beaumont

(Dioecesis Bellomontensis)

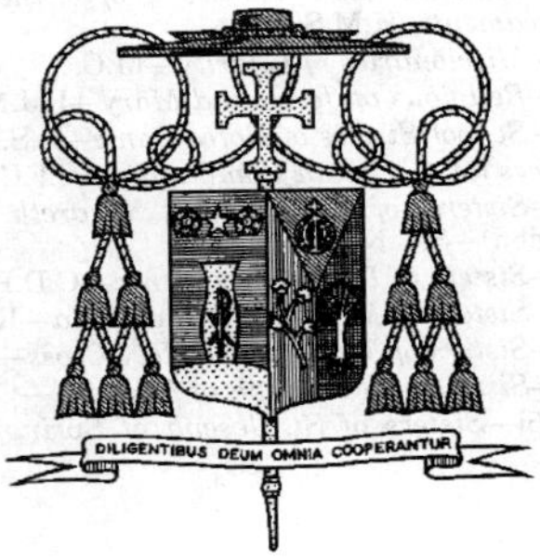

Most Reverend

CURTIS JOHN GUILLORY, S.V.D., D.D.

Bishop of Beaumont; ordained December 16, 1972; appointed Titular Bishop of Stagno and Auxiliary Bishop of Galveston-Houston December 29, 1987; consecrated February 19, 1988; appointed Bishop of Beaumont June 2, 2000; installed July 28, 2000. *Mailing Address: P.O. Box 3948, Beaumont, TX 77704-3948. Office: 703 Archie St., Beaumont, TX 77701-2899.* Tel: 409-838-0451, Ext. 130; Fax: 409-838-4511.

Diocesan Pastoral Center: 703 Archie St., Beaumont, TX 77701P.O. Box 3948, Beaumont, TX 77704-3948. Tel: 409-838-0451; Fax: 409-838-4511.

Web: www.dioceseofbmt.org

Email: chancery@dioceseofbmt.org

ESTABLISHED SEPTEMBER 29, 1966.

Square Miles 7,878.

Comprises the counties of Chambers, Hardin, Jasper, Jefferson, Liberty,Newton, Orange, Polk and Tyler.

Legal Title: For legal titles of parishes and diocesan institutions, consult the Diocesan Pastoral Office.

STATISTICAL OVERVIEW

Personnel	
Bishop	1
Priests: Diocesan Active in Diocese	31
Priests: Diocesan Active Outside Diocese	4
Priests: Retired, Sick or Absent	11
Number of Diocesan Priests	46
Religious Priests in Diocese	25
Total Priests in Diocese	71
Extern Priests in Diocese	4
Ordinations:	
Diocesan Priests	2
Permanent Deacons in Diocese	32
Total Brothers	1
Total Sisters	42
Parishes	
Parishes	45
With Resident Pastor:	
Resident Diocesan Priests	25
Resident Religious Priests	20
Missions	8
Pastoral Centers	2
New Parishes Created	1
Professional Ministry Personnel:	
Sisters	1
Lay Ministers	31
Welfare	
Catholic Hospitals	3
Total Assisted	360,739
Special Centers for Social Services	3
Total Assisted	54,792
Educational	
Diocesan Students in Other Seminaries	9
Total Seminarians	9
High Schools, Diocesan and Parish	1
Total Students	487
Elementary Schools, Diocesan and Parish	6
Total Students	1,396
Catechesis/Religious Education:	
High School Students	1,525
Elementary Students	6,990
Total Students under Catholic Instruction	10,407
Teachers in the Diocese:	
Sisters	5
Lay Teachers	163
Vital Statistics	
Receptions into the Church:	
Infant Baptism Totals	1,287
Adult Baptism Totals	170
Received into Full Communion	262
First Communions	1,359
Confirmations	826
Marriages:	
Catholic	204
Interfaith	164
Total Marriages	368
Deaths	850
Total Catholic Population	89,403
Total Population	599,139

Former Bishops—Most Revs. VINCENT M. HARRIS, D.D., ord. March 19, 1938; appt. Bishop of Beaumont, July 4, 1966; consecrated Sept. 28, 1966; installed as First Bishop of Beaumont, Sept. 29, 1966; appt. Titular Bishop of Rotaria and Coadjutor with right of succession to the Bishop of Austin, TX, April 21, 1971; succeeded to as Second Bishop of Austin, Nov. 16, 1971; died March 31, 1988; WARREN L. BOUDREAUX, J.C.D., D.D., ord. May 30, 1942; appt. Titular Bishop of Calynda and Auxiliary Bishop of Lafayette, LA, May 19, 1962; consecrated July 25, 1962; appt. second Bishop of Beaumont, June 4, 1971; installed Aug. 25, 1971; appt. first Bishop of Houma-Thibodaux, March 2, 1977; installed as first Bishop of Houma-Thibodaux, June 5, 1977; died Oct. 6, 1997; BERNARD J. GANTER, D.D., ord. May 22, 1952; appt. first Bishop of Tulsa, Dec. 19, 1972; consecrated and installed, Feb. 7, 1973; appt. third Bishop of Beaumont, Oct. 3, 1977; installed Dec. 13, 1977; died Oct. 9, 1993; JOSEPH A. GALANTE, D.D., J.C.D., ord. May 16, 1964; consecrated Dec. 11, 1992; appt. Bishop of Beaumont, April 5, 1994; installed May 9, 1994; appt. Coadjutor Bishop of Dallas, Nov. 23, 1999; installed Jan. 14, 2000.

Pastoral Center—703 Archie St., Beaumont, 77701-2899. Tel: 409-838-0451; Fax: 409-838-4511 Office Hours: 8-5. *P.O. Box 3948, Beaumont, 77704-3948.*

Vicar General and Moderator of the Curia—Rev. Msgr. MICHAEL A. JAMAIL, J.C.D., Ed.D., P.O. Box 3948, Beaumont, 77704-3948. Tel: 409-838-0451, Ext. 123; Fax: 409-838-4511.

Episcopal Vicars—Central Vicariate: Rev. Msgr. FRANCIS H. BURLTON, Our Lady of the Assumption, 4445 Ave. A, Beaumont, 77705. Eastern Vicariate: Very Rev. JAMES MCCLINTOCK, St. Henry Church, P.O. Box 427, Bridge City, 77611-0427. Northern Vicariate: Very Rev. RONALD B. FOSHAGE, M.S., St. Michael, P.O. Box 239, Jasper, 75951. Southern Vicariate: Very Rev. DONALD GOLASINSKI, Immaculate Conception Church, P.O. Box 967, Groves, 77619. Western Vicariate: Very Rev. JOSEPH KHANH HO, S.T.L., J.C.L., St. Louis Church, 315 W. Bucaneer, Winnie, 77665-9711.

Diocesan College of Consultors and Presbyteral Council—Rev. WILLIAM MANGER, Chm.; Rev. Msgrs. MICHAEL A. JAMAIL, J.C.D., Ed.D.; RICHARD A. DESTEFANO (Retired); Revs. MICHAEL MAI TRAN, C.M.C.; KEVIN BADEAUX, J.C.L.; ANDREW MOORE; BENNIE J. PATILLO; DAN MALAIN; STEPHEN MCCRATE; OLIVER OBELE, M.S.P.; SINCLAIR OUBRE, J.C.L.; LUONG QUANG TRAN.

Priests Personnel Board—Rev. BENNIE J. PATILLO, Chm., P.O. Box 3948, Beaumont, 77704-3948.

Chancellor—Sr. ESTHER DUNEGAN, I.W.B.S., J.C.L., Diocesan Offices, P.O. Box 3948, Beaumont, 77704-3948. Tel: 409-838-0451, Ext. 124; Fax: 409-838-4511.

Chief Financial Officer—RUSSELL J. CHIMENO, C.P.A., Diocesan Pastoral Center, P.O. Box 3948, Beaumont, 77704-3948. Tel: 409-838-0451, Ext. 134; Fax: 409-838-4511.

Diocesan Finance Council—RUSSELL J. CHIMENO, C.P.A., P.O. Box 3948, Beaumont, 77704-3948.

Tribunal—703 Archie St., P.O. Box 3948, Beaumont, 77704-3948. Tel: 409-838-0451, Ext. 140; Fax: 409-838-4511.

Judicial Vicar—Rev. LUONG QUANG TRAN.

Diocesan Judges—Rev. LUONG QUANG TRAN, Judicial Vicar; Rev. Msgr. KENNETH R. GREIG; Very Rev. JOSEPH KHANH HO, S.T.L., J.C.L.; Revs. KEVIN BADEAUX, J.C.L.; JOSEPH THUC NGUYEN, J.C.L.; SINCLAIR OUBRE, J.C.L.; BENNIE J. PATILLO; Sr. ESTHER DUNEGAN, I.W.B.S., J.C.L.

Promoter of Justice—Rev. Msgr. FRANCIS H. BURLTON.

Defenders of Bond—Rev. Msgrs. MICHAEL A. JAMAIL, J.C.D., Ed.D.; FRANCIS H. BURLTON; Rev. JOSEPH STRATMAN, M.Th. (Retired).

Advocate—Rev. MARTIN LESTER NELSON.

Psychologists for the Tribunal—RAY COXE, Ph.D.; Rev. Msgr. MICHAEL A. JAMAIL, J.C.D., Ed.D.; Mr. PATRICK BRADY, M.A., C.H.

Secretary-Notary—MARILYN PRICE; Sr. BARBARA ANNE OSTERHAUS, C.V.I., Sec.

Victim Assistance Coordinator—Bro. BERNARD PALMERI, C.S.C., L.P. Tel: 409-347-1316. Email: bpalmeri@aol.com.

Diocesan Departments

Apostleship of the Sea—Rev. SINCLAIR OUBRE, J.C.L., Diocesan Dir., 1500 Jefferson Dr., Port Arthur, 77642. Tel: 409-985-4545; Fax: 409-985-5945. Email: aosusa@stellamaris.net.

Lifelong Catholic Formation/Education—LORRAINE S. DELUCA, Ed.D., Dir., P.O. Box 3948, Beaumont, 77704-3948. Tel: 409-838-0451, Ext. 144; Fax: 409-838-4511.

Catholic Schools—GEORGE PRESSEY, M.A., Supt., P.O. Box 3948, Beaumont, 77704-3948. Tel: 409-838-0451, Ext. 150; Fax: 409-838-4511.

Communication, Information & Diocesan Press—Mrs. KAREN GILMAN, Exec. Dir., 1019 Colorado, Beaumont, 77705. Tel: 409-832-3944, Ext. 107; Fax: 409-832-4129. P.O. Box 3948, Beaumont, 77704-3948.

Diaconate, Permanent Diaconate—Rev. JEREMIAH MCGRATH, Vicar, St. Anthony Cathedral, P.O. Box 3309, Beaumont, 77704-3309. Tel: 409-833-6433; Fax: 409-833-6688; Deacon VERNON DRUMMOND, Dir., 3930 35th St., Port Arthur, 77642-4039. Tel: 409-982-6352.

Diaconate Formation—Rev. Msgr. MICHAEL A. JAMAIL, J.C.D., Ed.D., Dir., Diocese of Beaumont, P.O. Box 3948, Beaumont, 77704-3948. Tel: 409-838-0451, Ext. 123; Fax: 409-838-4511.

Stewardship & Development—LETTY LANZA, Dir., P.O. Box 3948, Beaumont, 77704. Tel: 409-838-0451,

Ext. 122; Fax: 409-838-4511.

Holy Childhood—LETTY LANZA, P.O. Box 3948, Beaumont, 77704-3948. Tel: 409-838-0451, Ext. 122; Fax: 409-838-4511.

Propagation of the Faith: Mission Coop—LETTY LANZA, P.O. Box 3948, Beaumont, 77704-3948. Tel: 409-838-0451, Ext. 138; Fax: 409-838-4511.

Hispanic Ministry, Diocesan—SR. AUGUSTINE SERRANO, O.S.F., Dir., P.O. Box 3948, Beaumont, 77704-3948. Tel: 409-838-0451, Ext. 153; Fax: 409-838-4511.

African American Ministry—Ms. JOSIE CURTIS, Dir., P.O. Box 3948, Beaumont, 77704-3948. Tel: 409-838-0451, Ext. 147; Fax: 409-838-4511.

Worship; Liturgical Commission; Diocesan Choir—Mrs. ROSALIND SANCHEZ, M.A., Dir., P.O. Box 3948, Beaumont, 77704-3948. Tel: 409-838-0451; Fax: 409-838-4511.

Principal Master of Episcopal Ceremonies—Deacon DAVID LUTHER.

Family Life Ministry & Respect Life Liaison—Mr. GLENN HITTER, M.Ed., Dir., P.O. Box 3948, Beaumont, 77704-3948. Tel: 409-838-0451, Ext. 147; Fax: 409-838-4511.

Criminal Justice Ministry—Deacon AL O'BRIEN, Dir., P.O. Box 3948, Beaumont, 77704-3948. Tel: 409-838-0451, Ext. 158; Fax: 409-838-4511.

Director of Seminarians—Rev. JOHN HUGHES, St. Jude Thaddeus Church, 6825 Gladys Ave., Beaumont, 77706. Tel: 409-866-5088; Fax: 409-866-1866.

Vocations—Rev. ANDREW MOORE, Dir., P.O. Box 10095 L.U.S., Beaumont, 77710. Tel: 409-835-5037; Fax: 409-832-4129.

Office of Youth & Campus Ministry—Mr. TOMMY CHATLOSH, Dir.; Ms. GINA DECUIR, Sec. & Coord. Campus Activities, P.O. Box 10095 L.U.S., Beaumont 77710. Tel: 409-835-3972; Fax: 409-832-4129.

Committees, Boards, Commissions

African American Advisory Committee, Diocesan—Ms. JOSIE CURTIS, Chm., P.O. Box 3948, Beaumont, 77704-3948. Tel: 409-838-0451, Ext. 147 Fax: 409-838-4511.

Boy Scouts—Rev. MICHAEL BALUYOT, Chap., Infant Jesus Church, P.O. Box 8180, Lumberton, 77657-8180.

Building Commission, Diocesan—Rev. Msgr. RICHARD A. DESTEFANO, Chm. (Retired), St. Peter, the Apostle Church, 2049 Taft Ave., Groves, 77619-4953. Tel: 409-962-8365.

Catholic Daughters of America—EVA ROBERTSON, District Deputy, 1190 Glasshouse, Beaumont, 77703. Tel: 409-832-8010.

Catholic Women, Council of—Very Rev. DONALD GOLASINSKI, Moderator, Immaculate Conception Church, P.O. Box 967, Groves, 77619-0967.

Charismatic Prayer Renewal—Rev. WILLIAM MANGER, Group Liaison, St. Anne Church, P.O. Box 3429, Beaumont, 77704-3429.

Commission for Continuing Education of Clergy & Religious—Rev. FRANCIS X. CONROY, Chm., St. Pius X Church, 5075 Bigner Rd., Beaumont, 77708-5299. Tel: 409-892-3316.

R.C.I.A. Commission—LORRAINE S. DELUCA, Ed.D., Chm., P.O. Box 3948, Beaumont, 77704-3948.

Diocese of Beaumont Retirement Committee—JOE BROUSSARD IV, J.D., Chm., P.O. Box 3948, Beaumont, 77704-3948. Tel: 409-838-0451, Ext. 135; Fax: 409-838-4511.

Diocesan School Board—DAVE MORROW, Pres.; JENNIFER THOMPSON, Vice Pres.

CLERGY, PARISHES, MISSIONS AND PAROCHIAL SCHOOLS

CITY OF BEAUMONT
(JEFFERSON COUNTY)

1—ST. ANTHONY CATHEDRAL (1879), Revs. Jeremiah McGrath; Chrysostom Plavunkunnathil, C.M.I. In Res., Rev. Antony Paulose.
Res.: 700 Jefferson St., P.O. Box 3309, 77704-3309. Tel: 409-833-6433; Fax: 409-833-8996.
School—Tel: 409-832-3486. Sisters 1; Lay Teachers 14; Students 183.

2—ST. ANNE (1937), Revs. William Manger; J.C. Coon; Robert Eathan Oakes; Deacon Joseph Scheurich. In Res., Rev. Msgr. Michael A. Jamail, J.C.D., Ed.D.
Res.: Calder Ave. & 11th, P.O. Box 3429, 77704-3429. Tel: 409-832-9963; Fax: 409-832-9964.
School— (Formerly St. Anne Tri-Parish School) Lay Teachers 47; Students 600.
Catechesis/Religious Program—Tel: 409-832-8107; Fax: 409-832-5099.

3—BLESSED SACRAMENT (1915), (African American), [CEM] Rev. Alfred Umagu, M.S.P.
Res.: 780 Porter St., 77701-7198. Tel: 409-833-6089; Fax: 409-833-6091.
Catechesis/Religious Program—Tel: 409-833-1909.

4—CRISTO REY (1951), (Hispanic), Rev. Luis Urriza, O.S.A.
Res.: 767 Ave. A, 77701. Tel: 409-835-7788; Fax: 409-835-7788.
Catechesis/Religious Program—Tel: 409-835-7240.

5—ST. JOSEPH (1905), (Italian—Vietnamese), Rev. Duc Duong, Admin.
Res.: 1115 Orange St., 77701-4392. Tel: 409-835-5662; Fax: 409-832-7717.

6—ST. JUDE THADDEUS (1978), Revs. John Hughes; Khue Si Bui; Deacon Alfred J. O'Brien.
Res.: 6825 Gladys, 77706-3239. Tel: 409-866-5088; Fax: 409-866-1866.
Catechesis/Religious Program—Tel: 409-866-9595.

7—OUR LADY OF THE ASSUMPTION (1951), Rev. Msgr. Francis H. Burlton.
Res.: 4445 Ave. A, 77705-4998. Tel: 409-835-5343; Fax: 409-835-5344.

8—OUR MOTHER OF MERCY (1937), (African American), Revs. Patrick S. Healy, S.S.J.; Harry Duffey, S.S.J.
Res.: 3390 Sarah St., 77705-3098. Tel: 409-842-5533; Fax: 409-842-4710.
School—Sisters 2; Lay Teachers 9; Students 92.
Catechesis/Religious Program—Tel: 409-842-0112.
Convent—Sisters of the Holy Spirit and Mary Immaculate, 3380 Sarah St.. Tel: 409-842-2940.

9—ST. PIUS X (1954), Rev. Francis X. Conroy; Deacon Robert Gros.
Res.: 5075 Bigner Rd. at East Lucas, 77708-5299. Tel: 409-892-3316; Fax: 409-892-8916.
Catechesis/Religious Program—Tel: 409-892-6052.

OUTSIDE THE CITY OF BEAUMONT

AMES, LIBERTY CO., OUR MOTHER OF MERCY (1903), (African American), [CEM] Rev. Paul Asih, M.S.P.
Res.: P.O. Box 264, Liberty, 77575-0264. Tel: 936-336-3004; Fax: 936-336-5955.

ANAHUAC, CHAMBERS CO., OUR LADY OF LIGHT (1938), Rev. Angelo Scolozzi, U.F.W., Parochial Admin.
Res.: Rte. 2, Box 1-F, 77514-9001. Tel: 409-267-3158; Fax: 409-267-4047.
Station— Smith Point.

BRIDGE CITY, ORANGE CO., ST. HENRY (1948), Very Rev. James McClintock; Deacons Eddie Blankenstein; Hazen Kenney.
Mailing Address: P.O.Box 427, 77611-0427.
Res.: 475 W. Round Bunch Rd., 77611-2448. Tel: 409-735-2422; Fax: 409-738-2158.
Catechesis/Religious Program—Tel: 409-735-8642; Fax: 409-697-1013.

BUNA, JASPER CO., ST. FRANCIS OF ASSISI MISSION (1968), Rev. Delphyn J. Meeks.
Mailing Address: P.O. Box 1688, 77612-1688. Tel: 409-994-3456; Fax: 409-994-2923.
Catechesis/Religious Program—Tel: 409-994-5516.

CHEEK, JEFFERSON CO., ST. MARTIN DE PORRES MISSION (1972), (African American), Rev. Jose Parackattu, C.M.I., Parochial Admin.
Mailing Address: 9894 Gilbert, 77705. Tel: 409-794-2548; Fax: 409-794-3411.
Catechesis/Religious Program—Tel: 409-794-1725.

CHINA, JEFFERSON CO., OUR LADY OF SORROWS (1918), Rev. Luong Quang Tran.
Res.: P.O. Box 38, 77613-0038. Tel: 409-752-3571; Fax: 409-752-5134.

CLEVELAND, LIBERTY CO., ST. MARY (1950), Rev. Paul Kahan, S.V.D.
Res.: P.O. Box 816, 77328-0816. Tel: 281-592-2985; Fax: 281-592-7247.

CORRIGAN, POLK CO., ST. MARTIN DE PORRES MISSION (1971), (Hispanic), Rev. Clifton Labbe, S.V.D.; Deacon Jose A. Vitela.
Mailing Address: P.O. Box 930, Livingston, 77351. Tel: 936-967-8385; Fax: 936-967-4657.
Hwy. 287, 75939.

DAYTON, LIBERTY CO., ST. JOSEPH THE WORKER (1945), [CEM] Rev. Joseph Malayampuram, C.M.I.
Res.: PO. Box 640, 77535-0640. Tel: 936-258-5735; Fax: 936-258-7220.

EASTGATE, LIBERTY CO., ST. ANNE MISSION (1918), Rev. Joseph Malayampuram, C.M.I.
Mailing Address: P.O. Box 640, Dayton, 77535-0640. Tel: 936-258-5735; Fax: 936-258-7220.

FANNETT, JEFFERSON CO., ST. MARY (1954), Formerly St. Mary, Hamshire (1899). Rev. Jose Parackattu, C.M.I., Parochial Admin.
Res.: 9894 Gilbert Rd., 77705-8878. Tel: 409-794-2548; Fax: 409-794-3411.
Catechesis/Religious Program—Tel: 409-794-1725; Fax: 409-794-3411.

GROVES, JEFFERSON CO.

1—IMMACULATE CONCEPTION (1928), Rev. Donald J. Golasinski.
Res.: 3250 Washington, P.O. Box 967, 77619-0967. Tel: 409-962-0255; Fax: 409-963-3464.

2—ST. PETER THE APOSTLE (1972), Rev. Msgr. Kenneth R. Greig. In Res., Rev. Msgr. Richard A. DeStefano (Retired).
Res.: 2049 Taft Ave., 77619-4953 Tel: 409-962-8365 Fax: 409-962-8366.
Catechesis/Religious Program—Tel 409-962-3661.

JASPER, JASPER CO., ST. MICHAEL (1952), Rev. Ronald Foshage, M.S.; Deacons John Charnisky; David Luther.
Res.: P.O. Box 239, 75951-0239. Tel: 409-384-2447; Fax: 409-384-2447.
Station—Toledo Village

KIRBYVILLE, JASPER CO., OUR LADY OF LA SALETTE MISSION (1948), Rev. Ronald Foshage, M.S.
Mailing Address: P.O. Box 239, Jasper, 75951-0239. Tel: 409-384-2447; Fax: 409-384-2447.

KOUNTZE, HARDIN CO., HOLY SPIRIT MISSION (1986), Rev. Michael Baluyot.
470 Monroe, 77625. Tel: 409-246-4457 (Office); Fax: 409-246-4623.

LIBERTY, LIBERTY CO., IMMACULATE CONCEPTION (1756), [CEM] Rev. Patrick Daniel Parcon (Philippines); Deacon Luther Wells.
Res.: 411 Milam, 77575-4730. Tel: 936-336-7267; Fax: 936-336-9740.

LIVINGSTON, POLK CO., ST. JOSEPH (1970), Rev. Clifton Labbe, S.V.D.; Deacons Rudy Cockburn; Jose A. Vitela; John G. Stanley.
Res.: P.O. Box 930, 77351-0930. Tel: 936-967-8385; Fax: 936-967-4657.

LUMBERTON, HARDIN CO., INFANT JESUS (1948), Rev. Michael Baluyot.
Res.: P.O. Box 8180, 77657-0180. Tel: 409-755-1734; Fax: 409-755-2833.

MAURICEVILLE, ORANGE CO., ST. MAURICE (1966), Rev. Delphyn J. Meeks.
Res.: P.O. Box 940, 77626-0940. Tel: 409-745-4060; Fax: 409-745-4272.

MONT BELVIEU, CHAMBERS CO., HOLY TRINITY (2003), Rev. Andrew Moore.
Mailing Address: 7419 Lone Oak Dr., Baytown, 77521-4915.
Church: 3515 Trinity.

NEDERLAND, JEFFERSON CO., ST. CHARLES BORROMEO (1923), Revs. Dan Malain; David A. Edwards; Louis Delarue; Deacons Vernon Drummond; Dallas Broussard.
Res.: 130 Hardy Ave., 77627-7326. Tel: 409-722-3413; Fax: 409-722-2020.
Catechesis/Religious Program—Tel: 409-722-0421.

ORANGE, ORANGE CO.

1—ST. FRANCIS OF ASSISI (1978), Revs. Thomas E. Phelan; George Kalappura, C.M.I.; Deacons Harvey Dubois; Stronnie McBride.
Church: 4300 Meeks Dr., 77632-4508. Tel: 409-883-9153; Fax: 409-883-9154.
Catechesis/Religious Program—Tel: 409-883-8232.

2—ST. MARY (1880), [CEM] Rev. Joseph P. Daleo; Deacon Melvin Payne.
Res.: 912 W. Cherry St., 77630-5017. Tel: 409-883-2883; Fax: 409-883-3547.
School—2600 Bob Hall Rd., 77630-2418. Tel: 409-883-8913; Fax: 409-883-0827. Sisters 1; Lay Teachers 20; Students 233.
Catechesis/Religious Program—Tel: 409-886-0841; Fax: 409-886-0841.

3—ST. THERESE (1924), (African American), Rev. Patrick Otor, M.S.P.; Deacon Julian Richard.
Res.: 1409 N. Sixth St., 77630-3927. Tel: 409-883-3783; Fax: 409-883-4918.

ORANGEFIELD, ORANGE CO., ST. HELEN (1938), Rev. Philip Neri Payyappilli, C.M.I., Parochial Admin.; Deacon Glen Hebert.
Res.: 8105 FM 1442, 77630. Tel: 409-735-2200 (Office); Fax: 409-735-7786.
Catechesis/Religious Program—Tel: 409-735-7028.

PORT ARTHUR, JEFFERSON CO.

1—ST. CATHERINE OF SIENA (1954), [CEM] Revs. Joseph J. Romero; Thuc Nguyen (Vietnam); Deacon Jim Gard.
Res.: 3706 Woodrow Dr., 77642-2320. Tel: 409-962-5715; Fax: 409-962-4775.
School—Lay Teachers 21; Students 155.

2—ST. JAMES (1929), Revs. Kevin Sumler; J.C. Coon. In Res., Rev. Kevin Badeaux, J.C.L.
Res.: 3617 Gulfway Dr., 77642-3693. Tel: 409-985-8865; Fax: 409-985-3847.

3—ST. JOHN (1951), (African American), Rev. Sinclair Oubre, J.C.L.; Deacon W. B. Goudeau Jr. In Res., Rev. Leonard Onwumere (Nigeria).
Res.: 620 53rd St., 77640-2351. Tel: 409-985-8010; Fax: 409-982-8691.

4—ST. JOSEPH (1951), Rev. D. Stephen McCrate; Deacon Luis Maganna.
Res.: 4600 Procter St., 77642-1365. Tel: 409-982-6409; Fax: 409-983-5383.
Catechesis/Religious Program—Tel: 409-982-0667.

5—ST. MARY (1903), (African American), Rev. Oliver Obele, M.S.P.; Deacon Roy Cormier Sr.

Office—545 Savannah Ave., 77640-6026. Tel: 409-985-9661; Fax: 409-985-9691.

6—OUR LADY OF GUADALUPE (1927), (Hispanic), Rev. Telesforo R. Blanco, O.S.A.; Deacon Jimmy Bourgeois.
Res.: 3648 S. Sgt. Lucian Adams Dr., 77642-6100. Tel: 409-962-6777; Fax: 409-963-0669.
Catechesis/Religious Program—Tel: 409-962-2247.

7—QUEEN OF VIETNAM (1977), (Vietnamese), Revs. Michael Mai Tran, C.M.C.; Bernard Hung Nguyen, C.M.C.
Res.: 801 Ninth Ave., 77642-3329. Tel: 409-983-7676; Fax: 409-982-1212.
Convent—1148 Ninth Ave., 77642. Tel: 409-985-5102; Fax: 409-985-5102. Dominican Sisters 6.

8—SACRED HEART (1915), (African American), Rev. Larry Leduff-Gutierrez, S.S.J.
Res.: 920 Booker Washington Ave., 77640-4923. Tel: 409-985-5104; Fax: 409-982-0106.

9—ST. THERESE THE LITTLE FLOWER OF JESUS (1928), Rev. Antony Moozhikuzhy, C.M.I.
Res.: 6412 Garnet Ave., 77640-1308. Tel: 409-736-1536; Fax: 409-736-2113.

PORT NECHES, JEFFERSON CO., ST. ELIZABETH (1922), Rev. Bennie J. Patillo.
Res.: 2006 Nall St., 77651-3714. Tel: 409-727-8874; Fax: 409-727-8875.
Catechesis/Religious Program—Tel: 409-722-5941.

RAYWOOD, LIBERTY CO., SACRED HEART (1952), (African American), [CEM] Rev. Charles Atuah, M.S.P., Parochial Admin.
Res.: P.O. Box 429, 77582. Tel: 936-587-4631; Fax: 936-587-1012.

SABINE PASS, JEFFERSON CO., ST. PAUL MISSION (1955), Rev. Sinclair Oubre, J.C.L.
Mailing Address: P.O. Box 123, Port Arthur, 77641-0123. Tel: 409-985-8010; Fax: 409-985-8691.

SAM RAYBURN, JASPER CO., ST. RAYMOND MISSION (1970), Rev. Ronald Foshage, M.S.
Mailing Address: P.O. Box 239, Jasper, 75951-0239. Tel: 409-384-2447.

SILSBEE, HARDIN CO., ST. MARK THE EVANGELIST (1940), Rev. Charles Sellars, O.M.I.
Res.: 905 N. Ninth St., 77656. Tel: 409-287-3287; Fax: 409-287-3271.

SOUR LAKE, HARDIN CO., OUR LADY OF VICTORY (1906), In Res., Rev. Martin Lester Nelson.
Res.: 140 Mitchell St., P.O. Box 1359, 77659. Tel: 409-287-3287; Fax: 409-287-3287.

VIDOR, ORANGE CO., OUR LADY OF LOURDES (1938), Rev. Paul Sumler.
Res.: 1600 N. Main, 77662. Tel: 409-769-2865; Fax: 409-769-4577.
Catechesis/Religious Program—Tel: 409-769-6758.

WINNIE, CHAMBERS CO., ST. LOUIS (1947), Very Rev. Joseph Khanh Ho, S.T.L., J.C.L.
Res.: 315 W. Buccaneer Dr., 77665-9711. Tel: 409-296-4200; Fax: 409-296-9715.
Catechesis/Religious Program—Tel: 409-296-4925.

WOODVILLE, TYLER CO., OUR LADY OF THE PINES (1950), Rev. Egidio Vecchio, M.S.; Deacon Paul Rachal.
Res.: P.O. Box 2029, 75979-2029. Tel: 409-283-5367; Fax: 409-283-2219.

Chaplains of Public Institutions

BEAUMONT. *Memoral Hermann Baptist Hospital*. Rev. Charles Atuah, M.S.P.

PORT ARTHUR. *Convalescent Home Ministry*. Rev. Chrysostom Plavunikunnathil, C.M.I.

Prisons

BEAUMONT. *Larry Gist State Jail*. Deacon Harry Davis, Chap.

DAYTON. *Plane State Jail*. Ms. Glory Siller, Chap.

LIVINGSTON. *Polunsky Unit*. Deacon Joe Vitela, Chap.

On Duty Outside the Diocese:
Revs.—
DeFrancisco, Joseph, St. Ambrose Univ., Davenport, IA
Shane, Michael, Pontifical North American College, 00120, Vatican City, Italy. (Special Assignment)

Educational Leave of Absence:
Rev.—
Baxter, Michael Shane, Pontifical North American College 01120 Vatican City State.

Military Chaplains:
Rev. Msgr.—
Marceaux, Sidney J., Chap. Col., 17th ASG, CM 4501, Box 2184, APO, AP 96338. U.S.A.
Rev.—
Beck, Robert P., Chap. Major, 28092 Mitchell Ave., Yigo.

Absent On Leave:
Rev.—
Paduch, Frank

Retired:
Rev. Msgrs.—
Culotta, Salvador J.
DeStefano, Richard A.
DiStefano, John
Revs.—
Dempsey, James
Iglesias, Clement
Montondon, Walter, Chap. Col.
Mudd, Earl
Pucar, August
Stratman, Joseph, M.Th.
Vanderholt, James

Permanent Deacons:
Blankenstein, Eddie, St. Henry, Bridge City
Bourgeois, Jimmy, Our Lady of Guadalupe, Port Arthur
Broussard, Dallas, St. Charles, Nederland
Charnisky, John, St. Michael, Jasper
Cockburn, Rudy, St. Joseph, Livingston
Cormier, Roy, Sr., St. Mary, Port Arthur
Davis, Harry, Our Lady of the Assumption & Larry Gist Jail, Beaumont
Drummond, Vernon, Dir. Permanent Diaconate, St. Charles Borromeo, Nederland
Dubois, Harvey, St. Francis, Orange
Gard, Jim, St. Catherine of Siena, Port Arthur
Goudeau, W. B., Jr., St. John, Port Arthur
Gros, Robert, St. Pius X, Beaumont
Hebert, Glen, St. Helen, Orangefield
Kenny, Hazen, St. Henry, Bridge City
Landry, Nolen
LeBlanc, E. R., Holy Trinity Church, Mont Belvieu; Our Lady of Light, Anahuac
Luther, David, St. Michael, Jasper; Our Lady of LaSalette, Kirbyville; St. Raymond, Rayburn
Maganna, Luis, St. Joseph Church, Pt. Arthur
McBride, Stronnie, St. Francis of Assisi and Southeast Texas Hospice, Orange
McKinney, Tom
O'Brien, Alfred J., Diocesan Dir. Office Criminal Justice Min., St. Jude Church, Beaumont
Payne, Melvin, St. Mary, Orange
Rachal, Paul, Our Lady of the Pines, Woodville
Richard, Julian, St. Therese, Orange
Rudolph, William
Scheurich, Joseph, (Asst. Director-Permanent Diaconate), St. Anne Church, Beaumont
Smith, Morris
Stanley, John G., St. Joseph, Livingston; State Jail, Travis City
Vitela, Joe, Chaplain-Polunsky Unit, Livingston
Wells, Luther, Immaculate Conception, Liberty
Wycliff, Wilbert
Wynn, Dow

INSTITUTIONS LOCATED IN THE DIOCESE

[A] HIGH SCHOOLS, DIOCESAN

BEAUMONT. *Monsignor Kelly Catholic High School*, 5950 Kelly Dr., 77707. Tel: 409-866-2351; Fax: 409-866-0917. Email: rbemis@kelly.beaumont.tx.us. Web: www.kelly.beaumont.tx.us. Mr. Roger Bemis, Prin.; Rev. Eathan Oakes, Chap. Sisters 1; Lay Teachers 40; Students 487.

[B] ELEMENTARY SCHOOLS, DIOCESAN

PORT ARTHUR. *Sr. Thea Bowman Academy* (Formerly Central Catholic Parochial School) , 3617 Gulfway Dr., 77642. Tel: 409-982-4140; Fax: 409-982-1850. Email: stbamtpg@aol.com. Mrs. Patricia Gougenheim, Dir. Lay Teachers 12; Students 109.

[C] GENERAL HOSPITALS

BEAUMONT. *CHRISTUS Health Southeast Texas* dba St. Elizabeth Hospital , 2830 Calder Ave., P.O. Box 5405, 77726-5405. Tel: 409-892-7171; Fax: 409-899-8191. Web: www.christusste.org. Mr. Ed Myers, CEO. Operated by CHRISTUS Health Southeast Texas Sisters 7; Bed Capacity 461; Patients Assisted Annually 214,367.

JASPER. *CHRISTUS Health Southeast Texas* dba Jasper Memorial Hospital , 1275 Martin Dr., 75951. Tel: 409-384-5461; Fax: 409-383-0622. Email: deborah.wieoand@christushealth.org. Deborah Wiegand, R.N., CEO Admin. Operated by CHRISTUS Health Southeast Texas. Bed Capacity 59; Patients Assisted Annually 33,717.

PORT ARTHUR. *CHRISTUS Health Southeast Texas* dba St. Mary Hospital , 3600 Gates Blvd., P.O. Box 3696, 77643. Tel: 409-985-7431; Fax: 409-985-9404. Web: www.christusstmary.org. Alice Baker, CEO; Sr. Maura Theriot, C.C.V.I., Treas.; Rev. Donald E. Donahugh (RCK), Chap. Operated by CHRISTUS Health Southeast Texas. Sisters 5; Bed Capacity 246; Patients Assisted Annually 110,000.

[D] MONASTERIES AND RESIDENCES OF PRIESTS AND BROTHERS

BEAUMONT. *Holy Cross Monastery*, 9920 N. Major Dr., 77713-7618. Tel: 409-899-3554; Fax: 409-899-3558. Email: porter@holycrossmonks.org. Web: www.holycrossmonks.org. Benedictine Monks

[E] NEWMAN CENTERS

BEAUMONT. *Lamar University-Catholic Student Center* 1010 E. Virginia, P.O. Box 10095, 77710. Tel: 409-835-3972; Fax: 409-832-4129. Email: youthandcampus@dioceseofbmt.org. Mr. Tommy Chatlosh, Dir.; Ms. Gina DeCuir, Sec. & Coord. of Campus Activities.

[F] RETREAT CENTERS

BEAUMONT. *Holy Family Retreat Center*, 9920 N. Major Dr., 77713-7618. Tel: 409-899-5617; Fax: 409-899-3161. Email: retreatcenter@dioceseofbmt.org. Web: www.dioceseofbmt.org/hfrc.htm. Rev. Peter C. Funk, Dir.; Bro. Michael Gallagher, Asst. Dir.

[G] SOCIAL AGENCIES - Catholic Charities of the Diocese of Beaumont, Inc.

BEAUMONT. *Catholic Charities of the Diocese of Beaumont, Inc.*, P.O. Box 829, 77704-0829.
Physical Address, 1410 North St., 77701-1741. Tel: 409-835-7118; Fax: 409-832-0145. Email: catholiccharities@catholiccharitiesbmt.org. Web: www.catholiccharitiesbmt.org. Dean Terrebonne, Exec. Dir.
Child Care Contractor Services, 304 Pearl St., 77701. Tel: 409-835-1411; Fax: 409-833-9706. Fran Hulsey, Dir.
Counseling Services, c/o St. Elizabeth Church, 2006 Nall, Port Neches, 77651. Tel: 409-724-0281; Fax: 409-727-8875. Gail P. Rexses, Dir.
Elijah's Place, P.O. Box 829, 77704. Tel: 409-727-1759; Fax: 409-727-8875. Gail P. Rexses, Dir.
Hospitality Center, 3959 Gulfway Dr., Port Arthur, 77642. Tel: 409-982-4842; Fax: 409-983-7145. Michael Perez, Dir.
Immigration Services, 1410 North St., 77701. Tel: 409-835-7118, Ext. 13; Fax: 409-832-0145. Alma Garza-Cruz, Dir.
Parenting Program, 1410 North St., 77701. Tel: 409-835-7118, Ext. 18; Fax: 409-832-0145. Joyce Coratti, Coord.
Parish Social Ministry, 1410 North St., 77701. Tel: 409-835-7118, Ext. 15; Fax: 409-832-0145. Ryan D. White, Dir.
Parish Social Ministry Southern Office, c/o St. James Church, 3617 Gulfway Dr., Port Arthur, 77642. Tel: 409-984-5204; Fax: 409-985-3847. Christina Vara, Coord.

[H] FOUNDATIONS, ENDOWMENTS AND TRUSTS

BEAUMONT. *St. Anne School Foundation, Inc.*, Formerly St. Anne's Catholic School Foundation375 N. 11th St., 77702. Tel: 409-832-5939; Fax: 409-832-4655. Web: www.stannecatholic.org.
St. Anthony School Foundation, Inc., Formerly St. Anthony Cathedral School Foundation850 Forsythe, 77701. Tel: 409-832-3486; Fax: 409-838-9051. Web: stanthonycathedralschool.org. Poncho Russell, Pres.
Catholic Clerical Student Fund, P.O. Box 3948, 77704-3948.
The Catholic Foundation of the Diocese of Beaumont, Inc, P.O. Box 3948, 77704-3948. Tel: 409-838-0451, Ext. 134; Fax: 409-838-4511. Rev. Msgr. Richard A. DeStefano, Pres. (Retired); Russell J. Chimeno, C.P.A., Sec. Treas.
Monsignor Kelly Catholic High School Foundation, Inc., 5950 Kelly Dr., 77707. Tel: 409-866-2351; Fax: 409-866-0917. Email: lmann@kelly.beaumont.tx.us. Lee Mann, Dir.

NEDERLAND. *Rev. Herman Vincent Scholarship Fund* Nederland , 130 Hardy St., 77627. Tel: 409-722-3413; Fax: 409-722-2020. Rev. Dan Malain, Admin.

ORANGE. *St. Mary School Foundation, Inc.*, Formerly St. Mary School Foundation912 Cherry St., 77630. Tel: 409-883-2883; Fax: 409-883-3547. Email: stmary@exp.net.

PORT ARTHUR. *St. Catherine School Foundation*, 3840 Woodrow Dr., 77642. Tel: 409-962-3011.
St. Mary Hospital Foundation, Formerly St. Mary Hospital Foundation of Port Arthur3619

Professional Dr., 77642. Tel: 409-983-5065; Fax: 409-983-5780. Email: brendadrago@christus.org. Brenda Drago, Exec. Dir., Pres.

[I] MISCELLANEOUS

BEAUMONT. *Abiding Place Catholic Charismatic Renewal Center*, 4440 Chaison, 77705. Tel: 409-839-8788. Ms. Nita Chavis, Dir.

St. Thomas More Society of Southeast Texas, 2195 Dowlen Rd., 77706. Tel: 409-866-3318; Fax: 409-866-5789. Email: patrick@heartfieldmcginnis.com. Mr. Patrick Connell McGinnis, Pres.; Rev. Luong Quang Tran, Chap.

ANAHUAC. *Third Order Missionaries of Charity Universal Fraternity of the Word*, P.O. Box 507, 77514. Tel: 409-267-3158; Fax: 409-267-4047. Rev. Angelo Scolozzi, U.F.W., Dir.

PORT ARTHUR. *Apostleship of the Sea of the United States of America (AOSUSA)*, 1500 Jefferson Dr., 77642-0646. Tel: 409-985-4545; Fax: 409-985-5945. Email: aosusa@stellamaris.net. Revs. Sinclair Oubre, J.C.L., Pres.; John A. Jamnicky (CHI), Natl. Dir.

RELIGIOUS INSTITUTES OF MEN REPRESENTED IN THE DIOCESE

For further details refer to the corresponding bracketed number in the Religious Institutes of Men or Women section.

[0140]—*The Augustinians* (Prov. of Castile, Spain)—O.S.A.

[0600]—*Brothers of the Congregation of Holy Cross* (Southwest Prov.)—C.S.C.

[0275]—*Carmelites of Mary Immaculate* (Chanda, India)—C.M.I.

[0275]—*Carmelites of Mary Immaculate* (Kerala, India)—C.M.I.

[0650]—*Congregation of the Holy Ghost*—C.S.Sp.

[]—*Congregation of the Mother Coredemptrix* (Missouri)—C.M.C.

[0720]—*The Missionaries of Our Lady of La Salette* (Prov. of Mary Queen)—M.S.

[]—*Missionaries of St. Paul*—M.S.P.

[0910]—*Oblates of Mary Immaculate* (Southern Prov.)—O.M.I.

[0420]—*Society of the Divine Word* (Southern Province of St. Augustin)—S.V.D.

[0700]—*St. Joseph's Society of the Sacred Heart* (Baltimore)—S.S.J.

RELIGIOUS INSTITUTES OF WOMEN REPRESENTED IN THE DIOCESE

[2190]—*Congregation of the Incarnate Word and Blessed Sacrament* (Houston, TX)—C.V.I.

[2200]—*Congregation of the Incarnate Word and Blessed Sacrament* (Victoria)—I.W.B.S.

[0470]—*Congregation of the Sisters of Charity of the Incarnate Word* (Houston, TX)—C.C.V.I.

[1070-19]—*Dominican Sisters*—O.P.

[1140]—*Eucharistic Missionaries of St. Dominic* (New Orleans)—O.P.

[]—*Sisters of Mercy* (St. Louis, MO)—R.S.M.

[1650]—*Sisters of St. Francis of Philadelphia*—O.S.F.

[]—*Sisters of the Holy Spirit and Holy Family* (Saltillo, Coahuila, Mexico)—M.E.S.S.F.

[2050]—*Sisters of the Holy Spirit and Mary Immaculate*—S.H.Sp.

[2205]—*Sisters of the Incarnate Word and Blessed Sacrament* (Corpus Christi)—I.W.B.S.

[]—*Vietnamese Dominican Sisters* (Houston)—O.P.

NECROLOGY

† Colbert, John—Died Dec. 6, 2002

† Turner, Patrick Arthur, Orange, TX St. Helen—Died March 31, 2003

Diocese of Belleville

(Dioecesis Bellevillensis)

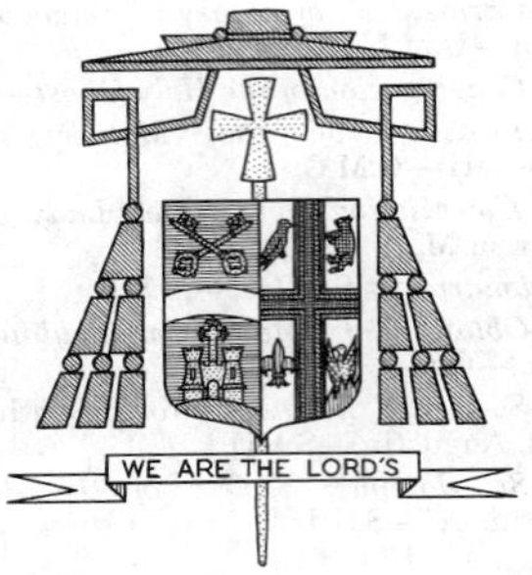

Most Reverend

WILTON D. GREGORY, S.L.D.

Bishop of Belleville; ordained May 9, 1973; appointed Auxiliary Bishop of Chicago and Titular Bishop of Oliva October 31, 1983; consecrated December 13, 1983; appointed Bishop of Belleville December 29, 1993; installed February 10, 1994 *Mailing Address: The Chancery*, 222 S. Third St., Belleville, IL 62220. Tel: 618-277-8181.

The Chancery: 222 S. Third St., Belleville, IL 62220-1985. Tel: 618-277-8181; 618-397-1279; Fax: 618-277-0387.

Web: www.diobelle.org

Email: info@diobelle.org

ERECTED JANUARY 7, 1887.

Square Miles 11,678.

Comprises Illinois south of the northern limits of the counties of St. Clair, Clinton, Marion, Clay, Richland and Lawrence.

For legal titles of parishes and diocesan institutions, consult the Chancery Office.

STATISTICAL OVERVIEW

Personnel	
Bishop	1
Priests: Diocesan Active in Diocese	80
Priests: Diocesan Active Outside Diocese	3
Priests: Retired, Sick or Absent	50
Number of Diocesan Priests	133
Religious Priests in Diocese	45
Total Priests in Diocese	178
Extern Priests in Diocese	6
Ordinations:	
Diocesan Priests	1
Transitional Deacons	1
Permanent Deacons in Diocese	28
Total Brothers	13
Total Sisters	224
Parishes	
Parishes	124
With Resident Pastor:	
Resident Diocesan Priests	76
Resident Religious Priests	1
Without Resident Pastor:	
Administered by Priests	35
Administered by Deacons	2
Administered by Religious Women	5
Administered by Lay People	5
Professional Ministry Personnel:	
Sisters	20
Lay Ministers	25
Welfare	
Catholic Hospitals	6
Total Assisted	607,037
Homes for the Aged	3
Total Assisted	299
Day Care Centers	5
Total Assisted	309
Specialized Homes	1
Total Assisted	150
Special Centers for Social Services	3
Total Assisted	26,835
Educational	
Diocesan Students in Other Seminaries	9
Total Seminarians	9
High Schools, Diocesan and Parish	3
Total Students	1,561
Elementary Schools, Diocesan and Parish	34
Total Students	6,181
Catechesis/Religious Education:	
High School Students	1,361
Elementary Students	6,837
Total Students under Catholic Instruction	15,949
Teachers in the Diocese:	
Priests	1
Brothers	1
Sisters	20
Lay Teachers	493
Vital Statistics	
Receptions into the Church:	
Infant Baptism Totals	1,464
Adult Baptism Totals	247
Received into Full Communion	257
First Communions	1,533
Confirmations	1,566
Marriages:	
Catholic	372
Interfaith	285
Total Marriages	657
Deaths	1,308
Total Catholic Population	103,818
Total Population	845,762

Former Bishops—Most Revs. JOHN JANSSEN, D.D., ord. Nov. 19, 1858; consecrated April 25, 1888; died July 2, 1913; HENRY J. ALTHOFF, D.D., ord. July 26, 1902; appt. Dec. 4, 1913; consecrated Feb. 24, 1914; died July 3, 1947; ALBERT R. ZUROWESTE, D.D. (Retired), ord. June 8, 1924; appt. Nov. 29, 1947; consecrated Jan. 29, 1948; retired Sept. 3, 1976; died March 28, 1987; WILLIAM M. COSGROVE, D.D. (Retired), ord. Dec. 18, 1943; Auxiliary Bishop of Cleveland June 19, 1968; consecrated Sept. 3, 1968; appt. Bishop of Belleville Sept. 3, 1976; installed Oct. 28, 1976; retired May 19, 1981; died Dec. 11, 1992; JOHN N. WURM, S.T.D., Ph.D., ord. April 3, 1954; Auxiliary Bishop of St. Louis June 25, 1976; consecrated Aug. 17, 1976; appt. Bishop of Belleville Sept. 19, 1981; installed Nov. 4, 1981; died April 27, 1984; JAMES P. KELEHER, S.T.D., M.Ed., ord. April 12, 1958; appt. Bishop of Belleville Oct. 23, 1984; consecrated Dec. 11, 1984; transferred to Kansas City, KS Sept. 8, 1993.

Diocese of Belleville Chancery Office—222 S. Third St., Belleville, 62220-1985. Tel: 618-277-8181; 618-397-1279; Fax: 618-277-0387.

Diocesan Pastoral Center—2620 Lebanon Ave., Belleville, 62221. Tel: 618-235-9601; Fax: 618-235-7416.

Vicar General—Rev. Msgr. JAMES E. MARGASON, V.G., M.Div., J.C.L.

Moderator of the Curia—Rev. Msgr. JAMES E. MARGASON, V.G., M.Div., J.C.L.

Chancellor—Rev. KENNETH J. YORK, J.C.L.

Vice-Chancellor—DAVID R. SPOTANSKI.

Secretary to the Bishop—Mrs. PATRICIA SCHILLING.

Archivist—Sr. MARY KENAN WOLFF, S.S.N.D., 220 W. Lincoln St., Belleville, 62220. Tel: 618-234-3157.

Diocesan Tribunal—Diocesan Pastoral Center, 2620 Lebanon Ave., Belleville, 62221. Tel: 618-212-0050; Fax: 618-212-0055. Address all rogatory commissions to the Chancellor at the Chancery.

Judicial Vicar—Rev. JAMES M. NALL, J.C.L.

Adjutant Judicial Vicar—Rev. PAUL R. WIENHOFF.

Judges—Rev. Msgr. JAMES E. MARGASON, V.G., M.Div., J.C.L.; Sr. MARY KATHLEEN KUENSTLER, P.H.J.C., J.C.D.

Promoter Justitiae—Rev. PAUL WIENHOFF, J.C.L.

Defensores Vinculi—Rev. Msgrs. DONALD W. EICHENSEER; THOMAS D. FLACH; Rev. PAUL WIENHOFF, J.C.L.; Mr. PATRICK MATHIS; Very Rev. MARK D. REYLING, V.F.

Advocate—Very Rev. JOHN T. MYLER, V.F., D.Min.

Notaries—RENEE QUIRIN; JACQUELINE MATT.

Diocesan Consultors—Rev. Msgrs. JAMES E. MARGASON, V.G., M.Div., J.C.L.; THEODORE J. BAUMANN; JEROME D. HARTLEIN; WILLIAM J. HITPAS; KENNETH J. SCHAEFER; MARVIN C. VOLK; Rev. BRIAN BARKER; Very Rev. JOHN T. MYLER, V.F., D.Min.; Revs. JAMES M. NALL, J.C.L.; PATRICK N. PETER; EUGENE H. WOJCIK.

Diocesan Deans—Very Revs. JOHN T. MYLER, V.F., D.Min., Belleville Deanery; MARK D. REYLING, V.F., East St. Louis Deanery; MARK D. STEC, V.F., East Deanery; DAVID M. DARIN, V.F., North Central Deanery; THOMAS STOUT, V.F., West Deanery; ROBERT B. FLANNERY, V.F., South Deanery.

Diocesan Finance Office—WILLIAM J. KNAPP, CFO; DAVID WAELTZ, Comptroller, Chancery Office. Tel: 618-277-8181; Fax: 618-277-0819.

Diocesan Finance Council—DEBI EDWARDS, Chm.; Rev. Msgr. JAMES E. MARGASON, V.G., M.Div., J.C.L.; WILLIAM J. KNAPP; J. ROY DEE III; ARTHUR HAMPTON; IRENE KRUSE; Rev. Msgrs. THOMAS MILLER; DONALD W. EICHENSEER; JEFF RENNER; Sr. JAN RENZ, A.S.C.; DENISE SCHABERG; JACKIE SETTLES; JOHN SMITH.

Diocesan Pastoral Council—Executive Committee: Sr. MARY CATHERINE CLARK, A.S.C.; MARGIE JONES; KATHY MULVIN. Tel: 618-277-8181; Fax: 618-277-0387.

Building Commission, Chancery Office—Rev. Msgr. JEROME D. HARTLEIN, Chm.

Campaign for Human Development—Rev. J. CLYDE GROGAN, Dir., 771 Vogel Pl., East St. Louis, 62205. Tel: 618-874-5025.

Catholic Charities of Southern Illinois—, Formerly Catholic Charities*222 S. Third St., Belleville, 62220.* ROBERT OTREMBIAK, Dir., 2620 Lebanon Ave., Belleville, 62221. Tel: 618-235-9601. Email: rotrembiak@diobelle.org.

Catholic Social Service of Southern Illinois—DAVID WENZEL, Dir., Office, 8601 W. Main St., Ste. 201, Belleville, 62223. Tel: 618-394-5900; Fax: 618-394-5909. Email: davew@cssil.org; Branch Offices, 216 S. University, Carbondale, 62901. Tel: 618-351-0743. 1 Doctor's Park Rd., Ste. H, Mt. Vernon, 62864. Tel: 618-244-0344. 120 W. Fifth St., P.O. Box 23, Mt. Carmel, 62863. Tel: 618-263-3863. 509 N. Second St., Breese, 62230. Tel: 618-526-2267.

Catholic Urban Programs—JOSEPH P. HUBBARD, Coord., 771 Vogel Pl., East St. Louis, 62205. Tel: 618-398-5616; Fax: 618-274-4659.

Holy Angels Shelter—PATRICIA LEWIS, Dir., 1410 N. 37th St., East St. Louis, 62204. Tel: 618-874-4079.

Griffin Center—Sr. JULIA HUISKAMP, D.C., Dir., 2630 Lincoln Ave., East St. Louis, 62204. Tel: 618-874-2500. De Shields-Robinson Center, 1235 McCasland, East St. Louis, 62201. Tel: 618-874-0637. Roosevelt Center, 400 Bunkum Rd., East

St. Louis, 62204. Tel: 618-271-9859. Weather-Owens Center, 1400 Missouri Ave., D-1 Bldg., East St. Louis, 62201. Tel: 618-875-0535.
Family Center—Sr. CAROL LEHMKUHL, O.P., 705 Summit, East St. Louis, 62201. Tel: 618-875-7295.
St. Regis Center After School Program—GLENDA DREW, Dir., After School Prog., 3500 Market St., East St. Louis, 62207.
Cemeteries—JOSEPH P. HUBBARD, Dir., Chancery Office.
Child Protection Office—LYNN MUSCARELLO, Dir. Tel: 618-277-8181.
Clergymen's Aid Society—Rev. Msgr. JEROME D. HARTLEIN, Pres., Holy Childhood of Jesus, 104 N. Independence, P.O. Box 160, Mascoutah, 62258. Tel: 618-566-2958.
Diocesan Development Office—MARTIN LEIFELD, Dir.; BARBARA MAYNARD, Assoc. Dir. Stewardship; JUDY PHILLIPS, Assoc. Dir. Foundations & Corporations, Chancery Office. Tel: 618-277-8181; Fax: 618-277-0387.
Diocesan Liturgical Commission—VACANT, Chm. Tel: 618-235-9601.
Diocesan Outreach Apostolate— Serving Alexander and Pulaski Counties. Daystar Community Program, *909 Washington Ave., Cairo, 62914*. Tel: 618-734-0178. JOHN KLEIN, Dir.; SHERRY MILLER, Assoc. Dir.
Diaconate, Office of Permanent—Rev. Msgr. MARVIN C. VOLK, Vicar for Deacons; Deacon RONALD KARCHER, Assoc. Vicar for Deacons, Diocesan Pastoral Center.
Diocesan Council of Catholic Women—Rev. DENNIS F. VOSS, Diocesan Moderator; JULIA "BETTY" VAHLKAMP, Pres., Diocesan Pastoral Center.
Ecumenical and Interreligious Affairs—Very Rev. ROBERT B. FLANNERY, V.F., 303 S. Poplar St., Carbondale, 62901. Tel: 618-457-4556.
Formation of Priests—Rev. JAMES R. DEITERS, Chm., 205 W. Third St., O'Fallon, 62269. Tel: 618-632-3562.
Office of Education—THOMAS H. POSNANSKI, Dir., Diocesan Pastoral Center.
Department of Elementary Education—Sr. KATHLEEN KOENEN, S.S.N.D., Dir.
Religious Education and Catechesis—RUSSELL PETERSON, Assoc. Dir.
Diocesan Board of Education—THOMAS H. POSNANSKI, Pres.
Guatemala Mission Society—JOSEPHINE FITCH, Chm., 803 Joliet Dr., Cahokia, 62206. Tel: 618-337-5981.
Hispanic Ministry—Sr. CECILIA MARIE HELLMANN, A.S.C., Dir., 2620 Lebanon Ave., Belleville, 62221. Tel: 618-235-9601.
Holy Childhood Association—Rev. KENNETH J. YORK, J.C.L., Dir., Chancery.
Hospitals—Rev. EUGENE J. NEFF, Delegate, Ministry to Sick and Aged, 2620 Lebanon Ave., Belleville, 62221. Tel: 618-235-9991.
Insurance Commission—WILLIAM J. KNAPP, Dir., Chancery Office.
Catholic Mutual Group—WILLIAM P. JOHNSON, Claims/ Risk Mgr., Diocesan Pastoral Center. Tel: 618-233-1090.
Ministry to Priests Office—Rev. WILLIAM HARTENBACH, C.M., Minister to Priests.
Pastoral Services—TOM SMITH, Dir.; SUE HUETT, Assoc. Dir. Worship & Family Life, Diocesan Pastoral Center; GREG ROHDE, Assoc. Dir. Lay Ministry.
Natural Family Planning—Catholic Social Services, 617 S. Belt W., Belleville, 62220-2414. Tel: 618-277-9200.
Newman Catholic Student Center—DONALD MARKOVITCH, Acting Dir., 715 S. Washington St., Carbondale, 62901. Tel: 618-529-3311; Ms. MARY MERTZLUFFT, Campus Min.
Newman Auxiliary—MARGE MANGAN, Pres., 9741 Stilley's Mill Dr., Marion, 62959. Tel: 618-982-2218.
Newspaper, "The Messenger"—LIZ QUIRIN, Editor, Diocesan Pastoral Center.
Ondessonk, Camp— Diocese of Belleville, Department of Outdoor Education: PATRICK R. HIGGINS, Exec. Dir., 3760 Ondessonk Rd., Ozark, 62972. Tel: 618-695-2489; Fax: 618-695-3593.
Priests Organizations—
Confraternity of Catholic Clergy—VACANT.
Southern Illinois Association of Priests—Rev. GEORGE A. MAUCK, Chm., 1171 Jefferson, Carlyle, 62231. Tel: 618-594-2225.
Pro-Life Office—ANN POLKA, Chm., Diocesan Pastoral Center.
Propagation of the Faith—Rev. KENNETH J. YORK, J.C.L., Dir., Chancery.
Office for Professional Fitness Review—PATRICIA KIEVLAN KEELEY, 222 South Third St., Belleville, 62220. Tel: 618-236-1812; 800-640-3044.
Office of Youth Ministry—COLETTE KENNETT, Dir.; Rev. BERNARD C. GOEDDE JR., Spiritual Moderator; JAMES KEIM, Athletic Dir., Diocesan Pastoral Center.
Rural Life Conference—Rev. ANDREW LINTKER, Dir., 7970 Primrose Rd., Venedy, 62214. Tel: 618-824-6346.
St. Vincent DePaul Society—RAY BERKEL, Admin., 3718 State St., East St. Louis, 62205. Tel: 618-397-3113.
Sick and Aged (Ministry)—Rev. EUGENE J. NEFF, Dir., Diocesan Pastoral Center. Tel: 618-235-9991.
Victim Assistance Coordinator—LYNN MUSCARELLO. Tel: 618-277-8181. Email: lmuscarello@diobelle.org.
Vocation Office—Rev. EUGENE H. WOJCIK, Dir., Diocesan Pastoral Center.

CLERGY, PARISHES, MISSIONS AND PAROCHIAL SCHOOLS

CITY OF BELLEVILLE
(ST. CLAIR COUNTY)

1—CATHEDRAL OF ST. PETER (1842), [CEM] Rev. Msgr. James A. Buerster, Rector; Rev. John Higgins; Deacons Robert Becker; Joseph Stock; Donald Deitz.
Res.: 200 W. Harrison, 62220-2090. Tel: 618-234-1166; Fax: 618-234-2957.
School—Cathedral School, 200 S. Second St., 62220. Tel: 618-233-6414; Fax: 618-233-3587. Sr. Ruth Ann Klauser, S.S.N.D., Prin. School Sisters of Notre Dame 1; Lay Teachers 21; Students 300.
Catechesis/Religious Program—Sr. Theresa Markus, S.S.N.D., D.R.E.; Miss Jane Stock, D.R.E. Students 165.
Convent—300 S. Second St., 62220. Tel: 618-233-3580.
2—ST. AUGUSTINE OF CANTERBURY (1955), Rev. Andrew J. Knopik.
Res.: 1910 W. Belle, 62226. Tel: 618-233-3813; Fax: 618-233-3946.
School—1900 Canterbury Dr., 62226. Tel: 618-234-4958; Fax: 618-234-3360. Sr. Ann Marie Bonvie, S.S.N.D., Prin. Lay Teachers 16; Students 200.
Catechesis/Religious Program—Students 34.
3—BLESSED SACRAMENT (1927), Rev. Msgr. Marvin C. Volk.
Res.: 8707 W. Main St., 62223. Tel: 618-397-2287; Fax: 618-397-2269.
School—8801 W. Main St., 62223 Tel: 618-397-1111; Fax: 618-397-8431. Ms. Claire Hatch, Prin. School Sisters of Notre Dame 2; Lay Teachers 13; Students 190.
Catechesis/Religious Program—Students 50.
Convent—8901 W. Main St., 62233. Tel: 618-397-0039.
4—CHAPEL OF ST. JOHN CHILDREN'S HOME, [CEM] Rev. Msgr. James E. Margason, V.G., M.Div., J.C.L. Mailing Address: Chancery Office, 222 S. Third St., 62220. Tel: 618-277-8181; Fax: 618-277-0387.
5—ST. HENRY (1925), Rev. Msgr. Bernard L. Voss.
Res.: 5315 W. Main St., 62223. Tel: 618-233-2423; Fax: 618-233-9879.
School—5303 W. Main St., 62223. Tel: 618-234-6061; Fax: 618-234-6801. Mr. Leo Hodapp, Prin. Lay Teachers 12; Students 101.
Catechesis/Religious Program—Students 78.
6—ST. LUKE (1883), Rev. Msgr. James E. Margason, V.G., M.Div., J.C.L.; Sr. Grace Marie Mueller, S.S.N.D., Pastoral Assoc. Tel: 618-236-1839; Fax: 618-236-1839; Deacon Robert Lanter.
Res.: 301 N. Church St., 62220. Tel: 618-236-1124; Fax: 618-236-1134.
Catechesis/Religious Program—Tel: 618-236-1839. Students 70.
7—ST. MARY (1893), Very Rev. John T. Myler, V.F., D.Min.
Res.: 1706 W. Main St., 62226. Tel: 618-233-2391; Fax: 618-233-9201.
School—1722 W. Main St., 62226. Tel: 618-234-2476; Fax: 618-234-0267. Mrs. Joan Dohle, Prin. Sisters 1; Lay Teachers 8; Students 115.
Catechesis/Religious Program—Students 68.
8—OUR LADY QUEEN OF PEACE (1955), Rev. John W. McEvilly.
Res.: 5923 N. Belt W., 62223. Tel: 618-234-6196; Fax: 618-234-6217.
School—5915 N. Belt W., 62223. Tel: 618-234-1206; Fax: 618-234-6123. Mrs. Frances Smith, Prin. Lay Teachers 18; Students 282.
Catechesis/Religious Program—Students 24.
9—ST. TERESA OF THE CHILD JESUS (1926),, (Little Flower) Very Rev. John L. Venegoni; Rev. Trevor Murry.
Res.: 1201 Lebanon Ave., 62221. Tel: 618-233-3500; Fax: 618-233-9703.
School—1108 Lebanon Ave., 62221 Tel: 618-235-4066; Fax: 618-235-7930. Sr. Kathleen Koenen, S.S.N.D., Acting Prin. Lay Teachers 20; Students 293.
Catechesis/Religious Program—Tel: 618-233-3550. Students 132.

OUTSIDE THE CITY OF BELLEVILLE

ALBERS, CLINTON CO., ST. BERNARD (1908), [CEM] Rev. Msgr. Donald W. Eichenseer.
Res.: 202 N. Broadway, P.O. Box 10, 62215. Tel: 618-248-5112; Fax: 618-248-5112.
Catechesis/Religious Program—Sr. Joan Stoverink, A.S.C., D.R.E. Students 144.
ANNA, UNION CO., ST. MARY (1857), Rev. Msgr. Thomas W. Miller; Sr. Joan Backes, S.S.N.D., Pastoral Assoc. & D.R.E.
Res.: 402 Freeman, 62906. Tel: 618-833-5835; Fax: 618-833-5835.
Catechesis/Religious Program—Tel: 618-833-3131. Students 105.
AVA, JACKSON CO., ST. ELIZABETH (1890), Rev. Leo J. Hayes.
Res.: 606 W. George St., P.O. Box 157, 62907. Tel: 618-426-3321; Fax: 608-426-3321.
Catechesis/Religious Program—Students 4.
AVISTON, CLINTON CO., ST. FRANCIS OF ASSISI (1865), (German), [CEM] Rev. Daniel L. Friedman; Deacons Gerald E. Stockman; Charles Litteken.
Res.: 251 S. Clinton, Box 93, 62216. Tel: 618-228-7219; Fax: 618-228-7320.
Catechesis/Religious Program—Tel: 618-228-7245; Fax: 618-228-7320. Students 250.
BARTELSO, CLINTON CO., ST. CECILIA (1885), (German), Rev. Henry J. Fischer.
Res.: 304 S. Washington St., P.O. Box 176, 62218. Tel: 618-765-2162; Fax: 618-765 2264.
Catechesis/Religious Program—Tel: 618-765-2163. Betty Budde, D.R.E.; Ellen Huegen, D.R.E. Students 248.
BEAVER PRAIRIE, CLINTON CO., ST. FELICITAS (1883), [CEM] Very Rev. David M. Darin, V.F., Canonical Pastor; Rev. Lawrence M. Nickels, O.F.M.; Sr. Diane M. Turner, S.S.N.D., Pastoral Life Coord. Mailing Address: 13322 Church Rd., Carlyle, 62231. Tel: 618-594-3040; Fax: 618-594-3040.
Catechesis/Religious Program—Students 46.
BECKEMEYER, CLINTON CO., ST. ANTHONY (1905), [CEM] Rev. Charles W. Tuttle; Deacon Robert Lippert.
Res.: P.O. Box 305, 62219. Tel: 618-227-8236; Fax: 618-227-8630.
Catechesis/Religious Program—Students 53.
BENTON, FRANKLIN CO., ST. JOSEPH (1872), [CEM] Rev. Joseph L. Trapp.
Res.: 506 W. Main, 62812. Tel: 618-438-9941; Fax: 618-438-9941.
Catechesis/Religious Program—Tel: 618-438-0009. Students 60.
BREESE, CLINTON CO.
1—ST. AUGUSTINE (1912), [CEM] Rev. Charles W. Tuttle; Deacon Robert Lippert.
Res.: 525 S. Third St., 62230. Tel: 618-526-4362; Fax: 618-526-4362.
Catechesis/Religious Program—Students 65.
2—ST. DOMINIC (1857), [CEM] Rev. Valentine J. Peter, S.T.D., J.C.D. (OM).
Res.: 493 N. Second St., 62230. Tel: 618-526-7746; Fax: 618-526-7755.
Catechesis/Religious Program—Tel: 618-526-8144. Mrs. Sue Darr, D.R.E. Students 117.
BRIDGEPORT, LAWRENCE CO., IMMACULATE CONCEPTION (1856), [CEM] Rev. Thomas Barrett.
Mailing Address: 1006 Collins, Lawrenceville, 62439. Tel: 618-943-5255.
Catechesis/Religious Program—Students 13.
CAHOKIA, ST. CLAIR CO.
1—ST. CATHERINE LABOURE (1959), Very Rev. Mark D. Reyling, V.F.
Res.: 913 Rome Ln., 62206. Tel: 618-337-4173; Fax: 618-337-1231.
School—Corpus Christi, 116 Church St., East St. Louis, 62206. Tel: 618-337-2880.
School—Day Care, 1826 Jerome Ln., East St. Louis, 62206. Tel: 618-337-3555.
Catechesis/Religious Program—Students 135.
2—HOLY FAMILY (1699), [CEM 3] Rev. Gerald R. Hechenberger.
Res.: 116 Church St., 62206. Tel: 618-337-4548; Fax: 618-332-1699.
Catechesis/Religious Program—Students 5.
CAIRO, ALEXANDER CO., ST. PATRICK (1838), [CEM] Rev. Jerome D. Fortenberry, C.M.
Res.: 312 Ninth St., 62914. Tel: 618-734-2061.
CARBONDALE, JACKSON CO., ST. FRANCIS XAVIER (1900), Very Rev. Robert B. Flannery, V.F.
Res.: 303 S. Poplar St., 62901. Tel: 618-457-4556; Fax: 618-457-7368.
Catechesis/Religious Program—Toni Intravaia,

D.R.E. Students 199.
CARLYLE, CLINTON CO., ST. MARY (1853), [CEM], (Immaculate Conception) Rev. George A. Mauck.
Res.: 12th St. & Jefferson St., Box 179, 62231. Tel: 618-594-2225; Fax: 618-594-4638.
Catechesis / Religious Program—Tel: 618-594-2284; Fax: 618-594-4638. Sr. Geraldine Neier, S.S.N.D., D.R.E. Students 322.
CARMI, WHITE CO., ST. POLYCARP (GERMAN) (1847), [CEM] Rev. Stephen A. Rudolphi.
Res.: 209 Fourth St., 62821. Tel: 618-382-7732.
Catechesis / Religious Program—Students 29.
CARTERVILLE, WILLIAMSON CO., CHURCH OF THE HOLY SPIRIT (1974), Rev. Msgr. William P. McGhee, Canonical Pastor; Sr. Carol Karnitsky, SSCM, Parish Life Coord.
Office: 300 N. Pine St., 62918. Tel: 618-985-2900; 618-925-5099; Fax: 618-985-9330.
Catechesis / Religious Program—Tel: 618-985-6929. Students 105.
CASEYVILLE, ST. CLAIR CO., ST. STEPHEN (1893), Rev. Joseph C. Rascher; Deacon William DeWolf.
Res.: 901 S. Main St., P.O. Box 458, 62232. Tel: 618-397-0666; Fax: 618-397-4430.
Catechesis / Religious Program—Students 47.
CENTRALIA, MARION CO., ST. MARY (1857), [CEM] Very Rev. David M. Darin, V.F.
Res.: 424 E. Broadway, 62801. Tel: 618-532-5041.
Church Office: 424 E. Broadway, 62801. Tel: 618-532-6291; Fax: 618-532-4758.
School—Tel: 618-532-3473; Fax: 618-532-5180. Sr. Barbara Habing, S.S.N.D., Prin. Sisters 1; Lay Teachers 8; Students 121.
Catechesis / Religious Program—Sr. Carol Markus, S.S.N.D., D.R.E. Students 55.
CENTREVILLE, ST. CLAIR CO., IMMACULATE CONCEPTION (1858), [CEM] Very Rev. Mark D. Reyling, V.F., Canonical Pastor; James Byrd, Parish Life Coord.
Res.: 6210 Church Rd., 62207. Tel: 618-337-5682; 618-337-7493; Fax: 618-337-7493.
CHESTER, RANDOLPH CO., ST. MARY HELP OF CHRISTIANS (1842), [CEM] Rev. Msgr. Dennis R. Schaefer.
Res.: 911 Swanwick St., 62233. Tel: 618-826-2444; Fax: 618-826-3486.
School—Tel: 618-826-3120; Fax: 618-826-3486. Mrs. Janelle Robinson, Prin. Lay Teachers 10; Pre-School 34; K-8 37.
Catechesis / Religious Program—Tel: 618-826-2526. Cheryl Gross, D.R.E. Students 45.
CHRISTOPHER, FRANKLIN CO., ST. ANDREW (1905), [CEM] Rev. Steven F. Poole.
Res.: 412 E. Washington St., 62822. Tel: 618-724-4114.
Catechesis / Religious Program—Elaine Polbinski, D.R.E. Students 59.
COBDEN, UNION CO., ST. JOSEPH (1883), [CEM] Rev. Federico Higuera; Deacon Patrick Patterson.
Res.: 101 Centennial St., P.O. Box 237, 62920. Tel: 618-893-2276.
Catechesis / Religious Program—Tel: 618-893-2368. Students 97.
COLUMBIA, MONROE CO., IMMACULATE CONCEPTION OF THE B.V.M. (1846), [CEM] Rev. Msgr. Carl E. Scherrer; Rev. Steve Gira, C.R.
Res.: 117 E. Madison, 62236. Tel: 618-281-5105; Fax: 618-281-6848.
School—Tel: 618-281-5353; Fax: 618-281-6044. Michael Kish, Prin. Lay Teachers 21; Students 358.
Catechesis / Religious Program—Students 151.
COULTERVILLE, RANDOLPH CO., ST. ANTHONY, Closed. For inquiries for parish records contact the chancery.
DAHLGREN, HAMILTON CO., ST. JOHN NEPOMUCENE (1893), (German), [CEM] Rev. Msgr. Joseph A. Lawlor.
Church: 7th & Main Sts., P.O. Box 220, 62828. Tel: 618-736-2879; 618-643-3552; Fax: 618-643-3112.
Res.: Rte. 3, Box 170, McLeansboro, 62859.
Catechesis / Religious Program—Tel: 618-643-3552. Rita Rapp, D.R.E. Students 58.
DAMIANSVILLE, CLINTON CO., ST. DAMIAN (1861), [CEM] Rev. Msgr. Donald W. Eichenseer.
One W. Main St., 62215. Tel: 618-248-5134; Fax: 618-248-5134.
Res.: 202 N. Broadway, Albers, 62215. Tel: 618-248-5112; Fax: 618-248-5112.
Catechesis / Religious Program—Students 108.
DU QUOIN, PERRY CO., SACRED HEART OF JESUS (1863), [CEM] Rev. Msgr. Harry J. Jerome.
Res.: 17 N. Walnut St., 62832. Tel: 618-542-3423; Fax: 618-542-2329.
School—Tel: 618-542-2335. Bonnie L. Paszkiewicz, Prin. Lay Teachers 6; Students 34.
Catechesis / Religious Program—Students 28.
DUBOIS, WASHINGTON CO., ST. CHARLES BORROMEO (1877), [CEM] Rev. Msgr. Melvin Vandeloo.
Res.: P.O. Box 6, 62831. Tel: 618-787-2781; Fax: 618-787-2171.
Catechesis / Religious Program—Students 22.
DUPO, ST. CLAIR CO., SACRED HEART OF JESUS (1914), Rev. Gerald R. Hechenberger.
100 S. 3rd St., 62239. Tel: 618-286-3224.
Catechesis / Religious Program—Tel: 618-337-4548. Students 35.
EAST ST. LOUIS, ST. CLAIR CO.
1—IMMACULATE CONCEPTION (1895), (Lithuanian), Rev. Kenneth J. York, J.C.L., Admin.
1509 Baugh Ave., 62205. Tel: 618-874-0162.
2—ST. JOHN FRANCIS REGIS (1901), Rev. J. Clyde Grogan.
3500 Market Ave., 62207. Tel: 618-874-5025.
3—ST. JOSEPH (1902), (African American), Rev. James A. Voelker.
Res.: 408 Columbia Pl., 62205. Tel: 618-274-0655.
4—ST. PATRICK (1861), [CEM] Rev. James Clyde Grogan; Deacon John Coates.
Res.: 771 Vogel Pl., 62205. Tel: 618-874-5025; Fax: 618-274-4659.
5—ST. PHILIP (1841), [CEM] Rev. James A. Voelker, Pastor.
Res.: 408 Columbia Pl., 62205. Tel: 618-274-0655.
Church: 8313 Church Ln., 62203. Tel: 618-397-1860.
ELDORADO, SALINE CO., ST. MARY (1900), [CEM] Rev. Donald E. Abell.
Res.: 1158 N. 2nd St., 62930. Tel: 618-273-6947; Fax: 618-273-3147.
Catechesis / Religious Program—Students 87.
ELIZABETHTOWN, HARDIN CO., ST. JOSEPH (1897), [CEM] Rev. Donald E. Abell.
Res.: IL 146-185 E Rd., Box 140, 62931-9711. Tel: 618-285-3332.
Catechesis / Religious Program—Tel: 618-287-4824. Students 16.
ELLIS GROVE, RANDOLPH CO., DIVINE MATERNITY OF THE B.V.M. (1933), Deacon Omer E. DuBois.
Res.: 7362 Shawneetown Tr., 62241. Tel: 618-859-3541.
Catechesis / Religious Program—Students 72.
ENFIELD, WHITE CO., ST. PATRICK (1830), (Irish), [CEM] Rev. Stephen A. Rudolphi.
St. Polycarp Church: 209 Fourth St., Carmi, 62821. Tel: 618-382-7732.
Catechesis / Religious Program—Students 16.
EQUALITY, GALLATIN CO., ST. JOSEPH (1873), [CEM] Very Rev. Mark D. Stec, V.F.
Mailing Address: P.O. Box 99, 62934. Tel: 618-276-4252; Fax: 618-272-5400.
Res.: P.O. Box 190, Ridgway, 62979. Tel: 618-272-7059; Fax: 618-272-5400.
Catechesis / Religious Program—Students 28.
EVANSVILLE, RANDOLPH CO., ST. BONIFACE (1860), [CEM] Rev. John J. Joyce.
Res.: 1007 Olive St., 62242. Tel: 618-853-4453; Fax: 618-853-4453.
Catechesis / Religious Program—Students 26.
FAIRFIELD, WAYNE CO., ST. EDWARD (1881), Rev. Henry R. Engelhart.
Res.: 300 N.W. 5th St., 62837. Tel: 618-847-7931; Fax: 618-842-7393.
Catechesis / Religious Program—Peggy Garrison, D.R.E. Students 46.
FAIRMONT CITY, ST. CLAIR CO., HOLY ROSARY (1922), Rev. David M. Wilke, Pastor.
Res.: 2716 N. 42nd St., 62201. Tel: 618-274-3486; Fax: 618-274-1814.
School—Tel: 618-271-8600; Fax: 618-271-7041. Mrs. Shirley Kurre, Prin. Sisters 1; Lay Teachers 8; Students 140.
Catechesis / Religious Program—Students 50.
FAIRVIEW HEIGHTS, ST. CLAIR CO.
1—HOLY TRINITY - EAST (1951), Rev. James T. Long; Deacon David Bigham.
Res.: 15 E. Lincoln Hwy., 62208. Tel: 618-632-5334; Fax: 618-632-0903.
School—Tel: 618-632-4937; Fax: 618-622-1386. Dr. Raymond Mack, Prin. Sisters 2; Lay Teachers 13; Students 190.
Catechesis / Religious Program—Tel: 618-632-8577. Students 125.
2—HOLY TRINITY - WEST, Rev. Raymond Schultz.
Res.: 9950 Bunkum Rd., 62208. Tel: 618-397-0121; Fax: 618-397-0396.
Catechesis / Religious Program—Students 44.
FAYETTEVILLE, ST. CLAIR CO., ST. PANCRATIUS (1837), [CEM] Rev. Kenneth J. York, J.C.L.
Res.: 2213 N. 2nd St., 62258. Tel: 618-677-2717.
FLORA, CLAY CO., ST. STEPHEN (1854), [CEM] Rev. Msgr. Hyacinth Mazuchowski.
Res.: 812 N. Main St., 62839. Tel: 618-662-6261.
Catechesis / Religious Program—Tel: 618-662-8121. Students 67.
FREEBURG, ST. CLAIR CO., ST. JOSEPH (1857), [CEM] Rev. Msgr. Theodore J. Baumann.
Res.: 9 N. Alton St., 62243. Tel: 618-539-3209.
School—Tel: 618-539-3930; Fax: 618-539-3930. Russell Hart, Prin. Sisters 1; Lay Teachers 10; Students 133.
Catechesis / Religious Program—Tel: 618-539-3209. Students 128.
GERMANTOWN, CLINTON CO., ST. BONIFACE (1837), [CEM] Rev. Stephen J. Humphrey.
Res.: 402 Munster St., Box 280, 62245. Tel: 618-523-4271; Fax: 618-523-4263.
Catechesis / Religious Program—Students 393.
GRAND CHAIN, PULASKI CO., ST. CATHERINE (1891), [CEM] Rev. Msgr. William P. McGhee.
517 N. Walnut St., Box 67, Mound City, 62963. Tel: 618-748-9113; Fax: 618-748-9113.
Catechesis / Religious Program—Students 14.
HARRISBURG, SALINE CO., ST. MARY (1906), [CEM] Rev. Donald E. Abell.
Res.: 2000 W. Poplar St., 62946. Tel: 618-253-7408; Fax: 618-252-7874.
Catechesis / Religious Program—Tel: 618-252-7874. Students 78.
HECKER, MONROE CO., ST. AUGUSTINE OF CANTERBURY (1824), [CEM] Rev. Joseph D. Hansmann.
Res.: 310 N. Main St., P.O. Box 126, 62248. Tel: 618-473-2217; Fax: 618-473-9141.
Catechesis / Religious Program—340 N. Main, 62248. Students 17.
HERRIN, WILLIAMSON CO., OUR LADY OF MOUNT CARMEL (1901), [CEM] Rev. Msgr. Kenneth J. Schaefer.
Res.: 316 W. Monroe St., 62948. Tel: 618-942-3114; Fax: 618-988-1375.
School—Tel: 618-942-4484; Fax: 618-942-2864. Mr. Brett Heinzman, Prin. Lay Teachers 17; Students 265.
Catechesis / Religious Program—Students 63.
JOHNSTON CITY, WILLIAMSON CO., ST. PAUL (1904), Rev. Msgr. Kenneth Schaefer; Sr. Catherine Wellinghoff, A.S.C., Parish Life Coord.
1103 Washington St., 62951. Tel: 618-983-5073.
Catechesis / Religious Program—Students 35.
KASKASKIA, RANDOLPH CO., IMMACULATE CONCEPTION (1675), (French—Native American), [CEM], (Independent Mission) , Mailing Address: 6450 Klein Lane, St. Mary's, MO 63673. Tel: 618-366-2633; Fax: 618-826-2667.
KINMUNDY, MARION CO., ST. ELIZABETH ANN SETON (1878), Darren Eultgen, M.Div., Parish Life Coord.
Mailing Address: 812 W. Main St., Salem, 62881. Tel: 618-548-0899; Fax: 618-548-0269.
Catechesis / Religious Program—N. Madison St., 62854. Tel: 618-245-6221. Denise Kramer, D.R.E. Students 12.
LAWRENCEVILLE, LAWRENCE CO., ST. LAWRENCE (1909), [JC] Rev. Thomas Barrett, Pastor.
Res.: 1006 Collins, 62439. Tel: 618-943-5255.
Catechesis / Religious Program—Students 34.
LEBANON, ST. CLAIR CO., ST. JOSEPH (1862), [CEM] Rev. Msgr. James E. Margason, V.G., M.Div., J.C.L.; Rev. Eugene J. Neff; Deacon Peter Cerneka III; Mrs. Brenda Pehle, Parish Life Coord.
901 N. Alton St., 62254. Tel: 618-537-2575; Fax: 618-537-0147.
Catechesis / Religious Program—Students 70.
LIVELY GROVE, WASHINGTON CO., ST. ANTHONY (1868), [CEM] Rev. Dennis F. Voss. Tel: 618-768-4921.
Church: 6101 St. Anthony Church Rd., Oakdale, 62268. Tel: 618-824-6271.
Catechesis / Religious Program—Tel: 618-824-6271. Students 46.
MADONNAVILLE, MONROE CO., IMMACULATE CONCEPTION (1833), Rev. Edwin H. Hustedde.
Mailing Address: 101 S. Meyer St., Valmeyer, 62295. Tel: 618-935-2247.
Catechesis / Religious Program—Students 7.
MARION, WILLIAMSON CO., ST. JOSEPH (1940), Rev. Richard G. Mohr.
Res.: 600 N. Russell St., P.O. Box 1679, 62959. Tel: 618-993-3194; Fax: 618-997-9391.
Catechesis / Religious Program—Tel: 618-997-7373; Fax: 618-997-9391. Sr. Anastasia Wehner, S.S.N.D., D.R.E. Students 214.
MARYDALE, CLINTON CO., ST. TERESA OF AVILA (1919), Very Rev. David M. Darin, V.F.; Rev. Lawrence M. Nickels, O.F.M.; Sr. Mary Catherine Clark, A.S.C., Parish Life Coord.
18021 Marydale Rd., Carlyle, 62231. Tel: 618-594-3266.
Catechesis / Religious Program—Students 24.
MASCOUTAH, ST. CLAIR CO., HOLY CHILDHOOD OF JESUS (1857), [CEM] Rev. Msgr. Jerome D. Hartlein.
Res.: 104 N. Independence St., P.O. Box 160, 62258. Tel: 618-566-2958; Fax: 618-566-4447.
School—Tel: 618-566-2922; Fax: 618-566-7720. Mr. Ronald Karcher, Prin. Lay Teachers 15; Students 163.
Catechesis / Religious Program—Tel: 618-566-2922. Students 118.
MCLEANSBORO, HAMILTON CO., ST. CLEMENT (1881), (German), [CEM] Rev. Msgr. Joseph A. Lawler.
Res.: 103 N. Hancock, 62859. Tel: 618-643-3552; Fax: 618-643-3112.
Catechesis / Religious Program—Tel: 618-643-3628. Students 83.
METROPOLIS, MASSAC CO., ST. ROSE OF LIMA (1872), Rev. Jose Ancheril.

Res.: 315 E. Third St., 62960-2229. Tel: 618-524-9006; Fax: 618-524-8637.
Catechesis/Religious Program—405 E. Third St., 62960. Students 25.

MILLSTADT, ST. CLAIR CO., ST. JAMES (1851), [CEM] Rev. Bernard C. Goedde Jr.; Deacon Ronald Karcher.
Res.: 405 W. Madison St., 62260. Tel: 618-476-3513; Fax: 618-476-3513 (call ahead).
School—Tel: 618-476-3510; Fax: 618-476-7357. Sr. Patricia Dalton, S.S.N.D, Prin. Sisters 3; Lay Teachers 10; Students 122.
Catechesis/Religious Program—Tel: 618-476-1923. Students 135.

MODOC, RANDOLPH CO., ST. LEO, [CEM] Rev. Richard J. Weidert, Admin.
Res.: #1 Pioneer Ln., Red Bud, 62278. Tel: 618-282-3176; Fax: 618-282-3176.

MOUND CITY, PULASKI CO., CHURCH OF THE IMMACULATE CONCEPTION-ST. MARY (1863), [CEM] Rev. Msgr. William P. McGhee.
Res.: 517 N. Walnut St., Box 67, 62963. Tel: 618-748-9113; Fax: 618-748-9113.
Catechesis/Religious Program—Students 35.

MOUNT CARMEL, WABASH CO., ST. MARY (1836), [CEM] Rev. William J. Rowe; Deacon Charles Speaks.
Res.: 125 W. Fifth St., 62863. Tel: 618-262-5337; Fax: 618-262-5333.
School—Tel: 618-263-3183; Fax: 618-263-3596. Mrs. Alice Wirth, Prin. Lay Teachers 13; Students 188.
Catechesis/Religious Program—Students 60.

MOUNT VERNON, JEFFERSON CO., ST. MARY (1871), [CEM] Revs. Daniel J. Jurek; Von C. Deeke.
Res.: 115 N. 14th St., 62864. Tel: 618-244-1559; Fax: 618-244-1793.
School—Tel: 618-242-5353; Fax: 618-242-5365. Susan Cunningham, Prin. Lay Teachers 10; Students 137.
Catechesis/Religious Program—Students 133.

MURPHYSBORO, JACKSON CO., ST. ANDREW (1868), [CEM] Rev. Gary P. Gummersheimer.
Res.: 724 Mulberry St., 62966. Tel: 618-687-2012; Fax: 618-684-3431.
School—Tel: 618-687-2013; Fax: 618-684-4969. Susan Sheffer, Prin. Lay Teachers 12; Students 136.
Catechesis/Religious Program—Tel: 618-684-6364; Fax: 618-684-3431. Mr. Bill Harper, D.R.E. Students 68.

NASHVILLE, WASHINGTON CO., ST. ANN (1874), [CEM] Rev. Paul R. Wienhoff, Admin.
Res.: 631 S. Mill St., 62263. Tel: 618-327-3232; Fax: 618-327-4904.
School—Tel: 618-327-8741. Laurie Klostermann, Prin. Lay Teachers 9; Students 130.
Catechesis/Religious Program—Tel: 618-327-3232. Students 104.
Convent—695 S. Mill St., 62263.

NEW ATHENS, ST. CLAIR CO., ST. AGATHA (1870), [CEM] Rev. James M. Nall, J.C.L.
Res.: 205 S. Market St., 62264. Tel: 618-475-2331.
School—Tel: 618-475-2170; Fax: 618-475-3177. Mrs. Charlotte Newbold, Prin. Lay Teachers 5; Students 52.
Catechesis/Religious Program—Tel: 618-295-2686. Students 60.

NEW BADEN, CLINTON CO., ST. GEORGE (1894), [CEM] Rev. Donald A. Blaes, Admin.
Res.: 200 N. 3rd St., 62265. Tel: 618-588-4323; Fax: 618-588-2413.
Catechesis/Religious Program—Tel: 618-588-3504. Martha Kruchten, D.R.E. Students 120.

O'FALLON, ST. CLAIR CO.
1—ST. CLARE (1867), [CEM] Rev. James E. Deiters.
Res.: 205 W. 3rd St., 62269. Tel: 618-632-3562; Fax: 618-632-9036.
School—214 W. 3rd St., 62269. Tel: 618-632-6327; Fax: 618-632-5587. Mr. Ken Pajares, Prin. Lay Teachers 26; Students 456.
Catechesis/Religious Program—Students 155.
2—ST. NICHOLAS (1982), Rev. Msgr. William J. Hitpas; Deacon Richard H. Olson.
Res.: 900 N. Smiley, 62269. Tel: 618-632-1997; Fax: 618-632-7703.
Church & Office: 625 St. Nicholas Dr., 62269. Tel: 618-632-1797; Fax: 618-632-7703.
Catechesis/Religious Program—Tel: 618-632-1007; Fax: 618-632-7703. Barbara Furdek, D.R.E. Students 320.

OKAWVILLE, WASHINGTON CO., ST. BARBARA (1867), [CEM] Rev. Paul Wienhoff.
Res.: 305 N. Front St., 62271. Tel: 618-243-6236; Fax: 618-243-5270.
Catechesis/Religious Program—Tel: 618-243-6236. Students 86.

OLNEY, RICHLAND CO., ST. JOSEPH (1857), [CEM] Rev. Jerry E. Wirth.
Res.: 215 S. Elliott St., 62450. Tel: 618-392-8181; Fax: 618-395-8500.
School—Tel: 618-395-3081; Fax: 618-395-8500. Linda Mastio, Prin. Lay Teachers 11; Students 167.
Catechesis/Religious Program—Students 45.

PADERBORN, ST. CLAIR CO., ST. MICHAEL (1843), (German), [CEM] Rev. Joseph D. Hansmann.
Church: 4576 Buss Branch Rd., Waterloo, 62298. Tel: 618-473-2798; Fax: 618-473-9180.
Catechesis/Religious Program—Tel: 618-473-2915. Jackie Billings, D.R.E. Students 53.

PINCKNEYVILLE, PERRY CO., ST. BRUNO (1872), [CEM] Rev. Brian Barker.
Res.: 204 N. Gordon Ave., 62274. Tel: 618-357-5510; Fax: 618-357-6050.
School—Tel: 618-357-8276; Fax: 618-357-6425. Ms. Marilyn Johnson, Prin. Lay Teachers 8 Students 113.
Catechesis/Religious Program—Tel: 618-357-8278. Sr. Joyce Engle, S.S.N.D., D.R.E. Students 94.

PIOPOLIS, HAMILTON CO., ST. JOHN THE BAPTIST (1841), [CEM] Rev. Msgr. Joseph A. Lawler; Deacon Gary D. Walsh.
Res.: Rte. 3, P.O. Box 170, McLeansboro, 62859. Tel: 618-648-2490.
Catechesis/Religious Program—Tel: 618-648-2586. Students 72.

POND SETTLEMENT, GALLATIN CO., ST. PATRICK (1842), Very Rev. Mark D. Stec, V.F.
Mailing Address: P.O. Box 579, Shawneetown, 62984. Tel: 618-269-3318; Fax: 618-272-5400.
Catechesis/Religious Program—Tel: 618-272-7059; Fax: 618-277-7059. Students 14.

POSEN, WASHINGTON CO., OUR LADY OF PERPETUAL HELP (1901), [CEM] Rev. James R. Van Oss.
Res.: 19824 Posen Rd., Nashville, 62263. Tel: 618-327-3556.

PRAIRIE DU ROCHER, RANDOLPH CO., ST. JOSEPH (1721), [CEM] Rev. Albert E. Kreher.
Res.: 802 Middle St., 62277. Tel: 618-284-3314.
Catechesis/Religious Program—Students 45.

RADDLE, JACKSON CO., ST. ANN (1875), Rev. Leo J. Hayes.
606 W. George St., P.O. Box 157, Ava, 62907. Tel: 618-426-3321; Fax: 618-426-3321.
Catechesis/Religious Program—Tel: 618-497-8124. Students 6.

RADOM, WASHINGTON CO., ST. MICHAEL (1874), (Polish), [CEM] Revs. Daniel J. Jurek; Von C. Deeke.
Church: 52 S. Third St., P.O. Box 15, 62876. Tel: 618-485-2265; Fax: 618-485-2272.
Res.: 115 N. 14th St., Mount Vernon, 62864. Tel: 618-244-1559; Fax: 618-244-1793.
School—Tel: 618-485-6461. Sr. Jacinta Willenborg, A.S.C., Prin. Lay Teachers 5; Students 53.

RED BUD, RANDOLPH CO., ST. JOHN THE BAPTIST (1862), [CEM] Very Rev. Thomas Stout, V.F.
Res.: 515 Locust St., 62278. Tel: 618-282-3222; Fax: 618-282-6867.
School—Tel: 618-282-3215; Fax: 618-282-6790. Sr. Aquinas Kurtz, O.S.F., Prin. Lay Teachers 9; Students 146.
Catechesis/Religious Program—Students 70.

RENAULT, MONROE CO., OUR LADY OF GOOD COUNSEL (1879), [CEM] Rev. Roger R. Karban, Admin.
Res.: P.O. Box 98, 62279. Tel: 618-458-7710; Fax: 618-458-7710.
Catechesis/Religious Program—Students 26.

RIDGWAY, GALLATIN CO., ST. JOSEPH (1870), [CEM] Very Rev. Mark D. Stec, V.F.
Res. 205 W. South St., P.O. Box 190, 62979. Tel: 618-272-7059; Fax: 618-272-5400.
Catechesis/Religious Program—Students 82.

ROYALTON-ZEIGLER, FRANKLIN CO., ST. ALOYSIUS/SACRED HEART (1919), [JC] Rev. Larry Lemay; Sr. Laura Reynolds, Pastoral Assoc.
Res.: 212 Pecan St., P.O. Box 100, 62983. Tel: 618-984-2146; Fax: 618-984-2146.
Catechesis/Religious Program—Students 18.

RUMA, RANDOLPH CO., ST. PATRICK (1818), [CEM] Rev. Richard J. Weidert, Admin.
Res.: #1 Pioneer Ln., Red Bud, 62278. Tel: 618-282-3176; Fax: 618-282-3176.

ST. FRANCISVILLE, LAWRENCE CO., ST. FRANCIS XAVIER (1836), (French), [CEM] Rev. Thomas M. Barrett.
Mailing Address: 1006 Collins St., Lawrenceville, 62439. Tel: 618-943-5255.
Catechesis/Religious Program—Students 5.

ST. LIBORY, ST. CLAIR CO., ST. LIBORIUS (1838), [CEM] Rev. Dennis F. Voss; Deacon Andrew Lintker.
Res.: P.O. Box 331, 62282. Tel: 618-768-4921; Fax: 618-768-4207.
Catechesis/Religious Program—Mona Mense, D.R.E.; Lynn Vasquez, D.R.E. Students 92.

ST. ROSE, CLINTON CO., ST. ROSE (1868), [CEM] Rev. Edward F. Schaefer.
Res.: 18010 St. Rose Rd., 62230-2506. Tel: 618-526-4118; Fax: 618-526-0004.
Catechesis/Religious Program—Tel: 618-526-4886. Sr. Justina Schaefer, A.S.C., D.R.E. Students 196.

ST. SEBASTIAN, WABASH CO., ST. SEBASTIAN (1871), [CEM] Rev. Henry R. Engelhart.
Church: 4921 N. 1400 Blvd., Mount Carmel, 62863. Tel: 618-298-2589.
Res.: 300 N.W. Fifth St., Fairfield, 62837. Tel: 618-847-7931; Fax: 618-872-7393.

Catechesis/Religious Program—Students 65.

SALEM, MARION CO., ST. THERESA OF AVILA (1868), [CEM] Darren Eultgen, M.Div., Parish Life Coord.
Res.: 812 W. Main St., 62881. Tel: 618-548-0899; Fax: 618-548-0269.
School—Tel: 618-548-3492; Fax: 618-548-9673. Sherri Beckham, Prin. Lay Teachers 7; Students 68.
Catechesis/Religious Program—Tel: 618-548-6316; Fax: 618-548-0899. Denise McGormack, D.R.E. Students 45.

SANDOVAL, MARION CO., ST. LAWRENCE (1871), [CEM] Very Rev. David M. Darin, V.F.; Sr. Jacklyn Marie Pritchard, C.D.P., Parish Life Coord.
Church: 311 W.M St., P.O. Box 278, 62882. Tel: 618-247-3300; Fax: 618-247-3837.
Res.: 1011 Alton Ave., Madison, 62060.
Catechesis/Religious Program—Students 33.

SCHELLER, JEFFERSON CO., ST. BARBARA (1898), Revs. Daniel Jurek; Von C. Deeke.
4281 N. Scheller Ln., 62883. Tel: 618-279-7207; Fax: 618-279-7209.
Catechesis/Religious Program—Students 24.

SESSER, FRANKLIN CO., ST. MARY (1909), Rev. Steven F. Poole, Admin.
Church: 100 N. Poplar St., P.O. Box 568, 62884. Tel: 618-625-5053.
Res.: 412 E. Washington St., Christopher, 62822. Tel: 618-724-4114.
Catechesis/Religious Program—Students 23.

SHAWNEETOWN, GALLATIN CO., ST. MARY (1842), [CEM] Very Rev. Mark D. Stec, V.F.
Mailing Address: 655 W. Marshall St., P.O. Box 579, 62984. Tel: 618-269-3318; Fax: 618-272-5400.
Catechesis/Religious Program—Tel: 618-272-7059. Students 27.

SHILOH, ST. CLAIR CO., CORPUS CHRISTI (1913), Rev. Msgr. Matthias Nyakatura.
Res.: 206 Rasp St., O'Fallon, 62269. Tel: 618-632-5631; Fax: 618-632-7614.
Catechesis/Religious Program—Tel: 618-632-7614. Students 70.

SMITHTON, ST. CLAIR CO., ST. JOHN THE BAPTIST (1867), [CEM] Rev. Kenneth J. York, J.C.L.; Deacon Donald R. Deitz.
Res.: 10 S. Lincoln St., 62285-1614. Tel: 618-234-2068; Fax: 618-234-0179.
School—Tel: 618-233-0581; Fax: 618-233-0581. Jane Spreng, Prin. Lay Teachers 9; Students 114.
Catechesis/Religious Program—Students 72.

SPARTA, RANDOLPH CO., OUR LADY OF LOURDES (1897), Rev. Msgr. Theodore J. Baumann, Admin.
Res.: 611 W. Broadway, 62286. Tel: 618-443-2811.
Catechesis/Religious Program—Tel: 618-443-2878. Lila Lehnherr, D.R.E. Students 70.

STONEFORT, WILLIAMSON CO., ST. FRANCIS DE SALES (1879), Rev. Jose Ancheril.
Mailing Address: 2020 State Rte. 146E., P.O. Box 1325, Vienna, 62995. Tel: 618-658-4501.

STRINGTOWN, RICHLAND CO., ST. JOSEPH (1841), [CEM] Rev. David L. Braun.
6342 N. Stringtown Rd., Olney, 62450. Tel: 618-752-5671 (Wendelin Rectory); 618-754-3676 (Wed.); Fax: 618-754-3356 (Parish Office).
Catechesis/Religious Program—Tel: 618-395-2862. Barbara Ochs, D.R.E. Students 73.

TAMAROA, PERRY CO., IMMACULATE CONCEPTION (1904), Rev. Msgr. Melvin Vandeloo.
Res.: 533 W. 2nd North St., 62888. Tel: 618-496-5867.
Catechesis/Religious Program—Tel: 618-787-2361. Students 30.

TIPTON, MONROE CO., ST. PATRICK (1850), [CEM] Rev. Eugene J. Wojcik.
Res.: 5675 LL Rd., Waterloo, 62298. Tel: 618-458-6875; Fax: 618-458-6875.
Catechesis/Religious Program—Students 22.

TODD'S MILL, PERRY CO., ST. MARY MAGDALEN (1868), [CEM] Rev. James R. Van Oss.
Res.: 5047 Todd's Mill Rd., Pinckneyville, 62274. Tel: 618-336-5414.

TRENTON, CLINTON CO., ST. MARY (1858), (German), [CEM] Rev. James R. Dougherty; Sr. Angela J. Schrage, A.S.C., Pastoral Assoc. & D.R.E.; Deacon John P. Dilley, (Retired).
Res.: 218 W. Kentucky St., 62293. Tel: 618-224-9335; Fax: 618-224-9346.
Catechesis/Religious Program—Students 195.

ULLIN, PULASKI CO., OUR LADY OF FATIMA (1949), [CEM] Rev. Msgr. William P. McGhee.
517 N. Walnut St., Box 67, Mound City, 62963. Tel: 618-748-9113; Fax: 618-748-9113.
Catechesis/Religious Program—Students 1.

VALMEYER, MONROE CO., SEVEN DOLORS OF THE B.V.M. (1921), Rev. Edwin H. Hustedde.
Res.: 101 Meyer Dr., P.O. Box 206, 62295. Tel: 618-935-2247.
Catechesis/Religious Program—Tel: 618-935-2521. Mrs. Caryl Sondag, D.R.E. Students 65.

VIENNA, JOHNSON CO., ST. PAUL (1895), [JC] Rev. Jose Ancheril.
Res.: P.O. Box 1325, 62995. Tel: 618-658-4501.

Catechesis/Religious Program—Tel: 618-658-4701. Students 29.

WALSH, RANDOLPH CO., ST. PIUS (1905), Rev. John J. Joyce.
7681 Walsh Rd., 62297. Tel: 618-853-4404.
Catechesis/Religious Program—Students 22.

WASHINGTON PARK, ST. CLAIR CO., ST. MARTIN OF TOURS, Closed. For inquiries for parish records contact the chancery.

WATERLOO, MONROE CO., SS. PETER AND PAUL (1843), [CEM] Rev. Msgr. Thomas D. Flach; Deacon Douglas L. Boyer; Jeanne Herzberg, Pastoral Assoc.
Res.: 204 W. Mill St., 62298. Tel: 618-939-6426; Fax: 618-939-2011.
School—Tel: 618-939-7217; Fax: 618-939-5994. Mr. Ben Fuehne, Prin. Lay Teachers 24; Students 408.
Catechesis/Religious Program—Sr. Mary Essner, S.S.N.D., D.R.E.; Rodney Brown, D.R.E. Students 215.

WENDELIN, CLAY CO., HOLY CROSS (1870), [CEM] Rev. David L. Braun.
Res.: 5782 Ingraham Ave., Newton, 62448. Tel: 618-752-5671; Fax: 618-752-6006.
Catechesis/Religious Program—Students 156.

WEST FRANKFORT, FRANKLIN CO., ST. JOHN THE BAPTIST (1916), [CEM] Rev. Larry Lemay.
Res.: 703 E. Main St., 62896. Tel: 618-932-2828; Fax: 618-932-2828.
School—Tel: 618-937-2017; Fax: 618-937-2287. Mr. Joseph Bierbaum, Prin. Franciscan Sisters of Our Lady of Perpetual Help 1; Lay Teachers 9; Students 83.
Catechesis/Religious Program—Peggy DeMaretti, D.R.E. Students 10.

WILLISVILLE, PERRY CO., ST. JOSEPH (1903), [CEM] Rev. Leo J. Hayes.
Mailing Address: 606 George St., P.O. Box 157, Ava, 62907. Tel: 618-426-3321; Fax: 618-426-3321.
Catechesis/Religious Program—Tel: 618-497-8115; Fax: 618-497-8115. Students 16.

ZEIGLER, FRANKLIN CO., SACRED HEART, Merged, with St. Aloysius, Royalton to form St. Aloysius/Sacred Heart, Royalton-Zeigler.

SACRAMENTAL RECORDS LOCATED IN CHANCERY ARCHIVES:
St. Adalbert Church, East St. Louis—
St. Augustine Church, East St. Louis—
SS. Cyril and Methodius Church, East St. Louis—
St. Elizabeth Church, East St. Louis—
St. Henry Church, East St. Louis—
Holy Angels Church, East St. Louis—
St. John's Orphanage, Belleville—
St. Anthony, Coulterville—
St. Joseph Church, Wetaug—
St. Anthony, Coulterville—
St. Martin of Tours, Washington Park—
St. Mary Church, East St. Louis—
Sacred Heart Church, East St. Louis—
St. Thomas Church, Millstadt—

Chaplains of Correctional Institutions and State Hospitals

ANNA. *Anna State Hospital*. Rev. Msgr. Thomas W. Miller, Chap. Tel: 618-833-5835. Attended from St. Mary Church, Anna.

CENTRALIA. *Centralia Correctional Center*, P.O. Box 1266, 62801. Rev. George A. Mauck.

CHESTER. *Chester Mental Health Center*, P.O. Box 31, 62233. Tel: 618-826-4571.
310 N. Main St., Hecker, 62248. Tel: 618-473-2217.

HARRISBURG. *Illinois Youth Center*, P.O. Box 300, 62946. (Vacant)

INA. *Big Muddy River Correctional Center*. (Vacant)

MARION. *Federal Maximum Security Prison*, P.O. Box 2000, 62959. Deacon Pat Patterson, Chap. Tel: 618-964-1441.
Veterans Hospital. Attended from St. Joseph, Marion.

MENARD. *Menard Correctional Center*, P.O. Box 711, 62259. Rev. Leo J. Hayes, Chap. Tel: 618-826-5071.

VIENNA. *Dixon Springs Work Camp* 62995. Rev. Msgr. Thomas W. Miller, Contact.
Shawnee Correctional Center, Box 400, 62995. Rev. Msgr. Thomas W. Miller, Chap.
Vienna Correctional Center. Rev. Msgr. Thomas W. Miller, Chap. Tel: 618-833-5835.

Military Chaplains:
Revs.—
Gegotek, Tadeusz, U.S.N.R.
Voelker, David A., U.S.A.F.

Special Assignment:
Rev.—
Geller, Charles H., Fort Stockton, TX

Leave of Absence:
Rev. Msgr.—
Blazine, James A.
Revs.—
Balestrieri, Edward
Chlopecki, Robert J.
Harbaugh, Paul E.
Kownacki, Raymond F.
Linnemann, Eugene C.
O'Guinn, Jon
Peterson, Louis P.
Rensing, William F.
Ruppert, Alan E.
Schrage, Joseph S.
Sebescak, Gary
Unverferth, Steven R.
Witte, Steven D.

Retired:
Most Rev.—
Schlarman, Stanley G., D.D. (DOD), Meredith Home, 16 S. Illinois, 62220. Tel: 618-277-6814
Rev. Msgrs.—
Dobkowski, Paulin J., Hincke Residence for Priests, 2620 Lebanon Ave., 62221.
Driscoll, Maurice F., McAuley Place, 3720 Dauphin St., Mobile, AL 36608.
Haselhorst, Vincent, Hincke Residence, 2620 Lebanon Ave., 62221.
Jansen, James H., Hincke Residence, 2620 Lebanon Ave., 62221.
Lombardo, Angelo J., Hincke Residence for Priests, 2620 Lebanon Ave., 62221.
Nebel, Charles A., Hincke Residence for Priests, 2620 Lebanon Ave., 62221.
Schwaegel, Joseph R., 222 S. Third St., 62220.
Revs.—
Arnold, J. Ralph, Rosewood Care Center, Rm. 314, Rosewood Village Dr., Swansea, 62226.
Bertsche, Conrad J., 6451 Fairlynn Blvd., Yorba Linda, CA 92686.
Crook, David G.
Daly, Richard L., Hincke Residence for Priests, 2620 Lebanon Ave., 62221.
Dollar, Robert J., 2175 Woods Creek Rd., Robertsville, MO 63072.
Frerker, Jack W., 7315 Henderson S.E., Olympia, WA 98501.
Haas, Ralph L., 9 S. 51st St., 62223.
Hays, Joseph C., Rosewood Care Center, Rosewood Village Dr., Swansea, 62226.
Hentschel, Cletus B., 5315 W. Main St., 62223.
Hibner, Jerome H., Rosewood Care Center, 100 Rosewood Village Dr., Swansea, 62226.
Hsu, Peter, 123 S. Pine, Ziegler, 62999.
Iffert, Wilbert J., 147 Juniper Dr., Oak Grove Terrace, Mount Vernon, 62864.
Kastner, Edwin H., 222 S. Third St., 62220.
Koehr, Louis, P. O. Box 56, 203 No. Franklin, Albers, 62215-0056.
Kopff, Herbert C., 4419 Taft, St. Louis, MO 63116.
Kribs, Charles R., Hincke Residence, 2620 Lebanon Ave., 62221.
Lenzini, Donald J., Hincke Residence for Priests, 2620 Lebanon Ave., 62221.
Lopardo, Vito R., Hincke Residence for Priests, 2620 Lebanon Ave., 62221.
MacPherson, Walter E., 222 S. Third St., 62220.
Malec, Raymond S., Hincke Residence for Priests, 2620 Lebanon Ave., 62221.
Meskenas, Vincent A., St. Isidore Church, 222 Clark Ave., Yuba City, CA 95991.
Miriani, Gerald C., 7158 E. Charro Cir., Tuscan, AZ 85715.
Misho, Lloyd P., Bohannon Nursing Home, 1201 N. Alton St., Lebanon, 62254.
O'Shea, Robert J., Sense Residence, 2620 Lebanon Ave., 62221.
Perjak, Edmond J., 210 Pelham Rd., Pier 1, Apt. 108-B, Fort Walton Beach, FL 32547.
Ratermann, Jerome B., 303 Hillcrest Dr., 62286-1203.
Reinhardt, Leo S., Hincke Residence for Priests, 2620 Lebanon Ave., 62221.
Stauder, Paul W., Hincke Residence for Priests, 2620 Lebanon Ave., 62221.
Thoonkuzhy, Joseph (TLS), 6526-E South Memorial Dr., Tulsa, OK 74133.
Vonnahmen, Robert J., 222 S. Third St., 62220.

Permanent Deacons:
Becker, Robert H.
Bigham, David
Boyer, Douglas
Cerneka, Peter
Coates, John
DeWolf, William
Dietz, Donald
Dilley, John P.
Dougherty, Michael
DuBois, Omer E.
DuPrey, John L.
Duff, James P., (On Sick Leave)
Hempen, John
Karcher, Ronald
Kirchgraber, Robert B., (Retired)
Lanter, Robert
Lintker, Andrew
Lippert, Robert
Litteken, Charles
Munie, George J.
Olson, Richard H.
Patterson, Pat
Rickert, Dennis
Speaks, Charles
Stock, Joseph E.
Stockmann, Gerald E.
Teaff, Joseph, (Retired)
Theis, Francis D., (On Leave of Absence)

INSTITUTIONS LOCATED IN THE DIOCESE

[A] HIGH SCHOOLS, DIOCESAN

BELLEVILLE. *Althoff Catholic High School*, 5401 W. Main St., 62226-4796. Tel: 618-235-1100; Fax: 618-235-9535. Email: althoff@norcom2000.com. Web: www.althoff.net. Sr. Jan Renz, A.S.C., Prin. Priests 1; Sisters 1; Lay Teachers 45; Students 681.

BREESE. *Mater Dei High School*, 900 N. Mater Dei Dr., 62230. Tel: 618-526-7216; Fax: 618-526-8310. Email: mda@lcls.org. Web: www.materdei.breese.il.us. Curt L. Winter, Pres.; Dennis Litteken, Prin.; Sr. Virginia Kampwerth, P.H.J.C., Asst. Prin., Academics; Rev. Charles W. Tuttle. Central Catholic High School for Clinton Co. Priests 1; Sisters 2; Lay Teachers 43; Students 544.

WATERLOO. *Gibault Catholic High School*, 501 Columbia Ave., 62298. Tel: 618-939-3883; Fax: 618-939-7215. Email: dbruegg@hTc.neT. Web: gibaulTonline.com. Mr. Daniel J. Brueggeman, Prin. Sisters 3; Students 335.

[B] ELEMENTARY SCHOOLS

BREESE. *All Saints Academy*, (Grades PreK-8), 295 N. Clinton St., 62230. Tel: 618-526-4323; Fax: 618-526-2547. Email: tvoss@asasaints.com. Web: www.asasaints.com. Terri Voss, Prin. Consolidated schools of Saint Augustine, Saint Dominic parishes, Breese, IL, and St. Anthony Parish, Beckemeyer, IL. Lay Teachers 26; Students 406.

CAHOKIA. *Corpus Christi Catholic School JDP*, Formerly Corpus Christi Catholic School *Diocese of Belleville*, 222 S. Third St., 62220. Tel: 618-337-2880; Fax: 618-337-7898. Email: corpuschristicahokia@yahoo.com. Dr. George Halsey, Prin. Lay Teachers 9; Students 127.

EAST ST. LOUIS. *Sister Thea Bowman Catholic School*, 8213 Church Ln., 62203. Tel: 618-397-0316; Fax: 618-397-0337. Email: belvsthea@yahoo.com. Alice Gardner, Prin. Sisters 3; Lay Teachers 11; Students 162.

FAIRVIEW HEIGHTS. *Holy Trinity Catholic School - West Campus*, Formerly Elizabeth Ann Seton Catholic School, 9940 Bunkum Rd., 62208. Tel: 618-398-3011; Fax: 618-398-3421. Email: easetono@setoncatholic.com. Dr. Raymond Mack, Prin. Consolidated schools of St. Stephen Parish, Caseyville, IL, and Our Lady of the Assumption Parish, Fairview Heights, IL. Sisters 1; Lay Teachers 10; Students 99.

[C] DAY CARE CENTERS

BELLEVILLE. *Don Bosco Children's Center*, 300 N. Church St., 62220. Tel: 618-277-7055; Fax: 618-277-7084. Web: cssil.org. Jayne Crader, Dir.
Administrative Office, 300 N. Charles St., 62220. Tel: 618-277-7055; Fax: 618-277-7084.
St. Henry Day Care Center, 5301 W. Main St., 62223. Tel: 618-233-3454; Fax: 618-233-3498. Email: sthdaycare2@peaknet.net. Judy Shovlin, Coord.; Linda Moyer, Coord. Children 89.
St. John Children's Home, 2620 Lebanon Ave., 62221.
Chancery Office, 222 S. Third St., 62220. Tel: 618-277-8181. Rev. Msgr. James E. Margason, V.G., M.Div., J.C.L.
St. John Day Care Center, 2620 Lebanon Ave., 62221. Tel: 618-235-6717; Fax: 618-235-8485. Donna M. Koderhandt, Dir. Lay Women 13; Children 62.

EAST ST. LOUIS. *Catholic Day Care Center*, 617 Summit Ave., 62201. Tel: 618-874-7178. Email: catholicdcc@htctech.net. Nursery and Kindergarten.; Conducted by the Cordi-Marian Sisters.
2417 Ridge Ave., 62205. Tel: 618-875-1447. Email:

irenejua@htctech.net. Sr. Gema Juarez, M.C.M., Dir. Brothers 2; Sisters 1; Lay Teachers 10; Children 71.

[D] GENERAL HOSPITALS

BELLEVILLE. *St. Elizabeth Hospital*, 211 S. Third St., 62220-1998. Tel: 618-234-2120; Fax: 618-222-4650. Web: www.steliz.org. Timothy Brady, Admin. Hospital Sisters of the Third Order of St. Francis, Clinically Affiliated with St. Louis University School of Medicine. Sisters 5; Bed Capacity 506; Patients Assisted Annually 165,002.

BREESE. *St. Joseph Hospital*, 9515 Holy Cross Ln., 62230. Tel: 618-526-4511; Fax: 618-526-8022. Email: dniemann@sjb.hshs.org. Web: www.stjoebreese.com. Jacolyn M. Schlautman, Exec. Vice Pres.; Sr. Dorothy Niemann, S.C.S.C., Pastoral Care. Hospital Sisters of the Third Order of St. Francis Sisters 2; Bed Capacity 85; Patients Assisted Annually 71,000.

CENTRALIA. **St. Mary's Hospital*, 400 N. Pleasant Ave., 62801. Tel: 618-436-8000; Fax: 618-436-8038. Web: www.smgsi.com. Mr. Bruce A. Merrell, Pres. Felician Sisters 5; Bed Capacity 233; Patients Assisted Annually 191,606.

EAST ST. LOUIS. *St. Mary Hospital of East St. Louis, Illinois Volunteers*, 129 N. 8th St., 62201 Tel: 618-274-1900; Fax: 618-482-7015. Email: sbarnett@ancilla.org. Web: www.ancilla.org/stmaryesl.htm.

St. Mary's Hospital, 129 N. 8th St., 62201 Tel: 618-274-1900; Fax: 618-482-7015. Email ascott@ancilla.org. Web: www.ancilla.org/stmaryesl.htm. Sponsored by the Poor Handmaids of Jesus Christ. Affiliate of Ancilla Systems, Inc. Sisters 2; Bed Capacity 169; Patients Assisted Annually 85,000.

MOUNT VERNON. **Good Samaritan Regional Health Center*, 605 N. 12th St., 62864. Tel: 618-242-4600. Leo F. Childers Jr., Pres.; Sr. Denise Sharp, S.S.J., Chap. Member of SSM Health Care. Sisters 2; Bed Capacity 175; Patients Assisted Annually 78,200.

MURPHYSBORO. *St. Joseph Memorial Hospital*, 2 S. Hospital Dr., 62966. Tel: 618-684-3156; Fax: 618-529-0529. Web: www.sih.net. J. Stephen Pautler, FACHE, Admin.; Sisters Mary Bede, A.S.C., Dir. of Pastoral Care; Clara Ternes, A.S.C., Corporate Dir. of Missions, Values & Ethics. Adorers of the Blood of Christ., A service of Southern Illinois Healthcare. Sisters 2; Bed Capacity 49; Patients Assisted Annually 16,229.

[E] HOMES FOR SENIOR CITIZENS

BELLEVILLE. *Charles and Bertha Hincke Residence for Priests and Sense Residence*, 2620 Lebanon Ave., 62221. Tel: 618-234-5722; Fax: 618-234-5792. Email: hinckehome@aol.com. Jolene Beck, Mgr. Owned by Diocese of Belleville. Guests 14.

Meredith Memorial Home, 16 S. Illinois St., 62220. Tel: 618-233-8780; Fax: 618-233-9602. Email: sueneuharth@aol.com. Web: www.ccsil.org. Sue Neuharth, Admin.; Rev. Robert D. Gore, Chap. Tel: 618-235-5226. Owned by the Diocese of Belleville. Guests 60.

Our Lady of the Snows Apartment Community Retirement Home, 726 Community Dr., 62223. Tel: 618-397-6400; Fax: 618-394-9051. Email: bob.mccardle@apartmentcommunity.org. Web: apartmentcommunity.org. D. Robert McCardle, Exec. Vice Pres.; Cathy Knowlton, Dir. Pastoral Care. Tel: 618-394-6258; Rev. Andrew G. Chalkey, O.M.I. Tel: 618-394-6264. Guests 225.

[F] MONASTERIES AND RESIDENCES OF PRIESTS AND BROTHERS

BELLEVILLE. *Missionary Oblates of Mary Immaculate - St. Henry's Oblate Residence*, 200 N. 60th St., 62223. Tel: 618-233-2991. Email: sthenryomi@peaknet.net. Revs. Real Bourque; Michael S. Deis, O.M.I.; Andrew G. Chalkey, O.M.I.; James Donovan, O.M.I.; Rene DuFour, O.M.I.; William Clark, O.M.I. (GAL); Vincent Fitzgerald, O.M.I.; Urban Figge, Supr. Oblate Community; Charles Giles, O.M.I.; Emil Helfrich, O.M.I.; Justin H. Huelsing, O.M.I.; George Kuryvial, O.M.I.; Elmar Mauer, O.M.I; Robert Morin, O.M.I.; Frank A. Ryan, O.M.I.; James E. Taylor, O.M.I.; Boniface Wittenbrink, O.M.I.; James Wynne, O.M.I.; Charles Zachman, O.M.I.; Bros. David Schell, O.M.I.; Francis Sullivan, O.M.I. Priests 19; Brothers 2.

Shrine of Our Lady of the Snows, 442 S. DeMazenod Dr., 62223-1023. Tel: 618-397-6700; Fax: 618-397-1210. Email: info@snows.org. Web: www.snows.org. Revs. Allen Maes, O.M.I., Area Supr.; Louis B. Studer, O.M.I., Dir.; Floyd B. Boeckman, O.M.I.; Joseph Pitts, O.M.I.; Robert Braun, O.M.I.; Leonard Baldus, O.M.I.; Eugene Glaub, O.M.I.; Leo Miller, O.M.I.; Raul Salas, O.M.I.; John Weissler, O.M.I.; Bro. Lorenzo Williams. Missionary Oblates of Mary Immaculate

EAST ST. LOUIS. *St. Benedict the Black Friary*, 404 N. 14th St., 62205. Tel: 618-482-5570; Fax: 618-482-5574. Revs. Fernand Cheri, O.F.M., Rel. Supr., Counselor; Christian Reuter, O.F.M., Diocesan Coord. of Prison Ministry; Carroll Mizicko, O.F.M., Chap., St. Elizabeth Hospital.

[G] CONVENTS AND RESIDENCES FOR SISTERS

BELLEVILLE. *Hospital Sisters of St. Francis*, 1036 Rutledge Dr., 62221. Tel: 618-235-5486; Fax: 618-235-5486. Web: www.springfieldfranciscans.org. Sisters 4.

Hospital Sisters of St. Francis, 1000 Royal Heights Rd., Apt. 58, 62226. Tel: 618-233-1687; Fax: 618-233-1687. Email: sistert@peaknet.net. Web: www.springfieldfranciscans.org.

Motherhouse and Novitiate of Ursuline Sisters of Belleville, 1026 N. Douglas Ave., 62220-4198. Tel: 618-235-3444; Fax: 618-235-3444. Email: OSUBELL@Juno.com. Sr. Dorothy Helbling, O.S.U., Community Leader. Total Membership of Congregation 10.

Poor Clare Monastery of Our Lady of Mercy, 300 N. 60th St., 62223. Tel: 618-235-4407; Fax: 618-235-4426. Web: www.poorclare.org/belleville. Sr. Mary Therese, P.C.C., Abbess; Rev. Robert D. Gore, Chap. Tel: 618-235-5226. Sisters 7.

CAIRO. *Mary Katherine Convent, Poor Handmaids of Jesus Christ*, 725 22nd St., 62914. Tel: 618-734-0778; Fax: 618-734-0778. Email: mkccairo@onemain.com. Sisters 3.

EAST ST. LOUIS. *St. Mary Convent, Poor Handmaids of Jesus Christ*, 5727 Warren St., 62204. Tel: 618-875-7570 Email: estlouis@Juno.com. Sisters 3.

RUMA. *Adorers of the Blood of Christ Ruma Center*, 2 Pioneer Ln., 62278. Tel: 618-282-3848 Fax: 618-282-3266. Email: rumacent@htc.net. Web: Adorers.org. Sr. Midred Gross, A.S.C., Dir., Community Life & Mission; Rev. Richard J. Weidert, Chap. Sisters 72; Total Membership of the Province 463.

[H] RETREAT HOUSES

BELLEVILLE. *King's House Retreat and Renewal Center*, 700 N. 66th St., 62223-3949. Tel: 618-397-0584; Fax: 618-397-5123. Email: Knghsebv@peaknet.net. Rev. Robert Aaron, O.M.I.; Bro. William Johnson, O.M.I., Dir.; Rev. David Kraus, O.M.I.; Bros. Victor Capek, O.M.I.; Edward Driggins, O.M.I.

[I] NEWMAN CENTERS

CARBONDALE. *The Newman Catholic Student Center* Southern Illinois University, 715 S. Washington, 62901. Tel: 618-529-3311; Fax: 618-549-9401. Web: www.siu.edu/~newman. Mr. Donald Markovitz, Acting Dir.; Ms. Mary Mertzlufft, Campus Min.

[J] MISCELLANEOUS LISTINGS

BELLEVILLE *Althoff Catholic High School Educational Endowment Trust*, 222 S. 3rd St., 62220. Tel: 618-277-8181. William Knapp, C.P.A., Contact Person.

Ancient Order of Hibernians, 1305 Doral Ct., O'Fallon, 62269. Tel: 618-632-7564. Bob Cunningham, Pres.

Ancient Order of Hibernians (LAOH), P.O. Box 23193, 62223. Tel: 618-277-9620. Jeanne Eisele, Pres.

Catholic Committee on Scouting of the Diocese of Belleville, John Sabo, 416 Chula Vista, 62221. Tel: 618-233-8031. Mr. John Sabo, Diocesan Chairman.

Catholic Community Foundation for the Diocese of Belleville, 222 South 3rd St., 62220-1985. Tel: 618-277-8181. Email: MLeifeld@diobelle.org. Martin Leifeld, Exec. Dir.

The Catholic Diocese of Belleville Custodial Fund, 222 S. Third St., 62220. Tel: 618-277-8181; Fax: 618-277-0819. Email: dwaeltz@diobelle.org. Web: diobelle.org. Most Rev. Wilton D. Gregory, S.L.D., Pres.; Rev. Msgr. James E. Margason, V.G., M.Div., J.C.L., Sec.; William Knapp, C.P.A., CFO.

The Catholic Diocese of Belleville Deposit and Loan Fund, 222 S. Third St., 62220. Tel: 618-277-8181; Fax: 618-277-0819. Email: dwaeltz@diobelle.org. Web: diobelle.org. Most Rev. Wilton D. Gregory, S.L.D., Pres.; Rev. Msgr. James E. Margason, V.G., M.Div., J.C.L., Sec.; William Knapp, C.P.A., CFO.

The Catholic Diocese of Belleville Group Health Insurance Fund, 222 S. Third St., 62220. Tel: 618-277-8181; Fax: 618-277-0819. Email: dwaeltz@diobelle.org. Web: diobelle.org. Most Rev. Wilton D. Gregory, S.L.D., Pres.; Rev. Msgr. James E. Margason, V.G., M.Div., J.C.L., Sec.; William Knapp, C.P.A., CFO.

The Catholic Diocese of Belleville Ministry Formation Fund, 222 S. Third St., 62220. Tel: 618-277-8181; Fax: 618-277-0819. Email: dwaeltz@diobelle.org. Web: diobelle.org. Most Rev. Wilton D. Gregory, S.L.D., Pres.; Rev. Msgr. James E. Margason, V.G., M.Div., J.C.L., Sec.; William Knapp, C.P.A., CFO.

The Catholic Diocese of Belleville Property Insurance Fund, 222 S. Third St., 62220. Tel: 618-277-8181; Fax: 618-277-0819. Email: dwaeltz@diobelle.org. Web: diobelle.org. Most Rev. Wilton D. Gregory, S.L.D., Pres.; Rev. Msgr. James E. Margason, V.G., M.Div., J.C.L., Sec.; William Knapp, C.P.A., CFO.

Catholic Fraternal Life, P.O. Box 327, 62222. Tel: 618-233-0286; Fax: 618-277-8257. Email: JohnL@cfllife.com. Web: www.cfllife.com.

Catholic Social Services of Southern Illinois, 8601 W. Main St., Suite 201, 62223. Tel: 618-394-5900; Fax: 619-394-5909. Web: www.cssil.org. David Wenzel, Dir.

Catholic War Veterans, 3535 State Rte. 159, Freeburg, 62243. Tel: 618-234-3074. Rev. Kenneth J. York, J.C.L., Chap.

Cursillos in Christianity, Belleville Diocese, 703 S. Jackson, 62220. Tel: 618-234-0456; Fax: 618-234-3168. John R. Bassett, Lay Dir.

Engaged Encounter, 120 N. 36th St., 62226. Tel: 618-277-1652; Fax: 618-237-7252. Gerry Bach, Coord.; Ann Bach, Coord.

St. Francis Thrift Shop, 800 E. Main St., 62220. Tel: 618-233-6998. Mrs. Catherine Heap, Mgr.

Health Care Endowment Fund of the Reverend Oblate Fathers, 726 Community Dr., 62223. Tel: 618-397-6700; Fax: 618-394-9051. Email: bob.mccardle@apartmentcommunity.org. D. Robert McCardle, Admin. & Contact Person.

Legal Title: *Health Care Endowment Fund of the Reverend Oblate Fathers at the Shrine of Our Lady of the Snows.*, Oblate Fathers and Trustees.

Missionary Association of Mary Immaculate-Missionary Oblates of Mary Immaculate Serving the missions of the Missionary Oblates, the National Shrine of Our Lady of the Snows, and the Tekakwitha Indian Missions. , 9480 N. De Mazenod Dr., 62223-1160. Tel: 618-398-4848; Fax: 618-398-0588. Email: mami@oblatesusa.org. Web: www.oblatesusa.org. Rev. Louis B. Studer, O.M.I., Oblate Dir.; Mrs. Lucille Green, Dir. Charitable Gifts; Revs. Floyd B. Boeckman, O.M.I., Charitable Gift Advisor; James E. Taylor, O.M.I., Charitable Gift Advisor; Mrs. Rosalee Cavataio, Charitable Gift Advisor; Ms. Colette Taylor, Charitable Gift Advisor.

Oblate Preaching Team, 200 N. 60th St., 62223. Tel: 618-233-2991; Fax: 618-233-9855. Revs. William Mason, O.M.I.; Robert Morin, O.M.I. Specializing in Parish Missions.

Radio Information Service for Blind and Print Handicapped, 9541 Church Circle Dr., 62223. Tel: 618-394-6221; Fax: 618-394-6438. Email: aschon@oblatesusa.org. Al Schon, Exec. Dir. Closed Circuit Radio for the blind and print handicapped.

Secular Franciscan Order, 200 W. Harrison, 62220. Tel: 618-476-1431; Fax: 618-234-2957. Email: Fransfo@aol.com. Ms. Mary Ellen Herman, S.F.O. St. Peter Fraternity

Serra Club of St. Clair County, P.O. Box 23017, 62220. John Kreisler, Pres.

7325 Stonewolf Ridge Ct., Fairview Heights, 62208. Tel: 618-632-7541. Rev. Msgr. Bernard L. Voss, Chap.

TEC (Teens Encounter Christ), 2620 Lebanon Ave., 62221. Email: crayola806@hotmail.com. Web: www.bellevilletec.com. Carol Underwood, Chairperson.

Victorious Missionaries, 442 S. DeMazenod Dr., 62223-1097. Tel: 618-394-6281 (Voice/TDD); Fax: 618-397-1210. Email: fsullivan@oblatesusa.org. Web: www.vmusa.org. Bro. Francis Sullivan, O.M.I., Natl. Dir. Spiritual Support Network for people with disabilities, chronic illness, and those who want to share the journey.

Western Catholic Union, Br. No. 59, 405 Southgate, 62223. Tel: 618-277-2892. Mrs. Marion Mueth, Pres.

World Apostolate of Fatima, The Blue Army, U.S.A., c/o 222 South 3rd St., 6220--985. Very Rev. John T. Myler, V.F., D.Min., Spiritual Advisor. Tel: 618-233-2391.

BREESE. *Daughters of Isabella, Precious Blood Circle #718*, 19000 St. Rose Rd., St. Rose, 62230. Tel: 618-526-4467. Helen Middeke, Diocesan Chairperson.

CARBONDALE. *Worldwide Marriage Encounter*, 205 Links Ln., Waterloo, 62298. Tel: 618-939-3846. Email: hermes@htc.net. John Hermes, Exec. Couple; Karen Hermes, Exec. Couple.

CARLYLE. *Carlyle Priest Center* Contact the Chancery, Tel: 618-277-8181. , 17440 Highline Rd., 62231.

CENTRALIA. **St. Mary's - Good Samaritan, Inc.*, 400 N. Pleasant Ave., 62801. Tel: 618-436-8000. Web: www.smgsi.com. James M. Sanger, Pres., CEO.

Co-Sponsored by the Franciscan Sisters of Mary and the Felician Sisters.

CHRISTOPHER. *Catholic Daughters of the Americas*, 805 S. Jesse, 62822. Tel: 618-724-4364. Mrs. Frances Furlin, Diocesan Chm.

EAST ST. LOUIS. *St. Mary Hospital of East St. Louis, Illinois Volunteers*, 129 N. 8th St., 62201. Tel: 618-274-1900; Fax: 618-482-7015. Email: ascott@ancilla.org. Web: www.ancilla.org/stmaryesl.htm.

St. Mary's Hospital Health Foundation, 129 N. 8th St., 62201. Tel: 618-482-7094; Fax: 618-482-7014. Email: mmaskal@ancilla.org. Web: www.ancilla.org/stmaryesl.htm.

O'FALLON. *ASC Health Services*, 6 Eagle Center, Ste. 4, 62269. Tel: 618-632-1284; Fax: 618-632-8063. Email: mldegenhart@compu-type.net. Sr. Meg Kapish, A.S.C., Exec. Dir.

Couple to Couple League, 338 Amy Dr.. Tel: 618-628-7759; Fax: 618-624-0902. Mike & Denise Terneus, Teaching Couple.

SCOTT AFB. *Scott Air Force Base*, Scott AFB Chapel, 375 AW/HC, 320 J St., Bldg. 1620, 62225-5256. Tel: 618-256-3303; Fax: 618-256-8010. Joseph S. Kuan, Ch. Col.; Robert Bruno, Ch. Col.

INCORPORATED CEMETERIES

BELLEVILLE. *Green Mount Catholic Cemetery of the Cathedral Congregation of Belleville*

BREESE. *St. Dominic Roman Catholic Cemetery of Breese*

EAST ST. LOUIS. *Holy Cross Cemetery of St. Henry Roman Catholic Church of East St. Louis*

Mount Carmel Cemetery of St. Patrick Roman Catholic Church

FAIRVIEW HEIGHTS. *St. Adalbert Association (An Illinois Religious Corporation)*

O'FALLON. *Mount Calvary Cemetery of St. Clare Roman Catholic Congregation*

VILLA RIDGE. *Calvary Cemetery of St. Patrick Roman Catholic Church of Cairo*

NECROLOGY

† Kuhl, Rev. Msgr. Urban B.—Died Aug. 25, 2003

† Haas, Melvin B., (Retired)—Died Sept. 11, 2003

Diocese of Biloxi

(Dioecesis Biloxiiensis)

Most Reverend

THOMAS J. RODI

Bishop of Biloxi; ordained May 20, 1978; appointed Bishop of Biloxi May 15, 2001; ordained and installed July 2, 2001. *Mailing Address: 1790 Popps Ferry Rd., Biloxi, MS 39532-2118.*

Most Reverend

JOSEPH LAWSON HOWZE, D.D.

Bishop Emeritus of Biloxi; ordained May 7, 1959; appointed Titular Bishop of Maxita and Auxiliary of Natchez-Jackson, November 8, 1972; ordained Bishop January 28, 1973; appointed Bishop of Biloxi March 1, 1977; installed June 6, 1977; retired May 15, 2001. *Mailing Address: P.O. Box 8152, Biloxi, MS 39535-8152.*

ESTABLISHED MARCH 1, 1977.

Square Miles 9,653.

Comprises 17 counties in southern Mississippi: Jackson, Harrison, Hancock, George, Stone, Pearl River, Greene, Perry, Forrest, Lamar, Marion, Walihall, Wayne, Jones, Covington, Jefferson Davis and Lawrence.

Legal Title: "Catholic Diocese of Biloxi".

For legal titles of parishes and diocesan institutions, consult the Chancery Office.

Chancery Office: 1790 Popps Ferry Rd., P.O. Box 1189, Biloxi, MS 39533-1189. Tel: 228-702-2100; Fax: 228-702-2125.

STATISTICAL OVERVIEW

Personnel	
Bishop	1
Retired Bishops	2
Priests: Diocesan Active in Diocese	39
Priests: Diocesan Active Outside Diocese	1
Priests: Diocesan in Foreign Missions	1
Priests: Retired, Sick or Absent	13
Number of Diocesan Priests	54
Religious Priests in Diocese	29
Total Priests in Diocese	83
Extern Priests in Diocese	12
Permanent Deacons in Diocese	26
Total Brothers	25
Total Sisters	46
Parishes	
Parishes	45
With Resident Pastor:	
Resident Diocesan Priests	34
Resident Religious Priests	7
Without Resident Pastor:	
Administered by Priests	4
Missions	13
Professional Ministry Personnel:	
Sisters	9
Lay Ministers	14
Welfare	
Homes for the Aged	7
Total Assisted	656
Special Centers for Social Services	10
Total Assisted	129,360
Other Institutions	1
Total Assisted	5,258
Educational	
Diocesan Students in Other Seminaries	10
Total Seminarians	10
High Schools, Diocesan and Parish	4
Total Students	1,023
High Schools, Private	1
Total Students	539
Elementary Schools, Diocesan and Parish	14
Total Students	3,073
Catechesis/Religious Education:	
High School Students	2,414
Elementary Students	3,299
Total Students under Catholic Instruction	10,358
Teachers in the Diocese:	
Brothers	5
Sisters	13
Lay Teachers	438
Vital Statistics	
Receptions into the Church:	
Infant Baptism Totals	782
Adult Baptism Totals	434
Received into Full Communion	179
First Communions	1,152
Confirmations	616
Marriages:	
Catholic	179
Interfaith	131
Total Marriages	310
Deaths	794
Total Catholic Population	72,158
Total Population	789,930

Former Bishop—Most Rev. JOSEPH LAWSON HOWZE, D.D. (Retired), ord. May 7, 1959; appt. Titular Bishop of Maxita and Auxiliary of Natchez-Jackson Nov. 8, 1972; ord. Bishop Jan. 28, 1973; appt. Bishop of Biloxi March 1, 1977; installed June 6, 1977; retired May 15, 2001.

Office of the Bishop—1790 Popps Ferry Rd., P.O. Box 1189, Biloxi, 39533-1189. Tel: 228-702-2111.

Vicar General and Moderator of the Curia—Rev. Msgr. ANDREW MURRAY, 1790 Popps Ferry Rd., P.O. Box 1189, Biloxi, 39533-1189. Tel: 228-702-2112.

Chancery Office—1790 Popps Ferry Rd., P.O. Box 1189, Biloxi, 39533-1189. Tel: 228-702-2100; Fax: 228-702-2125. Office Hours: Mon.-Fri. 8:30-5; All offices are at this address unless otherwise noted.

Pastoral Services—Rev. DOMINICK FULLAM, Dir. Tel: 228-702-2100.

Special Delegate for Matrimonial Dispensations—Rev. JOHN R. MCGRATH. Tel: 228-702-2116.

Chancellor—Sr. REBECCA RUTKOWSKI, O.S.F. Tel: 228-702-2137.

Office for Planning and Development—Deacon ROBERTO JIMENEZ, Dir. Tel: 228-702-2113.

Marriage Tribunal—

Judicial Vicar—Rev. JOHN R. MCGRATH. Tel: 228-702-2116.

Director of the Tribunal—Deacon RICK S. CONASON, J.D., J.C.L.

Promoter of Justice—Rev. Msgr. JAMES J. HANNON, J.C.D. (Retired).

Defenders of the Bond—Rev. Msgrs. JAMES J. HANNON, J.C.D. (Retired); RONALD P. HERZOG; Very Rev. THOMAS CONWAY, V.F.; Sr. JOYCE HOBEN, S.N.D.N., J.C.L.; Mr. PETER VERE, J.C.L., M.C.L.

Pro-Synodal Judges—Rev. Msgrs. JAMES J. HANNON, J.C.D. (Retired); JAMES P. MCGOUGH, J.C.D.

Advocates—Revs. LOUIS LOHAN; PATRICK MOCKLER; Deacons MARTIN FINNEGAN; LUCIEN MORAGAS.

Secretaries and Ecclesiastical Notaries (Court of First Instance)—Mrs. CLAIRE D. JONES; Mrs. CHARLENE GILES.

Deans—Very Revs. JOHN NOONE, V.F., West Coast Deanery; ANTONE LYNCH, V.F., Central Coast Deanery; PATRICK MCDERMOTT, V.F., East Central Coast Deanery; GERARD M. CLEARY, V.F., East Coast Deanery; THOMAS CONWAY, V.F., Northern Deanery.

College of Consultors—Rev. JOHN E. FORD, S.T.; Rev. Msgr. RONALD HERZOG; Rev. LOUIS LOHAN; Rev. Msgr. JAMES MCGOUGH, J.C.D.; Rev. PETER MOCKLER; Rev. Msgr. ANDREW MURRAY.

Diocesan Attorney—KEVIN J. NECAISE, P.O. Box 636, Gulfport, 39502. Tel: 228-586-0933.

Department of Administration and Finance Comptroller—TAMMY W. DILORENZO, C.P.A., Dir. Tel: 228-702-2118; BARBARA WATTERS, Accounting Specialist. Tel: 228-702-2118.

Office of Information Technology—THOMAS C. KESSLER, Dir. Tel: 228-702-2171.

Diocesan Risk Management for Property and Medical—Mr. A. J. SCARDINO, Contact Person. Tel: 228-702-2119; 228-452-3014.

Office of Human Resources—Deacon ROBERTO JIMENEZ, Dir. Tel: 228-702-2113.

Catholic Foundation of the Diocese of Biloxi, Inc.—Deacon ROBERTO JIMENEZ, Exec. Dir. Tel: 228-702-2113.

Mission Office—Rev. MICHAEL AUSTIN. Tel: 228-875-5419.

Department of Communication—

"Gulf Pine Catholic Newspaper"—SHIRLEY HENDERSON, Editor. Tel: 228-702-2126; 228-702-2127; Fax: 228-702-2128. Email: gulfpinecatholic@biloxidiocese.org.

Radio & Television—SHIRLEY HENDERSON. Tel: 228-702-2126; 228-702-2127; Fax: 228-702-2128. Email: shenderson@biloxidiocese.org.

Department of Education—

Office of Superintendent of Catholic Schools—Dr. LANNY ACOSTA. Tel: 228-702-2130; 228-702-2129.

Office of Resource Center—Dr. LANNY ACOSTA, Dir.; Mrs. ELIZABETH ECKERT, Coord. Tel: 228-702-2134.

Office of Special Education—Dr. LANNY ACOSTA.

Office of Religious Education—Mr. LEO TRAHAN, Dir. Tel: 228-702-2131.

Office of Youth Ministry—BRAGG MOORE, Dir. Tel: 228-702-2142.

Catholic Boy Scouts—JUDITH BRADFORD. Tel: 228-467-7452.

Campus Ministry—Very Rev. THOMAS CONWAY, V.F., Dir., 3117 W. Fourth St., Hattiesburg, 39401. Tel: 601-264-5192.

Priests' Continuing Education and Retreat Programs—Rev. CUTHBERT O'CONNELL, P.O. Box 10, Bassfield, 39421-0010. Tel: 601-943-5104.

Ecumenical & Interreligious Affairs—Mr. LEO TRAHAN, Contact Person. Tel: 228-702-2131.

Liturgy, Office of—Rev. Msgr. RONALD P. HERZOG, Dir., Immaculate Conception Church, 833 West Sixth, Laurel, 39440-3436. Tel: 601-426-3473.

Interim Diocesan Liturgical Commission—Rev. Msgr.

RONALD HERZOG; Revs. MICHAEL AUSTIN; PATRICK HAYES; Very Rev. ANTONE LYNCH, V.F.; Mrs. PEGGY ABSHIRE; Mr. PHIL BEINING; Mr. ROBERT DEJARDINS; Mrs. GINGER DELOROSA; Ms. JOY MEHRTENS; Mrs. PATRICIA SANCHEZ; Dr. RAPHAEL SANCHEZ.

Department of Social and Community Services—1790 Popps Ferry Rd., P.O. Box 1457, Biloxi, 39533-1457. Tel: 228-702-2137. Sr. REBECCA RUTKOWSKI, A.C.S.W., Diocesan Dir. All offices at this address unless otherwise noted. Legal Title: Catholic Social and Community Services, Inc.

Hattiesburg Regional Office—2410 O'Ferral St., Hattiesburg, 39401. Tel: 601-545-1616. POLLY SUMRALL, Office Mgr.; JANNIE GREENE, A.I.D.S. Ministry.

Pascagoula Regional Office—3512 Magnolia St., Pascagoula, 39567-3113. Tel: 228-769-8283; 228-769-8151. GAYLE OAKES, Dir.

Counseling Services—DENNIS CENAC, L.S.W.

Adoption Services—JENNIFER WILLIAMS, L.S.W., 1790 Popps Ferry Rd., P.O. Box 1457, Biloxi, 39533-1457. Tel: 228-702-2137.

Emergency Assistance—DELANE KRAUSE; JENNIFER KNUE, P.O. Box 1457, Biloxi, 39533-1457. Tel: 228-432-0045.

Morning Star Pregnancy Care Center— (Unplanned pregnancy services) NANCY LOFTUS, Maternity Caseworker; ANN RIVERA, Office Mgr., 2204 24th Ave., Gulfport, 39503. Tel: 228-864-4221.

12 Baskets Food Bank—SHIRLEY HEGGINS, Dir. Tel: 228-374-6884.

Refugee Resettlement—Mrs. MAGDA LELEAUX, Dir., P.O. Box 1457, Biloxi, 39533-1457. Tel: 228-374-6507.

Family Life Office—Tel: 228-702-2137.

Catholic Charities Housing Association of Biloxi, Inc.—

Santa Maria Retirement Apartments; Villa Maria Retirement Apartments—Most Rev. THOMAS J. RODI, Pres. Tel: 228-702-2100; Sr. REBECCA RUTKOWSKI, A.C.S.W., Contact Person. Tel: 228-702-2137.

Samaritan Housing, Inc.—Most Rev. THOMAS J. RODI, Pres. Tel: 228-702-2100; Sr. REBECCA RUTKOWSKI, A.C.S.W., Contact Person. Tel: 228-702-2137.

Notre Dame de la Mer, Inc.—Most Rev. THOMAS J. RODI, Pres. Tel: 228-702-2100; Sr. REBECCA RUTKOWSKI, A.C.S.W. Tel: 228-702-2137.

Gabriel Manor, Inc.—Most Rev. THOMAS J. RODI, Pres. Tel: 228-702-2100; Sr. REBECCA RUTKOWSKI, A.C.S.W. Tel: 228-702-2137.

Caritas Manor, Inc.—Most Rev. THOMAS J. RODI, Pres. Tel: 228-702-2100; Sr. REBECCA RUTKOWSKI, A.C.S.W. Tel: 228-702-2137.

Carlow Manor—Most Rev. THOMAS J. RODI, Pres. Tel: 228-702-2100; Sr. REBECCA RUTKOWSKI, A.C.S.W. Tel: 228-702-2137.

Gabriel Manor II, Inc.—Most Rev. THOMAS J. RODI, Pres. Tel: 228-702-2100; Sr. REBECCA RUTKOWSKI, A.C.S.W. Tel: 228-702-2137.

Apostleship of the Sea— Hancock County: Port Bienville Deacons LUCIEN MORAGAS, Harrison County: Port of Gulfport; DICK HENDERSON, Jackson County: Port of Pascagoula; WARREN GOFF.

Vietnamese Apostolate—Rev. DOMINIC PHAN, Church of the Vietnamese Martyrs, 171 Oak St., Biloxi, 39530. Tel: 228-374-3931.

Prison Apostolate—Jackson County Jails: Deacon VICTOR BAGLIONI, Dir. Tel: 228-475-5437. Harrison County Jails: Deacon THOMAS MILLER. Tel: 228-388-5467. South Mississippi Correctional Facility: VACANT.

Diocesan Boards and Committees—

Association of Priests (Diocese of Biloxi and Jackson)—Most Revs. THOMAS J. RODI, Bishop of Biloxi & Co-Chm.; JOSEPH LATINO, Bishop of Jackson & Co-Chm.; Very Rev. THOMAS CONWAY, V.F., Pres.; Rev. CHARLES BUCCIANTINI, Sec., Treas. & Pres. Elect. Trustees: Revs. PATRICK FARRELL; GEORGE MURPHY; KENNETH RAMON-LANDRY; ELVIN SUNDS.

Building and Real Estate Committee—Rev. Msgr. FRANCIS FARRELL, Chm. (Retired); CHUCK COLLINS; LEONARD COLLINS; WILLIAM H. CRAIG; KELEAL HASSIN JR.; GERALD HOPKINS; LLOYD MOON; BOB SLAUGHTER; ROBERT STARKS; STEPHEN STOJCICH; WESLEY TOCHE III; BOB USEY.

Catholic Foundation-Diocese of Biloxi—Most Rev. THOMAS J. RODI, Pres.; Rev. Msgr. ANDREW MURRAY, Vice Pres.; Deacon ROBERTO JIMENEZ, Exec. Dir.; Dr. HARRY SCHMIDT JR., Chm.; CHARLES HEWES; JOSEPH HUDSON; TED LONGO; DAVID LORD; ALFRED PARKER; ROBERT TUCEI; TAMMY W. DILORENZO, C.P.A., Advisor.

Catholic Housing Board—Most Rev. THOMAS J. RODI, Pres.; Sr. REBECCA RUTKOWSKI, A.C.S.W., Chm.; Rev. Msgr. ANDREW MURRAY; Rev. BERNARD FARRELL; TAMMY W. DILORENZO, C.P.A.; SALVADOR DOMINO; GEORGE WATSON; GERALD HOPKINS.

Finance Council—Most Rev. THOMAS J. RODI; WILLIAM PENEGUY, Chm.; Rev. Msgr. ANDREW MURRAY; RICHARD ECKERT; JOSEPH P. HUDSON; Deacon ROBERTO JIMENEZ; THEODORE LONGO; DAVID L. LORD; Rev. PETER MOCKLER; STEVE MONTAGNET; JOHN P. MYERS; DAVID A. TRUETEL.

Insurance Committee—Most Rev. THOMAS J. RODI; STEVE MONTAGNET, Chm.; Dr. LANNY ACOSTA; Rev. JOHN E. FORD, S.T.; Sr. DONELLA HARTMAN, R.S.M.; Rev. Msgr. ANDREW MURRAY; Sr. REBECCA RUTKOWSKI, A.C.S.W. Advisors: TAMMY W. DILORENZO, C.P.A.; Mr. A. J. SCARDINO.

Mission Board—Most Rev. THOMAS J. RODI; Rev. MICHAEL AUSTIN.

Personnel Board—Rev. PATRICK HAYES, Chm.; Rev. Msgr. ANDREW MURRAY; Revs. DENNIS CARVER; BERNARD FARRELL; GEORGE KITCHIN.

Presbyteral Council—Most Rev. THOMAS J. RODI, Pres.; Revs. ANTHONY ARGUELLES, Chm.; CUTHBERT O'CONNELL, Vice Chm.; DENNIS CARVER, Sec.; Rev. Msgrs. RONALD HERZOG; JAMES P. MCGOUGH, J.C.D.; ANDREW MURRAY; Very Revs. GERARD CLEARY, V.F.; THOMAS CONWAY, V.F.; ANTONE LYNCH, V.F.; PATRICK MCDERMOTT, V.F.; JOHN NOONE, V.F.; Revs. BERNARD FARRELL; JOHN FORD, S.T.; PATRICK HAYES; LOUIS LOHAN; PATRICK MOCKLER; PETER MOCKLER; MICHAEL SNYDER; JOSEPH TRUONG TRINH.

Miscellaneous Apostolates—

Campaign for Human Development—Rev. IVAN J. WEIS, Dir., St. John Parish, P.O. Box 347, Biloxi, 38533-0347.

Catholic Relief Services—Sr. REBECCA RUTKOWSKI, A.C.S.W., P.O. Box 1457, Biloxi, 39533-1457.

Catholic University, Friends of—Rev. Msgr. ANDREW MURRAY, P.O. Box 1189, Biloxi, 39533-1189.

Charismatic Renewal—Rev. GEORGE KITCHIN, Dir., St. James Parish, 366 Cowan-Lorraine Rd., Gulfport, 39507.

Council of the St. Vincent de Paul Society—Mr. FRED FIRTH, Pres. Tel: 228-388-1837.

Cursillo and Retreats—Rev. ANTHONY DOAN TRAN; BUCK O'GEA, Lay Dir., 14595 Vidalia Rd., Pass Christian, 39571. Tel: 228-255-7560.

Deaf and Disabled, Office of the—Mr. GREGORY K. CRAPO, Dir., de l'Epee Deaf Center, Inc., 1450 North St., Gulfport, 39507. Tel: 228-897-2280 (Voice-TDD); Fax: 228-897-2462.

Latin American Apostolate— Mission-Saltillo, Mexico, co-sponsored with Diocese of Jackson Rev. Msgr. MICHAEL THORNTON, Parroquia San Miguel Arcangel, Apdo. 52 Sucursal "A", 25000 Saltillo, Coah, Me.

Legion of Mary—Deacon VICTOR A. BAGLIONI, 3855 Riverpine Dr., Moss Point, 39563.

Permanent Diaconate Program—Deacon MARTIN FINNEGAN, Dir., 5713 Belle Fontaine Dr., Ocean Springs, 39564. Assoc. Directors: Deacons VICTOR BAGLIONI, (Formation); THOMAS LEBLANC, (Continuing Education & Formation).

Pontifical Association of the Holy Childhood—Rev. MICHAEL AUSTIN, Dir., Mailing Address, 502 Jackson Ave., Ocean Springs, 39564. Tel: 228-875-5419.

Propagation of the Faith—Rev. MICHAEL AUSTIN, Dir., Mailing Address, 502 Jackson Ave., Ocean Springs, 39564. Tel: 228-875-5419.

Vocations—Rev. DENNIS CARVER, Dir., P.O. Box 548, Pass Christian, 39571. Tel: 228-452-4586.

Victim Assistance Coordinator—Sr. MARY RIORDAN, R.S.M. Tel: 228-896-6302. Email: maryrb@worldnetatt.net.

CLERGY, PARISHES, MISSIONS AND PAROCHIAL SCHOOLS

CITY OF BILOXI
(HARRISON COUNTY)

1—CATHEDRAL OF THE NATIVITY OF THE BLESSED VIRGIN MARY (1843), Revs. I. Anthony Arguelles, Rector; Greg Barras; Deacons Rene J. Moniot; Ben Wimberly Jr.
Res.: 870 Howard Ave., P.O. Box 367, 39533. Tel: 228-374-1717; Fax: 228-374-1773.
School—(Grades K-6) Tel: 228-432-2269; Fax: 228-432-9421. Sr. Mary Jo Mike, O.S.F., Prin. Nativity 1; Lay Teachers 20; Students 241.
Catechesis/Religious Program—Students 130.

2—CHURCH OF THE VIETNAMESE MARTYRS (2000), (Vietnamese), [JC] Rev. Dominic Phan.
Res.: 171 Oak St., 39530. Tel: 228-374-1116.
Catechesis/Religious Program—Students 243.

3—ST. JOHN (1922), Rev. Ivan J. Weis.
Mailing Address: P.O. Box 347, 39533-0347. Tel: 228-374-0117; Fax: 228-374-0118.
Res.: 724 Bradford St., 39530. Tel: 228-374-0117; Fax: 228-374-0118.
Catechesis/Religious Program—P.O. Box 367, 39533. Tel: 228-374-1717. All programs held at Nativity B.V.M. Parish, Biloxi. Students 5.

4—ST. LOUIS (1957), Rev. Ivan J. Weis.
Mailing Address: P.O. Box 347, 39533-0347.
Office Address—St. John's, 724 Bradford St., 39533-0347. Tel: 228-374-0117; Fax: 228-374-0118.
Catechesis/Religious Program—P.O. Box 367, 39533. Tel: 228-374-1717. All programs held at Nativity B.V.M. Parish, Biloxi. Students 3.

5—ST. MARY (1973), Rev. Thomas White.
Res.: 8343 Woolmarket Rd., 39532. Tel: 228-392-7500; Fax: 228-392-1999.
Catechesis/Religious Program—Tel: 228-392-1999; Fax: 228-392-4552. Students 115.

6—ST. MICHAEL (1917), Rev. Patrick O'Shaughnessy.
Res.: 177 First St., P.O. Box 523, 39533. Tel: 228-435-5578; Fax: 228-435-5579.

7—OUR LADY OF FATIMA (1957), Rev. Patrick J. Mockler. In Res., Rev. Msgr. Francis Farrell (Retired).
Res.: 2090 Pass Rd., 39531. Tel: 228-388-3887; Fax: 228-388-7069.
School—(Grades PreK-6), 320 Jim Money Rd., 39531. Tel: 228-388-3602; Fax: 228-385-1140. Susie Bass, Prin. Lay Teachers 14; Students 245.
Catechesis/Religious Program—Tel: 228-388-5737. Students 222.

8—OUR MOTHER OF SORROWS (1914), (African American), Rev. Gregory Barras (JKS), Admin.
Res.: 803 Division St., 39530. Tel: 228-436-6503.

9—SACRED HEART (1921), Very Rev. Patrick M. McDermott, V.F. In Res., Rev. Denis Harlow.
Res.: 10446 Le Moyne Blvd., 39540. Tel: 228-392-4526; Fax: 228-396-3270.
School—(Grades PreK-6) Tel: 228-392-4180; Fax: 228-392-4859. Sr. Joan Landry, R.S.M., Prin. Sisters of Mercy 2; Lay Teachers 11; Students 188.
Catechesis/Religious Program—Tel: 228-392-4180. Sr. Julia Marie Burke, R.S.M., D.R.E. Students 442.

OUTSIDE THE CITY OF BILOXI

BASSFIELD, JEFFERSON DAVIS CO., ST. PETER (1904), (Irish), [CEM 2] [JC 2] Rev. Cuthbert O'Connell; Deacon Robert Everard.
Res.: 4143 Hwy. 42, P.O. Box 10, 39421. Tel: 601-943-5104; Fax: 601-943-8055.
Catechesis/Religious Program—Tel: 601-943-6259. Mrs. Mary E. Coulter, D.R.E. Students 60.
Mission—St. Elizabeth Carson, Jefferson Davis Co.
Mission—St. Mary's Prentiss, Jefferson Davis Co.
Mission—St. Lawrence P.O. Box 16, Monticello, Lawrence Co. 39654. Tel: 601-587-8017.

BAY ST. LOUIS, HANCOCK CO.

1—OUR LADY OF THE GULF (1847), [CEM] Revs. Michael Tracey (Ireland); Gary Nance, M.S.; Kathleen LeBlanc, Pastoral Assoc. In Res., Rev. John T. O'Brien (Retired).
Res.: 228 S. Beach Blvd., P.O. Box 208, 39520-0208. Tel: 228-467-6509; Fax: 228-467-6509.
School—Bay St. Louis Catholic Elementary, (Grades PreK-6) Tel: 228-467-5158; Fax: 228-467-9742. Dr. Randy Verret, Prin. Lay Teachers 20; Students 314.
High School—Tel: 228-467-7048; Fax: 228-467-1666. Sr. Donella Hartman, R.S.M., Prin. Sisters 3; Lay Teachers 19; Students 281.
Catechesis/Religious Program—Tel: 228-467-6509. Students 160.
Mission—St. Joseph's Chapel Dunbar & Blakemore, Hancock Co. 39520.

2—ST. ROSE DE LIMA (1924), (African American), Rev. Sebastian Myladiyil, S.V.D.
Res.: 301 S. Necaise Ave., 39520. Tel: 228-467-7357; Fax: 228-467-7740.
Catechesis/Religious Program—Tel: 228-466-2769. Mrs. Joan Thomas, D.R.E. Students 107.

CLERMONT HARBOR, HANCOCK CO., ST. ANN (1915), [CEM] Rev. John J. Kelly.
Res.: 5858 Lower Bay Rd., P.O. Box 1037, Lakeshore, 39558-1037. Tel: 228-467-4746; Fax: 228-467-2666.
Catechesis/Religious Program—Students 78.
Mission—St. John P.O. Box 1037, Lakeshore, Hancock Co. 39558.

COLUMBIA, MARION CO., MOST HOLY TRINITY (1959), Rev. Victor Seidel, S.T.
Res.: 1429 N. Park Ave., 39429. Tel: 601-736-3136; Fax: 601-736-1920.
Catechesis/Religious Program—Tel: 601-731-5120. Kathryn Stringer, D.R.E. (Holy Trinity); Tonya Sikes, D.R.E. (Holy Trinity); Betty Smet, D.R.E. (St. Paul the Apostle). Students 36.
Mission—St. Paul the Apostle 702 Union Rd., Tylertown, Walthall Co. 39667. Tel: 601-876-6422.

DELISLE, HARRISON CO., THE CATHOLIC CHURCH IN DELISLE (1874), Rev. John E. Ford, S.T.; Deacon Regis Brennan, S.T., Pastoral Assoc.
Res.: 25220 St. Stephen Rd., Pass Christian, 39571. Tel: 228-255-1294; Fax: 228-255-7479.
Catechesis/Religious Program—Shirley Callahan, D.R.E. Students 176.
Mission—St. Ann Vidalia Rd., Dubuisson, Harrison Co. 39571.
Mission—St. William Edwin Ladner Rd., Rotten Bayou, Harrison Co. 39571.

GAUTIER, JACKSON CO., ST. MARY (1968), Rev. Patrick Hayes.
Res.: 809 De La Pointe Rd., 39553. Tel: 228-497-2364; Fax: 228-497-5887.
Catechesis/Religious Program— Donna Harper, D.R.E. Students 240.

GULFPORT, HARRISON CO.

1—ST. ANN (1939), Rev. Peter Mockler.
Res.: 23529 Hwy. 53, 39503. Tel: 228-832-2560; Fax: 228-832-2560.
Catechesis/Religious Program—Tel: 228-831-9452. Robert Earl Lizana, D.R.E. Students 86.
Mission—Our Lady of Chartres Big Creek Road, Delmas Dedeaux, Harrison Co. 39503.

2—ST. JAMES (1898), [CEM] Rev. George Kitchin; Deacons John R. Henderson; Rick Conason.
Res.: 366 Cowan Rd., P.O. Box 7267, 39506. Tel: 228-896-6059; Fax: 228-896-5498.
School—(Grades PreK-6) Tel: 228-896-6631; Fax: 228-896-6638. Mrs. Linda Kremer, Prin. Sisters of Mercy (Ennis, Ireland) 3; Lay Teachers 17; Students 298.
Catechesis/Religious Program—Tel: 228-896-8047. Mr. Robert Russo, D.R.E. Students 385.

3—ST. JOHN THE EVANGELIST (1900), Rev. Msgr. Andrew Murray; Rev. Christopher Louis Munsch; Deacon Al Stockert.
Res.: 2414 17th St., P.O. Box 970, 39501. Tel: 228-864-2272; Fax: 228-864-2273.
School—(Grades PreK-6) Tel: 228-863-1606; Fax: 228-863-9677. Denise S. Barter, Prin. Lay Teachers 16; Students 167.
High School—Tel: 228-863-8141; Fax: 228-864-2788. Dr. William Heath, Prin. Lay Teachers 31; Students 293.
Catechesis/Religious Program—Sr. Mary Kealy, P.B.V.M., D.R.E.; Annette Seymour, D.R.E. Students 28.

4—ST. JOSEPH CATHOLIC CHURCH (Northwood Hills) (1966), Very Rev. Antone J. Lynch, V.F. (Retired).
Res.: 12290 DePew Rd., 39503. Tel: 228-832-3244; 228-832-1166; Fax: 228-832-1166.
Catechesis/Religious Program— Mrs. Bernice Engel, D.R.E. Students 265.

5—ST. THERESE (1932), (African American), Rev. Raymond P. Carignan, S.S.J.
Res.: 3521 19th St., 39501. Tel: 228-863-0624; Fax: 228-863-2531.
Catechesis/Religious Program—Tel: 228-863-7719. Sr. Carmelita Mulry, S.H.Sp., D.R.E.; Ms. Cynthia Graham, D.R.E. Students 92.

HATTIESBURG, FORREST CO.

1—HOLY ROSARY (1949), (African American), Rev. William Vollor.
Res.: 900 Dabbs St., 39401. Tel: 601-584-6528; Fax: 601-584-9533.

2—SACRED HEART (1900), Rev. George Murphy.
Res.: 313 Walnut St., P.O. Box 1027, 39401. Tel: 601-583-9404; Fax: 601-583-9486.
School—(Grades PreK-8) Tel: 601-583-8683; Fax: 601-583-8684. Dr. Maribeth Andereck, Prin. Lay Teachers 28; Students 317.
Catechesis/Religious Program—Tel: 601-583-9404; Fax: 601-583-9486. Students 157.

3—ST. THOMAS AQUINAS (1968),, (University of Southern Mississippi-Student Parish) Rev. Thomas Conway; Deacon Ralph Torrelli.
Res.: 3117 W. Fourth St., 39401. Tel: 601-264-5192; Fax: 601-264-0834.
Catechesis/Religious Program—Tel: 601-271-2919. Angie Box, D.R.E. Students 162.
Station—Danforth Chapel, U.S.M. University. (University of Southern Mississippi-Student Parish)

KILN, HANCOCK CO., ANNUNCIATION (1869), Very Rev. John Noone, V.F.
Res.: 5370 Kiln-DeLisle Rd., 39556. Tel: 228-255-1800; Fax: 228-255-1894.
Catechesis/Religious Program—Tel: 228-255-1869. Mrs. Alysia Ladner, D.R.E. Students 253.

LAUREL, JONES CO., IMMACULATE CONCEPTION (1887), Rev. Msgr. Ronald P. Herzog; Deacons Richard Hollingsworth; Larry Pressly; Mrs. Suzie Middleton, Youth Min.
Res.: 833 W. Sixth St., 39440. Tel: 601-426-3473; Fax: 601-426-3890.
School—(Grades PreK-6) Tel: 601-428-0129 Fax: 601-428-2056. Kathy Asmar, Prin. Lay Teachers 9; Students 108.
Catechesis/Religious Program—Tel: 601-426-3473. Students 125.

LONG BEACH, HARRISON CO., ST. THOMAS THE APOSTLE (1903), Rev. Louis Lohan; Sr. Teresa Baugh, P.B.V.M., Pastoral Assoc.; Deacon Bob Jones.
Res.: 720 E. Beach Blvd., 39560. Tel: 228-863-1610; Fax: 228-868-6068.
School—(Grades PreK-6) Tel: 228-863-6876; Fax: 228-863-9537. Mrs. Elizabeth Fortenberry, Prin. Lay Teachers 12; Students 252.
Catechesis/Religious Program—Tel: 228-868-3774. Mrs. Myrna Jordan, D.R.E. Students 506.

LUMBERTON, LAMAR CO., OUR LADY OF PERPETUAL HELP (1922), (German), [CEM] Rev. Ken Ramon-Landry; Deacon Harold Gaule; Mrs. Katie Murphy, Pastoral Assoc.
Res.: 379 W. Seneca Rd., 39455-7728. Tel: 601-796-3051 (Office); 601-769-3053 (Rectory); Fax: 601-796-3023.
Catechesis/Religious Program—Students 78.
Mission—St. Joseph P.O. Box 202, Poplarville, Pearl River Co. 39470. Tel: 601-795-9164

MOSS POINT, JACKSON CO., ST. JOSEPH (1950), Rev. Dominick Fullam; Deacons Victor A. Baglioni; Emery E. Elder.
Res.: 4114 First St., P.O. Box 8549, 39562-8549. Tel: 228-475-0777; Fax: 228-475-3672.
Catechesis/Religious Program— Mrs. Diane Stewart, D.R.E. (St. Ann). Tel: 228-441-3937. Students 130.
Mission—St. Ann P.O. Box 8549, Hurley Jackson Co. 39562-8549. Tel: 228-588-2224.

OCEAN SPRINGS, JACKSON CO.

1—ST. ALPHONSUS (1860), Revs. Henry McInerney; Michael Austin; Deacon Thomas Miller.
Res.: 502 Jackson Ave., 39564. Tel: 228-875-5419; Fax: 228-875-5410.
School—(Grades PreK-6) Tel: 228-875-5329; Fax: 228-875-3584. Sherrie McAllister, Prin. Lay Teachers 21; Students 293.
Catechesis/Religious Program—Tel: 228-872-2652. Sr. Eileen Lowney, D.R.E. Students 392.

2—ST. ELIZABETH ANN SETON (1975), Rev. Bernard Farrell; Deacon Tom Le Blanc, Pastoral Assoc.
Res.: 4900 Riley Rd., 39564. Tel: 228-875-0654; Fax: 228-875-6852.
Catechesis/Religious Program—Deacon Martin Finnegan, D.R.E. Students 245.

PASCAGOULA, JACKSON CO.

1—OUR LADY OF VICTORIES (1855), Very Rev. Gerard Cleary, V.F.
Res.: 510 Convent St., P.O. Box 368, 39568. Tel: 228-762-1653; Fax: 228-762-2546.
Catechesis/Religious Program—Tel: 228-497-6893. Michele Hill, D.R.E. Students 58.

2—ST. PETER THE APOSTLE (1907), (African American), [CEM] Rev. Charles E. McMahon, S.S.J., Admin.
Res.: 1715 Telephone Rd., P.O. Box 876, 39567. Tel: 228-762-1759; Fax: 228-762-4642.
School—(Grades K-6) Tel: 228-762-3766; Fax: 228-762-4642. Sr. Bernadette McNamara, S.H.Sp., Prin. Servants of the Holy Spirit 3; Lay Teachers 9; Students 94
Catechesis/Religious Program—Tel: 228-762-1759. Mrs. Angela Ashford, D.R.E. Students 90.

3—SACRED HEART (1963), Rev. Michael Kelleher; Deacon Warren Goff.
Mailing Address: P.O. Box 2190, 39569. Tel: 228-762-1837; Fax: 228-762-1958.
Res.: 3702 Quinn Dr., 39581. Tel: 228-762-1837.
School—Resurrection School-Elementary, (Grades PreK-6), 3709 Quinn Dr., 39581-2356. Tel: 228-762-7207; Fax: 228-762-0611. Elizabeth Benefield, Prin. Lay Teachers 20; Students 268.
Catechesis/Religious Program—Students 73.

PASS CHRISTIAN, HARRISON CO.

1—OUR MOTHER OF MERCY (1911), (African American), [JC] Rev. Bartholomew Enslow, S.S.J.
Res.: 222 E. Railroad Ave., 39571. Tel: 228-452-4514; Fax: 228-452-4514.
Catechesis/Religious Program—Tel: 228-452-4002. Students 93.
Convent—251 Saucier Ave., P.O. Box 157, 39571.

2—ST. PAUL (Dedeaux) (1847), [CEM] Revs. Dennis J. Carver; Joseph Truong Trinh.
Res.: 140 E. Beach Blvd., P.O. Box 548, 39571. Tel: 228-452-4686; Fax: 228-452-5488.
School—(Grades PreK-6) Tel: 228-452-7359; Fax: 228-452-5488. Mrs. J.B. Pike, Prin. Lay Teachers 12; Students 170.
Catechesis/Religious Program—Students 90.

3—SACRED HEART (Dedeaux) (1967), Rev. Anthony Doan Tran; Deacon Roberto Jiminez.
Res.: 14595 Vidalia Rd., 39571. Tel: 228-255-7453; Fax: 228-255-7560.
Catechesis/Religious Program—Students 152.
Station—Cursillo Center, Tel: 228-255-7560. Students 121

PEARLINGTON, HANCOCK CO., ST. JOSEPH (1939), [JC] Rev. James O'Bryan, S.T., M.A.
Mailing Address: P.O. Box 39, 39572. Tel: 228-533-7968; Fax: 228-533-0036.

PICAYUNE, PEARL RIVER CO., ST. CHARLES BORROMEO (1950), Rev. Michael E. Snyder.
Res.: 321 Juniper St., 39466. Tel: 601-798-4779.
Catechesis/Religious Program—Tel: 601-798-7574; Fax: 601-798-4749. Dorothy Ducote, D.R.E. Students 370.

PINEVILLE, HARRISON CO., OUR LADY OF LOURDES (Pass Christian) (1973), Rev. Thaddeus Searles, S.T.
Mailing Address: P.O. Box 508, Pass Christian, 39571. Tel: 228-452-7132; Fax: 228-452-2287.
Res.: 22342 Evangeline Rd., Pass Christian, 39571. Tel: 228-452-7132.
Catechesis/Religious Program—Students 36.

VANCLEAVE, JACKSON CO., HOLY SPIRIT CATHOLIC CHURCH (1980), Rev. John R. McGrath; Deacon John E. Jennings.
Res.: P.O. Box 5032, 39565. Tel: 228-826-4008.
Catechesis/Religious Program—Students 227.
Mission—Christ the King 10601 Daisy Vestry, Latimer, Jackson Co. 39565. Tel: 228-392-0340.

WAVELAND, HANCOCK CO., ST. CLARE (1919), Rev. Msgr. James P. McGough, J.C.D.
Res.: 236 S. Beach Blvd., P.O. Box 500, 39576. Tel: 228-467-9275; Fax: 228-466-3541.
School—Tel: 228-467-7071; Fax: 228-467-0584. Mr. Mark Camella, Prin. Lay Teachers 9; Students 138.
Catechesis/Religious Program— Noel Phillips, D.R.E. Students 112.

WAYNESBORO, WAYNE CO., ST. BERNADETTE (1977), [JC 2] Rev. Msgr. Ronald P. Herzog.
Res.: 401 Mississippi Dr., 39367. Tel: 601-735-9420.
Catechesis/Religious Program—Students 12.
Mission—Holy Trinity P.O. Box 896, Leakesville, Perry Co. 39451. Tel: 601-394-6761.

WHITE CYPRESS, HANCOCK CO., ST. MATTHEW THE APOSTLE (1982), Rev. Noel Fannon.
Mailing Address: P.O. Box 919, Kiln, 39556.
Res.: 27074 St. Matthew Church Rd., Perkinston, 39573. Tel: 228-255-7720; Fax: 228-586-0389.
Catechesis/Religious Program—Students 105.

WIGGINS, STONE CO., ST. FRANCIS XAVIER (1961), [JC] Rev. Fintan J. Kilmurray.
Res.: 1026 E. Central Ave., 39577. Tel: 601-928-2182; Fax: 601-928-2182.
Church: Tel: 601-928-2182.
Catechesis/Religious Program—Tel: 601-928-3267. Students 70.
Mission—St. Lucy CB6308, Lucedale, George Co. 39452. Tel: 601-947-9968. Deacon Caruba L. Merrill.
Station—Perkinston Junior College Perkinston.

Chaplains of Public Institutions

BILOXI. *Biloxi Regional Hospital, Gulf Coast Community Hospital*. Rev. Denis Harlow.
Keesler Airforce Base. Rev. Matthew J. Glaros (CLV), Lt.
V.A. Center. Rev. Joseph A. Dilettuso.

COLUMBIA. *Industrial and Training School*. Rev. Victor Seidel, S.T.

GULFPORT. *Naval Const. Bn. Center*. Rev. Michael Mikstay, LCDR.
U.S. Naval Home. (Vacant)
V.A. Hospital. Revs. Anthony E. Menz, Joseph Dilettuso.

HATTIESBURG. *University of Southern Mississippi*. Very Rev. Thomas Conway, V.F.

LEAKESVILLE. *South Mississippi Correctional Institution*. Vacant.

Special Assignment:
Rev.—
Dilettuso, Joseph, Veterans Affairs Hospital, 39531.

Military Chaplains:
Rev.—
Higginbotham, Robert, U.S.A.F.

Retired:
Most Rev.—
Howze, Joseph L.
Rev. Msgrs.—
Farrell, Francis
Hannon, James J., J.C.D.
Johnson, Gregory
Mercier, Joseph
Revs.—
Izral, John
Kozak, Remigius A.
O'Brien, John
Scott, Francis
Taylor, James B.

Permanent Deacons:
Baglioni, Victor A., St. Joseph, Moss Point
Bertucci, Chris, St. Stephen, DeLisle
Brennan, Regis S.T., DeLisle
Conason, Rick, St. James, Gulfport
Elder, Emery, St. Joseph, Moss Point

Everard, Robert, St. Peter, Bassfield
Finnegan, Martin, St. Elizabeth Seton, Ocean Springs
Gaule, Harold, Our Lady of Perpetual Help, Lumberton
Goff, Warren P., Sr., Sacred Heart, Pascagoula
Harper, Gayden R., St. Mary, Gautier
Henderson, John R., St. James, Gulfport
Hollingsworth, Richard A., Immaculate Conception, Laurel
Jennings, John E., Holy Spirit, Vancleave
Jimenez, Roberto, Sacred Heart, Pass Christian
Jones, Bob, St. Thomas, Long Beach
LeBlanc, Tom, St. Elizabeth Seton, Ocean Springs
Merrill, Caruba L., St. Lucy, Lucedale
Miller, Thomas M., St. Alphonsus, Ocean Springs
Moragas, Lucien F., Jr., Annunciation, Kiln
Pressly, Larry L., Immaculate Conception, Laurel
Stockert, Al, St. John the Evangelist, Gulfport.
Torrelli, Ralph
Vrazel, William, St. Paul, Pass Christian.
Wimberly, Ben, Jr., Nativity B.V.M. Cathedral, Biloxi

INSTITUTIONS LOCATED IN THE DIOCESE

[A] SEMINARIES, RELIGIOUS OR SCHOLASTICATES

BAY ST. LOUIS. *St. Augustine's*, 199 Seminary Dr., 39520. Tel: 228-467-6414; Fax: 228-466-4393. Priests 14; Brothers 4; Permanent Staff Priests 5; Permanent Staff Brothers 3.

St. Augustine's Retreat Center Tel: 228-467-9837; Fax: 228-466-4393. Very Rev. Joseph Guidry, S.V.D., Rector; Bro. Richard Chambers, S.V.D., Financial Admin.

Media Production Center Tel: 228-467-1097; Fax: 228-466-5640. Rev. James Pawlicki, S.V.D., Dir. Media Production Center. Priests 14; Brothers 3; Permanent Staff Priests 5; Permanent Staff Brothers 3. In Res. Revs. George Artis, S.V.D.; Joseph Detig, S.V.D.; Very Rev. Joseph Guidry, S.V.D.; Revs. Raymond Guidry, S.V.D.; Raymond Hannah, S.V.D.; Charles Heskamp, S.V.D.; John Kersten, S.V.D.; Michael Moody, S.V.D.; Brendan Murphy, S.V.D. (LAF); James Pawlicki, S.V.D.; Stanley Plutz, S.V.D.; Thomas Potts, S.V.D.; Peter Smits, S.V.D.; A. Francis Theriault, S.V.D.; Bros. Richard Chambers, S.V.D.; James Heeb, S.V.D.

[B] HIGH SCHOOLS, INTERPAROCHIAL

BILOXI. *Mercy Cross Inter-Parochial High School*, (Grades 7-12) , (Coed; includes junior high school) , 390 Crusader Dr., 39530. Tel: 228-374-4145; Fax: 228-374-8119. Email: mercycross@mercycross.com. Web: www.mercycross.com. Dr. Julie Wade, Prin. Lay Teachers 25; Students 312.

BAY ST. LOUIS. *Our Lady Academy*, (Grades 7-12) , (Girls) , 222 S. Beach Blvd., 39520-4320. Tel: 228-467-7048; Fax: 228-467-1666. Email: donella@ourladyacademy.com. Web: www.ourladyacademy.com. Sr. Mary Donella Hartman, R.S.M., Prin. Sisters of Mercy 3; Lay Teachers 20; Students 291.

GULFPORT. *St. John Inter-Parochial High School* (Coed) , 620 Pass Rd., 39501-6494. Tel: 228-863-8141; Fax: 228-864-2788. Email: stjohn1@cableone.net. Bill Heath, Ed.D., Prin. Lay Teachers 22; Students 294.

PASCAGOULA. *Resurrection School-Jr./Sr. School* (Coed) , 520 Watts Ave., 39567. Tel: 228-762-3353; Fax: 228-769-1226. Email: geolaird@aol.com. Web: www.rcseagles.com. George Laird, Ed.D., Pres. & Prin. Lay Teachers 16; Students 125.

[C] HIGH SCHOOLS AND ELEMENTARY SCHOOLS, PRIVATE

BAY ST. LOUIS. *St. Stanislaus College*, 304 S. Beach Blvd., 39520-4301. Tel: 228-467-9057; Fax: 228-466-2972. Email: ssc@ststan.com. Web: www.ststan.com. Bros. Ronald Talbot, S.C., Pres.; Ronald Hingle, S.C., Prin.; Dolores Richmond, Dir. Admissions. Brothers of the Sacred Heart, Boys boarding and day school, secondary and elementary. Brothers 10; Lay Teachers 54; Students 550.

[D] HOUSING FOR THE ELDERLY

BILOXI. *Gabriel Manor*, 2321 Atkinson Rd., 39531. Tel: 228-388-1013; Fax: 228-388-1176. Email: gab.apt@worldnet.att.net. Ms. Brenda Mulvaney, Mgr. Total Staff 3; Total in Residence 51.

Gabriel Manor II, Inc.

Santa Maria Retirement Apartments, 674 Beach, 39530. Tel: 228-432-1289; Fax: 228-435-0380. Email: santamar@datasync.com. Rhonda Meredith, Mgr. Total Staff 7; Total in Residence 200.

BAY ST. LOUIS. *Notre Dame de la Mer Retirement Apartments*, 292 Hwy. 90, 39520. Tel: 228-467-2885; Fax: 228-466-6300. Email: mftine@bellsouth.net. Ms. Michele Tine, Mgr. Total Staff 3; Total in Residence 64.

GULFPORT. *Carlow Manor*, 15195 Barbara Dr., 39503. Tel: 228-539-0707; Fax: 228-539-0704. Email: carlowmanor@digiscape.com. Connie Keech, Mgr. Total Staff 2; Total in Residence 40.

OCEAN SPRINGS. *Samaritan House*, 642 Jackson Ave., 39564. Tel: 228-875-1087; Fax: 228-872-9500. Email: samhouse@datasync.com. Ms. Sharon Ballow, Mgr. Total Staff 2; Total in Residence 52.

Villa Maria Retirement Apartments, 921 Porter Ave., 39564. Tel: 228-875-8811; Fax: 228-875-8889. Email: villacindy@aol.com. Mrs. Cindy A. Ladnier, Mgr. Total Staff 15; Total in Residence 225.

PETAL. *Caritas Manor*, 145 W. 10th Ave., 39465. Tel: 601-545-7744; Fax: 601-545-7740. Email: caritas@megagate.com. Total Staff 2; Total in Residence 32.

[E] MONASTERIES AND RESIDENCES OF PRIESTS AND BROTHERS

BILOXI. *St. John Neumann Residence*, 1044 Beach Blvd., 39530. Tel: 228-374-1800; Fax: 228-374-1829. Revs. Joseph Armshaw, C.Ss.R.; Albert Babin, C.Ss.R., Local Supr.; Warren Drinkwater, C.Ss.R.; Edward C. Cosgrove, C.Ss.R.; Earl Toups, C.Ss.R.; Gerard Siebold, C.SS.R.; Bro. John Bosco. Redemptorists

BAY ST. LOUIS. *Brothers of the Sacred Heart*, 114 Bookter St., 39520. Tel: 228-463-0282; Fax: 228-466-2972. Email: rtalbotsc@ststan.com. Bros. Adrian Gaudin, S.C., Dir.; Charles Schilling, S.C.; Harold Harris, S.C.; Ronald Hingle, S.C.; Ronald Talbot, S.C. Total in Residence 5.

Media Production Center "In A Word", 199 Seminary Dr., 39520. Tel: 228-467-1097; Fax: 228-466-5640. Email: editor@inaword.com. Web: www.inaword.com. Rev. James Pawlicki, S.V.D., Dir. & Editor.

Southern Province of St. Augustine - Provincial Residence, 201 Ruella Ave., 39520. Tel: 228-467-4322; Fax: 228-466-5618. Email: svduss@aol.com. Very Rev. Joseph D. Simon, S.V.D., Prov.; Rev. Thomas James, S.V.D., Vice Prov.; Bro. Richard Chambers, S.V.D., Treas. Society of the Divine Word Priests 56; Brothers 8; Parishes 23; Mission Stations 4; Elementary schools 5.

Province Development Office Tel: 228-467-3815; Fax: 228-466-5618. Rev. Thomas Potts, S.V.D., Dir.

Retreats Tel: 228-467-9837; Fax: 228-466-4393.

Saint Stanislaus Community, 109 Bookter St., 39520. Tel: 228-467-9102. Email: bcbouchereau@ststan.com. Bros. Carl Bouchereau, S.C., Dir.; Albert Ledet, S.C.; Donnan Berry, S.C., (Retired); Eduardo Baldioceda, S.C.; Francis Fleming, S.C.; Joseph Donovan, S.C.; Loyola Mattingly, S.C.; Mark Thornton, S.C., (Retired); Noel Lemmon, S.C.; Ramon Daunis, S.C.; Raymond Sylve, S.C.; Rian Messonnier, S.C., (Retired); Roy Reinecke, S.C., (Retired); Hubert Bonnette; Marcel Riviere; Nicholas Geisenberg, S.C., (Retired); Virgil Harris, S.C.; Alfred Kolb, S.C., (Retired). Brothers of the Sacred Heart Total in Residence 18.

[F] CONVENTS AND RESIDENCES FOR SISTERS

BILOXI. *Sisters of Mercy Convent*, 11454 Spring Ln., 39532. Tel: 228-392-2575; Fax: 228-392-2582. Sr. Kim Marie Lajoie, R.S.M., Contact Person. Religious Sisters of Mercy of the Americas 4.

LONG BEACH. *Congregation of the Holy Rosary* (Vietnamese) , 5122 N. Gates Ave., 39560. Tel: 228-863-3045. Sisters 4; Aspirants 7.

Presentation Sisters, 18091 Commission Rd., 39560. Tel: 228-864-8418. Email: pres18091@aol.com. Web: www.gnofn.org/~presis. Union of the Sisters of the Presentation of the Blessed Virgin Mary

PASCAGOULA. *St. Peter the Apostle Convent*, 1703 Telephone Rd., 39567. Tel: 228-762-3766; Fax: 228-762-4642. Email: Sstpeter13@aol.com. Sisters of the Holy Spirit and Mary Immaculate Consensus Community Sisters 3; Total Staff 3; Total in Residence 2.

[G] NEWMAN CENTERS

HATTIESBURG. *University of Southern Mississippi* St. Thomas Aquinas Chapel, 3117 W. Fourth St., 39401. Tel: 601-264-5192; Fax: 601-264-0834. Email: church@stthomas-usm.org. Web: www.stthomas-usm.org. Rev. Tommy Conway, Chap.

[H] MISCELLANEOUS

BILOXI. *Magnificat - Mississippi Gulf Coast Chapter*, P.O. Box 4344, 39531. Tel: 228-875-7407; Fax: 228-374-4157. Ms. Margie Fleming, Contact Person.

BAY ST. LOUIS. *St. Stanislaus College*, 304 S. Beach Blvd., 39520. Tel: 228-467-9057; 800-517-6257; Fax: 228-466-2972. Email: ssc@ststan.com. Web: www.ststan.com. Bro. Ronald Talbot, S.C., Pres. Day and resident Catholic boys school grades 6-12.

Camp Stanislaus Tel: 228-467-9057; 800-517-6257; Fax: 228-466-2972. Boys' summer program for ages 9-15.

RELIGIOUS INSTITUTES OF MEN REPRESENTED IN THE DIOCESE

For further details refer to the corresponding bracketed number in the Religious Institutes of Men or Women section.

[1100]—*Brothers of the Sacred Heart*—S.C.
[]—*Missionaries of the Infant Jesus of Good Health*
[0840]—*Missionary Servants of the Most Holy Trinity*—S.T.
[1070]—*Redemptorist Fathers*—C.Ss.R.
[0420]—*Society of the Divine Word*—S.V.D.
[0700]—*St. Joseph's Society of the Sacred Heart*—S.S.J.

RELIGIOUS INSTITUTES OF WOMEN REPRESENTED IN THE DIOCESE

[]—*Daughters of Our Lady of the Holy Rosary*—F.M.S.R.
[1070-11]—*Dominican Sisters*—O.P.
[2575]—*Institute of the Sisters of Mercy of the Americas*—R.S.M.
[]—*Missionaries of the Infant Jesus of Good Health*
[2790]—*Missionary Servants of the Most Blessed Trinity*—M.S.B.T.
[3530]—*Missionary Sisters Servants of the Holy Spirit*—S.H.Sp.
[3280]—*Presentation of the Blessed Virgin Mary Sisters*—P.B.V.M.
[3450]—*Religious of Jesus-Mary*—R.J.M.
[2970]—*School Sisters of Notre Dame*—S.S.N.D.
[]—*Sisters for Christian Community*—S.F.C.C.
[0430]—*Sisters of Charity of the Blessed Virgin Mary*—B.V.M.
[1510]—*Sisters of St. Francis*—O.S.F.
[2040]—*Sisters of the Holy Spirit*—S.H.S.

NECROLOGY

(No Deaths)

Diocese of Birmingham

(Dioecesis Birminghamiensis)

Most Reverend

DAVID E. FOLEY, D.D.

Bishop of Birmingham; ordained May 26, 1956; appointed Titular Bishop of Ottaba and Auxiliary Bishop of Richmond May 3, 1986; consecrated June 27, 1986; appointed Bishop of Birmingham 1994; installed May 13, 1994.

SURSUM CORDA

Chancery Office: Catholic Diocese of Birmingham, P.O. Box 12047, Birmingham, AL 35202-2047. Tel: 205-838-8322; Fax: 205-836-1910.

Web: www.bhmdiocese.org

ESTABLISHED JUNE 28, 1969.

Square Miles 28,091.

Comprises the Counties of North Alabama in an irregular line between the Counties (west to east) of Sumter and Choctaw and following the base of the following Counties: Marengo, Perry, Chilton, Coosa, Tallapoosa and Chambers or comprising the Counties of: Bibb, Blount, Calhoun, Chambers, Cherokee, Chilton, Clay, Cleburne, Colbert, Coosa, Cullman, DeKalb, Etowah, Fayette, Franklin, Greene, Hale, Jackson, Jefferson, Lamar, Lauderdale, Lawrence, Limestone, Madison, Marengo, Marion, Marshall, Morgan, Perry, Pickens, Randolph, St. Clair, Shelby, Sumter, Talladega, Tallapoosa, Tuscaloosa, Walker and Winston.

Legal Title: The Catholic Bishop of Birmingham in Alabama, a Corporation Sole.

For legal titles of institutions, consult the Chancery Office

STATISTICAL OVERVIEW

Personnel	
Bishop	1
Retired Bishops	1
Abbots	1
Retired Abbots	1
Priests: Diocesan Active in Diocese	53
Priests: Diocesan Active Outside Diocese	5
Priests: Diocesan in Foreign Missions	1
Priests: Retired, Sick or Absent	15
Number of Diocesan Priests	74
Religious Priests in Diocese	38
Total Priests in Diocese	112
Ordinations:	
Diocesan Priests	3
Religious Priests	1
Permanent Deacons in Diocese	41
Total Brothers	22
Total Sisters	129
Parishes	
Parishes	57
With Resident Pastor:	
Resident Diocesan Priests	38
Resident Religious Priests	15
Without Resident Pastor:	
Administered by Priests	12
Administered by Deacons	2
Administered by Religious Women	5
Administered by Lay People	2
Missions	17
Professional Ministry Personnel:	
Sisters	16
Lay Ministers	44
Welfare	
Catholic Hospitals	1
Total Assisted	168,315
Health Care Centers	1
Total Assisted	27,958
Special Centers for Social Services	13
Total Assisted	77,199
Educational	
Diocesan Students in Other Seminaries	9
Total Seminarians	9
High Schools Diocesan and Parish	5
Total Students	1,326
High Schools Private	1
Total Students	115
Elementary Schools, Diocesan and Parish	17
Total Students	5,342
Elementary Schools, Private	1
Total Students	238
Non-residential Schools for the Disabled	1
Total Students	121
Catechesis/Religious Education:	
High School Students	1,764
Elementary Students	6,625
Total Students under Catholic Instruction	15,540
Teachers in the Diocese:	
Priests	11
Brothers	2
Sisters	11
Lay Teachers	536
Vital Statistics	
Receptions into the Church:	
Infant Baptism Totals	1,829
Adult Baptism Totals	205
Received into Full Communion	494
First Communions	1,375
Confirmations	1,170
Marriages:	
Catholic	181
Interfaith	190
Total Marriages	371
Deaths	523
Total Catholic Population	74,777
Total Population	2,735,546

Former Bishops—Most Revs. JOSEPH G. VATH, ord. June 7, 1941; appt. Auxiliary Bishop of Mobile-Birmingham March 25, 1966; consecrated May 26, 1966; transferred to the Diocese of Birmingham Dec. 9, 1969; died July 14, 1987; RAYMOND J. BOLAND, D.D., ord. June 16, 1957; appt. Bishop of Birmingham Feb. 2, 1988; consecrated March 25, 1988; transferred to Kansas City-St. Joseph Sept. 9, 1993.

Chancery Office—Catholic Diocese of Birmingham, 2121 Third Ave. N., Birmingham, 35203. Tel: 205-838-8322; Fax: 205-836-1910. *P.O. Box 12047, Birmingham, 35202-2047*Web: www.bhmdiocese.org. Address all Diocesan Correspondence to the above Post Office Box unless otherwise indicated. Telephones listed below.

Office of the Bishop—ARLENE DEL BUENO, Sec. Tel: 205-838-8318; GERRY NABORS, Exec. Asst. Tel: 205-833-0175.

Moderator of the Curia—Very Rev. RICHARD E. DONOHOE. Tel: 205-838-8311.

Chancellor—Rev. JOHN HARTSFIELD. Tel: 205-776-7163.

Priests' Council—Most Rev. DAVID E. FOLEY, D.D., Pres.; Rev. RAY DUNMYER, Chm. Tel: 205-991-5488; Very Rev. ROBERT J. SULLIVAN, Vice Chm.; Rev. MARTIN MCGEOUGH, C.M., Sec. Members: Rev. Msgr. MICHAEL SEXTON, V.G.; Very Rev. RICHARD E. DONOHOE; Rev. Msgr. BRIAN EGAN, V.A.; Revs. JOHN FALLON; GREGORY BITTNER, J.C.L.; JOSEPH CULOTTA; JAMES NAUGHTON, S.D.B.; VERNON HUGULEY; J. THOMAS ACKERMAN; Rev. Msgr. PAUL ROHLING, V.C.; Very Revs. ROBERT SULLIVAN; JEREMIAH DEASY.

Diocesan College of Consultors—Rev. Msgr. MICHAEL SEXTON, V.G.; Very Revs. GREGORY BITTNER, J.C.L.; RICHARD E. DONOHOE, Moderator of the Curia; Revs. JOSEPH CULOTTA; RAYMOND DUNMYER; Rev. Msgr. BRIAN EGAN; Rev. JOHN FALLON; Very Revs. LOUIS GIARDINO, V.F.; ROBERT SULLIVAN; Rev. Msgr. PAUL ROHLING, V.C.

Diocesan College of Vicars—Rev. Msgr. MICHAEL SEXTON, V.G., Vicar General-Vicar for Northwest Deanery. Tel: 256-722-0130; Very Rev. ROBERT J. SULLIVAN, Vicar for Vocations; Rev. GREGORY BITTNER, J.C.L., Judicial Vicar. Tel: 205-838-8307; Rev. Msgrs. PAUL ROHLING, V.C., Vicar for Clergy. Tel: 205-822-4480; BRIAN EGAN, Vicar for Admin. Tel: 205-838-8309; Very Rev. RICHARD E. DONOHOE, Vicar for Hispanic Ministry; Rev. ROBERT CROSSMYER, C.P., Vicar for West Birmingham Deanery. Tel: 205-780-3440; Very Rev. MICHAEL MACMAHON, V.F., Vicar for Central Birmingham Deanery. Tel: 205-991-5488; Rev. Msgr. EUGENE O'CONNOR, Vicar for East Birmingham Deanery. Tel: 205-833-0334; Very Revs. MICHAEL MACMAHON, V.F., Vicar for Northeast Deanery. Tel: 205-881-4781; JEREMIAH DEASY, Vicar for Southwest Deanery. Tel: 205-553-9733; MATTHEW BRENNAN, Vicar for Southeast Deanery. Tel: 205-525-5161; PATRICK TIERNEY, Vicar for Northwest Deanery. Tel: 256-383-7207.

Diocesan Pastoral Council—Most Rev. DAVID E. FOLEY, D.D., Pres., Members include lay representatives of the Diocesan Deaneries, four Vicars for Deaneries, four religious and a staff representative.

Diocesan Finance Council—Most Rev. DAVID E. FOLEY, D.D., Pres.; Very Rev. RICHARD E. DONOHOE, Moderator of the Curia; Rev. Msgr. BRIAN EGAN, Vicar for Admin.; JIM FRANKLIN, Chm. Members: Rev. GREGORY BITTNER, J.C.L.; PAUL J. SHARBEL; LOUIS R. FORTIER; SHEILA BLAIR; RAY G. DYER JR., C.P.A.; ALAIN GALLET; J. STANLEY MACKIN JR. Staff Members: ROBERT M. SELLERS JR., Finance Officer; GERRY NABORS, Exec. Asst., Plus members of Diocesan Committees: Audit, Investment, Property, Personnel.

Tribunal—Rev. GREGORY T. BITTNER, J.C.L., Judicial Vicar. Tel: 205-838-8307; CYWILLA FABIJANIC, Case Mgt., Notary & Sec.; KATHY BRILL, Sec. & Notary; Sr. LYNN MCKENZIE, O.S.B., J.C.L., Second Instance, Defender of the Bond.

Judges—MARGARET S. POLL, J.D., J.C.D.; Very Revs. RICHARD DONOHOE; LOUIS GIARDINO, V.F.; Rev. Msgr. PAUL ROHLING, V.C.; Rev. JAMES MULVANNEY.

Defenders of the Bond—Deacon DANIEL J. LAURITA; Rev. Msgr. BRIAN EGAN; Rev. KEVIN M. BAZZEL; Deacon JAMES MACEY. Tel: 205-838-8307; Fax: 205-776-7165 Please address all Rogatory to the Office of the Tribunal, Catholic Diocese of Birmingham.

Catholic Social Services—ALBERT MANZELLA, Exec. Dir. Tel: 205-838-8316; Dr. MARIO G. MARTINEZ, Chm. Tel: 205-979-7676.

Catholic Family Services—TOM COOK, D.S.W., Rgnl. Dir., 2164 11th Ave. S., Birmingham, 35205. Tel: 205-324-6561.

Catholic Family Services Offices—LAURA DINWIDDIE, M.S.W., Rgnl. Dir., 1010 Church St., Huntsville, 35804. Tel: 256-536-0073; SUZANNA COLEMAN, M.S.W., Rgnl. Dir.; Sr. BERNADETTE SACHS, O.S.B., Dir., Catholic Family Service Center, 608 37th St., Tuscaloosa, 35405. Tel: 205-759-9384; ELLEN BEADLE, M.S.W., Social Worker, 1111 E. College St., Florence, 35630. Tel: 256-768-1550.

Catholic Centers of Concern— Birmingham; Anniston; Gadsden; Hamilton; Huntsville; Eutaw; Winfield; Sulligent; Fayette; Tuscaloosa.
Apostolate to the Aged—Deacon AL GERMANN, Dir., 369 Midwood Ave., Birmingham, 35228. Tel: 205-923-7108.
Engaged Encounter—BOB MARTIN; SUSAN MARTIN, 1633 Napoleon Dr., Alabaster, 35007. Tel: 205-663-9368.
Natural Family Planning—HAROLD GRAY; CATHY GRAY, 613 Bienville Ln., Birmingham, 35213. Tel: 205-590-1792.
Department of Education—FRANK X. SAVAGE, Dir., Catholic Education & Lifelong Formation.
Catholic Schools—Sr. M. LEANNE WELCH, P.B.V.M., Supt. Tel: 205-838-8303.
Religious Education—MICKY ZIELINSKI, Dir. Tel: 205-838-8312.
Apostolate with Mentally Retarded Persons—Rev. PATRICK CULLEN, Dir.; Sr. MARY VERNON GENTLE, R.S.M., Assoc. Dir., The Nazareth House, 7340 Cahaba Valley Rd., Birmingham, 35242. Tel: 205-980-1810; Fax: 205-980-9208. Email: mvgentle@aol.com.
Catholic Youth Ministry—DONALD SCHWARZHOFF, Dir. Tel: 205-838-8301.
Campus Ministry—Rev. GERALD HOLLOWAY, Dir., St. Francis University Parish, 811 Fifth Ave., Tuscaloosa, 35401. Tel: 205-758-5672.
Catholic Scouting—DONALD SCHWARZHOFF, Coord. Tel: 205-838-8301.
Toy Bowl Association—MICHAEL CAMMARATA, Dir., 222 73rd St. N., Birmingham, 35202. Tel: 205-838-2112.
Board of Education—DAN FLEMMING, Chm. Tel: 800-292-4847 (Office); 205-956-9300 (Res.).
Finance Office and Administration—
Diocesan Finance Officer—ROBERT M. SELLERS JR. Tel: 205-833-0173.
Annual Catholic Charities Appeal, Campaign for Human Development— Catholic Relief Services, and National and Special Collections Rev. Msgr. BRIAN EGAN, Dir. Tel: 205-838-8309.
Personnel—JAMES H. WARREN II, Dir. Tel: 205-838-8321.
Office of Pastoral Services—
Beginning Experience—TOM GARNER. Tel: 205-969-8509.
Children's Beginning Experience—JEANNETTE CAMPISI, 936 5th Ave., N.W., Alabaster, 35007. Tel: 205-664-0401.
Cursillo Program—Directors: DICK SWEENEY; JANE SWEENEY. Tel: 205-987-8038.
Hispanic Ministries—Sr. CANDELARIA HERNANDEZ, M.G.Sp.S., Dir. Tel: 205-838-8308.
Hispanic Social Services—BRENDA BULLOCK, Dir. Tel: 205-838-8306.
Multicultural Resource Center—KRISTIN S. COOMBES, M.S.W., L.G.S.W., Dir. Tel: 205-824-5046.
Lay Ministries Program—Sr. MARIE LEONARD, O.S.B., Dir. Tel: 205-838-8300.
Marriage Encounter—DEL FISHER; NANCY FISHER. Tel: 205-556-6471.
Black Catholic Ministry—Deacon WALTER HENDERSON, Dir. Tel: 205-838-8313.
Pro-Life Activities—Most Rev. DAVID FOLEY.
Propagation of the Faith and Holy Childhood—Rev. RAYMOND J. REMKE, Dir.; CATHY SCARVEY, Asst. Dir. Tel: 205-776-7181.
Serra Club of Birmingham—JANE SWEENEY, Pres. Tel: 205-987-8038.
Vocations—Dr. STEVE SMITH, Coord. Tel: 205-838-2184.
"One Voice"—MARY ALICE CROCKETT, Mng. Editor. Tel: 205-838-8305; ANN LANZI, Circulation, The Birmingham Catholic Press, Inc., P.O. Box 10822, Birmingham, 35202. Tel: 205-838-8305; Fax: 205-838-8319. Diocesan weekly
Assembly of Religious—Sr. CHRISTINE WILTRAKIS, M.S.B.T., Chm., Annunciation of the Lord Church, 3019 Spring Ave., S.W., Decatur, 35603. Tel: 256-353-2667.
Retrouvaille of Alabama, Inc.—Coordinators: FRAN HINES; LEE HINES. Tel: 205-967-3458.
Diocesan Council of Catholic Women—RUTH MAYS, Pres., 84 Muirfield Circle, Oneonta, 35121. Tel: 205-274-4101.
Priests' Retirement Fund—Mr. HENRY SMITH, c/o Priests' Retirement Fund, P.O. Box 10247, Birmingham, 35202-2047. Tel: 205-833-0173.
Victim Assistance Coordinator—AL MANZELLA. Tel: 205-776-7130. Email: amanzella@bhmdiocese.org.

CLERGY, PARISHES, MISSIONS AND PAROCHIAL SCHOOLS

CITY OF BIRMINGHAM
(JEFFERSON COUNTY)

1—ST. PAUL'S CATHEDRAL (1871), Very Rev. Richard E. Donohoe, Rector; Rev. Charles Alookaran; Deacon Hugh O'Brien.
Mailing Address: P.O. Box 10044, 35202-0044. Tel: 205-251-1279; Fax: 205-251-1284.
Res.: 2120 Third Ave. N., 35203. Tel: 205-328-7209.
Catechesis/Religious Program—Students 70.

2—ST. ANTHONY'S (1900), Closed., For inquiries for parish records contact St. Paul Cathedral, Birmingham.

3—ST. BARNABAS (1908), Rev. Msgr. Eugene O'Connor.
Mailing Address: P.O. Box 610304, 35261.
Res.: 7921 First Ave. N., 35206. Tel: 205-833-0334; 205-833-5695; Fax: 205-833-0272.
School—7901 First Ave. N., 35206. Tel: 205-836-5385; Fax: 205-833-0272. Tillie S. Barnhill, Prin. Lay Teachers 14; Students 197.
Mailing Address: P.O. Box 610347, 35261.
Catechesis/Religious Program—Tel: 205-836-4567. Rosemary Gagliano, D.R.E. Students 23.

4—ST. BERNARD'S (Inglenook) (1928), Closed., For inquiries for parish records contact St. Paul Cathedral, Birmingham.

5—BLESSED SACRAMENT (1910), [CEM] Very Rev. Gregory Bittner, J.C.L.; Rev. Bryan K. Lowe; Deacon J.S. Anzalone.
Res.: 1460 Pearson Ave., S.W., P.O. Box 110006, 35211. Tel: 205-785-9840.
Catechesis/Religious Program—Ann Nobln, D.R.E. Students 15.

6—ST. FRANCIS XAVIER (1953), Revs. Patrick J. Sullivan; John Michael Wrigley; Alan C. Mackey; Deacon George Mickwee; Sisters Jane Bishop, O.S.B., Pastoral Assoc.; Virginia Rohling, O.S.B., Pastoral Assoc.
Res.: P.O. Box 130669, 35213. Tel: 205-871-1153; Fax: 205-871-9831.
School—Tel: 205-871-1687; Fax: 205-871-1674. Sr. Judith Dianne McGowan, R.S.M., Prin. Sisters 1; Lay Teachers 16; Students 206.
Catechesis/Religious Program—Rev. Virginia E. Fisher, D.R.E. Students 251.

7—HOLY FAMILY (1938), (African American), Revs. Robert Crossmeyer, C.P.; Raymond McDonough, C.P.; Deacon Benjamin Jett.
Res.: 1910 19th St., 35218. Tel: 205-780-3440; Fax: 205-780-5272.
School—1916 19th St., Ensley, 35218. Tel: 205-785-5858; Fax: 205-785-2666. Sr. M. DePorres Collier, C.S.S.F., Prin. Sisters 1; Lay Teachers 15; Students 250.
Catechesis/Religious Program—Fax: 205-780-3440. Rose Sturdivant, D.R.E. Students 40.
Mission—St. Mary's (1943), 6101 Dr. Martin Luther King Dr., Fairfield, Jefferson Co. 35064. Tel: 205-923-0202 (Office); 205-780-3440 (Res.); Fax: 205-923-2276. Rev. Philip Paxton, C.P.; Deacon Walter Henderson.
Catechesis/Religious Program—Wade White, D.R.E.
School—6124 Myron Massey Blvd., Fairfield, 35064. Tel: 205-923-5161; Fax: 205-923-5166. Mr. Ron Bell, Prin. Lay Teachers 14; Students 205.

8—HOLY ROSARY (Gate City) (1889),, (See St. John Bosco, Birmingham for details.)

9—ST. JOHN BOSCO (1973), Rev. James J. Naughton, S.D.B., Admin.
Mailing Address: P.O. Box 321576, 35232. Tel: 205-595-0652.
Res.: 5224 First Ave. N., 35212. Fax: 205-702-4010.
Catechesis/Religious Program—Tel: 205-591-9964. Students 33.
Mission—Holy Rosary (Gate City) (1889), 7414 Georgia Rd., Jefferson Co. 35212. Tel: 205-595-0652. Revs. Anthony D'Angelo, S.D.B.; Kenneth Germaine, S.D.B.

10—ST. JOSEPH'S (1921), (Italian), Deacon Al Germann.
Res.: 3020 Avenue K, 35218. Tel: 205-788-5721; Fax: 205-788-7146.

11—KOREAN CATHOLIC COMMUNITY, ST. LUKE HWANG (1995), (Korean), Rev. Ru Ken-Bae Jerome.
Res.: 460 Park Ter., 35226. Tel: 205-823-6511; Fax: 205-823-6511.
Catechesis/Religious Program—Students 14.

12—ST. MARGARET'S, Closed., 1986. For inquiries for parish records contact Blessed Sacrament Parish, Birmingham.

13—ST. MARK THE EVANGELIST (1999), Rev. Patrick P. Cullen; Deacon Christopher J. Rosko.
Mailing Address: P.O. Box 380396, 35238-0396. Tel: 205-980-1810; Fax: 205-980-9208.
Catechesis/Religious Program—Dr. Joan Porter, D.R.E. Students 303.

14—ST. MARK'S (1904), Closed., For inquiries for parish records contact St. Paul's Cathedral, Birmingham.

15—OUR LADY OF FATIMA (1905), Rev. Paul Oberg, S.S.J.
Res.: 708 First St. S., 35205. Tel: 205-322-1205; Fax: 205-714-5056.
School—630 First St. S., 35205. Tel: 205-251-8395; Fax: 205-251-8393. Sr. Rita Radloff, S.B.S., Prin. Sisters of The Blessed Sacrament, PA 4; Lay Teachers 14; Students 226.
Catechesis/Religious Program—Tel: 205-251-8395. Mrs. Theresa Nalls, D.R.E. Students 85.

16—OUR LADY OF LOURDES (1959), Rev. Andrew Kennedy; Deacon Paul Yancey.
Res.: 980 Huffman Rd., 35215.
Office—Tel: 205-836-2274; Fax: 205-836-5436.
Catechesis/Religious Program—Robin Barron, D.R.E. Tel: 205-836-2274; Fax: 205-836-5436. Students 188.

17—OUR LADY OF SORROWS (1887), Rev. Msgr. Martin M. Muller; Revs. Michael J. Deering; Joseph Delano Lody Jr.; Sr. Pat Sullivan, M.S.B.T., Pastoral Assoc.
Mailing Address: P.O. Box 59447, 35259. Tel: 205-871-8121; Fax: 205-871-8180. In Res., Rev. Msgr. Brian Egan, V.A.
Res.: 1728 Oxmoor Rd., 35209. (Homewood)
School—Tel: 205-879-3237; Fax: 205-879-9332. Mary Jane Dorn, Prin. Lay Teachers 30; Students 481.
Catechesis/Religious Program—Tel: 205-871-1431; Fax: 205-871-1487. Anne Verchot, D.R.E.; Sr. Joan Harrington, C.S.J., D.R.E. Students 480.

18—OUR LADY OF THE VALLEY (1974), Rev. Raymond A. Dunmyer.
Res.: 5514 Double Oak Ln., 35242. Tel: 205-991-6288; Fax: 205-991-5181.
Church: Tel: 205-991-5488; Fax: 205-991-5181.
School—Tel: 205-991-5692; Fax: 205-991-1251. Lay Teachers 47; Students 541.
Catechesis/Religious Program—Tel: 205-991-5489; Fax: 205-991-5181. Deacon Dan Whitaker, D.R.E. Students 423.

19—OUR LADY QUEEN OF THE UNIVERSE (1955), (African American), Rev. Vernon Huguley.
Res.: 961 Center St. N., 35204. Tel: 205-328-7729; Fax: 205-328-7703.
Catechesis/Religious Program—Students 55.
Mission—Sacred Heart 3401 27th Ct. N., Collegeville, Jefferson Co. 35207. Tel: 205-252-8909.

20—ST. PETER THE APOSTLE (1962), Rev. Msgr. Paul L. Rohling, V.C.; Rev. Earl Gray Bean Jr. In Res., Rev. John Robinson.
Res.: 2061 Patton Chapel Rd., 35216. Tel: 205-822-4480; Fax: 205-822-4534.
Catechesis/Religious Program—Tel: 205-823-6324; Fax: 205-822-4534. Marcella Stobert, D.R.E.; Cynthia Armstrong, D.R.E. Students 437.

21—PRINCE OF PEACE (1984), Rev. John Fallon; Deacons Frank Iovino; Jerry Motherway; Jose Vasquez.
Church & Mailing Address: 4600 Moss Creek Blvd., Birmingham (Hoover), 35226. Tel: 205-822-9125; Fax: 205-822-9127.
Res.: 10-A Shades Crest Rd., 35226. Tel: 205-739-0070.
School—Tel: 205-824-7886; Fax: 205-827-2093. Connie Angstadt, Prin. Lay Teachers 15; Students 175.
Catechesis/Religious Program—Tel: 205-822-9125; Fax: 205-822-9127. Kathleen Dunne, D.R.E. Students 860.

22—SACRED HEART (1955),, (See Our Lady Queen of the Universe, Birmingham for details.)

23—ST. STANISLAUS (1914), Sr. Mary Humphries, P.B.V.M., Parish Dir.; Rev. Frank J. Muscolino (MRY).
Mailing Address: 904 Indiana St., 35224. Tel: 205-785-9625.
Convent—Tel: 205-674-7961.

24—ST. STEPHEN THE MARTYR (1991), Revs. Gregory T. Bittner, J.C.L.; Bryan T. Lowe; Deacon J.S. Anzalone; Sr. Karen Ann Lortscher, O.S.B., Campus Min.
Res.: 1515 12th Ave. S., 35205. Tel: 205-933-2500; Fax: 205-939-1500.

25—ST. THERESA'S, Closed., For inquiries for parish records contact St. Paul's Cathedral, Birmingham.

OUTSIDE THE CITY OF BIRMINGHAM

ADAMSVILLE, JEFFERSON CO., ST. PATRICK'S (1983), [CEM] Rev. Frank J. Muscolino (MRY); Sr. Maura Sampson, P.B.V.M., Pastoral Assoc. & D.R.E.
Res.: 301 Shamrock Tr., 35005. Tel: 205-674-1426.
Church: Tel: 205-798-5326; Fax: 205-798-5330.
Catechesis/Religious Program—Tel: 205-798-5326; Fax: 205-798-5330. Students 89.
Family Life Center—Tel: 205-798-0372.

ALEXANDER CITY, TALLAPOOSA CO., ST. JOHN THE APOSTLE (1948), (Hispanic—Vietnamese), Rev. Bruce J. Krause, C.M.; Deacon Mark Sullivan.
Res.: 454 N. Central St., 35010. Tel: 256-234-3631; Fax: 256-234-3789.
Catechesis/Religious Program—Tel: 256-329-8204; Fax: 256-234-3789. Mary Ellen Workman, D.R.E. Students 40.
Mission—St. Mark (1994), 460 Country Club Rd.,

Ashland, Clay Co. 36251. Tel: 256-354-3598; Fax: 256-354-3599. In Res., Revs. Alfred R. Pehrsson, C.M.; Thomas J. Hynes, C.M., Hispanic Min.

ANNISTON, CALHOUN CO.

1—ALL SAINTS (1939), B. Dianne Green, Parish Dir.
Mailing Address: P.O. Box 4862, 36204. 1112 W. 15th St., 36201. Tel: 256-237-9230; Fax: 256-237-9230.

2—SACRED HEART OF JESUS (1886), Very Rev. Robert J. Sullivan; Rev. John Jairo, Hispanic Min.; Deacons William Taffee; Michael Cova.
Res.: P.O. Box 5010, 36205. Tel: 256-237-3011; Fax: 256-241-2048.
School—16 Morton Rd., Fort McClellan, 36205. Tel: 256-237-4231; Fax: 256-241-2353. Paul M. Doty, Prin. Lay Teachers 16; Students 154.
Catechesis/Religious Program—Tel: 256-237-3011. Carla Keith, D.R.E. Students 62.

ASHLAND, CLAY CO., ST. MARK'S, , See St. John the Apostle, Alexander City for details.

ATHENS, LIMESTONE CO., ST. PAUL'S (1959), Rev. Joseph C. Allen.
Mailing Address: P.O. Box 998, 35612.
Res.: 1900 Hwy. 72 W., 35611. Tel: 256-232-4191; Fax: 256-232-4191 (call first).
Catechesis/Religious Program—Tel: 256-232-4191. Joanne Mandel, D.R.E. Students 104.

BESSEMER, JEFFERSON CO.

1—ST. ALOYSIUS CHURCH (1886), Rev. Ray W. Keiser; Deacon James A. Dunn; Stephanie Gerson, Pastoral Assoc.
Mailing Address: 751 Academy Dr., 35022. Tel: 205-424-2984; Fax: 205-426-5753.
Res.: Tel: 205-424-1839.
School—Tel: 205-425-0045; Fax: 205-425-0046. Mrs. Lisa Corona, Prin. Lay Teachers 17; Students 199.
Catechesis/Religious Program—Tel: 205-425-3448. Students 60.

2—ST. FRANCIS OF ASSISI (1940), (African American), Rev. Ray W. Keiser; Bobby Owens, Pastoral Assoc.
Res.: 2400 Seventh Ave. N., 35020. Tel: 205-425-0984; Fax: 205-428-4758.
Catechesis/Religious Program—2410 7th Ave. N., 35020. Tel: 205-428-4758; Fax: 205-428-4751. Students 41.

CULLMAN, CULLMAN CO., SACRED HEART (1877), (German), [CEM] Revs. Kevin D. McGrath, O.S.B.; John O'Donnell, O.S.B.; Deacon William Roberson.
Res.: 217 Second St. S.E., P.O. Box 1085, 35056. Tel: 256-734-3730; Fax: 256-734-3476.
School—Tel: 256-734-4563; Fax: 256-734-5882. Ms. Shawna W. Norman, Prin. Sisters 1; Lay Teachers 12; Students 157.
Catechesis/Religious Program—Mary Merritt, D.R.E. Students 165.
Mission—St. Boniface [CEM] P.O. Box 1085, Hanceville, Cullman Co. 35056. Tel: 256-734-3730; Fax: 256-734-3476.

DECATUR, MORGAN CO.

1—ST. ANN'S (1870), [JC], For more information please see Annunication of the Lord, Decatur.

2—ANNUNCIATION OF THE LORD (2003), Rev. Joseph Culotta; Sr. Christine Wiltrakis, M.S.B.T., Pastoral Assoc.
Res.: 3910 Spring Ave., S.W., 35603. Tel: 256-353-2667; Fax: 256-353-8994.
School—Tel: 256-353-6543. Janet Jensen, Prin. Lay Teachers 15; Students 225.
Catechesis/Religious Program—Jane Gile, D.R.E. Students 181.

DEMOPOLIS, MARENGO CO., ST. LEO (1936), Revs. Jose Maliakel; Thomas Anchanickal.
Res.: 307 Main Ave., P.O. Box 937, 36732. Tel: 334-289-2767; Fax: 334-289-6085.
Catechesis/Religious Program—Diane Busby, D.R.E. Students 40.
Mission—Our Lady of Lourdes 8 Erwin Woods Dr., Greensboro, Hale Co. 37644.
Mission—St. Mary (1948), 274 Wilson Ave., Eutaw, Greene Co. 35462. (African American)

EUTAW, GREENE CO., ST. MARY (1948), (African American),, See St. Leo, Demopolis for details.

FAIRFIELD, JEFFERSON CO., ST. MARY (1943),, See Holy Family, Birmingham for details.

FLORENCE, LAUDERDALE CO.

1—ST. JOSEPH'S (1898), Revs. Andrew A. Sullivan; Vincent Chembakassery; Kathie Franck, Youth Min.
Res.: 1111 E. College St., 35630. Tel: 256-764-3303; 256-767-9069 (Rectory); Fax: 256-718-0208.
School—Tel: 256-766-1923; 256-766-1955; Fax: 256-766-1713. Cathy Lennartz, Prin. Lay Teachers 21; Students 204.
Catechesis/Religious Program—Students 111.

2—ST. MICHAEL (1873), [CEM] Rt. Rev. Victor J. Clark, O.S.B. (Retired).
Res.: 2751 County Rd. 30, 35634. Tel: 256-764-1885; Fax: 256-764-8933.
Catechesis/Religious Program—Karen Holden, D.R.E., (High School). Students 45.

FORT PAYNE, DE KALB CO., OUR LADY OF THE VALLEY (1959), Sr. Deborah Kennedy, R.S.M., Parish Dir.
Mailing Address: 2907 Alabama Ave., 35967.
Church: 2910 Gault Ave., 35968-1615. Tel: 256-845-4774; Fax: 256-845-4708.
Catechesis/Religious Program—Students 214.

GADSDEN, ETOWAH CO.

1—ST. JAMES (1912), Rev. Thomas M. Kelly.
Mailing Address: P.O. Box 38, 35902.
Res.: 225 Carleen St., 35901. Tel: 256-549-0360; Fax: 256-546-2930.
Church: 622 Chestnut St., 35901. Tel: 256-546-2975; Fax: 256-546-2930.
School—Tel: 256-546-0132; Fax: 256-546 0134. Sr. M. Cecilia MacDermott, O.S.B., Prin. Lay Teachers 14; Students 170.
Catechesis/Religious Program—Michael Blood, D.R.E. Students 86.

2—ST. MARTIN DE PORRES, Closed., For inquiries for parish records contact St. James, Gadsden.

GARDENDALE, JEFFERSON CO., ST. ELIZABETH ANN SETON (1975), Rev. William Lucas; Margaret Wiley, Pastoral Assoc.
Mailing Address: 334 Main St., P.O. Box 1027, 35071. Tel: 205-631-9398 (Office); Fax: 205-631-5781.
Res.: 205 Powell Dr., P.O. Box 1027, 35071. Tel: 205-631-8582.
Catechesis/Religious Program—Fax: 205-631-5781. Michael Brasher, D.R.E. Students 124.
Mission—St. Henry [CEM] 211 5th St., Warrior, Jefferson Co. 35180.

GUNTERSVILLE, MARSHALL CO., ST. WILLIAM'S (1952), Rev. J. Thomas Ackerman; Deacon Hector Garcia.
929 Gunter Ave., 35976. Tel: 256-582-4245 (Office); 256-571-9905 (Hispanic Min); Fax: 256-582-7954.
Res.: 1002 Blount Ave., 35976. Tel: 256-582-4964.
Catechesis/Religious Program—Ms. Cecilia Hall, D.R.E. Students 275.

HUNTSVILLE, MADISON CO.

1—GOOD SHEPHERD (1981), Rev. Philip N. O'Kennedy; Deacons Ron Puent; Helmut Sassenfeld.
Res.: P.O. Box 4447, 35815-4447. Tel: 256-882-1844; Fax: 256-882-1841.
Catechesis/Religious Program—Tel: 256-882-1844. Katherine Maxwell, D.R.E. Students 557.

2—HOLY SPIRIT (1965), Very Rev. Michael MacMahon, V.F.; Rev. Kevin Bazzel; Bro. Benedict Stoegbauer, S.D.S.; Deacons Lee Roy Hoekenschnieder Sr.; Samuel Dias.
Res.: 625 Airport Rd., 35802. Tel: 256-881-4781; Fax: 256-881-5510.
School—Tel: 256-881-4852; Fax: 256-881-4904. James Bell, Prin. Lay Teachers 28; Students 437.
Catechesis/Religious Program—Tel: 256-881-0345. Mrs. Carolyn Brunty, D.R.E. Students 318.

3—ST. JOSEPH'S (1952), [CEM] Rev. Roman Mueller, S.D.S. In Res., Rev. Robert Wagner, S.D.S.
Res.: 2300 Beasley Ave., N.W., 35816. Tel: 256-534-8459; Fax: 256-534-8450.
School—Holy Family School, Tel: 256-539-5221; Fax: 256-533-0747. Mary Tomaine, Prin. Sisters of the Divine Savior 1; Lay Teachers 16; Students 167.
Catechesis/Religious Program—Tel: 256-534-1310; Fax: 256-534-3450. Carmen Amato, D.R.E. Students 167.

4—ST. MARY OF THE VISITATION (1861), Rev. Glen W. Sayers, S.D.S
Res.: 222 N. Jefferson St., 35801. Tel: 256-536-6349; Fax: 256-536-6349.
Catechesis/Religious Program—Tel: 256-536-6760. Mrs. Evelyn Jaap, D.R.E. Students 59.

5—OUR LADY QUEEN OF THE UNIVERSE (1965), Rev. Joy Chalissery; Deacon Daniel Melchoir; Terry Roehm, Pastoral Assoc.
Mailing Address: P.O. Box 3268, 35810.
Res.: 3701 Grizzard, 35810. Tel: 256-859-2353.
Church: 2421 Shady Lane Dr., N.W., 35810. Fax: 256-852-0199.
Catechesis/Religious Program—Tel: 256-852-0788. Susan Turner, D.R.E. Students 97.

JACKSONVILLE, CALHOUN CO., ST. CHARLES (1964), Rev. Alan C. Mackey; Sandra Herter, D.R.E.
Church: 308 Seventh St. N.E., 36265. Tel: 256-435-3238; Fax: 256-435-4942.
Res.: 400 Seventh St. N.E., 36265. Tel: 256-435-1307.
Catechesis/Religious Program—Students 82.
Mission—St. Joachim 308 7th St. N.E., Piedmont, Calhoun Co. 36265. Deacon Donald Ash.

JASPER, WALKER CO., ST. CECILIA (1964), Rev. David Buchanan.
Mailing Address: 2159 Hwy. 95, 35503.
Res.: 35503. Tel: 205-384-4800 (Office); Fax: 205-384-1009.
Catechesis/Religious Program—Brad Whitaker, D.R.E. Students 66.
Mission—Our Lady of Guadalupe Haleyville, Winston Co.

LANETT, CHAMBERS CO., HOLY FAMILY (1915), [CEM] Rev. Martin McGeough, C.M.; Deacon James A. Stagg.
Res.: 705 N. Third Ave., 36863-0325. Tel: 334-644-4405; Fax: 706-645-6783.
Catechesis/Religious Program—Cathie Green, D.R.E.; Jennifer Fiedler, D.R.E. Students 52.
Mission—Immaculate Conception 1256 Main St., Roanoke, Randolph Co. 36274. Tel: 334-853-4418.

LEEDS, JEFFERSON CO., ST. THERESA'S (1951), Rev. James Naughton, S.D.B.
Res.: P.O. Box 525, 35094. Tel: 205-699-8534; Fax: 205-702-4010.
Catechesis/Religious Program—Mary Kaye Gubenski, D.R.E. Students 56.

LIVINGSTON, SUMTER CO., ST. FRANCIS OF ASSISI (1972),, Administered by The Catholic Church in West Central Alabama. , Mailing Address: P.O. Box 1035, 35470. Tel: 334-289-2767; Fax: 334-289-6085. Church: Hwy. 28 E., 35470.

MADISON, MADISON CO., ST. JOHN THE BAPTIST (1973), Rev. Msgr. Michael Sexton, V.G.; Rev. Thomas Woods; Deacons Dan Laurita; Darrell Diem; Carmello Graffagnini; Terry Thompson, D.R.E.
Res.: 1055 Hughes Rd., 35758. Tel: 256-722-0130; Fax: 256-722-0303.
School—1057 Hughes Rd., 35758. Tel: 256-722-0772; Fax: 256-722-0151. Tommy Bridges, Prin. Lay Teachers 28; Students 442.
Catechesis/Religious Program—Tel: 256-722-8590. Students 758.

MONTEVALLO, SHELBY CO., ST. THOMAS THE APOSTLE (1951), Rev. Raymond J. Remke; Sr. Pat Hinton, O.S.F., Pastoral Assoc.
Res. & Mailing Address: 80 St. Thomas Way, 35115. Tel: 205-663-3936; Fax: 205-663-3929.
Catechesis/Religious Program—William Alexiou, D.R.E. Students 217.
Mission—Church of the Resurrection P.O. Box 735, Clanton, Chilton Co. 35046. Tel: 205-755-5498; Fax: 205-755-0715.
Catechesis/Religious Program—Sr. Maria Dina Puddu, M.C., Parish Dir. Students 176.

MOULTON, LAWRENCE CO., RESURRECTION CATHOLIC CHAPEL (1993), Deacon Robert Laremore, Admin.
Res.: 7363 Alabama Hwy. 33, 35650. Tel: 256-905-0330; Fax: 256-905-0330 (Call First).
Catechesis/Religious Program—Students 4.

ONEONTA, BLOUNT CO., CORPUS CHRISTI (1983), Unassigned. Rev. John Hartsfield.
Res.: 3019 County Hwy. 14, Altoona, 35952. Tel: 205-466-5161.
Church: 32015 State Hwy. 75, 35121. Tel: 205-625-6078; Fax: 205-625-6078.
Catechesis/Religious Program—Charlene Makofsky, D.R.E. Students 90.

PELL CITY, ST. CLAIR CO., OUR LADY OF THE LAKE (1969), Rev. Matthew Brennan; Deacon Terrence L. Rumore.
Mailing Address: Hwy. 231 S., P.O. Box 388, 35125.
Res.: 117 Ingram Lane, Cropwell, 35054. Tel: 205-525-5161 (Church); Fax: 205-525-5162.
Catechesis/Religious Program—Parma Boyle, D.R.E. Students 107.

RUSSELLVILLE, FRANKLIN CO., GOOD SHEPHERD CHURCH (1973), Rev. Bruce Bumbarger, M.SS.CC.
Res.: 1700 N. Jackson Ave., 35653. Tel: 256-332-0095; Fax: 256-332-4861.
Catechesis/Religious Program—Students 132.

SCOTTSBORO, JACKSON CO., ST. JUDE (1971), Rev. Vincent Lazar Chembakassery; Deacon Jerome P. Raispis.
Res.: P.O. Box 971, 35768. Tel: 205-259-2520.
Catechesis/Religious Program—Tel: 205-574-6156. Students 38.

SYLACAUGA, TALLADEGA CO., ST. JUDE (1947), Rev. Jose Manjaly; Sr. Therese Francis Walker, M.S.B.T., Parish Dir.
Res.: 310 W. Bay St., P.O. Box 111, 35150. Tel: 256-245-7741; Fax: 256-249-4781.
Catechesis/Religious Program—Students 47.
Mission—Holy Name of Jesus 4th St., S.W. at 5th Ave., Childersburg, Talladega Co. 35044.

TALLADEGA, TALLADEGA CO., ST. FRANCIS OF ASSISI (1951), [CEM] Rev. Jose Manjaly.
Res.: 722 S. East St., P.O. Box 1142, 35160. Tel: 256-362-5372; Fax: 256-362-5372.
Catechesis/Religious Program—Cindi Greene, D.R.E. Students 20.

TRUSSVILLE, JEFFERSON CO., HOLY INFANT OF PRAGUE (1941), Rev. Patrick O'Donoghue; Deacons Ed Pruet; E. Lee Robinson Sr., Pastoral Min.; Kathryn Williams, Pastoral Min. In Res., Rev. John Owens.
Res.: 215 Hewitt St., P.O. Box 43, 35173. Tel: 205-655-2541; Fax: 205-661-9231.
Catechesis/Religious Program—Terry Pruet, D.R.E. Students 342.

TUSCALOOSA, TUSCALOOSA CO.

1—ST. FRANCIS OF ASSISI UNIVERSITY PARISH (1929), Rev. Gerald Holloway; Deacon J. Adrian Straley; Stephanie Agro, Pastoral Assoc.
Res.: 811 Fifth Ave., 35401. Tel: 205-758-5672; Fax: 205-758-5673.
Catechesis/Religious Program—Nancy Woodbury, D.R.E. Students 167.

Mission—St. Robert Hwy. 175, Reform, Pickens Co. 35481. Tel: 205-375-8140.

2—HOLY SPIRIT (1961), Very Rev. Jeremiah Deasy, V.F.; Deacons Francis N. Viselli Jr.; Frank R. Slapikas; Sr. Madeline Contorno, O.S.B., Dir. Ministries.
Res.: 733 37th St. E., 35405. Tel: 205-553-9733; Fax: 205-553-7014.
School—711 37th St., 35405. Tel: 205-553-9630; Fax: 205-553-8880. Sr. Tonette Sperando, O.S.B., Pres. & Prin, (Grades K-6). Tel: 205-553-5606; Ana MacCrone, Prin. (Grades PreK); Steve Calabro, Prin. (Grades 7-12). Tel: 205-553-5606. Lay Teachers 42; Students 642.
Catechesis/Religious Program—Judi Hall, D.R.E.; Mary Jane Wagner, D.R.E. Students 107.
Mission—St. John c/o Rev. Jeremiah Deasy at Holy Spirit, 8th & Lurleen Wallace Blvd., Tuscaloosa Co. 35401.

TUSCUMBIA, COLBERT CO., OUR LADY OF THE SHOALS (1869), [CEM] Very Rev. Patrick J. Tierney, V.F.
Church & Res.: 200 N.E. Commons, 35674. Tel: 256-383-7207 (Church); 256-381-2699 (Res.); Fax: 256-383-7883.
Catechesis/Religious Program—Carolyn Wilson, D.R.E. Students 140.

WINFIELD, MARION CO., HOLY SPIRIT (1965), Rev. Michael Kerin, G.H.M.; Sr. Margaret Chambers, Pastoral Assoc.
2710 U.S. Hwy. 43 N., 35594. Tel: 205-487-3616; Fax: 205-487-3616.
Catechesis/Religious Program—Teresa Gray, D.R.E. Students 30.
Mission—Holy Family 423 19th St. N.W., Fayette, Fayette Co. 35555. Tel: 205-932-6242.

On Special or Other Diocesan Assignment:
Revs.—
Egan, Brian, Catholic Charities Appeal.
O'Donnell, John, O.S.B., 112 Second Ave., S.E., Cullman, 35055.

On Duty Outside the Diocese:
Rev. Msgr.—
Marino, Joseph, Second Section, Vatican City, Rome 00120 Italy. Tel: 39-6-698-83122 (Office); 698-97301 (Res.) Secretariat of State
Revs.—
Fisher, Albert, Chap., St. Joseph's Hospital, 11400 White Bluff Rd., # 88, Savannah, GA 31419.
Klauck, Michael, 6802 Edinborough Ct., Rapid City, SD 57702.
Reynolds, Jeffrie S., P.O. Box 51, Perry Point, MD 21902. Tel: 410-642-2411; 410-939-1548 (Res.)
Walsh, Edward P., 3600 N. Capitol St, N.W., USSAH #239, Washington, DC 20317. Tel: 202-730-3103

Absent on Leave:
Very Rev.—
Giardino, Louis, V.F.
Rev.—
Summitt, James A.

Retired:
Revs.—
Blazak, Camillus, 100 James Blvd., Apt. W-204, Signal Mountain, TN 37377-1876. Tel: 423-886-0343
DeFazio, Crescenzio, 2400 Rocky Ridge Rd., 35243. Tel: 205-824-8732
Donnelly, Paul J., Little Sisters of the Poor, Sacred Heart Residence, 1655 McGill Ave., Mobile, 36604. Tel: 251-476-8855
Hill, Timothy, #4 Annville, 13 Ballinlough Rd., Cork, Ireland. Tel: 011-353-21-323655
Kula, Joseph, Bethesda Gardens, 13825 N. Cavegreek Rd., Apt. 222, Phoenix, AZ 85022. Tel: 602-765-4225
Mulvaney, James J., 400 University Park Dr., Somerby, Apt. 203, 35209.
Murrin, Raymond J., 18 Merrion Ct., Ailesbury Rd., Dublin 4, Ireland.
Owen, John J., P.O. Box 259, Trussville, 35173. Tel: 205-655-9092
Regan, Desmond, 20 Cross Creek, 35213.
Sheehan, J. Peter, 653 S.E. Lakeview Dr., Sebring, FL 33870. Tel: 863-471-0378
Thorsen, Henry, 700 Connell Dr., Pensacola, FL 32507. Tel: 850-469-0919
Underwood, Joseph, 6520 Court K, 35228. Tel: 205-925-8329
White, Michael J., Pastor Emeritus, Our Lady of the Valley, 837 Greystone Highlands Dr., 35242-2651. Tel: 205-408-1034

Permanent Deacons:
Anzalone, J.S., Blessed Sacrament, Birmingham
Ash, Donald J., St. Joachim, Piedmont
Bodine, James G., St. Ann, Decatur
Cova, Michael A., Sacred Heart of Jesus, Anniston
Dias, Sam A., Holy Spirit, Huntsville
Diem, Darrell, St. John the Baptist, Madison
Dunn, James A., St. Aloysius, Bessemer
Garcia, Hector, St. William, Guntersville
Germann, Aloysius A., St. Joseph, Birmingham
Graffagnini, Carmello, St. John the Baptist, Madison
Henderson, Walter J., St. Mary, Fairfield
Hoekenschnieder, Lee Roy, Holy Spirit, Huntsville
Iovino, Frank, Prince of Peace, Birmingham
Jett, Benjamin, Holy Family, Birmingham
Joly, Walter Jerome, On Leave
Kelly, Alfred, (Retired)
Laremore, Robert, Glenmary Ministries, Moulton
Laurita, Dan, St. John the Baptist, Madison
Machus, Paul, (Retired)
Melchior, Daniel R., Our Lady, Queen of the Universe, Huntsville
Mickwee, George, St. Francis Xavier, Birmingham
Motherway, Gerald, Prince of Peace, Hoover
O'Brien, Hugh A., Cathedral of St. Paul, Birmingham
Pruet, Ed, Holy Infant of Prague, Trussville
Puent, Ron, Good Shepherd, Huntsville
Raispis, Jerome P., St. Jude, Scottsboro
Ritchey, Seraphim, St. George the Great Martyr, Birmingham
Roberson, William, Sacred Heart, Cullman
Robinson, E. Lee, Sr., Holy Infant of Prague, Trussville
Rosko, Christopher J., St. Mark the Evangelist, Birmingham
Rumore, Terrence L., Our Lady of the Lake, Pell City
Sassenfeld, Helmut, Good Shepherd, Huntsville
Slapikas, Frank R., Holy Spirit, Tuscaloosa
Stagg, James A., Holy Family, Lanett
Steltemeier, R. William, Diocese of Nashville
Stephens, Joseph R., Jr., St. Elias (Marionite Rite), Birmingham
Straley, J. Adrian, St. Francis University, Tuscaloosa
Sullivan, Paul Mark, (On leave of absence)
Taffee, William Francis, Jr., Sacred Heart of Jesus, Anniston
Vazquez, Jose R., Prince of Peace, Birmingham
Viselli, Francis N., Jr., Holy Spirit, Tuscaloosa
Whitaker, Dan, Our Lady of the Valley, Birmingham
Zieverink, Edward Walter, Jr., (Unassigned)

INSTITUTIONS LOCATED IN THE DIOCESE

[A] HIGH SCHOOLS, DIOCESAN

BIRMINGHAM. *John Carroll Catholic High School*, 300 Lakeshore Pkwy., P.O. Box 19907, 35219. Tel: 205-940-2400; Fax: 205-945-7429. Email: lwfisher@usit.net. Web: www.jcchs.org. Mr. Lee W. Fisher, Prin.; Revs. John Michael Wrigley; Earl Gray Bean Jr.; Michael Deering; Joseph Delano Lody Jr.; Bryan K. Lowe. Priests 5; Sisters 3; Lay Teachers 51; Students 744.

FORT MCCLELLAN. *Sacred Heart Catholic High School*, 16 Morton Rd., 36205. Tel: 256-237-4231; Fax: 256-237-4231. Email: PDoty209@aol.com. Paul M. Doty, Prin. Lay Teachers 17; Students 54.

HUNTSVILLE. *Catholic High School*, 4810 Bradford Dr., 35805. Tel: 256-430-1760; Fax: 256-430-1766. Email: vaquila@chsfalcons.org. Web: www.chsfalcons.org. Vince Aquila, Prin.; Revs. Kevin Bazzel; Tom Woods; Deacon Darrell Diem. Priests 2; Lay Teachers 24; Students 210.

TUSCALOOSA. *Holy Spirit High School*, 601 37th St. E., 35405. Tel: 205-553-5606; Fax: 205-556-7103. Email: scalabro@hshs.com. Web: www.hschs.com. Steve Calabro, Prin. Lay Teachers 22; Students 240.

[B] HIGH SCHOOLS, PRIVATE

BIRMINGHAM. *Holy Family High School*, 2001 19th St., 35218. Tel: 205-787-9937; Fax: 205-787-8530. Email: pbeckwith@holyfamilyhs.org. Web: www.hfhsschoolsinsites.com. Patricia Beckwith, Prin. Passionist Community of Chicago, IL Priests 1; Lay Teachers 19; Students 171.

CULLMAN. *St. Bernard Preparatory School*, 1600 St. Bernard Dr., SE, 35055. Tel: 256-739-6682; Fax: 256-734-2925. Email: sbprep@hiwaay.net. Web: www.stbernardprep.com. Revs. Marcus J. Voss, O.S.B., Pres.; Joel W. Martin, O.S.B., Headmaster. Priests 3; Sisters 1; Brothers 2; Lay Teachers 12; Students 115.

[C] ELEMENTARY SCHOOLS, PRIVATE

BIRMINGHAM. *St. Rose of Lima Academy*, (Grades K-8), 1401 S. 22nd St., 35219. Tel: 205-933-0549; Fax: 205-933-0591. Email: srmevelyn@saintroseacademy.com. Web: www.saintroseacademy.com. Sr. Mary Evelyn, O.P., Prin. Dominican Sisters of Nashville, TN Sisters 7; Lay Teachers 11; Students 238.

[D] GENERAL HOSPITALS

BIRMINGHAM. *Seton Health Corporation of North Alabama*, P.O. Box 12407, 35202-2407. Tel: 205-939-8600. Email: apurdy@stv.org. Curtis James Jr., Pres. & CEO. Daughters of Charity Patients Assisted Annually 27,958.
St. Vincent's Hospital, P.O. Box 12407, 35202-2407. Tel: 205-939-7000; Fax: 205-930-2157. Email: apurdy@stv.org. Web: www.stv.org. 810 St. Vincent's Dr., 35205. Curtis James Jr., Pres. & CEO. Sponsored by Daughters of Charity Sisters 8; Total Staff 1,711; Full-Time Nurses 348; Patients Assisted Annually 168,315; Bed Capacity 338.

[E] MONASTERIES AND RESIDENCES OF PRIESTS AND BROTHERS

BIRMINGHAM. *Franciscan Missionaries of the Eternal Word, A Public Association of the Christian Faithful*, 5821 Old Leeds Rd., 35210. Tel: 205-271-2937; Fax: 205-271-2949. Web: www.MFVA.info. Revs. Angelus M. Shaughnessy, O.F.M.Cap., Father Guardian; Joseph M. Wolfe, M.F.V.A.; Francis Mary Stone, M.F.V.A.; Anthony Mary Stelten, M.F.V.A.; Mark Mary Cristina, M.V.F.A. Professed 10; Total in Residence 13.

CULLMAN. *St. Bernard Abbey*, 1600 St. Bernard Dr., S.E., 35055. Tel: 256-734-8291; Fax: 256-734-3885. Email: abcletus@stbernardprep.com. Web: www.stbernardabbey.com. Rt. Revs. Cletus D. Meagher, O.S.B., Abbot; Victor J. Clark, O.S.B., Retired Abbot (Retired); Very Rev. Thomas J. O'Connor, O.S.B., Prior; Revs. Thomas J. Schnurr, O.S.B.; Roger R.S. Lott, O.S.B.; Francis M. Reque, O.S.B.; Edward P. Markley, O.S.B.; Ignatius B. Kane, O.S.B.; Marcus J. Voss, O.S.B.; Kevin D. McGrath, O.S.B.; Jose Ramon Mascareno, O.S.B.; John O'Donnell, O.S.B.; Joel W. Martin, O.S.B (Corporate Title: Benedictine Society of Alabama, Inc.) Total Priests of Abbey 12; Brothers 14.

[F] CONVENTS AND RESIDENCES OF SISTERS

BIRMINGHAM. *Sister Servants of the Eternal Word*, Casa Maria Retreat House, 3721 Belmont Rd., 35210. Tel: 205-956-6760; Fax: 205-951-0386. Sr. Mary Gabriel, Supr.

CULLMAN. *Sacred Heart Monastery*, P.O. Box 2040, 35056. Tel: 256-734-4622; 256-734-2199; Fax: 256-734-3835. Email: shmon@hiwaay.net. Sr. Veronica Ryan, O.S.B., Prioress. Benedictine Sisters Professed Sisters 48.

HANCEVILLE. *Our Lady of the Angels Monastery, Inc. and Shrine of the Most Blessed Sacrament*, 3222 County Rd. 548, 35077. Tel: 256-352-6267; Fax: 205-795-5702. Web: www.olamshrine.com. Sr. M. Angelica, P.C.P.A., Abbess & Pres. Poor Clare Nuns of Perpetual Adoration Sisters 41; Novices 6; Postulants 7.

[G] DIOCESAN SOCIAL SERVICE

BIRMINGHAM. *Catholic Center of Concern* (Div. of Catholic Charities) , 712 Fourth Ct. W., 35204. Tel: 205-786-4388; Fax: 205-786-6321. P.O. Box 12406, 35202. Sr. Adelangela Paita, M.C. Consolata Missionary Sisters Total Staff 7; Total Assisted 25,000.
Catholic Family Services, 2164 11th Ave. S., 35205. Tel: 205-324-6561; Fax: 205-323-0475. Email: cfsbham@bellsouth.net. Thomas Cook, D.S.W., Dir. Total Staff 6; Total Assisted 1,073.

ANNISTON. *All Saints Interfaith Center of Concern*, 1029 W. 15th St., 36201. Tel: 256-236-7793; Fax: 256-236-7793. Sr. Mary Roy, D.H.S., Dir. Tel: 256-238-1365. Total Staff 2; Total Assisted 12,200.

EUTAW. *Consolata Apostolate*, 331 Boligee St., P.O. Box 538, 35462. Tel: 205-372-3497; Fax: 205-372-2413. Sr. Zelita M. Bragagnolo, M.C., Dir. Total Staff 2; Total Assisted 7,307.

FAYETTE. *Christian Center of Concern*, P.O. Box 952, 35555. 210 1st St, N.W., 35555. Tel: 205-932-3218. Redonia Keeton, Dir. Staff 10; Total Assisted 6,403.

FLORENCE. *Catholic Family Services*, 1111 E. College St. P.O. Box 3633, 35630. Tel: 256-768-1550; Fax: 256-768-1551. Ellen Beadle, M.S.W., Social Worker.

GADSDEN. *Catholic Center of Concern*, 612 Chestnut St., 35901. Tel: 256-546-0028; Fax: 256-547-1730. Karen Knapp, M.S.W., Dir. Total Assisted 14,023.

HAMILTON. *Christian Center of Concern*, P.O. Box 973, 35570. Tel: 205-921-3470. Janis Griffin, Co-Dir.; Sonja Leonelli, Co-Dir. Total Assisted 1,794.

HUNTSVILLE. *Catholic Center of Concern*, 1010 Church St., N.W., P.O. Box 745, 35804. Tel: 256-536-0041; Fax: 256-534-3141. Email: shgcctr@bnalogy.net. Sr. Helen Gaffney, M.S.B.T., Dir. Total Assisted 3,987.

Catholic Family Services, 1010 Church St., N.W., P.O. Box 745, 35804. Tel: 256-536-0073; Fax: 256-534-3141. Email: hsvcfs@bellsouth.net. Laura Dinwiddie, M.S.W., Regl. Dir. Total Families Served 235.

SULLIGENT. *Christian Center of Concern*, P.O. Box 1154, 35586. Tel: 205-698-7197. Martha Richards, Dir. Staff 9; Total Assisted 807.

TUSCALOOSA. *Catholic Family Service Center*, 608 37th St. E., 35405. Tel: 205-759-1268. Suzanna Coleman, M.S.W., Regl. Dir. Total Assisted 779.

WINFIELD. *Christian Center of Concern*, 197 State Hwy. 253, 35594. Tel: 205-487-6230. Marie Weeks, Bookkeeper. Total Assisted 3,591.

[H] CAMPUS MINISTRY

BIRMINGHAM. *St. Stephen the Martyr Catholic Church and Catholic Campus Center* 1515 12th Ave. S., 35205. Tel: 205-933-2500; Fax: 205-939-1500. Email: saintst@bellsouth.com. Revs. Gregory T. Bittner, J.C.L.; Bryan K. Lowe; Sr. Karen Ann Lortscher, O.S.B., Campus Min. Parish Serves: University of Alabama at Birmingham, Samford University, Brimingham-Southern College. Total Staff 2; Students 300.

FLORENCE. *University of North Alabama* St. Joseph's Church, 1111 E. College St., 35630. Tel: 256-764-3303; Fax: 256-718-0208. Email: stjoseph@catholichill.com. Rev. Andrew A. Sullivan.

JACKSONVILLE. *Jacksonville State University* St. Charles Church, 308 Seventh St., N.E., 36265. Tel: 256-435-3238; Fax: 256-435-4942. Email: stcharleschurch@juno.com. Rev. Alan C. Mackey. Total Staff 2; Total in Program 15.

MONTEVALLO. *University of Montevallo* St. Thomas the Apostle Catholic Campus Ministry, 80 St. Thomas Way, 35115. Tel: 205-665-7379; Fax: 205-663-3929. Email: pastthomas@juno.com. Rev. Raymond J. Remke; Sr. Patricia Hinton, O.S.F., Pastoral Assoc.

TALLADEGA. *Talladega College Catholic Campus Ministry* St. Francis of Assisi, P.O. Box 1142, 35160. Tel: 256-362-5372; Fax: 256-362-5372. Email: frassisi@earthlink.net. Rev. Joy Chalissery.

TUSCALOOSA. *Diocesan Campus Ministry Office* St. Francis University Parish, 811 Fifth Ave., 35401. Tel: 205-758-5672; Fax: 205-758-5673. Email: stfrant@bellsouth.net. Web: stfrant.org. Rev. Gerald Holloway. Total Staff 1; Total in Residence 1.

University of Alabama in Tuscaloosa St. Francis University Parish, 811 Fifth Ave., 35401. Tel: 205-758-5672; Fax: 205-758-5673. Email: stfrant@bellsouth.net. Web: stfrant.org. Rev. Gerald Holloway, Campus Min.; Stephanie Agro, Campus Min. Total Staff 2; Total in Residence 1.

[I] MISCELLANEOUS LISTINGS

BIRMINGHAM. *St. Barnabas Regional School Educational Foundation*, 7921 First Ave. N., 35206. Tel: 205-833-0334; Fax: 205-833-0270. Email: tbarnhil@gte.net.

Bruno Family's Catholic Diocesan Trust, P.O. Box 12047, 35202-2047. Tel: 205-838-8322; Fax: 205-836-1910. Email: gnabors@bhmdiocese.org. Web: www.bhmdiocese.org.

Casa Maria Rereat House, 3721 Belmont Rd., 35210. Tel: 205-956-6760. Sr. Mary Gabriel, Dir.

Catholic Housing of Birmingham, Inc., P.O. Box 12047, 35202. Tel: 205-838-8309; Fax: 205-836-1910. 2121 3rd Ave. N., 35203. William M. Moran, Pres.; Rev. Msgr. Brian Egan, Vice Pres. & Sec.

Congregation of the Passion: Holy Family Community, Inc. (House of Religious Men) , 1910 19th St., Ensley, 35218. Tel: 205-780-3440; Fax: 205-780-5272. Email: rcrossmyer@aol.com. Rev. Robert Crossmeyer, C.P., Local Supr. Corporation for Holy Family Church, and Holy Family Elementary, Birmingham, and St. Mary's Church, Fairfield, St. Mary Elementary, Fairfield.

Contemplative Outreach Birmingham, Sacred Heart Monastery, P.O. Box 488, Cullman, 35056. Tel: 256-736-5820. Email: smmcgehee@hotmail.com. Web: www.bham.net/cobweb. Sr. Mary McGehee, O.S.B., Coord.; Aloysius Golden, Area Contact Person. Tel: 205-592-3930.

The Fatima Educational Foundation, 708 First St. S., 35205. Tel: 205-251-8395; Fax: 205-251-8393. Email: ritar@bellsouth.net. Web: olf.schoolinsites.com. Sr. Rita Radloff, S.B.S., Prin.

St. Francis Xavier Catholic School Education Foundation, 2 Xavier Cir., 35213. Tel: 205-871-1153; Fax: 205-871-1687. Email: srjdmcgowan@juno.com. Web: www.saintfrancisxavierschool.com. Sr. Judith Dianne McGowan, R.S.M., Prin. & Contact Person.

Holy Family Educational Foundation, 1910 19th St., 35218 Tel: 205-780-3440; Fax: 205-782-5272. Email: rcrossmyer@aol.com. Web: www.passionist.org. Melva Langford, Board Chair.

Holy Name of Jesus Hospital Trust (Senior Citizen Housing) c/o Regions Bank, P.O. Box 10247, 35202. Tel: 205-326-7219; Fax: 205-326-7052. Email: sroebuck@regionsbank.com. Sidney O. Roebuck Jr., Trustee, Vice Pres. & Senior Trust Officer, Regions Bank. Total Assisted 341

John Carroll Catholic High School Educational Foundation, Inc., 300 Lakeshore Pkwy., 35209. Tel: 205-940-2400; Fax: 205-945-7429. Email: mlconneryjcchs@yahoo.com. Web: www.jcchs.org. Mary Louise Connery, Dir.

Magnificat: Mary, Woman of Faith Chapter, 1341 Forest Ridge Ct., 35226. Tel: 205-941-0144; Fax: 205-942-7742. Email: carolynwright@msn.com. Web: www.angelfire.com/al4/cwright. Carolyn Mathis Wright, Coord.

Our Lady of Sorrows Educational School Foundation, 1728 Oxmoor Rd., 35209. Tel: 205-871-8121; Fax: 205-871-8180.

Our Lady of the Valley Educational Foundation, 5514 Double Oak Ln., 35242. Tel: 205-991-5488; Fax: 205-991-5181. Email: olvchurch@worldnet.att.net.

St. Peter's Endowment Foundation, 2061 Patton Chapel Rd., 35216. Email: stpeterapostle@bellsouth.net. Rev. Msgr. Paul Rohling, V.C. Total Assisted 200; Total Staff 7.

Villa Maria, 500 82nd St. S., 35206. Tel: 205-836-7839; Fax: 205-836-0664. Donna Faizson, Mgr. Total Staff 7; Total in Residence 63.

St. Vincent's Foundation, P.O. Box 12407, 35202-2407. Tel: 205-939-7825; Fax: 205-930-2525. Email: srmarydc@stv.org. Web: www.stvfoundation.org. Barbara Traylor, Dir. Devel.; William M. Moran, Exec. Dir.; Nita Rayburn, Exec. Asst.; Sr. Mary Cecilia Schlebecker D.C., Special Project Asst.; Susann Montgomery Clark, Dir. Planned Giving.

BESSEMER. *St. Aloysius Educational Foundation*, 751 Academy Dr., 35022. Tel: 205-424-2981; Fax: 205-426-5753. Email: aloysiusst@aol.com. Rev. Ray W. Keiser. Total Assisted Monthly 207.

CULLMAN. *Benedictine Manor Retirement Home, Inc.*, 200 Janeway Dr., 35055. Tel: 256-739-2853; Fax: 256-734-8302 (Call First). Email: shmon@hiwaay.net. Web: fly.hiwaay.net/~shmon. Sr. Bertha True O.S.B., Dir. Resident Capacity 35.

Benedictine Spirituality and Conference Center, P.O. Box 2040, 35056-2040. Tel: 256-734-8302; Fax: 256-734-8302 (Call First). Email: shmon@hiwaay.net. Web: www.shmon.org. Gloria Garrison, Dir. Bed Capacity 72; Total Staff 7.

St. Bernard Abbey Foundation, 1600 St. Bernard Dr., S.E., 35055. Tel: 256-734-8291; Fax: 256-734-3885. Rev. Cletus Meagher, O.S.B., Chm.

St. Bernard Preparatory School Educational Foundation, 1600 St. Bernard Dr., S.E., 35055. Tel: 256-739-6682; Fax: 256-734-2295. Email: mjvosb@hiwaay.net. Web: www.stbernardprep.com. Rt. Rev. Cletus Meagher, O.S.B., Chm.

Sacred Heart Monastery of Cullman, Alabama Foundation, P.O. Box 2040, 35056. Tel: 256-734-4622; Fax: 256-734-3835. Email: shmon@hiwaay.net. Sr. Veronica Ryan, O.S.B., Contact Person.

DECATUR. *St. Ann's Educational Foundation*, 240 Johnson St. S.E., 35601. Tel: 256-353-6543; Fax: 256-353-0705. Email: stann@hiwaay.net Web: sasd@schoolinsites.com. Janet Jensen.

FLORENCE. *St. Joseph School Foundation, Florence*, 115 Plum St., 35630. Tel: 256-766-1923. Email: barnescat@aol.com.

Society of St. Vincent de Paul, St. Joseph Conference, 659 S. Poplar St., 35630-6818. Tel: 256-718-0901; Fax: 256-718-0901. Email: svdpts@hiwaay.net. Rev. Andrew A. Sullivan, Spiritual Advisor; Mary Jane Thompson, Pres.; Peter A. Goudreau, Treas.

FORT MCCLELLAN. *Gertrude C. Luther, M.D. Charitable Trust*, 16 Morton Rd., 36205. Tel: 256-237-4231; Fax: 256-241-2353. Email: PDocy209@aol.com. Web www.cableone.net/shschool.

Sacred Heart of Jesus Charitable Trust, 16 Morton Rd., 36205. Tel: 256-237-4231; Fax: 256-241-2353. Email: pep1ermint@cs.com. Web: www.cableone.net/shschool.

GADSDEN. *St. James Educational Foundation*, 700 Albert Rains Blvd., 35901. Tel: 256-546-0132; Fax: 256-546-0134 Email: sjcs@microxl.com. Web: www.stjcs.org. Total Staff 18.

HUNTSVILLE. *Holy Spirit Regional School Foundation*, 625 Airport Rd., 35802. Tel: 256-881-4852, Ext. 137; Fax: 256-881-4904. Email: foundation89@comcast.net. Web: www.hstigers.net. Lee Dumbacher, Admin.

Society of St. Vincent dePaul, District Council of Huntsville 35802. Tel: 256-882-0040; Fax: 256-881-5510. Email: bakerhd@mindspring.com. Web: svdphsv.org. David J. Baker, Pres.; Sr. Treva Heinberg, O.S.B., Spiritual Advisor; Glen Anderson, Treas.

St. Vincent De Paul Thrift Store, 2140 Jonathan Dr., 35810-3453. Tel: 256-851-8881. Patricia Schuessler, Mgr.

MADISON. *St. John's Educational Foundation*, 1055 Hughes Rd., 35758. Tel: 256-722-0130; Fax: 256-722-0303. Rev. Msgr. Michael Sexton, V.G.

TUSCALOOSA. *The Harrison Family Endowment Trust for the Benefit of Holy Spirit School*, 711 37th St. E., 35405. Tel: 205-553-9630; Fax: 205-553-8880. Email: holyspiritelem@hselm.com. Very Rev. Jeremiah Deasy, V.F.

RELIGIOUS INSTITUTES OF MEN REPRESENTED IN THE DIOCESE

For further details refer to the corresponding bracketed number in the Religious Institutes of Men or Women section.

[0200]—*Benedictine Monks*—O.S.B.

[0820]—*Congregation of the Fathers of Mercy*—C.P.M.

[1330]—*Congregation of the Mission* (Eastern Prov.)—C.M.

[1000]—*Congregation of the Passion*—C.P.

[]—*Dominican Fathers*—O.P.

[]—*Franciscan Missionaries of the Eternal Word*—M.F.V.A.

[0570]—*Glenmary Home Missioners* (Cincinnati, OH)—G.H.M.

[1120]—*Missionaries of the Sacred Hearts of Jesus and Mary*—M.SS.CC.

[0910]—*Oblates of Mary Immaculate*—O.M.I.

[1190]—*Salesians of Don Bosco*—S.D.B.

[1200]—*Society of the Divine Savior*—S.D.S.

[]—*Society of the Divine Word*—S.V.D.

[0700]—*St. Joseph's Society of the Sacred Heart* (Baltimore, MD)—S.S.J.

RELIGIOUS INSTITUTES OF WOMEN REPRESENTED IN THE DIOCESE

[]—*A New Genesis*—A.N.G.

[0230]—*Benedictine Sisters of Pontifical Jurisdiction*—O.S.B.

[0260]—*Blessed Sacrament Sisters*—S.B.S.

[0720]—*Consolata Missionary Sisters*—M.C.

[0760]—*Daughters of Charity of St. Vincent de Paul*—D.C.

[0820]—*Daughters of the Holy Spirit*—D.H.S.

[1070-03]—*Dominican Sisters* (Adrian, MI)—O.P.

[1070-07]—*Dominican Sisters* (Nashville, TN)—O.P.

[1070-13]—*Dominican Sisters* (Sinsinawa, WI)—O.P.

[1170]—*Felician Sisters*—C.S.S.F.

[1310]—*Franciscan Sisters* (Little Falls, MN)—O.S.F.

[1845]—*Guadalupan Missionaries of the Holy Spirit*—M.G.Sp.S.

[2720]—*Mission Helpers of the Sacred Heart*—M.H.S.H.

[2790]—*Missionary Servants of the Most Blessed Trinity*—M.S.B.T.

[]—*Order of Consecrated Virgins*—O.C.V.

[3210]—*Poor Clares of Perpetual Adoration*—P.C.P.A.

[]—*Sister Servants of the Eternal Word*—S.S.E.W.

[2575]—*Sisters of Mercy of the Americas*—R.S.M.

[1650]—*Sisters of St. Francis of Philadelphia*—O.S.F.

[3840]—*Sisters of St. Joseph of Carondelet*—C.S.J.

[1030]—*Sisters of the Divine Savior*—S.D.S.

[3320]—*Sisters of the Presentation of the B.V.M.*—P.B.V.M

[4048]—*Society of Sisters Faithful Companions of Jesus*—F.C.J.

NECROLOGY

(No Deaths)

Diocese of Bismarck

(Dioecesis Bismarckiensis)

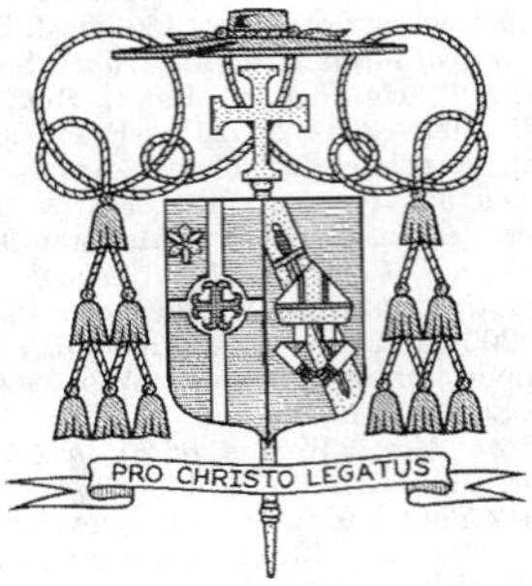

Most Reverend

PAUL A. ZIPFEL, D.D.

Bishop of Bismarck; ordained March 18, 1961; appointed Titular Bishop of Walla Walla and Auxiliary Bishop of St. Louis May 16, 1989; consecrated June 29, 1989; appointed Bishop of Bismarck December 31, 1996; installed February 20, 1997

ESTABLISHED DECEMBER 31, 1909.

Square Miles 34,268.

Comprises the Counties of Adams, Billings, Bowman, Burke, Burleigh, Divide, Dunn, Emmons, Golden Valley, Grant, Hettinger, McKenzie, McLean, Mercer, Morton, Mountrail, Oliver, Renville, Sioux, Slope, Stark, Ward and Williams in the State of North Dakota.

Legal Title: For legal titles of parishes and diocesan institutions, consult the Chancery Office.

Chancery Office: 420 Raymond St., Box 1575, Bismarck, ND 58502-1575. Tel: 701-223-1347; Fax: 701-223-3693.

STATISTICAL OVERVIEW

Personnel	
Bishop	1
Abbots	1
Retired Abbots	2
Priests: Diocesan Active in Diocese	41
Priests: Diocesan Active Outside Diocese	4
Priests: Retired, Sick or Absent	22
Number of Diocesan Priests	67
Religious Priests in Diocese	27
Total Priests in Diocese	94
Extern Priests in Diocese	5
Ordinations:	
Permanent Deacons	2
Permanent Deacons in Diocese	68
Total Brothers	24
Total Sisters	129
Parishes	
Parishes	62
With Resident Pastor:	
Resident Diocesan Priests	40
Resident Religious Priests	6
Without Resident Pastor:	
Administered by Priests	14
Administered by Deacons	2
Missions	38
Professional Ministry Personnel:	
Brothers	1
Sisters	6
Lay Ministers	31
Welfare	
Catholic Hospitals	4
Total Assisted	354,747
Homes for the Aged	4
Total Assisted	421
Specialized Homes	1
Total Assisted	160
Other Institutions	1
Total Assisted	6
Educational	
Diocesan Students in Other Seminaries	14
Total Seminarians	14
Colleges and Universities	1
Total Students	2,617
High Schools, Diocesan and Parish	3
Total Students	1,034
Elementary Schools, Diocesan and Parish	12
Total Students	1,557
Catechesis/Religious Education:	
High School Students	2,743
Elementary Students	5,906
Total Students under Catholic Instruction	13,871
Teachers in the Diocese:	
Sisters	7
Lay Teachers	175
Vital Statistics	
Receptions into the Church:	
Infant Baptism Totals	1,335
Adult Baptism Totals	140
Received into Full Communion	106
First Communions	1,105
Confirmations	1,177
Marriages:	
Catholic	235
Interfaith	172
Total Marriages	407
Deaths	754
Total Catholic Population	64,245
Total Population	259,479

Former Bishops—Most Revs. VINCENT DE PAUL WEHRLE, O.S.B., D.D. (Retired), appt. Bishop of Bismarck, April 9, 1910; consecrated May 19, 1910; retired Dec. 11, 1939; named Titular Bishop of Teos by Pope Pius XII; died Nov. 2, 1941; VINCENT J. RYAN, D.D., LL.D., appt. March 19, 1940; consecrated May 28, 1940; died Nov. 10, 1951; LAMBERT A. HOCH, D.D., L.L.D., appt. Jan. 23, 1952; consecrated March 25, 1952; transferred to Diocese of Sioux Falls, Dec. 5, 1956; died June 27, 1990; HILARY B. HACKER, D.D. (Retired), appt. Bishop, Dec. 29, 1956; retired June 28, 1982; died Nov. 6, 1990; JOHN F. KINNEY, D.D., J.C.D., appt. June 28, 1982;; Episcopal Ord. Jan. 25, 1977;; installed Aug. 23, 1982; transferred to Diocese of St. Cloud, July 6, 1995.

Vicar General—Rev. THOMAS E. KRAMER.

Chancery Office—420 Raymond St., Box 1575, Bismarck, 58502-1575. Tel: 701-223-1347; Fax: 701-223-3693.

Chancellor—Deacon JOEL MELARVIE.

Center for Pastoral Ministry Office—520 N. Washington St., P.O. Box 1137, Bismarck, 58502-1137. Tel: 701-222-3035.

Diocesan Tribunal—520 N. Washington St., P.O. Box 1137, Bismarck, 58502-1137. Tel: 701-222-3035.

Judicial Vicar—Rev. GENE E. LINDEMANN, J.C.L.

Defensor Vinculi—Revs. LEONARD A. ECKROTH; DAVID L. ZIMMER.

Pro-Synodal Judges—Revs. GEORGE A. DUKART; MARVIN J. KLEMMER; BRUCE D. KREBS; THOMAS E. KRAMER; MICHAEL T. KRANK (Retired); ALBERT R. LEARY; EDWIN P. WEHNER; GERALD RUELLE, O.S.B.

Procurator/Advocates—RUTH MOERICKE.

Advocate—HELEN GOLDADE.

Notary—JOLENE EMIL.

Presbyteral Council—Revs. WAYNE V. SATTLER, Chm.; GARY L. BENZ, Sec.; PAUL D. BECKER; JEFFREY A. ZWACK, Treas.; CHRIS B. WALTER; CHAD GION; AUSTIN VETTER, Vice Chm.; PATRICK MOORE, O.S.B.; THOMAS E. KRAMER.

Diocesan Corporate Board—Most Rev. PAUL A. ZIPFEL, Pres.; Revs. THOMAS E. KRAMER, Vice Pres.; PAUL D. BECKER; JAMES B. BRAATEN; Deacon JOEL MELARVIE, Sec.

Diocesan Finance Council—Most Rev. PAUL A. ZIPFEL, Pres.; Revs. THOMAS E. KRAMER, Chm.; JAMES B. BRAATEN; PAUL D. BECKER; Mr. RICHARD F. WHITE; ERNEST B. BORR; MIKE SCHWINDT; MARVIN HEINERT; JEFFREY J. TESCHER; Deacon JOEL MELARVIE; RON SCHATZ.

Diocesan Offices and Directors

Archives—MARGE GROSZ; Deacon JOEL MELARVIE, Box 1137, Bismarck, 58502-1137. Tel: 701-222-3035.

Boy Scouts—Deacon JOHN LAMONTAGNE, Chap., 1219 Eastwood St., Bismarck, 58504-6222.

Catholic Campaign For Human Development—Mr. RONALD SCHATZ, Dir., P.O. Box 1137, Bismarck, 58502-1137. Tel: 701-222-3035.

Catholic Charities North Dakota—BRISTON FERNANDEZ, Exec. Dir., 2537 University Dr. S., Fargo, 58103-5736. Tel: 701-235-4457. Other Locations, 1223 S. 12th St., Ste. 6, Bismarck, 58504-6626. Tel: 701-255-1793. 1809 S. Broadway, Ste. W, Minot, 58701-6567. Tel: 701-852-2854.

Catholic Relief—RONALD SCHATZ, Dir., P.O. Box 1137, Bismarck, 58502-1137. Tel: 701-222-3035.

Office of Vocations—Rev. THOMAS J. RICHTER, Dir., P.O. Box 1137, Bismarck, 58502-1137. Tel: 701-222-3035.

Vicar for Presbyters—Rev. MARVIN J. KLEMMER, P.O. Box 1137, Bismarck, 58502-1137. Tel: 701-222-3035.

Office of Worship—Rev. GENE LINDEMANN, J.C.L., Interim Dir., P.O. Box 1137, Bismarck, 58502-1137. Tel: 701-222-3035.

Continuing Education for Clergy—Rev. JOHN G. GUTHRIE, P.O. Box K, Williston, 58802-1115. Tel: 701-572-2116.

Ecumenism—Rev. MARVIN J. KLEMMER, 1905 S. Third St., Bismarck, 58504-7118. Tel: 701-223-3606.

Holy Childhood—RONALD M. SCHATZ, Dir., P.O. Box 1137, Bismarck, 58502-1137. Tel: 701-222-3035.

Newspaper—MARGE GROSZ, Editor, P.O. Box 1137, Bismarck, 58502-1137. Tel: 701-222-3035. "Dakota Catholic Action"

North Dakota Catholic Conference—CHRISTOPHER DODSON, 227 W. Broadway, Ste. 2, Bismarck, 58501-3737. Tel: 701-223-2519; Fax: 701-223-6075.

Permanent Diaconate Office—

Vicar for Deacons—Rev. DENNIS R. SCHAFER.

Director of Deacons—Deacon CHARLES L. KRAMER.

Director of Formation Program—Deacon ALVIN W. SCHWINDT, P.O. Box 1137, Bismarck, 58502-1137. Tel: 701-222-3035.

Priests' Benefit Association—Most Rev. PAUL A. ZIPFEL, Pres.; Revs. JAMES B. BRAATEN, Chm.; DAVID RICHTER; DANIEL BERG, Sec.; EDWIN P. WEHNER, Treas.; JEROME G. KAUTZMAN, Vice Chm. (Retired); MICHAEL T. KRANK (Retired); JEFFRY TESCHER, Agent of Record.

Priests' Personnel Board—Revs. THOMAS J. RICHTER, Ex Officio; GENE E. LINDEMANN, J.C.L., Chm.; PATRICK A. SCHUMACHER, S.T.L.; EDWIN P. WEHNER; JEFFREY A. ZWACK, Sec.; MARVIN J. KLEMMER, Ex Officio; Most Rev. PAUL A. ZIPFEL.

Propagation of the Faith—RONALD M. SCHATZ, P.O. Box 1137, Bismarck, 58502-1137. Tel: 701-222-3035.

Communications Office—Deacon JOEL MELARVIE, Dir., P.O. Box 1575, Bismarck, 58502-1575. Tel: 701-223-1347.

Office of Catechesis—Sr. KATHLEEN ATKINSON, O.S.B., Box 1137, Bismarck, 58502-1137. Tel: 701-222-3035.

Pro-Life—MARGE GROSZ, Dir., P.O. Box 1137, Bismarck, 58502-1137. Tel: 701-222-3035; Fax: 701-222-0269.

Provision for the Future—JEFFREY J. TESCHER, Contact Person, 520 N. Washington St., P.O. Box 1177, Bismarck, 58502. Tel: 701-222-3035; Fax: 701-222-0269. Email: jtescher@bismarckdiocese.com.

Stewardship and Resource Development Office—RONALD SCHATZ, Dir., Box 1137, Bismarck,

58502-1137. Tel: 701-222-3035.
Youth Ministry—KENNETH H. ROSHAU, Dir., 11010 41st St., S.W., Dickinson, 58601-9512. Tel: 701-225-5509.
Search Program—KENNETH H. ROSHAU, 11010 41st St., S.W., Dickinson, 58601-9512. Tel: 701-225-5509.
Victim Assistance Coordinator—Deacon JOEL MELARVIE. Tel: 701-223-1347. Email: jmelarvie@bismarckdiocese.com.

CLERGY, PARISHES, MISSIONS AND PAROCHIAL SCHOOLS

CITY OF BISMARCK
(BURLEIGH COUNTY)

1—CATHEDRAL OF THE HOLY SPIRIT (1947), [JC] Revs. Thomas E. Kramer; James P. Shea; Deacons Wilfred Wolf; Ralph von Reuden; Richard Fettig; Jim Ressler, (Retired).
Mailing Address: 519 Raymond St., 58501. Tel: 701-223-1033; Fax: 701-223-1438.
Res.: 308 West Ave., 58501. Tel: 701-223-1033 (Office); Fax: 701-223-1438.
School—Tel: 701-223-5484; Fax: 701-223-5485. Elizabeth Gross, Prin. Sisters of St. Benedict 1; Lay Teachers 19; Students 274.
Catechesis/Religious Program—Tel: 701-222-2259. Marie Gabel, D.R.E. Students 291.

2—ST. ANNE (1957), [JC] Rev. Edwin P. Wehner; Deacons Alvin Schmitz; Wayne Jundt; Joe Krupinsky; Betty E. Greff, Pastoral Assoc.; Edward Hartwig, Parish Admin. In Res., Rev. Thomas J. Richter, Dir. Office of Vocations.
Res.: 1321 Braman Ave., 58501. Tel: 701-223-1549; Fax: 701-250-9214.
School—(Grades PreK-8) Tel: 701-223-3373. Mrs. Laura Sturn, Prin. Lay Teachers 15; Students 192.
Catechesis/Religious Program—Tel: 701-224-0847. Mrs. Frances I. Roehrich, D.R.E. Students 390.

3—ASCENSION (1974), [JC] Rev. Marvin J. Klemmer; Deacons John Lamontagne; Ray Grabar; Edwin Wesolowski.
Res.: 1905 S. Third St., 58504-7118. Tel: 701-223-3606; Fax: 701-223-5783.
Catechesis/Religious Program—Tel: 701-258-5692. Cheryle Gagner, D.R.E. Students 632.

4—CORPUS CHRISTI (1964), [JC] Rev. Paul D. Becker; Sr. Ivo Schoch, Pastoral Assoc.; Deacons Lynn Clancy; Harry M. Deichert; Joseph J. Mathern; Rex McDowell; John Tharaldsen.
Res.: 1936 N. Second St., 58501. Tel: 701-255-4620; Fax: 701-255-4616.
Catechesis/Religious Program—Tel: 701-255-3104. Patricia Clark, D.R.E.; Mary Kay Vetter, D.R.E.; Patrick Hall, D.R.E. Students 431.

5—ST. MARY (1877), [JC] Rev. Bruce D. Krebs; Deacons Tony Dworshak; Kenneth Klein; Steve Braus, Admin.; Sr. Jeanette Hinds, O.S.B., Pastoral Min.; Kristi Gray, Pastoral Min.; Liz Braus, Pastoral Min.; Keven Wanuer, Pastoral Min.; Judy Erickstad, Pastoral Min.; Diane Huck, Pastoral Min.; Keven Wanuer, Pastoral Min.
Res.: 806 E. Broadway, 58501. Tel: 701-223-5562; Fax: 701-530-0864.
School—Tel: 701-223-0225; Fax: 701-250-9918. Gwyn Marback-Tschosik, Prin. Lay Teachers 16; Students 169.
Catechesis/Religious Program—Students 190.

OUTSIDE THE CITY OF BISMARCK

BEACH, GOLDEN VALLEY CO., ST. JOHN THE BAPTIST (1909), [CEM] Rev. David A. Richter; Deacons Samuel Larson; Donald Nistler; James Wosepka.
Res.: Box 337, 58621. Tel: 701-872-4153; Fax: 701-872-4695.
Catechesis/Religious Program—Karen Wojahn, D.R.E. Tel: 701-872-4895; Swenda Braden, D.R.E. Tel: 701-872-4333. Students 134.
Mission—St. Mary [CEM] P.O. Box 337, Golva, Golden Valley Co. 58621.

BELFIELD, STARK CO., ST. BERNARD (1910), [CEM] Rev. Shannon G. Lucht.
Res.: P.O. Box 38, 58622. Tel: 701-575-4295; Fax: 701-575-8457.
Catechesis/Religious Program—Tel: 701-575-4099. Diane Procive, D.R.E. (High School). Students 128.
Mission—SS. Peter and Paul New Hradec, Dunn Co.

BEULAH, MERCER CO., ST. JOSEPH (1915), (German—Russian), [CEM] Rev. Charles Zins.
Res.: P.O. Box 146, 58523. Tel: 701-873-5397; Fax: 701-873-5614.
Catechesis/Religious Program—Tel: 701-873-5006; 701-873-5622. Students 214.

BOWBELLS, BURKE CO., ST. JOSEPH (1905), (German—Scandinavian), Rev. Frank J. Schuster.
Res.: P.O. Box 488, Kenmare, 58746. Tel: 701-385-4311; Fax: 701-385-4321.
Church: 102 3rd St., N.W., 58721. Tel: 701-377-2611.
Catechesis/Religious Program—Tel: 701-377-2766. Roxanne Hanson, D.R.E. Students 13.

BOWMAN, BOWMAN CO., ST. CHARLES (1910), [CEM] [JC 2] Rev. Jeffrey Zwack.
Res.: 58623. Tel: 701-523-5292.
Catechesis/Religious Program—Tel: 701-523-5415. Rosemery Kadrmas, D.R.E. (Grades 1-6); Vivian Hernandez, D.R.E. (Grades 7-12). Students 158.
Mission—St. Mel P.O. Box 709, Rhame, Bowman Co. 58623. Tel: 701-523-5292.
Mission—Immaculate Heart of Mary P.O Box 709, Marmarth Slope Co. 58623.

BURLINGTON, WARD CO., ST. FRANCIS OF ASSISI, Closed. For inquiries for parish records contact the chancery., (Quasi-Parish)

CARSON, GRANT CO., ST. THERESA THE CHILD JESUS (1920), [JC] Rev. Gary Benz.
Res.: 421 Court St., Flasher, 58535-7216. Tel: 701-597-3570; 701-597-3228; Fax: 701-597-3228.
Catechesis/Religious Program—Tel: 701-597-3228. Students 55.

CENTER, OLIVER CO., ST. MARTIN (1914), [CEM 2] [JC] Rev. Chad D. Gion.
Res.: P.O. Box 2766, 58530. Tel: 701-794-3329; Fax: 701-794-3601.
Catechesis/Religious Program—Tel: 701-794-3191. Judith McNulty, D.R.E.; Alice Henderscheid, D.R.E. Students 77.
Mission—St. Edwin Washburn, Mercer Co. Rev. Edward F. Korte.

CROSBY, DIVIDE CO., ST. PATRICK (1912), [CEM 4] [JC 2] Rev. Daniel J. Berg.
Res.: P.O. Box 89, 58730. Tel: 701-965-6537; Fax: 701-965-6537.
Catechesis/Religious Program—Tel: 701-965-6600. Students 57.
Mission—St. Luke 304 Main St., Noonan, Divide Co. 58765. Tel: 701-925-5659.
Mission—St. John the Baptist [CEM] 201 1st Ave., P.O. Box 31, Portal, Burke Co. 58772. Tel: 701-926-4621.

CROWN BUTTE, MORTON CO., ST. VINCENT (1896), [CEM] Deacon Steve M. Brannan; Nancy J. Brannan, Pastoral Assoc. & D.R.E.
Mailing Address: 3180 36th St., Mandan, 58554. Tel: 701-255-9318.
Res.: 2119 S. 3rd St., 58504.
Catechesis/Religious Program—Students 19.

DICKINSON, STARK CO.

1—ST. JOSEPH (1902), (German—Russian), Revs. Kenneth Phillips; Dennis R. Schafer; Deacon Ralph Stockert.
Res.: 240 E. Broadway, 58601. Tel: 701-483-2223; Fax: 701-483-0648.
School—Tel: 701-225-6162. Sisters 1; Lay Teachers 8; Students 55.
Catechesis/Religious Program—Marlene Reisenauer, D.R.E. Students 164.

2—ST. PATRICK (1885), Revs. Austin Vetter; Claude Seeberger, O.S.B.; Deacons Joe Kappel; Anton Wanner; Ron Keller.
Res.: 229 Third Ave. W., 58601. Tel: 701-483-6700; Fax: 701-483-6702.
School—St Patrick Queen of Peace, 145 Third Ave. West, 58601. Tel: 701-225-8094; Fax: 701-225-8831. Patricia Hardy, Prin. Lay Teachers 11; Students 143.
Catechesis/Religious Program—Tel: 701-225-8831. Mary Agostini, D.R.E. Students 82.

3—ST. PIUS, Closed. For inquiries for parish records contact the chancery.

4—QUEEN OF PEACE CHURCH (1973), [JC] Rev. David G. Morman.
Office—725 12th St. W., 58601-3516. Tel: 701-483-2134; 701-483-2991 (Res.); Fax: 701-483-1379.
Catechesis/Religious Program—Tel: 701-483-9894. Dickie Jo Boespflug, D.R.E. Students 455

5—ST. WENCESLAUS (1912), (Bohemian), [CEM] [JC] Revs. James B. Braaten; Basil Atwell, O.S.B.; Deacons Joel Melarvie, Chancellor; Eugene F. Morman; Raymond Jilek.
Res.: 525 Third St. E., 58601. Tel: 701-225-3972; Fax: 701-225-4146.
School—Tel: 701-225-9463; Fax: 701-225-0474. Sr. Dorothy Zeller, S.S.N.D., Prin. Lay Teachers 10; Students 131.
Catechesis/Religious Program—Tel: 701-225-3972. Gini Zent, D.R.E. Students 214.

FLASHER, MORTON CO., ST. LAWRENCE (1912), [CEM] Rev. Gary Benz.
Res.: 421 Court St., 58535-7216. Tel: 701-597-3570.
Catechesis/Religious Program—Tel: 701-597-3228. Students 70.

FORT YATES, SIOUX CO., ST. PETER - CATHOLIC INDIAN MISSION (1878), (Native American), [CEM], (Standing Rock Indian Reservation) Rev. William P. Cosgrove.
Res.: P.O. Box 394, 58538. Tel: 701-854-3473; Fax: 701-854-3474.
School—St Bernard Mission School, Tel: 701-854-7413. Sr. Julie Brandt, S.S.N.D., Prin. Sisters 3; Lay Teachers 4; Students 69.
Catechesis/Religious Program—Tel: 701-854-3447. Sr. Frances M. Voigt, D.R.E. Students 34.
Mission—St. Elizabeth [CEM] P.O. Box 394, Cannon Ball, Sioux Co. 58538. Tel: 701-854-3474.
Mission—St. James [CEM] P.O. Box 394, Porcupine, Sioux Co. 58538.

FOXHOLM, WARD CO., ST. MARY (1887), [CEM] [JC] Rev. Keith N. Streifel.
Res.: 17901 128th Ave. N.W., 58718-9643. Tel: 701-468-5925.
Catechesis/Religious Program—Tel: 701-468-5648. Students 99.
Mission—St. Ann 217 Dewey St., Berthold, Ward Co. 58718. Tel: 701-453-3660.

GARRISON, MCLEAN CO., ST. NICHOLAS (1905), [JC 8] Rev. Francis X. Kalathiveettil (India).
Res.: 235 Second St. N.E., P.O. Box 870, 58540. Tel: 701-463-2327; Fax: 701-463-2323.
Catechesis/Religious Program—Students 133.
Mission—Immaculate Conception Max, McClean Co.
Mission—White Shield, Sacred Heart, St. Nicholas 58540.

GLEN ULLIN, MORTON CO., SACRED HEART OF JESUS (1883), (German—Russian), [CEM 2] Rev. Sebastian Schmidt, O.S.B.
Res.: Box 609, 58631. Tel: 701-348-3518.
Catechesis/Religious Program—Tel: 701-348-3527. Mrs. Kathy Schirado, D.R.E. Students 110.
Mission—St. Joseph, Grant Co. 58631-0609.

GLENBURN, RENVILLE CO., ST. PHILOMENA (1948), (German—Scandinavian), [CEM] Rev. Jacob Konath.
Res.: 302 Raymond St., Box 68, 58740. Tel: 701-362-7571; Fax: 701-362-7571.
Catechesis/Religious Program—1627 - 76th St., North Deering, 58731. Tel: 701-362-7367; 701-362-7419. Darla Johnson, D.R.E. Students 21.
Mission—St. John Rte. 2, Box 3, Lansford, Bottineau Co. 58750. Tel: 701-784-5421.

GRENORA, WILLIAMS CO., ST. BONIFACE (1912), [CEM 2] [JC] Rev. Raymond A. Aydt.
Church: P.O. Box 37, 58845. Tel: 701-694-3743.
Res.: 118 Fifth St. W., Williston, 58801. Tel: 701-572-6732.
Catechesis/Religious Program—Tel: 701-694-4285. Kathy Oster, D.R.E. Students 9.

HAGUE, EMMONS CO., ST. MARY (1890), (German—Russian), [CEM 2] Rev. Leonard A. Eckroth.
Church: P.O. Box 156, 58542. Tel: 701-336-7119.
Res.: Box 322, Strasburg, 58573. Tel: 701-336-2603; 701-336-7172.
Catechesis/Religious Program—Tel: 701-336-7102. Kathleen Kramer Nagel, D.R.E. Students 33.

HALLIDAY, DUNN CO., ST. PAUL (1952), [CEM] [JC], (Quasi-Parish) Rev. Gerald Ruelle, O.S.B.
Res.: P.O. Box 299, Killdeer, 58640. Tel: 701-764-5357; Fax: 701-764-6246.
Catechesis/Religious Program—Tel: 701-938-4504. Margaret Senger, D.R.E. Students 14.

HAZELTON, EMMONS CO., ST. PAUL (1905), Rev. Kenneth G. Phillips; Deacon Kenneth Wolbaum.
Church: 372 Harold St., 58544. Tel: 701-254-4588.
Res.: 613 N. Broadway St., Linton, 58552.
Catechesis/Religious Program—Tel: 701-782-6281. Charlotte Beastrom, D.R.E. Students 69.
Mission—St. Katherine [CEM 2] Linton. 613 N. Broadway, Braddock, Emmons Co. 58552-7311.

HAZEN, MERCER CO., ST. MARTIN (1914), (German—Russian), [CEM] Rev. Charles Zins.
Mailing Address: P.O. Box 387, 58545. Tel: 701-748-2121.
Res.: P.O. Box 146, Beulah, 58523. Tel: 701-873-5387; Fax: 701-873-5614.
Catechesis/Religious Program—Tel: 701-748-2121. Peg Rahn, D.R.E.; LuAnn Woeste, D.R.E. Students 163.

HEBRON, MORTON CO., ST. ANN (1906), (German), [CEM 3] Rev. Sebastian Schmidt, O.S.B.
Res.: P.O. Box 12, 58638. Tel: 701-878-4658; Fax: 701-878-4658.
Catechesis/Religious Program—Tel: 701-878-4686. Jane Scharf, D.R.E. Students 60.
Mission—St. Clement P.O. Box 12, Haymarsh, Morton Co. 58638.

HETTINGER, ADAMS CO., HOLY TRINITY (1916), (German), [CEM] [JC] Rev. John Mathai.
Res.: 405 3rd St. N., 58639. Tel: 701-567-2772; Fax: 701-567-2772.
Catechesis/Religious Program—Tel: 701-567-4635. Kathy Nagel, D.R.E.; Mary Kilwein, D.R.E. Tel: 701-567-2916; Deb Dewhirst, D.R.E. Tel: 701-567-2668. Students 132.
Mission—Sacred Heart 405-3rd St. N., Reeder, Adams Co. 58639. Tel: 701-853-2920.

Mission—Sacred Heart 405-3rd St. N., Scranton, Bowman Co. 58639. Tel: 701-275-8778.

KENMARE, WARD CO., ST. AGNES (1901), (Scandinavian—German), [CEM] Rev. Frank Schuster.
Res.: P.O. Box 488, 58746. Tel: 701-385-4311; Fax: 701-385-4321.
Catechesis/Religious Program—Tel: 701-386-2403. Evan and Deb Zeltinger, D.R.E. Students 78.
Mission—St. Anthony [CEM] Hwy. 52, Donnybrook, Ward Co. 58734.

KILLDEER, DUNN CO., ST. JOSEPH (1917), [CEM] [JC 2] Rev. Gerald Ruelle, O.S.B.; Deacons Edward J. Ziman; Herman Dukart.
Res.: P.O. Box 299, 58640. Tel: 701-764-5357; Fax: 701-764-6246.
Catechesis/Religious Program—Tel: 701-548-8068. Candice Benz, D.R.E. Students 114.

LEFOR, STARK CO., ST. ELIZABETH (1898), [CEM] Rev. Basil Atwell, O.S.B.
Res.: 18401 168th Ave. S.E., 58641-5010. Tel: 701-579-4312.

LINTON, EMMONS CO., ST. ANTHONY (1909), [CEM] Rev. Kenneth G. Phillips; Deacons Martin Schumacher, (Retired); Kenneth Wolbaum.
Res.: 613 N. Broadway, 58552-7311. Tel: 701-254-4588; Fax: 701-254-4589.
Catechesis/Religious Program—Tel: 701-254-4646. Susan Schumacher, D.R.E.; Denise Kautz, D.R.E. Students 201.
Mission—St. Michael 2315 79th St., S.E., Emmons Co. 58552.

MANDAN, MORTON CO.

1—CHRIST THE KING (1957), [CEM] Revs. Albert R. Leary; Casimir Paluck; Deacon Dennis Rohr.
Res.: 505-10th Ave., N.W., 58554-2599. Tel: 701-663-8842; Fax: 701-667-1730.
School—Tel: 701-663-6200; Fax: 701-667-1730. Rev. Albert R. Leary, Supt. Lay Teachers 13; Students 154.
Catechesis/Religious Program—Julie Schatz, D.R.E. Students 148.
Mission—St. Martin Huff, Morton Co.
Mission—St. Anthony St. Anthony, Morton Co.

2—ST. JOSEPH (1881), [CEM] Rev. Patrick A. Schumacher, S.T.L.; Deacons Peter Hoffman; Larry Dorrheim.
Res.: 108 Third St. N.E., 58554. Tel: 701-663-9562; Fax: 701-663-6522.
School—(Grades K-6) Tel: 701-663-9563; Fax: 701-663-0183. Lay Teachers 10; Students 132.
Catechesis/Religious Program—Al Shreve, D.R.E., (Grades K-7); Michele Himmelspach, D.R.E.; Randy Frohlich, D.R.E., (Confirmation Dir. Grade 8). Students 132.

3—SPIRIT OF LIFE (1978), Rev. Cyprian T. Meier; Deacons David Vaughn; Joel Melarvie.
Mailing Address: Box 247, 58554.
Res.: 801 First St. S.E., 58554. Tel: 701-663-1660; Fax: 701-667-2021.
Catechesis/Religious Program—Jim Fritzhuspen, D.R.E. Students 510.

MANDAREE, DUNN CO., ST. ANTHONY, (Native American), [CEM] Rev. Stephen Kranz, O.S.B.
Res.: Fr. Berthold Reservation, 9385 BIA Rte. 12, 58757-9269. Tel: 701-759-3412; Fax: 701-759-3412 (Call first).
Catechesis/Religious Program—Students 196.
Mission—St. Joseph Twin Buttes, Dunn Co. 58757.

MENOKEN, BURLEIGH CO., ST. HILDEGARD (1949), [JC] Rev. George A. Dukart.
Res.: 17200 Hwy. 10, 58558-9604. Tel: 701-673-3177; Fax: 701-673-3178.
Catechesis/Religious Program—Tel: 701-673-3452. Janice Aberle, D.R.E. Students 64.

MINOT, WARD CO.

1—ST. JOHN THE APOSTLE (1961), [JC] Rev. David L. Zimmer; Deacons Stephen B. Mays; Charles Kramer.
Res.: 109-25th St. N.W., 58703-2862. Tel: 701-837-0622.
Catechesis/Religious Program—Alicia Roman, D.R.E. Students 253.

2—ST. LEO (1886), (German), [CEM] Rev. Chris B. Walter.
Res.: 305 First St. S.E., 58701. Tel: 701-838-1026; Fax: 701-852-4683.
Catechesis/Religious Program—Tel: 701-838-1026. Rosie Workman, D.R.E. Students 349.

3—MINOT AIR FORCE BASE CHAPEL (1954), (Filipino), Rev. Ricardo P. Salditos (Philippines).
5 BW/HC: 230 Missile Ave., 58505-5003. Tel: 701-723-2456; Fax: 701-723-3052.
Catechesis/Religious Program—Tel: 701-723-6442. Students 127.

4—OUR LADY OF GRACE (1959), Rev. Gene E. Lindemann, J.C.L.
Res.: 715 16th Ave., S.W., 58701. Tel: 701-839-6834; 701-852-3002; Fax: 701-837-1080.
Catechesis/Religious Program—Darlene Demars, D.R.E., (Grades K-5); Beth Kathol, D.R.E., (Grades 6-12). Students 337.

5—ST. THERESE THE LITTLE FLOWER (1954), [JC] Rev. Paul L. Cervinski; Deacon Pat Cunningham.
Res.: 800 University Ave. W., 58703. Tel: 701-838-1520; Fax: 701-838-1520.
School—Tel: 701-839-5882. See separate listing under Institutions Located in the Diocese.
Catechesis/Religious Program—Tel: 701-839-8567. Deb Carroll, D.R.E. Students 127.

MOHALL, RENVILLE CO., ST. JEROME (1906), [CEM] [JC] Rev. Fred R. Harvey.
Mailing Address: P.O. Box 457, 58761.
Res.: 303 E. Main St., 58761. Tel: 701-756-6601; Fax: 701-756-6901.
Catechesis/Religious Program—Students 70.
Mission—St. James Sherwood, Renville Co. 58761. Tel: 701-756-6601.

MOTT, HETTINGER CO., ST. VINCENT DE PAUL (1907), [CEM] Rev. Kuriakose Nediakala, M.C.B.S.; Deacon Ervin Schneider.
Res.: 408 Iowa Ave., 58646. Tel: 701-824-2651; Fax: 701-824-2651.
Catechesis/Religious Program—Maureen Kautzman, D.R.E. Students 104.
Mission—St. John the Baptist New Leipzig, Grant Co. 58562.

NEW ENGLAND, HETTINGER CO., ST. MARY (1910), Rev. Basil Atwell, O.S.B.
Res.: 437 Main St., P.O. Box 369, 58647. Tel: 701-579-4312.
Catechesis/Religious Program—Lynn Dvorak, D.R.E. Students 91.
Mission—St. Elizabeth's [CEM] 18401 168th Ave., S.E., Lefor, Stark Co. 58641. Tel: 701-579-4312.
Mission—St. Thomas the Apostle 309 Cliff, Gladstone, Stark Co. 58630.

NEW SALEM, MORTON CO., ST. PIUS V (1912), [CEM] Rev. Chad O. Gion.
Res.: P.O. Box C, 58563. Tel: 701-843-7144; Fax: 701-843-7146.
Catechesis/Religious Program—Tel: 701-843-7061. Catherine Holle, D.R.E. Students 122.
Mission—St. Mary, Queen of Peace Almont, Morton Co. 58520.

NEW TOWN, MOUNTRAIL CO., ST. ANTHONY (1954), (Native American), [CEM 4] [JC] Rev. Stephen Kranz, O.S.B.; Deacon Daniel Barone.
Res.: P.O. Box 715, 58763. Tel: 701-627-4423.
Catechesis/Religious Program—Students 49.

PARSHALL, MOUNTRAIL CO., ST. BRIDGET (1917), (German—Norwegian), [CEM 4] [JC 3] Rev. Roger A. Synek.
Res.: 12 First Ave., N.E., Box 519, 58770-0519. Tel: 701-862-3484.
Catechesis/Religious Program—Tel: 701-862-3484. Students 34.
Mission—Sacred Heart Plaza, Mountrail Co. 58770-0519.
Mission—St. Elizabeth Makoti, Ward Co. 58770-0519.

RALEIGH, GRANT CO., ST. GERTRUDE (1913), [CEM] Rev. Gary Benz.
Res.: 421 Court St., Flasher, 58535-7216. Tel: 701-597-3570.
Catechesis/Religious Program—Tel: 701-597-3228. Students 20.

REGENT, HETTINGER CO., ST. HENRY (1913), [JC] Rev. Kuriakose Nediakala, M.C.B.S.; Deacon Don J. Gion.
Res.: P.O. Box 155, 58650-0155. Tel: 701-563-4595.
Catechesis/Religious Program—Tel: 701-563-4543. Karen Kouba, D.R.E. Students 50.

RICHARDTON, STARK CO., ST. MARY (1895), [CEM] Rev. Brian Wangler, O.S.B.
Res.: P.O. Box A, 58652. Tel: 701-974-3569.
Catechesis/Religious Program—Dennise Miller, D.R.E. (Grades K-11). Students 144.
Mission—St. Stephen Box A, Stark Co. 58652. Tel: 701-974-3332.

ST. MICHAEL, EMMONS CO., ST. MICHAEL'S, Closed. For inquiries for parish records contact the chancery.

SELFRIDGE, SIOUX CO., ST. PHILOMENA (1919), (German—Russian), [CEM] Rev. William P. Cosgrove.
Res.: P.O. Box 394, Fort Yates, 58538-0394. Tel: 701-854-3473; Fax: 701-854-3474.
Catechesis/Religious Program—Sr. Frances Marie Voigt, D.R.E. Students 28.
Mission—Sacred Heart Box 394, Fort Yates, Sioux Co. 58538.

SOUTH HEART, STARK CO., ST. MARY (1923), [CEM] Rev. Shannon G. Lucht.
Res.: P.O. Box 189, 58655. Tel: 701-677-5886; Fax: 701-677-5886.
Catechesis/Religious Program—Tel: 701-677-5365. Students 87.

STANLEY, MOUNTRAIL CO., QUEEN OF THE MOST HOLY ROSARY (1908), [JC] Rev. Wayne Sattler.
Res.: P.O. Box 159, 58784. Tel: 701-628-2323; Fax: 701-628-3405.
Catechesis/Religious Program—Fax: 701-628-3406. Students 87.
Mission—St. James [CEM] [JC] 8334 Hwy. 50, Powers Lake, Burke Co. 58773. Tel: 701-464-5771.

STRASBURG, EMMONS CO., STS. PETER AND PAUL (1889), (German—Russian), [CEM] Rev. Leonard A. Eckroth.
Res.: Box 322, 58573. Tel: 701-336-2603; 701-336-7172.
Catechesis/Religious Program—Tel: 701-336-4607. Kathleen Kramer Nagel, D.R.E. Students 114.

TIOGA, WILLIAMS CO., ST. THOMAS (1914), [CEM] [JC] Rev. Johnson Kuriappilly (India).
Res.: P.O. Box 667, 58852. Tel: 701-664-2445; Fax: 701-664-3531.
Catechesis/Religious Program—Students 20.
Mission—St. Michael Ray, Williams Co. 58849. Tel: 701-568-2252.

UNDERWOOD, MCLEAN CO., ST. BONAVENTURE (1913), Rev. Edward F. Korte.
Res.: P.O. Box 700, 58576. Tel: 701-442-5229.
Catechesis/Religious Program—Tel: 701-442-3412. Students 41.
Mission—St. Catherine [CEM] [JC] Main St., Turtle Lake, McLean Co. 58575. Tel: 701-488-9289.

WATFORD CITY, MCKENZIE CO., EPIPHANY (1915), Rev. John M. Pfeifer.
Res.: 112 6th Ave. N.E., P.O. Box 670, 58854. Tel: 701-842-3505.
Catechesis/Religious Program—Tel: 701-842-3791; 701-842-2483. Carol Garman, D.R.E. Students 117.
Mission—Our Lady of Consolation R.R. 1, Box 58, Alexander, McKenzie Co. 58831. Tel: 701-586-3720.
Mission—St. Peter Canisius HCO2, Box 27, Grassy Butte, McKenzie Co. 58634. Tel: 701-863-6759.

WILLISTON, WILLIAMS CO., ST. JOSEPH (1901), [JC] Revs. John G. Guthrie; Jacob Kayalaparambil (India).
Res.: 124 Sixth St. W., P.O. Box K, 58802. Tel: 701-572-6731; Fax: 701-572-4203.
School—Tel: 701-572-6384; Fax: 701-774-0998. Terry Buringrud, Prin. Lay Teachers 10; Students 189.
Catechesis/Religious Program—Tel: 701-572-0201. Ida Kirchmeier, D.R.E. Students 411.
Mission—St. John the Baptist P.O. Box K, Trenton, Williams Co. 58802. Tel: 701-572-6731; Fax: 701-572-0987.

WILTON, MCLEAN CO., SACRED HEART (1906), [CEM] [JC] Deacon James Nistler.
Res.: P.O. Box 128, 58579. Tel: 701-734-6384; Fax: 701-734-6377.
Catechesis/Religious Program—Tel: 701-734-8136; 701-734-6377. Debbie Smith, D.R.E. Students 43.

Chaplains of Public Institutions

BISMARCK. *North Dakota State Penitentiary*, P.O. Box 5521, 58506-5521. Tel: 701-328-6100. Deacon David Vaughn.

MANDAN. *North Dakota Youth Correctional Center*, 701-16th Ave. S.W., 58554-5800. Tel: 701-667-1400. Steve Brannan, Nancy Brannan.

On Duty Outside the Diocese:
Revs.—
Brown, Phillip, St. Mary's Seminary & Univ., 5400 Roland Ave., Baltimore, MD 21210-1994.
Deichert, Joseph, Bolling AFB, HQ 11th WG/HC, 310 Angel Way, Washington, DC 20332-5105.
Hill, Donald, Chap., Army National Guard, 807 N. Howard St., #114, Alexandria, VA 22304-5471.
Kuss, Allen R., Office of the Chaplain, 1018 Shoal Creek Tr., Chesapeake, VA 23320-9476.

Retired:
Rev. Msgr.—
Walsh, Gerald J., 3037 W. Avenida Destino, Tucson, AZ 85746-8268.
Revs.—
Bova, Eugene R., 360 Pinon Rd., Bailey, CO 80421-1837.
Dignan, Thomas L., 55747 Mountain View Tr., Yucca Valley, CA 99284-3403.
Dukart, Norman J., Dickinson, 58601.
Feeney, Robert E., 4629 Rebel Dr., 58503-7896.
Gustin, Theodore F., St. Vincent's Care Center, 1021 N. 26th St., 58501-3199.
Heidt, Charles A., 4198 13th St., N.W., Lot #28, Garrison, 58540-9423.
Kautzman, Jerome G., Benedict Court, 830 2nd Ave. E., #27, Dickinson, 58601-4475.
Kramer, Peter, St. Vincent's Care Center, 1020 N. 26th St., 58501-3199.
Krank, Michael T., 541-3rd Ave. S.W., Dickinson, 58601-5922.
Kuhn, John H., 1020 N. 26th St., 58501-3186.
O'Leary, John P., 1020 N. 26th St., Apt.6, 58501-3186.
Owens, John J., 520 N. Washington St., P.O. Box 1137, 58502-1137.
Reardon, James E., Emmaus Place, 1020 N. 26th St., Apt. 3, 58501-3186.

Rushford, William A., 1020 N. 26th St., Apt. 2, 58501-3186.
Schumacher, Jacob J., Emmaus Place, 1020 N. 26th St., Apt. 7, 58501-3186.
Spain, P. Arnold, 2881 B Warwick Loop, 58504-7640.
Sullivan, Thomas, 1005 Paul Pkwy. N.E. #12, Blaine, MN 55434-3926.
Wald, Kenneth J., 267 N. Rice Lake Rd., Douglas, 58735-9512.
Zastoupil, Stephen R., Little Knife Cottage Site, Box 14, New Town, 58763.

Permanent Deacons:
Barone, Daniel, St. Anthony, New Town
Berg, Melvin J., (Retired)
Brannan, Steve M., St. Vincent de Paul, Crown Butte
Bunce, Donald A., Billings, MT
Clancy, Lynn, Corpus Christi, Bismarck
Cunningham, Patrick M., Little Flower, Minot
Dangel, Robert A., Our Lady of Grace, Minot
Dean, Dennis L., St. John, Lansford
Deichert, Harry M., (Retired)
Dorrheim, Larry L., St. Joseph, Mandan
Dukart, Herman, St. Joseph, Killdeer
Dworshak, Anton T., (Retired)
Fettig, Richard H., Cathedral of the Holy Spirit, Bismarck
Gion, Donald J., St. Henry, Regent
Grabar, Ray A., (Retired)
Haga, James A., St. Joseph, Williston
Hibl, Albert W., (Retired)
Hoffman, Peter, (Retired)
Jilek, Raymond, (Retired)
Johnson, Ed J., Sr., Rolla, ND
Johnson, Ward A., (Retired)
Jundt, Wayne M., St. Anne, Bismarck
Kappel, Joseph, (Retired)
Keller, Ronald, St Patrick, Dickison
Klein, Kenneth M., St. Mary, Bismarck
Knopik, Martin, (Retired)
Kordonowy, Leonard J., Ukranian Church of St. Demetrius, Fairfield
Kramer, Charles L., Deacons Dir., St. John the Apostle, Minot
Krupinsky, Joseph M., St. Anne, Bismarck
Kuss, Leroy M., Colorado Springs, CO
Lamontagne, John H., Ascension, Bismarck
Larson, Samuel, St. John the Baptist, Beach
Lupo, Joseph G., (Retired)
Martin, Morris E., (Retired)
Mathern, Joseph J., Corpus Christi, Bismarck
Mattson, Joseph M., Holy Trinity, Hettinger
Maufort, George, Catholic Faith Communities of Sioux County, Fort Yates
Mays, Stephen B., St. John, Minot
McDowall Rexford R., Corpus Christi, Bismarck
Melarvie, Joel D., Spirit of Life, Mandan
Morgel, Edmund D., (Retired)
Morman, Eugene F., St. Wenceslaus, Dickinson
Nistler, Donald R., St. Mary, Golva
Nistler, James A., Coord., African Mission, Wilton
Olson, Robert C., (Retired)
Quintus, Terry B., St. Joseph, Dickinson
Ressler, James V., (Retired)
Riehl, Emil J., (Retired)
Ringwall, Kris, Queen of Peace, Dickinson
Rohr, Dennis, Christ the King, Madan
Rustand, Gerald T., St. Joseph, Williston
Schmitz, Alvin R., (Retired)
Schneider, Ervin H., St. Vincent de Paul, Mott
Schumacher, Martin, (Retired)
Schwindt, Alvin W., Deacon Formation Dir.
Stockert, Ralph F., (Retired)
Streitz, Steven F., Our Lady of Grace, Minot
Tharaldsen, John, Corpus Christi, Bismarck
Vaughn, David L., Spirit of Life, Mandan
Volk, Jerome, Queen of Peace, Dickinson
Von Ruden, Ralph, Cathedral of the Holy Spirit, Bismarck
Wanner, Anton, Jr., St. Patrick, Dickinson
Wesolowski, Edwin A., Ascension, Bismarck
Wolbaum, Kenneth J., St. Katherine, Braddock
Wolberg, Ronald R., Queen of Peace, Dickinson
Wolf, Wilfred P., (Retired)
Wosepka, James, St. John the Baptist, Beach
Ziman, Edward J., (Retired)

INSTITUTIONS LOCATED IN THE DIOCESE

[A] SEMINARIES, RELIGIOUS OR SCHOLASTICATES

RICHARDTON. *Assumption Abbey*, P.O. Box A, 58652. Tel: 701-974-3315; Fax: 701-974-3317. Email: monks@assumptionabbey.com. Web: www.assumptionabbey.com. Rt. Revs. Patrick Moore, O.S.B., Abbot; Robert West, O.S.B., Retired Abbot (Retired); Lawrence Wagner, O.S.B., Retired Abbot (Retired); Very Rev. Valerian Odermann, O.S.B., Prior; Bro. Basil Kirsch, O.S.B., Subprior; Revs. David Wolf, O.S.B., Business Mgr.; Eugene Hornstein, O.S.B.; Claude Seeberger, O.S.B.; Gerald Ruelle, O.S.B.; Wilfrid J. Splonskowski, O.S.B.; Raymond Dietlein, O.S.B.; John Odermann, O.S.B. (FAR); Stephen Kranz, O.S.B.; Raphael Stovik, O.S.B.; Damian Dietlein, O.S.B. (IND); Sebastian Schmidt, O.S.B.; Denis Fournier, O.S.B.; Francis Wehri, O.S.B., (Overseas); Terrence Kardong, O.S.B.; Victor Feser, O.S.B.; Odo Muggli, O.S.B.; Daniel Maloney, O.S.B.; Brian Wangler, O.S.B.; Philip Vanderlin, O.S.B., (Overseas); Francis dos Remedios, O.S.B. (Retired); Julian Nix, O.S.B.; Hugo L. Blotsky, O.S.B.; Efraim Villegas, O.S.B., (Overseas); Boniface Muggli, O.S.B.; Gonzalo Blanco, O.S.B., (Overseas); Thomas Wordekemper, O.S.B.; Nicolas Cano, O.S.B., (Overseas); James Kilzer, O.S.B.; Basil Atwell, O.S.B. Priests 33; Brothers 25.

[B] COLLEGES AND UNIVERSITIES

BISMARCK. *University of Mary*, 7500 University Dr., 58504-9652. Tel: 701-255-7500; Fax: 701-255-7687. Email: marauder@umary.edu. Web: www.umary.edu. Sr. Thomas Welder, O.S.B., Pres.; Dr. Diane Fladeland, Vice Pres. Academic Affairs; Revs. Daniel Maloney, O.S.B.; Denis Fournier, O.S.B.; Victor Feser, O.S.B.; Boniface Muggli, O.S.B.; Very Rev. Valerian Odermann, O.S.B., Chap. Priests 1; Sisters 3; Lay Teachers 88; Students 2,617.

[C] HIGH SCHOOLS, INTERPAROCHIAL AND PARISH

BISMARCK. *St. Mary's Central High School*, 1025 N. Second St., 58501. Tel: 701-223-4113; Fax: 701-223-8629. Email: smchs@smchs.org. Web: www.smchs.org. John Jankowski, Supt.; Tom Eberle, Prin. Priests 1; Lay Teachers 28; Students 362.

DICKINSON. *Trinity High School*, (Grades 7-12), 810 Empire Rd., P.O. Box 1177, 58602-1177. Tel: 701-483-6081; Fax: 701-483-1450. Web: www.trinityhighschool.com. Willie Thibault, Prin. Lay Teachers 20; Students 321; Total Staff 22.

MINOT. *Bishop Ryan High School*, 316 11th Ave. N.W., 58703-2260. Tel: 701-838-3355; Fax: 701-839-4651. Email: kevin.s.harmon@sendit.nodak.edu. Web: www.brhs.com. Kevin Harmon, Supt.; Terry Voiles, Prin. Priests 2; Full and part time 25; Students 351; Full time 18.

[D] GENERAL HOSPITALS

BISMARCK. *St. Alexius Medical Center*, P.O. Box 5510, 58506-5510. Tel: 701-530-7000; Fax: 701-530-7284. Web: www.st.alexius.org. Richard A. Tschider, Admin. & CEO; Sr. Renee Zastoupil, Dir. Pastoral Care. Sisters of St. Benedict Priests 1; Sisters 12; Bed Capacity 308; Total Staff 1,947; Patients Assisted Annually 173,984.

DICKINSON. *St. Joseph's Hospital and Health Center*, 30 W. Seventh St., 58601. Tel: 701-456-4271; Fax: 701-456-4300. Web: stjoeshospital.org. Allan Sonduck, Pres. & CEO. Nurses 190; Total Staff 370; Bed Capacity 109; Patients Assisted Annually 12,055.

GARRISON. *Garrison Memorial Hospital*, P.O. Box 39, 58540. Tel: 701-463-2275; Fax: 701-463-2886. Email: dgoebel@primecare.org. Dennis Goebel, Admin. Sisters of St. Benedict (Bismarck & 1 Benedictine of SD) 4; Nurses 50; Bed Capacity 46; Total Staff 112; Patients Assisted Annually 7,417.

WILLISTON. *Mercy Medical Center - Affiliate of Catholic Health Initiatives*, 1301 15th Ave. W., 58801. Tel: 701-774-7400; Fax: 701-774-7479. Web: www.mercy-williston.org. Kim Miller, Pres. & CEO. Bed Capacity 87; Patients Assisted Annually 61,291; Total Staff 541.

Mercy Medical Foundation, 1301 15th Ave. W., 58801. Tel: 701-774-7404; Fax: 701-774-7479. Email: dougblack@chi-midwest.org. Web: www.mercy-williston.org. Bed Capacity 87; Patients Assisted Annually 61,291; Total Staff 510.

[E] SPECIAL CARE FACILITIES

DICKINSON. *St. Benedict's Health Center*, 851 Fourth Ave. E., 58601. Tel: 701-456-7242; Fax: 701-456-7250. Email: Jon.frantsvog@bhshealth.org. Web: www.stbens.org. Jon Frantsvog, Admin. Operated by Benedictine Living Communities, Inc. Bed Capacity 172; Total Staff 245; Total Assisted 172.

Benedictine Assisting Living, Inc. dba Benedict Court, 830 2nd Ave. E., 58601. Tel: 701-456-7242; Fax: 701-456-7250. Email: Jon.frantsvog@bhshealth.org. Jon Frantsvog, Admin. & Contact Person.

GARRISON. *Benedictine Living Center of Garrison fka Garrison Nursing Center*, 609 4th Ave. N.E., P.O. Box 219, 58540. Tel: 701-463-2226; Fax: 701-463-2650. Email: scott.foss@bhshealth.org. Scott Foss, Admin. Operated by Benedictine Health System Long Term Care, Inc. Bed Capacity 63; Total Staff 85.

[F] PROTECTIVE INSTITUTIONS

SENTINEL BUTTE. *Home On The Range*, 16351 I-94, 58654-9500. Tel: 701-872-3745; Fax: 701-872-3748. Email: hotrnd@.midstate.net. Web: www.gohotr.org. Mr. Patrick J. Petermann, Exec. Dir.; Rev. David Richter, Chap. Total Staff 110; Total Assisted 160.

[G] HOMES FOR AGED

BISMARCK. *Emmaus Place*, 1020 N. 26th St., 58501. Tel: 701-258-2618. Revs. John O'Leary; James E. Reardon (Retired); John H. Kuhn (Retired); Albert R. Leary; William A. Rushford (Retired); Jacob J. Schumacher (Retired). Priests retirement home. Total Staff 5; Total Assisted 6; Total in Residence 6.

Marillac Manor, 1016 N. 28th St., 58501. Tel: 701-258-8702; Fax: 701-223-3127. Email: marillacadmin@mcleodusa.net. Sr. Phoebe Schwartze, O.S.B., Admin. Retirement Apartments 77; Total Staff 8; Total in Residence 85.

St. Vincent's Care Center, Inc., 1021 N. 26 St., 58501-3199. Tel: 701-223-6888; Fax: 701-223-3015. Email: lblakeman@mohs.org. Lynn Blakeman, Admin. Sisters of St. Benedict 1; Total Staff 167; Resident Patients 101; Total Assisted 156.

[H] CONVENTS AND RESIDENCES FOR SISTERS

BISMARCK. *Annunciation Monastery*, 7520 University Dr., 58504-9653. Tel: 701-255-1520; Fax: 701-255-1440. Web: www.annunciationmonastery.org. Sr. Susan Berger, O.S.B., Prioress; Rev. Daniel Maloney, O.S.B., Resident Chap. Motherhouse and Novitiate of the Benedictine Sisters of the Annunciation, B.M.V. Professed Sisters 81.

RICHARDTON. *Sacred Heart Monastery*, P.O. Box 364, 58652. Tel: 701-974-2121; Fax: 701-974-2124. Email: home@sacredheartmonastery.com. Web: www.sacredheartmonastery.com. Sr. Marie Hunkler, O.S.B., Prioress & Pres. Motherhouse and Novitiate of the Sisters of the Order of St. Benedict. Professed Sisters 32.

[I] MISCELLANEOUS

DICKINSON. *Subiaco Manor*, 2441 10th Ave. W., 58601. Tel: 701-483-2350. Email: reneeosb@pop.ctctel.com. Sr. Renee Branigan, O.S.B., Resident Mgr. Sponsored by the Benedictine Sisters of Sacred Heart Monastery in Richardton. Total Staff 3; Total in Residence 11.

MANDAN. *Blue Army, USA Bismarck Diocesan Division*, 802 Division St., N.E., 58554. Tel: 701-663-0812. Email: Bluearmy@bis.midco.net. Web: www.Bismarckbluearmy.org. Janet Helbing, Pres.

MINOT. *Minot Catholic Schools Corporation*, 316 11th Ave., N.W., 58703-2299. Tel: 701-852-4004; Fax: 701-839-4651. Email: kevin.s.harmon@sendit@nodak.edu. Web: www.brhs.com. Kevin Harmon, Supt. Total Staff 3; Total Assisted 4,300.

Bishop Ryan High School, 316 11th Ave., N.W., 58703-2260. Tel: 701-838-3355; Fax: 701-839-4651. Email: kevin.s.harmon@sendit.ondak.edu. Web: www.brhs.com. Kevin Harmon, Supt.; Terry Voiles, Prin. Priests 2; Lay Teachers 18; Students 351.

Little Flower School, 800 University Ave. W., 58703. Tel: 701-839-5882; Fax: 701-839-8567. Diane Zander, Prin. Lay Teachers 10; Students 73.

St. Leo's School, 305 First St., S.E., 58701. Tel: 701-838-2597; Fax: 701-838-2597. Gary Volk, Prin. Lay Teachers 11; Students 96.

RICHARDTON. *Sacred Heart Benedictine Foundation*, P.O. Box 364, 58652-0364. Tel: 701-974-2121; Fax: 701-974-2124. Email: home@sacredheartmonastery.com. Web: www.sacredheartmonastery.com. Sr. Marie Hunkler, O.S.B., Pres.

SENTINEL BUTTE. *Home On The Range Foundation*, 16351 I-94, 58654. Tel: 701-872-3745; Fax: 701-872-3748. Email: hotrnd@midstate.net. Web: www.gohotr.org. Rev. David G. Morman, Pres.

RELIGIOUS INSTITUTES OF MEN REPRESENTED IN THE DIOCESE

For further details refer to the corresponding bracketed number in the Religious Institutes of Men or Women section.

[0200]—*Benedictine Monks* (Richardton, ND)—O.S.B.

[]—*Missionary Congregation of the Blessed Sacrament* (Kerala, India)—M.C.B.S

[1200]—*Society of the Divine Savior* (Milwaukee, WI)—S.D.S.

RELIGIOUS INSTITUTES OF WOMEN REPRESENTED IN THE DIOCESE

[0230]—*Benedictine Sisters of Pontifical Jurisdiction* (Bismarck; Richardton, ND; Watertown, SD; Yankton, SD; Duluth, MN)—O.S.B.

[2970]—*School Sisters of Notre Dame* (Mankato Prov.; St. Louis, MO)—S.S.N.D.

[0990]—*Sisters of Divine Providence* (Alison Park, PA)—C.D.P.

[]—*Sisters of Mary of the Presentation* (Valley City, ND)—S.M.P.

[]—*Sisters of St. Francis of the Holy Family* (Dubuque, IA)—OSF

[]—*Sisters of the Presentation of the Blessed Vergin Mary* (Flargo, ND)—PBVM

NECROLOGY

† Backes, Hugo G., (Retired)—Died July 27, 2003

† Ryan, James W., Garrison, ND Church of St. Nicholas—Died Jan. 16, 2003

Diocese of Boise

(Dioecesis Xylopolitana)

Most Reverend

MICHAEL P. DRISCOLL, M.S.W., D.D.

Bishop of Boise; ordained May 1, 1965; appointed Titular Bishop of Massita and Auxiliary Bishop of Orange December 19, 1989; consecrated March 6, 1990; appointed Bishop of Boise January 19, 1999; installed March 18, 1999. *Res.: 303 Federal Way, Boise, ID 83705-5925.*

ESTABLISHED AS A VICARIATE-APOSTOLIC MARCH 3, 1868.

Square Miles 83,557.

Erected a Diocese by His Holiness Pope Leo XIII, August 26, 1893.

Comprises the State of Idaho, with a Total Population of 1,351,000.

Legal Title: "Roman Catholic Diocese of Boise".

For legal titles of parishes and diocesan institutions, consult the Chancery Office.

Chancery Office: 303 Federal Way, Boise, ID 83705-5925. Tel: 208-342-1311; Fax: 208-342-0224.

Email: aellis@rcdb.org

STATISTICAL OVERVIEW

Personnel	
Bishop	1
Priests: Diocesan Active in Diocese	44
Priests: Diocesan Active Outside Diocese	4
Priests: Retired, Sick or Absent	34
Number of Diocesan Priests	82
Religious Priests in Diocese	13
Total Priests in Diocese	95
Extern Priests in Diocese	5
Ordinations:	
Diocesan Priests	2
Transitional Deacons	2
Permanent Deacons in Diocese	52
Total Brothers	7
Total Sisters	91
Parishes	
Parishes	51
With Resident Pastor:	
Resident Diocesan Priests	43
Resident Religious Priests	2
Without Resident Pastor:	
Administered by Priests	6
Administered by Religious Women	2
Missions	31
Pastoral Centers	31
New Parishes Created	1
Closed Parishes	4
Professional Ministry Personnel:	
Sisters	8
Lay Ministers	65
Welfare	
Catholic Hospitals	5
Total Assisted	870,160
Day Care Centers	4
Total Assisted	152
Special Centers for Social Services	17
Total Assisted	284,000
Educational	
Diocesan Students in Other Seminaries	21
Total Seminarians	21
High Schools, Diocesan and Parish	1
Total Students	625
Elementary Schools, Diocesan and Parish	13
Total Students	2,563
Catechesis/Religious Education:	
High School Students	2,717
Elementary Students	7,056
Total Students under Catholic Instruction	12,982
Teachers in the Diocese:	
Sisters	1
Lay Teachers	187
Vital Statistics	
Receptions into the Church:	
Infant Baptism Totals	2,472
Adult Baptism Totals	290
Received into Full Communion	230
First Communions	2,353
Confirmations	1,034
Marriages:	
Catholic	341
Interfaith	165
Total Marriages	506
Deaths	736
Total Catholic Population	145,900
Total Population	1,351,000

Former Bishops—Rt. Revs. LOUIS LOOTENS, D.D., appt. first Vicar-Apostolic of Idaho, March 3, 1868; consecrated Bishop of Castabala, Aug. 9, 1868; resigned July 16, 1876; died Jan. 13, 1898; ALPHONSE JOSEPH GLORIEUX, D.D., appt. second Vicar-Apostolic of Idaho, Feb. 27, 1885; consecrated Titular Bishop of Apollonia, April 19, 1885; appt. first Bishop of the Diocese of Boise, Aug. 26, 1893; died Aug. 25, 1917; DANIEL MARY GORMAN, D.D., LL.D., consecrated May 1, 1918; died June 9, 1927; Most Revs. EDWARD JOSEPH KELLY, D.D., consecrated March 6, 1928; died April 21, 1956; JAMES J. BYRNE, D.D., S.T.D. (Retired), ord. June 3, 1933; appt. Titular Bishop of Etenna and Auxiliary of St. Paul, July 2, 1947; consecrated July 2, 1947; transferred to Boise June 16, 1956; appt. Archbishop of Dubuque, March 19, 1962; retired Aug. 23, 1983; died Aug. 2, 1996; SYLVESTER WILLIAM TREINEN, D.D. (Retired), ord. June 11, 1946; appt. May 19, 1962; consecrated July 25, 1962; retired Aug. 17, 1988; died Sept. 30, 1996; TOD D. BROWN, D.D., ord. May 1, 1963; appt. Dec. 27, 1988; ord. and installed April 3, 1989; appt. Bishop of Orange, June 30, 1998.

Executive Secretary to Bishop/Administration—BARBARA BIRD.

Moderator of the Curia—Very Rev. RONALD WEKERLE, V.G.

Vicars General—Very Revs. RONALD WEKERLE, V.G.; DENNIS WASSMUTH, V.G.

Administrative Assistant to Moderator of the Curia—SHARON RHODES.

Chancery Office—303 Federal Way, Boise, 83705-5925. Tel: 208-342-1311; Fax: 208-342-0224.

Chancellor—Sr. ARLENE ELLIS, S.S.C.

Office of Cultural Ministries—JOHN HITCHMAN, Dir.; ELEANOR SMITH, Sec. Programs Facilitator, 303 Federal Way, Boise, 83705-5925. Tel: 208-342-1311.

Notaries—LODICE GRANT; DOVE MIZELL.

Diocesan Tribunal—303 Federal Way, Boise, 83705-5925. Tel: 208-344-1344; Fax: 208-342-0224. (Direct all correspondence here.)

Director—VACANT.

Judicial Vicar—Very Rev. HENRY CARMONA, J.C.L.

Adjutant Judicial Vicars—Revs. JOSEPH F. MCDONALD III, J.C.L.; WILLIAM CROWLEY, J.C.B.; GERALD FUNKE, J.C.L.

Promoter of Justice—CARLOS VENEGAS, J.C.L.

Notaries—Very Rev. DENNIS WASSMUTH, V.G.; Sr. ARLENE ELLIS, S.S.C.; MARK RAPER; COLLEEN CUNNINGHAM; CAROLINE CARTHY-WICKHAM.

Judges—Very Rev. HENRY CARMONA, J.C.L.; Revs. JOHN W. MORGAN; WILLIAM CROWLEY, J.C.B.; SIMEON VAN DE VOORD, O.S.B. (Retired); SEAN CAULFIELD, J.C.L.; W. THOMAS FAUCHER, J.C.L.; GERALD FUNKE, J.C.L.; GEORGE KING, J.C.L.; Sr. ANN MARGUERITE SOUZA, C.S.J., J.C.L.

Defenders of the Bond—Revs. JOSEPH F. MCDONALD III, J.C.L.; ANDREW SCHUMACHER; JAIRO RESTREPO; Sr. BERNICE WESSELS, O.S.B., J.C.L.; CARLOS VINEGAS, J.C.L.

College of Consultors—Very Revs. ROGER LACHANCE, V.F., Chm.; WILLIAM CROWLEY, V.F.; JOSEPH DA SILVA, V.U.; JOSEPH MCDONALD III, V.F.; Revs. GERALD FUNKE, J.C.L.; WILLIAM GOULD; Very Revs. OSCAR JARAMILLO, V.F.; LES KISH, V.F.; JOHN KOELSCH, V.F.; Revs. ANDREW SCHUMACHER; WILLIAM TAYLOR; ENRIQUE TERRIQUEZ.

Ex Officio—Very Revs. DENNIS WASSMUTH, V.G.; RONALD WEKERLE, V.G.

Deans—Very Revs. ROGER LACHANCE, V.F., Northern Deanery; JOSEPH MCDONALD III, V.F., Eastern Deanery; OSCAR JARAMILLO, V.F., Western Deanery; JOSEPH DA SILVA, V.U., West Central Deanery; JOHN KOELSCH, V.F., Southern Deanery; LES KISH, V.F., North Central Deanery.

Presbyteral Council— See College of Consultors

Priest Personnel Commission—Rev. CAL BLANKINSHIP; Very Revs. HENRY CARMONA, V.F.; JOSEPH DASILVA, V.U.; Revs. DENNIS DAY; LEN MACMILLAN; ANDREW SCHUMACHER; PAUL WANDER; Very Revs. DENNIS WASSMUTH, V.G., Ex Officio; RONALD WEKERLE, V.G., Ex Officio.

Finance Council—Very Rev. DENNIS WASSMUTH, V.G., Chm.; JAMES BRUCE; LARRY HELLHAKE; STANLEY WELSH; CHARLES HUMMEL; SUSAN COPPLE; T. STEVE JOYCE; Very Rev. RONALD WEKERLE, V.G., Ex Officio; PATRICK CRISLER, C.P.A., Finance Office Consultant.

Building Commission—Very Rev. RONALD WEKERLE, V.G., Chm.; Deacon JACK PELOWITZ; DAVID DAVIES; MICHAEL JONES; ROBERT PETERS.

Priest Retirement Committee—Very Revs. DENNIS WASSMUTH, V.G., Chm.; JOHN KOELSCH, V.F.; Revs. TIMOTHY RITCHIE; JOHN WORSTER; FRANCISCO FLORES; JOSEPH MUHA, 303 Federal Way, Boise, 83705-5925. Tel: 208-342-1311.

Diocesan Offices and Directors

Apostleship of Prayer—VACANT.

Bureau of Information—303 Federal Way, Boise, 83705-5925. "Idaho Catholic Register"

Campaign for Human Development—Sr. ARLENE ELLIS, S.S.C., 303 Federal Way, Boise, 83705-5925.

Catholic Charities of Idaho, Inc.—MARIE D. HOFF, M.S.W., Ph.D., Exec. Dir.; Most Rev. MICHAEL P. DRISCOLL, D.D., M.S.W., Pres.; LYNNE TIDDENS, Admin. Mgr., 4202 W. Emerald St., Boise, 83706. Tel: 208-345-6031; Fax: 208-345-5674. Email: mhoff@ccidaho.org.

Catholic Communications Center—COLETTE COWMAN, 303 Federal Way, Boise, 53705-5925.

Catholic Relief Services—Sr. ARLENE ELLIS, S.S.C., 303 Federal Way, Boise, 83705-5925.

Catholic Scouts—DAVID L. DAVIS, Chm., 142 N. 9th St., Pocatelly, 83201. Tel: 208-232-2098; Rev. ROGER LACHANCE, Chap., St. Pius X, 625 E. Haycraft, Coeur d'Alene, 83815. Tel: 208-765-5108.

Catholic Daughters of the Americas—ARMELINA BERNHARDT, State Regent, P.O. Box 292, Osborn,

83840. Tel: 208-556-2302.
Catholic Schools—VACANT, Coord., 303 Federal Way, Boise, 83705-5925.
Catholic Hospitals—VACANT, 303 Federal Way, Boise, 83705-5925. Tel: 208-342-1311.
Catholic Liturgical Commission—LETICIA THORNTON, Chm.; Deacons RICK BONNEY; GERALD PERA; Very Rev. RONALD WEKERLE, V.G.; Rev. LEN MACMILLAN, Diocesan Liturgist; Sr. CLARISSA GOECKNER, O.S.B.; MARCIA BECKMAN; LARRY HARRISON; KATHY SELLS, 303 Federal Way, Boise, 83705. Tel: 208-342-1311.
Censor Librorum—Rev. ANDREW SCHUMACHER, P.O. Box 425, Cottonwood, 83522-0425. Tel: 208-962-3214.
Charismatic Renewal—VACANT.
Victim Assistance Coordinator—BOBBI K. DOMINICK, J.D., S.P.H.R. Tel: 208-342-1311, Ext. 137. Email: bdominick@rcdb.org.
Priest Retirement Plan— --Direct Inquiries to the Chancery, *303 Federal Way, Boise, 83705*.
Cursillo Movement—Deacon FRED SCHMIDT, Spiritual Dir. - English, 920 Cypress, Lewiston, 83501. Tel: 208-843-0632; Rev. MAURICIO MEDINA, Spiritual Dir. - Spanish (Retired), 931 Eastland Dr. N., Twin Falls, 83301. Tel: 208-670-2780.
Development/Stewardship Office—JIM HUGHES, Dir., 4202 W. Emerald St., Boise, 83706. Tel: 208-345-6031; Fax: 208-345-5674.
Diocesan Pastoral Council—TED VERMAS, Pres.; BOBBI DOMINICK, Pres.-Elect.
Ecumenical Commission—Very Rev. JOSEPH DA SILVA, V.U., 11511 Lake Hazel Rd., Boise, 83709.
Education Ministries Office—JACK CRAVEN, Dir.; PATRICIA THOMAS, Sec. & Events Coord., 303 Federal Way, Boise, 83705. Tel: 208-342-1311.
Coordinator of Schools—VACANT.
Coordinator Child and Family Catechesis,—Sr. CLARISSA GOECKNER, O.S.B.
Coordinator Youth Ministry—LAURA HENNING.
Coordinator of Adult Education—DAN MCGILL.
Resource Center Manager—GLORIA PETTINGER.
Finance Officer—PATRICK CRISLER, C.P.A.
Human Resources—BOBBI K. DOMINICK, J.D., S.P.H.R., Dir.
Idaho Council of Catholic Women—MARY FRANCES THOMPSON, Pres., 985 Hwy. 95, Weiser, 83672.
Idaho Catholic Foundation—Most Rev. MICHAEL P. DRISCOLL, D.D., M.S.W., Pres.
Knights of Columbus—AL MILLHOUSE, State Deputy, 647 Brandon Dr., Idaho Falls, 83402-2937; Rev. FRANCISCO FLORES, State Chap.
Campus Ministry—Deacon CHARLES L. SKORO, Dir., 1915 University Dr., Boise, 83706.
Newspaper—Most Rev. MICHAEL P. DRISCOLL, D.D., M.S.W., Publisher; COLETTE COWMAN, Exec. Editor; LEONARD GEORGE, Advertising/Business/Circulation; BARBARA HAMILTON, Artist & Production; LORETTA GOSSI, Sec., Library, 303 Federal Way, Boise, 83705. Tel: 208-342-1311. "Idaho Catholic Register"
Deacon Life and Ministry—Deacons RICHARD BONNEY, Dir., 145 9th St., Idaho Falls, 83404. Tel: 208-522-4366; GARY MCSWAIN, Asst. Dir., 625 E. Haycraft, Coeur d'Alene, 83815. Tel: 208-667-9233.
Deacon Formation Director—Sr. GRAYCE ROSS, S.N.J.M., 4450 N. Five Mile Rd., Boise, 83713-2709. Tel: 208-375-5487; Fax: 208-376-5787.
Prison Ministry—Rev. JESUS CAMACHO, 322 S. Manville St., Boise, 83705. Tel: 208-429-9196.
Propagation of Faith—Very Rev. RONALD WEKERLE, V.G., 303 Federal Way, Boise, 83705.
Respect Life Program—Deacon RALPH FLAGER, Dir., 5152 Burlington Dr., Boise, 83704. Tel: 208-375-2459.
St. Vincent de Paul Society—Rev. GERALD J. FUNKE, Diocesan Spiritual Dir., 1515 8th St., S., Nampa, 83651. Tel: 208-466-7031.
State Trustee—MARGO HENNING, 3717 Ticonderoga, Boise, 83706-5659. Tel: 208-344-0702.
Vocations—Rev. JAIRO RESTREPO, Dir., 804 N. 9th St., Boise, 83702. Tel: 208-342-1328.

CLERGY, PARISHES, MISSIONS AND PAROCHIAL SCHOOLS

CITY OF BOISE
(ADA COUNTY)

1—CATHEDRAL OF ST. JOHN THE EVANGELIST (1978), Very Rev. Henry Carmona, J.C.L., Rector; Rev. Brad Neely; Deacons Richard Henning; Ken Hiner; Tom Dominick.
Res.: 775 N. 8th St., 83702. Tel: 208-342-3511; 208-342-3512; Fax: 208-342-1564.
School—St. Joseph's School Ms. Antonia Bicandi, Prin. Lay Teachers 15; Students 312.
Catechesis/Religious Program—Kelley Kolpitcke, D.R.E. Students 320.

2—ST. MARK'S (1997), Revs. Steven Rukavina; Paul Materw, A.L.C.P.; Deacons Ralph Pierce; James Bowen; Bill Booth.
Res.: 7503 Northview St., 83704. Tel: 208-375-6651; Fax: 208-375-3211.
School—Dan Maloney, Prin. Lay Teachers 19; Students 297.
Catechesis/Religious Program—Students 530.

3—ST. MARY'S, Revs. W. Thomas Faucher, J.C.L.; Carlos Felipe Velez; Jesus Camacho; Deacons William Petzak; Rapelyea Howell; Francis Hess.
Res.: 2612 W. State St., 83702. Tel: 208-344-2597; Fax: 208-344-9337.
School—2620 W. State St., 83702. Tel: 208-342-7476; Fax: 208-345-5154. Marcia Beckman, Prin. Lay Teachers 11; Students 233.
Catechesis/Religious Program—Students 115.

4—OUR LADY OF THE ROSARY, Very Rev. Dennis Wassmuth, V.G.; Deacons Michael Dessert; Pierce Murphy; Chuck Skoro.
Res.: 1500 E. Wright, 83706. Tel: 208-343-9041; Fax: 208-343-2644.
Catechesis/Religious Program—Rosie Skoro, D.R.E. Students 405.
Chapel—Idaho City, St. Joseph's
Chapel—Boise, St. Paul's Student Center

5—ST. PAUL'S, Closed., See Our Lady of the Rosary, Boise for details.

6—RISEN CHRIST CATHOLIC COMMUNITY, Very Rev. Joseph da Silva, V.U.; Deacons Michael Eisenbeiss; C. J. Harris.
Res.: 11511 W. Lake Hazel Rd., 83709. Tel: 208-362-6584; Fax: 208-362-9545.
Catechesis/Religious Program—Students 155.

7—SACRED HEART, Sr. Betty Schumacher, Parish Life Dir.; Deacon James R. Kelly.
Mailing Address: 811 S. Latah St., 83705-0127. Tel: 208-344-8311; Fax: 208-343-1876.
School—3901 Cassia St., 83705. Tel: 208-344-9738; Fax: 208-343-1939. Joseph Baumann, Prin. Sisters 1; Lay Teachers 14; Students 258.
Catechesis/Religious Program—Deborah Fischer, D.R.E. Students 129.

OUTSIDE THE CITY OF BOISE

ABERDEEN, BINGHAM CO.

1—BLESSED SACRAMENT, Merged, with St. Mary, American Falls to form Presentation of the Lord, Aberdeen.

2—PRESENTATION OF THE LORD, Rev. Jorge Eugenia Garcia; Deacon Ed Souza.
Res.: Hwy. 39 & S. 4th W., P.O. Box 833, 83210. Tel: 208-397-7036; Fax: 208-226-1125.
Catechesis/Religious Program—Janice Bloom, D.R.E. Students 103.
Chapel—Pingree, St. John
Chapel—St. Mary P.O. Box 117, American Falls, 83211. Tel: 208-226-5217; Fax: 208-226-1125.
Chapel—Aberdeen, Blessed Sacrament P.O. Box 833, 83210. Tel: 208-397-7036.

AMERICAN FALLS, POWER CO., ST. MARY, Merged, with Blessed Sacrament, Aberdeen to form Presentation of the Lord, Aberdeen.

ARCO, BUTTE CO., ST. ANN'S, , See St. Charles, Salmon for details.

BLACKFOOT, BINGHAM CO., ST. BERNARD'S, Rev. Jose de Jesus Sierra Alfonso; Deacon Jack Pelowitz, Parish Life Dir.
Res.: 584 W. Sexton St., 83221. Tel: 208-785-1935; Fax: 208-785-7382.
Catechesis/Religious Program—Students 51.
Chapel—Blessed Kateri Tekakwitha Sheepskin Rd., Fort Hall, 83203.

BONNERS FERRY, BOUNDARY CO., ST. ANN'S, Rev. David Riffle; Deacon Joseph Nicholas; Margaret M. Mellett, Pastoral Assoc.
Res.: 6712 El Paso, 83805. Tel: 208-267-2852; Fax: 208-267-8222.
Catechesis/Religious Program—Students 86.

BUHL, TWIN FALLS CO., IMMACULATE CONCEPTION, Rev. V. Robb Keller.
Res.: 1701 Poplar, Box 626, 83316. Tel: 208-543-5136; Fax: 208-543-5714.
Catechesis/Religious Program—Jacqueline Machado, D.R.E. Students 139.
Station—Hagerman, St. Catherine's Hagerman.

BURLEY, CASSIA CO., ST. THERESA, Rev. Juan Maria Garatea.
Res.: 1601 Oakley, P.O. Box 1223, 83318. Tel: 208-678-5453; Fax: 208-678-5479.
Catechesis/Religious Program—Eugene Kramer, D.R.E. Students 140.

CALDWELL, CANYON CO.

1—ST. MARY'S, Merged, with St. Hubert's, Homedale and Sacred Hearts of Jesus and Mary, Parma to form Our Lady of the Valley, Caldwell.

2—OUR LADY OF THE VALLEY, Rev. Enrique Terriquez, Moderator; Very Rev. Oscar Jaramillo, V.F.
Office—616 Dearborn, P.O. Box 399, 83606. Tel: 208-459-3653; Fax: 208-454-8789.
Catechesis/Religious Program—Students 380.
Chapel—Marsing, Good Shepherd
Chapel—Caldwell, St. Mary's
Chapel—Homedale, St. Hubert's
Chapel—Parma, Sacred Hearts of Jesus & Mary

CHUBBUCK, BANNOCK CO., ST. PAUL'S, Merged, with St. Anthony's, Pocatello and St. Joseph, Pocatello to form Holy Spirit Catholic Community, Pocatello.

COEUR D'ALENE, KOOTENAI CO.

1—ST. PIUS X, Rev. Roger LaChance; Deacons Gary McSwain; Leonard Trueworthy; Walter Woznicki; William Sando, (Retired).
Res.: 625 E. Haycraft, 83715. Tel: 208-765-5108; Fax: 208-664-5325.
Catechesis/Religious Program—Deacon Gary McSwain, D.R.E. Students 330.

2—ST. THOMAS, Rev. James Rodenspiel.
Res.: 919 Indiana Ave., 83814. Tel: 208-664-9259; Fax: 208-667-8321.
Catechesis/Religious Program—Carol White, D.R.E. Students 76.

COTTONWOOD, IDAHO CO., ST. MARY'S, Rev. Andrew J. Schumacher.
Mailing Address: P.O. Box 425, 83522-0425. Tel: 208-962-3214; Fax: 208-962-5477.
Res.: 503 Garrett St., 83522.
Catechesis/Religious Program—June Behler, D.R.E. Students 136.
Chapel—Keuterville, Holy Cross

COUNCIL, ADAMS CO., ST. JUDE STATION, , See St. Agnes, Weiser for details.

DESMET, BENEWAH CO., SACRED HEART, Rev. Thomas Connolly, S.J.; Sr. Dolores Ellwart, S.P., Pastoral Assoc.
Res.: Box 306, 83824. Tel: 208-274-5871; Fax: 208-274-3015.
Station—Plummer, Our Lady of Perpetual Help Plummer.
Station—Worley, St. Michael's Worley.

EAGLE, ADA CO., ST. MATTHEW, Closed., Merged with Holy Spirit, Meridian to form Holy Apostles, Meridian.

EMMETT, GEM CO., SACRED HEART, Rev. Marcellus Fernandez; Deacon Alan Shaber.
Res.: 211 E. First, 83617. Tel: 208-365-4320; Fax: 208-365-0754.
Catechesis/Religious Program—Students 146.
Station—Garden Valley, St. Jude Garden Valley.

FERDINAND, IDAHO CO., ASSUMPTION, Rev. Andrew Schumacher.
Mailing Address: Rte. 1, Box 90, Greencreek, 83533. Tel: 208-962-3565; Fax: 208-962-3565.
Catechesis/Religious Program—June Behler, D.R.E. Students 49.

FRUITLAND, PAYETTE CO., CORPUS CHRISTI, Rev. Calvin Blankinship.
Res.: 1212 1st Ave., South Payette, 83661. Tel: 208-642-2261; Fax: 208-642-1099.
Catechesis/Religious Program—Students 150.
Chapel—New Plymouth, St. Aloysius
Chapel—Payette, Holy Family

GARDEN VALLEY, BOISE CO., ST. JUDE'S, , See Sacred Heart, Emmett for details.

GENESEE, LATAH CO., ST. MARY STATION, , See St. Mary's, Moscow for details. In Res., Rev. Robert Finucane (Retired).
Res.: 138 N. Jackson, P.O. Box 36, 83832. Tel: 208-285-1218; Fax: 208-285-1139.
Catechesis/Religious Program—Connie Esser, D.R.E. Students 29.

GLENNS FERRY, ELMORE CO., OUR LADY OF LIMERICK STATION, , See Our Lady of Good Counsel, Mountain Home for details. In Res., Rev. Eugene Esch, O.S.B.
Res.: 21 W. Arthur St., Box 216, 83623. Tel: 208-366-7721.
Catechesis/Religious Program—Justin Martell, D.R.E. Students 62.

GOODING, GOODING CO., ST. ELIZABETH'S, Rev. Carlos Perez; Deacons Marino Perea; Dee Ashett.
Res.: 1515 California St., Box 147, 83330-0147. Tel: 208-934-5634; Fax: 208-934-5634.
Catechesis/Religious Program—Theresa Patterson, D.R.E.; Bridget Arkoosh, D.R.E. Students 163.
Station—Wendell, St. Anthony's Wendell.

GRANDVIEW, OWYHEE CO., ST. HENRY CHAPEL, , See Our Lady of Good Counsel, Mountain Home for details.

GRANGEVILLE, IDAHO CO., SS. PETER AND PAUL, Rev. William Crowley; Deacon Don Sokolowski.
Res.: 318 S B St., 83530. Tel: 208-983-0403; Fax: 208-983-1152.
School—Tel: 208-983-2182. Milton Baelocher, Prin. Lay Teachers 4; Students 68.
Catechesis/Religious Program—Students 75.
Station—Nez Perce, Holy Trinity Nez Perce.

GREENCREEK, IDAHO CO., ST. ANTHONY'S, Rev. Andrew Schumacher.

Res.: Rte. 1, Box 90, 83533. Tel: 208-962-3565; Fax: 208-962-3565.
Catechesis/Religious Program—June Behler, D.R.E. Students 61.

HAGERMAN, GOODING CO., ST. CATHERINE'S, , See Immaculate Conception, Buhl for details.

HAILEY, BLAINE CO., ST. CHARLES BORROMEO, Rev. John W. Morgan; Sr. Regina Burrichter, R.S.M., Pastoral Assoc.
Res.: 311 1st. Ave. S., Box 789, 83333. Tel: 208-788-3024; Fax: 208-788-0726.
Catechesis/Religious Program—Students 85.
Chapel—Fairfield, Immaculate Conception

HOMEDALE, OWYHEE CO., ST. HUBERT, Merged, with St. Mary's, Caldwell and Sacred Hearts of Jesus and Mary, Parma to form Our Lady of the Valley, Caldwell.

HORSESHOE BEND, BOISE CO., OUR LADY QUEEN OF ANGELS CHAPEL, , See Holy Apostle, Meridian for details.

IDAHO CITY, BOISE CO., ST. JOSEPH'S CHAPEL, , See Our Lady of the Rosary, Boise for details.

IDAHO FALLS, BONNEVILLE CO.

1—CHRIST THE KING, Very Rev. Joseph F. McDonald III; Rev. Francisco Flores; Deacon Richard Bonney, Pastoral Assoc.
Res.: 1690 E. 17th St., 83404. Tel: 208-529-8170; Fax: 208-528-9164.
Catechesis/Religious Program—Susan Clark, D.R.E. Students 1,019.
Chapel—Shelley, Our Lady of Guadalupe

2—HOLY ROSARY, Very Rev. Joseph F. McDonald III; Rev. Francisco Flores; Deacon Richard Bonney, Pastoral Assoc.
Res.: 145 Ninth St., 83404-6392. Tel: 208-522-4366; Fax: 208-523-3827.
School—161 Ninth St., 83404. Tel: 208-522-7781; Fax: 208-522-7782. Gerald Chouinard, Prin. Lay Teachers 19; Students 191.
Catechesis/Religious Program—Sue Clark, D.R.E. Students 1,109.
Station—Roberts, St. Anthony's Roberts.
Station—Mud Lake, St. Ann's Mud Lake.

JEROME, JEROME CO., ST. JEROME'S, Very Rev. Ron Wekerle, V.G.; Deacons William Last; John Baumbach; Marino Perea.
Res.: 216 2nd Ave. E., Box 169, 83338. Tel: 208-324-8794; Fax: 208-324-4141.
Catechesis/Religious Program—Theresa May, Pastoral Assoc. Students 240.

KAMIAH, LEWIS CO., ST. CATHERINE'S OF SIENA, Rev. George L. King.
Res.: 407 7th St., Box 685, 83536. Tel: 208-935-2130; Fax: 208-935-7643.
Catechesis/Religious Program—Students 30.

KELLOGG, SHOSHONE CO., ST. RITA'S, Rev. Mel Sprute; Deacon David Beuerman.
Res.: 27 Kellogg Ave., 83837-2626. Tel: 208-784-7361; Fax: 208-784-7361.
Catechesis/Religious Program—Students 38.

KEUTERVILLE, IDAHO CO., HOLY CROSS, Merged, with St. Mary's, Cottonwood.

LAPWAI, NEZ PERCE CO.
CHAPEL—WHITE BIRD, SACRED HEART, See Our Lady of Lourdes, Lewiston for details.
Chapel—Elk City, Elk City Catholic Community

LEADORE, LEMHI CO., ST. JOSEPH'S CHAPEL, , See St. Charles, Salmon for details.

LEWISTON, NEZ PERCE CO.

1—ST. JAMES, Rev. Richard S. Haldane.
Office—1519 Ripon Ave., 83501. Tel: 208-743-8231; Fax: 208-798-8407.
Catechesis/Religious Program—Students 103.
Station—Lapwai, Sacred Heart Lapwai.

2—OUR LADY OF LOURDES, Rev. Leslie P. Kish; Deacon Fred Schmidt.
Church & Res.: 2015 13th Ave., 83501. Tel: 208-743-3238; 208-743-6101 (Church); Fax: 208-743-5301.
Catechesis/Religious Program—Students 246.

3—ST. STANISLAUS, Sr. Margie Schmidt, O.S.B., Parish Life Dir.
Res.: 633 5th Ave., 83501. Tel: 208-743-7331; Fax: 208-746-7134.
School—Tri-Parish School Marcia Ney, Prin. Lay Teachers 9; Students 172.
Catechesis/Religious Program—Students 78.

MCCALL, VALLEY CO., OUR LADY OF THE LAKE, Rev. Donald D. Fraser.
Res.: 501 Cross Rd., Box 821, 83638. Tel: 208-634-5474; Fax: 208-634-5475.
Catechesis/Religious Program—Students 37.
Station—St. Katherine Drexel P.O. Box 821, 83638-0821.
Chapel—Riggins, St. Jerome's

MERIDIAN, ADA CO.

1—HOLY APOSTLES, Rev. Timothy M. Ritchey; Deacons Ralph Flager; Gerald Pera; Charles Rasmussen.
Res.: Box 708, 83680. Tel: 208-888-1182; Fax: 208-884-1800.
Catechesis/Religious Program—Mary Ossenkop, D.R.E. Students 1,010.
Chapel—Horseshoe Bend, Our Lady Queen of Angels

2—HOLY SPIRIT, Closed., Merged with St. Matthew, Eagle to form Holy Apostles, Meridian.

MOSCOW, LATAH CO.

1—ST. AUGUSTINE'S, , (Catholic Center) Rev. Leonard MacMillan.
Res.: 628 Deakin St., P.O. Box 3457, 83843. Tel: 208-882-4613.
Station—Potlatch, St. Mary's Potlatch.

2—ST. MARY'S, Rev. Joseph F. Schmidt; Deacon Verne Geidl.
Res.: 618 E. First St., Box 9106, 83843. Tel: 208-882-4313; Fax: 208-883-0608.
School—412 N. Monroe, 83843. Tel: 208-882-2121. Sr. Margaret Johnson, O.S.U., Prin. Lay Teachers 12; Students 156.
School—Kindergarten & Preschool, St. Rose, 412 N. Howard, 83843. Tel: 208-882-4014; Fax: 208-882-0970. Owned by the Ursuline Nuns, affiliated with St. Mary's School.
Catechesis/Religious Program—Students 131.
Station—Genessee, St. Mary's Genessee.

MOUNTAIN HOME AIR FORCE BASE, ELMORE CO., ST. MARY'S, Rev. Msgr. John J. Cusack.
Res.: 366 FW/HC, 420 Gunfighter Ave., 83648. Tel: 208-828-6417; Fax: 208-828-4570.
Catechesis/Religious Program—Students 109.

MOUNTAIN HOME, ELMORE CO., OUR LADY OF GOOD COUNSEL, Rev. Raul R. Covarrubias.
Res.: 115 N. 4th St. E., Box 310, 83647. Tel: 208-587-3046; Fax: 208-587-5114.
Catechesis/Religious Program—Barbara Faneuf, D.R.E. Students 277.
Station—Bruneau, St. Bridget Bruneau.
Station—Glenns Ferry, Our Lady of Limerick Glenn's Ferry.
Chapel—Grandview, St. Henry's

NAMPA, CANYON CO.

1—OUR LADY OF GUADALUPE CHAPEL, Closed., See St. Paul's, Nampa for details.

2—ST. PAUL'S, Revs. Gerald J. Funke; Rob Cook; Sr. Evangelina Samaniego Gonzalez, H.M.R.F., Pastoral Assoc. & Hispanic Ministry.
Res.: 1515 8th St. S., 83651. Tel: 208-466-7031; Fax: 208-467-7203.
School—Tel: 208-467-3601; Fax: 208-467-6485. MaryAnn VandeBrake, Prin. Lay Teachers 13; Students 208.
Catechesis/Religious Program—Students 476.
Station—Melba, St. Joseph Melba.
Chapel—Silver City, Our Lady of Tears
Chapel—Oreana, Queen of Heaven

NEW PLYMOUTH, PAYETTE CO., ST. ALOYSIUS, Merged, with Holy Family, Payette to form Corpus Christi, Fruitland.

NEZPERCE, LEWIS CO., HOLY TRINITY, , See SS. Peter and Paul, Grangeville for details.
Res.: 506 Willow St., Box 65, Nez Perce, 83543. Tel: 208-937-2300.
Catechesis/Religious Program—Students 45.

OREANA, OWYHEE CO., QUEEN OF HEAVEN CHAPEL, , See St. Paul's, Nampa for details.

OROFINO, CLEARWATER CO., ST. THERESA'S, Rev. George L. King; Deacon Frank Phillips.
Res.: 446 Brown Ave., Box 1169, 83544. Tel: 208-476-5121.
Catechesis/Religious Program—Students 46.
Chapel—Pierce, Our Lady of Woodland

PARMA, CANYON CO., SACRED HEARTS OF JESUS AND MARY, Merged, with St. Mary's, Caldwell and St. Hubert's, Homedale to form Our Lady of the Valley, Caldwell.

PAYETTE, PAYETTE CO., HOLY FAMILY, Merged, with St. Aloysius, New Plymouth to form Corpus Christi, Fruitland.

POCATELLO, BANNOCK CO.

1—ST. ANTHONY'S, Merged, with St. Joseph, Pocatello and St. Paul, Chubbuck to form Holy Spirit Catholic Community, Pocatello.

2—HOLY SPIRIT CATHOLIC COMMUNITY, Revs. Joseph Muha; Camillus Temba, A.L.C.P.; Deacons Mel Hardy; Bill Duggan; Scott Pearhing, Pastoral Assoc.; Kathy Barkdull, Pastoral Assoc. In Res., Rev. Anthony Deiloreto (Retired).
Res.: 747 N. Hayes St., 83204. Tel: 208-232-1196; Fax: 208-232-1196. Web: www.bannockcatholic.net.
School—540 N. 7th Ave., 83205. Tel: 208-232-5763; Fax: 208-232-7142. Stephen Anderson, Lay Teachers 15; Students 171.
Catechesis/Religious Program—Ann Hysell, D.R.E. Students 240.
Chapel—St. John's Catholic Student Center 920 E. Lovejoy St., I.S.U., Box 8129, 83209 Tel: 208-233-0880; Fax: 208-233-5745.
Chapel—Pocatello, St. Anthony Chapel 504 N. 7th Ave., 83201. Fax: 208-234-2624.
Chapel—Pocatello, St. Joseph Chapel 439 N. Hayes St., 83204.
Chapel—Chubbuck, St. Paul Chapel 820 W. Chubbuck Rd., 83202. Tel: 208-237-7167.

3—ST. JOSEPH'S, Merged, with St. Anthony, Pocatello and St. Paul, Chubbuck to form Holy Spirit Catholic Community, Pocatello.

POST FALLS, KOOTENAI CO., ST. GEORGE'S, Revs. William R. Gould; Colman J. Nolan, S.T.; John V. Rizzo, F.S.S.P.
Res.: 2101 N. Lucas St., Box 10, 83877-0010. Tel: 208-773-4715; Fax: 208-777-1549.
Catechesis/Religious Program—Kristi Asburry, D.R.E. Students 182.
Chapel—Rathdrum, St. Stanislaus
Chapel—Spirit Lake, St. Joseph

POTLATCH, LATAH CO., ST. MARY'S STATION, , See St. Augustine's, Moscow for details.

PRIEST RIVER, BONNER CO., ST. CATHERINE'S, Rev. Lawrence L. Gooley, S.J., Admin.; Deacon Richard S. Hamm.
Res.: 206 Summit Blvd., Box 445, 83856. Tel: 208-448-2127.
Catechesis/Religious Program—Students 21.
Station—St. Blanche Priest Lake.

RATHDRUM, KOOTENAI CO., ST. STANISLAUS CHAPEL, , See St. George, Post Falls for details.

RUPERT, MINIDOKA CO., ST. NICHOLAS, Rev. Gabriel Vargas; Deacons Pete Rodriquez; Paul Henscheid; Orville Rathe.
Res.: 802 F St., Box 115, 83350. Tel: 208-436-3781; Fax: 208-436-0628.
School—P.O. Box 26, 83350. Tel: 208-436-6320. Suzette Miller, Prin. Lay Teachers 6; Students 137.
Catechesis/Religious Program—Students 230.

ST. ANTHONY, FREMONT CO., MARY IMMACULATE, Rev. Arnold J. Miller, Admin.
Res.: 328 W. First N., P.O. Box 527, 83445. Tel: 208-624-7459; Fax: 208-624-7991.
Catechesis/Religious Program—Mary Ann Leck, D.R.E. Students 173.
Station—Rexburg, St. Patrick's Rexburg.
Station—Driggs, Good Shepherd Driggs.
Chapel—Island Park, Chapel of the Pines Island Park.

SAINT MARIES, BENEWAH CO., ST. MARY'S, Rev. William Taylor.
Res.: 921 Jefferson St., Box 335, St. Maries, 83861. Tel: 208-245-2977; Fax: 208-245-4624.
Catechesis/Religious Program—Shannon Shepherd, D.R.E. Students 65.
Station—Harrison, Our Lady of Perpetual Help Harrison.

SALMON, LEMHI CO., ST. CHARLES, Revs. Paul Wander; Gordon A. Taylor (Retired).
Res.: 505 Hope Ave., 83467. Tel: 208-756-2432; Fax: 208-756-1190.
Catechesis/Religious Program—Mary Vander Schaaf, D.R.E. Students 72.
Station—Arco, St. Ann Arco.
Station—Challis, St. Louise Challis.
Station—Mackay, St. Barbara Mackay.
Chapel—Leadore, St. Joseph Leadore, 83464.

SANDPOINT, BONNER CO., ST. JOSEPH'S, Rev. Dennis C. Day; Deacon Ralph Arndt, (Retired).
Res.: 621 Oak St., P.O. Box 279, 83864-0279. Tel: 208-263-3720; Fax: 208-265-4974.
Catechesis/Religious Program—Irene Sundquist, D.R.E. Students 149.
Chapel—Clark Fork, Sacred Heart

SHOSHONE, LINCOLN CO., ST. PETER'S, Rev. Carlos Perez; Deacons Dee Aslett; Marino Perea.
Res.: 215 W. B St., Box 336, 83352. Tel: 208-886-2002; 208-934-5634.
Catechesis/Religious Program—Students 55.

SODA SPRINGS, CARIBOU CO., ST. MARY'S, Rev. John R. Worster.
Res.: 99 W. Center, 83276. Tel: 208-547-3200; Fax: 208-547-3200.
Catechesis/Religious Program—Students 67.
Chapel—Montpelier, Blessed Sacrament Montpelier.
Chapel—Soda Springs, St. Mary's
Chapel—Preston, St. Peter's Preston.
Chapel—Lava Hot Springs, Our Lady of Lourdes Lava Hot Springs.

SUN VALLEY, BLAINE CO., OUR LADY OF THE SNOWS, Rev. John W. Morgan; Teresa Gregory, Pastoral Assoc.
Res.: Sun Valley Rd., Box 1650, 83353. Tel: 208-622-3432; Fax: 208-622-4348.
Catechesis/Religious Program—Students 65.

TWIN FALLS, TWIN FALLS CO.

1—ST. EDWARD THE CONFESSOR, Rev. John Koelsch, Admin.; Deacons John McKinley; Lloyd LeClair; James Herrett; John Hurley; Robert Sass, (Retired).
Res.: 630 Falls Ave., 83301-3300. Tel: 208-734-2327; Fax: 208-734-4145.
School—Tel: 208-734-3872; Fax: 208-734-1214. Luke Schroeder, Prin. Lay Teachers 8; Students 166.
Catechesis/Religious Program—Deacon John McKinley, D.R.E. Students 240.

2—ST. EDWARD'S, Merged, with Our Lady of Guadalupe, Twin Falls to form St. Edward The Confessor, Twin Falls.

3—OUR LADY OF GUADALUPE, Merged, with St.

Edward's, Twin Falls to form St. Edward The Confessor, Twin Falls.

WALLACE, SHOSHONE CO., ST. ALPHONSUS, Rev. Thomas Loucks.
Res.: 214 Pine St., Box 970, 83873. Tel: 208-752-3551.
Catechesis/Religious Program—Students 43.
Chapel—Mullan, St. Michael's

WEISER, WASHINGTON CO., ST. AGNES, Rev. Nondier Zuleta; Deacon Francis Wander.
Res.: 214 E. Liberty, P.O. Box 87, 83672. Tel: 208-549-0088; Fax: 208-549-1080.
Catechesis/Religious Program—Students 257.
Station—Cambridge, Holy Rosary Cambridge.
Station—Council, St. Jude the Apostle Council.

WENDELL, GOODING CO., ST. ANTHONY'S, , See St. Elizabeth's, Gooding for details.

Chaplains of Public Institutions

BOISE. *Elks Rehabilitation*, 204 Fort Pl., 83702. Rev. Simeon Van De Voord, O.S.B. (Retired). 9th St., Boise, ID, 83702. Tel: 208-342-3511.
St. Luke's Medical Center, 190 E. Bannock, 83712. Attended by St. John Cathedral, 775 N. 8th St., Boise, ID, 83702. Tel: 208-342-3511. Vacant.
VA Hospital, 5th St. & Fort St., 83401. Attended by St. John Cathedral, 775 N. 8th St., Boise, ID, 83702. Tel: 208-342-3511. Vacant.

COTTONWOOD. *Monastery of St. Gertrude*, HC 3 Box 121, 83522. Tel: 208-962-3224. Rev. Meinrad Schallenberger, O.S.B.

On Duty Outside the Diocese:
Revs.—
Dolan, Raymond, Box 217, M.H. Station, Staten Island, NY 10303.
Legerski, John, Marist High School, 1900 Kingsley Rd., Eugene, OR 97401.
Segatta, Bruno, Gonzaga in Florence, Piazza Antinori No. 3, Florence, Italy.
Stravinskas, Peter M.J., 21 Fairview, Mt. Pocono, PA 18344.

Absent on Leave:
Revs.—
Anderson, B. Ernest
Anderson, Jude, O.S.B.
Dennis, Patrick
Schumacher, Mark R.

Retired:
Rev. Msgr.—
Hallissey, James T., 855 Galena Ct., Box 370, Mountain Home, 83647.
Revs.—
Carroll, William, 843 New York Ave., Hamilton, MT 59840-2055.
Caulfield, Sean, 505 7th Ave., Lewiston, 83501.
Daws, Dominic, 511 3rd Ave. E., Twin Falls, 83301.
DiLoreto, Anthony, 524 N. 7th Ave., Pocatello, 83202.
Dodds, Perry W., P.O. Box 264, Twin Falls, 83303-0264.
Dohman, William, J.C.L., 5972 Via Casitas Ave., Carmichael, CA 95608-6541.
Donoghue, John F., P.O. Box 5773, 83705.
Finucane, Robert, P.O. Box 36, Genesee, 83832.
Hebert, Francis, 465 W. Linden Way, Heppner, OR 97836.
McGoldrick, John T., 106 N. 12th St., #4C, Payette, 83661.
McNeill, Malachy, 6 Dublin Rd., Drogheda, Co. Louth, Ireland.
Medina, Mauricio, c/o St. Bernard's, 584 W. Sexton St., Blackfoot, 83221.
O'Donovan, Timothy John, 1802 W. Ontario St., Sand Point, 83864-6380.
O'Sullivan, John, 700 E. Fairview, #116, Meridian, 83642-3315.
Peterson, Francis A., Karcher Estates, 1127 Caldwell Blvd. Apt. 247, Nampa, 83651-1759.
Pu, Matthew, P.O. Box 9012, 83707.
Riffle, Donald J., 3110 Crescent Rim Dr., Apt. 305, 83706-2803.
Riffle, Douglas H., P.O. Box 456, Meridian, 83680-0456.
Scarcello, Michael S., 3427 W. Scarcello Rd., Rathdrum, 83858-3427.
Steinhoff, Henry, P.O. Box 626, Eureka, MT 59917.
Taylor, Gordon A., P.O. Box 161, Arco, 83213.
Van De Voord, Simeon, O.S.B., 1915 University Dr., 83706.
Waldmann, Robert J., P.O. Box 112, Ferdinand, 83526.
Wilson, James R., 4335 Rose Hill Ct., 83705.

Permanent Deacons:
Arndt, Ralph, (Retired)
Aslett, Devon H., St. Peter, Shoshone
Baumbach, John, St. Jerome's, Jerome
Bonney, Richard, Christ the King Holy Rosary, Idaho Falls
Booth, William, St. Mark's, Boise
Bowen, James E., St. Mark, Boise
Dessert, Michael, Our Lady of the Rosary, Boise
Dominick, Thomas, St. John's Cathedral, Boise
Duggan, Bill, Holy Spirit Catholic Community, Pocatello
Eisenbeiss, Michael, Risen Christ Catholic Community, Boise
Flager, Ralph, Holy Apostles, Meridian
Geidl, Verne, St. Mary's, Moscow
Hamm, Richard, St. Catherine of Siena, Priest River
Hardy, Melvin, Holy Spirit Catholic Community, Pocatello
Harris, C. J., Risen Christ Catholic Community, Boise
Henning, Richard, St. John Cathedral, Boise
Henscheid, Paul, St. Nicholas, Rupert
Herrett, James, St. Edward's, Twin Falls
Hess, Francis, St. Mary's, Boise
Hiner, Kenneth, St. John Cathedral, Boise
Howell, Rapelyea, St. Mary's, Boise
Hurley, John, St. Edward's, Twin Falls
Jacobs, Gary, St. Pius X, Coeur d'Alene
Kelly, James, Sacred Heart, Boise
Kelso, Richard
Kreilcamp, Ben, (Retired)
Last, William, St. Jerome, Jerome
Le Clair, Lloyd, St. Edward, Twin Falls
McKinley, John D., Jr., St. Edward, Twin Falls
McSwain, Gary, St. Pius X, Coeur d'Alene
Murphy, Pierce, Our Lady of the Rosary, Boise
Nicholas, Joseph, St. Ann's, Bonners Farry
Pelowitz, Jack, St. Bernard's, Blackfoot
Pera, Gerald D., Holy Apostles, Meridian
Perea, Marino, St. Jerome, Jerome
Petzak, William, St. Mary, Boise
Phillips, Frank, St. Theresa's, Orofino
Pierce, Ralph, St. Mark, Boise
Rasmussen, Charles, Holy Apostles, Meridian
Rathe, Orville, St. Nicholas, Rupert
Rodriguez, Pete, St. Nicholas, Rupert
Sando, William, St. Pius X, Coeur d'Alene
Sass, Robert, (Retired)
Schmidt, Fred, Our Lady of Lourdes, Lewiston
Shaber, Alan, Sacred Heart, Emmett
Skoro, Chuck, Our Lady of The Rosary, Boise
Sokolowski, Don, Sts. Peter & Paul, Grangeville
Solbrig, Charles W., (Retired)
Sousa, Ed, Presentation of The Lord, American Falls
Tamayo, Juan, Our Lady of the Valley, Caldwell
Trueworthy, Leonard, St. Pius X, Coeur d' Alene
Vietri, Nick, St. John's Cathedral, Boise
Wander, Francis, St. Agnes, Weiser
Woznicki, Walter, St. Pius X, Coeur D'Alene

INSTITUTIONS LOCATED IN THE DIOCESE

[A] HIGH SCHOOLS, INTER-PAROCHIAL

BOISE. *Bishop Kelly High School*, 7009 Franklin Rd., 83709-0998. Tel: 208-375-6010; Fax: 208-375-3626. Doug Stawdlee, Prin. Priests 2; Lay Teachers 49; Students 625.

COEUR D'ALENE. *Holy Family Catholic School of Coeur d'Alene*, 406 N. Tenth, Coeur D Alene, 83814. Tel: 208-765-4327; Fax: 208-664-2903. Karen Durgin, Prin. Lay Teachers 11; Students 194.

[B] GENERAL HOSPITALS

BOISE. *St. Alphonsus Regional Medical Center, Inc.*, 1055 N. Curtis Rd., 83706-1370. Tel: 208-367-2121. Sandra Bennett Bruce, Pres. & CEO.
Legal Title: *St. Alphonsus Regional Medical Center.*
Legal Title: *St. Alphonsus Building Co., Inc.*
Legal Title: *St. Alphonsus Diversified Care.* Sisters of the Holy Cross 5; Bed Capacity 359; Patients Assisted Annually 549,637.

COTTONWOOD. *St. Mary's Hospital* (Sub. of Benedictine Health System) , 701 N. Lewiston St., P.O. Box 137, 83522. Tel: 208-962-3251; Fax: 208-962-3722. Ms. Casey Meza, Admin.; Rev. Meinrad Schallberger, O.S.B., Chap.; Sr. Barbara Jo Glodowski, Dir., Mission Svc.; Iris Hawley, D.N.S., Dir., Nursing. Sponsored by Sisters of St. Benedict, Duluth, MN Sisters 2; Bed Capacity 28; Patients Assisted Annually 46,000.

JEROME. *St. Benedicts Family Medical Center*, 709 N. Lincoln, 83338-1851. Tel: 208-324-4301; Fax: 208-324-3878. Michael Cooper, Admin.; Sr. Claudia Rae Braun, O.S.B., Mission & Pastoral Svcs. Sponsored by St. Alphonsus Regional Medical Center, Boise, ID, Skilled Nursing Facility in connection with Medical Center. Sisters 1; Bed Capacity 65; Patients Assisted Annually 57,520.

LEWISTON. *St. Joseph Regional Medical Center*, 415 6th St., P.O. Box 816, 83501-0816. Tel: 208-743-2511; Fax: 208-799-5528. Howard A. Hayes, Admin. Nursing Education is in affiliation with Lewis-Clark State College and with Walla-Walla Community College, Clarkston Branch. Bed Capacity 161; Patients assisted annually 123,750.

NAMPA. *Mercy Medical Center*, 1512 12th Avenue Rd., 83686. Tel: 208-467-1171. Joseph A. Messmer, Pres. & CEO; Revs. Mark Bekkedahl, Vice Pres. Mission Integration; Joseph Newcomer, Chap.; Sr. Alice Marie Schmid, O.P.; Jim Hoff, Dir. Spiritual Care Resources & Chap.; Sr. Maura Clark, R.S.M., Chap. Sisters 2; Bed Capacity 152; Patients Assisted Annually 164,903.

[C] MONASTERIES AND RESIDENCES OF PRIESTS AND BROTHERS

JEROME. *Monastery of the Ascension*, 541 East, 100 South, 83338. Tel: 208-324-2377; Fax: 208-324-2377. Revs. Boniface Lautz, O.S.B., Prior; Norbert Novak, O.S.B., Subprior; Meinrad Schallberger, O.S.B.; Andrew Baumgartner, O.S.B.; Hugh Feiss, O.S.B.; Eugene Esch, O.S.B.; Simeon VanDeVoord, O.S.B. (Retired); Bros. Sylvester Sonnen, O.S.B.; Selby Coffman, O.S.B.; Tobiah Urrutia, O.S.B.; Jose Echanove, O.S.B.; David Cobos, O.S.B.; Maur Morneault, O.S.B.; Thien Vw, O.S.B.
Legal Title: *The Benedictine Monks of Idaho, Inc.* The Benedictine Monks of Idaho, Inc.

LEMHI. *Hermitage of St. Joseph*, Box 37, 83465. Bro. Maurice Mansfield, H.M.C. Hermits of Mt. Carmel

[D] CONVENTS AND RESIDENCES OF SISTERS

COTTONWOOD. *Monastery of St. Gertrude, Motherhouse and Novitiate*, HC3 Box 121, 83522-9408. Tel: 208-962-3224; Fax: 208-962-7212. Sisters Jean LaLande, O.S.B., Prioress; Meg Sass, O.S.B., Asst. Prioress. Sisters of St. Benedict 63.

MESA. *Marymount Hermitage, Inc., Hermit Sisters of Mary*, 2150 Hermitage Ln., 83643-5005. Tel: 208-256-4354 (msg. only). Sr. Mary Beverly Greger, H.S.M., Supr.; Rev. Robert E. Griffin, S.J. (SJ), Chap. Sisters 2.

[E] RETREAT HOUSES

BOISE. *Nazareth*, 4450 N. Five Mile Rd., 83713-2709. Tel: 208-375-2932; Fax: 208-376-5787. Sr. Grayce E. Ross, S.N.J.M., Exec. Dir.

[F] CAMPUS MINISTRY

BOISE. *Boise State University, St. Paul's Catholic Center* 1915 University Dr., 83706. Tel: 208-343-2128; Fax: 208-343-2142. Email: chuck@stpaulsboise.org. Deacon Charles L. Skoro, Dir.

CALDWELL. *Albertson's College of Idaho c/o Our Lady of The Valley*, 1122 W. Linden St., 83605. Tel: 208-459-3653; Fax: 208-454-8789. Rev. Enrique Terriquez.

COEUR D'ALENE. *North Idaho College* St Pius X, 625 E. Haycraft, 83815. Tel: 208-765-5108; Fax: 208-664-5325. Email: stpiusx@imbris.com. Rev. Roger LaChance.

LEWISTON. *Lewis and Clark State College* St. Stanislaus, 633 5th Ave., 83501. Tel: 208-743-7331; Fax: 208-746-7134. Sr. Margie Schmidt, O.S.B.

MOSCOW. *St. Augustine Catholic Center* , (Serving University of Idaho) , 628 Deakin, Box 3457, 83843-1911. Tel: 208-882-4613; Fax: 208-882-0810. Email: amondws@junp.com. Rev. Len MacMillan.

POCATELLO. *Idaho State University, St. John's Catholic Student Center* 920 E. Lovejoy, I.S.U. Box 8129, 83209. Tel: 208-233-0880; Fax: 208-233-5745. Email: stjohns@isu.edu. Web: www.bannockcatholic.net. Sr. Helene Higgins, C.S.J., Dir.

TWIN FALLS. *College of Southern Idaho* , Attended by St. Edward the Confessor, Twin Falls , 630 Falls Ave., 83301-3300. Tel: 208-734-2327; Fax: 208-734-4145. Rev. John Koelsch.

[G] MISCELLANEOUS

BOISE. *Catholic Charities of Idaho, Inc.*, 4202 Emerald St., 83706. Tel: 208-345-6031; Fax: 208-345-5674. Email: mhoff@ccidaho.org. Marie D. Hoff, M.S.W., Ph.D., Exec. Dir.; Most Rev. Michael P. Driscoll, D.D., M.S.W., Pres.; Lynne Tiddens, Admin. Mgr.
The Catholic Migrant Farmworker Network, Inc., 1915 University Dr., 83706-3022. Tel: 208-384-1778; Fax: 208-384-1879. Email: CMFNCC@aol.com. Web: www.cmfn.org. Hector R. Rodriquez, Exec. Dir.; Celine Caufield, Admin. Asst.
Society of St. Vincent de Paul - Southwest Idaho District Council, P.O. Box 8636, 83707. Tel: 208-331-2208. Margo Henning, Pres.

St. Vincent de Paul Society St. Francis of Assisi Conference. , 6464 W. State St., 83703. Tel: 208-853-4921; Fax: 208-853-4935. Email: stateSVDP@aol.com. Hope Ryan, Business Mgr.; Vicky Rowell, Store Mgr. Thrift Store.

St. Vincent de Paul Society St. John's Conference. , 5645 Hallmark Ct., 83703. Tel: 208-331-2208. Francis McDonnell, Pres.

St. Vincent de Paul Society Sacred Heart Conference. , 314 Jackson, 83705. Tel: 208-331-2208, Ext. 2. Ida Fisk, Pres.

St. Vincent de Paul Society Risen Christ Conference. , 5059 Silverspur, 83709. Tel: 208-331-2208, Ext. 3. Karen Knotts, Pres.

BLACKFOOT. *St. Vincent de Paul Thrift Store* St. Bernard Conference. , 206 S. Spruce, 83221. Tel: 208-785-0353; 208-785-0423; Fax: 208-782-0224. Charles Belmar, Pres.

CALDWELL. *Society of St. Vincent de Paul* Society of St. Vincent de Paul , 17281 Ustick Rd., 83607. Tel: 208-459-7658. John Ihli, Pres.; Jerry Phillips, Store Mgr.

COEUR D'ALENE. *St. Vincent de Paul Thrift Store* St. Thomas Conference. , 108 E. Walnut, 83814. Tel: 208-664-3095; Fax: 208-664-1772. Email: Lynnsvdp@yahoo.com. John O'Brien, Pres.; Lynn Peterson, Exec. Dir.

IDAHO FALLS. *St. Vincent de Paul Society of Idaho Falls*, P.O. Box 50951, 83405-0951. Dean M. Hallah, Pres.

KELLOGG. *Society of St. Vincent de Paul* St. Rita Conference. , 104 E. Riverside, 83837. Tel: 208-783-5551; Fax: 208-784-6041. Gary Strope, Pres.; Cindy Patton, Store Mgr.

LEWISTON. *Lewis and Clark District Council of St. Vincent de Paul*, 422 15th Ave., 83501. Tel: 208-746-2329; Fax: 798-758-9545. Mary Ropp, Board Pres.

NAMPA. *Mercy Housing Idaho, Inc.*, 1512 12th Avenue Rd., 83686-6008. Tel: 208-463-5858; Fax: 208-463-5859. Jeff Robinson, Regl. Vice Pres. Tel: 206-838-5700.

Mercy Properties II, Inc.
Mercy Idaho Properties, Inc.
Mercy Twin Falls, Inc.
Mercy Moscow, Inc.
Mercy Southeast Idaho, Inc.
Eagle Senior Village, Inc.

Our Lady of Guadalupe Conference, 1203 7th St. N., 83651. Tel: 208-442-3089. Jim Daniels, Pres. Tel: 208-466-3400 Message; 208-466-1000 (Food Pantry).

POCATELLO. *PortNeuf Valley Conference (St. Vincent de Paul)*, 335 N. Main, 83204-8359. Tel: 208-233-2555; Fax: 208-478-8359. Email: stvincent@if.rmci.net. Jerri Cole Baca, Pres.; Rita James, Social Svcs. Dir.

STAR. *Holy Apostles Conference*, 10453 W. Vega Ct., 83669. Tel: 208-888-2660. Karen Dhuyvetter, Pres.

TWIN FALLS. *St. Michael Conference (St. Vincent de Paul)*, 244 Main Ave. S., 83301. Tel: 208-734-9143. Email: svdp@lightcom.net. Mary Lou Howard, Pres.; Rick Mesaros, Store Mgr.

RELIGIOUS INSTITUTES OF MEN REPRESENTED IN THE DIOCESE

For further details refer to the corresponding bracketed number in the Religious Institutes of Men or Women section.

[]—*Apostolic Life Community of Priests*—A.L.C.P.

[0200]—*Benedictine Monks*—O.S.B.

[]—*Hermits of Mt. Carmel*—H.M.C.

[0690]—*Jesuit Fathers* (Oregon Prov.)—S.J.

[0840]—*Missionary Servants of the Most Holy Trinity*—S.T.

[1065]—*Priestly Fraternity of St. Peter*—F.S.S.P.

[1070]—*Redemptorist Fathers* (Oakland Prov.)—C.SS.R.

RELIGIOUS INSTITUTES OF WOMEN REPRESENTED IN THE DIOCESE

[0230]—*Benedictine Sisters of Pontifical Jurisdiction*—O.S.B.

[1920]—*Congregation of the Sisters of the Holy Cross*—C.S.C.

[1780]—*Congregation of the Sisters of the Third Order of St. Francis of Perpetual Adoration*—F.S.P.A.

[1070-21]—*Dominican Sisters*—O.P.

[]—*Hermit Sisters of Mary*—H.S.M.

[1250]—*Institute of the Franciscan Sisters of the Eucharist*—F.S.E.

[2575]—*Institute of the Sisters of Mercy of the Americas*—R.S.M.

[]—*Missionary Sisters of the Sacred Heart of the Rosary of Fatima*—H.M.R.F.

[]—*Religious of the Sacred Heart*—R.S.C.J.

[3340]—*Sisters of Providence*—S.P.

[3830]—*Sisters of St. Joseph*—C.S.J.

[1990]—*Sisters of the Holy Names of Jesus and Mary*—S.N.J.M.

[]—*Society of Sisters of the Church*—S.S.C.

[4110]—*Ursuline Nuns* (Western Prov.)—O.S.U.

NECROLOGY

† Shinnick, James F. (Retired)—Died Oct. 2, 2003

Archdiocese of Boston

(Archidioecesis Bostoniensis)

His Eminence

BERNARD FRANCIS CARDINAL LAW

Former Archbishop of Boston; ordained priest May 21, 1961; ordained Bishop of Springfield-Cape Girardeau December 5, 1973; appointed Archbishop of Boston January 11, 1984; installed March 23, 1984; named Cardinal Priest of Santa Susanna on May 25, 1985; resigned December 13, 2002. *Office: 2121 Commonwealth Ave., Boston, MA 02135-3193.*

Most Reverend

RICHARD GERARD LENNON, D.D., M.A.

Auxiliary Bishop of Boston; ordained priest May 19, 1973; appointed Auxiliary Bishop of Boston and Titular Bishop of Sufes June 29, 2001; ordained September 14, 2001; named Apostolic Administrator, December 13, 2002; secondary appointment ended July 1, 2003. *Office and Residence: 2121 Commonwealth Ave., Boston, MA 02135-3192.* Tel: 617-254-0100; Fax: 617-783-2947.

Most Reverend

WALTER JAMES EDYVEAN, D.D., S.T.D.

Auxiliary Bishop of Boston; ordained priest December 16, 1964; appointed Auxiliary Bishop of Boston and Titular Bishop of Aeliae June 29, 2001; ordained Bishop September 14, 2001. *Office: 5 Wilson St., Natick, MA 01760.* Tel: 508-647-0296; Fax: 508-647-1542. *Res.: Saint Patrick Rectory*, 44 E. Central St., Natick, MA 01760. Tel: 508-647-1860.

Most Reverend

SEAN P. O'MALLEY

Archbishop of Boston; ordained priest August 29, 1970; appointed Coadjutor Bishop of St. Thomas in the Virgin Islands May 30, 1984; installed August 2, 1984; succeeded to the See October 16, 1985; appointed sixth Bishop of Fall River June 16, 1992; installed August 10, 1992; appointed fourth Bishop of Palm Beach September 3, 2002; installed October 19, 2002; appointed Archbishop of Boston July 1, 2003; installed July 31, 2003. *Office: 2101 Commonwealth Ave., Boston, MA 02135-3193.* Tel: 617-782-2544; Fax: 617-782-8358.

Chancery Office: 2121 Commonwealth Ave., Boston, MA 02135-3193. Tel: 617-254-0100; Fax: 617-783-4564.

Web: www.rcab.org

Most Reverend

JOHN PATRICK BOLES, D.D., PH.D.

Auxiliary Bishop of Boston; ordained priest February 2, 1955; appointed Auxiliary Bishop of Boston and Titular Bishop of Nova Sparsa April 14, 1992; ordained May 21, 1992. *Office: 307 Bowdoin St., Boston, MA 02122-2245.* Tel: 617-436-3113; Fax: 617-436-7619. *Res.: St. Gregory Rectory*, 2223 Dorcehster Ave., Boston, MA 02124-5671. Tel: 617-298-2460.

Most Reverend

FRANCIS XAVIER IRWIN, D.D., A.C.S.W.

Auxiliary Bishop of Boston; ordained priest February 2, 1960; appointed Auxiliary Bishop of Boston and Titular Bishop of Ubaza July 24, 1996; ordained September 17, 1996. *Office: 99 Margin St., Peabody, MA 01960.* Tel: 978-531-1013; Fax: 978-531-5312. *Res.: Saint Mary Rectory*, 22 Conant St., Danvers, MA 01923. Tel: 978-774-0340.

Most Reverend

EMILIO SIMEON ALLUE, S.D.B., D.D., PH.D.

Auxiliary Bishop of Boston; ordained December 22, 1966; appointed Auxiliary Bishop of Boston and Titular Bishop of Croe July 24, 1996; installed September 17, 1996. *Office: 107 N. Main St., Westford, MA 01886.* Tel: 978-399-0000; Fax: 978-399-0123. *Res.: Saint Catherine of Alexandria Rectory*, 107 N. Main St., Westford, MA 01886. Tel: 978-692-6353.

Square Miles 2,465.

Created a Diocese April 8, 1808; Made Metropolitan Archdiocese February 12, 1875.

Comprises the Counties of Essex, Middlesex, Norfolk, Suffolk and Plymouth (excepting the towns of Marion, Mattapoisetts and Wareham) in the Commonwealth of Massachusetts.

For legal titles of parishes and archdiocesan agencies and institutions, consult the Chancery Office

STATISTICAL OVERVIEW

Personnel	
Retired Cardinals	1
Archbishops	1
Auxiliary Bishops	6
Abbots	1
Priests: Diocesan Active in Diocese	486
Priests: Diocesan Active Outside Diocese	32
Priests: Diocesan in Foreign Missions	7
Priests: Retired, Sick or Absent	334
Number of Diocesan Priests	859
Religious Priests in Diocese	670
Total Priests in Diocese	1,529
Extern Priests in Diocese	38
Ordinations:	
Diocesan Priests	5
Permanent Deacons in Diocese	239
Total Brothers	142
Total Sisters	2,601
Parishes	
Parishes	357
With Resident Pastor:	
Resident Diocesan Priests	330
Resident Religious Priests	27
Pastoral Centers	2
New Parishes Created	1
Closed Parishes	3
Professional Ministry Personnel:	
Sisters	41
Lay Ministers	16
Welfare	
Catholic Hospitals	8
Total Assisted	1,193,117
Health Care Centers	3
Total Assisted	6,868
Homes for the Aged	16
Total Assisted	3,016
Day Care Centers	11
Total Assisted	1,675
Specialized Homes	21
Total Assisted	1,722
Special Centers for Social Services	43
Total Assisted	206,000
Other Institutions	3
Total Assisted	35,410
Educational	
Seminaries, Diocesan	2
Students from This Diocese	31
Students from Other Diocese	100
Diocesan Students in Other Seminaries	11
Seminaries, Religious	2
Students Religious	51
Total Seminarians	93
Colleges and Universities	7
Total Students	22,400
High Schools, Diocesan and Parish	13
Total Students	5,335
High Schools, Private	20
Total Students	11,739
Elementary Schools, Diocesan and Parish	113
Total Students	34,725
Elementary Schools, Private	10
Total Students	2,558
Non-residential Schools for the Disabled	3
Total Students	348
Catechesis/Religious Education:	
High School Students	29,517
Elementary Students	111,501
Total Students under Catholic Instruction	218,216
Teachers in the Diocese:	
Priests	7
Brothers	35
Sisters	185
Lay Teachers	3,284
Vital Statistics	
Receptions into the Church:	
Infant Baptism Totals	22,287
Adult Baptism Totals	3,362
Received into Full Communion	214
First Communions	21,632
Confirmations	16,050
Marriages:	
Catholic	4,935
Interfaith	1,208
Total Marriages	6,143
Deaths	18,498
Total Catholic Population	2,077,487
Total Population	3,970,026

Former Bishops—His Eminence JOHN LEFEVRE CARDINAL DE CHEVERUS, ord. Dec. 18, 1790; appt. first Bishop of Boston, April 8, 1808; ord. Bishop Nov. 1, 1810; Apostolic Administrator of New York, NY (1810-1815); transferred to Montauban, May 3, 1823; appointed Archbishop of Bordeaux Oct. 2, 1826; named Cardinal, Feb. 1, 1836 (died before receiving red hat and titular church); died July 19, 1836; Most Revs. BENEDICT J. FENWICK, S.J., ord. June 11, 1808; appt. second Bishop of Boston, May 10, 1825; ord. Bishop Nov. 1, 1825; died Aug. 11, 1846; JOHN BERNARD FITZPATRICK, ord. June 13, 1840; appt. Titular Bishop of Callipolis and Coadjutor of Boston, Nov. 21, 1843; ord. Bishop March 24, 1844; appt. third Bishop of Boston, Aug. 11, 1846; died Feb. 13, 1866; JOHN JOSEPH WILLIAMS, D.D., ord. May 17, 1845; appt. Titular Bishop of Tripolis and Coadjutor of Boston, Jan. 8, 1866; ord. fourth Bishop of Boston, March 11, 1866; named first Archbishop of Boston, Feb. 12, 1875; died Aug. 30, 1907; His Eminence WILLIAM HENRY CARDINAL O'CONNELL, ord. June 7, 1884; appt. third Bishop of Portland, Maine, Feb. 8, 1901; ord. Bishop May 19, 1901; appt. Titular Archbishop of Constantia and Coadjutor with right of succession to the Archbishop of Boston, Feb. 8, 1906; appt. fifth Bishop and second Archbishop of Boston, April 30, 1907; named Cardinal, Nov. 27, 1911, Titular Church, San Clemente; died April 22, 1944; RICHARD JAMES CARDINAL CUSHING, ord. May 26, 1921; appt. Titular Bishop of Mela and Auxiliary of Boston, June 10, 1939; ord. June 29, 1939; appt. sixth Bishop and third Archbishop of Boston, Sept. 25, 1944; named Cardinal December 15, 1958, Titular Church, Santa Susanna; died Nov. 2, 1970; HUMBERTO SOUSA CARDINAL MEDEIROS, ord. June 15, 1946; appt. second Bishop of Brownsville, Texas April 14, 1966; ord. Bishop

June 9, 1966; named seventh Bishop and fourth Archbishop of Boston, Sept. 8, 1970; named Cardinal March 5, 1973, Titular Church, Santa Susanna; died Sept. 17, 1983; BERNARD FRANCIS CARDINAL LAW, ord. May 21, 1961; ord. Fourth Bishop of Springfield-Cape Girardeau, Oct. 22, 1973; ordained Bishop Dec. 5, 1973; appt. eighth Bishop and fifth Archbishop of Boston Jan. 11, 1984; installed March 23, 1984; named Cardinal Priest May 25, 1985; Titular Church, Santa Susanna; resigned Dec. 13, 2002.

Regional Bishops—Central Region: Most Rev. JOHN PATRICK BOLES, D.D., Ph.D., Regl. Bishop's Office, 307 Bowdoin St., Dorchester, 02122-2245. Tel: 617-436-3113; Fax: 617-436-7619. Merrimack Region: Most Rev. EMILIO SIMEON ALLUE, S.D.B., D.D., S.T.L., Ph.D., Regl. Bishop's Office, 107 N. Main St., Westford, 01886. Tel: 978-399-0000; Fax: 978-399-0123. North Region: Most Rev. FRANCIS XAVIER IRWIN, D.D., A.S.C.W., Regl. Bishop's Office, 99 Margin St., Peabody, 01960-1396. Tel: 978-531-1013; Fax: 978-531-5312. South Region: Most Rev. RICHARD JOSEPH MALONE, D.D., S.T.L., Th.D., Regl. Bishop's Office, 236 Pleasant St., Weymouth, 02190-2599. Tel: 781-337-4413; Fax: 781-337-3625. West Region: Most Rev. WALTER JAMES EDYVEAN, D.D., S.T.D., Regl. Bishop's Office, 44 E. Central St., Natick, 01760. Tel: 508-647-0296; Fax: 508-647-1542.

Vicars General—Most Revs. EMILIO SIMEON ALLUE, S.D.B., D.D., S.T.L., Ph.D.; JOHN PATRICK BOLES, D.D., Ph.D.; WALTER JAMES EDYVEAN, D.D., S.T.D.; FRANCIS XAVIER IRWIN, D.D., A.S.C.W.; RICHARD G. LENNON; RICHARD JOSEPH MALONE, D.D., S.T.L., Th.D.

Vicars—

CENTRAL REGION—Most Rev. JOHN PATRICK BOLES, D.D., Ph.D., Regional Bishop's Office, Boston. Tel: 617-436-3113; Fax: 617-436-7619; Rev. Msgr. CHARLES J. BOURQUE, V.F., Vicariate I, Pastor, Our Lady of Lourdes, Jamaica Plain. Tel: 617-524-0434; Fax: 617-524-1888; Very Revs. NICHOLAS C. CICCONE, V.F., Vicariate II, Pastor, St. Margaret, Dorchester. Tel: 617-436-2190; Fax: 617-282-5428; HUGH H. O'REGAN, V.F., Vicariate III, Admin., St. James the Greater, Boston. Tel: 617-542-8498; Fax: 617-542-1538; Rev. Msgr. DENNIS F. SHEEHAN, V.F., Vicariate IV, Pastor, St. Paul, Cambridge. Tel: 617-491-8400; Fax: 617-354-7092. MERRIMACK REGION: Most Rev. EMILIO SIMEON ALLUE, S.D.B., D.D., S.T.L., Ph.D., Regional Bishop's Office, Lowell. Tel: 978-459-4082; Fax: 978-452-5584; Very Revs. WILLIAM M. SULLIVAN, V.F., Chelmsford Vicariate, Pastor, St. Catherine of Alexandria, Westford. Tel: 978-692-6353; Fax: 978-392-0644; MARK S. SHEEHAN, V.F., Concord Vicariate, Pastor, St. Michael, Bedford. Tel: 781-275-6318; Fax: 781-271-9879; JAMES M. CARROLL, V.F., Haverhill Vicariate, Pastor, St. Mary, Georgetown. Tel: 978-352-2024; Fax: 978-352-5513; JAMES J. RONAN, V.F., Lawrence Vicariate, Pastor, Holy Rosary, Lawrence. Tel: 978-685-1711; Fax: 978-691-5927; JOHN F. HANLEY, O.M.I., V.F., Lowell Vicariate, Pastor, St. William, Tewksbury. Tel: 978-581-7381; Fax: 978-858-0544. NORTH REGION: Most Rev. FRANCIS XAVIER IRWIN, D.D., A.S.C.W., Regional Bishop's Office, Peabody. Tel: 978-531-1013; Fax: 978-531-5312; Very Revs. JOHN E. FARRELL, V.F., Gloucester Vicariate, Pastor, Our Lady of the Assumption, Lynnfield. Tel: 781-598-4313; Fax: 781-598-0055; RICHARD J. MEHM, V.F., Medford Vicariate, Pastor, Immaculate Conception, Malden. Tel: 781-324-4941; Fax: 781-397-8571; Rev. Msgr. PAUL V. GARRITY, V.F., Salem Vicariate, Pastor, St. Mary, Lynn. Tel: 781-598-2088; Fax: 781-599-2088; Very Rev. VINCENT P. MELLONE, V.F., Stoneham Vicariate, Pastor, St. Barbara, Woburn. Tel: 781-933-4130; Fax: 781-932-2536. SOUTH REGION: Most Rev. RICHARD JOSEPH MALONE, D.D., S.T.L., Th.D., Regional Bishop's Office, Weymouth. Tel: 781-337-4413; Fax: 781-337-3625; Very Rev. FRANCIS V. CLOHERTY, V.F., Brockton Vicariate, Pastor, St. Patrick, Brockton. Tel: 508-586-4840; Fax: 508-941-0639; Rev. Msgr. PETER V. CONLEY, V.F., Norwood Vicariate, Pastor, St. Jude, Norfolk. Tel: 508-528-0170; Fax: 508-528-1860; Very Rev. BRYAN K. PARRISH, V.F., Plymouth Vicariate, Pastor, St. Mary, Plymouth. Tel: 508-746-0426; Fax: 508-747-5886; Rev. Msgr. ROBERT P. DEELEY, V.F., J.C.D., Quincy Vicariate, Pastor, St. Ann, Quincy. Tel: 617-479-5400; Fax: 617-479-0955; Very Rev. JAMES J. RAFFERTY, V.F., Weymouth Vicariate, Pastor, St. Paul, Hingham. Tel: 781-749-0587; Fax: 781-749-8053. WEST REGION: Most Rev. WALTER JAMES EDYVEAN, D.D., S.T.D., Regional Bishop's Office, Natick. Tel: 508-647-0296; Fax: 508-647-1542; Rev. Msgr. FRANCIS V. STRAHAN, V.F., Framingham Vicariate, Pastor, St. Bridget, Framingham. Tel: 508-875-5959; Fax: 508-875-1270; Very Revs. MICHAEL J. BOVA CONTI, V.F., Marlborough Vicariate, Pastor, Our Lady of Fatima, Sudbury. Tel: 978-443-2647; Fax: 978-443-6264; THOMAS F. POWERS, V.F., Natick Vicariate, Pastor, St. John, Wellesley. Tel: 781-235-0045; Fax: 781-235-6990; O. WENDELL VERRILL, V.F., Newton Vicariate, Pastor, St. Mary, Waltham. Tel: 718-891-1730; Fax: 781-642-0604.

Archdiocesan Consultative Bodies—

Archdiocesan College of Consultors—Most Revs. SEAN P. O'MALLEY, O.F.M.Cap.; EMILIO SIMEON ALLUE, S.D.B., D.D., S.T.L., Ph.D.; JOHN PATRICK BOLES, D.D., Ph.D.; WALTER JAMES EDYVEAN, D.D., S.T.D.; FRANCIS XAVIER IRWIN, D.D., A.S.C.W.; RICHARD GERARD LENNON, D.D., M.A.; RICHARD JOSEPH MALONE, D.D., S.T.L., Th.D.; Rev. Msgr. ROBERT C. FICHTNER (Retired); Revs. ROBERT L. CONNORS; RICHARD S. DEVEER; OSCAR J. PRATT.

Finance Council—Most Rev. SEAN P. O'MALLEY, O.F.M.Cap., Pres. Members: Most Rev. RICHARD GERARD LENNON, D.D., M.A.; Ms. REGINA E. CAINES; Mr. JOHN CUNNINGHAM; Mr. THOMAS J. FLATLEY; Sr. THERESE HIGGINS, C.S.J.; Mr. JOHN A. KANEB; Mr. PETER S. LYNCH; Mr. WILLIAM F. MCCALL; Mr. JOHN A. MCNIECE; Mr. JAMES MOONEY; Mr. ROBERT J. MORRISSEY; Mr. GILES MOSHER; Mr. GERALD T. REILLY; Mr. DAVID W. SMITH; Mrs. MICHAEL A. VALERIO; Mr. FRANCIS M. WARD.

Vicar General and Moderator of the Curia—Most Rev. RICHARD G. LENNON, 2121 Commonwealth Ave., Boston, 02135-3193. Tel: 617-254-0100; Fax: 617-783-2947.

Assistant to the Moderator of the Curia for Canonical Affairs—Rev. MARK O'CONNELL, 2121 Commonwealth Ave., Boston, 02135-3193. Tel: 617-254-0100; Fax: 617-746-5920.

Delegate for Investigations—Ms. AMY JILL STRICKLAND, J.C.D. (Cand.), 2121 Commonwealth Ave., Boston, 02135-3193. Tel: 617-746-5922; Fax: 617-783-2947.

Healing and Assistance—Ms. BARBARA THORPE, Dir., 246 Walnut St., Ste. 103, Newton, 02460. Tel: 866-244-9603; 617-244-9603 Email: barbara_thorpe@healingandassistance.org. Web: www.rcab.org/oha/homepage.htm.

Planning and Research—Rev. ROBERT MCMILLAN, S.J.; Mr. HARRY FODEN, 2121 Commonwealth Ave., Boston, 02135-3193. Tel: 617-254-0100; Fax: 617-746-5754.

The Catholic Foundation—Mr. JAMES MOONEY, Chm., Bd. of Governors; KENNETH J HOKENSON, Exec. Dir., 2121 Commonwealth Ave., Boston, 02135-3193. Tel: 617-746-5632.

Annual Catholic Appeal—DAMIEN DEVASTO, Dir. Tel: 617-746-5630. Email: appeal@rcab.org.

Communications Office—ELIZABETH JENNINGS-WHITE, Dir. Tel: 617-746-5784.

Donor Relations—BETSY HIGGINS, Coord. Tel: 617-746-5794.

Parish Stewardship—KENNETH CHISHOLM, Dir. Tel: 617-746-5623. Email: stewardship@rcab.org.

Planned and Major Gifts Office—Gifts Officers: DICK MURPHY. Tel: 617-746-5929; MICHAEL RHODES. Tel: 617-746-5929. Email: giving@rcab.org.

Promise for Tomorrow—Tel: 617-746-5732. Email: promisefortomorrow@rcab.org.

Research—RITA CASEY, Coord. Grants. Tel: 617-746-5941; MERYL STOWNBRIDGE, Coord. Gift Planning. Tel: 617-746-5738.

Pontifical Association of the Holy Childhood—

Pontifical Society for the Propagation of the Faith—

Pontifical Society of St. Peter the Apostle—Rev. Msgr. ANDREW F. CONNELL, 49 Franklin St., Boston, 02110-1382. Tel: 617-542-1776; Fax: 617-542-1778.

Cabinet Secretaries

Secretary for Central Services—DAVID W. SMITH, 2121 Commonwealth Ave., Boston, 02135-3193. Tel: 617-746-5680; Fax: 617-783-4564.

Secretary for Child Advocacy, Implementation and Oversight—Deacon ANTHONY REZUTO, 2121 Commonwealth Ave., Boston, 02135-3192. Tel: 617-746-5994; Fax: 617-783-0766. Web: www.rcab.org/childadvocacy/homepage.html.

Secretary for Communications—Rev. Msgr. PAUL B. MCINERNY, J.C.L., 55 Chapel St., P.O. Box 9109, Newton, 02460-9109. Tel: 617-965-0050; Fax: 617-965-6587.

Secretary for Education—Sr. CLARE BERTERO, O.S.F., One Lake St., Boston, 02135-3800. Tel: 617-746-5855; Fax: 617-782-0213.

Secretary for Health Care Services—Mr. MICHAEL F. COLLINS, M.D., 736 Cambridge St., Boston, 02135-2997. Tel: 617-789-2500; Fax: 617-789-2124.

Secretary for Institutional Advancement—KENNETH J. HOKENSON, 2121 Commonwealth Ave., Boston, 02135-3193. Tel: 617-746-5632; Fax: 617-783-6366.

Secretary for Ministerial Personnel—Rev. ROBERT L. CONNORS, 2121 Commonwealth Ave., Boston, 02135-3193. Tel: 617-746-5750; Fax: 617-783-2947. Email: reverendrobertconnors@rcab.org.

Secretary for Pastoral Services—Rev. ARTHUR M. COYLE, 2121 Commonwealth Ave., Boston, 02135-3193. Tel: 617-746-5770; Fax: 617-746-5754.

Secretary for Public Relations—Rev. CHRISTOPHER J. COYNE, 2121 Commonwealth Ave., Boston, 02135-3193. Tel: 617-746-5775; Fax: 617-782-9416.

Secretary for Social Services—Rev. J. BRYAN HEHIR, 75 Kneeland St., Boston, 02111-1931. Tel: 617-451-7955; Fax: 617-451-0337.

Delegate for Religious—Sr. MARIAN BATHO, C.S.J., 2121 Commonwealth Ave., Boston, 02135-3193. Tel: 617-254-0100; Fax: 617-746-5754.

Chancery Office—2121 Commonwealth Ave., Boston, 02135-3193. Tel: 617-254-0100; Fax: 617-783-4564. Office Hours: Mon.-Fri. 9-5

Chancellor—Mr. DAVID W. SMITH, 2121 Commonwealth Ave., Boston, 02135-3193. Tel: 617-746-5680; Fax: 617-783-4564.

Archdiocesan Counsel—WILSON D. ROGERS, Esq., 2121 Commonwealth Ave., Boston, 02135-3193. Tel: 617-254-0100; Fax: 617-783-2947.

Archives—

Archivist—ROBERT JOHNSON-LALLY, Archivist Record Mgr.; MARGARET GONSALVES, Assoc. Archivist, 2121 Commonwealth Ave., Boston, 02135-3193. Tel: 617-746-5797; Fax: 617-783-5642.

Secretaries to the Archbishop and Masters of Ceremonies—Revs. JOHN J. CONNOLLY; ROBERT T. KICKHAM, Archbishop's Residence, 2101 Commonwealth Ave., Boston, 02135-3192. Tel: 617-782-2544; Fax: 617-782-8358.

Metropolitan Tribunal—One Lake St., Boston, 02135-3800. Tel: 617-746-5900; Fax: 617-783-2423. Office Hours: Mon.-Fri. 9-5

Judicial Vicar—Rev. Msgr. MICHAEL S. FOSTER, J.C.D.

Adjutant Judicial Vicars—Revs. MARK A. MAHONEY, J.C.L.; MARK O'CONNELL.

Archdiocesan Judges—Rev. Msgrs. RICHARD G. CUNNINGHAM, J.C.D.; ROBERT P. DEELEY, V.F., J.C.D.; MICHAEL S. FOSTER, J.C.D.; PAUL B. MCINERNY, J.C.L.; Revs. JAMES G. BURKE, J.C.L.; RODNEY J. COPP, J.C.L.; JOSEPH M. HENNESSEY, J.C.L.; JAMES J. LAUGHLIN, J.C.L.; MARK A. MAHONEY, J.C.L.; JAMES A. O'DONOHOE, J.C.D. (Retired); AIDAN J. WALSH, J.C.L.; Mr. ALEJANDRO ALVAREZ CAMPOS, J.C.D. (Cand.), J.D.; Ms. MARIA GALINDEZ DE BIANCO, J.C.L., J.D.; Ms. AMY JILL STRICKLAND, J.C.D. (Cand.); Sr. MARGARET L. SULLIVAN, C.S.J., J.C.L.

Defenders of the Bond—Rev. JAMES G. BURKE, J.C.L.; Mr. EMMETT G. WELLS, J.C.L., J.D.

Court Advocate—Rev. PETER G. GORI, O.S.A., J.C.D.

Court Guardian for Children— Consult the Tribunal Office.

Director of Case Administration—Ms. MARY-KATE TRACY, M.Div. (Cand.).

Court Staff Administrator—Ms. NANCY T. GAUDETTE, M.A.

Court Staff—Ms. ELIZABETH BALL; BRENDA FINCH; ELLEN OBSHATKIN; ANN MEDEIROS; MARSHA STAEN.

Court Experts for Languages—Revs. JOHN HOGAN, O.F.M., (French); CARMEL F. MIOTKE, O.F.M., (French, Italian, Spanish); GERALD MUDD, O.F.M., (Portuguese); BRIAN E. SMAIL, O.F.M., (French, Spanish); DAC TRAN, O.F.M., (Vietnamese).

Promoter of Justice—Rev. Msgr. RICHARD G. CUNNINGHAM, J.C.D.

Judge Auditor—Rev. JAMES W. DEADDER, S.T.D., Ph.D., J.D. (Retired).

Psychological Consultants— Family Counseling & Guidance Centers, Inc., Rev. THOMAS F. NESTOR, Ph.D.; NEIL J. CRONIN, L.I.C.S.W.; JOSEPH DOHERTY, Ed.D.; LEO FAHEY, L.I.C.S.W.; MARGARET L. HAGER, L.I.C.S.W.; THOMAS F. HIGGINS, Ed.D.; CHARLES H. HOGAN, Psy.D.; FRANCIS J. KELLY, L.I.C.S.W., M.S.W.; THOMAS H. KELLEY, Ph.D.; JOSEPH LIFTIK, Ph.D.; KERNAN T. MANION, M.D.; PAUL MCCORMICK, M.Div., Ph.D.; PATRICIA MORAN; A. EUGENE NEWMAN, Ph.D.; HELEN O'MEARA, L.I.C.S.W.; CLAIRE O'ROURKE, L.I.C.S.W.; DANIEL J. QUINN, L.I.C.S.W.; SYLVIA SACCHETTI, M.Ed.; MICHAEL ST. CLAIR, M.A., Ph.D.

Ecclesiastical Notaries—Ms. NANCY T. GAUDETTE, M.A.; MARSH STATEN.

Canonical Affairs Committee—Rev. Msgr. MICHAEL S. FOSTER, J.C.D., Chm.; Most Rev. RICHARD G. LENNON; Rev. Msgrs. ROBERT P. DEELEY, V.F., J.C.D.; PAUL B. MCINERNY, J.C.L.; Revs. JAMES G. BURKE, J.C.L.; RODNEY J. COPP, J.C.L.; JAMES M. DIPERRI, M.A., M.Div., J.C.L.; PETER G. GORI, O.S.A., J.C.D.; JAMES J. LAUGHLIN, J.C.L.; MARK A. MAHONEY, J.C.L.; MARK O'CONNELL; JAMES A.

O'DONOHUE, J.C.D.; Sr. MARGARET L. SULLIVAN, C.S.J., J.C.L.; Ms. MARIA GALINDEZ DE BIANCO, J.C.L., J.D.; Ms. AMY JILL STRICKLAND, J.C.D. (Cand.); Mr. ALEJANDRO ALVAREZ CAMPOS, J.C.D. (Cand.), J.D.; Mr. EMMETT G. WELLS, J.C.L., J.D.

Seminaries—

Blessed John XXIII National Seminary—Rev. Msgr. FRANCIS D. KELLY, S.T.L., Ph.D., Rector, 558 South St., Weston, 02493-2699. Tel: 781-899-5500; Fax: 781-899-9057.

St. John Seminary—Rev. JOHN A. FARREN, O.P., Rector, Lake St., Boston, 02135-3898. Tel: 617-254-2610; Fax: 617-787-2336.

Continuing Education and Spiritual Enrichment of Priests—Rev. JAMES P. MAHONEY, 5 Lake St., Boston, 02135-3899. Tel: 617-746-5415; Fax: 617-746-6498.

Central Services

Central Services—DAVID W. SMITH, Cabinet Sec., 2121 Commonwealth Ave., Boston, 02135-3193. Tel: 617-746-5680; Fax: 617-783-4564.

Cemeteries—Mr. ROB VISCONTI, Dir., 1175 Broadway, Malden, 02148-6097. Tel: 888-919-7926; Fax: 781-322-3801.

Planning Office for Urban Affairs—Ms. LISA ALBERGHINI, Dir., 185 Devonshire St., Boston, 02110-1407. Tel: 617-350-8885; Fax: 617-350-8889.

Volunteer Resources—Mrs. ANN LALLY, 2121 Commonwealth Ave., Boston, 02135-3193. Tel: 617-254-0100; Fax: 617-783-4564.

Child Advocacy, Implementation and Oversight—Deacon ANTHONY RIZZUTO, Cabinet Sec., 2121 Commonwealth Ave., Boston, 02315-3193. Tel: 617-746-5994; Fax: 617-783-0966. Web: www.rcab.org/childadvocacy/homepage.html.

Communications

Communications—Rev. Msgr. PAUL B. MCINERNY, J.C.L., Cabinet Sec., 55 Chapel St., Box 9109, Newton, 02460-9109. Tel: 617-965-0050; Fax: 617-965-6587.

Boston Catholic Directory—Rev. ROBERT M. O'GRADY, 2121 Commonwealth Ave., Boston, 02135-3193. Tel: 617-746-5873; Fax: 617-783-3904. Email: rmogrady@bostonpilot.org.

The Pilot—ANTONIO ENRIQUE, Editor, 2121 Commonwealth Ave., Boston, 02135-3193. Tel: 617-746-5895; Fax: 617-783-2684. Email: aerique@bostonpilot.org.

Radio Apostolate—Rev. ROBERT P. REED, Holy Ghost Parish, 518 Washington St., Whitman, 02382. Tel: 781-447-4421; Fax: 781-447-1375.

TV Apostolate—Rev. Msgr. PAUL B. MCINERNY, J.C.L., 55 Chapel St., P.O. Box 9109, Newton, 02460-9109. Tel: 617-965-0050; Fax: 617-965-6587.

Boston Catholic Television Center, Inc.—55 Chapel St., P.O. Box 9109, Newton, 02460-9109. Tel: 617-965-0050; Fax: 617-965-6587.

Education

Education—Sr. CLARE BERTERO, O.S.F., Cabinet Sec., One Lake St., Boston, 02135-3800. Tel: 617-746-5855; Fax: 617-782-0213.

Campus Ministry—Rev. RICHARD J. CLANCY, Dir., One Lake St., Boston, 02135-3800. Tel: 617-266-2635; Fax: 617-266-6148.

Catholic School Office—Sr. KATHLEEN CARR, C.S.J., Supt. Schools, 2200 Dorchester Ave., Boston, 02124-5607. Tel: 617-298-6555; Fax: 617-298-6622.

Ecumenical and Interreligious Affairs—Rev. EDWARD M. O'FLAHERTY, S.J., Dir., 2121 Commonwealth Ave., Boston, 02135-3193. Tel: 617-254-0100; Fax: 617-562-1104.

Religious Education—Sr. CLARE BERTERO, O.S.F., Dir., One Lake St., Boston, 02135-3800. Tel: 617-779-3625; Fax: 617-782-0213.

Liaison for Catholic-Jewish Relations—Rev. DAVID C. MICHAEL, St. Joseph Rectory, 345 Waverly St., Belmont, 02478-2418. Tel: 617-484-0279; Fax: 617-489-5445.

Social Justice—Rev. WILLIAM P. JOY, Dir., St. Angela Merici Parish, 1548 Blue Hill Ave., Boston, 02126-2187. Tel: 617-298-0080; Fax: 617-298-2388.

Health Care Services

Caritas Christi Health Care System—Mr. MICHAEL F. COLLINS, M.D., Pres., CEO & Cabinet Sec., 736 Cambridge St., Boston, 02135-2997. Tel: 617-789-2500; Fax: 617-789-2124 Caritas Carney Hospital, Boston; Caritas Christi Support Services, Inc., Boston; Caritas Good Samaritan Medical Center, Inc., Brockton; Caritas Holy Family Hospital Foundation, Inc., Methuen; Caritas Holy Family Hospital, Inc., Methuen; Caritas Norwood Hospital, Norwood; Caritas Southwood Hospital, Norfolk; Caritas St. Elizabeth Medical Center, Boston; Good Samaritan Hospice, Inc., Boston and Norwood; Metropolitan Boston Dialysis Center, Waltham; St. John of God Hospital, Boston; Valley Regional Health System, Inc., Methuen; Valley Regional Support Services, Inc., Methuen.

Archdiocesan Liaison with all other Catholic Hospitals in the Archdiocese— Bethany Hospital, Framingham; Franciscan Children's Hospital & Rehabilitation Center, Boston; Saints Memorial Medical Center, Inc., Lowell; Sancta Maria Hospital, Cambridge; Youville Hospital, Cambridge

Council of Nurses—ANNETTA L. ROMANO, R.N., Pres., 9 Nancia St., Boston, 02128-1261. Tel: 617-569-1726.

Guild of St. Luke—GERALD P. CORCORAN, M.D., 87 Chestnut St., Needham, 02492-2514. Tel: 781-444-5515; Fax: 781-444-1866.

Por Cristo—JOSEPH A. REARDON, Exec. Dir., 736 Cambridge St., Boston, 02135-2997. Tel: 617-562-7925; Fax: 617-562-7928.

Institutional Advancement

Institutional Advancement—KENNETH J. HOKENSON, Cabinet Sec., 2121 Commonwealth Ave., Boston, 02135-3193. Tel: 617-746-5632; Fax: 617-783-6366.

The Catholic Foundation—KENNETH J. HOKENSON, Exec. Dir., 2121 Commonwealth Ave., Boston, 02135-3193. Tel: 617-746-5632; Fax: 617-783-6366.

Ministerial Personnel

Ministerial Personnel—Rev. ROBERT L. CONNORS, Cabinet Sec., 2121 Commonwealth Ave., Boston, 02135-3193. Tel: 617-746-5750; Fax: 617-783-2947. Email: reverendrobertconnors@rcab.org.

Archdiocesan Institute for Ministry—WILLIAM DITTRICH, Interim Dir.; BARBARA RICHARDS, Registrar, One Lake St., Boston, 02135-3800. Tel: 617-746-5416; Fax: 617-254-8407. Email: barbararichards@rcab.org.

Clergy Personnel—Rev. RICHARD W. FITZGERALD, 2121 Commonwealth Ave., Boston, 02135-3193. Tel: 617-779-3685; Fax: 617-746-5754. Email: reverendrichardfitzgerald@rcab.org.

Delegate for Religious—Sr. MARIAN BATHO, C.S.J., 2121 Commonwealth Ave., Boston, 02135-3193. Tel: 617-746-5637; Fax: 617-783-5754. Email: sistermarianbatho@rcab.org.

Pastoral Ministries—Sr. DOROTHEA MASURET, C.S.J., One Lake St., Boston, 02135-3800. Tel: 617-779-3690; Fax: 617-254-8407. Email: sisterdorotheamasuret@rcab.org.

Pastoral Support for Priests—Rev. EDWARD M. O'FLAHERTY, S.J., 5 Lake St., Boston, 02135-3899. Tel: 617-746-5416; Fax: 617-746-5498. Email: reverend_edward-oflaherty@rcab.org.

Permanent Diaconate—Deacon LEO J. DONOGHUE, Dir., 2121 Commonwealth Ave., Boston, 02135-3193. Tel: 617-746-5648; Fax: 617-746-5699. Email: bosdiaconate@msn.com.

Priests Recovery Program—Rev. BRIAN M. CLARY, Interim Dir., 2121 Commonwealth Ave., Boston, 02135-3193. Tel: 617-746-5925; Fax: 617-782-9183. Email: frbrian2002@yahoo.com.

Regina Cleri, Inc.—Rev. Msgr. JAMES E. TIERNEY, 60 William Cardinal O'Connell Way, Boston, 02114. Tel: 617-523-1861; Fax: 617-720-0585. Email: jtierney@reginacleri.org.

Senior Priests—Rev. JAMES L. MCCUNE, Dir., Regina Cleri, 60 William Cardinal O'Connell Way, Boston, 02114. Tel: 617-723-3976; Fax: 617-523-0092. Email: nkowlton@reginacleri.org.

Society of St. James the Apostle—Rev. ROBERT F. THOMAS, Dir., 24 Clark St., Boston, 02109-1127. Tel: 617-742-4715; Fax: 617-723-7389.

Vocation Office—Rev. OSCAR J. PRATT, 127 Lake St., Boston, 02135-3898. Tel: 617-746-5436; Fax: 617-746-5468. Email: rcabvoc@aol.com.

Boards and Members

Clergy Fund Advisory Board—Most Rev. RICHARD G. LENNON, Sec. Members: Revs. Msgrs. WILLIAM M. HELMICK; FREDERICK J. MURPHY; Revs. JOHN E. MACINNIS; BRIAN F. MCMAHON; EUGENE P. SULLIVAN; WILLIAM C. BURCKHART (Retired); MARK O'CONNELL, Facilitator; ROBERT L. CONNORS, Auditor.

Clergy Personnel Board—Ex Officio: Most Rev. RICHARD G. LENNON; Revs. RICHARD W. FITZGERALD; ROBERT L. CONNORS; ROBERT G. MCMILLAN, S.J. Designated: Rev. BRIAN R. KILEY; Very Rev. MARK S. SHEEHAN, V.F. Selected: Revs. GEORGE F. EMERSON, Block I (Retired); TIMOTHY J. SHEA, Block II; BRIAN M. FLATLEY, Block III; ROBERT F. HENNESSEY, Block IV; KEVIN M. SEPE, Block V; KEVIN J. O'LEARY, Block VI.

Priestly Renewal Advisory Board—Rev. ROBERT L. CONNORS, Chm. Members: Revs. RICHARD W. FITZGERALD; ARTHUR M. COYLE; EDWARD M. O'FLAHERTY, S.J.

Pastoral Services

Pastoral Services—Rev. ARTHUR M. COYLE, Cabinet Sec., 2121 Commonwealth Ave., Boston, 02135-3193. Tel: 617-746-5770; Fax: 617-746-5754. Email: reverend_arthur_coyle@rcab.org.

Airport Chaplaincy—Rev. RICHARD J. UFTRING, Chap., Our Lady of the Airways Chapel, Logan International Airport, Boston, 02128. Tel: 617-567-2800; Fax: 617-569-6950.

Black Catholics—Ms. CHARLENE ROBERTS-HAYDEN, Interim Dir., 2121 Commonwealth Ave., Boston, 02135-3193. Tel: 617-746-5810; Fax: 617-746-5614.

Charismatic Renewal—Mr. DAVID THORP, Liaison, 30 Pond St., Waltham, 02451-4514. Tel: 781-891-3592; Fax: 781-891-3599.

Courage—Spiritual Directors:: Rev. Msgrs. LEONARD A. COPPENRATH; PAUL J. MCMANUS (Retired), 1573 Cambridge St., Cambridge, 02138-4398. Tel: 617-491-1297.

Cursillo—Rev. JOHN A. SASSANI, Spiritual Dir.; Mrs. MARY ANN MCLAUGHLIN, Lay Dir., 2121 Commonwealth Ave., Boston, 02135-3193. Tel: 617-779-3640; Fax: 617-254-6469.

Deaf Apostolate—Rev. MICHAEL J. MEDAS, 2121 Commonwealth Ave., Boston, 02135-3193. Tel: 617-746-5645; Fax: 617-746-5614. Email: frmichaelmedas@deafcatholic.org.

EnCourage—Rev. ALBERT A. SYLVIA, Spiritual Dir., 35 Newcastle Rd., Peabody, 01960-3627. Tel: 978-532-0272; Fax: 978-977-2991.

Ethnic Apostolates—Sisters NANCY CHARLESWORTH, S.S.M.M., Dir., Email: sister_nancy_charlesworth@rcab.org; MARY CORRIPIO, S.N.D., Assoc. Dir., 2121 Commonwealth Ave., Boston, 02135-3193. Tel: 617-746-5805; Fax: 617-746-5614. Email: mcorripio@rcab.org.

Apostolates—Brazilian, Rev. ANTONIO CARVALHO, C.S. Tel: 617-387-1393. *Cambodian*, Rev. ANTHONY GIANG NGUYEN. Tel: 617-889-2774; Deacon PETER AN ROS. Tel: 978-459-0561. *Cape Verdean, Capuchin Fathers*. Tel: 617-541-0462. Mr. JOHN BARROS. Tel: 617-442-9670. *Chinese*, Mr. PETER CHAN. Tel: 781-438-4772. *Filipino*, Rev. ERIC GENILO, S.J. Tel: 617-547-1086. *French, Office for Ethnic Apostolates*. Tel: 617-746-5805. *German*, Very Rev. HUGH H. O'REGAN, V.F. Tel: 617-426-6142. *Haitian*, Rev. GABRIEL MICHEL. Tel: 617-298-0080. *Hmong*, Mr. TER YANG. Tel: 508-583-7202. *Irish*, Rev. DANIEL J. FINN. Tel: 617-825-2852. *Italian, Office for Ethnic Apostolate*. Tel: 617-746-5805. *Korean*, Rev. SEUNG J. PARK. Tel: 617-244-9685. *Laotion*, Ms. PAULE VERDET. Tel: 617-965-2499. *Lithuanian*, Rev. STEPHAN ZUKAS. Tel: 617-268-0353. *Nigerian*, Rev. ANTHONY NGWUMOHAIKE. Tel: 617-442-4664. *Polish*, Rev. Msgr. STANISLAUS SYPEK. Tel: 617-361-0565. *Portuguese*, Mr. VICTOR MELO. Tel: 978-452-8751. *Vietnamese*, Mr. NGUYEN QUAN. Tel: 781-321-0228.

Communities—African, Congolese, Rev. HONORE KOMBO. Tel: 617-244-8960. *Eritrean*, Mrs. HIWET HUILESLUSSIE. Tel: 617-445-2044. *Ethiopian*, Mr. BESUFEDAD NEGEWO. Tel: 617-294-0471. *Ghanaian*, Dr. KWASI SARKODI-MENSAH. Tel: 617-552-4465. *Kenyan, Office for Ethnic Apostolates*. Tel: 617-746-5805. *Liberian, Office for Ethnic Apostolates*. Tel: 617-746-5805. *Rwandese*, Rev. BASILE BAZINA. Tel: 781-229-6884. *Ugandese*, Dr. ALOYSIUS LUGIRA; Mrs. AGNES LUGIRA. Tel: 781-937-3954. *Asian, Indian*, Mr. BRIAN SANTHUMAYOR. Tel: 781-482-3779. *Indonesian*, Mr. ANDREAS YULLIANNO. Tel: 857-891-6542. *Japanese*, Sr. FEDRE TANNO, P.D.D.M. Tel: 617-423-2629. *European, Croatian*, JOYCE GALANTIC. Tel: 617-484-2619.

Centers—

Brazilian Community Centers—Rev. JOSE MARIO RIBEIRO, Allston. Tel: 617-783-2121; Deacon MANUEL SOUZA, Framingham. Tel: 508-872-2781; Revs. PEDRO DAMAZIO, Lowell. Tel: 978-934-0622; JOSE G. FLORES, Marlborough. Tel: 508-480-8810; MOACIR BALEN, C.S., Somerville. Tel: 617-625-0288; FELIX I. FILHO, Stoughton. Tel: 781-341-3138.

Chinese Pastoral Center—Sr. MADELINE GALLAGHER, M.N.S.H., 78 Tyler St., Boston, 02111-1831. Tel: 617-482-2949; Fax: 617-482-2949.

Holy Union Multicultural Center—Sr. CHRISTINE LACROIX, S.U.S.C., 142 Chestnut St., Lowell, 01852-2429. Tel: 978-458-2061; Fax: 978-459-0823.

Irish Pastoral Center—Sr. VERONICA DOBSON, C.S.B., 953 Hancock St., Quincy, 02170-2322. Tel: 617-479-7404; Fax: 617-479-0541. Email: ipcboston@yahoo.com.

Saint Elizabeth Ann Seton Center—Sr. ELANA KILLILEA, S.C., One Ballard Way, Lawrence, 01843. Tel: 978-683-7316; Fax: 978-683-9075. Email: elanakilli@att.net.

Saint Julie Asian Center—Sr. JANET DEAETT, S.N.D., 236 Westford St., Lowell, 01851-2524. Tel: 978-454-7663; Fax: 978-454-7663.

Saint Patrick Asian Center—Mrs. ENGLY PEOU, 12 Orchard St., Lynn, 01905. Tel: 781-599-7750; Fax: 781-599-2201.

Family Life Office—Ms. JOANNE CURRY, Dir.

Marriage Ministries—Ms. KARI COLLELA.
Natural Family Planning—Ms. MARY FINNIGAN.
Young Adult Ministry—Ms. MARYANN POTTANT, 2121 Commonwealth Ave., Boston, 02135-3193. Tel: 617-746-5800; Fax: 617-783-5642.
Health Care Ministry—Ms. JEAN MARCHANT, St. Elizabeth Medical Center, 736 Cambridge St., Boston, 02135-2997. Tel: 617-789-2456; Fax: 617-789-2573. Email: jean_marchant@cchcs.org.
Hispanic Apostolate—Mrs. ANA MARIA PIATTI, Dir., 2121 Commonwealth Ave., Boston, 02135-3193. Tel: 617-746-5806; Fax: 617-746-5614. Email: ana_maria_piatti@rcab.org.
Holy Name Society—Rev. JOHN MCLAUGHLIN (Retired), 25 Arlington St., Somerville, 02145-3342. Tel: 617-625-0029; Fax: 617-666-5944.
Juvenile Court Chaplain—Rev. JAMES F. FRATUS, 15 Rita Rd., Boston, 02124. Tel: 617-436-0310; Fax: 617-436-1386.
League of Catholic Women—Rev. MARTIN J. CONNOR, Spiritual Dir., St. John Seminary, 127 Lake St., Boston, 02135-3898. Tel: 617-254-2610; Fax: 617-783-2336.
Legion of Mary—Rev. JOHN KILMARTIN, F.D.P., Spiritual Dir., 59 Ashley St., Boston, 02128. Tel: 617-569-0406; Fax: 617-569-8212.
Marian Devotions—Rev. WILLIAM R. CARROLL, 24 Medford St., Arlington, 02174-3197. Tel: 781-648-0220; Fax: 781-643-8955.
Persons with Disabilities—Ms. KAREN MURRAY, Dir., 2121 Commonwealth Ave., Boston, 02135-3193. Tel: 617-746-5679; Fax: 617-746-5646. Email: karen_murray@rcab.org.
Pilgrimages—Rev. WALTER H. CUENIN, Coord., 573 Washington St., Newton, 02158-1494. Tel: 617-527-7560; Fax: 617-527-1338.
Prison Ministry—Deacon WILLIAM F. KANE, Dir., 2121 Commonwealth Ave., Boston, 02135-3193. Tel: 617-746-5612; Fax: 617-746-5754.
Seaport of Boston— Waterfront Chapel, Rev. PHILIP LAPLANTE, S.M., 27 Isabella St., Boston, 02116-5262. Tel: 617-426-4448; Fax 617-482-1570.
Spiritual Development—Rev. JOHN E. SASSANI, 2121 Commonwealth Ave., Boston, 02135-3193. Tel: 617-799-3640; Fax: 617-254-6469 Email: spiritual_development@rcab.org.
Worship—Rev. BRIAN E. MAHONEY, 2121 Commonwealth Ave., Boston, 02135-3193. Tel: 617-746-5880; Fax: 617-746-5754.
Youth Ministry—Rev. THOMAS A. DUNNE, S.D.B., 139 Crescent St., Quincy, 02169-4040. Tel: 617-472-0333; Fax: 617-479-6298.
Public Relations—Rev. CHRISTOPHER J. COYNE, S.L.D., Cabinet Sec., 2121 Commonwealth Ave., Boston, 02135-3193. Tel: 617-746-5775; Fax: 617-782-9416.
Campaign for Human Development—Rev. WILLIAM F. JOY, St. Angela Parish, 1548 Blue Hill Ave., Boston, 02126-2187. Tel: 617-298-0080; Fax: 617-298-2388.
Labor Guild—Rev. EDWARD F. BOYLE, S.J., Dir., 883 Hancock St., Quincy, 02170-3860. Tel: 617-786-1822; Fax: 617-472-2486.
Massachusetts Catholic Conference—GERALD D'AVOLIO Exec. Dir., West End Place, 150 Staniford St., Boston, 02114-2511. Tel: 617-367-6060; Fax: 617-367-2767.

Social Services

Social Services—Rev. J. BRYAN HEHIR, Cabinet Sec., 75 Kneeland St., Eighth Fl., Boston, 02111-1431. Tel: 617-482-5440; Fax: 617-451-0337.
Catholic Social Services, Inc.—Rev. J. BRYAN HEHIR, Pres., 75 Kneeland St., Eighth Fl., Boston, 02111-1431. Tel: 617-482-5440; Fax: 617-451-0337.
Catholic Charitable Bureau of the Archdiocese of Boston, Inc.—Rev. J. BRYAN HEHIR, Pres., 75 Kneeland St., Eighth Fl., Boston, 02111-1431. Tel: 617-482-5440; Fax: 617-451-0337. Web: www.ccab.org.
Catholic Charities Brockton—SANDRA WITTED, Dir.
Catholic Charities Greater Boston - Somerville—VIVIAN SOPER, Dir.
Catholic Charities Merrimack Valley - Lowell, Lawrence—PATRICIA KIRWIN, Dir.
Catholic Charities North - Lynn, Peabody, Salem—VIRGINIA DOOCY, Dir.
Catholic Charities West - Framingham—PATRICIA DUNN, Dir.
El Centro Del Cardenal - Boston—SERGIO PLAZA, Interim Dir.
Laboure Center - South Boston—Sr. MARYADELE ROBINSON, D.C., Dir.
Haitian Multi-Service Center - Dorchester—PIERRE IMBERT, Dir.
Catholic Charities Behavioral Health Division - Brockton—VACANT, Dir.
Catholic Charities Child Care Division - Jamaica Plain—MARY ANN ANTHONY, Dir.
Catholic Charities Parish Social Ministries Division - Framingham & Franklin—PATRICIA DUNN, Dir.
Life Resources—WILLIAM CHIARADONNA, Pres., 5 Beale St., Quincy, 02170. Tel: 617-745-4114; Fax: 617-745-4196. Web: www.liferesourcesinc.org.
Nazareth—75 Kneeland St., Eighth Fl., Boston, 02111-1431. Tel: 617-482-5440; Fax: 617-451-0337.
Pro-Life Activities—MARIANNE LUTHIN, Dir., 159 Washington St., Boston, 02135. Tel: 617-783-5410; Fax: 617-787-7797. Email: prolifebos@aol.com.
St. Ann Home, Inc.—DENIS GRANDBOIS, Pres., 100-A Haverhill St., Methuen, 01844-4297. Tel: 978-682-5276; Fax: 978-688-4932. Web: www.stannshome.org.
Society of St. Vincent de Paul—PAUL MACNEIL, Dir., 1524 VFW Pkwy., Boston, 02132. Tel: 617-325-0124; Fax: 617-325-3075. Web: www.svdpboston.com.
Victim Assistance Coordinator—BARBARA THORP. Tel: 617-244-9603. Email: barbara_thorp@pastoralsupportandoutreach.com.

CLERGY, PARISHES, MISSIONS AND PAROCHIAL SCHOOLS

BOSTON
(SUFFOLK COUNTY)

1—CATHEDRAL OF THE HOLY CROSS (1788), Rev. Msgr. Frederick J. Murphy, Rector; Rev. Robert J Carr; Sr. Celeste Burgos, M.H.S.H., Pastoral Assoc.; Deacon Luis R. Casillas. In Res., Most Rev. Sean P. O'Malley, O.F.M.Cap.; Rev. Msgr. William H. Roche (Retired); Rev. Felix C. Ojimba (Nigeria).
Res.: 75 Union Park St., 02118. Tel: 617-542-5682; Fax: 617-542-5926.
School—Cathedral School, 595 Harrison Ave., 02118. Tel: 617-422-0042. Sisters 3; Lay Teachers 7; Students 191.

2—ST. ADALBERT (1913), (Polish), Rev. Msgr. Stanislaus T. Sypek.
Res.: 1450 River St., Hyde Park, 02136-2150. Tel: 617-361-0565; Fax: 617-361-7788.

3—ALL SAINTS (1894), Closed., For inquiries for parochial records contact St. Patrick, Roxbury.

4—ST. AMBROSE (1914), Rev. Vincent P. Von Euw; Sr. Mary Damien Powers, O.S.M., Pastoral Assoc.; Deacon Marcio O. Fonseca.
Res.: 240 Adams St., Dorchester, 02122-1380. Tel: 617-265-5302; Fax: 617-265-0886.
School—23 Leonard St., Dorchester, 02122. Tel: 617-825-9400. Sisters 5; Lay Teachers 9; Students 250.

5—ST. ANDREW (1918), Closed., For inquiries for parish records please see Sacred Heart Roslindale.

6—ST. ANGELA MERICI (1907), Revs. William P. Joy; Gabriel Michel (Haiti); Sr. Paula Coelho, S.U.S.C., Pastoral Assoc.
Res.: 1548 Blue Hill Ave., Mattapan, 02126. Tel: 617-298-0080; Fax: 617-298-2388.
School—120 Babson St., Mattapan, 02126. Tel: 617-296-1161. Lay Teachers 7; Students 222.

7—ST. ANN (1889), Revs. Walter F. Keymont; Thomas B. Corcoran; Deacon James B. Little.
Res.: 243 Neponset Ave., Dorchester, 02122-3239. Tel: 617-825-6180; Fax: 617-825-7869. Email: WallySaintAnn@aol.com.
School—239 Neponset Ave., Dorchester, 02122. Tel: 617-825-6262. Religious 5; Lay Teachers 12; Students 328.

8—ST. ANN (1945), Rev. John J. Unni; Elizabeth Chichak, Pastoral Assoc.; Hai Ok Hwang, Pastoral Assoc.
68 St. Stephen St., 02115. Tel: 617-266-2635; Fax: 617-266-9015. Email: stannparish@hotmail.com. Web: www.SaintAnnUniversityParish.org.

9—ST. ANNE (1919), Rev. William F. Joyce.
Res.: 79 W. Milton St., Readville, 02136-1929. Tel: 617-361-3443; Fax: 617-361-6690.
School—20 Como Rd., Readville, 02136. Tel: 617-361-3569. Lay Teachers 11; Students 225; Religious 1.

10—ST. ANTHONY (1896), Revs. Daniel P. Hegarty; Charles J. Higgins, Admin.
Res.: 43 Holton St., Allston, 02134-1397. Tel: 617-782-0775; Fax: 617-782-2008.
School—57 Holton St., Allston, 02134-1397. Tel: 617-782-7170. Lay Teachers 8; Students 119.

11—ST. AUGUSTINE (1868), Rev. Msgr. Thomas J. McDonnell; Rev. Donald S. Abbott.
Res.: 9 F St., South Boston, 02127-2898. Tel: 617-268-1230; Fax: 617-269-3831.
School—Tel: 617-269-2233. Sisters 2; Lay Teachers 9; Students 249.

12—BLESSED SACRAMENT (1891), Rev. Michael F. McLellan; Deacon Luciano Herrera.
Res.: 365 Centre St., Jamaica Plain, 02130-1240. Tel: 617-522-0650; Fax: 617-983-1407. Email: blsacjp@aol.com.
School—30 Sunnyside St., Jamaica Plain, 02130. Tel: 617-522-1870. Sisters 2; Lay Teachers 7; Students 198.
Catechesis/Religious Program—Jose Perez, D.R.E.; Awilda Perez, D.R.E. Students 210.

13—ST. BRENDAN (1929), Revs. James F. Fratus; Clifton M. Thuma.
Res.: 15 Rita Rd., Dorchester, 02124-5321. Tel: 617-436-0310; Fax: 617-436-1386.
School—29 Rita Rd., Dorchester, 02124-5321. Tel: 617-282-3388. Sisters 2; Lay Teachers 9; Students 245.
Catechesis/Religious Program—Tel: 617-825-8622. Jean Curley, D.R.E. Students 126.

14—ST. BRIGID (1908), Revs. Robert E. Casey; Daniel F. Hennessey. In Res., Revs. Daniel J. Sheehan (Retired); Richard F. Clancy; Sean M. Connor.
Res.: 841 E. Broadway, South Boston 02127-2302. Tel: 617-268-2122; Fax: 617-268-2666. Email: FrRobCasey@aol.com. Web: www.StBrigidSouthBoston.org.
School—866 E. Broadway, South Boston, 02127-2302. Tel: 617-268-2326. Sisters 2; Lay Teachers 7; Students 275.

15—ST. CATHERINE OF SIENA (1887), Rev. Robert J. Bowers.
Res.: 49 Vine St., Charlestown, 02129 Tel: 617-242-1750; Fax: 617-242-1899 Email: www.stcatherineparish.org.
School—Tel: 617-242-0169. Lay Teachers 8; Students 161.

16—ST. CECILIA (1888), Rev. Msgr. Michael F. Groden; Mr. Mark Donohoe, Pastoral Assoc. In Res., Revs. Pascal Begerimina; Romaine Rurangirwa.
Res.: 30 St. Cecilia St., 02115-3132. Tel: 617-536-4548; Fax: 617-536-1781. Email: www.rc.net/boston/stcecilia.
Catechesis/Religious Program—Scott MacDonald, D.R.E. Students 50.

17—ST. CHRISTOPHER (1956), Rev. George A. Carrigg, Admin.; Mary Fox, Pastoral Assoc.
Res.: 263 Mt. Vernon St., Dorchester, 02125-3182. Tel: 617-436-7273; Fax: 617-436-7273.

18—ST. COLUMBKILLE (1871), Revs. Richard J. Shmaruk; James J. O'Rourke; Deacon Eddy M. Montes. In Res., Rev. Carney E. Gavin.
Res.: 321 Market St., Brighton, 02135-2199. Tel: 617-782-5774; Fax: 617-782-7283.
School—25 Arlington St., Brighton, 02135-2199. Tel: 617-254-3110. Sisters 2; Lay Teachers 6; Students 200.

19—ST. FRANCIS DE SALES (1859), Rev. Daniel J. Mahoney. In Res., Revs. William J. McConnell (Retired); Celestino V. Pascual (Philippines).
Res.: 303 Bunker Hill St., Charlestown, 02129-1826. Tel: 617-242-0147; Fax: 617-242-3026. Email: stfran303@aol.com.

20—ST. FRANCIS DE SALES-ST. PHILIP (1867), Rev. Thomas F. Clark, S.J.; Sr. Mary Hart, R.G.S., Pastoral Assoc.; Mr. James Atkins, Pastoral Assoc.; Mr. Tipp Harris, Pastoral Assoc. In Res., Rev. Robert G. McMillan, S.J.
Res.: One Warwick St., Roxbury, 02120-2415. Tel: 617-445-8915; Fax: 617-445-6522.

21—ST. GABRIEL (1934), Rev. Justinian Manning, C.P. In Res., Revs. Brendan Breen, C.P.; Roger Gannon, C.P.; Bernardine Grande, C.P.
Res.: 139 Washington St., Brighton, 02135-4325. Tel: 617-254-6582; Fax: 617-783-1766.
Catechesis/Religious Program—Tel: 617-782-8683. Sr. Margaret T. Sullivan, O.S.F., D.R.E. Students 15.

22—GATE OF HEAVEN (1862), Revs. Robert E. Casey, Admin.; A. Paul White; Brian L. Flynn; Deacon Richard C. Martin. In Res., Rev. Richard A. Uftring.
Res.: 606 E. 4th St., South Boston, 02127-3092. Tel: 617-268-3344; Fax: 617-269-4299. Email: FrBobCasey@aol.com. Web: www.GateOfHeaven.net.
School—609 E. 4th, South Boston, 02127. Tel: 617-268-8431. Sisters 3; Lay Teachers 17; Students 483.

23—ST. GREGORY (1863), Rev. Msgr. Paul T. Ryan; Revs. James M. Larner; John F. O'Donnell. In Res., Most Rev. John Patrick Boles, D.D., Ph.D.; Rev. Dominic Kearns, S.M.A.
Res.: 2223 Dorchester Ave., Dorchester, 02124-5607. Tel: 617-298-2460; Fax: 617-298-9232.
School—2214 Dorchester Ave., Dorchester, 02124.

Tel: 617-296-1210. Sisters 2; Lay Teachers 8; Students 495.

24—HOLY FAMILY (1995), Rev. Msgr. William C. Francis; Deacon Francisco Guerrios.
Mailing Address: One Lingard St., Dorchester, 02125-2732. Tel: 617-445-9553; Fax: 617-445-2417. Email: HolyFamDor@aol.com.
School—516 Columbia Rd., Dorchester, 02125. Tel: 617-825-3883.

25—HOLY NAME (1927), Rev. Msgr. George F. Carlson; Rev. Anthony V. Luongo, S.D.B.; Deacon Ricardo M. Mesa; Fran M. Hauck, Pastoral Assoc. In Res., Rev. Oscar J. Pratt.
Res.: 1689 Centre St., West Roxbury, 02132-1292. Tel: 617-325-4865; Fax: 617-325-5571.
School—525 W. Roxbury Pkwy., West Roxbury, 02132. Tel: 617-325-9338. Sisters 10; Lay Teachers 19; Students 639.

26—HOLY TRINITY (1844), (German), Very Rev. Hugh H. O'Regan, V.F., Admin.
Res.: 140 Shawmut Ave., 02118-2227. Tel: 617-426-6142; Fax: 617-426-5409.

27—ST. JAMES THE GREATER (1854), Very Rev. Hugh H. O'Regan, V.F. In Res., Rev. Joseph J. Baggetta.
Res. and Parish: 135 Harrison Ave., 02111. Tel: 617-542-8498; Fax: 617-542-2708.

28—ST. JOHN BAPTIST (1921), (Portuguese), Closed., For inquiries for sacramental records contact Sacred Heart, East Boston.

29—ST. JOHN CHRYSOSTOM (1952), Rev. Paul A. Phinn; Sr. Maureen Taaffe, S.C.N., Pastoral Assoc.
Res.: 4740 Washington St., West Roxbury, 02132-2199. Tel: 617-323-4410; Fax: 617-323-0423.

30—ST. JOHN-ST. HUGH (1901), Rev. Russell W. Best; Deacon John W. McHugh.
Church: 517 Blue Hill Ave., Roxbury, 02121.
Res.: 26 Lawrence Ave., Dorchester, 02121. Tel: 617-442-1431; Fax: 617-442-2965. Email: stjohnssthughs@aol.com.

31—ST. JOSEPH (1845), Closed., For inquiries for parish records, please contact St. Patrick, Roxbury.

32—ST. JOSEPH (1862), Closed., For inquiries for parish records, please contact St. Patrick, Roxbury.

33—ST. JOSEPH (1938), Rev. William P. Joy, Admin.
Res.: 21 Chapel Rd., Hyde Park, 02136. Tel: 617-361-1314; Fax: 617-364-7129.

34—ST. JOSEPH-ST. LAZARUS (1892), Revs. John Kilmartin, F.D.P.; Miroslaw Kowalczyk, F.D.P.
Res.: 59 Ashley St., East Boston, 02128. Tel: 617-569-0406; Fax: 617-569-8212.

35—ST. KEVIN (1945), Closed., For inquiries for parish records, please contact Holy Family, Dorchester.

36—ST. LAZARUS (1892), Closed., For inquiries for parish records, please contact St. Joseph-St. Lazarus, Boston.

37—ST. LEO (1902), Closed., For inquiries for sacramental records, please contact St. Matthew, Dorchester.

38—ST. LEONARD OF PORT MAURICE (1873), (Italian), Revs. Rohwin Pais, O.F.M.; Aubert Manie Picardi, O.F.M. In Res., Revs. Dismas J. Centrella, O.F.M.; Ronald Siciliano, O.F.M.
Res.: 14 N. Bennet St., 02113-1913. Tel: 617-523-2110; Fax: 617-367-0456. Email: StLeonard@catholic-church.org. Web: www.catholic-church.org/stleonard.
Chapel—St. Mary 150 Endicott St., 02113.

39—ST. MARGARET (1893), Very Rev. Nicholas C. Ciccone, V.F.; Sr. Nancy Duffy, S.N.D., Pastoral Assoc. In Res., Revs. Raymond P. Benoit; Lazarus Anodee (Ghana).
Res.: 800 Columbia Rd., Dorchester, 02125-1710. Tel: 617-436-2190; Fax: 617-282-5428. Email: StMargaretDorchester@usa.net. Web: www.StMargaretDorchester.org.
School—790 Columbia Rd., Dorchester, 02125. Tel: 617-282-5621; Fax: 617-282-2212. Sisters of Charity 8; Lay Teachers 9; Students 316.
High School—Msgr. Ryan Memorial High School, Tel: 617-282-2818. Sisters 7; Lay Teachers 1; Girls 227.

40—ST. MARK (1905), Revs. Daniel J. Finn; Paul L. Ring.
Res.: 20 Roseland St., Dorchester, 02124. Tel: 617-825-2852; Fax: 617-825-0514.
School—197 Centre Ave., Dorchester, 02124. Tel: 617-282-2577. Sisters 7; Lay Teachers 15; Students 512.

41—ST. MARY, Closed., For inquiries for parochial records contact St. Leonard of Port Maurice, Boston.

42—ST. MARY (1828), Rev. Paul F. Coughlin.
Res.: One Monument Sq., 55 Warren St., Charlestown, 02129-3499. Tel: 617-242-4664; Fax: 617-242-0016. Email: StMaryRCC@aol.com.

43—ST. MARY OF THE ANGELS (1904), Rev. David H. Gill, S.J.; Sr. Virginia Mulhern, S.N.D. In Res., Revs. Joseph J. Bruce, S.J.; Michael D. Linden, S.J.
Res.: 377 Walnut Ave., Roxbury, 02119. Tel: 617-445-1524; Fax: 617-442-6455. Email: StMaryOfTheAngels@msn.com.
Catechesis/Religious Program—Tel: 617-524-0913. Aurea Pinto, D.R.E. Students 93.

44—ST. MARY, STAR OF THE SEA (1864), Revs. Robert R. Kennedy; Jose Benone (Brazil).
Res.: 63 Moore St., East Boston, 02128-1547. Tel: 617-567-0056; Fax: 617-569-8440.
School—58 Moore St., East Boston, 02128. Tel: 617-567-6609. Lay Teachers 10; Students 266.

45—ST. MATTHEW (1900), Revs. William P. Joy; Jean Gabriel Charles (Haiti); Jean-Michel Bolivar, Pastoral Assoc.; Immacula Bernard, Pastoral Assoc.
Res.: 33 Stanton St., Dorchester, 02124-3716. Tel: 617-436-3590; Fax: 617-287-2741.
School—29 Stanton St., Dorchester, 02124. Tel: 617-825-7955. Sisters 2; Lay Teachers 10; Students 247.

46—ST. MONICA (1907), Rev. Msgr. Thomas J. McDonnell; Rev. James H. Lane (Retired).
Res.: 9 F St., South Boston, 02127-3536. Tel: 617-268-1230; Fax: 617-269-3831.

47—MOST HOLY REDEEMER (1844), Rev. Robert F. Hennessey; Deacon Antonio M. Perea. Member Central Catholic School of East Boston.
St. Agnes Building: 65 London St., East Boston, 02128-1924. Tel: 617-567-3227; Fax: 617-569-6950.

48—MOST PRECIOUS BLOOD (1880), Rev. Peter P. Nolan, C.S.Sp.
Res.: 43 Maple St., Hyde Park, 02136-2738. Tel: 617-364-9500; Fax: 617-364-2590. Email: ppnmpb@aol.com.
School—Tel: 617-361-2162. Sisters 2; Lay Teachers 6; Students 187.

49—OUR LADY OF CZESTOCHOWA (1893), (Polish), Revs. Miroslaw Podymniak, O.F.M.Conv.; Adam Cieslik, O.F.M.Conv. In Res., Revs. Stephen Majewski, O.F.M.Conv.; Germain Kopaczynski, O.F.M.Conv.
Res.: 655 Dorchester Ave., South Boston, 02127-3551. Tel: 617-268-4355; Fax: 617-268-4599.
School—52 Boston St., South Boston, 02127. Tel: 617-268-3766. Felician Sisters 3; Lay Teachers 6; Students 202.
Convent—666 Dorchester Ave., 02127.

50—OUR LADY OF LOURDES (1908), Rev. Msgr. Charles J. Bourque, V.F.; Deacon Leonard F. De Coste. In Res., Rev. Michael F. McLellan.
Res.: 46 Brookside Ave., Jamaica Plain, 02130-2370. Tel: 617-524-0434; Fax: 617-524-1888. Email: ololjp@comcast.net. Web: www.OurLadyOfLourdesJPMA.org.
School—54 Brookside Ave., Jamaica Plain, 02130. Tel: 617-524-6136. Sisters 3; Lay Teachers 8; Students 220.

51—OUR LADY OF MT. CARMEL (1905), (Italian), Revs. Francis de Sales Paolo, O.F.M.; Kenneth Garofalo, O.F.M. Member East Boston Central Catholic School.
Res.: 128 Gove St., East Boston, 02128. Tel: 617-567-3215; Fax: 617-569-0552. Email: olmtcarmel1@aol.com.

52—OUR LADY OF PERPETUAL HELP (1868), Revs. Kevin Milton, C.SS.R.; Joseph Adamec, C.SS.R.; John Furey, C.SS.R.; Philip A. Cabasino, C.SS.R. In Res., Revs. Richard Bennett, C.SS.R.; Robert Lennon, C.SS.R.
Res.: 1545 Tremont St., Roxbury, 02120-2996. Tel: 617-445-2600; Fax: 617-445-1857. Email: www.TheMissionChurch.com.
School—94 St. Alphonsus St., 02120. Tel: 617-442-2660. (Grades 1-6) Sisters 4; Lay Teachers 3; Students 152.

53—OUR LADY OF THE ASSUMPTION (1869), Revs. Jose Manuel De La Pena (NEW); Owen F. Ince (NEW). Member East Boston Central Catholic School Consortium.
Res.: 404 Sumner St., East Boston, 02128. Tel: 617-567-1223; Fax: 617-561-6319. Email: ola_boston@familink.com.

54—OUR LADY OF THE PRESENTATION (1909), Rev. William F. Salmon.
Res.: 676 Washington St., Brighton, 02135-1612. Tel: 617-782-6260; Fax: 617-782-3303.
School—634 Washington St., Brighton, 02135-1612. Tel: 617-782-8670. Sisters 1; Lay Teachers 9; Students 226.

55—OUR LADY OF VICTORIES (1880), (French), Revs. Philip LaPlante, S.M.; Albert Dilanni, S.M. In Res., Rev. Kenneth Thibodeau, S.M.
Res.: 27 Isabella St., 02116-5216. Tel: 617-426-4448; Fax: 617-482-1570.

56—ST. PATRICK (1836), Revs. Walter J. Waldron; Jose A. Borja (Cape Verde); Sisters Gerard Ndagano, I.H.M.R., Pastoral Assoc.; M. Matthias Gallagher, S.B.S., Pastoral Assoc.; Christine Smith, S.B.S., Pastoral Assoc.; Mary Thomasine Twomey, M.S.B.T., Pastoral Assoc.; Luisa Vasconcelos, F.I.C., Pastoral Assoc.; Maria Macedo, F.I.C., Pastoral Assoc.; Antonia Suares, F.I.C., Pastoral Assoc.; Deacon Jacques A. McGuffie.
Res.: 10 Magazine St., Roxbury, 02119-2706. Tel: 617-445-7645; Fax: 617-445-6166.
School—131 Mt Pleasant Ave., Roxbury, 02119. Tel: 617-427-3881. Sisters 2; Lay Teachers 14; Students 349.

57—ST. PAUL (1907), Closed., For inquiries for parochial records contact Holy Family, Dorchester.

58—ST. PETER (1872), Rev. Daniel J. Finn, Admin.; Sisters Sally McLaughlin, S.C.H., Pastoral Assoc.; Glenna Connors, S.C.H., Pastoral Assoc.; Deacon Jesus Ortiz. In Res., Revs. Joseph M. Vu, C.M.C.; John Bosco Pham Trung Thuc, C.M.C.
Res.: 309 Bowdoin St., Dorchester, 02122-1834. Tel: 617-265-1132; Fax: 617-265-0463.
School—284 Bowdoin St., Dorchester, 02122-1834. Tel: 617-282-8573. Sisters 3; Lay Teachers 5; Students 210.

59—ST. PETER (1904), (Lithuanian), Rev. Stephen P. Zukas.
Res.: 50 Orton-Marotta Way, South Boston, 02127-2006. Tel: 617-268-0353; Fax: 617-268-2585. Email: klebonas@aol.com. Web: www.StPeterLithParish.CatholicWeb.com.
School—518 E. 6th St., South Boston, 02127. Tel: 617-268-0750. Sisters 3; Lay Teachers 8; Students 260.

60—SS. PETER AND PAUL (1844), Closed., For inquiries for parish records, please contact St. Vincent de Paul, South Boston.

61—ST. PHILIP, Closed., For inqueries for parish records, please contact St. Patrick, Roxbury.

62—ST. RICHARD, Closed., For inquiries for parish records, please contact St. Patrick, Roxbury.

63—SACRED HEART (1873), Rev. Wayne L. Belschner.
Res.: 303 Paris St., East Boston, 02128-3063. Tel: 617-567-5776; Fax: 617-567-3042.
School—East Boston Central Catholic School Consortium, 69 London St., East Boston, 02128. Tel: 617-567-7456. East Boston Catholic School Consortium. Sisters 1; Brothers 3; Lay Teachers 8; Students 229.

64—SACRED HEART (1888), (Italian), Rev. Vincenzo Rosato, C.S. In Res., Rev. Peter Bortolazzo, C.S.; Deacon Mario LoPriore.
Res.: 12 North Sq., 02113-2498. Tel: 617-523-5638; Fax: 617-227-4552.
School—St. John's School, 9 Moon St., 02113. Tel: 617-227-3143. Lay Teachers 11; Students 171.

65—SACRED HEART (1893), Rev. Msgr. Francis H. Kelley; Revs. John M. Mendicoa; Timothy E. Kearney; Sr. Virginia Bobrowski, S.S.N.D., Pastoral Assoc.; Deacon Francisco Quiles; John Scanion, Pastoral Assoc.
Res.: 169 Cummins Hwy., Roslindale, 02131-3739. Tel: 617-325-3322; Fax: 617-325-2145. Email: SacredHeartParish@verizon.net. Web: www.sh-roslindale.org.
School—1035 Canterbury St., Roslindale, 02131. Tel: 617-323-2500. Sisters 2; Lay Teachers 15; Students 464.
Catechesis/Religious Program—Midge Whelan, D.R.E. Students 395.

66—ST. THERESA OF AVILA (1895), Rev. Msgr. William M. Helmick; Revs. Charles J. Higgins; Richard S. Bradford. In Res., Rev. Raymond G. Helmick, S.J.
Res.: 10 St. Theresa Ave., West Roxbury, 02132-3499. Tel: 617-325-1300; Fax: 617-325-0380. Email: StTheresaRectory@msn.com. Web: www.rc.net/boston/st_theresa.
School—40 St. Theresa Ave., West Roxbury, 02132. Tel: 617-323-1050. Sisters 2; Lay Teachers 20; Students 589.

67—ST. THOMAS AQUINAS (1869), Rev. Gerald D. Perno. In Res., Rev. James J. Laughlin, J.C.L.
Res.: 97 South St., Jamaica Plain, 02130-3899. Tel: 617-524-0240; Fax: 617-524-1840. Email: StThomasQ@aol.com.

68—ST. VINCENT DE PAUL (1872), Rev. Richard E. Cannon; Nicole Feeley, Pastoral Assoc. In Res., Rev. Msgr. Andrew F. Connell.
Res.: 363 E. St., South Boston, 02127. Tel: 617-268-8100; Fax: 617-268-1277. Email: StVincentDePaul@comcast.net. Web: www.StVincentDePaulParish.org.

69—ST. WILLIAM (1909), Rev. Christopher J. Hickey; Deacon Stanley G. Pugsley.
Res.: 1048 Dorchester Ave., Dorchester, 02125-1750. Tel: 617-265-0100; Fax: 617-265-5464. Web: www.technobridge.com/stwill.
School—100 Savin Hill Ave., Dorchester, 02125. Tel: 617-265-7110. Lay Teachers 9; Students 193.

OUTSIDE THE CITY OF BOSTON

ABINGTON, PLYMOUTH CO.

1—ST. BRIDGET (1863), Revs. Allan L. Butler; Thomas C. Boudreau; Deacon James V. McLaughlin. In Res., Rev. Michael J. Regan.
Res.: 455 Plymouth St., 02351-1889. Tel: 781-878-0900; Fax: 781-878-6566. Web: www.rc.net/boston/saintbridget/.
School—455 Plymouth St., 02351-1889. Tel: 617-878-8482. Lay Teachers 11; Students 249.
Catechesis/Religious Program—Tel: 781-878-5950.

Anne Fennell, D.R.E. Students 1,159.
2—St. Nicholas (1964), Closed., For inquiries for parish records, contact St. Edith Stein, Brockton.
Acton, Middlesex Co., St. Elizabeth of Hungary (1945), Revs. Walter J. Woods; Sean M. McCarthy; Deacon John E. Bortz; Mr. Stephen J. Ryan, Pastoral Assoc.
Res.: 89 Arlington St., 01720. Tel: 978-263-4305; Fax: 978-263-9014. Email: office@seoh.org. Web: www.seoh.org.
Catechesis/Religious Program—Barbara Dane, D.R.E.; Cindy Harrington, D.R.E. Students 1,200.
Amesbury, Essex Co.
1—Holy Family (1998), [CEM] Revs. Thomas J. Buckley, Team Ministry; John W. Gentleman, Team Ministry.
School and Friend St., 01913. In Res., Rev. John D. Silk (Retired).
Res. & Parish Office: 9 Sparhawk St., 01913. Tel: 978-388-0330; Fax: 978-388-1451. Email: HFAmesbury@aol.com.
Catechesis/Religious Program—Tel: 978-388-3477. Doreen Keller, D.R.E. Students 698.
2—St. Joseph, Closed., For inquiries for parochial records contact Holy Family, Amesbury.
3—Sacred Heart, Closed., For inquiries for parochial records contact Holy Family, Amesbury.
Andover, Essex Co.
1—St. Augustine (1866), [CEM] Revs. Alfred J. Ellis, O.S.A.; Richard L. Foley, O.S.A.; Harry J Erdlen, O.S.A.; Deacon John J. Capomaccio. In Res., Rev. George R. Morgan, O.S.A.
Res.: 43 Essex St., 01810-3779. Tel: 978-475-0050; Fax: 978-475-3078.
School—26 Central St., 01810. Tel: 508-475-2414. Sisters 2; Lay Teachers 21; Students 405.
Mission—St. Joseph's (1881), Ballardville.
2—St. Robert Bellarmine (1961), Rev. Richard T. Conway. In Res., Rev. Francis C. O'Hare (Retired).
Res.: 198 Haggetts Pond Rd., 01810. Tel: 978-683-8922; Fax: 978-689-8878. Email: www.saintroberts-.net.
Arlington, Middlesex Co.
1—St. Agnes (1872), Revs. Brian M. Flatley; Shawn W. Allen. In Res., Rev. John A. Daley.
Res.: 51 Medford St., 02474. Tel: 781-648-0220; Fax: 781-643-7883. Email: parish@SaintAgnes.net. Web: www.SaintAgnes.net.
School—39 Medford St., 02474. Tel: 617-643-9031. Religious 1; Lay Teachers 20; Students 426.
High School—Arlington Catholic High School, 16 Medford St., 02472. Tel: 617-646-7770. Religious and Layteachers 46; Students 765.
2—St. Camillus (1950), Rev. James E. O'Leary.
Res.: 1175 Concord Tpke., 02476-7298. Tel: 781-643-3132; Fax: 781-643-8228.
Catechesis/Religious Program—Catherine Robinson, D.R.E. Students 123.
3—St. James the Apostle (1914), Rev. Francis E. Daley. In Res., Revs. Kenneth F. McAskill (Retired); Robert J. McAuliffe (Retired).
Res.: 22 Appleton St., 02476-5900. Tel: 781-643-0636; Fax: 781-643-7488. Email: stjamesarl@comcast.net.
Catechesis/Religious Program—Tel: 781-643-9258. Joyce Patriacca, D.R.E. Students 136.
4—St. Jerome (1934), Rev. Joseph P. Fratic.
Res.: 201 Lake St., 02474-8284. Tel: 781-648-2506; Fax: 781-648-2126. Email: saintjerome@rcn.com. Web: www.stjerome.net. Angela B. Jones, M.Div., D.R.E.
Ashland, Middlesex Co., St. Cecilia (1885), Revs. Paul F. Mulligan; Jeremy P. St. Martin.
Res.: 54 Esty St., 01721-2126. Tel: 508-881-1107; Fax: 508-881-8606. Email: business.stcecilia@comcast.com. Web: www.saintcecilia.org.
Avon, Norfolk Co., St. Michael (1908), Rev. Louis R. Palmieri.
Res.: 87 N. Main St., 02322-1286. Tel: 508-586-7210; Fax: 508-586-7211.
Catechesis/Religious Program—Francis Gammon, D.R.E. Students 304.
Ayer, Middlesex Co., St. Mary (1858), Rev. Richard R. Gosselin; Ms. Tammy Pacyna, Pastoral Assoc.
Res.: 31 Shirley St., 01432-1295. Tel: 978-772-2414; Fax: 978-772-0727.
Catechesis/Religious Program—Tel: 978-772-9907. Elizabeth C. Lewis, D.R.E. Students 265.
Bedford, Middlesex Co., St. Michael (1931), Very Rev. Mark S. Sheehan, V.F.; Rev. Michael L. Nolan. In Res., Revs. Joseph P. Robinson; Henry W. Gagnon (Retired).
Res.: 90 Concord Rd., 01730-1596. Tel: 781-275-6318; Fax: 781-271-9879. Email: office@SaintMichaelParishBedford.org. Web: www-.SaintMichaelParishBedford.org.
Bellingham, Norfolk Co.
1—Assumption (1927), Rev. Brian F. McMahon.
Parish Office: 370 Pulaski Blvd., 02019. Tel: 508-883-8226; Fax: 508-883-1713.
2—St. Blaise (1962), Rev. Brian F. McMahon, Admin. In Res., Rev. Daniel J. Gilmartin.
Res. & Office: 1158 Main St., 02019-1597. Tel: 508-966-1258; Fax: 508-966-0310.
3—St. Brendan (1945), Rev. David J. Mullen.
Res.: 384 Hartford Ave., 02019. Tel: 508-966-0260; Fax: 508-966-4404. Email: brendans@rcn.com. Web: users.rcn.com/brendans.
Belmont, Middlesex Co.
1—St. Joseph (1900), Rev. Albert M. Faretra. In Res., Rev. David C. Michael.
Res.: 345 Waverley St., 02478-2418. Tel: 617-484-0279; Fax: 617-489-5445. Email: frfaretra@atjoseph.belmont.ma.us. Web: www.stjoseph.belmont.ma.us.
Catechesis/Religious Program—Tel: 617-484-1770. Ann Marie Mahoney, D.R.E. Students 683.
2—St. Luke (1919), Revs. Gerard Petringa; John P. Kearns; Sr. Kathleen Moran, C.S.J., Pastoral Assoc.
Res.: 132 Lexington St., 02478-1239. Tel: 617-484-1996; Fax: 617-484-7831. Email: stlukesbelmont@yahoo.com. Web: www.stlukesbelmont.org.
Catechesis/Religious Program—Tel: 617-484-9357. Julie Voliton, D.R.E. Students 195.
3—Our Lady of Mercy (1926), Rev. James J. McGowan.
Res.: 15 Lawndale St., 02478-3451. Tel: 617-489-1160; Fax: 617-489-9682.
Beverly, Essex Co.
1—St. Alphonsus (1917), Rev. Robert W. Kirchmeyer. In Res., Rev. Edward D. Cowhig (Retired).
Res.: 488 Elliott St., 01915-2399. Tel: 978-777-0446; Fax: 978-922-8614.
2—St. John the Evangelist (1955), Rev. George J. Butera; Deacon Tomas E. Sanchez.
Res.: 552 Cabot St., 01915. Tel: 978-922-5542; Fax: 978-921-4563.
School—111 New Balch St., 01915. Tel: 508-922-0048. Sisters 1; Lay Teachers 8; Students 157.
3—St. Margaret (1905), Rev. James L. Fahey.
Res.: 672 Hale St., 01915-2119. Tel: 978-927-0069; Fax: 978-927-9359. Email: StMargaretBeverlyFarms@comcast.net.
Catechesis/Religious Program—Miss Mary Murray, M.S.Ed., D.R.E. Students 156.
4—St. Mary Star of the Sea (1870), Revs. Charles J. Hughes; Edward P. Geary; David J. Barnes; Sr. Julie Theresa Kane, S.N.D., Pastoral Assoc.; Deacon Joseph S. Easenenko.
Res.: 253 Cabot St., 01915-4597. Tel: 978-922-0113; Fax: 978-922-8501.
School—13 Chapman St., 01915. Tel: 508-927-3259. Sisters 4; Lay Teachers 6; Students 212.
Billerica, Middlesex Co.
1—St. Andrew (1868), Rev. Michael Parise.
Res.: 45 Talbot Ave., 01862-1414. Tel: 978-663-3624; Fax: 978-670-1433. Email: pastonmichael1@juno.com. Web: www.standrewbillerica.com.
Catechesis/Religious Program—Tel: 978-667-9024. Deborah E. Smith, D.R.E. Students 324.
2—St. Mary (1937), Revs. W. James Nyhan; Francis E. Sullivan; Deacon Allan R. Shanahan.
Res.: 796 Boston Rd., 01821. Tel: 978-663-2215; Fax: 978-663-0127. Email: StMarysParish@comcast.net. Web: www.StMarys-Parish.com.comcast.net.
3—St. Theresa of Lisieux (1945), Revs. Eugene D. Tully; John J. McCormick; Deacon Thomas F. Mullins.
Church: One Grace Ave., 01821-2504. Tel: 978-663-8816; Fax: 978-663-0577. Web: www.StTheresaParish.com.
Res.: 80 Concord Rd., 01821.
Braintree, Norfolk Co.
1—St. Clare (1959), Revs. Paul S. Sughrue; Thomas C. Foley (Retired); Deacon Michael J. Cavanaugh. In Res., Rev. Thomas C. Foley (Retired).
Res.: 1244 Liberty St., 02184-8299. Tel: 781-848-7480; Fax: 781-356-8380. Email: stclare@beld.net frpaul1@beld.net. Web: www.stclarebraintree.org.
2—St. Francis of Assisi (1903), Revs. Kevin M. Sepe; Robert W. Conole; Deacon Joseph G. Arsenault; Linda M. Muldoon, Pastoral Assoc. In Res., Rev. Charles I. Sheehy (Retired).
Res.: 856 Washington St., 02184-6464. Tel: 781-843-1332; Fax: 781-848-0976. Web: www.StFrancisBraintree.org.
School—850 Washington St., 02184. Tel: 617-848-0842. Lay Teachers 8; Students 193.
3—St. Thomas More (1938), Rev. James J. McCarthy; Deacon Charles P. Webb.
Res.: 8 Hawthorn Rd., 02184-1402. Tel: 781-843-1980; Fax: 781-843-7110. Web: www.stmparish.org.
Bridgewater, Plymouth Co., St. Thomas Aquinas (1853), Rev. Lawrence J. Drennan; Deacon Leo J. Donoghue. In Res., Rev. Edward J. McLaughlin (Retired).
Res.: 103 Center St., 02324-1397. Tel: 508-697-9528; Fax: 508-279-1859. Email: saquinaspar@aol.com. Web: www.StThomasAquinas.com.
Catechesis/Religious Program—Tel: 508-697-3632; Fax: 508-697-8907. Francine Bell, D.R.E. Students 1,813.
Brockton, Plymouth Co.
1—St. Casimir (1898), (Lithuanian), Rev. John P. Prusaitis.
Res.: 21 Sawtell Ave., 02302. Tel: 508-586-2226; Fax: 508-559-2761.
School—Tel: 508-587-7367. Sisters 1; Lay Teachers 5; Students 176.
2—St. Colman of Cloyne (1891), Rev. David P. O'Donnell.
Res.: 42 Wendell Ave., 02302. Tel: 508-586-1575; Fax: 508-586-9393. Email: staff@SaintColman.org. Web: www.SaintColman.org.
3—St. Edith Stein (2003), Revs. James A. Flavin; Brian P. Smith; Sr. Mary Lou McCarthy, C.S.J., Pastoral Assoc.
Res.: 71 E. Main St., 02301-2461. Tel: 508-586-6491; Fax: 508-587-1796. Email: StEdithSteinParish.org.
School—631 N. Main St., 02301-2461. Tel: 508-583-6231.
4—St. Edward (1897), Closed., For inquiries for parish records, contact St. Edith Stein, Brockton.
5—St. Margaret (1902), Rev. Richard C. Conway.
Parish Office: 335 Main St., East Mansfield, 02031-6657. Email: StMarg@shore.net. Web: www.StMargaretBrockton.com.
Res.: 917 Montello St., Box 3025, 02404-6657. Tel: 508-580-1295; Fax: 508-586-8443.
6—Our Lady of Lourdes (1931), Revs. Joseph H. Manning; Joseph F. Scorzello. In Res., Rev. Francis G. Goss (Retired).
Res.: 439 West St., 02301. Tel: 508-586-4715; Fax: 508-584-6257.
Catechesis/Religious Program—Tel: 508-588-1484; Fax: 508-584-6257. Sr. Marie Madigan, M.H.S.H., D.R.E. Students 514.
7—Our Lady of Ostrobrama (1914), (Polish), Closed., For inquiries for parish records, contact St. Edith Stein, Brockton.
8—St. Patrick (1856), Very Rev. Francis J. Cloherty, V.F.; Rev. Daniel R. Kayajan, C.S.C.; Jeanne Lafond, Pastoral Assoc. In Res., Rev. Msgr. Paul L. Moritz (Retired); Rev. Richard C. Conway.
Res.: 335 Main St., 02301-5396. Tel: 508-586-4840; Fax: 508-941-0639. Email: StPatrickBrockton@yahoo.com.
9—Sacred Heart (1891), (French), Rev. David P. O'Donnell, Admin.
Res.: 235 Court St., 02302. Tel: 508-586-1740; Fax: 508-584-8553. Email: shbrockton@comcast.net.
School—243 Court St., 02302. Tel: 508-588-4481. Sisters 3; Lay Teachers 6; Students 228.
Brookline, Norfolk Co.
1—St. Aidan (1911), Closed., For inquiries for parish records, please contact St. Mary of the Assumption, Brookline.
2—Infant Jesus (1938), Closed., For inquiries for parish records, please contact Infant Jesus-St. Lawrence, Brookline.
3—Infant Jesus-St. Lawrence (Chestnut Hill) (1999), Rev. James G. Burke, J.C.L.; Deacon John J. Mannion.
Res.: 774 Boylston St., Chestnut Hill, 02467. Tel: 617-566-3131; Fax: 617-738-3330. Email: ijsl@rcn.com. Web: www.ijsl.org.
Infant Jesus: 918 W. Roxbury Pkwy., 02467.
St. Lawrence: 774 Boyleston St., Chestnut Hill, 02467.
Catechesis/Religious Program—Mrs. Gail Corcoran, D.R.E. Students 81.
4—St. Lawrence (1898), Closed., For inquiries for parish records, please contact Infant Jesus-St. Lawrence, Brookline.
5—St. Mary of the Assumption (1852), Rt. Rev. John J. Ahern; Rev. Brian M. Clary; Deacons Richard F. Radford; Philip J. Newton. In Res., Rev. Charles J. Higgins.
Res.: 5 Linden Pl., 02445-7311. Tel: 617-734-0444; Fax: 617-734-3001. Web: www.StMaryBrookline.com.
School—67 Harvard St., 02445. Tel: 617-566-7184. Sisters 1; Lay Teachers 10; Students 185.
Catechesis/Religious Program—Julia Shanklin, M.Div., D.R.E. Students 208.
Burlington, Middlesex Co.
1—St. Malachy (1964), Rev. Leonard F. O'Malley; Mr. Ken Meltz, Pastoral Assoc.
Res.: 99 Bedford St., 01803. Tel: 781-272-5111; Fax: 781-270-9407. Email: office@saint-malachy.org. Web: www.saint-malachy.org.
2—St. Margaret (1945), Rev. John R. Crispo; Deacon Richard F. Bilotta. Burlington, MA St. Margaret
Res.: 111 Winn St., 01803-3124. Tel: 781-272-3111; Fax: 781-272-9204.
Cambridge, Middlesex Co.
1—St. Anthony (1902), (Portuguese), Rev. Jose S. Ferreira.

Res.: 400 Cardinal Medeiros Ave., 02141. Tel: 617-547-5593; Fax: 617-547-1505.
2—BLESSED SACRAMENT (1905), Rev. Michael J. Harkins, Admin.
Res.: 189 Pearl St., 02139-4087. Tel: 617-547-1669; Fax: 617-547-3220.
3—ST. FRANCIS OF ASSISI (1917), (Italian), Rev. Norbert DeAmato, O.F.M.; Joan DeGuglielmo, Pastoral Assoc.
Res.: 42 Sciarappa St., 02141-1204. Tel: 617-876-6754; Fax: 617-876-6753.
4—ST. HEDWIG (1907), (Polish), Closed., For inquiries for parochial records contact the Chancery.
5—IMMACULATE CONCEPTION (1910), (Lithuanian), Rev. Simeon W. Saulenas.
Res.: 432 Windsor St., 02141-1343. Tel: 617-547-1623; Fax: 617-547-0336.
6—IMMACULATE CONCEPTION (1926), Rev. Alexander J. Keenan; Sr. Phyllis O'Callaghan, C.S.J., Pastoral Assoc. In Res, Rev. George Roy, O.M.I. (Haiti).
Res.: 45 Alewife Brook Pkwy., 02140-1098. Tel: 617-547-3455; Fax: 617-354-8052.
Catechesis/Religious Program—Tel: 617-864-2319. Students 80.
7—ST. JOHN THE EVANGELIST (1893), Rev. Charles E. Collins. In Res., Revs. Thomas L. Leclerc, M.S.; Robert E. Nee.
Res.: 2254 Massachusetts Ave., 02140-1891. Tel: 617-547-4880; Fax: 617-441-8028. Email: SaintJohnChurch@aol.com.
School—Tel: 617-876-3589. Miss Marian Burns, Prin. Lay Teachers 10; Students 198.
8—ST. MARY OF THE ANNUNCIATION (1867), Revs. Joseph T. Canavan; Alonso E. Macias (Mexico); Deacon Stanley A. Straub. In Res., Rev. Andres G. Nino, O.S.A.
Res.: 134 Norfolk St., 02139-1805. Tel: 617-547-0120; Fax: 617-547-0232. Email: ParishInfo@StMaryOfTheAnnunciation.com. Web: www.StMaryOfTheAnnunciation.com.
9—OUR LADY OF PITY (1892), Closed., For inquiries for parochial records contact St. John the Evangelist, Cambridge.
10—ST. PATRICK (1908), Closed., For inquiries for parochial records contact Sacred Heart of Jesus, Cambridge.
11—ST. PAUL (1875), Rev. Msgr. Dennis F. Sheehan, V.F.; Rev. James W. Savage. In Res., Rev. George S. Salzmann, O.S.F.S.
Res.: 29 Mt. Auburn St., 02138. Tel: 617-491-8400; Fax: 617-354-7092. Email: info@StPaulParish.org. Web: www.StPaulParish.org.
School—Tel: 617-868-8658. Sisters 2; Lay Teachers 4; Students 49.
Catechesis/Religious Program—Katherine Hargadon, D.R.E. Students 98.
12—ST. PETER (1848), Rev. Kevin J. O'Leary; Janice Fitzgerald, Pastoral Assoc. In Res., Rev. Msgr. Michael S. Foster, J.C.D.
Res.: 31 Buckingham St., 02138-2297. Tel: 617-547-4235; Fax: 617-547-1525. Email: rectory@saint-peter-parish.org. Web: www.saint-peter-parish.org.
School—96 Concord Ave., 02138. Tel: 617-547-0101. Sisters 5; Lay Teachers 7; Students 201.
13—SACRED HEART OF JESUS (1842), Rev. John P. Tackney.
Res.: 47 Sixth St., 02141-1594. Tel: 617-547-0399; Fax: 617-441-8648.

CANTON, NORFOLK CO.
1—ST. GERARD MAJELLA (1960), Rev. Bernard P. McLaughlin.
Res.: 1860 Washington St., 02021-1642. Tel: 781-828-3420; Fax: 781-828-2520. Email: saintgerald@aol.com.
Catechesis/Religious Program—Eleanor George, D.R.E. Students 677.
2—ST. JOHN THE EVANGELIST (1861), Revs. Michael J. Doyle; Hal N. Obayashi; Deacon Edward M. Quigley. In Res., Rev. Robert G. LaBrie.
Res.: 700 Washington St., 02021-3036. Tel: 781-828-0090; Fax: 781-828-2480.
School—696 Washington St., 02021-3036. Tel: 617-828-2130. Sisters 1; Lay Teachers 11; Students 256.
Catechesis/Religious Program—Tel: 781-828-5130. Fran Crespi, D.R.E. Students 680.

CARLISLE, MIDDLESEX CO., ST. IRENE (1960), Rev. Thomas P. Donohoe. In Res., Rev. Winiko Luwanika (Malawi); Deacon Dean C. Bulpett.
Res.: 187 East St., 01741. Tel: 978-369-3940; Fax: 978-287-1440. Email: info@StIrenes.org. Web: www.stirenes.org.
Catechesis/Religious Program—Georgia Winfrey, D.R.E. Students 402.

CARVER, PLYMOUTH CO., OUR LADY OF LOURDES (1950), Revs. Anthony J. Medairos; Thomas P. Kelly, Admin.; Deacon Paul S. Jones.
Mailing Address: Box 68, 02355-0068.
Parish Office: 130 Main St., 02330-0068.
Res.: 192 Center St., 02355-0068. Tel: 508-866-4000; Fax: 508-866-5588. Email: ololcarver@aol.com.

CHELMSFORD, MIDDLESEX CO.
1—ST. JOHN THE EVANGELIST (1893), Revs. Paul E. Ritt; Paul J. Aveni; Deacon Joseph A. Donnelly; Joyce Wholey, Pastoral Assoc. In Res., Rev. Francis B. Leonard (Retired).
Res.: 115 Middlesex St., 01863-2030. Tel: 978-251-8571; Fax: 978-251-7873. Email: sjechurch@verizon.net. Web: www.mysite.verizon.net/sje.church/.
Catechesis/Religious Program—Tel: 978-251-4310. Elizabeth Webber, D.R.E. (Coord.). Students 930.
2—ST. MARY (1931), Revs. Leo E. Martel; Marc J. Bishop; Deacon Dennis Vandi.
Res.: 25 North Rd., 01824-2767. Tel: 978-256-2374; Fax: 978-256-0122. Web: www.saint-mary.org.

CHELSEA, SUFFOLK CO.
1—OUR LADY OF GRACE (1913), Rev. James J. Barry; Sr. Ann Kelley, S.N.D., Pastoral Assoc.
Res.: 59 Nichols St., 02150-1225. Tel: 617-884-0030; Fax: 617-884-0957. Web: www.olgo.net.
School—190 Nichols St., Everett, 02149. Tel: 617-387-8034. Lay Teachers 7; Students 147.
2—OUR LADY OF THE ASSUMPTION (1907), (French), Closed., For inquiries for sacramental records contact St. Rose of Lima, Chelsea.
3—ST. ROSE OF LIMA (1849), Revs. Terence J. Moran; Richard S. DeVeer; Anthony Giang Nguyen (Vietnam); Sisters Marcelina, M.S.H.J., Pastoral Assoc.; Innocentia, M.S.H.J., Pastoral Assoc.; Antonia, M.S.H.J., Pastoral Assoc.; Deacon Luis F. Rivera.
Res.: 601 Broadway, 02150-2998. Tel: 617-889-2774; Fax: 617-889-2854. Email: StRoseChelse@hotmail.com.
School—580 Broadway, 02150-2998. Tel: 617-884-2626. Sisters 8; Lay Teachers 10; Students 423.
4—ST. STANISLAUS (1905), (Polish), Rev. Andrew T. Grelak.
Res.: 163 Chestnut St., 02150. Tel: 617-889-0261; Fax: 617-889-2967.

COHASSET, NORFOLK CO., ST. ANTHONY (1873), Rev. John R. Mulvehill; Deacon Paul S. Rooney.
Res.: 129 S. Main St., 02025-2006. Tel: 781-383-0219; Fax: 781-383-2988 (Rectory); 781-383-9948 (Office).
Catechesis/Religious Program—Tel: 781-383-0630; Fax: 781-383-9948. Mrs. Virginia Macleod, D.R.E. Students 600.

CONCORD, MIDDLESEX CO.
1—ST. BERNARD (1863), Rev. John A. Murray; Deacons Alfred L. Murphy; Francis D. D'Ambrosio. In Res., Revs. Michael B. Medas; Peter J. Murphy.
Res.: 70 Monument Sq., 01742. Tel: 978-369-3778; Fax: 978-371-3346. Email: StBernard@StBernardsConcord.org. Web: www.StBernardsConcord.org.
2—OUR LADY HELP OF CHRISTIANS (1907), Rev. Austin H. Fleming; Deacon Charles I. Clough.
Office Address: 55 Church St., 01742-3040. Tel: 978-369-2810; Fax: 978-371-0853. Email: olhc@aol.com. Web: www.olhc.org.
Res.: 1004 Main St., 01742-2937.
Catechesis/Religious Program—Helen Cushman, D.R.E.; Colleen Brennan, D.R.E.; Claudette Chmura, D.R.E. Students 388.

DANVERS, ESSEX CO.
1—ST. MARY OF THE ANNUNCIATION (1871), Revs. Gerard L. Dorgan; William M. Walsh. In Res., Most Rev. Francis Xavier Irwin, D.D., A.S.C.W.
Res.: 24 Conant St., 01923-2968. Tel: 978-774-0340; Fax: 978-774-9407. Email: StMaryDanvers@comcast.net. Web: www.StMarysDanvers.org.
School—20 Otis St., 01923. Tel: 978-774-0307.
Catechesis/Religious Program—Tel: 978-774-8605. John Dillon, D.R.E.; Julie O'Hara, D.R.E. Students 557.
2—ST. RICHARD (1963), Revs. Bruce G. Flanagan; Henry M. Cunney; Deacon Norman R. St. Hilaire.
Res.: 90 Forest St., 01923-1806. Tel: 978-774-7575; Fax: 978-774-9543. Web: www.StRichardDanvers.org.

DEDHAM, NORFOLK CO.
1—ST. MARY (1866), Revs. John A. Dooher; Matthew M. Williams; Deacon Louis W. Sheedy.
Res.: 420 High St., 02026-2892. Tel: 781-326-0550; Fax: 781-326-1809.
2—ST. SUSANNA (1960), Rev. Stephen S. Josoma; Deacon Laurence J. Bloom; Karen MacDougall, Pastoral Assoc.
Res.: 262 Needham St., 02026-7009. Tel: 781-329-9575; Fax: 781-329-5966. Email: StSusanna@hotmail.com. Web: www.SaintSusanna.org.

DOVER, NORFOLK CO., MOST PRECIOUS BLOOD (1959), Rev. John J. Grimes.
Res.: 30 Center St., 02030-0812. Tel: 508-785-0305; Fax: 508-785-0432. Email: mpb.dover@comcast.com. Web: www.catholic-forum.com/mpdover.
Catechesis/Religious Program—Tel: 508-785-9909 (Grades 6-12). Regina O'Connor, D.R.E. (Grades 6-12); Kathleen Kimble, D.R.E. (Grades 1-5). Students 208.

DRACUT, MIDDLESEX CO.
1—ST. FRANCIS (1963), Rev. Robert M. Blaney.
Office: 115 Wheeler Rd., 01826-4254. Tel: 978-452-6611; Fax: 978-452-0772. Email: www.SaintFrancis.net.
Res.: 110 Percy St., 01826.
2—ST. MARGUERITE D'YOUVILLE (2001), Rev. Paul T. Clifford; Deacon Everett F. Penney.
Res.: 1340 Lakeview Ave., 01826. Tel: 978-957-0322; Fax: 978-957-5266. Email: StMar@comcast.net. Web: www.StMar.org.
3—ST. MARY OF THE ASSUMPTION (1909), Closed., For inquiries for parish records, please contact St. Marguerite D'Youville, Dracut.
4—ST. THERESE (1927), (French), Closed., For inquiries for parish records, please contact St. Marguerite D'Youville, Dracut.

DUXBURY, PLYMOUTH CO., HOLY FAMILY (1945), Rev. Msgr. William F. Glynn; Rev. Francis G. Chase; Deacons Arthur J. Keefe; Daniel R. Burns.
Church: 601 Tremont St., 02332-4450. Tel: 781-934-5055; Fax: 781-934-5796. Web: www.HolyFamily-Duxbury.org.

EAST BRIDGEWATER, PLYMOUTH CO., ST. JOHN (1903), Rev. Mark J. Riley; Deacons Brendan A. Fitzgerald; Lee A. Beatrice.
Res.: 210 Central St., 02333-1998. Tel: 508-378-4207; Fax: 508-378-7317. Email: StJohnEBridge@comcast.net. Web: www.geocities.com/StJohnsEB.

ESSEX, ESSEX CO., ST. JOHN THE BAPTIST (1931), Rev. Wallace E. Blackwood.
Res.: 52 Main St., 01929. Tel: 978-768-6284; Fax: 978-768-2533.

EVERETT, MIDDLESEX CO.
1—ST. ANTHONY (1927), (Italian), Revs. Camillo Lando, C.S.; Antonio Carvalho, C.S.; Luis A. Duque (Venezuela); Deacon Thomas W. Marchant.
Res.: 38 Oakes St., 02149. Tel: 617-387-0310; Fax: 617-387-1229.
School—54 Oakes St., 02149. Tel: 617-389-2448. Sisters 2; Lay Teachers 8; Students 213.
Catechesis/Religious Program—Doris DiTullio, D.R.E. Tel: 617-387-4806; Thomas Marchant. Tel: 617-387-2388. Students 106.
2—IMMACULATE CONCEPTION (1885), Rev. Gerald J. Osterman.
Res.: 489 Broadway, 02149-3603. Tel: 617-389-5660; Fax: 617-389-2456.
School—53 Summer St., 02149. Tel: 617-387-8304. Sisters 3; Lay Teachers 9; Students 270.
Catechesis/Religious Program—Sr. Janet McGilvray, R.C.E., D.R.E. Tel: 617-710-4963; Richard Randazzo, D.R.E. Tel: 617-387-7009. Students 348.
3—ST. JOSEPH (1912), Closed., For inquiries for parish records please see Immaculate Conception, Everett.
4—ST. THERESE (1927), Rev. Richard P. McLaughlin.
Res.: 20 Gledhill Ave., 02149-4007. Tel: 617-389-0412; Fax: 617-387-0052.

FOXBOROUGH, NORFOLK CO., ST. MARY (1859), Revs. Thomas J. Reilly; John R. McLaughlin; Ms. Lenore Danesco, Pastoral Assoc.
Res.: 83 Central St., 02035. Tel: 508-543-7726; Fax: 508-543-7728. Email: St.MaryFox@verizon.net. Web: www.StMarysFoxboro.org.
Catechesis/Religious Program—Tel: 508-543-4577. Lenore Danesco, D.R.E. Students 1,320.

FRAMINGHAM, MIDDLESEX CO.
1—ST. BRIDGET (1878), Rev. Msgr. Francis V. Strahan, V.F.; Rev. Mark E. Ballard; Mrs. Elizabeth Mingolelli, Pastoral Assoc.; Ms. Barbara Conlin, Pastoral Assoc.
Res.: 15 Wheeler Ave., 01702-2902. Tel: 508-875-5959; Fax: 508-875-1270. Email: stb@tiac.net. Web: www.home.tiac.net/stb.
School—832 Worcester Rd., 01702. Tel: 508-875-0181. Lay Teachers 14; Students 242.
2—ST. GEORGE (Saxonville) (1847), Rev. Francis E. O'Brien; Sr. Ann Marie McAndrews, S.N.D., Pastoral Assoc.; Deacon Neil F. Lacey. In Res., Rev. Albert C. Hughes (Retired).
Res.: 74 School St., 01701. Tel: 508-877-5130; Fax: 508-877-3080.
Catechesis/Religious Program—Leslee A. Willitts, D.R.E. Students 173.
3—ST. JEREMIAH (1958), Rev. Ronald G. Calhoun; Deacon William B. Koffel.
Res.: 41 Brook St., 01701-3996. Tel: 508-877-1428; Fax: 508-788-1592. Email: StJeremiah@aol.com.
4—ST. STEPHEN (1883), Revs. Laurence J. Borges, Team Ministry; Albert H. Stankard, Team Ministry; Deacons Guy J. Spiri; Pedro L. Torres. In Res., Rev. William T. Pearsall (Retired).
Res.: 221 Concord St., 01702. Tel: 508-875-4788; Fax: 508-875-2577.
Catechesis/Religious Program—James J. Drummey, D.R.E.; Maria Nieves, D.R.E. Students 300.
5—ST. TARCISIUS (1907), (Italian), Revs. Joseph F. Pranzo, C.S.; Cesare Ciceri, C.S.; Deacon Manoel

Souza (Brazil).
Res.: 35 Cedar St., 01702-6925. Tel: 508-875-8623; Fax: 508-875-6358. Email: StTarcis@aol.com.
School—560 Waverly St., 01702. Tel: 508-872-8188.
Catechesis/Religious Program—Students 120.

FRANKLIN, NORFOLK CO., ST. MARY (1877), Revs. Thomas J. Walsh; Carlos C. Kim; David C. Goodrow; Deacon Richard P. Delio.
Res.: One Church Sq., 02038-1896. Tel: 508-528-0020; Fax: 508-528-1641.

GEORGETOWN, ESSEX CO., ST. MARY (1874), Very Rev. James M. Carroll, V.F.
Church: 94 Andover St., 01833. Tel: 978-352-2024; Fax: 978-352-5513. Email: Rectory@StMaryParish.org.

GLOUCESTER, ESSEX CO.

1—ST. ANN (1855), Rev. Timothy A. Harrison; Deacon Daniel A. Dunn.
Res.: 60 Prospect St., 01930-5999. Tel: 978-283-0054; Fax: 978-283-5313.
School—Tel: 508-283-3455. Sisters 3; Lay Teachers 6; Students 185.
Catechesis/Religious Program—Tel: 978-283-2937. Susan Parsons, D.R.E. (Grades 1-5); Susanne Demetri, D.R.E. (Grades 6-10). Students 389.
Mission—St. Joseph's Chapel Magnolia, ID.

2—OUR LADY OF GOOD VOYAGE (1889), (Portuguese), Rev. Eugene L. Alves.
Res.: 142 Prospect St., 01930-3714. Tel: 978-283-1490; Fax: 978-283-0787.

3—ST. PETER (1928), Rev. C. Paul Rouse; Deacon George G. L'Italien.
Res.: One Brightside Ave., 01930-3217. Tel: 508-283-0874; Fax: 508-283-8223. Email: StPetersParish@pro-usa.net.
Chapel—Eastern Point, St. Anthony-by-the-Sea

4—SACRED HEART (1946), Rev. Myron F. Bullock.
Res.: 5 High St., 01930-1113. Tel: 978-283-4457; Fax: 978-281-7279.
Catechesis/Religious Program—Tel: 978-281-1455 (Sec.). Students 162.

GROTON, MIDDLESEX CO.

1—ST. JAMES (1945), Closed., For inquiries for parish records, contact Sacred Heart-St. James, Groton.

2—SACRED HEART, Closed., For inquiries for parish records, contact Sacred Heart-St. James, Groton.

3—SACRED HEART-ST. JAMES, Formerly Sacred Heart (2003), Merged, with St. James, Groton to form Sacred Heart-St. James, Groton. Rev. Michael A. Alfano; Ms. Joan Barclay, P.A.
Res.: 29 Old Orchard Rd., West Groton, 01472-0186. Tel: 978-448-6633; Fax: 978-448-2732. Email: shsjparish@charter.net. Web: www.shsjparish.org.

GROVELAND, ESSEX CO., ST. PATRICK (1946), Rev. Philip M. Conroy; Deacon Robert T. Hackett.
Res.: 728 Salem St., 01834. Tel: 978-372-6044; Fax: 978-374-9006. Email: StPat@mva.net. Web: www.StPatricksGroveland.org.

HALIFAX, PLYMOUTH CO., OUR LADY OF THE LAKE (1945), Rev. Thomas A. Kopp. In Res., Rev. Charles D. Logue (Retired).
Res.: 580 Monponsett St., Box 35, 02338-0035. Tel: 781-293-7971; Fax: 781-293-7969.

HAMILTON, ESSEX CO., ST. PAUL (1922), Rev. Louis D. Bourgeois; Deacons William H. James; James V. Manzi; Mrs. Elizabeth Reilly, Pastoral Assoc.
Res.: 50 Union St., 01982-2118. Tel: 978-468-2337; Fax: 978-468-6538.
Catechesis/Religious Program—Tel: 978-468-3617. Jeanne Abbott, D.R.E. Students 600.

HANOVER, PLYMOUTH CO., ST. MARY OF THE SACRED HEART (1907), Revs. Henry F. Doherty; Richard G. Curran; Ms. Marilyn Zedik, Pastoral Assoc.
Res.: 392 Hanover St., 02339-2215. Tel: 781-826-4303; Fax: 781-826-5203. Email: StMarysMass@comcast.net. Web: www.StMarysMass.org.
Catechesis/Religious Program—Tel: 781-826-2351. Joanne Jordan, D.R.E. Students 1,439.

HANSON, PLYMOUTH CO., ST. JOSEPH THE WORKER (1956), Rev. John M. Hannon; Deacon Gerald P. Ryan.
Res.: One Maquan St., 02341-0714. Tel: 781-293-3581; Fax: 781-294-1052. Web: www.StJoseph-TheWorker.org.

HAVERHILL, ESSEX CO.

1—ALL SAINTS (1998), Revs. Dennis T. Nason; Mark E. Ballard; Deacon Richard R. Bowley.
Res.: 120 Bellevue Ave., 01832-4711. Tel: 978-372-7721; Fax: 978-372-2085. Email: AllSaintsParish@earthlink.net. Web: www.AllSaintsParish.net.
School—St. Joseph, 56 Oak Ter., 01832. Tel: 978-521-4256. Sr. Maria Joseph Foley, Prin.
Catechesis/Religious Program—Tel: 978-373-5473. Carol Simone, D.R.E. Students 558.
St. Joseph's Early Childhood Ed. Center—100 Bellevue Ave., 01832. Tel: 978-372-0111.

2—ST. GEORGE (1961), Closed., For inquiries for parochial records contact All Saints, Haverhill.

3—ST. JAMES (1859), Rev. Francis X. Mawn; Deacon Jose Nelson Agudelo. In Res., Rev. Edward L. King (Retired).
Res.: 6 Cottage St., 01830-4920. Tel: 978-372-8537; Fax: 978-373-1505.
Catechesis/Religious Program—Tel: 978-372-2291. Larry N. Webster, D.R.E. Students 438.

4—ST. JOHN THE BAPTIST (1955), Rev. Keith P. LeBlanc.
Res.: 110 Lincoln Ave., 01830. Tel: 978-372-2780; Fax: 978-469-0947.

5—ST. JOSEPH (1876), Closed., For inquiries for parochial records contact All Saints, Haverhill.

6—ST. MICHAEL (1910), Closed., For inquiries for parochial records contact All Saints, Haverhill.

7—ST. RITA (1932), Closed., For inquiries for parochial records contact All Saints, Haverhill.

8—SACRED HEARTS (1908), Revs. Michael C. Randone; James T. Kelly; Deacon Robert J. Gaudreau; Miss Maria Fortune, Pastoral Assoc. In Res., Rev. James M. Broderick (Retired).
Parish Office: 6 Carleton Ave., 01835. Tel 978-373-1281; Fax: 978-374-3043. Web: www.SacredHearts.bradford.homestead.com.
Res.: 48 Chestnut St., 01835-7446.
School—31 S. Chestnut St., 01835. Tel: 508-372-5451. Sisters 1; Lay Teachers 9; Students 247.

HINGHAM, PLYMOUTH CO.

1—ST. PAUL (1871), Very Rev. James F. Rafferty, V.F.; Rev. Hoang Van Le; Deacon Timothy A. Lawless; Sr. Eleanor Ballantine, S.C., Pastoral Assoc.
Res.: 147 North St., 02043-3995. Tel: 781-749-0587; Fax: 781-749-8053.
School—18 Fearing Rd., 02043. Tel: 781-749-2407. Lay Teachers 9; Students 253; Religious 1.
Catechesis/Religious Program—Tel: 781-749-5568. Judy Tetreault Murphy, D.R.E. Students 788.

2—RESURRECTION OF OUR LORD AND SAVIOUR JESUS CHRIST (1957), Rev. Lawrence Pratt; Deacon John P. Steuterman.
Res.: 1057 Main St., 02043-3995. Tel: 781-749-3577; Fax: 781-740-0689. Email: resparish@res1057.org.
Catechesis/Religious Program—Janet Hickey, D.R.E. Students 649.

HOLBROOK, NORFOLK CO., ST. JOSEPH (1887), Rev. Joseph K. Raeke; Deacon John F. Boyle.
Res.: 153 S. Franklin St., 02343. Tel: 781-767-0605; Fax: 781-767-5225.
School—143 S. Franklin St., 02343. Tel: 781-767-1544. Sisters 2; Lay Teachers 14; Students 290.
Catechesis/Religious Program—Tel: 781-767-0650. Maura Murphy-Burke, D.R.E. Students 550.

HOLLISTON, MIDDLESEX CO., ST. MARY (1870), Revs. William J Haley; Brian G. Bachand; Deacons Martin E. Breinlinger; Philip M. Caruso.
Res.: 8 Church St., 01746-1741. Tel: 508-429-4427; Fax: 508-429-3324. Email: st.marys@verizon.net.
Catechesis/Religious Program—Tel: 508-429-6076. Andrea DeMayo, D.R.E.; Joan Cocchiarella, D.R.E. Students 1,385.

HOPKINTON, MIDDLESEX CO., ST. JOHN THE EVANGELIST (1866), Revs. James F. Degnan; Joseph Diem; Marie Buckley, Pastoral Assoc.
Res.: 20 Church St., 01748-1836. Tel: 508-435-3313; Fax: 508-435-5651. Email: StJohnHopkinton@aol.com. Web: www.StJohnTheEvangelist.com.
Catechesis/Religious Program—Tel: 508-435-3094. Carol Zani, D.R.E.; John O'Connor, D.R.E.; Ken Lysik, D.R.E. Students 1,168.

HUDSON, MIDDLESEX CO.

1—CHRIST THE KING (1927), Closed., For inquiries for parish records, please contact St. Michael, Hudson.

2—ST. MICHAEL (1870), Revs. Walter A. Carreiro; Steven W. Poitras; Sr. Yvonne Millman, S.S.A., Pastoral Assoc.
Res.: 20 High St., 01749-2315. Tel: 978-562-2552; Fax: 978-568-1761. Email: parish@StMikes.org. Web: www.StMikes.org.
School—18 High St., 01749. Tel: 978-562-2917. Lay Teachers 8; Students 119.
High School—Hudson Catholic High School, 198 Main St., 01749. Tel: 978-562-6701.

HULL, PLYMOUTH CO., ST. MARY OF THE ASSUMPTION (1938), Rev. William G. Williams; Deacon Edward L. Doyle.
Res.: 208 Samoset Ave., 02045-0565. Tel 781-925-0680; Fax: 781-925-0685.

IPSWICH, ESSEX CO.

1—ST. JOSEPH (1889), Closed., For inquiries for parochial records contact Our Lady of Hope, Ipswich.

2—OUR LADY OF HOPE (1997), Rev. John G Kiley.
Res.: One Pineswamp Rd., 01938-2909. Tel: 978-356-3944; Fax 978-356-9592. Email: RectoryIpswich-Catholics.org. Web: www.IpswichCatholics.org.

3—SACRED HEART (1908), (Polish), Closed., For inquiries for parochial records contact Our Lady of Hope, Ipswich.

4—ST. STANISLAUS (1910), (French), Closed., For inquiries for parish records, please contact Our Lady of Hope, Ipswich.

KINGSTON, PLYMOUTH CO., ST. JOSEPH (1908), Rev. Joseph M. Hennessey, J.C.L.; Deacons Richard G. Monroe; William V. Nagle.
Res.: 268 Main St., 02364-1922. Tel: 781-585-6679; Fax: 781-585-7104. Email: StJoseph@adelphia.net. Web: www.rc.net/boston/stjosephkingston/.
Catechesis/Religious Program—Tel: 781-585-6372. Margart M. Hall, D.R.E.; Ann M. Cussen, D.R.E. Students 1,036.

LAKEVILLE, PLYMOUTH CO., SAINTS MARTHA AND MARY (1958), Rev. Thomas J. Naughton; Sr. Carol Flaherty, F.M.M., Pastoral Assoc. In Res., Rev. Thomas J. Mooney (Retired).
Res.: 354 Bedford St., 02347-2107. Tel: 508-947-2107; Fax: 508-947-6543.

LAWRENCE, ESSEX CO.

1—ST. ANNE, Closed., For inquiries for parish records, please contact Sacred Heart, Lawrence.

2—ASUNCION DE LA VIRGEN MARIA (1993), (Hispanic), Rev. Paul G. McManus; Deacon Jose D. Naveo, Pastoral Assoc.; Mr. A. Felix Duran, Pastoral Assoc.
Res.: 216 Lawrence St., 01841-1715. Tel: 978-683-1069; Fax: 978-686-4677. Email: PadrePaul@comcast.net. Web: www.AsuncionLawrence.com.

3—ST. AUGUSTINE (1935), Closed., For inquiries for parish records, please contact Our Lady of Good Counsel, Lawrence.

4—ST. FRANCIS (1903), (Lithuanian), Unassigned.
Res.: 94 Bradford St., 01840-1003. Tel: 978-687-7356; Fax: 978-687-6480.

5—HOLY ROSARY (1904), (Italian), Closed., For inquiries for parish records, please contact Holy Rosary, Lawrence. Very Rev. James J. Ronan, V.F.; Revs. Richard T. Burton; Emilson de J. Aguirre (Colombia).
Res.: 35 Essex St., 01840-1797. Tel: 978-685-1711; Fax: 978-691-5927.

6—HOLY TRINITY (1905), (Polish), Revs. Conrad Salach, O.F.M.Conv.; Stanley Sobiech, O.F.M.Conv.
Res.: 30 Trinity St., 01841. Tel: 978-688-7226; Fax: 978-681-5356. Email: parish@holytrinity.mec.edu. Web: www.holytrinity-lawr.org.
School—31 Trinity St., 01841-2697. Tel: 978-686-3007. Sisters 2; Lay Teachers 7; Students 231.

7—ST. MARY IMMACULATE CONCEPTION (1848), Revs. William F. Waters, O.S.A.; Francis Barr, O.S.A.; Jorge A. Reyes, O.S.A.; Deacon John D. Harrison.
Res.: 300 Haverhill St., 01841. Tel: 978-685-1111; Fax: 978-686-5555.
School—301 Haverhill St., 01840. Tel: 978-685-2091. Sisters 2; Lay Teachers 8; Students 171.
Catechesis/Religious Program—Claudia Chase, D.R.E. Students 367.

8—ST. PATRICK (1872), Revs. Paul B. O'Brien; Francisco J. Anzoategui; Deacons Paul V. Specht; Silvio J. Menendez.
Res.: 118 S. Broadway, 01843-1427. Tel: 978-683-9416; Fax: 978-681-5808. Web: www.SaintPatrickParish.com.
School—101 Parker St., 01843. Tel: 978-683-5822. Sisters 6; Lay Teachers 11; Students 440.

9—SS. PETER AND PAUL (1907), (Portuguese), Very Rev. James J. Ronan, V.F.; Deacon Richard H. Rocha.
Res.: 125 Chestnut St., 01841-3844. Tel: 978-681-9080; Fax: 978-687-4112.

10—SACRED HEART (1905), (French), Revs. Normand J. Martin, S.M.; Roland Lacasse, S.M.; Clifton W. Moors, S.M.; Deacon Gerard E. Gagne. In Res., Revs. Laurence E. Ross, S.M.; Joel Grissom, S.M.
Res.: 321 S. Broadway, 01843-2691. Tel: 978-686-7921; Fax: 978-686-5687.
School—Tel: 978-682-8935. Sisters 1; Lay Teachers 13; Students 289.

LEXINGTON, MIDDLESEX CO.

1—ST. BRIGID (1848), Revs. Eugene P. Curtin; William P. Smith, O.M.I.; Deacons William H. Wildes; William E. Kerns; Francine Edwards, Pastoral Assoc.
Res.: 2001 Massachusetts Ave., 02421-4812. Tel: 781-862-0335; Fax: 781-862-1409. Email: StBrigid@verizon.net. Web: www.StBrigidLexington.org.
Catechesis/Religious Program—Francine Edwarde, D.R.E. Tel: 781-862-0319; Jaye Russo, D.R.E. Tel: 781-862-8724. Students 610.

2—SACRED HEART (1931), Rev. Arnold F. Coletti; Sr. Mary Nagle, C.S.J., Pastoral Assoc.
Res.: 21 Follen Rd., 02421. Tel: 781-862-4646; Fax: 781-863-5614. Email: shepherd@SacredHeatlLex.org. Web: www.SacredHeartLex.org.
Catechesis/Religious Program—Tel: 781-861-8385, Ext. 19. Mary Lipman, R.S.C.J., D.R.E. Students 437.

LINCOLN, MIDDLESEX CO., ST. JOSEPH (1946), Rev. Mark A. Mahoney, J.C.L.
Res.: 142 Lincoln Rd., Box 234, 01773-0234. Tel: 781-259-8364; Fax: 781-259-9331. Email: StJosephLincoln@aol.com.

LITTLETON, MIDDLESEX CO., ST. ANNE (1945), Rev. David P. Callahan; Deacon Daniel F. Crimmins.
Res.: 75 King St., Box 2246, 01460-3246. Tel: 978-486-4100; Fax: 978-952-6303.
Catechesis/Religious Program—Jacquelyn Butterfield, D.R.E.; Michelle Hatch, D.R.E. Students 492.

LOWELL, MIDDLESEX CO.

1—ST. ANTHONY (1901), (Portuguese), Rev. Francis M. Glynn; Victor Mello, Pastoral Assoc. In Res., Rev. Pedro J. Damazio (Brazil).
Res.: 893 Central St., 01852-3407. Tel: 978-452-1506; Fax: 978-458-9662. Email: GlynnFrank@hotmail.com. Web: www.StAnthony-.portoinc.com.

2—HOLY TRINITY (1904), (Polish), Rev. Msgr. Stanley Kempa; Joanne Faticanti, Pastoral Assoc.
Res.: 340 High St., 01852-2760. Tel: 978-452-2564; Fax: 978-452-4679. Email: www.HolyTrinity.org.
School—St. Stanislaus School, 368 High St., 01852-2760. Tel: 978-453-2360. Sisters 2; Lay Teachers 6; Students 224.

3—IMMACULATE CONCEPTION (1869), Revs. Patrick J. Hollywood, O.M.I.; John J. Hogan, O.M.I.; Francis J. Ouelette, O.M.I.; Claire Couillard, Pastoral Assoc.
Res.: 3 Fayette St., 01852-1298. Tel: 978-458-1474; Fax: 978-446-0790.
School—218 Merrimack St., 01852. Tel: 978-454-5339. Sisters 1; Lay Teachers 8; Students 175.

4—ST. JEAN BAPTISTE, Closed., For inquiries for parochial records contact St. Louis de France, Lowell.

5—SAINT JEANNE D'ARC (1922), (French), Revs. Donald G. Lozier, O.M.I.; Adhemar S. Deveau, O.M.I. In Res., Rev. Normand A. Fillion, O.M.I. (MAN).
Res.: 129 Fourth Ave., 01854-2904. Tel: 978-458-6316; Fax: 978-970-2299. Email: sjaparish@yahoo.com. Web: www.stjaparish.org.
School—68 Dracut St., 01854. Tel: 978-453-4114. Sisters 2; Lay Teachers 18; Students 466.

6—ST. JOSEPH (1908), (Lithuanian), Closed., For inquiries for sacramental records contact Immaculate Conception, Lowell.

7—ST. LOUIS DE FRANCE (1904), (French), Rev. Scott A. Euvard; Deacon Gerard J. Hardy.
Res.: 221 W. Sixth St., 01850. Tel: 978-454-0496; Fax: 978-446-7992. Email: StLouisChurch@comcast.net. Web: www.SaintLouisDeFrance.org.
School—77 Boisvert St., 01850. Tel: 978-458-7594. Sisters 5; Lay Teachers 6; Students 275.

8—ST. MARGARET (1910), [CEM] Rev. Thomas S. Domurat.
Res.: 374 Stevens St., 01851. Tel: 978-454-5143; Fax: 978-458-8472. Email: church@StMargaretParish.org. Web: www.StMargaretParish.org.
School—486 Stevens St., 01851. Tel: 978-453-8491; Fax: 978-453-1358. Sisters 1; Lay Teachers 19; Students 430.

9—ST. MARIE (1931), (French), Revs. Roger E. Lamoureux, O.M.I.; Gilmond C. Boucher, O.M.I. In Res., Rev. Norman E. Parent, O.M.I.
Res.: 80 Chamberlain St., 01852-5523. Tel: 978-453-2134; Fax: 978-446-0324. Email: SteMarieLowell@juno.com.

10—ST. MICHAEL (1883), Revs. Albert L. Capone; Mario J. Orrigo; Lisa K. Crowley, Pastoral Assoc.
Res.: 543 Bridge St., 01850-2098. Tel: 978-459-0713; Fax: 978-453-1123. Email: StMichaels.comcast.net. Web: www.saint-michael.com.
School—21 Sixth St., 01850. Tel: 978-453-9511. Lay Teachers 9; Students 260.

11—NOTRE DAME DE LOURDES (1908), (French), Rev. Richard Kulwiec, O.M.I.
Res.: 101 Smith St., 01851-2698. Tel: 978-459-2339; Fax: 978-446-0838.
Catechesis/Religious Program—Tel: 978-251-7065. Suzdnee Beebe, D.R.E. Students 53.

12—NUESTRA SENORA DEL CARMEN (1990), (Hispanic), Rev. James E. Taggart, O.M.I.
Res.: 725 Merrimack St., 01854-3978. Tel: 978-459-7829; Fax: 978-446-0442. Email: NSdCarmen@aol.com.

13—ST. PATRICK (1831), Revs. D. George Spagnolia; Anthony Giang Nguyen (Vietnam); R. Paul Cornell, Admin.; Deacon Peter An Ros.
Res.: 282 Suffolk St., 01854-4297. Tel: 978-459-0561; Fax: 978-446-0266.
School—311 Adams St., 01854-3799. Tel: 978-458-4232. Sisters 2; Lay Teachers 8; Students 231.
Catechesis/Religious Program—Tel: 978-441-0988. Sr. Linda Greenwood, D.R.E. Students 64.

14—ST. PETER (1841), Closed., For inquiries for parochial records contact Sacred Heart, Lowell.

15—ST. RITA (1910), Rev. Daniel D. Magni; Deacon Robert W. Dzuris.
Res.: 158 Mammoth Rd., 01854. Tel: 978-452-4812; Fax: 978-459-8969. Email: SaintRitaLowell@aol.com. Web: www.StRita@acomhosting.com.

16—SACRED HEART (1884), Revs. Roger E. Lamoureux, O.M.I.; Gilmond C. Boucher, O.M.I.; Pedro J. Damazio (Brazil); Sr. Joan Gregoire, S.N.D., Pastoral Assoc.; Mrs. Linda Burns, Pastoral Assoc.; Mrs. Carol Shepherd, Pastoral Assoc. In Res., Rev. Norman E. Parent, O.M.I.
Res.: 159 Moore St., 01852-5006. Tel: 978-453-3962; Fax: 978-454-3466.
School—122 Andrews St., 01852. Tel: 978-453-4751. Sisters 1; Lay Teachers 8; Students 255.

LYNN, ESSEX CO.

1—HOLY FAMILY (1922), (Italian), Rev. Gregory Mercurio; Deacon John M. Bresnahan.
Res.: 26 Bessom St., 01902-1205. Tel: 781-599-7200; Fax: 781-599-2202.
Catechesis/Religious Program—Tel: 781-596-2390; Fax: 781-599-2202. Catherine Raymond, D.R.E. Students 154.

2—ST. JEAN BAPTISTE (1886), (French), Closed., For inquiries for parochial records contact St. Mary, Lynn.

3—ST. JOSEPH (1874), Revs. James E. Gaudreau; J. Salvadore Quiroz (Ecuador); Deacons Finley H. Chisholm; Nelson J. Hidalgo.
Res.: 40 Green St., 01902-2905. Tel: 781-599-7040; Fax: 781-598-7439.
Convent—Sisters of St. Joseph 2.

4—ST. MARY (1862), Rev. Msgr. Paul V. Garrity, V.F.; Revs. Michael M. Ferraro; Lamartine Petit-Monsieur (Haiti); Deacon Timothy F. Dempsey.
Res.: 8 S. Common St., 01902-4489. Tel: 781-598-4907; Fax: 781-599-2088. Email: SaintMarysLynn@comcast.net.
High School—35 Tremont St., 01902. Tel: 781-595-7885; 781-599-6222 (Jr. High). Lay Teachers 16; Students 291.
Catechesis/Religious Program—Mary Jo Kelly-LaPointe, D.R.E. Tel: 781-599-2275. Students 168.

5—ST. MICHAEL (1906), (Polish), Rev. Kazimierz Zastawny.
Res.: 567 Summer St., 01905-2011. Tel: 781-593-4584; Fax: 781-599-7547.

6—ST. PATRICK (1906), Closed., For inquiries for parochial records contact St. Mary, Lynn.

7—ST. PIUS FIFTH (1912), Revs. Cornelius J. Mullaney, Team Ministry; Joseph M. Rossi, Team Ministry; Deacon Edward P. Elibero, Team Ministry; Sr. Kathleen Crowley, S.C., Pastoral Assoc.
Res.: 215 Maple St., 01904-2799. Tel: 781-595-7487; Fax: 781-595-7270. Web: www.shore.net/~stpiusv.
School—28 Bowler St., 01904. Tel: 781-593-8292. Sisters 2; Lay Teachers 8; Students 540.

8—SACRED HEART (1894), Revs. John P. McGinty; Tinh Van Nguyen; Deacon John W. Hardy. In Res., Rev. Thomas J. Fleming (Retired).
Res.: 571 Boston St., 01905-2160. Tel: 781-593-8047; Fax: 781-599-4040.
School—581 Boston St., 01905-2160. Tel: 781-592-7581. Sisters 1; Lay Teachers 8; Students 261.

LYNNFIELD, ESSEX CO.

1—ST. MARIA GORETTI (1960), Rev. Thomas J. Powers; Deacon Edward P. Elibero.
Res.: 112 Chestnut St., 01940. Tel: 781-334-2367; Fax: 781-334-9819. Email: smgpar@catholicfamilies.net.

2—OUR LADY OF THE ASSUMPTION (1937), Very Rev. John E. Farrell, V.F.; Rev. Mark G. Derrane.
Res.: 17 Grove St., 01940. Tel: 781-598-4313; Fax: 781-598-0055.
School—34 Grove St., 01940. Tel: 781-599-4422. Sisters 1; Lay Teachers 16; Students 457.
Catechesis/Religious Program—Judith Dixon, D.R.E. Students 1,198.

MALDEN, MIDDLESEX CO.

1—IMMACULATE CONCEPTION (1854), Very Rev. Richard J. Mehm, V.F.; Deacon Mark E. Rumley. In Res., Rev. James B. Caniff, C.M.
Res.: 10 Fellsway E., 02148-5313. Tel: 781-324-4941; Fax: 781-397-8571. Web: www.icmalden.com.
School—306 Highland Ave., 02148. Tel: 781-322-0129. Sisters 3; Lay Teachers 14; Students 426.
Catechesis/Religious Program—Tel: 781-324-5518. Sr. Margo Shen, C.S.J., D.R.E. Students 634.

2—ST. JOSEPH (1902), Revs. William J. Minigan; Richard T. Bakker, S.M.A.
Res.: 790 Salem St., 02148. Tel: 781-324-0402; Fax: 781-324-1790. Email: StJosephs2@comcast.net.

3—ST. PETER (1972), (Italian), Rev. John U. Paris, Admin.; Deacon Frank A. Valeri. In Res., Rev. Donald Howard, C.S.P.
Res.: 12 Thacher St., 02148. Tel: 781-322-6142; Fax: 781-321-6739.
Catechesis/Religious Program—Fax: 781-321-6739. Mary Ann DiMarco, D.R.E. Students 65.

4—SACRED HEARTS (1890), Rev. Daniel J. Hickey.
Res.: 297 Main St., 02148-7414. Tel: 781-324-0728; Fax: 781-324-2714.
School—30 Irving St., 02148. Tel: 781-324-6584. Sisters 2; Lay Teachers 17; Students 463.

MANCHESTER BY THE SEA, ESSEX CO., SACRED HEART (1905), Rev. Wallace E. Blackwood.
Res.: 60 School St., 01944-1342. Tel: 978-526-1263; Fax: 978-526-4335.

MARBLEHEAD, ESSEX CO., OUR LADY, STAR OF THE SEA (1859), Revs. Dennis J. Burns; William H. McLaughlin; Deacon John E. Whipple.
Res.: 85 Atlantic Ave., 01945-3036. Tel: 781-631-0086; Fax: 781-631-5668.

MARLBOROUGH, MIDDLESEX CO.

1—ST. ANN (1921), (Italian), Revs. G. Michael Bercik, O.F.M.; Michael MacInnis, O.F.M.; Deacon Richard C. Martino Sr.
Res.: 466 Lincoln St., 01752-2090. Tel: 508-485-1968; Fax: 508-481-7255. Email: StAnnParish@aol.com FrMikeFM@aol.com.

2—IMMACULATE CONCEPTION (1854), Revs. Michael W. MacEwen; Jose G. Flores (Brazil); David P. White; Deacon Douglas P. Peltak.
Res.: 17 Washington Ct., 01752. Tel: 508-485-0016; Fax: 508-480-9644. Email: icmarlboro42@comcast.net. Web: www.icmarlboro.org.
School—25 Washington Ct., 01752. Tel: 508-460-3400. Lay Teachers 14; Students 257.

3—ST. MARY (1870), (French), Rev. Laurier J. Martineau.
Res.: 26 Broad St., 01752-4098. Tel: 508-485-0390; Fax: 508-480-9835. Email: StMary1870@aol.com. Web: www.members.aol.com/stmary1870.

4—ST. MATTHIAS (1963), Rev. Francis P. O'Brien; Deacon Robert I. Hoaglund.
Res.: 409 Hemenway St., 01752-6710. Tel: 508-460-9255; Fax: 508-480-8801. Email: admin@st-mathias-church.com. Web: StMattPar.org.

MARSHFIELD, PLYMOUTH CO.

1—ST. ANN BY THE SEA (1945), Rev. Edward T. Serena.
Res.: 591 Ocean St., 02065. Tel: 781-834-4953; Fax: 781-834-7472. Web: www.StAnns.net.
Catechesis/Religious Program—Tel: 781-834-8223. Martha McLaughlin, D.R.E. Students 492.

2—ST. CHRISTINE (1945), Revs. Francis A. Regan; Henry M. Yanju; Mary Doolan, Pastoral Assoc.; Doretha Gurry, Pastoral Assoc.
Res.: 1295 Main St., 02051-0274. Tel: 781-834-6003; Fax: 781-834-0671.
Mission—St. Theresa's Humarock.

3—OUR LADY OF THE ASSUMPTION (1949), Rev. Donald P. Clifford; Deacon John P. Connor.
Res.: 40 Canal St., Box 368, 02041-0368. Tel: 781-834-6252; Fax: 781-834-5694. Email: assumchrch@aol.com. Web: www.AssumptionParish.com.

MAYNARD, MIDDLESEX CO.

1—ST. BRIDGET (1881), Rev. Kenneth B. Quinn; Deacon John W. Pepi.
Res.: One Percival St., 01754-1699. Tel: 978-897-2171; Fax: 978-897-5358. Web: www.SaintBridget-Maynard.com.

2—ST. CASIMIR (1912), (Polish), Closed., For inquiries for sacramental records contact St. Bridget, Maynard.

MEDFIELD, NORFOLK CO., ST. EDWARD THE CONFESSOR (1892), Rev. Leroy E. Owens.
Res.: 133 Spring St., Box 336, 02052-0003. Tel: 508-359-2633; Fax: 508-359-1846. Web: www.steward-ma.org.
Catechesis/Religious Program—Tel: 508-359-6150. Terry Ferraris, D.R.E. (1-6); Mrs. Lynn Kenney, D.R.E. (7-9). Students 1,353.

MEDFORD, MIDDLESEX CO.

1—ST. FRANCIS OF ASSISI (1921), Rev. Joseph F. Scorzello; Deacon Henry A. Mariani.
Res.: 441 Fellsway W., 02155. Tel: 781-396-3400; Fax: 781-396-3254.
School—Tel: 781-395-9170. Sisters 4; Lay Teachers 12; Students 347.
Catechesis/Religious Program—Tel: 781-395-4042; Fax: 781-306-0044. Mea Mustone, D.R.E. Students 345.

2—ST. JAMES (1919), Rev. James F. Darcy, Admin.; Deacon Arthur F. Rogers Jr. In Res., Rev. Stephen M. Boyle.
Res.: 779 Fellsway, 02155-4953. Tel: 781-396-0025; Fax: 781-396-2161.

3—ST. JOSEPH (1883), Revs. Robert J. Fountain, Team Ministry; Patrick J. McLaughlin, Team Ministry; Deacon Robert P. Amerault, Team Ministry.
Res.: 114 High St., 02155-3882. Tel: 781-396-0423; Fax: 781-391-2919. Email: StJosephParishMedfordMA@msn.com. Web: www.StJosephParishMedfordMA.org.
School—132 High St., 02155. Tel: 781-396-3636. Sisters 5; Lay Teachers 14; Students 342.
Catechesis/Religious Program—Donna Hardy, D.R.E. Students 245.

4—ST. RAPHAEL (1905), Rev. Kevin G. Toomey. In Res., Rev. David M. O'Leary.
Res.: 38 Boston Ave., 02155. Tel: 781-488-5444; Fax: 781-483-3375. Web: www.st-raphael-medford.org.

School—516 High St., 02155. Tel: 781-483-3373; Fax: 781-483-3097. Sisters of St. Joseph 2; Lay Teachers 11; Students 283.

5—SACRED HEART (1937), Rev. Robert J. Doherty.
Res.: 51 Winthrop St., 02155-5324. Tel: 781-396-2232; Fax: 781-396-3731.

MEDWAY, NORFOLK CO., ST. JOSEPH (1885), Rev. Msgr. Timothy J. Moran; Rev. Mark J. Coira.
Res.: 2 Barber St., Box 557, 02053-0557. Tel: 508-533-6500; Fax: 508-533-1236.
Catechesis/Religious Program—Tel: 508-533-7771; Fax: 508-533-0604. Sharon Moore, D.R.E. Students 1,180.

MELROSE, MIDDLESEX CO.

1—INCARNATION OF OUR LORD AND SAVIOR JESUS CHRIST (1958), Rev. James A. Field; Linda Swett, Pastoral Assoc.
Res.: 429 Upham St., 02176. Tel: 781-662-8844; Fax: 781-662-6653. Email: JamesField@aol.com. Web: www.IncarnationMelrose.org.

2—ST. MARY OF THE ANNUNCIATION (1894), Revs. John J. Ronaghan; John M. Sullivan; Sr. Mary Samson, S.H.C.J., Pastoral Assoc.; Deacon John W. Wise. In Res., Rev. Msgr. Alfonso G. Palladino (Retired).
Res.: 46 Myrtle St., 02176-3827. Tel: 781-665-0152; Fax: 781-665-2750.
School—4 Myrtle St., 02176. Tel: 781-665-5037. Lay Teachers 10; Students 198.

MERRIMAC, ESSEX CO., NATIVITY (1891), Revs. Edward F. Sherry; William T. Kremmell, Admin.
Res.: 4 Green St., 01860. Tel: 978-346-8604; Fax: 978-346-9970. Email: NativityParish@verizon.net.

METHUEN, ESSEX CO.

1—ST. LUCY (1958), Sr. Rena Brunetti, P.M., Pastoral Assoc.
Res.: 254 Merrimack St., 01844. Tel: 978-686-3311; Fax: 978-686-5343.
Catechesis/Religious Program—Tel: 978-794-0383. Michele MacEachern, D.R.E. Students 586.

2—ST. MONICA (1917), Revs. Jerome F. Gillespie; Joseph T. MacCarthy.
Res.: 214 Lawrence St., 01844-3852. Tel: 978-683-1193; Fax: 978-686-0249. Web: www.st-monica-parish.org.
School—212 Lawrence St., 01844. Tel: 978-686-1801. Sisters 4; Lay Teachers 12; Students 522.
Catechesis/Religious Program—Tel: 978-686-9573; Fax: 978-738-8898. Lorraine J. Toto, D.R.E.; Gayle C. Rousseau, D.R.E. Students 827.

3—OUR LADY OF MOUNT CARMEL (1937), Closed., For inquiries for parish records please see St. Monica Parish, Methuen.

4—ST. THERESA (1936), (French), Closed., For inquiries for parish records, please contact Our Lady of Good Counsel, Methuen.

MIDDLEBOROUGH, PLYMOUTH CO., SACRED HEART (1885), Revs. Richard P. Crowley; Martin J. McNulty; Deacon Charles H. Bower; Mary Q. Gallagher, Pastoral Assoc. In Res., Rev. Daniel F. Moran (Retired).
Res.: 340 Center St., 02346-2102. Tel: 508-947-0444; Fax: 508-947-2364. Web: www.sacredheart-middleboro.org.
Catechesis/Religious Program—M. Judith West, D.R.E. Tel: 508-947-2050; Fax: 508-947-2364; Mary Callagher, D.R.E. Tel: 508-947-2050; Michelle Sylvie, D.R.E. Tel: 508-923-1151. Students 324.

MIDDLETON, ESSEX CO., ST. AGNES (1945), Rev. Michael A. Hobson.
Res.: 22 Boston St., 01949-2199. Tel: 978-774-1958; Fax: 978-774-1964. Email: StAgnes@ParishMail.com. Web: www.StAgnesMiddleton.org.
Catechesis/Religious Program—Marie Lagace, D.R.E. Students 353.

MILLIS, NORFOLK CO., ST. THOMAS THE APOSTLE (1937), Rev. Henry G. Chambers.
Res.: 111 Exchange St., 02054-9998. Tel: 508-376-2621; Fax: 508-376-4308.

MILTON, NORFOLK CO.

1—ST. AGATHA (1922), Revs. Peter J. Casey; Joseph V. Keil; Sr. Helen Cornelia Lyons, S.N.D., Pastoral Assoc.; Deacon Daniel F. Sullivan; Mary Sheedy, Pastoral Assoc. In Res., Rev. William F. Kenneally (Retired).
Res.: 432 Adams St., 02186-4399. Tel: 617-698-2439; Fax: 617-698-1517. Email: rectory@StAgathaparish.org. Web: www.StAgathaParish.org.
School—440 Adams St., 02186. Tel: 617-696-3548. Sisters 2; Lay Teachers 15; Students 377.

2—ST. ELIZABETH (1946), Rev. Gilbert S. Phinn; Deacon Joseph P. MacDonald.
Res.: 350 Reedsdale Rd., 02186-3999. Tel: 617-696-6688; Fax: 617-698-4864. Email: office@StElizabethMilton.org. Web: www.StElizabethMilton.org.
Catechesis/Religious Program—Tel: 617-698-5763. Sr. Mary K. Walsh, C.S.T., D.R.E. Students 340.

3—ST. MARY OF THE HILLS (1931), Rev. Arthur J. Wright.
Res.: 29 St. Mary's Rd., 02186-2024. Tel: 617-696-0120; Fax: 617-696-7044. Email: smhrectory@aol.com. Web: www.SaintMaryoftheHills.org.
School—250 Brook Rd., 02186. Tel: 617-698-2464. Sisters 2; Lay Teachers 14; Students 307.

4—ST. PIUS TENTH (1954), Rev. David M. Burke; Marjorie Begin, Pastoral Assoc.
Res.: 865 Brush Hill Rd., 02186-1299. Tel: 617-333-0401; Fax: 617-333-0191.

NAHANT, ESSEX CO., ST. THOMAS AQUINAS (1902), Rev. Terence P. Curley.
Res.: 248 Nahant Rd., 01908-1340. Tel: 781-581-0023; Fax: 781-598-8860. Web: www.StThomasNahant.com.

NATICK, MIDDLESEX CO.

1—ST. LINUS (1950), Rev. Msgr. J. Robert Ciggi.
Res.: 119 Hartford St., 01760-2497. Tel: 508-653-5505; Fax: 508-655-4577.

2—ST. PATRICK (1858), Revs. Brian R. Kiely; Stephen S. Donohoe; Deacon James M. Crump; Denise Perreault, Pastoral Assoc. In Res., Most Rev. Walter James Edyvean, D.D., S.T.D.
Res.: 44 E. Central St., 01760-4639. Tel: 508-653-1093; Fax: 508-650-2922. Email: PatrickNat@aol.com. Web: www.StPatsNatick.org.

3—SACRED HEART (1891), Rev. Joseph W. Sylva.
Res.: 19 Eliot St., 01760-6092. Tel: 508-353-5113; Fax: 508-653-3051.
Catechesis/Religious Program—Carol O'Neil, D.R.E. Students 133.

NEEDHAM, NORFOLK CO.

1—ST. BARTHOLOMEW (1952), Rev. Philip E. McGaugh; Sr. Julie Connolly, S.N.D., Pastoral Assoc.
Res.: 1180 Greendale Ave., 02492-4706. Tel 781-444-3434; Fax: 781-449-7550. Email: StBarthomew@comcast.net.

2—ST. JOSEPH (1917), Revs. J. Michael Lawlor; Patrick S. Armano; Deacon Thomas A. Smith. In Res., Rev. Msgr. Francis J. McGann.
Res.: 1382 Highland Ave., 02192-2694. Tel 781-444-0245; Fax: 781-444-7713.
School—90 Pickering St., 02492. Tel: 781-444-4459. Sisters 1; Lay Teachers 18; Students 411.

NEWBURYPORT, ESSEX CO.

1—IMMACULATE CONCEPTION (1848), Revs. Marc A. Piche; Derek J. Borek. In Res., Rev. Paul W. Berube (Retired).
Res.: 7 Court St., 01950-2502. Tel: 978-462-2724; Fax: 978-463-6989. Web: www.NewburyportCatholic.org.
School—One Washington St., 01950. Tel: 978-465-7780; Fax: 978-234-7331. Sisters 2; Lay Teachers 7; Students 198.
Catechesis/Religious Program—Tel: 978-234-7420; Fax: 978-234-7399. Catherine Owens, S.N.D., D.R.E. Students 697.
Mission—St. James Plum Island.

2—ST. LOUIS DE GONZAGUE (1902), (French), Closed., For inquiries for sacramental records contact Immaculate Conception, Newburyport.

NEWTON, MIDDLESEX CO.

1—ST. BERNARD (1876), Revs. Paul E. Kilroy; Richard S. Moran; Mary Peterson, Pastoral Assoc. In Res., Rev. Daniel C. O'Connell.
Res.: 1529 Washington St., 02465-4419. Tel: 617-244-0608; Fax: 617-332-4951. Email: StBernard@StBernardNewton.org. Web: www.StBernardNewton.com.
Catechesis/Religious Program—Tel: 617-527-3364. Mary Belschner, D.R.E.; Mary Peterson, D.R.E. Students 351.

2—CORPUS CHRISTI (1922), Rev. Joseph F. McGlone; Cathi Duffy, Pastoral Assoc.
Res.: 45 Ash St., 02166. Tel: 617-244-9110; Fax: 617-558-7515.

3—ST. IGNATIUS (1926), Revs. Robert F. VerEecke, S.J.; Kenneth G. Loftus, S.J.; Sr. Diane Vallerio, O.S.F., Pastoral Assoc.
Res.: 28 Commonwealth Ave., Chestnut Hill, 02467-3849. Tel: 617-552-6100; Fax: 617-552-6101. Email: ignatius@bc.edu. Web: www.bc.edu/st-ignatius.

4—ST. JOHN THE EVANGELIST (1911), Closed., For inquiries for parochial records contact Our Lady Help of Christians, Newton.

5—MARY IMMACULATE OF LOURDES (1870), Rev. Kenneth A. Le Blanc.
Res.: 270 Elliot St., 02164-203. Tel: 617-244-0558; Fax: 617-965-4815. Email: donabed@aol.com. Web: www.MaryImmaculateOfLourdes.org.

6—OUR LADY HELP OF CHRISTIANS (1878), Rev. Walter H. Cuenin; Sr. Marie LaBollita, S.C., S.C., Pastoral Assoc.; Bridget Chamberas, Pastoral Assoc.; Mary Ellen Cocks, Pastoral Assoc.; Mr. Thomas Leahy, Pastoral Assoc. In Res., Revs. Thomas Doyle, C.S.C.; Sean McGraw, C.S.C. (CHI).
Res.: 573 Washington St., 02458-1494. Tel: 617-527-7560; Fax: 617-527-1338. Email: welcome@ourladys.com. Web: www.ourladys.com.
High School—Trinity Catholic High School, Formerly Trinity Catholic High School Interparish, 575 Washington St., 02458-1494. Tel: 617-244-1841. Sisters 3; Lay Teachers 10; Students 152.
Catechesis/Religious Program—Tel: 617-527-7560, Ext. 213. Maureen Cornell, D.R.E. Students 363.

7—ST. PHILIP NERI (1934), Rev. Charles J. McCoy. In Res., Rev. Seung J. Park (Korea, South).
Res.: 1518 Beacon St., 02168-1530. Tel: 617-244-0590; Fax: 617-558-7522. Email: SPNWaban@aol.com.
Catechesis/Religious Program—Tel: 508-270-0545. Chantal M. Aramati, D.R.E. Students 108.

8—SACRED HEART (1890), Rev. John J. Connelly; Winifred Murphy, Pastoral Assoc. Tel: 617-306-6231.
Res.: 1321 Centre St., Newton Center, 02459-2496. Tel: 617-969-2248; Fax: 617-965-7515. Email: parish@sacredheart.ws. Web: www.sacredheart.ws.

NORFOLK, NORFOLK CO., ST. JUDE (1949), Rev. Msgr. Peter V. Conley, V.F. In Res., Rev. Robert Rivard, F.M.S.I.
Res.: 86 Main St., Box 305, 02056-0305. Tel: 508-528-0170; Fax: 508-528-1860.

NORTH ANDOVER, ESSEX CO., ST. MICHAEL (1900), Revs. Paul T. Keyes; George G. Hogan; John W. Delaney.
Res.: 196 Main St., 01845. Tel: 978-686-4050; Fax: 978-686-5408.
School—80 Maple Ave., 01845. Tel: 978-686-1862. Sisters 8; Lay Teachers 8; Students 153.

NORTH READING, MIDDLESEX CO., ST. THERESA (1945), Revs. Thomas M. Gillespie; Thomas J. Powers; Daniel P. McCoy; Deacon Alfred O. Balestracci; Mary Ann Thomas, Pastoral Assoc.
Res.: 63 Winter St., 01864-2282. Tel: 978-664-3412; Fax: 978-276-0034. Email: STeresanr@earthlink.net.
Catechesis/Religious Program—Tel: 978-664-2962. Bridget Rao, D.R.E.; Nancy Cirone, D.R.E. Students 1,227.

NORWELL, PLYMOUTH CO., ST. HELEN (1950), Rev. Thomas H. Maguire.
Res.: 383 Washington St., 02061-2009. Tel: 781-659-2993; Fax: 781-659-7861.

NORWOOD, NORFOLK CO.

1—ST. CATHERINE OF SIENA (1890), Rev. Msgr. Cornelius M. McRae; Revs. John A. Currie; Edward M. Riley; Sr. Frances Sears, C.S.J.
Res.: 547 Washington St., 02062-0547. Tel: 781-762-6080; Fax: 781-255-9312.
School—249 Nahatan St., 02062. Tel: 781-769-5354. Sisters 1; Lay Teachers 20; Students 472.
Catechesis/Religious Program—Marybeth McDonough, D.R.E., Vice Prin. (Grades 1-5); R. Kerry Thompson, D.R.E. Prin. (Grades 6-12). Tel: 781-254-5087. Students 759.

2—ST. GEORGE (1912), (Lithuanian), Rev. William L. Wolkovich. In Res., Rev. William F. Lucey (Retired).
Res.: 36 St. George Ave., 02062-4420. Tel: 781-762-0979; Fax: 781-762-6389. Email: StGeorgeNorwood@aol.com.

3—ST. PETER (1918), (Polish), Closed., For inquiries for parochial records contact the Chancery.

4—ST. TIMOTHY (1963), Rev. John P. Culloty; Deacon Francis R. Tremblay. In Res., Rev. George F. Emerson (Retired).
Res.: 650 Nichols St., 02062. Tel: 781-769-2522; Fax: 781-769-9362. Email: StTim@StTim.net. Web: www.StTim.net.
Catechesis/Religious Program—Tel: 781-762-4868. Gudith Miley, D.R.E. Students 653.

PEABODY, ESSEX CO.

1—ST. ADELAIDE (1962), Revs. John C. Chaisson; Vincent J. Gianni, Admin.; Deacon Anthony J. Juliano. In Res., Rev. Francis H. Delaney (Retired).
Res.: 17 Bow St., 01960-3427. Tel: 978-535-1985; Fax: 978-535-4845. Email: chaiss6@aol.com.
Catechesis/Religious Program—Tel: 978-535-5376. Angela Federico, D.R.E. Students 685.

2—ST. ANN (1937), Deacon Martin J. Walsh.
Res.: 136 Lynn St., 01960-6432. Tel: 978-531-1480; Fax: 978-531-6683.
Catechesis/Religious Program—Tel: 978-531-5791. M. Ellen Fitzgerald, D.R.E. Students 565.

3—ST. JOHN THE BAPTIST (1871), Rev. John E. MacInnis; Deacons Valentin Rivera; Leo A. Martin. In Res., Rev. Msgr. Francis G. O'Sullivan (Retired); Rev. Charles R. Stanley.
Res.: 17 Chestnut St., 01960-5429. Tel: 978-531-0002; Fax: 978-531-5199.
School—19 Chestnut St., 01960-5429. Tel: 978-531-0444. Sisters 5; Lay Teachers 5; Students 578.
Catechesis/Religious Program—Tel: 978-532-1586. Karen E. Hinton, D.R.E.; Paula L. Colpitts, D.R.E. Students 670.

4—ST. JOSEPH (1927), Closed., For inquiries for parish records contact Our Lady of Hope, Ipswich.

5—OUR LADY OF FATIMA (1965), (Portuguese), Rev. Albert A. Sylvia; Sr. Ellen Dabrieo, S.N.D., Pastoral Assoc.
Res.: 35 Newcastle Rd., 01960. Tel: 978-532-0272; Fax: 978-977-2991. Email: OurLadyOfFatima@verizon.net. Web: www.tc.net/

boston/fatima.

PEMBROKE, PLYMOUTH CO., ST. THECLA (1964), Rev. Robert J. Sullivan.
Res.: 145 Washington St., 02358-0587. Tel: 781-826-9786; Fax: 781-826-3484.
Catechesis/Religious Program—Tel: 781-826-8042. Mary K. Doller, D.R.E. Students 933.

PEPPERELL, MIDDLESEX CO., ST. JOSEPH (1870), Rev. Robert J. Butler; Sr. Roberta Rzeznik, S.N.D., Pastoral Assoc.
Res.: 28 Tarbell St., Box 1486, 01463-3486. Tel: 978-433-5737; Fax: 978-433-9566. Email: StJoseph@sjpp.org. Web: www.sjpp.org.
Catechesis/Religious Program—Tel: 978-433-2591. Carole Babineau, D.R.E. Students 430.

PLAINVILLE, NORFOLK CO., ST. MARTHA (1953), Rev. John F. Walsh; Deacon Bertrand H. Guerin.
Res.: 219 South St., 02762. Tel: 508-699-8543; Fax: 508-699-6677.
Catechesis/Religious Program—Tel: 508-695-0054. Sharon Guerin, D.R.E. Students 523.

PLYMOUTH, PLYMOUTH CO.

1—BLESSED KATERI TEKAKWITHA (1982), Rev. James E. Braley; Deacon Edward F. Creutz.
Res.: 126 S. Meadow Rd., 02360-4740. Tel: 508-747-1568; Fax: 508-747-0616. Email: office@BlessedKateri.com. Web: www.BlessedKateri.com.
Catechesis/Religious Program—Tel: 508-747-5464. Joyce Hokanson, D.R.E. Students 369.

2—ST. BONAVENTURE (1950), Revs. Robert J. Deehan; Kenneth C. Overbeck; Deacon C. Michael Hickey.
Res.: 807 State Rd., Box 996, 02345-0996. Tel: 508-224-3636; Fax: 508-224-5889.
Catechesis/Religious Program—Tel: 508-224-6113; 508-224-6008; Fax: 508-224-6966. Karen Coughlin, D.R.E.; Paula Ryan, D.R.E. Students 1,097.
Mission—St. Catherine's Chapel White Horse Beach.

3—ST. MARY (1915), Very Rev. Byran K. Parrish, V.F.; Deacon Eugene V. Stenstrom. In Res., Rev. Paul F. Bailey (Retired).
Res.: 313 Court St., 02360-4336. Tel: 508-746-0426; Fax: 508-747-5886. Email: BParrish@St.MarysPlymouth.com. Web: www.StMarysPlymouth.org.
Catechesis/Religious Program—Linda Lennon, D.R.E.; Raymond Burton, D.R.E. Students 280.

4—ST. PETER (1876), Revs. Aidan J. Walsh, J.C.L.; Joseph S. McCarthy (Retired).
Res.: 81 Court St., 02360-3886. Tel: 508-746-0663; Fax: 508-747-1071.
Catechesis/Religious Program—Tel: 508-746-8174. Elizabeth Adey, D.R.E. Students 750.

QUINCY, NORFOLK CO.

1—ST. ANN (1922), Rev. Msgr. Robert P. Deeley, V.F., J.C.D.; Rev. Garrett J. Barry; Sr. Patricia Boyle, C.S.J., Pastoral Assoc.
Res.: 757 Hancock St., 02170. Tel: 617-479-5400; Fax: 617-479-0955.
School—One St. Ann Rd., 02170. Tel: 617-471-9071. Sisters 4; Lay Teachers 8; Students 176.

2—ST. BONIFACE (1956), Closed., For inquiries for parish records, please contact St. Elizabeth Ann Seton, Quincy.

3—ST. ELIZABETH ANN SETON (2001), Rev. Michael J. Kearney; Deacon John R. Menz. In Res., Rev. Albert J. Sallese (Retired).
Res.: 26 Shed St., 02169-5923. Tel: 617-479-9200; 617-472-1408; Fax: 617-479-5766. Email: StElizabethSeton@attbi.com.

4—ST. JOHN THE BAPTIST (1863), Revs. Peter F. Quinn; Raymond P. Kiley; Deacon Charles Bubello.
Res.: 21 Gay St., 02169-6602. Tel: 617-773-1021; Fax: 617-773-5608. Email: StJohns@StJohnsQuincy.org. Web: www.StJohns-Quincy.org.

5—ST. JOSEPH (1917), Rev. Vincent P. Doolan; Deacon John F. Jennette; Dorothy R. Ruggiero, Pastoral Assoc.
Res.: 556 Washington St., 02169-7216. Tel: 617-472-6321; Fax: 617-471-8849. Email: StJoeQuincy@comcast.net.
School—Tel: 617-773-8080. Sisters 3; Lay Teachers 9; Students 234.

6—ST. MARY (1840), Rev. John M. Rowan. In Res., Rev. F. Dominic Menna.
Res.: 115 Crescent St., 02169-4040. Tel: 617-773-0120; Fax: 617-786-9199.
School—121 Crescent St., 02169-4040. Tel: 617-773-5237. Lay Teachers 10; Students 226.

7—MOST BLESSED SACRAMENT (1915), Rev. William J. English; Deacon Paul G. Markey; Maureen C. Simons, Pastoral Assoc.
Res.: 1000 Sea St., 02169. Tel: 617-773-0233; Fax: 617-471-7143.

8—OUR LADY OF GOOD COUNSEL (1938), Closed., For inquiries for parish records, please contact St. Elizabeth Ann Seton, Quincy.

9—SACRED HEART (1903), Revs. John W. O'Brien; James E. Robertson; Deacon John D. Salenius.
Res.: 386 Hancock St., 02171-2414. Tel: 617-328-8666; Fax: 617-773-2522. Email: office@SacredHeartQuincy.org. Web: www.SacredHeartQuincy.org.
School—(Grades K-8), 370 Hancock St., 02171-2414. Tel: 617-328-3830. Sisters 5; Lay Teachers 16; Students 479.

10—STAR OF THE SEA (1945), Rev. Frederick L. Barr; Deacon James B. Little; Sr. Peggy Lowell, C.S.J., Pastoral Assoc.
Res.: 107 Bellevue Rd., 02171. Tel: 617-328-0866; Fax: 617-328-8457. Email: www.MaryStarOfThe-Sea.org.

RANDOLPH, NORFOLK CO.

1—ST. BERNADETTE (1937), Rev. Edward F Doughty; Deacons John J. Ego; Francis G. Gates. In Res., Rev. Richard F. Clancy.
Res.: 1026 N. Main St., 02368-3099. Tel: 781-963-1327; Fax: 781-963-0198.
Catechesis/Religious Program—Students 353.

2—ST. MARY (1851), Revs. Richard L. Harrington; Vincent R. Maffei; Michael K. Harvey; Deacons James H. Eames; Thomas P. Burke.
Res.: 211 N. Main St., 02368. Tel: 781-963-4141; Fax: 781-963-0884.

READING, MIDDLESEX CO.

1—ST. AGNES (1904), Revs. Arthur C. Flynn; Edward T. Malone; Carol A. Gaudette, Pastoral Assoc.
Res.: 186 Woburn St., 01867-3599. Tel: 617-944-0490; Fax: 617-944-4409. Email: saint.agnes@verizon.net. Web: www.st-agnes-reading.org.
Catechesis/Religious Program—Tel: 781-944-4552; Fax: 781-944-4403. Eileen A. McGrath, D.R.E. Students 873.

2—ST. ATHANASIUS (1961), Rev. Thomas D. Conway; William E. Lucey, Pastoral Assoc.
Res.: 27 Bainbridge Rd.., 01867-1810. Tel: 781-944-0330; Fax: 781-944-1266.

REVERE, SUFFOLK CO.

1—ST. ANTHONY OF PADUA (2001), Revs. R. Michael Guarino; Paul P. Soper; Deacon Joseph A. Belmonte.
Res.: 250 Revere St., 02151-4618. Tel: 781-289-1234; Fax: 781-289-6394.

2—IMMACULATE CONCEPTION (1888), Rev. Joseph A. Antonellis; Deacon Francis M. Gaffney; Linda De Cristoforo, Pastoral Assoc.
Res.: 22 Lowe St., 02151. Tel: 781-289-0735; Fax: 781-286-1124.
School—125 Winthrop Ave., 02151. Tel: 781-284-0519. Sisters 3; Lay Teachers 6; Students 269.
Catechesis/Religious Program—Tel: 781-289-8126. Judy-Ann E. Milan, D.R.E. Students 557.

3—ST. JOHN VIANNEY (1950), Closed., For inquiries for parish records, please contact St. Anthony of Padua, Revere.

4—ST. MARY OF THE ASSUMPTION (1947), Revs. William L. Butler; R. Michael Guarino, Admin.
Res.: 670 Washington Ave., 02151. Tel: 781-284-5252; Fax: 781-284-5801.

5—OUR LADY OF LOURDES (1905), Unassigned. Rev. Thomas E. Keyes, Admin.
Res.: One Endicott Ave., 02151. Tel: 781-284-0234; Fax: 781-284-0235.
Catechesis/Religious Program—Carole Smith, D.R.E. Tel: 781-286-2050. Students 250.

6—ST. THERESA (1937), Closed., For inquiries for parish records, please contact St. Anthony of Padua, Revere.

ROCHESTER, PLYMOUTH CO., ST. ROSE OF LIMA (1980), Revs. John P. Lyons; James F. Lanergan.
Res.: 282 Vaughan Hill Rd., Box 40, 02770-0040. Tel: 508-763-2244; Fax: 508-763-9877.

ROCKLAND, PLYMOUTH CO., HOLY FAMILY (1882), Revs. James F. Hickey; James B. Clark; Aroldo Schmoeller (Brazil); Sr. Anne Conway, C.S.J., Pastoral Assoc.
Res.: 403 Union St., 02370-1799. Tel: 781-878-0160; Fax: 781-871-6389.
School—6 Del Prete Ave., 02370. Tel: 781-878-1154. Religious 3; Lay Teachers 14; Students 315.
Catechesis/Religious Program—Tel: 781-871-1244. Helen Ulich, D.R.E. Students 995.

ROCKPORT, ESSEX CO., ST. JOACHIM (1849), Rev. Ronald J. Gariboldi; Deacon William F.X. Kane.
Res.: 9 Broadway Ave., 01966-1603. Tel: 978-546-6756; Fax: 978-546-2272. Email: joachim@parishmail.com. Web: www.StJoachim.org.

ROWLEY, ESSEX CO., ST. MARY (1945), Rev. James D. Lyons; Deacon Daniel E. McCarthy.
Res.: 202 Main St., 01969-1515. Tel: 978-948-3344; Fax: 978-948-3356. Email: pastor@StMaryRowley.org. Web: www.StMaryRowley.org.
Catechesis/Religious Program—James L. McKenney, D.R.E. Students 330.

SALEM, ESSEX CO.

1—ST. ANNE (1901), (French), Rev. George J. Dufour.
Res.: 290 Jefferson Ave., 01970-2895. Tel: 978-744-1930; Fax: 978-745-1190.
Catechesis/Religious Program—Tel: 978-745-8915. Mrs. Karen Moran, D.R.E.

2—IMMACULATE CONCEPTION (1826), Rev. Timothy J. Murphy.
Res.: 15 Hawthorne Blvd., 01970-3709. Tel: 978-745-6303; Fax: 978-744-4382.
Catechesis/Religious Program—Mary Louise Daly, D.R.E. Students 125.

3—ST. JAMES (1850), Rev. Lawrence J. Rondeau, Admin.; Deacon Norman P. LaPointe.
Res.: 161 Federal St., 01970-3297. Tel: 978-745-9060; Fax: 978-745-4229. Web: www.StJamesSalem.homestead.com.
Catechesis/Religious Program—Tel: 978-744-2230. Kathy Marques, D.R.E. Students 340.

4—ST. JOHN THE BAPTIST (1903), (Polish), Rev. Stanislaw Parfienczyk.
Res.: 28 St. Peter St., 01970. Tel: 978-744-1278; Fax: 978-744-2093.

5—ST. JOSEPH (1873), (French), Revs. Lawrence J. Rondeau; James D. Foley; Deacon Norman P. LaPointe.
Res.: 135 Lafayette St., 01970-5099. Tel: 978-744-0095; Fax: 978-744-3312.
School—Tel: 978-744-4773. Sisters 4; Lay Teachers 6; Students 232.

6—ST. MARY (1918), (Italian), Closed., For inquiries for parish records, contact Immaculate Conception, Salem.

7—ST. THOMAS THE APOSTLE (1927), Rev. David J. Bartley; Deacon Richard W. Cordeau.
Res.: One Margin St., Peabody, 01960-1999. Tel: 978-531-0224; Fax: 978-531-6517. Email: StThomas344p@aol.com. Web: www.SaintThomasParish.com.
Catechesis/Religious Program—Students 250.

SALISBURY, ESSEX CO., STAR OF THE SEA (1947), Rev. Thomas B. Morgan.
Res.: 18 Beach Rd., 01952-2007. Tel: 978-465-3334; Fax: 978-465-5524.

SAUGUS, ESSEX CO.

1—BLESSED SACRAMENT (1917), Rev. John F. Mulloy; Sr. Mary O'Rourke, C.S.J., Pastoral Assoc. In Res., Rev. Msgr. Edmund J. Sviokla (Retired).
Res.: 14 Summer St., 01906-2139. Tel: 781-233-2497; Fax: 781-231-5569. Web: www.BlessedSacramentParish.org.
Catechesis/Religious Program—Tel: 781-231-3699. Donna G. Zinna, D.R.E. Students 1,014.

2—ST. MARGARET (1949), Rev. George E. Morin; Gerri Milgroom, Pastoral Assoc.
Res.: 431 Lincoln Ave., 01906-3917. Tel: 781-233-1040; Fax: 781-233-7135. Web: www.StMargarets-Saugus.org.

SCITUATE, PLYMOUTH CO.

1—ST. FRANCES XAVIER CABRINI (1960), Rev. Paul V. MacDonald; Mary Fitzgerald, Pastoral Assoc.
Res.: 78 Mann Hill Rd., 02066-2117. Tel: 781-545-4585; Fax: 781-545-2497.

2—ST. MARY OF THE NATIVITY (1921), Revs. Brian F. Manning; James P. Seymour.
Res.: One Kent St., 02066-4215. Tel: 781-545-3335; Fax: 781-544-3678. Email: RectoryL@comcast.net.
Catechesis/Religious Program—Fax: 781-544-3678. Rosemary Lonborg, D.R.E. (Grades K-5); Jane Kuklis, D.R.E. (Grades 6-10). Students 1,050.

SHARON, NORFOLK CO., OUR LADY OF SORROWS (1906), Rev. Robert W. Bullock; Deacon Michael A. Iwanowicz.
Res.: 59 Cottage St., 02067-2132. Tel: 781-784-2265; Fax: 781-784-2540. Web: www.OurLadyOfSorrows.net.
Catechesis/Religious Program—Tel: 781-784-5091. Tami C. Ellis, D.R.E. Students 595.

SHERBORN, MIDDLESEX CO., ST. THERESA (1945), Rev. John E. Sassani, Admin.; Sr. Pauline Laurence, S.S.A., Pastoral Assoc.
Res.: 35 S. Main St., Box 176, 01770. Tel: 508-653-6253; Fax: 508-651-1318.
Catechesis/Religious Program—Elizabeth Yon, D.R.E.; Regina O'Connor, D.R.E. Students 212.

SHIRLEY, MIDDLESEX CO., ST. ANTHONY (1905), Rev. Edmond M. Derosier; Deacon Raymond A. Gagnon.
Res.: 14 Phoenix St., 01464. Tel: 978-425-4588; Fax: 978-425-2033.

SOMERVILLE, MIDDLESEX CO.

1—ST. ANN (1881), Revs. David A. Keene; Jean Pierre Aubin; Sr. Mary Gowern, C.S.J., Pastoral Assoc.; Deacon Charles E. Sullivan.
Parish Office & Res.: 100 Temple St., 02145. Tel: 617-625-1904; Fax: 617-625-7043.
School—50 Thurston St., 02145. Tel: 617-625-1108. Sisters 4; Lay Teachers 6; Students 235.

2—ST. ANTHONY (1915), (Italian), Rev. Moacir Balen, C.S.
Res.: 12 Properzi Way, 02143-3226. Tel: 617-625-4530; Fax: 617-625-2457.
School—480 Somerville, 02143. Tel: 617-623-0995. Sisters 5; Lay Teachers 5; Students 204.
Catechesis/Religious Program—Sr. Margaret Marie Murphy, S.N.D., D.R.E. Students 160.

3—ST. BENEDICT (1911), Revs. John E. McLaughlin;

David A. Doucet; Sr. Stephen Marie, C.S.J. Tel: 617-628-5997. In Res., Rev. Joaquin Martinez-Mari, S.J. (Bolivia).
Res.: 25 Arlington St., 02145-3235. Tel: 617-625-0029; Fax: 617-666-5944.
School—17 Franklin St., 02145. Tel: 617-628-7775. Sisters 5; Lay Teachers 4; Students 196.
Catechesis / Religious Program—Sr. Kathleen Carven, D.R.E. (English). Tel: 617-628-2117; Daisy Gomez, D.R.E. (Spanish). Tel: 617-825-4333. Students 660.

4—St. Catherine of Genoa (1891), Revs. Brian J. McHugh; Thomas P. Rossi.
Res.: 179 Summer St., 02143-2501. Tel: 617-666-2087; Fax: 617-666-5470. Email: secretary@stofg.com. Web: www.StCatherineSomerville.com.
School—192 Summer St., 02143-2501. Tel: 617-666-9116. Sisters 2; Lay Teachers 9; Students 225.
Catechesis / Religious Program—Amanda Adamczyk, D.R.E. (Grades 1-8); Jeanne Kiley, D.R.E (Grades 9 & 10). Students 152.

5—St. Clement (1912), Revs. Dennis A. Dever; James O'Driscoll; Deacon Andrew J. Goldy.
Res.: 71 Warner St., Medford, 02155. Tel: 781-396-3922; Fax: 781-396-2506.
School—589 Boston Ave., Medford, 02155. Tel: 781-396-3488. Sisters of St. Joseph 2; Lay Teachers 17; Students 421.
High School—579 Boston Ave., Medford, 02155. Tel: 781-393-5600. Sisters 2; Lay Teachers 3; Students 196.

6—St. Joseph (1869), Rev. Henry J. Jennings. In Res., Rev. John P. Kelly, Senior Priest (Retired).
Res.: 264 Washington St., 02143-3313. Tel: 617-666-4140; Fax: 617-628-0557. Email: StJoe1869@thecia.net.
Catechesis / Religious Program—Tel: 617-666-5678. John J. Piantedosi, D.R.E. Students 177.

7—St. Polycarp (1927), Closed., For inquiries for sacramental records contact St. Ann, Somerville.

Stoneham, Middlesex Co., St. Patrick (1868), Revs. William T. Schmidt; Ronald A. Barker; Robert M. Browne; Sr. Marylou A. Cassidy, C.S.J., Pastoral Assoc.; Deacons J. Robert Turner, Pastoral Assoc.; Cyril T. O'Neil, Pastoral Assoc.; Joan Puleo, Pastoral Assoc.
Res.: 9 Pomeworth St., 02180-2025. Tel: 781-438-0960; Fax: 781-438-6809. Email: StPatStone@aol.com. Web: www.catholic-church.org/st-patricks.
School—20 Pleasant St., 02180. Tel: 781-438-2593. Lay Teachers 10; Students 223.
Catechesis / Religious Program—Tel: 781-438-1093. Patricia O'Brien-Sluz, D.R.E.

Stoughton, Norfolk Co.

1—Immaculate Conception (1872), Revs. Joseph P. McDermott; Emile R. Boutin; Felix I. Filho (Brazil); Charles J. Ferrazzi; Deacon Francis X. Heffernan. In Res., Rev. Aroldo Schmoeller (Brazil).
Res.: 122 Canton St., 02072-2271. Tel: 781-344-2073; Fax: 781-344-2979.

2—St. James (1962), Rev. John E. Kelly.
Res.: 560 Page St., 02072. Tel: 781-344-9121; Fax: 781-341-9323. Email: SntJmsChurch@aol.com.
Catechesis / Religious Program—Tel: 781-297-7582. Mrs. Mary Ann Caldwell, D.R.E. Students 300.

3—Our Lady of the Rosary (1958), Rev. Maurice J. O'Connor.
Res.: 39 South St., 02072-3705. Tel: 781-341-6110; Fax: 781-344-3306.

Stow, Middlesex Co., St. Isidore (1961), Rev. Richard J. Butler; Deacon Charles A. Cornell.
Res.: 429 Great Rd., 01775-1101. Tel: 978-897-2710; Fax: 978-461-0577. Email: anna@StIsidoreStow.org. Web: www.StIsidoreStow.org.

Sudbury, Middlesex Co.

1—St. Anselm (1963), Rev. John P. Fitzpatrick, Admin.; Deacon Joseph R. Ramrath; Melinda B. Donovan, Pastoral Assoc.
Res.: 100 Landham Rd., 01776-0916. Tel: 978-443-8981; Fax: 978-443-7032. Email: info@StAnselmSudbury.org. Web: www.StAnselm-Sudbury.org.

2—Our Lady of Fatima (1955), Very Rev. Michael J. Bova Conti, V.F.; Deacon John D. Nicholson; Sr. Brenda Forry, C.S.J., Pastoral Assoc.
Res.: 160 Concord Rd., Box 916, 01776-0916. Tel: 978-443-2647; Fax: 978-443-6264. Email: PSecretary@FatimaSudbury.org. Web: www.Fatima-Sudbury.org.

Swampscott, Essex Co., St. John the Evangelist (1907), Revs. Joseph T. Sheehy; John F. Carmichael; Deacon Andrew J. Acampora.
Res.: 174 Humphrey St., 01907-2512. Tel: 781-593-2544; Fax: 781-593-3616. Web: www.StJohnSwamp-scott.com.

Tewksbury, Middlesex Co., St. William (1935), Very Rev. John W. Hanley, O.M.I., V.F.; Rev. Daniel Nassaney, O.M.I. (NOR); Deacon William R. Emerson.
Mailing Address: 1351 Main St., 01876-2098. In Res., Revs. William P. Smith, O.M.I.; George Croft, O.M.I.
Res.: 1351 Main St., 01876-2098. Tel: 978-851-7331; Fax: 978-858-0544.
Catechesis / Religious Program—Tel: 978-851-3471. Deborah M. Albano, D.R.E. Students 1,955.

Topsfield, Essex Co., St. Rose of Lima (1945), Rev. E. Paul Sullivan.
Res.: 17 Prospect St., Box 258, 01983-0458. Tel: 978-887-5505; Fax: 978-887-8201.

Townsend, Middlesex Co., St. John (1945), Rev. Clyde H. Chetwynde.
Res.: One School St., Box 533, 01469-0523. Tel: 978-597-2291; Fax: 978-597-3401.
Catechesis / Religious Program—Tel: 978-597-2183. Richard W. Myers, D.R.E. Students 653.

Tyngsborough, Middlesex Co., St. Mary Magdalen (1959), Rev. J. Garret Thomson; Deacon Barry V. Lloyd.
Res.: 93 Lakeview Ave., Box 100, 01879. Tel: 978-649-7515; Fax: 978-649-3796.
Catechesis / Religious Program—Tel: 978-649-2394. Jane G. Morency, D.R.E. Students 750.

Wakefield, Middlesex Co.

1—St. Florence (1947), Rev. H. Joseph Murphy.
Res.: 49 Butler Ave., 01880-5125. Tel: 781-245-2711; Fax: 781-245-4512. Email: StFlorence@cove.com. Web: www.StFlorence.org.

2—St. Joseph (1854), Revs. Michael L. Steele; David F. Ziomek.
Res.: 173 Albion St., 01880-3296. Tel: 781-245-5770; Fax: 781-246-2423.
School—15 Gould St., 01880-2700. Tel: 781-245-2081. Sisters 1; Lay Teachers 7; Students 167.

3—Most Blessed Sacrament (1931), Revs. William D. Coughlin; Nicholas A. Sanenella; Deacon Frank Valeri.
Res.: 11 Grove St., 01880-4222. Tel: 781-245-2080; Fax: 781-245-7981. Web: www.nexteon.com/mbsparish.

Walpole, Norfolk Co.

1—Blessed Sacrament (1874), Rev. Timothy J. Kelleher; Deacon Richard J. Brennan; Marie A. Martin, Pastoral Assoc.; Beverly Good Pastoral Assoc.
Res.: 796 East St., 02081. Tel: 508-668-4700; Fax: 508-668-3554. Email: www.BlessedSacrament.org.
School—808 East St., 02081. Tel: 508-668-2336. Sisters 3; Lay Teachers 17; Students 433.

2—St. Mary (1931), Rev. Donald R. Delay.
Res.: 176 Washington St., Box 131, 02032-0131. Tel: 508-668-4974; Fax: 508-668-3083.

Waltham, Middlesex Co.

1—St. Charles Borromeo (1909), Rev. Rodney J. Copp, J.C.L.; Deacon James C. Callahan.
Res.: 51 Hall St., 02453-5299. Tel: 781-893-0330; Fax: 781-893-2060.
Catechesis / Religious Program—Tel: 781-893-1438. Carol A. Gill, D.R.E. Students 130.

2—St. Joseph (1894), (French), Rev. Roger M. Jacques; Deacon Albert J. Aucoin.
Res.: 519 Main St., 02154-5524. Tel: 781-893-3185; Fax: 781-893-9681.

3—St. Jude (1949), Rev. William T. Leonard; Deacon Alfred E. Santosuosso.
Res.: 147-R Main St., 02453-6622. Tel: 781-893-3100; Fax: 781-893-2424.
School—175 Main St., 02453-6622. Tel: 781-899-3644. Sisters 2; Lay Teachers 8; Students 199.
Catechesis / Religious Program—Tel: 781-891-5718. Mrs. Barbara Keville, D.R.E. Students 255.

4—St. Mary (1839), Very Rev. O. Wendell Verrill, V.F.; Deacons Francisco Alicea; Eduardo Mora.
Res.: 133 School St., 02154. Tel: 781-891-1730; Fax: 781-642-0604.
Catechesis / Religious Program—Tel: 781-893-0917. Christopher Adams, D.R.E.; Debbie Cacciatore, D.R.E. Students 497.

5—Our Lady, Comforter of the Afflicted (1930), Revs. Joseph F. Byrne; Joseph M. White, Admin.; Deacon William E. MacKenzie.
Res.: 857 Trapelo Rd., 02154. Tel: 781-894-3481; Fax: 781-894-0021.
School—Tel: 781-899-0353. Lay Teachers 8; Students 180.

6—Sacred Heart (1922), (Italian), Rev. Dennis F. Wheatley, O.F.M.; Bro. Damian J. Johnson, O.F.M., Pastoral Assoc.
Res.: 311 River St., 02453. Tel: 781-899-0469; Fax: 781-899-0081.
Catechesis / Religious Program—Tel: 781-893-8461. Bernadette Scalese, D.R.E. Students 357.

Watertown, Middlesex Co.

1—St. Patrick (1847), Revs. Stephen J. Madden; Thomas A. Mahoney; Deacon Leo F. LaFrache.
Res.: 25 Chestnut St., 02472. Tel: 617-926-9680; Fax: 617-926-3715. Email: spats212@aol.com.

2—Sacred Heart (1893), Rev. Joseph L. Curran. In Res., Revs. John J. Stagnaro; Robert M. O'Grady.
Res.: 770 Mt. Auburn St., 02472. Tel: 617-924-9110; Fax: 617-926-3341.

3—St. Theresa of the Child Jesus (1927), Closed., For inquiries for sacramental records contact St. Patrick, Watertown.

Wayland, Middlesex Co.

1—St. Ann (1945), Rev. Frank J. Silva; Katherine Burbank, Pastoral Assoc. In Res., Rev. Francis M. Conroy.
Res.: 124 Cochituate Rd., 01778-2610. Tel: 508-358-2985; Fax: 508-358-3415. Email: parish@SaintAnn.org. Web: www.SaintAnn.org.
Catechesis / Religious Program—Judy Chaloux, D.R.E. Tel: 508-358-2985, Ext. 13. Students 240.

2—St. Zepherin (1889), Rev. Ronald L. Bourgault; Sr. Francis Thomas, R.S.M., Pastoral Assoc.
Res.: 99 Main St., 01778-4936. Tel: 508-653-8013; Fax: 508-655-6948. Email: 74044.320@compuserve.com. Web: www.rc.net/boston/st_zepherin.
Catechesis / Religious Program—Frances Thomas, R.S.M., D.R.E. Students 432.

Wellesley, Norfolk Co.

1—St. James the Great (1947), Rev. Daniel J. Crowley.
Res.: 900 Worcester St., 02482. Tel: 781-237-1160; Fax: 781-237-0497. Email: rectory@StJamestheGreat.org.
Catechesis / Religious Program—Corinne M. Monahan, D.R.E. Students 205.

2—St. John the Evangelist (1890), Very Rev. Thomas F. Powers, V.F.; Sr. Evelyn Ronan, S.N.D., Pastoral Assoc. In Res., Rev. Msgr. John J. Philbin (Retired); Deacon J. Scott Abercrombie.
Res.: 9 Glen Rd., Wellesley Hills, 02481-1600. Tel: 781-235-0045; Fax: 781-235-6990. Email: st-johns@comcast.net.
School—9 Ledyard St., 02481. Tel: 781-235-0300. Sisters 2; Lay Teachers 5; Students 187.
Catechesis / Religious Program—Tel: 781-235-5337. Joanne Pratt, D.R.E. Students 537.

3—St. Paul (1922), Revs. Richard W. Fitzgerald, Admin.; Michael C. Harrington; Deacon Paul M. Cloonan.
Res.: 502 Washington St., 02482. Tel: 781-235-1060; Fax: 781-235-4620. Email: StPaul_office@k12edu.com. Web: www.StPaulWellesley.com.
School—10 Atwood St., 02482. Tel: 781-235-1510. Sisters 3; Lay Teachers 7; Students 134.

West Bridgewater, Plymouth Co., St. Ann (1938), Rev. Edward C. McDonagh.
Res.: 103 N. Main St., Box 427, 02379-0427. Tel: 508-586-4880; Fax: 508-588-0239.

West Newbury, Essex Co., St. Ann (1945), Rev. John F. Leonard.
Res.: 46 Maple St., Box 237, 01985. Tel: 978-363-2303; Fax: 978-363-2046. Email: st.ann@greennet.net. Web: www.st-anns.west-newbury.ma.us.
Catechesis / Religious Program—Tel: 978-363-2685. Doreen O'Leary, D.R.E.; Barbara Gangi, D.R.E. Students 299.

Westford, Middlesex Co., St. Catherine of Alexandria (1922), Very Rev. William M. Sullivan, V.F.; Rev. Thomas J. Stanton; Deacons Russell W. Morey; Richard T. Joy. In Res., Most Rev. Emilio Simeon Allue, S.D.B., D.D., S.T.L., Ph.D.; Rev. Daniel F. Cronin (Retired).
Res.: 107 N. Main St., 01886-1219. Tel: 978-692-6353; Fax: 978-392-0644.

Weston, Middlesex Co., St. Julia (1919), Rev. Robert D. Tyrrell; Susan Bayard, Pastoral Assoc.
Res.: 374 Boston Post Rd., 02193. Tel: 781-899-2611; Fax: 781-899-8046.
Catechesis / Religious Program—Tel: 781-899-8434; Fax: 781-899-2611. Vincent G. Capodilupo, D.R.E. Students 500.

Westwood, Norfolk Co.

1—St. Denis (1949), Rev. Edwin D. Condon; Sr. Anne P. O'Connell, D.R.E. Tel: 781-326-2335; Deacon Joseph L. Delaney.
Res.: 157 Washington St., 02090-1336. Tel: 781-326-5858; Fax: 781-326-1232. Web: www.StDenisWestwood.com.

2—St. Margaret Mary (1931), Rev. T. Joseph Moynihan; Deacons Joseph E. Holderried; Joseph M. Messina.
Res.: 845 High St., Box 386, 02090-0386. Tel: 781-326-1071; Fax: 781-329-1879. Email: saintmm@comcast.net. Web: www.rc.net/boston/StMargMary.
Catechesis / Religious Program—Tel: 781-326-8005. Mary Lou Petty, D.R.E. Students 584.

Weymouth, Norfolk Co.

1—St. Albert the Great (1950), Rev. Ronald D. Coyne.
Res.: 1130 Washington St., 02189-1997. Tel: 781-337-8778; Fax: 781-335-5850.

2—St. Francis Xavier (1859), Rev. Eugene P. Sullivan; Deacon Joseph A. Canova.
Res.: 261 Pleasant St., 02190-2507. Tel: 781-337-2171; Fax: 781-331-4192.

School—234 Pleasant St., 02190. Tel: 781-335-6868. Religious 2; Lay Teachers 5; Students 172.
Catechesis/Religious Program—Tel: 781-331-6264. Marge Kearney, D.R.E.; Chris Gaffney, D.R.E. Students 1,064.

3—IMMACULATE CONCEPTION (1879), Revs. Paul Miceli; Linh T. Nguyen; Deacon Francis Corbett, Pastoral Assoc.
Res.: 1199 Commercial St., 02189. Tel: 781-337-0380; Fax: 781-340-3979.
Catechesis/Religious Program—Sr. Mary Reardon, D.R.E. Tel: 781-337-3024; Ruthann Sinibaldi, D.R.E. Tel: 781-335-3902. Students 840.

4—ST. JEROME (1928), Revs. Thomas F. Wyndham; Edward F Doughty. In Res., Rev. Msgr. Peter T. Martocchio (Retired).
Res.: 632 Bridge St., 02191-1845. Tel: 781-335-2038; Fax: 781-340-7165.
School—Tel: 781-335-1235. Sisters 1; Lay Teachers 9; Students 234.
Catechesis/Religious Program—Tel: 781-335-2786. Sr. Barbara Joyce, C.S.J., D.R.E. Students 590.

5—SACRED HEART (1871), Revs. Daniel J. Riley; Harry J. Kaufman. In Res., Rev. Arthur M. Calter (Retired).
Res.: 55 Commercial St., 02188-2604. Tel: 781-337-6333; Fax: 781-337-9192. Web: www.SacredHearthWeymouth.org.
School—75 Commercial St., 02188-2604. Tel: 781-335-6010. Sisters 2; Lay Teachers 7; Students 165.

WHITMAN, PLYMOUTH CO., HOLY GHOST (1897), Rev. Robert P. Reed; Deacon Joseph T. Nickley. In Res., Most Rev. Richard Joseph Malone, D.D., S.T.L., Th.D.; Rev. Paul E. Curran (Retired).
Res.: 518 Washington St., 02382. Tel: 781-447-4421; Fax: 781-447-1375. Email: mail@HolyGhostParish.com. Web: www.HolyGhost-Parish.com.

WILMINGTON, MIDDLESEX CO.

1—ST. DOROTHY (1954), Rev. Kevin P. Horrigan.
Res.: 11 Harnden St., 01887-3519. Tel: 978-988-0054; Fax: 978-658-2008. Web: www.SaintDorothy.2om.com.
Catechesis/Religious Program—Tel: 978-658-9713. Sr. Mildred Rothwell, O.S.F., D.R.E. Students 682.

2—ST. THOMAS OF VILLANOVA (1919), Revs. Philip B. Earley; Paul G. Flammia; Deacon Clifford D. King.
Res.: 126 Middlesex Ave., Box 397, 01887-2723. Tel: 978-658-4665; Fax: 978-658-4670.

WINCHESTER, MIDDLESEX CO.

1—ST. EULALIA (1966), Revs. Victor C. LaVoie; Thomas F. Nestor, Ph.D., Admin.; Mary Lou Burke, Pastoral Assoc.
Res.: 38 Ridge St., 01890-3633. Tel: 781-729-8220; Fax: 781-729-0919. Email: StEulalia@worldnet.att.net. Web: www.st_eulalia-.homestead.com.

2—IMMACULATE CONCEPTION (1931), Rev. Thomas S. Foley, Admin.
Res.: 1004 Main St., 01890-1929. Tel: 781-729-1858; Fax: 781-729-4253.

3—ST. MARY (1876), Revs. Richard C. Messina; Richard C. Beaulieu; Deacon James V. Kerrigan; Mr. Salvatore Caraviello, Pastoral Assoc.; Mr. Brian McCrohan, Pastoral Assoc. In Res., Rev. Paul G. Kelley (Retired).
Res.: 158 Washington St., 01890. Tel: 781-729-0055; Fax: 781-721-6542.
School—162 Washington St., 01890. Tel: 781-729-5515. Lay Teachers 7; Students 144.

WINTHROP, SUFFOLK CO.

1—HOLY ROSARY (1953), Rev. Thomas A. DiLorenzo, Admin.
Res.: 1015 Shirley St., 02152-2535. Tel: 617-846-1210; Fax: 617-539-4402. Web: www.HolyRosary-Parish.net.

2—ST. JOHN THE EVANGELIST (1907), Revs. Charles E. Bourke; Raymond Van De Moortell, S.J.; Sr. Jane Iannaccone, S.P., Pastoral Assoc.
Res.: 320 Winthrop St., 02152-3127. Tel: 617-846-7400; Fax: 617-539-0627. Web: www.StJohnsWinthrop.org.
Catechesis/Religious Program—Tel: 617-846-3100. Mrs. Geraldine Butters, D.R.E.; Mrs. Shirley Guthro, D.R.E. Students 948.

WOBURN, MIDDLESEX CO.

1—ST. ANTHONY (1945), Revs. Leo X. Lynch; John R. Carroll.
Res.: 80 Elm St., 01801-1855. Tel: 781-933-1323; Fax: 781-937-3233.
Catechesis/Religious Program—Tel: 781-933-6472. Salli Ford, D.R.E.; Joe Ford, D.R.E. Students 500.

2—ST. BARBARA (1954), Very Rev. Vincent P. Mellone, V.F.; Rev. Thomas J. Reilly. In Res., Rev. Edward G. Carroll.
Res.: 138 Cambridge Rd., 01801-4772. Tel: 781-933-4130; Fax: 781-932-2536.

3—ST. CHARLES BORROMEO, Formerly St. Charles (1862), Revs. Timothy J. Shea; Wayne L. Belschner; James M. Acadinha; Deacon Philip P. Hardcastle. In Res., Rev. Patrick J. Kelly (Retired).
Res.: 280 Main St., 01801. Tel: 781-933-0300; Fax: 781-932-7581.
School—Tel: 781-935-4635. Lay Teachers 19; Students 315.
Catechesis/Religious Program—Tel: 781-933-7595. Students 500.

4—ST. JOSEPH (1906), Rev. Harold E. LeBlanc.
Res.: 22 Central St., 01801-4616. Tel: 781-938-0473; Fax: 781-938-7818.

WRENTHAM, NORFOLK CO., ST. MARY (1928), Rev. John G. Connolly; Deacon Kenneth W. Oles.
Res.: 130 South St., Box 326, 02093-0326. Tel: 508-384-3373; Fax: 508-384-5747. Email: StMary@localnet.com. Web: StMarysWrentham.org.

Special Chaplaincies:
Revs.—
Bradford, Richard S., Chap., 192 Foster St., Brighton, 02135-4620. (Anglican Use)
Roy, George, O.M.I. (Haiti), Chap., 45 Alewife Brook Pkwy., Cambridge, 02140.

Chaplains of Public Institutions

BOSTON. *Health Care Ministry*, Our Lady Hall, St. Elizabeth Medical Center, 736 Cambridge St., 02135-2997. Tel: 617-789-2457; Fax: 617-789-2573. Ms. Kelly L. Dunn, Dir.

NEWTON. *Office of Prison Ministry*, 251 Watertown St., 02158. Tel: 617-244-7544; Fax: 617-244-7891. Vacant.

Health Care Ministry

BOSTON. *Arbour Hospital*, 49 Robinwood Ave., 02130. Tel: 617-522-4400. Attended by Our Lady of Lourdes, Jamaica Plain.
Beth Israel Deaconess Medical Center, 330 Brookline Ave., 02215. Tel: 617-667-4205. Revs. John P. Carroll, Spiritual Care Svcs. Tel: 617-667-4205, Peter Grover, O.M.V., Spiritual Care Svcs., Bruce Aguilar, Spiritual Care Svcs. Tel: 617-632-8103.
Boston Medical Center, University Campus, One Medical Center Pl., 02118-2393. Tel: 617-638-6851. Rev. Raymond P. Benoit, Spiritual Care Svcs.
Boston Medical Center, Boston City Campus, 818 Harrison Ave., 02118. Tel: 617-534-5336. Sr. Claire Hayes, C.D.P., Spiritual Care Svcs., Carmela D'Elia, Spiritual Care Svcs.
Brigham and Women's Hospital, 75 Francis St., 02115-6195. Tel: 617-732-7480; Fax: 617-232-2746. Rev. George P. Winchester, S.J., Spiritual Care Svcs.
Children's Hospital, 300 Longwood Ave., 02115. Tel: 617-355-4775. Rev. Mark J. Riley, Spiritual Care Svcs., Sr. Carlotta Gilarde, C.S.J., Spiritual Care Svcs.
Dana Farber Cancer Institute, 44 Binney St., 02115. Tel: 617-732-3000. Rev. John E. Doherty, C.SS.R., Spiritual Care Svcs.
St. Elizabeth's Medical Center, 736 Cambridge St., 02135-2997. Tel: 617-789-3045; Fax: 617-789-2124. Ms. Kelly L. Dunn, Dir., Our Lady Hall, Sr. Catherine O'Connor, C.S.B., Spiritual Care Svcs., Revs. Phillip M. Conroy, Spiritual Care Svcs., Garrett J. Thompson, Spiritual Care Svcs., Yaroslov Nalysnk, Spiritual Care Svcs., Matthew Perumpil, O.S.C., Spiritual Care Svcs., Sisters Susan Keating, Spiritual Care Svcs., MaryAnn Gallagher, O.S.F., Spiritual Care Svcs., Ivan Cadigan, C.S.J., Spiritual Care Svcs., Deacon Fran Bogle, Spiritual Care Svcs., Ann Cody, Spiritual Care Svcs., Edna Lezotte, Spiritual Care Svcs.
*St. Margaret's Center*Martha Sullivan.
Hebrew Rehabilitation Center, 1200 Centre St., 02131. Tel: 617-325-8000. Attended by Sacred Heart, Roslindale.
Jewish Memorial Hospital, 59 Townsend St., 02119. Tel: 617-442-8760. Attended by St. Joseph, Roxbury.
Massachusetts General Hospital, 32 Fruit St., 02114. Tel: 617-726-2222; Fax: 617-724-3401. Revs. Philip E. McGaugh, Spiritual Care Svcs., Felix C. Ojimba (Nigeria), Spiritual Care Svcs., Michael McElhinny, S.M., Spiritual Care Svcs.
New England Medical Center, 750 Washington St., 02111. Tel: 617-636-7500. Revs. Jan Hernick, O.F.M.Conv., Spiritual Care Svcs., Dac Tat Tran, O.F.M., Spiritual Care Svcs., James M. Shaughnessy, S.J., Spiritual Care Svcs., Amy Edmonds, Spiritual Care Svcs.
Shriners Burn Institute, 51 Blossom St., 02114. Tel: 617-722-3000. Attended by St. Joseph, Boston.
Spaulding Rehabilitation Hospital, 125 Nashua St., 02114-1198. Tel: 617-720-6400; Fax: 617-720-6960. Sr. Mary Samson, S.H.C.J., Spiritual Care Svcs.

ARLINGTON. *Medical Center at Symmes*, Hospital Rd., 02174. Tel: 781-646-1500. Attended by St. Agnes, Arlington.

AYER. *Deaconess-Nashoba Hospital*, 200 Groton St., 01432. Tel: 978-772-0200. Attended by St. Mary, Ayer.

BEDFORD. *Veterans Administration Hospital Bedford*, 200 Spring Rd., 01730. Tel: 781-687-2384. Revs. Joseph P. Robinson, Spiritual Care Svcs., Philip A. Cabasino, C.SS.R., Spiritual Care Svcs., Aidan J. Walsh, J.C.L., Spiritual Care Svcs., Deacon John Watson, Spiritual Care Svcs.

BELMONT. *Fernald Developmental Center*, Box 150, 02178. Tel: 781-894-3600, Ext. 2117. Rev. William T. Leonard, Spiritual Care Svcs., Deacon Eugene Counihan, Spiritual Care Svcs.
McLean Hospital, 115 Mill St., 02178. Tel: 617-855-2000. Attended by St. Luke, Belmont.

BEVERLY. *Beverly Hospital*, Herrick St., 01915. Tel: 978-922-3000, Ext. 2790. Joan Rossi, Spiritual Care Svcs.

BRAINTREE. *Healthsouth Braintree Hospital*, 250 Pond St., 02184. Tel: 781-848-5353. Attended by St. Francis of Assisi, Braintree.
Massachusetts Respiratory Hospital, 2001 Washington St., 02185. Tel: 781-848-2600. Attended by St. Clare, Braintree.

BRIGHTON. *Franciscan Children's Hospital*, 30 Warren St., 02135. Tel: 617-779-1644. Sisters Helen Mary McGonagle, C.S.J., Spiritual Care Svcs., Rena Foley, C.S.J., Spiritual Care Svcs., Patricia Huff Byrne, Spiritual Care Svcs.
St. John of God Hospital, 296 Allston St., 02135. Tel: 617-277-5750. Rev. Joseph K. Coleman, Spiritual Care Svcs., Sr. Alicia Brennan, D.C., Spiritual Care Svcs.
Vencor Hospital Boston, 1515 Commonwealth Ave., 02135. Tel: 617-254-1100. Rev. George Thekkummattathil, C.S.C., Spiritual Care Svcs.

BROCKTON. *Brockton Hospital*, 680 Centre St., 02402. Tel: 508-941-7000, Ext. 2550. Rev. David Murphy, Spiritual Care Svcs., Deacon John Connor, Spiritual Care Svcs.
Good Samaritan Medical Center, 235 N. Pearl St., 02401. Tel: 508-427-2376. Rev. Richard W. Visbisky, Spiritual Care Svcs., Sisters Margaret Crowley, S.C.N., Spiritual Care Svcs., George Powell, C.J.C., Spiritual Care Svcs., Helen Carpinelli, S.U.S.C., Spiritual Care Svcs., Eileen McCarthy, R.N., Spiritual Care Svcs.
Veterans Administration Hospital Brockton-West Roxbury, 940 Belmont St., 02402. Tel: 508-583-4500, Ext. 1125. Revs. Henry P. Nichols, Spiritual Care Svcs., Avelino R. Garcia, Spiritual Care Svcs.

BROOKLINE. *Bournewood Hospital*, 300 South St., 02146. Tel: 617-469-0300. Attended by Infant Jesus, Brookline.

BURLINGTON. *Lahey Hitchcock Medical Center*, 41 Mall Rd., 01805. Tel: 781-744-8800. Rev. Clif Moors, S.M., Spiritual Care Svcs., William W. Houghton, Spiritual Care Svcs.

CAMBRIDGE. *Cambridge Hospital*, 1493 Cambridge St., 02139. Tel: 617-498-1000. Attended by St. Mary, Cambridge.
Mount Auburn Hospital, 330 Mt. Auburn St., 02238. Tel: 617-499-5665, Ext. 4669. Revs. Lucien A. Sawyer, O.M.I., Spiritual Care Svcs., Celestino Vasquez Pascual, Spiritual Care Svcs., Sr. Margaret Holleran, Spiritual Care Svcs.
Youville Lifecare, Inc., 1575 Cambridge St., 02138-4398. Tel: 617-876-4344, Ext. 333. Revs. Ronald Paquin, Spiritual Care Svcs., William J. Mulligan, S.J., Spiritual Care Svcs., Sr. Virginia Murray, C.S.J., Spiritual Care Svcs., Patricia Kennedy, Spiritual Care Svcs., Elizabeth Walsh, Spiritual Care Svcs., Georgia Gojmerac Leiner, Spiritual Care Svcs.

CANTON. *Massachusetts Hospital School*, Randolph St., 02121. Tel: 781-828-2440. Attended by St. Gerard Majella, Canton.

CHELSEA. *Quigley Memorial Hospital*, 91 Crest Ave., 02150. Tel: 617-889-7146. Rev. Lawrence F. Sullivan, O.C.D., Spiritual Care Svcs.

CONCORD. *Emerson Hospital*, Rte. 2 ORNAC, P.O. Box 9120, 01742-9120. Tel: 978-287-3015. Joan Horgan, Spiritual Care Svcs.

DORCHESTER. *Carney Hospital*, 2100 Dorchester Ave., 02124-5666. Tel: 617-296-4000, Ext. 2187; Fax: 617-296-9513. Revs. Mikel Satcher, Spiritual Care Svcs., John J. Caskin, S.J., Spiritual Care Svcs., Sisters Paula Tinlin, S.N.D., Spiritual Care Svcs., Lillian McDonald, C.S.J., Spiritual Care Svcs., Ms. Jean Marchant, Spiritual Care Svcs.

EVERETT. *Whidden Memorial Hospital*, 103 Garland St., 02149. Tel: 617-389-6270, Ext. 2202. Sr. Agnes Melly, C.S.J., Spiritual Care Svcs.

FRAMINGHAM. *Metro West Medical Center*, Framingham Campus, 115 Lincoln St., 01701-9167. Tel: 508-383-1007. Rev. Robert E. Champagne, S.M., Spiritual Care Svcs., Sr. Ursula Tisdall, O.S.F., Spiritual Care Svcs., Deacon Augusto Diotalevi, Spiritual Care Svcs.

GLOUCESTER. *Addison Gilbert Hospital*, 298 Washington St., 01930. Tel: 978-283-4000. Attended by St. Ann, Gloucester.

HAVERHILL. *Hale Hospital*, 140 Lincoln Ave., 01830. Tel: 978-374-2000. Attended by St. John the

Baptist, Haverhill.

Whittier Rehabilitation Hospital, 76 Summer St., 01830. Tel: 978-372-8000. Attended by St. Joseph, Haverhill.

JAMAICA PLAIN. *Faulkner Hospital*, 1153 Centre St., 02130. Tel: 617-983-7000, Ext. 1556. Deacon Leonard F. DeCoste, Spiritual Care Svcs.

Jamaica Plain, 150 S. Huntington Ave., 02130. Tel: 617-232-9500. Revs. Philip Salois, Roger A. Sinclair.

Lemuel Shattuck Hospital, 170 Morton St., 02130. Tel: 617-522-8110, Ext. 463. Rev. Leonard J. Tighe, Spiritual Care Svcs.

Veterans Administration Hospital, 150 S. Huntington Ave., 02130. Tel: 617-232-9500. Revs. Philip Salois, Spiritual Care Svcs., Roger A. Sinclair, Spiritual Care Svcs.

LAWRENCE. *Lawrence General Hospital*, One General St., 01842. Tel: 978-683-4000, Ext. 2344. Maureen LaBelle, Spiritual Care Svcs.

LOWELL. *Lowell General Hospital*, 295 Varnum Ave., 01854. Tel: 978-937-6418. Sr. Eileen Auger, C.S.C., Spiritual Care Svcs.

Saints Memorial Medical Center, Hospital Dr. (Box 30), 01852. Tel: 978-458-1411. Revs. John J. Hogan, O.M.I., Spiritual Care Svcs., Romeo J. Murphy, O.M.I., Spiritual Care Svcs., Sr. Doris Brouillette, S.C.O., Spiritual Care Svcs., Dr. John Giannino, Spiritual Care Svcs., Patricia Hardy, Spiritual Care Svcs.

LYNN. *Atlanticare Medical Center*, 500 Lynnfield St., 01904. Tel: 781-581-9200. Deacon Lawrence R. McManus, Spiritual Care Svcs.

MARLBOROUGH. *Marlborough Hospital*, 57 Union St., 01752. Tel: 508-485-1121. Attended by St. Mary, Marlborough.

MEDFIELD. *Medfield State Hospital*, 45 Hospital Rd., 02052-2406. Tel: 508-359-7312, Ext. 4371. Rev. John J. Hever, Spiritual Care Svcs.

MEDFORD. *Lawrence Memorial Hospital of Medford*, 170 Governor's Ave., 02155. Tel: 781-306-6000. Rosemary Burke, Spiritual Care Svcs.

MELROSE. *Melrose-Wakefield Hospital*, 585 Lebannon St., 02176. Tel: 781-979-3011. Sr. Eunice Condrick, C.S.J., Spiritual Care Svcs.

METHUEN. *Holy Family Hospital, Inc.*, 70 East St., 01844. Tel: 978-687-0151, Ext. 2005. Sr. Claudia Blanchette, S.N.D., Spiritual Care Svcs., Rev. John T. Crabb, S.J., Chap. & Spiritual Care Svcs., Martha Byron, Nursing Svcs.

MILTON. *Milton Hospital*, 92 Highland St., 02186. Tel: 617-696-4600, Ext. 1801. Sr. Nora O'Connell, S.N.D., Spiritual Care Svcs.

NATICK. *Metro West*, Leonard Morse Campus, 67 Union St., 01760. Tel: 508-650-7331. Attended by St. Patrick, Natick

NEEDHAM. *Deaconess-Glover Hospital*, 148 Chestnut St., 02192. Tel: 781-444-5600. Attended by St. Joseph, Needham.

NEWBURYPORT. *Anna Jacques Hospital*, Highland Ave., 01950. Tel: 978-462-6601. Attended by Immaculate Conception, Newburyport.

NEWTON. *Newton-Wellesley Hospital*, 2014 Washington St., 02162. Tel: 617-243-6634. Ann Lomuto, Spiritual Care Svcs.

NORFOLK. *Caritas Southwood Hospital*, 111 Dedham St., 02056. Tel: 781-278-6045. Sr. Barbara Lavin, O.P., Spiritual Care Svcs.

NORWOOD. *Caritas Norwood Hospital*, 800 Washington St., 02062. Tel: 781-278-6045, Ext. 2012. Rev. Robert G. LaBrie, Spiritual Care Svcs., Sr. Barbara Lavin, O.P., Spiritual Care Svcs.

PEABODY. *Vencor-Boston Northshore*, 15 King St., 01960. Tel: 978-531-2900. Attended by St. John the Baptist, Peabody.

PLYMOUTH. *Jordan Hospital*, 275 Sandwich St., 02360. Tel: 508-746-2000, Ext. 2662. Nan Bouche, Spiritual Care Svcs.

QUINCY. *Quincy Hospital*, 114 Whitwell St., 02169. Tel: 617-773-6100, Ext. 5501. Rev. Theodore L. Fortier, A.A., Spiritual Care Svcs.

ROXBURY. *New England Baptist Hospital*, 91 Parker Hill Ave., 02120. Tel: 617-754-5160. Rev. Joseph O'Brien, Spiritual Care Svcs.

SALEM. *North Shore Medical Center*, 57 Highland Ave., 01970. Tel: 978-741-0631 (Rectory); 978-741-1215 (P.C. Dept.). Rev. Edward M. Keohan, Spiritual Care Svcs., Jane Korins, Spiritual Care Svcs., Christopher Junker, Spiritual Care Svcs.

SOMERVILLE. *Somerville Hospital*, 230 Highland Ave., 02143. Tel: 617-666-4400. Attended by St. Catherine, Somerville.

SOUTH WEYMOUTH. *South Shore Hospital*, 55 Frogg Rd., 02190. Tel: 781-340-8589; 781-340-8612. Rev. Daniel Crowley, Spiritual Care Svcs., Mary T. O'Connor, Spiritual Care Svcs.

STOUGHTON. *New England Sinai Hospital*, 150 York St., 02072. Tel: 781-344-0600, Ext. 302; Fax: 781-344-3226. Rev. Msgr. William A. Granville, Spiritual Care Svcs. (Retired), Rev. William O'Connor, Spiritual Care Svcs., Sr. Ellen Reilly, S.N.D., Spiritual Care Svcs.

TEWKSBURY. *Tewksbury Hospital*, East St., 01876. Tel: 978-851-7321, Ext. 288. Rev. Edward Lowney, O.M.I., Spiritual Care Svcs., John Carley, Spiritual Care Svcs.

WALTHAM. *Deaconess-Waltham Hospital*, Hope Ave., 02154. Tel: 781-647-6573. Elinor Quill, Spiritual Care Svcs., Arlene Larsen, Spiritual Care Svcs.

WESTWOOD. *Westwood Lodge Hospital*, 45 Clapboard St., 02090. Tel: 781-762-7764. Attended by St. Margaret Mary, Westwood.

WINCHESTER. *Winchester Hospital*, 41 Highland Ave., 01890. Tel: 781-729-9000. Sr. Geraldine DeFilippo, R.C.E., Spiritual Care Svcs.

WOBURN. *Healthsouth New England Rehabilitation Hospital*, Two Rehabilitation Way, 01801. Tel: 617-636-7500. Attended by St. Barbara, Woburn.

WRENTHAM. *Wrentham State School*, Box 144, 02093. Tel: 508-384-3114. Rev. John Fernz, Spiritual Care Svcs.

Prison Ministry

BRIDGEWATER. *Bridgewater State Hospital & Treatment Center*, 12 Administration Rd., 02324. Tel: 617-727-7672. Rev. James F. Lanergan.

Massachusetts Boot Camp, 12 Administration Rd., 02324. Tel: 617-727-7672. Deacon John W. McHugh.

Old Colony Correction Center, One Administration Rd., 02324. Tel: 617-727-3400. Deacon John W. McHugh.

Southeastern Correctional Center, 12 Administration Rd., 02324. Tel: 617-727-7672. Deacon Thomas H. Hanlon.

CARVER. *MCI-Plymouth*, Myles Standish State Forest, Box 207, 02355. Tel: 617-727-8938. Deacon John W. McHugh.

CONCORD. *MCI-Concord*, 965 Elm St., Box 00, 01742. Tel: 617-727-1950. Rev. Peter J. Murphy.

Northeast Correctional Center, Barretts Mill Rd., 01742. Tel: 617-727-0288. Deacon Arthur F. Rogers Jr.

FRAMINGHAM. *MCI-Framingham*, 99 Loring St., 01701. Tel: 617-727-5056. Sr. Maureen Clark, C.S.J.

South Middlesex Correctional Center, 135 Western Ave., Box 850, 01701. Tel: 617-727-5676. Sr. Maureen Clark, C.S.J.

JAMAICA PLAIN. *Shattuck Hospital Correctional Unit*, 180 Morton St., 02130. Tel: 617-727-6904. Rev. Leonard J. Tighe.

MATTAPAN. *Metropolitan Youth Service Center*, 591 Morton St., 02126. Tel: 617-288-9100. Rev. Joseph J. Baggetta.

NORFOLK. *Baystate Correctional Facility*, 28 Clark St., Box 73, 02056. Tel: 617-727-8474. Deacon John J. Mannion.

MCI-Norfolk, 2 Clark St., Box 43, 02056. Tel: 617-727-1480. Ms. Ruth Raichle, Sr. Kathleen Denevan, O.S.F., Deacon Gerald Rooney, Ms. Ruth Raichle.

Pondville Correctional Center, Box 146, 02056. Tel: 617-727-5203. Ms. Elizabeth Slaney, Catholic Co-ord., Sr. Kathleen Denevan, O.S.F., Ms. Ruth Raichle.

ROSLINDALE. *Judge John J. Connelly Youth Center*, 450 Canterbury St., 02131. Tel: 617-288-9100. Rev. Joseph J. Baggetta.

SHIRLEY. *MCI-Shirley*, Medium and Minimum Facilities, P.O. Box 1218, 01464. Tel: 978-425-4341. Rev. John Kilmartin, F.D.P., Deacons Carroll H. Taylor. Tel: 978-425-4341, Ext. 4818 Medium Facilities, Arthur F. Rogers Jr. Tel: 978-425-4341, Ext. 2267 Minimum Facilities

SOUTH WALPOLE. *MCI-Cedar Junction*, Rte. 1A, Box 100, 02071. Tel: 617-727-1686. Deacon John Mannion.

County Facilities

BOSTON. *Nashua Street Jail*, 200 Nashua St., 02114. Tel: 617-635-1100. Bro. George T. Williams, S.J.

Suffolk County House of Correction at South Bay, 20 Brandston St., 02118. Tel: 617-635-1000. Bro. George T. Williams, S.J.

BILERICA. *Middlesex County House of Correction*, Treble Pond Rd., Billerica, 01821. Deacon Harold E. Killam.

CAMBRIDGE. *Middlesex County Jail*, 40 Thorndike St., 02146. Tel: 617-494-4375. Deacon Harold E. Killam.

DEDHAM. *Norfolk County House of Correction*, 200 West St., 02026. Tel: 617-696-0593. Rev. Robert P. Beale.

MIDDLETON. *Essex County Correctional Facility*, 20 Manning Ave., 01949. Tel: 617-542-2564 978-750-1900. Rev. Jon C. Martin, Mr. Jack McCauley, Catholic Coord.

PLYMOUTH. *Plymouth County Correctional Facility*, 26 Long Pond Rd., 02360. Tel: 508-830-6200. Ms. Loraine Pietrantonio, Catholic Coord.

Absent on Leave:
For contact information please call or write: Clergy Personnel Office 2121 Commonwealth Ave., Boston, MA 02135-3193; Tel.:617-779-3685

Revs.—
De Angelis, Mark J.
Malloy, Stephen J.
McCarthy, Paul R.
Parker, Paul M.
Shay, James C.

Emergency Response Group:
For contact information please call or write: Clergy Personnel Office 2121 Commonwealth Ave., Boston MA 02135-3193; Tel.: 617-779-3685

Revs.—
John SwenckiT., (Permanent)
Casey, Richard L., (Temporary)
Kelleher, Robert N., (Temporary)
Kelley, Thomas P., (Temporary)
Sheridan, John E., (Temporary)

Graduate Studies:
For further information contact 617-779-3685

Rev. Msgr.—
McDonough, John P. (Retired)

Revs.—
Braley, James E.
Condon, Edwin A.
Connolly, John J.
Daily, Vincent E. (Retired)
Euvard, Scott A.
Kirwan, Christopher J., Jr., S.T.D.
Laughlin, James J., J.C.L.
Le, Hoang V.
Murphy, William F.
Thompson, Garrett J.

Higher Studies:
For contact information please call or write: Clergy Personnel Office 2121 Commonwealth Ave., Boston MA 02135-3193; Tel.: 617-779-3685

Revs.—
Mahoney, Brian E.
O'Connor, Christopher K.

Health Leave:
For contact information please call or write: Clergy Personnel Office 2121 Commonwealth Ave., Boston MA 02135-3193; Tel.: 617-779-3685

Revs.—
Ajemian, David J.
Andrade, Antonio L.
Bouton, Thomas F.
Flammia, Paul G.
Franz, Paul R.
Keane, John F.
Kelley, Laurence E.
Keville, Joseph F.
Reardon, John F.
St. Pierre, Ronald L.
Tyrrell, Robert D.
Walsh, William D.

Military & VA Chaplains:
For contact information please call or write: Clergy Personnel Office 2121 Commonwealth Ave., Boston MA 02135-3193; Tel.: 617-779-3685

Revs.—
Butler, Timothy A.
Crowley, Francis J.
Cuddy, William F.
Deeley, Kevin J.
Devine, William J.
Erickson, Richard M.
Hurley, Paul K.
Kennedy, William M.
Linehan, Stephen J.
McCabe, Edward D.
Monagle, Robert P.
Nichols, Henry P.
Raux, Redmond P.
Robinson, Joseph P.
Rock, Stephen B.
Russo, Lawrence J.

On Duty Outside the Archdiocese:
For contact information please call or write: Clergy Personnel Office 2121 Commonwealth Ave., Boston MA 02135-3193; Tel.: 617-779-3685

Rev. Msgrs.—
Abruzzese, John A.
Fay, William P.
Russell, Paul F.

Revs.—
Brown, Francis E.
Capuci, John M. (NO)
Donahue, Richard T.
Driscoll, Joseph J.
Galvin, John P., D.Th.

Kennedy, Arthur L.
McMahon, Gerard T.
McNeil, John R.
Moran, James F.
Picardi, John M.
Pucciarelli, George W.
Sullivan, Robert E.

Permanent Disability:
For Contact Information please call or write: Office for Senior Priests, Regina Cleri Residence, 60 William Cardinal O' Connell Way, Boston, MA 02114-2729, Tel.: 617-523-1861
Revs.—
Brennick, Stephen F.
Butler, James P.
DesRosiers, Philip J.
DiFruscio, John A.
Driscoll, Nicholas J.
Fraser, Gerald C.
Gomes, Ronald A.
Kane, Joseph M.
Kinsella, Charles R.
MacKenzie, William M.
McGrade, Kevin M.
Morris, John S. (Retired)
Mullin, William H.
Santerre, Richard R.
Scanlan, William A.
Walsh, Martin J.

Senior Priests:
For further information contact 617-523-1861
Rev. Msgrs.—
Abucewicz, John A. (Retired)
Alves, Joseph T. (Retired)
Anadore, Charles E. (Retired)
Boyle, Robert J. (Retired)
Collins, Russell J. (Retired)
Contons, Albert J. (Retired)
Coppenrath, Leonard (Retired)
Daly, Thomas J. (Retired)
Day, John D. (Retired)
Fichtner, Robert C. (Retired)
Finnegan, Thomas J. (Retired)
Forster, William J. (Retired)
Granville, William A. (Retired)
Haddad, James J. (Retired)
Lawler, John F. (Retired)
Lind, Joseph G. (Retired)
Martocchio, Peter T. (Retired)
McDonough, John P. (Retired)
McManus, Frederick R. (Retired)
McManus, Paul J. (Retired)
McNamara, Eugene P. (Retired)
Moritz, Paul L. (Retired)
O'Sullivan, Francis G. (Retired)
Palladino, Alfonso G. (Retired)
Philbin, John J. (Retired)
Roche, William H. (Retired)
Shea, William B. (Retired)
Sheehan, John J. (Retired)
Sullivan, William P. (Retired)
Sviokla, Edmund J. (Retired)
Very Rev.—
Craig, Richard J. (Retired)
Revs.—
Ahearn, Richard F. (Retired)
Anderson, William R. (Retired)
Bailey, Paul F. (Retired)
Barrett, Daniel J. (Retired)
Barry, Gerard B. (Retired)
Beksha, Francis W. (Retired)
Bergeron, Robert E. (Retired)
Bernatonis, John F. (Retired)
Bertelli, Ameilio J. (Retired)
Berube, Paul W. (Retired)
Billicky, Louis S. (Retired)
Blute, Robert H. (Retired)
Boivin, Henry P. (Retired)
Bonfiglio, David G. (Retired)
Brady, Richard J. (Retired)
Brady, Roger J. (Retired)
Brennan, Gerard M. (Retired)
Brennan, James F. (Retired)
Broderick, James M. (Retired)
Brown, Arthur A. (Retired)
Brudzynski, Peter F. (Retired)
Buckley, John K. (Retired)
Buckley, Thomas W. (Retired)
Burckhart, William C. (Retired)
Burns, John F. (Retired)
Calter, Arthur M. (Retired)
Campbell, William W. (Retired)
Canniff, James B. (Retired)
Carr, John F. (Retired)
Carr, Mark V. (Retired)
Carrigg, William J. (Retired)
Casey, Walter E. (Retired)
Cedrone, Laurence C. (Retired)
Clifford, Donald G. (Retired)
Clougherty, Paul L. (Retired)
Coffey, James H. (Retired)
Collins, Frederick J. (Retired)
Commane, William J. (Retired)
Connell, John K. (Retired)
Connolly, James H. (Retired)
Connolly, Maurice V. (Retired)
Corcoran, John W. (Retired)
Cormier, Leo G. (Retired)
Cormier, Roger C. (Retired)
Costello, Robert B. (Retired)
Cowhig, Edward D. (Retired)
Cronin, Daniel F. (Retired)
Curran, Paul E. (Retired)
Curtin, James F. (Retired)
Daily, John A. (Retired)
Daily, Vincent E. (Retired)
Daly, James J. (Retired)
Daniele, Anthony J. (Retired)
DeAdder, James W., S.T.D., Ph.D., J.D. (Retired)
Delaney, Francis H. (Retired)
DePietro, Arthur J. (Retired)
Desmond, Hubert E. (Retired)
Donovan, John L. (Retired)
Donovan, Joseph F. (Retired)
Doocey, Michael F. (Retired)
Downey, Joseph J. (Retired)
Doyle, John L. (Retired)
Doyle, Lawrence J. (Retired)
Doyle, Robert M. (Retired)
Driscoll, Arthur J. (Retired)
Driscoll, Richard A. (Retired)
Dufour, Louis C. (Retired)
Duggan, Charles T. (Retired)
Emerson, George F. (Retired)
Fallon, John F. (Retired)
Fallon, John J. (Retired)
Finnegan, John T. (Retired)
Fleming, Thomas J. (Retired)
Flynn, John H. (Retired)
Foley, Gerald J. (Retired)
Foley, John T. (Retired)
Foley, Thomas C. (Retired)
Francis, Paul R. (Retired)
Gagnon, Adelard J. (Retired)
Gagnon, Henry W. (Retired)
Gallagher, Edward L. (Retired)
Gallagher, Francis L. (Retired)
Gallagher, John E. (Retired)
Garrity, Francis D. (Retired)
Gaudet, Joseph A. (Retired)
Gibbons, James M. (Retired)
Gillis, Edward F. (Retired)
Gilmartin, Daniel J. (Retired)
Girardin, Peter T. (Retired)
Goss, Francis G. (Retired)
Gosselin, Robert H. (Retired)
Goulet, Raymond O. (Retired)
Grant, Frederick A. (Retired)
Guarcello, Russell V. (Retired)
Guerrette, William J. (Retired)
Hane, Howard S. (Retired)
Harrington, James J. (Retired)
Hession, James J. (Retired)
Hughes, Albert C. (Retired)
Janiunas, Albin F. (Retired)
Jennings, John J. (Retired)
Johnson, Richard G. (Retired)
Jusseaume, John E. (Retired)
Keane, Thomas F. (Retired)
Kelley, Paul G. (Retired)
Kelly, John P. (Retired)
Kelly, Patrick J. (Retired)
Kenneally, William F. (Retired)
Kierce, J. Joseph (Retired)
King, Edward L. (Retired)
King, Philip J. (Retired)
Koen, Stephen A. (Retired)
Kramer, George C. (Retired)
Lane, James H. (Retired)
LaRaia, Joseph P. (Retired)
Lawson, Harold F. (Retired)
Leonard, Clyde A. (Retired)
Leonard, Francis B. (Retired)
Lizio, John R. (Retired)
Logue, Charles D. (Retired)
Loiselle, Lucien H. (Retired)
Lucey, William F. (Retired)
Lukas, Joseph S. (Retired)
MacDonald, Stirling B. (Retired)
Mansfield, John L. (Retired)
Martin, Joseph I. (Retired)
McAskill, Kenneth F. (Retired)
McAuliffe, Robert J. (Retired)
McCarthy, Joseph S. (Retired)
McCarthy, William R. (Retired)
McConnell, William J. (Retired)
McConville, Philip G. (Retired)
McElroy, John W. (Retired)
McGahey, Charles R. (Retired)
McGann, Gerard J. (Retired)
McGann, Gerard J. (Retired)
McGowan, Frederick R. (Retired)
McLaughlin, Edward J. (Retired)
McLaughlin, Paul J. (Retired)
McMahon, Edward M. (Retired)
McPartland, Paul G. (Retired)
Meade, Henry J. (Retired)
Meade, Maurice P. (Retired)
Medeiros, Antonio S. (Retired)
Menna, Fiori D. (Retired)
Meskill, David B. (Retired)
Mooney, Thomas J. (Retired)
Moran, Daniel F. (Retired)
Moriarty, Thomas W. (Retired)
Morris, John S. (Retired)
Mottau, Robert S. (Retired)
Mulkern, John F. (Retired)
Murphy, Lawrence F. (Retired)
Murray, Frederick J. (Retired)
Murray, Thomas F. (Retired)
Nichols, John J. (Retired)
Noonan, Mark L., Ph.D. (Retired)
O'Brien, Frederick W. (Retired)
O'Connor, William B. (Retired)
O'Connor, William J. (Retired)
O'Donohoe, James A., J.C.D. (Retired)
O'Hara, Francis A. (Retired)
O'Hare, Francis C. (Retired)
O'Hearn, Paul V. (Retired)
O'Leary, Arthur P. (Retired)
O'Meara, Gerard J. (Retired)
O'Sullivan, Eugene M. (Retired)
Oliviera, Joel D. (Retired)
Parker, Edmund L (Retired)
Pearsall, William T. (Retired)
Perron, Richard J. (Retired)
Pied, Wilfrid L. (Retired)
Poirier, Vincent J. (Retired)
Pollis, Robert G. (Retired)
Powers, Richard J. (Retired)
Ready, Francis P. (Retired)
Regan, John J. (Retired)
Regan, Michael J. (Retired)
Reynolds, Thomas D. (Retired)
Riley, James H. (Retired)
Ronan, Henry T. (Retired)
Rothwell, Joseph T. (Retired)
Sallese, Albert J. (Retired)
Schatzel, John E. (Retired)
Shakalis, Peter A. (Retired)
Shea, John J. (Retired)
Sheehan, Daniel J. (Retired)
Sheehy, Charles I. (Retired)
Silk, John D. (Retired)
Smyth, Joseph P. (Retired)
Soucy, Robert P. (Retired)
Stocklosa, J. Walter (Retired)
Sullivan, James L. (Retired)
Sullivan, John L. (Retired)
Sullivan, Lawrence F. (Retired)
Sullivan, Michael D. (Retired)
Svirskas, Joseph J. (Retired)
Thomas, John E. (Retired)
Toland, Paul L. (Retired)
Toomey, John M. (Retired)
Vartzelis, George D. (Retired)
Vasaturo, Anthony J. (Retired)
Waldron, Robert J. (Retired)
Wasnewski, Richard P. (Retired)
Weber, Charles P. (Retired)
Wetterholm, Lawrence E. (Retired)
White, John J. (Retired)
Whittier, James E. (Retired)

Society of St. James the Apostle:
For contact information please write or call: Socierty of St. James the Apostle, 24 Clark St., Boston MA 02109-1127; Tel.: 617-742-4715
Revs.—
Kirke, Eugene K.
McCarthy, Jeremiah J.
O'Sullivan, Raymond S.
Oates, Thomas F.
Pashby, John J.
Thomas, Robert W.
Tynan, Desmond A.

Unassigned:
For contact Information please call or write: Clergy Personnel Office 2121 Commonwealth Ave., Boston MA 02135-3193; Tel.: 617-779-3685
Rev. Msgr.—
Groden, Michael F.
Revs.—
Byrne, Joseph F.
Conroy, Francis M.
Cordery, Robert J. (MO)
Healey, Stephen M.
McNamara, Michael J.
Ruggeri, Joseph A.
Sweeney, Frederick E.

Whalan, Thomas J.

Permanent Deacons:
Abercrombie, J. Scott, St. John the Evangelist, Wellesley
Acampora, Andrew J., St. John the Evangelist, Swampscott
Agudelo, Jose N., St. James, Haverhill
Albis, Leonard B., (Unassigned)
Alence, Robert W., (Unassigned)
Alexander, John F., St. Edith Stein, Brockton
Alicea, Francisco, St. Mary, Waltham
Amerault, Robert P., St. Joseph, Medford
Arsenault, Joseph G., St. Francis of Assisi, Braintree
Aucoin, Albert J., St. Joseph, Waltham
Balestracci, Alfred, St. Theresa, North Reading
Beatrice, Lee A., St. John, East Bridgewater
Belmonte, Joseph A., St. Anthony of Padua, Revere
Bilotta, Richard F., St. Margart, Burlington
Biron, R. Donald, (Unassigned)
Bloom, Laurence J., St. Susanna, Dedham
Borkush, George J., (Unassigned)
Bortz, John E., (Awaiting Assignment)
Bower, Charles H., Sacred Heart, Middleborough
Bowley, Richard R., All Saints, Haverhill
Boyle, John F., St. Joseph, Holbrook
Brady, Robert F., (Unassigned)
Breinlinger, Martin, St. Mary's, Holliston
Brennan, Richard J., Blessed Sacrament, Walpole
Bresnahan, John M., Holy Family, Lynn
Bubello, Charles M., St. John the Baptist, Quincy
Bulpett, Dean C., St. Irene, Carlisle
Burke, Thomas P., St. Mary, Randolph
Burns, Daniel R., Holy Family, Duxbury
Cabral, John F., (Unassigned)
Cabrera, Cresenzio A., (Retired)
Callahan, James C., St. Charles Borromeo, Waltham
Canova, Joseph A., St. Francis Xavier, Weymouth
Capomaccio, John J., (On Sick Leave)
Carey, John J., (Unassigned)
Caruso, Philip M., St. Mary, Holliston
Casillas, Luis, Cathedral of the Holy Cross, Boston
Cavanaugh, Michael J., St. Clare, Braintree
Chisholm, Finley H., St. Joseph, Lynn
Cloonan, Paul M., St. Paul, Wellesley
Clough, Charles I., Our Lady Help of Christians, Concord
Connelly, Milton E., (Retired)
Connor, John P., Our Lady of the Assumption, Marshfield
Corbett, Francis J., Immaculate Conception, Weymouth
Cordeau, Richard W., St. Thomas the Apostle, Salem
Cornell, Charles A., St. Isidore, Stowe
Counihan, Eugene A., Fernald Development Center, Waltham
Creutz, Edward F., Blessed Kateri Tekakwitha, Plymouth
Crimmins, Daniel F., St. Anne, Littleton
Crowley, Joseph I., (Unassigned)
Crump, James M., St. Patrick, Natick
D'Ambrosio, Francis A., M.D., St. Bernard, Concord
Dacey, Dennis J., Sick Leave
DeCoste, Leonard F., Our Lady of Lourdes, Jamaica Plain
Delaney, Joseph L., St. Denis, Westwood
Delio, Richard P., St. Mary, Franklin
Dempsey, Timothy F., St. Mary, Lynn
Donnelly, Joseph A., St. John the Evangelist, Chelmsford
Donoghue, Leo J., Office of the Permanent Diaconate, Director
Doyle, Edward L., St. Mary, Hull
Dunn, Daniel A., St. Ann, Gloucester
Dzuris, Robert W., St. Rita, Lowell
Eames, James H., St. Mary, Randolph
Egan, Francis G., (Unassigned)
Ego, John J., St. Bernadette, Randolph
Elibero, Edward P., St. Maria Goretti, Lynnfield
Farguheson, Wood Rowe, St. Joseph, Salem
Fenton, Jack H., (Unassigned)
Fernandez, Victor, (Unassigned)
Ferrazzi, Charles J., Immaculate Conception, Stoughton
Fitzgerald, Brendan A., St. John the Evangelist, East Bridgewater
Fonseca, Marcio O., St. Ambrose, Dorchester
Gaffney, Francis M., Immaculate Conception, Revere
Gagne, Gerard E., Sacred Heart, Lawrence
Gagne, Ronald D., (Unassigned)
Gagnon, Raymond A., St. Anthony of Padua, Shirley
Gallant, Robert J., (Leave of Absence)
Gardyna, Henry A., (On Sick Leave)
Gates, Francis G., St. Bernadette, Randolph
Gaudreau, Robert J., Sacred Hearts, Haverhill
Geneus, Alfred J., Our Lady of Pity, Cambridge
Goldy, Andrew J., St. Clement, Somerville
Grimley, Edward J., (Unassigned)
Guerin, Bertrand H., St. Martha, Plainville
Guerrini, Patrick E., (On Special Assignment)
Guerrios, Francisco, Holy Family, Dorchester
Hackett, Robert T., St. Patrick, Groveland
Hanson, Herbert C., St. Linus, Natick
Hardcastle, Philip P., St. Charles Borromeo, Woburn
Hardin, Howard P., (Unassigned)
Hardy, Gerard J., St. Louis de France, Lowell
Hardy, John W., Sacred Heart, Lynn
Harrison, John D., St. Mary-Immaculate Conception, Lawrence
Hassey, Richard J., (Unassigned)
Heffernan, Francis X., Immaculate Conception, Stoughton
Herrera, Luciano, Blessed Sacrament, Jamaica Plain
Hickey, C. Michael, St. Bonaventure, Plymouth
Hidalgo, Nelson S., St. Joseph, Lynn
Hoaglund, Robert, St. Matthias, Marlboro
Holderried, Joseph E., St. Margaret Mary, Westwood
Hunt, John C., Leave of Absence
Iwanowicz, Michael A., Our Lady of Sorrows, Sharon
James, William H., St. Paul, Hamilton
Jennette, John F., St. Joseph, Quincy
Johnson, Robert N., Sacred Heart, Watertown
Jones, Paul S., Our Lady of Lourdes, Carver
Joy, Richard T., St. Catherine of Alexandria, Westford
Juliano, Anthony J., (Unassigned)
Kaelin, Gerard J., (Unassigned)
Kane, William F.X., Office for Prison Ministry, Director
Kasenenko, Joseph S., St. Mary Star of the Sea, Beverly
Keefe, Arthur J., Holy Family, Duxbury
Kerns, William E., St. Brigid, Lexington
Kerrigan, James V., St. Barbara, Woburn
Killam, Harold E.
King, Clifford D., St. Thomas Villanova, Wilmington
Koffel, William B., St. Jeremiah, Framingham
Kramich, Robert A., St. Peter, Gloucester
L'Italien, George G., (Unassigned)
LaBrache, Leo F.
Lacey, Neil F., St. George, Framingham
LaPointe, Norman P., St. Joseph, Salem
Lauture, Albert, (Unassigned)
Leavitt, James P.
Little, James B., Star of the Sea, Quincy
Lloyd, Barry V., St. Mary Magdalen, Tyngsborough
LoPriore, Mario, Sacred Heart, Boston
MacDonald, Joseph P., St. Elizabeth, Milton
Machicado, Hernan
MacKenzie, William E., Our Lady Comforter of the Afflicted, Waltham
MacKinnon, William J., (Unassigned)
Mandosa, Francis A., St. Agnes, Arlington
Mannion, John J., Infant Jesus-St. Lawrence, Brookline
Manzi, James A., St. Paul, Hamilton
Marchant, Thomas W., St. Anthony, Everett
Mariani, Henry A., St. Francis of Assisi, Medford
Markey, Paul G., Most Blessed Sacrament, Quincy
Martin, Leo A., St. John the Baptist, Peabody
Martin, Richard C., Gate of Heaven, South Boston
Martinez, Orlando, (Unassigned)
Martino, Richard C., Sr., St. Ann, Marlborough
McCarthy, Daniel E., St. Mary, Rowley
McCarthy, William J., (Unassigned)
McDavitt, Thomas S., (Unassigned)
McGuffie, Jacques A., St. Patrick, Roxbury
McHugh, John W., St. John-St. Hugh, Boston
McLaughlin, James V., St. Briget, Abington
McLaughlin, Richard B., Hanscom AFB, Bedford
McManus, Lawrence R., St. Joseph, Lynn
Menendez, Silvio J., St. Patrick, Lawrence
Menz, John R., St. Elizabeth Ann Seton, Quincy
Mesa, Ricardo M., Holy Name, West Roxbury
Messina, Joseph M., Office of the Permanent Diaconate, Associate
Messinger, George H., (Unassigned)
Miles, Walter J., (Unassigned)
Mills, Chester P., (Unassigned)
Monroe, Richard G., St. Joseph, Kingston
Montes, Eddy M., St. Columbkille, Brighton
Mora, Eduardo R., St. Mary, Waltham
Morel, Pablo, St. Joseph, Lynn
Morey, Russell W., St. Catherine of Alexandria, Westford
Moschetto, Samuel J., (Unassigned)
Mullins, Thomas F., St. Theresa, Billerica
Murphy, Alfred L., St. Bernard, Concord
Murphy, Steven J., Our Lady of Good Counsel, Methuen
Nagle, William V., St. Joseph, Kingston
Naveo, Jose D., Asuncion de la Virgen Maria, Lowell
Nicholson, John D., Our Lady of Fatima, Sudbury
Nickley, Joseph T., Jr., Holy Ghost, Whitman
O'Brien, Donald V., (Unassigned)
O'Neil, Cyril T., St. Patrick, Stoneham
Oles, Kenneth W., St. Mary, Wrentham
Ortiz, Jesus M., St. Peter, Dorchester
Papile, Joseph A., St. Jerome, Weymouth
Patrick, Alexander J., (Unassigned)
Peltak, Douglas P., Immaculate Conception, Marlborough
Penney, Everett F., St. Marguerite D'Youville, Dracut
Pepi, John W., St. Bridget, Maynard
Perea, Antonio M., Most Holy Redeemer, East Boston
Pugsley, Stanley G., St. William, Dorchester
Quigley, Edward M., St. John the Evangelist, Canton
Quiles, Francisco, Sacred Heart, Roslindale
Quiles, Jesus, Blessed Sacrament, Jamaica Plan
Radford, Richard F., St. Mary of the Assumption, Brookline
Ramrath, Joseph R., St. Anselm, Sudbury
Rivera, Louis, St. Rose of Lima, Chelsea
Rivera, Valentin, St. John the Baptist, Peabody
Rizzuto, Anthony P., (On Special Assignment)
Rocha, Richard H., SS. Peter & Paul, Lawrence
Rodrigues, Pedro M., St. Anthony, Somerville
Rodriguez, Diego N., (Unassigned)
Rogers, Arthur F., Jr., Prison Ministry
Rooney, Paul S., St. Anthony, Cohassett
Ros, Peter An P., St. Patrick, Lowell
Rumley, Mark E., Immaculate Conception, Malden
Ryan, Gerald P., St. Joseph the Worker, Hanson
Ryan, John G., St. Joseph, Medway
Ryan, Kenneth N., (Unassigned)
Salenius, John D., Sacred Heart, Quincy
Sanchez, Tomas E., St. John the Evangelist, Beverly
Santosuosso, Alfred E., St. Jude, Waltham
Scamman, David R., (Unassigned)
Shanahan, Allan R., St. Mary, Billerica
Sheedy, Louis W., St. Mary, Dedham
Shrader, David J., (Unassigned)
Sicuso, Anthony C., (Leave of Absence)
Smith, Thomas M., St. Joseph the Worker, Needham
Specht, Paul V., St. Patrick, Lawrence
Spiri, Guy J., St. Stephen, Framingham
St. Hilaire, Norman R., St. Richard, Danvers
Stenstrom, Eugene V., St. Mary, Plymouth
Steuterman, John P., Resurrection, Hingham
Straub, Stanley A., St. Mary of the Annuciation, Cambridge
Sullivan, Charles E., St. Ann, Somerville
Sullivan, Daniel F., St. Agatha, Milton
Sullivan, John A., St. Thelca Parish, Pembroke
Taylor, Carroll H., Prison Ministry, Middleton
Torres, Pedro Luis, St. Stephen, Framingham
Tremblay, Francis R., St. Timothy, Norwood
Turner, John R., St. Patrick, Stoneham
Valeri, Frank A., Most Blessed Sacrament, Wakefield
Vandi, Dennis, St. Mary, Chelmsford
Vitello, Joseph V., St. Jerome, Weymouth
Walsh, Martin J., St. Ann, Peabody
Watson, John W.
Webb, Charles P., St. Thomas More, Braintree
Webb, Charles P.
Welch, Henry W., Sacred Heart, Weymouth
Whipple, John E., Our Lady Star of the Sea, Marblehead
Wildes, William H., St. Brigid, Lexington
Wise, John W., St. Mary of the Assumption, Melrose
Yanikoski, Florian F., St. Francis of Assisi, Braintree

INSTITUTIONS LOCATED IN THE ARCHDIOCESE

[A] SEMINARIES, ARCHDIOCESAN

BOSTON. *St. John Seminary School of Theology*, 127 Lake St., Brighton, 02135. Tel: 617-254-2610; Fax: 617-787-2336. Most Rev. Richard G. Lennon, Rector; Rev. John A. Farren, O.P., Rector; Rev. Msgrs. Laurence W. McGrath, M.S., M.A.; Richard G. Cunningham, J.C.D.; Revs. Martin P. Connor, S.T.L.; John L. Sullivan, S.S.L.; Stephen E. Salocks, S.S.L.; Thomas F. Nestor, Ph.D.; William B. Palardy, Ph.D.; Romanus Cessario, O.P., S.T.D.; Robert J. Congdon, S.T.D.; Christopher J. Coyne, S.L.D.; William T. Kelly, S.T.D.; Robin C. Ryan, C.P., Ph.D.; William F. Murphy, M.Div.; Robert W. Murray, M.Div.; Christopher J. Kirwan Jr., S.T.D.; James M. Mahoney, M.Div.; Vincent E. Daily,

S.T.D.; Robert W. Oliver, S.T.D., J.C.D. Priests 21; Lay Teachers 5; Students 108.

WESTON. *Blessed John XXIII National Seminary*, 558 South Ave., 02493. Tel: 781-899-5500; Fax: 781-899-9057. Email: seminary@blessedjohnxxiii.edu. Web: www.BlessedJohnXXIII.EDU. Rev. Msgr. Francis D. Kelly, S.T.L., Ph.D., Rector & Pres.; Revs. James M. DiPerri, M.A., M.Div., J.C.L.; Paul E. Fitzpatrick, S.M., S.T.L., S.T.D.; John J. Moriarty, S.J.; Joseph K. Fagan, M.Div.; Very Rev. Gregory J. Hoppough, C.S.S., M.Div., S.T.L., S.T.D.; Revs. Thomas F. Schmitt, S.T.L.; Charles J. Healey, S.J., S.T.L., S.T.D.; Peter J. Uglietto, M.Div., S.T.L., S.T.D.; Joseph C. Hencheu, C.S.S.; Sr. Rose Clarisse Gadoury, S.S.A., M.A., D.Min.; Leonard Maluf, S.T.D. A Major National Seminary open to men over thirty studying for the diocesan and religious priesthood. Priests 9; Sisters 1; Lay Teachers 1; Students 71.

[B] SEMINARIES, RELIGIOUS OR SCHOLASTICATES

BOSTON. *Oblate Provincialate*, 2 Ipswich St., 02215-3607. Tel: 617-536-4141; Fax: 617-536-7016. Email: omv.office@verizon.net. Web: www.oblatesofthevirginmary.org. Rev. William M. Brown, O.M.V., Prov.; Bro. Luigi Falbo, O.M.V., Treas. St. Ignatius Province of the Oblates of the Virgin Mary, Inc.
Priests of the Province on Special Assignment:
Philippines: Revs. Gregory Short, O.M.V.; Mark Yavarone, O.M.V. (MET).
Italy: Rev. Craig MacMahon, O.M.V.
U.S.A.: Rev. John Ferrara, O.M.V.
Trinidad: Rev. D. Clifford Graham, O.M.V.

Our Lady of Grace Seminary, 1105 Boylston St., 02215-3660. Tel: 617-266-5999; Fax: 617-247-7576. Web: www.oblatesofthevirginmary.org. Revs. S. Gregory Cleveland, O.M.V., Rector; David N. Beauregard, O.M.V., Dean of Studies; Timothy M. Gallagher, O.M.V., Formation Staff; Thomas Carzon, O.M.V., Formation Staff; Peter Grover, O.M.V., Vocation Dir.; Peter P. Gojuk, O.V.M. St. Ignatius Province of the Oblates of the Virgin Mary, Inc. Priests 6; Lay Teachers 4; Students 12.

CAMBRIDGE. *Weston Jesuit School of Theology*, 3 Phillips Pl., 02138. Tel: 617-492-1960; Fax: 617-492-5833. Email: rmanning@wjst.edu. Web: www.wjst.edu. Revs. Robert E. Manning, S.J., Pres.; John R. Sachs, S.J., Dean.
Legal Title: *Weston College Corporation* Priests 21; Sisters 4; Lay Teachers 11; Students 240.

DANVERS. *Xavier Center* House of Formation. , 21 Spring St., 01923. Tel: 978-777-1326. Bro. John D. Hamilton, C.F.X., Dir. Xaverian Brothers, USA Brothers Professed 4.

FRAMINGHAM. *Sylva Maria*, 567 Salem End Rd., 01702-5599. Tel: 508-879-2541; Fax: 508-879-7667. Email: sonsofmary@prodigy.net. Web: www.sonsofmary.com. Revs. Robert Rivard, F.M.S.I.; John Wallace, F.M.S.I. Motherhouse and Novitiate of the Sons of Mary, Health of the Sick. Priests 5; Brothers 4.
Council: Revs. John Murphy, F.M.S.I., Major Co-ord.; John Coss, F.M.S.I., Councilor; Deacon Kevin Courtney, F.M.S.I., Financial Coord.

HAVERHILL. *Sons of Divine Providence School for Exceptional Boys*, Groveland Rd., P.O. Box 205, 01835. Tel: 508-373-0461. Rev. Gino Marchesani, F.D.P.

[C] COLLEGES AND UNIVERSITIES

BOSTON. *Emmanuel College*, 400 The Fenway, 02115. Tel: 617-735-9715; Fax: 617-735-9877. Email: hatten@emmanuel.edu. Web: www.emmanuel.edu. Sr. Janet Eisner, S.N.D., Ph.D., Pres. Sisters of Notre Dame de Namur; Rev. Stephen Bayle, Co-Dir. Campus Ministry; Sr. Margaret Cummins, S.N.D., Dir. Campus Min. Priests 1; Sisters 3; Lay Teachers 49; Students 1,856.

Laboure College, Inc., 2120 Dorchester Ave., 02124. Tel: 617-296-8300; Fax: 617-296-7947. Web: www.labourecollege.org. Sr. Clarisse Correia, D.C., Pres. Two year college for nursing and allied health. Member of Caritas Christi Health Care System. Priests 1; Sisters 5; Lay Teachers 70; Students 450.

BRIGHTON. *St. John Seminary College*, College of Liberal Arts, 127 Lake St., 02135. Tel: 617-254-2610; Fax: 617-746-5499. Revs. Christopher J. Kirwan Jr., S.T.D., Dean of Students; Robert J. Congdon, S.T.D., Acting Dean; Mark L. Noonan, Ph.D. (Retired); William F. Murphy, M.Div.; Robert Oliver, B.H.; John J. Clabeaux, Ph.D., Academic Dean; Deborah DeChiara-Quenzer, Ph.D.; Michael Raiger, Ph.D. Priests 6; Lay Teachers 3; Students 32.

CHESTNUT HILL. **Boston College* (Coed) , 02467. Tel: 617-552-8000; Fax: 617-522-8828. Web: www.bc.edu. Rev. William P. Leahy, S.J., Pres.; Dr. John Neuhauser, Academic Vice Pres. Priests 40; Sisters 3; Lay Teachers 648; Students 14,379.

College of Arts and Sciences Tel: 617-552-3270; Fax: 617-552-1383. Joseph Quinn, Dean. Students 5,767.

Summer Session Tel: 617-552-3900; Fax: 617-552-3199. Rev. James A. Woods, S.J., Dean. Students 3,667.

Graduate School of Arts and Sciences Tel: 617-552-3268; Fax: 617-552-3700. Dr. Michael A. Smyer, Dean. Students 1,037.

School of Law Tel: 617-552-4340; Fax: 617-552-2851. John H. Garvey, Dean. Students 812.

College of Advancing Studies Tel: 617-552-3900; Fax: 617-552-3199. Rev. James A. Woods, S.J., Dean. Students 927.

Graduate School of Social Work Tel: 617-552-4020; Fax: 617-552-2374. Dr. Alberto Godenzi, Dean. Students 519.

School of Management Tel: 617-552-8420; Fax: 617-552-2593. Dr. M. Hossein Safizadeh, Interim Dean. Students 2,048.

Graduate School of Management Tel: 617-552-8420; Fax: 617-552-2593. Dr. M. Hossein Safizadeh, Interim Dean. Students 978.

School of Nursing Tel: 617-552-4250; Fax: 617-552-0745. Dr. Barbara Hazard Munro, Dean. Students 269.

School of Education Tel: 617-552-4200; Fax: 617-552-0812. Rev. Joseph M. O'Keefe, S.J., Interim Dean. Students 767.

Graduate School of Nursing Tel: 617-552-4250; Fax: 617-552-0745. Dr. Barbara Hazard Munro, Dean. Students 194.

Graduate School of Education Tel: 617-552-4200; Fax: 617-552-0812. Rev. Joseph M. O'Keefe, S.J., Interim Dean. Students 1,061.

NORTH ANDOVER. *Merrimack College* 01845. Tel: 978-837-5000; Fax: 978-837-5222. Web: www.merrimack.edu. Revs. Kevin F. Dwyer, O.S.A.; George R. Morgan, O.S.A.; Scott C. Ness, O.S.A.; James Wenzel, O.S.A.; Gary McCloskey, O.S.A.; Richard Piatt, O.S.A. Priests 9; Lay Teachers 120; Students 2,108; Continuing Education 800.

Our Mother of Good Counsel Monastery (1947), Tel: 978-837-5213; Fax: 978-837-5269. In Res. Revs. Kevin F. Dwyer, O.S.A.; William T. Garland, O.S.A (PH), Prior; Thomas C. Kenny, O.S.A.; Albert P. MacPherson, O.S.A.; Joseph X. O'Connor, O.S.A., Treas.; William J. Wynne, O.S.A., Librarian.

SWAMPSCOTT. *Marian Court College*, Little's Point Rd., 01907. Tel: 617-595-6768; Fax: 617-595-3560. Email: info@mariancourt.edu. Web: www.mariancourt.edu. Sr. Joanne Bibeau, R.S.M., Pres. Sisters 3; Lay Teachers 20; Lay Staff 37; Students 310.

WESTON. *Regis College*, 235 Wellesley St., 02493-1571. Tel: 781-768-7000; Fax: 781-768-8339. Email: postmaster@regiscollege.edu. Web: www.regiscollege.edu. Mary Jane England, M.D., Pres.; Rosemary Mulvihill, R.S.M., Campus Min. Sisters of St. Joseph 16; Lay Teachers 117; Students 1,470.

[D] HIGH SCHOOLS, ARCHDIOCESAN

BOSTON. *Cathedral High School*, 74 Union Park St., 02118. Tel: 617-542-2325; Fax: 617-542-1745. Web: www.cathedral.mec.edu. Christol Murch, Prin. Brothers 1; Sisters 6; Lay Teachers 18; Staff 7; Students 270.

BRAINTREE. *Archbishop Williams High School*, 80 Independence Ave., 02184. Tel: 781-843-3636; Fax: 781-843-3782. Email: mlsadowski@awhs.org. Web: www.awhs.org. Mary Louise Sadowski, Prin. Sisters 1; Lay Teachers 44; Students 633.

BROCKTON. *Cardinal Spellman High School*, 738 Court St., 02302. Tel: 508-583-6875; Fax: 508-580-1977. Email: cshs@spellman.pvt.k12.ma.us. Web: www.spellman.com. Sr. Thomasine Knowlton, C.S.J., Prin. Sisters of St. Joseph Brothers 2; Sisters 2; Deacons 1; Lay Teachers 41; Students 642.

CAMBRIDGE. *Matignon High School*, One Matignon Rd., 02140. Tel: 617-876-1212; Fax: 617-661-3905. Web: matignon-hs.org. Mr. Gary R. LeFave, Prin.; Mrs. Constance Skahan, Asst. Prin.; Maura Colleary, Campus Min. College Preparatory. Religious 1; Lay Teachers 38; Students 530.

North Cambridge Catholic High School, 40 Norris St., 02140. Tel: 617-876-6068; Fax: 617-576-1898. Email: sisterellen@hotmail.com. Web: www.ncc.mec.edu. Sr. Ellen Powers, C.S.J., Prin. Brothers 1; Sisters 2; Lay Teachers 24; Students 260.

EVERETT. *Pope John XXIII Central High School*, 888 Broadway, 02149. Tel: 617-389-0240; Fax: 617-389-2201. Email: popejohnhs@aol.com. Web: www.popejohn.mec.edu. Thomas P. Arria Jr., Prin. Sisters 5; Lay Teachers 33; Students 466.

FRAMINGHAM. *Marian High School*, 273 Union Ave., 01702. Tel: 508-875-7646; Fax: 508-875-0838. Email: ARBOSH78@connectinc.com. Web: www.marianhigh.net. Mr. Stephen D. Flynn, Prin. Sisters 1; Lay Teachers 20; Students 254.

PEABODY. *Bishop Fenwick High School*, 99 Margin St., 01960. Tel: 978-531-8200; Fax: 978-531-2483. Email: bfhs@fenwick.org. Web: www.fenwick.org. David J. Marion, Prin. Sisters 4; Lay Teachers 57; Students 875.

[E] HIGH SCHOOLS, PRIVATE

BOSTON. *Boston College High School & Jesuit Community*, 150 Morrissey Blvd., Dorchester, 02125. Tel: 617-436-3900; Fax: 617-282-7503. Email: hanwellsj@bchigh.edu. Web: www.bchigh.edu/. Revs. Joseph T. Bennett, S.J. Tel: 617-929-9482; Edward F. Boyle, S.J. Tel: 617-929-9483; William J. Hamilton, S.J. Tel: 617-929-9478; John J. Hanwell, S.J., Rector. Tel: 617-929-9413; James J. Hosie, S.J. Tel: 617-929-9488; Daniel C. Lewis, S.J. Tel: 617-929-9456; Joaquin Martinez-Mari, S.J. (Bolivia). Tel: 617-929-9463; Perard C. Monestime, S.J. Tel: 617-929-9424; James W. O'Neil, S.J. Tel: 617-929-9452; Francis J. O'Neill, S.J. Tel: 617-929-9494; Joseph P. O'Neill, S.J. Tel: 617-929-9425; Clement L. Pelletier, S.J. Tel: 617-929-9430; George A. Duffy, S.J. Tel: 617-929-9441; Peter D. Hickey, S.J. Tel: 617-929-9495; Kevin R. White, S.J. Tel: 627-929-9438; Stephen F. Dawber, S.J. Tel: 617-929-9423; Joseph R. Laughlin, S.J. Tel: 617-929-9470; John Joseph Walsh, S.J. Tel: 617-929-9462; William R. Campbell, S.J. Tel: 617-929-9442; John R. d'Anjou, S.J. Tel: 617-929-9427; Simon E. Smith, S.J. Tel: 617-929-9429; Bro. Cornelius C. Murphy, S.J. Tel: 617-929-9414; Deacons Rob Daifey, C.F.X. Tel: 677-929-9433; Mathew Manning, S.J. Tel: 677-929-9405; Bro. Donald J. Murray, S.J. Tel: 617-436-3900. Religious 25; Sisters 1; Lay Teachers 85; Students 1,294.

Jesuit Community Tel: 617-929-9400; Fax: 617-929-9459.

Catholic Memorial School, (Grades 7-12) , (Boys) Tel: 617-469-8000; Fax: 617-325-0888. Email: jmacdona@cath-mem.org. Web: www.cath-mem.org. 235 Baker St., West Roxbury, 02132-4395. Bro. James J. MacDonald, C.F.C., Pres.; Richard F. Chisholm, Prin. Congregation of Christian Brothers Brothers 4; Lay Teachers 57; Boys 860.

Mt. St. Joseph Academy, 617 Cambridge St., Brighton, 02135. Tel: 617-254-8383 (School Office); 617-783-4747 (Guidance Office); Fax: 617-254-0240. Email: mtstjoseph@mec.edu. Web: www.msja.mec.edu/. Kathleen Fraser, Prin. Sponsored by Sisters of St. Joseph of Boston Sisters 6; Lay Teachers 26; Girls 310.

Savio Preparatory High School Tel: 617-567-2710; Fax: 617-569-6883. Web: www.savioprep.org. 145 Byron St., East Boston, 02128. Tel: 617-567-2710; Fax: 617-569-6883. Mr. Edward Minor, Exec. Dir.; Revs. John J. Serio, S.D.B., Prin.; John DiFiore, S.D.B., Coord. Youth Min.; Jack Janko, S.D.B., Ph.D.; Angelo Bongiorno, S.D.B. A college preparatory school, sponsored by the Salesians of Don Bosco. Priests 4; Lay Teachers 33; Students 395.

DANVERS. *St. John's Preparatory School* 01923. Tel: 978-774-1050; Fax: 978-774-5069. Email: sshannon@stjohnsprep.org. Web: www.stjohnsprep.org. Albert J. Shannon, Ph.D., Headmaster. Day Students. Brothers 9; Lay Teachers 87; Boys 1,150.

DEDHAM. *Ursuline Academy Dedham, Inc.*, (Grades 7-12), 85 Lowder St., 02026-4299. Tel: 781-326-6161; Fax: 781-326-4898. Email: ursuline@attbi.com. Web: www.ursulineacademy.net. Sr. Mercedes Videira, O.S.U., Prin. Operated by Ursuline Convent. Ursuline Nuns. College Prep School for Girls. Sisters 9; Lay Teachers 33; Total Staff 62; Girls 398.

HINGHAM. *Notre Dame Academy*, 1073 Main St., 02043. Tel: 781-749-5930; Fax: 781-749-8366. Email: principal@ndahingham.pvt.k12.ma.us. Web: www.ndahingham.com. Sr. Janice Carmen, S.N.D., Prin. Total Staff 75; Girls 544.

KINGSTON. *Sacred Heart High School*, 399 Bishops Hwy., 02364. Tel: 781-585-7511; Fax: 781-585-7063. Email: shhs@adelphia.net. Web: www.sacredheart-hs.org. Mr. John Enos, Prin.; Mr. Douglas Trudeau, Asst. Prin.; Mrs. Anne Marie League, Asst. Prin. Sisters 7; Lay Teachers 37; Students 578.

LAWRENCE. *Central Catholic High School of Lawrence, Inc.*, 300 Hampshire St., 01841. Tel: 978-682-0260; Fax: 978-685-2707. Email: ddefillippo@centralcatholic.net. Web: www.centralcatholic.net. Deacon Thomas P. Long, F.M.S., Pres.; David M. DeFillippo, Prin. Conducted by the Marist Brothers of the Schools. Religious 8; Lay Teachers 55; Students 1,135.

LOWELL. *Lowell Catholic High School, Inc.*, 530

Stevens St., 01851. Tel: 978-452-1794. Email: ed2000@tiac.net. Mr. Edward J. Quinn, Prin. Sisters 2; Lay Teachers 18; Students 280.

MALDEN. *Malden Catholic High School*, 99 Crystal St., 02148. Tel: 781-322-3098; Fax: 781-397-0573. Email: greenr@maldencatholic.org. Web: www.maldencatholic.org. Bro. Robert J. Green, C.F.X., Headmaster. Xaverian Brothers Brothers 12; Lay Teachers 49; Boys 739.

METHUEN. *Presentation of Mary Academy*, 209 Lawrence St., 01844. Tel: 978-682-9391, Ext. 102; Fax: 978-975-3595. Email: pmacademy@comcast.net. Web: www.pmamethuen.org. Rose Maria Redman, Prin. Sisters of the Presentation of Mary Sisters 6; Lay Teachers 24; Total Staff 40; Girls 282.

MILTON. *Fontbonne Academy*, 930 Brook Rd., 02186. Tel: 617-696-3241; Fax: 617-696-7688. Web: www.fontbonneacademy.org. Sr. Marilyn McGoldrick, Pres. Sisters of St. Joseph 11; Lay Teachers 49; Students 644.

NEEDHAM. *St. Sebastian's School, Inc.*, (Grades 7-12), 1191 Greendale Ave., 02192. Tel: 617-449-5200; Fax: 617-449-5630. Web: www.stsebs.org. Mr. William L. Burke, III, Headmaster; Revs. John F. Arens; John U. Paris. Priests 2; Lay Teachers 48; Boys 341.

NEWTON. *Country Day School of the Sacred Heart*, (Grades 5-12), 785 Centre St., 02158. Tel: 617-244-4246; Fax: 617-965-5313. Email: postmaster@newtoncountryday.org. Web: www.newtoncountryday.org. Sr. Barbara Rogers, R.S.C.J., Prin.
Legal Title: *Boston Academy of the Sacred Heart* Religious of the Sacred Heart 1; Lay Teachers 70; Girls 365.

Mount Alvernia High School, (Grades 7-12), 790 Centre St., 02458. Tel: 617-964-5643 (Convent); 617-969-2260 (School); Fax: 617-969-4245. Email: MAHSinfo@mountalverniahs.org. Web: mountalverniahs.org. Mrs. Kathleen Kent, Prin. Missionary Franciscan Sisters of the Immaculate Conception Sisters 6; Lay Teachers 27; Total Staff 41; Girls 247.

READING. *Austin Preparatory School*, (Grades 6-12), 101 Willow St., 01867. Tel: 781-944-4900; Fax: 781-944-7530. Email: apadmit.@austinprepschool.org. Web: www.austinprepschool.org. Mr. Paul J. Moran, Headmaster; Revs. John D. Harrington (England); Kenneth Healey, S.M.; James Morris. Priests 3; Sisters 1; Lay Teachers 60; Administrators 11; Students 700.

TYNGSBOROUGH. *Academy of Notre Dame* 01879. Tel: 978-649-7611; Fax: 978-649-2909. Email: mfarren@ndatyngsboro.org. Web: www.ndatyngsboro.org. Sr. Mary M. Farren, S.N.D., Prin. Sisters of Notre Dame de Namur 2; Faculty 22; Girls 240.

WAKEFIELD. *Our Lady of Nazareth Academy*, 14 Winship Dr., 01880. Tel: 781-245-5210; Fax: 781-245-6648. Email: mkelley@ourladyofnazarethacademy.org. Web: www.ourladyofnazarethacademy.org. Mrs. Molly Kelley, Prin. Sisters of Charity of Nazareth Lay Teachers 17; Girls 180.

WESTWOOD. *Xaverian Brothers High School*, 800 Clapboardtree St., 02090. Tel: 781-326-6392; Fax: 781-320-0458. Email: admin@xbhs.com. Web: www.xbhs.com. Bro. Daniel Skala, C.F.X., Headmaster. Xaverian Brothers Brothers 4; Lay Teachers 76; Boys 1,050.

[F] ELEMENTARY SCHOOLS, ARCHDIOCESAN

DANVERS. *St. Mary of the Annunciation School*, 14 Otis St., 01923. Tel: 978-774-0307; Fax: 978-750-4852. Email: principal@stmaryschooldanvers.org. Web: stmaryschooldanvers.org. Mrs. Jennine D. Zito, M.Ed., Prin. (Grades PreK-8 & Extended Day Care). Sisters of Notre Dame de Namur 1; Lay Teachers 25; Students 534.

[G] MONTESSORI SCHOOLS

HAVERHILL. *The Merrimack Montessori School*, 55 Saltonstall Rd., 01830. Tel: 978-374-6103; Fax: 978-469-0730. Email: mmsronni@aol.com. Web: www.merrimackmontessori.org. Ronni George, Head of School. (For boys and girls aged 3-6) Lay Teachers 14; Students 131.

MARLBOROUGH. *The St. Anne Montessori School*, 720 Boston Post Rd. E., 01752. Tel: 508-485-3791. Sr. Doreen Scott, S.S.A., Dir. (For boys and girls aged 3-5) Religious 2; Lay Teachers 3; Students 72.

NEWTON. *Walnut Park Montessori School*, 47 Walnut Park, 02458. Tel: 617-969-9208; Fax: 617-969-6408. Email: walnutpk@gis.net. Web: www.walnutparkmontessori.org. Sr. Mary Ann Connolly, S.C., Prin. Religious 5; Lay Teachers 7; Students 145.

WENHAM. *Notre Dame Children's Class*, 74 Grapevine Rd., 01984 Tel: 508-468-1340; Fax: 508-468-0166. Email: notredcc@aol.com. Sisters Barbara Beauchamp, S.N.D., Dir.; Susan Raymc, S.N.D., Co-Dir. Religious 2; Lay Teachers 3; Primary Class 26; Preschool Students 48.

[H] ELEMENTARY SCHOOLS, PRIVATE

BOSTON. *Lt. Joseph P. Kennedy, Jr., Memorial School* (Under the patronage of Our Lady of Czestochowa.) Tel: 617-364-4975; Fax: 617-361-8820. Email: S.JoanneH@aol.com Web: www.rc.net/boston/kennedyschool. 17 Hale St., Hyde Park, 02136. Tel: 617-361-1726. Sisters Joanne Helen Grejdus, O.S.F., Prin.; M. de Lourdes Ckoniewski, O.S.F., Admin. Bernardine Sisters of the Third Order of St. Francis of Mass., Inc. Sisters 3; Lay Teachers 8; Students 161.

Mother Caroline Academy, 515 Blue Hill Ave., Dorchester, 02121. Tel: 617-427-1177; Fax: 617-427-7788. Email: info@mcaec.org. Web: www.mothercaroline.org. Carrie Maille Hickey, Exec. Dir.; Sr. Frances Butler, S.S.N.D., Prin.
Legal Title: *Mother Caroline Academy for Girls, Inc.* School Sisters of Notre Dame Sisters 3; Lay Teachers 10; Students 60.

Nativity Preparatory School, (Grades 5-8) Tel: 617-442-1993; Fax: 617-541-4148. Email: hicks@bchigh.edu. Web: www.nativityboston.org. 30 Raynor Cir., Roxbury, 02120. Tel: 617-442-1993; Fax: 617-541-4148. Revs. William R. Campbell, S.J., Exec Dir.; Alfred J. Hicks, S.J., Prin.; Simon E. Smith, S.J.
Legal Title: *Nativity-Boston, Inc.*, A Jesuit Middle School. Priests 3; Brothers 1; Lay Teachers 12; Boys 65.

BRAINTREE. *Cardinal Cushing Centers*, 85 Washington St., 02184. Tel: 617-848-6250; Fax: 617-848-0640. Email: PLarson@Coletta.org. Web: www.Coletta.org.
Legal Title: *St. Coletta's and Cardinal Cushing Schools of MA, Inc.*, Day School for multiple handicapped, developmentally delayed children, ages 4-22 years. Lay Teachers 10; Students 55.

GLOUCESTER. *St. Mel Independent Day School*, 8 Farrington Ave., 01930. Tel: 978-283-1700; Fax: 978-283-0422. Email: ARBOSE123082@connectinc.com. Web: www.marina.cove.com/index/stmels. Mrs. Rhonda Fears, Prin. Lay Teachers 10; Students 87.

GROTON. *Country Day School of the Holy Union*, 14 Main St. 01450. Tel: 978-448-5646; Fax: 978-448-2392. Email: cdsgroton@yahoo.com. Web: countrydayschooloftheholyunion.org. Sr. Lucille Guay, S.U.S.C., Prin. Sisters of the Holy Union 2; Lay Teachers 10; Students 220.

HANOVER. *Cardinal Cushing Centers, Inc.*, 400 Washington St., 02339. Tel: 781-826-6371; Fax: 781-826-1559. Email: skozaryn@coletta.org. Lawrence Sauer, Exec. Dir., Hanover; Pat Larson, Exec. Dir., Braintree; Jean Rogers, Exec. Dir. Adult Svcs. Sisters 6; Lay Staff 431; Students 208.

St. Coletta and Cardinal Cushing Schools of Massachusetts, Inc., 400 Washington St., 02339. Lay Teachers 1; Lay Staff 16; Students 20.

KINGSTON. *Sacred Heart Elementary School* (Day School), , 329 Bishops Hwy., 02364. Tel: 617-585-2114; Fax: 617-585-6993. Sr. Ann Therese Connolly, C.D.P., Prin. (Grades 1-6) Sisters of Divine Providence 6; Lay Teachers 21; Students 430.

Sacred Heart Pre-Primary School, 363 Bishops Hwy., 02364-2035. Tel: 781-585-3545; Fax: 781-582-1596. Sr. Angela Provost, C.D.P., Dir. Religious 1; Lay Teachers 3; Students 54.

LAWRENCE. *Blessed Stephen Bellesini, O.S.A., Academy, Inc.*, 94 Bradford St., 01840-1003. Tel: 978-989-0004; Fax: 978-989-9404. Email: info@bellesiniacademy.org. Web: www.bellesiniacademy.org. Ms. Julie DiFilippo, Exec. Dir. Total Staff 8; Students 45.

LOWELL. *Franco-American Private School*, 357 Pawtucket St., 01854. Tel: 978-458-0308; Fax: 978-458-0308. Email: faslowell@comcast.net. Web: ecommunity.uml.edu/fas. Sisters Lorraine Richard, S.C.Q., Prin.; Jane Holland, S.C.Q., Asst. Prin. Religious 2; Lay Teachers 18; Students 300.

MARLBOROUGH. *Our Lady Preschool Learning Center*, 197 Pleasant St., 01752. Tel: 508-481-0654; Fax: 508-481-0663. Email: olpreschool@hotmail.com. Sr. Jeanne Allard, S.S.Ch., Dir. Religious 1; Lay Teachers 1; Students ages 3-5 74.

NEWTON. *Jackson School Elementary*, (Grades K-6), 200 Jackson Rd., 02458-1428. Tel: 617-969-1537; Fax: 617-244-8596. Email: info@jacksonschool.org. Web: www.jacksonschool.org. Mrs Susan G. Niden, Prin. Sisters 9; Lay Teachers 22; Staff 5; Students 255.

Mount Alvernia Academy Tel: 617-527-7540; Fax: 617-527-7995. Email: webmaster@mountalverniaacademy.com. Web: mountalverniaacademy.com. 20 Manet Rd., Chestnut Hill, 02467. Tel: 617-527-7540; Fax: 617-527-7995. Joan T. Sullivan, Prin. Sisters 3; Lay Teachers 30; Students 348.
Tel: 617-244-3696.

TYNGSBOROUGH. *Academy of Notre Dame at Tyngsboro*, 180 Middlesex Rd., 01879. Tel: 978-649-7611; Fax: 978-649-2909. Email: mbillings@ndatyngsboro.org. Web: www.ndatyngsboro.org. Sr. Marcia Billings, S.N.D., Prin. Sisters of Notre Dame de Namur 2; Lay Teachers 26; Students 484.

[I] SPECIAL SCHOOLS

BOSTON. *Emmanuel House Kindergarten*, 11 Newcomb St., 02118. Tel: 617-445-2037; Fax: 617-445-2479. Email: esther_garcia@ccab.org. Sisters Esther Garcia, Dir.; Laurie MacDonald, Prog. Dir. Community Based Agency of Catholic Charitable Bureau of Archdiocese of Boston, Inc. Franciscan Sisters of the Atonement 4; Lay Teachers 4; Students 52.

METHUEN. *St. Ann's Home Special Needs School*, 100 A. Haverhill St., 01844. Tel: 978-682-5276; Fax: 978-688-4932. Email: dgrandbois@stannshome.org. Web: www.st.annshome.org. Denis Grandbois, Exec. Dir. Ungraded special needs school for emotionally disturbed and behaviorally disordered children. Lay Teachers 38; Psychotherapists 20; Counsellors 120; Administrators 11; Staff 23; Residential Students 103; Day Students 68.

PEABODY. *Holy Childhood Nursery & Kindergarten*, 5 Wheatland St., 01960. Tel: 508-531-4733; Fax: 978-531-2468. Sisters Benedetta Zaccardi, Coord.; Kathleen A. Bettencourt, O.Carm., Co-Dir. Sisters 5; Lay Teachers 6; Students 80.

WATERTOWN. *Rosary Academy Learning Center*, 2 Rosary Dr., 02172. Tel: 617-923-1935; Fax: 617-923-2993. Email: ROSARY1@erols.com. Karen Arena, Dir. Sisters of St. Dominic (St. Catherine, KY), Preschool & Day Care. Lay Teachers 12; Students 73.

[J] CATHOLIC CHARITIES

BOSTON. *Catholic Charitable Bureau of the Archdiocese of Boston, Inc.*, Central Office, 75 Kneeland St., 8th Fl., 02111. Tel: 617-482-5440; Fax: 617-451-0337. Email: www.ccab.org. Web: www.ccab.org. Dr. Joseph Doolin, Pres. Multi-Service Agency. Total Clients served 144,828.

El Centro Del Cardenal/Catholic Charities, 76 Union Park St., 02118. Tel: 617-542-9292; Fax: 617-542-6912. Ms. Elisabeth Zweig-Snippe, Contact Person.

Emmanuel House/Catholic Charities-Community, 11 Newcomb St., 02118. Tel: 617-445-2037; Fax: 617-445-2479. Email: esther_garcia@ccab.org. Community Based Agency of the Catholic Charitable Bureau of the Archdiocese of Boston, Inc.; Various Child Programs-Multi-Service. Franciscan Sisters of the Atonement 4; Total Assisted 2,377; Total Staff 14.

Haitian Multi-Service Center/Catholic Charitable Bureau of Boston, 12 Bicknell St., Dorchester, 02121. Tel: 617-436-2848. Mr. Jean Marc Jean-Baptiste, Dir. Education and Outreach, Day Care, Counseling and Advocacy.

HULL. *Children's Vacation House/Catholic Charities*, 138 Edgewater Rd., 02045. Tel: 617-925-0710. Conducted by the Catholic Charitable Bureau of Boston. Children 300.

[K] FAMILY COUNSELING AND GUIDANCE CENTERS

BOSTON. *Family Counseling and Guidance Centers* A Division of Catholic Charities. , *Admin. Headquarters*, 686 N. Main St., Brockton, 02301. Tel: 508-587-0815; Fax: 508-586-9446. Vivian Soper, L.I.C.S.W., Dir. Behavioral Health Div.
Local Clinics:

South Shore Braintree, 40 Independence Ave., Braintree, 02184. Tel: 617-848-7840; Fax: 781-849-1554.

North Shore-Danvers, 140 Commonwealth Ave., Ste. 202, Danvers, 01923. Tel: 978-774-6820; Fax: 978-777-4242.

Brockton, 686 N. Main St., Brockton, 02301. Tel: 508-587-0815; Fax: 508-586-9446.

[L] SOCIETY OF ST. VINCENT DE PAUL

BOSTON. *Society of St. Vincent DePaul, Central Office*, 1524 V.F.W. Pkwy., 02132. Tel: 617-325-0124; Fax: 617-325-3075. Email: resnick@SVDPBoston.com. Web: svdpboston.com. Paul MacNeil, Exec. Dir.

[M] CHILD CARE AGENCIES

BOSTON. *The Laboure Center/Catholic Charities*, 371 & 376 W. Fourth St., 02127. Tel: 617-268-9670. Sr. Maryadele Robinson, D.C., Dir., Laboure Center; Mrs. Margaret Kelly, Dir. Daughters of Charity of

St. Vincent de Paul, Early Childhood Services (includes Infant-Toddler, Preschool, Child Care, Special Needs). Sisters 1; Lay Teachers 12; Students 80.

Nazareth Child Care Center Tel: 617-522-4040; Fax: 617-983-0460. Email: pam-penton@ccab.org. 19 St. Joseph St., Jamaica Plain, 02130. Tel: 617-522-4040. Pamela J. Penton, Dir.

Legal Title: *Catholic Charities dba Nazareth Child Care Center* Capacity 83; Total Staff 18.

Nazareth Residence for Mothers and Children, 91 Regent St., Roxbury, 02119. Tel: 617-541-0100; Fax: 617-541-8781; Tel: 617-541-0100; Fax: 617-541-8781. Email: nazareth_residence@ccab.org. Sr. Mary Farren, R.G.S., Program Dir. Home for mothers and children who are HIV positive. Capacity 8; Total Staff 10; Total in Residence 22.

METHUEN. *St. Ann's Home, Inc.*, 100A Haverhill St., 01844. Tel: 978-682-5276; Fax: 978-688-4932. Email: dgrandbois@st.annshome.org. Web: www.st.annshome.org. Denis Grandbois, Exec. Dir.; Mrs. Sharon Cutter, Business Mgr. Total in Residence 100; Day Students 66; Total Staff 235; School Children 145.

Residential Treatment Center Tel: 978-692-5276; Fax: 978-688-4932. Children 85.

[N] GUIDANCE CENTERS

BOSTON. *St. Mary's Women and Infants Center*, 90 Cushing Ave., 02125. Tel: 617-436-8600. Email: jbeckler@SMWIC.org. Web: www.smwic.org. Judith Beckler, Exec. Dir. For pregnant, parenting women & their children.; Caritas Christi. Patients Assisted Annually 250; Total Staff 60.

Salesian Boys & Girls Club (Central Unit) , 189 Paris St., 02128. Tel: 617-567-0508; Fax: 617-567-0418. Email: sbgclub@juno.com. Salesians of St. John Bosco Total Assisted 3,000; Total Staff 20.

Orient Heights Unit, 145-150 Bryon St., 02128. Tel: 617-567-6626. Revs. Richard Crager, S.D.B., Exec. Dir. & Club Admin.; Jack Janko, S.D.B., Ph.D., Rector & Psychologist; Bro. John Robert Metell, S.D.B., Prog. Dir.

BROCKTON. *Phaneuf Center*, 104 Market St., 02401. Tel: 508-584-0500. Coed emergency shelter for 9 adolescents.

Phaneuf Out-Patient, 792 N. Main St., 02401. Tel: 508-588-2882. Drug and Alcohol outpatient counseling for all ages.

LAKEVILLE. *Bishop Joseph John Ruocco House*, 22 Highland Rd., 02347. Tel: 508-947-2823. Mr. Stephen Folino, Dir. Long term residential group home for 17 male adolescents. To provide comprehensive life skill services to residents and their families.

LITTLETON. *Life Resources/Alpha-Omega*, Four Omega Way, P.O. Box 922, 01460. Tel: 978-486-8919; Fax: 978-486-3990. Email: alphomeg@acunet.net. Web: www.liferesourcesinc.org. John C. Comeau, Prog. Dir. A long term residence for 17 adolescent boys. Total Staff 20; Total Assisted 30.

QUINCY. *Life Resources, Inc.*, 5 Beale St., 2nd Floor, 02170. Tel: 617-745-4114; Fax: 617-745-4196 (Admin.); 617-745-4195 (Office). Email: william_chiaradonna@liferesourcesinc.org. Web: www.liferesourcesinc.org. Mr. William J. Chiaradonna, L.I.C.S.W., D.C.S.W., Pres. Tel: 617-745-4114. Total in Residence 110; Total Staff 176; Total Assisted Annually 2,400.

[O] INFORMATION - CONFERENCE CENTERS

BOSTON. *Paulist Center*, 5 Park St., 02108. Tel: 617-742-4460; Fax: 617-720-5756. Email: fiveparkst@aol.com. Web: www.paulist.org/boston. Revs. John B. Ardis, C.S.P., Dir.; Joseph A. Ciccone, C.S.P.; Richard Colgan, C.S.P.; Susan Rutkowski, Pastoral Min.; Drew Deskur, Music Min.; Patricia Simpson, Admin.

ANDOVER. *Franciscan Center*, 475 River Rd., 01810. Tel: 978-851-3391; Fax: 978-858-0675. Email: franretc@aol.com. Web: www.franrcent.org. Rev. John D. Bavaro, O.F.M., Dir. & Guardian, Retreat Team. Order of Friars Minor Total in Residence 8; Total Staff 11.

Retreat Team: Revs. John C. DiMauro, O.F.M.; Justin J. Bailey, O.F.M.; Robert J. Caprio, O.F.M.; Michael Travaglione, O.F.M.; Bro. Gabriel Aceto, O.F.M.; Sr. Lorraine Pianka, S.S.N.D.; Mrs. Mildred Sheehan, Sec.; Jerrie Lou Buffo; Margaret McCarthy; Jackie Picken.

BROCKTON. *Chapel of Our Savior-Catholic Pastoral and Information Center*, 475 Westgate Dr., 02301-1819. Tel: 508-583-8357; Fax: 508-586-5510. Revs. Arthur Gouthro, S.A., Dir.; Malcolm Martin, S.A.; Henry Mair, S.A.; Boniface Riedmann, S.A.; Bros. DePorres Poncia, S.A.; Louis Marek, S.A.; Savio McNeice, S.A. Priests 4; Brothers 3.

PEABODY. *Catholic Information Center*, North Shore Shopping Center, 01960. Tel: 978-531-6145; Fax: 978-531-1359. Email: hjones@carmelnet.org. Revs. Herbert J. Jones, O.Carm., Prior & Dir.; Alan N. Crowley, O.Carm.; Peter Thomas Sherry, O.Carm.; Mario Lopez, O.Carm.; Felix Prior, O.Carm.; Bro. Damien Chong, O.Carm. Priests 5; Brothers 1.

[P] GENERAL HOSPITALS

BOSTON. *The Carney Hospital, Inc.*, 2100 Dorchester Ave., 02124-5666. Tel: 617-723-1100. Mr. Wilson D. Rogers Jr., Esq., Contact Person.

St. Elizabeth's Hospital of Boston, 736 Cambridge St., Brighton, 02135. Tel: 617-789-3900. Email: shagop@aol.com. Web: www.semc.org. Mr. Michael F. Collins, M.D., Pres.; Revs. Philip Conroy; Yaroslov Nalysnk; Matthew Perumpil, O.S.C.; Garrett J. Thompson; Sisters Ivan Cadigan, C.S.J.; Maryanne Gallagher, O.S.F.; Susan Keating, S.S.G.; Catherine O'Connor, C.S.B. Bed Capacity 350; Bassinets 50; Patients treated during the year 175,000.

BROCKTON. *Good Samaritan Medical Center*, 235 N. Pearl St., 02401. Tel: 508-427-3000; 508-427-3151. Frank J. Larkin, Pres. & CEO; Rev. Richard W. Visbisky, Chap. & Dir. of Pastoral Care; Rev. Suzanne Higgins, (Congregational); Mr. Richard Messing, (Rabbi). Total Assisted 107,500; Total Staff 1,350; Sisters of Charity of Nazareth 1; Sisters of Jesus Crucified 1; Holy Union Sisters 1.

LOWELL. *Saints Memorial Health System, Inc.*, One Hospital Dr., 01852. Tel: 978-458-1411; Fax: 978-458-8369. Email: info@stmmc.org. Web: www.saints-memorial.org. Thom Clark, Pres. & CEO. Sisters of Charity of Ottawa Bed Capacity 218; Total Assisted 214,000; Total Staff 1,352.

METHUEN. *Holy Family Hospital and Medical Center*, 70 East St., 01844-4597. Tel: 978-687-0151; Fax: 978-688-7689. Web: www.holyfamilyhosp.org. William L. Lane, Pres.; Rev. Richard O'Brien, Chap. Affiliating Hospital for: St. Anselm's Collegiate School of Nursing; Northern Essex Community College; UMass, Lowell; Salem State College; Boston University School of Public Health; Essex Agricultural School; New Hampshire Technical School; Massachusetts Bay Community College; Northeastern University; Rivier College; Greater Lowell Vocational School; Whittier Regional Vocational Technical School; Greater Lawrence Vocational School; and Salem High School. Bed Capacity 222; Bassinets 30; Patients Assisted Annually 230,000; Total Staff 1,844; Priests 1.

Holy Family Hospital Auxiliary, 70 East St., 01844-4597. Tel: 978-687-0156, Ext. 4023; Fax: 978-688-7689.

Holy Family Hospital Men's Guild, 70 East St., 01844-4597. Tel: 978-687-0156, Ext. 2362; Fax: 978-688-7689.

[Q] SPECIAL HOSPITALS

BOSTON. *Franciscan Children's Hospital and Rehabilitation Center* Tel: 617-254-3800; Fax: 617-779-1119. 30 Warren St., Brighton, 02135. Tel: 617-254-3800; Fax: 617-779-1119. Email: fch@fch.com. Web: www.fch.com. Paul Della Rocco, Pres. & CEO. General Pediatrics, Rehabilitation, Special Education, Mental Health Services & Home Care. Bed Capacity 100; Number under care 59,000; Day Program 90; Total Staff 750.

St. John of God Hospital, 296 Allston St., 02135. Tel: 617-277-5750; Fax: 617-731-3094. William K. Brinkert, Pres.; Rev. Joseph K. Coleman, Chap., Dir. Pastoral Care, Chronic & Rehabilitation Hospital. A member of Caritas Christi, the Catholic Health Care System of the Archdiocese of Boston. Bed Capacity 58; Total Staff 120; Total Assisted 575.

CAMBRIDGE. **Youville Hospital & Rehabilitation Center, Inc.*, 1575 Cambridge St., 02138-4398. Tel: 617-876-4344; Fax: 617-547-5501. Mr. Daniel Leahey, Pres. & CEO; Ms. Patricia Kennedy, Dir. Mission Integration; Rev. Ronald Paquin, Chap.; Ms. Patricia Kennedy, Dir. Pastoral Care Svcs.; Ms. Elizabeth Walsh, Chap.; Ms. Georgia Leiner, Chap. Member of Youville Lifecare, Inc. Priests 1; Sisters of Charity (Grey Nuns) 1; Bed Capacity 146; Patients Assisted Annually 2,285; Total Staff 517.

[R] SOCIAL SERVICES

BOSTON. *Chinese Catholic Pastoral Center*, 78 Tyler St., 02111-1831. Tel: 617-482-2949; Fax: 617-482-2949.

The Laboure Center/Catholic Charities, 371 & 376 W. Fourth St., 02127. Tel: 617-268-9670. Sr. Maryadele Robinson, D.C., Dir. Certified Home Health Services, Elderly Social Services, Early Childhood Services, Adult Day Health Program, Substance Abuse and Mental Health Counseling, Family Intervention Services, Emergency Assistance, Afterschool Programs, and Support Groups. Daughters of Charity of St. Vincent de Paul 5.

Little Sisters of the Assumption, Family Health Service, Inc. (Project Hope) , 45 Magnolia St., 02125. Tel: 617-442-1880; Fax: 617-442-1356. Email: mleonard@prohope.org. Web: www.prohope.org. A community based shelter for homeless families offering food pantry, education, child care and social services. Total Assisted 2,000; Staff 45; Sisters 3.

[S] PROTECTIVE INSTITUTIONS

BOSTON. *St. Mary's Women and Infants Center*, 90 Cushing Ave., 02125. Center for pregnant women.; (See Guidance Centers for more information.)

[T] HOMES FOR AGED-RESIDENTS & NURSING

BOSTON. *Don Orione Nursing Home*, 111 Orient Ave., East Boston, 02128-1006. Tel: 617-569-2100; Fax: 617-561-1138. Email: donorione@aol.com. Revs. Mario Guarino, F.D.P.; Rocco Crescenzi, F.D.P.; Gino Marchesani, F.D.P.; Marcelo Boschi, F.D.P.; Claudio Peters, F.D.P. Sons of Divine Providence (Don Orione Fathers) 5; Guests 190; Total Assisted 185; Total Staff 230.

St. Joseph Nursing Care Center, 321 Centre St., Dorchester, 02122. Tel: 617-825-6320; Fax: 617-825-7410. Gregory Karr, Admin. Member, Caritas Christi Healthcare System.; 123 Bed Nursing Care Center.; St. Joseph Nursing Care Center, Inc. Sisters 1; Total Staff 173.

Marian Manor (1954), 02111. 130 Dorchester St., South Boston, 02127. Tel: 617-268-3333; Fax: 617-268-4589. Email: joe@marianmanor.org. Web: www.marianmanor.org. Sr. Mark Louis, Admin.; Rev. Herbert J. Cleary, S.J., Chap. Priests 1; Carmelite Sister for the Aged and Infirm 10; Total Staff 520; Guests 366.

BROCKTON. *St. Joseph Manor Health Care Inc.*, 215 Thatcher St., 02302. Tel: 508-583-5834; Fax: 508-583-8551. Email: ateri@stjosephmanor.com. Anne M. Teri, CEO/Admin. Sisters of Jesus Crucified and the Sorrowful Mother 5; Residents 118; Total Staff 202.

Adult Day Health Center Tel: 508-583-8313; Fax: 508-588-7384. Total Assisted Per Day 40; Total Staff 10.

CAMBRIDGE. *Sancta Maria Nursing Facility*, 799 Concord Ave., 02138. Tel: 617-868-2200; Fax: 617-864-2801. Sr. Mary Mark, D.M., Admin. Daughter of Mary of the Immaculate Conception In-Patients/Residents 141; Bed Capacity 141; Sisters 5; Total Staff 235.

FRAMINGHAM. *Carmel Terrace*, 933 Central St., 01701. Tel: 508-788-8000; Fax: 508-626-1603. Web: www.carmelterrace.org. Sr. M. Joseph Augustine, Dir. Carmelite Sisters for the Aged and Infirm 3; Apartments for Assisted Living of the Elderly 62; Total Assisted 70; Total Staff 38.

St. Patrick's Manor, Inc., 863 Central St., 01701. Tel: 508-879-8000; Fax: 508-626-1604. Web: www.stpatricksmanor.org. Sr. Maureen McDonough, Admin. Carmelite Sisters for the Aged and Infirm 30; Total Staff 460.

IPSWICH. *St. Julie Billiart Residential Care Center, Inc.*, 30 Jeffreys Neck Rd., 01938. Tel: 978-356-4381; Fax: 978-356-1380. Email: lpakstis@greennet.net. Lee Pakstis, Admin.

LAWRENCE. **M.I. Adult Day Health Center, Inc.*, 189 Maple St., 01841. Tel: 978-682-7575; Fax: 978-691-5374. Email: lori_barrett@mihs.com. Barbara E. Grant, Pres. & CEO; Lori Barrett, R.N., Prog. Dir. Sisters of Charity of Montreal (Grey Nuns), Adult day health care for Senior Citizens; also, bilingual/bicultural (Spanish) adult day health care. Total in Residence 70; Total Staff 12.

M.I. Nursing-Restorative Center, Inc., 172 Lawrence St., 01841. Tel: 978-685-6321; Fax: 978-975-0050. Email: begrant@mihcs.com. Barbara E. Grant, Pres. & CEO; Michael D. Turpin, Admin. Covenant Health Systems.; Multi-level Skilled Nursing Facility.; Member of Convenant Health System, Lexington, MA. Unit of: Mary Immaculate Health Care Services. Residents 250; Total Staff 300.

M.I. Residential Community II, Inc., 191 Maple St., 01841. Tel: 978-682-7575; Fax: 978-691-5374. Barbara E. Grant, Pres. & CEO; Virginia Lynch, Mgr. Covenant Health Systems; Independent & assisted living for Elderly and Handicapped. Units 106; Total in Residence 120; Total Staff 35.

M.I. Residential Community III, Inc., 193 Maple St., 01841. Tel: 978-682-7575; Fax: 978-691-5374. Barbara E. Grant, Pres. & CEO; Virginia Lynch, Mgr. CHS, Independent & assisted living for Elderly and Handicapped. Units 88; Total in Residence 95; Total Staff 35.

M.I. Residential Community, Inc., 189 Maple St., 01841. Tel: 978-682-7575; Fax: 978-691-5374. Barbara E. Grant, Pres. & CEO; Virginia Lynch, Housing Mgr. Covenant Health Systems.; Assisted living for Elderly and Handicapped. Units 106; Total in Residence 121; Total Staff 35.

**M.I. Transportation, Inc.*, 189 Maple St., 01841. Tel: 978-682-7575; Fax: 978-691-5374. Barbara E. Grant, Pres. & CEO; Virginia Lynch, Mgr. Covenant Health Systems Total Assisted 75; Total Staff 5.

LOWELL. *D'Youville Manor Senior Care, Inc.*, 981 Varnum Ave., 01854. Tel: 978-454-5681; Fax: 978-453-3561. Email: dyouvill@dyouville.org. Web: www.dyouville.com. Janet B. Smith, CEO; Rev. Arnold Kelly, Chap. Sisters of Charity of Ottawa (Grey Nuns of the Cross) Priests 1; Sisters 5; Total Assisted 208; Total Staff 265; Adult Day Health Care Capacity 23; Total Staff 6.

MARLBOROUGH. *Marie Esther Health Center, Inc.*, 720 Boston Post Rd. E., 01752. Tel: 508-485-3791; Fax: 508-229-2294. Email: ecaron@sistersofsaintanne.org. Total Assisted 72; Total Staff 58.

SOMERVILLE. *Jeanne Jugan Pavilion*, 190 Highland Ave., 02143. Tel: 617-776-4420; Fax: 617-623-0707. Email: smmslsp@attglobal.net. 186 Highland Ave., 02143. Apartments for the Elderly 27; Residents 29; Total Staff 1.

Jeanne Jugan Residence, 186 Highland Ave., 02143. Tel: 617-776-4420; Fax: 617-623-0707. Email: smmslsp@attglobal.net. Rev. Joseph J. Downey, Chap. (Retired). Little Sisters of the Poor 15; Residents 84; Senior Citizen Total in Residence 84; Total Staff 105.

WALTHAM. *Maristhill Nursing & Rehabilitation Center*, 66 Newton St., 02453-6063. Tel: 781-893-0240; Fax: 781-894-6330. Email: jmurphy@maristhill.org. Janet C. Murphy, Admin. A member of Covenant Health Systems, offering skilled and rehabilitative nursing care. Priests 3; Sisters 10; Residents 123; Total Staff 154.

[U] PERSONAL PRELATURES

CAMBRIDGE. *Opus Dei, Prelature of the Holy Cross and Opus Dei*, 25 Follen St., 02138. Tel: 617-354-3204; Fax: 617-868-0349. Web: www.opusdei.org. Revs. Deogracias S. Rosales; David J. Cavanagh.

NEWTON. *Prelature of the Holy Cross and Opus Dei*, 481 Hammond St., 02167. Tel: 617-738-7348; Fax: 617-739-6001. Web: www.opusdei.org. Revs. Jose P. Ruisanchez; Richard W. Rieman; Raphael Caamano.

[V] MONASTERIES AND RESIDENCES OF PRIESTS AND BROTHERS

BOSTON. *Arrupe House*, 35 Creighton St., 02130. Tel: 617-524-9328; Fax: 617-522-1271. Revs. Paul F. Harman, S.J., Supr. & Novice Dir.; James P. Carr, S.J. Priests 2; Novices 7.

Assumptionist Center, 330 Market St., 02135. Tel: 617-783-0400; Fax: 617-783-8030. Email: sgoguen@assumpnon.org. Very Rev. John L. Franck, A.A., Prov. Supr.; Bro. Stephen Goguen, A.A., Prov. Treas. & Supr.; Revs. Joseph Fredette, A.A.; Claude Grenache, A.A.; Eugene LaPlante, A.A.; John Martin, A.A.; Richard E. Richards, A.A.; George Tavard, A.A.; Paul Vaudreuil, A.A. Total in Residence 9.

Assumption Guild, Inc.: Bro. Stephen Goguen, A.A., Dir.

Attached to Province:

St. Domenic's Rectory: 2517 John B. Dennis Hwy., Kingsport, TN 37660. Tel: 423-288-2773. Rev. Gregory Boisvert, A.A.

St. Vincent de Paul, 116 W. 24th St., New York, NY 10014. Tel: 212-242-8217. Rev. Gerard Messier, A.A.

3754 Glenn Haven Cir., Zephyrhills, FL 33541. Tel: 813-783-9969. Rev. Anselm Morrison, A.A.

Serving Abroad:

Ratisbonne Pontifical Institute, 26 Rehov Shmuel Hanagid, P.O. Box 7336, Jerusalem ISR 91072 Israel. Tel: 011-972-2-625-9171. Rev. Robert Fortin, A.A.

Paroisse Ste. Therese: Odos Eptanissoli 32, Athenes GR-13361 Greece. Tel: 82 14 846 (1). Rev. Theodore L. Fortier, A.A.

Parroquia Emperatriz de America, Mercaderes 99, 03900 Mexico D.F., Mexico. Tel: 525-593-2002; Fax: 525-651-2000. Rev. Gary Perron, A.A.

Parroquia de la Emperatriz, Mercaderes 99, Mexico D.F., Mexico. Tel: 525-593-2002; Fax: 525-651-2000. Rev. Camillus Thibault, A.A.

Montmartre Canadien, 1676 Chemin St. Louis, Quebec QUE GIS 165 Canada. Tel: 418-681-7357; Fax: 418-681-9644. Rev. Roger Tougas, A.A.

Haktari Songdang, 600-2 Hakgyio-Ri Hakgyio-Myon, Hamp Yong-Gun, Jeollan Amdo 525-812 Korea, South. Tel: 011-061-323-1337; Fax: 011-061-323-1337. Rev. Leo Brassard, A.A.

Austin House, P.O. Box 13230, Arusha, Tanzania. Tel: 011-255-57-2443. Revs. Richard Brunelle, A.A.; Oliver Blanchette, A.A.

Assumptionist Community, P.O. Box 58488, Nairobi 00200 Kenya. Tel: 011-254-2-567-698; Fax: 011-254-2-570-303. Rev. Luc Martel, A.A.

Padri Assuazionisti, Via San Piov 55, Rome 00165 Italy. Very Rev. Richard Lamoureux, A.A.

St. Bonaventure Friary, Franciscan Friars, 284 Foster St., 02135. Tel: 617-254-2447. Email: stbonafriary@aol.com. Rev. Francis Walter, O.F.M., Guardian and Novice Master; Bros. Mark Brown, O.F.M., Formation Staff; Juan Luis Rivera, O.F.M., Novice; Justin Morrisette, O.F.M., Novice. Priests 1; Total Staff 2.

Carmelite Monastery, 166 Foster St., 02135-3902. Tel: 617-797-5056; Fax: 617-783-1396. Revs. Emmanuel Sullivan, O.C.D.; Anthony Haglof, O.C.D.; Theodore Centala, O.C.D.; Lawrence F. Sullivan, O.C.D.; Terrence Dougherty, O.C.D.; Vincent Bowes, O.C.D.; John Grennon, O.C.D.; Bros. Robert Sentman, O.C.D.; Augustine Whart, O.C.D.; Sebastian Reale. Discalced Carmelite Friars Priests 7; Brothers 3; Total in Residence 10.

St. Christopher Friary, 18 N. Bennet St., 02113-1913. Tel: 617-742-4190; Fax: 617-725-0343. Bros. Juniper D. O'Connor, O.F.M., Guardian; Mark Brown, O.F.M. Brothers 2.

Divine Word Missionaries, 184 Beacon St., 02116. Tel: 617-267-5143; Fax: 617-267-0726. Revs. Donald P. Mulrenan, S.V.D., Supr. & Mission Dir.; Donald Skerry, S.V.D., Asst. Mission Dir.; Kenneth Feehan, S.V.D. Divine Word Missionaries

St. Gabriel Passionist Community, 139 Washington St., 02135-4235. Tel: 617-254-6582; Fax: 617-783-1766. Rev. Justinian Manning, C.P., Supr. & Pastor. The Congregation of the Passion (The Passionists) Priests 4. In Res. Revs. Brendan Breen, C.P.; Roger Gannon, C.P.; Bernadine Grande, C.P.

Jesuit Urban Center & Immaculate Conception Community, 775 Harrison Ave., 02118-2311. Tel: 617-536-8440; Fax: 617-536-2142. Email: info@jucboston.org. Web: www.jucboston.org. Revs. Thomas E. Carroll, S.J., Dir.; Jon D. Fuller, S.J.; Stephen F. Dawber, S.J.; Thomas J. Sheehan, S.J., Asst. Dir.; Mark S. Brown, Pastoral Assoc.; Dong-ill Shin, Music Ministry; Sr. Jeanne Ronayne, S.N.D., Receptionist. Total in Residence 4.

Little Brothers of St. Francis, 785-789 Parker St., 02120. Tel: 617-442-2556. Bro. James Curran, L.B.S.F., Servant General.

Legal Title: *Little Brothers of St. Francis Franciscan Fraternity of Peace and Love, Inc.*, Regional Fraternity and Novitiate. Brothers 4; Novices 2; Postulants 1.

Loyola House, 300 Newbury St., 02115-2801. Tel: 617-267-1008; Fax: 617-267-6672. Email: loybos@aol.com. Revs. Thomas F. Clark, S.J.; Herbert J. Cleary, S.J.; Charles B. Connolly, S.J., Min. & Treas.; Vincent F. Connolly, S.J.; Charles G. Crowley, S.J.; Joseph D. Devlin, S.J.; William F. Doyle, S.J.; Thomas J. Gallagher, S.J.; Walter J. Kane, S.J.; Robert G. McMillan, S.J.; William L. Mulligan, S.J.; Edward J. Murawski, S.J.; James F.X. Pratt, S.J.; Francisco A.S. Ribeiro, S.J.; Richard H. Roos, S.J.; James M. Shaughnessy, S.J., Supr.; Richard J. Stanley, S.J.; George P. Winchester, S.J.; Alfred O. Winshman, S.J. The Society of Jesus Priests 19; Total in Residence 19.

Marist Fathers and Brothers Provincial House, 27 Isabella St., 02116-5216. Tel: 617-426-5297; 617-426-4448; Fax: 617-482-1570. Email: rlajoie@aol.com. Web: users.aol.com/rlajoie/marists.htm. Very Rev. Kenneth Thibodeau, S.M., Prov.; Rev. James Strasz, S.M., Vicar Prov.

Marist Fathers Lourdes Residence, 698 Beacon St., 02215. Tel: 617-262-2271. Revs. Gerard Caron, S.M., Dir.; Marcel Lajoie, S.M. Priests 2.

Marist Fathers of Our Lady of Victories (Boston Prov.), 27 Isabella St., 02116. Tel: 617-426-4448; Fax: 617-482-1570. Email: rlajoie@aol.com. Web: members.aol.com/olofvictories. Very Rev. Kenneth Thibodeau, S.M.; Revs. Roland Lajoie, S.M.; Lucien Chasse, S.M.; Albert DiIanni, S.M., Supr.; Philip Laplante, S.M.; Armand Robichaud, S.M.; Armand Thibault, S.M.; Tuakapaw Tuipupotu (Tonga); Bros. Roland Bernier, S.M.; Leonard Haley, S.M.; Gregory Theriault, S.M. Priests 8; Brothers 3; Sisters 6.

*Ministry of the Word*Revs. Philip O'Shea, O.F.M.; John Anglin, O.F.M.; James Fitzmaurice, O.F.M.; Bro. Robert Frazzetta, O.F.M.

Paulist Fathers Residence, 5 Park St., 02108-4897. Tel: 617-742-4460; Fax: 617-723-2170. Email: JohnArdis@aol.com. Web: www.paulist.org/boston. Revs. John B. Ardis, C.S.P., Dir. & Supr.; Stanley F. MacNevin, C.S.P.; John P. Campbell, C.S.P.; Paul A. Reynolds, C.S.P.; Joseph A. Ciccone, C.S.P.; Francis M. Sweeney, C.S.P.; Thomas A. Kane, C.S.P. Total in Residence 8; Total Staff 2.

The Salesian Community, 145 Byron St., 02128. Tel: 617-569-6551; 617-569-6645; Fax: 617-568-3851. Email: jankoj@prodigy.net.

San Lorenzo Friary (the Province of St. Mary of the Capuchin Order, White Plains, New York), 15 Montebello Rd., Jamaica Plain, 02130-2370. Tel: 617-983-1919; 617-983-3692. Bro. John Shento, O.F.M.Cap., Guardian; Rev. John Rathschmidt, O.F.M.Cap., Vicar & Dir., Formation. Student Friars 9.

The Society of Jesus of New England-Provincial Offices, 85 School St., Watertown, 02472-4251. Tel: 617-607-2800; Fax: 617-607-2888. Email: nenprvsj@sjnen.org. Web: www.sjnen.org. P.O. Box 9199, Watertown, 02471-9199. Very Rev. Thomas J. Regan, S.J., Prov.; Revs. John P. Murray, S.J., Exec. Asst.; David I. Donovan, S.J., Asst. for Formation; James M. Hayes, S.J., Vocation Dir.; Michael D. Linden, S.J., Asst. for Intl., Pastoral, & Social Ministries; William C. McInnes, S.J., Liaison for Continuing Educ.; Thomas P. O'Malley, S.J., Asst. for Devel.; James M. Keegan, S.J., Liaison for Men in Apostolate of Spiritual Exercises; Dennis J. Yesalonia, Treas.

Priests of Province on Special Assignment: Revs. Robert J. Araujo, S.J.; John J. Begley, S.J.; I. Michael Bellafiore, S.J.; Aram J. Berard, S.J.; Richard D. Bertrand, S.J.; Stephen J. Bonian, S.J.; Richard P. Boyle, S.J.; Robert J. Braunreuther, S.J.; Scott N. Brodeur, S.J.; Joseph J. Bruce, S.J.; Mark J. Burke, S.J.; James P. Carr, S.J.; John J. Caskin, S.J.; Gregory C. Chisholm, S.J. (LA); Thomas F. Clark, S.J.; Richard T. Cleary, S.J.; Brian J. Conley, S.J.; Michael J. Connolly, S.J.; William J. Cullen, S.J.; John R. d'Anjou, S.J.; Richard A. Deshaies, S.J.; Michael J. Doody, S.J.; Robert R. Dorin, S.J.; Robert F. Drinan, S.J.; Michael A. Fahey, S.J.; Gerald F. Finnegan, S.J.; William B. Foley, S.J.; Anthony J. Forte, S.J.; John F. Gavin, S.J.; Francois Gick, S.J.; David H. Gill, S.J.; Richard K. Gross, S.J.; William J. Hamilton, S.J.; John B. Handrahan, S.J.; Robert M. Hanlon, S.J.; G. Simon Harak, S.J.; Edward F. Howard, S.J.; Daniel P. Jamros, S.J.; John J. Karwin, S.J.; Charles F. Kelley, S.J.; William J. Kennedy, S.J.; Daniel J. Lusch, S.J.; Frederic A. Maples, S.J.; James J. Martin, S.J.; Richard B. McCafferty, S.J.; Peter R. McGrath, S.J.; Frederick G. McLeod, S.J.; Robert G. McMillan, S.J.; Ronald A. Mercier, S.J.; John J. Moriarty, S.J.; John J. Mullen, S.J.; Joseph E. Mullen, S.J.; John F. Mullin, S.J.; Thomas R. E. Murphy, S.J.; Arthur H. Pare, S.J.; Ernest F. Passero, S.J.; Normand A. Pepin, S.J.; Philip A. Pusateri, S.J.; Robert F. Regan, S.J.; Richard W. Rousseau, S.J.; Stephen J. Sanford, S.J.; Solomon I. Sara, S.J.; Francis X. Sarjeant, S.J.; John D. Savard, S.J.; Joseph J. Schad, S.J.; James M. Shea, S.J.; John F.X. Sheehan, S.J.; Myles N. Sheehan, S.J.; Edward J. Small, S.J. (BGP); Lawrence C. Smith, S.J.; Walter J. Smith, S.J.; Paul M. Sullivan, S.J.; John E. Surette, S.J.; Robert F. Taft, S.J.; David O. Travers, S.J.; James F. Walsh, S.J.; John Joseph Walsh, S.J.; Terrance G. Walsh, S.J.; Robert L. Keane, S.J., Chap.

The Society of St. James the Apostle, Inc., 24 Clark St., 02109. Tel: 617-742-4715; Fax: 617-723-7389. Email: socjames@gte.net. Web: socstjames.com. Revs. Robert Thomas, Dir.; Hugh Joseph Shields (PH), Dir.; Milton Eggerling (OAK). Founded by His Eminence Richard Cardinal Cushing, in 1958 to recruit Priest volunteers for South America. See American Foreign Missions Section for Diocesan Priests serving in Latin America.

St. Benedict the Moor Friary (the Province of St. Mary of the Capuchin Order, White Plains, NY), 41 Harold St., 02119. Tel: 617-541-0465. Bro. Celestino Arias, O.F.M.Cap., Guardian; Revs. Zachary Grant, O.F.M.Cap., Vicar; Denilson Spironello, O.F.M.Cap.

ANDOVER. *St. Francis Friary*, 459 River Rd., 01810. Tel: 978-851-3391; Fax: 978-858-0675. Email: franretc@aol.com. Web: www.franrcent.org. Bro. Robert Artman, O.F.M., Guardian. Order of Friars Minor Total in Residence 7.

Community: Revs. John C. DiMauro, O.F.M.; Robert J. Caprio, O.F.M.; Roland Petinge, O.F.M., Retreat Dir.; Claude Scrima, O.F.M.; Deacon Charles Gingerich, O.F.M., Vicar, Vocational Dir.; Bros. Charles Trebino, O.F.M.; Gabriel Aceto, O.F.M., Retreat Team.

BROCKTON. *Chapel of Our Savior*, 475 Westgate Dr., 02301-1819. Tel: 508-583-8357; Fax: 508-586-5510. Revs. Arthur Gouthro, S.A., Dir.; Boniface Riedmann, S.A.; Malcolm Martin, S.A.; Henry Mair, S.A.; Bros. Savio McNeice, S.A.; Louis Marek, S.A.; DePorres Poncia, S.A. Franciscan Friars of the Atonement Priests 4; Brothers 3.

CAMBRIDGE. *Faber House*, 42 Kirkland St., 02138-2031. Tel: 617-497-5564. Revs. Christopher Frechette, S.J.; Kenneth J. Hughes, S.J.; John Privett, S.J.; Stephen Chow, S.J. (China); John Ghansah, S.J. (Nigeria) (NY); Paul C. Kenney, S.J.; Janez Sever, S.J. (Russia); Carlos Viana, S.J. (Brazil); John Murray, S.J.; Joaquin Martinez,

S.J.; Robert V. Poskey, S.J.; George Williams, S.J.; Patricuo Jascura, S.J. (Chile), Scholastics; Thomas E. Esselman, C.M. (STL). Residence for Jesuit Priests and Scholastics.

Weston Jesuit Community, 20 Sumner Rd., 02138. Tel: 617-547-3742; Fax: 617-868-8714. Rev. John A. Privett, S.J., Rector. Priests 58; Brothers 1; Scholastics 41.

Residences of Priests:

St. Edmunds House, 15 Avon St., 02138. Tel: 617-492-3908. Revs. John Baldovin, S.J.; Kevin Burke, S.J.

Faber House, 42 Kirkland St., 02138. Tel: 617-497-5564. Revs. Stephen Chow, S.J.; Christopher Frechette, S.J.; Kenneth J. Hughes, S.J.; John Privett.

7 Kirkland Rd., 02138. Tel: 617-661-4155. Revs. Richard J. Clifford, S.J.; John J. Kselman, S.S.; Robert E. Manning, S.J.

40 Kirkland St., 02138. Tel: 617-868-6568. Rev. Edward V. Vacek, S.J.

10 Martin St., 02138. Tel: 617-491-2155. Revs. Peter Dubovsky, S.J.; Manuel Francisco, S.J.; James Keenan, S.J.; John W. O'Malley, S.J.; Christopher Llanos; Edwin Vasquez.

6 Sumner Rd., 02138. Tel: 617-547-5310. Revs. Peter Fink, S.J.; John R. Sachs, S.J.

6 Manassas Ave., 02138. Tel: 617-547-1086. Revs. Eric Genilo, S.J.; William Ibach, S.J.

12 Linnaean St., 02138. Tel: 617-547-0931. Rev. Daniel J. Harrington, S.J.

3 Phillips Pl., 02138. Tel: 617-492-1960. Rev. Stanley B. Marrow, S.J.

66 Oxford St., 02138. Tel: 617-876-1233. Rev. Carlos Sergio Viana.

COHASSET. *Bellarmine House*, 150 Howard Gleason Rd., 02025. Tel: 781-383-0723; Fax: 781-383-3164. Rev. James M. Collins, S.J., Admin. (Summer Res. for Jesuits of New England Prov.).

DANVERS. *Xavier Center*, 21 Spring St., 01923. Tel: 978-777-1326. Bro. John D. Hamilton, C.F.X., Dir. of Formation, House of Formation. Xaverian Brothers, U.S.A. Brothers Professed 4.

DEDHAM. *African Mission House* Society of African Missions, Inc. , 269-337 Common St., 02026-4030. Tel: 781-326-3288; 781-326-4670; Fax: 781-326-7627. Email: smausa-d@ix.netcom.com. Web: www.smafathers.org. Rev. Ulick Bourke, S.M.A. Priests 1.

DOVER. *St. Stephen Priory*, 20 Glen St., Box 370, 02030. Tel: 508-785-0124; Fax: 508-785-1020. Email: thepriory@aol.com. Web: www.ststephenpriory.org. Bro. Ignatius Perkins, O.P., D.N.S., M.A.Ed., R.N.; Revs. E. Henry Gallagher, O.P.; Bruce A. Williams, O.P.; Richard A. Fleck, O.P.; John Stephen Fitzhenry, O.P.; Louis Roy, O.P. (Canada); Romanus Cessario, O.P.; Frank I. Sutman, O.P.; Frank Bede Shipps, O.P.; Bro. Patrick Foley, O.P. Spiritual Life Center and Retreat Center. Priests 8; Religious Brothers 1; Total Staff 9.

DUXBURY. *Society of the Divine Word*, 121 Parks St., P.O. Box M, 02331-0614. Tel: 781-585-2460; Fax: 781-585-3770. Email: miramarma@aol.com. Revs. Joseph Connolly, S.V.D.; Edward Dudink, S.V.D.; John J. Bergin, S.V.D.; Edward Tuohy, S.V.D.; Robert Mallonee, S.V.D.; Robert Jones, S.V.D., Rector; Bro. Donald Champagne, S.V.D.; Rev. Thomas Griffith, S.V.D. Priests 7; Brothers 1; Total Staff 22.

HINGHAM. *Glastonbury Abbey*, 16 Hull St., 02043. Tel: 781-749-2155; Fax: 781-749-6236. Email: office@glastonburyabbey.org. Web: www.glastonburyabbey.org. Rt. Revs. Nicholas J. Morcone, O.S.B., Abbot; Edward C. Campbell, O.S.B., Retired Abbot (Retired); Very Rev. Timothy J. Joyce, Prior; Revs. Andrew M. Quillen; Jonah P. Trombetta, O.S.B.; John P. Kelleher, O.S.B.; Gerald T. Leibenguth, O.S.B.; Thomas J. O'Connor; Roger Nolette; Bros. John Mark Carlin, O.S.B.; David K. Coakley, O.S.B.; James Crowley, O.S.B.; Daniel F. Walters, O.S.B. Benedictine Monks, Retreat Center. Priests 10; Brothers 4; Capacity 31; Conference Center Capacity 180.

Lincoln School Apartments for the Elderly, 02044. Tel: 781-749-2155; Fax: 781-749-6236. Email: office@glastonburyabbey.org. Web: www.glastonburyabbey.org.

HOLLISTON. *Xaverian Missionaries*, 101 Summer St., P.O. Box 5857, 01746-5857. Tel: 508-429-2144; Fax: 508-429-4793. Email: XAVMISSMA@yahoo.com. Web: www.sigmaweb.net/xavmissions. Revs. Kenneth V. Cannon, S.X., Supr.; Francis Signorelli, S.X.; Robert S. Maloney, S.X.; Gerard Furlan, S.X.; Tony Lalli, S.X.; Eugene Montesi, S.X. Priests 5.

LAWRENCE. *Marist Brothers*, 26 Leeds Ter., 01843. Tel: 978-686-7411; Fax: 978-686-6506. Bros. Kenneth Hogan, F.M.S.; Richard La Rose, F.M.S.; Jerry Dowsky, F.M.S. Brothers 3.

Marist Brothers Residence, 12 Sheridan St., 01841. Tel: 508-682-1163. Bros. William Lambert, F.M.S., Dir.; C. Vincent Dinnean, F.M.S.; Ernest Beland, F.M.S.; Richard Carey, F.M.S. Brothers 4.

LOWELL. *Missionary Oblates of Mary Immaculate*, 27 Kirk St., 01852-1004. Tel: 978-937-9594; Fax: 978-458-3603. Email: garin.residence@juno.com garin.residence@lowelloblates.us.

Andre Garin Retirement Residence Tel: 978-937-9594; Fax: 978-458-3603. Bro. Charles Gilbert, O.M.I., Dir. Tel: 978-441-1245; Revs. Roland Couture, Asst. Dir.; Charles Beausoleil, O.M.I.; Marcel Bolduc; Gilmond Boucher, O.M.I.; Adhemar Deveau, O.M.I.; Richard Kulwiec, O.M.I.; Roger E. Lamoureux, O.M.I.; James Taggart, O.M.I.; Bro. Thomas Cruise, O.M.I.

Missionary Oblates of Mary Immaculate, Northeast Area Office, 60 Wyman St., 01852-2841. Tel: 978-458-9912; Fax: 978-458-7274. Email: odomi@omiusa.org. Web: www.omiusa.org. Revs. William O'Donnell, O.M.I., Northeast Area Supr.; George Brown, O.M.I.; Norman Comtois, O.M.I.; Wilfred Harvey, O.M.I.; John King, O.M.I.; Michael Lauze, O.M.I.; Albert Lirette, O.M.I. (Retired); Roland St. Pierre, O.M.I.; Bro. Robert Dutil, O.M.I. Priests 90; Brothers 12; Total Staff 1; Serving Abroad 1; Total in Residence 8; Total Membership 102.

St. Eugene House (Residence), 60 Wyman St., 01852-2841. Tel: 978-441-0649; Fax: 978-454-0677. Revs. Bernard Belley, O.M.I.; Herve Gagnon, O.M.I.; Richard McAlear, O.M.I.; William O'Donnell, O.M.I.; George Protopapas, O.M.I.; Lucien Richard, O.M.I.; Lucien Sawyer, O.M.I.; Bro. Augustin Cote, O.M.I.

Contemplative Mission Center, 46 Mt. Washington St., 01854-3498. Tel: 978-454-0039; Fax: 978-452-9163. Email: jgd@juno.com. Revs. James Dukowski, O.M.I.; James Erving, O.M.I.; Roger Roy, O.M.I.; William Sheehan, O.M.I.

Oblate Foreign Mission Office, Northeast Area, 60 Wyman St., 01852-2841. Tel: 978-458-4380; Fax: 978-458-7274. Email: brogus@juno.com. Bro. Augustin Cote, O.M.I., Dir.

Oblate Vocation Office, Northeast Area, 60 Wyman St., 01852-2841. Tel: 978-458-9912; Fax: 978-458-7274. Email: jcerving@yahoo.com. Rev. James Erving, O.M.I., Dir.

LYNN. *Franciscan Community (Province of Immaculate Conception)*, 38 Michigan Ave., 01902. Tel: 617-592-7396; Fax: 617-593-8805. Revs. Alfonse Ferreira, O.F.M., Procurator & Guardian; Bede Ferrara, O.F.M.

"The Listening Place" (Counseling Center), 36 Michigan Ave., 01902. Tel: 781-592-7396; Fax: 781-593-8805. Rev. Alfonse Ferreira, O.F.M., Dir.; Sr. Jane Hogan, O.S.F., Assoc. Dir.

MILTON. *Oblate Residence (St. Joseph House)*, 65 Fr. Carney Dr., 02186-4206. Tel: 617-698-6785; Fax: 617-698-7621. Web: www.oblatesofthevirginmary.org. Revs. David Nicgorski, O.M.V.; Robert Lowrey, O.M.V.; James Montanaro, O.M.V.; Vincenzo Antolini, O.M.V.; Alan Hall, O.M.V.; Gerald Wright, O.M.V.; Bro. Joseph O'Connor, O.M.V. Congregation of the Oblates of the Virgin Mary Priests 6; Brothers 1.

NEWTON. *The Jesuit Community at Boston College* 02467. Tel: 617-552-8200; Fax: 617-552-2380. Web: www.bc.edu/sj/. Very Rev. Thomas J. Regan, S.J., Provincial; Revs. Paul F. Harman, S.J., Rector; James M. Collins, S.J., Admin. & Treas. & Asst. Rector; Francis J. Nicholson, S.J., Asst. Rector; Edward M. O'Flaherty, S.J., Asst. Rector; Ronald Anderson, S.J.; Joseph A. Appleyard, S.J.; J. Robert Barth, S.J. (New York); Charbel Batour, S.J. (N. East); James W. Bernauer, S.J. (New York); Stanley J. Bezuszka, S.J.; Richard Blake, S.J. (NY); James F. Bresnahan, S.J.; Joseph Bruce, S.J.; Michael Buckley, S.J. (California); Lawrence Daka, S.J. (Zim); John Butler, S.J.; Anselm Byun, S.J. (Korea, South); John F. Caulfield, S.J.; Richard T. Cleary, S.J.; Francis X. Clooney, S.J. (New York); Walter Conlan, S.J. (BAH); William Connolly, S.J.; Neil F. Decker, S.J.; Erroll D'Lima, S.J. (India); Robert J. Daly, S.J.; George Drury, S.J.; Joseph P. Duffy, S.J.; Harvey D. Egan, S.J.; Frederick Enman, S.J.; James Erps, S.J. (California); Robert Farrell, S.J.; Joseph F. X. Flanagan, S.J.; James Fleming, S.J.; Thomas F. Fleming, S.J.; David H. Gill, S.J.; Julio Giulietti, S.J.; Gerard Gallen, S.J. (England); Gary Gurtler, S.J. (New York); Edward J. Hanrahan, S.J.; James Hayes, S.J.; Charles J. Healey, S.J., S.T.L., S.T.D.; Raymond G. Helmick, S.J.; Francis R. Herrmann, S.J. (NY); Eduardo Henriques, S.J. (Brazil); David Hernandez-Correa, S.J.; Stephen Hess, S.J.; David Hollenbach, S.J. (Maryland); John W. Howard, S.J.; John Izzo, S.J. (California); Gregory Kalscheur, S.J. (MD); James Keenan, S.J. (NY); T. Frank Kennedy, S.J.; Kevin Kersten, S.J. (Wisconsin); Philip Kiley, S.J.; John Konicek, S.J. (NO); Arthur F. Liebscher, S.J. (SJ); William P. Leahy, S.J. (Wisconsin), Pres.; Michael Linden, S.J.; J. Allan Loftus, S.J. (BAL); Francis Liuima, S.J. (Lithuania); Kenneth Loftus, S.J.; Daniel J. Lusch, S.J.; Martin MacDonnell, S.J.; Francis C. Mackin, S.J.; Donald A. MacMillan, S.J.; Simon Makuru, S.J. (Zambia); James B. Malley, S.J.; Leo Manglaviti, S.J.; Douglas Marcouiller, S.J. (Missouri); Ageng Joseph Marwata, S.J. (Indonesia); Richard A. McGowan, S.J. (Maryland); William C. McInnes, S.J.; John P. McIntyre, S.J.; Paul McNellis, S.J. (NY); William W. Meissner, S.J. (New York); Paul A. Messer, S.J.; James Miracky, S.J. (NY); J. Donald Monan, S.J. (New York); James F. Morgan, S.J.; John J. Moriarty, S.J.; Francis J. Moy, S.J.; Abuchi Muoneme, S.J. (Nigeria); Bruce Morrill, S.J.; John F. Mullin, S.J.; William B. Neenan, S.J. (Wisconsin); Gerard C. O'Brien, S.J.; James C. O'Brien, S.J.; Joseph M. O'Keefe, S.J.; Martin O'Malley, S.J. (NY); Thomas P. O'Malley, S.J.; Charles Onyango, S.J. (Africa); Protas Opondo, S.J. (Africa); Cyril Opeil, S.J. (Maryland); Pyong Gwan Pak, S.J. (Korea, South); John Paris, S.J.; Frank J. Parker, S.J.; Sugiyo Pitoyo, S.J. (Indonesia); Donald J. Plocke, S.J.; William J. Richardson, S.J. (New York); Lubos Rojka, S.J. (Slovakia); Elisee Rutagambwa; William Russell, S.J.; Patrick J. Ryan, S.J.; Joop Schopman, S.J. (Netherlands); Stephen Schloesser, S.J. (MIL); James W. Skehan, S.J.; John Spencer, S.J.; Scott Steinkerchner, O.P.; Francis A. Sullivan, S.J.; Josef Stuchly, S.J.; Daniel Sweeney, S.J. (MD); Ronald K. Tacelli, S.J.; Leo Tagore, S.J. (India); Robert F. VerEecke, S.J.; James A. Woods, S.J.

QUINCY. *St. Columban's Foreign Mission Society*, 310 Adams St., 02169. Tel: 617-472-1494. Priests 8.

P.O. Box 227, Humarock, 02047. Rev. John S. Roche, S.S.C.

20 Frisbie Rd., Marshfield, 02050. Rev. Edward A. Roberts, S.S.C.

310 Adams St., 02169. Rev. James O'Brien, S.S.C., Supr.

St. John Chrystostom, 4750 Washington St., West Roxbury, 02132. Revs. Michael Breen, S.S.C.; Charles B. Flaherty, S.S.C.

Immaculate Conception, 487 Broadway, Everett, 02149. Rev. Joseph L. Crehan, S.S.C.

Presentation Apts., #54, 309 Church St., Clinton, 01510. Rev. Paul O'Malley, S.S.C.

SOMERVILLE. *Brotherhood of Hope*, 194 Summer St., 02143-2525. Tel: 617-623-9592; Fax: 617-625-1837. Email: brothers@brotherhoodofhope.org. Web: www.brotherhoodofhope.org. Total in Residence 13.

TEWKSBURY. *Oblate World/Missionary Association of Mary Immaculate*, 486 Chandler St., Box 680, 01876-0680. Tel: 978-858-0434; Fax: 978-858-3661. Email: oblateworld@omires.com. Rev. William O'Donnell, O.M.I., Editor & Dir.

WALPOLE. *Maryknoll Mission Promotion Department*, 80 Emerson Rd., 02032-1349. Tel: 508-668-6831; Fax: 508-660-0252. Email: mklboston@aol.com. Revs. Francis J. Breen, M.M., Dir.; Joseph W. Towle, M.M. Total in Residence 2; Staff 3.

WALTHAM. *Stigmatine Fathers & Brothers Provincial House*, 554 Lexington St., 02452. Tel: 718-209-3100; Fax: 781-894-9785. Web: www.stigmatines.com. Very Rev. Gregory J. Hoppough, C.S.S., M.Div., S.T.L., S.T.D., Prov. Supr.; Revs. Charles Dolan, C.S.S. (Thailand); Richard Woodarek, C.S.S. (Thailand); Robert Masciocchi, C.S.S. Total Staff 4.

Stigmatine House Bertoni Hall , 554 Lexington, 02452-3097. Tel: 781-209-3100. Web: www.stigmatines.com. Revs. Joseph Henchey, C.S.S., Supr.; Anthony Penna, C.S.S.; Nicholas Spagnolo, C.S.S.; Bro. Richard Spencer, C.S.S.

WESTON. *Campion Health Center, Inc.*, 319 Concord Rd., 02493. Tel: 781-788-6800; Fax: 781-894-5864. Revs. Ronald J. Amiot, S.J., Rector; Ronald E. Wozniak, S.J., Min.; David G. Boulton, S.J., Chap.; James T. Sheehan, S.J., Asst. Chap.; Dudley R. C. Adams, S.J.; John P. Banks, S.J.; Joseph F. Brennan, S.J.; John F. Broderick, S.J.; Robert R. Burke, S.J.; Robert B. Campbell, S.J.; Albert A. Cardoni, S.J.; Edward K. Cheney, S.J.; Richard J. Coakley, S.J.; Hubert F. Cunniff, S.J.; John F. Devane, S.J.; J. Frank Devine, S.J.; William G. Define, S.J.; John J. Diskin, S.J.; Joseph G. Fennell, S.J.; John F. Foley, S.J.; Paul P. Gilmartin, S.J.; Donald F. Grady, S.J.; William G. Guindon, S.J.; Philip K. Harrigan, S.J.; Alwyn C. Harry, S.J.; Robert J. Higgins, S.J.; Joseph J. LaBran, S.J.; William J. Larkin, S.J.; Victor F. Leeber, S.J.; Robert E. Lindsay, S.J.; Paul T. Lucey, S.J.; John MacDonnell, S.J.; George S. Mahan, S.J.; John L. Mahoney, S.J.; Joaquin Martinez-Mari, S.J. (Bolivia); James P. McCaffrey, S.J.; Martin F. McCarthy, S.J.; Paul T. McCarty, S.J.; Raymond E. McCluskey, S.J.; J. Joseph McGrath, S.J.; Frederick L. Moriarty, S.J.; Henry J. Murphy, S.J.; George W. Nolan, S.J.; Richard F. Olson, S.J.; Joseph P. O'Neill, S.J.; Joseph A.

Paquet, S.J.; Ignatius F. Pennisi, S.J.; William J. Power, S.J.; Leo F. Quinlan, S.J.; Martin E. Ryan, S.J.; Joseph S. Scannell, S.J.; Patrick A. Sullivan, S.J.; Robert J. Sullivan, S.J.; Wilfrid J. Vigeant, S.J.; Francis W. Vye, S.J.; James P. Walsh, S.J.; Maurice B. Walsh, S.J.; Bros. Edward P. Babinski, S.J.; H. Francis Cluff, S.J.; Peter J. Gabriel, S.J.; James P. McDavitt, S.J.; Edward L. Niziclek, S.J.; Italo A. Parnoff, S.J. Priests 57; Brothers 6.

Campion Jesuit Community, 319 Concord Rd., 02493. Tel: 781-788-6800; Fax: 781-894-5864. Revs. Ronald J. Amiot, S.J., Rector; Ronald E. Wozniak, S.J., Min.; Walter M. Abbott, S.J.; William A Barry, S.J.; Harry J. Cain, S.J.; Joseph H. Casey, S.J.; John J. Caskin, S.J.; Ned H. Cassem, S.J.; Lawrence E. Corcoran, S.J.; Robert G. Doherty, S.J.; Paul C. Kenney, S.J.; Joseph R. Laughlin, S.J.; John J. Mandile, S.J.; James R. Mattaliano; John J. McGrath, S.J.; Francis J. McManus, S.J.; John W. Michalowski, S.J., Dir., Renewal Center; John J. Mullen, S.J.; George B. Murray, S.J.; Ernest F. Passero, S.J.; Anthony R. Picariello, S.J.; James F. Talbot, S.J.; E. Corbett Walsh, S.J.; Bros. Vincent M. Brennan, S.J.; Calvin A. Clarke, S.J.; Deacon James J. Moran, S.J.; Bro. William M. Quegan, S.J.; Deacon William J. Spokesfield, S.J.

Legal Title: *Campion Residence & Renewal Center, Inc.* Priests 23; Brothers 5.

[W] CONVENTS AND RESIDENCES FOR SISTERS

BOSTON. *Archbishop's Residence* Tel: 617-782-2544; Fax: 617-782-8358. 2101 Commonwealth Ave., Brighton, 02135.

Bernardine Sisters, O.S.F., 17 Hale St., 02136. Tel: 617-361-1726; Fax: 617-361-8820. Email: sdelourdes@aol.com. Web: bfranciscan.org. Sr. Theresa Ann Rygiel, O.S.F., Contact Person.

Legal Title: *Bernardine Sisters of the Third Order of St. Francis of Mass., Inc.* Sisters 20.

Columban Sisters, 73 Mapleton St., 02135. Tel: 617-782-5683; Fax: 617-789-3569. Email: columbans@juno.com. Web: columbansisters.org. Sr. Ruth Dockert, U.S. Area Coord.

Legal Title: *Missionary Sisters of Saint Columban* Professed Sisters 8.

The Congregation of the Sisters of Our Lady of Mercy, 241 Neponset Ave., 02122. Tel: 617-288-1202; Fax: 617-265-9405. Email: mercy@sisterfaustina.org. Web: www.sisterfaustina.org. Sr. Saula M. Firer, Local Supr. Professed Sisters 5.

Daughters of St. Paul Inc., 50 St. Paul's Ave., 02130-3491. Tel: 617-522-8911; Fax: 617-524-8648. Email: usaprov@paulinemedia.org Web: www.pauline.org.

Legal Title: *Daughters of St. Paul, Inc. Novitiate, Juniorate, Provincialate Headquarters, and Technical Apostolate Center for U.S.* Prov. Community 7; Perpetually Professed Sisters 58; Novices 3; Initial Formation 4.

Pauline Book & Media Center, 885 Providence Hwy., Dedham, 02026. Tel: 781-326-5385; Fax: 781-461-1013.

Franciscan Missionary Sisters for Africa (USA Headquarters and only house.) , 172 Foster St., Box 35095, 02135. Tel: 617-254-4343; Fax: 617-787-8007. Email: sisters172@aol.com maurita172@aol.com. Web: www.members.aol.com/sisters172/fmsa.html. Serving in Uganda, Kenya, Zambia, Zimbabwe, and South Africa. Completely a Missionary congregation. Sisters 7.

Franciscan Monastery of St. Clare, The, 920 Centre St., 02130. Tel: 617-524-1760; Fax: 617-983-5205. Email: Bostonpoorclares@worldnet.att.net. Web: www.StAnthonyShrine.org/PoorClares. Sr. Teresa Dericks, O.S.C., Abbess. Franciscan Poor Clare Nuns, Solemn Vows. Cloistered Solemnly Professed 18; Extern Sisters 2.

Little Sisters of the Assumption Convent, 65 Magnolia St., 02125. Tel: 617-442-9411. Email: mleonard@prohope.org. Web: www.littlesisters.org.

Legal Title: *Little Sisters of the Assumption Family Health Services, Inc., dba Project Hope, Co-Opportunity, Inc.*

Monastery of Discalced Carmelites, 61 Mt. Pleasant Ave., 02119. Tel: 617-442-1411; Fax: 617-442-0203. Email: bostoncarmel@juno.com. Web: www.carmelitesofboston.org. Sr. Mary Teresa, O.C.D., Prioress. Cloistered. Professed 10.

Motherhouse of the Sisters of St. Joseph of Boston, 637 Cambridge St., 02135. Tel: 617-783-9090; Fax: 617-783-8246. Email: boscsj@aol.com. Web: www.CSJBoston.org. Renovation in process/no living quarters just Administration and Finance Offices.

Sacred Heart Convent, 286 Shawmut Ave., 02118-1613. Tel: 617-542-1143. Email: Joannemhsh@aol.com.

Legal Title: *Institute of Mission Helpers* Mission Helpers of the Sacred Heart Sisters 3.

Sister Disciples of the Divine Master, Convent and Eucharistic Center, 43 West St., 02111. Tel: 482-682-0978; 482-423-2629; Fax: 482-682-3779. Email: sddmboston@aol.com. Sr. Nieves Salinas, S.D.D.M., Supr. Sisters 10.

Sisters of Notre Dame de Namur (Boston Province Offices) Tel: 617-387-2500; Fax: 617-387-1303. Email: bo_admin@sndden.org. Web: www.sndden.org/boston. 351 Broadway Everett, 02149-3425. Total in Community 227.

Provincial Team: Sisters Theresa Carlow, S.N.D. de Namur; Catherine Fleming, S.N.D. de Namur; Patricia O'Malley, S.N.D. de Namur.

Sisters of the Good Shepherd, 35 Tyndale St., 02131. Tel: 617-469-2492; Fax: 617-469-9857. Email: smhvgs@verizon.net. Sisters 3.

St. Theresa House, 50 Brown Ave., 02131. Tel: 617-323-4644. Little Missionaries (A Pious Society) 1; Sisters 1; Lay Associates 12.

ANDOVER. *Monastery of St. Clare*, 445 River Rd., 01810-4213. Tel: 978-683-7599; Fax: 978-683-6085. Sr. Therese Lacroix, O.S.C., Abbess. Poor Clare Nuns Cloistered Solemnly Professed 12; Extern Perpetually Professed 2.

BROCKTON. *Our Lady of Sorrows Convent*, 261 Thatcher St., 02302-3997. Tel: 508-588-5070; Fax: 508-580-6770. Email: mjv@sisterscjcbrocktonma.org. Web: www.sisterscjcbrocktonma.org. Sr. Mary Valliere, C.J.C., Gen. Supr. Poor Sisters of Jesus Crucified and the Sorrowful Mother Sisters 34.

CAMBRIDGE. *Franciscan Missionaries of Mary*, 16 Lancaster St., 02140. Tel: 617-868-8036; Fax: 617-661-1835 Email: fmmvisit@aol.com. Sr. Mary Motte, F.M.M., Prov.

3305 Wallace Ave., Bronx, NY 10467-6599. Tel: 718-547-4693; Fax: 718-547-4607. Sr. Pauline Williams, F.M.M., Coord.

Sancta Maria Convent, 799 Concord Ave., 02138. Tel: 617-868-2200, Ext. 2950; Fax: 617-864-2801.

CHELSEA. *Don Guanella Center, Inc., Daughters of St. Mary of Providence*, 37 Nichols St., 02150. Tel: 617-889-0179; Fax: 617-889-3363. Email: dgcenterchelsea2@verizon.net. Web: www.donguanellacenter.com. Sr. Nancy McLennen, D.S.M.P., Dir. of Center. Family Support Respite for Developmentally Handicapped Ladies (Ages 18-65). Sisters 2; Families 100; Total Staff 20.

DANVERS. *Discalced Carmelite Monastery*, 15 Mt. Carmel Rd., 01923-3796. Tel: 978-774-3008; Fax: 978-774-7409. Sr. Anne of the Mother of God, O.C.D., Prioress. Total in Residence 16.

DEDHAM. *Ursuline Convent, Inc.*, 65 Lowder St., 02026-4205. Tel: 781-326-3158; Fax: 781-326-4428. Email: nestabeaudoin@msn.com. Sr. Mercedes Videira, O.S.U., Prioress. Sisters 10.

Ursuline Provincialate, 45 Lowder St., 02026-4200. Tel: 781-326-6219; Fax: 781-326-7296. Email: provosu@juno.com. Sr. Angela Krippendorf, O.S.U., Prov. Ursulines of the Roman Union, Northeastern Province 39.

EVERETT. *Pope John XXIII Convent*, 883 Broadway, 02149. Tel: 617-387-5165. Web: sndden.org. Sisters of Notre Dame de Namur 6.

The Sisters of Notre Dame de Namur Congregatonal Mission Office, Inc., 351 Broadway, 02149-3425.

FRAMINGHAM. *Fontbonne Hall*, 85 Bethany Rd., 01702. Tel: 508-879-1295; Fax: 508-424-1230. Email: fontfram@aol.com. Sr. Bernadette Kenney, C.S.J., Admin. Rev. Robert Graham, S.M., Chap. Professed Sisters 56.

US Federation of Sisters of St. Joseph 85 Bethany Rd., 01702. Tel: 508-424-1210; Fax: 508-424-1241. Email: cssifedkathy@aol.com. Web: www.sistersofsaintjosephfederation.org. Sr. Kathleen McCluskey, C.S.J., Exec. Dir.

HAVERHILL. *Sacred Hearts Convent*, 48 S. Chestnut St., 01835. Tel: 978-521-6867. Email: scimsh@juno.com. Sr. Claire Ouellette, Supr. Servants of the Immaculate Heart of Mary Good Shepherd Sisters of Quebec 4.

IPSWICH. *Sisters of Notre Dame de Namur Generalate Office*, 30 Jeffrey's Neck Rd., 01938. Tel: 978-356-2159; Fax: 978-356-1034. Email: JeanStoner@SNDDEN.org. Web: www.SNDdeN.org. Sr. Lorraine Connell, S.N.D.deN., Gen. Treas.

Casa Generalizia di Suore di Nostra Signora di Namur, Via Raffaello Sardiello, 20 Rome 00165 Italy. Tel: 39-06-6641-8704; Fax: 39-06-6641-8709. Sr. Camilla Burns, S.N.D.deN., Gen. Moderator. (Generalate)

The Sisters of Notre Dame de Namur Congregational Mission Office, Inc., 30 Jeffrey's Neck Rd., 01938. Tel: 978-356-2159; Fax: 978-356-1034.

Sisters of Notre Dame de Namur (Provincial Residence), 30 Jeffreys Neck Rd., 01938-1308. Tel: 978-356-4669; Fax: 978-356-9759. Email: prvncoff@aol.com. Web: www.sndden.org. Sisters 72; Total Staff 58.

Provincial Leadership Team: Sisters Eileen Burns, S.N.D. deN., Prov. Admin.; Maryalyce Gilfeather, S.N.D. deN.; Anne Stevenson, S.N.D. deN.

KINGSTON. *Congregation of the Sisters of Divine Providence*, Providence House, 363 Bishops Hwy., 02364. Tel: 781-585-7707; Fax: 781-582-1596. Email: cdpward@adelphia.net. Sr. Claudia Ward, C.D.P., Area Asst.

LEXINGTON. *Congregation of Armenian Catholic Sisters of Immaculate Conception, Inc.*, 6 Eliot Rd., 02173. Tel: 781-863-5962; Fax: 781-862-8479. Sisters 3.

Grey Nuns Regional Offices, 10 Pelham Rd., Ste. 1000, 02421-8499. Tel: 781-862-4704; Fax: 781-861-9641. Email: srjpoor@sgmlex.org. Web: www.sgmlex.org/. Headquarters (U.S.A. Region) of the Sisters of Charity of Montreal. "Grey Nuns".

General Administration, 138 Rue Saint-Pierre, Montreal QC H2Y 2L7 Canada. Tel: 514-842-9411; Fax: 514-842-7855. Sr. Jeanne Poor, S.G.M., Regl. Supr. Sisters 2.

LOWELL. *Convent of the Holy Union Retirement Home*, 142 Chestnut St., 01852-2429. Tel: 978-458-8862; 978-458-8835; Fax: 978-970-3780. Email: mtmbeaudoin@juno.com. Web: holyunionsisters.org. Holy Union Sisters Sisters 21.

Franciscan Sisters of Allegany, Region II Office, 282 Suffolk St., 01854. Tel: 978-452-2823; Fax: 978-452-9551. Email: fsaregion2@juno.com. Web: www.fsalleg.org. Sr. Mary Lou Lafferty, O.S.F., Region II Min.

St. Joseph Provincial House, 559 Fletcher St., 01854-3434. Tel: 978-453-4993; Fax: 978-441-1452. Email: pmalo@comcast.net. Sr. Prescille Malo, S.C.O., Prov. Supr. Sisters of Charity of Ottawa (Grey Nuns of the Cross) Sisters 33.

MARLBOROUGH. *Sisters of St. Anne, Provincialate*, 720 Boston Post Rd. E., 01752. Tel: 508-481-4934; Fax: 508-481-4939. Email: sydargy@hotmail.com. Web: www.sistersofsaintanne.org. Headquarters of American Province. Sisters 148.

Community of the Sisters of Saint Anne Tel: 508-481-4934; Fax: 508-481-4939.

St. Anne Convent, 720 Boston Post Rd. E., 01752. Tel: 508-485-3791; Fax: 508-481-4939. Sisters 68.

Sisters of St. Chretienne, 197 Pleasant St., 01752-1169. Tel: 508-485-0740; Fax: 508-481-0663. Email: marl@tiac.net. Sr. Lorraine Michaud, S.S.Ch., Local Coord. House of Retirement. Sisters 31.

Sisters of St. Chretienne, 207 Pleasant St., 01752-1169. Tel: 508-229-3505. Sr. Jeanne Allard, S.S.Ch., Local Coord.

Sisters of the Good Shepherd, 406 Hemenway St., 01752. Tel: 508-485-8610; Fax: 508-460-6372. Sr. Jane Amirault, Contact Person. Sisters 29.

METHUEN. *Our Lady of Mount Carmel Convent*, 82 Union St., 01844. Tel: 978-682-4833; Fax: 978-685-6290. Email: mtcarmel6@juno.com. Servants of the Immaculate Heart of Mary Good Shepherd Sisters of Quebec 4.

Provincial House, 209 Lawrence St., 01844. Tel: 978-687-1369; Fax: 978-975-1998. Email: prov.methuen@verizon.net. Web: www.presmarymethuen.org. Sr. Helene Bissonnette, Prov. Supr. Presentation of Mary Sisters 134; Total in Residence 89.

MILTON. *Franciscan Sisters of the Immaculate Conception, St. Mary of the Hills*, 260 Brook Rd., 02186. Tel: 617-698-3141. Sr. Rita Murray, F.M.A., Supr.

St. Mary of the Hills (Grades K-8)

Holy Union Sisters, Province Office, P.O. Box 410, 444 Centre St., 02186-0006. Tel: 617-696-8765; Fax: 617-696-8571. Web: www.holyunionsisters.org. Sisters Beverly Furtado, S.U.S.C., Province Mission Team; Gretchen Marlatt, S.U.S.C., Province Mission Team; Bernadette Sullivan, S.U.S.C., Province Mission Team.

NEWTON. *Immaculate Conception Provincialate*, 790 Centre St., 02458-2530. Tel: 617-527-1004; Fax: 617-527-2528. Email: usaprov@aol.com. Web: www.mficusa.org. Missionary Franciscan Sisters of the Immaculate Conception Total in Residence 4; Total Staff 5.

Mt. Alvernia Convent, 790 Centre St., 02458-2529. Tel: 617-969-4766; Fax: 617-527-2528. Email: mtalvercon@aol.com. Web: www.mficusa.org. Sisters 37.

PLAINVILLE. *Jesus and Mary Mission Center*, 92 School St., 02762-2033. Tel: 508-699-4427; Fax: 508-643-4179. Email: thpicard1@juno.com. Sr. Therese Picard, R.J.M., Admin. Total in Residence 14.

QUINCY. *Sisters of Charity (Halifax)* (Boston Office) ,

26 Phipps St., 02169. Tel: 617-773-6085; Fax: 617-472-7179. Email: spkelly@schalifax.com. Web: www.schalifax.ca. Sisters Patricia Kelly, Congregational Councilor; Joan Verner, Congregational Councillor/Sec.

Sisters of Charity (Halifax) Corporate Mission, Inc., 26 Phipps St., 02169. Tel: 617-773-6076; Fax: 617-472-7179. Email: dgerrnaert@schallfax.ca. Web: www.schalifax.ca. Sr. Donna Geernaert, Congregational Leader.

Sisters of Charity of Nazareth (Western Province), 169 Fenno St., 02170. Tel: 617-479-4909; Fax: 617-786-0767. Email: eleanormartin@msn.com. Web: www.scnazarethky.org. Sr. Eleanor Martin, S.C.N., Vice Provincial.
Legal Title: *Nazareth Literary and Benevolent Institution*

SOMERVILLE. *Medical Missionaries of Mary, Inc.*, 179 Highland Ave., 02143. Tel: 617-666-3223; Fax: 617-666-1877. Email: mmmdevof@comcast.net. Web: www.mmmusa.org. Congregation of the Medical Missionaries of Mary Motherhouse, Beechgrove, Drogheda, Ireland. Professed Sisters 10.

WAKEFIELD. *Mother Saint Joseph House*, 7 Emerson St., 01880. Tel: 617-387-2500; Fax: 781-224-0644. Email: sndmsjn@aol.com. Sisters Theresa Carlow, S.N.D., Pres.; Elizabeth Murtagh, S.N.D., Community Coord. Sponsored by the Sisters of Notre Dame de Namur. Sisters 12.

WALTHAM. *Marist Missionary Sisters* Tel: 781-893-0149; Fax: 781-899-6838. Email: maristsmsm@aol.com. Web: www.maristmissionarysmsm.org.
Legal Title: *Missionary Sisters of the Society of Mary, Inc., S.M.S.M.*

Provincial Offices, 349 Grove St., 02453-6018. Tel: 781-893-0149; Fax: 781-894-7610.

Residence for Senior Sisters, 62 Newton St., 02453-6058. Tel: 781-893-3960. Sisters 33.
Other Local Communities:
60 Newton St., 02453-6058. Tel: 781-899-1837. Sisters 4.
21 Beech St., Belmont, 02478-1299. Tel: 617-489-3587. Sisters 6.
4 Craig St., Framingham, 01701-7664. Tel: 508-877-7371. Sisters 3.
357 Grove St., 02453-6018. Tel: 781-899-3839. Sisters 7.
20 Bartlett Ave., Arlington, 02476-6418. Tel: 781-648-4341. Sisters 6.
88 Lexington St., 02452. Tel: 978-975-4375. Sisters 8.

Religious of Christian Education, Inc., 68 Lafayette St., Apt. A, 02453-6829. Tel: 781-899-6292; Fax: 781-899-6293. Email: yvettetrce@aol.com. Sr. Yvette Rivard, R.C.E., Contact Person.

Sisters of the Good Shepherd, 83-85 Lake St., 02451. Tel: 781-891-7688; Fax: 781-894-6183. Email: elishmcpar@aol.com. Sr. Elish McPartland, Contact Person.

WATERTOWN. *Rosary Manor*, One Rosary Dr., 02472. Tel: 617-924-1717; Fax: 617-924-8118. Email: rosmanor@juno.com. Sr. Eleanor Fabrizi, O.P., Coord. Total in Residence 25; Total Staff 3.

WELLESLEY. *Marillac Residence, Inc.*, 125 Oakland St., 02481. Tel: 781-237-0236; Fax: 781-237-8152. Email: aregan1211@aol.com. Web: www.schalifax.ca. Sr. Ann Regan, S.C., Pres. Sisters of Charity (Halifax)

Mount St. Vincent Retirement Community, 125 Oakland St., 02481. Tel: 781-237-2161; Fax: 781-237-8152. Email: bgr1938@aol.com. Web: www.schalifax.com. Sisters Ann Marie Barry, Community Leadership Team. Tel: 781-997-1165; Fax: 781-237-8152; Elizabeth Groome, Community Leadership Team. Tel: 781-997-1165; Fax: 791-237-8152; Ann Regan, Community Leadership Team. Tel: 781-997-1165; Fax: 781-237-8152. Sisters of Charity (Halifax)

Sisters of Charity (Halifax) Supporting Corporation, 125 Oakland St., 02481-5338. Tel: 781-237-0487; Fax: 781-235-8068. Sr. Donna Geernaert, Congregational Leader.

WELLESLEY HILLS. *Elizabeth Seton Residence, Inc.*, 125 Oakland St., 02481. Tel: 781-237-2161; Fax: 781-431-2589. Email: eseton@schalifax.org. Web: www.Elizabethseton.org. Phyllis A. Tedesco, Admin. Sisters of Charity of St. Vincent de Paul, Halifax, Nova Scotia, Canada., 84 bed Skilled Nursing & Rehab Facility. Medicare-Medicaid Certified. Accredited by Joint Commission on Accreditation of Healthcare Organizations (JCAHO).

WRENTHAM. *St. Chretienne Provincialate*, 297 Arnold St., 02093-1798. Tel: 508-384-7841; 508-384-8066; Fax: 508-384-3170. Email: ssch@tiac.net. Web: sistersofstchretienne.org. Sisters of St. Chretienne Sisters 4; Total in Residence 4.

Mount St. Mary's Abbey, 300 Arnold St., 02093. Tel: 508-528-1282; Fax: 508-528-5360. Email: sisters@msmabbey.org. Web: www.msmabbey.org. Sr. M. Agnes Day, O.C.S.O., Abbess.
Legal Title: *The Cistercians of the Strict Observance in Massachusetts, Inc.* The Cistercian Nuns of the Strict Observance (Trappistines) Professed Sisters 42; Total in Residence 47.

[X] RETREAT HOUSES

ANDOVER. *Franciscan Center - Retreat House*, 459 River Rd., 01810. Tel: 978-851-3391; Fax: 978-858-0675. Email: franretc@aol.com. Web: www.franrcent.org. Rev. Roland Petinge, O.F.M.; Deacon Robert Artman, O.F.M., Guardian; Revs. John C. DiMauro, O.F.M., Retreat Team; Claude Scrima, O.F.M., Retreat Team; Robert J. Caprio, O.F.M., Retreat Team; Deacon Charles Trebino, O.F.M., Retreat Team; Jerri Lou Buffo, Retreat Team; Mrs. Mildred Sheehan, Admin. Asst.; Bros. Charles Gingerich, O.F.M., Vocations; Gabriel Aceto, O.F.M., Retreat Team. Order of Friars Minor Total in Residence 7; Total Staff 8.

COHASSET. *St. Joseph Villa Retreat Center*, 339 Jerusalem Rd., 02025. Tel: 781-383-6024; 781-383-6029. Email: retreat.center@csj.boston.org. Sisters of St. Joseph 2.

DOVER. *St. Stephen Priory Spiritual Life Center*, 20 Glen St., Box 370, 02030-0370. Tel: 508-785-0124; Fax: 508-785-1020. Email: ThePriory@aol.com. Web: www.ststephenpriory.org. Revs. Joseph Barranger, O.P., Prior; Stephen Fitzhenry, O.P., Subprior; John E. Allard, O.P., Co-Dir. of Retreat & Renewal; Joseph Barranger, O.P., Co-Dir. of Retreat & Renewal; Stephen Fitzhenry, O.P., Co-Dir. of Retreat & Renewal; Sr. Maureen Casey, S.N.D., Co-Dir. of Retreat & Renewal. Dominican Priests 10; Religious Brother 3; Total in Residence 13; Total Staff 17.

DUXBURY. *Miramar Retreat Center*, 121 Parks St., P.O. Box M, 02331-0614. Tel: 781-585-2460; Fax: 781-585-3770. Email: miramarma@aol.com. Rev. Robert M. Jones, Rector. Total in Residence 8; Total Staff 22.

FRAMINGHAM. *The Marist House*, 518 Pleasant St., 01701. Tel: 508-879-1620; Fax: 508-879-1132. Email: director@themarists.org. Web: themarists.org. Revs. Raymond E. Coolong, S.M., Supr.; Michael J. Flynn, S.M., Retreat Dir.; Raymond J. Arsenault, S.M.; Robert E. Champagne, S.M.; Leo Bourdeau, S.M.; Henry Rancourt, S.M.; Raymond Boulanger, S.M.; Robert Graham, S.M.; Emile Guilmette, S.M.; Omer St. Onge, S.M.; Most Rev. George Szal, S.M.; Bros. Leo Lapointe, S.M.; James Dvorak, S.M. Total in Residence 13; Total Staff 2.

GLOUCESTER. *Eastern Point Retreat House*, Gonzaga, 37 Niles Pond Rd., 01930. Tel: 978-283-0013; Fax: 978-282-1989. Email: gonzaga@cove.com. Web: www.easternpoint.org. Revs. Francis H. Belcher, S.J.; John J. Bresnahan, S.J.; John T. Crabb, S.J.; Robert G. Gilroy, S.J.; John B. Kerdiejus, S.J.; James M. Keegan, S.J.; Richard J. Stanley, S.J.; Sr. Madeline Tiberii, S.S.J.; Frances Dixon Burden, Staff Member. Priests 7; Sisters 1; Total Staff 9.

HAVERHILL. *Don Orione Center*, Old Groveland Rd., P.O. Box 205, 08135. Tel: 573-373-0461. Rev. Gino Marchesani, F.D.P., Dir.

SCITUATE. *Foyer of Charity*, 74 Hollett St., 02066. Tel: 781-545-1080; Fax: 240-332-5826. Email: info@foyerofcharity.com. Web: www.foyerofcharity.com. Rev. Matthew Bradley, Dir. Total in Residence 1; Total Staff 6.

WALTHAM. *Espousal Retreat House and Conference Center*, 554 Lexington St., 02452. Tel: 781-209-3101; Fax: 781-893-0291. Email: espousalctrr@rcn.com. Web: www.espousal.org. Rev. Robert Masciocchi, C.S.S., Dir. Stigmatine Fathers and Brothers, Weekend and Weekly Retreats, Days-Evenings of Recollection. Total in Residence 2; Total Staff 10.

WESTON. *Campion Renewal Center*, 319 Concord Rd., 02493-1398. Tel: 781-788-6810; Fax: 781-894-5864. Email: acopponi@campioncenter.org. Web: www.campioncenter.org. Revs. John W. Michalowski, S.J., Dir.; Robert G. Doherty, S.J., Staff Member; Joseph F. Brennan, S.J., Staff Member; Lawrence E. Corcoran, S.J., Staff Member; James Mattaliano, S.J., Staff Member. Total in Residence 5; Total Staff 7.

[Y] RETIREMENT RESIDENCES FOR PRIESTS AND BROTHERS

BOSTON. *Saint Anthony Residence*, 103 Arch St., 02110-1102. Tel: 617-542-6454; Fax: 617-542-6659. Revs. Bernardine Kessing, O.F.M., Guardian & Supr.; Severin Brady, O.F.M., Vicar; Leo Clifford, O.F.M.; David J. Fleming, O.F.M.; Martin Hanhauser, O.F.M.; Wilfred A. Hept, O.F.M.; Robert B. Lynch, O.F.M.; Carmel F. Miotke, O.F.M.; Kenan Morris, O.F.M.; Gordon A. Murphy, O.F.M.; Reginald Redlon, O.F.M.; Robert White, O.F.M.; Bros. Francis J. Baggan, O.F.M.; Frederick A. Musser, O.F.M. (For Retired Franciscan Friars.) Total in Residence 14.

Regina Cleri Residence, 60 William Cardinal O'Connell Way, 02114. Tel: 617-523-1861; Fax: 617-720-0585. Email: jtierney@reginacleri.org. Rev. Msgr. James E. Tierney, Dir. Residence for Retired Archdiocesan Priests. Priests 48; Sisters 2.

TEWKSBURY. *Immaculate Heart of Mary Infirmary*, 486 Chandler St., 01876-2899. Tel: 978-851-7258; Fax: 978-851-3558. Email: macomi@aol.com. Revs. John F. Mc Hugh, O.M.I., Supr.; F. William Denzel, O.M.I.; Robert F. Kilroy, O.M.I.; Francis P. McCartin, O.M.I.; Francis X. Gorham, O.M.I.; Raymond Steen, O.M.I.; Joseph A. Ryan, O.M.I.; Francis Campbell, O.M.I.; Donald O'Brien, O.M.I.; Gerald Flater, O.M.I.; Lawrence Deery, O.M.I.; Gerald Forkin, O.M.I.; Leo Wetzel, O.M.I.; Chester J. Cappucci, O.M.I.; Edward Lowney, O.M.I.; Francis Demers, O.M.I.; Anatole Baillargeon, O.M.I.; Russell Nickerson, O.M.I.; George White, O.M.I.; Gerard McCormick, O.M.I.; Arthur J. King, O.M.I.; Patrick F. Healy, O.M.I.; Richard Bolduc, O.M.I.; Richard Harr, O.M.I.; Bros. Richard Schultz, O.M.I.; Joseph Gagne, O.M.I.; James H. Lucas, O.M.I. Priests 26; Brothers 1.

WALTHAM. *Stigmatine Fathers and Brothers*, St. Joseph's Hall, 554 Lexington St., 02452. Tel: 781-209-3100; 781-209-0006; Fax: 781-209-3070. Web: www.stigmatines.com. Very Rev. Gregory J. Hoppough, C.S.S., M.Div., S.T.L., S.T.D., Prov. Supr.; Revs. Joseph M. Connolly, C.S.S., Supr.; James Cunningham, C.S.S.; Paul Merrill, C.S.S.; James E. Flanagan, C.S.S.; Henry Linse, C.S.S.; David F Gallagher, C.S.S.; Vito Cannizzo, C.S.S.; Anthony Parcheski, C.S.S.; Joseph Welch, C.S.S.; Samuel Fayad, C.S.S.; Joseph Fellin, C.S.S.; Deacon Richard S. Spencer, C.S.S. Priests 12; Brothers 1.

[Z] RESIDENCES FOR MEN AND WOMEN

BOSTON. *St. Helena House*, 89 Union Park St., 02118. Tel: 617-426-2922; Fax: 617-542-3460. Lucille Becker, Property Mgr. Seniors, low income & disabled persons. Residents 89.

Our Lady's Guild House - Residence for Women, 20 Charlesgate W., 02215. Tel: 617-536-3000; Fax: 617-536-8508. Andrea Beall, Admin. Daughters of Mary of the Immaculate Conception 3; Residents 126.

BRIGHTON. *Archdiocesan Central High Schools, Inc.*, 2121 Commonwealth Ave., 02135. Tel: 617-746-5855; Fax: 617-782-0213. Most Rev. Sean P. O'Malley, O.F.M.Cap.

[AA] PUBLIC ORATORIES AND CHAPELS

BOSTON. *St. Anthony Shrine* 100 Arch St., 02110. Tel: 617-542-6440; Fax: 617-542-4225. Email: info@StAnthonyShrine.org. Web: www.StAnthonyShrine.org. Revs. David Convertino, O.F.M., Guardian & Exec. Dir.; John R. Ullrich, O.F.M.; Donan McGovern, O.F.M.; Stephen Doyle, O.F.M.; Fergus Healey, O.F.M.; Philip O'Shea, O.F.M.; Raphael Bonanno, O.F.M.; Stephen Walsh, O.F.M.; Brice Leavins, O.F.M.; Raymond Mann, O.F.M.; Myron McCormick, O.F.M.; Emeric Meier, O.F.M.; Colin O'Rourke, O.F.M.; Cyril Seaman, O.F.M.; Brian E. Smail, O.F.M.; Justin J. Bailey, O.F.M.; Francis McHugh, O.F.M.; Robert F. Nee, O.F.M.; Mathias Doyle, O.F.M.; Bros. Albert Aldrich, O.F.M.; John Capozzi, O.F.M.; Dominic Finneran, O.F.M.; Justus Frazier, O.F.M.; Edward Higgins, O.F.M.; John Jaskowiak, O.F.M.; Kevin Kriso, O.F.M.; John Maganzini, O.F.M.; Deacon Paul Chelus, O.F.M.; Bros. John Mahon, O.F.M.; Thomas McGowan, O.F.M.; Mark J. Murphy, O.F.M. Priests 19; Brothers 12.

Chapel of Our Lady of Lourdes 698 Beacon St., 02215. Tel: 617-536-2761. Marist Fathers Priests 2.

Marist Fathers Residence Tel: 617-262-2271. Revs. Gerard Caron, S.M., Dir.; Marcel Lajoie, S.M.

Chapel of the Holy Spirit Paulist Center, 5 Park St., 02108. Tel: 617-742-4460; Fax: 617-720-5756. Email: fiveparkst.@aol.com. Web: www.paulist.org/boston. Revs. John B. Ardis, C.S.P., Dir.; Joseph A. Ciccone, C.S.P.; Patricia Simpson, Admin.; Susan Rutkowski, Pastoral Min.; Drew Deskur, Music Min. Paulist Fathers

St. Clement Archdiocesan Eucharistic Shrine 1105 Boylston St., 02215. Tel: 617-266-5999; Fax: 617-247-7576. Email: petergrover@juno.com. Web: www.oblatesofthevirginmary.org. Revs. Peter Grover, O.M.V., Dir. of Shrine; David N. Beauregard, O.M.V. St. Ignatius Province of the Oblates of the Virgin Mary Priests 2.

St. Francis Chapel Prudential Center Plaza, 800 Boylston St., #21, 02199. Tel: 617-437-7117; Fax:

617-437-8420. Email: st.francis@chapel.as. Web: www.oblatesofthevirginmary.org. Revs. Thomas Carzon, O.M.V., Dir.; Alan Hall, O.M.V.; Robert Lowrey, O.M.V.; Vincenzo Antolini, O.M.V.; Bro. Joseph O'Connor, O.M.V. St. Ignatius Province of the Oblates of the Virgin Mary Priests 4; Brothers 1.

Madonna Queen Shrine 111 Orient Ave., 02128. Tel: 617-569-2100; Fax: 617-569-8701. Email: dofathers@aol.com. Rev. Mario Guarino, F.D.P., Rector. Don Orione Fathers

Our Lady of Good Voyage Chapel 65 Northern Ave., 02110. Tel: 617-268-8100; Fax: 617-268-1277. Email: REC7339@aol.com. *St. Vincent de Paul Rectory*, 363 E St., South Boston, 02127. Revs. Richard E. Cannon, Admin.; Philip La Plante, S.M., Chap. to Seaport.

Our Lady of the Airways Chapel First Floor, Tower Bldg., Logan International Airport, 02128. Tel: 617-567-2800; Fax: 617-569-6950. Email: fatherrichard@assport.com. Rev. Richard A. Uftring.

St. Stephen 24 Clark St., 02109. Tel: 617-523-1230; Fax: 617-723-7389. Email: socjames@gte.net. Robert Thomas, Dir.; Revs. Milton Eggerling; Hugh Joseph Shields (PH).

St. Thomas More Chapel 49 Franklin St., 02110. Tel: 617-542-1776; Fax: 617-542-1778. Email: propagationfaithboston.org. Web: propagationfaithboston.org. Rev. Msgr. Andrew F. Connell.

BROCKTON. *Chapel of Our Saviour* 475 Westgate Dr., 02301-1819. Tel: 508-583-8357; Fax: 508-586-5510. Revs. Arthur Gouthro, S.A., Dir.; Malcolm Martin, S.A.; Henry Mair, S.A.; Boniface Riedmann, S.A.; Bros. DePorres Poncia, S.A.; Savio McNiece, S.A.; Louis Marek, S.A. Priests 4; Brothers 3.

HOLLISTON. *Our Lady of Fatima Shrine* 101 Summer St., P.O. Box 5857, 01746-5857. Tel: 508-429-2144; Fax: 508-429-4793. Email: xavmissma@yahoo.com. Web: www.xaviermissionaries.org. Rev. Francis Signorelli, S.X. Xaverian Missionaries

LOWELL. *St. Joseph the Worker Shrine* 37 Lee St., 01852-1103. Tel: 978-458-6346; 978-459-9522; 800-287-9522 (Gift Shop); Fax: 978-441-0963; 978-323-0763 (Gift Shop). Email: info@stjosephshrine.org. Web: www.stjosephshrine.org.

St. Joseph the Worker Residence, 37 Lee St., 01852-1103. Tel: 978-454-6004. Revs. John Cox, O.M.I., Dir.; Charles Beausoleil, O.M.I.; John Morin, O.M.I.; Albert P. Martineau, O.M.I.; Norman Parent, O.M.I.

PEABODY. *St. Theresa Carmelite Chapel* North Shore Mall, 01960. Tel: 978-531-6145; Fax: 978-531-1359. Email: hjones@carmelnet.org. Revs. Herbert J. Jones, O.Carm., Prior & Dir.; Alan N. Crowley, O.Carm.; Peter Thomas Sherry, O.Carm.; Mario Lopez, O.Carm.; Felix Prior, O.Carm.; Bro. Damien Chong, O.Carm. Priests 5; Brothers 1.

[BB] CAMPUS MINISTRY

BOSTON. *The Catholic Center at Boston University* 211 Bay State Rd., 02215. Tel: 617-353-3632; Fax: 617-358-2049. Email: catholic@bu.edu. Web: www.bu.edu/CATHOLIC. Rev. Paul D. Helfrich, B.H.; Bros. Joseph Donovan, B.H.; Jason Zink, B.H.; Ms. Karen Mulholland.

Emmanuel College Campus Ministry 400 The Fenway, 02115. Tel: 617-735-9777. Web: emmanuel.edu. Sr. Margaret Cummins, S.N.D.

University of Massachusetts at Boston Campus Ministry 02125-3393. Tel: 617-287-5839. Email: maggie.cahill@umb.edu.

Harbor Campus, Dorchester, 02125. Tel: 617-287-5839.

BRIDGEWATER. *Bridgewater State College Catholic Center* 122 Park Ave., 02325. Tel: 508-531-1346; Fax: 508-531-6188. Email: mdow@bridgew.edu. Web: www.bridgew.edu/depts/cathcntrl. Sr. Mary Ellen Dow, S.N.D., Campus Min.

CAMBRIDGE. *Harvard Catholic Student Center* 20 Arrow St., 02138. Tel: 617-868-6585; Fax: 617-354-7092. Email: dsheehan@fas.harvard.edu. Web: www.hcs.harvard.edu/~csa. Rev. Msgr. Dennis F. Sheehan, V.F., Senior Chap.; Rev. George S. Salzmann, O.S.F.S., Chap.; Jacqueline L. Landry, Chap.; Joan Travers, Admin.

Massachusetts Institute of Technology Catholic Community 40 Massachusetts Ave., W-11, 02139. Tel: 617-253-2981; Fax: 617-253-3260. Email: catholic@mit.edu. Web: www.web.mit.edu/tcc/. Rev. Paul A. Reynolds, C.S.P.; Cyndi Aimo. Total Staff 2.

FRAMINGHAM. *Framingham State College Campus Ministry* 100 State St., 01701. Tel: 508-626-4610; Fax: 508-626-4939. Email: Bkremmell@frc.mass.edu. Rev. William T. Kremmell.

LOWELL. *The Catholic Center U Mass, Lowell* 52 Colonial Ave., 01854. Tel: 978-454-0151. Email: Catholic_Center@uml.edu. Web: www.uml.edu/student-services/ministry/catholic/. Email: Kenneth_Apuzzo@uml.edu. Bro. Kenneth Apuzzo, Campus Min. Total in Residence 4; Total Staff 1.

MEDFORD. *Tufts University Catholic Center* 58 Winthrop St., 02155-5300. Tel: 781-391-7272; Fax: 781-396-8779. Email: ann.penick@tufts.edu. Web: www.tuftslife.edu. Ms. Ann Penick, M.A., NCC. Total Staff 1; Total Assisted Annually 2,800.

NEWTON. *Boston College Campus Ministry* Tel: 617-552-3475; Fax: 617-552-3044. Email: ministry@bc.edu. Web: www.bc.edu/campus-ministry. Total in Residence 6; Total Staff 14.

McElroy 215, Chestnut Hill, 02467. Tel 617-552-3475; Fax: 617-552-3044. Rev. James Erps, S.J., Dir.

NORTH ANDOVER. *Merrimack College Campus Ministry Center* 350 Sakowich Center, 01845. Tel: 978-837-5450; Fax: 978-837-5004. Email: joseph.farrell@merrimack.edu. Revs. Joseph L. Farrell, O.S.A., Dir. & Campus Min.; Richard Piatt, O.S.A., Campus Min.; Ms. Peggy Agolino, Campus Min.

SALEM. *Salem State College, Catholic Campus Ministry* 352 Lafayette St., 01970. Tel: 978-542-6074; Fax: 978-744-0581. Email: muriel.lemoine@salemstate.edu. Sr. Muriel Lemoine, S.A.S.V.

WALTHAM. *Bentley College Spiritual Life Center* 175 Forest St., 02452-4705. Tel: 781-891-2754; Fax: 781-891-2839. Email: cgrenache@bentley.edu. Web: www.bentley.edu. Rev. Claude Grenache, A.A., Dir. Spiritual Life Center Chap.

Brandeis University Catholic Chaplaincy Mail stop 205, P.O. Box 549110, 02454-9110. Tel: 781-736-3574; Fax: 781-736-3577. Email: dmichael@brandeis.edu. Rev. David C. Michael.

WELLESLEY. *Babson College Campus Ministry* 9 Glen Rd., 02481. Tel: 617-235-1200. Sr. Frances Sheehey, O.S.F., Campus Coord.

Wellesley College Campus Ministry 02181. Tel: 781-283-2688 Fax: 781-283-3676. Email: vpoirier@wellesley.edu. Rev. Andres Nino, O.S.A.

WESTON. *Regis College Office of Campus Ministry* 235 Wellesley St., 02493. Tel: 781-768-7027; 781-768-7028; 781-768-7029; Fax: 781-768-8339. Email: ministry@regiscollege.edu. Web: www.regiscollege.edu. Sr. Rosemary Mulvihill, R.S.M., Dir.; Rev. Paul Kenney, S.J., Chap.; Maria DiLorenzo, Campus Min.

[CC] FOUNDATIONS, FUNDS & TRUSTS

BOSTON. *The Archdiocese of Boston Self-Insurance Group, Inc.*, Tel: 617-746-5740; Fax: 617-746-5421. Email: Joseph_McEnness@rcab.org. 2121 Commonwealth Ave., Brighton, 02135. Tel: 617-746-5740; Fax: 517-746-5421. Joseph McEnness, Admin.; Timothy McCrystal Esq., Counsel. Board of Directors: Rev. Philip B. Earley, Clerk; Mr. David Smith, Pres.; Mr. James Walsh Treas.; Mr. Steven Fischer; Mr. Joseph Welch; Mr. Robert Cantwell; Sr. Joan Duffy, C.S.J.

Chancery Office, 2121 Commonwealth Ave., Brighton, 02135. Tel: 617-254-0100; Fax: 617-783-4564. Web: www.rcab.org. Also see Miscellaneous Section for additional listings.

The Cardinal Medeiros Trust Tel: 617-254-0100.

Cardinal Cushing General Hospital Foundation, Brockton

The Carney Hospital Foundation, Inc., 2100 Dorchester Ave., 02124. Tel: 617-296-1788. J. Barry Driscoll, Pres.; Paul J. Kingston, Vice Pres.; Daniel J. McDevitt, Sec.; William F. Henderson, Exec. Dir. (Formerly The New Caritas Christi Hospital, Inc.)

**Catholic Schools Foundation, Inc.* Tel: 617-254-0100; Fax: 617-783-6366. (Formerly St. Anthony's Scholarship Fund, Inc.).

Clergy Benefit Trust Tel: 617-254-0100; Fax: 617-783-2947. Most Rev. Richard G. Lennon.

Clergy Fund Society Tel: 617-254-0100; Fax: 617-783-2947.

Clergy Medical-Hospitalization Trust Tel: 617-254-0100; Fax: 617-783-2947.

Archdiocese of Boston Clergy Retirement/Disability Trust Tel: 617-254-0100; Fax: 617-783-2947.

Family Counseling Endowment Fund, Inc., 141 Tremont St., 02111. Tel: 617-482-4355.

Marist Capital Trust Fund

c/o Financial Admin., The Missionary Sisters of the Society of Mary, Inc., 349 Grove St., Waltham, 02154 Tel: 617-893-0149. Sr. Virginia Fornasa, S.M.S.M., Trustee; John E. McCormack.

Metropolitan Boston Dialysis Center, Inc., 736 Cambridge St., Brighton, 02135.

Mission Promotion Missionary Sisters of the Society of Mary

c/o Mission Promoter, 349 Grove St., Waltham, 02453. Tel: 781-893-0149.

Roman Catholic Archdiocese of Boston Health Benefit Trust Tel: 617-746-5680; Fax: 617-783-4564. Mr. James Walsh, Admin.

Roman Catholic Archdiocese of Boston Insurance Trust Tel: 617-746-5640; Fax: 617-783-4564. Mr. James Walsh, Admin. Benefit Office,

Roman Catholic Archdiocese of Boston Pension Trust Tel: 617-746-5640; Fax: 617-746-4564. Mr. James Walsh, Admin. Benefit Office,

Roman Catholic Archdiocese of Boston Long Term Disability Trust Tel: 617-746-5640; Fax: 617-783-4564. Mr. James Walsh, Admin.

Roman Catholic Archdiocese of Boston Common Investment Fund Tel: 617-746-5680; Fax: 617-783-4564.

Roman Catholic Archdiocese of Boston Fixed Income Investment Fund Tel: 617-746-5680; Fax: 617-783-4564.

St. Charles Borromeo Educational Foundation, Inc.

Sacred Heart Trust Fund, c/o Society of Jesus, Trustee, 761 Harrison Ave., 02118. Tel: 617-536-5604. Bro. H. Francis Cluff, S.J.

St. Elizabeth's Hospital Foundation, Inc., 159 Washington St., Brighton, 02135.

Holy Family Hospital Foundation, Inc.

Catholic Foundation of the Archdiocese of Boston, 2121 Commonwealth Ave., Brighton, 02135. Tel: 617-746-5621; Fax: 617-783-6366. Mr. James Mooney, Pres.

The Xaverian Brothers Northeastern Community Support Charitable Trust Fund, 704 Brush Hill Rd., Milton, 02186.

Benefit Trust for Non-Incardinated Priests Tel: 617-254-0100; Fax: 617-783-2947.

Legal Title: *Benefit Trust for Non-Incardinated Priest Duly Assigned for Service in the Archdiocese of Boston*

St. Mary's High School Foundation, Inc., 2121 Commonwealth Ave., 02135. Tel: 617-746-5680. Mr. David W. Smith, Contact Person.

Clergy Assistance Trust, 2121 Commonwealth Ave., 02135. Tel: 617-746-5615; Fax: 617-783-2947.

FRAMINGHAM. *Senior Religious Trust Fund of Marist Fathers of Boston*, 518 Pleasant St., 01701-2898. Tel: 508-879-7223; Fax: 508-879-0719.

HANOVER. *St. Coletta and Cardinal Cushing Schools of MA*, 405 Washington St., 02339. Tel: 617-826-6371; Fax: 781-829-0881. Email: phudson@coletta.org. Web: www.coletta.org. Mr. Paul J. Hudson, Pres. & CEO.

IPSWICH. *Blin Charitable Trust*, 30 Jeffrey's Neck Rd., 01938. Tel: 978-356-4669, Ext. 303; Fax: 978-356-9759. Email: PRVNCOFF@aol.com. Web: www.SNDdeN.org. Sisters of Notre Dame de Namur

LEXINGTON. *Providential Prima*, 10 Pelham Rd., 02421-8499. Tel: 781-862-4700; Fax: 781-861-9641. Email: mlazdowsky@sgmlex.org. David Joy, Pres.

LOWELL. *D'Youville Senior Care Foundation, Inc.*, 981 Varnum Ave., 01854. Tel: 978-464-5681, Ext. 2053; Fax: 978-454-5681. Email: lcoulture@dyouville.org. Web: dyouville.org.

Saints Memorial Medical Center Foundation, P.O. Box 367, 01853-0367. Tel: 978-934-8334; Fax: 978-934-8479. Email: fund.kec@tmmc.org. Web: www.saints-memorial.org. Thom Clark, Pres. & CEO; Kevin E. Coughlin, Vice Pres.; D. Harold Sullivan, Chm.

METHUEN. *Holy Family Hospital Foundation, Inc.*, 70 East St., 01844-4597. Tel: 978-687-0151; Fax: 978-688-7689. Email: nmallen@cchcs.org. Web: www.holyfamilyhosp.org. Mrs. Noreen V. Mallen, Exec. Dir.

NEEDHAM. *St. Joseph Parish School Fund, Inc., Needham*, 1382 Highland Ave., 02492. Tel: 781-444-0245; Fax: 781-444-7713. Mr. James S. DiStasio, Treas.

[DD] LIFE RESOURCES

BRAINTREE. **Pilgrim Center for Boys*, 140 Adams St., P.O. Box 850907, 02185-0907. Tel: 617-848-5510. Total Staff 25; Students 24.

[EE] MISCELLANEOUS

BOSTON. *Caritas Christi - A Catholic Health Care System*, 736 Cambridge St., 02135. Tel: 617-789-2500; Fax: 617-789-2124. Web: www.caritaschristi.org. Mr. Michael F. Collins, M.D., Pres. & CEO. Caritas Carney Hospital, Boston; Caritas Good Samaritan Hospice, Inc., Boston and Norwood; Caritas Home Care, Boston and Norwood; Caritas Norwood Hospital, Inc., Norwood; Caritas Medical Groups, Boston; Caritas Rehabilitation Center, Boston; Caritas Southwood Hospital, Inc., Norfolk; Caritas Good Samaritan Medical Center, Inc., Brockton; Caritas Holy Family Hospital and Medical Center, Methuen; Laboure College, Boston; Por Cristo, Boston; Caritas St. Elizabeth's Medical Center of Boston; St. Joseph Nursing Care Center, Boston; and St. Mary's Women and Infants Center, Boston.

Caritas Christi Retirement Plan and Trust, 2121 Commonwealth Ave., 02135. Tel: 617-746-5857; Fax: 617-783-4564. James M. Walsh, Plan Admin.; Mary T. Regan, Plan Mgr.

Governing Board: Most Revs. Sean O'Malley; Richard Lennon; Mr. David W. Smith; Rev. Mark O'Connell; Anna-Marie Ferraro; John Gianino; Rev. Nicholas C. Ciccone Jr.; Lawrence McManus; Michael Metzler; Wilson D. Rogers Jr.; Lynn Wiatrowski.

The Catholic Lawyers Guild of the Archdiocese of Boston, Inc., One Union St., 02108. Tel: 617-523-2640; Fax: 617-720-4363. Hon. Joseph R. Nolan, Pres.

Corporation for the Sponsored Ministries of the Sisters of St. Joseph of Boston, 637 Cambridge St., 02135-2800. Tel: 617-746-2190; Fax: 617-746-2194. Email: suzanne.kearney@csjboston.org. Web: www.csjboston.org. Charles A. Schuetz, Pres.; Suzanne M. Kearney, Exec. Dir.

CSJ Ministries Connection, Inc., 637 Cambridge St., 02135-2800. Tel: 617-746-2190; Fax: 617-746-2194. Email: suzanne.kearney@csjboston.org. Web: www.csjboston.org. Charles A. Schuetz, Pres.; Suzanne M. Kearney, Exec. Dir.

Equestrian Order of the Holy Sepulchre of Jerusalem, Tel: 781-235-6291; Fax: 781-235-6291. Email: DennisJLooney@aol.com.

Northeastern Lieutenancy, 27 Southgate Rd., Wellesley, 02482. Tel: 781-235-6291; Fax: 781-235-6291. Dennis J. Looney Jr., KGCHS Lt.; Jonathan A. Noonan, KGCHS Chancellor.

**KOLBE Association, Inc.*, 2121 Commonwealth Ave., 02135. Tel: 617-746-5645; Fax: 617-746-5646. Email: Reverend_Michael_Medas@rcab.org. His Eminence Bernard Cardinal Law (WDC), Episcopal Mod.; Rev. Michael B. Medas, Exec. Dir.

Lanteri Charitable Trust, 1105 Boylston St., 02215-3660. Tel: 617-536-4141; Fax: 617-536-7016. Email: wbrownomv@aol.com. Laurence Flynn, Admin.

League of Catholic Women of the Archdiocese of Boston, 127 Lake St., 02135. Tel: 617-254-2610. Mrs. Daniel Sullivan, Pres.; Rev. Martin P. Connor, S.T.L., Spiritual Dir.

Lourdes Bureau, 698 Beacon St., 02215. Tel: 617-536-2761. Marist Fathers, Official Representatives in America for the Shrine of Lourdes, France.

Medaille Corporation, 637 Cambridge St., 02135. Tel: 617-783-9090; Fax: 617-783-8246. Email: boscsj@aol.com. Web: www.csjboston.org. Sisters Joan Duffy, C.S.J., Pres.; Maureen Doherty, C.S.J., Treas.

MI Management, Inc. Covenant Health Systems. Tel: 978-685-6321; Fax: 978-975-0050. Email: begrant@mihcs.com. 172 Lawrence St., Lawrence, 01841. Tel: 978-685-6321; Fax: 978-975-0050. Barbara E. Grant, Pres. & CEO. Management company for all Mary Immaculate Facilities.

Ministry of Evangelization and Catechesis, 286 Shawmut Ave., 02118-1613. Tel: 617-542-1143; Fax: 617-542-5926. Email: AmarilisJMD@aol.com. Sr. Celeste Burgos, Local Coord. & Contact Person.
Legal Title: *Institute of Mission Helpers* Mission Helpers of the Sacred Heart Total Staff 4.

Most Holy Name of Jesus Federation of Poor Clare Monasteries in the Eastern Region of the United Sta, Monastery of Saint Clare, 920 Centre St., 02130. Tel: 617-524-1760; Fax: 617-983-5205. Email: clarefrancesosc@aol.com. Sisters Claire Andre Gagliardi, O.S.C., Pres.; Clare Frances McAvoy, O.S.C., Vice Pres. Solemn Vows 124; Simple Professed 6.

National Catholic Bioethics Center, 159 Washington St., 02135. Tel: 617-787-1900; Fax: 617-787-4900. Email: postmaster@NCBCenter.org. Web: www.NCBCenter.org. John M. Haas, Ph.D., S.T.L., M.Div., Pres.; Rev. Albert S. Moraczewski, O.P., Ph.D., S.T.M., Pres. Emeritus, Distinguished Scholar in Residence; Bro. Ignatius Perkins, O.P., D.N.S., M.A.Ed., R.N., Exec. Vice Pres.; Chad D. McEachern, VP Operations & Devel.; Rev. Germain Kopaczynski, O.F.M.Conv., Ph.D., S.T.D., Dir. Education; Peter J. Cataldo, Ph.D., Dir. of Research; Edward J. Furton, M.A., Ph.D., Dir. Publications; Louise A. Mitchell, M.T.S., Managing Editor; Veronica McLoud Dort, M.A., M.T.S., Asst. Editor Publications and Research; J. Scott Abercrombie Jr., M.D., Senior Fellow in Medicine & Hospital Admin.; Richard M. Doerflinger, M.A., Adjunct Fellow in Bioethics & Public Policy; Thomas E. Gannoe, Systems & Graphic Design Dir.; Donald J. Powers, Vice Pres. for Finance; Kate Folan, Devel. Coord.; Bro. Ignatius Perkins, O.P., D.N.S., M.A.Ed., R.N., Adjunct Fellow in Healthcare Ethics & Life Sciences.

The Office of Outreach, Assistance, Education and Prevention of the Archdiocese of Boston, Inc., 2121 Commonwealth Ave., Brighton, 02135. Tel: 617-746-5680. Mr. David Smith, Contact Person & Sec.

Propagation of the Faith and Holy Childhood Association & Society of St. Peter the Apostle, 49 Franklin St., 02110. Tel: 617-542-1776; Fax: 617-542-1778. Email: propagationfaithboston.org. Web: propagationfaithboston.org. Rev. Msgr. Andrew F. Connell, Dir. Total Staff 12.

Sancta Maria House, Inc., 117 Waltham St., 02118-2162. Rev. Msgr. William H. Roche, Pres. (Retired).

St. Vincent Pallotti Center for Apostolic Development of Boston, Inc., 159 Washington St., Brighton, 02135. Tel: 617-783-3924; Fax: 617-787-7797. Email: VolService@aol.com. Web: www.pallotticenter.org.

**Women Affirming Life, Inc.*, P.O. Box 35532, 02135. Tel: 617-254-2277; Fax: 617-254-2299. Email: mail@affirmlife.com. Web: www.affirmlife.com. Frances X. Hogan, Pres.

ARLINGTON. *Fidelity House*, 25 Medford St., 02474-3105. Tel: 781-648-2005; Fax: 781-648-4604. Email: Fidelityhouse@rcn.com. Web: www.fidelityhouse.org. Edward F. Woods, Dir. Purpose: A community center sponsored by the Saint Agnes Parish providing quality services primarily for youth development with flexible and diverse services for people of all ages.

CAMBRIDGE. *Notre Dame Mission Volunteer Corporation*, 203 Erie St., 02139. Tel: 617-876-8818. Email: natloffice@ndmva.org. Web: www.ndmva.org.

Branch Office, 403 Markland Ave., Baltimore, MD 21212. Tel: 410-532-6864; Fax: 410-532-2418.

**The Youville House, Inc.*, 1575 Cambridge St., 02138-4398. Tel: 617-876-4344. Email: leaheyd@youville.org. Web: www.youville.org. Mr. T. Richard Quigley, Pres. & CEO; Ms. Marsha V. Whelan, Vice Pres. Mission Integration; Revs. William L. Mulligan, S.J., Chap.; Jennifer Casstevens, Chap.; Ms. Patricia Kennedy, Dir. of Pastoral Care Svcs. & Chap.; Ms. Elizabeth Walsh, Chap. Member of Youville Lifecare, Inc. Priests 1; Sisters of Charity (Grey Nuns) 3; Assisted Living Units 95.

**Youville Lifecare, Inc.*, 1575 Cambridge St., 02138-4398. Tel: 617-876-4344; Fax: 617-547-5501. Web: www.youville.org. Mr. Daniel Leahey, Pres. & CEO. Member of Covenant Health Systems, Lexington, MA.

FRAMINGHAM. *Bethany Health Care Center, Inc.*, 97 Bethany Rd., 01701. Tel: 508-872-6750; Fax: 508-875-5425. Email: jacquelyn.mccarthy@csjboston.org. Web: www.Bethanyhcc.org. Congregation of Sisters of St. Joseph of Boston, Skilled Nursing Facility. Residential Living Bed Capacity 169.

Bethany Hill School, Inc., 89 Bethany Rd., 01702. Tel: 508-875-1117; Fax: 508-875-2288. Email: dakcsj@aol.com. Sponsored by the Sisters of St. Joseph of Boston, 41 units of educational housing for low-income people with a variety of needs.

IPSWICH. *Cuvilly Arts and Earth Center, Inc.*, 10 Jeffrey Neck Rd., 01938. Tel: 508-356-4288. Email: cuvilly@shore.net. Sr. Eileen Burns, S.N.D., Pres. Total Assisted 95; Total Staff 12.

LAWRENCE. **Greater Lawrence Mental Health Center, Inc.*, 30 General St., 01841. Tel: 978-683-3128; Fax: 978-686-7856. Jeffrey Fox, Exec. Dir.

Notre Dame Education Center (1992), (Adult Literacy) , 301 Haverhill St., P.O. Box 1012, 01842-9998. Tel: 978-682-6441; Fax: 978-974-8940. Email: ndeclaw@aol.com. Sr. Gwynette Proctor, S.N.D., Exec. Dir. Sisters of Notre Dame de Namur, ESOL, External Diploma, Adult Basic Education, Job Counseling, Citizenship. Sisters 8; Adults 350; Total Staff 19.

LEXINGTON. *Covenant Health Systems, Inc.*, 420 Bedford St., 02420. Tel: 781-862-1634; Fax: 781-862-5477. Email: info@covenanths.org. Web: www.covenanths.org. David R. Lincoln, Pres. & CEO. Member organizations: Youville Hospital and Rehabilitation Center, Cambridge, MA; Youville House Assisted Living Residence, Cambridge, MA; St. Joseph Healthcare, Nashua, NH; Sisters of Charity Health System, Lewiston, ME; Marcotte Congregate Housing; St. Marguerite D'Youville Pavilion; St. Mary's Regional Medical Center, Lewiston, ME; Mary Immaculate Health/Care Services, Lawrence, MA; Maristhill Nursing Home, Waltham, MA; St. Joseph Manor Health Care, Brockton, MA; Fanny Allen Corp., Colchester, VT; St. Mary Health Care Center, Worcester, MA; St. Andre Healthcare Facility, Biddeford, ME.; Affiliate organizations: Santa Maria Nursing Facility, Cambridge, MA; Mont Marie Health Care Center, Holyoke, MA; Bethany Health Care Center, Framingham, MA; Notre Dame Long Term Care Center, Worcester, MA; Matulaitis Nursing Home, Putnam, CT; Lourdes Health Care Center, Wilton, CT; Holy Cross Health Center Manchester, NH; St. Joseph Healthcare, Bangor, ME.

Youville Place, Inc., 10 Pelham Rd., Ste. 2000, 02421-8408. Tel: 781-861-3535; Fax: 781-862-4289. Email: jscianna@erols.com. Web: youvilleplace.com. Sr. Jeanne Poor, S.G.M., Pres. Bd. of Directors. Assisted Living Facility.

LOWELL. *Saints Memorial Special Service, Inc.*, Saints Memoiral Medical Center, One Hospital Dr., 01852. Tel: 978-458-1411. Email: fs.soc@stmmc.org. Web: www.saints_memorial.org. Mr. Stephen O'Connor, Vice Pres. Finance.

MALDEN. *The Catholic Cemetery Association of the Archdiocese of Boston, Inc.*, 175 Broadway, 02148. Tel: 617-746-5680; Fax: 781-322-3801. Email: wo'connell@rcab.org. Web: www.ccemetery.org. David W. Smith, Sec.

METHUEN. *Holy Family Hospital Men's Guild*, 70 East St., 01844-4597. Tel: 978-687-0151, Ext. 2362; Fax: 978-688-7689. Web: www.holyfamilyhosp.org.

Valley Regional Health System, Inc., 70 East St., 01844-4597. Tel: 978-687-0151; Fax: 978-688-7689. Web: www.holyfamilyhosp.org.

Holy Family Hospital, Inc. Tel: 978-687-0151; Fax: 978-688-7689.

Holy Family Hospital Auxiliary Tel: 978-687-0151; Fax: 978-688-7689.

Valley Regional Support Services, Inc. Tel: 978-687-0151; Fax: 978-688-7689.

Holy Family Hospital Men's Guild Tel: 978-687-0151; Fax: 978-688-7689.

Holy Family Hospital Foundation, Inc. Tel: 978-687-0151; Fax: 978-688-7689.

Greater Lawrence Mental Health Center, Inc. Tel: 978-683-3128; Fax: 978-686-7856.

NEWTON. *Catholic Purchasing Services, Inc.*, 580 Washington St., 02458. Tel: 617-965-4343; Fax: 617-965-5430. Email: RJW@catholicpurchasing.org. Web: catholicpurchasing.org. Mr. Richard J. Wasilauskas, Pres.

Focolare Movement, Women's Branch, 31 Jackson Terr., 02458-1430. Tel: 617-965-4879; Fax: 617-965-4879. Email: ffbo@att.net. Web: www.rc.net/focolare. Total in Residence 5.

QUINCY. *The Good Shepherd: Maria Droste Services*, 1354 Hancock St., Ste. 209, 02169. Tel: 617-471-5686; Fax: 617-471-6622. Email: mariadroste@verizon.net. Thomas Tanguay, Dir.
Legal Title: *Madonna Hall* Total Staff 6; Volunteers 16; Total Assisted 290.

WALTHAM. *The Gathering Place*, 3 Common St., Ste. 3B, 02451-4401. Tel: 781-647-0012; Fax: 781-647-0055. Email: gather1997@aol.com. Web: www.hometown.aol.com/gather1997.

**Marist Missionary Sisters Senior Religious Trust*, 349 Grove St., 02453. Tel: 781-893-0149; Fax: 781-899-6838. Email: maristsmsm@aol.com. Web: www.maristmissionarysmsm.org.

RELIGIOUS INSTITUTES OF MEN REPRESENTED IN THE ARCHDIOCESE

For further details refer to the corresponding bracketed number in the Religious Institutes of Men or Women section.

[0130]—*Assumptionists*—A.A.
[1040]—*The Augustinians* (Villanova, PA)—O.S.A.
[0200]—*Benedictine Monks*—O.S.B.
[1350]—*Brothers of St. Francis Xavier*—C.F.X.
[0330]—*Brothers of the Christian Schools* (Long Island, New England Provs.)—F.S.C.
[0470]—*The Capuchin Friars* (Prov. of Mary)—O.F.M.Cap.
[0270]—*Carmelite Fathers & Brothers* (Prov. of Most Pure Heart of Mary)—O.Carm.
[0310]—*Congregation of Christian Brothers* (Eastern Prov.)—C.F.C.
[1210]—*Congregation of the Missionaries of St. Charles*—C.S.
[1000]—*Congregation of the Passion* (St. Paul of the Cross Prov.)—C.P.
[1140]—*Congregation of the Sacred Hearts of Jesus and Mary*—SS.CC.
[0480]—*Conventual Franciscans* (Buffalo, NY)—O.F.M.Conv
[0260]—*Discalced Carmelite Friars*—O.C.D.
[0520]—*Franciscan Friars* (Assumption of B.V.M., Holy Name, Immaculate Conception Provs.)—O.F.M.
[0530]—*Franciscan Friars of the Atonement*—S.A.
[0670]—*Hospitaller Brothers of St. John of God*—O.H.
[0690]—*Jesuit Fathers and Brother* (New England Prov.)—S.J.
[0770]—*The Marist Brothers* (Poughkeepsie, NY)—F.M.S.
[0780]—*Marist Fathers* (Boston Prov.)—S.M.
[0800]—*Maryknoll*—M.M.
[]—*Mekhitarist Fathers*—C.M.Vd.
[0720]—*The Missionaries of Our Lady of La Salette* (Eastern Prov.)—M.S.
[0910]—*Oblates of Mary Immaculate* (Eastern, St.

John the Baptist Provs.)—O.M.I.
[0430]—*Order of Preachers-Dominicans* (Prov. of St. Joseph)—O.P.
[1030]—*Paulist Fathers*—C.S.P.
[0610]—*Priests of the Congregation of Holy Cross* (Eastern Prov.)—C.S.C.
[1070]—*Redemptorist Fathers* (Baltimore Prov.)—C.SS.R.
[1190]—*Salesians of Don Bosco* (Prov. of St. Philip)—S.D.B.
[0110]—*Society of African Missions*—S.M.A.
[0420]—*Society of Divine Word* (Sacred Heart Prov.)—S.V.D.
[0850]—*Society of Missionaries of Africa*—M.Afr.
[0370]—*Society of St. Columban* (American Region)—S.S.C.
[0410]—*Sons of Divine Providence*—F.D.P.
[1270]—*Sons of Mary Missionary Society*—F.M.S.I.
[1280]—*Stigmatine Fathers and Brothers* (Rome, Italy)—C.S.S.
[1360]—*Xaverian Missionary Fathers*—S.X.

RELIGIOUS INSTITUTES OF WOMEN REPRESENTED IN THE ARCHDIOCESE

[1810]—*Bernardine Franciscan Sisters*—O.S.F.
[0330]—*Carmelite Sisters for the Aged and Infirm*—O.Carm.
[0670]—*Cistercian Nuns of the Strict Observance*—O.C.S.O.
[0270]—*Congregation of Bon Secours*—C.B.S.
[3110]—*Congregation of Our lady of the Retreat in the Cenacle*—R.C.
[]—*Congregation of the Armenian Catholic Sisters of the Immaculate Conception, Inc.*
[1920]—*Congregation of the Sisters of the Holy Cross*—C.S.C.
[0760]—*Daughters of Charity of St. Vincent de Paul*—D.C.
[0860]—*Daughters of Mary of the Immaculate Conception*—C.M.
[0420]—*Discalced Carmelite Nuns*—O.C.D.
[1070-01]—*Dominican Sisters*—O.P.
[1070-03]—*Dominican Sisters*—O.P.
[1070-13]—*Dominican Sisters*—O.P.
[1170]—*Felician Sisters*—C.S.S.F.
[1370]—*Franciscan Missionaries of Mary*—F.M.M.
[1320]—*Franciscan Missionary Sisters for Africa* (Co. Louth, Ireland)—O.S.F.
[1180]—*Franciscan Sisters of Allegany, New York*—O.S.F.
[1470]—*Franciscan Sisters of St. Joseph*—F.S.S.J.
[1840]—*Grey Nuns of the Sacred Heart*—G.N.S.H.
[2070]—*Holy Union Sisters*—S.U.S.C.
[0410]—*Institute of the Sisters of Our Lady of Mt. Carmel*—O.Carm.
[2290]—*Little Missionary Sisters of Charity*—L.M.S.C.
[2310]—*Little Sisters of the Assumption*—L.S.A.
[2320]—*Little Sisters of the Holy Family*—P.S.S.F.
[2340]—*Little Sisters of the Poor*—L.S.P.
[2420]—*Marist Missionary Sisters-Missionary Sisters of the Society of Mary*—S.M.S.M.
[2470]—*Maryknoll Sisters of St. Dominic*—M.M.
[2480]—*Medical Missionaries of Mary*—M.M.M.
[1360]—*Missionary Franciscan Sisters of the Immaculate Conception*—O.S.F.
[2790]—*Missionary Servants of the Most Blessed Trinity*—M.S.B.T.
[2880]—*Missionary Sisters of St. Columban*—S.S.C.
[2800]—*Missionary Sisters of the Most Sacred Heart of Jesus of Hiltrup*—M.S.C.
[3030]—*Oblates of the Most Holy Redeemer*—O.SS.R.
[3760]—*Order of St. Clare*—O.S.C.
[0950]—*Pious Society Daughters of St. Paul*—D.S.P.
[3240]—*Poor Sisters of Jesus Crucified and the Sorrowful Mother*—C.J.C.
[3410]—*Religious of Christian Education*—R.C.E.
[2070]—*Religious of the Holy Union of the Sacred Hearts*—S.U.S.C.
[2970]—*School Sisters of Notre Dame*—S.S.N.D.
[3550]—*Servants of the Immaculate Heart of Mary*—S.C.I.M.
[0980]—*Sisters Disciples of the Divine Master*—P.D.D.M.
[0490]—*Sisters of Charity of Montreal-Grey Nuns*—S.G.M.
[0500]—*Sisters of Charity of Nazareth*—S.C.N.
[0560]—*Sisters of Charity of Quebec-Grey Nuns*—S.C.Q.
[0590]—*Sisters of Charity of Saint Elizabeth, Convent Station*—S.C.
[0640]—*Sisters of Charity of St. Vincent de Paul, Halifax*—S.C.
[0540]—*Sisters of Charity, At Ottawa-Grey Nuns of the Cross*—S.C.O.
[0990]—*Sisters of Divine Providence*—C.D.P.
[2580]—*Sisters of Mercy of the Union in the United States of America*—R.S.M.
[3000]—*Sisters of Notre Dame de Namur*—S.N.D.deN.
[3360]—*Sisters of Providence of Saint Mary-Of-The-Woods, Indiana*—S.P.
[3950]—*Sisters of Saint Mary of Namur*—S.S.M.N.
[3720]—*Sisters of St. Anne*—S.S.A.
[3750]—*Sisters of St. Chretienne*—S.S.Ch
[1650]—*Sisters of St. Francis of Philadelphia*—O.S.F.
[3830]—*Sisters of St. Joseph*—C.S.J.
[3815]—*Sisters of Ste. Jeanne D'Arc*—S.J.A.
[0150]—*Sisters of the Assumption B.V.*—S.A.S.V.
[1830]—*Sisters of the Good Shepherd*—R.G.S.
[3310]—*Sisters of the Presentation of Mary*—P.M.
[1490]—*Sisters of the Third Franciscan Order*—O.S.F.
[1705]—*Sisters of the Third Order of St. Francis of Assisi*—O.S.F.
[4060]—*Society of the Holy Child Jesus*—S.H.C.J.
[4070]—*Society of the Sacred Heart*—R.S.C.J.
[4110]—*Ursuline Nuns* (Eastern Prov.)—O.S.U.

ARCHDIOCESAN CEMETERIES

BOSTON. *Diocesan Office*, 175 Broadway, Malden, 02148
ARLINGTON. *St. Paul*
BEVERLY. *St. Mary*
CAMBRIDGE. *North Cambridge Catholic*
CHARLESTOWN. *St. Francis de Sales*
HAVERHILL. *St. James, St. Joseph & St. Patrick*
LOWELL. *St. Patrick*
LYNN. *St. Mary, St. Joseph & St. Jean Baptiste*
MALDEN. *Holy Cross & St. Mary*
MARBLEHEAD. *Star of the Sea*
SALEM. *St. Mary*
SAXONVILLE. *St. George*
STONEHAM. *St. Patrick*
WALTHAM. *Calvary*
WATERTOWN. *Mount Auburn & St. Patrick*
WOBURN. *Calvary*

NECROLOGY

† Hart, Rev. Msgr. Peter F., (Senior Priest)—Died June 8, 2003
† Rossiter, Rev. Msgr. Francis S., Bilerica, MA Middlesex County Jail; Bilerica, MA Middlesex House of Corrections—Died Nov. 23, 2003
† Abracinskas, Albert C., (Senior Priest)—Died May 11, 2003
† Baltrushunas, Anthony P.—Died March 1, 2003
† Barry, Henry F., (Senior Priest)—Died Dec. 14, 2003
† Bryson, Robert C., (Senior Priest)—Died April 21, 2003
† Buckley, John E., Burlington, MA St. Margaret—Died Nov. 20, 2003
† Burke, Leonard J., (Senior Priest)—Died Sept. 20, 2003
† Collins, Joseph I.—Died Sept. 30, 2003
† Daley, Joseph D., (Senior Priest)—Died Oct. 2, 2003
† Donlon, William J.—Died Feb. 19, 2003
† Fitzgerald, Gerald J., Somerville, MA St. Ann—Died June 29, 2003
† Flaherty, Daniel E., Salem, MA St. James—Died Nov. 14, 2003
† Gaudette, Edward J., (Senior Priest)—Died June 16, 2003
† Greaney, Francis M., (Senior Priest)—Died June 30, 2003
† Jezowski, Anthony C.—Died Feb. 2, 2003
† Mahoney, James F.—Died March 9, 2003
† Motherway, Thomas F.—Died April 21, 2003
† O'Leary, Adrian P., (Senior Priest)—Died Sept. 21, 2003
† Piscitelli, Vincent J., (Senior Priest)—Died June 11, 2003
† Publicover, James L., (Senior Priest)—Died Nov. 18, 2003
† Ritchie, Francis J., (Senior Priest)—Died April 20, 2003
† Sullivan, Paul V., (Senior Priest)—Died March 7, 2003
† Sutton, John V., Weymouth, MA Sacred Heart—Died Feb. 10, 2003

Diocese of Bridgeport

(Dioecesis Bridgeportensis)

Most Reverend

WILLIAM E. LORI, S.T.D.

Bishop of Bridgeport; ordained May 14, 1977; appointed Titular Bishop of Bulla and Auxiliary of Washington April 20, 1995; appointed Bishop of Bridgeport January 23, 2001; installed March 19, 2001. *Office: 238 Jewett Ave., Bridgeport, CT 06606-2892.*

Chancery: The Catholic Center, 238 Jewett Ave., Bridgeport, CT 06606-2892. Tel: 203-372-4301; Fax: 203-371-8698.

Web: www.bridgeportdiocese.org

ESTABLISHED AUGUST 6, 1953.

Square Miles 633.

Corporate Title: The Bridgeport Roman Catholic Diocesan Corporation.

Comprises all of Fairfield County in the State of Connecticut.

Legal Title: For legal titles of parishes and diocesan institutions, consult the Chancery at The Catholic Center.

STATISTICAL OVERVIEW

Personnel	
Bishop	1
Priests: Diocesan Active in Diocese	181
Priests: Diocesan Active Outside Diocese	14
Priests: Diocesan in Foreign Missions	2
Priests: Retired, Sick or Absent	73
Number of Diocesan Priests	270
Religious Priests in Diocese	44
Total Priests in Diocese	314
Extern Priests in Diocese	14
Ordinations:	
Diocesan Priests	6
Transitional Deacons	4
Permanent Deacons in Diocese	93
Total Brothers	1
Total Sisters	403
Parishes	
Parishes	87
With Resident Pastor:	
Resident Diocesan Priests	82
Resident Religious Priests	5
Missions	1
Professional Ministry Personnel:	
Sisters	35
Lay Ministers	3,987
Welfare	
Catholic Hospitals	1
Total Assisted	139,407
Homes for the Aged	3
Total Assisted	843
Day Care Centers	1
Total Assisted	105
Specialized Homes	10
Total Assisted	40
Special Centers for Social Services	17
Total Assisted	9,336
Educational	
Seminaries, Diocesan	1
Students from This Diocese	17
Diocesan Students in Other Seminaries	10
Total Seminarians	27
Colleges and Universities	3
Total Students	11,196
High Schools, Diocesan and Parish	5
Total Students	2,598
High Schools, Private	3
Total Students	1,262
Elementary Schools, Diocesan and Parish	33
Total Students	8,717
Elementary Schools, Private	2
Total Students	504
Non-residential Schools for the Disabled	1
Total Students	11
Catechesis/Religious Education:	
High School Students	4,039
Elementary Students	31,675
Total Students under Catholic Instruction	60,029
Teachers in the Diocese:	
Priests	13
Brothers	1
Sisters	30
Lay Teachers	870
Vital Statistics	
Receptions into the Church:	
Infant Baptism Totals	6,036
Adult Baptism Totals	109
Received into Full Communion	97
First Communions	5,922
Confirmations	4,494
Marriages:	
Catholic	904
Interfaith	356
Total Marriages	1,260
Deaths	3,617
Total Catholic Population	410,304
Total Population	896,202

Former Bishops—His Eminence LAWRENCE J. CARDINAL SHEHAN, D.D., ord. Dec. 23, 1922; consecrated Dec. 12, 1945 as Auxiliary Bishop of Baltimore; installed as first Bishop of Bridgeport, Dec. 1, 1953; transferred to Archdiocese of Baltimore, July 10, 1961; created Cardinal, Feb. 22, 1965; died Aug. 26, 1984; Most Revs. WALTER W. CURTIS, S.T.D. (Retired), ord. Dec. 8, 1937; appt. Auxiliary Bishop of Newark and Titular Bishop of Bisica in Tunis; consecrated Sept. 24, 1957; appt. Bishop of Bridgeport, Sept. 23, 1961; installed Nov. 20, 1961; retired June 28, 1988; died Oct. 18, 1997; EDWARD M. EGAN, J.C.D., D.D., ord. Dec. 15, 1957; appt. Titular Bishop of Allegheny and Auxiliary Bishop of New York, April 1, 1985; consecrated May 22, 1985; appt. Bishop of Bridgeport, Nov. 8, 1988; installed Dec. 14, 1988; appt. Archbishop of New York, May 11, 2000; installed June 19, 2000; created Cardinal Feb. 21, 2001.

Vicars General—Rev. Msgrs. J. PETER CULLEN, V.G.; WILLIAM J. SCHEYD; THOMAS J. DRISCOLL, V.G., 238 Jewett Ave., Bridgeport, 06606-2892.

Moderator of the Curia—Rev. Msgr. J. PETER CULLEN, V.G.

Chancery—The Catholic Center, 238 Jewett Ave., Bridgeport, 06606-2892. Tel: 203-372-4301; Fax: 203-371-8698. Office Hours: Sept.-June Mon.-Fri. 9-5; July-Aug. 9-4

Chancellor—Mrs. NANCY B. MATTHEWS, Catholic Center, 238 Jewett Ave., Bridgeport, 06606-2892. Tel: 203-372-4301.

Vice Chancellor & Secretary to the Bishop—Rev. DARIUSZ J. ZIELONKA.

Episcopal Vicar for Religious—Rev. ERNEST T. ESPOSITO, D.Min.

Director for Clergy Personnel—Rev. FRANK C. MCGRATH.

Episcopal Vicar for Haitians—Rev. G. FRANTZ DESRUISSEAUX, J.C.L.

Episcopal Vicar for Hispanics—Rev. Msgr. ANICETO VILLAMIDE.

Finance Officer—Mr. GARY J. NIELSEN, C.P.A., CFO.

Diocesan Tribunal—The Catholic Center, 238 Jewett Ave., Bridgeport, 06606-2892. Tel: 203-372-4301.

Judicial Vicar—Rev. Msgr. JERALD A. DOYLE, Ph.D., J.C.D.

Judges—Rev. Msgrs. WILLIAM A. GENUARIO, P.A., J.C.D.; THOMAS J. DRISCOLL, V.G.; J. JAMES CUNEO, J.C.D.; GEORGE D. BIRGE; Rev. MICHAEL A. BOCCACCIO; Rev. Canon ALBERT W. WATTS, J.C.L.; REVS. JOSEPH K. PARAMPATH, J.C.D.; MICHAEL R. MOYNIHAN, J.C.L.

Defenders of the Bond—Revs. RICHARD F. FUTIE, J.C.D.; ALFRED F. PECARIC; WILLIAM F. VERRILLI.

Promoter of Justice—Rev. G. FRANTZ DESRUISSEAUX, J.C.L.

Notaries—MARY A. MOLLOY; KERRY PERILLE.

Diocesan General Counsel—MICHAEL T. DOLAN ESQ.

Diocesan Censors—Rev. Msgrs. LAURENCE R. BRONKIEWICZ, S.T.D.; THOMAS J. DRISCOLL, V.G.; Rev. CHRISTOPHER J. WALSH, Ph.D.

Diocesan Consultors—Rev. Msgrs. LAURENCE R. BRONKIEWICZ, S.T.D.; J. PETER CULLEN, V.G.; LOUIS A. DEPROFIO, P.A.; THOMAS J. DRISCOLL, V.G.; NICHOLAS V. GRIECO; WILLIAM J. SCHEYD; Revs. WALTER C. ORLOWSKI; ANDREW G. VARGA; Rev. Msgrs. ANICETO VILLAMIDE; KEVIN W. WALLIN; Rev. DARIUSZ J. ZIELONKA; Rev. Msgr. JERALD A. DOYLE, Ph.D., J.C.D.

Presbyteral Council—Most Rev. WILLIAM E. LORI, S.T.D., Presider; Rev. Msgrs. LAURENCE R. BRONKIEWICZ, S.T.D.; JERALD A. DOYLE, Ph.D., J.C.D.; WILLIAM J. SCHEYD, Vice Chm.; J. PETER CULLEN, V.G.; PETER P. DORA; ANICETO VILLAMIDE; KEVIN W. WALLIN; THOMAS J. DRISCOLL, V.G.; NICHOLAS V. GRIECO; STANLEY B. ROUSSEAU; Revs. MATTHEW BERNELLI; JAMES D. GROSSO; DONALD A. GUGLIELMI, S.T.D.; DAVID W. BLANCHFIELD; M. JUDE FAY; FRANCIS T. HOFFMAN; FRANK C. MCGRATH; DAVID C. LEOPOLD; JULIO LOPRESTI; GUSTAVO A. FALLA; RICHARD D. MURPHY; WALTER C. ORLOWSKI; PETER J. TOWSLEY; DARIUSZ J. ZIELONKA; ANDREW G. VARGA; WILLIAM R. MOYNIHAN.

Finance Council—Most Rev. WILLIAM E. LORI, S.T.D.; Rev. Msgrs. WILLIAM J. SCHEYD; J. PETER CULLEN, V.G.; THOMAS J. DRISCOLL, V.G.; Mrs. NANCY B. MATTHEWS; Mr. GARY J. NIELSEN, C.P.A.; Mr. DIGBY W. BARRIOS; Mr. RALPH A. BOSCH; Mrs. NANCY K. DOLAN; Mr. WILLIAM B. JAMES, C.F.A.; Mrs. MADELINE LACOVARA; Mr. DAVID LIPTAK; Mr. DENNIS NALLY; Mr. JOSEPH D. ROXE; WILLIAM J. TOTTEN.

Parochial Examiners—Rev. Msgrs. LOUIS A. DEPROFIO, P.A.; JOHN E. GILMARTIN; Rev. MICHAEL C. PALMER; Rev. Msgr. ANICETO VILLAMIDE.

Territorial Vicars—Vicariate I (Stamford, Darien, Glenbrook, Greenwich, Byram, Riverside): Rev. MICHAEL R. MOYNIHAN, J.C.L., St. Michael Rectory, 469 North St., Greenwich, 06830. Tel: 203-869-5421; Fax: 203-869-0169. Vicariate II (Norwalk, New Canaan, Wilton, Weston, Westport): Rev. Msgr. NICHOLAS V. GRIECO, St. Francis of Assisi Rectory, P.O. Box 1025, 35 Norfield Rd., Weston, 06883. Tel: 203-227-1341; Fax: 203-226-1154. Web: www.sfaparish.com.

Vicariate III (Fairfield, Easton, West Bridgeport): Rev. Msgr. KEVIN W. WALLIN, Vicar, Saint Augustine Cathedral, 359 Washington Ave., Bridgeport, 06604. Tel: 203-368-6777; Fax: 203-368-0386. Vicariate IV (East Bridgeport, Stratford, Trumbull, Monroe, Shelton): Rev. MATTHEW BERNELLI, St. Mary Rectory, 25 Sherman St., Bridgeport, 06608. Tel: 203-334-8811; Fax: 203-334-8574. Vicariate V (Bethel, Brookfield, Danbury, Georgetown, Newtown, New Fairfield, Redding, Ridgefield, Sherman): Rev. ROBERT E. WEISS, St. Rose of Lima Rectory, 46 Church Hill Rd., Newtown, 06470. Tel: 203-426-1014; Fax: 203-426-6222.

Office for Clergy Personnel—Revs. ERNEST T. ESPOSITO, D.Min., Episcopal Vicar for Religious; FRANK C. MCGRATH, Dir. Clergy Personnel; Deacon ANTHONY J. DETJE, Asst. Dir. Clergy Personnel.

The Catholic Center—238 Jewett Ave., Bridgeport, 06606. Tel: 203-372-4301; Fax: 203-372-9835. Web: www.bridgeportdiocese.org.

Finance Office—Mr. GARY J. NIELSEN, C.P.A., CFO; JOHN P. ROONEY, Dir., Parish Accounting & Finance, The Catholic Center, 238 Jewett Ave., Bridgeport, 06606-2892. Tel: 203-372-4301; Fax: 203-374-8628. Email: jrooney@diobpt.org.

Members of the Clergy Personnel Committee—Rev. Msgr. FRANCIS C. WISSEL; Revs. LAWRENCE J. CARROLL; J. BARRY FUREY.

Office for the Continuing Education of Clergy—Rev. ERNEST T. ESPOSITO, D.Min., Dir.

Office of Vocations—Rev. CHRISTOPHER J. WALSH, Ph.D., Dir., St. John Fisher Residence, 894 Newfield Ave., Stamford, 06905. Tel: 203-322-5331; Fax: 203-461-9876. Email: fatherwalsh@saintjohnfisher.org.

Pastors' Vocation Advisory Board—Rev. Msgrs. J. PETER CULLEN, V.G.; THOMAS J. DRISCOLL, V.G.; WILLIAM J. SCHEYD; EDWARD R. SURWILO; ANICETO VILLAMIDE; Revs. LAWRENCE J. CARROLL; RICHARD F. FUTIE, J.C.D.; FRANK T. HOFFMANN; FRANK C. MCGRATH; SAMUEL V. SCOTT.

Office of the Permanent Diaconate—Deacons ANTHONY J. DETJE, Dir. Formation; JOHN J. MORANSKI, Asst. Dir. Diaconate Formation; Rev. ERNEST T. ESPOSITO, D.Min., Spiritual Dir. Formation, The Catholic Center, 238 Jewett Ave., Bridgeport, 06606-2892. Tel: 203-372-4301; Fax: 203-371-8698. Email: fresposito@diobpt.org.

Office for Ecumenical and Interreligious Affairs—Rev. SAMUEL V. SCOTT, Dir., Saint Joseph Parish, 159 Whisconier Rd., P.O. Box 5072, Brookfield, 06804. Tel: 203-775-1035; Fax: 203-775-1684.

Diocesan Office of Divine Worship—Rev. JOSEPH C. LINCK, C.C.O. & Dir., Saint Theresa, 5301 Main St., Trumbull, 06611. Tel: 203-268-4060; Fax: 203-268-8723.

Office for Christian Formation—GLORIA F. ZAPIAIN, Dir., The Catholic Center, 238 Jewett Ave., Bridgeport, 06606-2892. Tel: 203-372-4301; Fax: 203-373-1418. Email: catechesis@diobpt.org.

Catechesis—GLORIA F. ZAPIAIN.

Clergy and Laity Formation Programs—ELIZABETH SIEGEL, Dir. Formation Program.

Adult Education and R.C.I.A.—Mrs. JEAN A. KECHEJIAN, Asst. Dir. Adult Education & R.C.I.A.

Youth Ministry—JOHN P. CAMPBELL, Asst. Dir.

Young Adult Ministry—BETTY ANNE CASARETTI, Asst. Dir.

Catholic Scouts—Deacon JOSEPH MELITA, Dir.

Office for Education—ARMAND R. FABBRI, Dir. & Supt., Schools; Dr. JOHN R. ALFONE, Asst. Supt. Elementary Education, 238 Jewett Ave., Bridgeport, 06606-2892. Tel: 203-372-4301; Fax: 203-372-1961. Email: afabbri@diobpt.org; WILLIAM J. ADAMS, Coord., Federal-State Programs, 238 Jewett Ave., Bridgeport, 06606. Tel: 203-576-7944.

Special Education—Sisters ELEACE KING, I.H.M., Ed.D., Asst. Supt., Special Education, The Catholic Center, 238 Jewett Ave., Bridgeport, 06606-2892. Tel: 203-372-4301, Ext. 330; Fax: 203-372-1961. Email: srking@diobpt.org; NANCY O'NEILL, C.N.D., Coord., Ministry to the Deaf. Tel: 203-372-4301, Ext. 335; 203-372-4782 (TTY); Fax: 203-372-1961. Email: sroneill@diobpt.org.

Catholic Charities of Fairfield County, Inc.—BRIAN A. CRONIN, A.C.S.W., C.I.S.W., Exec. Dir.; FRANK THIEL, Comptroller, Catholic Center, 238 Jewett Ave., Bridgeport, 06606-2892. Tel: 203-372-4301, Ext. 379 & 564; Fax: 203-372-5045. Email: ccfcexdir@aol.com; ccfcadmin@aol.com. Web: www.ccfc-ct.org.

Diocesan Offices and Directors

Ethnic and Cultural Services—Deacon JOSEPH J. FARLEY, Sec., 238 Jewett Ave., Bridgeport, 06606-2892. Tel: 203-372-4301, Ext. 226; Fax: 203-371-8698.

Aging, Diocesan Task Force—EDIE CASSIDY, Chm., 238 Jewett Ave., Bridgeport, 06606-2892. Tel: 203-372-4301, Ext. 386; Fax: 203-372-5045. Email: ecassidy@ccfc-ct.org.

Archives—Deacon WILLIAM J. BISSENDEN, Archivist, 238 Jewett Ave., Bridgeport, 06606-2892. Tel: 203-372-4301.

African Americans, Apostolate of—Rev. Msgr. JOHN C. SANDERS, Dir. (Retired), The Catherine Dennis Keefe Queen of the Clergy Retired Priests' Residence, 274 Strawberry Hill Ave., Stamford, 06902. Tel: 203-358-9906.

Catholic Lawyers—Rev. Msgr. J. JAMES CUNEO, J.C.D., Spiritual Moderator; JAMES J. RUANE ESQ., Coord., St. Thomas More Society of Fairfield Co., 238 Jewett Ave., Bridgeport, 06606-2892. Tel: 203-372-4301.

Catholic Physicians Guild—Dr. THOMAS G. FLYNN, Coord., 29 Old Studio Rd., New Canaan, 06840. Tel: 203-966-1959.

Catholic Women, Council of—Rev. MICHAEL R. MOYNIHAN, J.C.L., Diocesan Dir., St. Michael Rectory, 469 N. St., Greenwich, 06083. Tel: 203-869-5421; Mrs. HELEN F. CARROLL, Diocesan Pres., 1216 Noble Ave., Bridgeport, 06608. Tel: 203-335-7468 District Spiritual Directors:; Revs. ERNEST T. ESPOSITO, D.Min., (Bridgeport), Catholic Center, 238 Jewett Ave., Bridgeport, 06606. Tel: 203-372-4301, Ext. 314; Fax: 203-371-8698; MARTIN S. IGOE, (Greenwich), Sacred Heart Parish, 95 Henry St., Greenwich, 06830. Tel: 203-531-8730; Fax: 203-531-8794; Rev. Msgr. EDWIN F. BURKE, (Norwalk), Saint Ladislaus Parish, 25 Cliff St., South Norwalk, 06854. Tel: 203-866-1867; Fax: 203-866-7830; Rev. ROBERT G. POHLEY, (Stamford), Sacred Heart Parish, 37 Schuyler Ave., Stamford, 06902. Tel: 203-324-9544; Fax: 203-324-9202.

Cemeteries—RAY CAPO, Dir., 238 Jewett Ave., Bridgeport, 06606-2892. Tel: 203-372-4301; Fax: 203-374-7588. Email: raycapo@diobpt.org.

Communications—Dr. JOSEPH J. MCALEER, Editor & Dir., 238 Jewett Ave., Bridgeport, 06606-2892. Tel: 203-372-4301; Fax: 203-374-2044. Email: fcc@diobpt.org. Web: www.bridgeportdiocese.com; Rev. MARK CONNOLLY, Diocesan Dir., Radio & Television, P.O. Box 7466, Greenwich, 06836. Tel: 203-316-9394.

Connecticut Catholic Conference—Dr. MARIE HILLIARD, Exec. Dir., 134 Farmington Ave., Hartford, 06105. Tel: 203-524-7882.

Cursillos of Fairfield County, Inc.—Rev. PAUL F. MERRY, Advisor for English Language, Blessed Sacrament Church, 275 Union Ave., Bridgeport, 06607. Tel: 203-333-1202; Rev. Msgr. ANICETO VILLAMIDE, Advisor for Spanish Language, St. Peter Rectory, 695 Colorado Ave., Bridgeport, 06605. Tel: 203-366-5611.

Deaf, Apostolate for—Rev. PETER A. DEMARCO, Moderator, Res.: St. Catherine of Siena Rectory, 200 Shelton Rd., Trumbull, 06611. Tel: 203-261-3676 203-459-0484 (TTY); Fax: 203-377-1023. Email: pdem243377@aol.com.

Development, Office of—DONNA J. MARINO, Dir. Devel.; ROBERT MORGAN, Dir. Planned Giving; NICOLE M. ALFONE, Assoc. Dir., Annual Bishop's Appeal, 238 Jewett Ave., Bridgeport, 06606-2892. Tel: 203-372-4301.

Fairfield Foundation of the Diocese of Bridgeport, Inc.—MICHELLE JONES DELMHORST, Pres.; JOHN CROFFY, Exec. Dir., 238 Jewett Ave., Bridgeport, 06606-2892. Tel: 203-372-4301.

Inner-City Foundation for Charity and Education—Rev. Msgr. KEVIN W. WALLIN, Exec. Dir.; Mr. RICHARD T. STONE, Dir., 238 Jewett Ave., Bridgeport, 06606-2892. Tel: 203-372-4301; Fax: 203-371-8698. Email: innercity.foundation@snet.net.

Catholic Ministry for the Elderly—Rev. DAVID H. KRAHEL, Chap. (Greenwich, Darien, Stamford), Our Lady Star of the Sea Rectory, 1200 Shippan Ave., Stamford, 06902. Tel: 203-357-7956.

Haitian American Catholic Center of Greater Stamford—Rev. JEAN RIDLY JULIEN, Exec. Dir., 93 Hope St., Stamford, 06906. Tel: 203-406-0343; Fax: 203-406-0347.

Hispanic Apostolate, Episcopal Vicar for—Rev. Msgr. ANICETO VILLAMIDE, Vicar, The Catholic Center, 238 Jewett Ave., Bridgeport, 06606-2892. Tel: 203-372-4301.

Human Resources, Office of—LOUISE STEWART-SPAGNUOLO, Dir., 238 Jewett Ave., Bridgeport, 06606-2892. Tel: 203-372-4301; Fax: 203-371-0875. Email: lsspagnuolo@diobpt.org.

Insurance Office—JOSEPH G. BURTON, Claims & Risk Mgr., Catholic Mutual Group, 238 Jewett Ave., Bridgeport, 06606. Tel: 203-371-8471; Fax: 203-371-6139. Email: jburton@catholicmutual.org.

Nurses, Council of Catholic—Rev. STEPHEN J. GLEESON, Dir., St. Stephen Rectory, 6949 Main St., Trumbull, 06611. Tel: 203-268-6217; Fax: 203-268-9861.

Official Newspapers—Most Rev. WILLIAM E. LORI, S.T.D., Publisher; Dr. JOSEPH J. MCALEER, Editor & Dir. Communications, 238 Jewett Ave., Bridgeport, 06606. Tel: 203-372-4301; Fax: 203-374-2044. Email: jmcaleer@diobpt.org. Web: www.bridgeportdiocese.com; Mrs. PATRICIA HENNESSY, Asst. Editor. Tel: 203-372-4301; Fax: 203-374-2044. Email: phennessy@diobpt.org; VENESSA V. ANDERSON, Multimedia Editor. Tel: 203-372-4301, Ext. 454. Email: fccatholic@snet.net. "The Fairfield County Catholic", (Monthly),

Pilgrimages, Office of Diocesan—Rev. Msgr. WILLIAM J. LOUGHLIN (Retired), St. Thomas Rectory, 1719 Post Rd., Fairfield, 06824. Tel: 203-259-8717.

Pontifical Association of the Holy Childhood—Rev. Msgr. STANLEY B. ROUSSEAU, Dir.; ELIZABETH SAULNIER, Coord. for Schools; R.E. Programs, The Catholic Center, 238 Jewett Ave., Bridgeport, 06606-2892. Tel: 203-372-4301; Fax: 203-371-8698.

Portuguese-Speaking People, Apostolate for—Rev. Msgr. CONSTANTINO R. CALDAS, Dir. (Retired), 429 Huntington Rd., Bridgeport, 06608. Tel: 203-333-7575.

Propagation of the Faith—Rev. Msgr. STANLEY B. ROUSSEAU, Dir., The Catholic Center, 238 Jewett Ave., Bridgeport, 06606-2892. Tel: 203-372-4301; Fax: 203-371-8698. Email: frous@optonline.net.

Boy Scouts and Girl Scouts—Deacon JOSEPH MELITA, Dir., Catholic Center, 238 Jewett Ave., Bridgeport, 06606-2982. Tel: 203-372-4301; Rev. STEPHEN J. BALINT, Res.: St. Ladislaus Rectory, 25 Cliff St., South Norwalk, 06854. Tel: 203-866-1867.

Retired Priests—Rev. Msgrs. LOUIS A. DEPROFIO, P.A., Dir.; BERNARD S. SCANLON, Rector (Retired); VICKEY HICKEY, Admin., The Catherine Dennis Keefe Queen of the Clergy Retired Priests' Residence, 274 Strawberry Hill Ave., Stamford, 06904. Tel: 203-358-9906; Fax: 203-358-9524.

Office of Safe Environments—Ms. ERIN NEIL, Dir., 238 Jewett Ave., Bridgeport, 06606. Tel: 203-372-4301.

Victim Assistance Coordinator—Ms. LINDA MICHAUD, L.C.S.W., 238 Jewett Ave., Bridgeport, 06606. Tel: 203-650-3265. Email: lam472@cs.com.

CLERGY, PARISHES, MISSIONS AND PAROCHIAL SCHOOLS

CITY OF BRIDGEPORT
(FAIRFIELD COUNTY)

1—ST. AUGUSTINE CATHEDRAL (1842), Rev. Msgr. Kevin W. Wallin; Rev. Michael F. Dogali. In Res., Revs. Hernan D. Bohorquez; Alphonsus Tran Van Dong; Sr. Antoinette Mongkolrutana, S.L.C., Vietnamese Pastoral Assoc. Tel: 203-333-0837; Deacon John S. Moranski.

Res.: 359 Washington Ave., 06604. Tel: 203-368-6777; Fax: 203-368-6386.

School—Tel: 203-367-5896. See separate listing under Elementary Schools, Regional in the Institution section.

Catechesis/Religious Program—Students 147.

2—ST. AMBROSE (1928), Revs. Dennis G. Bludnicki; Richard A. Deshaies, S.J. (BO). In Res., Revs. Nello A. Barachini, C.M.; Evaristus Osuagwu (Nigeria); Deacon James Volpe.

Res.: 1596 Boston Ave., 06610. Tel: 203-333-1336; Fax 203-330-9085.

School— See separate listing under Elementary Schools, Regional in the Institution section.

Catechesis/Religious Program—Students 30.

Station—Bishop Curtis Homes, Tel: 203-366-4333.

Station—Success Park

3—ST. ANDREW (1961), Rev. Eugene R. Szantyr; Deacons Roland Blier; Edward Hendricks. In Res., Rev. William F. Verrilli, J.C.L.

Res.: 435 Anton St., 06606. Tel: 203-374-6171; Fax: 203-372-7709.

School—Tel: 203-372-4819; Fax: 203-396-0378. See separate listing under Elementary Schools, Regional in the Institution section.

Catechesis/Religious Program—Tel: 203-374-8118; Fax: 203-374-9450. Mrs. Jeanne Bisson, D.R.E. Students 359.

4—ST. ANN (1922), [CEM] Rev. David C. Leopold.

Res.: 481 Brewster St., 06605. Tel: 203-368-1607; Fax: 203-368-0859.

School—Tel: 203-334-5856; Fax: 203-333-8263. Mrs. Maria J. O'Neill, Prin. See separate listing under Elementary Schools, Regional in the Institution section.

Catechesis/Religious Program—Students 201.

5—ST. ANTHONY OF PADUA, Merged, with St. Peter,

Bridgeport. See separate listing.
6—BLESSED SACRAMENT (1917), Revs. Paul F. Merry; George M. Karcsinski; Deacons Ricardo Martinez; Donald P. Foust.
Res.: 275 Union Ave., 06607. Tel: 203-333-1202; Fax: 203-368-3502.
Catechesis/Religious Program—Students 36.
7—ST. CHARLES (1902), Revs. Joseph J. Saba; Juan G. Pineda (Columbia); Jean-Rony Philippe; Sergio da Silva; Sr. Antoinette Mongkolrutana, S.L.C., Laotian Pastoral Assoc. Tel: 203-333-0837; Deacons Santos Garcia; Fred Tetreault.
Res.: 391 Ogden St., 06608. Tel: 203-333-2147; Fax: 203-330-8316.
Catechesis/Religious Program—Tel: 203-576-1629. Rev. Juan G. Pineda (Colombia), D.R.E. Students 508.
8—SS. CYRIL AND METHODIUS (1907), (Slovak), Rev. Msgr. Joseph W. Pekar.
Res.: 79 Church St., 06608. Tel: 203-333-7003.
9—ST. GEORGE (1907), (Lithuanian), Rev. Julio Lopresti, I.V.E., Admin.
Res.: 443 Park Ave., 06604. Tel: 203-335-1797; Fax: 203-334-6359 9.
10—HOLY ROSARY (1903), (Italian), Rev. Matthew Mauriello. In Res., Revs. Andrew M. Walter; John Punnakunnel (India).
Res.: 365 E. Washington Ave., 06608. Tel: 203-334-2447; Fax: 203-335-5334.
Catechesis/Religious Program—Tel: 203-334-7000. Students 70.
11—ST. JOHN NEPOMUCENE, Closed., For inquiries for parish records contact Holy Name of Jesus, Stratford.
12—ST. JOSEPH'S, Closed., May 23, 1988. For inquiries for parish records contact St. Patrick, Bridgeport
13—ST. MARY (1857), (Spanish), [CEM] Rev. Matthew Bernelli.
Res.: 25 Sherman St., 06608. Tel: 203-334-8811; Fax: 203-334-8574.
Catechesis/Religious Program—Students 124.
14—ST. MICHAEL THE ARCHANGEL (1899), (Polish), [CEM] Revs. Martin Breski, O.F.M.Conv.; Stefan Morawski, O.F.M.Conv.
Catechesis/Religious Program—Students 56.
Res.: 310 Pulaski St., 06608. Tel: 203-334-1822; Fax: 203-696-0078.
15—OUR LADY OF FATIMA (1962), (Portuguese), Rev. Joseph De Brito Alves (Portugal), Admin. In Res., Rev. Msgr. Constantino R. Caldas (Retired); Deacon Gabriel A. Pereira.
Res.: 429 Huntington Rd., 06608. Tel: 203-333-7575; Fax: 203-333-7575.
Catechesis/Religious Program—Tel: 203-929-0780. Students 332.
16—OUR LADY OF GOOD COUNSEL (1955), [CEM] Rev. Martin J. Nikodem.
Res.: 163 Ortega Ave., 06606. Tel: 203-372-3533.
Catechesis/Religious Program— Noreen Franklin, D.R.E. Students 24.
17—ST. PATRICK CHURCH (1889), Revs. George F. O'Neill; Michael J. Bachman; Deacons William J. Bissenden; Alix Africot. In Res., Rev. Bernardo C. Rodriguez.
Res. and Business Office: 170 Thompson St., 06604-2816. Tel: 203-335-0106; Fax: 203-335-0107. Church: 851 North Ave., 06606.
Catechesis/Religious Program— Sandra Mihalek, D.R.E. Students 136.
Station—Connecticut State Correctional Institution
Station—St. Vincent Medical Center, Tel: 203-576-6000.
Station—Northbridge Health Care Center, Tel: 203-336-0232.
18—ST. PETER (1900), (Spanish), [CEM] Rev. Msgr. Aniceto Villamide; Rev. Greg J. Markey; Deacons Domingo Reveron; Luis Torres.
Res.: 695 Colorado Ave., 06605. Tel: 203-366-5611; Fax: 203-335-1924.
School—Tel: 203-333-2048; Fax: 203-333-2878. See separate listing under Elementary Schools, Regional in the Institution section.
Catechesis/Religious Program—Tel: 203-334-5681; Fax: 203-333-1590. Sr. Mirta Cruz, D.R.E. Students 275.
19—ST. RAPHAEL (1925), (Italian), Revs. Carducci S. D'Amico; Grazioso Artuso; Deacon Joseph Melita.
Res.: 162 Oak St., 06604. Tel: 203-333-3161; Fax: 203-368-1727.
School—Tel: 203-333-6818; Fax: 203-336-9205. See separate listing under Elementary Schools, Regional in the Institution section.
Catechesis/Religious Program—Students 268.
Convent—671 Oak St., 06604. Tel: 203-335-9817; Fax: 203-336-9205.
Chapel—St. Margaret's 2539 Park Ave., 06604. Tel: 203-368-4425.

OUTSIDE THE CITY OF BRIDGEPORT

BETHEL, FAIRFIELD CO., ST. MARY (1882), [CEM] Rev. Msgr. Edward B. Karl; Rev. Michael L. Dunn. In Res., Rev. Corey V. Piccinino.
Church & Office: 26 Dodgingtown Rd., 06801. Tel: 203-744-5777; Fax: 203-744-3740.
School—Tel: 203-744-2922; Fax: 203-798-8803. See separate listing under Elementary Schools, Regional in the Institution section.
Catechesis/Religious Program—Tel: 203-743-4557. Mary Ferri, D.R.E. Students 850.
Convent—Tel: 203-743-6985.

BROOKFIELD, FAIRFIELD CO.
1—ST. JOSEPH (1941), Revs. Lawrence J. Carroll; Miroslaw Stachurski; Deacons William Shaughnessy; Peter Kuhn.
Res.: 159 Whisconier Rd., P.O. Box 5072, 06804. Tel: 203-775-1035; Fax: 203-775-1684.
School— See separate listing under Elementary Schools, Regional in the Institution section.
Catechesis/Religious Program—Tel: 203-775-1035. Students 651.
2—ST. MARGUERITE BOURGEOYS (1982), [CEM] Revs. George S. Sankoorikal; Peter J. Towsley; Deacons Richard A. Fenton; Anthony J. Detje.
Res.: 138 Candlewood Lake Rd., 06804. Tel: 203-775-5117; Fax: 203-775-9254.
Catechesis/Religious Program—Tel: 203-775-2644. Students 384.

DANBURY, FAIRFIELD CO.
1—ST. GREGORY (1960), Revs. Angelo S. Arrando; John Stronkowski; Raymond M. Scherba; Deacons Robert Blankschen; William D. Murphy; Daniel N. Myott.
Res.: 85 Great Plain Rd., 06811. Tel: 203-797-0222; Fax: 203-743-5464.
School— See separate listing under Elementary Schools, Regional in the Institution section.
Catechesis/Religious Program—Tel: 203-743-5168. Mrs. Mary Ann Hauser, D.R.E. Students 901.
2—IMMACULATE HEART OF MARY, (Portuguese), [CEM] Rev. Antonio Carvalho de Azevedo, Admin.; Deacon Jose Rodrigues Cabral.
Res.: 149 Deer Hill Ave., 06811. Tel: 203-797-1821; Fax: 203-743-9146.
Catechesis/Religious Program—Students 113.
3—ST. JOSEPH (1905), Revs. Michael F. Dogali; John F. Pikulski, Ph.D.; Cyprian P. LaPastina. In Res., Rev. Raymond K. Petrucci.
Res.: 8 Robinson Ave., 06810. Tel: 203-748-8177; Fax: 203-748-2010.
School— See separate listing under Elementary Schools, Regional in the Institution section.
Catechesis/Religious Program—Tel: 203-778-1920. Students 355.
4—OUR LADY OF GUADALUPE (1985), (Spanish), [CEM] Revs. Frederick L. Saviano; Hector Leon (Colombia).
Res.: 29 Golden Hill Rd., 06811-4629. Tel: 203-743-1021; Fax: 203-798-8143.
Catechesis/Religious Program—Students 250.
5—ST. PETER (1851), [CEM] Rev. Albert D. Audette; Rev. Msgr. Pedro D. Diniz (Brazil); Revs. Thomas N. Haber; Tomi Thomas; Deacon Louis F. Howe, Sr. In Res., Rev. Michael Flynn.
Res.: 104 Main St., 06810. Tel: 203-743-2707; Fax: 203-794-1928.
School— See separate listing under Elementary Schools, Regional in the Institution section.
Catechesis/Religious Program—Tel: 203-743-1048; Fax: 203-797-9471. Joanne Durkin, D.R.E. (K-5); Louis Howe, Jr., D.R.E. (6-8). Students 230.
6—SACRED HEART (1925), Revs. Gerald Waterman, O.F.M.Conv.; Hilary Brzostowski, O.F.M.Conv.; Deacon John F. Esterheld. In Res., Rev. Thomas Gwozdz, O.F.M.Conv.
Res.: 12 Cottage St., 06810. Tel: 203-748-9029; Fax: 203-748-9168.
School—Tel: 203-792-6194. See separate listing under Elementary Schools, Regional in the Institution section.
Catechesis/Religious Program—Tel: 203-743-0689. Students 70.
Parish Center—46 Stone St., 06810. Tel: 203-743-6406.

DARIEN, FAIRFIELD CO.
1—ST. JOHN (1895), [CEM] Revs. Michael Jude Fay; Michael J. Madden; Deacon William K. Rowe. In Res., Rev. Msgr. Joseph J. Kohut (Retired).
Res.: 1986 Post Rd., 06820. Tel: 203-655-1145; Fax: 203-655-1048.
Catechesis/Religious Program—Tel: 203-655-8020. John Cunningham, D.R.E. Students 635.
2—ST. THOMAS MORE (1966), Revs. J. Barry Furey; Robert J. Post; Sr. Madeline McAdam, S.N.D., Pastoral Assoc.
Res.: 384 Middlesex Rd., 06820. Tel: 203-655-3303; Fax: 203-655-8901.
Catechesis/Religious Program—374 Middlesex Rd., 06820. Tel: 203-655-3077. Ms. Cornelia G. Dinnean, D.R.E. Lay Teachers 98; Students 970.
Convent—370 Middlesex Rd., 06820. Tel: 203-655-3580. Sisters of Notre Dame de Namur 1.

EASTON, FAIRFIELD CO., NOTRE DAME OF EASTON (1956), [CEM] Rev. Msgr. Thomas J. Driscoll, V.G.; Rev. Michael P. Lyons; Deacons Harold J. Lynch; Gerald F. Sabol.
Res.: 640 Morehouse Rd., 06612. Tel: 203-268-5838; Fax: 203-459-4940.
Church: 655 Morehouse Rd., 06612. Tel: 203-261-5596; Fax: 203-459-4940.
Catechesis/Religious Program—Tel: 203-261-5596; Fax: 203-459-4940. Students 523.

FAIRFIELD, FAIRFIELD CO.
1—ST. ANTHONY OF PADUA (1927), (Polish), [CEM] Rev. John P. Baran; Deacon Donald J. Ross.
Res.: 149 S. Pine Creek Rd., 06824. Tel: 203-259-0358; Fax: 203-259-5112.
Catechesis/Religious Program— Eleanor W. Sauers, D.R.E. Students 66.
2—ASSUMPTION (1922), [CEM] Rev. Msgr. Blase M. Gintoli; Revs. Frank Winn; Ernest T. Esposito, D.Min.
Res.: 545 Stratfield Rd., 06825. Tel: 203-333-9065; Fax: 203-333-2562.
School—Tel: 203-334-6271; Fax: 203-382-0399. See separate listing under Elementary Schools, Regional in the Institution section.
Catechesis/Religious Program—Tel: 203-367-1108; Fax: 203-367-0927. Frank Macari, D.R.E. Students 504.
Parish Center—605 Stratfield Rd., 06432. Tel: 203-336-3419.
3—ST. EMERY (1932), (Hungarian),, (United with St. Stephen's of Bridgeport 1897-1971) Rev. Louis M. Pintye, O.F.M. In Res., Rev. Emeric Szlezak, O.F.M.; Deacon Rudolph P. Trankovich.
Res.: 838 King's Hwy. E., 06825-5418. Tel: 203-334-0312; Fax: 203-579-9423. Email: SSEMERSTEP@aol.com.
Catechesis/Religious Program—108 Biro St., 06432. Tel: 203-335-4854. Students 80.
Convent—105 Biro St., 06825-5418. Tel: 203-334-3913. Congregation of Notre Dame 3.
4—HOLY CROSS (1913), (Slovenian), Rev. Milan Dimic, Admin.
Res.: 750 Tahmore Dr., 06825. Tel: 203-372-4595; Fax: 203-372-4668.
Catechesis/Religious Program—Tel: 203-373-0466. Students 117.
5—HOLY FAMILY (1938), Revs. Guido G. Montanaro; Henry J. Hoffman.
Res.: 700 Old Stratfield Rd., 06432. Tel: 203-336-1835; Fax: 203-336-0342.
School—Tel: 203-367-5409; Fax: 203-335-7317. See separate listing under Elementary Schools, Regional in the Institution section.
Catechesis/Religious Program—Tel: 203-579-4540. Stephen Sebestyen, D.R.E. Students 365.
Convent—70 Laurel St., 06432. Tel: 203-333-3423.
6—ST. PIUS X (1955), [CEM] Revs. Lawrence J. Carroll; Peter K. Smolik.
Res.: 834 Brookside Dr., 06824. Tel: 203-255-6134; Fax: 203-255-5232.
Catechesis/Religious Program—Tel: 203-259-4800; Fax: 203-255-5232. Students 479.
7—ST. THOMAS AQUINAS (1876), [CEM] Revs. Victor T. Martin; Christopher J. Samele; Deacon Daniel Ianniello; Sr. Catherine Leonard, C.N.D., Pastoral Asst.; Rev. Msgr. William J. Loughlin, Diocesan Pilgrimage Dir., (Retired).
Res.: 1719 Post Rd., 06824. Tel: 203-255-1097; Fax: 203-256-8177.
School—Tel: 203-255-0556; Fax: 203-255-0596. See separate listing under Elementary Schools, Regional in the Institution section.
Catechesis/Religious Program—Tel: 203-255-1984; Fax: 203-256-9305. Sr. Monica Leonard, C.N.D., D.R.E. Students 851.

GEORGETOWN, FAIRFIELD CO., SACRED HEART (1881), Revs. M. Joseph Joaquin; Mark E. Grimes.
Res.: 30 Church St., Box 388, 06829. Tel: 203-544-8345; Fax: 203-544-1246.
Catechesis/Religious Program—Tel: 203-544-8423. Students 275.

GREENWICH, FAIRFIELD CO.
1—ST. AGNES (1963), Rev. Stephen J. DeLuca.
Res.: 247 Stanwich Rd., 06830. Tel: 203-869-5396; Fax: 203-625-0596.
Catechesis/Religious Program—Students 74.
2—ST. MARY (1874), [CEM] Rev. Msgr. Frank C. Wissel, D.Min.; Revs. David A. Daigle; Richard J. Gemza; Deacons Matthew T. Ashe; Paul Tupper. In Res., Rev. German Martinez, O.S.B. (Spain).
Res.: 178 Greenwich Ave., 06830. Tel: 203-869-9393; Fax: 203-869-1032.
Catechesis/Religious Program—Tel: 203-869-9250; Fax: 203-625-4760. Sr. Patricia Wachter, S.S.N.D., D.R.E. Students 380.
3—ST. MICHAEL THE ARCHANGEL (1963), [CEM] Revs. Michael Robert Moynihan; William J. Kennedy, S.J.; Mark Connolly.
Res.: 469 North St., 06830. Tel: 203-869-5421; Fax: 203-869-0169.
Catechesis/Religious Program—Tel: 203-661-3088; Fax: 203-869-0169. Sr. Celine M. Flynn, S.S.N.D.,

D.R.E. Students 530.
Mission—St. Timothy's 469 North St., Fairfield Co. 06830. Tel: 203-869-5421; Fax: 203-869-0169.
4—ST. PAUL (1902), [CEM] Rev. William F. Platt; Deacon Wayne Malloy.
Res.: 84 Sherwood Ave., 06831. Tel: 203-531-8741; Fax: 203-532-1414.
Catechesis/Religious Program—Tel: 203-531-4265. Judy Mastoloni, D.R.E. Students 357.
5—ST. ROCH (1938), (Italian), Revs. Nicholas J. Calabro; Carlos Rodriques. In Res., Rev. Colin J. McKenna.
Catechesis/Religious Program—Jane Kowaleski, D.R.E. Students 144.
6—SACRED HEART (1890), [CEM] Rev. Martin S. Igoe.
Res.: 95 Henry St., 06830. Tel: 203-531-8730; Fax: 203-531-8794.
Catechesis/Religious Program—Tel: 203-531-4772. Joseph Mancusi, D.R.E. Students 150.

MONROE, FAIRFIELD CO., ST. JUDE (1973), Rev. Msgr. John B. Sabia; Rev. Joseph J. Karcsinski; Deacon Ian F. Black.
Res.: 707 Monroe Tpke., 06468. Tel: 203-261-6404; Fax: 203-261-7507.
School—Tel: 203-261-3619; Fax: 203-268-8748. See separate listing under Elementary Schools, Regional in the Institution section.
Catechesis/Religious Program—Tel: 203-261-6788. Mrs. Jean Paul, D.R.E. Students 1,868.

NEW CANAAN, FAIRFIELD CO., ST. ALOYSIUS (1896), Rev. Msgr. William J. Scheyd; Revs. Leszek P. Szymaszek; Samuel Martis; Deacons John H. Tugman; Joseph L. Rowan. In Res., Rev. William G. Carey.
Res.: 40 Maple St., 06840. Tel: 203-966-0020; Fax: 203-972-7691.
School—Tel: 203-966-0786; Fax: 203-972-6960. See separate listing under Elementary Schools, Regional in the Institution section.
Catechesis/Religious Program—30 Maple St., 06840. Tel: 203-966-4555; Fax: 203-801-0170. Students 1,100.

NEW FAIRFIELD, FAIRFIELD CO., ST. EDWARD THE CONFESSOR (1954), Rev. Msgr. Martin P. Ryan; Revs. Alfred Riendeau; Joseph Cervero; Deacons Henry Hein; David Vaughn. In Res., Rev. Brian M. Gray.
Res.: P.O. Box 8866, 06812. Tel: 203-746-2200; Fax: 203-746-4856.
Catechesis/Religious Program—Tel: 203-746-4270. Ms. Joan Marschall, D.R.E. Students 1,366.

NEWTOWN, FAIRFIELD CO., ST. ROSE OF LIMA (1859), [CEM] Revs. Robert E. Weiss; Milan Dimic; John J. Inserra; Deacons Thomas F. Curran; Donald Naiman.
Res.: 46 Church Hill Rd., 06470. Tel: 203-426-1014; Fax: 203-426-6222.
School—Tel: 203-426-5102; Fax: 203-426-5372. See separate listing under Elementary Schools, Regional in the Institution section.
Catechesis/Religious Program—Tel: 203-426-2333; Fax: 203-464-8074. Pam Arsenault, D.R.E. Students 1,685.

NORWALK, FAIRFIELD CO.
1—ST. JEROME (1960), [CEM] Revs. David W. Blanchfield; Joseph Palacino.
Church: 23 Half Mile Rd., 06851. Tel: 203-847-5349; Fax: 203-846-0238.
Catechesis/Religious Program—Tel: 203-846-2111. Students 468.
2—ST. JOSEPH (South Norwalk) (1895), Revs. David W. Howell; Gilbert P. D'Souza. In Res., Rev. G. Frantz Desruisseaux, J.C.L.; Deacon William O. Murphy.
Res.: 85 S. Main St., P.O. Box 443, 06856. Tel: 203-838-4171; Fax: 203-899-0007.
Catechesis/Religious Program—Tel 203-866-1225. Deacon William O. Murphy, D.R.E. Students 334.
Convent—14 Chestnut St., 06854. Tel: 203-866-9452.
3—ST. LADISLAUS (1907), (Hungarian), [CEM] Rev. Msgr. Edwin F. Burke. In Res., Rev. Stephen J. Balint.
Res.: 25 Cliff St., 06854. Tel: 203-866-1867; Fax: 203-866-7830.
Catechesis/Religious Program—Students 10.
4—ST. MARY (1848), [CEM] Revs. Gregory J. Huminski; Otoniel Lizcano; Deacon Stephan A. Genovese. In Res., Rev. Christopher J. Walsh, Ph.D.
Res.: 669 West Ave., 06850. Tel: 203-866-5546; Fax: 203-866-0464.
Catechesis/Religious Program—Tel: 203-866-7429; Fax: 203-866-0127. Mrs. Deborah Ruffin, D.R.E. Students 180.
5—ST. MATTHEW (1957), Revs. Walter C. Orlowski; Roy Henverson; Deacons David M. Sochacki; Mark T. Shine.
Res.: 216 Scribner Ave., 06854. Tel: 203-838-3788; Fax: 203-838-8195.
Catechesis/Religious Program—Tel: 203-838-0231. Virginia Codeanne, D.R.E. Students 608.
6—ST. PHILIP (1964), Rev. Michael A. Boccaccio; Sr. Mary Ann McPartland, C.N.D., Pastoral Assoc.; Deacons Frank J. Chiappetta; Paul J. Reilly.
Res.: One Fr. Conlon Pl., 06851. Tel: 203-847-4549 (Office); Fax: 203-847-4148.
Catechesis/Religious Program—Tel: 203-847-4286. Doris Chiappetta, D.R.E. Students 252.
7—ST. THOMAS THE APOSTLE (1935), Revs. Robert J. Crofut; Robert J. Boyd; Deacon Joseph Gagne.
Res.: 203 East Ave., 06855. Tel: 203-866-3141; Fax: 203-866-1219.
Malta House—5 Prowitt St., 06855. Tel: 203-857-0088; Fax: 203-857-0018.
Catechesis/Religious Program—Tel: 203-866-1189; Fax: 203-866-1219. Mrs. Patricia Postiglione, D.R.E. Students 371.

REDDING, FAIRFIELD CO., ST. PATRICK (1879), (Irish), Rev. Msgr. Russell Augustine; Deacon William C. Timmel.
Res.: 169 Black Rock Tpke., P.O. Box 119, Redding Ridge, 06876. Tel: 203-938-2253; Fax: 203-938-3396.
Catechesis/Religious Program—Tel: 203-938-2963. Roseann D' Aurelie, D.R.E. Students 175.

RIDGEFIELD, FAIRFIELD CO.
1—ST. ELIZABETH SETON (1976), Revs. Joseph A. Prince; David W. Franklin; Deacons Bart Mauceri; Terence Grant.
Res.: 520 Ridgebury Rd., 06877. Tel: 203-438-7292; Fax: 203-438-0600.
Catechesis/Religious Program—Tel: 203-438-9707; Fax: 203-438-7947. Carol Bates, D.R.E. Students 625.
2—ST. MARY (1882), [CEM] Rev. Msgr. Laurence R. Bronkiewicz, S.T.D., Pastor; Revs. Peter F. Lenox; Paul Murphy; Deacons Norman Roos; Frank Foyt.
Res.: 55 Catoonah St., P.O. Box 1109, 06877-4496. Tel: 203-438-6538; Fax: 203-438-4406.
School—Tel: 203-438-7288; Fax: 203-431-8742. See separate listing under Elementary Schools, Regional in the Institution Section.
Catechesis/Religious Program—Tel: 203-438-7335; Fax: 203-438-6876. Sr. Joan Brennan, D.R.E. Students 1,670.

RIVERSIDE, FAIRFIELD CO., ST. CATHERINE OF SIENA, Rev. Msgrs. William A. Genuario, P.A., J.C.D.; Alan F. Detscher; Rev. Marcel St. Jean; Deacons Renato Berzolla; Robert Henrey; Vincent Heidenreich.
Res.: 4 Riverside Ave., 06878. Tel: 203-637-3661; Fax: 203-637-8934.
Catechesis/Religious Program—6 Riverside Ave., 06878. Tel: 203-637-3661, Ext. 30; Fax: 203-637-2089. Barbara Glynn, D.R.E. Students 560.

SHELTON, FAIRFIELD CO.
1—ST. JOSEPH (1906), Revs. Francis T. Hoffmann; Jose Rebaque, S.A.C.; Joseph A. Marcello.
Res.: 50 Fairmont Pl., 06484. Tel: 203-924-8611; Fax: 203-924-9446.
School— See separate listing under Elementary Schools, Regional in the Institution section.
Catechesis/Religious Program—Tel: 203-924-9677. Mrs. Patricia Heller, D.R.E. Students 570.
Convent—Sisters of St. Joseph Chambery, 420 Coram Ave., 06484. Tel: 203-924-1545.
2—ST. LAWRENCE (1955), [CEM] Rev. Msgr. Joseph M. Fitzgerald; Revs. F. John Ringley; Nicholas A. Cirillo; Deacons James A. Brown; Joseph Filingeri; F. Robert Dwyer; Frank Masso.
Res.: 505 Shelton Ave., 06484. Tel 203-929-5355; Fax: 203-929-8939.
School—Tel: 203-929-4422; Fax: 203-929-3669. See separate listing under Elementary Schools, Regional in the Institution section.
Catechesis/Religious Program—Tel: 203-929-8421. Mrs. Barbara Pekar, D.R.E. Students 1,000.
3—ST. MARGARET MARY (1963), [CEM] Rev. Msgr. Thomas J. Whalen; Revs. Brian F Gannon; Nello Barachini; Deacon Matthew Skurat.
Res.: 380 Long Hill Ave., 06484. Tel: 203-924-4929; Fax 203-924-1849.
Catechesis/Religious Program—Tel: 203-924-2679. Mrs. Carol D'Amico, D.R.E. Students 370.

SHERMAN, FAIRFIELD CO., HOLY TRINITY (1985), [CEM] Rev Louis M. Dytkowski.
Res.: Rte. 37 & 39, P.O. Box 97, 06784. Tel: 860-354-1414; Fax: 860-355-9439.
Catechesis/Religious Program—Tel: 860-355-5189; Fax: 860-355-9439. Mrs. Karen Cardillo, D.R.E. Students 263.

STAMFORD, FAIRFIELD CO.
1—ST. BENEDICT (1930), (Slovak), Merged, with Our Lady of Montserrat, Stamford to form Saint Benedict and Our Lady of Montserrat, Stamford.
2—SAINT BENEDICT - OUR LADY OF MONTSERRAT (2000), [CEM] Rev. Gustavo A. Falla.
Mailing Address: One St. Benedict Cir., 06902. Tel: 203-327-7250; 203-323-7379; Fax: 203-323-0798.
Catechesis/Religious Program—Tel: 203-348-5531; Fax: 203-324-9638. Students 500.
3—ST. BRIDGET (1963), Rev. Gill C. Babeu.
Res.: 278 Strawberry Hill Ave., 06902. Tel: 203-324-2910; Fax: 203-363-0135.
Catechesis/Religious Program—Tel: 203-357-8157. Ms. Larrann Wilson, D.R.E. Students 130.
4—ST. CECILIA (1926), [CEM] Revs. David J. Riley; Richard D. Murphy.
Res.: 1184 Newfield Ave., 06905. Tel: 203-322-1562; Fax: 203-968-1550.
School—Tel: 203-322-6505; Fax: 203-322-6835. See separate listing under Elementary Schools, Regional in the Institution section.
Catechesis/Religious Program—Tel: 203-329-8783; Fax: 203-595-0519. Students 428.
5—ST. CLEMENT (1928), Rev. Joseph J. Malloy. In Res., Rev. Walter J. Seekamp.
Res.: 535 Fairfield Ave., 06902. Tel: 203-348-4206; Fax: 203-316-8131.
Catechesis/Religious Program—Tel: 203-348-1233; Fax: 203-316-8131. Students 208.
6—ST. GABRIEL (1963), Rev. Robert A. Uzzilio; Deacon Larry Buzzeo.
Res.: 914 Newfield Ave., 06905. Tel: 203-322-7426; Fax: 203-968-6266.
School— See separate listing under Elementary Schools, Regional in the Institution section.
Catechesis/Religious Program—Tel: 203-329-1978. Sr. Ann Marie Strileckis, C.N.D., D.R.E. Students 218.
7—HOLY NAME OF JESUS (1903), (Polish), Rev. Stanley Staniszewski, C.M., Temp. Admin.
Res.: 4 Pulaski St., 06902. Tel: 203-323-4967; Fax: 203-327-2229.
Catechesis/Religious Program—Tel: 203-359-3618; Fax: 203-323-4546. Sr. Donna Shatell, S.M.M.I., D.R.E. Students 187.
8—HOLY SPIRIT (1962), [CEM] Rev. Robert J. Hyl; Deacon Paul J. Jennings.
Res.: 403 Scofieldtown Rd., 06903-4009. Tel: 203-322-3722; Fax: 203-322-0543.
School—Tel: 203-329-1623; Fax: 203-595-0858. See separate listing under Elementary Schools, Regional in the Institution section.
Catechesis/Religious Program—Tel: 203-357-1094. Linda Dunn, D.R.E. Students 214.
9—ST. JOHN THE EVANGELIST (1854), [CEM] Rev. Msgr. Stephen M. Di Giovanni, H.E.D.; Rev. Paul N. Check.
Res.: 279 Atlantic St., 06901. Tel: 203-324-1553; Fax: 203-359-2660.
Catechesis/Religious Program—Students 124.
10—ST. LEO (1960), [CEM] Rev. Norman J. Guilbert, Admin.; Deacon Ralph Hammock.
Res.: 24 Roxbury Rd., 06902. Tel: 203-322-1669; 203-329-8884; Fax: 203-461-9761.
Catechesis/Religious Program—Tel: 203-348-0052; Fax: 203-357-9639. Mrs. Maureen Grosso, D.R.E. Students 556.
11—ST. MARY (1907), [CEM] Revs. Richard F. Futie, J.C.D.; Richard G. Cipolla; John Jairo Perez. In Res., Rev. Ciprian Bejan (Romania).
Res.: 566 Elm St., 06902. Tel: 203-324-7321; Fax: 203-323-9407.
Catechesis/Religious Program—Tel: 203-348-5196; Fax: 203-323-9401. Francesca Phillips, D.R.E. Students 305.
12—ST. MAURICE (1935), [CEM] Revs. Albert G. Pinciaro; Bernard A. Keefe.
Res.: 358 Glenbrook Rd., 06906-2198. Tel: 203-324-3434; Fax: 203-964-8023.
Catechesis/Religious Program—Tel: 203-348-8768; Fax: 203-964-8023. Janis Pataky, D.R.E. Students 198.
13—OUR LADY OF MONTSERRAT (1984), (Spanish), Merged, with St. Benedict, Stamford to form Saint Benedict and Our Lady of Montserrat, Stamford.
14—OUR LADY STAR OF THE SEA (1964), Rev. Msgr. Edward R. Surwilo. In Res., Rev. David H. Krahel.
Res.: 1200 Shippan Ave., 06902. Tel: 203-324-4634; Fax: 203-348-9963.
School— See separate listing under Elementary Schools, Regional in the Institution section.
Catechesis/Religious Program—Students 125.
Convent—1216 Shippan Ave., 06902. Tel: 203-359-1127.
15—SACRED HEART (1920), (Italian), [CEM] Revs. Robert G. Pohley; Alfred F. Pecaric; Rufin Kuveikis, O.F.M.Cap.; Carlos R. Rodrigues.
Res.: 37 Schuyler Ave., 06902. Tel: 203-324-9544; Fax: 203-324-9202.
School—Tel: 203-323-4844; Fax: 203-359-9859. See separate listing under Elementary Schools, Regional in the Institution section.
Catechesis/Religious Program—Tel: 203-323-3524. Students 175.
Convent—21 Schuyler Ave., 06902. Tel: 203-323-3524.

STRATFORD, FAIRFIELD CO.
1—HOLY NAME OF JESUS (1923), (Slovak), Rev. Msgrs. Peter P. Dora; Stanley Rousseau; J. James Cuneo, J.C.D.; Deacons Thomas Freibott; Michael Saranich.
Res.: 1950 Barnum Ave., 06614. Tel: 203-375-5815; Fax: 203-375-5954.

School— See separate listing under Elementary Schools, Regional in the Institution section.
Catechesis/Religious Program—Tel: 203-378-7407. Students 350.
Convent—2 Mary Ave., 06614. Tel: 203-378-1203.

2—ST. JAMES (1886), Revs. Thomas F. Lynch; Frank A. Winn; Gade Lourdu Marreddy; Deacon John Barton.
Res.: 2110 Main St., 06615. Tel: 203-375-5887; Fax: 203-378-1562.
School—Tel: 203-375-5994; Fax: 203-380-0749. See separate listing under Elementary Schools, Regional in the Institution section.
Catechesis/Religious Program—Therese LeFever, D.R.E. Students 530.

3—ST. MARK (1960), Revs. Donald A. Guglielmi, S.T.D.; Martin P. deMayo; Deacons T. Emmet Murray; F. Paul Kurmay; Andrew Dzujna.
Res.: 500 Wigwam Ln., 06614. Tel: 203-377-0444; Fax: 203-378-7913.
School—Tel: 203-375-4291; Fax: 203-375-4833. See separate listing under Elementary Schools, Regional in the Institution section.
Catechesis/Religious Program—Tel: 203-377-3158. Mr. Jon Ribeiro, D.R.E. Students 558.

4—OUR LADY OF GRACE (1954), [CEM] Rev. Msgr. William F. Schultz; Rev. Edward J. Small, S.J. In Res., Rev. Msgr. Jerald A. Doyle, Ph.D., J.C.D.; Deacon Robert W. McLaughlin.
Res.: 497 Second Hill Ln., 06614-2595. Tel: 203-377-0928; Fax: 203-377-5235.
Parish Center—345 Second Hill Ln., 06614-2595. Tel: 203-375-2005; 203-375-6610 (Preschool).
Catechesis/Religious Program—Tel: 203-375-6133. Mrs. Denise L. Bartelson, D.R.E. Students 283.

5—OUR LADY OF PEACE (1948), Rev. Msgr. John E. Gilmartin. In Res., Rev. Frank C. McGrath.
Res.: 230 Park Blvd., 06615. Tel: 203-377-4863; Fax: 203-378-5253.
Catechesis/Religious Program—Tel: 203-378-3053. Sr. Carolyn Stoe, S.S.N.D., D.R.E. Students 127.

TRUMBULL, FAIRFIELD CO.

1—ST. CATHERINE OF SIENA (1955), [CEM] Rev. Msgr. Richard J. Shea; Rev. Peter A. DeMarco. In Res., Rev. Peter J. Lynch.
Res.: 200 Shelton Rd., 06611. Tel: 203-377-3133; Fax: 203-377-1023.
School—Tel: 203-375-1947; Fax: 203-378-3935. See separate listing under Elementary Schools, Regional in the Institution section.
Catechesis/Religious Program—Tel: 203-377-3133, Ext. 22. Students 550.
Convent—110 Shelton Rd., 06611. Tel: 203-386-0267.

2—CHRIST THE KING (1962), [CEM] Revs. Bernard M. Dolan; Lawrence F. Carew; Deacon Frederick A. Harrity.
Res.: 4700 Madison Ave., 06611. Tel: 203-268-8695; Fax: 203-268-9265.
Catechesis/Religious Program—Tel: 203-261-2583. Students 512.

3—ST. STEPHEN (1953), Revs. Stephen J. Gleeson; Nicholas S. Pavia; Edward A. Colohan; Deacons Gary Carpenter; Michael Wolfer; Timothy Sullivan.
Res.: 6948 Main St., 06611-1340. Tel: 203-268-6217; Fax: 203-268-9861.
Catechesis/Religious Program—Tel: 203-268-6860. Deacon Timothy Sullivan, D.R.E. Students 566.

4—ST. THERESA (1934), [CEM] Rev. Msgr. Peter P. Dora; Revs. Joseph C. Linck; Bose Raja Selvaraj; Sr. Joan Flynn, R.S.M., Dir. Pastoral Min.; Deacons H. Paul Herman; Salvatore Clarizio, Ph.D. In Res., Rev. William F. Sangiovanni.
Res.: 5301 Main St., 06611. Tel: 203-261-3676; Fax: 203-268-8723.
School—Tel: 203-268-3236. See separate listing under Elementary Schools, Regional in the Institution section.
Catechesis/Religious Program—19 Rosemond Ter., 06611. Tel: 203-261-4706. Sr. Georgiana Miller, S.M.M.I., D.R.E. Students 1,005.
Convent—Tel: 203-261-3848. Sisters Minor of Mary Immaculate 3.

WESTON, FAIRFIELD CO., ST. FRANCIS OF ASSISI (1955), Rev. Msgr. Nicholas V. Grieco. In Res., Rev. Joseph K. Parampath, J.C.D.
Res.: 35 Norfield Rd, P.O. Box 1025, 06883. Tel: 203-227-1341; Fax: 203-226-1154.
Catechesis/Religious Program—Tel: 203-226-9474. Students 460.

WESTPORT, FAIRFIELD CO.

1—ASSUMPTION (1876), [CEM] Revs. Thomas P. Thorne; Lawrence A. Larson; Deacon John S. Fay. In Res., Rev. Msgr. Benedict F. Tighe.
Res.: 98 Riverside Ave., 06880. Tel: 203-227-5161; Fax: 203-227-1206.
Catechesis/Religious Program—Tel: 203-226-5448; Fax: 203-227-1209. Cathy Romano, D.R.E. Students 264.

2—ST. LUKE (1957), Revs. Andrew G. Varga; Gregg D. Mecca; Deacons Brian J. Kelly; Lance C. Fredricks.
Res.: 84 Long Lots Rd., 06880. Tel: 203-227-7245; Fax: 203-226-8063.
Catechesis/Religious Program—Tel: 203-226-0729; Fax: 203-226-5446. Deacon Lance C. Fredricks, D.R.E. Students 721.

WILTON, FAIRFIELD CO., OUR LADY OF FATIMA (1953), Revs. Michael C. Palmer; James C. Vattakunnel; Deacons Thomas K. Seith; Thomas J. McManus.
Res.: 229 Danbury Rd., 06897. Tel: 203-762-3928; Fax: 203-834-1261.
School—Tel: 203-762-8100; Fax: 203-834-0614. See separate listing under Elementary Schools, Regional in the Institution section.
Catechesis/Religious Program—Tel: 203-762-9080. Mrs. Kathleen Rooney, D.R.E. Students 1,382.

Chaplains of Public Institutions

BRIDGEPORT. *Bridgeport Community Correctional Facility*, 1106 North Ave., 06604. Tel: 203-579-6131. Deacon Carl M. Vecca. Tel: 203-582-6477.
Bridgeport Health Care, 600 Bond St., 06610. Tel: 203-384-6400. Rev. Michael A. D'Elia.
Bridgeport Hospital, 267 Grant St., 06610. Tel: 203-384-3311. Revs. Nello A. Barachini, C.M., Bernardo C. Rodriguez.

DANBURY. *Danbury Area Mental Health Authority*, 64 West St., 06810. Tel: 203-778-1640, Ext. 247. Vacant.
Danbury Hospital, 24 Hospital Ave., 06810. Tel: 203-797-7000. Revs. John F. Pikulski, Ph.D., Brian M. Gray.
Federal Correctional Institution 06811. Tel: 203-743-6471. Sr. Anne Marie Raftery, O.S.F., Dir. of Pastoral Care.

GREENWICH. *Greenwich Hospital* 06830. Tel: 203-863-3000. Revs. William F. Platt, David W. Franklin.

NORWALK. *Norwalk Hospital* 06856. Tel: 203-852-2000. Rev. Rufin Kuveikis, O.F.M.Cap.

STAMFORD. *Stamford Hospital* 06902. Tel: 203-325-7584. Rev. David W. Franklin.

On Duty Outside the Diocese:
Rev. Msgrs.—
Cusack, Andrew T., Ph.D., Dir. National Institute for Clergy Formation, Seton Hall University, 400 S. Orange Ave., South Orange, NJ 07079.
Green, Thomas J., J.C.D., Catholic University of America, Dept. of Canon Law, Washington, DC 20017.
Millea, William V., Via della Nocetta 63, Rome 00164 Italy.
Revs.—
Holbrook, Harold M., Padres de Santiago Apostol, Casilla 1021, Oruro, Bolivia.
Loftus, Robert A., St. Ann Rectory, 130 Boston Tpke., Shewsbury, PA 01545.
McDevitt, James A., St. Ann, 1220 Northway Rd., Williamsport, PA 17701.
McDonough, Roger F., St. Joan of Arc, 370 S.W. Third St., Boca Raton, FL 33432.
Mitchell, John C., P.O. Box 701, Carmel, NY 10072.
Posluszny, Francis, Parroquia San Juan Apostal, APTO 735, Chiclayo, Peru.
Smolko, John F., Catholic University of America, 9808 Dale Dr., Upper Marlboro, MD 20870.
Talar, Charles J.T., St. Mary Seminary & University, 5400 Roland Rd., Baltimore, MD 21210.
Terentieff, Robert J., Georgian Court College, 900 Lakewood Ave., Lakewood, NJ 08701.
Tracy, David W., University of Chicago, The Divinity School, 5521 S. University, Chicago, IL 60637.
Verrilli, William F., St. Mary Church, 520 Veirs Mill Rd., Rockville, MD 20852.

Graduate Studies:
Rev.—
Jones, Michael K.

Military Chaplains:
Revs.—
Carey, William F., U.S. Army
Gay, James A., U.S. Navy
Thompson, William D., U.S. Air Force

Leave of Absence:
Revs.—
Griffin, Paul D.
Hudanish, Jeffrey A.
Moore, Joseph P.
Yocis, David A.

Retired:
Rev. Msgrs.—
Botton, Pierre A.
Caldas, Constantino R.
Horgan-Kung, John V.
Jazowski, John F.
Kohut, Joseph J.
Laurello, Bartholomew J.
Medynski, Francis J.
Nagle, William A.
Potter, Joseph D.
Sanders, John C.
Scanlon, Bernard S.
Watts, Roger J.
Revs.—
Brady, Philip W.
Coyne, Edwin J.
Dennehy, Martin J.
Fernandez, Jose A.
Gregori, Emidio O.
Grise, J. Clifford
Hitchcock, Martin B.
Hribsek, Aloysius J.
Knurek, Dennis A.
Monahan, Richard J.
Morrissey, Philip T.
Onze, Robert E.
Rarus, Boleslaus J.
Rossitto, Joseph V.
Suwinski, Leo S.
Usenza, Robert J.

Permanent Deacons:
Africot, Alix, St. Patrick, Bridgeport
Ashe, Matthew, St. Mary, Greenwich
Barton, Jack, St. James, Stratford
Berzolla, Renato L., St. Catherine, Riverside
Bissenden, William J., St. Patrick, Bridgeport
Black, Ian F., St. Jude, Monroe
Blankschen, Robert, St. Gregory, Danbury
Blier, Roland, St. Andrew, Bridgeport
Brown, James, St. Lawrence, Huntington
Brunetto, Donald W., St. Stephen, Trumbull
Buzzeo, Michael L., St. Gabriel, Stamford
Cabral, Jose R., Immaculate Heart of Mary, Danbury
Calabrese, Robert P., St. Anthony Maronite, Danbury
Carpenter, Gary E., St. Stephen, Trumbull
Chiappetta, Frank, St. Philip, Norwalk
Clarizio, Salvatore, St. Theresa, Trumbull
Curran, Thomas F., St. Rose, Newtown
Detje, Anthony, St. Edward the Confessor, New Fairfield
Dwyer, F. Robert, St. Joseph, Shelton
Dzujna, Andrew W., St. Mark, Stratford
Esterheld, John, Sacred Heart, Danbury
Farley, Joseph J., St. Leo, Stamford
Fay, John S., Assumption, Westport
Filingeri, Joseph, St. Lawrence, Huntington
Finch, Dean, St. Jerome, Norwalk
Foust, Donald P., Blessed Sacrament, Bridgeport
Fredricks, Lance C., St. Luke, Westport
Freibott, Thomas, Holy Name, Stratford
Gagne, Joseph, St. Thomas, Fairfield
Garcia, Santos, Florida
Genovese, Stephan, St. Mary, Norwalk
Grant, Terence J., St. Elizabeth Seton, Ridgefield
Hammock, Ralph, St. Leo, Stamford
Harrity, Frederick A., Sacred Heart, Stamford
Heidenreich, Vincent, St. Catherine, Riverside
Hein, Henry R., St. Edward, New Fairfield
Hendricks, Edward R., St. Andrew, Bridgeport
Henrey, Robert, St. Catherine of Siena, Riverside
Herman, H. Paul, St. Teresa, Trumbull
Howe, Louis F., Sacred Heart, Stamford
Ianniello, Daniel, Holy Rosary, Bridgeport
Isidro, Ramon, Our Lady of Montserrat, Stamford
Kamper, Eugene P., Assumption, Westport
Kelly, Brian J., St. Luke, Westport
Kovacs, Richard, St. Joseph, Brookfield
Kuhn, Peter, St. Joseph, Brookfield
Kurmay, Paul, St. Mark, Stratford
Lynch, Harold, Notre Dame, Easton
Mack, D. Thomas, St. Stephen, Trumbull
Mann, John J., Our Lady Star of the Sea, Stamford
Martinez, Ricardo, Blessed Sacrament, Bridgeport
Masso, Frank J., St. Lawrence, Huntington
Mauceri, Bartholomew, St. Elizabeth Seton, Ridgefield
McLaughlin, Robert, Our Lady of Grace, Stratford
McMarcus, Thomas, Our Lady of Fatima, Wilton
Melita, Joseph, St. Raphael, Bridgeport
Moore, Kevin, Holy Cross, Fairfield
Moranski, John J., St. Ann, Bridgeport
Munson, David D., St. Joseph, Shelton
Murphy, William O., St. Joseph, Norwalk
Murphy, William D., St. Gregory the Great, Danbury
Murray, Emmet, St. Mark, Stratford
Myott, Daniel N., St. Gregory the Great, Danbury
Naiman, Donald, St. Gregory, Danbury
Nelson, Thomas E., Marguerite Bourgeoys, Brookfield
Pereira, Gabriel, Our Lady of Fatima, Bridgeport
Pilkington, Paul, St. Edward, New Fairfield
Pratt, Nicholas, St. Ann, Bridgeport
Reilly, Paul, St. Philip, Norwalk
Reveron, Domingo, St. Peter, Bridgeport

Ross, Donald J., Assumption, Fairfield
Ross, Norman, St. Mary, Ridgefield
Rowan, Joseph L., St. Thomas More, Darien
Rowe, William K., St. John, Darien
Sabol, Gerald, Notre Dame, Easton
Saymon, Richard F., Leave of Absence
Sebestyen, Stephen, Holy Family, Fairfield
Seith, Thomas K., Our Lady of Fatima, Wilton
Shaughnessy, William, St. Joseph, Brookfield
Shine, Mark, St. Matthew, Norwalk
Skurat, Matthew, St. Margaret Mary, Shelton
Sochacki, David, St. Matthew, Norwalk
Stenberg, S. Richard, St. Pius X, Fairfield
Stroud, Kenneth, St. Rose, Newtown
Sullivan, Timothy, St. Augustine Cathedral, Bridgeport
Timmel, William C., St. Patrick, Redding
Torres, Luis, St. Peter, Bridgeport
Tugman, John H., St. Aloysius, New Canaan
Tupper, Paul, St. Clement, Stamford
Vaughn, David J., St. Joseph, Danbury
Volpe, James, St. Ambrose, Bridgeport
Wolfer, Michael K., St. Stephen, Trumbull

INSTITUTIONS LOCATED IN THE DIOCESE

[A] SEMINARIES, DIOCESAN

STAMFORD. *St. John Fisher Seminary Residence*, 894 Newfield Ave., 06905. Tel: 203-322-5331; Fax: 203-461-9876. Email: info@saintjohnfisher.org. Web: www.saintjohnfisher.org. Revs. Kevin T. Royal, S.T.L., Rector; Thomas W. Powers, S.T.L., Spiritual Dir.; Christopher J. Walsh, Ph.D., Vocation Dir. Priests 3; Deacons 1; Lay Teachers 6; Lay Staff 4.

[B] COLLEGES AND UNIVERSITIES

BRIDGEPORT. *St. Vincent's College*, 2800 Main St., 06606. Tel: 203-576-5235; Fax: 203-576-5893. Email: dbrooks@stvincentscollege.edu. Web: www.stvincentscollege.edu. Anne T. Avallone, Ed.D., Pres.; Joanne R. Wolfertz, Vice Pres. Dean; Robert S. Trojanowski, M.B.A., J.D., CFO; Janice Nolan Faye, Dir. Admin. Svcs.; Joseph Macionus, M.P.A., Registrar; Anita K. McCain, Ed.D., Assoc. Dean of Academic Svcs.; Mary L. Rich, Financial Aid Dir.; Joan McTaggart Kayser, B.A., Dir. of Admissions & Mktg. Lay Teachers 12; Students 345.

FAIRFIELD. **Fairfield University* (Coed) , 1073 N. Benson Rd., 06824-5195. Tel: 203-254-4000; Fax: 203-254-4101. Email: pfitzpatrick@mail.fairfield.edu. Web: www.fairfield.edu. Very Rev. Aloysius P. Kelley, S.J., Pres.; Revs. John J. Higgins, S.J., Rector; James M. Bowler, S.J., Facilitator Catholic Jesuit Mission & Identity; Charles H. Allen, S.J., Exec. Asst. to Pres.; Dr. Orin L. Grossman, Academic Vice Pres.; Mr. Robert C. Russo, Univ. Registrar; Mr. Mark J. Guglielmoni, Dir. Human Resources; Rev. W. Laurence O'Neil, S.J., Dir. Student Support Svcs.; Dr. Norman A. Solomon, Dean Dolan School of Business; Dr. Jeanne M. Novotny, Dean School of Nursing; Dr. Timothy L. Snyder, Dean of Arts & Sciences; Dr. Evangelos Hadjimichael, Dean School of Engineering; Dr. Edna Wilson, Dean of University College; Dr. Margaret Deignan, Dean of Graduate School of Education & Allied Professions; Dr. Debnam Chappell, Dean of Freshmen; Ms. Marianne Gumpper, Interim Dir. Admissions; Mrs. Susan Kadir, Dir. Financial Aid; Mr. James Estrada, Vice Pres. Information Resources & Svcs. and Univ. Librarian; Mr. William P. Schimpf, Vice Pres. Student Svcs.; Mr. Mark C. Reed, Dean of Students; Ms. Martha Milcarek, Asst. Vice Pres., Public Rels.; Mr. James D. Fitzpatrick, Asst. Vice Pres. Students Svcs. Operations; Dr. Susan Birge, Asst. Vice Pres. Student Resources; Mr. Matthew Dinnan, Assoc. Dean of Students & Dir. Univ. Activities; Rev. Paul E. Carrier, S.J., Univ. Chap.; Ms. Carolyn Rusiackas, Assoc. Univ. Chap.; Rev. Terrence P. Devino, Assoc. Univ. Chap.; Mr. George E. Diffley, Vice Pres. Advancement; Ms. Janet Canepa, Dir. Alumni Rels.; Mr. Fredric Wheeler, Assoc. Vice Pres. Devel.; Mr. William J. Lucas, Vice Pres. Finance; Mr. Michael S. Maccarone, Assoc. Vice Pres. Finance; Mr. Kenneth R. Fontaine, Controller; Revs. Francis T. Hannafey, S.J.; Mark D. MacGregor, S.J.; John W. Elder, S.J.; Joseph F. MacDonnell, S.J.; James J. Mayzik, S.J. The Society of Jesus. College of Arts and Sciences; Dolan School of Business; University College; School of Nursing; School of Engineering; Graduate School of Education & Allied Professions; Graduate Program in Financial Management; Graduate Program in Nursing; Masters in Business Administration; Graduate Programs in Engineering and Masters in American Studies and Mathematics.; (See separate listing for Fairfield College Prep). Jesuits 12; Priests 5; Sisters 1; Lay Teachers 216; Students 5,023.

**Sacred Heart University*, 5151 Park Ave., 06432-1000. Tel: 203-371-7900; Fax: 203-365-7652. Email: weldonj@sacredheart.edu. Web: www.sacredheart.edu. Dr. Anthony J. Cernera, Pres.; Dr. Thomas Forget, Vice Pres. for Academic Affairs; Dr. Donna Dodge, S.C., Vice Pres. Mission & Planning; Mr. James M. Barquinero, Vice Pres. Enrollment Planning & Student Affairs; Dr. Paul K. Madonna, Vice Pres. Admin. & Finance. Coeducational and Comprehensive University. Courses offered year round, day & evening. Priests 2; Sisters 2; Deacons 1; Lay Teachers 429; Students 5,786.

[C] HIGH SCHOOLS, DIOCESAN

BRIDGEPORT. *Kolbe-Cathedral High School*, 33 Calhoun Pl., 06604. Tel: 203-335-2554; Fax: 203-335-2556. Email: cougars@kolbecaths.com. Web: www.kolbecaths.com. Mrs. Jo Anne Jakab, Prin.; Mr. Philip Broadhurst, Asst. Prin.; Sr. Karen Kane, S.S.N.D., Asst. Prin.; Rev. Hernan D. Bohorquez, Spiritual Dir. Priests 1; Sisters 1; Lay Teachers 23; Administrators 3; Students 300.

DANBURY. *Immaculate High School*, 73 Southern Blvd., 06810. Tel: 203-744-1510; Fax: 203-744-1275. Email: immacula@mail1.NAI.NET. Web: www.immaculatehs.org. Dr. Joseph Gerics, Prin.; Mr. Richard T. Stoops, Asst. Prin.; Rev. Corey V. Piccinino Spiritual Dir. & Asst. Prin. Priests 2; Lay Teachers 28; Students 423.

FAIRFIELD. *Notre Dame Catholic High School*, 220 Jefferson St., 06825. Tel: 203-372-6521; Fax: 203-374-0387. Email: info@notredame.org. Web: www.notredame.org. Rev. William F. Sangiovanni, Prin.; Mr. Carl Philipp, Asst. Prin. Priests 2; Lay Teachers 46; Students 650.

STAMFORD. *Trinity Catholic High School*, 926 Newfield Ave., 06905. Tel: 203-322-3401; Fax: 203-322-5330. Email: TCHS1@JUNO.COM. Web: www.trinitycatholic.org. Kevin Burke, Pres.; Robert D'Aquila, Prin.; Robert Chomiak, Asst. Prin.; Mrs. Connie McGoldrick, Admissions Coord.; Rev. Thomas Powers, Spiritual Dir.; Mr. Tracy Nichols, Athletic Dir.; Mrs. Mary D'Aquila, Reach Out. (Formerly Stamford Catholic High School) Records for Central Catholic High School, Norwich, and St. Mary's High School, Greenwich, located at Trinity. Priests 2; Lay Teachers 31; Students 414.

TRUMBULL. *St. Joseph High School*, 2320 Huntington Tpke., 06611-5099. Tel: 203-378-9378; Fax: 203-378-7306. Email: rbishop@sjhs.put.K12.ct.us. Web: www.sjhs.pvt.k12.ct.us. Richard A. Bishop, Pres.; Matthew R. Kenney, Ph.D., Prin.; Mrs. Laurene Collins, Asst. Prin.; Mrs. Suzanne Siano, Dir. Guidance; Rev. Peter J. Lynch, Spiritual Dir.; Mr. James Olayos Esq., Dir. Athletics; Mrs. Jackie Carlino, Dir. Devel.; Mrs. Maureen Anderson, Coord Student Activities; Mr. Kenneth Mayo, Dean of Students; Patricia Hayes, Ph.D., Dean of Students; Mrs. Margaret Marino, Admissions Dir.; Katherine Duerr, Dir. Campus Min.; Mr. Gerald DeForge, Registrar; Mrs. Doreen Rafferty, Bursar. Priests 1; Lay Teachers 59; Students 845.

[D] SPECIAL SCHOOLS, DIOCESAN

BRIDGEPORT. *St. Catherine Academy*, (Grades K-12), 238 Jewett Ave., 06606-2892. Tel: 203-372-1623; Fax: 203-373-0571. Email: srmuldoon@diobpt.org. Sr. Marilyn Muldoon, O.S.U., Prin. & Admin. Lay Teachers 3; Students 12.

[E] HIGH SCHOOLS, PRIVATE

FAIRFIELD. *Fairfield College Preparatory School*, 1073 N. Benson Rd., 06824. Tel: 203-254-4200; Fax: 203-254-4108. Email: raperrotta@campus.Fairfield.edu. Web: www.prep.fairfield.edu. Very Rev. Aloysius P. Kelley, S.J., Pres. Fairfield Univ. Revs. Michael Boughton, S.J., Pres.; Donald M. Barry, S.J.; William J. Eagan, S.J.; James J. Hederman, S.J.; George A. Gallarelli, S.J.; Walter R. Pelletier, S.J.; Ronald V. Perry, S.J.; Lawrence D. Ryan, S.J.; Martin G. Shaughnessy, S.J. Society of Jesus of New England, A preparatory day school for boys, established in 1942. Priests 10; Lay Teachers 62; Students 899.

STAMFORD. *Sacred Heart Academy of Stamford*, 200 Strawberry Hill Ave., 06902-2589. Tel: 203-323-3173; Fax: 203-975-7804. Email: sha200adm@aol.com. Web: www.shastamford.org. Sr. Jeanne Paolella, C.S.J., Prin. Sisters of St. Joseph Sisters 4; Lay Teachers 17; Students 126.

[F] ELEMENTARY SCHOOLS, REGIONAL

BRIDGEPORT. *Catholic Elementary Schools-Region X*, The Catholic Center, 238 Jewett Ave., 06606. Tel: 203-372-4301, Ext. 233; Fax: 203-372-0020. Email: rgaits@bless.com. Mr. Robert E. Gaits, Business Mgr.

St. Ambrose (Grades PreK-8), 461 Mill Hill Ave., 06610. Tel: 203-368-2835; Fax: 203-366-0599. Sr. Catherine Van Houten, S.S.J., Prin. Servants of the Immaculate of Mary 3; Lay Teachers 15; Students 313.

St. Andrew (Grades K-8), 395 Anton St., 06606. Tel: 203-372-4819; Fax: 203-373-0641. Mr. Michael Fettig, Prin. Lay Teachers 10; Students 215.

St. Ann (Grades PreK-8), 521 Brewster St., 06605. Tel: 203-334-5856; Fax: 203-333-8263. Mrs. Maria O'Neill, Prin. Daughters of the Holy Spirit 1; School Sisters of Notre Dame 1; Lay Teachers 11; Students 186.

St. Augustine Cathedral (Grades PreK-8), 63 Pequonnock St., 06604. Tel: 203-367-5896; Fax: 203-333-6694. Mrs. Barbara A. Coscio, Prin. Lay Teachers 13; Students 174.

St. Peter (Grades K-8), 659 Beechwood Ave., 06605. Tel: 203-333-2048; Fax: 203-333-2878. Miss Suzanna Zello, Prin. Sisters of the Company of the Savior 2; Lay Teachers 7; Students 192.

St. Raphael (Grades PreK-8), 324 Frank St., 06604. Tel: 203-333-6818; Fax: 203-336-9205. Sr. Kathleen Mary Coonan, A.S.C.J., Prin. Apostles of the Sacred Heart 2; Lay Teachers 10; Students 205.

DANBURY. *Catholic Elementary Schools-Region IX and XI*, Business Office, 3 Tammany Tr., 06811. Tel: 203-744-6248; Fax: 203-748-7603. Email: regionsixandxi@aol.com. Linda Barbosa, Business Mgr.

Region IX Tel: 203-744-6248; Fax: 203-748-7603. Rev. Msgr. Martin P. Ryan.

St. Gregory the Great (Grades K-8), 85 Great Plain Rd., 06811. Tel: 203-748-1217; Fax: 203-748-1217. Sr. Mary John O'Rourke, O.S.U., Prin. Lay Teachers 11; Students 259.

St. Joseph (Grades K-8), 370 Main St., 06810. Tel: 203-748-6615; Fax: 203-748-6508. Mrs. Sharon Quish, Prin. Lay Teachers 13; Students 259.

St. Peter (Grades K-8), 98 Main St., 06810. Tel: 203-748-2895; Fax: 203-748-5684. Mrs. Josephine P. Ferry, Prin. Lay Teachers 11; Students 178.

Sacred Heart (Grades K-8), 17 Cottage St., 06810. Tel: 203-792-6194; Fax: 203-778-4025. Email: shschool@snet.net. Web: www.danbury.org. Mary McCormack, Prin. Lay Teachers 10; Students 140.

Region XI Tel: 203-744-6248; Fax: 203-748-7603.

St. Mary (Grades K-8), 24 Dodgingtown Rd., Bethel, 06801. Tel: 203-744-2922; Fax: 203-798-8803. Sr. Anne McCarthy, Prin. Lay Teachers 9; Students 231.

St. Joseph (Grades K-8), Rte. 133, Brookfield, 06804. Tel: 203-775-2774; Fax: 203-775-5810. Mrs. Judith Shivy, Prin. Lay Teachers 9; Students 223.

St. Rose (Grades K-8), 40 Church Hill Rd., Newtown, 06470. Tel: 203-426-5102; Fax: 203-426-5374. Mrs. Mary Maloney, Prin. Lay Teachers 12; Students 227.

FAIRFIELD. *Catholic Elementary Schools-Region V*, 108 Biro St., P.O. Box 320358, 06825. Tel: 203-334-6327; Fax: 203-334-6497. Email: FERCSjec@aol.com. Mrs. Jean Correa, Business Mgr.

Holy Family (Grades PreK-8), Edison Ave., 06825. Tel: 203-367-5409; Fax: 203-335-7317. Mr. Larry Fitzgerald. Lay Teachers 14; Students 222.

Our Lady of the Assumption (Grades PreK-8), 591 Stratfield Rd., 06825. Tel: 203-334-6271; Fax: 203-334-1374. Ms. Gerri Desio, Prin. Augustinian Brothers 1; Lay Teachers 20; Students 261.

St. Thomas Aquinas (Grades PreK-8), 1719 Post Rd., 06824. Tel: 203-255-0556; Fax: 203-255-0596. Mrs. Mary Frances King, Prin. Lay Teachers 22; Students 439.

GREENWICH. *Greenwich Elementary Schools-Region I*

Greenwich Catholic School, 471 North St., 06830. Tel: 203-869-4000; Fax: 203-869-3405. Email: Greencath@aol.com info@greenwichcatholicschool.org. Web: www.greenwichcatholic.com. Mrs. Mary Flume, Business Mgr.; Mrs. Genevieve Madonna, Prin. Lay Teachers 35; Students 464.

NORWALK. *Catholic Elementary Schools-Region III*, All Saints Catholic School, 139 W. Rocks Rd., 06851. Tel: 203-847-3881. Email: ascnor@1stconnect.com. Web: www.ascs.net. Mrs. Patricia Stapleton, Business Mgr.

All Saints Catholic Elementary School (Grades Day Care-8), 139 W. Rocks Rd., 06851. Tel: 203-847-3881; Fax: 203-847-8055. Sr. Catherine Sheehy, R.S.M., Prin. Priests 1; Sisters 3; Lay Teachers 51; Students 876.

SHELTON. *Catholic Elementary Schools-Region VIII*

St. Lawrence Rectory/Shelton Catholic Regional School, 505 Shelton Ave., 06484. Tel: 203-924-4754;

Fax: 203-922-0161. Email: jsimpson@diobpt.org. Mrs. Joanne Simpson, Business Mgr.

St. Joseph (Grades PreK-8), 430 Coram Ave., 06484. Tel: 203-924-4669; Fax: 203-922-0161. Email: stjoseph.school@snet.net. Mrs. Cheryl Nelson, Prin. Lay Teachers 15; Students 324.

St. Lawrence (Grades PreK-8), 503 Shelton Ave., 06484. Tel: 203-929-4422; Fax: 203-929-3669. Email: Stlawrence.school@snet.net. Web: ctschools.net/stlawrenceschool. Mrs. Mary O'Connor, Prin. Sisters 1; Lay Teachers 11; Students 267.

STAMFORD. *Catholic Elementary Schools-Region II*, Catholic Regional School System, Inc., 926 Newfield Ave., P.O. Box 3127, 06905-0127. Tel: 203-968-2795; Fax: 203-968-8974. Email: kkcarty@crs-ct.org. Web: CRS-CT.Org. Mrs. Kathleen K. Carty, Business Mgr.

St. Aloysius (Grades K-8), 33 South Ave., New Canaan, 06840. Tel: 203-966-0786; Fax: 203-972-6960. Email: drwilcox@diobpt.org. Suzanne Dale Wilcox, Prin. Lay Teachers 17; Students 192.

Holy Spirit (Grades PreK-5), 403 Scofieldtown Rd., 06903. Tel: 203-329-1623; Fax: 203-595-0858. Email: drliotta@diobpt.org. Alfred Liotta, Prin. Lay Teachers 14; Students 145.

Our Lady Star of the Sea (Grades PreK-5), 1170 Shippan Ave., 06903. Tel: 203-348-1155; Fax: 203-324-6150. Email: gryanols@optonline.net. Mrs. Gail Ryan, Prin. Lay Teachers 9; Students 109.

Sacred Heart (Grades K-8), One Schuyler Ave., 06902. Tel: 203-323-4844; Fax: 203-359-9859. Email: pietrinash@aol.com. Sr. Pietrina Mazzola, M.P.F., Prin. Religious Teachers Filippini 2; Lay Teachers 11; Students 137.

St. Cecilia (Grades PreK-5), 1186 Newfield Ave., 06903. Tel: 203-322-6505; Fax: 203-322-6835. Email: jborcsc@aol.com. Mrs. Joann Borchetta, Prin. Sisters 1; Lay Teachers 18; Students 314.

St. Gabriel (Grades 6-8), 948 Newfield Ave., 06905. Tel: 203-322-7383; Fax: 203-322-4435. Email: rcavsg@juno.com. Mr. Robert J. Cavaliero, Prin. Religious 1; Lay Teachers 23; Students 213.

STRATFORD. *Catholic Elementary Schools-Region VI*, Stratford Catholic Regional School, St. James Campus, One Monument Pl., 06615. Tel: 203-380-1990; Fax: 203-380-0749. Email: info@stjamesstratford.com. Mrs. Natalia Zamachaj, Business Mgr.

St. James (Grades K-8), One Monument Pl., 06615. Tel: 203-375-5994; Fax: 203-380-0749. Mrs. Kathleen A. Lainey, Prin. Lay Teachers 28; Students 463.

St. Mark (Grades K-8), 500 Wigwam Ln., 06614. Tel: 203-375-4291; Fax: 203-375-4833. Mr. Phillip T. Adzima, Prin. Lay Teachers 11; Students 235.

TRUMBULL. *Catholic Elementary Schools-Region VII*, St. Catherine of Siena, 190 Shelton Rd., 06611. Tel: 203-375-1947; Fax: 203-378-3935. Email: office@stcatherineschool.org. Web: www.stcatherineschool.org. Mr. Ray LaLuna, Business Mgr.

St. Jude (Grades PreK-8), 707 Monroe Tpke., Monroe, 06468. Tel: 203-261-3619; Fax: 203-268-8748. Mrs. Linda Dunn, Prin. Lay Teachers 10; Students 220.

St. Catherine of Siena (Grades PreK-8), 190 Shelton Rd., 06611. Tel: 203-375-1947; Fax: 203-378-3935. Sr. Anne Marie Dorff, S.S.N.D., Prin. Lay Teachers 10; Students 281.

St. Theresa (Grades PreK-8), 55 Rosemond Ter., 06611. Tel: 203-268-3236; Fax: 203-268-7966. Sr. Carolyn Mary Cossack, S.M.M.I., Prin. Lay Teachers 9; Students 279.

WILTON. *Catholic Elementary Schools-Region IV*, Our Lady of Fatima School, 225 Danbury Rd., 06897. Tel: 203-762-8100; Fax: 203-834-0614. Email: lmkwsky@optonline.net. Web: www.wiltonCT.com/Fatima/. Mrs. Mary Gardiner, Business Mgr.

Our Lady of Fatima (Grades PreK-8), 225 Danbury Rd., 06897. Tel: 203-762-8100; Fax: 203-834-0614. Mrs. Mary Ann Bozzuti, Prin. Lay Teachers 22; Students 246.

Saint Mary's (Grades K-7), 183 High Ridge Ave., Ridgefield, 06877. Tel: 203-438-7288; Fax: 203-431-8742. Mrs. Marcie McDonald, Prin. Lay Teachers 17; Students 143.

[G] ELEMENTARY SCHOOLS, PRIVATE

GREENWICH. *Convent of the Sacred Heart*, (Grades PreSchool-12) , Day School for Girls , 1177 King St., 06831. Tel: 203-531-6500; Fax: 203-531-5206. Email: sacredheart@cshgreenwich.org. Web: www.cshgreenwich.org. Sr. Joan Magnetti, R.S.C.J., Headmistress. Sisters 6; Lay Teachers 107; Students 680.

STAMFORD. *Villa Maria Education Center*, 161 Sky Meadow Dr., 06903. Tel: 203-322-5886; Fax: 203-322-0228. Email: scarol@optonline.net. Web: villamariaedcenter.org. Sr. Carol Ann, O.S.F., Exec. Dir. Bernardine Sisters, School for Children with Learning Disabilities. Sisters 3; Lay Teachers 19; Students 63.

[H] CATHOLIC CHARITIES

BRIDGEPORT. *Catholic Charities of Fairfield County*, Catholic Center, 238 Jewett Ave., 06606-2892. Tel: 203-372-4301, Ext. 379;; Fax: 203-372-5045. Email: bcronin@ccfc-ct.org. Web: www.ccfc-ct.org. Brian A. Cronin, A.C.S.W., L.C.S.W., Exec. Dir.

Adoption Program, 238 Jewett Ave., 06606-2892. Tel: 203-372-4301, Ext. 370; Fax: 203-373-0835. Email: azajac@ccfc-ct.org. Domestic Adoptions and Home Studies.

Catholic Family Services, Bridgeport, 238 Jewett Ave., 06606-2892. Tel: 203-372-4301, Ext. 348; Fax: 203-373-0835. Email: bhoey@ccfc-cr.org. William Hoey, A.C.S.W, L.C.S.W., District Exec. Dir.

Catholic Family Services, Danbury, 30 Main St., Suite 503, Danbury, 06810. Tel: 203-743-4412; Fax: 203-744-3500. Email: dcampbell@ccfc-cr.org.

Ways to Work Family Loan Program, 30 Main St., Ste. 503, Danbury, 06810. Tel: 203-743-4412; Fax: 203-744-3500. Email: csilliman@ccfc-ct.org.

Catholic Family Services, Norwalk, One Park St., P.O. Box 2025, Norwalk, 06851. Tel: 203-750-9711; Fax: 203-750-9651. Email: swilliams@ccfc-ct.org. Susan Williams, L.C.S.W., District Exec. Dir.

Catholic Family Services, Stamford, 30 Myano Ln., Ste. 12, Stamford, 06902. Tel: 203-323-1105; Fax: 203-323-1108. Email: eeichler@ccfc-ct.org. Elaine Eichler, A.C.S.W, L.C.S.W., District Exec. Dir.

Catholic Family Services Outreach Offices: 1986 Post Rd., Darien, 06820. Tel: 203-655-2169; Fax: 203-323-1108. Email: eeichler@ccfc-ct.org.

Day Care Programs/Room to Grow, 208 East Ave., Norwalk, 06850. Tel: 203-831-8200; Fax: 203-855-0637. Email: nowens@ccfc-ct.org. Nancy Cook Owens, Prog. Dir.

Houses of Hospitality:

New Covenant House of Hospitality (Yerwood Center), 90 Fairfield Ave., Stamford, 06904. Tel: 203-964-8228; Fax: 203-375-0314. Email: dprice@ccfc-ct.org.

Thomas Merton Center, 43 Madison Ave., 06604. Tel: 203-367-9036; Fax: 203-367-8828. Email: mfurlong@ccfc-ct.org. Mary Ann Furlong, R.N., Dir.

Family Life Ministry, Diocesan Office, 238 Jewett Ave., 06606-2892. Tel: 203-372-4301, Ext. 320; Fax: 203-371-8698. Rev. Ernest T. Esposito, D.Min., Dir. Please call Rev. Ernest T. Esposito, Exec. Dir., Tel: 203-372-4301, Ext. 314, for the following programs: Ministry to Widows; Bereavement; Job Transition; Post-Abortion Support; Divorced and Separated; Marriage Profile; Marriage Preparation; Marriage Enrichment; and Family Enrichment.

Family Life/Respect Life Catholic Center, 238 Jewett Ave., 06606-2892. Tel: 203-372-4301, Ext. 314; Fax: 203-371-8698.

St. Stephen's Emergency Food Center, 43 Madison Ave., 06604. Tel: 203-394-6881.

Mental Health Outreach: Danbury, New Heights, 66 West Street, Danbury, 06810. Tel: 203-794-0819; Fax: 203-731-3260. Email: mgrasso@ccfc-ct.org. Mark Grasso, Prog. Dir.

Case Management Program, 24 Grassy Plain St., Bethel, 06801. Tel: 203-748-0848; Fax: 203-796-0046. Email: scole@ccfc-ct.org. Web: www.ccfc-ct.org. Sandy Cole, Dir.

Homeless Outreach Team, 24 Grassy Plain St., Bethel, 06801. Tel: 203-748-0848; Fax: 203-796-0046. Email: ewalsh@ccfc-ct.org. Web: www.ccfc-ct.org. Eileen Walsh, Dir.

Nutrition and Aging Services, 30 Myano Ln., Stamford, 06902. Tel: 203-324-6175; Fax: 203-323-1108. Email: cphelps@ccfc-ct.org. Cindy Phelps, B.S., B.S., Dir.

Table to Table Program, 30 Myano Ln., Ste. 10, Stamford, 06902. Tel: 203-323-3211; Fax: 203-323-1108. Email: mryan@ccfc-ct.org. Web: www.table2table.org. Mary Ryan, Prog. Dir.

Senior Citizen Outreach, 30 Main St., Ste. 503, Danbury, 06810. Tel: 203-743-4412; Fax: 203-744-3500. Lee Goldenberg, L.C.S.W., Prog. Coord.

Intensive Outreach and Monitoring, CFS Stamford, 30 Myano Ln., Stamford, 06902. Tel: 203-323-1105; Fax: 203-323-1108. Email: lobrien@ccfc-ct.org. (for adjudicated delinquents 10-16 years)

Intensive Outreach and Monitoring, 96 Catherine St., 06604. Tel: 203-366-0721, Ext. 386; Fax: 203-366-1143. Email: lobrien@ccfc-ct.org.

Intensive Outreach and Monitoring, One Park St., P.O. Box 2025, Norwalk, 06851. Tel: 203-750-9711; Fax: 203-750-9651. Email: lobrien@ccfc-ct.org. Larry O'Brien, B.S., M.S., Regl. Dir.

Social Issues Advocacy, 238 Jewett Ave., 06606-2892. Tel: 203-372-4301; Fax: 203-372-5045. Email: ecassidy@ccfc-ct.org. Edie Cassidy, R.N., Dir. Health, Aging Issues. Tel: 203-372-4301, Ext. 386.

Family Stages, 752 E. Main St., 06606. Tel: 203-576-7432; Fax: 203-332-4044. Email: mmedina@ccfc-ct.org. Maria Reyes Medina, M.S.W., Dir.

[I] DAY NURSERIES

BRIDGEPORT. *Daughters of Charity of the Most Precious Blood Day Nursery*, 1490 North Ave., 06604. Tel: 203-334-7000; Fax: 203-334-7000. Email: daughtersofcharity@yahoo.com. Sr. Theresa Tremblay, Dir.

STAMFORD. *Our Lady of Grace Day Nursery*, 635 Glenbrook Rd., 06906. Tel: 203-348-5531; Fax: 203-324-9638. Email: littleworkerposc@aol.com. Sr. Gesuina Gencarelli, P.O.S.C., Supr. Little Workers of the Sacred Hearts

Stepping Stones Preschool, Inc., (Grades PreSchool-K), Sacred Heart Academy, 200 Strawberry Hill Ave., 06902. Tel: 203-323-3173; Fax: 203-975-7804. Sisters of Saint Joseph

WILTON. *Notre Dame Child Development Center, Inc.*, 345 Belden Hill Rd., 06897. Tel: 203-762-2814. Sr. Mary Serafine Della Croce, S.S.N.D.

[J] GENERAL HOSPITALS

BRIDGEPORT. *St. Joseph Medical Center Foundation, Inc.*, Diocese of Bridgeport, 238 Jewett Ave., 06606-2852.

St. Vincent's Development Corporation, 2800 Main St., 06606. Tel: 203-576-5459; Fax: 203-576-5345. Web: www.stvincents.org. Ms. Jean LaVecchia, Chm.; John M. Ahle, Pres. & CEO. Bed Capacity 391; Total Annually Assisted 150,000; Total Staff 2,000.

St. Vincent's Health Services Corporation, 2800 Main St., 06606. Tel: 203-576-5455; Fax: 203-576-5345. Web: www.stvincents.org. Sr. Margaret John Kelly, D.C., Chm.; John M. Ahle, Interim Pres. & CEO. Bed Capacity 391; Total Annually Assisted 150,000; Total Staff 2,000.

St. Vincent's Medical Center, 2800 Main St., 06606. Tel: 203-576-6000; Fax: 203-576-5345. Web: www.stvincents.org. Sr. Margaret John Kelly, D.C., Chm.; John M. Ahle, Acting CEO; Revs. Daniel Kennelly; Simon Gicherhein. Daughters of Charity of St. Vincent de Paul (Albany, NY) Bed Capacity 350; Total Assisted Annually 18,000; Total Staff 1,965.

St. Vincent's College Tel: 203-576-5578; Fax: 203-576-5893. Students 345.

Saint Vincent's Special Needs Center, Inc., 95 Merritt Blvd., Trumbull, 06611. Tel: 203-375-6400; Fax: 203-380-1190.

St. Vincent's Medical Center Foundation, 2800 Main St., 06606. Tel: 203-576-5451; Fax: 203-576-5880. Email: rbianchi@svhs-ct.org. Mr. Arthur Laske Jr., Chm.; Mr. Ronald J. Bianchi, Pres. Bed Capacity 400; Total Assisted Annually 110,000; Total Staff 1,700.

[K] SPECIAL HOSPITALS

BRIDGEPORT. *Bridgeport Diocesan Health Care Corporation*, 238 Jewett Ave., 06606. Tel: 203-372-4301; Fax: 203-372-1817. Email: nygs@aol.com. Mr. Michael R. Bird, Exec. Dir.

St. Camillus Home Foundation, Inc., 238 Jewett Ave., 06606. Tel: 203-325-0200; Fax: 203-353-0550.

The Pope John Paul II Foundation, Inc., 238 Jewett Ave., 06606. Tel: 203-797-9300; Fax: 203-797-9300.

DANBURY. *The Pope John Paul II Center for Health Care, Inc.*, 33 Lincoln Ave., 06810. Tel: 203-797-9300; Fax: 203-790-4645. Email: onedee98@aol.com. Mrs. Diane A. Pimentel, Admin.; Sr. Frances Smalkowski, C.F.S.N., Co-Dir. Pastoral Care; Rev. Michael F. Flynn, Chap. Total Staff 198.

STAMFORD. *St. Camillus Health Center*, 494 Elm St., 06902. Tel: 203-325-0200; Fax: 203-353-0550. Email: jhalleran@stcamillushealth.org. Web: www.stcamillushealth.org. Mr. John Halleran, Admin.; T. LeBel, Asst. Admin.; Rev. Carlos Rodrigues, Chap. Total Staff 167.

St. Camillus Auxiliary Committee, 494 Elm St., 06902. Tel: 203-325-0200; Fax: 203-353-0550.

[L] HOMES FOR AGED

BRIDGEPORT. *Augustana Homes/Bishop Curtis Homes*, 525 Palisade Ave., 06610. Tel: 203-366-4333; Fax: 203-366-4756. Mr. James J. Casey, Mgr.; Mrs. Lillian Araujo, Site Mgr. Apartments 186; Total Staff 5.

Augustana Homes/Bishop Curtis Homes, 280 Jewett Ave., 06606. Tel: 203-374-5346. Mr. James J. Casey, Mgr.; Mrs. Nilda Alamo, Site Mgr.

Augustana Homes/Bishop Curtis Homes - East Bridgeport, 238 Jewett Ave., 06606. Tel: 203-372-4301; Fax: 203-371-8698. Mr. Larry W. Arszyla, Contact Person. Total Assisted 48; Total Staff 2.

Roncalli Apartments, 430 Grant St., 06610. Tel: 203-384-9984. Rev. Edward C. Doherty, M.SS.A., Pres.; Mariann Callahan, L.P.N., Admin. Affiliate of the Roncalli Institute, Supervised Apartments for the Elderly & Handicapped.

BETHEL. *Augustana Homes/Bishop Curtis Homes*, 28 Simeon Rd., 06801. Tel: 203-743-2508; Fax: 203-743-4570. Mr. Larry W. Arszyla, Exec. Dir.; Mr.

James J. Casey, SRAMCO Mgt. Co. Project Mgr. Total Staff 500.

DANBURY. *Augustana Homes Bishop Curtis Homes - Danbury*, 88 Main St., 06810. Tel: 203-791-8510; Fax: 203-791-8513. Mr. Larry W. Arszyla, Exec. Dir. Total Assisted 40; Total Staff 2.

FAIRFIELD. *Augustana Homes/Bishop Curtis Homes*, 1677 Post Rd., 06430. Mr. James J. Casey, Mgr. Tel: 203-576-0823.

RIVERSIDE. *Augustana Homes of Greenwich/Bishop Curtis Homes*, 1040 E. Putnam Ave., 06878. Tel: 203-637-8065; Fax: 203-637-8065. Mr. James J. Casey, Mgr. Tel: 203-576-0823. Total Assisted 33; Total Staff 2.

STAMFORD. *Augustana Homes/Bishop Curtis Homes - Glenbrook*, 352 Glenbrook Rd., 06902. Tel: 203-576-0823. Mr. James J. Casey, Pres. Total Assisted 35; Total Staff 2.

TRUMBULL. *Carmel Ridge*, 6454 Main St., 06611. Tel: 203-261-2229. Mr. Peter Cady, Site Mgr.

St. Joseph's Housing Corporation, Teresian Towers & Carmel Ridge Estates, 6448 Main St., 06611. Tel: 203-261-2229. Mr. Peter Cady, Site Mgr.

St. Joseph's Manor, 6448 Main St., 06611. Tel: 203-268-6204; Fax: 203-268-5271. Email: information@stjosephsmanor.org. Web: www.stjosephsmanor.org. Sr. Michelle Anne Reho, O.Carm., Admin.; Revs. Alfred E. Russo, Chap.; Patrick J. Speer (HRT) (Retired). Carmelite Sisters for the Aged and Infirm 8; Capacity 297; Total Staff 500.

[M] CONVALESCENT HOMES

NORWALK. *Notre Dame Convalescent Home*, 76 W. Rocks Rd., 06851. Tel: 203-847-5893; Fax: 203-849-1959. Sr. Edmond, S.S.T.V., Supr.; Mr. Kenneth B. Hugo, Admin.; Rev. Canon Albert W. Watts, J.C.L., Chap. Sisters of St. Thomas of Villanova Sisters 4; Patients Assisted Annually 75; Total Staff 85.

[N] SOCIAL PROGRAMS

BRIDGEPORT. *Social Issues Advocate-Parish Social Concerns*, 238 Jewett Ave., 06606. Tel: 203-372-4301, Ext. 386; Fax: 203-372-5045. Email: ecassidy@ccfc-ct.org. Web: ccfc-ct.org. Brian A. Cronin, A.C.S.W., L.C.S.W., Campaign for Human Devel.; Edith Cassidy, Social Concerns Dir.

[O] MONASTIC FOUNDATIONS

WEST REDDING. *The Benedictine Grange* 06896. Tel: 203-938-3689; Fax: 203-938-3689. Email: navj@optonline.net. Rev. John B. Giuliani, Dir.

[P] RESIDENCES OF PRIESTS AND BROTHERS

BRIDGEPORT. *Instituto Verbo Encarnado*, St. George Parish, 443 Park Ave., 06604-5493. Tel: 203-335-1797; Fax: 203-334-6359. Email st.georges@sbcglobal.net. Revs. Julio Lopresti I.V.E.; Julio Montagna, I.V.E.

Provincial Offices of the Priests and Brothers of Holy Cross, Eastern Province (Province of Our Lady of Holy Cross) , 835 Clinton Ave., 06604. Tel: 203-367-7252; Fax: 203-366-7886. Email: acolgan@hcep.com. Web: www.stonehill.Edu.HolyCross. Revs. Arthur J. Colgan, C.S.C., Prov.; James T. Preskenis, C.S.C., Asst. Prov. & Vicar; James Lackenmier, C.S.C., Prov. Steward & Treas.; James T. Donohue, C.S.C., (In Res.).

Legal Title: *Congregation of Holy Cross - Eastern Province, Inc.*

784 Columbus Ave., Apt. 14-C, New York, NY. Tel: 212-360-3948.

Brothers of Holy Cross, Valatie, NY. Tel: 518-784-9481; Fax: 518-784-9494. Rev. James P. Madden, C.S.C.

Congregazione Di Santa Croce, Via Framura, 85, 00168, Rome, Italy. Tel: 39-06-69-001-214. Rev. John M. Santone, C.S.C.

Cornell Medical Center, White Plains, NY. Tel: 914-997-5776; Fax: 914-682-6988. Rev. James L. Rebeta, C.S.C.

3455 Countryside Blvd., Clearwater, FL 33761. Tel: 813-854-1518; Fax: 813-891-1267. Rev. Edmund J. Sylvia, C.S.C.

Union Institute of Cincinnati, Sanbornville, NH 03872. Tel: 603-522-3728; Fax: 603-522-9244. Rev. Frank A. Toste, C.S.C.

Whiting Forensic Institute, Middletown. Tel: 860-262-5487; Fax: 860-262-5477. Rev. John L. Young, C.S.C.

45 North St., Apt. 33, Stoneham, MA 02180. Tel: 781-279-0991. Rev. James Burbank, C.S.C.

Via Framura, 85, Rome 00168 Italy. Tel: 39-06-612-962-11; Fax: 39-06-614-7547. Rev. Hugh W. Cleary, C.S.C., Supr. Gen.

St. Francis University, P.O. Box 600, Loretto, PA 15940. Tel: 814-472-3004. Rev. Anthony J. DeConciliis, C.S.C.

10 E. South St., Wikes-Barre, PA. Tel: 570-824-2049. Rev. Joseph A. Lorusso, C.S.C.

Fr. Patrick Peyton Center, Attymas, Balina Ireland. Tel: 353-96-45574. Rev. Bartholomew C. Salter, C.S.C.

FAIRFIELD. *The Augustinians*, Fairfield-Easton Regional Catholic School, 591 Stratfield Rd., 06825. Tel 203-334-6271; Fax: 203-382-0399.

The Fairfield Jesuit Community-Fairfield University, 86 Barlow Rd., 06824-5195 Tel: 203-256-2663; Fax: 203-255-5947. Email: jhiggins@mail.fairfield.edu. Web: www.faculty.fairfieldedu/faculty/jmac/fjc/fjcomm.htw. Revs. Charles H. Allen, S.J.; Francis R. Allen, S.J.; Donald M. Barry, S.J.; John V. Borgo, S.J. Michael Boughton S.J.; Gerhard H. Bowering, S.J. (Germany); James S. Bowler, S.J.; Vincent M. Burns, S.J.; William F. Carr, S.J.; Paul E. Carrier, S.J.; Richard D. Costello, S.J.; William J. Cullen, S.J. (BO); Richard A. Deshaies, S.J. (BO); Terrence P. Devino, S.J.; William J. Eagan, S.J.; John W. Elder, S.J.; George A. Gallarelli, S.J.; Andrew J. Garavel, S.J.; Francis T. Hannafey, S.J.; James J. Hederman, S.J.; John J. Higgins, S.J.; Very Rev. Aloysius P. Kelley, S.J.; Revs. William J. Kennedy, S.J.; Joseph F. MacDonnell, S.J.; Lucian C. Martinez, S.J.; James J. Mayzik, S.J.; Mark D. McGregor, S.J.; Joseph B. McHugh, S.J.; Barry C. Meehan, S.J.; W. Laurence O'Neil, S.J.; Walter R. Pelletier, S.J.; Ronald V. Perry, S.J.; Laurence D. Ryan, S.J.; Martin G. Shaughnessy, S.J.; Edward J. Small, S.J.

STAMFORD. *The Catherine Dennis Keefe Queen of the Clergy Retired Priests' Residence*, 274 Strawberry Hill Ave., 06902. Tel: 203-358-9906; Fax: 203-358-9524. Rev. Msgrs. Bernard S. Scanlon (Retired); John W. Horgan-Kung (Retired); Francis J. Medynski (Retired); Normand A. Methe; William A. Nagle (Retired); John C. Sanders (Retired); Revs. Joseph V. Rossito; James J. Breen; Rev. Msgr. Edward J. Howley. Home for Retired Priests

P.O. Box 1872, New Milford, 06776. Rev. Msgr. John F. Jazowski (Retired).

43 Harbor Dr., Unit 209, 06902. Tel: 203-357-0145. Rev. Francis J. Medynski.

43 Harbor Dr., Unit 209, 06902. Tel: 203-357-0145. Rev. Xavier F. Renda.

1270 N. High St., Apt. 116, East Haven, 06512. Deacon James Dennis.

Pope John Paul II Center, 33 Lincoln Ave., Danbury, 06810. Rev. Boleslaus J. Rarus (Retired).

St. Josephs Manor, 6448 Main St., Trumbull, 06611.

[Q] CONVENTS AND RESIDENCES FOR SISTERS

BRIDGEPORT. *Convent of Mary Immaculate, Missionary Sisters of the Blessed Sacrament and Mary Immaculate*. Prov. Headquarters. 1111 Wordin Ave., 06605. Tel: 203-334-5681; Fax 203-333-1590. Email: mssmi1896@aol.com. Sr. Angela Maria Zapata, Prov. Assisting the Apostolate to Spanish-Speaking People. Sisters 5.

Daughters of Charity of the Most Precious Blood Convent, 1482 North Ave., 06604. Tel: 203-334-7000. Fax: 203-334-7000. Email: daughtersofcharity@yahoo.com. Sr. Theresa Tremblay, Dir.

Holy Spirit Convent, Daughters of the Holy Spirit, 50 Pequonnock St., 06604. Tel: 203-334-6926; Fax: 203-334-6926. Email: sisters.holy.ghost@snet.net. Staffing & ministry work in public health.

Institute Servants of the Lord and the Virgin of Matara, 153 Linden Ave., 06601-5730. Tel: 203-330-8409; Fax: 203-334-6359. Email: stdamaris@sbcglobal.net. Sr. Myriam Alham, S.S.V.M., Supr.

Missionaries of Charity, 599 Beachwood Ave., 06604. Tel: 203-336-5626. Sr. Noreen Bilung, M.C., Contact Person.

Sisters of the Company of the Savior, 820 Clinton Ave., 06604. Tel: 203-368-1875; Fax: 203-368-1875. Sr. Araceli Fernandez, Supr. Spanish-Speaking Apostolate.

GREENWICH. *Sacred Heart Convent*, 38 Gold St., 06830. Tel: 203-531-8547. Franciscan Sisters of the Atonement 5.

MONROE. *Provincial House, Immaculate Heart of Mary Province, Sisters of the Holy Family of Nazareth, C.S.F.N*, 1428 Monroe Tpke., 06468. Tel: 203-268-7646; Fax: 203-452-9947. Email: dancenyc9@aol.com. Web: www.csfn/ct.org Sr. M. Agnese Palczynski, C.S.F.N., Prov. Supr.; Rev. James J. Cole, Chap. Professed 49.

NORWALK. *Regional House of Sisters of St. Thomas of Villanova*, 76 W. Rocks Rd., 06851. Tel: 203-847-2885; Fax: 203-847-3740. Email: vocationdirectorsstv@juno.com. Sr. Edmond, S.S.T.V., Supr. Notre Dame Convalescent Home; Rev. Canon Albert W. Watts, J.C.L., Chap. Professed 4.

RIDGEFIELD. *Provincial House, Congregation de Notre Dame*, 223 W. Mountain Rd., 06877. Tel: 203-438-5282; Fax: 203-894-9686. Email: provsec@juno.com. Sisters Anne C. Leonard, C.N.D., Prov. Leader; Kathleen Murphy, C.N.D., Local Community Leader. Tel: 203-438-3115; Rev. Michael J. McCarthy, Chap.

STAMFORD. *Franciscan Sisters of the Immaculate Heart of Mary*, 1216 Shippan Ave., 06902-7425. Tel: 203-359-1127. Sr. Pauline Josephinemary, F.I.H.M., Supr.

Heart of Mary Convent (Residence for Bernardine Sisters), 163 Sky Meadow Dr., 06903. Tel: 203-322-5920; Fax: 203-322-5491. Email: HMCSTAM@aol.com. Sr. Frances Michele Dunaj, O.S.F., Local Min. Tel: 203-322-8721. Bernardine Sisters 14.

Villa Maria Education Center, 161 Sky Meadow Dr.. Tel: 203-322-5886; Fax: 203-322-0228. Sr. Carol Ann Nawracaj, O.S.F., Exec. Dir. School for children with learning disabilities (Grades 1-8).

Our Lady of Grace Convent, 635 Glenbrook Rd., 06906. Tel: 203-348-5531; Fax: 203-324-9638. Email: sgesuina@aol.com. Sr. Gesuina Gencarelli, P.O.S.C., Supr. Motherhouse and Novitiate of Little Workers of Sacred Hearts.

Sisters Minor of Mary Immaculate, Holy Name of Jesus Convent, 305 Washington Blvd., 06902. Tel: 203-323-4546; Fax: 203-323-4546. Sisters 3.

St. Francis Villa Custody House, Immaculate Conception Custody, 138 Brushy Hill Rd., Danbury, 06810. Tel: 203-744-8041; Fax: 203-744-8041. Sr. Mary Elizabeth Lariviere, S.M.M.I., Delegate. Sisters 3.

Villa Divino Amore Convent, Little Workers of the Sacred Hearts of Jesus & Mary, 117 Hope St., 06906. Tel: 203-324-2449. Sr. Giacinta Scaramuzzo, P.O.S.C., Supr.

WILTON. *Lourdes Health Care Center, Inc.*, 345 Belden Hill Rd., 06897-3898. Tel: 203-762-3318, Ext. 3501; Fax: 203-762-2144. Email: Hfrostssnd@cs.com. Sr. Mary Henrita Frost, Pres.; Rev. Thomas Elliot, Resident Chap.

School Sisters of Notre Dame Motherhouse (Northeastern Province), 345 Belden Hill Rd., 06897. Tel: 203-762-3318; Fax: 203-761-9228. Web: www.SSND.ORG. Sr. Mary V. Maher, Prov. Supr.; Rev. Thomas Elliott, C.S.C. Tel: 203-762-3318. Priests 1; Professed 101.

[R] SECULAR INSTITUTES

BRIDGEPORT. *The Society of Our Lady of the Way*, 584 Capitol Ave., Apt. 6, 06606. Tel: 203-579-4531. Miss Margaret Gould, Unit Dir.; Rev. Timothy Curtin, S.J. A secular institute for women.

[S] FOUNDATIONS, TRUSTS AND FUNDS

BRIDGEPORT. *Fairfield Foundation of the Diocese of Bridgeport, Inc.*, 238 Jewett Ave., 06606-2892. Tel: 203-372-4301; Fax: 203-371-8698. Mrs. Michele H. Jones Delmhorst, Pres.; Mr. John Croffy, Exec. Dir.

Inner-City Foundation for Charity & Education, 238 Jewett Ave., 06606-2892. Tel: 203-372-4301; Fax: 203-371-8698. Email: innercity.foundation@snet.net. Rev. Msgr. Kevin W. Wallin, Exec. Dir.

[T] GUEST HOUSES

DARIEN. *Convent of St. Birgitta* 06820. Tel: 203-655-1068; Fax: 203-655-3496. Email: convent.st.birgitta@snet.net. Web: www.birgittines-us.com. Sr. M. Sabina Kavanadi, O.SS.S., Supr.; Rev. Robert F. McCormick, Chap.

[U] HOUSES OF STUDIES

BRIDGEPORT. *St. Peter's Parish, St. Maximillian Kolbe House of Studies*, 535 Colorado Ave., 06605. Tel: 203-335-4992. Email: st.m.kolbe.house@snet.net. Rev. Msgr. Francis C. Wissel, Dir.; Ms. Carmen Serrano, Supr.

[V] RETREAT HOUSES

BRIDGEPORT. *Queen of Saints, The Catholic Center*, 238 Jewett Ave., 06606. Tel: 203-372-4301, Ext. 217. School of Religion and Spirituality and Retreat Facility.

The Urban Center of St. Charles Parish, 1279 E. Main St., 06608. Tel: 203-366-4190; Fax: 203-333-8422.

St. Charles Outreach Program Tel: 203-333-8422; Fax: 203-333-8422. Sr. Ilona Mensik, S.S.N.D., Dir. of Outreach.

STAMFORD. *Villa Maria Retreat*, 159 Sky Meadow Dr., 06903. Tel: 203-322-0107; Fax: 203-595-0647. Email: villa.maria@juno.com. Sr. Maria J. Riedel, O.S.F., Dir.; Rev. Paul Lalic, Chap. Ecumenical Spirituality Center. Bernardine Franciscan Sisters 5.

[W] NEWMAN CENTERS

FAIRFIELD. *Fairfield University* , (Fairfield) , N. Benson Rd., 06824-5195. Tel: 203-255-4511; Fax:

203-254-4300. Phyllis A. Fitzpatrick, Dir., Office Mgmt. Information; Rev. Paul E. Carrier, S.J.; Mrs. Carolyn M. Rusiackas, Assoc. Univ. Chap.; Rev. Gregg H. Grovenburg, S.J., Asst. University Chap.; Melissa Reardon, Asst. University Chap.; Robert Cortigiano, Asst. University Chap.

[X] MISCELLANEOUS LISTINGS

BRIDGEPORT. *Blessed Brother Andre Charitable Trust*, 835 Clinton Ave., 06604. Tel: 203-367-7252; Fax: 203-366-7886. Email: acolgan@hcep.com.

Cardinal Shehan Center, Inc., 1494 Main St., 06604. Tel: 203-336-4468; Fax: 203-368-0901. Email: tjo@shehancenter.org. Web: shehancenter.org. Mr. Terry O'Connor, Exec. Dir.

Caroline House, Inc., 574 Stillman St., 06608. Tel: 203-334-0640; Fax: 203-334-0248. Email: schotzi@aol.com. Web: thecarolinehouse.org. Sisters Maureen Fleming, S.S.N.D., Dir.; Brenda Lynch, S.S.N.D., Dir.

The Diocesan Cemetery Care Fund, Inc., 238 Jewett Ave., 06606.

Faith in the Future Fund, Inc., 238 Jewett Ave., 06606. Tel: 203-372-4301; Fax: 203-373-6890. Email: schwipp@ibm.net. Thomas M. Sweeney, Dir. for Devel.

Hispanic Social Ministries of Fairfield County, Inc., 238 Jewett Ave., 06606-9990. Rev. Msgr. Aniceto Villamide, Contact Person.

Needle Fund, Inc., 238 Jewett Ave., 06606.

The Queen's Daughters, c/o Sr. Therese, D.H.S., 50 Pequonnock St., 06604. Tel: 203-334-6924; Fax: 203-334-6926. Email: sisters.holy.ghost@snet.net. Mrs. Mary Mazur, Pres. Sponsoring agency for Holy Spirit Convent. Care of the sick and poor in their homes by Daughters of the Holy Spirit.

FAIRFIELD. *The Institute for Religious Education and Pastoral Studies (REAPS)*, Sacred Heart University, 5151 Park Ave., 06825. Tel: 203-371-7843; 203-371-7867; Fax: 203-365-4798. Email: reaps@sacredheart.edu. Web: reaps.sacredheart.edu. Rev. Barry C. Meehan, S.J., Dir.; Mrs. Patricia A. Murphy, Coord. Graduate Catholic Schools & Religious Education Programs; Mr. William G. Joyce, Special Asst. to Dir.; Deacon Daniel Ianniello, Prog. Dir. Devel. & Operations; Mr. William Lyons, Coord. Electronic & Technological Learning; Mrs. Catherine Brewer, Admin. Sec.; Mr. Christopher Sheehan, Coord. Publicity; Mrs. Florence Wheeler, Data Programmer; Ms. Marion Radomski, Coord. Programs & Events; Mr. William Soisson, Coord. Payments.

GREENWICH. *Clemons Productions, Inc.* (In association with That's The Spirit Productions, Inc.) , P.O. Box 7466, 06836. Tel: 203-316-9394; Fax: 203-316-9396. Email: clemons10@aol.com. Web: www.spirituality.org. Rev. Mark Connolly, Pres. Tel: 203-316-9394.

Spirituality For Today Tel: 203-316-9394; Fax: 203-316-9396.

Radio Program: Thoughts for the Week Tel: 203-316-9394; Fax: 203-316-9396.

NORWALK. *Malta House of Good Counsel*, 5 Prowitt St., 06855-1203. Tel: 203-857-0088; Fax: 203-857-0018. Email: maltahouse@aol.com.

RIDGEFIELD. *The St. Mary's Endowment Trust*, 55 Catoonah St., 06877. Tel: 203-438-6538; Fax: 203-438-4406. Email: stmarysrcc@aol.com. Web: www.stmarysridgefield.org.

STAMFORD. *Haitian American Catholic Center of Greater Stamford*, 93 Hope St., 06906. Tel: 203-323-8391. Rev. Jean Ridly Julien, Exec. Dir.

Stamford Catholic Library, 566 Elm St., 06902. Tel: 203-348-4422. Rev. Msgr. John Terleckey, Pres.; Rev. Robert G. Pohley, Chap.; Mary Louise Flowers, Contact Person.

TRUMBULL. *Magnificat, A Ministry to Catholic Women-Triumphant*, 16 Stag Ln., 06611. Tel: 203-452-7040; Fax: 203-452-7043. Email: paxjc@aol.com. Fran Karpiej, Coord.

RELIGIOUS INSTITUTES OF MEN REPRESENTED IN THE DIOCESE

For further details refer to the corresponding bracketed number in the Religious Institutes of Men or Women section.

[0200]—*Benedictine Monks*—O.S.B.
[0470]—*The Capuchin Friars* (Prov. of St. Mary)—O.F.M.Cap.
[0270]—*Carmelite Fathers & Brothers* (St. Elias Prov. New York)—O.Carm.
[0480]—*Conventual Franciscans* (St. Anthony of Padua Prov.)—O.F.M.Conv
[0520]—*Franciscan Friars* (Commissariat of St. Stephen)—O.F.M.
[0650]—*Holy Ghost Fathers* (Irish Prov.)—C.S.Sp.
[]—*Instituto Verbo Encarnado*—I.V.E.
[0690]—*Jesuit Fathers and Brothers* (New England Prov.)—S.J.
[0870]—*Montfort Missionaries* (Haitian Prov.)—S.M.M.
[0610]—*Priests of the Congregation of Holy Cross* (Prov. of Our Lady of Holy Cross)—C.S.C.
[]—*The Augustinians*—O.S.A.

RELIGIOUS INSTITUTES OF WOMEN REPRESENTED IN THE DIOCESE

[0130]—*Apostles of the Sacred Heart of Jesus*—A.S.C.J.
[1810]—*Bernardine Sisters of the Third Order of St. Francis*—O.S.F.
[0280]—*Brigittine Sisters*—O.SS.S.
[0330]—*Carmelite Sisters for the Aged and Infirm*—O.Carm.
[0710]—*Company of the Savior*—C.S.
[4030]—*Congregation of Sisters of St. Thomas of Villanova*—S.S.T.V.
[0760]—*Daughters of Charity of St. Vincent de Paul*—D.C.
[0740]—*Daughters of Charity of the Most Precious Blood*
[0820]—*Daughters of the Holy Spirit*—D.H.S.
[1190]—*Franciscan Sisters of the Atonement*—S.A.
[]—*Franciscan Sisters of the Immaculate Heart of Mary*—F.I.H.M.
[2575]—*Institute of the Sisters of Mercy of the Americas*—R.S.M.
[]—*Institute Servants of the Lord and the Virgin of Matera*—S.S.V.M.
[2345]—*Little Workers of the Sacred Hearts of Jesus & Mary*—P.O.S.C.
[2780]—*Missionary Sisters of the Most Blessed Sacrament* (Spain)—M.SS.S.
[3760]—*Order of St. Clare*—O.S.C.
[3430]—*Religious Teachers Filippini*—M.P.F.
[2970]—*School Sisters of Notre Dame*—S.S.N.D.
[]—*Sisters Minor of the Mary Immaculate*—S.M.M.I.
[0590]—*Sisters of Charity of Saint Elizabeth, Convent Station*—S.C.
[0620]—*Sisters of Charity of St. Louis*—S.C.S.L.
[2990]—*Sisters of Notre Dame*—S.N.D.
[3000]—*Sisters of Notre Dame de Namur*—S.N.D.deN.
[3780]—*Sisters of Saints Cyril and Methodius*—SS.C.M.
[3850]—*Sisters of St. Joseph of Chambery*
[2980]—*Sisters of the Congregation de Notre Dame*—C.N.D.
[1970]—*Sisters of the Holy Family of Nazareth*—C.S.F.N.
[3480]—*Sisters of the Resurrection* (Eastern Prov.)—C.R.
[2160]—*Sisters, Servants of the Immaculate Heart of Mary*—I.H.M.
[4070]—*Society of the Sacred Heart*—R.S.C.J.
[4130]—*Ursuline Sisters of the Congregation of Tildonk, Belgium*—O.S.U.

DIOCESAN CEMETERIES

BRIDGEPORT. *St. Michael's*, 2205 Stratford Ave., 06497. Tel: 203-378-0404.

DANBURY. *St. Peter's*, Lake Ave. Exit, 06810. Tel: 203-743-9626.

GREENWICH. *St. Mary's*, 399 North St., 06830. Tel: 203-869-7026.

Putnam, 35 Parsonage Rd., 06830. Tel: 203-869-4828.

NEWTOWN. *Resurrection*, c/o St. Peter Cemetery, Lake Ave. Exit, 06810. Tel: 203-743-9626.

NORWALK. *St. John's & St. Mary's*, 223 Richards Ave., 06850. Tel: 203-838-4271.

STAMFORD. *St. John's*, 25 Camp Ave., 06820. Tel: 203-322-0455.

Queen of Peace, c/o St. John Cemetery, 25 Camp Ave., 06820. Tel: 203-322-0455.

TRUMBULL. *Gate of Heaven*, c/o St. Michael's, 2205 Stratford Ave., 06497. Tel: 203-378-0404.

WESTPORT. *Assumption Green Farms*, Kings Hwy., c/o St. John Cemetery, 223 Richards Ave., 06850. Tel: 203-838-4271.

NECROLOGY

† Hale, Rev. Msgr. Harry L., (Retired)—Died Jan. 15, 2003
† Tetreault, Rev. Msgr. Jean C., (Retired)—Died June 1, 2003
† Dennis, James J., (Retired)—Died June 7, 2003
† Hewitt, Charles L.—Died March 18, 2003
† Maglione, Joseph J., (Retired)—Died Sept. 20, 2003

Diocese of Brooklyn

(Dioecesis Bruklyniensis)

Most Reverend

NICHOLAS A. DIMARZIO

Seventh Bishop of Brooklyn; ordained May 30, 1970; appointed Titular Bishop of Mauriana and Auxiliary Bishop of Newark September 10, 1996 consecrated October 31, 1996; appointed Bishop of Camden June 18, 1999; installed July 22, 1999; appointed Bishop of Brooklyn August 1, 2003; installed October 3, 2003. *Office: 75 Greene Ave., P.O. Box C, Brooklyn, NY 11202.*

Chancery Office: 75 Greene Ave., P.O. Box C, Brooklyn, NY 11202. Tel: 718-399-5900; Fax: 718-399-5934.

Email: curia@diobrook.org

Most Reverend

THOMAS V. DAILY, D.D.

Retired Bishop of Brooklyn; ordained January 10, 1952; appointed Auxiliary to the Archbishop of Boston and Titular Bishop of Bladia December 31, 1974; consecrated February 11, 1975; appointed First Bishop of Palm Beach July 17, 1984; appointed Sixth Bishop of Brooklyn February 20, 1990; took possession April 16, 1990; installed April 18, 1990; retired August 1, 2003. *Mailing Address: 75 Greene Ave., P.O. Box C, Brooklyn, NY 11202.*

Most Reverend

JOSEPH M. SULLIVAN, M.S.W., M.P.A., V.E.

Tenth Auxiliary Bishop of Brooklyn; ordained June 2, 1956; appointed Titular Bishop of Suliana October 7, 1980; episcopal ordination November 24, 1980. *Mailing Address: 378 Clermont Ave., Brooklyn, NY 11238.*

Most Reverend

RENE A. VALERO, M.S.W.

Eleventh Auxiliary Bishop of Brooklyn; priestly ordination June 2, 1956; appointed Titular Bishop of Vicus Turris October 7, 1980; episcopal ordination November 24, 1980. *Res.: 34-43 93rd St., Jackson Heights, NY 11372.*

Most Reverend

IGNATIUS A. CATANELLO, PH.D.

Twelfth Auxiliary Bishop of Brooklyn; ordained May 28, 1966; appointed Titular Bishop of Deulto June 28, 1994; episcopal ordination August 22, 1994. *Res.: 175-20 74th Ave., Flushing, NY 11366.*

ESTABLISHED JULY 29, 1853.

Square Miles 179.

Comprises Kings and Queens Counties in the State of New York.

For legal titles of parishes and diocesan institutions, consult the Chancery Office.

STATISTICAL OVERVIEW

Personnel	
Bishop	1
Auxiliary Bishops	3
Retired Bishops	1
Priests: Diocesan Active in Diocese	365
Priests: Diocesan Active Outside Diocese	50
Priests: Retired, Sick or Absent	189
Number of Diocesan Priests	604
Religious Priests in Diocese	175
Total Priests in Diocese	779
Extern Priests in Diocese	94
Ordinations:	
Diocesan Priests	2
Transitional Deacons	1
Permanent Deacons in Diocese	159
Total Brothers	180
Total Sisters	1,097
Parishes	
Parishes	216
With Resident Pastor:	
Resident Diocesan Priests	184
Resident Religious Priests	22
Without Resident Pastor:	
Administered by Priests	10
Administered by Deacons	1
Closed Parishes	1
Professional Ministry Personnel:	
Brothers	18
Sisters	146
Lay Ministers	183
Welfare	
Catholic Hospitals	4
Total Assisted	662,211
Health Care Centers	17
Total Assisted	342,418
Homes for the Aged	6
Total Assisted	1,400
Residential Care of Children	6
Total Assisted	8,798
Day Care Centers	27
Total Assisted	2,867
Specialized Homes	35
Total Assisted	13,450
Special Centers for Social Services	96
Total Assisted	110,560
Residential Care of Disabled	75
Total Assisted	3,390
Other Institutions	29
Total Assisted	3,434
Educational	
Seminaries, Diocesan	1
Students from This Diocese	11
Students from Other Diocese	3
Diocesan Students in Other Seminaries	20
Seminaries, Religious	1
Students Religious	1
Total Seminarians	32
Colleges and Universities	3
Total Students	20,378
High Schools, Diocesan and Parish	4
Total Students	2,048
High Schools, Private	16
Total Students	15,528
Elementary Schools, Diocesan and Parish	152
Total Students	47,274
Elementary Schools, Private	2
Total Students	315
Non-residential Schools for the Disabled	1
Total Students	119
Catechesis/Religious Education:	
High School Students	2,200
Elementary Students	45,500
Total Students under Catholic Instruction	133,394
Teachers in the Diocese:	
Priests	13
Brothers	59
Sisters	253
Lay Teachers	3,753
Vital Statistics	
Receptions into the Church:	
Infant Baptism Totals	19,377
Adult Baptism Totals	1,003
Received into Full Communion	925
First Communions	14,543
Confirmations	12,298
Marriages:	
Catholic	3,222
Interfaith	412
Total Marriages	3,634
Deaths	10,869
Total Catholic Population	1,826,592
Total Population	4,694,705

Former Bishops—Rt. Revs. JOHN LOUGHLIN, D.D., First Bishop of Brooklyn; ord. Oct. 18, 1840; consecrated Oct. 30, 1853; died Dec. 28, 1891; CHARLES E. MCDONNELL, D.D., Second Bishop of Brooklyn; ord. May 19, 1878; consecrated April 25, 1892; died Aug. 8, 1921; Most Revs. THOMAS E. MOLLOY, D.D., Third Bishop of Brooklyn; ord. Sept. 19, 1908; consecrated Second Auxiliary Bishop of Brooklyn, Oct. 3, 1920; appt. Bishop of Brooklyn, Nov. 21, 1921; installed Feb. 15, 1922; died Nov. 26, 1956; BRYAN J. MCENTEGART, D.D., LL.D. (Retired), Fourth Bishop of Brooklyn; ord. Sept. 8, 1917; appt. Bishop of Ogdensburg, June 5, 1943; consecrated Aug. 3, 1943; appt. Rector of the Catholic University of America, Washington, DC, June 26, 1953; appt. Titular Bishop of Aradi, Aug. 19, 1953; appt. Bishop of Brooklyn, April 16, 1957; installed June 13, 1957; retired and appt. Titular Archbishop of Gabii, July 17, 1968; died Sept. 30, 1968; FRANCIS J. MUGAVERO, D.D. (Retired), Fifth Bishop of Brooklyn; ord. May 18, 1940; Bishop of Brooklyn; appt. July 15, 1968; consecrated Sept. 12, 1968; installed Sept. 12, 1968; retired Feb. 20, 1990; died July 12, 1991.

Central Offices—75 Greene Ave. Brooklyn, 11238. Mailing Address, P.O. Box C, Brooklyn, 11202-3604. Tel: 718-399-5900. Office Hours: Mon.-Fri. 9-4:30

Vicar General and Moderator of the Curia—Rev. Msgr. OTTO L. GARCIA, J.C.D., V.G., 75 Greene Ave., P.O. Box C, Brooklyn, 11202. Tel 718-399-5900; Fax: 718-399-5965.

Regional Bishop of Brooklyn West and Episcopal Vicar for Human Services—Most Rev. JOSEPH M. SULLIVAN, M.S.W., M.P.A., V.E., 191 Joralemon St., Brooklyn, 11201. Tel: 718-722-6000.

Regional Bishop of Queens North and Episcopal Vicar for Elderly and Racial Concerns—Most Rev. RENE A. VALERO, M.S.W., V.E., 7200 Douglaston Pkwy., Douglaston, 11362. Tel: 718-229-8001, Ext. 710.

Regional Bishop of Queens South and Episcopal Vicar for Evangelization and Spiritual Development—Most Rev. IGNATIUS A. CATANELLO, Ph.D., V.E., Holy Family Church, 175-20 74th Ave., Flushing, 11366. Tel: 718-380-6055.

Regional Bishop of Brooklyn East—VACANT.

Episcopal Vicars-Territorial—Brooklyn West: Rev. Msgr. MICHAEL J. BRENNAN, V.E., St. Cecilia, 84 Herbert St., Brooklyn, 11222. Tel: 718-389-0010. Brooklyn East: Rev. Msgr. FERNANDO FERRARESE, St. Therese of Lisieux, 1281 Troy Ave., Brooklyn, 11203. Tel: 718-451-1500. Queens South: Rev. Msgr. JAMES SPENGLER, V.E., St. Catherine of Sienna, 118-22 Riverton St., St. Albans, 11412. Tel: 718-528-1220. Queens North: Rev. SEAN OGLE, Resurrection-Ascension, 61-11 85th St., Rego Park, 11374. Tel: 718-424-5212.

Episcopal Vicar for Temporalities—Rev. Msgr. JOHN J. BRACKEN, 310 Prospect Park W., P.O. Box 159013, Brooklyn, 11215-0013. Tel: 718-965-7300; Fax: 718-965-7311.

Finance Officer—Mr. FRANCIS W. GALLIGAN, CFO; Mr. MARTIN J. MCMANUS, C.P.A., Comptroller. Tel: 718-965-7300, Ext. 1401; Fax: 718-965-7371.

Parish Services Corp.—Rev. Msgr. RAYMOND F. CHAPPETTO, Pres.; Mr. MARTIN J. MCMANUS, C.P.A., Treas.; BRIAN T. COSGROVE, Sec., 310

Prospect Park W., Brooklyn, 11215. Tel: 718-965-7300; Fax: 718-965-7382.

Peter Turner Insurance Co.—112 Lake St., Burlington, VT 05401. Tel: 802-658-9466; Fax: 802-658-5520. Rev. Msgr. RAYMOND F. CHAPPETTO, Pres.; Mr. FRANCIS W. GALLIGAN, Exec. Vice Pres.; Mr. MARTIN J. MCMANUS, C.P.A., Treas.; BRIAN T. COSGROVE, Sec.

Development Office—Rev. Msgr. JOHN J. BRACKEN, Dir. Tel: 718-965-7300; Fax: 718-965-7341.

Building and Property Administration—Mr. GERARD TANGREDI, Dir. Tel: 718-965-7300; Fax: 718-965-7353.

Institutional Services—Rev. MICHAEL HARDIMAN, Exec. Dir.; ROBERT RYMERS, Dir. of Oper., The Immaculate Conception Center, 7200 Douglaston Pkwy., Douglaston, 11362. Tel: 718-229-8001, Ext. 8290; Fax: 718-279-3004.

Episcopal Vicar for Education—VACANT, 310 Prospect Park W., P.O. Box 159013, Brooklyn, 11215-0013. Tel: 718-965-7300; Fax: 718-965-7323.

Chancery Office—75 Greene Ave., P.O. Box C, Brooklyn, 11202. Tel: 718-399-5990; Fax: 718-399-5934.

Chancellor—Rev. Msgr. ANDREW J. VACCARI, J.C.L.

Vice-Chancellors—Sr. JANE SCANLON, C.N.D., M.Div.; Rev. STEVEN J. AGUGGIA, J.C.L.

Diocesan Archivist—JOSEPH W. COEN, C.A.; PATRICK MCNAMARA, Asst., Mailing Address, 310 Prospect Park W., P.O. Box 159013, Brooklyn, 11215-0013. Tel: 718-965-7300, Ext. 1001.

Censors of Books—Rev. Msgrs. PETER I. VACCARI, S.T.L.; FRANK J. CAGGIANO, S.T.D.; BRYAN PATTERSON; JOHN CUSH, 75 Greene Ave., P.O. Box C, Brooklyn, 11202.

Secretary to the Diocesan Bishop—Rev. Msgr. RALPH J. MARESCA, M.Div. Tel: 718-399-5970; Fax: 718-399-5975.

Masters of Ceremonies to Bishops—Bishop Daily--: Rev. Msgr. FRANK J. CAGGIANO, S.T.D.; Revs. GEORGE HERNANDEZ; FRANK TUMINO. Bishop Sullivan--: Revs. MICHAEL A. CARRANO; ROBERT ADAMO; KEVIN MCBRIEN; JAMES CUNNINGHAM; RICHARD E. LONG, M.Div., M.B.A. Bishop Valero--: Revs. ROBERT ARMATO; ANTHONY HERNANDEZ; STEVEN J. AGUGGIA, J.C.L.; THOMAS C. MACHALSKI, J.C.L.; DAVID ESPINOSA. Bishop Catanello--: Rev. Msgr. THOMAS G. CASERTA, M.A., M.Div., D.Min.; Revs. JAMES KING; MARC SWARTVAGHER, S.T.B., S.T.L.; FRED MARANO; Very Rev. GREGORY C. WIELUNSKI, J.C.D.; Rev. CALEB BUCHANEN.

Tribunal—7200 Douglaston Pkwy., Douglaston, 11362. Tel: 718-229-8131; Fax: 718-631-1339.

Officialis-Judicial Vicar—Very Rev. GREGORY C. WIELUNSKI, J.C.D.

Vice Officiales-Associate Judicial Vicars—Revs. HUGO BEDOYA, S.T.L., J.C.D.; THOMAS CHENG, J.C.D., M.A.; JOSEPH GRIMALDI, J.C.L.; THOMAS C. MACHALSKI, J.C.L.; ANTHONY HERNANDEZ, J.C.L.

Diocesan Judge—EDWARD SCHARFENBERGER, J.C.L.

Defenders of the Marriage Bond—Rev. Msgrs. JOHN J. BROWN, S.T.L., J.C.L.; ANDREW J. VACCARI, J.C.L.; Rev. STEVEN J. AGUGGIA, J.C.L.

Promoter of Justice—Rev. Msgr. WILLIAM A. VARVARO, P.A., S.T.D., J.C.D.

Attorneys and Counselors at Canon Law—Rev. EDWARD G. BROPHY, M.Div.; Deacon JEROME KREBS; Sisters JOSITA WALSH, R.S.M., M.A.; MARY PARRY, O.P.; Revs. DAVID ESPINOSA; WITOLD MROZIEWSKI.

Senior Priests, Episcopal Vicar Delegate for—Rev. Msgr. GEORGE ZATARGA, 7200 Douglaston Pkwy., Douglaston, 11362. Tel: 718-229-8001, Ext. 411.

Religious, Episcopal Delegate for—Sr. MARYANN SETON LOPICCOLO, S.C., 75 Greene Ave., P.O. Box C, Brooklyn, 11202. Tel: 718-399-5900.

Cemeteries—Rev. Msgr. MICHAEL J. REID, Dir., 80-01 Metropolitan Ave., Middle Village, 11379. Tel: 718-894-4888.

Education, Offices— (See Institutions Located in the Diocese for details)

Family Life Office—Mrs. CATHERINE BALA, Dir.; Deacon LEON F. MILLER, Asst. Dir. for Hispanics, 7200 Douglaston Pkwy., Douglaston, 11362. Tel: 718-229-8001, Ext. 342.

Human Resources Office—ANNMARIE FAHEY, Admin., 310 Prospect Park W., P.O. Box 159013, Brooklyn, 11215-0013. Tel: 718-965-7300; Fax: 718-965-7363.

Pension Office—ANNMARIE FAHEY, Admin. Tel: 718-965-7300; Fax: 718-965-7363.

Medical Insurance Office—ANNMARIE FAHEY, Admin. Tel: 718-965-7300; Fax: 718-965-7363.

Diocesan Insurance Committee—310 Prospect Park W., Brooklyn, 11215. Tel: 718-965-7300; Fax: 718-965-7382. BRIAN T. COSGROVE, Dir. Insurance. Tel: 718-965-7300, Ext. 1351; FLORENCE FLYNN. Tel: 718-965-7300, Ext. 1353; CATHY FEMIA. Tel: 718-965-7300, Ext. 1352.

Liturgical Office—Rev. Msgr. JOHN C. TOSI, Exec. Sec.; Sr. BERNADETTE M. IZZO, O.P., Admin. Asst., 75 Greene Ave., P.O. Box C, Brooklyn, 11202. Tel: 718-399-5980; Fax: 718-399-5930.

Mediation and Arbitration, Board of—Rev. Msgr. EDWARD SCHARFENBERGER, Exec. Sec., Mailing Address, P.O. Box C, Brooklyn, 11202.

Ministerial Development Program—Rev. THOMAS CASERTA. Tel: 718-229-8001.

Newspaper "The Tablet"—Mr. FRANK DEROSA, Assoc. Publisher; ED WILKINSON, Editor, 310 Prospect Park W., P.O. Box 159013, Brooklyn, 11215-0013. Tel: 718-965-7300; Fax: 718-965-7339.

Permanent Diaconate Program—Rev. Msgr. FRANK CAGGIANO, Dir., 75 Greene Ave., P.O. Box C, Brooklyn, 11202. Tel: 718-399-5900.

Office of Clergy Personnel—Rev. Msgr. JOHN J. BROWN, S.T.L., J.C.L., Dir., 75 Greene Ave., P.O. Box C, Brooklyn, 11202. Tel: 718-399-5941; Fax: 718-399-7194.

Assignment Board—Rev. Msgrs. JOHN J. BROWN, S.T.L., J.C.L., Chm.; JAMES SPENGLER, V.E.; MICHAEL BRENNAN; FERNANDO FERRARESE; Rev. SEAN OGLE; Rev. Msgr. JOHN MCGUIRL; Rev. KEVIN MCBRIEN.

Personnel Board (Clergy)—Rev. Msgr. JOHN J. BROWN, S.T.L., J.C.L., Chm.; Revs. WILLIAM SWEENEY; EDWARD BROPHY; Rev. Msgr. PAUL SANCHEZ.

Propagation of the Faith—Rev. JOHN BROGAN, Office, 191 Joralemon St., P.O. Box 200, Brooklyn, 11202. Tel: 718-875-4375.

Holy Childhood, Pontifical Association—Rev. JOHN BROGAN, 191 Joralemon St., P.O. Box 200, Brooklyn, 11202.

Public Information Office—FRANK DEROSA, Dir., 75 Greene Ave., P.O. Box C, Brooklyn, 11202. Tel: 718-399-5955; Fax: 718-399-5957.

Retirement Board (Priests)—Most Rev. RENE A. VALERO, M.S.W., V.E., Chm., Mailing Address, 7200 Douglaston Pkwy., Douglaston, 11362.

Victim Assistance Coordinator—Sr. ELLEN PATRICIA FINN, O.P. Tel: 718-722-6050. Email: srepfinn@ccbq.org.

Vocations, Office of—Rev. JAMES F. FITZPATRICK, Dir.; Sr. REGINA WILSON, I.H.M., Assoc. Dir., 75 Greene Ave., P.O. Box C, Brooklyn, 11202. Tel: 718-399-5900.

Consultative Bodies

Presbyteral Council—Rev. Msgrs. PETER V. KAIN, Exec. Sec.; MICHAEL BRENNAN; JOHN O'BRIEN; FAUSTINO CORDERO; Most Revs. JOSEPH M. SULLIVAN, M.S.W., M.P.A., V.E.; RENE A. VALERO, M.S.W., V.E.; IGNATIUS A. CATANELLO, Ph.D., V.E.; Rev. Msgrs. OTTO L. GARCIA, J.C.D., V.G.; DAVID L. CASSATO, M.Div., M.S.Ed.; Revs. CALEB BUCHANAN; PETER GILLEN; Rev. Msgrs. NEIL MAHONEY; ANDREW VACCARI; Revs. THOMAS G. PETTEI; JAMES K. CUNNINGHAM; JOSEPH R. GRIMALDI, J.C.L.; JOSEPH G. FONTI, S.T.L.; RAYMOND C. GRUHN; THOMAS V. DOYLE; EDWARD BROPHY; JAMES KING; RUSSELL GOVERNALE, O.F.M.Conv.; LEONARD UGBOR; Rev. Msgr. JOHN F. CASEY, 75 Greene Ave., P.O. Box C, Brooklyn, 11202.

Diocesan Budget Committee—Rev. Msgr. JOHN J. BRACKEN, Chm.

Subcommittee for Assisted Schools and Parishes—Rev. THOMAS V. DOYLE.

Subcommittee for Agencies—Rev. Msgr. JOHN J. BRACKEN.

Subcommittee for Parishes—Rev. Msgr. RAYMOND W. KUTNER.

Subcommittee for Schools—Sr. KAREN LADEMANN, O.P.

Diocesan Consultors—Rev. Msgr. OTTO L. GARCIA, J.C.D., V.G., Sec.; Most Revs. RENE A. VALERO, M.S.W., V.E.; IGNATIUS A. CATANELLO, Ph.D., V.E.; Rev. Msgrs. MICHAEL BRENNAN; JOHN O'BRIEN; JOHN STRYNKOWSKI; ANDREW J. VACCARI, J.C.L.; Revs. NEIL MAHONEY; PETER GILLEN; WILLIAM HOPPE, 75 Greene Ave., P.O. Box C, Brooklyn, 11202.

Diocesan Pastoral Council—WILLIAM FARREN, Pres.; Rev. Msgr. GUY MASSIE, M.Div., Bishop's Liaison.

Brothers' Senate—Bro. LAWRENCE SEWARD, S.C., 71-06 31st Ave., East Elmhurst, 11370. Tel: 718-898-9600.

Commissions and Offices for Pastoral Services

Alcoholism Committee—Rev. Msgr. KIERAN MARTIN, Chm., 1550 Hendrickson St., Brooklyn, 11234. Tel: 718-951-7302; Fax: 718-951-7233.

Art and Architecture Commission—Rev. Msgr. JOHN C. TOSI, Exec. Sec.; Sr. MARY JANE KELLY, O.P., Chm.; Revs. ROBERT J. ARMATO; VITO BUONANNO; THOMAS V. DOYLE; THOMAS G. PETTEI, Office, 75 Greene Ave., P.O. Box C, Brooklyn, 11202.

Black Ministry, Office of—JOHN BAYNES, Exec. Dir., Immaculate Conception Center, 7200 Douglaston Pkwy., Douglaston, 11362. Tel: 718-229-8001.

Hispanic Ministry, Office of—Deacon JORGE A. GONZALEZ, 7200 Douglaston Pkwy., Douglaston, 11362. Tel: 718-229-8001, Ext. 741.

Catholic Charities—Most Rev. JOSEPH M. SULLIVAN, M.S.W., M.P.A., V.E., Episcopal Vicar, Human Svcs., 191 Joralemon St., Brooklyn, 11201. Tel: 718-722-6000; Fax: 718-643-0522 (See Institutions Located in the Diocese for details).

Catholic Migration and Refugee Office— (See Institutions Located in the Diocese for details)

Catholic Migration Services, Inc.—Rev. Msgr. RONALD T. MARINO, Dir. Tel: 718-236-3000.

Diocesan Institute of Languages—Rev. Msgr. MICHAEL J. HARDIMAN, M.Div., M.A., M.P.A., Dir., 7200 Douglaston Pkwy., Douglaston, 11362. Tel: 718-229-8001.

Chaplains and Uniformed Services, Official—Police Department: Rev. ROBERT ROMANO; Rev. Msgr. DAVID L. CASSATO, M.Div., M.S.Ed. Fire Department: Revs. JOHN DELENDICK; JOSEPH HOFFMAN. Sanitation Department: Rev. Msgrs. ROBERT THELEN, BMT Holy Name Society:; WILLIAM J. FLOOD.

Diocesan Building Commission—Rev. WILLIAM F. KRLIS, Chm., Mailing Address, 7200 Douglaston Pkwy., Douglaston, 11362.

Diocesan Real Estate Board—Rev. Msgr. RAYMOND W. KUTNER, Chm.; Rev. JOHN DELENDICK. Consultants: Rev. WILLIAM F. KRLIS; Mr. KEVIN KEARNEY; Mr. JOHN TYNAN, Mailing Address, 34-43 93rd St., Jackson Heights, 11372.

Diocesan Food Service—Mr. JAMES AUSTIN, Dir., 7200 Douglaston Pkwy., Douglaston, 11362. Tel: 718-229-8001, Ext. 100.

Ecumenical and Interreligious Affairs, Diocesan Commission for—Rev. Msgr. GUY MASSIE, M.Div., Exec. Sec.

Committee for Eastern Orthodox-Catholic Relations—Rev. STEVEN J. AGUGGIA, J.C.L., Chm.

Committee for Catholic-Protestant Relations—Rev. Msgr. GUY MASSIE, M.Div., Chm.

Committee for Catholic-Jewish Relations—Rev. Msgr. GUY MASSIE, M.Div.

Catholic Muslim Dialogue—Rev. Msgr. GUY MASSIE, M.Div., Chm.

Catholic Hindu/Buddhist Dialogue—Rev. ABRAHAM MATTHEW, Chm.

Evangelization Commission—Most Rev. IGNATIUS A. CATANELLO, Ph.D., Chm.; Dr. JAMES SHEEHAN.

Home School Association—Rev. Msgr. THOMAS A. GRAHAM. Tel: 718-525-9099.

Liturgical Commission—Rev. Msgr. JOHN C. TOSI, Exec. Sec.; Sr. THERESA AGLIARDI, R.S.M.; Revs. JOHN F. BROGAN; JOSEPH R. GIBINO; JOSEPH AGOSTINO, C.M.; DAVID ESPINOSA; Rev. Msgr. FERNANDO FERRARESE; Sr. ANGELA GANNON, C.S.J.; Rev. THADDEUS KAZANECKI; Deacon RONALD RIZZUTO; Mr. GREGORY JACK SR.; Sr. MARY JANE KELLY, O.P.; Rev. Msgr. JOHN E. MAHONEY; Dr. JULIE UPTON, R.S.M., Office, 75 Greene Ave., P.O. Box C, Brooklyn, 11202.

Music Commission—VACANT, Office, 75 Greene Ave., P.O. Box C, Brooklyn, 11202.

Pastoral Care of the Sick Office— (See Institutions Located in the Diocese for details)

Pastoral Communications, Office of—Rev. Msgr. MICHAEL J. DEMPSEY, Dir., 1712 10th Ave., Brooklyn, 11215. Tel: 718-499-9705 Legal Title: Trans Video Communications, Inc.

Pastoral Institute—Sr. ANGELA GANNON, C.S.J., 7200 Douglaston Pkwy., Douglaston, 11362. Tel: 718-631-4267.

Prison Ministries Office— (See Listing Under Catholic Charities)

Religious Education, Office of— Evangelization and Catholic Formation: Cultural and Ethnic Groups Dr. JAMES R. SHEEHAN, D.Min., Dir.; Deacon JOHN COFFEY, Regl. Dir., Brooklyn & Coord. Certification Courses; VACANT, Coord. Special Projects & Asst. Dir. Youth Ministry; Sr. ALICE MICHAEL, S.U.S.C., Dir. DRE Personnel, Coord. RCIA, & Dir. Religious Educ. for; RICHARD PIPCHINSKI, Rgnl. Dir., Queens & Coord. Curriculum; ELLEN RHATIGAN, Dir. Youth Ministry/Adolescent & Catechesis and Young Adult Ministry.

Cluster Planning and Collaboration, Office of—Rev. Msgr. CORNELIUS H. MAHONEY, Dir., Mailing Address, 7200 Douglaston Pkwy., Douglaston, 11362. Tel: 718-229-8001, Ext. 736; Fax: 718-428-4574.

Apostolic Organizations

Catholic Youth Organization, Diocesan—MICHAEL ABERNETHY, Dir., 191 Joralemon St., Brooklyn, 11201. Tel: 718-722-6117.

Charismatic Groups, Catholic—

Charismatic Renewal (English-speaking) of the

Diocese of Brooklyn—JOSEPHINE CACHIA, Dir.; JOSEPHINE MCNALLY, Sec., 240 Jay St., Brooklyn, 11201. Tel: 718-260-9121; Fax: 718-260-9121.

Renouveau Charismatique of the Diocese of Brooklyn— (serving the Haitian Charismatics of the Diocese) Rev. Msgr. JOSEPH MALAGRECA, Dir., 218-26 105th Ave., Queens Village, 11429. Tel: 718-465-0124; Fax: 718-479-3548.

Renovacion Carismatica of the Diocese of Brooklyn— (serving the Hispanic Charismatics of the Diocese) Rev. Msgr. JOSEPH MALAGRECA, Dir., 218-26 105th Ave., Queens Village, 11429. Tel: 718-465-0124; Fax: 718-479-3548.

Confraternity of the Guard of Honor and Confraternity of the Holy Hour—VACANT.

Confraternity of the Precious Blood—Rev. Msgr. AUSTIN P. BENNETT, Dir. (Retired), 5300 Fort Hamilton Pkwy., Brooklyn, 11219. Tel: 718-436-1120.

Courage Ministry—Rev. Msgr. WALTER C. MURPHY, Immaculate Conception Center, 7200 Douglaston Pkwy., Douglaston, 11362. Tel: 718-229-1748 (Hotline).

Guilds—

Accountants—Rev. Msgr. WALTER C. MURPHY, Dir.

Catholic Cemetery Guild—Rev. Msgr. MICHAEL J. REID, Moderator.

Lawyers—Rev. EDWARD B. SCHARFENBERGER, S.T.L., J.C.L., J.D., Kings Co.; Rev. Msgr. THOMAS F. DONOVAN, Queens Co.

Pharmacist—VACANT, Dir.

Physicians—Rev. Msgr. JOSEPH C. KONRAD, J.C.D., Kings Co. Chapter Moderator.

Teachers—Rev. Msgr. THOMAS F. NOONAN, M.S., Dir.

Holy Name Society—Rev. DENNIS FARRELL, Moderator.

Marriage Encounter—Coordinators: BOB NOBBS; MELINDA NOBBS. Tel: 718-805-7232.

National Council of Catholic Women—CLAIRE DUNNE, Pres.; Rev. Msgr. LAWRENCE J. MCALISTER, Spiritual Dir. (Retired), 35-60 158th St., Flushing, 11358.

Legion of Mary—Rev. Msgrs. VINCENT F. FULLAM, Dir.; JOSEPH ROSA, Spanish Curia; Deacon JEAN BAPTISTE BOURSIQUOT, Haitian Curia; Revs. JOSEPH AMN, Korean Curia; ALFRED WEINLICH, Flushing Curia; CHARLES REPOLE, O.F.M.Cap., N.W. Queens Curia; JOSEPH MARRIN, C.SS.R., Bay Ridge Curia, 82-00 35th Ave., Jackson Heights, 11372. Tel: 718-429-2333.

Nocturnal Adoration Society—VACANT.

Priests' Eucharistic League—VACANT.

Sodality Union—VACANT.

St. John's Priests Relief Society—Rev. Msgr. GEORGE M. SCHUSTER, Pres.

Apostleship of Prayer—Rev. Msgr. VINCENT KEANE.

CLERGY, PARISHES, MISSIONS AND PAROCHIAL SCHOOLS

CITY OF NEW YORK
BOROUGH OF BROOKLYN

1—THE CATHEDRAL-BASILICA OF ST. JAMES (Jay St. at Tillary) (1822), Rev. Msgr. John C. Tosi. In Res., Rev. Msgr. Otto L. Garcia, J.C.D., V.G.
Res.: 250 Cathedral Pl., 11201. Tel: 718-852-4002 (Office); 718-855-6390 (Rectory); Fax: 718-852-9452.
Catechesis/Religious Program—240 Jay St., 11201. Students 3.

2—ST. AGATHA'S (1912), Revs. James H. Sweeney; Juan J. Lopez (ARE); Lewis H. Maynard; Deacon Juan R. Vargas.
Res.: 702 48th St., 11220. Tel: 718-436-1080; Fax: 718-436-8870.
School—736 48th St., 11220. Tel: 718-435-3137; Fax: 718-437-7505. Sr. Francesca Portera, Prin. Sisters of St. Joseph 1; Lay Teachers 10; Students 245.
Catechesis/Religious Program—Tel: 718-438-4512. Zilia Hirsh, D.R.E. Students 400.

3—ST. AGNES (1878), Rev. William A. McLaughlin; Deacons Jaime Cobham; Aurelio Pagan, (Retired).
Res.: 433 Sackett St., 11231. Tel: 718-625-1717; Fax: 718-625-1929.
Catechesis/Religious Program—Sr. Denise Nolan, O.P., D.R.E. Students 31.

4—ALL SAINTS (1867), (Spanish), Rev. Donald J. Kenna.
Res.: 115 Throop Ave., 11206. Tel: 718-388-1951; Fax: 718-388-7712.
School—113 Throop Ave., 11206. Tel: 718-782-0569. Mrs. Martha Targes McNulty, Prin. Lay Teachers 11; Students 165.
Catechesis/Religious Program—Students 417.

5—ST. ALPHONSUS, Merged, 1976. Records at St. Anthony of Padua-St. Alphonsus.

6—ST. ANDREW THE APOSTLE (1971) Rev. Guy A. Massie; Deacons Gregory Dixon; William Wander; Bryon Amore.
Res.: 6713 Ridge Blvd., 11220. Tel: 718-680-1010; Fax: 718-680-3160.
Catechesis/Religious Program—7320 4th Ave., 11209. Tel: 718-748-6553. Christine Kemp, D.R.E. Students 327.

7—ST. ANN-ST. GEORGE (1860), Revs. James A. Hughes, Admin.; Christopher L. Coleman, Ph.D.
Res.: 207 York St., 11201. Tel: 718-625-0794; Fax: 718-625-4986.
Catechesis/Religious Program—Sharon Maze, D.R.E. Students 50.

8—ANNUNCIATION OF THE BLESSED VIRGIN MARY (1863), Revs. Joseph G. Fonti, S.T.L., Admin.; Juan A. Dielinikaitis (LIT).
Res. and Mailing Address: 275 N. Eighth St., 11211. Tel: 718-384-0223; Fax: 718-384-5838.
Church: 259 N. 5th St., 11211.
Catechesis/Religious Program—Tel: 718-384-0223; Fax: 718-384-5838. Margarita Duran, D.R.E.; Aurea Guzman, D.R.E. Students 12.

9—ST. ANSELM'S (1922), Rev. Msgr. Michael J. Phillips; Revs. Charles McLaughlin; Martin R. Kull; Joseph Vu; Deacon Thomas Davis. In Res., Rev. Herbert A. Travis (Retired).
Res.: 356 82nd St., 11209. Tel: 718-238-2900; Fax: 718-238-2902.
School—357 83rd St., 11209. Tel: 718-745-7643. Sr. Eileen Mary McMahon, S.S.N.D., Prin. Sisters of Notre Dame 2; Lay Teachers 28; Students 575.
Catechesis/Religious Program—Tel: 718-745-0077. Sisters Anne Bernadette, M.S.B.T., D.R.E.; Regina Corde, O.P., Pastoral Ministry. Tel: 718-836-0780; Mary Gilmore, O.P., Dir. of Spirituality. Tel: 718-238-2900. Students 155.
Missionary Cenacle—351 83rd St., 11209. Tel: 718-836-0957. Missionary Servants of the Most Blessed Trinity 2.

10—ST. ANTHONY OF PADUA-ST. ALPHONSUS (1856), Revs. Robert W. Czok; Raymond Roden; Bro. Richard O'Brien, C.S.C.
Res.: 862 Manhattan Ave., 11222. Tel: 718-383-3339; Fax: 718-383-6958.
School—725 Leonard St., 11222. Tel: 718-383-5860; Fax: 718-389-5953. Philip J. Ciani, Prin. Lay Teachers 13; Students 206.
Catechesis/Religious Program—Tel: 718-383-6935. Rose Acetta, Prin. Students 250.

11—ASSUMPTION OF THE BLESSED VIRGIN MARY (1852), Revs. Michael A. Carrano; Peter Mahoney; Sr. Maria Flosterman, F.S.P., Pastoral Assoc.
Res.: 64 Middagh St., 11201. Tel: 718-625-1161; Fax: 718-625-7223.
Catechesis/Religious Program—Sr. Maria Klosterman, F.S.P., D.R.E. Students 30.

12—ST. ATHANASIUS (1913), Rev. Msgr. David L. Cassato, M.Div., M.S.Ed.; Revs. Richard E. Long, M.Div., M.B.A.; Bryan Patterson; Godofrcoo Feliotas (Philippines); Deacon Frank Rosati John Fruner, Pastoral Assoc.
Res.: 2154 61st St., 11204. Tel: 718-236-0124; Fax: 718-236-4960.
School—6120 Bay Pkwy., 11204. Tel: 718-236-4791; Fax: 718-621-1423. Mrs. Lorraine Carone-Tesoro, M.A., M.S., Prin. Lay Teachers 12; Students 280.
Catechesis/Religious Program—Tel: 718-331-8811; Fax: 718-331-2582. Mrs. Nicoletta Milo, D.R.E. Students 350.
Convent—2201 62nd St., 11204. Tel: 718-236-2680.

13—ST. AUGUSTINE (1870), Rev. Robert J. Whelan; Deacon Joseph Bichotte. In Res., Revs. Robert Freul; Anthony Minielli (NY); Agnelo Pinto, (St. Boniface, Winnipeg, Canada); Peter A. Suvakeen (India); Terrence W. Klein (COL).
Res.: 116 Sixth Ave., 11217. Tel: 718-783-3132; Fax: 718-638-4669.
Catechesis/Religious Program—Students 100.

14—ST. BARBARA (1893), Rev. Msgr. John J. Powis; Revs. Frank Spacek; Adrian Alicea (Colombia).
Res.: 138 Bleecker St., 11221. Tel: 718-452-3660; Fax: 718-452-1279.
Catechesis/Religious Program—139 Menaham St., 11221. Tel: 718-453-1406. Carmen Morales, D.R.E.; Alberta Williams, D.R.E. Students 504.

15—ST. BENEDICT'S, Closed. For inquiries for parish records contact the chancery.

16—ST. BERNADETTE (1935), Revs. Robert J. Romano, M.Div.; Anthony V. Dell'Anno. In Res., Rev. Msgr. Cosmo G. Saporito, Pastor Emeritus; Revs. David J. Dettmer; Joseph K. Dolan.
Res.: 8201 13th Ave., 11228. Tel: 718-837-3400; Fax: 718-236-5883.
School—1313 83rd St., 11228. Tel: 718-236-1560; Fax: 718-236-3364. Religious Teachers Filippini 3; Lay Teachers 18; Students 369.
Catechesis/Religious Program—Tel: 718-232-7733. Students 217.

17—ST. BERNARD, Closed. For inquiries for parish records contact the chancery.

18—ST. BERNARD'S, Revs. Ralph J. Caputo; Frank Spacek; Deacon Frank J. D'Accordo. In Res., Rev. Marciano Caliwan.
Res.: 2055 E. 69th St., 11234. Tel: 718-763-5533; Fax: 718-763-0224.
School—2030 E. 69th St., 11234. Tel: 718-241-6040; Fax: 718-241-9653. Kathleen Buscemi, Prin. Religious 1; Lay Teachers 15; Students 300.
Catechesis/Religious Program—Tel: 718-444-4674; Fax: 718-241-7258. Rosanne Curry, D.R.E. Students 400.

19—ST. BLAISE, Merged, with St. Francis of Assisi in 1980. Records at St. Francis of Assisi-St. Blaise.

20—BLESSED SACRAMENT (1891), Revs. Thomas F. Brosnan; John E. Vesey; Sr. Catherine Thornton, O.P., Pastoral Assoc. In Res. Deacon Humberto Alvia.
Res.: 198 Euclid Ave., 11208 Tel: 718-827-1200; Fax: 718-827-2422.
School—187 Euclid Ave., 11208. Tel: 718-235-4863; Fax: 718-235-1132. Catherine Marlowe, Prin. Lay Teachers 15; Students 321.
Catechesis/Religious Program—Tel: 718-277-3231; Fax: 718-277-3231. Students 530.

21—THE ORATORY CHURCH OF ST. BONIFACE (1854), Rev. Mark J. Lane, C.O.; Very Rev. Dennis M. Corrado, C.O., Provost, Brooklyn Oratory; Rev. Joel M. Warden, C.O. In Res., Bro. James Simon, C.O., Dir. Devel.
Res.: 111 Willoughby St., 11201. Tel: 718-875-2096; Fax: 718-875-4678.
Catechesis/Religious Program—Students 180.

22—ST. BRENDAN'S (1907), Rev. Arthur D. Purcell. In Res., Rev. Msgr. Thomas C. Clancy (Retired).
Res.: 1525 E. 12th St., 11230. Tel: 718-339-2828; Fax: 718-339-5951.
Catechesis/Religious Program—Tel: 718-377-6932; Fax: 718-377-6374.

23—ST. BRIGID (1887), Rev. Msgr. James J. Kelly; Revs. George Hernandez; John H. Wilkinson; Deacon Philip J. Ehresmann.
Res.: 409 Linden St., 11237. Tel: 718-821-1690; Fax: 718-386-4302.
School—438 Grove St. E., 11237. Tel: 718-821-1477; Fax: 718-821-1079. Jean Flynn, Prin. Lay Teachers 11; Students 312.
Catechesis/Religious Program—Tel: 718-821-6401. Sr. Patricia Neary, O.P., D.R.E. Students 1,038.

24—ST. CASIMIR, (Polish), Merged, with Our Lady of Czestochowa in 1980. Records at Our Lady of Czestochowa-St. Casimir.

25—ST. CATHARINE OF ALEXANDRIA (1902), Revs. Michael J. Curran; Slawomir Sobiech; Sr. Barbara Mulken, O.P., Pastoral Assoc.; Deacon Genaro Medina.
Res.: 1119 41st St., 11218. Tel: 718-436-5917; Fax: 718-871-5140.
School—1053 41st St., 11219. Tel: 718-436-9721; Fax: 718-853-3347. Anna Marie Bartone, Prin. Sisters, Religious Sisters of the Sacred Heart of Mary 3; Lay Teachers 10; Students 167.
Catechesis/Religious Program—Tel: 718-438-2613. Sr. Rosalind Picciano, C.S.J., D.R.E. Students 360.

26—ST. CATHERINE OF GENOA (1911), Revs. Gerald Dumont; Anthony Iroh (Nigeria); Anthony Braiden-Amissah.
Res.: 520 Linden Blvd., 11203. Tel: 718-282-7162; Fax: 718-282-5568.
School—870 Albany Ave., 11203. Tel: 718-284-1050; Fax: 718-284-3461. Mary M. Blanchard, Co-Prin.; Patricia Maio, Co-Prin. Lay Teachers 14; Students 254.
Catechesis/Religious Program—Tel: 718-469-7505. Brigitte D. Bien-Aime, D.R.E. Students 69.

27—ST. CECILIA (1871), Revs. Patrick F. O'Toole; Matthew Ugwoji; Deacon Carlos Valderama. In Res., Rev. Msgr. Michael J. Brennan, V.E., Vicar of Brooklyn West; Rev. Kevin J. O'Donoghue.
Res.: 84 Herbert St., 11222. Tel: 718-389-0010; Fax: 718-389-5090.
School—Tel: 718-389-3161; Fax: 718-389-4333. Sr. Miriam Daniels, C.S.J., Prin. Sisters 3; Lay Teachers 21; Students 465.
Catechesis/Religious Program—1-15 Monitor St., 11222. Tel: 718-389-2546. Sr. Paul Maria, D.R.E. Students 100.

28—ST. CHARLES BORROMEO (1849), Revs. Charles A. Kraus; Thaddeus A. Grzelak. In Res., Rev. Ngozi Osuji; Bro. Becket Ryan, O.S.F.
Res.: 21 Sidney Pl., 11201. Tel: 718-625-1177; Fax: 718-624-1627.
School—23 Sidney Pl., 11201. Tel: 718-596-1362; Fax: 718-875-9471. Martha Accordino, Prin. Lay Teachers 14; Students 204.
Catechesis/Religious Program—Students 31.

29—ST. COLUMBA (1967), Revs. Charles J. Matonti; Paul K. Agyei, Pastoral Assoc.; Deacon Lawrence Coyle.
Res.: 2245 Kimball St., 11234. Tel: 718-338-6265; Fax: 718-377-6440.

Catechesis/Religious Program—Tel: 718-253-8840. Nancy Azzaro, D.R.E. Students 198.

30—St. Columbkille, Closed., Parochial records are located at SS. Cyril and Methodius. Became a mission in 1939.

31—SS. Cyril and Methodius (1917), (Polish), Revs. Roman Kmiec, C.M. (HRT); Joseph Wisniewski, C.M.
Res.: 150 Dupont St., 11222. Tel: 718-389-4424; Fax: 718-389-4191.
Catechesis/Religious Program—Students 160.

32—St. Dominic (1972), Rev. Gaetano J. Sbordone; Sr. Patricia Murphy, C.S.J., Pastoral Min.; Deacons Carlo V. Mellace; Dante Colandrea.
Res.: 2001 Bay Ridge Pkwy., 11204. Tel: 718-259-4636; 718-259-4637; Fax: 718-259-3066.
Catechesis/Religious Program—Tel: 718-621-0422. Maria Siragusa, D.R.E. Students 425.

33—St. Edmund's (1922), Rev. Edward Brophy; Deacon Ronald Rizzuto. In Res., Rev. Msgr. Thomas F. Noonan, M.S., Pastor Emeritus; Rev. Matthew Chacko, C.M.I. (India).
Res.: 2460 Ocean Ave., 11229. Tel: 718-743-0102; Fax: 718-891-7834.
School—1902 Avenue T, 11229. Tel: 718-648-9229. Patricia O'Connor, Prin. Lay Teachers 17; Students 295.
High School—Denis Maloney Institute/St. Edmund Preparatory High School, 2474 Ocean Ave., 11229. Tel: 718-743-6100; Fax: 718-743-5243. Mr. John Lorenzetti, Prin.; Mr. James Benson, Asst. Prin.; Sr. Barbara Doyle, C.S.J., Campus Min. Sisters 2; Lay Teachers 41; Students 670.
Catechesis/Religious Program—Tel: 718-743-8107. Deacon Ronald Rizzuto, D.R.E. Students 109.

34—St. Edward, Merged, with St. Michael Archangel in 1942. Parochial records are at St. Michael-St. Edward, 108 St. Edwards St., 11205.

35—St. Ephrem's (1921), Rev. Msgr. Peter V. Kain; Rev. Caleb Austin Pero Buchanan; Deacon Wilfred N. Horne.
Res.: 929 Bay Ridge Pkwy., 11228. Tel: 718-833-1010; Fax: 718-921-5232.
School—Tel: 718-833-1440; Fax: 718-745-5301. Sr. Nora Ashe, C.S.J., Prin. Sisters of St. Joseph and Servants of the Immaculate Heart of Mary 3; Lay Teachers 22; Students 405.
Catechesis/Religious Program—Tel: 718-745-7486. Diane Mosconi, D.R.E. Students 269.
Convent—935 Bay Ridge Pkwy., 11228. Tel: 718-833-1555.

36—Epiphany (1905), Rev. Richard Bucther, Admin.; Rev. Msgr. Matthew F. Foley, Pastor Emeritus.
Res.: 96 S. Ninth St., 11211. Tel: 718-387-6328; Fax: 718-387-2449.
Catechesis/Religious Program—Sr. Miriam Anne Morgan, D.R.E. Students 85.
Arriba Juntos--Forward Together, Inc. Center—96 S. Ninth St., 11211. Tel: 718-384-2121.

37—St. Finbar's (1880), Revs. Joseph T. Holcomb; Luke Wei; David F. Espinosa; Deacon Giovanni Rizzo.
Res.: 138 Bay 20th St., 11214. Tel: 718-236-3312; Fax: 718-236-3750.
School—1825 Bath Ave., 11214. Tel: 718-256-0818; Fax: 718-256-3766. Rosina Katsoulis, Prin. Lay Teachers 10; Students 178.
Catechesis/Religious Program—Tel: 718-837-3935. Sr. Ann Joachim, C.S.A.C., D.R.E. Students 225.

38—St. Fortunata (1934), Rev. Vincent F. Miceli. In Res., Rev. Msgr. James W. Ryan, Pastor Emeritus (Retired).
Res.: 2609 Linden Blvd., 11208. Tel: 718-647-2632; Fax: 718-647-1321.
School—26-35 Linden Blvd., 11208. Tel: 718-647-6440; Fax: 718-827-2166. Miss Marian J. Siconolfi, Prin. Lay Teachers 13; Students 309.
Catechesis/Religious Program—Tel: 718-827-0162. Carmen VanderPool, D.R.E. Students 117.

39—Fourteen Holy Martyrs, Merged, with St. Martin of Tours in 1976. Records at St. Martin of Tours-Fourteen Holy Martyrs.

40—St. Frances Cabrini (1963), Rev. Msgr. Richard E.. Marchese.
Res.: 1562 86th. St., 11228. Tel: 718-236-9165; Fax: 718-331-8139.
School—21 Bay 11th St., 11228. Tel: 718-232-6700; Fax: 718-234-5651. Sr. Martin Marie Doran, O.P., Prin. Sisters 2; Lay Teachers 13; Students 246.
Catechesis/Religious Program—Tel: 718-232-4228. Students 191.

41—St. Frances Cabrini Chapel, Closed. For inquiries for parish records contact the chancery.

42—St. Frances de Chantal (1891), Revs. Canon Andrzej Kurowski, S.A.C.; Slawomir Siok, S.A.C.; Piotr Karaszewski, S.A.C.
Res.: 1273 58th St., 11219. Tel: 718-436-6407; Fax: 718-854-2761.
Catechesis/Religious Program—Lay Teachers 18; Students 320.

43—St. Francis in the Fields, Closed. For inquiries for parish records contact the chancery.

44—St. Francis of Assisi-St. Blaise, Revs. John Bolduc, S.M.; Roger Bourgea, S.M.; Souvenir Jean Paul.
Res.: Tel: 718-756-2015; Fax: 718-756-1773.
Church: 319 Maple St., 11225.
School—400 Lincoln Rd., 11225. Tel: 718-778-3700; Fax: 718-778-7877. Sr. Theresa Scanlon, C.S.J., Prin. Lay Teachers 17; Students 382; Sisters 2.
Catechesis/Religious Program—335 Maple St., 11225. Tel: 718-778-1302. Ms. Myrmonde Dorismond, D.R.E. Students 206.

45—St. Francis of Paola (1918), (Italian), Rev. Andrew R. Varano; Deacon John P. Orlandello.
Res.: 219 Conselyea St., 11211. Tel: 718-387-0256; Fax: 718-387-6344.
Catechesis/Religious Program—Tel: 718-387-0256; Fax: 718-387-6344. Sr. Claudia Bradshaw, C.S.J., D.R.E. Students 80.

46—St. Francis Xavier (1886), Rev. Gregory A. Stankus; Deacons John Franca; James Ramos. In Res., Rev. Robert M. Powers.
Res.: 225 Sixth Ave., 11215. Tel: 718-638-1880; Fax: 718-638-2839.
School—763 President St., 11215. Tel: 718-857-2903. Sr. Kathleen Sullivan, C.S.J., Prin. Sisters of St. Joseph 3; Lay Teachers 19; Students 450.
Catechesis/Religious Program—Tel: 718-857-2903. Sr. Helene Conway, D.R.E. Students 150.

47—St. Gabriel The Archangel (1901), Revs. Marcelo Javier Navarro, I.V.E. (Argentina); Jose Agustin Orellana Lizana, I.V.E.
Res.: 749 Linwood St., 11208. Tel: 718-257-0612; Fax: 718-257-5258.
Catechesis/Religious Program—666 Essex St., 11208. Tel: 718-649-0450; Fax: 718-649-0450. Sr. Maria de Jesus Barruti, S.S.V.H., D.R.E. Students 656.

48—St. George, Merged, with St. Ann in 1986. Records at St. Ann-St. George.

49—Good Shepherd (1927), Rev. Msgr. Thomas F. Brady; Revs. Timothy J. Teahan; Abraham P. Mathew; Sr. Mary Lorraine.
Res.: 1950 Batchelder St., 11229. Tel: 718-998-2800; Fax: 718-382-5428.
School—1943 Brown St., 11229. Tel: 718-339-2745; Fax: 718-645-4513. Mr. Anthony Paparelli, Prin. Lay Teachers 25; Students 510.
Catechesis/Religious Program—Tel: 718-375-0899; Fax: 718-645-4513. Students 475.

50—St. Gregory the Great (1905), Rev. Gary P. Rogers; Deacons Roy N. George; Andres De Leon Jr.
Res.: 224 Brooklyn Ave., 11213-2505. Tel: 718-773-0100; Fax: 718-773-4198.
School—991 St. Johns Pl., 11213-2532. Tel: 718-774-3330; Fax: 718-774-3332. Cynthia O. Tege, Prin. Lay Teachers 15; Students 325.
Catechesis/Religious Program—Tel: 718-773-0100; Fax: 718-773-4198. Julia Bramwell, D.R.E. Students 100.

51—Guardian Angel (1885), Rev. Msgr. Perfecto Vazquez; Rev. Andrzej Lukianiuk; Deacon Anthony J. Russo.
Res.: 2978 Ocean Pkwy., 11235. Tel: 718-266-1561; Fax: 718-372-1603.
Catechesis/Religious Program—Tel: 718-372-1967. Olga Ortiz, D.R.E. Students 230.

52—Holy Cross (1848), Rev. Msgr. James F. Spengler, Admin.; Revs. Pascal Louis; David Attuanya, C.Ss.P.
Res.: 2530 Church Ave., 11226. Tel: 718-469-5900; Fax: 718-469-5901.
School—2520 Church Ave., 11226. Tel: 718-282-1710. Sr. Angela Patrice Murray, C.S.J., Prin. Lay Teachers 11; Students 206.
Catechesis/Religious Program—Tel: 718-941-5066. Catherine Hayes, D.R.E. Students 425.

53—Holy Family (1880), Rev. Thomas E. Fox; Deacon Hector Montalvo. In Res., Rev. Bartholomew Chidili, O.S.A.
Res.: 205 14th St., 11215. Tel: 718-768-0736; Fax: 718-832-2879.
School—Sisters 1; Lay Teachers 8; Students 99.
Catechesis/Religious Program—Sr. Doryne Bermoy, F.L.P., D.R.E. Students 93.

54—Holy Family (1880), Revs. John J. Amann; Edward R. Kane; Vitalis N. Opara (Nigeria). In Res., Rev. Msgr. Raymond F. Rau; Rev. John A. McShane (Retired).
Res.: 9719 Flatlands Ave., 11236. Tel: 718-257-4423; Fax: 718-257-4806.
School—Tel: 718-257-2954; Fax: 718-257-3043. Mary Lou Reitz, Prin. Lay Teachers 14; Students 265.
Catechesis/Religious Program—Tel: 718-257-8016; Fax: 718-272-2279. Elizabeth Mathew, D.R.E. Students 174.

55—Holy Family (1905), (Slovak), Rev. John Menonkari, C.M.I. (India).
Res.: 21 Nassau Ave., 11222. Tel: 718-388-5145; Fax: 718-387-1877.

56—Holy Innocents, Rev. Msgr. Rollin J. Darbouze; Revs. Luis Carlos Pisfil (Peru); Jean-Miguel Auguste.
Res.: 279 E. 17th St., 11226. Tel: 718-469-9500; Fax: 718-941-4931.
School—249 E. 17th St., 11226. Tel: 718-282-5294; Fax: 718-282-3490. Sr. Mary Immaculate, R.S.M., Prin. Sisters of Mercy 2; Lay Teachers 14; Students 228.
Catechesis/Religious Program—Tel: 718-469-8159. Students 232.

57—Holy Name (1878), Revs. Dennis J. Farrell; Henry Williams; Peter J. Rayder; Deacon Abel Torres.
Res.: 245 Prospect Park W., 11215. Tel: 718-768-3071; Fax: 718-369-2039.
School—241 Prospect Park W., 11215. Tel: 718-768-7629; Fax: 718-768-3007. Robert Hughes, Prin. & D.R.E. Sisters of St. Joseph 1; Lay Teachers 16; Students 229.
Catechesis/Religious Program—241 Prospect Park W., 11215. Tel: 718-768-7629; Fax: 718-768-3007. Students 229.

58—Holy Rosary (1889), (African American), Rev. William Smith.
Res.: 172 Bainbridge St., 11233. Tel: 718-493-8001; Fax: 718-493-8002.

59—Holy Spirit, Rev. Jerome T. Jecewiz; Deacons Wilfredo Hernandez; Louis Gonzalez. In Res., Rev. Bartholomew Okagbue.
Res.: 1712 45th St., 11204. Tel: 718-436-5565; Fax: 718-436-5586.
School—1668 46th St., 11204. Tel: 718-633-3959; Fax: 718-633-2830. Deacon Ronald Ruzzuto, Prin. Sisters of St. Joseph 1; Lay Teachers 9; Students 168.
Catechesis/Religious Program—Students 125.
Convent—1679 47th St., 11204.

60—St. Ignatius (1908), Revs. Rocco C. Danzi, S.J.; Carlos Quijano, S.J.; Deacons Berthal Beaubrun; Jean-Baptiste Boursiquot; Chris Cato, Pastoral Assoc.
Res.: 1101 Carroll St., 11225. Tel: 718-774-2102; Fax: 718-774-5821.
Catechesis/Religious Program—Tel: 718-774-2102; Fax: 718-774-5821. Lorraine Pierre, Ph.D., D.R.E. Students 170.

61—Immaculate Conception of the Blessed Virgin Mary (1853), Revs. Robert P. Morales; Luis David Pulido (Colombia).
Res.: 72 Maujer St., 11206. Tel: 718-384-0765; Fax: 718-384-2898.
Catechesis/Religious Program—Students 105.

62—Immaculate Heart of Mary (1893), Revs. John J. Costello; Joseph Gibino, Ph.D.; Deacon Thomas J. Devaney. In Res., Rev. Edward T. O'Connor, Pastor Emeritus (Retired).
Res.: 2805 Ft. Hamilton Pkwy., 11218. Tel: 718-871-1310; Fax: 718-633-1866.
School—3002 Ft. Hamilton Pkwy., 11218. Tel: 718-438-7373. Kathleen O'Sullivan-O'Donnell, Prin. Lay Teachers 12; Students 190.
Catechesis/Religious Program—Tel: 718-854-7326. Joyce Checkett, D.R.E. Tel: 718-854-7326. Students 200.

63—St. Jerome's (1901), Rev. Msgr. Guy Sansaricq; Deacon Magloire Marcel.
Res.: 2900 Newkirk Ave., 11226. Tel: 718-462-0223; Fax: 718-462-7753.
School—465 E. 29th St., 11226. Tel: 718-462-0211; Fax: 718-462-1828. Mrs. Satti Marchan, Prin. Lay Teachers 10; Students 240.
Catechesis/Religious Program—Paul Norman, D.R.E. Students 296.

64—St. John Cantius (1902), Rev. John A. Gurrieri; Deacon Rafael Marte; Sr. Mary Alice MacKenzie, S.C.
Res.: 479 New Jersey Ave., 11207. Tel: 718-342-2679; Fax: 718-342-4878.
School—692 Blake Ave.. Tel: 718-385-7494; Fax: 718-566-1928. Ms. Margaret Otunba, Prin. Sisters 5; Lay Teachers 10; Students 195.
Catechesis/Religious Program—Sr. Mary Alice Mackenzie, S.C., D.R.E. Students 180.

65—St. John the Baptist (1868), Revs. Joseph V. Agostino, C.M.; Eugene F. Sheridan, C.M.; Stephen F. Cantwell, C.M. (PH). In Res., Rev. Thomas S. Krafinski, C.M.
Res.: 75 Lewis Ave., 11206. Tel: 718-455-6864; Fax: 718-452-3738.
School—82 Lewis Ave., 11206. Tel: 718-453-1000; Fax: 718-453-1000. Cheryl Malcousu, Prin. Lay Teachers 24; Students 520.
Catechesis/Religious Program—Sr. Helen Gertrude Carroll, D.C., D.R.E. Students 205.

66—St. John the Evangelist (1849), Rev. Thomas M. Haggerty. In Res., Rev. James McDevitt.
Res.: 250 21st St., 11215. Tel: 718-768-3751; Fax: 718-768-4689.
Catechesis/Religious Program—Students 175.

67—St. John's Chapel, Closed. For inquiries for parish records contact the chancery.

68—St. Joseph Patron of the Universal Church

(1921),, (Scalabrini Fathers) Revs. Gianni Agostinelli, C.S.; Mariano Cisco.
Res.: 185 Suydam St., 11221. Tel: 718-386-0175; Fax: 718-821-1726.
School—St. Frances Cabrini, 181 Suydam St., 11221. Tel: 718-386-9277; Fax: 718-386-9064. Miss Maria Crifasi, Prin. Lay Teachers 10; Students 268.
Catechesis/Religious Program—Students 560.

69—ST. JOSEPH'S (1850), Rev. Robert Vitaglione; Sr. Juliet Duruanyaoha, D.D.L., Pastoral Assoc.
Res.: 856 Pacific St., 11238. Tel: 718-783-4500; Fax: 718-398-2410.
Catechesis/Religious Program—Students 50.

70—ST. LAURENCE (1964), Rev. Frank A. Black; Sisters Charlene Kay, O.P., Pastoral Assoc.; Judith Ann Flanagan, O.P., Pastoral Assoc.
Res.: 1020 Van Siclen Ave., 11207. Tel: 718-649-0545; Fax: 718-649-1606.
Catechesis/Religious Program—Tel: 718-927-3310. Sr. Mary Jareth, D.R.E. Students 120.

71—ST. LEONARD OF PORT MAURICE, , Closed 1978. Records at St. Joseph, Patron of the Universal Church.

72—ST. LOUIS, Closed., Became a Mission of St. Lucy in 1939. Parochial records are at St. Lucy-St. Patrick's, 285 Willoughby Ave., 11205. Tel: 718-622-8748; Fax: 718-622-6330.

73—ST. LUCY-ST. PATRICK (1843), Rev. Francis Shannon; Deacon Ronald Ronacher.
Res.: 285 Willoughby Ave., 11205. Tel: 718-622-8748; Fax: 718-622-6330.
Catechesis/Religious Program—Students 200.

74—ST. MALACHY'S (1854), Rev. Raymond J. Kelly; Remedios Guerrero, M.A., Pastoral Assoc. In Res., Rev. David Bertolotti.
Res.: 207 Hendrix St., 11207. Tel: 718-647-5900; Fax: 718-348-4744.
Catechesis/Religious Program—Tel: 718-235-3562. Remedios Guerrero, M.A., D.R.E. Students 183.

75—ST. MARGARET MARY (1920), Rev. Walter A. Mitchell.
Res.: 215 Exeter St., Manhattan Beach, 11235. Tel: 718-743-1824; Fax: 718-934-8226.
Catechesis/Religious Program—Students 25.

76—ST. MARK'S (1861), Revs. Joseph R. Grimaldi, J.C.L.; Edward M. Kachurka; Sr. Gloria Lepere, O.P., Pastoral Assoc. In Res., Revs. Joseph P. Quigley; Cyril J. Doody, Parochial Vicar (Retired).
Res.: 2609 E. 19th St., 11235. Tel: 718-891-3100; Fax: 718-891-9677.
Church: Ocean Ave. & Ave. Z, 11235.
School—2602 E. 19th St., 11235. Tel: 718-332-9604; Fax: 718-891-9677. Mary Ann DeMaso, Prin. Lay Teachers 11; Students 225.
Catechesis/Religious Program—Tel: 718-769-6311; Fax: 718-891-9677. Anne O'Brien, D.R.E. Students 164.

77—ST. MARTIN OF TOURS-FOURTEEN HOLY MARTYRS, Revs. Patrick G. Burns; Oliver A. Onwukbiko; Deacons Fausto Duran, P.D.; Pedro Leon. In Res., Rev. Dennis Klein.
Res.: 1288 Hancock St., 11221. Tel: 718-443-8484; Fax: 718-443-2968.
School—Tel: 718-386-4050; Fax: 718-386-1565. Cynthia Casciola Kitts, Prin. See St. Elizabeth Seton under Consolidated Elementary Schools in the Institutions located in the Diocese. Lay Teachers 10; Students 240.
Catechesis/Religious Program—Sr. Judy Fay, C.S.J., D.R.E. Students 160.

78—ST. MARY MOTHER OF JESUS (1889), Rev. Casper J. Furnari; Rev. Msgr. Rocco D. Villani, Pastor Emeritus; Revs. Reynolds Basilious, O.C.D.; Angelo A. Venuti.
Res.: 2326 84th St., 11214. Tel: 718-372-4000; Fax: 718-372-4002.
School—8401 23rd Ave., 11214. Tel: 718-372-0025; Fax: 718-265-6498. Sr. Elizabeth O'Neill, C.S.J., Prin. Sisters of St. Joseph 5; Lay Teachers 14; Students 309.
Catechesis/Religious Program—Tel: 718-449-8263; Fax: 718-265-6209. Sr. Patricia Conroy, R.S.M., D.R.E. Students 320.

79—ST. MARY OF THE ANGELS, (Lithuanian),, Closed 1981. Records at Annunciation Parish, Brooklyn.

80—MARY QUEEN OF HEAVEN (1927), Rev. Jamie J. Gigantiello; Sr. Joan J. Holmberg, S.C., Pastoral Assoc.; Rev. Msgr. John A. Burns, Pastor Emeritus (Retired). In Res.,
Res.: 1395 E. 56th St., 11234. Tel: 718-763-2330; Fax: 718-763-6592.
School—1326 E. 57th St., 11234 Tel: 718-763-2360. Sr. Donna Murphy, O.P., Prin. Lay Teachers 13; Students 280.
Catechesis/Religious Program—Tel: 718-763-2590. Elaine Bianchini, D.R.E. Students 210.

81—ST. MARY, STAR OF THE SEA (1851), Revs. Thomas Doyle; David Ihenacho; Sr. Denise Nolan, O.P.
Res.: 467 Court St., 11231. Tel: 718-625-2270; Fax: 718-624-9017.
Catechesis/Religious Program—Students 40.

82—ST. MATTHEW'S (1886), Revs. Andrew L. Struzzieri, D.Min.; Apollinaris Anyomi; Isaie Jean-Louis; Deacons Florencio Cruz; Dennis A. DaCosta; Herve Desdunes.
Res.: 1123 Eastern Pkwy., 11213. Tel: 718-774-6747; Fax: 718-953-4895.
Catechesis/Religious Program—1351 Lincoln Pl., 11213. Sr. Christine Scherer, D.W., D.R.E. Students 485.
Social Action Coord.—Sr. Dolores Augustine, P.V.M.I.

83—ST. MICHAEL ARCHANGEL AND ST. EDWARD (1891), Rev. James A. Hughes; Nelsa Elias, Pastoral Admin.
Res.: 108 St. Edward's St., 11205. Tel: 718-625-3017; Fax: 718-625-2536.
Catechesis/Religious Program—Students 70.

84—ST. MICHAEL'S (1870), Revs. John Delendick; Pedro Nel Ossa; Deacon Julio C. Mejia. In Res., Rev. Youssef Bochra Nasri; Sr. Dolores Ryan, C.S.J., Pastoral Assoc.
Res.: 352 42nd St., 11232. Tel: 718-768-6065; Fax: 718-768-3336.
School—4222 Fourth Ave., 11232. Tel: 718-768-3582; Fax: 718-768-9434. Mrs. Catherine Schiffer, Prin. Religious 1; Lay Teachers 10; Students 170.
Catechesis/Religious Program—Tel: 718-788-3442. Sr. Helene Jakubowski, R.S.M., D.R.E. Students 350.

85—ST. MICHAEL'S (1860), Revs. Luis Atencio, I.V.E.; Alexis Moronta, I.V.E.; Deacon Leon F. Miller; Sr. Rita Rompre, C.N.D.; Deacon Jorge Arturo Gonzalez.
Res.: 225 Jerome St., 11207. Tel: 718-647-1818; Fax: 718-647-2384.
School—235 Jerome St., 11207. Tel: 718-277-6766. Sisters 2; Lay Teachers 13; Students 306.
Catechesis/Religious Program—Tel: 718-647-1818; Fax: 718-647-2384. Students 254.

86—MOST HOLY TRINITY (1841), Revs. Russell Governale, O.F.M.Conv.; Vincent Rubino, O.F.M.-Conv.; Bro. Vincent Vivian, O.F.M.Conv.
Res.: 138 Montrose Ave., 11206. Tel: 718-384-0215; Fax: 718-384-3030.
School—140 Montrose Ave., 11206. Tel: 718-384-1101; Fax: 718-384-6567. Sr. Karen Lademann, O.P., Prin.
Catechesis/Religious Program—Tel: 718-486-6276; Fax: 718-384-3030. Students 165.

87—MOST PRECIOUS BLOOD (1927), (Italian), Rev. Msgr. Joseph Rosa; Rev. Joseph Attard.
Res.: 70 Bay 47th St., 11214. Tel: 718-372-8022; Fax: 718-996-6575.
School—133-157 27th Ave., 11214 Tel: 718-373-7343; Fax: 718-373-5887. Sisters 4; Lay Teachers 6; Students 231.
Catechesis/Religious Program—Sr. Isabel, D.R.E. Students 230.

88—NATIVITY OF OUR BLESSED LORD, Merged, with St. Peter Claver in 1973. Records at St. Peter Claver Church.

89—ST. NICHOLAS (1865), Rev. Kenneth J. Grande.
Res.: 26 Olive St., 11211. Tel: 718-388-1420; Fax: 718-388-9516.
School—287 Powers St., 11211. Tel: 718-388-7992; Fax: 718-388-7543. Sr. Joan Losson, O.P., Prin. Lay Teachers 14; Students 265.
Catechesis/Religious Program—Students 131.
Convent—312 De Voe St., 11211.

90—OUR LADY HELP OF CHRISTIANS (1927), Revs. Anthony M. Rucando; William A. With.
Res.: 1315 E. 28th St., 11210. Tel: 718-338-5242; Fax: 718-258-5341.
School—1340 E. 29th St., 11210. Tel: 718-377-1800; Fax: 718-377-6374. Ms. Joanne Adorisio, Prin. Lay Teachers 12; Students 174.
Catechesis/Religious Program—Tel: 718-377-6932; Fax: 718-258-5341. Stephen Rzonca, Pastoral Assoc. Students 85.

91—OUR LADY OF ANGELS (1891), Revs. James E. Devlin, Pastor; Kenneth J. Calder; Richard Lewkiewicz; Deacon Michael J. Troy. In Res., Rev. Thomas F. Kelly.
Res.: 7320 Fourth Ave., 11209. Tel: 718-836-7200; Fax: 718-238-2466.
School—Tel: 718-238-5045. Sr. Elizabeth Schroeder, C.S.J., Prin. Lay Teachers 17; Students 275.
Catechesis/Religious Program—Tel: 718-748-6553. Christine Kemp, D.R.E. Students 200.

92—OUR LADY OF CHARITY (1903), Deacon James J. Lacy, Admin.
Res.: 1669 Dean St., 11213. Tel: 718-774-5100; Fax: 718-778-3335.
Catechesis/Religious Program—Tel: 718-774-5100; Fax: 718-778-3338. Ethel Ancoh-Menson, D.R.E. Students 30.

93—OUR LADY OF CONSOLATION (1909), (Polish), Revs. Damian Tomiczek, S.D.S. (NEW); Pawel Dolinski, S.D.S.; Jacek Zebrowski, S.D.S. (Poland).
Res.: 184 Metropolitan Ave., 11211. Tel: 718-388-1942; Fax: 718-388-8993.

94—OUR LADY OF CZESTOCHOWA-ST. CASIMIR (1896), (Polish), Revs. Witold Mroziewski; Andrzej Gorczyca; Dariusz Blicharz.
Catechesis/Religious Program—Students 250.

95—OUR LADY OF GOOD COUNSEL, Rev. James W. Bukofsky; Deacon Isaac Duncan; Sr. Rosalina Garcia.
Res.: 915 Putnam Ave., 11221. Tel: 718-443-7211; Fax: 718-443-0121.
Catechesis/Religious Program—Mrs. Sonia Andrews, D.R.E. Students 160.

96—OUR LADY OF GRACE (1935), (Italian), Revs. Thomas F. Leach; Dominick F. Cutrone, Pastor Emeritus (Retired); John C. Miller; Deacon Philip Siani; Sr. Jane Talbot, Pastoral Min.
Res.: 430 Avenue W, 11223. Tel: 718-627-2020; Fax: 718-336-8033.
School—385 Avenue W, 11223. Tel: 718-375-2081; Fax: 718-376-7685. Mrs. Joan McMaster, Prin. Lay Teachers 16; Students 293.
Catechesis/Religious Program—Tel: 718-375-0404; Fax: 718-376-7685. Linda Nacinovich, D.R.E. Students 245.

97—OUR LADY OF GUADALUPE (1906), (Italian—Spanish), Rev. Msgr. Kevin B. Noone; Rev. Robert B. Adamo; Sr. Ann Elizabeth, O.P, Pastoral Assoc. In Res., Revs. Amiro Jimenez; Frank Mann.
Res.: 7201 Fifteenth Ave., 11228. Tel: 718-236-8300; Fax: 718-236-8119.
School—1518 73rd St., 11228. Tel: 718-236-5587; Fax: 718-236-5587. Sisters Lora Bannon, O.P., Prin.; Jean Fry, O.P., Asst. Prin. Sisters of St. Dominic 3; Sisters of St. Joseph 1; Lay Teachers 23; Students 609.
Catechesis/Religious Program—Tel: 718-331-4003. Mrs. Suzanne O'Connor, D.R.E. Students 280.

98—OUR LADY OF LORETO (1894), Rev. Fredi A. Rosales, Admin.
Res.: 124 Sackman St., 11233. Tel: 718-385-3740; Fax: 718-385-3446.
Catechesis/Religious Program—Our Lady of the Presentation, 1677 St. Nlarics Ave., 11233-4813. Tel: 718-345-2604; Fax: 718-245-4639. Students 56.

99—OUR LADY OF LOURDES (1872), Rev. William A. Smith.
Res.: 11 DeSales Pl., 11207. Tel: 718-452-2260; Fax: 718-452-6828.
School—2-12 Aberdeen St., 11207. Tel: 718-455-0037; Fax: 718-602-3348. Lay Teachers 11; Students 220.
Catechesis/Religious Program—Students 145.

100—OUR LADY OF MERCY (1961), Rev. Robert M. Powers.
Res.: 680 Mother Gaston Blvd., 11212. Tel: 718-346-3166; Fax: 718-346-5776.
Catechesis/Religious Program—Sr. Bernadette Sassone, D.W., D.R.E. Students 275.

101—OUR LADY OF MERCY, , Closed 1908. Second church at Schermerhorn & Bond closed April, Debevoise Place & DeKalb Ave. For inquiries for parish records contact the chancery.

102—OUR LADY OF MIRACLES (1936), Rev. Francis J. Hughes; Giovanna Piccioli, A.O., Pastoral Assoc.; Deacons Ernst Paul; Saint Charles Borno. In Res., Rev. Gordon P. Kusi (Ghana).
Res.: 757 E. 86th St., 11236. Tel: 718-257-2400; Fax: 718-257-4634.
School—Tel: 718-649-0271; Fax: 718-649-3113. Bruno Marchan, Prin. Lay Teachers 12; Students 280.
Catechesis/Religious Program—Tel: 718-649-1006. Sr. Vilma Orejola, F.L.P., D.R.E. Students 300.

103—OUR LADY OF MONSERRATE-ST. AMBROSE (1954), Rev. Francis Shannon; Sr. Maryellen Kane, C.S.J., Pastoral Assoc.; Deacon Ronald Ronacker, Pastoral Assoc. In Res., Revs. John Brogan; Christopher Cokman.
Res.: 134 Vernon Ave., 11206. Tel: 718-388-5196; Fax: 718-388-5153.
Catechesis/Religious Program—Students 190.

104—OUR LADY OF PEACE (1899), (Italian), Rev. Roderick A. Crispo, O.F.M. In Res., Revs. Bruno Ciardiello, O.F.M.; Samuel Karimi.
Res.: 522 Carroll St., 11215. Tel: 718-624-5122; Fax: 718-852-6149.
Catechesis/Religious Program—Students 125.
Convent—Hermanas Franciscanas de la Immaculada, 209 First St., 11215. Tel: 718-624-6720; Fax: 718-852-6149.

105—OUR LADY OF PERPETUAL HELP BASILICA (1893), Very Rev. Sean J. McGillicuddy, C.Ss.R., Pastor & Rector; Revs. Norman S. Bennett, C.SS.R.; Joseph Buono, C.SS.R.; Edward Byrne, C.SS.R.; Luis A. Caro, C.SS.R.; Martin Crowe, C.SS.R.; Edward Dunne, C.SS.R.; Sylvester E. Feeley, C.SS.R.; John Gauci, C.SS.R.; Thomas F. Hickey, C.SS.R.; Thomas Maceda, C.SS.R.; Ruskin Piedra, C.SS.R.; John Hamrogue, C.SS.R.; Pierce Kenny, C.SS.R.; John J. Travers, C.SS.R.; John Murray, C.SS.R.; Robert F. Wojtek, C.SS.R.; Sisters Bernard Loretto, C.S.J., Pastoral Assoc.; Noraleen Murphy, C.S.J.,

Pastoral Assoc.; Deacons Abdon Mejia (Peru), Pastoral Assoc.; Eduviges Lopez, Pastoral Assoc.; Jesus Soto, Pastoral Assoc.
Res.: 526-59th St., 11220. Tel: 718-492-9200; Fax: 718-439-8528.
School—Tel: 718-492-8067; Fax: 718-439-8081. Sr. Madeline Therese DiCarlo, C.S.J., Prin. Sisters 3; Lay Teachers 14; Students 289.
Catechesis/Religious Program—584 60th St., 11220. Tel: 718-492-9795; Fax: 718-439-8528. Students 350.

106—OUR LADY OF REFUGE (1911), Revs. Michael A. Perry; John Tobon; Judy Agard, Admin.
Res.: 2020 Foster Ave., 11210. Tel: 718-434-2090; Fax: 718-859-7411.
School—1087 Ocean Ave., 11230. Tel: 718-434-4117. Robert Thoering, Prin.; Judy Agard, Admin. Lay Teachers 17; Students 316.
Catechesis/Religious Program—Students 113.

107—OUR LADY OF SOLACE (1900), Revs. Patrick J. West; Robinson Sierra, S.A. (Colombia) (RVC); Deacon Dan J. Marley.
Res.: 2866 W. 17th St., 11224. Tel: 718-266-1612; Fax: 718-946-3651.
Catechesis/Religious Program—Mr. Augusto Lucero, D.R.E. Students 170.

108—OUR LADY OF SORROWS, Merged, with St. Leonard in 1942. Parochial records are at St. Joseph Patron of the Universal Church.

109—OUR LADY OF THE PRESENTATION (1887), Rev. Msgr. Joseph A. Nugent; Deacon Jaime Landron.
Res.: 1677 St. Marks Ave., 11233-4813. Tel: 718-345-2604; Fax: 718-345-4639.
Catechesis/Religious Program—Students 70.

110—OUR LADY OF THE ROSARY OF POMPEII (1900), (Hispanic), Rev. Frank Amato, S.A.C.
Res.: 225 Seigel St., 11206. Tel: 718-497-0614; Fax: 718-366-3236.
Catechesis/Religious Program—Students 170.

111—OUR LADY OF VICTORY (1868), Revs. Martin J. Carter, S.A.; Martin Madison, S.A.
Res.: 583 Throop Ave., 11216-2496. Tel: 718-574-5772; Fax: 718-919-2265.
Catechesis/Religious Program—Tel: 718-574-5772; Fax: 718-919-2265. Wendy Ratherford, D.R.E. Students 52.

112—ST. PATRICK (1849), Rev. Msgr. Martin Bannan, B.A., M.S.W.; Revs. Thomas Anastasio; Gerard J. Sauer; Sr. Jeanne Elaine, Pastoral Assoc. In Res., Rev. Msgr. Joseph K. Parks, Pastor Emeritus (Retired); Deacon Charles Postler.
Res.: 9511 Fourth Ave., 11209. Tel: 718-238-2600; Fax: 718-238-1508.
School—401 97th St., 11209. Tel: 718-833-0124; Fax: 718-238-6840. Mrs. Andrea D'Emic, Prin. Lay Teachers 21; Students 223.
Catechesis/Religious Program—Tel: 718-238-2600. Mrs. Nancy Lussier, D.R.E. Tel: 718-238-2600. Students 175.

113—ST. PATRICK'S, Merged, with St. Lucy's in 1974. Records at St. Lucy-St. Patrick's.

114—SS. PETER AND PAUL'S (1843), Rev. Msgr. Agustin Ruiz; Rev. Richard J. Beuther, Admin. In Res., Revs. Anthony Hernandez; James E. King (NTN) (Retired).
Res.: 71 S. Third St., 11211. Tel: 718-388-9576; Fax: 718-388-0714.
Catechesis/Religious Program—Tel: 718-387-1041. Sr. Maria Angelica. Students 366.

115—ST. PETER CLAVER, Rev. James J. Krische. In Res., Deacon Edward Aigbojie; Everett J. Wilson.
Res.: 29 Claver Pl., 11238. Tel: 718-622-4647; Fax: 718-622-3304.
Catechesis/Religious Program—Ms. Geneva Whitfield, D.R.E. Students 64.

116—ST. PETER-ST. PAUL-OUR LADY OF PILAR (1836), Rev. Kevin P. Cavalluzzi; Deacon Louis Gonzalez.
Res.: 234 Congress St., 11201. Tel: 718-624-3425; Fax: 718-834-0380.
Catechesis/Religious Program—Tel: 718-797-9262. Students 105.

117—QUEEN OF ALL SAINTS (1879), Rev. Msgr. John J. Brown, S.T.L., J.C.L., Admin. In Res., Rev. Steven J. Aguggia, J.C.L.; Sr. Eileen Sweeney, O.S.F., Pastoral Assoc.
Res.: 300 Vanderbilt Ave., 11205. Tel: 718-638-7625; 718-638-7626; Fax: 718-638-7393.
School—300 Vanderbilt Ave., 11205. Tel: 718-857-3114; Fax: 718-857-0632. Theresa Anttianese, Prin. Sisters 1; Lay Teachers 12; Students 290.
Catechesis/Religious Program—Theresa Attianese, D.R.E. Students 75.

118—REGINA PACIS VOTIVE SHRINE (1951), Attended by, St. Rosalia, 65 St. & 12th Ave. , 1230 65th St., 11219. Tel: 718-236-0909; Fax: 718-236-5357.
Catechesis/Religious Program—1201 66th. St.. Students 300.

119—RESURRECTION (1924), Rev. Msgr. Francis J. Fahy; Rev. Marciano Caliwan.
Res.: 2331 Gerritsen Ave., 11229. Tel: 718-743-7234; 718-743-7235; Fax: 718-743-0152.
School—2335 Gerritsen Ave., 11229. Tel: 718-332-9806; Fax: 718-743-3408. Ms. Diana C. Meringolo, Prin. Lay Teachers 10; Students 190.
Catechesis/Religious Program—Tel: 718-891-0888; Fax: 718-743-0152. Mrs. Angela Parente, D.R.E. Students 345.

120—RESURRECTION CATHOLIC COPTIC CHAPEL (1985), Rev. Youssef Bochra Nasri, (Coptic Catholic Patriarchate).
Mailing Address: 352 42nd St., 11232. Tel: 718-965-0422; Fax: 718-768-3336.
Church: 328 14th St., 11215. Tel: 718-499-6946.

121—ST. RITA'S (1913), (Spanish), Rev. Msgr. John T. Peyton; Deacons Luis Espinal; Marco Lopez.
Res.: 275 Shepherd Ave., 11208. Tel: 718-647-4910; Fax: 718-827-2767.
School—280 Shepherd Ave., 11208. Tel: 718-647-6040. William Geasor, Prin. Sisters 1; Lay Teachers 20; Students 632.
Catechesis/Religious Program—Mrs. Annemarie Ronacher, D.R.E. Students 345.

122—ST. ROCCO'S (1902), Rev. Msgr. Faustino Cordero.
Res.: 216 27th St., 11232. Tel: 718-768-9798; Fax: 718-768-7748.
Catechesis/Religious Program—Fax: 718-768-1742. Karen Reyes, D.R.E. Students 85.

123—ST. ROSALIA-REGINA PACIS (1904), Rev. Msgr. Dino M. Zeni; Revs. Edward A. Cassar; Timothy Hirten; Bro. Robert Ziobro, S.C.; Deacon Joseph Cafiero. In Res., Rev. Msgr. Ronald T. Marino.
Res.: 1230 65th St., 11219. Tel: 718-236-0909; Fax: 718-236-5357.
Center Regina Center, Inc.—1258 65th St., 11219. Tel: 718-232-4340.
Catechesis/Religious Program—Tel: 718-331-5465. Bro. Robert Ziobro, S.C., D.R.E. Students 300.
Mission—Regina Pacis Votive Shrine, Kings Co.

124—ST. ROSE OF LIMA (1870), Revs. Fred Marcano, Admin.; Giovanny Acosta; Wilson Maina, Pastoral Assoc.; Sr. Maureen Sullivan, C.S.J., Pastoral Assoc.
Res.: 269 Parkville Ave., 11230. Tel: 718-434-8040; Fax: 718-421-4223.
School—259 Parkville Ave., 11230. Tel: 718-434-1739; Fax: 718-421-7413. Sisters of St. Joseph 3; Lay Teachers 11; Students 135.
Catechesis/Religious Program—Students 150.

125—SACRED HEART (1871), Rev. John J. Gildea; Sr. Eileen Neary, R.S.M., Pastoral Assoc. & D.R.E.
Res.: 41 Adelphi St., 11205. Tel: 718-625-5115; Fax: 718-625-2918.
Catechesis/Religious Program—Students 200.

126—SACRED HEART CHAPEL, Closed., 1996. For inquiries for parish records contact the Chancery.

127—SACRED HEART MISSION, Closed., 1942. For inquiries for parish records contact the Chancery.

128—SACRED HEARTS OF JESUS AND MARY AND ST. STEPHEN (1866), Revs. Anthony J. Sansone; Simon Joseph. In Res., Rev. Charles P. Nichols (Retired).
Res.: 108 Carroll St., 11231. Tel: 718-596-7750; Fax: 718-260-9233.
School—135 Summit, 11231. Tel: 718-625-2267; Fax: 718-625-0916. Sr. Anna Desiderio, C.S.J., Prin. Lay Teachers 14; Students 181.
Catechesis/Religious Program—Students 181.

129—ST. SAVIOUR (1905), Rev. Msgr. Joseph P. Nagle; Revs. Antonius P. Gopaul; Robert Lawsine; Deacon William Williamsen; Sr. Patricia Hanvey, O.P., Pastoral Assoc. In Res., Rev. Joseph F. Mali (Nigeria).
Res.: 611 Eighth Ave., 11215. Tel: 718-768-4055; 718-768-7983; Fax: 718-768-4872.
School—701 Eighth Ave., 11215. Tel: 718-768-8000. Mr. James Flanagan, Prin. Lay Teachers 22; Students 446.
High School—588 Sixth St., 11215. Tel: 718-768-4406; Fax: 718-369-2688. Sr. Valeria Belanger, S.S.N.D., Prin. Students 358.
Catechesis/Religious Program—Tel: 718-768-4055; Fax: 718-768-4872. Students 125.

130—SHRINE CHURCH OF ST. JUDE (1961), Revs. Mateo J. Rizzo; Michael Tedone.
Res.: 1677 Canarsie Rd., 11236. Tel: 718-763-6300; Fax: 718-531-9655.
School—1696 Canarsie Rd., 11236. Tel: 718-241-6633. Lay Teachers 15; Students 289.
Catechesis/Religious Program—Tel: 718-241-4030. Mr. Vincent Tannacore, D.R.E. Students 200.

131—SHRINE OF OUR LADY OF MOUNT CARMEL (1887), (Italian), Revs. Joseph G. Fonti, S.T.L.; Juan A. Dielinikaitis (LIT); Deacon Everett Deming, Pastoral Assoc.; Giuditta Coccia, Pastoral Assoc. & Italian Apostolate. In Res., Rev. Michael O. Zunno, M.M.
Res.: 275 N. Eighth St., 11211. Tel: 718-384-0223; Fax: 718-384-5838.
School—Northside Catholic Academy at Mt. Carmel, 10 Withers St., 11211. Tel: 718-782-1110; Fax: 718-782-3344. John L. Mancini, Prin.
Catechesis/Religious Program—Rosemarie Walsh, D.R.E. Students 85.

132—SS. SIMON AND JUDE (1897), Revs. Donald A. Kavanagh; Paul Vazhapilly.
Res.: 185 Van Sicklen St., 11223. Tel: 718-375-9600; Fax: 718-375-6642.
Catechesis/Religious Program—Tel: 718-372-0733. Students 283.

133—ST.. AMBROSE, Merged, 1978. Records at Our Lady of Monserrate-St. Ambrose.

134—ST. STANISLAUS KOSTKA (1896), (Polish), Revs. Andraej Rafal Kopystynski, C.M.; Joseph Lachowski, C.M.; Edmund Gutowski, C.M.; Tadeusz Maciejewski, C.M.; Jan Urbaniak, C.M.; Jan Szylar, C.M.
Res.: 607 Humboldt St., 11222. Tel: 718-388-0170; Fax: 718-384-5290.
School—10 Newel St., 11222. Tel: 718-383-1970; Fax: 718-383-1711. Sr. Dorothea Jurkowski, Prin. Priests 6; Sisters of the Holy Family of Nazareth 5; Lay Teachers 17; Students 297.
Catechesis/Religious Program—Tel: 718-388-0170. Students 396.

135—ST. STANISLAUS MARTYR, Merged, with Holy Family (14th St.) in 1979. Records at Holy Family, 14th St., between Sixth and Seventh Aves.

136—ST. STEPHEN, Merged, with Sacred Hearts in 1941. Parochial records are at Sacred Hearts-St. Stephen Church, Carroll St.

137—ST. SYLVESTER (1923), (Spanish—Italian), Revs. Anthony F. Raso; Raymond C. Gruhn. In Res., Rev. Charles P. Vogel (Retired).
Res.: 416 Grant Ave., 11208. Tel: 718-647-1995; Fax: 718-348-4035.
School—396 Grant Ave., 11208. Tel: 718-235-4729; Fax: 718-235-4729. Carmen Padin, Prin. Lay Teachers 12; Students 275.
Catechesis/Religious Program—Sr. Elizabeth Folles, D.R.E. Students 317.

138—ST. TERESA OF AVILA (1874), Revs. Thomas W. Ahern, Pastor; James Yaro (Nigeria); Jose Lopez (JKS).
Res.: 563 Sterling Pl., 11238. Tel: 718-622-6500; Fax: 718-622-2234.
Catechesis/Religious Program—Sr. Doryne Bermoy, F.L.P., D.R.E. Students 141.

139—ST. THERESE OF LISIEUX (1926),, (The Little Flower) Revs. Alfred P. LoPinto; Francois Augustin. In Res., Rev. Msgr. Fernando Ferrarese; Deacons Mauclair Simon; Ronald Agnant.
Res.: 1281 Troy Ave., 11203. Tel: 718-451-1500; Fax: 718-451-1502.
School—4410 Avenue D, 11203. Tel: 718-629-9330; Fax: 718-629-6854. Sr. Paulette Pollina, R.S.M., Prin. Sisters of Mercy 3; Lay Teachers 18; Students 277.
Catechesis/Religious Program—Tel: 718-451-1671. Frances McCormick, D.R.E. Students 200.

140—ST. THOMAS AQUINAS (1884), Revs. Jesus Cuadros, Pastor; John Vgochukwa. In Res., Rev. Carlos Humberto Caceres.
Res.: 249 Ninth St., 11215. Tel: 718-768-9471; Fax: 718-965-4022.
School—211 Eighth St., 11215. Tel: 718-768-9007; Fax: 718-768-6046. Mrs. Elena Heimbach. Lay Teachers 10; Students 177.
Catechesis/Religious Program—Tel: 718-768-9471; Fax: 718-788-3390. Mrs. Elena Heimbach, D.R.E.; Mrs. Dorothy Negron, D.R.E. Students 87.

141—ST. THOMAS AQUINAS (1885), Revs. Thomas J. Lyons; Kieran E. Harrington; Rev. Msgr. Kieran J. Martin (Retired); Sr. Carole Fitzpatrick, C.S.J.
Res.: 1550 Hendrickson St., 11234. Tel: 718-253-4404; Fax: 718-951-7573.
School—1501 Hendrickson St., 11234. Tel: 718-377-0442; Fax: 718-677-4138. Sr. M. Alice Traynor, O.S.U., Prin. Religious Teacher 2; Lay Teachers 14; Students 255.
Catechesis/Religious Program—Tel: 718-338-3542. Margaret Tierney, D.R.E. Students 348.

142—TRANSFIGURATION (1874), Rev. Msgr. Bryan J. Karvelis; Deacon German Martinez.
Res.: 263 Marcy Ave., 11211. Tel: 718-388-8773; Fax: 718-388-8774.
School—250 Hooper St.. Tel: 718-388-1120; Fax: 718-388-2822. Sr. Mary Anne Ricioppo, Prin. Lay Teachers 8; Students 205.
Catechesis/Religious Program—Sr. Maryann Ricioppo, D.R.E. Students 202.
Southside Mission for Social Services—280 Marcy Ave., 11211. Tel: 718-388-3784. Sr. Kathryn Walsh, Dir.

143—ST. VINCENT DE PAUL, Rev. James W. King. In Res., Rev. Msgr. John P. McCullagh; Rev. Justo Beltran (Philippines).
Res.: 167 N. Sixth St., 11211. Tel: 718-388-4218; Fax: 718-486-0615.
School—Northside Catholic Academy, 180 N. 7th St., 11211. Tel: 718-384-3496; Fax: 718-384-6937. Sr. Helen Gulczynski, C.S.J., Prin. Lay Teachers 17; Students 187.
Catechesis/Religious Program—Students 6.

144—ST. VINCENT FERRER (1923), Rev. Coman V.

Brady; Mrs. Mary Anne Muller, Pastoral Assoc.
Res.: 1603 Brooklyn Ave., 11210-3495. Tel: 718-859-0041; 718-859-9009; Fax: 718-859-9032.
Church: E. 37th St. & Glenwood Rd., 11210.
School—Tel: 718-859-3505; Fax: 718-859-9545. Ms. Jean Guy, Prin. Lay Teachers 19; Students 380.
Catechesis/Religious Program—Tel: 718-859-9000. Mrs. Mary Anne Muller, D.R.E. Students 210.

145—VISITATION OF THE BLESSED VIRGIN MARY (1854), Rev. Neil Tiedemann, C.P.
Res.: 98 Richards St., 11231. Tel: 718-624-1572; Fax: 718-722-7748.
Catechesis/Religious Program—Milagros Almonte, D.R.E. Students 130.

BOROUGH AND COUNTY OF QUEENS

1—ST. ADALBERT (1892), (Polish), Revs. Paul Miskiewicz, O.F.M.Conv.; Paul Marut, O.F.M.Conv.; Jerzy Auquscik, O.F.M.Conv. (Poland).
Res.: 52-29 83rd St., Elmhurst, 11373. Tel: 718-639-0212; Fax: 718-651-1705.
School—52-17 83rd St., Elmhurst, 11373. Tel: 718-424-2376; Fax: 718-639-0465. Sr. Kathleen Maciej, C.S.F.N., Prin. Sisters 3; Lay Teachers 21; Students 420.
Catechesis/Religious Program—Tel: 718-429-2005. Mary Hellman, D.R.E. Students 160.
Office for Pastoral Care of the Sick—Tel: 718-429-2005.

2—ST. ALOYSIUS (1892), Revs. Christopher T. Cashman; Leonard Ugbor; Deacon Fabio Flam. In Res., Rev. Percival DeVera, Chap.
Res.: 382 Onderdonk Ave., Ridgewood, 11385. Tel: 718-821-0231; Fax: 718-628-7304.
School—360 Seneca Ave., Ridgewood, 11385. Tel: 718-821-7384; Fax: 718-821-6854. Virginia Daly, Prin. Lay Teachers 12; Students 320.
Catechesis/Religious Program—Tel: 718-417-6327. Blanche Ciangiulli, D.R.E. Students 99.
Pastoral Care Office—Tel: 718-963-7689.

3—AMERICAN MARTYRS (1948), Rev. Msgr. John F. Keppler; Rev. John J. Murray; Deacon Stanley J. Galazin. In Res., Rev. Anthony S. Ercolano.
Res.: 79-43 Bell Blvd., Bayside, 11364. Tel: 718-464-4582; Fax: 718-464-5488.
School—216-15 Peck Ave., Bayside, 11364. Tel: 718-776-3779. Sr. Maureen Coyne, O.P., Prin. Religious 1; Lay Teachers 12; Students 252.
Catechesis/Religious Program—Tel: 718-464-6411. Ms. Christine Rahner, D.R.E. Students 250.

4—ST. ANASTASIA (1919), Rev. Msgr. Michael J. Cantley; Rev. George J. Lutjen. In Res., Rev. John J. Gribbon.
Res.: 45-14 245th St., Douglaston, 11362. Tel: 718-631-4454; Fax: 718-631-1774.
School—45-11 245th St., Douglaston, 11362. Tel: 718-631-3153; Fax: 718-631-3945. Mrs. JoAnn Dolan, Prin. Lay Teachers 16; Students 280.
Catechesis/Religious Program—Tel: 718-225-5191. Janine Kramer, D.R.E. Students 265.

5—ST. ANDREW AVELLINO, Rev. Msgr. James P. Grace, S.T.L.; Revs. Michael J. McGee; Wilfred Dewan, C.S.P. In Res., Rev. Msgr. Lawrence J. McAlister, Pastor Emeritus (Retired); Rev. Matthew J. Diamond (Retired).
Res.: 35-60 158th St., Flushing, 11358. Tel: 718-359-0417; Fax: 718-539-2830.
School—35-50 158th St., Flushing, 11358. Tel: 718-359-7887; Fax: 718-359-2295. Lay Teachers 28; Students 420.
Catechesis/Religious Program—Tel: 718-445-7012; Fax: 718-539-2830. Students 233.

6—ST. ANN'S (1927), Revs. George A. Pfundstein, Pastor; Robert Kodwo Afful (Ghana); Jovito Carungay (Philippines); Deacon Sal Licata.
Res.: 142-30 58th Ave., Flushing, 11355. Tel: 718-886-3890; Fax: 718-358-4964.
School—142-25 58th Rd., Flushing, 11355. Tel: 718-463-1238; Fax: 718-539-6618. Mr. Robert Dinardo, Prin. Sisters 1; Lay Teachers 17; Students 272.
Catechesis/Religious Program—Tel: 718-359-8019; Fax: 718-358-4964. Sr. Patricia A. Anglin, O.P., D.R.E. Students 100.

7—ST. ANTHONY OF PADUA (1937), Revs. James J. Mueller; Thomas Muthukattil (India); Deacon J. Edward Joesten.
Res.: 133-25 128th St., South Ozone Park, 11420. Tel: 718-843-7410; 718-843-3356; Fax: 718-659-1478.
School—125-18 Rockaway Blvd., South Ozone Park, 11420. Tel: 718-641-0212; Fax: 718-641-8079. Jerry Sgambati, Prin. Lay Teachers 23; Students 396.
Catechesis/Religious Program—Tel: 718-848-1127; Fax: 718-738-7522. Marcella Slobodzian, D.R.E. Students 120.

8—ASCENSION (1945), Revs. Vito A. Buonanno; Peter Chidi Osuagwu; Francisco J. Walker.
Res.: 86-13 55th Ave., Elmhurst, 11373. Tel: 718-335-2626; Fax: 718-335-4181.
School—86-37 53rd Ave., Elmhurst, 11373. Tel: 718-335-9755; Fax: 718-335-2234. Sisters 1; Lay Teachers 12; Students 167.
Catechesis/Religious Program—Students 167.

9—ST. BARTHOLOMEW'S (1706), Revs. Joseph M. Hoffman; Clement Okono; Nelson Pichardo Diaz. In Res., Rev. Msgr. James E. Gotimer (Retired).
Res.: 43-22 Ithaca St., Elmhurst, 11373. Tel: 718-424-5400; Fax: 718-899-5257.
School—44-15 Judge St., Elmhurst, 11373. Tel: 718-446-7575. Sisters of St. Frances 2; Lay Teachers 25; Students 375.
Catechesis/Religious Program—Tel: 718-898-0096. Martha Canal, D.R.E. Students 650.

10—ST. BENEDICT JOSEPH LABRE (1892), (Spanish), Rev. Msgr. John H. O'Brien; Rev. Christopher O'Connor; Deacon Angel R. Rivera.
Res.: 94-40 118th St., Richmond Hill, 11419. Tel: 718-849-4048; Fax: 718-856-0732.
School—94-25 117th St., Richmond Hill, 11419. Tel: 718-441-6674; Fax: 718-441-4367. Sisters 2; Lay Teachers 18; Students 429.
Catechesis/Religious Program—Tel: 718-849-0246. Students 291.
Convent—94-24 118th St., Richmond Hill, 11419. Tel: 718-849-5571.

11—ST. BENEDICT, THE MOOR (1932), (African American), Rev. Paul C. Palmiotto.
Res.: 171-17 110th Ave., Jamaica, 11433. Tel: 718-526-4018; Fax: 718-526-4825.
Catechesis/Religious Program—Mrs. Angela Lewis, D.R.E. Students 42.

12—BLESSED SACRAMENT (1929), Rev. Msgr. Raymond W. Kutner; Revs. Edward J. Smith; Richard Conlon; Jose G. Zapata. In Res., Most Rev. Rene A. Valero, M.S.W., V.E.
Res.: 34-43 93rd St., Jackson Heights, 11372. Tel: 718-639-3888; Fax: 718-478-5536.
School—34-20 94th St., Jackson Heights, 11372. Tel: 718-446-4449; Fax: 718-446-5366 Grey Nuns of the Sacred Heart 2; Lay Teachers 16; Students 338.
Catechesis/Religious Program—93-15 35th. Ave., Jackson Heights, 11372. Tel: 718-639-6459. Students 984.

13—BLESSED VIRGIN MARY, HELP OF CHRISTIANS (1854), Revs. Noel Moyniltan, C.S.Sp.; Thomas Basquel, C.S.Sp.; Sr. Mary Conroy, C.S.J., Pastoral Assoc. Deacon Kevin Ryan.
Res.: 70-31 48th Ave., Woodside, 11377. Tel: 718-672-4848; Fax: 718-457-4055.
School—70-20 47th Ave., Woodside, 11377. Tel: 718-639-8042. Mary Basile, Prin. Lay Teachers 12; Students 171.
Catechesis/Religious Program—Tel: 718-672-4784. Patricia Wise, D.R.E. Students 195.

14—ST. BONAVENTURE'S (1930), Rev. Paul C. Palmiotto; Deacon Pascual Olivas.
Res.: 114-58 170th St., Jamaica, 11434. Tel: 718-526-0040; Fax: 718-526-4825.
Catechesis/Religious Program—Mrs. Angela Lewis, D.R.E. Students 130.

15—ST. CAMILLUS (1908), Rev. James M. Dunne. In Res., Rev. Robert Blauvelt.
Res.: 99-15 Rockaway Beach Blvd., Rockaway Beach, 11694. Tel: 718-634-8229; Fax: 718-634-8193.
School—185 Beach 99th St., Rockaway Beach, 11694. Tel: 718-634-5260; Fax: 718-634-8353. Sr. Agnes White, C.S.J., Prin. Sisters of St. Joseph 2; Lay Teachers 10; Students 230.
Catechesis/Religious Program—Tel: 718-474-3101. Sr. St. Claude, D.R.E. Students 155.

16—ST. CATHERINE OF SIENNA (1920), Rev. William F. Sweeney; Deacon Luis Taylor. In Res., Rev. Msgr. James F. Spengler, Vicar for Vicariate.
Res.: 118-22 Riverton St., St. Albans, 11412. Tel: 718-528-1220; Fax: 718-528-7907.
School—118-34 Riverton St.. Tel: 718-528-1857; Fax: 718-949-8739. Sr. Barbara Kradick, O.P., Prin. Lay Teachers 20; Religious 6; Students 369.
Catechesis/Religious Program—Mary Harris, D.R.E. Students 130.

17—CHRIST THE KING (1933), Rev. Jeffry T. Dillon; Deacon Winston M. Mayers.
Res.: 145-39 Farmers Blvd., Springfield Gardens, 11434. Tel: 718-528-6010; Fax: 718-949-3255.
Catechesis/Religious Program—Tel: 718-528-6010; Fax: 718-949-3255. Sr. Maryann Ambrose, C.S.J., D.R.E. Students 145.

18—ST. CLARE (1927), Revs. Kevin F. McBrien, S.T.L.; John J. O'Connor; Louis Uzoh.
Res.: 137-35 Brookville Blvd., Rosedale, 11422. Tel: 718-341-1018; Fax: 718-276-2001.
School—137-25 Brookville Blvd., Rosedale, 11422. Tel: 718-528-7174; 718-276-2001; Fax: 718-528-4389. Mrs. Mary Jane Finlay, Prin. Lay Teachers 25; Students 496.
Catechesis/Religious Program—Tel: 718-527-6153. Lorena DeFilippis, D.R.E. Students 186.

19—ST. CLEMENT POPE (1908), Rev. Joseph D. Diele; Deacon Nathaniel J. Smith.
Res.: 141-11 123rd Ave., Jamaica, 11436. Tel: 718-529-0273; Fax: 718-529-3089.
School—120-27 141 St., South Ozone Park, 11436. Tel: 718-659-9011. Bro. Gary Humes, S.C., Prin. Lay Teachers 10; Students 215.
Catechesis/Religious Program—Celia Brunn, D.R.E. Students 105.

20—CORPUS CHRISTI (1937), Rev. Msgr. Richard F. Dunn; Rev. Jose F. Herrera; Deacon Carlos Trochez. In Res., Rev. John O'Neill.
Res.: 31-30 61st St., Woodside, 11377. Tel: 718-278-8114; Fax: 718-278-3619.
School—31-29 60th St., Woodside, 11377. Tel: 718-721-2484; Fax: 718-721-4579. Lucetta A. Darragh, Prin. Lay Teachers 12; Students 220.
Catechesis/Religious Program—Patricia Carinci, D.R.E. Students 118.

21—ST. ELIZABETH'S (1873), Revs. Steven A. Ferrari; George Manchapilly. In Res., Rev. Thomas D. Dolan (Retired).
Res.: 94-20 85th St., Ozone Park, 11416. Tel: 718-296-4900; Fax: 718-296-1140.
School—Tel: 718-641-6990. William Ferguson, Prin. Lay Teachers 12; Students 275.
Catechesis/Religious Program—Students 220.

22—ST. FIDELIS (1856), Revs. Arthur G. Minichello; Ronald M. D'Antonio; Simon Nwachunkwu (Nigeria); Bro. Robert Russo; Sr. Helen Muhlbauer, O.P., Pastoral Min.; Deacon John Reichert; Angela DiPaola, Pastoral Assoc.
Res.: 123-06 14th Ave., College Point, 11356. Tel: 718-445-6164; Fax: 718-445-1623.
School—124-06 14th Ave., College Point, 11356. Tel: 718-539-2628. Bro. Robert Russo, C.S.C., Prin. Lay Teachers 23; Students 320.
Catechesis/Religious Program—Tel: 718-359-1249. Joan Colombo, D.R.E. Students 375.

23—ST. FRANCIS DE SALES (1906), Rev. Msgr. Martin T. Geraghty; Rev. Louis J. DeGaetano. In Res., Rev. Msgr. Howard B. Basler.
Res.: 129-16 Rockaway Beach Blvd., Belle Harbor, 11694. Tel: 718-634-6464; Fax: 718-634-0716.
School—216 Beach & 130th St., Belle Harbor, 11694. Tel: 718-634-2775; Fax: 718-634-6673. Sr. Patricia Chelius, C.S.J., Prin. Sisters of St. Joseph 3; Lay Teachers 30; Students 748.
Catechesis/Religious Program—Tel: 718-945-6911; Fax: 718-634-0716. Dr. Virginia Clark, D.R.E. Students 441.

24—ST. FRANCIS OF ASSISI (1930), Rev. Emilio J. Salerno. In Res., Revs. Charles P. Keeney; Francis Lynch; Deacons John Sucich; Savior Hili; Eileen Maguire, Pastoral Assoc.
Res.: 21-17 45 St., Long Island City, 11105. Tel: 718-728-7801; Fax: 718-728-7853.
School—21-18 46th St., Astoria, 11105. Tel: 718-726-9405; Fax: 718-721-2577. Barbara McArdle, Prin. Lay Teachers 20; Students 341.
Catechesis/Religious Program—Tel: 718-278-0259. Gerry Catoggio, D.R.E. Students 175.

25—ST. GABRIEL (1923), Rev. Robert F. Barclay. In Res., Revs. Celestine Anyanwu (Nigeria); James Fitzpatrick; William Chacon (Costa Rica); Deacon Eulogio S. Dupuy.
Res.: 26-26 98th St., East Elmhurst, 11369. Tel: 718-639-0474; Fax: 718-639-2810.
School—26-25 97th St., East Elmhurst, 11369. Tel: 718-426-7170; Fax: 718-426-1741. Bro. Edward Shields, F.S.C., Prin. Sisters 2; Brothers 3; Lay Teachers 21; Students 350.
Catechesis/Religious Program—Tel: 718-426-9577. Students 185.

26—ST. GENEVIEVE, Rev. John Cullinane.
Res.: 6 Beach 178 St., Breezy Point, 11697. Tel: 718-634-7276; Fax: 718-318-7905.
Catechesis/Religious Program—Tel: 718-634-9899. Rosemay Logan, D.R.E. Students 20.

27—ST. GERARD MAJELLA (1906), Rev. Edward P. Doran, Ph.D.; Deacons Guillermo Gomez; Luis Roman. In Res., Rev. Msgr. Eugene A. Feldhaus, Senior Priest (Retired).
Res.: 188-16 91st Ave., Hollis, 11423. Tel: 718-468-6565; Fax: 718-468-3136.
School—Tel: 718-468-1166. Lay Teachers 12; Students 120.

28—ST. GERTRUDE (1911), Rev. Brendan W. Downing; Deacon Alfred L. Whelan.
Res.: 336 Beach 38th St., Far Rockaway, 11691. Tel: 718-327-5673; Fax: 718-471-6405.
Catechesis/Religious Program—Students 70.

29—ST. GREGORY THE GREAT (1936), Revs. Joseph L. Cunningham, S.T.L.; Kevin F. McBrien, S.T.L.; Deacons Arthur Cutter; Robert Zeuner. In Res., Rev. Brendan Duggan, C.S.Sp.
Res.: 242-20 88th Ave., Bellerose, 11426. Tel: 718-347-3707; Fax: 718-347-0583.
School—244-44 87th Ave., Bellerose, 11426. Tel: 718-343-5053; Fax: 718-347-1142. Mrs. JoAnn DiNardo, Prin. Lay Teachers 24; Students 461.
Catechesis/Religious Program—Tel: 718-347-0525. Regina Joyce, D.R.E. Students 347.
Convent—88-19 Cross Island Pkwy., Bellerose, 11426.

30—ST. HELEN (1960), Rev. Msgr. Joseph C. Pfeiffer;

Revs. John P. Maloney (PIT); John P. Cush; Sr. Hannah Marie Cox, P.B.V.M., Pastoral Assoc.; Deacon Armand D'Accordo.
Res.: 157-10 83 St., Howard Beach, 11414. Tel: 718-738-1616; Fax: 718-835-5144.
School—83-09 157th Ave., Howard Beach, 11414. Tel: 718-835-5144; Fax: 718-738-0580. Religious 2; Lay Teachers 18; Students 334.
Catechesis/Religious Program—Tel: 718-835-6216; Fax: 718-848-4883. Students 560.

31—HOLY CHILD JESUS (1910), Revs. Daniel S. Murphy; Thomas M. Catania; Rev. Msgr. Lawrence E. Hinch; Deacon Dean Tully. Missionary Servants of the Most Blessed Trinity
Res.: 111-11 86th Ave., Richmond Hill, 11418. Tel: 718-847-1860; Fax: 718-847-2696.
School—112-02 86th Ave., Richmond Hill, 11418. Tel: 718-849-3988; Fax: 718-850-2842. Sisters of St. Joseph 2; Lay Teachers 23; Students 481.
Catechesis/Religious Program—Tel: 718-805-5771. Students 254.

32—HOLY CROSS (1913), (Polish), Revs. Peter Zendzian; Ryszard Koper (Poland); Jan Soliwoda.
Res.: 61-21 56th Rd., Maspeth, 11378-2498. Tel: 718-894-1387; Fax: 718-416-9245.
School—56-01 61st St., Maspeth, 11378-2499. Tel: 718-894-2356; Fax: 718-326-5194. Mrs. Margared Dandola, Prin. Lay Teachers 10; Students 191.
Catechesis/Religious Program—Students 277.

33—HOLY FAMILY (1940), Rev. Msgr. Joseph L. Stafford; Revs. Alexander Abugel, Pastoral Assoc.; Hilary J. Aidoo (Ghana), Pastoral Assoc. In Res., Rev. Edward M. Keane (Retired); Most Rev. Ignatius Catanello, D.D.
Res.: 175-20 74th Ave., Flushing, 11366. Tel: 718-969-2448; Fax: 718-591-6166.
School—75th Ave. & 175th St., Flushing, 11366. Tel: 718-969-2124; Fax: 718-380-2183. Mary Scheer, Prin. Sisters of St. Joseph 1; Lay Teachers 20; Students 398.
Catechesis/Religious Program—Tel: 718-591-6438. Barbara Makolin, D.R.E. Students 210.

34—HOLY TRINITY (1965), Revs. Marcello J. Latona; James F. Fraser; Joseph A. Pfaff, D.R.E. In Res., Rev. James E. Sullivan, Senior Priest (Retired).
Res.: 14-51 143rd St., Whitestone, 11357. Tel: 718-746-7730; Fax: 718-767-1368.
School—Tel: 718-746-1479; Fax: 718-746-4793. Eleanor Menna, Prin. Lay Teachers 19; Students 286.
Catechesis/Religious Program—Edward Duggan, D.R.E. Students 102.

35—IMMACULATE CONCEPTION (1924), Revs. Thomas Joyce, C.P.; Theophane Cooney, C.P.; Patrick Geizner, C.P.
Res.: 86-45 Edgerton Blvd., Jamaica, 11432. Tel: 718-739-0880; Fax: 718-657-0543.
School—179-14 Dalny Rd., Jamaica, 11432. Tel: 718-739-5933; Fax: 718-523-7436. Dr. Charlene Jaffie, Prin. Sisters of St. Joseph 5; Lay Teachers 22; Students 442.
Catechesis/Religious Program—86-16 Midland Pkwy., Jamaica, 11432. Tel: 718-291-3080. Sr. Elizabeth Gildea, C.S.J., D.R.E. Students 270.

36—IMMACULATE CONCEPTION (1924), Rev. Msgr. Charles P. Boccio. In Res., Revs. Vitalis D. Ozokpor (Nigeria); Raynald Nacino (Philippines); Leo V. Rosero (Philippines); Elvis Elano (Philippines).
Res.: 21-47 29th St., Long Island City, 11105. Tel: 718-728-1613; Fax: 718-956-9229.
School—21-63 29th St., Long Island City, 11105. Tel: 718-728-1969. Eileen Harnischfeger, Prin. Sisters 1; Lay Teachers 19; Students 415.
Catechesis/Religious Program—Tel: 718-956-4494. Marylyn Crum, D.R.E. Students 255.
Convent—21-60 31st St., Long Island City, 11105. Fax: 718-959-9229.

37—INCARNATION (1927), Revs. Joseph A. Ceriello; Dagoberto Noguera; Deacon Francois Innocent. In Res., Rev. Msgr. Edward J. Nolan, Pastor Emeritus (Retired).
Res.: 89-43 Francis Lewis Blvd., Queens Village, 11427. Tel: 718-465-8534; Fax: 718-465-3834.
School—89-15 Francis Lewis Blvd., Queens Village, 11427. Tel: 718-465-5066; Fax: 718-464-4128. Mary Sandoz, Prin. Sisters of St. Dominic (Amityville) 4; Lay Teachers 21; Students 458.
Catechesis/Religious Program—Tel: 718-776-8956. Elizabeth Bennett, D.R.E. Students 200.

38—SS. JOACHIM AND ANNE (1896), Rev. Msgr. Joseph P. Malagreca; Rev. John W. Byrnes (Retired).
Res.: 218-26 105 Ave., Queens Village, 11429. Tel: 718-465-0124; Fax: 718-479-3548.
School—218-19 105th Ave., Queens Village, 11429. Tel: 718-465-2230; Fax: 718-468-5698. Linda Freebes, Prin. Sisters of Notre Dame de Namur 1; Lay Teachers 22; Students 515.
Catechesis/Religious Program—Teresa Rosero, D.R.E. Students 326.

39—ST. JOAN OF ARC (1920), Rev. Msgr. John A. McGuirl; Revs. Stephen Valdazo; Barry Frazzita; Giovanni (John) Tino.
Res.: 82-00 35th Ave., Jackson Heights, 11372. Tel: 718-429-2333; Fax: 718-672-5881.
School—35-27 82nd St., Jackson Heights, 11372. Tel: 718-639-9020; Fax: 718-639-5428. Linda C. Kelly, Prin. Lay Teachers 25; Students 550.
Catechesis/Religious Program—Tel: 718-478-5593; Fax: 718-651-8485. Students 580.

40—ST. JOHN VIANNEY (1967), Rev. Brian P. Dowd; Deacon John McGreevey. In Res., Rev. Hugo Bedoya.
Res.: 140-10 34th Ave., Flushing, 11354. Tel: 718-762-7920; Fax: 718-460-8032.
Catechesis/Religious Program—Tel: 718-961-5092; Fax: 718-460-8032. Eileen Nesi, D.R.E. Students 180.

41—ST. JOSAPHAT (1910), (Polish), Rev. Richard J. McCormack. In Res., Revs. Thomas Machalski Jr., M.S.Ed., J.C.L.; Thomas Machalski Jr., M.S.Ed., J.C.L.
Res.: 34-32 210th St., Bayside, 11361. Tel: 718-229-1663; Fax: 718-229-8018.
Catechesis/Religious Program—Students 85.

42—ST. JOSEPH (1904), (Polish), Rev. Andrzej Kielkowski, S.D.S. (Poland); Bro. Piotr Bogawski, S.D.S.
Res.: 108-43 Sutphin Blvd., Jamaica, 11435. Tel: 718-739-4781; Fax: 718-658-5447.
Catechesis/Religious Program—Students 189.

43—ST. JOSEPH (1877), Revs. George J. Ryan; Robert J. Armato; Deacon Felipe J. Alvarez. In Res., Rev. William Farrugia; Bro. lawrence Larmann, O.S.F.
Res.: 43-19 30th Ave., Long Island City, 11103. Tel: 718-278-1611; Fax: 718-956-3589.
School—28-46 44th St., Long Island City, 11103. Tel: 718-728-0724; Fax: 718-728-8372. Luke Nawrock, Prin. Sisters of St. Dominic 1; Lay Teachers 28; Students 462.
Catechesis/Religious Program—Tel: 718-545-7338. Bro. lawrence Larmann, O.S.F., D.R.E. Students 245.

44—ST. KEVIN (1926), Rev. Msgrs. D. Joseph Finnerty; George V. Fogarty, Pastor Emeritus (Retired). In Res., Rev. Michael Parisi; Deacon Julio Barreneche.
Res.: 45-21 194 St., Flushing, 11358. Tel: 718-357-8888; Fax: 718-357-3671.
School—45-50 195th St., Flushing, 11358. Tel: 718-357-8110; Fax: 718-357-2519. Vacant (GB), Prin. Lay Teachers 24; Students 389.
Catechesis/Religious Program—Tel: 718-357-5317. Mrs. Laura Stroligo, D.R.E. Students 229.

45—ST. LEO (1903), (Hispanic—Italian), Revs. William Krlis; Joaquin Suran; Diego Villegas; Deacon Rafael Diaz, (Retired).
Res.: 104-05 49th Ave., Corona, 11368. Tel: 718-592-7569; Fax: 718-271-6726.
School—104-19 49th Ave., Corona, 11368. Tel: 718-592-7050; Fax: 718-592-0787. Mrs. Maureen Blaine, Prin. Lay Teachers 25; Students 452.
Catechesis/Religious Program—Tel: 718-699-8565. Students 358.
Mission—Our Lady of Mount Carmel Corona. 103-56 52nd Ave., Queens Co. 11368. Tel: 718-592-7569.

46—ST. LUKE (1870), Rev. Msgr. Nicholas J. Capua; Revs. Joseph F. Wilson; Joseph Cestaro; Deacon Harry A. Svebel. In Res., Rev. Leonard Stocker, O.M.I.
Res.: 16-34 Clintonville St., Whitestone, 11357. Tel: 718-746-8102; Fax: 718-746-3589.
School—16-01 150th Pl., Whitestone, 11357. Tel: 718-746-3833; Fax: 718-747-2101. Mrs. Barbara Reiter, Prin. Lay Teachers 23; Students 365.
Catechesis/Religious Program—Tel: 718-746-3409. Theresa Agrusa, D.R.E. Students 550.

47—ST. MARGARET (1860), Rev. Msgr. William A. Varvaro, P.A., S.T.D., J.C.D.; Revs. Leonard F. Badia, Ph.D.; Ralph Barile. In Res., Very Rev. Gregory Wielunski.
Res.: 66-05 79th Pl., Middle Village, 11379. Tel: 718-326-1911; Fax: 718-326-1883.
School—66-10 80th St., Middle Village, 11379. Tel: 718-326-0922. Sr. Bridget Olwell, O.S.U., Prin. Sisters of St. Dominic 1; Lay Teachers 23; Students 543.
Catechesis/Religious Program—Tel: 718-381-4048. Marie Vella, D.R.E. Students 140.

48—ST. MARGARET MARY (1961), Rev. Edmund P. Brady; Sr. Maryann McHugh, C.S.J., Pastoral Assoc.
Res.: 9-18 27th Ave., Long Island City, 11102. Tel: 718-721-9020; Fax: 718-721-3729.
Catechesis/Religious Program—Sr. Maryann McHugh, C.S.J., D.R.E. Students 140.

49—ST. MARY (1868), Rev. Ralph Barile.
Res.: 10-08 49th Ave., Long Island City, 11101. Tel: 718-786-0705; Fax: 718-482-7115.
Catechesis/Religious Program—Students 30.

50—ST. MARY GATE OF HEAVEN (1904), Revs. Matthew J. Considine, S.M.M.; Bernard Brault, S.M.M.; James Brady, S.M.M.; Bro. Paul Llorens, S.M.M.; Deacons Thomas Heaphy; Richard Gilligan.
Res.: 101-25 104th St., Ozone Park, 11416. Tel: 718-847-5957; Fax: 718-846-6489.
School—104-06 101st Ave., Ozone Park, 11416. Tel: 718-846-0689; Fax: 718-846-1059. Patrick Scannell, Prin. Sisters 1; Lay Teachers 27; Students 611.
Catechesis/Religious Program—Tel: 718-849-9329. Ann Farrell, D.R.E. Students 200.

51—ST. MARY MAGDALENE (1913), Rev. John Maloney; Deacon Lee C. Williams; Sr. Ave Regina Gould, C.S.J.
Res.: 218-12 136th Ave., Springfield Gardens, 11413. Tel: 718-949-4311; Fax: 718-528-7208.
Catechesis/Religious Program—Students 120.

52—ST. MARY STAR OF THE SEA (1857), Revs. James K. Cunnigham; Fulgencio Gutierrez. In Res., Rev. Samuel Arririatu; Deacon Antonia Bopoaoilla; Maria Christina Beyra, M.A., Pastoral Assoc.
Res.: 1920 New Haven Ave., Far Rockaway, 11691. Tel: 718-327-1133; Fax: 718-327-3276.
School—595 Beach 19th St., Far Rockaway, 11691. Tel: 718-327-2242. Miss Angela Brucia, Prin. Priests 2; Lay Teachers 13; Students 320.
Catechesis/Religious Program—1920 New Haven Ave., Far Rockaway, 11691. Tel: 718-327-1133, Ext. 25. Maria Christina Beyra, M.A., D.R.E. Students 300.

53—MARY'S NATIVITY (1926), Rev. James T. Rooney. In Res., Rev. Msgr. Edward J. Bottino; Rev. Thaddeus J. Kazanecki.
Res.: 46-02 Parsons Blvd., Flushing, 11355. Tel: 718-359-5996; Fax: 718-939-6737.
School—146-28 Jasmine Ave., Flushing, 11355. Tel: 718-359-1800. Mrs. Anne-Marie Baumis, Prin. Lay Teachers 13; Students 235.
Catechesis/Religious Program—Tel: 718-353-5961. Donna Marie Sticco, D.R.E. Students 226.

54—ST. MATTHIAS (1908), Rev. Msgr. Edward Scharfenberger; Revs. Philip J. Pizzo; Lukasz Pawel Trocha; Deacons John Sands; Lawrence Mule. In Res., Rev. Msgr. Joseph G. Konrad (Retired).
Res.: 58-15 Catalpa Ave., Ridgewood, 11385. Tel: 718-821-6447; 718-821-6448; 718-821-6449; Fax: 718-821-6876.
School—58-25 Catalpa Ave., Ridgewood, 11385. Tel: 718-381-8003; Fax: 718-381-5319. Miss Barbara Wehnes. Sisters of Notre Dame 5; Lay Teachers 10; Students 319.
Catechesis/Religious Program—Tel: 718-386-1077; Fax: 718-821-6876. Mrs. Carol E. Powell, D.R.E. Students 557.

55—ST. MEL (1941), Revs. Christopher J. Turczany; Victor Mbanisi, Pastoral Assoc.; William R. Dulaney, Pastoral Assoc.
Res.: 28-20 154th St., Flushing, 11354. Tel: 718-886-0201; 718-886-0881; Fax: 718-886-0882.
School—154-24 26th Ave., Flushing, 11354. Tel: 718-539-8211. Sr. Mary Spencer, O.P., Prin. Sisters 6; Lay Teachers 23; Students 547.
Catechesis/Religious Program—Tel: 718-461-9840; Fax: 718-886-0882. Theresa M. Spina, D.R.E. Students 263.

56—ST. MICHAEL (1833), Rev. Msgr. Edward V. Wetterer; Revs. Jose R. Aldegunde; Joseph Chavez (Philippines); Sr. Joan S. Dawber, S.C., Pastoral Asst.; Deacon Elias Yepes. In Res., Revs. Joseph Chavez (Philippines); Joseph H. Opoku.
Res.: 136-76 41st Ave., Flushing, 11355. Tel: 718-961-0295; Fax: 718-961-1403.
School—136-58 41st Ave., Flushing, 11355. Tel: 718-961-0246. Mrs. Maureen Rogone, Prin. Sisters of St. Joseph 1; Lay Teachers 16; Students 285.
Catechesis/Religious Program—Tel: 718-961-0312. Virginia DeLarosa, D.R.E. Students 456.

57—ST. MONICA, (Jamaican), Closed. For inquiries for parish records contact the chancery.

58—MOST PRECIOUS BLOOD (1922), Rev. Msgrs. Raymond W. Stafford; George T. Voiland (Retired); Revs. Michael J. McHugh; Robert Zubovic (Croatia); Deacon Giacomo Panessa.
Res.: 32-23 36th St., Long Island City, 11106. Tel: 718-278-3337; Fax: 718-278-4354.
School—32-52 37th St., Long Island City, 11103. Tel: 718-278-4081; Fax: 718-278-3089. Mr. Anthony Biscione, Prin. Sisters of St. Joseph 5; Lay Teachers 29; Students 624.
Catechesis/Religious Program—Tel: 718-721-9850. Students 260.
Convent—32-16 36th St., Long Island City, 11106. Tel: 718-278-4706.

59—NATIVITY OF THE BLESSED VIRGIN MARY (1906), Rev. Msgr. Robert J. Thelen; Revs. Angelo B. Pezzullo; Francis A. Colamaria; Deacon Andrew A. Marchello.
Res.: 101-41 91st St., Ozone Park, 11416. Tel: 718-845-3691; Fax: 718-845-8978.
School—101-60 92nd St., Ozone Park, 11416. Tel: 718-845-3074; Fax: 718-845-5068. Sr. Marguerite Torre, O.S.U., Prin. Sisters 3; Lay Teachers 21; Students 359.
Catechesis/Religious Program—101-41 91st St., Ozone Park, 11416. Tel: 718-845-1524. Michael

Rosa, D.R.E. Students 200.

60—ST. NICHOLAS OF TOLENTINE (1916), Revs. Robert J. McConnin; Kevin J. Sweeney; Deacons Lionel Knight; Josefino Bugay. In Res., Rev. Msgr. Thomas M. O'Brien, Pastor Emeritus.
Res.: 150-75 Goethals Ave., Jamaica, 11432. Tel: 718-969-3226; Fax: 718-380-0345.
School—80-22 Parsons Blvd., Jamaica, 11432. Tel: 718-380-1900; Fax: 718-591-6977. Sr. Elizabeth McNeela, S.C., Prin. Sisters of Charity (Halifax) 2; Lay Teachers 23; Students 430.
Catechesis/Religious Program—Tel: 718-591-6536. Students 132.

61—OUR LADY OF CHINA CHAPEL (1978), Rev. Antonius Ho, C.S.J.B. (Taiwan). See Monasteries and Residences for Priests and Brothers for the Religious Community.
Res.: 54-09 92nd St., Elmhurst, 11373. Tel: 718-699-1929; Fax: 718-592-5981.
Catechesis/Religious Program—Fax: 718-371-3215. Students 26.
School—Chinese School, Ming Yuan Chinese School. Tel: 718-278-6797; Fax: 718-278-6851.

62—OUR LADY OF FATIMA (1948), Rev. Msgr. Edward J. Breen; Revs. Eugene F. Donnelly (Retired); Michael S. Melendez. In Res., Rev. Patrick J. Frawley.
Res.: 25-02 80th St., Jackson Heights, 11370. Tel: 718-899-2801; Fax: 718-429-6404.
School—25-38 80th St., Jackson Heights, 11370. Tel: 718-429-7031; Fax: 718-899-2811. Mrs. Cassie Zelic, Prin. Lay Teachers 30; Students 673.
Catechesis/Religious Program—25-56 80th St.. Tel: 718-457-3457; Fax: 718-429-6404. Patricia Radice, D.R.E. Students 272.
Convent—25-56 80th St., Jackson Heights, 11370. Tel: 718-446-7097.

63—OUR LADY OF GRACE (1924), Rev. Msgr. William Flood; Rev. John Maduri; Deacon Joseph Campisi.
Res.: 100-05 159th Ave., Howard Beach, 11414. Tel: 718-843-6218; Fax: 718-738-8208.
School—158-12 101st St., Howard Beach, 11414. Tel: 718-848-7440; Fax: 718-641-3464. Elvira Anselmo, Prin. Lay Teachers 26; Students 389.
Catechesis/Religious Program—Tel: 718-835-2765; Fax: 718-835-4524. Sr. Ann Martha, O.P., D.R.E. Students 235.

64—OUR LADY OF HOPE (1960), Rev. Msgr. Nicholas W. Sivillo; Rev. Arthur A. Candreva, I.V.Dei; Deacon Robert F. Lavanco.
Res.: 61-27 71st St., Middle Village, 11379. Tel: 718-429-5438; Fax: 718-429-2764.
School—Tel: 718-458-3535; Fax: 718-458-9031. Sisters 4; Lay Teachers 27; Students 657.
Catechesis/Religious Program—Tel: 718-335-8394. Students 200.

65—OUR LADY OF LOURDES (1924), Rev. Msgr. Robert J. Pawson; Rev. Cuong M. Pham. In Res., Rev. Msgr. John F. Casey.
Res.: 92-96 220th St., Queens Village, 11428. Tel: 718-479-5111; Fax: 718-479-0826.
School—92-80 220th St., Queens Village, 11428. Tel: 718-464-1480; Fax: 718-740-4091. Sr. Josephine Barbiere, C.S.J., Prin. Lay Teachers 27; Students 502.
Catechesis/Religious Program—Tel: 718-740-4090. Joanne Russo, D.R.E. Students 305.

66—OUR LADY OF MERCY (1930), Rev. Msgr. Gerald J. Langelier; Rev. John J. Cremins; Deacon Edward Smolinski. In Res., Rev. August J. Iantosca.
Res.: 70-01 Kessel St., Forest Hills, 11375. Tel: 718-268-6143; Fax: 718-544-3764.
School—70-25 Kessel St., Forest Hills, 11375. Tel: 718-793-2086; Fax: 718-897-2144. Sr. Mary Ellen Malloy, I.H.M., Prin. Sisters Servants of the Immaculate Heart of Mary 1; Lay Teachers 13; Students 308.
Catechesis/Religious Program—Tel: 718-261-6285. Students 115.

67—OUR LADY OF MOUNT CARMEL (1841), Rev. Msgr. Paul R. Sanchez; Revs. Joseph Pham; Josephjude C. Gannon. In Res., Revs. Edmund P. Brady; Richard Bretone.
Res.: 23-25 Newtown Ave., Long Island City, 11102. Tel: 718-278-1834; Fax: 718-278-0998.
School—25-15 Newtown Ave., Long Island City, 11102. Tel: 718-728-8376; Fax: 718-278-3608. Ms. Angela Fazio, Prin. Lay Teachers 11; Students 216.
Catechesis/Religious Program—Tel: 718-545-7987; Fax: 718-278-0998. Students 130.

68—OUR LADY OF PERPETUAL HELP (1923), Revs. Donald M. Berran; John G. Garkowski, Pastoral Assoc. In Res., Rev. Edward W. Richards, Pastor Emeritus; Deacon Juan Carattini.
Res.: 111-50 115th St., South Ozone Park, 11420. Tel: 718-843-1212; Fax: 718-843-3554.
School—111-10 115th St., South Ozone Park, 11420. Tel: 718-843-4184; Fax: 718-843-6838. Mrs. Frances DeLuca, Prin. Religious 1; Lay Teachers 23; Students 512.
Catechesis/Religious Program—Tel: 718-641-6165. Thomas Columbia, D.R.E. Students 215.

69—OUR LADY OF SORROWS (1872), Revs. Thomas J. Healy; Kevin J. Sweeney; Raul O. Gelvez; Deacons Orlando Pascal; Francisco J. Tineo.
Res.: 104-11 37th Ave., Corona, 11368. Tel: 718-424-7554; Fax: 718-424-4910.
School—35-34 105th St., Corona, 11368. Tel: 718-426-5517; Fax: 718-651-5682. Sr. Katherine Hanrahan, C.S.J., Prin. Sisters of St. Joseph 2; Lay Teachers 18; Students 325.
Catechesis/Religious Program—Tel: 718-651-5682; Fax: 718-651-5682. Deacon Elias Yepes, D.R.E. Students 1,150.

70—OUR LADY OF THE ANGELUS (1938), Revs. John Mendonca; Lawrence Gellel, S.J.; Deacons Edwin Cancel; Julio Murillo. In Res., Rev. Msgr. William T. Hickey, Pastor Emeritus (Retired).
Res.: 63-63 98th St., Rego Park, 11374. Tel: 718-897-4444; Fax: 718-897-1453.
School—98-05 63rd. Dr., Rego Park, 11374. Tel: 718-896-7220; Fax: 718-896-5723. Ms. Mary Ann Rys, Prin. Lay Teachers 10; Students 226.
Catechesis/Religious Program—Tel: 718-896-4388; Fax: 718-897-1453. Sr. Jo Ann Schwarz, D.R.E. Students 210.

71—OUR LADY OF THE BLESSED SACRAMENT (1930), Rev. Msgr. John E. Mahoney; Revs. Gerard T. Walker; Peter A. DeSanctis.
Res.: 34-24 203rd St., Bayside, 11361. Tel: 718-229-5929; Fax: 718-229-3354.
School—34-45 202nd St., Bayside, 11361. Tel: 718-229-4434; Fax: 718-229-5820. Sisters 1; Lay Teachers 25; Students 371.
Catechesis/Religious Program—Tel: 718-225-6179. Mary Mullaney, D.R.E. Students 239.

72—OUR LADY OF THE CENACLE (1922), Rev. Msgr. Cornelius T. Kneafsey; Revs. Joseph Vella; Adnel T. Burgos. In Res., Revs. Pablo Sans (Retired); James Nunes, M.S., Hospital Chap. Tel: 718-206-6075; Deacon Eduardo Sencion.
Res.: 136-06 87th Ave., Richmond Hill, 11418. Tel: 718-291-2540; Fax: 718-291-6211.
School—Tel: 718-657-6690; Fax: 718-657-3497. Mrs. Rosemarie McGoldrick, Prin. Lay Teachers 14; Students 263.
Catechesis/Religious Program—Students 302.

73—OUR LADY OF THE MIRACULOUS MEDAL (1917), Rev. Msgrs. Edward A. Ryan; Anthony Danna; Rev. Al Barozzi; Deacon Jerome Krebs. In Res., Rev. Msgrs. Andrew J. Vaccari, J.C.L. George M. Schuster, Pastor Emeritus.
Res.: 62-81 60th Pl., Ridgewood, 11385. Tel: 718-366-3360; Fax: 718-456-0564.
School—Bleecker & 61st St., Ridgewood, 11385. Tel: 718-821-2221. Ms. Margaret A. Baxter, Prin. Lay Teachers 14; Students 289.
Catechesis/Religious Program—Tel: 718-456-3275. Mary Macchiaroli, D.R.E. Students 385.

74—OUR LADY OF THE SKIES CHAPEL (1955), Rev. James T. Devine, Admin.
Kennedy International Airport Terminal: International Arrivals Bldg., Fourth Floor, Jamaica, 11430. Tel: 718-656-5348; Fax: 718-656-8162.

75—OUR LADY OF THE SNOWS (1948), Rev. Msgr. Raymond F. Chappetto; Revs. Michael Ittykunju (India); John Wtulich; Deacons Henry J. Smith; Matthew Oellinger; Steven Borheck. In Res., Rev. James J. Reynolds.
Res.: 258-15 80th Ave., Floral Park, 11004. Tel: 718-347-6070; Fax: 718-343-3221.
School—79-33 258th St., Floral Park, 11004. Tel: 718-343-1346; Fax: 718-343-7303. Sr. Roberta Oberle, Prin. Lay Teachers 20; Students 515.
Catechesis/Religious Program—Tel 718-347-3511. Students 315.

76—OUR LADY, QUEEN OF MARTYRS (1917), Rev. Msgr. Joseph A. Funaro; Revs. Daniel Weiscopf; Frank L. Schwarz. In Res., Rev. Msgr. Michael J. Dempsey.
Res.: 110-06 Queens Blvd., Forest Hills, 11375. Tel: 718-268-6251; Fax: 718-793-2584.
School—72-55 Austin St., Forest Hills, 11375. Tel: 718-263-2622; Fax: 718-263-0063. Sr. Francis Marie Sheridan, Prin. Sisters 1; Lay Teachers 14; Students 312.
Catechesis/Religious Program—Tel: 718-263-0907. Mary Ellen O'Brien, D.R.E. Students 167.

77—ST. PANCRAS (1904), Revs. Vincent Gallo; William Rueger.
Res.: 72-22 68th St., Glendale, 11385. Tel: 718-821-2323; Fax: 718-417-8021.
School—Myrtle Ave. & 68th St., Glendale, 11385. Tel: 718-821-6721; Fax: 718-418-3991. Sr. Joseph Maureen, O.P., Prin. Lay Teachers 20; Students 374.
Catechesis/Religious Program—Tel: 718-479-0590. Margaret Walter, D.R.E. Students 270.

78—ST. PASCAL BAYLON (1930), (African American), Rev. Msgr. Robert R. McCourt; Sisters Mary Jane Rolston, O.P., Pastoral Assoc.; Dorothy Marie Seltwell, C.S.J., Pastoral Assoc. In Res., Rev. John W. Maloney.
Res.: 112-43 198th St., St. Albans, 11412. Tel: 718-468-3511; Fax: 718-479-2303.
Catechesis/Religious Program—Tel: 718-468-3511; Fax: 718-479-2403. Students 105.

79—ST. PATRICK (1869), Rev. Robert M. Robinson, S.T.B., M.A., Pastor. In Res., Rev. Jean-Pierre Ruiz, S.T.D.
Res.: 39-38 29th St., Long Island City, 11101. Tel: 718-729-6060; Fax: 718-729-1276.
Catechesis/Religious Program—Tel: 718-937-1239. Sr. Flora Marinelli, C.S.J., D.R.E. Students 165.

80—ST. PAUL CHONG HA-SANG ROMAN CATHOLIC CHAPEL (1985), (Korean), Revs. Sang Bong (Daniel) Suh; Heebong Nam; Deacon Paul M. Chin.
Office—32-15 Parsons Blvd., Flushing, 11354. Tel: 718-321-7676; Fax: 718-321-7005.
Catechesis/Religious Program—Sisters Jerome Lee, O.S.B.; Mos Park, O.S.B. Students 404.
Convent—Olivetan Benedictine Sisters, 32-15 Parsons Blvd., Flushing, 11354.
Chapel—St. Augustine Yu Chin-gil Chapel 2115 61st St., 11204. Tel: 718-729-0132; Fax: 718-729-0132.

81—ST. PAUL THE APOSTLE (1964), Rev. Paul W. Jervis. In Res., Rev. Jose Sanchez (Philippines); Sr. Grace Gately.
Res.: 98-16 55 Ave., Corona, 11368. Tel: 718-271-1100; Fax: 718-760-3496.
Catechesis/Religious Program—Ana Baratau, D.R.E. Students 190.

82—ST. PIUS V (1908), Revs. Richard J. Ahlemeyer; Luiz Antonio DeAguiar (Brazil).
Res.: 106-12 Liverpool St., Jamaica, 11435. Tel: 718-739-3731; Fax: 718-739-7086.
Catechesis/Religious Program—Students 200.

83—ST. PIUS X (1960), Rev. Msgr. Thomas A. Graham; Revs. James F. Marron; Joachim Fernando (Sri Lanka).
Res.: 148-10 249th St., Rosedale, 11422. Tel: 718-525-9099; Fax: 718-276-2467.
School—147-65 249th St., Rosedale, 11422. Tel: 718-525-7171. John Toomey, Prin. Lay Teachers 10; Students 212.
Catechesis/Religious Program—Marianne Gratto, D.R.E. Students 93.

84—PRESENTATION OF THE BLESSED VIRGIN MARY (1886), Rev. Stephen P. Lynch, Admin. In Res., Rev. Richard Ahlemeyer.
Res.: 88-19 Parsons Blvd., Jamaica, 11432. Tel: 718-739-0241; Fax: 718-739-2753.
Providence House III—159-23 89th Ave., Jamaica, 11432. Tel: 718-739-1348.
School—88-13 Parsons Blvd., Jamaica, 11432. Tel: 718-739-2003; Fax: 718-526-8153. Ms. Dorothea Breen, Prin. Lay Teachers 14; Students 200.
Catechesis/Religious Program—Tel: 718-739-0241, Ext. 11. Sr. Rosemary O'Connell, D.R.E. Students 397.

85—QUEEN OF ANGELS (1953), Revs. Vincent M. Daly; Gabriel Toro; Deacon Juan Calvo.
Res.: 44-04 Skillman Ave., Long Island City, 11104. Tel: 718-392-0011; 718-392-0012; Fax: 718-472-2625.
School—41-12 44th St., Long Island City, 11104. Tel: 718-786-2990; Fax: 718-472-4862. Sr. Adrienne Ryniewicz, R.S.M., Prin. Sisters of Mercy 2; Lay Teachers 13; Students 190.
Catechesis/Religious Program—Tel: 718-937-5174. Students 130.

86—QUEEN OF PEACE (1939), Rev. James Tighe. In Res., Rev. Msgr. Celsus O. Collini, Pastor Emeritus (Retired).
Res.: 141-36 77th Ave., Flushing, 11367. Tel: 718-380-5031; Fax: 718-969-2025.
School—141-25 77th Rd., Flushing, 11367. Tel: 718-969-3640; Fax: 718-969-5640. Mrs. Louise McNamara, Prin. Lay Teachers 15; Students 318.
Catechesis/Religious Program—Gregory J. Bizzoco Jr., D.R.E. Students 120.
Convent—Sisters of St. Dominic, Tel: 718-380-4293.

87—ST. RAPHAEL (1868), Revs. Thomas G. Pettei; Gabriel Lee; Deacon Ramon Lima.
Res.: 35-20 Greenpoint Ave., Long Island City, 11101. Tel: 718-729-8957; Fax: 718-729-5238.
School—48-25 37th St., Long Island City, 11101. Tel: 718-784-0482; Fax: 718-482-0214. Sr. Maureen Ahlemeyer, P.B.V.M., Prin. Sisters of the Presentation 1; Lay Teachers 12; Students 236.
Catechesis/Religious Program—Monica Gonzalez, D.R.E. Students 90.

88—RESURRECTION-ASCENSION (1926), Rev. Msgr. Vincent F. Fullam; Rev. Salvatore Amato. In Res., Very Rev. Sean G. Ogle.
Res.: 61-11 85th St., Rego Park, 11374. Tel: 718-424-5212; Fax: 718-639-8679.
School—85-25 61st Rd., Rego Park, 11374. Tel: 718-426-4963; Fax: 718-426-0940. Joann Heppt, Prin. Sisters 1; Lay Teachers 20; Students 280.
Catechesis/Religious Program—Tel: 718-533-7898. Students 206.

89—ST. RITA (1900), Revs. John P. Harrington; Jose Carlos Da Silva; Deacon Vincent Parisi.

Res.: 36-25 11th St., Long Island City, 11106. Tel: 718-361-1884; Fax: 718-786-4573.
Catechesis/Religious Program—Tel: 718-361-1884; Fax: 718-786-4573. Aida Alvarez, D.R.E. Students 120.

90—ST. ROBERT BELLARMINE (1939), Rev. Msgr. John B. Lavin; Revs. Edward R. Stewart; Andrew M. Kim; Deacon Andrew Ciccaroni. In Res., Rev. Henry A. Lang (Retired).
Res.: 56-15 213th St., Bayside, 11364. Tel: 718-229-6465; Fax: 718-229-8126.
School—56-10 214th St., Bayside, 11364. Tel: 718-225-8795; Fax: 718-423-5612. Sr. Mary Ann Carotenuto, C.S.J., Prin. Sisters of St. Joseph 4; Lay Teachers 18; Students 337.
Catechesis/Religious Program—Tel: 718-225-3181. Students 137.

91—ST. ROSE OF LIMA (1886), Rev. Peter D. Gillen. In Res., Revs. James T. Devine; Anthony C. Casey; Deacons Patrick Logue; Rafael Mejia.
Res.: 130 Beach 84th St., Rockaway Beach, 11693. Tel: 718-634-7394; Fax: 718-634-6591.
School—154 Beach 84th St., Rockaway Beach, 11693. Tel: 718-474-7079; Fax: 718-634-0524. Mrs. Theresa Andersen, Prin. Sisters 4; Lay Teachers 19; Students 334.
Catechesis/Religious Program—Tel: 718-945-4850. John O'Brien, D.R.E.; Ms. Antoinette Cammarata, D.R.E. Students 76.

92—SACRED HEART, Revs. Michael C. Gribbon; Calonge Lemaine; Felix Akpabio (Nigeria); Caleb A. Buchanan; Sisters Margaret Mary Igoe, O.P., Pastoral Assoc.; Carmele Nerette, F.D.M., Pastoral Assoc.; Deacons Paul Dorsinville; Roy Dudley. In Res., Rev. Joseph M. Nolan (Retired).
Res.: 115-58 222 St., Cambria Heights, 11411. Tel: 718-528-0577; Fax: 718-341-0253.
School—115-50 221st St., Cambria Heights, 11411. Tel: 718-527-0123; Fax: 718-527-1204. Lay Teachers 24; Students 390.
Catechesis/Religious Program—Elizabeth Wright, D.R.E. Students 90.

93—SACRED HEART (1931), Revs. John J. Fullum; Joseph A. Gancila. In Res., Rev. Romano Zanon.
Res.: 83-17 78th Ave., East Glendale, 11385. Tel: 718-821-6434; Fax: 718-497-2881.
School—84-05 78th Ave., East Glendale, 11385. Tel: 718-456-6636; Fax: 718-456-0286. Sisters of St. Dominic 1; Lay Teachers 14; Students 258.
Catechesis/Religious Program—Tel: 718-386-5616. Students 395.

94—SACRED HEART OF JESUS (1878), Rev. Msgr. Thomas F. Donovan; Rev. Daniel Agola; Sr. Kathleen Masterson, Pastoral Min. In Res., Revs. Coleman Costello; Kenneth J. Hand.
Res.: 215-35 38th Ave., Bayside, 11361. Tel: 718-428-2200; Fax: 718-428-5840.
School—216-33 38th Ave., Bayside, 11361. Tel: 718-631-4804. Dennis J. Farrell, Prin. Lay Teachers 32; Students 570.
Catechesis/Religious Program—Tel: 718-631-1307. Mrs. Georgette Lyons, D.R.E. Students 187.

95—ST. SEBASTIAN (1894), Rev. Msgr. Michael J. Hardiman, M.Div., M.A., M.P.A.; Revs. John Francis (Pakistan); Kevin P. Abels; Sabino Estrada; Deacons Stephen Damato; Julio Park; Richard Perez.
Res.: 39-63 57th St., Woodside, 11377. Tel: 718-429-4442; Fax: 718-429-7581.
School—39-68 58th St., Woodside, 11377. Tel: 718-429-1982; Fax: 718-446-7225. Robert J. Lowenberg, M.A., Prin. Sisters of Charity (Halifax) 1; Lay Teachers 22; Students 439.
Catechesis/Religious Program—39-66 58th St., Woodside, 11377. Tel: 718-899-3341. Ms. Martha Interiano, M.A., D.R.E. Students 250.

96—ST. STANISLAUS BISHOP AND MARTYR (1923), Rev. James J. Meszaros.
Res.: 88-10 102nd Ave., Ozone Park, 11416. Tel: 718-845-6206; Fax: 718-843-6408.
School—90-01 101st Ave., Ozone Park, 11416. Tel: 718-845-3188; Fax: 718-835-9447. Sr. Francis Marie Wystepek, C.S.F.N., Prin. Lay Teachers 9; Students 177.
Catechesis/Religious Program—Lee Grieco, D.R.E. Students 67.

97—ST. STANISLAUS KOSTKA (1872), Revs. Michael J. Walsh, S.T.D.; Joseph Palackal, C.M.I. (India).
Res.: 57-15 61st St., Maspeth, 11378. Tel: 718-326-2185; Fax: 718-416-2108.
School—61-17 Grand Ave., Maspeth, 11378. Tel: 718-326-1585; Fax: 718-326-1745. Sr. Rose Torma, C.S.J., Prin. Lay Teachers 11; Students 255.
Catechesis/Religious Program—Students 130.

98—ST. TERESA (1928), Rev. Msgr. Denis M. Herron; Rev. Darrell Da Costa; Deacons Martin Soraire; Roberto Abundo.
Res.: 50-20 45th St., Woodside, 11377. Tel: 718-784-2123; Fax: 718-706-6797.
School—50-15 44th St., Woodside, 11377. Tel: 718-784-0178; Fax: 718-784-3288. Martin C. Abruzzo, Prin. Sisters 1; Lay Teachers 9; Students 165.
Catechesis/Religious Program—Tel: 718-937-4819. Sr. Mary Jane Kelly, O.P., D.R.E. Students 339.

99—ST. TERESA OF AVILA (1929), Revs. Richard Hoare, Pastor; Hilaire Belizaire; Deacons Ramon Smith; Louis Panico; John Dennehy.
Res.: 109-26 130th St., South Ozone Park, 11420. Tel: 718-529-3587; Fax: 718-529-0324.
School—Tel: 718-641-1316; Fax: 718-843-0769. Ms. Loretta Rybacki, Prin. Lay Teachers 12; Students 326.
Catechesis/Religious Program—Tel: 718-641-5710. Douglas M. Blaine, D.R.E. Students 156.

100—ST. THOMAS APOSTLE (1910), Revs. William M. Hoppe; Felice J. De Laura; Deacon Okafor C. Uzoigwe.
Res.: 87-19 88th Ave., Woodhaven, 11421. Tel: 718-847-1353; Fax: 718-849-3776.
School—87-49 87th St., Woodhaven, 11421. Tel: 718-847-3904; Fax: 718-847-3513. Sisters 1; Lay Teachers 19; Students 328.
Catechesis/Religious Program—Tel: 718-441-8409. Jean Tuohy, D.R.E. Students 396.

101—ST. THOMAS MORE-ST. EDMUND (1937), Rev. Msgr. Michael J. Connelly; Rev. Vincent O'Connell, C.S.Sp.; Deacons Bernard M. Deschier; Richard G. Lee.
Res.: 204-25 Rockaway Point Blvd., Rockaway Point, 11697. Tel: 718-634-6357; Fax: 718-634-7900.
Catechesis/Religious Program—Sr. Joseph Amala, C.S.J., D.R.E. Students 115.

102—TRANSFIGURATION (1908), (Lithuanian), Revs. Paul A. Wood, Pastor; Vytas Volertas; Deacon William Oggeri. In Res., Most Rev. Paul A. Baltakis, O.F.M. (LIT), Bishop Emeritus.
Res.: 64-14 Clinton Ave., Maspeth, 11378. Tel: 718-326-2236; Fax: 718-326-2249.
Catechesis/Religious Program—Marija Wierzbicki, D.R.E. Students 75.

103—ST. VIRGILIUS (1914), Rev. Charles H. White.
Res.: 210 Noel Rd., Broad Channel, 11693-1091. Tel: 718-634-5680; Fax: 718-474-1538.
School—Tel: 718-634-6237; Fax: 718-634-2325. Diane M. Pizzo, Prin. Lay Teachers 10; Students 136.
Catechesis/Religious Program—Students 114.

Chaplains of Public Institutions

BROOKLYN. *Bernard Fineson Development Center*. Rev. Gordon Kusi.
Beth Israel Medical Center/Kings Hgwy. Elaine Chan.
Metropolitan Detention Center. Rev. James McDevitt.
Brookdale Hospital Medical Center.
Brooklyn Development Center. Rev. Gordon Kusi.
The Brooklyn Hospital. Michael Moran.
Coney Island Hospital. Rev. Joseph P. Quigley.
Downstate Medical Center. Sr. Karen O'Neil, C.S.J.
Kings County Hospital Center. Revs. Lucien Charlot, Roger Bourgea, S.M.
Kingsboro Psychiatric Center. Rev. Robert Frueh, M.S.
Long Island College Hospital. Has an interfaith Chaplain.
Lutheran Medical Center. Sr. Mary Ellen Vesey, C.S.J.
Maimonides Medical Center of Brooklyn. Sr. Mary Catherine Murphy, R.S.H.M.
Methodist Hospital. Sr. Therese Marie Camardella, C.S.J.
Veterans Administration Medical Center. Revs. Thomas Mullin, Luke Karpil, Vito Tiboni.
Victory Memorial Hospital. (Vacant)
Woodhull Medical & Mental Health Center. Rev. Justo Beltran Regado, Sr. Claudia Paredes, Rev. Cesar A. Rubiano, C.J.M. (MO).
Wyckoff Heights Hospital. Rev. Purcival DeVera.

QUEENS. *Creedmoor Psychiatric Center*. Revs. Paul Chenot, C.P., August J. Iantosca.
Elmhurst General Hospital. Revs. Alan Briceland, S.J., Jose Sanchez (Philippines).
Flushing Hospital and Medical Center. Sr. Florence Dippold, C.S.J.
Jamaica Hospital - Trump Pavilion. Rev. James Nunes, M.S.
Long Island Jewish Hospital. Sr. Benedicta Dega, F.S.S.J.
N.Y. Hospital Medical Center of Queens. Sr. Rosarine Quinn, C.S.J.
Peninsula Hospital Center. Deacon Thomas J. Devaney.
Queens Hospital Center--Pastoral Care Office. Rev. Jose Cadusale (Philippines).
Queensboro Correctional Facility. Deacon Frank DeTucci.
Veterans Affairs Extended Care Center, St. Albans, NY. Sr. Eleanor Woods.
Western Queens Community Hospital. (Vacant)

Special Assignment:
Rev. Msgrs.—
Maresca, Ralph, Sec. to Diocesan Bishop
Reilly, Philip J., Chap., Monastery of the Precious Blood, 5400 Ft. Hamilton Pkwy., 11219.
Rev.—
Leone, James M., Port Chap.

Military Chaplains:
Rev. Msgr.—
Gilhooley, John P. (Retired), 1260 Stevens Ave., Arbutus, MD 21227.
Revs.—
Dillon, James P., 1834 Tara Dr., Prattville, AL 36060.
Leibold, James C., Office of the Base Chap., MCB, Camp 5.D. Butler, Butler, AP 96373-5001.
Mulkerin, Terrence J., Chaplain's Office, USCG Reserve Training Center, Yorktown, VA 23690-9761.

Released from Diocesan Assignment:
Rev. Msgrs.—
Maksymowicz, John H., Apostolic Nunciature, 3339 Massachusetts Ave., N.W., Washington, DC 20008.
Sarno, Robert J., Congregation for the Causes of Saints 00120 Vatican City State.
Sherman, Anthony, USCCB, 3211 4th St., Washington, DC 20017.
Strynkowski, John J., National Conference of Catholic Bishops, 3211 Fourth St., Washington, DC 20017.
Vaccari, Peter I., S.T.L., Immaculate Conception Seminary, W. Neck Rd.-Lloyd Harbor, Huntington, 11743.
White, Leo J., St. George's Cathedral House, Westminster Bridge Rd., London SE1 7HY, England.
Revs.—
Bordeleau, Beau-Pierre G.
Boyd, James A., Chap., Dept. Naval Air Sta., Barbers Point, HI 96862-5050.
Caccavale, Charles, Seminary of the Immaculate Conception, Huntington, 11743.
D'Albro, Thomas G., 62A Widmer Rd., Wappingers Falls, 12590.
Finley, James F., Kath. Amerikanische Gemeinde, Huttenweig, 46, 14195 Berlin, Germany.
Folchetti, John T., Christian Brothers Academy, 850 Newman Springs Rd., Lincroft, NJ 07738.
Greene, Michael, C.P.
Hand, Kenneth J.
Heffernan, James F., Chap. (Retired), Veterans Admin. Medical Center, Northport, 11768.
Heffernan, Thomas A., Northwest Covenant Medical Center, Denville, NJ 07834.
Himes, Michael J., Department of Theology, Boston College, Chestnut Hill, MA 02167-3806.
Johnston, John F.
Lauder, Robert E., Cathedral Residence, 7200 Douglaston Pkwy., Douglaston, 11362.
Mariano, John M., 1620 S. Ocean Blvd. (9N), Pompano Beach, FL 33062.
Massa, James, Seminary of the Immaculate Conception, Huntington, 11743.
Nadine, Jerome E., St. Elizabeth Ann Seton Church, 18-11 Pueblo Vista Dr., Las Vegas, NV 89128.
Paterno, Salvatore D., St. Mary, 42 Goshen Ave., Washingtonville, 10992.
Penta, Leo J., Am Hegewinkel, 5B, D-14169 Berlin, Germany.
Pomilio, Matthew
Ruiz, Jean-Pierre, S.T.D., St. Patrick Rectory, 39-38 29th St., Long Island City, 11101.
Sears, William J., 1745 Padre Ln., Englewood, FL 34223.
Smith, LeRoy J., P.O. Box 23, Old Chatham, 12136.
Tivenan, John J., Mercy Medical Center, 1512 12th Ave. Rd., Nampa, ID 83686.
Trombetta, Paul N., 219 Old Oak Bucket Rd., Scituate, MA 02066.
Wulinski, Stanley F., 1701 N.E. 42nd St., Beacon Heights, FL 33064.

Graduate Studies:
Rev.—
Kazanecki, Thaddeus J.

On Leave/Unassigned:
Rev. Msgr.—
Tahaney, James
Revs.—
Acciarito, Anthony
Brown, Charles L.
Byrns, Joseph P.
Capellupo, Frank
Capolarello, Salvatore
Collins, Robert
Denzer, Joseph W.
Early, William F.
Fermeglia, Charles
Hannon, James

Javier, Nazareno
Keller, Brian
Mason, Edward J.
Newell, John J.
O'Brien, David G.
Perez, Jose
Placa, Stephen
Raveneau, Ricardo
Ryan, Barry
Sabatos, Daniel C.
Thompson, John
Valencia, Carlos
Vendetti, Michael A.
Waldron, John

Retired:
Rev. Msgrs.—
Adessa, Dominick J., 555 Albany Ave., Amityville, 11701.
Arella, Gerard J., Bishop Mugavero Residence, 7200 Douglaston Pkwy., Douglaston, 11362.
Asip, James W., 8255 Bridge Ln., Cutchogue, 11935.
Bednartz, August C., 130 Arcadia Walk, Rockaway Pt., 11697.
Bennett, Austin P., 378 Clermont Ave., 11238.
Burke, William F., Bishop Mugavero Residence, 7200 Douglaston Pkwy., Little Neck, 11362.
Burns, John A., 1395 E. 56th St., 11234.
Campbell, Thomas P., 1464 Forest Lake Blvd., Wantagh, 11793.
Clancy, Thomas C., 1525 E. 12th St., 11230.
Collini, Celsus O., 141-36 77th Ave., Kew Gardens Hills, 11367.
D'Anca, Achille, 274 Beachway Dr., Palm Coast, FL 32137.
Deas, George T., Bishop Mugavero Residence, 7200 Douglaston Pkwy., Little Neck, 11362.
Demski, Arthur A., P.O. Box 55129, Trenton, NJ 08638.
Ecker, Robert J., 300 Second St., Coronado, CA 92118.
Fagan, John T. (RVC), Little Flower Children's Services, N. Wading River Rd., Wading River, 11792.
Feldhaus, Eugene A., 188-16 91st Ave., Hollis, 11423.
Fitzpatrick, Franklin E., 91-18 86th Ave., Woodhaven, 11421.
Flanagan, Thomas J., P.O. Box 804, Beatrice Ct., Hampton Bays, 11946.
Florido, Raphael A., Ozanam Hall, 42-41 201st. St., Bayside, 11361.
Fogarty, George V., Bishop Mugavero Residence, 7200 Douglaston Pkwy., Little Neck, 11362.
Gotimer, James E., 43-22 Ithaca St., Elmhurst, 11373.
Gradilone, Thomas, 215 Exeter St., 11235.
HartmanN, John F., P.O. Box 1222, Madison, CT 06443.
Hendel, Thomas W., 104 Cassata Ct., Kings Park, 11754.
Hickey, William T., Our Lady of the Angelus, 63-63 98 St., Rego Pk., 11374.
Hickey, William T., 63-63 98th St., Rego Park, 11374.
Jolley, Edward W., Bishop Mugavero Residence, 7200 Douglaston Pkwy., Little Neck, 11363-0433.
King, James P., Bishop Mugavero Residence, 7200 Douglaston Pkwy., Little Neck, 11362.
Konrad, Joseph G., 5815 Catalpa Ave., Ridgewood, 11385.
Martin, Kieran J., 1550 Hendrickson St., 11234.
Martusciello, Joseph A., 7200 Douglaston Pkwy., Douglaston, 11362.
McAlister, Lawrence J., 1820 Briarwood Terr., South Belmar, NJ 07719-2906.
McMahon, James B., 7200 Douglaston Pkwy., Douglaston, 11362.
Mulhall, Francis X., Bishop Mugavero Residence, 7200 Douglaston Pkwy., Little Neck, 11362.
Nolan, Edward J., 89-43 Francis Lewis Blvd., Queens Village, 11427.
Noonan, Thomas F., St. Edmund, 2460 Ocean Ave., 11229.
Parks, Joseph K., St. Patrick, 9511 Fourth Ave., 11209.
Rau, Raymond F., 1302 Lantana St., Corpus Christi, TX 78407.
Rodgers, William J., Queen of Peace Residence, 110-30 221st St., Queens Village, 11429.
Ryan, James W., 2609 Linden Blvd., 11208.
Sapporito, Cosmo G., St. Bernadette, 8201 13th Ave., 11228.
Voiland, George T., 32-23 36th St., Long Island City, 11106.
Revs.—
Abrams, John L., Bishop Mugavero Residence, 7200 Douglaston Pkwy., Little Neck, 11362.
Angles, Sebastian, 2601 Muscatello St., Orlando, FL 32821.
Borzaga, Rinaldo, Manhattan College, Riverdale, 10471.
Buetow, Harold A., Bishop Mugavero Residence, 7200 Douglaston Pkwy., Little Neck, 11362.
Byrnes, Francis J., 7200 Douglaston Pkwy., Douglaston, 11362.
Byrnes, John W., 218-26 105th Ave., Queens Village, 11429.
Calderwood, Vincent T. (MET), McCarrick Care Center, 15 Dellwood Ln., Somerset, NJ 08893.
Collins, James, P.O. Box C, 11202.
Coyle, Eugene P., 7200 Douglaston Pkwy., Douglaston, 11362.
Cronin, John F., Bishop Mugavero Residence, 7200 Douglaston Pkwy., Little Neck, 11362.
Culkin, Harry M., Bishop Mugavero Residence, 7200 Douglaston Pkwy., P.O. Box 630433, Little Neck, 11363-0433.
Cushing, Charles B., Noreen McKeen Residence, 315 S. Flagler Dr., West Palm Beach, FL 33401.
Cutrone, Dominick F., Our Lady of Peache, 430 Ave. W., 11223.
D'Amato, James J., 1331 East 35th St., 11210.
Daly, Joseph F., Ozanam Hall Residence, 42-41 201st St., Bayside, 11361.
Dolan, Joseph, St. Bernadette, 8201 12 Ave., Brookly, 11228.
Dolan, Thomas D., 94-20 85th St., Ozone Park, 11416.
Donnelly, Eugene F., 25-02 80th St., Jackson Heights 11370.
Duran, Ernesto, Santa Beatriz 269, Apt. 503, Santiago 9, Chile.
Esposito, Joseph J., P.O. Box 370772, Las Vegas, NV 89137.
Flynn, Francis J., Sts. Joachim & Anne Residence, 2720 Surf Ave., 11224.
Frost, James, P.O. Box C., 11202.
Grant, Matthew, 204-13 Marshall Ave., Rockaway Point, 11697.
Guarracino, Ralph J., Mt. St. Mary Cemetary, 172-00 Booth Memorial Ave., Flushing, 11365.
Gural, Marion A., 123 Henry Rd., Southampton, 11968.
Guthrie, Alfred, Bishop Mugavero Residence, 7200 Douglaston Pkwy., Douglaston, 11362.
Harth, Charles F., Queen of Peace Residence, 110-30 221 St., Queens Village, 11429
Heffernan, James F., 146 Swan Lake, Poughkeepsie, 12605.
Keane, Edward M., 175-20 74th Ave., Flushing, 11366.
Keane, Joseph P., 204 E. Palm Dr., Rte. 10, Fort Myers, FL 33908.
Kelly, Thomas F., 7320 Fourth Ave., 11209.
Kenny, Albert N., 273 78th St., 11209.
Kirrane, James A., Holy Family, 5 Fordham Ave., Hicksville, 11801.
Labita, Francis J., 100-05 159th St., Howard Beach, 11414.
Lang, Henry A., 56-15 213th St., Bayside Hills, 11364.
Maceli, Anthony J., 6908 Stonesthrow Cir. N., St. Petersburg, FL 33710.
Malleck, Joseph L., 24 Steven St., Plainview, 11803.
Mankowski, Edmund A., 62357 St., 11220.
Mannion, Thomas F. (P), St. Charles, 94323 Gauntlett St., Gold Beach, OR 97444.
Mauer, Edward, P.O. Box C, 11202.
McCarren, William J., 8000 Roma N.E., Albuquerque, NM 87108.
McGovern, Eugene F., Bishop Mugavero Residence, 7200 Douglaston Pkwy., Douglaston, 11362.
Milde, Robert F., P.O. Box 610, Kerhonkson, 12446-0610.
Nichols, Charles P., Sacred Hearts of Jesus & Mary - St. Stephen, 108 Carroll St., 11231.
Nolan, Joseph M., 115-58 222nd St., Cambria Heights, 11411.
O'Brien, Thomas, 150-75 Goethals Ave., Jamaica, 11432.
O'Connor, Edward T., 6255 S.E. Charleston Pl., Hobe Sound, FL 33455.
Palubinskas, Vytautas A., Vilnius Seminary, Kalvariju 225B, LT2021, Vilnius, Lithuania.
Parisi, Michael R., St. Kevin, 45-21 194th St., Flushing, 11358.
Raila, Stanislaus, Bishop Mugavero Residence, 7200 Douglaston Pkwy., Little Neck, 11362.
Rizzi, Salvatore, 126 Pond Rd., Woodbury, 11797.
Salamone, Michael, P.O. Box C, 11202.
Sans, Pablo, 136-06 87th Ave., Richmond Hill, 11416.
Schmidt Jerome J., 5151 ackson Ct., Warrenton, VA 20187.
Schuck, Joseph J., Gilead House of Prayer, 1011 State Hwy. 7, Unadilla, 13849.
Schwind Donald F., 182 Monitor St., 11222.
Sheridan, Matthew W., Bishop Mugavero Residence, 7200 Douglaston Pkwy., Douglaston, 11362.
Smith, James, P.O. Box C, 11202.
Stack, George, P.O. Box C, 11202.
Sullivan, James E., 53-01 206 Street, Bayside, 11364.
Termine, Vincent J., 3736 Bayview Ave., 11224.
Travis, Herbert A., St. Anselm, 356 82nd St., 11209.
Tully, James J., 24 Brookway Dr., Greensboro, NC 27410.
Vivona, Anthony, 922 E. 96th St., 11236-2304.
Vogel, Charles P., 416 Grant Ave., 11208.
Wang, Barnabas, Bishop Mugavero Residence, 7200 Douglaston Pkwy., Douglaston, 11362.
Weinlich, Alfred J., Queen of Peace Residence, 110-30 221st St., Queens Village, 11429.
Wiseman, Joseph F., 46-02 Parsons Blvd., Flushing, 11355.
Young, Robert J., Bishop Mugavero Residence, 7200 Douglaston Pkwy, Little Neck, 11362.
Zaccagnigno, Raffaele, Dell Bono 48, 00122 Ostia Lido, Rome 5663580 Italy.

Permanent Deacons:
Abundo, Roberto S., St. Teresa, Woodside
Agnant, Ronald Y., St. Therese of Lisieux, Brooklyn
Aigbojie, Edward A., St. Peter Claver, Brooklyn
Almodovar, Ismael, Diocese of Orlando
Alvarez, Felipe J., St. Joseph, Long Island City
Alvia, Humberto R., Blessed Sacrament, Brooklyn
Amore, Bryan J., St. Andrew Apostle, Brooklyn
Arcand, Dennis A., Diocese of Savannah
Aris, Anthony J., (Inactive)
Baez, Angel, (Inactive)
Barreneche, Julio C., St. Kevin, Flushing
Beaubrun, Berthal, St. Ignatius, Brooklyn
Bichotte, Joseph, St. Augustine, Brooklyn
Bobadilla, Antonio, St. Mary Star of the Sea, Far Rockaway
Borheck, Steven J., Our Lady of the Snows, N. Floral Park
Boursiquot, Jean B., St. Ignatius, Brooklyn
Bugay, Josefino Y., St. Nicholas of Tolentine, Jamaica
Caceres, Ycelso, (Inactive)
Cajiao, Henry, Diocese of St. Petersburg
Cajoux, Francois G., Sacred Heart Cambria Hts.
Calvo, Juan, Queen of Angels, Sunnyside
Campisi, Joseph, Our Lady Grace, Howard Beach
Cancel, Edwin, Our Lady of the Angelus, Rego Park
Carattini, Juan M., Our Lady of Perpetual Help, South Ozone Park
Cardona, Ramon, Diocese of Mayaguez, PR
Casares, Gabriel, Diocese of St. Petersburg
Cederroth, Charles J., Diocese of Trenton
Chin, Paul M., St. Paul Chong Ha-Sang Chapel, Flushing
Ciccaroni, Andrew, St. Robert Bellarmine, Bayside
Cobham, Jaime A., St. Agnes, Brooklyn
Coffey, John P., Regional Director, Religious Education, Brooklyn
Colandrea, Dante, St. Athanasius, Brooklyn
Coyle, Lawrence J., St. Columba, Brooklyn
Cruz, Florencio, St. Matthew, Brooklyn
Cruz, Rafael, Archdiocese of Miami
Cutter, Arthur, St. Gregory the Great, Bellerose
D'Accordo, Armand C., St. Helen, Howard Beach
D'Accordo, Frank J., Saint Bernard, Brooklyn
Da Costa, Dennis A., St. Matthew, Brooklyn
Damato, Stephen T., St. Sebastian, Woodside
Daniel, Gordon V., St. Terese of Lisieux, Brooklyn
Davis, Thomas G., St. Anselm, Brooklyn
De Cola, Joseph P., Diocese of Palm Beach
De Tucci, Frank A., Catholic Charities Office for Prison Ministry and Our Lady of Mt. Carmel, Astoria
DeLeon, Andres, St. Gregory the Great, Brooklyn
Deming, Everett A., Our Lady of Mt. Carmel, Brooklyn
Dennehy, John P., St. Teresa of Avila, South Ozone Park
Deschler, Bernard M., St. Thomas More/St. Edmund, Rockaway Point
Desdunes, Herve, St. Matthew, Brooklyn
Devaney, Thomas J., Immaculate Heart of Mary, Brooklyn
Diaz, Ramon G., Immaculate Conception, Jamaica
Dixon, Gregory D., St. Andrew the Apostle, Brooklyn
Dorsinville, Paul C., Sacred Heart, Cambria Heights
Dudley, Roy A., Sacred Heart, Cambria Heights
Duncan, Isaac, Our Lady of Good Counsel, Brooklyn
Dupuy, Eulogio S., St. Gabriel, East Elmhurst
Duran, Juan R., Archdiocese of Minneapolis
Earley, George G., Diocese of Rockville Centre
Ehresmann, Philip J., St. Brigid, Brooklyn
Espinal, Luis J., St. Rita, Brooklyn
Felix, Antoine, Holy Innocents, Brooklyn
Flaim, Fabio, St. Aloysius, Ridgewood
Flannery, John A., St. Charles Borromeo, Brooklyn
Franca, John J., St. Francis Xavier, Brooklyn

Francis, John J., (Special Assignment: Simon's Ministries)
Galazin, Stanley J., American Martyrs, Bayside
Garamella, Robert, Diocese of Rockville Centre
George, Roy N., St. Gregory the Great, Brooklyn
Germain, Moliere
Gilligan, Richard J., St. Mary Gate of Heaven, Ozone Park
Gomez, Guillermo D., St. Gerard Majella, Hollis
Gonzalez, Jorge A., St. Michael, Brooklyn
Gonzalez, Louis A., St. Peter - St. Paul - Our Lady of Pilar, Brooklyn
Gonzalez, Rafael, Diocese of Orlando
Heaphy, Thomas F., St. Mary Gate of Heaven, Ozone Park
Hernandez, Rafael, Diocese of Orlando
Hernandez, Wilfredo, Holy Spirit, Brooklyn
Hili, Saviour, St. Francis of Assisi, Long Island City
Horne, Wilfred N., St. Ephrem, Brooklyn
Huckemeyer, Edward J., (On Leave)
Innocent, Francois, Incarnation, Queens Village
Joesten, F. Edward, St. Anthony of Padua, South Ozone Park
Kennedy, James F., Diocese of St. Petersburg, FL
Knight, Lionel A., St. Nicholas of Tolentine, Jamaica
Krebs, Jerome H., Our Lady Miraculous Medal, Brooklyn
Lacy, James J., Our Lady of Charity, Brooklyn
Landron, Jaime, Our Lady of the Presentation, Brooklyn
Lavanco, Robert F., Our Lady of Hope, Middle Village
Lee, Richard G., St. Thomas More-St. Edmund, Rockaway Point
Licata, Salvatore V., St. Ann, Flushing
Lima, Ramon, St. Raphael, Long Island City
Logue, Patrick J., St. Rose of Lima, Rockaway Beech
Lonergan, Robert P., St. Andrew Avellino, Flushing
Lopez, Eduvigis, Our Lady of Perpetual Help, Brooklyn
Lopez, Hiram, Archdiocese of New York
Lopez, Marco V., St. Rita, Brooklyn
Maldonado, Andres, Diocese of Ponce, PR
Malone, William F., Diocese of Trenton, NJ
Marcel, Magloire, St. Jerome, Brooklyn
Marchello, Andrew A., Nativity of the Blessed Virgin Mary, Queens
Marley, Daniel J., Our Lady of Solace, Brooklyn
Marte, Rafael, St. John Cantius, Brooklyn
Martinez, German, Transfiguration, Brooklyn
Mayers, Winston M., Christ the King, Springfield Gardens
Mazza, Nicholas, (Retired)
McCarthy, Thomas R., (Retired)
McGreevey, John F., St. John Vianney, Flushing
McGuire, Joseph P., (Retired)
Medina, Genaro, St. Catharine of Alexandria
Mejia, Abdon (Peru), Our Lady of Perpetual Help, South Ozone Park
Mejia, Julio C., St. Michael, Brooklyn
Mejia, Rafael A., Diocese of Orlando
Mellace, Carlo V., St. Dominic, Brooklyn
Miller, Leon F., St. Michael, East New York
Montalvo, Hector, Holy Family, Brooklyn
Morales, Julio A., Diocese of Orlando
Mule, Lawrence C., St. Matthias, Ridgewood
Munoz, Franklin G., Immaculate Conception, Long Island City
Murillo, Julio C., Our Lady of Angelus, Rrego Park
Murphy, John J., (Retired)
Occhiuto, Joseph J., (Inactive)
Oellinger, Matthew J., Our Lady of the Snows, North Floral Park
Oggeri, William, Transfiguration, Maspeth
Olivas, Pascual B., St. Bonaventure, Jamaica
Orlandello, John P., St. Francis of Paola, Brooklyn
Pagan, Aurelio, (Retired)
Panessa, Giacomo, Most Precious Blood, Astoria
Panico, Louis J., St. Teresa of Avila, South Ozone Park
Parisi, Vincent, St. Rita, Long Island City
Park, Julio, St. Sebastian, Woodside
Pascal, Orlando, Our Lady of Sorrows, Corona
Paul, Ernst, Our Lady of Miracles, Brooklyn
Postler, Charles A., St. Patrick, Brooklyn
Pouso, Roberto J., Blessed Sacrament, Jackson Heights
Proce, Horatio A., (Inactive)
Ramirez, Manuel, Diocese of Scranton
Ramos, James, St. Francis Xavier, Brooklyn
Ramos, Jose A., St. Lucy-St. Patrick, Brooklyn
Ramos, Pedro, Diocese of Caguas, PR
Reichert, John P., St. Fidelis, College Point
Rivera, Angel R., St. Benedict Joseph Labre, Richmond Hill
Rivera, Hector R., Archdiocese of San Juan, PR
Rizzo, Giovanni A., St. Finbar, Brooklyn
Rizzuto, Ronald, St. Edmund, Brooklyn
Roberts, Lionel V., Diocese of St. Petersburg, FL
Roman, Luis A., St. Gerard Majella, Hollis
Ronacher, Ronald M., St. Rita, Brooklyn
Rosati, Frank J., Chap., Holy Family Home for Aged
Ruiz, Jose D., Diocese of Ponce, PR
Russo, Anthony J., (Retired)
Ryan, Kevin F., Blessed Virgin Mary Help of Christians, Queens
Sands, John E., St. Matthias, Ridgewood
Sawney, Ira, Florida
Sclafani, Leonard A., St. Paul Center, Douglaston
Sencion, Eduardo, Our Lady of the Cenacle, Richmond Hill
Siani, Philip J., Our Lady of Grace, Brooklyn
Simon, Mauclair, St. Therese of Lisieux, Brooklyn
Sinisi, Henry C., (On Leave)
Smith, Charles J., Diocese of Trenton
Smith, Henry J., Our Lady of the Snows, North Floral Park
Smith, Nathaniel J., St. Clement Pope, South Ozone Park
Smith, Ramon, St. Teresa of Avila, South Ozone Park
Smolinski, Edward A., Our Lady of Mercy, Forest Hills
Soraire, Martin D., St. Teresa, Woodside
Soto, Jesus, Our Lady of Perpetual Help, Brooklyn
Sucich, John R., St. Francis of Assisi, Long Island City
Svebel, Harry A., St. Luke, Whitestone
Taylor, Luis C., St. Catherine of Sienna, St. Alban
Tejado, Ramon E., St. Mary Star of the Sea, Far Rockaway
Tierney, John A., Diocese of Albany
Tineo, Jose, Our Lady of Sorrows, Corona
Tokarcsik, George M., Pennsylvania
Torres, Abel, Holy Name, Brooklyn
Trochez, Carlos A., Corpus Christi, Woodside
Troy, Michael J., Our Lady of Angels, Brooklyn
Tully, Dean T., Holy Child Jesus, Richmond Hill
Uzoigwe, Okafor C., St. Thomas the Apostle, Woodhaven
Valderrana, Carlos, St. Cecilia, Brooklyn
Valle Valle, Esteban, Archdiocese of San Juan, PR
Van de Ven, Theodore, Diocese of Rockville Centre
Van Wassenhove, Raymond J., Diocese of Peoria
Varela, Jaime, Our Lady of Presentation and Our Lady of Loreto, Brooklyn
Vargas, Juan R., St. Agatha, Brooklyn
Vermilyea, Richard, (Inactive)
Vicinanza, Michael W., Queen of Peace, Kew Garden Hills
Wander, William H., St. Andrew the Apostle, Brooklyn
Whelan, Alfred L., St. Gertrude, Far Rockaway
Williams, Lee C., St. Mary Magdalene, Springfield Gardens
Williamsen, William, St. Saviour, Brooklyn
Yepes, Elias H., St. Michael, Flushing
Zeuner, Robert J., St. Gregory the Great, Bellerose

INSTITUTIONS LOCATED IN THE DIOCESE

[A] PASTORAL CENTERS

DOUGLASTON. *Immaculate Conception Center*, 7200 Douglaston Pkwy., 11362-1997. Tel: 718-229-8001; Fax: 718-229-2658. Email: sgalazin@iccdob.org. Web: www.iccdouglaston.org. Deacon Stanley J. Galazin, Dir.; Mr. Thomas D. Flynn, Asst. Comptroller; Mr. Gerard King, Asst. Dir. Bldg. Svcs. & Maintenance; Mr. James Austin, Dir. Diocesan Food Svcs. In Res. Rev. Msgrs. Frank Caggiano; Cornelius H. Mahoney; John E. Waldron; Revs. Francisco Ares; James Bradley; Joseph W. Denzer; Martin F. Kirby, M.A.; Robert E. Lauder; Joaquin Longres; Eugene Stoklie; Marc Swartvagher, S.T.B., S.T.L.

[B] SEMINARIES, DIOCESAN

DOUGLASTON. *Cathedral Seminary Residence of the Immaculate Conception*, 7200 Douglaston Pkwy., 11362. Tel: 718-229-8001; Fax: 718-224-0295. Rev. Msgrs. Octavio Cisneros, M.Div., Rector; Conrad R. Dietz (RVC), Academic Dean, Philosophy Prof.; Thomas G. Caserta, M.A., M.Div., D.Min., Spiritual Dir.; Vincent A. Keane, Adjunct Spiritual Dir.; Rev. Marc Swartvagher, S.T.B., S.T.L., Philosophy Prof. Residence for college level and post college level candidates for Priesthood. Priests 5; Lay Teachers 2; Seminarians 17. In Res. Rev. Msgr. Cornelius H. Mahoney; Revs. Martin F. Kirby, M.A.; Robert E. Lauder.

ELMHURST. *Cathedral Preparatory Seminary of the Immaculate Conception*, 56-25 92nd St., 11373. Tel: 718-592-6800; Fax: 718-592-5574. Email: revjpc@aol.com. Rev. Joseph P. Calise, Rector & Prin. Priests 2; Sisters 1; Lay Teachers 16; Seminarians 181. In Res. Rev. Sofronio LoFranco.

[C] SEMINARIES, RELIGIOUS

WHITESTONE. *St. Alphonsus Formation Residence*, 22-04 Parsons Blvd., 11357-3440. Tel: 718-321-1096; Fax: 718-321-1246. Email: paulbrow@aol.com. Web: www.baltcssr.com. Very Rev. Paul J. Borowski, C.SS.R., Rector & Dir. of Formation; Bro. Jeffrey Rolle, C.SS.R., Asst. Dir.; Revs. Philip Dabney, C.SS.R., Vocation Dir.; Robert Cheesman, C.SS.R. Priests 5; Students 9. In Res. Revs. Bao Vinh Luu Quang, C.SS.R.; Tuan Le Quang, C.SS.R.

[D] COLLEGES AND UNIVERSITIES

BROOKLYN. **St. Francis College*, 180 Remsen St., 11201. Tel: 718-489-5345; Fax: 718-237-8964. Web: www.stfranciscollege.edu. Dr. Frank Macchiarola, Pres. Brothers 3; Sisters 1; Students 2,525; Total Staff 70.

**St. Joseph's College*, 245 Clinton Ave., 11205. Tel: 718-636-6800; Fax: 718-636-7245. Email: fburns@sjcny.edu. Web: www.sjcny.edu. Under supervision of Board of Trustees.

Branch Campus, 155 West Roe Blvd., Patchoque, 11772. Tel: 631-447-3200; Fax: 631-654-1782. Sr. Elizabeth A. Hill, C.S.J., M.A., J.D., Pres.; Nancy J. Connors, M.S., Vice Pres. & Institute Advancement; John Roth, M.B.A., CFO; Joseph Spadaro, M.A., M.S., CIO; Sisters Loretta McGrann, C.S.J., Vice Pres. for Academic Affairs; Margaret Buckley, C.S.J., Ed.D., Academic Dean, School of Arts & Sciences, Brooklyn Campus; Randall Krieg, Ph.D., Academic Dean, School of Arts & Sciences, Patchogue Campus; Thomas G. Travis, Ph.D., Vice Pres. & Dean, School of Adult & Professional Education; Sr. John Raymond McGann, C.S.J., Asst. to Pres. Priests 1; Sisters 18; Lay Teachers 35; Students 1,226.

JAMAICA. *St. John's University*, 8000 Utopia Pkwy., 11439. Tel: 718-990-6161; Fax: 718-990-5723. Web: www.stjohns.edu. Rev. Donald J. Harrington, C.M., Pres. Sponsored by the Vincentian Priests and Brothers Eastern Province of the Congregation of the Mission. Priests 20; Sisters 3; Lay Teachers 566; Total Enrollment (undergraduate and graduate of Queens, Staten Island Campuses and Rome) 18,523; Queens Campus Enrollment 15,593.

Officers of Administration: Robert J. Crimmins, Exec. Vice Pres.; Tony H. Bonaparte, Ph.D., Provost; Rev. Michael J. Carroll, C.M., Vice Pres. Univ. Ministry & Graduate Center, Rome, Italy; Cecilia S. Chang, Ed.D., Vice Pres. Intl. Rels.; John P. Connolly Jr., Vice Pres. Admin. Svcs.; Rev. Joseph V. Daly, C.M., Ombudsman & Asst. to the Pres.; Susan L. Ebbs, Ed.D., Senior Vice Pres. Student Life; Dorothy E. Habben, Ph.D., Vice Pres., Univ. Sec. & Chief Assessment Officer; Suzanne M. Halpin, Vice Pres. Office of External Affairs; Rev. James F. Kiernan, C.M., Senior Vice Pres., Staten Island Campus; Dennis P. McAuliffe, Vice Pres. Univ. Affairs; James P. Pellow, Senior Vice Pres. & Treas.; Joseph A. Sciame, Vice Pres. Govt. & Community Rels.; Frank J. Sirianni, Ph.D., Vice Pres. & CIO; Rev. Bernard M. Tracey, C.M., Vice Pres. Institutional Advancement.

STATEN ISLAND. *St. John's University, Staten Island Campus*, 300 Howard Ave., 10301. Tel: 718-390-4545; Fax: 718-816-4520. Web: www.stjohns.edu. Rev. Donald J. Harrington, C.M., Pres. Sponsored by the Vincentian Priests and Brothers Eastern Province of the Congregation of the Mission. Priests 21; Sisters 2; Lay Teachers 559; Staten Island Campus Enrollment 2,382; Total Undergraduate & Graduate Enrollment 18,500.

Officers of Administration: James Pellow, Exec. Vice Pres.; Sr. Julie Upton, R.S.M., Provost; Rev. Michael J. Carroll, C.M., Vice Pres. Mission and Branch Campus; Cecilia S. Chang, Ed.D., Vice Pres. Intl. Rels.; Rev. Joseph V. Daly, C.M., Asst. to the Pres.; Susan L. Ebbs, Ed.D., Vice Pres. Student Life; Dorothy E. Habben, Ph.D., Vice Pres. & Univ. Sec.; Judy Ksher, Dir. of Media Relations; Thomas Nadell, Vice Pres. Finance & Treas.; Joseph Sciame, Vice Pres. Govt. & Community Rels.; Rev. Bernard M. Tracey, C.M., Vice Pres. Institutional Advancement.

[E] CATHOLIC EDUCATION OFFICES

BROOKLYN. *Office of Religious Education: Evangelization and Catholic Formation*, 310 Prospect Part West, 11215-7323. Tel: 718-965-7300; Fax: 718-965-7325. Email: jsheehan@diobrook.org. Web: www.dioceseofbrooklyn.org/catholic_ed/religious_ed. P.O. Box 159013, 11215. Dr. James Sheehan, Diocesan Dir.; Sr. Alice Michael, S.U.S.C., Dir. D.R.E. Personnel & Religious Educ. Cultural/Ethnic Groups & Coord. RCIA; Deacon John Coffey, Regl. Dir. Rel. Ed, Brooklyn; Richard Pipchinski, Regl. Dir. Rel. Ed.,

Queens; Ellen Rhatigan, Dir. Youth & Young Adult Min. & Dir. College Campus Min.; Dr. James Sheehan, Dir. College Campus Min.; Molly Barreto, Admin. Asst.; Millie Malone.

Campus Ministers and Ministry Centers Revs. Frank Mann, Brooklyn College; Paul Wood, Queens College; Richard Bretone, Pratt Institute of Technology; David Inhenacho Long Island University; Bro. Thomas Grady, O.S.F., St. Francis College; Sisters Joan Cahill, O.M., Kingsborough Community College; Alice Danaher, O.P., Queensborough Community College; Rev. James Mahar St. John's University; Sr. Susan Wilcox, C.S.J. Legal Titles & Corporations: Newman Apostolate, Inc.

Office of the Superintendent of Schools, 310 Prospect Park W., 11215-7323. Tel: 718-965-7300; Fax: 718-965-7323. Web: www.dioceseofbrooklyn.org/catholic-ed. Dr. Thomas Chadzutko, Interim Supt.; Dr. Patricia Kelly-Stiles, Assoc. Supt. Personnel; Mr. Michael Pizzingrillo, BRK, Assoc. Supt. Prog. Mgmt.; Sisters Jane Ellis, I.H.M., Assoc. Supt. Prin. Personnel; Sheila Conley, S.C., Assoc. Supt. Curriculum; Margaret Schmit, O.P., Asst. Dir. Personnel; Mr. William E. Slow, Assoc. Supt., Special Ed.; Mrs. Dorothy LaMere, Dist. Supt. - Queens North Schools; Sr. Miriam Blake, C.S.J., Dist. Supt. - Brooklyn E. Schools; Mr. Anthony Danile, Dist. Supt. - Queens South Schools; Bro. William Clifford, C.S.C., Dir. of Education Technology; Eileen King Dwyer, Exec. Dir. Prog. for the Devel. of Human Potential; Mrs. Margaret Sacca, Dir. St. Catherine LaBoure Special Education Prog.; Ms. Mary Jones, Asst. Dir. Curriculum. Priests 13; Brothers 59; Sisters 253; Lay Teachers 3,753; Total Enrollment 71,208.

Diocese of Brooklyn Education Offices Legal Titles & Corporations: Department of Education. Diocese of Brooklyn; Henry M. Hald High School Association; Saint John's Preparatory School, Brooklyn.

[F] HIGH SCHOOLS, DIOCESAN

BROOKLYN. *Bishop Loughlin Memorial High School*, 357 Clermont Ave., 11238. Tel: 718-857-2700; Fax: 718-398-4227. Email: dcronin@blmhs.org. Web: www.bishoploughlin.org. Bro. Dennis Cronin, F.S.C., Prin.; Nancy McKeeven, Asst. Prin. (Coed); Legal Corp.: Henry M. Hald Assoc. Brothers of the Christian Schools 8; Sisters 2; Lay Teachers 52; Students 876.

[G] HIGH SCHOOLS, PRIVATE

BROOKLYN. *Bishop Ford Central Catholic High School*, 500 19th St., 11215. Tel: 718-965-6400; Fax: 718-965-6405. Email: fbrancato@bishopfordhs.org. Web: www.bishopfordhs.org. Mr. Raymond P. Nash, Pres.; Mr. Frank V. Brancato, Prin.; Mr. Rocco V. Grella, Asst. Prin. (Coed) Sisters 3; Lay Teachers 45; Students 850.

Bishop Kearney High School, 2202 60th St., 11204-2599. Tel: 718-236-6363; Fax: 718-236-7784. Email: thomasine@bishopkearneyhs.org. Web: www.bishopkearneyhs.org. Sr. Thomasine Stagnitta, C.S.J., Prin. (Girls) Priests 1; Sisters of St. Joseph (Brentwood Community) 10 Sisters 1; Lay Teachers 57; Students 1,061.

Catherine McAuley, 710 E. 37th St., 11203. Tel: 718-462-7282; Fax: 718-462-7284. Sr. Peggy Lake, R.S.M., Prin.; Rev. John W. Maloney, Spiritual Dir. (Girls) Sisters of Mercy 7; Lay Teachers 21; Students 300.

Fontbonne Hall, 9901 Shore Rd., 11209. Tel: 718-748-2244; Fax: 718-745-3841. Email: clancy@fontbonne.org. Web: www.fontbonne.org. Sr. Anne P. Clancy, C.S.J., Prin. (Girls) Sisters of St. Joseph (Brentwood Community) 10; Lay Teachers 37; Students 515.

St. Joseph, 80 Willoughby St., 11201-5265. Tel: 718-624-3618; Fax: 718-624-2792. Email: admin@sjhsbridge.org. Web: www.sjhsbridge.org. Sr. Eugenia Calabrese, C.S.J., Prin. (Girls) Sisters of St. Joseph (Brentwood Community) 17; Other Religious 5; Lay Teachers 23; Students 300.

Nazareth Regional, 475 E. 57th St., 11203. Tel: 718-763-1100; Fax: 718-629-5382. Web: www.nazarethrhs.org. Peter M. Doran, Prin. (Coed) Lay Teachers 28; Students 560; Brothers 1.

Xaverian, 7100 Shore Rd., 11209. Tel: 718-836-7100; Fax: 718-836-7114. Email: jmarino@xaverian.org. Web: www.xaverian.org. Dr. Salvatore Ferrera, Pres.; Dr. Joseph Marino, Prin.; Mr. Nicholas Vendikos, Dir. of Devel.; Mr. George Donnelly, Asst. Prin. Academics; Mr. Daniel Sharib Dir. of Admissions; Ms. Johanna Motta, Asst. Prin. Staff Devel.; Domenick Laurendi, Asst. Prin. Discipline; Mr. Sigfried Heiles, Dir. of Alumni Affairs; Rev. David J. Dettmer, Chap. (Boys) Priests 1; Xaverian Brothers 5; Lay Teachers 83; Students 1,340.

Queens

ASTORIA

St. John Preparatory School, 21-21 Crescent St., 11105-3398. Tel: 718-721-7200; Fax: 718-545-3469. Web: www.stjohnsprepschool.org. Mr. William A. Higgins, Prin.; Rev. Charles P. Keeney Spiritual Dir. (Coed) Priests 2; Sisters 4; Lay Teachers 75; Students 1,329.

BRIARWOOD

Archbishop Molloy, 83-53 Manton St., 11435. Tel: 718-441-2100; Fax: 718-849-8251. Email: president@molloyhs.org. Web: www.molloyhs.org. Bros. Richard Van Houten, F.M.S., Pres.; Roy George, F.M.S., Prin. (Coed) Brothers 15; Sisters 1; Lay Teachers 68; Students 1,575.

COLLEGE POINT

St. Agnes Academic, 13-20 124 St., 11356-1814. Tel: 718-353-6276; Fax: 718-353-6068. Email: jmartin@stagneshs.org. Web: stagneshs.org. Sr. Joan Martin, O.P., Prin. (Girls) Sisters of St. Dominic (Amityville) 8; Lay Teachers 20; Students 400.

EAST ELMHURST

Monsignor McClancy, 71-06 31st Ave., 11370. Tel: 718-898-3800; Fax: 718-898-3929. Mr. James P. Carey, Prin. (Boys) Priests 1; Brothers 11; Sisters 1; Lay Teachers 28; Boys 530.

FLUSHING

Holy Cross High School, 26-20 Francis Lewis Blvd., 11358. Tel: 718-886-7250; Fax: 718-886-7257. Email: info@holycrosshs.org. Web: www.holycrosshs.org. Bro. Stephen LaMendola, C.S.C., Pres.; Mr. Joseph Giannuzzi Prin. (Boys) Brothers of Holy Cross 11; Lay Teachers 47; Students 960.

FRESH MEADOWS

St. Francis Preparatory School, 6100 Francis Lewis Blvd., 11365. Tel: 718-423-8810; Fax: 718-224-2108. Email: 21stcentury@stfrancisprep.org. Web: www.stfrancisprep.org. Bro. Leonard Conway, O.S.F., Prin.; Rev. William F. Sweeney, Chap. (Coed) Priests 1; Franciscan Brothers 10; Sisters 16; Lay Teachers 117; Students 2,713.

JAMAICA ESTATES

The Mary Louis Academy (College Preparatory), 176-21 Wexford Ter., 11432. Tel: 718-297-2120; Fax: 718-739-0037. Web: www.tmla.org. Sr. Kathleen McKinney, C.S.J., Prin. (Girls) Priests 1; Sisters of St. Joseph (Brentwood Community) 25; Sisters of St. Dominic (Amityville) 1; Lay Teachers 65; Students 1,038.

MIDDLE VILLAGE

Christ the King Regional High School, 68-02 Metropolitan Ave., 11379. Tel: 718-366-7400; Fax: 718-417-8830. Email: caldwell@ctkrhs.org. Web: www.ctkrhs.org. Mr. Michael J Lynch, Prin.; Rev. Anthony S. Ercolano, Chap. (Coed) Priests 1; Sisters 1; Lay Teachers 85; Students 1,568.

ROCKAWAY PARK

Stella Maris High School, Beach 112th St., 11694. Tel: 718-634-4994; Fax: 718-634-5267 Email: gmartinez@stellamarishigh.org. Web: www.stellamarishs.org. Miss Geri Martinez, Prin. (Girls) Sisters of St. Joseph (Brentwood) 5; Brothers 2; Lay Teachers 42; Students 477.

Maura Clarke Coed Jr. High Program Tel: 718-634-4994; Fax: 718-256-5761. Mrs. Ann Cordes.

[H] HIGH SCHOOLS PAROCHIAL

BROOKLYN. *Denis Maloney Institute/St. Edmund Preparatory High School*, 2474 Ocean Ave., 11229. Tel: 718-743-6100; Fax: 718-743-5243 Email: principal@stedmundhs.org. Web: www.stedmundhs.org. Mr. John P. Lorenzetti, Prin.; Mr. Jim Benson, Asst. Prin. (Coed Sisters 2; Lay Teachers 41; Students 670.

St. Saviour High School, 588 6th St., 11215. Tel: 718-768-4406; Fax: 718-369-2688. Email: belanger.sv@stsaviour.org. Web: www.stsaviour.org. Sr. Valeria Belanger, S.S.N.D., Prin.; Mrs. Margaret Bernstein, Asst. Prin. (Girls) Sisters 2; Lay Teachers 29; Students 358

[I] SPECIAL SCHOOLS

BROOKLYN. *Brooklyn Jesuit Prep*, 560 Sterling Pl., 11238. Tel: 718-638-5884; Fax: 718-638-5884. Email: vin@brooklynjesuit.org. Vacant (GB), Pres.

St. Catherine Laboure Special Education Program, Dept. of Education, 310 Prospect Park W., 11215. Tel: 718-965-7300, Ext. 1229; Fax: 718-965-7323. Mr. William E. Slow, Assoc. Supt. Program for mentally challenged students ages 5-21 and learning disabled students grades 6-8 Lay Teachers and Staff 24; Students 113.

St. Francis de Sales School for the Deaf, 260 Eastern Pkwy., 11225. Tel: 718-636-4573; Fax: 718-636-4577. Email: school@sfdesales.org. Web: www.sfdesales.org. Edward McCormack, M.A., Supt. Infant through Elementary Grades Sisters 3; Lay Teachers 45; Students 130.

St. Francis De Sales School for the Deaf Development Fund, 260 Eastern Pkwy., 11225. Tel: 718-626-4573; Fax: 718-636-4577 Email: school@sfdesales.org.

Robert F. Kennedy Incentive Program, 2635 Linden Blvd., 11208-4992. Tel: 718-235-0744; Fax: 718-235-0744. Email: rfkincentiveprogram@yahoo.com. Bro. Adrian Fannon, O.S.F., Prin. (Coed) Lay Teachers 6; Students 46.

Ryken Educational Center, Inc., 7100 Shore Rd., 11209. Tel: 718-836-7100. Email: sferrara@xaverian.org. Vacant (GB), Pres.

SPRINGFIELD GARDENS. *Martin de Porres School*, 136-25 218th St., 11413-2226. Tel: 718-525-3414; Fax: 718-525-0982. Email: mdpschool@metrocon.com. Web: www.mdp.org. Specialized day school for emotionally disturbed children, ages 7-21. Brothers 4; Sisters 1; Total Staff 125; Capacity 310.

[J] ELEMENTARY SCHOOLS PRIVATE

BROOKLYN. *St. Agnes Seminary*, 2221 Avenue R, 11229. Tel: 718-376-2756; Fax: 718-376-8834. Web: www.saintagnes seminary.org. Sr. Katherine Burke, C.S.J., Prin. Sisters of St. Joseph 2; Lay Teachers 14; Students 174.

St. Angela Hall Academy, 290 Washington Ave., 11205. Tel: 718-636-6919; Fax: 718-622-7005. Email: sfdssd@earthlink.net. Sr. Mary Sivillo, C.S.J., Prin. Under supervision of Sisters of St. Joseph. Sisters 3; Lay Teachers 50; Students 145.

Visitation Academy, 8902 Ridge Blvd., 11209. Tel: 718-680-9452; Fax: 718-680-4441. Email: dobsc261@impresso.com. Sr. Susan Kasprzak, Supr. & Pres.; Mrs. Arlene Figaro, Prin. Sisters of the Visitation 8; Lay Teachers 18; Girls 167.

[K] CONSOLIDATED ELEMENTARY SCHOOLS (REGIONAL)

BROOKLYN. *St. Elizabeth Seton*, 751 Knickerbocker Ave., 11221. Tel: 718-386-4050; Fax: 718-386-1565. Email: dobsc137@connectinc.com. Cynthia Kitts, Prin. Consolidated from Fourteen Holy Martyrs and St. Martin of Tours Lay Teachers 10; Students 244.

St. Frances Cabrini, 181 Suydam St., 11221. Tel: 718-386-9277; Fax: 718-386-9064. Email: mariacrifasi@aol.com. Maria Crifasi, Prin. Lay Teachers 10; Students 268.

St. Michael, 237 Jerome St., 11207. Tel: 718-277-6766; Fax: 718-348-0513. Sr. Margaret Merritt, O.P., Prin. Sisters 2; Brothers 1; Lay Teachers 13; Students 306.

[L] CATHOLIC CHARITIES

BROOKLYN. *Catholic Charities*, Central Office, 191 Joralemon St., 11201. Tel: 718-722-6000; Fax: 718-722-6096. Email: chorn@ccbq.org. Web: www.ccbq.org. Most Revs. Nicholas DiMarzio, D.D., Ph.D. (CAM); Joseph M. Sullivan, M.S.W., M.P.A., V.E., Exec. Vice Pres. & Episcopal Vicar for Human Svcs.; Mr. Robert Siebel, M.S.W., Exec. Dir. & CEO; Anthony Giugliano, C.F.O.; Carlo de Rege, M.U.P., Assoc. Exec. Dir.; Sr. Ellen Patricia Finn, O.P.; Emmie Glynn Ryan Esq., Dir. Legal Affairs; Thaddeus Taberski, M.S.W., M.B.A.; Sr. Frances Picone, R.S.M., Regl. Admin. Brooklyn East; Gladys Rodriguez, C.S.W., Regl. Admin. Brooklyn West; Robert Marquez, Regl. Admin. Queens North; Robert Mundy, Regl. Admin. Queens South; Rev. Msgr. Joseph A. Funaro, Special Asst. to Exec. Dir.; Sisters Lorna Colin, C.S.J., Special Asst. to Exec. Dir.; Kathleen Newell, B.V.M., Special Asst. to Exec. Dir.; Lynne Williams, Dir. Public Affairs; Donna Corrado, Dir. Govt. Rels. & Public Policy; Mary O'Reilly, Assoc. Dir. Family Svcs.; Fran Kommor, Assoc. Dir. Residential Svcs.; Rev. Peter Mahoney, Assoc. Dir. Evaluation; Lisa Rosen, Dir. Quality Assurance; Barbara Conley, M.S.W., Dir. Child Care & Planning; Michael Guglielmo, Dir. of Pastoral Svcs. & Prison Ministry; John Tynan, M.U.P., Dir. Housing; Gayle DeRienzis, M.S.W., Assoc. Dir. Behavioral Svcs.; Rev. Msgr. Howard B. Basler, Dir. Social Action & Campaign for Human Devel.; Rosalyn Ferguson, M.S.W., Employee Assistance Prog.; Edwin Colon, Human Resources; Richard Abrahamsen, Dir. Financial Affairs; Kenneth Haag, Dir. Financial Svcs., B.F.F.Y.; Frank Paterno, Dir. Computer Svcs.; Margaret Keaveney, Dir. Communications.

Aging Services:

Golden Age Clubs, 191 Joralemon St., 11201. Tel: 718-722-6022; Fax: 718-722-6039.

Human Services:

Center for Pregnant Women, 191 Joralemon St., 11201. Tel: 718-722-6121; Fax: 718-722-6233.

Family Centers:

Brooklyn West, 191 Joralemon St., 11201. Tel: 718-722-6002; Fax: 718-722-6045.

Brooklyn East, 1987 Flatbush Ave., 11234. Tel: 718-677-9848; Fax: 718-677-1869.

Queens North, 23-40 Astoria Blvd., Astoria, 11102. Tel: 718-726-9790; Fax: 718-725-8817.

Queens South, 90-39 189th St., Hollis, 11423. Tel:

718-217-1238; Fax: 718-464-1317.

Services For Disabled Persons:

Deafness Services, 191 Joralemon St., 11201. Tel: 718-722-6214; Fax: 718-722-6233.

Comprehensive Human Services:

Builders for the Family and Youth of the Diocese of Brooklyn, Inc. Tel: 718-722-6000; Fax: 718-722-6096. Most Rev. Joseph M. Sullivan, M.S.W., M.P.A., V.E., Pres.; Mr. Robert Siebel, Vice Pres. Operations; Thaddeus Taberski, M.S.W., M.B.A., Vice Pres. Svcs.; Anthony Giugliano, Vice Pres. Treasurer; Kenneth Haag, Exec. Sec.

B.F.F.Y. - Administration:

Regional Office - Brooklyn West, 191 Joralemon St., 11201. Tel: 718-722-6185; Fax: 718-722-6045.

Regional Office - Brooklyn East, 1987 Flatbush Ave., 11234. Tel: 718-677-9848; Fax: 718-677-1869.

Regional Office - Queens South, 90-39 189th St., Hollis, 11423. Tel: 718-217-1440; Fax: 718-464-1317.

Regional Office - Queens North, 23-40 Astoria Blvd., Astoria, 11102. Tel: 718-726-9790; Fax: 718-728-8817.

Aging Services:

Alzheimers Adult Day Care, 157-16 65th Ave., Flushing, 11357. Tel: 718-358-3541; Fax: 718-961-4712.

Bayside Senior Center, 221-15 Horace Harding Expwy., Bayside, 11364. Tel: 718-225-1144; Fax: 718-229-7320.

Bay Ridge Alzheimer Services, 255 Ovington Ave., 11220. Tel: 718-236-3205; Fax: 718-837-1957.

Northeast Queens Senior Services, Formerly BAYSIDE SENIOR SERVICES 45-50 195th St., Flushing, 11358. Tel: 718-357-4903; Fax: 718-357-5731.

Bensonhurst Senior Services Center Assistance Center , 1867 Bath Ave., 11241. Tel: 718-236-3205; Fax: 718-837-1957.

Hillcrest Senior Center, 168-01 B. Hillside Ave., Jamaica, 11432. Tel: 718-297-7171; Fax: 718-657-2247.

Pete McGuinnes Senior Center, 715 Leonard St., 11222. Tel: 718-383-1940; Fax: 718-383-1960.

Northeast Queens Senior Services, 45-50 195th St., Flushing, 11358. Tel: 718-357-4903; Fax: 718-357-5731.

Northside Senior Center, 179 N. 6th St., 11211. Tel: 718-387-2316; Fax: 718-387-3235.

Bay Senior Center, 3643 Nostrand Ave., 11230. Tel: 718-648-2053; Fax: 718-648-7213.

Catherine Sheridan Senior Center, 35-24 83rd St., Jackson Heights, 11372. Tel: 718-458-4600; Fax: 718-458-5665.

Glenwood Senior Center, 5701 Avenue H, 11234. Tel: 718-241-7711; Fax: 718-241-1936.

Narrows Senior Center, 1230 63rd St, 11219. Tel: 718-232-3211; Fax: 718-232-0512.

Ozone Park Senior Center, 103-02 101st Ave., Ozone Park, 11416. Tel: 718-847-2100; Fax: 718-847-2166.

Project Independence, 87-04 88th Ave., Woodhaven, 11421. Tel: 718-847-9200; Fax: 718-805-9496.

Peter J. Della Monica Center for Seniors, 23-56 Broadway, Astoria, 11106. Tel: 718-626-1500; Fax: 718-278-4432.

Richmond Hill Senior Center, 87-25 118th St., Richmond Hill, 11418. Tel: 718-846-2877; Fax: 718-849-0989.

Rockaway Senior Center, 307 Beach 37th St., Far Rockaway, 11691. Tel: 718-471-3906; Fax: 718-471-4216.

Sheepshead Bay Services for the Elderly, Formerly SHEEPSHEAD BAY SENIOR SERVICES 1215 Avenue O, 11230. Tel: 718-375-3377; Fax: 718-627-8640.

Sheepshead Bay Supportive Services (NORC), Formerly SHEEPSHEAD BAY SENIOR SUPPORT 3677 Nostrand Ave. #3-A, 11229. Tel: 718-769-3579; Fax: 718-769-4155.

Southwest Queens Senior Services, 87-04 88th Ave., Woodhaven, 11421. Tel: 718-847-9200; Fax: 718-805-9496.

Steinway Senior Center, 20-43 Steinway St., Astoria, 11105. Tel: 718-728-8473; Fax: 718-278-5301.

St. Charles Jubilee Center, 55 Pierrepont St., 11201. Tel: 718-855-0326; Fax: 718-852-5415.

St. Louis Senior Center, 230 Kingston Ave., 11213. Tel: 718-771-7945; Fax: 718-467-2524.

St. Mary's Senior Center, 10-15 49th Ave., Long Island City, 11101. Tel: 718-729-2688; Fax: 718-729-5377.

Wakefield Senior Center, 135-45 Lefferts Blvd., South Ozone Park, 11420. Tel: 718-641-0454; Fax: 718-641-2418.

Woodhaven Senior Center, 87-04 88th Ave., Woodhaven, 11421. Tel: 718-847-9200; Fax: 718-805-9496.

Woodside Senior Assistance Center, 61-20 Woodside Ave., Woodside, 11377. Tel: 718-799-1234; Fax: 718-779-7775.

B.F.F.Y. - Child Care & Head Start Programs:

Coney Island Child Care Center, 2757 W. 33rd St., 11224. Tel: 718-946-8759; Fax: 718-266-6879.

Farragut Child Care Center, 32 Navy St., 11201. Tel: 718-875-7555; Fax: 718-596-9649.

Growing Assets Child Care Development, 231 E. 17th St., 11226. Tel: 718-856-4738; Fax: 718-856-4871.

J. Di Marco Child Care Center, 36-49 11th St., Long Island City, 11106. Tel: 718-786-1166; Fax: 718-706-7198.

Joseph Di Marco Family Day Care, 36-49 11th St., Long Island City, 11106. Tel: 718-786-7309; Fax: 718-853-8671.

J.F. Kennedy Child Care Center, 103-15 Farragut Rd., 11236. Tel: 718-272-8751; Fax: 718-272-6035.

Msgr. Andrew Landi Daycare, 21-20 35th Ave., Long Island City, 11102. Tel: 718-784-2856; Fax: 718-784-9612.

John Oravecz Child Care Center, 25 Nassau Ave., 11222. Tel: 718-782-2727; Fax: 718-782-5166.

R.F. Kennedy Child Care Center, 741 Flushing Ave., 11206. Tel: 718-782-0766; Fax: 718-782-0767.

Vincent J. Caristo Child Care Center, 5901 13th Ave., 11219. Tel: 718-853-8300; Fax: 718-871-8186.

De Paul Head Start, 71 Lincoln Pl., 11217. Tel: 718-622-2060; Fax: 718-622-1941.

Madeline Jones Head Start, 3415 Neptune Ave., 11224. Tel: 718-266-5962; Fax: 718-266-5891.

Padre Kennedy Head Start, 288 Berry St., 11211. Tel: 718-387-3679; Fax: 718-599-3319.

St. Barbara's Head Start, 139 Menahan St., 11221. Tel: 718-443-9800; Fax: 718-443-1919.

St. Joseph's Head Start, 300 Vernon Ave., 11206. Tel: 718-455-5900; Fax: 718-455-7513.

Sunset Park Head Start, 4222 4th Ave., 11232. Tel: 718-768-1012; Fax: 718-768-1607.

St. Margaret Mary Head Start, 9-16 27th Ave., Long Island City, 11102. Tel: 718-721-8065; Fax: 718-721-7454.

Therese Cervini Head Start, 35-34 104th St., Corona, 11368. Tel: 718-478-2169; Fax: 718-478-0735.

Therese Cervini Family Day Care, 35-34 104th St., Corona, 11368. Tel: 718-334-0806; Fax: 718-334-0809.

St. Malachy Child Development Center, 220 Hendrix St., 11207. Tel: 718-647-0966; Fax: 718-647-1042.

St. Malachy Head Start, 220 Hendricks St., 11207. Tel: 718-443-9800; Fax: 718-647-1042.

B.F.F.Y. - Human Services:

Compeer, 165-15 88th Ave., Jamaica, 11432. Tel: 718-291-4848; Fax: 718-291-5485.

F.A.N. Program, 89-56 162nd St., Jamaica, 11432. Tel: 718-523-2220; Fax: 718-523-2333.

B.F.F.Y. - Mental Health Services:

Brooklyn Community Living, 2000 Flatbush Ave., 11234. Tel: 718-253-1366; Fax: 718-253-4893.

Corona - Elmhurst Clinic, 37-22 82 St., Jackson Heights, 11372. Tel: 718-779-1600; Fax: 718-803-0895.

Corona Elmhurst Community Support Systems, 37-22 82nd St. & 37-66 72nd St., Jackson Heights, 11372. Tel: 718-779-2803; Fax: 718-639-0167.

9/11 Disaster Relief Services, 1329 Beach Channel Dr., Far Rockaway, 11691. Tel: 718-337-6800; Fax: 718-237-0940.

Flatbush Addiction Treatment Center, 1463 Flatbush Ave., 11234. Tel: 718-951-9009; Fax: 718-951-9719.

Flatlands Guidance Clinic, 2000 Flatbush Ave., 11234. Tel: 718-377-5755; Fax: 718-377-0752.

Glendale Guidance Center, 67-29 Myrtle Ave., Glendale, 11385. Tel: 718-456-7001; Fax: 718-456-9470.

Human Outreach Mobile Exc., 200 Gold St., 11201. Tel: 718-875-5015; Fax: 718-875-4367.

Queens Homeless Outreach, 165-15 88th Ave., Jamaica, 11432. Tel: 718-658-8830; Fax: 718-291-1531.

Club Innovation, Formerly Innovation Club 80-45 Winchester Blvd., Bldg. #4, CBU #13, Queens Village, 11427. Tel: 718-468-4700; Fax: 718-464-5640.

Carona Elmhurst Clinic Satellite, King Solomon Manor Home for Adults, 160-11 89th Ave., Jamaica, 11432. Tel: 718-291-7173; Fax: 718-657-9480.

Jamaica Mental Health Continuing Day Treatment, Formerly JAMAICA MENTAL HEALTH 165-15 88th Ave., Jamaica, 11432. Tel: 718-291-4848; Fax: 718-291-5485.

Rockway Outreach Mobile Crisis Psychiatric Team, 13-29 Beach Channel Dr., Far Rockaway, 11691. Tel: 718-337-6800; Fax: 718-337-0940.

On-Site School Project, 67-29 Myrtle Ave., Glendale, 11385. Tel: 718-456-7001; Fax: 718-456-9470.

Partnership of Hope, 715 Dean St., 11238. Tel: 718-398-0153; Fax: 718-789-5050.

Queen Community Living Program Apartments, Formerly Queen Community Living Program 35-24 83rd St., Jackson Heights, 11372. Tel: 718-639-0700; Fax: 718-639-7684.

Rockaway Mental Health Screening Team, 13-29 Beach Channel Dr., Far Rockaway, 11691. Tel: 718-471-7586; Fax: 718-868-3782.

Freedom Village Psychosocial Club, 13-29 Beach Channel Dr., Far Rockaway, 11691. Tel: 718-337-0504; Fax: 718-868-3782.

Rockaway Community Life Skills - Cont. Treatment, 13-29 Beach Channel Dr., Far Rockaway, 11691. Tel: 718-337-6850; Fax: 718-868-3782.

Rockaway Mental Health Clinic, 13-29 Beach Channel Dr., Far Rockaway, 11691. Tel: 718-337-6800; Fax: 718-337-0940.

Woodside Clinic, 61-20 Woodside Ave., Woodside, 11377. Tel: 718-779-1234; Fax: 718-779-7775.

Rose House (RCCA), 80-45 Winchester Blvd., Bldg. #4, CBU #13, Queens Village, 11427. Tel: 718-468-4700; Fax: 718-464-5640.

Mercy Gardens SRO, 249 Classon Ave., 11205. Tel: 718-399-8141; Fax: 718-399-3208.

The Open Door, 2000 Flatbush Ave., 11234. Tel: 718-377-7757; Fax: 718-377-0752.

Monica House, 161-01 89th Ave., Jamaica, 11432. Tel: 718-262-8190; Fax: 718-739-4331.

Brownsville/E.N.Y. Family Support Center, 1165 Rockaway Ave., 11236. Tel: 718-385-2043; Fax: 718-385-2179.

B.F.F.Y. - Prevention of Foster Care:

New Vision Program, 161-06 89th Ave., Jamaica, 11432. Tel: 718-297-0496; Fax: 718-297-0539.

Family Support Center of East New York, 2635 Linden Blvd., 11208. Tel: 718-827-5700; Fax: 718-827-1226.

Jamaica Family & Youth Center, 120-09 141st. St., South Ozone Park, 11432. Tel: 718-738-2500; Fax: 718-529-8522.

B.F.F.Y. - Services for Disabled Persons:

Peter J. Connelly Residence, 15 Willow St., 11201. Tel: 718-625-5590; Fax: 718-625-4856.

Adessa House, 101-38 92 St., Ozone Park, 11416. Tel: 718-848-1940; Fax: 718-323-1250.

Alhambra Day Treatment Center, 11-29 Catherine St., 11211. Tel: 718-388-5900; Fax: 718-388-3927.

Caldwell House, 121-01 116th Ave., South Ozone Park, 11420. Tel: 718-845-1200; Fax: 718-323-1267.

Carmel Residence, 277 N. 8th St., 11211. Tel: 718-388-6109; Fax: 718-388-6522.

Cribbin House, 218-20 104th Ave., Queens Village, 11429. Tel: 718-776-4190; Fax: 718-464-4849.

Dawson Manor, 94-17 84th St., Ozone Park, 11416. Tel: 718-296-1172; Fax: 718-296-1247.

Donald Savio Residence, 104-22 48th Ave., Corona, 11368. Tel: 718-699-7800; Fax: 718-699-3773.

James Fitzpatrick Residence, Formerly Fitzpatrick Residence 240 McKinley Ave., 11208. Tel: 718-647-7070; Fax: 718-647-6458.

Garfield Manor, 305 Garfield Pl., 11215. Tel: 718-622-2100; Fax: 718-857-9308.

Golden Residence, 225 Brooklyn Ave., 11213. Tel: 718-953-4444; Fax: 718-953-0622.

Graci Residence, 132-14 90th St., Ozone Park, 11417. Tel: 718-848-1970; Fax: 718-323-7349.

Home & Community Based Services, 1469 Flatbush Ave., 11210. Tel: 718-253-4477; Fax: 718-253-0545.

Helen Owen Carey Residence, 174 Java St., 11222. Tel: 718-383-2451; Fax: 718-383-1488.

McLees House, 112-16 200th St., St. Albans, 11412. Tel: 718-217-0285; Fax: 718-217-9491.

Mugavero Manor, 145-16 Farmers Blvd., Rochdale Village, 11434. Tel: 718-712-9054; Fax: 718-723-2877.

Mulrooney Manor, 479 E. 29th St., 11226. Tel: 718-287-7553; Fax: 718-826-2519.

Senior F.U.N., 415 Bleeker St., 1121. Tel: 718-417-5316; Fax: 718-381-9407.

Jeanne Noel Hower Residence, 156 Midwood St., 11225. Tel: 718-282-8045; Fax: 718-469-2874.

Mary Wayrick Residence, 90-37 189th St., Hollis, 11423. Tel: 718-464-4090; Fax: 718-468-8919.

Straus Residence, 3730 Shore Pkwy., 11235. Tel: 718-769-8836; Fax: 718-368-0418.

Supportive Living Apartments, 479 E. 29 St., 11226. Tel: 718-287-7553; Fax: 718-826-2519.

The Francis De Falco Dental Clinic, 11-29 Catherine St., 11211. Tel: 718-384-0303; Fax: 718-388-3927.

B.F.F.Y. - Services for Persons Living with AIDS:

Circle of Hope, 90-50 Parsons Blvd., Ste. 207, Jamaica, 11432. Tel: 718-298-5780; Fax: 718-883-9137.

Circle of Hope, 2520 Flatbush Ave., Rm 7, 11234. Tel: 718-338-4716; Fax: 718-338-5383.

B.F.F.Y. - Youth Services:

Queens South Young Parents, 90-39 184th St., Hollis, 11423. Tel: 718-217-1238; Fax: 718-464-1317.

North West Queens. Parenting Partnership, 23-40 Astoria Blvd., Astoria, 11102. Tel: 718-726-9790; Fax: 718-728-8817.

Project Bridge, 144 Bleeker St., 11221. Tel: 718-455-4649; Fax: 718-455-9311.

Queens Helping Adolescents Reach Peers (HARP) 90-39 189th St., Hollis, 11423. Tel: 718-740-6733; Fax: 718-464-1317.

Housing Development and Management Services:
Progress of Peoples Development Corporation Tel: 718-722-6041; Fax: 718-722-6045. John Tynan, M.U.P., Dir.
Progress of Peoples Management Corporation Tel: 718-722-6155; Fax: 718-722-6134. Nancy Mayer, Dir., POP Fiscal.
Housing Corporations:
Bellerose Senior HDFC, Inc., 191 Joralemon St., 11201. Tel: 718-479-4739; Fax: 718-479-6612.
Bethlehem Community HDFC Inc., 191 Joralemon St., 11201. Tel: 718-722-6000; Fax: 718-722-6045.
Bishop Boardman Apartments HDFC, Inc., 191 Joralemon St., 11201. Tel: 718-965-4444; Fax: 718-965-3577.
Bishop Francis J. Mugavero HDFC, Inc., 191 Joralemon St., 11201. Tel: 718-643-6490; Fax: 718-643-6492.
Casa Betsaida HDFC, 191 Joralemon St., 11201. Tel: 718-722-6000.
Catherine Sheridan HDFC, Inc., 191 Joralemon St., 11201. Tel: 718-274-7200; Fax: 718-274-2333.
St. Teresa of Avila Senior HDFC, 191 Joralemon St., 11201. Tel: 718-722-6000.
Sr. Lucian Apartments HDFC, Inc., 191 Joralemon St., 11201. Tel: 718-417-4102; Fax: 718-381-9407.
Caring Communities Associates, HDFC, Inc., 191 Joralemon St., 11201. Tel: 718-857-2266; Fax: 718-857-5866.
Mary Star of the Sea HFDC, Inc., 191 Joralemon St., 11201. Tel: 718-858-7263; Fax: 718-858-7265.
Pierrepont HDFC, 191 Joralemon St., 11201. Tel: 718-722-6000; Fax: 718-722-6096.
Mary Immaculate, Inc., 191 Joralemon St., 11201. Tel: 718-722-6000; Fax: 718-722-6096.
Mary Immaculate HDFC, 191 Joralemon St., 11201. Tel: 718-722-6000; Fax: 718-722-6096.
Pierrepont Housing Development Fund Corporation, 55 Pierrepont St., 11201. Tel: 718-722-6000; Fax: 718-722-6096.
Mount Carmel Senior HDFC, 191 Joralemon St., 11201. Tel: 718-722-6000; Fax: 718-722-6045.
Pope John Paul II HDFC, Inc., 191 Joralemon St., 11201. Tel: 718-748-2882; Fax: 718-748-4455.
Pierrepont House for the Elderly, Inc., 191 Joralemon St., 11201. Tel: 718-852-3390; Fax: 718-852-3352.
Queens Rehab Corp., 191 Joralemon St., 11201. Tel: 718-722-6000; Fax: 718-722-6045.
St. Brendans HDFC, Inc., 191 Joralemon St., 11201. Tel: 718-645-7112; Fax: 718-645-7180.
St. Lucy/St.Patrick HDFC, 191 Joralemon St., 11201. Tel: 718-722-6000; Fax: 718-722-6045.
Msgr. John O'Brien HDFC, Inc., 191 Joralemon St., 11201. Tel: 718-972-4556; Fax: 718-972-9265.
St. Paul the Apostle Senior HDFC, 191 Joralemon St.., 11201. Tel: 718-722-6000; Fax: 718-722-6045.
Sunset Park HFDC, Inc., 191 Joralemon St., 11201. Tel: 718-438-1119.
Long Island City Senior Houses HFDC, Inc., 191 Joralemon St., 11201. Tel: 718-545-0816; Fax: 718-545-0817.
Families Together HDFC, Inc., 191 Joralemon St., 11201. Tel: 718-722-6000; Fax: 718-722-6045.
Parkville Senior Houses HDFC, Inc., 191 Joralemon St., 11201. Tel: 718-859-9248.
Holy Spirit HDFC, Inc., 191 Joralemon St., 11201. Tel: 718-854-0050; Fax: 718-854-8521.
Msgr. Joseph F. Stedman Residence HDFC, 191 Joralemon St., 11201. Tel: 718-722-6000; Fax: 718-722-6134.
161-01 89th Avenue Corp., 191 Joralemon St., 11201. Tel: 718-262-8190; Fax: 718-739-4331.
Our Lady of Fatima Apartments HDFC, Inc., 191 Joralemon St., 11201. Tel: 718-507-1933; Fax: 718-507-1214.
The David Minkin Residence HDFC, Inc., 191 Joralemon St., 11201. Tel: 718-438-7998; Fax: 718-438-0052.
Emmaus of the Diocese of Brooklyn, Inc., 191 Joralemon St., 11201. Tel: 718-722-6000; Fax: 718-722-6096.
St. Pius V Senior HDFC, 191 Joralemon St., 11201. Tel: 718-722-6000; Fax: 718-722-6045.
Youth Development and Recreation:
Catholic Youth Organization of the Diocese of Brooklyn, Inc., 191 Joralemon St., 11201. Tel: 718-722-6074; Fax: 718-722-6233.
Nursing Home:
Ss. Joachim & Anne Residence, 2720 Surf Ave., 11224. Tel: 718-714-4800; Fax: 718-714-0874.
Home Care for the Sick:
Care at Home for the Diocese of Brooklyn, Inc., 241 37th St., 11232-2409. Tel: 718-832-0550; Fax: 718-965-7010.
Residences for Women:
Providence House, Inc., Administrative Office, 703 Lexington Ave., 11221. Tel: 718-455-0197; Fax: 718-455-0692. P.O. Box 210529, 11221. Sr. Janet Kinney, C.S.J., Exec. Dir.
Providence House 1, 2518 Church Ave., 11226.
Providence House 2, 388 Prospect Ave., 11215.
Providence House 3, 159-23 89th Ave., Jamaica, 11432.
Providence House 4, 89 Sickles Ave., New Rochelle, 10801.
Providence House 5, 396 Lincoln Rd., 11225.
Providence House 6, 2876 W. 17 St., 11224.
Permanent Housing, 85 & 87 Sickles Ave., New Rochelle, 10801.
Community Centers:
Dr. White Community Center, 200 Gold St., 11201. Tel: 718-875-8801; Fax: 718-875-4367.
Other Affiliated Agencies:
Anthonian Hall, Inc. Tel: 718-722-6000; Fax: 718-722-6096 Sr. Ellen Patricia Finn, O.P., Treas.; Most Rev. Joseph M. Sullivan, M.S.W., M.P.A., V.E., Treas.
Catholic Guild for the Blind, Diocese of Brooklyn, Inc., 191 Joralemon St., 11201. Tel: 718-722-6000; Fax: 718-722-6096.
Ecclesial Consultants, Inc., 191 Joralemon St., 11201. Tel: 718-722-6000; Fax: 718-722-6096. Most Rev. Joseph M. Sullivan, M.S.W., M.P.A., V.E., Dir.; Rev. Msgrs. Emmet Fagan (RVC), Dir.; Charles J. Fahey (SY), Dir. A management service for Church agencies and organizations.
Ferrini Welfare League, 98-21 101 Ave., Ozone Park, 11416. Tel: 718-845-0539.
Flowers With Care, Diocese of Brooklyn, Inc., 23-40 Astoria Blvd., Astoria, 11102. Tel: 718-726-9790; Fax: 718-722-8817.
Italian Board of Guardians, 7808 18 Ave., 11214. Tel: 718-232-4242; Fax: 718-232-6402. Rev. Msgr. Fernando Ferrarese, Moderator; Maria Patalano, Exec. Dir.; Mrs. Beatrice Rizzo, Exec. Sec.
Mary's Hall, Inc., 191 Joralemon St., 11201. Tel: 718-722-6000; Fax: 718-722-6096. Most Rev. Joseph M. Sullivan, M.S.W., M.P.A., V.E., Pres.
Society of St. Vincent de Paul in Diocese of Brooklyn, Central Office, 191 Joralemon St., 11201. Tel: 718-625-1400; Fax: 718-625-1421. Most Rev. Thomas V. Daily, D.D. (PMB), Spiritual Advisor; Rev. Msgr. James W. Asip, Assoc. Spiritual Advisor (Retired); Mr. Joseph Martino, Pres.
District Council of Kings, 191 Joralemon St., 11201. Tel: 718-625-1400; Fax: 718-625-1421 Rev. Raymond J Kelly, Spiritual Advisor; Mr. Carlos Harris, Pres.
District Council of Queens, 191 Joralemon St., 11201. Tel: 718-625-1400; Fax: 718-625-1421. Rev. Msgr. James W. Asip, Spiritual Advisor (Retired); Mr. Vito Buccaria, Pres.
Bread & Life Soup Kitchen, 75 Lewis Ave., 11206. Tel: 718-574-0058. Larry Gile, Dir.; Rev. James J. Maher, C.M., Pres.

[M] NURSING SERVICES

BROOKLYN. *Nursing Sisters Home Visiting Service, Inc.*, 500 19th St., 11215. Tel: 718-768-7271; Fax: 718-965-2035. Sr. Mary Nadine Casey, C.I.J., Chair, Board of Directors; Keith Kertland, Pres. & CEO.
Nursing Service Offices, 500 19th St., 11215. Tel: 718-768-7271; Fax: 718-965-2035. Ms. Lillian Torres, Mgr. Branch Svcs.

[N] HOSPITALS

BROOKLYN. *St. Vincent's Catholic Medical Center*, 70 Buffalo Ave., 11213. Tel: 718-221-3000; Fax: 718-221-3179. Rev. Msgr. Austin P. Bennett, Chm. (Retired). Affiliated with Catholic Medical Centers. Bed Capacity 269.
JAMAICA. *Catholic Medical Centers of Brooklyn & Queens*, 88-25 153rd St., 11432. Tel: 718-558-6900; Fax: 718-558-7286.
Corporate Staff: Most Rev. Joseph M. Sullivan, M.S.W., M.P.A., V.E., Bd. Chm. Tel: 718-558-6921; William D. McGuire, Pres. & CEO. Tel: 718-558-6921; Ms. Kathleen Galvin, COO. Tel: 718-558-6959; Robert Nolan, Vice Pres. Human Resources. Tel: 718-459-4417; Daniel J. Rinaldi, CFO. Tel: 718-558-6940; Kathryn Anastos, M.D., Vice Pres. Ambulatory Care. Tel: 718-558-5962; Anthony Ferante Vice Pres. Home Health Care. Tel: 718-459-4600; Steven Wirth, Vice Pres. Mission Svcs. Tel: 718-558-7102; Stephen McClellan, Ph.D., Vice Pres. Public Relations & Mktg. Tel: 718-558-6925; G. Malcolm Murray, Vice Pres. Information Systems. Tel: 718-558-7048; Mildred A. Shanley, L.L.D., Senior Vice Pres., Chief Legal Officer. Tel: 718-558-6939; Margaret Fernandez, Admin. Asst. to the Pres. Tel: 718-558-6920.
Mary Immaculate Hospital Division, 152-11 89th Ave., 11432. Tel: 718-558-2000; Fax: 718-558-2524.
St. John's Queens Hospital Division, 90-02 Queens Blvd., Elmhurst, 11373. Tel: 718-558-1000; Fax: 718-558-1818.
St. Joseph's Hospital Division, 158-40 79th Ave., Flushing, 11366. Tel: 718-558-6200; Fax: 718-558-6209.
St. Mary's Hospital of Brooklyn Affiliate, 170 Buffalo Ave., 11213. Tel: 718-221-3000; Fax: 718-221-3971.
Mary Immaculate Hospital Home Health Agency, 95-25 Queens Blvd., Rego Park, 11374. Tel: 718-830-4500. Catherine Barbera, Dir., Home Care Agency.
St. Mary's Hospital of Brooklyn Home Health Agency, 170 Buffalo Ave., 11213. Tel: 718-221-3844. Catherine Barbera, Dir., Home Care Agency.
St. Mary's Hospital of Brooklyn Long Term Home Health Program, 170 Buffalo Ave., 11213. Tel: 718-221-3844. Catherine Barbera, Dir., Home Care Agency.
St. Anthony Health Professions & Nursing Institute, 175-05 Horace Harding Expwy., Fresh Meadows, 11365. Tel: 718-357-0500, Ext. 104. Joseph Skarzynski, M.D., Dir. Allied Health & Pre-Hospital Care.
Catholic Medical Center Physician Assistant Program, 175-05 Horace Harding Expwy., Fresh Meadows, 11365. Tel: 718-805-7599. JoAnn Deasy, M.P.H., PA-C, Dir.
Catholic Medical Center School of Nursing, 175-05 Horace Harding Expwy., Fresh Meadows, 11365. Tel: 718-805-5602. Genevieve Jensen, R.N., M.S., Dir.
Catholic Medical Centers Program of Medical Technology, 175-05 Horace Harding Expwy., Fresh Meadows, 11365. Tel: 718-357-0500, Ext. 111. Ann Paula Zero, Dir.
Catholic Medical Centers Program of Radiography, 175-05 Horace Harding Expwy., Fresh Meadows, 11365. Tel: 718-357-0500, Ext. 112. Albert Kish, Dir.
Catholic Medical Centers Emergency Medical Services Institute, 175-05 Horace Harding Expwy., Fresh Meadows, 11365. Tel: 718-357-0500, Ext. 181. Michael Tretola, Mgr. Allied Health Educ.
Catholic Medical Centers Pathology Assistants Program, 152-11 89th Ave., 11432. Tel: 718-558-6731. Usha Ruder, M.D., Dir.
Catholic Medical Centers Catholic Hospital Administration Personnel (CHAP) Program, 175-05 Horace Harding Expwy., Fresh Meadows, 11365. Tel: 718-357-0500, Ext. 173. Sr. Annelle Fitzpatrick, C.S.J., Ph.D., Dir. Co-sponsored with St. John's University.

[O] SPECIAL CARE FACILITIES

BROOKLYN. **Bishop Francis J. Mugavero Center for Geriatric Care, Inc.*, 155 Dean St., 11217. Tel: 718-694-6700; Fax: 718-694-6710. Paul Rosenfeld, Chm.; Ida Santos, Admin. Affiliated with Catholic Medical Centers. Bed Capacity 288.
St. Jerome's Health Services Corp. dba Holy Family Home , 1740 84th St., 11214. Tel: 718-232-3666. John Salandra, Chm.; Mary Ann Rose, Admin. Affiliated with Catholic Medical Centers. Bed Capacity 200.

[P] CHILD CARE AGENCIES

BROOKLYN. *Angel Guardian-St. Mary's Children and Family Services, Inc.*, 6301 12th Ave., 11219. Tel: 718-232-1500; Fax: 718-232-0331. Web: www.angelguardian.org. Liz Giordano, C.E.O. Sisters 4; Children in Care 750.
Foster Boarding Home Therapeutic Foster Boarding Home and Adoption Services , 6301 12th Ave., 11219. Tel: 718-232-1500; Fax: 718-232-0331.
Residences for Mother/Baby McAuley Residence , 372 Clinton Ave., 11238. Tel: 718-638-7424; Fax: 718-638-2287.
Virginia Residence, 263 9th St., 11215. Tel: 718-369-3812; Fax: 718-638-2287.
Supervised Independent Living Program Group Home, Agency Operated Boarding Home Preventive Program , 186 Montague St., 11201. Tel: 718-624-2100; Fax: 718-624-7740.
Family Support Center, 333 Avenue X, 11223. Tel: 718-375-7444; Fax: 718-375-2444. Group House. Agency Operated Boarding House, Adolescent Supervised Living Program, Therapeutic Foster Boarding Homes.
Angel Guardian Foundation, 6301 12th Ave., 11219. Tel: 718-232-1500; Fax: 718-232-0331. Sisters Eleanor Dobson, Pres.; Theresa Agliari, Sec.; William McGarry, Treas.
Catholic Child Care Society of the Diocese of Brooklyn, 540 Atlantic Ave., 11217. Tel: 718-797-6094; Fax: 718-797-6092. John J. Bennett Jr., Pres.; Belinda M. Conway, C.S.W., Exec. Dir.
St. Francis Home for Boys, 132 Eagle St., 11222. Tel: 718-383-9870; Fax: 718-349-1558. Email: yth2000ny@aol.com. Web: www.youth2000ny.com. Rev. Benedict J. Groeschel, C.F.R., Exec. Dir.; Mr. Joseph Campo, Dir. Residents 7.
Good Shepherd Services, 441 Fourth Ave., 11215. Tel: 718-788-0666; Fax: 718-965-0365. Email: plomonaco@goodshepherd.org. Web: www.GoodShepherds.org. Sr. Paulette LoMonaco, R.G.S., Exec. Dir. Provides a comprehensive range of neighborhood family services to individuals & youth from the South Brooklyn community. Services include educational support, counseling & crisis intervention & advocacy services to

children & families as well as foster care & adoption & residences for teenagers.

HeartShare Human Services of New York, Roman Catholic Diocese of Brooklyn, 191 Joralemon St., 4th Fl., 11201. Tel: 718-422-4200; Fax: 718-522-4506. Email: Heartshare@aol.com. Web: www.heartshare.org. William R. Guarinello, M.S., Pres. & CEO. Children and Family Services: Foster Boarding Home Program, Adoption Program, Family Services Centers, School-Based Beacon Program, Youth Services, Services for People with HIV/AIDS. Programs for the Developmentally Disabled: Group Homes, Supportive Apartments, Preschool Program (Early Childhood Centers), Respite & Recreation Program, Day Treatment/Day Habilitation Programs

Children and Family Services:

Brooklyn Office, 191 Joralemon St., 6th Fl., 11201. Tel: 718-422-4216; Fax: 718-422-4229.

Queens Office, 90-04 161st St., Jamaica, 11432. Tel: 718-739-5000; Fax: 718-739-6828.

Family Service Centers:

Bensonhurst Family and Youth Services, 138 Bay 20th St., 11214. Tel: 718-234-1717; Fax: 718-331-1541.

East Brooklyn Family Services, 3005 Glenwood Rd., 11210. Tel: 718-434-7900; Fax: 718-434-6715.

South Brooklyn Family Services, 266 Court St., 11201. Tel: 718-855-7766; Fax: 718-855-7999.

Family Services at P.S. 288, 2950 W. 25th St., 11224. Tel: 718-714-0103; Fax: 718-714-6738.

School-Based Beacon Programs:

McKinley Beacon Program-I.S. 259, 7301 Fort Hamilton Pkwy., 11228. Tel: 718-836-3620; Fax: 718-836-3683.

Beacon Program at P.S. 288, 2950 W. 25th St., 11224. Tel: 718-714-0103; Fax: 718-714-6738.

Youth Services/Summer Camps:

191 Joralemon St., 6th Fl., 11201. Tel: 718-422-4216; Fax: 718-422-4229.

Services for People with HIV/AIDS:

Community Follow-Up Program, 2882 W. 15th St., 11224. Tel: 718-372-0580; Fax: 718-372-0634.

Residential Housing Program, 87-16 101st Ave., Ozone Park, 11416. Tel: 718-323-2903; Fax: 718-323-4113.

Developmental Disabilities Services:

186 Joralemon St., 11201. Tel: 718-422-3306; Fax: 718-422-3324.

Adult Day Treatment Services:

Francis Aiello Center, 163 MacDonough St., 11216. Tel: 718-443-5071; Fax: 718-443-5741.

Harry Hoffman Center, 62-10 Northern Blvd., Woodside, 11377. Tel: 718-899-2752; Fax: 718-899-9365.

Eileen and William Lavin Center, 347 74th St., 11209. Tel: 718-745-7117; Fax: 718-745-3741.

Adult Day Habilitation Services:

Bay Ridge Day Habilitation, 347 74th St., 4th Fl., 11209. Tel: 718-745-7117; Fax: 718-745-3741.

Brooklyn Day Habilitation, 50 Court St., 9th Fl., 11201. Tel: 718-797-2020, Ext. 100; Fax: 718-797-2059.

Queens Day Habilitation, 61-58 Springfield Blvd., Bayside, 11364. Tel: 718-281-0480; Fax: 718-281-0478.

Early Childhood Services:

Angels on the Bay Early Childhood Evaluation Center, 162-30 Cross Bay Blvd., Howard Beach, 11414. Tel: 718-323-2877; Fax: 718-323-2897.

Matilda Raffa Cuomo, First Step Early Childhood Center, 115-15 101st. Ave., Richmond Hill, 11419. Tel: 718-441-5333; Fax: 718-805-0657.

Lefferts/Liberty Kiwanis, First Step Early Childhood Center, 82-12 151st Ave., Howard Beach, 11414. Tel: 718-848-0300; Fax: 718-835-2862.

Dolly and Frank Russo, Sr., First Step Early Childhood Center, 118-01/03 101st Ave., Richmond Hill, 11419. Tel: 718-805-7117; Fax: 718-805-7124.

Family Support Services Programs:

186 Joralemon St., 11201. Tel: 718-422-3271; Fax: 718-855-8302 186/2; 718-422-3324 186/10.

Group Homes:

Supportive Apartment Program:

50 Court St., 10th Fl., 11201. Tel: 718-797-0891.

Early Intervention Respite Reimbursement, 50 Court St., 9th Fl., 11210. Tel: 718-797-2020, Ext. 124; Fax: 718-522-2173.

Medicaid Service Coordination, 186 Joralemon St., 2nd Fl., 11201. Tel: 718-422-3336; Fax: 718-855-5821.

Options Project (Financial Assistance), 186 Joralemon St., 2nd Fl., 11201. Tel: 718-422-3290; Fax: 718-855-5821.

Parent Training/Non-Medicaid Case Management, 186 Joralemon St., 10th Fl., 11201. Tel: 718-422-3276; Fax: 718-422-3324.

Respite Recreation Programs, 186 Joralemon St., 2nd Fl., 11201. Tel: 718-422-3292; 718-422-3291; Fax: 718-855-8521.

Marian and Anthony Attardi Residence, 1341 78th St., 11228. Tel: 718-331-0570; Fax: 718-331-0634.

James and Kathleen Buckley Residence, 977-979 E. 92nd St., 11236. Tel: 718-272-1441; Fax: 718-234-5563.

Clermont Residence, 26 Clermont Ave., 11205. Tel: 718-834-9317; Fax: 718-834-9364.

Clinton Residence, 217 Clinton Ave., 11205. Tel: 718-638-2625; Fax: 718-638-2625.

Thomas J. Cuite Residence, 50-36 45th St., Woodside, 11377. Tel: 718-786-3113; Fax: 718-786-2949.

Doonan-Drake Residence, 300 E. 18th St., 11226. Tel: 718-469-5000; Fax: 718-469-5002.

Antonetta Ferraro Residence, 603 Beach 19th St., Far Rockaway, 11691. Tel: 718-327-9000; Fax: 718-327-9270.

Msgr. Thomas G. Hagerty Residence, 128 Montrose Ave., 11206. Tel: 718-387-3595; Fax: 718-387-3597.

Hart Street Residence, 689 Hart St., 11221. Tel: 718-919-7477; Fax: 718-919-7194.

Scibelli Residence, 19 Dongan Hills Ave., Staten Island, 10306. Tel: 718-668-2958; Fax: 718-668-2957.

Maureen Moore Residence, 119 End Pl., Staten Island, 10312. Tel: 718-605-2614; Fax: 718-608-1108.

John and Lillian Sharkey, Sr. Residence, 60-12 56th St., Maspeth, 11378. Tel: 718-417-6846; Fax: 718-417-6890.

Helen and John Sharkey Residence, 64-51 Cloverdale Blvd., Bayside, 11364. Tel: 718-746-4501; Fax: 718-746-4503.

Rita P. Short Residence, 296 Columbia St., 11231. Tel: 718-246-9114; Fax: 718-246-9109.

35th St. Residence, 172-07 35th Ave., Flushing, 11358. Tel: 718-961-7673; Fax: 718-961-7753.

Rocco Anthony Torre Residence, 1966 54th St., 11204. Tel: 718-259-4443; Fax: 718-259-1735.

Dr. Catherine White Residence, 175 Metropolitan Ave., 11211. Tel: 718-782-9104; Fax: 718-782-1394.

145th Street Residence, 29-41 145th St., Flushing, 11354. Tel: 718-460-0213; Fax: 718-460-4721.

Affiliate Programs:

Heartshare Wellness Ltd., 50 Court St., 9th Fl., 11201. Tel: 718-855-7707; Fax: 718-855-7717.

Neighborhood Heating Fund Tel: 718-522-6514; Fax: 718-694-9592. (Partnership with KeySpan Energy Delivery)

EnergyShare Tel: 877-480-7427; Fax: 866-764-3278. (Partnership with Consolidated Edison Company of New York)

Little Flower Children's Services, 186 Remsen St., 11201. Tel: 718-260-8840; Fax: 718-260-8863. Email: ryderm@lfchild.org. Web: www.LittleFlowerNY.org. Rev. Msgr. John T. Fagan (RVC), Exec. Vice Pres. (Retired); Mrs. Mary G. Ryder, Exec. Dir.; Sr. Rita Wasilewski, C.S.F.N., Supr. Foster Care, Adoption & Post Adoption Services, Services for Adult MR/DD clients; Residential Treatment Center, U.F.S.D., & Family Day Care at Wading River, NY; Teen Mothers & Infants in Foster Homes.

McAuley Residence for Mother & Baby, 372 Clinton Ave., 11238. Tel: 718-638-7424; Fax: 718-638-2287. Group Homes, 2 Mother/Child Residences, Agency Operated Boarding Home, 6 Adolescent Supervised Independent Living Apartments

Preventive Programs:

Fort Greene Family Services, 186 Montague St., 11201. Tel: 718-624-2100; Fax: 718-624-7740.

Gerard C. Durr Center, 333 Avenue X, 11223. Tel: 718-375-7444; Fax: 718-375-2444.

Mercy Home for Children, 243 Prospect Park W., 11215. Tel: 718-832-1075; Fax: 718-832-7612. Email: info@mercyhomeny.org. Sr. Catherine Crumlish. Under the sponsorship of the Sisters of Mercy.; Six Intermediate Care Facilities (Residences & 4 Individual Residential Alternatives) for adolescents & adults who are developmentally disabled: Visitation Residence; Harold Warren Residence, de Porres Residence; Littlejohn Residence; Santulli Residence; Kevin Keating Residence, Chrys Residence, Gail Addeo Residence, Rev. Michael J. McGivney Residence, and Augusta Residence. In Addition, we sponsor all day Saturday Recreation Programs, for adolescents and adjults with developmental disabilities. Sisters 5; Staff 188; Residents 97; Saturday Program 20.

St. Vincent's Services, Inc. (Formerly St. Vincent's Home for Boys and St. Vincent's Hall, Inc.) , 66 Boerum Pl., 11201. Tel: 718-522-3700; Fax: 718-875-8536. Web: www.svs.org. Rev. Msgr. Robert M. Harris, M.S.W., M.Phil., M.A., Pres. & CEO. Services include: Family Foster Boarding Homes, Adoption Services, Pediatric AIDS Program, Specialized Preventive Services for Medically Fragile Children, a Primary Care Medical Clinic, Residences for the Developmentally Disabled, Alcohol and Substance Abuse Treatment Programs & NY State Licensed Outpatient Mental Health Centers. Sisters 4; Priests 3; Children 850.

GLEN COVE. *St. Christopher-Ottilie*, 1 Alexander Pl., 11542. Tel: 516-671-1253; 718-895-2555; Fax: 516-671-2899. Email: bmcmahon@sco.org. Web: www.sco.org. Mr. Robert J. McMahon, Exec. Dir.; Mary Hall, Dir. of Intake and Placement. Residential Treatment Center for the profoundly & severely mentally retarded, Intermediate Care Facilities, Group Homes for Adolescent Teenage Boys and Girls, Teen Mother-Child Residence Program, Homeless Program for Teenage RS, Preventive Programs (3), EFBH Network, Supervised Independent Living Apartments, Therapeutic Foster Boarding Homes, Residential Treatment Facility, Article 81 School. Regular Foster Care Program for Mentally Retarded Individuals, Crisis Respite, Home & Community Based Waiver Services, Madonna Heights Services, Family dynamics, Center for Family Life. Children 5,000.

ROCKAWAY PARK. *St. John's Residence for Boys, Inc.*, 144-Beach 111 St., 11694. Tel: 718-945-2800; Fax: 718-945-4662. Email: stjohnsresidence@aol.com. Bro. Thomas N. Trager, S.M., Exec. Dir. Conducted by the Brothers of Society of Mary (Marianists). Residential care for adolescent boys. Diagnostic Reception Centers, Non-Secure Detention/Independent Living Program. Brothers 6; Residents 85.

[Q] GROUP HOMES FOR RETARDED CHILDREN

SPRINGFIELD GARDENS. *Martin De Porres Group Homes*, 136-25 218th St., 11413. Tel: 718-527-0606; Fax: 718-528-7475. Email: phiro@nyc.rr.com. Web: martindeporres.org. Bro. Philip Rofrano, F.S.C., Exec. Dir. Total Assisted Annually 24; Total Staff 13.

[R] SUMMER CAMPS AND DAY CAMPS

CENTERPORT. *Camp Alvernia*, 105 Prospect Rd., P.O. Box 301, 11721. Tel: 631-261-5730; Fax: 613-754-4204. Email: alvernia@juno.com camp1888@juno.com. Web: www.alvernia.org. Under the supervision of the Franciscan Brothers.

COMMACK. *Bishop McDonnell Camp, Society of St. Vincent de Paul*, 191 Joralemon St., 11201. Tel: 718-625-1400; Fax: 718-625-1421. Email: svdpbq@verizon.net. John Bittner, Dir. Day Outings for Senior Citizen Groups, Handicapped & Children from poor areas. Sponsored by the Society of St. Vincent de Paul Brooklyn Diocese.

[S] RESIDENCES FOR THE AGED

BROOKLYN. *Holy Family Home*, 1740 84th St., 11214. Tel: 718-232-3666; Fax: 718-259-9180. Email: aschlossberg@sucmeny.org. Sr. Theresita Sampson, Dir. Pastoral Care Office; Deacon Frank Rosati. Affiliated with Catholic Medical Center. Total Staff 274; Total Assisted Annually 274.

SS. Joachim & Anne Residence, Inc., 2720 Surf Ave., 11224. Tel: 718-714-4800. Marie Ferrara, Admin.

BAYSIDE. *Ozanam Hall of Queens Nursing Home, Inc.*, 42-41 201st St., 11361. Tel: 718-423-2000; Fax: 718-224-7598. Email: ozanamgen@ozanamhall.org. Web: www.ozanamhall.org. Sr. M. Philip Ann, O.Carm., Admin.; Rev. James M. Kelly, C.M., Chap. Carmelite Sisters for the Aged and Infirm Sisters 18; Residents 432.

JAMAICA. *Msgr. James H. Fitzpatrick Pavilion for Skilled Nursing Care*, 152-11 89th Ave., 11432. Tel: 718-558-2800; Fax: 718-558-2476. Michell A. Edwards, Admin. St. Vincent's Catholic Medical Centers of NY Total Staff 115; Total Assisted 115; Residents 115.

QUEENS VILLAGE. *Queen of Peace Residence*, 110-30 221st St., 11429. Tel: 718-464-1800; Fax: 347-626-2178. Sr. Margaret Regina, L.S.P., Supr.; Rev. Msgr. William J. Rodgers, Chap. (Retired).

Legal Title: *Home for the Aged, Little Sisters of the Poor* Sisters 20; Total Assisted Annually 84; Total Staff 110. In Res. Revs. Thomas P. Curry (Retired); Charles F. Harth (Retired); James Meade; Salvatore Rizzi (Retired); Alfred J. Weinlich (Retired).

[T] SETTLEMENT ASSOCIATIONS

GLENDALE. *Kolping Center*, 65-04 Myrtle Ave., 11385. Tel: 718-456-7727. Ms. Louise G. Conte, Pres.

Legal Title: *Catholic Kolping Society (Katholischer Gesellen Verein) of Brooklyn, Inc.*

[U] CATHOLIC MIGRATION AND REFUGEE OFFICES

BROOKLYN. *Catholic Migration & Refugee Office, Catholic Migration Services, Inc.*, 1258 65th St., 11219. Tel: 718-236-3000; Fax: 718-256-9707. Email: cmo112119@aol.com. Web:

www.catholicmigration.org. Rev. Msgr. Ronald T. Marino, Dir. Apostolate Coordinators.

Arab Speaking Tel: 718-965-0422. Rev. Yousseh Bochra Nasri.

Brazilian Apostolate Tel: 718-361-1884; Fax: 718-786-4573. Rev. Jose Carlos Da Silva.

Chinese Apostolate-Queens Tel: 718-699-1929; Fax: 718-271-3215. Rev. Antonius Ho, C.S.J.B. (Taiwan), Coord.

Chinese Apostolate-Brooklyn Rev. Norman Bennett, Asst. Tel: 718-492-9200; Fax: 718-439-8528.

Czech/Slovak Tel: 516-625-2682. Rev. Antonin Kocurek.

Croation Apostolate Tel: 718-278-3337; Fax 718-278-4354. Rev. Robert Zubovic, Coord.

Filipino Apostolate Tel: 718-728-1613; Fax 718-956-9229. Rev. Leo V. Rosero (Philippines).

Ghanaian Apostolate Tel: 718-282-0159. Mr. Francis Baidoo. Tel: 718-282-7162.

Haitian Apostolate Tel: 718-462-0223; Fax: 718-462-7753. Rev. Msgr. Guy Sansaricq, Coord.

Hispanic Ministry Office Tel: 718-229-8001, Ext. 741; Fax: 718-229-2658. Deacon Jorge A. Gonzalez.

Indian Apostolate Tel: 718-375-9600; Fax: 718-375-6642. Rev. Paul Vazhapilly, Coord.

Indonesian Apostolate Tel: 718-891-9691. Mr. Frans Samosir.

Irish Apostolate Tel: 718-429-4442; Fax 718-429-7581. Rev. Msgr. Michael J. Hardiman, M.Div., M.A., M.P.A., Coord.

Italian Apostolate Tel: 718-837-8670; 718-965-7300; Fax: 718-259-3066. Deacon Carlo Mellace, Coord.

Korean Apostolate Tel: 718-321-7676; Fax: 718-321-7005. Daniel Suh, Coord.

Knanaya Indian Apostolate Tel: 718-347-6070; Fax: 718-343-3221. Rev. Michael Ittykunju (India), Coord.

Lithuanuan Tel: 718-326-2236; Fax: 718-326-2249. Rev. Vytautas Volertas.

Nigerian Apostolate Tel: 718-341-1018; Fax: 718-276-2001. Rev. Louis Uzoh, Coord.

Pakistan Apostolate Tel: 718-357-8888; Fax: 718-357-3671. Rev. Anthony Sikandar, Coord.

Polish Apostolate Tel: 718-894-1387; Fax: 718-416-9245. Rev. Peter W. Zendzian, Coord.

Romanian Apostolate Tel: 718-386-7728; Fax: 718-628-6649. Mr. Ovidiu Iorgovan, Representative.

Russian Apostolate Tel: 212-226-8075. Rev. John Soles, Coord.

Vietnamese Apostolate Tel: 718-278-1834; Fax: 718-278-0998. Rev. Joseptan Tri-Pham.

West Indian Apostolate

Apostleship of the Sea Tel: 718-596-7750; Fax: 718-260-9233. Rev. James M. Leone.

Resources, Inc., 1258 65th St., 11219. Tel: 718-236-3000; Fax: 718-256-9707. Rev. Msgr. Ronald T. Marino, Dir.; Michael Campo, Mgr. Maintenance Dept.; Mr. James Casale, Business Devel.; Charles Hendershott, Mgr. Graphics Dept.

Catholic Immigrant Ministries, Inc., 1258 65th St., 11219. Tel: 718-236-3000; Fax: 718-256-9707. Rev. Msgr. Ronald T. Marino, Dir.

[V] MONASTERIES AND RESIDENCES OF PRIESTS AND BROTHERS

BROOKLYN. *Carmelites of Mary Immaculate, Inc.*, 21 Nassau Ave., 11222. Tel: 718-388-5145; Fax: 718-387-1877. Email: cmiusa@hotmail.com. Web: www.cmiusa.org. Rev. John Menonkari, C.M.I. (India), Supr. Regl. Coord.

St. Casimir's Monastery, Printing Plant and Cultural Center, 341 Highland Blvd., 11207. Tel: 718-235-5962; Fax: 718-827-2026. Most Rev. Paul Baltakis, O.F.M.; Rev. Francis Giedgaudas, O.F.M., Dir. Printery & Supr. Franciscan Fathers of the Lithuanian Province of St. Casimir Priests 1; Brothers 1.

Christian Brothers Residence, 367 Clermont Ave., 11238. Tel: 718-857-4311; Fax: 718-783-7576. Bros. Peter Bonventre, F.S.C.; David Carroll, F.S.C.; Robert Ferguson, F.S.C.; Richard Grieco, F.S.C.; John Guasconi, F.S.C.; Charles Guglielmo, F.S.C.; William Kemmerer, F.S.C.; Frederick Del Antonio, F.S.C.; Ralph Darmento, F.S.C.; Philip Zeller, F.S.C. Brothers 10.

Curial Residence, 378 Clermont Ave., 11238. Tel: 718-638-0697. Most Rev. Joseph M. Sullivan, M.S.W., M.P.A., V.E.; Rev. Msgr. Austin P. Bennett (Retired).

St. Francis Monastery-Generalate Offices of Franciscan Brothers, 135 Remsen St., 11201-4212. Tel: 718-858-8217; Fax: 718-858-8306. Email: bsb492003@yahoo.com francisca135@aol.com. Web: www.franciscanbrothers.org. Bros. Shane Burke, O.S.F., Ed.D., Supr. Gen.; Joseph Moloney, O.S.F., 1st Councilor; Joshua DiMauro, O.S.F., 2nd Councilor; Gabriel O'Brien, O.S.F., 3rd Councillor; William Boslet, O.S.F., 4th Councilor; Rev. Joseph L. Maloney, M.Div. (PH), Treas. Gen. Brothers 94.

St. John the Baptist Rectory, 75 Lewis Ave., 11206. Tel: 718-455-6864; Fax: 718-452-3738. Email: jagostino@stjohnthebaptistrec.org. Web: www.stjohnthebaptistrec.org. Revs. Joseph V. Agostino, C.M.; Stephen F. Cantwell, C.M. (PH), Parochial Vicar; Robert J. Stone, C.M. In Res. Rev. Thomas S. Krafinski, C.M.

Little Brothers of the Gospel, 554 Hart St., 11221. Bros. Rick Dixon; Jay McGowan; Giorgio Gonella.

St. Michael's Friary, 225 Jerome St., 11207. Tel: 718-827-6990; Fax: 718-827-5789. Email: stmikeca@ix.netcom.com. Revs. Raphael Iannone, O.F.M.Cap., Supr. & Co-Dir. of Capuchin Postulancy Prog.; Perry McDonald, O.F.M., Friary Vicar & Co-Dir. of Capuchin Postulancy Prog.; Knute Kenlon, O.F.M.Cap. (Retired); Gavin Reilly, O.F.M.Cap. (NY); Bro. John Conway, O.F.M.Cap. Priests 3.

Postulants: Bill Havican; James Crichton; Andrew Nowak.

Oratory of Saint Philip Neri, Congregation Pontifical Rite, 109 Willoughby St., 11201. Tel: 718-875-2096; Fax: 718-875-4678 Email: philipneri@aol.com. Web: Brooklyn-oratory.org. Very Rev. Dennis M. Corrado, C.O., Provost; Revs. Mark J. Lane, C.O.; Joel M Warden, C.O.; Bro. James Simon, C.O. Priests 3; Brothers 1.

Our Lady of Good Counsel Residence, 7509 Shore Rd., 11209. Tel: 718-833-1900; Fax: 718-630-5666. Web: www.redemptorists.net. Very Rev. Kevin J. Moley, C.SS.R., Prov. Supr.; Revs. Patrick F. Woods, C.SS.R., Prov. Vicar; Albert R Schreiber, C.SS.R., Sec. of Prov.; Lawrence E. Lover, C.SS.R., Curate; Francis P. Nelson, C.SS.R., Procurator; Gerard J. Knapp, C.SS.R., Asst. Procurator; Carl W. Hoegerl, C.SS.R., Prov. Archivist; Lawrence F. Dolan, C.SS.R., Curate; Alfred E. Bradley, C.SS.R. Provincial Residence for Redemptorist Fathers and Brothers Priests 8; Brothers 1.

ASTORIA. *Congregation of St. John the Baptist of China*, 23-15 Newtown Ave., 11102. Tel: 718-278-6797; Fax: 718-278-6851. Email: csjbny@catholic.org. Web: www.csjblb.org. Revs. Antonius Ho, C.S.J.B. (Taiwan), Regl. Supr.; Thomas Sung, C.S.J.B. (Taiwan); Dehua Zhang, C.S.J.B.; Bao Guo Ting, C.S.J.B. Priests 4; Brothers 10.

DOUGLASTON. *Bishop Mugavero Residence*, 7200 Douglaston Pkwy., 11362. Tel: 718-229-8001; Fax: 718-428-3070. Email: vicarofsrpriests@aol.com. Rev. Msgr. George F. Zatarga, Dir. In Res. Rev. Msgrs. Gerard Arella; William F. Burke; George T. Deas (Retired); George V. Fogarty (Retired); Edward W. Jolley (Retired); James P. King (Retired); Joseph A. Martusciello (Retired); James B. McMahon (Retired); Francis X. Mulhall (Retired); Walter Murphy; Revs. John L. Abrams (Retired); Francis P. Bien; Harold A. Buetow (Retired); Eugene P. Coyle (Retired); John F. Cronin (Retired); Harry M. Culkin (Retired); Alfred Guthrie; Francis J. Labita (Retired); Eugene McGovern; John A. McShane (Retired); Matthew W. Sheridan (Retired); Barnabas Wang (Retired); Robert J. Young (Retired).

Institutional Services Residence, 7200 Douglaston Pkwy., 11362-1997. Tel: 718-229-8290; Fax: 718-279-3004. Email: info@institutionalservices.org. Web: www.institutionalservices.org. Rev. Msgr. Michael J. Hardiman, M.Div., M.A., M.P.A., Exec. Dir.; Mr. Robert Rymers, Dir. Operations; Mr. Thomas D. Flynn, Controller.

JAMAICA. *Saint Charles House of Studies*, 168-41 84th Ave., 11432. Tel: 718-351-0232; Fax: 718-739-5515. Email: jfugolo@aol.com. Rev. Joseph Fugolo, C.S., Admin. & Dir.

Immaculate Conception Monastery, 86-45 Edgerton Blvd., 11432. Tel: 718-739-6502; Fax: 718-657-0578. Email: JDougcp@aol.com. Web: www.icmonastery.org. Very Rev. Jack Douglas, C.P., Rector; Revs. Stanislaus Watek, C.P., Vice Rector; Lawrence Bellew, C.P., Chap.; Jerome Bracken, C.P.; Paul Chenot, C.P., Chap.; Theophane Cooney, C.P., Asst. Pastor; Mario Gallipoli, C.P.; Thomas Griffiths, C.P.; Joseph D. Guzinski, C.P.; Colman Haggerty, C.P.; Ernest Hotz, C.P.; Thomas Joyce, C.P., Pastor; Owen Lally, C.P.; John Chrysostom Ryan, C.P.; Theodore Walsh, C.P.; Nicholas Zitz, C.P.; Neil Davin, C.P., Officialis; John R. Mescall, C.P.; Kenan Peters, C.P.; James Price, C.P., Retreat Dir.; Angelo Iacovone, C.P.; Henry Kavanagh, C.P.; David Roberts, C.P.; Isaias Powers, C.P.; Michael Greene, C.P.; Dominic Papa, Preaching Office; Xavier Hayes, C.P.; Kevin Dance, C.P.; Peter Grace, C.P.; Paul Wierichs; Alberto Cabrera, C.P.; Patrick Geinzer, C.P. (R); Paschal Smith, C.P. (NY); Bros. Vincent Basile, C.P.; Philip Maggiulli, C.P. Kenneth Pughe, C.P.; Terence Skorka, C.P., Econome; Angelo Sena, C.P.; Paul Joseph Morgan, C.P. Priests 30; Brothers 6.

Passionist Benefactor's Society Tel: 718-739-9337; Fax: 718-206-9284.

Parsons Manor, 88-25 153rd St., 11432. Tel: 718-558-6900; Fax: 718-558-7286. Revs. Louis D. Aufiero; Jose Cadusale (Philippines); James P. Sweeney; George J. Stack.

St. Vincent's House, 84-15 Kendrick Pl., 11432. Tel: 718-990-7900; Fax: 718-990-7933. Email: mckennaj@stjohns.edu. Revs. John H. McKenna, C.M., Supr.; Joseph V. Daly, C.M.; John B. Freund, C.M.; Donald J. Harrington, C.M.; James J. Maher, C.M.; Johnson Nedungadan, C.M.; Robert R. Vignola, C.M. Vincentian Fathers

Vincentian Residence, St. John's University, 8000 Utopia Pkwy., 11439. Tel: 718-990-6744; Fax: 718-990-5724. Email: traceyb@stjohns.edu. Revs. Bernard M. Tracey, C.M., Supr.; Michael J. Callaghan, C.M.; Michael J. Carroll, C.M.; Thomas V. Concagh, C.M.; James Dorr, C.M.; Peter D. Goldbach, C.M.; Walter F. Graham, C.M.; James M. Kelly, C.M.; Kevin G. Creagh, C.M.; John McDonnell, C.M.; John B. Murray, C.M.; Kenneth F. Slattery, C.M.; James E. Smith, C.M.; Robert J. Swain; Michael D. Whalen, C.M.; Charles T. Plock; Patrick S. Flanagan; Henry M. Bradbury.

JAMAICA ESTATES. *Paulist Fathers - Generalate*, 86-11 Midland Pkwy., 11432. Tel: 718-291-5995; Fax: 718-291-6646. Email: jfdcsp1@cs.com. Web: www.paulist.org. John F. Duffy, Pres.; Michael J. Kallock, Vice Pres.; Stephen J. Connor, Consultor.

LONG ISLAND CITY. *Holy Ghost Fathers of Ireland*, 48-49 37th St., 11101. Tel: 718-729-5273; Fax: 718-729-6949. Email: pdoody68@aol.com. Revs. Patrick Doody, C.S.Sp., Prov. Delegate; Michael J. McCarthy, C.S.Sp.; Patrick Holohan, C.S.Sp.; James Delaney, C.S.Sp.; Noel P. O'Meara, C.S.Sp.

OZONE PARK. *Montfort Missionaries Provincialate (Missionaries of the Company of Mary) - Formation Community*, 101-18 104th St., 11416. Tel: 718-849-5885; 718-849-1684 (Formation); 718-849-0071 (Vocations); Fax: 718-849-7518. Email: provincialusa@aol.com. Web: montfortmissionaries.com. Revs. Gerald J. Fitzsimmons, S.M.M., Prov. Supr.; Matthew J. Considine, S.M.M., Prov. Treas.; James Brady, S.M.M., Formation Dir.; Roy Tvrdik, S.M.M., Vocation Dir. Priests 4.

Priests of Province Serving Abroad: Revs. Everett Brown, S.M.M., Chontales, Nicaragua; Peter D'Abele, S.M.M., Chontales, Nicaragua; John Breslin, S.M.M., Dominican Republic; William J. Considine, S.M.M., Supr. Gen., Rome, Italy.

QUEENS VILLAGE. *DePaul Residence*, 80-14 217th St., 11427. Tel: 718-468-2900; Fax: 718-468-2903. Revs. Richard J. Devine, C.M.; Stephen C. Bicsko, C.M.; Michael J. Cummins, C.M.; Joseph P. Foley, C.M.

SOUTH OZONE PARK. *Sacred Heart Provincialate* (NY Province), 141-11 123 Ave., 11436-1426. Tel: 718-322-3309; Fax: 718-529-6004. Email: nyprovoffice@prodigy.net. Bro. Joseph Holthaus, S.C., Prov. Brothers 3.

SPRINGFIELD GARDENS. *Martin De Porres Brothers Community*, 136-01 219th St., 11413. Tel: 718-978-7155; Fax: 718-525-0982. Email: cbcmdp@nyc.rr.com. Web: www.mdp.org.

[W] CONVENTS AND RESIDENCES FOR SISTERS

BROOKLYN. *Discalced Carmelite Nuns*, The Chancery Office, P.O. Box C, 11202. Tel: 718-399-5900.

Franciscan Sisters of the Poor, Congregational Office, 133 Remsen St., 11201. Tel: 718-643-1919; Fax: 718-643-9710. Email: sfp@franciscansisters.org. Web: www.franciscansisters.org. Sr. Jeanne M. Glisky, S.F.P., Congregation Min.

Missionaries of Charity, Contemplative Our Lady of Lourdes Convent, 34 Aberdeen St., 11207. Tel: 718-443-2868. Sr. M. Taissa, M.C., Supr. Sisters 10.

Monastery of the Sisters Adorers of the Precious Blood, 54th St. and Ft. Hamilton Pkwy., 11219. Tel: 718-438-6371; Fax: 718-438-6381. Rev. Msgrs. Austin P. Bennett, Dir. Confraternity of the Precious Blood (Retired); Philip J. Reilly, Chap. Sisters 14.

Motherhouse and Convent of the Sisters of Mercy of the Americas, Brooklyn Regional Community, 273 Willoughby Ave., 11205-1487. Tel: 718-622-5840; Fax: 718-398-7866. Email: brooklynmercy@aol.com. Web: www.brooklynmercy.org. Sr. Mary Waters, R.S.M., Pres. Sisters 236.

Sisters of the Good Shepherd, 348 Ninth St., 11215. Tel: 718-499-9212; Fax: 718-369-1691. Sisters 2.

Provincial Office, 82-31 Doncaster Pl., Jamaica, 11432. Tel: 718-380-3270; Fax: 718-591-9376. Sr. Yvette Arnold, Prov. Officer.

Sisters of the Visitation of Brooklyn, NY, 8902 Ridge Blvd., 11209. Tel: 718-745-5151; Fax: 718-745-3680. Email: vamonastery@aol.com. Web: www.visitationsisters.org/mona/bro_main.asp. Sr. Susan Marie Kasprzak, V.H.M., Supr. Professed Sisters 20.

JAMAICA. *Provincialate of the Sisters of the Good Shepherd*, 82-31 Doncaster Pl., 11432. Tel: 718-380-3270; Fax: 718-591-9376. Email: yvettearnold@aol.com. Web: goodshepherdsistersna.com. Zenovia Jackson, Prov. Sec.
Legal Title: *Sisters of the Good Shepherd, Province of New York* Sisters 5.
Ursuline Provincial Administration Office, Glengarda, 81-15 Utopia Pkwy., 11432-1308. Tel: 718-591-0681; Fax: 718-969-4275. Email: taliaosu@juno.com. Web: tressy.tripod.com. Sr. Catherine Talia, O.S.U., Prov. Supr.

QUEENS VILLAGE. *St. Ann's Novitiate, Little Sisters of the Poor*, 110-39 Springfield Blvd., P.O. Box 280356, 11428. Tel: 718-464-4920; Fax: 718-479-3126. Email: mmnvtlsp@attglobal.net. Web: www.littlesistersofthepoor.org; www.lspusa.org. Sr. Mary Richard, L.S.P., Supr. & Mistress of Novices; Rev. James Pereda, C.R.C., Chap. Sisters 8; Novices 3; Postulants 5.
Little Sisters of the Poor, Provincial Residence, 110-30 221st St., 11429. Tel: 718-464-1800; Fax: 718-468-5132. Sr. Genevieve Regina, L.S.P., Prov. Sisters 150.

RIDGEWOOD. *Convent of the Sisters of Mary Reparatrix*, 62-67 60 Pl., 11385. Tel: 718-456-4242; 718-386-1107 (Altar Bread Department); Fax: 718-386-2254. Email: smrny@att.net. Web: www.smr.org. Sr. Patricia Mullen, S.M.R., Local Leader. Sisters 4.

ROCKAWAY PARK. *Stella Maris Convent, Sisters of St. Joseph* 11694-2497. Tel: 718-634-1886. Sisters 11.

[X] EVANGELIZATION AND RENEWAL CENTERS

BROOKLYN. *Centro Evangelizacion San Vicente de Paul*, 118 Congress St., 11201. Tel: 718-624-5670; Fax: 718-624-5806. Email: cesvip@aol.com. Revs. Victor Rodriguez, C.M. (Chile), Dir. & Dir. Cursillo Movement; Javier Antonio Serra, C.M. (Spain), Dir. Jornada Movement.

DOUGLASTON. *Immaculate Conception Center, St. Paul's Center*, 7200 Douglaston Pkwy., 11362. Tel: 718-229-8001, Ext. 310; Fax: 718-352-2490. Email: spc2135@aol.com. Rev. James Fitzpatrick, Dir. Staff: Mr. Phil Crivelli; Mr. Tom Leavens; Deacon Len Sclafani; Mrs. Cathie Sclafani; Ms. Maureen Powers, Sec.
St. Paul's Center Tel: 718-229-8001, Ext. 310; Fax: 718-352-2490. Email: spc2135@aol.com.

FLUSHING. *Cenacle Center for Spiritual Renewal*, 154-27 Horace Harding Expwy., 11367. Tel: 718-463-2073; Fax: 718-353-3514. Email: cenflushing@juno .com. Web: www.cenaclesisters.org. Sr. Judith Osterburg, R.C., Coord.

JAMAICA. *Bishop Molloy Retreat House for Laymen*, 86-45 Edgerton Blvd., 11432. Tel: 718-739-1229; Fax: 718-739-3421. Web: www.bishopmolloy.org. Revs. James Price, C.P., Retreat Dir.; Michael Greene, C.P., Assoc.; Sr. Maria Regina Loures, I.H.M., Assoc. Passionist Fathers

[Y] SECULAR INSTITUTES

BROOKLYN. *The Institute of Apostolic Oblates*, 730 E. 87th St., 11236. Tel: 718-649-0324; Fax: 718-272-5012. Email: apostolicoblates@msn.com. Giovanna Piccioli, Local Moderator.

FOREST HILLS. *Asociacion Misioneros Contemplativos Laicos* (Lay Association of Contemplative Missionaries) , P.O. Box 754267, 11375. Tel: 718-592-5458; 718-397-8648; Fax: 718-592-6930. Marta Herrera, Pres.; Maria Keany, Vice Pres.; Amparo Aponte, Sec.; Ana Luisa Ortega, Treas.

[Z] MISCELLANEOUS LISTINGS

BROOKLYN. *Alive in Hope Foundation of the Diocese of Brooklyn*, 310 Prospect Park West, 11215. Tel: 718-965-7300; Fax: 718-965-7341. Email: tflood@diobrook.org. Web: www.dioceseofbrooklyn.org. Rev. Msgr. John J. Bracken, Chm. of Alive in Hope Foundation Bd.; Thomas F. Flood, Exec. Dir.
Casa Betsaida Housing Development Fund Corp., 191 Joralemon St., 11201. Tel: 718-722-6086. Jeanne M. Diulio, Asst. Dir., Office of Legal Affairs.
Casa Betsaida-Home for people with AIDS, 267 Hewew St., 11211. Tel: 718-212-6869; Fax: 718-212-8264. Email: bedsaidany@aol.com. Dr. Francisco Quinteros.
The Cathedral Club of Brooklyn, P.O. Box 315, 11209-0315. Tel: 718-332-5796; Fax: 212-778-8294. Richard A. Re, Pres.
Centro Evangelization S. Vincente de Paul (Diocesan Cursillos Center) , 118 Congress St., 11201. Tel: 718-624-5670; Fax: 718-624-5806. Email: cesvip@aol.com. Revs. Robin E. Rodriguez, C.M., Dir.; Jose M. Sanchez, C.M.; Manuel Botet, C.M.
Compostela Fund of the Roman Catholic Diocese of Brooklyn, 310 Prospect Park W., 11215. Tel: 718-965-7300; Fax: 718-965-7311. Email: fgalligan@diobrook.org. Francis Galligan, Econome.
En El, Inc., 75 Greene Ave., 11238.
Franciscan Brothers Charitable Trust, 135 Remsen St., 11201. Tel: 718-858-8217; Fax: 718-858-8306. Email: bsb492003@yahoo.com franciscan135@aol.com. Web: www.francisanbrothers.org. Richard T. Arkwright, Trustees; Edwin Gill, Trustees; Robert Schaefer, Trustees; Michael Henning, Trustees.
Franciscan Sisters of the Poor Charitable Trust, 133 Remsen St., 11201. Tel: 718-643-1919; Fax: 718-643-9710. Email: sfp@franciscansisters.org. Web: www.franciscansisters.org. Sr. Jeanne M. Glisky, S.F.P., Contact Person.
The Futures in Education Foundation, Inc., 310 Prospect Park W., 11215. Tel: 718-965-7340; Fax: 718-965-7341. Ms. Jean O'Shea, Exec. Sec.
HeartShare Human Services of NY - Clermont Residence, 26 Clermont Ave., 11205. Tel: 718-834-9317; Fax: 718-834-9364. Miss Sharon Bewry, Resident Mgr. Residence for Developmentally Disabled Adults.
St. John's Bread & Life Program, Inc., 75 Lewis Ave., 11206. Tel: 718-574-0058. Mr. Hossein Saadat, M.S.A., Exec. Dir.; Sr. Bernadette Szyhczak, D.C., Soup Kitchen Coord. (Soup Kitchen, Employment Counseling, HIV/AIDS Support Group/Food Pantry, Counseling, Referrals and Advocacy)
Latvian Roman Catholic Mission (Our Lady of Aglona Center) , 361 Highland Blvd., 11207. Rev. Msgr. Leons Varna, S.T.D., Dir.
**The Maura Clarke Ita Ford Center*, 138 Bleecker St., 11221. Tel: 718-452-0167; Fax: 718-452-5173. Email: mcifcenter@aol.com. Sr. Mary Burns, S.C., Dir.
Mercy Home Foundation, 243 Prospect Park W., 11215. Tel: 718-832-1075; Fax: 718-832-7612. Sr. Virginia Farnam, Contact Person.
Mercy Montessori School, 1397 Brooklyn Ave., 11203. Tel: 718-469-2834. Sr. Mary Harvey, R.S.M., Dir.
National Center of the Haitian Apostolate, 455 E. 29th St., 11226. Tel: 718-856-3323; Fax: 718-703-0980. Email: haitiapost.com. Web: snaa.org. Rev. Guy Sansaricq, Exec. Dir.
Neighbors Together, P.O. Box 330-562, 11233. Tel: 718-498-7256. Ed Fowler, Exec. Dir. Services for the Poor. Soup Kitchen and Social Services Advocacy.
New Horizons Adult Education Program, Inc., St. John's Center, 75 Lewis Ave., 11206. Tel: 718-455-1166; 718-455-1033; Fax: 718-452-3047. Email: newhorizonsade@aol.com.
Pro Sanctity Movement, 730 E. 87th St., 11236. Tel: 718-649-0324; Fax: 718-272-5012. Email: prosanctityny@msn.com. Web: www.prosanctity.org. Miss Carla M. da Costa, Dir.; Rev. Msgr. Andrew J. Vaccari, Spiritual Advisor.
The Roman Catholic Pontifical Lay Association Memores Domini, 218 76 St., 11209. Tel: 718-833-3992; Fax: 718-833-7374.
Men's House, 218 76 St., 11209. Tel: 718-833-3992; Fax: 718-833-7374. Email: senator@ix.netcom.com. Christopher G. Bacich, Head of the House.
Women's House, 5757 Faraday Ave., Riverdale, 10471. Tel: 718-601-2349; Fax: 718-632-1926. Elvira Parravicini, Head of the House.
Ryken Educational Center, Inc., 7100 Shore Rd., 11209. Tel: 718-836-7100. Email: sferrara@xaverian.org. Dr. Salvatore Ferrara, Pres.
Society of the Immaculate Conception of Brooklyn (Missionary Society) , 191 Joralemon St., 11201-4306. Tel: 718-875-4375, Ext. 743; Fax: 718-875-2702. Rev. John F. Brogan, Exec. Dir. (Missionary Society)
St. Theresa of Avila Senior Housing Development Fund Corporation, 191 Joralemon St., 11201. Tel: 718-722-6086. Jeanne M. Diulio, Asst. Dir., Office of Legal Affairs.

ASTORIA. *Flowers With Care Youth Services, Diocese of Brooklyn, Inc.*, 23-40 Astoria Blvd., 11102. Tel: 718-726-9790; Fax: 718-728-8817. Email: fwcareyscc@yahoo.com. Paula Beltrone, Exec. Dir.

BAYSIDE. *Ozanam Geriatric Foundation*, 42-41 201 St., 11361. Tel: 718-971-2020; Fax: 718-971-2025. Email: godonovan@ozanamhall.org.

BRENTWOOD. *Congregation of the Sisters of St. Joseph*, Charitable Trust, Brentwood Rd., 11717-5587. Tel: 516-273-1187; Fax: 516-273-1345. Email: brentcsj@aol.com. Web: csjbrentwood.org. Sr. Joanne Feulner, Treas.

FLUSHING. *Cenacle of St. Regis of Flushing*, 154-25 Horace Harding Exwy., 11367-1296. Tel: 718-463-2073; Fax: 718-353-3514. Email: cenflushing@juno.com. Web: www.cenaclesisters.org. Sr. Judith Osterburg, R.C., Coord.
**Women Helping Women*, P.O. Box 580086, 11358-0086. Tel: 718-539-9111; Fax: 718-961-3322. Email: whwcol@aol.com.

HOLLIS HILLS. *Glencara, Inc.*, 86-05 218th St., 11427. Tel: 718-454-9804; Fax: 718-454-9806. Email: seanf662@aol.com. Sisters Sean Foley, R.S.M., Pres.; Kathleen Quinn, R.S.M., Vice Pres.; Patricia Hartigan, Esq.; Francene Horan, R.S.M., Sec.; Eileen Trainor, 2nd Vice Pres.; Regina Williams, Treas.

JAMAICA. *Global Women's Exchange*, 82-31 Doncaster Pl., 11432. Tel: 718-380-3270; Fax: 718-591-9376. Email: glbwmex@aol.com.
Immaculata Hall Housing Development Fund Corporation, 149-29 90th Ave., 11432. Tel: 718-818-5055. Email: Mditommaso@svcmcny.org.
Mary Immaculate, Inc., 88-25 153rd St., 11432. Tel: 718-558-6900.
Vincentian Service Corps.-East Inc. A program for laywomen and men willing to commit to one year of service to the poor. , Saint John's University - Annex 31, 8000 Utopia Pkwy., 11439. Tel: 718-990-6266; Fax: 718-990-2307. Email: vsceast@stjohns.edu. Web: vscorps.org.

LONG ISLAND CITY. *Hour Children*, 36-11A 12th St., 11106. Tel: 718-443-4724; Fax: 718-433-4728. Email: hourchildren@hourchildren.org. Sr. Teresa Fitzgerald, C.S.J., Exec. Dir.
World Compassion Link, P.O. Box 4279, 11104-9808. Tel: 301-933-4994; Fax: 301-933-4652. Email: omearanoel@aoc.com. Web: worldcompassionlink.org. 48-49 37th St., 11101. Revs. Noel P. O'Meara, C.S.Sp., Pres.; Patrick Doody, C.S.Sp., Vice Pres.; Michael J. McCarthy, C.S.Sp., Treas.; James Delaney, C.S.Sp., Dir. Devel.

MIDDLE VILLAGE. *National Italian Apostolate Conference*, 66-05 79th Pl., 11379. Tel: 718-326-1911; Fax: 718-326-1883. Email: wazo2@aol.com. Rev. Msgr. William A. Varvaro, P.A., S.T.D., J.C.D., Exec. Dir.

QUEENS. *Focolare Movement*
Queens Office, 6359 83rd St., Middle Village, 11379. Tel: 718-898-2611.

ROCKAWAY PARK. *Franciscan Missionary Brothers of North America*, 99-07 Rockaway Beach Blvd., 11694. Tel: 718-634-6476; Fax: 718-634-5833. Email: franciscanbr@netgero.net. Bro. Joseph Karimalayil, Pres.

SYOSSET. *Sisters of Mercy Housing, Inc* Sr. Terry Agliardi, Pres.Mailing Address: 273 Willoughby Ave., 11205.

RELIGIOUS INSTITUTES OF MEN REPRESENTED IN THE DIOCESE

For further details refer to the corresponding bracketed number in the Religious Institutes of Men or Women section.

[1350]—*Brothers of St. Francis Xavier* (Sacred Heart Prov.)—C.F.X.
[0330]—*Brothers of the Christian Schools*—F.S.C.
[0600]—*Brothers of the Congregation of Holy Cross*—C.S.C.
[1100]—*Brothers of the Sacred Heart*—S.C.
[0470]—*The Capuchin Friars* (Prov. of St. Mary)—O.F.M.Cap.
[0275]—*Carmelites of Mary Immaculate*—C.M.I.
[]—*Congregation of St. John the Baptist of China, Inc.*—C.S.J.B.
[0600]—*Congregation of the Holy Cross*—C.S.C.
[1330]—*Congregation of the Mission* (Eastern, New England, Spanish Provs.)—C.M.
[1330]—*Congregation of the Mission - Philadelphia (Vincentians)*—C.M.
[1330]—*Congregation of the Mission (Vincentian Fathers)*—C.M.
[1210]—*Congregation of the Missionaries of St. Charles*—C.S.
[]—*Congregation of the Missionary Brothrs of St.Francis of Assisi*—C.M.S.F.
[1000]—*Congregation of the Passion* (Prov. of St. Paul of the Cross)—C.P.
[0480]—*Conventual Franciscans* (Polish Prov.)—O.F.M.Conv
[0490]—*Franciscan Brothers of Brooklyn*—O.S.F.
[0520]—*Franciscan Friars* (Immaculate Conception Prov.; Lithuanian Vicariate)—O.F.M.
[0530]—*Franciscan Friars of the Atonement*—S.A.
[0610]—*Holy Cross Fathers*—C.S.C.
[0650]—*Holy Ghost Fathers*—C.S.Sp.
[]—*Institute of the Incarnate Word*—I.V.E.
[0690]—*Jesuit Fathers and Brothers* (New York Prov.)—S.J.
[]—*Little Brothers of the Gospel*—L.B.G.
[0770]—*The Marist Brothers*—F.M.S.
[0780]—*The Marist Fathers*—S.M.
[0870]—*Montfort Missionaries (Missionaries of the*

Company of Mary)—S.M.M.
[1330]—*New England Province of the Congregation of the Mission (Vincentian)*—C.M.
[0950]—*Oratorians* (Brooklyn)—C.O.
[0520]—*Order of St. Francis (Lithuanian)*—O.F.M.
[0990]—*Pallottine*—S.A.C.
[]—*Pallottine* (Polish Prov.)—S.A.C.
[1030]—*Paulist Fathers*—C.S.P.
[0610]—*Priests of the Congregation of Holy Cross* (Eastern Prov.)—C.S.C.
[1070]—*The Redemptorists*—C.SS.R.
[1200]—*Salvatorian Fathers*—S.D.S.
[1210]—*Scalabrini Fathers*—C.S.
[0690]—*Society of Jesus*—S.J.
[0690]—*Society of Jesus (The Pious Society for the Missionaries of St. Charles)*—S.J.
[0760]—*Society of Mary (Marianists)* (New York Prov.)—S.M.
[0990]—*Society of the Catholic Apostolate*—S.A.C.
[1200]—*Society of the Divine Savior*—S.D.S.
[1350]—*Xaverian Brothers U.S.A., Inc.*—C.F.X.

RELIGIOUS INSTITUTES OF WOMEN REPRESENTED IN THE DIOCESE

[0340]—*Carmelite Sisters of Charity*—C.C.V.
[0330]—*Carmelite Sisters of the Aged and Infirm*—O.Carm.
[2980]—*Congregation of Notre Dame*—C.N.D.
[2950]—*Congregation of Notre Dame de Sion*—N.D.S.
[]—*Congregation of Olivetan Benedictine Sisters* (Korea)
[3110]—*Congregation of Our Lady of the Retreat in the Cenacle*—R.C.
[2230]—*Congregation of the Infant Jesus*—C.I.J.
[3140]—*Congregation of the Sisters of the Catholic Apostolate (Pallottine)*—C.S.A.C.
[0760]—*Daughters of Charity of St. Vincent de Paul*—D.C.
[]—*Daughters of Divine Love*—D.D.L.
[]—*Daughters of Mary*—F.de.M.
[]—*Daughters of Mary Mother of Mercy*—D.M.M.M.
[0960]—*Daughters of Wisdom*—D.W.
[]—*Dominican Congregation of Our Lady of the Rosary (Sparkill Dominicans)*—O.P.
[1070-01]—*Dominican Sisters*—O.P.
[1070-02]—*Dominican Sisters*—O.P.
[1070-05]—*Dominican Sisters*—O.P.
[1105]—*Dominican Sisters of Hope*—O.P.
[1400]—*Franciscan Missionary Sisters of the Sacred Heart*—F.M.S.C.
[1180]—*Franciscan Sisters of Allegany, NY*—O.S.F.
[1425]—*Franciscan Sisters of Peace*—F.S.P.
[1420]—*Franciscan Sisters of Ringwood*—F.S.R.
[1470]—*Franciscan Sisters of St. Joseph*—F.S.S.J.
[1190]—*Franciscan Sisters of the Atonement*—S.A.
[]—*Franciscan Sisters of the Immaculate (Honduras)*—H.F.I.
[1440]—*Franciscan Sisters of the Poor*—S.F.P.
[1840]—*Grey Nuns of the Sacred Heart*—G.N.S.H.
[]—*Hermanas Franciscanos de la Immaculata*—H.F.I.
[2070]—*Holy Union Sisters*—S.U.S.C.
[2340]—*Little Sisters of the Poor*—L.S.P.
[2470]—*Maryknoll Sisters of St Dominic*—M.M.
[2710]—*Missionaries of Charity*—M.C.
[]—*Missionaries of Charity - Contemplative*—M.C.C.
[2790]—*Missionary Servants of the Most Blessed Trinity*—M.S.B.T.
[4190]—*Order of Visitation*—V.H.M.
[2950]—*Our Lady of Sion*—N.D.S.
[3160]—*Parish Visitors of Mary Immaculate*—P.V.M.I.
[2070]—*Religious of the Holy Union of the Sacred Hearts*—S.U.S.C.
[3465]—*Religious of the Sacred Heart of Mary*—R.S.H.M.
[3430]—*Religious Teachers Filippini*—M.P.F.
[2970]—*School Sisters of Notre Dame* (Wilton, CT; Baltimore, MD)—S.S.N.D.
[2970]—*School Sisters of Notre Dame*—S.S.N.D.
[]—*Servants of the Lord and the Virgin of Matara*—S.S.V.M.
[0110]—*Sisters Adorers of the Most Precious Blood*—A.P.B.
[0650]—*Sisters of Charity of St. Vincent de Paul of New York*—S.C.
[0640]—*Sisters of Charity of St. Vincent de Paul, Halifax*—S.C.
[0430]—*Sisters of Charity of the Blessed Virgin Mary*—B.V.M.
[1000]—*Sisters of Divine Providence of Kentucky*—C.D.P.
[2440]—*Sisters of Mary Immaculate* (Kenya)—S.M.I.
[2575]—*Sisters of Mercy of the Americas* (Brooklyn, NY; Dallas, TX)—R.S.M.
[3000]—*Sisters of Notre Dame de Namur*—S.N.D.deN.
[2670]—*Sisters of Our Lady of Mercy*—S.O.L.M.
[3830-05]—*Sisters of St. Joseph*—C.S.J.
[3830-01]—*Sisters of St. Joseph of Boston*—C.S.J.
[3140]—*Sisters of the Catholic Apostolate-Pallottine*—C.S.A.C.
[3180]—*Sisters of the Cross and Passion*—C.P.
[1830]—*Sisters of the Good Shepherd*—R.G.S.
[1970]—*Sisters of the Holy Family of Nazareth* (Immaculate Heart of Mary Prov.)—C.S.F.N.
[]—*Sisters of the Korean Martyrs*—S.K.M.
[3320]—*Sisters of the Presentation of the B.V.M.* (Newburgh)—P.B.V.M.
[2160]—*Sisters, Servants of the Immaculate Heart of Mary*—I.H.M.
[2460]—*Society of Mary Reparatrix*—S.M.R.
[4130]—*Ursuline Sisters of the Congregation of Tildonk, Belgium*—O.S.U.
[4190]—*Visitation Nuns*—V.H.M.

DIOCESAN CEMETERIES

BROOKLYN. *Holy Cross*, Brooklyn & Tilden Ave., 11203.
FARMINGDALE. *St. Charles*, Conklin St., 11735. Tel: 516-249-8700. Rev. Msgr. August C. Bednartz, Chap. (Retired).
Resurrection, Conklin St., 11735. Tel: 516-249-8700.
FLUSHING. *Mount St. Mary*, 172-00 Booth Memorial Ave., 11365. Tel: 718-353-1560. Rev. Romano Zanon, Chap.
MIDDLE VILLAGE. *St. John's*, 80-01 Metropolitan Ave., 11379. Tel: 718-894-4888. Rev. Ralph Guarracino, Chap. Administration Offices for the Diocesan Cemeteries.

PARISH CEMETERIES

AMITYVILLE. *Most Holy Trinity* Most Holy Trinity Parish, Brooklyn.
Trinity Most Holy Trinity Parish, Brooklyn.
ROCKAWAY. *St. Mary Star of the Sea*, Rockaway Blvd., 11691. Tel: 718-894-4888.

NECROLOGY

† Antoncic, Rev. Msgr. John J., Flushing, NY St. Mel—Died May 1, 2003
† Barretta, Rev. Msgr. Anthony J., Brooklyn, NY Holy Cross—Died Dec. 30, 2003
† Callahan, Rev. Msgr. Brian F., Brooklyn, NY St. Thomas Aquinas—Died Dec. 15, 2003
† Passarella, Rev. Msgr. Anthony F., (Retired)—Died Oct. 6, 2003
† Puglisi, Rev. Msgr. Guy, Brooklyn, NY Our Lady of the Angels—Died July 8, 2003
† Shevlin, Rev. Msgr. Raymond R. (Retired)—Died May 5, 2003
† Hughes, John F.—Died Feb. 20, 1903
† McNeill, John A., (Retired)—Died Sept. 26, 2003
† McNicholas, Edward J., (Retired)—Died Aug. 4, 2003
† Morgan, Raymond J., (Retired)—Died Oct. 24, 2003
† Mullen, Joseph A., (Retired)—Died Oct. 5, 2003
† Pupin, Vito A., (Retired)—Died April 11, 2003
† Reilly, John C., (Retired)—Died Aug. 30, 2003

Diocese of Brownsville

(Dioecesis Brownsvillensis)

Most Reverend

RAYMUNDO J. PEÑA, D.D.

Bishop of Brownsville; ordained May 25, 1957; appointed Titular Bishop of Trisipa and Auxiliary of San Antonio October 16, 1976; consecrated December 13, 1976; appointed Bishop of El Paso April 29, 1980; installed June 18, 1980; appointed Bishop of Brownsville May 23, 1995; installed August 6, 1995. *Mailing Address: P.O. Box 2279, Brownsville, TX 78522-2279.*

Most Reverend

JOHN J. FITZPATRICK, D.D.

Retired Bishop of Brownsville; ordained December 13, 1942; appointed Auxiliary of Miami June 24, 1968; consecrated August 28, 1968; appointed Bishop of Brownsville April 27, 1971; installed May 27, 1971; retired November 30, 1991. *P.O. Box 2279, Brownsville, TX 78522-2279.*

ESTABLISHED JULY 10, 1965.

Square Miles 4,226.

Comprises the four Counties of Cameron, Hidalgo, Starr and Willacy in the State of Texas.

For legal titles of parishes and diocesan institutions, consult the Catholic Pastoral Center.

Catholic Pastoral Center: 1910 E. Elizabeth St., P.O. Box 2279, Brownsville, TX 78522-2279. Tel: 956-542-2501; Fax: 956-542-6751.

Web: www.cdob.org

Email: cdob@cdob.org

STATISTICAL OVERVIEW

Personnel	
Bishop	1
Retired Bishops	1
Priests: Diocesan Active in Diocese	52
Priests: Diocesan Active Outside Diocese	1
Priests: Retired, Sick or Absent	15
Number of Diocesan Priests	68
Religious Priests in Diocese	43
Total Priests in Diocese	111
Extern Priests in Diocese	5
Ordinations:	
Diocesan Priests	2
Religious Priests	2
Transitional Deacons	5
Permanent Deacons in Diocese	64
Total Brothers	18
Total Sisters	131
Parishes	
Parishes	65
With Resident Pastor:	
Resident Diocesan Priests	40
Resident Religious Priests	22
Without Resident Pastor:	
Administered by Priests	4
Missions	44
Pastoral Centers	1
Professional Ministry Personnel:	
Brothers	3
Sisters	31
Lay Ministers	84
Welfare	
Health Care Centers	1
Total Assisted	114
Homes for the Aged	2
Total Assisted	581
Day Care Centers	2
Total Assisted	128
Special Centers for Social Services	5
Total Assisted	23,156
Other Institutions	2
Total Assisted	3,333
Educational	
Seminaries, Diocesan	1
Students from This Diocese	6
Diocesan Students in Other Seminaries	18
Total Seminarians	24
High Schools, Private	2
Total Students	1,001
Elementary Schools, Diocesan and Parish	8
Total Students	2,272
Elementary Schools, Private	2
Total Students	579
Catechesis/Religious Education:	
High School Students	7,515
Elementary Students	28,637
Total Students under Catholic Instruction	40,028
Teachers in the Diocese:	
Priests	3
Brothers	9
Sisters	11
Lay Teachers	270
Vital Statistics	
Receptions into the Church:	
Infant Baptism Totals	4,439
Adult Baptism Totals	682
Received into Full Communion	615
First Communions	7,354
Confirmations	2,905
Marriages:	
Catholic	790
Interfaith	106
Total Marriages	896
Deaths	2,373
Total Catholic Population	888,004
Total Population	1,044,711

Former Prelates—Rt. Revs. DOMINIC MANUCY, Titular Bishop of Delma and Vicar Apostolic of Brownsville; cons. Dec. 8, 1874; transferred to Mobile, March 9, 1884; reappointed to Vicariate Apostolic of Brownsville, Feb. 1, 1885; died Dec. 4, 1885; PETER VERDAGUER, Titular Bishop of Aulon and Vicar Apostolic of Brownsville; cons. Nov. 9, 1890; died Oct. 26, 1911; CLAUDE JAILLET, O.P., Administrator of Vicariate Apostolic of Brownsville, 1911-1913.

Former Bishops—Most Rev. ADOLPH MARX, D.D., J.C.D., First Bishop of Brownsville, ord. May 2, 1940; appt. Titular Bishop of Citrus and Auxiliary Bishop of Corpus Christi, July 6, 1956; consecrated Oct. 9, 1956; appt. first Bishop of Brownsville, July 19, 1965; installed Sept. 2, 1965; died in Cologne, Germany Nov. 1, 1965; His Eminence HUMBERTO CARDINAL MEDEIROS, D.D., second Bishop of Brownsville, appt. April 14, 1966; consecrated June 9, 1966; installed Bishop of Brownsville, June 29, 1966; appt. Archbishop of Boston, Sept. 8, 1970; installed Archbishop of Boston, Oct. 7, 1970; created Cardinal, March 5, 1973; died Sept. 17, 1983; Most Revs. JOHN J. FITZPATRICK, D.D., third Bishop of Brownsville (Retired), ord. Dec. 13, 1942; appt. Auxiliary Bishop of Miami, June 24, 1968; consecrated Aug. 28, 1968; appt. Bishop of Brownsville, April 27, 1971; installed May 27, 1971; retired Nov. 30, 1991; ENRIQUE SAN PEDRO, S.J., S.T.D., S.S.L., fourth Bishop of Brownsville, ord. March 18, 1957; appt. Auxiliary Bishop of Galveston-Houston April 1, 1986; consecrated June 29, 1986; appt. Coadjutor Bishop of Brownsville, Aug. 13, 1991; installed Sept. 26, 1991; succeeded to the See, Nov. 30, 1991; died July 17, 1994.

Office of the Bishop—Most Rev. RAYMUNDO J. PENA, D.D., 1910 E. Elizabeth St., P.O. Box 2279, Brownsville, 78522-2279. Tel: 956-550-1510; Fax: 956-550-1565. Email: rjpena@cdob.org; Rev. CARLOS A. VILLARREAL, Admin. Asst., Diocesan Liturgist & Ecclesiastical Notary. Tel: 956-550-1510. Email: cvillarreal@cdob.org; Mrs. INA L. PEREZ, Exec. Sec.. Email: iperez@cdob.org; Mrs. ISABEL SALAZAR, Asst. Sec.. Email: isalazar@cdob.org.

Bishop Emeritus—Most Rev. JOHN J. FITZPATRICK (Retired), St. Mary, Mother of the Church, 1914 Barnard Rd., Brownsville, 78520-8247. Tel: 956-546-3800.

Vicar General—Rev. ROBERT E. MAHER, V.G., Office, 400 Virgen de San Juan Blvd., San Juan, 78589. Tel: 956-781-5323; Fax: 956-784-5098. Email: rmaher@cdob.org; St. Joseph Parish, 122 W. Fay, Edinburg, 78539. Tel: 956-383-3728; Fax: 956-383-8737. Email: stjoseph@main.rgv.net.

Deans—Revs. HEBERTO M. DIAZ JR., Brownsville. Tel: 956-546-1982; MATTHIAS SHANLEY, SS.CC., Harlingen. Tel: 956-423-6341; LOUIS L. BRUM, McAllen. Tel: 956-787-2963; ROY LEE SNIPES, O.M.I., Mission. Tel: 956-585-2623; VACANT, Rio Grande City; Rev. EMMANUEL BIALONCIK, O.F.M., Weslaco. Tel: 956-262-1406.

Development Office—Mr. JESSE SALINAS, Dir.; Mr. EDGAR AGUILAR, Office Clerk. Tel: 956-550-1544. 1910 E. Elizabeth St., P.O. Box 2279, Brownsville, 78522-2279. Tel: 956-542-2501; Fax: 956-542-6751. Email: jsalinas@cdob.org.

Stewardship Office—VACANT, Dir.

Judicial Department (Diocesan Tribunal)—Rev. LUIS JAVIER GARCIA, J.C.L., Judicial Vicar. Email: lgarcia@cdob.org; Ms. CLARA M. MARTINEZ,

Notary. Email: cmartinez@cdob.org; Mrs. Irma Cantu, Sec.. Email: icantu@cdob.org; Main Office, 1910 E. Elizabeth St., P.O. Box 2279, Brownsville, 78522-2279. Tel: 956-550-1512; Fax: 956-542-6751. San Juan Office, 400 N. Virgen de San Juan Blvd., San Juan, 78589. Tel: 956-782-1728; Fax: 956-782-0418; Ms. Delia Flores, Sec.. Email: dflores@cdob.org; Rev. Ricardo Garcia, J.C.L., Adjutant Judicial Vicar. Email: rgarcia@cdob.org.

Presiding Judges—Most Rev. Raymundo J. Pena, D.D.; Revs. Luis Javier Garcia, J.C.L.; Ricardo Garcia, J.C.L.

Substitute Judge—Most Rev. John J. Fitzpatrick, D.D., Bishop Emeritus (Retired).

Promoter of Justice—Rev. Jose Rene Angel, J.C.L.; Rev. Msgr. Gustavo Barrera.

Procurators and Advocates—Bro. Francis J. Garza, F.M.S.; Revs. Mario Castro; Pedro Briseno.

Professional Court Expert—Sr. Norma Pimentel, M.J.

Associate Judges—Revs. Ariel O. Angel, J.C.L.; Herman J. Defler, M.S.F.; Thomas Kulleck; Bro. Manuel Enrique Ruiz, O.de.M., J.C.L.

Defenders of the Bond—Rev. Msgrs. F. Robert DaVola; Gustavo Barrera; Rev. Jose Rene Angel, J.C.L.

Office of the Chancellor—1910 E. Elizabeth St., P.O. Box 2279, Brownsville, 78522-2279. Tel: 956-550-1517; Fax: 956-542-6751. Revs. Heberto M. Diaz Jr., Chancellor. Email: hdiaz@cdob.org; Thomas G. Kulleck, Historical Archivist. Tel: 956-550-1526. Email: tkulleck@cdob.org; Mrs. Yolanda G. Escobar, Administrative Asst. Tel: 956-550-1559. Email: yescobar@cdob.org; Ms. Melissa A. Salinas, Sec. Tel: 956-550-1517. Email: msalinas@cdob.org; Miss Claudia Montemayor, Receptionist. Tel: 956-542-2501. Email: cmontemayor@cdob.org.

Moderator of the Curia, Lower Valley—Rev. Heberto M. Diaz Jr., 1910 E. Elizabeth St., P.O. Box 2279, Brownsville, 78522-2279. Tel: 956-550-1517; Fax: 956-542-6751. Email: hdiaz@cdob.org; Mrs. Yolanda G. Escobar, Administrative Asst.. Email: yescobar@cdob.org.

Moderator of the Curia, Upper Valley—Mrs. Ofelia Martinez, Office Mgr. Tel: 956-784-5010. Email: omartinez@cdob.org; Mrs. Michelle Lopez, Sec. Tel: 956-784-5012. Email: mlopez-gonzales@cdob.org; Ms. Terry DeLeon, Sec. Tel: 956-784-5013. Email: tdeleon@cdob.org; Mrs. Edna Garcia-Gonzalez, Sec. Tel: 956-784-5007. Email: egarcia@cdob.org; Mrs. Sandra Torres, Receptionist. Tel: 956-781-5323; 787-8571. Email: storres@cdob.org; Ms. Maey Latigo, Sec. Tel: 956-784-5051. Email: mlatigo@cdob.org; Mrs. Margot Martinez, Sec. Tel: 956-784-5055. Email: mmartinez@cdob.org; Mrs. Maria Juanita Reyes, Sec. Tel: 956-784-5067. Email: mreyes@cdob.org; 700 N. Virgen de San Juan Blvd., San Juan, 78589. Tel: 956-787-8571; Fax: 956-784-5081.

Secretariat for the Diocesan Synod—Mr. Luis Zuniga, Gen. Sec.. Email: lzuniga@cdob.org; Ms. Ninfa Cortina, Sec. Tel: 956-550-1519. Email: ncortina@cdob.org; Revs. Carlos Zuniga, Clergy Liaison. Tel: 956-682-5155; Ariel Oliver Angel, J.C.L., Canonical Peritus. Email: oangel@cdob.org; 1910 E. Elizabeth St., P.O. Box 2279, Brownsville, 78522-2279. Tel: 956-542-2501; Fax: 956-542-6751.

Diocesan Relations—700 N. Virgen de San Juan Blvd., San Juan, 78589. Tel: 956-781-5323; Fax: 956-784-5096. Mrs. Brenda Nettles Riojas, Dir.. Email: bnrpr@cdob.org.

Fiscal Office—1910 E. Elizabeth St., P.O. Box 2279, Brownsville, 78522-2279. Tel: 956-542-2501, Ext. 336; Fax: 956-550-1563. Mr. Jack Graham, Comptroller. Email: jgraham@cdob.org.

Accountant—Mr. Joel Ruiz. Tel: 956-550-1532. Email: jruiz@cdob.org.

Accounting Clerks—Ms. Gertrudis "Trudy" Contreras. Tel: 956-550-1538. Email: tcontreras@cdob.org.

Parish/School Accounting—Auditors: Mr. Ruben Olivares. Tel: 956-550-1537. Email: rolivares@cdob.org; Mrs. Socorro Padilla. Tel: 956-784-5019. Email: spadilla@cdob.org; Mrs. Sara Salas, Clerk. Tel: 956-550-1533. Email: ssalas@cdob.org.

Information Systems—1910 E. Elizabeth St., P.O. Box 2279, Brownsville, 78522-2279. Tel: 956-542-2501, Ext. 321; Fax: 956-550-1585. *700 N. Virgen de San Juan Blvd., San Juan, 78589.* Tel: 956-784-5004; Fax: 956-784-5097. Mr. Alberto Zavala, Dir. Tel: 956-550-1521. Email: azavala@cdob.org. Technicians: Mr. Daniel McGuffin. Tel: 956-784-5004. Email: dmcguffin@cdob.org; Mr. Leonardo Mendez. Tel: 956-550-1547. Email: lmendez@cdob.org.

Human Resources Office—1910 E. Elizabeth St., P.O. Box 2279, Brownsville, 78522-2279. Tel: 956-542-2501, Ext. 319; Fax: 956-542-6751. Mrs. Genoveva Trevino, Dir.. Email: gtrevino@cdob.org; Ms. Ninfa Cortina, Sec. Tel: 956-550-1519. Email: ncortina@cdob.org.

Insurance and Pensions—1910 E. Elizabeth St., P.O. Box 2279, Brownsville, 78522-2279. Tel: 956-542-2501, Ext. 349; Fax: 956-542-6751. Ms. Judy Plata, Dir.. Email: jplata@cdob.org; Mrs. Patricia Gomez, Insurance Asst. Tel: 956-550-1549. Email: pgomez@cdob.org; Mr. Edgar Aguilar, Clerk. Tel: 956-550-1557. Email: eaguilar@cdob.org.

Building/Property/Construction Management—700 N. Virgen de San Juan Blvd., San Juan, 78589. Tel: 956-781-5323; Fax: 956-784-5096. Mr. Javier Solis, Dir.. Email: jsolis@cdob.org.

Vicar for the Clergy—Rev. Gerard Barrett, O.M.I., Our Lady, Star of the Sea, Box 6504, Port Isabel, 78578. Tel: 956-943-1297; Fax: 956-943-1422.

Office for Vocations—5208 S. 494 Highway, Mission, 78572. Tel: 956-585-7078; Fax: 956-424-9851. Rev. Juan Victor Heredia. Email: jheredia@cdob.org.

Office for Seminarians—5208 S. 494 Hwy., Mission, 78572. Tel: 956-585-7078; Fax: 956-424-9851. Rev. Juan Victor Heredia, Dir.; Ms. Debbie Murillo, Sec.. Email: dmurillo@cdob.org; Ms. Patty Gonzalez. Email: pgonzalez@cdob.org.

Office for Permanent Deacons—Vacant, Dir.

Division for Communications—Rev. Pedro Briseno, Coord., P.O. Box 2147, Harlingen, 78551. Tel: 956-421-4111; Fax: 956-421-4150. Email: pbriseno@aol.com.

Division for Evangelization—Rev. Msgr. Juan Nicolau, Coord., 400 Virgen de San Juan Blvd., San Juan, 78589. Tel: 956-787-0033; Fax: 956-787-2908. Email: frnicolau@aol.com; Mr. Enrique de la Cruz, Asst. Coord. Tel: 956-371-3923. Email: kekahotejas@cs.com; Mrs. Julie Alvarado, Donor Correspondence.

Director for Hispanic Ministry—Mr. Enrique de la Cruz, 700 N. Virgen de San Juan Blvd., San Juan, 78589. Tel: 956-781-5323; Fax: 956-784-5081.

Episcopal Vicar for Religious—Rev. Louis Brum, P.O. Box 1159, Alamo, 78516. Tel: 956-787-2963; Fax: 956-787-6788; Sr. Norma Pimentel, M.J., Asst. Tel: 956-781-5323; Fax: 956-784-5096.

Division for Youth and Young Adult Ministry—Coordinator and Chaplain—Rev. Hilary Brzezinski, O.F.M.

UTB/TSC Campus—Mrs. Hilda Escandon, Campus Minister; Mr. Juan Pablo Cantu, Asst. Campus Minister; Miss Vanessa Serrano, Part-time Sec. & Clerk; Miss Jessica Alcantara, Part-time Sec. & Clerk, 1850 Ridgely Rd., Brownsville, Tx 78520. Tel: 956 542-3942; 956-541-9697; Fax: 956-542-3942.

UTPA Campus—Mr. Alfonso Liguez, Campus Minister; Ms. Hermelinda Salinas, Asst. Campus Minister; Ms. Dulce Cantu, Asst. Campus Minister, 1615 Kuhn St., Edinburg, 78539. Tel: 956-383-0133; Fax: 956-387-0738.

Division for Catholic Charities—Sr. Norma Pimentel, M.J., Dir.; Mr. Walter Lukaszek, L.M.S.W., Consultant, 700 N. Virgen de San Juan Blvd., San Juan, 78589. Tel: 956-702-4088; Fax: 956-784-5096.

Diocesan Campaign for Human Development—Rev. Carlos A. Villarreal, 1910 E. Elizabeth St., P.O. Box 2279, Brownsville, 78522-2279. Tel: 956-550-1510; Fax: 956-542-6751.

Diocesan Catholic Relief Services—Rev. Eduardo Ortega, 700 N. Virgen de San Juan Blvd., San Juan, 78589. Tel: 956-781-5323; Fax: 956-784-5081.

Catholic Social Services—700 N. Virgen de San Juan Blvd., San Juan, 78589. Tel: 956-702-4088; Fax: 956-784-5096. Sr. Norma Pimentel, M.J., Dir.; Mr. Silvestre Rodriguez, Counselor. Tel: 956-784-5070; Mrs. Yesenia Garcia, Case Worker. Tel: 956-784-5068. 47 W. Elizabeth St., P.O. Box 2282, Brownsville, 78520. Tel: 956-541-0220; Fax: 956-544-7580; Ms Matilde Bennett, M.Ed., Counselor; Mrs. Nora H. Rodriguez, Case Worker; Mr. Yolanda Perez, Sec.

Jail Ministry—47 W. Elizabeth St., Brownsville, 78520. Tel: 956-541-0220; Fax: 956-544-7580. Mr. Jaime Gomez, Coord.; Mr. Victor Villegas, Jail Minister. Chaplains: Revs. George Gonzalez, 412 South C St., Harlingen, 78550. Tel: 956-423-0855; Lionel Lopez, 1302 Champion, Edinburg, 78539. Tel: 956-383-5472; Bro. Manuel Enrique Ruiz, O.de.M., J.C.L., P.O. Box 9023, Mission, 78572. Tel: 956-585-8001; Rev. Jose Villalon, 606 W. Ocean Blvd., Los Fresnos, 78566. Tel: 956-233-5619.

Immigration Counseling Services—700 N. Virgen de San Juan Blvd., San Juan, 78589. Tel: 956-781-5323; Fax: 956-784-5096. *47 W. Elizabeth St., Brownsville, 78520.* Tel: 956-541-0220; Fax: 956-544-7580. Mrs. Santa Acuna, Coord.. Email: sacuna@cdob.org.

Division for Education and Formation—Tel: 956-787-8571; Fax: 956-784-5081.

Coordinator—Sisters Marcella Ewers, D.C., 700 N. Virgen de San Juan Blvd., San Juan, 78589-3042. Tel: 956-784-5050. Email: mewers@cdob.org; Charles Anne Solomon, O.P., Asst. Coord. Tel: 956-784-5052. Email: casolomon@cdob.org.

Media Resource/Library Coordinator—Sr. Maureen Crosby, S.S.D. Tel: 956-784-5041. Email: mcrosby@cdob.org.

San Juan Ministry Institute—Rev. Eduardo Ortega. Email: eortega@cdob.org.

Catholic Schools Office—700 N. Virgen de San Juan Blvd., San Juan, 78589-3042. Tel: 956-781-5323. Sisters Marcella Ewers, D.C., Supt.. Email: mewers@cdob.org; Charles Anne Solomon, O.P., Counselor & Asst. Supt.. Email: csolomon@cdob.org.

Family Life Office—700 N. Virgen de San Juan Blvd., San Juan, 78589-3042. Tel: 956-781-5323. Mrs. Lydia Pesina, Dir.. Email: lpesina@cdob.org; Ms. Elsa Cantu, Assoc. Dir.. Email: ecantu@cdob.org; Mrs. Willy Kopecky, Natural Family Planning, 1012 W. Third St., Weslaco, 78596. Tel: 956-969-3079.

Encuentro Matrimonial—Jesus Cano; Isabel Cano, 509 Orange Heights, Harlingen, 78550. Tel: 956-423-6431. Email: cano5_91@hotmail.com.

Engaged Encounter—Richard Loya; Rosie Loya, 2510 Lazy Lake, Harlingen, 78550. Tel: 956-428-4262.

Marriage Encounter—Tom Oaks; Angela Oaks, 513 E. Yarrow, McAllen, 78504. Tel: 956-994-3083.

Movimiento Familiar Cristiano—Jacinto Rodriguez; Marisela Rodriguez, (Fed West), 100 W. Moore Rd. #5, Pharr, 78577. Tel: 956-783-9682; Daniel Navarro; Alma Navarro, 5768 Paseo Real. Tel: 956-838-5417.

Office of Catechesis—700 N. Virgen de San Juan Blvd., San Juan, 78589-3042. Tel: 956-784-5040. Sr. Marguerite Broderick, D.C., Dir.. Email: mbroderick@cdob.org.

Division for Health Care Ministries—

Coordinator—Rev. Edouard Atangana, 700 N. Virgen de San Juan Blvd., San Juan, 78589. Tel: 956-781-5323; Fax: 956-784-5096.

Director for Pro-Life Activities—Rev. Matthias Shanley, SS.CC., 1509 New Combes Hwy., Harlingen, 78550. Tel: 956-423-6341.

Hospital Chaplains—Rev. Edouard Atangana, Coord., 700 N. Virgen de San Juan Blvd., San Juan, 78589. Tel: 956-781-5323; Fax: 956-784-5096.

Brownsville Medical Center—Sr. Gloria Morales, M.J., 1040 W. Jefferson, Brownsville, 78520. Tel: 956-544-1426; Fax: 956-541-0723.

Edinburg Regional Medical Center—Sr. Emma Marie Stillman, I.W.B.S., 1102 W. Trenton, Edinburg, 78541. Tel: 956-388-6235; Fax: 956-388-6020.

Knapp Medical Center—P.O. Box 1110, Weslaco, 78599. Tel: 956-968-8567; Fax: 956-968-6290.

McAllen Medical Center—Sr. Ebere Anosike, D.D.L.; Mr. Demetrio Tafoya, 301 W. Exwy. 83, McAllen, 78503. Tel: 956-632-4177; Fax: 956-632-4010.

McAllen Heart Hospital—Sr. Therese Anne Ridge, I.W.B.S., 1900 S. D St., McAllen, 78503. Tel: 956-994-2107; Fax: 956-994-2090.

Mission Hospital—Ms. Judy Krese, 900 S. Bryan Rd., Mission, 78572. Tel: 956-584-4562; Fax: 956-580-9430.

Rio Grande Regional Hospital—Sr. Helen Roper, S.S.N.D., 101 E. Ridge, McAllen, 78503. Tel: 956-632-6616; Fax: 956-632-6621.

Star Co. Memorial Hospital—Sr. Anne Miriam Landolt, S.S.N.D, P.O. Box 78, Rio Grande City, 78582. Tel: 956-487-5561, Ext. 2296; Fax: 956-487-0332. Valley Baptist Medical Center: Rev. Frank Clancy, S.C.J.; Sr. Theresa Han, O.S.F.; Deacon Ignacio R. Gonzales, 2101 Peace, Harlingen, 78550. Tel: 956-389-1194; Fax: 956-389-1189.

Valley Regional Medical Center—Dr. Ethel Winchester Didsbury, P.O. Box 5107, Brownsville, 78520. Tel: 956-350-7124.

Diocesan Attorney—Mr. David Garza, 680 E. St. Charles, Brownsville, 78520. Tel: 956-541-4914; Fax: 956-542-7403.

Presbyteral Council—Revs. Rodolfo Franco, Catholic Charities Commission; Robert E. Maher, V.G., Communications Commission; Pedro Briseno, Education & Formation Commission; Honecimo Figueroa, Evangelization Commission; Rev. Msgr. Gustavo Barrera, Health Care Commission; Rev. Samuel Arizpe, Justice & Peace Commission; Rev. Msgr. Juan Nicolau, Marriage & Family Life Commission; Revs. Carlos A. Villarreal, Basilica of the National Shrine of Our Lady of San Juan del Valle Commission; Philip Sosa,

M.S.F., Parish Needs Commission; GERARD BARRETT, O.M.I., Clergy Life & Ministry; EMMANUEL BIALONCIK, O.F.M., Vocations & Jr. College Seminarians; HORACIO CHAVARRIA, Liturgy & Worship Commission; HEBERTO M. DIAZ JR., Youth & Young Adult Ministry.

Ad Hoc Committee for Diocesan Insurance—Revs. LOUIS L. BRUM; PEDRO BRISENO; Rev. Msgr. JUAN NICOLAU; Revs. ROBERT E. MAHER, V.G.; GREGORY M. SPECK, S.C.J.; CARLOS ZUNIGA.

Diocesan College of Consultors—Revs. PEDRO BRISENO; GERARD BARRETT, O.M.I.; HEBERTO M. DIAZ JR.; RODOLFO FRANCO; ROBERT MAHER, V.G.

Parish Priests' Consultors & Priest Personnel Board—Revs. HEBERTO M. DIAZ JR.; ALFONSO GUEVARA; RODOLFO FRANCO; IGNACIO LUNA; Rev. Msgr. JUAN NICOLAU; Rev. THOMAS PINCELLI.

Diocesan Finance Council—Most Rev. RAYMUNDO J. PENA, D.D.; Mr. NOBLE ALLEN; Rev. PEDRO BRISENO; Mr. ALONZO CANTU; Mr. FRANK COSTILLA; Mr. CHARLES ELLARD; Mr. H. HUGH EMERSON; Ms. THELMA GARCIA; Mr. ED TAMAYO; Rev. ROBERT E. MAHER, V.G.

Catholic Foundation of the Rio Grande Valley—Ms. EVANA DAVIZ; Ms. HILDA ESCALON; Mr. RODOLFO GARCIA; Ms. GRACIELA GUTIERREZ; Mr. TOMAS REVESZ; Mr. PAUL RODRIGUEZ; Mr. RICHARD WALKER, P.O. Box 2279, Brownsville, 78522-2279. Tel: 956-542-2501; Fax: 956-542-6751.

Building Committee—Most Rev. RAYMUNDO J. PENA, D.D.; Revs. ROBERT E. MAHER, V.G.; LOUIS L. BRUM; Mr. JOSE A. CHANIN; Mr. OSCAR FALCON; Mr. CESAR R. PEREZ; Mr. MICHAEL E. VOURCOS; Mr. JIM MOFFITT; Mr. ARTURO GUERRA; Mr. ROEL RODRIGUEZ.

The Basilica of the National Shrine of Our Lady of San Juan Del Valle—

Board of Directors—Most Rev. RAYMUNDO J. PENA, D.D.; Rev. Msgr. JUAN NICOLAU; Mr. RICHARD ALANIZ; Judge ROBERTO GARZA; Mr. JORGE MEDINA; Mr. LOUIE TIJERINA; Rev. CARLOS A. VILLARREAL; Mr. BENITO MARTINEZ, Consultant.

Youth and Young Adult Steering Committee—Mr. FRANCISCO "PACO" CASTELLANOS; Ms. MERCEDES MEDINA; Mrs. BOBBIE PACHECO; Mr. SAM SALDANA; Rev. JOSE M. VILLALON; Mr. LUIS ZUNIGA; Ms. PURA REYNA.

Housing Board—Mr. RICARDO HERNANDEZ; Mr. OCTAVIANO GONZALEZ; Mr. ROEL A. RODRIGUEZ; Mr. RIGOBERTO SALINAS; Mrs. ANA ZAMARRIPA, Housing Mgr., El Rosario Homes, P.O. Box 971, Mission, 78572. Tel: 956-585-5051; Fax: 956-585-9938. La Merced Homes, P.O. Box 806, Mercedes, 78570. Tel: 956-565-2622; Fax: 956-565-4185.

Office for Propagation of the Faith—Rev. LUIS JAVIER GARCIA, J.C.L., P.O. Box 2279, Brownsville, 78522-2279. Tel: 956-542-2501. Email: lgarcia@cdob.org.

Office for the Church in Latin America—Rev. LUIS J. GARCIA, J.C.L., P.O. Box 2279, Brownsville, 78522-2279. Tel: 956-542-2501. Email: lgarcia@cdob.org.

Serra Club International—Mr. ED GARCIA, District Governor of Serra Club, P.O. Box 4348, McAllen, 78502. Tel: 956-618-3626. Brownsville: Mr. MANUEL VILLARREAL, Pres., 106 E. 8th St., Los Fresnos, 78566. Tel: 956-233-6781; Rev. CARLOS A. VILLARREAL, 1910 E. Elizabeth St., Brownsville, 78520. Tel: 956-542-2501. McAllen: Mr. AL BELTRAN, Pres., P.O. Box 4348, McAllen, 78502. Tel: 956-661-4001; Rev. BRIAN VAN HOVE, S.J., Chap., 5208 S. 494 Hwy., Mission, 78572. Rio Grande City: Ms. DOLORES S. GOMEZ, Pres., Rio Grande Serra Club, 506 E. Hidalgo, Rio Grande City, 78582. Tel: 956-487-3266; Rev. HONECIMO FIGUEROA, Chap., 5208 S. 494 Hwy., Mission, 78572. Harlingen: Mr. JOSE GUSTAVO GONZALEZ, Pres., 27218 McLelland Rd., Harlingen, 78552. Tel: 956-428-0624.

Boy Scouts—Rev. MARIO A. CASTRO, P.O. Box 451, Rio Hondo, 78583. Tel: 956-748-2327; Fax: 956-748-0089.

Knights of Columbus—Mr. WILBERT C. CARDENAS, Diocesan Deputy, 714 S. Texas Blvd., Weslaco, 78596. Tel: 956-968-0412. Email: wcard1148@aol.com; Mr. RENE RAMIREZ, Asst. Diocesan Deputy, 1500 Ebano St., San Benito, 78582. Tel: 956-399-7968.

District Deputies—JESUS D. HERNANDEZ, 125 N. McCullough, San Benito, 78582. Tel: 956-399-2776. Email: herjd@aol.com; JORGE A. PALACIOS, 1306 S. Kumquat, Pharr, 78577. Tel: 956-783-8506. Email: jorgepal@hotmail.com; Mr. FERNANDO RAMIREZ, 6351 Bocachica Blvd., Brownsville, 78521. Tel: 956-831-0086; Mr. DANIEL C. CAUER, 28823 McLelland Rd., Harlingen, 78552. Tel: 956-428-7954; RUBEN E. LOPEZ, P.O. Box 424, Mission, 78573. Tel: 956-585-0082. Email: jollyman2004@yahoo.com; ROMER FAJUTAG, 2805 Thunderbird Ave., McAllen, 78504. Tel: 956-682-0554. Email: fajutagr@asapogencytx.com; REYNALDO RIOJAS JR., 510 W. 12th, Weslaco, 78596. Tel: 956-968-0936; Mr. ROLANDO MARTINEZ, 1119 Bianca Ct., Alamo, 78516. Tel: 956-783-5758.

Victim Assistance Coordinator—Mr. WALTER LUKASZEK, L.M.S.W. Tel: 956-781-5323. Email: wlukaszek@cdob.org.

CLERGY, PARISHES, MISSIONS AND PAROCHIAL SCHOOLS

CITY OF BROWNSVILLE
(CAMERON COUNTY)

1—IMMACULATE CONCEPTION CATHEDRAL (1849), Revs. Pasquale Lanese, O.M.I.; Rufino Nava, O.M.I. (LA); Deacons John Kinch; Arturo Rodriguez.
Res.: 1218 E. Jefferson St., P.O. Box 311, 78522. Tel: 956-546-3178; Fax: 956-546-1284.
Catechesis/Religious Program—Mrs. Maria Galindo, D.R.E. Students 233.
Mission—St. Thomas 155 E. Jefferson St., Cameron Co. 78520.
Mission—Sacred Heart 602 E. Elizabeth St., Cameron Co. 78520.
Chapel—La Muralla D St., 78520.

2—CHRIST THE KING (1953), Revs. Heberto M. Diaz Jr.; Jean Olivier Mbodo Sambu; Deacon Roberto Cano.
2255 Southmost Rd., 78521. Tel: 956-546-1982; Fax: 956-546-7120.
Catechesis/Religious Program—Tel: 956-546-5147. Mrs. Elva Reyes, D.R.E. Students 400.
Mission—Blessed Juan Diego de Guadalupe 4180 S. Browne, Cameron Co. 78521.

3—CHURCH OF THE GOOD SHEPHERD (1968), Rev. Rafael Hernandez; Deacon Paul McArdle.
Res.: 2645 Tulipan, 78521. Tel: 956-542-5142; Fax: 956-542-5278.
Catechesis/Religious Program—Mrs. Arabella Garcia, D.R.E. Students 627.

4—ST. EUGENE DE MAZENOD (1996), Rev. Harry Schuckenbrock, O.M.I.
Res.: 5409 Austin Rd., 78251. Tel: 956-831-9923; Fax: 956-831-3110.
Catechesis/Religious Program—Ms. Rosario Rangel, D.R.E., (Grades K-6); Ms. Belinda Rodriguez, D.R.E., (Grades 7-12). Students 344.

5—HOLY FAMILY (1966), Rev. Martin de la Cruz; Deacon Alejandro Flores.
Res.: 2308 E. Tyler, 78520. Tel: 956-546-6975; Fax: 956-550-8884.
Catechesis/Religious Program—Tel: 956-550-9993. Ms. Cindy Gonzalez, D.R.E. Students 379.

6—ST. JOSEPH (1953), Rev. Jamie Cabanas; Deacon Felipe Trevino.
Mailing Address: P.O. Box 3407, 78523-3407.
Res.: 555 W. St. Francis St., 78520. Tel: 956-542-2709; Fax: 956-546-5162.
Catechesis/Religious Program—Tel: 956-546-4894. Mrs. Sandra Huerta, D.R.E. Students 273.

7—ST. LUKE (1974), Rev. Esteban Hernandez, M.S.F.; Deacon Andres Munoz.
Res.: 2800 Rockwell Dr., 78521. Tel: 956-541-1480; Fax: 956-542-8043.
School—2850 Price Rd., 78521. Tel: 956-544-7982; Fax: 956-544-4874. Dr. Christina Saavedra, Prin. Lay Teachers 17; Students 234.
Catechesis/Religious Program—Sr. Dorothy Carey, S.H.Sp., D.R.E. Students 719.

8—MARY, MOTHER OF THE CHURCH (1967), Rev. Msgr. Gustavo Barrera; Rev. Tom Kulleck; Deacons Gilbert Borja; Roberto Cano; Heriberto Solis; Heriberto Trevino; Juan Pablo Navarro. In Res., Most Rev. John J. Fitzpatrick (Retired).
Res.: 1914 Barnard Rd., 78520-8247. Tel: 956-546-3800; Fax: 956-546-1589.
School—1300 Los Ebanos Blvd., 78520. Tel: 956-546-1805; Fax: 956-546-0787. Mr. Juan Barreda, Prin. Religious 1; Lay Teachers 31; Students 549.
Catechesis/Religious Program—Mrs. Betty Bonnet, D.R.E. Students 685.

9—OUR LADY OF GOOD COUNSEL (1966), Rev. Larry Klein; Deacons Enrique Saldana; Alvino C. Olvera.
1055 Military Hwy., 78520. Tel: 956-541-8341; Fax: 956-548-0229.
Catechesis/Religious Program—Sisters Leticia Benavides, M.J., D.R.E.; Juliana Garcia, M.J., D.R.E. Students 433.
Mission—San Pedro San Pedro, Cameron Co.

10—OUR LADY OF GUADALUPE (1928), Rev. Francisco Acosta; Deacons Bruno Cedillo; Ramon G. Leal.
Res.: 1200 E. Lincoln St., 78521. Tel: 956-542-4823; Fax: 956-542-5944.
Catechesis/Religious Program—Tel: 956-542-3619. Miss Angelica Huerta, D.R.E. Students 269.

11—SAN FELIPE DE JESUS (1996), Rev. Michael Seifert, S.M.; Bro. Albert Phillipp, F.M.S., Pastoral Assoc.
Mailing Address: P.O. Box 8093, 78526-8093.
Res.: 2215 Avenida Rancho Viejo, 78521. Tel: 956-982-2007; Fax: 956-541-4177.
Catechesis/Religious Program—Fax: 956-982-2035. Ms. Isabel Velasquez, D.R.E. Students 222.

OUTSIDE THE CITY OF BROWNSVILLE

ALAMO, HIDALGO CO., RESURRECTION (1926),, (Formerly St. Joseph/Our Lady of Fatima) Revs. Louis L. Brum; Felix A. Cazares; Deacon Jesus P. Galvan.
Res.: 834 E. Citrus St., P.O. Box 1159, 78516. Tel: 956-787-2963; Fax: 956-787-6788.
Catechesis/Religious Program—Sr. Margarita Vargas, D.R.E. Students 611.

ALTON, HIDALGO CO., SAN MARTIN DE PORRES (1967), Rev. Julian Becerril, O.de.M.
Mailing Address: P.O. Box 9023, Mission, 78572.
Res.: 1111 W. Main St., 78572. Tel: 956-585-8001; Fax: 956-585-0715.
Catechesis/Religious Program—Tel: 956-585-3125. Students 625.

DONNA, HIDALGO CO., ST. JOSEPH (1928), Revs. Herman J. Defler, M.S.F.; Philip Sosa, M.S.F.; James Lienert, M.S.F.; James Beegan, M.S.F.; Deacon Eduardo Ovalle Sr.
Res.: 306 S. D Salinas Blvd., 78537. Tel: 956-464-3331; Fax: 956-464-6808.
Catechesis/Religious Program—Tel: 956-464-3472. Mrs. Liza G. Tobias, D.R.E. Students 765.
Mission—Christ the King S. FM 493, Colonia Nueva, Hidalgo Co.

EDCOUCH, HIDALGO CO., ST. THERESA OF THE INFANT JESUS (1948), Rev. Gregory M. Kuczmanski.
Res.: 200 P. Salazar, P.O. Box 307, 78538. Tel: 956-262-1347; Fax: 956-262-1348.
Catechesis/Religious Program—Miss Marta Martinez, D.R.E. Students 284.
Mission—Our Lady of Guadalupe 200 N. Laurel, La Villa, Hidalgo Co. 78562.

EDINBURG, HIDALGO CO.

1—HOLY FAMILY (1967), Rev. Lionel Lopez; Deacon Ruben Lopez.
Res.: 1302 E. Champion, 78539-4864. Tel: 956-383-5472; Fax: 956-383-5034.
Catechesis/Religious Program—Tel: 956-383-4593. Ms. Susie de la Garza, D.R.E. Students 519.

2—ST. JOSEPH (1948), Rev. Robert E. Maher, V.G.; Deacons Silvestre Garcia; Irineo Gonzalez Jr.
Res.: 122 W. Fay St., 78539. Tel: 956-383-3728; Fax: 956-383-8630.
School—119 W. Fay St., 78539. Tel: 956-383-3957; Fax: 956-318-0681. Sr. Kathleen Murray, D.C., Prin. Religious 1; Lay Teachers 17; Students 260.
Catechesis/Religious Program—Mrs. Ann Ameling, D.R.E. Students 619.

3—SACRED HEART (1927), Rev. Zdzislaw E. Swiniarski, S.S.; Deacons Jose Solis; Gilberto Lopez. In Res., Rev. Fredrick Meyer, SS.CC.
Res.: 215 N. 16th Ave., 78539. Tel: 956-383-3253; Fax: 956-383-7311.
Catechesis/Religious Program—Tel: 956-383-4631. Mrs. Elodia Espinosa, D.R.E.; Ms. Susan Mercado, D.R.E. Students 1,101.
Mission—Capilla de San Jose 4101 Fores St., Lull, Hidalgo Co.

ELSA, HIDALGO CO., SACRED HEART (1948), Revs. Emmanuel Bialoncik, O.F.M.; Hilary Brzezinski, O.F.M.
Res.: 1100 N. Broadway, P.O. Box 6, 78543. Tel: 956-262-1406; Fax: 956-262-4265.
Catechesis/Religious Program—Mrs. Frances Rocha, D.R.E. Students 1,049.
Mission—Christ the King, Holy Cross Catechetical Center Mile 15, Monte Alto, Hidalgo Co. 78538.

ESCOBARES, STARR CO., SACRED HEART (1967), Rev. Gabriel I. Ezeh.
Res.: P.O. Box 1180, Roma, 78584. Tel: 956-849-1741; Fax: 956-847-1502.
Catechesis/Religious Program—Mr. Rolando Munoz, D.R.E. Students 220.
Mission—Santa Rosa de Lima Rosita, Starr Co.
Mission—Our Lady of Guadalupe FM 649, El Sauz, Starr Co.

GRULLA, STARR CO., HOLY FAMILY (1967), Rev. Terrence Gorski, O.F.M.; Deacons Benito Saenz; Rodolfo Carlos Salinas.
Res.: P.O. Box 67, 78548. Tel: 956-487-3365; Fax: 956-487-4727.
Catechesis/Religious Program—Mrs. Norma Solis, D.R.E. Students 222.
Mission—La Victoria N. FM 2360, Cristo Rey, Starr Co.
Mission—Our Lady of the Peace FM 1430, La Casita, Starr Co.

HARLINGEN, CAMERON CO.

1—ST. ANTHONY (1940), Revs. Thomas L. Pincelli; Edouard Atangana.
Res.: 209 S. 10th, 78550. Tel: 956-428-6111; Fax:

956-428-4276.
School—1015 E. Harrison St., 78550. Tel: 956-423-2486; Fax: 956-412-0084. Ms. Margaret Van Nostrand, Prin. Religious 1; Lay Teachers 23; Students 257.
Catechesis/Religious Program—Tel: 956-428-2476; Fax: 956-425-8969. Mrs. Melba Gonzalez, D.R.E. Students 502.

2—IMMACULATE HEART OF MARY (1927), Revs. Pedro Briseno; Eusebio Martinez; Deacon Juan Valenzuela. In Res., Rev. George Gonzalez.
Res.: 412 S. C St., 78550. Tel: 956-423-0855; Fax: 956-421-1071.
Catechesis/Religious Program—Sr. Armida Rangel, D.R.E. Students 405.

3—OUR LADY OF THE ASSUMPTION (1958), Rev. Horacio Chavarria; Deacons Ignacio Gonzales; Jesus Reyes.
1313 W. Buchanan St., 78550. Tel: 956-423-4670; Fax: 956-423-5970.
Catechesis/Religious Program—Tel: 956-423-1765. Ms. Virginia Lopez, D.R.E. Students 832.
Mission— 1706 Rangerville Rd., San Felipe, Austin Co. 77473.

4—QUEEN OF PEACE (1967), Revs. Matthias Shanley, SS.CC.; Alphonsus McHugh, SS.CC.; Deacon Genaro Ibarra.
Res.: 1509 New Combes Hwy., 78550. Tel: 956-423-6341; Fax: 956-423-2864.
Catechesis/Religious Program—Tel: 956-425-2830. Mrs. Dora Schoonover, D.R.E. Students 461.

HIDALGO, HIDALGO CO., SACRED HEART (1967), Rev. Mario A. Aviles, C.O.
Res.: 308 E. Camelia St., P.O. Box 742, 78557. Tel: 956-843-2463; Fax: 956-843-2187.
Catechesis/Religious Program—Mrs. Eliza Garza, D.R.E. Students 253.

LA FERIA, CAMERON CO., ST. FRANCIS XAVIER (1930), Revs. Plutarco Belanggoy, C.I.C.M.; Andre B. Kazadi, C.I.C.M.
Res.: 500 S. Canal St., P.O. Box 116, 78559. Tel: 956-797-2666; Fax: 956-797-3387.
Catechesis/Religious Program—Tel: 956-797-5568. Mrs. San Juanita Betancourt, D.R.E. Students 621.

LA JOYA, HIDALGO CO., OUR LADY, QUEEN OF ANGELS (1960), Rev. Gerald W. Frank; Deacons Alberto Chapa; Lucio Flores.
Res.: 916 S. Leo Ave., P.O. Drawer D, 78560. Tel: 956-585-5223; Fax: 956-585-4878.
Catechesis/Religious Program—Sr. Emily Jocson, I.C.M., D.R.E. Students 629.
Mission—St. Mary Magdalene Abram, Hidalgo Co.
Mission—St. Anthony Penitas, Hidalgo Co.
Mission—St. Michael Los Ebanos, Hidalgo Co.
Mission—St. William Sullivan City, Hidalgo Co.

LOS FRESNOS, CAMERON CO., ST. CECILIA (1964), Rev. Jose M. Villalon; Deacon Augusto Chapa Jr.
Res.: 606 W. Ocean Blvd., 78566. Tel: 956-233-5619; Fax: 956-233-5565.
Catechesis/Religious Program—Tel: 956-233-5213. Mrs. Yolanda de la Rosa, D.R.E. Students 842.
Mission—Our Heavenly Father Old Hwy. 77 Parker & Mesqui, Olmito, Cameron Co. 78575.

LYFORD, WILLACY CO., PRINCE OF PEACE (1967), Revs. David Jackson, S.C.J.; Gregory Speck, S.C.J.; Anthony Kelly, S.C.J.
Res.: 1100 Park Ave., P.O. Box 460, 78569. Tel: 956-347-3580; Fax: 956-347-3649.
Catechesis/Religious Program—Students 317.
Mission—Santa Monica FM 1018 & 1420, Santa Monica, Willacy Co.
Mission—St. Martin Box 247/345, Sebastian, Willacy Co. 78594.

MCALLEN, HIDALGO CO.

1—HOLY SPIRIT (1981), Revs. Brian Van Hove, S.J.; Faustin Misakabo, O.Praem. (GE); Deacons Carlos S. Trevino; Alvin H. Gerbermann.
Res.: 2201 Martin Ave., 78504. Tel: 956-631-5295; Fax: 956-631-5460.
School—Preschool & Day Care Center, Tel: 956-682-6562. Mrs. Toni F. Espinoza, Dir. Lay Teachers 6; Students 76.
Catechesis/Religious Program—Tel: 956-664-2518. Mrs. Martha Sanchez, D.R.E. Students 1,137.

2—ST. JOSEPH THE WORKER (1967), Rev. Alfonso M. Guevara; Deacons Alejandro Gamboa; Salvador Rojas.
Res.: 2315 Ithaca St., 78501. Tel: 956-682-1351; Fax: 956-618-3317.
Catechesis/Religious Program—Tel: 956-686-6871. Sr. Maria T. Sanchez, M.C.D.P., D.R.E. Students 788.

3—SAINT JUAN DIEGO CUAUHTLATOAZIN (2002), Rev. Carlos Zuniga; Deacon Salvador Rojas.
Mailing Address: 3309 Helena St., 78503.
Res.: 3400 Idela St., 78503. Tel: 965-682-5155; Fax: 956-682-5472.
Catechesis/Religious Program—Mr. Jose A. Gutierrez, D.R.E.; Mrs. Rosa Gutierrez, D.R.E. Students 538.

4—OUR LADY OF PERPETUAL HELP (1967), Rev. Genaro Henriquez; Deacon Rene Villalon Sr.
Res.: 2209 Kendlewood Ave., 78501. Tel: 956-682-4238; Fax: 956-682-0289.
Catechesis/Religious Program—Tel: 956-682-3663. Students 528.

5—OUR LADY OF SORROWS (1941), Rev. Agostinho S. Pacheco; Deacons John Schwarz; Israel Sagredo.
Res.: 1108 Hackberry St., 78501-4304. Tel: 956-686-0251; Fax: 956-686-0322.
School—1100 Gumwood, 78501. Tel: 956-686-3651; Fax: 956-686-1996. Mrs. Jeanne L. Bruton, Prin. & Dir. of Day Care. Lay Teachers 29; Students 579.
School—Day Care
Catechesis/Religious Program—Sr. Jean Eloise Rodriguez, M.C.D.P., D.R.E. Students 947.

6—SACRED HEART (1917), Revs. Louis J Villarreal, O.M.I.; Henry Janssen, O.M.I.; Deacon Eduardo Reyna.
Res.: 306 S. 15th St., P.O. Box 370, 78505-0370. Tel: 956-686-7711; Fax: 956-686-2028.
Catechesis/Religious Program—Ms. Sandra Kent, D.R.E. Students 403.

MCCOOK, HIDALGO CO., IMMACULATE CONCEPTION (1950), Rev. Honecimo Figueroa.
28212 FM 2058, Edinburg, 78541. Tel: 956-842-3663; 956-481-3392.
Catechesis/Religious Program—Fax: 956-481-3392.

MERCEDES, HIDALGO CO.

1—OUR LADY OF MERCY (1909), Rev. George Kerketta.
Res.: 322 S. Vermont Ave., P.O. Box 805, 78570. Tel: 956-565-1141; Fax: 956-565-1640.
Catechesis/Religious Program—Tel: 956-565-3441. Mrs. Angie G. Garza, D.R.E. Students 462.

2—SACRED HEART CHURCH (1969), Rev. Celso Tabalanza, C.I.C.M.; Deacon Roberto Cantu.
Res.: 920 Anacuitas, 78570. Tel: 956-565-0271; Fax: 956-565-0272.
Catechesis/Religious Program—Mrs. Juanita Escandon, D.R.E. Students 447.

MISSION, HIDALGO CO.

1—OUR LADY OF GUADALUPE (1899), [CEM] Rev. Roy Lee Snipes, O.M.I.; Deacon Bill Castaneda.
Res.: 620 Dunlap St., P.O. Box 1047, 78572-1047. Tel: 956-585-2623; Fax: 956-584-5856.
Catechesis/Religious Program—Tel: 956-585-1376. Sr. Maria Guadalupe Lopez, M.C.P., D.R.E. Students 1,211.
Chapel—La Lomita

2—OUR LADY OF ST. JOHN OF THE FIELDS (1967), Rev. Francisco Castillo; Deacons Daniel Zamora; Peter Requenez.
Res.: 1052 Washington St., 78572. Tel: 956-585-2325; Fax: 956-585-7270.
Catechesis/Religious Program—Tel: 956-581-1289. Mrs Ana Maria Middlebrook, D.R.E. Students 591.

3—OUR LADY OF THE HOLY ROSARY (1968), Rev. Vicente Azcoiti.
Res: 923 Matamoros St., P.O. Box 1439, 78572. Tel: 956-581-2193; Fax: 956-581-1906.
Catechesis/Religious Program—Mrs. Olga Gomez, D.R.E. Students 205.
Mission—Our Lady of Lourdes Madero, Hidalgo Co.
Mission—Our Lady of Fatima 3634 El Camino Real, Granjeno, Hidalgo Co.

4—ST. PAUL (1915), Rev. Msgr. F. Robert DaVola; Deacons Ismael Garcia; Robert Ledesma.
Res.: 1119 Francisco Ave., 78572. Tel: 956-585-2701; Fax: 956-581-4801.
Catechesis/Religious Program—Tel: 956-585-2486. Mrs. Cindy Schaefer, D.R.E. Students 837.

PHARR, HIDALGO CO.

1—ST. ANNE, MOTHER OF MARY (1973), Rev. Ricardo Garcia, J.C.L.
Res.: 710 E. Lucas, 78577. Tel: 956-787-8122; Fax: 956-787-8272.
Catechesis/Religious Program—Tel: 956-787-5139. Sr. Bonnie McHugh, D.C., D.R.E. Students 446.

2—ST. FRANCES XAVIER CABRINI (1999), Rev. Eduardo Villa.
Mailing Address: P.O. Box 8538, Hidalgo, 78557-8538. Tel: 956-787-3554; Fax: 956-283-1354.
Church: 8001 S. Cage Blvd., 78577.
Catechesis/Religious Program—Students 270.

3—ST. JUDE THADDEUS (1951), Very Rev. Leo Francis Daniels, C.O.; Rev. Jose Encarnacion Losoya, C.O.
Res.: 505 S. Ironwood, 78577-1210. Tel: 956-781-2489; Fax: 956-783-4614.
School—Oratory Academy, P.O. Drawer ii, 78577. Tel: 956-781-3056; Fax: 956-702-3047. Mrs. G. Yvonne Perez, Dir. Religious 3; Lay Teachers 27; Students 440.
Catechesis/Religious Program—Tel: 956-781-3521. Mrs. Sochil J. Duran, D.R.E. Students 311.

4—ST. MARGARET MARY (1927) Rev. Jose Luis Garcia; Deacon Pedro F. Sanchez.
Res.: 224 N. Aster St., 78577. Tel: 956-787-8563; Fax: 956-702-4509.
Catechesis/Religious Program—Tel: 956-787-0832; Fax: 956-787-5385. Miss Diana Enriquez, D.R.E. Students 480.

PORT ISABEL, CAMERON CO., OUR LADY STAR OF THE SEA (1927), Rev. Gerard Barrett, O.M.I.
Res.: 705 S. Longoria St., Box 6504, 78578. Tel: 956-943-1297; Fax: 956-943-1422.
Catechesis/Religious Program—Tel: 956-943-6392. Mrs. Terri Lynn Hulsey, D.R.E. Students 263.

PROGRESO, HIDALGO CO., HOLY SPIRIT (1969), Rev. Thomas Matondo, C.I.C.M.; Deacon Salvador G. Saldivar.
Res.: 210 Watts Ave., P.O. Box 216, 78579. Tel: 956-565-6856; Fax: 956-565-3462.
Catechesis/Religious Program—Tel: 956-565-1572. Mrs. Yolanda Mora, D.R.E. Students 340.
Mission—St. Margaret Ann Military Hwy. 281, Santa Maria, Cameron Co. 78592.
Mission—Cristo Rey Bluetown, Cameron Co.

RANCHITO, CAMERON CO., ST. IGNATIUS (1967), Rev. Albert Lelo-Luemba, C.I.C.M.
24380 W. U.S. Hwy. 281, San Benito, 78586. Tel: 956-399-2022; Fax: 956-399-1213.
Catechesis/Religious Program—Ms. Lily Nunez, D.R.E. Students 374.
Mission—Our Lady of Lourdes La Paloma, Cameron Co.
Mission—Sacred Heart Las Rucias, Cameron Co.

RAYMONDVILLE, WILLACY CO.

1—ST. ANTHONY (1907), Revs. Pedro Briseno; Eusebio Martinez.
Res.: 464 S. First St., 78580. Tel: 956-689-3380; Fax: 956-689-3380.
Catechesis/Religious Program—Ms. Janie Garcia, D.R.E. Students 28.
Mission—St. Anne, Mother of Mary San Perlita, Willacy Co.

2—OUR LADY OF GUADALUPE (1927), Revs. Steve Pujdak, S.C.J.; Gregory M. Speck, S.C.J.; Anthony Kelly, S.C.J.; Charles Kelly, S.C.J. (GAL); Deacon Juan Francisco Gonzalez.
Res.: 693 N. Third St., 78580. Tel: 956-689-2408; Fax: 956-689-1687.
Catechesis/Religious Program—Miss Margaret Lopez, D.R.E. Students 935.
Mission—St. Patrick N. on Hwy. 1015, Lasara, Willacy Co. 78561.
Mission—St. Frances Xavier Cabrini 215 N. Couch St., Hargill, Hidalgo Co. 78549.

RIO GRANDE CITY, STARR CO., IMMACULATE CONCEPTION (1880), [CEM] Rev. Amador Garza.
Res.: 101 E. Third St., P.O. Box 1, 78582. Tel: 956-487-2317; Fax: 956-487-8246.
School—305 N. Britton Ave., 78582. Tel: 956-487-2558; Fax: 956-487-6478. Mrs. Rubirita Urbina, Prin. Religious 2; Lay Teachers 20; Students 216.
Catechesis/Religious Program—Ms. Jhune Urbina, D.R.E. Students 620.
Mission—St. Paul 5752 E. Hwy. 83, La Puerta, Starr Co. Tel: 956-487-8835.
Mission—Sacred Heart Old US Hwy. 83, Los Garcias Ranch, Starr Co. Deacon Benito Saenz.

RIO HONDO, CAMERON CO., ST. HELEN (1943), Rev. Mario A. Castro.
Res.: 228 Huisache, P.O. Box 451, 78583. Tel: 956-748-2327; Fax: 956-748-0089.
Catechesis/Religious Program—Mrs. Mary Kyser, D.R.E. Students 320.
Mission—St. Vincent de Paul Lozano, Cameron Co.

ROMA, STARR CO., OUR LADY OF REFUGE (1853), Revs. Richard Sheehan, O.M.I.; Richard Philion, O.M.I.
Res.: St. Eugene de Mazenod Ave., P.O. Box 156, 78584. Tel: 956-849-1455; Fax: 956-849-2257.
Catechesis/Religious Program—Tel: 956-849-7155. Mrs. Julia Salinas, D.R.E. Students 624.
Mission—Holy Trinity Falcon Heights, Starr Co.
Mission—St. Joseph Salineno, Starr Co.
Mission—Holy Family Los Saenz, Starr Co.
Mission—Lamb of God Fronton, Starr Co.

SAN BENITO, CAMERON CO.

1—ST. BENEDICT (1912), Rev. Ignacio Luna; Deacon Manuel Sanchez.
Res.: 351 S. Bowie, P.O. Box 1780, 78586. Tel: 956-399-2353; Fax: 956-399-5701.
Catechesis/Religious Program—Tel: 956-399-5975. Students 546.

2—OUR LADY, QUEEN OF THE UNIVERSE (1960), Rev. Msgr. Isaac Emeka Erondu; Deacon Margarito Briones.
Res.: 121 Garrison Dr., 78586. Tel: 956-399-2865; Fax: 956-399-2045.
Catechesis/Religious Program—Miss Estefana Garcia, D.R.E. Students 382.
Mission—St. Joseph 1001 W. Hwy. 77, Cameron Co. 78586. Tel: 956-399-2615.

3—ST. THERESA (1954), Rev. Rodolfo Franco; Deacons Benito Flores; Gilberto Perez; Bro. Hoss Anthony Alvarez.
Res.: 1300 Combes St., P.O. Box 1830, 78586. Tel: 956-399-3247; Fax: 956-276-0142.
St. Theresa Child Development—Tel: 956-361-0609; Fax: 956-276-0142. Mrs. Alma Sandoval, Dir.
Catechesis/Religious Program—Tel: 956-399-0571.

Bro. Hoss Anthony Alvarez, D.R.E. Students 364.
SAN CARLOS, HIDALGO CO., ST. JOSEPH THE WORKER (1970), Rev. Samuel Arizpe; Deacon Hector Perez.
Res.: 8310 Highland Ave., Edinburg, 78541. Tel: 956-383-5880; Fax: 956-383-0420.
Catechesis/Religious Program—Tel: 956-381-1888. Mrs. Consuelo Patino, D.R.E.; Miss Blanca Mata, D.R.E. Students 520.
Mission—St. Anne San Manuel, Hidalgo Co.
Mission—St. Theresa Faysville, Hidalgo Co.
SAN ISIDRO, STARR CO., ST. ISIDORE (1964), Rev. Honecimo Figueroa.
5160 FM 1017, P.O. Box 60, 78588. Tel: 956-481-3392; Fax: 956-481-3869.
Catechesis/Religious Program—Students 98.
SAN JUAN, HIDALGO CO.
1—THE BASILICA OF THE NATIONAL SHRINE OF OUR LADY OF SAN JUAN DEL VALLE, Rev. Msgrs. Juan Nicolau, Ph.D., S.T.L., Rector; Patrick Doherty. In Res., Rev. Ariel Oliver Angel, J.C.L.
Res.: 400 Virgen de San Juan Blvd., 78589. Tel: 956-787-0033; Fax: 956-787-2908.
2—ST. JOHN THE BAPTIST (1949), Rev. John Lasseigne, O.M.I.; Deacon Agapito L. Cantu; Rev. Michael Powell, O.M.I.; Deacon Julio Castilleja.
216 W. First St., P.O. Box 1196, 78589. Tel: 956-783-1196; Fax: 956-702-7447.
Catechesis/Religious Program—Mrs. Alva D. Pena, D.R.E. Students 1,593.
Mission—Immaculate Conception Lopezville, Hidalgo Co.
SANTA ROSA, CAMERON CO., ST. MARY (1967), Revs. Plutarco Belanggoy, C.I.C.M.; Andre B. Kazadi, C.I.C.M.
Res.: 101 San Antonio Ave., P.O. Box 365, 78593. Tel: 956-636-1211; Fax: 956-636-2941.
Catechesis/Religious Program—Mrs. Rosie Aguilar, D.R.E. Students 163.
WESLACO, HIDALGO CO.
1—ST. JOAN OF ARC (1929), Rev. Lee DaCosta; Deacon Francisco Caballero.
Res.: 109 S. Illinois Ave., 78596. Tel: 956-968-3670; Fax: 956-968-1872.
Catechesis/Religious Program—Tel: 956-968-6812. Mrs. Rosa Ochoa, D.R.E. Students 375.
2—ST. PIUS X (1955), Rev. Patrick K. Seitz; Deacon Jesus Aguayo.
Res.: 600 S. Oklahoma Ave., 78596. Tel: 956-968-7471; Fax: 956-968-3040.
Catechesis/Religious Program—Tel: 956-968-0317. Mr. John Trevino, D.R.E. Students 741.
3—SAN MARTIN DE PORRES (1967), Revs. Eduardo Ortega; Fernando Gonzalez; Deacons Juan Delgado; Jose G. Garza.
Res.: 901 N. Texas Blvd., 78596. Tel: 956-968-2691; Fax: 956-968-1473.
School—905 N. Texas Blvd., 78596. Tel: 956-973-8642; Fax: 956-973-0522. Sr. Helen Rottier, C.S.J., Prin. Religious 1; Lay Teachers 8; Students 120.
Catechesis/Religious Program—Tel: 956-968-1979. Ms. Maria Luisa Villanueva, D.R.E. Students 1,252.
Mission—St. Jude Chapel, Hidalgo Co.
Mission—Nuestra Senora de Guadalupe Expressway Heights, Hidalgo Co.

Chaplains of Public Institutions

BROWNSVILLE. *Bayview Detention Center*, 47 W. Elizabeth St., 78521. Tel: 956-541-0220. Mr. Jaime Gomez, Coord.
Brownsville Medical Center, 1040 W. Jefferson St., 78520. Tel: 956-544-1426. Sr. Gloria Morales, M.J., Chap.
Brownsville Valley Regional Medical Center, P.O. Box 5107, 78520. Tel: 956-350-7124. Dr. Ethel Winchester-Didsbury, Chap.
Cameron County Jail.
47 W. Elizabeth St., 78521. Tel: 956-541-0220. Mr. Jaime Gomez.
Ruben M. Torres I, 47 W. Elizabeth St., 78521. Tel: 956-541-0220. Mr. Jaime Gomez, Coord.
Ruben M. Torres II, 47 W. Elizabeth St., 78521. Tel: 956-541-0220. Mr. Jaime Gomez, Coord.
EDINBURG. *Boot Camp*.
47 W. Elizabeth St., 78521. Tel: 956-541-0220. Mr. Jaime Gomez, Coord.
Edinburg Regional Medical Center, 1102 W. Trenton, 78541. Tel: 956-388-6235; Fax: 956-388-6020. Sr. Emma Marie Stillman, I.W.B.S., Chap. Coord.
Evins Rg. Juvenile Ctr..
47 W. Elizabeth St., 78521. Tel: 956-541-0220. Mr. Jaime Gomez, Coord.
Hidalgo County Jail.
47 W. Elizabeth St., 78521. Tel: 956-541-0220. Mr. Jaime Gomez, Coord.
La Villa.
47 W. Elizabeth St., 78521. Tel: 956-541-0220. Mr. Jaime Gomez, Coord.
Lopez.
47 W. Elizabeth St., 78521. Tel: 956-541-0220. Mr. Jaime Gomez, Coord.
Segovia Unit (State).
47 W. Elizabeth St., 78521. Tel: 956-541-0220. Mr. Jaime Gomez, Coord.
HARLINGEN. *Valley Baptist Medical Center*, 2101 Pease St., 78550. Tel: 956-389-1194; Fax: 956-389-1189. Rev. Frank Clancy, S.C.J., Chap., Sr. Theresa Han, O.S.F., Chap., Deacon Ignacio R. Gonzalez, Chap. Asst.
MCALLEN. *McAllen Heart Hospital*, 1900 S. "D" St., 78503. Tel: 956-994-2107; Fax: 956-994-2090. Sr. Therese Ann Ridge, I.W.B.S., Chap.
McAllen Medical Center, 301 W. Expwy. 83, 78503. Tel: 956-632-4177; Fax: 956-632-4010. Mr. Demetrio Tafoya, Chap., Sr. Ebere Anisike, D.D.L.
Rio Grande Regional Hospital, 101 E. Ridge Rd., 78503. Tel: 956-632-6616; Fax: 956-632-6621. Sr. Helen Roper, S.S.N.D., Chap.
MISSION. *Mission Hospital*, 900 S. Bryan Rd., 78572. Tel: 956-584-4562; Fax: 956-580-9430. Mrs. Judy Krese, Chap.
RAYMONDVILLE. *Wackenhut St. Corrections*.
47 W. Elizabeth St., 78521. Tel: 956-541-0220. Mr. Jaime Gomez, Co-Coord.
RIO GRANDE CITY. *Memorial Hospital*, P.O. Box 78, 78582. Tel: 956-487-5561, Ext. 2296; Fax: 956-487-0332. Sr. Anne Miriam Landolt, S.S.N.D, Chap.
Starr County Jail.
304 N. East, 78582. Tel: 956-487-3112. Mr. Jaime Gomez, Coord., Deacon R. C. Salinas, Chap.
SAN BENITO. *Boot Camp*.
47 W. Elizabeth St., 78521. Tel: 956-541-0220. Mr. Jaime Gomez, Coord.
Darrell B. Hester Juvenile.
47 W. Elizabeth St., 78521. Tel: 956-541-0220. Mr. Jaime Gomez, Coord.
WESLACO. *Youth Village*.
47 W. Elizabeth St., 78521. Tel: 956-541-0220. Mr. Jaime Gomez, Coord.

On Assignment Outside the Diocese:
Rev.—
Mestas, Leonard J., St. Joseph the Worker Church, 10816 Mount View Ave., Loma Linda, CA 92354.

Retired:
Revs.—
Annunziato, Michael, SS.CC., 215 N. 16th Ave., Edinburg, 78539.
Diaz, Robert, P.O. Box 2279, 78520-227.
Escobedo, Armando, 615 Palo Blanco Ave., Mission, 78572.
Felion, Jerome (CR), 1171 FM 649, Rio Grande City, 78582.
Gomez, Frank, 5609 John Stockbauer, 8101, Victoria, 77904. Tel: 956-578-2376
Kelley, Donald, S.S.C. (OM), J-Five R-V Park, 3907 Taylor Rd., Mission, 78572.
Mateos, Tomas, S.F.O., P.O. Box 747, San Juan, 78589.
Meyers, Frederick, SS.CC., 215 N. 16 N. 16th Ave., Edinburg, 78539.
O'Malley, John A., P.O. Box 2576, San Juan, 78589. Tel: 956-783-1013
Ortiz, Benedicto, 2735 E. 31st St., 78521. Tel: 956-546-4510
Sweeney, Robert L., P.O. Box 4737, San Juan, 78589. Tel: 956-782-4371
Verboomen, Willy, C.I.C.M., 215 N. 16th Ave., Edinburg, 78539.
Wichmann, Edward, 1225 Central Blvd., Apt. 903, 78520.

Permanent Deacons:
Aguayo, Jesus, St. Pius X, Weslaco
Barrera, Ernesto, (Retired)
Borja, Gilberto, St. Mary, Mother of the Church, Brownsville
Briones, Margarito, Our Lady Queen of the Universe, San Benito
Caballero, Francisco, (Retired), St. Joan of Arc, Weslaco
Cano, Roberto, Christ the King, Brownsville
Cantu, Agapito L., St. John the Baptist, San Juan
Cantu, Roberto, Sacred Heart, Mercedes
Cardosa, Abraham, (Retired)
Castaneda, Bill, Our Lady of Guadalupe, Mission
Castilleja, Julio, St. John the Baptist, San Juan
Castro, Jose R., (Retired), St. Anne, Mother of Mary, Pharr
Cedillo, Bruno, Our Lady of Guadalupe, Brownsville
Chapa, Alberto X., Our Lady, Queen of Angels, La Joya
Chapa, Augusto, Jr., St. Cecilia, Los Fresnos
Crixell, Alfred V., Inactive
De la Cruz, Hugo
Delgado, Juan, San Martin de Porres, Weslaco
Flores, Alejandro, Holy Family, Brownsville
Flores, Benito, St. Theresa, San Benito
Flores, Lucio, Our Lady, Queen of Angels, La Joya
Galvan, Jesus P., Resurrection, Alamo
Gamboa, Alejandro, St. Joseph the Worker, McAllen
Garcia, Ismael, St. Paul, Mission
Garcia, Silvestre, St. Joseph, Edinburg
Garza, Francisco
Garza, Jose G., San Martin de Porres, Weslaco
Gerbermann, Alvin H., Holy Spirit, McAllen
Gonzales, Ignacio R., Our Lady of Assumption, Harlingen
Gonzalez, Irineo, Jr., St. Joseph, Edinburg
Gonzalez, Juan F., Our Lady of Guadalupe, Raymondville
Gonzalez, Leopoldo, Inactive
Grimaldo, Jose N., Inactive
Guerra, Jose, Our Lady Queen/Universe, San Benito
Ibarra, Genaro, Queen of Peace, Harlingen
Jurado, Mariano, St. Theresa (Mission), Edinburg
Kinch, John, Immaculate Conception Cathedral, Brownsville
Leal, Ramon G., Our Lady of Guadalupe, Brownsville
Ledesma, Robert, St. Paul, Mission
Lopez, Albert C., Administrative leave
Lopez, Gilberto, Sacred Heart, Edinburg
Lopez, Ruben, Holy Family, Edinburg
McArdle, Paul, Good Shepherd, Brownsville
Munoz, Andres, St. Luke, Brownsville
Navarro, Juan Pablo, St. Mary, Mother of the Church, Brownsville
Oden, Luis, Inactive
Olvera, Alvino C., Our Lady of Good Counsel, Brownsville
Ovalle, Eduardo, Sr., St. Joseph, Donna
Perez, Gilberto, St. Theresa, San Benito
Perez, Hector, St. Joseph the Worker, San Carlos
Requenez, Peter, Our Lady of St. John of the Fields, Mission
Reyes, Jesus H., Our Lady of Assumption, Harlingen
Reyna, Eduardo, Sacred Heart, McAllen
Rodriguez, Arturo, Immaculate Conception Cathedral, Brownsville
Rojas, Salvador, St. Juan Deigo Cuauhtlatoazin, McAllen
Rousset, Louis, Inactive
Saenz, Benito, Jr., Holy Family, Grulla
Sagredo, Israel, Our Lady of Sorrows, McAllen
Saldana, Enrique, Our Lady of Good Counsel, Brownsville
Saldivar, Salvador G., Holy Spirit, Progreso
Salinas, Rodolfo C., Holy Family, Grulla
Sanchez, Manuel, St. Benedict, San Benito
Sanchez, Pedro F., St. Margaret Mary, Pharr
Schwarz, John, Our Lady of Sorrows, McAllen
Solis, Heriberto, St. Mary, Mother of the Church, Brownsville
Solis, Jose, Sacred Heart, Edinburg
Trevino, Carlos S., Holy Spirit, McAllen
Trevino, Felipe, St. Joseph, Brownsville
Trevino, Heriberto, St. Mary, Mother of the Church, Brownsville
Trevino, Juan, Our Lady of Mercy, Mercedes
Valenzuela, Juan, Immaculate Heart of Mary, Harlingen
Villalon, Rene, Sr., S.F.O., Our Lady of Perpetual Help, McAllen
Villarreal, Arturo, (Retired)
Webre, Alfred L., Jr., (Retired)
Zamora, Daniel, Our Lady of St. John of the Fields, Mission

INSTITUTIONS LOCATED IN THE DIOCESE

[A] SEMINARIES

MISSION. *The Saint Joseph and Saint Peter Seminary*, 5208 S. 494 Hwy., 78572. Tel: 956-585-7078; Fax: 956-424-9851. Revs. Juan Victor Heredia, Rector; Jose Rene Angel, J.C.L., Dean of Men; Brian Van Hove, S.J., Spiritual Dir.; Honecimo Figueroa, Philosophy Prof.; Sr. Helena Nunes, Language Instructor; Ms. Debbie Murillo, Sec.

[B] HIGH SCHOOLS, PRIVATE

BROWNSVILLE. *St. Joseph Academy*, (Grades 7-12), 101 St. Joseph Dr., 78520. Tel: 956-542-3581. Bros. John Venturella, F.M.S., Pres.; Charles Imbergamo, F.M.S., Prin. Marist Brothers, Esopus Province. Religious 8; Lay Teachers 62; Students 784.

PHARR. *Oratory Athenaeum for University*

Preparation, 1407 W. Moore Rd., 78577. Tel: 956-781-3056; Fax: 956-702-3047. Email: oratoryacd@aol.com. Rev. Mario Alberto Aviles, C.O., Rector; Mrs. G. Yvonne Perez, Dir. Religious 3; Lay Teachers 9; Students 32.

[C] ELEMENTARY SCHOOLS, PRIVATE

BROWNSVILLE. *Guadalupe Regional Middle School*, 1214 E. Lincoln St., 78521. Tel: 956-504-5568. Mrs. Cathy Thomas, Prin.; Bro. Leo Shea, F.M.S., Pres. Religious 3; Lay Teachers 8; Students 57.

Incarnate Word Academy Elementary and Middle School (Convent Academy of the Incarnate Word) , 244 Resaca Blvd., 78520. Tel: 956-546-4486. Sr. Teresita Rodriguez, I.W.B.S., (Middle); Miss Christina Moreno, Prin. (Elementary). Sisters of the Incarnate Word and Blessed Sacrament Religious 3; Lay Teachers 25; Students 356.

PHARR. *Oratory Academy*, (Grades PreK-8), 507 S. Ironwood St., 78577-9999. Tel: 956-787-2052; Fax: 956-782-6374. Email: oratoryacd@aol.com. Rev. Mario A. Aviles, C.O., Rector. Lay Teachers 18; Students 408.

[D] CATHOLIC SOCIAL SERVICES

BROWNSVILLE. *Catholic Charities*, 700 N. Virgen de San Juan Blvd., San Juan, 78589. Tel: 956-702-4088; Fax: 956-784-5096. Email: npimentel@cdob.org. Web: www.cdob.org. Most Rev. Raymundo J. Pena, D.D., Chm.; Sr. Norma Pimentel, M.J., Dir.

Legal Title: *Catholic Charities of the Diocese of Brownsville, a Texas Non-Profit Corporation.*

Catholic Social Services, 47 W. Elizabeth St., 78520. Tel: 956-541-0220; Fax: 956-544-7580. Ms. Matilde Bennett, Counselor; Ms. Nora H. Rodriguez, Caseworker.

Jail Ministry, 47 W. Elizabeth St., 78520. Tel: 956-541-0220; Fax: 956-544-7580. Mr. Jaime Gomez, Coord.; Mr. Victor Villegas, Jail Min.; Revs. Lionel Lopez, Chap.; Jose M. Villalon, Chap.; George Gonzalez, Chap.

SAN JUAN. *Catholic Social Services*, 700 Virgen de San Juan Blvd., P.O. Box 128, 78589. Tel: 956-702-4088; Fax: 956-784-5098. Mr. Silvestre Rodriguez, Counselor; Mrs. Yesenia Garcia, Caseworker.

Immigration Counseling Services, 700 N. Virgen de San Juan Blvd., 78589. Tel: 956-702-4088; Fax: 956-784-5098. Mrs. Santa E. Acuna, Coord.

Jail Ministry, 700 N. Virgen de San Juan Blvd., 78589. Tel: 956-784-5022. Bro. Manuel Enrique Ruiz, O.de.M., J.C.L., Co-Coord., Upper Valley; Mr. Jaime Gomez, Coord.; Mr. Victor Villegas, Jail Min.

[E] HOMES FOR THE AGED

BROWNSVILLE. *Mother of Perpetual Help Nursing Home, Inc.*, 519 A East Madison St., 78520. Tel: 956-546-6745; Fax: 956-546-0711. Email: moph@sbcglobal.net. Ms. Laura G. Emmord, Admin. Owner: Sisters of the Holy Spirit and Mary Immaculate.; Chapel attended from Immaculate Conception Cathedral. Bed Capacity 38; Total Assisted 420; Total Staff 45.

SAN JUAN. *San Juan Nursing Home*, 300 N. Virgen de San Juan Blvd., P.O. Box 1238, 78589. Tel: 956-787-1771; Fax: 956-787-8091. Most Rev. Raymundo J. Pena, D.D.; Mrs. Olga Navarro, Admin.

Legal Title: *San Juan Nursing Home, Inc., of the Diocese of Brownsville, a Texas Non-Profit Corporation* Bed Capacity 122.

Board of Directors: Rev. Louis Brum; Hermila Anzaldua; Dr. Benjamin Bujanda, M.D.; Janice Kline; Ricardo Martinez; Mrs. Olga Navarro, Staff.

[F] RESIDENCES FOR PRIESTS AND BROTHERS

BROWNSVILLE. *Congregation of Christian Brothers* Our Lady of Guadalupe. , 1214 E. Lincoln St., 78521. Tel: 956-982-0614. Brothers 3.

Marist Brothers, Formerly Marist Brothers, St. Joseph Academy, 101 St. Joseph Dr., 78520. Tel: 956-546-2608. Brothers 13.

HARLINGEN. *Priests of the Sacred Heart*, 144 W. Spencer Ct., 78550. Tel: 956-428-8344. Rev. Frank Clancy, S.C.J.

PHARR. *Oratory of St. Philip Neri of Pontifical*, Formerly Oratory of St. Philip Neri, P.O. Box 1698, 78577. Tel: 956-843-8217; Fax: 956-843-2946. Very Rev. Leo Francis Daniels, C.O., Provost; Revs. Jose Encarnacion Losoya, C.O., Sec. & Treas.; Mario Alberto Aviles, C.O., Vicar.

[G] CONVENTS AND RESIDENCES FOR SISTERS

BROWNSVILLE. *Dominican Sisters of Charity of the Presentation*, 934 W. St. Charles St., 78520. Tel: 956-542-7225. Sisters 5.

Missionaries of Jesus, 1501 W. Adams, 78520. Tel: 956-542-2130. Sisters 8.

ALAMO. *Sisters of Mercy*, Rte. 2, Box 133A, 78516. Tel: 956-702-0824.

HARLINGEN. *Franciscan Sisters of Mary*, 3401 Business 83, #85, 78552-3517. Tel: 956-423-9447.

MISSION. *Misioneras Catequistas de los Pobres*, 615 Dunlap, 78572. Tel: 956-585-1376.

Sisters of St. Joseph of Carondelet, 1711 W. Gastel Cir., 78572-3037. Tel: 956-585-4870. Sisters 2.

PORT ISABEL. *Sisters of St. Francis*, 705 Manautau St., P.O. Box 6504, 78578. Tel: 956-943-2136.

[H] RETREAT HOUSES

SAN JUAN. *St. Eugene de Mazenod Christian Renewal Center*, P.O. Box 747, 78589. Tel: 956-787-0033.

[I] CAMPUS MINISTRY

BROWNSVILLE. *Young Adult Ministry/University of Texas at Brownsville-Texas Southmost College* 1850 Ridgely Rd., 78520. Tel: 956-542 3942; 956-541-9697; Fax: 956-542-3942. Hilda Escandon, Campus Min.

EDINBURG. *University of Texas Pan American Campus at Edinburg/Young Adult Ministry* 1615 W. Kuhn St., 78539. Tel: 956-383-0133. Sr. Hilary Brzezinski, O.F.M., Coord.

[J] MISCELLANEOUS

BROWNSVILLE. *Bishop Enrique San Pedro, S.J. Ozanam Center*, 656 N. Minnesota Ave., 78521. Tel: 956-831-6331; Fax: 956-831-8577. Alejandro Fuentes, Dir.

Villa Maria Language Institute, 224 Resaca Blvd., 78520. Tel: 956-546-7196; Fax: 956-546-8121. Sr. Mary Lelia Aguilar, I.W.B.S., Dir.

ALAMO. *Women Religious - Arise Inc.*, 306 N. Alamo Rd. (Tabor), P.O. Box 778, 78516. Tel: 956-702-0524; Fax: 956-783-0274. Sr. Gerrie Naughton, R.S.M., Pres.

Legal Title: *Women Religious-Arise, Inc.*

HARLINGEN. *KMBH-TV 60/KHID-FM 88.1/KMBH-FM 88.9*, P.O. Box 2147, 78551. Tel: 956-421-4111; Fax: 956-421-4150. Email: pbriseno@aol.com. Web: www.kmbh.org. Rev. Pedro Briseno, Gen. Mgr. & Pres.

MCALLEN. *Comfort House/Casa del Conseulo*, 617 Dallas Ave., 78501. Tel: 956-687-7367; Fax: 956-630-5423. Email: info@comforthouseservices.org. Web: www.comforthouseservices.com. Mary Rincones, Admin. AIDS Education & Outreach. Bed Capacity 10.

Secular Franciscan Order, Fraternity of Our Lady of Guadalupe, 3600 N. 23rd, Ste. 205, 78501. Tel: 956-687-6816. Juana Trujillo, Formator; Sr. Virginia Rivas, S.F.O., Vice Min.; Rosemary Hendricks, S.F.O., Treas.; Rev. Tomas Mateos, S.F.O., Spiritual Asst.; Sisters Paula Cortez, S.F.O., Sec.; Maria Celia Solis, S.F.O., Min.

MERCEDES. *La Merced Charitable Trust*, 413 S. Virginia, P.O. Box 806, 78570. Tel: 956-565-2622; Fax: 956-565-4185. Email: mercedhome@aol.com. Housing Board: Mr. Octaviano Gonzalez, Trustee; Mr. Ricardo Hernandez, Chairman of the Board; Mr. Roel A. Rodriguez, Trustee; Mr. Rigoberto Salinas, Trustee; Mrs. Ana Zamarripa, Housing Mgr.

MISSION. *El Rosario Charitable Trust*, 119 Retama, P.O. Box 971, 78572. Tel: 956-585-5051; Fax: 956-585-9938. Email: rosarioh@aol.com. Mrs. Ana Zamarripa, Housing Mgr.

SAN BENITO. *La Posada Providencia* (A program of Providence Ministry Corp.) A shelter for documented refugees seeking asylum or other residency. , 1610 Marydale Rd., 78586. Tel: 956-399-3826; Fax: 956-399-2898. Email: cdplaposada@aol.com. Web: www.divineprovidenceweb.org. Sr. Margaret Mertens, C.D.P., Dir.

SAN JUAN. *The Basilica of Our Lady of San Juan del Valle - National Shrine*, 400 Virgen de San Juan Blvd., 78589. Tel: 956-787-0033; Fax: 956-787-2908. Rev. Msgr. Juan Nicolau, Ph.D., S.T.L., Rector; Mr. Pablo H. Villescas, Admin. Assst. to the Rector; Rev. Msgr. Patrick Doherty In Res. Rev. Ariel Oliver Angel, J.C.L.

San Juan Retreat Center Tel: 956-787-0033, Ext. 350. Mrs. Maria Villanueva, Sec. of the Adm. Asst. to the Rector.

San Juan Pilgrim House/Hotel Tel: 956-787-0033, Ext. 249. Mrs. Aide Paz, Mgr.

Religious Gift & Book Store Tel: 956-787-0033, Ext. 339. Mrs. Vickie Flores, Mgr.

Human Resources Tel: 956-787-0033, Ext. 381. Ms. Melinda Singleterry, H.R. Clerk.

Finance Tel: 956-787-0033, Ext. 221. Mrs. Frida Hioe, C.P.L.

San Juan Cafeteria Tel: 956-787-0033, Ext. 252. Mrs. Miriam Arevalo, Mgr.

Worship Tel: 956-787-0033. Mr. Francisco Morales, Mgr.

Cursillos, 400 Virgen de San Juan Blvd., 78589. Tel: 956-787-0171; Fax: 956-787-2908. Rev. Juan Nicolau, Dir. Tel: 956-787-0033; Deacon Salvador Rojas Sr., Asst. Dir. Tel: 956-682-1351.

RELIGIOUS INSTITUTES OF MEN REPRESENTED IN THE DIOCESE

For further details refer to the corresponding bracketed number in the Religious Institutes of Men or Women section.

[0310]—*Congregation of Christian Brothers*—C.F.C.
[0630]—*Congregation of the Missionaries of the Holy Family*—M.S.F.
[1130]—*Congregation of the Priests of the Sacred Heart*—S.C.J.
[1140]—*Fathers of the Sacred Hearts*—SS.CC.
[0410]—*Franciscans-Assumption BVM Province*—O.F.M.
[0690]—*Jesuit Fathers and Brothers, Society of Jesus*—S.J.
[0770]—*The Marist Brothers*—F.M.S.
[0780]—*Marist Priests and Brothers of the Society of Mary*—S.M.
[0860]—*Missionhurst Congregation of the Immaculate Heart of Mary*—C.I.C.M.
[0910]—*Oblates of Mary Immaculate*—O.M.I.
[0950]—*Oratorians of St. Philip Neri*—C.O.
[]—*Third Order Penitence of St. Frances*—T.O.P.S.F.

RELIGIOUS INSTITUTES OF WOMEN REPRESENTED IN THE DIOCESE

[]—*Benedictine Sisters of Grand Rapids, Michigan*—O.S.B.
[]—*Benedictine Sisters of the Good Shepherd (Monastery)*—O.S.B.
[0990]—*Congregation of Divine Providence*—C.D.P.
[]—*Congregation of Divine Providence (Helotes)*—C.D.P.
[]—*Congregation of Notre Dame*—C.N.D.
[0470]—*Congregation of the Sisters of Charity of the Incarnate Word, Houston, Texas*—C.C.V.I.
[1920]—*Congregation of the Sisters of the Holy Cross*—C.S.C.
[0760]—*Daughters of Charity*—D.C.
[0760]—*Daughters of Charity of St. Vincent de Paul*—D.C.
[0793]—*Daughters of Divine Love*—D.D.L.
[]—*Dominican Sisters of Sinsinawa, WI*—O.P.
[]—*Dominican Sisters of St. Catherine of Kentucky*—O.P.
[1070-09]—*Dominican Sisters of St. Dominic* (Racine, WI)—O.P.
[1070-05]—*Dominican Sisters of the Presentation*—O.P.
[1070-19]—*Dominican Sisters, Congregation of the Sacred Heart* (Houston)—O.P.
[1200]—*Franciscan Sisters of Baltimore*—O.S.F.
[1415]—*Franciscan Sisters of Mary*—F.S.M.
[1150]—*Misioneras Eucaristicas Franciscanas*—M.E.F.
[2690]—*Missionary Catechists of Divine Providence*—M.C.D.P.
[]—*Missionary Daughters of the Most Pure Virgin Mary*—M.D.P.V.M.
[]—*Missionary Sisters of Jesus*—M.J.
[2750]—*Missionary Sisters of the Immaculate Heart of Mary*—I.C.M.
[]—*Missioneras Catequistas de los Pobres*—M.C.P.
[]—*Missioneras del Espiritu Santo Y la Sagrada Familia*—M.E.S.S.F.
[]—*Order of St. Benedict*—O.S.B.
[2970]—*School Sisters of Notre Dame* (Prov. of Dallas)—S.S.N.D.
[]—*Sisters for a Christian Community*—S.F.C.C.
[0460]—*Sisters of Charity of the Incarnate Word* (San Antonio, TX)—C.C.V.I.
[2575]—*Sisters of Mercy of the Americas* (St. Louis, MO; Cincinnati, OH)—R.S.M.
[2575]—*Sisters of Mercy of the Americas* (St. Louis)—R.S.M.
[]—*Sisters of Mercy (PA)*—R.S.M.
[3790]—*Sisters of St. Dorothy*—S.S.D.
[1720]—*Sisters of St. Francis of Our Lady of Lourdes*—O.S.F.
[3840]—*Sisters of St. Joseph of Carondelet* (St. Paul & St. Louis Provs.)—C.S.J.
[]—*Sisters of St. Joseph of Lyon*
[2980]—*Sisters of the Congregation of Notre Dame of Montreal*—C.N.D.
[]—*Sisters of the Franciscan Order*—S.F.O.
[2050]—*Sisters of the Holy Spirit and Mary Immaculate*—S.H.Sp.
[2200]—*Sisters of the Incarnate Word and Blessed Sacrament*—I.W.B.S.
[3320]—*Sisters of the Presentation of the Blessed*

Virgin Mary—P.B.V.M.

[3670]—*Sisters of the Sacred Heart of Jesus*—S.S.C.J.

[3670]—*Sisters of the Sacred Heart of Jesus of St. Jacut*—S.S.C.J.

[]—*Ursuline Sisters*—O.S.U.

[]—*Ursuline Sisters of Youngstown*

NECROLOGY

(No Deaths)

Diocese of Buffalo

(Dioecesis Buffalensis)

Most Reverend

EDWARD D. HEAD, D.D.

Bishop Emeritus of Buffalo; ordained January 27, 1945; appointed Titular Bishop of Ardstratha and Auxiliary of New York January 27, 1970; consecrated March 19, 1970; appointed to Buffalo January 17, 1973; installed March 19, 1973; retired June 12, 1995. *Res.: 795 Main St., Buffalo, NY 14203-1250.*

Most Reverend

BERNARD J. MCLAUGHLIN, D.D., V.G.

Retired Auxiliary Bishop of Buffalo; ordained December 21, 1935; appointed Auxiliary Bishop of Buffalo and Titular Bishop of Mottola December 28, 1968; consecrated January 6, 1969; retired January 15, 1988. *Res.: 204 Knoche Rd., Tonawanda, NY 14150.*

(VACANT SEE)

Chancery Office: 795 Main St., Buffalo, NY 14203. Tel: 716-847-5500; Fax: 716-847-5557.

Web: www.buffalodiocese.org

Email: dob@buffalodiocese.org

Most Reverend

EDWARD M. GROSZ, D.D.

Auxiliary Bishop of Buffalo; ordained May 29, 1971; appointed November 22, 1989; consecrated February 2, 1990. *Res.: St. Stanislaus Parish*, 123 Townsend St., Buffalo, NY 14212-1299.

ESTABLISHED APRIL 23, 1847

Square Miles 6,357.

Incorporated under the laws of the State of New York October 30th, 1897. Re-incorporated by special act passed April 5, 1951, Chapter 568 of the laws of 1951. Corporate Title: The Diocese of Buffalo, N.Y.

Comprises the Counties of Erie, Niagara, Genesee, Orleans, Chautauqua, Wyoming, Cattaraugus and Allegany in the State of New York.

For legal titles of parishes and diocesan institutions, consult the Chancery Office.

STATISTICAL OVERVIEW

Personnel	
Auxiliary Bishops	1
Retired Bishops	2
Priests: Diocesan Active in Diocese	248
Priests: Diocesan Active Outside Diocese	6
Priests: Retired, Sick or Absent	134
Number of Diocesan Priests	388
Religious Priests in Diocese	159
Total Priests in Diocese	547
Extern Priests in Diocese	9
Ordinations:	
Diocesan Priests	2
Transitional Deacons	5
Permanent Deacons	7
Permanent Deacons in Diocese	104
Total Brothers	48
Total Sisters	1,218
Parishes	
Parishes	265
With Resident Pastor:	
Resident Diocesan Priests	201
Resident Religious Priests	20
Without Resident Pastor:	
Administered by Priests	42
Administered by Deacons	1
Administered by Religious Women	1
Missions	9
Pastoral Centers	2
Professional Ministry Personnel:	
Sisters	73
Lay Ministers	158
Welfare	
Catholic Hospitals	6
Total Assisted	1,426,730
Health Care Centers	1
Total Assisted	1,100
Homes for the Aged	13
Total Assisted	2,050
Day Care Centers	3
Total Assisted	237
Specialized Homes	2
Total Assisted	965
Special Centers for Social Services	5
Total Assisted	235,650
Residential Care of Disabled	7
Total Assisted	46
Other Institutions	3
Total Assisted	12,849
Educational	
Seminaries, Diocesan	1
Students from This Diocese	23
Students from Other Diocese	5
Diocesan Students in Other Seminaries	2
Seminaries, Religious	1
Total Seminarians	25
Colleges and Universities	7
Total Students	16,393
High Schools, Private	16
Total Students	6,075
Elementary Schools, Diocesan and Parish	81
Total Students	19,306
Elementary Schools, Private	5
Total Students	1,021
Non-residential Schools for the Disabled	1
Total Students	489
Catechesis/Religious Education:	
High School Students	13,097
Elementary Students	35,324
Total Students under Catholic Instruction	91,730
Teachers in the Diocese:	
Priests	63
Scholastics	3
Brothers	12
Sisters	106
Lay Teachers	2,784
Vital Statistics	
Receptions into the Church:	
Infant Baptism Totals	6,226
Adult Baptism Totals	510
Received into Full Communion	433
First Communions	7,126
Confirmations	6,043
Marriages:	
Catholic	1,487
Interfaith	618
Total Marriages	2,105
Deaths	7,071
Total Catholic Population	707,981
Total Population	1,578,922

Former Bishops—Rt. Revs. JOHN TIMON, C.M., D.D., consecrated Oct. 17, 1847; died April 16, 1867; STEPHEN V. RYAN, C.M., D.D., consecrated Nov. 8, 1868; died April 10, 1896; JAMES EDWARD QUIGLEY, D.D., consecrated Bishop of Buffalo, Feb. 24, 1897; promoted to the Archdiocese of Chicago, Feb. 19, 1903; died July 10, 1915; CHARLES HENRY COLTON, D.D., consecrated Aug. 24, 1903; died May 9, 1915; His Eminence DENNIS CARDINAL DOUGHERTY, D.D., consecrated Bishop of Nueva Segovia, June 14, 1903; transferred to the Diocese of Jaro, April 19, 1908; transferred to the Diocese of Buffalo, Dec. 6, 1915; promoted to Archdiocese of Philadelphia, May 1, 1918; created Cardinal, March 7, 1921; died May 31, 1951; Most Revs. WILLIAM TURNER, D.D., consecrated March 30, 1919; died July 10, 1936; JOHN A. DUFFY, D.D., consecrated Bishop of Syracuse, June 29, 1933; transferred to the Diocese of Buffalo, April 14, 1937; died Sept. 27, 1944; His Eminence JOHN CARDINAL O'HARA, C.S.C., ord. Sept. 9, 1916; appt. Military Delegate of the Armed Forces and Titular Bishop of Mylasa, Dec. 11, 1939; consecrated Jan. 15, 1940; transferred to Buffalo, March 10, 1945; installed May 8, 1945; promoted to the Archdiocese of Philadelphia, Nov. 23, 1951; created Cardinal, Dec. 15, 1958; died Aug. 28, 1960; Most Revs. JOSEPH A. BURKE, D.D., consecrated Titular Bishop of Vita and Auxiliary, June 29, 1943; promoted to the See, Feb. 9, 1952; died Oct. 16, 1962; JAMES A. MCNULTY, D.D., consecrated Oct. 7, 1947; Titular Bishop of Methone and Auxiliary Bishop of Newark, NJ; appt. Bishop of Paterson, NJ April 9, 1953; transferred to Buffalo, Feb 12, 1963; died Sept. 4, 1972; EDWARD D. HEAD, D.D. (Retired), ord. Jan. 27, 1945; appt. Titular Bishop of Ardstratha and Auxiliary of New York, Jan. 27, 1970; consecrated March 19, 1970; appt. Bishop of Buffalo, Jan. 17, 1973; installed March 19 1973; retired June 12, 1995; HENRY J. MANSELL, D.D., ord. Dec. 19, 1962; appt. Titular Bishop of Marazane and Auxiliary of New York Nov. 24, 1992; ord. Jan. 6, 1993; appt. Bishop of Buffalo April 18, 1995; installed June 12, 1995; promoted to Archbishop of Hartford Oct. 20, 2003.

Vicars General—Most Rev. EDWARD M. GROSZ, D.D.; Rev. Msgr. ROBERT J. CUNNINGHAM, P.A., J.C.L.

Chancery Office—795 Main St., Buffalo, 14203. Tel: 716-847-5500; Fax: 716-847-5557. Email: dob@buffalodiocese.org. Office Hours: Mon.-Fri. 9-4:30

Chancellor—Rev. Msgr. ROBERT J. CUNNINGHAM, P.A., J.C.L.

Vice Chancellor—Rev. PAUL A. LITWIN.

Secretary to Diocesan Bishop and Vice Chancellor—Rev. DAVID G. LIPUMA.

Diocesan Tribunal—795 Main St., Buffalo, 14203. Tel: 716-847-8769; Fax: 716-847-8772. Email: tribunal@buffalodiocese.org. Send all rogatory commissions to the Tribunal.

Judicial Vicar—Rev. SALVATORE MANGANELLO.

Adjunct Judicial Vicar—Rev. PAUL P. SABO.

Defenders of the Bond—Revs. FRANCIS T. NOWAK (Retired); EDWARD R. CZARNECKI; FRANCIS X. MAZUR; GREGORY M. FAULHABER, S.T.D.; DENNIS A. FRONCZAK; Rev. Msgr. ROBERT J. CUNNINGHAM, P.A., J.C.L.

Advocates—Deacons DANIEL E. BRICK ESQ.; MICHAEL P. MCKEATING; Revs. RICHARD S. DIGIULIO; ROBERT W. VOGT (Retired); Sr. MARY HARTLEY, S.S.M.N.

Promoter of Justice—Rev. Msgr. W. JEROME SULLIVAN, J.C.D.

Judges—Rev. JAMES M. AUGUSTYN; Rev. Msgr. VINCENT J. BECKER; Rev. FRED D. INGALLS; Sr. JOLENE JASINSKI, C.S.S.F., J.C.L.; Revs. JOSEPH KLOS, J.C.L.; PAUL A. LITWIN; Sr. SANDRA MAKOWSKI, S.S.M.N., J.C.L.; Revs. SALVATORE MANGANELLO; HENRY A. ORSZULAK; PAUL P. SABO; Rev. Msgr. GEORGE B. YIENGST.

Notaries—Sr. AGNITA BROWN; LUCILLE BUCZEK; ROBIN COLVIN; DOROTHY MAY.

Consultors, College of—Most Rev. EDWARD M. GROSZ, D.D.; Rev. Msgrs. ROBERT J. CUNNINGHAM, P.A., J.C.L.; ALBERT W. CLODY; Revs. ROBERT M. MOCK;

THOMAS J. QUINLIVAN; RONALD W. SAMS, S.J.; JOSEPH J. SICARI; Rev. Msgr. ROBERT C. WURTZ, P.A.

Council of Priests—Most Rev. EDWARD M. GROSZ, D.D.; Rev. Msgrs. ROBERT J. CUNNINGHAM, P.A., J.C.L.; MATTHEW S. KOPACZ; Revs. JOSEPH F. BURKE, S.J., Ph.D.; JAMES C. CROGLIO; ROBERT S. HUGHSON; BARTHOLOMEW W. LIPIEC; JOSEPH D. PORPIGLIA; BERNARD U. NOWAK; MICHAEL J. PARKER; DENNIS G. WOLF; RICHARD E. ZAJAC; MATTHEW J. ZIRNHELD; THOMAS J. QUINLIVAN; LAWRENCE P. DAMIAN; Rev. Msgr. ALBERT W. CLODY; Rev. GREGORY M. FAULHABER, S.T.D.; Rev. Msgr. GERARD L. GREEN (Retired); Revs. JOSEPH A. GULLO; ROBERT M. MOCK; DANIEL F. FIEBELKORN; JACOB C. LEDWON; JOHN J. LEISING; STEWART M. LINDSAY, O.S.F.S.; RONALD W. SAMS, S.J.; JOSEPH J. SICARI; Rev. Msgr. W. JEROME SULLIVAN, J.C.D.; Revs. JOSEPH S. SPATORICO; JAMES VACCO, O.F.M.; JOSEPH E. VATTER; Rev. Msgr. JAMES E. WALL.

Finance Council—Most Rev. EDWARD M. GROSZ, D.D.; Rev. Msgrs. ROBERT J. CUNNINGHAM, P.A., J.C.L.; PAUL J.E. BURKARD; ANGELO M. CALIGIURI; JAMES F. CAMPBELL; Rev. RICHARD A. CSIZMAR; Rev. Msgr. THOMAS F. MALONEY; Rev. JOHN J. MITKA; Rev. Msgr. J. THOMAS MORAN; Mr. JOHN R. O'BRIEN; Rev. Msgr. RAYMOND F. PAA (Retired); Rev. DANIEL J. PALYS; Rev. Msgr. DAVID S. SLUBECKY; Mr. STEVEN D. TIMMEL; Revs. ROBERT W. WARDENSKI; MARK J. WOLSKI; Rev. Msgr. ROBERT C. WURTZ, P.A.

Vicariates—

Vicars—Revs. PAUL R. BOSSI, Northwest Buffalo; ROBERT L. GEBHARD, Central Buffalo; Most Rev. EDWARD M. GROSZ, Southeast Buffalo; Rev. Msgrs. ANGELO M. CALIGIURI, Northern Erie; DAVID S. SLUBECKY, Eastern Erie; Revs. LAWRENCE E. BURNS, Western Erie; DENNIS G. WOLF, Allegany; DANIEL P. WALSH, Tri-County; GREGORY J. DOBSON, Southern Cattaraugus; PATRICK H. ELIS, Northern Chautauqua; Rev. Msgrs. ANTOINE P. ATTEA, Southern Chautauqua; LEO F. MCCARTHY, Genesee; PAUL J. BELZER; VACANT, Western Niagara; Revs. RICHARD A. CSIZMAR, Orleans; RICHARD W. BLAZEJEWSKI, Wyoming.

The Diocese of Buffalo, N.Y.— A corporation under the laws of the State of New York. VACANT, Pres.; Most Rev. EDWARD M. GROSZ, D.D., Vice Pres.; Rev. Msgr. ROBERT J. CUNNINGHAM, P.A., J.C.L., Sec.

Diocesan Offices and Directors

All offices are located at: 795 Main St., Buffalo, NY 14203. Tel: 716-847-8700; Fax: 716-847-5557 (Unless otherwise noted).

Apostleship of Prayer—Rev. RICHARD M. POBLOCKI, Dir., 1955 Genesee St., Buffalo, 14211.

Apostleship of the Sea—Rev. Msgr. JOHN I. DUCETTE, Dir., Res.: 565 E. Park Dr., Tonawanda, 14150.

Archives—Sr. ANN LOUISE HENTGES, S.S.M.N. Tel: 716-847-5500.

Bishop's Committee for Christian Home and Family—Moderators: Deacon THOMAS SCHULTZ; GINI SCHULTZ. Tel: 716-847-2210.

Boy Scouts—Rev. JOHN E. KELLY, Chap. Tel: 716-847-8789; VINCENT J. HARMON, Lay Dir., 99 Clark St., Tonawanda, 14150. Tel: 716-693-7558.

Buildings and Properties—MICHAEL J. SULLIVAN, Dir. Tel: 716-847-8750; Fax: 716-847-8756.

Camp Turner—JOHN MANN. Tel: 716-847-8789.

Catechumenate Office—Mrs. JUDITH WAGGONER, Dir. Tel: 716-847-5546; Fax: 716-847-5593.

Catholic Alumni Club—ROBERT A. LIPOME, Pres.; Rev. RICHARD W. BLAZEJEWSKI, Chap., P.O. Box 87, Kenmore, 14223.

Catholic Charities—Rev. JOSEPH J. SICARI, Dir. & Pres.; DENNIS C. WALCZYK, CEO, 525 Washington St., Buffalo, 14203. Tel: 716-856-4494; Fax: 716-856-2005.

Catholic Charities Appeal—Rev. JOSEPH J. SICARI, Dir., Office, 525 Washington St., Buffalo, 14203. Tel: 716-856-4494.

Daybreak TV Productions—CLAIRE RUNG, Exec. Producer. Tel: 716-847-8734.

Catholic Relief Services—525 Washington St., Buffalo, 14203. Tel: 716-856-4494.

Chautauqua Catholic Community, Chautauqua Institution—Rev. Msgr. ANTOINE P. ATTEA, Spiritual Dir. & Diocesan Liaison.

Church Ministry, Office of—Mrs. KATHLEEN B. HEFFERN, Dir. Tel: 716-847-5531; Fax: 716-847-5593.

Council of Catholic Men—Rev. Msgr. WILLIAM A. SCHWINGER, Moderator (Retired).

Council of Catholic Women—Sr. MARY ANNE WELDON, R.S.M., Moderator.

Cemeteries—CARMEN A. COLAO, Dir., Mt. Olivet Cemetery, 4000 Elmwood Ave., Kenmore, 14217. Tel: 716-873-6500; Fax: 716-873-3247.

Censors--Board of Diocesan Censors of Books and Vigilance for the Faith—Rev. Msgrs. SAMUEL J. FAIOLA, S.T.D. (Retired); THOMAS E. CRANE.

Charismatic Renewal Program—Rev. RICHARD S. DIGIULIO, Dir.; Deacon JOHN T. SETERA, Asst. Dir.

Central Buffalo Ministries/Office of Black Ministry—BRENDA EASLEY WEBB, Dir. Tel: 716-847-8391; Fax: 716-847-2206.

Clergy Personnel Board—Rev. Msgrs. W. JEROME SULLIVAN, J.C.D., Coord. Tel: 716-847-5537; PAUL R. JUENKER (Retired); PAUL J. WHITNEY (Retired); Revs. RICHARD E. ZAJAC; JAMES C. CROGLIO.

Commission on Women in Church and Society—JANE DRISCOLL, Chm., 210 Smallwood Dr., Snyder, 14226.

Communications—Mr. KEVIN A. KEENAN, Dir. Tel: 716-847-8719; Fax: 716-847-8722.

Diocesan Directory—Sr. M. ANGELICA BIELSKI, C.S.S.F. Tel: 716-847-8723.

Public Relations, Assistant Director of Communications—KRISTINA M. CONNELL. Tel: 716-847-8749.

Assistant Director of Communications for Radio—GREGG PRINCE. Tel: 716-847-8744.

Coordinator of Telecommunications—LISA GIALLELLA. Tel: 716-847-8728.

Computer Services (Diocesan)—JAMES C. KAVANAGH, Dir. Tel: 716-847-5500.

Continuing Education for Clergy—Co-Directors: Rev. Msgr. JAMES E. WALL; Rev. RICHARD W. SIEPKA, M.A., S.T.L., Christ the King Seminary, P.O. Box 607, East Aurora, 14052. Tel: 716-652-8900; Fax: 716-652-8903.

Cursillo Movement—Deacon PETER WALDERS, Spiritual Dir. Tel: 716-675-1912.

Deaf—Rev. CONRAD P. STACHOWIAK, Chap., 425 Penora St., Depew, 14043-3721. Tel: 716-683-3038.

Development Office—DAVID KERSTEN, Exec. Dir., The Foundation of the Roman Catholic Diocese of Buffalo; JEANE HAWTHORNE, Asst. Dir. Tel: 716-847-8370.

Due Process—Rev. SALVATORE MANGANELLO, Chm., Catholic Center. Tel: 716-847-8769; Fax: 716-847-8772.

Ecumenism— (Ecumenical Liaison Committee): Revs. RICHARD E. ZAJAC; THOMAS D. DOYLE; JAMES C. CROGLIO; A. MARK ILLIG; JACOB C. LEDWON; BRENDA EASLEY WEBB; Sr. DIANE LOUTTIT, D.C.; Rev. FRANCIS X. MAZUR, Chm.

Catholic Education—Miss DENISE MCKENZIE, Sec. Education, 795 Main St., Buffalo, 14203-1250. Tel: 716-847-5520; Fax: 716-847-5593; Mrs. DIANE VIGRASS, Supt. Schools. Tel: 716-847-5512; Mrs. MARY BETH COATES, Diocesan Dir., Rel. Educ. Tel: 716-847-5505; Deacon WILLIAM J. WALKOWIAK, Regl. Dir., Rel. Educ. in Eastern Niagara, Orleans, Genesee & Wyoming Counties. Tel: 716-847-5516; Sr. JULIE UHRICH, O.S.F., Regl. Dir., Rel. Educ. in Allegany, Southern Cattaraugus and Southern Chautauqua Counties, Cuba. Tel: 585-968-5776; Mrs. SHARON URBANIAK, Regl. Dir., Rel. Educ. in Northern Chautauqua & Northern Cattaraugus Counties. Tel: 716-847-5514; Mrs. ELIZABETH SCHANBACHER, Dir. Educational Technology. Tel: 716-847-5512; Mrs. PATRICIA TRIMPER, Dir. Instruction & Assessment. Tel: 716-847-5517; Mr. THOMAS E. PETERS, Dir. Govt. Programs. Tel: 716-847-5511; Mrs. TINA TABERSKI, Office Mgr. Tel: 716-847-5520.

Evangelization Commission—Rev. DANIEL J. PALYS, Chm., 5271 Clinton St., Elma, 14059. Tel: 716-668-4017.

Family Life—Directors: Deacon THOMAS SCHULTZ; GINI SCHULTZ. Tel: 716-847-2210; Fax: 716-847-2206.

Finance Office—Mr. JOHN R. O'BRIEN. Tel: 716-847-5500; Fax: 716-847-5557.

Guild for the Blind, Inc.—Office, 525 Washington St., Buffalo, 14203. Tel: 716-856-4494.

Hispanic Apostolate—Rev. Msgr. DAVID M. GALLIVAN, Dir. Tel: 716-847-2217; Fax: 716-847-2206.

Holy Childhood (Pontifical) Association—Rev. Msgr. HAROLD WAGNER, Dir. Tel: 716-847-8773.

Holy Name Society—Rev. Msgr. FRANCIS B. JUCHNOWSKI, Moderator (Retired); RAYMOND ZIENTARA, Exec. Dir. Diocesan Union of Holy Name Societies. Tel: 716-847-2202.

Hospital Chaplains—Rev. RICHARD H. AUGUSTYN, Dir. Hospital Ministry, 100 High St., Buffalo, 14203. Tel: 716-859-5600.

Human Resources—PAUL C. EBERHARDT, Dir. Tel: 716-847-8376.

Insurance Services—JOHN SCHOLL, Dir. Tel: 716-847-8394; Fax: 716-847-5538.

Legion of Mary—Rev. DAVID W. BIALKOWSKI, Spiritual Dir. Tel: 716-847-5545.

Liturgical Commission—KAREN L. PODD, Chm.

Newman Club Chaplains—Rev. EUGENE P. ULRICH, Vicar Campus Ministry and Newman Club Centers, P.O. Box 1154, Alfred, 14802. Tel: 607-276-5304.

Newspaper—Mr. KEVIN A. KEENAN, Editor in Chief. Tel: 716-847-8719; RICK FRANUSIAK, Mng. Editor. Tel: 716-849-8738; Fax: 716-847-8722. "Western New York Catholic"

Pamphlet Society (Catholic) of Buffalo, Inc.—120 Old Maryvale Dr., Cheektowaga, 14225. Tel: 716-833-6617.

Pastoral Council—Mr. TOM LILLIS, Chm., 193 Briarhurst Dr., Tonawanda, 14150.

Peace and Justice (Diocesan Commission)—Rev. Msgr. JAMES G. KELLY, 1395 Hertel Ave., Buffalo, 14216.

Permanent Diaconate—Deacons THADDEUS P. MAY, Dir.; THADDEUS V. PIJACKI, Dir. Formation. Tel: 716-847-5543; Fax: 716-847-5593.

Priests, Vicar for—Rev. Msgr. JAMES E. WALL, 6892 Lake Shore Rd., Derby, 14047. Tel: 716-947-5449.

Pro-Life Activities—JUDITH A. GORMAN, Coord. Tel: 716-847-2205; Fax: 716-847-2206.

Propagation of the Faith—Rev. Msgr. HAROLD WAGNER. Tel: 716-847-8773; Fax: 716-847-2206.

Purchasing (Diocesan)—PETER M. MCKEE. Tel: 716-847-8711; Fax: 716-847-8702.

Research and Planning—Sr. REGINA MURPHY, S.S.M.N. Tel: 716-847-5539; Fax: 716-847-5593. Email: rmurphy@buffalodiocese.org.

Safe Environment—DONALD R. BLOWEY JR., Program Dir.

Service Corps—AMY FLEISCHAUER, Dir. Tel: 716-847-8384; Fax: 716-847-5593.

St. Peter Claver Youth Program, Inc.—BARBARA PITKIN, Exec. Dir., 185 Lang Ave., Buffalo, 14215. Tel: 716-893-4651.

St. Vincent de Paul Society—Mr. MARK S. ZIRNHELD, Exec. Dir., 1298 Main St., Buffalo, 14209. Tel: 716-882-3360; Fax: 716-882-3556.

Worship, Office Of—Rev. PAUL D. SEIL, Dir. Tel: 716-847-5545; Fax: 716-847-5593; ALAN D. LUKAS, Dir. Music, Christ the King Seminary, P.O. Box 607, East Aurora, 14052-0607. Tel: 716-652-6565; Fax: 716-652-8903.

Vicar for Religious—Sr. M. CHARLENE NOWAK, C.S.S.F.; Rev. JAMES J. RUDDICK, S.J., Assoc. Vicar. Tel: 716-847-5529; Fax: 716-847-5593.

Victim Assistance Coordinator—KATHRYN MARSH. Tel: 716-895-3010. Email: kathy.march@ccwny.org.

Vocations—Rev. LEON J. BIERNAT, Dir. Tel: 716-847-5535; Fax: 716-847-5593.

Youth Department - Diocese of Buffalo—DANIEL J. GREER, Dir. Tel: 716-847-8789; Fax: 716-847-8797.

Young Adult Ministry—PATRICIA BUBAR SPEAR. Tel: 716-847-8788; Fax: 716-847-8797.

Youth Department, Jamestown—KATHY NICASTRO, Prog. Coord., Southern Tier, 10 Prospect St., Jamestown, 14701. Tel: 716-484-9869.

CLERGY, PARISHES, MISSIONS AND PAROCHIAL SCHOOLS

CITY OF BUFFALO

(ERIE COUNTY)

1—ST. JOSEPH'S CATHEDRAL (1851), Rev. Msgr. James F. Campbell, Rector.
Res.: 50 Franklin St., 14202. Tel: 716-854-5855; Fax: 716-854-5861.
School—Catholic Academy of West Buffalo Regional School, Tel: 716-885-6111; Fax: 716-885-6452. See separate listing under Regional and Consolidated Elementary Schools in the Institutions located in the Diocese.

2—ST. ADALBERT'S BASILICA (1886), (Polish), [CEM] Rev. Thaddeus Nicholas Bocianowski.
Res.: 212 Stanislaus St., 14212. Tel: 716-895-8091; Fax: 716-895-8773.
Catechesis/Religious Program—130 Kosciuszko St., 14212. Tel: 716-894-8366. Students 31.
St. Adalbert Response to Love Center—130 Kosciuszko St., 14212. Tel: 716-894-7030; Fax: 716-891-5474. Sr. M. Johnice Rzadkiewicz, C.S.S.F., Dir. Total Assisted 40,167.

3—ST. AGATHA (1921), Rev. Adolph M. Kowalczyk.
Res.: 54 Alamo Pl., 14220. Tel: 716-822-2668; Fax: 716-828-1405.
School—Tel: 716-824-4510. Ms. Dolores Oakes, Prin. Lay Teachers 6; Students 106.
Catechesis/Religious Program—Students 52.

4—ST. AGNES (1883), Rev. James B. Cunningham.
Res.: 194 Ludington St., 14206. Tel: 716-893-0509; Fax: 716-896-0987.
School—Tel: 716-892-1441; Fax: 716-896-0934. Sr. Ann Helene Koenig, O.S.F., Prin. Lay Teachers 14; Students 192.

Catechesis/Religious Program—Mrs. Barbara Schmitt, D.R.E. Students 95.
Catholic Charities—Tel: 716-893-6418. Sr. Rose Therese Di Gregorio, O.S.F., TLCIM Project Dir.

5—ALL SAINTS (1911), Rev. Msgr. Albert W. Clody.
Res.: 127 Chadduck Ave., 14207-1531. Tel: 716-875-8183; Fax: 716-875-6597.
Catechesis/Religious Program—Ronald Szczerbiak, D.R.E. Students 120.

6—ST. AMBROSE (1930), Rev. Msgr. David M. Lee.
Res.: 65 Ridgewood Rd., 14220. Tel: 716-822-5962; Fax: 716-822-0966.
School—Tel: 716-824-6360; Fax: 716-826-5899. Laura Kazmierczak, Prin. Lay Teachers 22; Students 296.
Catechesis/Religious Program—Tel: 716-826-4125. Sr. Pauline Petruzzella, R.S.M., D.R.E. Students 200.

7—ST. ANN (1858), Revs. James F. Joyce, S.J.; Edward J. Durkin, S.J.; Sr. Marie Davis, O.S.F., Pastoral Assoc.
Office—491 Emslie St., 14212. Tel: 716-852-3316; Fax: 716-854-4131. In Res., Revs. James J. Ruddick, S.J.; Richard J. Zanoni, S.J.
Res.: 501 Emslie St., 14212. Tel: 716-854-3742; Fax: 716-854-4131.
School—Catholic Central Regional School See separate listing under Regional and Consolidated Elementary Schools in the Institutions located in the Diocese.
Catechesis/Religious Program—Students 20.

8—ANNUNCIATION (1885), Rev. Bartholomew W. Lipiec; Sr. Barbara Riter, S.S.M.N., Pastoral Assoc.
Res.: 18 Greenwood Pl., 14213. Tel: 716-885-2469; Fax: 716-885-3385.
Church: Lafayette Ave. & Grant St., 14213.
School—Catholic Academy of West Buffalo Regional School, Tel: 716-886-5384. See separate listing under Regional and Consolidated Elementary Schools in the Institutions located in the Diocese.
Catechesis/Religious Program—Tel: 716-881-2914. Darice Destino, D.R.E. Students 85.

9—ST. ANTHONY OF PADUA (1891), (Italian), Rev. Secondo Casarotto, C.S.
Res.: 160 Court St., 14202. Tel: 716-854-2563; Fax: 716-854-2564.
School—Catholic Academy of West Buffalo Regional School See separate listing under Regional and Consolidated Elementary Schools in the Institutions located in the Diocese.

10—ASSUMPTION (1888), (Polish),, Linked with St. Elizabeth, Buffalo. Rev. Richard Jedrzejewski. In Res., Rev. Msgr. John M. Ryan (Retired); Rev. Thomas P. Taton.
Res.: 435 Amherst St., 14207. Tel: 716-875-7626; Fax: 716-447-1027.
School—Our Lady of Black Rock Consolidated, 16 Germain St., 14207. Tel: 716-873-7497. Sr. Francianne Zielezinski, C.S.S.F., Prin. Felician Sisters 1; Students 144.
Catechesis/Religious Program—Tel: 716-873-7187. Mary Lou Wyrobek, D.R.E. Students 72.

11—ST. BARTHOLOMEW, , Closed 1993. Merged with Blessed Trinity Church. Records at the Catholic Center, 795 Main St., Buffalo, 14203.

12—ST. BENEDICT THE MOOR, Closed. For inquiries for parish records contact the chancery.

13—ST. BERNARD (1906), Rev. Francis J. Chmielewski. In Res., Rev. Msgr. Francis B. Juchnowski, Pastor Emeritus (Retired).
Res.: 414 S. Ogden, 14206. Tel: 716-822-8856; Fax: 716-822-7799.
School—Tel: 716-822-8057; Fax: 716-822-0280. Sr. M. Fredrica Polanski, C.S.S.F., Prin. Congregation of Sisters of St. Felix 1; Lay Teachers 14; Students 194.
Catechesis/Religious Program—Students 110.

14—BLESSED SACRAMENT (1887) Rev. Paul R. Bossi. In Res., Rev. Salvatore Manganello.
Res.: 1035 Delaware Ave., 14209-1605. Tel: 716-884-0053; Fax: 716-884-2279.
School—Catholic Academy of West Buffalo Regional School, Tel: 716-885-6111; Fax: 716-885-6452. See separate listing under Regional and Consolidated Elementary Schools in the Institutions located in the Diocese.
Catechesis/Religious Program—James J. Kennedy, D.R.E. Students 53.

15—BLESSED TRINITY (1906), Rev. George L. Reger.
Res.: 317 Leroy Ave., 14214. Tel: 716-833-0301; Fax: 716-834-4711.
School—Catholic Central Regional School See separate listing under Regional and Consolidated Elementary Schools in the Institutions located in the Diocese.
Catechesis/Religious Program—Students 15.

16—ST. BONIFACE, Closed. For inquiries for parish records contact the chancery.

17—ST. BRIGID, Merged, with St. Columba. For inquiries for parish records contact SS. Columba & Brigid, Buffalo.

18—ST. CASIMIR (1890), (Polish), Rev. Msgr Matthew S. Kopacz; Rev. James T. Bartnik.
Res.: 160 Cable St., 14206. Tel: 716-824-9589; Fax: 716-824-2004.
Catechesis/Religious Program—1833 Clinton St., 14206. Tel: 716-826-9338. Students 71.

19—SS. COLUMBA & BRIGID (1888), Rev. Roy T. Herberger, Admin.
Res.: 418 N. Division St., 14204. Tel: 716-852-3331; Fax: 716-852-3331.
School—Catholic Central Regional School See separate listing under Regional and Consolidated Elementary Schools in the Institutions located in the Diocese.

20—CORONATION OF THE BLESSED VIRGIN MARY (1950), In Res., Rev. Andrew Tu Minh Nguyen, Admin.; Rev. Msgr. Eugene M. Radon, Pastor Emeritus (Retired).
Res.: 348 Dewitt St., 14213. Tel: 716-882-2650.
School—Our Lady of Black Rock School, Tel: 716-875-7626. See separate listing under Regional and Consolidated Elementary Schools in the Institutions located in the Diocese.
Catechesis/Religious Program—Tel: 716-882-6360. Mr. Frank Antonnucci, D.R.E. Students 30.

21—CORPUS CHRISTI (1898), (Polish),, (St. Anthony's Convent) Revs. Anselm Chalupka, O.S.P.P.E.; Sebastian Hanks, O.S.P.P.E.; Bros. Peter Lisiecki; Thomas Fabiszewski, O.S.S.P.E.
Res.: 199 Clark St., 14212-1407. Tel: 716-896-1050; Fax: 716-896-1595.
Catechesis/Religious Program—Students 15.

22—ST. ELIZABETH OF HUNGARY (1906), (Hungarian), Attended by, Assumption, Buffalo. Rev. Richard Jedrzejewski, Admin.
Res.: 435 Amherst St., 14207. Tel: 716-875-6586; Fax: 716-876-3193.
Catechesis/Religious Program— Clustered with Assumption, Buffalo.

23—ST. FLORIAN (1917), (Polish), Rev. George Poltorak, S.A.C.
Res.: 567 Hertel Ave., 14207. Tel: 716-875-3246; Fax: 716-876-6410.
School—Our Lady of Black Rock Consolidated School See separate listing under Regional and Consolidated Elementary Schools in the Institutions located in the Diocese.
Catechesis/Religious Program—Tel: 716-882-4015. Students 38.

24—ST. FRANCIS OF ASSISI (1909), Rev. Richard S. DiGiulio; Deacon Roy P. Dibb.
Res.: 118 Schiller St., 14206. Tel: 716-895-6813; Fax: 716-891-4609.
Catechesis/Religious Program—Students 81.

25—ST. FRANCIS XAVIER (1849), (German), [CEM], Linked with St. John the Baptist, Buffalo. Rev. James M. Monaco, Admin.; Sr. Margaret Toohill, O.S.F., Pastoral Min.
Res.: 157 East St., 14207. Tel: 716-873-1911; Fax: 716-871-0623.
School—Our Lady of Black Rock Consolidated School, Tel: 716-873-7497. See separate listing under Regional and Consolidated Elementary Schools in the Institutions located in the Diocese.
Catechesis/Religious Program—Students 13.

26—ST. GERARD (1902), Rev. Francis X. Mazur.
Res.: 1190 E. Delavan Ave., 14215. Tel: 716-895-5761; Fax: 716-895-6311.
Catechesis/Religious Program—Tel: 716-895-3751. Debra Stafford, D.R.E. Students 35.

27—HOLY ANGELS (1852), Revs. Terrence O'Connell, O.M.I.; Dwight Hoeberechts, O.M.I. In Res., Revs. Eugene Tremblay, O.M.I.; Stephen Vasek, O.M.I.; George Kirwin, O.M.I.; Daniel F. O'Leary, O.M.I.; Bro. Richard Cote, O.M.I.
Res.: 348 Porter Ave., 14201. Tel: 716-885-3767; Fax: 716-882-8211.
School—Catholic Academy of West Buffalo Regional School, Tel: 716-885-6111; Fax: 716-885-6452. See separate listing under Regional and Consolidated Elementary Schools in the Institutions located in the Diocese.
Catechesis/Religious Program—Students 161.

28—HOLY APOSTLES SS. PETER AND PAUL (1909), (Polish), Rev. Ronald A. Bagienski.
Res.: 660 Smith St., 14210. Tel: 716-854-8971; Fax: 716-854-4458.
Catechesis/Religious Program—Tel: 716-856-5790; Fax: 716-856-4019. Joint program with SS. Rita and Patrick.

29—HOLY CROSS (1914),, Linked with Immaculate Conception Rev. Msgr. David M. Gallivan.
Res.: 345 Seventh St., 14201. Tel: 716-847-6930; Fax: 716-847-6934.
School—Catholic Academy of West Buffalo Regional School, Tel: 716-885-6111; Fax: 716-885-6452. See separate listing under Regional and Consolidated Elementary Schools in the Institutions located in the Diocese.
Catechesis/Religious Program—Jodi Miller, D.R.E.; Sr. Olivia Ortiz, C.S.S.F., D.R.E. Students 85.

30—HOLY FAMILY (1902), Rev. William R. Bigelow.
Res.: 1885 S. Park Ave., 14220. Tel: 716-822-0308; Fax: 716-826-6018.
School—Tel: 716-826-6017. Jane Driscoll, Prin. Sisters of Mercy 1; Lay Teachers 13; Students 117.
Catechesis/Religious Program—Students 83.

31—HOLY NAME OF JESUS (1887), Rev. Robert J. Hora.
Res.: 1947 Bailey Ave., 14211. Tel: 716-892-8056; Fax: 716-892-0836.
Catechesis/Religious Program—Tel: 716-897-4360. Students 5.

32—HOLY SPIRIT (1910), Rev. Joseph D. Wolf; Deacon William J. Hynes Jr.
Res.: 91 Dakota Ave., 14216. Tel: 716-875-8102; Fax: 716-875-4186.
School—85 Dakota Ave., 14216. Tel: 716-875-9478. Miss Karen Adamski, Prin. Lay Teachers 14; Students 101.
Catechesis/Religious Program—Tel: 716-875-8103. Students 70.

33—IMMACULATE CONCEPTION (1849), Attended by, Holy Cross, Buffalo Rev. Msgr. David M. Gallivan, Admin.
Office: 144 Edward St., 14201. Tel: 716-886-5627.
School—Catholic Academy of West Buffalo Regional School, Tel: 716-885-6111. See separate listing under Regional and Consolidated Elementary Schools in the Institutions located in the Diocese.
Catechesis/Religious Program—Giorgio Cappuzzello, D.R.E. Students 85.

34—IMMACULATE HEART OF MARY (1946), Rev. Richard H. Augustyn, Admin.
Res.: 381 Edison St., 14215. Tel: 716-894-6953; Fax: 716-892-1370.
Catechesis/Religious Program—Students 28.

35—ST. JAMES (1916), Rev. Robert L. Gebhard. In Res., Deacon Ronald Walker.
Res.: 10 Hastings Ave., 14215. Tel: 716-834-5601; Fax: 716-834-5601.
Catechesis/Religious Program—Tel: 716-832-7622. Len Rizzo, D.R.E. Students 33.
Convent—36 Davidson St., 14215. Tel: 716-836-7835.

36—ST. JOACHIM, Closed. For inquiries for parish records contact the chancery.

37—ST. JOHN KANTY (1892), (Polish), Rev. Anthony Lutostanski.
Res.: 101 Swinburne St., 14212. Tel: 716-893-0412; Fax: 716-893-9864.
Catechesis/Religious Program—Students 22.

38—ST. JOHN THE BAPTIST (1867), Attended by, St. Francis Xavier, Buffalo. Rev. James M. Monaco, Admin.
Res.: 60 Hertel Ave., 14207-2595. Tel: 716-873-1911.
Parish Center—410 East St., 14207. Tel: 716-873-8660.
School—Our Lady of Black Rock Consolidated School, Tel: 716-873-7497. See separate listing under Regional and Consolidated Elementary Schools in the Institutions located in the Diocese.
Catechesis/Religious Program— Combined with St. Francis Xavier, Buffalo

39—ST. JOHN THE EVANGELIST (1906), Rev. Robert M. Mock.
Res.: 2315 Seneca St., 14210. Tel: 716-822-2315; Fax: 716-822-2295.
Catechesis/Religious Program—Tel: 716-825-1252. Students 95.

40—ST. JOSEPH-UNIVERSITY (1850), Rev. Jacob C. Ledwon; Sr. Jeremy Midura, C.S.S.F., Pastoral Assoc.; Deacons Thaddeus V. Pijacki; Paul C. Emerson.
Res.: 3269 Main St., 14214. Tel: 716-833-0298; Fax: 716-833-7339.
School—3275 Main St., 14214. Tel: 716-835-7395; Fax: 716-833-6550. Sisters of St. Joseph 1; Sisters of St. Mary of Namur 2; Sisters of St. Francis of Penance and Christian Charity 1; Lay Teachers 20; Students 254.
Catechesis/Religious Program—Tel: 716-837-2971. Sr. Elizabeth Buchala, S.S.M.N., D.R.E. Students 301.

41—ST. LAWRENCE (1929), Rev. Paul D. Seil; Deacon Paul F. Weisenburger.
Res.: 1520 E. Delavan Ave., 14215. Tel: 716-892-2471; Fax: 716-892-1315.
School—Kolbe Catholic Regional School, Tel: 716-895-3127; Fax: 716-895-7347. See St. John Gualbert, Cheektowaga for details.
Catechesis/Religious Program—Tel: 716-896-0047. Sr. Bernadette Kapfer, C.S.S.F., D.R.E. Students 53.

42—ST. LOUIS (1829), Rev. Msgr. Robert J. Cunningham, P.A., J.C.L.
Res.: 35 Edward St., 14202. Tel: 716-852-6040; Fax: 716-853-9225.
School—Catholic Academy of West Buffalo Regional School See separate listing under Regional and Consolidated Elementary Schools in the Institutions located in the Diocese.

43—ST. LUKE, (Polish), Closed. For inquiries for parish records contact the chancery.
44—ST. MARGARET (1916), Rev. Msgr. James G. Kelly; Deacon Terrance P. Harter.
Res.: 1395 Hertel Ave., 14216. Tel: 716-876-5318; Fax: 716-875-9068.
School—Tel: 716-876-8885; Fax: 716-876-7553. Lay Teachers 14; Students 186.
Catechesis/Religious Program—Tel: 716-876-6122. Students 158.
45—ST. MARK (1908), Rev. Msgr. Francis Braun.
Res.: 401 Woodward Ave., 14214. Tel: 716-836-1600; Fax: 716-836-1611.
School—Tel: 716-836-1191; Fax: 716-836-0391. Sr. Jeanne Eberle, S.S.J., Prin. Sisters of St. Joseph 2; Lay Teachers 20; Students 305.
Catechesis/Religious Program—Students 50.
Convent—223 Summit Ave., 14214. Tel: 716-837-9055.
46—ST. MARTIN (1926), Revs. Vincent J. Becker; Michael Putich, O.F.M.; Deacons Lawrence D. Eschbach; Michael P. McKeating.
Res.: 1140 Abbott Rd., 14220. Tel: 716-823-7077; Fax: 716-823-4197.
School—Tel: 716-824-0726; 716-824-0727; Fax: 716-825-7685. Elaine Poleto, Prin. Lay Teachers 24; Students 379.
Catechesis/Religious Program—Students 70.
47—ST. MARTIN DE PORRES (1993), (African American), Rev. Ronald P. Sajdak; Deacon Ronald Walker; Sr. Philip Marie, S.S.J., Pastoral Assoc.
Office—555 Northampton St., 14208. Tel: 716-883-7729; Fax: 716-886-4101.
Res.: 26 Wyoming Ave., 14215. Tel: 716-893-6079.
School—Catholic Central Regional School, Tel: 716-852-6854. See Regional and Consolidated Elementary Schools under Institutions Located in the Diocese.
Catechesis/Religious Program—Students 54.
48—ST. MARY OF SORROWS (1872), Sisters Mary Augusta Kaiser, S.S.J., Parish Life Coord.; Jean Marie Zirnheld, S.S.J., Pastoral Assoc.; Deacon David R. Velasquez.
Church & Offices: 333 Guilford St., 14211. Tel: 716-892-4115; Fax: 716-892-4115.
School—Catholic Central Regional School, Tel: 716-852-6854; Fax: 716-852-8410. See separate listing under Regional and Consolidated Elementary Schools in the Institutions located in the Diocese.
Catechesis/Religious Program—Students 17.
Convent—Sisters of St. Joseph, 20 Rich St., 14211. Tel: 716-892-4116; Fax: 716-892-4116.
49—ST. MATTHEW, Closed., For inquiries for parish records contact St. Martin de Porres, Buffalo.
50—ST. MICHAEL (1851), Revs. Ronald W. Sams, S.J.; Francis Staebell, S.J.; Edward L. Guth, S.J.; John G. Sturm, S.J.; Joseph R. Spellerberg, S.J.; Richard J. Hoar, S.J.; H. James Roleke, S.J.; Bro. James Dennehy, S.J. In Res., Rev. John J. Mattimore, S.J.
Res.: 651 Washington St., 14203. Tel: 716-854-6726; Fax: 716-854-4616.
School—Catholic Academy of West Buffalo Regional School, Tel: 716-885-6111; 716-886-5384; Fax: 716-885-6452. See separate listing under Regional and Consolidated Elementary Schools in the Institutions located in the Diocese.
51—ST. MONICA, Closed. For inquiries for parish records contact the chancery.
52—THE NATIVITY OF THE BLESSED VIRGIN (1898), Rev. Angelo M. Chimera.
Res.: 20 Herkimer St., 14213. Tel: 716-885-1344; Fax: 716-885-2385.
School—Catholic Academy of West Buffalo Regional School, Tel: 716-885-6111; Fax: 716-885-6452. See separate listing under Regional and Consolidated Elementary Schools in the Institutions located in the Diocese.
Catechesis/Religious Program—Tel: 716-882-6360. Mr. Frank Antonnucci, D.R.E. Students 9.
53—OUR LADY OF LORETTO (1940), Rev. Norman P. McTigue; Deacon Roberto G. Miranda; Ronald Thaler, Pastoral Assoc.
Res.: 172 15th St., 14213. Tel: 716-885-7573; Fax: 716-885-0739.
School—Catholic Academy of West Buffalo Regional School See separate listing under Regional and Consolidated Elementary Schools in the Institutions located in the Diocese.
Catechesis/Religious Program—Tel: 716-881-2133. Elise McDowell, D.R.E. Students 81.
54—OUR LADY OF LOURDES, Closed. For inquiries for parish records contact the chancery.
55—OUR LADY OF PERPETUAL HELP (1897),, Linked with St. Valentine, Buffalo Rev. Donald J. Lutz, Admin.
Res.: 115 O'Connell Ave., 14204. Tel: 716-852-2671; Fax: 716-852-2672.
Catechesis/Religious Program—Students 45.
56—PRECIOUS BLOOD (1899), (Polish), Rev. Nicholas Swiatek, O.F.M.Conv.
Res.: 140 Lewis St., 14206. Tel: 716-854-4623; Fax: 716-854-3077.
Catechesis/Religious Program—Students 13.
57—QUEEN OF PEACE (1920), (Polish), Rev. Richard M. Poblocki, Admin.
Res.: 1955 Genesee St., 14211. Tel: 716-892-5646; Fax: 716-897-2411.
Catechesis/Religious Program—Students 9.
58—QUEEN OF THE MOST HOLY ROSARY, (Polish), Closed. For inquiries for parish records contact the chancery.
59—SS. RITA & PATRICK (1854), Revs. John Alderson, O.F.M.; Paul J. Osborne, O.F.M. (NY); Bro. Maurice V. Swartout, O.F.M., Pastoral Assoc. In Res., Revs. Robert Struzynski, O.F.M.; Gerald R. Mudd, O.F.M.; Bros. Timothy S. Dauenhauser, O.F.M.; Michael Oberst, O.F.M.
St. Patrick Friary: 102 Seymour St., 14210. Tel: 716-856-5790; Fax: 716-856-4019.
Catechesis/Religious Program—Students 128.
60—ST. ROSE OF LIMA (1925), Revs. Harry E. Winter, O.M.I.; Martin Walsh, O.M.I.
Res.: 500 Parker Ave., 14216. Tel: 716-834-6688; Fax: 716-834-6689.
School—201 Winston Rd., 14216. Tel: 716-833-4100; Fax: 716-834-3617. Joseph Duttweiler, Prin. Lay Teachers 14; Students 197.
Catechesis/Religious Program—Tel: 716-833-4130. Mrs. Mary Frances Mc Crorey, D.R.E.; Mrs. Amy V. Vukelic, D.R.E. Students 81.
61—ST. STANISLAUS (1873), (Polish), [CEM] Most Rev. Edward M. Grosz, D.D., V.G.
Res.: 123 Townsend St., 14212. Tel: 716-854-5511; Fax: 716-854-0170.
School—Tel: 716-854-1803. Felician Sisters 1; Lay Teachers 9; Students 65.
Catechesis/Religious Program—Students 31.
62—ST. STEPHEN (1875), Rev. Joseph Klos, J.C.L.
Res.: 193 Elk St., 14210-1499. Tel: 716-823-2358; Fax: 716-826-2168.
Catechesis/Religious Program—Students 80.
63—ST. TERESA (1897), Rev. John J. Mitka; Deacon Thomas M. Forcucci.
Res.: 1974 Seneca St., 14210. Tel: 716-822-0608.
School—Tel: 716-822-4546; Fax: 716-822-2576. Mrs. Eileen Coppola, Prin. Sisters 1; Lay Teachers 13; Students 147.
Catechesis/Religious Program—Tel: 716-822-2546. Students 129.
64—ST. THOMAS AQUINAS (1920), Rev. Arthur J. Smith; Deacon Thomas A. McDonnell.
Res.: 450 Abbott Rd., 14220-1796. Tel: 716-822-1250; Fax: 716-822-2594.
School—20 Athol St., 14220-1796. Tel: 716-824-5046; Fax: 716-824-2539. Eileen Landseadel, Prin. Lay Teachers 24; Students 322.
Catechesis/Religious Program—Tel: 716-826-0888; Fax: 716-822-2594. Students 120.
65—TRANSFIGURATION, (Polish), Closed. For inquiries for parish records contact the chancery.
66—ST. VALENTINE (1920), (Polish), Attended by, Our Lady of Perpetual Help, Buffalo. Rev. Donald J. Lutz, Admin.
Res.: 522 S. Park Ave., 14204. Tel: 716-854-7193; Fax: 716-852-2672.
Catechesis/Religious Program—Tel: 716-852-2671. Twinned with Our Lady of Perpetual Help, Buffalo.
67—ST. VINCENT DE PAUL, Closed. For inquiries for parish records contact the chancery.
68—THE VISITATION OF THE B.V.M. (1898), Rev. Paul P. Sabo.
Res.: 1040 Lovejoy St., 14206. Tel: 716-892-2289; Fax: 716-897-3310.
Catechesis/Religious Program—Students 17.

OUTSIDE THE CITY OF BUFFALO

AKRON, ERIE CO., ST. TERESA OF AVILA (1859), [CEM] Rev. Msgr. Robert J. Williamson; Rev. Karl E. Loeb, Admin.
Res.: 5771 Buell St., P.O. Box 168, 14001. Tel: 716-542-9103; Fax: 716-542-2444.
Catechesis/Religious Program—Tel: 716-542-9717; Fax: 716-542-2444. Sr. Mary Ruth Warejko, C.S.S.F., D.R.E. Students 256.
ALBION, ORLEANS CO.
1—ST. JOSEPH (1852), [CEM], Linked with St. Mary Assumption, Albion. Rev. Richard A. Csizmar; Deacon James L. Collichio.
Res.: 106 S. Main St., 14411. Tel: 585-589-4243; Fax: 585-589-0734.
Catechesis/Religious Program—Tel: 585-589-5236. Miss Nancy J. Sedita, D.R.E. Students 285.
2—ST. MARY ASSUMPTION (1891), (Polish), Attended by, St. Joseph, Albion. Rev. Richard A. Csizmar; Deacon James L. Collichio.
Res.: 47 Brown St., 14411. Tel: 585-589-4243; 585-589-5162; Fax: 585-589-0734.
Catechesis/Religious Program—Students 6.
ALDEN, ERIE CO., ST. JOHN THE BAPTIST (1850), [CEM] Rev. Robert A. Martin, Admin.; Deacon Richard J. Mahaney; Sr. Ellen McCarthy, S.S.J., Pastoral Assoc.
Res.: 2021 Sandridge Rd., 14004. Tel: 716-937-6959; Fax: 716-937-0075.
School—Tel: 716-937-9483; Fax: 716-937-9794. Ms. Marilynn Camp, Prin. Lay Teachers 15.
Catechesis/Religious Program—Tel: 716-937-3448. Margaret McCartin Orcutt, D.R.E. Students 557.
ALLEGANY, CATTARAUGUS CO., ST. BONAVENTURE (1854), Rev. Richard Husted, O.F.M.; Peggy Reitz, Pastoral Assoc.
Res.: 95 E. Main St., 14706. Tel: 716-373-1330; Fax: 716-373-4220.
School—Southern Tier Catholic Regional School See separate listing under Regional and Consolidated Elementary Schools in the Institutions located in the Diocese. Tel: 716-372-2891.
Catechesis/Religious Program—Holly Keenan, D.R.E. Students 283.
Mission—St. John the Baptist S. Nine Mile Rd., Vandalia, Cattaraugus Co. 14706.
ALMOND, ALLEGANY CO., SS. BRENDAN AND JUDE (1992), Rev. Eugene P. Ulrich; Susan M. Fowler, Pastoral Assoc.
Mailing Address: *St. Jude Chapel*, Lower College Dr., P.O. Box 1154, Alfred, 14802. Tel: 607-587-9411; Fax: 607-587-9431.
Church: 11 S. Main St., Box G, 14804. Tel: 607-276-5304.
Catechesis/Religious Program—Students 51.
AMHERST, ERIE CO., ST. LEO THE GREAT (1953), Rev. Msgr. Robert E. Zapfel; Sr. Jean Becker, O.S.F., Pastoral Assoc.
Res.: 885 Sweet Home Rd., 14226. Tel: 716-835-8905; Fax: 716-835-8997.
School—Tel: 716-832-6340. Mr. Patrick J. Brady, Prin. Sisters of Third Order of St. Francis 1; Lay Teachers 19; Students 167; Preschool Students 82.
Catechesis/Religious Program—Tel: 716-833-8359. Sr. Judith Beiswanger, O.S.F., D.R.E. Students 418.
ANDOVER, ALLEGANY CO., BLESSED SACRAMENT (1855), [CEM] Attended by, Immaculate Conception, Wellsville. Rev. Dennis G. Wolf.
Res.: 6 Maple Ave., Wellsville, 14895-1294. Tel: 585-593-4834; Fax: 585-593-7167.
Catechesis/Religious Program—Students 15.
ANGELICA, ALLEGANY CO., SACRED HEART (1848), Attended by, St. Mary, Belmont. Rev. Dennis J. Mancuso.
Res.: 5 Milton St., Belmont, 14813-1119. Tel: 585-268-7272; Fax: 585-268-9128.
Church: Park Cir., 14709.
Catechesis/Religious Program— Combined with St. Mary, Belmont.
ANGOLA, ERIE CO., MOST PRECIOUS BLOOD (1871), [CEM] Rev. Bernard U. Nowak.
Res.: 22 Prospect St., P.O. Box 153, 14006. Tel: 716-549-0420; Fax: 716-549-0425.
School—17 Prospect St., 14006. Tel: 716-549-1818; Fax: 716-549-3417. Franciscan Sisters of St. Joseph 2; Sisters of Mercy 1; Lay Teachers 8; Students 114.
Catechesis/Religious Program—Students 180.
ARCADE, WYOMING CO., SS. PETER AND PAUL (1907), [CEM], Linked with St. Mary, East Arcade. Rev. Czeslaw M. Krysa, Admin.
Res.: 417 Main St., 14009-1195. Tel: 585-492-5330; Fax: 585-492-1047.
School—St. Aloysius Regional School See separate listing under Regional and Consolidated Elementary Schools in the Institutions located in the Diocese.
Catechesis/Religious Program—Students 160.
ATHOL SPRINGS, ERIE CO., ST. FRANCIS OF ASSISI (1929), Revs. Steven G. Frenier, O.F.M.Conv.; Joseph Dorniak, O.F.M.Conv.; Mark David Skura, O.F.M.Conv.
Res.: S-4263 St. Francis Dr., 14010. Tel: 716-627-2710; Fax: 716-627-5263.
Catechesis/Religious Program—Tel: 716-627-3357. Annette Breen, D.R.E. Students 413.
ATTICA, WYOMING CO., ST. VINCENT DE PAUL (1857), [CEM] Rev. Stanley R. Chwalinski.
Res.: 50 East Ave., 14011. Tel: 585-591-1228; Fax: 585-591-1614.
School—Genesee-Wyoming Catholic Central Consolidated School See separate listing under Regional and Consolidated Elementary Schools in the Institutions located in the Diocese. Tel: 716-591-2515; Fax: 716-591-2516.
Catechesis/Religious Program—Students 217.
BARKER, NIAGARA CO., ST. PATRICK (1856), [CEM], Linked to St. Charles Borromeo, Olcott. Rev. James F. Hassett.
Res.: 1726 Quaker Rd., 14012. Tel: 716-795-3331; Fax: 716-795-3919.
Catechesis/Religious Program—Tel: 716-795-3459. Students 108.
BATAVIA, GENESEE CO.
1—ST. ANTHONY (1908), (Italian), Rev. Joseph S. Spatorico.
Res.: 122 Liberty St., 14020. Tel: 585-343-0914;

Fax: 585-344-8376.
School—Tel: 585-343-5561; Fax: 585-343-5653. Mrs. Kathleen E. Culik, Prin. Sisters of Mercy 1; Lay Teachers 13; Students 100.
Catechesis/Religious Program—Students 95.

2—ST. JOSEPH (1849), [CEM] Rev. Msgr. Leo F. McCarthy; Rev. Marek Gnidzinski; Deacon John Stone. In Res., Rev. John P. Mack.
Res.: 303 E. Main St., 14020. Tel: 585-343-5800; Fax: 585-345-9525.
School—Tel: 585-343-6154; Fax: 585-343-3911. Barbara Anderson, Prin. Lay Teachers 25; Students 259; Preschool Students 51.
Catechesis/Religious Program—Students 139.

3—ST. MARY (1906), Revs. Dennis G. Riter; Ivan R. Trujillo.
Res.: 18 Ellicott St., 14020. Tel: 585-343-5400; Fax: 585-344-0213.
School—Tel: 585-343-6866; Fax: 585-344-6603. Miss Nancy J. Sedita, Prin. Lay Teachers 12; Students 64.
Catechesis/Religious Program—40 Woodrow Rd., 14020. Tel: 585-343-6866. Students 180.

4—SACRED HEART (1904), (Polish), [CEM] Rev. Eugene S. Slomba.
Res.: 15 Sumner St., 14020. Tel: 585-343-1796; Fax: 585-344-3752.
Catechesis/Religious Program—Students 97.

BELFAST, ALLEGANY CO., ST. PATRICK (1859), [CEM] Attended by, St. Patrick, Fillmore. Rev. Michael P. Juran.
Res.: 31 E. Hughes St., 14711. Tel: 585-567-2282.
Catechesis/Religious Program—Students 48.

BELMONT, ALLEGANY CO., ST. MARY (1861),, Linked with Sacred Heart, Angelica. Rev. Dennis J. Mancuso, Admin.
Res.: 5 Milton St., 14813. Tel: 585-268-7272; Fax: 585-268-9128.
Catechesis/Religious Program— Twinned with Sacred Heart, Angelica, and St. Joseph Mission, Scio. Students 64.
Mission—St. Joseph (1844), [CEM] Rte. 19 at Day Brook Rd., Scio, Allegany Co. 14880. Tel: 585-268-7272; Fax: 585-268-7272.

BEMUS POINT, CHAUTAUQUA CO., OUR LADY OF LOURDES (1948), Rev. John L. Kuhlmann.
Res.: 41 Main St., P.O. Box 500, 14712. Tel: 716-386-2400; Fax: 716-386-5562.
School—Holy Family Catholic School See listing under Regional Consolidated Elementary Schools in the Institutions located in the Diocese.

BENNINGTON CENTER, WYOMING CO., SACRED HEART OF JESUS (1872), [CEM], Linked with Our Lady of Good Counsel, Darien Center. Rev. Joseph A. Fiore.
Res.: 1230 Clinton St., Attica, 14011. Tel: 585-591-0176; Fax: 585-591-4818.
School—Genesee-Wyoming Catholic Central Consolidated School See separate listing under Regional and Consolidated Elementary Schools in the Institutions located in the Diocese. Tel: 585-591-2515; Fax: 585-591-1614.
Catechesis/Religious Program—Tel: 585-591-0205. Mrs. Wendy Murray, D.R.E. Students 125.

BERGEN, GENESEE CO., ST. BRIGID (1861), [CEM] Rev. Robert J. Schober.
Res.: 18 Gibson St., P.O. Box 219, 14416. Tel: 585-494-1110; Fax: 585-494-1895.
Catechesis/Religious Program—Students 143.
Mission—St. Michael (1892), Byron-Stafford Rd., South Byron, Genesee Co. 14557. Tel: 585-494-1110; Fax: 585-494-1895.

BLASDELL, ERIE CO., OUR MOTHER OF GOOD COUNSEL (1905), Revs. Lawrence E. Burns; Edward R. Czarnecki.
Res.: 3688 S. Park Ave., 14219. Tel: 716-822-2630; Fax: 716-821-5980.
School—15 Oakwood Ave., 14219. Tel: 716-823-6286; Fax: 716-823-6286. Mrs. Bonnie Ryan, Prin. Sisters of St. Joseph 1; Lay Teachers 13; Students 145.
Catechesis/Religious Program—Alice Appenheimer, D.R.E. Students 357.

BLISS, WYOMING CO., ST. JOSEPH (1907), Attended by, St. Nicholas, North Java. Rev. Edward E. Muerder. St. Nicholas Rectory: Rte. 98, North Java, 14113. Tel: 585-535-7457.
Church: P.O. Box 80, 14024. Tel: 585-322-8866.
Catechesis/Religious Program—Students 44.

BLOSSOM, ERIE CO., ST. GABRIEL (1925), Rev. Daniel J. Palys; Sr. Joseph Marie Marczak, C.S.S.F., Pastoral Assoc.; Ann Bauman, Pastoral Assoc.
Res.: 5271 Clinton St., Elma, 14059-7617. Tel: 716-668-4017; Fax: 716-656-0616.
Catechesis/Religious Program—Tel: 716-668-2070. Rose Andrews, D.R.E. Students 1,330.

BOLIVAR, ALLEGANY CO., ST. MARY (1903), [CEM] Attended by, Our Lady of the Angels, Cuba. Rev. Jerome M. Dissek.
Res.: 50 South St., Cuba, 14727. Tel: 585-968-5885; Fax: 585-968-0123.
Church: 121 Wellsville St., 14715. Tel: 585-928-1024.

BOSTON, ERIE CO., ST. JOHN THE BAPTIST (1869), [CEM] Rev. Msgr. Fred R. Voorhes.
Res.: 6895 Boston Cross Rd., 14025-9601. Tel: 716-941-3549; Fax: 716-941-3030.
School—St. Aloysius Regional School, Springville See separate listing under Regional and Consolidated Elementary Schools in the Institutions located in the Diocese.
Catechesis/Religious Program—Tel: 716-941-6363. Students 263.

BOWMANSVILLE, ERIE CO., SACRED HEART (1920), [CEM] Rev. A. Mark Illig.
Res.: 5337 Genesee St., 14026-1098. Tel: 716-683-2375; Fax: 716-683-0412.
Catechesis/Religious Program—Tel: 585-894-0154. Students 190.

BRANT, ERIE CO., OUR LADY OF MT. CARMEL (1906), [CEM] Attended by, St. Anthony, Farnham. Rev. James W. Fliss.
Res.: 421 Commercial St., Farnham, 14061. Tel: 716-549-1159; Fax: 716-549-7742.
Church: 10708 Brant-Angola Rd., P.O. Box 225, 14027.
Catechesis/Religious Program—Students 48.

BROCTON, CHAUTAUQUA CO., ST. PATRICK (1922), Rev. Robert G. Beiter.
Res.: 12 Central Ave., P.O. Box P, 14716-0675. Tel: 716-792-4125; Fax: 716-792-4772.
School—Northern Chautauqua Catholic Regional School See separate listing under Regional and Consolidated Elementary Schools in the Institutions located in the Diocese.
Catechesis/Religious Program—Diana Giambra, D.R.E. Students 75.

CANASERAGA, ALLEGANY CO., ST. MARY (1855), [CEM] Attended by, Assumption B.V.M., Portageville. Rev. John J. Cullen, Admin.
Mailing Address: P.O. Box 404, Portageville, 14536-0404. Tel: 585-468-2643; Fax: 585-462-2126.
Catechesis/Religious Program—Students 14.

CASSADAGA, CHAUTAUQUA CO., IMMACULATE CONCEPTION, , Linked with St. John the Evangelist, Sinclairville. Rev. Patrick H. Elis.
Res.: 88 N. Main St., 14718. Tel: 716-595-3141; Fax: 716-595-3484.

CATTARAUGUS, CATTARAUGUS CO., ST. MARY (1863), Rev. William E. Frankhauser, S.J., Admin.
Res.: 36 Washington St., 14719. Tel: 716-257-9351.
Catechesis/Religious Program—Students 58.
Mission—St. Mary Little Valley, Cattaraugus Co.
Oratory—St. Isidore (1957), East Otto, Cattaraugus Co.

CHEEKTOWAGA, ERIE CO.

1—ST. ALOYSIUS GONZAGA (1940), Rev. Msgr. Peter J. Popadick.
Res.: 157 Cleveland Dr., 14215. Tel: 716-833-1715; Fax: 716-837-5703.
School—Tel: 716-836-4549; Fax 716-836-2191. Sr. Marilyn Ann Dudek, C.S.S.F., Prin. Sisters of St. Felix of Cantalice 2; Lay Teachers 17; Students 137.
Catechesis/Religious Program—Students 154.

2—INFANT OF PRAGUE (1946), Rev. Msgr. Angelo M. Caligiuri; Rev. James Hartwell.
Res.: 921 Cleveland Dr., 14225. Tel: 716-634-3660; Fax: 716-634-3661.
School—Tel: 716-632-5482; Fax: 716-632-5539. Mrs. Elizabeth Ryan, Prin. Lay Teachers 17; Students 183.
Catechesis/Religious Program—Sr. M. Antonita Sikorski, C.S.S.F., D.R.E. Students 310.

3—ST. JOHN GUALBERT (1917), (Polish), Revs. Daniel A. Pokornowski; David W. Bialkowski; Deacon Franklyn C. Steffen.
Res.: 83 Gualbert Ave., 14211. Tel: 716-892-5746; Fax: 716-897-3906.
School—Kolbe Catholic, Tel: 716-895-3127; Fax: 716-895-7347. Rose Mary Buscaglia, Prin. Lay Teachers 16; Students 193.
Catechesis/Religious Program—Tel: 716-897-2619. Mrs. Karen Pszczolkowski, D.R.E. Students 58.

4—ST. JOSAPHAT (1906), (Polish), Revs. Theodore C. Rog; Ryszard Lukomski, S.A.C.; Deacon Robert W. Badaszewski.
Res.: 20 Peoria Ave., 14206. Tel: 716-893-1086; Fax: 716-893-1099.
School—Tel: 716-893-6448; Fax: 716-893-0118. Margaret M. Smith, Prin. Lay Teachers 15; Students 202.
Catechesis/Religious Program—Tel: 716-896-5007. Maryanne Mann, D.R.E. Students 208.

5—MOST HOLY REDEEMER (1913), Rev. F. Norman Sullivan.
Res.: 25 Avery Pl., 14225. Tel: 716-895-7589; Fax: 716-895-7590.
School—Kolbe Catholic Regional School See separate listing under Regional and Consolidated Elementary Schools located in the Institution section.

6—MOTHER OF DIVINE GRACE (1946), Rev. Msgr. S. Paul Ayoub.
Res.: 120 Old Maryvale Dr., 14225. Tel: 716-834-8488; Fax: 716-834-0335.
Catechesis/Religious Program—Tel: 716-838-0551; Fax: 716-834-0335. Students 162.

7—OUR LADY HELP OF CHRISTIANS (1890), [CEM], (National Historic Site) Rev. Richard A. Jesionowski.
Res.: 4125 Union Rd., 14225. Tel: 716-634-3420; 716-634-3428; Fax: 716-634-3464.
School—Mary, Queen of Angels Catholic School See separate listing under Regional and Consolidated Elementary Schools located in the Institution section.
Catechesis/Religious Program—Tel: 716-632-3532. Denise Seeley, D.R.E. Students 248.

8—OUR LADY OF CZESTOCHOWA (1922), (Polish), Rev. Harry F. Szczesniak.
Res.: 23 Willowlawn Pkwy., 14206. Tel: 716-822-5590; Fax: 716-828-9001.
Catechesis/Religious Program—Tel: 716-826-3497. Students 45.

9—ST. PHILIP THE APOSTLE (1967), Most Rev. Joseph H. Penkaul; Rev. Fabian J. Maryanski; Deacons Walter N. Fudala; Raymond G. Corbin.
Res.: 950 Losson Rd., 14227. Tel: 716-668-8370; Fax: 716-668-3824.
Catechesis/Religious Program—Tel: 716-668-3344. Lorraine Cortina, D.R.E.; Judy Kogut, D.R.E. Students 794.

10—QUEEN OF MARTYRS (1946), Rev. Daniel A. Lapinski. In Res., Rev. John J. Sardina.
Res.: 180 George Urban Blvd., 14225-3095. Tel: 716-892-1746; Fax: 716-892-3005.
School—Mary, Queen of Angels Catholic School See separate listing under Regional and Consolidated Elementary Schools located in the Institution section.
Catechesis/Religious Program—Tel: 716-895-2162. Rita Sandage, D.R.E. Students 195.

11—RESURRECTION (1944), Revs. Walter L. Matuszak; George C. Maj, S.A.C.
Res.: 130 Como Park Blvd., 14227. Tel: 716-683-3712; Fax: 716-685-7487.
School—Tel: 716-683-8785; Fax: 716-683-4487. Mrs. Julie Watroba, Prin. Lay Teachers 11; Students 62.
Catechesis/Religious Program—Tel: 716-683-3422. Students 170.

CHERRY CREEK, CHAUTAUQUA CO., ST. ELIZABETH, Closed. For inquiries for parish records contact the chancery.

CLARENCE CENTER, ERIE CO., ST. AUGUSTINE (1949), Rev. Edward H. Schroeder.
Res.: 8700 Goodrich Rd., 14032. Tel: 716-741-2258; Fax: 716-741-5195.
Catechesis/Religious Program—Tel: 716-741-2026. Rosey Frost, D.R.E. Students 226.

CLARENCE, ERIE CO., OUR LADY OF PEACE (1922), Rev. Thomas D. Doyle.
Res.: 10950 Main St., 14031. Tel: 716-759-8554; Fax: 716-759-8537.
Catechesis/Religious Program—Students 505.

COLDEN, ERIE CO., OUR LADY OF THE SACRED HEART (1912), Rev. Richard C. Coveny.
Res.: 8428 Heath Rd., 14033. Tel: 716-941-5817; Fax: 716-941-5342.
School—St. Aloysius Regional School, Springville See separate listing under Regional and Consolidated Elementary Schools in the Institutions located in the Diocese.
Catechesis/Religious Program—Sr. Margaret Donner, S.S.M.N., D.R.E. Students 100.

COLLINS CENTER, ERIE CO., ST. FRANCES CABRINI (1955),, Linked with St. Martin, Langford and St. Mary, New Oregon. Rev. Peter J. Karalus, Admin.
Res.: 13940 Sisson Hwy., P.O. Box 332, 14035. Tel: 716-532-9431; Fax: 716-532-9431.
School—St. Aloysius Regional School, Springville See separate listing under Regional and Consolidated Elementary Schools.
Catechesis/Religious Program—Students 96.

CORFU, GENESEE CO., ST. FRANCIS OF ASSISI (1898), [CEM] Rev. Robert E. Waters.
Res.: P.O. Box 278, 18 W. Main St., 14036. Tel: 585-599-4833; Fax: 716-937-9883.
Catechesis/Religious Program—Students 108.
Mission—St. Patrick Alden-Crittenden Rd, Crittenden, Erie Co. 14038. Tel: 585-599-4833; Fax: 585-937-9883.

CRITTENDEN, ERIE CO., ST. PATRICK (1857),, Mission of St. Francis of Assisi, Corfu. Rev. Robert E. Waters.
Alden-Crittenden Rd., 14038. Tel: 585-599-4833; Fax: 716-937-9883.
18 W. Main St., P.O. Box 278, Corfu, 14036.

CUBA, ALLEGANY CO., OUR LADY OF THE ANGELS (1850), [CEM] Rev. Jerome M. Dissek; Deacon Francis W. Pasquale Jr.
Res.: 50 South St., 14727. Tel: 585-968-2885; Fax: 585-968-0123.
School—Southern Tier Catholic Regional School

See separate listing under Regional and Consolidated Elementary Schools in the Institutions located in the Diocese.
Catechesis/Religious Program—Students 30.
Oratory—Sacred Heart Friendship, Allegany Co.

DARIEN CENTER, GENESEE CO., OUR LADY OF GOOD COUNSEL (1911), [CEM] Attended by, Sacred Heart of Jesus, Bennington Center. Rev. Joseph A. Fiore. In Res., Rev. Francis P. Kowalewski (Retired).
Res.: 10675 Allegany Rd., 14040-9701. Tel: 585-547-3547; Fax: 585-547-3660.
School—Genesee-Wyoming Catholic Central Consolidated School See separate listing under Regional and Consolidated Elementary Schools in the Institutions located in the Diocese.
Oratory—Our Lady Help of Christians 1670 Church Rd., Bennington, Wyoming Co. 14040.

DAYTON, CATTARAUGUS CO., ST. PAUL OF THE CROSS, Closed., For inquiries for parish records contact St. John Fisher, South Dayton.

DELEVAN, CATTARAUGUS CO., BLESSED SACRAMENT (1947),, Linked with Holy Family, Machias. Rev. Raymond F. Uschold.
Res.: 10 N. Main St., P.O. Box 188, 14042. Tel: 716-492-2383; Fax: 716-492-3214.
School—St. Aloysius Regional School, Springville See separate listing under Regional and Consolidated Elementary Schools in the Institutions Located in the Diocese.
Catechesis/Religious Program—Tel: 716-353-4033. Willa Smith, D.R.E. Students 6.

DEPEW, ERIE CO.

1—ST. AUGUSTINE (1909), (Polish), [CEM] Rev. Conrad P. Stachowiak.
Res.: 425 Penora St., 14043. Tel: 716-683-3038; Fax: 716-683-9918.
Catechesis/Religious Program—Students 50.

2—ST. BARNABAS (1960), Rev. Msgr. John W. Madsen; Rev. Daniel J. Fawls; Deacon Thaddeus P. May. In Res., Rev. James H. Kasprzyk (Retired).
Res.: 2049 George Urban Blvd., 14043. Tel: 716-685-2350; Fax: 716-685-8679.
School—Tel: 716-684-1444; Fax: 716-685-2350. Sr. M. Rosa Mystica, O.S.F., Prin. Sisters 1; Lay Teachers 11; Students 168.
Catechesis/Religious Program—2099 George Urban Blvd., 14043. Tel: 716-685-2000; Fax: 716-685-2350. Judith Major, D.R.E. Students 450.

3—ST. JAMES (1897), Rev. David J. Borowiak.
Res.: 496 Terrace Blvd., 14043. Tel: 716-683-2746; Fax: 716-683-3121.
Catechesis/Religious Program—Janet Corda, D.R.E. Students 191.
Convent—Felician Nuns, 55 Westfield Ave., 14043. Tel: 716-685-1114.

4—OUR LADY OF THE BLESSED SACRAMENT (1965), Rev. Louis S. Dolinic; Deacon Gregory L. Feary Jr.
Res.: 10 French Rd., 14043. Tel: 716-684-6342; Fax: 716-684-1853.
School—20 French Rd., 14043. Tel: 716-685-2544; Fax: 716-685-9103. Felician Sisters 2; Lay Teachers 16; Students 210.
Catechesis/Religious Program—Tel: 716-685-2546. Students 434.

5—SS. PETER AND PAUL (1896), (Polish), Rev. Stanley F. Nowak.
Res.: 86 Burlington Ave., 14043. Tel: 716-683-1645; Fax: 716-685-6754.
Catechesis/Religious Program—Tel: 716-686-9501. Sr. Thaddeus Pogorzala, D.R.E. Students 172.

DUNKIRK, CHAUTAUQUA CO.

1—ST. ELIZABETH ANN SETON (1975), [CEM] Rev. Thomas J. Wopperer; Deacon Jose J. Ruiz. In Res., Rev. Walter Werbicki (STF).
Res.: 328 Washington Ave., 14048. Tel: 716-366-1750; Fax: 716-366-4398.
School—Northern Chautauqua Catholic Regional School, Tel: 716-366-0630. See separate listing under Regional and Consolidated Elementary Schools in the Institutions located in the Diocese.
Catechesis/Religious Program—Tel: 716-366-2827. Samuel Mancuso, D.R.E. Students 353.

2—ST. HEDWIG (1902), (Polish), [CEM] Rev. Joseph J. Janaczek.
Res.: 324 Townsend St., 14048. Tel: 716-366-1615; 716-366-2307 (Office); Fax: 716-363-0106.
School—Northern Chautauqua Catholic Regional School See separate listing under Regional and Consolidated Elementary Schools in the Institutions located in the Diocese.
Catechesis/Religious Program—Students 76.

3—HOLY TRINITY (1908), (Italian), [CEM] Rev. David A. Bellittiere.
Res.: 1032 Central Ave., 14048. Tel: 716-366-2306; Fax: 716-366-4738.
School—Northern Chautauqua Catholic Regional School See separate listing under Regional and Consolidated Elementary Schools in the Institutions located in the Diocese. Tel: 716-366-0630; Fax: 716-366-5101.
Catechesis/Religious Program—Tel: 716-366-0499. Roberta Coniglio, D.R.E.; Donna Seyedian, D.R.E. Students 163.

4—ST. HYACINTH (1875), (Polish), [CEM] Rev. Michael J. Parker; Deacon Daniel H. Mackowiak.
Res.: 295 Lakeshore Dr. E., 14048. Tel: 716-366-7266; Fax: 716-363-0031.
School—Tel: 716-366-1950; Fax: 716-366-1192. Felician Sisters 2; Lay Teachers 12; Students 130.
Catechesis/Religious Program—Tel: 716-366-5707. Students 84.

EAST ARCADE, WYOMING CO., ST. MARY'S (1846), [CEM] Attended by, SS. Peter and Paul, Arcade. Rev. Czeslaw M. Krysa, Admin.
Mailing Address: 6785 E. Arcade Rd., Arcade, 14009. Tel: 585-492-2282; Fax: 585-492-2282.
Res.: 417 Main St., Arcade, 14009. Tel: 585-492-5330; Fax: 585-492-1047.
Catechesis/Religious Program—Students 72.

EAST AURORA, ERIE CO., IMMACULATE CONCEPTION (1901), [CEM] Rev. Msgr. Kevin T. O'Neill; Rev. Andrzej Kozminski, S.A.C. (Poland); Deacon John M. Ruh.
Res.: 520 Oakwood Ave., 14052. Tel: 716-652-6400; Fax: 716-652-7168.
School—510 Oakwood Ave., 14052. Tel: 716-652-5855. Susan K. Gregg, Prin. Lay Teachers 16; Students 227.
Catechesis/Religious Program—Tel: 716-655-0067. Cheryl A. Bennett, D.R.E. Students 655.

EAST BETHANY, GENESEE CO., IMMACULATE CONCEPTION (1954), Rev. Thomas L. Kemp.
Res.: 5865 Ellicott St., 14054. Tel: 585-343-4537; Fax: 585-343-4537.
Catechesis/Religious Program—Students 95.

EAST EDEN, ERIE CO., ST. MARY (1835), [CEM] Rev. John E. Kelly.
Res.: 8175 E. Eden Rd., 14057. Tel: 716-992-4237; Fax: 716-992-2435.
Catechesis/Religious Program—Tel: 716-992-3123. Dorothy Zydel, D.R.E. Students 210.

EAST PEMBROKE, GENESEE CO., HOLY NAME OF MARY (1868), Rev. David J. Scheider.
Res.: P.O. Box 219, 14056. Tel: 716-762-9006; Fax: 716-762-9036.

EDEN, ERIE CO.

1—IMMACULATE CONCEPTION (1908), [CEM] Revs. Walter P. Grabowski; Francis Parella, S.S.P.; Deacon Richard H. Kelsey.
Res.: 8791 S. Main St., 14057. Tel: 716-992-3933; Fax: 716-992-2201.
Catechesis/Religious Program—Tel: 716-992-3508. Sharon Reed, D.R.E. Students 304.

2—ST. MARY OF IMMACULATE CONCEPTION (1858), [CEM] Attended by, St. Frances Cabrini, Collins Center.
Res.: 5107 Langford Rd. (New Oregon), 14057. Tel: 716-337-2291; Fax: 716-532-9431.
Catechesis/Religious Program—Students 120.

EGGERTSVILLE, ERIE CO., ST. BENEDICT (1920), Rev. Gary J. Bagley.
Res.: 1317 Eggert Rd., 14226. Tel: 716-834-1041; Fax: 716-835-5949.
School—Tel: 716-835-2518; Fax: 716-834-4932. Patricia Boyd, Prin. Sisters of St. Francis of Penance and Christian Charity 1; Lay Teachers 29; Students 259.
Catechesis/Religious Program—Tel: 716-836-6444. Sr. Virginia Judge, O.S.F., D.R.E. Students 415.

ELBA, GENESEE CO., OUR LADY OF FATIMA (1947), Rev. Ivan Skenderovic.
Res.: 65 S. Main St., P.O. Box 185, 14058-0185. Tel: 716-757-6891; Fax: 716-757-2472.
Catechesis/Religious Program—Students 138.

ELLICOTTVILLE, CATTARAUGUS CO., HOLY NAME OF MARY (1850), [CEM] Rev. Ronald B. Mierzwa.
Res.: P.O. Box 543, 14731. Tel: 716-699-2592; Fax: 716-699-8439.
Catechesis/Religious Program—Students 166.

ELMA, ERIE CO., ANNUNCIATION OF THE BLESSED VIRGIN MARY (1906), [CEM] Rev. Emil P. Swiatek; Deacons Joseph P. Mercurio; Dennis W. Kapsiak, Pastoral Assoc.
Res.: 7580 Clinton St., 14059. Tel: 716-683-5254; Fax: 716-685-6380.
School—Tel: 716-681-1327; Fax: 716-685-6380. Lay Teachers 18; Students 160; Preschool Students 60.
Catechesis/Religious Program—Tel: 716-683-5515. Students 510.

FALCONER, CHAUTAUQUA CO., OUR LADY OF LORETO (1912),, Linked with St. John, Jamestown. Rev. Joseph A. Gullo.
Res.: 309 W. Everett St., 14733. Tel: 716-665-4253; Fax: 716-664-9223.
School—Holy Family Catholic School See listing under Regional and Consolidated Elementary Schools in the Institutions located in the Diocese. Tel: 716-483-3245.
Catechesis/Religious Program—Tel: 716-665-3764. Mrs. Deborah C. Ognibene, D.R.E. Students 113.

FARNHAM, ERIE CO., ST. ANTHONY'S (1904), [CEM], Linked with Our Lady of Mt. Carmel, Brant. Rev. James W. Fliss; Deacon Frank Polizzi.
Mailing Address: P.O. Box A-9, 14061.
Res.: 421 Commercial St., 14061. Tel: 716-549-1159; Fax: 716-549-7722.
Catechesis/Religious Program—Tel: 716-549-2867; Fax: 716-549-7742. Kathy Brachmann, D.R.E. Students 161.

FILLMORE, ALLEGANY CO., ST. PATRICK (1881), [CEM], Linked with St. Patrick, Belfast. Rev. Michael P. Juran.
Res.: 109 W. Main St., P.O. Box 198, 14735. Tel: 585-567-2282; Fax: 585-567-4172.
Catechesis/Religious Program—Students 23.

FORESTVILLE, CHAUTAUQUA CO., ST. ROSE OF LIMA (1850), Attended by, St. John Bosco, Sheridan. Rev. Gerald P. Sheehan.
Res.: 2773 Main Rd., Sheridan, 14135. Tel: 716-679-4951; Fax: 716-679-4952.
Catechesis/Religious Program—Students 11.

FRANKLINVILLE, CATTARAUGUS CO., ST. PHILOMENA (1906), [JC] Rev. Michael D. O'Hara.
Res.: 26 N. Plymouth Ave., 14737. Tel: 716-676-3629; Fax: 716-676-2104.
Catechesis/Religious Program—Tel: 716-676-2123. Students 58.

FREDONIA, CHAUTAUQUA CO.

1—ST. ANTHONY (1905), Rev. Carlton J. Westfield.
Res.: 42 Orchard St., 14063. Tel: 716-679-4050; 716-679-4096 (Office); Fax: 716-672-8576 (Office); 716-679-0326 (Res.).
School—Northern Chautauqua Catholic Regional School See separate listing under Regional and Consolidated Elementary Schools in the Institutions located in the Diocese. Tel: 716-366-0630.
Catechesis/Religious Program—Tel: 716-674-1268. Mrs. Barbara O'Connell, D.R.E. Students 175.

2—ST. JOSEPH (1899), Rev. Charles J. Zadora; Deacon Michael C. Lemieux.
Res.: 145 E. Main St., 14063. Tel: 716-679-4116; Fax: 716-679-1352 (1-5 P.M.).
School—Northern Chautauqua Catholic Regional School See separate listing under Regional and Consolidated Elementary Schools in the Institutions located in the Diocese. Tel: 716-366-0630.
Catechesis/Religious Program—Tel: 716-672-2647. Students 108.

FRENCH CREEK, CHAUTAUQUA CO., ST. MATTHIAS (1873), [CEM], Linked with Our Lady of the Snows, Panama. Rev. Bernard C. Staszak.
Res.: 1762 French Creek Mina Rd., Clymer, 14724-0660. Tel: 716-355-8891; Fax: 716-355-2576.
School—Holy Family Catholic School See listing under Regional and Consolidated Elementary Schools in the Institutions located in the Diocese.
Catechesis/Religious Program—Students 70.

FREWSBURG, CHAUTAUQUA CO., OUR LADY OF VICTORY (1950), Attended by, St. James, Jamestown. Rev. Joseph A. Gullo.
Church: P.O. Box 533, 14738. Tel: 716-569-4725; Fax: 716-569-2292.
Res.: 27 Allen St., Jamestown, 14701. Tel: 716-487-0125; Fax: 716-661-3677.
School—Holy Family Catholic School See listing under Regional and Consolidated Elementary Schools in the Institutions located in the Diocese.
Catechesis/Religious Program—Elise Snyder, D.R.E. Students 54.

FRIENDSHIP, ALLEGANY CO., SACRED HEART (1912), [CEM], Oratory under Our Lady of Angels, Cuba

GASPORT, NIAGARA CO., ST. MARY (1968),, Linked with St. Stephen, Middleport. Rev. Joseph P. Badding.
Res.: 8110 West Ave., 14067. Tel: 716-772-7803; Fax: 716-772-7931.
Catechesis/Religious Program—Linda Griesbaum, D.R.E. Students 52.

GETZVILLE, ERIE CO., ST. PIUS X (1958), Rev. Msgr. George B. Yiengst; Deacons Brian C. Walkowiak; Donald E. Seyfried.
Res.: 1700 N. French Rd., P.O. Box 162, 14068-0162. Tel: 716-688-9143; Fax: 716-688-1203.
Catechesis/Religious Program—Tel: 716-688-5417. Students 583.

GOWANDA, ERIE CO., ST. JOSEPH (1898), [CEM] Rev. Daniel P. Walsh.
Res.: 26 Erie Ave., 14070. Tel: 716-532-5100; Fax: 716-532-4096.
School—Tel: 716-532-2520; Fax: 716-532-4172. Mr. Vincent George, Prin. Lay Teachers 10; Students 97.
Catechesis/Religious Program—Tel: 716-992-4151. Students 127.

GRAND ISLAND, ERIE CO., ST. STEPHEN (1862), [CEM] Revs. Paul M. Nogaro; Daniel F. Fiebelkorn.
Res.: 2100 Baseline Rd., 14072. Tel: 716-773-7647; Fax: 716-773-5792.
School—2080 Baseline Rd., 14072. Tel: 716-773-4347; Fax: 716-773-1438. Mrs. Donna Ende, Prin. Lay Teachers 22; Students 223.
Catechesis/Religious Program—Tel: 716-773-2002.

Angela Diebold, D.R.E.; Elizabeth Laski, D.R.E. Students 917.

HAMBURG, ERIE CO.

1—ST. MARY OF THE LAKE (1948), Rev. Msgr. W. Jerome Sullivan, J.C.D.; Deacon David R. Velasquez; Sr. Paula Zelazo, F.S.S.J., Pastoral assoc.
Res.: S-4737 Lake Shore Rd., 14075. Tel: 716-627-3123; Fax: 716-627-7062.
School—Tel: 716-627-7700. Mrs. Kristine Hider, Prin. Franciscan Sisters of St. Joseph 2; Lay Teachers 19; Students 164.
Catechesis/Religious Program—Tel: 716-627-7150. Sr. Catherine Taberski, S.S.M.N., D.R.E. Students 462.

2—SS. PETER AND PAUL (1844), [CEM] Revs. Mark J. Wolski; James D. Ciupek; James R. Bastian.
Res.: 66 E. Main St., 14075. Tel: 716-649-2765; Fax: 716-649-5218.
School—68 E. Main St., 14075. Tel: 716-649-7030. Daniel Grande, Prin. Lay Teachers 23; Students 331.
Catechesis/Religious Program—Tel: 716-649-0231. Mary Ann Senchyne, D.R.E.; Sr. M. Cynthia Kilian, C.S.S.F, D.R.E. Students 909.

HARRIS HILL, ERIE CO., NATIVITY OF THE BLESSED VIRGIN MARY (1954), Rev. Msgr. Frederick D. Leising; Deacon Francis R. Krahling In Res., Rev. Msgr. Raymond F. Paa, Pastor Emeritus (Retired).
Res.: 4375 Harris Hill Rd., Williamsville, 14221. Tel: 716-632-8838; Fax: 716-632-7898.
School—Tel: 716-633-7441. Mrs. Cherie M. Ansuini, Prin. Lay Teachers 17; Students 188.
Catechesis/Religious Program—8550 Main St., Williamsville, 14221. Tel: 716-634-3130. Mrs. Mary Ann Hoag, D.R.E. Students 942.

HINSDALE, CATTARAUGUS CO., ST. HELEN (1947), Rev. Barry J. Allaire, Admin.; Deacon Michael R. Bray.
Res.: 3826 Main St., P.O. Box 248, 14743-0248. Tel: 716-557-8841; Fax: 716-372-6707.
School—Southern Tier Catholic Regional School See separate listing under Regional and Consolidated Elementary Schools in the Institutions located in the Diocese.
Catechesis/Religious Program—Students 19.

HOLLAND, ERIE CO., ST. JOSEPH (1890), [CEM 2] Rev. Dennis A. Fronczak.
Res.: 46 N. Main St., 14080-9509. Tel: 716-537-9434; Fax: 716-537-9988.
Catechesis/Religious Program—Tel: 716-655-5728; Fax: 716-537-9988. Jill Trawinski, D.R.E. Tel: 716-992-9380. Students 275.

HOLLEY, ORLEANS CO., ST. MARY (1866), [CEM], Linked with St. Mark, Kendall. Rev. Joseph F. Kozlowski.
Res.: 11 S. Main St., 14470-1107. Tel: 585-638-6718; Fax: 585-638-3210.
Catechesis/Religious Program—Tel: 585-638-6027. Jean M. Mullins, D.R.E. Students 114.
Oratory—St. Rocco Hulberton, Orleans Co. 14470.

HUMPHREY, CATTARAUGUS CO., ST. PACIFICUS, MISSION OF ST. BONAVENTURE UNIVERSITY FRIARY (1855), [CEM] Rev. J. Gregory Brennan, O.F.M.
Res.: St. Bonaventure University, St. Bonaventure, 14778. Tel: 716-375-2545; Fax: 716-375-2424.
Catechesis/Religious Program— Joint program with Holy Name of Mary, Ellicottville.

JAMESTOWN, CHAUTAUQUA CO.

1—ST. JAMES (1910), (Italian), [CEM], Linked with Our Lady of Victory, Frewsburg Rev. Msgr. Antoine P. Attea; Revs. Ariel Cortes (Colombia); Robert A. Stolinski.
Res.: 27 Allen St., 14701. Tel: 716-487-0125; Fax: 716-661-3677.
School—Holy Family Catholic School See separate listing under Regional and Consolidated Elementary Schools under Institutions located in the Diocese.
Catechesis/Religious Program—Tel: 716-664-4237. Julie Rodriguez, D.R.E. Students 149.

2—ST. JOHN (1939),, Linked with Our Lady of Loreto, Falconer. Rev. Joseph A. Gullo.
Office—270 Newton Ave., 14701. Tel: 716-664-4556; Fax: 716-483-2108.
Parish Center—Tel: 716-434-1875.
School—Holy Family Catholic School See separate listing under Regional and Consolidated Elementary Schools under Institutions located in the Diocese.
Catechesis/Religious Program—Students 108.

3—SS. PETER AND PAUL (1854), [CEM 2] Rev. Dennis W. Mende.
Res.: 508 Cherry St., 14701. Tel: 716-664-5703; Fax: 716-664-5288.
School—Holy Family Catholic School See separate listing under Regional and Consolidated Elementary Schools under Institutions Located in the Diocese. Tel: 716-483-3245.
Catechesis/Religious Program—Tel: 716-484-8958. Students 198.

JAVA CENTER, WYOMING CO., ST. PATRICK (1838), Attended by, St. Nicholas, North Java. Rev. Edward E. Muerder; Louise Boucher, Pastoral Assoc.
Res.: 1468 Main St., 14082. Tel: 585-457-9532; Fax: 585-457-9532.
School—Genesee-Wyoming Catholic Central Consolidated School See separate listing under Regional and Consolidated Elementary Schools in the Institutions located in the Diocese.
Catechesis/Religious Program—Mary Agnes McCormick, D.R.E. Students 71.

KENDALL, ORLEANS CO., ST. MARK (1984), Attended by, St. Mary, Holley. Rev. Joseph F. Kozlowski. In Res., Rev. Msgr. Francis M. Skupien (Retired).
Res.: 11 S. Main St., Holley, 14470-1107. Tel: 585-638-6718; Fax: 585-638-3210.
Catechesis/Religious Program—Tel: 585-659-8631; Fax: 585-659-8631. Patricia Longrod, D.R.E. Students 150.

KENMORE, ERIE CO.

1—ST. ANDREW (1944), Revs. Charles E. Slisz; Gerald R. Mudd, O.F.M.; Deacons David P. McDermott; Stephen J. Swinarski; Sr. Mary Courts, G.N.S.H., Pastoral Assoc. In Res., Rev. Vincent J. Ferraro, Chap.
Res.: 1525 Sheridan Dr., 14217. Tel: 716-873-6716; Fax: 716-873-2214.
School—Tel: 716-877-0422; Fax: 716-877-3973. Lay Teachers 40; Students 522.
Catechesis/Religious Program—Tel: 716-877-3034. Students 341.

2—ST. JOHN THE BAPTIST (1836), [CEM] Revs. Richard A. Reina; Joseph A. Zalacca; Deacon Bernard M. Thomann.
Res. 1085 Englewood Ave., 14223-1982. Tel: 716-873-1122; Fax: 716-873-3305.
School—Englewood & Belmont, 14223. Tel: 716-877-6401; Fax: 716-877-9139. Cynthia Jacobs, Prin. Lay Teachers 44; Students 464.
Catechesis/Religious Program—Tel: 716-877-0474. Catherine Salzman, D.R.E. Students 412.

3—ST. PAUL (1897), Revs. John R. Gaglione; Richard E. Sowinski; Theresa Bornholdt, Pastoral Assoc.
Res.: 33 Victoria Blvd., 14217. Tel: 716-875-2730; Fax: 716-874-3475.
School—Tel: 716-877-6308; Fax: 716-877-3874. Louise Lopardi, Prin. Lay Teachers 24; Students 390.
Catechesis/Religious Program—Tel: 716-873-9429. Students 710.

KNAPP CREEK, CATTARAUGUS CO., SACRED HEART, MISSION OF ALLEGANY, Closed. For sacramental records contact St. Mary of the Angels, Olean.

LACKAWANNA, ERIE CO.

1—ST. ANTHONY (1917), Rev. Peter J. Drilling, Th.D.; Deacon Michael D. Quinn.
Res.: 306 Ingham Ave., 14218. Tel: 716-823-0782; Fax: 716-827-1381.
Catechesis/Religious Program—Tel: 716-827-8384. Students 105.

2—ASSUMPTION (1918), (Hungarian), Rev. Kalman Miskolczy, Sch.P., Admin. In Res., Rev. Nicholas Vitez Fodor, Sch.P.
Church: 80 Steelawanna Ave. 14218. Tel: 716-822-9828.

3—ST. BARBARA (1903), (Polish), Rev. Lawrence F. Cobel.
Res.: 551 Ridge Rd., 14218. Tel: 716-822-3470; Fax: 716-822-2412.

4—BASILICA OF OUR LADY OF VICTORY (1854), Rev. Msgrs. Robert C. Wurtz, P.A.; John H. Bugman (Retired); Revs. Matthew J. Zirnheld; Daniel J. Fawls. (National Shrine).
Res.: 767 Ridge Rd., 14218. Tel: 716-828-9444; Fax: 716-828-9429.
School—Tel: 716-828-9434; Fax: 716-828-9383. Sr. Ellen O'Keefe, Prin. Sisters 6; Lay Teachers 20; Students 325.
Catechesis/Religious Program—Tel: 716-828-9437; Fax: 716-828-9429. Sheila Flynn, D.R.E. Students 263.

5—ST. HYACINTH (1910), Polish), Rev. Henry A. Orszulak, Admin.
Res.: 253 Ridge Rd., 14218. Tel: 716-823-0845; Fax: 716-826-2292.

6—ST. MICHAEL THE ARCHANGEL (1921), (Polish), Rev. James M. Augustyn.
Res.: 144 Warsaw St., 14218. Tel: 716-826-0880; Fax: 716-828-1867.

7—OUR LADY OF BISTRICA (1917), (Croatian), Rev. Christopher Coric, O.F.M.Conv. (Croatia).
Res.: 1619 Abbott Rd., 14218. Tel: 716-822-0818; Fax: 716-822-0818.
Catechesis/Religious Program—Students 60.

8—QUEEN OF ALL SAINTS (1949), Merged, with St. Anthony, Lackawanna.

LAKE VIEW, ERIE CO., OUR LADY OF PERPETUAL HELP (1922), Rev. Msgr. John W. Zeitler; Sr. Sharon Erickson, R.S.M.; Deacon Mark J. Hooper.
Res.: 2052 Lake View Ave., 14085. Tel: 716-627-2910; Fax: 716-627-7972.
School—Southtowns Catholic Consolidated School See separate listing under Regional and Consolidated Elementary Schools in the Institutions located in the Diocese. Tel: 716-627-5011; Fax: 716-627-5335.
Catechesis/Religious Program—Tel: 716-627-9397. Mrs. Barbara Manley, D.R.E. Students 487.

LAKEWOOD, CHAUTAUQUA CO., SACRED HEART (1912), [JC] Rev. Msgr. Joseph M. Dowdell.
Res.: 380 E. Fairmount Ave., 14750-2197. Tel: 716-763-2815; Fax: 716-763-5646.
School—Holy Family Catholic School See separate listing under Regional and Consolidated Elementary Schools in the Institutions located in the Diocese. Tel: 716-483-3245.
Catechesis/Religious Program—Marilyn Wozneak, Pastoral Assoc. & D.R.E. Students 293.

LANCASTER, ERIE CO.

1—ST. MARY OF THE ASSUMPTION (1850), [CEM] Rev. Paul W. Steller.
Res.: 1 St. Mary's Hill, 14086-2094. Tel: 716-683-6445; Fax: 716-684-8446.
School—Tel: 716-683-2112; Fax: 716-683-2134. Sr. Barbara Jean Wajda, O.S.F., Prin. Sisters of Third Order of St. Francis 3; Lay Teachers 20; Students 367.
Catechesis/Religious Program—Tel: 716-683-8564. Mrs. Elaine Driscoll, D.R.E. Students 735.

2—OUR LADY OF POMPEII (1909), Rev. Jay W. McGinnis.
Res.: 158 Laverack Ave., 14086. Tel: 716-683-6522; Fax: 716-685-8066.
School—(Grades PreK-8) Tel: 716-684-4664; Fax: 716-684-4699. Mrs. Christine M. Schierer, Prin. Lay Teachers 15; Students 235.
Catechesis/Religious Program—Antoinette Duran, D.R.E., (Elementary); Joseph Blatz, D.R.E., (High School). Students 400.

LANGFORD, ERIE CO., ST. MARTIN (1851), [CEM] Attended by, St. Frances Cabrini, Collins Center. Rev. Peter J. Karalus, Admin.
Res.: 10893 Sisson Hwy. (Langford), North Collins, 14111. Tel: 716-337-2686; Fax: 716-532-9431.
School—St. Aloysius Regional School, Springville. See separate listing under Regional and Consolidated Schools in the Institutions located in the Diocese.
Catechesis/Religious Program—Students 50.

LE ROY, GENESEE CO.

1—ST. JOSEPH (1907), (Italian), [JC] Rev. Msgr. Emil P. Zupa.
Res.: 27 Lake St., 14482. Tel: 585-768-6600; Fax: 585-768-6136.
Catechesis/Religious Program—Students 63.

2—ST. PETER (1849), [CEM], Linked with St. Anthony, Lime Rock. Rev. Michael R. Rock, O.de.M.
Res.: 44 Lake St., 14482. Tel: 585-768-6543; Fax: 585-768-7093.
School—Holy Family School, Tel: 585-768-7390; Fax: 585-768-6680. Mrs. Olna Magill, Prin. Lay Teachers 13; Students 157.
Catechesis/Religious Program—Tel: 585-768-6720. Students 245.

LEWISTON, NIAGARA CO., ST. PETER (1851), Rev. Sebastian C. Pierro; Sr. Marcia Ann Fiutko, F.S.S.J., Pastoral Assoc.
Res.: 620 Center St., 14092. Tel: 716-754-4118; Fax: 716-754-4120.
School—Tel: 716-754-4470; Fax: 716-754-0167. Mr. James M. Allen, Prin. Lay Teachers 20; Students 222.
Catechesis/Religious Program—Tel: 716-754-2812. Students 397.
Convent—162 S. Seventh St., 14092. Tel: 716-754-4761.

LIME ROCK, GENESEE CO., ST. ANTHONY (1907), Attended by, St. Peter, Le Roy. Rev. Michael R. Rock, O.de.M.
E. Main Rd. & Church Rd..
Res.: 44 Lake St., Le Roy, 14482. Tel: 585-768-6543; Fax: 585-768-7093.
Catechesis/Religious Program—Tel: 585-768-6720. Combined with St. Peter, Le Roy.

LIMESTONE, CATTARAUGUS CO., ST. PATRICK (1875), [CEM] Attended by, St. Bonaventure Friary, Allegany. Rev. Jerome J. Stelmach, Admin. In Res., Deacon Don Radlinski.
Res.: 5823 Church St., 14753. Tel: 716-925-8596; Fax: 716-925-7319.
Catechesis/Religious Program—Students 21.

LITTLE VALLEY, CATTARAUGUS CO., ST. MARY (1874),, Mission of St. Mary's, Cattaraugus. Rev. William E. Frankhauser, S.J., Admin.
Mailing Address: 36 Washington St., Cattaraugus, 14719. Tel: 716-257-9351.
Catechesis/Religious Program—Students 20.

LOCKPORT, NIAGARA CO.

1—ST. ANTHONY (1928),, Linked with St. Joseph, Lockport. Rev. Joseph S. Rogliano.
Res.: 9 Bristol Ave., 14094. Tel: 716-434-5025; Fax: 716-434-6332.
School—DeSales Catholic Consolidated School See separate listing under Regional and Consolidated Elementary Schools in the Institutions located in

the Diocese.
Catechesis/Religious Program—Tel: 716-433-0179. Kathleen Wilson, D.R.E. Students 144.
Catechesis/Religious Program—
2—ST. JOHN THE BAPTIST (1834), Revs. Joseph C. Gatto, S.T.D.; Joseph C. Dumphrey, O.S.F.S.
Res.: 168 Chestnut St., 14094. Tel: 716-433-8118; Fax: 716-433-3562.
School—DeSales Catholic School See separate listing under Regional and Consolidated Elementary Schools in the Institutions located in the Diocese. Tel: 716-433-6422; Fax: 716-434-4002.
Catechesis/Religious Program—Tel: 716-438-9029. Sally Sayward, D.R.E. Students 700.
3—ST. JOSEPH (1912), (Italian), Attended by, St. Anthony, Lockport. Rev. Joseph S. Rogliano; Tamara Fitz-Arling, Pastoral Assoc.
Res.: 391 Market St., 14094. Tel: 716-433-5792; Fax: 716-438-5613.
School—DeSales Catholic School See separate listing under Regional and Consolidated Elementary Schools in the Institutions located in the Diocese. Tel: 716-433-6422.
Catechesis/Religious Program—Tel: 716-434-3194. Kim Perilli, D.R.E. Students 150.
4—ST. MARY (1859), (German), [JC] Rev. Gary R. Kibler; Sr. Patrice Yarborough, S.S.M.N., Pastoral Assoc.
Res.: 5 Saxton St., 14094. Tel: 716-434-6316; Fax: 716-438-5495.
School—DeSales Catholic School See separate listing under Regional and Consolidated Elementary Schools in the Institutions located in the Diocese. Tel: 716-433-6422; Fax: 716-434-4002.
Catechesis/Religious Program—Tel: 716-433-0340; Fax: 716-438-5495. Carol Costello, D.R.E. Students 170.
5—ST. PATRICK (1864), [CEM] Rev. Francis M. Schimscheiner, O.S.F.S. In Res., Rev. Gerald L. Bartko, O.S.F.S.
Res.: 76 Church St., 14094. Tel: 716-433-3707; Fax: 716-438-5608.
School—DeSales Catholic School See separate listing under Regional and Consolidated Elementary Schools in the Institutions located in the Diocese. Tel: 716-433-6422; Fax: 716-434-4002.
Catechesis/Religious Program—Tel: 716-433-6672. Sr. Rene Ruberto, S.S.M.N., D.R.E. Students 177.
Convent—138 N. Transit St., 14094. Tel: 716-433-9193.

LYNDONVILLE, ORLEANS CO., ST. JOSEPH (1962), Attended by, Sacred Heart, Medina. Rev. Joseph G. Fifagrowicz.
Res.: 38 Lake Ave., P.O. Box 496, 14098. Tel: 585-765-9722; Fax: 585-798-2833.
Catechesis/Religious Program—Students 60.

MACHIAS, CATTARAUGUS CO., HOLY FAMILY (1948), Attended by, Blessed Sacrament, Delevan. Rev. Raymond F. Uschold.
Res.: 10 N. Main St., P.O. Box 188, Delevan, 14042. Tel: 716-492-2383; Fax: 716-492-3214.
School—St. Aloysius Regional School See separate listing under Regional and Consolidated Elementary Schools in the Institutions located in the Diocese.
Catechesis/Religious Program—Tel: 716-492-0691. Students 17.

MAYVILLE, CHAUTAUQUA CO., ST. MARY (1925),, Linked with St. Isaac Jogues, Sherman. Rev. Raymond A.J. Donohue.
Res.: 24 E. Chautauqua St., Box 148, 14757. Tel: 716-753-2332; Fax: 716-753-3836.
School—Holy Family Catholic School See separate listing under Regional and Consolidated Elementary Schools in the Institutions located in the Diocese. Tel: 716-483-3245.
Catechesis/Religious Program—Students 92.

MEDINA, ORLEANS CO.
1—ST. MARY (1840), [CEM] Rev. Joseph E. Vatter.
Res.: 211 Eagle St., 14103. Tel: 585-798-0112; Fax: 585-798-2834.
Catechesis/Religious Program—Tel: 585-798-5399. Students 281.
2—SACRED HEART (1910), [CEM], Linked with St. Joseph, Lyndonville. Rev. Joseph G. Fifagrowicz.
Res.: 208 Ann St., 14103. Tel: 716-798-0356; Fax: 716-798-2833.
Catechesis/Religious Program—Students 64.

MIDDLEPORT, NIAGARA CO., ST. STEPHEN (1854), [CEM] Attended by, St. Mary, Gasport. Rev. Joseph P. Badding.
Res.: 21 Vernon St., 14105-1321. Tel: 716-735-9433; Fax: 716-735-9433.
Catechesis/Religious Program—Students 111.

NEWFANE, NIAGARA CO., ST. BRIDGET (1859), [CEM], Linked with Our Lady of the Rosary, Wilson. Rev. John J. Leising.
Res.: 3455 Ewings Rd., Box 87, 14108-0087. Tel: 716-778-9822; Fax: 716-778-8786.
Catechesis/Religious Program—Tel: 716-778-9822. Carol Piech, D.R.E. Students 225.

NIAGARA FALLS, NIAGARA CO.
1—ST. CHARLES BORROMEO (1970), Rev. Stewart M. Lindsay, O.S.F.S.
Res.: 5604 Lindbergh Ave., 14304-3111. Tel: 716-283-7602; Fax: 716-283-1371.
Catechesis/Religious Program—Tel: 716-283-1371. Students 141.
2—ST. GEORGE (1915), (Lithuanian), [JC] Rev. Sewerym J. Koszyk, S.A.C.
Res.: 1910 Falls St., 14303. Tel: 716-282-4587; Fax: 716-282-4587.
3—HOLY TRINITY (1902), (Polish), [CEM], Linked with St. Stanislaus, Niagara Falls. Most Rev. Slavomir Siok, S.A.C.
Res.: 1419 Falls St., 14303. Tel: 716-284-6628; Fax: 716-282-2297.
Catechesis/Religious Program—Tel: 716-284-8944. Students 14.
4—ST. JOHN DE LA SALLE (1907), Rev. Jerome E. Kopec; Deacon David P. Slish, Pastoral Assoc.
Res.: 8627 Buffalo Ave., 14304. Tel: 716-283-2238; Fax: 716-283-7973.
School—Tel: 716-283-3031; Fax: 716-283-4540. Jenny Muscarella, Prin. Lay Teachers 13; Students 143.
Catechesis/Religious Program—Tel: 716-283-8442. Students 220.
5—ST. JOSEPH (1903), (Italian), [CEM] Rev. Msgr. Richard S. Amico; Sr. Francis Marie Vallone, F.M.D.C., Pastoral Assoc.
Res.: 1413 Pine Ave., 14301. Tel: 877-864-7131 (Toll Free); 716-282-1379; Fax: 716-285-3704.
Catechesis/Religious Program—Tel: 716-283-8442. Mrs. Rae Pullo, D.R.E. Students 155.
6—ST. LEO (1957), Rev. David G. Griffin; Deacon Benjamin Marino, Pastoral Assoc.
Res.: 2748 Military Rd., 14304. Tel: 716-297-5010; Fax: 716-297-8314.
Catechesis/Religious Program—Tel: 716-297-3085. Students 321.
7—ST. MARY OF THE CATARACT (1847), Merged, with Our Lady of the Rosary, Niagara Falls. Rev. Michael H. Burzynski. In Res., Revs. Francis J. Zmozynski, Chap., Memorial Medical Center; Francis Gross, O.S.F.S.; Bro. Francis Murray, O.S.F.S.
Res.: 259 Fourth St., 14303. Tel: 716-282-0059; Fax: 716-282-3372.
Catechesis/Religious Program—Students 59.
8—OUR LADY OF LEBANON (1914), (Lebanese), Rev. Ronald A. Wiktor, C.M.
Res.: 1120 Niagara St., 14303. Tel: 716-282-0729; Fax: 716-282-4779.
Catechesis/Religious Program—Students 26.
9—OUR LADY OF MOUNT CARMEL (1949), Rev. Duane R. Klizek. In Res., Rev. William C. McGarry (Retired).
Res.: 2486 Grand Ave., 14301. Tel: 716-282-5546; Fax: 716-282-6395.
School—2499 Independence Ave., 14301. Tel: 716-282-0645; Fax: 716-282-7681. Jeannine Fortunate, Prin. Lay Teachers 12; Students 165.
Catechesis/Religious Program—Students 77.
10—OUR LADY OF THE ROSARY (1906), Attended by, St. Mary of the Cataract, Niagara Falls. Rev. Michael H. Burzynski.
Res.: 339 22nd St., 14303. Tel: 716-282-0264; Fax: 716-282-0264.
Catechesis/Religious Program—Tri-Parish Religious Education Program, 335 24th St., 14303. Tel: 716-284-8944.
11—PRINCE OF PEACE (1943), Rev. Robert S. Hughson.
Res.: 1040 Cayuga Dr., 14304. Tel: 716-283-2715; Fax: 716-283-5635.
School—(Grades PreK-5) Tel: 716-283-1455; Fax: 716-283-1355. Mr. Christopher Hope, Prin. Students 240.
Catechesis/Religious Program—Tel: 716-283-0569. Students 248.
12—SACRED HEART (1854), Rev. James J. Kasinski.
Res.: 1917 11th St., 14305. Tel: 716-282-1749; Fax: 716-282-1665.
Catechesis/Religious Program—Tel: 716-284-8581. Patricia McCarthy, D.R.E. Students 83.
13—ST. STANISLAUS KOSTKA (1917), (Polish),, Linked with Holy Trinity, Niagra Falls. Most Rev. Slavomir Siok, S.A.C.
Res.: 2437 Niagara St., 14303. Tel: 716-285-3604; Fax: 716-282-2297.
Catechesis/Religious Program—Tel: 716-284-8944. Students 39.
14—ST. TERESA OF THE INFANT JESUS (1930), Rev. Msgr. Leonard E. Biniszkiewicz.
Res.: 3840 Macklem Ave., 14305. Tel: 716-282-5583; Fax: 716-282-0453.
Catechesis/Religious Program—Tel: 716-282-0795; Fax: 716-282-2447. Catherine Halliday, D.R.E. Students 185.

NORTH COLLINS, ERIE CO., HOLY SPIRIT (1958), [CEM 2] Rev. James G. Judge.
Res.: 2017 Halley Rd., 14111. Tel: 716-337-2544; Fax: 716-337-3803.
Catechesis/Religious Program—Tel: 716-337-3701. Ellen Bowman, D.R.E. Students 150.

NORTH EVANS, ERIE CO., ST. VINCENT (1914), [CEM] Revs. William R. Tuyn; Brian M. Hatrick.
Res.: 2050 S. Creek Rd., 14112. Tel: 716-627-3382; Fax: 716-627-3176.
School—Southtowns Catholic Consolidated School See separate listing under Regional and Consolidated Elementary Schools in the Institutions located in the Diocese. Tel: 716-627-5011; Fax: 716-627-2455.
Catechesis/Religious Program—Tel: 716-627-7673. Ann Kirkpatrick, D.R.E. Students 355.

NORTH JAVA, WYOMING CO., ST. NICHOLAS (1890), [CEM], See separate listing under Regional and Consolidated Elementary Schools in the Institutions located in the Diocese. Rev. Edward E. Muerder.
Res.: 4316 Rte. 98, 14113. Tel: 585-535-7457.
School—Genesee-Wyoming Catholic Central Consolidated School See separate listing under Regional and Consolidated Elementary Schools in the Institutions located in the Diocese.

NORTH TONAWANDA, NIAGARA CO.
1—ST. ALBERT THE GREAT (1960), Rev. Msgr. Edward T. Fisher; Deacon Daniel E. Brick Esq.; Mr. Gary Copeland, Pastoral Assoc. In Res., Rev. Duane G. Fimbel.
Res.: 1520 Kingston Ave., 14120. Tel: 716-694-0540; Fax: 716-694-8943.
Catechesis/Religious Program—Tel: 716-694-4540. Students 807.
2—ASCENSION (1887), Rev. Gary Szczepankiewicz.
Res.: 168 Robinson St., 14120. Tel: 716-693-1211; Fax: 716-693-1263.
School—North Tonawanda Consolidated Catholic School See separate listing under Regional and Consolidated Elementary Schools in the Institutions located in the Diocese. Tel: 716-693-2828; Fax: 716-693-0169.
Catechesis/Religious Program—Tel: 716-694-3754. Kathleen Kocsis, D.R.E.; Suzanne Ruska, D.R.E. Students 212.
3—ST. JOSEPH (1947), Rev. Msgr. Thomas E. Crane.
Res.: 1451 Payne Ave., 14120. Tel: 716-693-2791; Fax: 716-743-1405.
School—North Tonawanda Catholic Consolidated School See separate listing under Regional and Consolidated Elementary Schools in the Institutions located in the Diocese. Tel: 716-693-4769; Fax: 716-693-0169.
Catechesis/Religious Program—Tel: 716-693-0421. Mrs. Lorraine Schintzius, D.R.E. Students 216.
4—OUR LADY OF CZESTOCHOWA (1903), (Polish), Rev. Dennis F. Fronckowiak; Deacon Michael R. Kopczynski.
Res.: 64 Center Ave., 14120. Tel: 716-693-3822; Fax: 716-693-3882.
School—North Tonawanda Catholic Consolidated School See separate listing under Regional and Consolidated Elementary Schools in the Institutions located in the Diocese. Tel: 716-694-3644; Fax: 716-693-0169.
Catechesis/Religious Program—Tel: 716-693-3855. Students 124.
Convent—Tel: 716-692-0276.

OAKFIELD, GENESEE CO., ST. CECILIA (1905), [CEM] Rev. John P. Mack.
Res.: 56 Maple Ave., 14125. Tel: 585-948-5344; Fax: 585-948-8239.
Catechesis/Religious Program—Students 133.
Mission—St. Patrick Lewiston Rd at Knowlesville Rd., Wheatville, Genesee Co. 14013. Tel: 585-948-5344; Fax: 585-948-8239.

OLCOTT, NIAGARA CO., ST. CHARLES BORROMEO (1912), [CEM] Attended by, St. Patrick, Barker. Rev. James F. Hassett. In Res., Rev. Eugene L. Wagner, Pastor Emeritus (Retired).
Res.: 5969 Washington St., 14126. Tel: 716-778-7592; 716-795-3331 (Church); Fax: 716-795-3919.
Catechesis/Religious Program—Tel: 716-778-0536. Students 112.

OLEAN, CATTARAUGUS CO.
1—ST. JOHN (1896), Rev. Msgr. William O. Wangler; Deacon Michael A. Gomola.
Res.: 931 N. Union St., 14760. Tel: 716-372-5313; Fax: 716-373-0919.
School—Southern Tier Catholic Regional School See separate listing under Regional and Consolidated Elementary Schools in the Institutions located in the Diocese. Tel: 716-372-2891; Fax: 716-373-1175.
Catechesis/Religious Program—Tel: 716-372-6633. Students 202.
2—ST. MARY OF THE ANGELS (1876),, Linked with Sacred Heart, Portville Rev. Gregory J. Dobson; Deacon Richard F. Matthews.
Res.: 202 S. Union St., 14760. Tel: 716-372-4841; Fax: 716-372-5905.
School—Southern Tier Catholic Regional School

See separate listing under Regional and Consolidated Elementary Schools in the Institutions located in the Diocese. Tel: 716-372-2891; Fax: 716-373-1175.
Catechesis/Religious Program—205 W. Henley St., 14760. Tel: 716-373-1855. Students 206.
3—TRANSFIGURATION (1902), (Polish), Rev. Jerome J. Stelmach.
Res.: 1102 Walnut St., 14760. Tel: 716-372-5430; Fax: 716-373-4719.
School—Southern Tier Catholic Regional School See separate listing under Regional and Consolidated Elementary Schools in the Institutions located in the Diocese. Tel: 716-372-2891; Fax: 716-373-1175.
Catechesis/Religious Program—Tel: 716-373-5446. Students 53.

ORCHARD PARK, ERIE CO.
1—ST. BERNADETTE (1957), Rev. Msgr. Richard T. Nugent; Revs. Raymond J. McNicholas, S.S.C.; Arthur E. Mattulke; Deacons Robert T. Ciezki; Edward Howard; Lawrence Markowski.
Res.: 5930 S. Abbott Rd., 14127-4516. Tel: 716-649-3090; Fax: 716-649-0211.
School—Tel: 716-649-3369. Sr. Diane Swanson, Prin. Lay Teachers 22; Students 254.
Catechesis/Religious Program—Tel: 716-648-1720. Joan Ersing, D.R.E. Students 933.
2—ST. JOHN VIANNEY (1958), Rev. Msgr. William J. Gallagher.
Res.: 2950 Southwestern Blvd., 14127. Tel: 716-674-9133; Fax: 716-674-9134.
School—Tel: 716-674-9232; Fax: 716-674-9248. Teresa A. Siuta, Prin. Lay Teachers 13; Students 167.
Catechesis/Religious Program—Tel: 716-674-9145. Sharon Kirsch, D.R.E. Students 830.
3—NATIVITY OF OUR LORD (1908), [CEM] Revs. Lawrence M. Milby; Eric L. Sikora.
Res.: 26 Thorn Ave., 14127. Tel: 716-662-9339; Fax: 716-662-2195.
School—Tel: 716-662-7572. Ruth Frost, Prin. Sisters of St. Francis of Penance and Christian Charity 1; Lay Teachers 29; Students 394.
Catechesis/Religious Program—Tel: 716-662-2169. Mary Ann Pietrzak, D.R.E. Students 851.
4—OUR LADY OF THE SACRED HEART (1920), Rev. Msgr. Paul J.E. Burkard; Rev. Patrick T. O'Keefe; Deacons William J. Walkowiak; Thomas G. Licata.
Res.: 3148 Abbott Rd., 14127. Tel: 716-824-2935; Fax: 716-827-7643.
School—3144 Abbott Rd., 14127. Tel: 716-824-8208; Fax: 716-827-7643. Mary Wood, Prin. Sisters of Mercy 2; Lay Teachers 33; Students 420.
Catechesis/Religious Program—Tel: 716-824-8209. Paula White, D.R.E.; Judy Quinn, D.R.E. Students 720.

PANAMA, CHAUTAUQUA CO., OUR LADY OF THE SNOWS (1946), Attended by, St. Matthias, French Creek. Rev. Bernard C. Staszak.
Mailing Address: P.O. Box 236, 14767.
Res.: 1762 French Creek Mina Rd., 14767. Tel: 716-355-8891; Fax: 716-355-2576.
School—Holy Family Catholic School See separate listing under Regional and Consolidated Elementary Schools in the Institutions located in the Diocese.
Catechesis/Religious Program—Students 38.

PAVILION, GENESEE CO., ST. MARY (1865), [CEM] Rev. Frederick M. Hinton, Admin.
Res.: 11095 Saint Mary St., 14525. Tel: 585-584-3280; Fax: 585-584-8628.
Catechesis/Religious Program—Mary Shaughnessy, D.R.E. Students 36.

PENDLETON, NIAGARA CO., GOOD SHEPHERD (1847), [CEM] Rev. Msgr. Paul J. Belzer. In Res., Rev. Samuel J. Venne.
Res.: 5442 Tonawanda Creek Rd., North Tonawanda, 14120-9699. Tel: 716-625-8594; Fax: 716-625-8365.
Catechesis/Religious Program—Tel: 716-625-8817 Roberta Spencer, D.R.E. Students 183.

PERRY, WYOMING CO.
1—ST. JOSEPH (1879), [CEM], Linked with St. Stanislaus Kostka, Perry. Rev. Richard W. Blazejewski; Deacon Daniel J. McGuire.
Res.: 8 Park St., 14530. Tel: 585-237-2625; Fax: 585-237-0150.
Catechesis/Religious Program—Students 91.
2—ST. STANISLAUS KOSTKA (1910), (Polish), [CEM] Attended by, St. Joseph, Perry. Rev. Richard J. Blazejewski; Deacon Daniel J. McGuire.
Res.: 8 Park St., 14530. Tel: 585-237-3869; Fax: 585-237-0150.
Catechesis/Religious Program—Tel: 585-237-2625. Students 21.

PERRYSBURG, CATTARAUGUS CO., ST. JOAN OF ARC (1950),, Linked with St. John the Fisher, S. Dayton Rev. Stanislaw Dudek, Admin.
Res.: P.O. Box 234, 14129-0222. Tel: 716-532-4556; Fax: 716-532-4556.
Catechesis/Religious Program— Twinned with St. John Fisher, S. Dayton.

PORTAGEVILLE, WYOMING CO., ASSUMPTION B.V.M. (1849), [CEM], Linked with St. Mary, Canaseraga. Revs. Robert M. Mock; John J. Cullen, Admin.
Res.: P.O. Box 404, 14536. Tel: 585-468-2643; Fax: 585-468-2126.
Catechesis/Religious Program—Students 33.

PORTVILLE, CATTARAUGUS CO., SACRED HEART (1909), Attended by, St. Mary of the Angels, Olean Rev. Robert J. Schober.
Res.: 205 S. Union St., Olean, 14760. Tel: 716-372-4841; Fax: 716-372-5905.
Church: 43 Maple Ave., P.O. Box 808, 14770. Tel: 716-933 6394; Fax: 716-933-0275.
School—Southern Tier Catholic Regional School See separate listing under Regional and Consolidated Elementary Schools in the Institutions located in the Diocese.

RANDOLPH, CATTARAUGUS CO., ST. PATRICK (1853), [CEM] Rev. Msgr. Leon M. Neu.
Res.: 189 Main St., 14772. Tel: 716-358-2991; Fax: 716-358-2122.
School—Holy Family Catholic School See separate listing under Regional and Consolidated Elementary Schools in the Institutions located in the Diocese.
Catechesis/Religious Program—Students 72.

RANSOMVILLE, NIAGARA CO., IMMACULATE CONCEPTION (1891), Revs. Herold M. Nuwer; Salvatore J. Piazza (Retired).
Res.: 4671 Townline Rd., Rte. 429, 14131-9740. Tel: 716-731-4822; Fax: 716-731-4911.
Catechesis/Religious Program—Tel: 716-731-5387. Mrs. Judith A. Kirkpatrick, D.R.E. Students 291.

RIPLEY, CHAUTAUQUA CO., ST. THOMAS MORE (1941), Rev. Daniel A. Young. Mission of St. James, Westfield.
66 E. Main St., Rte. 20, 14775. Tel: 716-736-5200; Fax: 716-326-2816.
Catechesis/Religious Program—15 Union St., Westfield, 14787. Tel: 716-326-2816. Twinned with St. James, Westfield.

RUSHFORD, ALLEGANY CO., ST. MARK (1948), Rev. Francis J. Jann (Retired).
Mailing Address: P.O. Box 37, 14777. Tel: 585-437-5332; Fax: 585-437-5532.
Res.: 7693 State Rte. 243, Caneadea, 14717. Tel: 585-365-9977.
Catechesis/Religious Program—Students 32.

SALAMANCA, CATTARAUGUS CO.
1—HOLY CROSS (1893), (Polish), Attended by, St. Patrick, Salamanca. Rev. Joseph D. Porpiglia; Deacon Michael L. Anderson.
Res.: 101 River St., 14779-1414. Tel: 716-945-2666; Fax: 716-945-0676.
Catechesis/Religious Program— Linked with St. Patrick, Salamanca.
2—ST. PATRICK (1868), [CEM], Linked with Holy Cross, Salamanca. Rev. Joseph D. Porpiglia; Deacon Michael L. Anderson.
Res.: 101 River St., 14779-1414. Tel: 716-945-5522; Fax: 716-945-0676.
Catechesis/Religious Program—Tel: 716-945-2666. Students 132.

SANBORN, NIAGARA CO., HOLY FAMILY (1953), [JC], (Tuscarora Native Americans) Rev. Peter M. Calabrese, C.R.S.P., Admin.
Mailing Address: P.O. Box 167, Youngstown, 14174-0167.
Res.: Tel: 716-754-7489; Fax: 716-754-9130.
Church: Chew Rd., 14132. Tel: 716-523-9114.
Catechesis/Religious Program—Students 22.

SARDINIA, ERIE CO., ST. JUDE (1953), [JC], Linked with St. John the Baptist, West Valley Rev. Alfons M. Osiander, Admin.
Res.: 12820 Genesee Rd., 14134-0267. Tel: 716-496-7535; Fax: 716-496-7535.
School—St. Aloysius Regional School, Springville See separate listing under Regional and Consolidated Elementary Schools in the Institutions located in the Diocese.
Catechesis/Religious Program—Tel: 716-537-2748. Students 29.

SCIO, ALLEGANY CO., ST. JOSEPH (1844),, Mission of St. Mary, Belmont. Rev. Dennis J. Mancuso.
Rte. 19 at Day Brook Rd., 14880. Tel: 585-268-7272; Fax: 585-268-9128.
Res.: 5 Milton St., P.O. Box 570, Belmont, 14813-1119.
Catechesis/Religious Program— Combined with St. Mary, Belmont.

SHELDON, WYOMING CO., ST. CECILIA (1848), [CEM 2] Attended by, St. Joseph, Varysburg Rev. Fred D. Ingalls, Admin.
Res.: 991 Centerline Rd., Strykersville, 14145-9553. Tel: 585-457-9437; Fax: 585-535-0477.
School—Genesee-Wyoming Catholic Central Consolidated School See separate listing under Regional and Consolidated Elementary Schools in the Institutions located in the Diocese. Tel: 585-591-2515; Fax: 585-591-2516.

SHERIDAN, CHAUTAUQUA CO., ST. JOHN BOSCO (1949),, Linked with St. Rose of Lima, Forestville. Rev. Gerald P. Sheehan.
Res.: Box 3, 14135. Tel: 716-679-4951; Fax: 716-679-4952.
Catechesis/Religious Program—Tel: 716-679-4116. Linked with St. Joseph, Fredonia.

SHERMAN, CHAUTAUQUA CO., ST. ISAAC JOGUES (1947), Attended by, St. Mary, Mayville. Rev. Raymond A.J. Donohue.
Res.: 24 E. Chautauqua St., Box 148, Mayville, 14757. Tel: 716-753-2332; Fax: 716-753-3836.
School—Holy Family Catholic School See separate listing under Regional and Consolidated Elementary Schools in the Institutions located in the Diocese.
Catechesis/Religious Program—Students 13.

SILVER CREEK, CHAUTAUQUA CO., OUR LADY OF MT. CARMEL (1882), [CEM] Rev. James E. Fitzgerald.
Res.: 165 Central Ave., 14136. Tel: 716-934-2233; Fax: 716-934-6216.
School—Northern Chautauqua Catholic Regional School See separate listing under Regional and Consolidated Elementary Schools in the Institutions located in the Diocese. Tel: 716-366-0630.
Catechesis/Religious Program—Tel: 716-934-4891. Students 196.

SILVER SPRINGS, WYOMING CO., ST. MARY (1892), [CEM] Rev. John J. Heigl, M.Afr.; Deacon John Kelly.
Res.: 23 Church St., Box 305, 14550. Tel: 585-493-5265.
Catechesis/Religious Program—Tel: 585-786-2400; Fax: 585-786-3977. Students 28.

SINCLAIRVILLE, CHAUTAUQUA CO., ST. JOHN THE EVANGELIST (1940), Attended by, Immaculate Conception, Cassadaga. Rev. Patrick H. Elis.
Res.: 88 N. Main St., Cassadaga, 14718. Tel: 716-962-3781; Fax: 716-595-3484.

SLOAN, ERIE CO., ST. ANDREW (1915), (Polish), Rev. Robert D. Moss.
Res.: 34 Francis St., 14212. Tel: 716-892-0425; Fax: 716-892-0425.
Catechesis/Religious Program—Students 83.

SNYDER, ERIE CO., CHRIST THE KING (1926), Rev. Msgr. James J. Lichtenthal. In Res., Rev. Joseph J. Sicari.
Res.: 30 Lamarck Dr., 14226. Tel: 716-839-1430; Fax: 716-839-1433.
School—Tel: 716-839-0473; Fax: 716-839-0473. Sr. Mary Ellen Tucker, O.S.F., Prin. Franciscan Sisters of Allegany 1; Lay Teachers 21; Students 268.
Catechesis/Religious Program—Tel: 716-839-0946. Students 472.

SOUTH BYRON, GENESEE CO., ST. MICHAEL (1892),, Mission of St. Brigid, Bergen. Rev. Robert J. Schober.
Res.: P.O. Box 219, Bergen, 14416. Tel: 585-494-1110; Fax: 585-494-1895.
Church: Rte. 237, 14557.

SOUTH DAYTON, CATTARAUGUS CO., ST. JOHN FISHER (1946),, Linked with St. Joan of Arc, Perrysburg. Rev. Stanislaw Dudek, Admin.
Res.: P.O. Box 243, Perrysburg, 14129. Tel: 716-532-4556; Fax: 716-532-4556.
Catechesis/Religious Program—Students 37.

SPRINGBROOK, ERIE CO., ST. VINCENT (1850), [CEM] Rev. James A. Walter; Deacon Richard Mackiewicz.
Res.: 6441 Seneca St., P.O. Box 290, 14140. Tel: 716-652-3972; Fax: 716-655-3048.
School—Tel: 716-652-8697. Ms. Jane Hibschweiler, Prin. Lay Teachers 9; Students 155.
Catechesis/Religious Program—Tel: 716-652-7242. Michael Morcelle, D.R.E. Students 530.

SPRINGVILLE, ERIE CO., ST. ALOYSIUS (1853), [CEM] Rev. John S. Kwiecien.
Res.: 190 Franklin St., 14141-1199. Tel: 716-592-2701; Fax: 716-592-4347.
School—St. Aloysius Regional School See separate listing under Regional and Consolidated Elementary Schools in the Institutions located in the Diocese.
Catechesis/Religious Program—Tel: 716-592-4869. Students 320.

STRYKERSVILLE, WYOMING CO., ST. MARY, QUEEN OF THE ROSARY (1885), [CEM] Rev. Michael P. McNicholl.
Res.: 3854 Main St., P.O. Box 9, 14145-0009. Tel: 585-457-3021; 585-457-3222; Fax: 585-457-1310.
Catechesis/Religious Program—Students 146.

SWORMVILLE, ERIE CO., ST. MARY (1849), [CEM] Revs. Robert M. Yetter; Paul S. Salemi; Deacons Howard J. Edbauer Jr.; Paul Snyder.
Res.: 6919 Transit Rd., Box 460, 14146. Tel: 716-688-9380; Fax: 716-688-6025.
School—Tel: 716-689-8424. Sisters of the Third Order of St. Francis 2; Lay Teachers 15; Students 260.
Catechesis/Religious Program—Tel: 716-688-0599. Students 1,300.

TONAWANDA, ERIE CO.
1—ST. AMELIA (1953), Rev. Msgr. Thomas F. Maloney;

Revs. Jorge H. Budez; Joseph C. Carlo (Retired); Sisters M. Jeanne Thomas, R.S.M., Pastoral Assoc.; Helen Buscarino, F.M.D.C., Pastoral Assoc. In Res., Rev. Donald L. Measer (Retired).
Res.: 210 St. Amelia Dr., 14150. Tel: 716-836-0011; Fax: 716-832-5439.
School—Tel: 716-836-2230; Fax: 716-832-9700. James Mule, Prin. Lay Teachers 34; Students 526.
Catechesis/Religious Program—Tel: 716-833-8647. Elaine Dankowski, D.R.E. Students 915.

2—ST. ANDREW KIM (1993),, Mission for Korean Catholics. Rev. Dominic Jung, C.PP.S., Chap.
Mailing Address: 9 O'Hara Rd., 14150. Tel: 716-693-7116; 716-693-1600; Fax: 716-693-7130.

3—BLESSED SACRAMENT (1929), Rev. Msgr. Robert K. Golombek. In Res., Rev. Leon J. Biernat.
Res.: 263 Claremont Ave., 14223. Tel: 716-834-4282; Fax: 716-834-9573.
School—Tel: 716-836-6360; Fax: 716-862-8101. Sr. M. Christelle Sawicki, C.S.S.F., Prin. Felician Sisters 3; Lay Teachers 15; Students 148.
Catechesis/Religious Program—Tel: 716-832-6161. Students 381.

4—ST. CHRISTOPHER (1928), Rev. Msgr. Francis G. Weldgen; Rev. Lynn M. Shumway; Deacon Francis A. Zwack.
Res.: 2660 Niagara Falls Blvd., 14150-1499. Tel: 716-692-2660; Fax: 716-693-5639.
School—Tel: 716-693-5604; Fax: 716-693-5127. Lay Teachers 26; Students 507.
Catechesis/Religious Program—Tel: 716-694-4310. Students 1,097.

5—ST. EDMUND (1965), Rev. Robert A. Wozniak; Deacon Robert Bauer.
Res.: 530 Ellicott Creek Rd., 14150. Tel: 716-694-5656; Fax: 716-694-5902.
School—Tel: 716-694-5900; Fax: 716-695-7248. Lay Teachers 10; Students 159.
Catechesis/Religious Program—Students 250.

6—ST. FRANCIS OF ASSISI (1858), [CEM] Rev. Michael G. Uebler; Deacon Paul J. Schnettler. In Res., Rev. James H. Kasprzyk (Retired).
Res.: 73 Adam St., 14150. Tel: 716-693-1150; Fax: 716-693-2025.
School—Tel: 716-692-7886. Lay Teachers 15; Students 114.
Catechesis/Religious Program—Tel: 716-694-5342. Students 282.

7—ST. TIMOTHY (1960), Rev. Msgr. John I. Ducette; Deacon Gordon J. Steinagle. In Res., Rev. Msgr. John Kempczynski (Retired).
Res.: 565 E. Park Dr., 14150. Tel: 716-875-9430; Fax: 716-874-3483.
Catechesis/Religious Program—Students 236.

VANDALIA, CATTARAUGUS CO., ST. JOHN THE BAPTIST (1900),, Mission of St. Bonaventure, Allegany. Rev. Richard Husted, O.F.M.
St. Bonaventure: 95 E. Main St., Allegany, 14706-1397. Tel: 716-373-1330; Fax: 716-373-1330.
School—Southern Tier Catholic Regional School See separate listing under Regional and Consolidated Elementary Schools in the Institutions located in the Diocese.
Catechesis/Religious Program—Fax: 716-373-4220. Students 20.

VARYSBURG, WYOMING CO., ST. JOSEPH (1910), [CEM] Rev. Fred D. Ingalls, Admin.
Res.: 2314 Attica Rd., 14167-9752. Tel: 716-535-7342; Fax: 716-535-7342.
School—Genesee-Wyoming Catholic Central Consolidated School See separate listing under Regional and Consolidated Elementary Schools in the Institutions located in the Diocese. Tel: 716-591-2515; Fax: 716-591-2516.
Catechesis/Religious Program—Students 66.

WARSAW, WYOMING CO., ST. MICHAEL (1858), [CEM] Rev. Lawrence P. Damian; Deacon John J. Kelly.
Res.: 171 N. Main St., 14569. Tel: 585-786-2400; Fax: 585-786-3977.
School—(Grades PreK-6), 16 North St., 14569. Tel: 585-786-8561; Fax: 585-786-8568. Mary Ann Moore, Prin. Lay Teachers 10; Students 79.
Catechesis/Religious Program—Students 154.

WELLSVILLE, ALLEGANY CO., IMMACULATE CONCEPTION (1850), [CEM], Linked with Blessed Sacrament, Andover Rev. Dennis G. Wolf.
Res.: 6 Maple Ave., 14895. Tel: 585-593-4834; Fax: 585-593-7167.
School—(Grades N-N), 24 Maple Ave., 14895. Tel: 585-593-5840; Fax: 585-593-5846. Sr. Alice Roach, Prin. Sisters of Mercy 1; Lay Teachers 14; Students 186.
Catechesis/Religious Program—Tel: 585-593-4834. Mrs. Carol Gardner, D.R.E. (Grades 9-11); Mrs. Karen Insley, D.R.E. (Grades PreK-8). Students 151.
Oratory—St. John of the Cross (1949), 540 Main St., Whitesville, 14897. Whitesville, NY

WEST FALLS, ERIE CO., ST. GEORGE (Jewettville) (1942), Rev. Walter J. Szczesny, Admin.
Res.: 74 Old Glenwood Rd., 14170. Tel: 716-652-3153; Fax: 716-687-1336.
Catechesis/Religious Program—Tel: 716-652-0126. Students 177.

WEST SENECA, ERIE CO.

1—ST. BONAVENTURE (1918), Revs. Ronald M. Bagley, C.J.M.; Benoit J. Drapeau, C.J.M., Asst.; J. Gregory Sampson, C.J.M.
Res.: 36 Flohr Ave., 14224. Tel: 716-823-1090; Fax: 716-825-4376.
School—Preschool Students 20.
School—2784 Seneca St., 14224. Tel: 716-822-7260; Fax: 716-824-3512. Lay Teachers 16; Students 160.
Catechesis/Religious Program—Tel: 716-825-5053. Madeleine Fuller, D.R.E. Students 189.

2—ST. CATHERINE OF SIENA (1967), Rev. Pascal D. Ipolito; Deacons Joseph M. Barr; Mark Nowak; Suzanne M. Buttino, Pastoral Assoc.
Res.: 4928 Seneca St., 14224. Tel: 716-675-0531; Fax: 716-675-8323.
Catechesis/Religious Program—Students 213.

3—FOURTEEN HOLY HELPERS (1864), [CEM] Rev. Msgr. David S. Slubecky; Rev. Edward F. Jost; Deacons James Waite; Thomas E. Scherr.
Res.: 1345 Indian Church Rd., 14224. Tel: 716-674-2374; Fax: 716-675-4864.
School—Tel: 716-674-1670. Ms. Susan Jagosh, Prin. Lay Teachers 18; Students 267.
Catechesis/Religious Program—Tel: 716-674-2180. Students 309.

4—QUEEN OF HEAVEN (1955), Revs. Thomas J. Quinlivan; Matt F. Nycz. In Res., Rev. Msgr. Joseph F. Coughlin (Retired); Deacon John M. Ruh.
Res.: 4220 Seneca St., 14224. Tel: 716-674-3468; Fax: 716-674-3475.
School—839 Mill Rd., 14224. Tel: 716-674-5206. Miss Barbara Ryan, Prin. Lay Teachers 24; Students 328.
Catechesis/Religious Program—Tel: 716-675-3714. Sr. Lori High, S.S.M.N., D.R.E.; Dorothy Flynn, D.R.E. Students 600.

5—ST. WILLIAM (1926), Rev. Robert W. Wardenski.
Res.: One Arcade St., 14224. Tel: 716-822-5449; Fax: 716-822-5457.
School—Tel: 716-822-7260 (St. Bonaventure); 716-674-1670 (Fourteen Holy Helpers); Fax: 716-822-7296 (St. Bonaventure); 716-675-4864. Affiliated with St. Bonaventure and Fourteen Holy Helpers, 1339 Indian Church Rd., West Seneca, NY 14224
Catechesis/Religious Program—Tel: 716-822-0439. Students 148.

WEST VALLEY, CATTARAUGUS CO., ST. JOHN THE BAPTIST (1904), [CEM] Attended by, St. Jude, Sardinia Rev. Alfons M. Osiander, Admin.
Res.: 5381 Depot St., P.O. Box 315, 14171-0315. Tel: 716-942-3259; Fax: 716-942-3259.
School—St. Aloysius Regional School, Springville See separate listing under Regional and Consolidated Elementary Schools in the Institutions located in the Diocese.
Catechesis/Religious Program—Tel: 716-942-6874. Janet Vant, D.R.E. Students 130.

WESTFIELD, CHAUTAUQUA CO., ST. JAMES MAJOR (1860), [CEM 2] Rev. Daniel A. Young.
Res.: 15 Union St., 14787-1494. Tel: 716-326-2816; Fax: 716-326-4863.
Catechesis/Religious Program—Tel: 716-326-3003. Denise Johnson, D.R.E. Students 110.
Mission—St. Thomas More 66 E. Main St., Rte 20, Ripley, Chautauqua Co. 14775. Tel: 716-736-5200; Fax: 716-326-2816.

WHEATVILLE, GENESEE CO., ST. PATRICK (1882),, Mission of St. Cecilia, Oakfield. Rev. John P. Mack.
Res.: 56 Maple Ave., Oakfield, 14125. Tel: 716-948-5344; Fax: 716-948-8239.
Catechesis/Religious Program— Combined with St. Cecilia, Oakfield.

WHITESVILLE, ALLEGANY CO., ST. JOHN OF THE CROSS (1949),, Subsidiary of Immaculate Conception, Wellsville.

WILLIAMSVILLE, ERIE CO.

1—ST. GREGORY THE GREAT (1958), Rev. Msgr. Rupert A. Wright; Revs. James R. Bastian; William J. Quinlivan; Robert J. Orlowski; Deacon Philip J. Amantia.
Res.: 260 St. Gregory Ct., 14221. Tel: 716-688-5678; 716-688-5679; Fax: 716-688-2315.
School—250 St. Gregory Ct., 14221. Tel: 716-688-5323; Fax: 716-688-6629. Mrs. Patricia Freund, Prin. Sisters 1; Lay Teachers 35; Students 645.
Catechesis/Religious Program—Tel: 716-688-5760; Fax: 716-639-8251. Mrs. Joan Rischmiller, D.R.E. Students 1,444.

2—SS. PETER AND PAUL (1836), [CEM 2] Rev. James C. O'Connor; Deacons George L. Klein; Alexander S. Molnar; Mrs. Linda Downey, Pastoral Assoc.
Res.: 5480 Main St., 14221. Tel: 716-632-2559; Fax: 716-626-0971.
School—Tel: 716-632-6146. Mrs. Marianne Maines, Prin. Lay Teachers 22; Students 429.
Catechesis/Religious Program—Tel: 716-632-2678. Ms. Denise Peplowski, D.R.E. (Grades K-5); Susan Cowan, D.R.E. (Grades 6-8, High School). Students 415.

WILSON, NIAGARA CO., OUR LADY OF THE ROSARY (1920), Attended by, St. Bridget, Newfane. Rev. John J. Leising.
Res.: 359 Lake St., Box 116, 14172-0116. Tel: 716-751-6459.
Catechesis/Religious Program—Mrs. Kathleen Higgins, D.R.E. Students 125.

WOODLAWN, ERIE CO., OUR LADY OF GRACE (1940), Rev. John F. Kasprzak.
Res.: S. 3319 Lake Shore Rd., 14219. Tel: 716-822-0607; Fax: 716-822-1366.
Catechesis/Religious Program—BettyLou Regueira, D.R.E. Students 140.

YOUNGSTOWN, NIAGARA CO., ST. BERNARD'S (1946), [CEM] Rev. Msgr. J. Thomas Moran.
Res.: 218 Hinman St., 14174. Tel: 716-745-7460; Fax: 716-745-1359.
Catechesis/Religious Program—Blanche Sylvester, D.R.E. Students 280.

Chaplains of Public Institutions

BUFFALO. *Buffalo General Hospital*. Revs. Patrick O. Fernandes, Richard H. Augustyn, Deacon Joseph Gill.
Buffalo Psychiatric Center, 400 Forest Ave., 14213. Rev. Norman P. McTigue.
Buffalo-Niagara International Airport. Rev. Msgr. Ronald P. Sciera.
Children's Hospital. Sr. Brenda Whelan, R.S.M.
Erie County Holding Center. Rev. Ivan R. Trujillo.
Erie County Juvenile Detention Center. Deacon Frank J. Shaughnessey.
Erie County Medical Center. Rev. Francis X. Mazur.
Genesee Memorial Hospital
Hospice of Buffalo. (Vacant)
Millard Fillmore Hospital. Rev. Thomas P. Taton.
Roswell Park Memorial Institute. Deacon Stephen J. Swinarski.
Sheehan Memorial Emergency Hospital. Rev. Roy T. Herberger.
Veterans Hospital. Revs. Richard E. Sowinski, Christopher Coric, O.F.M.Conv. (Croatia).

ALBION. *Albion Correctional Facility*. Rev. Eugene S. Slomba. Tel: 585-343-1796, Sr. Dolores Ann O'Dowd, G.N.S.H.
Orleans Correction Facility. Deacon Thomas Bringenberg Jr.

ALDEN. *Erie County Correctional Facility*, 11580 Walden Ave., 14004. Tel: 716-937-5693. Rev. Robert Moreno (STF).
Wende Correctional Facility. Deacons Gordon J. Steinagle, Timothy Maloney.

AMHERST. *Millard Fillmore Suburban Hospital*. Rev. Richard D. Bordonaro, Deacons Gary C. Ingold, Philip J. Amantia, Paul L. Snyder III.

ATTICA. *Attica Correctional Facility*. Rev. Ivan R. Trujillo, Sr. Rosalind Rosolowski, C.S.S.F.
Wyoming Correctional Facility. Deacon Brian C. Walkowiak.

BATAVIA. *Genesee Memorial Hospital*. Rev. Ivan Skenderovic.

COLLINS. *Collins Correctional Facility*. Deacons John H. Burke, Carlos W. Ramos, Sr. Mary Lou Schnitzer, S.S.J.

CUBA. *Cuba Memorial Hospital and Adult Day Care Facility*. Deacon Francis W. Pasquale Jr.

DUNKIRK. *Brooks Memorial Hospital*. Deacon Jose J. Ruiz.

GOWANDA. *Gowanda Correctional Facility*. Deacon Carlos W. Ramos.

LAKEVIEW. *Lakeview Shock Incarceration Correctional Facility*. Rev. Walter Werbicki, S.T.F.

MEDINA. *Medina Memorial Hospital*. Deacon Nelson Darroch.

NIAGARA FALLS. *Niagara Falls Memorial Medical Centers*. Rev. Francis J. Zmozynski.

NORTH TONAWANDA. *DeGraff Memorial Hospital*, 1520 Kingston Ave., 14120. Tel: 716-694-4500. Rev. Duane G. Fimbel.

OLEAN. *Olean General Hospital*. Deacons Michael L. Anderson, Michael R. Bray.

WEST SENECA. *Development Center*. Deacon Albert F. Fox, Carol Ann Corey.

On Duty Outside the Diocese:
Rev. Msgr.—
Sciera, Ronald P., Rome, Italy.
Revs.—
Conoscenti, Frederick M., 605 Grove St., D4, Clifton, NJ 07013.
Enright, James C., Auburn Correctional Facility, 135 State St., Auburn, 13021.
Nielsen, Kenneth M., Kentwood Village Apts., 246 Kentwood Blvd., Brook, NJ 08724.
Wild, Robert A., S.J. (MIL), Madonna House, Combermere ON Canada.

Military Chaplains:
Revs.—
Koester, Timothy J., P.O. Box 25771, Havelock, NC 28532.
Zuffoletto, Michael P., Naval Activities U.K.-London, PSC 821 Box 1, FPO, AE 09421-0001. U.S. Navy

Absent on Leave:
Revs.—
Blesnuk, Donald J.
Gresock, Thomas G.
Levan, Donald E..
Moreno, Joseph F.
Swartz, Michael R.

Retired:
Rev. Msgrs.—
Berg, Theodore S., 14 North Shore Dr., Blasdell, 14219.
Boruszewski, Joseph A., 348 Atlantic Ave., 14212.
Brennan, George J., 4 Lockwood Ln., Orchard Park, 14127-2713.
Bugman, John H., Our Lady of Victory, 767 Ridge Rd., Lackawanna, 14218-1697.
Cahill, Richard M., 1825 Alberta Dr., Clearwater, FL 33756.
Caine, Martin J., 4000 Ridgeline Dr., Austin, TX 78731-1326.
Caligiuri, Anthony J., O'Hara Residence, 69 O'Hara Rd., Tonawanda, 14150-6227.
Connelly, James N., O'Hara Residence, 69 O'Hara Rd., Apt. 3, Tonawanda, 14150-6227.
Conniff, John J., 1088 Delaware Ave., Apt. 15C, 14209-1627.
Coughlin, Joseph F., Queen of Heaven Rectory, 4220 Seneca St., 14224-3199.
Cronin, Paul T., Sheehan Residence, 330 Linwood Ave., 14209-1689.
Crumlish, Richard C., Holy Family Home, 410 Mill St., Williamsville, 14221.
DelVecchio, Michael E., P.O. Box 22, Orchard Park, 14127.
Duggan, John M., 127 Keil St., North Tonawanda, 14120-6921.
Engelhardt, Herbert G., 43 Circle End Dr., 14224-3925.
Faiola, Samuel J., S.T.D., 72B Lexington Ct., Lockport, 14094-5365.
Gill, Richard, 103 E. 7th St., Dunkirk, 14048-2650.
Green, Gerard L., 9686 Oak Grove Dr., Angola, 14006-8904.
Griffin, Charles T., O'Hara Residence, 69 O'Hara Rd., Tonawanda, 14150-6227.
Hammerl, Leo E., O'Hara Residence, 69 O'Hara Rd., Tonawanda, 14150-6227.
Higgins, Grant J., 170 Countryside Ln., Apt. #4, Orchard Park, 14127.
Jasinski, Anthony J., Bishop Head Residence, 10 Rosary Ave., Lackawanna, 14218.
Juchnowski, Francis B , 414 S. Ogden St., 14206-3396.
Juenker, Paul R., O'Hara Residence, 69 O'Hara Rd., Tonawanda, 14150-6227.
Kempczynski, John, St. Timothy Rectory, 565 E. Park Dr., Tonawanda, 14150-6705.
Kern, Walter O., Holy Family Home, 410 Mill St., Williamsville, 14221.
Klein, Stanley H., Chap. Col., St. Francis Home, 147 Reist St., Williamsville, 14221.
Kozminski, Max M., 150 Brush Creek Rd., Williamsville, 14221-2743.
Letourneau, Paul R., O'Hara Residence, 69 O'Hara Rd., Tonawanda, 14150-6227.
Lorenzetti, Dino J., O'Hara Residence, 69 O'Hara Rd., Tonawanda, 14150-6227.
Mack, Robert A., 53 Hinman Ave., 14216.
Meloch, Chester A., 6613 Hunters Creek Rd., South Wales, 14139.
Myszka, Daniel J., 391 Bristol St., 14206-3721.
O'Loughlin, Eugene E., St. Elizabeth Home, 5539 Broadway, Lancaster, 14086.
Paa, Raymond F., 4375 Harris Hill Rd., Williamsville, 14221-6203.
Radon, Eugene M., Coronation of BVM, 348 Dewitt St., 14213-1191.
Ronald, Roy K., 200 Boncroft Dr., 14224-2829.
Ryan, John M., 435 Amherst St., 14207-2891.
Scanlan, Edward J., 4421 Lower River Rd., Stella Niagara, 14144.
Schneider, Arnold J., Sheehan Residence, 330 Linwood Ave., 14209.
Schwab, Robert C., 2164 N.E. 36th St., Apt. 49, Lighthouse Point, FL 33064-7555.
Schwinger, William A., Bishop Head Residence, 10 Rosary Ave., Lackawanna, 14218.
Skupien, Francis M., P.O. Box 424, Kendall, 14476-0424.
Smiraldo, Onofrio R., Bishop Head Residence, 10 Rosary Ave., Lackawanna, 14218.
Sobierajski Edward J., O'Hara Residence, 69 O'Hara Rd., Tonawanda, 14150-6299.
Sorci, Francis P., 34 Loch Lee, Williamsville, 14221-4934.
Stachewicz, Henry J., 103 Kokomo, Depew, 14043-3705.
Stengel, Paul F., Bishop Head Residence, 10 Rosary Ave., Lackawanna, 14218.
Stillwell, William J., Nazareth Nursing Home, 291 North St., 14201.
Swiatkowski, Francis M., O'Hara Residence, 69 O'Hara Rd., Tonawanda, 14150-6227
Szostak, Daniel J., 10665 Walnut St., P.O. Box 233, North Collins, 14111.
Ulaszeski, Edward J., 2035 Bush Rd., Grand Island, 14072.
Waclawski, Joseph P., 81 Forest View Rd., Depew, 14043-1715.
Wangler, Donald R., 7360 Rochester Rd., Lockport, 14094-1626.
Weimer, John C., 153 Nassau Ave., Kenmore, 14217-2141.
Wendzikowski, Mecislaus S., 142 Phyllis Ave., 14215-2826.
Wetter, Richard L., O'Hara Residence, 69 O'Hara Rd., Tonawanda, 14150-6227.
Whitney, Paul J., 5B Lexington CT., Lockport, 14094.
Yunk, Michael J., 47 Linwood Ave., Williamsville, 14221-6501.
Zak, Casimir A., O'Hara Residence, 69 O'Hara Rd., Tonawanda, 14150-6227.
Revs.—
Amico, Charles R., Ph.D., S.T.D. Christ the King Seminary, P.O. Box 607, East Aurora, 14052-1689.
Becker, Donald, P.O. Box 48, Java Center, 14082.
Besinger, Robert J., Sheehan Residence, 330 Linwood Ave., 14209-1689.
Bosack, Albert J., Bishop Head Residence, 10 Rosary Ave., Lackawanna, 14218.
Carlo, Joseph C., 1317 Norwood Ave., Niagara Falls, 14305.
Coppola, Paul R., Sacred Heart Home, Brothers of Mercy, 4520 Ransom Rd., Clarence, 14031-2199.
Crowley, Thomas J., Sheehan Residence, 330 Linwood Ave., 14209-1689.
Cusimano, Salvatore J., O'Hara Residence, 69 O'Hara Rd., Tonawanda, 14150-6227.
Czechowicz, Bernard J., Father Baker Manor, 6400 Powers Rd., Orchard Park, 14127.
Daley, James M., Quaker Towne Apartments, 150 Countryside Ln., #1, Orchard Park, 14127-1349.
Della Neve, Louis, 6A Lexington Ct., Lockport, 14094-5365.
Fafinski, Donald S., 137 Serval St., Dunkirk, 14048.
Faraci, Douglas F., 182 Wilmington Ave., Tonawanda, 14150.
Federico, Ralph P., 83 Wilderness Park, Clarendon, PA 16313-9747.
Ferens, Boniface D., Suwalki, Noniewicza 95 M8, 16-400, Woj Podlaskie, Poland.
Fitzgerald, Donald J., Box 3100, Bonita Springs, FL 33959.
Fox, John J., P.O. Box 882, Amherst, 14226-1297.
Friel, Mark M., 259 Fourth St., Niagara Falls, 14303-1208.
Gagliardo, Anthony F., 1301 Wynkoop Dr., Colorado Springs, CO 80909-3243.
Grimmer, James A., Bishop Head Residence, 10 Rosary Ave., Lackawanna, 14218.
Haran, James E., 81 South St., Cattaraugus, 14719-1216.
Hogan, Francis T., 2792 N. Breeze Rd., Melbourne, FL 32935-2010.
Jann, Francis J., P.O. Box 37, Rushford, 14777-0037.
Kasprzyk, James H., St. Barnabas Rectory, 2049 George Urban Blvd., Depew, 14043-1823.
Kaukus, Edwin J., 245 Richmond Ave., 14222.
Keppeler, Ricfhard J., 1358 McKinley Pkwy., Lackawanna, 14218.
Kibuka, Matthias W., P.O. Box 218, Niagara Falls, 14304.
Klos, Walter, Albertine Home, 1501 Hoffman St., Hammond, IN 46327-1764.
Kowalewski, Francis P., Our Lady of Good Counsel, 10675 Allegany Rd., Darien Center, 14040-9701.
Kwiatkowski, Constantine, 26 Sanford Dr., Jamestown, 14701-7410.
Kwolek, Joseph, Sheehan Residence, 330 Linwood Ave., 14209-1689.
Lex, Henry V., Sheehan Residence, 330 Linwood Ave., 14209-1689.
Lowry, Joseph E., 124 Division St., Salamanca, 14779-1759.
Mahar, Raymond J., Sheehan Residence, 330 Linwood Ave., 14209-1689.
Martlock, Loville N., P.O. Box 10, Jemez Springs, NM 87025.
Massar, Richard A., Bishop Head Residence, 10 Rosary Ave., Lackawanna, 14218.
McCarthy, Thomas J., P.O. Box 2082, Blasdell, 14219.
McGarry, William C., 2486 Grand Ave., Niagara Falls, 14301-2426.
McGrath, James R., 536 St. Lawrence Ave., 14216-1529.
Measer, Donald L., St. Amelia, 210 St. Amelia Dr., Tonawanda, 14150-7126.
Mergenhagen, John J., P.O. Box 36, South Wales, 14139-0036.
Naber, John T., P.O. Box 868, 14205-0868.
Nowak, Francis T., 25 Euclid Ave., 14211.
O'Shea, John T., 3178 Merchant Rd., Warsaw, 14569-9320.
Orsolits, Norbert F., P.O. Box 91, Springville, 14141.
Paa, Joseph F., 21 Foxwood Row, Depew, 14043-5019.
Pavlock, Martin L., 407 Herr Rd., P.O. Box 63, Angola, 14006.
Peter, David J., 339 22nd St., Niagara Falls, 14303-1745.
Piazza, Salvatore J., 501 Greensward Ln., Apt. C # 202, Delray Beach, FL 33445.
Pulikoottil, Berard, 297 Collins Ave., 14224-1109.
Roche, David V., Sheehan Residence, 330 Linwood Ave., 14209-1689.
Rodriguez, Antonio L., Bishop Head Residence, 10 Rosary Ave., Lackawanna, 14218.
Rossello, Nicholas A., 118 Old Niagara Rd., Apt. 3, Lockport, 14094-1520.
Russell, Raymond R., Sheehan Residence, 330 Linwood Ave., 14209-1689.
Schreck, Paul C., Sheehan Residence, 330 Linwood Ave., 14209.
Selzler, Norbert E., 5020 Carpenter Rd., Hamburg, 14075-6618.
Siracuse, Guy F., Brothers of Mercy, 10570 Bergtold Rd., Clarence, 14031.
Sokolowski, Bernard T., Bishop Head Residence, 10 Rosary Ave., Lackawanna, 14218.
Staebell, James A., 12428 Barone Dr., Silver Creek, 14136-1204.
Vallone, Louis A., 17140 S.E. 115 Terrace Rd., Summerfield, FL 34491-7823.
Vogt, Robert W., 128 Kinsey Ave., Kenmore, 14217.
Wagner, Eugene L., St. Charles Borromeo, 5969 Washington St., Olcott, 14126-9998.
Ward, William G., Sheehan Residence, 330 Linwood Ave., 14209-1689.
Weber, Donald C., Bishop Head Residence, 10 Rosary Ave., Lackawanna, 14218.
Werth, Charles M., 108 Wellington Ct., 14221-6750.
Wood, Robert W., c/o 795 Main St., 14203.
Wright, Vincent L., Bishop Head Residence, 10 Rosary Ave., Lackawanna, 14218.
Zancan, Robert D., P.O. Box 261065, Lakewood, CO 80226.

Permanent Deacons:
Amantia, Philop J., Sr.
Anderson, Michael L.
Badaszewski, Robert W.
Barr, Joseph M.
Bauer, Robert A.
Bedard, Peter J.
Boyd, Jimmie L., Sr.
Bray, Michael R.
Brick, Daniel E., Esq.
Bringenberg, Thomas B.
Burke, John H.
Burns, Robert E.
Carmody, Paul F.
Casey, Christopher T.
Ciezki, Robert T.
Collichio, James L.
Crimi, Victor
Dains, Ronald
Darroch, Nelson
Dibb, Roy P.
Edbauer, Howard J., Jr.
Emerson, Paul C.
Eschbach, Lawrence D.
Eschrich, Paul C.
Feary, Gregory L., Jr.
Forcucci, Thomas M.
Foster, Norman E.
Fox, Albert F.
Friedman, Heinz H.
Fudala, Walter N.
Gill, Joseph J.
Gomola, Michael A.
Griesbaum, Charles J., Jr.
Hart, Thomas J.
Harter, Terrance P.
Hooper, Mark J.
Houck, William
Howard, Edward R.
Hynes, William
Jerome, David R.
Kapsiak, Dennis W.
Kelly, John J.

Kelsey, Richard H.
Klein, George L.
Kopczynski, Michael R.
Krahling, Francis R.
Lankes, George A.
Lemieux, Michael C.
Licata, Thomas G.
Mackiewicz, Richard
Mackowiak, Daniel H.
Mahaney, Richard J.
Maloney, Timothy
Marino, Benjamin
Markowski, Lawrence
Matthews, Richard F.
May, Thaddeus P.
McDermott, David P.
McDonnell, Thomas A.
McGuire, Daniel G.
McKeating, Michael P.
Meister, Alan A.
Mercurio, Joseph P.
Miranda, Roberto G.
Molik, Daniel J.
Molnar, Alexander S.
Moses, Robert J.
Nowak, Mark
O'Connell, Edward G.
Parker, Richard W.
Pasquale, Francis W., Jr.
Penksa, Daniel M.
Pijacki, Thaddeus V.
Polizzi, Frank
Quinn, Michael D.
Radlinski, Donald
Ramos, Carlos W.
Ruh, John M.
Ruiz, Jose J.
Santana, Reinaldo
Scherr, Thomas E.
Schnettler, Paul J.
Schultz, Thomas E.
Setera, John T.
Seyfried, Donald E.
Shaughnessey, Frank J.
Slish, David P.
Snyder, Paul L., III
Stahl, Raymond H.
Steffen, Franklyn C.
Steinagle, Gordon J.
Stone, John G.
Swinarski, Stephen J.
Terrana, Gary C.
Thomann, Bernard M.
Velasquez, David R.
Walders, Peter J.
Walek, Edward S.
Walker, Ronald
Walkowiak, Brian C.
Walkowiak, William J.
Weisenburger, Paul F.
Wetter, Donald A.
Wick, John G.
Willis, William W.
Zwack, Francis A.

INSTITUTIONS LOCATED IN THE DIOCESE

[A] SEMINARIES

BUFFALO. *Pope John Paul II Residence*, 217 Winston Rd., 14216. Tel: 716-836-5526; Fax: 716-836-3303. Email: ejsheedy72@aol.com. Rev. Edward J. Sheedy, Dir. Students 4; Priests 1; Total Staff 1.

EAST AURORA. *Christ the King Seminary*, Graduate School of Theology, 711 Knox Rd., P.O. Box 607, 14052. Tel: 716-652-8900; Fax: 716-652-8903. Email: cksacad@cks.edu. Web: www.cks.edu. Interdiocesan Theologate. Owned and operated by the Diocese of Buffalo. Seminarians are assigned by the Bishop of any diocese for preparation for ordination to Priesthood.
Administration and Faculty: Revs. Richard W. Siepka, M.A., S.T.L., Pres. Rector; Gregory M. Faulhaber, S.T.D., Vice Rector & Dir. of Formation; Edward J. Sheedy, Academic Dean; Rev. Lynn R. Morgan, M.Div., Academic Svcs. Coord.; Mr. Douglas George, M.A.P.M., Dir. of Lay Formation; Mrs. Nancy Ehlers, Treas.; Mr. Thomas V. Kane, Dir. of Institutional Advancement; Mr. William DeWitt, Dir. of Facilities; Mrs. Teresa Lubienecki, B.A., M.L.S., Dir. Library.
Faculty: Revs. Charles R. Amico, Ph.D., S.T.D. (Retired); Richard Cassidy, Ph.D.; Scott Detisch, Ph.D.; Gabriel Scarfia, O.F.M., S.T.D.; Joseph F. Burke, S.J., Ph.D.; Walter J. Szczesny; Paul L. Varuvel, S.T.D.; Alan D. Lukas, Dir. of Music; Rev. Thomas Sheehan, O.F.M., M.Div., Dir. of Alumni; Sr. M. Tiburtia Gorecki, F.S.S.J., M.L.S., Librarian; Rev. Peter J. Drilling, Th.D.; Dennis Castillo, Ph.D.; Kathy Castillo, M.A.
Adjunct Faculty: Rev. Joseph C. Gatto, S.T.D.; Rev. Msgr. David M. Lee; Revs. Gwarek Leslaw, S.A.C.; Alfons M. Osiander; Paul A. Litwin; Edward J. Sheedy; E. Christine Moll, Ph.D.; Sr. M. Charlene Nowak, C.S.S.F.; Mark Hammer, M.A.

[B] SEMINARIES, RELIGIOUS

YOUNGSTOWN. *St. Anthony M. Zaccaria Seminary*, The Barbabite Fathers, Inc. 981 Swann Rd., P.O. Box 167, 14174-0167. Tel: 716-754-7489; Fax: 716-754-9130. Email: office@fatimashrine.com. Web: www.fatimashrine.com. Revs. Peter M. Calabrese, C.R.S.P.; Paul M. Keeling, C.R.S.P.; Very Rev. Julio M. Ciavaglia, C.R.S.P., Shrine Dir. & Comm. Supr.; Revs. Ubaldo M. Fior, C.R.S.P.; Joseph M. Gariolo, C.R.S.P.; Luciano M. Visconti, C.R.S.P. Priests 6; Total Staff 8.

The National Shrine Basilica of Our Lady of Fatima, 1023 Swann Rd., P.O. Box 167, 14174-0167. Tel: 716-754-7489; Fax: 716-754-9130. Email: office@fatimashrine.com. Web: www.fatimashrine.com. Very Rev. Julio M. Ciavaglia, C.R.S.P., Rector; Revs. Paul M. Keeling, C.R.S.P., Assoc. Dir.; Peter M. Calabrese, C.R.S.P., Assoc. Dir. Priests 3; Total Staff 18.

[C] COLLEGES AND UNIVERSITIES

BUFFALO. *Canisius College*, 2001 Main St., 14208-1098. Tel: 716-883-7000; Fax: 716-888-2525. Email: cookev@canisius.edu. Web: www.canisius.edu. Revs. Vincent M. Cooke, S.J., Pres.; John P. Bucki, S.J., Dir. Campus Min.; Dr. Ellen O. Conley, Vice Pres. for Student Affairs; Mr. John J. Hurley, Vice Pres. for College Relations and Sec. Bd. Trustees; Dr. Laurence W. Franz, Vice Pres., Business & Finance & Treas.; Dr. Herbert J. Nelson, Vice Pres. for Academic Affairs; Dr. Paula M. McNutt, Dean College of Arts & Sciences; Dr. Antone F. Alber, Dean Wehle School of Business; Dr. Margaret C. McCarthy, Dean School of Education & Human Svcs.; Dr. Joel A. Cohen, Dir., Assoc. Vice Pres. for Library & Information Svcs. Priests 10; Lay Teachers 202; Total Enrollment 5,051.

**D'Youville College*, 320 Porter Ave., 14201. Tel: 716-881-3200; Fax: 716-881-7780. Email: Brayjd@dyc.edu. Web: www.dyc.edu. Sr. Denise A. Roche, G.N.S.H., Ph.D., Pres.; Rev. Jan Mahle, Chap. (Dir. Campus Ministry). Grey Nuns of the Sacred Heart. Sisters 6; Lay Teachers 158; Total Staff 350; Students 2,471.

Trocaire College, 360 Choate Ave., 14220. Tel: 716-827-2423; Fax: 716-828-6109. Email: hurleyp@trocaire.edu. Web: www.trocaire.edu. Paul B. Hurley Jr., Ph.D., Pres. Sisters 7; Lay Teachers 120; Students 1,003; Total Staff 41.

Villa Maria College of Buffalo, 240 Pine Ridge Rd., 14225-3999. Tel: 716-896-0700; Fax: 716-896-0705. Email: info@villa.edu. Web: www.villa.edu. Sr. Marcella Marie Garus, Pres.; Natalie J. Moudgil, Ph.D., Vice Pres. Academic Affairs; Sisters Mary De Angelis Nowak, Vice Pres. Business Affairs; Mary Marcine Borowiak, Vice Pres. Devel.; Mary Louis Rustowicz, Vice Pres. Student Affairs. Sisters 2; Lay Teachers 63; Students 459; Total Staff 128.

HAMBURG. *Hilbert College*, 5200 S. Park Ave., 14075. Tel: 716-649-7900; Fax: 716-558-6380. Email: edmunette@hilbert.edu. Web: www.hilbert.edu/. Sr. Edmunette Paczesny, F.S.S.J., Pres.; Rev. Bernard Olszewski, O.F.M.Conv., Chap.; Sr. Jacqueline Benbenek, C.S.S.F., Campus Min. Franciscan Sisters of Saint Joseph Priests 2; Sisters 3; Lay Teachers 92; Students 1,055; Total Staff 137.

NIAGARA UNIVERSITY. *Niagara University*, Lewiston Rd., 14109-2015. Tel: 716-285-1212; Fax: 716-286-8355. Email: jbm@niagara.edu. Web: www.niagara.edu. Revs. Joseph L. Levesque, C.M., Pres.; Dennis H. Holtschneider, C.M., Exec. Vice Pres. & COO; Bonnie Rose, Ph.D., Vice Pres. for Academic Affairs; Michael S. Jaszka, Vice Pres. for Admin.; Rev. Francis X. Prior, C.M., Vice President Emeritus; Sheila L. Hausrath, M.S.Ed., Vice Pres. for Student Life; Patrick A. Hanley, Vice Pres. for Univ. Advancement; Judith S. Willard, Ph.D., Asst. Pres. for Planning; Dolores A. Bower, R.N., Ph.D., Dean Emerita, College of Nursing; Nancy E. McGlen, Ph.D., Dean College of Arts & Sciences; John A. Helmuth, Ph.D., Dean College of Business Admin.; Debra A. Colley, Ph.D., Dean College of Education; George C. Pachter Jr., M.S.Ed., Dean of Enrollment Mgmt.; Gary Praetzel, Ph.D., Dean College of Hospitality & Tourism Mgmt.; Jay Stockslader, Dir. Center for Continuing & Community Education; Patricia G. Kinner, M.A., Dir. Academic Support; David M. Schoen, M.L.S., Dir. Library; Laurene Buckley, Ph.D., Dir. Castellani Art Museum; Maureen Salfi, M.S.Ed., Dir. Financial Aid; John B. Stranges, Ph.D., Univ. Prof.; Mati Ortiz, Dir., Campus Activities; Sr. Nora Gatto, D.C., Dir. Campus Min.; Joseph H. Cuda, M.A., Dean Student Affairs; Ilona Yungblut, Dir. Health Svcs.; David Blackburn, Dir. Multicultural Student Affairs; Rev. Thomas J. McDermott (DUB), Dir. Counseling Svcs.; Martha E. Troia, M.S., Dir. Career Devel.; Kimberly J. Zukowski, M.S.Ed., Dir. University Housing; Scott Stuart, B.S., Dir. Alumni Relations; Linus L. Ormsby, M.S.Ed., Dir. Public Rels.; Jeannine Brown Miller, M.A., Dir. Human Resources; Revs. Joseph G. Hubbert, C.M., Assoc. Prof. Rel. Studies; Thomas Casella, C.M., Supr. of Vincentian Community; Gregory L. Klein, O.Carm., Assoc. Prof. of Rel. Studies; William M. Allegretto, C.M., Univ. Chap.; Stephen J. Denig, C.M., Supvr. of Clinical Practice in Admin.; Michael T. Mazurchuk, C.M., Campus Ministry; Daniel F. O'Leary, O.M.I., Assoc. Vice Pres. for Academic Affairs; Thomas P. McGourty, C.M., Assoc. Prof. of Rel. Studies; Louis P. Trotta, C.M., Asst. Pres. Alumni Relations; Bros. Stephen J. Kennedy, C.M., Dir. St. Vincent de Paul; Martin J. Schneider, C.M., Coord. Conv. & Admin. Asst. of Theatre & Fine Arts; Augustine D. Towey, C.M., Prof. Theatre & Fine Arts.
Meade Hall: In Res. Rev. Michael J. Tumulty, C.M.

ST. BONAVENTURE. *St. Bonaventure University* 14778. Tel: 716-375-2000; Fax: 716-375-2055. Email: fstorms@sbu.edu. Web: www.sbu.edu. Franciscan Friars, Province of the Holy Name, Order of Friars Minor., School of Arts and Sciences, School of Education, School of Business, School of Journalism/Mass Communication; School of Franciscan Studies and the Franciscan Institute; Graduate Studies.
Administration: Rev. Dominic V. Monti, O.F.M., Ph.D., Interim Pres.; Sr. Margaret Carney, O.S.F., S.T.D., Senior Vice Pres.; Frank E. Saal, Ph.D., Vice Pres. Academic Affairs; Brenda McGee Snow, B.S., Vice Pres. Business & Finance; George F. Solan, M.S., Vice Pres. Student Life; David P. Ferguson, M.S., Vice Pres. Mktg. & Public Rels. and Acting V.P. for Advancement; Rev. Francis Storms, O.F.M., M.A., Asst. to Pres.; Michael J. Fischer, Ph.D., Dean Graduate Studies; Stephen D. Stahl, Ph.D., Dean School of Arts & Sciences; Sr. Margaret Carney, O.S.F., S.T.D., Dir. Franciscan Institute; Rev. Michael F. Cusato, O.F.M., Ph.D., Dean School of Franciscan Studies; Michael J. Fischer, Ph.D., Dean School of Business; Peggy Y. Burke, Ed.D., Dean School of Education; Lee Coppola, J.D., Dean Russel J. Jandoli School of Journalism & Mass Communication; Michael V. Chiariello, Ph.D., Dean Clare College; James M. Dirisio, B.A., Dir. Admissions; Mary K. Piccioli, M.B.A., Dir. Financial Aid; Heather L. Jackson, M.A., Registrar; Stephen Plesac, M.S., Dir. Student Activities; Nichole J. Gonzalez, B.A., Dir. Residence Life; Joseph V. Flanagan, M.S., Dir. Alumni Svcs.; June T. Solan, M.S., Dir. Human Resources; Margaret T. Bryner, M.S., Dir. Higher Education Opportunities Prog. (HEOP); Jean T. Ehman, M.A., Dir. The Teaching & Learning Center; John G. Watson, Ph.D., Dir. Leadership Prog.; Alice F. Sayegh, M.S., Advisor, International Student Advisement; John A. Lympany, M.Ed., Dir. Technology Svcs.; Paul J. Spaeth, M.L.S., M.A., Dir. Library; Constance F. Whitcomb, M.S.Ed., Dir. Career Devel.; Robert M. Donius, M.A., Vice Pres. University Ministries; Rev. Thomas D. Blow, O.F.M., M.A., M.Div., Guardian of the Friary.

Friar Community, 14778. Tel: 716-375-2416; Fax: 716-375-2424. Bros. Scott F. Brookbank, O.F.M.; David Haack, O.F.M.; Gregory P. Jakubowicz, O.F.M.; Anthony J. LoGalbo, O.F.M., Vicar; Adrian A. Riester, O.F.M.; Julian Riester, O.F.M.; Basil J. Valente, O.F.M.; Revs. David D. Blake, O.F.M.; Michael Blastic, O.F.M.Conv.; Thomas D. Blow, O.F.M., M.A., M.Div., Guardian; J. Gregory Brennan, O.F.M.; Michael D. Calabria, O.F.M.; Michael F. Cusato, O.F.M., Ph.D.; Regis A. Duffy, O.F.M.; David Flood, O.F.M.; Robert Karris, O.F.M.; Dominick V. Monti, O.F.M.; Peter Schneible, O.F.M.; Francis Storms, O.F.M., M.A.; Alphonsus A. Trabold, O.F.M.; Patrick E. Tuttle, O.F.M.; James Vacco, O.F.M.; Allen Weber, O.F.M.; William J. Weiksnar, O.F.M.

Holy Peace Friary, Mt. Irenaeus, West Clarksville, 14786-0100. Tel: 716-973-2470; Fax: 716-973-2400. Bro. Joseph A. Kotula, O.F.M.; Revs. Daniel A. Hurley, O.F.M.; Louis M. McCormick, O.F.M.; Daniel P. Riley, O.F.M., Guardian, Dir.

[D] HIGH SCHOOLS, PRIVATE

BUFFALO. *Bishop Timon-St. Jude High School*, 601 McKinley Pkwy., 14220. Tel: 716-826-3610; Fax: 716-824-5833. Web: www.bishoptimon.com. Rev.

Joel A. Campbell, O.F.M.; Mr. James Rzad, Acting Pres.; Mr. Thomas J. Sullivan, Prin. Owned and operated by Bishop Timon Board of Trustees. Franciscans 2; Lay Teachers 30; Students 350; Total Staff 40.

Canisius High School, 1180 Delaware Ave., 14209. Tel: 716-882-0466; Fax: 716-883-1870. Email: higgins@canisiushigh.org. Web: www.canisiushigh.org. Mr. Frank Tudini, Prin. Society of Jesus Priests 10; Lay Teachers 53; Students 839; Total Staff 80.

Holy Angels Academy, 24 Shoshone Dr., 14214-1097. Tel: 716-834-7120; Fax: 716-834-7121. Email: jagrippi@holyangelsacademy.org. Web: www.holyangelsacademy.org. Jo Anne Grippi, Prin. Priests 1; Grey Nuns of the Sacred Heart 5; Lay Teachers 35; Religious 1; Students 326; Total Staff 48.

St. Joseph's Collegiate Institute, 845 Kenmore Ave., 14223-3195. Tel: 716-874-4024; Fax: 716-871-0956. Email: wbatt@sjci.com. Web: www.sjci.com. Robert Scott, A.F.S.C., Prin.; Rev. James C. Croglio, Chap. of School and Brothers' Community; Bros. William Batt, F.S.C., Pres.; Peter Henderson, F.S.C., Community Dir.; Edward Martin, F.S.C.; Luke Wittmann, F.S.C.; John Griffin, F.S.C.; Daniel Goeddeke, F.S.C.; Peter Killeen, F.S.C.; Deacons Thaddeus V. Pijacki; Gregory Feary; William Hynes. Brothers of the Christian Schools. (De La Salle Christian Brothers) Priests 1; Deacons 3; Brothers 7; Lay Teachers 60; Students 851; Total Staff 68.

Mt. Mercy Academy, 88 Red Jacket Pkwy., 14220. Tel: 716-825-8796; Fax: 716-825-0976; 716-825-0129 (Devel. Fax). Email: pgaske@mtmercy.org. Web: www.mtmercy.org. Mrs. Paulette Gaske, Prin. Sisters of Mercy Students 451; Total Staff 62.

Nardin Academy High School, 135 Cleveland Ave., 14222. Tel: 716-881-6262; Fax: 716-881-0086. Email: highschool@nardin.org. Web: www.nardin.org. Sr. Barbara Rapier, D.H.M., Pres.; Rebecca R. Reeder, Prin. Lay Teachers 53; Girls 476.

Villa Maria Academy, 600 Doat St., 14211. Tel: 716-894-0398; Fax: 716-894-0468. Email: adm@villamariaacademy.org. Web: www.vmabuffalo.org. Sr. Paul Marie Baczkowski, C.S.S.F., Prin. Felician Sisters Sisters 11; Lay Teachers 25; Students 181; Total Staff 36.

ATHOL SPRINGS. *St. Francis High School*, 4129 Lake Shore Road, 14010-0185. Tel: 716-627-1200; Fax: 716-627-4610. Email: principal@stfrancishigh.org. Web: stfrancishigh.org. Revs. Joseph Benicewicz, O.F.M.Conv., Pres.; Charles Jagodzinski, O.F.M.Conv.; Stephen King, O.F.M.Conv.; Michael Lasky, O.F.M.Conv.; Michael Sajda, O.F.M.Conv., Prin.; Mark David Skura, O.F.M.Conv.; Bros. Joseph Colarossi, O.F.M.Conv.; Lawrence LaFlame, O.F.M.Conv. St. Anthony Province of the Order of Friars Minor Conventual Priests 6; Brothers 2; Sisters 1; Lay Teachers 42; Total Staff 65; Students 582.

BATAVIA. *Notre Dame High School of Batavia*, 73 Union St., 14020. Tel: 585-343-2783; Fax: 585-343-7323. Email: ndhs@ndhsbatavia.com. Web: www.ndhsbatavia.com. Mr. John Jakubowski, Prin.; Mr. Mike Rapone, Dean Students; Rev. Robert A. Martin. Owned and operated by Notre Dame Board of Trustees. Priests 1; Lay Teachers 21; Students 210; Total Staff 35.

EGGERTSVILLE. *Buffalo Academy of the Sacred Heart*, 3860 Main St., 14226. Tel: 716-834-2101; Fax: 716-834-2944. Email: Info@sacredheartacademy.org. Web: www.sacredheartacademy.org. Barbara E Ochterski, Ph.D., Prin. Sisters of St. Francis of Penance and Christian Charity. Sisters 8; Lay Teachers 38; Students 380; Total Staff 67.

HAMBURG. *Immaculata Academy*, 5138 S. Park Ave., 14075. Tel: 716-649-6161; Fax: 716-646-1782. Email: dchristian@immaculataacademy.com. Sr. Lynne Anne Schimminger, F.S.S.J., Pres.; David T. Christian, Prin. Franciscan Sisters of St. Joseph Sisters 4; Lay Teachers 18; Students 167; Total Staff 36.

KENMORE. *Mt. St. Mary Academy*, 3756 Delaware Ave., 14217. Tel: 716-877-1358; Fax: 716-877-0548. Email: driggie@mt-st-marys.org. Web: mt-st-marys.org. Mrs. Dawn Riggie, Prin. Owned and operated by the Mt. St. Mary Academy Board of Trustees. Lay Teachers 38; Girls 350; Day Care Center 100.

LANCASTER. *St. Mary's High School*, 142 Laverack Ave., 14086. Tel: 716-683-4824; Fax: 716-683-4996. Email: lancer@smhlancers.org. Web: www.smhlancers.org. Joseph A. Casimino, Ed.D., Prin. Owned and operated by St. Mary's Board of Trustees. Sisters 1; Lay Teachers 33; Students 361; Total Staff 53.

NIAGARA FALLS. *Niagara Catholic High School*, 520-66th St., 14304. Tel: 716-283-8771; Fax: 716-283-8774. Email: rdifrancesco@niagaracatholic.org. Web: www.niagaracatholic.org. Robert M. DiFrancesco, Prin.; Rev. Gerald L. Bartko, O.S.F.S. Owned and operated by Niagara Catholic Board of Trustees. Priests 1; Lay Teachers 18; Students 226.

OLEAN. *Archbishop Walsh High School*, 208 N. 24th St., 14760-1985. Tel: 716-372-8122; Fax: 716-372-6707. Email: sbrady@archbishopwalsh.org. Web: www.archbishopwalsh.org. Kathy Baker, Prin.; Rev. Barry J. Allaire. Owned and operated by Archbishop Walsh Board of Trustees Priests 1; Lay Teachers 10; Students 91; Total Staff 26.

TONAWANDA. *Cardinal O'Hara High School*, 39 O'Hara Rd., 14150. Tel: 716-695-2600; Fax: 716-692-8697. Email: mpowers@cardinalohara.com. Web: www.cardinalohara.com. Michael P. Powers, Prin. Owned and operated by Cardinal O'Hara Board of Trustees. Lay Teachers 27; Students 240.

[E] ELEMENTARY SCHOOLS, PRIVATE

BUFFALO. *Ss. Columba-Brigid Montessori School*, 75 Hickory St., 14204-1920. Tel: 716-842-6213; Fax: 716-842-1454. Email: dbernbeck@catholic.org. Sr. Diane Bernbeck, O.S.F., Prin. Students 62.

Mount St. Joseph Academy Web: www.msja.org.

Elementary Division, 2064 Main St., 14208. Tel: 716-883-1515; Fax: 716-882-9053. Email: msjaprinc@adelphia.net. Mr. John E. Kingston, Prin. Sisters 1; Lay Teachers 21; Students 185.

Nardin Academy, 135 Cleveland Ave., 14222. Tel: 716-881-6262; Fax: 716-881-4130. Email: br@nardin.org. Web: www.nardin.org. (Montessori-Grade 12) Priests 1; Sisters 1; Lay Teachers 107; Students 960.

LEWISTON. *Sacred Heart Villa School*, (Grades PreK-5), 5269 Lewiston Rd., 14092. Tel: 716-284-8273; 716-285-9257 (school); Fax: 716-284-8273. Email: shvschool@adelphia.net. Sr. Elizabeth Domin, S.S.H.J., Prin. Sisters 8; Lay Teachers 5; Students 90; Total Staff 13.

STELLA NIAGARA. *Stella Niagara Education Park*, 4421 Lower River Rd., 14144. Tel: 716-754-4314; Fax: 716-754-2964. Sr. Margaret Sullivan, O.S.F., Prin. Sisters of St. Francis of Penance and Christian Charity Sisters 3; Lay Teachers 23; Students 200.

[F] ELEMENTARY SCHOOLS, SPECIAL

BUFFALO. *Cantalician Center for Learning, Inc.*, 3233 Main St., 14214. Tel: 716-833-5353; Fax: 716-833-0108. Email: cc3@cantalician.com. Web: www.cantalician.org. Sr. Patricia Tomasik, C.S.S.F., Exec. Dir.; Rev. Msgr. Harold Wagner, Chap. Program for the disabled: Infant, Toddler and Preschool; Elementary and Secondary. Workshop for adult individuals with disabilities, day treatment-lite program, & day habilitation for retired, disabled adults. Group homes/I.R.A. for adult individuals with disabilities; Daycare. Priests 1; Sisters 5; Laystaff 277; Students 489; Total Staff 283.

[G] REGIONAL AND CONSOLIDATED ELEMENTARY SCHOOLS

BUFFALO. *Catholic Academy of West Buffalo* Email: gglen@cawb.org. Sponsoring parishes: Annunciation, St. Anthony, Blessed Sacrament, Holy Angels, Holy Cross, Immaculate Conception, St. Joseph's Cathedral, St. Louis, St. Michael, Nativity, Our Lady of Loretto.

Delaware Campus (Grades 3-8), 1069 Delaware Ave., 14209. Tel: 716-885-6111; Fax: 716-885-6452. Email: gglen@cawb.org.

Lafayette Campus (Grades PreK-2), 279 Lafayette Ave., 14213. Tel: 716-886-5384; Fax: 716-886-5393. Sr. Gail Glenn, S.S.J., Prin.; Mrs. Geraldine Kizielewicz, Bldg. Prin., (Lafayette Campus). Sisters 2; Lay Teachers 25; Students 306; Total Staff 28.

Catholic Central School, (Grades PreK-8), 476 Emslie St., 14212. Tel: 716-852-6854; Fax: 716-852-8410. Email: catholicentre@catholic.org. Patricia G. Duffy, Prin. Sponsoring parishes: St. Ann, Blessed Trinity, SS. Columba & Brigid, St. Mary of Sorrows, & St. Martin de Porres. Sisters 5; Lay Teachers 19 Students 155; Total Staff 33.

Our Lady of Black Rock, 16 Germain St., 14207. Tel: 716-873-7497; Fax: 716-447-9926. Email: es15@buffalodiocese.org. Sr. Mary Francianne Zielezinski, C.S.S.F., Prin. Sponsoring parishes: Assumption, St. Florian, St. Francis Xavier, Coronation, St. Elizabeth, St. John the Baptist, All Saints. Sisters 1; Lay Teachers 12; Students 145; Total Staff 13.

ATTICA. *Genesee-Wyoming Catholic Central Consolidated School*, 72 East Ave., 14011. Tel: 585-591-2515; Fax: 585-591-2516. William F. Schofield, Prin. Sponsoring parishes: Attica, St. Vincent; Bennington Center, Sacred Heart; Darien Center, Our Lady of Good Counsel; Java Center, St. Patrick; North Java, St. Nicholas; Sheldon, St. Cecelia; Varysburg, St. Joseph; Warsaw, St. Michael. Lay Teachers 11; Students 62.

CHEEKTOWAGA. *Kolbe Catholic Regional School*, 120 Alexander Ave., 14211. Tel: 716-895-3127; Fax: 716-895-7347. Email: rbuscaglia@juno.com. Rose Mary Buscaglia, Prin. Sponsoring Parishes: St. Lawrence, Holy Name, St. Gerard, St. John Kanty, St. John Gualbert, Most Holy Redeemer. Lay Teachers 16; Students 193; Total Staff 30.

Mary Queen of Angels School, (Grades K-8), 170 Rosewood Terr., 14225. Tel: 716-895-6280; Fax: 716-895-6359. Sr. Diane Marie Szylkowski, C.S.S.F., Prin.; Rev. Daniel A. Lapinski, Canonical Admin. Sponsoring Parishes: Queen of Martyrs, Our Lady Help of Christians.

Preschool Center (3-4 yr. olds), 4115 Union Rd., 14225. Tel: 716-632-4199; Fax: 716-632-4298. Linda Gladwell, Dir. Sisters 2; Lay Teachers 13; Students 209.

DUNKIRK. *Northern Chautauqua Catholic*, 336 Washington Ave., 14048. Tel: 716-366-0630; Fax: 716-366-5101. Email: nccs@netsync.net. Kathy Y. Moser, Prin. Sponsoring parishes: Brocton: St. Patrick; Dunkirk: St. Elizabeth Ann Seton, St. Hedwig, Holy Trinity; Fredonia: St. Anthony, St. Joseph; Silver Creek: Our Lady of Mt. Carmel; Cassadaga: Immaculate Conception; Sinclairville: St. John the Evangelist; Westfield: St. James Major; Ripley: St. Thomas More; Sheridan: St. John Bosco; Forestville: St. Rose of Lima. Lay Teachers 17; Students 178; Total Staff 26.

JAMESTOWN. *Holy Family Catholic School*, 1135 N. Main St., 14701-3199. Tel: 716-483-3245; Fax: 716-483-3245. Email: holyfamilyjt@catholic.org. Tina Rosage, Prin. Sponsoring parishes: Jamestown, St. James, St. John, SS. Peter & Paul; Bemus Point, Our Lady of Lourdes; Falconer, Our Lady of Loreto; Frewsburg, Our Lady of Victory; French Creek, St. Matthias; Lakewood, Sacred Heart; Mayville, St. Mary; Panama, Our Lady of the Snows; Randolph, St. Patrick; Sherman, St. Isaac Jogues; Sinclairville, St. John the Evangelist. Lay Teachers 20; Students 160; Total Staff 27.

LAKE VIEW. *Southtowns Catholic*, 2052 Lakeview Rd., Box 86, 14085. Tel: 716-627-5011; Fax: 716-627-5335. Email: catholic@buffnet.net. Web: www.southtownscatholic.org. Judith M. MacDonald, Prin. Sponsoring parishes: St. Vincent de Paul, North Evans; Our Lady of Perpetual Help, Lake View. Lay Teachers 20; Students 277; Total Staff 31.

LOCKPORT. *DeSales Catholic School*, 6914 Chestnut School, 14094. Tel: 716-433-6422; Fax: 716-434-4002. Email: desalesp@aol.com. Web: www.desalescatholicschool.org. Sr. Carol Kleindinst, S.S.M.N. Sponsoring parishes: Lockport, St. Anthony, St. John the Baptist, St. Joseph, St. Mary, St. Patrick; Gasport, St. Mary; Middleport, St. Stephen; Newfane, St. Bridget, Wilson, Our Lady of the Rosary; Barker, St. Patrick; Olcott, St. Charles Borromeo; Ransomville, Immaculate Conception; N. Tonawanda, Good Shepherd; Clarence Center, St. Augustine. Sisters 4; Lay Teachers 36; Students 544; Total Staff 45.

NIAGARA FALLS. *St. Dominic Savio Middle School*, (Grades 6-8), 504 66th St., 14303. Tel: 716-215-1461; Fax: 716-215-1465. Email: stdominic@catholic.org. Rev. Stewart M. Lindsay, O.S.F.S., Canonical Admin.; Patricia M. Muscatello, Prin. Lay Teachers 15; Students 193.

Niagara Falls Catholic Schools Network, 1413 Pine Ave., 14301. Rev. Stewart M. Lindsay, O.S.F.S., Chm.

NORTH TONAWANDA. *North Tonawanda Catholic* Email: office@ntcatholic.org. Web: www.ntcatholic.org. Sponsoring parishes: Ascension, Our Lady of Czestochowa, St. Albert the Great and St. Joseph.

Ascension Campus (Grades 4-8), 75 Keil St., 14120. Tel: 716-693-2828; Fax: 716-693-0169. Email: RKutsko@catholic.org. Sr. Rosemarie Kutsko, C.S.S.F., Supervising Prin.

OLC Campus (Grades K-3), 57 Center Ave., 14120. Tel: 716-694-3644.

St. Joseph Campus (Grades PreSchool-PreSchool), 1469 Payne Ave., 14120. Tel: 716-693-4769. Sisters 2; Lay Teachers 21; Students 277; Total Staff 23.

OLEAN. *Southern Tier Catholic*, 205 W. Henley St., 14760. Tel: 716-372-2891; Fax: 716-373-1175. Email: SOTIERCS@adelphia.net. Luella Potter, Bldg. Prin. Sponsoring parishes: Allegany, St. Bonaventure; Cuba, Our Lady of the Angels; Hinsdale, St. Helen; Portville, Sacred Heart; Olean, St. Mary of the Angels; St. John; Transfiguration; Vandalia; St. John the Baptist. Lay Teachers 17; Students 171; Total Staff 23.

SPRINGVILLE. *St. Aloysius Regional School*, 186

Franklin St., 14141-1198. Tel: 716-592-7002; Fax: 716-592-7002. Email: es72@buffalodiocese.org. Web: www.staloysiusweb.org. Bonnie Renzi, Prin. Sisters 1; Lay Teachers 16; Students 140.

[H] CATHOLIC CHARITIES

BUFFALO. *The Catholic Charities of the Diocese of Buffalo*

Central Office, 525 Washington St., 14203. Tel: 716-856-4494; Fax: 716-856-2005. Email: revj.sicari@ccwny.org. Web: www.ccwny.org. Rev. Joseph J. Sicari, Diocesan Dir.

Finance Dept. Tel: 716-856-4494; Fax: 716-856-2005. Theodore S. Lesinski, Comptroller. Tel: 716-856-4494; Gregory Thrun, Human Resources Dir. Tel: 716-856-4494; Rose Caldwell, Dir. Communications & Public Rels.

Catholic Charities Program Services Rev. Joseph J. Sicari, Interim Diocesan Dir. Tel: 716-856-4494; Dennis C. Walczyk, CEO. Tel: 716-856-4494.

Central Intake Mrs. Kathryn Heavey, Supvr.

Kenfield Office, 188 Oakmont Ave., 14215. Tel: 716-835-6894; Fax: 716-832-8286. Jesselyn Garcia, Supvr.

Mount St. Mary's Housing Development Fund Company, Inc., 525 Washington St., 14203. Rev. Joseph J. Sicari, Diocesan Dir., Catholic Charities.

Black Rock/Riverside Office, 819 Tonawanda St., 14207. Tel: 716-877-4716; Fax: 716-447-1180. Cindy Manne, Supvr.

West Side Family Counseling Center, 412 Niagara St., 14201. Tel: 716-854-3622; Fax: 716-842-1366. Marjorie Quartley, Supvr.

Lackawanna Family Counseling Center, 33-37 Wilkesbarre Ave., Lackawanna, 14218. Tel: 716-822-6877; Fax: 716-827-1726. Judith Perry, Supvr.

Preventive Services & Batterer's Intervention Program, 1581 Bailey Ave., 14212. Tel: 716-896-6390; Fax: 716-896-4236. Greg White, Supvr.

Legal Title: *Preventive Services and Batterer's Intervention Program, and Therapeutic Supervised Visitation Program*

School Intervention Service, 3370 Delaware Ave., Kenmore, 14217. Tel: 716-877-8822; Fax: 716-874-5245. Cindy Manne, Supvr.

9 E. Union, P.O. Box 94, Hamburg, 14075. Tel: 716-648-6515; Fax: 716-648-7101.

3719 Union Rd., Ste. 214, Cheektowaga, 14225. Tel: 716-681-7394; Fax: 716-685-9087. Jerry Kelly, Supvr.

4498 Main St., Amherst, 14226. Tel: 716-839-4066; Fax: 716-839-4082.

Department of Workforce Development, 170 Kerns Ave., 14211. Tel: 716-893-3500; Fax: 716-893-0807. Michael Talluto, Dir.

Diocesan Resettlement Division, 394 Franklin St., Ste. 200, 14202. Tel: 716-842-6816; Fax: 716-842-0509. Ann Brittain, Supvr.

Youth Careers Program, 170 Kerns Ave., 14211. Tel: 716-893-3500; Fax: 716-893-0807. Michael Talluto, Dir.

Department of Parish Based Social Services Tel: 716-856-4494; Fax: 716-856-2005. Sr. Mary Anne Weldon, R.S.M., Dir.

Office of Pastoral Ministry With Handicapped Persons Tel: 716-856-4494; Fax: 716-856-2005. Rosemary Walter, Prog. Coord.

Chautauqua Elderly Project, 741 Falconer St., Jamestown, 14701. Tel: 716-665-4374; Fax: 716-488-9233. Francine Lloyd, Supvr.

Adoptions, Child Care Division and Young Parents Program Tel: 716-856-4494; Fax: 716-855-1312. Gail Sunshine-May, Supvr.

GIFTS Program, Grand Island Families, Town & Schools, 2255 Baseline Rd., Grand Island, 14072. Tel: 716-773-9690; Fax: 716-773-9653. Sue Novits, Coord.

GIFTS Advantage After School Program, Veronica E. Connors Middle School, 1100 Ransom Rd., Grand Island, 14072. Tel: 716-773-6604; Fax: 716-773-8983. Kim Auger, Supvr.

Cattaraugus & Allegany Co. Offices: Jon Anderson, County Dir.

Cattaraugus County Multi-Systematic Therapy (MST), 520 W. State St., P.O. Box 554, Olean, 14760. Tel: 716-372-0101; Fax: 716-372-3886. Margot Myers, Supvr.

Cattaraugus Intensive Case Management (ICM), 284 Broad St., Salamanca, 14779. Sara Terrano, Supvr. Salamanca Drop-In Center

Chautauqua Co. Offices: Patricia Williams, County Dir.

314 Central Ave., Ste. 207, Dunkirk, 14048. Tel: 716-366-3533; Fax: 716-363-1184.

413 N. Main St., Jamestown, 14701. Tel: 716-484-9188; Fax: 716-484-0766.

Genesee, Orleans & Wyoming Co. Offices: Margaret Meyer, County Dir.

Genesee and Orleans County Multi-Systemic Therapy (MST), 25 Liberty St., Ste.7, Batavia, 14020. Tel: 585-343-0614; Fax: 585-344-3868. Kristin Hallbauer, Supvr.

Niagara County Offices: Kathleen Hall, County Dir.

345 Third St., Ste. 515, Niagara Falls, 14303. Tel: 716-282-2351; Fax: 716-282-0146.

Niagara County Multi-Systemic Therapy (MST), 644 Park Pl., Niagara Falls, 14301. Tel: 716-282-4991; Fax: 716-804-0273. Maria Picone, Coord.; Laura Chatfield, Supvr.; Kimberly Pascucci, Supvr.

Lockport MST, 331 Bewley Bldg., Lockport, 14094. Tel: 716-478-0035. Dan Greene, Supvr.

Women, Infants & Children (W.I.C.) of Niagara County, 237 Fourth St., Niagara Falls, 14303. Tel: 716-285-0975; Fax: 716-282-7015. Rev. John J. Ward, C.S.B. (DET), Supvr.

Lockport W.I.C., Bewley Bldg. (Market at Main), Ste. 200, Lockport, 14094. Tel: 716-439-4712; Fax: 716-439-5109.

Kenmore - Tonawanda W.I.C., 3200 Elmwood Ave., Rm. 118, Kenmore, 14217. Tel: 716-874-9530; Fax: 716-874-7318.

Catholic Charities Satellite Offices:

Blackrock-Riverside, 819 Tonawanda St., 14207. Tel: 716-877-4716; Fax: 716-447-1180.

Bailey-Broadway Office, 1581 Bailey Ave., 14212. Tel: 716-896-6390; Fax: 716-896-4236.

Grider Street, 359 Grider St., 14215. Tel: 716-895-7715 (DDFSP); 716-895-7718 (GOTT); Fax: 716-895-1544 (DDFSP); 716-893-1692 (GOTT).

Oakmont Avenue, 188 Oakmont Ave., 14215. Tel: 716-835-6894; Fax: 716-832-8286.

Fulton Street, 170 Fulton St., 14204. Tel: 716-856-4456; Fax: 716-852-2343.

South Buffalo, 2315 Seneca St., 14210. Tel: 716-821-1929; Fax: 716-825-2199.

Albion, 243 S. Main St., Albion, 14411. Tel: 585-589-7477; Fax: 585-344-3868.

Amherst, 4498 Main St., Amherst, 14226. Tel: 716-839-4066; Fax: 716-839-4082.

Cheektowaga, 3719 Union Rd., Cheektowaga, 14225. Tel: 716-681-7394; Fax: 716-685-9087.

Hamburg, 9 E. Union St., 14075. Tel: 716-648-6515; Fax: 716-648-7101.

Kenmore, 3370 Delaware Ave., Kenmore, 14217. Tel: 716-877-8822; Fax: 716-874-5245.

Lockport, Bewley Bldg., Ste. 200, Lockport, 14094. Tel: 716-433-0246; Fax: 716-433-0246.

North Tonawanda, 1089 Kinkead Ave., Ste. 203, North Tonawanda, 14120. Tel: 716-692-1440.

Southtowns Office, 34 Barnstead Dr., Springville, 14141. Tel: 716-592-3420.

Warsaw, 4 W. Buffalo St., Ste. B, Warsaw, 14569. Tel: 585-786-3440; Fax: 585-344-3868.

Wellsville, 25 E. Pearl St., Box 106, Wellsville, 14895. Tel: 716-593-2015.

West Seneca, 4105 Seneca St., P.O. Box 244, West Seneca, 14224. Tel: 716-675-3785; Fax: 716-677-0289.

Catholic Charities Appeal Tel: 716-856-4494; Fax: 716-856-2005. Rev. Joseph J. Sicari, Diocesan Dir.; Judy Larsen, Appeal Supvr.

Department of Clinical Services:

Msgr. Carr Institute Tel: 716-835-9745. Brian T. O'Herron, M.Ed., M.B.A., Dept. Head.

Msgr. Carr Institute Satellite Tel: 716-895-7715. Arry Green, Coord.

Community Outreach Treatment Team Tel: 716-895-7715. Arry Green, Coord.

Chemical Dependency, Substance Abuse Prevention & Counseling Program Tel: 716-332-3910. Judith M. Vogtli, Ph.D., M.Ed., C.A.S.A.C., P.P.C., Prog. Dir.

Abstinence Until Marriage Character-Based Education Program Tel: 716-332-3910. Judith M. Vogtli, Ph.D., M.Ed., C.A.S.A.C., P.P.C., Prog. Dir.

Chemical Dependency Program Tel: 716-835-9745. Jean Brighton, C.S.W., Supvr.

Children's Enhanced Mental Health Program Tel: 716-845-9745. William Reynolds, Ph.D., Supvr.

St. Joseph's Psychosocial Club Tel: 716-896-6038. Marsha Sladeski, Supvr.

Senior Advocacy Services Tel: 716-895-7905. Marsha Sladeski, Supvr.

Senior Social Integration Program Tel: 716-891-7401. Eileen Hothow, CRC, ATR-BC, Supvr.

Creative Edge Art Studio, 2495 Main St., Tri Main Bldg., Ste. 410, 14214. Tel: 716-862-0367.

Turner-Carroll Family Support Center Tel: 716-893-3500. Lori Ricupito, Ph.D., Supvr.

Diocesan Counseling Center for Clergy and Religious Tel: 716-894-2743. Rev. James C. Croglio, Dir.

Marriage Counseling Center Tel: 716-839-4406. David Catalano, C.S.W., Supvr. (Marital, premarital, post-marital counseling)

Department of Services to the Aging Tel: 716-856-4494; Fax: 716-856-2005. Ms. Mary Jo Giambelluca, Dir.

Family Focus Program, 30 Rich St., 14211. Tel: 716-896-8262; Fax: 716-894-3088. Kathleen Pharris, Supvr.

Senior Day Center, 30 Rich St., 14211. Tel: 716-896-6388; Fax: 716-894-3088. Kathleen Pharris, Dir.

Guardian Angel Day Care, 1193 Delaware Ave., 14209. Tel: 716-882-9146; Fax: 716-881-7051. Dana M. Cassiano, Supvr.

Holy Innocents Day Care, 30 Rich St., 14211. Tel: 716-896-6386; Fax: 716-894-3088. Mrs. Deborah L. Coyne, Supvr.

Housing and Supportive Services Tel: 716-856-4494; Fax: 716-856-2005. Marie Bakowski, Supvr.

Foster Grandparents Program Tel: 716-856-4494; Fax: 716-856-2005. Dorothy Turchiarelli, Supvr.

Friendly Phones Tel: 716-856-4494; Fax: 716-856-2005. Dorothy Turchiarelli, Supvr.

Volunteer Agencies:

Catholic Guild for the Blind Tel: 716-856-4494; Fax: 716-856-2005. Sr. Michael Jordan, Prog. Dir.

Guild of St. Apollonia Tel: 716-856-4494; Fax: 716-856-2005. Rev. Richard M. Poblocki, Spiritual Dir.

Ladies of Charity, 1122 Broadway, 14212. Tel: 716-895-4001. Rev. Joseph J. Sicari; Mrs. Eileen Nowak, Prog. Dir.

Society of St. Vincent de Paul, 1298 Main St., 14209. Tel: 716-852-7415. Rev. Msgr. John J. Conniff, Spiritual Dir. (Retired); Mr. Mark S. Zirnheld, Dir.

Delta Development Low Income Housing Development & Management Tel: 716-856-4494; Fax: 716-856-2005. Total Assisted 210; Total Staff 39.

[I] ORPHANAGES AND INFANT HOMES

BUFFALO. *German Roman Catholic Orphan Home*, 795 Main St., 14203. Inactive.

[J] PROTECTIVE INSTITUTES

BUFFALO. *The Franciscan Center, Inc.*, 1910 Seneca St., 14210-1842. Tel: 716-822-8017; Fax: 716-822-8537. Rev. Joseph Bayne, O.F.M.Conv., Exec. Dir. Emergency & Transitional Shelters for Adolescent Males 16-20. Total Assisted 135; Total Staff 20.

LACKAWANNA. *Baker Victory Services* (formerly known as Baker Hall, Our Lady of Victory Infant Home, St. Joseph Orphanage and St. John's Protectory) , 780 Ridge Rd., 14218. Tel: 716-828-9500; 888-287-9986; Fax: 716-828-9526. Email: baker@buffnet.net. Web: www.bakervictoryservices.org. Rev. Msgr. Robert C. Wurtz, P.A., Pres. of the Bd.; James J. Casion, CEO; Joseph J. Cozzo, COO; Alan Nelson, Personnel Dir. Staff 800; Total Assisted 3,500.

Educational Services:

Early Intervention (ages birth to 7) Tel: 716-828-9560; Fax: 716-828-9460.

Therapeutic Preschool (ages 3-5) Tel: 716-828-9560; Fax: 716-828-9460.

Baker Hall School (ages 12-21) Tel: 716-828-9737; Fax: 716-828-9798.

Baker Academy (ages 6-18) Tel: 716-447-2500; Fax: 716-447-2502.

Residential Services:

Dorothy Miler House (mother & child group residence) Tel: 716-828-9500; Fax: 716-828-9526.

Foster Family Boarding Home Care Tel: 716-828-9500; Fax: 716-828-9526.

Residential Treatment Facilities (psychiatric adolescent and young adult residence) Tel: 716-828-9500; Fax: 716-828-9526.

Special Services Program (emotionally disturbed young adult residence) Tel: 716-828-9500; Fax: 716-828-9526.

Institutional Program Tel: 716-828-9500; Fax: 716-828-9526.

Group/Boarding Home Program Tel: 716-828-9500; Fax: 716-828-9526.

Services For The Developmentally Disabled:

Residential Services Tel: 716-828-9500; Fax: 716-828-9526.

Respite Program Tel: 716-828-9500; Fax: 716-828-9526.

Care Management Tel: 716-828-9500; Fax: 716-828-9526.

Other Services:

Family Pointe Evaluation Center Tel: 716-892-9323; Fax: 716-892-9307. Early Identification of delays in ages birth to five.

Domestic and International Adoption Services Tel: 716-828-9500; Fax: 716-828-9526.

Preventive Services Tel: 716-828-9755; Fax: 716-828-9685.

Outpatient Clinic Tel: 716-828-9700; Fax: 716-828-9745.

Day Treatment Program Tel: 716-828-9651; Fax: 716-828-9745.

Baker Victory Dental Center Tel: 716-828-9334; Fax: 716-828-9335. (Fully owned subsidiary of Baker Victory Services) Full service family dental care.

[K] GENERAL HOSPITALS

BUFFALO. *Catholic Health System, Inc.*

Marian Professional Center, 515 Abbott Rd., Ste. 508, 14220. Tel: 716-828-2750; Fax: 716-828-2703. Email: webmaster@WNYCHS.org. Web: www.chsbuffalo.org. Joseph D. McDonald, Pres. & CEO.

Bed Capacity 868; Patients Assisted Annually 1; Total Staff 7,800.

McAuley Mercy Corporation, 515 Abbott Rd., 14220. Tel: 716-828-2750. Email: Briody@CHSBuffalo.org. Sr. Sally Maloney, R.S.M., Chairperson. A holding company for Mercy Home Care of Western New York. Sponsored by the Catholic Health System, Inc.

Mercy Hospital, 565 Abbott Rd., 14220. Tel: 716-826-7000; Fax: 716-828-2700. Email: JPD@chsbuffalo.org. Mr. John P. Davanzo, Pres. & CEO; Mary Beth Farruggio, Nursing Svcs. Sponsored by the Catholic Health System, Inc. Sisters of Mercy 4; Patients Assisted Annually 263,744; Outpatients 247,374; Admissions 13,370; Bed Capacity 349; Skilled Nursing Beds 74; Bassinets 60; Total Staff 1,883.

Sisters Hospital Foundation, Inc., 2130 Main St., 14214. Tel: 716-862-1990; Fax: 716-835-8643. Email: jsnyder@chsbuffalo.org. Web: www.sistershospitalfoundation.org.

Sisters of Charity Hospital of Buffalo, NY, 2157 Main St., 14214. Tel: 716-862-1000; Fax: 716-862-1899. Email: mdougherty@wnychs.org. Web: www.sisters-buffalo.org. Revs. Louis S. Klein, Chap.; Richard E. Zajac, Chap.; Sisters Margaret Dougherty, D.C., Dir., Clinical Pastoral Education & CPE Supvr.; Janet Bielmann, R.S.M., CPE Supvr.; Mr. Tyler Dudley, D.Min., CPE Supvr.; Sisters Ann Paul Chenard, D.C., Chap.; Kathleen Simpson, D.C., Chap.; Rev. Ernest Williams, Chap.; Ms. Judith Miller, M.A., Chap.; Ms. Teresa Maikisch, Chap.; Ms. Pearl Cutlaw, Chap.; Thunder Silk, Chap. Sponsored by the Catholic Health System, Inc. Daughters of Charity of St. Vincent de Paul 10; Bed Capacity 398; Bassinets 60; Patients Assisted Annually 647,062; Total Staff 1,381.

CHEEKTOWAGA. *St. Joseph Hospital*, 2605 Harlem Rd., 14225-4097. Tel: 716-891-2400; Fax: 716-891-2616. Email: webmaster@chsbuffalo.org. Web: www.chsbuffalo.org. Franciscan Sisters of St. Joseph, Sponsored by the Catholic Health System, Inc. Bed Capacity 208; Patients Assisted Annually 145,545; Total Staff 531.

McAuley-Seton Home Care, 14 Appletree Business Park, 14227. Tel: 716-685-4870; Fax: 716-651-9613. Email: mek@chsbuffalo.org. Mark Sullivan, Pres. & CEO. Patients Assisted Annually 10,091; Staff 243; Home Care 2,312; Staff 200; Long Term Hospital Patients 446; Staff 18.

KENMORE. *Kenmore Mercy Foundation Inc.*, 2950 Elmwood Ave., 14217. Tel: 716-447-6204; Fax: 716-447-6052. Email: PFilocam@chsbuffalo.org.

Kenmore Mercy Hospital, 2950 Elmwood Ave., 14217. Tel: 716-447-6100; Fax: 716-447-6090. Joseph D. McDonald, CEO; Rev. Vincent J. Ferraro, Chap. Sponsored by the Catholic Health System, Inc. Bed Capacity 184; Total Staff 719; Outpatient Visits 138,546; Admissions 6,937.

LACKAWANNA. *Our Lady of Victory Hospital*, 55 Melroy at Ridge Rd., 14218. Tel: 716-828-3830; Fax: 716-823-1342. Web: www.chsbuffalo.org. Mr. John P. Davanzo, Pres. & CEO; Rev. Robert J. McArtney, Dir. Pastoral Care. Sponsored by the Catholic Health System, Inc. Sisters of St. Joseph 3; Patients Assisted Annually 30,500; Total Staff 100.

Our Lady of Victory Hospital Auxiliary, 55 Melroy at Ridge Rd., 14218. Tel: 716-825-8000.

LEWISTON. *Mount St. Mary's Hospital of Niagara Falls*, 5300 Military Rd., 14092-1997. Tel: 716-297-4800; Fax: 716-298-2333 (Gen.); 716-298-2001 (Pres.). Web: www.msmh.org. Angelo G. Calbone, Pres. & CEO; Rev. Francis J. Zmozynski, Chap.; Sisters Helen Edward Dodd, Chap.; Maureen Huet, O.S.F., Chap.; Diane Louttit, D.C., Chap. Ascension Health, St. Louis, MO Capacity 175; Patients Assisted Annually 194,396; Total Staff 887.

[L] HEALTH CARE FACILITIES

BUFFALO. *St. Francis of Buffalo, Inc.* (Formerly known as St. Francis Hospital). , 34 Benwood Ave., 14214. Tel: 716-862-2500; Fax: 716-862-2505. Email: sperry@wnychs.org. Sheila Perry, Admin.; Rev. Robert Mack, Chap.; Sr. Marilyn Perkins, D.C., Chm. & Prov. Supr. Sisters of St. Francis 1; Total Assisted 288; Total Staff 195.

[M] HOMES FOR AGED

BUFFALO. *Nazareth Nursing Home*, 291 North St., 14201. Tel: 716-881-2323; Fax: 716-881-1578. Email: Dcrispel@chsbuffalo.org. Sr. Evelyn McCarte, D.C., Board Chair; Darlene Jones Crispell, Admin.

Legal Title: *Nazareth Nursing Home of the Franciscan Sisters of the Immaculate Conception*, Chapel attended by Oblate Fathers of Holy Angels Church. Franciscan Sisters of the Immaculate Conception 2; Bed Capacity 125; Patients Assisted Annually 363; Total Staff 185.

BATAVIA. *St. Luke Manor*, 17 Wiard St., 14020. Tel: 716-343-8806; Fax: 716-343-0959. Sheila Perry, Admin. Bed Capacity 20; Patients Assisted Annually 30.

CLARENCE. *Brothers of Mercy Housing Co., Inc.*, 10500 Bergtold Rd., 14031. Tel: 716-759-2122; Fax: 716-759-8030. Email: len@brothersofmercy.org. Web: www.brothersofmercy.org. Leonard Krufka, Admin.; Bro. Jude Holzfoerster, F.M.M., Pres. Apartments 100; Total in Residence 100; Total Staff 6.

Brothers of Mercy Nursing & Rehabilitation Center, 10570 Bergtold Rd., 14031. Tel: 716-759-6985; Fax: 716-759-6223. Email rich@brothersofmercy.org. Web: www.brothersofmercy.org. Mr. Richard C. Cleland, Admin. Bro. Jude Holzfoerster, F.M.M., Pres.; Rev. John J. Sardina, Chap. Bed Capacity 240; Total Assisted Annually 1,100; Staff 500. In Res. Sr. Jean Thompson, O.S.F., Dir. Spiritual Care.

Brothers of Mercy Sacred Heart Home, Inc., 4520 Ransom Rd., 14031. Tel: 716-759-2644; Fax: 716-759-6433. Email: geri@brothersofmercy.org. Web: www.brothersofmercy.org. Geri Pfohl Admin.; Bro. Jude Holzfoerster, F.M.M., Pres. of Board; Rev. John J. Sardina, Chap. Bed Capacity 80; Total in Residence 80; Total Staff 56.

DUNKIRK. *St. Vincent's Home for the Aged*, 319 Washington Ave., 14048. Tel: 716-366-2066; Fax: 716-366-0545. Email: dsmith@chsbuffalo.org. Deborah smith, Admin. Catholic Charities of Buffalo, Inc. Residents 40; Total Staff 25.

KENMORE. *Kenmore Mercy Homes, Inc.* dba McAuley Residence , Administrative Offices, 2950 Elmwood Ave., 14217. Tel: 716-447-6101; Fax 716-447-6090. Shari Hutchison, Admin. Residential Health Care Facility; Sponsored by the Catholic Health System, Inc. Bed Capacity 160; Total Assisted 160; Total Staff 221.

LANCASTER. *St. Elizabeth's Home*, 5539 Broadway, 14086. Tel: 716-683-5150; Fax: 716-683-4049. Email: bsiener@chsbuffalo.org. Bartholomew J. Siener, Admin. Sisters of Mercy 1; Daughters of Charity 1; Residents 117; Total Staff 58.

LEWISTON. *Our Lady of Peace, Inc.*, 5285 Lewiston Rd., 14092. Tel: 716-298-2900; Fax: 716-298-2800. Henry M. Sloma, Exec. Dir.; Sr. Marilyn Perkins, D.C., Bd. Chm. Total Assisted Annually 300.

OLEAN. *St. Joseph Manor*, 2211 W. State St., 14760. Tel: 716-372-7810; Fax: 716-373-4375. Email: bcampbell@wnychs.org. Web: www.chsbuffalo.org. Brenda Campbell, Admin. Bed Capacity 22; Total Assisted 30; Total Staff 37.

ORCHARD PARK. *W.N.Y. Catholic LongTerm Care, Inc.* dba Father Baker Manor , 6400 Powers Rd., 14127. Tel: 716-667-0001; Fax: 716-667-0028. Email: bakermanor@aol.com. Michael McRae, Admin. Nursing facility sponsored by the Catholic Health System, Inc. Bed Capacity 160; Total Assisted 160; Total Staff 247.

SILVER CREEK. *St. Columbans on the Lake, Home for the Aged*, 2546 Lake Rd., 14136. Tel: 716-934-4515; Fax: 716-934-3919. Sr. Corona Colleary, Admin. Columban Sisters 9; Aged Residents 50; Total Staff 36. In Res. Rev. Peter Cronin, S.S.C.

WILLIAMSVILLE. *St. Francis of Williamsville*, 147 Reist St., 14221. Tel: 716-633-5400; Fax: 716-663-6404. Email: rzito@chsbuffalo.org. Ronald F. Zito, Admin.

Legal Title: *St. Francis of Williamsville*, Skilled Nursing Facility Residents 142; Total Assisted 220; Total Staff 194.

Holy Family Home, 410 Mill St., 14221. Tel: 716-634-5400; Fax: 716-634-5730. Email: holyfamginny@aol.com. Web: www.wmsvlfranciscans.org. Sr. Virginia Balk, O.S.F., Admin. Sisters of St. Francis of the Third Order Regular 7; Residents 75; Total Staff 50.

Mount St. Mary's LTC Facility, Inc., 201 Reist St., 14221. Tel: 716-632-2155; Fax: 716-632-0339. Email: jweisbeck@osfwmsv.org. Sr. Jeanne Weisbeck, Chair, Bd. of Dir.; Bonnie Gifford, Dir. Nursing Svcs. Sponsored by the Sisters of St. Francis.

[N] DAY CARE CENTERS

BUFFALO. *Guardian Angel Day Care Center*, 1193 Delaware Ave., 14209. Tel 716-882-9146; Fax: 716-881-7051. Dana M. Cassiano, Admin. Lay Staff 15; Children 68; Total Staff 15.

Holy Innocents Day Care Center, 30 Rich St., 14211. Tel: 716-896-6386; Fax: 716-894-3088. Email: debbiecoyne@ccwny.org. Web: www.ccwny.org. Mrs. Deborah L. Coyne, Dir Day care for children age 6 weeks to 12 yrs. Children 109; Total Staff 25.

[O] MONASTERIES AND RESIDENCES OF PRIESTS AND BROTHERS

BUFFALO. *Bishop's Residence*, 77 Oakland Pl., 14222. Tel: 716-883-7707; Fax: 716-883-7702. Revs. David G. LiPuma; Paul A. Litwin.

Canisius Jesuit Community, 2001 Main St., 14208. Tel: 716-883-7000; Fax: 716-886-6506. Email: lynchp@canisius.edu. Web: www.canisius.edu. Revs. Patrick J. Lynch, S.J., Rector; Frederick G. Betti, S.J.; John P. Bucki, S.J.; Joseph F. Burke, S.J., Ph.D.; Bro. Thomas J. Casey, S.J.; Revs. Vincent M. Cooke, S.J.; Paul J. Dugan, S.J.; Edward T. Dunn, S.J.; Benjamin Fiore, S.J.; Louis T. Garaventa, S.J.; Robert A. Haus, S.J.; James P. Higgins, S.J.; Richard D. Hunt, S.J.; Daniel P. Jamros, S.J.; Ladislaus F. Juhasz, S.J. (Hungary); Joseph J. Kamiensky, S.J.; Mark G. Kriz, S.J.; Daniel P. Liderbach, S.J.; Joseph W. Lux, S.J.; Edward C. Lynch, S.J.; Michael J. McCarthy, C.S.Sp. (BRK); William J. McCurdy, S.J.; Vincent M. McNally, S.J.; Martin X. Moleski, S.J.; Paul W. Nochelski, S.J.; Thomas A. O'Connor, S.J.; Michael H. Pastizzo, S.J.; John J. Ryan, S.J.; Frederick J. Reisert, S.J.; Ronald W. Sams, S.J., Min.; Edward P. Sullivan, S.J.; Michael F. Tunney, S.J.; David F. White, S.J.; Eugene A. Zimpfer, S.J.; Daniel J. Lusch, S.J.

Legal Title: *The Jesuits of Canisius College, Inc.*

Elmwood 4, 4845 Transit Rd., 14043. Tel: 716-668-3251; Fax: 716-886-6506. Total in Residence 31; Total Staff 9.

Maryknoll House, 127 Chadduck Ave., 14207. Tel: 716-875-0005; Fax: 716-875-2322. Email: mklbuffalo@aol.com. Web: www.maryknoll.org. Mr. Paul Bork, Dir. Total in Residence 1; Total Staff 2.

Sheehan Residence for Priests Residence for retired priests , 330 Linwood Ave., 14209-1689. Tel: 716-884-9679; Fax: 716-881-3268. Rev. Robert J. Biesinger (Retired); Rev. Msgrs. Paul T. Cronin (Retired); Arnold J. Schneider (Retired); Revs. Raymond J. Mahar (Retired); Thomas J. Crowley (Retired); Mark M. Friel (Retired); Henry V. Lex (Retired); Joseph Kwolek (Retired); David V. Roche (Retired); Raymond R. Russell (Retired); Paul C. Schreck (Retired); William G. Ward (Retired).

ATHOL SPRINGS. *St. Francis of Assisi Friary*, 4129 Lake Shore Rd., 14010-0185. Tel: 716-627-5762; Fax: 716-627-4610. Email: president@stfrancishigh.org. Web: www.stfrancishigh.org. Revs. Aurelian W. Brzezniak, O.F.M.Conv.; Bernard Olszewski, O.F.M.Conv.; Charles Jagodzinski, O.F.M.Conv.; Joseph Benicewicz, O.F.M.Conv., Guardian & Pres.; Michael Lasky, O.F.M.Conv.; Michael Sajda, O.F.M.Conv., Vicar & Prin.; Stephen King, O.F.M.Conv.; Roman Siola, O.F.M.Conv.; Francis Lombardo, O.F.M.Conv.; Anthony M. Konieczny, O.F.M.Conv.; Bros. Lawrence LaFlame, O.F.M.Conv.; Joseph Colarossi, O.F.M.Conv. Faculty Residence for St. Francis High School Priests 10; Brothers 2; Total in Residence 12.

St. Maximilian Kolbe Friary, 4190 St. Francis Dr., 14010. Tel: 716-627-3861; Fax: 716-627-4059. Email: office@rosaryhour.net. Web: www.rosaryhour.net. Bro. Daniel Geary, O.F.M.Conv., Guardian; Revs. Ronald Sermak, O.F.M.Conv.; Wladek Mezyk, O.F.M.Conv. (Poland), Dir. Total Staff 4; Total in Residence 4; Total in Residence 3; Total Staff 3.

Staff to the Rosary Hour Apostolate: Anne Holmes; Joanna Makula; Jerry Kornowicz, Office Mgr.; Alice Preteroti; Teresa Sokolowski; Eleanor Filipski.

CLARENCE. *Provincial Motherhouse of Brothers of Mercy*, 4520 Ransom Rd., 14031. Tel: 716-759-8341; Fax: 716-759-8341. Email: jude@brothersofmercy.org. Web: www.brothersofmercy.org. Bro. Jude Holzfoerster, F.M.M., Prov.; Rev. John J. Sardina, Chap.

Legal Title: *Brothers of Mercy, Inc.* Brothers 16; In Formation 1.

LACKAWANNA. *Bishop Head Residence*, 10 Rosary Ave., 14218. Tel: 716-824-4644; Fax: 716-824-4844. Sr. Marguerite Gendreau, S.S.M.N., Admin.; Rev. Msgrs. Anthony J. Jasinski (Retired); William A. Schwinger (Retired); Onofrio R. Smiraldo (Retired); Revs. Albert J. Bosack (Retired); James A. Grimmer (Retired); Richard A. Massar (Retired); Paul F. Stengel; Bernard T. Sokolowski (Retired); L. Antonio Rodriguez; Vincent Wright; Donald C. Weber (Retired).

Piarist Fathers Residence, Assumption of the Blessed Virgin Mary, 80 Steelawanna Ave., 14218-0343. Tel: 716-822-9828; Fax: 716-822-9828. Email: maurice_1921@lasernational.com. Revs. Kalman Miskolczy, Sch.P., Treas.; Nicholas Vitez Fodor, Sch.P., Supr. Total in Residence 2; Total Staff 2.

LEROY. *Order of the BVM of Mercy/Mercedarian Friars*, Mercygrove, 7758 E. Main Rd., 14482-9701. Tel: 585-768-7110; Fax: 585-768-4803. Web: www.orderofmercy.org. Revs. Wayn Genereux, O.de.M., Local Supr. & Master of Postulants; Michael Donovan, O.de.M., Master of

Novices; Paul Pietrzyk, O.de.M., Retreat Dir.; Michael R. Rock, O.de.M., Pastor of St. Peter and St. Anthony. United States headquarters for the community. Pre-novitiate and Novitiate formation community. Total in Community: Professed Religious 4; Postulants 6; Novices 2.

St. Raymond Nonnatus Novitiate Order of the BVM of Mercy. , Mercygrove, 7758 E. Main Rd., 14482-9701. Tel: 585-768-7110; Fax: 585-768-4803. Web: www.orderofmercy.org. Rev. Michael Donovan, O.de.M., Novice Master. Novices 2.

NIAGARA UNIVERSITY. *Vincentian Community at Niagara University*, Meade Hall, 14109-2209. Tel: 716-286-8110; Fax: 716-286-8766. Email: tcasella@niagara.edu. Rev. Thomas A. Casella, C.M., Supr.; Bros. Martin J. Schneider, C.M., Asst.; Augustine D. Towey, C.M., Sub Asst.; Revs. William M. Allegretto, C.M.; Stephen J. Denig, C.M.; Dennis H. Holtschneider, C.M.; Joseph G. Hubbert, C.M.; Joseph L. Levesque, C.M.; Michael T. Mazurchuk, C.M.; Thomas P. McGourty, C.M.; Daniel F. O'Leary, O.M.I.; Francis X. Prior, C.M.; Louis P. Trotta, C.M.; Michael J. Tumulty, C.M.; Bro. Stephen J. Kennedy, C.M. Total in Residence 3.

NORTH TONAWANDA. *Society of the Catholic Apostolate*, Infant Jesus Delegature, 3452 Niagara Falls Blvd., P.O. Box 563, 14120-0563. Tel: 716-694-4313; Fax: 716-743-5430. Revs. Leslaw M. Gwarek, S.A.C., Supr. & Prov. Delegate; John Posiewala, S.A.C.

ST. BONAVENTURE. *St. Bonaventure Friary* 14778. Tel: 716-375-2000; Fax: 716-375-2424. Email: Fstorms@SBu.edu. Web: www.sbu.edu. Revs. Thomas D. Blow, O.F.M., M.A., M.Div., Guardian; Michael Blastic, O.F.M.Conv.; David D. Blake, O.F.M.; J. Gregory Brennan, O.F.M.; Michael D. Calabria, O.F.M.; Michael F. Cusato, O.F.M., Ph.D.; Regis A. Duffy, O.F.M.; Richard C. Flaherty, O.F.M.; David Flood, O.F.M.; Robert Karris, O.F.M.; Dominick V. Monti, O.F.M.; Francis Storms, O.F.M., M.A., Treas.; Peter Schneible, O.F.M.; Alphonsus A. Trabold, O.F.M.; Patrick E. Tuttle, O.F.M.; James Vacco, O.F.M.; Allen Weber, O.F.M.; William J. Weiksnar, O.F.M.; Robert H. White, O.F.M.; Bros. Scott F. Brookbank, O.F.M.; David Haack, O.F.M.; Gregory P. Jakubowicz, O.F.M.; Anthony J. LoGalbo, O.F.M., Vicar; Adrian A. Riester, O.F.M.; Julian Riester, O.F.M.; Basil J. Valente, O.F.M. Fathers 17; Brothers 7.

TONAWANDA. *O'Hara Residence*, 69 O'Hara Rd., 14150-6227. Tel: 716-743-0037; Fax: 716-743-8772. Rev. Msgrs. Anthony J. Caligiuri (Retired); James N. Connelly (Retired); Rev. Salvatore J. Cusimano (Retired); Rev. Msgrs. Charles T. Griffin (Retired); Leo E. Hammerl (Retired); Paul R. Juenker, Admin. (Retired); Paul R. Letourneau (Retired); Dino J. Lorenzetti (Retired); Robert C. Schwab (Retired); Edward J. Sobierajski (Retired); Francis M. Swiatkowski (Retired); Richard L. Wetter (Retired); Casimir A. Zak (Retired). Total in Residence 13; Total Staff 5.

WEST SENECA. *The Eudists, St. John Eudes Center*, St. Bonaventure Church, 36 Flohr Ave., 14224-1818. Tel: 716-825-4319; Fax: 716-825-4376. Email: EudesCenter@cs.com. Web: www.parishrenewal.org. Revs. Benoit J. Drapeau, C.J.M., Supr.; Ronald M. Bagley, C.J.M.; J. Gregory Sampson, C.J.M.; Mr. Dennis Mahaney, Dir., St. John Eudes Center. Total in Residence 3; Total Staff 5.

WILLIAMSVILLE. *Consolata Fathers*, 35 Brompton Rd., P.O. Box 570, 14221. Tel: 716-634-5678; 716-634-3793. Revs. John N. Reuther, I.M.C., Supr.; Robert Rezac, I.M.C.; James Kingori, I.M.C. (Kenya).

[P] CONVENTS AND RESIDENCES FOR SISTERS

BUFFALO. *Congregation of the Sisters of St. Joseph Generalate*, Administrative Offices, 23 Agassiz Cir., 14214-2611. Tel: 716-838-4400; Fax: 716-838-4102. Email: Buffssj@ssjbuffalo.org. Web: www.ssjbuffalo.org. Professed Sisters 134.

Discalced Carmelite Monastery of St. Teresa of the Child Jesus (1920), 75 Carmel Rd., 14214. Tel: 716-837-6499; Fax: 716-837-3517. Sr. Mother Miriam of Jesus, O.C.D., Prioress. Cloistered Professed Sisters 18; Extern Professed Sisters 2; Novices 2.

Holy Name Province - Provincial Motherhouse Tel: 716-754-4311; Fax: 716-754-1223. Email: stella@buffnet.net. Web: www.franciscans-stella-niagara.org.

Sisters of St. Francis of Holy Name Province, Inc., 4421 Lower River Rd., Stella Niagara, 14144-1001. Tel: 716-754-4312, Ext. 764; Fax: 716-754-7657. Email: dorothymueller@intotem.net. Sr. Dorothy Mueller, O.S.F., Prov. Min.

Center of Renewal, Inc., 4421 Lower River Rd., Stella Niagara, 14144. Tel: 716-754-7376; Fax: 716-754-1223. Sr. Dorothy Mueller, O.S.F., Prov. Min.

Francis Center, 1301 Ferry Ave., Niagara Falls, 14301. Tel: 716-282-3783; Fax: 716-754-7657. Sr. Dorothy Mueller, O.S.F., Prov. Min.

Stella Niagara Education Park, Inc., 4421 Lower River Rd., Stella Niagara, 14144. Tel: 716-754-4311; Fax: 716-754-1223. Sr. Dorothy Mueller, O.S.F., Prov. Min.

The Stella Niagara Education Park Endowment Foundation, 4421 Lower River Rd., Stella Niagara, 14144. Tel: 716-754-4311; Fax: 716-754-1223. Sr. Dorothy Mueller, O.S.F., Prov. Min.

The Sisters of St. Francis Retirement Fund, 4421 Lower River Rd., Stella Niagara, 14144. Tel: 716-754-4312; Fax: 716-754-7657. Sr. Dorothy Mueller, O.S.F., Prov. Min.

The Providence Fund, 4421 Lower River Rd., Stella Niagara, 14144. Tel: 716-754-4312; Fax: 716-754-7657. Sr. Dorothy Mueller, O.S.F., Prov. Min.

Buffalo Academy of the Sacred Heart, Inc., 3860 Main St., 14226-3398. Tel: 716-834-2101; Fax: 716-834-2944. Email: shalib@buffnet.net. Web: www.sacredheartacademy.org.

Immaculate Heart of Mary Provincial House and Convent, Villa Maria, 600 Doat St., 14211. Tel: 716-892-4141; Fax: 716-892-4177. Email: cssfbuffalo@catholic.org. Sr. Mary Ambrose Wozniak, C.S.S.F., Prov. Min. Felician Sisters 243.

Mercy Center, 625 Abbott Rd., 14220. Tel: 716-825-5531; Fax: 716-826-1518. Email: mercybuf@buffnet.net. Web: www.bflorsm.com. Total in Residence 67.

Monastery of Our Lady of the Rosary, 335 Doat St., 14211-2199. Tel: 716-892-0066; Fax: 716-892-8846. Email: MTNOP3@aol.com. Sr. Mary Thomas, O.P., Prioress; Rev. Salvatore B. Matarazzo, O.P., Chap.

Legal Title: *Legal Title: Legal Title: Legal Title: Dominican Nuns of the Perpetual Rosary, Buffalo, NY* Professed Nuns 29; Sisters in Temporary Vows 2; Novices 1.

Sisters of Mercy of the Buffalo Diocese Retirement Corp., 625 Abbott Rd., 14220. Tel: 716-825-5531; 716-826-6248; Fax: 716-826-1518. Email: mercybuf@buffnet.net. Web: www.bflorsm.com. Sr. Nancy Hoff, R.S.M., Pres.

Sisters of Mercy-Regional Community Offices, 625 Abbott Rd., 14220. Tel: 716-826-5051; 716-826-6248; Fax: 716-826-1518. Email: mercybuf@buffnet.net. Web: www.bflorsm.com. Sr. Nancy Hoff, R.S.M., Pres. Sisters of Mercy Sisters Professed 167; Temporary Vows 4; Candidates 5.

Sisters of Social Service District Residence & Novitiate, 296 Summit Ave., 14214. Tel: 716-834-0197; Fax: 716-834-6168. Email: sssbuffalo@wzrd.com. Sr. Agnes Pataki, S.S.S., Dist. Moderator. Sisters 3.

Other Convents:

Generalate, Bathori Laszlo u 10, Budapest H-1029 Hungary. Tel: 011-361-275-7057; Fax: 011-361-275-7057. Email: sss.gen@hcbc.hu. Sr. Franciska Berkecz, S.S.S., Gen. Moderator.

St. Scholastica House, 210 Winston Rd., 14216. Tel: 716-833-7412; Fax: 716-833-7412. Email: Scholastica@pcom.net. Sisters 1; Sisters Living Alone 4; Sisters in Nursing Home 1.

Sara House, 42 Linden Ave., 14214. Tel: 716-836-0685. Sisters 3.

Bethany House, 152 Kinsey Ave., Kenmore, 14217. Tel: 716-873-6179. Sisters 2.

Sisters of St. Mary of Namur St. Mary Center , St. Mary Center, 241 Lafayette Ave., 14213. Tel: 716-884-8221; Fax: 716-884-6598. Email: ssmnprov@intotem.net. Web: www.ssmn.org. Sisters Mary Veronica White, S.S.M.N., Prov. Supr.; Katherine Marie Bogner, S.S.M.N., Prov. Councillor. Provincial House of the Sisters of St. Mary of Namur Professed Sisters 103.

ALLEGANY. *Franciscan Sisters of Allegany, New York, Inc.*, 115 E. Main St., 14706. Tel: 716-373-0200; Fax: 716-372-5774. Email: fsaalleg@adelphia.net. Web: www.fsalleg.org/sem.htm; www.franciscansister.com. Sr. Margaret Mary Kimmins, O.S.F., Pres.

St. Elizabeth Motherhouse, 115 E. Main St., 14706. Tel: 716-373-0200; Fax: 716-372-5774. Sisters Margaret Mary Kimmins, O.S.F., Gen. Min.; Noella Lachat, O.S.F., Local Min. Sisters 94.

Region 1 Office, Franciscan Sisters of Allegany, 115 E. Main St., 14706. Tel: 716-373-1888; Fax: 716-373-6514. Email: rfbrunner@adelphia.net. Web: www.franciscansister.com. Sr. Roberta Brunner, O.S.F., Region 1 Min.

BELMONT. *Immaculate Conception Convent*, 5173 State Rte. 244, 14813. Tel: 585-268-5524.

CLARENCE. *Sisters of St. Joseph*, Clarence Residence, 4975 Strickler Rd., 14031. Tel: 716-759-6893; Fax: 716-759-2488. Email: ssjbuffalo@msn.com. Sisters Madelene Stauring, Coord.; Carol Morgan, Coord.; Marie Kerwin, Coord.; Judith Hutson, Admin. Total in Residence 55; Total Staff 41.

CUBA. *Mt. Pamfilo - Franciscan Sisters of Allegany*, 7905 Mt. Monroe Rd., 14727. Tel: 716-373-0200; Fax: 716-372-5774. Email: fsaalleg@adelphia.net. Web: www.franciscansister.com. Sr. Edward Catherine Barrett, O.S.F., Contact Person.

HAMBURG. *Immaculate Conception Convent*, 5286 S. Park Ave., 14075. Tel: 716-649-1205; Fax: 716-649-5958. Rev. Mark David Skura, O.F.M.Conv., Chap.; Sr. M. Paulette Tirone, F.S.S.J., Gen. Min. Motherhouse of the Franciscan Sisters of St. Joseph Sisters 95. In Res. Rev. Ronald Sermak, O.F.M.Conv.

North American Union of the Sisters of Our Lady of Charity, 3800 Howard Rd., 14075. Tel: 716-648-4988; Fax: 716-648-3062. Sr. Rosemary Toth, Local Supr.

Legal Title: *Sisters of Our Lady of Charity of the Refuge, Inc.* Sisters 8.

LE ROY. *Sisters of Our Lady of Mercy (SOLM) (Mercedarians)*, 14 W. Main St., 14482. Tel: 716-768-8053. Email: Mercy@Rochester.rr.com. Sr. Leonilla Puggioni, S.O.L.M., Supr. Sisters 4.

LEWISTON. *Sisters of the Sacred Heart of Jesus (S.S.H.J.)*, Sacred Heart School & Convent, 5269 Lewiston Rd., 14092. Tel: 716-284-8273; Fax: 716-284-8273. Email: shvschool@adelphia.net. Sr. M. Ambrogia Alderuccio, S.S.H.J., Supr. Sisters 9.

SILVER CREEK. *Missionary Sisters of St. Columban, St. Columban's on the Lake*, 2546 Lake Rd., 14136. Tel: 716-934-4515; Fax: 716-934-3919. Rev. Peter Cronin, S.S.C., Chap. Professed Sisters 9.

WEST SENECA. *Sisters of Charity of St. Vincent de Paul of Zagreb, Croatia*, 171 Knox Ave., 14224. Tel: 716-825-5859; 716-822-6841; Fax: 716-822-2841. Sr. Stella Simetich, V.Z., Supr.

Legal Title: *Sisters of Charity of St. Vincent de Paul of Zagreb, Croatia - U.S.A. Delegacy Headquarters* Professed Sisters 13.

WILLIAMSVILLE. *Sisters of St. Francis of the Third Order Regular, St. Mary of the Angels*, P.O. Box 275, 14231-0275. Tel: 716-632-2155; Fax: 716-632-0339. Email: mnachreiner@osfwmsv.org. Web: www.wmsvlfranciscans.org. Sr. Marian Rose Mansius, Gen. Min.; Rev. Richard D. Bordonaro, Chap. Motherhouse of the Sisters of St. Francis of the Third Order Regular. Sisters 139.

[Q] RETREAT HOUSES

DERBY. *St. Columban Center*, 6892 Lake Shore Rd., P.O. Box 816, 14047-0816. Tel: 716-947-4708; Fax: 716-947-5759. Email: columban@buffnet.net. Web: www.stcolumbancenter.org/. Rev. Msgr. James E. Wall, Dir.; Sisters Mary Leah Krauth, O.S.F., Assoc. Dir.; Mary Catherine Cummins, O.S.U., Assoc. Dir. Total in Residence 3; Total Staff 20.

LEROY. *St. Peter Nolasco Spiritual Center*, Mercygrove, 7770 E. Main Rd., 14482-9701. Tel: 585-768-7110; 585-768-6408; Fax: 585-768-4803. Web: www.orderofmercy.org. Rev. Paul Pietrzyk, O.de.M., Dir. Offering directed or private retreats. Facility available for overnight programs.

WEST CLARKSVILLE. *Mount Irenaeus, Franciscan Mountain Retreat & Holy Peace Friary*, P.O. Box 100, 14786. Tel: 585-973-2470; Fax: 585-973-2400. Email: mmarc@sbu.edu. Web: www.mounti.com. Revs. Daniel P. Riley, O.F.M., Pres. & Guardian; Daniel A. Hurley, O.F.M.; Bro. Joseph A. Kotula, O.F.M., Vicar; Rev. Louis M. McCormick, O.F.M. Order of Friars Minor Holy Name Province Total in Residence 4.

[R] CAMPUS MINISTRY AND NEWMAN CENTERS

ALFRED. *Campus Ministry* P.O. Box 1154, 14802. Tel: 607-587-9411; Fax: 607-587-9431. Email: stjude@znet.net. Rev. Eugene P. Ulrich, Vicar of Campus Ministry.

Canisius College:

Campus Ministry Office, 2001 Main St., 14208. Tel: 716-888-2420; Fax: 716-888-3144. Email: buckij@canisius.edu. Revs. John P. Bucki, S.J., Dir.; Thomas A. O'Connor, S.J., Assoc. Campus Min.; Sr. Patricia Brady, S.S.M.N., Assoc. Campus Min.; Ms. Susan Fischer, Assoc. Campus Min.; Mr. Joseph VanVolkenburg, Assoc. Campus Min.; Mr. Dennis McCunney, Assoc.Campus Min.

Daemen College:

Campus Ministry Office, 4380 Main St., Snyder, 14226. Tel: 716-839-3600, Ext. 237. Rev. A. Mark Illig; Rae Dzialak.

D'Youville College:

320 Porter Ave., 14201. Tel: 716-881-7693; Fax: 716-881-7760. Leandra Kosmoski; Sr. Eileen Spanier, G.N.S.H.; Rev. Thomas Ribits, O.S.F.S.; Rev. Jan Mahle.

Erie Community College:

City Campus, 121 Ellicott St., 14203. Tel: 716-260-2668. Sr. Ruth Marie Penksa, G.N.S.H., Dir. Campus Ministry.

North Campus, Newman Center, 6325 Main St., Williamsville, 14221. Tel: 716-632-8898. Sr. Francis Gangloff, O.S.F., Dir.

South Campus, Newman Center Tel: 716-649-6186. Email: smfran@aol.com. Sr. Francis Gangloff, O.S.F., Dir.

Medaille College:

Campus Ministry, 18 Agassiz Cir., 14214. Tel: 716-884-3281.

Niagara University, Lewiston Rd., Niagara University, 14109. Tel: 716-286-8400; Fax: 716-286-8477. Rev. Thomas P. McGourty, C.M.; Sr. Nora Gatto, D.C., Dir.; Rev. Patrick J. Zengierski, Dir.; Ms. Monica Saltarelli; Mr. Jeff Klein.

State University College at Buffalo:

Newman Center, 1219 Elmwood Ave., 14222. Tel: 716-882-1080; Fax: 716-882-6914. Rev. Msgr. John C. Weimer, Dir. (Retired); Sr. Charlene Fontana, S.S.J., Assoc. Dir.; Jonathan Neureuther, Assoc. Dir.

State University of New York at Buffalo (Main St. South Campus), St. Joseph's University Parish, 3269 Main St., 14214. Tel: 716-833-0298; Fax: 716-833-7339. Rev. Jacob C. Ledwon, Dir.; Ms. Rebecca Calvo; Mr. Greg Coogan.

Trocaire College, 360 Choate Ave., 14220. Tel: 716-827-2489; Fax: 716-828-6107. Sr. Marie Andre Main, R.S.M., Dir.

Villa Maria College, 240 Pine Ridge Rd., 14225. Tel: 716-896-0700; Fax: 716-896-0705. Mr. Frank Antonnucci, Dir.

St. Jude's Chapel at Alfred University & Alfred State College, Box 1154, Lower College Dr., 14802. Tel: 607-587-9411; Fax: 607-587-9431. Rev. Eugene P. Ulrich, Dir.; Susan M. Fowler.

State University of New York at Buffalo (North Campus) Newman Center, UB Commons-Ste. 209, Amherst, 14228. Tel: 716-636-7495; Fax: 716-568-0692. Rev. Msgr. J. Patrick Keleher, Dir.; Anne Tupper; Maria Clare.

State University College at Fredonia, 222 Temple St., Fredonia, 14063. Tel: 716-679-4686; Fax: 716-679-3486. Rev. Michael J. Parker, Dir.; Karen Sampson.

Hilbert College:

Campus Ministry Office, 5200 S. Park Ave., Hamburg, 14075. Tel: 716-649-7900; Fax: 716-649-0702. Rev. Bernard Olszewski, O.F.M.Conv.; Sr. Jacqueline Benbenek, C.S.S.F., Dir.

St. Bonaventure University, P.O. Box AR, St. Bonaventure, 14778. Tel: 716-375-2600; Fax: 716-375-2618. Robert M. Donius, M.A., Vice Pres.; Revs. Daniel A. Hurley, O.F.M.; Daniel P. Riley, O.F.M.; Patrick E. Tuttle, O.F.M.; Jud Weiksnar, O.F.M.; Bro. Joseph A. Kotula, O.F.M.; Rev. Cheryl Parris; Ms. Sarah Nies; Mr. Peter Ghiloni; Mr. Doug Looney; Ms. Donna Wysokenski.

[S] CAMPS AND COMMUNITY CENTERS

ANGOLA. *St. Vincent de Paul Camp* Tel: 716-549-2950; Fax: 716-882-3556. Email: info@svdpwny.org. Web: www.SVDPWNY.org. (Camp for needy boys and girls).

Office, 1298 Main St., 14209. Tel: 716-882-3360; Fax: 716-882-3556. Rev. Msgr. John J. Conniff, Spiritual Dir. (Retired).

SALAMANCA. *Camp Turner* Tel: 716-354-4555. (Coed).

Office, 795 Main St., 14203. Tel: 716-847-8789; Fax: 716-847-8789. Email: Director@CampTurner.com. Web: www.campturner.com. John Mann, Dir.

[T] MISCELLANEOUS

BUFFALO. *158 Chenango Street Housing Development Fund Company, Inc., dba St. John Bosco Apartments*, 525 Washington St., 14203. Tel: 716-847-1635; Fax: 716-856-7201. Email: bernadette.harlan@ccwny.org. Web: www.deltadevelopmentwny.com. Rev. Joseph J. Sicari, Contact Person. Low income housing for the elderly age 62 and over Staff 2; Residents 12.

50-60 Kosciuzko Street Housing Development Fund Company, Inc., 525 Washington St., 14203. Tel: 716-847-1635; Fax: 716-856-7201. Email: bernadette.harlan@ccwny.org. Web: www.deltadevelomentwny.com. Rev. Joseph J. Sicari, Contact Person. Special Purpose Housing for the chronically mentally ill

Catholic Charities of Buffalo, NY, Foundation, Inc., 525 Washington St., 14203. Tel: 716-856-4494; Fax: 716-856-2005. Email: david.kersten@ccwny.org. Web: www.ccwny.org.

Catholic Communications of Western New York, Inc., 795 Main St., 14203. Tel: 716-847-8719; Fax: 716-847-8722. Email: comm@buffalodiocese.org. Catholic Communications of Western New York produces and distributes Catholic print and electronic programs.

Catholic Union Store, 795 Main St., 14203. Tel: 716-847-8715; Fax 716-847-8702. Email: cus@buffalodiocese.org. Peter M. McKee, Dir.

Chestnut Ridge Medical Supplies, Inc., 515 Abbott Rd., Ste. 306, 14220. Tel: 716-828-2750; Fax: 716-828-3720. Email: cnrdme@chsbuffalo.org. Nancy Lampkin, Dir.

St. Clare Apartments Housing Development Fund, c/o Delta Development of Western New York, 525 Washington St., 14203. Tel: 716-856-4494; Fax: 716-526-2005. Rev. Joseph J. Sicar, Contact Person.

The Foundation of the Roman Catholic Diocese of Buffalo, NY, Inc., 795 Main St., 14203-1250. Tel: 716-847-5500; Fax: 716-842-5557. Email: devoffice@buffalodiocese.org. Web: www.frcdb.org. David Kersten, Exec. Dir.

Franciscan Mystery Players, Inc., 102 Seymour St., 14210. Rev. Francis Pompei, Dir.

Gerard Place Housing Development Fund Company, Inc., 2515 Bailey Ave., 14215. Tel: 716-897-9948; Fax: 716-897-9953. Email: gerardhdfc@aol.com. Mary E. Moriarty Kienzle, C.S.W., Pres.

Good Counsel Apartments, 525 Washington St., 14203. Tel: 716-847-1635; Fax: 716-856-7201. Email: bernadette.harlan@ccwny.org. Web: www.deltadevelopmentwny.com. Rev. Joseph J. Sicari, Contact Person. Housing for mobility impaired & elderly of low income. Total in Residence 39; Total Staff 2.

Immaculate Heart of Mary Home for Children, Inc., 600 Doat St., 14211. Tel: 716-892-4141; Fax: 716-892-4177. Email: cssfbuffalo@catholic.org.

Kolping Catholic Young Men's Association of Buffalo, NY dba Kolping Society of Buffalo, 25 Delphi Dr., 14227-3605. Tel 716-668-0077. Norman Kuerzdoerfer, Pres.; Rev. Msgr. Paul R. Letourneau, Moderator (Retired).

La Casa Del Tainos Housing Development Fund Company, Inc., 525 Washington St., 14203. Tel: 716-847-1635; Fax: 716-856-7201. Email: bernadette.harlan@ccwny.org. Web: www.deltadevelopmentwny.com. Rev. Joseph J. Sicari, Contact Person. Low income housing for the elderly age 62 and over Residents 49.

Monsignor Adamski Village Housing Development Fund Company, Inc., 123 Townsend St., 14212. Tel: 716-854-5510; Fax: 716-854-0170.

Monsignor Adamski Village, Inc., 123 Townsend St., 14212. Tel: 716-854-5510; Fax: 716-854-0170. Facility for elderly and handicapped persons of low income

Monsignor Carr Institute, 76 W. Humboldt Pkwy., 14214. Tel: 716-835-9745; Fax: 716-835-6785. Web: www.ccwny.org. Brian T. O'Herron, M.Ed., M.B.A., Dir. Licensed outpatient mental health and substance abuse treatment community outreach team, senior advocacy and socialization, marriage counseling, school-based drug prevention, adult psychosocial club, abstinence until marriage education,creative arts studio. Total Assisted 38,621; Saff 90.

Monsignor Kirby Apartments Housing Development Fund Company, Inc., 525 Washington St., 14203. Tel: 716-847-1635, Ext. 3095; Fax: 716-856-7201. Email: bernadette.harlan@ccwny.org. Web: www.deltadevelopmentwny.com. Rev. Joseph J. Sicari, Contact Person. Low income housing for the elderly age 62 and over. Total in Residence 39; Total Staff 2.

Mother of Divine Grace Housing Development Fund Company, Inc., 3233 Main St., 14214. Tel: 716-833-5353; Fax: 716-833-0108. Email: cc3@cantalician.com. Web: www.cantalician.org. Sr. Mary Patricia Tomasik, Exec. Dir. Purpose: To provide housing for persons of low income, particularly handicapped mentally retarded and developmentally disabled adults. Total in Residence 10; Total Staff 10.

Nativity Housing Development Fund Company, Inc., 3233 Main St., 14214. Tel: 716-833-5353; Fax: 716-833-0108. Email cc3@cantalician.com. Web: www.cantalician.org. Sr. Mary Patricia Tomasik, Exec. Dir. Purpose: To provide housing for persons of low income, particularly handicapped mentally retarded and developmentally disabled adults. Total in Residence 11; Total Staff 5.

Our Lady of Peace Housing Development Fund Company, Inc., 3323 Main St., 14214. Tel: 716-833-5353; Fax: 716-833-0108. Email: cc3@wzrd.com. Web: www.cantalician.org. Purpose: To provide housing for persons of low income, particularly handicapped mentally retarded and developmentally disabled adults. Total Residents 5; Total Staff 30.

Our Lady of Victory Community Housing Development Organization, Inc., 515 Abbott Rd., Ste. 306, 14220. Tel: 716-828-2975; Fax: 716-828-3720. Email: agb@chsbuffalo.org. Aimee Gomlak Brace, Pres.

Our Lady of Victory Renaissance Corporation, 515 Abbott Rd., Ste. 306, 14220. Tel: 716-828-2975; Fax: 716-828-3720. Email: agb@chsbuffalo.org. Aimee Gomlak Brace, Pres.

St. Rita's Home, Inc., 600 Doat St., 14211. Tel: 716-892-4141; Fax: 716-892-4117. Email: cssfbuffalo@catholic.org.

Salesian Studios, 152 Plymouth Ave., 14201-1214. Tel: 716-886-6597. Rev. Thomas Ribits, O.S.F.S.

Santa Maria Towers, 525 Washington St., 14203. Tel: 716-847-1635; Fax: 716-856-7201. Email: bernadette.harlan@ccwny.org. Web: www.deltadevelopmentwny.com. Rev. Joseph J. Sicari, Contact Person. Housing for mobility impaired and elderly of low income Total in Residence 113.

Monsignor Gambino Tower, Ltd.

Timon Towers Housing Development Fund Company, Inc., 525 Washington St., 14203. Tel: 716-847-1635; Fax: 716-856-7201. Email: bernadette.harlan@ccwny.org. Web: deltadevelopmentwny.com. Rev. Joseph J. Sicari, Contact Person. Low income housing for the mobility impaired and elderly. Total Staff 5; Total in Residence 124.

St. Timothy's Park Villa Housing Development Fund Company, Inc., 525 Washington St., 14203. Tel: 716-847-1635, Ext. 3095; Fax: 716-856-7201. Email: bernadette.harlan@ccwny.org. Web: www.deltadevelopmentwny.com. Rev. Joseph J. Sicari, Contact Person. Low income housing for the elderly age 62 and over. Total in Residence 49; Total Staff 2.

Wheatfield Housing Development Fund Company, Inc., 525 Washington St., 14203. Tel: 716-847-1635; Fax: 716-856-7201. Email: bernadette.harlan@ccwny.org. Web: www.deltadevelopmentwny.com. Rev. Joseph J. Sicari, Sec. & Treas. Low income housing for the elderly age 62 and over. Apartments 50.

ALLEGANY. *Canticle Farm, Inc.*, 115 E. Main St., 14706. Tel: 716-373-0200. Email: canticle.farm@fsalleg.org. Sr. Margaret Mary Kimmins, O.S.F., Pres.; Linda Matthews, Bd. Chairperson; Sr. Frances Cardillo, O.S.F., Farm Dir.

Dr. Lyle F. Renodin Foundation, Inc., 115 E. Main St., 14706. Tel: 716-373-0200; Fax: 716-372-5774. Email: fsalleg@eznet.net. Web: www.fsalleg.org. Sr. Margaret Mary Kimmins, O.S.F., Pres.

St. Elizabeth Mission Society, Inc., 115 E. Main St., 14706. Tel: 716-373-1130; Fax: 716-373-9324. Email: stelizmission@adelphia.net. Web: www.stelizabethmissionsociety.com. Sr. Marie Dolores Gionta, O.S.F., Dir.

KENMORE. *K M H Homes, INC.*, 2950 Elmwood Ave., 14217. Tel: 716-828-2696. J. Thomas Briody, Vice Pres., Catholic Health System. A holding company of the Catholic Health System

LACKAWANNA. *Our Lady of Victory Homes of Charity*, 780 Ridge Rd., 14218. Tel: 716-828-9648; Fax: 716-828-9643. Email: olv@buffnet.net. Web: www.OurLadyofVictory.org. Rev. Msgr. Robert C. Wurtz, P.A., Exec. Vice Pres. & Treas.

Legal Title: *Our Lady of Victory Homes of Charity*

Legal Title: *Society for the Protection of Destitute Roman Catholic Children at Buffalo, NY*

Legal Title: *Father Baker's*, (Formerly Association of Our Lady of Victory); Includes the following Institutions: Baker Victory Services 716-828-9500 or 1-888-287-9986 (Formerly Baker Hall, Our Lady of Victory Infant Home, St. Joseph Orphanage and St. John's Protectory). Total Assisted 3,000; Total Staff 100.

Western New York Catholic Healthcare Corporation, Our Lady of Victory Hospital, 55 Melroy Ave., 14218.

NEW YORK. *St. Bonaventure Lake House West Bank Perimeter Road at Kinzua South Valley, N.Y.*, 158 W. 27th St., 6th Fl., 10001-6206. Tel: 212-967-6300; Fax: 212-967-6344. Email: hnp@hnp.com. Web: www.ofm.org.

NIAGARA FALLS. *Catholic Worker Center*, 931 Niagara Ave., P.O. Box 297, 14305. Tel: 716-282-8683; Fax: 716-282-3545. Email: cwniagara@sysr.com. Patricia J. Merino, Mng. Dir.

NIAGARA UNIVERSITY. *Our Lady of Angels Association*, Marian House, 14109-1918. Tel: 716-754-0035; Fax: 716-754-0137. Email: novena@niagara.edu. Web: www.ourladyofangels.net. Deborah Korzak, Dir. of Devel. Development Office for the Congregation of the Mission, Eastern Province. Total Staff 7.

NORTH TONAWANDA. *Shrine of the Infant Jesus* Administered by the Pallottine Fathers. , 3452 Niagara Falls Blvd., P.O. Box 563, 14120-0563. Tel: 716-694-4313; Fax: 716-743-5430.

STELLA NIAGARA. *DeSales Resources and Ministries*, 4421 Lower River Rd., 14144-1001. Tel: 716-754-4948; 800-782-2270; Fax: 716-754-4948. Email: desales@desalesresource.org. Web: www.desalesresource.org. Rev. John Graden, O.S.F.S., Dir.; Joanne Kinney, Admin. Asst.; Darlene Dixon, Business Mgr. Total Staff 3.

WEST SENECA. *St. John Eudes Center*, 36 Flohr Ave., 14224-1818. Tel: 716-825-4319; Fax: 716-825-4376.

Email: eudesctr@parishrenewal.org. Web: www.parishrenewal.org. Mr. Dennis Mahaney, Dir.

Victorious Missionaries, 791 Seneca Creek Rd., 14224. Tel: 716-675-5891. Deacon William W. Willis, Spiritual Dir. A spiritual and social movement for the handicapped and chronically ill.

WILLIAMSVILLE. *400 Mill Street, Inc.* (Formerly Mount St. Mary's Hospital of Niagara Falls) , P.O. Box 275, 14231-0275. Tel: 716-632-2155; Fax: 716-632-0339. Email: mnachreiner@osfwmsv.org. Web: www.wmsvlfranciscans.org.

Annabachmann, Inc. (Formerly St. Francis Geriatric & Healthcare Services, Inc.) , P.O. Box 275, 14231-0275. Tel: 716-632-2155; Fax: 716-632-0339. Email: mnachreiner@osfwmsv.org. Web: www.wmsvlfranciscans.org.

RELIGIOUS INSTITUTES OF MEN REPRESENTED IN THE DIOCESE

For further details refer to the corresponding bracketed number in the Religious Institutes of Men or Women section.

[0810]—*Brothers of Mercy*—F.M.M.
[0330]—*Brothers of the Christian Schools* (New York Prov.)—F.S.C.
[0160]—*Clerics Regular of St. Paul*—C.R.S.P.
[1330]—*Congregation of the Mission* (Eastern Prov.)—C.M.
[0390]—*Consolata Missionaries*—I.M.C.
[0480]—*Conventual Franciscans* (St. Anthony of Padua)—O.F.M.Conv
[0450]—*The Eudists - Congregation of Jesus and Mary*—C.J.M.
[0520]—*Franciscan Friars* (Holy Name Prov.)—O.F.M.
[0690]—*Jesuit Fathers and Brothers* (New York Prov.)—S.J.
[0800]—*Maryknoll* (Buffalo)—M.M.
[0850]—*Missionaries of Africa*—M.Afr.
[1210]—*Missionaries of St. Charles-Scalabrinians*—C.S.
[0910]—*Oblates of Mary Immaculate* (Eastern Prov.)—O.M.I.
[0920]—*Oblates of St. Francis De Sales*—O.S.F.S.
[0270]—*Order of Carmelites*—O.Carm.
[0970]—*Order of Our Lady of Mercy* (Le Roy)—O.deM.
[0430]—*Order of Preachers-Dominicans* (Provs. of St. Joseph; St. Albert the Great)—O.P.
[1010]—*Pauline Fathers*—O.S.P.P.E.
[1040]—*Piarist Fathers*—Sch.P.
[0370]—*Society of St. Columban*—S.S.C.
[0990]—*Society of the Catholic Apostolate* (Annunciation Prov.)
[1060]—*Society of the Precious Blood*—C.P.P.S.
[0560]—*Third Order Regular of St. Francis*—T.O.R.

RELIGIOUS INSTITUTES OF WOMEN REPRESENTED IN THE DIOCESE

[1810]—*Bernadine Franciscan Sisters*—O.S.F.
[0760]—*Daughters of Charity of St. Vincent de Paul*—D.C.
[0810]—*Daughters of the Heart of Mary*—D.H.M.
[0420]—*Discalced Carmelite Nuns*—O.C.D.
[1060]—*Dominican Contemplative Sisters*—O.P.
[1170]—*Felician Sisters*—C.S.S.F.
[1180]—*Franciscan Sisters of Allegany, New York*—O.S.F.
[1470]—*Franciscan Sisters of St. Joseph*—F.S.S.J.
[1280]—*Franciscan Sisters of the Immaculate Conception*—O.S.F.
[1840]—*Grey Nuns of the Sacred Heart*—G.N.S.H.
[2575]—*Institute of the Sisters of Mercy of the Americas*—R.S.M.
[2480]—*Medical Missionaries of Mary*—M.M.M.
[2830]—*Missionary Sisters of Our Lady of Mercy*—M.O.M.
[2880]—*Missionary Sisters of St. Columban*—S.S.C.
[3040]—*Oblate Sisters of Providence*—O.S.P.
[0570]—*Sisters of Charity of Seton Hill*—S.C.
[0630]—*Sisters of Charity of St. Vincent de Paul of Zagreb*—S.V.Z.
[3000]—*Sisters of Notre Dame de Namur* (Ohio Prov.)—S.N.D.deN.
[3070]—*Sisters of Our Lady of Charity*—N.A.U.-O.L
[]—*Sisters of Our Lady of Mercy (Mercedarians)*—S.O.L.M.
[3950]—*Sisters of Saint Mary of Namur*—S.S.M.N.
[4090]—*Sisters of Social Service*—S.S.S.
[1620]—*Sisters of St. Francis of Millvale, PA*—O.S.F.
[1630]—*Sisters of St. Francis of Penance and Christian Charity*—O.S.F.
[1650]—*Sisters of St. Francis of Philadelphia*—O.S.F.
[1660]—*Sisters of St. Francis of the Providence of God*—O.S.F.
[1800]—*Sisters of St. Francis of the Third Order Regular* (Williamsville, NY)—O.S.F.
[3830-06]—*Sisters of St. Joseph* (Buffalo, NY)—S.S.J.
[3830-09]—*Sisters of St. Joseph* (Erie, PA)—S.S.J.
[3830-13]—*Sisters of St. Joseph* (Baden, Pa)—C.S.J.
[3840]—*Sisters of St. Joseph of Carondelet*—C.S.J.
[3658]—*Sisters of the Sacred Heart of Jesus*—S.S.H.J.
[4120]—*Ursuline Sisters of Cleveland*—O.S.U.

DIOCESAN CEMETERIES

CHEEKTOWAGA. *Holy Sepulchre*

GRAND ISLAND. *Assumption*

KENMORE. *Mount Olivet*, 4000 Elmwood Ave., 14217. Tel: 716-873-6500; Fax: 716-873-3247. Email: ccolas@buffalodiocese.org. Web: www.cathcemsbflo.com. Carmen A. Colao, Dir.

LACKAWANNA. *Holy Cross*

LOCKPORT. *Queen of Heaven*

NIAGARA FALLS. *Gate of Heaven*

NECROLOGY

† Beasley, Rev. Msgr. Thomas J., (Retired)—Died June 11, 2003
† Gabalski, Rev. Msgr. John R., Buffalo, NY St. Stanislaus Parish—Died Oct. 9, 2003
† Kreuzer, Rev. Msgr. Gerald J., (Retired)—Died Oct. 27, 2003
† LaRusch, Rev. Msgr. Alton J., (Retired)—Died March 22, 2003
† Stanton, Rev. Msgr. William G.—Died 2003
† Streng, Rev. Msgr. James E., (Retired)—Died May 24, 2003
† Sutherland, Rev. Msgr. William J., 4350 McCullough St., Port Charlotte, FL 33948—Died Aug. 17, 2003
† Hansen, Albert M., Tonawanda, NY St. Francis of Assisi Parish—Died March 23, 2003
† Hughes, Donald R.—Died Feb. 24, 2003
† Pulikoottil, Abraham, (Retired)—Died April 8, 2003

Diocese of Burlington

(Dioecesis Burlingtonensis)

Most Reverend

KENNETH A. ANGELL, D.D.

Bishop of Burlington; ordained May 26, 1956; appointed Auxiliary Bishop of Providence August 9, 1974; consecrated October 7, 1974; Transferred to Bishop of Burlington October 6, 1992; installed November 9, 1992. *Mailing Address: 351 North Ave., P.O. Box 489, Burlington, VT 05402-0489*. Fax: 802-658-0436.

Chancery Office: 351 North Ave., P.O. Box 489, Burlington, VT 05402-0489. Tel: 802-658-6110; Fax: 802-658-0436.

Web: www.vermontcatholic.org

Email: kangell@vermontcatholic.org

ESTABLISHED JULY 29, 1853.

Square Miles 9,135.

Comprises the State of Vermont.

Legal Title: For legal titles of parishes and diocesan institutions, consult the Chancery Office.

STATISTICAL OVERVIEW

Personnel	
Bishop	1
Priests: Diocesan Active in Diocese	65
Priests: Diocesan Active Outside Diocese	2
Priests: Retired, Sick or Absent	47
Number of Diocesan Priests	114
Religious Priests in Diocese	47
Total Priests in Diocese	161
Extern Priests in Diocese	8
Ordinations:	
Transitional Deacons	2
Permanent Deacons in Diocese	41
Total Brothers	16
Total Sisters	184
Parishes	
Parishes	83
With Resident Pastor:	
Resident Diocesan Priests	58
Resident Religious Priests	15
Without Resident Pastor:	
Administered by Priests	10
Missions	41
Pastoral Centers	1
Professional Ministry Personnel:	
Brothers	1
Welfare	
Homes for the Aged	4
Total Assisted	200
Special Centers for Social Services	1
Total Assisted	5,751
Educational	
Diocesan Students in Other Seminaries	9
Total Seminarians	9
Colleges and Universities	2
Total Students	3,139
High Schools, Diocesan and Parish	2
Total Students	618
Elementary Schools, Diocesan and Parish	11
Total Students	1,704
Elementary Schools, Private	4
Total Students	819
Catechesis/Religious Education:	
High School Students	2,687
Elementary Students	8,262
Total Students under Catholic Instruction	17,238
Teachers in the Diocese:	
Sisters	12
Lay Teachers	38
Vital Statistics	
Receptions into the Church:	
Infant Baptism Totals	1,375
Adult Baptism Totals	126
Received into Full Communion	131
First Communions	1,499
Confirmations	1,179
Marriages:	
Catholic	420
Interfaith	185
Total Marriages	605
Deaths	1,526
Total Catholic Population	149,154
Total Population	608,827

Former Bishops—Rt. Revs. LOUIS DE GOESBRIAND, D.D., consecrated Oct. 30, 1853; died Nov. 3, 1899; JOHN S. MICHAUD, D.D., consecrated Coadjutor Bishop with right of succession June 29, 1892; succeeded to Nov. 3, 1899; died Dec. 22, 1908; Most Revs. JOSEPH J. RICE, D.D., consecrated April 14, 1910; died April 1, 1938; MATTHEW F. BRADY, D.D., consecrated Oct. 26, 1938; transferred to Manchester, NH, Nov. 11, 1944; died Sept. 20, 1959; EDWARD F. RYAN, D.D., consecrated Jan. 3, 1945; died Nov. 3, 1956; ROBERT F. JOYCE, D.D. (Retired), consecrated Auxiliary Bishop Oct. 28, 1954; installed Diocesan Bishop Feb. 26, 1957; retired Jan. 24, 1972; died Sept. 2, 1990; JOHN A. MARSHALL, D.D., consecrated and installed January 25, 1972; transferred to Springfield, MA, Dec. 27, 1991; died July 3, 1994.

Vicar General—Rev. WENDELL H. SEARLES, V.G., 351 North Ave., P.O. Box 489, Burlington, 05402-0489. Tel: 802-658-6110; Fax: 802-658-0436.

Vicar for Administration—Rev. WALTER D. MILLER, J.C.D., 351 North Ave., P.O. Box 489, Burlington, 05402-0489. Tel: 802-658-6110; Fax: 802-658-0436.

Vicar for Ministries—Rev. MICHAEL W. DEFORGE, The Catholic Center at UVM, 390 S. Prospect St., Redstone Campus, Burlington, 05401. Tel: 802-862-8403; Fax: 802-865-9480.

Chancery Office—Rev. WALTER D. MILLER, J.C.D., Chancellor, 351 North Ave., P.O. Box 489, Burlington, 05402-0489. Tel: 802-658-6110; Fax: 802-658-0436 Office Hours: Mon.-Fri. 9-12 & 1-5.

Finance Office—Mr. KEVIN J. HEFFERNAN, C.P.A., CFO, 351 North Ave., P.O. Box 489, Burlington, 05402-0489. Tel: 802-658-6110; Fax: 802-658-0436.

Secretary to the Most Rev. Bishop—Rev. WALTER D. MILLER, J.C.D., 351 North Ave., P.O. Box 489, Burlington, 05402-0489. Tel: 802-658-6110.

Office of the Tribunal—351 North Ave., P.O. Box 489, Burlington, 05402-0489. Tel: 802-658-6110; Fax: 802-658-0436.

Judicial Vicar—Rev. WALTER D. MILLER, J.C.D.

Case Director—Mr. TODD THIBAULT.

Judges—Rev. Msgr. JOHN R. MCSWEENEY, J.C.L. (Retired); Rev. THOMAS V. MATTISON.

Auditors—Revs. JOHN J. MCDERMOTT; DANIEL J. JORDAN.

Promoter of Justice—Rev. BERNARD F. DEPEAUX (Retired).

Defenders of the Bond—Revs. ROGER L. CHARBONNEAU; JOHN G. FELTZ; DANIEL J. JORDAN.

Advocates—Revs. RAYMOND A. GIROUX (Retired); PETER A. ROUTHIER.

Notaries—Mr. TODD THIBAULT; Revs. JOHN J. MCDERMOTT; DANIEL J. JORDAN.

Diocesan Administrative Board—Most Rev. KENNETH A. ANGELL, D.D., Chm.; Revs. WENDELL H. SEARLES, V.G.; MICHAEL W. DEFORGE; Sr. SHIRLEY DAVIS, S.S.J.; Mrs. MARY MCCLINTOCK; Mr. MICHAEL J. MITIGUY.

Diocesan Consultors—Rev. Msgr. JOHN R. MCSWEENEY, J.C.L. (Retired); Revs. BERNARD E. GAUDREAU; WENDELL H. SEARLES, V.G.; WALTER D. MILLER, J.C.D.; MAURICE J. ROY; MICHAEL W. DEFORGE; FRANCIS M. HOLLAND; MARCEL R. RAINVILLE, S.S.E.

Deans—Revs. JOHN W. HAMILTON; PIERRE A. LAVALLEE; RICHARD G. LAVALLEY; ROBERT W. LOZINSKI, C.S.C.; STEPHEN J. NICHOLS; ROLAND J. RIVARD; PETER A. ROUTHIER; MAURICE J. ROY; YVON J. ROYER; RONALD SAUNDERS, S.M.; RICHARD W. TINNEY; FREDERICK E. MCLACHLAN, S.S.E.

Canon 1742 Panel of Pastors—Revs. MICHAEL E. AUGUSTINOWITZ; ROGER L. CHARBONNEAU; DONALD J. RAVEY.

Diocesan Offices and Directors

Apostolate for the Deaf—VACANT.

Apostolate for the Handicapped—Office of Catholic Formation, Special Needs Ministry, 351 North Ave., P.O. Box 489, Burlington, 05402-0489. Tel: 802-658-6110.

Bishop's Commission on Women—VACANT, Chm., 351 North Ave., P.O. Box 489, Burlington, 05402-0489. Tel: 802-658-6110.

Bishop's Fund Office—Mr. MARTIN A. HOAK, 351 North Ave., P.O. Box 489, Burlington, 05402-0489. Tel: 802-658-6110.

The Blue Army (World Apostolate of Fatima)—Mrs. CLAIRETTE BERARD, Pres., 302 Colchester Rd., Essex Junction, 05452. Tel: 802-878-3214.

Scouting Program—Deacon IVAN O. HAWK III, Mailing Address, 81 Brook Dr., Burlington, 05401. Tel: 802-863-8163.

Building Commission—Mr. RICHARD WIEMANN, Chm., Chancery Office, 351 North Ave., P.O. Box 489, Burlington, 05402-0489. Tel: 802-658-6110.

Vermont Catholic Charities, Inc.—Mrs. MARY M. MCNAMARA, Dir., Central Office, 351 North Ave., P.O. Box 489, Burlington, 05402-0489. Tel: 802-658-6110; Fax: 802-860-0451. Rutland Office, 24 1/2 Center St., Rutland, 05701. Tel: 802-773-3379.

Campaign for Human Development—Mrs. MARY M. MCNAMARA, Dir., 351 North Ave., P.O. Box 489, Burlington, 05402-0489. Tel: 802-658-6110; Fax: 802-860-0451.

Catholic Daughters of The Americas—Rev. PATRICK J. FORMAN, Chap., St. John the Evangelist Rectory, 49 Winter St., St. Johnsbury, 05819-2144. Tel: 802-748-8129.

Catholic Relief Services—Mrs. MARY M. MCNAMARA, 351 North Ave., P.O. Box 489, Burlington, 05402-0489. Tel: 802-658-6110; Fax: 802-860-0451.

Catholic Women, Vermont Council of—Rev. GEORGE H. DUPUIS, St. Margaret Mary Rectory, 3938 Rte. 7A, Arlington, 05250-0039. Tel: 802-375-2849.

Censor Librorum—Rev. WALTER D. MILLER, J.C.D.,

351 North Ave., P.O. Box 489, Burlington, 05402-0489. Tel: 802-658-6110.

Charismatic Renewal—Rev. LANCE W. HARLOW, St. Anthony Parish, P.O. Box 63, Church St., Bethel, 05032. Tel: 802-234-9916.

Chief Administrator for Catholic Formation—Sr. MARIANNE READ, R.S.M., M.Ed., C.A.E.S., Office of Catholic Formation, 351 North Ave., P.O. Box 489, Burlington, 05402-0489. Tel: 802-658-6110.

Diocesan Archives—Mr. DAVID BLOW, 351 North Ave., P.O. Box 489, Burlington, 05402-0489. Tel: 802-658-6110.

Diocesan Coordinator of the Vietnamese Ministry—Rev. ROBERT B. KOLAKOWSKI, The Catholic Center at U.V.M., 390 S. Prospect St., Redstone Campus, Burlington, 05401-3534. Tel: 802-862-8403.

Office of Communications—Ms. GLORIA J. GIBSON, Dir., 351 North Ave., P.O. Box 489, Burlington, 05402-0489. Tel: 802-658-6110.

Daughters of Isabella—Rev. JOHN M. MILANESE, Chap., Sts. Donatian & Rogatian Rectory, 25 S. Pleasant St., Randolph, 05060. Tel: 802-728-3227.

Diocesan Board of Vicars—

Vicar General—Rev. WENDELL H. SEARLES, V.G.

Vicar for Administration—Rev. WALTER D. MILLER, J.C.D.

Vicar for Ministries—Rev. MICHAEL W. DEFORGE.

Chief Administrator for Catholic Formation—Sr. MARIANNE READ, R.S.M., M.Ed., C.A.E.S.

Chief Financial Officer—Mr. KEVIN J. HEFFERNAN, C.P.A.

Diocesan Cemeteries—Mr. PETER WELLS, Chancery Office, 351 North Ave., P.O. Box 489, Burlington, 05402-0489. Tel: 802-658-6110; Mr. PATRICK JENNINGS, Chm., 45 Morrill Dr., Burlington, 05401. Tel: 802-864-5071. Resurrection Park, South Burlington, 05403. Tel: 802-862-1530. St. Joseph's Cemetery, Burlington, 05401.

Diocesan Finance Council—Ex Officio Members: Most Rev. KENNETH A. ANGELL, D.D.; Mr. KEVIN J. HEFFERNAN, C.P.A., CFO & Chm. Board Members: Mr. RICHARD COUTURE, Chm.; Mr. JAMES STROUSE; Mr. MARK KELLEY; Ms. LAURIE DAWSON.

Diocesan Insurance Office—Mr. PETER WELLS, Dir., 351 North Ave., P.O. Box 489, Burlington, 05402-0489. Tel: 802-658-6110.

Ecumenical Commission—Mr. JAMES G. CASE, 1818 Richmond Rd., Hinesburg, 05461.

Education, Board of—Sr. ROSEMARIE RYAN, S.N.D., Chm., 57 Jackson Ave., Rutland, 05701.

Evangelization—Rev. JOSEPH T. SULLIVAN, Dir., P.O. Box 18, Fairfield, 05455. Tel: 802-827-3203.

Office of Marriage, Family Life/Respect Life—Mrs. MARGARET WEHRUNG, P.O. Box 225, Bennington, 05201-0225. Tel: 802-447-5718.

Engaged Encounter—Rev. RICHARD M. MYHALYK, S.S.E. Coordinating Couple: ANDREA PEDEN; MICHAEL PEDEN, 351 North Ave., P.O. Box 489, Burlington, 05402-0489. Tel: 802-658-6110.

Finance Office—Mr. KEVIN J. HEFFERNAN, C.P.A., CFO, 351 North Ave., P.O. Box 489, Burlington, 05402-0489. Tel: 802-658-6110.

Liturgical Commission—Rev. PETER A. ROUTHIER, St. Monica, 79 Summer St., Barre, 05641. Tel: 802-479-3253.

Holy Childhood Association—Rev. FRANCIS M. HOLLAND, 351 North Ave., P.O. Box 489, Burlington, 05402-0489. Tel: 802-658-6110.

House of Discernment—Rev. MICHAEL W. DEFORGE, Dir., The Catholic Center at UVM, 390 S. Prospect St., Redstone Campus, Burlington, 05401. Tel: 802-862-8403; Fax: 802-865-9480.

Knights of Columbus—Rev. JUSTIN J. BAKER, State Chap., St. Mary Parish, 326 College St., Middlebury, 05753. Tel: 802-388-2943.

State Friar—Rev. JOHN M. MILANESE, 25 S. Pleasant St., Randolph, 05060. Tel: 802-728-3227.

Leap—Rev. MARCEL R. RAINVILLE, S.S.E., St. Michael's College, Winooski Park, Colchester, 05439. Tel: 802-654-2332.

Marriage Encounter, Vermont—JOHN AUBIN; SHEILA AUBIN, P.O. Box 301, West Hartford, 05084. Tel: 802-295-5484.

Diocesan Master of Ceremonies—Rev. WALTER D. MILLER, J.C.D., 351 North Ave., P.O. Box 489, Burlington, 05402-0489. Tel: 802-658-6110; Fax: 802-658-0436.

Office of Continuing Education for Clergy—Rev. BENEDICT KIELY, Dir., St. John the Baptist Parish, P.O. Box 563, Enosburg Falls, 05450. Tel: 802-933-4464; Fax: 802-933-4225.

Misconduct Review Board—KEVIN SCULLY, Chm.; GAIL ENGELS; Revs. STEPHEN W. HORNAT, S.S.E.; JOHN J. MCDERMOTT; Dr. WILLIAM CUNNINGHAM; MARGARET FOSTER.

Victim Assistance Committee—Mrs. MARY M. MCNAMARA. Email: mmcnamara@vermontcatholic.org; Sr. SUSAN FORTIER, R.S.M.. Email: sfortier@vermontcatholic.org; ELLIE CALABRESE. Email: ecalabrese@vermontcatholic.org; Rev. WENDELL H. SEARLES, V.G.. Email: wsearles@vermontcatholic.orgTel: 802-658-6110.

National Catholic Conference for Interracial Justice—Rev. WALTER D. MILLER, J.C.D., Diocesan Coord., 351 North Ave., P.O. Box 489, Burlington, 05402-0489. Tel: 802-658-6110; Fax: 802-658-0436.

National Shrine of the Immaculate Conception, Washington—Rev. ROGER L. CHARBONNEAU, Holy Cross Rectory, 416 Church Rd., Colchester, 05446. Tel: 802-863-3002.

Office of Catholic Formation—Mr. CHRISTOPHER FOUNTAIN, 351 North Ave., P.O. Box 489, Burlington, 05402-0489.

Youth Ministry—RICHARD P. O'DONNELL.

Office of Diocesan Pastoral Planning—Rev. JOHN J. MCDERMOTT, Dir., St. Thomas Parish, P.O. Box 3, Underhill Center, 05490. Tel: 802-899-4632.

Office of Ministerial Formation and Permanent Diaconate—Rev. BERNARD E. GAUDREAU, Dir., Blessed Sacrament Rectory, Mountain Rd., P.O. Box 27, Stowe, 05672. Tel: 802-253-7536; Fax: 802-253-4445.

Diocesan Presbyteral Council—Members Ex Officio: Most Rev. KENNETH A. ANGELL, D.D.; Revs. WENDELL H. SEARLES, V.G.; WALTER D. MILLER, J.C.D.; MICHAEL W. DEFORGE; BERNARD E. GAUDREAU. Elected Members: Rev. Msgr. JOHN R. MCSWEENEY, J.C.L. (Retired); Revs. MICHAEL E. AUGUSTINOWITZ; WILFRED ANDRE HOULE; ROBERT W. LOZINSKI, C.S.C.; ROGER L. CHARBONNEAU; PETER A. ROUTHIER; STANLEY DERESIENSKI, S.S.E.; ALBERT G. BALTZ; LANCE W. HARLOW; MAURICE J. ROY; DONALD J. RAVEY; FRANCIS M. HOLLAND; DANIEL J. RUPP; MARCEL R. RAINVILLE, S.S.E.

Newspaper—Most Rev. KENNETH A. ANGELL, D.D., Publisher; Mrs. PATRICIA GORE, Editor, Editorial & Business Office, 351 North Ave., P.O. Box 489, Burlington, 05402-0489. Tel: 802-658-6110; Fax: 802-658-3866. "The Vermont Catholic Tribune"

Priests' Benefit Fund—Rev. FRANCIS R. PRIVE, Chm., 351 North Ave., P.O. Box 489, Burlington, 05402-0489. Tel: 802-658-6110.

Prison Ministry—Deacon STEPHEN J. RATTE, 351 North Ave., P.O. Box 489, Burlington, 05402-0489. Tel: 802-658-6110.

Propagation of the Faith—Rev. FRANCIS M. HOLLAND, 351 North Ave., P.O. Box 489, Burlington, 05402-0489. Tel: 802-658-6110.

Rural Life—Mrs. JANE CLIFFORD, 6147 Rte. 116, Starksboro, 05487. Tel: 802-453-3810.

Office of Catholic Schools—Sisters MARIANNE READ, R.S.M., M.Ed., C.A.E.S., Supt. of Schools; SHIRLEY DAVIS, S.S.J., Asst. Supt., 351 North Ave., P.O. Box 489, Burlington, 05402-0489. Tel: 802-658-6110; Fax: 802-658-0436.

Diocesan Coordinator of the Retirement Fund—Sr. RUTH RAVEY, R.S.M., 50 Fletcher Pl., Burlington, 05401. Tel: 802-658-5494.

Senate of Sisters—VACANT.

Vermont Cursillo—Rev. STEPHEN J. NICHOLS, St. Elizabeth, P.O. Box 141, Lyndonville, 05851. Tel: 802-626-5267.

Lay Director—DAN DAIGLER, P.O. Box 91, West Dummerston, 05357. Tel: 802-257-7395.

Vocations and Seminarians—Rev. MICHAEL W. DEFORGE, Dir., The Catholic Center at UVM, 390 South Prospect St., Redstone Campus, Burlington, 05401. Tel: 802-862-8403; Fax: 802-865-9480.

CLERGY, PARISHES, MISSIONS AND PAROCHIAL SCHOOLS

CITY OF BURLINGTON
(CHITTENDEN COUNTY)

1—CATHEDRAL OF THE IMMACULATE CONCEPTION (1830), Rev. Thomas J. Ball, Rector; Deacon William Glinka.
Res.: 20 Pine St., 05401. Tel: 802-658-4333.
Catechesis/Religious Program—Tel: 802-862-3258. JoAnn Lafayette, D.R.E. Students 28.

2—ST. ANTHONY'S (1903), Rev. Roland J. Rivard; Deacon Louis A. Meunier.
Res.: 305 Flynn Ave., 05401. Tel: 802-864-0478.

3—CHRIST THE KING (1940), Rev. Roland J. Rivard; Deacon Timm Taylor.
Res.: 136 Locust St., 05401-4849. Tel: 802-862-5784; Fax: 802-651-3021.
School—Tel: 802-862-6696; Fax: 802-658-6553. Lay Teachers 17; Students 205.
Catechesis/Religious Program—Students 86.

4—ST. JOSEPH'S (1850), [CEM] Revs. Stephen W. Hornat, S.S.E.; Raymond J. Doherty, S.S.E.
Res.: 85 Elmwood Ave., 05401. Tel: 802-863-2388; Fax: 802-863-2380.
School—Tel: 802-864-5623; Fax: 802-860-2627. Lay Teachers 16; Students 167.
Catechesis/Religious Program—Tel: 802-862-5102. Monica Morano-Aurigemma, D.R.E. Students 59.

5—ST. MARK'S (1940), Revs. Francis M. Holland; Peter P. O'Leary; Daniel J. Jordan; Deacon Eugene Herrick.
Res.: 1251 North Ave., 05401. Tel: 802-864-7686; Fax: 802-651-9391.
Catechesis/Religious Program—Students 255.
Convent—*Franciscan Sisters of the Atonement*, 21 Dodds Ct., 05401. Tel: 802-862-8288. Sr. Frances Flynn, S.A., Coord.

OUTSIDE THE CITY OF BURLINGTON

ALBURG, GRAND ISLE CO., ST. AMADEUS (1886), [CEM 2] Rev. Maurice U. Boucher, S.S.E.
Res.: P.O. Box 49, 05440. Tel: 802-796-3481; Fax: 802-796-3481.
Catechesis/Religious Program—Aline Wahburn, D.R.E. Students 92.
Mission—*St. Joseph* Isle La Motte, Grand Isle Co.
Chapel—*Isle La Motte, St. Anne's Shrine*

ARLINGTON, BENNINGTON CO., ST. MARGARET MARY (1946), [CEM] Rev. George H. Dupuis.
Res.: 3938 Route 7A, Box 39, 05250-0039. Tel: 802-375-2849; Fax: 802-375-2849.
Catechesis/Religious Program—Students 56.

BARRE, WASHINGTON CO., ST. MONICA (1892), Revs. Peter A. Routhier; Henry P. Furman; Deacons Fernand R. Rivard; David Bisson; Daniel Pudvah.
Res.: 79 Summer St., 05641. Tel: 802-479-3253; Fax: 802-479-3154.
School—Tel: 802-476-5015; Fax: 802-476-0861. Lay Teachers 14; Students 166.
Catechesis/Religious Program—Tel: 802-476-4020; Fax: 802-479-3154. Marybeth Hebert, D.R.E. Students 335.

BARTON, ORLEANS CO., CONVERSION OF ST. PAUL (1893), [CEM] Rev. Daniel J. Rupp, Admin.
Res.: 85 St. Paul Lane, 05822. Tel: 802-525-3711; Fax: 802-525-1292.
School—Tel: 802-525-6578. Lay Teachers 5; Students 62.
Catechesis/Religious Program—Students 105.

BELLOWS FALLS, WINDHAM CO.

1—ST. CHARLES (1871), [CEM] Rev. Ernest F. Passero, S.J.
Res.: 31A Cherry Hill St., 05101. Tel: 802-463-3128; Fax: 802-463-8179.
Catechesis/Religious Program—Students 53.

2—SACRED HEART (1909), [CEM] Rev. Felix J. Reczek, O.F.M., Admin.; Deacon John Blicharz.
Res.: 39 Green St., 05101. Tel: 802-463-4110.
Catechesis/Religious Program—Students 8.

BENNINGTON, BENNINGTON CO., SACRED HEART ST. FRANCIS DE SALES (1995), Revs. Robert W. Lozinski, C.S.C.; Vincent J. Coppola, C.S.C. In Res., Rev. Douglas W. Hawkins, C.S.C. (Retired).
Parish Office—238 W. Main St., 05201. Tel: 802-442-3141; Fax: 802-442-3142.
School—*Sacred Heart School*, 307 School St., 05201. Tel: 802-442-2446; Fax: 802-442-3584. Mr. David B. Estes, Prin. Lay Teachers 10; Students 181.
Catechesis/Religious Program—Tel: 802-447-0223; Fax: 802-442-3142. Janet Lucy, D.R.E. Students 152.
Mission—*Our Lady of Lourdes* North Pownal, Bennington Co.

BETHEL, WINDSOR CO., ST. ANTHONY (1912), Rev. Lance W. Harlow, Admin.
Res.: P.O. Box 63, Church St., 05032. Tel: 802-234-9916; Fax: 802-234-9916.
Catechesis/Religious Program—Tel: 802-234-9522. Rosemary Brown, D.R.E. Students 27.
Mission—*St. Elizabeth* Rochester, Windsor Co.

BRADFORD, ORANGE CO., OUR LADY OF PERPETUAL HELP (1945), Rev. Philip R. LaMothe; Deacon Kelly Fitzpatrick.
Res.: 113 Upper Plain, 05033. Tel: 802-222-5268; Fax: 802-222-9049.
Catechesis/Religious Program—Students 72.
Mission—*St. Francis of Assisi* Norwich, Windsor Co.
Mission—*St. Eugene* Wells River, Orange Co.
Mission—*Our Lady of Light* South Strafford, Orange Co.

BRANDON, RUTLAND CO., ST. MARY'S (1867), [CEM 2] Rev. Albert G. Baltz; Deacon Gary Griffin.
Res.: 38 Carver St., 05733. Tel: 802-247-6351; Fax: 802-247-6396.
Catechesis/Religious Program—Students 84.
Mission—*St. Agnes* Leicester, Addison Co.

BRATTLEBORO, WINDHAM CO., ST. MICHAEL (1855), [CEM] Rev. Stanley Deresienski, S.S.E. In Res., Rev. Francis X. McMahon, S.S.E. (Retired).

Res.: 47 Walnut St., 05301. Tel: 802-257-5101; 802-254-5229; Fax: 802-257-5102.
School—Tel: 802-254-5666; Fax: 802-254-5229. Mr. Frank J. Vara, Prin. Lay Teachers 23; Students 250.
Catechesis/Religious Program—Students 251.
Convent—77 Grove St., 05301. Tel: 802-254-9431.

Bristol, Addison Co., St. Ambrose (1893), [CEM] Rev. Pierre A. LaVallee.
Res.: 11 School St., 05443. Tel: 802-453-2488; Fax: 802-453-7712.
Catechesis/Religious Program—Students 103.

Cambridge, Lamoille Co., St. Mary (1914), Rev. John J. McDermott.
P.O. Box 129, 05444. Tel: 802-644-5073; Fax: 802-644-2546.
Catechesis/Religious Program—Tel: 802-899-1005. Sharon Hallman, D.R.E. Students 61.

Canaan, Essex Co., Assumption of the Blessed Virgin Mary (1950), [CEM] Revs. Daniel R. Deveau, Pastor; Craig Cheney.
Res.: P.O. Box 176, Beecher Falls, 05902. Tel: 603-246-8829; Fax: 603-246-7167.
Catechesis/Religious Program—Students 46.

Castleton, Rutland Co., St. John the Baptist (1899), Rev. Charles R. Danielson.
Res.: P.O. Box 128, 05735. Tel: 802-468-5706; Fax: 802-468-2777.
Catechesis/Religious Program—Tel: 802-468-2155. Tina Rampone, D.R.E. Students 70.

Charlotte, Chittenden Co., Our Lady of Mount Carmel (1858), [CEM] Rev. David Cray, S.S.E.
Res.: P.O. Box 158, 2894 Spear St., 05445. Tel: 802-425-2637.
Catechesis/Religious Program—Students 110.

Chester, Windsor Co., St. Joseph (1946), Rev. Raymond A. Fournier, S.M.
Res.: 96 S. Main St., P.O. Box 1129, 05143. Tel: 802-875-2610; Fax: 802-875-2745.
Catechesis/Religious Program—Students 41.
Station—*St. Joseph Chapel* Londonderry.

Chittenden, Rutland Co., St. Robert (1965), Closed., For inquiries for parish records please see St. Alphonsus Liguori, Pittsford.

Colchester, Chittenden Co.
1—Holy Cross (1950), [CEM] Rev. Roger L. Charbonneau; Deacon Ivan O. Hawk III.
Res.: 416 Church Rd., 05446. Tel: 802-863-3002; Fax: 802-862-5687.
Catechesis/Religious Program—Peggy Hawk, D.R.E. Students 243.
2—Our Lady of Grace (1966), Rev. Jay C. Haskin.
Res.: 800 Main St., 05446. Tel: 802-878-5987; Fax: 802-878-9308.
Catechesis/Religious Program—Students 253.

Derby Line, Orleans Co., St. Edward (1946), [CEM] Rev. Yvon J. Royer, Admin.; Deacon John P.E. Gratton.
Res.: 250 Main St., P.O. Box 397, 05830. Tel: 802-873-3522; Fax: 802-873-3299.
Catechesis/Religious Program—Students 176.
Mission—*St. Benedict Labre* West Charleston, Orleans Co.

East Dorset, Bennington Co., St. Jerome (1868), Closed., See St. Paul's, Manchester.

Enosburg Falls, Franklin Co., St. John the Baptist (1874), [CEM] Rev. Benedict Kiely, Admin.
Res.: P.O. Box 563, 05450. Tel: 802-933-4464; Fax: 802-933-4225.
Catechesis/Religious Program—Students 138.

Essex Center, Chittenden Co., St. Pius X (1957), Rev. William P. Giroux.
Res.: 20 Jericho Rd., Essex Junction, 05452-2707. Tel: 802-878-5997; Fax: 802-878-7793.
Catechesis/Religious Program—Tel: 802-878-1182. Gail Tisseur, D.R.E. Students 359.

Essex Junction, Chittenden Co.
1—Holy Family (1893), [CEM] Rev. Charles H. Ranges, S.S.E.
Res.: 4 Prospect St., 05452. Tel: 802-878-5331; Fax: 802-878-5332.
Catechesis/Religious Program—Tel: 802-878-5331, Ext. 202. John McMahon, D.R.E. Students 180.
2—St. Lawrence, Martyr (1968), Rev. Charles H. Ranges, S.S.E.
Res.: 4 Prospect St., 05452. Tel: 802-878-5331; Fax: 802-878-5332.
Catechesis/Religious Program—Students 80.

Fair Haven, Rutland Co., Our Lady of Seven Dolors (1866), [CEM] Rev. Richard W. Tinney.
Res.: 10 Washington St., 05743. Tel: 802-265-3135.
Catechesis/Religious Program—Tel: 802-265-8049. Claudia Stacey, D.R.E. Students 110.
Mission—*St. Matthew of Avalon* West Castleton, Rutland Co.
Mission—*St. Frances Cabrini* West Pawlet, Rutland Co. 05775.

Fairfax, Franklin Co., St. Luke (1943), [CEM] Rev. Francis E. Connors; Deacon Stephen J. Ratte.
Res.: 17 Huntville Rd., P.O. Box 7, 05454. Tel: 802-849-6205; Fax: 802-849-6078.
Catechesis/Religious Program—Students 480.
Mission—*Ascension* Georgia, Franklin Co.

Fairfield, Franklin Co., St. Patrick (1858), [CEM] Rev. Joseph T. Sullivan.
Res.: P.O. Box 18, 05455. Tel: 802-827-3203; Fax: 802-827-9840.
Catechesis/Religious Program—Students 122.
Mission—*St. Anthony-St. George* East Fairfield, Franklin Co.

Graniteville, Washington Co., St. Sylvester (1895), [CEM] Rev. Donald J. Roy.
Res.: 217 Church Hill Rd., 05654. Tel: 802-476-3913; Fax: 802-476-1332.
Catechesis/Religious Program—Students 51.
Mission—*St. Cecilia & St. Frances Cabrini* East Barre, Washington Co.

Hardwick, Caledonia Co., St. Norbert (1902), [CEM 2] Rev. Michael E. Augustinowitz.
Mailing Address: 193 S. Main St., P.O. Box 496, 05843.
Res.: 193 S. Main St., 05843. Tel: 802-472-5544; Fax: 802-472-5543.
Catechesis/Religious Program—Students 147.
Mission—*St. Michael* Greensboro Bend, Orleans Co.
Mission—*Our Lady of Fatima* Craftsbury, Orleans Co.

Highgate Center, Franklin Co., St. Louis (1886), [CEM 2] Rev. John J. Meagher, S.S.E.
Mailing Address: P.O. Box 78, 05459. Tel: 802-868-4517; Fax: 802-868-4262.
Res.: 65 Canada St., Swanton 05488. Tel: 802-862-4502.
Catechesis/Religious Program—Students 114.

Hinesburg, Chittenden Co., St. Jude the Apostle (1943), Rev. David Cray, S.S.E.
Res.: P.O. Box 69, 05461-0069. Tel: 802-482-2290; Fax: 802-482-5263.
Catechesis/Religious Program—Students 143.

Island Pond, Essex Co., St. James the Greater (1871), [CEM] Rev. William P. Morgan, Admin.
Res.: P.O. Box 407, 05846. Tel: 802-723-4312; Fax: 802-723-4275.
Catechesis/Religious Program—Students 19.
Mission—*St. Bernard* Norton, Essex Co.

Ludlow, Windsor Co., Annunciation of the Blessed Virgin Mary (1885), Revs. George A. Paulin; William R. Beaudin.
Res.: 7 Depot St., 05149. Tel: 802-228-3451; Fax: 802-228-7012.
Catechesis/Religious Program—Students 75.
Mission—*Holy Name of Mary* Proctorsville, Windsor Co.

Lyndonville, Caledonia Co., St. Elizabeth (1891), [CEM] Rev. Stephen J. Nichols; Deacon Alfred Toborg.
Res.: 630 Hill St., P.O. Box 141, 05851-0141. Tel: 802-626-5267; Fax: 802-626-3924.
Catechesis/Religious Program—Students 177.
Mission—*Our Lady Queen of Peace* Danville, Caledonia Co.

Manchester Center, Bennington Co., St. Paul's (1896), Rev. John Whalen, Admin.; Deacon Peter Putis.
Res.: 398 Bonnet St., 05255. Tel: 802-362-1380; Fax: 802-366-1168.
Catechesis/Religious Program—Students 98.
Mission—*St. Jerome* East Dorset, Bennington Co.
Mission—*Holy Trinity* Danby, Rutland Co.

Middlebury, Addison Co., Assumption of the Blessed Virgin Mary (1855), [CEM] Rev. Justin J. Baker, Admin.
Res.: 326 College St., 05753. Tel: 802-388-2943; Fax: 802-388-2943.
School—*St. Mary's*, 86 Shannon St., 05753. Tel: 802-388-8392. Lay Teachers 8; Students 93.
Catechesis/Religious Program—Students 171.
Mission—*St. Bernadette* Bridport, Addison Co.
Mission—*St. Genevieve* Shoreham, Addison Co. 05770.

Middletown Springs, Rutland Co., St. Anne (1963), Rev. Adam J. Krempa; Deacon Richard Perkins; Rev. Robert J. Moran.
Res.: P.O. Box 1098, 05757.
Catechesis/Religious Program—Students 3.
Mission—*St. Frances Cabrini* West Pawlet, Rutland Co.

Milton, Chittenden Co., St. Ann (1866), [CEM] Rev. John G. Feltz.
Res.: P.O. Box 1, 05468. Tel: 802-893-2487; Fax: 802-893-3701.
Catechesis/Religious Program—Tel: 802-893-8482. Angela Barsalow, D.R.E. Students 252.

Montpelier, Washington Co., St. Augustine (1850), [CEM] Rev. Thomas L. Mosher; Deacons Regis E. Cummings; Walter Brenneman Jr.
Res.: 16 Barre St., 05602. Tel: 802-223-5285; Fax: 802-223-3621.
School—*St. Michael School*, 46 Barre St., 05602. Tel: 802-223-6430; Fax: 802-229-4827. Sisters 1; Lay Teachers 10; Students 130.
Catechesis/Religious Program—Students 175.
Mission—*North American Martyrs* (1963), Marshfield, Washington Co.

Morrisville, Lamoille Co., Holy Cross (1913), [CEM] Rev. Paul C. Houde; Deacon Thomas Cooney.
Res.: P.O. Box 339, 05661. Tel: 802-888-3318; Fax: 802-888-6177.
Catechesis/Religious Program—Students 64.
Mission—*St. John the Apostle* Johnson, Lamoille Co.
Mission—*St. Gabriel* Eden, Lamoille Co.
Mission—*St. Teresa* Hyde Park, Lamoille Co.

Newport, Orleans Co., St. Mary Star of the Sea (1873), [CEM] Revs. Yvon J. Royer; Lawrence P. Ridgley.
Res.: 191 Clermont Ter., 05855. Tel: 802-334-5066; Fax: 802-334-5067.
Catechesis/Religious Program—Tel: 802-334-6240. Dennis De La Bruere, D.R.E.; Aline De La Bruere, D.R.E. Students 90.

North Bennington, Bennington Co., St. John the Baptist (1885), [CEM] Deacon Edward R. Howard.
Res.: 3-5 Houghton St., P.O. Box 219, 05257. Tel: 802-447-7504; Fax: 802-442-6620.
Catechesis/Religious Program—Eileen M. Flynn, D.R.E. Students 117.

North Troy, Orleans Co., St. Vincent de Paul (1939), [CEM] Revs. Joseph H. Blattner, Admin.; Jerome Mercure, Temp. Admin.
Res.: Pleasant St., 05859. Tel: 802-988-2608.
Catechesis/Religious Program—Students 19.

Northfield, Washington Co., St. John the Evangelist (1865), [CEM] Rev. Kevin E. Rooney.
Res.: 206 Vine St., 05663. Tel: 802-485-8313; Fax: 802-485-3043.
Catechesis/Religious Program—Marguerite Moore, D.R.E. Students 109.
Mission—*St. Edward* Williamstown, Orange Co.

Orleans, Orleans Co., St. Theresa of Child Jesus (1942), [CEM 2] Rev. Daniel J. Rupp.
Res.: 5 Willoughby Ave., 05860. Tel: 802-754-6049.
Mission—*St. John Vianney* Irasburg, Orleans Co.

Orwell, Addison Co., St. Paul (1886), [CEM] Rev. Charles R. Danielson.
Res.: P.O. Box 128, Castleton, 05735. Tel: 802-468-5706.
Catechesis/Religious Program—Tel: 802-948-2408. Regina Charron, D.R.E. Students 20.

Pittsford, Rutland Co., St. Alphonsus Liguori (1893), [CEM] Rev. James A. Lawrence.
Res.: 2918 U.S. Rte. 7, 05763-9499. Tel: 802-483-2301; Fax: 802-483-2136.
Catechesis/Religious Program—Lisa Adamsen, D.R.E. Students 94.
Mission—*St. Robert* Chittenden, Rutland Co.

Poultney, Rutland Co., St. Raphael (1884), [CEM] Rev. Adam J. Krempa.
Res.: 21 E. Main St., 05764-1107. Tel: 802-287-5703.
Catechesis/Religious Program—Students 46.

Proctor, Rutland Co., St. Dominic (1888), [CEM] Rev. Joseph Romano.
Res.: 45 South St., 05765. Tel: 802-459-2221.
Catechesis/Religious Program—Tel: 802-459-2122. Jan Horner, D.R.E. Students 67.

Putney, Windham Co., Our Lady of Mercy (1931), Revs. John T. Scully, S.S.E.; Frederick E. McLachlan, S.S.E. In Res., Rev. James R. Coombs, S.S.E. (Retired).
Res.: 52 Old Depot Rd., P.O. Box 246, 05346. Tel: 802-387-5861; Fax: 802-387-5968.
Catechesis/Religious Program—Students 27.
Mission—*St. Edmund of Canterbury* Saxtons River, Windham Co.
Mission—*Chapel of the Snows* Stratton Mountain, Windham Co.
Mission—*Our Lady of the Valley* Townshend, Windham Co.
Mission—*Our Lady of Hope* Wardsboro, Windham Co.

Randolph, Orange Co., SS. Donatian and Rogatian (1903), [CEM] Rev. John M. Milanese.
Res.: 25 S. Pleasant St., P.O. Box 428, 05060. Tel: 802-728-3227; Fax: 802-728-3570.
Catechesis/Religious Program—Students 30.

Readsboro, Bennington Co., St. Joachim (1895), Rev. Joseph H. Tate.
Res.: 342 Tunnel St., 05350-9738. Tel: 802-423-5267; 802-423-9961; Fax: 802-423-5267.
Catechesis/Religious Program—Students 68.
Mission—*St. John Bosco* Stamford, Bennington Co.

Richford, Franklin Co., All Saints (1899), [CEM] Rev. Francis C. Eksterowicz; Deacons Clifford Chagnon; Jon Ramey.
Res.: 152 Main St., 05476. Tel: 802-848-7741; Fax: 802-848-3150.
Catechesis/Religious Program—Students 135.
Mission—*Our Lady of Lourdes* East Berkshire, Franklin Co.
Mission—*St. Isidore* Montgomery Center, Franklin Co.

Richmond, Chittenden Co., Our Lady of the Holy

ROSARY (1860), [CEM 2] Rev. Ronald H. Benoit.
Res.: 64 W. Main St., P.O. Box 243, 05477. Tel: 802-434-2521.
Catechesis/Religious Program—Students 140.

RUTLAND, RUTLAND CO.
1—CHRIST THE KING (1907), Revs. Reid C. Mayo; Thomas V. Mattison.
Res.: 66 S. Main St., 05701. Tel: 802-773-6820; Fax: 802-773-6820.
School—Tel: 802-773-6820, Ext. 117. Sisters 2; Lay Teachers 26; Students 298.
Catechesis/Religious Program—Students 183.
2—IMMACULATE HEART OF MARY (1869), [CEM] Revs. Francis R. Prive; Paul Sackerch.
Res.: 18 Lincoln Ave., 05701. Tel: 802-775-0846; Fax: 802-775-9640.
Catechesis/Religious Program—Tel: 802-775-0845. Ciny Tuomisto, D.R.E. Students 169.
3—ST. PETER (1855), [CEM] Revs. Wilfred Andre Houle; John J. Herbert; Bro. James Moran, S.J.
Res.: 134 Convent Ave., 05701. Tel: 802-775-1994; Fax: 802-775-0178.
Catechesis/Religious Program—Students 155.

ST. ALBANS BAY, OUR LADY OF THE LAKE, Closed., For inquiries for parish records, please contact the chancery office.

ST. ALBANS, FRANKLIN CO.
1—HOLY ANGELS (1872), [CEM] Revs. Maurice J. Roy; David Kiyingi.
Res.: 246 Lake St., 05478. Tel: 802-524-2585; Fax: 802-524-2586.
Catechesis/Religious Program—Students 343.
2—IMMACULATE CONCEPTION (1847), [CEM] Rev. Leonidas B. Laroche; Deacon John Rixon.
Res.: 45 Fairfield St., 05478. Tel: 802-527-7775; Fax: 802-527-1667.
Catechesis/Religious Program—Tel: 802-524-9416; 280--. Donna Corrigan, D.R.E. Students 172.

ST. JOHNSBURY, CALEDONIA CO., ST. JOHN THE EVANGELIST (1896), [CEM] Rev. Patrick J. Forman; Deacons Bruce Burk; Raymond J. Desilets; Bernier L. Mayo; William J. Brown III.
Res.: 49 Winter St., 05819. Tel: 802-748-8129; Fax: 802-748-7863.
Catechesis/Religious Program—Tel: 802-748-8038 (PreK-8). Marie Hagan, D.R.E. (PreK-8); Debra Priest, D.R.E. (High School). Students 133.
Mission—St. Theresa Gilman, Essex Co.
Mission—St. Leo Lunenburg, Essex Co.

SHELBURNE, CHITTENDEN CO., ST. CATHERINE OF SIENA (1906), [CEM] Rev. Leopold J. Bilodeau.
Res.: 72 Church St., P.O. Box 70, 05482. Tel: 802-985-2373; Fax: 802-985-9181.
Catechesis/Religious Program—Dorothea F. Penar, D.R.E. Students 246.

SHELDON SPRINGS, FRANKLIN CO., ST. ANTHONY (1906), [CEM 2] Rev. Bernard J. Bechard, S.S.E.
Res.: P.O. Box 97, 05485-0097. Tel: 802-933-8921; Fax: 802-933-8921.
Catechesis/Religious Program—Students 50.
Mission—St. Mary Franklin, Franklin Co.

SOUTH BURLINGTON, CHITTENDEN CO., ST. JOHN VIANNEY (1940), Rev. John W. Hamilton; Deacons Joseph Lane; Anthony Previti.
Res.: 160 Hinesburg Rd., 05403. Tel: 802-864-4166; Fax: 802-863-6065.
Catechesis/Religious Program—Tel: 802-658-2344. Patricia Soychak, D.R.E. Students 424.

SOUTH HERO, GRAND ISLE CO., ST. ROSE OF LIMA (1895), Rev. Philip J. Branon.
Res.: 501 Rte. 2, 05486. Tel: 802-372-4092; Fax: 802-372-4770.
Catechesis/Religious Program—Students 69.
Mission—St. Joseph Grand Isle, Grand Isle Co.
Mission—St. Benedict Joseph Labre North Hero, Grand Isle Co.

SPRINGFIELD, WINDSOR CO., MATERNITY OF THE BLESSED VIRGIN MARY (1900), [CEM] Rev. Peter Y. Williams.
Res.: 40 Summer St., 05156. Tel: 802-885-3400; Fax: 802-885-2250.
Catechesis/Religious Program—Students 61.

STOWE, LAMOILLE CO., BLESSED SACRAMENT (1954), Rev. Bernard E. Gaudreau.
Res.: 728 Mountain Rd., P.O. Box 27, 05672. Tel: 802-253-7536; Fax: 802-253-4445.
Catechesis/Religious Program—Tel: 802-253-7536, Ext. 13. Joan Mattila, D.R.E.; Ann Spearing, D.R.E. Students 111.

SWANTON, FRANKLIN CO., NATIVITY OF THE BLESSED VIRGIN MARY (1854), [CEM] Rev. John J. Meagher, S.S.E.
Res.: 65 Canada St., 05488. Tel: 802-868-4517; 802-868-4262; Fax: 802-868-9202.
Catechesis/Religious Program—Students 175.

TROY, ORLEANS CO., SACRED HEART OF JESUS (1931), [CEM] Rev. Jerome Mercure, Admin.
Res.: P.O. Box 109, 05868. Tel: 802-744-2239; Fax: 802-744-2239.
Catechesis/Religious Program—Julie Ste. Marie, D.R.E. Tel: 802-744-6552; Gail Sicotte, D.R.E. Tel: 802-744-2446. Students 61.
Mission—St. Ignatius Loyola Lowell, Orleans Co.

UNDERHILL CENTER, CHITTENDEN CO., ST. THOMAS (1856), [CEM 3] Rev. John J. McDermott.
Res.: P.O. Box 3, 05490-0003. Tel: 802-899-4632; Fax: 802-899-5120.
Catechesis/Religious Program—Tel: 802-899-4770. Sr. Yvette Rainville, D.R.E. Students 425.

VERGENNES, ADDISON CO., ST. PETER (1881), [CEM] Rev. Gerard P. Leclerc.
Res.: 85 S. Maple St., P.O. Box 324, 05491. Tel: 802-877-2367; Fax: 802-877-1063.
Catechesis/Religious Program—Nancy R. Hess, D.R.E.; Kathleen Krayewsky, D.R.E. Students 91.

WAITSFIELD, WASHINGTON CO., OUR LADY OF THE SNOWS (1964), Closed., See St. Andrew, Waterbury.

WALLINGFORD, RUTLAND CO., ST. PATRICK (1910), [CEM] Rev. Robert J. McKnight.
Res.: 218 N. Main St., P.O. Box 99, 05773-0099. Tel: 802-446-2161; Fax: 802-446-2161.
Catechesis/Religious Program—Students 30.
Mission—Our Lady of Mercy Mount Holly, Rutland Co.

WATERBURY, WASHINGTON CO., ST. ANDREW (1869), [CEM] Rev. Bernard W. Bourgeois.
Res.: 109 S. Main St., 05676. Tel: 802-244-7734; Fax: 802-244-7934.
Catechesis/Religious Program—Dianne Bilodeau, D.R.E. Students 179.
Mission—Our Lady of the Snows Waitsfield, Washington Co.
Mission—St. Patrick Moretown, Washington Co.

WEST RUTLAND, RUTLAND CO.
1—ST. BRIDGET (1857), [CEM 2] Rev. Robert B. Whalen.
Res.: 28 Church St., 05777-0087. Tel: 802-438-2490; Fax: 802-438-2710.
Catechesis/Religious Program—Tel: 802-438-2232. Lorraine Davis, D.R.E. Students 73.
2—ST. STANISLAUS KOSTKA (1904), (Polish), [CEM] Rev. Frank S. Warzocha.
Res.: 23 Barnes St., 05777. Tel: 802-438-5671.
Catechesis/Religious Program—Students 25.

WHITE RIVER JUNCTION, WINDSOR CO., ST. ANTHONY (1869), [CEM 2] Revs. Ronald Saunders, S.M.; Adrien O. Pelletier, S.M.; Deacon John P. Guarino.
Res.: 15 Church St., 05001. Tel: 802-295-2225; Fax: 802-296-6008.
Religious Education Center—53 Church St., 05001. Tel: 802-295-6607.
Catechesis/Religious Program—Linda James, D.R.E.; Michelle Filardi, D.R.E.; Donna Porter, D.R.E.; Jackie Pierce, D.R.E. Students 205.

WILLISTON, CHITTENDEN CO., IMMACULATE HEART OF MARY (1951), Rev. Donald J. Ravey.
Res.: P.O. Box 1047, 05495. Tel: 802-878-4513.
Catechesis/Religious Program—Students 350.

WILMINGTON, WINDHAM CO., OUR LADY OF FATIMA (1959), Rev. Charles L. Wallen, C.S.C.; Deacon Paul Mello.
Res.: P.O. Box 188, 05363. Tel: 802-464-7329; Fax: 802-464-5256.
Catechesis/Religious Program—Students 74.

WINDSOR, WINDSOR CO., ST. FRANCIS OF ASSISI (1886), [CEM] Rev. Paul Belhumeur, M.S.
Res.: 30 Union St., P.O. Box 46, 05089. Tel: 802-674-2157; Fax: 802-674-9416.
Catechesis/Religious Program—Joyce K. Corbin, D.R.E. Students 130.

WINOOSKI, CHITTENDEN CO.
1—ST. FRANCIS XAVIER (1868), [CEM] Rev. Richard G. LaValley; Deacon John F. Place.
Res.: 3 St. Peter St., Ste. 2, 05404. Tel: 802-655-2290; Fax: 802-655-3036.
School—Tel: 802-655-2600; Fax: 802-655-3096. Sisters 1; Lay Teachers 15; Students 160.
Catechesis/Religious Program—Students 113.
Convent—Tel: 802-655-2395; Fax: 802-655-3888.
St. Vincent de Paul Center—Tel: 802-655-3006.
School—Day Care, Tel: 802-655-4660.
2—ST. STEPHEN (1882), [CEM] Rev. Paul F. St. James.
Res.: 115 Barlow St., 05404. Tel: 802-655-0318; Fax: 802-655-4779.
Catechesis/Religious Program—Roland Dion, D.R.E. Students 46.

WOODSTOCK, WINDSOR CO., OUR LADY OF THE SNOWS (1894), Rev. Charles P. Davignon, Admin.
Res.: 7 South St., P.O. Box 397, 05091-0397. Tel: 802-457-2322; Fax: 802-457-5805.
Catechesis/Religious Program—Claire Ruch, D.R.E.; Betsey Frates, D.R.E. Students 51.
Mission—Our Lady of the Mountains Killington, Rutland Co.

Chaplains of Public Institutions

BURLINGTON. *Fletcher Allen Health Care* 05401. Tel: 802-656-2770. Revs. John Nuagbaraocha, D.S., Fidelis Agughara, Sr. Monica Rock, R.H.S.J., Pastoral Assoc.

WATERBURY. *State Hospital*. Rev. Bernard W. Bourgeois.

WHITE RIVER JUNCTION. *Veterans Administration Hospital*. Rev. Adrien O. Pelletier, S.M.

On Duty Outside the Diocese:
Rev.—
Dowd, Barry G., Mary Queen of the Universe Shrine, 8300 Vineland Ave., Orlando, FL 32821.

On Special or Other Diocesan Assignment:
Rev.—
Miller, Walter D., J.C.D., Chancery Office

Other Residence:
Rev.—
Bruder, John W., O.C.S.O., 800 Waldon Hill Rd., Danville, 05828.

Retired:
Rev. Msgrs.—
Flanagan, Francis B., Mt. View Genesis Nursing Home, 9 Haywood Ave., Rutland, 05701.
Gelineau, Edward J., St. Joseph's Home, 243 N. Prospect St., 05401. Tel: 802-865-9240
McSweeney, John R., J.C.L., 125 Kennedy Dr., Unit #36, South Burlington, 05403. Tel: 802-863-6017
Revs.—
Bean, Donald A., Michaud Manor, 47 Herrick Rd., Derby Line, 05830.
Beauregard, James E.
Brackett, Anthony H., 9854 Wildginger Dr., S.W., Fort Myers, FL 33919. Tel: 941-482-5749
Bransfield, Thomas A., Holy Cross Senior Housing, 468 Church Rd., Apt. 103, Colchester, 05446. Tel: 802-658-5277
Brochu, Gerard H., P.O. Box 4268, North Fort Myers, FL 33918.
Chant, William S., P.O. Box 3192, 05401-0031.
Couture, Bernard G., c/o Mrs. Gisele Fournier, Box 202, East Barre, 05639.
Demasi, Michael A., 212 Autumn Acres, Bennington, 05201. Tel: 802-447-4864
Depeaux, Bernard F., 351 North Ave., P.O. Box 489, 05402-0489. Tel: 802-658-6110
Duquette, Lucien G., 1241 W. Bourgainvillea Cir., Barefoot Bay, FL 32916. Tel: 407-664-8442
Falvella, Richard J., 100 Bluff View Ave., Apt. 510C, Largo, FL 33770.
Fowler, Richard A., P.O. Box 5637, Apache Jct., AZ 85278. .
Giroux, Raymond A., 9 Florida Ave., Winooski, 05404. Tel: 802-655-3658
Guischard, John A., The Kervick Home, 131 Convent Ave., Rutland, 05701. Tel: 802-773-8263
Hart, Edward J., St. Joseph's Home, 243 N. Prospect St., 05401.
Hawkins, Douglas W., C.S.C., Sacred Heart St. Francis de Sales, 238 W. Main St., Bennington, 05201. Tel: 802-442-3141
Kennedy, David G., P.O. Box 846, Dewey, AZ 86327-0846.
Kenney, John B., 8 Hullcrest Ln., Shelburne, 05482. Tel: 802-985-2333
LaFlamme, Julien J., 239 Rte. 67 W., North Bennington, 05257.
Lagor, Joseph J., P.O. Box 4696, White River Jct., 05001. Tel: 802-296-3010
Laliberte, William F., 113 Robbins St., Rutland, 05701. Tel: 802-773-2989
Laplante, Jean-Paul, 64 N. Elm St., St. Albans, 05478.
Lively, Joseph A., 257 Peacham Pond Rd., Marshfield, 05658.
McCarthy, Joseph, 130 Curtis Ave., 05401. Tel: 802-862-3183
Moore, Edward F., 86 Westview Heights Dr., Stowe, 05672-4361. Tel: 802-253-5085
Mulligan, William R., 20 N. 28th Ave., Longport, NJ 08403. Tel: 609-823-1901
Murtagh, George O., 5001 S.W. 20th St., #7102, Ocala, FL 34474. Tel: 352-236-3202
Pagliuca, Joseph P., 21 Via Trieste, 67057 Pescino (AQ), Italy.
Pray, Joseph N., P.O. Box 85, Castleton, 05735. Tel: 802-273-2621
Ritchie, Donald E., 8213 Cagel Rd., Fort Washington, MD 20744. Tel: 301-567-6116
Rousseau, Peter A., 16 Clover Dr., B1, Essex Jct., 05452. Tel: 802-879-6934
Shea, James M., 792 Capri Isles Blvd., Venice, FL 34292. Tel: 941-483-4361
Soutiere, Ronald A., 37 Gamelin Ct., Winooski, 05404.
St. Pierre, Michel J., Mont Marie Health Ctr., Inc., 34 Lower Westfield Rd., Holyoke, MA 01040.
Vignoe, Joseph M., 109 Preston Ln., P.O. Box 532, Bomoseen, 05732. Tel: 802-468-5349
Von Fauer, Stephen C., Mary Theotokos Center, P.O. Box 88, West Burke, 05871. Tel: 802-467-1132
Walsh, Raymond D., The Loretto Home, 59 Meadow St., Rutland, 05701. Tel: 802-773-8840

Ward, Donal, P.O. Box 56, East Calais, 05650.

Permanent Deacons:
Moran, Robert J., St. Anne, Middletown Springs
Adams, Carl J., Jr., (On Duty Outside the Diocese)
Allen, Eugene, Jr., St. Joseph, Chester
Bisson, David, St. Monica, Barre
Blicharz, John, Sacred Heart, Bellow Falls
Brenneman, Walter, St. Augustine, Montpelier
Brooks, Peter T., St. Thomas, Underhill Ctr.
Brown, William J., III, St. Theresa, Gilman
Burk, Bruce, St. John, St. Johnsbury
Chagnon, Clifford, All Saints, Richford
Cooney, Thomas, Holy Cross, Morrisville
Cummings, Regis E., St. Augustine, Montpelier
Degnon, Robert, (On Duty Outside the Diocese)
Desilets, Raymond J., St. John, St. Johnsbury
Fitzpatrick, Kelly, Our Lady of Perpetual Help, Bradford
Glinka, William, Cathedral of the Immaculate Conception, Burlington
Graden, William, St. James, Island Pond
Gratton, John P.E., St. Benedict, West Charleston
Griffin, Gary, St. Mary, Brandon
Guarino, John P., St. Anthony, White River Junction
Hawk, Ivan O., III, Holy Cross, Colchester
Krawczyk, Eugene, (On Duty Outside the Diocese)
Lane, Joseph W., Sr., St. John Vianney, South Burlington
Lissandrello, Paul, (On Duty Outside the Diocese)
Mayo, Bernier L., St. John, St. Johnsbury
Mello, Paul, Our Lady of Fatima, Wilmington
Meunier, Louis A., St. Anthony and Christ the King, Burlington
Moore, Dennis, Ascension, Georgia
Nadeau, Thomas, Graduate Studies
O'Brien, David M., St. John the Baptist, North Bennington
Perkins, Richard, St. Frances Cabrini, West Pawlet
Place, John F., St. Francis Xavier, Winooski
Previti, Anthony, St. John Vianney, South Burlington
Pudvah, Daniel, St. Monica, Barre
Putis, Peter, St. Paul, Manchester Center
Ramey, Jon, St. Isidore, Montgomery Center
Ratte, Stephen J., St. Luke, Fairfax
Rivard, Fernand R., St. Monica, Barre
Rixon, John, St. Mary, St. Albans
Rock, James E., (On Duty Outside the Diocese)
Scilla, Gerald, St. Pius X, Essex Ctr.
Toborg, Alfred, St. Elizabeth, Lyndonville
Vincelette, Alan, St. Amadeus, Alburg

INSTITUTIONS LOCATED IN THE DIOCESE

[A] COLLEGES AND UNIVERSITIES

COLCHESTER. *St. Michael's College*, Winooski Park, 05439. Tel: 802-654-2000; 802-654-2386; Fax: 802-654-2701. Email: mcormier@smcvt.edu. Web: www.smcvt.edu. Dr. Marc A. vanderHeyden, Pres.; Mr. James H. Wall, Chm. of the Bd.; Ms. Lisa Powlison, Asst. to Pres.; Ms. Marilyn Cormier, Dir. Community Rels.; Dr. Janet Sheeran, Vice Pres. Academic Affairs; Mr. Michael D. Samara, Vice Pres. Student Affairs; Mr. Neal Robinson, Vice Pres. Finance; Ms. Anne W. Hansen, Vice Pres. Institutional Advancement; Dr. John P. Kenney, Dean of the College; Mr. Jerry E. Flanagan, Vice Pres. Enrollment & Mktg.; Mr. John D. Sheehey, Registrar; Dr. Bonnie Tangalos, Dean Intl. Students; Dr. Edward Mahoney, Dir. Graduate Theology & Pastoral Ministry Prog.; Rev. Marcel R. Rainville, S.S.E., Dir. Edmundite Campus Min.; Ms. Ann Giombetti, Assoc. Dir. Community Svcs. Priests 5; Sisters 1; Lay Teachers 140; Students 2,630.

RUTLAND. *College of St. Joseph in Vermont*, 71 Clement Rd., 05701-3899. Tel: 802-773-5900; Fax: 802-773-5900. Email: fmiglcrie@csj.edu. Web: www.csj.edu. Dr. Frank G. Miglorie Jr., Pres. Lay Teachers 12; Students 509.

[B] CENTRAL HIGH SCHOOLS, DIOCESAN AND PAROCHIAL

RUTLAND. *Mt. St. Joseph Academy*, 127 Convent Ave., 05701. Tel: 802-775-0151; Fax: 802-775-0424. Email: principal@msjvt.org. Web: www.msjvermont.org. Sr. Kathryn Gallagher, S.S.J., Prin.; Mr. Anthony J. Cirelli, Asst. Prin.; Charles Stevens, Guidance Dir.; Eleanor Chiccarelli, Admissions Dir.; Gail Wetzler, Librarian; Bro. James Moran, S.J., Community Svc. Sisters of St. Joseph Lay Teachers 20; Students 180; Brothers 1; Sisters of St. Joseph 1.

SOUTH BURLINGTON. *Rice Memorial High School*, 99 Proctor Ave., 05403. Tel: 802-862-6521; Fax: 802-864-9931. Web: www.ricehs.org. Dr. Alan J. Crowley, Prin.; Mr. Lloyd Hulburd, Asst. Prin. Priests 1; Sisters 1; Lay Teachers 29; Students 438.

[C] ELEMENTARY SCHOOLS, PAROCHIAL

BURLINGTON. *Christ The King*, (Grades PreK-8), 136 Locust St., 05401. Tel: 802-862-6696; Fax: 802-658-6553. Email: ajlonge@christthekingburlington.org. Web: www.christthekingburl.org. Mary Beth Davidson, Prin. Lay Teachers 17; Students 205.

St. Joseph, (Grades PreK-8), 20 Allen St., 05401. Tel: 802-864-5623; Fax: 802-860-2627. Email: sjsoffice@adelphia.net. Web: www.stjosephvermont.com. Evelyn Rogerson, Prin Sisters 1; Lay Teachers 15; Students 167.

Mater Christi School, 50 Mansfield Ave., 05401. Tel: 802-658-3992; Fax: 802-863-1197. Email: bgaida@sover.net. Web: www.mcschool.org. Barbara Gaida, Prin. Sisters 2; Lay Teachers 33; Students 394.

BARRE. *St. Monica's*, (Grades PreK-8), 73 Summer St., 05641. Tel: 802-476-5015; Fax: 802-476-0861. Mrs. Betty Foley, Prin. Lay Teachers 14; Students 165.

BARTON. *St. Paul's*, (Grades K-8), 54 Eastern Ave., 05822. Tel: 802-525-6578; Fax: 802-525-3839. Email: stpaul@surfglobal.com. Peter T. Close, Prin. Lay Teachers 5; Students 62.

BENNINGTON. *Sacred Heart*, (Grades K-8), 307 School St., 05201. Tel: 802-442-2446; Fax: 802-442-3584. Email: estesd@adelphia.net. Web: www.sacredheartschool@sover.net. Mr. David B. Estes, Prin. Lay Teachers 10; Students 181.

BRATTLEBORO. *St. Michael's*, (Grades PreK-8), 48 Walnut St., 05301. Tel: 802-254-5666; Fax: 802-254-5229. Email: stmikesb@adelphia.net. Mr. Frank J. Vara, Prin. Sisters 1; Lay Teachers 17; Students 217.

MIDDLEBURY. *St. Mary School*, (Grades PreK-6), 86 Shannon St., 05753. Tel: 802-388-8392; Fax: 802-388-8392. Deborah Nason Foster, Prin. Lay Teachers 8; Students 93.

MONTPELIER. *St. Michael's School*, (Grades K-6), 46 Barre St., 05602. Tel: 802-223-6430; Fax: 802-229-4827. Web: www.saintmikes.org. Coleen Reynolds, Prin. Sisters 1; Lay Teachers 7; Students 120.

MORRISVILLE. *Bishop John A. Marshall School*, (Grades K-8), 680 La Porte Rd., 05661. Tel: 802-888-4758; Fax: 802-888 3137. Web: www.bjams.org. Mr. Bruce A. Batchelder, Prin. Sisters 2; Lay Teachers 10; Students 144.

NEWPORT. *Sacred Heart Schools Inc.*, (Grades PreK-8), 47 Clermont Ter., 05855-2194. Tel: 802-334-8185; Fax: 802-334-7803. Email: main@sacredheartnewport.org. Web: www.sacredheartnewport.org. Mrs. Kateri Stokes, Admin. Coord./Prin. Lay Teachers 11; Students 142.

RUTLAND. *Christ the King*, (Grades PreK-8), 60 S. Main St., 05701. Tel: 802-773-6820; Fax: 802-773-6820. Mrs. RoseMaria Doran, Prin. Sisters 2; Lay Teachers 4; Students 285.

ST. JOHNSBURY. *Good Shepherd School*, (Grades PreK-8), P.O. Box 384, 05819. Tel: 802-751-8111; Fax: 802-751-8223. Email: goodshepherd@kingcon.com. Mr. Robert Gessner, Prin. Lay Teachers 20; Students 139.

SPRINGFIELD. *Holy Family Catholic School*, 38 Pleasant St., 05156. Tel: 802-885-4733; Fax: 802-885-3699. Web: www.hfs-vt.org. Jacqueline P. Hughes, Prin. Lay Teachers 10; Students 48.

WINOOSKI. *St. Francis Xavier*, (Grades PreK-8), 5 St. Peter St., 05404. Tel: 802-655-2600; Fax: 802-655-3096. Email: mhorton@sfxwinooski.org. Web: www.SFXWinooski.org. Maria Horton, Co-Prin.; Simon Lewis, Co-Prin.; Kathryn LaVigne, Co-Prin. Sisters 1; Lay Teachers 15; Students 160.

[D] HOMES FOR AGED

BURLINGTON. *St. Joseph's Home*, 243 N. Prospect St., 05401. Tel: 802-864-0264; Fax: 802-864-5640. Mrs. Mary M. McNamara, Dir.; Esther MacPherson, Admin.; Rev. Msgr. Edward J. Gelineau (Retired); Revs. Edward J. Hart (Retired); James E. Beauregard (Retired); Brian E. Mead. Managed by Vermont Catholic Charities. Guests 35.

DERBY LINE. *Michaud Memorial Manor* 05830. Tel: 802-873-3152; Fax: 802-873-9206. Email: manor@together.net. Web: www.vermontcatholic.org. Mrs. Mary M. McNamara, Dir.; Rachel Ducharme, Admin. Managed by Vermont Catholic Charities. Guests 30.

RUTLAND. *St. Joseph's Kervick Residence*, 131 Convent Ave., 05701. Tel: 802-775-5133; Fax: 802-747-0617. Mrs. Terry Dion Cavacas, Admin.; Mrs. Mary M. McNamara, Dir.; Rev. John A. Guischard, Chap. (Retired). Managed by Vermont Catholic Charities. Guests 43

Loretto Home for Aged 05701. Tel: 802-773-8840; Fax: 802-773-9638. Email: lhometc@sover.net. Mrs. Mary M. McNamara, Dir.; Mrs. Terry Dion Cavacas, Admin.; Rev. Raymond E. Walsh, Resident Chap. Managed by Vermont Catholic Charities. Guests 47.

[E] MONASTERIES AND RESIDENCES OF PRIESTS AND BROTHERS

ARLINGTON. *Carthusian Foundation in America, Inc., Charterhouse of the Transfiguration*, 1800 Beartown Rd., 05250. Tel: 802-362-2550; Fax: 802-362-3584. Email: carthusians_in_america@juno.com. Web: www.chartreux.org. Revs. Johan de Bruijn, O.Cart. (Holland); Philip Dahl, O.Cart. (Norway); Lorenzo Maria Tolentino de la Rosa Jr., O.Cart. (Philippines), Prior; Mary Joseph Kim, O.Cart (Korea, South), Novice Master of Cloister Monks & Brothers, Antiquior; Mary Paul Chapeau, O.Cart. (France), Vicar. Carthusian Foundation, Association Fraternelle Romande. Choir Monks: Solemn Professed 5; Converse Brothers: Solemn Professed 5; Perpetual Donates 2.

COLCHESTER. *Society of St. Edmund* (Edmundite Generalate) , 270 Winooski Park, 05439. Tel: 802-654-3400; Fax: 802-654-3409. Email: generalate@aol.com. Web: www.sse.org. Revs. Richard M. Myhalyk, S.S.E., Supr. Gen.; Edward J. Dubriske, S.S.E. (Venezuela); Philippe Simonnet, S.S.E. (France). Central Offices, Society of Saint Edmund.

Society of St. Edmund, P.O. Box 272, 05439. Tel: 802-654-2000; Fax: 802-654-3409. Revs. Michael P. Cronogue, S.S.E., Supr.; Marcel R. Rainville, S.S.E.; Richard N. Berube, S.S.E.; Paul E. Couture, S.S.E.; Brian J. Cummings, S.S.E.; Raymond J. Doherty, S.S.E.; Joseph M. McLaughlin, S.S.E.; Romeo A. Trahan, S.S.E.; Richard L. VanderWeel, S.S.E. (Edmundite Community at St. Michael's College)

WESTON. *Priory of Benedictine Monks*, 58 Priory Hill Rd., 05161-6400. Tel: 802-824-5409; Fax: 802-824-3573. Email: brothers@westonpriory.org. Web: www.westonpriory.org. Very Rev. Richard Iaquinto, O.S.B., Prior; Revs. Peter Claude Anctil, O.S.B.; Robert J. Kiernan, O.S.B.; Mark Ronald Nicolosi, O.S.B.; John Hammond, O.S.B. Priests 5; Brothers 10.

[F] CONVENTS AND RESIDENCES OF SISTERS

BURLINGTON. *Franciscan Sisters of the Atonement Convent*, 21 Dodds Ct., 05401. Tel: 802-862-8288. Sr. Frances Flynn, S.A., Coord. Sisters 3.

Mount St. Mary Convent, 100 Mansfield Ave., 05401. Tel: 802-863-6835; Fax: 802-863-1486. Email: rsmvermont@hotmail.com. Sr. Jeannine Mercure, R.S.M., Pres. Motherhouse and Novitiate of Sisters of Mercy. Ministry in the field of: Education, Parish Ministry, Social Services and Spirituality. Sisters 69. In Res. Rev. Wendell H. Searles, V.G., Chap.

BRADFORD. *The Carmelite Nuns of Vermont, Inc., St. Joseph's Carmelite Monastery*, 113 Upper Plain, 05033. Tel: 802-222-5268. Sr. Diane Gauthier, O.C.D., Contact Person. Sisters 2.

COLCHESTER. *Religious Hospitallers of St. Joseph*, 786 College Pkwy., 05446-3007. Tel: 802-655-1160; Fax: 802-847-2690. Email: rhsjrt@msn.com. Sr. Adrienne Desjardins, R.H.S.J., Supr. Sisters 15.

NEWPORT. *Sacred Heart Convent* (Daughters of Charity of the Sacred Heart) , 119 Clermont Ter., 05855. Tel: 802-334-7058. Sisters 5.

RUTLAND. *Congregation of the Sisters of St. Joseph of Springfield, MA*, Formerly Sisters of St. Joseph Society, Inc.
Residences:
St. Francis Residence, 11 Clement Rd., 05701. Tel: 802-773-8513; Fax: 802-773-8513.
Avila Hall Residence, Formerly Avila Hall 7 Clement Rd., 05701. Tel: 802-775-0665; Fax: 802-775-0105.
Marion Hall Residence, Formerly Marion Hall 9 Clement Rd., 05701. Tel: 802-775-0665.
Fontbonne Hall (Residence), 13 Clement Rd., 05701. Tel: 802-775-4231.
Clementwood Spiritual Life Center, Formerly St. Joseph Assisted Living Residence - Kervick Home Clement Rd., 05701. Tel: 802-775-5133.

WESTFIELD. *Monastery of the Immaculate Heart of Mary*, 4103 VT Rte. 100, 05874. Tel: 802-744-6525; Fax: 802-744-6236. Sisters Laurence A. M. Couture, O.S.B., Prioress; Marie-Bernard N. Lavoie, O.S.B., Subprioress; Rev. Dom Lawrence Brown, O.S.B., Resident Chap., Monk of Clear Creek, OK. Benedictine Cloistered Nuns, Congregation of Solesmes Professed Nuns 14;

Novices 1; Postulants 1.

WINOOSKI. *Missionary Sisters of Our Lady of Africa (M.S.O.L.A.)*, 47 W. Spring St., 05404. Tel: 802-655-4003; Fax: 802-655-3888. Email: msolanger@aol.com. Sr. Claire Bernier, Sec. Sisters 5.

Our Lady of Providence Convent, 47 W. Spring St., 05404. Tel: 802-655-2395; Fax: 802-655-3888. Email: olopr@aol.com. Sr. Rita Bourassa, S.P., Supr. Sisters 28.

[G] SUMMER CAMPS

BURLINGTON. *Camp Holy Cross, Inc.*, P.O. Box 489, 05402-0489. Tel: 802-658-6110 (Winter); 802-863-5986 (Summer); Fax: 802-951-2471. Email: pwells@vermontcatholic.org. Mr. Peter Wells, Exec. Dir. Summer Camp for Boys. Day Camp for Boys and Girls. Diocesan institution under direction of Board of Trustees. Capacity 100.

Camp Holy Cross, P.O. Box 489, 05402-0489.

Camp Tara, Catholic Charities Central Office, 351 North Ave., P.O. Box 489, 05402-0489. Tel: 802-658-6110; Fax: 802-860-0451. Email: charities@vermontcatholic.org. Web: www.vermontcatholic.org. Summer camp for needy Vermont children. Diocesan program under direction of Vermont Catholic Charities. Capacity 49.

[H] NEWMAN CENTERS

BURLINGTON. *University of Vermont-The Catholic Center at UVM* 390 S. Prospect St., Redstone Campus, 05401. Tel: 802-862-8403; Fax: 802-865-9480. Email: cathuvm@together.net. Web: www.uvm.edu/~catholic/. Revs. Michael W. DeForge, Chap.; Robert B. Kolakowski, Asst. Chap.

Castleton State College, St. John Rectory, P.O. Box 128, Castleton, 05735. Tel: 802-468-5706; Fax: 802-468-5299. Rev. Charles R. Danielson, Chap.

Goddard College (Plainfield) Tel: 802-223-5285; Fax: 802-223-3621. Rev. Thomas L. Mosher. Attended by St. Augustine, 16 Barre St., Montpelier, VT 05602

Green Mountain College, St. Raphael Rectory, Main St., Poultney, 05764. Tel: 802-287-5703. Rev. Adam J. Krempa.

Johnson State College (Johnson), P.O. Box 339, Morrisville, 05661. Tel: 802-888-3318; Fax: 802-888-6177. Rev. Paul C. Houde. Attended by Holy Cross, Morrisville

Lyndon State College, Lyndon Center, 05850. Tel: 802-656-5267; Fax: 802-656-3324. Rev. Stephen J. Nichols.

St. Elizabeth Church, P.O. Box 141, Lyndonville, 05851. Tel: 802-626-5267; Fax: 802-656-3324.

Middlebury College, St. Mary Rectory, 326 College St., Middlebury, 05753. Tel: 802-388-2943; Fax: 802-388-2943. Rev. Justin J. Baker.

Norwich Newman Apostolate, Norwich University, Northfield, 05663. Tel: 802-862-8403; Fax: 802-865-9480. Rev. Michael W. DeForge, Chap.

The Catholic Center at UVM, 390 S. Prospect St., Redstone Campus, 05401. Tel: 802-862-8403; Fax: 802-865-9480. Rev. Richard G. LaValley, Chap.

St. Francis Xavier Rectory, 3 St. Peter St., Winooski, 05404. Tel: 802-655-2290; Fax: 802-655-3036.

Vermont Technical College, Sts. Donatian and Rogatian Rectory, 25 S. Pleasant St., Randolph, 05060. Tel: 802-728-3227; Fax: 802-728-3570. Rev. John M. Milanese, Chap.

[I] MISCELLANEOUS

BURLINGTON. *Institute for Spiritual Development, Inc.*, Formerly Institute for Spiritual Development346 Shelburne Rd., 05401. Tel: 802-846-7084; Fax: 802-846-7237. Email: claireboissy@hotmail.com. Web: www.spiritvt.org. Sr. Claire Boissy, R.S.M., Admin. Coord.

Mercy Connections, Inc., 346 Shelburne Rd., 05401. Tel: 802-846-7062; Fax: 802-846-7237. Email: lindoracabral@mercyconnections.org. Web: www.mercyconnections.org. Sr. Lindora Cabral, R.S.M., Exec. Dir.

Mercy Investment Program, Inc., Formerly Mercy Consolidated Asset Management Program (MCAMP)Sisters of Mercy of the Americas, 100 Mansfield Ave., 05401. Tel: 802-863-6835; Fax: 802-863-1486. Sisters Patricia McDermott, R.S.M., (Silver Spring, MD); Catherine McGroarty, R.S.M., (Dallas, PA); Barbara Wheeley, R.S.M., (Baltimore, MD); Jeannine Mercure, R.S.M., (Burlington, VT); JoAnne Courneen, R.S.M., (Erie, PA); Patricia Combies, R.S.M., (Cumberland, RI); Patricia Forret, R.S.M., (Omaha, NE); Suzanne Elliott, R.S.M., (Hartsdale, NY); Mary Waters, R.S.M., (Brooklyn, NY). MIP Members & Regional Communities.

BENSON. *Lumen Christi Retreat House*, 56 Howard Hill Rd., P.O. Box 300, 05731. Tel: 802-537-4531. Sr. Judy Fortune, R.S.M., Spiritual Dir. Reservations for retreat call Tel: 802-846-7084

BRATTLEBORO. *Neringa, Inc.*, 600 Liberty Hwy., Putnam, CT 06260. Tel: 978-582-5592. Email: info@neringa.org. Web: www.neringa.org.

COLCHESTER. *Fanny Allen Hospital*, 790 College Pkwy., 05446. Tel: 802-847-6448; Fax: 802-847-6464. Email: irene.duchesneau@vtmed.net.org. Sr. Irene Duchesneau, R.H.S.J., Corporate Sponsor Liaison. Fanny Allen Hospital has the oversight responsibility to assure that the Fletcher Allen Health Care Corporation does not conduct actions on the Fanny Allen Campus that conflict with the teachings, traditions, Canons or other laws of the Roman Catholic Church or the Constitutions and Directives of the Religious Hospitallers of St. Joseph.

ISLE LA MOTTE. *St. Anne's Shrine* 05463. Tel: 802-928-3362; Fax: 802-928-3305. Email: fstanne@aol.com. Web: www.sse.org. Rev. Maurice U. Boucher, S.S.E., Spiritual Dir. Conducted by Fathers of Society of St. Edmund.; Open May 15-Oct. 15.

RANDOLPH. *Prelature of the Holy Cross and Opus Dei*, Wynnview Center, R.D. 1, 05060. Tel: 802-728-5414; Fax: 802-728-3334. Web: www.opusdei.org. Legal Names: Opus Dei; The Work of God.

RELIGIOUS INSTITUTES OF MEN REPRESENTED IN THE DIOCESE

For further details refer to the corresponding bracketed number in the Religious Institutes of Men or Women section.

[0200]—*Benedictine Monks*—O.S.B.
[0300]—*Cistercian Order of the Strict Observance (Trappists)*—O.C.S.O.
[0520]—*Franciscan Friars*—O.F.M.
[0780]—*Marist Fathers*—S.M.
[0720]—*The Missionaries of Our Lady of La Salette* (Prov. of the Immaculate Heart of Mary)—M.S.
[0280]—*Order of Carthusians*—O.Cart.
[0610]—*Priests of the Congregation of Holy Cross* (Eastern Prov.)—C.S.C.
[]—*Society of Jesus of New England*—S.J.
[0440]—*Society of Saint Edmund*—S.S.E.

RELIGIOUS INSTITUTES OF WOMEN REPRESENTED IN THE DIOCESE

[0170]—*Benedictine Cloistered Nuns of the Congregation of Solesmes*—O.S.B.
[0750]—*Daughters of the Charity of the Sacred Heart of Jesus*—F.C.S.C.J.
[0820]—*Daughters of the Holy Spirit*—D.H.S.
[0960]—*Daughters of Wisdom*—D.W.
[0420]—*Discalced Carmelite Nuns*—O.C.D.
[1070]—*Dominican Sisters*—O.P.
[1190]—*Franciscan Sisters of the Atonement*—S.A.
[2820]—*Missionary Sisters of Our Lady of Africa*—M.S.O.L.A.
[3440]—*Religious Hospitallers of Saint Joseph*—R.H.S.J.
[1930]—*Sisters of Holy Cross*—C.S.C.
[2575]—*Sisters of Mercy*—R.S.M.
[3000]—*Sisters of Notre Dame de Namur*—S.N.D.deN.
[3350]—*Sisters of Providence*—S.P.
[3830-01]—*Sisters of St. Joseph (Boston, MA)*—C.S.J.
[3830-07]—*Sisters of St. Joseph (Springfield, MA)*—S.S.J.
[4130]—*Ursuline Sisters of the Congregation of Tildonk, Belgium*—O.S.U.

DIOCESAN CEMETERIES

BURLINGTON. *St. Joseph's Cemetery* 05401.

SOUTH BURLINGTON. *Resurrection Park Cemetery* 05403.

NECROLOGY

† Bresnehan, Rev. Msgr. Paul M., Proctor, VT St. Dominic—Died July 23, 2003
† Dennigan, Patrick J., (Retired)—Died May 20, 2003
† Foley, James F., (Retired)—Died Nov. 27, 2002
† Gallagher, William P., Woodstock, VT Our Lady of the Snows—Died Oct. 13, 2003
† Hackett, John P., St. Albans, VT Our Lady of the Lake—Died Nov. 21, 2002
† Lapan, Robert, (Retired)—Died April 1, 2003

Diocese of Camden

(Dioecesis Camdensis)

Most Reverend

JOSEPH A. GALANTE, D.D., J.C.D.

Bishop of Camden; ordained May 16, 1964; appointed Titular Bishop of Equilum and Auxiliary Bishop of San Antonio October 13, 1992; consecrated December 11, 1992; appointed Bishop of Beaumont April 5, 1994; installed Bishop of Beaumont May 9, 1994; appointed Coadjutor Bishop of Dallas November 23, 1999; installed January 14, 2000; appointed Bishop of Camden March 23, 2004; installed May 30, 2004

Chancery Office: Camden Diocesan Center, 631 Market St., P.C. Box 708, Camden, NJ 08101. Tel: 856-756-7900; Fax: 856-963-2655.

ESTABLISHED DECEMBER 9, 1937.

Square Miles 2,691.

Legal Corporate Title: "The Diocese of Camden, New Jersey."

Comprises six Counties in the State of New Jersey--viz., Atlantic, Camden, Cape May, Cumberland, Gloucester and Salem.

For legal titles of parishes and diocesan institutions, consult the Chancery Office.

STATISTICAL OVERVIEW

Personnel	
Priests: Diocesan Active in Diocese	184
Priests: Diocesan Active Outside Diocese	32
Priests: Diocesan in Foreign Missions	5
Priests: Retired, Sick or Absent	84
Number of Diocesan Priests	305
Religious Priests in Diocese	45
Total Priests in Diocese	350
Extern Priests in Diocese	39
Ordinations:	
Diocesan Priests	4
Transitional Deacons	2
Permanent Deacons in Diocese	115
Total Brothers	18
Total Sisters	344
Parishes	
Parishes	125
With Resident Pastor:	
Resident Diocesan Priests	120
Resident Religious Priests	5
Missions	10
Pastoral Centers	34
Professional Ministry Personnel:	
Brothers	18
Sisters	341
Lay Ministers	78
Welfare	
Catholic Hospitals	1
Total Assisted	298,136
Health Care Centers	2
Total Assisted	12,662
Homes for the Aged	5
Total Assisted	1,257
Residential Care of Children	1
Total Assisted	7
Day Care Centers	2
Total Assisted	211
Specialized Homes	1
Total Assisted	962
Special Centers for Social Services	1
Total Assisted	7,372
Residential Care of Disabled	1
Total Assisted	444
Other Institutions	1
Total Assisted	6,200
Educational	
Diocesan Students in Other Seminaries	29
Total Seminarians	29
High Schools, Diocesan and Parish	10
Total Students	6,121
High Schools, Private	3
Total Students	1,434
Elementary Schools, Diocesan and Parish	56
Total Students	12,666
Elementary Schools, Private	1
Total Students	47
Non-residential Schools for the Disabled	2
Total Students	653
Catechesis/Religious Education:	
High School Students	550
Elementary Students	36,464
Total Students under Catholic Instruction	57,964
Teachers in the Diocese:	
Priests	10
Brothers	8
Sisters	85
Lay Teachers	1,346
Vital Statistics	
Receptions into the Church:	
Infant Baptism Totals	6,192
Adult Baptism Totals	1,056
First Communions	6,647
Confirmations	5,560
Marriages:	
Catholic	1,222
Interfaith	1,304
Total Marriages	2,526
Deaths	4,421
Total Catholic Population	442,389
Total Population	1,337,416

Former Bishops—Most Revs BARTHOLOMEW J. EUSTACE, S.T.D., First Bishop of Camden; consecrated March 25, 1938; died Dec. 11, 1956; JUSTIN J. MCCARTHY, S.T.D., LL.D., Second Bishop of Camden; consecrated June 17, 1954; appt. to Camden, Jan. 27, 1957; died Dec. 26, 1959; CELESTINE J. DAMIANO, D.D., Third Bishop of Camden; consecrated Feb. 11, 1953; transferred to Camden, Jan. 24, 1960, with the personal title of Archbishop; died Oct. 2, 1967; GEORGE H. GUILFOYLE, D.D., J.D. (Retired), ord. March 25, 1944; appt. Titular Bishop of Marazanae and Auxiliary Bishop of New York, Oct. 17, 1964; consecrated Nov. 30, 1964; appt. Fourth Bishop of Camden, Jan. 2, 1968; installed March 4, 1968; retired May 22, 1989; died June 11, 1991; JAMES T. MCHUGH, S.T.D., ord. May 25, 1957; appt. Titular Bishop of Morosbisdo and Auxiliary Bishop of Newark, Nov. 20, 1987; consecrated Jan. 25 1988; appt. Fifth Bishop of Camden, May 13, 1989; installed June 20, 1989; appt. Coadjutor Bishop of Rockville Centre, Dec. 7, 1998; installed Third Diocesan Bishop, Jan. 4, 2000; died Dec. 10, 2000; NICHOLAS A. DIMARZIO, Ph.D., D.D., ordained May 30, 1970, appointed Titular Bishop of Mauriana and Auxiliary Bishop of Newark, Sept. 10, 1996; consecrated Oct. 31, 1996; appointed Sixth Bishop of Camden June 8, 1999; installed July 22, 1999; appointed Bishop of Brooklyn, Aug. 1, 2003; installed Oct. 3, 2003.

Diocesan Offices

Camden Diocesan Center—631 Market St., Camden, 08102. Tel: 856-756-7900; Fax: 856-963-2655. Some offices are listed at separate locations.

The Diocese of Camden— A corporation under the laws of the State of New Jersey

Officers—Rev. Msgrs. THOMAS J. MORGAN, Apostolic Admin.; JOSEPH W. POKUSA, J.C.D., Sec.

Diocesan Bishop—Rev. Msgr. THOMAS J. MORGAN, Apostolic Admin., 631 Market St., Camden, 08102. Tel: 856-756-7900, Ext. 5432; Fax: 856-338-0376.

Chancellor and Episcopal Vicar for Canonical Affairs—Rev. Msgr. JOSEPH W. POKUSA, J.C.D., 631 Market St., Camden, 08102. Tel: 856-756-7900, Ext. 5216.

Vice Chancellor—Rev. PETER M. JOYCE, J.C.L., 631 Market St., Camden, 08102. Tel: 856-756-7900, Ext. 5451.

Assistant Chancellor for Marriage Preparation—Deacon ROBERT WILLSON, 631 Market St., Camden, 08102. Tel: 856-756-7900, Ext. 5263.

Judicial Vicar—Rev. Msgr DOMINIC J. BOTTINO, J.C.L., 631 Market St., Camden, 08102. Fax: 856-756-0113; Tel: 856-756-7900, Ext. 5452.

Episcopal Vicar for Priestly Life & Development—Rev. Msgr. JOHN T. FREY, V.E., 631 Market St., Camden, 08102. Tel: 856-964-2776, Ext. 5266.

Episcopal Vicar for Hispanics—Rev. Msgr. VICTOR S. MURO, Immaculate Heart of Mary, 410 S. 8th St., Vineland, 08360. Tel: 856-692-8992.

Deaneries and Vicars Forane—

Atlantic Deanery—Rev. Msgr. DONALD D. VELOZO, V.F., St. Bernadette, 1421 New Rd., Northfield, 08225. Tel: 609-646-5611; Fax: 609-484-8345.

Cape May Deanery—Rev. Msgr. WILLIAM QUINN, St. Paul, 9910 Third Ave., Stone Harbor, 08247. Tel: 609-368-3091; Fax: 609-368-2775.

Camden City Deanery—Rev. Msgr. MICHAEL DOYLE, V.F., St. Joseph Pro Cathedral, 2907 Federal St., Camden, 08105. Tel 856-964-2776; Fax: 856-964-0044.

Camden North Deanery—Rev. Msgr. WILLIAM P. BRENNAN, V.F., St Pius X, 344 Kresson Rd., Cherry Hill, 08034. Tel: 856-429-1330; Fax: 856-429-8679.

Camden South Deanery—Rev. Msgr. WILLIAM P. GRAHAM, St. Lawrence, 100 South Ave., Lindenwold, 08021. Tel: 856-627-2222; Fax: 856-627-8210.

Camden West Deanery—Rev. GEORGE C. SEITER, V.F., St. Aloysius, 37 W. Haddon Ave., Oaklyn, 08107. Tel: 856-854-2352; Fax: 856-854-4189.

Central Deanery—Rev. CARMEN A. CARLONE, V.F., St. Mary, 32 Carrol Ave., Williamstown, 08094. Tel: 856-629-6142; Fax: 856-875-2097.

Cumberland Deanery—Rev. JOHN H. BURTON, V.F., St. Isidore, 1655 Magnolia Rd., Vineland, 08360. Tel: 856-691-9077; Fax: 856-692-3305.

Gloucester Deanery—Rev. Msgr. JAMES R. TRACY, V.F., St. Charles Borromeo, 176 Stagecoach Rd., Sicklerville, 08081. Tel: 856-629-0411; Fax: 856-629-0412.

Southwest Deanery—Rev. Msgr. ROCCO A. CONTINILLO, V.F., Corpus Christi, 369 Georgetown Rd., Carneys Point, 08069. Tel: 856-299-3833; Fax: 856-299-3834.

Diocesan Tribunal

Diocesan Tribunal—Tel: 856-756-7900, Ext. 5452.

Judicial Vicar—Rev. Msgr. DOMINIC J. BOTTINO, J.C.L. Tel: 856-756-7900, Ext. 5452; Fax: 856-756-0113.

Presiding Judge for Court of Second Instance Cases—Rev. Msgr. EUGENE J. FITZSIMMONS, J.C.D. Tel: 856-756-7900, Ext. 5446.

Adjutant Judicial Vicars—Revs. DAVID J. KLEIN, J.C.L. Tel: 856-756-7900, Ext. 5462; PETER M. JOYCE, J.C.L. Tel: 856-756-7900, Ext. 5462; JAMES M. MAGGART, J.C.L. Tel: 856-756-7900, Ext. 5462.

Director of the Tribunal—GLENN CARROZZA, J.C.D. Tel: 856-756-7900, Ext. 5462.

Promoter of Justice—Rev. JOSEPH A. SALERNO, J.C.L.

Judges—Rev. Msgr. EDWARD D. ALLEYNE (Retired); GLENN CARROZZA, J.C.D.; Rev. Msgr. EUGENE J.

FITZSIMMONS, J.C.D.; Revs. FRANCIS P. GAFFNEY, J.C.L.; DAVID J. KLEIN, J.C.L.; EDWARD J. LIPINSKI; JOSEPH A. SALERNO, J.C.L.; Rev. Msgr. THOMAS F. SHARKEY, J.C.D.

Defenders of the Bond—Revs. JAMES F. BARRY; HERMAN N. BURGER, J.C.L.; Deacons W. LEO MCBLAIN; JAMES H. ROCKS.

Advocates—Revs. CHRISTOPHER BAKEY; JAMES F. BETZ; Rev. Msgr. DOMINIC J. BOTTINO, J.C.L.; Revs. THOMAS S. CAPPERELLA; CHARLES J. COLOZZI; MICHAEL P. HEGARTY; ROBERT J. KANTZ; EDWARD R. KOLLA; ALLEN B. LOVELL; ALBERT J. MCLAVERTY; DANIEL J. MELENDEZ; RONAN B. MURPHY; JOSEPH PHAM; JOSEPH-CUONG M. PHAM; STEPHEN RAPPOSELLI; JASON T. ROCKS; MICHAEL G. SPAGNOLA; Deacons JOSEPH COSTELLO; GERALD DEMURO; MICHAEL HARKINS; FELIX MIRANDA; DAVID M. MURNANE; WILLIAM NORQUEST; ERNEST F. PICKNALLY; RICHARD SAMPSON; WILLIAM SCOTT; JACK WERNER; ROBERT WILLSON; Sisters CATHERINE KANE, O.S.F.; RITA MCGURK, R.S.M.; MARIE ST. LEGER, S.S.J.; Mr. BRIAN AYSCUE; Ms. KATHY BENNETT; Mr. JOHN CONTINO; Mrs. CATHERINE COSTELLO; Mr. THOMAS DOYLE; Ms. ANNE MARIE GAVIN; Mr. CHARLES GIRARD, Esq.; Mr. JAMES HALLEY; Ms. NANCY HARRIGAN; Mr. JOHN HARRINGTON JR.; Mr. JAMES HOGAN; Mr. GERALD JAJBLONOWSKI; Mr. ANTHONY JADICK; Mrs. CAROL A. JENNINGS; Mr. THOMAS E. JENNINGS; FRANCIS J. KARDOS, C.P.A.; Mr. JOSEPH B. MCGARRITY; Mr. THOMAS MOLESKI; Mr. PAUL M. PARCHINSKI; Mr. THOMAS ROBITAILLE; Mr. HUGH SWEENEY; Mr. VINCENT TRAINER; Mr. JAMES H. TRYON; Mrs. KATALINA UYEHARA; Mr. ROBERT UYEHARA; Mr. GERALD WASHKO; Ms. KATHRYN ANN WINTERLE, Esq.

Diocesan Delegate for Women Religious—Sr. PHILOMENA NOWICKA, L.S.I.C., Provincialate, 1000 Cropwell Rd., Cherry Hill, 08003. Tel: 856-751-1212; Fax: 856-751-1855. Email: pnowicka@camdendiocese.org.

Sisters' Council—Sisters PHILOMENA NOWICKA, L.S.I.C., Chm.; JOANNE BURZICHELLI, R.S.M.; CATHERINE KANE, O.S.F.; CYNTHIA LUDWICK, S.S.J.; MARIANNE MCCANN, M.P.F.; MARIE ST. JAMES, I.H.M.; CONNIE TRAYNOR, S.S.J.

Vicariate for Priestly Life and Development—Rev. Msgr. JOHN T. FREY, V.E., Vicar. Tel: 856-756-7900, Ext. 5266.

Office of Priest Personnel—Mr. ROD J. HERRERA, L.C.S.W., Exec. Sec. Tel: 856-756-7900, Ext. 5261; Fax: 856-966-5957; MARCIA FIAMINGO, Coord. Tel: 856-756-7900, Ext. 5215.

Priests Personnel Board—Mr. ROD J. HERRERA, L.C.S.W., Ex Officio; Rev. Msgr. ANDREW E. MARTIN, Chm.; Rev. JOSEPH J. ADAMSON; Rev. Msgr. JAMES P. CURRAN; Revs. JOSEPH R. FERRARA; WILLIAM H. HART (Retired); PETER M. JOYCE, J.C.L.; ROGER E. MCGRATH; TERRY M. ODIEN; ROBERT V. SMITH.

Continuing Education & Spiritual Formation of Priests (CESF)—Rev. KENNETH JOHNSTON, Dir. Tel: 856-756-7900, Ext. 5266. Members: Revs. MARK R. CAVAGNARO; JOHN A. DELDUCA; Rev. Msgrs. J. FRANCIS FLAHERTY; JOHN FREY; Revs. ROBERT J. GREGORIO, S.T.D.; PAUL D. HARTE; Mr. ROD J. HERRERA, L.C.S.W.; Revs. WILLIAM A. HODGE; ROBERT E. HUGHES; PETER M. IDLER; JULIAN A. KARCZEWSKI; RICHARD J. LODGE; JAMES M. MAGGART, J.C.L.; EDWARD J. MAHER; CADMUS D. MAZZARELLA; PAUL A. OLSZEWSKI; STEPHEN J. RAPPOSELLI; JOSEPH T. SZOLACK, M.Div.; Rev. Msgr. JAMES R. TRACY, V.F.

Advanced Studies for Priests—Rev. Msgr. JOHN T. FREY, V.E., Vicar. Tel: 856-756-7900, Ext. 5266.

Liaison with Retired Priests—Rev. Msgr. RICHARD J. CALLAHAN (Retired). Tel: 856-691-9077.

Vicar for Men Religious—Very Rev. STEPHEN LAROSA, O.S.A. Tel: 856-697-9660.

Priests Assistance Program—Rev. MARCEL TABONE. Tel: 609-263-8696.

Clergy Health Panel—Rev. MARCEL TABONE, Chm. Members: Rev. Msgr. ROBERT T. MCDERMOTT; Rev. LEWIS A. BATTISTI; Rev. Msgr. ANDREW MARTIN; Revs. THOMAS A. NEWTON; FRED VOLTAGGIO; JOSEPH D. WALLACE; Mr. ROD J. HERRERA, L.C.S.W.; Dr. JOSEPH W. SOKOLOWSKI.

Sacred Heart Residences—200 St. Mary's Dr., Cherry Hill, 08003. Tel: 856-751-2010; Fax: 856-489-8999. Rev. Msgr. HARRY J. JORDAN, Dir. (Retired).

Vianney Villa—230 St. Mary's Dr., Cherry Hill, 08003. Tel: 856-424-2035.

Neumann House—250 St. Mary's Dr., Cherry Hill, 08003. Tel: 856-424-1741.

Vocations Apostolate—Rev. CADMUS D. MAZZARELLA, Dir.; Sr. DOROTHY ALOSIO, Assoc. Dir.; Rev. CHRISTOPHER BAKEY, Dir., Recruitment of Priestly & Religious Vocations, Nazareth House, 300 Cuthbert Blvd., Cherry Hill, 08002. Tel: 856-910-4930; Fax: 856-662-8917.

Vocation Advisory Board—Rev. CADMUS D. MAZZARELLA; Sr. DOROTHY ALOISIO; Rev. Msgrs. JOHN T. FREY, V.E.; THOMAS FITZSIMMONS; Revs. CHRISTOPHER BAKEY; WILLIAM A. HODGE; KENNETH JOHNSTON; JOSEPH PHAM; JOSEPH T. SZOLACK, M.Div.

Assistant Vocation Directors for Recruitment—Revs. JOSEPH BYERLEY; JAMES A. CASADIA; CHARLES CONATY; WALTER GUASP-SANTOS; PETER IDLER; ALLEN B. LOVELL; ALBERT J. MCLAVERTY; PAUL A. OLSZEWSKI; ROBERT C. PASLEY; JASON T. ROCKS.

Amicus—Rev. Msgr. JOHN T. FREY, V.E., Chap.

Nazareth House of Discernment—Rev. CADMUS D. MAZZARELLA, Dir. Tel: 856-910-4900.

Friends of the Sacred Heart—Rev. Msgr. CHARLES P. BARTH, Chap. Tel: 856-663-1371, Ext. 5216.

Serra Clubs International— District 35: Mr. THOMAS HALPIN, Governor. Tel: 856-756-7900, Ext. 6125. Atlantic County East: Mr. JAMES STECHER, Pres.; Rev. BRENDAN V. SULLIVAN, Chap. Cape May County: Mr. JOHN DWYER, Pres.; Rev. MARK CAVAGNARO, Chap. Cumberland County: Mr. PHILIP BORGESE, Pres.; Rev. RAYMOND GORMLEY, Chap.

Apostolic Administrator—Rev. Msgr. THOMAS J. MORGAN. Tel: 856-756-7900, Ext. 5432; Fax: 856-338-0376.

Chancellor and Episcopal Vicar for Canonical Affairs—Rev. Msgr. JOSEPH W. POKUSA, J.C.D. Tel: 856-756-7900, Ext. 5216; Fax: 856-338-0376.

Vicars Forane, Presbyteral Council, Censor Librorum, Diocesan Historian—Rev. JAMES BETZ. Tel: 856-467-0037.

Offices Reporting to the Apostolic Administrator

Diocesan Finance Officer—WILLIAM J. MURRAY. Tel: 856-756-7900, Ext. 5240.

College of Consultors—Mr. LAWRENCE READER, Exec. Sec. Tel: 856-756-7900, Ext. 5206; WILLIAM J. MURRAY, Recording Sec. Tel: 856-756-7900, Ext. 5240.

Members—Rev. Msgrs. WILLIAM P. BRENNAN, V.F.; JOSEPH V. DIMAURO; HARRY J. JORDAN (Retired); THOMAS J. MCINTYRE; JOSEPH W. POKUSA, J.C.D.; WILLIAM QUINN; RUSSELL L. ROCK; PATRICK M. TIERNEY; JAMES R. TRACY, V.F.; DONALD VELOZO.

Diocesan Finance Council—Rev. Msgrs. THOMAS FITZSIMMONS; JOSEPH P. HERRON (Retired); THOMAS J. MORGAN; WILLIAM CONWAY; PATRICK HARKER; WILLIAM LEAHY; JERRY PONTILLO; WILLIAM RENNIE.

Diocesan Self-Insurance Plan (DSIP) & Pension Funds—WILLIAM MURRAY. Tel: 856-756-7900, Ext. 5240.

Office of Mission Awareness—Directors: Revs. JOHN C. MUSCAT; GEORGE C. SEITER, V.F. Tel: 856-756-7900, Ext. 5464.

Propagation of the Faith & Holy Childhood Association—Rev. GEORGE C. SEITER, V.F. Tel: 856-756-7900, Ext. 5464.

Brazilian Missions & Catholic Relief Services—Rev. JOHN C. MUSCAT. Tel: 856-756-7900, Ext. 5464.

Operation Rice Bowl—Tel: 856-756-7900, Ext. 5464.

Campaign for Human Development—Rev. KENNETH P. HALLAHAN, S.T.D., Coord.

Office of Development—Rev. Msgr. LOUIS A. MARUCCI, D.Min., Dir. Tel: 856-756-7900, Ext. 6125.

House of Charity/Bishop's Annual Appeal—MARIANN GETTINGS, Dir. Tel: 856-756-7900, Ext. 6128.

Planned Giving—JAMES LANAHAN, Asst. Dir. Devel. Tel: 856-756-7900, Ext. 6134.

Stewardship—JOHN D'AMICO, Coord.

Fund for Educational Development—JAMES LANAHAN, Coord. Tel: 856-756-7900, Ext. 6134.

Jubilate Deo Chorale and Orchestra—Rev. Msgr. LOUIS A. MARUCCI, D.Min., Exec. Dir. Tel: 856-756-7900, Ext. 6122.

Secretariat for Communications—ANDREW WALTON, Sec. Tel: 856-756-7900, Ext. 5282.

Office of Communications—ANDREW WALTON, Dir. Tel: 856-756-7900, Ext. 5282; STEPHANIE LODER, Asst. Tel: 856-756-7900, Ext. 5281.

Office of Community Affairs—

Special Collections—

Diocesan Newspaper—P.O. Box 708, Camden, 08101. Tel: 856-756-7900; Fax: 856-756-7938. CARL D. PETERS, Mng. Editor. Tel: 856-756-7900, Ext. 6218. "The Catholic Star Herald"

Office for Pastoral Planning and Research—

Diocesan Pastoral Planning—SHARON A. TUMULTY, Ph.D., Dir. Tel: 856-756-7900, Ext. 5275.

Pastoral Planning for Parish Life—Rev. JOHN STABENO, Dir. Tel: 856-756-7900, Ext. 5201.

Statistics and Technology—Rev. ROBERT J. KANTZ, Coord. Tel: 856-756-7900, Ext. 5265.

Secretariat for Temporal Services—LAWRENCE READER, Sec., 631 Market St., Camden, 08102. Tel: 856-756-7900, Ext. 5206.

Bishop's Representative to Labor Unions—Rev. Msgr. THOMAS A. GUENTHER.

Cemeteries—ROBERT GUERRIERI, Dir. Tel: 856-756-7900, Ext. 5411.

Facilities—ART BASCIANO, A.I.A., Dir. Tel: 856-756-7900, Ext. 5277; THOMAS BECHARD, Diocesan Engineer. Tel: 856-756-7900, Ext. 5289; JOSEPH MARTIN, Plant Facilities Mgr. Tel: 856-756-7900, Ext. 5400.

Financial Services—EDWARD J. LOCASALE, C.P.A., Dir. Tel: 856-756-7900, Ext. 5234; Fax: 856-963-2655.

Budgeting—THOMAS J. ARDECKI, Dir. Tel: 856-756-7900, Ext. 5268; MICHAEL R. PORTER, Analyst. Tel: 856-756-7900, Ext. 5429.

Comptrollers—LISA M. CILIBERTO, C.P.A., Comptroller. Tel: 856-756-7900, Ext. 5274; CAROLYNN THOMPSON, Asst. Comptroller. Tel: 856-756-7900, Ext. 5280; MARIE E. PELUSO, Account Supvr. Tel: 856-756-7900, Ext. 5249.

Parish Services—MAUREEN M. AUSTIN, Analyst. Tel: 856-756-7900, Ext. 5238; J. ROWELL REYES, C.P.A., Parish Auditor. Tel: 856-756-7900, Ext. 5267.

Human Resources—JOHN RAFTERY, Dir. Tel: 856-756-7900, Ext. 5203; JOSEPH P. HIGGINS, Benefits Admin. Tel: 856-756-7900, Ext. 5246; CANDY NEWHOUSE, Health Insurance. Tel: 856-756-7900, Ext. 5253.

Diocesan Liability & Insurance Program—CATHY JAMES. Tel: 856-756-7900, Ext. 5203.

Management Information Services—MARIANNE LINKA, Dir. Tel: 856-756-7900, Ext. 5232.

Real Estate—KENNETH MCILVAINE, Consultant. Tel: 856-756-7900, Ext. 5257.

Vicariate for Pastoral Life—

Vicar for Pastoral Life—Rev. ROBERT E. HUGHES, 631 Market St., Camden, 08102. Tel: 856-756-7900, Ext. 6208; Fax: 856-225-0096.

Assistant to Vicar General for Pastoral Life—Deacon LEO MCBLAIN. Tel: 856-756-7900, Ext. 6230.

Offices Reporting to the Vicar for Pastoral Life

Secretariate for Catholic Schools—Rev. ROBERT E. HUGHES, Sec. Tel: 856-756-7900, Ext. 6208.

Superintendent of Schools—VACANT. Tel: 856-756-7900, Ext. 6295; Fax: 856-756-0225.

Personnel and School Support Services—Sr. DAWN GEAR, G.N.S.H., Asst. Supt. Tel: 856-756-7900, Ext. 6256.

Religious Education and School Marketing—Curriculum and Educational Services Sr. THERESA BRUNO, Asst. Supt. Tel: 856-756-7900, Ext. 6271.

Educational and Government Programs—Sr. ROSE DIFLURI, I.H.M. Tel: 856-756-7900, Ext. 6296.

Tuition Assistance Programs—BETTY PASTORE, Coord. Tel: 856-756-7900, Ext. 6265.

Parent-Teachers Association—Rev. Msgr. JAMES P. CURRAN, Moderator. Tel: 856-881-0909; PATRICIA WIRBICK, Pres. Tel: 856-456-4839, Ext. 6230.

Board of Education—MARK D'ONOFRIO, Pres.

Secretariat for Parish Life and Worship—

Secretary—Deacon LEO MCBLAIN. Tel: 856-756-7900, Ext. 6230.

Permanent Diaconate—Rev. FREDERICK LINK, Chap. Tel: 856-756-7900, Ext. 6210.

Office of Family Life—Deacon LEO MCBLAIN, Exec. Dir. Tel: 856-756-7900, Ext. 6230; Fax: 856-964-3401.

Marriage and Family Enrichment—STEVEN BOZZA. Tel: 856-756-7900, Ext. 6221.

Natural Family Planning—CECILIA LECHEVALLIER, Coord. Tel: 856-756-7900, Ext. 6315.

Chastity Education—MARY ANN CHEZIK, Ph.D. Tel: 856-756-7900, Ext. 6314.

Singles Never Married/Bereavement—VACANT, Co-ord. Tel: 856-756-7900, Ext. 6242.

Marriage Preparation—Rev. STEPHEN RAPPOSELLI, Coord. Tel: 856-756-7900, Ext. 6257.

Office of Pro Life—WILLIAM KLATT, Dir. Tel: 856-756-7900, Ext. 6298.

Office of Worship—Rev. JAMES M. MAGGART, J.C.L., Dir. Tel: 856-756-7900, Ext. 5251.

School of Liturgy—TRUDY CRANSTON, Coord. Tel: 856-756-7900, Ext. 5248.

Liturgical Commission—Rev. JOHN H. BURTON, V.F., Chm. Tel: 856-965-4021, Ext. 6151.

Choir Master—THEODORE KIEFER. Tel: 856-756-7900, Ext. 5355.

Church Architectural Commission—Rev. ROBERT E. HUGHES, Chm. Tel: 856-756-7900, Ext. 6151.

Office of Ecumenical and Interreligious Affairs—Rev. JOSEPH D. WALLACE, Coord. Tel: 856-429-3334, Ext. 5446.

Commission on Ecumenical and Interreligious Affairs—Rev. Msgr. EUGENE J. FITZSIMMONS, J.C.D., Chm. Tel: 856-756-7900, Ext. 5446.

St. Pius X Retreat Center—1840 Peter Cheeseman Rd.,

Blackwood, 08012. Tel: 856-227-1436; Fax: 856-227-2907. Rev. THOMAS J. BARCELLONA, Dir.

Catholic Family Health and Recreation Center—P.O. Box 250, Blackwood, 08012. Rev. THOMAS BARCELLONA, Exec. Dir. & Spiritual Moderator; BETH ANN CULKIN, Dir. Tel: 856-227-1259; Fax: 856-227-1840.

Office of Youth Ministry—St. Pius X Retreat House, 1840 Peter Cheeseman Rd., Blackwood, 08012. Rev. THOMAS J. BARCELLONA, Exec. Dir. & Moderator. Tel: 856-227-1436; KATHLEEN A. EBNER, Dir. Tel: 856-227-8250; Fax: 856-227-2907.

Office of Youth and Young Adult Activities—St. Pius X Retreat House, 1840 Peter Cheeseman Rd., Blackwood, 08012. Rev. THOMAS J. BARCELLONA, Exec. Dir. & Moderator. Tel: 856-227-1436.

Young Adult Ministry—Rev. TIMOTHY E. BYERLEY, Dir. Tel: 856-227-2623.

Youth Ministry—PAT WIRBICK, West Coord. Tel: 856-227-8250; Fax: 856-227-2907 (Camden, Gloucester, Salem); VACANT, East Coord., (Atlantic, Cape May, Cumberland).

Scouting—Rev. ALBERT E. HARSHAW, Chap. Tel: 609-861-3771; ANSON WAGER, Chm. Tel: 856-547-3197, Ext. 6290.

Secretariate for Evangelization and Catechetical Formation

Secretary—VACANT. Tel: 856-756-7900, Ext. 6290.

Office for Lay Leadership Development—VACANT, Dir. Tel: 856-756-7900, Ext. 6290; Fax: 856-338-1581.

Office for Religious Education—Sr. MARY BETH COYLE, I.H.M., Dir. Tel: 856-756-7900, Ext. 6284; Fax: 856-541-9644.

Office of Hispanic Apostolate—Sr. KATHLEEN BROWN, I.H.M., Dir. Tel: 856-756-7900, Ext. 6112; Rev. Msgr. VICTOR S. MURO, Episcopal Vicar, 414 S. 8th St., Vineland, 08360. Tel: 856-692-3992; Fax: 856-692-1259.

Office of Black Catholic Ministry—Deacon WILLIAM JOHNSON, Dir. Tel: 856-756-7900, Ext. 6363.

Office of Deaf and Disabilities—Rev. BRIAN E. O'NEILL, Dir. Tel: 856-784-4090; Fax: 856-784-6371.

Office of Ethnic Ministries—Rev. RONALD S. FALOTICO. Tel: 609-641-0285; Fax: 609-641-0385.

Office of Evangelization and Adult Faith Formation—FRANCIS BLEE, Ph.D., Dir. Tel: 856-756-7900, Ext. 6227; Fax: 856-541-9644.

English Cursillo—Rev. Msgr. JOHN T. FREY, V.E., Spiritual Dir. Tel: 856-547-0564.

Spanish Cursillo—Rev. ALVERO DIAZ, Spiritual Dir. Tel: 609-641-0285, Ext. 6247.

R.C.I.A. Office—VACANT, Coord. Tel: 856-756-7900, Ext. 6247.

Campus Ministry—Rev. MICHAEL T. MANNION, Coord. Tel: 856-225-1077; Fax: 856-757-0438.

Rutgers University - Camden—Rev. MICHAEL T. MANNION, Campus Minister Tel: 856-963-6568; Fax: 856-966-5955.

Rowan University - Glassboro—Rev. CADMUS D. MAZZARELLA, Dir.; ANN POLO, Asst. Dir. Tel: 856-881-5642; Fax: 856-881-4183.

Stockton College of New Jersey - Pomona—Rev. JEFFRIES BURTON, S.J., Campus Minister. Tel: 609-652-0230.

Camden County Community College—Sr. KAREN MCCONNELL, Campus Minister. Tel: 856-227-7200, Ext. 4552.

Atlantic Cape Community College - Mays Landing—Rev. JEFFRIES BURTON, S.J., Campus Minister. Tel: 609-652-0230, Ext. 6346.

Diocesan Media and Resource Center—CONSTANCE TEESDALE, Coord. Tel: 856-756-7900, Ext. 6346; Fax: 856-338-1581.

Men's Ministry—Rev. DAVID A. GROVER. Tel: 856-478-2294, Ext. 6223.

Charismatic Renewal—Rev. CHRISTOPHER BAKEY, Moderator. Tel: 856-910-4900; Fax: 609-886-9415; 856-662-8918; Deacon JOSEPH COSTELLO, Diocesan Liaison. Tel: 609-522-6586.

Hispanic Charismatic Renewal—Rev. FELIPE MOYANO. Tel: 609-641-0285; Fax: 609-641-8385.

Marian Commission—Rev. WILLIAM A. HODGE, Chm. Tel: 609-344-1040; Fax: 609-344-2471.

Legion of Mary—Rev. WILLIAM A. HODGE, Spiritual Dir. Tel: 609-344-1040; Fax: 609-344-2471

Holy Name Society—Rev. JEROME C. ROMANOWSKI, Dir. Tel: 856-694-2576; Fax: 856-694-4636.

Vicariate for Human Services—Rev. THOMAS A. NEWTON, Vicar, 1845 Haddon Ave., Camden, 08103. Tel: 856-342-4101; Fax: 856-342-4180; FRANCIS J. KARDOS, C.P.A., C.F.O., 1845 Haddon Ave., Camden, 08103. Tel: 856-342-4123 Fax: 856-342-4180; KEVIN H. HICKEY, M.S.W., Exec. Dir., Catholic Charities, 1845 Haddon Ave., Camden, 08103. Tel: 856-342-4102; Fax: 856-342-4180; MARTIN IDLER, Exec. Dir., Diocesan Health Services Corp., 1845 Haddon Ave. Camden, 08103. Tel: 856-342-4131; Fax: 856-342-4180; CURTIS H. JOHNSON JR., Exec. Dir., Diocesan Housing Services Corp., 1845 Haddon Ave., Camden, 08103. Tel: 856-342-4130; Fax: 856-342-4180; JOSEPH TORRIERI, Dir., Information Technology Dept., 1845 Haddon Ave., Camden, 08103. Tel: 856-342-4130; Fax: 856-342-4180; JOAN M. VALK, Dir., Human Resources Dept., 1845 Haddon Ave., Camden, 08103. Tel: 856-342-4103; Fax: 856-342-4180.

Catholic Charities, Diocese of Camden, Inc.—KEVIN H. HICKEY, M.S.W., Exec. Dir., Catholic Charities, 1845 Haddon Ave., Camden, 08103. Tel: 856-342-4102; Fax: 856-342-4180; JOSEPH BARTLEY, C.P.A., 1845 Haddon Ave., Camden, 08103 Tel: 856-342-4129; Fax: 856-342-4180.

Offices Reporting to the Executive Director of Catholic Charities

Emergency Service Centers—

Camden County—CEREIDA MEDINA, Coord., 1484-86 Mt Ephraim Ave., Camden, 08104. Tel: 856-964-2133; Fax: 856-225-1384; LAURA CARABALLO, Case Mgr. Aide, St. Joseph Pro-Cathedral, 2907 Federal St., Camden, 08105. Tel: 856-964-2776; LAURA CARABALLO, Case Mgr. Aide, St. Anthony of Padua, 2814 River Rd., Camden, 08105. Tel: 856-963-5884.

Atlantic County—Sr. GRACE NOLAN, R.S.M., B.A., Coord., 9 N. Georgia Ave, Atlantic City, 08401. Tel: 609-345-3448; Fax: 609-345-7180.

Cape May County—CHERYL KING, Acting Coord., 1304 Hwy. 47 S., Rio Grande 08242. Tel: 609-886-2662; Fax: 609-886-3583.

Cumberland County—JOHN DESPARROIS, C.S.W., Regl. Coord., 810 Montrose Ave., Vineland, 08360. Tel: 856-691-1841; Fax: 856-692-6575.

Gloucester County—MARCIA HOFFMAN, Acting Coord., 1200 Delsea Dr., Ste. One, Westville, 08093. Tel: 856-845-9200; Fax: 856-845-8905.

Salem County—JOHN DESPARROIS, C.S.W., Regl. Coord., 14-16 W. Main St., Penns Grove, 08069. Tel: 856-299-1296; Fax: 856-299-4010.

Division of Mental Health Services—

Administrative—1845 Haddon Ave., Camden, 08103. Tel: 856-342-4110; Fax: 856-342-4180.

Mental Health Services—Tel: 856-682-2166; Fax: 856-691-6084.

Victim Assistance Coordinator—BARBARA ANN GONDEK, L.C.S.W. Tel: 856-524-4552.

Crisis Pregnancy and Adoption Services—JAN BONO, Dir., 810 Montrose Ave., Vineland, 08360. Tel: 856-691-1909; Fax: 856-692-6575.

Project Rachel— (Post-Abortion Counseling and Support)-- Tel: 856-342-4108.

AIDS Ministry—Sr. ELISE GITTRICH, S.C., B.A., B.S., Dir., 2825 Concorde Ave., Camden, 08105. Tel: 856-542-3155; Fax: 856-966-5145.

Job Development—JOHN MARCANTUONO, L.C.S.W., Dir., 1845 Haddon Ave. Camden, 08103. Tel: 856-342-4167; Fax: 856-342-4180.

Special Education—EILEEN MURTHA, M.A., Dir., 1845 Haddon Ave., Camden, 08103. Tel: 856-342-4163; Fax: 856-342-4180

Disaster Relief—JENNIFER DYER, B.A., Dir., 1845 Haddon Ave., Camden, 08103. Tel: 856-342-4107; Fax: 856-342-4180.

Migration and Refugee Services—TUAN "TIMMY" NGUYEN, Dir., 1845 Haddon Ave., Camden, 08105. Tel: 856-342-4156; Fax: 856-342-4180.

School-Based Family Support Program—CHERYL DUNICAN, A.C.S.W., L.C.S.W., Dir., 1845 Haddon Ave., Camden, 08103 Tel: 856-342-4148; Fax: 856-342-4180.

Faith Families Case Management—CAROLE PARKER, B.A., Dir., 1845 Haddon Ave., Camden, 08103. Tel: 856-342-4142; Fax: 856-342-4180.

Prison Ministry—VACANT, 1845 Haddon Ave., Camden, 08103. Tel: 856-342-4106; Fax: 856-342-4180.

Catholic Charities' Community Liaison—Rev. JOSEPH MESSINA. Tel: 856-342-4104.

St. John Prenatal Clinic—PATRICIA A. CHICO, L.P.N., Coord., 6th and Erie Sts., Camden, 08102. Tel: 856-757-9540.

Guadalupe Family Services—Sr. HELEN COLE, S.S.J., L.C.S.W., Dir., 511 State St., Camden, 08102. Tel: 856-365-8081.

Immigration Services and Legal Assistance to the Poor—Rev. WALTER A. NORRIS; VINCENT G. GUEST ESQ., Camden Center for Law and Social Justice, 509 State St., Camden, 08102. Tel: 856-966-8896. Camden Center for Law and Social Justice - Romero Center, 1845 Haddon Ave., Camden, 08103. Tel: 856-362-4160; Fax: 856-342-4180. Camden Center for Law and Social Justice - Our Lady Star of the Sea, 15 N. California Ave., Atlantic City, 08401. Tel: 609-348-2111.

The Diocesan Health Services Corporation of the Diocese of Camden, Inc.—MARTIN IDLER, Exec. Dir., 1845 Haddon Ave., Camden, 08103. Tel: 856-342-4131; Fax: 856-342-4180; JUDY GUNDERSHEIM, Finance Dir., Health Affairs, 1845 Haddon Ave., Camden, 08103. Tel: 856-342-4132; Fax: 856-342-4180.

Offices Reporting to the Executive Director of the Diocesan Health Services Corporation

Long Term Care Facilities—

St. Mary's Catholic Home—Sr. BEATRIX WIECZOREK, L.S.I.C., L.N.H.A., Admin., 220 St. Mary Dr., Cherry Hill, 08003. Tel: 856-424-9521.

Our Lady's Residence—ANNA TOSTI, L.N.H.A., Acting Dir., 1100 Clematis Ave., Pleasantville, 08232. Tel: 609-646-2450.

Bishop McCarthy Residence—Sr. LUCY MAROOR, H.S.M., L.N.H.A., Admin., 1045 E. Chestnut Ave., Vineland, 08360. Tel: 856-692-2850.

Mater Dei Nursing Home—Sr. ANNE EBERSOLD, M.S.C., L.N.H.A., Admin., 176 Rte. 40, Newfield, 08344. Tel: 856-358-2061.

Manor at St. Mary's—Sr. FRANCIS M. SZYMANSKA, L.S.I.C., C.A.L.A., Admin., 220 St. Mary's Dr., Cherry Hill, 08003. Tel: 856-424-3817.

Clinics—

St. Luke Catholic Medical Services—LESLY D'AMBOLA, D.O., Dir., 511 State St., Camden, 08102. Tel: 856-365-4642.

Health Care Ministry—Rev. DAVID J. KLEIN, J.C.L., Coord. Tel: 856-342-4109; Fax: 856-342-4180.

The Diocesan Housing Services Corporation of the Diocese of Camden, Inc.—CURTIS H. JOHNSON JR., Exec. Dir., 1845 Haddon Ave., Camden, 08103. Tel: 856-342-4130; Fax: 856-342-4180.

Offices Reporting to the Executive Director of the Housing Services Corporation

Senior Housing—

Victorian Towers, Inc.—

Victorian Towers Management Corp.—MAUREEN FARRELL, Office Mgr., 608 Washington St., Cape May, 08204. Tel: 609-884-5883.

Village Apartments of Cherry Hill, NJ—THERESA MOSTEIG, Assoc. Exec. Dir., 212 Lourdes Ct., Cherry Hill, 08003. Tel: 856-424-7913.

Family Housing—

Domicilium Corporation—

Davenport Village—Site Manager, 301 Davenport Ave., Hainesport, 08060. Tel: 609-702-0138.

Other Human Services Vicariate Ministries—

Representative to Archbishop Damiano School and St. John of God—Rev. THOMAS A. NEWTON, Vicar.

Apostleship of the Sea—Rev. Msgr. MICHAEL J. DOYLE. Tel: 856-966-6700.

Ladies of Charity—Rev. JAMES J. DURKIN, Spiritual Dir. Tel: 856-783-5555; Sr. ELISE GITTRICH, S.C., B.A., B.S., Sister Moderator. Tel: 856-910-8723.

St. Vincent De Paul Society—MARY ANN CARLSON, Pres.; Deacon MICHAEL HARKINS, Spiritual Dir.

The Cathedral Soup Kitchen, Inc.—KAREN TALARICO. Tel: 856-964-6771; Fax: 856-964-6772.

CLERGY, PARISHES, MISSIONS AND PAROCHIAL SCHOOLS

CITY OF CAMDEN
(CAMDEN COUNTY)

1—IMMACULATE CONCEPTION CATHEDRAL (1864), [CEM] Rev. Michael T. Mannion, Rector.

Res.: 642 Market St., 08102. Tel: 856-964-1580; Fax: 856-757-0438.

2—ST. ANTHONY OF PADUA (1945), (Hispanic), Revs. Todd Carpenter, O.F.M.; John C. Coughlin, O.F.M.; Patrick Sieber, O.F.M.; Bro. Frank B. Waywood, O.F.M.; Deacon Felix Miranda.

Res.: 2818 River Ave. 08105. Tel: 856-963-5884; Fax: 856-635-1286.

School—Tel: 856-966-6791; Fax: 856-966-1616. Mrs. Linda Meehan, Prin. Lay Teachers 11; Students 212.

Catechesis/Religious Program—Students 2,002.

3—ST. BARTHOLOMEW'S (1940), (African American), Rev. Gerard C. Marable.

Res.: 751 Kaighns Ave., 08103. Tel: 856-365-0573; Fax: 856-365-0744.

Catechesis/Religious Program—Students 29.

4—HOLY NAME (1913), (Hispanic), Revs. William J. Kelley, S.J. (CHL); Donald M. Ward, S.J.; Sr. Linda Stilling, S.S.N.D., Pastoral Assoc. School Sisters of Notre Dame (Baltimore) In Res., Revs. Charles G. Gonzalez, S.J.; Francis X. Moan, S.J.; Jeffrey P. Puttoff, S.J.

Res.: 522 State St., 08102-1919. Tel: 856-963-1621; Fax: 856-338-0793.

School—Tel: 856-365-7930; Fax: 856-365-8041. Mrs.

Patricia Munyan, Prin. Lay Teachers 11; Students 200.
Catechesis/Religious Program—Students 335.
Convent—Sisters of St. Joseph (Chestnut Hill), 517 State St.. Tel: 856-964-1233; 856-488-3540.
5—St. Joan of Arc (1920), Rev. Kenneth P. Hallahan, S.T.D. In Res., Rev. Gerard C. Marable.
Res.: 3107 Alabama Rd., 08104. Tel: 856-962-8642; Fax: 856-962-7123.
Catechesis/Religious Program—Students 41.
6—St. Joseph's (1892), (Polish), [CEM] Rev. Piotr Szamocki.
Res.: 1010 Liberty St., 08104. Tel: 856-963-1285; Fax: 856-963-2466.
7—St. Joseph's Pro-Cathedral (1893), Rev. Msgr. Robert T. McDermott; Sisters Margaret Mary Schmicker, O.S.F., Pastoral Min.; Clarisa Vazquez, S.S.T., Hispanic Min. Tel: 856-964-4336, Ext. 503; John Klein, Business Admin.; Ms. Patricia Slater, Dir., Romero Ctr.; Evelin Ciarrocca. In Res., Rev. Msgr. Andrew E. Martin; Rev. James Creedon, O.S.A.
Res.: 2907 Federal St., 08105. Tel: 856-964-2776; Fax: 856-964-0044.
School—Tel: 856-964-4336; Fax: 856-964-1080. Mrs. Kathleen Shiflet, Prin. Lay Teachers 20; Students 291.
St. Joseph Child Development Center—17 Church St.. Tel: 856-963-9202; Fax: 856-963-8940. Betty Mitchell, Dir. Children 75.
Catechesis/Religious Program—Tel: 856-541-4944, Ext. 502. Mrs. Sue Ann Jeral, D.R.E. Tel: 856-541-4944, Ext. 502. Students 190.
8—Our Lady of Mount Carmel/Fatima, (Hispanic—Italian), Rev. Salvatore A. Scuderi, M.SS.CC.; Deacon Aladino Velez. In Res., Bro. David Graber, M.SS.CC.
Res.: 832 S. 4th St., 08103. Tel: 856-541-7618; Fax: 856-541-2835.
Catechesis/Religious Program—Students 443.
9—Sacred Heart (1885),, Records for St. George kept at Sacred Heart, Camden. Records for Sts. Peter and Paul kept at the Cathedral of the Immaculate Conception, Camden. Records for St. John the Baptist kept at St. Joseph Pro-Cathedral, Camden. Rev. Michael Doyle.
Res.: 1739 Ferry Ave., 08104. Tel: 856-966-6700; Fax: 856-756-0102.
School—Fourth & Jaspers Sts., 08104. Tel: 856-963-1341; Fax: 856-963-3551. Mrs. Janet Williams, Prin. Lay Teachers 14; Students 254.
Catechesis/Religious Program—Students 254.

OUTSIDE THE CITY OF CAMDEN

Absecon, Atlantic Co., St. Elizabeth Ann Seton (1975), Revs. Robert V. Smith; Carlton C. Stoegbauer; Deacons Joseph Becker; William Peters.
Res.: 591 New Jersey Ave., 08201. Tel: 609-641-1480; Fax: 609-641-7396.
School—Assumption Regional School, Pomona, Tel: 609-652-7134; Fax: 609-965-4149. See separate listing.
Catechesis/Religious Program—Tel: 609-641-7043; Fax: 609-641-5709. Students 589.
Atco, Camden Co., Assumption (1947), Revs. John O'Leary; John T. Gavin, O.S.F.S.; Deacons Charles McAleer; Charles Smith.
Res.: 318 Carl Hasselhan Dr., 08004. Tel: 856-753-4161; Fax: 856-753-7917.
School—Tel: 856-767-0569; Fax: 856-753-7917. Mr. Paul Ricci, Prin. Tel: 856-767-0569. Lay Teachers 10; Students 178.
Catechesis/Religious Program—Tel: 856-767-3414. Students 425.
Atlantic City, Atlantic Co.
1—Holy Spirit (1908), Closed., For requests for ecclesiastical documents please refer to St. Nicholas of Tolentine, Atlantic City.
2—St. Michael's (1904), (Italian), Rev. Michael H. D'Amico.
Res.: 10 N. Mississippi Ave., 08401. Tel: 609-344-8536; Fax: 609-344-5304.
3—St. Monica's (1925), Revs. Paul C. Wise, Admin.; Victorino Coronado.
Res.: 108 N. Pennsylvania Ave., 08401. Tel: 609-345-1786; Fax: 609-344-5090.
Catechesis/Religious Program—Students 52.
4—St. Nicholas of Tolentine (1855), Revs. William A. Hodge; Joseph V. Jurkowski.
Res.: 1409 Pacific Ave., 08401. Tel: 609-344-1040; Fax: 609-344-2471.
Catechesis/Religious Program—Students 8.
5—Our Lady Star of the Sea (1894), Revs. Patrick J. Brady; Gustavo Agudelo; Joseph Luong Pham; Deacon James Tully.
Res.: 2651 Atlantic Ave., 08401. Tel: 609-345-1878; Fax: 609-348-0248.
School—Tel: 609-345-0648. Sr. Mary Shamus, R.S.M., Prin. & Supr. Sisters 6; Lay Teachers 9; Students 320.
Catechesis/Religious Program—Tel: 609-340-0116. Students 330.
Convent—Sisters of Mercy, 15 N. California Ave.. Tel: 609-347-0434.
Audubon, Camden Co., Church of the Holy Maternity (1957), Rev. A. Robert Cairone.
Res.: 431 W. Nicholson Rd., 08106. Tel: 856-547-0444; Fax: 856-547-0045.
School—Annunciation Regional School, Bellmawr, Tel: 609-931-0122; Fax: 609-931-0155.
Catechesis/Religious Program—Students 120.
Avalon, Cape May Co., Maris Stella (1961), Rev. Msgr. Patrick M. Tierney.
Res.: 5012 Dune Dr., 08202. Tel: 609-967-3746; Fax: 609-967-8172.
School—Bishop McHugh Regional Catholic School of Dennis Twp., Tel: 609-624-1900. See separate listing.
Catechesis/Religious Program—Tel: 609-967-3017. Students 80.
Barrington, Camden Co., St. Francis de Sales (1955), Rev. Francis J. Gramigna; Deacon Michael Harkins. In Res., Rev. Msgr. William F. Poyatt (Retired).
Res.: 199 Willmont Ave., 08007. Tel: 856-547-2313; Fax: 856-547-8225.
School—St. Francis de Sales Regional School, Tel: 856-547-7958; Fax: 856-547-0472. See separate listing.
Catechesis/Religious Program—Students 170.
Convent—424 Browning Rd., Bellmawr, 08031. Tel: 856-931-8973.
Bellmawr, Camden Co.
1—Annunciation (1951), Revs. James O. Dabrowski; Perry A. Cherubini, Part-time; Deacon Michael J. DiGirolamo.
Res.: 601 W. Browning Rd., 08031. Tel: 609-931-6307; Fax: 609-931-0155.
School—Tel: 856-931-0122; Fax: 856-931-4390. Sr. Lorraine DeArros, I.H.M., Prin. Sisters 3; Lay Teachers 12; Students 265.
Catechesis/Religious Program—Tel: 856-931-8590. Students 107.
Convent—Sisters Servants of Immaculate Heart of Mary, 603 W. Browning Rd.. Tel: 856-931-7192.
2—Mary, Mother of the Church (1965), Rev. Msgr. Joseph C. Downing; Rev. Joseph T. Szolack, M.Div.; Deacon Ron Olesiewicz.
Res.: 20 Braisington Ave., 08031. Tel: 856-931-0204; Fax: 856-933-5120.
School—St. Francis de Sales Regional, Barrington, Tel: 856-547-7958. See separate listing.
Catechesis/Religious Program—Students 135.
Berlin, Camden Co., Our Lady of Mt. Carmel (1903), Revs. Fred Voltaggio; Stanley L. Witcoskie; Deacon Joseph Beebe.
Res.: 178 W. White Horse Pike, 08009. Tel: 856-767-2563; Fax: 856-767-8791.
School—Our Lady of Mt. Carmel Regional School, Tel: 856-767-1751; Fax: 856-767-1293. See separate listing.
Catechesis/Religious Program—Tel: 856-767-1537; Fax: 856-767-3304. Students 525.
Blackwood, Camden Co.
1—St. Agnes (1946), Rev. Msgr. Joseph V. DiMauro; Revs. Raymond P. Gormley; Michael G. Spagnolo; Deacons Henry S. Custodio; Joseph Buccilli; John Werner.
Res.: 701 Little Gloucester Rd., 08012. Tel: 856-228-4331; Fax: 856-227-0743.
School—St. Agnes Regional School, Blackwood, Tel: 856-228-7076; Fax: 856-228-7527. See separate listing.
Catechesis/Religious Program—Tel: 856-227-0555. Students 1,014.
2—St. Jude's (1961), Revs. Daniel M. Rocco; Joseph Panthackal; Deacons William J. Drum; Michael McDonaugh.
Res.: 402 S. Black Horse Pike, 08012. Tel: 856-227-0572; Fax: 856-227-1276.
School—St. Jude Regional School, Blackwood, Tel: 856-227-4442; Fax: 856-401-1622. See separate listing.
Catechesis/Religious Program—Tel: 856-227-8558. Students 425.
Blue Anchor, Camden Co., Blessed John the Twenty-Third (1925), (Italian), [CEM] Revs. Robert J. Gregorio, S.T.D.; Jose Ainikkal, C.M.I.
Res.: 250 S. Rte. 73, 08037-2317. Tel: 609-561-6116; Fax: 609-561-9305.
(1925), St. Lucy: Hammonton, 08037.
(1904), Sacred Heart: Cedar Brook, 08018.
School—St. Joseph Regional School, Hammonton, Tel: 609-704-2400. See separate listing.
Catechesis/Religious Program—Students 255.
Bridgeton, Cumberland Co.
1—Immaculate Conception (1874), (Italian), [CEM] Revs. James P. Rush; Peter M. Idler; Jesus A. Gonzalez-Ovalle; Deacons C. J. Achee; Carmen Bischer. In Res., Rev. Robert P. Weber.
Res.: 312 N. Pearl St., 08302. Tel: 856-451-0254; Fax: 856-451-7842.
School—Immaculate Conception Regional School, Bridgeton, Tel: 856-451-2134; Fax: 856-451-8268. See separate listing.
2—St. Teresa of Avila (1961), Rev. Michael M. Signiski; Deacon William Johnson.
Res.: 46 Central Ave., 08302. Tel: 856-455-2323; Fax: 856-455-7291.
School—Immaculate Conception Regional School, Bridgeton, Tel: 856-451-2134; Fax: 856-451-8268. See separate listing.
Brigantine, Atlantic Co., St. Thomas (1958), Rev. Edward J. Lipinski. In Res., Rev. Joseph A. Perreault; Deacon Joseph D. Long.
Res.: 331 8th St. S., 08203. Tel: 609-266-2123; Fax: 609-266-6416.
Catechesis/Religious Program—Tel: 609-266-3154. Students 400.
Brooklawn, Camden Co., St. Maurice's (1955), Rev. Thomas E. Ploude.
Res.: 401 Community Rd., 08030. Tel: 856-456-9039; Fax: 856-456-0161.
Catechesis/Religious Program—Students 38.
Buena Borough, Atlantic Co., Queen of Angels (2001), Rev. John J. Vignone; Deacon Joseph A. Perella.
Res.: 202 N.W. Blvd., Landisville, 08326. Tel: 856-697-1450; Fax: 856-697-6996.
School—Notre Dame Regional School, Landisville, Tel: 856-697-3456; Fax: 856-697-8540. See separate listing.
Catechesis/Religious Program—Tel: 856-697-6320. Students 180.
Cape May Court House, Cape May Co., Our Lady of the Angels (1956), Unassigned.
Res.: 106 Mechanic St., P.O. Box 324, 08210. Tel: 609-465-5245; Fax: 609-465-7822.
School—Bishop McHugh Regional Catholic School, Dennis Township
Cape May, Cape May Co., Our Lady Star of the Sea (1878), [CEM] Rev. Msgr. Timothy A. Ryan; Rev. Gerald M. Dolan, O.F.M.; Bro. Robert Carson, S.J.; Deacon William Lauth.
Res.: 525 Washington St., 08204. Tel: 609-884-5311; Fax: 609-884-0162.
School—Our Lady Star of the Sea School, Cape May, Tel: 609-884-4437; Fax: 609-898-4253. See separate listing.
Catechesis/Religious Program—Tel: 609-884-7736. Students 246.
Chapel—Cape May Point, St. Agnes, (Summer)
Carneys Point, Salem Co., Corpus Christi (1966), Rev. Msgr. Rocco A. Continillo, V.F.
Res.: 369 Georgetown Rd., 08069. Tel: 856-299-3833; Fax: 856-299-3834.
School—Bishop Guilfoyle Regional Catholic School, Carney's Point., Tel: 856-299-0400; Fax: 856-299-6556.
Catechesis/Religious Program—Students 127.
Cedarville, Cumberland Co., St. Michael's (1942), Rev. William James Bleiler.
Res.: 367 Main St., P.O. Box 327, 08311. Tel: 856-447-3480; Fax: 856-447-3480.
School—Immaculate Conception Regional School, Bridgeton See separate listing.
Catechesis/Religious Program—Students 59.
Mission—St. Anthony (1913), 1560 Main St., Port Norris, Cumberland Co. 08349.
Station—NJ State Medium Security Prison, Bayside Prison Rte. 47, Leesburg, 08327. Tel: 856-785-0040, Ext. 5458.
Station—Ancora Bayside Prison Winslow Twp..
Mission—Our Lady of the Lake Chapel Battle Ln., Laurel Lake, 08332.
Cherry Hill, Camden Co.
1—Holy Rosary (1958), Rev. Msgr. Leonard G. Scott, Pastor; Deacon Raymond Radziak.
Res.: 99 Burnt Mill Rd., 08003. Tel: 856-428-9456 (Office); Fax: 856-428-9152.
School—Tel: 856-428-4855; Fax: 856-428-0249. Mrs. Patricia Connell, Prin. Lay Teachers 9; Students 185.
Catechesis/Religious Program—Mrs. Anita D'Imperio, D.R.E. Students 250.
Convent—Sisters of Saint Joseph, Tel: 856-429-1364.
Mission—St. Yi Yun Il John Korean Catholic Mission, Tel: 856-427-4229. Rev. Chong Hyo Lee.
2—St. Mary's (1961), Revs. John C. Killeen; Francis Gaffney.
Res.: 2001 Springdale Rd., 08003. Tel: 856-424-1454; Fax: 856-424-8270.
School—Holy Rosary Regional School, Cherry Hill, Tel: 856-428-4855; Fax: 856-428-9152. See separate listing.
Catechesis/Religious Program—Tel: 856-424-2679. Students 650.
3—St. Peter Celestine (1961), Revs. Thomas A. Newton; Edward M. Friel; Nestor Lisondra; Deacons W. Leo McBlain; William Watts; William Iannuzzi; Paul Lee; Deacon Joseph F. Seaman.
Res.: 402 N. Kings Hwy., 08034. Tel: 856-667-2440; Fax: 856-482-0332.
School—Tel: 856-667-3034; Fax: 856-667-9160. Mrs.

Camille Forrest, Prin. Sisters of St. Joseph (Chestnut Hill, PA) 2; Lay Teachers 24; Students 308; Special Education Students 24.
Catechesis/Religious Program—Tel: 856-667-4250. Students 487.

4—St. Pius X (1961), Rev. Msgr. William P. Brennan, V.F.; Deacon Peter J. Powell. In Res., Revs. Allen B. Lovell; E. Joseph Byerley; Sr. Janice Firn, I.H.M.
Res.: 344 Kresson Rd., 08034. Tel: 856-429-1330; Fax: 856-429-8679. Email: stpiusx@comcast.net.
School—Christ the King Regional School, Haddonfield See separate listing.
Catechesis/Religious Program—Tel: 856-428-9207. Students 605.

5—Queen of Heaven (1955), Revs. Joseph D. Wallace; James L. Bartoloma, Chap. & Part-time Assoc.; Bruno Dongo; Deacons Charles C. Reiss; James H. Rocks.
Res.: 700 W. Marlton Pike, 08002. Tel: 856-429-3334; Fax: 856-795-3318.
School—Tel: 856-428-2890; Fax: 856-428-4640. Sr. Rita Marotta, I.H.M., Prin. Sisters 6; Lay Teachers 9; Students 202.
Catechesis/Religious Program—Students 281.
Convent—10 Massachusetts Ave., 08002. Tel: 856-428-8818. Queen of Heaven Convent.

6—St. Thomas More (1968), Rev. Msgr. Thomas J. Morgan; Revs. Thomas S. Donio; Dasam F. Don Bosco.
Res.: 1439 Springdale Rd., 08003. Tel: 856-424-3212; Fax: 856-424-2411.
School—Holy Rosary Regional School, Cherry Hill, Tel: 856-428-4855; Fax: 856-428-0249. See separate listing.
Catechesis/Religious Program—Students 238.

Clayton, Gloucester Co., St. Catherine's (1943), Rev. Edward F. Heintzelman; Deacon Matthew J. Hanrahan.
Res.: 49 W. North St., 08312. Tel: 856-881-9155; Fax: 856-881-9166.
School—51 W. North St., 08312. Tel: 856-881-0067; Fax: 856-881-4064. Miss Janice Bruni, Prin. Lay Teachers 10; Students 193.
Catechesis/Religious Program—Tel: 856-881-8707. Students 149.

Collings Lakes, Atlantic Co., Our Lady of the Lakes (1976), Rev. John A. Cavagnaro.
Res.: 19 Malaga Rd., 08094. Tel: 609-561-8313; Fax: 609-561-8374.
School—Notre Dame Regional School, Landisville See separate listing.
Catechesis/Religious Program—Tel: 609-561-3999. Students 125.

Collingswood, Camden Co., St. John's (1903), Rev. Msgr. Martin J. Mannion; Rev. Davis Madavana.
Res.: 809 Park Ave., 08108. Tel: 856-858-0298; Fax: 856-858-2796.
School—Tel: 856-858-1562; Fax: 856-858-2943. Miss Joan Simpson, Prin. Lay Teachers 16; Students 255.
Catechesis/Religious Program—Students 350.

Delair, Camden Co., St. Veronica's (1961), Rev. Max S. Fasciglione.
Res.: 8329 Holman Ave., 08110. Tel: 856-662-8050; Fax: 856-662-9477.
Catechesis/Religious Program—Students 95.

Deptford, Gloucester Co., St. John Vianney (1971), Deacon John Berstecher. In Res., Rev. Timothy E. Byerley, Admin.
Res.: 2901 Good Intent Rd., 08096. Tel: 856-227-2623; Fax: 856-228-1823.
School—St. Agnes Regional School, Blackwood, Tel: 856-228-7076; Fax: 856-228-7527. See separate listing.
Catechesis/Religious Program—Fax: 856-228-1823. Students 240.

Egg Harbor City, Atlantic Co., St. Nicholas (1864), Revs. James F. Betz; James F. Barry, Admin.; Bernard J. Gannon; Deacon Michael H. Guerrieri.
Res.: 525 St. Louis Ave., 08215-2224. Tel: 609-965-0350; Fax: 609-804-1313.
School—526 Chicago Ave.. Tel: 609-965-2398; Fax: 609-804-1658. Joan Dollinger, Prin. Lay Teachers 16; Students 190.
Catechesis/Religious Program—Tel: 609-965-0720. Students 260.

Egg Harbor Township, Atlantic Co., St. Katharine Drexel (2000), Rev. Joseph R. Ferrara; Deacon John A. Leone.
6075 W. Jersey Ave., 08234. Tel: 609-645-3719; Fax: 609-645-3719.
Catechesis/Religious Program—Students 440.

Elmer, Salem Co., St. Ann's (1961), Rev. Julian A. Karczewski; Deacons Edward J. Harkins; Robert Fanelli.
Res.: 115 Broad St., 08318. Tel: 856-358-3106; Fax: 856-358-3117.
School—Notre Dame Regional School Newfield/Landisville See separate listing.
Catechesis/Religious Program—Students 70.

Franklinville, Gloucester Co., Nativity (1961), Rev. Paul D. Harte.
Res.: P.O. Box 249, 08322. Tel: 856-694-2349; Fax: 856-694-4131.
School—St. Catherine of Siena Regional School, Clayton, 08312. Tel: 856-881-0067; Fax: 856-881-9166. See separate listing.
Catechesis/Religious Program—Students 241.

Gibbsboro Camden Co., St. Andrew the Apostle (1963), Rev. Msgr. Ciaran P. Omeadin; Revs. Robert W. Kunze; Sebastian Chelat; Deacon Paul Johnson
Res.: 120 United States Ave., 08026. Tel: 856-784-3878; Fax: 856-435-7508.
School—Our Lady of Mt. Carmel Regional School, Berlin, Tel: 609-767-2563; Fax: 609-767-8791. See separate listing.
Catechesis/Religious Program—Tel: 856-783-0550; Fax: 856-783-7935. Students 1,058.

Gibbstown, Gloucester Co., St. Michael's (1940), Rev. John E. Bruni; Deacons James Kiley; Robert Willson.
Res.: 313 Memorial Ave., 08027. Tel: 856-423-0007; Fax: 856-423-1445.
School—Guardian Angel Regional School 08027. Tel: 856-423-9440; Fax: 856-423-9445. See separate listing.
Catechesis/Religious Program—Tel: 856-423-9337. Students 250.
Convent—320 Memorial Ave., 08027. Tel: 856-423-8680; Fax: 856-423-8681.

Glassboro, Gloucester Co.

1—St. Bridget's (1887), (Italian), [CEM] Rev. Wayne Patrick Lavin; Deacon Joseph W. Laungo.
Res. 125 Church St., 08028. Tel: 856-881-2753; Fax: 856-881-9697.
School—St. Bridget's Regional School, Glassboro, Tel: 856-881-2578; Fax: 856-881-8771. See separate listing.
Catechesis/Religious Program—Students 280.

2—Our Lady of Lourdes (1966), Revs. Vincent G. Carpinelli; Joseph C. Pham; Deacons Nicholas Martelliti; Michael J. Carter. In Res., Rev. Msgr. James J. Gaffney (Retired).
Res.: 500 Greentree Rd., 08028. Tel: 856-881-0909; Fax: 856-881-5457.
School—St. Bridget Regional School, Glassboro See separate listing.
Catechesis/Religious Program—Tel: 856-881-1552. Students 629.

Gloucester, Camden Co., St. Mary's (1848), [CEM] Rev. Msgr. James P. Curran (RIC); Rev. Ronan B. Murphy; Deacon Frank Crossor.
Res.: 426 Monmouth St., 08030 Tel: 856-456-0052; Fax: 856-456-1837.
School—Tel: 856-456-0913; Fax: 856-456-7382. Sr. Nora Foley, O.P., Prin. Dominican Sisters of Hope 3; Lay Teachers 15; Students 334.
Catechesis/Religious Program—Students 230.

Haddon Heights, Camden Co., St. Rose's (1896), Rev. Msgr. John T. Frey, V.F.; Revs. Paul A. Olszewski; Michael P. Hegarty; Deacons Frank A. Iula, M.D.; Gerald DeMuro.
Res.: 300 Kings Hwy, 08035-1397. Tel: 856-547-0564; Fax: 856-547-7311.
School—Tel: 856-546-6166; Fax: 856-546-6601. Dr. Mary Burke, Prin. Sisters of St. Dominic (Newburgh, NY) 1; Lay Teachers 17; Students 390.
Catechesis/Religious Program—Tel: 856-546-0564, Ext. 103. Students 535.

Haddon Township, Camden Co., St. Vincent Pallotti (1963), Rev. Msgr. Louis A. Marucci, D.Min. In Res., Rev. Msgr. Eugene J. Fitzsimmons, J.C.D.; Rev. Thomas S. Capperella.
Res.: 901 Hopkins Rd., Haddonfield, 08033. Tel: 856-858-1313; 856-858-1314; Fax: 856-869-9010.
Catechesis/Religious Program—Students 200.

Haddonfield, Camden Co., Christ the King (1927), Rev. Msgr. Joseph W. Pokusa, J.C.D.; Rev. Edward J. Maher. In Res., Rev. David J. Klein, J.C.L.
Res.: 200 Windsor Ave., 08033. Tel: 856-429-1600; Fax: 856-429-2734.
School—Christ the King Regional School, Haddonfield, Tel: 856-429-2084; Fax: 856-429-4959. See separate listing. Lay Teachers 24; Students 349.
Catechesis/Religious Program—Tel: 856-354-5030. Students 520.
Convent—St. Mary of the Angels Convent, 134 Kings Hwy. W., 08033. Tel: 856-428-0824.

Hammonton, Atlantic Co.

1—St. Anthony of Padua (1964), Rev. Msgr. Charles P. Barth; Deacon Rocco A. Mangino. In Res., Rev. John M. Fleming.
Res.: 285 Rte. 206, 08037. Tel: 609-561-3313; Fax: 609-567-7764.
School—St. Joseph Regional School, Hammonton, Tel: 908-704-2400. See separate listing.
Catechesis/Religious Program—Students 143.

2—St. Joseph's (1886), [CEM] Revs. Robert Nolan, S.A.C.; Louis Rojas, S.A.C.; Deacon Ismael Perez Tavarez. In Res., Rev. Michael Parente, S.A.C.
Res.: 226 French St., 08037. Tel: 609-561-0180; Fax: 609-561-6808.
School—St. Joseph Regional School, Hammonton See separate listing.
Catechesis/Religious Program—Students 200.

3—St. Martin de Porres (1962), Rev. John A. DelDuca. In Res., Rev. Charles Conaty.
Res.: 129 Park Ave., 08037. Tel: 609-561-4322; Fax: 609-561-4433.
School—St. Joseph Regional School, Hammonton, Tel: 609-704-2400. See separate listing.
Catechesis/Religious Program—Students 400.

Landisville, Atlantic Co., Our Lady of Victories (1952), Merged, with St. Michael, Minotola to form Queen of Angels, Buena Borough.

Lindenwold, Camden Co., St. Lawrence's (1896), Rev. Msgr. William P. Graham; Rev. Thomas R. Kiely. In Res., Rev. Josekutty Manjakunnel.
Res.: 100 South Ave., 08021. Tel: 856-627-2222; 856-627-7522; Fax: 856-627-8210.
School—Tel: 856-783-0710. Mrs. Lynn Domenico, Prin. Lay Teachers 13; Students 293.
Catechesis/Religious Program—Tel: 856-346-0902. Students 305.

Linwood, Atlantic Co., Our Lady of Sorrows (1965), Revs. Malcolm C. MacLeod, M.SS.CC.; John Perdue, M.SS.CC.
Res.: 724 Maple, 08221. Tel: 609-927-1154; Fax: 609-927-0398.
Catechesis/Religious Program—Tel: 609-927-0121. Students 538.

Longport, Atlantic Co., Epiphany (1954), Rev. Msgr. Thomas M. Flynn.
Res.: 2801 Ventnor Ave., 08403. Tel: 609-822-8940; Fax: 609-822-1050.
School—Blessed Sacrament Regional School, Margate, Tel: 609-822-7105. See separate listing.
Catechesis/Religious Program—Students 30.

Magnolia, Camden Co., St. Gregory's (1955), Rev. Brian E. O'Neill; Rev. Msgrs. Edward L. Korda, Pastor Emeritus (Retired); Joseph P. Joynes; Deacon Leonard P. Carlucci.
Res.: 340 E. Evesham Ave., 08049. Tel: 856-784-4090; Fax: 856-784-6371.
School—Our Lady of Grace Regional School, Somerdale, Tel: 856-784-0372. See separate listing.
Catechesis/Religious Program—230 E. Evesham Ave., 08049. Tel: 856-784-1440. Students 180.
Convent—230 E. Evesham Ave., 08049. Tel: 856-784-1576.

Malaga, Gloucester Co., St. Mary's (1961), Rev. Jerome C. Romanowski.
Res.: Dutch Mill Rd., P.O. Box M, 08328. Tel: 856-694-2576; Fax: 856-694-4636.
School—Notre Dame Regional School, Newfield See separate listing.
Catechesis/Religious Program—Students 132.

Mantua, Gloucester Co., Incarnation (1956), Revs. Joseph A. Salerno, J.C.L.; Joseph J. Adamson; Deacons Thomas F. O'Brien; John Schiavo.
Res.: 234 Shadow Pl., 08051. Tel: 856-468-1314; Fax: 856-468-4886.
School—St. Margaret Regional School, Woodbury Heights, Tel: 856-845-5200. See separate listing.
Catechesis/Religious Program—Tel: 856-468-7566. Students 850.

Margate, Atlantic Co., Blessed Sacrament (1945), Rev. Lewis A. Battisti. In Res., Rev. Perry A. Cherubini.
Res.: 11 N. Kenyon Ave., 08402. Tel: 609-822-7105; Fax: 609-822-3817.
School—Blessed Sacrament Regional School, Margate, Tel: 609-822-9243; Fax: 609-822-2036. See separate listing.
Catechesis/Religious Program—Tel: 609-822-8810. Students 223.
Convent—14 N. Jerome Ave., 08402. Tel: 609-822-5543. Sr. Kathryn Rush, O.S.F., Local Supr.

Marmora, Cape May Co., The Church of the Resurrection (1975), Revs. Mark R. Cavagnaro; John Kennedy.
Res.: 200 W. Tuckahoe Rd., 08223. Tel: 609-390-0664; Fax: 609-390-8717.
School—Bishop McHugh Regional School, Cape May Court House, Tel: 609-624-1900; Fax: 609-624-9696.
Catechesis/Religious Program—Tel: 609-390-2203. Students 868.

Mays Landing, Atlantic Co., St. Vincent de Paul (1906), [CEM] Revs. John F. Sugrue; Edward R. Kolla; Deacon Richard Wigglesworth.
Res.: 114 Rte. 50, 08330. Tel: 609-625-2124; Fax: 609-625-8718.
School—Tel: 609-625-1565; Fax: 609-625-4703. Miss Linda Pirolli, Prin. Lay Teachers 11; Students 237.
Catechesis/Religious Program—5809 Main St., 08330. Tel: 609-625-1567. Students 451.
Convent—Sisters of St. Joseph of Chestnut Hill, 5807 Main St., 08330. Tel: 609-625-1566.
Mission—St. Bernard [CEM] Dorothy, Atlantic Co.

Merchantville, Camden Co., St. Peter's (1903),

Revs. Anthony J. Manuppella; John P. Connors; John J. Byrnes; Deacon Peter J. Gilmartin.
Res.: 43 W. Maple Ave., 08109. Tel: 856-663-1373; Fax: 856-488-0647.
School—Tel: 856-665-5789; Fax: 856-665-4943. Sr. Alice Ivanyo, M.P.F., Prin. Lay Teachers 18; Students 434.
Catechesis / Religious Program—Tel: 856-663-4490. Sheila O'Boyle, D.R.E. Students 320.

MILLVILLE, CUMBERLAND CO.

1—ST. JOHN BOSCO (1966), In Res., Rev. William C. Pierce; Deacon Francis Duffy.
Res.: 2 Hillcrest Ave., 08332. Tel: 856-825-1513; Fax: 856-765-9489.
Catechesis / Religious Program—Students 175.

2—ST. MARY MAGDALEN'S (1864), [CEM] Revs. Carmel Polidano; David V. Minniti; Deacon Hipolito Lagares.
Res.: 621 Dock St., 08332. Tel: 856-825-0021; Fax: 856-825-4338.
School—3 W. Powell St., 08332. Tel: 856-825-3600; Fax: 856-825-9119. Sr. Armida Fabela, M.D.P.V.M., Prin. Sisters 4; Lay Teachers 15; Students 232.
Catechesis / Religious Program—Tel: 856-825-0373. Sr. Armida Fabela, M.D.P.V.M., Supr. Students 138.
Convent—Missionary Daughters of the Most Pure Virgin Mary, 3 W. Powell St., 08332. Tel: 856-327-2235. Sr. Armida Fabela, M.D.P.V.M., Supr.

MINOTOLA, ATLANTIC CO., ST. MICHAEL (1902), Merged, with Our Lady of Victories, Landisville to form Queen of Angels, Buena Borough.

MOUNT EPHRAIM, CAMDEN CO., SACRED HEART (1939), Rev. Robert J. Dunphy; Deacon William Norquist.
Res.: 11 N. Black Horse Pike, 08059. Tel: 856-931-1441; Fax: 856-931-9433.
Catechesis / Religious Program—Tel: 856-931-9444. Students 177.

MULLICA HILL, GLOUCESTER CO., HOLY NAME OF JESUS (1901), [CEM] Revs. Anthony DiBardino; David A. Grover; Deacons Sam Nastasi; Phillip Giordano.
Res.: 17 Earlington Ave., 08062. Tel: 856-478-2294; Fax: 856-478-0222.
Catechesis / Religious Program—Tel: 856-478-9694. Students 1,000.

NATIONAL PARK, GLOUCESTER CO., ST. MATTHEW'S (1915), Revs. Edward F. Sobolewski; Walter Norris; Deacon William J. Rumaker.
Res.: 307 Wesley Ave., 08063. Tel: 856-845-2523; Fax: 856-251-0822.
School—St. Matthew Regional School, Verga, 08093. Tel: 856-845-7203; Fax: 856-853-7711. See separate listing.
Catechesis / Religious Program—Tel: 856-845-3891. Students 235.
Convent—Hessian Ave., Verga, 08093. Tel: 856-845-7204; Fax: 856-853-7771.

NEWFIELD, GLOUCESTER CO., ST. ROSE OF LIMA (1922), Revs. John Joseph Tumosa; Paul C. Amakiri.
Res.: 104 Catawba Ave., 08344. Tel: 856-697-3232; Fax: 856-697-1455.
School—Notre Dame Regional School, Newfield, Tel: 856-697-0155; Fax: 856-697-8540. See separate listing.
Catechesis / Religious Program—108 Church St., 08344. Students 105.

NORTH CAPE MAY, CAPE MAY CO., ST. JOHN OF GOD (1966), Rev. Richard L. Forbes. In Res., Revs. Valentine Awoyemi; James R. Ryan.
Res.: 680 Town Bank Rd., 08204. Tel: 609-884-1656; Fax: 609-898-0673.
School—St. Raymond Regional School, Villas, Tel: 609-856-5366; Fax: 609-856-9415. See separate listing.
Catechesis / Religious Program—Students 101.

NORTHFIELD, ATLANTIC CO., ST. BERNADETTE (1966), Rev. Msgr. Donald D. Velozo, V.F.; Revs. Sung Heum (John) Kim; Albert J. McLaverty.
Res.: 1421 New Rd., 08225. Tel: 609-646-3499; 609-646-5611; Fax: 609-484-8345.
School—Blessed Sacrament Regional School, Margate, Tel: 609-822-9243; Fax: 609-822-3817. See separate listing.
Catechesis / Religious Program—Tel: 609-484-0249. Students 495.

OAKLYN, CAMDEN CO., ST. ALOYSIUS (1935), Revs. George C. Seiter, V.F.; Warren Rector, O.F.M.
Res.: 37 W. Haddon Ave., 08107. Tel: 856-854-2352; Fax: 856-854-4189.
School—St. John Regional School, Collingswood See separate listing.
Catechesis / Religious Program—Students 120.

OCEAN CITY, CAPE MAY CO.

1—ST. AUGUSTINE'S (1894), Rev. Michael P. Rush; Rev. Msgr. Andrew Duignan.
Res.: 1310 Ocean Ave., 08226. Tel: 609-399-0648; Fax: 609-399-0063.
School—St. Augustine Regional School, Ocean City, Tel: 609-399-1435; Fax: 609-399-8675. See separate listing.
Catechesis / Religious Program—Tel: 609-399-2316. Students 185.

2—ST. FRANCES CABRINI (1966), Rev. Msgr. Patrick A. McCabe.
Res.: 114 Atlantic Ave., 08226. Tel: 609-399-4776; Fax: 609-391-9412.
School—St. Augustine Regional School, Ocean City, Tel: 609-399-1435; Fax: 609-399-0063. See separate listing.
Catechesis / Religious Program—Tel: 609-399-2643. Students 150.
Convent—712 2nd St., 08226. Tel: 609-398-6713.

3—OUR LADY OF GOOD COUNSEL (1961), Rev. Msgr. Thomas A. Guenther.
Res.: 3948 Central Ave., 08226. Tel: 609-399-2085; 609-398-3654 (Office); Fax: 609-399-3761.
School—St. Augustine Regional School, Ocean City, Tel: 609-399-1435; Fax: 609-399-8675. See separate listing.

PAULSBORO, GLOUCESTER CO., ST. JOHN'S (1904), (Italian—Irish), Revs. Anthony L. Minniti; Robert J. Fritz; Deacon Joseph Lopes.
Res.: 647 Beacon Ave., 08066. Tel: 856-423-0086; Fax: 856-423-0123.
Catechesis / Religious Program—712 Mantua Ave., 08066. Tel: 856-423-0099. Students 78.

PENNS GROVE, SALEM CO., ST. JAMES (1901), Rev. Robert J. Kantz; Deacon Joseph A. Ganci.
Res.: 114 State St., 08069. Tel: 856-299-0399; Fax: 856-299-3728.
Catechesis / Religious Program—Students 67.

PENNSAUKEN, CAMDEN CO.

1—ST. CECILIA'S (1939), Revs. William F. Moore; Walter Guasp-Santos; Deacons D. Eugene Burns; Miguel A. Rivera.
Res.: 4824 Camden Ave., 08110. Tel: 856-662-2721; Fax: 856-486-2089.
School—Day Care Center, 48th St. & Camden Ave., 08110. Tel: 856-662-9228. Vickie Caracciolo, Dir.
School—49th t. & Camden Ave., 08110. Tel: 856-662-0149. Mr. John Strada, Prin. Lay Teachers 10; Students 225.
Catechesis / Religious Program—49th & Camden Ave., 08110. Tel: 856-661-9489. Students 86.

2—ST. STEPHEN (1952), Rev. Msgr. Dominic J. Bottino, J.C.L. In Res., Rev. Msgr. J. Francis Flaherty; Deacon Ernest Picknally.
Res.: 6306 Browning Rd., 08109. Tel: 856-662-9338; Fax: 856-662-4679.
School—Tel: 856-662-5935; Fax: 856-662-6128. Sr. Kathleen M. Boyle, S.S.J., Prin. Sisters of St. Joseph 1; Lay Teachers 14; Students 199.
Catechesis / Religious Program—Students 85.

PENNSVILLE, SALEM CO., QUEEN OF THE APOSTLES (1955), Rev. Dennis W. Bajkowski.
Res.: 391 S. Broadway, 08070. Tel: 856-678-5400; Fax: 856-678-4153.
School—Bishop Guilfoyle Regional School, Carney's Point, Tel: 856-299-0400.
Catechesis / Religious Program—Students 251.

PINE HILL, CAMDEN CO., ST. EDWARD'S (1953), Revs. John P. Ward; Joseph P. Rush.
Res.: 500 Erial Rd., 08021. Tel: 856-783-2670; Fax: 856-627-9373.
Catechesis / Religious Program—Tel: 856-783-0293; Fax: 856-783-2090. Students 548.

PITMAN, GLOUCESTER CO., OUR LADY QUEEN OF PEACE (1949), Rev. Msgr. John F. Cooke; Rev. R. Douglas Smith, O.S.F.S.
Res.: 161 Pitman Ave., 08071. Tel: 856-589-5673; Fax: 856-589-0102.
School—St. Bridget Regional School, Glassboro See separate listing.

PLEASANTVILLE, ATLANTIC CO., ST. PETER'S (1896), Revs. Ronald S. Falotico; Alvaro Diaz. In Res., Rev. Felipe Moyano.
Res.: 25 Black Horse Pike, 08232. Tel: 609-641-0285; Fax: 609-641-0385.
School—Tel: 609-646-3057; Fax: 609-646-3467. Sr. Romana Stepnik, L.S.I.C., Prin. Lay Teachers 9; Students 153.
Catechesis / Religious Program—Students 220.

POMONA, ATLANTIC CO., ASSUMPTION (1938), Revs. Michael J. Matveenko; Peter A. McLaughlin; Deacon James Teeney. In Res., Rev. C. Jeffries Burton, S.J. (BAL).
Res.: 276 W. White Horse Pike, 08240. Tel: 609-965-4021; Fax: 609-965-4149.
School—Assumption Regional School, Pomona, Tel: 609-652-7134; Fax: 609-652-2544. Sr. Mary Jude Filep. See separate listing.
Catechesis / Religious Program—Tel: 609-965-7368. Students 850.

ROSENHAYN, CUMBERLAND CO., ST. MARY'S (1914), [CEM] Rev. John C. Muscat. In Res., Rev. Sebastian V. Annino.
Res.: Morton Ave., P.O. Box 376, 08352-0376. Tel: 856-451-8763; Fax: 856-453-8831.
School—Immaculate Conception Regional School, Bridgeton, Tel: 856-451-2134; Fax: 856-451-8268. See separate listing.
Catechesis / Religious Program—Students 206.

RUNNEMEDE, CAMDEN CO.

1—ST. MARIA GORETTI (1965), Rev. Msgr. Russell L. Rock.
Res.: 321 Orchard Ave., 08078. Tel: 856-933-0037; Fax: 856-933-0036.
School—St. Teresa Regional School, Runnemede See separate listing.
Catechesis / Religious Program—Tel: 856-939-5121. Students 140.

2—ST. TERESA OF THE INFANT JESUS (1927), Revs. Kenneth J. Johnston; Krzysztof Wtorek.
Res.: 13 E. Evesham Rd., 08078. Tel: 856-939-1681; Fax: 856-939-3878.
School—St. Teresa Regional School, Runnemede, Tel: 856-939-0333; Fax: 856-939-1204. See separate listing.
Catechesis / Religious Program—Tel: 856-939-0592. Students 263.

SALEM, SALEM CO., ST. MARY'S (1864), [CEM] Rev. Joseph F. Ganiel; Sr. Carol Adams, C.S.J.P., Pastoral Assoc.
Res.: 25 Oak St., 08079. Tel: 856-935-0288.
Catechesis / Religious Program—Students 96.

SEA ISLE CITY, CAPE MAY CO., ST. JOSEPH'S (1884), Revs. Stephen Carey; Marcel M. Tabone; Deacons Liam C. O'Clisham; Norbert Klimaszewski.
Res.: 4308 Landis Ave., 08243. Tel: 609-263-8696; Fax: 609-263-7884.
Catechesis / Religious Program—Tel: 609-263-2087. Students 275.
Convent—132 44th St., 08243. Tel: 609-263-6228.

SICKLERVILLE, CAMDEN CO., ST. JOHN NEUMANN (1977), Rev. Glenn Hartman; Deacon John Schiavo.
Res.: 234 Sicklerville Rd., Box G, 08081-0438. Tel: 856-728-1060; Fax: 856-728-2480.
Catechesis / Religious Program—Students 263.

SOMERDALE, CAMDEN CO., OUR LADY OF GRACE (1954), Revs. Roger E. McGrath; James M. Maggart, J.C.L.
Res.: 35 N. White Horse Pike, 08083. Tel: 856-783-2256; Fax: 856-435-1722.
School—Our Lady of Grace Regional School, Somerdale, Tel: 856-784-0372; Fax: 856-784-5496. See separate listing.
Catechesis / Religious Program—Tel: 856-627-3036. Students 220.

SOMERS POINT, ATLANTIC CO., ST. JOSEPH'S (1946), Revs. Josef A. Wagenhoffer; Hugh J. Bradley. In Res., Rev. Robert T. Matysik.
Res.: 606 Shore Rd., 08244. Tel: 609-927-3568; Fax: 609-653-8707.
School—St. Joseph Regional School, Tel: 609-927-2228; Fax: 609-927-7834. Sr. Grace Christi Costello, Prin. Regionalized with Our Lady of Sorrows Parish, Linwood. Sisters 7; Lay Teachers 24; Students 428.
Catechesis / Religious Program—Tel: 609-927-3302. Students 522.
Convent—Sisters of St. Joseph, 580 Shore Rd., 08244. Tel: 609-926-9127.

STONE HARBOR, CAPE MAY CO., ST. PAUL'S (1911), Rev. Msgr. William Quinn.
Res.: 9910 Third Ave., 08247. Tel: 609-368-3091; Fax: 609-368-2775.
School—Bishop McHugh Regional School, Cape May Court House, Tel: 609-624-1900; Fax: 609-624-9696. See separate listing.
Catechesis / Religious Program—5012 Dune Dr., 08247. Tel: 609-967-3746; Fax: 609-967-8172. Students 36.

STRATFORD, CAMDEN CO., ST. LUKE (1961), Revs. James J. Durkin; Michael J. Coffey; Rev. Msgr. Edward F. Mullen (Retired).
Res.: 55 Warwick Rd., 08084. Tel: 856-783-5555; Fax: 856-782-8336.
School—Tel: 856-783-3088; Fax: 856-783-9302. Mrs. Kathleen A. Dugan, Prin. Lay Teachers 16; Students 285.
Special Education— Lay Teachers 2; Students 20.
Catechesis / Religious Program—Tel: 856-783-6144; Fax: 856-783-6144. Students 378.

SWEDESBORO, GLOUCESTER CO., ST. JOSEPH'S (1854), [CEM 2] Revs. Michael J. Field, D.Min.; Vincent Orum; Deacon Pablo Berrios.
Res.: 140 N. Broad St., 08085. Tel: 856-467-0037; Fax: 856-467-0038.
School—Bishop Guilfoyle Regional School, 350 Georgetown Rd., Carneys Point, 08069. Mrs. Claire Whitaker, Prin.
Catechesis / Religious Program—Tel: 856-467-3123. Students 495.

VENTNOR, ATLANTIC CO., ST. JAMES (1922), Revs. Brendan V. Sullivan; Danilo Quiray; Deacon Agatino Garufi.
Res.: 6415 Atlantic Ave., 08406. Tel: 609-822-2176; Fax: 609-487-8137.
School—Tel: 609-822-2234. Sr. Joan Mary Baldridge, O.P., Prin. Sisters 4; Lay Teachers 8; Students 234.
Catechesis / Religious Program—Students 95.
Convent—Dominican Sisters (Sinsinawa, WI), Portland & Atlantic Ave., 08406. Tel: 609-487-8110.

VILLAS, CAPE MAY CO., ST. RAYMOND (1937), Revs. William S. Vandegrift; Robert Sadlack; Deacon George Del Rossi.
Res.: 25 E. Hudson Ave., 08251. Tel: 609-886-5366; Fax: 609-886-9415.
School—St. Raymond Regional School, Villas, Tel: 609-886-2893; Fax: 609-889-8335. See separate listing.
Catechesis/Religious Program—Tel: 609-886-7640. Students 189.

VINELAND, CUMBERLAND CO.
1—ST. FRANCIS OF ASSISI (1961), Revs. Ernest R. Soprano; Sergio Bicomong.
Res.: 23 W. Chestnut Ave., 08360. Tel: 856-691-9181; Fax: 856-794-9029.
School—Tel: 856-691-9184; Fax: 856-691-2043. Sr. Kathryn Chesnut, Prin. Lay Teachers 10; Students 157.
Catechesis/Religious Program—Tel: 856-691-9181, Ext. 13. Students 106.
Convent—Daughters of Mercy, W. Chestnut Ave., 08360. Tel: 856-691-8129.
2—IMMACULATE HEART OF MARY, Rev. Msgr. Victor S. Muro. Tel: 856-692-5022; Rev. Ariel Hernandez; Deacons Bernardino Quiles; Angel Gonzalez.
1010 E. Landis Ave., 08360. Tel: 856-692-5022.
Office—410 S. 8th St., 08360. Tel: 856-692-8992; Fax: 856-692-1259.
Catechesis/Religious Program—Students 225.
3—ST. ISIDORE (1962), Rev. John H. Burton, V.F. In Res., Rev. Msgr. Richard J. Callahan (Retired); Deacon Robert Andreacchio.
Res.: 1655 Magnolia Ave., 08361-6598. Tel: 856-691-9077; Fax: 856-692-3305.
School—Sacred Heart Regional School, Vineland, Tel: 856-691-4490; Fax: 856-691-1516. See separate listing.
Catechesis/Religious Program—Tel 856-563-0482; Fax: 856-692-3305. Sr. Catherine Kane, O.S.F., D.R.E. Students 278.
4—ST. MARY'S (1887), [CEM], For inquiries please see St. Padre Pio, Vineland.
5—OUR LADY OF POMPEII (1909),, For inquiries please see St. Padre Pio.
6—ST. PADRE PIO (1978), Revs. Peter M. Saporito; Faustino Parisi.
736 S. Union Rd., 08060. Tel: 856-691-9721; Fax: 856-696-8872.
Rectory: 4680 Dante Ave., 08360-6810. Tel: 856-691-7526; Fax: 856-692-2686.
Church: 736 S. Union Rd., 08360.
School—735 S. Union Rd., 08060. Tel: 856-692-8537. Sr. Margaret Curcio, D.M., Prin.
Catechesis/Religious Program—Students 274.
7—SACRED HEART (1874), (Italian), [CEM] Revs. Patsy C. Amabile; Pawel Kryszkiewicz; George Punnolil; Edward F. Namiotka.
Res.: 1010 Landis Ave., 08360. Tel: 856-691-0420; Fax: 856-691-1516.
School—Sacred Heart Regional School, Vineland, Tel: 856-691-4490; Fax: 856-691-5579. See separate listing.
Catechesis/Religious Program—922 E. Landis Ave.. Tel: 856-696-0325. Students 737.

WASHINGTON TOWNSHIP, GLOUCESTER CO.
1—ST. CHARLES BORROMEO (1965), Rev. Msgr. James R. Tracy, V.F.; Rev. James A. Casadia; Deacon Joseph B. Chandler.
Res.: 176 Stagecoach Rd., Sicklerville, 08081. Tel: 856-629-0411; Fax: 856-629-9109.
School—St. Jude Regional School, Blackwood See separate listing.
Catechesis/Religious Program—Tel: 856-228-5694. Mrs. Mary Ann Exler, D.R.E. Students 1,000.
2—HOLY FAMILY (1974), Revs. Robert E. Hughes; Charles J. Colozzi; Stephen Rapposelli; Deacons George M. Ferland; Frank Pepe.
Res.: 226 Hurffville Rd., Sewell, 08080. Tel: 856-228-1616; Fax: 856-228-6332.
School—St. Jude Regional School, Blackwood, Tel: 856-227-4442; Fax: 856-227-1276. See separate listing.
Catechesis/Religious Program—Tel: 856-228-2215; Fax: 856-401-1817. Students 1,135.
3—SS. PETER AND PAUL (1973), Rev. Msgr. John A. Clarke; Rev. Brendan J. Meaney. In Res., Rev. Howard E. Muhlbaier.
Res.: 362 Ganttown Rd., P.O. Box 1022, Turnersville, 08012. Tel: 856-589-3366; Fax: 856-256-1964.
School—St. Jude Regional School, Blackwood See separate listing.
Catechesis/Religious Program—Tel: 856-589-6451. Students 1,016.

WATERFORD, CAMDEN CO., ST. ANTHONY (1966), Rev. John F. Bourke; Deacon Nicholas P. Ludovich.
Res.: 436 Pennington Ave., 08089. Tel: 856-767-7535; Fax: 856-767-7372.
School—St. Joseph Regional School, Hammonton See separate listing.
Catechesis/Religious Program—Students 137.

WEST COLLINGSWOOD, CAMDEN CO., TRANSFIGURATION (1950), Rev. Richard J. Lodge; Deacon William C. Robinson.
Res.: 445 White Horse Pike, 08107. Tel: 856-854-0364; Fax: 856-869-5129.
Catechesis/Religious Program—Students 124.

WESTMONT, CAMDEN CO., HOLY SAVIOUR (1928), Rev. Terry M. Odien.
Res.: 50 Emerald Ave., 08108. Tel: 856-854-0022; Fax: 856-854-5741.
School—30 Emerald Ave., 08108. Tel: 856-858-1966. Sisters Janice Novak, Prin.; Bianca, Supr. Sisters, Franciscan Missionaries of the Immaculate Heart of Mary 2; Lay Teachers 9; Students 239.
Catechesis/Religious Program—Tel: 856-854-1516. Students 290.

WESTVILLE GROVE, GLOUCESTER CO., MOST HOLY REDEEMER (1958), Revs. Neal F. Dante; Julian A. Karczewski.
Res.: 1219 Delsea Dr., 08093. Tel: 856-848-6779; Fax: 856-848-6208.
School—Tel: 856-848-6826; Fax: 856-251-0344. Mrs. Patricia Mancuso, Prin.; Sr. Cynthia Ludwick, S.S.J., Supr. Lay Teachers 10; Students 189.
Catechesis/Religious Program—Tel: 856-384-6070. Mrs. Nancy Jerome, D.R.E. Students 150.
Convent—1211 Delsea Dr., 08093. Tel: 856-848-2729.

WESTVILLE, GLOUCESTER CO., ST. ANNES (1921), Revs. Andrew J. Bolcar; Frederick G. Link.
Res.: 213 Woodbine Ave., 08093. Tel 856-456-4136; Fax: 856-456-7502.
School—St. Matthew Regional School, National Park Tel: 856-845-7203; Fax: 856-853-7711. See separate listing.
Catechesis/Religious Program—Tel 856-456-4136. Students 140.

WILDWOOD CREST, CAPE MAY CO., ASSUMPTION B.V.M. (1961), Rev. Msgr. Joseph P. Herron (Retired); Revs. Richard J. Hadyka; Daniel A. Donardo; Deacons Joseph A. Costello; Ralph M. Catanese.
Res.: 7110 Seaview Ave., 08260. Tel: 609-522-4114; 609-522-6071; Fax: 609-523-9069.
School—St. Ann Regional School, Wildwood, Tel: 609-522-2704. See separate listing under St. Ann's Parish.
Catechesis/Religious Program—Tel: 609-827-9587. Students 107.

WILDWOOD, CAPE MAY CO., ST. ANN'S (1895), Rev. Msgr. Thomas B. Fitzsommons; Rev. Jason T. Rocks; Deacon Joseph Pierce.
Res.: 2900 Pacific Ave., 08260. Tel: 609-522-2709; Fax: 609-522-9375.
School—St. Ann Regional School Regionalized with Assumption Parish, Wildwood Crest, 2901 New Jersey Ave., 08260. Tel: 609-522-2704; Fax: 609-522-5229. Sr. Sheila Murphy, S.S.J., Prin. Sisters of St. Joseph 2; Lay Teachers 12; Students 293.
Catechesis/Religious Program—Tel: 609-827-9587. Students 137.
Convent—119 E. Glenwood Ave., 08260. Tel: 609-522-5721.

WILLIAMSTOWN, GLOUCESTER CO., ST. MARY'S (1906), [CEM] Revs. Carmen A. Carlone, V.F.; Prosper Pael; Jaromir Michalek; Deacons John J. Leyden; John Kirk; John Kacy.
Res.: 32 Carrol Ave., 08094. Tel 856-629-6142; Fax: 856-875-2097.
School—Tel: 856-629-6190; Fax: 856-728-1437. Miss Judith McBride, Prin. Lay Teachers 36; Students 602.
Catechesis/Religious Program—Tel: 856-629-0614. Students 995.
Convent—St. Joseph Sisters 640 S. Main St., 08094. Tel: 856-262-1358.

WOODBINE, CAPE MAY CO., ST. CASIMIR'S (1939), [CEM] Rev. Albert E. Harshaw.
Res.: 304 Clay St., P.O. Box 533, 08270. Tel: 609-861-3771; Fax: 609-861-7112.
School—Bishop McHugh Regional School, Dennis Township, Tel: 609-624-1900; Fax: 609-624-9696. See separate listing.
Catechesis/Religious Program—Tel: 609-861-1601. Students 145.
Mission—St. Elizabeth [CEM] Rte. 47, Goshen, Cape May Co. 08218. Tel: 609-861-5218.

WOODBURY HEIGHTS, GLOUCESTER CO., ST. MARGARET'S (1961), Revs. Calogero N. LaVerde; Daniel J. Melendez; Deacons Robert M. Kenney; Nicholas A. Danze.
Res.: 334 Beech Ave., 08097. Tel: 856-848-0047; Fax: 856-384-8123.
School—St. Margaret Regional School, Woodbury Heights, Tel: 856-845-5200; Fax: 856-845-2405. See separate listing.
Catechesis/Religious Program—Tel: 856-845-5251; Fax: 856-845-5251. Students 560.

WOODBURY, GLOUCESTER CO., ST. PATRICK'S (1877), Revs. J. Gerald Gallagher; William F. Ryan; John M. Stabeno; Deacons David Murnane; Albert J. Riviello.
Res.: 64 Cooper St., 08096. Tel: 856-845-0123; Fax: 856-845-7409.
School—Tel: 856-845-1660; Fax: 856-845-4605. Mrs. Dorice Palumbo, Prin. Lay Teachers 11; Students 210.
Catechesis/Religious Program—Tel: 856-853-6681. Students 348.

WOODLYNNE, CAMDEN CO., IMMACULATE HEART OF MARY (1949), (Vietnamese), Rev. Joseph An Nguyen.
Res.: 201 Cooper St., 08107. Tel: 856-962-8610; Fax: 856-962-9438.

WOODSTOWN, SALEM CO., ST. JOSEPH'S (1895), [CEM] Rev. Stephen F. Cervoni.
Res.: 51 Broad St., 08098. Tel: 856-769-0004; Fax: 856-769-9904.
Catechesis/Religious Program—Students 237.

Chaplains of Public Institutions

CAMDEN. *Camden County Jail* 08104. Rev. Charles S. Gonzalez, S.J., Chap. Tel: 856-963-1621.
Riverfront Prison 08102.
Holy Name: Tel: 856-963-1621. Rev. Jeffrey Puttoff, S.J., Chap.

ANCORA. *New Jersey State Mental Hospital*.
2239 Carolyn Ave., Atco, 08004. Tel: 856-768-8630. Deacon Charles Smith.

BRIDGETON. *Southwoods State Prison* 08302.
Immaculate Conception 08302. Tel: 856-451-0254. Rev. Robert P. Weber, Chap.

CAPE MAY. *United States Coast Guard, Command Chaplain's Office*, 1 Monroe Ave., 08204-5001. Tel: 609-898-6974. Rev. Sam Ferretti.

DELMONT. *Southern State Correctional Facility*, Tel: 856-451-0254. Rev. Robert P. Weber.

FAIRTON. *Federal Correctional Institution*, P.O. Box 280, 08320. Tel: 856-227-1436. Rev. Sergio Bicomong, Chap.

LAKELAND. *Camden County Hospital at Lakeland*, St. Joseph's Chapel, Blackwood Post Office, 08012. Tel: 856-227-3000, Ext. 444. Rev. Paul C. Amakiri, Chap.

LEESBURG. *New Jersey State Medium Security Prison* 08327. Tel: 856-447-3480. Rev. William James Bleiler.

VINELAND. *Vineland State School*.
Chaplaincy, St. Isidore. Tel: 856-691-9077.

WOODBINE. *State Colony*.
St. Casimir's Church: 304 Clay St., 08270. Tel: 609-861-3771.

On Duty Outside the Diocese:
Rev. Msgrs.—
Checchio, James F., Pontifical North American College 60120 Vatican City State.
Daiber, Sean J., Central Mailing Address, Paroguia de Sao Jose Rua 107, Setor Sul, Caiza Postal 716, 74,000 Goiania Goias, Brazil. Brazilian Missions
Revs.—
Beebe, David E., Saint Gabriel, 2559 40th Ave., San Francisco, CA 94116. Tel: 415-731-6161
Davis, Charles J. (Retired), 73 Joy Dr., Bath, NH 03740. Tel: 603-747-3776
Gomes, Robert (SP), St. Cecilia, 820 Jasmine Way, Clearwater, FL 33756-4095. Tel: 727-447-3494
Hubbs, Timothy L., Chap. (Major), HHB/1 - 15 FA, Apo, AP 96224.
Kocik, Francis W., St. Patrick, Pincourt, Ile Perrot, Province of Quebec, Canada.
Kunzman, Richard T., 450 Paradise Isle Blvd #203, Hallandale, FL 33009.
Nwoga, Laserian, (Air Force)
Orsi, Michael P., Ave Maria School of Law, 3475 Plymouth Rd., Ann Arbor, MI 48105.
Pastore, Peter J. (Retired), 12111 Eucalyptus St., San Antonio, TX 78245-3309.
Reese, Donald B., P.O. Box 8173, Asheville, NC 28814.
Wade, Edward C., Queen of Peace, 3011 Telephone Rd., Houston, TX 77023.

On Sick Leave:
Revs.—
Burger, Herman N., J.C.L.
Fallon, William J.
Rosinski, Edward B.
Trinh, Paul

On Leave of Absence:
Revs.—
Hudson, Frank X.
Marucci, Carl J.
Zito, Thomas M.

Disabled:
Revs.—
Bean, Charles S. (Retired)
Fallon, William J.
McArdle, Sean A. (Retired)
Orsini, Joseph E. (Retired)

Weber, George A. (Retired)

Retired:
Rev. Msgrs.—
Alleyne, Edward D., Sacred Heart Residence for Priests, 200 St. Mary's Dr., Cherry Hill, 08003-5217. Tel: 856-449-7503
Budney, David F., 62 Trent Rd., Turnersville, 08012. Tel: 856-589-5385
Callahan, Richard J., St. Isidore, 1655 Magnolia Rd., Vineland, 08360.
Carr, James A., Sacred Heart Residence for Priests, Cherry Hill, 08003.
Casey, John H., 925 West Calle Del Regalo, Green Valley, AZ 85614.
Chiarilli, Patrick S., 222 N. Genessee St., Geneva, NY 14456.
Clark, John J., 644 Pleasure Ave., Ocean City, 08226.
Coyne, Michael J., P.O. Box 95, Leeds Point, 08220.
Flaherty, J. Francis, St. Stephen, 6306 Browning Rd., Pennsauken, 08109.
Gaffney, James J., Our Lady of Lourdes, 500 Green Tree Rd., Glassboro, 08028-1427.
Herron, Joseph P., Assumption of the B.V.M., 7110 Seaview Ave., Wildwood Crest, 08260-3826. Tel: 609-522-4114
Hewitt, Bernard P., Sacred Heart Residence, 200 St. Mary's Drive, Cherry Hill, 08002.
Jordan, Harry J., Sacred Heart Residence, 200 St. Mary's Dr., Cherry Hill, 08002. Tel: 856-751-4910
Kennedy, Edward J., Sacred Heart Residence for Priests, 200 St. Mary's Dr., Cherry Hill, 08003.
Kernan, Eugene J., 91 Geneva Ave., Westmont, 08108.
Kloskowski, Stanley E., 4027 Fleetwood Dr., Hamilton Square, 08690.
Korda, Edward L., St. Gregory, 340 Evesham Ave., Magnolia, 08049.
Mullen, Edward F., St. Luke Rectory, 65 Warwick Rd., Stratford, 08084.
O'Connell, Joseph F., 555 Monmouth Ave., Spring Lake Heights, 07762.
O'Connor, Edward J., Sacred Heart Residence, 200 St. Mary's Dr., Cherry Hill, 08002.
O'Connor, Paul, 23 N. Wissahickan Ave., Ventnor, 08406.
O'Leary, Cornelius P., 25098 Jaclyn Ave., Moreno Valley, CA 92557-5703. Tel: 909-242-6939
O'Neill, Felix M., 717 S. Columbus Blvd., Apt 518, Philadelphia, PA 19147. Tel: 215-925-7001
Poyatt, William F., Saint Francis de Sales, 199 Willmont Ave., Barrington, 08007-1238. Tel: 856-547-2313
Robertson, Glendon E., 3851 Boardwalk # 1002, Atlantic City, 08401. Tel: 609-347-0546
Rynne, James J., Sacred Heart Residence for Priests, 200 St. Mary's Dr., Cherry Hill, 08003-5217. Tel: 856-751-2010
Sharkey, Thomas H., 3 Catherine Pl., Northfield, 08225.
Sprecace, Francis A., 856 Palermo Rd., St. Augustine, FL 32086.
Stoerlein, Joseph G., 97 Hobart Ave., Absecon, 08201.
Welsh, James F., Sacred Heart Residence for Priests, 200 St. Mary's Dr., Cherry Hill, 08003.
Revs.—
Anderson, Arthur T., Sacred Heart Residence for Priests, 200 St. Mary's Dr., Cherry Hill, 08003.
Barr, Stanley J., 3 South Wissahickon Ave., Ventnor, 08406.
Bean, Charles S., Saint Mary's Catholic Home, 210 St. Mary's Dr., Cherry Hill, 08003-2517. Tel: 856-791-2010
Bober, Marjan L., 791 Burman Lane, N.E., Melbourne, FL 32902.
Campuzano, J. Eduardo, Puerto del Carmen 4-A, Maspalomas 35100 (Las Palmas), Spain.
Collins, William F., 216 Leeds Ave., Bellmawr, 08031.
Davis, Charles J., 73 Joy Rd., Bath, NH 03740. Tel: 603-747-3776
Delelse, Salvatore, 618 W. Glenside Ave., Glenside, PA 19038.
Eckert, William F., P.O. Box 1601, Pittsfield, MA 01202-1601.
Hart, William H., 504-A Mulberry Ct., Mt. Laurel, 08054.
Hayden, Joseph M., 5050 Asbury Park Dr., Apt 103, Lakeland, FL 33805-9588.
Hewett, Alfred J., St. Rose of Lima, 300 Kings Hwy., Haddon Heights, 08035-1397.
Hope, Abbott J., Sacred Heart Residence for Priests, 200 St. Mary's Dr., Cherry Hill, 08003.
Jarka, Thomas H., 4-A Oakview Mobile Leisure Village, Shamong, 08088.
Jones, J. Overton, 447 N. Tennessee Ave., Atlantic City, 08401.
Kolton, Stanislaus J., 117 Brown Ave., Spring Lake, 07762-1017. Tel: 908-449-6364
Lambert, Cornelius F., Ocean Reef Condos, 109 Tarpon Ct., Ocean City, 08226.
Lyons, Edward D., 5 Bonita Ct., Ocean City, 08226.
McArdle, Sean A., Our Lady's Residence, 1100 Clematis Ave., Pleasantville, 08232.
McBride, Henry J., Sacred Heart Residence, 200 St. Mary's Dr., Cherry Hill, 08003.
Newton, John G., 579 Keolu Dr., Kailua, HI 96734.
Onufer, Paul P., 1402 S. Rte. #9, GLP #196-L, Cape May Court House, 08201.
Pastore, Peter J., 12111 Eucalyptus St., San Antonio, TX 78245-3309. (Military)
Plummer, James, 216 N. Jerome Ave., Margate, 08402.
Selleck, John P., 5012 Whitaker St., Panama City, FL 32404.
Stout, O. Hugh, Holy Ghost, 2015 Louisiana Ave., New Orleans, LA 70015.
Tovar, Ireneo Lopez, 121 Country Club Dr., Tower II, Apt. 403, Lake Placid, FL 33852.
Tracey, Thomas S., 17 Rehoboth Bay, Rehoboth Beach, DE 19971. Tel: 302-227-3063
Weber, George A., Box 272114, Tampa, FL 33688-2114.
Yori, Robert O., 13 W. 4th St., Hazleton, PA 18201.

Permanent Deacons:
Achee, C. J.
Andreaccho, Robert A.
Becker, Joseph F.
Beebe, Joseph F.
Berrios, Pablo
Berstecher, John L.
Bischer, Carmen M.
Buccilli, Joseph C.
Burns, D. Eugene
Carlucci, Leonard P.
Carson, Robert L., S.J.
Carter, Michael J.
Catanese, Ralph A.
Chandler, Joseph B.
Como, Anthony C., (Retired)
Costello, Joseph A., (Retired)
Crosson, Francis W.
Custodio, Henry S., (Retired)
Danze, Nicholas A.
DeMuro, Gerard V.
Del Rossi, George C.
Demarest, Kenneth H., (Retired)
DiGirolamo, Michael V.
Drum, William J., (Retired)
Duffy, Francis A., (Retired)
Fanelli, Robert M.
Ferland, George M., (Retired)
Ferrario, Raymond C., (Retired)
Gallimore, John R., (Retired)
Ganci, Joseph A.
Garufi, Agatino A.
Gilmartin, Peter J.
Giordano, Philip
Gonzalez, Angel A.
Guerrieri, Michael H.
Hafner, Thomas J., (Retired)
Hanrahan, Matthew J.
Hardy, Robert, (Retired)
Harkins, Edward J., (Retired)
Harkins, Michael
Iannuzzi, William P.
Iula, Frank A., M.D.
Johnson, Paul F.
Johnson, William G.
Kacy, John J.
Kearney, J. Brian, (Retired)
Kenney, Robert M.
Kijonka, Anthony V., (Retired)
Kiley, James W.
Kirk, John T.
Klimaszewski, Norbert J.
Lagares, Hipolito
Lauth, William
Lee, Paul K.
Leone, John A.
Leyden, John J.
Liss, George R.
Long, Joseph D.
Lopes, Joseph S.
Loungo, Joseph W.
Ludovich, Nicholas P.
Majewski, Walter, (Retired)
Mangino, Rocco A.
McAleer, Charles L.
McBlain, W. Leo
McCarthy, Richard F., (Retired)
McDonaugh, Michael L.
McHugh, Joseph
McLeer, Eugene L., (Retired)
Miranda, Felix T.
Mortelliti, Nicholas V.
Murnane, David W.
Nastasi, Santo A.
Norquist, William V.
O'Brien, Thomas F.
O'Clisham, Liam C.
Olesiewicz, Ronald J.
Pepe, Frank J.
Perella, Joseph A.
Peters, William L.
Picknally, Ernest F.
Pierce, Joseph R.
Porowicz, Alfred T., (Retired)
Powell, Peter J.
Quiles, Bernardino S.
Radziak, Raymond R.
Ralbusky, Emil A.
Reiss, Charles C.
Rivera, Miguel A.
Riviello, Albert J.
Robinson, William C.
Rocks, James H.
Rumaker, William J.
Sampson, Richard T.
Schiavo, John A.
Scott, Michael F.
Smith, Charles L.
Tankard, Gary
Tavarez, Ismael P.
Teeney, James J.
Tully, James M., (Retired)
Vargo, Frank T., (Retired)
Vega, Angel Ramos
Velez, Aladino
Watts, William L.
Werner, John F.
Wigglesworth, Richard J.
Willson, Robert F.
Seaman, Joseph F.

INSTITUTIONS LOCATED IN THE DIOCESE

[A] HIGH SCHOOLS, DIOCESAN

ABSECON. *Holy Spirit High School*, New Rd., 08201. Tel: 609-646-3000; Fax: 609-646-1770. Rev. Joseph A. Perreault, Prin. Sisters of Mercy 1; Priests 2; Lay Teachers 41; Students 833.

CHERRY HILL. *Camden Catholic High School*, Rte. 38 and Cuthbert Rd., 08002. Tel: 856-663-2247; Fax: 856-661-0632. Email: camdencatholic@aol.com. Web: www.camdencatholic.org. Rev. Msgr. Andrew E. Martin, Pres.; Mr. Albert G. Colleluori, Prin. Priests 2; Sisters of Mercy 1; Lay Teachers 55; Students 1,038.

HADDONFIELD. *Paul VI High School*, 901 Hopkins Rd., Ste. B, 08033. Tel: 856-858-4900; Fax: 856-858-6832. Email: principal@pvihs.org. Web: pvihs.org. Dr. David Coughlin, Pres.; Sr. Marianne McCann, M.P.F., Prin.; Revs. E. Joseph Byerley; Allen B. Lovell. Priests 3; Religious Teachers Filippini 3; Lay Teachers 54; Students 1,004.

[B] HIGH SCHOOLS, PAROCHIAL

HAMMONTON. *St. Joseph High School*, 133 N. 3rd St., 08037. Tel: 609-704-2400; Fax: 609-561-4940. James J. Cavalieri, Prin. Priests 1; Religious Sisters Filippini 1; Lay Teachers 25; Students 410.

GLOUCESTER. *Gloucester Catholic High School*, 333 Ridgeway St., 08030. Tel: 856-456-4400; Fax: 856-456-0506. Email: Pmurphy@gchsrams.org. Web: www.gchsrams.org. Mr. John T. Colman, Prin. Priests 2; Dominican Sisters 1; Lay Teachers 42; Students 793.

NORTH WILDWOOD. *Wildwood Catholic High School*, 1500 Central Ave., 08260. Tel: 609-522-7257; Fax: 609-522-2453. Email: wchs@capemayschools.com. Mr. Richard J. Turco, Prin.; Mr. Frank Smith, Vice Prin.; Bro. Robert Carson, S.J., Asst. Prin. Brothers 1; Lay Teachers 19; Students 365.

VINELAND. *Sacred Heart High School*, 15 N. East Ave., 08360. Tel: 856-691-4491; Fax: 856-563-1644. Web: www.sacredhearthighvineland.org. Rev. Edward F. Namiotka, Prin. Priests 1; Lay Teachers 29; Students 350.

[C] HIGH SCHOOLS, PRIVATE

NEWFIELD. *Our Lady of Mercy Academy*, 1001 Main Rd., 08344. Tel: 856-697-2008; Fax: 856-697-2887. Email: srgrace@aol.com. Web: www.olmanj.org. Sr. Grace Marie, D.M., Prin. Daughters of Our Lady of Mercy Sisters 2; Lay Teachers 18; Students 230.

PENNSAUKEN. *Bishop Eustace Prep School*, 5552 Rte. 70, 08109-4798. Tel: 856-662-2160, Ext. 214; Fax: 856-662-0802. Web: www.eustace.org. Revs. Joseph Capella, S.A.C., Rector; Nicholas Rinaldi, S.A.C., (In Res.); Bro. James Beamesderfer, S.A.C. Society of the Catholic Apostolate, Province of the Immaculate Conception Priests 2; Brothers 1; Lay Teachers 70; Students 750.

RICHLAND. *St. Augustine Preparatory School* 611 N. Cedar Ave., P.O. Box 279, 08350. Tel: 856-697-2600; 856-697-2612 (Monastery); Fax: 856-697-8389. Email: admin@hermits.com. Web: www.hermits.com. Revs. Paul W. Galetto, O.S.A., Pres. & Prin.; Stephen J. La Rosa O.S.A.; Cherubin Kerr, O.S.A.; Ronald A. Hamaday, O.S.A.; Martin L. Smith, O.S.A.; Bros. Frank Cucinotta, O.S.A.; David Graber, M.SS.CC. Order of St. Augustine, Province of St. Thomas of Villanova Priests 4; Brothers 1; Deacons 2; Lay Teachers 38; Students 469.

[D] ELEMENTARY SCHOOLS, PRIVATE

CAMDEN. *San Miguel School, Inc.*, (Grades 6-8), 836 S. 4th St., 08103. Tel: 856-342-6707; Fax: 856-342-6708. Email: sanmiguel3@juno.com. Web: www.fscbaltimore.org/sanmiguel. Bro. William Johnson, F.S.C., Pres.; Vacant (GB), Prin. De La Salle Christian Brothers 3; Lay Teachers 6; Students 45.

[E] REGIONAL SCHOOLS, ELEMENTARY

BARRINGTON. *St. Francis de Sales*, West Gloucester Pike, 08007. Tel: 856-547-7958; Fax: 856-547-0472. Email: sistercatherine@hotmail.com. Web: www.erols.com/sfdsale. Sisters Patricia Burns, Supr.; Catherine Mulcahy, F.D.N.S.C., Supr. & Prin. Serving St. Francis de Sales, Barrington and Mary, Mother of the Church, Bellmawr. Daughters of Our Lady of the Sacred Heart 12; Sisters 5; Lay Teachers 1; Students 330.

BERLIN. *Our Lady of Mt. Carmel*, One Maple Ave., 08009. Tel: 856-767-2115; Fax: 856-767-2115. Email: SMinnockO@aol.com. Web: www.olmcparish.net. Sr. Carmel Buckley, R.S.M., Prin. Serving Our Lady of Mt. Carmel, Berlin and St. Andrew, Gibbsboro. Sisters of Mercy (American Province) 5; Lay Teachers 15; Students 313.

BLACKWOOD. *St. Agnes School*, 117 W. Church St., 08012. Tel: 856-228-7076. Email: jtcafagna@yahoo.com. Web: www.stagnesnj.org. Mr. John T. Cafagna, Prin. Serving St. Agnes, Blackwood; St. John Vianney, Deptford. Lay Teachers 15; Students 280.

St. Jude, 420 S. Black Horse Pike, 08012. Tel: 856-227-4442; 856-401-1622. Sr. Paula Marie Randow, O.S.F., Prin. Serving St. Jude, Blackwood; SS. Peter & Paul, St. Charles Borromeo, & Holy Family, Washington Township. Franciscan Sisters 2; Lay Teachers 20; Students 483

BRIDGETON. *Immaculate Conception Regional School*, 398 N. Pearl St., 08302. Tel: 856-451-2134; Fax: 856-451-8268. Mrs. Kathleen Bischer, Prin. Serving Immaculate Conception, St. Teresa of Avila, Bridgeton; St. Michael, Cedarville; St. Mary, Rosenhayn. Lay Teachers 10; Students 160.

CAPE MAY. *Our Lady, Star of the Sea School*, 520 Lafayette St., 08204. Tel: 609-884-4437; Fax: 609-898-4253. Email: olsos@capemayschools.com. Ms. Barbara Byrne, Prin. Serving Our Lady, Star of the Sea, Cape May. Sisters of St. Joseph 1; Lay Teachers 15; Students 236.

CAPE MAY COURT HOUSE. *Bishop McHugh Regional School*, 2221 NJSH Rte. 9, 08210. Tel: 609-624-1900; Fax: 609-624-9696. Sr. Rosalie Pronsati, R.S.M., Prin. Lay Teachers 22; Students 412.

CARNEYS POINT. *Bishop Guilfoyle Regional School*, 350 Georgetown Rd., 08069. Tel: 856-299-0400; Fax: 856-299-6556. Web: www.bgrcs.org. Claire Whittaker, Prin. Serving parishes of: Corpus Christi, Carney's Point; Queen of Apostles, Pennsville; St. Mary, Salem; St. James, Penns Grove; St. Joseph, Woodstown; St. Joseph, Swedesboro. Lay Teachers 15; Students 340.

COLLINGSWOOD. *St. John School*, 100 Lees Ave., 08108. Tel: 856-858-1562; Fax: 856-858-2943. Miss Joan Simpson, Prin. Serving St John, Collingswood; St. Aloysius, Oaklyn. Lay Teachers 10; Students 226; PreK 32.

GIBBSTOWN. *Guardian Angels Regional School*, 150 S. School St., 08027. Tel: 856-423-9440; Fax: 856-423-9445. Email: gars@comcast.net. Sr. Jerilyn Einstein, F.M.I.J., Prin. Sisters 3; Lay Teachers 3; Students 86.

GLASSBORO. *St. Bridget Regional School*, 25 W. High St., 08028. Tel: 856-881-2578; Fax: 856-881-8771. Email: tgregal@stbridget.net. Web: www.stbridget.net. Jane Dickerman, Prin. Serving St. Bridget, Our Lady of Lourdes, Glassboro; Our Lady, Queen of Peace, Pitman. Lay Teachers 15; Students 265.

HADDONFIELD. *Christ the King Regional School*, 164 Hopkins Ave., 08033. Tel 856-429-2084; Fax: 856-429-4959. Email: principal@ckrs.org. Mrs. Marianne Gaffney, Prin. Serving Christ the King, Haddonfield; St. Pius X, Cherry Hill. Franciscan Sisters of Allegany 1; Lay Teachers 25; Students 380.

HAMMONTON. *St. Joseph School*, 133 N. 3rd St., 08037. Tel: 609-704-2400; Fax: 609-561-4940. Email: msullivan@stjoek12.org. Web: www.stjoek12.org. Sr. Barbara Ranere, M.P.F., Prin. Serving St. Joseph, St. Martin de Porres, St. Anthony of Padua, Hammonton; St. Anthony, Waterford; Blessed John XXIII, Blue Anchor. Religious Teachers Filippini 4; Lay Teachers 14 Students 313.

MARGATE. *Blessed Sacrament School*, 14 N. Jerome Ave., 08402. Tel: 609-822-9243; Fax: 609-822-2036. Sr. Rosaline Walters, O.S.F., Prin. Serving Blessed Sacrament, Margate; St. Bernadette, Northfield; Epiphany, Longport. Sisters of St. Francis of Syracuse, NY 2; Lay Teachers 8; Students 254.

NEWFIELD. *Notre Dame Regional School*, 108 Church St., 08344. Tel: 856-697-0155 (Newfield, Grades K-4); 856-697-3456 (Landisville, Grades 5-8); Fax: 856-697-5114; 856-697-8546. Email: ndrsnj@aol.com Web: www.asd.com. Mrs. Mary Brogan, Prin. Serving Queen of Angels, Landisville; St. Michael, Minotola; Our Lady of the Lakes, Collings Lakes; St. Rose, Newfield; St. Mary, Malaga; St. Ann, Elmer. Lay Teachers 19; Students 259.

OCEAN CITY. *St. Augustine Regional School*, 1337 Asbury Ave., 08226-3299. Tel: 609-399-1435; Fax: 609-399-8675. Web: www.staugustineoc.org. Sr. de Paul Juliano, O.S.F. Serving St. Augustine, St. Frances Cabrini & Our Lady of Good Counsel, Ocean City. Sisters of St. Francis 1 Lay Teachers 9; Students 150.

POMONA. *Assumption Regional School* White Horse Pike, 08240. Tel: 609-652-7134; Fax: 609-652-2544. Email: jfilep@atlantica-a.org. Web: www.assumptionregional.org. Sr. Mary Jude Filep, Prin. Serving Assumption, Pomona; St. Elizabeth Ann Seton, Absecon. Lay Teachers 14; Students 256.

RUNNEMEDE. *St. Teresa School*, 18 Ardmore Rd., 08078. Tel: 856-939-0333; Fax: 856-939-1204. Email: schooloffice@stteresa.xohost.com. Web: www.stteresa.xohost.com. Sr. Anne Francine Windle, I.H.M., Prin. Serving St. Teresa & St. Maria Goretti, Runnemede. Sisters Servants of the Immaculate Heart of Mary 7; Lay Teachers 12; Students 252.

SOMERDALE. *Our Lady of Grace School*, 105 N. White Horse Pike, 08083. Tel: 856-784-0372; Fax: 856-784-5496. Email: olgssec@yahoo.com. Mrs. Patricia Krohn, Prin. Serving Our Lady of Grace, Somerdale; St. Gregory, Magnolia. Lay Teachers 18; Students 205.

WESTVILLE. *St. Matthew School*, 1210 Hessian Ave., 08093. Tel: 856-845-7203; Fax: 856-853-7711. Email: marial@hotmail.com. Web: www.stmatthewrs.net. Sr. Maria Liber, Prin. Serving St. Matthew, National Park; St. Anne, Westville; West Deptford Township. Little Servant Sisters of the Immaculate Conception 3; Lay Teachers 8; Students 138.

VILLAS. *St. Raymond School*, 25 E Ocean Ave., 08251. Tel: 609-886-2893; Fax: 609-889-8335. Email: strayprincipal@saintraymonds.capemayschools.com. Sr. Kathleen Nuckols, I.H.M., Supr. & Prin. Serving St. Raymond, Villas; St. John of God, North Cape May. Sisters, Servants of the Immaculate Heart of Mary 6; Lay Teachers 8; Students 181.

VINELAND. *St. Mary's Regional School*, 735 Union Rd., 08360. Tel: 856-692-8537; Fax: 856-692-5034. Email: smrschool@aol.com. Web: www.smrschool.org. Sr. Margaret Curcio, D.M., Prin. Serving St. Mary; St. Joseph Mission, Richland; St Padre Pio, East Vineland. Daughters of Our Lady of Mercy 1; Lay Teachers 22; Students 359.

Sacred Heart School, 922 E. Landis Ave., 08360. Tel: 856-691-4490; Fax: 856-691-5579. Email: shgsmainoffice@snip.net. Web: school.nj.com/school/sacredheart. Patrice DeMartino, Prin. Serving Sacred Heart, St. Isidore. Lay Teachers 29; Students 381.

WOODBURY HEIGHTS. *St. Margaret School*, 773 Third St., 08097. Tel: 856-845-5200; Fax: 856-845-2405. Web: www.stmargarets-rs.org. Sr. Lorraine Klein, F.M.I.J., Prin. & Supr. Serving St. Margaret, Woodbury Heights; Incarnation, Mantua. Sisters 3; Lay Teachers 18; Students 626.

[F] SCHOOLS FOR SPECIAL CHILDREN

WESTVILLE GROVE. *Archbishop Damiano School/St. John of God Community Services*, 1145 Delsea Dr., 08903. Tel: 856-848-4700; Fax: 856-848-3965. Email: ads@jersey.net. Web: www.sjogcs.org. Ms. Muncie Buckalew, Exec. Dir. Brothers 3; Sisters 2; Lay Teachers 74; Students 636; Total Staff 226.

[G] CATHOLIC FOUNDATIONS

CAMDEN. *Francis , Elizabeth and Edward Roger Welsh Scholarship Trust*, 631 Market St., 08102. Tel: 856-756-7900. Rev. Msgr. Joseph W. Pokusa, J.C.D., Advisory Committee Chair.

The Frank J. and Rosina W. Suttill Catholic Foundation, 631 Market St., 08102. Rev. Msgr. Joseph P. Herron, Sec. (Retired).

The Tuition Assistance Fund, Inc., 631 Market St., 08102. Tel: 856-756-7900; Fax: 856-756-0225. Email: bpastore@camdendiocese.org. Betty Pastore, Admin.

NORTHFIELD. *The Sharkey Family Charitable Trust*, Three Catherine Pl., 08225-2503. Tel: 609-407-6863. Rev. Msgr. Thomas H. Sharkey, Trustee (Retired).

[H] GENERAL HOSPITALS

CAMDEN. *Our Lady of Lourdes Health Care Services, Inc.*, 1600 Haddon Ave., 08103. Tel: 856-757-3500; Fax: 856-757-3611. Web: www.lourdesnet.org. Alexander J. Hatala, Pres. & CEO. Bed Capacity 663; Total Staff 2,511; Patients Assisted Annually 335,030.

Our Lady of Lourdes Medical Center (Formerly Our Lady of Lourdes Hospital)(Parent Corporation: Our Lady of Lourdes Health Care Services, Inc.) , 1600 Haddon Ave., 08103. Tel: 856-757-3500; Fax: 856-757-3611. Rev. Warren Rector, O.F.M., Chap. Franciscan Sisters of Allegany

Our Lady of Lourdes Health Foundation, Inc., 1600 Haddon Ave., 08103. Tel: 856-482-4950; Fax: 856-482-4960.

Lourdes Cardiovascular Foundation, Inc., 1600 Haddon Ave., 08103. Tel: 856-482-4950; Fax: 856-482-4960.

Lourdes Home Health Services, Inc., 900 Haddon Ave., Ste. 316, 08103. Tel: 856-869-0900; Fax: 856-869-0311.

Osborn Family Health Center, Inc., 1600 Haddon Ave., 08103. Tel: 856-757-3700; Fax: 856-365-7972.

Our Lady of Lourdes School of Nursing, Inc., 1600 Haddon Ave., 08103. Tel: 856-782-2101.

Our Lady of Lourdes Medical Center, Inc. Auxiliary, 1600 Haddon Ave., 08103. Tel: 856-482-4950; Fax: 856-482-4960.

[I] NURSING HOMES

CHERRY HILL. *St. Mary's Catholic Home*, 210 St. Mary's Dr., 08003. Tel: 856-874-5300; Fax: 856-424-5143. Email: sr.beatrix@vhscd.org. Sr. M. Beatrix Wieczorek, Admin. & Supr.; Mr. James J. Heinz, Assoc. Admin.; Rev. Aleksy Kowalski, Chap. Little Servant Sisters of the Immaculate Conception Sisters 11; Total Staff 293; Total Assisted Annually 305.

NEWFIELD. *Mater Dei Nursing Home*, 176 Rte. 40, 08344. Tel: 856-358-2061; Fax: 856-358-0403. Sr. Anne Ebersold, Admin.; Rev. Sebastian V. Annino, Chap. Marianites of Holy Cross Sisters 4; Bed Capacity 64; Total Staff 104; Total Assisted Annually 97.

PLEASANTVILLE. *Our Lady's Multi-Care Center*, 1100 Clematis Ave., 08232. Tel: 609-646-2450; Fax: 609-646-7569. Anna Tosti, Acting Admin.; Sr. Elizabeth Rani Gnanapragasam, H.S.M., Supr.; Rev. Anthony Patricio, M.SS.CC., Chap. Hospitaler Sisters of Mercy Sisters 13; Bed Capacity 214; Patients Assisted Annually 214; Total Staff 240.

VINELAND. *Bishop McCarthy Residence*, 1045 E. Chestnut Ave., 08360. Tel: 856-692-2850; Fax: 856-696-5770. Email: srlucia.maroor@uhscd.org. Sr. Lucia Maroor, L.N.H.A., Admin.; Rev. George Punnolil, Chap. Hospitaler Sisters of Mercy Sisters 4; Bed Capacity 182; Patients Assisted Annually 182.

[J] VISITING NURSES

EGG HARBOR TOWNSHIP. *Holy Redeemer Visiting Nurse Agency, Inc.*, 6727 Delilah Rd., 08234. Tel: 609-625-2200; Fax: 609-625-2992.

SWAINTON. *Holy Redeemer Visiting Nurse Agency, Inc.* Subsidiary of Holy Redeemer Health System, Inc. , 1801 Rte. 9 N., 08210. Tel: 609-465-2082; 800-745-4693; Fax: 609-463-6121. Sr. Mary Anne McDonagh. Sponsored by Sisters of the Holy Redeemer, C.S.R.

[K] HOUSING FOR AGED

CAPE MAY. *Victorian Towers Associates*, 608 Washington St., 08204. Tel: 609-884-5883; Fax: 609-884-5625. Email: victoriantowers@snip.net. Total in Residence 262; Total Staff 7.

CHERRY HILL. *The Manor at St. Mary's*, 220 St. Mary's Dr., 08003. Tel: 856-424-3817; Fax: 856-424-5128. Sr. Frances Szymanska, L.S.I.C., Admin. Total in Residence 92; Total Staff 50.

Marian Residence, 1000 Cropwell Rd., 08003. Tel: 856-424-1131; Fax: 856-424-5333. Sr. M. Melchior, L.S.I.C., Supvr. Total in Residence 5; Total Staff 2.

Village Apartments of Cherry Hill, NJ, Inc., 212

Lourdes Ct., 08003. Tel: 856-424-7913; Fax: 856-424-9211. Email: theresa@villageaptscherryhill.com. Theresa Mosteig, On-site Manager. Total in Residence 164; Total Staff 7.

[L] CHILD CARE CENTERS

CAMDEN. *St. Joseph's Child Development Center*, 17 Church St., P.O. Box 1443, 08105. Tel: 856-963-9202; Fax: 856-963-8940. Betty Mitchell, Dir. Children 75.

CHERRY HILL. *Blessed Edmund Early Childhood Education Center*, 1000 Cropwell Rd., 08003. Tel: 856-424-3063.

[M] MONASTERIES AND RESIDENCES OF PRIESTS AND BROTHERS

CAMDEN. *Dominican Sisters of the Perpetual Rosary Chaplain's Residence*, 1500 Haddon Ave., 08103. Tel: 856-635-1179. Rev. Anthony I. Cataudo, O.P.; Sr. Mary Ann, O.P., Prioress.

BLACKWOOD. *Bishop's Residence*, Marywood, 1600 Peter Cheeseman Rd., 08012. Tel: 856-227-7565; Fax: 856-228-6082. In Res. Rev. Peter M. Joyce, J.C.L.

CHERRY HILL. *Sacred Heart Residences*, 200 St. Mary's Dr., 08003. Tel: 856-751-2010; Fax: 856-489-8999. Rev. Msgr. Harry J. Jordan, Dir. (Retired).

Neumann House, 250 St. Mary's Dr., 08003. Tel: 856-424-1741; Fax: 856-424-2896. Rev. Msgr. Harry J. Jordan, Dir. (Retired).

Vianney Villa, 230 St. Mary Dr., 08003. Tel: 856-424-2035. Rev. Msgr. Harry J. Jordan, Dir. (Retired).

LINWOOD. *Villa Pieta. Missionaries of the Sacred Hearts of Jesus & Mary*, 2249 Shore Rd., 08221. Tel: 609-927-5600; Fax: 609-927-5262. Email: shsusa@aol.com. Revs. Anthony Patrizio, M.SS.CC., Rector; Leonard Carrieri, M.SS.CC.; John Cavanaugh, M.SS.CC.; Frederick Clement, M.SS.CC.; Robert McDade, M.SS.CC., Vice Rector.

MARGATE. *Franciscan Friary* Holy Name Province. , 118 S. Mansfield Ave., 08402-2516. Tel: 609-822-9552; Fax: 609-822-0601. Revs. Bernard Splawski, O.F.M., Curator; Boniface Hahley, O.F.M. Total Staff 2.

OCEAN CITY. *Augustinian Friars*, St. Rita of Cascia Cottage, 823 5th St., 08226. Tel: 609-398-1299; Fax: 609-398-1229.

Ocean Rest Summer School and Retreat House, 3045 Central Ave., 08226. Tel: 609-399-6480; Fax: 609-398-7520. *Brother Provincial*, P.O. Box 29, Adamstown, MD 21710-0029. Tel: 301-874-5188. Brothers of Christian Schools Summer Home and Retreat House.

VENTNOR. *St. Benilde Community*, 107 S. Derby Ave., 08406. Tel: 609-487-6995; Fax: 609-487-6881. Web: www.delasallebrothers.org. Brothers of the Christian Schools & De La Salle Christian Brothers.

Provincialate, P.O. Box 29, Adamstown, MD 21710. Tel: 301-874-5188; Fax: 301-874-5674. Bro. Andrew Bartley, F.S.C., Dir.

WESTVILLE GROVE. *Hospitaller Order of St. John of God*, 1145 Delsea Dr., 08093. Tel: 856-848-4700; Fax: 856-848-7305. Email: sjogprior@aol.com. Web: www.sjogbrothers.com. Bro. Thomas Osorio, O.H., Supr. Brothers 5.

[N] CONVENTS AND RESIDENCES FOR SISTERS

CAMDEN. *Monastery of the Dominican Nuns of the Perpetual Rosary*, 1500 Haddon Ave., 08103. Tel: 856-342-8340. Sr. Mary Anne, O.P., Prioress; Rev. Anthony I. Cataudo, O.P., Chap. Sisters 6.

ATLANTIC CITY. *St. John's Retreat House and Rest Home*, 128 S. Dover Ave., 08401. Tel: 609-345-7361; Fax: 609-345-7361. Sr. Halina Aurelia Jackiewicz, Supvr. Little Servant Sisters of the Immaculate Conception Sisters 4.

CHERRY HILL. *Franciscan Missionary Sisters of the Infant Jesus*Sisters 4.

U.S. Province and Novitiate, 1215 Kresson Rd., 08003. Tel: 856-428-8834; Fax: 856-428-7930. Email: fmijusdel@worldnet.att.net. Sr. Angela Pia Camillotti, F.M.I.J., Delegate Supr.

Little Servant Sisters of the Immaculate Conception Provincialate and Novitiate. , 1000 Cropwell Rd., 08003. Tel: 856-424-1962; Fax: 856-424-5333. Email: LSICProv@aol.com. Web: www.geocities.com/lsiccherry. Sr. M. Leonarda, L.S.I.C., Prov. Professed Sisters 22.

ELMER. *The Sisters of Mary Immaculate of Nyeri, Inc.*, 400 State St., 08318. Tel: 856-358-4030; Fax: 856-358-4570. Email: smi21sep1999@aol.com. Sr. Mary Jennifer Wandia, S.M.I., Pres. & Contact Person.

HADDONFIELD. *St. Mary of the Angels Convent* Formation House , 134 Kings Hwy. W., 08033. Tel: 856-428-0824. Email: jterrameoosf@aol.com. Sr. Ann Caldwell, Treas. Franciscan Sisters of Allegany Sisters 8.

NEWFIELD. *Villa Rossello* Provincial House and Novitiate of Daughters of Our Lady of Mercy. , 1009 Main Rd., 08344. Tel: 856-697-2983; Fax: 856-697-8595. Email: dmnewfield@yahoo.com. Sr. M. Ambrogina, D.M., Prov. Sisters 21.

PLEASANTVILLE. *Hospitaler Sisters of Mercy Novitiate*, 915 S. Main St., 08232. Tel: 609-272-7659; Fax: 609-645-9600. Email: villaraffaella@msn.com. Total in Residence 5.

Hospitaler Sisters of Mercy Convent, 909 S. Main St., 08232. Tel: 609-272-7659; Fax: 609-645-9600. Sisters 5.

Villa Raffaella, 917 S. Main St., 08232. Tel: 609-645-9300; Fax: 609-645-9600. Senior Assisted Living Community, Hospitaler Sisters of Mercy. Total Staff 15; Bed Capacity 40.

SEA ISLE CITY. *The Sisters of St. Francis of Philadelphia*, 55th & Landis Ave., 08243. Tel: 610-558-7676; Fax: 610-558-6122. Email: roconnor@osfphila.org. Web: www.osfphila.org. *Our Lady of Angels Convent*, 609 S. Convent Rd., Aston, PA 19014.

STONE HARBOR. *Villa Maria by the Sea* 08247. Tel: 609-368-3621. Summer retreat house for Sisters Servants of the Immaculate Heart of Mary. (Immaculata, PA)

SWAINTON. *Sisters of the Holy Redeemer*, Our Lady of Peace Convent, 8 Brooks Ave., 08210. Tel: 609-465-3549; Fax: 609-463-6121. Email: srmO@holyredeemer.com. Web: www.sistersholyredeemer.org. Total in Residence 2.

VENTNOR. *The Benedictine Sisters of Elizabeth, NJ*, 114 S. Troy Ave., 08406. Tel: 609-823-9843.

Holy Family, Seaside Convent, 110 S. Dorset Ave., 08406. Tel: 609-822-5127. Sisters of St. Dominic (Blauvelt, NY)

McAuley House, 102 S. Derby Ave., 08406. Tel: 609-822-7944; 410-435-4400 Sisters of Mercy (Baltimore Regl. Community). Sisters of Mercy (Baltimore Regl. Community)

Mercy By-the-Sea, 114 S. Portland Ave., 08406. Sisters of Mercy (Plainfield - Watchung)

Mercy Villa, 104 S. Derby Pl., 08406. Sisters of Mercy (Prov. of New York)

VINELAND. *Bishop McCarthy Residence Convent*, 1045 E. Chestnut Ave., 08360. Tel: 856-692-2850; Fax: 856-696-5770. Email: hsm@aol.com. Sr. Lucia Maroor, Supr. Hospitaler Sisters of Mercy 4.

[O] RETREAT HOUSES

BLACKWOOD. *St. Pius X Retreat House*, 1840 Peter Cheeseman Rd., 08012. Tel: 856-227-1436; Fax: 856-227-2907. Revs. Thomas J. Barcellona, Exec. Dir.; Gerald J. Fitzpatrick, S.J., Spiritual Dir.; Bro. Nicholas Crosby, S.D.S.

VINELAND. *Pope John Paul II Retreat Center*, 414 S. 8th St., 08360. Tel: 853-692-8360; Fax: 856-691-1259. Email: sccpjIIrc@aol.com. Rev. Msgr. Victor Muro, Dir.

[P] APOSTOLIC CENTERS

BERLIN. *Mater Ecclesiae Chapel*, 261 Cross Keys Rd., 08009-9431. Tel: 856-753-3408; Fax: 856-753-2671. Email: rector@materecclesiae.org. Web: www.materecclesiae.org. Revs. Robert C. Pasley, Rector; Aleksy Kowalski; Paul Trinh.

CAPE MAY POINT. *Marianist Family Retreat Center*, 417 Yale Ave., Box 488, 08212-0488. Tel: 609-884-3829; Fax: 609-884-0545. Email: mfrc@capemaymarianists.org. Web: www.capemaymarianists.org. Rev. Theodore Cassidy, S.M., Local Community Dir.; James Fitzgibbons, S.M.; Mr. Anthony Fucci, Center Dir.; Bros. Albert Koch, S.M.; Edward Underdorfer, S.M.

GLASSBORO. *Collegium Center for Faith and Culture*, 5 Redmond Ave., 08028. Tel: 856-227-2623. Rev. Timothy E. Byerley, Contact Person.

[Q] EMERGENCY SERVICES CENTERS OF CATHOLIC CHARITIES

PENNSAUKEN. *Catholic Charities* Administrative Office , 2830 Marlton Pike, 08105. Tel: 856-663-9800; Fax: 856-663-0253. Email: css4@snip.net. Web: www.catholiccharitiescamden.org. Kevin H. Hickey, M.S.W., Exec. Dir.; Sr. Elise Gittrich, S.C., B.A., B.S., Dir. Tel: 856-964-1191; Fax: 856-966-5145. Aids Ministry.

Catholic Charities - Camden County, 1484-86 Mt. Ephraim Ave., 08104. Tel: 856-964-2133; Fax: 856-225-1384. Cereida Medina, Coord.

Catholic Charities - Atlantic County, 9 N. Georgia Ave., Atlantic City, 08401. Tel: 609-345-3448; Fax: 609-345-7180. Sr. Grace Nolan, R.S.M., Coord.

Catholic Charities - Cape May County, Village Shoppes, 1304 Rte. 47 S., Rio Grande, 08242. Tel: 609-886-2662; Fax: 609-886-3583. Cheryl King May, Acting Coord.

Catholic Charities - Cumberland County, 810 Montrose St., Vineland, 08360. Tel: 609-691-1841; Fax: 609-692-6575. John Desparrois, Regl. Coord.

Catholic Charities - Salem County, 14-16 W. Main St., Penns Grove, 08069. Tel: 609-299-1296; Fax: 609-299-4010. Email: cc11@snip.net. John Desparrois, Regl. Coord.

Catholic Charities of Gloucester County, 1200 N. Delsea Dr., Ste. One, Westville, 08093. Tel: 856-845-9200; Fax: 856-845-8905. Marcia Hoffman, Coord.

Catholic Charities, Camden/Gloucester Counseling Center, 141 S. Black Horse Pike, Blackwood, 08012. Tel: 856-227-9002; Fax: 856-227-9005. Email: cc7@snip.net. Ed Rosado, L.C.S.W., Center Dir.

Catholic Charities, 21 W. Verona Ave., Pleasantville, 08232. Tel: 609-383-0909; Fax: 609-383-2084. Cape/Atlantic Counseling Center

Catholic Charities Counseling Center in Newfield/Salem, 951 Main Rd., Vineland, 08360. Tel: 856-697-0744; Fax: 856-697-0742. Sylvia Loumeau, L.C.S.W., Center Dir.

[R] CAMPUS MINISTRIES

CAMDEN. *Rutgers University - Camden Campus* 126 Broadway, 08102. Tel: 856-963-6568; Fax: 856-966-5955. Email: mtmannion@comcast.net. Web: www.cathedralministries.com. Rev. Michael T. Mannion, Diocesan Campus Ministry Coord.

BLACKWOOD. *Camden County College Community Center College Community Center*, P.O. Box 20C, 08012. Tel: 856-227-7200, Ext. 4552; Fax: 856-347-2230. Email: kmcconnell@camdencc.edu. Sr. Karen McConnell, F.M.I.H.M., Campus Min.

GLASSBORO. *Rowan University* Newman Center, Rte. 322 and Bowe Blvd., 08028. Tel: 856-881-5642; Fax: 856-881-4183. Email: frmazz@erols.com. Rev. Cadmus D. Mazzarella, Campus Min. & Dir.; Ann Polo, Asst. Dir.

MAYS LANDING. *Atlantic Community College* 08330.

Assumption Rectory, P.O. Box 517, Pomona, 08240. Tel: 609-652-0230. Email: frjeffsj@bellatlantic.com. Rev. C. Jeffries Burton, S.J. (BAL), Chap.

POMONA. *Richard Stockton College of New Jersey* Jim Leeds Rd., 08240. Tel: 609-652-0230; Fax: 609-965-4149.

Catholic Campus Ministry Center at Stockton P.O. Box 1003, 08240. Tel: 609-804-0200; Fax: 609-804-9135. Rev. C. Jeffries Burton, S.J. (BAL).

[S] MEDICAL CLINICS

CAMDEN. *St. John the Baptist Pre-Natal Clinic*, 6th St. & Erie St., 08102. Tel: 856-757-9540; Fax: 856-757-9541. Patricia A. Chico, L.P.N., Admin. Patients Assisted Annually 1,750.

Saint Luke's Catholic Medical Services, Inc., 511 State St., 08102. Tel: 856-365-4642; Fax: 856-365-0539. Lesly A. D'Ambola, D.O., Medical Dir. Patients Assisted Annually 4,500; Staff 3.

[T] LEGAL SERVICES

CAMDEN. *Camden Center for Law and Social Justice, Inc.*, 509 State St., 08102. Tel: 856-966-8896; Fax: 856-541-8826. Email: vguest@superlink.net. Vincent G. Guest Esq. Patients Assisted Annually 5,000; Total Staff 6.

[U] FOOD CENTERS

CAMDEN. *The Cathedral Soup Kitchen, Inc.*, 642 Market St., 08102. Tel: 856-964-6771 (Office); Fax: 856-964-6772. Email: cathedralkitchen@aol.com. Edward Clark, Pres. Tel: 856-783-2479; Karen Talarico, Exec. Dir. Total Assisted 56,000; Total Staff 8.

[V] MISCELLANEOUS

CAMDEN. *The Diocesan Health Sevices Corporation of The Diocese of Camden, Incorporated*, 1845 Haddon Ave., 08103. Tel: 856-342-4131; Fax: 856-342-4172. Email: martin.idler@vhscd.org. Martin B. Idler, Exec. Dir.

The Diocesan Housing Services Corporation of The Diocese of Camden, Incorporated, 1845 Haddon Ave., 08103. Tel: 856-342-4101; Fax: 856-342-4180. Email: Curtis.Johnson@vhscd.org. Curtis H. Johnson Jr., Exec. Dir.

Diocese of Camden Historic Preservation Corporation, 631 Market St., 08102. Rev. Peter M. Joyce, J.C.L., Trustee.

Guadalupe Family Services, 509 State St., 08102. Tel: 856-365-8081; Fax: 856-365-8247. Sr. Helen Cole, Admin. Dir.

Holy Spirit Housing, Inc., 1845 Haddon Ave., 08103. Tel: 856-342-4130. Curtis H. Johnson Jr. Corporation formed to design, build, administer & operate the senior housing facility in Atlantic City.

Padre Pio Shrine, Buena Borough, N.J., Inc., 631 Market St., 08102. Rev. Peter M. Joyce, J.C.L., Contact Person.

The Vicariate for Human Services of The Diocese of Camden Corporation, 1845 Haddon Ave., 08103.

Tel: 856-342-4101; Fax: 856-342-4180. Email: kzmuda@vhsco.org. Rev. Thomas A. Newton, Vicar.

CAPE MAY. *Victorian Towers, Inc.*, 608 Washington St., 08204. Tel: 609-884-5883; Fax: 609-884-5625.

Victorian Toewrs Management Corporation, 608 Washington St., 08204. Email: VictorianTowers@Snip.net. Maureen Farrell, Office Mgr.

CHERRY HILL. *Village Apartments of Cherry Hill, N.J., Inc.*, 212 Lourdes Ct., 08003. Tel: 856-424-7913; Fax: 856-424-9211. Email: theresa@villageaptscherryhill.com. Theresa Mosteig, Office Mgr.

HAINESPORT. *Domicilium Corporation Davenport Village*, 301 Davenport Ave., 08060. Tel: 609-702-5817. Email: Davenport@Pennrose.com.

NORTH CAPE MAY. *Christ Child Society, Cape May County Chapter*, P.O. Box 882, 08204. Tel: 609-884-4054. Email: circle@dandy.net.

PENNSAUKEN. *Catholic Charities, Diocese of Camden, Inc.*, 2830 Marlton Pike, 08110. Tel: 856-663-9800; Fax: 856-663-0253. Kevin H. Hickey, M.S.W., Exec. Dir.

PLEASANTVILLE. *Pleasantville Multicultural Corporation*, 25 W. Black Horse Pike, 08232-2639. Tel: 609-641-0285; Fax: 609-641-0385. Corporation accepts and administers funds received from the Casino Reinvestment Development Authority (CRDA) for the improvement of certain buildings owned by St. Peter's Catholic Church, Pleasantville, NJ.

RELIGIOUS INSTITUTES OF MEN REPRESENTED IN THE DIOCESE

For further details refer to the corresponding bracketed number in the Religious Institutes of Men or Women section.

[0140]—*The Augustinians* (Province of St. Thomas of Villanova, Villanova, PA)—O.S.A.

[0330]—*Brothers of the Christian Schools*—F.S.C.

[0480]—*Conventual Franciscans* (Syracuse, NY)—O.F.M.Conv

[0520]—*Franciscan Friars* (Prov. of the Most Holy Name of Jesus)—O.F.M.

[0670]—*Hospitaller Brothers of St. John of God*—O.H.

[0690]—*Jesuit Fathers and Brothers*—S.J.

[1120]—*Missionaries of the Sacred Hearts of Jesus and Mary*—M.SS.CC.

[0920]—*Oblates of St. Francis De Sales* (Wilmington-Philadelphia)—O.S.F.S.

[0430]—*Order of Preachers-Dominicans* St. Joseph Prov., New York)—O.P.

[0760]—*Society of Mary*—S.M.

[0990]—*Society of the Catholic Apostolate*—S.A.C.

[1200]—*Society of the Divine Savior*—S.D.S.

[0560]—*Third Order Regular of Saint Francis*—T.O.R.

RELIGIOUS INSTITUTES OF WOMEN REPRESENTED IN THE DIOCESE

[2410]—*Congregation of the Marianites of Holy Cross*—M.S.C.

[0890]—*Daughters of Our Lady of Mercy*—D.M.

[0900]—*Daughters of Our Lady of the Sacred Heart*—F.D.N.S.C.

[1050]—*Dominican Contemplative Nuns*—O.P.

[1070-03]—*Dominican Sisters*—O.P.

[1105]—*Dominican Sisters of Hope*—O.P.

[]—*Franciscan Missionaries of the Immaculate Heart of Mary*—F.M.I.H.M.

[1365]—*Franciscan Missionary Sisters of the Infant Jesus*

[1180]—*Franciscan Sisters of Allegany, New York*—O.S.F.

[]—*Franciscian Sisters of Syracuse*—O.S.F.

[1840]—*Grey Nuns of the Sacred Heart*—G.N.S.H.

[]—*Hospitaler Sisters of Mercy* (Pleasantville, NJ)—H.S.M.

[2575]—*Institute of the Sisters of Mercy of the Americas* (Merion, PA; Baltimore, MD)—R.S.M.

[2300]—*Little Servant Sisters of the Immaculate Conception*—L.S.I.C.

[2490]—*Medical Mission Sisters*—M.M.S.

[]—*Missionary Daughters of the Most Pure Virgin Mary*—M.D.P.V.M.

[2790]—*Missionary Servants of the Most Blessed Trinity*—M.S.B.T.

[3430]—*Religious Teachers Filippini* (Morristown, NJ)—M.P.F.

[2970]—*School Sisters of Notre Dame*—S.N.D.

[0590]—*Sisters of Charity of St. Elizabeth*—S.C.

[0650]—*Sisters of Charity of St. Vincent de Paul, of New York*—S.C.

[0660]—*Sisters of Christian Charity*

[]—*Sisters of Mary Immaculate* (Pleasantville, NJ)—S.M.I.

[3893]—*Sisters of Saint Joseph of Chestnut Hill, Philadelphia*—S.S.J.

[1650]—*Sisters of St. Francis of Philadelphia*—O.S.F.

[3890]—*Sisters of St. Joseph of Peace*—C.S.J.P.

[2000]—*Sisters of the Holy Redeemer*—C.S.R.

[1490]—*Sisters of the Third Franciscan Order*—O.S.F.

[2170]—*Sisters, Servants of the Immaculate Heart of Mary*—I.H.M.

[4060]—*Society of the Holy Child Jesus*—S.C.J

NECROLOGY

† Lubicky, Rev. Msgr. John R., (Retired)—Died April 30, 2003

† Wieckowski, Rev. Msgr. John F., (Retired)—Died Aug. 6, 2003

† Darby, Bernard M., (Retired)—Died Nov. 24, 2002

† Melvin, James M., (Retired)—Died Nov. 16, 2002

† Mroczkowski, Leonard A., (Retired)—Died Dec. 24, 2002

† Walsh, Edward J., (Retired)—Died June 2, 2003

Diocese of Charleston

(Dioecesis Carolopolitana)

Most Reverend

ROBERT J. BAKER, S.T.D.

Bishop of Charleston; ordained March 21, 1970; appointed July 13, 1999; consecrated September 29, 1999. *Res.: 114 Broad St., Charleston, SC 29401. Office: 119 Broad St., Charleston, SC 29401. Mailing Address: P.O. Box 818, Charleston, SC 29402.* Tel: 843-853-2130; Fax: 843-724-6387.

Most Reverend

DAVID B. THOMPSON, D.D., J.C.L.

Retired Bishop of Charleston; ordained May 27, 1950; appointed Coadjutor Bishop of Charleston April 22, 1989; ordained May 24, 1989; succeeded to Bishop of Charleston February 22, 1990; retired July 13, 1999. *Res.: 4479 Downing Pl., Mount Pleasant, SC 29466.* Tel: 843-971-2810.

ESTABLISHED JULY 11, 1820.

Square Miles 31,055.

Comprises the State of South Carolina.

For legal titles of parishes and diocesan institutions, consult the Chancery Office.

Chancery Office: 119 Broad St., P.O. Box 818, Charleston, SC 29402. Tel: 843-853-2130; Fax: 843-724-6387.

Web: www.catholic-doc.org

Email: jim@catholic-doc.org

STATISTICAL OVERVIEW

Personnel	
Bishop	1
Retired Bishops	1
Priests: Diocesan Active in Diocese	59
Priests: Diocesan Active Outside Diocese	3
Priests: Diocesan in Foreign Missions	1
Priests: Retired, Sick or Absent	30
Number of Diocesan Priests	93
Religious Priests in Diocese	43
Total Priests in Diocese	136
Extern Priests in Diocese	29
Permanent Deacons in Diocese	96
Total Brothers	26
Total Sisters	145
Parishes	
Parishes	94
With Resident Pastor:	
Resident Diocesan Priests	82
Resident Religious Priests	25
Without Resident Pastor:	
Administered by Priests	2
Administered by Deacons	1
Administered by Professed Religious Men	1
Administered by Religious Women	6
Missions	25
Pastoral Centers	10
New Parishes Created	1
Welfare	
Catholic Hospitals	3
Total Assisted	334,890
Homes for the Aged	1
Total Assisted	15
Special Centers for Social Services	7
Total Assisted	39,604
Educational	
Diocesan Students in Other Seminaries	21
Total Seminarians	21
High Schools, Diocesan and Parish	2
Total Students	1,256
High Schools, Private	2
Total Students	344
Elementary Schools, Diocesan and Parish	26
Total Students	6,176
Catechesis/Religious Education:	
High School Students	2,918
Elementary Students	10,411
Total Students under Catholic Instruction	21,126
Teachers in the Diocese:	
Priests	1
Brothers	1
Sisters	6
Lay Teachers	644
Vital Statistics	
Receptions into the Church:	
Infant Baptism Totals	2,793
Adult Baptism Totals	964
Received into Full Communion	475
First Communions	2,484
Confirmations	1,988
Marriages:	
Catholic	386
Interfaith	320
Total Marriages	706
Deaths	1,057
Total Catholic Population	152,413
Total Population	4,054,890

Former Bishops—Rt. Revs. JOHN ENGLAND, D.D., first Bishop; consecrated Sept. 21, 1820; died April 11, 1842; WILLIAM CLANCY, D.D., consecrated Dec. 21, 1834, Coadjutor; made Vicar-Apostolic of British Guiana, April 12, 1837;; died June 19, 1847; IGNATIUS A. REYNOLDS, D.D., second Bishop; consecrated March 19, 1844; died March 6, 1855; PATRICK N. LYNCH, D.D., third Bishop; consecrated March 14, 1858; died Feb. 26, 1882; HENRY P. NORTHROP, D.D., fourth Bishop; consecrated Titular-Bishop of Rosalia and Vicar-Apostolic of North Carolina, Jan. 8, 1882; transferred to Charleston, by brief dated Jan. 27, 1883; died June 7, 1916; WILLIAM T. RUSSELL, D.D., fifth Bishop; consecrated March 15, 1917; died March 18, 1927; Most Revs. EMMET M. WALSH, D.D., sixth Bishop; consecrated Sept. 8, 1927; transferred to Youngstown, Ohio, as Coadjutor Bishop, Sept. 8, 1949; JOHN J. RUSSELL, D.D., seventh Bishop; consecrated March 14, 1950; transferred to Bishop of Richmond, July 10, 1958; PAUL J. HALLINAN, D.D., eighth Bishop; consecrated Oct. 28, 1958; transferred to Archbishop of Atlanta, Feb. 21, 1962; FRANCIS F. REH, S.T.L., J.C.D. (Retired), ninth Bishop; consecrated June 29, 1962; appt. Titular Bishop of Macriana in Mauretania and Rector of North American College, Rome, Italy, Sept. 5, 1964; transferred to Saginaw, Dec. 18, 1968; installed Feb. 26, 1969; retired April 29, 1980; ERNEST L. UNTERKOEFLER, D.D., J.C.D., S.T.L., tenth Bishop; ord. May 18, 1944; appt. Titular Bishop of Latopolis and Auxiliary Bishop of Richmond, Dec. 13, 1961; consecrated Feb. 22, 1962; appt. Bishop of Charleston, Dec. 12, 1964; resigned Feb. 22, 1990; died Jan. 4, 1993; DAVID B. THOMPSON, D.D., J.C.L. (Retired), eleventh Bishop; ord. May 27, 1950; appt. Coadjutor Bishop of Charleston April 22, 1989; ord. May 24, 1989; succeeded to Bishop of Charleston Feb. 22, 1990; retired July 13, 1999.

Vicar General's Office—Rev. Msgr. JAMES A. CARTER, V.G., P.A. , 119 Broad St., P.O. Box 818, Charleston, 29402. Tel: 843-853-2130. Email: jac@catholic-doc.org; Deacon ALFRED PAYNE, Asst. to Vicar Gen. & Vice Chancellor. Tel: 843-853-2130, Ext. 206. Email: acp@catholic-doc.org; DOROTHY FISHER, Admin. Asst. Tel: 843-884-5587; Fax: 843-884-7086. Christ Our King Catholic Church, 1122 Russell Dr., Mount Pleasant, 29465. Email: dfisher@pal-metto.com; BONNIE SIGERS, Coord., Office of Vicar Gen. Tel: 843-853-2130, Ext. 206; Fax: 843-724-6387; 843-723-1649 (screening). Email: bonnie@catholic-doc.orgFax: 843-724-6387 (Chancery); Rev. Msgr. JOSEPH R. ROTH, D.D., V.G., 120 Broad St., Charleston, 29401. Tel: 843-724-8395; Fax: 843-724-6386. Email: jrr@catholic-doc.org; LEANNE THOMAS, Admin. Asst. Tel: 843-724-8395, Ext. 236. Email: leanne@catholic-doc.org; Cathedral of St. John the Baptist, 120 Broad St., Charleston, 29407.

Chancery Office—119 Broad St., P.O. Box 818, Charleston, 29402. Tel: 843-853-2130; Fax: 843-724-6387. Web: www.catholic-doc.org/index.html.

Chancellor—Rev. H. GREGORY WEST, J.C.L., 119 Broad St., P.O. Box 818, Charleston, 29402. Tel: 843-853-2130, Ext. 214. Email: gwest@catholic-doc.org; Deacon ALFRED C. PAYNE JR., Asst. to Vicar Gen. & Vice Chancellor. Tel: 843-853-2130, Ext. 209. Email: acp@catholic-doc.org.

Chancery West—1662 Ingram Rd., Charleston, 29407. Tel: 843-402-9115; Fax: 843-402-9071; 843-402-7724 (Christian Formation).

Diocesan Web Page—Web: www.catholic-doc.org.

Archivist—MARY GILES, C.A. Tel: 843-724-8372. Email: mgiles@catholic-doc.org.

Bishop's Office—SALLY WOOTEN, Admin. Asst. Tel: 843-853-2130, Ext. 203. Email: sally@catholic-doc.org; ANDREA A. CRAWFORD, Sec. Tel: 843-853-2130, Ext. 202. Email: andrea@catholic-doc.org; YULONDA V. WILKINSON, Receptionist. Tel: 843-853-2130, Ext. 201. Email: yulonda@catholic-doc.org (Chancery).

Office of Finance—Mr. DENNIS F. ATWOOD, K.S.G., CFO. Tel: 843-402-9115, Ext. 12. Email: dennis@

catholic-doc.org; BERNADETTE W. FARETRA, Controller. Tel: 843-402-9115, Ext. 12. Email: bernadette@catholic-doc.org; DANIEL TORLAY, Asst. Controller. Tel: 843-402-9115, Ext. 55. Email: daniel@catholic-doc.org; PAT SHRADER, Admin. Asst. Tel: 843-402-9115, Ext. 12. Email: pat@catholic-doc.org; JANETTE CARAVIELLO, Accounts Payable. Tel: 843-402-9115, Ext. 30. Email: janette@catholic-doc.org; CAROLYN CORDER, Payroll. Tel: 843-402-9115, Ext. 31. Email: carolyn@catholic-doc.org; WANDA ELROD, Staff Accountant. Tel: 843-402-9115, Ext. 33. Email: wanda@catholic-doc.org; LAURIE MCGUCKIN, Staff Accountant. Tel: 843-402-9115, Ext. 34. Email: laurie@catholic-doc.org; CALUNDRA SAMPSON, Staff Accountant. Tel: 843-402-9115, Ext. 32. Email: calundra@catholic-doc.orgFax: 843-402-9071 (Chancery West).

Campus Ministry— (See Christian Formation)

Canonical Consultant—Rev. Msgr. THOMAS X. HOFMANN, J.C.L. Tel: 843-724-8363.

Carter-May Home—JANINE BAUDER, Admin., 1660 Ingram Rd., Charleston, 29407. Tel: 843-556-8314; Fax: 843-556-6879.

Office of Computer Services—MARK T. HOUPT, Dir. Tel: 843-402-9115, Ext. 24. Email: mthoupt@catholic-doc.org; MOSHEERA ABDUL KAREEM, Coord. Data Mgmt. Tel: 843-402-9115, Ext. 25. Email: mosheera@catholic-doc.org. (Chancery West).

Continuing Education for Priests—Rev. JAY SCOTT NEWMAN, J.C.L., St. Mary Catholic Church, 111 Hampton Ave., Greenville, 29601. Tel: 864-271-8422; Fax: 864-370-9880.

Diocesan Curia—Rev. Msgrs. JAMES A. CARTER, V.G., P.A. ; JOSEPH R. ROTH, D.D., V.G.; Mr. DENNIS F. ATWOOD, K.S.G., CFO; Very Rev. STEVEN L. BROVEY, V.F., Piedmont Dean; Rev. Msgr. THOMAS R. DUFFY, V.F., Pee Dee Dean; DOROTHY GRILLO, Dir. Social Ministry; Very Rev. JOSEPH HANLEY, V.F., Coastal Dean; Rev. Msgr. E. CHRISTOPHER LATHEM, V.F., Vicar for Priests; Rev. JAMES L. LEBLANC, Dir. Family Life; Rev. Msgr. LEIGH A. LEHOCKY, V.F., Midlands Dean; Rev. MARTIN T. LAUGHLIN, V.F., Lowcountry Dean; DEIRDRE C. MAYS, Editor, The Catholic Miscellany; Rev. JAMES PARKER, Vicar, Retired Clergy; KATHLEEN MERRITT, Dir. Ethnic Ministries; LISA M. RAWLINS, Dir. Planning; Rev. Msgr. CHARLES H. ROWLAND, J.C.L., Vicar, Judicial Affairs; Rev. C. ALEXANDER MCDONALD, Vicar for Ecumenical Affairs; Sr. PAT KEATING, O.P., Liaison for Religious.

Office of Tribunal—P.O. Box 818, Charleston, 29402. Tel: 843-724-8363 Phone inquiries are accepted from 10:30-11:30 & 1:30-4:30. Rev. Msgrs. CHARLES H. ROWLAND, J.C.L., Judicial Vicar; THOMAS X. HOFMANN, J.C.L., Adjutant Judicial Vicar; MARY E. MCKENZIE, Dir. Tribunal; LUCINDA BRYAN, Procurator & Advocate; MARGARET VERGARA, Ecclesiastical Notary. All petitions for a sanatio, declarations of nullity, and other questions related to divorced persons should be sent to the Office of Tribunal; All prenuptial matters, requests for dispensations and permissions should be sent to the: Office for Matrimonial Concerns and Dispensations, P.O. Box 818, Charleston, SC 29402. Tel: 843-853-2130

Judges—Rev. Msgrs. ROBERT J. KELLY; JOSEPH R. ROTH, D.D., V.G.; Most Rev. DAVID B. THOMPSON, D.D., J.C.L. (Retired); Rev. H. GREGORY WEST, J.C.L.

Defenders of the Bond—Rev. Msgr. THOMAS R. DUFFY, V.F.; Revs. EDWARD FITZGERALD, J.C.L.; JAMES LEBLANC; MARY MCKENZIE; Sr. CHRISTINA MURPHY, S.N.D.deN.

Promoter of Justice—Rev. DENNIS B. WILLEY.

Case Instructor—RAPHAEL S. FRACKIEWICZ, 114 Rear Broad St., Charleston, 29402. Tel: 843-724-8363.

College of Consultors—Rev. Msgrs. JAMES A. CARTER, V.G., P.A. ; JOSEPH R. ROTH, D.D., V.G.; Very Rev. STEVEN L. BROVEY, V.F.; Rev. PETER CLARKE, S.T.D.; Rev. Msgr. THOMAS R. DUFFY, V.F.; Very Rev. JOSEPH F. HANLEY JR., V.F.; Rev. Msgrs. ROBERT J. KELLY; E. CHRISTOPHER LATHEM, V.F.; LEIGH A. LEHOCKY, V.F.; LAWRENCE B. MCINERNY, J.C.L.; CHARLES H. ROWLAND, J.C.L.

Deans—Very Rev. JOSEPH F. HANLEY, V.F., Coastal Deanery. Tel: 843-556-0801; Fax: 843-556-2851. Email: blessac@wpmedia.com; Rev. Msgrs. LEIGH A. LEHOCKY, V.F., Midlands Deanery. Tel: 803-779-0036; Fax: 803-799-2438. Email: stpeterschurch@logicsouth.com; THOMAS R. DUFFY, V.F., Pee Dee Deanery. Tel: 843-651-3737; Fax: 843-651-6316. Email: stmichl13@aol.com; Very Rev. STEVEN L. BROVEY, V.F., Piedmont Deanery. Tel: 864-268-4352; Fax: 864-322-2239. Email: taylorspop@juno.com; Rev. MARTIN T. LAUGHLIN, V.F., Lowcountry Deanery. Tel: 843-785-2895; Fax: 843-842-7494. Email: holyfamily@isle.net.

Family Life Services—Rev. JAMES L. LEBLANC, Dir., 219 York St., S.E., Aiken, 29801. Tel: 803-649-4777; Fax: 803-642-6421.

Finance Council—Rev. Msgrs. JAMES A. CARTER, V.G., P.A. ; JOSEPH R. ROTH, D.D., V.G.; Mr. DENNIS F. ATWOOD, K.S.G.; BERNADETTE W. FARETRA; JOSEPH GRIFFITH SR., K.S.G.; JAY KEENAN; CHRISTINA MYERS; WYATT PRINGLE, K.S.G.; Sr. M. BRIDGET SULLIVAN, O.L.M.; ESTHER TECKLENBURG; JOHN WARD.

Office of Ethnic Ministries—KATHLEEN MERRITT, Dir., 4810 Frontage Rd., Greenville, 29607. Tel: 864-234-9009, Ext. 121; Fax: 864-672-1190. Email: kathleen@catholic-doc.org; MARIA HENAO, Sec. Tel: 864-234-9009, Ext. 118.

Vicar for African-American Catholics—Rev. PAUL M. WILLIAMS, O.F.M., 2229 Hampton St., Columbia, 29204. Tel: 803-254-6862. Email: pw4ofm@aol.com.

Vicar for Hispanic Ministry—Rev. FILEMON JUYA.

Vicar for Vietnamese Ministry—Rev. DAC T. TRAN, O.F.M., 307 Gower St., Greenville 29611-4390. Tel: 864-233-7717. Email: dacofm@yahoo.com.

Presbyteral Council—Rev. Msgrs. JAMES A. CARTER, V.G., P.A. , Facilitator; JOSEPH R. ROTH, D.D., V.G.; Very Rev. STEVEN L. BROVEY, V.F.; Revs. BERNARD J. CAMPBELL, C.S.P.; PETER CLARKE, S.T.D.; D. ANTHONY DROZE; Rev. Msgr. THOMAS R. DUFFY, V.F.; Very Rev. JOSEPH F. HANLEY JR., V.F.; Rev. Msgrs. ROBERT J. KELLY; E CHRISTOPHER LATHEM, V.F.; Very Rev. MARTIN LAUGHLIN, V.F.; Rev. Msgr. LEIGH A. LEHOCKY, V.F.; Rev. C. ALEXANDER MCDONALD; Rev. Msgr LAWRENCE B. MCINERNY, J.C.L.; Rev. GEORGE F. MOYNIHAN; Rev. Msgr. CHARLES H. ROWLAND, J.C.L.; Sr. M. BRIDGET SULLIVAN, O.L.M., Sec.

Bishop's Missionary Support Committee—Rev. Msgr. ROBERT J. KELLY, P.O. Box 1257, Folly Beach, 29439. Tel: 843-588-2336.

Building & Renovation Commission—Rev. Msgrs. JAMES A. CARTER, V.G., P.A. , Chm.; JOSEPH R. ROTH, D.D., V.G.; CHESTER M. MOCZYDLOWSKI; Very Rev. STEVEN L. BROVEY, V.F.; DENNIS ATWOOD, K.S.G.; Deacon JOSEPH CAHILL; MIKE GOCSIK; NORMAN HAFT, K.S.G.; Rev. RICHARD D. HARRIS; Rt. Rev. FRANCIS KLINE, O.C.S.O.; ROSS KUYKENDALL; LISA RAWLINS; JIM POSDA; WILLIAM ROBERTS; KATHY SWEENEY, Sec. Tel: 843-884-5587. Email: ksweeney@pal-metto.com.

Catholic Charities—

Main Office—DOROTHY GRILLO, Dir.. Email: dorothy@catholic-doc.org; LINDA COLLINS, Admin. Asst. Tel: 843-402-9115, Ext. 15. Email: linda@catholic-doc.org.

Counseling Services—MARA CALDERON, Ph.D. Tel: 843-402-9115, Ext. 17 Services in English and Spanish.

Elderly Services—JANINE BAUDER, Coord. Tel: 843-556-6879; Fax: 843-402-9071 (Chancery West).

Coastal Deanery—Sr. PATRICIA KEATING, O.P., Regl. Coord., St. John Church, 3921 St. John's Ave., North Charleston, 29405. Tel: 843-308-9361; Fax: 843-402-9071. Email: srpat@catholic-doc.org; DEBORAH CUSHER, Sec. Tel: 843-402-9115, Ext. 16. Email: debbie@catholic-doc.org.

Midlands Deanery—TRACY KROLL, Regl. Coord.. Email: thkroll@bellsouth.net; P.O. Box 7245, Columbia, 29202-7245. Tel: 803-254-9776; Fax: 803-252-7605.

Pee Dee Deanery—DIANE C. BULLARD, Regl. Coord., P.O. Box 3091, Conway, 29528. Tel: 843-347-5157; Fax: 843-347-9546. Email: dcb@sccoast.net.

Piedmont Deanery—Sr. MARGIE HOSCH, O.S.F., Regl. Coord., P.O. Box 216, Greenville, 29602-0216. Tel: 864-242-2233; Fax: 864-370-9880. Email: smargie@greenville.infi.net

Catholic Women, Council of—Rev. WILLIAM F. PENTIS, C.O., Moderator, P.O. Box 11586, Rock Hill, 29731. Tel: 803-327-2097.

Cemeteries—WARREN STUCKEY Dir., Holy Cross Cemetery. Tel: 843-795-2111; Fax: 843-402-9071; JIMMY LYLES, St. Lawrence Cemetery. Tel: 843-723-8228.

Charismatic Renewals and Prayer Groups—JOSEPH BALAZS JR., Diocesan Liaison, 114 Horseshoe Cove, Sumter, 29150. Tel: 803-773-1160.

Chief Financial Officer—DENNIS ATWOOD, K.S.G. Tel: 843-402-9115, Ext. 12. Email: dennis@catholic-doc.org. (Chancery West).

Divine Worship & Sacraments, Vicar for—Very Rev. STEVEN L. BROVEY, V.F., 1209 Brushy Creek Rd., Taylors, 29687-4103. Tel: 864-268-4352; 864-322-2233; Fax: 864-322-2239. Email: SursumCordaChas@earthlink.net.

Christian Formation—Fax: 843-402-7724. Rev. Msgr. JOSEPH R. ROTH, D.D., V.G. Tel: 843-402-9115, Ext. 20. Email: jrr@catholic-doc.org; CATHY ROCHE, Admin. Asst. Tel: 843-402-9115, Ext. 20. Email: cathy@catholic-doc.org.

Catholic Schools Office—MARGARET E. ADAMS, Ph.D., Dir. Tel: 843-402-9115, Ext. 19. Email: madams@catholic-doc.org; SUSANNE DUNIPACE-FISHTER, Admin. Asst. Tel: 843-402-9115, Ext. 19. Email: susanne@catholic-doc.org.

Evangelization, Catechesis & Christian Initiation—Rev. RONALD R. CELLINI, Dir. Tel: 843-402-9115, Ext. 37. Email: rcellini@catholic-doc.org.

Youth & Young Adults Ministry Office—JERRY WHITE, Dir. Tel: 843-402-9115, Ext. 38. Email: jerry@catholic-doc.org. (Chancery West).

Campus Ministry—Revs. JEFFREY A. KENDALL, Dir., MSC 58 The Citadel, 171 Moultrie St., Charleston, 29409. Tel: 843-953-7692; JOSEPH WAHL, C.O., Dir., (See Institute for Parish Leadership Development).

Holy Childhood Association—Rev. Msgr. ROBERT J. KELLY, Dir., P.O. Box 1257, Folly Beach, 29439. Tel: 843-588-2336; Fax: 843-588-3478.

Human Resources—MARY LOUISE HUDSON, Dir. Tel: 843-402-9115, Ext. 21. Email: mlhudson@catholic-doc.org; MELISSA KUHNELL, Coord. Tel: 843-402-9115, Ext. 56 (Chancery West).

Institute for Parish Leadership Development—Very Rev. JOSEPH A. WAHL, C.O., S.T.D., Dir.. Email: wahl@catholic-doc.org; CATHY ROCHE, Admin. Support. Email: cathy@catholic-doc.org; Charleston Office: Tel: 843-402-9115, Ext. 35; Fax: 843-402-7724 (Chancery West). Rock Hill Office: The Oratory. Tel: 803-327-2097; Fax: 803-327-6264.

Insurance—TRACY KONICKE, Claims/Risk Mgr., Catholic Mutual. Tel: 843-402-9115, Ext. 23. Email: tracy@catholic-doc.org; MELISSA ESTRADA, Asst. Tel: 843-402-9115, Ext. 42. Email: melissa@catholic-doc.org. (Chancery West).

Investment Council—Rev. Msgrs. JAMES A. CARTER, V.G., P.A. ; JOSEPH R. ROTH, D.D., V.G.; Mr. DENNIS F. ATWOOD, K.S.G.; SCOTT CRACRAFT; BERNADETTE W. FARETRA; JAY KEENAN; JOHN SPRAGUE; JOHN WARD.

Marian Programs—Rev. D. ANTHONY DROZE, Moderator, 111 Hampton Ave., Greenville, 29601. Tel: 864-271-8422; Fax: 864-370-9880.

Diocesan Master of Ceremonies—Rev. GREGORY WILSON, Cathedral of St. John the Baptist, 120 Broad St., Charleston, 29401. Tel: 843-724-8395; Fax: 843-724-6386.

Ministry for People with Disabilities—Office of Social Ministry. Tel: 843-402-9115, Ext. 15; Fax: 843-402-9071 (Chancery West).

Office of Prayer & Worship—Very Rev. STEVEN L. BROVEY, V.F., 1209 Brushy Creek Rd., Taylors, 29687. Tel: 864-268-4352.

Newspaper—DEIRDRE C. MAYS, Editor. Email: deirdre@catholic-doc.org; MARIE THROWER, Asst. Editor; NANCY SCHWERIN, Graphic Designer. Email: nancy@catholic-doc.org; STEPHANIE D. PAETSCH, Circulation Coord.. Email: stevie@catholic-doc.orgTel: 843-724-8375; Fax: 843-724-8368. "The Catholic Miscellany"

Parish Priest Consultors—Rev. Msgr. JAMES A. CARTER, V.G., P.A. ; Rev. PETER CLARKE, S.T.D.; Rev. Msgrs. THOMAS R. DUFFY, V.F.; ROBERT J. KELLY; JOHN A. SIMONIN (Retired).

Pastoral Council—Most Rev. ROBERT J. BAKER, S.T.D.; Rev. RICHARD D. HARRIS, Moderator; Rev. Msgrs. JAMES A. CARTER, V.G., P.A. , Ex Officio; JOSEPH R. ROTH, D.D., V.G., Ex Officio; LISA M. RAWLINS, Ex Officio; TINA BOYLE; SIMON BULA; MARTA CONWAY; JOSEPH CONWAY; Sr. MARYJANE GOLDEN, S.S.M.N.; RICHARD KOEHLER; MICHAEL MCGRADY; The Honorable A. GENE MOREHEAD III; YVONNE ORR; JOSEPH PARSONS; MARY REIMER; BOB SHEHEEN; VERA WRIGHT; WILLIAM MEANY.

Pilgrimages, Diocesan Coordinator for—Rev. BASIL P. CONGRO, St. Patrick Church, P.O. Box 20726, Charleston, 29413. Tel: 843-723-6066; Fax: 843-853-8114.

Propagation of the Faith—Rev. Msgr. ROBERT J. KELLY, Dir., P.O. Box 1257, Folly Beach, 29439. Tel: 843-588-2336; Fax: 843-588-3478.

Office of Communications & Information—MARIA A. ASELAGE, Dir.. Email: maselage@catholic-doc.org; STEPHANIE D. PAETSCH, Admin. Asst.. Email: stevie@catholic-doc.orgTel: 843-724-8375; Fax: 843-724-8368.

Respect Life— (Please see Catholic Charities Regional Offices)

Project Rachel—Tel: 843-815-3100.

Road Signs for Parishes—NANCY SCHWERIN, Communications & Information. Tel: 843-724-8375; Fax: 843-724-8368 (Chancery).

Social Ministry, Office of—DOROTHY GRILLO, Dir.. Email: dorothy@catholic-doc.org; LINDA COLLINS, Admin. Asst.. Email: linda@catholic-doc.orgTel: 843-402-9115, Ext. 15; Fax: 843-402-9071 (Chancery West).

Vocations—Revs. H. GREGORY WEST, J.C.L., Co Dir.. Email: vocdirsc@catholic-doc.org; RICHARD D. HARRIS, Co Dir.; Deacon JOSEPH F. CAHILL, Asst. Dir.. Email: joe@catholic-doc.org; AMY RODRIGUEZ,

Admin. Asst.. Email: amy@catholic-doc.orgTel: 843-402-9115, Ext. 22; Fax: 843-402-9071 (Chancery West).

Bishop's Missionary League—P.O. Box 818, Charleston, 29402. Tel: 843-853-2130, Ext. 0.

Cursillo Movement—Ms. SHARON THOMAS, Lay Dir., 233 Gaillard Rd., Moncks Corner, 29461. Tel: 843-899-5741; Rev. HAYDEN J. VAVEREK, Spiritual Advisor. Email: gale@spbcc.org.

Diaconate, Office of—Rev. Msgr. JOSEPH R. ROTH, D.D., V.G., Dir.; LEANNE THOMAS, Admin. Asst., 120 Broad St., Charleston, 29401. Tel: 843-724-8395. Email: jrr@catholic-doc.org.

Campaign for Human Development—Office of Social Ministry. Tel: 843-402-9115, Ext. 15; Fax: 843-402-9071. (Chancery West)

Office of Stewardship & Mission Advancement—MICHAEL J. GOCSIK, Sec. Stewardship & Mission Advancement, P.O. Box 300, Charleston, 29402. Tel: 843-853-2130, Ext. 211. Email: mike@catholic-doc.org; JAMES T. MYERS, Ph.D., Dir. Stewardship. Tel: 803-256-9070. Email: jmyers7462@aol.com; LILIA SANCHEZ, Bishop Stewardship Appeal Asst. Tel: 843-853-2130, Ext. 212. Email: lilia@catholic-doc.org; JOAN M. SILO, Mission Advancement Coord. Tel: 843-853-2130, Ext. 226. Email: joan@catholic-doc.org; KRISTA LEMASTERS, Admin. Asst. Tel: 843-853-2130, Ext. 211. Email: krista@catholic-doc.org.

Personnel Committee—Rev. Msgrs. E. CHRISTOPHER LATHEM, V.F., Chm.; JAMES A. CARTER, V.G., P.A. , Ex Officio; JOSEPH R. ROTH, D.D., V.G.; Bro. EDWARD BERGERON SR., C.F.C.; Sr. ANNE FRANCIS CAMPBELL, O.L.M.; Revs. JAMES PARKER; D. ANTHONY DROZE; Rev. Msgr. ROBERT J. KELLY; Rev. FREDERICK LABRECQUE; Rev. Msgr. LAWRENCE B. MCINERNY, J.C.L.; Rev. GEORGE F. MOYNIHAN; PETER SHAHID; Revs. DENNIS B. WILLEY; PAUL M. WILLIAMS, O.F.M.

Priests' Retirement—P.O. Box 818, Charleston, 29402. Tel: 843-853-2130, Ext. 206.

Scouting Programs—Deacon SAMUEL E. HANVEY, P.O. Box 639, Charleston, 29402. Tel: 843-722-2614.

Sites & Boundaries Committee—Rev. Msgr. JAMES A. CARTER, V.G., P.A. ; DENNIS ATWOOD, K.S.G., (Chancery).

Office of Planning—LISA M. RAWLINS, Dir. Tel: 843-853-2130, Ext. 215. Email: rawlins@catholic-doc.org; ALLISON K. JONES, Admin. Asst. Tel: 843-853-2130, Ext. 230; Fax: 843-965-4990. Email: allison@catholic-doc.org.

Vietnamese Apostolate— (See Office of Ethnic Ministries)

African-American Catholics— (See Office of Ethnic Ministries)

Vicar for Ecumenical & Interreligious Affairs—Rev. SANDY MCDONALD; MELISSA WALKER, Admin., P.O. Box 2048, Columbia, 29202-2048. Tel: 803-779-1801.

Education, Dept. of— (See Christian Formation)

Hispanic Ministry— (See Office of Ethnic Ministries)

Office of Black Catholic Ministry— (See Office of Ethnic Ministries)

Vicar for Clergy—Rev. Msgr. E. CHRISTOPHER LATHEM, V.F.. Email: clathem@sc.rr.com; CARLA DEMILLE, Priest Personnel Coord. Tel: 843-853-2130, Ext. 208. Email: carla@catholic-doc.org; BONNIE SIGERS, Coord.. Email: bonnie@catholic-doc.orgTel: 843-853-2130, Ext. 206. Chancery, 119 Broad St., P.O. Box 818, Charleston, 20402. Mail can be sent to their attention at:.

Victim Assistance Coordinator—Deacon ALFRED C. PAYNE. Tel: 843-853-2130. Email: al@catholic-doc.org.

Vocations Board—Rev. DENNIS B. WILLEY, Dir.; Sr. DEANNA BARTOLOMEI, O.S.F.; Very Rev. STEVEN L. BROVEY, V.F.; Deacon JOSEPH F. CAHILL; Rev. RONALD J. FARRELL; Sr. JULIENNE GUY, O.S.U.; Dr. RONALD KASPER; Revs. JEFFREY A. KENDALL; ROBERT J. SAYER; Deacon ROBERT WATERS.

Volunteers, Office of—Most Rev. ROBERT J. BAKER, S.T.D., Admin., 34 Wentworth St., Charleston, 29401. Tel: 843-723-5758. Email: volunteers@catholic-doc.org.

Youth Ministry— (See Christian Formation)

CLERGY, PARISHES, MISSIONS AND PAROCHIAL SCHOOLS

GREATER CHARLESTON
(CHARLESTON COUNTY)

1—CATHEDRAL OF ST. JOHN THE BAPTIST (1821), Rev. Msgr. Joseph R. Roth, D.D., V.G.; Rev. Gregory B. Wilson; Deacons Thomas Baranoski; Philip M. Meyer.
Mailing & Res. Address: 120 Broad St., 29401. Tel: 843-937-8504 (Res.); 843-724-8395; Fax: 843-724-6386.
School—Charleston Catholic School, Tel: 843-577-4495; Fax: 843-577-6662. See Sacred Heart for details.
Catechesis/Religious Program—Students 117.

2—BLESSED SACRAMENT (1944), Revs. Joseph F. Hanley; John M. Zimmerman.
Res.: 5 St. Teresa Dr., 29407. Tel: 843-556-0801; Fax: 843-556-2851.
School—7 St. Teresa Dr., 29407. Tel: 843-766-2128; Fax: 843-766-2154. Sr. Linda Marie Bolinski, SS.C.M., Prin. Lay Teachers 25; Students 475.
Catechesis/Religious Program—Students 118.
Convent—O Moore Dr., 29407. Tel: 843-766-5120.

3—CHRIST OUR KING (1971), Rev. Msgr. James A. Carter, V.G., P.A. ; Rev. Thomas Kingsley.
Res.: 1122 Russell Dr., P.O. Box 724, Mount Pleasant, 29465. Tel: 843-884-5587; Fax: 843-884-7086.
School—Christ Our King-Stella Maris School, 1183 Russell Dr., Mount Pleasant, 29464. Tel: 843-884-4721; Fax: 843-971-9666. Sr. Stella Maris Craven, O.L.M., Prin. Sisters 1; Lay Teachers 35; Students 710.
Catechesis/Religious Program—Students 380.

4—CHRIST THE DIVINE TEACHER (1968), Rev. Jeffrey A. Kendall.
Mailing Address: *MSC 58, The Citadel*, 171 Moultrie St., 29409-0058. Tel: 843-953-7692; 843-722-7018 (Res.); Fax: 843-953-4811 (Res.).
Catechesis/Religious Program—

5—CHURCH OF THE HOLY SPIRIT (1938), [CEM] Rev. James Parker.
Mailing Address: P.O. Box 719, Johns Island, 29457.
Res.: 2545 Bohicket Rd., Johns Island, 29455. Tel: 843-559-0353; Fax: 842-559-4364.
Catechesis/Religious Program—Students 24.

6—CHURCH OF THE NATIVITY (1959), Rev. Dennis B. Willey.
Mailing Address: 1061 Folly Rd., 29412. Tel: 843-795-3821; Fax: 843-795-2714. In Res., Rev. Nicholas R. Bayard (Retired).
Res.: 1129 Pittsford Cir., 29412. Tel: 843-795-5525; Fax: 843-795-2714.
School—Tel: 843-795-3975; Fax: 843-795-7575. Mrs. Rosann Greiner, Prin. Lay Teachers 13; Students 160.
Catechesis/Religious Program—Students 150.

7—DIVINE REDEEMER (1956), Rev. Edward W. Fitzgerald, J.C.L.
Office—1106 Fort Dr., Hanahan, 29406. Tel: 843-553-0340; Fax: 843-553-0346.
School—1104 Fort Dr., Hanahan, 29406. Tel: 843-553-1521; Fax: 843-553-7109. Jean Steinhoff, Prin. Lay Teachers 13; Students 220.
Catechesis/Religious Program—Students 50.

8—ST. JOHN'S (1929), Rev. Ernest E. Kennedy, Moderator; Bro. Edward E. Bergeron, C.F.C., Parish Life Facilitator.
Res.: 3921 St. John's Ave., North Charleston, 29405-7158. Tel: 843-744-6201; Fax: 843-744-2792.
School—Tel: 843-744-3901; Fax: 843-744-3689. Ms. Carole Anne White, Prin. Lay Teachers 10; Students 76.
Catechesis/Religious Program— Bro. Leonard A. Quinn, C.F.C., D.R.E. Students 15.

9—ST. JOSEPH (1966), Revs. Gabriel J. Smith; Wilbroad Mwape, Admin. Pro Tem.
Mailing Address: 1695 Wallenberg Blvd., 29407. Tel: 843-556-4611; Fax: 843-556-4612.
Res.: 1549 Montclair St., 29407.
Catechesis/Religious Program—Students 85.

10—ST. JOSEPH'S, Closed., For inquiries for parish records please contact Diocesan Archive, P.O. Box 818, Charleston, SC 29402. Tel: 843-724-8372

11—ST. MARY'S (1789), [CEM] Rev. Msgr. Joseph R. Roth, D.D., V.G.
Res.: 89 Hasell St., 29401. Tel: 843-722-7696; Fax: 843-577-5036.
Catechesis/Religious Program—Tel: 843-577-0903; Fax: 843-853-9074. Students 48.

12—OUR LADY OF MERCY (1928), (African American), Rev. Peter S. Kulandai.
Res.: 77 America St., 29403. Tel: 843-723-6066; Fax: 843-853-8114.
School—Tel: 845-577-4495; Fax: 843-577-6662. See Sacred Heart for details.
Catechesis/Religious Program—Tel: 843-723-6088. Students 5.

13—ST. PATRICK'S (1837), (African American), [CEM] Rev. Peter S. Kulandai.
Res.: 125 St. Philip St., P.O. Box 20726, 29413. Tel: 843-723-6066; Fax: 843-853-8114.
School—Charleston Catholic School, Tel: 843-577-4495; Fax: 843-577-6662. See Sacred Heart for details.
Catechesis/Religious Program—Tel: 843-723-6088. Students 58.

14—ST. PETER'S, Closed., For inquiries for parish records contact St. Patrick, P.O. Box 20726, Charleston, SC 29413.

15—SACRED HEART (1920), Rev. Jeffrey A. Kendall.
Res.: 888 King St., 29403-4139. Tel: 843-722-7018; Fax: 843-579-9604.
School—Charleston Catholic School, Tel: 843-577-4495; Fax: 843-577-6662. Yvonne Tolley Orr, Prin. Lay Teachers 14; Students 164; Religious 1.
Catechesis/Religious Program—St. Patrick Church, 134 St. Philip St.. Tel: 843-723-6066; Fax: 843-853-8114. Students 9.
Catechesis/Religious Program—The Citadel, 171 Moultrie St.. Tel: 843-953-7692; Fax: 843-953-4811.

16—STELLA MARIS (1845), Rev. Msgr. Lawrence B. McInerny, J.C.L.; Deacons Walter S. Pezanowski; R. Michael Osbourne.
Res.: 1204 Middle St., P.O. Box 280, Sullivan's Island, 29482. Tel: 843-883-3108 (Office); 843-883-9158 (Rectory); Fax: 843-883-3160.
Catechesis/Religious Program—Christian Formation/CCD, Tel: 843-883-9040. Students 261.

17—ST. THOMAS THE APOSTLE (1966), Rev. William F. Leonard (MET); Deacon Jorge V. Ramirez.
Res.: 6650 Dorchester Rd., North Charleston, 29418. Tel: 843-552-9045; 843-552-2223; Fax: 843-552-9077.
Catechesis/Religious Program—Students 130.

OUTSIDE OF THE CITY OF CHARLESTON

ABBEVILLE, ABBEVILLE CO., SACRED HEART (1885), Revs. Richard Harris, Admin.; Allam Marreddy (India).
Res.: 206 N. Main St., P.O. Box 812, 29620. Tel: 864-459-5150; Fax: 864-465-3615.
Catechesis/Religious Program—Students 11.
Mission—Good Shepherd P.O. Box 1468, McCormick, McCormick Co. 29835. Tel: 864-465-3615.
Station—McCormick Correctional Institution McCormick.

AIKEN, AIKEN CO.

1—ST. GERARD (1943), Rev. Justin S. Upkong, Admin.
Res.: 640 Edrie St., N.E., 29801. Tel: 803-649-3030; Fax: 803-649-3030.
School— Merged with St. Mary's School.

2—ST. MARY, HELP OF CHRISTIANS (1853), [CEM] Revs. James L. Le Blanc; Gade Show Reddy (India); Deacons Donald V. Roseborough; Robert A. Pierce.
Res.: 219 York St. S.E., P.O. Box 438, 29802. Tel: 803-649-4777; Fax: 803-642-6421.
School—118 York St., 29801. Tel: 803-649-2071; Fax: 803-643-0092. Mr. Keith Darr, Prin. Lay Teachers 30; Students 308.
Catechesis/Religious Program—Robert Pierce, D.R.E. Students 245.

ANDERSON, ANDERSON CO.

1—ST. JOSEPH'S (1868), Rev. James N. Dubrouillet; Deacon Robert Jacobi. In Res., Rev. Louis J.P. Kennedy.
Office—1303 McLees Rd., 29621. Tel: 864-225-5341; Fax: 864-225-6432.
Res.: 1107 McLees Rd., 29621. Tel: 864-224-0538.
Church: 1200 Cornelia Rd., 29621.
School—1200 Cornelia Rd., 29621. Tel: 864-225-2143. Mary Ann Groves, Prin. Lay Teachers 7; Students 105.
Catechesis/Religious Program—Students 140.

2—ST. MARY OF THE ANGELS (1943), Rev. David L. Hyman, O.F.M. In Res., Rev. Thomas F. Vigliotta, O.F.M.
Res.: 1821 White St., P.O. Box 3, 29622. Tel: 864-226-8621; Fax: 864-226-2536.
Catechesis/Religious Program—Tel: 864-226-3881. Students 85.

AWENDAW, CHARLESTON CO., ST. BENEDICT (1999), Rev. Paul A. Brenninkmeijer (England), Admin.
Church: 1280 15 Miles Landing Rd., 29429-5915. Tel: 843-216-0039; Fax: 843-928-3447.
Catechesis/Religious Program—Students 140.

BARNWELL, BARNWELL CO., ST. ANDREW, Rev. Michael J. Oenbrink.
Mailing Address: 168 Madison St., 29812. Tel: 803-259-7593.
Church: 110 Madison St., 29812.
Mission—Sacred Heart Blackville, Barnwell Co.
Mission—St. Theresa Springfield, Orangeburg Co.

BATESBURG, LEXINGTON CO., ST. JOHN OF THE CROSS (1959), Revs. Robert J. Sayer; Filemon Juya.
Res.: 320 W. Columbia Ave., P.O. Box 2279, Batesburg-Leesville, 29070-2279. Tel: 803-532-1208.
Catechesis/Religious Program—Tel: 803-532-6777. Students 75.

BEAUFORT, BEAUFORT CO., ST. PETER'S (1846), [CEM] Rev. Ronald R. Cellini (PIT).
Res.: 70 Lady's Island Dr., 29907. Tel: 843-522-9555; Fax: 843-522-0667.
School—Tel: 843-522-2163; Fax: 843-522-6513. Mr. Eugene Cahill, Prin. Sisters 1; Lay Teachers 18; Students 214.
Catechesis/Religious Program—Students 206.

Mission—Holy Cross St. Helena Island, Beaufort Co.

BLUFFTON, BEAUFORT CO., ST. GREGORY THE GREAT (1960), Rev. H. Gregory West, J.C.L.
Mailing Address: 333 Fording Island Rd., 29909.
Res.: 232 Pinckney Colony Rd., 29909. Tel: 843-815-3100; Fax: 843-815-3150.
Catechesis/Religious Program—Students 150.
Chapel—St. Andrew 220 Pinckney Colony Rd., 29910.

BLYTHEWOOD, RICHLAND CO., TRANSFIGURATION (1998), Rev. Arul Joseph Rayappan (India), Admin.
Church: 9720 Wilson Blvd., 29016. Tel: 803-735-0512; Fax: 803-735-1742.
Catechesis/Religious Program—Students 95.
Mission—St. Theresa 321 Bypass, P.O. Box 1004, Winnsboro, Fairfield Co. 29180.

CAMDEN, KERSHAW CO., OUR LADY OF PERPETUAL HELP (1914), Rev. James M. Crowley.
Res.: 1709 Lyttleton St., 29020. Tel: 803-432-6131; Fax: 803-432-3440.
Catechesis/Religious Program—Tel: 803-432-8808. Students 121.

CHAPIN, LEXINGTON CO., OUR LADY OF THE LAKE (1989), [CEM] Rev. Andrew J. Vollkommer.
Mailing Address: 195 Amicks Ferry Rd., P.O. Box 549, 29036. Tel: 803-345-3962; Fax: 803-345-8933.
Res.: 2 Oak Stand Ct., Irmo, 29063. Tel: 803-781-8767.
Catechesis/Religious Program—Students 410.

CHERAW, CHESTERFIELD CO., ST. PETER'S (1842), [CEM] Rev. Bernardino S. Yebra (Philippines).
Res.: 602 Market St., P.O. Box 905, 29520. Tel: 843-537-7351.
Catechesis/Religious Program—Students 3.
Mission—St. Denis Bennettsville, Marlboro Co.
Mission—St. Ernest [CEM] Pageland, Chesterfield Co.

CHESTER, CHESTER CO., ST. JOSEPH'S (1854), Rev. John T. O'Holohan, S.J.; Deacon James P. Hyland, Parish Life Facilitator.
Res.: 110 West End, P.O. Box 869, 29706. Tel: 803-377-4695; Fax: 803-581-7848.
Catechesis/Religious Program—Students 20.

CLEMSON, PICKENS CO., ST. ANDREW (1935), Revs. Bernard J. Campbell, C.S.P.; Gerard J. Aylward, C.S.P.; William L. Edens, C.S.P.
Res.: 123 Folger St., P.O. Box 112, 29633. Tel: 864-654-1757; Fax: 864-654-2950.
Catechesis/Religious Program—Students 600.
Mission—St. Paul the Apostle 130 Bounty Ln., Seneca, Oconee Co. 29672. Tel: 864-882-8551.
Mission—St. Francis of Assisi Mauldin St., Walhalla, Oconee Co. 29691. Tel: 864-638-2958.
Station—Clemson University, Tel: 864-654-7804.

COLUMBIA, RICHLAND CO.

1—GOOD SHEPHERD (1984), Rev. William D. Ladkau.
Mailing Address: P.O. Box 1298, 29202.
Res.: 1625 Granby Rd., Cayce, 29033. Tel: 803-765-1334 (Office); Fax: 803-765-2208.
Catechesis/Religious Program—Students 16.

2—ST. JOHN NEUMANN (1979), Rev. Frederick F. Masad.
Res.: 2816 Bancroff Rd., P.O. Box 23689, 29224. Tel: 803-788-1274; 803-788-0811 (Office); Fax: 803-788-1501 (Office).
Church: 100 Polo Rd., 29223. Tel: 803-788-1478.
School—721 Polo Rd., 29223. Tel: 803-788-1367; Fax: 803-788-7330. Barbara Cole, Prin. Lay Teachers 33; Students 370.
Catechesis/Religious Program—Students 277.

3—ST. JOSEPH (1948), Rev. Msgr. Charles H. Rowland, J.C.L.; Revs. Lee A. Selzer; Ralph C. Robinson.
Office—3512 Devine St., 29205. Tel: 803-254-7646; Fax: 803-799-7607.
Res.: 3451 Blossom St., 29205. Tel: 803-540-1910.
Church: 3600 Devine St., 29205.
School—3700 Devine St., 29205. Tel: 803-254-6736; Fax: 803-540-1913. Sr. Christina Murphy, S.N.D.deN., Prin. Ursuline Nuns of the Congregation of Paris 3; Lay Teachers 33; Students 373.
Catechesis/Religious Program—Students 223.

4—SAINT MARTIN DE PORRES (1935), (African American), Rev. Paul M. Williams, O.F.M.
Res.: 2229 Hampton St., 29204. Tel: 803-254-6862; Fax: 803-799-4720.
School—Tel: 803-254-5477; Fax: 803-254-7335. Mrs. Sandra Leatherwood, Prin. Lay Teachers 7; Students 129.
Catechesis/Religious Program—Students 75.
Station—Correctional Institutions in the Greater Columbia Area

5—OUR LADY OF THE HILLS (1972), Rev. D. Anthony Droze.
Mailing Address & Religious Educ. Center: 2700 Ashland Rd., 29210. Tel: 803-772-7400; Fax: 803-798-8030.
Res.: 120 Marydale Ln., 29210. Tel: 803-772-6692.
Catechesis/Religious Program—Students 410.

6—ST. PETER'S (1824), [CEM 3] Rev. Msgr. Leigh A. Lehocky, V.F.; Rev. Carson Bush.
Mailing Address: P.O. Box 1896, 29202.
Res.: 2125 Raven Tr., West Columbia, 29169. Tel: 803-791-9552.
Church: 1529 Assembly St., 29201. Tel: 803-779-0036; Fax: 803-799-2438.
School—Tel: 803-252-8285. Mrs. Madeline McMillion, Prin. Lay Teachers 18; Students 163.
Catechesis/Religious Program—Students 382.
Station—South Carolina State Hospital

CONWAY, HORRY CO., ST. JAMES (1945), Rev. Frederick LaBrecque.
Church, Office & Mailing Address: 1071 Academy Dr., 29526. Tel: 843-347-5168; Fax: 843-347-1212.
Catechesis/Religious Program—Students 133.

DILLON, DILLON CO., ST. LOUIS (1943), Rev. Anthony Pasala (India), Admin.; Deacon John S. Larkin, Parish Life Facilitator.
Res.: 207 E. Roosevelt St., 29536. Tel: 843-774-1582; 843-774-0255 (Office); Fax: 843-774-0257.
Catechesis/Religious Program—Students 16.
Mission—Infant Jesus 4534 Hwy. 501 N., Marion, Marion Co. 29571. Tel: 843-423-1823; Fax: 843-423-3987.

EDGEFIELD, EDGEFIELD CO., ST. MARY'S (1856), [CEM] Rev. Robert W. Ninedorf (Retired). Tel: 803-637-2079.
Office—302 Jeter St., 29824. Tel: 803-637-6248; Fax: 803-637-6248.
Church: 305 Buncombe St., 29824.
Catechesis/Religious Program—Students 11.

FLORENCE, FLORENCE CO.

1—ST. ANN (1940), (African American), [JC] Rev. Michael T. Corrigan (GAL).
Res.: 113 S. Kemp St., 29506. Tel: 843-662-1736; Fax: 843-661-5012.
Catechesis/Religious Program—Tel: 843-662-8727. Students 50.

2—ST. ANTHONY'S ALL SOULS MEMORIAL (1872), Revs. Arturo O. Dalupang; John D. O'Donnell; Deacon Reginald A.T. Armstrong.
Res.: 2536 W. Hoffmeyer Rd., P.O. Box 5327, 29502. Tel: 843-665-5853; 843-662-5674; Fax: 843-662-4800.
School—Tel: 843-662-1910; Fax: 843-662-5335. Ms. Phyllis Brandis, Prin. Priests 1; Lay Teachers 22; Students 257.
Catechesis/Religious Program—Students 173.

FOLLY BEACH, CHARLESTON CO., OUR LADY OF GOOD COUNSEL (1950), Rev. Msgr. Robert J. Kelly; Rev. Thomasiah Reddimasu, Admin.
Church: 56 Center St., P.O. Box 1257, 29439. Tel: 843-588-2336; Fax: 843-588-3478.
Catechesis/Religious Program—Students 50.

FORT MILL, YORK CO., ST. PHILIP NERI (1993), [CEM] Revs. John P. Giuliani, C.O.; Joseph Francis Pearce, C.O.; Deacon Jon Dwyer.
Church: 292 Munn Rd., 29715. Tel: 803-548-7282; Fax: 803-547-2999.
Catechesis/Religious Program—Students 558.

GAFFNEY, CHEROKEE CO., SACRED HEART (1955), Rev. Raymond J. Carlo.
Res.: 407 Grace St., 29340. Tel: 864-489-9453; Fax: 864-488-2302.
Catechesis/Religious Program—Students 61.

GARDEN CITY, HORRY CO., ST. MICHAEL (1975), Rev. Msgr. Thomas R. Duffy, V.F.; Rev. Michael William (India).
Mailing Address: P.O. Box 2639, Murrells Inlet, 29576.
Res.: 572 Cypress Ave., 29576. Tel: 843-651-3737; Fax: 843-651-6316.
School—(Grades K-8) Tel: 843-351-6795; Fax: 843-651-6803. Sr. Roberta Thoen, S.S.M.N., Prin. Lay Teachers 9; Students 164.
Catechesis/Religious Program—Tel: 843-651-3737; Fax: 843-651-6316. Students 396.

GEORGETOWN, GEORGETOWN CO.

1—ST. CYPRIAN (1950), (African American—Hispanic), Rev. Ronald J. Farrell, Admin.; Sr. Kathleen Driscoll, D.C., Parish Life Facilitator.
Center & Mailing Address: 1905 Front St., P.O. Box 2037, 29442. Tel: 843-546-1470; Fax: 843-527-2139.
Catechesis/Religious Program—Students 4.

2—ST. MARY'S, [JC] Rev. Ronald J. Farrell, Admin.; Deacon Anthony A. De Blasio.
Mailing Address: 317 Broad St., 29440. Tel: 843-546-7416; Fax: 843-546-7003. (Our Lady of Ransom)
Res.: 810 Highmark St., 29442.
Catechesis/Religious Program—Students 40.
Mission—St. Leo the Great Andrews, Georgetown Co.

GLOVERVILLE, AIKEN CO., OUR LADY OF THE VALLEY (1954), Revs. John L. Lawlor, C.M.; Robert J. Waters, Parish Life Facilitator (Retired).
Mailing Address: P.O. Box 419, 29828. Tel: 803-593-2241; Fax: 803-593-2241.
Res.: 2429 Augusta Rd., 29828. Tel: 803-593-2241.
Parish Community Center—Tel: 803-593-2623; Fax: 803-593-0873.
Catechesis/Religious Program—Students 29.
Convent—Horsecreek Valley Convent, P.O. Box 358, 29828. Tel: 803-593-9862. Daughters of Charity 2.

GOOSE CREEK, BERKELEY CO., IMMACULATE CONCEPTION (1976), Revs. Frank Palmieri, C.R.M.; Edgardo Enverga, C.R.M.
Res.: 510 St. James Ave., 29445. Tel: 843-553-1386 (Rectory); 843-572-1270 (Office); Fax: 843-572-3128.
Catechesis/Religious Program—Tel: 843-569-7162. Students 295.

GREENVILLE, GREENVILLE CO.

1—ST. ANTHONY OF PADUA (1939), (African American), Rev. Steven Pavignano, O.F.M.
Res.: 307 Gower St., 29611. Tel: 864-233-7717; Fax: 864-233-2852.
School—309 Gower St., 29611. Tel: 864-271-0167; Fax: 864-271-2936. Sr. Catherine Noecker, O.S.F., Prin. Sisters of St. Francis of Williamsville 4; Lay Teachers 8; Students 112.
Catechesis/Religious Program—Students 86.

2—ST. MARY'S (1852), Revs. Jay Scott Newman, J.C.L.; Francisco Cruz; Deacons Frank Farina; John Karandisevsky; George Tierney; Diego Ferro.
Mailing Address: 111 Hampton Ave., 29601. Tel: 864-271-8422; Fax: 864-370-9880.
School—101 Hampton Ave., 29601. Tel: 864-271-3870. Sr. Veronica Janas, O.L.M., Prin. Sisters of Charity of Our Lady of Mercy 1; Lay Teachers 18; Students 344.
Catechesis/Religious Program—Students 264.

3—OUR LADY OF THE ROSARY (1952), Rev. Dac T. Tran, O.F.M., Admin.
Res.: 3710 Augusta Rd., P.O. Box 8396, 29604. Tel: 864-422-1648; Fax: 864-277-5969.
School—Tel: 864-277-5350; Fax: 864-277-7745. Mrs. Mary Louque, Prin. Lay Teachers 16; Students 231.
Catechesis/Religious Program—Students 69.

GREENWOOD, GREENWOOD CO., OUR LADY OF LOURDES (1920), Revs. Richard D. Harris; Allam Marreddy (India).
Office & Mailing Address: 110 E. Laurel Ave., 29649. Tel: 864-223-8410; Fax: 864-223-7555.
Res.: 120 Colonial Dr., 29649. Tel: 864-223-3003.
Catechesis/Religious Program—Tel: 864-223-4406. Students 221.

GREER, GREENVILLE CO., BLESSED TRINITY (1974), Very Rev. Steven L. Brovey, V.F., Admin.; Revs. Louis Philip Manuel, S.J. (India); Santiago Avila-Mora, C.M.F. (Colombia); Marcian Thet-Kyaw (Burma); Deacon Gabriel Cuervo.
Mailing Address: 901 River Rd., P.O. Box 1371, 29652-1371. Tel: 864-879-4225; Fax: 864-879-4225.
Catechesis/Religious Program—Students 100.

HARTSVILLE, DARLINGTON CO.

1—ST. JOSEPH'S, Closed., For inquiries for parish records contact St. Mary's, 363 N. 5th St., Hartsville, SC 29550.

2—ST. MARY THE VIRGIN MOTHER (1941), Rev. Karl J. Roesch, O.S.B.
Res.: 115 Church St., 29550. Tel: 843-332-7773; 843-332-3136; Fax: 843-332-2812.
Church: 363 N. 5th St., 29550.
Catechesis/Religious Program—Students 91.
Mission—St. Joseph the Worker SC 52 Bus, Darlington, Darlington Co. 29532.

HILTON HEAD ISLAND, BEAUFORT CO.

1—ST. FRANCIS BY THE SEA (1984), [CEM] Rev. Michael F. McCafferty.
Res.: 45 Beach City Rd., 29926-2423. Tel: 843-681-6350; Fax: 843-689-5502.
School— 29926. Tel: 843-689-5502; Fax: 843-689-3725. Mrs. Mary T. Fallon, Prin. Lay Teachers 16; Students 230.
Catechesis/Religious Program—Tel: 843-681-6350, Ext. 248. Students 400.

2—HOLY FAMILY (1966), Rev. Martin T. Laughlin, V.F.
Res.: 24 Pope Ave., P.O. Box 5397, 29938. Tel: 843-785-2895; 843-785-2876; Fax: 843-842-7494.
Catechesis/Religious Program—Students 99.

HOLLY HILL, ORANGEBURG CO., ST. ANN (1945), Rev. Carl E. Kaltreider (CHL).
Church: 8305 Old State Rd., P.O. Box 1520, 29059. Tel: 803-496-7636.
Catechesis/Religious Program—Students 8.

JOANNA, LAURENS CO., ST. BONIFACE (1949), Rev. Jose Rodolfo Lache Avila; Sr. Karen R. Pourby, O.S.F., Parish Life Facilitator.
Office—403 N. Main St., P.O. Box 188, 29351. Tel: 864-697-6745; Fax: 864-697-6745.
Catechesis/Religious Program—Students 32.
Mission—Holy Spirit (1963), 1040 W. Main St., P.O. Box 864, Laurens, Laurens Co. 29360. Tel: 864-984-2880; Fax: 864-984-2880. Sr. Karen R. Pourby, O.S.F., Parish Life Facilitator.
Station—Whitten Center Clinton. Tel: 864-833-2733.

KINGSTREE, WILLIAMSBURG CO., ST. ANN'S (1947), Rev. Michael C. Okere, Admin.
Res.: 300 Aston Ave., Kingtree, 29556. Tel: 843-354-7798; Fax: 843-354-7798.
Church & Mailing Address: 330 Main St., P.O. Box 529, 29556. Tel: 843-354-7798.
Center—908 Thorne Ave., 29556. Tel: 843-354-9415; Fax: 843-354-9093.

Catechesis/Religious Program—Students 21.
Convent—908 Thorne Ave., 29556. Tel: 843-354-9415. Felician Sisters 2.

LAKE CITY, FLORENCE CO., ST. PHILIP'S (1952), [JC] Rev. Michael C. Okere, Admin.
Res.: 146 Anderson St., P.O. Box 399, 29560. Tel: 843-394-8343; Fax: 843-394-8343.
Catechesis/Religious Program—Fax: 843-394-1814. Students 10.
Mission—St. Patrick P.O. Box 399, Johnsonville, Florence Co. 29560.

LANCASTER, LANCASTER CO., ST. CATHERINE'S (1948), Rev. John T. O'Holohan, S.J.
Res.: 720 W. Meeting St., 29720. Tel: 803-283-3362; Fax: 803-283-3363.
Catechesis/Religious Program—Students 35.
Mission—St. Michael 310 Chester Ave., Great Falls, Chester Co. 29055.

LEXINGTON, LEXINGTON CO., CORPUS CHRISTI (1977), Rev. Robert J. Sayer.
Res.: 2350 Augusta Hwy., 29072. Tel: 803-359-4391; Fax: 803-359-8885.
Catechesis/Religious Program—Students 356.

MAULDIN, GREENVILLE CO., ST. ELIZABETH ANN SETON (1972), Revs. Patrick E. Cooper; Howard L. Coughlin, Pastor Emeritus (Retired).
Mailing Address: P.O. Box 672, 29662-0672. Tel: 864-963-3959; Fax: 864-967-9726.
Res.: 110 Woodtrace Cir., Greenville, 29615. Tel: 864-627-9693.
Catechesis/Religious Program—Students 205.

MONCKS CORNER, BERKELEY CO., ST. PHILIP BENIZI (1965), Rev. Hayden J. Vaverek.
Res.: 1404 Old Hwy. 52 S., 29461. Tel: 843-761-3777; Fax: 843-761-0905.
Catechesis/Religious Program—Students 66.
Mission—Our Lady of Peace 224 Murray's Ferry Rd., Bonneau, Berkeley Co. 29431.

MURPHY VILLAGE, EDGEFIELD CO., ST. EDWARD (1964), Rev. Cherian Thalakulam, C.M.I.
Res.: 1370 Edgefield Rd., P.O. Box 6340, North Augusta, 29861. Tel: 803-279-1837; Fax: 803-279-9655.
Catechesis/Religious Program—Tel: 803-279-1441. Students 184.

MYRTLE BEACH, HORRY CO., ST. ANDREW'S (1946), Rev. Msgr. Chet M. Moczydlowski.
Pastoral Center—512 36th Ave. N., 29577. Tel: 843-448-5428; Fax: 843-626-9630.
Parish Administration Office—503 37th Ave. N., 29577. Tel: 843-448-5930; Fax: 843-448-3947.
Res.: 503 37th Ave. N., 29577. Tel: 843-445-7731.
School—3601 N. Kings Hwy., 29577. Tel: 843-448-6062; Fax: 843-626-8644. Mrs. Mary M. Halasz, Prin. Lay Teachers 14; Students 222.
Catechesis/Religious Program—Students 102.

NEWBERRY, NEWBERRY CO., ST. MARK (1956), [JC] Rev. Jose Rodolfo Lache Avila; Deacon Gerald Loignon Jr.
Res.: 928 Boundary St., 29108. Tel: 803-276-6446; Fax: 803-276-0856.
Catechesis/Religious Program—Students 83.

NORTH AUGUSTA, AIKEN CO., OUR LADY OF PEACE (1948), Revs. C. Alexander McDonald; Teofilo Trujillo, O.F.M.
Res.: 856 Old Edgefield Rd., P.O. Box 6605, 29861-6605. Tel: 803-279-0315; Fax: 803-279-5247.
School—Karen Wilcox, Prin. Lay Teachers 15; Students 155.
Catechesis/Religious Program—Students 171.

NORTH MYRTLE BEACH, HORRY CO., OUR LADY STAR OF THE SEA (1964), Rev. George F. Moynihan.
Office—1100 Eighth Ave. N., 29582. Tel: 843-249-2356; Fax: 843-249-8514.
Res.: 1105 Golf View Dr., 29582. Tel: 843-249-8049.
Catechesis/Religious Program—Students 162.

ORANGEBURG, ORANGEBURG CO.
1—CHRIST THE KING, Closed., For inquiries for parish records contact Holy Trinity, 2202 Riverbank Dr., N.W. 29118-4044. Tel: 803-534-8177.
2—HOLY TRINITY (1917), Revs. Michael J. Polewczak (ALB); Abdenago Vargas Rodriguez.
Mailing Address: 2202 Riverbank Dr., 29118-4044. Tel: 803-534-8177; Fax: 802-535-0012.
Res.: 2161 Griffith Dr., N.W., 29118-4009. Tel: 803-534-5900; Fax: 803-539-0206.
Brothers Residence—1710 Amelia St., N.E., 29115-6074. Tel: 803-534-2302. Xaverian Brothers (St. Joseph Prov.) 2.
Catechesis/Religious Program—Students 95.
Mission—St. Mary Allendale, Barnwell Co. Rev. Abdenago Vargas Rodriguez.

PAWLEYS ISLAND, GEORGETOWN CO., PRECIOUS BLOOD OF CHRIST (1986), [CEM] Rev. Patrick J. Stenson, M.S.C.
Res.: 100 Arcadia Rd., 29585. Tel: 843-237-0906.
Office—1633 Waverly Rd., 29585. Tel: 843-237-3428; Fax: 843-237-2293.
Catechesis/Religious Program—Students 115.

PICKENS, PICKENS CO., HOLY CROSS (1965), Rev. Francis J. Travis.
Res.: 416 John St., P.O. Box 855, 29671. Tel: 864-878-0574.
Church: 558 Hampton Ave., 29671. Tel: 864-878-0574; Fax: 864-878-0028.
Catechesis/Religious Program—Students 175.
Mission—St. Luke 4408 Hwy. 86, Easley, Anderson Co. 29642. Tel: 864-855-9039; Fax: 864-855-9038. Deacon Eugene Egendoerfer.

RIDGELAND, JASPER CO., ST. ANTHONY'S (1963), Rev. Michael J. Hussey, O.M.I.
Res.: 700 S. Jacob Smart Blvd., 29936. Tel: 843-726-3606; Fax: 843-726-3606.
Catechesis/Religious Program—Students 17.
Mission—St. Mary 703 5th St. E., Hampton, Hampton Co. 29924. Tel: 803-941-4019.
Mission— P.O. Box 487, Hardeeville, 29927. Tel: 843-487-2943; Fax: 848-784-5338.

ROCK HILL, YORK CO.
1—ST. ANNE'S (1919), Revs. William F. Pentis, C.O.; Adilso Coelho, C.O.; Deacons Ray Moore; Guillermo Nunez.
Office & Mailing Address: 1694 Bird St., 29730. Tel: 803-329-2662; Fax: 803-329-2190.
Res.: 434 Charlotte Ave., 29731. Tel: 803-327-3236.
School—Tel: 803-324-4814; Fax: 803-324-0189. Mr. Frederick S. McKay Jr., Prin. Lay Teachers 24; Students 350.
Catechesis/Religious Program—Students 340.
2—ST. MARY'S (1946), Revs. Joseph Wahl, C.O., Moderator; David D. Valtierra, C.O.; Bro. David Boone, C.O., Parish Life Facilitator; Sr. Francis K. Saring, M.S.B.T., Parish Life Facilitator.
Mailing Address: Bannon Hall, 902 Crawford Ave., P.O. Box 11982, 29731. Tel: 803-329-1008; Fax: 803-329-3799.
Catechesis/Religious Program—Students 75.
Convent—St. Mary's Missionary Cenacle, 915 Crawford Rd., 29730. Tel: 803-329-7450. Missionary Servants of the Most Blessed Trinity.
Saint Martin de Porres Recreation Center—911 Crawford Rd., 29730.

SIMPSONVILLE, GREENVILLE CO., ST. MARY MAGDALENE (1989), Revs. Herbert K. Conner, S.J.; John T. O'Holohan, S.J.; J. Robert Falabella; Deacon Matthew A. Mannino.
Res.: 107 Wickersham Dr., 29681. Tel: 864-234-5323.
Church & Office: 2252 Woodruff Rd., 29681. Tel: 864-288-4884; Fax: 864-297-5804.
Catechesis/Religious Program—Tel: 864-288-4884, Ext. 205. Students 578.

SPARTANBURG, SPARTANBURG CO.
1—JESUS OUR RISEN SAVIOR (1978), Revs. Basil P. Congro; Charles J. Snopek, Admin.; Bartholomew Leon, O.S.B. (SAM).
Res.: 2575 Reidville Rd., 29301. Tel: 864-576-1164; 864-576-0726; 864-574-8117; Fax: 864-576-0860.
Catechesis/Religious Program—Students 426.
2—ST. JOSEPH'S, Closed., For inquiries for parish records contact St. Paul the Apostle, Spartanburg.
3—ST. PAUL THE APOSTLE (1883), Rev. Michael R. DeAntonio.
Res.: 161 N. Dean St., 29302. Tel: 864-582-0674; Fax: 864-582-0716.
School—Tel: 864-582-6645; Fax: 864-582-1225. Patricia Lanthier, Prin. Lay Teachers 18; Students 150.
Catechesis/Religious Program—Tel: 864-585-1858; Fax: 864-582-0716. Students 186.

SUMMERTON, CLARENDON CO., ST. MARY'S (1914), Rev. Carl E. Kaltreider (CHL).
Res.: 10 N. Cantey St., P.O. Box 1110, 29148. Tel: 803-485-2925 (Rectory Center); 803-473-5111 (Parish Office); Fax: 803-485-2925.
Catechesis/Religious Program—Tel: 803-496-7636. Students 4.
Mission—Santee Catholic Community 1592 Village Square Blvd., Santee, Orangeburg Co. 29412.
Mission—Our Lady of Hope Mission 2451 Raccoon Rd., P.O. Box 395, Manning, Clarendon Co. 29102.

SUMMERVILLE, DORCHESTER CO.
1—ST. JOHN THE BELOVED (1898), Rev. Msgr. E. Christopher Lathem, V.F.; Rev. Francis Obong.
Res.: 28 Sumter Ave., 29483. Tel: 843-873-0631; Fax: 843-873-1431.
School—Summerville Regional Catholic School, (Grades K-8), 226 Black Oak Blvd., 29483. Tel: 843-873-9310; Fax: 843-873-5709. Paul Schroeder, Prin. Sisters 1; Lay Teachers 21; Students 265.
Catechesis/Religious Program—Students 235.
2—ST. THERESA THE LITTLE FLOWER (1984), Rev. Msgr. Edward D. Lofton.
Res.: 11001 Dorchester Rd., 29485. Tel: 843-875-5002; 843-875-6911; Fax: 843-875-4884.
Catechesis/Religious Program—Students 214.
Station—MacDougall Correction Center

SUMTER, SUMTER CO.
1—ST. ANNE'S (1911), [CEM] Revs. Daniel J. Carboy, C.SS.R.; Karl Aschmann, C.SS.R.
Res.: 216 E. Liberty St., 29150. Tel: 803-773-3524; Fax: 803-778-1644.
School—Tel: 803-775-3632. Mr. Peter Lawrence, Prin. Lay Teachers 13; Students 180.
Catechesis/Religious Program—Tel: 803-755-0764. Students 120.
2—ST. JUDE (1939), Rev. Alistair McKay, C.SS.R.
Res.: 611 W. Oakland Ave., P.O. Box 1589, 29150. Tel: 803-773-9244; Fax: 803-775-6913.
Catechesis/Religious Program—Tel: 803-778-6404. Students 125.

TAYLORS, GREENVILLE CO., PRINCE OF PEACE (1975), Very Rev. Steven L. Brovey, V.F.; Revs. Louis Philip Manuel, S.J. (India); Marcian Thet-Kyaw (Burma); Deacons Gary Walczak; Gerald W. Grismore.
Mailing Address: 1209 Brushy Creek Rd., 29687. Tel: 864-268-4352; Fax: 864-322-2239.
Res.: 1201 Brushy Creek Rd., 29687. Tel: 864-244-7799.
Catechesis/Religious Program—Tel: 864-322-2233, Ext. 219. Students 697.

UNION, UNION CO., ST. AUGUSTINE'S (1967), Rev. Raymond J. Carlo.
Mailing Address: 103 E. South St., 29379. Tel: 864-489-9453.
Res.: 407 Grace St., Gaffney, 29379. Tel: 864-437-7240; Fax: 864-488-2302.
Catechesis/Religious Program—Students 10.

WALTERBORO, COLLETON CO.
1—ST. ANTHONY'S (1917), [CEM] Rev. C. Thomas Miles.
Res.: 925 S. Jefferies Blvd., P.O. Box 933, 29488. Tel: 843-549-5230; Fax: 843-549-9176.
Catechesis/Religious Program—Students 52.
Mission—St. James the Greater [CEM] 3087 Ritter Rd., Colleton Co. 29488. Tel: 843-844-2454.
2—ST. JOSEPH'S, Closed., For inquiries for parish records contact St. Anthony's, P.O. Box 933, Walterboro, SC 29488.

WARD, SALUDA CO., ST. WILLIAM'S (1895), [CEM] Rev. Robert W. Ninedorf (Retired); Deacon John P. Klein, Parish Life Facilitator.
Res.: 1199 Ridge Spring Hwy., 29166. Tel: 864-445-7215; Fax: 864-445-1150.
Catechesis/Religious Program—Students 24.

YONGES ISLAND, CHARLESTON CO., ST. MARY (1890), Rev. William G. Kinney.
Res.: 4255 State Hwy. 165, 29449. Tel: 843-889-8549; Fax: 843-889-8549.
Catechesis/Religious Program—Students 14.
Mission—SS. Frederick & Stephen P.O. Box 602, Edisto Island, Charleston Co. 29438. Tel: 843-869-0124; Fax: 843-869-0124.

YORK, YORK CO., DIVINE SAVIOUR (1938), Rev. Edward P. McDevitt, C.O.; Deacon Melvin W. Carroll.
Res.: P.O. Box 11586, Rock Hill, 29731. Tel: 803-327-0106; 803-327-2097; Fax: 803-327-6264.
Catechesis/Religious Program—Students 70.
Mission—All Saints P.O. Box 341, York Co. 29745. Tel: 803-684-3431; Fax: 803-684-3431.

Chaplains of Public Institutions

LEXINGTON. *Correctional Institutions in the Greater Columbia Area*, 4214 Grand St., 29203. Tel: 803-786-7177. Mr. Roland L. Thomas.

Special Assignment:
Revs.—
Juya, Filemon (Colombia), 1000 Windsor Dr., Apt. 26 B, Columbia, 29223.
Kennedy, Ernest E., 105 Driftwood, Bonneau, 29431.

On Duty Outside the Diocese:
Rev. Msgr.—
Gorski, J. Donald, Casa Parroquial, Zorritos-Tumbes, Peru.
Revs.—
Abbott, Donald S., St. Dorothy's Church, 11 Harnden St., Wilmington, MA 01887-3519.
Dilley, Gary D., Diocese of Youngstown, Youngstown, OH.

Military Chaplains:
Revs.—
Linsky, Gary S., U.S. Air Force
Spencer, Robert A., U.S. Navy
Torm, Agustin, U.S. Army

Absent On Leave:
Revs.—
Congro, Basil P.
Davino, Michael J.
Morrison, Thomas F.
Sorce, John J.
Watters, Timothy J.

Retired:
Rev. Msgrs.—
Aiken, Roy F., P.O. Box 1728, Columbia, 29202.
Hamburger, Donald C., c/o Donald J. Hamburger, 1347 Edgewater Dr., 29407.
McManus, J. Fleming, 1809 Mepkin Dr., 29407.

Simonin, John A., 826 N. Shem Dr., Mt. Pleasant, 29464-4009.

Revs.—

Bayard, Nicholas R., 1129 Pittsford Cir., 29412.
Burke, Henry J., 720 Garden Lake St., Murrells Inlet, 29576.
Burn, William C., 2107 Westchase Dr., 29407-8829.
Cilwick, Theodore T., 2225 Ashley River Rd., Apt. 182, 29414.
Clarke, Peter, S.T.D., P.O. Box 6337, North Augusta, 29861.
Coughlin, Howard L., P.O. Box 672, Mauldin, 29662.
Day, Charles J.
Dumouchel, Raymond E., P.O. Box 12410, 29422.
Fix, Robert H., 3512 Devine St., Columbia, 29205.
Leonard, Eugene A., 201 E. Blackstock Rd., Apt. 74, Spartanburg, 29301.
McCaffrey, Edmund M., Ph.D.
Mullen, Edward F., 11 E. Augusta Pl., Apt. 235, Greenville, 20605.
Ninedorf, Robert W., 302 Jeter St., Edgefield, 29824.
Powers, Jerome C., 606 Muller Ave., Columbia, 29203.
Riplog, Duane T., 298 Summerset Ln., Summerville, 29483-8338.
Seitz, Paul F.X.
Ward, Jerome A., O.M.I., 2585 Lorentz Dr., Sumter, 29154-7073.

Permanent Deacons:

Anderson, Ronald J., St. Peter, Columbia
Anonie, Joseph A., Immaculate Conception Church, Goose Creek
Armstrong, Reginald, St. Anthony, Florence
Baranoski, Thomas, Cathedral of St. John the Baptist, Charleston
Beeler, Michael A., St. Peter, Beaufort
Bellavance, Peter, St. Mary Magdalene, Simpsonville
Biviano, Joseph P., Our Lady of the Lake Church, Chapin
Bower, William, St. Augustine, Union
Brown, John H., St. Joseph, Charleston
Cahill, Joseph F., Christ Our King Church, Mount Pleasant
Carmody, Joseph E., (Retired), St. John the Beloved Church, Summerville
Carroll, Melvin W., Divine Saviour, York
Cassandra, Anthony J., Our Lady of the Rosary Church, Greenville
Collins, James, Church of the Resurrection, Loris
Corum, Lawrence, St. Jude, Sumter
Crocker, Dr. Jack L., Corpus Christi, Columbia
Cuervo, Gabriel, Blessed Trinity, Greer
Cuomo, Nicholas G., (Retired)
Dashnaw, Donald R., Ph.D., Divine Redeemer, Hanahan; Charleston County Jail
Davis, Thomas E., St. Theresa the Little Flower, Summerville
De Blasio, Anthony A., Our Lady of Ransom, Georgetown
DeNitto, Donald, Church of the Infant Jesus, Marion
DeWolfe, John, St. Francis by the Sea, Hilton Head
Delmonte, Richard, (Retired), St. John the Beloved, Summerville
DiRusso Charles R., Our Lady of the Hills, Columbia
Dillard, Henry, St. Anthony, Greenville
Dotson, Robert E., St. Andrew, Bluffton
Drinkwater, Oscar, St. Andrew, Myrtle Beach
Dwyer, Jon E., St. Philip Neri, Fort Mill
Easterling, Charles M., St. Peter, Columbia
Efken, Donald C., St. Michael, Garden City
Egendoerfer, Eugene, St. Luke, Easley
Ellis, Billy J., St. Anne, Sumter
Farina, Frank J., St. Mary, Greenville
Ferro, Diego, St. Mary, Greenville
Fiore, Charles, St. Michael, Garden City
Gerald, Robert, Jr., St. Anne, Florence
Gorman, Chester E., St. Andrew, Myrtle Beach
Graham, Shane, St. Theresa the Little Flower, Summerville
Grismore, Gerald W., Prince of Peace, Taylors
Hand, Gerald, St. Francis by the Sea, Hilton Head
Hanvey, Samuel E., (Retired)
High, Raymond, Corpus Christi, Lexington
Hollis, Walter W., Our Lady of Peace, North Augusta
Hyland, James P., St. Joseph, Chester
Jackson, Harold I., St. Ann, Kingstree
Jacobi, Robert, St. Joseph, Anderson
Johnson, James H., St. Ann, Florence
Jones, Dennis N., Our Lady of the Hills, Columbia
Karandisevsky, John F., St. Mary, Greenville
Kemper, Joseph G., (Retired)
Klein, John P., St. William, Ward
Kronyak, Robert C., St. Ann Church, Holly Hill
LaCombe, William, St. Peter, Beaufort
Larkin, John S., St. Mary, Hartsville
Lenny, William P., (Retired)
Loignon, Gerald, Jr., St. Mark, Newberry
Lozado, Mariano, (Retired)
Mahaffey, Robert L., Jr., St. Paul the Apostle, Spartanburg
Mannino, Matthew A., St. Mary Magdalene, Simpsonville
McDonald, Thomas F., (Retired), Divine Redeemer, Hanahan
Mevissen, Jeffrey P., St. James, Conway
Meyer, John P., St. James, Conway
Meyer, Philip M., Cathedral of St. John the Baptist, Charleston
Mirande, August J., (On Duty Outside the Diocese)
Moore, James R., (On Duty Outside the Diocese)
Moore, Oliver R., St. Anne, Rock Hill
Murtaugh, Richard J., Jr., St. Elizabeth Ann Seton, Mauldin
Nazzaro, Joseph J., St. Francis by the Sea, Hilton Head
Nunez, Guillermo, St. Anne, Rock Hill
O'Donnell, John D., St. Anthony, Florence
Osbourne, R. Michael, Stella Maris, Sullivan's Island
Palmer, Orean D., Corpus Christi, Lexington
Parks, Coleman T., Corpus Christi, Lexington
Payne, Alfred C., Christ Our King, Mt. Pleasant
Pecko, Harry, St. Augustine, Union
Peitlier, Edward, St. Peter, Beaufort
Petrusak, Frank T., St. Thomas the Apostle, North Charleston
Pezanowski, Walter S., Stella Maris, Sullivan's Island
Pierce, Robert, St. Mary Help of Christians, Aiken
Poole, Charles P., Jr., St. Joseph, Columbia
Ramirez, Jorge V., St. Thomas, North Charleston
Richardson, David W., Holy Spirit, Johns Island
Rock, Paul J., (Retired)
Roseborough, Donald, St. Mary Help of Christians, Aiken
Sams, Gregory W., St. Gregory the Great, Bluffton
Shook, Paul F., (Retired)
Sturm, Robert M., Jesus, Our Risen Savior, Spartanburg
Thomas, Roland L., St. Martin de Porres Church, Columbia
Tierney, George, St. Mary, Greenville
Traxler, Harold G., Jr., St. Andrew, Clemson
Tyson, Robert, Our Lady Star of the Sea, North Myrtle Beach
Walczak, Gary, Prince of Peace, Taylors
Walsh, Charles Michael, Lexington-Richland Project, Manning
Waters, Robert J. (Retired), Our Lady of the Valley, Gloverville; St. Mary Help of Christians, Aiken
West, James L., On Duty Outside the Diocese
Whitford, James E., Sr., Immaculate Conception, Goose Creek
William, W. James, III, St. Anthony of Padua, Greenville
Wright, Winston C., St. Anthony of Padua, Greenville

INSTITUTIONS LOCATED IN THE DIOCESE

[A] HIGH SCHOOLS, DIOCESAN

CHARLESTON. *Bishop England High School*, 363 Seven Farms Dr., 29492-7534. Tel: 843-849-9599; Fax: 843-849-9221. Email: dheld@behs.com. Web: www.behs.com. Rev. Msgr. Robert J. Kelly; Mr. David F. Held, Prin. Priests 1; Lay Teachers 65; Students 871.

COLUMBIA. *Cardinal Newman High School*, (Grades 7-12), 4701 Forest Dr., 29206. Tel: 803-782-2814; Fax: 803-782-9314. Email: jimmcintyrecns@hotmail.com. Web: www.cnhs.org. Mr. Jim McIntyre, Prin. Priests 1; Sisters 1; Lay Teachers 42; Students 380.

[B] HIGH SCHOOLS, PRIVATE

GREENVILLE. *St. Joseph's High School*, 100 St. Joseph's Dr., 29607. Tel: 864-234-9009; Fax: 864-234-5516. Email: info@sjhigh.org. Web: www.sjhigh.org. Keith F. Kiser, Headmaster. Lay Teachers 18; Staff 12; Students 258.

SUMTER. *St. Francis Xavier High School*, 15 School St., 29150. Tel: 803-773-0210; Fax: 803-775-0119. Email: sfxhs@ftc-i.net. Web: www.sfxhs.com; www.saintfrancisxavier.com. Dianne Trapini, Prin. Lay Teachers 3; Students 41.

[C] GENERAL HOSPITALS

CHARLESTON. *Bon Secours St. Francis Hospital*, 2095 Henry Tecklenburg Dr., 29414. Tel: 843-402-1000; Fax: 843-402-1945. Email: petercampbell@ropersaintfrancis.com. Web: www.ropersaintfrancis.com. Sr. Alice Talone, C.B.S., Pres., Sisters of Bon Secours USA; Mr. Allen P. Carroll, Admin.; Sr. Patricia O'Donovan, R.S.M., Dir. Clinical Pastoral Education. Sponsored by the Sisters of Bon Secours, Marriottsville, MD. Bed Capacity 141; Staff 968; Patients Assisted Annually 74,378.

GREENVILLE. **Bon Secours St. Francis Health System, Inc.*, One St. Francis Dr., 29601. Tel: 864-255-1000; Fax: 864-255-1137. Web: stfrancishealth.org.

**St. Francis Hospital, Inc.* Tel: 864-255-1000; Fax: 864-255-1034. Mrs. Valinda Rutledge, CEO; Michael Doiron, Ph.D., Vice Pres. Mission. Sisters of Bon Secours 1; Bed Capacity 319 Patients Assisted Annually 134,373.

[D] HOMES FOR AGED

CHARLESTON. *Carter-May Home*, 1660 Ingram Rd., 29407. Tel: 843-556-8314; Fax: 843-402-9071. Email: janine@catholic-doc.org. Mrs. Janine N. Bauder, Admin. Residents 15.

[E] MONASTERIES AND RESIDENCES OF PRIESTS AND BROTHERS

MONCKS CORNER. *Mepkin Abbey* (Trappist Monks), 1098 Mepkin Abbey Rd., 29461-4796. Tel: 843-761-8509; Fax: 843-761-6719 Email: community@mepkinabbey.org. Web: www.mepkinabbey.org. Rt. Revs. Francis Kline, O.C.S.O.; Christian Aidan Carr, O.C.S.O. (Retired); Revs. Kevin V. Walsh (HRT); Leonard A. Cunningham, O.C.S.O.; Aelred Hagan, O.C.S.O., Novice Dir. & Contact Person; Guerric Frederick A. Heckel; Feliciano Manalili, O.C.S.O.; Richard G. McGuire, O.C.S.O.; Bros. Stephen Petronek, O.C.S.O., Prior; Stan Gumula, O.S.C.O., Business Mgr. Professed Monks 19; Priests 9; Novices 4; Number in Community 23.

ROCK HILL. *Oratory of St. Philip Neri, Congregation of the Oratory of Pontifical Rite*, 434 Charlotte Ave., Box 11586, 29730. Tel: 803-327-2097; Fax: 803-327-6264. Email: oratory@cetlink.net. Web: www.rockhilloratory.com. P.O. Box 11586, 29731-1586. Very Rev. Joseph A. Wahl, C.O., S.T.D., Provost; Revs. William F. Pentis, C.O., First Deputy, Vicar; Edward P. McDevitt, C.O., Sec.; Bro. David Boone, C.O., Treas.; Revs. Robert S. Dell, C.O.; John P. Giuliani, C.O.; James Moran, C.O.; Halbert Weidner, C.O., Ph.D.; Clarence Edward Jones, C.O.; Joseph Francis Pearce, C.O.; David D. Valtierra, C.O.; Adilso Coelho, C.O. Fathers 11; Brothers 5; Scholastics 3.

[F] CONVENTS AND RESIDENCES FOR SISTERS

CHARLESTON. *Convent of the Franciscan Sisters*, 5 Riverside Dr., 29403.

Daughters of St. Paul Convent, 243 King St., 29401. Tel: 843-577-0175; Fax: 843-577-9833. Email: charleston@pauline.org. Web: www.pauline.org. Sr. Maria Bernard Tran, Local Supr. Sisters 4.

Sisters of Charity of Our Lady of Mercy, 424 Ft. Johnson Rd., 29412. Tel: 843-795-6083; Fax: 843-795-6083. Email: olm@home.com. P.O. Box 12410, 29422. Sr. Anne Francis Campbell, O.L.M., Gen. Supr. Tel: 843-795-2866. Professed Sisters in Community 24.

GREENVILLE. *Monastery of St. Clare*, 1916 N. Pleasantburg Dr., 29609-4080. Tel: 864-244-4514; Fax: 864-268-9379. Email: oscgreenville@juno.com. Web: www.poorclaresc.com. Sr. Carolyn Forgette, O.S.C., Abbess. Franciscan Poor Clare Nuns Cloistered Nuns in Solemn Vows 14; Novices 1; Simple Vows 1; Extern in Perpetual Vows 1.

ST. HELENA ISLAND. *Franciscan Center*, 85 Mattis Rd., U.S. Hwy. 21, P.O. Box 682, 29920. Tel: 843-838-3924; Fax: 843-838-2152. Email: franctr@islc.net. Web: www.islc.net/~franctr. Sisters of St. Francis of Philadelphia, Glen Riddle-Aston, PA 2.

[G] CATHOLIC CHARITIES

CHARLESTON. *Catholic Charities of the Diocese of Charleston*, 1662 Ingram Rd., 29407. Tel: 843-402-9115, Ext. 15; Fax: 843-402-9071. Email: dorothy@catholic-doc.org. Web: www.catholic-doc.org/catholiccharities. Dorothy Grillo, Dir.

Coastal Regional Office, 3921 St. John's Ave, North Charleston, 29405-7158. Tel: 843-308-9361, Ext. 16; Fax: 843-308-9361. Sr. Pat Keating, O.P., Regl. Coord.

Midlands Regional Office, 1012 Taylor St., P.O. Box 7245, Columbia, 29202-7245. Tel: 803-254-9776; Fax: 803-252-7605. Mrs. Tracy Kroll, Regl. Coord.

Pee Dee Regional Office, 407 Blossom St., P.O. Box 3091, Conway, 29528. Tel: 843-488-2112; Fax: 843-488-0658. Mrs. Diane Bullard, Regl. Coord.

Piedmont Regional Office, P.O. Box 216, Greenville, 29602-0216. Tel: 864-242-2233; Fax: 864-242-1387.

Sr. Margie Hosch, O.S.F., Regl. Coord.

Echo House-Inner City Apostolate, 1911 Hackemann Ave., 29405. Tel: 843-554-7319; Fax: 843-554-1244.

Neighborhood House-Inner City Apostolate, 77 America St., 29403. Tel: 843-723-5129.

[H] CAMPUS MINISTRIES

CHARLESTON. *The Catholic Campus Ministry of the College of Charleston; Medical University of South Carolina* c/o 119 Broad St., 29401.

Charleston Southern University Email: emcdermo@csuniv.edu. c/o 6650 Dorchester Rd., Charleston Heights, 29418. Tel: 843-552-2223. Rev. William F. Leonard (MET).

The Citadel MSC 58, The Citadel, 171 Moultrie St., 29409-0058. Tel: 843-953-7692; 843-722-7018; Fax: 843-953-4811. Email: kendallj@citadel.edu. Rev. Jeffrey A. Kendall.

AIKEN. *University of South Carolina, Aiken Extension* P.O. Box 438, 29802. Tel: 803-649-4777. Rev. Gade Show Reddy (India).

BEAUFORT. *University of South Carolina, Beaufort Extension* 70 Lady's Island Dr., 29902. Tel: 843-522-9555. Rev. Ronald R. Cellini (PIT).

CLEMSON. *Clemson University, Southern Wesleyan University* 209 Sloan St., P.O. Box 112, 29633. Tel: 864-654-7804; 864-654-1757; 864-654-9670; Fax: 864-654-2950. Email: csa@clemson.edu. Web: www.clemson.edu/~csa. Rev. William L. Edens, C.S.P.; Ms. Marilyn Angoli, Campus Min.

Legal Title: *Clemson University - Catholic Campus Ministry at St. Andrew's Church and the Catholic Student Association.*

CLINTON. *Presbyterian College* Tel: 864-984-2880; Fax: 864-984-2880. 1040 Main St., Newberry, 29108.

COLUMBIA. *Allen University, Benedict College* c/o St. Martin de Porres Church, 2229 Hampton St., 29204. Tel: 803-254-6862; Fax: 803-799-4720. Email: deporres@yahoo.com. Deacon Roland L. Thomas.

University of South Carolina, St. Thomas More Center 1610 Greene St., 29201. Tel: 803-799-5870; Fax: 803-765-0800. Email: tlijewski@aol.com. Web: www.stthomasmoreusc.org. Rev. Timothy M. Lijewski.

CONWAY. *Coastal Carolina University* P.O. Box 1754, 29526. Tel: 843-349-2026; Fax: 843-349-2127. Timothy McCormick, Prof.

DUE WEST. *Erskine College* P.O. Box 812, Abbeville, 29620. Tel: 864-459-5150; Fax: 864-459-5150. Rev. Richard Harris.

FLORENCE. *Francis Marion University* 113 S. Kemp St., 29501. Tel: 843-662-1736; Fax: 843-676-9001. Rev. Michael T. Corrigan (GAL).

GAFFNEY. *Limestone College* 407 Grace St., 29340. Tel: 864-489-9453; Fax: 864-488-2302. Rev. Raymond J. Carlo.

GREENVILLE. *Furman University Campus Ministry*, Formerly Furman University *St. Mary's Catholic Church*, 111 Hampton Ave., 29601. Tel: 864-271-8422; Fax: 864-370-9880. Email: churchoffice@stmarysgvl.org. Web: www.stmarysgvl.org. Rev. Jay Scott Newman, J.C.L.

GREENWOOD. *Lander University* Office, 110 E. Laurel Ave., 29649. Tel: 864-223-8410; Fax: 864-223-7555. Email: RE@OLOL.org. Rev. Richard D. Harris.

HARTSVILLE. *Coker College* 115 Church St., 29550. Tel: 843-332-7773; 843-332-3136; Fax: 843-332-2812. Email: stmary2@earthlink.net. Rev. Karl Roesch, O.S.B.

NEWBERRY. *Newberry College* 928 Boundry St., 29108. Tel: 803-276-6446; Fax: 803-276-0856.

ORANGEBURG. *South Carolina State University & Claflin College c/o Holy Trinity Catholic Church*, 2202 Riverbank Dr., 29118-4044. Served by Xaverian Brothers

ROCK HILL. *Winthrop University, York Co. Tech Center* 434 Charlotte Ave., Box 11586, 29731. Tel: 803-327-6450; Fax: 803-327-6450. Email: valtiera@cetlink.net. Rev. David D. Valtierra, C.O.

SPARTANBURG. *Converse College, Spartanburg Methodist College* 161 N. Dean St., 29302. Tel: 864-582-0674. Deacon Robert L. Mahaffey Jr.

Wofford College 429 N. Church St., 29303-3668. Tel: 864-597-4180. Mr. Doyle Boggs, Advisor.

[I] RETREAT CENTERS

EDISTO ISLAND. *Sea of Peace House of Prayer*, 59 Palmetto Pointe Rd., 29438. Tel: 843-869-0513; Fax: 843-869-0513. Email: condone@bellsouth.net or barbarahubbard@bellsouth.net. Web: www.retreatsintl.org/list.htm#sc.

KINGSTREE. *Springbank Retreat Center-Dominican Retreat House*, 1345 Springbank Rd., 29556. Tel: 843-382-3426; 800-671-0361; Fax: 843-382-5340. Email: springbank@mindspring.com. Web: www.springbankspirit.org.

[J] MISCELLANEOUS

CHARLESTON. *Ladies of Charity of Sacred Heart Church*, 888 King St., 29403-4138. Tel: 843-722-7018.

Pauline Books & Media, 243 King St., 29401. Tel: 843-577-0175; Fax: 843-577-9833. Email: charleston@pauline.org. Web: www.pauline.org. Daughters of St. Paul

The Sisters of Charity of Our Lady of Mercy Charitable Trust, 424 Ft. Johnson Rd., P.O. Box 12410, 29422. Tel: 843-795-2866; Fax: 843-795-6083.

COLUMBIA. *Family Honor, Inc.*, 2927 Devine St., Ste. 130, 29205. Tel: 803-929-0858; Fax: 803-771-2379. Email: famhonor@aol.com. Web: www.familyhonor.org. Brenda Cerkez, Exec. Dir.

Sisters of Charity Foundation of South Carolina, 2711 Middleburg Dr., Ste. 115, 29204-2413. Tel: 803-254-0230; Fax: 803-748-0444. Web: www.sistersofcharitysc.com.

Sisters of Charity Ministry Development Corporation, 2711 Middlebury Dr., Ste. 115, 29204-2413. Tel: 216-696-5560; Fax: 216-696-2204. Web: www.CSAHealthSystems.org. Sr. Judith Ann Karam, C.S.J., Pres. & CEO.

Sisters of Charity Providence Hospitals, 2435 Forest Dr., 29204. Tel: 888-223-1816; Fax: 216-696-2204.

GILBERT. *Society of St. Vincent de Paul*, 206 Evans Addy Rd., 29054. Tel: 803-892-2553; Fax: 803-892-2553. Email: svdpsc@pbtcomm.net. Eleanor Serra, Diocesan Council Pres.; Thomas V. Serra, Midlands District Council Pres.

Society of St. Vincent de Paul, 107 Springhill Dr., Simpsonville, 29681. Tel: 864-963-5086. Philip Cunningham, Piedmont Pres.

GREENVILLE. *SFH, Inc.*, One St. Francis Dr., 29601. Tel: 864-255-1000; Fax: 864-255-1137.

JOHNS ISLAND. *Our Lady of Mercy Community Outreach Services, Inc.*, 1684 Brownswood Rd., 29455. Tel: 843-559-4109; Fax: 843-559-8819. Email: olmoutreach@aol.com. Web: olmoutreach.org. P.O. Box 607, 29457. Tel: 843-559-4109; Fax: 843-558-8819. Sponsored by Sisters of Charity of Our Lady of Mercy.

RELIGIOUS INSTITUTES OF MEN REPRESENTED IN THE DIOCESE

For further details refer to the corresponding bracketed number in the Religious Institutes of Men or Women section.

[0100]—*Adorno Fathers*—C.R.M.
[0200]—*Benedictines*—O.S.B.
[1350]—*Brothers of St. Francis Xavier* (St. Joseph Prov.)—C.F.X.
[0350]—*Cistercians Order of the Strict Observance-Trappist*—O.C.S.O.
[0310]—*Congregation of Christian Brothers*—C.F.C.
[1330]—*Congregation of the Mission* (Eastern Prov.)—C.M.
[0520]—*Franciscan Friars* (Prov. of the Most Holy Name)—O.F.M.
[0690]—*Jesuit Fathers and Brothers* (New Orleans; New England Provs.)—S.J.
[1110]—*Missionaries of the Sacred Heart*—M.S.C.
[0910]—*Oblates of Mary Immaculate* (Eastern American Prov.)—O.M.I.
[0950]—*Oratorians*—C.O.
[1030]—*Paulist Fathers*—C.S.P.
[1070]—*Redemptorist Fathers* (Richmond Vice Prov.)—C.SS.R.

RELIGIOUS INSTITUTES OF WOMEN REPRESENTED IN THE DIOCESE

[0270]—*Congregation of Bon Secours*—C.B.S.
[1000]—*Congregation of Divine Providence* (KY)—C.D.P.
[1730]—*Congregation of the Sisters of the Third Order of St. Francis* (Oldenburg, IN)—O.S.F.
[0760]—*Daughters of Charity of St. Vincent de Paul*—D.C.
[0960]—*Daughters of Wisdom* (American Prov.)—D.W.
[1070-03]—*Dominican Sisters* (Sinsinawa, WI)—O.P.
[1070-04]—*Dominican Sisters* (San Rafael, CA)—O.P.
[1070-11]—*Dominican Sisters* (Sparkill, NY)—O.P.
[1070-13]—*Dominican Sisters* (Adrian, MI)—O.P.
[1170]—*Felician Sisters*—C.S.S.F.
[1415]—*Franciscan Sisters of Mary*—F.S.M.
[1425]—*Franciscan Sisters of Peace*—F.S.P.
[1440]—*Franciscan Sisters of the Poor*—S.F.P.
[1360]—*Missionary Franciscan Sisters of the Immaculate Conception*—M.F.I.C.
[2790]—*Missionary Servants of the Most Blessed Trinity*—M.S.B.T.
[3760]—*Order of St. Clare*—O.S.C.
[0950]—*Pious Daughters of St. Paul*—F.S.P.
[2970]—*School Sisters of Notre Dame*—S.S.N.D.
[0500]—*Sisters of Charity of Nazareth*—S.C.N.
[0510]—*Sisters of Charity of Our Lady of Mercy*—O.L.M.
[0580]—*Sisters of Charity of St. Augustine*—C.S.A.
[2575]—*Sisters of Mercy of the Americas* (Chicago, IL; Pittsburgh, PA;)—R.S.M.
[3000]—*Sisters of Notre Dame* (Baltimore, MD)—S.N.D.deN.
[3950]—*Sisters of Saint Mary of Namur*—S.S.M.N.
[3780]—*Sisters of Saints Cyril and Methodius*—SS.C.M.
[1540]—*Sisters of St. Francis* (Clinton, IA)—O.S.F.
[1620]—*Sisters of St. Francis of Millvale, Pennsylvania*—O.S.F.
[1650]—*Sisters of St. Francis of Philadelphia*—O.S.F.
[1570]—*Sisters of St. Francis of the Holy Family*—O.S.F.
[1800]—*Sisters of St. Francis of the Third Order Regular* (Williamsville, New York)—O.S.F.
[3840]—*Sisters of St. Joseph of Carondelet* (Prov. of St. Louis)—C.S.J.
[2110]—*Sisters of the Humility of Mary*—H.M.
[]—*Sisters of the Sacred Heart of Jesus* (Mexico)—H.C.J.S.
[1720]—*Sisters of the Third Order of St. Francis of the Congregation of Our Lady of Lourdes* (Rochester)—O.S.F.
[1890]—*Society of Helpers*—H.H.S.
[4048]—*Society of Sisters Faithful Companions of Jesus*—F.C.J.
[4120-03]—*Ursuline Nuns, of the Congregation of Paris*—O.S.U.

DIOCESAN CEMETERIES

CHARLESTON. *St. Lawrence and Holy Cross*, 604 Ft. Johnson Rd., 29412. Tel: 843-795-2111. Mr. Warren R. Stuckey Jr., Dir.

NECROLOGY

† Evatt, Rev. Msgr. Thomas A. (Retired)—Died July 18, 2003

Diocese of Charlotte

(Dioecesis Carolinana)

Most Reverend

PETER J. JUGIS

Bishop of Charlotte; ordained June 12, 1983; appointed Bishop of Charlotte August 1, 2003; consecrated October 24, 2003.

Chancery: P.O. Box 36776, Charlotte, NC 28236. Tel: 704-370-6299; Fax: 704-370-3379.

Web: charlottediocese.org

Email: chancery@charlottediocese.org

ESTABLISHED JANUARY 12, 1972.

Square Miles 20,470.

Comprises the Counties of Alexander, Alleghany, Anson, Ashe, Avery, Buncombe, Burke, Cabarrus, Caldwell, Catawba, Cherokee, Clay, Cleveland, Davidson, Davie, Forsyth, Gaston, Graham, Guilford, Haywood, Henderson, Iredell, Jackson, Lincoln, Macon, Madison, McDowell, Mecklenberg, Mitchell, Montgomery, Polk, Randolph, Richmond, Rockingham, Rowan, Rutherford, Stanley, Stokes, Surry, Swain, Transylvania, Union, Watauga, Wilkes, Yadkin and Yancey in the State of North Carolina.

For legal titles of parishes and diocesan institutions, consult the Chancery.

STATISTICAL OVERVIEW

Personnel	
Bishop	1
Retired Bishops	1
Abbots	1
Retired Abbots	1
Priests: Diocesan Active in Diocese	61
Priests: Diocesan Active Outside Diocese	6
Priests: Retired, Sick or Absent	38
Number of Diocesan Priests	105
Religious Priests in Diocese	62
Total Priests in Diocese	167
Extern Priests in Diocese	7
Ordinations:	
Diocesan Priests	3
Transitional Deacons	3
Permanent Deacons in Diocese	75
Total Brothers	9
Total Sisters	106
Parishes	
Parishes	68
With Resident Pastor:	
Resident Diocesan Priests	46
Resident Religious Priests	22
Missions	23
Pastoral Centers	4
Professional Ministry Personnel:	
Brothers	3
Sisters	18
Lay Ministers	84
Welfare	
Health Care Centers	13
Total Assisted	289,700
Homes for the Aged	1
Total Assisted	205
Day Care Centers	13
Total Assisted	996
Specialized Homes	2
Total Assisted	43
Residential Care of Disabled	1
Total Assisted	170
Other Institutions	1
Total Assisted	104
Educational	
Diocesan Students in Other Seminaries	17
Total Seminarians	17
Colleges and Universities	2
Total Students	863
High Schools, Diocesan and Parish	2
Total Students	1,510
Elementary Schools, Diocesan and Parish	16
Total Students	5,723
Catechesis/Religious Education:	
High School Students	3,232
Elementary Students	15,048
Total Students under Catholic Instruction	26,393
Teachers in the Diocese:	
Priests	3
Brothers	1
Sisters	8
Lay Teachers	503
Vital Statistics	
Receptions into the Church:	
Infant Baptism Totals	5,677
Adult Baptism Totals	245
First Communions	3,836
Confirmations	2,352
Marriages:	
Catholic	457
Interfaith	361
Total Marriages	818
Deaths	935
Total Catholic Population	138,583
Total Population	1,696,148

Former Bishops—Most Revs. MICHAEL J. BEGLEY (Retired), ord. May 26, 1934; appt. Nov. 30, 1971; consecrated first Bishop of Charlotte Jan. 12, 1972; retired 1984; died Feb. 9, 2002; JOHN F. DONOGHUE, D.D., ord. June 4, 1955; appt. Nov. 6, 1984; consecrated Dec. 18, 1984; appt. Archbishop of Atlanta June 22, 1993; consecrated Aug. 19, 1993; WILLIAM G. CURLIN (Retired), ord. May 25, 1957; appt. Auxiliary Bishop of Washington Nov. 2, 1988; consecrated Dec. 20, 1988; appt. Bishop of Charlotte, Feb. 22, 1994; installed April 13, 1994; retired Sept. 10, 2002.

Chancery—P.O. Box 36776, Charlotte, 28236. Tel: 704-370-6299; Fax: 704-370-3379.

Vicar General, Chancellor, and Moderator in Curia—Rev. Msgr. MAURICIO W. WEST, P.O. Box 36776, Charlotte, 28236. Tel: 704-370-6299; 704-370-3326.

Vice Chancellors—Rev. Msgr. ANTHONY J. MARCACCIO, St. Pius Tenth Church, 2210 N. Elm St., Greensboro, 27408; Deacon CURTISS P. TODD, 1123 S. Church St., Charlotte, 28203. Tel: 704-370-3339.

Chief Financial Officer—WILLIAM G. WELDON, 1123 S. Church St., Charlotte, 28203. Tel: 704-370-3313.

Controller—STELLA NELL, 1123 S. Church St., Charlotte, 28203. Tel: 704-370-3312.

Diocesan Properties—Deacon GUY A. PICHE, Dir., 1123 S. Church St., Charlotte, 28203. Tel: 704-370-3304.

Employee Benefits—TERRI WILHELM, 1123 S. Church St., Charlotte, 28203. Tel: 704-370-3338.

Diocesan Tribunal—1123 S. Church St., Charlotte, 28203. Tel: 704-370-3343.

Judicial Vicar—Rev. JOHN T. PUTNAM, J.C.L.; MARY L. HILDRETH, 1123 S. Church St., Charlotte, 28203.

Education—Rev. JAMES HAWKER, Vicar, 1123 S. Church St., Charlotte, 28203 Tel: 704-370-3210; Fax: 704-370-3291.

Diocesan Consultors—Rev. Msgrs. MAURICIO W. WEST; ANTHONY J. MARCACCIO; RICHARD BELLOW; Very Revs. MICHAEL BUTTNER; PAUL GARY; Rev. IGNATIUS ZAMPINO, O.F.M.Cap.

Office for Religious—Sr. M. TIMOTHY WARREN, R.S.M., 1123 S. Church St., Charlotte, 28203. Tel: 704-370-3213.

Diocesan Offices and Directors

Airport Chaplain—Deacon BERNARD W. WENNING JR., 1123 S. Church St., Charlotte, 28203. Tel: 704-370-3344; Fax: 704-370-3378.

Archives—CYNTHIA BARNES, Dir., 1123 S. Church St., Charlotte, 28203. Tel: 704-370-3215; Fax: 704-370-3378.

Boy Scouts—Deacon JAMES R. JOHNSON, St. Charles Borromeo Church, 714 W. Union St., Morganton, 28655. Tel: 828-437-3461.

Campus Ministry—Ms. MARY WRIGHT, Dir., 1123 S. Church St., Charlotte, 28203. Tel: 704-370-3212; Fax: 704-370-3378.

Campus Ministry - UNC-Greensboro—Rev. JOHN FRAMBES, O.F.M., ACM Center, P.O. Box 26170, Greensboro, 27402-6170. Tel: 336-334-4264.

Cursillo—Rev. JOHN T. PUTNAM J.C.L., Spiritual Dir.; ALAN M. BROWN, Lay Dir., 128 N. Fulton St., Salisbury, 28144.

Evangelization—Mr. FRANK VILLARONGA, Dir., 1123 S. Church St., Charlotte, 28203. Tel: 704-370-3274.

Office of Faith Formation—Dr. CRIS VILLAPANDO, Program Dir., 1123 S. Church St., Charlotte, 28203. Tel: 704-370-3246; Fax: 704-370-3378.

Youth Ministry—PAUL KOTLOWSKI, 1123 S. Church St., Charlotte, 28203. Tel: 704-370-3211.

Development—JAMES K. KELLEY, Dir.; BARBARA GADDY, Assoc. Dir., 1123 S. Church St., Charlotte, 28203. Tel: 704-370-3301; 704-370-3302; Fax: 704-370-3378.

Foundation of the Roman Catholic Diocese of Charlotte, Inc., The—JAMES KELLEY, Exec. Dir., 1123 S. Church St., Charlotte, 28203. Tel: 704-370-3301.

Office of Hispanic Ministry—Sr. ANDREA INKROTT, O.S.F., Dir., 1123 S. Church St., Charlotte, 28203. Tel: 704-370-3269; Fax: 704-370-3291. Our Lady of Guadalupe Hispanic Center, 6212 Tuckaseegee Rd., Charlotte, 28214. Tel: 704-391-3732; Fax: 704-391-6594.

Human Resources—Deacon CURTISS P. TODD, Dir.; TERRI WILHELM, Assoc., 1123 S. Church St., Charlotte, 28203. Tel: 704-370-3338; 704-370-3339; Fax: 704-370-3378.

Korean Catholic Cultural Center—Rev. SOO-TAE BAK, Dir., 7109 Robinson Church Rd., Charlotte, 28215. Tel: 704-531-8417.

Lay Ministry—FRANK VILLARONGA, Dir., 1123 S. Church St., Charlotte, 28203. Tel: 704-370-3274; Fax: 704-370-3291.

African-American Ministry—Deacon CURTISS P. TODD, Coord., 1123 S. Church St., Charlotte, 28203. Tel: 704-370-3339.

Media Resource Center—Sr. PATRICIA DURBIN, R.S.M., 1123 S. Church St., Charlotte, 28203. Tel: 704-370-3242.

Cathedral Publishing Corporation—P.O. Box 37267, Charlotte, 28237. Tel: 704-370-6299. *1123 S.*

Church St., Charlotte, 28203. Tel: 704-370-3336.

Newspaper: "Catholic News & Herald"—KEVIN MURRAY, Editor, P.O. Box 37267, Charlotte, 28237. Tel: 704-370-3333; 704-370-3334; Fax: 704-370-3382.

Permanent Diaconate—Rev. Msgr. MAURICIO W. WEST; Deacon BERNARD W. WENNING JR., Assoc., P.O. Box 36776, Charlotte, 28236. Tel: 704-370-6299; Fax: 704-370-3379.

Planning—GEORGE COBB, Dir., 1123 S. Church St., Charlotte, 28203. Tel: 704-370-3328; Fax: 704-370-3378.

Propagation of the Faith—Rev. Msgr. ANTHONY KOVACIC, 1123 S. Church St., Charlotte, 28203. Tel: 704-370-6299; Fax: 704-370-3378.

School—LINDA CHERRY, Supt.; Dr. JANICE RITTER, Asst. Supt., 1123 S. Church St., Charlotte, 28203. Tel: 704-370-3271; Fax: 704-370-3291.

Mecklenburg Area Catholic Schools—1123 S. Church St., Charlotte, 28203. Tel: 704-370-3270; Fax: 704-370-3291.

Prison Ministry— Contact Permanent Diaconate Office: *1123 S. Church St., Charlotte, 28203.* Tel: 704-370-3344; Fax: 704-370-3378.

Social Services—ELIZABETH THURBEE, A.C.S.W., Diocesan Dir., 1123 S. Church St., Charlotte, 28203. Tel: 704-370-3228.

Campaign for Human Development—TERRY JARINA, Diocesan Dir., 1123 S. Church St., Charlotte, 28203. Tel: 704-370-3234; Fax: 704-370-3288.

Justice and Peace—JOSEPH PURELLO, Dir., 1123 S. Church St., Charlotte, 28203. Tel: 704-370-3225; Fax: 704-370-3288.

Victim Assistance Coordinator—NANCY M. CAMPBELL. Tel: 704-370-3217; DAVID W. HAROLD, A.C.S.W. Tel: 336-714-3202. Email: dwharold@charlottediocese.org; MICHELLE SHEPPARD. Tel: 828-255-0146. Email: mmsheppard@charlottediocese.org.

Vietnamese Apostolate—4929 Sandy Porter Rd., Charlotte, 28273. Tel: 704-504-0907. Rev. TAN VAN LE, Chap.

Vocations—Rev. JOHN ALLEN, Dir., Newman House, 2951 Brookridge Lane, Charlotte, 28211. Tel: 704-364-1130.

Worship—Dr. LARRY STRATEMEYER, St. Patrick Cathedral, 1621 Dilworth Rd., E., Charlotte, 28203. Tel: 704-334-2283; Fax: 704-377-6403.

CLERGY, PARISHES, MISSIONS AND PAROCHIAL SCHOOLS

CITY OF CHARLOTTE
(MECKLENBURG COUNTY)

1—ST. PATRICK CATHEDRAL (1939),, (Phelan Memorial) Very Rev. Paul Q. Gary; Rev. Lawrence LoMonaco; Deacons Nicholas Fadero; Carlos Medina.
Res.: 1621 Dilworth Rd., E., 28203. Tel: 704-334-2283; Fax: 704-377-6403.
Catechesis/Religious Program—Tel: 704-334-2283, Ext. 27; Fax: 704-377-6403. Students 280.

2—ST. ANN (1955), Rev. Conrad Hoover.
Church: 3635 Park Rd., 28209. Tel: 704-523-4641; Fax: 704-527-8671.
Res.: 632 Hillside Ave., 28209.
Catechesis/Religious Program—Tel: 704-527-0122; Fax: 704-527-8671. Students 110.
Convent—3430 Willow Oak Rd., 28209. Tel: 704-523-0331.

3—ST. GABRIEL (1957), Rev. Msgr. Richard Bellow; Revs. Tien Duong; Matthew Buettner; Deacons Bernard Wenning; Robert Gettelfinger; Louis A. Pais; Curtiss Todd.
Res.: 3016 Providence Rd., 28211. Tel: 704-364-5431; Fax: 704-362-5049.
Catechesis/Religious Program—Tel: 704-366-2738; Fax: 704-362-5049. Susan Krasniewski, D.R.E. Tel: 704-362-5047, Ext. 271. Students 733.

4—ST. JOHN NEUMANN (1977), Revs. Thomas J. Meehan, O.S.A.; Arthur D. Johnson, O.S.A. (NY); Deacon Joseph Mack. In Res., Rev. James Cassidy, O.S.A.
Res.: 8451 Idlewild Rd., 28227. Tel: 704-536-6520; Fax: 704-536-3147.
Catechesis/Religious Program—Tel: 704-535-4197. Students 710.

5—ST. LUKE (1987), Rev. James Hawker.
Res.: 13700 Lawyers Rd., 28227. Tel: 704-545-1224; Fax: 704-545-7288.
Catechesis/Religious Program—Tel: 704-545-0065. Students 421.

6—ST. MATTHEW (1986), Rev. Msgr. John J. McSweeney; Revs. Duc Duong; Carmen Malacari; Sr. Jeanne Marie Kienast, R.S.M., Pastoral Assoc.; Deacons James Hamrlik; Jeffrey Evers.
Office—8015 Ballantyne Commons Pkwy., 28277. Tel: 704-543-7677; Fax: 704-542-7244.
Res.: 5726 Ballantyne Commons Pkwy., 28277. Tel: 704-846-6311; Fax: 704-846-6311.
Catechesis/Religious Program—Tel: 704-541-8362; Fax: 704-542-7244. Patricia Tomlinson, D.R.E. Students 2,797.

7—OUR LADY OF CONSOLATION (1955), Rev. Jude Duffy, O.F.M.Cap.; Deacon Charles Knight. In Res., Rev. Martin Schratz, O.F.M.Cap.
Res.: 1224 Dearborn Ave., 28206-2491. Tel: 704-375-4339; Fax: 704-375-8039.
Catechesis/Religious Program—Students 120.
Mission—St. Helen 341 Dallas-Spencer Mountain Rd., Spencer Mountain, Gaston Co. 28059.

8—OUR LADY OF THE ASSUMPTION (1949), Rev. Gregory Littleton; Deacons Stephen J. Horai; Peter Duca.
Res.: 4207 Shamrock Dr., 28215. Tel: 704-535-9965; 704-535-9970; Fax: 704-535-3621.
Catechesis/Religious Program—Tel: 704-535-3310. Pamela Miller, D.R.E. Students 198.

9—ST. PETER (1851), Revs. Joseph A. Sobierajski, S.J.; James J. Kelly, S.J. In Res., Revs. Vincent P. Alagia, S.J.; Thomas P. McDonnell, S.J.
Res.: 507 S. Tryon St., 28202. Tel: 704-372-6808; Fax: 704-358-0050.
Catechesis/Religious Program—Tel: 704-332-2901; Fax: 704-358-0050. Students 125.

10—ST. THOMAS AQUINAS (1978), Revs. Ignatius Zampino, O.F.M.Cap.; Martin Schratz, O.F.M.Cap.; Stanley Kobel, O.F.M.Cap.; Deacons Carl Macero Sr.; Mark D. Nash.
Res.: 1400 Suther Rd., 28213. Tel: 704-549-1607; Fax: 704-549-1614.
Catechesis/Religious Program—Tel: 704-549-0199. Sr. Anastacia Pagulayan, O.P., D.R.E. Students 851.

11—ST. VINCENT DE PAUL (1965), Revs. Mark Lawlor, Admin.; Richard N. Hanson; Patrick Winslow (ALB); Deacon Gerald P. Hickey.
Res.: 6828 Old Reid Rd., 28210. Tel: 704-554-7088; Fax: 704-554-0490.
Catechesis/Religious Program—Tel: 704-554-1622; Fax: 704-554-0490. Joan Mahony, D.R.E. Students 293.

OUTSIDE THE CITY OF CHARLOTTE

ALBEMARLE, STANLY CO., OUR LADY OF THE ANNUNCIATION (1934), Rev. Lawrence W. Heiney.
Res.: 416 N. Second St., 28001. Tel: 704-982-2910; Fax: 704-982-0881.
Catechesis/Religious Program—Tel: 704-982-1048. Jane Snyder, D.R.E.; Cyndi Norton, D.R.E. Students 122.
Mission—Our Lady of the Americas 105 Hyde St., P.O. Box 1187, Biscoe, Montgomery Co. 27209. Tel: 910-428-3051; Fax: 910-428-1136. Rev. Ricardo Sanchez, Admin.

ANDREWS, CHEROKEE CO., HOLY REDEEMER (1962), Rev. Michael Kottar, Admin.
Res.: 214 Aquone Rd., 28901. Tel: 828-321-4463.
Mission—Prince of Peace 704 Talluah Rd., Rte. #129, Robbinsville, Graham Co. 28771.
Catechesis/Religious Program—Students 9.

ARDEN, BUNCOMBE CO., ST. BARNABAS (1964), Rev. Roger Arnsparger; Deacon Arthur J. Kingsley.
Mailing Address: P.O. Box 38, 28704. Tel: 828-684-6098; Fax: 828-684-6152.
Res.: 109 Crescent Hill Rd., 28704.
Catechesis/Religious Program—Miss Sheryl Peyton, D.R.E. Students 288.

ASHEBORO, RANDOLPH CO., ST. JOSEPH (1948), Rev. Joseph W. Mack.
Res.: 512 W. Wainman Ave., 27203. Tel: 336-629-0221; Fax: 336-629-6968.
Catechesis/Religious Program—Students 227.

ASHEVILLE, BUNCOMBE CO.

1—BASILICA OF ST. LAWRENCE (1869), Revs. Wilbur N. Thomas; Joseph Long Dinh.
Res.: 97 Haywood St., 28801. Tel: 828-252-6042; Fax: 828-254-0414.
Catechesis/Religious Program—Tel: 828-252-8816; Fax: 828-254-0414. Mrs. Elizabeth Girton, D.R.E. Students 120.

2—ST. EUGENE (1957), Rev. Francis T. Cancro; Deacon Michael Zboyovski Sr.
Office & Mailing Address: 72 Culvern St., 28804. Tel: 828-254-5193; Fax: 828-254-5797.
Catechesis/Religious Program—Students 487.

3—ST. JOAN OF ARC (1928), Rev. John M. Pagel.
Res.: 919 Haywood Rd., 28806. Tel: 828-252-3151; Fax: 828-252-4154.
Catechesis/Religious Program—Students 68.

BELMONT, GASTON CO., QUEEN OF THE APOSTLES (1965), Rev. Joseph Zuschmidt, O.S.F.S.; Sisters Mary John Madden, Pastoral Assoc.; Josephine Thomas, Pastoral Assoc.
Church: 503 N. Main St., 28012. Tel: 704-825-9600; Fax: 704-825-1413.
Res.: 2121 Ferncliff Ln., Cramerton, 28012. Tel: 704-825-9907.
Catechesis/Religious Program—Tel: 704-825-9600, Ext. 21. Students 125.

BOONE, WATAUGA CO., ST. ELIZABETH (1954), Rev. John Schneider; Deacon Alec Lyerly.
Mailing Address: P.O. Box 1052, 28607.
Office—259 Pilgrim's Way, 28607. Tel: 828-264-8338; Fax: 828-262-3721.
Res.: 333 Poplar Hill Dr., 28607. Tel: 828-264-4503.
Catechesis/Religious Program—Carol Brown, D.R.E. Students 180.
Mission—Epiphany 163 Galax Ln., Blowing Rock, 28607.

BREVARD, TRANSYLVANIA CO., SACRED HEART (1949), Rev. Carl Del Giudice.
Res.: 4 Brian Berg Ln., 28712. Tel: 828-883-9572; Fax: 828-883-9587.
Catechesis/Religious Program—Tel: 828-883-4572. Students 111.
Mission—St. Jude Cashiers. P.O. Box 3126, Sapphire Valley, Jackson Co. 28717. Tel: 828-743-5717. Rev. William Morris Evans.

BRYSON CITY, SWAIN CO., ST. JOSEPH (1941), Rev. Shawn O'Neal, Admin.
Res.: P.O. Box 727, 28713. Tel: 828-488-6766; Fax: 828-488-0586.
Catechesis/Religious Program—Tel: 828-479-8014; Fax: 828-488-0586. Students 9.
Mission—Our Lady of Guadalupe P.O. Box 202, Cherokee, Swain Co. 28719. Tel: 828-497-9755.

CLEMMONS, FORSYTH CO., HOLY FAMILY (1980), Very Rev. Michael J. Buttner; Rev. Adrian Porras; Deacons Gerard Schumacher; Michael Langsdorf.
Office Address—P.O. Box 130, 27012. Tel: 336-778-0600.
Res.: 2890 Knobb Hill Dr., 27012. Tel: 336-766-1882.
Church: 4820 Kinnamon Rd., Winston-Salem, 27103. Fax: 336-766-2918.
Catechesis/Religious Program—Tel: 336-766-0600, Ext. 214; 336-766-0600, Ext. 204. Mrs. Mary Langsdorf, D.R.E.; Mrs. Margaret Schumacher, D.R.E. Students 507.
Mission—Cristo Rey Catholic Hispanic Center of Yadkin Valley U.S. Hwy. 601 & Hoot Rd., P.O. Box 788, Yadkinville, Yadkin Co. 27055. Tel: 336-367-7067.

CONCORD, CABARRUS CO., ST. JAMES (1969), Revs. James H. Geiger, C.SS.R.; Edward J. Gray, C.SS.R.; Alvaro A. Riquelme, C.S.R.; Darrell L. Cevasco, C.SS.R.; Deacon J. Daniel Carl.
Mailing Address: P.O. Box 123, 28026. Tel: 704-720-0600; Fax: 704-720-0610.
Res.: 251 Union St. N., 28025. Tel: 704-720-0608.
Catechesis/Religious Program— Patti Andruzzi, D.R.E. (St. James); Claudine Caabral, D.R.E. (St. Joseph Mission). Students 643.
Mission—St. Joseph 108 St. Joseph St., P.O. Box 220, Kannapolis, Cabarrus Co. 28082. Tel: 704-932-4607; Fax: 704-932-0566.

DENVER, LINCOLN CO., HOLY SPIRIT (1988), Rev. Joseph Ayathupadam; Deacon Richard Kauth.
Church: 537 N. Hwy. 16, 28037-9235. Tel: 704-483-6448; Fax: 704-483-6898.
Res.: 6789 Hawks Nest Ln., Stanley, 28164. Tel: 704-820-0153.
Catechesis/Religious Program—Students 210.

EDEN, ROCKINGHAM CO., ST. JOSEPH OF THE HILLS (1938), Rev. Thomas Selvaraj (India).
Res.: 316 Boone Rd., 27288. Tel: 336-623-2661.
Catechesis/Religious Program—Tel: 336-623-1538. Students 61.

FOREST CITY, RUTHERFORD CO., IMMACULATE CONCEPTION (1950), Rev. Herbert Burke; Deacon Andrew Cilone.
Res.: 1024 W. Main St., 28043. Tel: 828-245-4017.
Catechesis/Religious Program—Students 75.

FRANKLIN, MACON CO., ST. FRANCIS OF ASSISI (1953), Rev. Matthew Kauth, Admin.
Res.: 299 Maple St., 28734. Tel: 828-524-2289; Fax: 828-369-0809.
Catechesis/Religious Program—Tel: 828-369-8131. Sharon Edwards, D.R.E.; Ron Brahmer, D.R.E. Students 90.
Mission—Our Lady of the Mountains P.O. Box 2729, Highlands, Macon Co. 28741. Tel: 828-526-2418. Rev. William Morris Evans.

GASTONIA, GASTON CO., ST. MICHAEL (1903), Rev. Joseph Mulligan.
Res.: 708 St. Michael's Ln., 28052. Tel: 704-853-8808.
Church: Tel: 704-867-6212; Fax: 704-867-6379.
School—Tel: 704-865-4382. Lay Teachers 18; Students 200.
Catechesis/Religious Program—Tel: 704-867-6212, Ext. 114. Students 110.

GREENSBORO, GUILFORD CO.

1—ST. BENEDICT (1901), Rev. Robert Ferris, Admin.; Deacon Philip Killian.
Res.: 109 W. Smith St., 27401. Tel: 336-272-0303.
Catechesis/Religious Program—Tel: 336-272-0301. Students 33.

2—ST. MARY (1928), Revs. Robert J. Prior, C.M. (GR); Michael M. Nguyen, C.M.; Robert J. Stone, C.M.

(BRK); Deacons Vincent Shaw; Pierre M. K'Briuh.
Mailing Address: P.O. Box 21012, 2742.
Res.: 812 Duke St., 27401. Tel: 336-272-8650.
Catechesis/Religious Program—Fax: 336-272-3594. Students 172.

3—OUR LADY OF GRACE (1952), Revs. Francis J. O'Rourke; Luis S. Osorio; Deacons Timothy Rohan; Paul Teich.
Mailing Address: 201 S. Chapman St., 27403-1611. (Ethel Clay Price Memorial)
Res.: 207 S. Chapman St., 27403. Tel: 336-274-6520 (Office); 336-275-5376 (Rectory); Fax: 336-274-7326.
Church: 2205 W. Market St., 28203.
School—Tel: 336-275-1522; Fax: 336-279-8824. Roberta Hutchcraft, Prin. Lay Teachers 27; Students 418.
Catechesis/Religious Program—Tel: 336-274-6520. James D. McCullough, D.R.E. Students 291.

4—ST. PAUL THE APOSTLE (1974), Revs. Thomas Murphy, O.S.F.S.; Anthony J. Larry, O.S.F.S. (WIL); Deacon Gordon L. Forester.
Res.: 2715 Horsepen Creek Rd., 27410. Tel: 336-294-6160; 336-294-4696 (Office); Fax: 336-294-6149.
Catechesis/Religious Program—Students 605.

5—ST. PIUS X (1960), Rev. Msgr. Anthony J. Marcaccio; Sr. Phyllis Tierney, S.S.J., M.S.W., Pastoral Assoc.; Mr. Tracy Earl Welliver, M.T.S., Pastoral Assoc.; Mrs. Patricia Spivey, Pastoral Assoc.
Office—2210 N. Elm St., 27408. Tel: 336-272-4681; 336-272-8598; Fax: 336-274-8112.
School—Tel: 336-273-9865; Fax: 336-273-0199. Mr. Mark Akerman, Prin. Lay Teachers 32; Students 485.
Catechesis/Religious Program—Tel: 336-273-9860. Students 260.
Catholic Campus Connection (Thea House)—1009 Bluford St., 27401. Tel: 336-272-5868.

HAMLET, RICHMOND CO., ST. JAMES (1910), Rt. Rev. Patrick Shelton, O.S.B., V.F.; Rev. David Draim, O.S.B.
Mailing Address: P.O. Box 1208, 28345. Tel: 910-582-0207; 910-582-8776 (Rectory).
Catechesis/Religious Program— Ann Peters, D.R.E. Students 112.
Mission—Sacred Heart 205 Rutherford St., Wadesboro, Anson Co. 28710. Tel: 704-674-5183.

HENDERSONVILLE, HENDERSON CO., IMMACULATE CONCEPTION (1912), Revs. John C. Aurilia, O.F.M.Cap.; John Salvas, O.F.M.Cap.
Parish Office—208 7th Ave., W., 28791-3602. Tel: 828-693-6901; Fax: 828-697-1656
Res.: 717 Buncombe St., 28791-3609. Tel: 828-692-0550.
School—Immaculata, 711 Buncombe St., 28791-3609. Tel: 828-693-3277; Fax: 828-696-3677. Mr. William Meehan, Prin. Lay Teachers 20; Students 185.
Catechesis/Religious Program—Tel: 828-697-7420. Sandy Donecho, D.R.E. Students 138.

HICKORY, CATAWBA CO., ST. ALOYSIUS (1913), Revs. Edward J. Sheridan; Jose Enrique Gonzalez-Gayton; Deacons Hugo L. May; Thomas A. Rasmussen.
Res.: 921 Second St., N.E., 28601. Tel: 828-327-2341; Fax: 828-327-3376.
Catechesis/Religious Program—Students 898.

HIGH POINT, GUILFORD CO.

1—CHRIST THE KING (1940), Rev. Philip Kollithanath.
Res.: 1505 Kivett Dr., 27260. Tel: 336-884-0244; Fax: 336-887-1200.
Catechesis/Religious Program—Students 105.

2—IMMACULATE HEART OF MARY (1947), Revs. John Kelly, O.S.F.S.; Anthony Gilborges, O.S.F.S.; Deacons Thomas Kak; Joseph T. Smith; Frederick Scarletto.
Mailing Address: 605 Barbee Ave., 27262. Tel: 336-884-5212.
Church: 4145 Johnson St., 27265. Tel: 336-869-7739; Fax: 336-869-1059.
Res.: 512 Montlieu Ave., 27262. Tel: 336-884-5436; Fax: 336-884-1849.
School—500 Montlieu Ave., 27262. Tel: 336-887-2613; Fax: 336-884-1849. Ned Forney, Prin. Lay Teachers 24; Students 252.
Catechesis/Religious Program—Tel: 336-885-5210. Sr. Johanna Orlet, O.S.F., D.R.E. Students 1,180.

HUNTERSVILLE, MECKLENBURG CO., ST. MARK (1997), Revs. Mark Lamprich, Admin.; Christopher Alan Roux.
Res.: 14740 Stumptown Rd., 28078. Tel: 704-948-0231; Fax: 704-948-8018.
Catechesis/Religious Program—Tel: 704-948-1306. Donna Smith, D.R.E. Students 1,238.

JEFFERSON, ASHE CO., ST. FRANCIS OF ASSISI (1962), Rev. C. Morris Boyd, Temp. Admin.
Mailing Address: P.O. Box 1, 28640. Tel: 336-246-9151; Fax: 336-246-5925.
Catechesis/Religious Program—Students 81.
Mission—St. Frances of Rome P.O. Box 367, Sparta, Alleghany Co. 28675. Tel: 336-372-8846.

KERNERSVILLE, FORSYTH CO., HOLY CROSS (1973), Rev. Joseph E. Tustin, O.S.F.S.
Res.: 616 S. Cherry St., 27284. Tel: 336-996-5109; Fax: 336-996-5669.
Child Developmental Center—Tel: 336-996-5144; Fax: 336-996-5115. Diana Morgan, Dir.
Catechesis/Religious Program—Tel: 336-996-5109; Fax: 336-996-5115. Marie Kinney, D.R.E. Students 346.

LENOIR, CALDWELL CO., ST. FRANCIS OF ASSISI (1936), Rev. Matthew Leonard; Deacon Ronald Caplette.
Res.: 328-B Woodsway Ln., N.W., 28645-4356. Tel: 828-754-5281; Fax: 828-754-5281.
Catechesis/Religious Program—Students 89.
Mission—Holy Trinity Hwy. 90 W., 655 W. Main Ave., Taylorsville, Alexander Co. 28681. Tel: 828-632-8009; Fax: 828-632-8009.

LEXINGTON, DAVIDSON CO., OUR LADY OF THE ROSARY (1944), Rev. Albert J. Gondek, O.S.F.S
Res.: 619 S. Main St., 27292. Tel: 336-248-2463; Fax: 336-238-3241.
Catechesis/Religious Program—Students 50.

LINCOLNTON, LINCOLN CO., ST. DOROTHY (1944), Rev. Thomas Stott.
Res.: 148 St. Dorothy Ln., 28092. Tel: 704-735-5575.
Catechesis/Religious Program—Students 188.

MAGGIE VALLEY, HAYWOOD CO., ST. MARGARET (1968), Rev. Francis J. Doyle, O.S.A.
Mailing Address: P.O. Box 1359, 28751. Tel: 828-926-0106; Fax: 828-926-0855. In Res., Rev. William C. Harkin, O.S.A.; Deacon Jerry LaPointe.
Res.: 37 Murphy Dr., 28751. Tel: 828-926-0025.
Catechesis/Religious Program—Students 14.

MARS HILL, MADISON CO., ST. ANDREW THE APOSTLE (1985), Rev. David Brzoska, Admin.
Mailing Address: P.O. Box 1406, 28754-1406. Tel: 828-689-3719; Fax: 828-689-3719.
Res. & Church: 149 Brook St., 28754.
Mission—Sacred Heart Burnsville Yancey CoP.O. Box 1406, 28754.
Mission—Chapel of the Redeemer P.O. Box 7, Hot Springs, Madison Co. 28743. Tel: 828-622-7366; Fax: 828-622-3586. Revs. Joseph J McGovern, S.J.; Francis X. Reese, S.J. Jesuit House of Prayer.
Catechesis/Religious Program—Fax: 828-689-3719. Students 45.

MOCKSVILLE, DAVIE CO., ST. FRANCIS OF ASSISI (1958), Rev. Andrew Draper, T.O.R.; Deacon John O. Zimmerle.
Mailing Address: P.O. Box 642, 27028. Tel: 336-751-2973; Fax: 336-751-9929.
Church: 862 Yadkinville Rd., 27028.
Catechesis/Religious Program—Students 93.

MONROE, UNION CO., OUR LADY OF LOURDES (1945), Rev. James W. Cassidy, O.S.A.; Deacons Edwin Rodriguez; Jesus Reyes.
Res.: 725 Deese St., 28112. Tel: 704-289-2773; Fax: 704-283-7210.
Catechesis/Religious Program—Tel: 704-289-2773; Fax: 704-283-7210. Students 355.

MOORESVILLE, IREDELL CO., ST. THERESE (1946), Revs. James F. McAndrews, S.J.; Joseph B. Kappas, S.J. (CLV); Gabriel L. Rajendra, S.J. (India). In Res., Revs. James Keogh, S.J.; William J. Lynch, S.J.; Deacon John Sims.
Res.: 217 Brawley School Rd., 28117. Tel: 704-664-3992; Fax: 704-660-6321.
Catechesis/Religious Program—Tel: 704-664-7762. Students 736.

MORGANTON, BURKE CO., ST. CHARLES BORROMEO (1947), Rev. Kenneth L. Whittington; Deacon James R. Johnson.
Res.: 728 W. Union St., 28655. Tel: 828-437-3108; Fax: 828-437-6262.
Catechesis/Religious Program— Terri Martino, D.R.E. Students 221.
Mission—Our Lady of the Angels 258 N. Garden St., Marion, McDowell Co. 28752. Tel: 828-652-8690. Rev. Gnana Pragasam Mariasoosai.

MOUNT AIRY, SURRY CO., HOLY ANGELS (1921), Rev. Eric Kowalski, Admin.
Res.: 1208 N. Main St., Mt. Airy, 27030. Tel: 336-786-8147.
Catechesis/Religious Program—Tel: 336-786-8315. Linda Gallasetti-Simmons D.R.E. Students 110.

MURPHY, CHEROKEE CO., ST. WILLIAM (1952), Rev. George M. Kloster; Deacon Carl Hubbel.
Res.: 763 Andrews Rd., P.O. Box 546, 28906. Tel: 828-837-2000; Fax: 828-835-9889.
Catechesis/Religious Program—Students 51.
Mission—Immaculate Heart of Mary U.S.Hwy. 64 W., Hayesville, Clay Co. 28906.

NEWTON, CATAWBA CO., ST. JOSEPH (1978), Rev. James M. Collins; Deacon Scott D. Gilfillan.
Church: 720 W. 13th St., 28658-3899. Tel: 828-464-9207; Fax: 828-464-9880
Holy Family Parish Center—Tel: 828-465-2878.
Catechesis/Religious Program—Tel: 828-465-2878. Students 162.

NORTH WILKESBORO, WILKES CO., ST. JOHN BAPTIST DE LASALLE (1952), Rev. John D. Hanic; Deacon Frank Aversa.
Res.: 275 C.C. Wright School Rd., 28659. Tel: 336-838-5562.
Catechesis/Religious Program—Tel: 336-670-2792. Students 105.
Mission—St. Stephen 101 Hawthorne, Elkin, Surry Co. 28621. Tel: 336-835-3007.

REIDSVILLE, ROCKINGHAM CO., HOLY INFANT (1961), Rev. Christopher Davis.
Res.: 1042 Freeway Dr., P.O. Box 1197, 27323. Tel: 336-342-1448.
Catechesis/Religious Program—Students 54.

SALISBURY, ROWAN CO., SACRED HEART (1882), Revs. John T. Putnam, J.C.L.; Julio Dominguez; Deacons Patrick Vallandingham; James Mazur.
Res.: 128 N. Fulton St., 28144. Tel: 704-633-0591; Fax: 704-647-0126.
School—Tel: 704-633-2841; Fax: 704-633-6033. Mrs. Kathleen Miller, Prin. Lay Teachers 18; Students 157.
Catechesis/Religious Program—Tel: 704-638-0172. Students 275.
Convent—Sisters of Mercy, 425 W. Council St., 28144. Tel: 704-636-4070.

SHELBY, CLEVELAND CO., ST. MARY'S (1935), Very Rev. Eric Houseknecht, V.F.
Res.: 818 McGowan Rd., 28150. Tel: 704-487-7697; Fax: 704-487-0187.
Catechesis/Religious Program—Meg Nichter, D.R.E. Students 99.
Mission—Christ the King 714 Stone St., Kings Mountain, Cleveland Co. 28086.

SPRUCE PINE, MITCHELL CO., ST. LUCIEN (1940), Rev. Christopher Gober, Admin.
Res.: 695 Summit Ave., P.O. Box 688, 28777. Tel: 828-765-2224; Fax: 828-765-0086.
Mission—St. Bernadette P.O. Box 1252, Linville, Avery Co. 28646. Tel: 828-898-6900.
Catechesis/Religious Program—Students 10.

STATESVILLE, IREDELL CO., ST. PHILIP THE APOSTLE (1898), Rev. Kurt Fohn, Admin.; Deacon Charles Brantley.
Mailing Address: P.O. Box 882, 28687-0882. In Res., Rev. James M. Byer.
Office—Tel: 704-872-2579; Fax: 704-872-2579.
Res.: 525 Camden Dr., 28677. Tel: 704-873-8641.
Catechesis/Religious Program—Tel: 704-872-2579; Fax: 704-872-2579. Students 228.

SWANNANOA, BUNCOMBE CO., ST. MARGARET MARY (1936), Rev. Frank J. Seabo, Admin.
Office—Tel: 828-686-8833; Fax: 828-686-8832.
Res.: 102 Andrews Pl., 28778. Tel: 828-686-5300.
Catechesis/Religious Program— Bea Madden, D.R.E. Students 40.

SYLVA, JACKSON CO., ST. MARY (1955), Rev. W. Ray Williams.
Res.: 22 Bartlett St., 28779. Tel: 828-586-9496.
Catechesis/Religious Program—Tel: 828-586-9496. Students 85.

THOMASVILLE, DAVIDSON CO., OUR LADY OF THE HIGHWAYS (1953), Rev. Thomas J. Fitzpatrick, O.S.F.S.; Deacons Wayne Adams; David E. King.
Res.: 943 Ball Park Rd., 27360. Tel: 336-475-2667; Fax: 336-476-3337.
Catechesis/Religious Program—Tel: 336-475-2732. Students 65.

TRYON, POLK CO., ST. JOHN THE BAPTIST (1911), Rev. Dean Cesa.
Mailing Address: 180 Laurel Ave., 28782. Tel: 828-859-9574; Fax: 828-859-5932.
Res.: 222 Winner's Cir., 28782. Tel: 828-859-5287.
Church: 120 Laurel Ave., 28782.
Catechesis/Religious Program—Tel: 828-859-9574, Ext. 7; Fax: 828-859-3732. Students 80.

WAYNESVILLE, HAYWOOD CO., ST. JOHN THE EVANGELIST (1926), Rev. Dennis M. McGowan, O.S.A.
Res.: 234 Church St., 28786. Tel: 828-456-6707; Fax: 828-456-4329.
Catechesis/Religious Program—Tel: 828-456-7450. Students 78.
Mission—Immaculate Conception 42 Newfound Rd., Canton, Haywood Co. 28716.

WINSTON-SALEM, FORSYTH CO.

1—ST. BENEDICT THE MOOR (1940), Rev. Lawrence J. Hunt, S.J.
Res.: 1625 E. Twelfth St., 27101. Tel: 336-725-9200; Fax: 336-722-4264.
Mission—Good Shepherd P.O. Box 1149, King, Stokes Co. 27021. Tel: 336-983-2680.
Catechesis/Religious Program—Tel: 336-725-1801; Fax: 336-725-1801. Students 138.

2—ST. LEO'S (1891), Revs. Thomas Kessler; Johnathan Hanic; Deacons Dennis O'Madigan; Robert DeSautels.
Res.: 334 Springdale Ave., 27104. Tel: 336-724-5314.
Church: 335 Springdale Ave., 27104. Tel: 336-724-0561; Fax: 336-724-7036.
School—333 Springdale Ave., 27104. Tel: 336-748-8252; Fax: 336-748-9005. Sisters of St. Joseph 1; Lay Teachers 18; Students 270.
Catechesis/Religious Program—Tel: 336-724-0561; Fax: 336-724-7036. Students 669.

Convent—1975 Georgia Ave., 27104. Tel: 336-723-3639.

3—OUR LADY OF MERCY (1954), Revs. William Robinson, O.F.M.Conv.; Conall McHugh, O.F.M-.Conv.; Deacon Joseph Schumacher; Sr. Kathy Ganiel, Pastoral Assoc. In Res., Rev. Jude T. DeAngelo, O.F.M.Conv.

Res.: 1910 S. Main St., 27127. Tel: 336-724-6806.

Church: 1918 S. Main St., 27127. Tel: 336-722-7001; Fax: 336-722-0465.

School—Tel: 336-722-7204; Fax: 336-725-2294. Sandra McMonagle, Prin.; Sr. Geri Rogers, S.S.J., Asst. Sisters of St. Joseph 2; Lay Teachers 18; Students 206.

Catechesis/Religious Program—Tel: 336-722-7001; Fax: 336-722-0465. Students 180.

Convent—1922 S. Main St., 27127. Tel: 336-727-0925.

Mission—Our Lady of Fatima 211 W. 3rd St., Forsyth Co. 27101. Tel: 336-723-8238; Fax: 336-723-8290.

Special Assignment:
Rev. Msgr.—
West, Mauricio W., Vicar Gen. & Chancellor
Revs.—
Allen, John A., Vocations Dir.
Hoover, John P.

On Duty Outside the Diocese:
Revs.—
Kaltreider, Carl E., Diocese of Charleston
Valentine, Joseph R., F.S.S.P., Fraternity of St. Peter
Wilderotter, Paul C., Archdiocese of Miami

Military Chaplains:
Revs.—
Fitzgibbons, Peter L., U.S. Army
Klepacki, Michael S., U.S. Navy

Unassigned:
Revs.—
Pham, Peter
Tarasi, Carlo D.

On Sabbatical:
Rev.—
Hokanson, Richard P.

Absent On Leave:
Revs.—
Baker, Donald P.
Choquet, Alexei H.
DeAguilar, Arturo
Farrell, William
Kuhn, Dennis R.
Tice, Cecil
Williamson, Thomas

Retired:
Most Rev.—
Curlin, William G., 1521 Dilworth Rd., 28203.
Rev. Msgrs.—
Allen, Richard F.
Kerin, Joseph A.
Kovacic, Anthony, 411 Dogwood Ln., Belmont, 28012.
Pharr, William N.
Showfety, Joseph
Walsh, Thomas R., 12 N. 6th St., Allegany, NY 14706.
Revs.—
Cahill, James, P.O. Box 1856, Sylva, 28779-1856.
Cintula, Francis M., 45 S.E. 13th St., A-1, Boca Raton, FL 33432.
Clements, Thomas P., P.O. Box 5086, Statesville, 28687.
Connolly, Francis T., 164 Ceekside Ln., # C-2, Boone, 28607.
D'Silva, Aloysius, 1406 Maryfield Ct., High Point, 27260.
Erb, Vincent I., St. Joseph Villa, 110 W. Wissahickon Ave., Room 345, Flourtown, PA 19031.
Gavigan, P. Patrick, Maryfield Nursing Home, 1315 Greensboro Rd., High Point, 27270.
Hourihan, Raymond B., 507 Fulton St., Elmira, NY 14904.
Kelleher, Joseph, 1525 Woods Rd., #101, 27106.
Kimbrough, Conrad, 620 S. Ellis St., Salisbury, 28144.
Latsko, Andrew, 1414 Maryfield Ct., High Point, 27260.
Manley, Bernard A., 420 Lakeshore Dr., Asheville, 28804.
McCarthy, Joseph L., Maryfield Nursing Home, 1315 Greensboro Rd., High Point, 27270.
McCue, Richard T., P.O. Box 153, Hampton, NH 03842.
Meehan, Gabriel, 805 Foxwood Ct. S.W., Lenoir, 28645.
Reese, Charles T., 800 Bay Dr., No. 25, Niceville, FL 32578.
Solari, James K., 30 Lorraine Ave., Asheville, 28804-2529.
Sullivan, D. Edward, 3400 Eastern Blvd., H-3, York, PA 17402-3113.
Tuller, John, P.O. Box 794, Saluda, 28773.
Waters, Joseph, 5646-A W. Market St., Greensboro, 27409.

Permanent Deacons:
Adams, Wayne, Our Lady of the Highways, Thomasville
Aversa, Frank, St. John, North Wilkesboro
Brantley, Charles, St. Philip the Apostle, Statesville
Burke, John, (Unassigned)
Caplette, Ronald, St. Francis of Assisi, Lenoir
Carl, Daniel, St. James, Concord
Chirico, Neil, Leave of Absence
Cilone, Andrew, Immaculate Conception, Forest City
Cooper, Philip, St. Pius X, Greensboro
DeSautels, Charles, St. Leo, Winston-Salem
Dotson, Robert E., (Living Outside of the Diocese)
Duca, Peter, Our Lady of the Assumption, Charlotte
Eckoff, Ralph R., St. Margaret Mary, Maggie Valley
Evers, Jeffrey, St. Matthew, Charlotte
Fadero, Nick, (Retired), St. Patrick Cathedral, Charlotte
Forester, Gordon L., St. Paul the Apostle, Greensboro
Gettlefinger, Robert, St. Gabriel, Charlotte
Gilfillan, Scott D., St. Joseph, Newton
Gillis, Eugene J., (Unassigned)
Hamrlik, James, St. Matthew, Charlotte
Harkin, William, St. Margaret, Maggie Valley
Haslett, Bruce H., (Living Outside of Diocese)
Heine, Charles, Our Lady of the Mountains, Highlands
Hickey, Gerald P., (Retired), St. Vincent de Paul, Charlotte
Horai, Stephen J., (Retired), Our Lady of the Assumption, Charlotte
Hubbell, Carl, St. William, Murphy
Johnson, James R., St. Charles, Morganton
K'Briuh, Pierre M., St. Mary, Greensboro
Kak, Thomas, Immaculate Heart of Mary, High Point
Kauth, Richard, Holy Spirit, Denver
Killian, Philip, Jr., St. Benedict, Greensboro
King, David E., Our Lady of the Highways, Thomasville
Kingsley, Arthur J., St. Barnabas, Arden
Knight, Charles, Our Lady of the Consolation, Charlotte
Kolodziej, Keith M., (Living Outside of Diocese)
La Pointe, Gerard P., St. Margaret, Maggie Valley
Langsdorf, Michael, Holy Family, Clemmons
Lyerly, R. Alexander, St. Elizabeth, Boone
Macero, Carl, Sr., St. Thomas Aquinas, Charlotte
Mack, Joseph H., Jr., (Retired), St. John Neumann, Charlotte
Manning, Franklin L., Sr., (Retired), Christ the King, High Point
Marini, Anthony, Immaculate Conception, Hendersonville
Markle, Harold, (Retired-Hispanic Ministry, Boonville)
May, Hugo L., (Retired), St. Aloysius, Hickory
Mazur, James, Sacred Heart, Salisbury
McMahon, George, St. Joseph, Newton
Medina, Carlos A., Sr., St. Patrick, Charlotte
Nash, Mark D., St. Thomas Aquinas, Charlotte
O'Madigan, Dennis T., St. Leo, Winston-Salem
Pais, Louis, St. Gabriel, Charlotte
Parrish, John N., St. John Neumann, Charlotte
Piche, Guy, Chap., St. Helen, Spencer Mountain
Potkay, Gerald, Holy Infant, Reidsville
Rasmussen, Thomas, St. Aloysius, Hickory
Reyes, Jesus, Our Lady of Lourdes, Monroe
Rinkus, Louis, (Retired), St. Eugene, Asheville
Rodriguez, Edwin, Our Lady of Lourdes, Monroe
Rohan, Timothy, Our Lady of Grace, Greensboro
Scarletto, Frederick C., Immaculate Heart of Mary, High Point
Schumacher, Gerard A., Holy Family, Clemmons
Schumacher, Joseph N., (Retired), Our Lady of Mercy, Winston-Salem
Shaw, Vincent H., Jr., St. Mary, Greensboro
Shaw, William S., (Unassigned)
Sims, John E., St. Therese, Mooresville
Smith, Joseph T., Immaculate Heart of Mary, High Point
Steinkamp, Ronald F., St. Pius Tenth, Greensboro
Szalony, George, St. Ann, Charlotte
Teich, Paul A., Our Lady of Grace, Greensboro
Todd, Curtiss, St. Gabriel, Charlotte
Torres, Rafael, Our Lady of Guadalupe Hispanic Center, Charlotte
Triana, Rudolph J., (Unassigned)
Vallandingham, Patrick, Sacred Heart, Salisbury
Weisenhorn, John P., St. Michael, Gastonia
Wenning, Bernard W., Jr., St. Gabriel, Charlotte
Zboyovski, Michael J., Sr., St. Eugene, Asheville
Zimmerle, John O., St. Francis of Assisi, Mocksville

INSTITUTIONS LOCATED IN THE DIOCESE

[A] COLLEGES AND UNIVERSITIES

BELMONT. **Belmont Abbey College*, 100 Belmont-Mount Holly Rd., 28012-1802. Tel: 704-825-6748; Fax: 704-825-6743. Email: donaldbeagle@bac.edu. Web: belmontabbeycollege.edu. Rt. Rev. Placid D. Solari, O.S.B., Pres.& Chancellor; Dean De La Motte, Ph.D., Academic Dean; Heather Metress, Registrar; Rev. Kieran Neilson, O.S.B., Chap. Campus Ministry; Karen Van Norman, Dean, Student Life; Mr. James Schuppenhauer, Vice Pres. Admin. & Finance; Mr. Michael Poll, Vice Pres. Enrollment Mgmt.; Donald Beagle, Dir. Library. (Coed) Liberal Arts Senior College. Priests 2; Brothers 1; Sisters 2; Lay Teachers 40; Students 863.

The Ecumenical Institute of Wake Forest University and Belmont Abbey College Tel: 704-825-6748; Fax: 704-825-6743.

Ecumenical Institute, Wake Forest University, P.O. Box 7363, Winston-Salem, 27109. Tel: 336-759-5800.

Sacred Heart College, 101 Mercy Dr., 28012-4805. Tel: 704-829-5100; Fax: 704-829-5137. Sr. M. Rosalind Picot, R.S.M., Pres. Sisters of Mercy, College ceased academic operation, effective August 1987. Corporation intact.

[B] HIGH SCHOOLS

KERNERSVILLE. *Bishop McGuinness Catholic High School*, 1725 N.C. Hwy. 66 S., 27284. Tel: 336-564-1010; Fax: 336-564-1060. Email: grepass@bmhs.us. Web: www.bmhs.us. George L. Repass, M.Ed., Prin. Sisters of St. Joseph 2; Lay Teachers 32; Students 467.

[C] ELEMENTARY SCHOOLS, INTERPAROCHIAL

ASHEVILLE. *Asheville Catholic School*, 12 Culvern St., 28804. Tel: 828-252-7896; Fax: 828-252-5708. Email: info@ashevillecatholic.org. Web: www.ashevillecatholic.org. Virginia C. Hutton, Ed.S., Prin. Lay Teachers 13; Students 231.

[D] REGIONAL SCHOOLS

CHARLOTTE. *Mecklenburg Area Catholic Schools (M.A.C.S.)*, 1123 S. Church St., 28203. Tel: 704-370-0405; Fax: 704-370-3292. Linda Cherry, Supt.

Charlotte Catholic High School (Bishop Hafey Memorial), 7702 Matthews-Mint Hill Rd., 28226. Tel: 704-543-1127; Fax: 704-543-1217. Gerald A. Healy, Prin.; Rev. John Allen, Chap. Clergy 1; Lay Teachers 79; Students 1,041.

Charlotte Catholic High School Athletic Association Tel: 704-543-1127; Fax: 704-543-1217.

Charlotte Catholic High School Alumni Association Tel: 704-543-9118; Fax: 704-543-1217.

Charlotte Catholic High School Home School Association Tel: 704-543-1127; Fax: 704-543-1217.

Holy Trinity Middle School, 3100 Park Rd., 28209. Tel: 704-527-7822; Fax: 704-525-7288. Carole Breerwood, Prin. Lay Teachers 60; Students 949.

St. Matthew School, Formerly All Saints Catholic School 11525 Elm Ln., 28277. Tel: 704-544-2070; Fax: 704-544-2184. Kevin O'Herron, Prin. Lay Teachers 36; Students 621.

Our Lady of the Assumption School, 4225 Shamrock Dr., 28215. Tel: 704-531-0067; Fax: 704-531-7633. Mrs. Patricia Murphy, Prin. Lay Teachers 16; Students 160.

St. Ann School, 600 Hillside Ave., 28209. Tel: 704-525-4938; Fax: 704-525-2640. Sr. Helene Nagle, S.S.J., Prin. Clergy 1; Lay Teachers 20; Students 253.

St. Gabriel School, 3028 Providence Rd., 28211. Tel: 704-366-2409; Fax: 704-362-5063. Sharon Broxterman, Prin. Lay Teachers 33; Students 529.

St. Mark School, 14750 Stumptown Rd., Huntersville, 28078. Tel: 704-766-5000; Fax: 704-875-6377. Dr. Walter Przygocki, Prin. Lay Teachers 30; Students 469.

St. Patrick School, 1125 Buchanan St., 28203. Tel: 704-333-3174; Fax: 704-333-3178. Angela Montague,

Prin. Lay Teachers 21; Students 280.

[E] GENERAL HOSPITALS

ASHEVILLE. *Sisters of Mercy Services Corporation*, 445 Biltmore Ave., Ste. 501, 28801. Tel: 828-281-1303; Fax: 828-254-4102. Email: colleen@somsc.org. G. John Coli, Ph.D., Pres. & CEO.

Sisters of Mercy Urgent Care, Inc., 445 Biltmore Ave., Ste. 501, 28801. Tel: 828-281-2598; Fax: 828-254-4102. Email: bill@somc.org. Patients Assisted Annually 286,000.

[F] SPECIAL CARE FACILITIES

BELMONT. **Holy Angels, Inc.*, 6600 Wilkinson Blvd., P.O. Box 710, 28012. Tel: 704-825-4161; Fax: 704-825-0553. Email: info@holyangelsnc.org. Web: www.holyangelsnc.org. Mrs. Regina P. Moody, M.Ed., Pres. & CEO. Residential and developmental programs and services for children and adults with mental retardation and physical disabilities. Sisters of Mercy 2; Capacity (All Programs) 174.

Holy Angels Specialized Community Residential Center (Children 0-20)

Little Angels Child Development Center On-site integrated day care.

Great Adventures Social Club Adults with mental retardation.

South Point Adult group home.

Lakewood Adult group home.

Fox Run ICF/MR Group Homes Bed Capacity 26.

Cherubs Cafe, Gifts & Candy Bouquets by Holy Angels Tel: 704-825-0418; Fax: 704-825-0416. (Age 18+); Job coaching, work options.

Supported Living (Age 18+)

Camp Hope Recreational Opportunities for Individuals with Developmental Disabilities.

Carrabaun Adult group home.

Gary Home Adult group home. Total Assisted Annually 170.

[G] CATHOLIC SOCIAL SERVICES

CHARLOTTE. *Catholic Social Services of the Diocese of Charlotte, Inc.*

The Catholic Center, 1123 S. Church St., 28203. Tel: 704-370-3228; Fax: 704-370-3277. Email: EKTHURBEE@Charlottediocese.org. Web: www.c-ssnc.org. Elizabeth K. Thurbee, A.C.S.W., A.C.S.W, Acting Dir.

Area Offices:

Asheville-Smoky Mountain Vicariates, 50 Orange St., Asheville, 28801. Tel: 828-255-0146; Fax: 828-253-7339. Elizabeth K. Thurbee, A.C.S.W., A.C.S.W, Acting Dir.

Albemarle-Charlotte-Gastonia Vicariates, 1123 S. Church St., 28203. Tel: 704-370-3232; Fax: 704-370-3377. Geri King, M.S.W., Dir.

Boone-Greensboro-Hickory-Winston-Salem Vicariates

P.O. Box 10962, Winston-Salem, 27108. Tel: 336-714-3201; Fax: 336-714-3232.

621 W. Second St., Winston-Salem, 27101. Tel: 336-714-3201; Fax: 336-714-3232. David W. Harold, A.C.S.W, Dir.

Catholic Social Services Refugee Office, 1123 S. Church St., 28203. Tel: 704-370-3260; 704-370-3296. Cira Ponce, Dir.

Special Ministries:

Adoption Contact the Domestic Adoption Unit at CSS offices. Tel: 828-255-0146, (Asheville); Tel: 336-714-3201, (Winston-Salem); Tel: 704-370-3232, Fax: 704-370-3377, (Charlotte).

Adoption International, Asheville. Tel: 828-255-0146; 888-990-4199; Fax: 828-253-7339. Carol Meyerriecks, M.S.W.

Elder Services Contact Diocesan Office. Tel: 704-370-3220; 704-370-3228; Fax: 704-370-3377. Sandra Breakfield, Contact Person.

Disaster Contact the Office of Justice and Peace, Diocesan Office. Tel: 704-370-3225; Fax: 704-370-3377. Joseph Purello, Contact Person.

Marriage Preparation Contact Diocesan Office. Tel: 704-370-3228; Fax: 704-370-3377. Amy Coburn Contact Person.

Family Life Contact the Office of Special Ministries, Diocesan Office. Tel: 704-370-3250; Fax: 704-370-3377. Gerard Carter, Dir.

Hand to Hand Contact Winston-Salem Office. , Winston-Salem. Tel: 336-725-4263; Fax: 336-714-3232. Connie McVey, Contact Person.

High Point Hispanic Center, 210 Gatewood Ave., High Point, 27260. Tel: 336-884-5858; 336-727-0705 or Contact the Winston-Salem Office; Fax: 336-714-3232. Irene Agudello, Contact Person.

Hispanic/Migrant Outreach Contact Asheville, Winston-Salem, or Charlotte Offices. Tel: 828-255-0146 (Asheville); 336-727-0705 (Winston-Salem); 704-370-3235 (Charlotte); Fax: 704-370-3377 (Charlotte).

Host Homes Contact Winston-Salem Office. , Winston-Salem. Tel: 336-725-4678; Fax: 336-727-9333. Mable Stevenson, Contact Person.

Natural Family Planning Contact the Diocesan Office. Tel: 704-370-3250; Fax: 704-370-3377. Cathy Tepper, Contact Person.

Office of Justice and Peace, 1123 S. Church St., 28203. Tel: 704-370-3225; Fax: 704-370-3377. Joseph Purello, Dir.

Catholic Campaign for Human Development Contact Office of Justice and Peace. Tel: 704-370-3234; Fax: 704-370-3377. Terri Jarina, Contact Person.

Catholic Relief Services Contact Office of Justice and Peace. Tel: 704-370-3225; Fax: 704-370-3377. Joseph Purello, Contact Person.

Operation Rice Bowl Contact Office of Justice and Peace. Tel: 704-370-3234; Fax: 704-370-3377. Terri Jarina, Contact Person.

Office of Economic Opportunity, 27 Hatchett St., Murphy, 28906. Tel: 828-835-3535. Joan Furst, Dir.

Support Pregnancy, Formerly Problem Pregnancy Contact the pregnancy support worker at any of the CSS offices. Tel: 704-370-3232 (Charlotte); 828-255-0146 (Asheville); 336-727-0705 (Winston); Fax: 704-370-3377 (Charlotte).

Respect Life Contact the Diocesan Office. Tel: 704-370-3229; Fax: 704-370-3377. Maggi Nadol, Contact Person.

HAMPTONVILLE. *Well of Mercy Inc.*, 131 Mercy Ln., 27020. Tel: 704-539-5449; Fax: 704-539-4487. Email: mercy@yadtel.net. Sisters Brigid McCarthy, R.S.M., Co-Dir.; Donna Marie Vaillancourt, R.S.M., Co-Dir. Retreats and psycho-spiritual development programs.

[H] HOME HEALTH CARE

ROSMAN. **Frances Warde Health Service*, HC73, Box 581, 28772. Tel: 828-884-7990; Fax: 828-966-9609. Email: jdewarrsm@juno.com. Sr. Gretchen Hermanny, R.S.M., M.D., Medical Dir. Sisters 3; Total Assisted 3,700.

[I] NURSING HOMES

HIGH POINT. *Maryfield Nursing Home*, 1315 Greensboro Rd., 27260. Tel: 336-886-2444; Fax: 336-886-4036. Email: srlucy@npe_infi.net. Web: www.greensboro.com/mnh. Sr. Lucy Hennessy, S.M.G., Admin. Poor Servants of the Mother of God 6; Bed Capacity 115.

Pennybyrn at Maryfield Tel: 336-886-2444; Fax: 336-886-4036. Retirement Homes 29.

[J] MONASTERIES AND RESIDENCES OF PRIESTS AND BROTHERS

BELMONT. *Belmont Abbey*, 100 Belmont-Mount Holly Rd., 28012-1802. Tel: 704-825-6675; Fax: 704-825-6680. Email: AbbotPlacid@bac.edu. Web: www.bac.edu/monastery. Rt. Revs. Placid D. Solari, O.S.B.; Oscar C. Burnett, O.S.B. (Retired); Rev. Arthur J. Pendleton, O.S.B., Prior; Very Rev. David G. Brown, O.S.B., Subprior; Revs. Raymond J. Geyer, O.S.B.; Matthew T. McSorley, O.S.B.; John A. Oetgen, O.S.B.; Kenneth A. Geyer, O.S.B.; David R. Kessinger, O.S.B.; Kieran A. Neilson, O.S.B.; Francis P. Forster, O.S.B.; Arthur J. Pendleton, O.S.B.; Lawrence R. Willis, O.S.B.; William F. George, O.S.B.; Paschal M. Baumstein, O.S.B.; Christopher A. Kirchgessner, O.S.B.; Bros. Paul Shanley, O.S.B.; Agostino Fernandez, O.S.B., Sub-Prior; Emmanuel Slobodzian, O.S.B.; Boniface Hamilton, O.S.B.; Michael Boes, O.S.B.

Legal Title: *Southern Benedictine Society of North Carolina, Inc.* Abbots 2; Monk Priests of Abbey 13; Priests in Residence 12; Brothers 5.

GREENSBORO. *Franciscan Friary*, 613 Kimberly Dr., 27408-5198. Tel: 336-379-7568; Fax: 336-379-7568. Email: j_frambe@aoluncg.edu. Revs. Louis Canino, O.F.M., Dir.; John Frambes, O.F.M.

The Franciscan Center, 233 N. Greene St., 27401. Tel: 336-273-2554; Fax: 336-273-2441.

MOORESVILLE. *Jesuit Community*, 217 Brawley School Rd., 28117-9103. Tel: 704-664-3992; Fax: 704-660-6321. Email: stccoo@altel.net. Revs. Vincent P. Alagia, S.J.; Lawrence J. Hunt, S.J.; Joseph B. Kappes, S.J. (DET); James J. Kelly, S.J.; James Keogh, S.J.; William J. Lynch, S.J.; James F. McAndrews, S.J., Supr.; Joseph J. McGovern, S.J.; Gabriel L. Rajendra, S.J. (India); Francis X. Reese, S.J.; Joseph A. Sobierajski, S.J.

Legal Title: *Jesuit Community in Western North Carolina*

[K] CONVENTS AND RESIDENCES FOR SISTERS

CHARLOTTE. *Coolock House*, 2328 Red Barn Ln., 28210. Tel: 704-554-1967; Fax: 704-554-1967. Email: therese_galligan@yahoo.com. Parish and bereavement care. Sisters of Mercy of the Americas 2.

Missionaries of Charity, 236 S. Torrence St., 28204. Tel: 704-344-8685 Ministry for poor. Sisters 4.

Sisters' of Mercy Residence, Carmel House, 3035 Carmel Rd., 28226. Tel: 704-552-2899; Fax: 704-552-2899. Sisters Paulette Williams, R.S.M.; Joann Ury, R.S.M., Admin. Administration; Caregiver Assisted Living and Shut-ins Sisters 2.

ASHEVILLE. *Sisters of Mercy Convent*, 428 Biltmore Ave., 28801. Tel: 828-232-0084; Fax: 828-232-0084. Email: smg@somsc.org. Web: www.urgentcares.org. Sisters 3; Health Care 2; Parish 1.

BELMONT. *Sisters of Mercy of North Carolina, Inc.*, Sacred Heart Convent, 100 Mercy Dr., 28012-4805. Tel: 704-829-5100; Fax: 704-829-5137. Email: ncreg@mercync.org. Web: www.mercync.org. Sisters Mary Rosalind Picot, R.S.M., Pres.; Mary Andrew Ray, R.S.M., Motherhouse Coord. Motherhouse of Sisters of Mercy of the Americas, Regional Community of North Carolina, Connected with the Motherhouse are Holy Angels, Inc., the McAuley Center, House of Mercy, Inc., and Catherine's House, Inc. Sisters in Motherhouse 31; Professed Sisters in Community 113.

HIGH POINT. *Congregation of the Sisters of Charity of St. Vincent De Paul*, St. Vincent Convent, 1507 E. Kivett Dr., 27260. Tel: 336-884-1441; Fax: 336-887-1200. Email: FrPhilipk@aol.com. Sisters Phillo, S.C.V., Pres.; Liza, S.C.V., Vice Pres.; Pushpa, S.C.V., Secretary; Archana, S.C.V., Treasurer; David Long, ESQ, Bd. Chair.

VALE. *Maryvale Motherhouse*, 2522 June Bug Rd., 28168. Tel: 704-276-2626; Fax: 704-276-2626. Sr. Mary Louis, Foundress and Supr. Congregation of Our Lady Help of the Clergy, (Maryvale Sisters). Parish ministry, day-care center, spiritual/retreat center, religious education and pastoral ministry. Sisters 5.

[L] CAMPUS MINISTRY CENTERS

CHARLOTTE. *Diocesan Office of Campus Ministry* Mary Wright, Dir.; Sr. Antonette Schmidt, R.S.M., Dir., Young Adult Min.; Terri McKendry, Prog. Coord. Young Adult Ministry.

Res.: 1123 S. Church St., 28203. Tel: 704-370-3212; Fax: 704-370-3291. Email: aschmidt@charlottediocese.org mmwright@charlottediocese.org. Web: www.charlottediocese.org.

University of North Carolina-Charlotte, ORA, 9201 University City Blvd., UNC-Charlotte, 28223-0001. Tel: 704-547-4069; Fax: 704-370-3291. Mary Wright, Catholic Campus Min.

University of North Carolina-Asheville, Catholic Campus Ministry, UNC-Asheville, 24 Hyannis Dr., Asheville, 28804. Tel: 828-250-3841. Email: wenphil@ioa.com. Mrs. Wendy Murray, Catholic Campus Ministry; Justin Schumacher, Campus Min. Intern.

Belmont Abbey College, 100 Belmont-Mount Holly Rd., Belmont, 28012. Tel: 704-829-7196; Fax: 704-825-6680. Email: ruthpayne@bac.edu fatherkieran@bac.edu. Ruth Payne, Dir. Campus Ministry; Rev. Kieran A. Neilson, O.S.B., Chap. Tel: 704-825-6836.

Appalachian State University, 232 Faculty St., Boone, 28607. Tel: 828-264-7087; Fax: 828-262-0970. Email: jpaul_60@hotmail.com. Paul Welsh, Catholic Campus Min.

Western Carolina University, Catholic Student Center, P.O. Box 364, Cullowhee, 28723-0364. Tel: 828-293-9374; Fax: 828-262-3721. Email: wcucatholic@wcu.edu. Gloria Schweizer, Catholic Campus Min.

Davidson College, P.O. Box 314, Davidson, 28036. Tel: 704-894-2917. Email: BB195@aol.com. Barbara Bagnall, Catholic Campus Min. (Davidson)

Gardner Webb University, c/o St. Mary Church, 818 McGowan Rd., Shelby, 28150. Tel: 704-406-4437. David Carscaddon, Campus Min.

NC Agricultural and Technical State University & Bennett College, 1009 Bluford St., Greensboro, 27401. Tel: 336-272-5868. Email: theahouse1@juno.com. Alberta Hairston.

University of North Carolina-Greensboro, Greensboro College & Guilford College, UNG-G ACM Center, P.O. Box 26170, Greensboro, 27402-6170. Tel: 336-334-4264; Fax: 336-334-4264. Email: j_frambe@uncg.edu. Rev. John Frambes, O.F.M.

High Point University, Immaculate Heart of Mary Parish, 605 Barbee Ave., High Point, 27262. Tel: 336-884-5352; Fax: 336-884-1849. Email: taiken@ihmchurch.org. Terry Aiken, Parish Contact.

Lenoir-Rhyne College, Hickory, 28754. Tel: 828-328-7186. Dr. Phil Blosser, Faculty Dir. Newman Club.

Catawba College and Livingston AME, 128 N. Fulton St., Salisbury, 28144. Tel: 704-633-0591; Fax: 704-647-0126. Chris Beal, Catholic Campus Min.

Wake Forest University and Winston-Salem University, P.O. Box 7204, Reynolda Station, Winston-Salem, 27109. Tel: 336-758-5018; Fax:

336-758-4462.

Salem College and N.C. School of the Arts, Reynolda Station, P.O. Box 7204, Winston-Salem, 27109. Tel: 336-758-5018; Fax: 336-758-4462. Email: Deangeit@wfu.edu ostergjm@wfu.edu. Rev. Jude T. DeAngelo, O.F.M.Conv., Catholic Campus Min.; Julianne Ostergaard, Catholic Campus Min.

Johnson C. Smith University/Barber Scotia College, 6517 Wickville Dr., 28215. Tel: 704-536-2340; Fax: 704-375-8039. Mrs. Nannette Lide, Parish Contact.

Brevard College, 4 Brian Berg Ln., Brevard, 28712. Tel: 828-883-9572; Fax: 828-883-9587. Email: gallivant@citcom.net. Christine Baglio, Parish Contact.

[M] RETREAT CENTERS

HOT SPRINGS. **Jesuit House of Prayer*, P.O. Box 7, 28743. Tel: 828-622-7366. Email: vpaul@madison.main.nc.us. Web: www.geocities.com/~jesuit_housenc. Sr. Margaret Verstege, R.S.M., Dir.; Revs. Joseph J. McGovern, S.J.; Francis X. Reese, S.J. Ignation directed, private individual retreats and small group retreats for men and women, as well as ecumenical.

[N] REFLECTION CENTERS

BELMONT. *The McAuley Center* Center for Adult Religious Education. , 100 Mercy Dr., 28012. Tel: 704-829-5113; Fax: 704-829-5137. Sr. Mary Hugh Mauldin, R.S.M., Dir.

MAGGIE VALLEY. *Living Waters Catholic Reflection Center*, 103 Living Waters Ln., 28751. Tel: 828-926-3833; Fax: 828-926-1997. Email: lwcrc@main.nc.us. Web: www.catholicretreat.org. Rev. Terrance W. Hyland, O.S.A., Dir. Retreats, days of recollection, and continuing education.

[O] HISPANIC MINISTRY

CHARLOTTE. *Diocesan Hispanic Ministry*, 1123 S. Church St., 28203. Tel: 704-370-3269; Fax: 704-370-3291. Email: aminkrott@charlottediocese.org. Sr. Andrea Inkrott, O.S.F., Dir. Hispanic Ministry.

Our Lady of Guadalupe Hispanic Center, 6212 Tuckaseegee Rd., 28214. Tel: 704-391-3732; Fax: 704-391-6594. Revs. Vincent Finnerty, C.M.; Joseph Elzi, C.M.; Jaime Gonzalez, C.M.; Deacon Rafael Torres.

[P] CONFERENCE CENTERS

HICKORY. *Catholic Conference Center*, 1551 Trinity Lane, 28602-9049. Tel: 828-327-7441; 888-536-7441 (Toll Free); Fax: 828-327-0872. Email: info@catholicconference.org. Web: www.catholicconference.org. Deacon Guy A. Piche, Dir. & Chap.

[Q] MISCELLANEOUS

CHARLOTTE. *Catholic Diocese of Charlotte Housing Corp.* Rev. Msgr. Mauricio W. West, Pres.; Mrs. Elizabeth Thurbee, Vice Pres.; William G. Weldon, Treas.; Gerard Carter, Staff1123 S. Church St., 28203. Tel: 704-370-3227; Fax: 704-370-3298. Email: ekthurbee@charlottediocese.org. Provides housing facilities and services for individuals and families with special needs.

**Room at the Inn, Inc.*, 3737 Weona Ave., 28209. Tel: 704-525-4673; Fax: 704-521-2751. Email: iroomattheinn@carolino.rr.org. Web: www.rate.org. Cindy Brown, Exec. Dir. Room at the Inn-Charlotte, 3737 Weona Ave., Charlotte, NC 28209. Tel: 704-525-4673. Long-term maternity and aftercare home for single, pregnant women, with their babies.

**Seton Media House, Inc.*, 7421 Carmel Executive Park, Ste. 214, 28226. Tel: 704-544-2077; Fax: 704-542-0867. Email: setonhouse@aol.com. Richard G. Hoefling, Pres. & CEO; Stephen M. Wilfong, Exec. Dir. Purpose: Distribution of printed materials reflective of Catholic teaching to Catholic schools, and religious education programs at no cost to students, family or school.

Sisters of Mercy of North Carolina Foundation, Inc., 2115 Rexford Rd., Ste. 401, 28211. Tel: 704-366-0087; Fax: 704-366-8850. Web: www.somncfdn.org. Sr. Mary Jerome Spradley, R.S.M., Pres.

ASHEVILLE. *McAuley Foundation, Inc.*, 445 Biltmore Ave., Ste. 501, 28801. Tel: 828-281-1268; Fax: 828-254-4102. Email: colleen@somsc.org.

Sisters of Mercy Thrift Store, Inc., 445 Biltmore Ave., Ste. 501, 28801. Tel: 828-281-1303; Fax: 828-281-0455. Email: colleen@somsc.org. Ms. Colleen Epp, Admin. Dir.

BELMONT. **Catherine's House*, 400 Mercy Dr., P.O. Box 1633, 28012. Tel: 704-825-9599; Fax: 704-825-2734. Email: patsyfullerl@yahoo.com. Web: www.geocities.com/catherineshouse/index.html. Sr. Bernadette McNamara, R.S.M., Pres. & CEO. Transitional housing for women and women with children who are homeless.

House of Mercy, Inc., 701 Mercy Dr., 28012. Tel: 704-825-4711; Fax: 704-825-9976. Email: hse4mercy@aol.com. Web: www.thehouseofmercy.org. P.O. Box 808, 28012. Stan Patterson, Pres. & CEO. Provides a home for persons living with AIDS in the advanced stages who have no other housing alternative in an 11 county region. Bed Capacity 6.

Mercy Community Housing North Carolina (MCHNC), 101 Mercy Dr., 28012-2898. Tel: 704-829-5264, Ext. 1230; Fax: 704-829-5267. Email: kbrownlee@mercyhousing.org. Web: www.mercyhousing.org. Kathleen Brownlee, Pres.; Patricia O'Roark, Vice Pres.

Mercy Housing, South East, Inc., 101 Mercy Dr., 28012-2898. Tel: 704-829-5260, Ext. 123; Fax: 704-829-5267. Email: kbrownlee@mercync.org. Web: www.mercyhousing.org. Purpose: provide housing and supportive services to low income, special needs populations and seniors.

Mercy Place Belmont Ms. Kathleen R. Brownlee, Pres.; Patricia M. O' Roark, Vice Pres.; Chuck Wehrwein, Treas.101 Mercy Dr., 28012-2898. Tel: 704-829-5260; Fax: 704-829-5267. Provides housing and support services for very low-income seniors.

Sisters of Mercy of North Carolina, Inc., 101 Mercy Dr., 28012-2898. Tel: 704-829-5260; Fax: 704-829-5267. Email: ncreg@mercync.org. Web: www.mercync.org. Sr. M. Rosalind Picot, R.S.M., Pres.

GREENSBORO. *Franciscan Center*, 233 N. Greene St., 27401. Tel: 336-273-2554; Fax: 336-273-2441. Email: fransprings@aol.com. Revs. Louis Canino, O.F.M., Dir.; John Frambes, O.F.M.

Society of St. Vincent De Paul, 201 S. Chapman St., 27403. Tel: 336-272-0336. Financial assistance, food and clothing.

HIGH POINT. *Poor Servants of the Mother of God Inc.*, 1315 Greensboro Rd., 27260. Tel: 336-886-2444; Fax: 336-886-4036. Email: sisterlucy@maryfieldliving.org. Sr. Lucy Hennessy, S.M.G., Pres. & Admin.

RELIGIOUS INSTITUTES OF MEN REPRESENTED IN THE DIOCESE

For further details refer to the corresponding bracketed number in the Religious Institutes of Men or Women section.

[0140]—*Augustinians* (Villanova, PA)—O.S.A.
[0200]—*Benedictine Monks* (Belmont, NC)—O.S.B.
[0470]—*The Capuchin Friars Province of the Stigmata*—O.F.M.Cap.
[1330]—*Congregation of the Mission* (Eastern Prov.)—C.M.
[0480]—*Conventual Franciscans* (Union City, NJ)—O.F.M.Conv
[0520]—*Franciscan Friars* (New York, NY)—O.F.M.
[0690]—*Jesuit Fathers and Brothers* (Maryland Prov.)—S.J.
[0920]—*Oblates of St. Francis De Sales* (Wilmington-Philadelphia)—O.S.F.S.
[1070]—*Redemptorist Fathers* (Baltimore Prov.)—C.SS.R.
[0560]—*Third Order Regular of St. Francis* (Pittsburg, PA)—T.O.R.

RELIGIOUS INSTITUTES OF WOMEN REPRESENTED IN THE DIOCESE

[2980]—*Congregation de Notre Dame*—C.N.D.
[3080]—*Congregation of Our Lady, Help of the Clergy*—C.L.H.C.
[]—*Congregation of the Sisters of St. Vincent DePaul* (India)—S.C.V.
[1110]—*Dominican Sisters of St. Catherine of Sienna*—O.P.
[]—*Glenmary Lay Missioners*—G.L.M.
[2470]—*Maryknoll Sisters*—M.M.
[2710]—*Missionaries of Charity*—M.C.
[3640]—*Poor Servants of the Mother of God*—S.M.G.
[]—*School Sisters of St. Francis* (Milwaukee, WI)—O.S.F.
[0590]—*Sisters of Charity of Saint Elizabeth, Convent Station*—S.C.
[0660]—*Sisters of Christian Charity*—S.C.C.
[2575]—*Sisters of Mercy of the Americas* (Belmont, NC; Dallas, PA; Detroit, MI; Watchung, NJ; Cincinatti, OH)—R.S.M.
[]—*Sisters of St. Francis* (Tiffin, OH)—O.S.F.
[]—*Sisters of St. Francis* (Rochester, MN)—O.S.F.
[1570]—*Sisters of St. Francis of the Holy Family*—O.S.F.
[3893]—*Sisters of St. Joseph* (Chestnut Hill, PA)—S.S.J.
[3830-14]—*Sisters of St. Joseph* (Rochester, NY)—S.S.J.
[4060]—*Society of the Holy Child Jesus* (Drexel Hill)—S.H.C.J.

NECROLOGY

† Berg, Ramon A., (Retired)—Died May 15, 2003
† Bradley, John P., (Retired)—Died Nov. 8, 2003
† Orlando, Samuel, (Retired)—Died April 2, 2003

Diocese of Cheyenne

(Dioecesis Cheyennensis)

Most Reverend

DAVID LAURIN RICKEN, D.D., J.C.L.

Bishop of Cheyenne; ordained September 12, 1980; appointed Coadjutor Bishop of Cheyenne December 14, 1999; Episcopal Ordination January 6, 2000; succeeded to See September 26, 2001. *Res.: P.O. Box 1468, Cheyenne, WY 82003.*

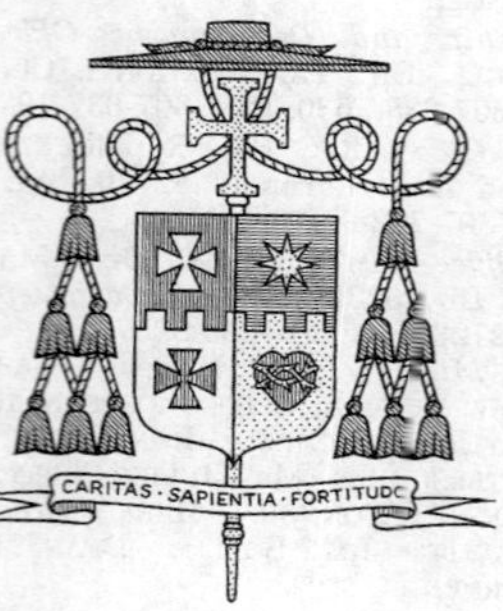

Most Reverend

JOSEPH HART, D.D.

Retired Bishop of Cheyenne; ordained May 1, 1956; appointed July 1, 1976; appointed Titular Bishop of Timida Regia; Episcopal Ordination August 31, 1976; installed June 12, 1978; retired September 26, 2001. *Res.: P.O. Box 1468, Cheyenne, WY 82003.*

ESTABLISHED AUGUST 2, 1887.

Square Miles 97,548.

Comprises the State of Wyoming and Yellowstone National Park.

For legal titles of parishes and diocesan institutions, consult the Chancery Office.

Chancery Office: 2121 Capitol Ave., P.O. Box 1468, Cheyenne, WY 82003-1468. Tel: 307-638-1530; Fax: 307-637-7936.

Web: www.dioceseofcheyenne.org

Email: bishopr@dioceseofcheyenne.org

STATISTICAL OVERVIEW

Personnel	
Bishop	1
Retired Bishops	1
Priests: Diocesan Active in Diocese	32
Priests: Retired, Sick or Absent	14
Number of Diocesan Priests	46
Religious Priests in Diocese	13
Total Priests in Diocese	59
Extern Priests in Diocese	5
Ordinations:	
Diocesan Priests	2
Permanent Deacons in Diocese	15
Total Brothers	2
Total Sisters	22
Parishes	
Parishes	35
With Resident Pastor:	
Resident Diocesan Priests	27
Resident Religious Priests	6
Without Resident Pastor:	
Administered by Priests	2
Missions	42
Professional Ministry Personnel:	
Brothers	2
Sisters	21
Welfare	
Homes for the Aged	2
Total Assisted	119
Residential Care of Children	1
Total Assisted	106
Day Care Centers	2
Total Assisted	100
Specialized Homes	13
Special Centers for Social Services	9
Total Assisted	15,940
Educational	
Diocesan Students in Other Seminaries	14
Students Religious	5
Total Seminarians	19
High Schools, Private	1
Total Students	18
Elementary Schools, Diocesan and Parish	7
Total Students	1,005
Catechesis/Religious Education:	
High School Students	1,415
Elementary Students	8,082
Total Students under Catholic Instruction	10,539
Teachers in the Diocese:	
Sisters	2
Lay Teachers	101
Vital Statistics	
Receptions into the Church:	
Infant Baptism Totals	870
Adult Baptism Totals	173
Received into Full Communion	132
First Communions	905
Confirmations	1,117
Marriages:	
Catholic	154
Interfaith	140
Total Marriages	294
Deaths	582
Total Catholic Population	50,979
Total Population	498,703

Former Bishops—Rt. Revs. MAURICE F. BURKE, D.D., consecrated Oct. 28, 1887; transferred to the See of St. Joseph, MO, June 19, 1893; died March 17, 1923; THOMAS M. LENIHAN, D.D., consecrated Feb. 24, 1897; died Dec. 15, 1901; Most Revs. JAMES J. KEANE, D.D., consecrated Bishop of Cheyenne Oct. 28, 1902; raised to the archiepiscopal dignity and transferred to Archdiocese of Dubuque, Aug. 11, 1911;; died Aug. 2, 1929; PATRICK A. MCGOVERN, D.D., LL.D., ord. Aug. 18, 1895; assistant at the Pontifical Throne;; appt. Jan. 19, 1912; consecrated April 11, 1912; died Nov. 8, 1951; HUBERT M. NEWELL, D.D., LL.D. (Retired), ord. June 15, 1930; appt. Coadjutor Aug. 2, 1947; consecrated Sept. 24, 1947; succeeded to the See Nov. 8, 1951; retired Jan. 3, 1978; died Sept. 8 1987; HUBERT JOSEPH HART, D.D. (Retired), ord. May 1, 1956; appt. Titular Bishop of Timida Regia July 1, 1976; consecrated Aug. 31, 1976; installed June 12, 1978; retired Sept. 26, 2001.

Chancery Office—2121 Capitol Ave., P.O. Box 1468, Cheyenne, 82003-1468. Tel: 307-638-1530; Fax: 307-637-7936.

Catholic Ministries Office—623 S. Wolcott, Casper, 82601. Tel: 307-237-2723; Fax: 307-235-9157.

Vicar General—Very Rev. MICHAEL CARR, Mailing Address, 604 S. Center, Casper, 82601. Tel: 307-266-2666; Fax: 307-266-4127.

Chancellor—CAROL DELOIS, P.O. Box 1468, Cheyenne, 82003-1468. Tel: 307-638-1530; Fax: 307-637-7936.

College of Consultors—Very Rev. MICHAEL CARR, V.G.; Revs. VERNON CLARK; ROBERT COOK; THOMAS E. CRONKLETON JR.; ANDREW DUNCAN; CARL GALLINGER.

Presbyteral Council—Most Rev. DAVID LAURIN RICKEN, D.D., J.C.L.; Very Rev. MICHAEL CARR, V.G., Ex Officio; Revs. DREW DUNCAN, Chm.; JOHN SAVIO, Vice Chm.; ROBERT COOK, Sec.; VERNON CLARK; THOMAS E. CRONKLETON JR.; CARL GALLINGER; JAN SANTICH.

Episcopal Vicar for Priests—Rev. VERNON CLARK, 1333 Monument, Cody, 82414. Tel: 307-587-3388.

Vicars Forane—Very Revs. MICHAEL CARR, Casper Deanery; KEVIN KOCH, Cheyenne Deanery; JOHN MURRAY, Rock Springs Deanery; THOMAS OGG, Sheridan Deanery; SAMUEL HAYES, Thermopolis Deanery.

Finance Officer—Mr. JAMES S. VANCE, P.O. Box 1468, Cheyenne, 82003-1468. Tel: 307-638-1530; Fax: 307-637-7936.

Finance Council—Most Rev. DAVID LAURIN RICKEN, D.D., J.C.L. Ex Officios, Voting: Very Rev. MICHAEL CARR, V.G.; Rev. GARY RUZICKA; The Honorable MIKE SULLIVAN; Mr. HOWARD BAKER. Ex Officios, Non-Voting: Rev. THOMAS E. CRONKLETON JR.; Very Rev. THOMAS OGG; Mr. JAMES S. VANCE; Mr. THOMAS L. PRINGLE; Mrs. VICKI LOUGEE. Appointed Members, Voting: JANE SCHNAUBER; JAMES T. DINNEEN; WILLIAM DOWNES; FRANK ROTELLINI, Chm.; Rev. JOHN SAVIO; CHUCK HARKINS; DEBBIE ROBBINS; JOSEPH STANBURY; PAUL VAN MAREN; STEVE BIANDO.

Tribunal Office— All marriage correspondence is to be directed to: *The Tribunal Office, P.O. Box 1468, Cheyenne, 82003-1468.* Tel: 307-638-1530; 800-788-4606; Fax: 307-637-7936.

Judicial Vicar—Rev. THOMAS E. CRONKLETON JR.

Coordinator of the Tribunal—DARLENE FLYNN.

Auditors—DARLENE FLYNN; CONNIE KASSAHN.

Administrative Assistant/Ecclesiastical Notary—CONNIE KASSAHN.

Bookkeeper/Clerk/Ecclesiastical Notary—LESLIE CONNAGHAN.

Promoter of Justice—Rev. CHARLES F. TAYLOR.

Judges—Very Rev. MICHAEL CARR, V.G.; Revs. GERALD F. CHLEBORAD, J.C.L.; THOMAS E. CRONKLETON JR.; DARLENE FLYNN.

Defenders of the Bond—Very Rev. SAMUEL HAYES; Rev. Msgr. GERALD A. SULLIVAN; Revs. CHARLES F. TAYLOR; CARL GALLINGER; THOMAS KADERA.

Advocates—SUSAN SIMON; BONNIE BAUMBERGER; Rev. AUGUST KOEUNE; DIANE BARR, J.D., J.C.D.; Deacon EDWARD MCCARTHY; Mrs. PAT MCCARTHY; DORENE MCINTYRE.

Diocesan Administrative Offices and Boards

Catholic Charities of Wyoming, Inc.—ELIZABETH E.

GROOM, M.S.W., Dir., P.O. Box 1468, Cheyenne, 82003-1468. Tel: 307-638-1530; Fax: 307-637-7936. Board of Directors: Most Rev. DAVID LAURIN RICKEN, D.D., J.C.L.; Very Rev. MICHAEL CARR, V.G.; BOBBIE CLONINGER, Chm.; ELIZABETH E. GROOM, M.S.W., Agency Dir. Board of Trustees: BOBBIE CLONINGER, Pres.; PAT NOVAK, Sec.; BILL SNIFFIN, Vice Pres.; ELIZABETH E. GROOM, M.S.W., Dir.; NANCY SNIFFIN; GEORGE BURNS; LES CLONINGER; MIKE CHADEY, Treas.; LYNN CHADEY; FRANCES MAKESHINE; MARY GUENZEL; Rev. ROBERT FOX; CINDY KEINERT.

Education Office—Deacon ED MCCARTHY, Dir.; MARY SUTTON, Media Librarian, 623 S. Wolcott, Casper, 82601. Tel: 307-237-2723; Fax: 307-235-9157.

Education Office Board—Most Rev. DAVID LAURIN RICKEN, D.D., J.C.L.; Deacon ED MCCARTHY, Supt. Educ.; Revs. ANDREW DUNCAN; ROBERT G. LYNCH, S.J.; MARY SUTTON, Media Librarian; ANDREA CHOJNACKY, (Glenrock); MARY ANN CUMMINS, (Buffalo); DONNA DUNCAN, (Torrington); JANE JOHNSON, (Gillette); Mrs. PAT MCCARTHY, Dir., Family & Respect Life Ministries; JIM ZIERDEN, Youth Dir.

Catholic Family and Respect Life Ministries—Mrs. PAT MCCARTHY, Dir., 623 S. Wolcott, Casper, 82601. Tel: 307-237-2723; Fax: 307-235-9157.

Catholic Family and Respect Life Ministries Board—Most Rev. DAVID LAURIN RICKEN, D.D., J.C.L.; Revs. VERNON CLARK; RAY ROGRIGUEZ; TERRY CASSIDY; BOB ADAMS; JANE ADAMS; RUTHIE HALVORSEN; LINDA HURLESS; CHARLIE LUX; TOM CRULL; MARILYN CRULL; CARLOS SAUCEDO; RALPH SPECHT; CAROL SPECHT; DICK WILLIAMS; JOANN WILLIAMS.

Catholic Family and Respect Life Divisions—Mrs. PAT MCCARTHY, Dir.

Beginning Experience for Divorced or Widowed—LINDA HURLESS; LAVERNE LESTER, P.O. Box 9953, Casper, 82609. Tel: 307-265-3509; 307-237-7333.

Bereavement Ministry—TERRY CASSIDY. Tel: 307-635-4965.

Divorced/Separated/Widowed Ministry—LINDA HURLESS. Tel: 307-265-3509.

Engaged Encounter—JAN MARTIN; STEVE MARTIN, 1340 Nottingham Dr., Casper, 82609. Tel: 307-577-3009.

Marriage Encounter—MIKE WINGERT; ANN WINGERT, 2005 Apache St., Cheyenne, 82009. Tel: 307-637-0441.

Marriage Preparation—Mrs. PAT MCCARTHY.

Marriage and Family Enrichment—Mrs. PAT MCCARTHY.

Natural Family Planning—Mrs. PAT MCCARTHY.

Rainbows for All God's Children—JULIE PETERSEN, 1334 Juniper Dr., Rock Springs, 82901. Tel: 307-362-7595.

Respect Life Catholic Pro-Life Ministry—Mrs. PAT MCCARTHY.

Retrouvaille, Ministry for Hurting Marriages—Mrs. PAT MCCARTHY.

Newspaper "Wyoming Catholic Register"—PAULA GLOVER, Editor, P.O. Box 1468, Cheyenne, 82003-1468. Street Address, 2121 Capitol Ave., Cheyenne, 82001. Tel: 307-638-1530; Fax: 307-637-7936.

Newspaper, Wyoming Catholic Register Board—Most Rev. DAVID LAURIN RICKEN, D.D., J.C.L.; PAULA GLOVER, Editor; Very Rev. MICHAEL CARR, V.G.; Rev. KEVIN KOCH; WYOMA GROENENBERG; ELIZABETH MCCLAIN; THOMAS L. PRINGLE; LAURA PRINGLE.

Stewardship and Development Office—THOMAS L. PRINGLE, Dir., P.O. Box 1468, Cheyenne, 82003. Tel: 307-638-1530; Fax: 307-637-7936.

Vocation Office—Rev. RAY RODRIGUEZ, Dir., 1800 E. Grand Ave., Laramie, 82070. Tel: 307-742-6001; Fax: 307-742-0521.

Youth Office—JIM ZIERDEN, Dir.; MARY O'CONNOR, Asst. Dir., 623 S. Wolcott, Casper, 82601. Tel: 307-237-2723; Fax: 307-235-9257.

Youth Ministry Board—Revs. CARL GALLINGER; DREW DUNCAN; CLIFF JACOBSON; RAY RODRIGUEZ; Mr. RAY PACHECO; RON MCGINLEY; DOMINIC LITTLESHIELD; Ms. JULIE PERRY; JENN WOOD; MARY O'CONNOR; MARK HORAN; LORRAINE LEAVITT; JIM SCALIA; DEAN MENARDI; JIM ZIERDEN.

Other Diocesan Boards, Councils and Programs

Diocesan of Cheyenne, Board of Directors—Most Rev. DAVID LAURIN RICKEN, D.D., J.C.L.; Very Rev. MICHAEL CARR, V.G.; Rev. GARY RUZICKA; Mr. HOWARD BAKER; The Honorable MIKE SULLIVAN.

Wyoming Catholic Ministries Foundation Board of Directors—Most Rev. DAVID LAURIN RICKEN, D.D., J.C.L.; Very Rev. MICHAEL CARR, V.G.; ATTILIO BEDONT; Ret. Major Gen. CHARLES WING.

Bishop's Annual Campaign, "Bishop's Appeal"—Mr. THOMAS L. PRINGLE; Mr. JAMES S. VANCE, P.O. Box 1468, Cheyenne, 82003-1468. Tel: 307-638-1530; Fax: 307-637-7936.

Boy and Girl Scouts—THOMAS RYDER, 29 Meandering Way, Lander, 82520. Tel: 307-332-9816.

Building Committee—Most Rev. DAVID LAURIN RICKEN, D.D., J.C.L.; Very Rev. MICHAEL CARR, V.G.; ROGER BAALMAN, A.I.A., Chm.; Revs. GERALD F. CHLEBORAD, J.C.L.; JOHN SAVIO; CAROL DELOIS; JOHN STEIL; VIRGIL SLOUGH; Mr. JAMES S. VANCE, Sec.

Catholic Relief Services—ELIZABETH E. GROOM, M.S.W., P.O. Box 1468, Cheyenne, 82003-1468. Tel: 307-638-1530.

Catholic Telecommunications—VACANT.

Confraternity of Christian Doctrine—Deacon ED MCCARTHY, Dir., 623 S. Wolcott, Casper, 82601. Tel: 307-237-2723.

Council of Religious—Sisters HOPE RODENBORN, O.S.B.; GLADYS NOREEN, O.S.B.

Cursillo Board—Rev. ANDREW DUNCAN; Deacon DAVID ZELENKA; VICTOR VILLALVA, Pres.; CURTIS WEST; BOBBY JO WEST; CHARLIE RANDO; VIRGINIA SPINDLER.

Diaconate Program, Permanent—Rev. RAY RODRIGUEZ, 1800 E. Grand Ave., Laramie, 82070. Tel: 307-742-6001; Fax: 307-742-0521.

Diaconate Board—Most Rev. DAVID LAURIN RICKEN, D.D., J.C.L.; Very Rev. MICHAEL CARR, V.G.; Revs. RAY RODRIGUEZ, Bishop's Delegate and Dir. Deacons; CLIFF JACOBSON; KARL MILLIS; Deacon ROLLAND RABOIN; Mrs. BECKY STEWART.

Ecumenism Commission—Revs. PETER JOHNSON, Chm.; GERALD F. CHLEBORAD, J.C.L.; Mrs. PAT MCCARTHY.

Holy Child Pontifical Association—Deacon ED MCCARTHY, Dir., 623 S. Wolcott, Casper, 82601. Tel: 307-237-2723.

Housing—LEAANN PESTOTNIK, Admin., St. Anthony Manor, 211 E. 6th, Casper, 82601. Tel: 307-237-0843; Sr. RUTH ANN HEHN, S.C.L., Admin., Holy Trinity Manor, 2516 E. 18th St., Cheyenne, 82001. Tel: 307-778-8850.

Information Office—PAULA GLOVER, P.O. Box 1468, Cheyenne, 82003-1468. Tel: 307-638-1530; Fax: 307-637-7936.

Liturgical Commission—Most Rev. DAVID LAURIN RICKEN, D.D., J.C.L.; Revs. GARY RUZICKA, Exec. Sec.; GERALD F. CHLEBORAD, J.C.L.; THOMAS CRONKLETON JR.; BETTY MCCARTHY; BRENDA WILKING.

Propagation of the Faith—PAULA EPPERSON, Dir., 623 S. Wolcott, Casper, 82601. Tel: 307-237-2723.

Rural Life Ministry—Rev. PETER JOHNSON, Dir., P.O. Box 818, Powell, 82435.

St. Joseph's Society for Priests (Clergy Mutual Benefit Society)—Most Rev. DAVID LAURIN RICKEN, D.D., J.C.L.; Very Rev. THOMAS OGG, Pres.; Revs. CARL BEAVERS; THOMAS E. CRONKLETON JR., Sec.; Very Rev. KEVIN KOCH, Vice Pres.; Rev. Msgr. GERALD A. SULLIVAN; Mr. LEO RILEY, Admin.

Retirees' Representative—VACANT.

Victim Assistance Coordinator—Deacon ROLLAND RABOIN. Tel: 307-532-8296. Email: rraboin@ewc.wy.edu.

CLERGY, PARISHES, MISSIONS AND PAROCHIAL SCHOOLS

CITY OF CHEYENNE
(LARAMIE COUNTY)

1—ST. MARY'S CATHEDRAL (1868), [CEM] Revs. Gary J. Ruzicka; Peter James Mwaura Kamau; Peter Auer, S.O.L.T.; Deacon Lee Pico.
Mailing Address: P.O. Box 1268, 82003-1268. Tel: 307-635-9261; Fax: 307-635-5723.
School—Tel: 307-638-9268; Fax: 307-635-2847. Kristina Giger, Prin. Lay Teachers 28; Students 306.
Catechesis/Religious Program—Tel: 307-637-4009; 307-635-9261. Roserita DuFresne, D.R.E. (Grades PreK-5); Rob Zlomke, D.R.E. (Grades 9-12); Vicki Yeoman, D.R.E. (Grades 6-8). Students 520.
Convent—2102 Warren Ave., 82001. Tel: 307-638-6005.

2—HOLY TRINITY (1957), Rev. Thomas E. Cronkleton Jr.; Deacon David Zelenka. In Res., Rev. Msgr. William Delaney (Retired); Rev. James Doudican (Retired).
Res.: 1836 Hot Springs Ave., 82003-5337. Tel: 307-632-5872; 307-637-7150; Fax: 307-632-1810.
Catechesis/Religious Program—Tel: 307-632-4482. Martha Thein, D.R.E.; Terri Mercer, D.R.E. Students 275.

3—ST. JOSEPH'S (1929), (Hispanic), Rev. Raymond B. Moss.
Mailing Address: P.O. Box 1141, 82003-1141. Tel: 307-634-4625; Fax: 307-635-4700.
Office—314 E. Sixth St., 82007.
Res.: 515 House, 82007. Tel: 307-638-3133.
Church: 300 E. 6th St., 82007.
Catechesis/Religious Program—Tel: 307-778-7107. Eva Estorga, D.R.E. Students 145.

OUTSIDE CITY OF CHEYENNE

BUFFALO, JOHNSON CO., ST. JOHN THE BAPTIST (1885), (Basque), [JC] Rev. Charles F. Taylor.
Res.: 532 N. Lobban, 82834. Tel: 307-684-7268; Fax: 307-684-5490.
Catechesis/Religious Program—Tel: 307-684-7217. Mary Ann Cummins, D.R.E. Students 130.
Mission—St. Mary Clearmont, Johnson Co. 82834.
Mission—St. Hubert Kaycee, Johnson Co. 82834.

CASPER, NATRONA CO.

1—ST. ANTHONY OF PADUA (1903), Very Rev. Michael Carr; Deacon Don Stewart.
Office—604 S. Center, 82601. Tel: 307-266-2666; Fax: 307-266-4127.
School—St. Anthony Tri-Parish School, 218 E. Seventh, 82601. Tel: 307-234-2873; Fax: 307-235-4946. Jane Smith, Prin. Lay Teachers 14; Students (K-9) 158; Preschool 11.
Catechesis/Religious Program—Students 180.
Mission—St. Francis Mission 17 Navy Row, Midwest, Natrona Co. 82643. Tel: 307-266-2666.

2—OUR LADY OF FATIMA (1954), Rev. Robert W. Cook; Deacon Ed McCarthy.
Res.: 1401 CY Ave., 82604. Tel: 307-265-5586; Fax: 307-266-2958.
Catechesis/Religious Program—Tel: 307-473-2076; Fax: 307-266-2958. Teresa Sears, D.R.E. Students 128.

3—SAINT PATRICK'S (1963), (Irish), Rev. August Koeune; Rev. Msgr. James O'Neill (Retired); Deacon Russ Humphreys.
Res.: 425 S. Illinois, Box 50397, 82605-0397. Tel: 307-235-5535; 307-266-2495; Fax: 307-237-7244.
Catechesis/Religious Program—Sam Carrick, D.R.E. Students 205.

CODY, PARK CO., ST. ANTHONY (1942), Rev. Vernon F. Clark.
Res.: 1333 Monument Dr., 82414-3406. Tel: 307-587-3388; Fax: 307-587-3383.
Catechesis/Religious Program—Tel: 307-587-2567; Fax: 307-587-3383. Rick Moser, D.R.E. Students 130.
Mission— 1333 Monument, Yellowstone National Park, Park Co. 82414. Tel: 307-587-3388. Sunday Services at Old Faithful, Lake Lodge, Canyon Junction, and Grant Village in summer only.
Mission—St. Therese 1406 State, Meeteetse, Park Co. 82433.

DOUGLAS, CONVERSE CO., ST. JAMES (1907), Rev. Clifford Jacobson.
Res.: P.O. Box 1500, 82633-1500. Tel: 307-358-2338; Fax: 307-358-5540.
Catechesis/Religious Program—Fax: 307-358-8498. Mayme Hofland, D.R.E. Students 116.
Mission—Our Lady of Lourdes 423 A St., Glendo, Platte Co. 82213. Tel: 307-358-2338.

EVANSTON, UINTA CO., ST. MARY MAGDALEN (1878), [JC] Rev. Robert Fox.
Mailing Address: Box 163, 82931-0163. Tel: 307-789-2189; Fax: 307-789-2788.
Catechesis/Religious Program—Students 106.
Mission—St. Helen P.O. Box 183, Fort Bridger, Uinta Co. 82933. Tel: 307-782-6190.
Catechesis/Religious Program—Tel: 307-787-6590. Students 28.

GILLETTE, CAMPBELL CO., ST. MATTHEW'S (1926), [JC] Revs. Thomas Kadera; Karl Millis.
Res.: 900 Butler Spaeth Rd., 82716. Tel: 307-682-3319; Fax: 307-682-6386.
Catechesis/Religious Program—Tel: 307-682-5321. Students 675.
Mission—Blessed Sacrament 624 Wright Blvd., Wright, Campbell Co. 82732. Tel: 307-464-0809.
Mission—St. Patrick 216 N. Belle Fourche, Moorcroft, Crook Co. 82721. Tel: 307-756-9478.

GLENROCK, CONVERSE CO., ST. LOUIS (1920), [JC] Rev. Ralph H. Talkin, S.J.
Mailing Address: P.O. Box 27, 82637-0027. Tel: 307-436-9529.
Catechesis/Religious Program—Tel: 307-436-5769. Andrea Chojnacky, D.R.E. Students 63.

GREEN RIVER, SWEETWATER CO., IMMACULATE CONCEPTION (1884), [JC] Rev. Tom Sheridan.
Mailing Address: P.O. Box 70, 82935-0070. Tel: 307-875-2441; Fax: 307-875-2184 (Office hours only).
Catechesis/Religious Program—Tel: 307-875-2184. Michele Harris, D.R.E. Students 266.

GREYBULL, BIG HORN CO., SACRED HEART (1919), Rev. Michael Ehiemere.

Mailing Address: P.O. Box 231, 82426-0231. Tel: 307-765-2438; Fax: 307-765-2438.
Catechesis/Religious Program—Jeanette Nicholson, D.R.E. Students 40.
Mission—St. Philip Ave. D, Basin, Big Horn Co. 82410. Tel: 307-568-2616.

GUERNSEY, PLATTE CO., ST. ANTHONY'S (1969), Rev. Robert H. Cousineau, S.J.
Res.: P.O. Box 430, 82214-0430. Tel: 307-836-2586.
Catechesis/Religious Program—Lori Ibarra, D.R.E. Students 23.

JACKSON, TETON CO., OUR LADY OF THE MOUNTAINS (1955), (Hispanic), [JC] Revs. Carl A. Beavers; Jaime Bueno (Colombia); Deacons Robert Miller; Doug Vlchek.
Mailing Address: P.O. Box 992, 83001-0992. Tel: 307-733-2516; Fax: 307-739-1478.
Catechesis/Religious Program—Tel: 307-733-7326. J.D. Chism, D.R.E. Students 165.
Mission—Holy Family P.O. Box 231, Afton, Lincoln Co. 83110.
Chapel—Moran, Sacred Heart

KEMMERER, LINCOLN CO., ST. PATRICK'S (1901), (Italian—Slovak), [JC] Very Rev. John E. Murray.
Mailing Address: Box 311, 83101-0311. Tel: 307-877-4573; Fax: 307-877-3354.
Catechesis/Religious Program—Students 100.
Mission—St. Dominic P.O. Box 296, Cokeville, Lincoln Co. 83114. Tel: 307-279-3426.
Mission—La Barge Catholic Community Center P.O. Box 42, La Barge, Lincoln Co. 83123. Tel: 307-386-9257.

LANDER, FREMONT CO., HOLY ROSARY (1882), [JC] Rev. David H. Gau, S.J. In Res., Rev. Robert K.C. Siu (HON).
Res.: 163 Leedy Rd., P.O. Box 1047, 82520-1047. Tel: 307-332-4952; Fax: 307-332-6141.
Catechesis/Religious Program—Tel: 307-332-4803. Sr. Delores Herbeck, D.R.E. Students 101.
Mission—Ascension P.O. Box 72, Hudson, Fremont Co. 82515.
Mission—St. Brendan Jeffrey City, Freemont Co.

LARAMIE, ALBANY CO.
1—ST. LAURENCE O'TOOLE (1872), [JC] Rev. James Schumacher.
Mailing Address: 617 S. Fourth St., 82070-1045. Tel: 307-745-3115; Fax: 307-745-3131.
School—(Grades K-6) Tel: 307-742-6363; Fax: 307-745-3131. Mr. Thomas Wilhelm, Prin. Lay Teachers 7; Students 82.
Catechesis/Religious Program—Students 144.
2—ST. PAUL'S NEWMAN CENTER (1957), Rev. Carl J. Gallinger; Lincoln A. Wood, Pastoral Assoc.
Mailing Address: Parish, 1800 E. Grand Ave., 82070-4316. Tel: 307-745-5461; Fax: 307-742-0521.
Catechesis/Religious Program—Students 88.

LOVELL, BIG HORN CO., ST. JOSEPH'S (1979), Rev. Peter Johnson.
Res. and Church: 1141 Shoshone Ave., P.O. Box 185, 82431-0185. Tel: 307-548-2282; Fax: 307-548-2395.
Catechesis/Religious Program—Students 45.

LUSK, NIOBRARA CO., ST. LEO'S (1911), (German—Irish), [JC] Rev. Evan P. Shea.
Res.: 900 W. Fifth St., Box 959, 82225-0959. Tel: 307-334-2702; Fax: 307-334-3161.
Catechesis/Religious Program—Tel: 307-334-2504; Fax: 307-334-2428. Cindy Wurdeman, D.R.E.; Bob Brown, D.R.E. Students 32.

NEWCASTLE, WESTON CO., CORPUS CHRISTI (1890), [JC] Rev. Bruce R. Clapham; Deacons Kenneth Pitlick, Pastoral Assoc.; Peter Kim Carroll, Pastoral Assoc.
Res.: 19 W. Winthrop, 82701. Tel: 307-746-4219; Fax: 307-746-9909.
Catechesis/Religious Program—Students 45.
Mission—St. Paul P.O. Box 28, Sundance, Crook Co. 82729. Tel: 307-283-2383; Fax: 307-283-2383.
Catechesis/Religious Program—Students 14.
Mission—St. Anthony P.O. Box 177, Upton, Weston Co. 82730.
Catechesis/Religious Program—Students 29.
Mission—St. Matthew's 26 Hunter, Hulett, Crook Co. 82720.
Catechesis/Religious Program—Students 37.

PINE BLUFFS, LARAMIE CO., ST. PAUL'S (1913), Rev. Hugo L. Blotsky, O.S.B.
Res.: P.O. Box 97, 82082-0097. Tel: 307-245-3761.
Catechesis/Religious Program—Tel: 307-245-3104. Nancy Malcolm, D.R.E. Students 58.
Mission—St. Joseph Albin, Laramie Co.
Mission—St. Peter 316 4th St., Carpenter, Laramie Co.

PINEDALE, SUBLETTE CO., OUR LADY OF PEACE (1940), Rev. Robert G. Lynch, S.J.
Mailing Address: P.O. Box 70, 82941-0070. Tel: 307-367-2359; Fax: 307-367-3553.
Catechesis/Religious Program—Tel: 307-367-2802. Elizabeth Roulean, D.R.E. Students 47.
Mission—St. Anne Big Piney, Sublette Co. 83113. Tel: 307-276-3227.
Mission—St. Christopher Eden, Sweetwater Co. 82926.

POWELL, PARK CO., ST. BARBARA (1910), Rev. Peter Johnson.
Res.: 115 E. Third, P.O. Box 818, 82435-0818. Tel: 307-754-2480; Fax: 307-754-5018.
Catechesis/Religious Program—Tel: 307-754-3361. Tom Spiering, D.R.E.; Janet Spiering, D.R.E. Students 120.
Mission—Our Lady of the Valley P.O. Box 818, Clark, Park Co. 82435. Tel: 307-754-2480.

RAWLINS, CARBON CO., ST. JOSEPH'S (1867), [JC] Rev. Malcolm Reid; Deacon Jesus P. Juarez.
Mailing Address: P.O. Box 68, 82301-0068. Tel: 307-324-4631; Fax: 307-324-3288.
Catechesis/Religious Program—Tel: 307-324-4033. Catherine Faber, D.R.E. Students 132.
Mission—Our Lady of the Sage P.O. Box 26, Baggs, Carbon Co. 82321. Tel: 307-383-2695.

RIVERTON, FREMONT CO., ST. MARGARET'S (1908), Revs. Andrew D. Duncan; Clifford J. Stevens, O.M. Res.: 622 E. Park, 82501. Tel: 307-856-3757; Fax: 307-856-8533.
School—(Grades PreK-5) Tel: 307-856-5922; Fax: 307-857-5892. Janet R. Melia, Prin. Lay Teachers 12; Students 104.
Catechesis/Religious Program—Tel: 307-856-3724; Fax: 307-857-5892. Janet R. Melia, D.R.E. Students 146.
Mission—St. Joseph 211 Wyoming St., Shoshoni, Fremont Co. 82649. Tel: 307-876-2760.
Mission—Our Lady of the Woods 4 S. Riverton St., P.O. Box 1134, Dubois, Fremont Co. 82513. Tel: 307-455-2533.
Mission—St. Edward Kinnear Rectory, 11350 US Hwy. 26, P.O. Box 34, Kinnear, Fremont Co. 82516. Tel: 307-856-5502.

ROCK SPRINGS, SWEETWATER CO.
1—SS. CYRIL AND METHODIUS (1910), Consolidated, with Our Lady of Sorrows Church, Rock Springs to form Holy Spirit Catholic Community.
2—HOLY SPIRIT CATHOLIC COMMUNITY (1887), Revs. John Savio; Dennis Cloonan; Deacons Randal Hruska; Charles Lux.
Mailing Address: 116 Broadway, 82901. Tel: 307-362-2611; Fax: 307-382-4911.
Res.: 333 Bridger Ave., 82901. Tel: 307-362-3493.
School—Holy Spirit Catholic School, Tel: 307-362-6077; Fax: 307-362-2177. Sr. Lucia Daluz, Prin. Religious 2; Lay Teachers 10; Students 115.
Catechesis/Religious Program—(Grades K-12) Fax: 307-382-4911. Elaine Menardi, D.R.E. Students 330.
Mission—St. Vivian Superior, Sweetwater Co.
Mission—St. Anthony Wamsutter, Sweetwater Co.
3—OUR LADY OF SORROWS, Consolidated, with SS. Cyril and Methodius to form Holy Spirit Catholic Community.

ST. STEPHENS, FREMONT CO., ST. STEPHEN'S (1884), (Native American), [CEM], Indian Mission for the Shoshone and Arapahoe Indians. St. Stephen's Indian Mission, Inc. Revs. J. Robert Hilbert, S.J.; Daniel J. Gannon, S.J.; Sisters Florence Petsch, Pastoral Assoc.; Teresa Frawley, Pastoral Assoc.
Mailing Address: Box 250, 82524-0250. Tel: 307-856-5937; Fax: 307-857-1802. In Res., Rev. David H. Gau, S.J.
Catechesis/Religious Program—Tel: 307-856-7806. Jean Watt, D.R.E. Students 32.
Mission—St. Joseph Box 8358, Ethete, Fremont Co. 82520. Tel: 307-332-4415.
Mission—Blessed Sacrament Box 307, Fort Washakie, Fremont Co. 82514-0307.

SARATOGA, CARBON CO., ST. ANN'S (1957), Rev. Gerald Chleborad.
Mailing Address: P.O. Box 667, 82331-0667. Tel: 307-326-5461; Fax: 307-326-5461
Catechesis/Religious Program—Tel: 307-326-8190. Marilyn Verplancke, D.R.E. Students 45.
Mission—St. Joseph P.O. Box 782, Hanna, Carbon Co. 82327. Tel: 307-325-9712.
Mission—St. Malachy P.O. Box 223, Medicine Bow, Carbon Co. 82329. Tel: 307-379-2597.

SHERIDAN, SHERIDAN CO., HOLY NAME (1885), (European), [JC] Very Rev. Thomas Ogg; Rev. Ronald Stolcis.
Mailing Address: 9 S. Connor, 82801. Tel: 307-672-2848; Fax: 307-672-5105.
School—121 S. Connor, 82801. Tel: 307-672-2021; Fax: 307-672-2021. Toni Wendt, Prin. Sisters of Charity (Leavenworth) 1; Lay Teachers 22; Students 120.
Catechesis/Religious Program—Tel: 307-672-2848, Ext. 17. Cel Hope, D.R.E. Students 201.
Mission—Our Lady of the Pines Story, Sheridan Co. Tel: 307-672-2848.
Mission—St. Edmund P.O. Box 197, Ranchester, Sheridan Co. 82839. Tel: 307-655-2357.

THERMOPOLIS, HOT SPRINGS CO., ST. FRANCIS (1906), Rev. Lawrence Fedor.
Mailing Address: P.O. Box 272, 82443-0272. Tel: 307-864-2674.
Catechesis/Religious Program—Tel: 307-864-9408. Andrew Stropko, D.R.E. Students 25.

TORRINGTON, GOSHEN CO., ST. ROSE (1906), Very Rev. Kevin A. Koch; Deacon Rolland Raboin.
Res.: 605 E. 22nd Ave., 82240. Tel: 307-532-5556; Fax: 307-534-2329.
Catechesis/Religious Program—Tel: 307-532-3125. Lynette Saucedo, D.R.E. Students 225.

WHEATLAND, PLATTE CO., ST. PATRICK'S (1891), Rev. Jan Joseph Santich.
Res.: 1009 Ninth St., 82201. Tel: 307-322-2070.
Catechesis/Religious Program—Tel: 307-322-4213. Students 106.
Mission—Mary Queen of Heaven 401 5th St., Chugwater, Platte Co. 82201. Tel: 307-322-2070.

WORLAND, WASHAKIE CO., ST. MARY MAGDALEN (1949), [JC] Very Rev. Sam Hayes.
Mailing Address: Box 901, 82401-0901. Tel: 307-347-2820; Fax: 307-347-2450. *Shipping Address*, 1099 Charles Ave., 82401.
Catechesis/Religious Program—Tel: 307-347-6441. Students 143.
Mission—St. Brigid's 216 2nd St., Ten Sleep, Washakie Co. 82442. Tel: 307-366-2345.

Chaplains of Public Institutions

CHEYENNE. *U.S. Veterans Administration Hospital 1*, 90 MW/HC, F.E. Warren AFB, 82005. Rev. Eugene Theisen. Tel: 307-773-3434.

EVANSTON. *Wyoming State Hospital*. Vacant.

RAWLINS. *Wyoming State Penitentiary*, P.O. Box 468, 82301-0068. Tel: 307-324-4631. Rev. Malcolm Reid.

SHERIDAN. *U.S. Veterans Administration Hospital*. (Vacant)

In Residence:
Revs.—
Halvey, William, S.V.D., P.O. Box 510, Dayton, 82836.
Powell, Harold, 720 E. 17th St., 82001.
Siu, Robert K.C., Holy Rosary Church, P.O. Box 1047, Lander, 82520-1047.
Stevens, Clifford, Our Lady of the Woods, 4 S. Riverton St., Dubois, 82513.

Retired:
Rev. Msgrs.—
Delaney, William, 1836 Hot Springs Ave., 82001-5337.
Godley, James, Ballyheige, County Kerry Ireland.
O'Neill, James, P.O. Box 50397, Casper, 82605-0397. Tel: 307-235-5535
Sullivan, Eugene, 1416 Trent Ct., 82009.
Sullivan, Gerald, 1416 Trent Ct., 82009.
Revs.—
Caspers, William A., #1 Easy St., 3990 S. 136 W., Mountain Home, ID 83647.
Colibraro, Daniel, P.O. Box 1368, Casper, 82602-1368.
Colibraro, Philip, P.O. Box 2025, Casper, 82602-2025.
Daley, Joseph A., 2919 Bass Ave., Cody, 82414.
Doudican, James, 1836 Hot Springs Ave., 82001-5337.
Fahey, Thomas C., O.F.M., Chap., Victory Noll Sisters, 1900 W. Park Dr., Box 109, Huntington, IN 46750.
Fraher, Joseph P., 412 Kearney St., Laramie, 82070.
Gianola, William, 650 Mooring Line Dr., Naples, FL 34102.
Wright, John A., 454 Sunlight Ct., Powell, 82435.

Permanent Deacons:
Bradley, Patrick, UMC Chap.; St. Joseph, Cheyenne
Carroll, Kim, Corpus Christi, Newcastle
Hruska, Randy, Holy Spirit, Rock Springs
Humphreys, Russ, St. Patrick's Church, Casper
Juarez, Jesus, St. Joseph, Rawlins
Kristufek, Joseph M., Holy Name Church, Sheridan
Lux, Charles, Holy Spirit, Rock Springs
McCarthy, Ed, Our Lady of Fatima, Casper
Miller, Robert, Our Lady of the Mountains, Jackson
Nash, Wes, Immaculate Conception, Green River
Pico, Lee, St. Mary's Cathedral, Cheyenne
Pitlick, Ken, Corpus Christi, Newcastle
Raboin, Rolland, St. Rose of Lima, Torrington
Stewart, Don, St. Anthony's Church, Casper
Vlchek, Douglas, Our Lady of the Mountains, Jackson
Zelenka, David, Holy Trinity, Cheyenne

INSTITUTIONS LOCATED IN THE DIOCESE

[A] PROTECTIVE INSTITUTIONS

TORRINGTON. *St. Joseph's Children's Home*, Box 1117, 82240-1117. Tel: 307-532-4197; Fax: 307-532-8405. Email: bmayor@stjoseph-wy.org. Web: www.stjoseph-wy.org. Robert C. Mayor, Exec. Dir. Children 62; Total Staff 132; Total Assisted 191.

[B] HOUSING FOR THE ELDERLY (LOW INCOME)

CHEYENNE. *Holy Trinity Manor*, 2516 E. 18th St., 82001. Tel: 307-778-8850; Fax: 307-778-8850. Email: holytrinitymanor@qwest.net. Sr. Ruth Ann Hehn, S.C.L., Admin. Total Staff 1; Total in Residence 34; Total Assisted 41.

CASPER. *St. Anthony Manor*, 211 E. Sixth St., 82601. Tel: 307-237-0843; Fax: 307-237-3516. Rev. Michael Carr; Lea Ann Pestotnik, Admin. Total Staff 3; Total in Residence 64.

[C] MONASTERIES AND RESIDENCES FOR PRIESTS AND BROTHERS

ST. STEPHENS. *St. Stephens Mission - Jesuit Community*, Box 250, 82524. Tel: 307-866-5937; Fax: 307-857-1802. Email: rhilbert@wyoming.com. Revs. J. Robert Hilbert, S.J.; Daniel J. Gannon, S.J.

[D] CONVENTS AND RESIDENCES FOR SISTERS

DAYTON. *Benedictine Sisters of Perpetual Adoration*, San Benito Monastery, P.O. Box 510, 82836-0520. Tel: 307-655-9013; Fax: 307-655-9052. Email: sanbenit@fiberpipe.net. Web: www.benedictinesisters.org/b6.html. Sr. Josetta Grant, O.S.B., Supr. Sisters 4.

[E] CAMPUS MINISTRY

CASPER. *Casper Community College* St. Francis Newman Center, 1732 S. Elm St., 82601. Tel: 307-577-1421. Email: davidandanitamartin@hotmail.com. Anita Martin, Dir. Attended by St. Anthony of Padua, Casper. Total Staff 1.

LARAMIE. *University of Wyoming* St. Paul's Newman Center, University Catholic Parish, 1800 E. Grand Ave., 82070-4316. Tel: 307-745-5461; Fax: 307-742-0521. Email: newman@newmancenter.org. Web: www.newmancenter.org. Rev. Carl J. Gallinger. Total Staff 8.

POWELL. *NorthWest College* John Henry Newman Center, 674 N. Absaroka, 82435. Tel: 307-754-9220. Email: joebush@catholicexchange.com. Rev. Peter Johnson; Joe Bush, Dir. Attended by St. Barbara, Powell.

[F] MISCELLANEOUS LISTINGS

CHEYENNE. *Catholic Schools Endowment Fund, Seminarian Education Endowment*, P.O. Box 1468, 82003-1468. Tel: 307-638-1530.

Mall at St. Vincent DePaul, c/o St. Mary Cathedral, P.O. Box 1268, 82003. Tel: 307-432-0253. Mary Genereux, Mgr. Total Staff 5; Total Assisted 885.

St. Mary's Goods Bookstore, 100 W. 21st St., 82001. Tel: 307-635-4228. Total Staff 1; Total Assisted 150.

St. Mary's School Foundation, P.O. Box 1268, 82003. Tel: 307-635-9261; Fax: 307-635-5723. Email: gruzicka@stmarycathedral.com. Rev. Gary Ruzicka; Kristina Giger, Prin.

The Wyoming Catholic Ministries Foundation, P.O. Box 1468, 82003. Tel: 307-638-1530; Fax: 307-637-7936. Email: jim@dioceseofcheyenne.org.

CASPER. *St. Anthony Tri-Parish School Foundation*, 218 E. 7th St., 82601. Tel: 307-234-2873; Fax: 307-235-4946. Email: jsmith2724@attbi.com. Very Rev. Michael Carr; Jane K. Smith, Prin.; Debbie Frankenberger, Contact Person.

**Holy Cross Food Center, Inc.*, 1030 N. Lincoln, 82601. Tel: 307-577-1041. Bro. Francis Kjeldgaard, C.S.C., Dir. Operated by Holy Cross Center, Inc. Total Staff 33; Total Assisted 12,113.

Knights of Columbuis Charitable Trust for Seminarian Education and Priests' Retirement, 623 S. Wolcott, 82601. Tel: 307-237-2723. Paula Epperson; Thomas Pringle, P.O. Box 1468, 82003. Tel: 307-638-1530.

**Mother Seton Housing, Inc.*, 906 N. Beech St., 82601. Tel: 307-577-8026; Fax: 307-577-8026. Email: setonh@trib.com. Pam Kozola, Exec. Dir. Emergency/Transitional Housing for Homeless Women and Children/Homeless Men and Children.

Shelter, 324 E. H St., 82601. Tel: 307-234-1119. Total Assisted 60; Individuals 417.

St. Vincent De Paul Thrift Store, 301 H St., 82601. Tel: 307-237-2607. Shirley Watson, Dir.

LARAMIE. *St. Laurence School Foundation*, 608 S. 4th, 82070. Tel: 307-742-6363; Fax: 307-745-3131. Email: STLOS@wyomail.com. Tom Wilhelm, Prin.; Rev. James Schumacher, Contact Person.

ROCK SPRINGS. *Rock Springs Catholic School Foundation*, P.O. Box 6038, 82901-0038. Tel: 307-362-2611; Fax: 307-382-4911. Email: holyspirit@wyoming.com. Rev. John Savio; Sr. Lucia Daluz, Prin.

ST. STEPHENS. *St. Stephens Indian Mission Foundation* (1974), P.O. Box 278, 82524-0278. Tel: 307-856-6797; Fax: 307-857-1802. Email: smif@wyoming.com. Rev. Ronald S. Seminara, S.J. (RC), Dir.

RELIGIOUS INSTITUTES OF MEN REPRESENTED IN THE DIOCESE

For further details refer to the corresponding bracketed number in the Religious Institutes of Men or Women section.

[0200]—*Benedictine Monks*—O.S.B.

[0690]—*Jesuit Fathers and Brothers Jesus*—S.J.

[0975]—*Society of Our Lady of the Most Holy Trinity*—S.O.L.T.

[0420]—*Society of the Divine Word*—S.V.D.

RELIGIOUS INSTITUTES OF WOMEN REPRESENTED IN THE DIOCESE

[0230]—*Benedictine Sisters of Pontifical Jurisdiction*—O.S.B.

[1070-03]—*Dominican Sisters* (Sinsinawa)—O.P.

[]—*Dominican Sisters of Hope*—O.P.

[1430]—*Franciscan Sisters of Our Lady of Perpetual Help*—O.S.F.

[3130]—*Our Lady of Victory Missionary Sisters*—O.L.V.M.

[1680]—*School Sisters of St. Francis* (Milwaukee, WI)—O.S.F.

[0480]—*Sisters of Charity of Leavenworth, Kansas*—S.C.L.

[1650]—*Sisters of St. Francis of Philadelphia*—O.S.F.

[3830]—*Sisters of St. Joseph*—C.S.J.

DIOCESAN CEMETERIES

CHEYENNE. *Olivet Cemetery*

NECROLOGY

(No Deaths)

Liturgical Design

St. Elizabeth Ann Seton Church
Transformation of Hall into Church

St. Francis of Assisi Church
Renovation

St. Patrick Church
Restoration Renovation

St. Patrick Shrine

St. John Vianney Church

Church of St. Margaret
Restoration Renovation

Archdiocese of Chicago

(Archidioecesis Chicagiensis)

His Eminence

FRANCIS CARDINAL GEORGE, O.M.I., PH.D., S.T.D.

Archbishop of Chicago; Profession of Perpetual Vows September 8, 1961; ordained December 21, 1963; appointed Bishop of Yakima July 10, 1990; Episcopal Ordination and Installation September 21, 1990; appointed Archbishop of Portland in Oregon April 30, 1996; installed May 27, 1996; appointed Archbishop of Chicago April 8, 1997; installed May 7, 1997; created Cardinal Priest February 21, 1998 *Res.: 1555 N. State Pkwy., Chicago, IL 60610.*

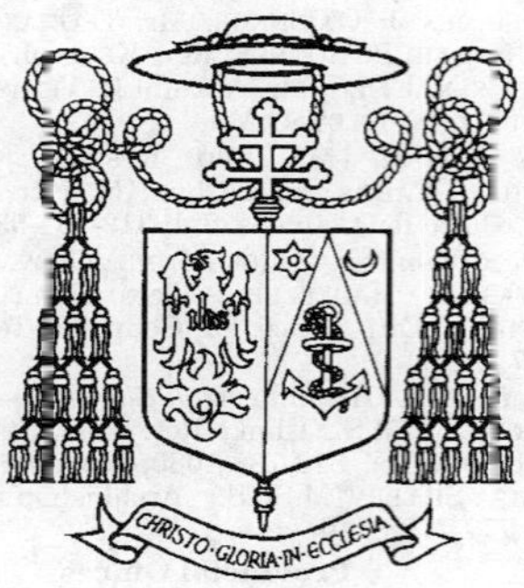

The Pastoral Center: P.O. Box 1979, Chicago, IL 60690. Tel: 312-751-8200.

Web: www.archchicago.org

Most Reverend

TIMOTHY J. LYNE

Retired Auxiliary Bishop of Chicago; ordained May 1, 1943; appointed Auxiliary Bishop of Chicago and Titular Bishop of Vamalla October 31, 1983; consecrated December 13, 1983; retired January 24, 1995. *Res.: Holy Name Cathedral*, 730 N. Wabash, Chicago, IL 60611.

Most Reverend

THAD J. JAKUBOWSKI

Retired Auxiliary Bishop of Chicago; ordained May 3, 1950; appointed Auxiliary Bishop of Chicago and Titular Bishop of Plestia February 16, 1988; consecrated April 11, 1988; retired January 24, 2003. *Res.: 6002 W. Berteau Ave., Chicago, IL 60634-1630.* Tel: 773-202-7720; Fax: 773-202-7725.

Most Reverend

JOHN R. GORMAN

Retired Auxiliary Bishop of Chicago; ordained May 1, 1952; appointed Auxiliary Bishop of Chicago and Titular Bishop of Catula February 16, 1988; consecrated April 11, 1988; retired January 24, 2003. *Res.: Our Lady of the Woods*, 10731 W. 131st St., Orland Park, IL 60462. Tel: 708-361-4754.

Most Reverend

RAYMOND E. GOEDERT

Retired Auxiliary Bishop of Chicago; ordained May 1, 1952; appointed Auxiliary Bishop of Chicago and Titular Bishop of Tamazeni July 8, 1991; consecrated August 29, 1991; retired January 24, 2003. *Res.: 1555 N. State Pkwy., Chicago, IL 60610.*

Most Reverend

EDWIN M. CONWAY

Auxiliary Bishop of Chicago; ordained May 3, 1960; appointed Auxiliary Bishop of Chicago and Titular Bishop of Auguro January 24, 1995; consecrated March 20, 1995. *Res.: 1555 N. State Pkwy., Chicago, IL 60610.*

Most Reverend

FRANCIS J. KANE

Auxiliary Bishop of Chicago; ordained May 14, 1969; appointed Auxiliary Bishop of Chicago and Titular Bishop of Sault Sainte Marie in Michigan January 24, 2003; consecrated March 19, 2003. *Mailing Address: 1651 W. Diversey, Chicago, IL 60614.* Tel: 773-388-8670; Fax: 773-388-8676.

Most Reverend

JOHN R. MANZ

Auxiliary Bishop of Chicago; ordained May 12, 1971; appointed Auxiliary Bishop of Chicago and Titular Bishop of Mulia January 23, 1996; consecrated March 5, 1996. *Mailing Address: 1820 S. Leavitt St., Chicago, IL 60608.* Tel: 312-243-4655; Fax: 312-243-4970.

Most Reverend

JOSEPH N. PERRY

Auxiliary Bishop of Chicago; ordained May 24, 1975; appointed Auxiliary Bishop of Chicago and Titular Bishop of Lead May 5, 1998; consecrated June 29, 1998. *Mailing Address: P.O. Box 733, South Holland, IL 60473-0733.* Tel: 708-339-2474; Fax: 708-339-2477.

Most Reverend

JEROME E. LISTECKI

Auxiliary Bishop of Chicago; ordained May 14, 1975; appointed Auxiliary Bishop of Chicago and Titular Bishop of Nara November 7, 2000; consecrated January 8, 2001. *Mailing Address: 200 N. Milwaukee Ave., Ste. 200, Libertyville, IL 60048.* Tel: 847-549-0160; Fax: 847-549-0163.

Most Reverend

THOMAS J. PAPROCKI

Auxiliary Bishop of Chicago; ordained May 10, 1978; appointed Auxiliary Bishop of Chicago and Titular Bishop of Vulturara January 24, 2003; consecrated March 19, 2003. *Mailing Address: 1400 S. Austin Ave., Cicero, IL 60804.* Tel: 708-329-4040; Fax: 708-222-8854.

Most Reverend

GUSTAVO GARCIA-SILLER, M.SP.S.

Auxiliary Bishop of Chicago; ordained June 22, 1984; appointed Auxiliary Bishop of Chicago and Titular Bishop of Esco January 24, 2003; consecrated March 19, 2003. *Mailing Address: 2330 W. 118th St., Chicago, IL 60643.* Tel: 773-779-8440; Fax: 773-779-8469.

ESTABLISHED NOVEMBER 28, 1843; CREATED 1880.

Square Miles 1,411.

Comprises the Counties of Cook and Lake in the State of Illinois.

Legal Title: The Catholic Bishop of Chicago, a Corporation Sole.

For legal titles of institutions, consult The Pastoral Center.

STATISTICAL OVERVIEW

Personnel	
Cardinals	1
Auxiliary Bishops	7
Retired Bishops	4
Priests: Diocesan Active in Diocese	564
Priests: Diocesan Active Outside Diocese	20
Priests: Diocesan in Foreign Missions	2
Priests: Retired, Sick or Absent	265
Number of Diocesan Priests	851
Religious Priests in Diocese	837
Total Priests in Diocese	1,688
Extern Priests in Diocese	157
Ordinations:	
Diocesan Priests	16
Religious Priests	11
Transitional Deacons	14
Permanent Deacons	30
Permanent Deacons in Diocese	632
Total Brothers	323
Total Sisters	2,618
Parishes	
Parishes	373
With Resident Pastor:	
Resident Diocesan Priests	297
Resident Religious Priests	52
Without Resident Pastor:	
Administered by Priests	23
Administered by Religious Women	1
Missions	10
Pastoral Centers	7
New Parishes Created	1
Closed Parishes	2
Professional Ministry Personnel:	
Brothers	14
Sisters	159
Lay Ministers	608
Welfare	
Catholic Hospitals	20
Total Assisted	3,026,371
Health Care Centers	2
Total Assisted	17,500
Homes for the Aged	37
Total Assisted	5,413
Residential Care of Children	3
Total Assisted	3,500
Day Care Centers	27
Total Assisted	2,280
Specialized Homes	5
Total Assisted	1,112
Special Centers for Social Services	120
Total Assisted	371,255
Residential Care of Disabled	6
Total Assisted	1,008
Other Institutions	10
Total Assisted	146,470
Educational	
Seminaries, Diocesan	3
Students from This Diocese	334
Students from Other Diocese	128
Diocesan Students in Other Seminaries	2
Seminaries, Religious	1
Students Religious	175
Total Seminarians	511
Colleges and Universities	5
Total Students	45,122
High Schools, Diocesan and Parish	6
Total Students	1,701
High Schools, Private	34
Total Students	27,180
Elementary Schools, Diocesan and Parish	238
Total Students	81,815
Elementary Schools, Private	3
Total Students	680
Non-residential Schools for the Disabled	6
Total Students	500
Catechesis/Religious Education:	
High School Students	11,713
Elementary Students	104,255
Total Students under Catholic Instruction	273,477
Teachers in the Diocese:	
Priests	65
Scholastics	5
Brothers	50
Sisters	225
Lay Teachers	5,600
Vital Statistics	
Receptions into the Church:	
Infant Baptism Totals	39,927
Adult Baptism Totals	1,831
Received into Full Communion	1,670
First Communions	30,940
Confirmations	21,316
Marriages:	
Catholic	7,243
Interfaith	1,481
Total Marriages	8,724
Deaths	17,199
Total Catholic Population	2,442,000
Total Population	6,104,000

Former Bishops—Rt. Revs. WILLIAM QUARTER, D.D., consecrated March 10, 1844; died April 10, 1848; JAMES O. VAN DE VELDE, D.D., consecrated Feb. 11, 1849; transferred to Natchez, July 29, 1853; died Nov. 13, 1855; ANTHONY O'REGAN, D.D., consecrated July 25, 1854; resigned 1858; died Nov., 1866; JAMES DUGGAN, D.D., consecrated Bishop of Antigone, and Coadjutor to the Archbishop of St. Louis, May 1, 1857; transferred to Chicago, Jan. 21, 1859; hospitalized, 1869; died March 27, 1899; THOMAS FOLEY, D.D., Coadjutor-Bishop and Administrator of the diocese; cons. Bishop of Pergamus, Feb. 27, 1870; died Feb. 19, 1879; Most Revs. PATRICK A. FEEHAN, D.D., First Archbishop of Chicago; cons. Bishop of Nashville, Nov. 1, 1865; promoted to Chicago, Sept. 10, 1880; died July 12, 1902; JAMES EDWARD QUIGLEY, D.D., Archbishop of Chicago; ord. April 12, 1879; consecrated Bishop of Buffalo, Feb. 24, 1897; promoted to Archbishop of Chicago, Jan. 8, 1903; died July 10, 1915; His Eminence GEORGE CARDINAL MUNDELEIN, Archbishop of Chicago; ord. June 8, 1895; consecrated Titular Bishop of Loryma and Auxiliary Bishop of Brooklyn, Sept. 21, 1909; promoted to the See of Chicago, Dec. 9, 1915; created Cardinal Priest, March 24, 1924; died Oct. 2, 1939; SAMUEL CARDINAL STRITCH, Archbishop of Chicago; ord. May 21, 1910; appt. Bishop of Toledo, Aug. 10, 1921; promoted to Archbishop of Milwaukee, Aug. 26, 1930; transferred to Archbishop of Chicago, Dec. 27, 1939; created Cardinal Priest Feb. 18, 1946; elevated to the Roman Curia, Sacred Congregation for the Propagation of the Faith, March 1, 1958; died in Rome, May 27, 1958; ALBERT CARDINAL MEYER, Archbishop of Chicago; ord. July 11, 1926; appt. Bishop of Superior, Feb. 18, 1946; promoted to Archbishop of Milwaukee, July 21, 1953; transferred to Archbishop of Chicago, Sept. 19, 1958; created Cardinal Priest, Dec. 24, 1959; died April 9, 1965; JOHN CARDINAL CODY, Archbishop of Chicago; ord. Dec. 8, 1931; appt. Auxiliary Bishop of St. Louis, May 14, 1947; consecrated July 2, 1947; promoted to Coadjutor of St. Joseph, Jan. 27, 1954; transferred to Kansas City-St. Joseph, Aug. 29, 1956; promoted to Coadjutor Archbishop of New Orleans, Aug. 14, 1961; acceded to the the See of New Orleans, Nov. 8, 1964; transferred to the Archdiocese of Chicago, June 16, 1965; created Cardinal Priest in the Consistory, June 26, 1967; died April 25, 1982; JOSEPH CARDINAL BERNARDIN, D.D., Archbishop of Chicago; ord. April 26, 1952; appt. Auxiliary Bishop of Atlanta, March 9, 1966; consecrated April 26, 1966; appt. Archbishop of Cincinnati, Nov. 21, 1972; appt. Archbishop of Chicago, July 10, 1982; installed Aug. 25, 1982; created Cardinal Priest, Feb. 2, 1983; died Nov. 14, 1996.

Vicar General—Most Rev. EDWIN M. CONWAY.

Episcopal Vicars—Most Revs. JEROME E. LISTECKI, Vicariate I (Deaneries A, B); FRANCIS J. KANE, Vicariate II (Deaneries A, B, C, D, E, F); JOHN R. MANZ, Vicariate III (Deaneries A, B, D, E); THOMAS J. PAPROCKI, Vicariate IV (Deaneries A, B, C); GUSTAVO GARCIA-SILLER, M.Sp.S., Vicariate V (Deaneries A, BE, BW, C, D, E); JOSEPH N. PERRY, Vicariate VI (Deaneries A, B, C, D).

Deans—Revs. FARRELL KANE, O.Carm., Deanery I-A; WILLIAM J. ZAVASKI, Deanery I-B; EDWARD D. GRACE, Deanery II-A; HAROLD B. MURPHY, Deanery II-B; ROBERT J. HEIDENREICH, Deanery II-C; DANIEL G. MAYALL, Deanery II-D; RONALD N. KALAS, Deanery II-E (Retired); MICHAEL A. WULSCH, Deanery II-F; VACANT, Deanery III-A; Revs. MICHAEL DANEK, C.R., Deanery III-B; KENNETH M. BRIGHAM, Deanery III-D; DONALD J. NEVINS, Deanery III-E; WILLIAM J. HASTINGS, Deanery IV-A; CLAUDIO HOLZER, C.S., Deanery IV-B; RICHARD P. HYNES, Deanery IV-C; BRUCE WELLEMS, C.M.F., Deanery V-A; STANLEY G. RATAJ, Deanery V-B Midway-East; MARCEL J. PASCIAK, Deanery V-B Midway-West; LAWRENCE R. DOWLING, Deanery V-C; GERALD F. MULCAHY, Deanery V-D; EDWARD F. UPTON, Deanery V-E; DAVID A. JONES, Deanery VI-A; JAMES J. MARTIN, Deanery VI-B; MICHAEL P. ENRIGHT, Deanery VI-C; THOMAS E. CIMA, Deanery VI-D.

College of Consultors—Revs. JEREMIAH M. BOLAND; GINO DALPIAZ, C.S.; LAWRENCE R. DOWLING; EDWARD R. FIALKOWSKI; PATRICK R. LAGGES, J.C.D.; PETER B. MCQUINN; PATRICK J. POLLARD; GEORGE J. RASSAS; FRANCIS ROG, C.R.; DONALD SENIOR, C.P., S.T.D.; Mr. JIMMY M. LAGO, Sec.

Presbyteral Council—Revs. EDWARD R. FIALKOWSKI, Chm.; JOHN COLLINS, Vice Chm.; MICHAEL S. MICHELINI, Treas.; PATRICK LAGGES, Sec.

Administrative Council—Most Rev. EDWIN M. CONWAY; Mr. JIMMY M. LAGO; Most Revs. FRANCIS J. KANE; JOHN R. MANZ; JOSEPH N. PERRY; JEROME E. LISTECKI; THOMAS J. PAPROCKI; GUSTAVO GARCIA-SILLER, M.Sp.S.; Dr. NICHOLAS M. WOLSONOVICH, Ph.D.; Rev. MICHAEL M. BOLAND; Mr. THOMAS M. BRENNAN; Mr. RAYMOND P. COUGHLIN; Dr. CAROL L. FOWLER; Mr. JAMES W. VODAK.

Finance Council—Vice Chairmen: Mr. FRANK W. CONSIDINE; Mr. JAMES M. DENNY; Mr. JIMMY M. LAGO. Members: Ms. MARY SUE BARRETT; Mr. JOHN A. BUCK; Most Rev. EDWIN M. CONWAY; Miss EILEEN T. CORCORAN; Mr. JOHN W. CROGHAN; Mr. WILLIAM M. GOODYEAR; Mr. DONALD GOSS; Mr. RICHARD J. GUZIOR; Revs. RICHARD M. HOMA; DAVID A. JONES; Hon. GEORGE N. LEIGHTON; Mr. WILLIAM A. MCINTOSH; Mr. ANDREW J. MCKENNA SR.; Mr. JAMES J. MCNULTY; Mr. KENNETH MEYER; Mr. R. MICHAEL MURRAY JR.; Mr. OLIVER NICKLIN; Mr. JAMES J. O'CONNOR; Mr. THOMAS H. QUINN; Mr. PHILLIP B. ROONEY; Rev. KEVIN J. SPIESS; Mr. FIDELIS N. UMEH; Mr. ARTHUR R. VELASQUEZ; Rev. RUFUS J. WHITLEY, O.M.I.

Pastoral Council—Mr. TED ROSEAN, Chm.; Mr. MICHAEL CAHILL, Vice Chm.; Ms. RITA KATTNER, Dir., Office for Councils. Tel: 312-751-5357.

Women's Committee—CHERI LYNN GLOVACKI, Chm.; ELIZABETH HADERLEIN, Vice Chm.; Ms. RITA KATTNER, Dir., Office for Councils. Tel: 312-751-5357.

Consejo Pastoral Hispano Arquidiocesano—Mr. JAIME BASCUNAN, M.S., Chm.; Rev. ESEQUIEL SANCHEZ, Exec. Dir. Tel: 312-738-1080; Most Rev. GUSTAVO GARCIA-SILLER, M.Sp.S., Archbishop's Delegate. Tel: 773-779-8440.

Provincial Offices

The Catholic Conference of Illinois—ROBERT F. GILLIGAN, 65 E. Wacker Pl., Ste. 1620, Chicago, 60601. Tel: 312-368-1066; Fax: 321-368-1090.

Provincial Court of Appeals—20 N. Wacker Dr., Ste. 3420, Chicago, 60606. Tel: 312-553-4080; 800-572-7835 (In Illinois); Fax: 312-553-4085.

Archdiocesan Offices

All Archdiocesan Departments can be contacted through *Street & Package Delivery Address: The Pastoral Center, 155 E. Superior St., Chicago, 60611. Address all mail to: P.O. Box 1979, Chicago, 60690.* Tel: 312-751-8200.

Office of the Archbishop—Rev. DANIEL A. FLENS, Personal Sec. to the Archbishop. Tel: 312-751-8129; Most Rev. J. BASIL MEEKING, D.D., Special Assistant. Tel: 312-337-5952; Mrs. MARIE FELLER-KNOLL, Special Assistant. Tel: 773-751-8299; Mrs. MARY HALLAN FIORITO, Special Assistant. Tel: 312-751-8211; Rev. RAYMOND C. BAUMHART, S.J., Personal Consultant to the Cardinal. Tel: 312-751-8346.

The Chancery— See Office of the Chancellor

The Metropolitan Tribunal— See Office for Canonical Services.

Vicar General

Vicar General—Most Rev. EDWIN M. CONWAY. Tel: 312-751-8271.

Vicar for Priests—Revs. THOMAS A. TIVY; JAMES T. KACZOROWSKI, 645 N. Michigan Ave., Ste. 543, Chicago, 60611. Tel: 312-642-1837.

Commission on the Mission and Life of the Diocesan Priest—Rev. JAMES KACZOROWSKI, Chm., 645 N. Michigan Ave., Ste. 543, Chicago, 60611. Tel: 312-642-1837.

Priests' Placement Board—Rev. JOHN W. CLEMENS, Exec. Sec. Tel: 312-751-5270; Fax: 312-751-5281.

Archbishop's Delegate for Extern and International Priests—Rev. JERIMIAH BOLAND, Archbishop's Delegate. Tel: 312-751-5237.

Mundelein Seminary—Very Rev. JOHN F. CANARY, Rector; Revs. THOMAS A. BAIMA, Provost; RAYMOND J. WEBB, Ph.D., Academic Dean; KEVIN J. FEENEY, M.A.S., M.Div., Dean of Formation, 1000 E. Maple Ave., Mundelein, 60060. Tel: 847-566-6401.

St. Joseph College Seminary at Loyola University—Rev. JAMES PRESTA, Rector, 6551 N. Sheridan Rd., Chicago, 60626. Tel: 773-973-9700.

Archbishop Quigley Preparatory Seminary—Revs. PETER SNIEG, Rector; DAVID A. JONES, Pres., 103 E. Chestnut, Chicago, 60611. Tel: 312-787-9343.

Bishop Abramowicz House—Rev. ANDREW IZYK, 1447 W. Superior, Chicago, 60622. Tel: 312-455-0598.

Casa Jesus—Rev. ALEJANDRO GARRIDO, Dir.; Ms. KAREN HERMAN DEMURO, Dir. Devel., 1335 W. Harrison St., Chicago, 60607. Tel: 312-738-0700; Fax: 312-738-2090.

The Tuite House at St. Columbanus Church—Rev. MATTHEW EYERMAN, Dir., 331 E. 71st St., Chicago, 60619. Tel: 773-224-1022; Fax: 773-224-1477.

Office of the Chancellor

Chancellor—Mr. JIMMY M. LAGO. Tel: 312-751-8220; Fax: 312-751-5381.

Department Directors—VACANT, Evangelization, Catechesis & Worship; Mr. RAYMOND P. COUGHLIN, Stewardship and Development; Rev. MICHAEL M. BOLAND, Human Svcs.; Mr. THOMAS M. BRENNAN, Financial Svcs.; Mr. JAMES W. VODAK, Communication & Public Rels.; Dr. CAROL L. FOWLER, Personnel Svcs.; Dr. NICHOLAS M. WOLSONOVICH, Ph.D., Catholic Schools.

Racial Justice—Sr. ANITA P. BAIRD, D.H.M., Dir.; Mr. RICARDO TOVAR, Assoc. Dir. Workshops on Racism & Ethnic Sensitivity. Tel: 312-751-8336.

Legal Services—Mr. JOHN C. O'MALLEY, Dir. Tel: 312-751-5379.

Information Technology—Ms. ELLEN M. ANDERSON, Dir. Tel: 312-751-5330; Fax: 312-751-3888; Mr. GANG CHEN, Mgr. Tel: 312-751-8331; Fax: 312-751-5346; Mr. HUGH O'NEILL, Mgr. Technical Svcs. Tel: 312-751-5249; Fax: 312-751-3888.

Research & Planning—Ms. JEAN WELTER, Dir. Tel: 312-751-8345; Fax: 312-751-8766; Mr. DAVID F. SCHWARTZ, Assoc. Dir., Research. Tel: 312-751-8344.

Archives and Records—Mr. JOHN J. TREANOR, 711 W. Monroe St., Chicago, 60661. Tel: 312-831-0711; Fax: 312-831-0610.

Office of Canonical Services

Canonical Services—Rev. PATRICK R. LAGGES, J.C.D., Vicar. Tel: 312-751-8250. Associate Vicars: Revs. RICHARD B. SAUDIS. Tel: 312-751-8382; WILLIAM H. WOESTMAN, O.M.I., J.C.D. Tel: 312-751-8362; JEFFREY GROB, J.C.D. Tel: 312-751-5256; Sr. MARIAN RUSSO, A.S.C., Admin. Asst. Tel: 312-751-8207; Fax: 312-751-8314.

Metropolitan Tribunal—Tel: 312-751-8280.

Judicial Vicar—Rev. PATRICK R. LAGGES, J.C.D. Tel: 312-751-8384. Email: Tribunal@Archdiocese-Chgo.org.

Adjutant Judicial Vicar—Rev. DANIEL A. SMILANIC, J.C.D. Tel: 312-751-8206.

Applications Coordinator—GLENDA MCFADDEN. Tel: 312-751-8253.

Promoter of Justice—Rev. WILLIAM WOESTMAN, O.M.I., J.C.D.

Judges—Rev. MICHAEL A. HACK, J.C.D.; Sr. JOYCE HOBEN, S.N.D.N., J.C.L.; Revs. STANLEY DREWNIAK; JOHN GRIFFITHS, J.C.D.; JOHN C. HERGENROTHER; PATRICK R. LAGGES, J.C.D.; DANIEL SMILANIC, J.C.D.; DAVID M. HYNOUS, O.P.; MARK SIMPSON; MICHAEL BRADLEY, J.C.L.; ALEC WOLFF, J.C.L.; Sisters CARMEN GONZALES, C.D.P., J.C.L.; CHRISTINE KUB, O.P., J.C.L.; MONICA MAVRIC.

Defenders of the Bond—Revs. WILLIAM O. WOESTMAN, O.M.I., J.C.D.; JOHN A. ROLEK, B.A.; W. ARTHUR MARAT; Mr. OLEGARIO CASTILLO, J.C.L.

Delegate of the Archbishop for Privilege Cases—Rev. JOHN A. ROLEK, B.A.

Auditors—Ms. SUSAN MILLER; Sr. ANNELLE PASZYNA, C.S.S.F.

Advocates—Rev. JOSEPH MOL; Sr. DIONETTE WERNER, C.S.S.F.

Office of Conciliation—RALPH BONACCORSI, Exec. Dir. Tel: 312-751-8291.

Department of Evangelization, Catechesis and Worship

Evangelization, Catechesis and Worship—VACANT, Dir. Tel: 312-751-8388; Sr. MARILYN KOFLER, S.P., Exec. Asst. Tel: 312-751-8385; Fax: 312-751-3856.

Office for Catechesis—MARIA SEDANO, Dir.; Sr. JUDITH DIETERLE, S.S.L., Assoc. Dir., 1025 W. Fry St., Chicago, 60622. Tel: 312-243-3700; Fax: 312-243-3801.

Catechetical Ministry—Coordinators: SUZANNE BORDENARO; ELZBIETA CHUDZIK; Mr. JUAN CARLOS FARIAS-GONZALES; LIBIA PAEZ-HOWARD; Mrs. MARY CATHERINE MEEK; Sr. M. ALVERNA HOLLIS, O.P.; Mr. STEPHANE KALONJI; Mr. FRANK KOOB; MARILYN KRAWCZYK; Mr. PAT REDINGTON.

Office of Catholic Youth Ministry—Mr. ANGUS MCDONELL, 155 E. Superior St., Chicago, 60611. Tel: 312-751-5316; Fax: 312-751-3856.

Special Religious Education (SPRED)—Rev. JAMES H. MCCARTHY, Dir., 2956 S. Lowe, Chicago, 60616. Tel: 312-842-1039; Fax: 312-842-4449; Sisters MARY THERESE HARRINGTON, S.H.; SUSANNE GALLAGHER, S.P.

Ministry in Higher Education—Mr. NICHOLAS C. LUND-MOLFESE, M.A., J.D., Coord., 700 S. Morgan, Chicago, 60607. Tel: 312-335-3366; Fax: 928-396-9281.

Office for Evangelization—Rev. JOSEPH KRUSZYNSKI, O.F.M.Conv., Dir. Tel: 312-751-5353; Fax: 312-787-1554; KEITH BORCHERS, Assoc. Dir., .: Tel: 312-751-5288.

Family Ministries—Mr. FRANCIS P. HANNIGAN, Dir. Tel: 312-751-8351.

Cana Conference—Mr. FRANCIS P. HANNIGAN, Contact. Tel: 312-751-8340.

Marriage Education—Mr. ANDREW LYKE. Tel: 312-751-8264.

Annulment Support—ELSIE RADTKE. Tel: 312-751-8353.

Hispanic Family Ministries—VALENTIN ARAYA, Contact. Tel: 312-751-8240.

Natural Family Planning—MARIA GARCIA, Contact. Tel: 312-751-5298 (Spanish); 312-751-8273 (English).

Elizabeth Ministry & Family Advocates—KIM HAGERTY, Contact. Tel: 312-751-8351.

Divorce Ministry—ELSIE RADTKE. Tel: 312-751-8353.

Ecumenical and Interreligious Affairs, Office for—Sisters JOAN MCGUIRE, O.P., Dir. Tel: 312-751-5325; MARY ELLEN COOMBE, N.D.S., Assoc. Dir. Tel: 312-751-5324.

Institute for Catholic Jewish Education—Sr. MARY ELLEN COOMBE, N.D.S., Dir. Tel: 312-251-8800, Ext. 316.

Catholic Youth Organization—Revs. JOHN P. SMYTH, Dir.; DAVID RYAN, Asst. Exec. Dir. Tel: 312-491-3530.

Divine Worship, Office for—Mr. TODD WILLIAMSON, Dir.; Mr. CHARLES KESSELL, Dir., Liturgical Music; Mr. BRIAN LEPACEK, Dir., Parish Liturgy Program; Mr. JOSE CASTILLO, Coord. Hispanic Programming; Ms. ROSARIO CAMACHO, Programming Asst.; Revs. PHILIP HORRIGAN, Dir., Art & Environment; ROBERT TUZIK, Special Project Coord.

Young Adult Ministry/Singles—Rev. JOHN C. CUSICK, Dir.; Ms. KATHERINE F. DEVRIES, Assoc. Dir., 711 W. Monroe St., Chicago, 60661. Tel: 312-466-9473; Fax: 312-466-9474.

Office for Peace & Justice—Mr. BILL PURCELL, Dir. Tel: 312-751-8390; Fax: 312-787-1554.

Catholic Campaign for Human Development—Ms. ELENA SEGURA. Tel: 312-751-5333.

Catholic Relief Services—Ms. ADRIENNE CURRY. Tel: 312-751-8367.

Housing Coordinator—Mr. JONATHAN NJUS. Tel: 312-751-8367.

Parish Sharing Program—Mr. BILL PURCELL. Tel: 312-751-8390.

Catholic Missions Office—Propagation of the Faith: Sr. MARIA BURKE, S.Sp.S., Dir., 721 N. LaSalle St., Chicago, 60610. Tel: 312-382-3322.

Respect Life/Pro-Life Activities—MARY-LOUISE KUREY, Dir. Tel: 312-751-5355; Fax: 312-787-1554.

Project Rachel—Tel: 312-337-1962; 800-456-4673 (800-456-HOPE).

Chastity Education Initiative—Tel: 312-751-5355.

Prison Ministry/Kolbe House—Rev. LAWRENCE J. CRAIG, Dir., 2434 S. California, Chicago, 60608. Tel: 773-247-0700.

Councils, The Archdiocesan Office for—

Parish Pastoral Councils—Ms. RITA KATTNER, Dir. Tel: 312-751-8364; Fax: 312-751-3883.

Christ Renews His Parish—Ms. RITA KATTNER, Spiritual Dir. Tel: 312-751-8364.

Amate House/Young Adult Volunteer Program—Mr. MARK LABOE, Dir., 2601 N. Sayre Ave., Chicago, 60635. Tel: 773-745-0002.

Archdiocesan Vocations—Rev. JOSEPH NOONAN, Dir. Tel: 847-970-4845; Fax: 847-566-7330.

Vocation Office—Sr. PETER MARY HETTLING, C.S.J. Tel: 312-751-5245; Fax: 312-751-8372.

Ethnic Offices—Mrs. SHEILA ADAMS, Dir., Office for Black Catholics. Tel: 312-751-8377; Mrs. TERESITA L. NUVAL, Dir., Office for Asian Catholics. Tel: 312-751-8305; Fax: 312-751-5207; Mrs. KRYSTYNA ZAMBRZYCKI FLAHERTY, Dir., Office for European Catholics. Tel: 312-751-8301; Rev. ESEQUIEL SANCHEZ, Dir., Office for Hispanic Catholics; Mr. JORGE RIVERA, Hispanic Young Adult Ministry, 1838 S. Throop St., Chicago, 60608. Tel: 312-738-1080; Fax: 312-243-3459.

Vicariate Hispanic Coordinators—

Vicariate I—GRACIELA CONTRERAS, 200 N. Milwaukee Ave., Ste. 212, Libertyville, 60048. Tel: 847-549-0164.

Vicariate VI—CARLOS SALMERON, 16160 Seton Rd., South Holland, 60473. Tel: 708-339-5044.

Ethnic Apostolates—

Anawim Center (Native American Apostolate)—Sr. PATRICIA ANN MULKEY, Anawin Center, 4750 N. Sheridan Rd., Chicago, 60640. Tel: 773-561-6155.

Czech Catholic Mission—Rev. DUSAN HLADIK, 2340 S. 61st Ave., Cicero, 60804. Tel: 708-656-1050.

Haitian Catholic Apostolate—Rev. JOSEPH ERNEST, Dir., 7851 S. Jeffery Blvd., Chicago, 60649. Tel: 773-721-6365.

Indochinese Catholic Center—Rev. PETER HUNG, Dir., 4827 N. Kenmore, Chicago, 60640. Tel: 773-784-1932.

Irish Catholic Apostolate—VACANT, Chicago Chap. to the Young Irish, 721 N. LaSalle St., Chicago, 60610. Tel: 312-337-8445.

Italian Catholic Apostolate—Rev. GINO DALPIAZ, C.S., 1621 N. 39th Ave., Stone Park, 60165. Tel: 708-345-3842.

Korean Catholic Mission of Chicago (Kedvale)—Rev. JOHN SMITH, S.S.C., Dir., 4115 N. Kedvale, Chicago, 60641. Tel: 773-283-3979.

Chaplaincies/Chaplain Affairs—Most Rev. JEROME LISTECKI, Liaison, 200 N. Milwaukee Ave., Ste. 200, Libertyville, 60048-2250. Tel: 847-549-0160; Fax: 847-549-0163.

The Catholic Ministry at Chicago O'Hare International Airport—Rev. MICHAEL G. ZANIOLO, Chap.; Deacon JAMES O'MALLEY, Assoc. Chap., P.O. Box 66353, Chicago, 60666-0353. Tel: 773-686-2636.

Airport Midway—Chaplains: Revs. GEORGE P. MCKENNA (Retired); MICHAEL J. WANDA. Tel: 708-352-7388.

Fire Department Chaplain—Rev. THOMAS A. MULCRONE, Chap., 1140 W. Jackson Blvd., Chicago, 60607. Tel: 312-738-9246.

Police Department Chaplain—Rev. THOMAS R. NANGLE, Dir., 1140 W. Jackson Blvd., Chicago, 60607. Tel: 312-738-7588; Fax: 312-738-2825.

Archdiocesan Council of Catholic Women (ACCW)—MARY ANN ROSSO, Pres.; Rev. STAN JANKOWSKI, O.F.M., Moderator. Tel: 312-751-8325.

Archdiocesan Council of Catholic Men—Rev. JOHN C. CUSICK, 711 W. Monroe St., Chicago, 60661. Tel: 312-466-9473; Fax: 312-466-9474.

Department of Stewardship and Development

Department of Stewardship and Development—Mr. RAYMOND F. COUGHLIN, Dir. Tel: 312-655-7910.

Vicariate Stewardship Coordinators—MICHAEL J. GLEASON. Tel: 312-655-7830; ANNE MARIE TIRPAK. Tel: 312-655-7713.

Development Services—Mr. TIMOTHY DOCKERY. Tel: 312-655-7928.

Planned Giving/Annuities—Mr. RICHARD S GOODE, Dir. Tel: 312-655-7848.

Seminary Development-Archbishop Quigley Preparatory—PATRICIA HERMAN. Tel: 312-787-9343.

St. Joseph Seminary—MARIE COMPOSTO. Tel: 773-973-9721.

St. Mary of the Lake, Mundelein—MARK TEFESI, Vice Pres., Institutional Advancement. Tel: 847-970-4817.

Big Shoulders Fund—Rev. Msgr. KENNETH VELO, Pres. Tel: 312-751-5395; HEIDI WALTNER-PEPPER. Tel: 312-751-5395.

Department of Human Services

Director—Most Rev. MICHAEL M. BOLAND, 126 N. Desplaines St., Chicago, 60661. Tel: 312-655-7460; Fax: 312-655-0219.

Catholic Charities of Chicago—Most Rev. MICHAEL M. BOLAND, Admin.; Rev. CHARLES T. RUBEY, Dir. Programs; Mr. WALTER OUSLEY, Dir. Operations; CYNTHIA D. SMETANA, Dir. Admin. Svcs. Associate Administrators: Revs. RICHARD E. BULWITH; FRANCIS A. CIMARRUSTI; ROGER J. COUGHLIN (Retired); GERARD KELLY; WAYNE F. WATTS. Consultant: Most Rev. EDWIN M. CONWAY, D.D., 126 N. Desplaines St., Chicago, 60661-2357. Tel: 312-655-7000 (Refer to Catholic Charities section under the Institutions Located in the Archdiocese for further listings.).

Maternity Fund—Rev. ROGER J. COUGHLIN (Retired), 721 N. LaSalle St., Chicago, 60610. Tel: 312-655-7596.

Catholic Office of the Deaf—Rev. JOSEPH A. MULCRONE, Dir.; Ms. NANCY HUBER, Rel. Educ. Dir., 721 N. LaSalle, Chicago, 60610. Tel: 312-655-7899; Fax: 312-751-0394.

Health/Hospital Affairs and Bio-Ethics Commission—Most Revs. EDWIN M. CONWAY, Liaison. Tel: 312-751-8270; JEROME LISTECKI, Assoc. Liaison. Tel: 847-549-0610.

Mercy Home for Boys and Girls—Revs. JAMES J. CLOSE, Pres. Tel: 312-738-7563; SCOTT DONAHUE, Assoc. Pres., 1140 W. Jackson, Chicago, 60607. Tel: 312-738-9240.

Office for Persons with Disabilities—Rev. CHARLES T. RUBEY, 721 N. LaSalle St., Chicago, 60610. Tel: 312-655-7445.

Victim Assistance Coordinator—RALPH BONACCORSI. Tel: 312-751-8267; Fax: 312-751-8307. Email: rbonaccorsi@archchicago.org.

Department of Financial Services

Director—Mr. THOMAS M. BRENNAN. Tel: 312-751-8218.

Facilities and Construction—C. GREGORY VEITH, Mgr. Tel: 312-751-8342.

Controller's Operations—MARK COSENTINO, Mgr. Tel: 312-751-5266.

Insurance—MATTHEW KAMINSKI, Mgr. Tel: 312-751-8295.

Real Estate—Ms. MAUREEN O'BRIEN, Mgr. Tel: 312-751-8221.

Parish Operations—TAFFIE IWANICKI, Parish Operations Mgr. Tel: 312-751-5312; JASON BERTRAND, Parish Operations Coord. Tel: 312-751-5399.

Vicariate I—MICHAEL GIBBS. Tel: 312-751-5364. Vicariate Office. Tel: 847-549-0165.

Vicariate II—GENE MYERS. Tel: 312-751-5321. Vicariate Office. Tel: 773-388-8673.

Vicariate III—JESSE ESTRADA. Tel: 312-751-5323. Vicariate Office. Tel: 312-243-1135.

Vicariate IV—PATRICIA POMYKALSKI. Tel: 312-751-5384. Vicariate Office. Tel: 773-202-7722.

Vicariate V—DENNIS ROBAK. Tel: 312-751-5318. Vicariate Office. Tel: 773-779-9165.

Vicariate VI—PAMELA GUTTER. Tel: 312-751-5342. Vicariate Office. Tel: 708-333-6132.

Catholic Cemeteries—Rev. PATRICK J. POLLARD, Dir.; Mr. ROMAN SZABELSKI, Exec. Dir., 1400 S. Wolf Rd., Hillside, 60162. Tel: 708-449-6100; Fax: 708-449-3419.

Department of Communications and Public Relations

Department of Communications and Public Relations—Mr. JAMES W. VODAK. Tel: 312-751-8289; Fax: 312-751-5306.

Communications, Office of—JAMES DWYER, Dir. Communication. Tel: 312-751-8233; MARY MCDONOUGH, Asst. Dir. Tel: 312-751-8393.

Hispanic Communications—ALEJANDRO CASTILLO, Dir. Tel: 312-751-8287; Fax: 312-751-5307.

Chicago Catolico—MARIA DEL CARMEN MACIAS, Editor. Tel: 312-655-7880; Fax: 312-642-7310.

New World Publications—THOMAS H. SHERIDAN, Editor & Gen. Mgr., 721 N. LaSalle St., Chicago, 60610. Tel: 312-655-7577.

Office of Radio & Television—Mr. JIM DISCH, Dir. Tel: 312-751-8277; Mr. MICHAEL MAY, Audio/Visual Coord. Tel: 312-751-8282; Fax: 312-751-5307; Bro. EDWARD HOWE, C.R., Television Engineer Specialist. Tel: 312-751-8374.

Department of Personnel Services

Director—Dr. CAROL FOWLER. Tel: 312-751-8349.

Human Resources—FRED VAN DEN HENDE, Mgr. Tel: 312-751-5352.

Lay Ecclesial Ministry, Office for—Ms. KEIREN O'KELLY, Dir. Tel: 312-751-5263; ALICE ALTIVEROS-LADAO, Ministry Openings. Tel: 312-751-5262; 312-751-7999, Ext. 3 (Hotline); Fax: 312-751-5281.

Office of Ministeral Evaluation—KATHLEEN LEGGDAS, Dir. Tel: 312-751-5265; Fax: 312-751-5281.

Religious, Office for—Sisters JOAN MCGLINCHEY, M.S.C., Dir. Tel: 312-751-8360; MARGARET COLEMAN, O.S.F., Retirement Collection. Tel: 312-751-8234.

Priests' Retirement and Mutual Aid Association (PRMAA)—Mr. ALEX BECKER, Admin., 4951 Harrrison St., Hillside, 60162. Tel: 708-449-8026.

Vicar for Senior Priests—Most Revs. TIMOTHY J. LYNE, Co-Vicar. Tel: 312-787-8040; 312-787-9113; THAD J. JAKUBOWSKI, D.D., Co-Vicar. Tel: 773-202-7720; Rev. JOHN A. KUZINSKAS, Asst. Vicar (Retired).

Co-Vicars for the Diaconate Community—Revs. EDWARD P. SALMON, 816 Marengo, Forest Park, 60130. Tel: 708-366-8900; MICHAEL P. AHLSTROM, 816 Marengo, Forest Park, 60130. Tel: 708-366-8900; THOMAS MCGOREY, Assoc. Dir. Personnel; CHARLES O'DONNELL, Assoc. Dir. Ministerial Devel.

Diaconate Formation Program—Mundelein Seminary, 1000 E. Maple, Mundelein, 60060-1174. Tel: 847-837-4563; Fax: 847-837-4565. Deacon RICHARD BAUM, Dir.; Rev. DAVID DOWDLE, Dir. Spiritual Formation.

Office of Professional Responsibility—Ms. LEAH MCCLUSKEY, Admin., 676 N. St. Clair, Ste. 1910, Chicago, 60611. Tel: 312-751-5205; 800-994-6200; Fax: 312-751-5279.

Office for Protection of Children and Youth—Ms. JAN SLATTERY, Dir. Tel: 312-751-5388; Fax: 312-751-9806.

Assistance Ministry—RALPH BONACCORSI, Dir.; Dr. MICHAEL BLAND, 676 N. St. Clair, Ste. 1910, Chicago, 60611. Tel: 312-751-8267; Fax: 312-751-8307.

Cardinal Stritch Retreat House—Revs. LOUIS J. CAMELI, Dir.; ANTHONY M. TALARICO, Admin.; EDMUND J. SIEDLECKI, Retired Admin. (Retired); Mr. DONALD E. WICHLIN, Facilities Mgr., P.O. Box 455, Mundelein, 60060. Tel: 847-566-6060; Fax: 847-566-6082.

Lay Ministry Programs—GRAZIANO MARCHESCHI, Dir., 1000 E. Maple Ave., Mundelein, 60060-1174. Tel: 847-837-4550; Fax: 847-837-4565.

Instituto De Liderazgo Pastoral (Hispanic Programs

for Lay Ministry and Permanent Diaconate)—Mr. JAIME BASCUNAN, M.S., Dir.; Rev. GERARDO CARCAR, Dir., Spiritual Formation. Assoc. Directors: Mrs. ANA M. RIVAS; Mrs. REBECCA VILLANUEVA; Sr. NATALIA E. CAMPOS-SOLIS, R.S.C.J. Tel: 847-837-4556; Fax: 847-837-4565.

Ongoing Formation for Priests—Rev. LOUIS J. CAMELI, Dir., 1641 W. Diversey, Chicago, 60614-027. Tel: 773-281-1087; Fax: 773-281-1051.

Ongoing Formation in Ministry—Sr. JUDY VALLIMONT, S.S.P.S., 4419 N. Kedzie, Chicago, 60625. Tel: 773-478-7543; 773-566-6060.

Department of Catholic Schools

Department of Catholic Schools—Dr. NICHOLAS M. WOLSONOVICH, Ph.D., Supt. Tel: 312-751-5200.

Marketing—Sr. DAWN TOMASZEWSKI, S.P., Dir. Tel: 312-751-5334.

Other Archdiocesan Agencies

Rev. RAYMOND C. BAUMHART, S.J., Personal Consultant to the Cardinal. Tel: 312-751-8346.

Food Service Professionals, Archdiocese—Mr. RON HUNTER, Dir., 5150 Northwest Hwy., Chicago, 60638. Tel: 773-385-5100.

Liturgy Training Publications (LTP)—JOHN A. THOMAS, 1800 N. Hermitage Ave., Chicago, 60622. Tel: 773-486-5153 (ODW); 773-486-8970 (LTP); Fax: 773-486-5158 (ODW); 773-486-7094 (LTP).

CLERGY, PARISHES, MISSIONS AND PAROCHIAL SCHOOLS

CITY OF CHICAGO
(COOK COUNTY)

1—CATHEDRAL OF THE HOLY NAME, Revs. Daniel G. Mayall, Rector & Pastor of Parish; John Boivin; Thomas R. Rzepiela; Ronald T. Kunkel; Ms. Kristin Sadie, Pastoral Assoc.; Mrs. Ann Klocke, Pastoral Assoc.; Ms. Cathleen Mika, Pastoral Assoc.; Ms. Judith Horak, Pastoral Min.; Deacons Michael McCloskey, Pastoral Assoc.; Stan Strom, Pastoral Assoc.; Mary Ann Hoban, D.Min., Coord. of Ministry of Care; Mr. Matthew Walsh, Dir. Music; H. Ricardo Ramirez; Mrs. Rosalie V. Clifford, Business Mgr.; Ms. Allegra Rogers, Parish Sec.; Mr. Joseph A. Konen. In Res., Most Revs. Timothy J. Lyne, Pastor Emeritus & Auxiliary Bishop of Chicago (Retired); Michael M. Boland; Revs. William J. Moriarity; Eugene F. Durkin (Retired); Patrick Lagges.
Rectory—730 N. Wabash Ave., 60611. Tel: 312-787-8040; Fax: 312-787-9113.
Cardinal's Residence—1555 N. State Pkwy., 60610. His Eminence Francis Cardinal George, O.M.I., Ph.D., S.T.D., Archbishop of Chicago; Most Revs. Raymond E. Goedert, Auxiliary Bishop (Retired); Basil Meeking, D.D. (Retired), Christchurch, New Zealand; Rev. Daniel A. Flens, Sec. to the Archbishop.
School—Frances Xavier Warde School, 751 N. State St., 60611. Tel: 312-466-0700; Fax: 312-337-7180. Dr. John Sloan, Exec. Dir. Religious 1; Lay Teachers 56; Students 664.
Catechesis/Religious Program—Tel: 312-787-8040. Ms. Sharon Kinsley, D.R.E. Students 55.
Convent—Sisters of Charity of the Blessed Virgin Mary, 750 N. Wabash Ave., 60611. Tel: 312-664-1462.
Convent—Oblate Sisters of Jesus the Priest, 740 N. Wabash Ave., 60611. Tel: 312-787-8040; Fax: 312-787-9113.

2—ST. ADALBERT, Revs. Michael S. Michelini; Walter Yepes; Deacon Joseph Mally. In Res., Revs. Alejandro Garrido; Dennis R. Karamitis, S.J.
Res.: 1650 W. 17th St., 60608. Tel: 312-226-0340; Fax: 312-266-0194.
Catechesis/Religious Program—Students 265.

3—ST. ADRIAN, Rev. Theodore L. Ostrowski.
Res.: 7000 S. Fairfield Ave., 60629. Tel: 773-434-3223.
Church: 70th and S. Washtenaw Ave., 60619.

4—ST. AGATHA, Rev. Daniel J. McCormack; Deacon Gregory Shumpert.
Res.: 3147 W. Douglas Blvd., 60623. Tel: 773-522-3050; Fax: 773-522-3842.
School—Campus No. One--Our Lady of the Westside Catholic School, Tel: 773-762-1809. Serving the following parishes: St. Agatha and Presentation. Totals represent two campuses. Sisters 6; Lay Teachers 23; Students 609.
Convent—3143 W. Douglas Blvd., 60623. Tel: 773-762-7969.

5—ST. AGNES OF BOHEMIA, Revs. Matthew E. Foley; Diego F. Cadavid; Felipe Vaglienty; Sisters Yesenia Ortiz, Pastoral Assoc.; Veronica Cortez, Pastoral Assoc.; Deacon Angel Favila, Pastoral Assoc.
Res.: 2651 S. Central Park Ave., 60623. Tel: 773-522-0142; Fax: 773-522-0172.
School—2643 S. Central Park Ave., 60623. Tel: 773-522-0143; Fax: 773-522-0132. Lay Teachers 35; Students 560.
Catechesis/Religious Program—Tel: 773-277-5446. Students 605.
Convent—Misioneras de San Pio X, 2658 S. Central Park Ave., 60623. Tel: 773-762-3229.

6—ST. AILBE, Rev. John S. Breslin; Deacon Bruce T. McElrath.
Res.: 9015 S. Harper Ave., 60619. Tel: 773-374-2345; Fax: 773-374-7096.
School—9037 S. Harper Ave., 60619. Tel: 773-734-1386; Fax: 773-734-1440. Sr. Kathryn Hartnett, Prin. Sisters of St. Dominic (Adrian, MI) 2; Lay Teachers 15; Students 250.
Catechesis/Religious Program—Students 147.

7—ALL SAINTS-ST. ANTHONY, Revs. Raymond P. Devereux; John W. Parker; Oscar Dario Colorado Montoya (Colombia); Deacons Peter Liberti; Duke Vemich; Saul Vazquez.
Res.: 518 W. 28th Pl., 60616. Tel: 312-842-2744; Fax: 312-842-2791.
School—Participant in Bridgeport Catholic Academy See separate listing for Consolidated Elementary Schools.
Catechesis/Religious Program—Students 160.

8—ST. ALOYSIUS, Rev. Nicholas R. Desmond; Deacons Adolph Lopez; Dennis Ramos.
Res.: 2300 W. Le Moyne St., 60622. Tel: 773-278-4808; Fax: 773-278-4898.
Catechesis/Religious Program—Students 192.

9—ST. ALPHONSUS, (German), Revs. James F. Hurlbert; John Blazek; Deacon Joseph Riffner.
Res.: 1429 W. Wellington Ave., 60657. Tel: 773-525-0709; Fax: 773-525-3238.
School—Tel: 773-348-4629; Fax: 773-348-4829. Lay Teachers 12; Students 137.
Catechesis/Religious Program—Students 70.

10—ST. AMBROSE, Rev. David A. Jones.
Res.: 1012 E. 47th St., 60653. Tel: 773-624-3695; Fax: 773-624-3697.
Catechesis/Religious Program—

11—ST. ANDREW, Revs. John A. Farry; Francis Li.
Res.: 3546 N. Paulina St., 60657. Tel: 773-525-3016; Fax: 773-525-4124.
School—1710 W. Addison, 60613. Tel: 773-248-2500; Fax: 773-248-2709. Lay Teachers 16; Students 310.
Catechesis/Religious Program—Students 30.

12—ST. ANGELA, Rev. Kenneth M. Brigham; Sr. Joseph Ellen Keitzer, S.P., Pastoral Assoc.; Deacon Jose Uroza. In Res., Revs. Magnus Anokwuru, (Extern); Jerome Onwugalu, C.S.Sp.
Res.: 5758 W. Potomac Ave., 60651. Tel: 773-379-7700; Fax: 773-379-7701.
School—Tel: 773-626-2655. Sisters 4; Lay Teachers 29; Students 350.
Catechesis/Religious Program—1332 N. Massasoit Ave., 60651. Tel: 773-626-2656. Students 37.

13—ST. ANN, Most Rev. John R. Manz, Admin.; Rev. John J. Keehan, (On Leave); Deacons Rodrigo Silva; Jesus Blanco. In Res., Rev. Louis J. Zake.
Res.: 1840 S. Leavitt St., 60608. Tel: 312-733-7486; Fax: 312-733-5681.
School—2211 W. 18th Pl., 60608. Tel: 312-829-4153. Sr. Michael Marie Franzak, Prin. Lay Teachers 8; Students 300.
Catechesis/Religious Program—Students 120.

14—ANNUNCIATA, Revs. Paul M. Cullen, O.S.M.; Dennis Kriz, O.S.M.; Bro. Brian Fitzpatrick, O.S.M., Pastoral Assoc.; Mr. Mike Schnabel, Business Mgr. In Res., Revs. Conrad M. Borntrager, O.S.M.; James M. Dore, O.S.M.
Res.: 11128 S. Avenue G, 60617. Tel: 773-221-1040; Fax: 773-221-1556.
School—Tel: 773-375-5711; Fax: 773-375-5704. Lay Teachers 10; Students 270.
Catechesis/Religious Program—Students 164.

15—ST. ANSELM, Rev. Mark Weber, S.V.D.; Bro. Vinh Trinh, S.V.D., Pastoral Assoc. In Res., Rev. Donald J. Ehr, S.V.D.
Res.: 6045 S. Michigan Ave., 60637. Tel: 773-493-5959; Fax: 773-363-1887.
Catechesis/Religious Program—Students 37.

16—ST. ANTHONY, (Italian), Revs. Bideri Nyagasaza, S.X., Admin.; Mario Merino Rodriguez, M.C.C.J.; Deacons Edward Ryan; Juan Mo...es.
Res.: 11530 S. Prairie Ave., 60628. Tel: 773-468-1200; Fax: 773-468-3570.
School—Lay Teachers 11; Students 155.

17—ASSUMPTION, Revs. Lawrence J. Craig; Arturo Perez Rodriguez; Deacons Ronald DeRose; John W. Harrington.
Res.: 2434 S. California Ave., 60608. Tel: 773-247-6644; Fax: 773-247-0569.
Convent—2831 W. 24th St. Blvd., 60623. Tel: 773-247-3560.
Kolbe House—Tel: 773-247-0070. Rev. Lawrence J. Craig, Dir. Catholic Prison Ministry.
Catechesis/Religious Program—Students 227.

18—ASSUMPTION OF THE B.V.M./ST. CATHERINE OF GENOA, Closed., Consult Archives and Records Center for parish and school records.

19—ASSUMPTION OF THE BLESSED VIRGIN MARY, Rev. John M. Dowd, O.S.M. In Res., Very Rev. Anthony M. O'Connell, O.S.M.; Revs. John M. Pawlikowski, O.S.M., Ph.D.; David M. Brown, O.S.M.; Paul M. Novak, O.S.M.; Damian M. Charbonneau, O.S.M.
Res.: 323 W. Illinois St., 60610. Tel: 312-644-0036; Fax: 312-644-1838.

20—ST. BARBARA, Revs. Robert C. Behnke; Dennis A. Ziomek. In Res., Rev. Dennis A. Ziomek.
Res.: 2859 S. Throop St., 60608. Tel: 312-842-7979; Fax: 312-842-7978.
School—2867 S. Throop St., 60608. Tel: 312-326-6243. Sisters of St. Joseph of the Third Order of St. Francis (Chicago, IL) 2; Lay Teachers 11; Students 240.
Catechesis/Religious Program—Students 20.

21—ST. BARNABAS, Revs. Raymond J. Tillrock; John T. Noga; Gene F. Smith; Mr. Bernard Cissell, Pastoral Assoc.; Deacons James Temple; William Sullivan; James L. Conway; Andrew Neu. In Res., Rev. Anthony M. Leany (Retired).
Res.: 10134 S. Longwood Dr., 60643. Tel: 773-779-1166; Fax: 773-445-9671.
School—10121 S. Longwood Dr., 60643. Tel: 773-445-7711; Fax: 773-445-9815. Dominican Sisters (Sinsinawa, WI) 1; Lay Teachers 29; Students 530.
Catechesis/Religious Program—Tel: 773-445-3450. Students 200.

22—ST. BARTHOLOMEW, Revs. George F. Cerny; Jason A. Malave; Sr. Geraldine Moorman, B.V.M., Pastoral Assoc.; Deacon Saul Gonzalez; Mrs. Lenore Gonzalez, Lay Min. In Res., Revs. Casimir J. Kozien (Retired); J. Edward Duggan (Retired); Eduardo Pinzon, S.J.
Res.: 4949 W. Patterson Ave., 60641. Tel: 773-286-7871; Fax: 773-286-4808.
School—4941 W. Patterson Ave., 60641. Tel: 773-282-9373; Fax: 773-282-4757. Sisters 1; Lay Teachers 22; Students 360.
Catechesis/Religious Program—Tel: 773-725-1413. Students 254.
Convent—Tel: 773-545-2119.

23—ST. BASIL/VISITATION, Rev. Brian G. Walker, O.P. In Res., Revs. David F. Wright, O.P.; Thomas D. Noesen, O.P.
Res.: 843 W. Garfield Blvd., 60621. Tel: 773-846-3570; Fax: 773-783-3348.
School—Visitation School, 900 W. Garfield Blvd., 60609. Tel: 773-373-5200; Fax: 773-373-5201. Sisters 5; Lay Teachers 14; Students 260.
Catechesis/Religious Program—Students 14.

24—ST. BEDE THE VENERABLE, Revs. Brian Lisowski; Marion Soprych; Michael F. Wheaton.
Res.: 8200 S. Kostner Ave., 60652. Tel: 773-582-9100; Fax: 773-582-0026.
School—4440 W. 83rd St., 60652. Tel: 773-582-8800; Fax: 773-582-3366. Lay Teachers 27; Students 697.
Catechesis/Religious Program—Tel: 773-767-2186; Fax: 773-767-9254. Students 750.

25—ST. BENEDICT, Revs. Robert A. Heidenreich; John F. Kratje; John F. Kartje; Deacons Robert Jacob; Paul Guzman, Pastoral Assoc.; Philip Bertolani. In Res., Rev. John W. Clemens.
Res.: 2215 W. Irving Park Rd., 60618. Tel: 773-588-6484; Fax: 773-588-4927.
School—3920 N. Leavitt St., 60618. Tel: 773-463-6797; Fax: 773-463-0782. Lay Teachers 17; Students 250.
High School—3900 N. Leavitt St., 60618. Tel: 773-539-0066; Fax: 773-539-3397. Sisters 6; Lay Teachers 30; Students 373.
Catechesis/Religious Program—Students 193.

26—ST. BENEDICT THE AFRICAN (EAST), Rev. David E. Baldwin; Sisters Mary Pokorny, Pastoral Assoc.; Joanne Delehanty, Pastoral Assoc.; Eileen Hauswald, Pastoral Assoc.
Res.: 340 W. 66th St., 60621. Tel: 773-873-4464; Fax: 773-873-2354.
School—Academy of St. Benedict the African Total Students for 3 Sites: 903.
Stewart Site—6547 S. Stewart, 60636. Tel: 773-944-6100.
Catechesis/Religious Program—Students 75.

27—ST. BENEDICT THE AFRICAN (WEST), Rev. David R. Straub; Sr. Joann Sambs, Pastoral Assoc.; Deacon Louis Constanopolis.
Worship Site—7033 S. Honore, 60636.
Office—6012 S. Laflin St., 60636. Tel: 773-476-4831; Fax: 773-925-1010.
Rectory—1818 W. 71st St., 60636. Tel: 773-925-2535.
School—Academy of St. Benedict the African Total Students for 3 Sites: 903.
Honore Site—7033 S. Honore St., 60636. Tel: 773-476-2258; Fax: 773-476-0753.
Laflin Site—6020 S. Laflin St., 60636. Tel: 773-776-3316; Fax: 773-776-3715.
Stewart Site—6547 S. Stewart St., 60636. Tel:

773-994-6100; Fax: 773-994-1433.
Catechesis/Religious Program—Students 138.
28—BLESSED ALOJZIJE CARDINAL STEPANIC MISSION, Rev. Nicholas Dugandzic, O.P., Admin. (Independent Mission)
Res.: 6346 N. Ridge, 60660. Tel: 773-262-0535; Fax: 773-262-4603.
29—BLESSED SACRAMENT, Revs. William Bueche, C.Ss.R.; Steven N. Wilson, C.Ss.R.; Bros. Eugene Patin, C.Ss.R.; Paul Jorns, C.Ss.R. In Res., Rev. John Phelps, C.Ss.R.
Res.: 2153 S. Millard Ave., 60623. Tel: 773-521-5595; Fax: 773-521-6076.
30—ST. BONAVENTURE, Rev. James A. Heneghan; Sr. Patricia Doody, O.S.F., Pastoral Assoc.; Deacon Antero Santos. In Res., Revs. Richard E. Bulwith; Louis J. Cameli.
Res.: 1641 W. Diversey Pkwy., 60614. Tel: 773-281-6588; Fax: 773-281-1051.
School—Cardinal Bernardin Early Childhood Center, 1651 W. Diversey Pkwy., 60614. Tel: 773-975-6330; Fax: 773-975-6339. Sr. Barbara Jean Ciszek, C.S.J., Prin.
31—ST. BRIDE, Unassigned.
Res.: 7811 S. Coles Ave., 60649. Tel: 773-731-8822.
School—7760 South Shore Dr., 60649. Tel: 773-721-5459; Fax: 773-721-0673. Lay Teachers 11; Students 202.
32—ST. BRONISLAVA, Revs. Michael J. Bonner, S.V.D., Admin.; Jesus Puentes (Colombia).
Res.: 8708 S. Colfax Ave., 60617. Tel: 773-734-0776; Fax: 773-734-1429.
Catechesis/Religious Program—Students 200.
33—ST. BRUNO, Revs. Waldemar Aleksander Kilian; Antoni Bury (Poland); Deacons Sal Villa; Lawrence Chyba. In Res., Rev. Ernest D. Ciemiega (Retired).
Res.: 4751 S. Harding Ave., 60632. Tel: 773-523-3467; Fax: 773-523-4253.
School—Tel: 773-847-0697; Fax: 773-847-1620. Lay Teachers 14; Students 320.
Catechesis/Religious Program—Students 230.
34—ST. CAJETAN, Revs. John H. Barkemeyer; Edward Pelrine; Brigid Wolff, Pastoral Assoc.
Parish Center Office—2445 W. 112th St., 60655. Fax: 773-474-7878.
Res.: 11234 S. Artesian Ave., 60655. Tel: 773-238-4100.
School—2447 W. 112th St., 60655. Tel: 773-233-8844. Lay Teachers 27; Students 528.
Catechesis/Religious Program—Students 160.
35—ST. CAMILLUS, Revs. Waclaw L. Lech O.C.D. (GRY); Michael G. Veneklase, O.C.D. (GRY). In Res., Rev. Norman M. Czajka, Pastor Emeritus (Retired).
Res.: 5426 S. Lockwood Ave., 60638. Tel: 773-767-8183; Fax: 773-284-3812.
School—5434 S. Lockwood Ave., 60638. Tel: 773-767-6977; Fax: 773-767-2633. Albertine Sisters 3; Lay Teachers 12; Students 165.
Catechesis/Religious Program—Students 460.
36—CHRIST THE KING, Revs. Patrick J. Pollard; William Wilkosz; Deacons Larry Antonsen; William Hurley. In Res., Rev. Thomas J. Raftery (Retired).
Res.: 9235 S. Hamilton Ave., 60620. Tel: 773-238-4877; Fax: 773-238-4963.
School—9240 S. Hoyne Ave., 60620. Tel: 773-779-3329. Lay Teachers 23; Students 303.
37—CHRIST THE REDEEMER BYZANTINE BIELARUSIAN, Closed., Consult Archives and Records Center for parish records.
38—ST. CHRISTINA, Revs. Martin E. O'Donovan; Charles Balskus; Wayne A. Svida; Deacon Thomas Ryan.
Res.: 11005 S. Homan Ave., 60655. Tel: 773-779-7181; Fax: 773-238-2942.
School—Tel: 773-445-2969; Fax: 773-445-0444. Lay Teachers 31; Students 783.
Catechesis/Religious Program—3333 W. 10th St., 60655. Tel: 773-445-2969; Fax: 773-238-2942. Students 783.
39—ST. CLARE OF MONTEFALCO, Rev. Ramiro Trejo, O.F.M.Cap.; Deacon Gregorio Bustos. In Res., Rev. Michael Sullivan, O.F.M.Cap.
Res.: 5443 S. Washtenaw Ave., 60632. Tel: 773-436-4422; Fax: 773-476-1888.
Catechesis/Religious Program—Students 207.
40—ST. CLEMENT, Revs. Thomas E. Hickey; Mark Greschel. In Res., Rev. Thomas Dennis (SFD).
Res.: 642 W. Deming Pl., 60614. Tel: 773-281-0371; Fax: 773-281-2509.
School—2524 N. Orchard St., 60614. Tel: 773-348-8212; Fax: 773-348-4712. Anne Rog, Prin. Lay Teachers 22; Students 237.
Catechesis/Religious Program—Students 150.
41—ST. CLOTILDE, Rev. John B. Atoyebi.
Res.: 8430 Calumet Ave., 60619. Tel: 773-874-1022; Fax: 773-874-1736.
School—321 E. 84th St., 60619. Tel: 773-488-4214. Ms. Shirley Hackney-DeSadier, Prin. Lay Teachers 10; Students 165.
Catechesis/Religious Program—
42—ST. COLUMBA, Rev. Kilian Knittel.
Res.: 13323 S. Greenbay Ave., 60633. Tel 773-646-2660; Fax: 773-646-6821.
Catechesis/Religious Program—
43—ST. COLUMBANUS, Rev. Matthew S. Eyerman; Deacons William McKinnis; George Borha.
Res.: 331 E. 71st St., 60619. Tel: 773-224-1022; Fax: 773-224-1477.
School—7120 S. Calumet, 60619. Tel: 773-224-3811; Fax: 773-224-3810. Lay Teachers 25 Students 425.
Catechesis/Religious Program—Students 35.
44—ST. CONSTANCE, Revs. Thaddeus Dzieszko; Tomasz Radecki, S.V.D.; Marek Kaskperczuk (Poland); Jacek Wrona (Poland); Sr. Marie Ellen Sullivan, Pastoral Assoc.; Deacons Ted Lisowski; George Griech, Pastoral Assoc.; James Schiltz, Pastoral Assoc. In Res., Rev. Thomas J. Paprocki.
Res.: 5843 W. Strong St., 60630. Tel: 773-545-8581; Fax: 773-545-0227.
School—5841 W. Strong St., 60630. Tel: 773-283-2311. Lay Teachers 17; Students 269.
45—ST. CORNELIUS, Revs. Edwin D. Pacocha; Thomas Refermat, S.T.L., M.Div., M.A.; Deacons Carl D. Olson; Edward Condon.
Res.: 5205 N. Lieb Ave., 60630. Tel: 773-283-5222; Fax: 773-283-8484.
School—Tel: 773-283-2192; Fax: 773-283-1377. Lay Teachers 21; Students 350.
Catechesis/Religious Program—Students 100.
46—CORPUS CHRISTI, Revs. Donatus Anosike, M.S.P.; Charles Atuah, M.S.P. In Res., Rev. Cajetan Ebuziem (Nigeria).
Corpus Christi Friary: 4920 King Dr., 60615-2306. Tel: 773-285-7720; Fax: 773-285-2572.
Catechesis/Religious Program—Students 20.
47—ST. DANIEL THE PROPHET, Revs. Lawrence J. Malcolm; Jacek Dada (Poland); Sr. Eileen Tierney, C.N.D., Pastoral Assoc.; Deacons Albert Malec; Chester Golab. In Res., Rev. John M. Cassidy (Retired).
Res.: 5330 S. Nashville Ave., 60638. Tel: 773-586-1223; Fax: 773-586-1238.
School—5337 S. Natoma Ave., 60638. Tel: 773-586-1225; Fax: 773-586-1232. Lay Teachers 31 Students 722.
Catechesis/Religious Program—Tel: 773-586-0660.
48—ST. DENIS, Rev. Lawrence R. Dowling; Sr. Norine Burns, O.P., Pastoral Assoc.; Deacons Thomas Ewers; Thomas Solon.
Res.: 8301 S. St. Louis Ave., 60652. Tel: 773-434-3313; Fax: 773-776-3922.
Catechesis/Religious Program—Sr. Elizabeth Lynch, O.P., D.R.E. Students 80.
49—ST. DOROTHY, Revs. James J. Martin; James D. Beath; Longinus Obasi (Nigeria); Deacons Roscoe Dixon; Wallace Harris.
Res.: 450 E. 78th St., 60619. Tel: 773-651-7000; Fax: 773-651-0969.
School—7740 S. Eberhart Ave., 60619. Tel 773-783-0555; Fax: 773-783-3736. Sisters of the Presentation of the Blessed Virgin Mary 1; Lay Teachers 15; Students 271.
Catechesis/Religious Program—Tel: 773-651-7000; Fax: 773-651-0969. Students 75.
50—ST. EDWARD, Revs. John M. Murphy; Henry C. Kricek. In Res., Rev. Joseph C. Taylor (Retired).
Res.: 4350 W. Sunnyside Ave., 60630-4147. Tel: 773-545-6496; Fax: 773-545-1136.
School—4343 W. Sunnyside Ave., 60630-4147. Tel: 773-736-9133; Fax: 773-736-9280. Dominican Sisters (Springfield, IL) 7; Lay Teachers 22; Students 404.
Catechesis/Religious Program—Students 175.
51—ST. ELIZABETH, Rev. Richard Andrus, S.V.D.
Res.: 50 E. 41st St., 60653. Tel: 773-268-1518; Fax: 773-268-2640.
School—4052 S. Wabash, 60653. Tel: 773-548-4100; Fax: 773-373-8642. Sisters 7; Lay Teachers 18; Students 315.
Catechesis/Religious Program—Students 315.
52—EPIPHANY, Revs. Peter B. McQuinn; Daniel Long, L.C.
Res.: 2524 S. Keeler Ave., 60623. Tel: 773-521-1112; Fax: 773-521-4394.
School—4225 W. 25th St., 60623. Tel: 773-762-1542. Sr. Elizabeth Pardo, I.H.M., Prin. Sisters 1; Lay Teachers 13; Students 190.
Catechesis/Religious Program—Sr. Berta Lopez, M.H.S.P.X. D.R.E. Students 400.
53—ST. ETHELREDA, Rev. James F. Nallen.
Res.: 8754 S. Paulina St., 60620. Tel: 773-238-6118; Fax: 773-238-6059.
School—8734 S. Paulina St., 60620. Tel: 773-238-1757; Fax: 773-238-6059. Lay Teachers 12 Students 164.
54—ST. EUGENE, Revs. James J. O'Brien; Philip J. Grib, S.J.; William J. Costello; Deacons Gerard Kwasegroch; Edward O'Leary. In Res., Rev. Peter M. Yangas (Retired).
Res.: 7958 W. Foster Ave., 60656-1698. Tel: 773-775-6659; Fax: 773-775-2832.
School—7930 W. Foster Ave., 60656. Tel: 773-763-2235; Fax: 773-763-2775. Sisters of Charity B.V.M. 1; Lay Teachers 23; Students 518.
Catechesis/Religious Program—Students 163.
55—ST. FELICITAS, Revs. John T. Boyle; Augustine Ogumere, C.S.Sp.; Casimir Eke, C.S.Sp.; Deacons James Hubbard; John Cook. In Res., Rev. Casimir Eke, C.S.Sp.
Res.: 1526 E. 84th St., 60619. Tel: 773-734-2300; Fax: 773-731-5381.
School—1501 E. 83rd Pl., 60652. Tel: 773-721-0858; Fax: 773-731-0142. Lay Teachers 13; Students 226.
Catechesis/Religious Program—Students 40.
56—ST. FERDINAND, Revs. David J. Cortesi; Roman Rataj (Poland); William M. Holbrook (Retired); Marek Jurzyk (Poland); Mr. Daniel P. Costigan, Business Mgr.; Deacons Irwin Hotcaveg; Ron Weiner. In Res., Rev. Joseph Kromenaker.
Res.: 5900 W. Barry Ave., 60634. Tel: 773-622-5900; Fax: 773-622-5903.
School—3131 N. Mason Ave., 60634. Tel: 773-622-3022; Fax: 773-622-2807. Dr. Lucine Mastalerz, Prin. Lay Teachers 24; Students 369.
Catechesis/Religious Program—Tel: 773-622-5900, Ext. 366. Students 118.
57—ST. FIDELIS, Sr. Leonette Kaluzny, S.Sp.S., Pastoral Coord.; Deacon Jose Alvarez.
Res.: 1406 N. Washtenaw Ave., 60622. Tel: 773-486-8700; Fax: 773-486-8944.
Catechesis/Religious Program—Students 165.
58—FIVE HOLY MARTYRS, Revs. Gerald Grupczynski, S.Ch.; Julian Kaczowka, S.Ch.; Boguslaw Burgat, S.Ch.; Deacon Richard Wieczorek. In Res., Rev. Adam Bobola, S.Ch.
Res.: 4327 S. Richmond St., 60632. Tel: 773-254-3636; Fax: 773-254-3609.
School—Pope John Paul II School, Five Holy Martyrs Campus, 4325 S. Richmond St., 60632. Tel: 773-523-6161; Fax: 773-254-9194. Sisters 4; Lay Teachers 26; Students 433.
Catechesis/Religious Program—Students 208.
59—ST. FLORIAN, Rev. James A. Mezydlo.
Res.: 13145 S. Houston Ave., 60633. Tel: 773-646-4877; Fax: 773-646-5965.
School—Tel: 773-646-2868; Fax: 773-646-2891. Lay Teachers 12; Students 177.
60—ST. FRANCIS BORGIA, Revs. Andrew P. Wypych; Gerald Walsh; Deacons Robert Cnota; Casimir Fronczek; Ralph Hinch; Charles Huber; Emil L. Melkovitz; William Lehman. In Res., Revs. Joseph A. Mulcrone; Joseph P. Grembla (Retired).
Res.: 8033 W. Addison St., 60634. Tel: 773-625-1118; Fax: 773-625-1110.
School—Tel: 773-589-1000. Lay Teachers 22; Students 455.
Catechesis/Religious Program—Tel: 773-625-1705. Students 200.
Convent—3521 N. Panama St., 60634. Tel: 773-625-8063.
61—ST. FRANCIS DE SALES, Revs. Juan Sanchez-Espinoza; Phillip C. Kiley; Francis Javier Maciel (Mexico); Deacon Joseph Pastirik, (Retired). In Res., Revs. James P. Keating, Pastor Emeritus (Retired); Ildephonse Skorup, O.F.M.
Res.: 10201 S. Ewing Ave., 60617. Tel: 773-734-1383; Fax: 773-734-3022.
Catechesis/Religious Program—Students 335.
62—ST. FRANCIS OF ASSISI, (Hispanic), Rev. Donald J. Nevins; Deacons Zeferino Ochoa; Manuel Rodriguez; Arturo Velasco.
Res.: 813 W. Roosevelt Rd., 60608. Tel: 312-226-7575; Fax: 312-226-6283.
Catechesis/Religious Program—Tel: 312-226-7575; Fax: 312-226-6283. Students 355.
63—ST. FRANCIS OF ASSISI/OUR LADY OF THE ANGELS, Rev. Tirso S. Villaverde; Deacon Sabino Sanchez.
Res.: 932 N. Kostner, 60651. Tel: 773-235-3132; Fax: 773-486-7726.
Catechesis/Religious Program—4418 W. Walton, 60651. Students 150.
64—ST. GABRIEL, Rev. John P. McNalis.
Res.: 4522 S. Wallace St., 60609. Tel: 773-268-9595; Fax: 773-268-9586.
Church: 45th St. and Lowe Ave., 60609.
School—4500 S. Wallace St., 60609. Tel: 773-268-6636; Fax: 773-268-2501. Lay Teachers 12; Students 250.
Catechesis/Religious Program—Students 150.
65—ST. GALL, Revs. John W. Dearhammer; Marco Farfan (Colombia); Deacons Michael Slajchert; Albert Herrera; John Bumbul. In Res., Rev. Robert Tuzik.
Res.: 5511 S. Sawyer Ave., 60629. Tel: 773-737-3113; Fax: 773-737-0272.
School—5515 S. Sawyer Ave., 60629. Tel: 773-737-3454. Lay Teachers 13; Students 365.
Catechesis/Religious Program—Students 511.
66—ST. GELASIUS, Closed., Consult Archives and Records Center for parish and school records.
67—ST. GENEVIEVE, Revs. Leoncio S. Santiago; Jose

Alberto Barreto (Argentina); Sr. Jean Michael Rafferty, S.P., Pastoral Assoc.; Deacon Benito Centeno.
Res.: 4835 W. Altgeld St., 60639. Tel: 773-237-3011; Fax: 773-237-3043.
School—4854 W. Montana St., 60639. Tel: 773-237-7131; Fax: 773-237-7265. Lay Teachers 17; Students 297.
Catechesis/Religious Program—Tel: 773-637-6086; Fax: 773-237-3043. Students 326.

68—St. George, (Slovenian), Revs. Juan Sanchez-Espinoza; Phillip C. Kiley; Francisco Javier Maciel Estrada (Mexico).
Res.: 9546 S. Ewing Ave., 60617. Tel: 773-734-0554; Fax: 773-734-3327.
Catechesis/Religious Program—Tel: 773-734-1383. Students 225.

69—St. Gertrude, Rev. William G. Kenneally; Mr. Peter Buttitta, Pastoral Assoc.
Res.: 1420 W. Granville Ave., 60660. Tel: 773-764-3621; Fax: 773-761-4164.
School—Northside Catholic Academy, 6216 N. Glenwood Ave., 60660. Tel: 773-743-6277; Fax: 773-743-6174. Lay Teachers 17; Students 300.
Catechesis/Religious Program—Students 50.

70—Good Shepherd, Revs. Marco A. Mercado; William E. Zimmer.
Res.: 2719 S. Kolin Ave., 60623. Tel: 773-762-2322; Fax: 773-762-4885.
School—2733 S. Kolin Ave., 60623. Lay Teachers 15; Students 246.
Catechesis/Religious Program—Students 390.

71—St. Gregory, Revs. Bartholomew S. Winters; Brian J. Fischer; Sr. Barbara Quinn, S.N.D.deN., Pastoral Assoc. In Res., Revs. John P. Moulder; Donatus Chukwu (Nigeria).
Res.: 1634 W. Gregory St., 60640. Tel: 773-561-3546; Fax: 773-728-3827.
High School—1677 W. Bryn Mawr Ave., 60660. Tel: 773-907-2100; Fax: 773-907-2120. Lay Teachers 24; Students 261.
Catechesis/Religious Program—Students 118.

72—St. Hedwig, Revs. Gary Hogan, C.R.; Casimir V. Polinski, C.R. In Res., Revs. Walter Wilczek, C.R. (Retired); Eugene Szarek, C.R.; Deacons Gilberto Cintron; Salomon Villegas.
Res.: 2226 N. Hoyne Ave., 60647. Tel: 773-486-1660; Fax: 773-486-1684.
Catechesis/Religious Program—Students 105.

73—St. Helen, Rev. Richard Milek; Deacon Francisco Serna.
Res.: 2315 W. Augusta Blvd., 60622. Tel: 773-235-3575; Fax: 773-235-3810.
School—2347 W. Augusta Blvd., 60622. Tel: 773-486-1055. Lay Teachers 13; Students 198.
Catechesis/Religious Program—Fax: 773-235-3810. Students 10.

74—St. Helena, Rev. Thomas J. Kaminski; Deacons Daniel Sutton; Tommy West; Clayton Kort.
Res.: 10121 S. Parnell Ave., 60628. Tel: 773-779-2243; Fax: 773-779-2749.
School—10115 S. Parnell Ave., 60628. Tel: 773-238-5432; Fax: 773-238-6026. Lay Teachers 11; Students 242.
Catechesis/Religious Program—Students 247.

75—St. Henry, Rev. Dominic Vinh Van Ha; Deacon Frank G. Duffy.
Res.: 6335 N. Hoyne Ave., 60659. Tel: 773-764-7413; Fax: 773-764-5994.
School—Northside Catholic Academy, 6325 N. Hoyne, 60659. Tel: 773-274-5227; Fax: 773-274-2157.
Convent—1956 W. Devon, 60660.

76—St. Hilary, Rev. Robert G. Darow; Deacons Edmund Tryba, (Retired); Donald Wehling.
Res.: 5600 N. Fairfield Ave., 60659. Tel: 773-561-3474; Fax: 773-561-1129.
School—5614 N. Fairfield Ave., 60659. Tel: 773-561-5885; Fax: 773-561-6409. Lay Teachers 22; Students 405.
Catechesis/Religious Program—Students 100.

77—Holy Angels, Revs. Robert J. Miller, O.P., Admin.; John W. Calicott, (On Leave); Deacons Jasper Roy; Dexter Watson. In Res., Rev. David Kusi.
Res.: 607 E. Oakwood Blvd., 60653. Tel: 773-624-5375.
School—545 E. Oakwood Blvd., 60653. Priests 1; Sisters 18; Lay Teachers 30; Students 1,000.

78—Holy Cross/Immaculate Heart of Mary, Revs. Bruce Wellems, C.M.F.; George Ruffolo, C.M.F.; Thomas Joyce, C.M.F.
Res.: 4557 S. Wood St., 60609. Tel: 773-376-3900; Fax: 773-376-8929.
Catechesis/Religious Program—Students 760.

79—Holy Family, Rev. Jerimiah M. Boland, Admin.; Deacon Rudolph Kotleba.
Res.: 1019 S. May St., 60607. Tel: 312-492-8442; Fax: 312-492-8430.
Catechesis/Religious Program—Students 20.

80—Holy Innocents, Revs. Richard J. Klajbor; Stanislaus Kuca (Poland); Jose Luis Castillo (Mexico).
Res.: 743 N. Armour St., 60622. Tel: 312-666-3675; Fax: 312-666-0714.
Catechesis/Religious Program—Tel: 312-243-9887; Fax: 312-243-4524. Students 150.

81—Holy Name of Mary, Rev. James F. Flynn.
Res.: 11159 S. Loomis St., 60643. Tel: 773-238-6800; Fax: 773-238-7304.
Mission—Sacred Heart 11652 S. Church St., Cook Co. 60643. Tel: 773-233-3955.
Catechesis/Religious Program—Students 58.

82—Holy Rosary, Rev. Richard C. Creagh. In Res., Rev. Ronald L. Kondziolka.
Res.: 351 E. 113th St., 60628. Tel: 773-568-4455; Fax: 773-568-4456.
Catechesis/Religious Program—Students 40.

83—Holy Rosary, Most Rev. Lawrence Sabatini, C.S.; Deacon Jorge Rozo. In Res., Rev. William Woestman, O.M.I.
Res.: 612 N. Western Ave., 60612. Tel: 773-278-4820; Fax: 773-278-3770.
Catechesis/Religious Program—Students 76.

84—Holy Trinity, (Croatian), Rev. Esquiel Sanchez.
Res.: 1850 S. Throop St., 60608. Tel: 312-226-2736; Fax: 312-243-3459.
Catechesis/Religious Program—1850 S. Throop St., 60608. Sr. Maria del Rayo Cuaya-Castillo, S.H., D.R.E.

85—Holy Trinity Mission, (Polish), Revs. Pawel Bandurski, S.Ch.; Rafal Dygula, S.Ch.; Wieslaw Berdowicz, S.Ch.
Res.: 1118 N. Noble St., 60622-4015. Tel: 773-489-4140; Fax: 773-489-5918.
Catechesis/Religious Program—Students 650.

86—St. Hyacinth Basilica, Revs. Michael Osuch, C.R.; Francis Rog, C.R.; Chester Mitoraj, C.R.; Stanislaw Jankowski, C.R.; Jerzy Jedynak, C.R.; Jacek Junak, C.R.; Deacon Frank Girjatowicz; Bro. Thomas Iwicki, C.R.
Res.: 3636 W. Wolfram St., 60618. Tel: 773-342-3636; Fax: 773-342-3638.
School—3640 W. Wolfram St., 60618. Tel: 773-342-7550; Fax: 773-384-0581. Sisters of the Holy Family of Nazareth (Des Plaines) 2; Lay Teachers 14; Students 207.
Catechesis/Religious Program—Students 15.

87—St. Ignatius, Rev. Joseph M. Jackson. In Res., Revs. William P. Grogan; Gerardo Carcar (Paraguay); Patrick J. McAteer, S.J.; Andrew Hoolan (Ireland), Extern.
Res.: 6559 N. Glenwood Ave., 60626. Tel: 773-764-5936; Fax: 773-764-4360.
Catechesis/Religious Program—Students 118.

88—Immaculate Conception, Revs. Michael J. Hoolahan, C.P.; Eric Meyer, C.P.; Ronan Newbold, C.P.; Deacon Richard Moritz.
Res.: 7211 W. Talcott Ave., 60631. Tel: 773-775-3833; Fax: 773-631-1024.
School—7263 W. Talcott Ave., 60631. Tel: 773-775-0545; Fax: 773-775-3822. Lay Teachers 36; Students 576.
Catechesis/Religious Program—Tel: 773-775-0545, Ext. 216. Students 160.

89—Immaculate Conception, (Lithuanian), Revs. Thomas R. Koys; Edward J. Maza; Deacons Vincente Estrada; Roberto Rivas. In Res., Rev. Jaunius Kelpsas (Lithuania).
Res.: 2745 W. 44th St., 60632-1999. Tel: 773-523-1402; Fax: 773-523-8465.
School—Tel: 773-523-6161; Fax: 773-254-9194. Consolidated with Five Holy Martyrs to form Pope John Paul II School. See Five Holy Martyrs, Chicago for details.
Catechesis/Religious Program—Students 150.

90—Immaculate Conception of the Blessed Virgin Mary, Rev. Patrick J. Lee. In Res., Rev. Mark Kalema.
Res.: 1431 N. North Park Ave., 60610. Tel: 312-944-1230; Fax: 312-944-0673.
Catechesis/Religious Program—Students 95.

91—Immaculate Conception of the Blessed Virgin Mary, Rev. Michael P. Enright.
Parish Office and Rectory—2944 E. 88th St., 60627. Tel: 773-768-2100.
Church: 88th & Commercial Ave., 60617.
School—8739 S. Exchange, 60617. Tel: 773-375-4674. Sr. Maria de Jesus Nunez, Prin.
Catechesis/Religious Program—Tel: 773-221-1423. Students 230.

92—Immaculate Heart of Mary, Revs. James F. Blazek; Joji Thanugundla; Deacons John Kearney; Kenneth Jenney Jr.; David Reyes. In Res., Revs. Robert Onofrey, C.PP.S.; Phillip Thodukayil.
Res.: 3817 N. Christiana Ave., 60618. Tel: 773-478-1157; Fax: 773-478-6044.
School—3820 N. Spaulding Ave., 60618. Tel: 773-478-6554. Lay Teachers 13; Students 250.
Catechesis/Religious Program—Students 100.

93—Immaculate Heart of Mary Vicariate, Closed., See Holy Cross, Wood St.

94—Saint Ita, Revs. Steven W. Patte; Claudio Diaz. In Res., Rev. Matthias Ocamuna (Uganda).
Res.: 1220 West Catalpa Ave., 60640. Tel: 773-561-5343; Fax: 773-561-5609.
School—Northside Catholic Academy, 5525 N. Magnolia Ave., 60640. Tel: 773-271-2008; Fax: 773-271-3101. Lay Teachers 12; Students 135.
Catechesis/Religious Program—Students 230.

95—St. James, Revs. Edward Linton, O.S.B.; Jamels James (India). In Res., Rev. Anselm Russell, O.S.B. (IND).
Res.: 2942 S. Wabash Ave., 60616. Tel: 312-842-1919; Fax: 312-842-3612.
School—2920 S. Wabash Ave., 60616. Sisters 2; Lay Teachers 12; Students 270.
Catechesis/Religious Program—Students 14.

96—St. James, Revs. Wojciech Kwiecien; John L. Wodniak, Pastor Emeritus (Retired); Piotr Wasek (Poland); Jose del Carmen Mendez.
Res.: 5730 W. Fullerton Ave., 60639. Tel: 773-237-1474; Fax: 773-237-1546.
Catechesis/Religious Program—Tel: 773-237-1474; Fax: 773-237-1546. Students 900.

97—St. Jane de Chantal, Rev. Joseph J. Wojcik; Deacon Ron Morowczynski.
Res.: 5252 S. Austin Ave., 60638. Tel: 773-767-2411; Fax: 773-767-2769.
School—5201 S. McVicker Ave., 60638. Tel: 773-767-1130. Lay Teachers 13; Students 236.
Catechesis/Religious Program—Students 92.

98—St. Jerome, Rev. Jeremy Thomas (Wales), Admin.; Deacons Fritz Jean-Pierre; Sigifredo Hernandez; Victor LaCoursiere; Robert Murphy; Raymond Ward; Elisco Ramos; Francisco Marin.
Res.: 1709 W. Lunt Ave., 60626. Tel: 773-262-3170; Fax: 773-262-2834.
Catechesis/Religious Program—1706 W. Morse Ave., 60626. Tel: 773-262-9880; Fax: 773-262-2834. Students 205.

99—St. Jerome, (Croatian), Revs. Jozo Grbes, O.F.M.; Tomislav Puljic, O.F.M.
Res.: 2823 S. Princeton Ave., Cardinal Stepinac Way, 60616. Tel: 312-842-1871; Fax: 312-842-6427.
School—2813 S. Princeton Ave., 60616. Tel: 312-842-7668; Fax: 312-842-6427. Lay Teachers 19; Students 211.
Catechesis/Religious Program—1706 W. Morse Ave., 60616. Tel: 773-262-9880; Fax: 773-262-2834. Students 45.

100—St. Joachim, Rev. John M. Collins. In Res., Rev. Modest Odama (Uganda).
Res.: 700 E. 91st St., 60619. Tel: 773-488-4488; Fax: 773-994-8945.

101—St. John Berchmans, Rev. Eugene W. Gratkowski; Deacons Virgilio Bonifazi; Jorge Cabrera; Guillermo Mendizabal.
Res.: 2517 W. Logan Blvd., 60647. Tel: 773-486-4300.
School—2509 W. Logan Blvd., 60647. Tel: 773-486-1334; Fax: 773-486-1782. Dominican Sisters (St. Catherine, KY) 1; Lay Teachers 21; Students 537.
Catechesis/Religious Program—Students 263.

102—St. John Bosco, Revs. William Bucciferro, S.D.B.; Serges Lamaute, S.D.B.; Juan Bosco Jiminez, S.D.B.; Thomas Provenzano, S.D.B.; Slawomir Walczak, S.D.B.; Oswaldo Guillen, S.D.B. (Venezuela) (WDC); Deacon Ronald Swiatek.
Res.: 2250 N. McVicker Ave., 60639. Tel: 773-622-4620; Fax: 773-622-5040.

103—St. John Cantius, (Polish), Revs. C. Frank Phillips, C.R.; Burns K. Seeley; Albert Tremari.
Res.: 825 N. Carpenter St., 60622. Tel: 312-243-7373; Fax: 312-666-4545.
Catechesis/Religious Program—Students 50.

104—St. John de la Salle, Rev. Michael P. Knotek.
Res.: 10205 King Dr., 60628. Tel: 773-785-2022.
School—Tel: 773-785-2331. Linda Bond, Prin. Lay Teachers 12; Students 280.
Catechesis/Religious Program—Students 8.

105—St. John Fisher, Revs. Robert J. Kyfes; Thomas J. Purtell, Pastor Emeritus; Frank Latzko; Daniel F. Costello; Deacons Sidney Mench; Raymond Reilly; Clayton Kort; Martin Mongan.
Res.: 10234 S. Washtenaw Ave., 60655. Tel: 773-445-6565; Fax: 773-445-1644.
School—10200 S. Washtenaw Ave., 60655. Tel: 773-445-4737; Fax: 773-233-3012. Sisters of St. Joseph (LaGrange, IL) 2; Lay Teachers 41; Students 820.
Catechesis/Religious Program—Tel: 773-238-1851. Students 175.

106—St. Josaphat, Rev. Dominic J. Grassi; Deacon Daniel Welter. In Res., Rev. Michael J. Bradley.
Res.: 2311 N. Southport Ave., 60614. Tel: 773-327-8955; Fax: 773-327-2047.
School—2245 N. Southport Ave., 60614. Tel: 773-549-0909; Fax: 773-549-3127. Lay Teachers 17; Students 252.
Catechesis/Religious Program—Students 50.

107—St. Joseph, Rev. Patrick J. Lee.
Res.: 1107 N. Orleans St., 60610. Tel: 312-787-7174; Fax: 312-787-9825.
Catechesis/Religious Program—Students 15.

108—ST. JOSEPH, Revs. Edward Shea, O.F.M.; Rogelio Martinez, O.F.M.
Res.: 4821 S. Hermitage Ave., 60609. Tel: 773-254-2366; Fax: 773-254-2640.
Catechesis/Religious Program—

109—ST. JULIANA, Revs. Philip J. Dressler; Donald J. Ahearn, Pastor Emeritus (Retired); Robert Grib, S.J.; Michael McGovern; Ms. Pam Francisco, Pastoral Assoc.; Deacons Michael Finnegan; Robert Ryan; Edward Dolan; Louis Wojtowicz.
Res.: 7142 N. Osceola Ave., 60631. Tel: 773-631-4127; Fax: 773-631-4150.
School—7400 W. Touhy, 60648. Tel: 773-631-2256. Lay Teachers 35; Religious 2; Students 714.
Catechesis/Religious Program—Students 160.

110—ST. KEVIN, Rev. Alfredo Gundrum, O.F.M.Cap. In Res., Rev. Campion R. Baer, O.F.M.Cap.
Res.: 10509 S. Torrence Ave., 60617. Tel: 773-721-2563; Fax: 773-721-2208.
Catechesis/Religious Program—Tel: 708-862-6292; Fax: 773-721-2563.

111—ST. KILIAN, Revs. William E. Vanecko; John W. Shirey (Retired); Deacon Warren Allen.
Res.: 8725 S. May St., 60620. Tel: 773-651-4000; Fax: 773-651-5876.
Catechesis/Religious Program—Students 20.

112—ST. LADISLAUS, Revs. Stephen F. Kanonik; Andrzej Bartos (Poland); Mariusz Nawalaniec (Poland). In Res., Rev. John Hergenrother.
Res.: 5345 W. Roscoe St., 60641. Tel: 773-725-2300; Fax: 773-725-6042.
School—3330 N. Lockwood Ave., 60641. Tel: 773-545-5600; Fax: 773-545-5676. Sisters of the Holy Family of Nazareth (Des Plaines, IL) 3; Lay Teachers 10; Students 170.
Catechesis/Religious Program—Tel: 773-545-5809; Fax: 773-545-4340. Students 100.

113—ST. LAURENCE, Closed., Consult Archives and Records Center for parish and school records.

114—ST. LEO THE GREAT, Closed., Consult Archives and Records Center for parish and school records.

115—ST. MALACHY, Rev. Patrick T. Casey, O.M.I.
Res.: 2251 W. Washington Blvd., 60612. Tel: 312-733-1068; Fax: 312-491-9164.
School—2252 W. Washington Blvd., 60612. Tel: 312-733-2252; Fax: 312-733-5703. Sisters 1; Lay Teachers 12; Students 350.
Catechesis/Religious Program—Students 325.

116—ST. MARGARET MARY, Revs. Mark B. Sorvillo; John R. Lynch; Ha Nam Thanh Dao.
Res.: 2324 W. Chase Ave., 60645. Tel: 773-764-0615; Fax: 773-764-0641.
School—Tel: 773-764-0641; Fax: 773-764-1095. Lay Teachers 27; Students 300.
Catechesis/Religious Program—Students 65.

117—ST. MARGARET OF SCOTLAND, Revs. Daniel J. Mallette; Claude Souffrant, S.J.
Res.: 9837 S. Throop St., 60643. Tel: 773-779-5151; Fax: 773-779-6198.
School—9833 S. Throop St., 60643. Tel: 773-238-1088; Fax: 773-238-1049. School Sisters of Notre Dame 2; Lay Teachers 25; Students 480.
Shelter—Maryville/St. Margaret of Scotland. Tel: 773-371-2500; Fax: 773-371-2515. Students 35.
Catechesis/Religious Program—Students 110.

118—ST. MARK, Rev. Michael J. Shanahan; Deacons Jorge Gutierrez; Ignacio Ortega; Antonio Villalobos; Mel Maldonado; Antonio Navarro. In Res., Most Rev. Enrique Hernandez; Rev. Daniel J. Cassidy.
Res.: 1048 N. Campbell Ave., 60622. Tel: 773-342-1516; Fax: 773-342-1372.
School—2510 W. Cortez St., 60622. Tel: 773-486-0430; Fax: 773-342-7118. Sisters of Providence 3; Lay Teachers 9; Students 270.

119—ST. MARTIN DE PORRES, Rev. Kenneth M. Brigham; Deacon Anthony Llorens. In Res., Rev. Michael Okoye (Africa).
Res.: 5112 W. Washington Blvd., 60644. Tel: 773-287-0206; Fax: 773-261-2344.
School—5072 W. Jackson Blvd., 60661. Tel: 773-261-6061; Fax: 773-626-0780. Lay Teachers 18; Students 320.

120—ST. MARY MAGDALENE, Rev. Daniel L. Walsh, C.S.Sp. In Res., Revs. James Okoye, C.S.Sp.; Bernard A. Kelly, C.S.Sp.
Res.: 8426 S. Marquette Ave., 60617. Tel: 773-768-1700; Fax: 773-734-8518.
Catechesis/Religious Program—Students 30.

121—ST. MARY OF PERPETUAL HELP, Rev. Donald R. Craig.
Res.: 1039 W. 32nd St., 60608. Tel: 773-927-6646; Fax: 773-523-4565.
Catechesis/Religious Program—Students 110.

122—ST. MARY OF THE ANGELS, Revs. Hilary F. Mahaney; John P. Debicki. In Res., Rev. Charles M. Ferrer.
Res.: 1850 N. Hermitage Ave., 60622. Tel: 773-278-2644; Fax: 773-278-8904.
School—1810 N. Hermitage Ave., 60622. Tel: 773-486-0119. Sisters of the Resurrection (Chicago, IL) 1; Lay Teachers 12; Students 200.
Catechesis/Religious Program—Students 200.

123—ST. MARY OF THE ASSUMPTION, Rev. John L. Harvey; Deacon John Amberg.
Res.: 310 E. 137th St., 60827. Tel: 773-568-1611; Fax: 773-568-6268.
School—*Our Lady of the Gardens*, 13300 S. Langley Ave., 60627. Tel: 773-568-4099; Fax 773-568-4718. Daughters of Charity 3; Lay Teachers 11.
Catechesis/Religious Program—Students 50.

124—ST. MARY OF THE LAKE, Rev. James A. Colleran; Deacons Paul Spalla; John Navolio; Romeo Munoz, Pastoral Assoc. In Res., Revs. Daniel J. Collins (Retired); Thomas A. Tivy; Robert Grodnicki, O.S.A.
Res.: 4200 N. Sheridan Rd., 60613. Tel: 773-472-3711; Fax: 773-327-2899.
School—1026 W. Buena Ave., 60613. Tel 773-281-0018; Fax: 773-281-0112. Lay Teachers 11 Students 285.
Catechesis/Religious Program—Students 150.

125—ST. MARY OF THE WOODS, Revs. Gregory Sakowicz; Leo T. Mahon, Pastor Emeritus (Retired); Deacons William Mages; George Hennig. In Res., Revs. Thomas F. Maher (Retired); Donald J. Headley (Retired); Marcia Mahoney, Pastoral Assoc.
Res.: 7033 N. Moselle Ave., 60646. Tel: 773-763-0206; Fax: 773-763-4968.
School—Tel: 773-763-7577; Fax: 773-763-4293. Religious 1; Lay Teachers 25; Students 498.
Catechesis/Religious Program—Students 155.

126—ST. MARY, STAR OF THE SEA, Revs. John J. McDonnell Michael J. Adams, Pastor Emeritus (Retired); Antony Aravindassery (India); Daniel Jarosewic; Deacons Jesse Navarro; Gregory Serratore.
Res.: 6435 S. Kilbourn Ave., 60629. Tel: 773-767-1246.
School—6424 S. Kenneth Ave., 60629. Tel: 773-767-6160. Lay Teachers 26; Students 575.
Catechesis/Religious Program—Tel: 773-767-7078. Students 147.

127—MATERNITY OF THE BLESSED VIRGIN MARY, Revs. Thomas Paxton; Manuel G. Padilla; Deacons Jorge Garcia; Felipe Gonzalez; Floro Hita; Milton Rodriguez; Jose Vazquez; Benito Velasco.
Res.: 3647 W. North Ave., 60647. Tel: 773-772-9401; Fax: 773-772-7454.
School—1537 N. Lawndale Ave., 60651. Tel: 773-227-1140; Fax: 773-227-2939. Sisters of Providence of Saint Mary-of-the-Woods, IN 2; Lay Teachers 12; Students 202.
Catechesis/Religious Program—Students 445.

128—ST. MATTHIAS, Revs. Terence M. Keehan; Elmer Romero; Deacons John Fay; D.J. Shinkle In Res., Rev. Francis A. Cimarrusti.
Res.: 2310 W. Ainslie St., 60625. Tel: 773-506-2191; Fax: 773-506-2418.
School—4910 N. Claremont Ave., 60625. Tel: 773-784-0999; Fax: 773-784-3601. Sisters 5; Lay Teachers 9; Students 222.
Catechesis/Religious Program—5044 N. Rockwell. Students 169.

129—ST. MAURICE, Revs. Richard J. Martin Admin.; Oscar Dario Colorado Montoya (Colombia); Deacon Dismas Fernandez.
Res.: 3615 S. Hoyne Ave., 60609. Tel: 773-847-3357; Fax: 773-847-3804.
Catechesis/Religious Program—Students 90.

130—ST. MICHAEL, Revs. John Schmidt, C.Ss.R.; Kenneth Sedlak, C.SS.R.; Michael Quinn, C.Ss.R. In Res., Revs. Edward Wilhelm, C.Ss.R.; John Paul Andree, C.SS.R.; John Dowd, C.Ss.R.; Peter Schavitz, C.Ss.R.; Robert Halter, C.Ss.R.; Daniel Andree, C.Ss.R.
Res.: 1633 N. Cleveland Ave., 60614. Tel: 312-642-2498; Fax: 312-642-9283.
Perpetual Help Confraternity Office—Tel: 312-642-9399; Fax: 312-642-9283. Bro. Patrick Considine, C.Ss.R.
Catechesis/Religious Program—Tel: 312-664-4655. Students 70.

131—ST. MICHAEL, Rev. Robert R. Perez. In Res., Rev. Paul J. Kalchik.
Res.: 8237 South Shore Dr., 60617. Tel: 773-734-4921; Fax: 773-734-8723.
School—8231 South Shore Dr., 60617. Tel: 773-221-0212. Sr. Judine Hilbing, O.P., Prin. Lay Teachers 13; Students 320.
Catechesis/Religious Program—Students 125.

132—ST. MICHAEL ARCHANGEL, (Italian), Closed., Consult Archives and Records Center for parish records.

133—ST. MICHAEL THE ARCHANGEL, (Slovak), Revs. John E. Tiford; Alfredo del Toro, M.C.C.J.; Sr. Rosemary Bell, D.S.M.P., Pastoral Assoc.
Res.: 4821 S. Damen Ave., 60609. Tel: 773-523-1248; Fax: 773-523-0955.
Catechesis/Religious Program—Students 441.

134—ST. MONICA, Revs. Michael A. Wulsch; Edward B. Panek; Sr. Kathleen Maloney, O.S.B., Pastoral Assoc.
Office—5136 N. Nottingham Ave., 60656. Tel: 773-763-1661; Fax: 773-763-4917.
Res.: 5135 N. Mont Clare Ave., 60656.
School—Tel: 773-631-7880; Fax: 773-631-3266. Sisters 2; Lay Teachers 21; Students 397.
Catechesis/Religious Program—Tel: 773-631-7810; Fax: 773-763-4917. Students 125.

135—NATIVITY OF OUR LORD, Rev. James P. Kehoe; Deacon Francis Henry. In Res., Rev. Michael Flynn, O.Carm.
Res.: 653 W. 37th St., 60609. Tel: 773-927-6263.
School—*Participant in Bridgeport Catholic Academy*, Tel: 773-376-6223. See separate listing under Consolidated Elementary Schools in the Institutions section.
Catechesis/Religious Program—Students 94.

136—NATIVITY OF THE BLESSED VIRGIN MARY, Rev. Rimantas Gudelis. In Res., Rev. Vito E. Mikolaitis (Retired).
Res.: 6812 S. Washtenaw Ave., 60629. Tel: 773-776-4600; Fax: 773-776-0677.
School—6820 S. Washtenaw Ave., 60629. Tel: 773-476-0571; Fax: 773-476-0065. Sisters of St. Casimir 2; Lay Teachers 9; Students 230.
Convent—6804 S. Washtenaw Ave., 60629. Tel: 773-476-5135.

137—ST. NICHOLAS OF TOLENTINE, Revs. Stanley G. Rataj; Francis P. Cassidy (Retired); Miguel Angel Martinez; Deacons Edwin Hill; Joaquin Verela.
Res.: 3721 W. 62nd St., 60629. Tel: 773-735-1121; Fax: 773-735-1135.
School—3743 W. 62nd St., 60629. Tel: 773-735-0772; Fax: 773-735-5414. Lay Teachers 12; Students 270.
Catechesis/Religious Program—Tel: 773-284-2635. Students 270.

138—NOTRE DAME, Rev. A. Paul Reicher; Sr. Kathleen Brazda, C.S.J., Pastoral Assoc.; Deacons Candelario Rodriguez; Eduardo Zavala. In Res., Rev. Alejandro Garrido.
Res.: 1335 W. Harrison St., 60607-3318. Tel: 312-243-7400; Fax: 312-243-7614.
Catechesis/Religious Program—Students 60.

139—OLD ST. MARY, Revs. Francis P. DeSiano, C.S.P.; Charles J. Brunick, C.S.P.; David Farnum, C.S.P.; Deacon Timothy Donovan.
Res.: 1500 S. Michigan, 60605. Tel: 312-922-3444; Fax: 312-922-3447.
Catechesis/Religious Program—Students 42.

140—OUR LADY GATE OF HEAVEN, Rev. Mel Hermanns, O.F.M.Cap.
Res.: 2338 E. 99th St., 60617. Tel: 773-375-3059; Fax: 773-375-3091.
School—2330 E. 99th St., 60617. Tel: 773-375-7350; Fax: 773-375-4756. Mr. Charles Carroll, Prin. Religious 1; Lay Teachers 7; Students 155; Preschool 26.
Catechesis/Religious Program—Students 35.

141—OUR LADY HELP OF CHRISTIANS, Revs. Kenneth M. Brigham; Maurice Mamba Ngalamulume, Extern; Deacon Abrom Salley.
Res.: 832 N. Leclaire Ave., 60651. Tel: 773-287-0244; Fax: 773-287-1258.
Catechesis/Religious Program—Students 68.

142—OUR LADY OF AGLONA, (Latvian), Revs. Boleslaus Baginskis, M.I.C.; Dainis Kass.
Res.: 2541 W. Wabansia, 60647. Tel: 773-276-9566.

143—OUR LADY OF FATIMA, Revs. Pierre J. Barr, Pastor Emeritus (Retired); Marco Cardenas, C.M.F.; Deacon Candido Torres.
Res.: 2751 W. 38th Pl., 60632. Tel: 773-927-2421.
School—*Pope John Paul II School, Our Lady of Fatima Campus*, 2744 W. Pershing Rd., 60632. Lay Teachers 12; Students 200.

144—OUR LADY OF GOOD COUNSEL, Revs. James M. Hyland; Richard J. O'Donnell, Pastor Emeritus (Retired).
Res.: 3528 S. Hermitage Ave., 60609. Tel: 773-523-3917; Fax: 773-247-9285.
Catechesis/Religious Program—Students 170.

145—OUR LADY OF GRACE, Rev. Jose Leonardo Gomez; Sr. Florence Norton, S.P., Pastoral Assoc.; Deacons James Kwasigroch; Enrique Alonso; Ernesto Robles. In Res., Most Rev. John R. Manz; Rev. Lawrence E. Gorski.
Res.: 2455 N. Hamlin Ave., 60647. Tel: 773-772-5900; Fax: 773-276-4469.
School—2446 N. Ridgeway Ave., 60647. Tel: 773-341-0170. Dominican Sisters (Springfield, IL) 7; Lay Teachers 12; Students 268.
Catechesis/Religious Program—Students 430.

146—OUR LADY OF GUADALUPE, Revs. James F. Maloney, C.M.F.; Thomas Moran, C.M.F.; Edmundo Andres, C.M.F.; Thomas Brummel, C.M.F.; Deacon Raul Nunez.
Res.: 3200 E. 91st, 60617. Tel: 773-768-0793; Fax: 773-768-3245.
School—Tel: 773-768-0999; Fax: 773-768-0529. Lay Teachers 16; Students 275.
Shrine—*National Shrine of St. Jude*, Tel: 312-236-7782; Fax: 312-236-7230. (Claretian Missionaries)

Catechesis/Religious Program—9049 S. Brandon, 60617. Tel: 773-734-0605. Students 370.

147—OUR LADY OF LOURDES, Revs. Curtis Lambert; Nester Saenz (Peru); Deacons Roy Henry; John Klemanovic; Daniel Patino; Bill Conway. In Res., Rev. James T. Kaczorowski.
Res.: 4640 N. Ashland Ave., 60640. Tel: 773-561-2141; Fax: 773-561-9853.
School—4641 N. Ashland Ave., 60640. Tel: 773-561-9348. Ms. Noel Ferrera, Prin. Lay Teachers 12; Students 150.
Catechesis/Religious Program—Students 425.

148—OUR LADY OF LOURDES, Rev. Ramon Dompke, C.SS.R.; Sr. Caritas Wehrman, S.S.N.D., Pastoral Assoc.
Res.: 1444 S. Keeler Ave., 60623. Tel: 773-762-5700; Fax: 773-762-5960.
Catechesis/Religious Program—Students 22.

149—OUR LADY OF MERCY, Revs. Joseh Tito; William Vanagas, Extern; Deacons Manuel R. Del Llano, Pastoral Assoc.; Robert Janega, Pastoral Assoc.; Ms. Theresita Perez, Pastoral Assoc. In Res., Rev. Patrick Rugen.
Res.: 4432 N. Troy St., 60625. Tel: 773-588-2620; Fax: 773-866-1838.
Catechesis/Religious Program—Students 622.

150—OUR LADY OF MOUNT CARMEL, Revs. Thomas E. Srenn; Thomas I. Healy, Pastor Emeritus (Retired); Joseph Thai Nguyen; Deacons Edmund Gronkiewicz; Thomas Lambert. In Res., Rev. Peter Snieg.
Res.: 690 W. Belmont Ave., 60657. Tel: 773-525-0453; Fax: 773-525-9438.
School—708 W. Belmont Ave., 60657. Tel: 773-525-8779; Fax: 773-525-7810. Lay Teachers 14; Students 230.
Catechesis/Religious Program—Tel: 773-348-4932. Students 64.

151—OUR LADY OF PEACE, Revs. Lawrence M. Duris; Natale Ezama (Uganda); Rev. Msgr. John Mary Kayanga (Uganda). In Res., Rev. Maximus Ssekiwala, Extern.
Res.: 7851 S. Jeffrey Ave., 60649. Tel: 773-768-0105; Fax: 773-721-3835.
Catechesis/Religious Program—Students 40.

152—OUR LADY OF POMPEII, , See St. Patrick, Shrine of Our Lady of Pompeii See St. Patrick, Shrine of Our Lady of Pompeii

153—OUR LADY OF SORROWS, BASILICA OF, Rev. Donald M. Siple, O.S.M.; Deacons Joseph Lewis; Alfred Bouey. In Res., Rev. Vidal M. Martinez, O.S.M.
Res.: 3121 W. Jackson Blvd., 60612. Tel: 773-638-0159; Fax: 773-638-3036.
Catechesis/Religious Program—

154—OUR LADY OF TEPEYAC, Revs. Robert G. Casey; Pedro Compos; Deacon Ramon Echaverria; Maria Brito-Ramos, Pastoral Assoc.
Res.: 2226 S. Whipple St., 60623. Tel: 773-521-8400; Fax: 773-521-4890.
School—2235 S. Albany, 60623. Tel: 773-522-0024; Fax: 773-522-4577. Lay Teachers 13; Students 210.
High School—2228 S. Whipple St., 60623. Tel: 773-522-0023; Fax: 773-522-0508. Sisters 4; Lay Teachers 14; Students 220.
Catechesis/Religious Program—Tel: 773-277-0320. Students 632.

155—OUR LADY OF THE SNOWS, Rev. Robert J. Wielosinski.
Res.: 4858 S. Leamington Ave., 60638. Tel: 773-582-2266; Fax: 773-582-3363.
School—4810 S. Leamington Ave., 60638. Tel: 773-735-4810; Fax: 773-582-3363. Lay Teachers 11; Students 250.
Catechesis/Religious Program—Tel: 773-582-4904. Students 101.

156—OUR LADY OF VICTORY, Revs. Philip E. Cyscon; Eugene R. Winkowski; Deacons Robert Leck; Rudolph Schoewe; Michael Ahern. In Res., Revs. Norbert J. Zawistanowicz (Retired); Abraham Mutholath Jacob (SYM).
Res.: 5212 W. Agatite Ave., 60630. Tel: 773-286-2950; Fax: 773-286-8579.
School—4434 N. Laramie, 60630. Tel: 773-283-2229; Fax: 773-283-0842. Sr. Bernadette Matheison, O.P., Prin. Dominican Sisters of St. Celicia 3.
Convent—5244 W. Cullom St., 60641. Tel: 773-427-6570. Dominican Sisters of St. Cecilia 4.
Catechesis/Religious Program—Mary Beth Frystak, D.R.E. Students 115.

157—OUR LADY, MOTHER OF THE CHURCH, Rev. Daniel R. Fallon.
Res.: 8747 W. Lawrence Ave., 60656. Tel: 773-625-3369; Fax: 773-625-0226.

158—ST. PANCRATIUS, Rev. Bronislaus Chmiel.
Res.: 4025 S. Sacramento Ave., 60632. Tel: 773-523-5666; Fax: 773-523-3115.

159—ST. PASCAL, Revs. Gary J. Lewanski; Thomas J. Campana; Deacons Eugene Dorgan; Thomas Stubstad.
Res.: 3935 N. Melvina Ave., 60634. Tel: 773-725-7641; Fax: 773-725-9368.
School—6143 W. Irving Park Rd., 60634. Tel: 773-736-8806; Fax: 773-725-3461. Lay Teachers 18; Students 292.
Ciezadlo Center—3954 N. Meade Ave., 60634. Tel: 773-545-9453.
Catechesis/Religious Program—Tel: 773-725-7641, Ext. 22. Students 127.

160—ST. PATRICK, Revs. John J. Wall; John C. Cusick; Thomas J. Hurley.
Res.: 700 W. Adams St., 60606. Tel: 312-782-6171.
Shrine—Shrine of Our Lady of Pompeii, Tel: 312-421-3757; Fax: 312-421-3756.

161—ST. PAUL, Revs. Peter Rodriguez, C.M.F.; Marino Novoa, C.M.F.; Richard J. Todd, C.M.F.; Milton Alarez, C.M.F.
Res.: 2127 W. 22nd Pl., 60608. Tel: 773-847-7622; Fax: 773-847-8687.
School—2114 W. 22nd Pl., 60608. Tel: 773-847-6078. Sisters 2; Lay Teachers 8; Students 270.
Catechesis/Religious Program—Students 293.

162—SS. PETER AND PAUL, Revs. Bruno B. Grinis, Pastor Emeritus (Retired); John Velutis. In Res., Rev. John Baptist Kiberu.
Res.: 12433 S. Halsted St., 60628. Tel: 773-785-1200.

163—SS. PETER AND PAUL, Revs. James M. Hyland; Stephen F. Lesniewski.
Res.: 3745 S. Paulina St., 60609. Tel: 773-523-3410; Fax: 773-523-0540.
Convent—1640 W. 38th St., 60608. Tel: 773-523-0916. Felician Sisters 3; Poor Handmaids of Jesus Christ 1.
Catechesis/Religious Program—Students 70.

164—ST. PETER CANISIUS, Rev. Tirso S. Villaverde; Deacon Leopoldo Cervantes. In Res., Rev. John T. Hillenbrand.
Res.: 5057 W. North Ave., 60639-4565. Tel: 773-637-2075; Fax: 773-889-3929.
Catechesis/Religious Program—Students 94.

165—ST. PETER'S, Rev. William Spencer, O.F.M. (For complete listing of residents see Section N - Residences of Priests and Brothers.) In Res., Rev. Thomas Aldworth, O.F.M.
St. Peter's Friary: 110 W. Madison St., 60602. Tel: 312-372-5111; Fax: 312-853-2361. For further details, see Residences of Priests and Brothers located in the Institutions section. Priests 16; Brothers 5.

166—ST. PHILIP NERI, Rev. Lawrence M. Duris; Deacons Wilmer Hatch; Aaron Pressie. In Res., Most Rev. Joseph N. Perry; Revs. William H. Sheridan (Retired); Albert Gavamukulya (East Africa).
Res.: 2132 E. 72nd St., 60649. Tel: 773-363-1700.
School—2110 E. 72nd St., 60649. Lay Teachers 13; Students 200.

167—ST. PHILOMENA, Revs. Dennis O'Mara, S.S.C.; Clarence Beckley, S.S.C.; Thomas Shaughnessy, S.S.C.; Deacons Francisco Ramos; Israel Valentin; Edwin Martinez; Benjamin Diaz.
Res.: 1921 N. Kedvale Ave., 60639. Tel: 773-489-1100; Fax: 773-489-1088.
School—4131 W. Cortland Ave., 60639. Tel: 773-235-0120; Fax: 773-235-0646. Lay Teachers 16; Students 330.
Catechesis/Religious Program—Tel: 773-342-3462. Students 471.

168—ST. PIUS V, Revs. Charles W. Dahm, O.P.; Matthias R. Mueller, O.P.; Brendan A. Curran, O.P.
Res.: 1914 S. Ashland Ave., 60608. Tel: 312-829-1931; Fax: 312-226-6119.
School—1919 S. Ashland Ave., 60608. Tel: 312-226-1590; Fax: 312-226-7265. Mrs. Nancy Nasko, Prin. Dominican Sisters 1; Lay Teachers 9; Students 268.
Shrine—Shrine of St. Jude Thaddeus, Tel: 312-226-0020.

169—PRECIOUS BLOOD, Rev. Patrick T. Casey, O.M.I.; Deacon Mario Avila. In Res., Rev. George Knab, O.M.I. (MIA).
Res.: 2411 W. Congress Pkwy., 60612. Tel: 312-733-5331; Fax: 312-733-1285.
Catechesis/Religious Program—Students 200.

170—PRESENTATION, Rev. Thomas P. Walsh.
Res.: 734 S. Springfield Ave., 60624. Tel: 773-533-2820; Fax: 773-638-2803.
School—Campus No. Two--Our Lady of the Westside School, Tel: 773-638-6555.
Catechesis/Religious Program—Students 375.

171—ST. PRISCILLA, Revs. Idzi Stacherczak; John J. Cunningham, Pastor Emeritus; Andrzej Chludzinski, O.F.M.Cap.; Deacon Fred Spitzerri.
Res.: 6949 W. Addison St., 60634. Tel: 773-545-8840; Fax: 773-545-8919.
School—7011 W. Addison St., 60634. Tel: 773-685-3581. Lay Teachers 22; Students 383.
Catechesis/Religious Program—Tel: 773-685-3785. Students 321.

172—ST. PROCOPIUS, Revs. Timothy A. Howe, S.J.; Jeremiah W. Lynch, S.J. In Res., Rev. John P. Foley, S.J.
Res.: 1641 S. Allport St., 60608. Tel: 312-226-7887; Fax: 312-226-0812.
School—Tel: 312-421-5135; Fax: 312-492-8368. Lay Teachers 10; Students 243.
Catechesis/Religious Program—Students 250.

173—PROVIDENCE OF GOD, Rev. Donald J. Nevins, Admin.; Deacon Max Carrizales.
Res.: 717 W. 18th St., 60616. Tel: 312-226-2929; Fax: 312-226-3694.
Catechesis/Religious Program—1814 S. Union, 60616. Students 75.

174—QUEEN OF ALL SAINTS BASILICA, Revs. Wayne F. Prist; Kenneth J. Baker; George Koeune; Deacons Michael Monnelly; Raymond Ward; William Malloy; Mrs. Charlene Keane, Pastoral Assoc. In Res., Revs. Wayne F. Watts; John M. Michet.
Res.: 6280 N. Sauganash Ave., 60646. Tel: 773-736-6060; Fax: 773-736-6099.
School—Tel: 773-736-0567. Sisters 3; Lay Teachers 33; Students 792.
Catechesis/Religious Program—Students 237.

175—QUEEN OF ANGELS, Revs. William J. O'Brien; Thomas E. Lamping; Deacons Richard Hankett; Bienvenido Nieves. In Res., Rev. John M. Griffiths.
Parish Office—4412 N. Western Ave., 60625. Tel: 773-539-7510; Fax: 773-539-3408.
Res.: 2330 W. Sunnyside Ave., 60625.
School—4520 N. Western Ave., 60625. Tel: 773-769-4211; Fax: 773-769-4289. Lay Teachers 23; Students 315.
Catechesis/Religious Program—Students 157.

176—QUEEN OF THE UNIVERSE, Rev. George Velloorattil; Deacons Marcial Herrera; Angelo Cordoba.
Res.: 7114 S. Hamlin Ave., 60629. Tel: 773-582-4662; Fax: 773-581-3313.
School—7130 S. Hamlin Ave., 60629. Tel: 773-582-4266; Fax: 773-585-7254. Lay Teachers 13; Students 286.
Catechesis/Religious Program—Students 210.

177—ST. RENE GOUPIL, Rev. Thomas R. Kasputis; Deacon Owen Boehm.
Res.: 6949 W. 63rd Pl., 60638. Tel: 773-229-8523; Fax: 773-229-1252.
School—6340 S. New England Ave., 60638. Tel: 773-586-4414; Fax: 773-586-3747. Marlene DeSantis, Prin. Lay Teachers 13; Students 216.
Catechesis/Religious Program—Students 87.

178—RESURRECTION, Rev. James W. Miller; Deacons Paul Bovyn; George Fuller, (Retired); Uriol Rodriguez; Guido Pozo.
Business Office—3043 N. Francisco Ave., 60618. Tel: 773-478-9705; Fax: 773-478-1387.
Res.: 2840 W. Nelson St., 60618. Tel: 773-478-1441.
School—2845 W. Barry, 60618. Tel: 773-478-9191; Fax: 773-478-9920. Lay Teachers 10; Students 181.
Catechesis/Religious Program—Tel: 773-478-8399. Students 175.

179—ST. RICHARD, Revs. Thomas A. Bernas; Robert Lojek; Rev. Msgr. Zdzislaw Wyrowinski (Poland).
Res.: 5032 S. Kostner Ave., 60632. Tel: 773-585-1221; Fax: 773-585-4959.
School—5025 S. Kenneth Ave., 60632. Tel: 773-582-8083; Fax: 773-582-8330. Lay Teachers 15; Students 305.
Catechesis/Religious Program—Students 309.

180—ST. RITA OF CASCIA, Revs. Christopher Howe, O.S.A.; Edward J. Kersten, O.S.A.; Deacons Ignacio Alarez; Jesus Ochoa; Jorge Terrazas; Francisco Torres. In Res., Revs. Robert F. Dueweke, O.S.A.; Gerardo M. Garcia, O.S.A.; William E. Lego, O.S.A.; Bro. William Wiegel, O.S.A.
Res.: 6243 S. Fairfield Ave., 60629. Tel: 773-434-9600; Fax: 773-434-9668.
Catechesis/Religious Program—Tel: 773-434-5599. Students 298.

181—ST. ROBERT BELLARMINE, Rev. Michael A. Goergen; Deacon Ben Aurelio. In Res., Rev. L. Scott Donahue.
Res.: 4646 N. Austin Ave., 60630. Tel: 773-777-2666; Fax: 773-777-2770.
School—6036 W. Eastwood Ave., 60630. Tel: 773-725-5133; Fax: 773-777-2770. Sisters 6; Lay Teachers 20; Students 405.
Catechesis/Religious Program—Tel: 773-286-0956. Students 180.

182—ST. ROMAN, Rev. David P. Pavlik; Deacon Jose Marrero.
Res.: 2311 S. Washtenaw Ave., 60608. Tel: 773-247-6645; Fax: 773-927-1610.
Catechesis/Religious Program—Students 384.

183—ST. SABINA, Rev. Michael L. Pfleger.
Res.: 1210 W. 78th Pl., 60620. Tel: 773-483-4300; Fax: 773-483-7583.
School—7801 S. Throop St., 60620. Tel: 773-483-5000; Fax: 773-483-7583. Dominican Sisters (Sinsinawa, WI) 1; Congregation of Mother of Carmel 1; Lay Teachers 27; Students 592.
Catechesis/Religious Program—Students 201.

184—SACRED HEART, (Croatian), Rev. Stephen Bedenikovic, O.F.M.
Res.: 2864 E. 96th St., 60617. Tel: 773-768-1423; Fax: 773-768-3750.

School—2906 E. 96th St., 60617. Tel: 773-773-3728; Fax: 773-768-5034. School Sisters of St. Francis 3; Lay Teachers 9; Students 196.
Catechesis/Religious Program—Students 31.

185—SACRED HEART MISSION OF HOLY NAME OF MARY, Unassigned.
Res.: 11652 S. Church St., 60643. Tel: 773-233-3955.
Catechesis/Religious Program—Students 36.

186—SANTA LUCIA-SANTA MARIA INCORONATA, Rev. Nicholas A. Marro, C.S.
Res.: 3022 S. Wells St., 60616. Tel: 312-842-6115; Fax: 312-842-0103.
School—3017 S. Wells St., 60616. Tel: 312-326-1839; Fax: 312-326-1945. Geraldine Maratea, Prin. Lay Teachers 12; Students 244.
Catechesis/Religious Program—Students 50.

187—SANTA MARIA ADDOLORATA, Rev. Vincent Gennardo, C.S.; Deacons Arthur DeLuna; James Cozzo Jr.; Luis Perez.
Res.: 528 N. Ada St., 60622. Tel: 312-421-3122; Fax: 312-421-4814.
School—1337 W. Ohio St., 60622. Tel: 312-421-5482. Sisters of the Holy Family of Nazareth 1; Lay Teachers 8; Students 165.
Catechesis/Religious Program—Students 220.

188—ST. SIMON THE APOSTLE, Rev. Francis Q. Kub; Laura L. Zbella, Pastoral Assoc. In Res., Rev. Charles J. Kouba (Retired).
Res.: 5157 S. California Ave., 60632. Tel: 773-436-1045; Fax: 773-436-4684.
School—5135 S. California Ave., 60632. Tel: 773-434-5036; Fax: 773-436-4667. Lay Teachers 13; Students 220.
Catechesis/Religious Program—Students 190.

189—ST. STANISLAUS KOSTKA, (Polish—Spanish), Revs. Anthony Bus, C.R.; Edmund Jastrzebski, C.R.; Deacons Nicolas Flores; Miguel Garcia.
Res.: 1351 W. Evergreen Ave., 60622. Tel: 773-278-2470; Fax: 773-278-2471.
School—1255 N. Noble St., 60622. Tel: 773-278-4560; Fax: 773-278-9097. Sisters 1; Lay Teachers 12; Students 220.
Catechesis/Religious Program—Students 119.

190—ST. STANISLAUS, BISHOP AND MARTYR, Revs. Anthony Dziorek, C.R.; Richard Balazs, C.R. Marion Wroblewski, C.R.; Jerzy Matuscak, C.R.; Deacons Zygfryd Oborski; Mitchell Szady. In Res., Rev. Francis Grzechowiak, C.R. (Retired).
Res.: 5352 W. Belden Ave., 60639. Tel: 773-237-5800; Fax: 773-237-7029.
School—2318 N. Lorel Ave., 60639. Tel: 773-622-3342; Fax: 773-622-9160. Lay Teachers 12; Students 243.
Catechesis/Religious Program—Students 150.

191—ST. STEPHEN, KING OF HUNGARY, Revs. Michael E. Danek, C.R.; Laszlo Vas (Romania), Admin.
Res.: 2015 W. Augusta Blvd., 60622. Tel: 773-486-1896; Fax: 773-486-1902.
Catechesis/Religious Program—Students 7.

192—ST. SYLVESTER, Revs. Michael T. Herman; Paul Maina Waithaka; Deacons Sigifredo Ortiz; Santos Soto; Carlos Soria; Hipolito Crespo.
Res.: 2157 N. Humboldt Blvd., 60647. Tel: 773-235-3646; Fax: 773-489-0974.
School—Tel: 773-772-5222; Fax: 773-722-0352. Lay Teachers 18; Students 200.
Catechesis/Religious Program—Tel: 773-772-9082. Students 550.

193—ST. SYMPHOROSA AND SEVEN SONS, Revs. Marcel J. Pasciak; Francis N. Maniola, Pastor Emeritus (Retired); Norman J. Trela; Waclaw Jamroz, S.D.S.
Res.: 6135 S. Austin Ave., 60638. Tel: 773-767-1523; Fax: 773-767-6135.
School—6125 S. Austin Ave., 60638. Lay Teachers 19; Students 385.
Catechesis/Religious Program—Students 290.

194—ST. TARCISSUS, Revs. Daniel P. McCarthy; John J. Grace, Pastor Emeritus (Retired); Rodolfo Gaytan; Simon Braganza (India); Michael Leonard (Ireland); Deacon Gregory M. Bzdon.
Res.: 6020 W. Ardmore Ave., 60646. Tel: 773-763-8228; Fax: 773-774-8461.
School—6040 W. Ardmore Ave., 60646. Tel: 773-763-7080; Fax: 773-775-3593. Lay Teachers 35; Students 631.
Catechesis/Religious Program—Students 95.

195—ST. TERESA, Rev. John R. Hoffman; Sr. Joan Granzeier, S.H., Pastoral Assoc.; Deacon Hector Rivera. In Res., Rev. Padraig Gallagher, C.SS.R. (Scotland).
Res.: 1037 W. Armitage Ave., 60614. Tel: 773-528-6650; Fax: 773-871-6766.
School—Cardinal Bernardin Early Childhood Center, 1651 W. Diversey Pkwy., 60614. Tel: 773-975-6330; Fax: 773-975-6339. Sr. Barbara Jean Ciszek, C.S.J., Prin.
Catechesis/Religious Program—Students 104.

196—ST. THADDEUS, Rev. Frank M. Sasso; Deacon Jimmie Flewellen.
Res.: 9540 S. Harvard Ave., 60628. Tel: 773-568-7077; Fax: 773-928-5447.

197—ST. THECLA, Revs. Kenneth A. Buczikowski; Andrzej Bartosz (Poland).
Res.: 6725 W. Devon Ave., 60631. Tel: 773-792-3077; Fax: 773-792-3820.
School—6323 N. Newcastle Ave., 60631. Tel: 773-763-3380; Fax: 773-763-6151. Lay Teachers 12; Students 230.
Catechesis/Religious Program—Students 120.

198—ST. THERESE CATHOLIC CHINESE CHURCH, Rev. Michael Davitti, S.X. In Res., Rev. Aniello Salicone, S.X.
Res.: 218 W. Alexander St., 60616. Tel: 312-842-6777; Fax: 312-567-1389.
School—247 W. 23rd St., 60616. Tel: 312-326-2837; Fax: 312-326-6068. Sisters 4; Lay Teachers 14; Students 296.
Catechesis/Religious Program—Students 254.

199—ST. THOMAS APOSTLE, Revs. Michael Mulhall, O.Carm.; Thomas J. Fitzgerald, Pastor Emeritus (Retired); Thomas R. Seitz (Retired); Ferdinand Lansang, O.Carm. (LA); Deacons Robert Monica; James Morgan.
Res.: 5472 S. Kimbark Ave., 60615. Tel: 773-324-2626; Fax: 773-753-7415.
School—5467 S. Woodlawn Ave., 60615. Tel: 773-667-1142; Fax: 773-753-7434. Lay Teachers 26; Students 365.
Catechesis/Religious Program—Students 120.

200—ST. THOMAS MORE, Revs. Anthony J. Brankin; Gerald K. O'Reilly; Theodore McNulty. In Res., Revs. John P. Frawley (Retired); J. Austin Graff (Retired); John McGrath (Retired).
Res.: 2825 W. 81st St., 60652. Tel: 773-436-4444; Fax: 773-778-9087.
School—8130 S. California Ave., 60652. Tel: 773-434-4575; Fax: 773-434-2026. Congregation of the Mother of Carmel 6; Lay Teachers 10; Students 310.
Catechesis/Religious Program—Students 310.

201—ST. THOMAS OF CANTERBURY, Revs. Richard T. Simon; Trinh Peter Hung, (Vietnamese Apostolate); Deacons Orlando Perez; Duc Nguyen; John Green.
Res.: 4827 N. Kenmore Ave., 60640. Tel: 773-878-5507.
School—Tel: 773-271-8655. Lay Teachers 13; Students 275.
Catechesis/Religious Program—Students 285.

202—ST. TIMOTHY, Revs. Harold B. Murphy; Gilbert A. Carroll, Pastor Emeritus (Retired). In Res., Rev. Sammy Alvaro (Philippines).
Res.: 6326 N. Washtenaw Ave., 60659. Tel: 773-262-6600; Fax: 773-262-9214.
Catechesis/Religious Program—Tel: 773-761-1368; Fax: 773-262-9214. Students 50.

203—TRANSFIGURATION OF OUR LORD, Revs. John J. Rudnik; Terence M. Keehan; Elmer Romero. In Res., Revs. Robert A. Florido (Philippines) Rene L. Pareja (Philippines).
Res.: 2609 W. Carmen Ave., 60625. Tel: 773-561-7953; Fax: 773-561-7635.
School—4910-20 N. Claremont Ave., 60625. Tel: 773-334-0239; Fax: 773-334-0107. Lay Teachers 14; Students 260.
Catechesis/Religious Program—Students 65.

204—ST. TURIBIUS, Revs. Ralph H. Zwirn; Paul Stein; Andrew Godlewski (Poland).
Res.: 5646 S. Karlov Ave., 60629. Tel: 773-581-2730.
School—4120 W. 57th St., 60629. Tel: 773-585-5150; Fax: 773-585-5328. Felician Sisters 4; Lay Teachers 19; Students 470.

205—ST. VICTOR, Revs. Robert M. Egan, C.S.V.; John E. Eck, C.S.V.; Robert T. Bolser, C.S.V.; Deacon Joseph Cascino.
Res.: 4170 W. Addison St., 60641. Tel: 773-286-4040; Fax: 773-286-4122.
School—4140 W. Addison St., 60641. Tel: 773-545-2173; Fax: 773-794-1697. Lay Teachers 28; Students 370.
Catechesis/Religious Program—Students 98.

206—ST. VINCENT DE PAUL, Rev. Donald Ours, C.M.; Sr. Marie Orf, C.PP.S., Pastoral Assoc.
Res.: 1010 W. Webster Ave., 60614. Tel: 773-327-1113; Fax: 773-327-2326.

207—ST. WALTER, Rev. Peter J. Heidenrich. Deacon Thomas O'Connell.
Res.: 11722 S. Oakley Ave., 60643. Tel: 773-779-1515; Fax: 773-779-0381.
School—11741 S. Western Ave., 60643. Tel: 773-445-8850. Sisters 3; Lay Teachers 9; Students 250.
Catechesis/Religious Program—Students 50.

208—ST. WENCESLAUS, Revs. Michael E. Danek, C.R.; Gerald Watt, C.R.; Jacek Praski. In Res., Rev. Gregory Helminski, C.R.
Res.: 3400 N. Monticello Ave., 60618. Tel: 773-588-1135; Fax: 773-588-3735.
Catechesis/Religious Program—Students 244.

209—ST. WILLIAM, Revs. William J. Hastings; Daniel J. Brandt; Duy Cao; Deacon Dennis Colgan.
Res.: 2600 N. Sayre Ave., 60707. Tel: 773-637-6565; Fax: 773-637-7042.
School—2559 N. Sayre Ave., 60707. Tel: 773-637-5130; Fax: 773-745-4208. Lay Teachers 15; Students 250.
Catechesis/Religious Program—Students 90.

OUTSIDE THE CITY OF CHICAGO

ALSIP, COOK CO., ST. TERRENCE, Rev. Edward J. Barrett.
Res.: 4300 W. 119th Pl., 60803. Tel: 708-597-0970; Fax: 708-597-9118.
Catechesis/Religious Program—Tel: 708-597-0754. Students 624.

ANTIOCH, LAKE CO., ST. PETER, Revs. Ronald H. Anglim; Roland H. Folger; Deacons Robert A. Gagnon; Paul M. Neurauter; Scott Keenan.
Res.: 557 W. Lake St., 60002. Tel: 847-395-0274; Fax: 847-395-4553.
School—Tel: 847-395-0037; Fax: 847-395-2532. Lay Teachers 15; Students 235.
Catechesis/Religious Program—559 Elizabeth, 60002. Tel: 847-395-0246; Fax: 847-395-2532. Students 529.

ARGO, COOK CO., ST. BLASE, Revs. Michael L. Zoufal; Jan Henk; Deacon Raymundo Diaz DeLeon.
Res.: 6101 S. 75th Ave., 60501. Tel: 708-458-0007; Fax: 708-458-0276.
Catechesis/Religious Program—Tel: 708-458-0246. Students 795.

ARLINGTON HEIGHTS, COOK CO.

1—ST. EDNA, Revs. Jerome Jacob; Steven G. Dombrowski; Deacons Raymond Graffia Jr.; James Gaughan. In Res., Revs. John J. Hurley, O.S.F.S. (WIL), Pastor Emeritus; Eugene J. Faucher (Retired).
Res.: 2525 N. Arlington Heights Rd., 60004. Tel: 847-398-3362; Fax: 847-394-5226.
Catechesis/Religious Program—Students 957.

2—ST. JAMES, Revs. William J. Zavaski; Theodore J. Schmitt; John P. Chrzan; Sr. Kathleen A. Donohoe, O.S.F., Pastoral Assoc.; Deacons Robert Plantz, (Retired); Louis Lekan; Armand Ferrini; Matt Hennessy. In Res., Rev. Abraham Vettuvelil (India).
Office—820 N. Arlington Heights Rd., 60004. Tel: 847-253-6305; Fax: 847-253-0269.
School—821 Arlington Heights Rd., 60004. Tel: 847-255-6746; Fax: 847-259-4223. Lay Teachers 57; Students 910.

3—OUR LADY OF THE WAYSIDE, Revs. Vincent F. Costello; Ignatius I. Anaele; Deacons Robert Duffy; Donald Grossnickle; Brendan Foley; Donna Cunningham, Pastoral Assoc.
Res.: 432 W. Park St., 60005. Tel: 847-253-5353; Fax: 847-253-7175.
School—Tel: 847-253-0050; Fax: 847-253-0543. Lay Teachers 42; Students 757.
Catechesis/Religious Program—423 S. Mitchell, 60005. Tel: 847-398-5011. Students 715.

BARRINGTON, LAKE CO., ST. ANNE, Revs. John W. Dewes; Britto Berchmans; Fred Licciardi, C.PP.S.; Deacons Richard Baum; Robert C. Brauch; James Condill; Richard Seveska; James Crane; Sisters Lauretta Leipzig, Pastoral Assoc.; Lorraine Menheer, Pastoral Assoc.
Res.: 120 N. Ela St., 60010. Tel: 847-382-5300; Fax: 847-382-5363.
School—319 E. Franklin St., 60010. Tel: 847-381-0311; Fax: 847-381-0384. School Sisters of St. Francis 6; Lay Teachers 30; Students 600.
Catechesis/Religious Program—Students 1,050.

BARTLETT, COOK CO., ST. PETER DAMIAN, Rev. Thomas Hoffman. In Res., Rev. Martin R. Borowczyk (Retired).
Res.: 109 S. Crest Ave., 60103. Tel: 630-837-5411; Fax: 630-837-9424.
Catechesis/Religious Program—Tel: 630-830-2295. Students 806.

BELLWOOD, COOK CO., ST. SIMEON, Rev. John J. McCarville. In Res., Rev. Joseph Ekpo.
Res.: 430 Bohland Ave., 60104. Tel: 708-547-6868.
Catechesis/Religious Program—Students 58.

BERWYN, COOK CO.

1—ST. LEONARD, Revs. William J. Curran; Michael E. Flynn; David Sajdak, S.D.B.; Deacons Joel Chrastka; Peter Morrissey; Jose Cisneros. In Res., Rev. John A. Rolek, B.A.
Res.: 3318 S. Clarence Ave., 60402. Tel: 708-484-0015; Fax: 708-484-6982.
School—3322 S. Clarence Ave., 60402. Tel: 708-749-3666; Fax: 708-749-7981. Lay Teachers 20; Students 284.
Convent—Sisters of St. Joseph (La Grange, IL), 6634 W. 34th St., 60402. Tel: 708-788-2681.
Catechesis/Religious Program—Tel: 708-795-5919. Students 277.

2—ST. MARY OF CELLE, Revs. Richard J. Prendergast; William J. Clavey.
Res.: 1428 Wesley Ave., 60402. Tel: 708-788-0876; Fax: 708-788-0242.
School—1448 S. Wesley Ave., 60402. Tel: 708-749-1989; Fax: 708-749-2120. Lay Teachers 13; Students 192.
Catechesis/Religious Program—Tel: 708-795-6460. Students 200.

3—ST. ODILO, Revs. Peter J. Cyscon; Ryszard Gron (Poland). In Res., Revs. Richard B. Saudis; Thomas J. Kaveney (Retired).
Res.: 2244 S. East Ave., 60402. Tel: 708-484-2161; Fax: 708-788-0565.
School—2301 S. Clarence Ave., 60402. Tel: 708-484-0755. William Donegan, Prin. Sisters of Charity B.V.M. 2; Lay Teachers 13; Students 288.
Catechesis/Religious Program—Students 136.
Shrine—Poor Souls, Tel: 708-484-2161; Fax: 708-788-0565.

BLUE ISLAND, COOK CO.

1—ST. BENEDICT, Revs. George L. Schopp; Ismael Sandoval-Manzo; Deacons Juan Limon; Abundio Valadez; Dan Carroll. In Res., Rev. Henry Sanni.
Res.: 2339 York St., 60406. Tel: 708-385-8510; Fax: 708-371-2631.
School—2324 New St., 60406. Tel: 708-385-2016; Fax: 708-385-4490. Lay Teachers 14; Students 235.
Catechesis/Religious Program—Students 220.
Mission—St. Peter Claver 14125 Claire Blvd., Robbins, Cook Co. 60472. Tel: 708-389-2434; Fax: 708-389-2434.

2—ST. DONATUS, Revs. Louis Gasparini, M.C.C.J.; Hugo Riva, M.C.C.J. In Res., Rev. Archimede Fornasari, M.C.C.J., Ph.D.
Res.: 1939 Union St., 60406. Tel: 708-385-2890; Fax: 708-385-4708.
Catechesis/Religious Program—Tel: 708-388-7886. Students 350.

3—ST. ISIDORE, Rev. Gregory A. Rom.
Res.: 1811 W. Burr Oak Ave., 60406. Tel: 708-388-0807; Fax: 708-388-5077.

BRIDGEVIEW, COOK CO., ST. FABIAN, Revs. Walter J. Turlo; Gregory W. Warmuz, O.Cist; Deacons Charles Tipperreiter; Sal Lema.
Res.: 8300 S. Thomas Ave., 60455. Tel: 708-599-1110; Fax: 708-599-0673.
Catechesis/Religious Program—7450 83rd St., 60455. Tel: 708-458-6150; Fax: 708-458-2398. Students 1,300.

BROOKFIELD, COOK CO., ST. BARBARA, Revs. John M. Murphy; Maurice J. Kissane, Pastor Emeritus; Sr. Margaret Halligan, C.S.J., Pastoral Assoc.; Deacons John Debnar; Dave Brencic. In Res., Rev. Michael P. Ahlstrom.
Res.: 4008 Prairie Ave., 60513. Tel: 708-485-0589; Fax: 708-485-2343.
School—8900 Windemere Ave., 60513. Tel: 708-485-0806; Fax: 708-485-2343. Lay Teachers 13; Students 220.
Catechesis/Religious Program—Tel: 708-485-4610. Students 320.

BUFFALO GROVE, LAKE CO., ST. MARY, [CEM] Revs. Marc W. Reszel; Gerald E. Rogala; Michael F. McMahon; Deacons I. James Young, M.D.; Eugene Kukla; Bruce Peters; Gary Long.
Res.: 10 N. Buffalo Grove Rd., 60089. Tel: 847-541-1450; Fax: 847-541-2443.
School—50 N. Buffalo Grove Rd., 60089. Tel: 847-459-6270; Fax: 847-537-2810. Lay Teachers 46; Students 620.
Catechesis/Religious Program—Tel: 847-537-9423; Fax: 847-808-0548. Students 1,150.

BURBANK, COOK CO., ST. ALBERT THE GREAT, Revs. Robert A. Stepek; Bruno Janik; Marek B. Grzela; Deacon Irvin Bryce.
Res.: 5555 W. State Rd., 60459. Tel: 708-423-0321; Fax: 708-425-4329.
School—5535 W. State Rd., 60459. Tel: 708-424-7757. Dominican Sisters (Adrian, MI) 2; Lay Teachers 22; Students 325.
Catechesis/Religious Program—Tel: 708-636-0406. Students 600.

BURNHAM, COOK CO., MOTHER OF GOD, Rev. Edmund F. Guz.
Res.: 14207 S. Green Bay Ave., 60633. Tel: 708-862-8777; Fax: 708-891-1349.

CALUMET CITY, COOK CO.

1—ST. ANDREW THE APOSTLE, Revs. Martin E. Michniewicz; Michael J. Weidman; Deacon Robert Banet.
Res.: 768 Lincoln Ave., 60409. Tel: 708-862-4165; Fax: 708-862-4124.
School—331-155th Pl., 60409. Tel: 708-862-4143; Fax: 708-862-4148. Sisters of the Holy Family of Nazareth (Des Plaines, IL) 2; Lay Teachers 13; Students 215.
Catechesis/Religious Program—Tel: 708-758-4945. Students 75.

2—OUR LADY OF KNOCK, Revs. Patrick M. Lyons; Donald J. Fenske, Pastor Emeritus (Retired); Sr. Alban Hermes, O.P., Pastoral Assoc.; Deacon Edward Ryan.
Res.: 501 163rd St., 60409. Tel: 708-862-3011; Fax: 708-862-9618.
School—497 163rd St., 60409. Tel: 708-862-0275. Lay Teachers 12; Students 165.
Catechesis/Religious Program—Tel: 708-868-1711; Fax: 798-862-3011. Students 95.

3—ST. VICTOR, Rev. Thomas E. Cima; Deacon Daniel Ragonese.
Res.: 553 Hirsch Ave., 60409. Tel: 708-891-8920; Fax: 708-891-8943.
School—Tel: 708-891-8930; Fax: 708-891-8943. Lay Teachers 14; Students 223.
Catechesis/Religious Program—Tel: 708-891-8931. Students 40.

CALUMET PARK, COOK CO., SEVEN HOLY FOUNDERS, Rev. Thomas Michael Vermigilio, M.C.C.J.
Res.: 12400 S. Ada St., 60827. Tel: 708-385-8459; Fax: 708-385-2143.
Catechesis/Religious Program—Tel: 708-385-8498. Students 75.

CHICAGO HEIGHTS, COOK CO.

1—ST. AGNES, Rev. John S. Siemianowski; Deacons Thomas Nowak; David Brothers; Charlene Klabacha, Pastoral Assoc.
Res.: 1501 Chicago Rd., 60411. Tel: 708-709-2694; Fax: 708-709-2693.
School—1501 Chicago Rd., 60411. Tel: 708-709-2333; Fax: 708-709-2693. Lay Teachers 18; Students 312.
Catechesis/Religious Program—Students 110.

2—ST. KIERAN, Rev. William A. Eddy; Deacons Eugene La Belle; Bernard Halper, (Retired); David Dutko.
Res.: 724 W. 195th St., 60411. Tel: 708-755-0074; Fax: 708-754-2246.
School—700 W. 195th St., 60411. Tel: 708-754-8999; Fax: 708-754-9007. Lay Teachers 14; Students 225.
Catechesis/Religious Program—Tel: 708-754-0484. Students 208.

3—ST. PAUL, Rev. John S. Siemianowski, Admin., Chicago Heights, IL St. Paul; Deacon Juan L. Garza.
Res.: 206 E. 25th St., 60411. Tel: 708-754-3120; Fax: 708-754-0076.
Catechesis/Religious Program—Tel: 708-754-7720. Students 512.

CHICAGO RIDGE, COOK CO., OUR LADY OF THE RIDGE, Revs. Paul Burak; Anthony L. Markus; Charles W. Watkins; Deacons Michael Krapez; Terris Albano.
Res.: 10811 S. Ridgeland Ave., 60415. Tel: 708-425-3800; Fax: 708-425-2792.
School—10859 S. Ridgeland Ave., 60415. Tel: 708-424-4409. Lay Teachers 8; Students 221.
Catechesis/Religious Program—Tel: 708-424-4949. Students 339.

CICERO, COOK CO.

1—ST. ANTHONY, Revs. James J. Kastigar; Dionisio Zabala (Bolivia); Deacons Alfonso Salgado; Claude Hensley.
Res.: 1515 S. 50th Ave., 60804. Tel: 708-652-0231; Fax: 708-652-0228.
St. Anthony Center—1510 S. 49th Ct., 60804. Tel: 708-652-0231; Fax: 708-652-0228.
Catechesis/Religious Program—Students 430.

2—ST. FRANCES OF ROME, Rev. Mark A. Bartosic. In Res., Rev. Educardo Rivera, S.S.P.
Res.: 1428 S. 59th Ct., 60804. Tel: 708-652-2140; Fax: 708-652-6513.
School—1400 S. Austin Blvd., 60804. Tel: 708-652-2277. Lay Teachers 12; Students 220.
Catechesis/Religious Program—Tel: 708-656-8632. Students 310.

3—ST. MARY OF CZESTOCHOWA, (Polish—Spanish), Revs. Walter Juszczak, C.Ss.R.; Thaddeus J. Makuch, Pastor Emeritus (Retired); Walderma Wieladek, C.SS.R.; Zbigniew Pienkos, C.SS.R.
Res.: 3010 S. 48th Ct., 60804. Tel: 708-652-0948; Fax: 708-652-0646.
School—3001 S. 49th Ave., 60804. Tel: 708-656-5010; Fax: 708-656-4043.
Catechesis/Religious Program—Tel: 708-652-0948; Fax: 708-652-0646. Students 232.

4—MARY, QUEEN OF HEAVEN, Rev. John W. Hurley, Admin.; Deacons Julio Rosado; Armando Herrera. In Res., Rev. William P. Fegan.
Res.: 5300 W. 24th St., 60804. Tel: 708-863-6608; Fax: 708-863-2349.

5—OUR LADY OF CHARITY, Revs. Jose Sequeira; Robert J. Burnell; Deacon Antonio Ponce.
Res.: 3600 57th Ct., 60804. Tel: 708-863-1207; Fax: 708-863-1209.
School—3620 57th Ct., 60804. Tel: 708-652-0262; Fax: 708-652-0601. Lay Teachers 11; Students 231.
Catechesis/Religious Program—Students 168.

6—OUR LADY OF THE MOUNT, Rev. Lawrence E. Collins; Deacons Robert E. Devereux; Antonio Llano. In Res., Rev. Dusan Hladik (Czech Republic).
Res.: 2414 S. 61st Ave., 60804. Tel: 708-652-2791; Fax: 708-863-6014.
School—2400 S. 61st Ave., 60804. Lay Teachers 10; Students 265.
Catechesis/Religious Program—Students 372.

COUNTRY CLUB HILLS, COOK CO., ST. EMERIC, Revs. Paul G. Seaman; John J. Rochford, Pastor Emeritus (Retired); Deacons James Detloff; Thomas O'Brien, (Retired); Philip DuBrownik.
Res.: 4330 W. 180th St., 60478. Tel: 708-798-0757; Fax: 708-798-0799.
Catechesis/Religious Program—Tel: 708-799-4430; Fax: 708-798-0799. Students 75.

DEERFIELD, LAKE CO., HOLY CROSS, Revs. Harold B. Stanger; Laurence J. Dunn; Deacons Jerome Kasimatis; James Carroll; Edward Melton; Mary Ann Spina, Pastoral Assoc.
Res.: 724 Elder Ln., 60015. Tel: 847-945-0430; Fax: 847-945-7651.
School—720 Elder Ln., 60015. Tel: 847-945-0135; Fax: 847-945-0705. Mr. David Burke, Prin. Lay Teachers 24; Students 416.
Catechesis/Religious Program—Tel: 847-945-0581; Fax: 847-945-0582. Sr. Jeanne Landry, S.S.N.D., D.R.E. Students 645.

DES PLAINES, COOK CO.

1—ST. MARY, Revs. Gene J. Dyer; Charles H. Schlax; Flavio V. Gonzales.
Res.: 794 Pearson St., 60016. Tel: 847-824-8144; Fax: 847-824-3906.
School—Our Lady of Destiny (North Campus), 795 Center St., 60016. Tel: 847-824-2762; Fax: 847-824-3465. Lay Teachers 15; Students 217.
Catechesis/Religious Program—Tel: 847-298-1435; Fax: 847-824-3906. Students 420.

2—ST. PAUL CHONG HASANG, Rev. Robert Kim.
Res.: 675 Dursey Ln., 60016. Tel: 847-699-6334; Fax: 847-699-1281.
Catechesis/Religious Program—Students 190.

3—ST. STEPHEN PROTOMARTYR, Revs. Michael A. Olivero; Leonard T. Mezydlo, Pastor Emeritus (Retired); Flavio V. Gonzalez; Deacons Donald J. Telposky; Anthony Towey.
1267 Everett Ave., 60018-2398. Tel: 847-824-2026; Fax: 847-824-3842. In Res., Revs. Haldane Mysliwiec; Michael G. Zaniolo.
School—Our Lady of Destiny (South Campus), 1880 Ash St., 60018-2343. Tel: 847-827-2900; Fax: 847-827-0475. Lay Teachers 6; Students 100.
Catechesis/Religious Program—1253 Everett Ave., 60018. Tel: 847-297-3844; Fax: 847-824-3842. Students 175.

4—ST. ZACHARY, Revs. John S. Plotkowski; Victor Miranda; Deacons Peter N. Lagges; John J. Smith; Sam Pincich. In Res., Rev. Lawrence F. Springer.
Res.: 567 W. Algonquin Rd., 60016. Tel: 847-956-7020; Fax: 847-981-1148.
School—Tel: 847-437-4022. Lay Teachers 15; Students 190.
Catechesis/Religious Program—Tel: 847-956-1175. Students 350.

ELK GROVE VILLAGE, COOK CO.

1—ST. JULIAN EYMARD, Rev. Leon J. Rezula.
Res.: 601 Biesterfield Rd., 60007. Tel: 847-956-0130; Fax: 847-956-0189.
Catechesis/Religious Program—Tel: 847-593-8938. Students 909.

2—QUEEN OF THE ROSARY, Revs. Arthur J. Fagan; Francis J. Cerniglia, Pastor Emeritus (Retired); John A. Robinson; Deacon Ted Czarnecki. In Res., Rev. Robert L. Ebrom.
Res.: 750 Elk Grove Blvd., 60007. Tel: 847-437-0403; Fax: 847-437-0336.
School—690 Elk Grove Blvd., 60007. Tel: 847-437-3322; Fax: 847-437-8961. Lay Teachers 21; Students 436.
Catechesis/Religious Program—680 Elk Grove Blvd., 60007. Tel: 847-437-3346. Students 521.

ELMWOOD PARK, COOK CO., ST. CELESTINE, Rev. Lawrence J. Sullivan; Deacons James Devine; Michael DeLarco. In Res., Rev. Bernard C. White (Retired).
Res.: 3020 N. 76th Ct., 60707. Tel: 708-453-2555; Fax: 708-462-0560.
School—Tel: 708-453-8234; Fax: 708-452-0237. Lay Teachers 22; Students 534.
Catechesis/Religious Program—3017 N. 77th Ave., 60707. Tel: 708-452-7370; Fax: 708-452-0560. Students 216.

EVANSTON, COOK CO.

1—ST. ATHANASIUS, Revs. Thomas A. Libera; James Heyd; Deacon Richard S. Jay.
Res.: 1615 Lincoln St., 60201. Tel: 847-328-1430; Fax: 847-328-1809.
School—2510 Ashland, 60201. Tel: 847-864-2650; Fax: 847-475-7385. Lay Teachers 24; Students 329.
Catechesis/Religious Program—Tel: 847-328-5931; Fax: 547-475-7385. Students 327.

2—ST. MARY, Revs. Michael J. Solazzo; Jason Torba (Poland).
Res.: 1012 Lake St., 60201. Tel: 847-864-0333; Fax: 847-864-0354.
Parish Center—Tel: 847-864-0333; Fax: 847-864-0354.
School—Tel: 847-475-5678; Fax: 847-475-5683. Consolidated with St. Nicholas Parish to form Pope John XXIII School. See St. Nicholas for further details.
Catechesis/Religious Program—Students 125.

3—ST. NICHOLAS, Rev. Robert H. Oldershaw. In Res., Revs. James R. Halstead, O.S.A.; Joseph Kabari (Nigeria).

Res.: 806 Ridge Ave., 60202. Tel: 847-864-1185; Fax: 847-864-7810.
School—1120 Washington, 60202. Tel: 847-475-5678. Mrs. Rosalie Musiala, Prin. Consolidated with St. Mary Parish to form Pope John XXIII School. Lay Teachers 22; Students 294.
Catechesis/Religious Program—Students 345.

EVERGREEN PARK, COOK CO.

1—ST. BERNADETTE, Rev. Gary M. Miller.
Res.: 9343 Francisco Ave., 60805. Tel: 708-422-8995; Fax: 708-422-8699.
School—9311 S. Francisco Ave., 60805. Tel: 708-422-6429; Fax: 708-422-6484. Dominican Sisters (Springfield, IL) 2; Lay Teachers 22; Students 342.
Catechesis/Religious Program—Tel: 708-425-7697. Students 285.

2—MOST HOLY REDEEMER, Revs. Michael G. Foley; Mark J. Walter. In Res., Rev. Albert R. Adamich (Retired); Deacon Richard Kulleck.
Res.: 9525 S. Lawndale Ave., 60805. Tel: 708-425-5354; Fax: 708-346-8182.
School—9535 S. Millard Ave., 60805. Tel: 708-422-8280; Fax: 708-422-4193. Lay Teachers 25; Students 455.
Catechesis/Religious Program—Tel: 708-346-8185. Students 463.

3—QUEEN OF MARTYRS, Revs. Edward M. Mikolajczyk; William P. Murphy, Pastor Emeritus (Retired); JoAndre Beltran.
Res.: 10233 S. Central Park, 60805-3799. Tel: 708-423-8110; Fax: 708-423-7372.
School—3550 W. 103rd St., 60655. Lay Teachers 25; Students 558.
Catechesis/Religious Program—Tel: 708-422-1647. Students 101.

FLOSSMOOR, COOK CO., INFANT JESUS OF PRAGUE, Revs. Michael A. Hack, J.C.D.; Andrew J. Santos; John J. Doyle; Deacon George Brooks. In Res., Rev. William J. Finnegan (Retired).
Res.: 1131 Douglas Ave., 60422. Tel: 708-799-5400.
School—1101 Douglas Ave., 60422. Lay Teachers 22; Students 500.

FOREST PARK, COOK CO., ST. BERNARDINE, Revs. Patrick M. Tucker; Phillip F. Cioffi; Deacons Timothy Rehor; John Walters. In Res., Rev. Francis J. Grady, S.S.C.
Res.: 7246 Harrison St., 60130. Tel: 708-366-0839; Fax: 708-366-3136.
School—815 Elgin Ave., 60130. Tel: 708-366-6890; Fax: 708-366-8015. Lay Teachers 16; Students 245.
Catechesis/Religious Program—Tel: 708-366-3553. Students 107.

FRANKLIN PARK, COOK CO., ST. GERTRUDE, Revs. Alfred P. Corbo; Aldo Pozza, M.C.C.J.; Julian de Jesus Hernandez Herrera (Colombia); Deacons Robert Murphy; Lorenzo Chaidez.
Res.: 9613 Schiller Blvd., 60131. Tel: 847-455-1100; Fax: 847-455-1209.
Catechesis/Religious Program—9617 Schiller Blvd, 60131. Tel: 847-455-5810.

GLENVIEW, COOK CO.

1—ST. CATHERINE LABOURE, Revs. Robert G. Mair; Alfredo J. Salera; Deacons Ray Gavin; Michael Bretz; Frank Beil.
Res.: 3535 Thornwood Ln., 60025. Tel: 847-729-1414; Fax: 847-729-5184.
School—3425 Thornwood Ln., 60025. Tel: 847-724-2240; Fax: 847-724-5805. Sisters 1; Lay Teachers 20; Students 302.
Catechesis/Religious Program—Students 260.

2—OUR LADY OF PERPETUAL HELP, Revs. John E. Flavin; Thomas Bishop; John M. Thinnes; Patrick Tyrell, S.J. (Ireland); Deacons James Revord; Alan Sedivy.
Res.: 1775 Grove St., 60025. Tel: 847-729-1525; Fax: 847-724-7025.
School—1123 Church St., 60025. Tel: 847-724-6990. School Sisters of St. Francis 4; Lay Teachers 74; Students 1,060.
Catechesis/Religious Program—Tel: 847-998-5289. Students 1,050.

GLENWOOD, COOK CO., ST. JOHN, Rev. John J. Sullivan.
Res.: 301 S. Cottage Grove Ave., 60425. Tel: 708-758-5098; Fax: 708-758-0408.
Catechesis/Religious Program—Students 225.

GRAYSLAKE, LAKE CO., ST. GILBERT, Revs. Robert W. Beaven; Dean F. Semmer; Deacons Chester Kozuchowski; Henry Iwan; Chris Mondello; Richard Globis.
Res.: 301 E. Belvidere Rd., 60030. Tel 847-223-4731; Fax: 847-223-5840.
School—251 E. Belvidere Rd., 60030. Tel: 847-223-8600. Gloria Petraitis, Prin. Lay Teachers 39; Students 735.
Catechesis/Religious Program—Tel: 847-223-3071. Students 790.

GURNEE, LAKE CO., ST. PAUL THE APOSTLE, Revs. Farrell J. Kane, O.Carm.; Raymond Clennon, O.Carm.; Deacon Michael Penich.
Res.: 6401 Gages Lake Rd., 60031. Tel: 847-918-0600; Fax: 847-918-0640.
Catechesis/Religious Program—Tel: 847-816-8677; Fax: 847-918-0640. Students 1,882.

HANOVER PARK, COOK CO., ST. ANSGAR, Rev. John W. Murray; Deacons Louis Barone; Nick Tereza; Robert Ziomek; Oscar Monterroso; Ronald Weber.
Res.: 2040 Laurel Ave., 60133. Tel: 630-837-5553; Fax: 630-837-9847.
Catechesis/Religious Program—Students 322.

HARVEY, COOK CO.

1—ASCENSION-ST. SUSANNA, Revs. Joseph W. Altman; Christopher Vodzogbe (Africa); Robert J. Gilbert; Deacons Thomas R. Carvlin; Henry Burke Jr.; Terrence Collins.
Res.: 15234 Myrtle Ave., 60426. Tel: 708-333-0931; Fax: 708-333-3281.
Catechesis/Religious Program—Students 30.

2—ST. JOHN THE BAPTIST, (Polish), Revs. Edward Romanski (Poland), Admin.; Clarence J. Jachcinski, Pastor Emeritus (Retired); Michael Wasiel (Retired).
Res.: 15743 Union Ave., 60426. Tel: 708-333-0184; Fax: 708-333-0861.
Catechesis/Religious Program—Students 90.

HARWOOD HEIGHTS, NORRIDGE, COOK CO., ST. ROSALIE, Revs. Jerzy Maj, O.S.P.; Basil Cendrowicz, O.S.P. In Res., Rev. Richard J. Ehrens (Retired).
Res.: 4401 N. Oak Park Ave., Harwood Heights-Norridge, 60706. Tel: 708-867-8817; Fax: 708-867-8615.
Catechesis/Religious Program—6750 W. Montrose, Harwood Hts., 60706. Tel: 708-867-4588; Fax: 708-867-0774. Students 275.

HAZEL CREST, COOK CO., ST. ANNE, Revs. Leonard A. Dubi; Robert J. Keener; Deacons John Leonas, (Retired); Herman Benthey; Steven Moore; William Churilla.
Res.: 16802 S. Lincoln St., 60429. Tel 708-335-3221; Fax: 708-335-1953.
School—Early Learning Center, (Grades PreK-Day Care), 16777 Dixie Hwy., 60429. Tel: 708 335-4831. Students 32.
Catechesis/Religious Program—Tel: 708-335-2286. Students 60.

HICKORY HILLS, COOK CO., ST. PATRICIA, Revs. Gerald F. Mulcahy; Darrio L. Boscutti; Deacons Charles Keegan; Norbert Weitendorf. In Res., Rev. Joseph C. Mol.
Res.: 9050 S. 86th Ave., 60457. Tel: 708-598-5222; Fax: 708-598-5280.
School—9000 S. 86th Ave., 60457. Tel 708-598-8200; Fax: 708-598-8233. Sisters of the Holy Family of Nazareth (Des Plaines, IL) 4; Lay Teachers 20; Students 452.
Catechesis/Religious Program—Tel: 708-599-1221; Fax: 708-598-8233.

HIGHLAND PARK, LAKE CO., IMMACULATE CONCEPTION, Rev. Terrence A. McCarthy; Deacons James Fruge; Louis Vignocchi; Luis Lara; Stewart Adams; Ellsworth Cordesman. In Res., Revs. Edward J. Norkett (Retired); Alec J. Wolff; Simon Sang-il Lee, S.J.
Res.: 770 W. Deerfield Rd., 60035. Tel: 847-433-0130; Fax: 847-433-0669.
Catechesis/Religious Program—Tel: 847-433-2224. Students 298.

HIGHWOOD, LAKE CO., ST. JAMES, Revs. James O'Malley, Pastor Emeritus; Timothy J. O'Malley; Deacons Bruno Pagliai; James Gallagher Ellsworth Cordesman. In Res., Rev. John E. Mulvihill.
Res.: 134 North Ave., 60040. Tel: 847-433-1494; Fax: 847-433-2011.
School—140 North Ave., 60040. Tel: 847-432-2277; Fax: 847-432-1321. Lay Teachers 18; Students 185.
Catechesis/Religious Program—Tel: 847 432-2570. Students 227.

HILLSIDE, COOK CO., ST. DOMITILLA, Rev. Peter Galek; Deacons Angelo Marotto; Kenneth Bell.
Res.: 4940 Washington St., 60162. Tel: 708-449-8430; Fax: 708-449-2009.
School—601 Hillside Ave., 60162. Tel: 708-449-7420. Sisters 3; Lay Teachers 10; Students 300.
Catechesis/Religious Program—Tel: 708-449-1558. Students 130.

HOFFMAN ESTATES, COOK CO., ST. HUBERT, Rev. Eugene J. Nowak; Deacons James Knippen, (Retired); Richard Lawson; Thomas Hayden; Steven Baldasti.
Res.: 729 Grand Canyon St., 60194. Tel: 847-885-7700; Fax: 847-885-4631.
School—Tel: 847-885-7702; Fax: 847-885-0604. Lay Teachers 42; Students 760.
Catechesis/Religious Program—Tel: 847-855-7703. Students 671.

HOMETOWN, COOK CO., OUR LADY OF LORETTO, Rev. James J. Donovan; Deacon Thomas Meehan, (Retired). In Res., Revs. John J. Mackin (Retired); Andrew Beltkowski (Poland).
Res.: 8925 S. Kostner Ave., 60456. Tel: 708-424-7471; Fax: 708-424-7588.
School—Tel: 708-636-8668. Lay Teachers 15; Students 234.
Catechesis/Religious Program—Tel: 708-499-0832. Students 138.

HOMEWOOD, COOK CO., ST. JOSEPH, Revs. Richard J. Kozak; James M. Sayers, Pastor Emeritus (Retired); Samson Ngatia Mukundi; Deacons Jack O'Leary; George Maddock.
Res.: 17951 Dixie Hwy., 60430. Tel: 708-798-0622; Fax: 708-798-6137.
School—17949 Dixie Hwy., 60430. Tel: 708-798-0467; Fax: 708-957-5659. Lay Teachers 24; Students 313.
Catechesis/Religious Program—Tel: 708-798-3567. Students 410.

INDIAN CREEK, LAKE CO., ST. MARY OF VERNON, Rev. Joseph C. Curtis; Deacons Mark R. Zwolski; Dante D. Virgilio; James Wogan; Philip Pagnotta Jr.; John Glenn; Frank DeFrank.
Res.: 236 U.S. Hwy. 45, 60061. Tel: 847-362-1005; Fax: 847-362-6375.
Catechesis/Religious Program—Tel: 847-362-0653. Students 1,117.

INGLESIDE, LAKE CO., ST. BEDE, Rev. Timothy J. Fairman; Deacons John McMahon; Edward Quackenbush. In Res., Rev. Robert J. Fitzpatrick, Pastor Emeritus (Retired).
Res.: 36455 N. Wilson Rd., 60041. Tel: 847-587-2251; Fax: 847-973-1765.
School—36399 N. Wilson Rd., 60041. Tel: 847-587-5541; Fax: 847-587-2713. Lay Teachers 20; Students 340.
Catechesis/Religious Program—Tel: 847-587-2301. Students 187.

INVERNESS, COOK CO., HOLY FAMILY, Revs. Patrick J. Brennan; Fred Licciardi, C.PP.S.; Deacons Robert Antiss; James Multeri; Dawn Mayer, Pastoral Assoc.
Res.: 2515 W. Palatine Rd., 60067. Tel: 847-359-0042; Fax: 847-359-0639.
Catechesis/Religious Program—Tel: 847-359-0572. Students 1,700.

LA GRANGE PARK, COOK CO., ST. LOUISE DE MARILLAC, Revs. Fred W. Tomzik; Robert Marchwiany; Deacons Michael McLynn; David Kowalski.
Res.: 1144 Harrison Ave., 60526. Tel: 708-352-7388; Fax: 708-352-0714.
School—Tel: 708-352-2202; Fax: 708-352-6654. Lay Teachers 18; Students 262.
Youth Ministry—1144 Harrison Ave., 60526. Tel: 708-352-7388; Fax: 708-352-0714.
Catechesis/Religious Program—1125 Harrison Ave., LaGrange Park, 60526. Tel: 708-482-8814. Students 364.

LA GRANGE, COOK CO.

1—ST. CLETUS, Revs. Raymond F. Klees; Charles Gallagher, Pastor Emeritus; Patrick J. O'Neill.
Res.: 600 W. 55th St., 60525. Tel: 708-352-6209; Fax: 708-352-6774.
School—700 W. 55th St., 60525. Tel: 708-352-4820; Fax: 708-352-0707. Lay Teachers 25; Students 500.
Catechesis/Religious Program—Tel: 708-352-2383. Students 500.

2—ST. FRANCIS XAVIER, Revs. William J. Stenzel; Terrence M. Johnson; Robert A. Bacchi.
Res.: 124 N. Spring Ave., 60525. Tel: 708-352-0168; Fax: 708-352-4904.
School—145 N. Waiola Ave., 60525. Tel: 708-352-2175; Fax: 708-352-2057. Lay Teachers 47; Students 688.
Catechesis/Religious Program—Tel: 708-352-4555. Students 827.

LAKE FOREST, LAKE CO.

1—ST. MARY, Revs. George J. Rassas; Christopher M. Gustafson; Deacons James L. Kenney; Joseph G. Krakora; Joan O'Keefe, Pastoral Assoc.; Patricia Moran, Pastoral Assoc. In Res., Rev. Stephen E. Grunow.
Res.: 175 E. Illinois Rd., 60045. Tel: 847-234-0205; Fax: 847-234-9860.
School—185 E. Illinois Rd., 60045. Tel: 847-234-0371; Fax: 847-234-9593. Lay Teachers 57; Students 680.
Catechesis/Religious Program—Tel: 847-234-0090; Fax: 847-234-2755. Students 660.

2—ST. PATRICK, Rev. William J. McNulty.
Res.: 991 S. Waukegan Rd., 60045. Tel: 847-234-1401; Fax: 847-234-1433.
Catechesis/Religious Program—Tel: 847-234-2179; Fax: 847-234-1433. Students 700.

LAKE VILLA, LAKE CO., PRINCE OF PEACE, Revs. Richard M. Yanos; Steven G. Dombrowski; Deacons Timothy Leonard; Jeff Barton. In Res., Rev. Daniel F. Sullivan (Retired).
Res.: 135 S. Milwaukee Ave., 60046. Tel: 847-356-7915; Fax: 847-265-1678.
School—Tel: 847-356-6111; Fax: 847-356-6121. Lay Teachers 12; Students 228.
Catechesis/Religious Program—Tel: 847-356-5850; Fax: 847-265-1678. Students 740.

LAKE ZURICH, LAKE CO., ST. FRANCIS DE SALES, Revs. Ronald J. Gollatz; Roger Corrales-Diaz.

Res.: 135 S. Buesching Rd., 60047. Tel: 847-438-6622; Fax: 847-438-6638.
School—11 S. Buesching Rd., 60047. Tel: 847-438-7921; Fax: 847-438-7114. Lay Teachers 27; Students 504.
Catechesis/Religious Program—Tel: 847-438-3233; Fax: 847-438-7114. Students 1,691.

LANSING, COOK CO., ST. ANN, Revs. Michael A. Gabriel; Kurt D. Boras; Sr. Julie Flynn, O.P., Pastoral Assoc.
Parish Office—3010 Ridge Rd., 60438. Tel: 708-895-6700; Fax: 708-895-6877.
Res.: 3026 Ridge Rd., 60438. Tel: 708-895-6700; Fax: 708-895-6877.
School—3014 Ridge Rd., 60438. Tel: 708-895-1661. Lay Teachers 36; Students 657.
Catechesis/Religious Program—Tel: 708-895-5970. Students 473.

LEMONT, COOK CO.

1—ST. ALPHONSUS, Revs. Francis C. Jenks; Fred C. Pesek.
Res.: 210 E. Logan, 60439. Tel: 630-257-2414; Fax: 630-257-2476.
School—St. Alphonsus-St. Patrick Consolidated, (Grades K-8), Admin. Office: 20 W. 145 Davey Rd., 60439. Tel: 630-783-2220. Sisters 2; Lay Teachers 18; Students 338.
Catechesis/Religious Program—Tel: 630-257-2371; Fax: 630-257-2381. Students 440.

2—BLESSED JURGIS MATULAITIS, Rev. Algirdas Paliokas, S.J. In Res., Rev. Msgr. Ignatius L. Urbonas (GRY) (Retired).
Lithuanian Catholic Mission: 14915-127th St., Unit 101, 60439. Tel: 630-257-5613.
Catechesis/Religious Program—

3—SS. CYRIL AND METHODIUS, Revs. Lawrence M. Lisowski; Franciszek Florczyk (Poland); Deacon Norbert Lesnieski; Sr. Sandra Zorko, O.S.F., Pastoral Assoc.
Res.: 608 Sobieski St., 60439. Tel: 630-257-2776; Fax: 630-257-9372.
School—607 Sobieski St., 60439. Tel: 630-257-6488; Fax: 630-257-6465. Lay Teachers 18; Students 600.
Catechesis/Religious Program—Tel: 630-257-9314; Fax: 630-257-5806. Students 440.

4—ST. JAMES AT SAG BRIDGE, [CEM] Rev. Edward D. Gleeson, (CHC, USN Retired).
Res.: 10600 Archer Rd., 60439. Tel: 630-257-7000; Fax: 630-257-7912.
Catechesis/Religious Program—Students 124.

5—ST. PATRICK, Rev. Michael J. Cronin; Deacon Joseph Winblad.
Res.: 200 Illinois St., 60439. Tel: 630-257-6134; Fax: 630-257-0401.
School—St. Alphonsus-St. Patrick Consolidated, (Grades PreK-8), Admin. Office: 20 W. 145 Davey Rd., 60439. Tel: 630-783-2220; Fax: 630-783-2230. Lay Teachers 14; Students 322.
Catechesis/Religious Program—Tel: 630-257-8012; Fax: 630-257-0401. Students 355.

6—SLOVENIAN CATHOLIC MISSION, , (Dedicated to Bl A.M. Slomsek) Rev. Metod Ogorevc, O.F.M.; Deacon John Vidmar.
Res.: 14246 Main St., P.O. Box 608, 60439-0608. Tel: 630-257-2068; Fax: 630-257-2359.

LIBERTYVILLE, LAKE CO., ST. JOSEPH, Revs. John E. Hennessey; Kenneth Kiepura; Valerian Laini (Africa); Deacons Dennis I. Mudd; Dennis J. Dunn; Robert E. Matthews; William Sands; Jeffrey Newman. In Res., Rev. Victor J. Ivers (Retired).
Res.: 121 E. Maple Ave., 60048. Tel: 847-362-2073; Fax: 847-362-6821.
School—221 Park Pl., 60048. Tel: 847-362-0730; Fax: 847-362-8130. Lay Teachers 28; Students 562.
Catechesis/Religious Program—116 Hurlburt Ct., 60048. Tel: 847-362-5797; Fax: 847-362-6821. Students 1,356.

LYONS, COOK CO., ST. HUGH, Revs. Thomas A. Moran; Joseph Sellas (India); Deacon Willaim Rueth.
Res.: 7939 W. 43rd St., 60534. Tel: 708-447-3108; Fax: 708-447-9870.
Catechesis/Religious Program—Tel: 708-447-5711. Students 80.

MARKHAM, COOK CO., ST. GERARD MAJELLA, Rev. Joseph W. Altman, Admin.
Res.: 16130 Clifton Park, 60426. Tel: 708-331-8400; Fax: 708-596-0770.
Catechesis/Religious Program—Students 48.

MATTESON, COOK CO., ST. LAWRENCE O'TOOLE, Revs. Michael A. Nacius; Joseph T. Cook; Deacons Ronald Zanardo; Thomas Dehler; Rossini Alcos; John Rangel; Edward Winter.
Res.: 4101 St. Lawrence Ave., 60443. Tel: 708-748-6090; Fax: 708-748-4055.
School—Tel: 708-748-6090; Fax: 708-747-4099. Lay Teachers 18; Students 431.
Catechesis/Religious Program—Tel: 708-748-6090. Students 225.

MAYWOOD, COOK CO.

1—ST. EULALIA, Rev. James V. Quinlan; Rev. Msgr. William J. Quinn, Pastor Emeritus (Retired); Deacons Ben Bacchi; Giulio Camerini; George Lambert. In Res., Rev. Michael Adaickalam.
Res.: 1851 S. 9th Ave., 60153. Tel: 708-343-6120.
School—815 Lexington St., 60153. Tel: 708-343-5652. Sisters 4; Lay Teachers 10; Students 225.

2—ST. JAMES, Rev. Herbert J. Meyr; Deacons Antonio Maney; Roman Revering; Norberto Ojeda.
Res.: 305 S. 6th Ave., 60153. Tel: 708-343-5210; Fax: 708-343-9317.
Catechesis/Religious Program—611 Maple, 60153. Tel: 708-343-4542. Students 250.

MELROSE PARK, COOK CO.

1—ST. CHARLES BORROMEO, Revs. Claudio Holzer, C.S.; Michele DeSalvia, C.S.; Deacon Dominic Marella. In Res., Rev. Gino Dalpiaz, C.S.
Res.: 1637 N. 37th Ave., 60160. Tel: 708-343-7646; Fax: 708-343-3527.

2—OUR LADY OF MOUNT CARMEL, (Italian), Revs. Louis Gandolfi, C.S.; Hector Palos, C.S. In Res., Rev. John DiVito, C.S.
Res.: 1101 N. 23rd Ave., 60160. Tel: 708-344-4140; Fax: 708-344-0902.
Catechesis/Religious Program—Nereida Pareda, D.R.E. Students 350.

3—SACRED HEART, Revs. Cosmo F. Militello; Erwin J. Friedl; Deacons Raymond Behrendt; Victor Colucci. In Res., Rev. Peter Kunnalakatt (India).
Res.: 819 N. 16th Ave., 60160. Tel: 708-344-0757; Fax: 708-344-5906.
School—1503 W. Rice St., 60160. Tel: 708-344-4960. Sisters of the Third Order of St. Francis of the Holy Family 1; Lay Teachers 20; Students 201.
Catechesis/Religious Program—Tel: 708-681-0307. Students 80.

MIDLOTHIAN, COOK CO., ST. CHRISTOPHER, Revs. William E. Killeen; Michael V. Kalck; Deacons Joseph Brady, Pastoral Assoc.; Michael Smith. In Res., Rev. John Jesu Sagaya (India).
Res.: 14641 S. Keeler Ave., 60445. Tel: 708-388-8190; Fax: 708-388-0072.
School—14611 S. Keeler Ave., 60445. Tel: 708-385-8776; Fax: 708-385-8102. Sisters 1; Brothers 1; Lay Teachers 20; Students 348.
Catechesis/Religious Program—Tel: 708-388-4040. Students 358.

MORTON GROVE, COOK CO., ST. MARTHA, Rev. Dennis B. O'Neill; Deacons Bernard Berquist; Peter Meehan.
Res.: 8523 Georgiana Ave., 60053. Tel: 847-965-0262; Fax: 847-965-2535.
Catechesis/Religious Program—Tel: 847-965-8062. Students 220.

MT. PROSPECT, COOK CO.

1—ST. CECILIA, Revs. Daniel J. Brady; John W. Tapper. In Res., Rev. Elzear Gehlen, S.V.D.
Res.: 700 S. Meier Rd., 60056. Tel: 847-437-6208; Fax: 847-437-2520.
Catechesis/Religious Program—Tel: 847-437-6310; Fax: 847-437-5730. Students 243.

2—ST. EMILY, Revs. Dennis Stafford; Mark P. Canavan; Deacons Bill DiCanio; James R. Sanford; Sr. Joanne Marie Schutz, S.S.C.M., Pastoral Assoc.
Res.: 101 N. Horner Ln., 60056. Tel: 847-824-5049; Fax: 847-297-0358.
School—1400 E. Central Rd., 60056. Tel: 847-296-3490; Fax: 847-296-1155. Sisters of the Holy Family of Nazareth 3; Lay Teachers 32; Students 546.
Catechesis/Religious Program—Tel: 847-299-5865. Students 520.

3—ST. RAYMOND DE PENAFORT, Revs. Bernard J. Pietrzak; Phillip Henseler Jr.; Thomas F. Baldonieri; Deacon John Lorbach. In Res., Rev. Charles J. Skach (Retired); Sr. Dee Peppard, Pastoral Assoc.
Res.: 311 S. Ioka St., 60056. Tel: 847-253-8600; Fax: 847-253-0023.
School—300 S. Elmhurst Rd., 60056. Tel: 847-253-8555; Fax: 847-253-8939. Lay Teachers 37; Students 588.
Catechesis/Religious Program—Tel: 847-253-8600, Ext. 150. Students 792.

4—ST. THOMAS A BECKET, Rev. John W. Roller; Sr. Marylyn Welter, S.S.F., Pastoral Assoc.
Res.: 1321 Burning Bush Ln., 60056. Tel: 847-827-9220; Fax: 847-827-0370.
Catechesis/Religious Program—Tel: 847-296-9051. Students 208.

MUNDELEIN, LAKE CO.

1—ST. MARY OF THE ANNUNCIATION (Fremont Center), Revs. Ronald J. Lewinski; Salvador Den Hallegado; Deacons Robert A. Poletto; Albert Dietz.
Res.: 22333 W. Erhart Rd., 60060. Tel: 847-223-0010; Fax: 847-223-5960.
School—Tel: 847-223-4021; Fax: 847-223-3489. Lay Teachers 13; Students 224.
Catechesis/Religious Program—Tel: 847-223-0011. Students 510.

2—SANTA MARIA DEL POPOLO, Revs. Robert G. Aguirre; James W. Kinn, (Pastor Emeritus) (Retired); Jackson Colomb; M. David Arcilia, O.D.C. (Colombia); Edgar Rodriguez; Deacons John Simmons; Bill Dunn; Dave Auld. In Res., Revs. William J. Shields (Retired); Edgar Cardinas, O.D.C.
Res.: 116 N. Lake St., 60060. Tel: 847-949-8300; Fax: 847-949-2339.
School—126 N. Lake St., 60060. Tel: 847-949-2335; Fax: 847-949-9721. Lay Teachers 24; Students 405.
Catechesis/Religious Program—Tel: 847-949-2327. Students 580.
Convent—133 N. Lincoln Ave., 60060. Tel: 847-566-7343.

NILES, COOK CO.

1—ST. ISAAC JOGUES, Revs. Edward R. Fialkowski; Roman Zbieranski, O.F.M.; Deacons Frederick W. Ray, (Retired); Robert C. O'Keefe; Paul Stanton; Rod Ranola.
Res.: 8149 Golf Rd., 60714. Tel: 847-967-1060; Fax: 847-967-1070.
Catechesis/Religious Program—Tel: 847-966-1180; Fax: 847-966-0159. Students 343.

2—ST. JOHN BREBEUF, Revs. Thomas P. May; Arthur J. Olsen; Adams S. Galek (Poland); Deacons John Perkowitz; Thomas Paluch, Pastoral Assoc.; Lawrence Skaja.
Res.: 8307 N. Harlem Ave., 60714. Tel: 847-966-8145; Fax: 847-966-0014.
School—8301 Harlem Ave., 60714. Tel: 847-966-3266; Fax: 847-966-5351. Sisters 2; Lay Teachers 16; Students 465.
Catechesis/Religious Program—Tel: 847-966-3269. Students 486.

3—OUR LADY OF RANSOM, Revs. John R. Hall; Xamie M. Reyes; Deacons Robert Crandall; Charles O'Donnell.
Ministry Center—8624 W. Normal, 60714. Tel: 847-823-2550; Fax: 847-823-4291.
School—8350 N. Greenwood, 60714. Tel: 847-696-4413; Fax: 847-696-0031. Felician Sisters 3; Lay Teachers 15; Students 245.
Catechesis/Religious Program—Tel: 847-696-2994. Students 327.

NORRIDGE, COOK CO., DIVINE SAVIOR, Rev. Stephen J. Tebes; Deacons Gus Jeffery; Ronald Gronek.
Res.: 7740 W. Montrose, 60706. Tel: 708-456-9000; Fax: 708-456-7838.
School—7750 W. Montrose, 60706. Tel: 708-456-9074; Fax: 708-456-7856. Sisters 2; Lay Teachers 12; Students 120.
Catechesis/Religious Program—Students 255.

NORTH CHICAGO, LAKE CO., QUEEN OF PEACE, Rev. James E. Merold; Deacons Gary Munda Sr.; Irvin Boppart.
Res.: 910 14th St., 60064. Tel: 847-473-4079; Fax: 847-473-4143.
Catechesis/Religious Program—Tel: 847-473-1238. Students 635.

NORTH RIVERSIDE, COOK CO., MATER CHRISTI, Rev. M. Cyril Nemecek; Deacon Richard Gordus.
Res.: 2431 S. 10th Ave., 60546. Tel: 708-442-5611; Fax: 708-442-1306.
School—2400 S. 10th Ave., 60546. Tel: 708-442-7115; Fax: 708-447-1062. Lay Teachers 11; Students 158.
Catechesis/Religious Program—Students 70.

NORTHBROOK, COOK CO.

1—ST. NORBERT, Revs. Richard J. Mueller; Robert J. Lutz, Pastor Emeritus (Retired); Don Woznicki; Susan Martin, Pastoral Assoc. In Res., Rev. Richard J. Valker (Retired).
Res.: 1809 Walters Ave., 60062. Tel: 847-272-7090; Fax: 847-272-7771.
School—1817 Walters Ave., 60062. Tel: 847-272-0051; Fax: 847-272-5274. Maureen M. Brennen, Prin. Lay Teachers 31; Students 425.
Catechesis/Religious Program—Tel: 847-272-3086; Fax: 847-272-7771. Students 580.

2—OUR LADY OF THE BROOK, Rev. Richard E. Sztorc.
Res.: 3700 W. Dundee Rd., 60062. Tel: 847-272-5686; Fax: 847-498-0899.
Catechesis/Religious Program—Tel: 847-272-5131; Fax: 847-498-0899. Students 245.

NORTHFIELD, COOK CO., ST. PHILIP THE APOSTLE, Rev. Msgr. Robert J. Dempsey.
Res.: 1962 Old Willow Rd., 60093. Tel: 847-446-8383; Fax: 847-446-8338.
Catechesis/Religious Program—1962 Old Willow Rd., 60093. Tel: 847-446-9390. Students 190.

NORTHLAKE, COOK CO., ST. JOHN VIANNEY, CURE OF ARS, Revs. Charles V. Fanelli; Victor Rual de la Cruz (Peru), Extern; Martin Azhikkakath (India); Deacons John Zurawski; James Sinacore.
Res.: 46 N. Wolf Rd., 60164. Tel: 708-562-0500; Fax: 708-562-1824.
School—Tel: 708-562-1466; Fax: 708-562-1958. Lay Teachers 20; Students 206.
Catechesis/Religious Program—Tel: 708-562-2580. Students 393.

OAK FOREST, COOK CO., ST. DAMIAN, Revs. Michael G. Meany; Francis G. Scanlan; Robert Stuglik; Deacons Len Steinbeigle; Thomas Hipelius; William Stearns; Richard Werner.

Res.: 5220 W. 155th St., 60452. Tel: 708-687-1370; Fax: 708-687-1377.
School—5300 W. 155th St., 60452. Tel: 708-687-4230. Barbara Wesolowski, Prin. Lay Teachers 22; Students 777.
Catechesis/Religious Program—Tel: 708-687-7788. Students 976.

OAK LAWN, COOK CO.

1—ST. CATHERINE OF ALEXANDRIA, Revs. Patrick J. Henry; William J. Lion, Pastor Emeritus (Retired); John R. Dolehide, O.P.; Sr. Mary Cullen, O.P., Pastoral Assoc.; Deacon Richard Feltes.
Res.: 4100 W. 107th St., 60453. Tel: 708-425-2850; Fax: 708-425-2313.
School—10621 S. Kedvale Ave., 60453. Tel: 708-425-5547; Fax: 708-425-3701. Lay Teachers 22; Students 584.
Catechesis/Religious Program—Tel: 708-425-5747; Fax: 708-425-3701. Students 184.

2—ST. GERALD, Revs. Richard J. LoBianco; Martin T. Marren. In Res., Revs. William J. Buhrfeind (Retired); John L. White, S.M. (Retired).
Parish Office—9310 S. 55th Ct., 60453. Tel: 708-422-0234; Fax: 708-422-0822.
Res.: 9349 S. Central Ave., 60453. Tel: 708-422-0234; Fax: 708-422-0822.
School—9320 S. 55th Ct., 60453. Tel: 708-422-0121; Fax: 708-422-9216. Sisters of St. Francis (Clinton, IA) 2; Lay Teachers 24; Students 411.
Catechesis/Religious Program—Tel: 708-423-0458. Students 377.

3—ST. GERMAINE, Revs. William E. Malloy William O. Goedert, Pastor Emeritus (Retired); Michael J. Furlan; Deacons John Flanagan; Donald Daum; John L. Malone; Everett Helmer.
Res.: 9711 S. Kolin, 60453. Tel: 708-636-5060; Fax: 708-636-8007.
School—9735 S. Kolin, 60453. Tel: 708-425-6063. Lay Teachers 18; Students 390.

4—ST. LINUS, Rev. William T. Corcoran; Rev. Msgr. John I. Cardiff, Pastor Emeritus (Retired); Rev. Len Kruzel; Deacons Edward Gadomski; James Reinhart. In Res., Rev. William Browne (Jamaica).
Res.: 10300 S. Lawler Ave., 60453. Tel: 708-422-2400; Fax: 708-422-2707.
School—10400 S. Lawler Ave., 60453. Tel: 708-425-1656. Felician Sisters 2; Lay Teachers 26; Students 495.
Catechesis/Religious Program—Tel: 708-636-4373. Students 228.

5—ST. LOUIS DE MONTFORT, Rev. Frank J. Burek; Deacons Michael Karnoski; Michael Sharwarko; William Sullivan.
Res.: 8808 S. Ridgeland, 60453. Tel: 708-599-5300; Fax: 708-599-2678.
School—Tel: 708-599-5781; Fax: 708-599-5782. Lay Teachers 11; Students 202.
Catechesis/Religious Program—8840 S. Ridgeland, 60453. Tel: 708-598-1092. Students 190.

OAK PARK, COOK CO.

1—ASCENSION, Rev. William A. Burke.
Res.: 815 S. East Ave., 60304. Tel: 708-848-2703; Fax: 708-848-2773.
School—601 Van Buren, 60304. Tel: 708-386-7282; Fax: 708-524-4796. Lay Teachers 25; Students 475.
Catechesis/Religious Program—Tel: 708-848-3099. Students 330.

2—ST. CATHERINE OF SIENA-ST. LUCY, Revs. Daniel Whiteside; John J. Carolan, Pastor Emeritus (Retired); Deacon Bruce Bardford; James Hargadon, Pastoral Assoc.
Res.: 38 N. Austin Blvd., 60302. Tel: 708-386-8077; Fax: 708-386-5190.
School—27 Washington Blvd., 60302. Tel: 708-386-5286; Fax: 708-386-7328. Sr. Marion Cypser, R.S.M., Prin. Sisters of Mercy 1; Lay Teachers 12; Students 200.
Catechesis/Religious Program—Students 125.

3—ST. EDMUND, Rev. Joseph B. Ruiz; Sr. Madeleva Deegan, R.S.M., Pastoral Assoc.; Deacons James Przepasniak; Edward P. DeLorenzo. In Res., Revs. John P. Lucas; Edward C. Dufficy (Retired).
Res.: 188 S. Oak Park Ave., 60302. Tel: 708-848-4417; Fax: 708-848-0049.
School—200 S. Oak Park Ave., 60302. Tel: 708-386-5131; Fax: 708-386-5616. Lay Teachers 14; Students 250.
Catechesis/Religious Program—Tel: 708-848-7220. Students 260.

4—ST. GILES, Revs. Thomas M. Dore; Leroy A. Wickowski; Livingstone Kombo; Deacons Loretto J. Madonia; John A. Henricks. In Res., Rev. Edward P. Salmon.
Res.: 1045 Columbian Ave., 60302. Tel: 708-383-3430; Fax: 708-383-8644.
School—1030 Linden Ave., 60302. Tel: 708-383-6279; Fax: 708-383-9952. Lay Teachers 29; Students 432; PreK 43.
Catechesis/Religious Program—Tel: 708-383-4185; Fax: 708-383-8669. Students 305.

ORLAND HILLS, COOK CO., ST. ELIZABETH SETON, Revs. Lawrence P. McBrady; Tan Nguyen; Deacon Frank Gildea. In Res., Rev. William B. Gubbins (Retired).
Res.: 9300 W. 167th St., 60477. Tel: 708-403-0101; Fax: 708-403-0105.
School—Cardinal Joseph Bernardin, 9250 W. 167th St., 60477 Tel: 708-403-6525; Fax: 708-403-8621. Inter-Parish School serving St. Elizabeth Seton, St. Francis of Assisi, St. Julie Billiart and St. Stephen, Deacon and Martyr.
Catechesis/Religious Program—Tel: 708-403-0101; Fax: 708-403-9810. Students 2,407.

ORLAND PARK, COOK CO.

1—ST. FRANCIS OF ASSISI, Revs. Edward F. Upton; Kevin M. Birmingham.
Res.: 15050 S. Wolf Rd., 60467. Tel: 708-460-0042; Fax: 708-460-0136.
Catechesis/Religious Program—Tel: 708-460-0155. Students 1,762.

2—ST. MICHAEL, Revs. Edward J. McLaughlin; Robert J. Clark; Sr. Marietta Umlor, C.S.C., Pastoral Assoc.; Deacons Michael McDonough; Thomas Bartholomew; Tony Cocco. In Res., Rev. Michael J. Adams (Retired).
Res.: 14327 Highland Ave., 60462. Tel 708-349-0903; Fax: 708-349-6015.
School—14355 Highland Ave., 60462. Tel: 708-349-0068; Fax: 708-349-2658. Sisters 1; Lay Teachers 30; Students 764.
Catechesis/Religious Program—14345 Highland Ave., 60462. Tel: 708-349-0769. Students 722.

3—OUR LADY OF THE WOODS, Rev. Michael W. O'Connell; Deacon John Macarol.
Res.: 10731 W. 131st St., 60462. Tel: 708-361-4754; Fax: 708-361-5965.
Catechesis/Religious Program—Tel: 708-361-9435. Students 907.

PALATINE, COOK CO.

1—MISSION SAN JUAN DIEGO, Rev. Moises Marin, Admin.
Res.: 2323 North Wilke Rd., Arlington Heights, 60004. Tel 847-590-9332; Fax: 847-590-9333.
Catechesis/Religious Program—

2—ST. THERESA, Revs. Richard M. Zborowski; Christopher Ciomek; James E. Schmaus; Deacons Stephen Norys; Richard Pizzato; Lou Riccio; Jeffrey Shaw. In Res., Rev. Paul F. Rosemeyer (Retired).
Res.: 455 N. Benton, 60067. Tel: 847-705-2080; Fax: 847-202-8941.
Church: 465 N. Benton, 60067. Tel: 847-358-7760.
Ministry Center—455 N. Benton, 60067. Tel: 847-359-2846.
School—465 N. Benton, 60067. Tel: 847-359-1820; Fax: 847-705-2084. Lay Teachers 40; Students 670.
Catechesis/Religious Program—Tel: 847-358-2846. Students 748.

3—ST. THOMAS OF VILLANOVA, Revs. Raymond A. Yadron; Edward A. Carlson; Deacons Edward Kaczmarek; Thomas Maloney; Thomas Dunne; Richard Willer; Mark Duffey; John Pistone; William Karstenson.
Office—1152 E. Anderson Dr., 60074. Tel: 847-358-6999; Fax: 847-934-4919.
School—1141 E. Anderson Dr., 60074. Tel: 847-358-2110; Fax: 847-776-1435. Lay Teachers 15; Students 245.
Catechesis/Religious Program—Tel: 847-358-2386. Students 650.

PALOS HEIGHTS, COOK CO.

1—ST. ALEXANDER, Revs. Edward J. Cronin; Frank A. Kurucz.
Res.: 7025 W. 126th St., 60463. Tel: 708-448-4861; Fax: 708-448-0039.
School—126th St. at 71st Ave., 60463. Tel: 708-448-0408; Fax: 708-448-5947. Lay Teachers 30; Students 442.
Catechesis/Religious Program—Tel: 708-448-6624. Students 610.

2—INCARNATION, Revs. Ronald J. Mass; David J. Byrne; Deacons John Seitz; James Langwell.
Res.: 5757 W. 127th St., 60463. Tel: 708 597-3180; Fax: 708-597-2452.
School—Tel: 708-385-6250; Fax: 708-597-0588. Lay Teachers 20; Students 304.
Catechesis/Religious Program—Tel: 708 388-4004; Fax: 708-597-0588. Students 306.

PALOS HILLS, COOK CO., SACRED HEART, Revs. Richard M. Homa; Robert F. McGinnity, Pastor Emeritus (Retired); Brian Ardagh; Deacon William Barker. In Res., Rev. Robert G. Herne (Retired).
Res.: 8245 W. 111th St., 60465. Tel: 708-974-3336; Fax: 708-974-3556.
Catechesis/Religious Program—Students 470.

PARK FOREST, COOK CO., ST. IRENAEUS, Rev. Daniel J. O'Sullivan.
Res.: 78 Cherry St., 60466. Tel: 708-748-3891; Fax: 708-748-7998.
Catechesis/Religious Program—Tel: 708-748-7997.

PARK RIDGE, COOK CO.

1—MARY, SEAT OF WISDOM, Revs. Robert E. McLaughlin; Ronald N. Kalas, Pastor Emeritus (Retired); Michael J. Wanda. In Res., Rev. Theodore Stone (Retired).
Res.: 920 Granville Ave., 60068. Tel: 847-825-3153; Fax: 847-825-3484.
School—1352 S. Cumberland, 60068. Tel: 847-825-2500; Fax: 847-825-1943. Lay Teachers 33; Students 675.
Catechesis/Religious Program—Tel: 847-825-8763; Fax: 847-825-3484. Students 648.

2—ST. PAUL OF THE CROSS, Revs. Carl Morello; Robert C. Rizzo; Neil E. Fackler; Deacons Aloysius J. Memmel; Robert T. Bulger. In Res., Rev. Daniel A. Smilanic, J.C.D.
Res.: 320 S. Washington St., 60068. Tel: 847-825-7605; Fax: 847-825-5186.
School—Tel: 847-825-6366; Fax: 847-825-2466. Sisters 2; Lay Teachers 29; Students 682.
Catechesis/Religious Program—Tel: 847-692-2758. Students 1,193.

POSEN, COOK CO., ST. STANISLAUS BISHOP AND MARTYR, Rev. Ralph E. Starus; Deacons Joseph Wilczynski; Daniel Dutkiewicz.
Res.: 14414 McKinley Ave., 60469. Tel: 708-597-4910; Fax: 708-597-4841.
School—14418 McKinley Ave., 60469. Tel: 708-388-9211; Fax: 708-388-8755. Lay Teachers 10; Students 253.
Catechesis/Religious Program—Students 12.

PROSPECT HEIGHTS, COOK CO., ST. ALPHONSUS LIGUORI, Revs. Robert P. Heinz; Richard J. Maginot, Pastor Emeritus (Retired); Deacon Norbert Ciesil. In Res., Rev. Raymond A. Dunne, S.J.
Res.: 411 N. Wheeling Rd., 60070. Tel: 847-255-7452; Fax: 847-255-7520.
School—Tel: 847-255-5538. Sisters 1; Lay Teachers 20; Students 341.
Catechesis/Religious Program—Tel: 847-255-9490. Students 325.

RIVER FOREST, COOK CO.

1—ST. LUKE, Revs. Kenneth J. Fischer; Thomas G. Aschenbrener; Deacons Terrance Norton; John O'Neill; Thomas Coffey; Paul Faherty; Robert Zima; Robert Slobig.
Res.: 528 Lathrop Ave., 60305. Tel: 708-771-8250; Fax: 708-771-8809.
School—519 Ashland Ave., 60305. Tel: 708-366-8587; Fax: 708-366-3831. Lay Teachers 25; Students 351.
Catechesis/Religious Program—Tel: 708-771-5959; Fax: 708-771-5960. Students 415.

2—ST. VINCENT FERRER, Revs. Thomas D. Noesen, O.P.; Robert Kilbridge, O.P.; Albert P. Judy, O.P. In Res., Revs. Vincent I. Zarlenga, O.P.; John J. O'Malley, O.P.; John J. Meany, O.P.; Kevin O'Rourke, O.P.; Kevin R. Fane, O.P.; Peter J. Hereley, O.P.; Paul Whittington, O.P.; Bro. Jordan Kelly, O.P.; Deacons Robert C. Sassetti; Jerome Trakszelis.
Res.: 1530 Jackson Ave., 60305. Tel: 708-366-7090; Fax: 708-366-7092.
Church: 1530 Jackson Ave., 60305.
School—1515 Lathrop Ave., 60305. Tel: 708-771-5907; Fax: 708-771-7114. Dominican Sisters 2; Lay Teachers 26; Students 372.
Catechesis/Religious Program—Tel: 708-771-0322. Students 160.

RIVER GROVE, COOK CO., ST. CYPRIAN, Rev. Ronald W. Navoy; Deacons James Platt; Gerald Zych.
Res.: 2601 Clinton St., 60171. Tel: 708-453-4800; Fax: 708-453-6141.
School—2561 Clinton St., 60171. Tel: 708-453-6300; Fax: 708-453-6141. Religious 1; Lay Teachers 10; Students 165.
Catechesis/Religious Program—Tel: 708-453-5719; Fax: 708-453-6141.

RIVERDALE, COOK CO., QUEEN OF APOSTLES, Rev. Daniel M. Tomich; Deacon Gerald Hahn.
Res.: 207 W. 145th St., 60827. Tel: 708-849-4901; Fax: 708-849-5903.
School—14419 S. Atlantic, 60827. Tel: 708-849-3848; Fax: 708-849-5903. Lay Teachers 10; Students 240.
Catechesis/Religious Program—Tel: 708-841-0252. Students 7.

RIVERSIDE, COOK CO., ST. MARY, Revs. Gerald T. Gunderson; Robert S. Banzin; Sr. Margaret Sannasardo, B.V.M., Pastoral Assoc.
Res.: 126 Herrick Rd., 60546. Tel: 708-447-1020; Fax: 708-447-3309.
School—97 Herrick Rd., 60546. Tel: 708-442-5747; Fax: 708-442-0125. Sisters 6; Lay Teachers 25; Students 466.
Catechesis/Religious Program—Tel: 708-447-6812. Students 448.

ROLLING MEADOWS, COOK CO., ST. COLETTE, Revs. Dennis M. Zalecki; Ricardo Castillo-Castillo; Deacons John Connor; Eddies Ortiz. In Res., Rev. Joseph F. Ognibene (Retired).
Res.: 3900 S. Meadow Dr., 60008. Tel: 847-394-8100; Fax: 847-394-8102.
School—Tel: 847-392-4098; Fax: 847-392-8155. Lay Teachers 14; Students 217.

Catechesis / Religious Program—Tel: 847-394-0274. Students 413.

ROSEMONT-DES PLAINES, COOK CO., OUR LADY OF HOPE, Revs. William D. Mannion; Thomas E. Schwab, Pastor Emeritus (Retired); Deacon James J. Ernst. In Res., Rev. Kenneth J. Velo.
Res.: 9711 W. Devon Ave., 60018. Tel: 847-825-4673; Fax: 847-825-4631.
Catechesis / Religious Program—Students 75.

ROUND LAKE, LAKE CO., ST. JOSEPH, Revs. Joseph P. Allen; Donald J. Lund; Deacons John Brooks; David Kamka.
Res.: 114 N. Lincoln Ave., 60073. Tel: 847-546-3610; Fax: 847-546-3449.
School—Tel: 847-546-1720. Lay Teachers 23; Students 443.
Catechesis / Religious Program—Tel: 847-546-3554. Students 600.

SAUK VILLAGE, COOK CO., ST. JAMES, Rev. David B. Krolczyk. In Res., Rev. Paul E. Schwartz (Retired).
Res.: 22400 S. Torrence Ave., 60411-5144. Tel: 708-757-2170; Fax: 708-757-2176.
Catechesis / Religious Program—Tel: 708-757-2174; Fax: 708-757-2176. Students 215.
Convent—21903 Orion St., 60411. Tel: 708-758-5431.

SCHAUMBURG, COOK CO.

1—CHURCH OF THE HOLY SPIRIT, Rev. William Tkachuk; Deacons Raymond Doud; Lowell Taylor, (Retired); Timothy Kryszak Sr.; Luis Trevino; Wayne Beyer; Mario Contreras; Mike Enger; Sung Han; Xavier Carrera.
Res.: 1451 W. Bode Rd., 60194. Tel: 847-882-7580; Fax: 847-882-1845.
Catechesis / Religious Program—Tel: 847-882-7584. Students 1,188.

2—ST. MARCELLINE, Revs. Denis Condon; Sergio Romo; Deacons Edward Boggio; Joe Garcia; John Zeller; Phil Ontiveros; Thomas LaMantia.
Res.: 822 Springinsguth, 60193. Tel: 847-524-4429; Fax: 847-524-4597.
Catechesis / Religious Program—Tel: 847-524-3960. Students 593.

3—ST. MATTHEW, Revs. Joseph M. Wilk; Kenneth R. Bratko, C.R.; Deacon Thomas Duszynski.
Res.: 1001 E. Schaumburg Rd., 60194. Tel: 847-891-1220; Fax: 847-891-3140.
Catechesis / Religious Program—1005 Schaumberg Rd., Schaumberg, 60194. Tel: 847-891-8408; Fax: 847-891-4291. Students 925.

SCHILLER PARK, COOK CO.

1—ST. BEATRICE, Rev. John J. Bresnahan.
Res.: 4157 Atlantic Ave., 60176. Tel: 847-678-0138; Fax: 847-678-3974.
School—Tel: 847-678-1752; Fax: 847-678-1033. Lay Teachers 14; Students 209.
Catechesis / Religious Program—4141 N. Atlantic, 60176. Students 178.

2—ST. MARIA GORETTI, Rev. Thomas C. McNeff.
Res.: 3929 N. Wehrman Ave., 60176. Tel: 847-678-3988; Fax: 847-678-3901.
School—Tel: 847-678-2560; Fax: 847-678-2919. Lay Teachers 13; Students 240.
Catechesis / Religious Program—Students 123.

SKOKIE, COOK CO.

1—ST. JOAN OF ARC, Rev. James L. Barrett.
Res.: 9248 N. Lawndale Ave., Evanston, 60203. Tel: 847-673-0409; Fax: 847-673-9626.
School—Tel: 847-679-0660; Fax: 847-673-0689. Lay Teachers 18; Students 249.
Catechesis / Religious Program—Students 250.

2—ST. LAMBERT, Revs. Andrew E. Luczak; William P. Welsh; Deacons John O'Leary; David Baez.
Res.: 8148 Karlov Ave., 60076. Tel: 847-673-5090; Fax: 847-677-5135.
Catechesis / Religious Program—Tel: 847-329-1201. Students 160.

3—ST. PETER, Revs. Edward D. Grace; Jerome Twarog, C.R.; Deacon James Wills. In Res., Rev. Thomas A. Baima.
Res.: 8116 Niles Center Rd., 60077. Tel: 847-673-1492; Fax: 847-673-6979.
School—8140 Niles Center Rd., 60077. Tel: 847-673-0918; Fax: 847-673-6469. Lay Teachers 20; Students 300.
Catechesis / Religious Program—Tel: 847-679-1202; Fax: 847-673-6469. Students 340.

SOUTH HOLLAND, COOK CO.

1—HOLY GHOST, Rev. Joseph R. Bennett.
Res.: 700 E. 170th St., 60473. Tel: 708-333-7011; Fax: 708-333-1996.
School—Tel: 708-333-7010; Fax: 708-333-1693. Lay Teachers 10; Students 209.
Catechesis / Religious Program—Tel: 708-333-7011. Students 39.

2—ST. JUDE THE APOSTLE, Revs. Thomas S. Cabala; John J. Powers, Pastor Emeritus (Retired); Deacons Herbert Drazba; Arthur Nylen; Mel Stasinski; Romeo Munoz.
Res.: 880 E. 154th St., 60473. Tel: 708-333-3550; Fax: 708-339-3336.
School—900 E. 154th St., 60473. Tel: 708-333-8173. Sisters 3; Lay Teachers 19; Students 300.
Catechesis / Religious Program—Tel: 708-225-1180. Students 125.

STICKNEY, COOK CO., ST. PIUS X, Rev. Neil Van Dyke; Deacon Marvin Kocar.
Res.: 4314 S. Oak Park Ave., 60402. Tel: 708-484-7951; Fax: 708-749-8515.
Catechesis / Religious Program—Tel: 708-788-6090; Fax: 708-749-8518. Students 140.

STREAMWOOD, COOK CO., ST. JOHN THE EVANGELIST, Revs. Robert F. Tonelli; Martin Educardo Bedoya; Deacons Earl Dahl; Louis Farinella; James Furey; Robert DeFiore; Larry Rybicki.
Res.: 427 Cedarcrest Dr., 60107. Tel: 630-837-6500; Fax: 630-483-3153.
School—Tel: 630-289-3040; Fax: 630-289-3026. Lay Teachers 14; Students 232.
Catechesis / Religious Program—Tel: 630-837-1060; Fax: 630-289-3026. Students 496.

SUMMIT, COOK CO., ST. JOSEPH, Revs. Thaddeus J. Bojczuk; Gerald C. Kroeger, O.P.; Henry Pozdol (Retired); Deacons Ben Michalowski; Peter Manning.
Res.: 7240 W. 57th St., 60501. Tel: 708-458-0501.
School—5641 S. 73rd Ave., 60501. Tel: 708-458-2927. Sisters 1; Lay Teachers 9; Students 200.

TINLEY PARK, COOK CO.

1—ST. GEORGE, Revs. Kenneth J. Fleck; Michael Novick; Christopher E. Doering; Deacons Richard Kristinat; Paul Gilbert; Dominick Dattoli; John Ficker; Joseph Panek. In Res., Rev. Blaise Coelho.
Res.: 6707 W. 175th St., 60477. Tel: 708-532-2243; Fax: 708-532-2055.
School—6700 W. 176th St., 60477. Tel: 708-522-2626; Fax: 708-532-2025. Mantellate Sisters 2; Felician Sisters 1; Lay Teachers 22; Students 584.
Catechesis / Religious Program—Tel: 708-532-8211. Students 825.

2—SAINT JULIE BILLIART, Revs. Steven M. Lanza; Anthony C. Puchenski; Deacons Richard Miska; Michael Kiley.
Res.: 7399 W. 159th St., 60477. Tel: 708-429-6767; Fax: 708-429-6788.
Catechesis / Religious Program—Tel: 708-429-1044. Students 1,200.

3—ST. STEPHEN, DEACON AND MARTYR, Revs. James Finno; Waldemar Stawiarski; Deacons Joseph Stalcup Sr.; Kenneth Zawadzki; William Engler.
Res.: 17500 S. 84th Ave., 60477. Tel: 708-342-2400; Fax: 708-342-1545.
Catechesis / Religious Program—Students 870.

VOLO, LAKE CO., ST. PETER, Rev. Donald Dietz, O.M.I., Admin.
Res.: 27551 Volo Village Rd., 60073. Tel: 815-385-5496.
Catechesis / Religious Program—Students 124.

WADSWORTH, LAKE CO., ST. PATRICK, Revs. Patrick G. Cecil; George J. Dyer, Pastor Emeritus (Retired); Ronald C. Lewandowski; Deacons Dennis Brown, Pastoral Assoc.; John Richardson; Louis Abboud; Phillip Fragassi; Edward Tomkowiak; David Egan; Daniel Simmet.
Res.: 15000 Wadsworth Rd., 60083. Tel: 847-244-4161; Fax: 847-336-0630.
School—Tel: 847-623-8446; Fax: 847-623-3119. Marcella Bosnak, Prin. Lay Teachers 26; Students 580.
Catechesis / Religious Program—Tel: 847-236-9131; Fax: 847-336-0630. Students 505.

WAUCONDA, LAKE CO., TRANSFIGURATION, Revs. Thomas M. Enright; Jan F. Kaplan (Poland); Deacons Marion Omiatek; John Zimmermann; Feliks Pezowicz; Gilberto Vasquez; Marilyn Omiatek, Pastoral Min.; Dee Zimmermann, Pastoral Min.; Josette Pezowicz, Pastoral Min.; Carolina Vazquez, Pastoral Min. In Res., Rev. John Mendonca (Pakistan).
Res.: 316 W. Mill St., 60084. Tel: 847-526-2400; Fax: 847-526-2961.
School—Tel: 847-526-6311; Fax: 847-526-4637. Lay Teachers 25; Students 340.
Catechesis / Religious Program—Tel: 847-526-6400. Students 526.

WAUKEGAN, LAKE CO.

1—ST. ANASTASIA, Rev. Aloysius Funtila.
Res.: 624 Douglas Ave., 60085. Tel: 847-623-2875; Fax: 847-623-4882.
School—Lay Teachers 20; Students 368.
Catechesis / Religious Program—Students 78.

2—ST. BARTHOLOMEW, Merged, with St. Joseph. See Holy Family for details.

3—ST. DISMAS, Rev. John M. Ryan; Deacons Anthony Sacramento; Michael Sanzone.
Res.: 2600 Sunset Ave., 60087. Tel: 847-623-5050; Fax: 847-623-5292.
Catechesis / Religious Program—2226 McAree Rd., 60087. Tel: 847-244-9510; Fax: 847-623-5092. Students 190.

4—HOLY FAMILY, Revs. Gary M. Graf; Sergio Solis; Deacons Euesbio Mareno; Edward Scarbalis; Angel Velazquez. In Res., Rev. Michael Boehm.
Res.: 450 S. Keller Ave., 60085. Tel: 847-623-2655; Fax: 847-623-9479.
School—501 S. Utica St., 60085. Participant in Lake Shore Catholic Academy.
Catechesis / Religious Program—Students 100.

5—IMMACULATE CONCEPTION B.V.M., Rev. Frank W. Plotka; Deacons Victor Ruiz; Pedro Martinez; Rev. Antoni J. Kretowicz (Poland). In Res., Rev. James P. Shields (Retired).
Res.: 508 Grand Ave., 60085. Tel: 847-336-3684; Fax: 847-336-9040.
School—Tel: 847-336-4110; Fax: 847-336-9040. Lay Teachers 16; Students 200.
Catechesis / Religious Program—Tel: 847-360-7065; Fax: 847-336-9040. Students 270.

6—ST. JOSEPH, Merged, with St. Bartholomew. See Holy Family listing for details.

WESTCHESTER, COOK CO.

1—DIVINE INFANT, Revs. Gerald P. Joyce; Thomas Winikates.
Res.: 1601 Newcastle Ave., 60154. Tel: 708-865-8071; Fax: 708-865-8032.
School—Tel: 708-865-0122; Fax: 708-865-9495. Lay Teachers 14; Students 230.
Catechesis / Religious Program—Students 210.

2—DIVINE PROVIDENCE, Rev. Thomas E. Unz; Mr. Marco Matonich, Pastoral Assoc.; Deacons Frank DeVita, (Retired); Jerry Fox.
Res.: 2550 S. Mayfair Ave., 60154. Tel: 708-562-3364; Fax: 708-562-3134.
School—2500 S. Mayfair Ave., 60154. Tel: 708-562-2258; Fax: 708-562-9171. Lay Teachers 13; Students 197.
Catechesis / Religious Program—Tel: 708-562-3422; Fax: 708-562-3134. Students 114.

WESTERN SPRINGS, COOK CO., ST. JOHN OF THE CROSS, Revs. Richard P. Hynes; Joseph F. McDonnell, Pastor Emeritus (Retired); John W. McGivern; Sr. Jeanne Bonneau, C.N.D., Pastoral Assoc.; Deacons Thomas McGorey; Joseph Pepitone.
Res.: 5005 Wolf Rd., 60558. Tel: 708-246-4404; Fax: 708-246-4566.
School—705 51st St., 60558. Tel: 708-246-4454; Fax: 708-246-9010. Lay Teachers 42; Students 764.
Catechesis / Religious Program—51st St. & Wolf Rd., 60558. Tel: 708-246-6760; Fax: 708-246-9010. Students 1,239.

WHEELING, COOK CO., ST. JOSEPH THE WORKER, Rev. Frederick L. Brandstrader; Deacons Perry Duderstadt; Steve Stecker.
Res.: 181 W. Dundee Rd., 60090. Tel: 847-537-2740; Fax: 847-537-7914.
Catechesis / Religious Program—Tel: 847-537-4182. Students 800.

WILMETTE, COOK CO.

1—ST. FRANCIS XAVIER, Revs. William J. Sheridan; Edward F. Harnett, Pastor Emeritus (Retired); George W. Klein; Sr. Joyce Shanabarger, O.S.F., Pastoral Assoc.; Dr. Patty Jane Pelton, Pastoral Assoc.; Deacon William Thesing, Pastoral Assoc. In Res., Rev. Richard Jakubik.
Office—524 Ninth St., 60091. Tel: 847-256-4250; Fax: 847-256-4254.
School—808 Linden Ave., 60091. Tel: 847-256-0644. Sr. Mary K. O'Brien, B.V.M., Prin. Sisters 1; Lay Teachers 27; Students 380.
Catechesis / Religious Program—Tel: 847-251-6730; Fax: 847-256-4254. Students 660.

2—ST. JOSEPH, Revs. John E. Pollard; Robert Schultz; Ms. Dana McKenna, D.R.E. In Res., Rev. Thomas M. Powers (Retired).
Res.: 1747 Lake Ave., 60091. Tel: 847-251-0771; Fax: 847-251-5715.
School—1757 Lake Ave., 60091. Tel: 847-256-7870. Ronald Berger, Prin. Lay Teachers 24; Students 314.
Catechesis / Religious Program—Tel: 847-251-3254. Students 375.

WINNETKA, COOK CO.

1—SS. FAITH, HOPE AND CHARITY, Revs. Kevin J. Spiess; Louis J. Tylka; Deacons Terrence Levins; Roger Mullaney. In Res., Revs. William J. Flaherty (Retired); Jeffrey S. Grob.
Res.: 191 Linden St., 60093. Tel: 847-446-7646; Fax: 847-446-7630.
School—180 Ridge Ave., 60093. Tel: 847-446-0031; Fax: 847-446-9064. Sisters 1; Lay Teachers 32; Students 436.
Catechesis / Religious Program—Students 750.

2—SACRED HEART, Revs. Robert E. Ferrigan; Mark Simpson; Deacons Michael McNulty; John Fay.
Res.: 905 Burr Ave., 60093. Tel: 847-446-0856; Fax: 847-501-5311.
Parish Center—1077 Tower Rd., 60093. Tel: 847-446-0856.
School—1095 Gage St., 60093. Tel: 847-446-0005. Lay Teachers 35; Students 276.
Catechesis / Religious Program—Tel: 847-446-6535; Fax: 847-446-1969. Students 565.

ZION-BEACH PARK, LAKE CO., OUR LADY OF HUMILITY, Revs. David J. Mulvihill; Jan Krutewicz; Deacons James Askew; Philip Horne; Max Jinkens; Michael Mercure; Robert Ochsner.

Res.: 10655 Wadsworth Rd., 60099. Tel: 847-872-8778; Fax: 847-872-8780.
School—10601 Wadsworth Rd., 60099. Tel: 847-746-3722; Fax: 847-731-2870. Ms. Deborah Poturalski, Prin. Lay Teachers 13; Students 245.
Catechesis/Religious Program—Tel: 847-746-3744; Fax: 847-872-8780. Students 340.

Syro-Malabar Rite

BELLWOOD, COOK CO., SYRO-MALABAR CATHOLIC MISSION OF THE ARCHDIOCESE OF CHICAGO, See Separate Listing, Under the Diocese of St. Thomas Syro-Malabar

CHICAGO, COOK CO., KNANITE SYRO-MALABAR CATHOLIC MISSION OF THE ARCHDIOCESE OF CHICAGO, Rev. Philip Joseph Thodukayil, Dir.
Immaculate Heart of Mary: 3834 N. Spaulding, 60618. Tel: 773-509-9147.

Malankara Rite

CHICAGO, COOK CO., SYRO-MALANKARA CATHOLIC MISSION OF THE ARCHDIOCESE OF CHICAGO,
Divine Liturgy—1208 Ashland St., Evanston, 60202. Tel: 847-332-1794. Rev. Thomas Varghese, Dir.

Chaplains of Public Institutions

CHICAGO. *Chicago Airports Catholic Chaplaincy*, Formerly CHICAGO O'HARE INTERNATIONAL AIRPORTP.O. Box 66353, 60666. Rev. Michael G. Zaniolo.
Hines V.A. Hospital. Rev. Max Ernesto M. Saldua (Philippines) (MO).
John H. Stroger, Jr. Hospital of Cook County, Formerly COOK COUNTY HOSPITALTel: 312-633-6000. Revs. Eugene J. Nevins, S.J., Dir., James Chambers, S.J., Robert Finn, S.J., Sr. Marie Louise Jilk, S.Sp.S.

NORTH CHICAGO. *Veterans Affairs Medical Center*. Rev. William F. Vander Heyden (GB).

OAK FOREST. *Oak Forest Hospital*, 4700 W. 159th St., 60452. Tel: 708-687-2035. Rev. Wayne H. Wurst.

On Duty Outside the Archdiocese:
Rev. Msgr.—
Trisco, Robert F., Hist.Eccl.D., Curley Hall, Catholic University of America, Washington, DC 20064.
Revs.—
Barnum, Martin, Sacred Heart School of Theology, 7335 S. Hwy. 100, P.O. Box 429, Hales Corners, WI 53130-0429.
Brankin, Patrick M., St. Theresa, P.O. Box 297, Collinsville, OK 74021-0297.
Broccolo, Gerard T., 1011 S. Valentia St., #135, Denver, CO 80231.
Clements, George H., 1522 K St., Ste. 450 NE, Washington, DC 20005.
Coughlin, Daniel P., Office of the Chaplain, U.S. House of Representatives, H B 25 The Capitol, Washington, DC 20004.
Jamnicky, John A., Mobility Apostolates, 3211 Fourth St., NE, Washington, DC 20017.
Kiley, J. Cletus, Bishop's Staff House, 4001 14th St., N.E., Washington, DC 20017.
Krylowicz, Mark J., Immaculate Conception, P.O. Box Copperton, Bingham Canyon, UT 84006.
Lorenz, Matthais E., 5531 E. Lake Dr., #31C, Lisle, 60532.
Place, Michael D., S.T.D., The Catholic Health Association of the United States, 4455 Woodson Rd., P.O. Box 5889A, St. Louis, MO 63134-9916.

Military Chaplains:
Rev. Msgr.—
Dobes, George E., J.C.L., Archdiocese for the Military Services U.S.A., P.O. Box 4469, Washington, DC 20017-0469.
Revs.—
Falkenthal, Thomas W., P.O. Box 55001, MCAS, Beaufort, SC 29904-5001.
Hannigan, John T., Marine Corps Recruit Depot, Bldg 854 P.O. Box 4469, Parris Island, SC 29905.
Joslyn, James W., 655 Riverside Dr., Apt. 401S, Memphis, TN 38103-4630.
Kloak, David G., Chap. of Marine Corp, 2 Navy Annex Room 3024, Washington, DC 20380-1775.
Simpson, Brian L., U.S. Naval Support Activities, Psc 816, Box 1795, FPO, AE 09612.
Stake, Ronald P., 11204 Terrel Lane, Hampton, VA 23666-5839.

Graduate Studies:
Revs.—
Fiala, Timothy R., International Theological Institute, Kartause Maria Thron A-3292 Gaming, Germany.
Huitrado, Juan, Planzuela De Villa Seca #102, Colonia Centro, Zacatecas, Zac 98000 Mexico.

Missionary Work:
Revs.—
Cleary, Philip C., Nuestros Pequenos Hermanos, Apartado Postal 333, 62000 Cuernavaca, Morelos, Mexico.
Hays, Kevin W., Society of St. James the Apostle, Ap # 136, Moquegua, Peru.

Other Assignments:
Rev. Msgr.—
Sarauskas, R. George
Revs.—
Alcantara, Miguel B., 2702 N. Artesian, 60647.
Bonin, Harold A., 2040 Laurel Ave., Hanover Park, 60133.
Buck, Daniel P., P.O. Box 455, Mundelein, 60060.
Burke, William A., 9427 S. Utica Ave., Evergreen Park, 60805.
Carlson, Kenneth F., 2801 O.W. Curry Dr., APT 621, Killeen, TX 76542.
Clair, John J., Misericordia-North, 6300 N. Ridge Ave., 60660.
Coleman, Robert P., Apartado 1951, Acapulco Guerrero 39581 Mexico.
Egan, Gerard P., Loyola University, 820 N Michigan, 60611.
Englert, Anthony A., 7033 1/2 N. Sheridan Rd. - 2W, 60626.
Franzman, Thomas R., 8237 South Shore Dr., 60617.
Galivan, James F., 1039 W. 32nd St., 60608.
Gilligan, Michael J., San Rocco Oratory of St. Agnes, 315 E. 22nd St & San Rocco Pl., Chicago Hts., 60411.
Holihan, Daniel M., P.O. Box 455, Mundelein, 60060.
Hurtado-Badillo, Domingo, 916 N. Noble, 60622.
Kealy, Robert L., P.O. Box 455, Mundelein, 60060.
Kleiber, Kenneth R., 15202 N. 40th St., #223-2, Phoenix, AZ 85032-4652.
LaChance, Charles P., 810 W. Montrose Ave., 60613.
Laz, Medard P., P.O. Box 300415, 60630
Lefebure, Leo D., Christ the King, 740 N. Broadway, Yonkers, NY 10701.
Maday, Norbert J., P.O. Box 455, Mundelein, 60060.
McCarthy, James H., 2953 S. Lowe, 60616. Special Religious Ed. Div.
McGlinn, Robert J., Cristo Rey Parish, 800 Wisconsin Ave., Racine, WI 53403.
McKenna, Edward J., P.O. Box 648, Beverly Shores, IN 46301.
Mulsoff, Donald J., P.O. Box 455, Mundelein, 60060.
Nangle, Thomas R., Police Chaplaincy, 1140 W. Jackson, 60607.
Ngyuen, Phien T., O.L. Queen of Angels, 2046 Mar Vista Dr., Newport Beach, CA 92660.
O'Keefe, Millard, Alvernia Manor, 13950 Main St., Lemont, 60439.
O'Reilly, Gerald K., c/o Ellen O'Reilly-Garcia, 5434 N. Magnolia, 60640.
Price, John R., 6054 W. 64th Place, 60638.
Ray, James M., P.O. Box 455, Mundelein, 60060.
Robinson, John A., P.O. Box 455, Mundelein, 60060.
Roll, Robert J., 3745 S. Paulina St., 60609.
Sevick, John M., 75-246 Malulani Dr., Kailuna-Kona, HI 96740.
Snieg, Marion J., 645 N. Michigan Ave., Ste. 543, 60611-2814.
Stefanski, Gery W., 837 Mulford St., Apt. 1, Evanston, 60202.
Steiner, Daniel R., Villa Scalabrini, 480 N. Wolf Rd., Northlake, 60164.
Strand, Ralph S., P.O. Box 455, Mundelein, 60060.
Strus, Walter A., 1039 W. 32nd St., 60608.
Swade, Thomas J., P.O. Box 455, Mundelein, 60060.
Szabelski, Joseph R., Queen of Peace Retirement Center, 24955 N. Hwy. 12, Lake Zurich, 60047.
Tabor, Kenneth F., St. Benedict Home, 6930 W. Touhy, Niles, 60714.
Vitro, Thomas J., P.O. Box 932, Lake Geneva, WI 53147.

Retired:
Most Revs.—
Goedert, Raymond E., 1555 N. State Pkwy., 60610.
Gorman, John R., 2330 W. 118th St., 60643.
Jakubowski, Thad J., 6002 W. Berteau Ave., 60634-1630.
McDonald, Andrew J., D.D., J.C.D. (LR)
Rev. Msgrs.—
Bergin, Clifford E., 5912 Cleveland, Morton Grove, 60053.
Cardiff, John I., St. Linus, 10300 S. Lawler Ave., Oak Lawn, 60453.
McDermott, Ignatius D., The McDermott Foundation, 932 W. Washington St., 60607.
Mroczkowski, Joseph J., 1501 Hoffman St., Hammond, IN 46327.
Quinn, William J., St. Eulalia, 1851 S. 9th Ave., Maywood, 60153.
Revs.—
Adamich, Albert R., Most Holy Redeemer, 9525 S. Lawndale Ave., Evergreen Park, 60042.
Ahearn, Donald J., St. Juliana, 7142 N. Osceola, 60063.
Auer, Joseph E., Bishop Lyne Home, 12210 S. Will-Cook Rd., Lemont, 60439.
Baldwin, John F., CHC, USN , 5100 Marine Dr., #27-M, 60640.
Ballweber, Eugene L., 2302 Julie S.W., Albuquerque, NM 87105.
Barr, Pierre J., 3825 S. California Ave., 60633.
Bohula, Edwin V., St. James (Sag Bridge), 10600 Archer Rd., Lemont, 60439.
Borowczyk, Martin R., St. Peter Damian, 109 S. Crest Ave., Bartlett, 60103-4279.
Bowler, Michael J., 3211 S. Racine Ave., 1st Fl. Front, 60608.
Bowman, R. Peter, 645 N. Michigan Ave., Ste. 543, 60611-2814.
Boyle, Thomas S., Bishop Lyne Home, 12210 S. Will-Cook Rd., Lemont, 60439.
Brzozowski, Edward J., 13356 Buffalo Ave., 60633.
Buhrfeind, William J., St. Gerald, 9349 S. Central, Oak Lawn, 60453.
Burns, Eugene P., 797 Waverly Rd., LaPorte, IN 46350.
Bykowski, Norbert H., 1318 Millstream Dr., McHenry, 60050.
Caplis, Robert J., P.O. Box 656, Williams Bay, WI 53191-0656.
Carolan, John J., St. Catherine of Siena-St. Lucy, 38 N. Austin Blvd., Oak Park, 60302.
Carroll, Gilbert A., St. Timothy, 6326 N. Washtenaw, 60659.
Cassidy, Frank P., St. Nicholas of Tolentine, 3721 W. 62nd St., 60629-4099.
Cassidy, John M., St. Daniel, 5330 S. Nshville, 60638.
Cerniglia, Francis J., Queen of the Rosary, 750 Elk Grove Blvd., Elk Grove, 60007-4298.
Chapell, Norbert A., 7737 Golf View Dr., Palos Heights, 60463.
Chen, Anthony K., Chung-jen, School of Nursing, 217 Hung Mao PI, Chiayi 600, Taiwan.
Ciemiega, Ernest D., St. Bruno, 4751 S. Harding, 60632.
Coffey, Edward N., St. Andrew Home, 7000 N. Newark, Niles, 60714.
Conley, Thomas P., Bishop Lyne Home, 12230 S. Will-Cook Rd., Lemont, 60439.
Corcoran, Edward G., P.O. Box 28232, San Diego, CA 92128.
Coughlin, Roger J., 721 N. LaSalle St., 60610.
Cowell, Raymond, Paraoquia Nuest, Sen De Fatima, El Pari Casilla 919, Santa Cruz, Bolivia.
Cross, Robert A., 700 Ashland, River Forest, 60305.
Cull, Paul J., 920 Vose Dr., Apt. #212, Gurnee, 60031.
Cullen, George H., St. Benedict Home, 6930 W. Touhy, Niles, 60714.
Czajka, Norman M., 5426 S. Lockwood, 60638.
Devine, William J., P.O. Box 53, Worth, 60482.
Dilla, Francis E., P.O. Box 88, New Carlisle, IN 46552.
Dillon, Arthur J., St. Benedict Home, 6930 W. Touhy, Niles, 60714.
Dolciamore, John V., J.C.L., Mundelein Seminary of the University of St. Mary of the Lake, 1000 E. Maple, Mundelein, 60060-1174.
Donohue, John J., 282 Woodstone Circle, Buffalo Grove, 60089-6701.
Dovick, Robert E., Alvernia Manor, 13950 Main St., Lemont, 60439.
Downes, Thomas J., 2630 Sierra Dr., Colorado Springs, CO 80917.
Doyle, James P., Bishop Lyne Home, 12230 S. Will-Cook Rd., Lemont, 60439.
Dufficy, Edward C., St. Edmund, 188 S. Oak Park Ave., Oak Park, 60302.
Duffy, Donald J., Resurrection Life Center, 7370 W. Talcott, 60631.
Duggan, J. Edward, St. Bartholomew, 4949 W. Patterson Ave., 60641.
Durkin, Eugene F., Holy Name Cathedral, 730 N. Wabash Ave., 60611.
Dyer, George J., 239 Bechview Ln., Barrington, 60010.
Ehrens, Richard J., St. Rosalie, 4401 N. Oak Park Ave., Harwood Hts., 60706.
Enright, John P., 1801 W. 35th St., #1217, Oakbrook, 60521.
Fassbinder, Richard W., 645 N. Michigan Ave., Ste. 543, 60611-2814.
Faucher, Eugene J., St. Edna, 2525 N. Arlington Heights Rd., Arlington Heights, 60004.
Felczak, Leonard J., 4325 S. Spaulding, 60632.
Feller, Richard J., 1201 Bonita, Park Ridge, 60068.
Fenske, Donald J., Our Lady of Knock, 501 163rd St., Calumet City, 60409.

Festle, Robert H., 5046 N. Ashland Ave., 60640.
Finnegan, John P., 660 Chandler Rd., Gurnee, 60031.
Finnegan, William J., Infant Jesus of Prague, 1131 Douglas Ave., Flossmoor, 60422.
Fitzgerald, Edward P., Mercy Hospital and Medical Center, 2525 S. Michigan Ave., 60616.
Fitzgerald, Thomas J., 5472 S. Kimbark, 60615.
Fitzpatrick, Edmund J., 444 Fullerton, #1604, 60614.
Fitzpatrick, Robert J., St. Bede Parish, 36455 N. Wilson Rd., Ingleside, 60041-9609.
Flaherty, William J., 191 Linden St., Winnetka, 60093-3832.
Fraser, Gerald D., 207 Rivershire Ln. #306, Lincolnshire, 60069.
Frawley, John P., 2825 W. 81st St., 60652-2722.
Gallagher, Charles G., St. Cletus, 600 W. 55th St., La Grange, 60525.
Gerrity, Raymond J., 917 S. 8th Ave., #2, LaGrange, 60525.
Goedert, William O., St. Germaine, 4240 W. 98th St., Oak Lawn, 60453.
Grace, James N., 1833 E. Wildberry Dr., Glenview, 60025.
Grace, John J., St. Tarcissus, 6020 W. Ardmore Ave., 60646.
Graff, J. Austin, St. Thomas More, 2825 W. 81st St., 60652.
Greeley, Andrew M., N.O.R.C., 1155 E. 60th St., 60637.
Grembla, Joseph P., St. Francis Borgia, 8033 W. Addison St., 60634.
Grinis, Bruno B., 12433 S. Halsted St., 60628.
Gruchot, Stanley J., 7000 N. Newark, 60714.
Gubbins, William B., 9440 Seton Pl., Orland Park, 60459.
Gunia, Edward S., 904 Joliet Rd., Room #2, Countryside, 60525.
Hanley, Lawrence F., 7112 Concord Cir., Fox Lake, 60020.
Harnett, Edward F., St. Francis Xavier, 524 Ninth St., Wilmette, 60091.
Headley, Donald J., St. Mary of the Woods, 7033 N. Moselle Ave., 60646.
Healy, Thomas I., Our Lady of Mount Carmel, 690 W. Belmont Ave., 60657.
Hefferan, John E., Bishop Lyne Home, 12210 S. Will-Cook Rd., Lemont, 60439.
Helfrich, George J., St. Benedict Home, 6930 W. Touhy Ave., Niles, 60714.
Herne, Robert G., Sacred Heart Parish, 8245 W. 111th St., Palos Hills, 60465.
Hills, Richard L., St. Benedict Home, 6930 W. Touhy Ave., Niles, 60714.
Hoffman, Matthias H., 1131 Douglas Ave., Flossmoor, 60422.
Hosty, Thomas J., 8419 Bailey Rd., Darien, 60561.
Huppenbauer, Walter E., 645 N. Michigan Ave., Ste. 543, 60611-2814.
Hurley, John J., St. Edna, 2525 N. Arlington Hts. Rd., Arlington Hts., 60004.
Huske, Leonard G., 347 Daffodil Ln., Matteson, 60443.
Ivers, Victor J., St. Joseph, 121 E. Maple Ave., Libertyville, 60048-2283.
Jabusch, Willard F., 5040 Warren St., Apt. 404, Skokie, 60077.
Jasinski, Raymond J., Rosary Hill Nursing Home, 9000 W. 81st /st., Justice, 60458.
Jozwiak, Richard M., 19717 S. Edinburg, Frankfort, 60423.
Juchcinski, Clarence J., 16001 Lowe Ave., Harvey, 60426.
Kalas, Ronald N., Mary Seat of Wisdom, 920 W. Granville Ave., Park Ridge, 60068.
Kane, George J., 1700 Cambourne, Schaumburg, 60194.
Kash, Robert J., 21 S. Spring Ave., Unit A, LeGrange, 50525-2272.
Kastigar, John J., 1774 Lexington Dr., Sierra Vista, AZ 85635.
Kauzlarich, John, 9997 Cambridge Ct. D, Mokena, 60448-7095.
Kaveney, Thomas J., St. Odilo, 2244 S. East Ave., Berwyn, 60402.
Keating, James P., 10201 S. Ewing Ave., 60617.
Keating, James W., St. Benedict Home, 6930 W. Touhy Ave., Niles, 60714.
Kelly, Charles F., Box 455, Powers Lake, WI 53155-0455.
Kelly, William J., c/o Jones, 3332 S. 59th Ave., Cicero, 60650.
Keusal, Eugene, Our Lady of Mt. Carmel, 48-422 Kamehameha Hwy., Waikane, HI 96744.
Kinane, Joseph J., 2222 W. 113 th Pl., 60643.
Kinn, James W., Sta Maria Del Popolo, 116 N. Lake St., Mundelein, 60060.
Kirkilas, Michael, 6666 20th Ave., N.E., St. Petersburg, FL 33710.
Klug, Jerome G., 26166 W. Mattalina Ct., Ingleside, 60041.
Kouba, Charles J., 5157 S. California, 60632.
Kozien, Casimir J., 4949 W. Patterson Ave., 60641.
Krebs, John F., 6540 245 th Ave., Salem, WI 53168-9784.
Kuzinskas, John A., 12375 McCarthy Rd., Lemont, 60438.
Lambert, Rollins E., 5404 Montgomery, Apt. 504A, Alburquerque, NM 87109-1371.
Laske, Kenneth S., 4032 W. Nelson St., 60641.
Lee, Joseph, 6157 N. Leavitt St., 60659.
LeVoy, Joseph T., St. Benedict Home, 6930 W. Touhy Ave., W4, Niles, 60714.
Lion, William J., Catherine of Alexandria, 4100 W. 107th St., Oak Lawn, 60453.
Lisowski, William J., 15714 Old Orchard Ct., Orland Park, 60462.
Lutz, Robert J., St. Norbert, 1809 Walters Ave., Northbrook, 60062.
Lynch, Cletus J., 1010 American Eagle Blvd., #609, Sun City Center, FL 33573.
Lynch, Joseph P., 14130 Green Valley Dr., Orland Park, 60462.
Lyons, Leo J., 14226-84th Ave., Orland Park, 60462.
Lyons, William J., Bishop Lyne Home, 12230 S. Will-Cook Rd., Lemont, 60439.
Mackin, John J., 8925 S. Kostner, Hometown, 60456.
Maddock, Laurence F., St. Joseph Seminary College at Loyola University, 6551 N. Sheridan Rd., 60626.
Maginot, Richard J., St. Alphonsus Liguori, 411 N. Wheeling Rd., Prospect Heights, 60070.
Maher, Byron G., 416 E. Jefferson, Burlington, WI 53105.
Maher, Thomas F., St. Mary-of-the-Woods, 7033 N. Moselle Ave., 60646.
Mahon, Leo T., St. Mary of the Woods, 7033 N. Moselle Ave., 60646.
Makuch, Thaddeus J., St. Mary Czestochowa, 3010 S. 48th Ct., Cicero, 60804.
Maloney, Edward J., 7417 Channahon Ct., Fox Lake, 60020.
Maniola, Francis N., 6135 S. Austin, 60638.
Maraczewski, Edward S., 1516 E. Lowden, Mt. Prospect, 60056.
Marszalek, Paul B., 15103 Quail Hollow Dr., Unit #601, Orland Park, 60462.
McCaig, John J., Vilas de Golf, #6103, Largo, FL 33774. (Sept.-April)
McCarthy, Warren J., 1080 W. Irving Park Rd., Schaumburg, 60172.
McDonald, Matthew D., Resurrection Retirement Community, 7260 W. Peterson, 60631.
McDonnell, Joseph F., 17 W. 706 Butterfield Rd., Oakbrook Terrace, 60181.
McGinnity, Joseph P., Bishop Lyne Home, 12230 S. Will-Cook Rd., Lemont, 60439.
McGinnity, Robert F., Sacred Heart, 8245 W. 111th St., Palos Hills, 60465.
McGrath, John F., St. Thomas More, 2825 W. 81st St., 60652.
McHugh, Thomas J., St. Benedict Home, 6930 W. Touhy Ave., Niles, 60714.
McKenna, George P., Chaplain Midway Airport, 9720 S. Kedzie, Evergreen Park, 60805.
McKiernan, Thomas M., St. Benedict Home, 6930 W. Touhy Ave., Niles, 60714.
McMahon, John J., 660 Garland Ave., Winnetka, 60093-3912.
McNamara, John P., Bishop Lyne Home, 12230 South Will-Cook Rd., Lemont, 60439.
Meyer, Charles R., Mundelein Seminary, University of St. Mary-of-the-Lake, Mundelein, 60060.
Mezydlo, Leonard T., St. Stephen Protomartyr Parish, 1267 Everett St., Des Plaines, 60018.
Michalek, Henry J., 7264 W. Peterson Ave., C-605, 60631.
Mikolaitis, Vito E., 6812 S. Washtenaw, 60629.
Millea, Thomas V., P.O. Box 48623, Niles, 60714.
Mollan, Ralph R., Bishop Lyne Home, 12230 Will-Cook Rd., Lemont, 60439-7332.
Moriarty, James F., Bishop Lyne Home, 12230 Will-Cook Rd., Lemont, 60439-7332.
Murphy, William P., Queen of Martyrs, 10233 S. Central Pk., Evergreen Park, 60642.
Nicola, John J., Belle Meade, 400 Waters Dr., Apt. D1-13, Southern Pines, NC 28387.
Norkett, Edward J., 770 W. Deerfield, Highland Park, 60035.
Novak, Robert J., 2960 N. Lake Shore Dr., Apt. 1209, 60657.
O'Brien, John E., 12365 First Ct., Pleasant Prairie, WI 53158-5308.
O'Brien, Joseph J., 300 N. State St., #2627, 60610.
O'Connor, James T., 447 N. Dover Ave., LaGrange Park, 60526.
O'Donnell, Richard J., 3528 S. Hermitage, 60609.
O'Malley, James F, St. James, 134 North Ave., Highwood, 60040-1522.
O'Malley, Patrick J., Mundelein Seminary, 1000 E. Maple, Mundelein, 60060.
Ognibene, Joseph F., St. Colette, 3900 S. Meadow Dr., Rolling Meadows, 60008.
Orozco, Raphael R., 200 W. Wood St., Palatine, 60067-5346.
Ouletta, James F., 141 S. Lake Shore, #E6, Racine, WI 53403.
Pastick, Joseph A., 4939 Floramar Ter., #608, New Port Richey, FL 34652-3310.
Paurazas, Peter P., Maria H.S. Convent, 6727 S. California Ave., 60629.
Peng, John B., 3420 N. Kolmar, 60641.
Powers, John J., St. Jude the Apostle, 880 E. 154th St., South Holland, 60473.
Powers, Thomas M., St. Joseph, 1747 Lake Ave., Wilmette, 60091.
Pozdol, Henry, 7240 W. 57th St., Summit, 60501.
Raftery, Thomas J., Christ the King, 9235 S. Hamilton, 60620.
Riley, Dennis S., 1952 Carlsbad Cir. #104, Naperville, 60563-8853.
Roache, James P., P.O. Box 58, Lyons, WI 53148-0058.
Rochford, John J., Bishop Lyne Home, 12230 S. Will-Cook Rd., Lemont, 60439.
Rodell, Jeremiah J., 7330 Galeview Ln., Frankfort, 60423.
Rosemeyer, John C., P.O. Box 455, Powers Lake, WI 53159.
Rosemeyer, Paul F., St. Theresa, 467 Benton, Palatine, 60067.
Rudcki, Stanley R., 7712 W. Oak Ridge Ct., #2B, Palos Heights, 60463.
Sayers, James M., St. Joseph, 17951 Dixie Hwy., Homewood, 60430.
Scarlata, Ronald E., 1662 Willow Circle Dr., Cresthill, 60435.
Schouten, Francis L., 3755 W. 112th Pl., 60655.
Schroeder, Richard F., 7216 Oxford Cir., Fox Lake, 60020.
Schwab, Thomas E., 9711 W. Devon Ave., Rosemont, 60018.
Schwartz, Paul E., St. James, 22244 S. Torrence Ave., Sauk Village, 60411-5144.
Seitz, Joseph W., 9131 S. Sacramento, Evergreen Park, 60805.
Seitz, Thomas R., St. Thomas the Apostle, 5472 S. Kimbark, 60615.
Shaunessy, Francis W., St. Benedict Home, 6930 W. Touhy Ave., Niles, 60714.
Sheridan, William H., 2132 E. 72nd St., 60649.
Shields, James P., Immaculate Conception, 508 Grand Ave., Waukegan, 60085.
Shields, William J., 116 N. Lake St., Mundelein, 60060.
Shirey, John W., 8725 S. May, 60620.
Siedlecki, Edmund J., Cardinal Stritch House, 1000 E. Maple, P.O. Box 455, Mundelein, 60060.
Siwek, Jerome S., St. Benedict Home, 6930 W. Touhy Ave., Niles, 60714.
Skach, Charles J., 301 S. I-Oka Ave., Mt. Prospect, 60056.
Slosarcik, Edward A., 13950 Main St., Lemont, 60439.
Somerville, Walter F., Handmakers, 2221 N. Rosemont #413, Tuscon, AZ 85715.
Stefanski, Walter, 12556 E. Richton Rd., Crete, 60417.
Stockus, Edward S., 10508 S. Keeler, Oak Lawn, 60453.
Sullivan, Daniel J., 3217 W. 184th St., Homewood, 60430.
Sullivan, Daniel F., 129 E. Mill St., Apt. 203, Wauconda, 60084.
Szlanga, Edmund S., Bishop Lyne Home, 12230 Will-Cook Rd., Lemont, 60439-7332.
Taylor, Joseph C., 4350 W. Sunnyside Ave., 60630.
Tessmer, Richard A., 800 W. Biesterfield Rd., Elk Grove Village, 60007.
Thomas, Joseph S., 645 N. Michigan Ave., Ste. 543, 60611-2814.
Tlapa, Richard J., 6350 S. Taft Ave., Merrillville, IN 46410.
Tuite, Howard A., 700 S. Paulina, #922, 60612.
Vader, Anthony J., 11652 S. Church St., 60643.
Valker, Richard J., St. Norbert, 1809 Walters Ave., Northbrook, 60062.
Velutis, John, 11129 S. Homan, 60655.
Vita, Mariano L., 1809 E. 31st St., La Grange Park, 60525.
Wagner, Leon R., 2435 Seabrook Island Rd., John Island, SC 29455.
Walsh, Michael J., Bishop Lyne Home, 12230 S. Will-Cook Rd., Lemont, 60439.
Wasiel, Michael J., 546 E. 155th St., Harvey, 60426.
Waszak, Norbert J., St. Benedict's Home, 6930 W. Touhy Ave., Niles, 60714.
Weber, Gerard P., 4316 Lanai Rd., Encino, CA 91436.

White, Bernard C., 3020 N. 76th Ct., Elmwood Park, 60707.
White, William J., 10418 S. Keating Ave., #3D, Oak Lawn, 60453.
Winters, Martin N., Benedictine Monastery of Our Lady of Sorrows, 5800 W. 147th St., 60452.
Wodniak, John L., 5730 W. Fullerton, 60639.
Wojcik, Richard J., M.C.G., Mundelein Seminary of the University of St. Mary-of-the-Lake, 1000 E. Maple, Mundelein, 60060.
Yangas, Peter M., St. Eugene, 7958 W. Foster Ave., 60656.
Zakarauskas, Anthony J., P.O. Box 42915, Evergreen Park, 60805.
Zawistanowicz, Norbert J., Our Lady of Victory Parish, 5212 W. Agatite Ave., 60630.

Permanent Deacons:
Abboud, Louis, St. Patrick, Wadsworth
Adams, Stewart, Immaculate Conception, Highland Park
Ahern, Michael, Our Lady of Victory
Albano, Terris, Our Lady of the Ridge, Chicago Ridge
Alcos, Rossini, St. Lawrence O'Toole, Matteson
Allen, Warren, St. Kilian, Chicago
Alonso, Enrique, Our Lady of Grace, Chicago, Office of the Diaconate
Alvarez, Ignacio, St. Rita, Chicago
Alvarez, Jose, St. Fidelis, Chicago
Alvarez, Margarito, St. Kevin, Chicago
Amberg, John, (Retired), St. Mary of the Assumption, Chicago
Antiss, Robert S., Holy Family, Inverness
Antonsen, Larry, Christ the King, Chicago
Arvidson, Robert, St. Francis de Sales, Lake Zurich
Askew, James, Our Lady of Humility, Beach Park/Zion
Auld, David D., Santa Maria del Popolo, Mundelein
Aurelio, Benjamin, Jr., St. Matthew, Schaumburg
Avila, Mario, Precious Blood, Chicago
Baez, David, St. Lambert, Skokie
Baldasti, Steven, St. Hubert, Hoffman Estates
Banet, Robert, St. Andrew the Apostle, Calumet City
Barker, William, Sacred Heart, Palos Hills
Bartholomew, Thomas, St. Michael, Orland Park
Barton, Jeffrey, Prince of Peace, Lake Villa
Baum, Richard, St. Anne, Barrington
Behrendt, Raymond J., Sacred Heart, Melrose Park
Beil, Frank, St. Catherine Laboure, Glenview
Belanger, James, (Retired)
Bell, Kenneth, St. Domitilla, Hillside
Benthey, Herman, St. Anne, Hazel Crest
Bergquist, Bernard, (Retired), St. Tarcissus, Chicago
Bertolani, Philip, St. Benedict, Chicago
Beyer, Wayne, Church of Holy Spirit, Schaumburg
Bishop, Joseph, St. James, Sauk Village
Blais, Emile, St. Mary of the Angels
Blanco, Jesus, St. Ann
Boehm, Owen, St. Rene, Chicago
Boggio, Edward, St. Marcelline, Schaumburg
Bohannon, Morris E., (Retired), St. Clotilde, Chicago
Boharic, Robert, St. Mary, Riverside
Bonifazi, Virgilio, (Retired), St. John Berchmans, Chicago
Borha, George, St. Columbanus, Chicago
Bouey, Alfred, Our Lady of Sorrows Basilica
Bovyn, Paul, Resurrection, Chicago
Bradford, Bruce, St. Catherine of Siena/St. Lucy, Oak Park
Brady, Joseph, St. Christopher, Midlothian
Brauch, Robert, St. Anne, Barrington
Brencic, David, St. Barbara, Brookfield
Bretz, Michael, St. Mary, Des Plaines
Brooks, George, Infant Jesus of Prague, Flossmoor
Brooks, John, (Retired), St. Joseph, Round Lake
Brothers, David, St. Agnes, Chicago Heights
Brown, Dennis G., St. Patrick, Wadsworth
Bryce, Irvin, St. Albert the Great, Burbank
Buissereth, Rameau, Our Lady of Peace
Bulger, Robert, St. Paul of the Cross, Park Ridge
Bumbel, John, St. Gall, Chicago
Burke, Henry, Ascension/St. Susanna, Harvey
Burns, James, St. Donatus, Blue Island
Bustos, Gregorio, St. Clare of Montefalco, Chicago
Bzdon, Gregory M., St. Tarcissus, Chicago
Cabrera, Daniel, St. Hedwig
Cabrera, Jorge, St. John Berchmans, Chicago
Camerini, Guilio, St. Eulalia, Maywood
Carerra, Xavier, Holy Spirit, Schaumburg
Carrillo, Martin, St. Joseph, (Hermitage Ave.)
Carrizales, Maximiliano, Providence of God, Chicago
Carroll, Daniel, St. Benedict, Blue Island
Carroll, James, Holy Cross, Deerfield
Carroll, Roberto, Jr., St. John Fisher, Chicago
Carvlin, Thomas, Ascension/St. Susanna, Harvey
Cascino, Joseph, Jr., St. Viator, Chicago
Castanon, Toribio, Holy Cross-Immaculate Heart of Mary, Chicago
Cavanaugh, Michael, Ss. Faith, Hope and Charity, Winnetka
Cervantes, Leopoldo, St. Peter Canisius, Chicago
Cesario, Carmen, (Retired), Our Lady, Mother of the Church
Chaidez, Lorenzo, St. Gertrude, Franklin Park
Chairez, Victor, St. Simeon, Bellwood
Chappel, Dorsey, (Retired), St. Leo the Great, Chicago
Chausse, Joseph, (Retired), St. Francis Borgis; Center for the Deaf, Chicago
Chavez, Abraham, St. Simeon, Bellwood
Chrastka, Joel, St. Leonard, Berwyn
Churilla, William, St. Anne, Hazelcrest
Chyba, Lawrence J., St. Bruno
Ciesil, Norbert, St. Alphonsus, Prospect Heights
Cintron, Gilberto, St. Hedwig, Chicago
Cisneros, Jose, St. Leonard, Berwyn
Clark, William, Queen of Peace, North Chicago
Cocco, Anthony, St. Michael, Orland Park
Coffey, Thomas W., St. Luke, River Forest
Coleman, Alfred, II, St. Basil/Visitation, Chicago
Colgan, Dennis L., St. William, Chicago
Collins, Terrence, Ascension-St. Susanna, Harvey
Colucci, Victor, (Retired), Sacred Heart, Melrose Park
Condill, James, St. Anne, Barrington
Condon, Edward, St. Cornelius, Chicago
Connor, John, St. Colette, Rolling Meadows
Constanopolis, Louis
Contreras, Mario, Church of the Holy Spirit, Schaumburg
Conway, James, St. Barnabas, Chicago
Conway, William, (Retired), Our Lady of Lourdes, Ashland
Cook, John, St. Felicitas
Cooper, Willie, (Retired)
Corcoran, Thomas, Our Lady of the Wayside, Arlington Hts.
Cordesman, Ellsworth, (Retired), St. James, Highwood
Cordoba, Angelo, Queen of the Universe, Chicago
Cozzo, James, Santa Maria Addolorata
Crandall, Robert, (Retired), Our Lady of Ransom, Niles
Crane, Walter James, St. Ann, Barrington
Crespo, Feliciano, St. Wencelaus, Chicago
Crespo, Hipolito, St. Sylvester, Chicago
Czarnecki, Thaddeus, Queen of the Rosary, Elk Grove Village
Dahl, Earl, St. John the Evangelist, Streamwood
Dattoli, Dominick, St. George, Tinley Park
Daum, Donald, St. Germaine, Oak Lawn
Davis, James, (Retired), St. Martin de Porres, Chicago
Deabel, Raymond, St. James Hospital, Chicago Heights
Debnar, John, St. Barbara, Brookfield
DeFiore, Robert, St. John the Evangelist, Streamwood
DeFrank, Frank, St. Mary of Vernon, Indian Creek
Dehler, Thomas, St. Lawrence O'Toole, Matteson
Deiters, James, Sr., St. Walter, Chicago
Del Llano, Manuel, Our Lady of Mercy, Chicago
Delaney, James, (Retired), St. Bede the Venerable, Chicago
DeLarco, Michael, St. Celestine, Elmwood Park
DeLorenzo, Edward, St. Edmund, Oak Park
DeLuna, Arthur, Sta. Maria Addolorata, Chicago
DeRose, Ronald, Kolbe House, Chicago
Detloff, James, St. Emeric, Country Club Hills
Devereux, Robert, Our Lady of the Mount, Cicero
Devine, James, St. Celestine, Elmwood Park
DeVita, Frank, (Retired), Divine Providence, Westchester
Diaz, Benjamin, St. Philomena, Chicago
Diaz De Leon, Raymundo, St. Blase, Argo
DiCanio, Vito W., St. Emily, Mt. Prospect
Dienberg, Clifford, St. Mary of Celle, Berwyn
Dietz, Albert, St. Mary, Fremont Center
Disparte, Philip, O'Hare Airport Chapel
DiVirgilio, Dante, St. Mary of Vernon, Indian Creek
Dixon, Roscoe B., St. Benedict, Blue Island
Dolan, Edward, St. Juliana, Chicago
Donovan, Timothy, Old St. Mary's, Chicago
Dorgan, Eugene J., St. Pascal, Chicago
Doud, Raymond, Church of the Holy Spirit, Schaumburg
Drazba, Herbert, St. Jude the Apostle, South Holland
Dubrownik, Phillip, St. Emeric, Country Club Hills
Duderstadt, Peery, St. Joseph the Worker, Wheeling
Duffy, Frank, St. Henry, Chicago
Duffy, Mark, St. Thomas of Villanova, Palatine
Duffy, Robert, Our Lady of the Wayside, Arlington Heights
Dulen, John, (Retired), St. John Brebeuf, Niles
Dunn, Dennis, St. Joseph, Libertyville
Dunn, William F., Jr., Santa Maria del Popolo, Mundelein
Dunne, Thomas, St. Thomas of Villanova, Palatine
Duszynski, Thomas, St. Matthew, Schaumburg
Dutkiewicz, Daniel, St. Stanislaus, Bishop & Martyr, Posen
Dutko, David, St. Kieran, Chicago Heights
Dwyer, James T., (Retired), Church of the Holy Spirit, Schaumburg
Echevarria, Ramon, Our Lady of Tepeyac, Chicago
Egan, David, St. Patrick, Wadsworth
Ende, Gilbert, Special Ministry
Enger, Michael, Church of the Holy Spirit, Schaumburg
Engler, William, St. Stephen, Deacon & Martyr, Tinley Park
Ernst, James, Our Lady of Hope, Rosemont
Esposito, Robert, St. Peter Damian, Bartlett
Estrada, Vincente, Immaculate Conception, Chicago
Ewers, Thomas, St. Denis, Chicago
Faherty, Paul, St. Luke, River Forest
Fair, Davis, Presentation BVM
Farinella, Louis A., St. John the Evangelist, Streamwood
Favila, Angel, St. Agnes of Bohemia, Chicago
Feltes, Richard, St. Catherine of Alexandria, Oak Lawn
Fernandez, Dismas, St. Maurice, Chicago
Ficker, John, St. George, Tinley Park
Figueroa, Roberto, St. Gregory, Chicago
Filipucci, Michael, St. Marcelline, Schaumburg
Finnegan, Michael, St. Juliana, Chicago
Flanagan, John, St. Germaine, Oak Lawn
Flewellen, James, (Retired), St. Thaddeus, Chicago
Flores, Nicolas, St. Stanislaus Kostka, Chicago
Foley, Brendan, Our Lady of the Wayside, Arlington Heights
Fox, Gerald, (Retired), Divine Providence, Westchester
Fragassi, Phillip, St. Patrick, Wadsworth
Fronczek, Casimir, St. Francis Borgia Deaf Center, Chicago
Fruge, James, Immaculate Conception, Highland Park
Fuller, George, (Retired), Resurrection, Chicago
Furey, James P., St. John the Evangelist, Streamwood
Gadomski, Edward, St. Linus, Oak Lawn
Gagnon, Robert, St. Peter, Antioch
Gallagher, James, St. James, Highwood
Garcia, Jose, St. Marcelline, Schaumburg
Garcia, Miguel, St. Stanislaus Kostka, Chicago
Garza, Juan L., St. Paul, Chicago Heights
Gaughan, James, St. Edna, Arlington Hts.
Gavin, Raymond, St. Catherine Laboure, Glenview
Gembara, Emil, (Retired), St. Alexander, Palos Heights
Gianatasio, Philip, St. Mary of Celle, Berwyn
Gilbert, Paul, St. George, Tinley Park
Gildea, Francis, St. Elizabeth Seton, Orland Park
Girjatowicz, Frank, St. Theresa, Palatine
Glatz, John, St. Cajetan, Chicago
Glenn, John, St. Mary of Vernon, Indian Creek
Globis, Richard J., St. Gilbert, Grayslake
Gniech, George, St. Constance, Chicago
Golab, Chester J., St. Daniel the Prophet, Chicago
Gonzalez, Felipe, Maternity, B.V.M.
Gonzalez, Juan, Resurrection, Chicago
Gordus, Richard, Mater Christi, North Riverside
Graffia, Raymond, St. Edna, Arlington Heights
Green, John, St. Thomas of Canterbury
Green, Richard, St. Turibius, Chicago
Gronek, Ronald, Divine Savior, Norridge
Gronkiewicz, Edmund, Our Lady of Mount Carmel, Chicago
Grossnickle, Donald R., Our Lady of the Wayside, Arlington Heights
Gutierrez, Jorge, St. Mark, Chicago
Guzman, Paul, St. Benedict
Hahn, Gerald E., Queen of Apostles, Riverdale
Halper, Bernard, (Retired), St. Kieran, Chicago Heights
Han, Sung, Church of the Holy Spirit, Schaumburg
Hankett, Richard G., Queen of Angels, Chicago
Hare, Martin, (Retired), Holy Rosary, Chicago
Harrington, John, Kolbe House
Harris, Wallace, St. Dorothy, Chicago
Hart, Vernon, Seven Holy Founders, Calumet Park
Hatch, Wilmer, (Retired), St. Philip Neri, Chicago
Hayden, Thomas L., St. Hubert, Hoffman Estates
Helmer, Everett, (Retired), St. Germaine, Oak Lawn
Hempen, Harold, St. Irenaeus, Park Forest
Hennessy, Matthew, St. James, Arlington Heights
Henning, George J., St. Mary of the Woods
Henricks, John, St. Giles, Oak Park
Henry, Francis, Nativity of Our Lord, Chicago
Hensley, Claude, St. Anthony, Cicero
Hernandez, Sigifredo, St. Jerome, Chicago
Herrera, Albert, St. Gall, Chicago

Herrera, Armando, Mary Queen of Heaven, Chicago
Herrera, Marcial, Queen of the Universe, Chicago
Hess, Rudolf, Our Lady of Good Counsel
Hill, Edwin, St. Nicholas of Tolentine, Chicago
Hinch, Ralph, St. Francis Borgia Deaf Center, Chicago
Hipelius, Thomas, St. Damian, Oak Forest
Hita, Floro, Maternity BVM, Chicago
Horne, Philip G., Our Lady of Humility, Zion
Hotcaveg, Irwin E., St. Ferdinand, Chicago
Howard, Samuel E., Infant Jesus of Prague, Flossmoor
Hubbard, James, St. Felicitas, Chicago
Huber, Charles, St. Francis Borgia, Chicago
Hudzik, Richard, St. Maria Goretti, Schiller Park
Hurley, William, Christ the King, Chicago
Hyde, Thomas, St. Joseph, Summit
Ibarra, Juan, St. Stanislaus Kostka, Chicago
Iwan, Henry, St. Gilbert, Grayslake
Jacob, Robert, St. Benedict, Chicago
Janega, Robert, Our Lady of Mercy
Jay, Richard, (Retired), St. Athanasius, Evanston
Jean-Pierre, Fritz, St. Jerome, Chicago
Jeffrey, August, Divine Savior, Norridge
Jenney, Kenneth, Jr., Immaculate Heart of Mary, Chicago
Jinkens, Max R., Our Lady of Humility, Zion
Juncer, Bart, St. John Cantitus
Kaczmarek, Edward, St. Thomas of Villanova, Palatine
Kalivoda, Bill, Addolorata Villa, Wheeling
Kancler, Lawrence, Special Ministry
Karnoski, Michael, St. Louis de Montfort, Oak Lawn
Karstenson, William, St.Thomas of Villanova, Palatine
Kasimatis, Jerome, (Retired), Holy Cross, Deerfield
Kearney, John, Immaculate Heart of Mary, Chicago
Keating, Timothy, Our Lady of the Snows, Chicago
Keegan, Charles, St. Patricia, Hickory Hills
Keenan, Scott, St. Peter, Antioch
Kenney, James, St. Mary, Lake Forest
Kiley, Michael E., St. Julie Billart, Tinley Park
Klemanovic, John, Our Lady of Lourdes, Chicago
Knippen, James, (Retired), St. Hubert, Hoffman Esttes
Kocar, Marvin, St. Pius X, Stickney
Kort, Clayton, St. Helena of the Cross, Chicago
Kotleba, Rudolf, Holy Family/St. Francis Assisi, Chicago
Kowalski, David J., St. Louise de Marillac, LaGrange Park
Kozuchowski, Chester, (Retired), St. Gilbert, Grayslake
Krakora, Joseph, St. Mary, Lake Forest
Kristinat, Richard L., St. George, Tinley Park
Kryszak, Timothy, Holy Spirit, Schaumburg
Kukla, Eugene, St. Mary, Buffalo Grove
Kulleck, Richard, Most Holy Redeemer, Evergreen Park
Kwasegroch, Gerald, St. Eugene, Chicago
Kwasigroch, James, Our Lady of Grace, Chicago
La Belle, Eugene, St. Kieran, Chicago Heights
LaCoursiere, Victor, St. Jerome, Chicago
Lagges, Peter, St. Zachary, Des Plaines
LaMantia, Thomas, St. Marcelline Schaumburg
Lambert, George, (Retired), St. Eulalia, Maywood
Lambert, Thomas, Our Lady of Mt. Carmel, Chicago
Langwell, James E., Incarnation, Palos Heights
Lara, Luis, Immaculate Conception, Highland Park
Lawson, Richard, St. Hubert, Hoffman Estates
Leck, Robert, (Retired), Our Lady of Victory, Chicago
Lehman, William B., St. Francis Borgia, Chicago
Lekan, Louis, St. James, Arlington Heights
Lema, Salvatore, St. Fabian, Bridgeview
Leo, Kevin, St. Alphonsus Ligouri, Prospect Heights
Leonard, Timothy, Prince of Peace, Lake Villa
Leonas, John, (Retired), St. Anne, Hazel Crest
Lesnieski, Norbert, SS. Cyril & Methodius, Lemont
Levins, Terrence, SS. Faith, Hope & Charity, Winnetka
Lewis, Joseph, Our Lady of Sorrows, Chicago
Liberti, Peter, All Saints-St. Anthony, Chicago
Lilly, Leroy, (Retired), St. Simeon, Bellwood
Limon, Juan, St. Benedict, Blue Island
Limon, Vincente, Our Lady of Tepeyac, Chicago
Lisowski, Thaddeus, St. Constance, Chicago
Llano, Antonio, Our Lady of the Mount, Cicero
Llorens, Anthony, St. Martin de Porres, Chicago
Lohmann, Rudolph, St. Matthew, Schaumburg
Long, Gary, St. Mary, Buffalo Grove
Lopez, Adolf, St. Aloysius, Chicago
Lorbach, John, St. Raymond de Penafort, Mt. Prospect
Macarol, John, Our Lady of the Woods, Orland Park
Maddock, George, St. Joseph, Homewood
Madonia, Loretto, St. Giles, Oak Park
Mages, William, St. Mary of the Woods, Chicago
Maldonado, Meliquides, (Retired), St. Mark, Chicago
Malec, Albert, St. Daniel the Prophet, Chicago
Malloy, William, Queen of All Saints Basilica
Mally, Joseph, St. Adalbert, Chicago
Malone, Jack, St. Germaine, Oak Lawn
Maloney, Thomas J., St. Thomas of Villanova, Palatine
Maney, Antonio, St. James, Maywood
Manning, Peter, St. Joseph, Summit
Marin, Francisco, St. Jerome, Chicago
Marotto, Angelo, St. Domitilla, Hillside
Marquez, J. Frank, (Retired), St. Pascal, Chicago
Marrero, Jose, (Retired), St. Roman, Chicago
Matthews, Robert, St. Joseph, Libertyville
Maune, William, (Retired), St. Irenaeus, Park Forest
McAllister, Dennis F., Our Lady of the Brook, Northbrook
McCloskey, Michael, Holy Name Cathedral, Chicago
McDonough, Michael, St. Michael, Orland Park
McElrath, Bruce, St. Ailbe, Chicago
McGorey, Thomas, Office of the Diaconate
McGuire, Terrence, St. Alphonsus, Lemont
McKinnis, William, St. Columbanus, Chicago
McLynn, Michael, St. Louis de Marillac, La Grange Park
McMahon, John, St. Bede, Ingleside
McNulty, Michael, Sacred Heart, Winnetka
Meehan, Peter, St. Martha, Morton Grove
Meehan, Thomas, (Retired), Our Lady of Loretto, Hometown
Melkovitz, Emil, (Retired), St. Francis Borgia, Chicago
Melton, Edward, Holy Cross, Deerfield
Memmel, Aloysius, St. Paul of the Cross, Park Ridge
Mench, Sidney, (Retired), St. John Fisher, Chicago
Mendez, Genaro, Area Hispanic Ministry
Mendizabal, Guillermo, St. John Berchmans, Chicago
Merced, Rolando, Transfiguration of Our Lord
Mercure, Michael, Our Lady of Humility, Zion-Beach Park
Metallo, Arthur, Resurrection Hospital, Chicago
Michalowski, Benedict, St. Joseph, Summit
Migala, Paul, St. Marcelline, Schaumberg
Miska, Richard, St. Julie Billiart, Tinley Park
Mondello, Christopher, St. Gilbert, Grayslake
Mongan, Martin, St. John Fisher, Chicago
Monica, Robert, St. Thomas the Apostle, Chicago
Monnelly, Michael, Queen of All Saints, Chicago
Monterroso, Oscar, St. Ansgar, Hanover Park
Moore, Steven, St. Anne, Hazel Crest
Morales, Juan, St. Anthony, Chicago
Moran, Charles, (Retired), St. John the Evangelist, Streamwood
Moreno, Eusebio, Holy Family, Waukegan
Morgan, James, St. Thomas the Apostle, Chicago
Moritz, Richard H., Immaculate Conception (Talcott Rd.)
Morowczynski, Romuald, St. Jane de Chantal, Chicago
Morrissey, Henry, St. Leonard, Berwyn
Mudd, Dennis, St. Joseph, Libertyville
Mujica, Ines, (Retired)
Mullaney, Roger, SS. Faith, Hope & Charity, Winnetka, Catholic Charities
Multeri, James R., Holy Family, Inverness
Munda, Gary, Sr., Queen of Peace, North Chicago
Munoz, Romeo, St. Jude the Apostle, South Holland
Munoz, Romeo, St. Mary of the Lake
Murphy, Robert, St. Jerome, Chicago
Murphy, Robert, St. Gertrude, Franklin Park
Murray, Michael, (Retired), Our Lady of the Brook, Northbrook
Navarro, Anthonio, St. Mark, Chicago
Navarro, Jesse, St. Mary, Star of the Sea, Chicago
Navolio, John, St. Mary of the Lake
Nazario, Carlos, Our Lady of Grace, Chicago
Negron, Julio A., Queen of Peace, North Chicago
Neu, Andrew, St. Barnabas
Neurauter, Paul, St. Peter, Antioch
Newhall, Redondo, St. Cajetan, Chicago
Newman, Jeffrey, St. Joseph, Libertyville
Newton, Robert, St. Peter Damian, Bartlett
Nguyen, Duc Van, St. Thomas of Canterbury, Chicago
Nieves, Bienvenido, Queen of Angels, Chicago
Nimietz, James, (Retired), St. John the Evangelist, Streamwood
Nolan, John, St. Julian Eymard, Elk Grove Park
Norton, Terrence, St. Luke, River Forest
Norys, Stephen, St. Theresa, Palatine
Nowak, Thomas, St. Agnes, Chicago Heights
Nunez, Raul, Our Lady of Guadalupe, Chicago
Nylen, Arthur A., St. Jude the Apostle, South Holland
O'Brien, Thomas, (Retired), St. Emeric, Country Club Hills
O'Connell, Thomas, St. Walter, Chicago
O'Donnell, Charles, Our Lady of Ransom, Niles
O'Donnell, Patrick, (Retired), St. Damian, Oak Forest
O'Keefe, Robert C., St. Isaac Jogues, Niles
O'Leary, Edward, St. Eugene, Chicago
O'Leary, John, St. Lambert, Skokie
O'Leary, John A., St. Joseph, Homewood
O'Malley, James, (Retired)
O'Malley, Michael, St. Emily, Mt. Prospect
O'Neill, John, St. Luke, River Forest
Oborski, Zygfryd, St. Stanislaus Bishop & Martyr, Chicago
Ochoa, Jesus, St. Rita, Chicago
Ochoa, Zeferino, Holy Family/St. Francis of Assisi, Chicago
Ochsner, Robert, Our Lady of Humility, Beach Park & Zion
Odegard, Robert, St. Priscilla, Chicago
Ojeda, Norberto, St. James, Maywood
Olson, Carl, St. Cornelius, Chicago
Omiatek, Marion, Transfiguration, Wauconda
Ontiveros, Philip, St. Marcelline, Schaumburg
Ortega, Ignacio, St. Mark, Chicago
Ortiz, Eddies, St. Colette, Rolling Meadows
Ortiz, Sigifredo, St. Sylvester, Chicago
Pagliai, Bruno, St. James, Highwood
Pagnotta, Philip, Jr., St. Mary of Vernon, Indian Creek
Palacios, Freddy, St. Charles Borromeo, Melrose Park
Palmer, Donald, St. Joseph (Orleans St.), Chicago
Palmer, Lawrence, St. Benedict, Blue Island
Paluch, Thomas M., St. John Brebeuf, Niles
Panek, Joseph, St. George, Tinley Park
Paskauskas, Vitas, Nativity, B.V.M.
Pastirik, Joseph, (Retired), St. Francis de Sales, Chicago
Patino, Daniel, Our Lady of Lourdes
Pena, Leonardo, Area Hispanic Ministry
Pencich, Samuel, St. Zachary, Des Plaines
Penich, Michael, Jr., St. Paul the Apostle, Gurnee
Pepitone, Joe, St. John of the Cross, Western Springs
Perez, Alphonse M., (Retired), Assumption, Chicago
Perez, Carlos, (Retired)
Perez, Luis, Santa Maria Addolorata, Chicago
Perez, Miguel, St. Pius V., Chicago
Perez, Orlando, St. Thomas of Canterbury, Chicago
Perkowitz, John, (Retired), St. John Brebeuf, Niles
Peters, Bruce, St. Mary, Buffalo Grove
Peterson, George A., (Retired)
Pezowicz, Feliks, Transfiguration, Wauconda
Pineda, Javier, St. Francis of Rome, Cicero
Pistone, John, St. Thomas of Villanova, Palatine
Pizzato, Richard, St. Theresa, Palatine
Platt, James, St. Cyprian, River Grove
Poletto, Robert, St. Mary, Fremont Center, Mundelein
Ponce, Antonio, Our Lady of Charity, Cicero
Powers, Robert, St. Anne, Barrington
Pozo, Guido, Resurrection
Puhala, Robert, St. Philip, Northfield
Quackenbush, Edward, St. Bede, Ingleside
Ragonese, Dan, St. Victor, Calumet City
Ramirez, Juan, St. Pancratius, Chicago
Ramos, Dennis, St. Aloysius, Chicago
Ramos, Eliseo, St. Jerome
Ramos, Francisco, St. Philomena, Chicago
Rangel, John, St. Lawrence O'Toole, Matteson
Ranke, Dennis, Our Lady of Victory, Chicago
Ranola, Rodrigo, St. Isaac Jogues, Niles
Rehor, Timothy, St. Bernardine, Forest Park
Reinert, William, St. James, Arlington Heights
Reinhart, James, St. Linus, Oak Lawn
Renwick, James, St. Ann, Lansing
Revering, Roman, (Retired), St. James, Maywood
Revord, James, Our Lady of Perpetual Help, Glenview
Reyes, David, Immaculate Heart of Mary
Reynolds, Kevin, St. Barbara, Brookfield
Riccio, Louis, Charismatic Renewal Office; St. Theresa, Palatine
Richardson, John, St. Patrick, Wadsworth
Richardson, Leonard M., St. Sabina, Chicago
Riffner, Joseph, (Retired), St. Alphonsus, Chicago
Rios, Jamie, St. Wenselaus, Chicago
Rivas, Roberto, Immaculate Conception, Chicago
Rivera, Francisco, Resurrection, Chicago
Rivera, Hector, St. Teresa of Avila, Chicago
Robles, Ernesto, Our Lady of Grace, Chicago
Rodriguez, Candelario, Notre Dame, Chicago
Rodriguez, Emiliano, (Retired), St. Bonaventure, Chicago
Rodriguez, Manuel, St. Francis of Assisi, Chicago
Rodriguez, Milton, Maternity of B.V.M., Chicago
Rodriguez, Uriol, Resurrection, Chicago
Rodriguez, Wilmer, St. Hedwig

Roman, Francisco, St. Sylvester, Chicago
Romano, Michael, St. Joseph Hospital, Chicago
Rottman, John, St. Thecla
Rozo, Jorge, Holy Rosary, Chicago
Rueth, William, St. Hugh, Lyons
Ryan, Edward, St. Anthony, Chicago
Ryan, Robert E., Sr., St. Juliana, Chicago
Ryan, Thomas, St. Christina, Chicago
Rybicki, Lawrence, St. John the Evangelist, Streamwood
Sacramento, Anthony, St. Dismas, Waukegan
Salgado, Alfonso, St. Anthony, Cicero
Salley, Abrom, Our Lady Help of Christians
Sanchez, Sabino, St. Francis and Our Lady of the Angels, Chicago
Sanchez, Salvador, St. Francis of Assisi/Our Lady of the Angels, Chicago
Sandoval, Jose M., Immaculate Conception
Sands, William, St. Joseph, Libertyville
Sanford, James, St. Emily, Mount Prospect
Santos, Antero, St. Bonaventure
Sanzone, Michael, St. Dismas, Waukegan
Sassetti, Robert C., St. Vincent Ferrer, River Forest
Sattler, David, St. Peter Damien, Bartlett
Scarbalis, Edward, Holy Family, Waukegan
Schiltz, James, St. Constance, Chicago
Schmidt, Paul, St. James, Arlington Hts.
Schoewe, Rudolph, (Retired), Our Lady of Victory, Chicago
Schultz, Ronald, (Retired), St. Victor, Calumet City
Sedano, Pedro, St. Franics of Assisi, Chicago
Sedivy, Alan, Our Lady of Perpetual Help, Glenview
Seitz, John, Incarnation, Palos Heights
Serna, Francisco, St. Helen
Serratore, Gregory, St. Mary Star of Sea, Chicago
Seveska, Richard, St. Anne, Barrington
Sharwarko, Michael, St. Louis de Monfort, Oak Lawn
Shaw, Ralph, (Unassigned)
Sheehan, Patrick P., St. James, Arlington Heights
Shinkle, Derald, St. Joseph, Willmette
Shumpert, Gregory, St. Agatha
Silva, Rodrigo, St. Ann, Chicago
Simmet, Daniel, St. Patrick, Wadsworth
Simmons, John, Santa Maria del Popolo, Mundelein
Sinacore, James M., St. John Vianney, Northlake
Siranovic, Joseph, St. Domitilla, Hillside
Skaja, Lawrence, St. John Brebeuf, Niles
Slajchert, Michael, St. Gall, Chicago
Slobig, Robert, St. Luke, River Forest
Smith, John J., St. Zachary, Des Plaines
Smith, Michael E., St. Christopher, Midlothian
Smith, Robert S., Jr., Ss. Faith, Hope and Charity, Winnetka
Solon, Thomas, St. Denis, Chicago
Soria, Carlos, (Retired), St. Sylvester
Soto, Santos, St. Sylvester, Chicago
Spalla, Paul, St. Mary-of-the-Lake, Chicago
Spitizzeri, Fred, St. Priscilla, Chicago
Spohr, Lawrence, St. Bede, Ingleside
Staddler, Ted, Queen of the Rosary, Elk Grove Village
Stalcup, Joseph, Sr., St. Stephen, Tinley Park
Stanton, Paul, St. Isaac Jogues, Niles
Starr, Robert, Sr., St. Dismas, Waukegan
Stasinski, Melvin, St. Jude the Apostle, South Holland
Stearns, William, St. Damian, Oak Forest
Stecker, Stephen, St. Joseph the Worker, Wheeling
Steinbeigle, Francis, St. Damian, Oak Forest
Strom, Stanley, Holy Name Cathedral, Chicago
Stubstad, Thomas, St. Pascal, Chicago
Sullivan, William, St. Louis de Montfort, Oak Lawn
Sullivan, William, St. Barnabas, Chicago
Sutton, Daniel, (Retired), St. Ailbe, Chicago
Swiatek, Ronald, St. John Bosco, Chicago
Swiech, Edward, (Retired), St. Robert Bellarmine, Chicago
Szady, Mitchell, St. Stanislaus B & M, Chicago
Tamayo, Mario, St. Nicholas, Evanston
Taylor, Lowell, (Retired), Church of the Holy Spirit, Schaumburg
Telle, Paul, Holy Family, Waukegan
Telposky, Donald, St. Stephen, Des Plaines
Temple, James, St. Barnabas, Chicago
Tereza, Nick, St. Ansgar, Hanover Park
Terrazas, Jorge, St. Rita of Cascia
Thesing, William, St. Francis Xavier, Wilmette
Threet, Michael, St. Sabina
Tipperreiter, Charles, St. Fabian, Bridgeview
Tomkowiak, Edward, St. Patrick, Wadsworth
Torres, Candido, Our Lady of Fatima, Chicago
Torres, Francisco, St. Rita of Cascia
Towey, Anthony, St. Stephen Protomartyr, Des Plaines
Trakszelis, Jerome, St. Vincent Ferrer, River Forest
Trevino, Luis, Chicago-O'Hare International Airport
Truesdale, Joseph, St. Francis of Assisi, Orland Park
Tryba, Edmund, (Retired), St. Hilary, Chicago
Uroza, Jose, St. Angela, Chicago
Valadez, Abundio, St. Benedict, Chicago
Valadez, Asuncion, St. Mary of Celle, Berwyn
Valentin, Israel, St. Philomena, Chicago
Valle, Miguel Angel, St. Genevieve, Chicago
Varela, Joaquim, St. Nicholas of Tolentine
Vargas, Miguel, Mision Juan Diego, Palatine
Vazquez, Gilberto, Transfiguration, Wauconda
Vazquez, Jose, Maternity B.V.M., Chicago
Vazquez, Saul, St. Sainta & St. Anthony
Velasco, Arturo, St. Francis of Assisi, Chicago
Velasco, Benito, Maternity B.V.M., Chicago
Velazquez, Angel, Holy Family, Waukegan
Vellurattil, Matthew, St. Ladislaus
Vemich, Duke, All Saints-St. Anthony, Chicago
Vidmar, John, Bl. A.M. Slomsek Slovenian Catholic Mission, Lemont
Vignocchi, Louis, Immaculate Conception, Highland Park
Villa, Salvatore, St. Bruno, Chicago
Villalobos, Antonio, St. Mark, Chicago
Villasenor, Faustino, St. Mary, Des Plaines
Villegas, Salomon, St. Hedwig, Chicago
Virruso, Christopher, Our Lady, Mother of the Church, Chicago
Walters, John, St. Bernardine, Forest Park
Ward, Raymond E., St. Jerome, Chicago
Ward, Raymond, (Retired), Queen of All Saints, Chicago
Warfield, Richard, Special Ministry
Watson, Dexter, Holy Angels, Chicago
Weber, Ronald J., St. Ansgar, Hanover Park
Wegner, Albin J., Jr., St. Michael, Chicago
Wehling, Donald, St. Hilary, Chicago
Weiner, Ronald, St. Ferdinand, Chicago
Weitendorf, Norbert, St. Patricia, Hickory Hills
Welter, Daniel, St. Josaphat, Chicago
Werner, Richard, St. Damian, Oak Forest
West, Tommy, St. Helena of the Cross, Chicago
White, Philip, St. Eulalia, Maywood
Wilkinson, John, St. James at Sag Bridge, Lemont
Willer, Richard, St. Thomas of Villanova, Palatine
Wills, James, St. Peter, Skokie
Winblad, Joseph, St. Patrick, Lemont
Winter, Edward, St. Lawrence O'Toole, Matteson
Wogan, James, St. Mary of Vernon, Indian Creek
Young, Irving, (Retired), St. Mary, Buffalo Grove
Zadruzny, Wieslaw, St. Pancratius, Chicago
Zanardo, Ronald, St. Lawrence O'Toole, Matteson
Zaragoza, Luis, Mission Juan Diego, Palatine
Zavala, Eduardo, Notre Dame
Zawadzki, Kenneth, St. Stephen, Deacon & Martyr, Tinley Park
Zeller, John, St. Marcelline, Schaumburg
Zima, Robert, St. Luke, River Forest
Zimmerman, Edward, (Retired), Our Lady of the Snows, Chicago
Zimmermann, John, Transfiguration, Wauconda
Ziomek, Robert, St. Ansgar, Hanover Park
Zurawski, John, St. John Vianney, Northlake
Zwolski, Mark, St. Mary of Vernon, Mundelein
Zych, Gerald, St. Cyprian, River Grove

INSTITUTIONS LOCATED IN THE ARCHDIOCESE

[A] SEMINARIES, ARCHDIOCESAN

CHICAGO. *Archbishop Quigley Preparatory Seminary*, 103 E. Chestnut St., 60611. Tel: 312-787-9343; Fax: 312-787-9167. Email: info@quigley.org. Web: www.quigley.org. Revs. Paul J. Kalchik; David A. Jones, Pres.; Peter Snieg, Rector; Mark Kalema; Louis J. Zake; Dennis A. Ziomek. Priests 6; Lay Teachers 23; Students 205.

St. Joseph College Seminary, The Seminary College at Loyola University, 6551 N. Sheridan Rd., 60626. Tel: 773-973-9700; Fax: 773-973-9718. Email: jpresta@orion.it.luc.edu. Web: www.stjoseph.luc.edu.

Seminary Administration: Revs. James Presta, M.Div., S.T.B., S.T.L., M.Div., S.T.B., S.T.L., S.T.D (Cand.), Rector-Pres.; Ronald A. Hicks, B.A., M.Div., D. Min., (Cand.) Dean of Formation; Thomas P. Conde, M.Div., S.T.B., M.B.A., Dir. of Vocation; Laurence F. Maddock, Spiritual Dir. (Retired); Patrick J. Rugen, S.T.L., M.Div., M.A., Academic Dean; William Vollmer, M.Div., Dir. Liturgy.

Full-Time Faculty: Dr. Dennis M. Composto, Ph.D., Ed.D., Comptroller, M.P.A., M.Ed., Ph.D., Comptroller; Mr. John A. Houlihan, M.A., M.S., J.D., Dir. Information Technologies; Mr. Jesus Huerta, M.P.S., (Cand.), Dir. Pastoral Formation; Mrs. Maria Anabella Mora, B.S., Academic Admin., Spanish; Mr. Michael D. Martino, M.A., Dir. English Proficiency Prog.; Revs. James Presta, M.Div., S.T.B., S.T.L., (Cand.), Theology; William Vollmer, M.Div., Theology.

Part-Time Faculty: Mr. Scott Arkenberg, B.M., M.M., Music; Dr. Elizabeth Browne, Ph.D., English & Philosophy; Rev. William M. Frigo, O.F.M.Cap., M.S.W., Dir. Capuchin; Dr. Kathleen G. Burke, Ph.D., English; Revs. Joseph M. Jackson, Psychology; James J. Kastigar, Spanish; Mr. Thomas Kleeman, M.A., Physical Education; Revs. Henry Kricek, M.A., S.T.L., Philosophy; Thomas Refermat, S.T.L., M.Div., M.A., (Cand.), Mathematics & Theology; Dr. Charles F. Schmidt, Ph.D., Anthropology, Natural & Social Science; Rev. Richard T. Simon, Classics; Mrs. Cheryl Wollin, American Studies & Political Science.

Administrative Staff: Mrs. Marie Composto, Dir. Office of Institutional Advancement; Mrs. Yuvanka Juarez-Zavala, B.A., Financial Aid Admin., Human Resources Manager, Student Business Manager; Mrs. Eileen Mullin, B.A., Dir. of Grant Writing; Ms. Melissa Rabelhoffer, B.A., Admin. Asst. to Dir. of Ins. Advancement; Mrs. Sally Walsh, Sec. to the Rector.

MUNDELEIN. *University of St. Mary of the Lake-Mundelein Seminary*, 1000 E. Maple Ave., 60060. Tel: 847-566-6401; Fax: 847-566-7330. Email: rectorusml@vocations.org. Web: www.vocations.org. Priests 33; Brothers 1; Sisters 2; Lay Teachers 5; Students 203.

Resident Faculty: Very Rev. John F. Canary, Rector, Pres.; Revs. John G. Lodge, M.Div., M.A., S.T.L., S.T.D., S.S.L., Ecclesiastical Dean; Lawrence R. Hennessey, Ph.D.; Kevin J. Feeney, M.A.S., M.Div., Dean of Formation; Sr. Linda Sevcik, S.M., S.T.L., Dir. Field Education; Revs. Raymond J. Webb, Ph.D., Academic Dean Dir. Newly Ordained Prog. Dir. Pastoral Internship Program; Thomas W. McQuaid, Dir. of Chicago & International Students; August J. Belauskas, Ph.D. (Cand.), Admissions Dir.; Patrick J. Boyle, S.J., Ph.D.; Dennis J. Lyle, S.T.L.; Robert E. Barron, S.T.D. (Cand.); John V. Dolciamore, J.C.L. (Retired); David P. Dowdle, Deacon Formation Program; Stephen Giorno, S.T., B.A., M.A.; W. Scott Hebden, M.Div., S.T.D., S.T.L.; Charles R. Meyer, Prof. Emeritus (Retired); James P. McIlhone, Ph.D.; Patrick O'Malley, M.A., S.T.L.; Martin Zielinski, Ph.D.; Joseph C. Mol, Canonical Recorder; Arlene Michna, B.Mus., M.Mus.; Dr. C. Colt Anderson, M.A., Ph.D.; Bro. Henry Baldwin, F.S.C., M.A., M.L.S., M.Ed., Dir. of Cultural and Language Programs; Revs. Peter Damian Akpunonu, S.S.L., S.T.D.; Thomas A. Baima, A/SC., A.B., M.Div., M.B.A., S.T.D., (Cand.); Jacque B. Beltran, B.A., S.T.B., D.Min., (Cand.); Emery DeGaal, D.Theol., Ph.D., V.D.; Michael J. Fuller, M.Div., S.T.L., S.T.D.; Douglas A. Martis, M.Div., S.T.L., S.T.D., P.; Joseph T. Noonan, B.A., C.P.A., M.Div., Vocation Dir.; Edward T. Oakes, S.J., Ph.D.; Alberto Rojas, M.Div.; Robert L. Schoenstene, S.S.L. (JOL); Daniel S. Siwek, S.T.L.; John S. Szmyd, B.S., M.Div., S.T.B.; Walter J. Takuski, B.A., M.Div.; Paul H. Wachdorf, M.C.Sp.; Richard J. Wojcik, M.C.G., Prof. Emeritus (Retired); Mary Ocasek, B.A., M.L.S., Dir. Librarian; Dr. Daniel G. VanSlyke, B.A., M.A., Ph.D.; Sr. Kathleen Mulchay, B.A., M.A.; Dr. Denis G. McNamara, B.A., Ph.D., H., M.Arch.

Convent Tel: 847-566-6401; Fax: 847-566-7330. Sr. Consuelo Vazquez, Supr. Oblate Sisters of Jesus the Priest 7.

The Liturgical Institute, 1000 E. Maple Ave., 60060. Tel: 847-837-4542; Fax: 847-837-4545. Web: www.usml.edu/liturgicalinstitute. Rev. Msgr. Roy Klister, S.T.D., J.C.L., S.T.L. (GB), Dir.

[B] SEMINARIES, RELIGIOUS OR SCHOLASTICATES

CHICAGO. *The Catholic Theological Union at Chicago*, 5401 S. Cornell Ave., 60615. Tel: 773-324-8000; Fax: 773-324-8490. Email: mcassidy@ctu.edu. Web: www.ctu.edu. Revs. Donald Senior, C.P., S.T.D., Pres.; Gary L. Riebe-Estrella, S.V.D., Vice Pres. & Academic Dean; Kenneth O'Malley, C.P., Ph.D., Dir. Library; Mr. Michael D. Marback, C.P.A., J.D., Vice Pres. Admin. & Finance; Mr. William Booth, Dir. Devel.; Ms. Priscilla Sporrong, M.B.A., Dir. Mktg. & Communications; Ms. Kathy Van Duser, Dir. Admissions & Recruitment; Ms. Vanessa White, M.T.S., Dir. Augustus Tolton Prog.; Ms. Sheila McLaughlin, Dir. Bernardin Center; Sr. Barbara Dohery, S.P., Ph.D., Dir. Institute for Rel. Formation; Rev. Eugene Lauer, Dir. Hesburgh Center, Continuing Formation in Ministry; Mrs. Maria de Jesus Lemus, Registrar; Mr. Carlos Salmeron, Dir. Romero Prog.; Rev. Leslie J. Hoppe, O.F.M., Dir. Israel Study Prog.; Ms. Opal Easter, Ed.D., Dir. Continuing Education & Ministeral Formation; Ms. Judy

Logue, M.A., Dir. Emmaus Prog. Major Seminary. Serving the following: Franciscans, Servites, Passionists, Augustinians, Norbertines, Society of the Divine Word, Missionaries of the Precious Blood, Claretians, Crosier Fathers, Spiritans, Sacred Heart Missionaries, Viatorians, Comboni Missionaries, Franciscans Capuchins, Sacred Heart Fathers and Brothers, Ukrainian Catholic Diocese, Congregation of the Blessed Sacrament, Columban Missionaries, Redemptorist Fathers, Oblates of Mary Immaculate, Xaverian Missionaries, Maryknoll Missionaries, Conventual Franciscans, Oratorians, Scalabrinians, Discalced Carmelites, Vincentians Priests 20; Sisters 6; Lay Teachers 6; Lay Administrators 10; Non-Catholic Clergy 2; Students 500.

Faculty: Mr. Michel Andraos, Ph.D., Prof. Cross Cultural Studies; Mr. Scott C. Alexander, Ph.D., Prof. & Dir. Catholic-Muslim Studies; Rev. Claude-Marie Barbour, S.T.D.; Sr. Dianne Bergant, C.S.A., Ph.D.; Rev. Stephen B. Bevans, S.V.D., Dir. M.A. Prog.; Sr. Barbara Bowe, R.S.C.J., Th.D.; Avis Clendenen, M.A.P.S. Prog. & Dir. Field Educ.; Sr. Eleanor Doidge, L.O.B., D.Min.; Mr. Richard E. McCarron, Ph.D., Prof. Liturgy; Revs. Richard Fragomeni, Ph.D.; Edward Foley, O.F.M.Cap., Ph.D., M.Mus., D. Min. Dir.; Archimede Fornasari, M.C.C.J., Ph.D.; Ms. Mary Frohlich, Ph.D.; Ms. Linda Strozdas, Psy.D., Prof. Pastoral Care; Revs. Anthony Gittins, C.S.Sp., Ph.D.; Zachary Hayes, O.F.M., Ph.D.; Leslie J. Hoppe, O.F.M.; Thomas Nairn, O.F.M., Ph.D., Dir. Health Care Mission; James C. Okoye, C.S.Sp., BLL Chair; Sr. Carolyn Osiek, R.S.C.J., Th.D.; Revs. Gilbert Ostdiek, O.F.M., S.T.D.; John M. Pawlikowski, O.S.M., Ph.D., Dir. Jewish Chair; Sisters Barbara Reid, O.P., Ph.D.; Dawn Nothwehr, O.S.F., Ph.D., M.Div. Dir.; Revs. Gary L. Riebe-Estrella, S.V.D.; Robert Schreiter, C.PP.S., Th.D.; Roger P. Schroeder, S.V.D.; Donald Senior, C.P., S.T.D.; Gilberto Cavazos-Gonzales, O.F.M., S.L.T.

TECHNY. *Divine Word Residence*, P.O. Box 6000, 60082-6000. Tel: 847-272-2700; Fax: 847-272-2873. Email: uscsvd1@aol.com. Web: www.divineword.org. Revs. Walter Bracken, S.V.D., Rector; John Beemster, S.V.D.; James Bergin, S.V.D.; Michael J. Bonner, S.V.D.; Edward Borkowski, S.V.D.; James Braband, S.V.D.; Joseph Bugner, S.V.D.; John Cannuli, S.V.D.; Thomas Commons, S.V.D.; Joseph Connors, S.V.D.; Sonny DeRivera, S.V.D.; John Donaghey, S.V.D.; John Farley, S.V.D.; Joaquin Ferrer, S.V.D.; Sunny Francis, S.V.D.; Dariusz Garbaciak, S.V.D.; Kazimierz Garbacz, S.V.D.; Gerald Garry, S.V.D.; Gilbert Gawlik, S.V.D.; Elzear Gehlen, S.V.D.; Joseph Gunning, S.V.D. (TR); Thomas Halleran, S.V.D.; William Hegarty, S.V.D.; Leo Hotze, S.V.D.; Francis J. Kamp, S.V.D.; Robert Kelly, S.V.D.; John Koster, S.V.D.; Anthony Krajci, S.V.D.; Very Rev. Thomas A. Krosnicki, S.V.D.; Revs. Paschal LoBianco, S.V.D.; Matthias Lunzer, S.V.D.; Louis Luzbetak, S.V.D.; Adam MacDonald, S.V.D.; Andrew Masters, S.V.D.; John Musinsky, S.V.D.; Robert Myers, S.V.D.; Edward Norton, S.V.D.; Chester Nowicki, S.V.D.; Carlos Paniagua, S.V.D.; Lawrence Poetz, S.V.D.; Raymond Quetchenbach, S.V.D.; Eugene Rochford, S.V.D.; Frederick Rudolph, S.V.D.; Raymond Sanders, S.V.D.; Charles Scanlon, S.V.D.; Otto Schellenberger, S.V.D.; Charles Schneider, S.V.D.; Werner Shadeg, S.V.D.; Peter Silvester, S.V.D.; Eugene Stoll, S.V.D.; John Swift, S.V.D.; Aloysius Turbek, S.V.D.; Harrie Vanderstappen, S.V.D.; Wilbert Wagner, S.V.D.; Edward Wald, S.V.D.; John Wald, S.V.D.; Ralph Wiltgen, S.V.D.; Richard Winters, S.V.D.; Bros. Leonard Bauer, S.V.D.; Rene Gawlik, S.V.D.; George Haegele, S.V.D.; Patrick Hogan, S.V.D.; Herman Thomas Joseph, S.V.D.; Brian McLauchlin, S.V.D.; Dennis Newton, S.V.D.; Joachim Oros, S.V.D.; Stephen Pardy, S.V.D.; Gerard Pashia, S.V.D.; Cyril Schroeder, S.V.D.; Joseph Urban, S.V.D.; Kenneth Valois, S.V.D.; Vincent Webb, S.V.D.; Mathew Zemel, S.V.D.

Legal Title: *Divine Word Techny Community Corporation*, (Formerly Divine Word Seminary-St. Mary's Mission House)

Divine Word Theologate, 5342 S. University Ave., 60615. Tel: 773-288-2777; Fax: 773-288-6307. Rev. Edward Peklo, S.V.D., Rector. Major Seminary of the Chicago Province. Priests 10.

Staff: Revs. Stephen B. Bevans, S.V.D.; Lloyd Cunningham, S.V.D.; Quang Duc Dinh, S.V.D.; Gary L. Riebe-Estrella, S.V.D.; Roger P. Schroeder, S.V.D.; Derek Simons, S.V.D.; Mark Schramm, S.V.D.

Edward McGuinn, S.V.D. Residence, 5712 S. Kenwood, Unit 3, 60657. Tel: 773-643-1518. Revs. Stephen B. Bevans, S.V.D.; Gary L. Riebe-Estrella, S.V.D.; Henryk Slusarczyk, S.V.D.

Midwest District, 5420 S. Cornell Ave., #501, 60615. Tel: 773-493-2103. Bro. Stephen Pardy, S.V.D. Religious Brothers Conference

Angels Studio, 319 S. Jefferson, Suite 200, 60661. Tel: 312-583-9560; Fax: 312-583-9561. Rev. Derek Simons, S.V.D.

[C] COLLEGES AND UNIVERSITIES

CHICAGO. *De Paul University*, One E. Jackson Blvd., 60604. Tel: 312-362-8000; Fax: 312-362-6606. Web: www.depaul.edu. Revs. John P. Minogue, C.M., Pres.; John T. Richardson, C.M., Chancellor; Edward R. Udovic, C.M., Senior Exec. Univ. Mission, Sec. Vice Pres. Admin.; Dr. John J. Kozak, Exec. Vice Pres. Academic Affairs; Dr. Scott L. Scarborough, Exec. Vice Pres. Operations. Sponsored by the Priests of the Congregation of the Mission (Vincentian Fathers and Brothers), Campuses: Downtown, Lincoln Park, Barat, Oak Forest, O'Hare, Naperville, Lake Forest, Rolling Meadows, Lake County.

Administrative Officers of the University: Ms. Bridget K. Butwin, acting Vice Pres. and General Counsel; Mr. David O. Dabney, Treasurer; Mr. James R. Doyle, Vice Pres. Student Affairs; Ms. Bonnie Hirsch, Controller; Mr. Robert Janis, Vice Pres. Facilities Operations; Mr. David O. Justice, Vice Pres. Lifelong Learning & Suburban Campuses; Dr. David Kalsbeek, Vice Pres. Enrollment Mgmt.; Mr. Vincent Kellen, acting Vice Pres. Information Services; Mr. Robert L. Kozoman, Vice Pres. Financial Affairs; Mr. William Seithel, Vice Pres. Human Resources; Mr. Brenda Wilson-Hale, Assoc. Vice Pres. Devel.

College of Liberal Arts and Sciences, 900 W. Fullerton Ave., 60614. Tel: 773-325-7310; Fax: 773-325-7304. Dr. Michael L. Mezey, Dean.

College of Law, 931 Lewis Center, 25 E. Jackson Blvd., 60604. Tel: 312-362-8701; Fax: 312-362-5826. Mr. Glen Weissenberger, Dean.

College of Commerce, Kellstadt Graduate School of Business, 7103 DePaul Center, One E. Jackson Blvd., 60604. Tel: 312-362-6783; Fax: 312-362-6677. Mr. Arthur Kraft, Dean.

Academic Officers of the University:

School of Music, 200 Music Bldg., 804 W. Belden, 60614. Tel: 773-325-7260; Fax: 773-325-7263. Dr. Donald E. Casey, Dean.

Barat College, Barat College of DePaul University, 700 E. Westleigh Rd., Lake Forest, 60045. Tel: 847-243-3000; Fax: 847-574-4299. Dr. Katherine C. Delaney, Dean.

School for New Learning, 212 Lewis Center, 25 E. Jackson Blvd., 60604. Tel: 312-362-8001; Fax: 312-362-8809. Dr. Susanne M. Dumbleton, Dean.

School of Computer Science, Telecommunication and Information Systems, 450 CS & T Center, 243 S. Wabash Ave., 60604-2302. Tel: 312-362-8381; Fax: 312-362-6116. Dr. Helmunt P. Epp, Dean.

The Theatre School, 214 Theatre School Bldg., 2135 N. Kenmore Ave., 60614. Tel: 773-325-7917; Fax: 773-325-7920. Mr. John Culbert, Dean.

School of Education, 458 Schmitt Academic Center, 60614. Tel: 773-325-7740; Fax: 773-325-7713. Quintin Vargas III, Dean. Faculty 775; Staff 1,440; Students 23,610.

Jesuit Community at Loyola University Chicago, Jesuit Residence, 6525 N. Sheridan Rd., 60626. Tel: 773-508-8800; Fax: 773-508-2098. Web: www.luc.edu. Revs. John J. O'Callaghan, S.J., Rector; Bonaventura Balige, S.J.; Raymond C. Baumhart, S.J.; Frans J. van Beeck, S.J.; Fred F. Bergewisch, S.J.; Robert L. Bireley, S.J.; Mark G. Bosco, S.J. (SFR); Bro. Brutus J. Clay, S.J.; Revs. David J. Collins, S.J.; Richard F. Costigan, S.J.; William E. Creed, S.J.; Matthew E. Creighton, S.J.; Dariusz Dankowski, S.J.; Gene M. Donatelli, S.J.; Eugene F. Dwyer, S.J.; Keith J. Esenther, S.J.; Michael Garanzini, S.J.; Donal Godfrey, S.J. (Ireland) (SFR); David A. Godleski, S.J.; Daniel F. Hartnett, S.J.; John C. Haughey, S.J.; John J. Kilgallen, S.J.; Steven E. Kimmons, S.J.; Allan F. Kirk, S.J.; Walter P. Krolikowski, S.J.; Peter Lah, S.J.; John F. Libens, S.J.; Patrick J. McAteer, S.J.; Jerome T. Overbeck, S.J.; Eduardo Pinzon, S.J.; John E. Reilly, S.J.; Lawrence Reuter, S.J.; Paul V. Robb, S.J.; Charles E. Ronan, S.J.; Donald F. Rowe, S.J.; Maria Augustine Selvan, S.J.; Myles N. Sheehan, S.J.; J. Michael Sparough, S.J.; David J. Stagaman, S.J.; Richard P. Salmi, S.J.; Robert T. Sears, S.J.; James A. Stoeger, S.J.; Thomas H. Tobin, S.J.; Theodore J. Tracy, S.J.; J. Richard VandeVelde, S.J.; George E. Von Kaenel, S.J.; Gerald C. Walling, S.J.; Earl A. Weis, S.J.; Chang Son Yu, S.J.; Bro. Haile-Mehari Tesfa-Michael, S.J.

Legal Title: *The Jesuit Community Corporation at Loyola University* Priests 55; Brothers 1.

Loyola University-Chicago Tel: 312-915-6000; 773-274-3000. Web: www.luc.edu.

Legal Title: *Loyola University of Chicago, Illinois*

President's Office, 820 N. Michigan Ave., 60611. Tel: 312-915-6400; Fax: 312-915-6414. Web: http://www.luc.edu. Michael R. Quinlan, Bd. Chm.; Rev. Michael J. Garanzini, S.J., Pres.; Dr. Anthony L. Barbato, Pres. & CEO, Loyola Univ. Medical Center; Mr. Johnathan Heintzelman, Acting Vice Pres. Advancement; Rev. Richard P. Salmi, S.J., Vice Pres. Student Affairs; Mr. Jerry Sanders, Assoc. Provost/C.I.O.; Dr. Lucien Roy, Vice Pres. Mission and Ministry; Dr. Peter A. Facione, Provost; Dr. John Fendreis, Vice-Provost; Mr. Phil Kosiba, Vice Pres., Facilities; Dr. Tom Kelly, Vice Pres. Human Resources; Dr. Richard S. Hurst, Dir. Institutional Research; Mr. Terry Richards, Assoc. Vice Pres. Enrollment Management; Ms. April Hansen, Dir. Undergraduate Admissions; Mr. Eric Weems, Dir. Student Financial Assistance; Ms. Claire Korinek, Dir. Registration and Records; Mr. Leaf McGregor, Asst. Dir. Registration and Records; Mr. Warren Hale, Dir. Residence Life; Mr. Bud Jones, Assoc. Vice Pres. Public Relations; Mr. Paul Roberts, Vice Pres., Officer of Professional Student Recruitment; Mr. Richard Ward, Dir., Alumni and Special Events; Ms. Kay Geary, University Controller; Dr. Marjorie Beane, University Planning; Mr. William Laird, Vice Pres. Finance/C.F.O.; Mr. Wayne Magdziarz, Strategic Initiatives; Mrs. Ellen Kane Munro, Vice Pres. & Gen. Counsel.

The following are the Schools and Colleges which compose the University:

The College of Arts and Sciences (1870), Tel: 773-508-3500; Fax: 773-508-3514.

Lake Shore Campus, 6525 N. Sheridan Rd., 60626. Tel: 773-274-3000. Dr. Isiaah Crawford, Dean. Tel: 773-508-3500.

The School of Law (1908), 1 E. Pearson St., 60611. Tel: 312-915-7120; Fax: 312-915-7201. Nina Appel, Dean.

The Stritch School of Medicine (1909), 2160 S. First Ave., Maywood, 60153. Tel: 708-216-3223; Fax: 708-216-4305. Dr. Stephen Slogoff, Dean.

School of Social Work (1914), 820 N. Michigan Ave., 60611. Tel: 312-915-7005; Fax: 312-915-7645. Dr. Joseph Walsh, Dean.

School of Professional Studies, 6525 N. Sheridan Rd., 60626. Tel: 312-915-6800; Fax: 312-915-6660. Dr. Robert L. Hasenstab, Dean.

The School of Business Administration (1922), 820 N. Michigan Ave., 60611. Tel: 312-915-6113; Fax: 312-915-6118. Mr. Robert L. Parkinson, Dean.

The Graduate School (1926), 6525 N. Sheridan Rd., 60626. Tel: 773-508-3396; Fax: 773-508-2460. Dr. William Yost, Dean.

The School of Nursing (1935), 6525 N. Sheridan Rd., 60626. Tel: 773-508-3249; Fax: 773-508-3241. Dr. Sheila Haas, Dean.

The School of Education (1969), 820 N. Michigan Ave., 60611. Tel: 312-915-6000. Dr. Margaret Fong-Bloom, Dean. Total University Enrollment 13,061; Total full-time faculty 615.

St. Joseph's Seminary, 6551 N. Sheridan Rd., 60626. Tel: 773-973-9700; Fax: 773-973-9718. Rev. Patrick Rugen, Academic Dean.

Saint Xavier University, 3700 West 103rd St., 60655. Tel: 773-298-3000. Dr. Richard A. Yanikoski, Pres. Sisters of Mercy of the Union in the U.S. 10; Order of St. Francis 1; Sisters of Charity of Blessed Virgin Mary 1; Full Time Faculty 169; Students 4,916.

RIVER FOREST. *Dominican University (Formerly Rosary College)*, 7900 W. Division St., 60305. Tel: 708-366-2490; Fax: 708-524-5990. Email: webmaster@email.dom.edu. Web: www.dom.edu. Dr. Donna M. Carroll, Pres.; Sr. Elwyn McHale, O.P., Prioress; Dr. Norman Carroll, Provost.

Legal Title: *Dominican University* Dominican Sisters of Sinsinawa, WI Priests 1; Sisters 5; Lay Teachers 91; Students 2,900.

Rosary College of Arts and Sciences at Dominican University Tel: 708-524-6816; Fax: 708-524-5990. Dr. Jeffrey Carlson, Dean.

School of Business Tel: 708-524-6826; Fax: 708-524-6939. Dr. Molly Burke, Dean.

School of Education Tel: 708-524-6830; Fax: 708-524-6665. Sr. Colleen McNicholas, Dean.

Graduate School of Library and Information Science Tel: 708-524-6472; Fax: 708-524-6657. Dr. Prudence Dalrymple, Dean.

Graduate School of Social Work Tel: 708-366-3463; Fax: 708-366-3446. Dr. Vimala Pillari, Dean.

Institute for Adult Learning Tel: 708-714-9125; Fax: 708-714-9126. Bryan Watkins, Exec. Dir. Priests 1; Sisters 5; Lay Teachers 91; Total Enrollment 2,900.

[D] HIGH SCHOOLS, PRIVATE

CHICAGO. *Brother Rice High School*, 10001 S. Pulaski Rd., 60655-3356. Tel: 773-779-3410; Fax: 773-779-5239. Email: kwalczak@brrice.chi.il.us. Web: www.brrice.chi.il.us. Bro. Karl J. Walczak, C.F.C., Pres.; Mr. James P. Antos, Prin. Congregation of Christian Brothers Priests 2; Brothers 10; Lay Teachers 64; Students 1,180.

Cristo Rey Jesuit High School, Inc., 1852 W. 22nd Pl., 60608. Tel: 773-890-6800; Fax: 773-890-6801. Email: jfoley@cristorey.net. Web:

www.cristorey.net. Rev. John P. Foley, S.J., Pres.; Patricia Garrity, Prin. Priests 3; Sisters 1; Brothers 1; Lay Teachers 26; Students 497.

Cristo Rey Work/Study Program, Inc., 1852 W. 22nd Pl., 60608. Tel: 773-890-6800; Fax: 773-890-6880. Preston Kendall, Vice Pres.

De La Salle Institute, 3455 S. Wabash Ave., 60616. Tel: 312-842-7355; Fax: 312-842-4142. Email: webmaster@dls.org. Web: www.dls.org. Bro. Michael Quirk, F.S.C., Pres.

Legal Title: *De La Salle Institute* Brothers of the Christian Schools Brothers 6; Lay Teachers 85; Students 849.

De LaSalle Institute, West Campus (Lourdes Hall), 1040 W. 32nd Pl., 60608. Tel: 773-650-6800; Fax: 773-650-9722. Email: webmaster@dls.org. Web: www.dls.org. Bro. Michael Quirk, F.S.C., Pres.; Mr. James Krygier, Prin.; Ms. Diane Brown, Assoc. Prin.; Sr. Josita Krzeminski, Assoc. Prin. Sisters 5; Lay Teachers 34; Students 335.

St. Francis de Sales High School, 10155 S. Ewing Ave., 60617. Tel: 773-731-7272; Fax: 773-731-7888. Dennis Moller, Pres.; Richard D. Hawkins, Prin. Lay Teachers 26; Students 348.

Gordon Tech High School, 3633 N. California Ave., 60618-4602. Tel: 773-539-3600; Fax: 773-539-9158. Email: jglab@gordontech.org. Web: www.gordontech.org. Rev. Joseph Glab, C.R., Pres.; Dr. William Watts, Ph.D., Prin.; Revs. Fred Ciesla, C.R.; Thomas Kubik, C.R.; Joseph Malczyk, C.R.; Donald Zinn, C.R.; Bro. Ed Jaszkowski, C.R. Priests 5; Brothers 1; Lay Teachers 33; Students 640.

**Hales Franciscan High School, Inc.*, 4930 Cottage Grove Ave., 60615. Tel: 773-285-8400; Fax: 773-285-7025. Robert Anderson, Pres.; Ms. Avis Wright, Acting Prin.; Revs. John Paul Cafiero, O.F.M., D.Min., Dir. Campus Ministry; Phil D. Hogan, O.F.M., Coord. Student Activities & Special Programs; David Rodriguez, O.F.M., M.F.A., Fine Arts & Theology Chair; Bro. Fred Smith, O.F.M., Mgr. Bookstore. Priests 3; Brothers 1; Lay Teachers 28; Students 400.

Hales Services, Inc., 4930 S. Cottage Grove, 60615. Tel: 773-285-8400, Ext. 255; Fax: 773-285-7025. Sylvia Lottie, Dir.

Holy Spirit Friary Tel: 773-285-8402, Ext. 257. Revs. Charles E. Payne, O.F.M., Ph.D.; Thomas Nairn, O.F.M., Ph.D.; Gilberto Canazos, O.F.M., Ph.D.; Frank Folinio, O.F.M., M.A.; Michael Ward, O.F.M., B.A.

Holy Trinity High School, 1443 W. Division St., 60622. Tel: 773-278-4212; Fax: 773-278-0144. Email: tbednar@holytrinity-hs.org. Mr. Thomas Bednar, Pres. Brothers of Holy Cross Priests 2; Brothers 6; Sisters 4; Lay Teachers 28; Students 400.

St. Ignatius College Prep, 1076 W. Roosevelt Rd., 60608-1594. Tel: 312-421-5900; Fax: 312-829-5846. Email: brian.paulson@ignatius.org. Web: ignatiuschicago.com. Revs. Brian G. Paulson, S.J., Pres.; Joseph T. Brennan, S.J., Rector; Ms. Carole Manning, Prin.; Revs. Joseph T. Brennan, S.J.; Patrick Fairbanks, S.J.; Ross Pribyl, S.J.; Robert C. Thul, S.J.; James S. Vorwoldt, S.J. Priests 7; Scholastics 2; Sisters 1; Lay Teachers 80; Students 1,325.

St. Ignatius Jesuit Community, 1025 W. Taylor, 60607. Tel: 312-829-2297; Fax: 312-829-9552. Revs. Joseph T. Brennan, S.J., Rector; David Barry, S.J.; Louis E. Busemeyer, S.J.; James E. Chambers, S.J.; John P. Coakley, S.J.; James J. Creighton, S.J.; Patrick A. Fairbanks, S.J.; Philip J. Grib, S.J.; Eugene Nevine, S.J.; Brian G. Paulson, S.J.; Ross Pribyl, S.J.; Robert C. Thul, S.J.; James F. Vorwoldt, S.J.; Bros. Anthony R. Kreutzjans, S.J.; Peter Nguyen, S.J. Priests 4; Sisters 2; Lay Teachers 80.

Josephinum, 1501 N. Oakley Blvd., 60622. Tel: 773-276-1261; Fax: 773-292-3963. Email: martha.roughhan@josephinum.org. Web: www.josephinum.org.

Legal Title: *Josephinum, Inc.*, Middle School and High School (Grades 6-12) Sisters 3; Lay Teachers 25; Girls 163.

Leo High School, 7901 S. Sangamon, 60620. Tel: 773-224-9600; Fax: 773-224-3856. Email: admin@leohighschool.org. Web: www.leohighschool.org. Mr. Robert W. Foster, Pres.; Mr. Peter W. Doyle, Prin. Boys 322.

Maria High School (Formerly St. Casimir Academy), 6727 S. California Ave., 60629. Tel: 773-925-8686; Fax: 773-925-8885. Email: maria-hs@archchicago.org. Web: www.mariahighschool.org. Sisters Margaret Zalot, S.S.C., Pres.; Nancy Gannon, S.F.C.C., Prin. Sisters of St. Casimir Sisters 2; Lay Teachers 35; Students 547.

Marist High School, 4200 W. 115th St., 60655-4306. Tel: 773-881-6360; Fax: 773-881-0595. Email: Klaurencell@marist.net. Web: www.marist.net.

Marist Brothers Tel: 773-881-5300; Fax: 773-881-0595. Bro Richard J. Carey, F.M.S., Pres.; Larry F. Tucker, Prin. Brothers 11; Lay Teachers 80; Students 1,381.

Mother McAuley Liberal Arts High School, 3737 W. 99th St., 60655. Tel: 773-881-6500; Fax: 773-881-6562. Email: rwiorek@mothermcauley.org. Web: www.mothermcauley.k12.il.us. Sr. Rose Wiorek, R.S.M. Sisters of Mercy Sisters 8; Lay Teachers 105; Students 1,710.

Mt. Carmel High School, 6410 S. Dante Ave., 60637. Tel: 773-324-1020; Fax: 773-324-9235. Email: principal@mchs.org. Web: www.mchs.org.

Carmelites:

Res.: 6401 S. Harper Ave., 60638. Revs. Benjamin Aguilar, O.Carm.; Carl J. Markelz, O.Carm., Prin.; Daniel Carroll, O.Carm.; Mark Schaffer O.Carm.; Leander Troy, O.Carm.; J. Gerald Williams, O.Carm.; Peter McGarry, O.Carm. (NEW); John Knoernschild, O.Carm.; Bro. Daryl Moresco, O.Carm. (Australia). Carmelites in Residence 9; Lay Teachers 55; Students 755.

Notre Dame High School, 3000 N. Mango Ave., 60634. Tel: 773-622-9494; Fax: 773-622-8511. Email: bmurphy@ndhs4girls.org. Web: www.ndhs4girls.org. Sr. Mary Bridget Murphy, Pres. Emeritus; Richard Hussmann; Mrs. Karen F. Brown, Prin. Sisters of Notre Dame de Namur Sisters 3; Lay Teachers 28; Girls 400.

St. Patrick High School, 5900 W. Belmont Ave., 60634. Tel: 773-282-8844; Fax: 773-282-2361. Web: www.stpatrick.org. Bro. Konrad Diebold, F.S.C., Pres.; Dr. Joseph Schmidt, Prin.; Mr. Charles Schmidt, Asst. Prin.

Legal Title: *St. Patrick High School* Brothers of the Christian Schools Brothers 2; Lay Teachers 64; Students 990.

Resurrection High School, 7500 W. Talcott Ave., 60631. Tel: 773-775-6616; Fax: 773-775-0611. Web: www.reshs.org. Email: hs.resurrection@archchicago.org. Mrs. Jo Marie Yonkus Prin.; Sr. Stephanie Blaszczynski, C.R., Pres. Sisters of the Resurrection Sisters 8; Lay Teachers 56; Girls 920.

St. Rita of Cascia High School, 7740 S. Western Ave., 60620. Tel: 773-925-6600. Email: strita@stritahs.com. Web: www.stritahs.com. Revs. Thomas R. McCarthy, O.S.A., Pres./Principal; Bernard Danber, O.S.A. (See Section N for Monastery listing) Priests 5; Brothers 4; Sisters 2; Lay Teachers 40; Students 803.

St. Scholastica Academy, 7416 N. Ridge Blvd., 60645. Tel: 773-764-5715; Fax: 773-764-0304. Email: amatz@scholastica.us. Web: www.scholastica.us. Ms. Anne Matz, Prin. Sisters 5; Lay Teachers 29; Students 250.

Convent, 7430 N. Ridge Blvd., 60645. Tel: 773-764-2413; Fax: 773-761-5131.

ARLINGTON HEIGHTS. *St. Viator High School*, 1213 E. Oakton St., 60004. Tel: 847-392-4050; Fax: 847-392-8305. Email: tvonbehren@svhs.viator.il.us. Web: www.saintviator.com. Revs. Thomas R. von Behren, C.S.V., Pres./Principal; Daniel R. Hall, C.S.V.; Arnold E. Perham, C.S.V.; John E. VanWiel, C.S.V.; Bros. James E. Lewnard, C.S.V.; Robert Fuhl, C.S.V.; Michael Gosch, C.S.V.; Rob Robertson, C.S.V.; Daniel J. Triparier, C.S.V. Clerics of St. Viator Priests 4; Brothers 5; Lay Teachers 65; Students 1,030.

BURBANK. *St. Laurence High School, Inc.*, 5556 W. 77th St., 60459. Tel: 708-458-6900; Fax: 708-458-6908. Email: vikings@stlaurence.com. Web: www.stlaurence.com. Bro. Michael Segrich, C.F.C., Prin. Congregation of Christian Brothers Priests 1; Brothers 8; Lay Teachers 46; Students 776.

Queen of Peace High School (Girls). , 7659 S. Linder Ave., 60459. Tel: 708-458-7600; Fax: 708-458-5734. Email: info@queenofpeacehs.org. Web: www.queenofpeacehs.org. Dr. Catherine Karl, Pres.; Ms. Patricia Nolan Fitzgerald, Prin. Sisters 2; Lay Teachers 69; Students 900.

CHICAGO HEIGHTS. *Marian Catholic High School*, 700 Ashland Ave., 60411. Tel: 708-755-7565; Fax: 708-756-9758. Email: mchsinfo@marianchs.com. Web: www.marianchs.com. Sisters M. Paul McCaughey, O.P., Pres.; M. Joan Sorge, O.P., Prin Dominican Sisters (Springfield, IL) Sisters 14; Lay Teachers 86; Students 1,655.

LAGRANGE PARK. *Nazareth Academy*, 1209 W. Ogden Ave., 60526. Tel: 708-354-0061; Fax: 708-354-0109. Email: ccrepeau@nazarethacademy.com. Web: www.nazarethacademy.com. Ms. Deborah Vondrasek, Prin.; Sr. Carol Crepeau, C.S.J., Pres. Sisters of St. Joseph Sisters 8; Lay Teachers 42; Students 776.

LAKE FOREST. *Woodlands Academy of the Sacred Heart*, 760 E. Westleigh Rd., 60045-3298. Tel: 847-234-4300; Fax: 847-234-4348. Email: info@woodlands.lfc.edu. Web: www.woodlands.lfc.edu. Sr. Carol Campbell, R.S.C.J., Head of School. Religious of Sacred Heart Sisters 3; Lay Teachers 43; Students 197.

LEMONT. *Mt. Assisi Academy*, 13860 Main St., 60439. Tel: 630-257-7844; Fax: 630-257-6362. Sr. Mary Francis Werner, O.S.F. Sisters of St. Francis of Christ the King Sisters 8; Lay Teachers 25; Students 350.

MUNDELEIN. *Carmel High School*, One Carmel Pkwy., 60060. Tel: 847-566-3000; Fax: 847-566-8465. Email: (name)@carmelhs.org. Web: www.carmelhs.org. Sr. Mary Frances McLaughlin, B.V.M., Pres.; Rev. Robert Carroll, O.Carm., Prin. Priests 1; Sisters 3; Brothers 2; Lay Teachers 68; Students 1,352.

NILES. *Notre Dame High School* (Boys) , 7655 Dempster St., 60714. Tel: 847-965-2900; Fax: 847-965-2975. Web: www.ndhsdons.org. Revs. Michael M. DeLaney, C.S.C., Pres./Religious Superior; W. Patrick Hannan, C.S.C., Prin.; Sr. Carole Cierniak, O.S.F., Asst. Prin. Academics; Mr. Michael Hennessey, Asst. Prin. Student Life; Mr. James Boylan, Dean of Men; Ms. MaryAnne Malartsik, Business Mgr.; Dr. Charles Pistonio, Dir. Guidance & Counseling; Mr. Michael Hennessey, Dir. Athletics; Revs. David Scheidler, Dir. Campus Ministry; William Brinker, C.S.C. (Retired); Richard Conyers, C.S.C.; Jerome Esper, C.S.C.; Christopher A. Kuhn, C.S.C.; Don McNeill, C.S.C.; Leonard Rozario, C.S.C.; Mr. Phil Donner; Mr. Charles McNulty, Vice Pres. Financial Affairs; Bro. Paul Badnarczryk, C.S.C. Priests 9; Retired Priests 1; Brothers 2; Sisters 2; Seminarian 1; Lay Teachers 56; Students 790.

OAK PARK. *Fenwick High School*, 505 Washington Blvd., 60302. Tel: 708-386-0127; Fax: 708-386-3052. Email: admin@fenwickfriars.com. Web: www.fenwickfriars.com. Revs. Richard C. LaPata, O.P., Pres.; William J. Bernacki, O.P.; Joseph Ekpo; Thomas Saucier, O.P.; Michael A. Winkels, O.P.; Joseph I. Hren, O.P.; Paul Whittington, O.P.; Bro. Gabriel J. Dault, O.P. Dominican Order Priests 8; Brothers 3; Lay Teachers 71; Students 1,159.

RIVER FOREST. *Trinity High School*, 7574 W. Division St., 60305. Tel: 708-771-8383. Web: www.trinityhs.org. Sr. Michelle Germanson, O.P., Pres.; Mrs. Michele Whitehead, Prin. Dominican Sisters (Sinsinawa, WI) Sisters 1; Lay Teachers 36; Students 516.

RIVER GROVE. *Holy Cross High School*, 3000 North 80th Ave., 60171-1202. Tel: 708-456-5110; Fax: 708-456-9647. Email: bjspoonercsc@yahoo.com. Web: www.holycross-hs.org. Bro. James Spooner, C.S.C., Pres./ Prin.; Rev. Steven Bartczyszyn, C.R., Prin.; Mr. Tom Spoleti, Dir. Campus Ministry. Brothers of Holy Cross, (See Section N for Residence Listing) Priests 2; Brothers 4; Sisters 1; Lay Teachers 35; Students 400.

Mother Theodore Guerin High School, 8001 Belmont Ave., 60171. Tel: 708-453-6233; Fax: 708-453-6296. Email: nnolan@mtguerin.org. Web: www.mtguerin.org. Sisters Nancy Nolan, S.P., Pres.; Elisabeth Brown, Prin. Sisters of Providence Sisters 5; Lay Teachers 48; Students 567.

SOUTH HOLLAND. *Seton Academy*, 16100 Seton Rd., 60473-1899. Tel: 708-333-6300; Fax: 708-333-1534. Email: seton@seton-academy.org. Web: www.seton-academy.org. Lay Teachers 24; Students 325.

WAUKEGAN. *St. Martin de Porres High School*, 1 N. Genesee St., 60085. Tel: 847-623-5500; Fax: 847-623-5604. Email: mmcgowan@osalaw.com. Web: www.smdpwaukegan.org. Mr. R. J. McMahon, Pres.; Rev. Paul Sims, C.R., Prin.

SMDP Work Study, Inc., 1 N. Genesee St., 60085. Tel: 847-623-5500; Fax: 847-623-5604.

WESTCHESTER. *Immaculate Heart of Mary High School*, 10900 W. Cermak Rd., 60154. Tel: 708-562-3115; Fax: 708-531-0036. Web: www.ihmhs.net. Karen M. Ristau, Pres.; Clara Jurivich, Exec. Dir. Operations; Bridget O'Malley, Prin. Sisters, Servants of the Immaculate Heart of Mary, Office of the President. Sisters 1; Lay Teachers 30; Students 445.

IHM Corporate Connections, Inc., 10900 W. Cermak Rd., 60154. Tel: 708-531-9044; Fax: 708-531-0036. Mary Panik, Dir. Student work/study program.

St. Joseph High School, 1840 Mayfair, 60154-4299. Tel: 708-562-4433; Fax: 708-562-4459. Email: stjoehs@mediaone.net. Web: stjoehs.org. Mr. David McCreery, Pres.; Mr. Thomas J. Geraghty, Vice Pres.; Dr. JoAnn Rapp; Ms. Donna Keil. Brothers of the Christian Schools Brothers 2; Lay Teachers 28; Students 510.

WILMETTE. *Loyola Academy*, 1100 N. Laramie Ave., 60091. Tel: 847-256-1100; Fax: 847-256-1724. Email: dmcnulty@loy.org. Web: www.goramblers.org. Revs. Theodore G. Munz, S.J., Pres.; Peter W. Breslin, S.J., Rector; Terrence A. Baum, S.J., Headmaster; Mr. John E. Hoerster, Athletic Dir.; Ms. Tanya Johnson, Assoc. Athletic Dir.; Dr. Lorraine Ozar, Academic Dean; Mr. Kenneth Maziarka, Dean of Students; Mr. David

McNulty, D.C., CFO; Revs. Robert Ytsen, S.J.; Steven F. Hurd, S.J.; Paul J. Faulstich, S.J.; John J. Foley, S.J.; Bros. James W. Small, S.J.; Kent Beansoleil, S.J. Priests 7; Brothers 2; Lay Teachers 136; Students 2,000.

Regina Dominican High School, 701 Locust Rd., 60091. Tel: 847-256-7660; Fax: 847-256-3726. Web: www.rdhs.org. Sr. Adrienne Piennette, O.P., Pres.; Kathy Rzany, Prin. Sisters of St. Dominic (Adrian, MI) Sisters 8; Lay Teachers 35; Students 439.

[E] ELEMENTARY SCHOOLS, PRIVATE

CHICAGO. *Sacred Heart Schools (Academy of the Sacred Heart for Girls, Hardey Prep. for Boys)*, (Grades K-8), 6250 N. Sheridan Rd., 60660-1799. Tel: 773-262-4446; Fax: 773-262-6178. Email: sacred.heart@shschicago.org. Web: www.shschicago.org. Sr. Susan Maxwell, R.S.C.J., Dir. Schools; Mrs. Janet Underwood, Head of Lower School. (Grades 2-4); Mr. Daniel Flaherty, Head of Middle School, (Grades 5-8); Ms. Meg Steele, Dir. of Kindergarten and First Grade. Religious of the Sacred Heart Sisters 2; Lay Teachers 61; Students 547.

[F] CONSOLIDATED ELEMENTARY SCHOOLS

CHICAGO. *Bridgeport Catholic Academy*, 3700 S. Lowe, 60609. Tel: 773-376-6223. Mrs. Lillian Buckley, Prin. Serving the following parishes: All Saints-St. Anthony (518 W. 28th Pl.); Nativity of Our Lord (653 W. 37th St.). Lay Teachers 10; Students 200.

[G] CATHOLIC CHARITIES

CHICAGO. *Catholic Charities of the Archdiocese of Chicago-Archdiocesan Offices*, 126 N. Desplaines St., 60661. Tel: 312-655-7000; Fax: 312-655-0219. Web: catholiccharities.net. Most Rev. Michael M. Boland, Admin.; Mr. Walter H. Ousley, Dir. Operations; Rev. Charles T. Rubey, Dir. Programs; Ms. Ellen E. Gorney, Assoc. Dir. Programs; Cynthia Smentana, Dir. of Administrative Services; Revs. Roger J. Coughlin, Assoc. Admin. (Retired); Richard E. Bulwith, Assoc. Admin.; Gerard P. Kelly, C.M., Staff Chap.; Francis A. Cimarrusti, Assoc. Admin.; Charles T. Rubey, Assoc. Admin.; Wayne F. Watts, Assoc. Admin.; Most Rev. Edwin M. Conway, Episcopal Consultant. Administers charitable activities of the Archdiocese.

Administration:

Communications, 126 N. Desplaines St., 60661. Tel: 312-655-7024; Fax: 312-441-0529. William L. Sullivan Jr., Dir.

Development, 126 N. Desplaines St., 60661. Tel: 312-655-7289; Fax: 312-655-0605. Mary Perrotti, Dir.

Facilities Operations, 126 N. Desplaines St., 60661. Tel: 312-655-7044; Fax: 312-879-0289. Arlene Norton-White, Dir.

Finance, 721 N. LaSalle St., 60610. Tel: 312-655-7326; Fax: 312-266-4276. Elida Hernandez, Dir.

Human Resources, 126 N. Desplaines St., 60661. Tel: 312-651-2077; Fax: 312-831-1321. Ed Guerrero, Dir.

Government Relations, 721 N. LaSalle, 60610. Tel: 312-655-7314; Fax: 312-751-2350. Laurie Barretto, Dir.

Legal Services, 721 N. LaSalle, 60610. Tel: 312-655-7538; Fax: 312-654-0849. Michele Bianchi, Dir.

Board Relations, 126 N. Desplaines St., 60661. Tel: 312-655-7171; Fax: 312-930-0425. Laina Lurito, Dir.

Research and Quality Improvement, 721 N. LaSalle, 60610. Tel: 312-655-7492; Fax: 312-266-2142. Jean Mirabella, Dir.

Cook County Regional Services:

Chicago Services, 126 N. Desplaines, 60621. Tel: 312-655-7298; Fax: 312-263-4290. Arlene Jackson-Ervin, Regl. Svcs. Rep.

North Suburban Services, 1717 Rand Rd., Des Plaines, 60016. Tel: 847-376-2100; Fax: 847-390-8214. Mary Beth Hartmann, Regl. Svcs. Rep.

Northwest Suburban Services, 1717 Rand Road, Des Plaines, 60016. Tel: 847-376-2100; Fax: 847-390-8214. Cheryl Margiewicz, Regl. Svcs. Rep.

South Suburban Services, 16100 Seton Dr., South Holland, 60473. Tel: 708-333-8379; Fax: 708-333-9514. Frederick Shannon, Regl. Svc. Rep.

Southwest Suburban Services, 10661 Roberts Rd., Palos Hills, 60465. Tel: 708-430-0428; Fax: 708-430-0502. Cosima Dean, Regl. Svc. Rep.

West Suburban Services, 1400 S. Austin Blvd., Cicero, 60804. Tel: 708-222-1491; Fax: 708-222-1495. Dalia Rocotello, Regl. Svc. Rep.

Lake County Regional Services:, 671 S. Lewis Ave., Waukegan, 60085. Tel: 847-782-4000; Fax: 847-782-1040. Teresa Denny, Community Liaison & Business Mgr. Joseph Cardinal Bernardin Center for Lake County Services

Division of Community Development and Outreach Services, 721 N. La Salle, 60610. Tel: 312-655-7482; Fax: 312-642-9716. Dennis E. McSwain, Div. Mgr.; Sunnye Fredia, Assoc. Div. Mgr.

Brothers and Sisters of Love, 721 N. LaSalle St., 60610. Tel: 312-655-7474; Fax: 312-642-9716. Jim Fogarty, Program Dir.

Commodity and Food Supplemental Program (CFSP), 4970 W. Flournoy, 60644. Tel: 773-378-6643; Fax: 773-261-0536. Eliu Irizarry, Prog. Dir.

Mother and Child Food and Nutrition Program (MAC), 10 N. Cicero, 60644. Tel: 773-378-6643; Fax: 773-261-0536. Eliu Irizarry, Prog. Dir.

Respond Now, 1439 Emerald Ave., Chicago Heights, 60412. Tel: 708-755-4357; Fax: 708-755-4381. Dennis Condon, Prog. Dir.

Women Infant Children Food Centers Program, 907 N. Larrabee, 60610. Tel: 312-655-7480; Fax: 312-943-8295. Phil Parson, Dir. WIC Food Centers: 907 N. Larrabee, Chicago, IL 60610; 2907 S. Wabash Ave., Chicago, IL 60616; 416 E. 43rd St., Chicago, IL 60653; 5060 S. State St., Chicago, IL 60609; 6202 S. Halsted St., Chicago, IL 60621; 2310 W. Roosevelt Rd., Chicago, IL 60608; 5332 S. Western, Chicago, IL 60609; 3110 W. Armitage, Chicago, IL 60647; 4500 W. Chicago Ave., Chicago, IL 60651; 1643 W. Cermak Rd., Chicago, IL 60608; 1734 W. Chicago Ave., Chicago, IL 60622; 3932 W. Madison St., Chicago, IL 60624; and at 5125 W. Chicago, Chicago, IL 60651; 1802 E. 71st St., Chicago IL 60649; 11255 S. Michigan Ave., Chicago, IL 60628; 4622 W. Diversey Ave., Chicago, IL 60639; 8959 S. Commercial Ave., Chicago , IL 60617; 2400 S. Kedzie Ave., Chicago, IL; 1106 W. 79th St., Chicago, IL.

Division of Family and Parish Support Services, 126 N. Desplaines St., 60661. Tel: 312-655-7136; Fax: 312-427-3130. Kathy Donahue, Div. Mgr.; Veronica Glodowski, Assoc. Div. Mgr.

Addiction Consultation and Educational Services, 721 N. La Salle, 60610. Tel: 312-655-7450; Fax: 312-335-9853. Mary Ellen Flynn, Prog. Dir.

Central Information and Referral Services, 126 N. Desplaines St., 60661. Tel: 312-655-7700; Fax: 312-655-0678. Linda Hoag, Dept. Dir.

Central States Institute for Addiction, 721 N. LaSalle, 60610. Tel: 312-655-7530; Fax: 312-266-9027. Kevin J. Doyle, Dept. Dir.

Community Family Service Center, 1100 S. May, 60607. Tel: 312-733-5661; Fax: 312-733-5211. Sandra Villwocks, Prog. Dir.

Cooke's Manor Transitional Housing For Men, 126 N. Desplaines, 60661. Tel: 773-224-5607; Fax: 773-483-5301. Rev. Richard E. Bulwith, Chap.; Harry Francisco, Dir.

Emergency Assistance Program, 721 N. LaSalle St., 60610. Tel: 312-655-7500; Fax: 312-654-9861. Christene Dykes-Sorrells, Prog. Dir.

Family and Aged Services, 126 N. Desplaines St., 60661. Tel: 312-655-7299; Fax: 312-879-0208. Robert Haennicke, Dept. Dir.

Forever Free, 8235 S. Shore Dr., 60621. Tel: 773-374-8165; Fax: 312-374-2177. Josephine Abi-Rached, Prog. Dir.

Archdiocesan AIDS Ministry Office Tel: 312-655-7294; Fax: 312-263-4290.

Holbrook Center for Counseling and Psychotherapy, 721 N. LaSalle, 60610. Tel: 312-655-7550; Fax: 312-655-5490.

Lake County HIV/AIDS Case Management, 671 S. Lewis, Waukegan, 60085. Tel: 847-782-4000; Fax: 847-782-1030. Amy Hennings, Dir.; Linda Hoag, Dept. Dir.

Immigration & Naturalization Services, 126 N. Desplaines St., 60661. Tel: 312-382-2707; Fax: 312-427-3130. Nancy Gavilanes, Prog. Dir.

Refugee Resettlement Program, 126 N. Desplaines St., 60661. Tel: 312-655-7356; Fax: 312-427-3130. Elmida Kulovic, Prog. Dir.

Lake County Community Casework Emergency Services, 671 S. Lewis Ave., Waukegan, 60085. Tel: 847-782-4000; Fax: 847-782-1030. Amy Hennings, Prog. Dir.

Lake County Holbrook Center for Counseling & Psychotherapy, 998 E. Maple Street, Mundelein, 60060. Tel: 847-566-5168; Fax: 847-566-5178. Cornelia Zerban, Prog. Dir.

LOSS (Loving Outreach to Survivors of Suicide), 126 N. Desplaines St., 60661. Tel: 312-655-7283; Fax: 312-655-0219. Rev. Charles T. Rubey, Prog. Dir.

Joseph Cardinal Bernardin Family Shelter Program, 126 N. Desplaines St., 60661. Tel: 773-224-5607; Fax: 773-483-5301. Mildred Lincoln, Dept. Dir.

St. Peter Claver Senior Housing Corporation, 721 N. LaSalle Dr., 5th Floor, 60610.

Assumption BVM Family Shelter, 7020 S. Aberdeen, 60661. Tel: 773-874-4000, Ext. 2280; Fax: 773-483-5301. Derrolyn Steele. Scattered site housing

St. Francis de Paula Hospitality House, 7811 S. Ellis, 60619. Tel: 773-487-8615; Fax: 773-651-0857. Jean Stratton, Supvr.

St. Susanna Family Shelter, 14926 S. Honore, Harvey, 60426. Tel: 708-331-8211; Fax: 708-339-4398. Sr. Lois Bromark, Supvr.

St. Sylvester Family Shelter, 2915 W. Palmer St., 60647. Tel: 773-278-8253; Fax: 773-862-9388. Mary Fuqua, Admin.

St. Stanislaus Kostka Soup Kitchen, 1351 W. Evergreen, 60622. Tel: 773-278-2470; Fax: 773-278-2471. Sr. Ann Schaffer, Dir.

Transition to the Workplace, 126 N. DesPlaines, 60610. Tel: 312-651-2007; Fax: 312-906-8265. Eileen Higgins, Dept. Dir.

Lake County Samaritan House, 671 S. Lewis Ave., Waukegan, 60085. Tel: 847-782-4000; Fax: 847-782-1030. Jackie Small, Supvr.

North/Northwest Suburban Family Shelter Program, 1717 N. Rand Rd., Des Plaines, 60016. Tel: 847-376-2100; Fax: 847-390-8214. Millicent Ntiamoah, Dir.

Project Hope, 10661 S. Roberts Rd., Palos Hills, 60465. Tel: 708-430-0428; Fax: 708-430-0502. Millicent Ntiamoah, Dir.

Division of Non-Residential Services for Children and Youth, 651 W. Lake St., 60661. Tel: 312-655-7646; Fax: 312-879-0293. Sylvia Flory, Div. Mgr.; George Thibeault, Assoc. Div. Mgr.; Mary Grimes, Assoc. Div. Mgr.

Child Abuse/Neglect Investigations, 641 W. Lake, 60661. Tel: 312-382-2583; Fax: 312-879-0760.

671 S. Lewis Ave., Waukegan, 60085. Matthew Hunnicutt, Pro. Dir.

Child Welfare Counseling and Therapeutic Services, 651 W. Lake, 60661. Tel: 312-655-7191; Fax: 312-236-5384. Asela Paredes, Dept. Dir.

Foster Care Intake and Assessment, 651 W. Lake, 60661. Tel: 312-655-7243; Fax: 312-236-5384. Heidi Jesswein-Darville, Dept.Dir.

Foster Care, 651 W. Lake, 60661. Tel: 312-655-7995; Fax: 312-236-5384. Mary Grimes, Assoc. Div. Mgr.

Intact Family Services, 651 W. Lake St., 60661. Tel: 312-655-7601; Fax: 773-292-5713. Patricia Green, Dept. Dir.

In-Home Protective Services, 651 W. Lake St., 60661. Tel: 312-655-7601; Fax: 773-292-5713. Patricia Green, Dept. Dir.

Lake County Foster Care, 671 S. Lewis, Waukegan, 60085. Tel: 847-782-4221; Fax: 847-782-1040. Darlene Shappee, Contact Person.

Maternity/Adoption Services, 651 W. Lake St., 60661. Tel: 312-655-7071; Fax: 312-236-5384. Norene Chesebro, Dept. Dir.

Medicaid Specialized Foster Care, 651 W. Lake, 60661. Tel: 312-655-7995; Fax: 312-236-5384. Lynn Lyon, Dept. Dir.

Specialized Adolescent Foster Care, 651 W. Lake, 60661. Tel: 312-655-7995; Fax: 312-236-5384. James Scherrer, Ph.D., Dept. Dir.

Lake County Child Abuse/Neglect Investigations, Waukegan, 60085. Tel: 847-782-4000; Fax: 847-782-1040. Matthew Hunnicutt, Dept. Dir.

Jadonal E. Ford Center for Adolescent Parenting, 11255 S. Michigan Ave., 60628. Tel: 773-995-1737; Fax: 773-995-0125. Velma Brown-Walker, Dir.

Children & Adolescent Parent Program, 651 W. Lake St., 60661. Tel: 312-655-7222; Fax: 312-236-5384. James Scherrer, Ph.D., Dept. Dir.

Arts of Living Institute, 651 W. Lake St., 60661. Tel: 312-948-3610; Fax: 312-236-5384. Alice Wyatt, Prog. Dir.

Division of Residential Housing, 721 N. LaSalle St., 60610. Tel: 312-655-7490; Fax: 312-944-1550. Email: wdarcy@catholiccharities.net. William G. D'Arcy, Div. Mgr.; Lawrence Brozek, Assoc. Division Mgr.

Catholic Charities Housing Development Corporation, 721 N. LaSalle, 60610. Tel: 312-655-7975; Fax: 312-337-8793. William D'Arcy, COO.

Legal Title: *Ailbe Assisted Housing Corporation-Brendan Senior Housing CorporationGoedert Senior Housing CorporationHayes Senior Housing CorporationRoseland Senior Housing Corporation-Sabina Senior Housing CorporationSt. Peter Claver Senior Housing Corporation*, Under Development: St. Katharine Drexel Senior Housing, Chicago; St. Brendan Senior Housing, Chicago; Cortland Manor LLC, Chicago; St. Peter Claver Senior Housing, Robbins; St. Brendan Senior Housing, Chicago; Bishop Goedert Senior Housing, Chicago

Legal Titles:

Ailbe Assisted Housing Corporation
Brendan Senior Housing Corporation
Goedert Senior Housing Corporation
Hayes Senior Housing Corporation
Roseland Senior Housing Corporation
Sabina Senior Housing Corporation
St. Peter Claver Senior Housing Corporation

Under Development:

St. Peter Claver Senior Housing, Robbins
St. Brendan Senior Housing, Chicago
Bishop Goedert Senior Housing

Senior Housing Institutions:

Bishop Edwin M. Conway Residence, 1900 N. Karlov, 60639. Tel: 773-722-4510; Fax: 773-722-4515. Maureen Scholle, Admin.

Hayes Manor, 1211 W. Marquette Rd., 60636. Tel: 773-873-7400; Fax: 773-873-1709. Delores Davis, Admin.

Matthew Manor, 271 N. Albany Ave., 60612. Tel: 773-533-0001; Fax: 773-533-0622. Margaret Bridgmon, Admin.

Ozanam Village, 271 N. Albany Ave., 60612. Tel: 773-533-0001; Fax: 773-533-0622. Margaret Bridgmon, Admin.

Roseland Manor, 11717 S. State St., 60628. Tel: 773-995-9000; Fax: 773-995-1310.

Goedert Senior Housing Corporation, 721 N. La Salle Dr., 5th Flr., 60610. Tel: 312-655-7492. Shirley Caldwell, Admin.

St. Ailbe Faith Apartments, 1244 E. 93rd St., 60619. Tel: 773-721-0903; Fax: 773-721-0920. Jocelyne McGlorthan, Admin.

St. Ailbe Love Apts., 9240 S. Kimbark. Tel: 773-721-0903; Fax: 773-721-0920. Jocelyne McGlorthan, Admin.

St. Ailbe Hope Apts., 9101-9103 S. Harper. Tel: 773-721-0903. Jocelyne McGlorthan, Admin.

St. Brendan Apts., 6717 S. Elizabeth St., 60636. Tel: 773-846-8600; Fax: 773-846-0531. Sylvia Moore, Admin.

St. Sabina Elders Village, 1222 W. 79th St., 60620. Tel: 773-994-7850; Fax: 773-994-7945. Yvonne Plummer, Admin.

St. Theodore Apts., 6209 S. Paulina St., 60636. Tel: 773-776-0200; Fax: 773-846-8600. Sylvia Moore, Admin.

Tolton Manor, 6345 S. Stewart, 60621. Tel: 773-783-7800; Fax: 773-783-6362. Lee Cole, Admin.

Frances Manor, 1270 E. Golf Rd., Des Plaines, 60016. Tel: 847-390-1270; Fax: 847-390-9331. Dottie Fursek, Admin.

Lawrence Manor, 21425 Southwick, Matteson, 60443. Tel: 708-481-1200; Fax: 708-481-3168. Ron Zanardo, Admin.

Bernardin Manor, 1700 Memorial Dr., Calumet City, 60409. Tel: 708-832-1700; Fax: 708-832-9160. Cynthia Grinage, Admin.

Senior Care Institutions:

Senior Care Institutions:

Holy Family Villa, 12375 McCarthy Rd., Lemont, 60439. Tel: 630-257-2291; Fax: 630-257-2334. Roberta Magurany, Admin.

Bishop T.J. Lyne Residence for Retired Priests, 12230 S. Will-Cook Rd., Lemont, 60439. Tel: 630-257-9510; Fax: 630-257-2334. Roberta Magurany, Contact Person.

Division of Senior Social Services, 721 N. La Salle Dr., 60610. Tel: 312-655-7572; Fax: 312-640-1589. Wendy S. Siefert, Div. Mgr.; Janis Ahlgrim, Assoc. Div. Mgr.

Northeast/Northwest Chicago Case Management Services, 5801 N. Pulaski, Bldg. A, 60646. Tel: 773-583-9224; Fax: 773-583-2373. Sarah Cohen, Dept. Dir.

South Suburban Senior Services and Senior Activity Center, 15300 S. Lexington, Harvey, 60426. Tel: 708-596-2222; Fax: 708-596-6329. Margaret Latham, Dept. Dir.

Lake County Senior Case Management Services, 116 N. Lincoln, Round Lake, 60073. Tel: 847-546-5733; Fax: 847-546-7114. Jan Ahlgrin, Dept. Dir.

Maplehurst Congregate Senior Housing, 2312 Elisha, Zion, 60099. Tel: 847-872-7527; Fax: 847-782-4296. Frank Phillps, Dept. Dir.

Lake County Senior Community Services & Nutrition Program Sites, 414 S. Lewis Ave., Waukegan, 60085. Tel: 847-662-0085; Fax: 847-662-0747. Frank Phillips, Dept. Dir.

Antioch Area Center, 817 Holbeck St., Antioch, 60002. Tel: 847-395-7120; Fax: 847-395-7647.

Ela Township Area Center, 99 E. Main St., Lake Zurich, 60047. Tel: 847-438-0303. Mary Matzl, Ctr. Dir.

Lake County Nutrition Programs for Seniors:

Round Lake Senior Center, 814 Hart Rd., Round Lake, 60073. Tel: 847-546-0056.

Northwest Suburban Senior Services, 1801 W. Central, Arlington Heights, 60005. Tel: 847-253-5500; Fax: 847-253-9597. Ms. Cindy Gunderson, Prog. Dir.

Cook County Senior Community Services, 6412 S. Halsted, 60612. Tel: 773-994-8923; Fax: 773-488-5878. Barbara Carlo, Dept. Dir.

Ada S. Niles Senior Center and Adult Day Care Services, 7849 S. Aberdeen, 60620. Tel: 773-874-2400; Fax: 773-488-5878. Denise King, Senior Center Dir.; Norma Nalls, Day Care Senior Center Supvr.

Senior Aides Employment Program Tel: 773-874-2400; Fax: 773-488-5878. Victor Dodd, Supr.

Catholic Home Care, Inc., 721 N. La Salle St., 60610. Tel: 312-655-7415; Fax: 312-337-2705. Greta Brown, Dir.

Division of Early Childhood and Self Sufficiency, 721 N. LaSalle St., 60610. Tel: 312-655-7492; Fax: 312-335-9853. Guadalupe Preston, Div. Mgr.

Latin American Youth Center/El Centro De La Causa, 731 W. 17th St., 60616. Tel: 312-243-8508; Fax: 312-243-8414. Mr. Felip (Phil) Ayala, Dept. Dir.

Street Intervention Program, 4541 S. Wood, 3rd Flr., 60609. Tel: 773-376-0982; Fax: 773-376-5756. Oscar Contreras.

Early Childhood Development Programs, Day Care/Head Start, 721 N. LaSalle St., 60610. Tel: 312-655-7875; Fax: 312-255-0068.

Chicago Lawn Early Childhood Center, 3001 W. 59th St., 60629. Tel: 773-925-1085; Fax 773-925-1170. Marcela Gomez, Dir.

Cordi-Marian Early Childhood Center, 1100 S. May St., 60607. Tel: 312-666-3787; Fax: 312-666-3562. Frances Fister, Dir.

Ebenezer Head Start, 1652 W. Foster Ave., 60640. Tel: 773-878-9925; Fax: 773-784-6214. Lelia Coleman, Dir.

Grace Mission Early Childhood Center 5332 S. Western Ave., 60609. Tel: 773-476-1990; Fax: 773-476-2421. Francine Johnson, Dir.

Latin American Youth After School Program, 731 W. 17th St., 60616. Tel: 312-243-8508; Fax: 312-243-8414. Anita Riojas-Garcia, Dir.

Maria's Garden Head Start, 7320 S. Yale, 60621. Tel: 773-994-3016; Fax: 773-994-7509. Katherine Bacon, Dir.

Our Lady of Guadalupe Early Childhood Center, 9129 S. Burley, 60617. Tel: 773-978-8320; Fax: 773-221-5475. Stephanie Newsome, Dir.

Our Lady of Lourdes Early Childhood Center, 1449 S. Keeler, 60623. Tel: 773-521-3126; Fax: 773-522-3753. Valerie Jones, Acting Dir.

Our Lady of Tepeyac Head Start, 2414 S. Albany, 60623. Tel: 773-277-5888; Fax: 773-522-3403. Felicima Gosien, Dir.

Providence of God Early Childhood Center, 1100 S. May St., 60606. Tel: 312-666-3787; Fax: 312-666-3562. Frances Fister, Dir.

St. Blase Early Childhood Center, 7438 W. 61st Pl., Summit, 60501. Tel: 708-496-1193; Fax: 708-496-1246. Virginia Carrillo, Acting Dir.

St. James Early Childhood Center, 611 Maple St., Maywood 60153. Tel: 708-343-2878; Fax: 708-343-5783. Karen Evans, Dir.

St. Joseph Early Childhood Center, 4800 S. Paulina, 60609. Tel: 773-927-2524; Fax: 773-927-2122. Maira Monteiro Dir.

St. Kevin Early Childhood Center, 10509 S. Torrence, 60617. Tel: 773-374-6466; Fax: 773-221-7451. InaRay Moss, Dir.

St. Mark Head Start, 1041 N. Campbell, 60622. Tel: 773-772-6606; Fax: 773-252-3007. Deborah O'Brien, Asst. Dir.

St. Mel Early Childhood Center, 4215 W West End Ave., 60624. Tel: 773-533-1550, Ext 51; Fax: 773-533-1556. Janice Williams-Gathings, Dir.

St. Michael Early Childhood Center, 8235 S. Shore Dr., 60617. Tel: 773-933-7676; Fax: 773-221-4180. Karen Moore, Dir.

St. Philomena Head Start, 4131 W. Cortland, 60639. Tel: 773-486-6466; Fax: 773-227-6594. Corazon Navarro, Dir.

Santa Maria Head Start, 1337 W. Ohio St., 60622. Tel: 312-421-7322; Fax: 312-563-1754. Carol Christensen, Dir.

Non-Division Listing:

Christ Child Society of Chicago, 1616 Sheridan Rd., Wilmette, 60091. Tel: 847-251-9253. Mrs. Jane Helmer, Contact Person.

Keenager News, 126 N. Desplaines, 60610. Tel: 312-655-7425; Fax: 312-441-0529. William Sullivan, Dir.

Little Mexico, Inc., 115 N. Wolf Rd., Wheeling, 60090. Tel: 847-419-8935. Sr. Teresa Mary Martinez, Contact Person.

Mission of the Holy Cross, 126 N. Desplaines St., 60606. Tel: 312-655-7000; Fax: 312-655-0219. Rev. Michael M. Boland.

Shelter for the Homeless, Inc., 721 N. LaSalle St., 60610. Tel: 312-655-5312. Paul W. Thompson, Contact Person.

Society of St. Vincent De Paul of Chicago, 645 W. Randolph St., 60661. Tel: 312-655-7181; Fax: 312-454-0101. Web: www.svdpchicago.org. Claudia Pieske, Exec. Dir.; Mrs. Mary Van Wazer, Pres.

Affiliated Agencies:

Boys Hope/Girls Hope Of Illinois, 1100 N. Laramie, Wilmette, 60091. Tel: 847-254-9595; Fax: 847-256-5959. Sr. Carol Fleming, Exec. Dir.

Maryville Academy, 1150 N. River Rd., Des Plaines, 60016. Tel: 847-824-6126; Fax: 847-824-7190. Revs. John Smyth, Exec. Dir.; David Ryan, COO.

Mercy Home for Boys & Girls, 1140 W. Jackson Blvd., 60607. Tel: 312-738-7590; Fax: 312-738-0484. Revs. James Close, Pres.; Scott Donahue, Pres.

Misericordia Home, North: Heart of Mercy Village, Marian Center, 6900 N. Ridge, 60660. Tel: 773-973-6300; Fax: 773-973-5214. Sr. Rosemary Connelly, R.S.M., Exec. Dir.

South: 2916 W. 47th St., 60632. Tel: 773-254-9595; Fax: 773-254-6856. Betty Flynn, Admin.

St. Coletta's of Illinois, 18350 Crossing Dr., Tinley Park, 60477. Tel: 708-342-5200; Fax: 708-342-2579. Wayne A. Kottmeyer, Exec. Dir.

St. Joseph's Carondelet Child Center, 739 E. 35th St., 60616. Tel: 773-624-7443. Mr. James B. McLaughlin, Pres. & CEO.

[H] RESIDENTIAL CHILD-YOUTH CARE

CHICAGO. *Mission of Our Lady of Mercy-Mercy Home for Boys and Girls*, 1140 W. Jackson Blvd., 60607. Tel: 312-738-7560; Fax: 312-738-1545. Email: info@mercyhome.org. Web: www.mercyhome.org. Revs. James J. Close, Pres. & CEO; L. Scott Donahue, Assoc. Pres.; Cheryl Murphy, CFO; Tita Yutuc, Vice Pres. Youth Prog.; Mark Mroz, Vice Pres. Communications & CQI Planning; Mimi LeClair, Vice Pres. Devel.; Barbara Moran, Asst. to Pres.; Larry Kruszynski, Vice Pres. Information Systems & Mission Press. Staff 110; Full Time Religious 5; Youths 306.

DES PLAINES. *Maryville Academy*, 1150 N. River Rd., 60016. Tel: 847-824-6126; Fax: 847-824-7190. Rev. John P. Smyth, Exec. Dir.

Legal Title: *Maryville Academy* Patients Assisted Annually 16,500.

[I] DAY NURSERIES, SETTLEMENTS AND SOCIAL CENTERS

CHICAGO. *Marillac Social Center*, 212 S. Francisco Ave., 60612. Tel: 773-722-7440; Fax: 773-722-1469. Email: Marillac1@aol.com. Web: Marillachouse.org. Sr. Yvonne Thranow, D.C., Exec. Dir. Day care for children ages 2 1/2 to 12 years; Recreation programs for ages 6 to 25 years; emergency assistance food and clothing for poor families; day shelter for the homeless; child abuse and neglect treatment; counselling services; programs for pregnant & parenting teens and their babies; home bound elderly; services for teenage mothers. Day Care capacity 422.

**Port Ministries* A Franciscan outreach of the Assumption of the Blessed Virgin Mary Province, Pulaski, WI. Soup Kitchen, food pantry, overnight shelters (men, women & family), GED, ESL, family services, mobile soup kitchen, neighborhood gym. , 5013 S. Hermitage Ave., 60609. Tel: 773-778-5955; Fax: 773-778-2451. Email: port532857@aol.com. Web: www.theportministries.org. Rev. Augustin Milon, O.F.M., Founder & Pres. Total Staff 30; Total Assisted 120,130.

Resurrection Day Care Center, 1849 N. Hermitage Ave., 60622. Tel: 773-384-7142. Sr. Paulette Pieta, C.R., Admin. & Supr. Sisters of the Resurrection Sisters 4; Daily Attendance 23.

St. Rose Center, 4911 S. Hoyne, 60609. Tel: 773-436-1433; Fax: 773-436-2280. Email: strosecenter@aol.com. Sr. Theresa Tamburo, D.S.M.P., Admin. Day training program for mentally impaired adults Sisters 2; Q.M.R.P. 2; Developmental Trainers 5; Work Activity Director 1; Capacity 50.

**San Miguel Febres Cordero School, Inc.* Operated by DeLaSalle Christian Brothers. Gratuitous Catholic Middle School with two campuses for at risk youth; Adult education (ESL); after school and evening youth programs, ages 11-18; parenting skills classes. Mentoring, tutoring and scholarship assistance to graduates who study in Catholic high schools. , 1949 W. 48th St., 60609-4145. Tel: 773-890-1481; Fax: 773-254-3382. Email: sanmiguelchgo@hotmail.com. Web: www.san-miguel.org. Bros. Edwin Dupre, F.S.C.; Ed Siderewicz, F.S.C.; Michael Ferenbach, F.S.C.; Martin Spellman, F.S.C. Total Staff 37; Total Assisted Annually 300.

St. Vincent de Paul Center, 2145 N. Halsted St., 60614. Tel: 312-943-6776. Sr. Cathrine Mary Norris, D.C., Admin. Day care for children 4 mos. to 11 yrs.; family social services; Provides youth and adult recreational and athletic programs for ages 18 years through adult.; Provides case management, counseling and emergency relief for senior citizens. Provides intergenerational living quarters for 15 seniors (low income) and 5 young adults.; Provides outreach to the homeless in the form of case management and other concrete services. Daughters of Charity 2; Capacity 468; Individual registration 468; Individual registration 175; Individuals served 60.

[J] HOSPITALS

CHICAGO. *St. Anthony Hospital* Ascension Health & Missionary Sisters of the Sacred Heart of Jesus. ,

2875 W. 19th St., 60623. Tel: 773-521-1710. Mr. Peter Faxio, Board Chm.; Ms. Kathleen DeVine, COO; Sr. Benigna Morais, M.S.C., Chap.; Revs. Donatus Chukwu, Extern Priest; Marco Cardenas, C.M.F., Extern Priest; Michael Adaiuckalam, S.S.S., Extern Priest; David Petraitis, O.S.A., Extern Priest; Bernard Okafor, Extern Priest; Joseph Varkey Kattackal, Extern Priest; Thomas Varughese, Extern Priest; Magnus Anokwuru, Extern Priest.

Legal Title: *Catholic Health Partners Services* Sisters 6; Bassinets 26; Bed Capacity 150; Patients Assisted Annually 66,200.

St. Bernard Hospital & Health Care Center, 326 W. 64th St., 60621. Tel: 773-962-3900; Fax: 773-873-8247. Email: elizvs@aol.com. Web: stbernardhospital.com. Sisters Janet Wahleithner, R.H.S.J., Supr.; Elizabeth Van Straten, R.H.S.J., Pres. & CEO; Janet Wahleithmer, R.H.S.J., Dir. Pastoral Care Dept.

Legal Title: *St. Bernard Hospital* Religious Hospitallers of St. Joseph Sisters 2; Bed Capacity 226; Patients Assisted Annually 105,000.

Saint Elizabeth's Hospital, 1431 N. Claremont Ave., 60622. Tel: 773-278-2000; Fax: 312-850-5970. Joseph F. Toomey, Pres.; Ms. Margaret McDermott, CEO; Revs. John Kobus, Coord. & Spiritual Svcs.; Robert Florido; Sr. Maureen Dolan, O.S.F.; Mary Mallon, Lay Chap.; Kathy Ponce, Lay Chap. Sponsored by Sisters of the Holy Family of Nazareth & Sisters of the Resurrection., Operated by Resurrection Health Care. Bed Capacity 276; Patients Assisted Annually 145,742.

Holy Cross Hospital, 2701 W. 68th St., 60629. Tel: 773-884-9000. Web: www.holycrosshospital.org. Brian L. Lemon, CEO; Sr. Dolores Cavalli, O.P., Chap.; Revs. Thomas Griffin, O.S.A., Chap.; Mark Mengel, S.S.C., Chap.; Thomas A. Morrison, O.P., Chap.; Sr. Agnese Chapp, Patient Visitor.

Legal Title: *Holy Cross Hospital* Sisters of St. Casimir of Chicago. Sisters 6; Licensed Beds 311; Patients Assisted Annually 175,300.

Holy Cross Hospital and Sisters of St. Casimir Foundation

Saint Joseph Hospital Missionary Sisters of the Sacred Heart of Jesus. , 2900 N. Lake Shore Dr., 60657. Tel: 773-665-3000; Fax: 773-665-4859. Joseph F. Toomey, Pres.; Ron Struxness, Group Vice Pres., Exec. Vice Pres. & CEO; Ms. Margaret McDermott, COO; Revs. Theodore Ploplis, Coord. Spiritual Svcs.; Anthony J. Adducci, Chap.; Deacon Michael Romano, Chap.; Sr. Alverda Bonifas, O.P., Chap. Sponsored by Sisters of the Holy Family of Nazareth & Sisters of the Resurrection, Operated by Resurrection Health Care Bassinets 31; Bed Capacity 403; Patients Assisted Annually 76,800.

Saint Mary of Nazareth Hospital Center, 2233 W. Division, 60622. Tel: 312-770-2000; Fax: 312-770-3391. Web: www.reshealth.org. Joseph F. Toomey, Pres.; Sr. Sally Marie Kiepura, C.S.F.N., Exec. Vice Pres. & CEO; Rev. John Kobus, Chap., Coord. & Spiritual Svcs.; Most Rev. Enrique Rivera Hernandez, Chap.; Rev. Abraham Miller, Chap.; Sr. Blanche Zalewski, C.S.F.N., Chap. Sponsored by Sisters of the Holy Family of Nazareth & Sisters of the Resurrection, Operated by Resurrection Health Care Bed Capacity 387; Bassinets 32; Patients Assisted Annually 182,031.

Mercy Hospital and Medical Center, 2525 S. Michigan Ave., 60616-2477. Tel: 312-567-2100; Fax: 312-567-6575. Web: www.mercy-chicago.org. Sr. Sheila Lyne, R.S.M., Pres. & CEO. Tel: 312-567-2580; Fax: 312-567-6575; Rev. Martin J. Hebda, Vice Pres., Spirituality & Community. Tel: 312-567-2045; Fax: 312-328-7741. Sisters 4; Bed Capacity 475; Bassinets 30; Patients assisted annually 343,456.

Affiliates:

Mercy Diagnostic & Treatment Center

Mercy Services Corp.

Mercy Foundation, Inc.

Mercy Health Care & Rehabilitation Center

Mercy Health System of Chicago Liability Self-Insurance Trust

Mercy Medical at Presidential Towers, Tower Three, 614 W. Madison St., 60661. Tel: 312-902-2523. (Outpatient Satellite Facility & Alcohol-Drug Dependency Program)

Mercy Works at Presidential Towers, Tower Three, 614 W. Monroe St., 60661. Tel: 312-902-2489; Fax: 312-902-4022.

Mercy Medical in Chinatown, 2347 S. Wentworth, 60616. Tel: 312-842-0100. (Outpatient Satellite Facility)

Mercy Medical on Pulaski, 5525 S. Pulaski, 60629. Tel: 773-585-1955. (Outpatient Satellite Facility)

Mercy Works on Pulaski, 5635 S. Pulaski Rd., 60629. Tel: 773-284-5278; Fax: 773-585-0395.

Mercy Medical on Michigan, 2930 S. Michigan Ave., 60616. Tel: 312-808-0400.

Mercy Works on Ashland, 3316 S. Ashland, 60608. Tel: 773-254-2133.

Mercy Medical in Chatham, 8541 S. State St., 60619. Tel: 773-994-2300.

Mercy Works Bryn Mawr, 8619 W. Bryn Mawr, 60631. Tel: 773-380-0400.

**Our Lady of the Resurrection Medical Center*, 5645 W. Addison, 60634. Tel: 773-282-7000; Fax: 773-794-7671. Web: www.reshealth.org. Joseph F. Toomey, Pres.; Ivette Estrada, CEO; Revs. Robert Walsh, Chap.; Abraham Jacob, Chap.; Sr. Mary Hedwig Kuczynski, C.R., Chap.; Mary Mallon, Chap.; Kathleen Ponce, Chap. Sponsored by Sisters of the Holy Family of Nazareth & Sisters of the Resurrection, Operated by Resurrection Health Care Bed Capacity 286; Patients Assisted Annually 100,979.

Resurrection Medical Center, 7435 Talcott Ave., 60631. Tel: 773-774-8000; Fax: 773-792-9926. Web: www.reshealth.org. Joseph F. Toomey, Pres.; Sisters Donna Marie, C.R., Group Vice Pres., Exec. Vice Pres. & CEO; Mary Leonette, C.R., Supr.; Rev. Bonaventure Baliege, S.J., Chap.; Deacons Frank Biel, Chap.; Vito DeCanio, Chap.; Sisters Rose Mary Carney, O.S.F., Chap.; Kathryn Komarek, O.P., Chap.; Leszek Baczkura, Lay Chap.; M. Katherine Biesterfield, Lay Chap.; Conceicao Mesquita, Lay Chap.; James Croegaert, Coord. Sponsored by Sisters of the Holy Family of Nazareth & Sisters of the Resurrection, Operated by Resurrection Health Care Bed Capacity 434; Patients Assisted Annually 184,645; Student Nurses affiliated with Nurses-Triton College 40; Student Nurses, Oakton Community College 20; Chicago Board of Education 12.

BLUE ISLAND. *St. Francis Hospital and Health Center*, 12935 S. Gregory St., 60406. Tel: 708-597-2000; Fax: 708-389-9480. Web: www.stfrancisblueisland.com. Ms. Colleen L. Kannaday, Pres.; Sr. Doris Ashcraft, F.S.M., Chap.; Rev. Philita Carney; Sr. Vivian Custo, O.P., Chap.; Jeanne Tatum, Chap.; Joel Sanchez, Chap.; Revs. Steven Kovacevich, Chap.; Parath-Undyil T. Thomas (India), Chap.; Bro. Patrick Varilla, C.F.C., Chap.; Rev. Orlando Toledo, Chap., Baptist Min.; Mary McShane, Dir. Spiritual Care & Mission. Member of SSM Health Care Sisters 1; Bed Capacity 410; Patients Assisted Annually 110,485; Total Staff 1,500.

CHICAGO HEIGHTS. *St. James Hospital and Health Centers*, 1423 Chicago Rd., 60411. Tel: 708-756-1000; Fax: 708-756-6863. Web: www.stjameshhc.org. 20201 S. Crawford Ave., Olympia Fields, 60461. Tel: 708-747-4000; Fax: 708-503-3270.

Legal Title: *Sisters of St. Francis Health Services, Inc., Mishawaka, Indiana* Sisters 5; Bed Capacity 561; Patients Assisted Annually 260,369; Total Staff 2,373.

Chicago Heights Mr. Peter J. Murphy, Pres. & CEO; Sr. Marlene Shapley, O.S.F., Vice Pres.; Rev. Ronald L. Kondziolka, Chap. Sisters of St. Francis of Perpetual Adoration Sisters 4; Bed Capacity 561; Patients Assisted Annually 252,846; Total Staff 1,581.

DES PLAINES. *Holy Family Medical Center*, 100 N. River Rd., 60016. Tel: 847-297-1800; Fax: 847-297-1863. Web: www.reshealth.org. Joseph F. Toomey, Pres.; Sisters Donna Marie Wolowicki, C.R., Group Vice Pres., Exec. Vice Pres. & CEO; Rita Marie Kocanda, C.S.F.N., Spiritual Svcs. Coord.; Rev. Haldane Mysliwiec, Chap.; Deacons Jack Smith, Chap.; Don Wehling, Chap. Sponsored by Sisters of the Holy Family of Nazareth & Sisters of the Resurrection., Operated by Resurrection Health Care Bed Capacity 252; Patients Assisted Annually 98,233.

ELK GROVE VILLAGE. *Alexian Brothers Medical Center*, 800 Biesterfield Rd., 60007-3397. Tel: 847-437-5500. Email: johnson@alexian.net. Web: www.wswwalexian.org. Roger W. Johnson, Pres. & CEO; Robert Creighton, Chap.; Rosemary A. Kimpel, Chap.; Revs. Stan Fernando, Chap.; William E. Veith, Chap.; Andrew Beltowski, Chap.; Rian Clancy, C.P., Chap.; James Gullickson, Chap. Congregation of Alexian Brothers, Immaculate Conception Province, Parent Institution: Alexian Brothers Hospital Network; Associated with Stritch School of Medicine of Loyola University. Brothers 14; Licensed Beds 387; Lay Staff 2,800; Patients Assisted Annually 135,808.

EVANSTON. *Saint Francis Hospital*, 355 Ridge Ave., 60202. Tel: 847-316-4000; Fax: 847-316-7733. Web: www.reshealth.org. Joseph F. Toomey, Pres.; Sherlyn Hailstone, Exec. Vice Pres. & CEO; Revs. James E. Dunlap, Spiritual Svcs. Coord., (Presbyterian); Thomas Varugese, Chap.; Sharon S. Barcham, Chap.; Rabbi Ilene Melemad, Chap. Sponsored by Sisters of the Holy Family of Nazareth & Sisters of the Resurrection, Operated by Resurrection Health Care Bed Capacity 300; Patients Assisted Annually 250,000.

EVERGREEN PARK. *Little Company of Mary Hospital and Health Care Centers*, 2800 W. 95th St., 60805. Tel: 708-422-6200; Fax: 708-425-9756. Web: www.lcmh.org. Sr. Kathleen McIntyre, L.C.M., Bd. Chm.; Dennis Reilly, Pres.; Ms. Roseann Keller, Dir. Pastoral Care Svcs.; Rev. James R. Gallagher, Chap.; Rev. Dale Lawson, Chap. & Baptist Min.; Sr. Jean Stickney, L.C.M., Chap.; Deacon Richard Warfield, Chap.; Margaret Schneider, Chap.; Carol Ehler, Chap.; Sandra Dieckmann, Chap.; Sr. Sharon Ann Walsh, L.C.M., Chap.; Christa Henrich, Chap.; Peg Radakovitz, Chap.; Karen Rushen, Chap.

Legal Title: *The Little Company of Mary Hospital and Health Care Centers* Sisters of the Little Company of Mary 26; Bed Capacity 294; Bassinets 24; Patients Assisted Annually 242,900.

Affiliates:

Little Company of Mary Auxiliary, 2800 W. 95th St., 60805. Tel: 708-229-5447.

Little Company of Mary Affiliated Services, Inc., 2800 W. 95th St., 60805. Tel: 708-422-6200, Ext. 5100; Fax: 708-425-9369.

Oak Lawn Care Station, 5660 W. 95th St., Oak Lawn, 60453. Tel: 708-499-2273; Fax: 708-857-3705.

Burbank Care Station, 4901 W. 79th St., Burbank, 60459. Tel: 708-424-2273; Fax: 708-857-3713.

Mary Potter Pavilion, 2850 W. 95th St., 60805. Tel: 708-857-9524.

Little Company of Mary Hospital Foundation, 2800 W. 95th St., 60805. Tel: 708-229-5022; Fax: 708-229-6525. Mary Jo May, Exec. Dir.

HOFFMAN ESTATES. *Alexian Brothers Behavioral Health Hospital*, 1650 Moon Lake Rd., 60194. Tel: 847-755-8001; Fax: 847-755-8060. Email: mark.frey@abbhh.net. Web: abbhh.org. Mark A. Frey, Pres. & CEO; Rev. Stan Kedzior, Dir. Mission Integration. Congregation of Alexian Brothers, Immaculate Conception Province Brothers 1; Licensed Beds 95; Patients Assisted Annually 7,476.

Parents:

Alexian Brothers Health System Tel: 847-981-0627; Fax: 847-981-5561.

Alexian Brothers of Illinois Tel: 847-640-7551; Fax: 847-981-5561.

St. Alexius Medical Center, 1555 Barrington Rd., 60194. Tel: 847-843-2000; Fax: 847-490-2570. Email: larry.kancler@stalexius.net. Edward M. Goldberg, Pres. & CEO; Sr. Laurette Betz, Chap.; Rev. Domingo Hurtado-Badillo, Chap.; Deacon Lawrence Kancler, Chap. Congregation of Alexian Brothers, Immaculate Conception Province Brothers 1; Licensed Beds 321; Lay Staff 1,663; Patients Assisted Annually 141,300.

Parent Institutions:

Alexian Brothers Health System Tel: 847-437-5500; Fax: 847-981-5561.

Alexian Brothers of Illinois Tel: 847-437-5500; Fax: 847-981-5561.

MAYWOOD. *Foster G. McGaw Hospital of Loyola University of Chicago*, 2160 S. First Ave., 60153. Tel: 708-216-9056; Fax: 708-216-1121. Email: mcoglia@lumc.edu. Marie Coglianese, M.P.S., Dir. Pastoral Care & Education; Revs. Thomas M. Heskin, O.S.M.; John P. Coakley, S.J.; Mr. Jerry Kaelin, M.Div., M.A., Chap. SIT Supvr., CPE Mgr.; Rev. James J. Creighton, S.J., CPE Supvr.; Ms. Janet McCabe, M.Div., Chap. & SIT Supvr.; Mr. David Corcoran, M.Ed.; JoElla Doggett, M.P.S.; Deacon Albin Wegner; Ms. Kathleen Brannigan, M.T.S.; Mr. John Grubba, M.Div., M.A.; Mrs. Adrienne Zervos, M.P.S.; Revs. Gino Donatelli, S.J., D.Min.; Lee Smits, M.Div. Bed Capacity 520; Patients Assisted Annually 350,000.

MELROSE PARK. **Westlake Hospital*, 1225 Lake St., 60160. Tel: 708-938-7670; Fax: 708-938-7975. Web: www.reshealth.org. Joseph F. Toomey, Pres.; M. Patricia Shehorn, Group Vice Pres., Exec. Vice Pres. & CEO; Revs. Janet Lundblad, Chap. & Coord. Spiritual Svcs. (Covenant Min.); Peter Kunnalakat, Chap.; Michael Adaickalam, Chap.; Sr. Mary Dominic Russell, C.R., Chap. Sponsored by Sisters of the Holy Family of Nazareth & Sisters of the Resurrection., Operated by Resurrection Health Care; Student Nurses affiliated with Nurses-Triton College, Student Nurses, Elmhurst College Licensed Beds 304; Total Assisted Annually 9,807; Total Staff 906.

OAK PARK. *Rush Oak Park Hospital*, 520 S. Maple Ave., 60304. Tel: 708-383-9300; Fax: 708-660-6658. Email: mmay_oph17@hotmail.com. Web: www.oakparkhospital.org. Mr. Bruce M. Elegant, Pres. & CEO; Bro. Michael May, O.F.M., Chap. & Dir.; Sylvia Fromme, Chap.

Legal Title: *Rush Oak Park Hospital* Wheaton

Franciscan Sisters Bed Capacity 176; Patients Assisted Annually 94,947.

Oak Park Hospital Endowment Fund Affiliate.

[K] HEALTH CARE CENTERS

CHICAGO. *St. Basil Health Service - Free People's Clinic*, 1850 W. Garfield, 60609. Tel: 773-436-4758; Fax: 773-436-2749. Patients Assisted Annually 5,000.

BROADVIEW. **Proviso Family Services* dba ProCare Centers , 1820 S. 25th Ave., 60160. Tel: 708-681-2324; Fax: 708-681-1289. Web: www.reshealth.org. Joseph F. Toomey, Pres.; Mr. J. Melvin Smith, Vice Pres., ProCare Centers. Sponsored by the Sisters of the Holy Family of Nazareth & Sisters of the Resurrection., Operated by Resurrection Health Care Total assisted annually 7,500.

[L] PROTECTIVE INSTITUTIONS

CHICAGO. *Big Sisters*, 721 N. LaSalle St., Room 386, 60610. Tel: 312-751-0111; Fax: 312-751-1385. Mrs. Elizabeth J. Brennan, Pres.; Ms. Mary A. Courtney, Past Pres.

House of the Good Shepherd, 1114 W. Grace St., 60613. Tel: 773-935-3434; Fax: 773-935-3523.
Legal Title: *House of the Good Shepherd* Sisters of The Good Shepherd, Shelter for abused women with children. Sisters 6; Part time social workers 4; Capacity: 14 Families 0.

St. Joseph's Carondelet Child Center, 739 E. 35th St., 60616. Tel: 773-624-7443; Fax: 773-624-7676. Email: jbmc@stjcc.org. Web: www.stjcc.org. Mr. James B. McLaughlin, Pres. & CEO; Rev. Charles T. Rubey, Chap.
Legal Title: *St. Joseph's Carondelet Child Center* Sisters of St. Joseph of Carondelet, Treatment, rehabilitation and education of the dependent emotionally disturbed children and youth. Sisters 1; Children 220.

**L'Arche Chicago*, 1049 S. Austin Blvd., 60644. Tel: 773-287-8249. Email: larchechicago@hotmail.com. Web: www.larchechicago.org. Deborah G. Seles, Dir. A Christian Community concerned with life sharing between persons with a developmental disability and persons who assist them.

St. Mary of Providence, 4200 N. Austin Ave., 60634. Tel: 773-545-8300; Fax: 773-545-8035. Email: commsmop@aol.com. Sisters Rita Butler, Dir.; Janet Kosman, Admin.; Rev. Thomas A. Mulcrone, Chap.
Legal Title: *Daughters of St. Mary of Providence* Operated by the Daughters of St. Mary of Providence., Developmental Training and residential care of developmentally disabled adults. Sisters 11; Total Staff 150; Adults 96.

Misericordia Home South, 2916 W. 47th St., 60632. Tel: 773-254-9595; Fax: 773-254-6856. Sr. Rosemary, R.S.M., Dir. Sisters of Mercy 9; Patients Assisted Annually 110; Respite Beds 2; Handicapped children under 22 years of age: Bed Capacity for Children 110.

Misericordia/Heart of Mercy Center, 6300 N. Ridge, 60660. Tel: 773-973-6300; Fax: 773-973-5214. Web: www.misericordia.com. Sr. Rosemary Connelly, R.S.M., Exec. Dir. Children and adults with Developmental disabilities. Sisters 14; Residents 550.

BARTLETT. *Bartlett Learning Center*, 801 W. Bartlett Rd., 60103. Tel: 630-289-4221; Fax: 630-289-4390. Samuela Bovelli, Exec. Dir.
Legal Title: *Barlett Learning Center, Inc. DBA Clarewoods Academy and Cupertino Home* Sponsored by the Sisters of St. Joseph, Third Order of St. Francis., Operates Bartlett Learning Center Day School Program and the Cupertino Home, Warrenville, IL. Day School program serves developmentally delayed and multiple handicapped individuals ages 3 to 21. Day Shool Program accepts youth identified LD, BD, EMH, TMH, and TBI Speech/Language Impaired, Autistic. Community Integrated Living Arrangement Serves developmentally delayed gentlemen ages 18 to 45. Sisters 5; Lay Staff 100; Patients Assisted Annually 140.

LAKE ZURICH. *Mt. St. Joseph Home*, 24955 North Hwy. 12, 60047. Tel: 847-438-5050; Fax: 847-438-6313. Email: msjlz@aol.com. Rev. Aloysius Romanski, O.F.M.Conv.; Sr. Sharon Williams, Supr./Admin. Operated by the Daughters of St. Mary of Providence., Intermediate care for developmentally disabled women. Sisters 8; Lay Assistants 166; Residents 130.

PALOS PARK. *St. Coletta's of Illinois*, 18350 Crossing Dr., Tinley Park, 60477. Tel: 708-342-5200; Fax: 708-342-3579. Wayne A. Kottmeyer, Exec. Dir. Sponsored by the Sisters of St. Francis of Assisi. Residential care, education, job training & job placement for developmentally disabled children and adults. Residents 168; Students 70; Job Training Clients 207.
Divisions:

Lt. Joseph P. Kennedy Jr. School, Tinley Park Tel: 708-342-5200; Fax: 708-342-3579.

Vocational Job Training Center, Tinley Park Tel: 708-342-5200; Fax: 708-342-3579.

St. Coletta's of Illinois Foundation Tel: 708-342-5200; Fax 708-342-3579. Affiliate

[M] SENIOR CARE INSTITUTIONS

CHICAGO. *Cortland Manor Retirement Home*, 1900 N. Karlov, 60639. Tel: 773-235-3670. Maureen Scholle, Admin. Catholic Charities Housing Development Corporation. Capacity 48.

Franciscan Communities St. Joseph Home of Chicago, 2650 N. Ridgeway Ave., 60647 Tel: 773-235-8600; Fax: 773-235-2933. Email: rbracken@franciscancommunities.com. Richard Bracken, Admin.; Rev. Charles Mrowinski, C.R., Chap. Sisters 8; Licensed Beds 173.

Jugan Terrace, 2300 N. Racine, 60614. Tel: 773-935-9600; Fax: 773-935-4291. Email: mschlsp@attglobal.net.
Legal Title: *Little Sisters of the Poor of Chicago, Inc.* Senior Housing Apts. 50.

Little Sisters of the Poor Center for the Aging, 2325 N. Lakewood Ave., 60614. Tel: 773-935-9600; Fax: 773-935-9514. Sr. Patricia Friel, L.S.P., Supr.
Legal Title: *Little Sisters of the Poor of Chicago, Inc.*, Intermediate and skilled care facility. Sisters 11; Residents 69.

Resurrection Life Center, 7370 W. Talcott Ave., 60631. Tel: 773-594-7400; Fax: 773-594-7402. Web: www.reshealth.org. Joseph F. Toomey, Pres.; Frances Lachowicz, Admin.; Sisters M. Leonette Klafeta, C.R., Chap.; Ann O'Hara, O.F., Chap. & Spiritual Svcs. Coord. A division of Resurrection Senior Services, Resurrection Health Care; Skilled intermediate and sheltered nursing care Bed Capacity 159.

Resurrection Retirement Community, 7262 W. Peterson Ave., 60631. Tel: 773-792-7930; Fax: 773-792-8316 Email: kstadler@reshealthcare.org. Web: www.reshealth.org. Joseph F. Toomey, Pres.; Sr. Kathleen Ann Stadler, C.S.F.N., Exec. Dir.; Ann Murphy, Spiritual Svcs. Coord.; Lawrence Valentine, Lay Chap. A division of Resurrection Senior Services, Resurrection Health Care Apartments 472.

DES PLAINES. *Holy Family Nursing and Rehabilitation Center*, 2380 Dempster, 60016. Tel: 847-296-3335; Fax: 847-296-2027. Web: www.reshealth.org. Joseph F. Toomey, Pres.; Sr. M. Elizabeth Trembczynski, C.S.F.N., Admin.; Anne Murphy, Spiritual Svcs. Coord.; Deacon Jack Smith, Chap. Sponsored by the Sisters of the Holy Family of Nazareth and the Sisters of Resurrection., A division of Resurrection Senior Services, Resurrection Health Care; Intermediate and skilled nursing facility Licensed Bed Capacity 337.

Nazarethville, 300 N. River Rd., 60016. Tel: 847-297-5900; Fax: 847-297-0504. Sr. M. Lucille Madura, C.S.F.N., Admin. Sponsored by the Sisters of the Holy Family of Nazareth Total under care 83.

EVANSTON. *Saint Francis Nursing and Rehabilitation Center*, 500 Ashbury Ave., 60202. Tel: 847-316-3320; Fax: 847-316-3337. Web: www.reshealth.org. Joseph F. Toomey, Pres.; Gary Mellman, Admin.; Anne Murphy, Chap., Spiritual Svcs. Coord.; Sarah Hinojosa, Lay Chap. A division of Resurrection Senior Services, Resurrection Health Care; Comprehensive nursing, rehabilitation and social services Bed Capacity 127.

FRANKLIN PARK. *Scalabrini Life Center* 10500 W. Grand Ave., 60131. Tel: 847-451-1520. Web: www.reshealth.org. Joseph F. Toomey, Pres.; Mary Ann Lacy, Admin.; Bro. Kenney Gorman, C.F.X., Chap. & Spiritual Svcs. Coord.; Richard Heatley, Lay Chap. A division of Resurrection Senior Services, Resurrection Health Care; Comprehensive nursing, rehabilitation and social services Bed Capacity 146.

GLENVIEW. *Maryhaven Nursing and Rehabilitation Center*, 1700 East Lake Ave., 60025. Tel: 847-729-1300; Fax: 847-729-9620. Web: www.reshealth.org. Joseph F. Toomey, Pres.; Judy Pitzele, Admin.; Anne Murphy, Chap. & Spiritual Svcs. Coord. A division of Resurrection Senior Services, Resurrection Health Care; Home for Aged, intermediate and skilled care facilities, Medicare, Therapy. Capacity 138.

JUSTICE. *Rosary Hill Home*, 9000 W. 81st St., 60458. Tel: 708-458-3040; Fax: 708-458-7230. Email: rosaryhill@southchicago.net. Sr. M. Natalie, O.P., Supr.; Rev. Raymond J. Jasinski (Retired). Operated by the Dominican Sisters of Chicago Sisters 12; Bed Capacity 48; Number under care 48.

LAGRANGE PARK. *Bethlehem Woods Retirement Community*, 1571 Ogden Ave., 60526. Tel: 708-579-3663; Fax: 708-579-7159. Web: www.reshealth.org. Joseph F. Toomey, Pres.; Jim Kouzios, Exec. Dir.; Bro. Kenney Gorman, C.F.X., Chap. & Spiritual Svcs. Coord.; Sr. Elizabeth Gillis, O.S.F., Chap. A division of Resurrection Senior Services, Resurrection Health Care Residents 316.

LEMONT. *Alvernia Manor*, 13950 Main St., 60439. Tel: 630-257-7721; Fax: 630-257-0338. Email: am13950@aol.com. Sr. Georgine Hroma, O.S.F., Admin. Sisters of St. Francis of Christ King 6; Guests 50.

Holy Family Villa, 12220 S. Will-Cook Rd., 60439. Tel: 630-257-2291; Fax: 630-257-2334. Email: hfv12375@aol.com. Roberta Magurany, Admin. Sisters of St. Casimir Sisters 2; Residents 99.

Mother Theresa Home, 1270 Franciscan Dr., 60439. Tel: 630-243-3400; Fax: 630-257-5823. Email: rcoon@franciscancommunities.com. Robert E. Coon, Exec. Dir. Sponsored by the Franciscan Sisters of Chicago., Continuing Care Retirement Community Independent Living 202; Assisted Living 30; Nursing Home 150.

NILES. *Saint Andrew Life Center*, 7000 N. Newark Ave., 60714-4497. Tel: 847-647-8332; Fax: 847-647-7073. Web: www.reshealth.org. Joseph F. Toomey, Pres.; Anthony Madl, Admin.; Rev. Stanley Gruchot, Chap.; Bro. Kenney Gorman, C.F.X., Chap. & Spiritual Svcs. Coord.; Deb Heen, Lay Chap. A division of Resurrection Senior Services, Resurrection Health Care

Saint Benedict Nursing and Rehabilitation Center, 6930 W. Touhy Ave., 60714. Tel: 847-647-0003; Fax: 847-647-1936. Web: www.reshealth.org. Joseph F. Toomey, Pres.; Peter E. Goschy, Admin.; Bro. Kenney Gorman, C.F.X., Spiritual Svcs. Coord.; Deacon Ed O'Leary. A division of Resurrection Senior Services, Resurrection Health Care Residents 99.

NORTHLAKE. *Casa San Carlo Retirement Community*, 420 N. Wolf Rd., 60164. Tel: 708-562-4300; Fax: 708-562-5677. Web: www.reshealth.org. Joseph F. Toomey, Pres.; Nick Papp, Campus Admin.; Bro. Kenney Gorman, C.F.X., Spiritual Svcs. Coord.; Mary Fox, Chap. A division of Resurrection Senior Services, Resurrection Health Care Residents 200.

Villa Scalabrini Nursing and Rehabilitation Center, 480 N. Wolf Rd., 60164-1667. Tel: 708-562-0040; Fax: 708-562-5180. Web: www.reshealth.org. Joseph F. Toomey, Pres.; Nick Papp, Campus Admin.; Bro. Kenney Gorman, C.F.X., Spiritual Svcs. Coord.; Rev. Daniel Steiner; Sisters Maria Cigolini, M.S.C.S.; Ruth Marostica, M.S.C.S. A division of Resurrection Senior Services, Resurrection Health Care Residents 259.

OLYMPIA FIELDS. *Mercy Residence at Tolentine Center*, 20300 Governors Hwy., 60461. Tel: 708-748-9500; Fax: 708-481-2090. Email: mercyresidence@aol.com. Sr. Conleth Foley, R.S.M., Admin. Senior citizen housing. Sisters 4; Residents 48.

PALATINE. *St. Joseph's Home for the Elderly*, 80 W. Northwest Hwy., 60067. Tel: 847-358-5700; Fax: 847-358-5763. Sr. Benedict Armstrong, Supr.; Most Rev. Andrew J. McDonald, D.D., J.C.D. (LR) (Retired).
Legal Title: *Little Sisters of the Poor of Palatine, Inc.* Operated by the Little Sisters of the Poor Sisters 15; Guests 100.

PARK RIDGE. *Resurrection Nursing and Rehabilitation Center*, 1001 N. Greenwood, 60068. Tel: 847-692-5600; Fax: 847-692-2305. Web: www.reshealth.org. Joseph F. Toomey, Pres.; Nikki Curth, Admin.; Anne Murphy, Chap. & Spiritual Svcs. Coord. & Chap.; Rev. Leon Grantz, C.P., Chap.; Sisters Fidelis Rolfes, S.L.W., Chap.; Rita Mary Ganser, C.R., Chap.; Shirley Jean Short, Lay Chap. A division of Resurrection Senior Services, Resurrection Health Care Skilled Care Bed Capacity 295.

WHEELING. **Addolorata Villa*, 555 McHenry Rd., 60090-3899. Tel: 847-537-2900; Fax: 847-215-5805. Email: Bskonieczny@franciscancommunities.com. Web: www.franciscancommunities.com. Mr. Lawrence D. Carlson, Exec. Dir.; Ms. Dawn Cohn, Dir. Campus Oper.; Mrs. Betty Skonieczny, Dir. Mission Integration & Pastoral Care; Rev. Richard J. Ehrens (Retired). Sponsored by the Franciscan Sisters of Chicago, a continuing retirement community. Servants of Mary 17; Skilled 88; Intermediate 10; Sheltered 42; Assisted Living 61; Independent Living Apartments 100.

[N] MONASTERIES AND RESIDENCES OF PRIESTS AND BROTHERS

CHICAGO. *The Blessed Sacrament House of Studies*, Home House, Apt. 95, 5300 South Shore Dr., 60615-5708. Tel: 773-684-1969. Revs. John Keenan, S.S.S., Psy.D., Ph.D.; Robert Rousseau, S.S.S.

Brandsma House, 1036 W. Loyola Ave., #3, 60626-5233. Tel: 773-761-5139; Fax: 773-761-8599.

Revs. Michael O'Keefe, O.Carm.; Garvin Grech, O.Carm.

Carmelite Priory of St. Cyril, 6401 S. Harper Ave., 60637. Tel: 773-684-0112; Fax: 773-684-4713. Revs. John Knoernschild, O.Carm., Prior; Leander Troy, O.Carm.; Daniel Carroll, O.Carm. (Retired). Residing here are all the priests who teach at Mt. Carmel High School.

Residing here are all the priests who teach at Mt. Carmel High School: Revs. Carl Markelz, O.Carm., Prin.; Peter McGarry, O.Carm.; John Knoernschild, O.Carm.; Benjamin Aguilar, O.Carm; Mark Schaffner, O.Carm; Gerald Williams, O.Carm.; Bro. Daryl Moresco, O.Carm. (Australia).

Chicago Province of the Society of Jesus-Provincial Office, 2050 N. Clark St., 60614. Tel: 773-975-6363; Fax: 773-975-0230. Email: chgprov@jesuits-chi.org. Web: www.jesuits-chi.org. Very Rev. Edward W. Schmidt, S.J., Prov.; Revs. Michael J. Class, S.J., Socius; George E. Von Kaenel, S.J., Asst. Intl. Apostolates, Jesuit Intl. Missions, & Social Ministries; James A. Stoeger, S.J., Asst. Secondary Education & Pastoral Ministries; Paul V. Robb, S.J., Asst. Treas.; Daniel L. Flaherty, S.J., Asst. for Business & Finance; Paul J. Faulstich, S.J., Asst. Records & Res.; David A. Godleski, S.J., Asst. for Vocation Promotion; William L. Verbryke, S.J., Asst. Formation.

Jesuits Serving Abroad:

Apartado 595, Arequipa, Peru. Tel: 51147-27-2570. Revs. Kevin E. Gallagher, S.J., Interprovince Liaison; Robert E. Beckman, S.J. (Peru); Kevin H. Flaherty, S.J. (Peru); Jeffrey L. Klaiber, S.J. (Peru); Lewis C. Murtaugh, S.J. (Peru); James M. O'Leary, S.J. (Peru); John R. Sima, S.J. (Peru).

Residing elsewhere in the U.S.: Revs. Paul V. Mankowski, S.J. (Vatican City State); John R. Crocker, S.J. (Rome); Philip J. Chmielewski, S.J.; William L. Verbryke, S.J.; David V. Meconi, S.J. (England); Bernard F. McAniff, S.J. (BOS); James M. McCann, S.J. (WDC); William P. O'Brien, S.J. (OAK); Mitchell C. Pacwa, S.J. (BIR); Robert J. Ochs, S.J. (OAK); Denis A. Dirscherl, S.J. (BAL); Bradley M. Schaeffer, S.J. (WDC); Thomas W. Florek, S.J. (DET); Henry T Chamberlain, S.J. (Vatican City State); Robert J. Geisinger, S.J. (Vatican City State); Michael W. Cooper, S.J. (SP); Lester E. Love, S.J. (OAK); Thomas C. Widner, S.J. (WDC).

Clark Street Jesuit Residence, 2050 N. Clark St., 60614. Tel: 773-935-3947; Fax: 773-975-0230. Revs. John F. Costello, S.J.; Michael E. Dorrler, S.J.; James P. Gschwend, S.J.; Patrick J. McAteer, S.J.; Richard H. McGurn, S.J.; Francis P. O'Donnell, S.J.; John F. Pennington, S.J.; Very Rev. Edward W. Schmidt, S.J. Priests 12.

Woodlawn Jesuit Community, 5554 S. Woodlawn, 60637. Tel: 773-667-1395; Fax: 773-667-2089. Revs. Robert J. Bueter, S.J.; Robert E. Finn, S.J.; Lawrence P. Herrera, S.J.; George A. Lane, S.J.; Paul P. Mariani, S.J.; Donald J. McGuire, S.J.; Paul R. Mueller, S.J.; J-Glenn Murray, S.J.; Paul J. Nienaber, S.J.; James W. Schulz, S.J.

St. Clare Friary, 3407 S. Archer Ave., 60608-6817. Tel: 773-890-1238; Fax: 773-847-7409. Web: www.capuchinfranciscans.org. Rev. Mark Joseph Costello, O.F.M.Cap., Local Min.; Friars Lawrence Groeschel, O.F.M.Cap; Brian Luense, O.F.M.Cap; Bro. Robert Roemer, O.F.M.Cap.; Revs. William Frigo, O.F.M.Cap.; John Holly, O.F.M.Cap; Gerald Pehler, O.F.M.Cap.

Claretian Missionaries, St. Jude League, Inc., 205 W. Monroe, 60606. Tel: 312-236-7782; Fax: 312-236-7230. Web: www.claretians.org. Revs. John Molyneux, C.M.F., Dir.; Mark J. Brummel, C.M.F., Dir. Editorial Offices: "U.S. Catholic" and other Claretian Publications.

Columban Fathers Mission Center, 6449 N. Magnolia Ave., 60626. Tel: 773-274-9111; Fax: 773-274-9053. Revs. Thomas P. Reynolds, S.S.C.; Thomas G. Glennon, S.S.C.; Sean Conneely, S.S.C.

Columban Fathers Theologate, 5103 S. Ellis Ave., 60615. Tel: 773-955-0660; Fax: 773-955-0805. Rev. Mark Mengel, S.S.C., Rector. Priests 3; Columban Seminarians 6.

Comboni Missionaries Theologate (M.C.C.J.), Verona Fathers, 5512 Hyde Park Blvd., 60637. Tel: 773-667-8920; Fax: 773-667-6414. Email: chicombtheo@ameritech.net. Revs. Mario Malaerida, M.C.J. (Italy); Raphael Wokorach (Uganda). Theology students 18.

Congregation of Christian Brothers, Brother Rice Community, 10001 S. Pulaski Rd., 60655. Tel: 773-445-5048. Bros. Eugene O. Carty, C.F.C., Community Leader; Robert E. Beckstrom, C.F.C.; Thomas J. Collins, C.F.C.; George G. Gremley, C.F.C.; Charles E. Joyce, C.F.C.; James A. Houlihan, C.F.C.; John B. Moore, C.F.C.; Patrick B. Martin, C.F.C.; John Toole, C.F.C.; Patrick T. Varilla, C.F.C.; John S. O'Keefe, C.F.C.; William L. McInerney, C.F.C. Brothers 12.

Congregation of Marian Fathers of the Immaculate Conception, 6336 S. Kilbourn Ave., 60629-5588. Tel: 773-582-8191 (Provincial Office); 773-767-1687 (Religious House); Fax: 773-582-8961 (Provincial Office). Email: promic@aol.com. Web: www.marians.org. Very Rev. Donald S. Petraitis, M.I.C., Prov.; Revs. Timothy Roth, M.I.C., Councilor I; Jerome A. Zalonis, M.I.C., Councilor II; Daniel Cambra, M.I.C., Councilor III; Bros. Donald Schaefer, M.I.C., Prov. Treas.; Brian Manian, M.I.C., Councilor IV; Revs. Jonas Duoba, M.I.C., Local Supr.; Victor Rimselis, M.I.C.; Jonas Sakevicius, M.I.C. Priests 4.

Conventual Franciscans of St. Bonaventure Province, 6107 N. Kenmore Ave., 60660. Tel: 773-274-7681; Fax: 773-274-9751. Very Rev. Anthony Labedis, O.F.M.Conv., Prov.; Revs. Joseph Kruszynski, O.F.M.Conv.; Hippolite Kuras, O.F.M.Conv.; Justin Kusibab, O.F.M.Conv.; Robert Melnick, O.F.M.Conv.

Legal Title: *The Conventual Franciscans of Saint Bonaventure Province Corporation; The Conventual Franciscans of Saint Bonaventure Province Charitable Continuing Care Trust Fund; Franciscan Friars Educational Corporation; St. Hedwig Cemetery and Mausoleum Corporation; Franciscan Friars Retirement Corporation*

Sacred Heart Friary, 6107 N. Kenmore Ave., 60660. Tel: 773-764-8811. Rev. Joseph Kruszynski, O.F.M-.Conv.; Bros. Joseph Graff; George Searles.

Assigned but serving elsewhere:

St. Michael's: 13270 Maple Dr., St. Louis, MO 63127. Rev. Francis Kiley, O.F.M.Conv.

Mount St. Joseph Institute - Chaplaincy, 24955 N. Highway 12, Lake Zurich, 60047-9752. Rev. Aloysius Romanowski, O.F.M.Conv.

Apostolate for Family Consecration, 3375 County Rd. 36, Bloomingdale, OH 43910-7903. Rev. Bernard Geiger, O.F.M.Conv.

St. Bonaventure Friary, 1 Friary Circle, St. Bonaventure, NY 14778. Rev. Michael Blastic, O.F.M. Conv.

St. Mary's Parish, 501 NW 25th St., Corvallis, OR 97330. Most Rev. John Henderson, O.F.M.Conv., O.F.M. Conv.

Friars of the Province Serving Abroad: Revs. John Calgaro, O.F.M.Conv. (Mexico); Abraham Crisostomo, O.F.M.Conv. (Mexico); Bros. Paschal Metzger, O.F.M.Conv. (Mexico); Stanley Sabkiewicz, O.F.M.Conv. (Zambia).

Legal Titles:

The Conventual Franciscans of Saint Bonaventure Province Corporation

The Conventual Franciscans of Saint Bonaventure Province Charitable Continuing Care Trust Fund

Franciscan Friars Educational Corporation

St. Hedwig Cemetery and Mausoleum Corporation

Franciscan Friars Retirement Corporation

Croatian Dominican Fathers, 6346 N. Ridge, 60660. Tel: 773-262-0535; Fax: 773-262-4603. Revs. Nicholas Dugandzic, O.P., Asst. Chap., Croatian Catholic Mission Blessed Alojzije Stepinac; Zvonko Dzankic, O.P., Asst. Chap.

Croatian Franciscan Custody of the Holy Family, 4851 S. Drexel Blvd., 60615. Tel: 773-536-0552; Fax: 773-536-2094. Email: croatiancustody@aol.com. Rev. Marko Puljic, O.F.M., Custos, Croatia Franciscan Custody of the Holy Family.

St. Anthony's Friary, 4848 S. Ellis Ave., 60615. Tel: 773-373-3463; Fax: 773-268-7744. Revs. Jerome Kucan, O.F.M., Guardian; Vjekoslav Bambir, O.F.M.; Timothy Majic, O.F.M.; Miron Lasic, O.F.M.; Kvirin Vasilj, O.F.M.; Theodore Benkovic, O.F.M.; Bruno Raspudic, O.F.M.; Stephen Raich, O.F.M.; Sr. Ljubo Krasic, O.F.M., Vicar; Revs. Vincent Cvitkovic, O.F.M.; Philip Pavich, O.F.M.

Crosier Community of Chicago, 5401 S. Cornell Ave., 60615. Tel: 773-684-6975; Fax: 773-684-8357. Revs. Thomas Enneking, O.S.C.; John Neville, O.S.C.; Bro. David Donnay, O.S.C.

Daneo Hall (Passionist Retirement Wing) , 5700 N. Harlem, 60631. Tel: 312-631-5179. Email: chundcp@visioni.com. Revs. Leo Brady, C.P.; William Browning, C.P.; Myron Gohmann, C.P.; Damian McHale, C.P.; Bros. Joachim Saunders, C.P.; Carl Hund, C.P., Dir. Priests 4; Brothers 2.

DePaul Vincentian Residence, 2233 N. Kenmore Ave., 60614-3594. Tel: 773-880-2968. Rev. Paul Sisul, C.M.; Mr. Michael Walsh, Treas.

Legal Title: *Society of Priests of the Congregation of the Mission of Chicago*

Members of the Vincentian Community (Congregation of the Mission): Bros. Paul P. Joseph, C.M.; Leo Keigher, C.M.; Revs. Patrick Flanagan, C.M.; Thomas J. Meik, C.M.; John P. Minogue, C.M.; Thomas P. Munster, C.M.; Andres Rey, C.M.; Manuel J. Pelleteri, C.M.; Mark Pranaitis, C.M.; Donald Ours, C.M.; Anthony Dosen, C.M.; John F. Cawley, C.M.; Tesfamariam Texlemariam, C.M.; Edward J. Tomasiewicz, C.M.; Charles J. Welter, C.M.; Raymond F. White, C.M.; Jose Nazhianpara, C.M.; Robertus Wijanarko, C.M.

Discalced Carmelite Friars; Edith Stein House of Studies, 5345 S. University Ave., 60615. Tel: 773-752-6943; 773-493-6066; Fax: 773-752-6594. Email: djcocld@aol.com. Revs. Kevin Culligan, O.C.D.; Daniel Chowning, O.C.D.; Michael Dodd, O.C.D.; George Wangiarala; Bros. Michale Berry, Friar; Fred Hickey, Friar; Frank Salamone, O.C.D., Friar. Priests 3; Students 2.

Divine Word Theologate, 5342 S. University, 60615. Tel: 773-288-2777 (office); 773-288-7923 (residence); Fax: 773-288-6307. Email: theologate@aol.com. Web: www.dwtusc.org. Revs. Edward Peklo, S.V.D., Rector; Mark Schramm, S.V.D., Vice-Rector; Roger S. Arnold, S.V.D., Dir. Formation; Gary L. Riebe-Estrella, S.V.D.; Peter De Ta Vo, S.V.D.; Stephen B. Bevans, S.V.D.; Lloyd Cunningham, S.V.D.; Bernard Latus, S.V.D.; Roger P. Schroeder, S.V.D.; Derek Simons, S.V.D. Priests 10; Students 52.

Dominican Community, 1914 S. Ashland Ave., 60608. Tel: 312-829-1931; Fax: 312-226-6119. Email: brendancurran@yahoo.com. Revs. Charles W. Dahm, O.P.; Matthias R. Mueller, O.P.; Brendan Curran, O.P.

Dominicans (Provincial Office), St. Pius V. Priory, 1909 S. Ashland Ave., 60608. Tel: 312-226-0074; Fax: 312-829-8471. Email: domcenprov@dominicans.org. Web: www.op.org/domcentral.

Legal Title: *Dominicans, Province of St. Albert the Great, U.S.A. (Central Dominican Province)*

Provincial Office Tel: 312-666-3244; Fax: 312-829-8471. Email: domcenprov@dominicans.org.

Provincial Staff: Very Rev. Michael A. Mascari, O.P., Prior Prov.; Revs. Jerome M. Walsh, O.P., Dir. Shrine of St. Jude; Donald J. Goergen, O.P., Regent Studies; John J. Meany, O.P., Syndic & Vicar Prov.; David F. Wright, O.P., Socius & Vicar Prov., Prov. Archivist; Andrew-Carl Wisdon, O.P., Dir. Vocations & Vocational Support; Bede R. Jagoe, O.P., Dir. St. Dominic Mission; Dennis C. Woerter, O.P., Promoter of Social Justice; James R. Motl, O.P., Promoter of Dominican Laity; Vincent I. Zarlenga, O.P., Dir., Fra Angelico Art Foundation; Bro. Edward J. Van Marriemboer, O.P.

St. Pius V Priory Tel: 312-226-0074; Fax: 312-226-6199. Very Rev. Michael A. Mascari, O.P., Prior Prov.; Revs. Jordan R. Aumannm, O.P.; Robert L. Barry, O.P.; Roderick M. Brown, O.P.; Rapael A. Fabish, O.P.; Joseph A. Fogarty, O.P.; Michael A. Garcia, O.P.; Robert A. Goedert, O.P.; Gilbert J. Graham, O.P.; James C. Hahn, O.P.; Jacob J. Joerger, O.P.; Thomas J. Johnston, O.P.; Lawrence T. Kearney, O.P.; Arthur L. Kinsella, O.P.; Robert J. Miller, O.P.; Gregory J. Moore, O.P.; Thomas A. Morrison, O.P.; Walter T. O'Connell, O.P.; Jerome M. Walsh, O.P.; Andrew-Carl Wisdom, O.P.; Deacon J. Reid Perkins-Buzo, O.P.; Bros. Benedict G. Baer, O.P.; Carlos Griego, O.P.; Reginald W. Neu, O.P.; Gerald Pidcock, O.P.

Legal Title: *Spirituality Today Journal, Inc.; Shrine of St. Jude Thaddeus; Society for Vocational Support, Inc.; St. Dominic Mission Society; Dominican Social Action Fund; Dominican Laity; Fra Angelico Art Foundatioin; The Bolivian Trust of the Dominicans; Office for Mission Advancement*

Assigned but Serving Elsewhere: Revs. Richard de Ranitz, O.P.; John R. Dolehide, O.P.; Thomas P. Doyle, O.P.; Francis X. Dyer, O.P.; John C. Fabian, O.P.; Ricard R. Farmer, O.P.; James M. Karepin, O.P.; Gerald C. Kroeger, O.P.; Alfred A. Lopez, O.P.; C. Thomas Moore, O.P.; Daniel W. Morrissey, O.P.; Frank M. Nouza, O.P.; Bros. Henry A. Denier, O.P.; Joachim M. Thiel, O.P.

Priests of the Province Serving Abroad: Revs. Gerard B. Cleator, O.P. (Mexico); Eric deWasseige, O.P., Bolivia; Thomas P. Lynch, O.P., Bolivia; Joseph P. Kenny, O.P., Nigeria; Thomas K. McDermott, O.P., Nigeria; Peter Otillio, O.P., Nigeria; Mark R. Paraday, O.P., Bolivia; Justus M. Pokrzewinski, O.P., Nigeria; Edward H. Riley, O.P., Nigeria; Lewis M. Shea, O.P., Kenya; Gerald L. Stookey, O.P., Italy; Gilbert J. Thesing, O.P., Nigeria; Benedict T. Viviano, O.P., Switzerland; Bro. Stephen D. Lucas, O.P., Nigeria.

Franciscan House of Studies, 6107 N. Kenmore Ave., 60660. Tel: 773-764-8811; Fax: 773-274-9751. Rev. Robert Melnick, O.F.M.Conv. A Formation House of Conventual Franciscan Friars.

Holy Evangelists Friary Order of Friars Minor. , 4513 N. Ashland Blvd., 60650-5401. Tel: 773-878-3723. Email: rfpawell@aol.com. Revs. Fred Radtke; Robert Pawell; Eulogio Roselada. Priests 3.

Holy Name Friary, Assumption BVM Province, 1200 E. Madison Park #2, 60615-2961. Tel: 773-285-1388. Revs. Leslie J. Hoppe, O.F.M., Prof. Catholic Theological Union, Guardian; Lawrence Janowski, O.F.M., Faculty, Wright College, Vicar; Bro. Craig Wilking, O.F.M.

St. John Stone Friary, 1165 E. 54th Pl., 60615-5109.

Tel: 773-684-6510; Fax: 773-684-9830. Web: www.midwestaugustinians.org. Rev. James Thompson, O.S.A., Dir. Formation, Prior; Bro. Fred Kaiser, O.S.A., Treas.; Most Rev. David Petraitis, O.S.A.; Revs. John Szura, O.S.A.; Anthony Pizzo, O.S.A.

St. Joseph Interprovincial Post-Novitiate Formation House (A Franciscan House of the Sacred Heart Province) , 5495 S. Hyde Park Blvd., 60615. Tel: 773-363-0072; Fax: 773-363-0076. Revs. Gilberto Cavazos Gonzales, O.F.M., Formation Staff; E. John Stein, O.F.M., Guardian & Formation Staff; Louis Davino, O.F.M., Formation Staff; Zachary Hayes, O.F.M., Ph.D., Prof. CTU; Gil Ostdiek, O.F.M., Prof. CTU. Professed 16.

St. Joseph's Priory, 4747 S. Dorchester Ave., 60615. Tel: 773-268-9745. Rev. David Murphy, O.Carm. (VEN); Bro. Timothy Sklopan, O.Carm.

Korean Catholic Center, 4115 N. Kedvale, 60641. Tel: 773-283-3979. Rev. John Smith, S.S.C., Dir.

Lithuanian American Jesuits (Della Strada Residence and Lithuanian Youth Center) , 2345 W. 56th St., 60636. Tel: 773-737-8400; Fax: 773-737-0486. Email: lithjesuit@aol.com.

Legal Title: *Jesuit Fathers of Della Strada Inc.*

Baltic Jesuits Advancement Office, 2345 W 56th St., 60636-1040. Tel: 773-737-9891; Fax: 773-737-0486. Rev. Antanas Saulaitis, S.M., Lithuanian and Latvian Jesuit Prov.

Members of the Community: Revs. Kazimieras Ambrasas, S.J.; Vaclovas Gutauskas, S.J.; Algirdas Paliokas, S.J., Chap. Dir.

Blessed Jurgis Matulaitis Mission 14911 E. 127th St., Lemont, 60439. Tel: 630-257-5613. Priests 4.

Lithuanian Youth Center Inc., 5620 S. Claremont Ave., 60636. Tel: 773-778-7500.

Marist Brothers, Monastery Community, 4200 W. 115th St., 60655. Tel: 773-881-6380; Fax: 773-881-0595. Email: brown.gerard@marist.net. Web: www.marist.net. Bros. Gerard Brown, Dir.; M. Oswald Ouellette; Philip McEnaney; Kevin Moran; Julian Roy; Paul Forgues; Richard Grenier; Christopher Shannon.

Marist Brothers, St. Ann Residence, 10114 S. Leavitt, 60643. Tel: 773-239-4116. Bros. Timothy Brady, Dir.; Vito Aresto; Louis Richard; Hugh Turley; Henry Hammer; Brendan Brennan.

Maryknoll Fathers & Brothers, 5128 S. Hyde Park, 4S,, 60615-4217. Tel: 773-493-3367; Fax: 773-493-3427. Email: mklchicago@aol.com. Web: www.maryknoll.org. Revs. Herbert T. Gabba, M.M., Dir.; Gerard T. McCrane, M.M.; Bro. Adrian R. Mazuchowski, M.M.

Legal Title: *The Catholic Foreign Mission Society of America*

Miguel Pro Jesuit Community, 1611 S. Allport St., 60608. Tel: 312-226-6496; Fax: 312-226-2915. Revs. Richard J. Baumann, S.J.; John P. Foley, S.J.; Charles W. Niehaus, S.J.; James G. Gartland, S.J., Local Supr.; Timothy A. Howe, S.J.; James W. Schulz, S.J.; Sean A. O'Sullivan, S.J.; Bros. David L. Henderson, S.J.; Michael T. Conley, S.J.

Monastery of the Holy Cross, 3111 S. Aberdeen St., 60608-6503. Tel: 773-927-7424; Fax: 773-927-5734. Email: porter@chicagomonk.org. Web: www.chicagomonk.org. Revs. Thomas-Benedict Baxter, O.S.B., Prior; Brendan D. Creeden, O.S.B., Novice Master; Edward J. Gianzmann, O.S.B., Guest Master; Bros. Peter Funk, O.S.B.; Antonio Bravo, O.S.B. Benedictine Monks (Subiaco Congregation) Novice 1.

The Oblate House of Theology, 5535 S. Kenwood Ave., 60637. Tel: 773-493-3590; Fax: 773-493-6239. Revs. James P. Brobst, O.M.I., Supr.; Philip Singarayar, O.M.I., Assoc.; Francis Zabala, O.M.I., (In Res.). Scholastics 7.

Order of Friar Servants of Mary (Servites) United States of America Province, Inc., Servite Provincial Center, 3121 W. Jackson Blvd., 60612-2729. Tel: 773-533-0360; Fax: 773-533-8307. Email: bromikeosm@hotmail.com. Web: www.servite.org. Very Rev. Anthony M. O'Connell, O.S.M., Prior Prov.; Revs. Paul M. Novak, O.S.M., Asst. Prov.; James M. Dore, O.S.M., Prov. Councilor; John M. Fontana, O.S.M., Prov. Councilor; Luke M. Stano, O.S.M., Prov. Councilor; Bros. Edmund Baran, O.S.M., Prov. Treas.; Michael M. Callary, O.S.M., Prov. & Corp. Sec. Mission Procurator; Revs. Robert M. Anderson, O.S.M. (P), Province St. Peregrine Ministry, Portland, OR; Conrad M. Borntrager, O.S.M., Prov. Archivist & Historian; Paul M. Gins, O.S.M., Servite Vocation Dir., Seven Holy Founders Priory, 1922 W. La Palma Ave., Anaheim, CA 92801-3544. Tel: 714-491-8598; Fax: 714-774-6792; Christopher M. Krymski, O.S.M., Province St. Peregrine Ministry; Vidal M. Martinez, O.S.M., Natl. Asst. for Servite Secular Order; Philip M. McGlynn, O.S.M., Prov. Devel. Dir.; John M. Topper, O.S.M., Dir., The Sanctuary of Our Sorrowful Mother "The Grotto", Portland, OR; Robert M. Warsey, O.S.M., Dir. Marian Center; Bros. Martin M. Doherty, O.S.M., Prov. Sacristan; Joel A. Lechner, O.S.M., Pres. Servite High School, Anaheim, CA.

Servite Marian Center, 3121 W. Jackson Blvd., 60612-2729. Tel: 773-638-5800, Ext. 19; Fax: 773-533-8307. Rev. Robert M. Warsey, O.S.M., Dir.

Servite Secular Order, 3121 W. Jackson Blvd., 60612-2729. Tel: 773-638-5800, Ext. 55. Rev. Vidal M. Martinez, O.S.M., General & National Asst.

Monastery of Our Lady of Sorrows, 3121 W. Jackson Blvd., 60612-2729. Tel: 773-638-5800; Fax: 773-533-8307. Bros. Edmund M. Baran, O.S.M.; Robert M. Fandel, O.S.M.; Joseph Fundak, O.S.M.; Bonfilius M. McGovern, O.S.M.; Revs. Charles M Brennan, O.S.M.; Lawrence M. Choate, O.S.M.; Donald Duplessis, O.S.M.; Matthew M. Ford, O.S.M.; Thomas M. Greaney, O.S.M.; Christopher M. Krymski, O.S.M.; Augustine M. Kulbis, O.S.M.; Vidal M. Martinez, O.S.M.; Donald M. Siple, O.S.M.; Robert M. Warsey, O.S.M.

Annunciate Priory, 11128 S. Avenue G, 60617. Tel: 773-221-1043; Fax: 773-221-1556. Bro. Brian M. Fitzpatrick, O.S.M.; Revs. Conrad M. Borntrager, O.S.M.; Paul M. Cullen, O.S.M.; James M. Dore, O.S.M.; Dennis Kriz, O.S.M.

Assumption Priory, 323 W. Illinois St., 60610. Tel: 312-644-0392; Fax: 312-644-1838. Very Rev. Anthony M. O'Connell, O.S.M.; Revs. David M. Brown, O.S.M.; Damian M. Charboneau, O.S.M.; John M. Dowd, O.S.M.; Paul M. Novak, O.S.M.; John M. Pawlikowski, O.S.M., Ph.D.

St. Bonfilius Priory, 3401 S. Home Ave., Berwyn, 60402-3327. Tel: 708-484-2595; Fax: 708-484-0064. Rev. Michael M. Guimon, O.S.M.; Bro. Robert M. Lee, O.S.M.; Revs. Frank M. Falco, O.S.M.; Thomas M. Heskin, O.S.M.; Peter M. Rookey, O.S.M.

Servants of Mary (Servite) Development Office, 1439 S. Harlem Ave., Berwyn, 60402. Tel: 708-795-8885; Fax: 708-795-8892. Rev. Philip M. McGlynn, O.S.M., Dir.

Members of the Province Located Elsewhere in the Archdiocese of Chicago and Other Locations in the U.S.: Revs. Robert M. Anderson, O.S.M. (P), Sanctuary of Our Sorrowful Mother, Portland, OR; Bernard M. Barnes, O.S.M., Resurrection Life Center, Chicago, IL; Richard Boyle, O.S.M., Our Lady of Perpetual Help Parish, Cottage Grove, OR; Louis M. Breton, O.S.M., Sanctuary of Our Sorrowful Mother, Portland, OR; Joseph M. Carbone, O.S.M., Our Lady of Mount Carmel Priory, Denver, CO; Joseph M. Chamblain, O.S.M., Seven Holy Founders Priory, Afton, MO; Joseph M. Cheah, O.S.M., Paolo Sarpi Priory, Berkeley, CA; Thomas M. Crotty, O.S.M., Seven Holy Founders Priory, Anaheim, CA; Mark M. Dennehy, O.S.M., Holy Family Villa, Lemont, IL; Patrick M. Donovan, O.S.M., St. Juliana Falconieri Priory Fullerton, CA; Lawrence Michael Doyle, O.S.M., Seven Holy Founders Proiry, Affton, MO; Carl M. Feil, O.S.M., Our Lady of Lourdes, Melbourne, FL; John M. Fontana, O.S.M., Seven Holy Founders Priory, Affton, MO; Mark M. Franceschini, O.S.M., Our Lady of Mount Carmel Priory, Denver, CO; Albert M. Gallegos, O.S.M., Our Lady of Guadalupe Parish, Peralta, NM; David M. Gallegos, O.S.M., Our Lady of Belen Priory, Belen, NW; Anthony M. Gaydos, O.S.M., St. Marie du Lac Parish, Ironton, MO; Paul M. Gins, O.S.M., Seven Holy Founders Priory, Anaheim, CA; Loren M. Gonzales, O.S.M., Seton Catholic High School, Chandler, AZ; Peregrine M. Graffius, O.S.M., Seven Holy Founders Priory, Anaheim, CA; Hugh Guentner, O.S.M., Sanctuary of Our Sorrowful Mother, Portland, OR; Michael M. Guimon, O.S.M., Servite Residence, Berkeley, CA; Jude M. Herlihy, O.S.M., St. Juliana Falconieri Priory, Fullerton, CA; Gerald M. Horan, O.S.M., Servite Reisence, Buena Park, CA; Ignatius M. Kissel, O.S.M., St. Philip Benizi Priory, Fullerton, CA; Bruce M. Klikunas, O.S.M., Paolo Sarpi Priory, Berkeley, CA; Damian M. Kobus, O.S.M., Sanctuary of Our Sorrowful Mother Priory, Portland, OR; Timothy M. Kremen, O.S.M., Our Lady of Mount Carmel Priory, Denver CO; George M. Luzmicky, O.S.M., St. Juliana Falconieri Priory, Fullerton, CA; Manuel Maya-Chavez O.S.M., St. Philip Benizi Priory, Fullerton, CA; Perry M. McCoy, O.S.M., Our Lady of Sorrows Priory, El Paso, TX; Patrick M. McNamara, O.S.M., Sanctuary of Our Sorrowful Mother, Portland, OR; George M. O'Connell, O.S.M., Little Sisters of the Poor, Chicago, IL; Vincent M. O'Shea, O.S.M., Little Sisters of the Poor, Chicago, IL; Edward M. Penonzek, O.S.M., Paolo Sarpi Priory, Berkeley, CA; Justin M. Pisciotta, O.S.M., St. Philip Benizi Priory, Fullerton, CA; Michael M. Pontarelli, O.S.M., Seven Holy Founders Priory, Anaheim, CA; Gabriel M. Ramacciotti, O.S.M., Our Lady of Mount Carmel Priory, Denver, CO; Stephen M. Ryan, O.S.M., Paolo Sarpi Priory, Berkeley, CA; Philip M. Scherer, O.S.M., Mother of Sorrows Convent, Blue Island, IL; Eugene M. Smith, O.S.M., Seven Holy Founders Priory, Anaheim, CA; Luke M. Stano, O.S.M., St. Juliana Falconieri Priory, Fullerton, CA; John M. Topper, O.S.M., The Sanctuary of Our Sorrowful Mother, Portland, OR; Lawrence M. Walling, O.S.M., Our Lady of Mount Carmel Priory, Denver, CO; Gabriel M. Weber, O.S.M., Our Lady of Mount Carmel Priory, Denver, CO; Bros. Michael M. Callary, O.S.M., Servite Reisdence, Chicago, IL; Gregory M. Atherton, O.S.M., The Sanctuary of Our Sorrowful Mother, Portland, OR; Martin M. Doherty, O.S.M., Servite Residence, Chicago, IL; Philip M. Eikmeyer, O.S.M., St. Juliana Falconieri Priory, Fullerton, CA; Joel A. Lechner, O.S.M., Seven Holy Founders Priory, Anaheim, CA; Christopher Moran, O.S.M., Our Lady of Guadalupe Parish, Peralta, NM; Andrew M. Motsko, O.S.M., Resurrection Life Center, Chicago, IL; Arnaldo M. Sanchez, O.S.M., Severn Holy Founders Priory, Anaheim, CA.

Members of the Province Serving Abroad: Revs. Patrick M. Boyle, O.S.M., Tuart Hill, Australia; Frank M. Christie, O.S.M., Tuart Hill, Australia; Declan M. Doherty, O.S.M., Kwazulu-Natal, Republic of South Africa; John M. LeMay, O.S.M., Kwazulu-Natal, Republic of South Africa; Sean M. Lennon, O.S.M., Benburb, Ireland; Mel M. Loftus, O.S.M., Kwazulu-Natal, Republic of South Africa; Myles M. Lynch, O.S.M., Parkville, Australia; Liam M. Mackle, O.S.M., Parkville, Australia; Carlo M. Marchetti, O.S.M., Tuart Hill, Australia; Camillus M. McGrane, O.S.M., Kwazulu-Natal, Republic of South Africa; Mafanisa Mthembu, O.S.M., Kwazulu-Natal, Republic of South Africa; Thulani Ntsele, O.S.M., Kwazulu-Natal, Republic of South Africa; Most Rev. Michael M. O'Shea, O.S.M., Kwazulu-Natal, Republic of South Africa; Revs. Christopher M. Ross, O.S.M., Tuart Hill, Australia; Leo M. Spicer, O.S.M., Tuart Hill, Australia; Charles M. Toland, O.S.M., Kwazulu-Natal, Republic of South Africa; Amideus M. Wickers, O.S.M., Dusseldorf-Nord, Germany; Robert M. Zivkovic, O.S.M., Tuart Hill, Australia; Bros. Oscar M. Aguilera Acosta, O.S.M., Rome, Italy; Stephen M. Barker, O.S.M., Tuart Hill, Australia.

Passionist Community-CTU, 5401 S. Cornell Ave., 60615-5698. Tel: 773-324-2704; Fax: 773-324-2557. Email: omalleyK@ctu.lib.il.us. Revs. Kenneth O'Malley, C.P., Ph.D., Supr.; Francis Landry, C.P., Dir. Students; Donald Senior, C.P., S.T.D.; Lee Harvey, C.P., Scholastic; Daniel Turner, C.P., Scholastics.

Legal Title: *Congregation of the Passion: St. Vincent Strambi Community* Priests 10; Scholastics 2.

Passionist Community-Immaculate Conception Monastery, 5700 N. Harlem Ave., 60631-2342. Tel: 773-631-1686; Fax: 773-631-8059. Email: jkschork@juno.com. Web: www.passionist.org. Revs. John Schork, C.P., Supr.; Myron Gohmann, C.P.; Luke Connolly, Dir., Passionist Missions Appeals; Frederick Sucher, C.P.; Warren Womack, C.P.; Donald Webber, C.P., Prov. Consultor; Louis Doherty, C.P.; Michael J. Hoolahan, C.P., Pastor, Immaculate Conception Parish; Paul I. Bechtold, C.P.; Robert Bovenzi, C.P.; Rian Clancy, C.P.; Damian McHale, C.P.; John T. Render, C.P.; Leon Grantz, C.P., Chap., Our Lady of the Resurrection Hospital; Francis X. Keenan, C.P., Chap., Lutheran General Hospital; John F. Kobler, C.P.; Eric Meyer, C.P., Assoc. Pastor, Immaculate Conception Parish; Very Rev. Michael Higgins, C.P., Prov. Supr.; Revs. Philip Schaefer, C.P.; Leo Patrick Brady, C.P.; William Browning, C.P.; Ronan Newbold, C.P., Assoc. Pastor, Immaculate Conception Parish; Bros. Raymond Sanchez, C.P., Chap. Cook Co. Jail; Carl Hund, C.P.; Joachim Saunders, C.P.

Legal Title: *Congregation of the Passion: Immaculate Conception Community* Priests 22; Brothers 3.

Passionist Provincial Office, 5700 N. Harlem Ave., 60631-2342. Tel: 773-631-6336; Fax: 773-631-8059. Email: mail@passionist.org. Web: passionist.org. Very Rev. Michael Higgins, C.P., Prov.; Revs. Donald Webber, C.P., Asst. Prov.; James Strommer, C.P., Consultor; Alexander Steinmiller, C.P., Consultor; Philip Paxton, C.P., Consultor.

Legal Title: *Congregation of the Passion (Holy Cross Province)*

Special Assignment:

Bishop of Mandeville, P.O. Box 8, Mandeville, Jamaica, West Indies. Tel: 876-962-1269; Fax: 876-962-1297. Most Rev. Paul M. Boyle, C.P.

20120 N. Key Dr., Boca Raton, FL 33498. Tel: 561-470-5828. Rev. Richard Johnson, C.P.

984 E. Camino Diestro, Tucson, AZ 85737. Tel: 618-558-4261. Rev. John Gabriel R. Mulnix, C.P.

Curia Generalizia Dei Passionisti, Piazza SS. Giovanni e Paolo 13, Rome 00184 Italy. Tel: 011-39-06-772-71232; Fax: 011-39-06-700-8454. Rev. Robert Coward, C.P.

Curia Generalizia Dei Passionisti, Piazza SS. Giovanni e Paolo 13, Rome 00184 Italy. Tel: 011-39-06-772-71214; Fax: 011-39-06-700-8454. Rev. Arthur Carrillo, C.P.

Jnan Nilaya-Passionist Community, Seminary Hills P.O., Nagpur, Maharashtra 440-006 India. Tel: 011-91-712-511-071. Rev. Blaise Czaja, C.P.

Passionist Theologate Community, Thambuchettypalya Post, K.R. Puram, Bangalore 560-036 India. Tel: 011-91-80-561-1944. Rev. David Colhour, C.P.

St. Blaise Parish, 3130 Parkwood Ln., Maryland Heights, MO 63043. Tel: 314-739-0230; Fax: 314-739-0237. Rev. John P. Day, C.P.

RR #2, Box 36, Pierce City, MO 65723. Tel: 417-476-2281. Rev. Louis Doherty, C.P.

Ashram J.X.P., Pallichal Rd. - Palluruthy, Kochi 682-006, Kerala, India. Tel: 011-91-484-231-309; Fax: 011-91-484-223-652. Rev. Joseph Van Leeuwen, C.P.

Our Lady of Lourdes Parish: 2808 Lakeshore Ave., Oakland, CA 94610. Tel: 510-451-1225. Rev. Joseph Mitchell, C.P.

Christian Brothers University, Box 32-650 E., Pkwy. S., Memphis, TN 38104-5581. Tel: 901-321-3964; Fax: 901-321-3505. Bro. John Monzyk, C.P.

Stauros U.S.A., 5401 S. Cornell Ave., 60615-5698. Tel: 773-752-5732; Fax: 773-752-5741. Amy Florian, Exec. Dir.

Catholic Theological Union, 5401 S. Cornell Ave., 60615-5698. Tel: 773-752-5732; Fax: 773-752-5741.

Passionist Missions of India 5700 N. Harlem Ave., 60631. Tel: 773-631-6336; Fax: 773-631-8059. Rev. Walter Kaelin, C.P., Procurator.

Congregation of the Passion, 5700 N. Harlem Ave., 60631. Tel: 773-631-1686; Fax: 773-631-1705. Mother of Good Counsel Community

Passionist Missions, Inc., 5700 N. Harlem Ave., 60631. Tel: 773-631-1686; Fax: 773-631-1705. Laura Hoffmann, Act. Exec. Dir.; Rev. Luke Connolly, C.P., Mission Appeals.

Province Development Office, 5700 N. Harlem Ave., 60631-2342. Tel: 847-518-8844; Fax: 847-518-0461. Laura Hoffmann, Act. Exec. Dir.

Planned Giving, 5700 N. Harlem Ave., 60631-2342. Tel: 847-518-8844; Fax: 847-518-0461. Mrs. Kathi Grummel.

Province Finance Office, 5700 N. Harlem Ave., 60631-2342. Tel: 773-631-6336; Fax: 773-631-8059. Mr. Keith Zekind, Dir. Finance; Mrs. Susan Arvanitis, Controller; Rev. Michael Hoolahan, Province Treas.

Passionist Archives, 5700 N. Harlem Ave., 60631-2342. Tel: 773-631-1686; Fax: 773-631-1705. Mr. Damian Schaab, Archivist.

Legal Title: *Congregation of the Passion (Holy Cross Province)*

St. Patrick's Missionary Society, 1347 W. Granville Ave., 60660. Tel: 773-973-3737; Fax: 773-973-6049. Email: spsil@spms.org. Web: spms.org. Rev. Karl Langsdorf, Supr.

St. Peter's Friary, 110 W. Madison St., 60602-4196. Tel: 312-372-5111; Fax: 312-853-2361. Web: www.stpetersloop.org. Revs. William Spencer, O.F.M.; Elric Sampson; Lawrence Janezic, O.F.M.; Bros. John Bush, O.F.M.; Fred Smith, O.F.M.; Revs. Vincent Callahan; Wenceslaus Church; Michael Clarahan; Bro. Sammy Danna; Revs. Thomas Ess; Charles Faso; Thomas Fratus; Francis Jerome Gray; Robert Hutmacher; Robert Karris, O.F.M.; Bros. Clarence Klingert; Thomas Krull; William Lanning; Revs. Clement Leahy; George Musial; Fred Radtke; Bro. Raymond Shuhert; Rev. Joseph Windolph. Order of Friars Minor

Premonstratensian Fathers and Brothers (Norbertines), 4841 S. Woodlawn Ave., 60615. Tel: 773-548-8020; Fax: 773-548-8023. Web: www.norbertines.org. Revs. Timothy Shillcox, O.Praem, Supr.; Laurence A. Mayer, O.Praem; Andrew Ciferni, O.Praem; Frater Robert Campbell, O.Praem. Holy Spirit House of Studies. Priests 3; Students 3; Simply Professed 2.

Priests of the Sacred Heart, 1417 East 53rd St., 60615-4501. Tel: 773-493-3080; Fax: 773-493-3120. Rev. Michael Burke, S.C.J., S.C.J. Coord., College Formation Dir. SCJ College Program Priests 4; Brothers 2; Scholastics 4; College Candidates 8.

SCJ Novitiate, 5310 S. Blackstone, 60615. Tel: 773-363-1326; Fax: 773-493-3120. Revs. John Czyzynski, S.C.J., Novice Dir.; Robert W. Bossie, S.C.J.

SCJ Theology Program, 5306 S. Blackstone, 60615. Tel: 773-752-2305; Fax: 773-493-3120. Bros. Michael Fette, S.C.J., Theology Formation Dir.; Peter Mankins, S.C.J., Treasurer.

5728 N. Talman, 60659. Tel: 773-994-5448 (residence); 630-883-1400, Ext. 44968 (work). Rev. Michael McMillen, S.C.J.

Provincial Office of the Congregation of the Resurrection, 7050 N. Oakley Ave., 60645-3426. Tel: 773-465-8320; Fax: 773-465-8314. Email: jhnowakcr@aol.com. Very Rev. John H. Nowak, C.R., Prov.

Legal Title: *Weber High School, Inc., Tel: 773-465-8320*

Legal Title: *Weber Endowment Fund, Tel: 773-465-8320*

Priests serving abroad:

Via San Sebastianello 11, 00187, Rome, Italy. Tel: 011-39-06-679-5908; Fax: 011-39-06-678-4397. Very Rev. Norbert W. Raszeja, C.R.; Rev. James Gibson, C.R.

Resurrection Retreat Center, 2710 S. Country Club Rd., Woodstock, 60098-8012. Tel: 815-338-1032; Fax: 815-338-1017.

Resurrection Center Retreat House, 2710 S. Country Club Rd., Woodstock, 60098. Tel: 815-338-1032; Fax: 815-338-1017. Revs. Stephen Glab, C.R.; Richard Grek, C.R.

Resurrection Parish: 2918 S. Country Club Rd., Woodstock, 60098. Tel: 815-338-7330; Fax: 815-338-7365. Revs. Jerzy Zieba, C.R.; Dennis Sanders, C.R.

Resurrection Health Care, 5910 N. Odell Ave., 60645-3426. Tel: 773-792-2208; Fax: 773-763-8285.

St. Wenceslaus Parish: 3400 N. Monticello Ave., 60618. Tel: 773-588-1135; Fax: 773-588-3735.

Archbishop Weber House, 7050 N. Oakley Ave., 60645-3426. Tel: 773-465-8320, Ext. 742; Fax: 773-465-8314. Rev. Steven Bartczyszyn, C.R.

The Redemptorist Fathers of Chicago, 1633 N. Cleveland Ave., 60614. Tel: 312-642-2498; Fax: 312-642-9283. Email: stmichael-cleveland@archchicago.org. Web: www.st-mikes.org. Revs. John Schmidt, C.Ss.R.; Kenneth Sedlak, C.SS.R.; Michael Quinn, C.Ss.R.; Edward Wilhelm, C.Ss.R.; John Paul Andree, C.SS.R.; John Dowd, C.SS.R.; Peter Schavitz, C.Ss.R.; Daniel Andree, C.Ss.R.; Robert Haltere, C.SS.R.

Redemptorist Theology Residence, 1027 E. Hyde Park Blvd., 60615-2807. Tel: 773-363-2094; Fax: 773-363-2095. Email: bcarlin114@aol.com. Revs. Paul Binh Ta, C.SS.R., Formation Dir.; Bernard L. Carlin, C.SS.R., Formation Dir. & Supr.; Vincent Minh, C.SS.R.; J. Robert Fenili, C.SS.R.; Maurice J. Nutt, C.SS.R.; Bros. Vitus Gerard Boomershine, C.SS.R.; Nghia Cao, C.SS.R.; Thong Ngo, C.SS.R; Denis Ryan, C.SS.R.; Tat Thang Hoang, C.SS.R.; Jeremy Kritt, C.SS.R. Priests 7; Students 6. In Res. Revs. Joseph P. Dorcey, C.SS.R.; Stephen Rehrauer, C.SS.R. (DEN).

The Redemptorists of Blessed Sacrament, 2153 S. Millard Ave., 60623. Tel: 773-521-5595; Fax: 773-521-6076. Revs. William Bueche, C.SS.R.; Steven N. Wilson, C.Ss.R.; John Phelps, C.Ss.R.; Ramon Dompke, C.SS.R.; Bros. Eugene Patin, C.SS.R.; Paul Jorns, C.Ss.R.

St. Rita Monastery, 7740 S. Western Ave., 60620-5867. Tel: 773-476-3879; Fax: 773-925-2451. Revs. Wes E. Benak, O.S.A.; Bernard R. Danber, O.S.A., Prior; Thomas McCarthy, O.S.A.; Walter F. McNicholas, O.S.A.; John J. Molnar, O.S.A.; Bros. John M. Hibbard, O.S.A.; Gary L. Hresil, O.S.A. (See High Schools, Private)

Sacred Heart Mission House, 4105 N. Avers Ave., 60618. Tel: 773-588-7476; Fax: 773-588-6517. Email: polmes@jezuicichicago.org. Web: jezuici.org. Revs. Pawel Kosinski, S.J., Editor, The Messenger of The Sacred Heart in Polish language; Wieslaw Krupinski, S.J.; Stanislaw Czarnecki, S.J.; Mariusz Han, S.J.; Bro. Jerzy Piskorek, S.J.; Sem. Krzysztof Pietruszkiewicz, S.J.

Legal Title: *The Polish Messenger of The Sacred Heart, Inc.* Priests 4; Brothers 1; Seminarians 1.

Jesuit Millenium Center, 5835 W. Irving Park Rd., 60636. Tel: 773-777-7000; Fax: 773-588-6517.

Jan Beyzym Society, Inc., 4105 N. Avers Ave., 60618. Tel: 773-588-7476; Fax: 773-588-6517. Rev. Pawel Kosinski, S.J. (Polish Jesuit Foreign Missions)

Scalabrini House of Theology, 5121 S. University Ave., 60615. Tel: 773-684-5230; 773-684-4340; Fax: 773-684-5240. Email: gerardogarciap@hotmail.com. Revs. Gerardo Garcia, C.S., Rector; Mauro Lazzarato, C.S., Animator; Luigi Gandolfi, C.S., Spiritual Dir. Priests 3; Students 15.

Viatorian Residence, 1201 W. Belden, 60614. Email: dannolan@viatorians.com. Web: www.viatorians.com. Revs. Daniel T. Nolan, C.S.V. Tel: 773-871-6342; Kenneth R. Morria, C.S.V. Tel: 773-871-6379; Bro. Donald P. Houde, C.S.V. Tel: 773-871-6523. Priests 2; Brothers 1.

Vincentian Community, Congregation of the Mission, Midwest Province, 2210-12 N. Racine Ave., 60614. Tel: 773-880-2968; Fax: 773-348-4802. Email: tcroak@wppost.depaul.edu. Revs. Thomas Croak, C.M., Supr.; Joseph C. Geders, C.M.; Robert Lucas, C.M.; Edward R. Udovic, C.M.; J. Patrick Murphy, C.M.; David Nygren, C.M.; Milton Ryan; Daniel Theiss, C.M.; Gerard P. Kelly, C.M.; Bros. Mark Elder, C.M.; Timothy Opferman, C.M.

Xaverian Missionaries (S.X.), 1347 E. Hyde Park Blvd., 60615-2924. Tel: 773-643-5745; Fax: 773-643-6907. Email: rndpsx@hotmail.com. Web: www.xaviermissionaries.org. Revs. Rocco N. Puopolo, S.X., Rector; Pascal Kasanziki, S.X.

ARLINGTON HEIGHTS. *Viatorian Province Center-Clerics of St. Viator*, 1212 E. Euclid St., 60004. Tel: 847-398-1350; Fax: 847-394-4507. Web: www.viatorians.com. Revs. George Auger, C.S.V.; William C. Mayer, C.S.V.; Charles L. Maranto, C.S.V.; Thomas P. McCarthy, C.S.V.; John C. Puisis, C.S.V.; Thomas F. McMahon, C.S.V.; Robert E. Erickson, C.S.V.; Donald J. Fitzsimmons, C.S.V.; Donald F. Lund, C.S.V.; Arnold E. Perham, C.S.V.; John A. Toolan, C.S.V.; John E. VanWiel, C.S.V.; Thomas F. Wise, C.S.V.; Bro. Leo V. Ryan, C.S.V.

Priests of the Province Serving Abroad: Revs. Carlos L. Claro, C.S.V.; Brian G. Cooper, C.S.V.; Pedro E. Herrera, C.S.V.; Luis E. Lopez, C.S.V.; Felipe Montes, C.S.V.; John A. Pisors, C.S.V.; Rafael Sanabria, C.S.V.; Albeyro Vanegas, C.S.V.

Colegio San Viator, Kilmetro 14, Autopista del Norte, Bogota, D.C. 54-11-62 Colombia. Tel: 011-57-1-676-0957; Fax: 011-57-1-676-5883. Bros. Fredy Santos, C.S.V.; Edgar Orlando Suarez, C.S.V.; Carlos Florez, C.S.V.; Rev. Christopher Glancy, C.S.V.

Catholic Mission Corozal P.O. Box 34, Corozal Town, Belize. Tel: 011-501-422-; Fax: 011-501-422-. Rev. John N. Peeters.

Priests Serving Elsewhere In U.S.A.:

North Little Rock, AR. Tel: 501-791-0078; Fax: 501-257-2157. Rev. Victor E. Bertrand.

428 S. Indiana Ave., Kankakee, 60901. Tel: 815-932-3001; Fax: 815-932-2585. Rev. Joseph B. Tremonti.

800 N. County Club Rd., Tucson, AZ 85717. Tel: 520-326-4302. Rev. Donald W. Huntimer, C.S.V.

5 Mountain Ash Ln., Apt. 345, Goffstown, NH 03045. Tel: 603-627-6726. Rev. Thomas G. Kass, C.S.V.

240 River St. #11, Santa Cruz, CA 95060. Tel: 831-458-4102. Rev. Alan M. Syslo, C.S.V.

BLUE ISLAND. *Marist Brothers*, 12212 Irving Ave., 60406. Tel: 708-385-1488. Email: fmsbi@aol.com. Bro. Richard Carey, F.M.S.

COUNTRYSIDE. *St. Gratian Friary, Franciscan Friars*, 5536 S. Edgewood Ave., 60525-3426. Tel: 708-482-4546; Fax: 708-481-8676. Email: stgratian@aol.com. Revs. James Walton, O.F.M.; Dennis Koopman, O.F.M.; James A. Hoffman, O.F.M.; Ildephonse Skorup, O.F.M.; Kieran Kemner, O.F.M.; Donald P. Blaeser, O.F.M.; Bro. Leon Beranek, O.F.M. Priests 6; Brothers 1.

ELK GROVE VILLAGE. *Congregation of Alexian Brothers Immaculate Conception Province, Inc.*, 600 Alexian Way, 60007. Tel: 847-640-7550; Fax: 847-981-6099. Email: krueger1@alexian.net. Bro. Lawrence Krueger, C.F.A., Prov.

Provincial Councilors: Bros. Thomas Keusenkothen, C.F.A.; James Classon, C.F.A.; Richard Dube, C.F.A.; Theodore Loucks, C.F.A.; Patrick Gaughan, C.F.A., Vocations Dir.; Daniel McCormick, C.F.A., Community Dir.

Res.: 801 Gloucester Dr., 60007. Tel: 847-439-5845.

Brothers of St. Alexius Health and Welfare Fund, Inc. Tel: 847-640-7550; Fax: 847-981-5561.

EVANSTON. *Canisius House*, 201 Dempster St., 60201-4704. Tel: 847-475-1825; Fax: 847-475-1869. Revs. Daniel L. Flaherty, S.J., Supr.; F. Michael Perko, S.J.; Thomas L. Kenealy, S.J.; Gene D. Phillips, S.J.

GLENVIEW. *The Redemptorists of Glenview, Illinois* North American Redemptorist Novitiate and Redemptorist Foreign Mission Office , 1111 N. Milwaukee Ave., P.O. Box 6, 60025. Tel: 847-724-0425; Fax: 847-724-8953. Email: pobcssr@aol.com. Revs. Patrick O'Brien, C.Ss.R., Local Supr.; Joseph T. Hurley, C.Ss.R., Novice Dir.; Henry Novak, C.Ss.R., Treas.; Kevin Fraher, C.Ss.R., Asst. Novice Dir.; Bros. Thomas Sanhuber, C.Ss.R.; Daniel Hall, C.Ss.R.

Redemptorist Denver Province Foreign Mission Office Tel: 847-724-0425; Fax: 847-724-8953. Rev. Patrick O'Brien, C.Ss.R., Dir.

LA GRANGE PARK. *Comboni Missionaries*, 1615 E. 31st St., 60526-1377. Tel: 708-354-1999; Fax: 708-354-2006. Email: combonislagrangeg@qwest.net combonilmp@qwest.net. Web: www.combonimmionaries.org; www.laymission-comboni.org. Revs. Sixtus Agostini, M.C.C.J., Supr., Lay Miss. Prog.; Maurizio Binaghi, M.C.C.J., Peace Corner, West-side; Provvido Crozzoletto, M.C.C.J., Comboni Mission Center; Alfredo Del Toro, M.C.C.J., at St. Michael the Archangel; Paul Longo, M.C.C.J., Prof.; Aldo Pozza, M.C.C.J., at St. Gertrude; Valentino Saoncella, M.C.C.J., Bursar. Priests 7.

LEMONT. *Legion of Christ*, 89 W. Logan, 60439. Tel: 630-243-6389; Fax: 630-243-6388. Email: chicago@legionaries.org. Rev. Andre LaSana, L.C., Supr.; Bros. John Szymanski, L.C.; Jasen Brooks, L.C.; Stephen Walther, L.C.

The Slovene Franciscan Fathers, Order of Friars Minor, Commissariat of the Holy Cross, 14246 Main St., P.O. Box 608, 60439. Tel: 630-257-2494; Fax: 630-257-8559. Revs. Blase Chemazar, O.F.M., Pres.; Metod Ogorevc, O.F.M., Guardian; Vendelin Spendov, O.F.M.; Bernardin Susnik, O.F.M.; Martin Stepanich, O.F.M.; Athanasius Lovrencic, O.F.M. Priests 6.

LIBERTYVILLE. *Marytown, Our Lady of Fatima Friary*, 1600 W. Park Ave., 60048-2593. Tel: 847-367-7800; Fax: 847-367-7831. Email: max63@marytown.com. Web: www.consecration.com. Bro. Juniper Kriss, O.F.M.Conv., Vicar; Revs. Patrick Greenough, O.F.M.Conv., Guardian & Prov. Asst., J.I. Editorial Office for Immaculata Magazine & Prow Books; Gabriel Ignaszek, O.F.M.Conv.; John Grigus, O.F.M.Conv.; Anthony J. Jelinek; Phillip Wozniak; James Ciaramitaro, O.F.M.Conv.

Conventual Franciscan Friars of Marytown Tel: 847-367-7800; Fax: 847-367-7831.

Shrine of St. Maximilian Kolbe Tel: 847-367-7800; Fax: 847-367-7831. Conventual Franciscan Friars 19.

MATTESON. *Austin Friary*, 5245 Stoneridge Ct., 60443-2269. Tel: 708-747-2732; Fax: 708-747-3549. Revs. G. Jerome Kines, O.S.A.; John A. Kret, O.S.A.; Donald J. Bates, O.S.A.; Terry A. Deffenbaugh, O.S.A., Prior; Bros. David W. Adelsbach, O.S.A.; Thomas P. Taylor, O.S.A. Priests 4; Brothers 2.

MUNDELEIN. *Carmelite Monastery*, 999 E. McKinley Ave., 60060. Tel: 847-566-4070. Bro. Dominic Saganich, O.Carm., Prior; Rev. Robert Carroll, O.Carm.; Bro. Thomas Murphy, O.Carm.

OAK PARK. *Claretian Fathers Headquarters of U.S.A. Eastern Province*, 400 N. Euclid, 60302. Tel: 708-848-2076; Fax: 708-848-2069. Email: usaeastprov@claret.org. Web: www.claretians.org. Revs. Leonard J. Brown, C.M.F., Prov. Supr.; Wayne Barron, C.M.F.; Robert Fath, C.M.F.; George Morgan, C.M.F.; Wayne Schimmelmann, C.M.F.; Bro. Richard Wilga, C.M.F.

Priests serving outside Province:

Dominguez Retreat Renewal Center, 18127 S. Alameda St., Rancho Dominguez, CA 90220. Tel: 213-636-6030; Fax: 310-631-3518. Rev. Donald Lavelle, C.M.F.

Members serving abroad:

Our Lady of the Angels Parish: 75 A Molynes Rd., Kingston, Jamaica, WI. Tel: 520-445-3141; Fax: 520-717-1074. Revs. Thomas McGann; Stephen Keusenkothen, C.M.F.; Bro. Thomas Haerle, C.M.F. Priests 44; Scholastics 7; Brothers 3.

Claretian Missionaries Community Support Trust, 400 N. Euclid Ave., 60302. Tel: 708-848-2076; Fax: 708-848-2069. Revs. Leonard J. Brown, C.M.F., Pres.; Mark J. Brummel, C.M.F., Vice Pres.; Carl Quebedeaux, C.M.F., Vice Pres.; Bruce Wellems, C.M.F., Vice Pres.; James F. Maloney, C.M.F., Vice Pres.

Dominican Community of St. Martin de Porres, 204 S. Humphrey, 60302. Tel: 708-848-4271; Fax: 708-445-0581. Email: stmartin@dominicans.org. Web: www.dominicans.org; digitalfriars.net. Revs. Michael Winkels, O.P.; James Marchionda, O.P.; Thomas Saucier, O.P.; Bro. Gabriel Dault, O.P.

Missionaries of Saint Charles, Provincial Residence, 546 N. East Ave., 60302. Tel: 708-386-4430; Fax: 708-386-4457. Email: provoff@comcast.net. Rev. Antonio Tapparello, C.S., Prov.

Legal Title: *Fathers of St. Charles*

Scalabrini Development Office, 546 N. East Ave., 60302. Tel: 708-848-1616; Fax: 708-848-2525. Rev. Aldo Vendramin, C.S.

Scalabrinians Community Support Corporation, Oak Park Tel: 708-386-4430; Fax: 708-386-4457.

Scalabrinians Community Formation Corporation, Oak Park Tel: 708-386-4430; Fax: 708-386-4457.

OLYMPIA FIELDS. *The Augustinians-Provincialate*, Tolentine Center, 20300 Governors Hwy., 60461-1081. Tel: 708-748-9500; Fax: 708-481-2090. Email: secretary@midwestaugustinians.org. Web: www.midwestaugustinians.org. Very Rev. David L. Brecht, O.S.A., Prior Prov.; Bros. Thomas Taylor, O.S.A., Prov. Sec.; John J. Stobba, O.S.A., Mission Dir.; Revs. G. Jerome Knies, O.S.A., Vicar Prov. & Personnel Dir.; William E. Lego, O.S.A., Prov. Treas.; John D. Merkelis, O.S.A., Vocation Dir.

Tolentine Monastery at Tolentine Center, 20300 Governors Hwy., 60461. Tel: 708-748-9500; Fax: 708-481-2090; 708-748-0018. Web: www.midwestaugustinians.org. Very Rev. Robert F. Prevost, O.S.A., Prior Gen., Curia Agostiniana, Rome; Rev. James Friedel, O.S.A., Prior; Very Rev. David L. Brecht, O.S.A., Prior Prov.; Revs. Alfred M. Burke, O.S.A.; James V. Corrigan, O.S.A.; Edward G. Grace, O.S.A.; Donald W. Harkabus, O.S.A.; John P. Tasto, O.S.A.; Gerald J. Van Overbeek, O.S.A.; John R. Mabarak, O.S.A.; John J. Flaherty, O.S.A.; Reinhard Sternemann, O.S.A.; Bros. Daniel L. Gridley, O.S.A.; Anthony Schander, O.S.A.; John Stobba, O.S.A., Sacristan; Angelo Sturn, O.S.A.

RIVER FOREST. *St. Thomas Aquinas Priory*, 7200 Division St., 60305. Tel: 708-771-3030; Fax: 708-714-9002. Revs. Thomas F. O'Meara, O.P., Prior; David M. Hynous, O.P.; William J. Bernacki, O.P., Vicar & Pres.; Francis R. Crowe, O.P.; John M. Gambro, O.P.; Joseph I. Hren, O.P.; Bede R. Jagoe, O.P.; Jordan A. McGrath, O.P.; Richard C. LaPata, O.P., Vicar; Richard J. Woods, O.P. Legal Subsidiaries and holdings: The Priory Press, theology texts for high schools; "Listening", journal of Religion and Culture; Vestments and Vessels; Dominican Conference Center; Carpentier Art Collection. Priests 13; Brothers 3.

Assigned, but not living at the Priory: Revs. David J. Santoro O.P.; Michael Ruthenberg, C.P.; Bros. Terence G. Bullock, O.P., (Assigned, but living elsewhere) Joseph Kilikevich, O.P.

American Friends of the Ecole Biblique: Rev. Peter J. Hereley, O.P., Pres.

RIVER GROVE. *Brothers of Holy Cross*, 3000 N. 80th Ave., 60171. Tel: 708-452-5535. Email: d_allen46@aol.com. Bros. Donald Allen, C.S.C.; Walter Duda, C.S.C.; Roberto Jimenez, C.S.C.; Anthony Jorae, C.S.C.; Joseph Walter Olszowka, C.S.C.; Julian Przybla, C.S.C.; James Reddy, C.S.C.; John Schuszler, C.S.C.; John Ptaszek, C.S.C.; Roy Smith, C.S.C.; James Spooner, C.S.C.; James Van Dyke, C.S.C.; Ralph Heppe, F.S.C. (See High Schools, Private for Holy Cross High School listing)

TECHNY. *Society of the Divine Word, Provincial Headquarters-Chicago Prov.* (Province of Saint Joseph Freinademetz, S.V.D.) , 1985 Waukegan Rd., P.O. Box 6038, 60082-6038. Tel: 847-272-2700; Fax: 847-272-2517. Email: uscsvd1@aol.com. Web: www.divineword.org. Very Rev. Thomas A. Krosnicki, S.V.D., Prov.; Bro. Dennis Newton, S.V.D., Vice Prov.; Revs. Dariusz Garbaciak, S.V.D., Treas.; James Braband, S.V.D. Sec. of Education/Recruitment Formation.

Vocation Office Tel: 800-553-3321. Email: dwm@mvcinet. Web: www.svd.org.

Divine Word Missionaries, Inc. Tel: 847-272-7600; Fax: 847-272-8572. Email: www.svdmissions.org.

Divine Words Funds, Inc. Tel: 847-272-7600; Fax: 847-272-8572.

Catholic Universities, Inc. Tel: 847-272-7600; Fax: 847-272-8572. Bros. Dennis Newton, S.V.D., Mission Center Dir.; Brian McLauchlin, S.V.D., Delegated Supr. for Missionaries on Home Leave.

Blessed Arnold Charitable Trust Tel: 847-272-2700; Fax: 847-753-7464. Email: dgarbaciak@uscsvd.org. Web: www.divineword.org. Rev. Dariusz Garbaciak, S.V.D., Sec

DWTCRE Charitable Trust, 1901 Waukegan Rd., 60082. Tel: 847-272-2700; Fax: 847-753-7464. Email: dgarbaciak@uscsvd.org. Web: www.divineword.org. Rev. Dariusz Garbaciak, S.V.D., Sec.

S.V.D. Funds, Inc. Tel: 847-272-2700; Fax: 847-272-2517. Very Rev. Thomas A. Krosnicki, S.V.D., Pres.; Rev. Dariusz Garbaciak, S.V.D., Treas.

Divine Word International, 2001 Waukegan Rd., P.O. Box 176, 60082-0176. Tel: 847-272-1100; Fax: 847-272-9353. Bro. Patrick Hogan, S.V.D., Dir.

House of Religious Men: Divine Word Theologate, 5342 University Ave., 60615. Tel: 773-288-2777; Fax: 773-288-6307. Revs. Edward Pekle, S.V.D., Rector; Quang Duc Dinh, S.V.D., Dir. of Formation; Lloyd Cunningham, S.V.D.; Mark Schramm, S.V.D., Ministry Dir.; Roger P. Schroeder, S.V.D.; Derek Simons, S.V.D. Attending Catholic Theological Union 38; Participating in overseas and other ministry programs 15.

Edward McGuinn House of Studies, 5487 S. Hyde Park, #1N, 60615. Tel: 773-643-1518; Fax: 773-288-6307. Revs. Stephen B. Bevans, S.V.D.; Gary L. Riebe-Estrella, S.V.D.

Divine Word Novitiate, 1940 Waukegan Rd., 60082-6000. Tel: 847-272-0299; Fax: 847-272-2873. Rev. James Bergin, S.V.D., Novice Dir. Novices 16.

Divine Word Residence, 1901 Waukegan Rd., P.O. Box 6000, 60082-6000. Tel: 847-272-2700; Fax: 847-272-2873. Rev. Walter Bracken, S.V.D., Rector. Fathers 54. Brothers 14.

WILLOW SPRINGS. *Cistercian Fathers, Our Lady Mother of the Church*, 8121 Archer Rd., 60480. Tel: 708-839-6808; Fax: 708-839-6808. Box 334, Argo, 60501. Revs. Michael Blicharski, O.Cist.; Alberic Lipinski, O.Cist.; John Muc, O.Cist.

Legal Title *Cistercian Fathers, Our Lady Mother of the Church*, Cistercian Priory dependant monastery of the Abbey in Szczyrzyc Poland (Polish Congregation) est. 1982. Priests 3.

[O] CONVENTS AND RESIDENCES FOR SISTERS

CHICAGO. *Academy of Our Lady Convent*, 9535 S. Loomis St., 60643. Tel: 773-445-0403; Fax: 773-233-1752. School Sisters of Notre Dame (Chicago Prov.) Sisters 37.

Administrative Center of the Sisters of Mercy of the Americas, Regional Community of Chicago, 10024 S. Central Park, 60655-3132. Tel: 773-779-6011; Fax: 773-779-6094. Email: rsm@mercychicago.com. Sr. Joy Clough, R.S.M., Pres. Sisters 4.

Sisters of Mercy of the Americas, Regional Community of Chicago Charitable Trust Tel: 773-779-6011; Fax: 773-779-6094.

Benedictine Sisters of Chicago, St. Scholastica Monastery, 7430 N. Ridge Blvd., 60645. Tel: 773-764-2413; Fax: 773-761-5131. Email: jsmith@osbchicago.org. Sr. Jane Smith, O.S.B., Prioress. Sisters 70.

Congregation of the Albertine Sisters, 1550 N. Astor, 60610. Tel: 312-642-5838.

Daughters of St. Mary of Providence, Provincialate: 4200 N. Austin Ave., 60634-1615. Tel: 773-205-1313; Fax: 773-205-1316. Email: dsmpchi@aol.com. Sr. Patricia McCafferty, Prov.

Daughters of St. Paul, 172 N. Michigan, 60601. Tel: 312-346-4228; 312-346-3240; Fax: 312-346-3554. Email: fspchicago@aol.com. Web: www.rc.net/org/littlesisters. Sr. Michelle Jane Black, F.S.P., Supr. Sisters 4.

St. Elizabeth Convent, 1356 N. Claremont, 60622. Tel: 312-633-5840. Poor Handmaids of Jesus Christ.

Little Sisters of Jesus, 1529 S. Sawyer St., 60623. Tel: 773-277-5061. Email: littlesrs.chg@juno.com. Sisters 4.

Little Sisters of the Poor, The, 2325 N. Lakewood Ave., 60614. Tel: 773-935-9600; Fax: 773-935-9614. Sr. Patricia Friel, L.S.P., Supr.

Legal Title: *Little Sisters of the Poor of Chicago, Inc.* Sisters 11.

Medical Missionaries of Mary, 3410 W. 60th Pl., 60629. Tel: 773-737-3458; Fax: 773-737-4582. Email: mmmchi@aol.com. Web: www.medical-missionaries.com. Sisters 5.

Mercy Convent, 10044 S. Central Park, 60655. Tel: 773-238-4887; Fax: 773-238-0024. Sr. Ann Sullivan, R.S.M., Coord. Sisters 55.

Missionaries of Charity, 2234 W. Washington Blvd., 60612. Tel: 312-421-0038.

Missionary Sisters of Christ the King, 1118 N. Noble St., 60622. Tel: 773-489-0714. Sr. Bernadetta Gosciniak, Supr. Sisters 31.

5936 W. Barry Ave., 60634-5130. Tel: 773-889-7979. Sr. Katarzyna Zaremba, Supr.

2441 N. Menard Ave., 60639-2334. Tel: 773-637-9187. Sr. Beata Koltun, Supr.

3651 W. George St., 60618. Tel: 773-395-3520. Sr. Marta Cichon, Supr.

6101 S. 75th Ave., Summit, 60501. Tel: 708-458-8556. Sr. Renata Bochenek, Supr.

64 S. Pershing Ave., Mundelein, 60060. Tel: 847-949-0552. Sr. Gertruda Szymanska, Supr.

Missionary Sisters of the Sacred Heart, 434 W. Deming Pl., 60614. Tel: 773-883-7302; Fax: 773-525-0513. Sr. Antonia Lanzone, M.S.C., Treas.

Mother of Good Counsel Provincialate, 3800 Peterson Ave., 60659. Tel: 773-463-3020; Fax: 773-463-3567. Email: cssf@felicianschicago.org. Web: www.felicianschicago.org. Sr. Mary Barbara Ann Bosch, C.S.S.F., Prov. Min.; Revs. Stanley Janowski, O.F.M.; Anselm Zupka, O.S.B. (CLV).

Legal Title: *The Felician Sisters of the United States of America, Incorporated, Chicago Province*, Provincialate of the Felician Sisters, Novitiate, Our Lady of the Angels, Bl. Angela, St. Colette, St. Elizabeth of Hungary, *Felician Services, Inc.

The Felician Sisters of the United States of America, Incorporated, Chicago Province

Felician Volunteers in Mission, Inc. Professed Sisters 208.

Good Counsel High School, Inc.

North American Province of the Congregation of Our Lady of the Cenacle, Inc., 513 W. Fullerton Pkwy., 60614-5999. Tel: 773-528-6300; Fax: 773-549-0554. Email: cenacleprovincialate@usa.net. Web: www.cenaclesisters.org. Sr. Mary Peters, R.C., Prov. Professed Sisters 159.

Cenacle Sisters, 513 W. Fullerton Pkwy., 60014-5999. Tel: 773-528-6300; Fax: 773-528-2456. Sr. Ann Wylder, R.C., Coord. Professed Sisters 22.

Queen of the Resurrection House of Prayer, 7430 W. Talcott Ave., 60631. Sr. M. Therese Yokiel, Supr. Sisters 20.

Religious Hospitallers of St. Joseph of Delaware, Inc., 326 W. 64th St., 60621. Tel: 773-962-3900; Fax: 773-873-8247. Email: elizvs@aol.com. Sr. Janet Wahleither, R.H.S.J., Local Contact.

Sisters of Our Lady of LaSalette, 4220 N. Sheridan Rd., 60613. Tel: 773-248-4047. Email: np737@

aol.com. Sisters Saturnina Pascual, S.N.D.S., Provincial; Saturnina Pascual, S.N.D.S.

Sisters of St. Casimir, Motherhouse and Novitiate, 2601 W. Marquette Rd., 60629-1817. Tel: 773-776-1324; Fax: 773-776-8755. Web: www.ssc2601.com. Sr. M. Immacula Wendt, S.S.C., Gen. Supr. Sisters 136.

Sisters of the Good Shepherd, 1114 W. Grace St., 60613. Tel: 773-935-3434; Fax: 773-935-3523. Email: rgs@rcn.com. Sr. Dorothy Renckens, R.G.S., Supr. Sisters 6.

Sisters of the Holy Cross, 7422 N. Harlem, 60631-4409. Tel: 773-774-5449.
Other Residences:
5140 S. Hyde Park Blvd., 60615. Tel: 773-684-2995.
9964 W. 153rd St., Orland Park, 60462. Tel: 708-403-5134. Sisters of the Holy Cross 6.

Sisters of the Resurrection Provincial House and Novitiate, 7432 Talcott Ave., 60631. Tel: 773-792-6363; Fax: 773-792-9590. Sr. Mary Barbara Sniegowski, C.R., Prov. Supr.
Legal Title: *Sisters of the Resurrection* Congregation of the Sisters of the Resurrection, Chicago Province, Attended by Passionist Fathers. Sisters 61.

Society of Helpers, Provincial Office, 3206 S. Aberdeen, 60608. Tel: 773-523-8638; Fax: 773-523-8715. Email: margaret_nimbley@claret.org. Sr. Margaret Nimbley, S.H., Prov. Professed Sisters 38.
Other residences:
2043 N. Humboldt Blvd., 60647. Tel: 773-384-7707; Fax: 773-278-6629.
4721 S. Woodlawn, 60615. Tel: 773-548-5026; Fax: 773-548-3471.
4541 S. Wood, 60609. Tel: 773-927-7033; Fax: 773-376-8929.
2258 S. Marshall Blvd., 60623. Tel: 773-522-9160; Fax: 773-522-9161.
303 W. Barry, 60657. Tel: 773-248-8646; Fax: 773-248-0547.
1536 W. Wellington, 60614. Tel: 773-975-1197.
3257 S. Archer, 60608. Tel: 773-376-6168.

Wright Hall-Sisters of Charity B.V.M., 6364 Sheridan Rd., 60660. Tel: 773-761-7550; Fax: 773-761-4341. Email: wh6364@aol.com. Professed Sisters B.V.M. 65.

ARLINGTON HEIGHTS. *Missionaries of the Sacred Heart of Jesus and Our Lady of Guadalupe M.S.C.Gpe.*, 1212 E. Euclid Ave., 60004. Tel: 847-255-5616.

Sisters of Charity of Seton Hill Generalate, Seton House International, 4238 N. Walnut St., 60004. Tel: 847-398-1891; Fax: 847-398-1896. Email: marlenemondalek@hotmail.com. Sr. Marlene Mondalek, S.C., Gen. Supr. Seton House International

Sisters of the Living Word, 800 N. Fernandez Ave. B, 60004-5336. Tel: 847-577-5972; Fax: 847-577-5980. Email: slw@slw.org. Web: www.slw.org. Sr. Barbara Mass, S.L.W., Supr. Gen. & Coord. of Spiritual Life. Sisters 75.

BARTLETT. *Immaculata Congregational Home*, 801 W. Bartlett Rd., 60103-4401. Tel: 630-837-3502; Fax: 630-837-0052. Email: ssj801@aol.com. Congregational Home of the Sisters of St. Joseph, T.O.S.F. Sisters in Residence 24.
Management Team: Sisters Lydia Bilecki, S.S.J.-T.O.S.F.; Patricia Schafke, S.S.J.-T.O.S.F.

BERWYN. *Poor Handmaids of Jesus Christ*, 1916 S. Clarence Ave., 60402. Tel: 708-749-0125. Email: jiffert@juno.com. Sisters 4.

School Sisters of Notre Dame, 1431 Euclid Ave., 60402. Tel: 708-749-1380; 708-749-1381; Fax: 708-749-9446. Email: barb.bowers@juno.com. Web: www.ssndchicago.org. Sr. Barbara Bowers, S.S.N.D., Prov. Leader. (Chicago Province) Professed Sisters 127.

BLUE ISLAND. *Franciscan Sisters of Mary*, 12101 Artesian Ave., 60406-1047. Tel: 708-597-2720. Sisters 2.

Mother of Sorrows Convent, 13811 S. Western Ave., 60406. Tel: 708-385-2103; Fax: 708-385-4051. Sr. M. Eleanor Carella, O.S.M., Regl. Supr.
Legal Title: *Mantellate Sisters Servants of Mary*, Motherhouse of the Servants of Mary. Sisters 16.

BURBANK. *Adrian Dominican Sisters, Dominican Midwest Mission Chapter*, 8000 Linder Ave., 60459-2099. Tel: 708-636-7566; Fax: 708-636-0031. Email: sallyafop@aol.com. Web: www.adriansisters.org. Sr. Sarah Ann Fergus, O.P., Chapter Prioress.

DES PLAINES. *Monastery of Discalced Carmelities*, 1101 N. River Rd., 60016. Tel: 847-298-4241; Fax: 847-298-4242. Sr. Marie Andre of the Holy Spirit, Prioress. Attended by Holy Cross Fathers.

Provincial House of the Sisters of the Holy Family of Nazareth, 310 N. River Rd., 60016-1211. Tel: 847-298-6760; Fax: 847-803-1941. Sr. Marie Kielanowicz, C.S.F.N., Prov. Supr. Professed Sisters 42.

EVERGREEN PARK. *American Province of Little Company of Mary Sisters* (Little Company of Mary Sisters) , 9350 S. California, 60805. Tel: 708-422-0130; Fax: 708-422-2212. Email: cpacini@lcmh.org. Web: www.lcmglobal.org. Sr. Carol Pacini, Prov. Leader. Charitable Trust: American Province of Little Company of Mary Sisters Charitable Trust. Total in Community 25.

HIGHWOOD. *Daughters of Divine Love Congregation*, 140 North Ave., 60040. Tel: 847-432-4946 (office); 847-432-9003 (convent); Fax: 847-681-8974. Email: ddloveus@aol.com. Sr. Maria Uche Chukwu, D.D.L., Regl. Supr. A Pontifical Religious Institute

HOFFMAN ESTATES. *Poor Handmaids of Jesus Christ, Annunciation Convent*, 1480 Ashley Rd., 60195. Tel: 847-519-1384; Fax: 847-885-2757. Email: phjcashley@aol.com. Web: poorhandmaids.org.

JUSTICE. *Immaculate Conception Prov. House and Novitiate of the Dominican Sisters*, 9000 W. 81st St., 60458. Tel: 708-458-3040; Fax: 708-458-7230. Email: rosaryhill@cometlink.com. Sr. Natalie, O.P., Prov. Sisters 39.

LA GRANGE PARK. *Sisters of St. Joseph of La Grange*, 1515 W. Ogden Ave., 60526. Tel: 708-354-9200; Fax: 708-354-9573. Email: mrace@csjlagrange.org. Web: www.csjlagrange.org. Sr. Marianne Race, C.S.J., Pres.
Legal Title: *Nazareth Academy, Sisters of St. Joseph Charitable Trust.*, Sponsored ministries include secondary education, Christ in the Wilderness (retreat center) and School on Wheels, an adult literacy program. Total in Community 94.

LAKE VILLA. *Handmaids of the Precious Blood-Priory of the Heart of Mary*, 724 W. Petite Lake Rd., 60046-9619. Tel: 847-356-7729. Sr. Mary Genevieve, H.P.B., Prioress. Sisters 3.

LEMONT. *Franciscan Sisters of Chicago, General Administration Building*, 11500 Theresa Dr., 60439-0856. Tel: 630-243-3600; Fax: 630-243-3576. Web: www.chicagofranciscans.org. Sr. Diane Marie Collins, Gen. Min.
Legal Title: *Franciscan Sisters of Chicago* Sisters 74; Professed Sisters 74.

Our Lady of Victory Convent, 11400 Theresa Dr., 60439-0856. Tel: 630-243-3600; Fax: 630-243-3601. Email: dcollins@chicagofranciscans.com. Web: www.chicagofranciscans.org. Sr. Diane Marie Collins, Gen. Min. General Motherhouse and Novitiate of the Franciscan Sisters of Chicago.

Madonna Foundation Tel: 708-647-3127; Fax: 708-647-6982.

Poor Clare Monastery of the Immaculate Conception of Illinois, 12210 S. Will Cook Rd., 60439. Tel: 708-361-1810; Fax: 708-361-1816. Sr. M. Teresita Vicaress.

MELROSE PARK. *Sisters of St. Charles Borromeo* Provincialate. , 1414 N. 37th Ave., 60160. Tel: 708-343-2162; Fax: 708-343-6452. Email: mdaltoe@core.com. Sr. Marissonia Daltoe, M.S.C.S., Prov. Supr. Missionary Sisters of St. Charles Borromeo (Scalabrinians) Sisters 64.

Charitable Trust: Tel: 708-343-2162; Fax: 708-343-6452. Sisters of St. Charles Borromeo, Province of Our Lady of Fatima Charitable Trust.

OAK FOREST. *Missionary Sisters of St. Benedict of Illinois, Inc.*, 5900 W. 147th St., 60452. Tel: 708-535-9623; Fax: 708-535-3625. Email: missionarysis@aol.com. Sr. Teresa Strus Estera, Supr. In Res. Rev. Martin N. Winters (Retired).

OAK PARK. *Daughters of the Heart of Mary*, 140 N. Euclid Ave., # 401, 60302-1684. Tel: 708-386-0190; Fax: 708-383-1327. Sr. Marianna Mercurio.
Legal Title: *Ephpheta Center* Under the direction of the Daughters of the Heart of Mary.

TECHNY. *Provincial House of the Missionary Sisters Servants of the Holy Spirit*, 319 Waukegan Rd., P.O. Box 6026, 60082-6026. Tel: 847-441-0126; Fax: 847-441-5587. Email: manorris@claret.org. Sr. Margaret Anne Norris, Prov. Supr. Professed Sisters 80.

Arnold Janssen Foundation

Helena Stollenwerk Foundation

WAUKEGAN. *Franciscan Missionaries of Mary*, 726 S. Lincoln St., 60085. Tel: 847-662-8439. Sr. Noreen Murray, F.M.M., Coord. Sisters 4.

WILMETTE. *Maria Immaculata Convent-The Province Center* The Society of the Sisters of Christian Charity, Corporation of Mallinckrodt College of the North Shore , 2041 Elmwood Ave., 60091-1431. Tel: 847-920-9341; Fax: 847-920-9346. Email: sccmaryclement@hotmail.com. Web: www.sccwilmette.org. Sr. Mary Clement Eiden, S.C.C., Prov. Supr. Sisters 6.

Sacred Heart Convent, 2221 Elmwood Ave., 60091-1435. Tel: 847-251-3770; Fax: 847-251-8040. Sr. Harriette Stieber, S.C.C., Supr. A home for aged and infirm Sisters of Christian Charity. Motherhouse in Wilmette, Illinois. Sisters in Residence 58.

[P] SECULAR INSTITUTES

RIVER FOREST. *Caritas Christi*, P.O. Box 5162, 60305. Tel: 419-222-8411. Email: mjm1152@wcoil.com. Web: www.ccinfo.org.
Legal Title: *Cultural Crossroads, Inc.*, An International Secular Institute of Pontifical Rite, which forms and gives to the Church laywomen who according to their callings, talents, and professional skills seek to respond to the love of Christ in their providential environment by following the demands of the Gospel.

[Q] PIOUS UNIONS AND OTHER SOCIETIES

CHICAGO. **Society of Saint John Cantius*, 825 N. Carpenter St., 60622-5405. Tel: 312-243-7373; Fax: 312-243-4545. Email: kolinskid@yahoo.com. Web: www.societycantius.org. Revs. C. Frank Phillips, C.R., Moderator; Burns K. Seeley; Albert Tremari. A public diocesan association of the Christian Faithful

LIBERTYVILLE. *Marytown, U.S. National Center of the Militia of the Immaculata Movement*, Shrine of St. Maximilian Kolbe, 1600 W. Park Ave., 60048-2593. Tel: 847-367-7800; Fax: 847-367-7831. Email: max63@marytown.com. Web: www.marytown.com. Rev. Patrick Greenough, O.F.M.Conv., Prov. Asst. for M.I. International Latin name: Militia Immaculatae (M.I.).; An association of clergy, religious and laity dedicated to Catholic evangelization, founded 1917 in Rome by St. Maximilian Kolbe.

[R] VISITING AND NURSING OF THE SICK IN THEIR HOMES

CHICAGO. *Catholic Home Care*, 721 N. LaSalle St., 60610. Tel: 312-655-7415. Home health agency, Medicare certified, JCAHO accredited, providing health care to individuals in their homes in Cook and Lake Counties.

Catholic Home Care Home Services, 721 N. LaSalle St., 60610. Tel: 312-655-7415. Home health agency, private duty, JCAHO accredited

SKOKIE. **Resurrection Home Health Services*, 4930 W. Oakton St., 60077. Tel: 877-742-7447 (toll free); Fax: 847-568-8537. Web: www.reshealth.org. Joseph F. Toomey, Pres.; Mrs. Marie Cleary-Fishman, Senior Vice Pres., Home Health Svcs. Sponsored by Sisters of the Holy Family of Nazareth & Sisters of the Resurrection, Operated by Resurrection Health Care Patients Assisted Annually 72,795.

[S] SOCIETIES, CLUBS AND RESIDENCES

CHICAGO. *Kolping Center*, 5826 N. Elston, 60646. Tel: 773-792-2190; Fax: 773-792-0062. Email: chicagokolping@aol.com. Web: www.kolping.org. Rev. Anthony A. Englert. The Catholic Kolping Society of Chicago.

WILMETTE. *Equestrian Order of the Holy Sepulchre of Jerusalem* North Central Lieutenancy , 2350 Schiller, 60091. Tel: 847-853-0996; Fax: 847-853-0997. Email: nclhs@aol.com. Web: holysepulchre.net. H.E. Thomas J. McCabe, K.G.C.H.S., Lieutenant; Sir Thomas Mulligan, K.H.S., Sec.

[T] RETREAT HOUSES

CHICAGO. *Ascension Guest House*, 3111 S. Aberdeen St., 60608. Tel: 773-927-7424; 888-539-4261 (toll free); Fax: 773-927-5734. Email: porter@chicagomonk.org. Web: www.chicagomonk.org. (Benedictine Bed & Breakfast)

Cenacle Retreat and Conference Center, 513 Fullerton Pkwy., 60614. Tel: 773-528-6300; Fax: 773-528-2456. Email: crcc@cenaclechicago.org ministryoffice@cenaclechicago.org (ministry office) prayercardoffice@cenaclechicago.org (prayer enrollment office). Web: www.cenaclechicago.org/chicago.htm. Mr. Robert J. Raccuglia, Dir.

Focolare Movement-Mariapolis Center, 5001 S. Greenwood Ave., 60615. Tel: 773-285-2746; Fax: 773-536-5054. Email: midwest.focolare@att.net. Web: www.rc.net/focolare. Daytime Capacity 60; Overnight Capacity 30.

BARRINGTON. *Bellarmine Hall*, 175 W. County Line Rd., 60011. Tel: 847-381-1261; Fax: 847-381-4695. Email: bellarmine@bellarminehall.org. Web: www.bellarminehall.org. Rev. John T. Dillon, S.J., Dir.; Bro. William R. Haas, S.J. Jesuit Retreat House serving laity (High School, College & Adults), priests and religious. Overnight Capacity 68.

The Jesuit Retreat League of Chicago Tel: 847-381-1261; Fax: 847-381-4695. Revs. George W. Steenken, S.J.; Robert C. Dressman, S.J.; Mark W. Andrews, S.J.; Donald J. Hayes, S.J. (CLV); Mark J. Link, S.J.

DES PLAINES. *Cabrini Retreat Center* (Formerly St. Frances Cabrini Retreat House) , 9430 Golf Rd., 60016. Tel: 847-297-6530; Fax: 847-297-6544.

Email: cabriniretreat@aol.com. Web: www.cabriniretreat.org. Sr. Bridget Zanin, M.S.C., Development Dir.; Mr. Robert J. Moynihan, Exec. Dir.; Ms. Irma Herrera, Hospitality Coord. Retreats for priests, religious, laity & youth. Staffed by Missionary Sisters of the Sacred Heart of Jesus. Sisters 1.

LEMONT. *St. Mary's Retreat House*, 14230 Main St., P.O. Box 608, 60439. Tel: 630-257-5102; Fax: 630-257-6432. Rev. Blase Chemazar, O.F.M., Dir.

MUNDELEIN. *Cardinal Stritch Retreat House*, 1000 E. Maple, P.O. Box 455, 60060. Tel: 847-566-6060; Fax: 847-566-6082. Email: csrhouse@aol.com. Revs. Louis J. Cameli, Dir.; Edmund J. Siedlecki, Retired Admin. (Retired); Anthony M. Talarico, Admin.; Mr. Donald E. Wichlin, Facilities Mgr. Serves the clergy of Chicago and Region VII. Retreatants during year 1,600.

[U] NATIONAL INSTITUTIONS

CHICAGO. *Catholic Church Extension Society, aka Catholic Extension*, 150 S. Wacker Dr., 20th Fl., 60606-4200. Tel: 312-236-7240; Fax: 312-236-5276. Email: mail@catholic-extension.org. Web: www.catholic-extension.org. His Eminence Francis E. George, O.M.I., Chancellor; Most Rev. William R. Houck (JKS), Pres. (Retired); Mr. Richard A. Ritter, Gen. Sec., V.P.; James Williams, Treas.

Legal Title: *The Catholic Church Extension Society of the United States of America*

**Catholic Guild for the Blind* Provides devotional services including large print Mass, library, scholarships for Catholic Students; the liturgy of the Hours in large print or audio cassette; the sacramental rites in large print; and large print Bibles. , 180 N. Michigan Ave., Ste. 1700, 60601-7463. Tel: 312-236-8569; Fax: 312-236-8128. Email: guild@guildfortheblind.org. Web: www.guildfortheblind.org. Mr. David J. Tabak, Exec. Dir.

Catholic Kolping Society of America-National Endowment Fund, 5826 N. Elston Ave., 60646-5544. Tel: 877-659-7237; Fax: 973-478-8049. Email: edfarkas@aol.com. Web: www.Kopling.org. Ken Oshita, Treas.

Catholic League for Religious Assistance to Poland, Headquarters, 6002 W. Berteau Ave., 60634-1630. Tel: 773-202-7720; Fax: 773-202-7725. Most Rev. Thad J. Jakubowski, D.D., Exec. Dir.; Rev. Thaddeus Dzieszko, Asst. Dir.

Legal Title: *Catholic League for Religious Assistance to Poland*

Center for the Study of Religious Life, 5401 S. Cornell Ave., 60615-5698. Tel: 773-752-2720; Fax: 773-752-2723. Email: csrl@visioni.com. Web: www.csrlonline.org. Sr. Mary Charlotte Chandler, Dir. Sponsored by the Conference of Major Superiors of Men, the Leadership Conference of Women Religious and Catholic Theological Union at Chicago to conduct interdisciplinary and intercultural reflection on U.S. religious life questions and serve as a resource to religious leadership.

Jan Beyzym Society, Inc., 4105 N. Avers Ave., 60618. Tel: 773-588-7476; Fax: 773-588-6517. Email: polmes@jezuicichicago.org. Web: jezuici.org. Polish Jesuits Foreign Missions

**The National Center for the Laity*, P.O. Box 291102, 60629. Tel: 773-776-9036; Fax: 773-776-9036. Email: wdroel@cs.com. Mr. Vaile Scott, Pres. Founded in 1977, the NCL is dedicated to advancing a key insight of Vatican II: that the church is the people of God in service to the modern world. NCL publishes a newsletter, INITIATIVES, furnishes a weekly e-mail message, gfapierce@aol.com, hosts conferences and retreats and maintains a speakers' bureau.

National Coalition for Church Vocations, 5420 S. Cornell, #105, 60615. Tel: 773-955-5453; Fax: 773-363-5530. Email: NCCV400@aol.com. Web: www.nccv-vocations.org. Sr. Diane Poplawski, O.P., Exec. Dir.

National Organization for Continuing Education of Roman Catholic Clergy, Inc., 1337 W. Ohio, 60622. Tel: 312-226-1890; Fax: 312-829-8915. Email: nocercc@nocercc.org. Web: www.nocercc.org. Rev. Mark R. Hession, Pres.; Mr. James Alphen, Exec. Dir. An association of dioceses and religious communities supporting continuing formation for priests. Founded in 1973, membership includes over 220 Roman Catholic dioceses and religious provinces in the United States and 90 other organizations and individuals around the world. Professional services offered include an annual convention, regional meetings, specialized workshops, a bimonthy newsletter, practical resources in diverse media, and individual consultation.

National Religious Vocation Conference, 5420 S. Cornell, #105, 60615. Tel: 773-363-5454; Fax: 773-363-5530. Email: NRVC@aol.com. Web: nrvc.net. Bro. Paul Bednarczyk, C.S.C., Exec. Dir.

Radio Maryja, P.O. Box 39565, 60639-0595. Tel: 773-385-8472; Fax: 773-385-5631. Email: radiomaryja@core.com. Web: www.radiomaryja.pl. 6965 W. Belmont Ave., 60634. Redemptorist religious radio

**Trinity House*, 5300 S. Shore, Apt. 98, 60615. Tel: 773-684-5770. Email: ssspsyd@enteract.com. Rev. John Keenan, S.S.S., Psy.D., Ph.D., Dir. Treatment Center for Clergy and Religious

**Zambian Rehabilitation Institute* Organized to raise funds and recruit volunteers in the U.S. to assist in the establishment of an addictions treatment center for clergy, religious and laity. Initial location of center in Zambia will also serve Eastern and South Africa. , 5414 N. Lina Ave., 60630-1310. Tel: 773-792-2380; Fax: 773-792-9093. Email: zamrehab@aol.com. Thomas E. Healy, Contact Person.

EVANSTON. **Solidarity Bridge, Inc.*, 1577 Florence Ave., 60201. Tel: 847-328-7748; Fax: 547-328-6860. Email: solidbridge@aol.com. Web: www.solidaritybridge.org. Dr. Juan Hinjosa, Exec. Dir. Provides short term international mission opportunities utilizing secular callings as vehicles of service to the poor in partnership with local counterparts in Bolivia through the Chicago Catholic Medical Mission, the Chicago Catholic Enterprise Mission and the Chicago Catholic Education Mission

GURNEE. **Caritas For Children, Inc.*, 5250 Grand Ave., PMB 105, 60031-1877. Tel: 888-227-4827; Fax: 614-771-3528. Email: cthoar@caritasforchildren.org. Web: www.caritasforchildren.org. Christopher T. Hoar, Contact Person. Promotes and supports inter-country adoptions from Poland through Catholic Charities of Chicago and provides financial assistance for the health, education and general welfare of orphaned and other disadvantaged children through the services of Catholic religious communities

RIVER FOREST. **American Friends of the Ecole Biblique*, 7200 W. Division St., 60305-1294. Tel: 708-771-3030; Fax: 708-771-4510. Email: ecolebibli@aol.com. Web: www.op.org/op/ebaf/index-eng.htm. Rev. Peter J. Hereley, O.P., Pres.; Judy Valentine Gerth, Mng. Dir. Tel: 847-475-4114. Organized to raise funds in the U.S. to support the work of the Ecole Biblique et Archeologique Francaise de Jerusalem and promote the dissemination of biblical scholarship and archeological research through newsletters, receptions, and seminars with biblical scholars.

Dominican Leadership Conference, 7200 W. Division St., 60305-1294. Tel: 708-771-0909; Fax: 708-914-9002. Email: dlc@dom.edu. Web: www.op.org/dlc. Sr. Mary Ellen O'Grady, O.P., Exec. Dir.

Legal Title: *Dominican Leadership Conference of Dominican Men and Women Religious in the United States of America*

Conferences:

Parable Conference for Dominican Life and Mission Tel: 708-771-0088; Fax: 708-914-9002.

Opus: A History of the Order of Preachers in the United States Tel: 708-921-2538; Fax: 708-921-2207.

STICKNEY. **Ministry Potential Discerner, Inc.*, St. Pius X Campus, 4314 S. Oak Park Ave., 60402. Tel: 708-795-1221; Fax: 708-795-1226. Email: ray@mpdinc.org Web: www.mpdinc.org. Charles Planek, Pres. A self-assessment evangelizing vocational tool designed to aid vocation recruitment in discerning individuals for service to the church as priest or religious.

TECHNY. *Divine Word Missionaries, Inc., Divine Word Funds, Inc.*, 1835 Waukegan Rd., Box 6099, 60082-6099. Tel: 847-272-7600; Fax: 847-272-8572. Email: info@svdmission.org. Web: www.svdmissions.org. Bro. Dennis Newton, S.V.D.; Mr. David Gallagher, Treas.

S.V.D., Catholic Universities, Inc., 1835 Waukegan Rd., Box 6099, 60082-6099. Tel: 847-272-7600; Fax: 847-272-8572. Email: info@svdmissions.org. Web: www.svdmissions.org. Bro. Dennis Newton, S.V.D., Pres.; Mr. David Gallagher, Treas.

[V] MINISTRY IN HIGHER EDUCATION

CHICAGO. *Ministry in Higher Education*, 700 S. Morgan St., 60607. Tel: 312-355-3366; Fax: 928-396-9281. Email: nclm@faithandculture.us. Mr. Nicholas C. Lund-Molfese, M.A., J.D., Coord.

Non-Catholic Institutions:

Northwestern University/Kendall College, Sheil Center, 2110 N. Sheridan Rd., Evanston, 60201. Tel: 847-328-4648; Fax: 847-328-4660. Rev. Kenneth C. Simpson, E.S., M.Div., D.Min., Dir.

University of Chicago Calvert House, 5735 S. University Ave., 60637. Tel: 312-288-2311; Fax: 773-288-1124. Rev. Michael T. Yakaitis, Dir.

University of Illinois at Chicago - John Paul II Newman Center, 700 S. Morgan St., 60607-3429. Tel: 312-226-1880; Fax: 312-226-2361. Rev. Patrick M. Marshall, Dir.

[W] PERSONAL PRELATURE

CHICAGO. *Midtown Center* Prelature of the Holy Cross and Opus Dei , 1825 N. Wood St., 60622. Tel: 773-292-5450; 773-292-0660; Fax: 773-292-0996. Web: www.opusdei.org. Revs. John P. Debicki; Charles M. Ferrer; Hilary F. Mahaney; Fred Piegl.

Northview University Center Prelature of the Holy Cross and Opus Dei , 7225 N. Greenview Ave., 60626. Tel: 773-465-3468; Fax: 773-465-1195. Web: www.opusdei.org. Rev. Joseph Landauer (PIT).

Prelature of the Holy Cross and Opus Dei, 5800 N. Keating Ave., 60646. Tel: 773-283-5800; Fax: 773-202-8179. Web: www.opusdei.org. Very Rev. Peter V. Armenio, Vicar for the Midwest; Revs. John Agnew; Frank Hoffman; Edward G. Maristany. Office of the Vicar for the Midwest.

OAK PARK. *Oak Park Study Center* Prelature of the Holy Cross and Opus Dei , 831 S. Euclid Ave., 60304. Tel: 708-383-0928; Fax: 708-386-2612. Web: www.oakparkstudy.org. Revs. Richard L. Schendt; Martin Miller; James Socias.

[X] MISCELLANEOUS LISTINGS

CHICAGO. **Aid for Women* Dedicated to upholding the principles of Humanae Vitae and Evangelium Vitae, the organization maintains a crisis center where any pregnant woman will find help and encouragement to choose life for her unborn child through pregnancy testing, confidential counseling and referral to community resources. , 8 S. Michigan Ave., Ste. 1100, 60603-3311. Tel: 312-621-1100; Fax: 312-621-1972. Email: info@aidforwomen.org. Web: www.aidforwomen.org. Elaine M. Kindler, Dir.

Alexian Brothers Bonaventure House, 825 W. Wellington Ave., 60657. Tel: 773-327-9921; Fax: 773-327-9113. Email: information@bonaventurehouse.org. Web: www.bonaventurehouse.org. Mr. Robert N. Pfeiffer, CEO. Congregation of Alexian Brothers, Immaculate Conception Province, Residences for persons with AIDS.

Apostolate of the Handicapped, 721 N. LaSalle, 60610. Tel: 312-655-7188. Active membership 750.

St. Daniel the Prophet, 5330 S. Nashville, 60638. Robert Roeder, Pres.; Rev. Charles F. Kelly (Retired).

The Aquin Guild, 1025 W. Fry St., 60622. Tel: 312-280-9199. Rev. John W. Clemens, Dir. Provides spiritual direction to Catholics engaged in public and parochial education.

Aquinas Literacy Center (ESL), 3525 S. Hermitage Ave., 60609. Tel: 773-927-0512; Fax: 773-927-8980. Email: aquinaslit@aol.com. Sr. Kathy McNulty, O.S.F., Dir.

The Bolivian Trust of the Dominicans, 1909 S. Ashland Ave., 60608. Tel: 312-666-3244; Fax: 312-829-8471.

**Brother David Darst Center for Justice, Peace and Spirituality Education*, 2834 S. Normal, 60616. Tel: 312-225-3099. Email: brdaviddarstcenter@juno.com. Web: www.brdaviddarstcenter.org. Bro. Denis Murphy, F.S.C., Contact Person.

Catholic Chaplaincy at O'Hare, Chicago O'Hare International Airport, P.O. Box 66353, 60666-0353. Tel: 773-686-2636; Fax: 773-686-0130. Email: ORDchapel@aol.com. Web: ohareairportchapel.org. Rev. Michael G. Zaniolo, Chap.

Catholic Conference of Illinois, 65 E. Wacker Pl., Ste. 1620, 60601. Tel: 312-368-1066; Fax: 312-368-1090. Email: rfgcci@aol.com. Web: www.catholicconferenceofillinois.org. Mr. Robert Giligan, Exec. Dir.

The Catholic Education Institute, P.O. Box 597524, 60659. Tel: 718-823-8565. Email: johnpiderit@msn.com. Web: www.catholicexcellence.org. Rev. John J. Piderit, S.J., Pres.

Catholic Health Partners Services, 2875 W. 19th St., 60623. Tel: 773-484-4300; Fax: 773-521-7902. Web: www.cath-health.org. Sponsored by Ascension Health and the Missionary Sisters of the Sacred Heart of Jesus to operate St. Anthony Hospital

Catholic Health Partners Development Corporation Tel: 773-484-4300; Fax: 773-521-7902.

Catholic Health Partners Medical Network Tel: 773-484-4300; Fax: 773-521-7902.

Partners Occupational Health Tel: 773-484-4300; Fax: 773-521-7902.

Partners Support Services Tel: 773-484-4300; Fax: 773-521-7902.

St. Anthony Health Affiliates, 2875 W. 19th St., 60623. Tel: 773-484-4300; Fax: 773-521-7902.

The Catholic New World, 721 N. LaSalle St., 60610. Tel: 312-655-7777; Fax: 312-642-7350. Email:

mail@catholicnewworld.com. Web: www.catholicnewworld.com. Thomas H. Sherdian, Editor & Gen. Mgr.; Dawn Vidmar, Advertising & Mktg. Mgr.; Ann DeFrisco, Office Mgr. Publishers of The Catholic New World; Chicago Catolico; and the Archdiocesan Directory.

Catholic Office of the Deaf, 721 N. LaSalle, 60610. Tel: 312-655-7899 (Voice); 312-751-8368 (TDD); Fax: 312-751-0394. Email: cathdeafch@archchicago.org. Rev. Joseph A. Mulcrone, Dir.

**Central American Martyrs Center (Su Casa Catholic Worker Community)*, 5045 S. Laflin, 60609. Tel: 773-376-9263; Fax: 773-376-9241. Email: sucasacw@juno.com. Sr. Mary Davis, I.H.M.; Dorothy Dvorachek; Daniel DelaPava; Tamara Davis; Stephanis Schandel; Edward Casarez.

Charis Ministries, 1400 Devon Ave., Box 14, 60660. Tel: 773-508-3237; Fax: 773-508-2844. Email: charis@jesuits.net. Web: www.jesuits.net/charis. Provides opportunities for spiritual growth utilizing the gifts of Ignatian Spirituality

The Chicago Marian Center, 7262 W. Foster Ave., 60656. Tel: 773-774-7700; Fax: 773-774-1630. Email: chicagomarian@aol.com. Web: chicagomarian.com/org. Kathleen Long, Contact Person.

Claret Center, 5536 S. Everett, 60637. Tel: 773-643-6259; Fax: 773-643-6929. Email: claret_center@claret.org. Web: www.claret.org. Pauline LaMothe, O.P., Admin. Resources for Counseling and Spiritual Direction.

Claretian Associates, Inc. Organization to provide affordable housing and encourage neighborhood improvement in South Chicago. , 9108 S. Brandon Ave., 60617. Tel: 773-734-9181; Fax: 773-734-9221. Email: kateg@claretiamassociates.org. Web: www.claretianassociates.org. Kate Graham, Assoc. Dir.

Claretian Volunteers and Lay Missionaries, 205 W. Monroe St., 60606. Tel: 312-236-7782; Fax: 312-236-7230. Email: comovol@claret.org. Web: www.claret.org. John Dimucci, Dir.

Co-Redemptorist Association Office, 3700 N. Ashland Ave., 60613-3602. Tel: 773-472-8509; Fax: 773-472-8515. Email: cocssr@aol.com. Web: www.redemptorists-denver.org. Rev. John Paul Andree, C.SS.R., Dir.

Court of Appeals-Province of Chicago, 20 N. Wacker Dr., Ste. 3420, 60606. Tel: 312-553-4080; Fax: 312-553-4085. Email: johnplucas@msn.com. The Court of Second Instance in matrimonial cases for the Tribunals of the Province of Chicago.

**Dominican Literacy Center*, 2436 N. Ridgeway Ave., 60647.

**Felician Services, Inc.*, 3800 W. Peterson Ave., 60659-3116. Tel: 773-463-3806; Fax: 773-463-2059. Email: fsichgo@fs-inc.net. Sr. Mary Clarette Stryzewski, C.S.S.F., Pres. & CEO.

Felician Volunteers in Mission, Inc., 3800 W. Peterson Ave., 60659. Tel: 773-523-0916. Sr. Margaret Mary Eder, Dir.

Focolare Movement, P.O. Box 53426, 60653. Tel: 773-285-2746; Fax: 773-536-5054. Email: midwest.focolare@att.net. Web: www.rc.net/focolare. Work of Mary founded in Trent, Italy in 1943. International headquarters are in Rome, Italy; national formation center in New York.

Women, 5017 S. Greenwood Ave., 60615. Tel: 773-536-7873; Fax: 773-536-5054. Ms. Paola Santostefano, Contact Person.

Men, 1112 S. Oak Park Ave., Oak Park, 60304. Tel: 708-848-6576; Fax: 708-848-6950. Mr. Marco Desalvo, Contact Person.

Foundation for Adult Catechetical Teaching Aids, 6007 N. Sheridan Rd., Ste. 22A, 60660. Tel: 773-334-6774; Fax: 773-334-6806. Rev. Robert E. McLaughlin, Pres.; M. E. Buckley, Contact Person.

Franciscan Friars Retirement Corporation, 6107 Kenmore Ave., 60660-2797. Tel: 773-274-7681; Fax: 773-274-9751.

Franciscan Outreach Association, 1645 W. LeMoyne St., 60622. Tel: 773-278-6724; Fax: 773-278-7120. Email: mail@franoutreach.org. Web: www.franoutreach.org. Rev. Larry Janezic, O.F.M., Exec. Dir. Owns & operates: Marquard Center, Franciscan House of Mary & Joseph and a Case Management Program for the homeless in Chicago.

Friends of the Metropolitan Andrew Sheptysky Hospital, P.O. Box 1979, 60690-1979. Tel: 312-751-8270; Fax: 312-337-6397. Most Rev. Edwin Conway, Pres.

General Assistance, Inc., 30 N. LaSalle St., Ste. 4100, 60602. Tel: 312-422-9140; Fax: 312-621-0297. Email: dancoyne@okeefe-law.com. Daniel W. Coyne, Contact Person. Support organization for the Daughters of Charity.

Holy Family Church, Inc., 2050 N. Clark St., 60614. Tel: 773-975-6363; Fax: 773-975-0230.

Ignatius Productions, Inc, 2050 N. Clark St., 60614. Tel: 773-975-6363; Fax: 773-975-0230.

Illinois Catholic Health Association, 65 E. Wacker Pl., Ste. 1620, 60601. Tel: 312-368-0011; Fax: 312-368-1701. Email: pkarst@il-cha.org. Web: www.il-cha.org. Philip J. Karst, Exec. Dir.

The Illinois Patrons of the Arts in the Vatican Museums, 221 N. LaSalle St., Ste. 1000, 60601. Tel: 312-782-5681; Fax: 312-782-6904. His Eminence Francis E. George, O.M.I.; Mr. Edmund M. Burke, Pres.

Institute for Spiritual Leadership, 5498 S. Kimbark Ave., P.O. Box 53147, 60653-0147. Tel: 773-752-5962; Fax: 773-752-5964. Email: islusa@aol.com. Web: www.spiritleader.org. Sr. Patricia M. Bombard, B.V.M., Exec. Dir. Education Center for Spiritual Direction and Renewal.

**The Institute on Religious Life*, 3051 N. Christiana, 60618. Tel: 773-267-1195; Fax: 773-267-2044. Email: mail@religiouslife.com. Web: www.religiouslife.com. P.O. Box 410007, 60641. Rev. Thomas Nelson, O.Praem., Exec. Dir.; Michael D. Wick, Dir. of Operations.

Jesuit International Missions, Inc., 2050 N. Clark St., 60614. Tel: 773-975-6881; Fax: 773-975-0230. Email: vonkaenel@chicagoprovincejesuits.org. Rev. George E. Von Kaenel, S.J.

Jesuit Seminary Association, 2050 N. Clark St., 60614. Tel: 773-975-6363; Fax: 773-975-0230. Web: www.jesuits-chi.org.

Kolbe House, 2434 S. California Ave., 60608. Tel: 773-247-0070; Fax: 773-247-0569. Email: khjailmin@aol.com. Revs. Lawrence J. Craig, Exec. Dir.; David A. Kelly, C.PP.S.; Arturo Perez-Rodriguez; Deacons James Morgan; Ronald DeRose; George Brooks; John Harrington; Charles Huber; John Richardson; Jack Malone. Catholic prison ministry.

Loyola Press, 3441 N. Ashland Ave., 60657. Tel: 773-281-1818; Fax: 773-281-0555. Email: lane@loyolapress.com. Web: www.loyolapress.org. Rev. George A. Lane, S.J., Dir.

Lumen Christi Institute, 5735 S. University Ave., 60637-1507. Tel: 773-955-5887; Fax: 773-955-5233. Web: lumenchristi.org. The Lumen Christi Institute promotes Catholic thought through formation programs, lectures, courses and conferences. Events are organized in Chicago or, through collaboration with other scholarly church organizations, elsewhere in the Midwest, as well as nationally and internationally.

Marist Volunteer Program, 4200 W. 115th St., 60655. Tel: 773-881-6360, Ext. 5367; Fax: 773-881-0595. Email: mvp@marist.net. Web: www.marist.net/~mvp. Bro. Robert Clark, F.M.S., Exec. Dir.

Martin de Porres House, 3322 Washington Blvd., 60624. Tel: 773-826-9336. Margaret Brooks, Pres.; Cathryn Peters, Vice Pres.; Claire Cummings, Sec.

Mercy Housing Corporation, 10024 S. Central Park, 60655-3132. Tel: 773-779-6011; Fax: 773-779-6094. Email: rsm@mercychicago.com. Sr. Lois Graver, R.S.M., Contact Person. Sisters of Mercy of the Americas, Regional Community of Chicago

Miles Jesu, Tel: 773-262-0861; Fax: 773-267-1093. Email: chicagomen@milesjesu.com. Web: milesjesu.com.

Men's Formation Center, 1128 W. Morse Ave., 60626. Tel: 773-262-0861; Fax: 773-262-1093. Mr. David Rey, Vocation Dir.; Rev. Christopher Foeckler, M.J., Formation Dir.

Women's Formation Center, 1126 W. Morse Ave., 60626. Tel: 773-262-0806; Fax: 773-262-1093. Mary Pat Cross, Vocation Dir.

Mother Cabrini League, 434 W. Deming Pl., 60614. Tel: 773-388-7329. Sr. Antonia Lanzone, M.S.C., Business Mgr. The purpose of the League is to spread devotion to St. Frances Xavier Cabrini.

Mundelein College, Office of the General Counsel of Loyola University-Chicago, 820 N. Michigan Ave., 60611. Tel: 312-915-6195. 6525 N. Sheridan Rd., 60626. Tel: 773-508-3029; Fax: 312-915-6208; Tel: 312-915-6195; Fax: 312-915-6208. Email: emunro@luc.edu. Web: luc.edu. Mr. Wayne Magdziarz, Pres. & Chm. Bd. Trustees; Ms. Ellen Kane Munro, Sec.; Philip R. Kosiba, Vice Pres. & Treas.; Loretta A. Namovic, Trustee.

National Catholic AIDS Network, 1400 W. Devon Ave., #502, 60660. Tel: 713-508-7080. Email: info@ncan.org. Web: www.ncan.org. Mr. Daniel T. Lunney, Interim Exec. Dir.

Nowe Zycie Association, 7015 W. Diversey Ave., 60707. Tel: 773-637-7312; Fax: 773-637-7430. Email: redakcja@nowezycie.com. Web: www.nowezycie.com. Mr. Roman Harmata, Contact Person.

Oblates for International Pastoral aka Oblate International Pastoral Investment Trust, 5535 S. Kenwood Ave., 60637-1755. Email: whitley@omigen.org. Revs. Thomas Singer, O.M.I., Trustee; Rufus J. Whitley, O.M.I., Trustee; David Ullrich, O.M.I., Trustee; Robert Moosbrugger, O.M.I., Trustee.

Office for Mission Advancement Dominicans: Province of St. Albert the Great. , 1909 S. Ashland Ave., 60608. Tel: 312-226-0020; Fax: 312-226-6440. Email: dominicans@preachers.org. Web: www.op.org.

Order of Friar Servants of Mary United States of America Province, Inc., 3121 W. Jackson Blvd., 60612. Tel: 773-533-0360; Fax: 773-533-8307. Email: bromikeosm@hotmail.com. Web: www.servite.org. The Order of Friar Servants of Mary-U.S.A. Province, Inc., Chicago, IL

Precious Blood Ministry of Reconciliation, P.O. Box 09379, 60609-0379. Tel: 773-579-0781; Fax: 773-579-0782. Email: pbreconciliation@sbcglobal.net. Revs. David Kelly, C.PP.S.; Dennis Kinderman, C.PP.S.; Joseph Nassal, C.PP.S.; William Nordenbrock, C.PP.S. (CIN), Exec. Dir.; Sr. Mary Louise Degenhart, A.S.C. A ministry of the Cincinnati and Kansas City provinces of the Missionaries of the Precious Blood that responds to violence and conflict in the Back of the Yards neighborhood of Chicago (1936 W. 48th Street-Rear) and fosters renewal of the church through reconciliation programs, retreats and training workshops for church communities.

Resurrection Health Care, 7435 W. Talcott Ave., 60631. Tel: 773-774-8000; Fax: 773-792-9926. Web: www.reshealth.org. Joseph F. Toomey, Pres. & CEO; Sisters Clara Francis Kusek, C.R., Exec. Vice Pres., Mission; Mary Paul Schultz, C.R., Mission Representative; Rev. Romulo Manching, Dir. Clinical Pastoral Education; Deacons Robert Bulger, Mission Sinior Vice Pres.; N. Arthur Metallo, Dir. Spiritual Svcs.

Other members of Resurrection Health Care:

**Resurrection Behavioral Health*, 7435 W. Talcott Ave., 60631. Tel: 708-681-2324; Fax: 708-681-1289. (Provisio Family Services, d.b.a. ProCare Centers)

Resurrection Development Foundation Tel: 773-792-7924; Fax: 773-792-5872.

**Partners Home Care Foundation d/b/a/ Resurrection Home Health Foundation*, 7435 W. Talcott Ave., 60631.

**Resurrection Home Health Foundation*, 7000 N. Newark, Ste. 144, Niles, 60714. Tel: 847-647-2383; Fax: 847-647-2762.

**Resurrection Home Health Services* Tel: 847-568-8536; Fax: 847-568-8537.

Resurrection Senior Services Tel: 708-579-8950; Fax: 708-579-8956.

Resurrection Services Tel: 773-774-8000; Fax: 773-792-9926.

Retirement Plan of the Order of Friar Servants of Mary-U.S.A. Province, Inc., 3121 W. Jackson Blvd., 60612. Tel: 773-533-0360; Fax: 773-533-8307. Email: bromikeosm@hotmail.com. Web: www.servite.org.

S.F.V., Inc., 1645 W. LeMoyne St., 60622. Tel: 773-278-6724; Fax: 773-278-7021. Rev. Kurt Hartrich, O.F.M., Pres. Sponsor corporation of St. Francis Village (a retirement village) in Crowley, TX.

School Sisters of Notre Dame of North America, Inc., c/o NAMA Coordinating Center, 9535 S. Loomis St., 60643. Tel: 773-233-1181; Fax: 773-233-1609. Email: mcgoeyssnd@aol.com. Web: www.ssnd.org. Sr. Maureen McGoey, S.S.N.D., Dir.

Serra International, 220 S. State St., Ste. 1703, 60604. Tel: 312-588-0700; 800-488-4008 (toll free); Fax: 312-588-0600; 800-377-7877 (toll free). Email: serra@serrainternational.org. Web: www.serrainternational.org. Mr. John W. Woodward, Exec. Dir., Serra International & Serra International Foundation.

USA Council of Serra International Tel: 312-201-6549; 888-777-6681 (toll free); Fax: 312-201-6548; 888-777-6803 (toll free). Email: serraus@serraus.org. Web: www.serraus.org. Mr. E. V. Verbeke, Exec. Dir.

Shelters for the Homeless, Inc., 126 N. Desplaines St., 60661. Tel: 773-224-5607; Fax: 773-483-5301.

**Society of Friends of the John Paul II Foundation*, P.O. Box 34618, 60634. Email: mskawski@furkon.com.

**Society of Jesus Worldwide*, 2050 N. Clark St., 60614.

St. Thomas Aquinas Foundation (STAF) (St. Albert the Great Prov.) , 1909 S. Ashland Ave., 60608-2994. Tel: 312-666-3244; Fax: 312-829-8471. Very Rev. Edward M. Ruane, O.P., Sec. & Treas.

United Stand Family Center, 3731 W. 62nd St., 60629. Tel: 773-585-4499. Sr. Kim Mis, C.S.S.F., Exec. Dir. Education, Prevention, Problem Identification, Consultation, and Intervention with Children and Families Staff 55.

Villa Guadalupe Senior Services Corporation, 3201 E. 91st St., 60617. Tel: 773-933-0344; Fax: 773-933-0827. Barbara Kilbourne, Chairwoman; Rev. Mark Brummel, C.M.F., Treas. Organization to provide affordable housing and related services for

Senior Citizens in South Chicago.

Youth Ministry Office, Archdiocese of Chicago, 155 E. Superior, 60611. Tel: 312-751-8716; Fax: 312-751-3856. Email: Amcdonell@archchicago.org. Mr. Angus McDonell, Dir.; Joanne Walczynski, Youth Ministry Coord. of Vicariate I. Tel: 847-549-0166; Fax: 847-549-0163; Patrick Pacer, Youth Ministry Coord. of Vicariate II. Tel: 773-388-8674; Fax: 773-388-8674; Eduardo Rivera, Youth Ministry Coord. of Vicariate III. Tel: 312-243-4063; Fax: 312-243-4970; Dave Melzer, Youth Min. Coord. of Vicariate IV. Tel: 773-282-3270; Fax: 773-282-4809; Patti Melzer, Youth Min. Coord. of Vicariate IV; Maria Perez Eraci, Youth Ministry Coord. of Vicariate V. Tel: 708-370-3674; Fax: 708-352-2482 Joyce Gillie, Youth Ministry Coord. of Vacariate VI. Tel: 708-889-0573; Fax: 708-889-0206.

Zaccheus House (2002), 12242 S. Parnell, 60628. Tel: 773-568-7822; Fax: 773-287-1258. Web: www.zacchaeushouse.org. Most Rev. Joseph N. Perry, Moderator; Deacon Abrom Salley, Dir. A ministry of Deacons offering hospitality and life skills education to men in transition to stability in their lives.

ARLINGTON HEIGHTS. *Living Word Charitable Trust*, 800 N. Fernandez Ave.-B, 60004-5316. Tel: 847-577-5972; Fax: 847-577-5980. Email: slw@slw.org. Web: slw.org. Mary Ann Zrust, S.L.W., Chair.

BERWYN. *Academy of Our Lady, Chicago, Inc.*, 1431 Euclid Ave., 60402. Tel: 708-749-1380; Fax: 708-749-9446. Email: barb.bowers@juno.com.

BLUE ISLAND. *St. Francis Health Care Foundation*, 12935 S. Gregory St., 60406. Tel: 708-824-4810; Fax: 708-389-9480. Email: bryant_krauss@ssmhc.com. Member of SSM Health Care.

ELK GROVE VILLAGE. *Alexian Brothers Community Services*, 600 Alexian Way, 60007. Tel: 847-640-7550; Fax: 847-981-5561.

Alexian Brothers Community Services of St. Louis, 600 Alexian Way, 60007. Tel: 847-640-7550; Fax: 847-981-5561.

Alexian Brothers Health System, 600 Alexian Way, 60007. Tel: 847-640-7550; Fax: 847-981-5561. Congregation of Alexian Brothers, Immaculate Conception Province, d.b.a. Alexian Brothers Health System Foundation

**Alexian Brothers Health System, Inc. Investment Trust*, 600 Alexian Way, 60007. Tel: 847-640-7500; Fax: 847-981-5561.

Alexian Brothers of America, Inc., 600 Alexian Way, 60007. Tel: 847-640-7550; Fax: 847-981-5561. Congregation of Alexian Brothers, Immaculate Conception Province

Alexian Brothers of the Midwest, 600 Alexian Way, 60007. Tel: 847-640-7550; Fax: 847-981-5561. Congregation of Alexian Brothers, Immaculate conception Province

**Chicago Catholic Healthcare System, Inc.*, 600 Alexian Way, 60007. Tel: 847-640-7550; Fax: 847-981-5561. Congregation of Alexian Brothers, Immaculate Conception Province

EVANSTON. *Intercommunity Housing Corporation*, 2859 Central St., 60201. Tel: 847-864-1206. Janet Bilandic, Exec. Dir.

**Mission FIDES*, P.O. Box 5250, 60204-5250. Tel: 773-262-6370; Fax: 773-262-6370. Web: www.missionfides.com.

EVERGREEN PARK. *American Province of Little Company of Mary Sisters Charitable Trust*, 9350 S. California, 60805. Tel: 708-422-0130; Fax: 708-422-2212. Email: cpacini@lcmh.org. Web: 222.lcmglobal.org.

Little Company of Mary Hospital and Health Care Centers, 2800 W. 95th St., 60642.

GLENVIEW. *Redemptorist Fathers of St. Alphonsus Parish of Chicago*, c/o Redemptorists of Glenview, Illinois 1111 N. Milwaukee Ave., P.O. Box 6, 60025. Tel: 847-724-0425; Fax: 847-724-8953.

Villa Redeemer, c/o Redemptorists of Glenview, Illinois, 1111 N. Milwaukee Ave., P.O. Box 6, 60025. Tel: 847-724-0425; Fax: 847-724-8953.

HOMEWOOD. *Madonna Foundation*, 1055 W. 175th St., Ste. 202, 60430. Tel: 708-647-3127; Fax: 708-647-6982. Email: jsisler@franciscanservices.com. Web: www.madonnafoundation4girls.org. Sr. M. Francis Clare Radke, O.S.F., Pres.; Janet Sisler, Exec. Dir. Sponsored by the Franciscan Sisters of Chicago, A charitable foundation focused on increasing access to Catholic high schools by young women in urban areas through scholarships and program enhancement

INVERNESS. **Alexian Brothers Northwest Mental Health Association*, 1606 Colonial Pkwy., 60067. Tel: 847-952-7460; Fax: 847-991-3065. Web: alexian-northwest.org. 1616 N. Arlington Heights Rd., Arlington Heights, 60004. Tel: 847-925-7460; Fax: 547-392-2047. 3350 Salt Creek Ln., Ste. 110, Arlington Heights, 60005. Tel: 847-952-7460; Fax: 847-259-5771. Congregation of Alexian Brothers, Immaculate Conception Province

**Alexian Brothers Northwest Mental Health Center*, 1606 Colonial Pkwy., 60067. Tel: 847-952-7460; Fax: 847-991-3065. Web: alexian-northwest.org. 1616 N. Arlington Heights Rd., Arlington Heights, 60004. Tel: 847-952-7460; Fax: 847-392-2047. 3350 Salt Creek Ln., Ste. 110, Arlington Heights, 60005. Tel: 847-952-7460; Fax: 847-259-5771. Congregation of Alexian Brothers, Immaculate Conception Province

LAGRANGE PARK. **Joyful Again* Support program for widowed men and women. , P.O. Box 1365, 60526. Tel: 708-354-7211; Fax: 708-354-7519 Email: joyful@megsinet.net. Rev. Medard P Laz, Exec. Dir.; Charlotte Hrubes, Dir.

Sisters of St. Joseph of LaGrange Charitable Trust, 1515 W. Ogden Ave., 60525. Tel: 708-354-9200; Fax: 708-354-9573. Email: gsbr@juno.com

LAKE FOREST. *Barat Education Foundation* 700 E. Westleigh Rd., 60045. Tel: 847-574-4246; Fax: 847-574-6070. Email: dimengo@thebaratfoundation.org. Web: www.thebaratfoundation.org. Michael G. Dimengo, Senior Vice Pres. & Admin.

LEMONT. *Franciscan ElderCare Services/Illinois, Inc.*, 14700 Main St., 60439. Tel: 708-647-6500; Fax: 708-647-6500.

MUNDELEIN. *Civitas Dei Foundation*, P.O. Box 665, 60060. Tel: 847-382-5853. Rev. George J. Dyer (Retired). The Journal is named Chicago Studies.

NORTHLAKE. *Italian Catholic Federation*, 46 N. Wolf Rd., 60164. Tel: 708-562-0500; Fax: 708-562-1824. Email: sjvchurch@aol.com. Web: www.icf.org. Rev. Charles V. Fanelli, Chap.

Scalabrini Village, 420-480 N. Wolf Rd., 60164. Tel: 708-562-0040; Fax: 708-562-5180.

OAK LAWN. **Pope John Paul II Eucharistic Adoration Association, Inc.*, P.O. Box 702, 60454. Tel: 773-582-9222. Web: www.pj2ea.org. Mary Ann Scott, Contact Person.

RIVER FOREST. **Dominican Volunteers USA*, 7200 W. Division St., 60305. Tel: 708-524-5984; 708-524-5985; Fax: 708-714-9002. Email: sgreen@dom.edu. Web: www.dvusa.org. Shannon D. Green, Exec. Dir. Dominican volunteers USA providedes full-time volunteer opportunities for lay people. Volunteers live and work with Dominican(Order of Preachers) ministries and communities across the United States, serving those who are in most need.

**Education and Intervention, Inc.*, 7777 W. Lake St., 60305-1734. Tel: 708-488-9770; Fax: 708-488-9774. Email: sister.close@2icap.org. Web: www.2icap.org. Sr. Letitia Close, Pres. & Exec. Dir.
Legal Title: *Education and Intervention, Inc.*, d.b.a. ICAP(Inter Congregational Addictions Program); National and International network for women religious recovering in 12 step programs; services of intervention, referral, follow-up and education to communities of women religious.

ROLLING MEADOWS. *Rainbows for All God's Children, Inc.*, 2100 Golf Rd., 60008. Tel: 800-266-3206; Fax: 847-952-1774 Email: info@rainbows.org. Web: www.rainbows.org. Mrs. Suzy Yehl Marta, Founder & Pres.

TECHNY. *Blessed Arnold Religious Charitable Trust*, 1985 Waukegan Rd., P.O. Box 6067, 60082-6067. Tel: 847-272-2700; Fax: 847-753-7464. Email: dgarbaciak@uscsvd.org. Web: www.divineword.org. Society of the Divine Word

DWTCRE Charitable Trust, 1901 Waukegan Rd., 60082. Tel: 847-272-2700; Fax: 847-753-7464. Email: tlc1670@aol.com. Web: www.divineword.org. Rev. Francis J. Kamp, S.V.D., Trustee.

WAUKEGAN. *Alexian Brothers The Harbor*, 826 W. North Ave., 60085. Tel: 847-782-8015; Fax: 847-782-0822. Email: information@theharborwaukegan.org. Web: www.theharborwaukegan.org. Mr. Merrill Kenna, CEO. Congregation of Alexian Brothers, Immaculate Conception Province, Operated by Alexian Brothers Bonaventure House, Inc.; Residences for persons with AIDS.

Lake Shore Catholic Academy, 510 Tenth St., 60085. Tel: 847-623-4070; Fax: 847-623-5169. Email: lakeshore@ameritech.net. Web: www.lsca.pvt.k12.il.us. Sr. Miriam Patrick Cummings, S.S.N.D., Admin.

Provena Saint Therese Medical Center, 2615 Washington St., 60085. Tel: 847-249-3900 Fax: 847-249-5897. Timothy Selz, Pres.; Sr. Jeanette Pierce, Dir. Pastoral Care. Chaplains 3 Bed Capacity 386; Patients Assisted Annually 155,000.

Provena Physical Medicine, 222 S. Greenleaf Ave., Gurnee, 60031. Tel: 847-599-0400; Fax: 847-599-1054.

Provena Work Power Center, 1005 Butterfield Rd., Vernon Hills, 60061. Tel: 847-816-9998; Fax: 847-816-4771. Bed Capacity 386; Patients Assisted Annually 150,000.

WILMETTE. *Loyola Recreational Facility Corp.*, 1100 North Laramie, 60091. Tel: 847-256-1100; Fax: 847-920-2421. Web: goramblers.org. Rev. Theodore G. Munz, S.J.

Musica Pacis, Office of the Treasurer, P.O. Box 969, 60091-0969. Tel: 708-624-2559. Email: musicapacis@attglobal.net. Revs. Willard F. Jabusch, Pres. (Retired); Robert H. Festle, Sec. (Retired); Alec J. Wolff, Treas.

[Y] CLOSED INSTITUTIONS

CHICAGO. *Archdiocese of Chicago's Joseph Cardinal Bernardin Archives and Records Center*, 711 W. Monroe St., 60661. Tel: 312-831-0711; Fax: 312-831-0610. Email: info@chgocatholicarchives.org. Web: www.archdiocese-chgo.org/archives/home.htm. The following parish, school or institution records may be found at the above address unless otherwise indicated. Notations to sacramental records of closed parishes held by the Archives and Records Center should be directed to the Archives and Records Center and should specify the name of the parish. The location of records periodically changes. Inquiries for records of parishes, schools or institutions not on this list should be directed to the above address.

Academy of St. Benedict the African (May St.)
Academy of the Sacred Heart, 6250 N. Sheridan Rd., 60660. Tel: 773-262-4446. Sacred Heart Schools
Academy of Our Lady
St. Adalbert School and Commercial High School, St. Adalbert Parish, 1650 W. 17th St., 60608. Tel: 312-226-0340.
St. Adrian School
St. Agatha School
Blessed Agnes Commercial High School and School, St. Agnes of Bohemia School, 2643 S. Central Park, 60623. Tel: 773-522-0143.
Blessed Agnes of Bohemia Church & School, St. Agnes of Bohemia, 2643 S. Central Park, 60623. Tel: 773-522-0143.
St. Agnes (39th St.) (Pershing Rd.)
St. Agnes School (39th St.)
St. Agnes High School (Unknown)
Alexine Learning Center School
All Saints (State St.)
All Saints School (State St.)
All Saints (Wallace St.), at All Saints/St. Anthony, 518 W. 28th Pl., 60616. Tel: 312-842-2744; Fax: 312-842-2791.
All Saints School (Wallace St.)
All Saints/St. Anthony School (Wallace)
St. Aloysius School
St. Aloysius Commercial High School (Boys), St. Aloysius Parish. (Boys)
St. Aloysius High School (Boys) (Unknown)
St. Alphonsus School (Lemont), St. Alphonsus/St. Patrick, 205 Cass St., Lemont, 60439. Tel: 630-257-2380; Fax: 630-257-4648.
St. Alphonsus Commercial High School (Chicago)
St. Alphonsus Commercial High School (Lemont) (Unknown)
Alvernia Conservatory of Music (Unknown)
Alvernia High School
St. Ambrose School (47th St.)
St. Ambrose See St. Louis de France (117th St.)
St. Andrew High School
St. Andrew Misson , (Wadsworth), St. Patrick Parish, 15000 Wadsworth Rd., Wadsworth, 60083. Tel: 847-244-4161; Fax: 847-336-0630.
Angel Guardian Croatian Catholic Mission 6346 N. Ridge Ave., 60660. Tel: 773-262-0535; Fax: 773-262-4603. at Blessed Alojzije Cardinal Stetinac Mission
Angel Guardian Orphanage
St. Ann (Chicago Heights)
St. Ann School (Chicago Heights)
St. Ann High School (Leavitt St.), St. Ann, 2211 W. 18th Pl., 60608. Tel: 312-829-4153; Fax: 312-829-4155.
St. Ann Hospital, St. Elizabeth Hospital, 1431 N. Claremont Ave., 60622. Tel: 773-278-2000.
St. Anne (Garfield Blvd.)
St. Anne School (Garfield Blvd.)
St. Anne School (Hazel Crest) Archives
St. Anne (Waukegan), Immaculate Conception, 508 Grand Ave., Waukegan, 60085. Tel: 847-336-3684; Fax: 847-336-9040.
St. Anne Mission Chapel , (Richton), St. Liborius, 71 W. 35th St., Steger, 60475. Tel: 708-754-1363.
Annunciation (Wabansia)
Annunciation School (Wabansia)
St. Anselm School
St. Anthony of Padua (24th Pl.), All Saints-St. Anthony, 518 W. 28th Pl., 60616. Tel: 312-842-2744; Fax: 312-842-2791. (Parish)
St. Anthony of Padua School (24th Pl.)
St. Anthony School (Cicero) Archives
St. Anthony High School & Commercial High School (24th Pl.)
St. Anthony School (Prairie)
Aquinas Catholic High School

Aquinas Dominican High School
Aquinas High School
Ascension (Harvey), at Ascension-St. Susanna, 15234 Myrtle Ave., Harvey, 60426-3194. Tel: 708-333-0931; Fax: 708-333-3281.
Ascension School (Harvey)
Ascension-St. Susanna School (Harvey)
Ascension of Our Lord (Evanston)
Ascension of Our Lord School (Evanston)
Assumption School (24th St.)
Assumption (Marshfield Ave.)
Assumption School (Marshfield Ave.)
Assumption BVM (123rd St.)
Assumption BVM School (123rd St.)
Assumption School (Illinois St.) (Unknown)
Assumption / St. Catherine of Genoa School and Parish
St. Attracta (Cicero)
St. Attracta School (Cicero)
St. Attracta-St. Valentine Church (Cicero)
St. Augustine (S. Laflin)
St. Augustine School & High School
St. Barbara High School
St. Bartholomew, Holy Family, 501 S. Utica, Waukegan, 60079-0440. Tel: 847-623-2655. (Waukegan)
St. Bartholomew School (Waukegan)
St. Basil, St. Basil/Visitation 5443 S. Honore, 60609.
St. Basil School
Bellarmine School of Theology-Loyola University of Chicago, Dean of Students of the Graduate School, 820 N. Michigan Ave., 60611.
St. Benedict High School (Co-ed) (Unknown)
St. Bernard (65th St.)
St. Bernard School
Bishop Quarter Boarding School for Motherless Boys

Bishop Quarter Junior Military School aka Bishop Quarter School for Little Boys
St. Blase School, St. Joseph School, 5641 S. 73rd St., Summit, 60501. Tel: 708-458-2927; Fax: 708-458-7635. (Argo)
Blessed Agnes Commercial High School St. Agnes of Bohemia School
Blessed Sacrament School
Blessed Sacrament / Our Lady of Lourdes School
SS. Benedict and Scholastica Academy St. Scholastica High School
St. Bonaventure School (Diversey)
St. Boniface (N. Noble)
St. Boniface School (N. Noble)
St. Boniface High School (Unknown)
St. Brendan (Racine)
St. Brendan School (Racine)
St. Bridget
St. Bridget School & High School
Bridgeport Industrial School for Boys See Illinois Industrial School for Boys
Bridgeport Catholic Academy Middle School
Bridgeport Catholic Academy North Campus
Bridgeport Catholic Academy South Campus open, Pre-2000
St. Bronislava School
Brother Candidates High School (Techny), Divine Word Missionaries, Box 107, East Troy, WI 53120. Tel: 414-642-3300.
Cabrini Green Alternate High School Archives
Cabrini Hospital Sacramental records - St. Anthony Hospital (Chicago); Medical records - St. Anthony Hospital
St. Callistus Church at Norte Dame Parish, 1335 W. Harrison, 60607. Tel: 312-243-7400; Fax: 312-243-7614.
St. Callistus School
Cardinal Stritch High School
Carmel High School, Carmel High School, One Carmel Pkwy., Mundelein, 60060-2499. Tel: 847-566-3000. (Boys and Girls).
St. Carthage (73rd St.)
St. Carthage School
St. Casimir Academy, Maria High School, 6727 S. California Ave., 60629-1887. Tel: 773-925-8686.
St. Casimir (Chicago Heights)
St. Casimir School (Chicago Heights)
St. Casimir (Whipple St.)
St. Casimir School (Whipple St.)
St. Casimir High School, Our Lady of Tepeyac High School, 2228 S. Whipple St., 60623. Tel: 773-522-0023; Fax: 773-522-0508. (Whipple St.)
St. Catherine Academy (See Siena High School)
St. Catherine High School (See Siena High School)
Cathedral College
Cathedral High School
Chrysalis Program
Corpus Christi School
St. Catherine of Genoa
St. Catherine of Genoa School
St. Catherine of Siena (Oak Park)
School Records:
St. Catherine / St. Lucy School, 27 W. Washington Blvd., Oak Park, 60302. Tel: 708-386-5286.
Sacramental Records:
St. Catherine/St. Lucy Parish: 38 N. Austin Blvd., Oak Park, 60302. Tel: 708-386-8077; Fax: 708-386-5190.
St. Cecelia (Wells St.)
St. Cecelia School (Wells St.)
St. Charles Borromeo (Hoyne Ave.)
St. Charles Borromeo School (Hoyne Ave.)
St. Charles Borromeo School (Melrose Park)
St. Charles Lwanga (W. Garfield)
St. Charles Lwanga School (W. Garfield)
Christ the Redeemer Church Archives
St. Clara (Woodlawn Ave.)
St. Clara School (Woodlawn)
St. Clara-St. Cyril (S. Woodlawn)
St. Clara-St. Cyril School
St. Clare of Montefalco School
St. Clement High School
St. Columba School (134th St.)
St. Columbkille (Paulina)
St. Columbkille School & Commercial High School
St. Columbkille High School, Mother Guerin High School, 8001 Belmont Ave., River Grove, 60171. Tel: 708-453-6233. (Girls)
Columbus Hospital Sacramental Records - Archives, Medical Records - St. Anthony Hospital
Columbus Hospital School of Nursing
St. Constance High School
Convent of the Sacred Heart, Sacred Heart Schools, 6250 N. Sheridan Rd., 60660. Tel: 773-262-4446. (Chicago)
Convent of the Sacred Heart (Lake Forest), Woodlands Academy of the Sacred Heart, 760 E. Westleigh Rd., Lake Forest, 60045-3298. Tel: 847-234-4300.
Corpus Christi High School, Hales Franciscan High School, 4930 S. Cottage Grove, 60615. Tel: 773-285-8400.
Cuneo Hospital Medical Records - St. Anthony Hospital; Sacramental-Archives
St. Cyril (Dante Ave.)
St. Cyril College, Mt. Carmel High School.
St. Cyril School
Ss. Cyril & Methodius Church & School (Hermitage Ave.)
Ss. Cyril & Methodius Church & School (Walton St.)
St. David School
St. David Church, All Saints-St. Anthony, 518 W. 28th Pl., 60616. Tel: 312-842-2744; Fax: 312-842-2791.
De Lourdes College (Des Plaines), Holy Family College, Registrar's Office, Grant Ave. & Frankford Ave., Philadelphia, PA 19114. Tel: 215-637-4851.
St. Denis School
DePaul Academy, DePaul University, Registrar's Office, 243 S. Wabash, 60604. Tel: 312-341-8610.
DePaul High School (Unknown)
DePaul University Loop High School (Unknown)
St. Dionysius (Cicero)
St. Dionysius School (Cicero)
St. Dominic (Locust)
St. Dominic School & High School
St. Donatus School (Blue Island)
St. Elizabeth High School (41st St.)
St. Emeric Church (Washtenaw Ave.), St. Stephen King of Hungary, 2015 W. Augusta Blvd., 60622-4947. Tel: 773-486-1896; Fax: 773-486-1902.
St. Emeric School (County Club Hills)
Englewood Catholic Academy (Honore St.)
Englewood Catholic Academy (Laflin St.)
Englewood Catholic Academy (May St.)
Englewood Catholic Academy (Princeton St.)
Ephpheta School for the Deaf
St. Eulalia School (Open pre-1989)
Felician College
St. Felicitas High School (Unknown)
St. Fidelis School (N. Washtenaw)
St. Finbarr Church (14th St.)
St. Finbarr High School and School (Unknown)
Five Holy Martyrs School
St. Florian Commerical High School (Unknown)
St. Florian Mission, (52nd & Archer), St. Camillus, 5426 S. Lockwood Ave., 60638. Tel: 773-767-8183.
Ford City Catholic Center
Fornier Institute, DePaul University, Registrar's Office, 243 S. Wabash, 60604. Tel: 312-341-8610.
Fornier Institute Viatorian Preparatory (Lemont), Viatorian Archives, Arlington Heights.
St. Frances Xavier Cabrini (Lexinton St.)
St. Frances Xavier Cabrini School (Lexinton St.)
St. Frances Xavier Commercial High School (Unknown)
St. Francis de Paula
St. Frances de Paula School (S. Ellis)
St. Francis de Sales School
St. Francis of Assisi Church (Kostner Ave.), St. Francis of Assisi/Our Lady of the Angels, 3808 W. Iowa St., 60651. Tel: 773-235-3132; Fax: 773-486-7726.
St. Francis of Assisi School (Kostner Ave.)
St. Francis of Assisi School (Roosevelt Ave.)
St. Francis Xavier (Nelson), Resurrection, 2840 W. Nelson, 60618-7012. Tel: 773-478-9705; Fax: 773-478-1387.
St. Francis Xavier School (Nelson)
St. Gabriel Commercial High School
Garfield Alternative High School Archives
St. Gelasius Parish and School
St. George (Wentworth Ave.)
St. George School & Commercial High School (Lituanica Ave.)
St. George School (Wentworth Ave.)
St. George (Lituanica)
St. George School (Ewing St.)
St. George High School (Evanston)
St. Gerard Majella School (Markham)
St. Gertrude School (Chicago)
St. Gertrude School (Franklin Park)
Good Counsel High School Archives
Good Shepherd Chapel, (Illinois Technical School for Colored Girls).
St. Gregory the Great School
Hardey Preparatory, Sacred Heart Schools, 6250 N. Sheridan Rd., 60660. Tel: 773-262-4446.
Heart of Mary High School
St. Hedwig Mission St. John Berchmans, 2517 W. Logan Blvd., 60647. Tel: 773-486-4300; Fax: 773-252-5346. (Washtenaw Ave.)
St. Hedwig Orphanage (Niles)
St. Hedwig School
St. Henry School
St. Henry Commercial High School Archives
Holy Child High School (Waukegan), St. Anastasia School, 629 Glen Flora, Waukegan, 60685. Tel: 847-623-8320; Fax: 847-623-4882.
Holy Cross (65th St.)
Holy Cross School (65th St.)
Holy Cross School (Wood St.)
Holy Cross, Holy Cross/Immaculate Heart of Mary, 4541 S. Wood St., 60609. Tel: 773-376-3900; Fax: 773-376-8929. (46th St.)
Holy Family (North Chicago)
Holy Family School (North Chicago)
Holy Family School (May St.)
Holy Family Academy (Division St.)
Holy Family Extension High School (Des Plaines), Sisters of Holy Family of Nazareth, Provincial Archives, 310 N. River Rd., Des Plaines, 60016. Tel: 847-298-6760.
Holy Family Orphanage (Unknown)
Holy Ghost Church & School
Holy Ghost Academy, Convent of the Holy Spirit (Techny). (Techny)
Holy Guardian Angel (Arthington/Cabrini)
Holy Guardian Angel School
Holy Innocents School
Holy Name Cathedral School
Holy Name of Mary School
Holy Rosary Slovak (108th St.)
Holy Rosary Slovak School (108th St.)
Holy Rosary School (113th St.)
Holy Rosary (North Chicago)
Holy Rosary School (North Chicago)
Holy Rosary School (Western Ave.)
Holy Trinity Church, Holy Trinity Polish Mission, 1118 N. Noble St., 60622-4015. Tel: 773-489-4140; Fax: 773-489-5918.
Holy Trinity School (Noble St.)
Holy Trinity (Wolcott)
Holy Trinity School (Wolcott)
Holy Trinity School (Throop)
Holy Trinity School (Taylor, Deaf Children)
House of the Good Shepherd
St. Hugh (Lyons)
St. Hyacinth Mission, (Spaulding), St. Hyacinth Parish, 3636 N. Wolfram, 60618. Tel: 773-342-3636; Fax: 773-342-3638.
St. Ignatius College, St. Ignatius College Prep., 1073 W. Roosevelt Rd., 60608. Tel: 312-421-5900.
St. Ignatius School
Illinois Industrial School for Boys (Unknown)
Illinois Technical School for Colored Girls
Immaculata High School
Immaculate Conception School (Exchange Ave.)
Immaculate Conception Commercial High School (Aberdeen St.)
Immaculate Conception-St. Bridget School
Immaculate Conception (Aberdeen St.)
Immaculate Conception School (Aberdeen St.)
Immaculate Conception School (44th St.)
Immaculate Conception School (Highland Park)
Immaculate Conception School (North Park Ave.)
Immaculate Conception (Highland Park); (Unknown)
Immaculate Conception Parish (Buffalo Grove) St. Mary Parish (Buffalo Grove)
Immaculate Heart of Mary Vicariate (Ashland Ave.), Holy Cross-Immaculate Heart of Mary Parish, 4541 S. Wood St., 60609. Tel: 773-376-3900; Fax: 773-376-8929.
St. Irenaeus School (Park Forest)

St. Isaac Jogues School (Niles)

St. Isidore the Farmer School (Blue Island)

St. Ita School

St. James School (Maywood)

St. James (Mundelein), St. Mary, 22333 W. Erhart Rd., Mundelein, 60060. Tel: 847-223-0010; Fax: 847-223-5960.

St. James Commercial (Maywood); (Unknown)

St. James School (Fullerton and Menard)

St. James School (Sauk Village)

St. James High School (Wabash)

St. Jarlath (Jackson)

St. Jarlath School (Jackson)

St. Jean Baptiste Church (33rd Pl.)

St. Jerome School

Jesuit School of Theology, 820 N. Michigan Ave,, 60611. Loyola University of Chicago, Office of the Dean of Graduate School,

Jesus, Our Brother School

St. Joachim School

St. John Bosco School

Old St. John (18th St.)

Old St. John School, Christian Brothers University, 2455 Avery Ave., Memphis, TN 38112.

St. John Cantius School

St. John Chrysostom (Bellwood)

St. John Chrysostom School (Bellwood)

St. John Nepmucene Church & School

St. John of God Church & School (S. Throop)

St. John the Baptist (50th Pl.)

St. John the Baptist Church (Burley Ave.)

St. John the Baptist School (50th Pl.)

St. John the Baptist School (Harvey)

St. Josaphat School (Open pre 1961)

St. Josaphat Parish Orphanage (Unknown)

St. Joseph Bohemian Orphanage, Maryville Academy, 1150 N. River Rd., Des Plaines, 60016. Tel: 708-824-6126; Fax: 847-824-7277. (Lisle)

St. Joseph Commercial Business College (Waukegan)

St. Joseph the Worker School

St. Joseph High School (Hermitage)

St. Joseph's Institute

St. Joseph (17th Pl.)

St. Joseph School (17th Pl.)

St. Joseph Parish and School (38th Pl.) (See St. Joseph and St. Anne Parish)

St. Joseph School (Orleans)

St. Joseph School (Hermitage)

St. Joseph (Chicago Heights)

St. Joseph School (Chicago Hts.)

St. Joseph (Saginaw St.)

St. Joseph School (Saginaw St.)

St. Joseph's Orphan Asylum (Unknown)

St. Joseph Orphanage for Boys (destroyed by fire)

St. Joseph Parish Orphanage (Unknown)

St. Joseph Provident Orphanage (Unknown)

St. Joseph Military Academy (See St. Joseph's Institute)

St. Joseph Academy (LaGrange Park) (See St. Joseph's Institute)

St. Joseph Commercial High School (Waukegan); (Unknown)

St. Joseph & SS. Joseph & Bartholomew (Waukegan), Holy Family, 501 S. Utica, Waukegan, 60079-0440. Tel: 847-623-2655.

St. Joseph School (Waukegan)

St. Joseph & St. Anne Church, Our Lady of Fatima, 2751 W. 38th Pl., 60632-1686. Tel: 773-927-2421; Fax: 773-247-1737.

St. Joseph & St. Anne Commercial High School and School (Unknown)

St. Joseph Mission, (13th St.)

St. Joseph Mission School, (13th St.)

St. Joseph Servite Seminary (Elgin-St. Charles), Provincial Archives, Servite Provincial Center, 3121 W. Jackson Blvd., 60612. Tel: 773-533-0360.

St. Joseph's Home for the Friendless, St. Joseph's Corondelet Child Center, 739 E. 35th St., 60616. Tel: 773-624-7443.

St. Joseph Technical High School (Techny), Divine Word Missionaries, East Troy, WI.

St. Josaphat Commercial High School

Josephinum Academy, Josephinum High School.

St. Justin Martyr (71st St.)

St. Justin Martyr School

St. Kevin School, 10509 S. Torrence, 60617. Tel: 773-721-2563. St. Kevin Parish,

St. Kilian School

St. Lambert School (Skokie); Archives

St. Laurence School and Parish

St. Leo High School, Mother Guerin Convent, 8001 Belmont Ave., River Grove, 60171. Tel: 708-453-6233.

St. Leo the Great School and Parish

St. Leonard Commercial High School (Berwyn), St. Leonard School, 3322 S. Clarence, Berwyn, 60402. Tel: 708-749-1989; Fax: 708-749-7981.

Lewis Memorial Maternity Hospital

Little Flower School see St. Therese of the Infant Jesus School

Little Flower High School

Longwood Academy see Academy of Our Lady

Loretto Academy (Woodlawn)

Loretto Academy (Englewood)

Loretto Adult Center (Englewood), Kennedy King College, 6800 S. Wentworth, 60621.

Loretto Extension Service (Unknown)

St. Louis de France (117th St.)

St. Louis de France School (117th St.)

St. Louis (Polk St.) (School Unknown)

St. Louis Academy (117th Ave.), St. Jude the Apostle Convent, 890 E. 154th St., South Holland, 60473. Tel: 708-333-7595.

Loretto High School (Englewood)

Loyola Academy, 1100 N. Laramie Ave., Wilmette, 60091. Tel: 847-256-1100. (Chicago) at Loyola Academy (Wilmette)

St. Lucy, St. Catherine-St. Lucy, 38 N. Austin Blvd., Oak Park, 60302. Tel: 708-386-8077; Fax: 708-386-5190. Sacramental Records:

St. Lucy School Records

St. Ludmilla

St. Ludmilla School

St. Louise Marillac High School

Madonna High School

St. Malachy High School, St. Malachy School, 2252 W. Washington, 60612. Tel: 312-733-2252; Fax: 312-733-5703.

Mallinckroat High School

Mallinckroat College (Wilmette)

St. Margaret's Home & Hospital (Unknown)

Marian School for Deaf (Unknown)

Maria Immaculata Academy (Wilmette)

St. Mark the Evangelist School

Marquette Institute (Clark St.)

St. Martha School (Morton Grove)

St. Martin (Princeton St.)

St. Martin de Porres Academy

St. Martin School & Commerical High School (Princeton

St. Mary School (Des Plaines)

St. Mary (Riverside)

St. Mary School (Evanston)

St. Mary (Lemont), St Patrick, 200 Illinois St., Lemont, 60439. Tel: 708-257-6134; Fax: 630-257-0401.

St. Mary (Waukegan), Immaculate Conception, 508 Grand Ave., Waukegan, 60085. Tel: 847-336-3684; Fax: 847-336-9040.

St. Mary Center for Learning (Grenshaw); Archives

St. Mary High School (Grenshaw)

St. Mary Alternative High School (Grenshaw) (to 1976); Archives

St. Mary (Seeley) (Byzantine Rite)

St. Mary's Mission, (90th St.) (Byzantine Rite)

Annunciation Byzantine, 14610 Will-Cook Rd., Lockport, 60441-9212. Tel: 708-645-0214.

St. Mary Magdalen School

St. Mary of the Assumption School (137th St.)

St. Mary of the Lake Mission, (Ingleside), St. Bede, 36455 N. Wilson Rd., Ingleside, 60041-9609. Tel: 847-587-2251; Fax: 847-973-1765.

St. Mary of Mt. Carmel (Hermitage St.)

St. Mary of Mt. Carmel School (Hermitage)

St. Mary of Nazareth School (Harvey)

St. Mary of Perpetual Help School

St. Mary of Perpetual Help High School

St. Mary of the Woods (Highland Park), Immaculate Conception, 700 W. Deerfield Rd., Highland Park, 60035. Tel: 847-433-0130; Fax: 847-433-0669.

St. Mary Mission Seminary (Techny), Catholic Theological Union, 5401 S. Cornell, 60615-5698. Tel: 773-324-8000.

St. Mary Orphanage for Girls (destroyed in fire)

Mary, Queen of Heaven School (Cicero)

St. Mary Training School, Maryville Academy, 1150 N. River Rd., Des Plaines, 60016. Tel: 847-824-6126; Fax: 847-824-7277.

St. Mary School of Nursing (Des Plaines), Holy Family College, Registrar's Office, Grant Ave. & Frankford Ave., Philadelphia, PA 19114. Tel: 215-637-4851.

Marywood High School (Evanston), Mother Guerin High School, 8001 Belmont Ave., River Grove, 60171. Tel: 773-625-3278; 708-453-6233.

Mater Dolorosa Seminary (Hillside), 3121 W. Jackson Blvd., 60612. See Servite Seminary, Servite Provincial Archives.

St. Matthew (Walnut St.)

St. Matthew Commercial High School (Unknown)

St. Matthew School (Walnut St.)

St. Matthias School Archives

St. Maurice School

St. Mel & St. Mel-Holy Ghost

St. Mel & St. Mel-Holy Ghost School

St. Mel High School (up to 1969),

Mendel High School

Mercy High School

Mercy Mission High School

St. Michael School (Cleveland & Hudson)

St. Michael Central High School (Cleveland & Hudson)

St. Michael School (South Shore Dr.); Archives

St. Michael (Wabansia St.)

St. Michael School (Wabansia St.)

St. Michael School (24th Pl.)

St. Michael the Archangel School

St. Michael Commercial High School (South Shore Dr.)

Misericordia Hospital Sacramental Records in registers of St. Agnes, 39th St.

Client Records & Adoption Placements, Catholic Charities, 126 N. Des Plaines, 60606. Tel: 312-876-2288; 312-236-5172.

Mission of the Holy Ghost, (Northbrook), St. Norbert, 1809 Walters Ave., Northbrook, 60062. Tel: 847-272-7090; Fax: 847-272-7771.

St. Monica (36th St.) (School Unknown); Parish-Archives

Monastery of Mt. St. Phillip Servite Novitiate, Provincial Archives, Servite Provincial Center, 3121 W. Jackson Blvd., 60612. Tel: 773-533-0360. (Granville, WI),

Montay College

Mother of God (Waukegan)

Mother of God School & High School (Waukegan)

Mother of Sorrows Grade and High School (Blue Island)

Mount Carmel School (Chicago Heights) (served St. Rocco)

Mundelein College,, Office of Registration & Records, 820 N. Michigan Ave., Room 504, 60611. Tel: 312-915-7221. Loyola University,

Mundelein High School

Municipal Tuberculosis Sanitarium (Sacred Heart Chapel).

Nativity of Our Lord School & Commercial High School

Nazareth Academy (LaGrange) Renamed Our Lady of Bethlehem Academy

St. Nicholas School (Evanston)

St. Nicholas (State St.)

St. Nicholas School (State St.)

Niles College at St. Joseph Seminary College

Notre Dame de Chicago School

Our Lady of Bethlehem Academy

Our Lady of Fatima Mission, (Christina Ave.), St. Hyacinth Parish, 3636 N. Wolfram, 60618. Tel: 773-342-3636; Fax: 773-342-3638.

Our Lady of Fatima School (39th/Pershing Rd.)

Our Lady of the Garden, St. Mary of the Assumption, 310 E. 137th St., 60627-1896. Tel: 773-568-1611; Fax: 773-568-6268.

Our Lady of Good Counsel (Western Ave.)

Our Lady of Good Counsel School (Western Ave.)

Our Lady of Good Counsel School (Hermitage Ave.)

Our Lady of Guadalupe Chapel Holy Cross-Immaculate Heart of Mary, 4541 S. Wood St., 60609. Tel: 773-376-3900; Fax: 773-376-8929.

Our Lady Help of Christians School

Our Lady of Hope School (Des Plaines)

Our Lady of Hungary (93rd St.)

Our Lady of Hungary School (93rd St.)

Our Lady of Lourdes Commercial High School (Keeler St.)

Our Lady of Lourdes School (Keeler St.)

Our Lady of Lourdes High School (Ashland Ave.); (Unknown)

Our Lady of Mercy School Archives

Our Lady of Mt. Carmel School (Melrose Park)

Our Lady of Peace School

Our Lady of Perpetual Help Vicariate (13th St.)

Our Lady of Perpetual Help Vicariate School (13th St.)

Our Lady of Providence Academy (Records destroyed in flood)

Our Lady of Solace (Sangamon)

Our Lady of Solace School (Sangamon)

Our Lady of Sorrows School

Our Lady of Sorrows Seminary, Servite Provincial Archives, 3121 W. Jackson, 60612. Tel: 773-638-0159; Fax: 773-638-3036.

Our Lady of the Angels, St. Francis of Assisi/Our Lady of the Angels, 3808 W. Iowa St., 60651. Tel: 773-235-3132; Fax: 773-486-7726.

Our Lady of Angels School

Our Lady of the Cross Mission Chapel St. Margaret Mary, 2324 W. Chase, 60645. Tel: 773-764-0615; Fax: 773-764-0941.

Our Lady of Pompeii School

Our Lady of Pompeii Church, Our Lady of Pompeii Shrine, 1224 W. Lexington, 60607. Tel: 312-421-3757; Fax: 312-421-3756.

Our Lady of Vilna (23rd St.)

Our Lady of Vilna School (23rd St.), St. Paul/Our Lady of Vilna School, 2114 W. 22nd Pl., 60608. Tel: 773-847-6078; Fax: 773-847-2118.

St. Pancratius School

St. Patrick Academy (Chicago) (Girls)

St. Patrick High School (Belmont Ave.)

St. Patrick School (Adams St.) (pre 1967)
St. Patrick School (Lemont), St. Alphonsus-St. Patrick School, 205 Cass St., Lemont, 60439. Tel: 630-257-2380.
St. Patrick (Commercial Ave.)
St. Patrick School (Commercial Ave.); (Unknown)
St. Patrick Academy (Boys); at St. Patrick High School (Belmont Ave.), McAuley High School, 3737 W. 99th St., 60642. Tel: 773-881-6522.
St. Patrick High School (Adams St.); at St. Patrick High School (Belmont Ave.)
St. Patrick High School (Adams St.) (Girls)
St. Paul School (Chicago Heights)
St. Paul School (22nd St.), St. Paul/Our Lady of Vilna School (22nd St.), 2114 W. 22nd Pl., 60608. Tel: 773-847-6078; Fax: 773-847-2118.
St. Paul High School (Midway)
St. Paul (12th St.) (Records destroyed in 1871 fire)
St. Peter School (Volo), St. Peter, 27551 W. Hwy. 120, Round Lake, 60073. Tel: 815-385-5496; Fax: 631-514-4647.
St. Peter School (Madison) (Unknown)
St. Peter Canisius School
SS. Peter and Paul (Exchange St.)
SS. Peter and Paul School (Exchange St.)
St. Peter & Paul School (Halsted St.)
Ss. Peter & Paul School (Paulina St.)
SS. Peter & Paul (Libertyville), St. Joseph, 121 E. Maple, Libertyville, 60048. Tel: 847-362-2073; Fax: 847-362-6821.
SS. Peter & Paul High School (Exchange Ave.), St. Francis de Sales High School, 10155 S. Ewing, 60617. Tel: 773-731-7272.
St. Peter & Paul Church (Central Park Ave.), St. Nicholas (Byzantine Rite), 8103 Columbia Ave., Munster, IN 46321-1802. Tel: 219-838-9380.
St. Philip Benizi (Maypole St.) (later named St. Mel)
St. Philip Benizi (Oak St.)
St. Philip Benizi School (Oak St.)
St. Philip Evening School (Unknown)
St. Philip Basilica High School
St. Philip the Apostle School (Northfield); Archives
St. Philomena Commercial High School, St. Philomena School, 4131 W. Cortland, 60639. Tel: 773-235-0120; Fax: 773-235-0646.
St. Pius V Commercial High School, St. Pius V School, 1919 S. Ashland, 60608. Tel: 312-226-1590; Fax: 312-226-7265.
St. Pius X School (Stickney)
Precious Blood School
Presentation School
Presentation-Precious Blood Unit School, 2401 W. Congress, 60612. Tel: 773-421-6157. Our Lady of the West Side Catholic, Precious Blood Campus,
St. Procopius School (open) (pre 1983)
St. Procopius High School
Providence Academy & High School, Mother Guerin High School, 8001 Belmont Ave., River Grove, 60171. Tel: 312-625-3278.
Providence of God School and Commercial High School
Providence-St. Mel High School, 119 S. Central Park Blvd., 60624. Tel: 773-722-4600.
Quigley Preparatory Seminary North
Quigley Preparatory Seminary South Tel: 321-787-9343.
Quigley Preparatory Seminary
St. Raphael (60th St.)
St. Raphael School (60th St.)
Resurrection (Jackson Blvd.) (Church and School)
St. Rita College, St. Rita High School, 7740 S. Western Ave., 60620. Tel: 773-925-6600.
St. Rita of Cascia School
St. Rocco (Chicago Heights) (For school records, see Mt. Carmel School.)
St. Roman School
St. Rosalie School (Harwood Heights)
Rosary House High School (River Forest), 7574 W. Division St., River Forest, 60305. Tel: 708-771-8383. Trinity High School
Rosary College, Dominican University, 7900 W. Division St., River Forest, 60305. Tel: 708-366-2490.
St. Rose of Lima (W. 48th St.)
St. Rose of Lima School
Sacred Heart (19th St.)
Sacred Heart School & High School (19th St.)
Sacred Heart (May St.)
Sacred Heart School & High School (May St.)
Sacred Heart (Oakley Blvd.)
Sacred Heart School (Oakley Blvd.)
Sacred Heart (Church St.), Sacred Heart Mission, 11652 S. Church St., 60643. Tel: 773-233-3955.
Sacred Heart of Jesus (46th St.)
Sacred Heart of Jesus School (46th St.)
Sacred Heart of Jesus High School (46th St.)
Sacred Heart of Mary High School (Arlington Heights), St. Viator High School, 1213 E. Oakton St., Arlington Heights, 60004. Tel: 847-392-4050.
Sacred Heart Seminary (Melrose Park) (Stone Park), Scalabrini Mission Center, 3800 W. Division St., Stone Park, 60165. Tel: 708-345-8270.
St. Salomea (S. Indiana)
St. Salomea School (S. Indiana)
San Callisto Mission
San Marcello Mission, (Evergreen), Immaculate Conception, 1415 N. North Park, 60610. Tel: 312-944-1230; Fax: 312-944-0673.
Santa Lucia Mission *Sacramental Records*, Santa Lucia-Santa Maria Incoranata, 3022 S. Wells, 60616. Tel: 312-842-6115; Fax: 312-842-0103. Santa Lucia School, 3017 S. Wells, 60616. Tel: 312-326-1839; Fax: 312-842-0103. (School Records)
Santa Maria Incoranata, Santa Lucia-Santa Maria Incoranata, 3022 S. Wells, 60616. Tel: 312-842-6115; Fax: 312-842-0103. Sacramental Records: Santa Lucia School, 3017 S. Wells, 60616. Tel: 312-326-1839; Fax: 312-842-0103. (School Records)
Santa Teresita Vicariate (Palatine), Mision Juan Diego, 35 W. Wood St., Palatine, 60067. Tel: 847-358-6337; Fax: 847-202-4603.
St. Sebastian (W. Wellington)
St. Sebastian School & High School
Servite Seminary (Hillside), Provincial Archives, Servite Provincial Center, 3121 W. Jackson Blvd., 60612. Tel: 773-533-0360.
Seven Holy Founders School (Calumet Park)
Sheil Institute
Siena High School, McAuley High School, 3737 W. 99th St., 60642. Tel: 773-881-6522.
St. Simeon School (Bellwood)
St. Stanislaus College, Gordon Technical High School, 3633 N. California, 60618. Tel: 773-539-3600.
St. Stanislaus Kostka High School, St. Stanislaus Kostka Elementary, 1255 N. Noble, 60622. Tel: 773-278-4560; Fax: 773-278-2471.
St. Stephen School (22nd Pl.)
St. Stephen Protomartyr School (Des Plaines)
St. Stephen Church (22nd Pl.), St. Stephen Shrine, 2242 S. Wolcott Ave., 60608. Tel: 773-376-4334.
Old St. Stephen (Ohio St.)
Old St. Stephen School (Ohio St.)
St. Susanna (Harvey), Ascension-St. Susanna, 15234 Myrtle, Harvey, 60426-3194. Tel: 708-333-0931.
St. Susanna School (Harvey)
St. Sylvester Commercial
St. Thaddeus School Archives
St. Theodore (S. Paulina)
St. Theodore School
St. Teresa of Avila School
St. Therese of the Infant Jesus Church (Wood St.)
St. Therese of the Infant Jesus School (See Little Flower School)
St. Thomas Aquinas (Washington Blvd.) (Church and School)
St. Thomas Mission, (River Forest), St. Luke, 528 Lathrop, River Forest, 60305. Tel: 708-771-8250; Fax: 708-771-8809.
St. Thomas the Apostle High School, St. Thomas the Apostle School, 5467 S. Woodlawn, 60615. Tel: 773-667-1142; Fax: 773-753-7434.
St. Timothy School
Transfiguration of Our Lord School
Unity Catholic High School
Unity High School
St. Valentine (Cicero)
St. Valentine School (Cicero)
St. Veronica, Resurrection, 2840 W. Nelson, 60618. Tel: 773-478-9705.
St. Veronica School (Whipple St.)
St. Victor High School (Addison) (Unknown)
St. Victor High School (Calumet City) (Unknown)
Villa Nazareth High School (Des Plaines)
St. Vincent de Paul School
St. Vincent de Paul Academy (Girls) (Depaul High School & St. Vincent Academy) (Location of records, Unknown)
St. Vincent de Paul High School Seminary (Lemont), Perryville, MO 63775. Tel: 314-547-6533. St. Mary Seminary
St. Vincent Orphanage Client & School Records: Catholic Charities, Division of Services for Children and Youth, 126 N. Desplaines, Chicago, IL 60606 Tel: 312-876-2288; 236-5172 Ext. 330; Sacramental Records: Holy Name Cathedral, 730 N. Wabash, Chicago, IL 60611 Tel: 312-787-8040 Fax: 312-787-9113
St. Vincent Ferrer Orphanage (Unknown) For Sacramental records, please contact Cathedral of the Holy Name, 730 N. Wabash Ave., Chicago, IL 60611. Tel: 312-787-8040; Fax: 312-787-9113.
St. Vincent Infant Hospital School of Child Care, St. Vincent de Paul Center, 2145 N. Halsted, 60614. Tel: 312-943-6776.
Visitation Church (Garfield Blvd.)
St. Basil-Visitation, 5443 S. Honore, 60609. Tel: 773-625-6311; Fax: 773-783-3348.
Visitation Academy (Evanston) See Marywood High School. (Records destroyed in flood.)
Visitation High School
St. Vitus
St. Vitus School
Weber High School, Gordon Technical High School, 3633 N. California Ave., 60618. Tel: 773-539-3600.
St. Wenceslaus School (Monticello St.)
St. Wenceslaus Church (DeKoven St.)
St. Wenceslaus School (DeKoven St.) (Unknown)
St. Willibrord (114th St.)
St. Willibrord School (114th St.)
Willibrord Catholic High School
St. Willibrord High School
St. Xavier Academy, Mother McAuley High School, 3737 W. 99th St., 60655. Tel: 773-881-6500.

RELIGIOUS INSTITUTES OF MEN REPRESENTED IN THE ARCHDIOCESE

For further details refer to the corresponding bracketed number in the Religious Institutes of Men or Women section.

[0120]—*Alexian Brothers*—C.F.A.
[0140]—*The Augustinians* Chicago—O.S.A.
[0200]—*Benedictine Monks*—O.S.B.
[0330]—*Brothers of the Christian Schools (Midwest Province)* (Burr Ridge, IL)—F.S.C.
[0600]—*Brothers of the Congregation of Holy Cross*—C.S.C.
[0900]—*Canons Regular of Premontre* (U.S. Circary)—O.Praem.
[0400]—*Canons Regular of the Order of the Holy Cross* (Prov. of St. Odilia, Minneapolis, MN)—O.S.C.
[0470]—*The Capuchin Friars*—O.F.M.Cap.
[0270]—*Carmelite Fathers & Brothers* (Most Pure Heart of Mary)—O.Carm.
[0340]—*Cistercian Fathers* (Polish Congr.)—O.Cist.
[0360]—*Claretian Missionaries*—C.M.F.
[1320]—*Clerics of St. Viator* (Chicago, IL)—C.S.V.
[0380]—*Comboni Missionaries of the Heart of Jesus-Verona*—M.C.C.J.
[0310]—*Congregation of Christian Brothers*—C.F.C.
[0750]—*Congregation of Marianhill Missionaries*—C.M.M.
[0220]—*Congregation of the Blessed Sacrament* (Rome, Italy)—S.S.S.
[]—*Congregation of the Holy Spirit* (Eastern Prov.)—C.S.Sp.
[1330]—*Congregation of the Mission* (Western Prov.)—C.M.
[1210]—*Congregation of the Missionaries of St. Charles* (Western Prov.)—C.S.
[1000]—*Congregation of the Passion* (Western Prov.)—C.P.
[1130]—*Congregation of the Priests of the Sacred Heart*—S.C.J.
[1080]—*Congregation of the Resurrection* (Chicago Prov.)—C.R.
[0480]—*Conventual Franciscans* (St. Bonaventure, Our Lady of Consolation Provs.)—O.F.M.Conv.
[0260]—*Discalced Carmelite Friars*—O.C.D.
[0520]—*Franciscan Friars* (Sacred Heart, Assumption of B.V.M. Provs.; Commissariats of the Holy Cross, Holy Family)—O.F.M.
[0690]—*Jesuit Fathers and Brothers* (Chicago, Polish, Lithuanian Provs.)—S.J.
[0730]—*Legionnaires of Christ*—L.C.
[0740]—*Marian Fathers*—M.I.C.
[0770]—*The Marist Brothers*—F.M.S.
[0780]—*Marist Fathers*—S.M.
[0800]—*Maryknoll*—M.M.
[0830]—*Mill Hill Missionaries*—M.H.M.
[0860]—*Missionhurst Congregation of the Immaculate Heart of Mary*—C.I.C.M.
[0910]—*Oblates of Mary Immaculate*—O.M.I.
[0430]—*Order of Preachers-Dominicans*—O.P.
[1030]—*Paulist Fathers* (New York Prov.)—C.S.P.
[0610]—*Priests of the Congregation of Holy Cross* (Notre Dame, IN)—C.S.C.
[1070]—*Redemptorist Fathers* (Denver)—C.SS.R.
[1190]—*Salesians of Don Bosco*—S.D.B.
[1220]—*Servants of Charity*—S.C.
[1240]—*Servites* (Chicago, IL)—O.S.M.
[1260]—*Society of Christ*—S.Ch.
[0760]—*Society of Mary*—S.M.
[0370]—*Society of St. Columban*—S.S.C.
[1200]—*Society of the Divine Savior*—S.D.S.
[0420]—*Society of the Divine Word*—S.V.D.
[1060]—*Society of the Precious Blood* (Kansas City Prov.)—C.PP.S.
[1170]—*St. Patrick Missionary Society*—S.P.S.
[1360]—*Xaverian Missionary Fathers*—S.X.

RELIGIOUS INSTITUTES OF WOMEN REPRESENTED IN THE ARCHDIOCESE

[0100]—*Adorers of the Blood of Christ*—A.S.C.
[0230]—*Benedictine Sisters of Pontifical Jurisdiction*

(Chicago, IL; Duluth, MN)—O.S.B.
[0690]—*Comboni Missionary Sisters*—C.M.S.
[3110]—*Congregation of Our Lady of the Retreat in the Cenacle*—R.C.
[1860]—*Congregation of the Handmaids of the Precious Blood*—H.P.B.
[2100]—*Congregation of the Humility of Mary*—C.H.M.
[]—*Congregation of the Mother of Carmel*—C.M.C.
[0460]—*Congregation of the Sisters of Charity of the Incarnate Word*—C.C.V.I.
[3710]—*Congregation of the Sisters of Saint Agnes*—C.S.A.
[1920]—*Congregation of the Sisters of the Holy Cross*—C.S.C.
[1780]—*Congregation of the Sisters of the Third Order of St. Francis of Perpetual Adoration*—F.S.P.A.
[1710]—*Congregation of the Third Order of St. Francis of Mary Immaculate, Joliet, IL*—O.S.F.
[1730]—*Congregation of the Third Order of St. Francis, Oldenburg, IN*—O.S.F.
[0760]—*Daughters of Charity of St. Vincent de Paul*—D.C.
[0793]—*Daughters of Divine Love*—D.D.L.
[0940]—*Daughters of St. Mary of Providence*—D.S.M.P.
[0810]—*Daughters of the Heart of Mary*—D.H.M.
[0420]—*Discalced Carmelite Nuns*—O.C.D.
[1070-01]—*Dominican Sisters*—O.P.
[1070-07]—*Dominican Sisters*—O.P.
[1070-13]—*Dominican Sisters*—O.P.
[1070-27]—*Dominican Sisters*—O.P.
[1070-10]—*Dominican Sisters*—O.P.
[1070-03]—*Dominican Sisters*—O.P.
[1170]—*Felician Sisters*—C.S.S.F.
[1370]—*Franciscan Missionaries of Mary*—F.M.M.
[1210]—*Franciscan Sisters of Chicago*—O.S.F.
[1230]—*Franciscan Sisters of Christian Charity*—O.S.F.
[1310]—*Franciscan Sisters of Little Falls, Minnesota*—O.S.F.
[1415]—*Franciscan Sisters of Mary*—F.S.M.
[1430]—*Franciscan Sisters of Our Lady of Perpetual Help*—O.S.F.
[1450]—*Franciscan Sisters of the Sacred Heart*—O.S.F.
[1240]—*Franciscan Sisters, Daughters of the Sacred Hearts of Jesus and Mary*—O.S.F.
[2370]—*Institute of the Blessed Virgin Mary (Loretto Sisters)*—I.B.V.M.
[2330]—*Little Sisters of Jesus*—L.S.J.
[2320]—*Little Sisters of the Holy Family*—P.S.S.F.
[2340]—*Little Sisters of the Poor*—L.S.P.
[3570]—*Mantellate Sisters, Servants of Mary of Blue Island*—O.S.M.
[2420]—*Marist Missionary Sisters*—S.M.S.M.
[2430]—*Marist Sisters Congregation of Mary*—S.M.
[2470]—*Maryknoll Sisters of St. Dominic*—M.M.
[2480]—*Medical Missionaries of Mary*—M.M.M.
[2680]—*Misericordia Sisters*—S.M.
[2710]—*Missionaries of Charity*—M.C.
[2865]—*Missionaries of the Sacred Heart of Jesus and Our Lady of Guadalupe*—M.S.C.Gpe.
[2790]—*Missionary Servants of the Most Blessed Trinity*—M.S.B.T.
[2715]—*Missionary Sisters of Christ the King for Polonia*—M.S.C.K.
[2900]—*Missionary Sisters of St. Charles Borromeo*—M.S.C.S.
[3990]—*Missionary Sisters of St. Peter Claver*—S.S.P.C.
[2860]—*Missionary Sisters of the Sacred Heart*—M.S.C.
[3530]—*Missionary Sisters Servants of the Holy Spirit*—S.Sp.S.
[3040]—*Oblate Sisters of Providence*—O.S.P.
[3130]—*Our Lady of Victory Missionary Sisters*—O.L.V.M.
[0950]—*Pious Society Daughters of St. Paul*—F.S.P.
[3230]—*Poor Handmaids of Jesus Christ*—P.H.J.C.
[3440]—*Religious Hospitallers of Saint Joseph*—R.H.S.J.
[2970]—*School Sisters of Notre Dame*—S.S.N.D.
[1680]—*School Sisters of St. Francis*—O.S.F.
[3590]—*Servants of Mary (Servite Sisters)*—O.S.M.
[3520]—*Servants of the Holy Heart of Mary*—S.S.C.M.
[0440]—*Sisters of Charity of Cincinnati, Ohio*—S.C.
[0570]—*Sisters of Charity of Seton Hill, Greensburg, Pennsylvania*—S.C.
[0630]—*Sisters of Charity of St. Vincent de Paul*—S.V.Z.
[0430]—*Sisters of Charity of the Blessed Virgin Mary*—B.V.M.
[0660]—*Sisters of Christian Charity*—S.C.C.
[0990]—*Sisters of Divine Providence*—C.D.P.
[2360]—*Sisters of Loretto at the Foot of the Cross*—S.L.
[2575]—*Sisters of Mercy of the Americas* (Chicago, IL)—R.S.M.
[3000]—*Sisters of Notre Dame de Namur*—S.N.D.deN.
[3080]—*Sisters of Our Lady Christian Doctrine*—R.C.D.
[3350]—*Sisters of Providence*—S.P.
[3360]—*Sisters of Providence of Saint Mary-of-the-Woods, IN*—S.P.
[1620]—*Sisters of Saint Francis of Millvale, Pennsylvania*—O.S.F.
[1540]—*Sisters of Saint Francis, Clinton, Iowa*—O.S.F.
[3780]—*Sisters of Saints Cyril and Methodius*—SS.C.M.
[3740]—*Sisters of St. Casimir*—S.S.C.
[1520]—*Sisters of St. Francis of Christ the King*—O.S.F.
[1640]—*Sisters of St. Francis of Perpetual Adoration*—O.S.F.
[1570]—*Sisters of St. Francis of the Holy Family*—O.S.F.
[1800]—*Sisters of St. Francis of the Third Order Regular*—O.S.F.
[3830-02]—*Sisters of St. Joseph*—C.S.J.
[3830-15]—*Sisters of St. Joseph*—C.S.J.
[3840]—*Sisters of St. Joseph of Carondelet*—C.S.J.
[3930]—*Sisters of St. Joseph of the Third Order of St. Francis*—S.S.J.-T.O.S.F.
[0260]—*Sisters of the Blessed Sacrament for Indians and Colored People*—S.B.S.
[2980]—*Sisters of the Congregation de Notre Dame*—C.N.D.
[1030]—*Sisters of the Divine Savior*—S.D.S.
[1830]—*Sisters of the Good Shepherd*—R.G.S.
[1970]—*Sisters of the Holy Family of Nazareth*—C.S.F.N.
[2140]—*Sisters of the Immaculate Conception of the Blessed Virgin Mary* (Lithuanian)
[2270]—*Sisters of the Little Company of Mary*—L.C.M.
[2350]—*Sisters of the Living Word*—S.L.W.
[3320]—*Sisters of the Presentation of the B.V.M.*—P.B.V.M.
[3480]—*Sisters of the Resurrection*—C.R.
[1705]—*Sisters of the Third Order of St. Francis of Assisi*—C.S.F.
[1720]—*Sisters of the Third Order of St. Francis of the Congregation of Our Lady of Lourdes*—O.S.F.
[2150]—*Sisters, Servants of the Immaculate Heart of Mary*—I.H.M.
[1890]—*Society of Helpers*—H.H.S.
[4060]—*Society of the Holy Child Jesus*—S.H.C.J.
[4070]—*Society of the Sacred Heart*—R.S.C.J.

ARCHDIOCESAN CEMETERIES

CHICAGO. *St. Boniface*
St. Casimir
Central Office
Catholic Cemeteries, 1400 S. Wolf Rd., Hillside, 60162-2197. Tel: 708-449-6100; Fax: 708-449-3419. Web: www.cathcemchgo.org. Rev. Patrick J. Pollard, Archdiocesan Dir.; Mr. Roman Szabelski, Exec. Dir.
St. Henry
Mt. Olivet
CALUMET CITY. *Holy Cross*
CRESTWOOD. *St. Benedict*
DES PLAINES. *All Saints*
EVANSTON. *Calvary*
EVERGREEN PARK. *St. Mary*
FOX LAKE. *St. Bede*
FREMONT CENTER. *St. Mary*
GLENWOOD. *Assumption*
HIGHLAND PARK. *St. Mary*
HILLSIDE. *Mt. Carmel*
Our Lady of Sorrows
Queen of Heaven
JUSTICE. *Resurrection*
LAKE FOREST. *St. Mary*
LEMONT. *St. Alphonsus*
SS. Cyril & Methodius
St. James, Sag Bridge
St. Patrick
LIBERTYVILLE. *Ascension*
NILES. *St. Adalbert*
Maryhill
NORTHBROOK. *Sacred Heart*
OAK FOREST. *St. Gabriel*
ORLAND PARK. *St. Michael*
PALATINE. *St. Michael the Archangel*
PARK FOREST. *St. Anne*
RIVER GROVE. *St. Joseph*
ROSENCRANS. *St. Patrick*
ROUND LAKE. *St. Joseph*
SAUK VILLAGE. *St. James*
SKOKIE. *St. Peter*
STEGER. *Calvary*
VOLO. *St. Peter*
WAUCONDA. *Transfiguration*
WAUKEGAN. *St. Mary*
WEST LAKE FOREST. *St. Patrick*
WILMETTE. *St. Joseph*
WORTH. *Holy Sepulchre*

NECROLOGY

† Hardiman, Rev. Msgr. James C., (Retired)—Died April 30, 2003
† Ahern, John J., (Retired)—Died April 25, 2003
† Bednarz, Matt A., (Retired)—Died Aug. 25, 2003
† Bull, Albert D., (Retired)—Died March 6, 2003
† Cain, John C. (Retired)—Died July 2, 2003
† Chisek, Anthony S., (Retired)—Died June 14, 2003
† Curley, Thomas J., (Retired)—Died Dec. 20, 2002
† Ezerskis, Charles E., (Retired)—Died Oct. 12, 2003
† Hayes, Peter F., (Retired)—Died Aug. 4, 2003
† Henkel, William A., (Retired)—Died June 15, 2003
† Hock, William T., (Retired)—Died Nov. 26, 2003
† Kyle, John M., (Retired)—Died Oct. 9, 2003
† Lyons, James W., (Retired)—Died June 3, 2003
† Nallen, Michael J.—Died May 3, 2003
† O'Connor, William T., Chicago Heights, IL St. Paul—Died Oct. 5, 2003
† Olejniczak, Henry A., (Retired)—Died Jan. 1, 2003
† Quinn, William J., Oak Lawn, IL St. Louis De Montfort—Died July 20, 2003
† Schreiber, Edmund J., (Retired)—Died July 7, 2003

Archdiocese of Cincinnati

(Archidioecesis Cincinnatensis)

Most Reverend

DANIEL E. PILARCZYK, S.T.D., PH.D.

Archbishop of Cincinnati; ordained December 20, 1959; appointed Titular Bishop of Hodelm and Auxiliary Bishop of Cincinnati November 12, 1974; consecrated December 20, 1974; appointed Archbishop of Cincinnati November 2, 1982; installed December 20, 1982. *Res.: 100 E. Eighth St., Cincinnati, OH 45202-2129.*

Most Reverend

CARL K. MOEDDEL, M.A., M.DIV., D.D.

Auxiliary Bishop of Cincinnati; ordained August 15, 1962; appointed Titular Bishop of Bistue and Auxiliary Bishop of Cincinnati August 24, 1993. *Res.: 100 E. Eighth St., Cincinnati, OH 45202-2129.*

Square Miles 8,543.

Erected Diocese June 19, 1821; Archdiocese July 19, 1850.

Comprises that part of the State of Ohio lying south of 40 degrees, 41 minutes, being the 19 Counties south of the northern line of Mercer, Auglaize, and Logan, all west of the eastern line of Logan, Champaign, Clark, Greene, Clinton, Highland and Adams Counties.

For legal titles of parishes and archdiocesan institutions, consult the Chancery Office.

Archdiocesan Offices: 100 E. Eighth St., Cincinnati, OH 45202-2129. Tel: 513-421-3131; Fax: 513-421-6225.

Web: www.archdiocese-cinti.org

STATISTICAL OVERVIEW

Personnel	
Archbishops	1
Auxiliary Bishops	1
Priests: Diocesan Active in Diocese	196
Priests: Diocesan Active Outside Diocese	5
Priests: Diocesan in Foreign Missions	1
Priests: Retired, Sick or Absent	87
Number of Diocesan Priests	289
Religious Priests in Diocese	247
Total Priests in Diocese	536
Extern Priests in Diocese	5
Ordinations:	
Diocesan Priests	6
Religious Priests	1
Transitional Deacons	6
Permanent Deacons in Diocese	138
Total Brothers	146
Total Sisters	1,127
Parishes	
Parishes	224
With Resident Pastor:	
Resident Diocesan Priests	164
Resident Religious Priests	21
Without Resident Pastor:	
Administered by Priests	34
Administered by Deacons	1
Administered by Religious Women	3
Administered by Lay People	1
Pastoral Centers	1
New Parishes Created	5
Professional Ministry Personnel:	
Brothers	13
Sisters	78
Lay Ministers	317
Welfare	
Catholic Hospitals	9
Total Assisted	995,000
Health Care Centers	2
Total Assisted	400
Homes for the Aged	13
Total Assisted	2,451
Residential Care of Children	1
Total Assisted	26
Special Centers for Social Services	6
Total Assisted	1,500
Residential Care of Disabled	1
Total Assisted	29
Other Institutions	6
Total Assisted	1,220
Educational	
Seminaries, Diocesan	1
Students from This Diocese	32
Students from Other Diocese	8
Diocesan Students in Other Seminaries	9
Total Seminarians	41
Colleges and Universities	4
Total Students	24,597
High Schools, Diocesan and Parish	17
Total Students	12,526
High Schools, Private	4
Total Students	3,122
Elementary Schools, Diocesan and Parish	106
Total Students	37,684
Elementary Schools, Private	4
Total Students	1,706
Non-residential Schools for the Disabled	1
Total Students	124
Catechesis/Religious Education:	
High School Students	6,505
Elementary Students	31,555
Total Students under Catholic Instruction	117,860
Teachers in the Diocese:	
Priests	19
Scholastics	2
Brothers	13
Sisters	78
Lay Teachers	3,094
Vital Statistics	
Receptions into the Church:	
Infant Baptism Totals	7,280
Adult Baptism Totals	830
Received into Full Communion	864
First Communions	8,576
Confirmations	8,442
Marriages:	
Catholic	1,592
Interfaith	1,000
Total Marriages	2,592
Deaths	4,473
Total Catholic Population	512,146
Total Population	2,951,228

Former Bishops—Rt. Rev. EDWARD D. FENWICK, O.P., D.D., consecrated Jan. 13, 1822; died Sept. 26, 1832; Most Revs. JOHN BAPTIST PURCELL, D.D., consecrated Oct. 13, 1833; appt. Archbishop, July 19, 1850; died July 4, 1883; WILLIAM HENRY ELDER, D.D., consecrated Bishop of Natchez May 3, 1857; appt. Titular Bishop of Avar, and Coadjutor to the Archbishop of Cincinnati cum jure successionis, Jan. 30, 1880; succeeded to the See of Cincinnati, July 4, 1883; died Oct. 31, 1904; HENRY K. MOELLER, D.D., consecrated Bishop of Columbus, Aug. 25, 1900; promoted to Archiepiscopal See of Areopolis and made Coadjutor to the Most Rev. William Henry Elder cum jure successionis, April 27, 1903; succeeded to the See of Cincinnati, Oct. 31, 1904; died Jan. 5, 1925; JOHN T. MCNICHOLAS, O.P., S.T.M., consecrated Bishop of Duluth, MN Sept. 8, 1918; promoted to Archiepiscopal See of Cincinnati, July 8, 1925; appt. Assistant at the Pontifical Throne, Feb. 18, 1923; died April 22, 1950; KARL J. ALTER, D.D. (Retired), consecrated Bishop of Toledo, June 17, 1931; appt. Assistant to the Pontifical Throne, May 30, 1950; elevated to Archbishop of Cincinnati, June 21, 1950; retired July 23, 1969; died Aug. 23, 1977; PAUL F. LEIBOLD, D.D., J.C.D., appt. Titular Bishop of Trebenna and Auxiliary of Cincinnati, April 10, 1958; consecrated June 17, 1958; installed as Bishop of Evansville, June 15, 1966; transferred to Archdiocese of Cincinnati, July 23, 1969; installed Oct. 2, 1969; died June 1, 1972; His Eminence JOSEPH CARDINAL BERNARDIN, D.D., appt. Titular Bishop of Lugura and Auxiliary Bishop of Atlanta, March 9, 1966; consecrated April 26, 1966; appt. Archbishop of Cincinnati, Nov. 21, 1972; installed Dec. 19, 1972; appt. Archbishop of Chicago, July 10, 1982; installed Aug. 25, 1982; created Cardinal Priest, Feb. 2, 1983; died Nov. 14, 1996.

Vicar General—Most Rev. CARL K. MOEDDEL.

Archdiocesan Department Directors—ROBERT DAVIS, Dir., Community Svcs.; Bro. JOSEPH KAMIS, S.M., Dir., Educational Svcs.; Revs. JOSEPH R. BINZER, Dir., Exec. Svcs.; HOWARD P. PECQUET, Dir., Financial Svcs.; Most Rev. CARL K. MOEDDEL, Dir., Pastoral Svcs.; VINCENT FRASHER, Dir., Personnel Svcs.

Presbyteral Council—Ex Officio Members: Most Revs. DANIEL E. PILARCZYK, S.T.D., Ph.D.; CARL K. MOEDDEL; Rev. ERWIN J. BERTKE (Retired); Rev. Msgr. EUGENE A. FELDHAUS (Retired); Revs. STANLEY H. NEIHEISEL; JAMES E. SHAPPELLE; TERRANCE W. SMITH; RICHARD W. WALLING. Priest Councilors: Revs. THOMAS BRENBERGER, C.PP.S.; JOSEPH FOLZENLOGEN, S.J.; MARK J. BURGER; JOHN R. CIVILLE; JAMES S. DUELL; JOHN P. FISCHER; RICHARD FRIEBEL, C.PP.S.; JOSEPH W. GOETZ (Retired); EDWARD F. HASKAMP; CARL J. LANGENDERFER, O.F.M.; GEORGE P. JACQUEMIN; THOMAS M. SHEARER; EDWARD M. JACH, S.M.; JOHN E. WALL (Retired); JAMES J. WALSH.

Vicarri Foranei (Deans)—Revs. JOSEPH A. ROBINSON, Cathedral Deanery; MARK J. BURGER, St. Andrew Deanery; GILES PATER, St. Francis de Sales Deanery; EDWARD L. RUDEMILLER, St. Lawrence Deanery; GEORGE JACQUEMIN, St. Margaret Mary Deanery; TIMOTHY S. BUNCH, Hamilton Deanery; THEODORE C. KOSSE, St. Martin Deanery; DAVID E. BRINKMOELLER, Dayton Deanery; RICHARD M. WALLING, Springfield Deanery; GERALD E. BENSMAN, Sidney Deanery; JAMES C. SEIBERT, C.PP.S., St. Mary's Deanery.

Consultors—Most Rev. CARL K. MOEDDEL, Auxiliary Bishop; Revs. ERWIN J. BERTKE (Retired); MARK J. BURGER; JOHN R. CIVILLE; JOHN P. FISCHER; JOSEPH W. GOETZ (Retired); STANLEY H. NEIHEISEL; JAMES E. SHAPPELLE; THOMAS M. SHEARER; TERRANCE W. SMITH; RICHARD W. WALLING.

Archdiocesan Offices

Unless otherwise indicated, all Archdiocesan Offices and Directors are located at: *100 E. Eighth St., Cincinnati, 45202*. Tel: 513-421-3131; Fax: 513-421-6225.

Office of the Archbishop—Rev. MALCOLM S. GRAD, Vice Chancellor; LINDA CHOUTEAU, Exec. Sec. to the Archbishop; GAYLE SCOTTI, Sec.

Office of Mediation—JOSEPH B. CROWE, Admin. Tel: 513-421-3131, Ext. 408.

Department of Executive Services

Director—Rev. JOSEPH R. BINZER.

Chancery—

Chancellor—Rev. JOSEPH R. BINZER.

Vice Chancellor—Rev. MALCOLM S. GRAD.

Archivist—DON H. BUSKE (Special Address & Phone No. for Historical Archives Only), 6616 Beechmont Ave., Cincinnati, 45230. Tel: 513-231-0810.

Censors—Revs. RICHARD L. KLUG; RALPH J. LAWRENCE (Retired); ROBERT L. HAGEDORN (Retired); CHRISTOPHER R. ARMSTRONG, J.C.D.; TIMOTHY P. SCHEHR, Ph.D.; GILES H. PATER; ROBERT A. STRICKER (Retired); RICHARD W. WALLING; DAVID L. ZINK; LORENZO RUIZ, Spanish.

Communications Office—DAN ANDRIACCO, Dir.

Newspaper--"The Catholic Telegraph"—Most Rev. DANIEL E. PILARCZYK, S.T.D., Ph.D., Publisher.

Tribunal-Archdiocese of Cincinnati—Tel: 513-421-3131; Fax: 513-723-1035.

Director—Sr. VICTORIA VONDENBERGER, R.S.M., J.C.L.

Judicial Vicar—Rev. EDWIN F. GEARHART, J.C.L.

Adjutant Judicial Vicars—Revs. JOSEPH R. BINZER; BARRY M. WINDHOLTZ, J.C.L.; THOMAS A. SNODGRASS, J.C.L.

Judges—Deacon MICHAEL A. ASCOLESE; Rev. Msgr. LAWRENCE K. BRESLIN; Revs. CHRISTOPHER R. ARMSTRONG, J.C.D.; MICHAEL D. BEATTY; JAMES A. BRAMLAGE; JOHN L. CAVANAUGH, J.C.D. (Retired); DENNIS J. CAYLOR, J.C.L.; J. RAYMOND FAVRET; DAVID E. FAY; JOHN P. FISCHER; MICHAEL T. FLAHERTY; GERALD R. HAEMMERLE, M.A.; TIMOTHY S. KALLAHER, J.C.L.; RAYMOND C. KELLERMAN; RICHARD L. KLUG; EMIL J. LABBE, C.PP.S., J.C.D.; FRANCIS G. LAMMEIER (Retired); NORMAN W. LANGENBRUNNER; RALPH J. LAWRENCE (Retired); THOMAS C. NOLKER; ROBERT A. OBERMEYER; EDWARD L. RUDEMILLER; OSCAR H. SEGER; R. MARC SHERLOCK; TERRANCE W. SMITH; LARRY P. THARP; FRANCIS W. VOELLMECKE, Ph.D.; JOHN R. WHITE, J.C.L.

Defenders of the Bond—Revs. HERMAN H. KENNING (Retired); WILLIAM H. WYSONG, J.C.L.; Sr. VICTORIA VONDENBERGER, R.S.M., J.C.L.

Promoter of Justice—Sr. VICTORIA VONDENBERGER, R.S.M., J.C.L.

Assessors—Mrs. ELVA E. BRUNNER; Mrs. KELLY M. TERRY; Miss CHRISTINE GATELY.

Auditors—Mrs. CANDY L. ENGELKE; Mrs. BETTY L. MEDER; Mrs. AMI R. TENNER.

Secretary/Auditor—Mrs. PAMELA J. JASPERS.

Department of Community Services

Director—ROBERT L. DAVIS.

Archdiocesan Office of Catholic Charities—ROBERT L. DAVIS, Dir.

Association of Ladies of Charity—LENORA WRIGHT, Pres. Tel: 513-421-3131.

Catholic Federation for the Mentally Retarded—BOB STONE, Pres. Tel: 513-522-0006 Catholic Residential Services of Archdiocese of Cincinnati with People with Mental Retardation; Ms. CHARMAINE KESSINGER, Exec. Dir., 100 E. Eighth St., Cincinnati, 45202. Tel: 513-784-0400; Fax: 513-333-3172.

Catholic Social Services of Hamilton—JUDITH FULCHER, Exec. Dir., 140 N. Fifth St., Hamilton, 45011. Tel: 513-863-6129.

Catholic Social Services of Miami Valley—RONALD A. ECKERLE, Exec. Dir., 922 W. Riverview Dr., Dayton, 45407. Tel: 937-223-7217.

Catholic Social Services of Southwestern Ohio—KATHLEEN DONNELLAN, Exec. Dir. Tel 513-241-7745.

Catholic Social Services of Springfield—VINCENT CHASE, Exec. Dir., 641 High St., Springfield, 45505. Tel: 937-325-8715.

Cemeteries—ROBERT DAVIS, Dir.; DAVE BONDI, Dir., 11000 Montgomery Rd., Cincinnati, 45242. Tel: 513-489-0300.

Ecumenical and Interfaith Relations—LOUISE VERA, Program Coord.

St. Vincent de Paul Society—PATRICK WHITE, Pres.; Rev. LOUIS HOHLMAYER, Spiritual Dir., (See Special Listing: St. Vincent de Paul Society).

Health Affairs—ROBERT DAVIS. Tel: 513-241-7745.

Rural Life Conference—266 Bainbridge St., Dayton, 45402. Tel: 937-224-3026.

Catholic Social Action—CORI THIBODEAU, Acting Dir.; CONNIE WIDMER, Assoc. Dir. Dayton Office: CORI THIBODEAU, 266 Bainbridge St., Dayton, 45402. Tel: 937-224-3026.

Department of Educational Services

Director—Bro. JOSEPH KAMIS, S.M.

School Office—Bro. JOSEPH KAMIS, S.M., Supt., Archdiocesan Schools, 100 E. Eighth St., Cincinnati, 45202. Tel: 513-421-3131; Ms. ANNE BATTES KIRBY, Deputy Supt., Archdiocesan Schools Office, 266 Bainbridge St., Dayton, 45402. Tel: 937-223-5151.

Religious Education Office—KENNETH GLEASON, Archdiocesan Dir., 100 E. Eighth St., Cincinnati, 45202. Tel: 513-421-3131; DAVID RILEY, Regl. Dir., Dayton Religious Education Office, 226 Bainbridge St., Dayton, 45402. Tel: 937-223-4075; JANE PIERRON, Regl. Dir., 119 E. Water St., Sidney, 45365. Tel: 937-498-1192.

Department of Financial Services

Treasurer & Director—HOWARD P. PECQUET.

Office of Property Management-Central Services—GARY RAFFEL, Dir.

Office for Financial Development—JOAN SCHROEDER, Dir.

Department of Pastoral Services

Director—Most Rev. CARL K. MOEDDEL.

Campus Ministry—Dr. JANE STEINHAUSER, Dir., 444 W. Third St., Dayton, 45402. (See Special Listing: Campus Ministry).

African American Catholic Ministries—GEORGE C. FINDLEY, Dir.

Family Life—MARGARET BLACK, Dir. Dayton: MARY EHRET, Assoc. Dir., 266 Bainbridge St., Dayton, 45402. Tel: 937-222-0227. Northern Area: VELMA JEAN BORGERT, 119 E. Water St., Sidney, 45365. Tel: 937-492-4449.

Missions—

Pontifical Mission Aid Societies—Most Rev. CARL K. MOEDDEL.

Missions Office—Mr. MIKE GABLE, Dir.

Pastoral Council Secretariat—Rev. MALCOLM S. GRAD, Exec. Sec.

Hispanic Catholic Ministry, Dayton—Sr. MARIA FRANCINE STACY, S.N.D., 266 Bainbridge St., Dayton, 45402. Tel: 937-222-1340.

Archdiocesan Office of Hispanic Ministry—Rev. WILLIAM JANSEN, M.C.C.J., Dir., 115 W. Seymour Ave., Cincinnati, 45216. Tel: 513-948-1760.

Planning and Research—VACANT.

Worship—Ms. KAREN KANE, Dir.

Youth—Mr. SEAN REYNOLDS, Dir., 100 East Eighth St., Cincinnati, 45202. Tel: 513-421-3131; TIMOTHY E. COLBERT, Regl. Dir., Dayton & Northern Area: 266 Bainbridge St., Dayton, 45402. Tel: 937-223-1001.

Department of Personnel Services

Director—VINCENT FRASHER.

Office of Religious—Sr. MARY GARKE, C.PP.S., Dir.

Permanent Diaconate Office—BERNARD J. MERSMANN.

Personnel Office for Archdiocesan Administrative Offices—VINCE FRASHER, Dir.

Priestly Formation—Rev. THOMAS P. DIFOLCO, Dir.

Priests' Personnel Director—Most Rev. CARL K. MOEDDEL, Dir.

Victim Assistance Coordinator—Rev. JOSEPH R. BINZER. Tel: 513-421-3131, Ext. 401. Email: jbinzer@catholiccincinnati.org.

Vocations Office—Rev. MARK T. WATKINS, Dir.

CLERGY, PARISHES, MISSIONS AND PAROCHIAL SCHOOLS

GREATER CINCINNATI (HAMILTON COUNTY)

1—ST. PETER IN CHAINS CATHEDRAL (1822), Rev. James A. Bramlage. In Res., Revs. Mark T. Watkins; Thomas A. Snodgrass, J.C.L.; Patrick D. Duffy.
Res.: 325 W. Eighth St., 45202. Tel: 513-421-5355. Church: Eighth & Plum St., 45202. Tel: 513-421-5354; Fax: 513-241-9517.

2—ST. AGNES (Bond Hill) (1892), (African American), Rev. Thomas P. DiFolco; Deacon Royce Winters.
Res.: 1619 California Ave., 45237. Tel: 513-242-4747; Fax: 513-242-4748.
Catechesis/Religious Program—Students 26.

3—ALL SAINTS (Kenwood) (1948), Rev. J. Dennis Jaspers; Mr. Amado Lim, Pastoral Assoc.; Mr. Lou Elefante, Business Mgr.
Res.: 8939 Montgomery Rd., 45236. Tel: 513-791-6351; Fax: 513-792-4730.
School—Tel: 513-792-4732; Fax: 513-792-7990. Mrs. Mary E. Stratford, Prin. Sisters of Charity 1; Lay Teachers 28; Students 482.
Catechesis/Religious Program—Tel: 513-791-6351, Ext. 103; Fax: 513-792-4730. Mrs. Wilma McGlasson, D.R.E. Students 216.

4—ST. ALOYSIUS GONZAGA (Bridgetown) (1866), Rev. James M. Schmitmeyer; Sr. Josetta Boeing, S.C., Pastoral Assoc.; Deacon Jerry Schneider.
Res.: 4366 Bridgetown Rd., 45211. Tel: 513-574-4840; Fax: 513-574-4402.
School—4390 Bridgetown Rd., 45211. Tel: 513-574-4035; Fax: 513-574-5421. Sr. Carol Ann Mause, O.S.F., Prin. Lay Teachers 19; Students 325.
Catechesis/Religious Program—Tel: 513-574-4840; Fax: 513-574-4402. Ms. Kathy Robinson, D.R.E. Students 76.

5—ST. ALOYSIUS-ON-THE-OHIO (1873), Rev. Donald R. Rettig.
Res.: 134 Whipple St., 45233. Tel: 513-941-3445; Fax: 513-941-2257.
School—6207 Portage, 45202. Tel: 513-941-7831; Fax: 513-941-7831. Lay Teachers 13; Students 153.
Catechesis/Religious Program—Tel: 513-941-3445; Fax: 513-941-2257. Students 30.

6—ST. ANDREW (1874), (African American), Rev. Jerry Steinbrunner, C.PP.S.
3401 Reading Rd., P.O. Box 29064, 45229. Tel: 513-281-7504; Fax: 513-281-7504.

7—ST. ANN (Groesbeck) (1953), Revs. Thomas J. Dennemann; Anthony Muller.
Res.: 2900 Galbraith Rd., 45239. Tel: 513-521-8440; Fax: 513-521-7221.
School—2940 W. Galbraith Rd., 45239. Tel: 513-931-3070; Fax: 513-931-3071. Mariane Rosemond, Prin. Lay Teachers 22; Students 377.
Catechesis/Religious Program—Tel: 513-729-2810. Diane C. Ferrier, D.R.E. Students 156.

8—ANNUNCIATION OF THE BLESSED VIRGIN MARY (1910), Rev. Richard L. Klug. In Res., Rev. Edward G. Trippel (Retired).
Res.: 3547 Clifton Ave., 45220. Tel: 513-861-1295; Fax: 513-281-8009.
School—3545 Clifton Ave., 45220. Tel: 513-221-1230; Fax: 513-281-8009. Sr. Lawrence Sickman, O.S.U. Prin. Lay Teachers 12; Students 165.
Catechesis/Religious Program—Tel: 513-861-1295. Students 35.

9—ST. ANTHONY (Madisonville) (1858), [CEM] Rev. Leonard C. Wenke; Sr. Jean Masterson, C.S.J., Pastoral Assoc.
Res.: 6104 Desmond St., 45227. Tel: 513-271-0920; Fax: 513-271-6630.
School—Prince of Peace, Tel: 513-271-8288; Fax: 513-272-1740.
Catechesis/Religious Program—Tel: 513-271-0920; Fax: 513-271-6630. Rita Balcom, D.R.E. Students 148.

10—ST. ANTONINUS (1944), Revs. Christopher R. Armstrong, J.C.D.; Lawrence J. Mick; Deacon William J. Petrie.
Res.: 1500 Linneman Rd., 45238. Tel: 513-922-5400; Fax: 513-451-5871.
School—5425 Julmar Dr., 45238. Tel: 513-922-2500; Fax: 513-922-5519. Mr. James Leisring, Prin. Lay Teachers 29; Students 539.
Catechesis/Religious Program—Tel: 513-922-4759. Deacon Robert Schroeder, D.R.E. Students 32.

11—ASSUMPTION (Mount Healthy) (1854), [CEM] Rev. William M. Kennedy.
Res.: 7711 Joseph St., 45231. Tel: 513-521-7274; Fax: 513-521-3728.
School—1500 McMakin Ave., Mt. Healthy, 45231. Tel: 513-522-0071; Fax: 513-728-4946. William J. Walborn, Prin. Lay Teachers 20; Students 307.
Catechesis/Religious Program—Tel: 513-728-4941. Sr. Marietta Sharkey, O.S.F., D.R.E. Students 49.

12—ASSUMPTION OF THE BLESSED VIRGIN MARY (Walnut Hills) (1872), Rev. Thomas Bokenkotter.
Res.: 2622 Gilbert Ave., 45206. Tel: 513-961-3242; 513-271-0016.

13—ST. BARTHOLOMEW (1961), Rev. Robert J. Farrell; Sr. Janet Schneider, Pastoral Assoc.; Skip Borgman, Business Mgr.
Res.: 9375 Winton Rd., 45231. Tel: 513-522-3680; Fax: 513-728-3141.
School—St. Bartholomew Consolidated School, Tel: 513-521-0860; Fax: 513-728-3110. See separate listing.
Catechesis/Religious Program—Tel: 513-728-3146, Ext. 105; Fax: 513-728-3141. Patricia B. Douglas, D.R.E. Students 345.

14—ST. BERNARD (1919), Revs. James Shappelle; Michael Paraniuk.

Res.: 740 Circle Ave., 45232. Tel: 513-541-3732; Fax: 513-541-0362.
Catechesis/Religious Program— Twinned with Mother of Christ. Students 25.

15—ST. BERNARD (Taylor's Creek) (1867), [CEM] Rev. Stanley D. Doerger.
Res.: 7130 Harrison Rd., 45247. Tel: 513-353-4207; Fax: 513-353-9600.
School—Tel: 513-353-4224; Fax: 513-353-3958. Lay Teachers 9; Students 241.
Catechesis/Religious Program—Students 85.

16—ST. BONAVENTURE (1869), Closed., For inquiries for parish records, see St. Leo, Cincinnati.

17—ST. BONIFACE (1863), Rev. Joseph A. Robinson; Deacons Ted Schmidt; Jerry Yetter.
Res.: 1750 Chase Ave., 45223. Tel: 513-541-1563; Fax: 513-541-1514.
School—St. Boniface Consolidated, Tel: 513-541-5122; Fax: 513-541-3939. See separate listing.
Catechesis/Religious Program—Students 10.

18—ST. CATHARINE (1903), Rev. Anthony M. Dattilo; Therese Bower Hibdon, Pastoral Min.
Res.: 2848 Fischer Pl., P.O. Box 111115, 45211. Tel: 513-661-0651; Fax: 513-661-0652.
School—3324 Wunder Ave., 45211. Tel: 513-481-7683; Fax: 513-481-9438. Harry Meyer, Prin. Lay Teachers 19; Students 362.
Catechesis/Religious Program—Students 30.

19—ST. CECILIA (Oakley) (1908), Rev. Elmer W. Smith; Deacon John Slattery.
Res.: 3105 Madison Rd., 45209. Tel: 513-871-5757; Fax: 513-533-6066.
School—4115 Taylor Ave., 45209. Tel: 513-533-6060; Fax: 513-533-6068. Ms. Lori Heffner, Prin. Lay Teachers 12; Students 198.
Catechesis/Religious Program—Billie Jean Schimian, D.R.E. Students 40.
Parish Center—4030 Gilmore Ave., 45209. Tel: 513-553-6067.

20—ST. CLARE (College Hill) (1908), Rev. George Jacquemin. In Res., Rev. Robert J. Hater (Retired).
Res.: 1443 Cedar Ave., 45224. Tel: 513-541-2100; Fax: 513-541-2101.
School—5800 Salvia Ave., 45224. Tel: 513-541-5751; Fax: 513-541-2101. Mrs. Michael Kirry, Prin. Lay Teachers 12; Students 120.
Catechesis/Religious Program—Tel: 513-541-2100. Students 35.

21—ST. CLEMENT (St. Bernard) (1850), Revs. Donald E. Holtgrewe, O.F.M.; Carl J. Langenderfer, O.F.M.; Bro. Joel Soldenski, O.F.M., Pastoral Assoc.
St. Clement Friary: 4536 Vine St., 45217. Tel: 513-641-3176; 513-641-2257 (Friary); Fax: 513-641-2262.
School—4534 Vine St., 45217. Tel: 513-641-2137; Fax: 513-242-6036. Mrs. Cathy Stover, Prin. Tel: 513-641-2137, Ext. 802. Sisters 1; Lay Teachers 16; Students 205.
Catechesis/Religious Program—Tel: 513-641-2137, Ext. 808; Fax: 513-641-0149. Colleen Gerke, D.R.E. Students 286.

22—CORPUS CHRISTI (1958), Rev. James Meade. In Res., Rev. Robert Bruening; Connie Leyendecker, Business Mgr.
Res.: 2014 Springdale Rd., 45231. Tel: 513-825-0618; Fax: 513-825-0182.
School—St. Bartholomew Consolidated, Tel: 513-521-0860; Fax: 513-728-3110. See separate listing.
Catechesis/Religious Program—Tel: 513-825-0182. Barbara Conway, D.R.E. Students 172.

23—ST. DOMINIC (Delhi Hills) (1933), Revs. Jim J. Walsh; Chris Lack; Deacon Mark A. Bardonaro.
Res.: 4551 Delhi Pike, 45238. Tel: 513-471-7741; Fax: 513-471-0363.
School—371 Pedretti Ave., 45238. Tel: 513-251-1276; Fax: 513-251-6428. Aloysius H. Grote, Prin. Lay Teachers 31; Students 654.
Catechesis/Religious Program—Tel: 513-471-7741, Ext. 481. Students 152.

24—ST. FRANCIS DE SALES (1849), [CEM], Collaborative cluster - see St. Robert, Bellarmine. Rev. Edward M. Jach, S.M.; Bro. David Betz, S.M.
Res.: 1600 Madison Rd., 45206. Tel: 513-961-1945; Fax: 513-221-4907.
School—Tel: 513-961-1953; Fax: 513-961-2900. William Shula, Ed.D., Prin. Brothers 1; Lay Teachers 11; Students 214.
Catechesis/Religious Program— Collaborative Cluster, see St. Robert Bellarmine.

25—ST. FRANCIS SERAPH (1859), Rev. Gil Wohler, O.F.M.; Bros. Josef Anderlohr, O.F.M.; Ronald Bolfeta, O.F.M.
St. Francis Friary: 1615 Vine St., 45202. Tel: 513-721-4700; Fax: 513-421-9672.
School—14 E. Liberty St., 45210. Tel: 513-721-7778; Fax: 513-721-5445. Ms. Wanda W. Hill, Prin. Sisters 1; Lay Teachers 12; Students 140.

26—ST. FRANCIS XAVIER (1819), Revs. Robert J. Thesing, S.J.; Paul A. Huber, S.J.; John P. Murphy, S.J.; Carl J. Moell, S.J.; Robert C. O'Connor, S.J.; Mr. Thomas Choquette, Pastoral Assoc.
Res.: 607 Sycamore St., 45202. Tel: 513-721-4045; Fax: 513-723-0451.

27—ST. GABRIEL (Glendale) (1857), Rev. David E. Fay; Sr. Mary Doeker, O.S.U., Pastoral Assoc.; Deacon Herman H. Bryant.
Res.: 48 W. Sharon Ave., 45246. Tel: 513-771-4700; Fax: 513-612-4545.
School—St. Gabriel Consolidated School, Tel: 513-771-5220; Fax: 513-771-5133. See separate listing.
Catechesis/Religious Program—Fax: 513-621-4545. Rose Voulgarakis, D.R.E. Students 59.

28—ST. GERTRUDE (Madeira) (1923), Revs. Kenneth R. Letoile, O.P.; Walter Wagner, O.P., Novice Master; Michael Detemple, O.P.; Stephen Alcott, O.P.; Charles Farrell, O.P. In Res., Rev. J. Vincent Watson, O.P.
Res.: 7630 Shawnee Run Rd., 45243. Tel: 513-561-5954; Fax: 513-527-3971.
School—6551 Miami Ave., 45243. Tel: 513-561-8020; Fax: 513-561-7184. Sr. Maria Christi, O.P., Prin. Dominican Sisters (Nashville, TN) 4; Lay Teachers 33; Students 433.
Catechesis/Religious Program—Tel: 513-561-8369; Fax: 513-561-8369. Students 652.

29—GOOD SHEPHERD (1973), Rev. Robert E. Schmitz; Deacon Raymond Grismer; Stephen P. Lindner, Pastoral Assoc.; Patricia Lindner, Pastoral Assoc.; Elmer H. Fischesser, Pastoral Assoc.; Scott Mussari, Pastoral Assoc.; Jim Crosby, Pastoral Assoc.; Jeanie Wolf, Pastoral Assoc.; Jen Crosby, Pastoral Assoc.; Jerry DiCristoforo, Pastoral Assoc.
Res.: 8815 E. Kemper Rd., 45249. Tel: 513-489-8815; Fax: 513-489-8521.
Catechesis/Religious Program—Students 1,010.

30—GUARDIAN ANGELS (Mt. Washington) (1892), Revs. Thomas M. King; Michael L. Cordier; Deacon Rick Novick. In Res., Rev. Carl J. Wollering.
Res.: 6531 Beechmont Ave., 45230. Tel: 513-231-7440; Fax: 513-624-3145.
School—6539 Beechmont Ave., 45230. Tel: 513-624-3141; Fax: 513-624-3150. Mr. David A. Reker, Prin. Lay Teachers 34; Students 647.
Catechesis/Religious Program—Tel: 513-624-3146. Students 282.

31—HOLY ANGELS (1859), Merged, with St. Francis de Sales, Cincinnati.

32—HOLY CROSS-IMMACULATA (Mount Adams) (1859), Rev. Stanley H. Neiheisel.
Res.: 30 Guido St., 45202. Tel: 513-721-6544; Fax: 513-721-6177.

33—HOLY FAMILY (Price Hill) (1883),, Includes the consolidation of Our Lady of Grace, Our Lady of Perpetual Help Parishes, Blessed Sacrament and St. Michael. Rev. Steve Angi.
Parish Office—3006 W. 8th St., 45205.
Res.: 814 Hawthorne Ave., 45205. Tel: 513-921-7527; Fax: 513-921-6033.
School—(Grades K-8), 3001 Price Ave., 45205. Tel: 513-921-8483; Fax: 513-921-2460. Sr. Brenda Busch, S.C., Prin. Sisters 7; Lay Teachers 6; Students 174.
Catechesis/Religious Program—Students 211.

34—HOLY NAME (1904), Rev. Al Hirt, O.F.M.; Sr. Mary Gallagher, S.C., Pastoral Admin.
Res.: 2448 Auburn Ave., 45219. Tel: 513-721-5608; Fax: 513-721-5608 (call first).
Catechesis/Religious Program—Students 17.

35—HOLY TRINITY CHURCH (Norwood) (1994), Rev. Raymond C. Kellerman.
Res.: 2420 Drex Ave., 45212. Tel: 513-366-4400; Fax: 513-366-4404.
School—Holy Trinity School, Tel: 513-366-4406; Fax: 513-366-4420. Lay Teachers 20; Students 220.
Catechesis/Religious Program—Tel: 513-366-4400; Fax: 513-366-4404. Students 19.

36—ST. IGNATIUS LOYOLA (Monfort Heights) (1946), Revs. Thomas L. Bolte; Donald G. McCarthy (Retired); John E. Wall (Retired); Barb Campbell, Business Mgr.
Res.: 5222 N. Bend Rd., 45247. Tel: 513-661-6565; Fax: 513-389-3241.
School—Tel: 513-389-3242; Fax: 513-389-3255. Timothy Reilly, Prin. Lay Teachers 40; Students 818.
Catechesis/Religious Program—Tel: 513-389-3247. Kris Schoettmer, D.R.E. Students 152.

37—IMMACULATE HEART OF MARY (Forestville) (1944), Rev. Jan Kevin Schmidt; Deacons Bill Mullaney; Dave Shea.
Res.: 7820 Beechmont Ave., 45255. Tel: 513-388-4466; Fax: 513-388-4097.
School—Tel: 513-388-4086; Fax: 513-388-4097. Mrs. Mary Hedger, Prin. Brothers 1; Lay Teachers 24; Students 675.
Catechesis/Religious Program—Tel: 513-388-4093; Fax: 513-388-4097. Leisa Anslinger, D.R.E.; Matthew Cohen, D.R.E. Students 645.

38—ST. JAMES OF THE VALLEY (Wyoming) (1886), Revs. James R. Collins; James E. Ulrich.
Res.: 411 Springfield Pk., 45215. Tel: 513-948-1218; Fax: 513-948-1225.
School—Tel: 513-821-9054; Fax: 513-821-9556. Mrs. Melissa Mathis, Prin. Lay Teachers 12; Students 208.
Catechesis/Religious Program—Ms. JoAnn Menne, D.R.E. Students 200.

39—ST. JAMES THE GREATER (White Oak) (1843), [CEM] Rev. Thomas C. Nolker; Sr. Joan Roach, O.S.U., Pastoral Assoc.; Deacon Paul J. Kluener.
Res.: 3565 Hubble Rd., 45247. Tel: 513-741-5300; Fax: 513-741-5302.
School—6111 Cheviot Rd., 45247. Tel: 513-741-5333; Fax: 513-741-5312. Kevan Hartman, Prin. Lay Teachers 50; Students 1,062.
Catechesis/Religious Program—Tel: 513-741-5335; Fax: 513-741-5302. Students 122.

40—ST. JEROME (1853), Rev. Carl J. Wollering.
Church: 131 Rohde St., 45228.
Res.: 5858 Kellogg Ave., 45228. Tel: 513-231-7042; Fax: 513-231-7042.
Catechesis/Religious Program—Guardian Angels, 6531 Beechmont Ave., 45230. Tel: 513-624-3146; Fax: 513-624-3145. Students 30.

41—ST. JOHN FISHER (Newtown) (1947), Rev. Giles H. Pater.
Office—3227 Church St., 45244. Tel: 513-561-9431; Fax: 513-561-7513.
Catechesis/Religious Program—Students 190.

42—ST. JOHN NEUMANN (Springfield Township) (1978), Rev. John Porter; Deacon John R. Gobbi, Pastoral Assoc.; Martha M. Barnes, Pastoral Assoc.; Ms. Courtney Watson, Pastoral Assoc.
Res.: 12191 Mill Rd., 45240. Tel: 513-742-0953; Fax: 513-742-5875.
School—St. Bartholomew Consolidated, Tel: 513-521-0860. See separate listing.
Catechesis/Religious Program—Tel: 513-742-0953; Fax: 513-742-5875. Students 260.

43—ST. JOHN THE BAPTIST (Dry Ridge) (1860), [CEM] Rev. Timothy S. Kallaher, J.C.L.
Res.: 5361 Dry Ridge Rd., 45252. Tel: 513-385-8010; Fax: 513-385-8080.
School—5375 Dry Ridge Rd., 45252. Tel: 513-385-7970; Fax: 513-699-6964. Mr. Thomas Bailey, Prin. Sisters 1; Lay Teachers 26; Students 455.
Catechesis/Religious Program—Students 710.

44—ST. JOHN THE BAPTIST (Harrison) (1851), [CEM] Revs. Edward J. Shine; William J. Dorrmann (Retired).
Res.: 110 N. Hill St., Harrison, 45030. Tel: 513-367-9086; Fax: 513-367-6864.
School—Tel: 513-367-6826; Fax: 513-367-6864. Sisters 1; Lay Teachers 23; Students 397.
Catechesis/Religious Program—Tel: 513-367-9878. Students 323.

45—ST. JOHN THE EVANGELIST (1891), Revs. Thomas Espelage; Dale C. Peterka.
Res.: 7121 Plainfield Rd., 45236. Tel: 513-791-3238; Fax: 513-686-2720.
School—7131 Plainfield Rd., 45236. Tel: 513-686-2727; Fax: 513-686-2729. Patricia Sand, Prin. Lay Teachers 17; Students 209.
Catechesis/Religious Program—Mr. Tim Cronin, D.R.E. Students 72.

46—ST. JOHN VIANNEY (Madison Pl.) (1949), Rev. Leonard F. Fecko. In Res., Rev. William H. Cross.
Res.: 4448 Berwick, 45227. Tel: 513-271-5490; Fax: 513-271-0470.
School—Prince of Peace, Tel: 513-289-7657; Fax: 513-271-0470. Mr. Barry Thomas, Prin. Lay Teachers 11; Students 140.
Catechesis/Religious Program—Tel: 513-272-6347. Students 21.

47—ST. JOSEPH (1846), (African American), Rev. Patrick D. Duffy; Deacon Raphael Simmons.
Res.: 745 Ezzard Charles Dr., 45203. Tel: 513-381-4526; Fax: 513-381-5244.
School—Tel: 513-381-2126; Fax: 513-381-6513. Sr. Mary Lou Smith, Prin. Lay Teachers 13; Students 152.
Catechesis/Religious Program—Tel: 513-381-4526, Ext. 16. Margaret Grizzard, D.R.E. Students 9.

48—ST. JOSEPH (North Bend) (1860), Rev. Michael A. Savino.
Mailing Address: P.O. Box 219, 45052.
Res.: 25 E. Harrison Ave., 45052. Tel: 513-941-3661; Fax: 513-941-8559.
Catechesis/Religious Program—Susan K. Rensing, D.R.E. Students 156.

49—ST. JUDE THE APOSTLE (1956), Rev. Richard E. Dressman; Deacon James Sunderman.
Res.: 5924 Bridgetown Rd., 45248. Tel: 513-574-1230; Fax: 513-598-2109.
School—5940 Bridgetown Rd., 45248. Tel: 513-598-2100; Fax: 513-598-2118. Jay McNitt, Prin. Lay Teachers 28; Students 484.
Catechesis/Religious Program—Tel: 513-598-2100, Ext. 30; Fax: 513-598-2109. Students 200.

50—ST. LAWRENCE (Price Hill) (1868), Rev. Ralph A. Westerhoff; Sr. Helen Julia Hahn, S.C., Pastoral Assoc.
Res.: 3680 Warsaw Ave., 45205. Tel: 513-921-0328; Fax: 513-921-5108.

School—1020 Carson Ave., 45205. Tel: 513-921-4996. Mrs. Alma Lee Joesting, Prin. Lay Teachers 17; Students 293.
Catechesis/Religious Program—Students 350.

51—ST. LEO THE GREAT (1886), Rev. Edwin F. Gearhart, J.C.L.
Res.: 2573 St. Leo Pl., 45225-1960. Tel: 513-921-1044; Fax: 513-921-8048.
School—St. Boniface Consolidated, Tel: 513-541-5122; Fax: 513-541-3939. See separate listing.
Catechesis/Religious Program—Students 6.

52—ST. LOUIS (1870), (German), Rev. Joseph R. Binzer.
Res.: 29 E. Eighth St., 45202-2086. Tel: 513-263-6621.

53—ST. MARGARET MARY (North College Hill) (1920), Rev. Jerome J. Gardner; Deacon Raymond S. Burger.
Res.: 1830 W. Galbraith Rd., 45239. Tel: 513-521-7387; Fax: 513-521-7388.
School—1820 W. Galbraith Rd., 45239. Tel: 513-521-8619; Fax: 513-521-8620. Patricia Kennedy, Prin. Lay Teachers 17; Students 211.
Catechesis/Religious Program—Tel: 513-729-1551. Al Cuchetti, D.R.E. Students 296.

54—ST. MARGARET OF CORTONA (Madisonville) (1921), Rev. Leonard F. Fecko; Deacon William Aufderheide.
Res.: 4100 Watterson St., 45227. Tel: 513-271-0856; Fax: 513-271-1513.
School—Prince of Peace, Tel: 513-271-8288; Fax: 513-272-1740. Mr. Barry Thomas, Prin. Lay Teachers 11; Students 138.
Catechesis/Religious Program—Fax: 513-272-1540. Students 28.

55—ST. MARK (1904), Rev. Jerry Steinbrunner, C.PP.S.; Bro. Hugh Henderson, C.PP.S., Pastoral Assoc.
Res.: 3500 Montgomery Rd., 45207. Tel: 513-961-0472; Fax: 513-961-0492.

56—ST. MARTIN DE PORRES (Lincoln Heights) (1935), (African American), Rev. Thomas P. DiFolco.
Res.: 9927 Wayne Ave., 45215. Tel: 513-554-4010; Fax: 513-554-4191.
School—St. Gabriel Consolidated School, Tel: 513-771-5220. See separate listing.
Catechesis/Religious Program—Students 17.

57—ST. MARTIN OF TOURS (Cheviot) (1911), Revs. George C. Kunkel; George Schmitz.
Res.: 3720 St. Martin Pl., 45211. Tel: 513-661-2000; Fax: 513-661-1432.
School—3729 Harding Ave., 45211. Tel: 513-661-7609; Fax: 513-661-8102. Mrs. Kathryn Lawrence, Prin. Lay Teachers 19; Students 353.
Catechesis/Religious Program—Students 34.

58—ST. MARY (Hyde Park) (1898), Rev. David C. Robisch; Deacon John Thamann; Mrs. Judy Wickert, Pastoral Assoc.; Mrs. Emily Besl Henry, Pastoral Assoc.; Mr. Keith Pfaller, Pastoral Assoc.
Res.: 2853 Erie Ave., 45208. Tel: 513-321-1207; Fax: 513-533-5518.
School—2845 Erie Ave., 45208. Tel: 513-321-0703; Fax: 513-533-5517. Jane Welling, Prin. Lay Teachers 24; Students 515.
Catechesis/Religious Program—Tel: 513-321-0703; Fax: 513-533-5518. Students 120.

59—ST. MATTHIAS (Forest Park) (1967), Revs. David E. Fay; Gerard A. Evers (Retired); Deacon Raymond George.
Res.: 1050 W. Kemper Rd., 45240. Tel: 513-851-1930; Fax: 513-589-3850.
Catechesis/Religious Program—Tel: 513-851-1930, Ext. 14; Fax: 513-589-3850. Students 25.

60—ST. MICHAEL (1919), Rev. Michael U. Pucke; Cindy Wurzelbacher, Pastoral Assoc.; Deacon Francis Wagner; Brian Bisig, Dir. Music; Scott Hungler, Business Mgr.
Res.: 11144 Spinner Ave., 45241. Tel: 513-563-6377; Fax: 513-554-3543.
School—Tel: 513-554-3555; Fax: 513-554-3551. Jody Farrell, Prin. Lay Teachers 22; Students 420.
Catechesis/Religious Program—Tel: 513-554-3547. Anna Geoppinger, D.R.E. Students 194.

61—ST. MONICA-ST. GEORGE PARISH NEWMAN CENTER (1993), Revs. Alan Hirt, O.F.M.; Tom Speier, O.F.M.
Res.: 328 W. McMillan St., 45219. Tel: 513-381-6400; Fax: 513-381-2540.
Church: Tel: 513-381-6400.
Catechesis/Religious Program—Students 20.

62—MOTHER OF CHRIST (1946), (African American), Rev. James Shappelle; Sr. Mary Macke, O.S.U., Pastoral Admin.
Church and Res.: 5301 Winneste Ave., 45232. Tel: 513-242-0164 (Church); 513-541-3732 (Res); Fax: 513-242-0164 (Church); 513-541-0362 (Res).
Catechesis/Religious Program—Students 10.

63—NATIVITY OF OUR LORD (Pleasant Ridge) (1917), Rev. R. Marc Sherlock.
Res.: 5935 Pandora Ave., 45213-2017. Tel: 513-531-3164; Fax: 513-458-6761.
School—5936 Ridge Ave., 45213-1699. Tel: 513-458-6767; Fax: 513-458-6769. Robert C. Herring, Prin. Lay Teachers 20; Students 390.
Catechesis/Religious Program—Tel: 513-531-3164, Ext. 310. Students 30.

64—OLD ST. MARY (1842), Revs. Stanley H. Neiheisel, Admin.; Lawrence Juarez.
Res.: 123 E. 13th St., 45202. Tel: 513-721-2988; Fax: 513-721-0436.

65—OUR LADY OF LOURDES (Westwood) (1927), Revs. Edward L. Rudemiller; Lawrence M. Gearhart; Deacon Thomas E. Westerfield; Sr. Maria Hill, Pastoral Assoc.; Catherine Lucas, Business Mgr. In Res., Revs. Robert R. Wolfer (Retired); Paul J. Wolfer (Retired).
Res.: 2832 Rosebud Dr., 45238. Tel: 513-922-0715; 513-347-2641 (Res.); Fax: 513-347-2644.
School—5835 Glenway Ave., 45238. Tel 513-347-2660; Fax: 513-347-2663. Ms. Karen A. Rusche, Prin. Lay Teachers 30; Students 605.
Catechesis/Religious Program—Tel: 513 347-2646. Carol Grealich, D.R.E. Students 79.

66—OUR LADY OF THE ROSARY (Greenhills) (1938), Rev. Charles J. Bowes.
Res.: 17 Farragut Rd., 45218. Tel: 513-825-8626; Fax: 513-825-2783.
School—Tel: 513-825-2336; Fax: 513-825-3410. Ms. Judith Hoferkamp, Prin. Lay Teachers 12; Students 189.
Catechesis/Religious Program—19 Farragut Rd., 45218. Tel: 513-825-2338; Fax: 513-825-3410. Mr. David Nissen, D.R.E. Students 130.

67—OUR LADY OF THE SACRED HEART (Reading) (1874), Rev. Jack W. Wehman; Deacons James Geraci; Robert Glassmeyer.
Res.: 177 Siebenthaler Ave., 45215. Tel: 513-733-4950; Fax: 513-733-0973.
School—Tel: 513-733-5225; Fax: 513-733-0186. Ms. Barbara Adelmann, Prin. Lay Teachers 18; Students 335.
Catechesis/Religious Program—Students 135.

68—OUR LADY OF VICTORY (Delhi Hills) (1842), [CEM] Revs. George Schmitz; Thomas E. Meyer; Deacons Charles Jenkins; Joseph Schultheis.
Res.: 810 Neeb Rd., 45233. Tel: 513-922-4460; Fax: 513-922-5476.
School—808 Neeb Rd., 45233. Tel: 513-347-2072; Fax: 513-922-5476. Mrs. Sally Hicks Prin. Lay Teachers 37; Students 730.
Catechesis/Religious Program—Tel: 513-347-2071; Fax: 513-922-5476. Mrs. Doris Steille, D.R.E. Students 135.

69—OUR LADY OF VISITATION (Mack) (1947), Rev. Anthony M. Brausch; Sr. Marla Gipson, C.P.P.S., Pastoral Assoc.; Deacon William A. Dehmer.
Res.: 3172 South Rd., 45248. Tel: 513-922-2056; Fax: 513-347-2238.
School—3180 South Rd., 45248. Tel: 513-347-2222; Fax: 513-347-2225. Mr. Terry P. Chapman, Prin. Sisters 1; Lay Teachers 40; Students 834.
Catechesis/Religious Program—Tel: 513-347-2228; Fax: 513-347-2225. Sr. Mary Tewes, O.S.B., D.R.E. Students 63.

70—OUR LORD, CHRIST THE KING (Mt. Lookout) (1926), Revs. Robert A. Obermeyer; Lawrence Tabi (Ghana).
Res.: 3223 Linwood Rd., 45226. Tel: 513-321-4121; Fax: 513-871-3978.
School—Cardinal Pacelli, 927 Ellison, 45226. Tel: 513-321-1048; Fax: 513-533-6118. Kim Roy, Prin. Lay Teachers 24; Students 409.
Catechesis/Religious Program—Students 50.

71—OUR MOTHER OF SORROWS (Roselawn) (1941), Rev. Steven P. Walter; Deacon Michael A. Ascolese.
Res.: 7243 Eastlawn Dr., 45237. Tel: 513-731-6480; Fax: 513-731-4640.
School—Tel: 513-731-8838; Fax: 513-731-4640. Catie Blum, Prin. Lay Teachers 12; Students 130.
Catechesis/Religious Program— Combined with St. Robert Bellarmine, Cincinnati

72—STS. PETER AND PAUL (Reading) (1850), [CEM] Rev. Michael F. Leshney.
330 W. Vine St., Reading, 45215. Tel: 513-554-1010; 513-554-0700 (Rectory); Fax: 513-554-0190.
School—Tel: 513-554-1311; Fax: 513-554-4667. Mrs. Sharon Willmes, Prin. Lay Teachers 12; Students 189; Sisters 1.
Catechesis/Religious Program—Tel: 513-733-5542. Jane Gorton, D.R.E. Students 297.

73—RESURRECTION OF OUR LORD (1919), Rev. Robert L. Keller.
Res.: 1744 Iliff Ave., 45205. Tel: 513-471-2700; Fax: 513-471-2703.
School—1740 Iliff Ave., 45205. Tel: 513-471-6600; Fax: 513-471-6600. Kathleen Sparks, Prin. Sisters 3; Lay Teachers 10; Students 140.
Catechesis/Religious Program—Tel: 513-471-2431. Students 5.

74—ST. ROBERT BELLARMINE (1927), Revs. Richard W. Bollman, S.J.; Albert J. Bischoff, S.J.; Lauren McDonough Renneker, Dir. Social Mission. Tel: 513-745-3398; Scott Buzza, Dir. Music Min. Tel: 513-745-3270; Marcia L. Peebles, Dir. Youth Min. Tel: 513-745-4224; Karen Brandstetter, Pastoral Assoc.
Xavier University: 3800 Victory Pkwy., 45207. Tel: 513-745-3398; Fax: 513-745-2031.
Catechesis/Religious Program—Tel: 513-745-3317. Rosemary G. Conrad, D.R.E. Students 81.

75—ST. ROSE OF LIMA (1867), Rev. Barry Windholtz.
Res.: 2501 Eastern Ave., 45202. Tel: 513-871-1162; Fax: 513-871-2851.

76—SACRED HEART (1870), (Italian), Rev. Mario Rauzi, C.S.
Res.: 2733 Massachusetts Ave., 45225. Tel: 513-541-4654; Fax: 513-541-4662.
School—Corryville Catholic Elementary School, Tel: 513-281-4856; Fax: 513-281-6497. See separate listing.

77—ST. SAVIOUR (Blue Ash) (1947), Rev. Patrick H. Crone.
Res.: 4136 Myrtle Ave., 45236. Tel: 513-791-9004; Fax: 513-791-6530.
Catechesis/Religious Program—Tel: 513-791-0119. Students 60.

78—ST. SIMON THE APOSTLE (1966), Rev. Michael D. Beatty.
Res.: 825 Pontius Rd., 45233. Tel: 513-941-3656; Fax: 513-941-1562.
Catechesis/Religious Program—Tel: 513-941-6173; Fax: 513-641-1562. Carolyn Meyers, D.R.E. Students 221.

79—ST. STEPHEN (1867), Rev. Ronald J. Averbeck.
Res.: 320 Donham Ave., 45226. Tel: 513-871-3373.

80—ST. TERESA (1916), Rev. Larry R. Tharp; Deacon Michael Davenport.
Res.: 1175 Overlook Ave., 45238. Tel: 513-921-9200; Fax: 513-921-0307.
School—1194 Rulison Ave., 45238. Tel: 513-471-4530. William Cavanaugh, Prin. Lay Teachers 23; Students 418.
Catechesis/Religious Program—Tel: 513-471-4530. David L. Donovan, D.R.E. Students 63.

81—ST. THERESE, THE LITTLE FLOWER (Mt. Airy) (1926), Revs. Robert W. Goebel; Robert A. Stricker (Retired).
Res.: 5560 Kirby Ave., 45239. Tel: 513-541-5560; Fax: 513-681-2631.
School—5555 Little Flower Ave., 45239. Tel: 513-542-6787; Fax: 513-542-3658. Ms. Linda Westendorf, Prin. Lay Teachers 19; Students 407.
Catechesis/Religious Program—Tel: 513-541-5560. Sr. Francis Margaret Maag, C.D.P., D.R.E. Students 602.

82—ST. VINCENT DE PAUL (1861), Rev. Gregory J. Lockwood.
Res.: 4044 River Rd., 45204. Tel: 513-451-5714; Fax: 513-451-3830.
School—Tel: 513-451-5656. Mrs. Diane Reder, Prin. Lay Teachers 8; Students 73.

83—ST. VINCENT FERRER (Kenwood) (1946), Rev. Terence J. Hamilton; Judith Verny, Pastoral Assoc.
Res.: 7754 Montgomery Rd., 45236. Tel: 513-791-9030; Fax: 513-791-7405.
School—Tel: 513-791-6320; Fax: 513-791-7405. Joan Tessarolo, Prin. Lay Teachers 17; Students 218.
Catechesis/Religious Program—Tel: 513-791-6321; Fax: 513-791-7405. Sr. Kaye Lednik, C.S.J., D.R.E. Students 200.

84—ST. VIVIAN (1943), Rev. John Kroeger; Kathleen Rothschild, Business Mgr. In Res., Rev. Paul L. Gebhardt; Deacon Larry Maag; Tim McManus, Dir. of Music and Devel.
Res.: 7600 Winton Rd., 45224. Tel: 513-728-4331; Fax: 513-728-4335.
School—885 Denier Pl., 45224. Tel: 513-522-6858; Fax: 513-728-4336. Jean Margello, Prin. Lay Teachers 27; Students 408.
Catechesis/Religious Program—Tel: 513-728-4339; Fax: 513-728-4335. Jodie A. Bender, D.R.E. Students 79.

85—ST. WILLIAM (1909), Rev. Paul A. Bader; Deacons George Bruce; Thomas Faeth. In Res., Rev. Paul L. Rehling (Retired).
Res.: 4108 W. Eighth St., 45205. Tel: 513-921-0247; Fax: 513-921-2810.
School—4125 St. William Ave., 45205. Tel: 513-471-2989; Fax: 513-471-8226. Mr. Jeffrey Finke, Prin. Sisters 1; Lay Teachers 22; Students 325.

OUTSIDE THE CITY OF CINCINNATI

AMELIA, CLERMONT CO., ST. BERNADETTE'S (1944), Rev. Hans H. Gruenbauer.
Res.: 1479 Locust Lake Rd., 45102. Tel: 513-753-5566; Fax: 513-753-7664.
School—1453 Locust Lake Rd., 45102. Tel: 513-753-4744; Fax: 513-753-9018. Mr. Thomas Salerno, Prin. Lay Teachers 13; Students 198.
Catechesis/Religious Program—Tel: 513-753-5466. Kelly Lafferty, D.R.E. Students 93.

ARNHEIM, BROWN CO., ST. MARY (1837), Rev. Dohrman W. Byers.
Res.: 6647 Van Buren St., Georgetown, 45121. Tel: 937-446-2555; Fax: 937-446-2555.
Catechesis/Religious Program—Tel: 937-446-1854. Linda Mulaney. Combined with St. Elizabeth,

Sardinia, OH Students 59.
BATAVIA, CLERMONT CO., HOLY TRINITY (1906), Rev. William R. Stockelman; Deacon James Hennessey.
Res.: 140 N. 6th St., 45103. Tel: 513-732-2024; Fax: 513-732-0049.
Catechesis/Religious Program—Tel: 513-732-2024. Patricia Bruce, D.R.E. Students 92.
BEAVERCREEK, GREENE CO., ST. LUKE (1955), Rev. William J. Kramer; Deacon Gerry Dupree.
Res.: 1440 N. Fairfield Rd., 45432. Tel: 937-426-1733; Fax: 937-426-3965.
School—(Grades K-8), 1442 N. Fairfield Rd., 45432. Tel: 937-426-8551; Fax: 937-426-6435. Mrs. Leslie Vondrell, Prin. Lay Teachers 20; Students 444.
Catechesis/Religious Program—1444 N. Fairfield Rd., 45432. Tel: 937-426-5656. Students 261.
BELLEFONTAINE, LOGAN CO., ST. PATRICK'S (1852), [CEM] Rev. Patrick L. Sheridan; Deacon Harold Dipple.
Res.: 328 E. Patterson Ave., 43311. Tel: 937-592-1656; Fax: 937-592-0971.
Catechesis/Religious Program—320 E. Patterson Rd., 43311. Tel: 937-592-6621. Mrs. Barbara Daly, D.R.E. Students 218.
BETHEL, CLERMONT CO., ST. MARY (1941), Rev. Don J. West; Deacon Jerry Etienne.
Res.: 3398 S.R. 125, 45106. Tel: 513-734-4041; Fax: 513-734-3588.
Catechesis/Religious Program—Tel: 513-734-3676; Fax: 513-734-3588. Students 206.
BLANCHESTER, CLINTON CO., HOLY NAME (1853), Closed., For inquiries for parish records, see St. Angela Merici, Fayetteville.
BOTKINS, SHELBY CO., IMMACULATE CONCEPTION (1865), (German), [CEM] Rev. Patrick L. Sloneker.
Res.: 116 N. Mill St., P.O. Box 519, 45306. Tel: 937-693-2561; Fax: 937-693-2561.
Catechesis/Religious Program—Students 292.
BRADFORD, MIAMI CO., IMMACULATE CONCEPTION (1875), [JC] Rev. James S. Duell.
Res.: 5874 N. Buckneck Rd., R.R. 2, 45308. Tel: 937-448-6220; Fax: 937-473-2476.
Catechesis/Religious Program—Tel: 937-448-6220. Students 75.
BURKETTSVILLE, MERCER CO., ST. BERNARD (1874), Rev. Matthew W. Jozefiak, C.PP.S.
Res.: 71 W. Main St., P.O. Box 146, 45310. Tel: 419-375-2333; Fax: 419-375-9413.
St. Henry Catechetical Center—Tel: 419-678-3811. See St. Henry, St. Henry for details.
Catechesis/Religious Program—Students 115.
CAMDEN, PREBLE CO., ST. MARY'S (1942),
Res.: 5304 Jacksonburg Rd., Trenton, 45067. Tel: 513-726-6294.
Church: 7721 N. Main St., 45311. Tel: 937-452-3352.
Catechesis/Religious Program—Students 39.
CARTHAGENA, MERCER CO., ST. ALOYSIUS (1865), (German), [CEM] Rev. David A. Hoying, C.PP.S.
Res.: 1509 Cranberry Rd., St. Henry, 45883. Tel: 419-925-4776. Email: stfranc@bright.net.
Church: 6036 State Rte. 274, Celina, 45822.
St. Henry Catechetical Center— For details call Tel: 419-678-3811. Students 65.
CASSELLA, MERCER CO., NATIVITY OF THE BLESSED VIRGIN MARY (1847), [CEM] Revs. Kenneth J. Schroeder, C.PP.S.; Harry M. Cavanaugh, C.PP.S. ((TOL)).
Office—7428 State Rte. 119, Maria Stein, 45860. Tel: 419-925-4775; Fax: 419-925-1745.
Catechesis/Religious Program—Tel: 419-925-4812. Kathy Broering, D.R.E. Students 114.
CELINA, MERCER CO., IMMACULATE CONCEPTION OF THE BLESSED VIRGIN MARY (1864), (German), [CEM] Revs. Thomas Brenberger, C.PP.S.; Richard R. Riedel, C.PP.S.; Deacon Thomas Huff.
Res.: 229 W. Anthony St., 45822. Tel: 419-586-6648; Fax: 419-586-6649.
School—Tel: 419-586-2379; Fax: 419-586-6649. Ms. Kathryn Mescher, Prin. Sisters of the Precious Blood 1; Lay Teachers 14; Students 165.
Catechesis/Religious Program—Wayne & Walnut Sts.. Tel: 419-586-2370; Fax: 419-586-6649. Students 381.
CENTERVILLE, MONTGOMERY CO.
1—ST. FRANCIS OF ASSISI (1969), Rev. Thomas W. Schmidt; Deacon Mark Stasiak; Marilyn Hutter, Parish Sec.; Frances Obringer, Sec. of Rel. Educ.
Res.: 6245 Wilmington Pike, 45459. Tel: 937-433-1013; Fax: 937-433-1699.
Catechesis/Religious Program—Tel: 937-433-0128; Fax: 937-433-1699. Mary Ellen Singer, D.R.E. Students 352.
2—INCARNATION (1945), Revs. Lawrence E. Mierenfeld; Christopher J. Worland; Deacon Robert Zinck; Tim Niesel, Pastoral Assoc.; Marilyn Porcino, Pastoral Assoc.
Res.: 55 Williamsburg Ln., 45459. Tel: 937-433-1188; Fax: 937-433-3263.
School—45 Williamsburg Ln., 45459. Tel: 937-433-1051; Fax: 937-433-9796. Cheryl Reichel, Prin. Lay Teachers 41; Students 722.
Catechesis/Religious Program—Tel: 937-433-3377; Fax: 937-433-3263. Paula Weckesser, D.R.E. Students 720.
CHICKASAW, MERCER CO., MOST PRECIOUS BLOOD (1903), (German), [CEM] Rev. John L. Bensman.
Res.: Box 26, 35 S. Maple St., 45826-0026. Tel: 419-925-4391.
Catechesis/Religious Program—Margie Ronnebaum, D.R.E. Students 203.
COLDWATER, MERCER CO., HOLY TRINITY (1867), [CEM] Revs. Ronald H. Wilker; Thomas E. Dorn; Deacon Virgil Lochtefeld.
Res.: 116 E. Main St., 45828. Tel: 419-678-4802; Fax: 419-678-4803.
Catechesis/Religious Program—110 N. Second St., 45828. Tel: 419-678-3328. Deacon Virgil Lochtefeld, D.R.E. Students 1,024.
COVINGTON, MIAMI CO., ST. TERESA (1950), (German—French), [JC] Rev. James S. Duell.
Res.: 6925 W. U.S. 36, 45318. Tel: 937-473-2970; Fax: 937-473-2476.
Catechesis/Religious Program—Tel: 937-473-2970; Fax: 937-473-2476. Ms. Linda Poast, D.R.E.; Mrs. Elaine Christian, Prin. Students 43.
CRANBERRY PRAIRIE, MERCER CO., ST. FRANCIS (1858), (German), [CEM] Rev. David A. Hoying, C.PP.S.
Res.: 1509 Cranberry Rd., St. Henry, 45883. Tel: 419-925-4776. Email: stfranc@bright.net.
St. Henry Catechetical Center— See St. Henry, St. Henry for details. Tel: 419-678-3811. Students 71.
DAYTON, GREENE CO., QUEEN OF APOSTLES (1973), Rev. H. James Bartlett, S.M., Priest Coord.; Deacon Greg Cecere.
Church: 4400 Shakertown Rd., 45430-1075. Tel: 937-429-0510; Fax: 937-429-0510.
Catechesis/Religious Program— Terri Nordmeyer, D.R.E. Students 87.
DAYTON, MONTGOMERY CO.
1—ST. ADALBERT (1903), (Polish), Rev. Michael J. Holloran.
Office—1511 Valley St., 45404. Tel: 937-228-8782.
Catechesis/Religious Program—1509 Valley St., 45404. Arlene Bottenfield, D.R.E. Students 24.
2—ST. AGNES (1915), Rev. James R. Schutte; Mary Reaman, Pastoral Admin.
Res.: 811 N. Paul L. Dunbar St., 45407. Tel: 937-274-2212; Fax: 937-274-0976.
School—Dayton Catholic Elementary Consolidated, Tel: 937-275-8114. See separate listing.
Catechesis/Religious Program—Students 20.
3—ST. ALBERT THE GREAT (1939), Revs. James J. Manning; Martin E. Fox. In Res., Rev. Thomas Beischel, C.PP.S.
Res.: 3033 Far Hills Ave., 45429. Tel: 937-293-1191; Fax: 937-293-1848.
School—Tel: 937-293-9452; Fax: 937-293-1848. Mrs. Lucianne Lilienthal, Prin. Lay Teachers 31; Students 577.
Catechesis/Religious Program—104 Dorothy Ln., Kettering, 45429. Tel: 937-298-2402; Fax: 937-293-1848. Barbara Leibold, D.R.E. Students 430.
4—ST. ANTHONY OF PADUA (1913), Rev. Jeffrey M. Fulmer; Janet Gaier, Pastoral Assoc.
Res.: 820 Bowen St., 45410. Tel: 937-253-9132; Fax: 937-253-6658. Rev. George V. Uralikunnel (India) (MO).
School—Tel: 937-253-6251; Fax: 937-253-1541. Lay Teachers 21; Students 307.
Catechesis/Religious Program—Students 7.
5—ASCENSION (1955), Revs. David E. Brinkmoeller; James A. Hoffbauer; Ronald P. Combs; Sisters Florence Seifert, C.PP.S., Pastoral Assoc.; Agnes Kramer, C.D.P., Pastoral Assoc.; Deacon Victor B. Hildebrand, Pastoral Assoc.; Tom Platfoot, Business Mgr.
Res.: 2025 Woodman Dr., Kettering, 45420. Tel: 937-253-5171; Fax: 937-253-0886.
School—Tel: 937-245-5411; Fax: 937-254-1105. Brent Devitt, Prin. Sisters 2; Lay Teachers 21; Students 424.
Catechesis/Religious Program—Tel: 937-254-0622. Maryellen Fargey, D.R.E. Students 307.
6—ASSUMPTION (1949), Merged, with Our Lady of Mercy, Dayton.
7—ST. CHARLES BORROMEO (1962), Rev. Msgr. Lawrence K. Breslin; Rev. Ronald E. Williams Jr.; Deacon Leonard Baltes; Mary Schulz, Business Mgr.
Res.: 4500 Ackerman Rd., 45429. Tel: 937-434-6081; Fax: 937-434-6251.
School—Tel: 937-434-4933; Fax: 937-434-6692. Miss Judy Ellerbrock, Prin. Sisters 3; Lay Teachers 30; Students 600.
Catechesis/Religious Program—Tel: 937-434-9272. Anne Trick, D.R.E. Students 218.
8—CORPUS CHRISTI (1911), Rev. James R. Schutte.
Res.: 224 Squirrel Rd., 45405. Tel: 937-228-6672; Fax: 937-461-0611.
School—200 Homewood Ave., 45405. Tel: 937-228-3091; Fax: 937-449-2440. Lay Teachers 13; Students 180.
Catechesis/Religious Program—Tel: 937-224-7952. Students 34.
9—EMMANUEL (1837), Revs. Lee L. Sciarrotta, S.M.; Charles T. Bergedick, S.M.
Res.: 149 Franklin St., 45402. Tel: 937-228-2013; Fax: 937-228-5354.
Catechesis/Religious Program—Tel: 937-228-5354. Students 77.
10—ST. HELEN (1953), Rev. Paul F. DeLuca; Deacons John J. Jachimowicz; Susano Mascorro; Roy Deardorff; Ralph O'Bleness.
Res.: 605 Granville Pl., 45431. Tel: 937-254-6233; Fax: 937-256-6117.
School—Tel: 937-256-1761; Fax: 937-254-4614. Mr. Richard Harrmann, Prin. Lay Teachers 22; Students 365.
Catechesis/Religious Program—Tel: 937-256-8815. Joan Torres, D.R.E. Students 141.
Convent—Sisters of Notre Dame, 5098 Burkhardt Rd., 45431. Tel: 937-252-7972.
11—ST. HENRY (1960), Rev. Thomas M. Shearer; Michael Montgomery, Pastoral Assoc.
Res.: 6696 Springboro Rd., 45449. Tel: 937-434-9231; Fax: 937-434-6798.
School—Bishop Leibold Consolidated, Tel: 937-434-9343. See separate listing.
Catechesis/Religious Program—Tel: 937-433-8220; 937-434-9416 (Youth Ministry). Students 630.
12—HOLY ANGELS (1902), Rev. Daniel J. Meyer; Sr. Annette Grisley, O.S.F., Pastoral Assoc.
Parish Office—218 K St., 45409. Tel: 937-222-7807; Fax: 937-222-8167.
Church: Brown & L Sts., 45409.
School—Tel: 937-222-0365; Fax: 937-222-1580. Louise P. Moore, Prin. Lay Teachers 22; Students 274.
Catechesis/Religious Program—Tel: 937-222-2641. Jeanne Fairbanks, D.R.E. Students 237.
13—HOLY CROSS (1914), (Lithuanian), Rev. Michael J. Holloran.
Res.: 22 Notre Dame Ave., 45404. Tel: 937-228-8802.
Catechesis/Religious Program—1511 Valley St., 45404. Tel: 937-228-8782; Fax: 937-443-0969. Students 5.
14—HOLY FAMILY (1905), Rev. John E. Krumm. In Res., Revs. Edward Haggerty; Charles Kanai (Kenya).
Res.: 140 S. Findlay St., 45403. Tel: 937-253-1109; Fax: 937-253-2172.
School—121 S. Monmouth St., 45403. Tel: 937-253-4859; Fax: 937-253-8534. G. Janell Klippel, Prin. Lay Teachers 11; Students 175.
Catechesis/Religious Program—St. Mary Church, 310 Allen St., 45410. Tel: 937-256-5633; Fax: 937-256-7138. Students 21.
15—HOLY TRINITY (1860), [JC] Rev. Rick Friebel, C.PP.S.; Deacon George Zvonar; Mary C. Wlodarski, Christian Formation Min.; Judith L. Trick, Business Mgr.
Res.: 272 Bainbridge St., 45402. Tel: 937-228-1223; Fax: 937-445-0232.
Catechesis/Religious Program—Students 64.
16—ST. JAMES (1919), Merged, with Resurrection of Our Lord, Dayton to form St. James/Resurrection of Our Lord, Dayton.
17—ST. JAMES/RESURRECTION OF OUR LORD (1919), (African American), Rev. Francis Tandoh, C.S.Sp.; Deacon Jacob Jerigan.
Office—130 Gramont Ave., P.O. Box 17219, 45417. Tel: 937-268-6697; Fax: 937-268-6698.
Res.: 719 Edgemont Ave., 45408. Tel: 937-228-7023.
School—Tel: 937-268-6391; Fax: 937-268-9775. Ms. Debra Johnson, Prin. Lay Teachers 16; Students 220.
Catechesis/Religious Program—Students 67.
18—ST. JOSEPH (1847), Rev. Louis Osterhage, C.PP.S.
Res.: 411 E. Second St., 45402. Tel: 937-228-9272; 937-228-9522; Fax: 937-228-6144.
19—ST. MARY'S (1859), Rev. John E. Krumm; Deacon William Saluke; Margot Lebreton Merz, Pastoral Assoc.
Res.: 310 Allen St., 45410. Tel: 937-256-5633; Fax: 937-256-7138.
Catechesis/Religious Program—Tel: 937-256-5633; Fax: 937-256-7138. Dr. Robert Obach, D.R.E. Students 20.
20—OUR LADY OF MERCY (1928), Revs. P. Del Staigers; Walter Macpherson (Retired); Sr. Ann Clark, C.PP.S., Pastoral Assoc.; Deacon Thomas Platfoot; Pam Long, Pastoral Assoc.
Res.: 220 W. Siebenthaler Ave., 45405. Tel: 937-274-2107; Fax: 937-274-4363.
School—Tel: 937-278-5483. Ann Vogel, Prin. Lay Teachers 11; Students 175.
Catechesis/Religious Program—Students 30.
21—OUR LADY OF THE IMMACULATE CONCEPTION (1938), Rev. Anthony J. Geraci. In Res., Rev. Satish Joseph Antony.
Res.: 2300 S. Smithville Rd., 45420. Tel: 937-252-9919; Fax: 937-252-0890.
School—Tel: 937-253-8831; Fax: 937-252-8832. Mr. Walter Klimaski, Prin. Lay Teachers 19; Students

322.
Catechesis/Religious Program—Students 24.
22—OUR LADY OF THE ROSARY (1887), Rev. Michael J. Holloran; Deacon Henry B. Beck.
Res.: 22 Notre Dame Ave., 45404. Tel: 937-228-8802; Fax: 937-443-0969.
School—40 Notre Dame Ave., 45404. Tel: 937-222-7231; Fax: 937-222-7393. Genevieve S. Ritzel, Prin. Lay Teachers 10; Students 235.
Catechesis/Religious Program—St. Adalbert, 1511 Valley St., 45404. Tel: 937-228-8782. Students 34.
23—ST. PETER (Huber Heights) (1959), Revs. Earl Francis Simone; Stephen S. Mondiek; Deacons Allen K. Miller; Robert Borgerding; John E. Gould; Timothy J. Harris; Robert M. Correale; Charles O. Wright.
Res.: 6161 Chambersburg Rd., 45424. Tel: 937-233-1503; Fax: 937-237-3523.
School—Tel: 937-233-8710; Fax: 937-237-3974. Feliza Poling, Prin. Lay Teachers 43; Students 749.
Catechesis/Religious Program—Tel: 937-237-3516; Fax: 937-233-5717. Ms. Joy Blaul, D.R.E. Students 469.
24—PRECIOUS BLOOD (1948), Rev. William O'Donnell, C.PP.S.; Deacon Richard Janowiecki; Joseph Murr, Business Mgr. In Res., Rev. Ken Schnipke, C.PP.S.; Bro. Jerome Schulte, C.PP.S.
Gaspar House: 4880 Denlinger Rd., 45426. Tel: 937-278-3265.
School—4870 Denlinger Rd., 45426. Tel: 937-277-2291; Fax: 937-277-2217. Antonio Ferraro, Prin. Lay Teachers 23; Students 273.
Catechesis/Religious Program—Tel: 937-276-5955; Fax: 937-276-5955. Timothy Clarke; Mark Moorman. Students 218.
25—QUEEN OF MARTYRS (Northridge) (1948), Rev. Del Staigers; Deacon Skip Royer; Jane Bensman, Pastoral Assoc.
Res.: 4144 Cedar Ridge Rd., 45414. Tel: 937-277-2092; Fax: 937-277-2773.
School—Tel: 937-274-5592; Fax: 937-274-4852. Frances Moore, Prin. Sisters 2; Lay Teachers 7; Students 137.
Catechesis/Religious Program—Tel: 937-277-2092. Students 6.
26—ST. RITA (1922), Rev. Kenneth R. Baker; Deacon James C. Olinger.
Res.: 5401 N. Main St., 45415. Tel: 937-278-5815; Fax: 937-275-3302.
School—Tel: 937-277-8978; Fax: 937-277-8979. Mary Ann Eismann, Prin. Sisters 1; Lay Teachers 14; Students 261.
Catechesis/Religious Program—Jenny Terbay, D.R.E. Students 79.
27—ST. STEPHEN (North Dayton) (1906), (Hungarian), Rev. Michael J. Holloran.
Parish Office—114 Troy St., 45404. Tel: 937-228-8802; Fax: 937-443-0969.
Catechesis/Religious Program— Refer to St. Adalbert, Dayton. Tel: 937-228-8782.

EATON, PREBLE CO., VISITATION OF THE BLESSED VIRGIN MARY (1853), Rev. J. Thomas Fitzsimmons; Deacon Joseph James.
Res.: 407 E. Main St., 45320. Tel: 937-456-3380.
Catechesis/Religious Program—Tel: 937-456-3395. Sharon Stump, D.R.E. Students 147.

EGYPT, AUGLAIZE CO., ST. JOSEPH (1852), [CEM], Clustered with St. Augustine, Minister. Rev. Louis Schmit, C.PP.S.
Res.: 02441 SR 364, 45865. Tel: 419-628-2614; Fax: 419-628-2958.
Catechesis/Religious Program—Tel: 419-628-3434. Clustered with St. Augustine, Minster. Students 57.

ENGLEWOOD, MONTGOMERY CO., ST. PAUL'S (1972), Rev. Todd Grogan; Deacon Joseph Subler.
Res.: 1000 W. Wenger Rd., 45322. Tel: 937-836-7535; Fax: 937-836-1130.
Catechesis/Religious Program—Tel: 937-836-2337. Dr. Sandra Chakeres, D.R.E.

FAIRBORN, GREENE CO., MARY HELP OF CHRISTIANS (1862), [CEM] Rev. Charles F. Lang; Deacon Max Roadruck; Pat Scanlon, Pastoral Assoc.
Res.: 954 N. Maple Ave., 45324-5498. Tel: 937-878-8353; Fax: 937-879-8800.
School—934 N. Maple Ave., 45324-5499. Tel: 937-878-9152; Fax: 937-879-8804. Anne Steck, Prin. Lay Teachers 13; Students 172.
Catechesis/Religious Program—1030 N. Maple Ave., 45324. Tel: 937-878-7325; Fax: 937-879-8800. Molly Hynes Collinsworth, D.R.E. Students 91.

FAIRFIELD, BUTLER CO., SACRED HEART OF JESUS (1957), Rev. Norman Langenbrunner
Church: 400 Nilles Rd., 45014. Tel: 513-829-4383; Fax: 513-858-4211.
Res.: 5202 Mississippi Dr., 45014. Tel: 513-863-5318; Fax: 513-863-5318.
School—Tel: 513-858-4215; Fax: 513-858-4218. Joseph Nagle, Prin. Lay Teachers 21; Students 450.
Catechesis/Religious Program—Tel: 513-858-4213; Fax: 513-858-4211. Students 150.

FAYETTEVILLE, BROWN CO.
1—ST. ANGELA MERICI (2003), Rev. Ronald C. Cooper; Sr. Rita Hawk, S.C., D.R.E.
130 Stone Alley, P.O. Box 279, 45118. Tel: 513-875-5020; Fax: 513-875-5022.
Catechesis/Religious Program—Tel: 513-875-3860; Fax: 513-875-3861. Refer to St. Martin, Martin.
Chapel—Holy Name Chapel Blanchester, 45107.
Chapel—St. Patrick Chapel 45118.
Chapel—St. Martin Chapel Martin, 43445.
2—ST. PATRICK (1837), [CEM] Closed., For inquiries for parish records, see St. Angela Merici, Fayetteville.

FELICITY, CLERMONT CO., OUR MOTHER OF GOOD COUNSEL, Closed., For inquiries for parish records please see St. Mary Church, Bethel.

FORT LORAMIE, SHELBY CO., ST. MICHAEL'S (1838), [CEM] [JC 3] Rev. Steven L. Shoup; Deacon Werner Bensman.
Res.: 33 Elm St., P.O. Box 7, 45845. Tel: 937-295-2891; Fax 937-295-3349.
Catechesis/Religious Program—Tel: 937-295-2179; Fax: 937-295-3349. Madeline Maurer, D.R.E.; Frank Turner, D.R.E. Students 587.

FORT RECOVERY, MERCER CO.
1—MARY HELP OF CHRISTIANS (1881), [CEM] Revs. Paul W. Wohlwend, C.PP.S.; Norbert Loshe, C.PP.S.; Deacon John Parker.
Res.: 403 Sharpsburg Rd., 45846. Tel: 419-375-4153.
Catechesis/Religious Program—Tel: 419-375-4153; Fax: 419-375-4154. Students 408.
2—ST. PETER (1860), (German), [CEM] Rev. Kenneth G. Alt, C.PP.S.
Res.: 1477 Philothea Rd., St. Peter, 45846. Tel: 419-375-4344; Fax: 419-375-4030.
Catechesis/Religious Program—Tel: 419-375-4344. Lisa Roessner, D.R.E.; Virginia Fortkamp, D.R.E. Students 164.

FRANKLIN, WARREN CO., ST. MARY (1867), Rev. Charles E. Mentrup.
Res.: 115 S. Main St., 45005. Tel: 937-746-5404; Fax: 937 746-5470.
Catechesis/Religious Program—Tel: 937-746-1404. Students 280.

FRENCHTOWN, DARKE CO., HOLY FAMILY (1846), [CEM] Rev. David P. Vincent; Deacon Jack Borgerding.
Res.: 14 E. Wood St., Versailles, 45380. Tel: 937-526-4945; Fax: 937-526-4893.
Catechesis/Religious Program—Tel: 419-336-7875. Mary Hartke, D.R.E. Students 78.

FRYBURG, AUGLAIZE CO., ST. JOHN (1850), (German), [CEM 2] Rev. Oscar H. Seger.
Res.: 11519 Van Buren St., Wapakoneta, 45895-8467. Tel: 419-738-6043; Fax: 419-738-4364.
Catechesis/Religious Program—Tel: 419-738-6268. Ann Limbert, D.R.E. Students 45.

GEORGETOWN, BROWN CO., ST. GEORGE (1902), Rev. John P. Fischer.
Parish Office & Mailing Address: 16 N. 4th St., Ripley, 45167. Tel: 937-392-1116; Fax: 937-392-1699.
Res.: 109 S. Elm St., 45121. Tel: 937-378-4376.
Church 501 E. State St. & Elm St., 45121.
Catechesis/Religious Program—Tel: 937-378-9616. Joan St. Clair, D.R.E. Students 68.

GERMANTOWN, MONTGOMERY CO., ST AUGUSTINE (1941), Rev. John R. Kummer.
Res.: 6891 Weaver Rd., 45327-9378. Tel: 937-855-2289; Fax: 937-855-1109.
Catechesis/Religious Program—Tel: 937-855-2289. Students 79.

GLYNWOOD, AUGLAIZE CO., ST. PATRICK (1857), (Irish), [CEM] Rev. Oscar H. Seger.
Res.: 05959 Glynwood Rd., St. Marys, 45885. Tel: 419-738-6043; Fax: 419-738-7113.
Catechesis/Religious Program—Tel: 419-394-8458. Margaret Oen, D.R.E. Students 44.

GREENFIELD, HIGHLAND CO., ST. BENIGNUS (1856), [CEM] Rev. Francis X. Klamet (CLV)
Res.: 218 S. Second St., 45123. Tel: 937-981-2785; Fax: 937-981-4483.
Catechesis/Religious Program—Kathy Henry, D.R.E. Students 62.

GREENVILLE, DARKE CO., ST. MARY (1853), [CEM] Rev. John R. White, J.C.L.
Res.: 233 W. 3rd St., 45331. Tel: 937-548-1616; Fax: 937-548-0352.
School—238 W. Third St., 45331. Tel: 937-548-2345; Fax: 937-548-0878. Lay Teachers 9; Students 102.
Catechesis/Religious Program—Students 201.

HAMILTON, BUTLER CO.
1—ST. ANN (1909), Rev. Dennis Dettenwanger; Deacon Mark E. Brunner; Pat Miller, Pastoral Assoc.
Res.: 646 Clinton Ave., 45015. Tel: 513-863-4963; Fax: 513-863-2017.
School—3064 Pleasant Ave., 45015. Tel: 513-863-0604. Mrs. Donna L. Weber, Prin. Sisters 1; Lay Teachers 11; Students 177.
Catechesis/Religious Program—Tel 513-863-4963. Students 41.
Convent—Sisters of the Third Order Regular of St. Francis (Oldenburg, IN) , 646 Clinton Ave., 45015. Tel: 513-863-1701.
2—ST. JOSEPH (1867), (German), Rev. Dennis Dettenwanger; Deacon James Kowalski, Pastoral Admin.
Res.: 171 Washington St., 45011. Tel: 513-863-1424; Fax: 513-863-1451.
School—Tel: 513-863-8758; Fax: 513-863-5253. Joseph Pyfrin, Prin. Lay Teachers 12; Students 219.
Catechesis/Religious Program—Students 250.
3—ST. JULIE BILLIART (1989), [CEM 2], (This parish is the successor in interest to St. Mary, St. Stephen and St. Veronica parishes, formerly located in Hamilton, OH.) Rev. Jeffrey P. Silver; Deacons William B. Renneker, Pastoral Assoc.; Thomas Strodtbeck; Mrs. Betty Meiner, Business Mgr.
Church: 224 Dayton St., 45011. Tel: 513-863-1040; Fax: 513-863-1132.
School—(Grades K-8), 1206 Shuler Ave., 45011. Tel: 513-867-8477; Fax: 513-867-0139. Mr. Edward Lenney, Prin. Lay Teachers 12; Students 190.
Catechesis/Religious Program—Mrs. Lynne Briggs, D.R.E. Students 100.
4—ST. PETER IN CHAINS (1894), (German), Rev. Timothy S. Bunch.
Res.: 382 Liberty Ave., 45013. Tel: 513-863-3938; Fax: 513-863-1257.
School—451 Ridgelawn Ave., 45013. Tel: 513-863-0685; Fax: 513-863-1859. Lay Teachers 23; Students 325.
Catechesis/Religious Program—Tel: 513-863-3344. Students 78.

HILLSBORO, HIGHLAND CO., ST. MARY (1853), [CEM] Rev. Stanley E. Luehrmann; Deacon Leonard Parker, Pastoral Assoc.
Res.: 212 S. High St., 45133-1445. Tel: 937-393-1742; Fax: 937-393-1742.
School—Tel: 937-840-9932; Fax: 937-840-9932. Lay Teachers 5; Religious 1; Students 66.
Catechesis/Religious Program—Kathy Henry, D.R.E. Students 61.

JAMESTOWN, GREENE CO., ST. AUGUSTINE (1870), Rev. William V. Thomas.
Res.: 31 S. Chillicothe St., P.O. Box F, South Charleston, 45368-0806. Tel: 937-462-8971; Fax: 937-462-9184.
Catechesis/Religious Program—Rita Canty, D.R.E. Tel: 937-675-3219. Students 28.

LEBANON, WARREN CO., ST. FRANCIS DE SALES (1883), Rev. Bernard J. Weldishofer; Deacons Herschel Steward; John Taylor; Mark Anthony, Admin.
Parish Office: 20-A DeSales Ave., 45036.
Res.: 15 DeSales Ave., 45036. Tel: 513-932-2601; Fax: 513-932-9144.
Oratory— 20 DeSales Ave., 45036. Tel: 513-932-6501; Fax: 513-932-9919. Jo Anne Fischesser, Prin. Lay Teachers 12; Students 247.
Catechesis/Religious Program—Tel: 513-933-0307. Students 250.

LIBERTY TOWNSHIP, BUTLER CO., ST. MAXIMILIAN KOLBE (1989), Revs. Terrance W. Smith; Bryan T. Reif.
Church & Mailing: 5720 Hamilton-Mason Rd., 45011.
Res.: 7168 St. Albans Way, Hamilton, 45011. Tel: 513-777-4322; Fax: 513-777-7264.
School—St. Gabriel Consolidated School See separate listing.
Catechesis/Religious Program—Students 1,514.

LOVELAND, CLERMONT CO., ST. COLUMBAN (1859), Rev. Lawrence R. Tensi; Deacons Joseph Coll; James Miller; Edward Reising; Harry Walker.
Office & Mailing Address: 894 Oakland Rd., 45140. Tel: 513-683-7903; Fax: 513-683-1389.
Res.: 855 Oakland Rd., 45140. Tel: 513-677-8084.
School—896 Oakland Rd., 45140. Fax: 513-683-7904. Sr. Mary Dennise, S.N.D., Prin. Sisters 2; Lay Teachers 24; Students 679.
Catechesis/Religious Program—Tel: 513-683-0105; Fax: 513-683-1389. Students 237.
Convent—Sisters of Notre Dame (Covington, KY) , 896 Oakland Rd., 45140. Tel: 513-683-0255.

MANCHESTER, ADAMS CO., ST. MARY OF THE ASSUMPTION (1878), Closed., For inquiries for parish records please contact Holy Trinity, West Union.

MARIA STEIN, MERCER CO., ST. JOHN THE BAPTIST (1836), [CEM] Revs. Kenneth J. Schroeder, C.PP.S.; Harry M. Cavanaugh, C.PP.S. ((TOL)); Deacons Carl Franzer; Omer Bertke.
Office—7428 State Rte. 119, 45860. Tel: 419-925-4775; Fax: 419-925-1745.
Res.: 8533 State Rte. 119, 45860. Tel: 419-925-4522; Fax: 419-925-7522.
Catechesis/Religious Program—Tel: 419-925-4235. Students 304.

MASON, WARREN CO., ST. SUSANNA (1938), Revs. Harry J. Meyer; J. Daniel Schuh; Sr. Angela Jarboe, O.S.B., Pastoral Assoc.; Deacons James A. Merritt; Daniel L. Rader; Karen Gottschall, Pastoral Assoc.; Chris Kreger, Pastoral Assoc.; Rosie Leugers, Pastoral Assoc.; Herb Keil, Business Mgr.
Office—305 Fourth Ave., 45040. Tel: 513-398-3821;

Fax: 513-398-2254.
School—500 Reading Rd., 45040. Tel: 513-398-3821; Fax: 513-398-1657. Julie Heyob, Prin. Lay Teachers 22; Students 499.
Catechesis/Religious Program—Tel: 513-398-3821. Students 1,300.

MCCARTYVILLE, SHELBY CO., SACRED HEART OF JESUS (1882), Rev. Patrick J. Welsh.
Res. and Mailing Address: 9333 State Rte. 119 W., Anna, 45302. Tel: 937-394-3823; 419-628-2502; Fax: (Call for fax number).
Catechesis/Religious Program—Tel: 937-394-3823; Fax: 973-394-3823 (call first). Barbara Riethman, D.R.E. Students 445.

MECHANICSBURG, CHAMPAIGN CO., ST. MICHAEL'S (1865), Rev. Clarence G. Heis.
Res.: 40 Walnut St., 43044. Tel: 937-834-2413; Fax: 937-834-2413.
Catechesis/Religious Program—Students 39.

MIAMISBURG, MONTGOMERY CO., OUR LADY OF GOOD HOPE (1852), [CEM] Rev. Thomas A. Nevels; Deacon Richard Martin.
Res.: 6 S. Third St., 45342. Tel: 937-866-1432; Fax: 937-859-5035.
School—Bishop Leibold Consolidated, Dayton, Tel: 937-866-3021; Fax: 937-859-5035. See separate listing.
Catechesis/Religious Program—Tel: 937-866-1492. Students 209.

MIDDLETOWN, BUTLER CO., HOLY FAMILY (1991), [JC], (This parish is the successor in interest to Holy Trinity, St. John the Baptist and St. Mary parishes, formerly located in Middletown, OH) Rev. John R. Civille; Sr. Jean Sora, O.S.F., Pastoral Assoc. In Res., Deacons Thomas Coyle; William Krumm.
Office—201 Clark St., 45042. Tel: 513-422-0602; Fax: 513-424-7416.
School—John XXIII Consolidated, Middletown, Tel: 513-424-0838; Fax: 513-424-8568. See separate listing.
Catechesis/Religious Program—Tel: 513-422-0602; Fax: 513-424-7416. Students 140.

MILFORD, CLERMONT CO., ST. ANDREW (1854), [CEM] Revs. Robert C. Waller; Edward P. Smith.
Res.: 552 Main St., 45150. Tel: 513-831-3353; Fax: 513-831-6597.
School—St. Andrew-St. Elizabeth Seton, (Grades K-8), 555 Main St., 45150. Tel: 513-831-5277; Fax: 513-831-8436. Donna J. Beebe, Prin. Consolidated. Lay Teachers 24; Students 617.
Catechesis/Religious Program—Tel: 513-831-3812; Fax: 513-831-6597. Barbara Aluotto, D.R.E. Students 193.

MILLVILLE, BUTLER CO., QUEEN OF PEACE (1941), Rev. W. Michael Hay; Deacon Bill Brunsman.
Res.: 2550 Millville Ave., Hamilton, 45013. Tel: 513-863-4344; Fax: 513-863-4364.
School—Tel: 513-863-8705; Fax: 513-863-4310. Bernadette Zimmerman, Prin. Lay Teachers 15; Students 242.
Catechesis/Religious Program—Tel: 513-863-3428; Fax: 513-863-4364. Cindy Smith, D.R.E. Students 147.

MINSTER, AUGLAIZE CO., ST. AUGUSTINE (1832), (German), [CEM] Revs. Louis Schmit, C.PP.S.; Mark Armstrong; Deacons John J. Schmiesing; Hal Belcher; Rev. Mark Armstrong.
Res.: 48 N. Hanover St., P.O. Box 93, 45865. Tel: 419-628-2614; Fax: 419-628-1078.
Catechesis/Religious Program—47 N. Lincoln St., P.O. Box 93, 45865. Tel: 419-628-3434; Fax: 419-628-1078. Jane Boeke. Students 689.

MONROE, BUTLER CO., OUR LADY OF SORROWS (1883), Rev. Terrance A. Meehan.
Mailing Address: 330 Lebanon St., 45050.
Res.: 416 Lebanon St., 45050. Tel: 513-539-8383; Fax: 513-539-0443.
Catechesis/Religious Program—330 Lebanon St., 45050. Tel: 513-539-8061; Fax: 513-539-0443. Corinne Butera, D.R.E. Students 97.

MONTEZUMA, MERCER CO., OUR LADY OF GUADALUPE (1903), [CEM] Rev. James H. Dugal, C.PP.S.
Res.: P.O. Box 69, 45866. Tel: 419-268-2312; Fax: 419-268-1602.
Catechesis/Religious Program—Tel: 419-268-2312. Ruth Wynk; Ron Niekamp, D.R.E. Students 140.

MORROW, WARREN CO., ST. PHILIP THE APOSTLE (1965), [CEM] Rev. Ronald J. Piepmeyer.
Res.: 944 East U.S. 22-3, 45152-9690. Tel: 513-899-3601; Fax: 513-899-3601.
Catechesis/Religious Program—Tel: 513-899-3785; Fax: 513-899-3785. Sr. Mary William Luxford, O.S.U. Students 181.

MOUNT CARMEL, CLERMONT CO., ST. VERONICA (1949), Revs. Michael T. Flaherty; Benedict O'Cinnsealaigh, S.T.L.; Deacon Walter Srode.
Res.: 4473 Mt. Carmel-Tobasco Rd., 45244. Tel: 513-528-1622; Fax: 513-528-1622.
School—Tel: 513-528-0442; Fax: 513-528-0513. Mr. Paul McLaughlin, Prin. Sisters 2; Lay Teachers 19; Students 470.
Catechesis/Religious Program—Tel: 513-528-8723. Students 176.

MOUNT ORAB, BROWN CO., ST. MICHAEL (1944), Rev. Dohrman W. Byers.
Res.: 6647 Van Buren St., Georgetown, 45121-9563. Tel: 937-446-2555; Fax: 937-446-2555.
Church: 220 S. High St., 45154. Tel: 937-444-3944.
Catechesis/Religious Program—Tel: 937-444-3770; 937-446-2555. Connie Carroll, D.R.E. Students 25.

MOUNT REPOSE, CLERMONT CO., ST. ELIZABETH ANN SETON (1976), Rev. David A. Sunberg.
Res.: 5890 Buckwheat Rd., Milford, 45150. Tel: 513-575-0119; Fax: 513-575-0957.
School—5900 Buckwheat Rd., Milford, 45150. Tel: 513-575-0093; Fax: 513-575-1078. Ms. Donna Beebe, Prin. Lay Teachers 25; Students 436.
School—Preschool, Tel: 513-575-9900; Fax: 513-575-1078. Mrs. Terri Imming, Dir. Lay Teachers 10; Students 150.
Catechesis/Religious Program—Tel: 513-575-0119; Fax: 513-575-0957. Ed Alten, D.R.E. Students 290.

NEW BREMEN, AUGLAIZE CO., HOLY REDEEMER (1948), Rev. Thomas M. Mannebach; Deacon Gregory Bornhorst.
Res.: 120 S. Eastmoor Dr., P.O. Box 67, 45869. Tel: 419-629-2543; Fax: 419-629-2543.
Catechesis/Religious Program—Students 457.

NEW CARLISLE, CLARK CO., SACRED HEART (1950), Deacon Robert Kozlowski.
Res.: 476 N. Scott St., 45344. Tel: 937-845-3121; Fax: 937-846-1223.
Catechesis/Religious Program—Tel: 937-845-1373; Fax: 937-846-1223. Joan Steinlage, D.R.E. Students 209.

NEW PARIS, PREBLE CO., ST. JOHN THE EVANGELIST (1870), Rev. J. Thomas Fitzsimmons.
Res., Visitation: 407 E. Main St., Eaton, 45320. Tel: 937-456-3380.
Catechesis/Religious Program—Students 12.

NEW RICHMOND, CLERMONT CO., ST. PETER (1850), [CEM] Rev. Gary J. Witsken.
Res.: 1192 Bethel-New Richmond Rd., 45157. Tel: 513-553-3267; Fax: 513-553-4321.
Catechesis/Religious Program—Tel: 513-553-4321. Rosanne Thomas, D.R.E. Students 130.

NEW VIENNA, CLINTON CO., ST. MICHAEL (1874), Closed. For inquiries for parish records contact the chancery.

NEWPORT, SHELBY CO., SS. PETER AND PAUL (1856), [CEM] Rev. Anthony E. Cutcher.
Res.: 6788 State Rte. 66, Fort Loramie, 45845. Tel: 937-295-3001; Fax: 937-295-2536.
Catechesis/Religious Program—Tel: 937-295-2536. Jan Stockman, D.R.E. Students 135.

NORTH LEWISBURG, CHAMPAIGN CO., IMMACULATE CONCEPTION (1869), Rev. Clarence G. Heis.
Res.: 40 Walnut St., Mechanicsburg, 43044. Tel: 937-834-2413; Fax: 937-834-2413.
Catechesis/Religious Program—Students 8.

NORTH STAR, DARKE CO., ST. LOUIS (1891), [CEM] Rev. David L. Zink.
Parish Office—P.O. Box 9, Osgood, 45351. Tel: 419-582-2531; Fax: 419-582-2015.
Catechesis/Religious Program—Linda Wehrkamp, D.R.E. Students 172.

OSGOOD, DARKE CO., ST. NICHOLAS (1909), [CEM] Rev. David L. Zink.
Office—128 Church St., P.O. Box 9, 45351. Tel: 419-582-2531; Fax: 419-582-2015.
Catechesis/Religious Program—Linda Kuether, D.R.E. Students 202.

OWENSVILLE, CLERMONT CO., ST. LOUIS (1856), [CEM] Rev. Gerard P. Hiland.
Res.: 210 N. Broadway, 45160. Tel: 513-732-2218; Fax: 513-732-2368.
School—250 N. Broadway, 45160. Tel: 513-732-0636; Fax: 513-732-1748. Mrs. Margaret Noonan Hunsberger, Prin. Ursuline Sisters 1; Lay Teachers 13; Students 208.
Catechesis/Religious Program—Tel: 513-732-2580. Students 53.

OXFORD, BUTLER CO., ST. MARY CHURCH AND CATHOLIC CAMPUS MINISTRY (Miami U.) (1853), [CEM] Rev. Terrance L. Schneider; Roberta L. Kinne, Pastoral Assoc.; Christopher E. Cotter, Pastoral Assoc.
Res.: 111 E. High St., 45056. Tel: 513-523-2153; Fax: 513-523-0559.
Catechesis/Religious Program—Students 136.

PEEBLES, ADAMS CO., ST. MARY QUEEN OF HEAVEN (1952),, (Vicariate) Rev. Theodore C. Kosse.
Holy Trinity: 612 E. Mulberry St., West Union, 45693. Tel: 937-544-2757; Fax: 937-544-1430.
Catechesis/Religious Program—Tel: 937-446-9294. Students 22.

PHILOTHEA, MERCER CO., ST. MARY (1851), (German), [CEM] Rev. Ronald H. Wilker.
Res.: 116 E. Main St., P.O. Box 93, Coldwater, 45828. Tel: 419-678-4802; Fax: 419-678-4803.
Catechesis/Religious Program—Cathy Bruns, D.R.E. Students 83.

PIQUA, MIAMI CO.
1—ST. BONIFACE (1855), Rev. James A. Hoffbauer.
Res.: 310 S. Downing St., 45356. Tel: 937-773-1656; Fax: 937-773-2665. Rev. Angelo C. Caserta (Retired). Tel: 513-778-9526.
School—Piqua Catholic School, Piqua (Consolidated) See separate listing. Tel: 937-773-3876; Fax: 937-773-5875.
Catechesis/Religious Program—Students 97.
2—ST. MARY (1843), Rev. Thomas J. Grilliot; Sr. Joan Stewart, Pastoral Assoc. In Res., Rev. Anselm F. Boeke (Retired).
Res.: 528 Broadway, 45356. Tel: 937-773-1327; Fax: 937-773-2313.
School—Piqua Catholic School, Piqua, Tel: 937-773-1564; Fax: 937-773-0380. See separate listing.
Catechesis/Religious Program— Michael Worland, D.R.E. Students 59.

RHINE, SHELBY CO., ST. LAWRENCE (1856), (German), [CEM] Rev. Patrick L. Sloneker.
Res.: 16053 Botkins Rd., P.O. Box 519, Botkins, 45306. Tel: 937-693-2561; Fax: 937-693-2561.
Catechesis/Religious Program—Tel: 937-693-2571. Students 123.

RIPLEY, BROWN CO., ST. MICHAEL (1840), Rev. John P. Fischer; Maureen Harvey, Pastoral Assoc.
Church & Parish Office: 16 N. Fourth St., 45167. Tel: 937-392-1116; Fax: 937-392-1699.
Res.: 109 S. Elm St., Georgetown, 45121. Tel: 937-378-4376.
School—Tel: 937-392-4202; Fax: 937-392-4248. Mrs. Ann Boley, Prin. Lay Teachers 6; Students 58.
Catechesis/Religious Program—Tel: 937-392-1840. Trisha Hannah, D.R.E. Students 52.

ROCKFORD, MERCER CO., ST. TERESA (1936), Rev. Thomas Brenberger, C.PP.S.
Res.: 213 S. Franklin St., P.O. Box 445, 45882. Tel: 419-363-2633; Fax: 419-363-2633.
Catechesis/Religious Program— Denise Myers, D.R.E. Students 72.

RUSSELLS POINT, LOGAN CO., ST. MARY OF THE WOODS (1927), Rev. Harold W. Kist; Deacon Steve Brown.
Res.: 464 Madison Ave., P.O. Box 329, 43348. Tel: 937-843-3127; Fax: 937-843-3866.
Catechesis/Religious Program—Madison Ave., 43348. Tel: 937-843-4227. Dona Fischer. Tel: 937-592-6621. Students 198.
Mission—St. George Chapel Marianists of Ohio 9636 Lake Shore Dr., East Huntsville, Logan Co. 43324. Tel: 937-842-4902.

RUSSIA, SHELBY CO., ST. REMY (1846), Rev. Frank Amberger.
Res.: 108 E. Main St., 45363. Tel: 937-526-3437; Fax: 937-526-5326.
Catechesis/Religious Program—Tel: 937-526-3437. Karen Rosenbeck, D.R.E. Students 316.

ST. ANTHONY, MERCER CO., ST. ANTHONY (1852), (German), [CEM] Rev. Kenneth G. Alt, C.PP.S.
Res.: 471 St. Anthony Rd., Fort Recovery, 45846. Tel: 419-942-1795.
Catechesis/Religious Program—Tel: 419-942-1795. Students 95.

ST. HENRY, MERCER CO., ST. HENRY (1839), [CEM] Rev. Larry Wyen, C.PP.S.; Deacon Jerry Buschur.
Res.: Box 301, 272 E. Main St., 45883. Tel: 419-678-4118; Fax: 419-678-8285.
Inter-parish Center—162 S. Walnut, 45883. Tel: 419-678-3811; Fax: 419-678-8285.
Catechesis/Religious Program—Tel: 419-678-3811. Connie Bargdill, D.R.E. Students 968.

ST. JOSEPH, MERCER CO., ST. JOSEPH (1839), (German), [CEM] Rev. Kenneth G. Alt, C.PP.S.
Res.: 1477 Philothea Rd., St. Peter, 45846. Tel: 419-375-4344; Fax: 419-375-4030.
Church: 1689 St. Joe Rd., Fort Recovery, 45846.
Catechesis/Religious Program—Students 96.

ST. MARYS, AUGLAIZE CO., HOLY ROSARY (1852), Rev. David A. Heinl. In Res., Rev. James O. Byrne (Retired).
Res.: 511 E. Spring St., 45885. Tel: 419-394-5050; Fax: 419-394-0184.
School—Tel: 419-394-5291; Fax: 419-394-6585. Anna Mae Saum, Prin. Lay Teachers 11; Students 153.
Catechesis/Religious Program—Tel: 419-394-5291. Sandi Rammel, D.R.E. Students 222.

ST. PARIS, CHAMPAIGN CO., SACRED HEART (1868), Rev. Gregory J. Konerman.
Res.: 231 Washington Ave., Urbana, 43078-1728. Tel: 937-653-1375; Fax: 937-653-1383.
Catechesis/Religious Program—Tel: 937-653-1375. Twinned with St. Mary, Urbana. Students 8.

ST. ROSE, MERCER CO., ST. ROSE (1839), (German), [CEM] Revs. Kenneth J. Schroeder, C.PP.S.; Harry M. Cavanaugh, C.PP.S. ((TOL)).
Office—7428 State Rte. 119, Maria Stein, 45860. Tel: 419-925-4775; Fax: 419-925-1745.
Res.: 8533 State Rte. 119, Maria Stein, 45860. Tel: 419-925-4522; Fax: 419-925-7522.
Catechesis/Religious Program—Tel: 419-925-4542. Joyce Hartings, D.R.E. Students 94.

ST. SEBASTIAN, MERCER CO., ST. SEBASTIAN (1852),

(German), [CEM] Rev. John L. Bensman.
Precious Blood Church: 35 S. Maple St., Box 26, Chickasaw, 45826-0026. Tel: 419-925-4391.
Church: 3280 Co. Rd. 716-A, Celina, 45822. Tel: 419-925-4391.
Catechesis/Religious Program—Nancy Broering, D.R.E. Students 65.

ST. WENDELIN, MERCER CO., ST. WENDELIN (1856), [CEM] Rev. Matthew W. Jozefiak, C.PP.S.
Res.: 517 Meiring Rd., Fort Recovery, 45846. Tel: 419-375-2603; Fax: 419-375-9413.
Catechesis/Religious Program—Students 53.

SAINT MARTIN, BROWN CO., SAINT MARTIN (1830), [CEM] Closed., For inquiries for parish records, see St. Angela Merici, Fayetteville.

SARDINIA, BROWN CO., ST. ELIZABETH PARISH (1955), Rev. Dohrman W. Byers.
Res.: 6647 Van Buren St., Georgetown, 45121. Tel: 937-446-2555; Fax: 937-446-2555.
Church: 122 N. Main St., 45171.
Catechesis/Religious Program—Tel: 937-446-1854; Fax: 937-446-2555. Linda Mulvaney. Combined with St. Mary, Arnheim, OH. Students 37.

SHANDON, BUTLER CO., ST. ALOYSIUS (1867), [CEM] Rev. David F. Reilly.
Res.: P.O. Box 95, 45063. Tel: 513-738-1014; Fax: 513-738-2084.
Catechesis/Religious Program—Tel: 513-738-4641. Joan Mills, D.R.E.; Mary Bahner, D.R.E. Tel: 513-738-9928. Students 230.

SHARPSBURG, MERCER CO., ST. PAUL (1868), [CEM] Rev. Matthew W. Jozefiak, C.PP.S.
Res.: 517 Meiring Rd., Fort Recovery, 45846. Tel: 419-375-2603; Fax: 419-375-9413.
Catechesis/Religious Program—Tel: 419-375-2308. Helen Lefevre, D.R.E. Students 169.

SIDNEY, SHELBY CO., HOLY ANGELS (1848), Revs. Gerald E. Bensman; Earl K. Fernandes; Deacons Philip Myers; John Holthaus.
Res.: 324 S. Ohio Ave., 45365-3012. Tel: 937-498-2308; Fax: 937-498-2308.
School—120 E. Water St., 45365-3199. Tel: 937-492-9293; Fax: 937-492-8578. Harold Schmiesing, Prin. Lay Teachers 21; Students 411.
Catechesis/Religious Program—c/o Office 121 E. Water St., 45365-3199. Tel: 937-498-0433; Fax: 937-498-1448. Erica Kerg. Students 320.

SOUTH CHARLESTON, CLARK CO., ST. CHARLES BORROMEO (1866), [CEM] Rev. William V. Thomas.
Res.: 31 S. Chillicothe St., P.O. Box F, 45368-0806. Tel: 937-462-8971; Fax: 937-462-9184.
Catechesis/Religious Program—Tel: 937-462-7311; Fax: 937-462-9184. Susan Severt, D.R.E. Tel: 937-883-2168. Students 38.

SPRINGFIELD, CLARK CO.

1—ST. BERNARD (1860), (German), [CEM] Rev. Paul F. Hurst.
Res.: 910 Lagonda Ave., 45503. Tel: 937-322-5243; Fax: 937-322-3788.
School—800 Lagonda Ave, 45503. Tel: 937-324-4551; Fax: 937-324-4070. Lay Teachers 10; Students 187.
Catechesis/Religious Program—Tel: 937-324-2870; Fax: 937-322-3788. Trish Evans, D.R.E. Students 101.

2—ST. JOSEPH (1882), Rev. Dennis J. Caylor, J.C.L.; Deacon Norman G. Horstman; Rev. Marvin R. Hackman.
Church: 225 E. High St., 45505. Tel: 937-323-7523; Fax: 937-324-1512.
School—Holy Trinity Catholic School, Springfield, Tel: 937-322-8781; Fax: 937-323-2790. See separate listing.
Catechesis/Religious Program— Twinned with St. Raphael, Springfield. Students 54.

3—ST. MARY (1921), Closed., For inquiries for parish records please see St. Raphael, Springfield.

4—ST. RAPHAEL (1849), Rev. Dennis J. Caylor, J.C.L.; Deacon Norman G. Horstmann; Rev. Marvin R. Hackman.
Res.: 225 E. High St., 45505. Tel: 937-323-7523; Fax: 937-324-1512.
School—Holy Trinity Catholic School, Springfield, Tel: 937-322-8781; Fax: 937-323-2790. See separate listing.
Catechesis/Religious Program—Tel: 937-323-7523. Twinned with St. Joseph, Springfield. Students 231.

5—ST. TERESA OF THE CHILD JESUS (1931), Rev. Richard W. Walling.
Res.: 1827 N. Limestone St., 45503. Tel: 937-342-8861; Fax: 937-399-6971.
School—Tel: 937-399-5451; Fax: 937-342-0042. Mrs. Martha Szczesny, Prin. Lay Teachers 11; Students 220.
Catechesis/Religious Program—Tel: 937-399-5451; Fax: 937-399-6971. Students 80.

STONELICK, CLERMONT CO., ST. PHILOMENA (1837), [CEM] Rev. Gerard P. Hiland.
Res.: 210 N. Broadway, Box 85, Owensville, 45160. Tel: 513-732-2218; Fax: 513-732-2368.

TIPP CITY, MIAMI CO., ST. JOHN THE BAPTIST (1858), [CEM] Rev. Eugene F. Vonderhaar (Retired).
Res.: 218 S. Third St., 45371. Tel: 937-667-3419; Fax: 937-667-9267.
Catechesis Religious Program—Tel: 937-667-6092. Nelda Schwab, D.R.E. Students 380.

TRENTON, BUTLER CO., HOLY NAME (187[illegible]), [CEM] Rev. George W. Klein; Deacon William Martin.
Res.: 222 Hamilton Ave., 45067. Tel: 513-988-6335; Fax: 513-988-9900.
Catechesis/Religious Program—Tel: 513-988-9348. Students 127.

TROY, MIAMI CO., ST. PATRICK (1857), Revs. John D. MacQuarrie; Charles B. Rohrkemper (Retired); Joseph Kozar, S.M.; Deacons Michael Knight; John Carlin; Mark Chaplin.
Res.: 409 E. Main St., 45373. Tel: 937-335-2833; Fax: 937-335-1453.
School—Tel: 937-339-3705; Fax: 937 339-1158. James O'Leary, Prin. Lay Teachers 7; Students 167.
Catechesis/Religious Program—409 E. Main St., 45373. Tel: 937-339-5517. Students 402.

TWENTY MILE STAND, WARREN CO., ST. MARGARET OF YORK (1984), Revs. Thomas W. Kreidler; James L. Simons; Deacon Raymond Kroger.
Res.: 9483 Columbia Rd., Loveland, 45140. Tel: 513-683-7100; Fax: 513-683-7101.
School—Tel: 513-683-7100, Ext. 222. Sisters Mary Ann Trotta, R.S.M., Educ. Admin. Team; Bernadine Stone, Educ. Admin. Team; Mrs. Nancy Shula, Educ. Admin.Team. Lay Teachers 27; Students 708.
Catechesis/Religious Program—Susan Gravely, D.R.E. Students 940.

URBANA, CHAMPAIGN CO., ST. MARY (1853), Rev. Gregory J. Konerman.
Res.: 231 Washington Ave., 43078. Tel: 937-653-1375; Fax: 937-653-1383.
School—Tel: 937-653-1370; Fax: 937-653-1376. Anthony Frierott, Prin. Lay Teachers 10; Students 100.
Catechesis/Religious Program—Tel: 937-653-1383. Students 51.

VANDALIA, MONTGOMERY CO., ST. CHRISTOPHER (1957), Rev. Francis J. Keferl; Deacon Stephen Bermick.
Res.: 435 E. National Rd., 45377. Tel: 937-898-3542; Fax: 937-898-1017.
School—(Grades K-8) Tel: 937-898-5104; Fax: 937-454-4790. Lay Teachers 23; Students 392.
Catechesis/Religious Program—Tel: 937-898-2155. Students 430.

VERSAILLES, DARKE CO., ST. DENIS (1839), [CEM] Rev. David P. Vincent; Deacon Jack Borgerding.
Res.: 14 E. Wood St., 45380. Tel: 937-526-4945; Fax: 937-526-4893.
Catechesis/Religious Program—Tel: 937-526-3957. Arlene Niekamp, D.R.E.; Linda Meyer, D.R.E. Students 586.

WAPAKONETA, AUGLAIZE CO., ST. JOSEPH (1839), [CEM] Rev. Henry F. Albietz; Deacon Richard L. Westbay.
Res.: 309 S. Perry St., 45895. Tel: 419-738-2115; Fax: 419-738-4525.
School—1101 Lincoln Hwy., 45895. Tel: 419-738-3311; Fax: 419-738-7706. Lay Teachers 13; Students 268.
Catechesis/Religious Program—Tel: 419-738-2115; Fax: 419-738-4525. Students 222.

WAYNESVILLE, WARREN CO., ST. AUGUSTINE (1876), [JC] Rev. Raymond Kammerer.
Res.: 5715 Lytle Rd., 45068. Tel: 513-897-2821; Fax: 513-897-2821.
Catechesis/Religious Program—Tel: 937-433-7114. Pat Ebright, D.R.E. Students 80.

WEST CHESTER, BUTLER CO., ST. JOHN (1880), Revs. Mark Burger; J. Raymond Favret; Steven Klode.
Res.: 9080 Cincinnati-Dayton Rd. 45069. Tel: 513-777-6433; Fax: 513-777-9741.
School—Tel: 513-771-5220; Fax: 513-771-5133. Consolidated. See St. Gabriel.
Catechesis/Religious Program—Tel: 513-755-4974. Students 748.

WEST MILTON, MIAMI CO., TRANSFIGURATION (1950), Rev. John D. MacQuarrie; Deacon Robert Huffman.
Res.: 972 S. Miami St., 45383. Tel: 937-698-4520; Fax: 937-698-4500.
Catechesis/Religious Program—Students 190.

WEST UNION, ADAMS CO., HOLY TRINITY (1950), Rev. Theodore C. Kosse.
Res.: 612 E. Mulberry St., 45693. Tel: 937-544-2757; Fax: 937-544-1430.
Catechesis/Religious Program—Tel: 937-446-9294. Students 64.

WILLIAMSBURG, CLERMONT CO., ST. ANN (1947), Rev. William R. Stockelman.
Res.: 140 N. Sixth St., Batavia, 45103. Tel: 513-732-2024 Fax: 513-732-0049.
Catechesis/Religious Program—Carla Simpson, D.R.E. Students 67.

WILMINGTON, CLINTON CO., ST. COLUMBKILLE (1866), Rev. James M. Wedig; Deacons Robert G. Baker; Robert E. Meyer; Edward B. Ostendorf.
Res.: 73 N. Mulberry St., 45177-2277. Tel: 937-382-2236; Fax: 937-382-0676.
Catechesis/Religious Program—Tel: 937-382-1596. Students 260.

WITHAMSVILLE, CLERMONT CO., ST. THOMAS MORE (1940), Revs. William C. Wagner; Joseph A. Bruemmer (Retired); Deacons Gene Miller; Jerry Cain; Mr. Michael Thomas, Pastoral Assoc.
Res.: 800 Ohio Pike, 45245-2299. Tel: 513-752-2080 (Office); 513-752-2080 (Pastor); Fax: 513-753-2542.
School—788 Ohio Pike, 45245. Tel: 513-753-2540, Ext. 22; Fax: 513-753-2554. Mrs. Peggy Fischer, Prin. Lay Teachers 13; Students 278.
Catechesis/Religious Program—Tel: 513-752-2080, Ext. 28; Fax: 513-753-2542. Mrs. Becky Ready, D.R.E. Students 239.

XENIA, GREENE CO., ST. BRIGID (1849), [CEM] Rev. Kenneth Schartz.
Res.: 258 Purcell Ave., 45385. Tel: 937-372-3193; Fax: 937-374-3622.
School—Tel: 937-372-3222. Sr. Lois Jean Goettke, S.C., Prin. Sisters 1; Lay Teachers 10; Students 244.
Convent—Sisters of Charity of Cincinnati, OH, 216 Purcell Ave., 45385. Tel: 937-372-0994.
Catechesis/Religious Program—Tel: 937-372-3222. Students 99.

YELLOW SPRINGS, GREENE CO., ST. PAUL (1856), [CEM] Rev. Joseph R. Raudabaugh; Deacon Paul E. Richardson.
Res.: 308 Phillips St., 45387. Tel: 937-767-7450; Fax: 937-767-7465.
Catechesis/Religious Program—Carole Grady, D.R.E. Students 120.

Closed and Merged Parishes

GREATER CINCINNATI

1—ST. ALOYSIUS CHURCH (Elmwood Place), Closed., For inquiries for parish records, contact St. Clement, (St. Bernard).

2—ST. CHARLES BORROMEO CHURCH (Carthage), Closed., For inquiries for parish records, contact St. James of the Valley, (Wyoming).

3—COMMUNITY OF HOPE, Consolidated, with Holy Family Parish. Records at the Chancery.

4—ST. ELIZABETH CHURCH (Norwood), Merged, with St. Matthew Church, Norwood and Sts. Peter & Paul Church, Norwood to form Holy Trinity Church, Norwood.

5—ST. GEORGE PARISH & NEWMAN CENTER, Closed., For inquiries for parish records contact St. Monica-St. George Newman Center.

6—ST. MATTHEW CHURCH (Norwood), Merged, with St. Elizabeth Church, Norwood and Sts. Peter & Paul Church, Norwood to form Holy Trinity Church, Norwood.

7—ST. MICHAEL CHURCH, Closed., For inquiries for parish records, contact Holy Family Parish.

8—OUR LADY OF GRACE (Price Hill), Consolidated, with Holy Family Parish.

9—OUR LADY OF LORETTO, Merged, with St. Margaret of Cortona

10—OUR LADY OF PERPETUAL HELP (Sedamsville), Consolidated, with Holy Family Parish.

11—OUR LADY OF PRESENTATION, Closed., For inquiries for parish records contact St. Leo the Great, Cincinnati.

12—ST. PATRICK (Northside), Merged, with St. Boniface, Cincinnati. See listing for details.

13—STS. PETER AND PAUL CHURCH (Norwood), Merged, with St. Elizabeth Church, Norwood and St. Matthew Church, Norwood to form Holy Trinity Church, Norwood.

14—ST. PIUS CHURCH, Closed., For inquiries for parish records, contact St. Joseph Parish, Ezzard Charles Dr.

15—ST. RICHARD OF CHICHESTER (College Hill), Merged, with St. Therese, the Little Flower, Cincinnati. See listing for details.

16—SAN ANTONIO DI PADOVA, (Italian),, Refer to St. Leo for records.

17—ST. THOMAS AQUINAS, Closed., For inquiries for parish records, contact St. Clement, (St. Bernard).

BLUE CREEK, ADAMS CO., ST. JOSEPH, Closed., For inquiries for parish records contact Holy Trinity, West Union.

DAYTON, MONTGOMERY CO., SACRED HEART, Closed., For inquiries for parish records contact Emmanuel, Dayton.

FELICITY, CLERMONT CO., OUR MOTHER OF GOOD COUNSEL, Closed., For inquiries for parish records, contact St. Mary, (Bethel).

HAMILTON, BUTLER CO.

1—ST. MARY, Merged, now known as St. Julie Billiart.

2—ST. STEPHEN, Merged, now known as St. Julie Billiart.

3—ST. VERONICA, Merged, now known as St. Julie Billiart.

MIDDLETOWN, BUTLER CO.

1—HOLY TRINITY, Merged, now known as Holy Family.

2—St. John the Baptist, Merged, now known as Holy Family.
3—St. Mary, Merged, now known as Holy Family.
New Miami, Butler Co., St. Lawrence, Closed., For inquiries for parish records please see St. Julie Billiart, Hamilton.
St. Patrick, Shelby Co., St. Patrick, Closed., For inquiries for parish records contact St. Michael, Fort Loramie.
Vera Cruz, Brown Co., Holy Ghost (Vicariate), Closed., For inquiries for parish records contact St. Angela, Fayetteville.

On Special and Archdiocesan Assignment:
Revs.—
Breaker, Donald J., P.O. Box 627, Fort Leonard Wood, MO 65473.
DeVore, David G., c/o Priests' Personnel Office, 100 E. Eighth St., 45202.
Elsbernd, James H., 6700 Dawson Rd., 45243.
Grad, Malcolm S., Admin. Asst., Archbishop's Office, 100 E. 8th St., 45202.
Lemkuhl, David E., 9375 Winton Rd., 45231. Tel: 513-522-3680
Mick, Lawrence E., 3103 Observation Trail, Dayton, 45449. Tel: 937-434-4689
Nguyen, Huan Tien, 314 Township Ave., 45216. Tel: 513-242-2933
Peterka, Dale C., 7121 Plainfield Rd., 45236. Tel: 513-791-3238
Schmieder, Mark C., 1413 Garden Pl., 45246. Tel: 513-771-1877

On Duty Outside the Archdiocese:
Revs.—
Kelly, William T., P.O. Box 299., Danbury, TX 77534-0299.
Lemkuhl, David A., P.O. Box 43058, Nairobi, Kenya.
McGuire, Frederick J., Blessed Trinity, 1600 54th Ave., St. Petersburg, FL 33712.
Meyer, Mark A., c/o Rev. Joseph Binzer, 29 E. 8th St., 45202.

Military Chaplains:
Revs.—
Janning, Timothy J., 6451 Crescent Way, #107, Norfolk, VA 23513.
Niemeier, Dennis A., CH LTC, 307-A Sudut St., Wahiawa, HI 96786.
St. George, Peter T., LT, USS Kearsarge, Fpo, AE 09534-1662.

Medical Leave of Absence:
Revs.—
Gaeke, Thomas M., Ste. 129-257, 3225 S. MacDill Ave., Tampa, FL 33629-8171.
Mahoney, Michael T., 4644 Burkardt Rd., Dayton, 45431.

Leave of Absence:
Rev.—
Anh, Tuan

Retired:
Rev. Msgr.—
Kennedy, Francis B., 1960 Madison Rd., 45206. Tel: 513-861-5108
Revs.—
Aichele, Raymond P., 2472 Picnic Woods, Bright, IN 47025. Tel: 812-637-2490
Allison, Joseph C., 6019 Woodford Ct., #3, 45213. Tel: 513-731-5273
Andres, Joseph P., P.O. Box 54458, 45254. Tel: 513-231-0508
Axe, Thomas R.
Ballman, Thomas J., 8100 Clyo Rd., Centerville, 45458.
Beckman, Joseph F., 6616 Beechmont Ave., 45230. Tel: 513-624-0554
Behler, Donald A., Mercy Franciscan at West Park, 2950 West Park Dr. #374, 45238.
Bertke, Erwin J., 5662 Rapid Run #8, 45238. Tel: 513-922-3089
Birarelli, Carl A., Villa St. Francis, 3618 Trado Dr., Sarasota, FL 34235. Tel: 941-358-1225
Boeke, Aloysius B., St. Charles Seminary, 2860 St., Rte. 127, Carthegena, 45822-9591.
Boeke, Anselm F., 528 Broadway, Piqua, 45356. Tel: 937-773-1327
Bruemmer, Joseph A., 5440 Moeller Ave., 45212. Tel: 513-351-4661
Bruening, Bernard H., 41550 Henke Rd., Miamisburg, 45342. Tel: 937-866-1550
Bruening, Joseph B., 5900 Delhi Rd., Mount Saint Joseph, 45051. Tel: 513-347-5311
Buening, Robert B., Corpus Christi, 2014 Springdale Rd., 45231. Tel: 513-825-0618
Byrne, James O., 511 Spring St., St. Marys, 45885. Tel: 513-394-5050
Caserta, Angelo C., P.O. Box 1636, Piqua, 45356. Tel: 937-778-9526
Caserta, Charles W., 133 Douglas, Lewisburg, 45338. Tel: 937-962-3059
Cavanaugh, John L., J.C.D., 100 Compton Rd., 45215. Tel: 513-821-3927
Dorenbusch, Thomas A., 8184 Chambersburg Rd., Dayton, 45424. Tel: 937-235-9342
Dorrmann, William J., 110 N. Hill St., Harrison, 45030. Tel: 513-367-9086
Edrich, Paul J., 4991 Dry Ridge Rd., 45252. Tel: 513-245-9073
Evers, Gerard A., 1044 W. Kemper Rd., 45240. Tel: 513-851-1930
Favret, Raymond J., St. Margaret Hall, 1960 Madison Rd., 45206. Tel: 513-787-3509
Gerdes, Harry J., Bayley Place, 928 Bayley Place Dr., 45233. Tel: 513-347-5647
Goetz, Joseph W., 1528 Turnberry Village Dr., Dayton, 45458. Tel: 937-432-6589
Guntzelman, Louis J., 10709 Adventure Ln., 45242.
Hagedorn, Robert L., 6210 Cleves-Warsaw Ave. #104, 45233. Tel: 513-467-2724
Hater, Robert J., 1443 Cedar Ave., 45224. Tel: 513-541-4611
Henz, Kenneth W., 1805 John Glenn Rd., Dayton, 45420. Tel: 937-253-2829
Hohlmayer, Louis R., 3505 Calumet Rd., Ludlow Falls, 45339. Tel: 937-698-6757
Hoying, Leo A., 6-A Green Hills Dr., Minster, 45865. Tel: 419-628-2078
Huebner, Donald C., 3505 Calumet Rd., Ludlow Falls, 45339. Tel: 937-698-6696
Hussey, Edmund M., 3714 Falls Circle Dr., Hilliard, 43026. Tel: 614-771-2736
Keller, Neil J., 836 N. Hill Ln., 45224. Tel: 513-522-5578
Kenning, Herman H., 60 Compton Rd., 45215. Tel: 513-821-1886
Kneipp, August J., Leibold Home, 476 Riddle Rd., 45220. Tel: 513-281-2648
Lammeier, Francis G., 12120 Regency Run #7, 45240. Tel: 513-742-9982
Lawrence, Ralph J., 140 Ewing Dr., #C, Fairfield, 45014. Tel: 513-939-2363
Leurck, Raymond J., 119 Everett Ln., Nancy, KY 42544. Tel: 606-636-5559
Lutmer, Joseph H., 4688 Largo Dr., 45236. Tel: 513-793-9937
Macpherson, Walter, 4144 Cedar Ridge Rd., Dayton, 45414.
Mattscheck, John J., 3468 Robb Ave., 45211. Tel: 513-389-9366
Mauntel, Robert J., 19 Mohave Dr., Sardinia, 45171. Tel: 513-446-3491
McCarthy, Donald G., N. Bend Rd., 45247. Tel: 513-661-6565
Metz, Earl O., 2497 Eastern Ave., 45202. Tel: 513-861-0740
Mick, Lawrence J., 1500 Linneman Rd., 45238. Tel: 513-922-5400
Mick, Robert, 3720 St. Martin Pl., 45211. Tel: 513-661-2000
Miller, Francis J., 4988 Lord Alfred Ct., 45241-2196. Tel: 513-247-0966
Minic, John F., 1273 Chickadee Ct., Centerville, 45458. Tel: 937-434-1007
Monnin, Robert J., 3505 Calumet Rd. #2B, Ludlow Falls, 45339. Tel: 937-689-6785
Mueller, Eugene J., 3055 Inwood Dr., 45241. Tel: 513-769-4908
Niehaus, Francis H., P.O. Box 727, Florence, KY 41022.
O'Connor, James J., 319 Mulberry Pl., Sidney, 45365. Tel: 937-492-9577
Perin, Glen W., 3505 Calumet Rd., #1-B, Ludlow Falls, 45339. Tel: 937-698-6713
Perryman, John E., 138 Heritage Dr., Urbana, 43078. Tel: 937-652-3540
Powers, Alfred J., 2344 N. Limestone #1, Springfield, 45503. Tel: 937-399-7757
Poynter, Gail A., 6509 Azure Way, West Carrollton, 45449. Tel: 513-438-9001
Rehling, Paul L., 4108 W. Eighth St., 45205. Tel: 513-921-6739
Rivers, Clarence J., 17 Erkenbrecher Ave., 45220. Tel: 513-221-5538
Rohrkemper, Charles B., 109 Freedom Ct., Sidney, 45365. Tel: 937-492-3010
Schutte, Robert W., 3001 Middle Urbana Rd., #225, Springfield, 45502.
Schwartz, William H., 350 Thomas Blvd., Apt. 207, Hamilton, 45013. Tel: 513-894-5747
Seher, Philip O., 5272 Farmhouse Ln., 45238. Tel: 513-602-7875
Shelander, Donald E., 4249 Duneden Ave., 45236. Tel: 513-936-9003
Stolz, Paul L., 100 Compton Rd., 45215.
Stricker, Robert A., 5560 Kirby Rd., 45239. Tel: 513-541-5560
Thorsen, Robert J., 5002 Lord Alfred Ct., 45241. Tel: 513-469-0921
Trick, James F., 11562 Channelview Dr., Lakeview, 43331. Tel: 937-842-5560
Trippel, Edward G., 3547 Clifton Ave., 45220. Tel: 513-861-1295
Urbain, Joseph V., 3480 N. McMullen Booth Rd., Clearwater, FL 33761.
Vonderhaar, Eugene F., 10560 Blocker Rd., Bradford, 45308. Tel: 937-743-3985
Wall, John E., 5222 N. Bend Rd., 45247. Tel: 513-661-6565
Wessling, John E., 10095 Wayside Dr., #259, 45241. Tel: 513-779-5350
Wiemeyer, Raymond G., 5367 Julmar Dr., 45238. Tel: 513-922-2791
Wolfer, Paul J., 2832 Rosebud Dr., 45238. Tel: 513-922-0715
Wolfer, Robert R., 2832 Rosebud Dr., 45238. Tel: 513-922-0715

Permanent Deacons:
Arber, Alan W., (Retired)
Ascolese, Michael A., Our Mother of Sorrows, Cincinnati
Aufderheide, William, St. Margaret of Cortona, Cincinnati
Baker, Robert, St. Columbkille, Wilmington
Baltes, Leonard W., St. Charles, Kettering
Bardonaro, Mark A., St. Dominic, Cincinnati
Barney, Gerald L., St. John, West Chester
Beck, Henry B., Our Lady of the Rosary, Dayton
Belcher, Halver L., St. Augustine, Minster
Bensman, Werner, SS. Peter & Paul, Newport; St. Michael, Ft. Laramie
Bermick, Stephen C., III, St. Christopher, Vandalia
Bertke, Omer H., St. John the Baptist, Maria Stein
Blum, Raymond, (Retired)
Borgerding, Jonathan P., St. Denis (Versailles); Holy Family (Frenchtown)
Borgerding, Robert H., St. Peter, Dayton
Bornhorst, Gregory A., Holy Redeemer, New Bremen
Brodeur, Wilfred J., St. Cecilia, Ft. Meyers, FL
Brown, Steven R., St. Mary of the Woods, Russells Point
Bruce, George A., St. William, Cincinnati
Brunner, Mark E., St. Ann, Hamilton
Brunsman, Willard, Queen of Peace, Millville
Bryant, Herman, St. Gabriel, Cincinnati
Burger, Raymond S., St. Margaret Mary, Cincinnati
Buschur, Jerome L., St. Henry, St. Henry
Cain, Jerome J., St. Thomas More, Withamsville
Camele, David G., (Retired)
Carlin, John K., St. Patrick, Troy
Cecere, Gregory, Queen of Apostles, Dayton
Chaplin, Mark, St. Patrick, Troy
Coll, Joseph J., St. Columban, Loveland
Coomes, Gerald L., (Retired)
Correale, Robert M., St. Peter, Huber Heights
Couzins, Jerome, Unassigned
Coyle, Thomas J., Holy Family, Middletown
Davenport, Michael D., St. Teresa of Avila, Cincinnati
Dawson, David A., (Unassigned)
Deardorff, Roy L., St. Helen, Dayton
Dehmer, William A., Our Lady of Visitation, Cincinnati
Dipple, Harold I., St. Patrick, Bellefontaine
Dupree, Gerald M., St. Luke, Beavercreek
Etienne, Jerald F., St. Mary, Bethel
Faeth, Thomas J., St. William, Cincinnati
Fischesser, Elmer, New Jerusalem Community, Cincinnati
Franzer, Carl C., St. John the Baptist, Maria Stein
George, Raymond W., St. Matthias, Cincinnati
Geraci, James L., Our Lady of the Sacred Heart, Reading
Glassmeyer, Robert A., Our Lady of the Sacred Heart, Reading
Gobbi, John R., St. John Neumann, Cincinnati
Gould, John E., St. Peter, Huber Heights
Grismer, Raymond L., Good Shepherd, Cincinnati
Haas, Frederick J., St. Leo & St. Bonaventure, Cincinnati
Harris, Timothy J., St. Peter, Huber Heights
Hennessey, James F., Holy Trinity, Batavia
Hildebrand, Victor B., Ascension, Kettering
Holthaus, John G., Holy Angels, Sidney
Homan, Cletus H., St. Anthony, Fort Recovery
Horstman, Norman G., St. Raphael & St. Joseph, Springfield
Huff, Thomas, (Retired)
Huffman, Robert J., Transfiguration, West Milton
Jachimowicz, John J., St. Helen, Dayton
Janowiecki, Richard J., Precious Blood, Dayton
Jenkins, Charles J., Our Lady of Victory, Cincinnati
Jernigan, Jacob, Resurrection, Dayton

Jones, James E., Good Shepherd, Cincinnati
Keller, David R., (Leave of Absence)
Kluener, Paul J., St. James, White Oak
Knight, Michael R., St. Patrick, Troy
Kolis, Conrad C., St. James of the Valley, Wyoming
Kostic, Nicholas V., Jr., St. Brigid, Xenia
Kowalski, James, St. Joseph, Hamilton
Kozlowski, Robert R., Sacred Heart, New Carlisle
Kraus, Daniel E., Ascension, Kettering
Kroger, Raymond, St. Margaret of York, Twenty Mile Stand
Kronenberger, Arthur, (Retired)
Krumm, William T., Holy Family, Middletown
Lochtefeld, Virgil V., Holy Trinity, Coldwater
Maag, Lawrence A., St. Vivian, Cincinnati
Martin, Richaed W., Our Lady of Good Hope, Miamisburg
Martin, William, Holy Name, Trenton
Mascorro, Susano, St. Helen, Dayton
Merritt, James A., St. Susanna, Mason
Meyer, Robert E., St. Columbkille, Wilmington
Miller, Allen K., St. Peter, Dayton
Miller, James A., St. Columban, Loveland
Mullaney, William M., Immaculate Heart of Mary, Cincinnati
Myers, Philip B., Holy Angels, Sidney
Novick, Rick, Guardian Angels, Cincinnati
Obleness, Ralph F., St. Helen, Dayton
Olinger, James C., St. Rita, Dayton
Orlando, Vincent, (Retired)
Ostendorf, Edward B., St. Columbkille, Wilmington
Parker, John G., Mary, Help of Christians, Fort Recovery
Parker, Leonard B., St. Mary, Hillsboro
Perry, Robert W., Our Lady, Queen of Peace, Wright Patterson Air Force Base
Perryman, Clifton, St. James, Mequon, WI
Petrie, William J., St. Antoninus, Cincinnati
Platfoot, Thomas F., Our Lady of Mercy, Dayton
Rader, Daniel L., St. Susanna, Mason
Reder, Richard P., Assumption, Mt. Healthy
Reeves, Paul S., (Retired)
Reising, Edward B., St. Columban, Loveland
Renneker, William B., St. Julie Billiart, Hamilton
Richardson, Paul E., St. Paul, Yellow Springs
Riva-Saleta, Luis O., St. Ignatius, Cincinnati
Roadruck, Max, Mary Help of Christians, Fairborn
Royer, Milton W., Queen of Martyrs, Dayton
Runnels, Arthur, (Retired)
Saluke, William M., St. Mary, Dayton
Schmidt, Joseph Ted, St. Boniface, Cincinnati
Schmiesing, John J., St. Augustine, Minster
Schneider, Jerry R., St. Aloysius Gonzaga, Cincinnati
Schroeder, Robert J., St. Antoninus, Cincinnati
Schultheis, Joseph R., Our Lady of Victory, Cincinnati
Shea, David J., Immaculate Heart of Mary, Cincinnati
Simmons, Raphael, St. Joseph, Cincinnati
Slattery, John M., St. Cecilia, Cincinnati
Sonnenberg, James J., (Unassigned)
Srode, Walter, St. Veronica, Mt. Carmel
Stasiak, Mark, St. Francis of Assisi, Centerville
Steward, Herschel R., St. Francis De Sales, Lebanon
Strodtbeck, Thomas M., St. Julie Billiart, Hamilton
Subler, Joseph, St. Paul, Englewood
Sunderman, James P., St. Jude the Apostle, Cincinnati
Taylor, John, St. Francis de Sales, Lebanon
Thamann, John D., St. Mary, Cincinnati
Vilaboy, Manuel D., (Retired)
Wagner, Francis X., St. Michael, Cincinnati
Walker, Harry S., St. Columban, Loveland
Wallace, Forrest, St. Antoninus, Cincinnati
Wersching, J. Phillip, (Retired)
Westbay, Richard L., St. Joseph, Wapakoneta
Westerfield, Thomas E., Our Lady of Lourdes, Cincinnati
Winters, Royce E., St. Agnes, Cincinnati
Woeste, James H., St. Elizabeth Seton, Rockford, IL
Wright, Charles O., St. Peter, HuberHeights
Yetter, Jerry J., St. Boniface, Cincinnati
Zinck, Robert C., Jr., Incarnation, Centerville
Zvonar, George J., Holy Trinity, Dayton

INSTITUTIONS LOCATED IN THE ARCHDIOCESE

[A] THE ATHENAEUM OF OHIO

CINCINNATI. *The Athenaeum of Ohio*, Mt. St. Mary's Seminary, 6616 Beechmont Ave., 45230. Tel: 513-231-2223; Fax: 513-231-3254. Email: ath@athenaeum.edu. Web: www.athenaeum.edu. Most Rev. Daniel E. Pilarczyk, D.D., Archbishop of Cincinnati, Chancellor, Chm. of Bd. of Trustees; Rev. Gerald R. Haemmerle, M.A.; Dr. Terrance D. Callan, Ph.D., Dean, Athenaeum of Ohio; Dennis K. Eagan, B.B.A., Vice Pres., Finance Admin. Incorporated March 24, 1928 by the State of Ohio and presently has three divisions: Mt. St. Mary's Seminary of the West; the Lay Pastoral Ministry Program and the Special Studies Division.

Lay Pastoral Ministry Program, 6616 Beechmont Ave., 45230. Tel: 513-231-1200; Fax: 513-231-3254. Ms. Mary Sue O'Donnell, M.A.R., Dir.; Dr. Susan McGurgan, M.A.R., Assoc. Dir.; Sr. Nancy McMullen, C.PP.S., Prog. Coord.; Mr. Thomas Giordano, M.Div., Assoc. Dir.

The St. Gregory Seminary Trust, 100 E. Eighth St., 45202.

[B] SEMINARIES

CINCINNATI. *Mt. St. Mary's Seminary of the West* (Diocesan), 6616 Beechmont Ave., 45230. Tel: 513-231-2223; Fax: 513-231-3254. Email: ath@mtsm.org. Web: www.athenaeum.edu. Rev. Gerald R. Haemmerle, M.A., Rector; Dr. Terrance D. Callan, Ph.D., Athenaeum Academic Dean; Revs. Jeffrey M. Kemper, Ph.D., Seminary Dean; Andrew Umberg, S.T.L., Dir. of Field Educ. Prog.; Mr. Thomas Giordano, M.Div., Dir. of Pastoral Internship; Rev. Edward Smith, M.A., Dir. of Formation; Michael E. Sweeney, M.A., Registrar; Dennis K. Eagan, B.B.A., Vice Pres., Finance & Admin.; William Wester, Ed.D., Dir. Pastoral Counseling Degree. Major seminary for students in Theology. In Res. Most Rev. Carl K. Moeddel; Revs. Joseph F. Beckman (Retired); Gerald R. Haemmerle, M.A.; J. Robert Jack, M.A.; Jeffrey M. Kemper, Ph.D.; Benedict O'Cinnsealaigh, S.T.L.; Theodore Ross, S.J., S.T.L.; Timothy P. Schehr, Ph.D.; Michael Seger, S.T.D.; Edward Smith, M.A.; Andrew Umberg, S.T.L.; Francis W. Voellmecke, Ph.D.

Non-Resident Faculty: Sr. Betty Jane Lillie, Ph.D.; Mr. Terrance Callan, Ph.D.; Mr. Anthony Dicello, M.M.; Mrs. Tracy Koenig, M.A., M.L.S.

CARTHAGENA. *St. Charles*, Society of the Precious Blood, 45822. Tel: 419-925-4516; Fax: 419-925-4800. Web: ma.noacsc.org/stcharl/. Revs. James C. Seibert, C.PP.S., Dir.; George Albers, C.PP.S.; Clement Alt, C.PP.S.; Joseph Anthamatten, C.PP.S.; Milton Ballor, C.PP.S.; Louis Barga, C.PP.S.; John Behen, C.PP.S.; Aloysius B. Boeke (Retired); Paul Buehler, C.PP.S.; Robert Contant (FTW); Raymond Cera, C.PP.S.; Bernard Diekhoff, C.PP.S.; William Donohoe, C.PP.S.; David Dougherty, C.PP.S.; William Dougherty, C.PP.S.; Cornelius Fenton, C.PP.S.; Anthony Gamble, C.PP.S.; Joseph Hajduch, C.PP.S.; John Herber, C.PP.S.; Alphonse Jungwirth, C.PP.S.; Leonard A. Kistler, C.PP.S. (TOL); Gerold Koller, C.PP.S.; William Kramer, C.PP.S.; Clement Kuhns, C.PP.S.; Emil Labbe, C.PP.S.; Vincent Lengerich (Gary); Paul Link, C.PP.S.; Henry Langhals, C.PP.S.; Joseph Lima, C.PP.S.; James McCabe, C.PP.S.; Arnold Meiring, C.PP.S.; James Miller, C.PP.S.; Alfred Naseman, C.PP.S.; William O'Neill, C.PP.S.; Joseph Pax, C.PP.S.; Daniel Raible, C.PP.S.; Albert Reed, C.PP.S.; Charles Rueve, C.PP.S.; Frederick Ryder, C.PP.S.; Paul Schaaf, C.PP.S.; Raymond Schultheis, C.PP.S.; Raymond Seifert, C.PP.S.; Emil Schuwey, C.PP.S.; John Spatt, C.PP.S.; Leonard Sudhoff, C.PP.S.; Werner Verhoff, C.PP.S.; Carl Wise, C.PP.S. Priests 47; Brothers 10.

[C] NOVITIATES AND HOUSES OF STUDY

CINCINNATI. *St. Anthony Shrine, Francisan Candidacy*, St. John the Baptist Province, 5000 Colerain Ave., 45223. Tel: 513-541-2146; Fax: 513-541-9347. Revs. Donald A. Miller, O.F.M., Ph.D. (Y), Prov. Vocation Dir.; Clyde Young, O.F.M., Vicar; Louis Bartko, O.F.M., Hospital Chap.; Aquinas Schneider, O.F.M., Hospital Chap.; Kenan Freson, O.F.M., Prov. Treas.; Frank Geers, O.F.M., Dir. of Candidates; Bros. Gabriel Balassone, O.F.M., Porter; Scott Obrecht, O.F.M., Dir. Franciscan Mission Office; Donald Rewers, O.F.M., Assoc. Prov. Archivist; Gene Mayer, O.F.M., Local Min., Sec. of the Prov. Priests 6; Brothers 4; Candidates 1.

Dominican Novitiate, 7630 Shawnee Run Rd., 45243. Tel: 513-527-3972; Fax: 513-527-3973. Email: wcw93@earthlink.net. Web: www.op-stjoseph.org/. Rev. Walter C. Wagner O.P., Novice Master & Contact Person. Novices 1.

DAYTON. *Marianist Novitiate*, 4435 E. Patterson Rd., 45430-1095. Tel: 937-426-5721; Fax: 937-429-4686. Email: joseph.tedesco@notes.udayton.edu. Revs. Joseph P. Tedesco, S.M., Dir.; David McGuigan, S.M. Priests 3; Brothers 7; Novices 4.

[D] COLLEGES AND UNIVERSITIES

CINCINNATI. *College of Mount St. Joseph*, 5701 Delhi Rd., 45233-1670. Tel: 513-244-4200; Fax: 513-244-4601. Email: greg_grady@mail.msj.edu. Web: www.msj.edu. Sr. Francis Marie Thrailkill, O.S.U., Pres.; Cynthia Zane, Ph.D., Academic Dean; Rev. Angelo A. della Picca (Italy). Coed. Chartered by the State of Ohio. Priests 1; Sisters 7; Lay Teachers 109; Students 5,199; Total Staff 117.

Xavier University, 3800 Victory Pkwy., 45207. Tel: 513-745-3000; Fax: 513-745-4223. Email: vezina@xavier.edu. Web: www.xu.edu. Rev. Michael J. Graham, S.J., Pres. College of Arts & Sciences Enrollment 1,749; Williams College of Business Administration 937; College of Social Sciences Enrollment 1,048; Center for Adults & Part-time Students Enrollment 181; Graduate Program Enrollment 2,711; Permanent Staff: Priests 18; Sisters 3; Faculty (full-time): Priests 4; Lay Teachers 269.

Vice Presidents: Revs. Richard W. Bollman, S.J., Pastor & Rector, Bellarmine Chapel; Thomas P. Kennealy, S.J., Assoc. Dean College of Arts & Sciences and College of Social Sciences; J. Leo Klein, S.J., Vice Pres. Mission and Ministry; Dr. James Brodzinski, Assoc. Dean Williams College of Business; Mr. Allen Cole, Registrar; Dr. Roger A. Fortin, Vice Pres. Academic Affairs; Dr. Neil R. Heighberger, Dean College of Social Sciences; Robert Hill, Assoc. Vice Pres. Mktg. & Public Rels.; Dr. J. Richard Hirte, Vice Pres. Financial Devel.; Mr. John F. Kucia, Admin. Vice Pres.; Dr. Ali Malekzadeh, Dean Williams College of Business; Mr. Gary R. Massa, Vice Pres. Univ. Rels.; Dr. Linda Naimi, Vice Pres. Information Resources; Dr. Ronald Slepitza, Vice Pres. Student Devel.; Jackie Vezina, Contact Person; Dr. Janice Walker, Dean College of Arts & Sciences; Ms. Susan G. Wideman, Assoc. Academic Vice Pres. Non-Traditional Programs.

DAYTON. *The University of Dayton* (1850), (Coed), 300 College Park Ave., 45469-1624. Tel: 937-229-1000; Fax: 937-229-4000. Web: www.udayton.edu. Dr. Daniel J. Curran, Pres.; Rev. James L. Heft, S.M., Chancellor & Univ. Prof. of Faith and Culture; Dr. Fred P. Pestello, Senior Vice Pres. for Academics and Provost; Prof. Joseph Untener, Assoc. Provost, Faculty & Academic Affairs; Mr. Thomas E. Burkhardt, Vice Pres. for Finance Affairs & Admin. Svcs.; Mr. Ted L. Kissell, Vice Pres. & Dir. of Athletics; Dr. William C. Schuerman, Vice Pres. Student Devel. & Dean of Students; Rev. Eugene Contadino, S.M., Rector; Mr. S. Ted Bucaro, Govt. & Regl. Rels. Dir.; Ms. Lynnette Heard, Exec. Dir. Pres. Office; Mr. Richard G. Perales, Dir. Facilities Mgmt.; Mr. Thomas J. Westendorf, Registrar; Mrs. Joyce J. Wilkins, Dir. Financial Aid; Ms. Patricia J. Whitney, Vice Pres. Human Resources; Dr. Gordon A. Sargent, Vice Pres. Graduate Studies & Research & Dean Graduate School; Ms. Frances W. Evans, Vice Pres. Univ. Advancement; Dr. Deborah J. Bickford, Asst. Provost Learning & Pedagogy & Dir.; Dr. Thomas D. Skill, Asst. Provost Academic Technology & Dir. Learning Village; Mr. Thomas S. Danford, Assoc. Provost & Chief Information Officer; Revs. James H. Bartlet, S.M.; Norbert C. Burns, S.M.; Gerald T. Chinchar, S.M.; Christopher W. Conlon, S.M.; Eugene Contadino, S.M.; Matthew F. Kohmescher, S.M.; Joseph F. Kozar, S.M.; James L. Heft, S.M.; Paul M. Marshall, S.M.; Paul F. Vieson, S.M.; Thomas A. Schoen, S.M.; Thomas A. Thompson, S.M.; John S. Putka, S.M.; Bertrand A. Buby, S.M.; John A. McGrath, S.M.; Johann B.G. Roten, S.M.; Joseph D. Massucci; Christopher T. Wittmann, S.M., Dir. Campus Min.; Bros. Philip T. Aaron, S.M.; Edward M. Brink, S.M.; William M. Fackovec, S.M.; Raymond L. Fitz, S.M.; Victor M. Forlani, S.M.; Donald Geiger, S.M.; Robert H. Hughes, S.M.; Daniel L. Klco, S.M.; M. Gary Marcinowski, S.M.; Raymond E. Martin, S.M.; Thomas J. Pieper, S.M.; Alex J. Tuss, S.M.; Thomas A. Wendorf, S.M.; Sisters Leanne Jablonski, F.M.I.; Laura M. Leming, F.M.I., (On Leave); Kathleen A. Rossman, O.S.F.; Judith G. Martin, S.S.J.; Jody O'Neil, S.P.; Pamela L. Thimmes, O.S.F.; Angela Ann Zukowski, M.H.S.H.; Mary Louise Foley, F.M.I. Society of Mary (Marianists)

College of Arts and Sciences Tel: 937-229-2611; Fax: 937-229-2615. Dr. Paul J. Morman, Dean; Dr. Patricia A. Johnson, Assoc. Dean Connected Learning; Dr. Linda J. Snider, Assoc. Dean Humanities & Fine Arts; Dr. F. Thomas Eggemeier, Assoc. Dean Science & Social Studies. Professors 224; Students 3,261.

Graduate Studies and Research Tel: 937-229-2390; Fax: 937-229-4545. Dr. Gordon A. Sargent, Vice Pres. Graduate Studies & Research, Dir. of UDRI & Dean of Graduate School; Dr. Katy E. Marre, Assoc. Vice Pres. Graduate Studies & Research.

Students 2,583.

School of Business Administration Tel: 937-229-3731; Fax: 937-229-3301. Dr. Patricia Meyers, Dean; Dr. Charles E. Wells, Assoc. Dean Academic Affairs; Dr. Janice M. Glenn, Dir. M.B.A. Prog.; Dr. Richard J. Walsh, Exec. Dir., Business Outreach and Exec. Devel. Professors 45; Students 1,588.

School of Education Tel: 937-229-3146; Fax: 937-229-3199. Dr. Thomas J. Lasley, Dean; Dr. C. Daniel Raisch, Dean Admin.; Dr. H. Roberta Weaver, Asst. Dean Community Outreach; Dr. Patricia Hart, Assoc. Dean Prog. Dev. Professors 44; Students 877.

School of Engineering, 45469. Tel: 937-229-2736; Fax: 937-229-2756. Dr. Blake E. Cherrington, Dean; Dr. Donald L. Moon, Assoc. Dean for Graduate Programs, Research & Technology; Dr. Malcolm W. Daniels, Assoc. Dean Undergrad. Programs; Most Rev. Carol M. Shaw, Assoc. Dean & Dir. Center Competitive Change. Professors 63; Students 1,191.

School of Law Tel: 937-229-3211; Fax: 937-229-4769. Lisa A. Kloppenberg, Dean; Mr. Kelvin H. Dickinson, Assoc. Dean for Academic Affairs; Mr. Timothy P. Stonecash, Asst. Dean External Rels.; Ms. Janet L. Hein, Asst. Dean & Dir., Admission & Financial Aid; Ms. Laurel A. Hajek, Asst. Dean and Dir. Career Svcs. Professors 21; Students 457.

Libraries and Information Technologies Tel: 937-229-4265. Dr. Edward D. Garten, Dean of Libraries and Information Technology; Lori E. Shaw, Dean of Studies, Prof. & Asst. Dean of Student Affairs. Faculty 407; Total Enrollment 10,125.

The Marian Library / International Marian Research Institute (IMRI) Tel: 937-229-4124; Fax: 937-229-4258. Revs. Johann B.G. Roten, S.M., Dir.; Thomas A. Thompson, S.M., Dir. & Curator.

Institute for Pastoral Initiatives Tel: 937-229-3126; Fax: 937-229-3130. Sr. Angela Ann Zukowski, M.H.S.H., Dir.

University of Dayton, 45469-1390. Tel: 937-229-4214.

SAINT MARTIN. *Chatfield College*, Brown County Ursulines, 20918 State Rte. 251, St. Martin, 45118. Tel: 937-875-3344; Fax: 937-875-3912. Email: nlinenkuge1@chatfield.edu. Web: www.chatfield.edu. Sr. Nancy Linenkugel, O.S.F., Pres. Students 245.

[E] HIGH SCHOOLS, INTER-PAROCHIAL

CINCINNATI. *Elder High School*, 3900 Vincent Ave., 45205-1699. Tel: 513-921-3744; Fax: 513-921-8123. Email: otten.t@elderhs.org. Web: www.elderhs.org. Tom Otten, Prin. & Contact Person; Revs. Anthony M. Brausch; Donald R. Rettig. Priests 2; Lay Teachers 59; Students 1,036.

LaSalle High School, 3091 N. Bend Rd., 45239-7696. Tel: 513-741-3000; Fax: 513-741-2666. Web: www.cincinnatilasalle.net/. Mr. Thomas Luebbe, Prin. Priests 1; Lay Teachers 66; Students 832.

McAuley High School, 6000 Oakwood Ave., 45224. Tel: 513-681-1800; Fax: 513-681-1802. Email: sucherc@mcauleyhs.net. Web: www.mcauleyhs.net. Ms. Cheryl A. Sucher, Prin. & Contact Person; Mrs. Connie Kampschmidt, Asst. Prin.; Mrs. Nicole Brainard, Asst. Prin. Sisters of Mercy 2; Lay Teachers 59; Girls 820.

Convent: 1768 Cedar Ave., 45224.

Convent: 5925 Oakwood Ave., 45224.

Convent: 5764 Belmont Ave., 45224.

McNicholas High School, 6536 Beechmont Ave., 45230. Tel: 513-231-3500; Fax: 513-231-1351. Email: ddugan@mnhs.org. Web: www.mcnhs.org. Mr. Thomas R. Bill, Prin. Lay Teachers 72; Students 900.

Moeller High School, 9001 Montgomery Rd., 45242. Tel: 513-791-1680; Fax: 513-792-3343. Email: bbalbach@moeller.org. Web: www.moeller.org. Mr. Blane Collison, Prin.; William J. Balbach, Treas. & Contact Person. Sisters of Mercy 1; Marianist 6; Lay Teachers 50; Students 970.

Mother of Mercy High School, 3036 Werk Rd., 45211. Tel: 513-661-2740; Fax: 513-661-1842. Email: merkle_n@therofmercy.org. Web: www.motherofmercy.org. Sr. Nancy Merkle, R.S.M., Prin. Sisters of Mercy 2; Lay Teachers 50; Girls 611.

Mt. Notre Dame High School, 711 E. Columbia Ave., 45215. Tel: 513-821-3044; Fax: 513-821-6068. Web: www.mndhs.org. Mrs. Maureen Baldock, Prin. Sisters 4; Lay Teachers 65; Girls 788.

Purcell Marian High School (East Walnut Hills) , 2935 Hackberry St., 45206. Tel: 513-751-1230; Fax: 513-751-1395. Email: jankennedy@purcellmarian.org. Web: www.purcellmarian.org. Janis M. Kennedy, Prin.; Terry Meinking, Business Mgr.; Ms. Jen Meinking, Dir. Ministry. Priests 1; Brothers 3; Sisters 2; Lay Teachers 49; Students 600.

Roger Bacon High School, 4320 Vine St., 45217. Tel: 513-641-1300; Fax: 513-641-0498. Email: wfarris@rogerbacon.org. Web: www.rogerbacon.org. Tom Devolve, Prin. & Contact Person; Rev. William Farris, O.F.M., Pres.; Bro. Christopher Cahill, O.F.M., Computer Network Coord. Teacher; Rev. Mark J. Hudak, O.F.M., Teacher & Chap. Franciscan Friars of the Cincinnati Province of St. John the Baptist Priests 2; Brothers 1; Sisters 2; Lay Teachers 51; Students 764.

Seton High School (Price Hill) , 3901 Glenway Ave., 45205. Tel: 513-471-2600; Fax: 513-471-0529. Email: gibbons_s@hccanet.org. Web: www.setoncincinnati.org. Ms. Susan M. Gibbons, Prin.; Mr. Gordon MacIntosh, Assoc. Prin. Academics; Mrs. Nora Spencer, Assoc. Prin. Student Life; Mrs. Janice Linz, Campus Min. Sisters of Charity of Cincinnati 7; Lay Teachers 48; Students 640.

DAYTON. *Archbishop Alter High School*, 940 E. David Rd., 45429. Tel: 937-434-4434; Fax: 937-434-0507. Email: npalter@mdeca.org. Web: www.alterhighschool.com. Mr. Albert Early, Prin. Sisters 1; Lay Teachers 51; Students 750.

Carroll High School, 4524 Linden Ave., 45432. Tel: 937-253-8188; Fax: 937-258-7001. Email: jsens@carrollhs.org. Web: www.carrollhs.org. Mr. Joseph R. Sens, Prin. Sisters 1; Lay Teachers 64; Students 1,032.

Chaminade-Julienne High School, 505 S. Ludlow St., 45402. Tel: 937-461-3740; Fax: 937-461-6256. Email: gocjeagles@aol.com. Web: www.cjeagles.org. Mr. Lorcan Barnes, Pres.; Mr. Mike Trainor, Prin.; Ms. Jennifer Yarnell, Asst. Prin., Academics; Mrs. Jeannie Horn, Asst. Prin. Student Svcs.; Mr. Matt Ernst, Dir. Admin. Svcs. & Contact; Mr. James Pera, Dir. Campus Ministry; Sr. Damienne Grismer, S.N.D.deN. Conducted by the Society of Mary (Marianists) and Sisters of Notre Dame de Namur. Brothers 2; Sisters 3; Lay Teachers 59; Students 978.

HAMILTON. *Stephen T. Badin High School*, 571 New London Rd., 45013. Tel: 513-863-3993; Fax: 513-785-2844. Email: fmargello@mail.badinhs.org. Web: badinhs.org. Mr. Frank Margello, Prin. Lay Teachers 35; Total Staff 68; Students 651.

MIDDLETOWN. *Bishop Fenwick High School*, 3800 Manchester Rd., 45042. Tel: 513-423-0723; Fax: 513-420-8690. Email: c1_birck@swoca.ohio.gov. Web: www.bishop-fenwickcnd.pvt.k12.oh.us. Rev. Charles E. Mentrup, Prin. Priests 1; Deacons 1; Lay Teachers 32; Students 438.

SIDNEY. *Lehman Catholic High School*, 2400 St. Mary's Ave., 45365. Tel: 937-498-1161; Fax: 937-492-9877. Email: LE_mbarhors@woco-k12.org. Web: www.lehmancatholic.com. Mr. Michael Barhorst, Prin. Sisters 1; Lay Teachers 25; Students 369.

SPRINGFIELD. *Catholic Central High School*, 1200 E. High St., 45505-1124. Tel: 937-325-9204; Fax: 937-328-7426. Email: tlaengle@yahoo.com. Web: www.cchsirish.org. Sr. Teresa Marie Laengle, S.C., Prin. Sisters 1; Lay Teachers 18; Students 200.

[F] HIGH SCHOOLS, PRIVATE

CINCINNATI. *St. Ursula Academy High School*, 1339 E. McMillan St., 45206. Tel: 513-961-3410; Fax: 513-961-3856. Email: fromweber@saintursula.org. Web: www.saintursula.org. Judith A. Wimberg, Pres.; Frances Romweber, Prin. Lay Teachers 72; Girls 678.

Ursuline Academy of Cincinnati Senior High School. , 5535 Pfeiffer Rd., 45242. Tel: 513-791-5791; Fax: 513-791-3170. Email: dcastelli@ursulineacademy.org. Web: www.ursulineacademy.org. Rev. John E. Wessling (Retired); Dr. Diane Castelli, Pres.; Sharon Redmond, Prin. & Contact Person. Ursuline Sisters of Brown Co. Saint Martin, OH Priests 1; Sisters 3; Lay Teachers 69; Girls 653.

St. Xavier High School, 600 N. Bend Rd., 45224. Tel: 513-761-7600; Fax: 513-761-3811. Mr. David B. Mueller, Prin.; Janet Reder, Contact Person; Rev. Walter C. Deye, S.J., Pres.; Mr. William Sandquist Jr., Asst. Prin.; Revs. John J. Beckman, S.J.; R. Michael Brophy, S.J.; Edward L. Pigott, S.J.; Dennis P. Ahern, S.J.; Francis J. Daly, S.J., Rector; William Murphy, S.J., Scholastics; Charles Rodrigues, S.J., Scholastics. Priests 5; Sisters 1; Lay Teachers 105; Students 1,452.

[G] CONSOLIDATED ELEMENTARY SCHOOLS

CINCINNATI. *St. Bartholomew*, (Grades K-8), 9375 Winton Rd., 45231. Tel: 513-521-0860; Fax: 513-728-3110. Email: carver_m@hccanet.org. Web: www.hccanet.org/sbcs. Ms. Mary R. Carver, Prin.; Ms. Lynn Mowery, Asst. Prin. Consolidated school serving the parishes of St. Bartholomew, Corpus Christi and St. John Neumann, Cincinnati. Lay Teachers 31; Students 620.

St. Boniface School, 4305 Pitts Ave., 45223. Tel: 513-541-5122; Fax: 513-541-3939. Email: agormanrsm@juno.com. Sr. Ann Gorman, R.S.M., Prin. & Contact Person. Serving the parishes of St. Boniface, St. Leo and Mother of Christ, Cincinnati. Sisters 2; Lay Teachers 13; Students 160.

Corryville Catholic Elementary School, 108 Calhoun St., 45219. Tel: 513-281-4856; Fax: 513-281-6497. Email: smith-ma@corryvillecatholic.org. Sr. Marie Smith, S.N.D., Prin. & Contact Person. Consolidated school serving the parishes of St. George, St. Monica, Holy Name, St. Andrew, Assumption and Sacred Heart. Sisters 6; Lay Teachers 10; Students 185.

St. Gabriel Consolidated School, (Grades K-8), 18 W. Sharon Ave., 45246. Tel: 513-771-5220; Fax: 513-771-5133. Email: j.epplen@stgabeschool.org. Web: www.st.gabeschool.org. Joseph Epplen, Prin. & Contact Person. Consolidated school serving the parishes of St. Gabriel, Glendale; St. John, West Chester; St. Martin de Porres, Lincoln Heights; St. Matthias, Forest Park; St. Maximilian Kolbe, West Chester. Lay Teachers 21; Students 418.

DAYTON. *Bishop Leibold School*Students 606.

West Campus (Grades K-3), 24 S. Third St., Miamisburg, 45342. Tel: 937-866-3021; Fax: 937-866-5680. Email: NPBishop@mdeca.org.

East Campus (Grades 4-8), 6666 Springboro Rd., 45449. Tel: 937-434-9343; Fax: 937-436-3048. Mr. Christopher Judge, Prin.; Julie Wehner, Sec. West Campus; Laura Eiken, Sec. East Campus. Lay Teachers 35; Students 606.

Dayton Catholic Elementary School, (Grades K-8), 3805 King's Hwy., 45406. Tel: 937-275-8114; Fax: 937-275-5737. Email: KarynDCES@aol.com. Web: www.daycath.cnd.pvt.k12.oh.us. Mrs. Karyn J. Hecker, Prin. Serving the parishes of St. Agnes, and St. James, Dayton. Lay Teachers 11; Students 187.

HAMILTON. *St. Joseph Consolidated School*, (Grades K-8), 925 S. Second St., 45011. Tel: 513-863-8758; Fax: 513-863-5253. Email: 08_stenger@swocai.swoca.net. Joseph Pyfrin, Prin. Serving the parishes of St. Aloysius, Shandon and St. Joseph, Hamilton. Lay Teachers 11; Students 216; Total Staff 15.

MIDDLETOWN. *John XIII Catholic Elementary School* Serving the parishes of Holy Family, Middletown and St. Mary, Franklin.

East Campus (Grades K-5), 3907 Central Ave., 45044. Tel: 513-424-0838; Fax: 513-424-8568.

North Campus (Grades 6-8), 3806 Manchester Rd., 45042. Tel: 513-424-1196; Fax: 513-420-8480. Email: c2_krista@swocai.swoca.net. Sr. Nancy Krista, S.N.D., Prin. & Contact Person. Sisters 1; Lay Teachers 25; Students 471.

PIQUA. *Piqua Catholic School* Serving the parishes of St. Boniface and St. Mary.

North St. Campus (Grades 4-8), 503 W. North St., 45356. Tel: 937-773-1564; Fax: 937-773-0380. Email: olearyr@piquacatholic.org. Web: www.piquacatholic.org.

Downing St. Campus (Grades K-3), 218 S. Downing St., 45356. Tel: 937-773-3876; Fax: 937-773-5875. Mr. Robert O'Leary, Prin.; Linda Lange, Contact Person. Sisters 1; Lay Teachers 19; Students 367.

SPRINGFIELD. *Holy Trinity Catholic School*, (Grades PreSchool), 1035 W. High St., 45506. Tel: 937-322-8781; Fax: 937-323-2790. Email: hlty_sblank@k12server.mveca.org. Web: www.holytrinity.cnd.pvt.k12.oh.us. Sr. Sharon Blank, Prin. Serving the parishes of St. Joseph and St. Raphael. Lay Teachers 10; Students 136.

[H] ELEMENTARY SCHOOLS, PRIVATE

CINCINNATI. *Summit Country Day School*, (Grades PreK-12), 2161 Grandin Rd., 45208-3300. Tel: 513-871-4700; Fax: 513-533-5373. Email: summitinfo@summitcds.org. Web: www.summitcds.org. Joseph T. Devlin, Head of School. Priests 1; Lay Teachers 148; Support Staff 52; Students 1,100.

St. Ursula Villa, (Grades PreK-8), 3660 Vineyard Pl., 45226. Tel: 513-871-7218; Fax: 513-871-0082. Email: p.loechle@stursulavilla.org. Web: www.stursulavilla.org. Paul Loechle, Prin. & Contact Person. Lay Teachers 44; Students 474.

LIBERTY TOWNSHIP. *Mother Teresa Catholic Elementary School*, (Grades K-5), 6085 Jackie Dr., 45044-9426. Tel: 513-779-6585; Fax: 513-779-6468. Email: mtces2@yahoo.com. Web: www.mtces.org. Tony Reed, School Bd. Chm.; Sr. Anne Mary Schulz, C.PP.S., Prin. Sisters 1; Lay Teachers 8; Students 172.

[I] CHILD CARE INSTITUTIONS

CINCINNATI. *St. Aloysius Orphanage*, 4721 Reading Rd., 45237. Tel: 513-242-7600; Fax: 513-242-2845. Email: pgoulet@staloysiuscincinnati.org. Web: www.staloysiuscincinnati.org. Pank Goulet, Exec. Dir.; Tim Sillaman, Chief Operating Officer & Int.

Prin. Crisis group home girls/boys ages 5-17. Children 20.

St. Joseph Infant and Maternity Home dba St. Joseph Home , 10722 Wyscarver Rd., 45241. Tel: 513-563-2520; Fax: 513-563-1958. Email: smvanvurst@sjh-cincy.com. Web: www.sjh-cincy.com. Sr. Marianne Van Vurst, Admin. Sisters of Charity of Cincinnati, OH Respite Beds 5; Residential 47.

St. Joseph Orphanage Archdiocesan Children's Residential Center. , 5400 Edalbert Dr., 45239-7695. Tel: 513-741-3100; Fax: 513-741-5656. Email: sjo@one.net. Web: www.stjosephorphanage.org. Robert J. Wehr, Ph.D., Exec. Dir.

A.C.T. Child Case Management, 7611 Cheviot Rd., Bldg. C, 45211. Tel: 513-385-1900; Fax: 513-245-7970. Robert J. Wehr, Ph.D., Exec. Dir. Employees 57; Children Served 350.

St. Joseph Villa, 5400 Edalbert Dr., 45239. Tel: 513-741-3100; Fax: 513-741-5686. Robert J. Wehr, Ph.D., Exec. Dir. Residential Treatment Children 6-18. Staff 81; Residents 350.

Altercrest, 274 Sutton Rd., 45230. Tel: 513-231-5010; Fax: 513-231-8651. Robert J. Wehr, Ph.D., Exec. Dir. Residential Treatment for Boys ages 12-18. Staff 72; Residents 123.

C.A.R.E. Child Case Management, 90 Lawn Ave., Hamilton, 45013. Tel: 513-887-2100; Fax: 513-887-2101. Robert J. Wehr, Ph.D., Exec. Dir. Staff 21; Children Served 276.

Family Ties Therapeutic Foster Care, 3425 N. Bend Rd., Unit D, 45239. Tel: 513-421-7350; Fax: 513-481-7360. Robert J. Wehr, Ph.D., Exec. Dir. Staff 23; Total Assisted 107.

Home-Based Therapy, 7611 Cheviot Rd., Bldg. C, 45211. Tel: 513-385-1900; Fax: 513-245-7972. Robert J. Wehr, Ph.D., Exec. Dir. Staff 26; Total Assisted 135.

[J] SPECIAL SCHOOLS

CINCINNATI. *St. Rita School for the Deaf*, 1720 Glendale-Milford Rd., 45215. Tel: 513-771-7600; Fax: 513-326-8264. Email: ernst_g@hccanet.org. Web: www.srsdeaf.org. Mr. Gregroy R. Ernst, Exec. Dir.; Ms. Mary Ann Stansfield, Dir. Special Svcs.; Rev. William H. Wysong, J.C.L. Residential and day school for deaf and hard of hearing children. Sisters of Charity 2; Lay Teachers 33; High School Students 33; Elementary Students 46; Pre-School 42.

[K] GENERAL HOSPITALS

CINCINNATI. *Good Samaritan Hospital*, 375 Dixmyth Ave., 45220. Tel: 513-872-1400; Fax: 513-872-1190. Web: www.trihealth.com. Mr. John Prout, Pres. & CEO; David Dornheggen, Contact Person; Rev. Gerald R. Niklas. Catholic Health Initiative (CHI). Bed Capacity 643; Bassinets 65; Long-term Care 15; Patients Assisted Annually 375,000.

Registered Training College of Nursing Tel: 513-872-2631; Fax: 513-872-3572. Students 300.

Mercy Hospital Anderson, 7500 State Rd., 45255. Tel: 513-624-4500; Fax: 513-624-3299. Web: www.e-mercy.com. Patrica A. Schroer, Pres.; Sr. Eileen Wrobleski, C.S.C., Vice Pres., Mission Svcs. Sisters of Mercy Bed Capacity 186; Patients Assisted Annually 159,580; Total Staff 1,022.

Mercy Hospitals West dba Mercy Franciscan Hospital Mt. Airy , A member of the Mercy Health Partners. , 2446 Kipling Ave., 45239 Tel: 513-853-5000; Fax: 513-853-9141. Web: www.e-mercy.com. Rodney Reider, Pres.; Sr. Eileen Wrobleski, C.S.C., Vice Pres. Mission Svcs.; Don Rohling, Dir. Mission Svcs.; Rev. Mike Paraniuk, Chap.; Sisters Donna De Mange, O.S.F., Chap.; Louise Zaplitny, S.C., Chap. Bed Capacity 269; Patients Assisted Annually 198,349; Total Staff 949.

Mercy Hospitals West dba Mercy Franciscan Hospital-Western Hills , A member of the Mercy Health Partners. , 3131 Queen City Ave., 45238. Tel: 513-389-5000; Fax: 513-389-9141. Web: www.e-mercy.com. Rodney Reider, Int. Pres.; Don Rohling, Dir. Mission Svcs.; Sr. Adrienne Colson, O.P., Chap.; Ms. Alberta Utrup, Chap.; Sally Koester, Chap.; Rev. Aquinas Schneider, O.F.M., Chap. Sisters 1; Bed Capacity 267; Patients Assisted Annually 102,952; Total Staff 905.

BATAVIA. *The Sisters of Mercy Of Clermont County, Ohio* dba Mercy Hospital Clermont , 3000 Hospital Dr., 45103. Tel: 513-732-3200; Fax: 513-732-8537. Web: www.e-mercy.com. Mark Shugarman, Pres.; Sisters Eileen Wrobleski, C.S.C., Vice Pres., Mission Svcs.; Joan Nemann, R.S.M., Dir. Mission Svcs.; Rev. R. Gwinn Lacy. Bed Capacity 157; Patients Assisted Annually 89,004; Total Staff 580.

DAYTON. *Good Samaritan Hospital*, 2222 Philadelphia Dr., 45406. Tel: 937-278-2612. Web: www.goodsamdayton.org. Mr. Douglas Deck, Pres. Affiliate with Catholic Health Initiative. Bed Capacity 560; Patients Assisted Annually 300,000.

FAIRFIELD. *Sisters of Mercy of Hamilton* dba Mercy Hospital Fairfield , 3000 Mack Rd., 45014. Tel: 513-870-7000; Fax: 513-870-7065. Web: www.e-mercy.com. Mark Hood, Pres.; Sr. Sharon Wiedmar, R.S.M., Dir. Mission Svcs. Bed Capacity 165; Total Assisted Annually 159,416; Total Staff 967.

HAMILTON. *The Sisters of Mercy of Hamilton, Ohio* dba Mercy Hospital of Hamilton-Fairfield , 100 Riverfront Plaza, P.O. Box 418, 45011. Tel: 513-867-6400; Fax: 513-867-9043. Web: www.e-mercy.com. Thomas S. Urban, Pres.; Sr. Sharon Wiedmar, R.S.M., Dir. of Mission Svcs.

SPRINGFIELD. *Mercy Health Systems - Western Ohio*, One South Limestone, 45501-0688. Tel: 937-390-5000; Fax: 937-890-5507. Email: lynncasey@health-partners.org. Web: www.mercy-health.org. Mr. Andrew McCulloch, Pres. & CEO Sr. Lynn Casey, S.C.L., Mission Svcs.; Rev. Marvin R. Hackman, Chap.; Patricia O'Connor, Ph.D., Regl. Dir., Spiritual Care. Sisters of Mercy Sisters 7; Bed Capacity 902; Patients Assisted Annually 150,000.

URBANA. *Mercy Memorial Hospital*, 904 Scioto St., 43078. Tel: 937-653-5231; Fax: 937-484-6150. Email: kzalar@health-partners.org. Sisters of Mercy Sisters 2; Bed Capacity 25; Total Assisted 4,573.

[L] SENIOR RESIDENCES

CINCINNATI. *Archbishop Leibold Home for the Aged*, 476 Riddle Rd., 45220-2493. Tel: 513-281-8001; Fax: 513-281-4943. Email: msinclsp@mindspring.com. Revs. Cyprian Berens, O.F.M., Chap.; Jovian C. Weigel, O.F.M.; August J. Kniepp; Charles Miller, O.F.M.; Sr. Joseph Grenon, L.S.P., Supr. The Little Sisters of the Poor Sisters 10; Residents 87; Total Staff 112.

St. Margaret Hall, 1960 Madison Rd., 45206-1896. Tel: 513-751-5880; Fax: 513-751-9813. Email: administrator@stmargarethall.com. Sr. Norah Michael, O.Carm., Admin. & Contact Person; Rev. James Favret. Carmelite Sisters for the Aged and Infirm ; Residents 133; Total Staff 195.

Mercy Franciscan Senior Health and Housing Services Inc. dba Mercy St. Theresa Center , 7010 Rowan Hill Dr., 45227. Tel: 513-271-7010; Fax: 513-527-0143. Web: www.e-mercy.com. Brian E. Forschner, Pres.; Jamie J. Houseman, Exec. Dir.; Rev. Stephen J. Emerick, Chap.; Deacon Jerry Schneider. Bed Capacity 174; Permanent Residents 154; Total Assisted 286; Total Staff 174.

Mercy Franciscan Senior Health and Housing Services, Inc. dba Mercy Franciscan at West Park , 2950 West Park Dr., 45238. Tel: 513-451-8900; Fax: 513-451-3728. Web: www.e-mercy.com. Brian E. Forschner, Pres. Bed Capacity 338; Total Assisted Annually 214; Residents 340; Total Staff 267.

Mercy Franciscan Senior Health and Housing Services, Inc. dba Mercy Franciscan Terrace , 100 Compton Rd., 45215. Tel: 513-761-9036; Fax: 513-761-5199. Web: www.e-mercy.com. Brian E. Forschner, Pres.; Beth A. Luken, Exec. Dir.; Rev. Howard Hudepohl, O.F.M., Pastoral Care; Joan Owens, Pastoral Care. Licenced Beds 169; Total Assisted 111; Staff 175.

Sisters of Charity Senior Care Corp. dba Bayley Place , 990 Bayley Place Dr., 45233. Tel: 513-347-5500; Fax: 513-347-5553. Email: bayleyplace@srcharitycinti.org. Web: www.bayleyplace.org. Sr. Jeanne Roach, Pres. & CEO. Also includes Eldermount Adult Day Program and The Village at Bayley Place. Total Assisted 85; Independent Cottages 78; Nursing Beds 100.

CENTERVILLE. *St. Leonard*, 8100 Clyo Rd., 45458. Tel: 937-433-0480; Fax: 937-439-7165. Email: horvathe@stleonard.net. Web: www.stleonard.net. Rev. Msgr. Anthony Giannamore, Moderator & Chap., Sunday Community; Rev. Joseph Rigali, O.F.M., Chap. A facility of the Franciscan Services Corporation, sponsored by the Sisters of St. Francis, Sylvania, OH. A residence for Senior Citizens. Residents 690; Total Staff 356.

DAYTON *The Maria Joseph Living Care Center*, 4830 Salem Ave., 45416. Tel: 937-278-2692; Fax: 937-278-9016. Email: mariajoseph@mariajoseph.org. Web: www.mariajoseph.org. Sharon Thornton, Pres. & CEO; Sr. Alice Schoettelkotte, C.PP.S., Spiritual Care Coord. Skilled Nursing-Intermediate Nursing; Independent Living, Alzheimer's Unit, Skilled Rehab. Licensed/Certified Nursing Care 384; Independent Living 56; Total Assisted Annually 930; Total Staff 421.

Mercy Siena Springs, 6215 N. Main St., 45415. Tel: 937-279-6114; Fax: 937-279-6870. Deb Pauley, Resident Mgr. Sponsored by the Sisters of Mercy, Apartments, Independent Living for the Elderly. Residents 45; Total Staff 3.

Mercy Siena Springs II, 6217 N. Main St., 45415. Tel: 937-279-6114; Fax: 937-279-6870. Debra Pauley, Mgr. Residents 35.

Mercy Siena Woods, 6125 N. Main St., 45415. Tel: 937-278-8211; Fax: 937-278-8046. Email: shayes@health-partners.org. Susan M. Hayes, Admin. & CEO. Nursing Home, nonsectarian. A member of Catholic Healthcare Partners. Specialized Alzheimer's Center, Skilled Nursing Center. Assisted living and Independent Cottages. Sponsored by the Religious Sisters of Mercy. 58 years of ministry. Sisters 2; Residents 99.

HAMILTON. *Mercy Franciscan Senior Health and Housing Services, Inc.* dba Mercy Franciscan at Schroder , 1302 Millville Ave., 45013. Tel: 513-867-1300; Fax: 513-867-1415. Web: www.e-mercy.com. A Facility of the Mercy Health Partners. Sponsored by the Catholic Healthcare Partners. Special unit for Alzheimer Treatment. Bed Capacity 138; Residents 125; Total Assisted 203; Total Staff 150.

SPRINGFIELD. *Oakwood Village Retirement Community*, 1500 Villa Rd., 45503. Tel: 937-390-9000; Fax: 937-390-9333. Email: razechiel@health-partners.org. Web: www.oakwoodvillage.com. Total in Residence 200; Total Assisted Annually 250; Total Staff 160.

URBANA. *Mercy McAuley Center-Mercy Health Systems*, 906 Scioto St., 43078. Tel: 937-653-5432; Fax: 937-652-2072. Email: kzalar@health-partners.org. Karl P. Zalar Jr., Admin. Residents 129; Total Staff 155.

[M] MONASTERIES AND RESIDENCES OF PRIESTS AND BROTHERS

CINCINNATI. *St. Ann Friary*, 2936 W. Galbraith Rd., 45239. Tel: 513-522-7420; Fax: 513-522-1752. Email: joeric@fuse.net. Revs. Joseph Rayes, O.F.M.; Joseph Ricchini, O.F.M., Guardian & Contact Person; Bros. Phillip Robinette, O.F.M.; Kevin Schroeder, O.F.M.

The Catholic Foreign Mission Society of America, Inc., 6930 Greenfield Dr., 45224-1626. Tel: 513-681-7888; Fax: 513-681-7893 (Call first). Email: mklcin@aol.com. Web: www.maryknoll.org. Revs. Leslie F. Blowers, M.M., Dir.; Peter L. Chabot, M.M. Maryknoll Fathers

St. Clare Friary, 5831 Saranac Ave., 45224. Tel: 513-541-5742; Fax: 513-541-5774. Rev. Patrick McCloskey, O.F.M.; Bros. Francisco Meyer, O.F.M.; John Schreck, O.F.M.

Claver Jesuit Community, 3731 Borden Ave., 45223-2310. Tel: 513-542-2312; Fax: 513-542-0889. Email: claver@fuse.net. Web: home.fuse.net/claver. Revs. James A. Hasse, S.J., Supr.; Joseph D. Folzenlogen, S.J. (IND); J. Timothy Hipskind, S.J.; Louis J. Lipps, S.J.; Bro. Michael J. O'Grady, S.J. Priests 4; Brothers 1.

St. Clement Friary St. John the Baptist Province. Residence for Retired Friars, Pastors of St. Clement Parish and other Friars. , 4536 Vine St., 45217. Tel: 513-641-2257; Fax: 513-641-2262. Email: langender@aol.com. Revs. Donald E. Holtgrewe, O.F.M.; Carl J. Langenderfer, O.F.M., Local Min.; Bede Clancy, O.F.M. (Retired); Stanley Bir, O.F.M., Prov. Personnel Advisor; Joel Byrne, O.F.M. (Retired); William Farris, O.F.M., Pres., Roger Bacon High School; Alphonse A. Hoff, O.F.M. (Retired); Howard Hudepohl, O.F.M., Chap., Mercy Franciscan Terrrace; Marcan Hetteberg, O.F.M., Asst. Archivist & Prov. Librarian; Chris Schneider, O.F.M. (Retired); Fridolin Voegele, O.F.M. (Retired); Valens J. Waldschmidt, O.F.M. (Retired); Roman Pfalzer, O.F.M. (Retired); Paul Wild, O.F.M. (Retired); Bros. Conrad F. Rebmann, O.F.M., (Retired); Louis Lamping, O.F.M., Treas. & Fraternal Svc.; Linus Border, O.F.M., Fraternal Svcs.; David W. Crank, Dir. of Office of Senior Friars; Bernard Jennings, O.F.M., (Retired); Kenneth Beetz, O.F.M., Maintenance; Joel Soldenski, O.F.M., Sacristan; Stephen Richter, O.F.M., (Retired); Jerry Jackson, O.F.M., (Retired). Priests 14; Brothers 9.

Comboni Missionaries (Verona Fathers)-Comboni Mission Center Houses Comboni Missionaries of the Heart of Jesus, Inc., The Offices of the Province of North America, including the Office of the Provincial. , 1318 Nagel Rd., 45255-3120. Tel: 513-474-4997; Fax: 513-474-0382. Email: info@combonimissionaries.org. Web: www.combonimissionaries.org. Revs. Dennis Conway, M.C.C.J., Prov. Tel: 513-474-3818; Joseph Bragotti, M.C.C.J., Dir. of Mission Office; Sergio Contran, M.C.C.J., Prov. Treas.; Sr. Roseanne White, O.S.U., Finance Dir.; Revs. Mario Ongaro, M.C.C.J., Personnel Dir.; Paul Donohue, M.C.C.J., Editor Comboni Missions Newsletter & Comboni Press Feature Svc., Temporary Vocation Dir.; Cindy Browne, Mgr. & Editor, CPN Newsletter; Mgr., Peace & Justice Resource Ctr.; Tom Keller, C.F.R.E, Devel. Dir.; Revs. Kenneth Gerth,

M.C.C.J.; William Jansen, M.C.C.J. Priests 8.

De Sales Crossings Marianist Community, 1600 Madison Rd., 45206-1815. Tel: 513-961-1945; Fax: 513-221-3911. Bros. Lawrence W. Corbin, S.M., Dir.; David K. Betz, S.M.; Giancarlo Bonutti, S.M.; Joseph H. Kamis, S.M.; Robert A. Politi, S.M.; Daniel R. Stupka, S.M.; Robert N. Wiethorn, S.M., Dir.; William I. Grundish, S.M.; Rev. Edward M. Jach, S.M. Priests 1; Brothers 8.

Faber Jesuit Community, 790 Clinton Springs Ave., 45229. Tel: 513-961-7700; Fax: 513-569-4582. Email: fabrjes@cinci.rr.com. Revs. Donald Nastold, S.J.; John M. Ferone, S.J., Supr.; Robert J. Hagee, S.J.; Donald O'Shaughnessy, S.J.; Herbert J. Raterman, S.J.; Harold Sommer, S.J.; Peter Sharkey, S.J.; John Beckman, S.J.

4105 Hoffman Ave., 45236. Tel: 513-791-4735. Rev. Robert J. Ross, S.J.

2028 Mackoy Ave., Covington, KY 41014. Tel: 859-261-0498. Bros. Donald H. Bengert, S.J.; John P. Martin, S.J. Priests 9; Brothers 2.

St. Francis Seraph Friary Provincial Headquarters of the Province of St. John the Baptist of the Order of Friars Minor. , 1615 Vine St., 45202. Tel: 513-721-4700; Fax: 513-421-9672. Email: secsjb@franciscan.com. Web: www.franciscan.org. Revs. Donald Miller, O.F.M., Vocation Dir.; Fred Link, O.F.M., Prov. Min.; Jeremy Harrington, O.F.M., Publisher & CEO St. Anthony Messenger Press; Hilarion Kistner, O.F.M., Educ. Homily Helps, Assoc. Chap, The Christ Hospital; Jeffrey Scheeler, O.F.M., Vicar Prov.; Kenan Freson, O.F.M., Prov. Treas.; James M. Bok, O.F.M., Dir. Devel.; Francis S. Tebbe, O.F.M., Dir. Ongoing Formation; Gil Wohler, O.F.M., Pastor of St. Francis Seraph Parish; Peter Paul James, O.F.M. (Retired); Simeon Cleves, O.F.M., Chap., Christ Hospital; Varin Slacke, O.F.M. (Retired); Thomas Speier, O.F.M. (GRY), Part time Assoc. at St. Monica - St. George Parish and Newman Ctr./ Part time Word Ministry; Bruno Kremp, O.F.M., Vocation Dir.; Loren Connell, O.F.M., Prov. Spiritual Dir. for Secular Franciscan Order; Sr. Donna Graham, O.S.F., Office of Justice, Peace and Integrity of Creation; Ms. Toni Cashnelli, Dir. Communications; Bros. Scott Obrecht, O.F.M., Dir. Franciscan Mission Office & Missionary Union; Gene Mayer, O.F.M., Prov. Sec.; Josef Anderlohr, O.F.M., Assoc. Pastor, Liturgical Design Consultant, & Guardian; John Carey, O.F.M., Assoc., Mission Office; David Crank, O.F.M., Office for Senior Friars; Robert Lucero, O.F.M., SAM Production Mgr. & Vicar; Ronald Bolfeta, O.F.M., Parish Admin., Prov. Councilor, Exec. Dir., O.F.M. English-Speaking Conference; Chris Cahill, O.F.M., Instructor, Roger Bacon High School. Priests 8; Brothers 5.

Friars of the Province Serving Abroad:

St. Anthony Church: 51 Yafet St., P.O. Box 8423, 61083 Jaffa 00165 Israel. Tel: 011-972-3-822667. Rev. Malachy Brogan, O.F.M.

Franciscan Renewal Center, Tungkop, Minglanilla, 6046 Cebu, Philippines. Tel: 011-63-32-272-8555; Fax: 011-63-32-272-8585. Rev. Carl Kemphues, O.F.M.

Parroquia de San Francisco, Ciudad, Juarez, Mexico. Tel: 011-52--56-6. Rev. Francis Wendling, O.F.M.

Parroquia San Vincente de Paul, Ciudad, Juarez, Mexico. Rev. Justus Wirth, O.F.M.

Saint Anthony Shrine 254 Manrique St., Sampaloc 1008, Manila, Philippines. Tel: 011-63-2-734-6526; Fax: 011-63-2-734-6527. Bro. Cletus Riederer, O.F.M.

69 San Pedro Bautista St., San Francisco del Monte, 1104 Quezon City, Philippines. Tel: 011-63-02-373-2973; Fax: 011-63-02-373-2972. Rev. Daniel Kroger, O.F.M.

Mt. Laverna, 6501 Palo Leyte, Philippines. Tel: 011-63-053-323-6158. Rev. Harold Geers, O.F.M.

Sanctuario de San Antonio, P.O. Box 3215 MCC, Forbes Park, Makati, Metro Manila 1299 Philippines. Tel: 011-63-02-843-8830; Fax: 011-63-02-843-9223. Bro. Philip Wilhelm, O.F.M.

Saint Francis of Assisi Formation House, 14 Capricorn St., Pleasant Home Subdivision, 6000 Cebu City, Philippines. Bro. Roger Covero, O.F.M.

Franciscans International, 37-39 rue de Vermont, P.O. Box 104, CH 1211 Geneva 20, Switzerland. Tel: 011-41-22-919-4010; Fax: 011-41-22-740-2430. Rev. John Quigley, O.F.M.

Ainmillerstr. 5 Whg. 608, Munich 80801 Germany. Tel: 011-49-89-399081; Fax: 011-49-33-019087. Rev. James Fehrenbach, O.F.M.

Mary, Gate of Heaven Friary, P.O. Box 2654, Negril, Westmoreland, Jamaica. Bro. Vincent Delorenzo, O.F.M. Tel: 876-957-4900; Fax: 876-957-4625.

Mary, Gate of Heaven Friary, P.O. Box 2654, Negril, Westmoreland, WI. Tel: 876-957-4900; Fax: 876-957-4625.

St. Joseph Friary, P.O. Box 66, Savanna-la-mar, Westmoreland, WI. Tel: 876-955-2648. Bro. Mark Gehret, O.F.M.

Sts. Philip and James Friary, 31 Watson Stylor Dr., P.O. Box 31, Lucea- Hanover, Jamaica. Tel: 876-955-2648. Bro. Louis Zant, O.F.M.; Rev. John Joseph Gonchar, O.F.M.

Franciscanos, Templo de San Frandisci y Santa Clara, Uxmal #2300, Colonia Guajardo, Mexicali, Baja California CP21050 Mexico. Tel: 011-52-6-555-2286; Fax: 011-52-6-555-1342. Rev. Matthew Krempel, O.F.M.

Friars on Special Assignment in the U.S.A.:

The Catholic University of America, Washington, DC 20064. Tel: 202-269-3491; Fax: 202-319-5719. Revs. Arthur Espelage, O.F.M., Exec. Coord., Canon Law Society; Matthias Crehan, O.F.M., Chap.,Veteran's Affairs Med. Ctr. Phoenix AZ.

Friars in Retirement Homes in the Archdiocese of Cincinnati: Revs. Charles Miller, O.F.M.; Jovian Weigel, O.F.M.

Archbishop Leibold Home for the Aged, 476 Riddle Rd., 45220-2493. Tel: 513-281-8001; Fax: 513-281-4943. Revs. Aloys Held, O.F.M.; Theobald Hattrup, O.F.M.; Vincent Dieckman, O.F.M.

Mercy Franciscan Terrace, 100 Compton Rd., 45215-5152. Tel: 513-761-9036. Bro. Jude Sukup, O.F.M.

St. Margaret Hall, 1960 Madison Rd., 45206-1828. Tel: 513-751-5880; Fax: 513-751-9813. Bro. Francis Williams, O.F.M.

St. Gertrude Priory, 7630 Shawnee Run Rd., 45243. Tel: 513-561-5954; Fax: 513-527-3971. Email: frkenop@juno.com. Web: www.stgertrude.org. Revs. Walter Wagner, O.P., Novice Master; Kenneth R. Letoile, O.P., Prior; Michael Detemple, O.P., Subprior; Stephen Alcott, O.P.; Charles A. Farrell, O.P.; J. Vincent Watson, O.P., (Part-time).

Headquarters of Glenmary Home Missioners, P.O. Box 465618, 45246-5618. Tel: 513-874-8900; Fax: 513-874-1690. Email: info@glenmary.org. Web: www.glenmary.org. Also known as The Home Missioners of America.

4119 Glenmary Trace, Fairfield, 45014. Tel: 513-874-8900; Fax: 513-874-1690. Revs. Dan Dorsey, G.H.M., Pres.; Bob Poandl, G.H.M., 1st Vice Pres. & Dir. of Educ.; Dominic R. Duggins, G.H.M., 2nd Vice Pres. & Dir. of Devel.; Steve Pawelk, G.H.M., Dir. of Vocations.

Senior Members: Revs. Bob Bond, G.H.M.; Joseph Dean, G.H.M.; Tom Field, G.H.M.; Joseph Gartner, G.H.M.; Ed Gorny, G.H.M.; Edward Haggerty, G.H.M.; Robert Healy, G.H.M.; Charles Hughes, G.H.M.; James Kelly, G.H.M.; John Marquardt, G.H.M.; George Mathis, G.H.M.; John McNearney, G.H.M.; Joseph O'Donnell, G.H.M.; Patrick O'Donnell, G.H.M.; Raymond Orlett, G.H.M.; John Otterbacher, G.H.M.; Gerald Peterson, G.H.M.; Robert Rademacher, G.H.M.; Francisco Schenk, G.H.M.; Leo Schloemer, G.H.M.; William Smith, G.H.M.; Bros. Robert Hoffman, G.H.M.; Lawrence Jochim, G.H.M.; Thomas Kelly, G.H.M.; Charles Kennedy, G.H.M.; Bernie Stern, G.H.M. In Res. Revs. August Guppenberger; Richard Kreimer; Bros. Dennis Craig, Senior Member Coordinator; Del Homes, G.H.M.; Bill Wright, G.H.M.

On Special Assignment: Revs. Bruce C. Brylinski, G.H.M. (COV), Artist-Evangelizer/Sacramental Min. (Olive Hill, KY); Jerry Dorn, G.H.M., Sabbatical; John Rausch, G.H.M., Human Economics Ministry (Stanton, KY).

Jesuit Community at Xavier University, Jesuit Community Residence, 3844 Victory Pkwy., 45207. Tel: 513-745-3591; Fax: 513-745-3858. Revs. Frederick J. Benda, S.J.; Joseph A. Bracken, S.J.; Albert J. Bischoff, S.J.; Robert C. Baumiller, S.J.; Richard W. Bollman, S.J., Rector; Eugene J. Carmichael, S.J.; Glen Chun, S.J.; Michael J. Graham, S.J.; James E. Hoff, S.J.; Thomas P. Kennealy, S.J.; William F. King, S.J.; J. Leo Klein, S.J.; John J. LaRocca, S.J.; Theodore C. Thepe, S.J.; Benjamin J. Urmston, S.J.; Joseph Wagner, S.J.; George B. Wilson, S.J. Members of the Jesuit Community (Society of Jesus, S.J.) Priests 17.

Jesuit Community at St. Xavier High School, Jesuit Community, 7361 View Pl., 45224. Tel: 513-761-5522; Fax: 513-761-0514. Revs. Francis J. Daly, S.J., Rector; Dennis P. Ahern, S.J.; Michael Brophy, S.J.; Walter C. Deye, S.J.; Edward L. Pigott, S.J.; Robert J. Thesing, S.J.; William Murphy, S.J., Scholastics; Charles Rodrigues, S.J., Scholastics.

St. John the Baptist Friary, 10722 Wyscarver Rd., 45241-3803. Tel: 513-769-1613; Fax: 513-769-1650. Email: jvv@fuse.net. Revs. Loren Connell, O.F.M.; Melvin Holtel, O.F.M.; Bruno Kremp, O.F.M.; Joachim Lux, O.F.M.; Bill Reichel, O.F.M.; James VanVurst, O.F.M., Local Min.; Warren Zeisler, O.F.M.; Bro. Dominic Lococo, O.F.M.

Marianist Community, 9025 Montgomery Rd., 45242-7711. Tel: 513-793-4777; Fax: 513-792-3343. Email: rflaherty@moeller.org. Web: www.moeller.org. Bro. Robert M. Flaherty, S.M., Dir.; Rev. Lawrence L. Schoettelkotte, S.M. Priests 1; Brothers 8.

Marianist Community, 118 Findlay St., Apt. #1, 45202-7702. Tel: 513-369-0388. Rev. Michael L. Lisbeth, S.M.; Bros. James H. Abel, S.M.; J. Mitchell Schweickart, S.M.; Paul Hoffman, S.M., Acting Dir. Brothers 3; Priests 1.

Pleasant Street Friary, 1723 Pleasant St., 45210. Tel: 513-621-0599; Fax: 513-621-0519. Email: dja@franciscan.org. Revs. James M. Bok, O.F.M.; Mark J. Hudak, O.F.M.; Daniel J. Anderson, O.F.M.; Jack R. Wintz, O.F.M.; Murray L. Bodo, O.F.M.

DAYTON. *Marianist Community*, 100 Chambers St., 45409-2817. Tel: 937-627-8998. Revs. Christopher W. Conlon, S.M., Dir.; Eugene Contadino, S.M. Priests 2; Brothers 3.

Marianist Community, 149 Franklin St., 45402-2598. Tel: 937-228-2013; Fax: 937-228-5354. Revs. Lee L. Sciarrotta, S.M., Dir.; Francis J. Kenney, S.M. Priests 2; Brothers 2.

Marianist Community, Meyer Hall, 4435 E. Patterson Rd., 45430-1095. Tel: 937-426-7852; Fax: 937-426-7858. Revs. Richard K. Knuge, S.M., Dir.; John Mulligan, S.M. Priests 1; Brothers 7.

Marianist Community, Novitiate, 4435 E. Patterson Rd., 45430-1095. Tel: 937-426-5721; Fax: 937-429-4686. Revs. Joseph P. Tedesco, S.M., Acting Dir. & Master of Novices; H. James Bartlett, S.M.; Bro. Thomas Redmond, S.M. Priests 1; Brothers 7.

Marianist Community, 141 Washington St., 45402-2530. Tel: 937-224-9978. Revs. John A. McGrath, S.M., Dir.; Charles T. Bergedick, S.M.; Thomas A. Schroer, S.M. Priests 3; Brothers 8.

Marianist Community, 62 Indiana Ave, 45410-2308. Tel: 937-258-3212. Bro. Raymond Martin, S.M., Dir.; Rev. Norbert C. Burns, S.M. Priests 1; Brothers 3.

Marianist Community, 312 Stonemill Rd., 45409-2543. Tel: 937-627-1553. Revs. Gerald T. Chinchar, S.M.; Paul M. Marshall, S.M., Dir.; Bertrand A. Buby, S.M. Priests 3; Brothers 3.

Marianist Community, 121 Sawmill Rd., 45409-2524. Tel: 937-222-4928. Bro. Alex J. Tuss, S.M., Dir.; Revs. Matthew F. Kohmescher, S.M.; Thomas A. Schoen, S.M.; Kenneth J. Sommer, S.M. (STL), 4213 Romain Dr. #19, 45209; Bros. Robert Donovan, S.M., 1516 Elm St. #10, 45202. Tel: 513-259-1179; Joseph Spehar, 5440 Moeller Ave., 45212. Tel: 513-351-5414; Paul Merland, 3751 Eastern Hills Lane #1709, 45209. Priests 2; Brothers 2.

Marianist Community, 1903 Trinity Ave., 45409-2445. Tel: 937-293-9744. Revs. James L. Heft, S.M.; Christopher T. Wittmann, S.M., Dir. Priests 2; Brothers 2.

Marianist Community, Alumni Hall, University of Dayton, 45469-0300. Tel: 937-229-4695; 937-229-4703 (Office). Revs. Paul F. Vieson, S.M., Dir.; Robert E. Hughes, S.M.; Joseph F. Kozar, S.M.; James R. McKay, S.M.; John S. Putka, S.M.; Johann B.G. Roten, S.M.; Joseph P. Tedesco, S.M.; Thomas A. Thompson, S.M.; Adolf M. Windisch, S.M. Priests 9; Brothers 13.

Mercy Siena Village, 6105 N. Main St. Apt 139, 45415-3110. Revs. Donald F. Bracht, S.M.; John Mueller, S.M.; John Mulligan, S.M. Priests 7; Brothers 6.

Mercy Siena Woods, Nursing Care, 6125 N. Main St., 45415-3110. Revs. Edmund L. Rhodes, S.M.; Cyril G. Middendorf, S.M.

Mercy Siena Gardens, 6105 N. Main St., 45415-3110. Revs. Robert J. Hoeper, S.M.; Philip C. Hoelle, S.M.; Robert Backherms, S.M. (NY).

Marianist Community, 301 Kiefaber St., 45409. Tel: 937-627-8091. Bro. Thomas J. Pieper, S.M., Dir.; Rev. David McGuigan, S.M. Priests 2; Brothers 1.

Marianist Network for the Arts Tel: 937-320-5450; Fax: 937-429-3195. Religious 3; Total Staff 3.

North American Center for Marianist Studies Tel: 937-429-2521; Fax: 937-429-3195. Religious 2; Total Staff 9.

Marianist Mission, 119 Franklin St., 45402-2599. Tel: 937-222-4641; 800-348-4732; Fax: 937-222-3038. Bro. Ron L. Overman, S.M. Religious 5; Total Staff 62.

Marianist Environmental Education Center Tel: 937-429-3582; Fax: 937-429-3195. Religious 2; Total Staff 6.

Provincial Office of the Cincinnati Province of the Society of the Precious Blood, 431 E. Second St., 45402-1764. Tel: 937-228-9263; Fax: 937-228-6878. Email: prodirsec@cpps-preciousblood.org. Web: www.cpps-preciousblood.org. Very Rev. Angelo Anthony, C.PP.S., Prov. Dir.; Bro. Joseph J. Fisher, C.PP.S., Treas.; Revs. Kenneth Schnipke, C.PP.S., Dir. Vocations. Tel: 937-228-6224; Larry J. Hemmelgarn, C.PP.S., Prov. Sec.

Members of the Provincial Council: Revs. Kenneth Schnipke, C.PP.S., Vice Prov., Gaspar House: 4880 Denlinger Rd., 45426-2012. Tel: 937-278-3365; Fax: 937-228-6878; Kenneth Schroeder, C.PP.S., 1st Councilor, St. John/St. Rose/Nativity BVM: 7428

State Rte. 119, Maria Stein, 45860-9730. Tel: 419-925-4775; Fax: 419-925-1745; Thomas Hemm, C.PP.S., 2nd Councilor, St. Peter and Paul Church: 307 N. Locust St., Ottawa, 45875-1452. Tel: 419-523-5216; Fax: 419-523-4048; James Dugal, C.PP.S., 3rd Councilor, Our Lady of Guadalupe: 6701 State Rte. 219, P.O. Box 69, Montezuma, 45866-0069. Tel: 419-268-2312; Fax: 419-268-1602; Bros. Thomas Bohman, C.PP.S., 4th Councilor, St. Adalbert, 2347 E. 83rd St., Cleveland, 44104-2103. Tel: 216-881-7647; Fax: 216-881-7670; Joseph J. Fisher, C.PP.S., 5th Councilor, Provincial House, 431 E. Second St., 45402-1764. Tel: 973-228-9263, Ext. 12; Fax: 937-228-6878.

Military: Revs. Eugene H. Schnipke, C.PP.S., 2121 Prudence Dr., Beavercreek, 45431-3346. Tel: 937-429-6842; 937-257-4943 (Work); John S. Srode, C.PP.S., PSC 41 Box 3003, Apo, AE 09464-2801.

Priests of the Province Serving Abroad: Very Rev. Barry J. Fischer, C.PP.S., Moderator Gen., Viale di Porta Ardeatina, 66, Rome 1-00154 Italy. Tel: 011-39-06-574-1656; Fax: 011-39-06-574-2874.

Foreign Mission:

Casilla 619, Valdivia, Chile. Tel: 011-56-63-214200; Fax: 011-56-63-224528. Rev. Richard L Beischel, C.PP.S.

Parroguia Sangre de Cristo, Apartado Postal 2483, 01901 Guatemala City, Guatemala. Tel: 011-502-364-1135; Fax: 011-502-364-1324. Rev. William J. Beuth, C.PP.S.

Nuestra Senora de la Luz, Apartado 2348, Lima, 100, Peru. Tel: 011-51-1-536-9592; Fax: 011-51-1-537-5107. Rev. Joseph F. Deardorff, C.PP.S.

Apartado 07-0148, Lima 07, Peru. Tel: 011-51-1-539-5285; Fax: 011-51-1-546-0285. Rev. Gerald G. Dreiling, C.PP.S.

Iglesia Del Sagrado Corazon de Jesus, Calzada San Lorenzo 749, Col San Juan Xalpa, Iztapalapa 09850DF Mexico. Tel: 011-525-612-23-22. Rev. Edgar Jutte, C.PP.S.

Parroguia Sangre de Cristo, Casilla 619, Valdivia, Chile. Tel: 011-56-63-222124. Rev. John F. Falter, C.PP.S.

San Francisco de Borja, Apartado 1983, Lima, Peru. Tel: 011-51-1-476-5181; Fax: 011-51-1-475-6266. Rev. James E. Gaynor, C.PP.S.

Parroquia Cristo Rey, Apartado 36, La Oroya, Peru. Tel: 011-51-64-39-1675; Fax: 011-51-64-39-1675. Rev. James W. Bender, C.PP.S.

Casilla 619, Valdivia, Chile. Tel: 011-56-63-371339. Rev. Daniel J. Mangen, C.PP.S.

San Francisco de Borja, Apartado 1983, Lima, 100, Peru. Tel: 011-51-1-476-5181; Fax: 011-51-1-475-6266. Rev. Ernest W. Ranly, C.PP.S.

N.S. de la P. Sangre, Casilla 176 Correa 2, Santiago, Chile. Tel: 011-56-2-643-7042; Fax: 011-56-2-643-7042. Rev. Donald J. Thieman, C.PP.S.

Returned to U.S.A.:

In Residences Not Listed Elsewhere:

315 Brick Ln., New Oxford, PA 17350-9050. Tel: 717-624-2562. Rev. Paul Aumen, C.PP.S.

St. Albert the Great Church: 3033 Far Hills Ave., Kettering, 45429-2509. Tel: 937-294-5624. Rev. Thomas Beischel, C.PP.S.

16359 Emerald Dr., Middleburg Heights, 44130. Tel: 440-526-3030, Ext. 6265. Rev. John Bolan, C.PP.S.

4835 S. Marshfeld Ave., 2nd Floor, Chicago, IL 60609. Tel: 773-927-1664. Rev. David A. Kelly, C.PP.S. (CHI).

1936 W. 48th St. - Rear, P.O. Box 09379, Chicago, IL 60609. Tel: 773-579-0781. Rev. Dennis Kinderman, C.PP.S. (CHI).

45 Second St., Frackville, PA 17931. Tel: 570-874-1101. Rev. George Kuzara, C.PP.S. (TOL).

120 N. Ela St., Barrington, IL 60010. Tel: 847-382-5300. Rev. Fred Licciardi, C.PP.S. (CHI).

1114 Troy St., 45404-2719. Tel: 973-223-8306. Bro. Timothy Cahill, C.PP.S.

5326 S. Cornell Ave., Chicago, IL 60615. Tel: 773-643-4221. Rev. Dennis Chriszt, C.PP.S.

3321 Acadia Ct., Bloomington, IN 47401-8119. Tel: 812-336-6846. Rev. Donald Davison, C.PP.S.

431 E. Second St., 45402. Rev. Diego Gettig, C.PP.S.

St. James the Less Church, 1652 Oakland Park Ave., Columbus, 43224-3552. Tel: 614-262-1179. Rev. Mark Hoying, C.PP.S.

407 S. Blackhoof St. #120, Wapakoneta, 45895-2148. Rev. William Hoying, C.PP.S.

Precious Blood Center, 2140 Hughes Rd., Liberty, MO 64068-9376. Tel: 816-792-2637. Bro. Joseph Mary Hrezo, C.PP.S.

14037 Fairway Island Dr., Apt. 226, Orlando, FL 32837-5250. Tel: 407-251-0909. Rev. Robert Hunt, C.PP.S.

22866 Montalvo Rd., Laguna Niguel, CA 92677-2740. Tel: 714-493-2800. Rev. Edward Joyce, C.PP.S.

2444 Madison Rd. #1409, 45208-1228. Tel: 513-871-2361. Bro. William Kapitan, C.PP.S.

3908 Cardinal Blvd., Daytona Beach, FL 32127-6504. Tel: 386-322-3275. Rev. Sante J. Reale C.PP.S. (ORL).

3505 Calumet Rd. Apt. 3B, Ludlow Falls, 45339. Tel: 973-698-6191. Rev. Peter Chiodo, C.PP.S.

300 W. Forest Ave., Ypsilanti, MI 48197-2451. Tel: 734-337-4619. Rev. Robert Conway, C.PP.S.

10315 Burgess Rd., Colorado Springs, CO 80908-4149. Rev. Frederick Lang, C.PP.S.

P.O, Box 09379, Chicago, IL 60609-0379. Tel: 773-579-0781; Fax: 773-579-0782. Rev William Nordenbrock, C.PP.S.

100 Bluff View Dr., #106C, Belleair Bluffs, FL 33770-1322. Rev. Robert Onofrey, C.PP.S. (CHI).

7963 Brookwood Ln. #913, North Royalton, 44133. Tel: 440-526-3030, Ext. 6265. Rev. Joseph Rodak, C.PP.S.

1410 Baxter Ave., Superior, WI 54880. Tel: 715-392-2024. Rev. Leon Flaherty, C.PP.S.

652 Stewart Ct., Whiting, IN 46394-1464. Tel: 219-473-4351. Rev. Alphonse Spilly, C.PP.S.

4880 Denlinger Rd., 45426-2012. Tel: 937-278-3265. Bro. Jerome Schulte, C.PP.S.

HAMILTON. *St. Francis Friary*, 723 Main St., 45013-2548. Tel: 513-896-5326; Fax: 513-896-5226. Email: franciscanbrscfp@aol.com. Bros. Eric Lauer, C.F.P.; Howard Parent, C.F.P.; Julian Lane, C.F.P., Contact Person. Brothers of the Poor of St. Francis

HUNTSVILLE. *St. George Chapel of Marianist Community*, 9636 Lakeshore Dr., E., 43324-9520. Tel: 937-842-4902. Bros. Paul F. Bredestege, S.M., Dir. & Contact Person; William A. Deanhoffer, S.M.; Stanley G. Mathews, S.M.; Rev. James A. Russell, S.M. Priests 1; Brothers 3.

[N] CONVENTS AND RESIDENCES FOR SISTERS

CINCINNATI. *Central Office of Sisters of St. Joseph of Medaille*, 1821 Summit Rd., Ste. 210, 45237-2819. Tel: 513-761-2888; Fax: 513-761-9957. Email: patti@sistersofstjoseph.org. Web: www.sistersofstjoseph.org. Sisters Phyllis Manda, C.S.J., Pres.; Eleanor Bernstein, Vice Pres.; Caroline Benken, C.S.J., Gen. Councilor; Anne Meridier, C.S.J., Gen. Councilor. Sisters in Archdiocese 20; Total Congregation 151.

St. Clare Convent, Franciscan Sisters of the Poor U.S. Regional Office Franciscan Sisters of the Poor, 60 Compton Rd., 45215. Tel: 513-761-9040; Fax: 513-948-9116. Email: theusregionsfp@fuse.net. Web: www.franciscansisters.org. Sisters Anne Cecile Albers, S.F.P., Community Min.; Mary Jacinta Doyle, S.F.P., Regl. Min & Contact Person; Rev. Herman H. Kenning, Resident Chap. (Retired). Sisters 20.

Convent of St. Dominic, 916 York St., 45214. Tel: 513-621-5899. Email: gaia916@juno.com. Dominican Sisters of Hope 3.

Franciscan Monastery of St. Clare (Poor Clares), 1505 Miles Rd., 45231-2427. Tel: 513-825-7177; Fax: 513-825-4071. Email: pccinti@juno.com. Web: www.poorclare.org/cincinnati. Sr. Anna M. Covely, O.S.C., Abbess. Sisters 9.

McAuley Convent, 1768 Cedar Ave., 45224. Tel: 513-681-2100; Fax: 513-354-5051. Email: knoonanrsm@mcauley.org. Sr. Kathleen Marie Noonan, R.S.M., Dir. Sisters of Mercy 41.

Mercy Center Convent, 2335 Grandview Ave., 45206. Tel: 513-221-1800; Fax: 513-221-0207. Email: mercycin@aol.com. Sr. Eileen Veeley, R.S.M., Local Coord. Professed Sisters 4.

Mercy Hall, 2317 Grandview Ave., 45206. Tel: 513-475-3726; Fax: 513-221-0207. Email: esm@mercycincinnati.org. Web: www.mercycincinnati.org. Professed Sisters 4.

Provincial House, Health Center of Sisters of Notre Dame de Namur, 699 E. Columbia Ave., 45215-3945. Tel: 513-821-7448; Fax: 513-821-7476. Web: www.sndohio.org. Sisters Elizabeth Marie Bowyer, S.N.D.deN., Prov.; Colette Quinn, S.N.D.deN., Local Moderator; Donna Wisowaty, S.N.D.deN., Admin. Sisters 80.

Sisters of Charity of Cincinnati, Ohio, 5900 Delhi Rd., 45051. Tel: 513-347-5201; Fax: 513-347-5228. Email: spm@scexec.org. Web: www.srcharitycinti.org. Sr. Barbara Hagedorn, S.C., Pres. Sisters in Congregation 525; Sisters in Archdiocese 390.

Sisters of Mercy, Administrative Offices, 2335 Grandview Ave, 45206. Tel: 513-221-1800; Fax: 513-221-0207. Email: rsm@mercycincinnati.org. Web: www.mercycincinnati.org. Represented in: Archdioceses of Cincinnati, Boston, Detroit, Louisville, Washington; Dioceses of Brownville, Charlotte, Cleveland, Knoxville, Lansing, Las Cruces, Memphis, Nashville, Newark, Oakland, Orlando, Lexington, Omaha, Owensboro, Portland (ME), Richmond, Toledo and Jamaica, (WI). Institute of the Sisters of Mercy of the Americas 3

Sisters of Mercy of the Americas Regional Community of Cincinnati, 2335 Grandview Ave., 45306. Tel: 513-221-1800; Fax: 513-221-0207. Email: rsm@mercycincinnati.org. Web: www.mercycincinnati.org. Sisters Marjorie Rudemiller, R.S.M., Pres. Regl. Community of Cincinnati; Carol Ann Wenning, Inc. Min. Co-sponsors: Catholic Health Partners. Professed Sisters 314.

Sisters of the Good Shepherd, 2108 Hatmaker St., 45204. Tel: 513-921-5923.

Ursulines of Cincinnati, 1339 E. McMillan St., 45206-2164. Tel: 513-961-3410, Ext. 139; Fax: 513-872-7177. Email: selang@juno.com or ursofcinti@juno.com. Ursuline Sisters, Sisters of this community sponsor one high school, one elementary school, counseling, social service, health care, communications, adult education, parish work and Hispanic Ministry. Sisters 21.

BATAVIA. *Sisters of Mercy*, Clermont, 4315 Elizabeth Dr., 45103. Tel: 513-732-6335; Fax: 513-732-8686 (Clermont Mercy Hospital).

DAYTON. *Sisters of the Precious Blood Generalate*, 4000 Denlinger Rd., 45426. Tel: 937-837-3302; Fax: 937-837-8825. Email: srs.cpps@spbdo.com. Web: www.bright.net/~cppsnews. Sisters Maryann Bremke, C.P.P.S., Pres.; Jeanette Buehler, C.P.P.S., Vice Pres. & Councilor & Sec.; M. Elise Calmus, C.P.P.S., Treas.; Nadine Kaschalk, C.P.P.S., Councilor; Edna Hess, C.P.P.S., Councilor; Madonna Ratermann, C.P.P.S., Councilor; Noreen Jutte, C.P.P.S., Archivist.

Sisters of the Precious Blood, Salem Heights Convent, 4960 Salem Ave., 45416-1797. Tel: 937-278-0871; Fax: 937-278-8722. Email: sbbodnar@salemheights.com. Web: www.bright.net/~cppsnews. Kathryn Shafer, Admin.; Sr. Beverly Bodnar, C.P.P.S., Asst. Admin. Resident Life & Contact Person; Rev. Donald C. Huebner (Retired). Sisters 76.

SAINT MARTIN. *Ursulines of Brown County*, Ursuline Center, 20860 State Rte. 251, St. Martin, 45118-9705. Tel: 513-875-2020, Ext. 27; Fax: 513-875-2311. Email: nvollman@tds.net. Web: www.ursulinesofbc.org. Sr. Patricia Homan, O.S.U., Congregational Min. Ursuline Order, Congregation of Paris Sisters 36.

[O] RESIDENCES FOR ADULTS AND YOUTHS

CINCINNATI. *Friars Club*, 65 W. McMillan St., 45219. Tel: 513-381-5432; Fax: 513-381-7909. Email: tcaldwell@friarsclubinc.org. Web: www.friarsclubinc.org. Tina Caldwell, Int. Exec. Dir.; Mike Besl, Pres. Bd. of Trustees. Residential programs for male teens, residency for men, transitional living for mentally ill, counseling, education for teen school dropouts, youth sports, and community outreach for high risk youth, family resource center, housing & support for homeless families.

[P] RETREAT HOUSES, CONFERENCE AND RENEWAL CENTERS

CINCINNATI. *Friarhurst Retreat Center*, 8136 Wooster Pike, 45227. Tel: 513-561-2270; Fax: 513-561-0367. Email: frhurst@one.net. Revs. Lambert R. Dannenfelser, O.F.M. (Retired); Paul Desch, O.F.M., Local Min.

DAYTON. *Bergamo*, 4400 Shakertown Rd., 45430-1075. Tel: 937-426-2363; Fax: 937-426-1090. Email: info@bergamocenter.org. Web: www.bergamocenter.org. Mr. Dick Flack, Exec. Dir.; Kevin Kozlowski, Dir. Youth Programs; Barbara Kozlowski, Prog. Dir.; Patricia O'Grady, Dir. Conference Svcs. & Guest Rels.

MILFORD. *Milford Spiritual Center*, 5361 S. Milford Rd., 45150-9746. Tel: 513-248-3500; Fax: 513-248-3503. Email: milfordspiritualcenter@zoomtown.com. Web: www.milfordspiritualcenter.org. Revs. Richard W. Anderson, S.J., Supr.; Frank M. Oppenheim, S.J.; George W. Traub, S.J.; Thomas J. Diehl, S.J.; Steven F. Hurd, S.J. (CHI); Bro. Paul F. Mattingly, S.J.; Daniel O. Roche, Exec. Dir.; David Deye, Chm.

[Q] CAMPUS MINISTRY AND NEWMAN CENTERS

CINCINNATI. *College of Mt. St. Joseph Campus Ministry* 5701 Delhi Rd., 45233-1670. Tel: 513-244-4844; Fax: 513-244-4594. Email: monica_gundler@mail.msj.edu. Web: www.msj.edu. Sr. Monica Gundler, S.C., Dir. of Campus Min. Tel: 513-244-4844.

University of Cincinnati Newman Center 328 W. McMillan St., 45219-1224. Tel: 513-381-6400; Fax: 513-381-2540. Email: st.monica-st.george@fuse.net. Web: home.fuse.net/StMonica-StGeorge. Revs. Alan Hirt, O.F.M.; Thomas Speier, O.F.M. (GRY); Ms. Mickey Sheibley, Campus Min.; Mrs. Jill Kreinbrink, Music Min.; Mr. Lee Allard, Faith Formation; Ms. Linda Martin, Business Mgr.

Xavier University Campus Ministry 3800 Victory Pkwy., 45207-2411. Tel: 513-745-3567; Fax: 513-745-1959. Email: goetz@xu.edu. Web: www.xu.edu/spiritual. Ms. Chris Potter-Wroblewski, Dir.; Mr. Scot Buzza, Coord. Liturgical Music; Pam Goetz, Sec.; Rev. Albert J. Bischoff, S.J., Campus Min.; Ms. Kelly Albanix-Jenei, Campus Min.; Ms. Megan Halverson, Assoc. Dir.; Mr. Gregory Carpinello, Campus Min.

DAYTON. *Sinclair Community College Campus Ministry* 444 W. Third St., 45402. Tel: 937-512-2768. Email: jane.steinhauser@sinclair.edu. Dr. V. Jane Steinhauser, Archdiocesan Dir. of Campus Ministry.

University of Dayton Campus Ministry 45469-0408. Tel: 937-229-3339; Fax: 937-229-2035. Email: campus-ministry@udayton.edu. Web: www.udayton.edu/~campmin/. Revs. Christopher T. Wittmann, S.M., Dir. Tel: 937-229-3339; Gerald T. Chinchar, S.M. Tel: 937-229-2725; Christopher W. Conlon, S.M. Tel: 937-229-4767; Sisters Mary Louise Foley, F.M.I. Tel: 937-229-2093; Jody O'Neil, S.P. Tel: 937-229-2574; Kathleen Rossman, O.S.F. Tel: 937-229-4587; Bros. Philip Aaron, S.M. Tel: 937-229-2575; Thomas Pieper, S.M. Tel: 937-229-2211; Karl Penn, Campus Min, African American Students, Baptist Min. Tel: 937-229-3973; Nick Cardilino, Assoc. Dir./Center of Social Concern & Coord. Community Outreach & Svc. Clubs. Tel: 937-229-2576; Yolanda Copeland, Sec. Center of Social Concern. Tel: 937-229-2524; Bridget Ebbert, Campus Min., Marycrest Hall & Campus S. Tel: 937-229-1754; Terri Lauer, Admin. Asst. to the Dir. & Office Mgr. Tel: 937-229-3339; Peggy Matley, Chapel & Wedding Coord. Tel: 937-229-2019; Mary Niebler, Retreats & Faith Devel. Coord. Tel: 937-229-2012; Andrea Stiles, Coord. Community Outreach/Center Social Concern. Tel: 937-229-2516; Allen Stock, Dir. of Music Min. Tel: 937-229-2019; Patti Stock, Asst. Dir. of Music Min. Tel: 937-229-2019; Jen Violi, Dir. Retreats and Faith Devel. Tel: 937-229-2010; Sr. Linda Jackson, O.P., Neighborhood Faith Dir. Coord. Tel: 937-229-3570; Marta Robinson, Coord. Latin-American Students.

FAIRBORN. *Catholic Campus Ministry* 3650 Colonel Glenn Hwy., 45324-2096. Tel: 937-426-1836; Fax: 937-426-3490. Email: christian.rohmiller@wright.edu. Web: www.ccmwsu.org. Rev. Christian A. Rohmiller, Campus Min.; Ms. Joan Marquis, Campus Min.

OXFORD. *Miami University Catholic Campus Ministry* 111 E. High St., 45056. Tel: 513-523-2153; Fax: 513-523-0559. Email: stmary1@woh.rr.com. Web: stmary1-ccm.com. Rev. Terrance L. Schneider; Christopher E. Cotter, Pastoral Assoc.; Roberta L. Kinne, Pastoral Assoc.; Michael Puglielli, D.R.E.

SPRINGFIELD. *Mercy Medical Center* 1343 N. Fountain Blvd., 45501. Tel: 937-390-5000. Rev. Marvin R. Hackman, Regl. Priest Chap.

WILMINGTON. *Wilmington College Campus Ministry* 73 N. Mulberry St., 45177. Tel: 937-382-2236; Fax: 937-382-0672 (*2). Email: saintcolumbkille@yahoo.com. Web: www.stcolumbkille.org. Rev. James M. Wedig. Pastoral care available through St. Columbkille Parish.

YELLOW SPRINGS. *Antioch College Campus Ministry* St. Paul Catholic Church, 308 Phillips St., 45387-1724. Tel: 937-767-7450; Fax: 937-767-7465. Email: stpaulpastor@woh.rr.com. Rev. Joseph R. Raudabaugh. Pastoral care available through St. Paul Parish.

[R] COMMUNITY CENTERS

CINCINNATI. *Mercy Connections*, 1602 Madison Rd., 2nd Flr., 45206-1815. Tel: 513-221-7331; Fax: 513-221-5498. Email: mconnections@mercycon.org. Web: www.mercycon.org. Sr. Sarah Marie Sherman, R.S.M., Exec. Dir.; Beverly McCarthy, Sec.; Mary Farris, Vice Pres.; Ms. Christine Wheatley, Pres.; Ms. Adriene Phillips, Treas.

Mercy Franciscan Social Ministries, Inc., dba Mercy Franciscan at St. John, P.O. Box 14368, 45250. Tel: 513-241-2186; Fax: 513-651-6476. Web: www.e-mercy.com. 1212 Sycamore St., 45202. Tel: 513-241-2186; Fax: 513-651-6476. Ericka Copeland, Exec. Dir.; Sr. Eileen Wrobleski, C.S.C., Vice Pres. Mission Svcs. Provides emergency assistance, temporary shelter for families, job training classes, shared housing for seniors, a senior center and program for male responsibility.

Program for the Medically Underserved of Cincinnati, 3131 Queen City Ave., 45238. Tel: 513-389-5295; Fax: 513-389-5548. Email: hmbdirector@nuvox.net. Kathleen Brogle, M.S.W., Exec. Dir. Annual Participants 3,500.

HAMILTON. *Mercy Franciscan Social Ministries dba Mercy Franciscan at St. Raphael*, 610 High St., 45011. Tel: 513-863-3184; Fax: 513-887-6163. Web: www.e-mercy.com. Sr. Eileen Wrobleski, C.S.C., Vice Pres. Mission Svcs. Assist Social Service. Provides food and other emergency services and self-sufficiency programs to over 10,000 clients annually.

SPRINGFIELD. *Mercy-St. John's Center*, 100 W. McCreight Ave., 45504. Tel: 937-399-9910; Fax: 937-399-9449. Email: rmgiles@health-partners.org. Richard M. Giles II, Admin. Day care center for adults. Four Levels of Care: 1. Adult Day (Pottigrew Ctr.); 2. High Functioning Unit (The Gardens); 3. Intermediate Unit (The Bridge); 4. End Stage (the Rainbow). Skilled & intermediate long term care facility for all ages, Alzheimer's unit, ventilator unit. Total Assisted 242; Total Staff 210.

[S] ST. VINCENT DE PAUL SOCIETY

CINCINNATI. *Archdiocesan Central Council of Cincinnati*, 1125 Bank St., 45214. Tel: 513-562-8841; 513-562-8842; Fax: 513-562-8843. Patrick White, Pres.

District Council of Cincinnati and Subordinate Parish Conferences, 45214.
1125 Bank St., 45214. Tel: 513-562-8841; Fax: 513-562-8843. Mr. Edward J. Wenstrup, Pres.; Ms. Liz Carter, Exec. Dir.; Deacon George Bruce, Spiritual Advisor.

District Council of Dayton and Subordinate Parish Conferences, Dayton, 45408.
1133 Edwin C. Moses Blvd., Ste. 300, Dayton, 45408. Tel: 937-222-7349; Fax: 937-222-7944. Deacon Robert Zinck, Spiritual Advisor; Mr. Robert Young, Pres.; Mr. James H. Butler, Exec. Dir. & Contact; Jim Sturtevant, Treas.

District Council of Hamilton and Subordinate Parish Conferences, 401 N. Washington Blvd., Hamilton, 45013. Tel: 513-863-5091. Mr. Howard Hetterich, Pres.

District Council of Springfield and Subordinate Parish Conferences, 2425 E. High St., Springfield, 45505. Tel: 937-322-2643. Deacon Norman G. Horstman, Spiritual Advisor; Mr. Anthony Bickers, Pres.

District Council of Saint Martin and Subordinate Parish Conferences, 254 Saddleback Dr., Loveland, 45140. Tel: 513-677-1189. David Cherry, Pres.; Mr. Bert Reihle, Spiritual Advisor.

St. Vincent de Paul Stores, Inc., 1125 Bank St., 45214. Tel: 513-621-3265; Fax: 513-562-8843. Ms. Elizabeth Carter, Exec. Dir.

St. Vincent de Paul Stores of Dayton, Ohio, Inc., 45214. Tel: 937-222-5555; Fax: 937-222-0754.
945 S. Edwin C. Moses Blvd., Dayton, 45408. Mr. James H. Butler, Exec. Dir. & Contact. Tel: 937-222-7349.

St. Vincent de Paul Store of Springfield, OH, 2425 E. High St., Springfield, 45505. Tel: 937-325-9111; 937-325-8880; Fax: 937-525-0794.

St. Vincent Hotel, Inc., 1133 Edwin C. Moses Blvd., Ste. 300, Dayton, 45408. Tel: 937-222-7349; Fax: 937-222-7944. Mr. James H. Butler, Exec. Dir. Active Programs: De Paul Center and St Vincent Supportive Housing.

St. Martin Ozanam House, 56 Main St., Milford, 45150. Mr. Greg Oliver, Contact Person. Tel: 513-831-0191.

[T] HEALTH CARE SYSTEMS

CINCINNATI. *Catholic Healthcare Partners*, 615 Elsinore Pl., 45202. Tel: 513-639-2800; Fax: 513-639-2700. Web: www.health-partners.org. Mr. Michael Connelly, Pres. & CEO. 31 acute care hospitals, 16 long-term care facilities, 14 elderly housing projects. Catholic Healthcare Partners is co-sponsored by the Sisters of Mercy, Cincinnati Regional Community; Sisters of Mercy, Dallas (PA) Regional Community; Covenant Health System, Sisters of the Humility of Mary, Franciscan Sisters of the Poor. Patients Assisted Annually 4; Residence for Senior Citizens 585.

Mercy Health Partners of Southwest Ohio dba Mercy Health Partners , 4600 McAuley Pl., 45242. Tel: 513-981-6000; Fax: 513-981-6133. Web: www.mercy.health-partners.org. Thomas S. Urban, Pres. & CEO.

Mercy Medical Associates, 4600 Mc Auley Pl., 45242. Tel: 513-981-6375; Fax: 513-981-6375. Email: pchiltz@health-partners.org. Web: www.e-mercy.com. Paul C. Hiltz, Vice Pres. Group Practice Operations & Physician Svcs.

DAYTON. *Franciscan Health System of the Ohio Valley operations in Dayton, OH*, One Franciscan Way, 45408. Tel: 937-229-6000. Jim Alund, Post Admin.

Franciscan Health System of the Ohio Valley, Inc., One Franciscan Way, 45408. Tel: 937-229-6000; Fax: 937-229-7093. Jim Alund, Post Admin.

Samaritan Health Partners, 2222 Philadelphia Dr., 45406. Tel: 937-278-2612. Web: www.goodsamdayton.org. Affiliate of Catholic Health Initiative.

SPRINGFIELD. *Mercy Health Partners, Sisters of Mercy*, One S. Limestone St., P.O. Box 688, 45501-0688. Tel: 973-328-7013; Fax: 937-328-7010. Web: www.mercy-health.org; www.mercy-allyourcare.org. Andrew R. McCulloch, Pres. & CEO; Pat O'Connor, Regl. Dir. Spiritual Svcs.; Sr. Lynn Casey, S.C.L., Mission Svcs.

[U] FOUNDATIONS AND ENDOWMENTS

CINCINNATI. *Community Support Charitable Trust*, 1615 Vine St., 45210. Tel: 513-721-4700; Fax: 513-421-9672. Revs. Kenan Freson, O.F.M., Trustee; Jeremy Harrington, O.F.M., Trustee; Bart Pax, O.F.M., Trustee.
Legal Title: *Community Support Charitable Trust for the Province of St. John the Baptist of the Order of Friars Minor*

Friars Club Foundation, Inc., 1615 Vine St., 45210. Tel: 513-721-4700; Fax: 513-287-8488. Mr. Thomas Klinedinst Jr., Trustee & Pres.; Rev. Kenan Freson, O.F.M., Trustee & Treas.; Mr. John O'Connor, Vice Pres., Sec. & Trustee.

Good Samaritan Hospital Foundation of Cincinnati, Inc., 375 Dixmyth Ave., 45220-2489. Tel: 513-872-3786; Fax: 513-872-3788. Email: mary_rafferty@trihealth.com. Mary L. Rafferty, Contact Person.

Mercy Health Partners of Southwest Ohio Foundation, 4600 Mc Auley Pl., 45242. Tel: 513-981-6329; Fax: 513-981-6104. Web: www.e-mercy.com. Kenneth C. Page, Int. Pres. A Subsidiary of Mercy Health Partners of Southwest Ohio.

Roger Bacon High School Endowment, 4320 Vine St., 45217. Tel: 513-641-1300; Fax: 513-641-0498. Email: wfarris@rogerbacon.org. Web: www.rogerbacon.org. Rev. William Farris, O.F.M., Pres. & Contact Person; Mr. Thomas Devolve, Prin.

SC Ministry Foundation, Inc., 345 Neeb Rd., 45233. Tel: 513-347-1122; Fax: 513-347-1017. Email: jwasser@scministryfdn.org. Web: www.scministryfdn.org. Sr. Maryanna Coyle, S.C., Exec. Dir.

Seton High School Foundation, 3901 Glenway Ave., 45205. Tel: 513-471-2600; Fax: 513-471-0529. Email: mckiernan@fuse.net. Mr. Thomas E. McKiernan, K.S.G., Chm. Emerituas; Mrs. Mary Sullivan Schultz, J.D. Chm.; Ms. Susan M. Gibbons, Pres.

Sisters of Charity of Cincinnati-Charitable Trust, 5900 Delhi Rd., 45051. Tel: 513-347-5201; Fax: 513-347-5228. Web: www.srcharitycinti.org. Sr. Barbara Hagedom, S.C., Pres. A designated trust fund to primarily support older and infirmed members of the congregation.

Sisters of Notre Dame De Namur, Ohio Province, Charitable Trust, 701 E. Columbia Ave., 45215-3999. Tel: 513-761-7636; Fax: 513-761-6159. Email: ohprovoff@aol.com. Web: www.sndohio.org. Sisters Elizabeth Marie Bowyer, S.N.D.deN., Prov.; Dorothy Kiley, S.N.D.deN., Contact Person.

The Summit Country Day School Foundation, 2161 Grandin Rd., 45208. Tel: 513-871-4700; Fax: 513-871-6558. Email: martin_r@summitcds.org. Thomas D. Grote Jr., Pres.; Christopher Vollner, Vice Pres.; Roger T. Martin, Contact Person.

Ursulines of Cincinnati, Ohio Charitable Trust, 1339 E. McMillan St., 45206-2164. Tel: 513-961-3410, Ext. 140; Fax: 513-872-7177. Email: Buchert@zoomtown.com. Sr. Mary Jerome Buchert, O.S.U.

DAYTON. *Community Support Charitable Trust*, 431 E. Second St., 45402. Tel: 937-228-9263; Fax: 937-228-6878. Revs. Albert A. Reed, C.PP.S., Trustee; Thomas R. Brenberger, C.PP.S., Trustee; Scott T. Kramer, C.PP.S., Trustee; Thomas J. Beischel, C.PP.S., Trustee; Bros. Joseph J. Fisher, C.PP.S., Trustee; Thomas R. Bohman, C.PP.S., Trustee.

**Samaritan Health Foundation*, 2222 Philadelphia Dr., 45406. Tel: 937-278-5770; Fax: 937-278-5140. Email: ktormey@shp-dayton.org. Web: www.samaritanhealthfoundation.org. J. Kay Tormey, Pres. Affiliate of Catholic Health Initiatives and Samaritan Health Partners.

FAIRFIELD. *Glenmary Home Missioners Charitable Trust*, 4119 Glenmary Trace, 45014. Tel: 513-874-8900; Fax: 513-874-1690. Revs. George Mathis, Trustee; Dominic R. Duggins, G.H.M., Sec. & Trustee; Bro. Curt Kedley, Trustee.

[V] MISCELLANEOUS LISTINGS

CINCINNATI. *St. Andrew Kim Korean Catholic Community*, 3171 Struble Rd., 45251. Tel: 513-851-3065; Fax: 513-521-3728. Web: www.cincinnatikoreancatholic.org. Rev. Mateo Hong Dae Choi, S.J., Chap./Admin.; Luke Sang Ho Ryhu, Chmn. Pastoral Council.

St. Anthony Messenger, St. Anthony Messenger Press and Franciscan Communications, 28 W. Liberty St., 45202. Tel: 513-241-5615; Fax: 513-241-0399. Email: st.anthony@americancatholic.org. Web: www.americancatholic.org. Thomas A. Shumate, Contact Person. Operated by the St. John the

Baptist Province of the Franciscan Friars.

Apostleship of Prayer, 607 Sycamore St., 45202. Tel: 513-721-4045; Fax: 513-723-0451. Rev. Paul A. Huber, S.J.

Catholic Alumni Club (Cincinnati Chapter), 100 E. 8th St., 45202. Tel: 513-421-3131.

Catholic Charismatic Renewal Liaison, 5924 Bridgetown Rd., 45248. Tel: 513-574-1230; Fax: 513-598-2109. Email: fredress@aol.com. Rev. Richard E. Dressman.

Catholic Cursillo of Cincinnati, P.O. Box 317655, 45231. Tel: 513-931-7382. Email: tperazzo@cinci.rr.com. Web: www.cincinnati-cursillo.org. Mr. Thomas Perazzo, Dir. Tel: 937-323-5409; Deacon Manuel D. Vilaboy, Dir. Tel: 513-321-8326.

Cincinnati Catholic Women's Association, 958 Marion Ave., 45229. Tel: 513-961-3563. Carol Harten, Pres.

The Comboni Lay Missionaries Association, 1318 Nagel Rd., 45255-3120. Tel: 513-474-4997; Fax: 513-474-0382. Web: www.combonimissionaries.org; www.laymission-comboni.org. Mr. James G. Lindsay, Pres.; Mr. Don Toomey, Vice Pres.; Ann Sassett, Treas.; Caren Wilkie, Sec.

The Comboni Missionaries Auxiliary, Inc., 1318 Nagel Rd., 45255-3120. Tel: 513-474-4997; Fax: 513-474-0382. Email: info@combonimissionaries.org. Web: www.combonimissionaries.org. Jane Tate, Pres.; Catherine Myer, Vice Pres.; Jane Mentzel, Treas.; Jo DeSalvo, Sec.; Rev. Paul Donohue, M.C.C.J., Spiritual Advisor.

Concerned Catholics for Gay/Lesbian Inclusion - Within Archdiocese of Cincinnati, 328 W. McMillan St., 45219-1224. Tel: 513-381-5400; Fax: 513-381-2540. Rev. Alan Hirt, O.F.M., Contact Person.

**The Couple to Couple League International*, P.O. Box 111184, 45211. 4290 Delhi Pk., 45238. Tel: 513-471-2000; Fax: 513-557-2449. Email: ccli@ccli.org. Web: www.ccli.org. Andrew B Alderson, Exec. Dir.

St. Dymphna Ministry, Summit Behavioral Healthcare, P.O. Box 16061, 45216. Tel: 513-641-2257; Fax: 513-641-2262. *St. Clement Friary*, 4536 Vine St., St. Bernard, 45217. Rev. Valens J. Waldschmidt, O.F.M. (Retired).

St. Francis Bookshop Conducted by the St. John the Baptist Province of the Franciscan Friars. , 1618 Vine St., 45202. Tel: 513-241-7304; 800-241-6392; Fax: 513-241-7654. Email: bookshop@stfrancisonline.com. Web: www.stfrancisonline.com.

Franciscan Central Purchasing, St. Clement Friary, 4536 Vine St., 45217. Tel: 513-641-2257; Fax: 513-641-2262. Rev. Maynard Tetreault, O.F.M., Dir.

Franciscan Missionary Union, 1615 Vine St., 45202. Tel: 513-721-4700, Ext. 3222; Fax: 513-421-9672. Email: sjbfmu@franciscan.org. Web: www.franciscan.org. Bro. Scott Obrecht, O.F.M., Exec. Dir.; Dolores Schmitz, Sec. & Contact Person.

Franciscans Network, 4820 Glenway Ave., 48238. Tel: 513-541-7740; Fax: 513-541-7740. Email: dhlmercy@aol.com. Web: www.franciscansnetwork.org. Ms. Diane H. Laake, Contact Person; Revs. John Quigley O.F.M., Bd. of Trustees; Murray Bodo, O.F.M., Bd. of Trustees; Alan Hartman, S.F.O., Bd. of Trustees.

Good Samaritan College of Nursing and Health Science, 375 Dixmyth Ave., 45220. Tel: 513-569-6062; Fax: 513-569-6062. Email: donnanienaber@trihealth.com. Web: www.trihealth.com; goodsamaritancollege.com. Morris Cohen, Pres. Tel: 513-872-2491; Fax: 513-872-3572; Donna S. Nienaber, Sec.

Hispanic Ministries at St. Charles, Archdiocese of Cincinnati, 115 W. Seymour Ave., 45216. Tel: 513-948-1760; Fax: 513-948-1823. Email: wjansen@catholiccincinnati.org. Web: www.archdiocese-cinti.org. Rev. William J. Jansen, M.C.C.J., Dir.

HIV/AIDS Ministry Team, Archdiocese of Cincinnati, 100 E. Eighth St., 45202. Tel: 513-357-6187. Ms. Kathy Cox, Coord.

Jesuit Development Office, 2245 Gilbert Ave., 45206. Tel: 513-751-6688; Fax: 513-751-2340. Email: mike@chicagoprovincejesuits.org. Web: www.jesuits-chi.org. Michael P. Murray, Dir.

Legion of Mary, 3105 Madison Rd., 45209. Tel: 513-871-5757; Fax: 513-533-6066. Rev. Elmer W. Smith, Spiritual Dir.

Living Monuments of Reparation, P.O. Box 29372, 45229. Tel: 513-569-4587; Fax: 513-569-4582. Rev. Herbert J. Raterman, S.J., Dir.

Marian Center of Cincinnati, 5365 Cleves Warsaw, 45238. Tel: 513-922-1250; Fax: 859-441-0641. Mr. Robert E. Hater, Lay Dir.

Mercy Franciscan Social Ministries, Inc. dba Franciscan Home Development A member of Mercy Health Partners. , 1300 Main St., 45210. Tel: 513-651-6457; Fax: 513-651-6472. Web: www.e-mercy.com. Kenneth C. Page, Pres.; Linda Fox, Exec. Dir. Provides housing to over 270 persons in over 201 residential units.

Ministers of Service, 745 Ezzard Charles, 45203. Tel: 513-381-0630; Fax: 513-742-9096 Email: 3824churches@cs.com. Mr. Jack D. McWilliams, Dir. The Ministers of Service Program, which began in 1979, provides training in urban ministry, primarily but not exclusively for African American laypersons. The Ministers of Service Program focuses on parish/community ministry to prepare laypersons to take active roles in church ministry.

New Jerusalem Community, 745 Derby Ave., 45232. Tel: 513-541-4748; Fax: 513-541-4748. Email: njcommunity@juno.com. Mary Heimert, Leadership Council; Debby Carrico, Leadership Council; Karen Healy, Leadership Council; Mike Frick, Leadership Council; Terri Coleman, Admin. & Coord. Community Life; William A. Zins, Bookkeeper.

North American Ursuline Education Services, 5535 Pfeiffer Rd., 45242. Tel: 314-966-7725; Fax: 314-966-9850. Email: lcastillon@ursulinestl.org. Web: www.ursuline-ed.net. Sisters Lois Castillon, O.S.U., Exec. Dir.; Patricia Homan, O.S.U., Representative. N.A.U.E.S. is a service to all Ursuline Schools.

Priests Eucharistic League, 100 E. Eighth St., 45202. Tel: 513-421-3131; Fax: 513-421-3225. Web: www.catholiccincinnati.org. Rev. Joseph R. Binzer, Dir.

Secular Franciscan Order Holy Trinity Regional Fraternity, Inc. , 8497 Pringle Dr., 45231. Tel: 513-522-7430. Email: anitabid@aol.com. Anita Bidleman, Min., (Cincinnati, OH); Don Lipps, Vice Min., (Cincinnati, OH); Rosemary Menetrey, (Ft. Thomas, KY); Pattie Normile, Formation Dir., (Cincinnati, OH). Founded by St. Francis of Assisi before A.D. 1215.

Seton Family Center, 712 Purcell Ave., 45205. Tel: 513-471-3169; Fax: 513-251-7922. Email: setonfam@aol.com. Web: members.aol.com/setonfam. Sisters Jacqueline Kowalski, S.C., Pres. & Contact Person; Elizabeth Finn, S.C., Board Chair; Barbara Jean Krekeler, S.C., Vice Chair. Sponsored by: Sisters of Charity of Mt. St. Joseph.. Purpose: Individual and Family Therapy, Children's Play Therapy and Diagnostic Services

Sisters of Mercy H.O.M.E. Program, 1602 Madison Rd., 45206. Tel: 513-221-1080; Fax: 513-221-1904. Email: mafuerstrsm@aol.com. Sr. Mary Ann Fuerst, R.S.M., Contact Person.

Stimuli, Inc., 17 Erkenbrecher Ave., 45220-2202. Tel: 513-221-5538; 513-221-3889. Email: stimuli@eos.net Rev. Clarence Rufus J. Rivers, Ph.D., Pres. The inculturation of African American culture with Catholic worship.

Su Casa Hispanic Center, 7036 Fairpark Ave., 45216. Tel: 513-761-1588; Fax: 513-761-9538. Email: sucasa@fuse.net. Mr. Michael Flynn, Dir. Affiliated with Hispanic Ministries at St. Charles, Archdiocese of Cincinnati.

Vietnamese Catholic Community of Our Lady of Lavang, 314 Township Ave., 45216. Tel: 513-242-2933. Rev. Huan Tien Nguyen, Chap. & Contact Person.

St. Xavier Church Property Corporation, 607 Sycamore St., 45202. Tel: 513-721-4045; Fax: 513-723-0451. Rev. Robert J. Thesing, S.J., Contact Person & Trustee; Very Rev. Edward W. Schmidt, S.J. (CHI), Pres.

CENTERVILLE. *St. Leonard Faith Community*, 8100 Clyo Rd., 45458. Tel: 937-435-3626; 937-433-7224 (Friary); Fax: 937-435-3626. Email: faithcom@bright.net. Web: www.bright.net. Rev. Msgr. Anthony J. Giannamore, Moderator & Chap.

DAYTON. *Catholic Alumni Club (Dayton Chapter)*, 51 Regina Dr., Fairborn, 45324. Tel: 937-878-4268. Email: greggo63@aol.com. Web: www.caci.org/cac/dayton. Kathy Rainer, Contact Person. Tel: 937-298-3399, Ext. 54729; Rev. Daniel J. Meyer, Chap., 218 K St., 45409.

Samaritan Behavioral Health, Inc., 50 E. Woodbury Ave., 45415. Tel: 937-276-8333. Email: smcgatha@shp-dayton.org. Sue McGatha, Pres. & CEO.

MARIA STEIN. *Maria Stein Center Shrine of the Holy Relics*, 2291 St. Johns Rd., 45860. Tel: 419-925-4532; Fax: 513-925-5044. Email: mscadmin@dtnspeed.net. Web: www.mariasteincenter.org. Sr. Barbara Ann Hoying, C.PP.S., Dir. Includes The National Marian Shrine of the Holy Relics, The Heritage Museum, and The Pilgrim Gift Shop.

RELIGIOUS INSTITUTES OF MEN REPRESENTED IN THE ARCHDIOCESE

For further details refer to the corresponding bracketed number in the Religious Institutes of Men or Women section.

[0460]—*Brothers of the Poor of St. Francis*—C.F.P.
[0380]—*Comboni Missionaries of the Heart of Jesus (Verona)*—M.C.C.J.
[0650]—*Congregation of the Holy Spirit* (Eastern Province)—C.S.Sp.
[0520]—*Franciscan Friars* (Province of St. John the Baptist)—O.F.M.
[0570]—*Glenmary Home Missioners*—G.H.M.
[0690]—*Jesuit Fathers and Brothers* (Chicago Province)—S.J.
[0800]—*Maryknoll*—M.M.
[1210]—*Missionaries of St. Charles (Scalabrinians)*—C.S.
[0430]—*Order of Preachers (Dominicans)* (St. Joseph Province)—O.P.
[0760]—*Society of Mary (Marianists)* (Cincinnati Province)—S.M.
[1060]—*Society of the Precious Blood* (Cincinnati Province)—C.PP.S

RELIGIOUS INSTITUTES OF WOMEN REPRESENTED IN THE ARCHDIOCESE

[0230]—*Benedictine Sisters of Pontifical Jurisdiction* (Beech Grove, IN; Covington, KY)—O.S.B.
[0330]—*Carmelite Sisters for the Aged and Infirm*—O.Carm.
[0870]—*Congregation of the Daughters of Mary Immaculate (Marianist Sisters)*—F.M.I.
[1920]—*Congregation of the Sisters of the Holy Cross*—C.S.C.
[1730]—*Congregation of the Sisters of the Third Order of St. Francis, Oldenburg, IN*—O.S.F.
[1710]—*Congregation of the Third Order of St. Francis of Mary Immaculate, Joliet, IL*—O.S.F.
[1070-07]—*Dominican Sisters* (Adrian, MI)—O.P.
[1070-13]—*Dominican Sisters* (St. Mary of the Springs, Columbus, OH)—O.P.
[1070-16]—*Dominican Sisters* (Nashville, TN)—O.P.
[1070-15]—*Dominican Sisters of Hope*—O.P.
[]—*Franciscan Sisters of Mary*—F.S.M.
[1440]—*Franciscan Sisters of the Poor*—S.F.P.
[2340]—*Little Sisters of the Poor*—L.S.P.
[2470]—*Maryknoll Sisters of St. Dominic*—M.M.
[2490]—*Medical Mission Sisters*—M.M.S.
[2790]—*Mission Helpers of the Sacred Heart*—M.H.S.H.
[3760]—*Order of St. Clare-Poor Clares*—O.S.C.
[3130]—*Our Lady of Victory Missionary Sisters*—O.L.V.M.
[3230]—*Poor Handmaids of Jesus Christ*—P.H.J.C.
[0440]—*Sisters of Charity of Cincinnati, Ohio*—S.C.
[0570]—*Sisters of Charity of Seton Hill, Greensburg, Pennsylvania*—S.C.
[1000]—*The Sisters of Divine Providence of Kentucky*—C.D.P.
[2575]—*Sisters of Mercy of the Americas* (Regional Community of Cincinnati, OH; Regional Community of Cedar Rapids, IA
[2630]—*Sisters of Mercy of the Holy Cross*—S.C.S.C.
[2990]—*Sisters of Notre Dame* (Covington Prov.)—S.N.D.
[2990]—*Sisters of Notre Dame* (Toledo Prov.)—S.N.D.
[3000]—*Sisters of Notre Dame de Namur*—S.N.D.deN.
[3360]—*Sisters of Providence of Saint Mary-of-the-Woods, Indiana*—S.P.
[1530]—*Sisters of St Francis of the Congregation of Our Lady of Lourdes* (Sylvania,OH)—O.S.F.
[1630]—*Sisters of St. Francis of Penance and Christian Charity, Stella Niagara, NY*—O.S.F.
[3840]—*Sisters of St. Joseph of Carondolet* (Latham, NY)—C.S.J.
[3880]—*Sisters of St. Joseph of Medaille* (Cincinnati Prov.)—C.S.J.
[0260]—*The Sisters of the Blessed Sacrament for Indians and Colored People*—S.B.S.
[1830]—*The Sisters of the Good Shepherd*—R.G.S.
[2110]—*Sisters of the Humility of Mary*—H.M.
[3260]—*Sisters of the Precious Blood* (Dayton, OH)—C.PP.S.
[2150]—*Sisters, Servants of the Immaculate Heart of Mary*—I.H.M.
[4120]—*Ursuline Nuns of the Congregation of Paris* (Saint Martin)—O.S.U.
[]—*Ursuline Nuns of the Congregation of Paris* (Louisville, KY)—O.S.U.
[4120-01]—*Ursuline Nuns of the Congregation of Paris (Cincinnati, OH)*—O.S.U.
[4110]—*Ursuline Nuns (Roman Union)*—O.S.U.

CEMETERIES

CINCINNATI. *Calvary*, 1721 Duck Creek Rd., 45207. Tel: 513-961-2179; Fax: 513-961-8006.

Gate of Heaven, 11000 Montgomery Rd., 45242. Tel: 513-489-0300; Fax: 513-489-1817.

St. John, 701 Ross Ave., 45217. Tel: 513-242-4191.

St. Joseph, Eighth St. & Seton Ave., 45205. Tel: 513-921-3050.

St. Joseph New, 4500 Foley Ave., 45238. Tel: 513-251-3110; Fax: 513-251-1075.

St. Mary, 701 Ross Ave., 45217. Tel: 513-242-4191.

DAYTON. *Calvary*, Calvary & Dixie Ave., 45409. Tel: 937-293-1221.

SPRINGFIELD. *Calvary*, 3155 E. Possum Rd., 45502. Tel: 937-323-7474.

NECROLOGY

† Amann, Rev. Msgr. Robert J., (Retired)—Died Aug. 17, 2003

† Buerger, Francis J., (Retired)—Died Dec. 15, 2003

† Filippine, John E. Cincinnati, OH St. Vivian—Died Jan. 11, 2003

† Haskamp, Edward F., Norwood, OH Holy Trinity Church—Died Aug. 29, 2003

† Jaekle, Lawrence E., (Retired)—Died Dec. 15, 2002

† McWilliam, James J., (Retired)—Died Jan. 16, 2003

† Mick, Rev. Robert, Cincinnati, OH St. Martin of Tours—Died June 10, 2003

† Monnig, Francis R., Trenton, OH St. Mary—Died Dec. 28, 2003

† Pater, Thomas G., (Retired)—Died Feb. 25, 2003

† Ries, Victor F., (Retired)—Died Jan. 30, 2003

† Stolze, Edward B., Morrow, OH St. Philip the Apostle—Died Feb. 16, 2003

† Will, Carl G., (Retired)—Died March 24, 2003

† Williams, Edward T., (Retired)—Died Jan. 22, 2003

† Zugelter, Alvin T., (Retired)—Died Dec. 2, 2003

Diocese of Cleveland

(Dioecesis Clevelandensis)

Most Reverend

ANTHONY M. PILLA, D.D., M.A.

Bishop of Cleveland; ordained May 23, 1959; appointed Auxiliary and Titular Bishop of Scardona June 30, 1979; consecrated August 1, 1979; named Apostolic Administrator of Cleveland July 29, 1980; appointed Bishop of Cleveland November 18, 1980; installed January 6, 1981 *Office: 1027 Superior Ave., Cleveland, OH 44114.* Tel: 216-696-6525; 800-869-6525 (Ohio only); Fax: 216-696-6547.

Most Reverend

A. JAMES QUINN, J.C.D., J.D.

Auxiliary Bishop of Cleveland; ordained May 24, 1958; appointed Auxiliary and Titular Bishop of Socia October 14, 1983; consecrated December 5, 1983 *Office: 2500 Elyria Ave., Lorain, OH 44055.* Tel: 440-244-2120; 216-579-0326 (Cleveland Line); Fax: 216-899-1122.

Most Reverend

ROGER W. GRIES, O.S.B.

Auxiliary Bishop of Cleveland; ordained May 16, 1963; appointed Auxiliary and Titular Bishop of Presidio April 3, 2001; consecrated June 7, 2001 *Office: 5135 Superior Ave., Cleveland, OH 44103.* Tel: 216-361-0873; Fax: 216-361-0877.

Most Reverend

A. EDWARD PEVEC, PH.D.

Retired Auxiliary Bishop of Cleveland; ordained April 29, 1950; appointed Auxiliary and Titular Bishop of Mercia April 13, 1982; consecrated July 2, 1982; retired September 1, 2002 *Office: Center for Pastoral Leadership,* 28700. Euclid Ave., Wickliffe, OH 44092. Tel: 216-944-1400; Fax: 216-943-7577.

Most Reverend

MARTIN JOHN AMOS

Auxiliary Bishop of Cleveland; ordained May 25, 1968; appointed Auxiliary and Titular Bishop of Meta April 3, 2001; consecrated June 7, 2001 *Office: 795 Russell Ave., Akron, OH 44307.* Tel: 330-762-9651; 877-406-1049; Fax: 330-762-9655.

Chancery Building: 1027 Superior Ave., Cleveland, OH 44114. Tel: 216-696-6525; 800-869-6525 (Ohio only); Fax: 216-621-7332.

Web: www.dioceseofcleveland.org

Email: chancellor@dioceseofcleveland.org

ESTABLISHED APRIL 23, 1847.

Square Miles 3,414.

Comprises since July 22, 1943, eight Counties in the north-central part of the State of Ohio, namely Ashland, Cuyahoga, Geauga, Lake, Lorain, Medina, Summit and Wayne Counties.

For legal titles of parishes and diocesan institutions, consult the Chancery Office.

STATISTICAL OVERVIEW

Personnel	
Bishop	1
Auxiliary Bishops	3
Retired Bishops	1
Abbots	1
Priests: Diocesan Active in Diocese	317
Priests: Diocesan Active Outside Diocese	9
Priests: Diocesan in Foreign Missions	5
Priests: Retired, Sick or Absent	111
Number of Diocesan Priests	442
Religious Priests in Diocese	137
Total Priests in Diocese	579
Extern Priests in Diocese	35
Ordinations:	
Diocesan Priests	9
Transitional Deacons	3
Permanent Deacons	9
Permanent Deacons in Diocese	189
Total Brothers	57
Total Sisters	1,325
Parishes	
Parishes	234
With Resident Pastor:	
Resident Diocesan Priests	206
Resident Religious Priests	14
Without Resident Pastor:	
Administered by Priests	5
Administered by Deacons	4
Administered by Professed Religious Men	1
Administered by Religious Women	4
Missions	1
Pastoral Centers	2
Professional Ministry Personnel:	
Brothers	3
Sisters	83
Lay Ministers	180
Welfare	
Catholic Hospitals	3
Total Assisted	491,548
Homes for the Aged	26
Total Assisted	4,395
Residential Care of Children	1
Total Assisted	225
Day Care Centers	8
Total Assisted	981
Specialized Homes	7
Total Assisted	927
Special Centers for Social Services	23
Total Assisted	732,639
Residential Care of Disabled	2
Total Assisted	324
Other Institutions	3
Total Assisted	49,796
Educational	
Seminaries, Diocesan	2
Students from This Diocese	53
Students from Other Diocese	1
Students Religious	10
Total Seminarians	63
Colleges and Universities	3
Total Students	6,681
High Schools, Diocesan and Parish	6
Total Students	3,414
High Schools, Private	17
Total Students	10,772
Elementary Schools, Diocesan and Parish	122
Total Students	42,288
Elementary Schools, Private	9
Total Students	2,388
Non-residential Schools for the Disabled	2
Total Students	154
Catechesis/Religious Education:	
High School Students	6,407
Elementary Students	42,985
Total Students under Catholic Instruction	115,152
Teachers in the Diocese:	
Priests	15
Brothers	12
Sisters	181
Lay Teachers	3,647
Vital Statistics	
Receptions into the Church:	
Infant Baptism Totals	9,355
Adult Baptism Totals	944
Received into Full Communion	781
First Communions	11,176
Confirmations	10,751
Marriages:	
Catholic	2,271
Interfaith	1,219
Total Marriages	3,490
Deaths	8,530
Total Catholic Population	812,675
Total Population	2,852,331

Former Bishops—Rt. Revs. AMADEUS RAPPE, D.D., consecrated Oct. 10, 1847; resigned July 29, 1870; died Sept 8, 1877; RICHARD GILMOUR, D.D., consecrated April 14, 1872; died April 13, 1891; IGNATIUS F. HORSTMANN, D.D., consecrated Feb. 25, 1892; died May 13, 1908; JOHN P. FARRELLY, D.D., consecrated May 1, 1909; died Feb. 12, 1921; Most Revs. JOSEPH SCHREMBS, S.T.D., Archbishop-Bishop of Cleveland consecrated Feb. 22, 1911; transferred to the See of Cleveland, June 16, 1921; installed Sept. 8, 1921; appt. Archbishop, March 25, 1939; died November 2, 1945; EDWARD F. HOBAN, S.T.D., Ph.D., L.L.D., Archbishop-Bishop of Cleveland; consecrated Dec. 21, 1921; transferred to Cleveland as Coadjutor Bishop "cum jure successionis" Nov. 14, 1942; succeeded to See of Cleveland, Nov. 2, 1945; appt. Archbishop, July 23, 1951; died Sept. 22, 1966; CLARENCE G. ISSENMANN, S.T.D. (Retired), consecrated May 25, 1954; transferred to Cleveland as Coadjutor Bishop "cum jure successionis" and Titular Bishop of Filaca. Apadm. Oct. 7, 1964; succeeded to See of Cleveland, Sept. 22, 1966; retired June 5, 1974; died July 27, 1982; JAMES A. HICKEY, S.T.D , J.C.D. (Retired), consecrated April 14, 1967; appt. Bishop of Cleveland, June 5, 1974; installed July 16, 1974; appt. Archbishop of Washington, DC June 17, 1980; created Cardinal by Pope John Paul II in the consistory on June 28, 1988; retired Jan. 4, 2001.

Vicars General—Most Revs. A. JAMES QUINN, J.C.D., J.D., 2500 Elyria Ave., Lorain, 44055. Tel: 440-244-2120; 216-579-0326 (Cleveland Line); ROGER W. GRIES, O.S.B., D.D., M.Ed., St. Andrew, 5135 Superior Ave., Cleveland, 44103-1239. Tel: 216-361-0873; MARTIN J. AMOS, Akron Catholic Center, 795 Russell Ave., Akron, 44307-1115. Tel: 330-762-9651; A. EDWARD PEVEC, Ph.D. (Retired), Center for Pastoral Leadership, 28700 Euclid Ave., Wickliffe, 44092. Tel: 440-944-1400; Rev. RALPH E. WIATROWSKI, Chancellor, 1027 Superior Ave., Cleveland, 44114. Tel: 216-696-6525, Ext. 2080.

College of Consultors—Rev. CHARLES T. DIEDRICK; Most Rev. ROGER GRIES, O.S.B.; Revs. JOHN R. HENGLE; LAWRENCE N. MARTELLO; THOMAS V. O'DONNELL; DOUGLAS M. PROEHL; PAUL J. ROSING; R. STEPHEN VELLENGA; RALPH E. WIATROWSKI, Sec.

Presbyteral Council—Most Rev. ANTHONY M. PILLA, D.D., M.A., Pres.; Revs. MARK LATCOVICH, Moderator; THOMAS HAREN; LAWRENCE JURCAK, J.C.L.; TIMOTHY P. KESICKI, S.J.; THOMAS MAHONEY; JOHN MANNING; STEPHEN MORAN; PAUL J. ROSING; SALVATOR RUGGERI; KEVIN SHEMUGA;

THOMAS WOOST. Presbyteral Conveners: Revs. EDWARD A. BURBA; MARK DINARDO; DANIEL R. FICKES; JOHN R. HENGLE; DENNIS J. KLEINWEBER; JOHN KUMSE; LAWRENCE N. MARTELLO; NEIL O'CONNOR; THOMAS V. O'DONNELL; DONALD P. OLEKSIAK; DOUGLAS PROEHL; JOHN G. VRANA.

Diocesan Finance Advisory Committee—Most Rev. ANTHONY M. PILLA, D.D., M.A., Pres.; JOSEPH H. SMITH, Financial & Legal Sec./CFO; PETER CARFAGNA; ANGELA CARLIN; THOMAS GARVEY; ANTHONY LANG; PAT MCCARTAN; JOHN P. MCGINTY; KEVIN O'DONNELL; DOMINIC OZANNE; THOMAS J. PERCIAK; WILLIAM J. REIDY.

Diocesan Pastoral Council—Most Rev. ANTHONY M. PILLA, D.D., M.A.; Mrs. MARY PAT FREY, Chm.; ANDY STRADA, Vice Chm.; RICHARD S. KRIVANKA, Exec. Sec.

Conference of Religious Leadership—Co Chm.: Sisters MARIAN DURKIN, C.S.A., 6571 Second Ave., Independence, 44131. Tel: 440-328-9716; MARY ALICE JAROSZ, S.S.F.-T.O.S.F., 11907 Granger Rd., Garfield Heights, 44125-2911. Tel: 216-475-3866; ANNE VICTORY, H.M., Sec. & Treas., 5945 Rhonda Dr., North Ridgevelle, 44039. Tel: 440-356-5707.

Diocese of Cleveland—

Chancery Building—1027 Superior Ave., Cleveland, 44114.

Catholic Center—1031 Superior Ave., Cleveland, 44114.

All Diocesan Offices in the Chancery Building or in the Catholic Center may be reached at: Tel: 216-696-6525; 800-869-6525 (Ohio only); Fax: 216-781-8243.

Address dispensations and all business communication to the Chancery Office

Chancellor—Rev. RALPH E. WIATROWSKI, Office: Chancery Building. Fax: 216-621-7332.

Vice-Chancellor—Rev. DAVID J. WALKOWIAK, J.C.D. Office: Chancery Building.

Assistant Chancellors—Revs. EDWARD T. ESTOK Office: Catholic Center; PAUL J. ROSING, Office, 795 Russell Ave., Akron, 44307. Tel: 330-434-4114; Sr. LAURA BOUHALL, O.S.U. Office: Chancery Building.

Secretary to Bishop Pilla—Rev. EDWARD T. ESTOK Office: Catholic Center.

Judicial Offices—

Office of Mediation—Sr. DONNA MIKULA, O.S.U., Chancery Building. Tel: 216-696-6525; 800-869-6525.

Tribunal—Office, 1027 Superior Ave., Ste. 500, Cleveland, 44114. Tel: 216-696-6525,; 800-869-6525 (Ohio only); 800-676-4431 (Outside Ohio); Fax: 216-696-3226.

Judicial Vicar—Rev. GARY D. YANUS.

Adjutant Judicial Vicars—Revs. MARK Q. FEDOR, J.C.D.; WILLIAM M. JERSE; LAWRENCE JURCAK, J.C.L.; PETER D. WASLO, J.C.L.

Judges—Deacon LOUIS G. PECEK, Ph.D.; Sisters MARY ANN ANDREWS, C.S.A., J.C.L.; THERESE GUERIN SULLIVAN, S.P., J.C.L.; Ms. LYNETTE TAIT, J.C.L.

Defenders of the Bond—Rev. JOSEPH A. BACEVICE; Sr. CHRISTINE M. RODY, V.S.C., J.C.L.; Revs. MICHAEL J. TROHA; ALLEN F. CORRIGAN.

Associate Judicial Vicars—Revs. MIRKO HLADNI, J.C.L.; EDWARD J. LUCA; JOHN R. OLSAVSKY; WILLIAM P. O'NEILL; ROBERT F. PFEIFFER; ROBERT J. SANSON; DAVID J. WALKOWIAK, J.C.D.; EDWARD F. WEIST; ROBERT M. WENDELKEN; RALPH E. WIATROWSKI.

Associate Judges—Deacon JAMES L. AGRIPPE; Most Rev. MARTIN J. AMOS; Revs. CHARLES T. DIEDRICK; JEROME J. DUKE; JOHN R. HENGLE; EDWARD J. KORDAS; ALAN R. LAUBENTHAL, S.T.D.; JOHN E. MANNING; LAWRENCE N. MARTELLO; THOMAS W. MCCANN; PAUL J. ROSING; THOMAS R. SMITH; DONALD E. SNYDER; CHARLES J. STOLLENWERK; ALBERT J. TESEK (Retired); ANTHONY W. ZEPP.

Auditor/Assessor—Ms. ALICE HINKEL; Sr. DONNA MIKULA, O.S.U.; Deacon THOMAS B. DAW; Revs. CHARLES F. STREBLER; DAVID R. TRASK; Ms. CYNTHIA M. QUINLAN; Ms. PATRICIA DAW.

Procurators—Revs. EDWARD T. ESTOK; JOSEPH HILINSKI, M.Div.; THEODORE MARSZAL, S.T.D.

Promoters of Justice—Sr. CHRISTINE RODY, V.S.C., J.C.L.; Rev. MARK Q. FEDOR, J.C.D.

Ecclesiastical Notaries—Ms. MARY M. BRYAN, Notary Public; Ms. LEE ANN CALVERT, Notary Public; Ms. AMANDA L. JOHNS; Ms. TERESA LASCIO.

Translators—Revs. RICHARD R. BOBER, Ph.D.; EDWARD ESTOK, M.A., M.Div.; BEDE KOTLINSKI, O.S.B.; AUGUSTINE PHAM VAN LAN; JOHN F. WESSEL (Retired); MICHAEL J. TROHA; MARION BENDYK.

Administrator of Buildings—WILLIAM HUDSON, Financial & Legal Secretariat.

Archivist—Rev. RALPH E. WIATROWSKI; CHRISTINE L. KROSEL, Archival Research Dir.; PHILIP HAAS, Archives Admin., Chancery Building.

Catholic Cemeteries Association—Rev. JOHN J. WRIGHT, CEO & Dir.; ANDREJ LAH, COO, 10000 Miles Ave., Box 05310, Cleveland, 44105. Tel: 216-641-7575.

Callistian Guild—P.O. Box 605044, Cleveland, 44105. Tel: 216-641-7575.

Central Purchasing—JAMES P. TERESI, Dir., 3020 Superior Ave., Cleveland, 44114. Tel: 216-696-4811; 800-362-9016.

Communications Department—ROBERT D. TAYEK, Dir., Media & Pub. Rel., Chancery Building. Tel: 216-696-6525, Ext. 4460.

"Catholic Universe Bulletin"—Most Rev. ANTHONY M. PILLA, D.D., M.A., Publisher; JOSEPH M. POLITO, Assoc. Publisher & CEO, Chancery Building. Tel: 216-696-6525, Ext. 5870; 216-696-6525, Ext. 2770 (after 5 p.m.).

Catholic Universe Bulletin Publishing Company, Inc.—Chancery Building.

Diocesan Pastoral Planning Office—RICHARD S. KRIVANKA, Dir.; DAVID DE LAMBO, Ph.D., Assoc. Dir.; V. GAIL ROUSSEY, Consultant for Pastoral Planning & Stewardship; MARY PAT FREY, Office Coord., Office. Tel: 216-696-6525, Ext. 4210.

Mission Office, Society for the Propagation of the Faith—Rev. R. STEPHEN VELLENGA, Dir., Office: The Catholic Center. Tel: 216-696-6525, Ext. 4240.

Pontifical Programs— Society for the Propagation of the Faith; Society of St. Peter the Apostle; Missionary Union of the Clergy; Holy Childhood Assoc.

National Programs— Latin-American Program; Lay Mission Volunteers

Diocesan Programs— Missionary Cooperation Plan; St. Francis Xavier Mission Assoc.; Cleveland Diocesan Mission, C.A.

National Shrine of Immaculate Conception—Washington, DC. Rev. RALPH E. WIATROWSKI, Chancellor, Chancery Building.

Financial and Legal

Financial and Legal Secretariat—JOSEPH H. SMITH, Financial & Legal Sec. & CFO, 1404 E. 9th St., 8th Fl., Cleveland, 44114.

Legal—JOSEPH H. SMITH, 1404 E. 9th St., 8th Fl., Cleveland, 44114.

Diocesan Budget Committee—THOMAS LANGE, Chm., 1404 E. 9th St., 8th Fl., Cleveland, 44114.

Diocesan Building Commission—KEVIN T. BURKE, Coordinator.

Diocesan Financial Advisory Committee—Most Rev. ANTHONY M. PILLA, D.D., M.A., Chm.; JOSEPH H. SMITH, Financial & Legal Sec./CFO.

Property/Casualty Office/DISC—PALMIRA JURAS; J. THOMAS HANNON, 1404 E. 9th St., 8th Fl., Cleveland, 44114.

Benefit Plans - Health Benefits, Group Life, and Pension—PALMIRA JURAS, 1404 E. 9th St., 8th Fl., Cleveland, 44114.

Workers' Compensation Office—ANTHONY GIELTY, 1404 E. 9th St., 8th Fl., Cleveland, 44114.

Secretariat for Education

Secretary—Sr. CAROL ANNE SMITH, H.M., The Catholic Center. Tel: 216-696-6525, Ext. 3280; Fax: 216-696-6217.

Departments—

School Food Services/Summer Food Service Program—Mr. EDWARD MOREL, Dir., Catholic Center.

Buildings and Grounds/Technology—DANIEL BRODNIK, Dir., Catholic Center.

Catholic Education Endowment Trust—Catholic Center.

Inner-City School Fund—Catholic Center.

Office of Catechetical Services—JOYCE M. KELLEHER, Dir., Catholic Center. Tel: 216-696-6525, Ext. 2880.

Newman Campus Ministry—Ms. MAUREEN MASTERSON, Assoc. Dir., Catholic Center. Tel: 216-696-6525, Ext. 8920.

Ministers—GREGORY STEVENS, Akron University. Tel: 330-773-7621; KRISTEN KOLOJA, Case Western Reserve University, Hallinan Center. Tel: 216-421-1522; Rev. KEVIN M. CONROY, Ashland University. Tel: 419-994-4396; TIMOTHY BARRON, College of Wooster. Tel: 216-263-2096; EMILY HOLTEL-HOAG, Baldwin-Wallace College. Tel: 216-243-4955; JOYCE KELLEHER, Dir., Newman Commuter Faith Community for Cleveland State, Lorain Community, Lakeland Community and Cuyaho. Tel: 216-421-1522, Ext. 2880.

Religious Education Office—JOYCE M. KELLEHER, Dir., Catholic Center. Tel: 216-696-6525, Ext. 2880.

Catechetical Consultants—DENISE SMITHBERGER; PATRICIA FLAHERTY, Southern Area, 1025 Clay St., Akron, 44301. Tel: 330-773-7621; MARY LOU NECKEL-JAMES, Eastern Area Office, Hallinan Center, 11303 Euclid Ave., Cleveland, 44106. Tel: 216-421-1522.

Media Consultant—JEFF STUTZMAN, Catholic Center. Tel: 216-696-6525, Ext. 4330.

Office of Catholic Education—MARGARET LYONS, Supt. Schools, Catholic Center. Tel: 216-696-6525, Ext. 1022.

Administrative Support Services—JANET POLEVACIK, Dir., Catholic Center. Tel: 216-696-6525, Ext. 4150.

Curriculum—CATHERINE COLLINS, Coord. Tel: 216-696-6525, Ext. 3330.

Educational Support Services—KATHLEEN O'BRIEN, Dir., Catholic Center. Tel: 216-696-6525, Ext. 1148.

Assistant Superintendents—JEAN TAKACS, Eastern Area Office, Hallinan Center, 11303 Euclid Ave., Cleveland, 44106. Tel: 216-421-1522; Sr. LUCIA BUCHOLTZ, S.S.J.-T.O.S.F., Western Area Office, 2500 Elyria Ave., Lorain, 44055. Tel: 440-244-1612; 440-871-5246 (Cleveland line).

Associate Superintendent—Sr. PATRICIA KIDDER, I.H.M., Southern Area Office, 1025 Clay St., Akron, 44301. Tel: 330-773-7621, Ext. 3780.

Special Projects—MARY LOU TOLER, Dir., Catholic Center. Tel: 216-696-6525, Ext. 3250.

School Planning Process—Sr. ANNE GLASER, S.N.D., Dir., Catholic Center. Tel: 216-696-6525, Ext. 3780.

Catholic Parent Teacher League—NANCY MASKOW, Pres., 19406 Stony Point Dr., Strongsville, 44136. Tel: 440-572-8777; ROSA ESPARRA BUCHANAN, Corresponding Sec. Tel: 440-886-1324.

Finance—CECILIA FREW, Dir., Catholic Center. Tel: 216-696-6525.

Secondary Education—WAYNE UCHLEIN, Assoc. Supt., Catholic Center. Tel: 216-696-6525, Ext. 2450.

Government Programs—MICHAEL VOINOVICH, Dir., Catholic Center. Tel: 216-696-6525, Ext. 3350.

Teacher Support Services—MICHELE SCHREFLER, Dir. Mandates Services - Consultants: JOHN KASTELIC; KRISTEN MITCH; PAMELA OUTZ, Catholic Center.

Secretariat for Parish Life and Development

Secretary—Sr. RITA MARY HARWOOD, S.N.D., Catholic Center. Tel: 216-696-6525, Ext. 3500.

African Ministry—Sr. RITA MARY HARWOOD, S.N.D., Catholic Center. Tel: 216-696-6525, Ext. 3500.

Apostleship of the Sea Chaplain for the Diocese of Cleveland (Port Chaplain)—Rev. MARK A. DINARDO, St. Patrick Church, 3602 Bridge Ave., Cleveland, 44113-3314.

Asian Ministry—Sr. RITA MARY HARWOOD, S.N.D., Catholic Center. Tel: 216-696-6525, Ext. 3500.

Blue Army of Our Lady of Fatima—Marian Center, 6626 Pearl Rd., Parma Heights, 44130-3808. Tel: 440-888-8553.

Catholic Renewal Ministries—Rev. ROBERT FRANCO, 1878 Abbe Rd., Sheffield, 44054-2322. Tel: 440-934-4227. Bishop's Delegate, Presentation House, 28706 Euclid Ave., #4, Wickliffe, 44092. Tel: 440-944-9445.

Central City Ministry with Poor—Rev. JAMES P. O'DONNELL, 2186 E. 35th St., Cleveland, 44115. Tel: 216-566-0531.

Cleveland Diocesan Council, NCCW—DOROTHY KLODNICKI, Pres., Catholic Center; Rev. RALPH HUDAK, Moderator, 6700 Lansing Ave., Cleveland, 44105-3797. Tel: 216-341-2734, Ext. 5110.

Diocesan Interfaith Commission—Rev. JOSEPH J. HILINSKI, Delegate, Catholic Center. Tel: 216-696-6525, Ext. 5110.

Enthronement of the Sacred Heart—Diocesan Center, St. John Cathedral Rectory, 1007 Superior Ave., Cleveland, 44114. Tel: 216-267-4713, Ext. 4300. MARGARET OLLE, Sec.

Ethnic Ministries—

Diocesan Hispanic Office—Sr. ALICIA ALVARADO, O.P., Dir., Catholic Center. Tel: 216-696-6525, Ext. 4300.

Korean Catholic Apostolate—Rev. JOHN BYONG KWON AHN, St. Andrew Kim (Korean Pastoral Center), 2310 West 14th St., Cleveland, 44113. Tel: 216-861-4630.

Lay Apostolate for Immigrant Catholic Indians of America, Inc.—Dr. ABRAHAM C. KUTTOTHARA, M.D., Dir., P.O. Box 349, Loudonville, 44842. Tel: 419-994-3983; Fax: 419-994-3982. Email: laicia@yahoo.com. Web: layapostolate.org.

Native American Ministry—Sr. JOAN LANG, C.S.J., Dir., Catholic Center. Tel: 216-696-6525, Ext. 3500.

Office of Ministry to African American Catholics—VANESSA GRIFFIN CAMPBELL, Dir., Catholic Center. Tel: 216-696-6525, Ext. 3020.

Philippine-American Ministry—Rev. CIRILO A. NACORDA, Dir., 1007 Superior Ave., Cleveland, 44114. Tel: 216-771-6666.

Vietnamese-American Apostolate—Rev. AUGUSTINE

PHAM VAN LAN, Dir., 3545 W. 54th St., Cleveland, 44102. Tel: 216-961-2713, Ext. 2540
For all other ethnic ministries, please contact the Parish Life Office, Sr. Rita Mary Harwood, S.N.D., Dir., Ext. 3500.

Office of Evangelization—Sr. MARGARET MACH, V.S.C., Dir., Catholic Center. Tel: 216-696-6525, Ext. 2540.

Holy Name Societies, Cleveland Diocesan Union—Rev. THOMAS HAREN, Spiritual Dir., 15000 Lake Shore Blvd., Cleveland, 44110-1298. Tel: 216-481-8200.

Pastoral Ministry Office—KATHLEEN HAASE-FALBO, Dir., Center for Pastoral Leadership, 28700 Euclid Ave., Wickliffe, 44092. Tel: 440-943-7669, Ext. 3070.

Legion of Mary—Rev. HERMAN B. PETERS, Spiritual Dir. (Retired), Office, 1007 Superior Ave., Cleveland, 44114.

Office for Pastoral Liturgy—Rev. J-GLENN MURRAY, S.J., Dir., Catholic Center. Tel: 216-696-6525, Ext. 4120.

Office for Women in Church and Society—DEBRA MARSEY, Dir., Catholic Center. Tel: 216-696-6525, Ext. 3070.

St. Joseph Christian Life Center—Rev. WALTER J. HYCLAK, Exec. Dir., 18485 Lake Shore Blvd., Cleveland, 44119. Tel: 216-531-7370.

Secretariat for Clergy and Religious

Secretary—Rev. JOHN F. MURPHY, Vicar for Clergy and Religious, The Catholic Center.

Borromeo Seminary— See Seminaries.

Clergy Personnel Board—Rev. LAWRENCE JURCAK, J.C.L., Dir., The Catholic Center.

Continuing Education and Formation of Ministers—Rev. EDWARD T. ESTOK, Dir. Associate Directors:: Rev. THOMAS DRAGGA; Deacon JEROME ZIEMKIEWICZ; Mrs. KAREN ROMAN, The Center for Pastoral Leadership, 28700 Euclid Ave., Wickliffe, 44092.

Office for Religious—Sr. MARIETTA STARRIE, C.S.J., Delegate, The Catholic Center.

Diaconate Office—Deacon KENNETH PIECHOWSKI, Dir., The Center for Pastoral Leadership, 28700 Euclid Ave., Wickliffe, 44092.

Retirement Board—Revs. THOMAS H. WEBER, Chm. (Retired), Center for Pastoral Leadership, 28700 Euclid Ave., Wickliffe, 44092. Tel: 440-943-7600; THOMAS L. WEBER, Recording Sec., St. Bernadette, 2256 Clague Rd., Westlake, 44145. Tel: 440-734-1300.

St. Mary Seminary— See Seminaries.

Senior Priests—Rev. LAWRENCE JURCAK, J.C.L., Delegate, The Catholic Center.

Vocations Office—Rev. ROBERT STEC, M.A., M.Div.

Avilas of the Diocese of Cleveland—BETTY CLARK, Pres., The Catholic Center.

Parents of Priests—DONALD TRASK, Pres., The Catholic Center.

Secretariat for Catholic Charities Health and Human Services

Catholic Charities Health and Human Services—J. THOMAS MULLEN, Pres. & CEO. Tel: 216-696-6525, Ext. 4160; JOHN KLEE, Exec. Vice Pres. Tel: 216-696-6525, Ext. 4170; PATRICIA BROWNLIE, Deputy Sec., 1027 Superior Ave., Cleveland, 44114. Tel: 216-696-6525, Ext. 4410; Fax: 216-861-9795.

Catholic Charities Parish Services—TERRENCE FLANAGAN, Senior Dir., 1031 Superior Ave., Cleveland, 44114. Tel: 216-696-6525, Ext. 5030; Fax: 216-536-0963.

Camp Corde—2901 Ridgewood Ave., Parma, 44134. Tel: 440-884-3950; Fax: 440-884-3950.

Special Ministry to the Aged—6804 Lansing Ave., Cleveland, 44105-1521. Tel: 216-441-5402; Fax: 216-441-4510. Sr. ANNA KASZUBA, S.S.M.I., Dir.

Pro Life Office—MARY E. COLLINGWOOD, Dir., 1031 Superior Ave., Cleveland, 44114. Tel 216-696-6525, Ext. 5230; Fax: 216-781-8243.

Office of Ministry for Persons with Disabilities—Rev. JOSEPH MCNULTY, M.Div., M.Th., Exec. Dir., St. Augustine Church, 2486 W. 14th St., Cleveland, 44113. Tel: 216-781-5530; Fax: 216-781-1124.

Marriage and Family Office—Rev. STEPHEN J. DOHNER Dir., 1031 Superior Ave., Cleveland, 44114. Tel: 216-696-6525, Ext. 3570.

Catholic Information and Referral Service (CIRS)—CAROLE TOYODA, Coord., 1027 Superior, Cleveland, 44114. Tel: 216-696-6525, Ext. 1001. CIRS (Lorain County), 928 Poplar St., Elyria, 44035. Tel: 440-366-6255.

Youth and Young Adult Ministry and CYO Office—GREG MOSER, Dir., 1031 Superior Ave., Cleveland, 44114. Tel: 216-696-6525, Ext. 1070.

Migration and Refugee Services—MARJEAN PERHOT, Dir., 7300 Detroit Ave., Cleveland, 44102. Tel: 216-287-7005.

Catholic Charities Services Corporation—THOMAS W. WOLL, Exec. Dir.; MICHAEL HAGGERTY, Assoc. Exec. Dir., 1111 Superior Ave., Cleveland, 44114. Tel: 216-696-6525, Ext. 8020; Fax: 216-344-9962.

Children and Family Services—MICHAEL HAGGERTY, Dir. Tel: 216-696-6525, Ext. 1019.

Disabilities Services—DENNIS MCNULTY, Senior Dir. Tel: 216-696-6525, Ext. 2490.

Emergency Assistance Services—GAYLE DOUCETTE, Dir. Tel: 216-696-6525, Ext. 1083.

Other Adult Services—DAVE MODARSKY, Senior Dir. Tel: 216-631-3499; Fax: 216-631-3654.

Pastoral Care Services—Rev. FRANK GODIC, 1027 Superior Ave., Cleveland, 44114. Tel: 216-696-6525, Ext. 2380.

Catholic Charities Facilities Corp.—LAWRENCE E. MURTAUGH, Admin. Tel: 216-696-6525, Ext. 5540; CAROLYN SCHUEMANN, CFO, 1111 Superior Ave., Cleveland, 44114. Tel: 216-696-6525, Ext. 8970; Fax: 216-861-1176.

Catholic Charities Housing Corporation—1111 Superior Ave., Cleveland, 44114.

Catholic Charities Corporation—JOHN P. KLEE, Exec. Dir., 1027 Superior Ave., Cleveland, 44114. Tel: 216-696-6525, Ext. 4170; Fax: 216-861-9795.

Diocesan Social Action Office—THOMAS J. ALLIO, Exec. Dir., 1031 Superior Ave., Cleveland, 44114. Tel: 216-696-6525, Ext. 3740; Fax: 216-781-8243.

Commission on Catholic Community Action—LEONARD M. CALABRESE, Exec. Dir., The Chancery Bldg., 1027 Superior Ave., Cleveland, 44114.

Catholic Action Commission of Lorain County—SHARON KLEPPEL, Dir., 2500 Elyria Ave., Lorain, 44055. Tel: 216-244-6037; Fax: 216-899-1122.

Catholic Commission of Lake and Geauga Counties—PETER HOKKY, Dir., Schrembs Hall, 28706 Euclid Ave., Wickliffe, 44092. Tel: 216-585-7745; Fax: 216-585-7747.

Catholic Commission (Summit County)—THOMAS J. ALLIO, Dir., 729 Russell Ave., Akron, 44307. Tel: 330-535-2787; Fax: 330-535-9040.

Catholic Commission of Wayne, Ashland and Medina Counties—PATRICK O'BRIEN, Dir., 521 Beall Ave., P.O. Box 15, Wooster, 44691. Tel: 330-263-6176; Fax: 330-262-4633.

Campaign for Human Development—ROCKY ORTIZ, Coord.

Catholic Relief Services—ROCKY ORTIZ, Dir., 2500 Elyria Ave., Lorain, 44055. Tel: 440-245-5043.

Bishop William M. Cosgrove Family Center—1736 Superior Ave., Cleveland, 44114. Tel: 216-781-8262; Fax: 216-566-9161.

CYO and Community Services of Summit County—812 Birutha St., Akron, 44307. Tel: 330-762-2961; Fax: 330-762-2001. *Camp Christopher, Ira & Hametown Rd., Bath, 44210.* Tel: 800-CYO-CAMP; Fax: 330-762-2001. Affiliated Corporations within the Secretariat for Catholic Charities Health & Human Services (Under membership structure of Bishop, Secretary for Health & Human Services & Chairperson of Board of Trustees).

Catholic Community Care—7801 Detroit Ave., Cleveland, 44102. Tel: 216-939-7720; Fax: 216-634-7483. Email: amhorne@worldnet.att.net.

Catholic Social Services of Summit County—640 N. Main St., Akron, 44310. Tel: 330-762-7481; Fax: 330-762-7484.

Rose-Mary, The Johanna Grasselli Rehabilitation and Education Center—19350 Euclid Ave., Cleveland, 44102. Tel: 216-634-7400; Fax: 216-634-7483.

St. Augustine Corporation—7801 Detroit Ave., Cleveland, 44102. Tel: 216-634-7400; Fax: 216-634-7483.

The Society of St. Vincent de Paul—1027 Superior Ave., Cleveland, 44114. Tel: 216-696-6525; Fax: 216-589-4772.

The Catholic Diocese of Cleveland Foundation—ANTHONY F. LANG, Dir., 1111 Superior Ave., Cleveland, 44114. Tel: 216-696-6525, Ext. 6100; Fax: 216-861-1176.

Catholic Lawyers' Guild of Cleveland— The Catholic Diocese of Cleveland Foundation.

Catholic Lawyers' Guild of Cleveland Endowment Trust— The Catholic Diocese of Cleveland Foundation.

Victim Assistance Coordinator—Sr. LAURA BOUHALL, O.S.U. Tel: 216-696-6525, Ext. 2060. Email: lbouhall@dioceseofcleveland.org.

CLERGY, PARISHES, MISSIONS AND PAROCHIAL SCHOOLS

CITY OF CLEVELAND
(CUYAHOGA COUNTY)

1—CATHEDRAL OF ST. JOHN THE EVANGELIST (1848), Revs. Edward T. Estok, Admin.; Cirilo A. Nacorda; Kenneth J. Jakubowski; Sr. Marie Gillich, C.S.J.; Deacon John P. Sferry Sr., Pastoral Assoc. In Res., Rev. Lawrence Jurcak, J.C.L.
Res.: 1007 Superior Ave., N.E., 44114-2582. Tel: 216-771-6666; Fax: 216-781-5646.
Church: E. 9th St. & Superior Ave. N.E., 44114.

2—ST. ADALBERT (1883), Rev. Kenneth F. Pleiman, C.PP.S. In Res., Bro. Thomas R. Bohman, C.PP.S.
Res.: 2347 E. 83rd St., 44104-2198. Tel: 216-881-7647; Fax: 216-881-7670.
School—2345 E. 83rd St., 44104. Tel: 216-881-6250; Fax: 216-881-9030. Mr. Kevin James, Prin. Lay Teachers 11; Students 172.
Catechesis/Religious Program—Students 194.

3—ST. AGNES - OUR LADY OF FATIMA (1980), Rev. Michael K. Barth, S.T.
Res.: 6800 Lexington Ave., 44103-3297. Tel: 216-391-3947; 216-391-1655 (Office); Fax: 216-391-7919.
Church: 6800 Lexington Ave., 44103. Tel: 216-391-1655.

4—ST. ALOYSIUS - ST. AGATHA (1975), Revs. William Behringer, S.M.; Eldon Reichert, S.M.; Bro. Michael O'Grady, S.M., Admin.; Deacon James Paul Jr.
Res.: 10932 St. Clair Ave., 44108-1939. Tel: 216-451-3262; 216-451-3263; Fax: 216-268-3830.
School—640 Lakeview Rd., N.E., 44108. Tel: 216-451-2050; Fax: 216-541-1601. Sr. Sandra Sabo, S.S.J.-T.O.S.F., Prin. Sisters 3; Lay Teachers 9; Students 217.
School—St. Joseph School, Tel: 216-451-2143; Fax: 216-451-8832. Sisters 2; Lay Teachers 10; Students 231.
Catechesis/Religious Program—Students 39.

5—ST. ANDREW (1906), (Slovak), Rev. Ronald Mahnke, O.S.B., Admin. In Res., Most Rev. Roger W. Gries, O.S.B.
Res.: 5135 Superior Ave., 44103-1239. Tel: 216-431-2057.

6—ST ANDREW KIM (1988), (Korean), Rev. John Byong Kwon Ahn, Admin.; Deacon Charles C. Shin.
Res.: 2310 West 14th St., 44113-3613. Tel: 216-861-4630; Fax: 216-241-6366.
Catechesis/Religious Program—Students 61.

7—ANNUNCIATION (1924), Rev. Timothy M. Daw, Presbyteral Moderator; Sisters Janet Bednar, C.S.J., Parish Life Coord.; Marilyn Nicko , C.S.J., Pastoral Assoc.
Res.: 4697 W. 130th St., 44135-3798. Tel: 216-671-2015; Fax: 216-941-1014.

8—ASCENSION (1946), Rev. Joseph J. Fortuna; Ms. Laurel S. Jurecki, Pastoral Assoc.; Deacon John Koch, Pastoral Assoc.
Res.: 14040 Puritas Ave., 44135-2822. Tel: 216-671-5890; 216-671-5891; Fax: 216-671-2320.
School—4400 W. 140th St., 44135. Tel: 216-941-3715; Fax: 216-941-6051. Sr. Laura Bregar, O.S.U., Prin. Sisters 2; Lay Teachers 12 Students 230.

9—ST. AUGUSTINE (1860), Revs. Joseph D. McNulty; Benjamin P. Jimenez, S.J.; Sisters Corita Ambro, C.S.J., Pastoral Assoc.; Audrey Koch, C.S.J., Pastoral Assoc.; Miriam Fidelis Pinchot, O.S.U., Pastoral Assoc.; Deacons John M. Rivera, Pastoral Assoc.; Edmund J. Karecki, Pastoral Assoc.; Louis Woyton, Pastoral Assoc.; Mary Ellen Czelusniak, Pastoral Assoc.; Mary Smith, Pastoral Assoc.; Peggy Driscoll, Pastoral Assoc.; Sr. Corita Ambro, C.S.J.
Res.: 2486 W. 14th St., 44113-4498. Tel: 216-781-5530; Fax: 216-781-1124.
Catechesis/Religious Program—Mrs. Sheila Gelzinis, D.R.E. Students 362.
Convent—2432 W. 14th St., 44113. Tel: 216-579-1306.

10—ST. BARBARA (1905), (Polish), Revs. Michael S. Dyrcz, Admin.; Chester C. Cudnik, Pastor Emeritus (Retired).
Res.: 1505 Denison Ave., 44109-2890. Tel: 216-741-2067.
Catechesis/Religious Program—Students 15.
Convent—3855 W. 16th St., 44109. Tel: 216-661-0547.

11—ST. BENEDICT, Closed. For inquiries for parish records contact the chancery.

12—BLESSED SACRAMENT (1903), Rev. Matthew A. Ischay.
Mailing Address: P.O. Box 602776, 44109.
Res.: P.O. Box 602776, 44109. Tel: 216-741-8338; Fax: 216-741-9397.
Catechesis/Religious Program—Students 26.

13—ST. BONIFACE (1903), Rev. Augustine Pham Van Lan.
Res.: 3545 W. 54th St., 44102. Tel: 216-961-2713; 216-961-2714; Fax: 216-961-1859.
School—Metro Catholic Parish School See Separate Listing Under Elementary Schools, Parochial and Private Diocesan.
Convent—3588 W. 52nd St., 44102. Tel: 216-961-0669.

14—ST. CASIMIR (1891), (Polish), Rev. Msgr. Leo

Telesz. In Res., Rev. John M. Wachala.
Res.: 8223 Sowinski Ave., 44103-2298. Tel: 216-361-4322.
Convent—1116 East 82nd St., 44103.

15—ST. CATHERINE (1898), Rev. William Dickinson, Admin.; Sisters M. Kathleen McCafferty, S.N.D., Pastoral Assoc.; Mary Janeta Stamper, S.N.D., Pastoral Assoc.
Res.: 9412 Heath Ave., 44104-5512. Tel: 216-341-3353; 216-341-5542; Fax: 216-341-5542.
Church: E. 93rd & St. Catherine Ave., 44104.
School—Tel: 216-341-7212; Fax: 216-641-8184. See Archbishop Lyke School.
Catechesis/Religious Program—Students 36.

16—ST. CECILIA (1915), Revs. Daniel L. Begin; Herman B. Peters, Pastor Emeritus (Retired); Sr. Rosella Holloman, C.S.A., Pastoral Assoc.; Deacon William Ansley Love.
Res.: 3476 E. 152nd St., 44120-4272. Tel: 216-921-3310; 216-921-3311; Fax: 216-921-2932.
Church: Kinsman Rd. & E. 152nd St., 44120.
Catechesis/Religious Program—Students 63.

17—ST. COLMAN (1880), Rev. Robert T. Begin, Sacramental Min.; Deacon William H. Corrigan; Sisters Ann Kilbane, C.S.J., Parish Life Coord.; Carol English, C.S.J., Pastoral Assoc.; Lucy Dragonette, C.S.J., Pastoral Assoc.; Linda Dlugo, Pastoral Assoc.; Eileen Kelly, Pastoral Assoc.; Jerry Brandt, Pastoral Assoc.; Sisters Wilma Apack, C.S.J., Pastoral Assoc.; Audrey Koch, C.S.J., Pastoral Assoc.
Res.: 2027 W. 65th St., 44102-4394. Tel: 216-651-0550; Fax: 216-651-1663.
Catechesis/Religious Program—Students 33.
Convent—2007 W. 65th St., 44102. Tel: 216-961-1550.

18—COMMUNITY OF ST. MALACHI (1975),, (Personal Parish) Revs. Anthony J. Schuerger; Paul J. Hritz, Pastor Emeritus (Retired).
Res.: 2459 Washington Ave., 44113-2380. Tel: 216-781-3110; Fax: 216-861-5340.
Church: W. 25th & Detroit Ave., 44113.
Catechesis/Religious Program—Students 123.

19—CONVERSION OF ST. PAUL (1931), Rev. Robert Marva, O.F.M.Cap. In Res., Revs. Andrew Hohman, O.F.M.Cap.; Eric Gauchet, O.F.M.Cap.
Res.: 4120 Euclid Ave., 44103-3728. Tel: 216-431-8854; 216-431-8855; Fax: 216-361-1951. Connected with the monastery of the Poor Clares of Perpetual Adoration.
Convent—4108 Euclid Ave., 44103-3728. Tel: 216-361-0783.

20—CORPUS CHRISTI (1935), Rev. Ronald J. Szudarek; Deacons David J. Lundeen; Charles Zawadzki.
Res.: 5204 Northcliff Ave., 44144-4065. Tel: 216-351-8738; 216-351-8739; Fax: 216-741-5620.
School—4850 Pearl Rd., 44109. Tel: 216-351-2974; Fax: 216-661-9188. Mr. Raymond Welling, Prin. Lay Teachers 15; Students 158.
Catechesis/Religious Program—Students 12.

21—CRISTO REY, CAPILLA DE (1983), (Hispanic), Closed., For inquiries for parish records contact La Sagrada Familia.

22—ST. ELIZABETH OF HUNGARY (1892), (Hungarian), Rev. Andras Antal, Admin.
Mailing Address: P.O. Box 20175, 44120-0175. Tel: 216-231-0325; Fax: 216-421-0461.
Church: 9016 Buckeye Rd., 44104.
Catechesis/Religious Program—Students 14.

23—ST. EMERIC (1904 & Territorial 1964), (Magyar), Rev. Sandor Siklodi, Admin.
Res.: 1860 W. 22nd St., 44113. Tel: 216-861-1937.

24—EPIPHANY (1944), Rev. Daniel L. Begin; Sr. Sheila Marie Tobbe, O.S.U., Pastoral Assoc.
Res.: 11901 Oakfield Ave., 44105-1803. Tel: 216-561-3975; Fax: 216-561-2794.
School—3845 E. 131st St., 44105. Tel: 216-991-1615. See Mount Pleasant Catholic Elementary Education Center,

25—ST. FRANCIS (1887), Rev. R. Stephen Vellenga; Sr. Geraldine M. Tengler, S.N.D., Parish Life Coord.; Deacon Frank Lozada.
Office—7206 Myron Ave., 44103-1951. Tel: 216-361-4133; Fax: 216-361-1673.
School—Tel: 216-361-4858; Fax: 216-361-1673. Sr. Karen Sommerville, S.N.D., Prin. Sisters of Notre Dame 5; Lay Teachers 12; Students 260.
Catechesis/Religious Program—Students 17.
Convent—7119 Superior Ave., 44103. Tel: 216-361-5094.

26—ST. GEORGE (1895), (Lithuanian), Rev. Joseph A. Bacevice.
Res.: 6527 Superior Ave., 44103-2698. Tel: 216-431-5794; Fax: 216-391-8233.
Hunger Center—Tel: 216-431-5794.

27—ST. HENRY (1946), Rev. Robert J. Kropac; Gerry Kynkor, Pastoral Assoc.; Ms. Barbara Price, Pastoral Assoc. In Res., Rev. J. Glenn Murray, S.J.; Deacon Shelby M. Friend.
Res.: 18200 Harvard Ave., 44128-1796. Tel: 216-921-0725; 216-921-0726; 216-921-7030; Fax: 216-767-0454.
School—Archbishop James P. Lyke Elementary School, Tel: 216-991-9644; Fax: 216-991-9470. See Elementary Schools, Parochial and Diocesan under Institutions Located in the Diocese.
Catechesis/Religious Program—Students 37.

28—HOLY FAMILY (1911), Closed. For inquiries for parish records contact the chancery.

29—HOLY NAME (1854), Rev. Thomas V. O'Donnell. In Res., Revs. John C. Dalton, Pastor Emeritus; Norbert Oloya Atimnedi, A.J.; Deacon Frank Tatulinski.
Res.: 8328 Broadway Ave. S.E., 44105-3931. Tel: 216-271-4242; 216-271-4243; 216-271-6995; Fax: 216-271-0886.
School—Tel: 216-341-0084; Fax: 216-341-1122. Penelope Lins, Prin. Lay Teachers 13; Students 235; Religious 1.
Catechesis/Religious Program—Students 51.

30—HOLY REDEEMER (1924), (Italian), Rev. Martin F. Polito; Sr. Carmen Hocevar, O.S.U., Pastoral Assoc.
Res.: 15712 Kipling Ave., 44110-3104. Tel: 216-531-3313; Fax: 216-531-4717.
Catechesis/Religious Program—Students 11.
Convent—924 Ruple Rd., 44110. Tel: 216-481-2740.

31—HOLY ROSARY (1892), (Italian), Rev. Philip G. Racco; Sr. Mary Ann Isabella, S.N.D., Pastoral Assoc. In Res., Rev. Joselito de los Reyes.
Res.: 12021 Mayfield Rd., 44106-1996. Tel: 216-421-2995; 216-421-2996; Fax: 216-421-2258.
Catechesis/Religious Program—Students 102.

32—HOLY TRINITY - ST. EDWARD (1975), Rev. Robert Marva, O.F.M.Cap.
Res.: 7211 Woodland Ave., 44104-3026. Tel: 216-431-1134; 216-431-8854; Fax: 216-361-1951.
Catechesis/Religious Program—Students 11.

33—ST. HYACINTH (1906), (Polish), Rev. Theodore Marszal; Deacon Kenneth J. Piechowski, Parish Life Coord.
Res.: 6114 Francis Ave., 44127. Tel: 216-641-3944.
Convent—2971 E. 61st St., 44127. Tel: 216-641-1508.

34—ST. IGNATIUS OF ANTIOCH (1902), Rev. James R. McGonegal; Rev. Msgr. James P. McIntyre, Pastor Emeritus (Retired); Sr. Dianne Piunno, S.N.D., Pastoral Assoc.; Deacon Billy Malcolm. In Res., Rev. Gary D. Yanus.
Res.: 10205 Lorain Ave., 44111-5470. Tel: 216-251-0300; 216-251-0301; 216-251-0302; Fax: 216-251-0302.
School—Tel: 216-671-0535; Fax: 216-671-0536. Joyce M. Needham, Prin. Lay Teachers 21; Students 394.
Catechesis/Religious Program—Students 20.

35—IMMACULATE CONCEPTION (1865), Revs. Frank G. Godic; Albert J. Mackert, Pastor Emeritus (Retired). In Res., Rev. John J. Hayes.
Res.: 4129 Superior Ave., 44103-1179. Tel: 216-431-5900; Fax: 216-431-0463.
School—Tel: 216-361-1883; Fax: 216-881-4274. Miss Rosemary DiPietro, Prin. Ursuline Sister of Cleveland 1; Lay Teachers 12; Students 193.

36—IMMACULATE HEART OF MARY (1894), (Polish), [CEM] Revs. Ralph Hudak; Andrew Knapik.
Res.: 6700 Lansing Ave., 44105-3797. Tel: 216-341-2734; 216-341-2735; Fax: 216-341-7200.
Convent—6804 Lansing Ave., 44105. Tel: 216-641-7121.

37—ST. JEROME (1919), Revs. Thomas A. Haren; Anthony Cassese; Deacon Peter Travalik. In Res., Rev. Joseph A. Goebel (Retired).
Res.: 15000 Lake Shore Blvd., 44110-1298. Tel: 216-481-8200; Fax: 216-481-6459.
School—15100 Lake Shore Blvd., 44110. Tel: 216-486-3587; Fax: 216-486-4288. Margaret Cosgriff, Prin. Lay Teachers 13; Students 228; Religious 1.
Convent—15025 Ridpath Ave., 44110. Tel: 216-531-6118.

38—ST. JOHN CANTIUS (1898), (Polish), Revs. Lucjan Stokowski; Ralph A. Bodziony, Pastor Emeritus (Retired).
Res.: 906 College Ave., S.W., 44113-4494. Tel: 216-781-9095; Fax: 216-696-6065.

39—ST. JOHN NEPOMUCENE (1902), (Bohemian), Rev. Robert J. Jasany. In Res., Deacon William A. Donlin.
Res.: 3785 Independence Rd., 44105-3357. Tel: 216-641-8444; 216-641-8445; Fax: 216-641-8824.
Church: Fleet Ave. & E. 50th St., 44105. Tel: 216-641-8444.
School—3777 Independence Rd., 44105. Tel: 216-341-1347; Fax: 216-341-4466. Mrs. Roswitha Wunker, Prin. Lay Teachers 14; Students 200.
Catechesis/Religious Program—Students 54.
Convent—Tel: 216-341-6393.

40—ST. JOSAPHAT (1908), Closed. For inquiries for parish records contact the chancery.

41—ST. JOSEPH (Woodland), Closed. For inquiries for parish records contact the chancery.

42—ST. JOSEPH (Collinwood) (1877), Closed., For inquiries for parish records contact St. Aloysius, Cleveland.

43—ST. LAWRENCE (1901), (Slovenian), Revs. Anthony Rebol, Pastor Emeritus; Dominic Mondzelewski, O.S.B., Admin.
Res.: 3547 E. 80th St., 44105-1521. Tel: 216-341-3886; Fax: 216-341-0496.
Church: 3532 E. 81st St., 44105.
Catechesis/Religious Program—Students 8.
Convent—3551 E. 80th St., 44105. Tel: 216-341-1235.

44—ST. LEO THE GREAT (1948), Revs. Robert M. Bielek; Thomas E. Stock; Sr. Kathleen Lyons, S.N.D., Pastoral Assoc.
Res.: 4940 Broadview Rd., 44109-5799. Tel: 216-661-1006; 216-661-1007; 216-661-1008; Fax: 216-661-0887.
School—4900 Broadview Rd., 44109. Tel: 216-661-2120; Fax: 216-661-7125. Michael Fasciano, Prin. Lay Teachers 23; Students 534.
Catechesis/Religious Program—Students 182.

45—ST. MALACHI (1865), Revs. Anthony J. Schuerger; Paul J. Hritz, Pastor Emeritus (Retired); Mary Jane Treichel, Pastoral Assoc.; Sr. M. Francis Borgia Allwine, O.S.U., Pastoral Assoc.
Res.: 2459 Washington Ave., 44113-2380. Tel: 216-861-5343; 216-861-5344; Fax: 216-861-5340.
School—Urban Community School, 2401 Washington Ave., 44113. Tel: 216-771-8014; Fax: 216-771-7888. Sr. Maureen Doyle, O.S.U., Dir. (Intermediate Level) (See St. Wendelin listing for Primary Level) Sisters 3; Lay Teachers 25; Students 411.
Convent—2456 Vermont Ave., 44113. Tel: 216-781-3481.

46—ST. MARK (1945), Revs. Douglas H. Koesel; Anthony J. Muzic, Pastor Emeritus (Retired); Joseph F. Wagner, Pastor Emeritus (Retired); Deacon Joseph McGraw; Donna M. Wimbiscus, Pastoral Assoc.
Res.: 15800 Montrose Ave., 44111-1084. Tel: 216-226-7577; 216-226-7578; Fax: 216-226-7578.
School—15724 Montrose Ave., 44111. Tel: 216-521-4115; Fax: 216-221-8664. Dr. Marilyn Kurnath, Prin. Lay Teachers 23; Students 443.
Catechesis/Religious Program—Students 136.

47—ST. MARY (1905), (Slovenian), Revs. John M. Kumse; Victor N. Tomc, Pastor Emeritus (Retired).
Res.: 15519 Holmes Ave., 44110-2497. Tel: 216-761-7740; 216-761-1837; 216-761-5524 (Ministry House); Fax: 216-761-6673.
School—716 E. 156th St., 44110. Tel: 216-451-1717; Fax: 216-451-7911. Luis Pla, Prin. Religious 1; Lay Teachers 13; Students 209.
Catechesis/Religious Program—Students 18.

48—ST. MARY OF CZESTOCHOWA (1913), (Polish), Closed. For inquiries for parish records contact the chancery.

49—ST. MEL (1945), Rev. Mark Q. Fedor, J.C.D.; Allison M. Miller, Pastoral Assoc.
Res.: 14436 Triskett Rd., 44111-2263. Tel: 216-941-4313; 216-941-4314; Fax: 216-941-1093.
School—14440 Triskett Rd., 44111. Tel: 216-941-6879; Fax: 216-941-1005. Patricia Kelly, Prin. Lay Teachers 19; Students 377.
Catechesis/Religious Program—Students 41.
Convent—Tel: 216-941-6589.

50—ST. MICHAEL THE ARCHANGEL (1882), Revs. James H. McCreight; Dennis R. O'Grady, Pastor Emeritus; Sr. Mary Reean Coyne, S.N.D., Pastoral Assoc.; Deacon Miquel Figueroa.
Res.: 3114 Scranton Rd., 44109-1689. Tel: 216-861-6297; 216-861-6298; 216-621-3847 (Spanish); Fax: 216-696-9351.
School—Metro Catholic Parish School See Separate Listing Under Elementary Schools, Parochial and Diocesan.
Catechesis/Religious Program—Students 89.

51—NATIVITY OF THE BLESSED VIRGIN MARY, Closed. For inquiries for parish records contact the chancery.

52—OUR LADY OF ANGELS (1922), Rev. John J. Cregan; Deacon Thomas J. Senn. In Res., Rev. John Lyons.
Res.: 3644 Rocky River Dr., 44111. Tel: 216-252-2332; Fax: 216-252-2383.
School—Tel: 216-251-6841; Fax: 216-251-7831. Miss Kathleen A. Lynch, Prin. Lay Teachers 29; Students 480.

53—OUR LADY OF GOOD COUNSEL (1873), Revs. Leroy Moreeuw, C.PP.S.; Anthony T. Fortman, C.PP.S.; Deacon Patrick F. Berigan.
Res.: 4423 Pearl Rd., S.W., 44109-4266. Tel: 216-749-2323; 216-749-2324; Fax: 216-741-7183.
School—4419 Pearl Rd., 44109. Tel: 216-741-3685; Fax: 216-741-7183. Helen D. Bykowski, Prin. Lay Teachers 14; Students 209.
Catechesis/Religious Program—Students 68.

54—OUR LADY OF LOURDES (1883), (Bohemian), Rev. James J. Masek; Diana Llipfird, Pastoral Assoc.
Res.: 3395 E. 53rd St., 44127-1692. Tel: 216-641-2829; 216-641-2830; Fax: 216-641-0043.
Church: E. 53rd St. & Hamm Ave., 44127-1692.
Catechesis/Religious Program—Students 3.
Convent—3401 E. 53rd St., 44127.

55—OUR LADY OF MERCY (1922), (Slovak), Rev. Joseph T. Hilinski.
Res.: 2425 W. 11th St., 44113-4496. Tel: 216-781-8277 (Parish House); 216-781-7928 (Laheta Hall).
Catechesis/Religious Program—Students 2.

56—OUR LADY OF MOUNT CARMEL (East) (1936), (Italian),, Officially closed as a parish on July 29, 1990, however, still in existence as an Oratory. Mrs. Rose Marie Criniti, Admin.
Res.: 2615 Martin Luther King Blvd., 44104-2553. Tel: 216-421-0140.
Oratory— 11501 Mount Carmel Rd., 44104.

57—OUR LADY OF MOUNT CARMEL (West) (1926), (Italian), Revs. Richard Rasch, O.de.M.; Marino Frascati, O.de.M.; Joseph K. Horvath, O.de.M.; Arcangelo Manzi, O.de.M. In Res., Bro. John M. Zyckowski, O.de.M.
Res.: 6928 Detroit Ave., 44102-3093. Tel: 216-651-5043; 216-651-2547; 216-651-1611; Fax: 216-651-6641.
School—1355 W. 70th St., 44102. Tel: 216-281-7146; Fax: 216-281-6651. Sr. Rosario Vega, H.M.S.S., Prin. Sisters of Most Holy Trinity 7; Lay Teachers 11; Students 286.
Catechesis/Religious Program—Students 10.
Convent—1355 W. 70th St., 44102.

58—OUR LADY OF PEACE (1919), Rev. Gary D. Chmura; Deacon William E. Dirk; Mrs. Nancy McIntosh, Pastoral Assoc.
Res.: 12503 Buckingham Ave., 44120-1498. Tel: 216-421-4211; 216-421-4212; Fax: 216-421-1612.
Church: Shaker Blvd. & E. 126th St., 44120.
School—12406 Buckingham Ave., 44120-1419. Tel: 216-795-7161; Fax: 216-795-7370. Mrs. Sheila Bolek, Prin. Lay Teachers 12; Students 241.
Catechesis/Religious Program—Students 53.

59—OUR LADY OF PERPETUAL HELP (1929), (Lithuanian), Rev. Gediminas Kijauskas, S.J.; Nijole Kersnauskas, Pastoral Assoc.; Stasys Ignatavicius, Pastoral Assoc.
Res.: 18022 Neff Rd., 44119-2644. Tel: 216-531-4263; Fax: 216-531-8441.
Convent—18021 Marcella Rd., 44119.

60—ST. PATRICK (1853), Rev. Mark A. DiNardo; Mary Jane Treichel, Pastoral Assoc.; Deacon William Merriman.
Res.: 3602 Bridge Ave., 44113-3314. Tel: 216-631-6872; 216-631-6873; 216-631-6874; Fax: 216-631-0267.
School—Urban Community School, Tel: 216-771-8014. See St. Malachi listing.
Catechesis/Religious Program—Students 234.

61—ST. PATRICK (West Park) (1848), [CEM] Revs. Thomas J. Hagedorn; Robert W. Wisniewski; Joseph C. Pednekar, M.S.F.S.; Deacons Richard C. Beercheck; William Staab. In Res., Rev. Joseph C. Pednekar, M.S.F.S.
Res.: 4427 Rocky River Dr., 44135-2551. Tel: 216-251-8286; 216-251-8287; Fax: 216-251-8555.
School—17720 Puritas Ave., 44135. Tel: 216-671-4314; Fax: 216-671-5277. Catherine White, Prin. Sisters 1; Lay Teachers 20; Students 400.
Catechesis/Religious Program—Students 15.
Convent—17712 Puritas Ave., 44135. Tel: 216-941-1088.

62—ST. PAUL (1902), (Croatian), Revs. Mirko Hladni; Zvonko Blasko.
Res.: 1369 E. 40th St., 44103-1194. Tel: 216-431-1895; Fax: 216-431-1128.
Catechesis/Religious Program—Students 151.

63—ST. PETER (1853), (German), Rev. Robert J. Marrone.
Res.: 1533 E. 17th St., 44114. Tel: 216-861-1798; Fax: 216-861-1799.
Catechesis/Religious Program—Students 38.

64—SS. PHILIP AND JAMES (1950), Revs. J. Brendan McNulty; Joseph R. Sdolnu, Admin. In Res., Rev. William H. Severt.
Res.: 10812 Adeline Rd., 44111-4806. Tel: 216-941-6808; 216-941-6809; Fax: 216-941-3808.
Church: 3727 Bosworth Rd., 44111.

65—ST. PHILIP NERI (1914), Rev. Norman N. Smith; Deacon Carl Varga, Parish Life Coord.; Rose Marie Egensperger, Pastoral Assoc.; Ms. Linda Teare, Pastoral Assoc.
Res.: 8215 St. Clair Ave., 44103-3728. Tel: 216-431-2583; Fax: 216-431-0224.
School—St. Thomas Aquinas-St. Philip Neri, 9101 Superior Ave., 44106. Tel: 216-421-4668; Fax: 216-721-8444. Althea Cheatham, Prin. Lay Teachers 15; Students 183.
Catechesis/Religious Program—Students 32.
Convent—799 E. 82nd St., 44103. Tel: 216-431-0224.

66—ST. PROCOP (1872), (Bohemian), Rev. Gary D. Yanus; Sr. Annette Amendolia, S.N.D., Parish Life Coord.
Res.: 3181 W. 41st St., 44109-1275. Tel: 216-631-0365; 216-631-0367.
Catechesis/Religious Program—Students 8.

67—ST. ROCCO (1922), (Italian), Very Rev. Michael Contardi, O.de.M.; Revs. Paschal Rosca, O.de.M.; Timothy J. Brady, O.de.M. In Res., Bro. Martin J. Jarocinski, O.de.M.
Res.: 3205 Fulton Rd., 44109-1495. Tel: 216-961-8331; Fax: 216-961-1845.
School—Tel: 216-961-8557; Fax: 216-961-1112. Sr. Judith Wilk, O.SS.T., Prin. Sisters of Most Holy Trinity 4; Lay Teachers 7; Students 218.
Catechesis/Religious Program—Students 26.
Convent—Tel: 216-961-2378.

68—ST. ROSE OF LIMA (1899), Revs. James A. Viall, Administrative Leave; Michael J. Troha, Admin.
Res.: 11411 Detroit Ave., 44102-2399. Tel: 216-521-0133; Fax 216-521-1306.
Church: Detroit Ave. & W. 114th St., 44102.
Catechesis/Religious Program—Students 37.
Convent—1418 W. 114th St., 44102.

69—SACRED HEART OF JESUS (1888), (Polish), Rev. Joseph S. Mecir.
Res.: 6916 Krakow Ave., 44105-5737. Tel: 216-341-2828; 216-341-8525; Fax: 216-271-6287.
Church: E. 71st & Kazimier Ave., 44105.

70—SAGRADA FAMILIA (1997), (Hispanic), Rev. David F. Fallon; Deacons Ceferino Medina; Epifanio Torres; Victor Colon; Ignacio Miranda; Frederick Simon; Marilyn Hernandez, Pastoral Assoc.
Church: 7719 Detroit Ave., 44102-2811. Tel: 216-631-6817; 216-631-2888; 216-631-2889; Fax: 216-631-2305.
Catechesis/Religious Program—Students 226.

71—SAN JUAN BAUTISTA (1975), (Spanish), Closed., For inquiries for Parish Records contact La Sagrada Familia.

72—ST. STANISLAUS (1873), (Polish), Revs. Michael Surafka, O.F.M., Admin.; George Kusy; Joachim Studwell, O.F.M.
Res.: 3649 E. 65th St., 44105-1293. Tel: 216-341-9091; 216-341-9092; Fax: 216-341-2683.
Church: Forman Ave. & E. 65th St., 44105.
School—6615 Forman Ave., 44105. Tel: 216-883-3307; Fax: 216-883-0514. Mrs. Alice Torrence, Prin. Sisters 2; Lay Teachers 17; Students 330.
Catechesis/Religious Program—Students 306.
Convent—6615 Forman Ave., 44105. Tel: 216-341-0934.

73—ST. STEPHEN (1869), (German), Rev. S. Michael Franz; Mrs. Ana Matos, Pastoral Assoc.
Res.: 1930 W. 54th St., 44102-3298. Tel: 216-631-5633; Fax: 216-631-5634.
School—Metro Catholic Parish School Sr. Anne Mary Maline, S.N.D., Prin. See Separate Listing under Elementary Schools, Parochial and Diocesan.
Catechesis/Religious Program—Students 10.
Convent—1891 W. 57th St., 44102. Tel: 216-631-0754.

74—ST. THOMAS AQUINAS, Closed. For inquiries for parish records contact the chancery.

75—TRANSFIGURATION (1943), Closed. For inquiries for parish records contact the chancery.

76—ST. VINCENT DE PAUL (1922), Revs. John E. Manning; Urban A. Reichlin, Pastor Emeritus (Retired); Deacons Kenneth J. Hill; Billy Malcolm. In Res., Revs. Charles F. Strebler; Robert R. Vieweg.
Res.: 13400 Lorain Ave., 44111-3470. Tel: 216-252-2626; Fax: 216-251-0455.
Church: Lorain Ave. & Berea Rd., 44111.
School—13442 Lorain Ave., 44111. Tel: 216-251-3932. Sr. Caroline Kocur, O.S.U., Prin. Sisters 1; Lay Teachers 20; Students 352.
Catechesis/Religious Program—Students 45.

77—ST. VITUS (1893), (Slovenian), Rev. Joseph P. Boznar; Sr. Mary Avsec, S.N.D., Pastoral Assoc.
Res.: 6019 Lausche Ave., 44103-1455. Tel: 216-361-1444; 216-361-1445; Fax: 216-361-1145.
Catechesis/Religious Program—Students 191.

78—ST. WENDELIN (1903), (Slovak), Rev. Jerome M. Lajack; Deacon James J. Armstrong.
Res.: 2281 Columbus Rd., 44113-4230. Tel: 216-861-1141; Fax: 216-861-1141.
School—Urban Community School, 2281 Columbus Rd., 44113-4230. Tel: 216-861-4706; Fax: 216-781-0034. Joy Smith, Prin. (Primary and Junior High) (See St. Malachi listing for Intermediate Level)
Catechesis/Religious Program—Students 3.
Convent—2259 Columbus Rd., 44113. Tel: 216-241-1773.

OUTSIDE THE CITY OF CLEVELAND

AKRON, SUMMIT CO.

1—ANNUNCIATION (1907), Rev. Edwin M. Leonard; Jean J. Jordan, Pastoral Min.; Diana Herhold, Pastoral Min. In Res., Rev. James J. Berardi.
Res.: 87 Broad St., 44305-2591. Tel: 330-535-4141; Fax: 330-762-8456.
Church: Broad St. & Kent St., 44305.
School—Annunciation-St. John the Baptist, 88 Kent St., 44305. Tel: 330-253-5311; Fax: 330-762-8456. Barbara Mesko, Prin. Lay Teachers 14; Students 193.
Catechesis/Religious Program—Students 94.

2—ST. ANTHONY OF PADUA (1933), (Italian), Revs. James V. Ragnoni; Robert Labella.
Res.: 83 Mosser Pl., 44310-3184. Tel: 330-762-7277; Fax: 330-762-2229.
School—80 E. York St., 44310. Tel: 330-253-6918. Sr. Elizabeth Szilvasi, M.P.F., Prin. Religious Teachers Filippini 1; Lay Teachers 9; Students 162.
Catechesis/Religious Program—Students 30.
Convent—93 Mosser Pl., 44310. Tel: 216-376-1735.

3—ST. BERNARD (1861), [CEM] Rev. Paul E. Schindler; Sr. Catherine Walsh, C.S.A., Pastoral Assoc.; Deacon Daniel J. Matusicky. In Res., Revs. Norman K. Douglas; Frances Ejimofor, C.S.Sp.; Albert I. Reymann, M.M.; Wilhelm Malasi (Tanzania); Bernard E. Okafor (Nigeria).
Res.: 44 University Ave., 44308-1609. Tel: 330-253-5161; 330-253-5162; 330-253-5265; 330-253-5364; Fax: 330-253-6949.
Catechesis/Religious Program—Students 95.

4—CHRIST THE KING (1935), Revs. Francis J. Basa; Victor J. Cimperman, Pastor Emeritus (Retired).
Res.: 1584 Creighton Ave., 44310-2699. Tel: 330-633-8418; Fax: 330-633-4512.
School— Closed. For further information please refer to North Akron Catholic School under Elementary Schools located in the Institution section.
Catechesis/Religious Program—Students 3.
Convent—Tel: 330-633-8217.

5—ST. FRANCIS DE SALES (1948), Revs. James R. Schleicher; Robert E. Stein; Deacon Richard C. Butz. In Res., Rev. Thomas B. Zeisig (Retired).
Res.: 4019 Manchester Rd., 44319-2193. Tel: 330-644-2225; 330-644-2226; Fax: 330-644-2225.
School—4009 Manchester Rd., 44319. Tel: 330-644-0638; Fax: 330-644-2663. Carol Trifonoff, Prin. Sisters Servants of Immaculate Heart of Mary 1; Lay Teachers 20; Students 377.
Catechesis/Religious Program—Students 224.

6—ST. HEDWIG (1912), (Polish), Rev. Thaddeus M. Swirski.
Res.: 215 E. Glenwood Ave., 44310-3837. Tel: 330-376-6979.
Catechesis/Religious Program—Students 8.

7—ST. HILARY (1958), Revs. Gordon A. Yahner; Salvatore M. Ruggeri; Deacon Lee F. Hindersheid; Sr. Marlene LoGrasso, O.S.U., Pastoral Assoc.; Mrs. Mary Lou Grossman, Pastoral Assoc.; Mrs. Patricia Schnee, Pastoral Assoc.
Mailing Address: 2750 W. Market St., Fairlawn, 44333-4236. In Res., Rev. Patrick Nicanda Allala.
Res.: 615 Moorfield Rd., Fairlawn, 44333. Tel: 330-867-1055; 330-867-1056; Fax: 330-869-2312.
Church: 2750 W. Market St., Fairlawn, 44333.
School—645 Moorfield Rd., Fairlawn, 44333. Tel: 330-867-8720; Fax: 330-867-5081. Dr. Patricia Nugent, Prin. Religious 1; Lay Teachers 38; Students 715.
Catechesis/Religious Program—Students 485.

8—IMMACULATE CONCEPTION (1923), Rev. Michael B. Smith; Melissa Keegan, Pastoral Assoc. In Res., Rev. Samuel R. Ciccolini.
Res.: 2101 17th St. S.W., 44314-2315. Tel: 330-753-8429; Fax: 330-753-7440.
Church: 2100 16th St. S.W., 44314.
Catechesis/Religious Program—Students 44.

9—ST. JOHN THE BAPTIST (1907), (Slovak), Rev. Ralph V. Coletta.
Res.: 1034 Brown St., 44301-1596. Tel: 330-773-9114; Fax: 330-773-3613.
School—Annunciation-St. John the Baptist School, 88 Kent St., 44305. Tel: 330-253-5311; Fax: 330-762-8456. Barbara Mesko, Prin. Lay Teachers 14; Students 210.
Catechesis/Religious Program—Students 14.

10—ST. MARTHA (1919), Rev. Michael A. Matusz; Sr. Mercia Madigan, O.S.U., Pastoral Assoc.; Mrs. Kathleen Lux, Pastoral Assoc.
Res.: 300 E. Tallmadge Ave., 44310-2399. Tel: 330-376-5144; 330-376-5145; 330-374-6909; Fax: 330-376-5311.
School— Closed. For further information please refer to North Akron Catholic School under Elementary Schools located in the Institution section.
Catechesis/Religious Program—Students 92.

11—ST. MARY (1887), Rev. Edward A. Burba.
Res.: 750 S. Main St., 44311-1094. Tel: 330-762-9247; Fax: 330-252-1768.
School—Tel: 330-253-1233; Fax: 330-253-1472. Kathleen Allio, Prin. Religious 1; Lay Teachers 13; Students 218.
Catechesis/Religious Program—Students 24.

12—ST. MATTHEW (1943), Revs. Michael Williamson; Thomas A. McGovern, Pastor Emeritus (Retired); Deacon James A. White.
Res.: 2603 Benton St., 44312-1694. Tel: 330-733-9944; Fax: 330-733-9424.
Church: Berne & Woolf St., 44312.
School—2580 Benton St., 44312. Tel: 330-784-1711; Fax: 330-733-1004. Mr. Thomas S. Maroon, Prin. Lay Teachers 23; Students 375.
Catechesis/Religious Program—Students 166.

13—NATIVITY OF THE LORD JESUS (1977), Rev. David

J. Halaiko; Deacon Dennis L. Smith; Rosemary Frey, Pastoral Assoc. In Res., Rev. Joachim Oforchukwu, C.S.Sp. (Nigeria).
Res.: 2425 Myersville Rd., 44312-4951. Tel: 330-699-5086; Fax: 330-699-4299.
Catechesis/Religious Program—Students 268.

14—ST. PAUL (1919), Revs. John M. Jenkins; Ralph W. Thomas; Therese Nesline, Pastoral Assoc.; Deacon Francis R. Lonteen.
Res.: 433 Mission Dr., 44301-2798. Tel: 330-724-1263; Fax: 330-724-7680.
School—1580 Brown St., 44301-2798. Tel: 330-724-1253; Fax: 330-724-1127. Mrs. Rosemary Capotosto, Prin. Lay Teachers 19; Students 295.
Catechesis/Religious Program—Students 100.

15—ST. PETER (1917), Closed., For inquiries for parish records contact St. Mary Parish, Akron.

16—SACRED HEART OF JESUS (1915), (Hungarian), Rev. Robert E. Clancy, Admin.; Deacon Geza Balassy.
Res.: 212 E. Voris St., 44311-1508. Tel: 330-434-4348.
Church: 734 Grant St., 44311.

17—ST. SEBASTIAN (1928), Revs. William D. Karg; John T. McDonough, Pastor Emeritus (Retired); Robert H. Jackson; Deacon Terry W. Peacock.
Res.: 476 Mull Ave., 44320-1299. Tel: 330-836-2233; 330-836-2234; Fax: 330-836-2235.
School—500 Mull Ave., 44320. Tel: 330-836-9107; Fax: 330-836-7690. Mr. Howard J. Sheetz, Prin. Lay Teachers 28; Students 467.
Catechesis/Religious Program—Students 77.

18—ST. VINCENT (1837), [CEM] Rev. Joseph H. Kraker; Sr. Joan Radar, O.P., Pastoral Assoc. In Res., Most Rev. Martin J. Amos.
Res.: 164 W. Market St., 44303-2395. Tel: 330-535-3135; Fax: 330-535-4160.
Church: W. Market St. & Maple St., 44303.
School—17 S. Maple St., 44303. Tel: 330-762-5912; Fax: 330-535-2515. William D. Hackman, Prin. Lay Teachers 19; Students 259.
Catechesis/Religious Program—Students 101.

AMHERST, LORAIN CO., ST. JOSEPH (1864), [CEM] Revs. Lawrence N. Martello; Joseph A. Warner; Sr. Mary Ann Burke, S.N.D., Pastoral Assoc.; Deacons Daniel Hancock; Paul Heise. In Res., Rev. Thomas V. Rath (Retired).
Res.: 200 St. Joseph Dr., 44001-1663. Tel: 440-988-2848; 440-988-2849; 440-871-4415 (Cleveland); Fax: 440-984-2301.
School—175 St. Joseph Dr., 44001. Tel: 440-988-4244. Mrs. Karen Casper, Prin. Lay Teachers 18; Students 313.
Catechesis/Religious Program—Students 491.
Convent—151 St. Joseph Dr., 44001. Tel: 440-988-2621.

ASHLAND, ASHLAND CO., ST. EDWARD (1853), [JC] Rev. James M. Cassidy; Deacon James A. Kaniecki.
Res.: 501 Cottage St., 44805-2167. Tel: 419-289-7224; 419-289-8333; Fax: 419-289-0515.
Administration Center—149 Pleasant St., 44805.
School—433 Cottage St., 44805. Tel: 419-289-7456; Fax: 419-289-9474. Suellen Valentine, Prin. Lay Teachers 15; Students 191.
Catechesis/Religious Program—Students 55.

AVON LAKE, LORAIN CO.

1—HOLY SPIRIT (1965), Rev. James H. Beatty; Deacons James A. Smallhoover; Robert Walling.
Res.: 410 Lear Rd., 44012-2004. Tel: 440-933-3777; 440-871-8157 Cleveland Line; Fax: 440-871-8157.
Catechesis/Religious Program—Tel: 440-933-8818. Students 442.

2—ST. JOSEPH'S (1949), Rev. Timothy J. O'Connor; Deacon Howard Masony.
Res.: 32929 Lake Rd., 44012-1497. Tel: 440-933-3152; Fax: 440-933-8919.
School—Tel: 440-933-6233; Fax: 440-933-2463. Mrs. Patricia Vaccaro, Prin. Lay Teachers 20; Students 390.
Catechesis/Religious Program—Students 367.
Convent—32911 Lake Rd., 44012. Tel: 216-933-5769.

AVON, LORAIN CO.

1—HOLY TRINITY (1833), [CEM] Revs. John A. Misenko; John J. Gorski, Pastor Emeritus (Retired).
Res.: 33601 Detroit Rd., 44011-1999. Tel: 440-937-5363; Fax: 440-937-5128.
School—2610 Nagel Rd., 44011. Tel: 440-937-6420; Fax: 440-937-6420. Sr. Sean Groh, S.N.D., Prin. Notre Dame Sisters 1; Lay Teachers 16; Students 340.
Catechesis/Religious Program—Students 377.
Convent—2620 Nagel Rd., 44011. Tel: 440-937-5005.

2—ST. MARY OF THE IMMACULATE CONCEPTION (1841), [CEM] Revs. C. Thomas Cleaton; Arthur B. Egan, Pastor Emeritus (Retired).
Res.: 2640 Stoney Ridge Rd., 44011-1899. Tel: 440-934-4212; Fax: 440-934-0507.
School—2680 Stoney Ridge Rd., 44011. Tel: 440-934-6246; Fax: 440-934-6250. Miss Linda A. Kenzik, Prin. Sisters of Notre Dame 3; Lay Teachers 10; Students 171.
Catechesis/Religious Program—Students 259.
Convent—2680 Stoney Ridge Rd., 44011. Tel: 440-934-5173.

BARBERTON, SUMMIT CO.

1—ST. AUGUSTINE (1898), Revs. Richard Burchell; David J. Majikas; Paul J. Clines, Pastor Emeritus (Retired); Karen Bellett, Pastoral Assoc.; Deacon Robin Adair.
Res.: 204 Sixth St., N.W., 44203-2198. Tel: 330-745-0011; Fax: 330-745-0012.
Church: Sixth St. & Lake St., 44203.
School—195 Seventh St., N.W., 44203. Tel: 330-753-6435; Fax: 330-753-4095. Michael Ziegelhofer, Prin. Lay Teachers 22; Students 336.
Catechesis/Religious Program—Students 215.

2—SS. CYRIL AND METHODIUS (1906), (Slovak), Rev. Edward F. Lajack.
Res.: 189 15th St. N.W., 44203-7052. Tel: 330-825-7089; 330-825-7081; Fax: 330-825-7181.
Church: 183 15 St. N.W., 44203.

3—HOLY TRINITY (1911), (Magyar), Rev. Carl A. Ciprian.
Res.: 398 Van St., 44203-2329. Tel: 330-745-4735.
Church: 380 Wooster Rd. N., 44203-2329.

4—ST. MARY'S (1912), (Polish), Closed. For inquiries for parish records contact the chancery.

5—PRINCE OF PEACE, Rev. Richard A. Arko; Deacon Harold R. Krause.
Res.: 1263 Shannon Ave., 44203-6792. Tel: 330-825-9543.
Catechesis/Religious Program—Students 105.

6—SACRED HEART (1916), (Slovenian), Closed. For inquiries for parish records contact the chancery.

BAY VILLAGE, CUYAHOGA CO., ST. RAPHAEL (1946), Revs. Timothy W. Gareau; Nelson J. Callahan, Pastor Emeritus (Retired); Craig M. Hovanec; Barbara Moore, Pastoral Assoc.
Res.: 525 Dover Center Rd., 44140-2366. Tel: 440-871-1100; Fax: 440-899-2911.
School—Tel: 440-871-6760; Fax: 440-871-1358. Ann Miller, Prin. Lay Teachers 35; Students 744.
Catechesis/Religious Program—Students 619.

BEDFORD HEIGHTS, CUYAHOGA CO., HOLY TRINITY (1965), Revs. Albert Veigas; Ernest C. Hepner, Pastor Emeritus; Deacon William Starkey; Sr. Nina Vitale, O.S.U., Pastoral Assoc.
Res.: 24821 Columbus Rd., 44146-2599. Tel: 440-232-2044; 440-232-2045; Fax: 440-232-3720.
Catechesis/Religious Program—Students 20.

BEDFORD, CUYAHOGA CO.

1—ST. MARY (1910), Rev. Thomas J. Winkel.
Res.: 300 Union St., 44146-4594. Tel: 440-232-9393; 440-232-9394; Fax: 440-232-7752.
Church: 340 Union St., 44146.
School—270 Union St., 44146. Tel: 440-232-2303; Fax: 440-439-4419. Michelle Nowakowski, Prin. Religious 1; Lay Teachers 15; Students 180.
Catechesis/Religious Program—Students 42.
Convent—36 Paul St., 44146. Tel: 216-439-1667.

2—ST. PIUS X (1952), Rev. Thomas D. Mahoney; Sr. Irene Mraz, V.S.C., Pastoral Assoc.
Res.: 400 Center Rd., 44146-2296. Tel: 440-232-8166; 440-232-8167; Fax: 440-786-9929.
School—370 Center Rd., 44146-2297. Tel: 440-232-1531; Fax: 440-232-1534. Mrs. Mary Ann Murnyack, Prin. Lay Teachers 12; Students 137.
Catechesis/Religious Program—Students 67.

BEREA, CUYAHOGA CO.

1—ST. ADALBERT (1873), (Polish), [CEM] Rev. Gerald J. Keller; Deacon Donald P. Butkovic.
Res.: 66 Adalbert St., 44017-1799. Tel: 440-234-6830; Fax: 440-234-2588.
School—56 Adalbert St., 44017. Tel: 440-234-5529; Fax: 440-234-2881. Miss Margaret Ricksecker, Prin. Lay Teachers 15; Students 158.
Catechesis/Religious Program—Students 147.
Convent—24 Adalbert St., 44017. Tel: 440-234-1096.

2—ST. MARY (1852), [CEM] Revs. George A. Vrabel; John C. Retar; Mrs. Anne Chadwoski, Pastoral Assoc.
Res.: 250 Kraft St., 44017-1449. Tel: 440-243-3877; 440-243-3878; Fax: 440-891-9417.
School—265 Baker St., 44017-1515. Tel: 440-243-4555; Fax: 440-243-6214. Nancy C. Kaesgen, Prin. Lay Teachers 25; Students 410.
Catechesis/Religious Program—Students 609.

BRECKSVILLE, CUYAHOGA CO., ST. BASIL THE GREAT (1960), Revs. Walter H. Jenne; William R. Dickinson; Paul Choo; Sr. Susan Imburgia, C.S.J., Pastoral Assoc.; Deacon David Pecot; Mrs. Carol Gaby, Pastoral Assoc. In Res., Rev. Lloyd J. Boymer (Retired).
Res.: 8700 Brecksville Rd., 44141-1999. Tel: 440-526-1686; 440-526-1687; Fax: 440-526-2373.
Catechesis/Religious Program—Tel: 440-526-3520; 440-526-3587. Students 1,251.
Convent—6901 Mill Rd., 44141. Tel: 440-526-2850.

BROADVIEW HEIGHTS, CUYAHOGA CO., ASSUMPTION (1857), Revs. Christopher Schwartz, O.S.B.; Justin Drywal, O.S.B.; Sr. Therese Horan, Pastoral Assoc.; Deacon Robert C. Bubnick Sr.
Res.: 9183 Broadview Rd., 44147-2596. Tel: 440-526-1177; 440-526-1178; Fax: 440-526-2838.
School—Tel: 440-526-4877; Fax: 440-526-3752. Sr. Carol Tobler, S.I.W., Prin. Sisters of Incarnate Word 2; Lay Teachers 19; Students 274.
Catechesis/Religious Program—Students 292.
Convent—9139 Broadview Rd., 44147. Tel: 216-526-4069.

BROOK PARK, CUYAHOGA CO.

1—ASSUMPTION OF MARY (1860), [CEM] Rev. Thomas A. Boone; Deacons Francis B. Wilson; Douglas P. Bewley. In Res., Rev. Adelbert J. Gassert (Retired).
Res.: 5445 Smith Rd., 44142-2077. Tel: 216-267-0630; Fax: 216-267-3064.
Church: 5555 Smith Rd., 44142. Tel: 216-267-1775.
Catechesis/Religious Program—Fax: 216-267-0665. Students 88.

2—ST. PETER THE APOSTLE (1968), Rev. James R. Stenger; Deacon James C. Vincent. In Res., Rev. Dismas Boeff, O.S.B.
Res.: 6455 Engle Rd., 44142-3503. Tel: 216-433-1440; 216-433-1441; Fax: 216-433-1434.
Catechesis/Religious Program—Students 303.

BROOKLYN, CUYAHOGA CO., ST. THOMAS MORE (1946), Revs. James J. Vesely; John S. Juhas; Russell P. Lowe; Sr. Elaine Theresa Burrows, S.I.W., Pastoral Assoc.; Deacons Rudolph Jarosh Jr.; Martin A. Thiel.
Res.: 4170 N. Amber Dr., 44144-1399. Tel: 216-749-0414; Fax: 216-749-1001.
School—4180 N. Amber Dr., 44144. Tel: 216-749-1660; Fax: 216-398-4265. Nancy D. Brewer, Prin. Sisters 1; Lay Teachers 25; Students 429.
Catechesis/Religious Program—Students 208.

BRUNSWICK, MEDINA CO.

1—ST. AMBROSE (1957), Revs. Robert C. Hilkert; Sean J. Donnelly; John A. Valencheck; Deacons Clement J. Belter; John Miklosovic; Thomas J. Sheridan.
Res.: 929 Pearl Rd., 44212-2597. Fax: 330-220-1748.
School—923 Pearl Rd., 44212. Tel: 330-225-2116; Fax: 330-225-5425. Denise Modic Urban, Prin. Sisters of Humility of Mary 1; Lay Teachers 19; Students 426.
Catechesis/Religious Program—Students 1,262.

2—ST. COLETTE (1977), Rev. Thomas G. Montavon.
Res.: 330 W. 130th St., 44212-2309. Tel: 330-273-5500; Fax: 330-225-7909.
Catechesis/Religious Program—Students 331.

CHAGRIN FALLS, CUYAHOGA CO.

1—HOLY ANGELS (1977), Rev. Daniel F. Schlegel, Admin.; Sr. Susan Javorek, S.N.D., Pastoral Assoc.
Mailing Address: 18205 Chillicothe Rd., 44023-4879.
Res.: 8390 Stoney Brook Dr., 44023-4879. Fax: 440-708-0787.
Church: 18046 Chillicothe Rd., 44023-4879. Tel: 440-708-0000.
Catechesis/Religious Program—Tel: 440-708-0808. Students 973.

2—ST. JOAN OF ARC (1948), Revs. John R. Olsavsky; John J. Kinkopf, Pastor Emeritus (Retired); Christopher H. Weber; Mrs. Rosemary Amor, Pastoral Assoc.; Sisters Bernadette Bacho, S.N.D.; Ann Marie Kanusek, S.N.D., Pastoral Assoc.; Deacons Louis J. Capek; Jeffrey Dunlop.
Res.: 496 E. Washington St., 44022-2999. Tel: 440-247-7183; Fax: 440-247-2327.
School—498 E. Washington St., 44022-2998. Tel: 440-247-6530; Fax: 440-247-2045. Shelley DiBacco, Prin. Lay Teachers 16; Students 259.
Catechesis/Religious Program—Tel: 440-247-3606. Students 486.
Convent—456 E. Washington St., 44022. Tel: 440-247-4419.

CHARDON, GEAUGA CO., ST. MARY (1909), Revs. Thomas C. Gilles; Gregory F. Schaut; Deacons Edward J. McCarthy Jr.; Lawrence Boehnlein.
Res.: 401 North St., 44024-1087. Tel: 440-285-7051; Fax: 440-286-3886.
School—Tel: 440-286-3590; Fax: 440-286-3590. Sr. Mary Sandra Nativio, S.N.D., Prin. Sisters of Notre Dame 2; Lay Teachers 21; Students 350.
Catechesis/Religious Program—Students 530.
Convent—315 North St., 44024. Tel: 440-286-5641.

CHESTERLAND, GEAUGA CO., ST. ANSELM (1961), Revs. Thomas M. Sweany; John F. Anderson, Pastor Emeritus (Retired); Barry T. Gearing; Deacons Dale A. Bacik; Donald E. Sill; Jean Fitzgerald, Pastoral Assoc.
Res.: 12969 Chillicothe Rd., 44026-3199. Tel: 440-729-9575; Fax: 440-729-9103.
Church: 13013 Chillicothe Rd., 44026.
School—Tel: 440-729-7806; Fax: 440-729-3524. Mrs. Patricia Zaranec, Prin. Sisters of Notre Dame 1; Lay Teachers 23; Students 355.
Catechesis/Religious Program—Students 603.
Convent—13055 Chillicothe Rd., 44026. Tel: 440-729-0292.

CHIPPEWA LAKE, MEDINA CO., JESUS DIVINE REDEEMER

(1976), Attended by, Our Lady Help of Christians, Litchfield.

CLEVELAND HEIGHTS, CUYAHOGA CO.

1—ST. ANN (1915), Rev. James E. Singler; Ms. Renee Barber, Pastoral Assoc.
Res.: 2175 Coventry Rd., 44118-2898. Tel: 216-321-0024; Fax: 216-321-7702.
School—2160 Stillman Rd., 44118. Tel: 216-932-4177; Fax: 216-932-7439. Sr. Anne McGreevey, O.S.B., Prin. Sisters 1; Lay Teachers 21; Students 316.
Catechesis/Religious Program—Students 94.

2—ST. LOUIS (1947), Rev. Leonard J. Zamborsky; Sr. Marie Manning, S.N.D., Pastoral Assoc.; Deacon Richard E. Woods. In Res., Rev. Stephen J. Dohner.
Res.: 2475 N. Taylor Rd., 44118-1397. Tel: 216-382-0440; 216-382-0441; 216-382-1071; Fax: 216-382-1605.
Church: 2463 N. Taylor Rd., 44118.
School—2463 N. Taylor Rd., 44118. Tel: 216-382-0033; Fax: 216-382-5933. Julie Dougherty, Prin. Lay Teachers 16; Students 146.
Catechesis/Religious Program—Students 146.

CLINTON, SUMMIT CO., ST. GEORGE (1908), Rev. Msgr. Robert E. Bacher.
Res.: 7615 Second Ave. N., 44216-9105. Tel: 330-882-3353; Fax: 330-882-3353.
Church: 7609 Second Ave. N., 44216.
Catechesis/Religious Program—Students 35.

COLUMBIA STATION, LORAIN CO., ST. ELIZABETH ANN SETON (1976), Rev. Charles J. Ryba.
Mailing Address: P.O. Box 968, 44028-0968.
Res.: 25777 Royalton Rd., 44028-0968.
Church: 25801 Royalton Rd., 44028. Tel: 440-236-5095; Fax: 440-236-5804.
Catechesis/Religious Program—Tel: 440-236-3711. Students 170.

CONCORD TWP., LAKE CO., ST. GABRIEL (1966), Revs. Frederick F. Pausche; John G. Vrana; Gary J. Malin; Deacon Ronald Adkins; Carolyn Jablonski, Pastoral Assoc.
Res.: 9925 Johnnycake Ridge Rd., 44060-6294. Tel: 440-352-8282; 440-953-3867 (Cleveland); Fax: 440-354-7558.
School—9935 Johnnycake Ridge Rd., 44060. Tel: 440-352-6169; Fax: 440-639-0143. Sr. Josephmarie Bunosky, S.N.D., Prin. Sisters of Notre Dame 1; Lay Teachers 34; Students 901.
Catechesis/Religious Program—Students 647.
Convent—9918 Johnnycake Ridge Rd., 44060. Tel: 440-354-7553.

COPLEY, SUMMIT CO., GUARDIAN ANGELS (1964), Revs. James F. Kramer; J. Norman Riley, Pastor Emeritus; Rev. Msgr. Robert C. Wolff, Pastor Emeritus (Retired).
Church and Res.: 1686 Cleveland-Massillon Rd., 44321-1976. Tel: 330-666-1373; Fax: 330-666-8189.
Catechesis/Religious Program—Students 203.

CUYAHOGA FALLS, SUMMIT CO.

1—ST. EUGENE (1963), Revs. Neil A. Crosby; B. Thomas Zeisig.
Res.: 1821 Munroe Falls Ave., 44221-3699. Tel: 330-923-5244; Fax: 330-923-8436.
Catechesis/Religious Program—Students 145.

2—IMMACULATE HEART OF MARY (1952), Revs. Thomas W. McCann; John R. Rathfon, Pastor Emeritus (Retired); A. Jonathan Zingales; Deacon J. David Seal. In Res., Rev. Robert E. Pahler (Retired).
Res.: 1905 Portage Trail, 44223-1792. Tel: 330-929-8361; 330-929-8362; 330-929-8399; Fax: 330-929-8496.
School—2859 Lillis Dr., 44223. Tel: 330-923-1220; Fax: 330-929-4373. Anita Nagel, Prin. Lay Teachers 24; Students 453.
Catechesis/Religious Program—Students 287.

3—ST. JOSEPH (1831), Rev. James J. Marsick; Deacon Robert Kochanski.
Res.: 215 Falls Ave., 44221-3999. Tel: 330-928-2173; Fax: 330-928-3082.
Church: 1761 Second St., 44221.
School—1909 Third St., 44221-3894. Tel: 330-928-2151; Fax: 330-928-3139. Robert Kochanski, Prin. Deacons 1; Lay Teachers 23; Students 446.
Catechesis/Religious Program—Students 83.

DOYLESTOWN, WAYNE CO., SS. PETER AND PAUL (1827), [CEM] [JC] Rev. David J. McCarthy; Deacon Dale A. Youngblood.
Res.: 161 W. Clinton St., 44230-1297. Tel: 330-658-2145.
School—169 W. Clinton St., 44230. Tel: 330-658-2804; Fax: 330-658-2287. Marian Gillen, Prin. Lay Teachers 13; Students 164.
Catechesis/Religious Program—Students 134.

EAST CLEVELAND, CUYAHOGA CO.

1—CHRIST THE KING (1928), Rev. Michael A. Wittman; Sr. Marietta Rohr, C.S.A., Pastoral Assoc.; Deacon Raymond Daull.
Res.: 1862 Noble Rd., 44112-1636. Tel: 216-851-4388; 216-851-4389; Fax: 216-851-4040.
Catechesis/Religious Program—Students 6.
Convent—16005 Terrace Rd., 44112.

2—ST. PHILOMENA (1902), Rev. Dennis J. Kleinweber; Delores Breckenridge, Pastoral Assoc. In Res., Rev. John R. McCarthy (STU).
Res.: 13824 Euclid Ave., 44112-4299. Tel: 216-541-3540; Fax: 216-541-3545.

EASTLAKE, LAKE CO., ST. JUSTIN MARTYR (1962), Revs. Kevin M. Liebhardt; David R. Ireland; Joanne E. Novak, Pastoral Assoc.
Mailing Address: 35781 Stevens Blvd., 44095-5095. Tel: 440-946-1177; Fax: 440-946-9126.
Administration Center—Tel: 440-946-1177.
Res.: 35701 Stevens Blvd., 44095.
School—35741 Stevens Blvd., 44095. Tel: 440-946-5414; Fax: 440-946-2074. Sr. Mary Quinlan, S.N.D., Prin. Sisters of Notre Dame 2; Lay Teachers 15; Students 263.
Catechesis/Religious Program—Students 440.
Convent—35711 Stevens Blvd., 44095. Tel: 440-946-1013.

ELYRIA TOWNSHIP, LORAIN CO., ST. VINCENT DE PAUL (1949), Revs. James R. Ols; Liam J. Kitt, Pastor Emeritus; Deacons John K. Slatcoff; Donald M. Jankowski.
Res.: 41295 N. Ridge Rd., 44035-1098. Tel: 440-324-4212; 440-277-5285; Fax: 440-324-2892.
School—41315 N. Ridge Rd., 44035-1098. Tel: 440-277-6208; Fax: 440-324-9552. Mrs. Margaret Malenich, Prin. Lay Teachers 13; Students 218.
Catechesis/Religious Program—Students 258.

ELYRIA, LORAIN CO.

1—ST. AGNES (1914), Rev. Albert A. Krupp.
611 Lake Ave., 44035-3541. Tel: 440-322-5622; Fax: 440-322-0251.
Catechesis/Religious Program—Tel: 440-366-5999. Students 53.

2—HOLY CROSS (1922), (Polish), Rev. James D. Schorr, Admin.
Church & Res.: 1417 West Ave., 44035-7337. Tel: 440-323-1022; Fax: 440-323-8277.
Catechesis/Religious Program—Students 30.

3—ST. JUDE (1943), Revs. Frank P. Kosem; Edward J. Smith; Sr. Jennifer Kramer, S.N.D., Pastoral Assoc.; Deacon Patrick J. Humphrey.
Res.: 590 Poplar St., 44035-3999. Tel: 440-366-5711; 440-366-6052; Fax: 440-366-1916.
School—594 Poplar St., 44035. Tel: 440-366-1681; Fax: 440-366-5238. Sr. Mary Berigan, S.N.D., Prin. Lay Teachers 26; Students 497.
Catechesis/Religious Program—Students 335.
Convent—342 Longford, 44035. Tel: 440-366-1551.

4—ST. MARY (1845), [CEM] Revs. Joseph C. Weigand; Patrick J. Shields; Edmund Goldbach, O.F.M.Conv. (GR); Deacons Frank A. Humphrey III; Clement G. Klingshirn Jr.
Res.: 320 Middle Ave., 44035-5796. Tel: 440-323-5530; 440-323-5539; Fax: 440-322-2329.
School—237 Fourth St., 44035. Tel: 440-322-2808; Fax: 440-323-0886. Mr. Fred A. Visci, Prin. Lay Teachers 23 Students 334.
Catechesis/Religious Program—Tel: 440-322-3054. Students 230.
Convent—255 Fourth St., 44035-5796. Tel: 440-322-1423.

5—SACRED HEART OF JESUS (1922), (Hungarian), Unassigned. Sr. Marietta Starrie, C.S.J., Co-Parish Coord.; Deacon Edward R. Dillon, Co-Parish Coord.
Res.: P.O. Box 417, 44036-0417. Tel: 440-323-3382; Fax: 440-323-1434.
Church: 162 Irondale St., 44036.
Catechesis/Religious Program—Students 80.

EUCLID, CUYAHOGA CO.

1—ST. CHRISTINE (1925), Rev. Patrick Henry, Admin.
Res.: 840 E. 222nd St., 44123-3317. Tel: 216-261-1410; 216-261-6210; 216-261-6144; 216-261-6383; Fax: 216-261-9039.
School—860 E. 222nd St., 44123. Tel: 216-731-6244; Fax: 216-261-6003. Mrs. Mary Benns, Prin. Lay Teachers 13; Students 188.
Catechesis/Religious Program—Students 71.

2—ST. FELICITAS (1950), Revs. Richard J. Bober, Pastoral Team Coord.; Dennis J. Kristancic; Deacon Thomas B. deHaas Jr.; MaryBeth Muehle, Pastoral Team.
Res.: 140 Richmond Rd., 44143-1299. Tel: 216-289-0770; Fax: 216-289-0740.
School—Tel: 216-261-1240; Fax: 216-261-5843. Anne Marie Woyma, Prin. Lay Teachers 24; Students 462.
Catechesis/Religious Program—Students 201.

3—HOLY CROSS (1924), Revs. John P. McNulty; William G. Bouhall; Sr. Kathleen Flannery, O.S.U., Pastoral Assoc.; Deacons Jerome B. Vrabel, Pastoral Assoc.; James Croniger, Pastoral Assoc.
Res.: 19951 Lake Shore Blvd., 44119-1066. Tel: 216-486-0850; 216-486-0853; Fax: 216-486-0851.
Church: Lake Shore Blvd. & E. 200th St., 44119.
School—175 E. 200th St., 44119. Tel: 216-481-6824; Fax: 216-481-9841. Patricia Patterson, Prin. Ursuline Nuns of Cleveland 2; Lay Teachers 19; Students 434.
Catechesis/Religious Program—Students 137.
Convent—177 E. 201st St., 44123. Tel: 216-486-0088.

4—ST. PAUL (1860), [CEM] Rev. Francis C. Mulvanity; Deacon Louis G. Pecek, Ph.D.; Barbara Pallo, Pastoral Assoc. In Res., Rev. William M. Jerse.
Res.: 1231 Chardon Rd., 44117-1192. Tel: 216-531-0900; 216-531-0901; Fax: 216-531-5117.
School—1200 E. 200th St., 44117. Tel: 216-481-6060; Fax: 216-481-0919. Mrs. Mary Petelin, Prin. Lay Teachers 13; Students 148.
Catechesis/Religious Program—Students 26.
Convent—1050 E. 200th St., 44117. Tel: 216-531-9178.

5—ST. ROBERT BELLARMINE (1950), Rev. Dennis M. McNeil.
Res.: 23802 Lake Shore Blvd., 44123-1200. Tel: 216-731-2606; 216-731-2607; Fax: 216-731-2607.
School—Tel: 216-731-2108; Fax: 216-731-2109. Mary M. Pittinger, Prin. Lay Teachers 13; Students 199.

6—ST. WILLIAM (1946), Revs. Leonard G. Obloy; David G. Baugh, Pastor Emeritus (Retired); James T. Klein; Sr. Irene Charette, O.S.U., Pastoral Assoc. In Res., Rev. Jerome A. Lukachinsky (Retired).
Res.: 367 E. 260th St., 44132-1495. Tel: 216-731-1515; Fax: 216-731-7611.
School—351 E. 260th St., 44132. Tel: 216-731-3060; Fax: 216-731-0300. Mary Heramb, Prin. Lay Teachers 18; Students 266.
Catechesis/Religious Program—Students 89.
Convent—321 E. 260th St., 44132. Tel: 216-731-5645.

FAIRPORT HARBOR, LAKE CO., ST. ANTHONY OF PADUA (1887), Rev. Peter M. Mihalec; Deacon John T. Wenzel; Dorothy M. Trepal, Pastoral Assoc.
Res.: 316 Fifth St., 44077-5696. Tel: 440-354-4525; Fax: 440-354-8313.
Catechesis/Religious Program—Students 79.

FAIRVIEW PARK, CUYAHOGA CO., ST. ANGELA MERICI (1923), Revs. Douglas M. Proehl; Curtis L. Kondik; Anthony Iezzi, Ph.D., Pastoral Assoc.; Laura Campbell, Pastoral Assoc.; Carole Dlouhy, Pastoral Assoc. In Res., Rev. David L. Mami.
Res.: 20970 Lorain Rd., 44126-2096. Tel: 440-333-2133; Fax: 440-333-8061.
School—20830 Lorain Rd., 44126. Tel: 440-333-2126; Fax: 440-333-8480. Susan Jelenic, Prin. Lay Teachers 31; Students 593.
Catechesis/Religious Program—Tel: 216-333-2133. Students 405.

GARFIELD HEIGHTS, CUYAHOGA CO.

1—ST. MONICA (1952), Revs. Donald P. Oleksiak; William A. Smith; Deacon Ralph W. Netzband, Pastoral Team; Sisters Helen Weis, S.J.S.M., Pastoral Team; Mary Dorothy Tecca, C.S.A., Pastoral Assoc.
Res.: 13623 Rockside Rd., 44125-5197. Tel: 216-662-8685; 216-662-8686; 216-662-8687; 216-662-8625; Fax: 216-662-1245.
School—13633 Rockside Rd., 44125. Tel: 216-662-9380; Fax: 216-662-3137. Sr. Helen Weis, S.J.S.M., Prin. Sisters of St. Joseph Third Order of St. Francis 5; Lay Teachers 17; Students 520.
Catechesis/Religious Program—Students 196.
Convent—Tel: 216-581-0810.

2—SS. PETER AND PAUL (1927), (Polish), Revs. Theodore Marszal; Anthony W. Zepp, Pastor Emeritus; Marion Bendyk.
Res.: 4750 Turney Rd., 44125-1448. Tel: 216-429-1515; 216-429-1516; Fax: 216-429-1889.
School—4740 Turney Rd., 44125. Tel: 216-271-6564; Fax: 216-271-0504. Mrs. Mary Tetlak, Prin. Lay Teachers 14; Students 234.
Catechesis/Religious Program—Students 82.
Convent—Tel: 216-429-2666.

3—ST. THERESE (1927), Revs. Norman A. Gajdzinski; Eric Orzech; Deacons Frank Tatulinski; Lawrence Cermak.
Res.: 5276 E. 105th St., 44125-2698. Tel: 216-581-2852; 216-581-2853; Fax: 216-581-5091.
School—10608 Penfield Ave., 44125. Tel: 216-581-3080; Fax: 216-581-3031. Sr. Jane Morgan, O.S.U., Prin. Ursuline Nuns of Cleveland 2; Lay Teachers 15; Students 233.
Catechesis/Religious Program—Students 174.

4—ST. TIMOTHY (1923), Rev. John J. Wright; Deacon Joseph H. Newman; Sr. Peter Claver Walter, S.N.D., Pastoral Assoc.
Res.: 4341 E. 131st St., 44105-5563. Tel: 216-581-0981; 216-581-0982; Fax: 216-581-8222.
School—Archbishop James P. Lyke Elementary School, Tel: 216-581-3517; Fax: 216-581-6204. See Elementary Schools, Parochial and Diocesan under Institutions Located in the Diocese.

GATES MILLS, CUYAHOGA CO., ST. FRANCIS OF ASSISI (1943), Revs. James L. Caddy; Sylvester W. Fridrich, Pastor Emeritus (Retired); Zachary M. Kawalec; Deacons Leo F. McNulty; William T. Elwood; Maureen Dowd, Pastoral Assoc.
Res.: 6850 Mayfield Rd., 44040-9635. Tel: 440-461-0066; Fax: 440-461-9053.
School—Tel: 440-442-7450; Fax: 440-446-1132. Mr.

William DiBacco, Prin. Religious 1; Lay Teachers 23; Students 454.
Catechesis/Religious Program—Students 321.

GRAFTON, LORAIN CO.
1—ASSUMPTION (1894), (Polish), Rev. John P. Seabold.
Res.: 1033 Elm St., 44044-1449. Tel: 440-926-2364.
Catechesis/Religious Program—Students 112.
2—IMMACULATE CONCEPTION (1835), [CEM] Revs. Robert R. Vieweg, Pastor Emeritus; John P. Seabold.
Res.: 708 Erie St., 44044-1308. Tel: 440-926-2268.
Catechesis/Religious Program—Students 220.

HIGHLAND HEIGHTS, CUYAHOGA CO., ST. PASCHAL BAYLON (1953), Revs. Michael J. Arkins, S.S.S.; Donald J. Jette, S.S.S.; Roger Bourgeois, S.S.S.; Thomas J. Smithson, S.S.S.; Mrs. Annette Cicatelli, Pastoral Assoc.; Deacons Robert J. Bowers; Joseph Bourgeois. In Res., Rev. Scott Haig, S.S.S.
Res.: 5384 Wilson Mills Rd., 44143-3092. Tel: 440-442-3410; 440-449-7532; 440-449-7758; Fax: 440-442-2001.
School—5360 Wilson Mills Rd., 44143. Tel: 440-442-6766; Fax: 440-446-9037. Mr. John V. Bednar, Prin. Lay Teachers 29; Students 490.
Catechesis/Religious Program—Students 195.

HINCKLEY, MEDINA CO., OUR LADY OF GRACE (1965), Rev. William P. O'Neill. In Res., Rev. John T. McDonough (Retired).
Res.: 1088 Ridge Rd., 44233-9602. Tel: 330-278-4121; Fax: 330-278-2834.
Catechesis/Religious Program—Students 312.

HUDSON, SUMMIT CO., ST. MARY (1860), [CEM] Revs. Edward J. Kordas; Damian J. Ference; Sr. Barbara Einloth, S.C., Pastoral Assoc.; Rose Gordyan, Pastoral Assoc.
Res.: 340 N. Main St,, 44236-2242. Tel: 330-653-8118; 330-656-2558; 330-463-5753 (Cleveland); 330-650-0722 (Akron); Fax: 330-463-5759.
Church: 340 N. Main St., 44236.
Catechesis/Religious Program—Students 1,732.

INDEPENDENCE, CUYAHOGA CO., ST. MICHAEL (1851), [CEM] Revs. Carl L. D'Agostino; Adelbert J. Gassert, Pastor Emeritus (Retired); Peter Colletti; Deacons Robert Weniger; James Vincent.
Res.: 6912 Chestnut Rd., 44131-3399. Tel: 216-524-1394; 216-524-1395; Fax: 216-328-8537.
Church: Brecksville Rd., 44131.
School—6906 Chestnut Rd., 44131. Tel: 216-524-6405; Fax: 216-524-7538. Sr. Carol Marek, S.N.D., Prin. Sisters of Notre Dame 2; Lay Teachers 25; Students 417.
Catechesis/Religious Program—Tel: 216-447-4406. Students 351.
Convent—6800 Chestnut Rd., 44131-3399. Tel: 216-447-4406.

KIRTLAND, LAKE CO., DIVINE WORD (1977), Rev. Norman N. Smith; Deacon Carl M. Varga, Pastoral Assoc. In Res., Revs. John J. Kinkopf (Retired); Joseph McMahon.
Res.: 8100 Eagle Rd., 44094-9714. Tel: 440-256-1412; 440-256-1413; 440-256-1417; Fax: 440-256-4929.
School—Peaceful Children Montessori, Tel: 440-256-1976; Fax: 440-256-4370. Mary Potosky, Prin. Lay Teachers 7; Students 90.
Catechesis/Religious Program—Students 254.

LAKEWOOD, CUYAHOGA CO.
1—ST. CLEMENT (1922), Rev. Alfred H. Winters; Sr. Mary Jane Masterson, C.S.J., Pastoral Assoc.
Res.: 2022 Lincoln Ave., 44107-6099. Tel: 216-226-5116; Fax: 216-226-5117.
Church: Madison & Lincoln Aves., 44107.
School—14505 Madison Ave., 44107. Tel: 216-226-1942; Fax: 216-226-9459. Barbara Pollock, Prin.; Susan Seeds, Prin. Lay Teachers 14; Students 146.
Catechesis/Religious Program—Students 150.
Convent—14505 Madison Ave., 44107.
2—SS. CYRIL AND METHODIUS (1902), (Slovak), Revs. Richard J. Ondreyka, M.S., Pastor Emeritus (Retired); Jerome J. Duke.
Res.: 12608 Madison Ave., 44107-4997. Tel: 216-521-7288; 216-521-9091; Fax: 216-521-7005.
Church: Madison Ave. & Lakewood Ave., 44107.
School—1639 Alameda Ave., 44107. Tel: 216-221-9409. Carol Shakarian, Prin. Lay Teachers 12; Students 144.
Catechesis/Religious Program—Tel: 216-221-9402. Students 78.
Convent—1635 Alameda Ave., 44107. Tel: 216-221-3164.
3—ST. HEDWIG (1905), (Polish), Rev. John J. Bryk.
Res.: 12903 Madison Ave., 44107-4939. Tel: 216-521-5086; 216-521-4463.
Church: 12905 Madison Ave., 44107-4939.
4—ST. JAMES (1908), Revs. John J. Weigand; Thomas J. Behrend; Deacon James R. Stewart; Miss Kathryn Haag, Pastoral Assoc. In Res., Rev. Thomas P. Kowatch.
Res.: 17514 Detroit Ave., 44107-3498. Tel: 216-221-0233; Fax: 216-221-2431.
Church: Detroit & Granger Ave., 44107.
School—17415 Northwood Ave., 44107. Tel: 216-221-1225; Fax: 216-529-7950. Miss Sheila Mannix, Prin. Lay Teachers 19; Students 247.
Catechesis/Religious Program—Students 254.
5—ST. LUKE (1922), Revs. Francis P. Walsh; John W. Krasen; Sr. Karen Shimko, S.S.J.-T.O.S.F., Pastoral Assoc.; Deacon David A. Streeter. In Res., Rev. Ralph E. Wiatrowski.
Res.: 1212 Bunts Rd., 44107-2699. Tel: 216-521-0184; 216-521-0185; 216-521-0186; Fax: 216-521-9360.
School—13889 Clifton Blvd., 44107. Tel: 216-521-7033; Fax: 216-521-9127. Mr. Mark Dudek, Prin. Lay Teachers 20; Students 286.
Catechesis/Religious Program—Students 172.

LITCHFIELD, MEDINA CO., OUR LADY HELP OF CHRISTIANS PARISH (1976), Rev. Ronald J. Bryda, Coord. Pastoral Team; Deacons Michael F. Jervis Sr.; John M. Buda; Revs. Edward F. Weist, Pastoral Team; Daniel R. Fickes, Pastoral Team; Sisters Margaret Duffy, O.S.U., Pastoral Team; Mary Lou Misciasci, C.S.J., Pastoral Team; Sandra J. Lynn, Pastoral Team.
Administration Center—9608 Norwalk Rd., 44253-9598. Tel: 330-722-1180; 330-273-1500 (Cleveland); Fax: 330-723-5891.
Catechesis/Religious Program—Students 278.
Convent—9608 Norwalk Rd., 44253.
Mission—Jesus the Christ Child, Medina Co.
Mission—Jesus Divine Redeemer Chippewa Lake, Medina Co.
Mission—Jesus the Good Shepherd 356 N. Main St., Nova-Savannah, Medina Co.
Mission—Jesus Emmanuel 60 High St., Seville-Creston, Medina Co.
Mission—Jesus Our Savior Spencer, Medina Co.
Mission—Jesus Our Teacher Lodi, Medina Co.

LODI, MEDINA CO., JESUS OUR TEACHER (1976), Attended by, Our Lady Help of Christians, Litchfield.

LORAIN, LORAIN CO.
1—ST. ANTHONY OF PADUA (1923), Rev. Joseph West, O.F.M.Conv. In Res., Rev. Charles Henkle, O.F.M-.Conv.; Deacons Dennis Moses, O.F.M. Conv.; James K. Debrason.
Res.: 1305 E. Erie Ave., 44052-2299. Tel: 440-288-0106; 440-288-0107; Fax: 440-288-0143.
School—1339 E. Erie Ave., 44052. Tel: 440-288-2155; Fax: 440-288-2159. Robert Halloway, Prin. Lay Teachers 14; Students 232.
Catechesis/Religious Program—Students 96.
2—SS. CYRIL AND METHODIUS (1905), (Slovenian), Rev. Paul Krajnik.
Res.: 1709 E. 31st St., 44055-1719. Tel: 440-277-8286.
Church: 1705 E. 31st St., 44055.
Catechesis/Religious Program—Students 4.
3—HOLY TRINITY (1906), (Slovak), Rev. David A. Novak.
Res.: 2428 Elyria Ave., 44055-1366. Tel: 440-244-1253; 440-244-2418.
Catechesis/Religious Program—Students 4.
4—ST. JOHN THE BAPTIST (1900), Revs. Thomas V. Rath, Pastor Emeritus (Retired); Thomas R. Smith.
Res.: 2143 Homewood Dr., 44055-2799. Tel: 440-277-7266.
Catechesis/Religious Program—Students 76.
5—ST. JOSEPH (1896), (German), Rev. Kevin C. Shemuga; Deacon Luis Maldonado, Pastoral Admin.
Res.: 317 W. 15th St., 44052-3488. Tel: 440-244-2179.
Church: Reid Ave. & 15th St., 44052.
Catechesis/Religious Program—Students 11.
6—ST. LADISLAUS (1890), (Hungarian), Rev. James P. Schmitz.
Res.: 1412 E. 29th St., 44055-1696. Tel: 440-277-8187.
7—ST. MARY (1873), Revs. Daniel O. Divis; John J. Kline, Pastor Emeritus (Retired); Mrs. Patricia Shullick, Pastoral Assoc.
Res.: 309 Seventh St., 44052-1879. Tel: 440-245-5283; Fax: 440-246-0804.
School—307 Seventh St., 44052. Tel: 440-244-1697; Fax: 440-244-3423. Jane Bauman, Prin. Lay Teachers 13; Students 161.
Administration Center—309 Seventh St., 44052.
Catechesis/Religious Program—Students 36.
8—NATIVITY OF THE BLESSED VIRGIN MARY (1898), (Polish), Rev. Robert J. Glepko; Deacon Robert J. Dybo.
Res.: 418 W. 15th St., 44052-3597. Tel: 440-244-9090; 216-621-6445 (Cleveland); Fax: 440-244-0421.
Church: 1454 Lexington Ave., 44052.
9—ST. PETER (1909), Revs. Kenneth J. Wolnowski; David G. Woost; Deacon Ralph Krupp.
Res.: 3655 Oberlin Ave., 44053-2759. Tel: 440-282-9103; 440-282-9104; 440-282-8104; 440-892-8641 (Cleveland); Fax: 440-282-9490.
School—3601 Oberlin Ave., 44053. Tel: 440-282-9909; Fax: 440-282-9320. Ms. Emily Fabanich, Prin. Lay Teachers 38; Students 506.
Catechesis/Religious Program—Students 233.
Convent—3651 Oberlin Ave., 44053. Tel: 440-282-2378.
10—SACRED HEART CHAPEL (1952), (Hispanic), Rev. William A. Thaden; Sr. Theresa Stegman, C.D.P., Pastoral Assoc.; Deacons Tomas Badillo; Jose A. Flores; Carlos Rivera; Jose A. DeGracia; Jose Luis Piniero; Juan Ortiz.
Mailing Address: 4301 Pearl Ave., 44055-2634.
Res.: 3921 Seneca Ave., 44055. Tel: 440-277-7231; 440-277-7232; 440-277-7379 (Rectory); Fax: 440-277-4886.
Church: 4301 Pearl Ave., 44055.
Catechesis/Religious Program—Students 386.
11—ST. STANISLAUS (1908), (Polish), Rev. Kevin C. Shemuga; Deacon William E. Schill.
Res.: 2702 Elyria Ave., 44055-1337. Tel: 440-244-4185; Fax: 440-244-4212.
Catechesis/Religious Program—Tel: 440-244-4580. Students 37.
12—ST. VITUS (1922), (Croatian), Rev. Simon J. Nekic.
Res.: 1785 E. 32nd St., 44055-1721. Tel: 440-277-8210.
Catechesis/Religious Program—Students 7.

LOUDONVILLE, ASHLAND CO., ST. PETER (1870), [CEM] Rev. Kevin M. Conroy.
Res.: 132 N. Wood St., 44842-1235. Tel: 419-994-4396; Fax: 419-994-5263.
Catechesis/Religious Program—Tel: 419-994-3329. Students 84.

LYNDHURST, CUYAHOGA CO., ST. CLARE (1944), Revs. Stanley J. Klasinski; Edward J. Janoch; Deacons Ross C. DeJohn Sr.; Robert J. Matoney Jr.
Res.: 5659 Mayfield Rd., 44124-2981. Tel: 440-449-4242; Fax: 440-646-9648.
School—5655 Mayfield Rd., 44124. Fax: 440-449-1497. Miss Ruth Downey, Prin. Lay Teachers 19; Students 291.
Catechesis/Religious Program—Students 397.

MACEDONIA, SUMMIT CO., OUR LADY OF GUADALUPE (1967), Revs. David R. Trask; Lloyd J. Boymer, Pastor Emeritus (Retired); Deacon Mario Vinciguerra; Mrs. Nancy Freibott, Pastoral Assoc.
Res.: 9080 Shepard Rd., 44056-1450. Tel: 330-468-2194; Fax: 330-468-2196.
Catechesis/Religious Program—Students 223.

MADISON, LAKE CO., IMMACULATE CONCEPTION (1863), Deacons Thomas G. Hupertz; Kenneth C. Meade; Richard F. Kuhlman; Johnna Kopczak, Parish Life Coord. In Res., Rev. Wilfred T. Smith.
Res.: 2846 Hubbard Rd., 44057-2998. Tel: 440-428-5164; 440-428-5165; 440-428-3988; 440-975-0729 (Cleveland); Fax: 440-428-3075.
Catechesis/Religious Program—Students 350.

MAPLE HEIGHTS, CUYAHOGA CO.
1—ST. MARTIN OF TOURS (1960), [CEM] Rev. Luigi C. Miola; Deacons John R. Bender; Thaddeus C. Bizon Jr.
Res.: 14600 Turney Rd., 44137-4788. Tel: 216-475-4300; 216-475-4301; Fax: 216-475-8242.
School—Tel: 216-475-3633; Fax: 216-475-2484. Miss Mary Mackin, Prin. Lay Teachers 14; Students 193.
Catechesis/Religious Program—Students 98.
2—ST. WENCESLAS (1923), Rev. Clyde K. Foster; Rev. Msgr. Joseph C. Heruday, Pastor Emeritus (Retired); Deacon Daniel C. Terrion.
Res.: 17825 Libby Rd., 44137-1598. Tel: 216-475-2477; 216-475-2478; 216-475-3304; Fax: 216-475-3304.
Church: Libby Rd. & Cato St., 44137.
School—5254 Arch St., 44137. Tel: 216-662-0180; Fax: 216-662-8101. Mrs. Sharon Vejdovec, Prin. Lay Teachers 14; Students 138.

MEDINA, MEDINA CO.
1—ST. FRANCIS XAVIER (1860), [CEM] Revs. Mark L. Hollis; Stephen K. Brunovsky; Stephen J. Kaminski; Russell G. Rauscher; Deacons Joseph E. Loutzenhiser; James T. Schlund; Daniel E. Norris; Paul Kipfstuhl.
Res.: 606 E. Washington St., 44256-2183. Tel: 330-725-4968; 330-225-3940 (Cleveland); Fax: 330-723-6234.
Church: 600 E. Washington St., 44256.
School—612 E. Washington St., 44256. Tel: 330-725-3345; Fax: 330-721-8626. Sandra Bevec, Prin. St. Felix of Cantalice 1; Lay Teachers 32; Students 535.
Catechesis/Religious Program—Tel: 330-722-7700. Students 935.
2—HOLY MARTYRS (1980), Rev. Robert F. Pfeiffer; Deacon Alfred J. Koch; Mary Frances Ehlinger, Pastoral Assoc.; Suzanne Kozub, Pastoral Assoc.
Res.: 3100 S. Weymouth Rd., 44256-9207. Tel: 330-722-6633; 330-722-8951; 330-273-1188 (Cleveland); Fax: 330-725-2193.
Catechesis/Religious Program—Students 905.

MENTOR, LAKE CO.
1—ST. BEDE THE VENERABLE (1964), Rev. John J. Sullivan; Mrs. Karen J. Roman, Pastoral Assoc.; Deacons Robert P. Ulman, Pastoral Assoc.; John Burke Jr., Pastoral Assoc.; Kenneth Knight, Pastoral Assoc. In Res., Rev. Michael Woost.
Res.: 9114 Lake Shore Blvd., 44060-1697. Tel:

440-257-5544; 440-257-5545; Fax: 440-257-2318.
Catechesis/Religious Program—Tel: 440-257-6988. Students 562.

2—ST. JOHN VIANNEY (1969), Revs. Robert W. Kline, Pastor Emeritus (Retired); Thomas W. Johns; Anthony F. Sejba; John D. Betters; Deacons Wayne W. Snyder; James J. Duffy; Mary Kovach, Pastoral Assoc.
7575 Bellflower Rd., 44060-3997. Tel: 440-943-3445 (Cleveland); 440-255-0600; Fax: 440-255-6482.
School—All Saints of St. John Vianney, Wickliffe, Tel: 440-943-1395; Fax: 440-944-3341. See separate listing under Institutions Located in the Diocese.
Catechesis/Religious Program—Tel: 440-255-7266. Students 872.

3—ST. MARY OF THE ASSUMPTION (1857), Revs. Thomas G. Elsasser; Wilfred T. Smith, Pastor Emeritus; Robert Wenz; Deacon Joseph R. Kovitch.
Res.: 8560 Mentor Ave., 44060-5853. Tel: 440-255-3404; 440-255-3405; 440-942-1774 (Cleveland); Fax: 440-974-8107.
School—8540 Mentor Ave., 44060. Tel: 440-255-9781; Fax: 440-974-8107. Mrs. Candice Konicki, Prin. Lay Teachers 32; Students 456.
Catechesis/Religious Program—Students 364.

MIDDLEBURG HEIGHTS, CUYAHOGA CO., ST. BARTHOLOMEW (1956), Revs. John A. Leahy, Pastor Emeritus (Retired); Leonard M. Bacik; Kenneth J. Jakubowski; Deacon Robert G. Sabol.
Res.: 14865 E. Bagley Rd., 44130-5502. Tel: 440-842-5400; 440-842-5401; Fax: 440-842-2691.
School—Academy of St. Bartholomew, 14875 E. Bagley Rd., 44130-5502. Tel: 440-845-6660; Fax: 440-845-6672. Mrs. Donna Hujarski, Prin. Sisters 1; Lay Teachers 24; Students 525.
Catechesis/Religious Program—Students 278.

MIDDLEFIELD, GEAUGA CO., ST. LUCY (1958), Revs. John T. Burkley, Admin.; Harry S. Winca, Pastor Emeritus; Deacon Gregory C. Frania.
Church & Mailing Address: 16280 Kinsman Rd., 44062-9405. Tel: 440-632-5824; 440-548-8091.
Catechesis/Religious Program—Students 69.

NEWBURY, GEAUGA CO., ST. HELEN (1949), Rev. James G. McPhillips; Deacons Willard Payne; Lawrence Somrack.
Res.: 12060 Kinsman Rd., 44065-9678. Tel: 440-564-5805; 440-338-3358 (Cleveland); Fax: 440-564-7969.
School—Tel: 440-564-7125. Sr. Christin Alfieri, S.N.D., Prin. Sisters of Notre Dame 2; Lay Teachers 14; Students 249.
Catechesis/Religious Program—Students 300.

NORTH OLMSTED, CUYAHOGA CO.

1—ST. BRENDAN (1964), Revs. Cornelius J. Murray; Vincent J. Hawk; Deacon Stanley J. Fulton; Sr. Mary Ann Phillip, O.P., Pastoral Assoc.; Deborah Rayle, Pastoral Assoc.
Church & Mailing Address: 4242 Brendan Ln., 44070-2999.
Res.: 3920 Brendan Ln., 44070. Tel: 440-777-7222; 440-777-7223; Fax: 440-779-7997.
School—Tel: 440-777-8433; Fax: 440-779-7997. Miss Julie Onacila, M.A., Prin. Lay Teachers 14; Students 252.
Catechesis/Religious Program—Students 276.

2—ST. CLARENCE (1978), Revs. Thomas A. Flynn (Retired); Allan R. Laubenthal; Neil P. Kookoothe; Sr. Donna M. Bradesca, O.S.U., D.Min., Pastoral Assoc.; Deacons Wayne A. Bosau; Homer L. Sherman.
Res.: 30106 Lorain Rd., 44070-3986. Tel: 440-734-2414; Fax: 440-734-4255.
Catechesis/Religious Program—Students 530.
Convent—30072 Lorain Rd., 44070. Tel: 440-777-5258.

3—ST. RICHARD (1950), Rev. Charles J. Stollenwerk; Deacon John Zdolshek; Sr. M. Jerome Fitzgerald, S.I.W., Pastoral Assoc.; Mrs. Janet O'Donnell; Mrs. Kathleen Huber, Pastoral Assoc.
Res.: 26855 Lorain Rd., 44070-3260. Tel: 440-777-5050; 440-777-5051; 440-777-5052; Fax: 440-777-3577.
School—Tel: 440-777-2922; Fax: 440-777-7374. Mr. Michael Cappabianca, Prin. Sisters 1; Lay Teachers 26; Students 514.
Catechesis/Religious Program—Students 179.
Convent—5053 Whitethorn Ave., 44070. Tel: 440-777-2168.

NORTH RIDGEVILLE, LORAIN CO.

1—ST. JULIE BILLIART (1978), [JC] Rev. Richard A. Gonser; Deacon John M. Rivera; Maureen Coughlin, Pastoral Assoc. In Res., Rev. Elmer E. Marquard.
Res.: 5545 Opal Dr., 44039-2025. Tel: 440-327-1978; 440-327-1979; Fax: 440-327-1994.
Church: 5500 Lear Nagle Rd., 44039.
Catechesis/Religious Program—Students 166.

2—ST. PETER (1875), [CEM] Rev. Stephen J. Kaminski. In Res., Rev. Thomas J. Hyland, Pastor Emeritus (Retired).
Res.: 35777 Center Ridge Rd., 44039-3097. Tel: 440-327-2201; 440-327-2204; Fax: 440-327-2204.
School—35749 Center Ridge Rd., 44039. Tel: 440-327-3212; Fax: 440-327-6843. Sr. Mary Patricia Vovk, S.N.D., Prin. Sisters of Notre Dame 2; Lay Teachers 13; Students 352.
Catechesis/Religious Program—Students 481.
Convent—7209 Wil-Lou Ln.. Tel: 440-327-8713.

NORTH ROYALTON, CUYAHOGA CO., ST. ALBERT THE GREAT (1959), Revs. John L. Viall; Daniel P. Redmond. In Res., Rev. Albert J. Tesek (Retired); Laura Kuhn, Pastoral Assoc.
Res.: 6667 Wallings Rd., 44133-3067. Tel: 440-237-6760; 440-237-6761; Fax: 440-237-5945.
School—Tel: 440-237-1032; Fax: 440-237-3308. Mr. Thomas Brownfield, Prin. Lay Teachers 36; Students 859.
Catechesis/Religious Program—Students 946.

NORTHFIELD, SUMMIT CO., ST. BARNABAS (1956), Revs. Charles T. Diedrick; G. David Bline; Deacons Gerald Butler; James Hostutler; Marie Mikovsky, Pastoral Assoc.
Res.: 9451 Brandywine Rd., 44067-2499. Tel: 330-467-7959; 330-467-7941; 330-467-6424; Fax: 330-467-6424.
School—9200 Olde Eight Rd., 44067. Tel: 330-467-7921; Fax: 330-468-1926. Miss Beverly Tabacco, Prin. Lay Teachers 37; Students 793.
Catechesis/Religious Program—Students 758.

NORTON, SUMMIT CO., ST. ANDREW THE APOSTLE (1951), Revs. James G. Maloney; John A. Wittreich, Pastor Emeritus (Retired).
Res. & Church: 4022 Johnson Rd., 44203-5998. Tel: 330-825-2617; Fax: 330-825-5309.
Catechesis/Religious Program—Tel: 330-825-8264. Students 177.

OBERLIN, LORAIN CO., SACRED HEART (1880), Revs. William B. Padavick; Robert A. Bonnel, Pastor Emeritus (Retired).
Res.: 410 W. Lorain St., 44074-1002. Tel: 440-774-6791; 440-774-1337; Fax: 440-775-1306.
Catechesis/Religious Program—Students 114.

OLMSTED FALLS, CUYAHOGA CO., ST. MARY OF THE FALLS (1854), [CEM] Revs. Robert J. Cole; Mark S. Ott; Deacons Richard Mueller; Thomas Daw; P. Robert Martin.
Res.: 25615 Bagley Rd., 44138-1915. Tel: 440-235-2222; 440-235-2223; Fax: 440-235-2937.
School—8262 Columbia Rd., 44138-2242. Tel: 440-235-4580; Fax: 440-235-6833. Mrs. Priscilla Shields, Prin. Lay Teachers 13; Students 266.
Catechesis/Religious Program—Tel: 440-235-2808. Students 608.

ORANGE VILLAGE, CUYAHOGA CO., ST. MARGARET OF HUNGARY (1921), (Hungarian), Rev. Ladislaus Rosko.
Res.: 4680 Lander Rd., 44022-1704. Tel: 440-248-2618; 440-248-8148; Fax: 440-248-8706.
Catechesis/Religious Program—Students 11.

ORRVILLE, WAYNE CO., ST. AGNES (1879), Rev. Ronald J. Turek, Admin.
Res.: 541 Spring St., 44667-2414. Tel: 330-682-3606; 330-682-2611.
Church: E. Oak St. & Lake St., 44667.
Catechesis/Religious Program—Students 185.

PAINESVILLE, LAKE CO., ST. MARY (1848), [CEM] Revs. R. Stephen Vellenga; Michael J. Stalla; John T. Ostrowski; Sr. Regina Tevis, V.S.C., Pastoral Assoc.
Res.: 242 N. State St., 44077-4095. Tel: 440-354-4381; 440-354-4382; 440-358-9741; Fax: 440-354-9174.
School—268 N. State St., 44077. Tel: 440-352-9414; Fax: 440-352-8712. Ms. Beverly Moore, Prin. Vincentian Sisters of Charity 1; Lay Teachers 17; Students 228.
Catechesis/Religious Program—Students 533.
Convent—339 Erie St., 44077-4095. Tel: 440-354-3762.

PARKMAN, GEAUGA CO., ST. EDWARD (1928), Revs. John T. Burkley; Harry S. Winca, Pastor Emeritus; Deacon Gregory C. Frania.
Res.: P.O. Box 709, 44080-0709. Tel: 440-548-8091; 440-548-3812.
Church: 16150 Center St., 44080.
Catechesis/Religious Program—Students 50.

PARMA, CUYAHOGA CO.

1—ST. ANTHONY OF PADUA (1959), Revs. Dale W. Staysniak; Thomas G. Woost; Sisters Karen Kellereski, C.S.F.N., Pastoral Assoc.; Roberta Goebel, O.S.U., Pastoral Assoc.; Kathryn Mary O'Brien, O.S.U., Pastoral Assoc.
Res.: 6750 State Rd., 44134-4518. Tel: 440-842-2666; 440-842-2667; 440-842-2668; Fax: 440-845-9549.
School—6800 State Rd., 44134-4632. Tel: 440-845-3444; Fax: 440-884-4548. Mr. Frank M. Kuhar, Prin. Religious 1; Lay Teachers 23; Students 485.
Catechesis/Religious Program—Students 359.
Convent—6834 State Rd., 44134. Tel: 440-842-2211.

2—ST. BRIDGET (1956), Revs. Lawrence J. Bayer; Stephen M. Spisak.
Res.: 5620 Hauserman Rd., 44130-1698. Tel: 440-886-4434; 440-886-4435; Fax: 440-886-4431.
School—Tel: 440-886-1468; Fax: 440-886-5121. Mrs. Karen A. Lamson, Prin. Lay Teachers 21; Students 290.
Catechesis/Religious Program—Students 127.
Convent—

3—ST. CHARLES BORROMEO (1923), Revs. John T. Carlin; Timothy D. Kalista; Joseph M. Koopman; Deacon John A. Talerico; Sr. Denise Marie Vlna, O.S.U., Pastoral Assoc. In Res., Revs. James A. Conry; J. Norman Riley.
Res.: 5891 Ridge Rd., 44129-3642. Tel: 440-884-3030; 440-884-3031; 440-884-3232; Fax: 440-884-5326.
School—7107 Wilber Ave., 44129-3445. Tel: 440-886-5546; Fax: 440-886-1163. Mr. James E. Flynn, Prin. Ursuline Nuns of Cleveland 1; Lay Teachers 31; Students 720.
Catechesis/Religious Program—Students 416.
Convent—6818 Charles Ave., 44129. Tel: 440-886-0390.

4—ST. COLUMBKILLE (1956), Revs. Neil D. O'Connor; Joseph E. Lehane; Michael J. Lanning; Richard A. Evans; Deacons Edward A. Telepak; Paul C. Kutolowski.
Res.: 6740 Broadview Rd., 44134-4898. Tel: 216-524-1987; 216-524-1988; 216-524-1516; Fax: 216-524-9146.
School—6740 Broadview Rd., 44134-4899. Tel: 216-524-4816; Fax: 216-524-4153. Miss Rita Klement, Prin. Lay Teachers 23; Students 569.
Catechesis/Religious Program—Students 380.

5—ST. FRANCIS DE SALES (1931), Revs. Robert L. Hoban; Douglas T Makowski; Deacon Robert J. Piskach.
Res.: 3434 George Ave., 44134-2904. Tel: 440-884-2319; 440-884-2320; 440-884-2321; Fax: 440-884-1661.
Church: State & Snow Rd., 44134.
School—3421 Snow Rd., 44134-2596. Tel: 440-884-2340; Fax: 440-884-8211. Anne Sweeney, Prin. Lay Teachers 18; Students 267.
Catechesis/Religious Program—Students 208.
Convent—3425 Snow Rd., 44134. Tel: 440-884-7242.

6—HOLY FAMILY (1872), [CEM] Revs. James P. Costello; Edward Holland; Kenneth F. Wallace; Edward N. Schwet; James F. Mazanec; Deacons Russell J. Glorioso; Joseph P. Litke.
Res.: 7367 York Rd., 44130-5162. Tel: 440-842-5533; Fax: 440-842-3090.
School—Tel: 440-842-7785; Fax: 440-842-3634. Kathleen Hrutkay, Prin. Lay Teachers 31; Students 503.
Catechesis/Religious Program—Students 390.

7—ST. JOHN BOSCO (1963), Revs. David D. Liberatore; John A. Ocilka; Deacon Roger Polefko.
Res.: 6480 Pearl Rd., Parma Heights, 44130. Tel: 440-886-3500; 440-886-3501; 440-886-3502; Fax: 440-886-0966.
School—6460 Pearl Rd., Parma Heights, 44130. Tel: 440-886-0061; Fax: 440-884-4115. Mrs. Martha K. Jacobs, Prin. Religious 2; Lay Teachers 21; Students 443.
Catechesis/Religious Program—Students 422.
Convent—12213 Denver Dr., 44130. Tel: 216-267-0133.

8—ST. MATTHIAS (1980), Rev. Raymond A. Sutter; Deacon Geza J. Balassy.
Res.: 1200 W. Sprague Rd., 44134-6801. Tel: 440-888-8220; 440-888-8221; Fax: 440-888-8146.
Catechesis/Religious Program—Students 274.

PENINSULA, SUMMIT CO., MOTHER OF SORROWS (1882), Revs. John D. Terzano; Robert W. Donohoe, Pastor Emeritus.
Res.: 6034 S. Locust St., 44264-9726. Tel: 330-657-2631; 330-657-2075; 330-467-5549 (Cleveland Line); Fax: 330-657-2423.
Catechesis/Religious Program—Students 79.

PERRY, LAKE CO., ST. CYPRIAN (1968), Revs. James J. Patton; Anthony F. Alexander, Pastor Emeritus (Retired); Deacons Andrew Novak; Paul Hlabse Sr.; James F. Daley Jr.
Res.: 4223 Middle Ridge Rd., 44081-9794. Tel: 440-259-2344; Fax: 440-259-2255.
Catechesis/Religious Program—Students 373.

RICHFIELD, SUMMIT CO., ST. VICTOR (1964), Revs. Allen F. Corrigan, Admin.; Arthur A. Bacher, Pastor Emeritus.
Church & Res.: 3435 Everett Rd., 44286-0461. Tel: 330-659-6591; 330-659-6321; 330-659-3398; Fax: 330-659-3618.
Catechesis/Religious Program—Students 241.

RITTMAN, WAYNE CO., ST. ANNE (1855), [CEM] Rev. Phillip P. Pritt.
Res.: 139 S. First St., 44270-1492. Tel: 330-927-2941; Fax: 330-927-3002.
Church: E. Ohio & S. First St., 44270.
Catechesis/Religious Program—Students 21.

ROCKY RIVER, CUYAHOGA CO., ST. CHRISTOPHER (1922), Revs. John C. Chlebo; Edward F. Prendergast, Pastor Emeritus (Retired); Richard Bona; Timothy

M. Daw; Mrs. Marianne Betters, Pastoral Assoc.; Ms. Gayle Cilimburg, Pastoral Assoc.
Res.: 20141 Detroit Rd., 44116-2420. Tel: 440-331-4255; 440-331-4256; Fax: 440-331-3885.
School—1610 Lakeview Ave., 44116-2409. Tel: 440-331-3075; Fax: 440-331-0674. Sr. Patricia Twohig, C.S.J., Prin. Sisters 1; Lay Teachers 26; Students 533.
Catechesis/Religious Program—Tel: 440-331-6226. Students 513.

SEVILLE-CRESTON, MEDINA-WOOSTER COUNTIES, JESUS EMMANUEL (1976), Attended by, Our Lady Help of Christians, Litchfield.

SHAKER HEIGHTS, CUYAHOGA CO., ST. DOMINIC (1945), Rev. Thomas G. Fanta; Deacon Robert Matoney Jr.
Res.: 3450 Norwood Rd., 44122-4967. Tel: 216-991-1444; 216-991-1445; Fax: 216-491-0190.
Church: 19000 Van Aken Blvd., 44122.
School—3455 Norwood Rd., 44122-4901. Tel: 216-561-4400; Fax: 216-561-1573. Joan Agresta, Prin. Lay Teachers 17; Students 229.
Catechesis/Religious Program—Students 316.

SHEFFIELD LAKE, LORAIN CO., ST. THOMAS THE APOSTLE (1962), Rev. Stephen L. Shields.
Res.: 521 Harris Rd., 44054-1409. Tel: 440-949-7744; Fax: 440-949-8611.
School—719 Harris Rd., 44054. Tel: 440-949-6275; Fax: 440-949-5183. Ms. Evaristas Maesas, Prin. Lay Teachers 6; Students 76.
Catechesis/Religious Program—Students 162.
Convent—37954 French Creek Rd., 44054. Tel: 440-934-6964.

SHEFFIELD, LORAIN CO., ST. TERESA OF AVILA (1845), [CEM] Revs. Robert J. Franco; Edward J. Luca, Pastor Emeritus.
Church: 1878 Abbe Rd., 44054-2322. Tel: 440-934-4227; Fax: 440-934-4500.
Catechesis/Religious Program—Students 7.

SOLON, CUYAHOGA CO.
1—RESURRECTION OF OUR LORD (1971), Revs. J. Mark Hobson, Coord., Pastoral Team; Louis J. Trivison, Pastor Emeritus (Retired); Sr. Mary Jeanette Brown, S.N.D., Pastoral Team; Ms. Elisabeth Frey, Pastoral Team; Theresa Battaglia, Pastoral Team.
Res. & Church: 32001 Cannon Rd., 44139-1699. Tel: 440-248-0980; 440-248-0981; Fax: 440-248-0992.
Catechesis/Religious Program—Students 363.
2—ST. RITA (1929), Revs. Robert M. Wendelken; Timothy J. Plavac; Sr. Beth Rancourt, S.N.D., Pastoral Assoc.; Deacons Robert Anderson; Robert H. Payne; Mr. Albert E. Leko, Pastoral Assoc.
Res.: 32820 Baldwin Rd., 44139-4098. Tel: 440-248-1350; Fax: 440-248-2094.
School—33200 Baldwin Rd., 44139. Fax: 440-248-9442. Ms. Beverly Moore, Prin. Lay Teachers 26; Students 506.
Catechesis/Religious Program—Students 723.

SOUTH AMHERST, LORAIN CO., NATIVITY OF BLESSED VIRGIN MARY (1933), Rev. Denis L. St. Marie. In Res., Rev. John M. Tezie.
Res.: 333 S. Lake St., 44001-2013. Tel: 440-986-7011; Fax: 440-986-7012.

SOUTH EUCLID, CUYAHOGA CO.
1—ST. GREGORY THE GREAT (1922), Revs. Mark J. Peyton; Francis G. Van Bergen; Deacon John P. Sferry Sr. In Res., Rev. John G. Crawford (Retired).
Res.: 1545 S. Green Rd., 44121-4085. Tel: 216-382-7601; 216-382-7602; 216-382-7603; Fax: 216-382-4992.
School—4478 Rushton Rd., 44121-4084. Tel: 216-381-0363; Fax: 216-382-4604. Miss Lucy Iemmolo, Prin. Sisters of Notre Dame 3; Lay Teachers 33; Students 666.
Catechesis/Religious Program—Students 167.
2—ST. MARGARET MARY (1948), Revs. Richard E. Hudak; Thomas J. Lusoski, Pastor Emeritus (Retired).
Res.: 4217 Bluestone Rd., 44121-3427. Tel: 216-382-4114; 216-382-4115; Fax: 216-381-8730.
Catechesis/Religious Program—Students 81.
Convent—4215 Bluestone Rd., 44121. Tel: 216-381-8787.

SPENCER, MEDINA CO., JESUS OUR SAVIOR (1976), Attended by, Our Lady Help of Christians, Litchfield.

STOW, SUMMIT CO., HOLY FAMILY (1946), Rev. Paul J. Rosing, Admin.; Deacon Philip P. Kamlowsky; Joan Skalak, Pastoral Assoc. In Res., Revs. Michael D. Ausperk; Thomas A. McGovern (Retired).
Res.: 3450 Sycamore Dr., 44224-3999. Tel: 330-688-6411; Fax: 330-689-0186.
Church: 3179 Kent Rd., 44224.
School—3163 Kent Rd., 44224. Tel: 330-688-3816; Fax: 330-688-3474. Mrs. Michelle Noack, Prin. Lay Teachers 36; Students 704.
Catechesis/Religious Program—Students 529.

STRONGSVILLE, CUYAHOGA CO.
1—ST. JOHN NEUMANN (1977), Revs. Robert J. Kraig; Steven H. Breck; Neil G. Walters; Sisters Mary Popoczy, S.N.D., Pastoral Assoc.; Patricia Sylvester, S.N.D., Pastoral Assoc.; Deacon Thomas Grasson; Sandy Zorn, Pastoral Assoc.
Res.: 16271 Pearl Rd., 44136-6095. Tel: 440-238-1770; 440-238-1771; Fax: 440-238-2030.
School—SS. Joseph & John Interparochial, Tel: 440-238-4877; Fax: 440-238-8745. See St. Joseph, Strongsville.
Catechesis/Religious Program—Students 1,254.
2—ST. JOSEPH (1946), Revs. Robert J. Sanson; John P. Miceli; Deacons Pete Moore; Gerald J. Ziemkiewicz.
Res.: 12700 Pearl Rd., 44136-3484. Tel: 440-238-5555; 440-238-5556; 440-238-1038; Fax: 440-238-1059.
School—SS. Joseph and John Interparochial, 12580 Pearl Rd., 44136-3422. Tel: 440-238-4877; Fax: 440-238-8745. Mrs. Darlene Thomas, Prin. Sisters of St. Joseph 1; Lay Teachers 31; Students 747.
Catechesis/Religious Program—Tel: 440-238-5231. Students 716.
Convent—12600 Pearl Rd., 44136. Tel: 440-238-6352.

TALLMADGE, SUMMIT CO., OUR LADY OF VICTORY (1944), Rev. John R. Hengle; Deacon Gregory Perkowski; Diane Hardick, Pastoral Assoc.
Mailing Address: *Administration Center*, 73 North Ave., 44278-1996. Tel: 330-633-3637; 330-633-3672; Fax: 330-633-6978.
Rectory—55 North Ave., 44278.
Church: 105 North Ave., 44278.
Catechesis/Religious Program—Students 464.

THOMPSON, GEAUGA CO., ST. PATRICK (1854), [CEM] Rev. Paul F. Smith; Deacon James T. Martin; Debra S. McCready, Pastoral Assoc.
Res.: 16550 Rock Creek Rd., Rte. 166, 44086-8753. Tel: 440-298-1327; Fax: 440-298-1846.
Catechesis/Religious Program—Students 153.

TWINSBURG, SUMMIT CO., SS. COSMAS AND DAMIAN (1963), Revs. John P. Singler; Robert E. Friedel, Pastor Emeritus (Retired); Deacon Vincent L. Belsito.
Res.: 10419 Ravenna Rd., 44087-1726. Tel: 330-425-8141; 330-425-8142; Fax: 330-963-6597.
Church: 10439 Ravenna Rd., 44087-1726.
School—10429 Ravenna Rd., 44087. Tel: 330-425-4279; Fax: 330-405-2947. Mrs. Susan Kohut, Prin. Religious 1; Lay Teachers 12; Students 162.
Catechesis/Religious Program—Students 518.

UNIONTOWN, SUMMIT CO., QUEEN OF HEAVEN (1964), Revs. David R. Durkee; Robert E. Pahler, Pastor Emeritus (Retired); Deacons Robert Bender; Louis Centric.
Res.: 1800 Steese Rd., 44685-9555. Tel: 330-896-2345; 330-896-3332; Fax: 330-896-8882.
Catechesis/Religious Program—Students 618.

UNIVERSITY HEIGHTS, CUYAHOGA CO., GESU (1926), Revs. James E. Von Tobel, S.J.; Lorn Snow, S.J.; Mark George, S.J.; Deacon James K. O'Donnell. In Res., Rev. Robert J. Welsh, S.J.
Res.: 2470 Miramar Blvd., 44118-3896. Tel: 216-932-0616; 216-932-0617; 216-932-0618; Fax: 216-932-0731.
Church: 2490 Miramar Blvd., 44118.
School—2450 Miramar Blvd., 44118. Tel: 216-932-0620; Fax: 216-932-8326. Sr. Linda Martin, O.S.U., Prin. Sisters of Notre Dame 1; Lay Teachers 40; Students 801.
Catechesis/Religious Program—Students 280.
Convent—4070 Meadowbrook Blvd., 44118. Tel: 216-932-1660.

VALLEY CITY, MEDINA CO., ST. MARTIN OF TOURS (1840), [CEM] Rev. Thomas R. Dunphy.
Res.: 1824 Station Rd., 44280-9522. Tel: 330-483-3808; Fax: 330-483-3848.
Catechesis/Religious Program—Tel: 330-483-5925. Students 367.

WADSWORTH, MEDINA CO., SACRED HEART OF JESUS (1866), [JC] Revs. Joseph L. Labak; James A. Conry, Pastor Emeritus; Deacon Roger N. Klaas; Mrs. Karla Bellinger.
Res.: 260 Broad St., 44281-2113. Tel: 330-336-3049; Fax: 330-336-0143.
School—110 Humbolt Ave., 44281. Tel: 330-334-6272; Fax: 330-334-3236. Mrs. Tracy Arnone, Prin. Vincentian Sisters of Charity 1; Lay Teachers 19; Students 313.
Catechesis/Religious Program—Students 418.
Convent—268 Broad St., 44281. Tel: 330-334-5063.

WARRENSVILLE HEIGHTS, CUYAHOGA CO., ST. JUDE (1945), Rev. Thomas Carolan, O.F.M.; Susan Horvath, Pastoral Assoc. In Res., Bro. Joseph DiSanto, O.F.M.; Rev. Emmanuel Beunen, O.F.M.
Res.: 4761 Richmond Rd., 44128-5986. Tel: 216-292-6600; 216-292-6601; 216-292-6602; Fax: 216-292-0454.
Catechesis/Religious Program—Students 20.

WELLINGTON, LORAIN CO., ST. PATRICK (1851), Rev. James J. Reymann.
Res.: 512 N. Main St., 44090-1198. Tel: 440-647-4375; Fax: 440-647-4675.
Catechesis/Religious Program—Students 300.

WEST SALEM, WAYNE CO., ST. STEPHEN (1952), Rev. Carl A. Uhler; Deacon Peter J. Foradori.
Res.: 44 Britton St., 44287-9318. Tel: 419-853-4946; Fax: 419-853-7037.
Catechesis/Religious Program—Students 130.

WESTLAKE, CUYAHOGA, CO.
1—ST. BERNADETTE (1950), Revs. Thomas L. Weber; Robert A. Lorkowski; Mrs. Diane Portorreal, Pastoral Assoc.; Mrs. Judy Head, Pastoral Assoc.; Mrs. Christine Krysiak, Pastoral Assoc.
Res.: 2256 Clague Rd., 44145-4328. Tel: 440-734-1300; 440-734-1301; 440-734-1302; 440-734-3220; Fax: 440-734-1584.
School—2300 Clague Rd., 44145. Tel: 440-734-7717; Fax: 440-734-9198. Denise King, Prin. Religious 1; Lay Teachers 25; Students 457.
Catechesis/Religious Program—Students 493.
2—ST. LADISLAS (1973), Revs. Donald E. Snyder; Thomas F. Cullen, Pastor Emeritus (Retired); Deacons David L. Kinzel, Pastoral Assoc.; William Gorman, Pastoral Assoc.; Robert C. Hertl, Pastoral Assoc.; Coletta Fratus, Pastoral Assoc. In Res., Most Rev. A. James Quinn.
Res. & Church Address: 2345 Bassett Rd., 44145-2999. Tel: 440-835-2300; Fax: 440-835-5895.
Catechesis/Religious Program—Students 422.

WICKLIFFE, LAKE CO., OUR LADY OF MOUNT CARMEL (1921), Revs. David L. McCafferty; Joseph Cappelletti; Michael K. Gurnick; Sr. Rosemary Diba, V.S.C., Pastoral Assoc.; Deacon John W. Strmac. In Res., Revs. John M. Richards; David G. Baugh (Retired).
Res.: 1730 Mount Carmel Dr., 44092-1896. Tel: 440-585-0700; Fax: 440-585-0870.
Church: 29850 Euclid Ave., 44092.
School—29840 Euclid Ave., 44092. Tel: 440-585-0800; Fax: 440-585-9391. Susan Pohly, Prin. Lay Teachers 22; Students 312.
Catechesis/Religious Program—Students 195.

WILLOUGHBY HILLS, LAKE CO., ST. NOEL (1980), Rev. George Smiga; Alice M. Hinkel, Pastoral Assoc.; Anthony Camino, Pastoral Assoc.
Res.: 35200 Chardon Rd., 44094-9193. Tel: 440-946-0887; Fax: 440-946-4331.
Catechesis/Religious Program—Mrs. Marianne Slattery, D.R.E. Students 354.

WILLOUGHBY, LAKE CO., IMMACULATE CONCEPTION (1866), Revs. Francis D. Curran; Louis A. Pizmoht.
Res.: 37935 Wright St., 44094-5899. Tel: 440-942-4500; Fax: 440-942-1540.
School—37940 Euclid Ave., 44094-5997. Tel: 440-942-2121; Fax: 440-942-6766. Mrs. Rosalie A. Lewis, Prin. Ursuline Nuns of Cleveland 1; Lay Teachers 22; Students 339.
Catechesis/Religious Program—Students 281.

WILLOWICK, LAKE CO., ST. MARY MAGDALENE (1949), Revs. Ronald Wearsch, Pastoral Team; Theodore Lucas, Pastoral Team; Sr. Joan Franklin, O.P., Pastoral Team; Deacon Carl Toomey, Pastoral Team; Darlene Bednarz, Pastoral Team.
Res.: 460 East 321 St., 44095-3663. Tel: 440-943-2133; Fax: 440-943-3780.
Church: 32114 Vine St., 44095.
School—Tel: 440-944-7222; Fax: 440-944-8416. Ms. Judy Nakasian, Prin. Lay Teachers 17; Students 293.
Catechesis/Religious Program—Tel: 440-944-2523. Students 526.
Convent—32010 Vine St., 44095. Tel: 440-944-1134.

WOOSTER, WAYNE CO., ST. MARY OF THE IMMACULATE CONCEPTION (1846), [CEM] Revs. John J. Mueller, Pastor Emeritus; Stephen P. Moran; Deacon Bernard E. Hosfeld, Parish Life Coord.; Mrs. Jacquelynn Lee, Pastoral Assoc.
Res.: 527 Beall Ave., P.O. Box 109, 44691-0109. Tel: 330-264-8824; 330-264-8822; Fax: 330-262-4633.
Church: 527 Beall Ave., 44691.
School—535 E. Bowman St., P.O. Box 109, 44691. Tel: 330-262-8671; Fax: 330-262-0990. Cathleen Mark, Prin. Lay Teachers 14; Students 222.
Catechesis/Religious Program—Students 350.

Cleveland Diocesan Mission

EL SALVADOR, C.A.. *Casa Parroquial Inmaculada Concepcion*. Rev. Richard C. Antall, Carol Savage. La Libertad dept La Libertad El Salvador, Central America.
Casa Parroquial San Pedro Teotepeque. Rev. John D. King, Sr. Mary Lou Tadsen, O.S.U. La Libertad El Salvador, Central America.
Casa Parroquial Santo Domino. Rev. Robert J. Reidy, Judith Arzuaga. Chiltiupan, La Libertad El Salvador, Central America.
The Catholic Center. Rev. Denis L. St. Marie, Dir., Society for the Propagation of the Faith.
Nuestra Senora de Guadalupe. Rev. Joseph H. Callahan. Chirilagua Depto San Miguel El Salvador, Central America.

Chaplains of Public Institutions

CLEVELAND. *Airport, Cleveland Hopkins International*. Deacon Charles Doerpers. Tel: 216-433-0411.
Cleveland Clinic Foundation. Revs. William Young,

S.S.S. Tel: 440-442-6311, Joseph S. Mecir. Tel: 216-341-2828.
Cleveland House of Correction. Rev. Emmanuel Beunen, O.F.M. Tel: 216-292-6602.
Cuyahoga County Detention Home. Rev. James P. O'Donnell. Tel: 216-566-9953.
Cuyahoga County Jail. Deacon Martin Thiel. Tel: 216-351-8802.
Cuyahoga Hills Boys School. Rev. James Masek. Tel: 216-641-2829.
Deaconess Hospital. Rev. Norbert Oloya Atimnedi, A.J., Holy Name. Tel: 216-271-4242.
Euclid Hospital, Tel: 216-481-8200. Rev. Joseph A. Goebel (Retired). Tel: 216-486-0850.
Fairview General Hospital. Rev. John F. Lyons, Our Lady of Angels. Tel: 216-252-2332.
Grace Hospital, Tel: 216-781-5530. Attended from St. Augustine.
Health Hill Hospital for Children, Tel: 216-721-5300. Attended from St. Andrew Abbey.
Hillcrest Hospital, Tel: 216-461-0066. Attended from St. Francis of Assisi.
Huron Road Hospital, Tel: 216-541-3540. Attended by St. Philomena.
Kaiser Foundation Hospital, Snow Rd., 44129. Tel: 216-886-4434. Attended from St. Bridget.
Lakewood Hospital, Tel: 216-226-5116. Rev. Thomas P. Kowatch.
Lutheran Medical Center. Rev. Michael Donovon, O. de M. Tel: 216-961-8331.
Metro Health Medical Center & Rehabilitation Center. Rev. Arthur Snedeker, Chap. Tel: 216-781-8277. (Hospital)
Metzenbaum Children's Center, Tel: 216-781-5330. Attended from St. Augustine.
St. Michael Hospital. Rev. Norbert Oloya Atimnedi, A.J.
Northcoast Behavioral Healthcare System North Campus. Rev. Gary Chmura. Tel: 216-421-4211.
Northeast Pre Release Center. Rev. James O'Donnell. Tel: 216-566-9953.
Parma Community Hospital. Rev. James R. Semonin. Tel: 216-843-8781.
Rainbow Hospital. (See University Hospitals)
Richmond Heights Hospital, Tel: 216-289-0770. Attended from St. Felicitas.
South Pointe Hospital. Attended from St. Jude. Tel: 216-292-6602
SouthWest General Hospital. Rev. Dismas Boeff. Tel: 216-433-0696.
University Hospitals. Rev. William Severt. Tel: 216-941-6808.
University Hospitals Bedford Medical Center. Attended from St. Pius X. Tel: 440-232-8166
Veterans Administration Hospitals, Brecksville V.A., 1000 Brecksville Rd., 44141. Tel: 440-526-3030, Ext. 6265. Revs. John E. Bolan, C.PP.S., Chap., Robert Chukwu. Tel: 440-232-9393, Joseph Rodak, C.PP.S. (CIN), 1000 Brecksville Rd., Brecksville, 44141. Tel: 440-582-1194, Jose Bengco. Tel: 440-526-2431, David Mani. Tel: 440-333-2133.
Cleveland V.A., 10701 East Blvd., 44106. Tel: 216-791-3800, Ext. 305. Rev. Joseph Rodak, C.PP.S. (CIN). Tel: 440-582-1194.

AKRON. *Akron City Hospital*. Rev. James J. Berardi. Tel: 330-535-4141.
Akron General Hospital. Rev. Robert E. Clancy. Tel: 330-434-4348.
Edwin C. Shaw Hospital, Tel: 440-669-5086. Attended from Nativity of the Lord Jesus.
Summit County Jail, Tel: 330-724-8043. Deacon Daniel Matusicky.

AMHERST. *Amherst Hospital*, Tel: 440-988-2848. Attended from St. Joseph.

APPLE CREEK. *Apple Creek State Institute*, Tel: 216-696-6525, Ext. 2700. Apostolate for Persons with Developmental Disabilities.

ASHLAND. *Ashland County Jail*, Tel: 419-289-7224. Attended from St. Edward.
Samaritan Hospital, Tel: 419-289-0491. Attended from St. Edward.

AVON. *Our Lady of the Wayside*, Tel: 216-651-0550. Rev. Robert T. Begin.

BARBERTON. *Barberton Citizens Hospitals*, Tel: 330-745-0011. Attended from St. Augustine.

CHAGRIN FALLS. *Windsor Hospital*, Tel: 440-247-7183. Attended from St. Joan of Arc.

CHARDON. *Geauga Community Hospital*, Tel: 440-564-5805; 440-338-3358 (Cleveland). Attended from St. Helen, Newbury.
Geauga County Jail, Tel: 440-834-8055. Deacon Frederick Giel.

CUYAHOGA FALLS. *Fallsview Mental Health Center*, Tel: 330-923-5244. Attended from St. Eugene
General Hospital, Tel: 330-928-2173. Attended from St. Joseph.

ELYRIA. *Elyria Memorial Hospital*, Tel: 440-329-7680. Sr. Joan Tomchey, O.S.U., Chap., Pastoral Care. Tel: 440-329-7680. Sacred Heart, Elyria.

GRAFTON. *Grafton Correctional Institution*. Rev. Charles J. Ryba. Tel: 440-236-5095, Deacon John Rivera. Tel: 440-327-4426.

HUDSON. *Youth Development Center*, Tel: 216-721-5300. Attended from St. Andrew Abbey.

LODI. *Lodi Hospital*, Tel: 216-722-1180; 216-273-1500 (Cleveland). Attended from Our Lady Help of Christians.

LORAIN. *Lorain Correctional Institution*, Tel: 440-236-5095. Rev. Charles J. Ryba.

LOUDONVILLE. *Kettering Hospital*, Tel: 419-994-4396. Attended from St. Peter.

MEDINA. *Medina Community Hospital*, Tel: 330-725-4968. Attended from St. Francis Xavier.
Medina County Jail, Tel: 330-725-4968. Deacon Daniel Norris.

NORTHFIELD. *Northcoast Behavioral Healthcare System South* 44067. Rev. Gary Chmura. Tel: 216-421-4211.

OBERLIN. *Allen Memorial Hospital*, Tel: 330-774-6791. Attended from Sacred Heart.

ORRVILLE. *Dunlap Memorial Hospital*, Tel: 330-682-3606. Attended from St. Agnes.

PAINESVILLE. *Lake County Jail*, Tel: 440-953-3867. Deacon Norman Davis.
Lake County Memorial Hospital-East, Tel: 330-585-0700. Rev. John M. Richards.

SMITHVILLE. *Boys Village of Ohio*, Tel: 330-264-8824. Attended from St. Mary, Wooster.

WADSWORTH. *Wadsworth Health Care Center*, Tel: 330-336-3049. Attended from Sacred Heart of Jesus.
Wadsworth-Rittman Hospital, Tel: 330-336-3049. Attended from Sacred Heart of Jesus.

WILLOUGHBY. *Lake County Memorial Hospital-West*. Rev. John M. Richards. Tel: 440-585-0700.

WOOSTER. *Wayne County Jail*, Tel: 330-264-8824. Attended from St. Mary of the Immaculate Conception.
Wooster Community Hospital, Tel: 330-264-8824. Attended from St. Mary.

Released from Diocesan Assignment:
Revs.—
Cozzens, Donald, John Carroll University, 20700 N. Park Blvd. University Heights, 44118.
Klamet, Francis X., 1050 Glenn Ave., Washington Courthouse, 43160-2603.
Patrick, William J., St. Jude Hospital & Rehabilitation Center, 3733 N. Harbor #15, Fullerton, CA 92835.
Valley, John, P.O. Box 5302, Willowick, 44094.

Military Chaplains:
Revs.—
Buckon, Neal J.
Czech, Edward M.
Glaros, Matthew J.
Sheil, James

Absent on Leave:
Revs.—
Baranek, Raymond
Bartnikowski Raymond
Dimengo, Michael
Enzman, David
Lonteen, Daniel
Weaver, Jeffrey

Administrative Leave:
Revs.—
Banner, Russell
Bartnikowski, Raymond
Berthiaume, Gary
Brickman, Donald
Brodnick, Joseph
Bruening, Allen
Labbe, Joseph
Lang, Joseph
Lieberth, Joseph
McBride, Daniel
McNulty, J. Brendan
Mueller, John
O'Connor, Patrick, M.A.
Rebol, Anthony
Romansky, Joseph
Rupp, Edward
Seminatore, Joseph
Viall, James A.
Weber, David

Retired:
Rev. Msgrs.—
Heruday, Joseph C., 6765 State Rd., Parma, 44134.
McIntyre, James P., St. Augustine Towers, 7821 Lake Ave., 44102.
Spitzig, Joseph, 1264 Tupelo Ln., West Salem, 44287.
Wolff, Robert C., 4516 Rex Lake Dr., Akron, 44319.
Revs.—
Alexander, Anthony F., 344 Sanford St., Painesville, 44077.
Anderson, John F., 12969 Chillicothe Rd., Chesterland, 44026.
Bacher, Arthur, 5269 Mill Creek Blvd., Brunswick Hills, 44212.
Baugh, David G., 1730 Mt. Carmel Dr., Wickliffe, 44092.
Becherer, James R., 4963 E. Lake Rd., Sheffield Lake, 44054.
Bodziony, Ralph A., 5159 Everett Rd., Richfield, 44286.
Bonnell, Robert A., 143 E. College St., Apt. 313, Oberlin, 44074.
Boymer, Lloyd J., 7831 Lave Ave., 44102.
Burge, Robert
Callahan, Nelson J., 12550 Lake Rd., Apt. 1309, Lakewood, 44107.
Cimperman, Victor J., 6114 Lausche Ave., Apt. 311, 44103.
Clines, Paul J., St. Augustine Parish, 965 Norton Ave., Barberton, 44203.
Conroy, James A., 5891 Ridge Rd., Parma, 44129.
Conway, Neil
Crawford, John G., 1545 Green Rd., South Euclid, 44121.
Cudnik, Chester C., 886 Eastlawn Dr., Highland Hts., 44143.
Cullen, Thomas F., 19517 Horsax Ave., 44135.
Dalton, John, Regina Health Care, 5232 Broadview Rd., Richfield, 44286.
Donohue, Robert W., St. Augustine Manor, 7801 Detroit Rd., 44102.
Egan, Arthur B., 800 Brick Mill Run #519, Westlake, 44145.
Flynn, Thomas A., 7268 Lilac Ct., North Olmsted, 44070.
Fridrich, Sylvester W., 33882 Maple Ridge Blvd., Avon, 44011.
Friedel, Robert E., 2943 Country Club Ln., Twinsburg, 44087.
Gaebelein, Claude J., 4291 Richmond Rd., Warrenville Heights, 44122.
Gallagher, Thomas J., 1344 Weathervane La., 1-B, 44143.
Gassert, Adelbert J., 5445 Smith Rd., Brook Park, 44142.
Goebel, Joseph A., 15000 Lakeshore Blvd., 44110-1298.
Gorski, John J., 2935 N. Bay Dr., Apt. H-14, Westlake, 44145.
Hayes, John, 4129 Superior Ave., 44103.
Hepner, Ernest, 101 Single Tree Ln., Aiken, SC 29803.
Horley, Ray, 4291 Richmond Rd., Warrensville Heights, 44122.
Hritz, Paul J., 10202-B Granger Rd., Garfield Heights, 44125.
Hyland, Thomas J., 35777 Center Ridge Rd., North Ridgeville, 44039.
Johnson, William J., Regina Health Care Center, 5232 Broadview Rd., Richfield, 44286.
Kilcoyne, John, 7821 Lake Ave., 44102.
Kinkopf, John J., Divine Word, 8100 Eagle Rd., Kirtland, 44094.
Kitt, William J., Castleblakeney, Ballinasloe, Co. Galway Ireland.
Kline, John J., 33803 Electric Blvd., #E-6, Avon Lake, 44012.
Kline, Robert W., 28700 Euclid Ave., Wickliffe, 44092.
Kunkle, Albert A., 39 N. Portage Path, Akron, 44303.
Leahy, John A., 12700 Lake Ave., Unit 213, Lakewood, 44107.
Luca, Edward J, 1535 Elmwood Ave., Lakewood, 44107.
Lukachinsky, Jerome A., 367 E. 260th St., Euclid, 44132.
Lusoski, Thomas J., 21108 Franklin Rd., Maple Hts., 44137.
Mackert, Albert J., 13719 Tartan Dr., Sun City West, AZ 85375. Winter Months, 3644 Rocky River Dr., 44111.
McDonough, John T., 1088 Ridge Rd., Hinckley, 44233.
McGovern, Thomas A., 3450 Sycamore Dr., Stow, 44224.
McMahon, Joseph W., 8100 Eagle Rd., Kirtland, 44095.
McShane, Patrick E., 10 Linda Ln. #3-2, Dorchester, MA 02125.
Mulica, James
Muzic, Anthony J., 1160 Broadway Ave., Bedford, 44146.
O'Grady, Dennis, 7096 Pearl Rd., Parma Heights, 44130.
Ondreyka, Richard J., M.S., P.O. Box 1132, Norton, 44203.
Pahler, Robert E., 1905 Portage Tr., Cuyahoga Falls, 44223-1792.
Peters, Herman B., Regina Healthcare, 5232 Broadview Ln., Richfield, 44286.

Piskura, Joseph, 29050 Detroit Rd., Ste. 129, Westlake, 44145.
Prendergast, Edward F., 29591 Detroit Rd., Ste. 1, Westlake, 44145.
Rath, Thomas V., 200 St. Joseph Dr., Amherst, 44001.
Rathfon, John R., 273 Robinhood Circle #102, Naples, FL 34104-9404.
Rebol, Anthony, 6705 Lansing Rd., 44105.
Reichlin, Urban A., 76 Westshore Dr., Avon Lake, 44012.
Riley, Norman, 5891 Ridge Rd., Parma, 44129-3642.
Sheehan, Thomas W.
Silva, David E., 2899 E. Ridgewood Dr., Seven Hills, 44131.
Smith, Raymond, 39 N. Portage Path, Akron, 44303.
Smith, Wilfred, 2846 Hubbard Rd., Madison, 44057-2998.
Tesek, Albert J., 6667 Wallings Rd., North Royalton, 44133-3099.
Tezie, William F., 4242 Brendan Ln., North Olmsted, 44070.
Tomc, Victor N., 20654 Centuryway Rd., Maple Heights, 44137.
Tomicky, Ronald
Trivison, Louis J., 283 Union St., Bedford, 44146.
Valentini, Francis M., 2749 Orchid Oaks Dr., #302-A, Sarasota, FL 34239.
Vituj, George L., 4291 Richmond Rd., Warrensville Heights, 44122.
Wagner, Joseph F., 7821 Lake Ave., 44102.
Weber, Thomas H., 28700 Euclid Ave., Wickliffe, 44092.
Wessel, John F., 2451 Crimson Dr., Westlake, 44145.
Winca, Harry, 1620 Windrow La., Broadview Heights, 44147.
Wittreich, John A., 3131 Smith Rd., Fairlawn, 44333.
Wysocki, Paul, 8274 Kellogesville/Stanhope Rd., Williamsfield, 44093.
Zeisig, Thomas B., 100 Brookmont Rd., Apt. 139, Akron, 44105.
Zepp, Anthony, 6705 Lansing Ave., 44105.

Permanent Deacons:
Adair, Robin, St. Augustine, Barberton
Adkins, Ronald M., St. Gabriel, Concord Township
Agrippe, James L., (Retired)
Anderson, Robert C., St. Rita, Solon
Armstrong, James J., Diaconate Staff, St. Wendelin, Cleveland
Bacik, Dale A., St. Anselm, Chesterland
Badillo, Tomas, Sacred Heart Chapel, Lorain
Balassy, Geza J., Sacred Heart, Akron; St. Matthias, Parma
Bals, Jerry J., St. Matthias, Parma
Beebe, Raymond C., (Retired)
Beercheck, Richard C., St. Patrick, (Rocky River), Cleveland
Belsito, Vincent L., Sts. Cosmas and Damian, Twinsburg
Belter, Clement J., St. Ambrose, Brunswick
Bender, John R., St. Martin of Tours, Maple Heights
Bender, Robert C., Queen of Heaven, Green
Berigan, Patrick F., Our Lady of Good Counsel, Cleveland
Bewley, Douglas P., Assumption of Mary, Brook Park
Bizon, Thaddeus C., Jr., St. Martin of Tours, Maple Heights
Boehnlein, Lawrence A., St. Mary, Chardon, Diaconate Staff
Bosau, Wayne A., St. Clarence, North Olmsted
Bowers, Robert J., St. Paschal Baylon, Highland Heights
Broering, J. Harry, Jr., (Retired)
Bubnick, Robert C., Sr., Apostolate for the Mentally Retarded, Assumption, Broadview Heights
Buda, John M., Our Lady Help of Christians, Litchfield
Burke, John Jr., St. Bede the Venerable, Mentor
Butkovic, Donald P., St. Adalbert, Berea
Butz, Richard C., St. Francis de Sales, Akron
Capek, Louis J., Representative Diocesan Vocation Council, St. Joan of Arc, Chagrin Falls
Cermak, Lawrence, St. Therese, Garfield Heights
Colon, Victor R., Sagrada Familia, Cleveland
Corrigan, William H., St. Colman, Cleveland
Croniger, James D., Holy Cross, Euclid
Daley, James F., Jr., St. Cyprian, Perry
Daull, Raymond L., Christ the King, Cleveland
Davis, Norman H., (Retired)
Davison, John H., Leave of Absence
Daw, Thomas B., St. Mary of the Falls, Olmsted Falls
Debrason, James K., St. Anthony of Padua, Lorain
DeGracia, Jose A., Sacred Heart Chapel, Lorain
DeHaas, Thomas B., Jr., St. Felicitas, Euclid
DeJohn, Ross C., Sr., St. Clare, Lyndhurst
Dillon, Edward R., Sacred Heart of Jesus, Elyria
Dirk, William E., Our Lady of Peace, Cleveland; St. Luke Hospital
Doerpers, Charles B., Cleveland Hopkins Airport
Donlin, William A., St. John Nepomucene, Cleveland
Duffy, James J., (Retired)
Duhlop, Jeffrey F., St. Joan of Arc, Chagrin Falls
Dybo, Robert J., Nativity of the Blessed Virgin Mary, Lorain
Elwood, William T., St. Francis of Assisi, Gates Mills; Youth & Family Ministry, Eastern Region
Feldkamp, Edward J., (Retired)
Figueroa, Miguel A., St. Michael, Cleveland
Flores, Jose A., Sacred Heart Chapel, Lorain
Foradori, Peter J., St. Stephen, West Salem
Frania, Gregory C., St. Lucy Mission, Middlefield
Friend, Shelby M., St. Henry, Cleveland
Fulton, Stanley J., St. Brendan, North Olmstead
Giel, Frederick F., The Villages, FL
Girard, Charles C., Tuscon, AZ
Glorioso, Russell J., Holy Family, Parma
Golanka, Kenneth A., St. Felicitas, Euclid
Grasson, Thomas J., St. John Neumann, Strongsville
Hancock, Daniel J., St. Joseph, Amherst
Heise, Paul R., St. Joseph, Amherst
Hill, Kenneth J., St. Vincent de Paul, Cleveland
Hinderscheid, Lee F., St. Hilary, Fairlawn
Hlabse, Paul J., St. Cyprian, Perry; St. Mary, Painesville
Hosfeld, Bernard E., St. Mary of the Immaculate Conception, Wooster
Humphrey, Frank A., III, St. Mary, Elyria
Humphrey, Patrick J., St. Jude, Elyria
Hupertz, Thomas G., Immaculate Conception, Madison
Jankowski, Donald M., St. Vincent De Paul, Elyria Township
Jarosh, Rudolph, Jr., St. Thomas More, Brooklyn
Jervis, Michael F., Our Lady Help of Christians, Litchfield
Johnson, Charles O.
Johnson, Joseph W., Jacksonville, FL
Kamlowsky, Philip P., Holy Family, Stow
Kaniecki, James A., St. Edward, Ashland
Karecki, Edmund J., St. Augustine, Cleveland
Kinzel, David L., St. Ladislas, Westlake
Kipstuhl, Paul J., St. Francis Xavier, Medina
Klaas, Roger N., Sacred Heart, Wadsworth, Diaconate Staff
Klingshirn, Clement G., Jr., St. Mary, Elyria
Knight, Kenneth, St. Bede the Venerable, Mentor
Koch, Alfred J., Holy Martyrs, Medina
Koch, John A., Ascension, Cleveland
Kochanski, Robert M., St. Joseph, Cuyahoga Falls
Kovitch, Joseph R., DPC Representative, St. Mary, Mentor
Krupp, Ralph J., St. Peter, Lorain
Kuhlman, Richard F., Immaculate Conception, Madison
Kutolowski, Paul C., St. Columbkille, Parma
Litke, Joseph P., Holy Family, Parma
Lobdell, Donald W., Waupaca, Wisconsin
LoCascio, Phillip A., Phoenix, AZ
Lonteen, Francis R., St. Paul, Akron
Loutzenhiser, Joseph E., St. Francis Xavier, Medina
Lozada, Frank, St. Francis, Cleveland
Lundeen, David J., Corpus Christi, Cleveland
Malcolm, Billy J., St. Ignatius of Antioch & St. Vincent De Paul, Cleveland
Maldonado, Louis, St. Joseph Lorain
Martin, Hardin M., Epiphany, Cleveland
Martin, James T., St. Patrick, Thompson
Martin, P. Robert, St. Mary of the Falls, Olmsted Falls
Masony, Howard J., Diaconate Staff, St. Joseph, Avon Lake
Matoney, Robert, Jr., St. Dominic, Shaker Heights
Matusicky, Daniel J., St. Bernard, Akron
McCarthy, Edward J., Jr., Diaconate Staff, St. Mary, Chardon
McGraw, Joseph E., St. Mark, Cleveland
McNulty, Leo F., St. Francis of Assisi, Gates Mills, St. Joseph Christian Life Center
Meade, Kenneth C., Immaculate Conception, Madison
Medina, Ceferino, Sagrada Familia, Cleveland
Merriman, William C., St. Patrick, Cleveland
Miklosovic, John, St. Ambrose, Brunswick
Miranda, Ignacio, Sagrada Familia, Cleveland
Mueller, Richard A., St. Mary of the Falls, Olmstead Falls
Netzband, Ralph W., St. Monica, Garfield Heights
Newman, Joseph H., St. Timothy, Garfield Heights
Norris, Daniel F., St. Francis Xavier, Medina.
Novak, Andrew J., St. Cyprian, Perry
O'Connell, Frank J., Louisville, KY
O'Donnell, James K., Gesu, University Heights
Ortiz, Juan, Sacred Heart Chapel, Lorain
Paul, James, St. Aloysius-St. Agatha, Cleveland
Payne, Robert H., St. Rita, Solon
Payne, Willard C., St. Helen, Newbury
Peacock, Terry W., (Retired)
Pecek, Louis G., Ph.D., St. Paul, Euclid
Pecot, David E., St. Basil the Great, Brecksville
Perkowski, Gregory A., (On Leave)
Piechowski, Kenneth J., Dir. Diaconate & St. Hyacinth, Cleveland
Pineiro, Jose L., Sacred Heart Chapel, Lorain
Piskach, Robert J., St. Francis de Sales, Parma
Polefko, Roger F., St. John Bosco, Parma Heights
Quiles, Rafael, (Retired)
Ramos, Jose L., (On Leave)
Rapp, Robert, Garrettsville, OH
Reiland, George J., Jr., (Retired)
Rivera, Carlos, (Retired)
Rivera, John M., St. Augustine, Cleveland; St. Julie Billiart, North Ridgeville
Rodriguez, Alfonso, (Retired)
Sabol, Robert G., St. Bartholomew, Middleburg Heights
Savage, Joseph J., (Retired)
Schad, Kenneth E., (On Leave)
Schill, William E., St. Stanislaus, Lorain
Seal, J. David, Immaculate Heart of Mary, Cuyahoga Falls
Senn, Thomas J., (On Leave)
Sferry, John P., Sr., Diaconate Staff, St. Gregory, South Euclid; Cathedral of St. John the Evangelist, Cleveland
Sheridan, Thomas, St. Ambrose, Brunswick
Sherman, Homer L., St. Clarence, North Olmsted
Shin, Charles C., St. Andrew Kim Pastoral Center, Cleveland
Sill, Donald E., St. Anselm, Chesterland
Simon, Frederick F., Diaconate Staff, Sagrada Familia, Cleveland
Skrha, Joseph W., Dir., Pastoral Care Dept., St. Michael Hospital, Cleveland
Slatcoff, John K., St. Vincent De Paul, Elyria Township
Smallhoover, James A., Holy Spirit, Avon
Smith, Dennis L., Immaculate Conception, Akron
Snyder, Wayne W., St. John Vianney, Mentor
Somrack, Lawrence A., St. Helen, Newbury
Staab, William M., St. Patrick, Cleveland
Starkey, William R., Holy Trinity, Bedord Heights
Stewart, James R., St. James, Lakewood
Stokes, Troy F., (On Leave)
Streeter, David A., St. Luke, Lakewood
Strmac, John W., Our Lady of Mount Carmel, Wickliffe
Talerico, John A., St. Charles Borromeo, Parma
Tatulinski, Frank E., Holy Name, Cleveland
Telepak, Edward A., St. Columbkille, Parma
Terrion, Daniel C., St. Wenceslas, Maple Heights
Thiel, Martin A., St. Thomas More, Brooklyn
Toomey, Carl M., St. Mary Magdalene, Willowick
Torres, Epifanio, Sagrada Familia, Cleveland
Travalik, Peter M., St. Jerome, Cleveland
Ulman, Robert P., St. Bede the Venerable, Mentor
Varga, Carl M., Divine Word, Kirtland; St. Philip Neri, Cleveland
Vicens, Prudo, (Retired)
Vincent, James C., St. Peter the Apostle, Brook Park; St. Michael, Independence
Vinciguerra, Mario J., Our Lady of Guadelupe, Macedonia
Volek, Ronald J., Seiverville, TN
Vrabel, Jerome B., Holy Cross, Euclid
Waken, Thomas J., Lexington, Kentucky
Walling, Robert K., Holy Spirit, Avon
Weglicki, Frank L., Jr., St. Ambrose, Brunswick
Weniger, Robert L., St. Michael, Independence
Wenzel, John T., St. Anthony of Padua, Fairport Harbor
Wilson, Francis B., Assumption of Mary, Brook Park
Woods, Richard E., St. Louis, Cleveland Heights
Woyton, Louis M., St. Augustine, Cleveland
Youngblood, Dale A., S.S. Peter and Paul, Doylestown
Zawadzki, Charles W., Corpus Christi, Cleveland
Zdolshek, John R., St. Richard, North Olmstead
Ziemkiewicz, Gerard J., NADO Representative, Diaconate Staff, St. Joseph, Strongsville; Associate Director Office of Continuing Education and Formation of Ministers

INSTITUTIONS LOCATED IN THE DIOCESE

[A] SEMINARIES, DIOCESAN

WICKLIFFE. *Borromeo Seminary*, 28700 Euclid Ave., 44092-2585. Tel: 440-943-7600; Fax: 440-943-7577. Email: tmd@dioceseofcleveland.org. Web: www.a-full-life.com. Very Rev. Thomas M. Dragga, D.Min., Pres. & Rector; Rev. Robert Stec, M.A., M.Div., Vocation Dir.; Mrs. Paulette M. Begin, B.A., Registrar; Rev. John F. Loya, M.Div., M.A., Spiritual Dir.; Bro. Charles McElroy, O.F.M.Cap., Religious Studies; Mr. Brian F. Houlahan, Treas.; Sr. Rosemarie Carfagna, O.S.U., Ph.D., Academic Dean; Revs. Donald Dunson, Formation Advisor; Robert E. McCreary, O.F.M.Cap., Formation Advisor; John Murphy, Formation Advisor; Ed Kaczuk, M.M., Lay Teacher; Ray Leopold, M.Lit., Lay Teacher; William Tighe, B.S., Lay Teacher. Priests 5; Brothers 1; Sisters 1; Lay Teachers 3; Seminarians 25. In Res. Rev. Robert W. Kline (Retired).

St. Mary Seminary and Graduate School of Theology (Our Lady of the Lake) , 28700 Euclid Ave., 44092-2585. Tel: 440-943-7600; Fax: 440-943-7577. Email: twt@dioceseofcleveland.org. Web: stmarysem.edu. Revs. Thomas W. Tifft, Ph.D., Pres./Rector; Mark A. Latcovich, Ph.D., Vice Pres.-Vice Rector, Academic Dean; David J. Walkowiak, J.C.D., Dean of Students; John F. Loya, M.Div., M.A., Spiritual Dir.; Mrs. Paulette M. Begin, B.A., Registrar; Sisters Therese Dugan, S.N.D., Ph.D.; Mary McCormick, O.S.U., Ph.D.; Revs. Gerald J. Bednar, Ph.D.; Donald Dunson, Ph.D.; Very Rev. Thomas M. Dragga, D.Min.; Revs. Michael G. Woost, S.T.L.; Lorenzo Tosco, S.S.D., S.S.L.; Mr. Edward J. Kaczuk, M.M.; Mr. Alan K. Rome, M.L.S., Librarian; Mr. Brian F. Houlahan, Treas. Priests 9; Sisters 2; Adjunct Faculty 10; Students for Priesthood, Diocesan 28; Permanent Diaconate 31; Other 89.

[B] COLLEGES AND UNIVERSITIES

CLEVELAND. *Notre Dame College of Ohio*, 4545 College Rd., South Euclid, 44121. Tel: 216-381-1680; Fax: 216-381-3802. Email: mkovach@ndc.edu. Web: www.notredamecollege.edu. Andrew P. Roth, Ph.D., Pres.; Marilyn Jones, Ph.D., Vice Pres. Academic Affairs. Priests 1; Sisters of Notre Dame 4; Lay Teachers 82; Total Staff 195; Students 1,000.

Ursuline College, 2550 Lander Rd., Pepper Pike, 44124. Tel: 440-449-4200; Fax: 440-646-8102. Web: www.ursuline.edu. Diana Stano, O.S.U., Ph.D., Pres.; JoAnne Podis, Ph.D., Vice Pres. Academic Affairs; David Steiner, Vice Pres. & CFO; Deanne Hurley, Vice Pres. Student Affairs; Sisters Anna Margaret Gilbride, O.S.U., Ph.D., Asst. to the Pres.; Patricia McCaffrey, Vice Pres. Enrollment Mgmt.; Charles Sweeney, Vice Pres. Facilities Mgmt.; Kevin Gladstone, Vice. Pres. Institutional Advancement. Ursuline Sisters of Cleveland 11; Lay Professors 58; Students 1,409.

UNIVERSITY HEIGHTS. *John Carroll Jesuit Community* Tel: 216-397-1886; Fax: 216-397-4228. Email: jesuits@jcu.edu. Web: www.jcu.edu.

John Carroll University, University Heights, 44118. Tel: 216-397-1886; Fax: 216-397-4228. Web: www.jcu.edu/jesuit. Rev. Howard J. Gray, S.J., Rector; Bro. Michael L. Nusbaum, S.J., Min.; Revs. William M. Bichl, S.J.; Casimir R. Bukala, S.J.; Harry J. Gensler, S.J.; Edward Glynn, S.J.; John A. Knapek, S.J.; Stephen T. Krupa, S.J.; Francis P. Lihvar, S.J.; Francis X. Ryan, S.J.; Gerald J. Sabo, S.J.; Joseph O. Schell, S.J.; Thomas L. Schubeck, S.J.; Francis J. Smith, S.J.; Ernest G. Spittler, S.J. Priests 14; Brothers 1; Total Enrollment 4,242.

John Carroll University, 20700 N. Park Blvd., 44118. Tel: 216-397-1886; Fax: 216-397-4256. Web: www.jcu.edu. Revs. Edward Glynn, S.J., Pres.; Howard Gray, S.J., Asst. to Pres. for Univ. Mission & Identity; Ms. Janetta Hammock, Asst. to Pres & Sec. to Brd.; Mr. Patrick Rombalski, Vice Pres. Student Affairs; Mr. Peter Anagnostos, Vice Pres. Devel. & Alumni Rels.; Mr. Jonathan Ivec, Vice Pres. Finance & Admin. Svcs.; Dr. David M. La Guardia, Academic Vice Pres.; Dr. James H. Krukones, Assoc. Academic Vice Pres.; Mr. John Gladstone, Assoc. Academic Vice Pres. for Enrollment Svcs.; Dr. Frank J. Navratil, Dean Boler School of Business; Dr. Nick Baumgartner, Dean College of Arts & Sciences; Dr. Mary Beadle, Dean of Graduate School; Dr. Joseph B. Miller, Assoc. Dean College of Arts & Sciences; Rev. William M. Bichl, S.J., Asst. Dean College of Arts & Sciences; Ms. Sophie Kus-Patena, Asst. Dean College of Arts & Sciences; Dr. Darrell Radson, Assoc. Dean Boler School of Business; Ms. Laura Atkins, Asst. Dean Boler School of Business; Dr. Edward Peck, Asst. Dean Graduate School. Priests 10; Sisters 1; Lay Faculty 235; Students 4,242; Total Staff 625.

[C] HIGH SCHOOLS, DIOCESAN

CLEVELAND. *Cleveland Central Catholic High School*, Forman Campus, 6550 Baxter Ave., 44105. Tel: 216-441-4700; Fax: 216-441-8353. Email: TDEdwards68@hotmail.com. Web: www.centralcatholichs.org. Terry D. Edwards, Prin.

**St. Martin de Porres High School*, 6111 Lausche Ave., 44103.

Villa Angela-St. Joseph High School, 18491 Lake Shore Blvd., 44119. Tel: 216-481-8414; Fax: 216-486-1035. Email: roccojtr@aol.com Web: www.VASJ.com. James J. Sukys, Pres. Email: jsukys@vasj.com; Janice T. Roccosalva, Prin. Marianists 3; Ursuline Nuns 3; Lay Teachers 43; Students 511.

BEDFORD. *St. Peter Chanel High School*, 480 Northfield Rd., 44146. Tel: 440-232-5900; Fax: 440-232-9283. Email: smiroglotta@stpeterchanel.com. Web: www.stpeterchanel.com. Mr. Sal Miroglotta, Prin. Sisters 1; Lay Teachers 24; Students 371.

ELYRIA. *Elyria Catholic High School* (Coed) , 725 Gulf Rd., 44035. Tel: 440-365-1821; Fax: 440-365-7536. Web: www.elyriacatholic.com. Mr. Andrew G. Krakowaik, M.A., Prin. Serving Elyria, Avon, Sheffield, North Ridgeville, Grafton, Oberlin, Amherst, Lorain and Wellington. Lay Teachers 32; Students 500.

LORAIN. *Lorain Catholic High School*, (Grades 9-12), 760 Tower Blvd., 44052. Tel: 440-282-8216; Fax: 440-282-8123. Email: cpaul@leeca.org. Web: www.loraincatholic.org. Mrs. Chris Paul, Prin.; Mr. James W. Lawhead, Asst. Prin./Athletic Dir.; Rev. Giampietro Gasparin, C.S.J., Chap. Lay Teachers 19; Students 210.

MENTOR. *Lake Catholic High*, 6733 Reynolds Rd., 44060. Tel 440-951-0077; Fax: 440-974-9087. Email: lakecatholic@hotmail.com. Sr. St. Ann Waldron, O.S.U., Prin. Ursuline Sisters of Cleveland (O.S.U.) 2; Lay Teachers 54; Students 826.

PARMA HEIGHTS. *Holy Name High School* (Coed) , 6000 Queens Hwy., 44130. Tel: 440-886-0300; Fax: 440-886-1267. Email: rramicone@schoolone.com. Web: www.greenwave.org. Raymond R. Ramicone, Pres.; Benjamin Farmer, Prin.; Rev. William R. Krinzner, Chap. Priests 1; Sisters 3; Lay Teachers 59; Administration 4; Students 836.

[D] HIGH SCHOOLS, PRIVATE

CLEVELAND. *Becumont School*, 3301 N. Park Blvd., Cleveland Heights, 44118. Tel: 216-321-2954; Fax: 216-321-3947. Email: Info@beaumontschool.org. Web: www.beaumontschool.org. Ursuline Sisters Sisters 10; Lay Teachers 32; Students 455.

Beaumont Convent, 3240 Fairmount Blvd., 44118. Tel: 216-321-2157; Fax: 216-321-3947. Sr. Ritamary Welsh, O.S.U., Pres.; Mrs. Margaret Connell, Prin. Sisters 11; Lay Teachers 32; Students 448.

Benedictine High School, 2900 Martin Luther King Dr., 44104-3898. Tel: 216-421-2080; Fax: 216-421-1100. Email: cbhs@cbhs.net. Web: www.cbhs.net. Rt. Rev. Clement Zeleznik, O.S.B., Pres.; Rev. Gerard Gonda, O.S.B., Prin.; Mr. August Pisa, Asst. Prin. & Academic Dean; Mr. Ronald Vojacek, Dir. Devel.; Mr. Anthony Russ, Dean Student Affairs; Revs. Paschal Petcavage, O.S.B.; Michael Brunovsky, O.S.B.; Timothy Buyansky, O.S.B.; Gary Hoover, O.S.B., School Chap.; Bede Kotlinski, O.S.B.; Anselm Zupka, O.S.B.; Dominic Mondzelewski, O.S.B.; Bros. Nichalas Spisak, O.S.B.; Patrick Ryan, O.S.B.; Mario Parisi, O.S.B. Priests 8; Brothers 3; Lay Teachers 28; Students 445.

St. Edward High School (Boys) , 13500 Detroit Ave., Lakewood, 44107. Tel: 216-221-3776; Fax: 216-221-4609. Email: sehs.net. Web: www.sehs.net. Bro. Peter Graham, C.S.C., Pres. Brothers 6; Lay Teachers 62; Students 900; Total Staff 100.

St. Ignatius High School, 1911 W. 30th St., 44113. Tel: 216-651-0222; Fax: 216-651-6313 Web: www.ignatius.edu. Revs. Timothy Kesicki, S.J., Pres.; John V. White, S.J., Rector; Peter H. Corrigan Jr., Prin.; Thomas J. Bain, S.J.; Robert J. Dietrich, S.J.; James E. Farrell, S.J.; Raymond P. Guiao, S.J.; Benjamin P. Jimeinez, S.J.; John H. Kleinhenz, S.J.; James V. Lewis, S.J.; Lawrence M. Ober, S.J.; Bernard J. Streicher, S.J.; Kenneth A. Styles, S.J.; Michael A. Vincent, S.J. Priests 12; Lay Teachers 93; Students 1,379.

St. Joseph Academy, 3430 Rocky River Dr., 44111. Tel: 216-251-6788; Fax: 216-251-5809. Email: kasper2@apk.net. Web: www.stjoeacademy.org. Jacqualine Kasprowski, Pres. & Prin. Sisters 5; Lay Teachers 49; Students 610; Total Staff 54.

Magnificat High School (Girls) , 20770 Hilliard Blvd., 44116. Tel: 440-331-1572; Fax: 440-331-7257. Email: smpcook@magnificaths.org Web: www.magnificaths.org. Sisters Carolyn Marshall, H.M., Pres.; Mary Pat Cook, H.M., Prin. Sisters 3; Lay Teachers 70; Students 837.

Regina High School (Girls) , 1857 S. Green Rd., 44121. Tel: 216-382-2110; Fax: 216-382-3555. Email: rhs@stratos.net. Web: www.reginahigh.com. Sr. Maureen Burke, S.N.D., Prin. Sisters of Notre Dame Sisters 10; Lay Teachers 20; Students 280.

**St. Martin de Porres High School*, 6111 Lausche Ave., 44103. Richard F. Clark, Pres.

AKRON. *Archbishop Hoban High School* (Coed) , One Holy Cross Blvd., 44306. Tel: 330-773-6658; Fax: 330-773-9100. Email: beitingm@hoban.org. Web: www.hoban.org. Bro. Kenneth Haders, C.S.C., Pres.; Mrs. Mary Anne Beiting, Prin. Brothers of Holy Cross Brothers 7; Sisters 1; Lay Teachers 54; Students 826.

Our Lady of the Elms School, (Grades 7-12), 1375 W. Exchange St., 44313-7697. Tel: 330-867-0880; Fax: 330-864-6488. Email: mdfriedman@elms.k12.oh.us. Web: www.ourladyoftheelms.org. Margaret Duffy-Friedman, Pres.; Katherine Bush, Prin. Please see complete listing under Elementary Schools. Sisters 2; Lay Teachers 35; Students 223.

St. Vincent-St. Mary High School, 15 N. Maple St., 44303. Tel: 330-253-9113; Fax: 330-996-0000. Email: webmaster@stvm.com. Web: www.stvm.com. David V. Rathz, Headmaster; Sue M. Garlando, Dir. of Devel.; Joanne Wiseman, Dir. of Admissions; Ranoi Bostick, Business Mgr.; Dan Nichols, Dean of Students; Ken McDonald, Campus Min.; Revs. Robert H. Jackson, Chap.; Salvatore Ruggerio, Chap. Priests 2; Lay Teachers 36; Students 645.

CHARDON. *Notre Dame-Cathedral Latin School*, 13000 Auburn Rd., 44024. Tel: 440-286-6226; 888-214-8108 (toll free); Fax: 440-286-7199. Email: nd_hschool@lgca.org. Web: www.ndcl.org. Sr. Margaret M. Gorman, S.N.D., Prin. Sisters of Notre Dame Sisters 8; Lay Teachers 58; Students 766.

CUYAHOGA FALLS. *Walsh Jesuit High School*, 4550 Wyoga Lake Rd., 44224. Tel: 330-929-4205; 800-686-4694 (Cleveland); Fax: 330-929-9749. Email: peppardp@walshjesuit.org. Web: www.walshjesuit.onlinecommunity.com. Revs. Michael J. Marco, S.J., Pres.; Patrick F. Peppard, S.J., Religious Supr.; James S. Prehn, S.J., Prin.; Vincent A. Hagarman, S.J.; Emmett P. Holmes, S.J.; James J. King, S.J.; Paul D. Panaretos, S.J.; Timothy J. Shepard. Priests 8; Lay Teachers 66; Students 879.

GARFIELD HEIGHTS. *Trinity High School*, 12425 Granger, 44125. Tel: 216-581-1644; Fax: 216-581-9348. Email: tmaher@ths.org. Web: www.ths.org. Sr. Shawn Lee, S.S.J.-T.O.S.F., Pres.; Patrick J. Riley, D.Min., Asst. to the Pres.; Thomas M. Maher, Ph.D., Prin.; Mr. Daniel J. Thomeier, Business Mgr.; Mr. Joseph A. Waler, M.A., M.Ed., Assoc. Prin. Sisters of St. Joseph of the Third Order of St. Francis Sisters of St. Joseph 4; Lay Teachers 46; Students 625.

GATES MILLS. *Gilmour Academy*, (Grades PreK-12) , Private. , 34001 Cedar Rd., 44040-9356. Tel: 440-473-8000; Fax: 440-473-8010. Email: laveller@gilmour.org. Web: www.gilmour.org. Mr. Murlan J. Murphy Jr., Chm., Bd. of Trustees; Bro. Robert Lavelle, C.S.C., Headmaster; J. Brian Horgan, Dir. of Upper School; Yvonne Saunders, Dir. Middle School; Dr. Monica Veto, Dir. of Lower School; Rev. John Blazek, C.S.C., Campus Min.; Sr. Rosemary Hammer, H.M., Dir. Pastoral Ministry. Congregation of Holy Cross, Day and Resident College Preparatory School. Priests 1; Brothers 1; Sisters 3; Students 757; Residents 47; Lay Teachers 66.

LAKEWOOD. *St. Augustine Academy*, 14808 Lake Ave., 44107. Tel: 216-221-4227; Fax: 216-221-7453. Email: splen@aol.com. Web: www.st-aug-academy.org. Sr. Patricia Lenard, C.S.F.N., Dir. Sisters of the Holy Family of Nazareth 4; Lay Teachers 22; Total Staff 34; Girls 211.

PARMA. *Padua Franciscan High School*, 6740 State Rd., 44134. Tel: 440-845-2444; Fax: 440-845-5710. Email: padua@paduafranciscan.com. Web: www.paduafranciscan.com. Rev. Theodore Haag, O.F.M., Pres.; Gerald R. Jindra, Vice Pres. for Institutional Advancement; Christopher W. Keavy, Prin.; David Stec, Min.; Bro. Tom Carroll, O.F.M., Academic Dean. Priests 2; Sisters 2; Brothers 1; Lay Teachers 70; Students 1,068.

[E] ELEMENTARY SCHOOLS

CLEVELAND. *Incarnate Word Academy*, 6618 Pearl Rd., 44130. Tel: 440-842-6818; Fax: 440-888-1377. Email: incarnword@leeca.org. Web: incarnatewordacademy.org. Sr. Eileen Fitzgerald,

S.I.W., Prin.; Rev. Kenneth J. Katricak, O.S.B. Sisters 9; Lay Teachers 18; Students 492.

Villa Montessori Center, 5620 Broadway Ave., 44127. Tel: 216-641-4770; Fax: 216-641-4771. Email: villageecc@aol.com. Sr. Marie Veres, H.M., Dir. & Prin.

AKRON. *North Akron Catholic School*, 1570 Creighton Ave., 44310. Tel: 330-633-1383; Fax: 330-633-4512. Christine Lackney, Prin.

Our Lady of the Elms School, (Grades 1-6), 1290 W. Market St., 44313-7108. Tel: 330-864-7210; Fax: 330-867-1262. Email: mdfriedman@elms.k12.oh.us. Web: www.ourladyoftheelms.org. Mrs. Margaret Duffy-Friedman, Pres.; Michelle Thomas, Prin. Sisters 1; Lay Teachers 18; Students 120.

CHARDON. *Notre Dame Elementary School*, 13000 Auburn Rd., 44024. Tel: 440-279-1129; Fax: 440-279-1127. Email: lpetelin@ndec.org. Sr. Mary Lisette Petelin, S.N.D., Prin. Sisters of Notre Dame 12; Lay Teachers 25; Students 530.

Notre Dame PreSchool, 13000 Auburn Rd., 44024. Tel: 440-286-7101, Ext. 5920; Fax: 440-286-9364. Email: mmcgovern@ndec.org. Sr. Margaret McGovern, S.N.D., Dir. Sisters of Notre Dame 1; Lay Teachers 3; Aides 2; Students 61.

HUDSON. *Seton Catholic School*, 6923 Stow Rd., 44236. Tel: 330-342-4200; Fax: 330-342-4276. Email: seton@lecca.org. Web: www.setoncatholicschool.org. Sr. Marie Damicone, Prin.; Mark Corr, Treas. Sisters 1; Lay Teachers 12; Students 218.

KIRTLAND. *Peaceful Children Montessori School*, 8100 Eagle Rd., 44094. Tel: 440-256-1976; Fax: 440-256-4370. Marilyn Wright, Dir. Lay Teachers 7; Total Enrollment 90; Total Staff 9.

PARMA HEIGHTS. *Incarnate Word Academy (IWA)*, 6618 Pearl Rd., 44130. Tel: 440-842-6818; Fax: 440-888-1377. Email: info@incarnatewordacademy.org. Web: www.incarnatewordacademy.org. Sisters 9; Lay Teachers 21; Total Enrollment 494; Total Staff 30.

[F] ELEMENTARY SCHOOLS, PAROCHIAL AND DIOCESAN

CLEVELAND. *Archbishop James P. Lyke Elementary School* St. Henry, St. Timothy and St. Catherine Schools consolidated to form Archbishop James P. Lyke Elementary School. , 18230 Harvard Ave., 44128. Tel: 216-991-9644; Fax: 216-991-9470. Email: lykesthenry@leeca.org. Web: www.cleveland.catholicnet.com. Sr. Brigetta Waldron, O.S.U., Dir. Lay Teachers 29; Students 500.

St. Catherine Campus (Grades K-1), 3443 E. 93rd St., 44104. Tel: 216-341-7212; Fax: 216-641-8184. Sr. Mary Beth Daly, S.N.D., Prin. Students 84.

St. Henry Campus (Grades 2-4), 18230 Harvard Ave., 44128. Tel: 216-991-9644; Fax: 216-991-9470. Ms. Mary Pat Hable, Prin. Students 196.

St. Timothy Campus (Grades 5-8), 4351 E. 131st St., Garfield Heights, 44105. Tel: 216-581-3517; Fax: 216-641-8184. Mrs. Margarete W. Smith, Prin. Students 220.

Metro Catholic School Tel: 216-281-4044; Fax: 216-634-2853. Email: metro@leeca.net.

St. Stephen Bldg. (Grade 5-8), 1910 W. 54th St., 44102. Tel: 216-281-4044; Fax: 216-234-2853.

St. Michael Bldg. (Grades 2-4), 1903 W. 57th St., 44102. Tel: 216-281-4044; Fax: 216-634-2853.

St. Boniface Bldg. (PreK-1), 3555 W. 54th St., 44102. Tel: 216-631-5733; Fax: 216-634-2853. Sr. Anne Malene, Prin. Sisters of Notre Dame 13; Ursuline Nun 2; Lay Teachers 24; Students K-8 531; Pre-School 63.

Urban Community School, 2401 Washington Ave., 44113. Tel: 216-771-8014; Fax: 216-771-7888. Email: mdoyle2401@aol.com. Sr. Maureen Doyle, O.S.U., Dir. Ursuline Nuns 3; Lay Teachers 22; Students 412.

WICKLIFFE. *All Saints of St. John Vianney School*, (Grades PreK-8), 28702 Euclid Ave., 44092. Tel: 216-943-1395; Fax: 216-943-4468. Email: allsaints@leeca.org. Web: www.cleveland.catholivnet.com/school/allststjohnvianney. Mrs. Rosemary Wilson, Prin. Sisters 1; Lay Teachers 20; Students 364.

[G] SPECIAL SCHOOLS AND CENTERS For Exceptional Children

CLEVELAND

Julie Billiart, 4982 Clubside Rd., Lyndhurst, 44124-2596. Tel: 216-381-1191; Fax: 216-381-2216. Email: aloporto@juliebilliartschool.org. Web: www.juliebilliartschool.org. Sr. Agnesmarie, S.N.D., Prin. Non-graded school for children having learning problems. Sisters 10; Lay Teachers 9; Students 110.

OLA-St. Joseph Center, 2346 W. 14th St., 44113. Tel: 216-621-3451; Fax: 216-621-6104. Email: olasjc@dioceseofcleveland.org. Mrs. Pamela Delly, Prin. Non-graded school for developmentally handicapped children, ages 6-16. Lay Teachers 7; Students 55.

[H] PRESCHOOL AND DAY CARE CENTERS

CLEVELAND. *Catholic Charities Services/Head Start*, 1031 Superior Ave., 6th Floor, 44114. Tel: 216-696-6525, Ext. 2870; Fax: 216-696-3631. Email: rdlovejoy@dioceseofcleveland.org. Lay Teachers 26; Children 1,168.

AKRON. *Our Lady of the Elms* PreSchool , 1295 W. Exchange St., 44313-7696. Tel: 330-864-6817; Fax: 330-867-1322. Email: mdfriedman@elms.k12.oh.us. Web: www.ourladyoftheelms.org. Mrs. Margaret Duffy-Friedman, Pres.; Suzanne Scarpitti, Prin. Lay Teachers 6; Students 70.

GARFIELD HEIGHTS. *Marymount Child Care Center*, 12215 Granger Rd., 44125. Tel: 216-581-3540; Fax: 216-581-4264. Email: felmann@aol.com. Sr. Felicia Mann, S.S.J.-T.O.S.F., Dir. Total Assisted Annually 150; Total Staff 14.

[I] GENERAL HOSPITALS

(For information on other Catholic related hospitals please contact the Chancery Office.)

CLEVELAND

St. John Hospital, 2351 E. 22nd St., 44115. Tel: 216-696-5560; Fax: 216-696-2204. Web: www.csahealthsystem.org. Sisters Mary Patricia Barrett, C.S.A., Chm. Bd. of Trustees; Judith Ann Karam, C.S.J., Pres. & CEO.

Marymount Hospital, Inc., 12300 McCracken Rd., 44125. Tel: 216-587-8080; Fax: 216-587-8212. Email: dkilarski@marymount.org. Web: www.marymount.org. Mr. David J. Kilarski, Pres. & CEO; Judith Shemkovitz, Dir. Mission Svcs.; Rev. Joseph O'Donnell, Priest Chap. & Coord. Sacramental Svcs. & Priest Chaplains; Sr. Betty Gulick, S.S.J., Staff Chap. Sisters of St. Joseph of Third Order of St. Francis 5; Bed Capacity 312; Med/surg 274; Skilled Nursing 20; Bassinets 18; Patients Assisted Annually 158,548; Total Staff 1,160.

LORAIN

Community Health Partners Health System, (East Campus), 205 W. 20th St., 44052. Tel: 440-233-1053; Fax: 440-246-5390. *(West Campus)*, 3700 Kolbe Rd., 44053-1697. Tel: 440-960-4000; Fax: 440-960-4630. Email: karen_yacobucci@hmis.org. Web: www.community-health-partners.com. Mr. Brian C. Lockwood, Pres. & CEO. Bed Capacity 250; Patients Assisted Annually 330,000; Total Staff 2,019.

[J] TRAINING SCHOOLS FOR NURSES

CLEVELAND. *Marymount School of Practical Nursing* Tel: 216-587-8160; Fax: 216-587-8632. Email: kknittel@marymount.org. 12300 McCracken Rd., Garfield Heights, 44125. Tel: 216-587-8160; Fax: 216-587-8632. Email: vbowden@marymount.org. Students 40.

[K] SPECIAL HOSPITALS

CLEVELAND. *Holy Family Home*, 6707 State Rd., 44134. Tel: 440-885-3100; Fax: 440-885-0644. Email: donations@holyfamilyhome.com. Web: www.holyfamilyhome.com. Sr. M. Christopher, O.P., Supr.; Rev. Nikomedius Mwacha, Chap. Tel: 440-842-1436.

Legal Title: *The Servants of Relief for Incurable Cancer, Inc.*, Free nursing home for terminal cancer patients who are unable to pay.; Administered by Dominican Sisters of the Third Order, Congregation of St. Rose of Lima. Sisters 10; Total Staff 55; Bed Capacity 37; Patients Assisted Annually 157.

Rose Mary, The Johanna Grasselli Rehabilitation and Education Center, 19350 Euclid Ave., 44117. Tel: 216-481-4823; Fax: 216-481-4154. Ms. Patricia A. Colombo, Exec. Dir. Children 42; Residents 86; Bed Capacity 88; Total Staff 250.

[L] PROTECTIVE INSTITUTIONS

CLEVELAND. *Christ Child - DePaul Day Care Center*, 2320 E. 24th St., 44115. Tel: 216-687-0000, Ext. 17; Fax: 216-687-0403. Email: depaul@dioceseofcleveland.org. Elbert W. Clark Jr., M.A., L.S.W., Dir. of Early Childhood Education Programs; Deborah Baker, Day Care Admin. Day Care program sponsored by Catholic Charities Services Corp. Funded by United Way & Catholic Charities. Students 102; Total Assisted Annually 172; Total Staff 17.

PARMA. *CCSC/Parmadale*, 6753 State Rd., 44134. Tel: 440-845-7700; Fax: 440-845-5910. Email: pdale@dioceseofcleveland.org. Web: www.clevelandcatholiccharities.com. Anne Mengerink, Dir. Specialized Residential Services; Intensive Treatment Services; Partial Hospitalization; Community Flexible Clinical Response; Specialized Foster Care; Whole Family Treatment; In-Home Services; Outpatient Services; Day Care; Training and Consultation Services; and Volunteer Program; Adoption Services; Head Start. Capacity 102; Children in Foster Care 213; Total Assisted Annually 1,379; Total Staff 260. In Res. Rev. James R. Semonin.

[M] HOMES FOR AGED

CLEVELAND. *St. Augustine Manor*, 7801 Detroit Ave., 44102. Tel: 216-634-7400; Fax: 216-634-7483. Email: pgareau@st-aug.org. Web: www.staugustinemanor.org. Mr. John Cooney, Chm., Bd. of Trustees; Mr. Patrick Gareau, Pres. & CEO. Affiliated with Catholic Charities. Provider of rehabilitation services, subacute care, skilled nursing, assisted living and child day care. Bed Capacity 347; Patients Assisted Annually 750; Total in Residence 340; Total Staff 450.

Coterie of St. Augustine Manor, The, 7801 Detroit Ave., 44102. Tel: 216-634-7400; Fax: 216-634-7483. Mrs. Margaret Lynch, Pres. (Operates the Coterie Boutique)

Jennings Center for Older Adults, 10204 Granger Rd., 44125. Tel: 216-581-2900; Fax: 216-581-4505; 216-581-1517. Email: martha.kutik@jenningscenter.org. Web: jenningscenter.org. Mrs. Martha M. Kutik, Pres. & CEO; Rev. Kestutis Zemaitis (Lithuania), Chap. Tel: 216-581-2900. Continuum of Services Campus for older adults, including a skilled nursing facility independent, congregate and assisted living apartments, an adult day center, and intergenerational child day care center for 75 children. Under the sponsorship of the Sisters of the Holy Spirit. Sisters 5; Residents 156; Total Assisted Annually 351; Total Staff 240.

Jennings Hall Nursing Home Tel: 216-581-2900; Fax: 216-581-4505. Skilled and Intermediate Care Bed Capacity 156.

Jennings Manor Housing Corporation Tel: 216-587-0842; Fax: 216-587-0875. Independent Housing Apartments 61; HUD 202.

Holy Spirit Villas Tel: 216-587-0842; Fax: 216-587-0875. Independent Housing Units 4.

St. Agnes Terrace Apartments Independent Housing Tel: 216-587-3450. Apartments 42.

Eva L. Bruening Adult Day Center Tel: 216-581-2900. Clients Per Day 42.

The Learning Circle Child Day Care Center Infant to before/and/after school care. Capacity 75.

Sts. Mary and Joseph Home for the Aged, 4291 Richmond Rd., 44122-6199. Tel: 216-464-1222; Fax: 216-292-2364. Sr. Marie Edward, L.S.P. Little Sisters of the Poor Sisters 11; Association Members 18; Nursing 62; Independent Living 22; Bed Capacity 123; Total Assisted Annually 39; Total Staff 140. In Res. Revs. Leo A. Boyle; Edward J. Corrigan, S.M.; Paul A. Duzinski, O.F.M.Conv.; Claude J. Gaebelein (Retired); Ray J. Horley, Chap.; George L. Vituj (Retired).

Mount St. Joseph, 21800 Chardon Rd., 44117. Tel: 216-531-7426; Fax: 216-531-4033. Email: mountstjoe@aol.com. Sr. M. Cecilia Illig, NHA. Conducted by Sisters of St. Joseph of St. Mark - Mount St. Joseph. Sisters 10; Bed Capacity 100; Residents 100; Total Assisted Annually 100; Total Staff 165.

AKRON. *Francesca Residence*, 39 N. Portage Path, 44303. Tel: 330-867-6334; Fax: 330-867-6334. Email: ddcakron@ameritech.net. Sr. M. Martin Green, F.D.C., Admin.; Rev. Albert A. Kunkel, Chap. Daughters of Divine Charity 5; Total Assisted Annually 41; Total in Residence 34; Total Staff 11.

BEACHWOOD. *Villa Sancta Anna Home for the Aged, Inc.*, 25000 Chagrin Blvd., 44122-5665. Tel: 216-464-9250; Fax: 216-464-9274. Email: lscherger@en.com. Linda Scherger, R.N., Admin. Residents 68; Total Assisted 68; Total Staff 91.

BEDFORD. *Light of Hearts Villa, Inc.*, 283 Union St., 44146. Tel: 216-232-1991; Fax: 440-232-1782. Email: lightofhearts@sbcglobal.net. Web: www.lightofheartsvilla.org. Sisters Helen Therese Scasny, V.S.C., Exec. Dir.; Kathryn Thomas, C.S.J., Asst. Dir.; Barbara Hammrel, Asst. Dir. Total in Residence 109; Total Assisted 109; Total Staff 70.

FAIRLAWN. *St. Edward Home* dba The Village at St. Edward Nursing Care and Assisted Living , 3131 Smith Rd., 44333. Tel: 330-666-1183; Fax: 330-666-2721. Email: jhennelly@vased.org. Web: www.vased.org. John J. Hennelly, Pres. & CEO; Rev. James F. Flood, Chap. Sisters 2; Nursing Care Residents 100; Assisted Living Residents 26; Total Staff 147.

St. Edward Home dba The Village at St. Edward Independent Living , 3125 Smith Rd., 44333. Tel: 330-668-2828; Fax: 330-666-6636. John J. Hennelly, Pres. & CEO; Rev. James F. Flood, Chap. Total in Residence 160; Total Staff 33.

PARMA. *Franciscan Communities - Mount Alverna*

Home, 6765 State Rd., 44134. Tel: 440-843-7800; Fax: 440-843-7107. Web: www.franciscancommunities.com/facilities/mtalverna. Patrick M. Welsh, Exec. Dir.; Rev. Jerome Dunn, O.F.M.Cap. Capacity 203; Residents 203; Total Assisted 203; Total Staff 350.

RICHFIELD. *Regina Health Center*, 5232 Broadview Rd., 44286-9608. Tel: 330-659-4161; Fax: 330-659-5113. Email: bflannery@reginahealthcenter.org. Sr. Miriam Erb, C.S.A., Congregational Leader. Sponsored by Sisters of Charity of St. Augustine. Nursing Home Beds 101; Assisted Living Units 54; Total in Residence 141; Total Assisted 41; Total Staff 180.

[N] RESIDENCE FOR RETIRED PRIESTS

BROOKLYN. *St. Anthony of Padua Friary*, 4185 Brookway Ln., 44144. Tel: 216-661-1470. William Brady, Asst. Admin. Franciscan Friary of St. Anthony of Padua, St. Louis, MO Total in Residence 5; Total Staff 2.

[O] MONASTERIES AND RESIDENCES OF PRIESTS AND BROTHERS

CLEVELAND. *Benedictine Order of Cleveland*, St. Andrew Abbey, 10510 Buckeye Rd., 44104. Tel: 216-721-5300; Fax: 216-721-1253. Email: clement@wviz.org. Web: www.bocohio.org. Most Rev. Roger W. Gries, O.S.B., Auxiliary Bishop of Cleveland. Priests 20; Brothers 14.

5135 Superior Ave., 44103. Tel: 216-361-0873; Fax: 216-361-0877. Rt. Rev. Clement Zeleznik O.S.B., Abbot of St. Andrew Abbey; Revs. Bede Kotlinski, O.S.B., Subprior; Albert Marflak, O.S.B., Vocation Dir.; Joachim Pastirik, O.S.B.; Gerard Gonda, O.S.B.; Timothy Buyansky, O.S.B.; Dominic Mondzelewski, O.S.B.; Placid Pientek, O.S.B.; Gary Hoover, O.S.B.; William T. Matyas, O.S.B.; Paschal Petcavage, O.S.B.; Benedict Sellers, O.S.B.; Lawrence Sevcik, O.S.B.; Anselm Zupka, O.S.B.; Justin Dyrwal, O.S.B.

Assumption Church: 9183 Broadview Rd., Broadview Heights, 44147. Tel: 440-526-1177; Fax: 440-526-2838.

Other Assignments:

St. Vincent Hospital, Billings, MT 59107-5200. Tel: 406-657-7000. Rev. Anthony J. Ozimek, O.S.B.

Assumption Church: 9183 Broadview Rd., 44147. Tel: 440-526-1177; Fax: 440-526-2838. Rev. Christopher Schwartz, O.S.B.

St. Andrew: 5135 Superior Ave., 44103. Tel: 216-431-2057. Rev. Ronald Mahnke, O.S.B.

St. Peter: 6455 Engle Rd., 44142. Tel: 216-433-1440; Fax: 216-433-1434. Revs. Michael Brunovsky, Novice Master; Dismas Boeff, O.S.B., Chap., Southwest General Hospital.

Incarnate Word: 6618 Pearl Rd., Parma Heights, 44130. Tel: 440-886-6996; Fax: 440-888-1377. Rev. Kenneth J. Katricak, O.S.B., Chap.

Blessed Sacrament Community, 5384 Wilson Mills Rd., 44143-3092. Tel: 440-442-3411; Fax: 440-442-2001. Web: blessedsacrament.com. Very Rev. Norman Pelletier, S.S.S., Prov. Supr. Revs. Michael Arkins, S.S.S., Pastor; Roger Bourgeois, S.S.S., Supr.; Donald J. Jette, S.S.S.; Michael Noreika, S.S.S.; Walter A. Riendeau, S.S.S.; John Dowling, S.S.S.; Thomas Smitson, S.S.S.; Dominic Luong, S.S.S.; Robert Pittman, S.S.S.; William T. Young, S.S.S.; Deacon Joseph Bourgeois; Bros. Eugene Blee, S.S.S.; Edmund Hardy, S.S.S.; Gerard Hickey, S.S.S.; Thomas F. Flanagan, S.S.S.; Gary L. Laverdiere, S.S.S.; Michael J. O'Leary, S.S.S.; Allen Boeckman, S.S.S.; Michael Galligan, S.S.S.; Ignatius J. Montgomery, S.S.S. Priests 11; Deacons 1; Brothers 9.

Regina Health Center, 5232 Broadview Rd., Richfield, 44286-9608. Tel: 330-659-4161. Revs. George Evans, S.S.S.; Edmund Slattery, S.S.S.; Lionel Lavigne, S.S.S.; Raymond Dubois, S.S.S.; Frederick Roberge, S.S.S.; Roger Pageot, S.S.S.; Martin Hayes, S.S.S. Priests 6; Brothers 1.

Congregation of the Blessed Sacrament Provincial House Province of St. Ann.

5384 Wilson Mills Rd., Highland Heights, 44143-3092. Tel: 440-442-6311; Fax: 440-442-4752. Web: www.blessedsacrament.com. Very Rev. Norman B. Pelletier, S.S.S., Prov. Supr.; Rev. Edward J. Stapleton, S.S.S., Prov. Treas.

Priests Serving Outside Country: Rev. Ralph Roberts, S.S.S., Parrocchia S. Marco Evangelista, Via Del Modiano 1/1, Trieste 34148 Italy. Tel: 011-39-040-941218; Fax: 011-39-040-938-1987.

Priests attached to Provincialate:

11487 Kerridale Ave., Spring Hill, FL 34608-3111. Tel: 352-686-8078. Rev. Andrew Beaudoin, S.S.S.

58 Dudley St., New Bedford, MA 02744-1503. Tel: 508-993-3717. Rev. Rene A. Belanger, S.S.S.

Holy Cross Diocesan Center, 3710 East Ave. S., P.O. Box 4004, La Crosse, WI 54602-4004. Tel: 608-787-8739. Rev. Peter Cops, S.S.S.

36 Monument Sq., Apt. 4, Charlestown, MA 02129-3429. Tel: 617-241-9121. Rev. Edward Roberts, S.S.S.

P.O. Box 1419, Gretna, LA 70053-1419. Tel: 504-392-1630; Fax: 504-392-5440. Revs Joachim Viet-Chau S.S.S., Vietnamese Apostolate; Nicholas Zohnerowicz, S.S.S., 584 Landers Dr., S.W., Mableton, GA 30126-2353; John Kamas, S.S.S., Our Lady of Good Counsel Church, 230 E. 90 St., New York, NY 10128-3503. Tel: 212-289-1742; Thomas O'Mahony, S.S.S., 78 Third Street, Providence, RI 02906-2729; Dennis Ruane, S.S.S., 11715 State St., Apt. D, Draper, UT 84020-6922. Tel: 801-495-3691.

Regina Health Center, 5232 Broadview Rd., Richfield, 44286-9608. Tel: 330-659-4161. Revs. George Evans, S.S.S.; Lionel Lavigne, S.S.S.; Edmund J. Slattery, S.S.S.; Raymond Dubois, S.S.S.; Frederick Roberge, S.S.S. In Res. Revs. Paul Bernier, S.S.S.; Mario Marzocchi, S.S.S., St. Vincent De Paul, P.O. Box 3865, Holiday, FL 34690. Tel: 727-938-1974; Roger Pageot, S.S.S.; Robert S. Pittman, S.S.S., Blessed Sacrament Community, 5384 Wilson Mills Rd., 44143. Tel: 440-442-3410; Bro. Maurice (Martin) Hayes, S.S.S.

St. Jude Friary, 4761 Richmond Rd., 44128. Tel: 216-292-6602; Fax: 216-292-0454. Revs. Emmanuel Beunen, O.F.M.; Thomas Carolan, O.F.M., Supr.; Bro. Joseph Di Santo, O.F.M. Priests 2; Brothers 1; Total Assisted 60.

Marianist Community, 18340 Marcella Rd., 44119-2622. Tel: 216-481-1007. Email: jpjdempsey@vasj.com. Bro. John P. Dempsey, S.M., Dir.; Rev. George J. Abmayr, S.M.; Bros. David L. Conrad, S.M.; William G. Halloway, S.M.; David F. Murphy, S.M.; Rev. Eldon G. Reichert, S.M.; Bros. Richard Roesch, S.M.; Joseph A. Scheible, S.M. Priests 2; Brothers 6.

Maryknoll Fathers, 10309 Edgewater Dr., 44102. Tel: 216-651-2121; Fax: 216-651-8242. Email: mklcleve@aol.com. Web: www.maryknoll.org. Revs. James H. Huvane, M.M., Dir.; Richard S. Kardian, M.M. Total in Residence 2; Total Staff 1.

Mercedarians, 6928 Detroit Ave., 44102-3093. Tel: 216-651-5043; Fax: 216-651-6641. Email: mtcarmel@megsinet.net. Web: www.massintransit.com. Rev. Richard S. Rasch, O.de.M. Order of the BVM of Mercy Priests 4; Brothers 1. In Res. Revs. Marino Frascati, O.de.M.; Joseph K. Horvath, O.de.M.; Arcangelo Manzi, O.de.M., Supr.; Bro. John Michael Zyckowski, O.de.M.

Missionary Servants of the Most Holy Trinity Tel: 216-391-3947; Fax: 216-391-7919. Email: frmikeb@cs.com. Web: www.cleveland.catholicnet.com.

St. Agnes-Our Lady of Fatima: 6800 Lexington Ave., 44103. Tel: 216-391-1655; Fax: 216-391-7919. Rev. Michael K. Barth, S.T.

St. Paul Friary, 4120 Euclid Ave., 44103. Tel: 216-431-8854; Fax: 216-361-1951. Email: Stpaulshrine@aol.com. Revs. Michael Joyce, O.F.M.Cap. Andrew Hohman, O.F.M.Cap.; Eric Gauchat, O.F.M.Cap.; Robert Marva, O.F.M.Cap. Priests 4.

St. Stanislaus Friary (Please see St. Stanislaus, Cleveland in the parish section for additional information.) , 3649 E. 65th St., 44105-1293. Tel: 216-341-9091; Fax: 216-341-2688. Email: ststans@ameritech.net. Web: www.ststanislaus.org. Revs. Michael Surufka, O.F.M.; Joachim Studwell, O.F.M. The Franciscan Friars, Province of the Assumption of the Blessed Virgin

Marymount Convent, Garfield Heights, 44125. Tel: 516-581-2225. Rev. George Jaskulski, O.F.M. (Pulaski, WI), Chap.

University of Akron, Akron, 44325-3908. Tel: 330-972-7163; Fax: 330-972-8445. Rev. Lazarus Macior, O.F.M. (Pulaski, WI), Prof. Priests 4.

AVON. *Congregation of St. Joseph*, 4076 Case Rd., 44011. Tel: 440-934-6270; Fax: 440-934-6270. Email: avon@murialdo.org. Web: www.murialdo.org. Revs. Lawrence Tosco, C.S.J.; Leo Dechant, C.S.J.; Libero Ballestrazzi, C.S.J.; Gaetano Menegatto, C.S.J.; Giampietro Gasparin, C.S.J. Fathers and Brothers of St. Joseph Priests 5.

BROOKLYN. *Padua Franciscan Friary*, 4185 Brookway Ln., 44144. Tel: 216-661-7138; Fax: 216-845-5710. Revs. Walter Dolan, O.F.M.; Theodore Haag, O.F.M., Guardian; James McManamon, O.F.M.; Bro. Thomas Carroll, O.F.M., Vicar. Priests 3; Brothers 1.

[P] CONVENTS AND RESIDENCES FOR SISTERS

CLEVELAND. *Carmel of the Holy Family*, 3176 Fairmount Blvd., 44118-4199. Tel: 216-321-6568. Email: carmelite@csnmail.net. Sr. Anne Joan Boyle, O.C.D., Prioress. Discalced Carmelite Nuns Professed Nuns 14.

Marymount Congregational Home Tel: 216-581-3535; Fax: 216-581-3564. Email: srmaslanka@aol.com. Web: www.ssj-tosf.org. 12215 Granger Rd., Garfield Heights, 44125. Tel: 216-581-3535; Fax: 216-581-3564. Sr. Anne Maslanka, Contact; Rev. George Jaskulski, O.F.M., Chap. & Contact Person. Residence of the Sisters of St. Joseph, Third Order of St. Francis. Sisters 60.

Monastery of the Poor Clares Poor Clare Nuns (Colettine) , 3501 Rocky River Dr., 44111-2998. Tel: 216-941-2820. Observing the Primitive Rule of St. Clare (strictly cloistered solemn vows). Perpetual exposition of the Blessed Sacrament. Cloistered Nuns 21; Extern Sisters 3.

Motherhouse and Novitiate of the Sisters of the Holy Spirit, 10102 Granger Rd., 44125. Tel: 216-581-2941; Fax: 216-581-1207. Email: sistermarywahoo@ameritech.net. Sr. Assumpta Zabas, C.S.Sp., Supr. Gen. Professed Sisters 8.

Motherhouse and Novitiate of the Ursuline Sisters, 2600 Lander Rd., 44124. Tel: 440-449-1200; Fax: 440-449-3588. Email: vdevinne@ursulinesisters.org. Web: www.ursulinesisters.org. Sr. Virginia DeVinne, O.S.U., Gen. Supr.

Legal Title: *The Ursuline Academy of Cleveland* Professed Nuns 232.

Motherhouse of the Sisters of St. Joseph, 3430 Rocky River Dr., 44111. Tel: 216-252-0440; Fax: 216-941-3430. Email: info@csjcleveland.org. Web: www.csjcleveland.org. Sisters Mary Brinkman, C.S.J., Leadership Team; Patricia Kozak, C.S.J., Leadership Team; Mary Schrader, C.S.J., Leadership Team. Sisters 131.

St. Joseph Wellness Center Tel: 216-251-7062; Fax: 216-251-2886. Email: sjwellnesscenter@yahoo.com. Sisters 3; Associates 1.

Seeds of Literacy Tel: 216-651-4302; Fax: 216-651-4305. Total Staff 2.

Wellspring Bookstore & Gift Shop Tel: 440-323-4466; Fax: 440-323-1761. Email: wscsjgog@aol.com. Total Staff 2.

St. Joseph Conference & Learning Center Tel: 216-688-1111; Fax: 216-688-1116. Email: stjosconf@aol.com. Total Staff 2.

Poor Clares of Perpetual Adoration, 4108 Euclid Ave., 44103. Tel: 216-361-0783; Fax: 216-361-0979. Sr. Mary James, P.C.P.A., Supr. Monastery adjoins Conversion of St. Paul Church, where they maintain Perpetual Adoration. Cloistered Sisters 16.

Provincial House of Sisters of the Most Holy Trinity, 21281 Chardon Rd., 44117. Tel: 216-481-8232; Fax: 216-481-6577. Email: trinitarian@srstrinity.com. Web: www.srstrinity.com. Sr. Phyllis Ann Lavalle, O.SS.T., Regl. Delegate. Attended from Center for Pastoral Leadership. Sisters 22; Total in Residence 13.

Sisters of St. Joseph of St. Mark General Motherhouse and Novitiate of Sisters of St. Joseph of St. Mark-Generalate, Diocese of Cleveland., 21800 Chardon Rd., 44117. Tel: 216-531-7426; Fax: 216-531-4033. Email: mountstjoe@aol.com. Sr. M. Therese Trunk, Gen. Supr. Sisters 12.

Sisters of the Incarnate Word and Blessed Sacrament, 6618 Pearl Rd., 44130-3808. Tel: 440-886-6440; Fax: 440-842-6391. Email: sctobler@yahoo.com. Sr. Carol Tobler, S.I.W., Congregational Leader.

Legal Title: *Motherhouse and Novitiate of the Sisters of the Incarnate Word and Blessed Sacrament* Final Professed Sisters 32.

6634 Pearl Rd., Parma Heights, 44130-3808. Tel: 440-886-6996. In Res. Rev. Kenneth J. Katricak, O.S.B.

AKRON. *Motherhouse of the Sisters of St. Dominic of the Immaculate Heart of Mary*, Our Lady of the Elms Convent, 1230 W. Market St., 44313-7108. Tel: 330-836-4908; Fax: 330-836-5913. Email: ssd1230@akronop.org. Web: www.akronop.org. Sisters 88.

Provincial Motherhouse and Novitiate of the Daughters of Divine Charity, 39 N. Portage Path, 44303-1183. Tel: 330-867-4960; Fax: 330-867-6334. Email: ddcakron@ameritech.net. Sr. Mary Coffelt, F.D.C., Prov. Supr.; Rev. Albert Kunkel, Chap. Tel: 330-867-2618. Sisters 20.

BEDFORD. *Motherhouse and Novitiate of the Vincentian Sisters of Charity*, Villa San Bernardo, 1160 Broadway, 44146-4523. Tel: 440-232-4755; Fax: 440-232-7832. Email: a.vscoffice@.att.net. Web: www.vsc.catholicweb.com. Sisters Christine Rody, Gen. Supr.; Regina Kusnir, Formation; Anita Maroun, Vocation-Contact Person. Sisters 51.

CHARDON. *Provincial House of the Sisters of Notre Dame, Juniorate, Novitiate*, Notre Dame Educational Center, 13000 Auburn Rd., 44024. Tel: 440-286-7101; Fax: 440-286-3377. Email: msvoboda@ndec.org. Web: www.snd1.org. Rev. Paul J. Sciarrotta, Chap. Sisters 398.

INDEPENDENCE. *Contemplative Sisters of the Good Shepherd* (Infirmary) , 7800 Brookside Rd., 44131.

Tel: 216-524-4578; Fax: 216-524-5699. Email: cgs2000@ameritech.com. Contemplative Sisters of the Good Shepherd 13; Religious Sisters of the Good Shepherd 2.

Sisters of the Good Shepherd dba Marycrest of the City of Cleveland , 7800 Brookside Rd., 44131. Tel: 216-524-4578; Fax: 216-524-5699. Sisters 16.

RICHFIELD. *Mount Augustine, Motherhouse of the Sisters of Charity of St. Augustine*, 5232 Broadview Rd., 44286-9608. Tel: 330-659-5100; Fax: 330-659-3899. Email: sme@srsofcharity.org. Web: www.srsofcharity.org. Sr. Miriam Erb, C.S.A., Congregational Leader. Finally Professed Sisters 77.

Regina Health Center Tel: 330-659-4161; Fax: 330-659-5113. Religious Congregations 22; Total Assisted Care 54; Skilled Nursing Beds 101.

Saint Ann Foundation Tel: 216-241-9300; Fax: 216-241-9345.

[Q] SECULAR INSTITUTES

CLEVELAND HEIGHTS. *Society of Our Lady of the Way*, c/o Mary Ann Tady, 1064 Oxford Rd., 44121. Tel: 216-381-5502. Email: matslow@aol.com. Web: www.secularinstitutes.org. Secular Institute for Single Women.

[R] HOMES FOR WOMEN

AKRON. *Leonora Hall*, 39 N. Portage Path, 44303. Tel: 330-867-1752; Fax: 330-867-6334. Sr. M. Antoinette, F.D.C., Exec. Dir. Residence for Young Women, providing residential and support services to individuals with mild or moderate mental retardation/developmental disabilities in addition to providing a "Home Away From Home" for students and other young women in need of independent or semi-independent living. Daughters of Divine Charity 2; Residents 21.

[S] LAY ASSOCIATIONS

CLEVELAND. *Community of Little Brothers and Sisters of the Eucharist, Inc.*, 2186 East 35th St., 44115-3039. Tel: 216-566-0531; Fax: 216-566-9370. Email: lsismags@stratos.net. Maggie Conrad, Dir.

[T] RETREAT HOUSES

CLEVELAND. *Jesuit Retreat House*, 5629 State Rd., 44134. Tel: 440-884-9300; Fax: 440-885-1055. Email: jrhcleve@worldnet.att.net. Web: www.jrh-cleveland.org. Revs. Clem Metzger, S.J., Dir.; James Farrell, S.J., Spirituality Team; Thomas W. Gedeon, S.J., Spirituality Team.

St. Joseph Christian Life Center, 18485 Lake Shore Blvd., 44119-1299. Tel: 216-531-7370; Fax: 216-531-0629. Email: frontdesk@stjosephchristianlife.org. Web: stjosephchristianlife.org. Rev. Walter J. Hyclak, Exec. Dir.; Jackie Cherep, Operations Mgr. & Finance Coord.; Pat Kassay, Prog. Dir.; Carol Jauch, Facility Coord.; Deacon Leo McNulty. Total Staff 30.

AKRON. *Loyola of the Lakes Jesuit Retreat House, Inc.* Tel: 800-827-1416; Fax: 330-896-0858. Email: lotljrh@aol.com. Web: www.loyolaofthelakes.com. 700 Killinger Rd., Clinton, 44216-9653. Tel: 330-896-2315; 800-827-1416; Fax: 330-896-0858. Mr. Elizabeth R. Haller, Exec. Dir.; Theresa M. Nieman, Office Mgr. In Res. Revs. Vincent A. Hagarman, S.J.; Paul D. Panaretos, S.J., Retreat Master.

AVON. *St. Leonard Youth Retreat Center*, 4076 Case Rd., 44011. Tel: 440-934-6735; Fax: 440-934-6270. Email: frgiampietro@aol.com. Web: www.stleonard-yrc.org. Rev. Giampietro Gasparin, C.S.J., Dir.

BEDFORD. *Poustinia*, 1160 Broadway, 44146-4523. Tel: 440-232-4755; Fax: 440-232-7832. Email: a.vscoffice@att.net. Web: www.vsc.catholicweb.com. Judy Kendrick, Contact Person. Vincentian Sisters of Charity

Tabor Center, 1160 Broadway, 44146-4523. Tel: 440-232-4755; Fax: 440-232-7832. Email: a.vscoffice@att.net. Web: www.vsc.catholicweb.com. Judy Kendrick, Contact Person. Vincentian Sisters of Charity Maximum Capacity 5.

[U] SOCIAL SERVICE AGENCIES AND INSTITUTIONS

For information call Catholic Information and Referral Services (CIRS) Tel: 216-696-HELP (4357).

CLEVELAND

Bishop William M. Cosgrove Family Center, 1736 Superior Ave., 44114. Tel: 216-781-8262; Fax: 216-566-9161. Email: nxevans@dioceseofcleveland.org. Nicole Evans, Prog. Dir. Total Assisted 22,000; Total Staff 6.

Catholic Charities Corporation, 1027 Superior Ave., 44114. Tel: 216-696-6525; 216-696-6525, Ext. 4170 (Catholic Charities Appeal); Fax: 216-861-9795. Email: JPKlee@dioceseofcleveland.org. Web: www-.ClevelandCatholicCharities.org. John P. Klee, Pres.

Catholic Charities Facilities Corporation (CCFC), 1111 Superior Ave., 44114. Tel: 216-696-6525, Ext. 5540; Fax: 216-861-1176. Email: lxmurtaugh@dioceseofcleveland.org. Lawrence E. Murtaugh, Pres. & CEO.

Catholic Charities Services Corporation, Eaton Center, 1111 Superior Ave., Ste. 420, 44114. Tel: 216-696-6525; Fax: 216-344-9962. Email: txwoll@dioceseofcleveland.org. Web: www.clevelandcatholiccharities.org. Thomas Woll, Exec. Dir. Tel: 216-696-6525, Ext. 416; Michael Haggerty, Assoc. Exec. Dir.; Bernadette Washington, Asst. Exec. Dir., Family Center Svcs.; Maureen Dee, Asst. Exec. Dir., Chemical Dependency Svcs.; James Clements, Asst. Exec. Dir., County Services. Catholic Charities Services Corporation is part of the health and human services delivery system of the Diocese. Utilizing a holistic approach to healing, the system focuses on four service groups: children and families, persons with disabilities, older adults and persons with emergency and transitional needs.

Catholic Charities Services Corporation, 1111 Superior Ave., Ste. 420, 44114. Tel: 216-696-6525; Fax: 216-344-9962. Email: txwoll@dioceseofcleveland.org. Maureen Dee, Dir.

Catholic Charities Services of Medina County, 246 Northland Dr., Medina, 44256. Tel: 330-723-9615 (Medina); Fax: 330-764-8795 (Medina); Tel: 419-289-1903 (Ashland); Fax: 419-281-8342 (Ashland); Tel: 330-262-7386 (Wayne); Fax: 330-262-2867 (Wayne). Timothy Putka, Dir.

Catholic Charities Services of Cuyahoga County, 7800 Detroit Ave., 44102. Tel: 216-631-3499; Fax: 216-631-3654. Email: towers@dioceseofcleveland.org. Web: www.cle-dioc.org. Mike Haggerty, Assoc. Exec. Dir.

Catholic Charities Services of Geauga County, 1077 Mayfield Rd., 44024-9323. Tel: 800-242-9755; Fax: 440-285-4909. Anthony J. Marjenin, M.S.S.A., L.I.S.W., Dir.

Catholic Charities Services of Lake County, 8 N. State St., Suite 455, Painesville, 44077-3954. Tel: 440-946-7264; Fax: 440-953-1608. Anthony Marjenin, Dir.

Catholic Charities Services of Lorain County, 628 Poplar St., Elyria, 44035. Tel: 440-366-1106; 877-566-1106; Fax: 440-366-5645. Mary Lou Wellman, Dir.

Chemical Dependency Services - Midtown Professional Center, 3135 Euclid Ave., Room 202, 44115-2507. Tel: 216-391-2064; Fax: 216-391-8946.

DePaul Family Center, 2320 E. 24th St., 44115. Tel: 216-687-0000; Fax: 216-687-0403. E. Clark, Dir.

Employment & Training Services - Midtown Professional Center, 3135 Euclid Ave., Room 203, 44115-2507. Tel: 216-426-9870; Fax: 216-426-9932. Beverly Cinouzc, Dir.

Fatima Family Center, 6600 Lexington Ave., 44103. Tel: 216-391-0505; Fax: 216-391-1118. LaJean Ray, Dir.

Head Start, 1031 Superior Ave., 44114. Tel: 216-696-6525; Fax: 216-696-3631. Rhonda Lovejoy, Dir.

Hispanic Senior Center, 7800 Detroit Ave., 44102. Tel: 216-631-3599; Fax: 216-631-3654. Edna Fuentes-Casiano, Prog. Dir.

LaProvidencia Family Center, 2012 W. 25th St., 44113. Tel: 216-696-2089; Fax: 216-696-2088. Ramonita Johnson, Dir.

Matt Talbot Inn, 2270 Professor Ave., 44113-4489. Tel: 216-781-0288; Fax: 216-781-6270. Terry Morris, Prog. Dir.

Matt Talbot for Women at St. Vincent Charity Hospital, 2351 E. 22nd St., 44115. Tel: 216-592-2800; Fax: 216-592-2854. Colleen McKenna, Dir.

OLA / St. Joseph Center, 2346 W. 14th St., 44113-3697. Tel: 216-621-3451; Fax: 216-621-6104. Pamela Delly, Prin.

Parmadale, 6753 State Rd., Parma, 44134-4596. Tel: 440-845-7700; Fax: 440-845-5910. Anne Mengerink, Dir.

St. Martin de Porres Family Center, 1264 E. 123rd St., 44108-4042. Tel: 216-268-3909; Fax: 216-268-0207. Kevin Hodges, Dir.

LaProvidencia Family Center, 7800 Detroit Ave., 44102. Tel: 216-631-3955; Fax: 216-631-3654. Ramonita Johnson, Dir.

Catholic Charities Parish Services:

Camps:

Camp Corde, 2901 Ridgewood Ave., Parma, 44134. Tel: 440-884-3950; Fax: 440-884-3950.

Camp Christopher, Ira & Hametown Rd., Bath, 44210. Tel: 800-CYO-CAMP; Fax: 330-762-2001.

Affiliated Corporations within the Secretariat for Catholic Charities Health & Human Services (Under membership structure of Bishop, Secretary for Health & Human Services & Chairperson of Board of Trustees.

Catholic Community Care, 7801 Detroit Ave., 44102. Tel: 216-939-7720; Fax: 216-634-7483. Email: amhorne@worldnet.att.net.

Catholic Social Services of Summit County, 640 N. Main St., Akron, 44310. Tel: 330-762-7481; Fax: 330-762-7484.

CYO & Community Services of Summit County, 812 Birutha St., Akron, 44307. Tel: 330-762-2961; Fax: 330-762-2001.

Matt Talbot For Women, a St. Vincent Charity Hospital, 2351 E. 22nd St., 44115. Tel: 216-592-2800; Fax: 216-592-2854.

Rose-Mary, The Johanna Grasselli Rehabilitation and Education Center, 19350 Euclid Ave., 44117. Tel: 216-481-4823; Fax: 216-481-4158.

Special Ministry to the Aged, 6804 Lansing Ave., 44105-1521. Tel: 216-441-5402; Fax: 216-441-4510. Sr. Anna Kaszuba, S.S.M.I., Dir.

St. Augustine Corporation, 7801 Detroit Ave., 44102. Tel: 216-634-7400; Fax: 216-634-7483.

The Society of St. Vincent de Paul (not under membership structure), 1027 Superior Ave., 44114. Tel: 216-696-6525; Fax: 216-589-4772. Total Staff 3; Total Assisted 20,000.

Bishop William M. Cosgrove Family Center, 1736 Superior Ave., 44114. Tel: 216-781-8262; Fax: 216-566-9161. Sharon Fields, Dir.

Catholic Charities Services of Ashland County, 1260 S. Center St., Ashland, 44805-2000. Tel: 419-289-1903; Fax: 419-281-8342. Cathy Thiemens, Dir.

Catholic Charities Services of Wayne County, 521 Beall Ave., Wooster, 44691-3523. Tel: 330-262-7836; Fax: 330-262-2867.

Catholic Charities Services of Ashland, Medina, and Wayne Counties, 246 Northland Dr., Medina, 44256-1598. Tel: 330-723-9615; Fax: 330-764-8795. Email: medina@dioceseofcleveland.org. Provides counseling, casework, and family life education in Ashland, Wayne, and Medina Counties.

Medina. Tel: 330-723-9615; Fax: 330-764-8795.

Ashland. Tel: 419-289-1903; Fax: 419-281-8342.

Brunswick-Cleveland. Tel: 330-225-7100.

Wadsworth-Akron. Tel: 330-336-6657.

Wooster. Tel: 330-262-7836; Fax: 330-262-2867. Timothy J. Putka, M.S., Dir.

Catholic Charities Services of Cuyahoga County, St. Augustine Towers, 7800 Detroit Ave., 44102-2895. Tel: 216-631-3499; Fax: 216-631-3654. Email: towers@dioceseofcleveland.org. Web: www.clevelandcatholiccharities.org. Michael Haggerty, Assoc. Exec. Dir. A multi-function social service agency which offers social service programs. Individual, family, and group counseling; marital counseling, psychiatric consultations; and outpatient psychiatric services for children, youth, and adults. Chemical dependency assessments and outpatient counseling for youth and families having alcohol and other drug-related problems. Bilingual services for Hispanic youth and families. Child day care; school for pregnant teens; pregnancy counseling and planning; adoption; older adult programs, senior citizens counseling and respite care; employment services.

Midtown Center, 3135 Euclid Ave., Ste. 202, 44115-2507. Tel: 216-391-2061; Fax: 216-391-8946. Chemical Dependency Svcs.

3135 Euclid Ave., Ste. 203, 44115-2507. Tel: 216-426-9870; Fax: 216-426-9932. Employment & Training Svcs.

Parmadale, 6753 State Rd., Parma, 44134. Tel: 440-845-7700; Fax: 440-845-5610.

Hispanic Services, 2012 W. 25th St., Rm. 517, 44113. Tel: 216-696-2089; Fax: 216-696-2088.

Catholic Charities Services of Geauga County, 10771 Mayfield Rd., Chardon, 44024-9323. Tel: 440-285-3537 (TDD); 800-242-9755 (Ohio); Fax: 440-285-4909. Email: geauga@dioceseofcleveland.org. Anthony J. Marjenin, M.S.S.A., L.I.S.W., Dir. Outpatient counseling for families and individuals. Substance abuse counseling. Parenting programs. Services for the elderly. Services to strengthen and enrich the valued relationships of families and individuals for effective and healthy living. Employment programs for youth and for disabled adults.

St. Malachi Center, Inc., 2416 Superior Viaduct, 44113. Tel: 216-771-3036; Fax: 216-771-3659. Email: st-malachi@ameritech.net. Web: www.StMalachi-Center.org. Total Assisted 150 per day (Neighborhood Center); 30 per Monday (Health Services) Total Staff 14.

Malachi House, Inc., 2810 Clinton Ave., 44113. Tel: 216-621-8831; Fax: 216-621-8841. Email: st_malachi@ameritech.net. Web: www.malachihouse.org. Malachi House provides unskilled, family-like care to the dying poor without cost. Serves individuals who need an available caregiver, who have limited or no financial resources and are in need of special home care in the final stages of life. A trained staff and volunteers provide spiritual , emotional and physical support with the assistance of a hospice team. Acceptable only if care is manageable in a home setting. Handicapped access. Total Assisted Annually 90; Total Staff 25.

Society of St. Vincent de Paul, Diocesan Central Council, Chancery Bldg., 1027 Superior Ave., 44114. Tel: 216-696-6525, Ext. 3580; Fax: 216-589-4772. Email: lglauter@dioceseofcleveland.org. Web: www.svdpcle.org. Frank J. Fearon, Diocesan Pres.; Lawrence Lauter, A.C.S.W, L.I.S.W., M.Div., Exec. Sec.; Rev. James R. Schleicher, Spiritual Dir.
1031 Superior Ave., 44114. Tel: 216-696-6525, Ext. 2540. Email: mmach@diocessofcleveland.org. Sr. Margaret Mach, V.S.C., Diocesan Spiritual Advisor.

Akron District Council, 4533 Pineridge Dr., Stow, 44224. Tel: 330-929-9230. Leonard Sikora, Pres.

Cleveland District Council, Chancery Building, 1027 Superior Ave., 44114. Tel: 216-696-6525, Ext. 3580; Fax: 216-589-4772. Lawrence Lauter, Exec. Dir.; James F. Mullen, Asst. Exec. Dir. Tel: 216-696-5720; Fax: 216-589-4772.

Lorain District Council, 6587 Lake Ave., Elyria, 44035. Tel: 440-324-4589. James Fischer, Interim Pres., 36300 Behm Drive, North Ridgeville, 44039. Tel: 440-327-8235.

St. Vincent de Paul Thrift Stores, 875 E. 70th, 44103. Tel: 216-391-9655; Fax: 216-391-8910.
16730 Lorain Ave., 44111. Tel: 216-252-8764.
5700 Broadway Ave., 44127. Tel: 216-341-3445.

AKRON

Catholic Social Services of Summit County, Inc., 640 N. Main St., 44310-3098. Tel: 330-762-7481; Fax: 330-762-7484. Email: susans@csssc.org. Web: www.csssc.org. Patrick A. McGrath, M.S.S.W., Exec. Dir. Service sites throughout Summit County. Total Assisted 17,000; Total Staff 38.

CYO & Community Services, 812 Biruta St., 44307-1104. Tel: 330-762-2961; Fax: 330-762-2001. Email: DFinn@akroncyo.org. Web: www.akroncyo.org.
CYO Adult Day Services:
812 Biruta St., 44307. Tel: 330-762-2000; Fax: 330-762-2001. Donald P. Finn, Exec. Dir. Total Assisted 252; Total Staff 25.

Interval Brotherhood Home Alcohol-Drug Rehabilitation Center, 3445 S. Main St., 44319. Tel: 330-644-4095; Fax: 330-645-2031. Email: sam@ibh.org. Web: www.ibh.org. Rev. Samuel R. Ciccolini, Dir. Total in residential treatment 430; Total Staff 94.

Leonora Hall (Refer to Homes for Women)

**St. Patrick Manor, Inc. c/o Humility of Mary Housing, Inc.*, 3250 W. Market St., Ste. 204, 44333. Tel: 330-384-1555; Fax: 330-384-2144. Email: kenhmhi@earthlink.net. Web: www.humilityofmary.com/frame_ministries.html. Kenneth W. Radigan, Pres.; Patricia Lindley, Sec.

ELYRIA

Catholic Charities Services of Lorain County, 628 Poplar St., 44035. Tel: 440-366-1106; Fax: 440-366-5645. Email: lorain@dioceseofceleveland.org. Mary Lou Wellman, Dir.

Catholic Charities Adult Day Services Center, St. Joseph Community Center 3B, 205 West 20th St., Lorain, 44055. Tel: 440-245-3275; Fax: 440-245-3277. Nancy Carrell, Prog. Admin.

Catholic Charities Family Center, 203 Eighth St., Lorain, 44052. Tel: 440-244-9915; Fax: 440-245-1057. James Gepperth, Prog. Admin.

GARFIELD HEIGHTS

Brendan Manor, Inc., 13401 Cranwood Dr., 44105. Tel: 216-475-5230; Fax: 216-475-5852. Email: dlkalchert@hotmail.com. Web: www.brendanmanor.org. Diane Kalchert, Exec. Dir. Licensed non-profit, nondenominational shared living home for low to moderate income older adults. Total in Residence 16; Total Staff 9.

NORTHFIELD

St. Barnabas Villa, Inc., 9234 Olde Eight Rd., 44067. Tel: 330-467-3758; Fax: 330-467-4044. Sr. M. Germaine Maximovich, V.S.C., Mgr. A shared living facility for 10 people over 60 years of age. Total in Residence 10; Total Staff 2.

PAINESVILLE

Catholic Charities Services of Lake County, 8 N. State St., No. 455, 44077-3954. Tel: 440-352-6191; 440-946-7264; Fax: 440-953-1608. Email: lake@dioceseofcleveland.org. Anthony J. Marjenin, M.S.S.A., L.I.S.W., Dir. Satellite Offices-Adoption/ Foster Care/Maternity Services to birth parents.

St. Anthony Center, 28700 Euclid Ave., Wickliffe, 44092. Tel: 440-943-7800; Fax: 440-943-7893. (Adult Day Care)

[V] SHRINES

CLEVELAND. *Our Lady of Lourdes Shrine* , Euclid, (U.S. Rtes. 20 & 6). Administered by the Sisters of the Most Holy Trinity. , 21281 Chardon Rd., 44117. Tel: 216-481-8232; Fax: 216-481-6577. Email: Trinitarian@srstrinity.com. Web: www.srstrinity.com. Sr. Phyllis Ann Lavalle, O.SS.T., Regnl. Supr. Total in Residence 13.

BEDFORD. *Our Lady of Levocha Shrine* , (Ohio Rte. 14). Administered by the Vincentian Sisters of Charity (V.S.C.). , 1160 Broadway, 44146-4523. Tel: 440-232-4755; Fax: 440-232-7832. Email: a.vscoffice@att.net. Web: www.vsc.catholicweb.com. Sr. Christine Rody, V.S.C., Contact Person.

GARFIELD HEIGHTS. *Our Lady of Czestochowa Shrine* , (Ohio Rte. 17). Administered by the Sisters of St. Joseph Third Order of St. Francis (S.S.J.-T.O.S.F.) , 12215 Granger Rd., 44125. Tel: 216-581-3535; Fax: 216-581-3564. Email: MCH125@.com. Sr. Thomasine Antenucci, Shrine Contact.

PARMA. *Our Lady, Queen of the Holy Rosary* , (U.S. Rte. 42). Administered by the Sisters of the Incarnate Word and Blessed Sacrament (S.I.W.). , 6618 Pearl Rd., 44130-3808. Tel: 440-886-6440; Fax: 440-842-6391. Email: sctobler@yahoo.com.

[W] MINISTRY TO THE SPANISH SPEAKING

CLEVELAND. *Office of Hispanic Ministry*, Diocese of Cleveland, 1031 Superior Ave., 44114-2519. Tel: 216-696-6525, Ext. 2530; Fax: 216-781-8243. Email: aalvarado@dioceseofcleveland.org. Web: mail-now.com. Sr. Alicia Alvarado, O.P., Dir.

Hispanic Parishes: Iglesia La Sagrada Familia, 7719 Detroit Ave., 44102. Tel: 216-631-6317; Fax: 216-631-3305. Rev. David F. Fallon.

Sacred Heart Chapel 4301 Pearl Ave., Lorain, 44055. Tel: 440-277-7231; 440-277-7379; Fax: 440-277-7232. Rev. William A. Thaden, Admin.

Parishes with Ministry to Spanish Speaking: St. Bernard, 47 University Ave., Akron, 44308. Tel: 330-253-5161; Fax: 330-253-6949. Rev. Paul E. Schindler.

St. Francis, 7119 Superior Ave., 44103. Tel: 216-361-4133; Fax: 216-361-1673. Sr. Geraldine Tengler, S.N.D., Parish Life Coord.; Deacon Frank Lozada.

St. Michael, 3114 Scranton Rd., 44109. Tel: 216-861-6297; Fax: 216-696-9351. Rev. James H. McCreight.

St. Mary's - Painesville, 242 N. State St., Painesville, 44077. Tel: 440-354-4381; Fax: 440-354-9174. Revs. R. Stephen Vellenga; Michael J. Stalla.

[X] NEWMAN CENTERS

CLEVELAND. *Office of Newman Campus Ministry* 1031 Superior Ave., 44114. Tel: 440-243-4955; Fax: 440-243-4955. Web: www.DioceseOfCleveland.org. Joyce M. Kelleher, Dir.
170 E. Center St., Berea, 44017. Tel: 440-243-4955; Fax: 440-243-4955. Email: mmasterson@dioceseofcleveland.org. Web www.nccm.org. Ms. Maureen Masterson, Assoc. Dir.; Emily Holtel-Hoag, Campus Min.

Case-Western Reserve University Tel: 216-421-1522; Fax: 216-421-2925. Kirsten Kolja, Campus Min.

University of Akron, Newman Center, 44 University Ave., Akron, 44308. Tel: 330-376-3585; Fax: 330-253-6949. Gregory Stevens, Campus Min. (Akron)

Baldwin-Wallace College Newman Center, 170 E. Center St., Berea, 44017. Tel: 216-243-4955; Fax: 216-243-0354. Mrs. Emily Holtel, Hoag Campus Min.; Ms. Maureen Masterson, Hoag Campus Min. (Berea)

Oberlin College, Office of Chaplains, 217 Wilder Hall, Oberlin, 44074. Tel: 440-775-8103. Mr. William Miller (Oberlin)

The College of Wooster, Box C-3135, Wooster, 44691. Tel: 330-263-2096; Fax: 440-243-4955. Mr. Tim Barron, Campus Min. (Wooster)

Ashland Tel: 449-994-4396. Rev. Kevin Conroy. Total Staff for 5 Newman Centers 5.

[Y] ENDOWMENT TRUSTS

CLEVELAND. *The Benedictine High School Endowment Trust*, 2900 Martin Luther King Jr. Dr., 44104. Tel: 216-721-5300, Ext. 207; Fax: 216-721-1253. Email: abbotclement@csnmail.net. Web: www.cbhs.net. Rev. Albert M. Marflak, O.S.B., Bd. Chm.; Rt. Rev. Clement L. Zeleznik, O.S.B.

St. John Cathedral Endowment Trust, 1007 Superior Ave., 44114. Tel: 216-771-6666; Fax: 216-781-5646. Email: stjohns@dioceseofcleveland.org. Web: www.dioceseofcleveland.org/stjohncathedral. Revs. Edward T. Estok, Admin.; Kenneth J. Jakubowski, Assoc. Pastor; Cirilo A. Nacorda, Assoc. Pastor; Deacon John P. Sferry Sr. Pastoral Assoc.

Sisters of St. Joseph Community Support Charitable Trust, 3430 Rocky River Dr., 44111-2997. Tel: 216-252-0440; Fax: 216-941-3430. Email: info@csjcleveland.org. Web: www.csjcleveland.org. Sr. Jeanne Cmolik, C.S.J., Contact Person.

The Thomas C. and Sandra S. Sullivan Foundation, c/o The Catholic Diocese of Cleveland Foundation, 1111 Superior Ave., 44114. Tel: 216-696-6525, Ext. 6040; Fax: 216-861-1173. Email: tlang@dioceseofcleveland.org. Web: www.cdcf.org. Anthony F. Lang, Dir.

Villa Angela - St. Joseph High School Education Endowment Foundation, 18491 Lake Shore Blvd., 44119. Tel: 216-481-8414; Fax: 216-486-1035. Email: jroccosalva@vast.com. Web: www.vasj.com.

AKRON. *The Daughters of Divine Charity, St. Mary Province, Charitable Trust*, 39 N. Portage Path, 44303-1183. Tel: 330-867-4960; Fax: 330-867-6334. Email: gaburick@ameritech.net.

Our Lady of the Elms-Sisters of St. Dominic Foundation, 1230 W. Market St., 44313. Tel: 330-836-4908; Fax: 330-836-5913. Email: ssd1230@akronop.org. Web: www.akronop.org.

St. Vincent-St. Mary High School Endowment Trust (1983), 15 N. Maple St., 44303. Tel: 330-253-9113; Fax: 330-996-0000. Email: sgarlando@stvm.com. Web: www.stvm.com. Sue M. Garlando, Dir. Devel.

CHARDON. *The Sisters of Notre Dame Charitable Trust*, 13000 Auburn Rd., 44024. Tel: 440-942-6716; Fax: 440-286-3377. Email: msvoboda@ndec.org. Web: www.snd1.org; www.sndchardon.org. Sr. Melannie Svoboda, S.N.D., Chm.

FAIRLAWN. **St. Hilary Parish Foundation*, 2750 W. Market St., 44333. Tel: 330-867-1055; Fax: 330-869-2312. Mr. Edward F. Carter, Pres.

LYNDHURST. *Julie Billiart School Foundation*, 4982 Clubside Rd., 44124. Tel: 216-381-1191. Email: aloporto@juliebilliartschool.org. Sr. Agnesmarie LoPorto, S.N.D., Dir.

MENTOR. *St. Mary of the Assumption Parish Endowment Trust*, 8560 Mentor Ave., 44060-5853. Tel: 440-255-3404; Fax: 440-255-4194. Web: www.stmarysmentor.org.

PARMA HEIGHTS. *Incarnate Word Academy Student and Faculty Advancement Endowment (IWA Endowment)*, 6618 Pearl Rd., 44130. Tel: 440-842-6818; Fax: 440-888-1377. Email: incarnate@leeca.org. Web: www.incarnatewordacademy.com. Sr. Eileen Fitzgerald, S.I.W.

Incarnate Word Endowment Trust, 6618 Pearl Rd., 44130-3808. Tel: 440-886-6440; Fax: 440-842-6391. Email: sctobler@yahoo.com. Sr. Carol Tobler, S.I.W., Chm.

SEVEN HILLS. *Sisters Servants of Mary Immaculate Endowment Fund in Memory of Sr. Amelia Kuska*, 285 Panorama Dr., 44131. Tel: 216-441-5402; Fax: 216-441-4510. Sr. Anna Kaszuba, S.S.M.I., Pres.

SHAKER HEIGHTS. *St. Dominic Endowment Fund*, 3450 Norwood Rd., 44122. Tel: 216-991-1444; Fax: 216-491-0190. Email: stdominic@csnmail.net. Rev. Thomas Fanta, Pres.

WELLINGTON. *St. Patrick Church Endowment Trust*, 512 N. Main St., 44090. Tel: 440-647-4375; Fax: 440-647-4675.

WOOSTER. *St. Mary of the Immaculate Conception Elementary Day School Endowment Trust*, 527 Beall Ave., P.O. Box 109, 44691. Tel: 330-264-8824; Fax: 330-262-4633. Email: stmwoost@bright.net.

[Z] MISCELLANEOUS

CLEVELAND. **St. Augustine Services Corporation*, 7801 Detroit Ave., 44102. Tel: 216-634-7400; Fax: 216-634-7483. Email: pgareau@st-aug.org. Mr. Patrick Gareau, Pres. Total Staff 15.

Caritas Connection, 2351 E. 22nd St., 44114. Tel: 216-875-4613; Fax: 216-696-2204. Email: william.mergerink@csauh.com. William Mengerink, Pres.

Catholic Charities Housing Corporation (CCHC), 1111 Superior Ave., 44114. Tel: 216-696-6525, Ext. 5540; Fax: 216-861-1176. Email: lxmurtaugh@dioceseofcleveland.org. J. Thomas Mullen, Pres.; Lawrence E. Murtaugh, Vice Pres.; Mary Ellen Staab, Sec.

Catholic Community Care, 7801 Detroit Ave., 44102. Tel: 216-939-7720; Fax: 216-939-7614. Email: A.M.Horn@worldnet.att.net. Web: www.catholiccommunitycare.org. Antoinette Horn, Pres. & CEO.

**Christ Child Society of Cleveland*, 16306 Detroit Ave., 44107. Tel: 216-521-2457; Fax: 216-288-9482. Email: ccs1cleve@aol.com. Web: community.cleveland.com/cc/christchildsoc. Mrs. Mary Graves, Contact Person.

Cleveland Slovenian Community Center, 15519 Holmes Ave., 44110-2497. Tel: 216-761-7740; Fax: 216-761-6673. Email: johnkumse@yahoo.com. Rev. John M. Kumse.

COAR Peace Mission, Inc., 4395 Rocky River Dr., 44135-2569. Tel: 216-252-5572; 800-340-6862; Fax: 216-252-5573. Email: coarpm@earthlink.net. Teodosio Feliciano, Exec. Dir. Nilda Ramos, Admin. Asst.

COAR Children's Village Tel: 011-503-314-0824. Sr. Mary Pat Driscoll, C.C.V.I., Dir. (Zaragoza, El Salvador, C.A.); Comunidad Oscar Arnulfo Romero (COAR) provides housing, education and health care for orphaned, abandoned and street children in Zaragoza, El Salvador, Central America. The Children's Village can house up to 120 children under the supervision and guidance of a housemother in fifteen home-like cottages. The COAR school provides a kindergarten to grade twelve school education to about 800 children from Zaragoza and neighboring villages. State approved vocational training is offered to high school students. The Santa Teresita Clinic, a quality medical clinic in an area with little other access to health care, serves the health and dental needs of up to 75-100 patients (adults and children) weekly. The Sisters of Charity of the Incarnate Word administer COAR Children's Village. The COAR Peace Mission in Cleveland, OH is the support and development office for the children's Village in El Salvador. COAR was founded in August 1980 by Rev. Ken Myers.

CSA Health Network, 2351 East 22nd St., 44115. Tel: 216-659-5560; Fax: 216-696-2204. Web: www.csahealthsystem.org. Sr. Judith Ann Karam, C.S.J., Pres. & CEO. Serves as the general partner to the joint venture ownership of Catholic healthcare providers.

CSA St. John Ministries fka St. John West Shore Hospital, 2351 E. 22nd St., 44115. Tel: 888-223-1816; Fax: 216-696-2204. Web: www.csahealthsystem.org. Sr. Judith Ann Karam, C.S.J., C.S.A. Pres. & CEO.

CSA St. Vincent Charity Ministries fka St. Vincent Charity Hospital, 2351 E. 22nd St., 44115. Tel: 888-223-1816; Fax: 216-696-2204. Web: www.csahealthsystem.org. Sr. Judith Ann Karam, C.S.J., C.S.A. Pres. & CEO.

First Friday Club of Cleveland, Inc., P.O. Box 6302, 44101. Tel: 440-526-4382; Fax: 216-861-0503. Gregory Szuter, Trustee; Jane Dinda, Sec.

The Greater Cleveland/Akron Corporation United for Education, 1404 E. Ninth St., 8th Fl., 44114-1722. Tel: 216-696-6525, Ext. 436; Fax: 216-696-8084. Rev. John J. Wright, Exec. Dir.; Andrej N. Lah, Attorney; Joseph Smith, Treas.

Healing Prayer Institute, P.O. Box 200404, 44120. Tel: 216-371-5133; Fax: 216-321-3097. Email: info@healingprayerinstitute.com. Web: www.healingprayerinstitute.com. Judith Pamula, Board Member.

L'Arche, Cleveland, P.O. Box 20450, 44120. Tel: 216-721-2614; Fax: 216-229-2311. Email: rebecca_larchecleveland@juno.com. An ecumenical community providing homes for adults with mental retardation and developmental disabilities. Residents 14; Total Staff 20.

National Catholic Ministry to the Bereaved, Inc., 28700 Euclid Ave., 44092-2527. Tel: 440-943-3480; Fax: 440-943-3500. Email: NCMBereave@aol.com. Web: www.griefwork.org. Mary Ann Wachtel, Exec. Dir.; Deacon Ray Deabel, Pres. (2003-2005). N.C.M.B. offers pastoral and spiritual support to the bereaved, caregivers, agencies, dioceses, congregations, and parishes through education and resources toward the development of grief support groups and a training program & manual for ministers. Total Staff 2; Total Assisted 10,000.

Ninth Street CDC, 1404 E. Ninth St., 8th Fl., 44114-1722. Tel: 216-696-6525; Fax: 216-696-8084. Joseph H. Smith, Pres.

St. Philip Neri/Divine Word Church in the City Partnership Inc., 8215 St. Clair Ave., 44103. Tel: 216-431-2583; Fax: 216-431-2583. Email: dw-carl@lightstream.net. Deacon Carl Varga, Contact Person.

Pulaski Franciscan Community Development Corp., 3649 E. 65th St., 44105. Tel: 216-883-4432; Fax: 216-271-6364. Email: pfcdccleveland@aol.com. Rev. Michael Surufka, O.F.M., Pres.

Sisters of Charity Foundation of Cleveland, The Hanna Building, #425, 1422 Euclid Ave., 44115-1901. Tel: 216-241-9300; Fax: 216-241-9345. Web: www.socstannfdn.org. Susanna H. Krey, Interm. Exec. Dir.

Sisters of Charity of St. Augustine Health System, 2351 E. 22nd St., 44115. Tel: 216-696-5560; Fax: 216-696-2204. Web: www.csahealthsystem.org. Sr. Judith Ann Karam, C.S.J., Pres. & CEO. Serves as the Member of foundations and health and human service corporations sponsored by the Sisters of Charity of St. Augustine, Richfield, OH. Serves as one of two members of the joint venture corporation operating St. John West Shore Hospital, St. Luke Medical Center and St. Vincent Charity Hospital, Ohio Health Choice, and Professional Medical Equipment.

**St. Vitus Development Corporation*, 6019 Lausche Ave., 44103. Tel: 216-361-1444; Fax: 216-361-1445. Email: skuhar@hotmail.com. Stane Kuhar, Sec. & Contact Person; Rev. Joseph P. Boznar, Pastor, St. Vitus Church; Joseph V. Hocevar, Business Mgr., St. Vitus Church.

AKRON. *First Friday Club of Greater Akron*, 795 Russell Ave., 44307. Tel: 330-535-7668; Fax: 330-535-9040. Frank C. Comunale, Pres.

H.M. Housing Development Corporation, 3250 W. Market St., Ste. 204, 44333. Tel: 330-384-1555; Fax: 330-384-2144. Email: kenhmhi@earthlink.net. Web: www.humilityofmary.com/frame_ministries.html. Kenneth W. Radigan, Exec. Dir.

H.M. Life Opportunity Services, Box 22490, 44302. Tel: 330-376-5600; Fax: 330-376-2277. Email: hmlife@hmlife.org.

Central Office, 321 W. Exchange St., 44302. Tel: 330-376-5600; Fax: 330-376-2277. Angela Tucker Cooper, Exec. Dir.

Humility of Mary Housing, Inc., 3250 W. Market St., Ste. 204, 44333. Tel: 330-384-1555; Fax: 330-384-2144. Email: kenhmhi@earthlink.net. Web: www.humilityofmary.com/frame_ministries.html. Kenneth W. Radigan, Exec. Dir. Affordable housing and housing related services for low and moderate income individuals. Total Assisted 450; Total Staff 19.

Saint Joseph Parenting Center of Akron, P.O. Box 5344, 44333. Tel: 330-864-3804. Catherine Klie, Dir.

BEDFORD. *Emmaus Conference Center*, Vincentian Sisters of Broadway, 1160 Broadway, 44146-4523. Tel: 440-232-4755; Fax: 440-232-7832. Email: a.vscoffice@att.net. Web: www.vsc.catholicweb.com. Judy Kendrick, Contact Person.

CHARDON. *Christ Child Society-Geauga Chapter*, P.O. Box 1133, 44024. Tel: 440-338-8060. Patricia McHenry, Pres.

COPLEY. *Faith and Light U.S.A., Inc.*, 1518 Sunside Dr., 44321. Tel: 330-666-6816. Email: ac282@acorn.net. W. Kirt Bromley, Contact Person.

EUCLID. *St. Robert's Holy Name Society Boosters*, 23802 Lakeshore Blvd., 44123. Tel: 216-731-2606; Fax: 216-731-2607. Rev. Dennis M. McNeil, Pastor.

GARFIELD HEIGHTS. *Jennings Manor Housing Corporation*, 10204 Granger Rd., 44125. Tel: 216-581-2900; Fax: 216-581-4505. Web: www.jenningscenter.org. Mrs. Martha M. Kutik, Pres. & CEO; Allison Salopeck, Admin. & COO; Jane Carbeck, Housing Dir. 60 unit apartment building - HUD 202 Supportive Housing for Older Adults.

Marymount Health Care Systems, 12300 McCracken Rd., 44125. Tel: 216-587-8080; Fax: 216-587-8212. Email: dkilarski@marymount.org. Web: www.marymount.org. Provides comprehensive health and human services in response to the needs of the local community by owning, leasing, and operating health care facilities and services, including Marymount Place, a 104-unit Senior Living Community for the Well-Elderly/Assisted Living and operates Clare Hall, a 28 bed Third Order of St. Francis within the philosophy and objectiver of the Sisters of St. Joseph of the Third Order of St. Francis and is the Special Member of Marymount Hospital, Inc.

MHCS Real Estate Holding Company, 12300 McCracken Rd., 44125-2975. Tel: 216-587-8080; Fax: 216-587-8212. Email: dkilarski@marymount.org. Mr. William D. Keckan, COO. To assist in the provision of comprehensive health care services by acquiring, holding, owning, and leasing real estate (and interests therein) and health care facilities, including but not limited to leasing such as real estate and facilities to Marymount Hospital, consistent with the philosophy and objectives of the Roman Catholic Church as promulgated by the National Conference of Catholic Bishops and the local Ordinary. Holds the Title to Marymount Hospital as a part of the Marymount Health Care Systems Special Member responsibility.

HUDSON. **Laurel Lake Retirement Community, Inc.*, 200 Laurel Lake Dr., 44236. Tel: 330-650-0681; Fax: 330-655-1700. Email: george-paulson@hmis.org. Web: www.laurellake.com. George Paulson, Pres. Independent Living Residents 350; Assisted Living Residents 20; Skilled Nursing Residents 75; Total Staff 280.

INDEPENDENCE. *UHHS/CSAHS - Cuyahoga, Inc.*, 2 Summit Park Dr., Summit Two Office Building, Ste. 425, 44131. Tel: 216-436-4640; Fax: 216-436-4646. Mary C. Morrison, Pres. & CEO.

LOUDONVILLE. *Lay Apostolate for Immigrant Catholic Indians of America, Inc.*, P.O. Box 349, 44842. Tel: 419-994-3983; Fax: 419-994-3982. Email: LAICIA@yahoo.com. Web: www.layapostolate.org. Dr. Abraham C. Kuttothara, M.D., Dir.

OBERLIN. *Common Ground Center for Community Renewal*, 14240 Baird Rd., 44074. Tel: 440-965-5551; Fax: 440-965-5570. Email: cgroun@commongrouncenter.org. Web: www.commongroundcenter.org. Sr. Rose Bator, H.M., Pres.

PARMA. *Society of St. Joseph the Worker*, 7033 State Rd., 44134-4952. Tel: 440-888-4872; Fax: 440-888-6825. Email: bsjw@msn.com. Web: www.bsjw.org. Lawrence R. Verbiar, Dir.

PEPPER PIKE. *New Ventures Network*, 2600 Lander Rd., 44124. Tel: 440-442-4160, Ext. 226; Fax: 440-442-4587. Email: DCAPUANO@ursulinesophiacenter.com. Web: www.newventuresnetwork.com. Sr. Donna Capuano, O.S.U.

Ursuline Child Care/Learning Center, Ursuline Educational Center, 2600 Lander Rd., 44124. Tel: 440-449-1200, Ext. 280. Email: uil@ursulinesisters.org. Sr. Angelita Zawada, O.S.U., Dir.

**Ursuline Sophia Center*, 2600 Lander Rd., 44124. Tel: 440-442-4160; Fax: 440-442-4587. Email: info@ursulinesophiacenter.com. Web: www.ursulinesophiacenter.com. Sr. Donna Capuano, O.S.U., Dir. Total Staff 20; Total Assisted Annually 5,000.

ROCKY RIVER. *Heartbeats*, 20015 Detroit Rd., 44116. Tel: 440-356-8601; Fax: 440-356-8078. Email: heartbt@en.com. Web: www.heartbeatscatalog.org. Sr. Jo Marie Chrosniak, H.M., Dir.

SOLON. *The O'Neill Brothers Foundation*, 30000 Aurora Rd., Suite 250, 44139. Tel: 440-248-2027; Fax: 440-248-2153. Email: lstopar@aol.com. Mr. Robert K. Healey, Pres.

WESTLAKE. *The Center for Learning*, Editorial/Prepress Office, 24600 Detroit Rd., Ste. 201, 44145. Tel: 440-331-9341; Fax: 440-250-9715. Sr. Rose Schaffer, H.M., Pres. & CEO. Educational Publisher of values-based curriculum: Religion for Catholic schools and parishes; English/Language Arts, Social Studies, and Novel/Drama Curriculum Units for all schools.; Owned and operated by the Sisters of Humility of Mary. Directed by an Ecumenical Lay Board.

Administrative/Customer Service Office, Evergreen Rd., P.O. Box 910, Villa Maria, PA 16155. Tel: 800-767-9090; 724-964-8083; Fax: 888-767-8080. Email: rschaffer@centerforlearning.org. Web: www.centerforlearning.org.

WICKLIFFE. *Center for Pastoral Leadership Services, Inc.*, 28700 Euclid Ave., 44092-2585. Tel: 440-943-7600; Fax: 440-943-7577. Email: bfhcpl@dioceseofcleveland.org. Deacon Kenneth Piechowski; Mr. Brian F. Houlahan, COO.

RELIGIOUS INSTITUTES OF MEN REPRESENTED IN THE DIOCESE

For further details refer to the corresponding bracketed number in the Religious Institutes of Men or Women section.

[]—*Apostles of Jesus* (Karen, Kenya)—A.J.
[0200]—*Benedictine Monks* (St. Andrew Abbey)—O.S.B.
[0600]—*Brothers of the Congregation of Holy Cross* (Midwest Prov.)—C.S.C.
[0470]—*The Capuchin Friars*—O.F.M.Cap.
[1150]—*Congregation of St. Joseph*—C.S.J.
[0220]—*Congregation of the Blessed Sacrament*—S.S.S.
[0650]—*Congregation of the Holy Ghost and of the Immaculate Heart of Mary*—C.S.Sp.
[0520]—*Franciscan Friars* (Provs. of Our Lady of Consolation & Assumption)—O.F.M.
[0480]—*Franciscan Friars (Conv.)*—O.F.M.Conv
[0690]—*Jesuit Fathers and Brothers* (Maryland Prov.)
[0690]—*Jesuit Fathers and Brothers (Society of Mary)* (Detroit Prov.)
[0780]—*Marist Fathers (Society of Mary)* (Washington Prov.)—S.M.
[0800]—*Maryknoll*—M.M.
[]—*Missionaries of St. Francis de Sales*—M.S.F.S.
[0840]—*Missionary Servants of the Most Holy Trinity*—S.T.
[0910]—*Oblates of Mary Immaculate*—O.M.I.
[0970]—*Order of Our Lady of Mercy*—O.de.M.
[0610]—*Priests of the Congregation of the Holy Cross* (Indiana Prov.)—C.S.C.
[0760]—*Society of Mary-Marianists* (Dayton, OH)—S.M.
[1060]—*Society of the Precious Blood* (Cincinnati Prov.)—C.PP.S.

RELIGIOUS INSTITUTES OF WOMEN REPRESENTED IN THE DIOCESE

[0230]—*Benedictine Sisters of Pontifical Jurisdiction* (Erie, PA)—O.S.B.
[]—*Byzantine Nuns of St. Clare*—B.N.S.C.
[1710]—*Congregation of the Third Order of St. Francis of Mary Immaculate, Joliet, IL*—O.S.F.
[1830]—*Contemplative Sisters of the Good Shepherd*—C.G.S.
[0790]—*Daughters of Divine Charity*—F.D.C.
[0420]—*Discalced Carmelite Nuns*—O.C.D.
[1070-14]—*Dominican Sisters*—O.P.
[1070-23]—*Dominican Sisters*—O.P.
[1070-28]—*Dominican Sisters*—O.P.
[1170]—*Felician Sisters*—C.S.S.F.

[]—*Felician Sisters-Mother of Good Counsel Province* Chicago—C.S.S.F.
[1210]—*Franciscan Sisters of Chicago*—O.S.F.
[]—*Handmaids of Nazareth*—HN
[2340]—*Little Sisters of the Poor*—P.S.D.P.
[3760]—*Order of St. Clare-Poor Clare Colettine Nuns*—P.C.C.
[3130]—*Our Lady of Victory Missionary Sisters*—O.L.V.M.
[3210]—*Poor Clares of Perpetual Adoration*—P.C.P.A.
[3420]—*Religious of the Eucharist*—R.E.
[1830]—*Religious of the Good Shepherd*—R.G.S.
[3430]—*Religious Teachers Filippini*—M.P.F.
[0440]—*Sisters of Charity of Cincinnati, Ohio*—S.C.
[0570]—*Sisters of Charity of Seton Hill*—SC
[0580]—*Sisters of Charity of St. Augustine*—C.S.A.
[0990]—*Sisters of Divine Providence*—C.D.P.
[]—*Sisters of Divine Redeemer*—S.D.R.
[2580]—*Sisters of Mercy of the Americas* (Cincinnati)—R.S.M.
[2590]—*Sisters of Mercy of the Blessed Sacrament*—H.M.S.S.
[2990]—*Sisters of Notre Dame*—S.N.D.
[3360]—*Sisters of Providence*—S.P.
[1530]—*Sisters of St. Francis* (Sylvania)—O.S.F.
[]—*Sisters of St. Francis of Millvale, PA*—O.S.F.
[3830-08]—*Sisters of St. Joseph*—C.S.J.
[3910]—*Sisters of St. Joseph of St. Mark*—S.J.S.M.
[3930]—*Sisters of St. Joseph of the Third Order of St. Francis*—S.S.J.-T.O.S.F.
[1970]—*Sisters of the Holy Family of Nazareth*—C.S.F.N.
[2030]—*Sisters of the Holy Spirit*—C.S.Sp.
[2110]—*Sisters of the Humility of Mary*—H.M.
[2210]—*Sisters of the Incarnate Word and Blessed Sacrament*—S.I.W.
[2350]—*Sisters of the Living Word*—S.L.W.
[2060]—*Sisters of the Most Holy Trinity*—O.SS.T.
[3730]—*Sisters of the Order of St. Basil the Great*—O.S.B.M.
[3260]—*Sisters of the Precious Blood* (Dayton, Ohio)—C.PP.S.
[1710]—*Sisters of the Third Franciscan Order*—O.S.F.
[2160]—*Sisters Servants of the Immaculate Heart of Mary* (Scranton)—I.H.M.
[3620]—*Sisters Servants of Mary Immaculate*—S.S.M.I.
[2150]—*Sisters Servants of the Immaculate Heart of Mary*—I.H.M.
[]—*Social Mission Sisters*—S.M.
[4120-04]—*Ursuline Nuns of the Congregation of Paris*—O.S.U.
[4120-07]—*Ursuline Nuns of the Congregation of Paris*—O.S.U.
[4170]—*Vincentian Sisters of Charity* (Bedford, OH)—V.S.C.

DIOCESAN CEMETERIES

CLEVELAND. *Assumption of Mary*, 14900 Brookpark Rd., 44135.
Calvary, 10000 Miles Ave., P.O. Box 605310, 44105.
St. John, 7000 Woodland Ave., 44104.
St. Joseph, 7916 Woodland Ave, 44104.
St. Mary, 267* W. 41st St., 44113.

AKRON. *Holy Cross*, 100 E. Waterloo Rd., 44319.

AVON. *Holy Trinity*, 33601 Detroit Rd., 44011. P.O. Box 326, 44011-0326.
Holy Trinity, Jaycox Rd.. P.O. Box 326, 44011-0326.
St. Joseph, 32787 Detroit Rd., 44011. P.O. Box 326, 44011-0326.

BEREA. *St. Mary of the Falls*, 1260 Bagley Rd., 44017.

BROOK PARK. *Holy Cross*, 14609 Brookpark Rd., 44142.

CHARDON. *All Souls*, 10366 Chardon Rd., P.O. Box 11, 44024.

CUYAHOGA HEIGHTS. *St. Mary*, 4720 E. 71st St., 44125.

ELYRIA. *St. Mary*, 7284 Lake Ave., 44035.

LORAIN. *Calvary*, 555 N. Ridge Rd. W., 44053.

NORTHFIELD. *All Saints*, 480 Highland Rd., 44067.

VALLEY CITY. *Resurrection*, 6303 Center Rd., 44280.

NECROLOGY

† Englert, William J., Fairport Harbor, OH St. Anthony of Padua—Died Nov. 23, 2003
† Gerrity, John J., Maple Heights, OH St. Martin of Tours—Died Nov. 2, 2003
† Grismer, Raymond J., Sheffield, OH St. Theresa of Avila—Died Nov. 14, 2003
† Gulas, William E., Cleveland, OH St. Stanislaus Friary—Died 2003
† Hanzo, Robert G., Painesville, OH St. Mary Parish—Died Jan. 6, 2003
† Laheta, Andrew P., Cleveland, OH Our Lady of Mercy Parish—Died April 4, 2003
† Minoggio, Ferrando, Wickliffe, OH Borromeo Seminary; Rome, Italy, North American College—Died June 14, 2003
† Paik, Francis M., Euclid, OH St. Christine Parish—Died June 17, 2003
† Peir, Andrew, Benedictine Order of Cleveland, Cleveland—Died March 18, 2003
† Scharf, Joseph, Cleveland, OH Jesuit Retreat House—Died 2003
† Sterk, Francis R., Euclid, OH St. Christine—Died June 26, 2003
† Woll, Peter J., Cleveland, OH Holy Trinity-St. Edward—Died July 29, 2003

Diocese of Colorado Springs

Most Reverend

MICHAEL J. SHERIDAN

Bishop of Colorado Springs; ordained May 29, 1971; appointed Titular Bishop of Tibiuca and Auxiliary Bishop of Saint Louis July 9, 1997; ordained September 3, 1997; appointed Coadjutor Bishop of Colorado Springs December 4, 2001; succeeded to the See January 30, 2003.

Diocesan Offices: 228 N. Cascade Ave., Colorado Springs, CO 80903-1498. Tel: 719-636-2345; Fax: 719-636-1216.

Most Reverend

RICHARD C. HANIFEN, D.D., J.C.L.

Bishop Emeritus of Colorado Springs; ordained June 6, 1959; appointed Titular Bishop of Abercorn and Auxiliary of Denver July 6, 1974; consecrated September 20, 1974; appointed First Bishop of Colorado Springs November 10, 1983; installed January 30, 1984; retired January 30, 2003. *Office: 228 N. Cascade Ave., Colorado Springs, CO 80903-1498.*

ESTABLISHED AND CREATED A DIOCESE JANUARY 30, 1984.

Square Miles 15,500.

Comprising the Counties of Chaffee, Cheyenne, Douglas, Elbert, El Paso, Kit Carson, Lake, Lincoln, Park and Teller.

Legal Title: Diocese of Colorado Springs.

For legal titles of parishes and diocesan institutions, consult the Diocesan Offices.

STATISTICAL OVERVIEW

Personnel	
Bishop	1
Retired Bishops	1
Priests: Diocesan Active in Diocese	25
Priests: Diocesan Active Outside Diocese	2
Priests: Retired, Sick or Absent	11
Number of Diocesan Priests	38
Religious Priests in Diocese	30
Total Priests in Diocese	68
Extern Priests in Diocese	7
Permanent Deacons in Diocese	28
Total Brothers	3
Total Sisters	128
Parishes	
Parishes	34
With Resident Pastor:	
Resident Diocesan Priests	21
Resident Religious Priests	7
Without Resident Pastor:	
Administered by Priests	2
Administered by Deacons	2
Administered by Lay People	1
Completely Vacant	1
Missions	9
Professional Ministry Personnel:	
Lay Ministers	75
Welfare	
Catholic Hospitals	2
Total Assisted	254,000
Health Care Centers	2
Total Assisted	109
Homes for the Aged	2
Total Assisted	103
Educational	
Diocesan Students in Other Seminaries	8
Total Seminarians	8
High Schools, Private	1
Total Students	350
Elementary Schools, Diocesan and Parish	5
Total Students	1,487
Catechesis/Religious Education:	
High School Students	2,831
Elementary Students	2,976
Total Students under Catholic Instruction	7,652
Teachers in the Diocese:	
Sisters	1
Lay Teachers	116
Vital Statistics	
Receptions into the Church:	
Infant Baptism Totals	1,555
Adult Baptism Totals	132
Received into Full Communion	145
First Communions	1,529
Confirmations	1,032
Marriages:	
Catholic	191
Interfaith	115
Total Marriages	306
Deaths	339
Total Catholic Population	136,814
Total Population	855,088

Former Bishops—Most Rev. RICHARD C. HANIFEN, D.D., J.C.L. (Retired), ord. June 6, 1959; appt. Titular Bishop of Abercorn and Auxiliary of Denver July 6, 1974; consecrated Sept. 20, 1974; appt. first Bishop of Colorado Springs Nov. 10, 1983; installed Jan. 30, 1984; retired Jan. 30, 2003.

Diocesan Offices—228 N. Cascade Ave., Colorado Springs, 80903-1498. Tel: 719-636-2345; Fax: 719-636-1216. Office Hours: Mon.-Fri. 8:30-4:30

Vicar General—Very Rev. DONALD F. DUNN, V.G.

Vicar for Clergy—Rev. ROBERT E. JAEGER.

Executive Assistant to the Bishop—PETER HOWARD, S.T.L.

Chancellor—Rev. KARL J. USELDINGER, J.C.L., 228 N. Cascade Ave., Colorado Springs, 80903. Tel: 719-636-2345.

Archivist—Sr. JOSEPH MARIE JACOBSEN, O.S.B.

Diocesan Consultors—Very Rev. DONALD F. DUNN, V.G.; Revs. ERNEST W. BOND; GEORGE V. FAGAN, J.C.L.; ROBERT E. JAEGER; JAY JUNG, C.M.; PAUL WICKER; JOHN AUER.

Finance Officer—ROBERT G. DOERFLER JR.

Judicial Vicar—Rev. KARL J. USELDINGER, J.C.L.

Associate Judges—Revs. JAMES I. DONLON, J.C.D.; JOSEPH KOURY, S.J., J.C.D.

Defenders of the Bond—Rev. Msgr. MARK PLEWKA, J.C.L.; Rev. GEORGE V. FAGAN, J.C.L.

Procurator-Advocates—Rev. ERNEST W. BOND; Sr. JOSEPH MARIE JACOBSEN, O.S.B.; Deacon GEORGE D. LINEHAN JR.

Ecclesiastical Notary—Mrs. SHIRLEY WELLS.

Catholic Charities of Colorado Springs, Inc.—ROBERT G. DOERFLER JR., Interim Dir.

Office of Pastoral Administration—ROBERT G. DOERFLER JR., Dir.

Office of Pastoral Services—EDWARD GAFFNEY, Dir.; TERRI SORTOR, Human Resources Mgr.

Office of Stewardship and Development—Dr. JAY CAMPBELL, Dir.

Office of Total Catholic Education—Sr. MARY MULLALY, F.M.A., Ed.D., Dir.; KATHERINE CAMPBELL, TCE Ministries Asst.; DONNA GAFFNEY, Resource Ctr. Coord.

Continuing Formation of Priests—Rev. KARL J. USELDINGER, J.C.L., Dir.

Propagation of the Faith—Rev. JAMES WILLIAMS, Dir.

Seminarian Formation—Rev. WILLIAM JAREMA, Dir.

Vocations Office—Very Rev. DONALD DUNN, V.G., Dir. Seminarians & Vocations.

Regionalization—Metro-Central Region (Colorado Springs): Very Rev. DONALD F. DUNN, V.G., Vicar. Metro-North Region (Colorado Springs): Rev. PAUL WICKER, Vicar, Metro-South Region (Colorado Springs). Metro-South Region (Colorado Springs): Rev. JOHN AUER, Vicar. Eastern Region: Rev. GEORGE V. FAGAN, J.C.L., Vicar. Northern Region: Rev. ERNEST W. BOND, Vicar. Western Region: Rev. JAY JUNG, C.M., Vicar.

Victim Assistance Coordinator—BARBARA MAHONEY. Tel: 719-633-8182.

CLERGY, PARISHES, MISSIONS AND PAROCHIAL SCHOOLS

CITY OF COLORADO SPRINGS

(COUNTY OF EL PASO)

1—ST. MARY'S CATHEDRAL (1887), Very Revs. Donald F. Dunn, V.G., Rector; Theodore A. Haas, Rector Emeritus; Rev. John P. Cousins, O.F.M.Cap. (DEN); Deacons Charles W. Specht; Patrick Bidon; Leroy M. Kuss.

Office—22 W. Kiowa St., 80903. Tel: 719-473-4633; Fax: 719-473-5248.

Catechesis/Religious Program—Kerry Susser, D.R.E. Students 175.

Mission—Immaculate Conception, El Paso Co. Tel: 719-635-2379. Rev. Thomas Fritschen, F.S.S.P., Chap.

2—ST. ANDREW KIM QUASI PARISH (1981), (Korean), Rev. Chul-Hyun Kang.

Office—4515 E. Pikes Peak Ave., 80916. Tel: 719-638-0100; 719-638-0105 (Rectory); Fax: 719-638-0101.

3—CORPUS CHRISTI (1916), Rev. Stephen J. Parlet; Deacon Benedict Cruise.

Res.: 2318 N. Cascade Ave., 80907. Tel: 719-633-1457; Fax: 719-473-7567.

School—2410 N. Cascade Ave., 80907. Tel: 719-632-5092; Fax: 719-578-9124. Norm Hale, Prin. Lay Teachers 35; Students 451.

Catechesis/Religious Program—Tel: 719-633-1457, Ext. 17. Mary Kellison, D.R.E. Students 250.

4—DIVINE REDEEMER (1950), [JC] Revs. William Jarema; Jaimes Ponce; Deacon Ray Milberg.

Res.: 1520 E. Yampa St., 80909. Tel: 719-633-5559; Fax: 719-234-0358.

School—901 N. Logan, 80909. Tel: 719-471-7771;

Fax: 719-234-0300. Sarah Miller, Prin. Lay Teachers 24; Students 445.
Catechesis/Religious Program—Tel: 719-234-0342. Bernadette Tittle, D.R.E. Students 164.

5—St. Francis of Assisi (1981), Revs. Jen P. Jensen, Parish Admin.; Karl J. Useldinger, J.C.L.; Deacon Michael Ciletti.
Office—2650 Parish View, 80919. Tel: 719-599-5031; Fax: 719-599-3360. Email: parish@pcisys.net.
Catechesis/Religious Program—Terri Kowalczyk, D.R.E. Students 472.

6—St. Gabriel the Archangel (1998), Rev. August Stewart; Deacon Robert Hunter.
Office—3470 Briargate Blvd., 80920. Tel: 719-528-8407; Fax: 719-598-1696.
Catechesis/Religious Program—Students 250.

7—Holy Apostles (1973), Revs. Paul F. Wicker; Luis Alfredo Garcia Chavez; Deacons Michael Leverington; Charles Matzker.
Res.: 4925 N. Carefree Cir., 80917. Tel: 719-597-4249; Fax: 719-591-1816.
School—Preschool, 4925 N. Carefree, 80917. Tel: 719-591-1566; Fax: 719-591-1816. Mary Parsons, Dir. Lay Teachers 11; Students 145.
Catechesis/Religious Program—Tel: 719-597-4249. Gail Murphy, D.R.E. Students 670.

8—Holy Trinity (1968), CoCo Soper, Parish Dir.
Office—3122 Poinsetia Dr., 80907. Tel: 719-633-2132; Fax: 719-633-0975.
School—3115 Larkspur Dr., 80907. Tel: 719-634-1029; Fax: 719-634-4875. Ron Sebben, Prin.; Sara Frese, Asst. Prin. Lay Teachers 12; Students 177.
Catechesis/Religious Program—Terri Beabes, D.R.E. Students 200.

9—St. Joseph's (Southgate) (1968), Revs. James M. Williams; Francis Maher (JOL) (Retired); Warren Heidjen, OSB (Retired); Randall Brungardt, Assoc. Pastor.
Res.: 1830 S. Corona Ave., 80906. Tel: 719-632-9903; Fax: 719-632-9170.
Catechesis/Religious Program—Tel: 719-635-3166. Students 794.

10—Our Lady of Guadalupe (1948), (Hispanic), Rev. Robert Sullivan, S.J.; Deacon Ernest Romero.
Res.: 2715 E. Pikes Peak, 80909. Tel: 719-633-7204; Fax: 719-630-3184.
Catechesis/Religious Program—Students 282.

11—Our Lady of the Pines-Black Forest (1965), Revs. Gerald Borer, SJ; Joseph Damhorst, S.J. (STL); Deacons David Camous; Gene Eastham; Lynn Sherman, Parish Dir.
Res.: 11020 Teachout Rd., 80908. Tel: 719-495-2351; Fax: 719-495-9062.
Catechesis/Religious Program—Tel: 719-495-2352. Vickie Welsh, D.R.E. Students 269.

12—St. Patrick's (1981), Revs. Bradford Noonan; Michael Butler; Deacons Richard Brown; Norm Ridder.
Office—6455 Brookpark Dr., 80918. Tel: 719-598-3595; Fax: 719-599-5741.
Catechesis/Religious Program—Angelita M. Dykes, D.R.E. Students 775.

13—Saint Paul (1925), Rev. John Auer; Rev Msgr. Richard Bowles (Retired).
Office—9 El Pomar Rd., 80906. Tel: 719-471-9700; Fax: 719-471-3009.
School—Pauline Memorial Catholic School, Tel: 719-632-1846; Fax: 719-632-0495. Sr. Marilyn Beyers, Prin. Lay Teachers 15; Students 308.
Catechesis/Religious Program—Students 308.

14—Sacred Heart (1891), Revs. Thomas Lemos, C.S.C.; Eric J. Schimmel, C.S.C. In Res., Rev. Thomas A. Stella, C.S.C.
Office—2021 W. Pikes Peak Ave., 80904. Tel: 719-633-8711; Fax: 719-633-1859.
Catechesis/Religious Program—Kathleen Moriarty, D.R.E.; Tena Jelinek, D.R.E. Students 170.
Mission—Our Lady of Perpetual Help 218 Ruxton Ave., Manitou Springs, El Paso Co. 80829.
Mission—Holy Rosary 4435 Holiday Tr., Cascade, El Paso Co. 80809.

15—The Vietnamese Holy Martyrs Quasi-Parish (1993), (Vietnamese), [CEM] Rev. Matthew Minh Thanh Tran.
Res. & Mailing Address: 2902 Airport Rd., #214, 80910. Tel: 719-635-6892.
Church: 1131 N. Wahsatch Ave., 80903. Tel: 719-635-0679.

OUTSIDE THE CITY OF COLORADO SPRINGS

Bailey, Park Co., St. Mary of the Rockies (1990), Rev. Ernest W. Bond.
Res.: P.O. Box 319, 80421-8319. Tel: 303-838-2375; Fax: 303-816-2399.
Catechesis/Religious Program—Students 50.

Buena Vista, Chaffee Co., St. Rose of Lima (1880), Rt. Rev. R. William Rhinehart, C.M.; Deacon Richard Willburn.
Res.: 114 S. Gunnison, P.O. Box 458, 81211. Tel: 719-395-8424; Fax: 719-395-8424.
Catechesis/Religious Program—Students 90.
Mission—St. Joseph 5th & Castello, Fairplay, Park Co. 80440. Tel: 719-395-8424. (Send all correspondence to Buena Vista address.)

Burlington, Kit Carson Co., St. Catherine of Siena (1916), Rev. Frank Quezada.
Res.: 450 3rd St., 80807. Tel: 719-346-7156.
Catechesis/Religious Program—Students 80.

Calhan, El Paso Co., St. Michael's (1920), Unassigned.
Res.: Box 199, 80808. Tel: 719-347-2290; Fax: 719-347-2848.
Catechesis/Religious Program—Students 25.

Castle Rock, Douglas Co., St. Francis of Assisi (1888), Revs. Herbert Hayek, O.P., Admin.; George Reynolds, O.P.
Res.: 2746 E. Hwy. 86, 80104. Tel: 303-688-3025; Fax: 303-688-4016.
Catechesis/Religious Program—Students 700.

Cheyenne Wells, Cheyenne Co., Sacred Heart (1918), Rev. Khanh Pham Nguyen.
Res.: P.O. Box 819, 80810. Tel: 719-767-5272; Fax: 719-767-5272.
Mission—St. Augustine P.O. Box 82, Kit Carson, Cheyenne Co. 80825. Tel: 719-962-3552.
Catechesis/Religious Program—Students 34.

Elizabeth, Elbert Co., Our Lady of the Visitation Quasi-Parish, Rev. Dennis E. Dwyer, Pastoral/Parish Admin.
34201 County Rd. 33, P.O. Box 1689, 80107. Tel: 303-646-4964; Fax: 303-646-4964.
Catechesis/Religious Program—Students 246.

Fountain, El Paso Co., St. Joseph (1970), Rev. W. Lawrence Carmody.
101 N. Main St., P.O. Box 277, 80817. Tel: 719-382-7086.
Catechesis/Religious Program—Students 67.

Highlands Ranch, Douglas Co.
1—St. Mark, Rev. Lawrence T. Solan.
9961 S. Silver Maple Rd., 80129. Tel: 720-348-9700; Fax: 720-344-6847.
Catechesis/Religious Program—Students 275.
2—Pax Christi Catholic Church (1988), Rev. Kenneth Przybyla.
Office—5761 McArthur Ranch Rd., Littleton, 80124. Tel: 303-799-1036; Fax: 303-799-1072.
Catechesis/Religious Program—Sue Giudici, D.R.E. Students 850.

Leadville, Lake Co., Catholic Community of Leadville, Annunciation (1879) & St. Joseph (1899), [CEM] [JC] Rev. Jay Jung, C.M.; Deacon Charles Moss III; Bro. Kenneth J. Lund, C.M., Dir. Hispanic Min.
Res.: 609 Poplar St., 80461. Tel: 719-486-1382; Fax: 719-486-3930.
Catechesis/Religious Program—Students 118.

Limon, Lincoln Co., Our Lady of Victory (1925), Rev. George V. Fagan, J.C.L.
Res.: 425 H Ave., P.O. Box 790, 80828. Tel: 719-775-2118; Fax: 719-775-9230.
Catechesis/Religious Program—Limon & Missions, Fax: 719-775-9406. Students 68.
Mission—St. Anthony of Padua 133 Fifth St., P.O. Box 275, Hugo, Lincoln Co. 80821. (Send all correspondence to Limon address.)
Mission—St. Mary [CEM] Flagler, Kit Carson Co. (Send all correspondence to Limon address.)

Monument, El Paso Co., St. Peter (1911), Revs. Robert E. Jaeger; Mark Zacker; Deacon Rollo Watkins; Rev. Jaimes Ponce.
Mailing Address: P.O. Box 827, 80132. Tel: 719-481-3511; Fax: 719-481-9606.
Res.: 55 N. Jefferson, 80132. Tel: 719-481-3511; Fax: 719-481-9606.
Catechesis/Religious Program—Connie Proffitt, D.R.E. Students 800.

Parker, Douglas Co., Ave Maria (1983), Revs. Donald P. Brownstein; James J. Klein; Deacon George D. Linehan Jr.
Res.: 9056 E. Parker Rd., 80138-7209. Tel: 303-841-3750; Fax: 303-841-2412.
School— (2000),Tel: 720-842-5400; Fax: 720-554-7700. Sr. Margaret Ghomas, O.P., Prin. Lay Teachers 13; Students 250.
Catechesis/Religious Program—Lynne K. Lane, D.R.E. Students 1,045.

Salida, Chaffee Co., St. Joseph (1907), Rev Henry Grodecki, C.M. In Res., Rev. Anthony C. Uh, Chap. Colorado Dept. of Corrections (Retired).
Res.: P.O. Box 847, 81201. Tel: 719-539-6419; Fax: 719-539-7127.
Catechesis/Religious Program—Students 110.

Security, El Paso Co., Holy Family (1957), Revs. Lawrence W. Carmody; Boleslaw Kuzma (Poland); Deacon Albert E. Kimminau.
Res.: 331 Main St., 80911. Tel: 719-392-7653; Fax: 719-392-1651.
Catechesis/Religious Program—Cathy Jane King, D.R.E. Students 505.

Stratton, Kit Carson Co., St. Charles Borromeo (1910), Revs. R. William Rhinehart, C.M.; Frank Quezada (SAT).
Church: P.O. Box 57, 80836. Tel: 719-348-5336; Fax: 719-348-5336.
Res.: 450 3rd St., Burlington, 80807.
Catechesis/Religious Program—Students 70.

Woodland Park, Teller Co., Our Lady of the Woods (1954),, (Teller Co. Catholic Community) Rev. John Slattery; Deacon Roger Eberwein, Parish Dir.
Res.: P.O. Box 416, 80866. Tel: 719-687-9345; Fax: 719-687-0893.
Catechesis/Religious Program—Students 204.
Mission—St. Peter's 3rd & Golden, Cripple Creek, Teller Co. 80813. (Send all correspondence to Woodland Park address.)
Mission—St. Victor's 2nd & Portland, Victor, Teller Co. 80860. (Send all correspondence to Woodland Park address.)

On Duty Outside Diocese:
Revs.—
Grabrian, Dennis, 7172 Regional St., PMB 434, Dublin, CA 94568.
Khanh, San Hoag, St. Jude Parish, 94-455 Makakila Dr., Kapolei, HI 96707.

On Leave of Absence:
Rev.—
Battiato, Patrick, 5710 Snow Creek Pt., #305, 80915.

Retired:
Most Rev.—
Hanifen, Richard C.
Revs.—
Bruggeman, Gerald H., Chap., 2215 N. Cascade Ave., 80907. Penrose Hospital
Dresen, Arthur G., 4559 Sunnyhill Dr., 80916.
Haas, Theodore, 1719 E. Bijou St., 80909.
Halloran, James, Castle West Apartments, 3770 E. Uintah A32, 80909.
Halloran, Joseph H., Fountain Terrace Apartments, 3211 E. Fountains Blvd., #103, 80910.
Krenzke, John, c/o Christ the King, 845 Fairfax St., Denver, 80220.
McHugh, Owen, 7161 White Buffalo Rd., 80919.
Myers, Rawley, St. Mary's Cathedral, 22 W. Kiowa, 80903.
Slattery, John, Res.: 7665 Assisi Heights, 80919-3836. Our Lady of the Woods, Woodland Park, CO;
Vollmer, William C., 35 Tilly Ln., Castle Rock, 80104.

Permanent Deacons:
Bidon, Patrick, Dir. Office of the Dioconate; Coord. Jail Ministry, St. Mary's Cathedral, Colorado Springs
Bowles, Richard, St. Paul & Fort Carson, Colorado Springs
Breaux, Allen, (Retired)
Brown, Richard, St. Patrick, Colorado Springs
Camous, Dave, Parish Dir., Our Lady of the Pines, Colorado Springs
Ciletti, Michael, National Chap., Faith and Light, USA, Ministry to & with people who have a mental disability; St. Francis of Assisi, Colorado Springs
Cruise, Ben, Corpus Christi, Colorado Springs
Eastham, Eugene S., Our Lady of the Pines, Colorado Springs
Eberwein, Roger, Parish Dir., Our Lady of the Woods, Woodland Park
Henry, Jake, On sabbatical
Huber, Robert A., (Retired)
Hunter, Robert, St. Gabriel the Archangel, Colorado Springs
Kimminau, Albert E., Holy Family, Security
Kuss, Al, Hospice Min., St. Mary's Cathedral, Colorado Springs
Leverington, Michael, Holy Apostles, Colorado Springs
Linehan, George D., Jr., Ave Maria, Parker
Matzker, Charles, Holy Apostles, Colorado Springs and contact person for Catholic Charismatic Renewal Services
McKee, Anthony, Our Lady of the Woods, Woodland Park
McLean, Arthur J., (Retired)
Milberg, Raymond, Divine Redeemer, Colorado Springs
Moss, Charles J., Catholic Community of Leadville, Leadville
Ridder, Norm, St. Patrick's, Colorado Springs
Romero, Ernest, Our Lady of Guadalupe, Colorado Springs
Sherpa, Lee, (Retired)
Specht, Charles W., St. Mary's Cathedral, Colorado Springs
Watkins, Rollo, St. Peter's, Monument

Willburn, Richard, St. Rose of Lima, Buena Vista

Sherman, Lynn, Our Lady of the Pines, Colorado Springs

INSTITUTIONS LOCATED IN THE DIOCESE

[A] HIGH SCHOOLS

COLORADO SPRINGS. **St. Mary's High School*, 2501 E. Yampa, 80909. Tel: 719-635-7540; Fax: 719-471-7623. Email: klevi@smhscs.org. Web: www.smhscs.org. Ms. Karen Levi, Contact Person; Patty Beckert, Prin. Students 350; Lay Teachers 29.

[B] EDUCATIONAL INSTITUTIONS

COLORADO SPRINGS. **The Center at Benet Hill Monastery*, 2577 N. Chelton Rd., 80909. Tel: 719-633-0655; Fax: 719-471-0403. Email: benet@quest.net. Web: www.benethillmonastery.org. Sr. Diane Liston, O.S.B., Contact Person. Sisters 5; Lay Staff 20; Assisted Annually 700.

[C] GENERAL HOSPITALS

COLORADO SPRINGS. *St. Francis Health Center* Catholic Health Initiatives , 825 E. Pikes Peak Ave., 80903. Tel: 719-776-5000; Fax: 719-776-8767. Diana Moore, Chap.; Mary Jo Bay, Chap.; Sarah Parino, Chap.

Penrose-St. Francis Health Services, 2215 N. Cascade Ave., P.O. Box 7021, 80907. Tel: 719-776-5000; Fax: 719-776-2770. Email: LucilleKrippel@centura.org. Web: www.centura.org. Sr. Lucille Krippel, O.S.F., Dir., Mission & Ministry.

Penrose Hospital, 2215 N. Cascade Ave., 80907. Tel: 719-776-5000; Fax: 719-776-2770. Rev. Gerald H. Bruggeman, Sacramental Min. (Retired); Rev. Alan Filippi, Protestant Chap.; Rev. Tom Stella, Sacramental Min.; James H. Gunn, Protestant Chap.; Dianna Moore, Protestant Chap.; Michael Crino, Chap.; Theresa Gregoire, Chap.; Sisters Jane Grosheider, S.C., Chap.; Lucille Krippel, O.S.F., Chap. & Dir. Spiritual Care; Immaculata Park, O.S.F., Chap.; John Zay, Chap. Sponsored by Catholic Health Initiatives. Sisters 3.

Penrose Community Hospital, 3205 N. Academy Blvd., 80917. Tel: 719-776-5000; Fax: 719-591-3477. Rev. Bruce DePenning, Protestant Chap. Sponsored by Catholic Health Initiatives. Bed Capacity 522; Patients Assisted Annually 254,000; Staff 2,944.

[D] NURSING HOMES

COLORADO SPRINGS. **St. Francis Nursing Center*, 7550 Assisi Heights, 80919. Tel: 719-598-1336; Fax: 719-598-6472. Rick Grimaldi, Spiritual Svcs. Dir.; Vivian Booker, Admin. Sisters of St. Francis of Perpetual Adoration Staff 182; Beds 110.

[E] SPECIAL CARE FACILITIES

COLORADO SPRINGS. *Catholic Health Initiatives Colorado Foundation*, 961 E. Colorado Ave., 80903. Tel: 719-634-6725; Fax: 719-630-0873. Email: jaymaloney@centura.org.

Namaste Alzheimer Foundation, 2 Penrose Blvd., 80906. Tel: 719-634-2046; Fax: 719-630-0832. Email: jerrybagg@centura.org. A division of Catholic Health Initiatives Colorado Foundation Staff 4.

Medalion Foundation, 1719 E. Bijou St., 80909. Tel: 719-634-2046; Fax: 719-630-0832. Email: jerrybagg@centura.org. A division of Catholic Health Initiatives Colorado Foundation Staff 4.

Penrose-St. Francis Health Foundation, 961 E. Colorado Ave., 80903. Tel: 719-634-2046; Fax: 719-630-0832. Email: jerrybagg@centura.org. A division of Catholic Health Initiatives Colorado Foundation Staff 4.

[F] RESIDENCES FOR MEN RELIGIOUS

COLORADO SPRINGS. *Padre Pio Friary*, 2415 Canticle Hts., 80919. Tel: 719-955-3749. Revs. Gene Emrisek, O.F.M.Cap., Guardian; Curtis Caslson, O.F.M.Cap; Myron Flax, O.F.M.

Solanus Casey Friary, 15 W. View Place, 80901. Tel: 719-632-7584; Fax: 719-632-7718. Revs. John P. Cousins, O.F.M.Cap. (DEN); Matthew Gross, O.F.M.Cap.

CASCADE. *Holy Cross Novitiate*, 7872 W. Hwy. 24, Box 749, 80809. Tel: 719-684-9277; Fax: 719-684-2485. Email: dlguffey@aol.com. Revs. David L. Guffey, C.S.C., Dir. Novices & Supr.; Jeffrey A. Cooper, C.S.C.; Bro. Thomas Moser, C.S.C., Asst. Supr. Congregation of Holy Cross Priests 3; Brothers 1; Novices 5. In Res. Rev. Wilfred A. Menard, C.S.C.

SEDALIA. *Sacred Heart Jesuit Community*, Box 185, 80135-0185. Tel: 303-688-5198; Fax: 303-688-9633. Email: shrinformation@quest.net. Web: www.sacredheartretreat.org. Revs. Louis J. McCabe, S.J., Supr.; Vincent E. Hovley, S.J.; Richard W. Dunphy, S.J.; Vernon R. Heinz, S.J.; E. Eugene Arthur, S.J.; Bro. Richard P. May, S.J.

[G] RESIDENCES FOR WOMEN RELIGIOUS

COLORADO SPRINGS. **Benet Hill Monastery*, 2555 N. Chelton Rd., 80909. Tel: 719-633-0655. Email: benet@quest.net. Web: www.benethillmonastery.org. Sisters Rose Ann Barmann, O.S.B., Prioress; Diane Liston, O.S.B., Community Archivist. Motherhouse of the Sisters of St. Benedict (1963).; Properties owned: The Center at Benet Hill Monastery and Benet Pines. Professed Sisters 40; Temporary Professed 2.

Mount St. Francis, 7665 Assisi Hts., 80919-3836. Tel: 719-598-5486; Fax: 719-598-1518. Email: stephanie@stfrancis.org. Web: www.stfrancis.org. Sr. Stephanie McReynolds, O.S.F., Prov.; Rev. John Slattery, Chap. Provincial and Formation House. Sisters of St. Francis of Perpetual Adoration, Province of St. Joseph (The Sisters of St. Francis of Colorado Springs). Professed Sisters 87.

Spirit of Life Monastery, 2430 N. Murray Blvd., 80915. Tel: 719-550-3716. Sr. Katherine Wawersich, O.S.B., Prioress.

[H] RETREAT CENTERS

COLORADO SPRINGS. **Benet Pines*, 15780 Hwy. 83, 80921. Tel: 719-495-2574; Fax: 719-495-4469. Email: bpinescs@hotmail.com. Sisters Marie Therese Summers, O.S.B., Admin.; Jose Sanchez, O.S.B., Center Dir. Total in Residence 3; Total Staff 4.

Franciscan Retreat Center at Mount St. Francis, 7740 Deer Hill Grove, 80919-3836. Tel: 719-955-7025; Fax: 719-260-8044. Email: frc@stfrancis.org. Web: www.franciscanretreatcenter.org. Sr. Joanne Moeller, F.S.P.A., Dir. Total Guests 11,000; Total Staff 7.

SEDALIA. *Sacred Heart Jesuit Retreat House*, Box 185, 80135-0185. Tel: 303-688-4198; Fax: 303-688-9633. Email: shrinformation@quest.net. Web: www.sacredheartretreat.org. Revs. Louis J. McCabe, S.J.; Richard W. Dunphy, S.J.; Vernon R. Heinz, S.J.; E. Eugene Arthur, S.J.; Vincent E. Hovley, S.J.; Bro. Richard P. May, S.J.; Sr. Eleanor Sheehan, C.S.J. Total in Residence 5.

[I] MISCELLANEOUS LISTINGS

COLORADO SPRINGS. *Ave Maria Catholic School Corporation*, 228 N. Cascade Ave., 80903. Tel: 719-636-2345; Fax: 719-636-1216. Sr. Mary Mullaly, F.M.A., Ed.D., Contact Person.

Catholic Center at the Citadel, 750 Citadel Dr. E., Ste. 3046, 80909. Tel: 719-573-7364. Revs. Gene Emrisek, O.F.M.Cap.; Myron Flax, O.F.M.; Matthew Gross, O.F.M.Cap.; Curtis Carlson, O.F.M.Cap.

Catholic Charismatic Renewal Services c/o Holy Apostles Church (CCRS) , 4925 N. Carefree Cir., 80917. Tel: 719-597-4249; Fax: 719-591-1816. Email: freshfire@adelphia.net. Deacon Chuck Matzker, Liaison to Bishop Hanifen for Charismatic Renewal.

Catholic Charities of Colorado Springs, Inc., 228 N. Cascade Ave., 80903. Tel: 719-636-2345; Fax: 719-636-1216. Email: info@ccharitiescs.org. Web: www.ccharitiescs.org. Krzysztof M. Myszkowski, Exec. Dir.; Robert G. Doerfler Jr., Interim Dir.

The Catholic Foundation of the Diocese of Colorado Springs, Inc., 228 N. Cascade Ave., 80903. Tel: 719-636-2345; Fax: 719-636-1216. Email: jay@diocs.org. Web: www.diocs.org. Robert G. Doerfler Jr., Pres. & Exec. Dir.

Colorado Springs Council of Black Catholics, 228 N. Cascade Ave., 80903.

Colorado Springs Diocesan Council of Catholic Women, 228 N. Cascade Ave., 80903.

Franciscan Community Counseling, 7665 Assisi Heights, 80919. Tel: 719-598-5486, Ext. 7720; Fax: 719-598-0346.

Franciscan Family Wellness Program, Inc. DBA Franciscan Community Counseling, 7665 Assisi Hts., 80919. Tel: 719-598-5486, Ext. 7720; Fax: 719-598-0346. Email: sharonccompono@stfrancis.org. Web: www.ffwpinc.com. Sharon Compono, Exec. Dir. Total Assisted 2,100; Total Staff 7.

The Franciscan Foundation of Colorado Springs, 7665 Assisi Hts., 80919-3836. Tel: 719-598-5486; Fax: 719-532-0567. Email: stephanie@stfrancis.org. Sr. Stephanie McReynolds, O.S.F., Contact Person.

Jail Ministries, c/o Diocese of Colorado Springs, 228 N. Cascade Ave., 80903. Tel: 719-636-2345. Deacon Patrick Bidon, Coord.

**St. Mary's Catholic Education Foundation*, 2501 Yampa St., 80809. LeRoy K. Hoelting, Contact Person.

**Mercy Center, Inc.*, 520 W. Buena Ventura St., 80907. Tel: 719-633-2302; Fax: 719-633-1031. Web: www.mercycenter.com. Mr. Timothy J. Fogle, Exec. Dir.

**Partners in Housing, Inc.*, 7 E. Bijou St., Ste. 211, 80903. Tel: 719-473-8890; Fax: 719-635-9360. Web: www.partnersinhousing.org. Kathy Robertson, Dir. of Family Svcs. Staff 9; Total Assisted Annually 57.

**S.E.T. of Colorado Springs*, 825 E. Pikes Peak Ave., Bldg. 29, 80903. Tel: 719-328-0908; Fax: 719-328-0910. Email: maureenmcgrain@setofcs.org. Web: www.setofcs.org. Maureen McGrain, Pres. & CEO.

**Society of Missionaries of Mercy*, 520 W. Buena Ventura St., 80907. Tel: 719-633-2302; Fax: 719-633-1031. Rev. William Jarema, Founder.

Theresian Foundation, 2577 N. Chelton Rd., 80909. Tel: 719-471-0345. Email: cynthiatremaroli@att.net. Cynthia Tremaroli, Attorney.

**Villa San Jose, Inc.*, 1810 S. Corona, 80906. Tel: 719-632-7444; Fax: 719-520-0177. Email: villas@hotmail.com. Web: www.freeservers.villasinsouthgate.com. Mike Gabriel, Admin. Total in Residence 50; Total Staff 10.

**Villa Santa Maria, Inc.*, 405 E. St. Elmo Ave., 80906. Tel: 719-520-9344; Fax: 719-520-0177. Email: villas@hotmail.com. Mike Gabriel, Admin. Staff 10; Total in Residence 50.

NECROLOGY

(No Deaths)

Diocese of Columbus

(Dioecesis Columbensis)

Most Reverend

JAMES A. GRIFFIN, J.D., J.C.L.

Bishop of Columbus; ordained May 28, 1960; consecrated Titular Bishop of Holar and Auxiliary to the Bishop of Cleveland August 1, 1979; appointed Tenth Bishop of Columbus February 7, 1983; installed April 25, 1983 *Res.: 198 E. Broad St., Columbus, OH 43215.* Tel: 614-224-2251.

Chancery Office: 198 E. Broad St., Columbus, OH 43215. Tel: 614-224-2251; 614-224-8718; Fax: 614-224-6306.

ESTABLISHED 1868.

Square Miles 11,310.

Comprises the following 23 Counties in the State of Ohio: Hardin, Marion, Morrow, Knox, Holmes, Tuscarawas, Union, Delaware, Licking, Coshocton, Madison, Franklin, Muskingum, Fayette, Pickaway, Fairfield, Perry, Ross, Hocking, Pike, Jackson, Vinton and Scioto.

Legal Title: For legal titles of parishes and diocesan institutions, consult the Chancery Office.

STATISTICAL OVERVIEW

Personnel	
Bishop	1
Priests: Diocesan Active in Diocese	121
Priests: Diocesan Active Outside Diocese	6
Priests: Retired, Sick or Absent	55
Number of Diocesan Priests	182
Religious Priests in Diocese	41
Total Priests in Diocese	223
Extern Priests in Diocese	11
Ordinations:	
Diocesan Priests	1
Transitional Deacons	6
Permanent Deacons in Diocese	77
Total Brothers	5
Total Sisters	341
Parishes	
Parishes	107
With Resident Pastor:	
Resident Diocesan Priests	94
Resident Religious Priests	6
Without Resident Pastor:	
Administered by Priests	6
Administered by Religious Women	1
Missions	4
Professional Ministry Personnel:	
Brothers	3
Sisters	29
Lay Ministers	79
Welfare	
Catholic Hospitals	4
Total Assisted	972,123
Homes for the Aged	20
Total Assisted	1,595
Day Care Centers	1
Total Assisted	178
Special Centers for Social Services	7
Total Assisted	402,884
Residential Care of Disabled	1
Total Assisted	98
Educational	
Seminaries, Diocesan	1
Students from This Diocese	13
Students from Other Diocese	123
Diocesan Students in Other Seminaries	8
Total Seminarians	21
Colleges and Universities	1
Total Students	2,566
High Schools, Diocesan and Parish	11
Total Students	4,882
Elementary Schools, Diocesan and Parish	44
Total Students	12,601
Elementary Schools, Private	2
Total Students	316
Catechesis/Religious Education:	
High School Students	2,296
Elementary Students	16,526
Total Students under Catholic Instruction	39,208
Teachers in the Diocese:	
Priests	1
Brothers	1
Sisters	7
Lay Teachers	1,242
Vital Statistics	
Receptions into the Church:	
Infant Baptism Totals	3,760
Adult Baptism Totals	511
Received into Full Communion	795
First Communions	4,197
Confirmations	3,630
Marriages:	
Catholic	571
Interfaith	605
Total Marriages	1,176
Deaths	1,673
Total Catholic Population	240,682
Total Population	2,408,079

Former Bishops—Rt. Revs. SYLVESTER HORTON ROSECRANS, D.D., consecrated Titular Bishop of Pompeiopolis and Auxiliary to the Bishop of Cincinnati, March 25, 1862; transferred to Columbus, March 3, 1868; died Oct. 21, 1878; JOHN AMBROSE WATTERSON, D.D., consecrated Aug. 8, 1880; died April 17, 1899; Most Revs. HENRY MOELLER, D.D., consecrated Bishop of Columbus, Aug. 25, 1900; promoted to the Archiepiscopal See of Areopolis and made Coadjutor to the Archbishop of Cincinnati, with the right of succession, April 27, 1903 succeeded to the See of Cincinnati, Oct. 31, 1904; died Jan. 5, 1925; JAMES JOSEPH HARTLEY, D.D., consecrated Feb. 25, 1904; died Jan. 12, 1944; MICHAEL JOSEPH READY, D.D., consecrated Dec. 14, 1944; died May 2, 1957; CLARENCE GEORGE ISSENMANN, S.T.D., consecrated Titular Bishop of Phytea and Auxiliary Bishop of Cincinnati May 25, 1954; appt. Bishop of Columbus Dec. 5, 1957; transferred to Cleveland as Apostolic Administrator. "cum jure successionis," Oct. 7, 1964; died July 27, 1982; His Eminence JOHN CARDINAL CARBERRY, D.D., appt. Titular Bishop of Elis and Coadjutor of Lafayette in Indiana "cum jure successionis," May 3, 1956; consecrated July 25, 1956; succeeded to See Nov. 20, 1957; transferred to Columbus Jan. 20, 1965; transferred to the Archdiocese of St. Louis, March 24, 1968; created Cardinal April 28, 1969; Most Revs. CLARENCE E. ELWELL, D.D., consecrated Dec. 21, 1962; appt. to Columbus May 29, 1968; died Feb. 16, 1973; EDWARD J. HERRMANN, D.D. (Retired), appt. Auxiliary Bishop of Washington and Titular Bishop of Lamzella, March 4, 1966; consecrated April 26, 1966; appt. Ninth Bishop of Columbus, June 26, 1973; installed Aug. 21, 1973; retired Sept. 18, 1982; named Apostolic Administrator Sept. 1982 to April 1983; died Dec. 22, 1999.

Vicar General/Chancellor—Rev. Msgr. STEPHAN J. MOLONEY, M.A., M.Div., J.C.L.

Episcopal Vicar for Charities and Social Concerns—MARK H. HUDDY, J.D.

Episcopal Vicar for Education—LUCIA D. MCQUAIDE, M.S.Ed. M.Rel.Ed.

Episcopal Vicar for Church Ministry—Sr. JOAN M. HARPER, C.D.P.

Episcopal Vicar for Spiritual Life—Deacon JAMES A. ROUSE, M.Sc.

Chancery Office—198 E. Broad St., Columbus, 43215. Tel: 614-224-2251 (Sat.-Sun.); 614-224-8718 (other times); Fax: 614-224-6306. Office Hours: Mon.-Fri. 8-4:30

Chancellor—Rev. Msgr. STEPHAN J. MOLONEY, M.A., M.Div., J.C.L.

Vice Chancellor—Deacon JAMES A. ROUSE, M.Sc.

Assistant Chancellor—Mr. THOMAS M. BERG JR., B.A., M.J., M.P.S.

Diocesan Consultors—Most Rev. JAMES A. GRIFFIN, J.D., J.C.L.; Rev. Msgr. STEPHAN J. MOLONEY, M.A., M.Div., J.C.L.; Revs. JAMES A. KLIMA; WILLIAM A. METZGER, B.A.; SHAWN CORCORAN; JOHN E. STATTMILLER; Rev. Msgr. A. ANTHONY FRECKER, M.Div., MTh; Revs. MICHAEL F. NIMOCKS; ROBERT E. WILLMANN, J.C.L.

Parochial Examiners—Rev. Msgrs. WILLIAM A. DUNN; PAUL P. ENKE; JAMES L.T. RUEF; Revs. JOHN E. STATTMILLER; PAUL A. NOBLE, M.A., Ph.D.; MARK J. HAMMOND, J.C.L., S.T.L.

Vicars Forane—Vicariate 1: Center City Rev. DAVID A. POLIAFICO, St. Joseph Cathedral, 212 E. Broad St., Columbus, 43215. Vicariate 2: Northwest: Rev. Msgr. DAVID R. FUNK, B.A., S.T.B., St. Agatha Church 1860 Northam Rd., Columbus, 43221-2299. Vicariate 3: North High: Rev. Msgr. JAMES L.T. RUEF, Holy Name Church, 154 E. Patterson Ave., Columbus, 43202-3047. Vicariate 4: Northland: Rev. RICHARD NIEBERDING, C.PP.S., St. James the Less Church, 1652 Oakland Park Ave., Columbus, 43224-3552. Vicariate 5: West: Rev. PATRICK A. TONER, St. Joseph Church, 140 West Ave., P.O. Box 166, Plain City, 43064-0166. Vicariate 6: South: Rev. MARK J. HAMMOND, J.C.L., S.T.L., St. Mary Church, 684 S. Third St., Columbus, 43206-1094. Vicariate 7: East: VACANT. Vicariate 8: Marion: Rev. JOHN BARRY BENTZ, Our Lady of Lourdes Church, 1033 W. 5th St., Marysville, 43040-9282. Vicariate 9: Zanesville: Rev. S. JORDAN MCCONWAY, O.P., St. Thomas Aquinas Church, 130 N. 5th St., Zanesville, 43701-3583. Vicariate 10: Knox Licking: Rev. F. RICHARD SNOKE, St. Luke Church, 307 S. Market St., P.O. Box P, Danville, 43014-0616. Vicariate 11: Tusc-Holmes: Rev. Msgr. GEORGE J. SCHLEGEL, B.A., Sacred Heart Church, 139 3rd St., N.E., New Philadelphia, 44663. Vicariate 12: Lancaster: Rev. JUSTIN J. REIS, St. Bernadette Church, 1343 Wheeling Rd., Lancaster, 43130. Vicariate 13: Chillicothe: Rev. JAMES P. BLACK, St. Peter Church, 122 Church St., Chillicothe, 45601. Vicariate 14: Scioto County: Rev. PETER M. GIDEON, St. Peter Church, 2167 Lick Run Lyra Rd., Wheelersburg, 45694-8882. Vicariate 15: Perry County: Rev. FRANCIS M. STANTON, Church of the Atonement, 320 Winter St., Crooksville, 43731-1347.

Priests' Senate—Revs. DAVID E. YOUNG, B.A., M.Div., Chm.; LEO L. CONNOLLY, Vice Chm.; SHAWN CORCORAN, Sec.; RICHARD F. ENGLE (Retired); G. MICHAEL GRIBBLE, M.Div.; ANTHONY DINOVO JR.; CHARLES E. COTTON; RICHARD C. WEYLS, M.A., M.Div., S.T.L.; WILLIAM H. DEVILLE; DAVID W. SIZEMORE; LEO L. CONNOLLY; C. THEODORE THOMAS; HOMER D. BLUBAUGH; JONATHAN F. WILSON; JOHN E. STATTMILLER. Appointed

Members: Rev. Msgr. STEPHAN J. MOLONEY, M.A., M.Div., J.C.L.; Rev. ROBERT E. WILLMANN, J.C.L.

Diocesan Pastoral Council—AMY TAULBEE, Chm.; MARY BURNS, Exec. Sec., 197 E. Gay St., Columbus, 43215. Tel: 614-228-1646.

Tribunal—Ste. 500, 197 E. Gay St., Columbus, 43215-3290. Tel: 614-241-2500.

Judicial Vicar—Rev. JOSEPH N. BAY, M.A., M.Div., J.C.L.

Adjutant Judicial Vicars—Rev. Msgrs. JOHN K. CODY, B.A., M.Div., J.C.L.; JAMES LEROY TONKINSON RUEF, M.A., M.Div., J.C.L.

Presiding Judges of First Instance—Rev. Msgr. JOHN K. CODY, B.A., M.Div., J.C.L.; Revs. MARK J. HAMMOND, J.C.L., S.T.L.; DENNIS E. STEVENSON, J.C.L.

Presiding Judge in Second Instance—Rev. Msgr. JAMES LEROY TONKINSON RUEF, M.A., J.D., J.C.L.

Promoter of Justice—Rev. Msgr. STEPHAN J. MOLONEY, M.A., M.Div., J.C.L.

Defenders of the Bond—Rev. Msgr. JOHN G. JOHNSON, J.C.D.; Sr. WANDA SCHERER, O.S.F., M.A.; Mr. PHILLIP L. WEBSTER II, M.A., J.C.L.

Medical Experts—Dr. WILLIAM B. BENNINGER, Ph.D.; Dr. FRANK OROSZ, Ph.D.; Rev. STEPEHN G. VIRGINIA, Ph.D.; Sr. MARIALEIN ANZENBERGER, O.P., M.A.

Diocesan Judges—Rev. WILLIAM ARNOLD, M.E., M.Ed.; Rev. Msgr. ANTHONY BORRELLI, J.C.L.; Revs. THOMAS CADDEN, M.A.; LEO CONNOLLY, M.Div.; Rev. Msgrs. JOHN T. DITTOE, S.T.D., S.T.B. (Retired); JOHN DREESE, S.S.L., S.T.L.; A. ANTHONY FRECKER, M.Div., MTh; DAVID R. FUNK, B.A., S.T.B.; F. THOMAS GALLEN, B.A., C.G.M. (Retired); Revs. JAMES GEIGER, A.M., Ph.D.; G. MICHAEL GRIBBLE, M.Div.; TIMOTHY M. HAYES, S.T.L.; KEVIN KAVANAGH, S.S.L., M.Div.; W. THOMAS KESSLER, Ph.D.; DENIS S. KIGOZI, M.Div.; CHARLES F. KLINGER, B.A., M.A., M.Div., Ph.D.; Rev. Msgr. FRANK P. LANE, B.A., M.A., M.Th., M.Div.; Revs. WILLIAM A. METZGER, B.A.; DANIEL MILLISOR, M.Div.; PAUL A. NOBLE, M.A., Ph.D.; Rev. Msgr. GEORGE J. SCHLEGEL, B.A.; Rev. THEODORE K. SILL, M.Div., M.Th.; Rev. Msgr. DAVID V. SOROHAN, M.A., S.T.L., Ph.D.; Rev. CHARLES T. THOMAS, B.A., M.Div., M.A.; Rev. Msgr. EDWARD F. TRENOR, J.C.L.; Revs. MICHAEL B. WATSON, M.Div.; RICHARD C. WEYLS, M.A., M.Div., S.T.L.; ROBERT E. WILLMANN, J.C.L.; Rev. Msgr. JOHN V. WOLF, S.T.D. (Retired); Rev. DAVID E. YOUNG, B.A., M.Div.

Tribunal Staff—Sr. RAYMUNDA BROOKS, O.P., M.A.; Mrs. JOANNE WILLIS, B.A.; Ms. MARY BETH KRECSMAR; Sr. MARY LINDA LORENZ, O.P., M.A.; Ms. PATRICIA SMITH.

Advocates—Hon. PEGGY BRYANT, J.D.; Mr. THOMAS LONG ESQ., J.D.; Mrs. BARBARA KEGELMEYER, B.A.

Black Catholic Ministries of Columbus—WILLIE MOORE, Chm., 244 E. Rich St., Columbus, 43215-5232. Tel: 614-228-0024; Fax: 614-221-1787.

Building Commission—Rev. Msgr. EDWARD F. TRENOR, J.C.L., Christ the King, 2770 Dover Rd., Columbus, 43209.

Catholic Campaign for Human Development—ERIN CORDLE, Dir., Department of Social Concerns, 197 E. Gay St., Columbus, 43215-3229. Tel: 614-241-2540; Fax: 614-228-7302. Email: ecordle@colsdioc.org.

Catholic Center—Diocesan Office Building, 197 E. Gay St., Columbus, 43215. Tel: 614-228-2453.

Catholic Charities and Social Concerns—MARK H. HUDDY, J.D., Vicar, 197 E. Gay St., Columbus, 43215. Tel: 614-241-2540.

Catholic Conference of Ohio—TIMOTHY V. LUCKHAUPT, Dir., 9 E. Long St., Ste. 201, Columbus, 43215. Tel: 614-224-7147; Fax: 614-224-7150. Email: cco@cdeducation.org. Web: cdeducation.org/cco.

Catholic Record Society—DONALD SCHLEGEL, Sec., 197 E. Gay St., Columbus, 43215. Tel: 614-241-2571.

Catholic Relief Services—ERIN CORDLE, Diocesan Dir., Dept. of Social Concerns, 197 E. Gay St., Columbus, 43215. Tel: 614-241-2540.

Catholic Social Services—DONALD S. WISLER, Pres., 197 E. Gay St., Columbus, 43215. Tel: 614-221-5891.

Cemeteries—RICHARD FINN, Dir., 6440 S. High St., Lockbourne, 43137. Tel: 614-491-2751; Fax: 614-491-4264. Email: ccocrfinn@aol.com.

Censor of Books—Rev. Msgr. JOHN V. WOLF, S.T.D. (Retired); Rev. WILLIAM THOMAS KESSLER.

Central Purchasing Service, Inc.—Deacon JOHN VELLANI, Dir., 1567 Loretta Ave., Ste. 212, Columbus, 43211. Tel: 800-842-8319; 614-262-0010.

Catholic Charismatic Renewal, Inc.—Rev. JUSTIN J. REIS, Bishop's Liaison, St. Bernadette, 1343 Wheeling Rd., Lancaster, 43130-8701. Tel: 740-654-1893; MAXINE POWERS, Exec. Dir.; DOREEN MCCULLOUGH, Asst. Dir., Catholic Charismatic Center, 4207 E. Broad St., Ste. C, Columbus, 43213-1200. Tel: 614-237-7080; Fax: 614-237-6847. Email: columbus_ccr@juno.com.

St. Vincent Family Centers—MICHELLE WARD, L.S.W., Pres. & C.E.O., Main Campus, 1490 E. Main St., Columbus, 43205. Tel: 614-252-0731; 614-252-2069 (TDD & TTY); Fax: 614-252-8468.

Franklinton Office—ROSEMARY STANDISH, L.I.S.W., Program Dir., 840 W. State St., Columbus, 43222. Tel: 614-221-7855; Fax: 614-221-8797.

Wayne Office—REJEANNA HAYNES, L.I.S.W., Program Dir., 880 S. Wayne Ave., Columbus, 43204. Tel: 614-351-1080; Fax: 614-351-0891.

Lincoln Park West Office—JUAN VAZQUEZ, Community Service Provider, 4343 W. Port Rd., Columbus, 43228. Tel: 614-279-8511; Fax: 614-351-8645.

Department of Communications—ROBIN A. MILLER, Dir., 197 E. Gay St., Columbus, 43215. Tel: 614-241-2555; Fax: 614-241-2557.

Council of Religious—Sr. NADINE OVERBECK, O.S.F., 861 Grove Rd., Zanesville, 43701-1359.

Deaf Apostolate—Rev. STANLEY BENECKI, St. Mary Magdalene, 473 S. Roys Ave., Columbus, 43204-2598. Tel: 614-358-7323 (TDD); 614-274-1121 (Voice); Fax: 614-274-1122.

Department of Education—LUCIA D. MCQUAIDE, M.S.Ed., M.Rel.Ed., Vicar-Supt., 197 E. Gay St., Columbus, 43215. Tel: 614-221-5829.

Diocesan Board of Review for the Protection of Children—Rev. Msgr. STEPHAN J. MOLONEY, M.A., M.Div., J.C.L., Victims Asst. Coord.; LESLIE A. BOSTIC, Ph.D.; YVETTE MCGEE BROWN, Chm.; Mrs. MARILYN DONO; Dr. MARIAN SCHUDA; Rev. Msgr. DAVID V. SOROHAN, M.A., S.T.L., Ph.D.; LINDA DAY-MACKESSY; Dr. JUANITA MURAWSKI, 198 E. Broad St., Columbus, 43215. Tel: 614-224-2251.

Diocesan Council of Catholic Women—LOIS MURPHY, Pres., 197 E. Gay St., Columbus, 43215. Tel: 614-228-8601.

Development Office—RICK H. JERIC, Dir. Devel., 197 E. Gay St., Columbus, 43215. Tel: 614-241-2550.

Diocesan Finance Council—Most Rev. JAMES A. GRIFFIN, J.D., J.C.L.; Rev. Msgr. STEPHAN J. MOLONEY, M.A., M.Div., J.C.L.; W. MATTHEW BROWN; Deacon JAMES A. ROUSE, M.Sc.; FRANK BETTENDORF, Chm.; THOMAS MCAULIFFE; HUGH DORRIAN; Rev. Msgr. EDWARD TRENOR; JAMES CSASZAR; TIMOTHY BOTTS; TIMOTHY KELLEY; CHRISTOPHER FIDLER; LUCIA MCQUAIDE; MARK HUDDY; Sr. JOAN HARPER, C.D.P., 198 E. Broad St., Columbus, 43215. Tel: 614-224-1221; Fax: 614-224-6306.

Priests Personnel Board—Rev. DANIEL J. MILLISOR, Chm., 222 E. Highland Ave., Ada, 45810-1122. Tel: 419-634-2626.

Diocesan Retirement Plans for Priests, Lay Employees and Lay Teachers—Rev. Msgr. EDWARD F. TRENOR, J.C.L., Chm. Admin. Board for Plans. Tel: 614-237-0401.

Family Life Office—STEPHANIE JENEMANN, Dir., 197 E. Gay St., Columbus, 43215. Tel: 614-241-2560. Email: flomailbox@colsdioc.org.

Finance Office—W. MATTHEW BROWN, Dir., 198 E. Broad St., Columbus, 43215. Tel: 614-224-1221; 614-224-1235.

Foundation of the Catholic Diocese of Columbus—KATHLEEN SPENCER, Exec. Dir., 1071 S. High St., Columbus, 43206. Tel: 614-443-8893; Fax: 614-443-8894.

Health Affairs Department (Hospitals)—Rev. MARK J. HAMMOND, J.C.L., S.T.L., Coord., 197 E. Gay St., Columbus, 43215. Tel: 614-445-9668.

Insurance—Diocesan Finance Office, 198 E. Broad St., Columbus, 43215. Tel: 614-224-1221.

Catholic Charities of Columbus—

J.O.I.N. (Joint Organization for Inner-City Needs)—Mrs. RUTH BECKMAN, Dir., 196 E. Gay St., Columbus, 43215. Tel: 614-241-2530.

Legion of Mary—Rev. Msgr. CHARLES J. FOELLER, Dir., Sacred Hearts Church, 4680 U.S. Rt. 42, Cardington, 43315. Tel: 419-946-3611. Email: foeller@bright.net.

Liturgical Commission—Sr. RENE SIMONELIC, O.S.F., 197 E. Gay St., Columbus, 43215. Tel: 614-221-4640.

Liturgy Office—Sr. RENE SIMONELIC, O.S.F., Dir., 197 E. Gay St., Columbus, 43215. Tel: 614-221-4640.

Ministry Formation Office—LESLIE J. YOUNG, Ph.D., Dir.; JIMMY HATFIELD, Prog. Coord., 197 E. Gay St., Columbus, 43215. Tel: 614-241-2544.

Newspaper—MARK MORETTI, Editor, 197 E. Gay St., Columbus, 43215. Tel: 614-224-5195. "The Catholic Times"

Pastoral Services, Office of—MARY E. BURNS, Dir., 197 E. Gay St., 4th Floor, Columbus, 43215. Tel: 614-228-1646.

Office of the Diaconate—Deacons FRANK A. IANNARINO, Dir.; THOMAS V. JOHNSTON, Assoc. Dir., Office, 197 E. Gay St., Columbus, 43215. Tel: 614-241-2545. Email: fiannarino@colsdioc.org; School, 7625 N. High St., Columbus, 43235. Tel: 614-885-5585.

Personnel Services—JOAN THORNTON PALKUTI, Sec., 197 E. Gay St., Columbus, 43215. Tel: 614-241-2590.

Priests Continuing Education—Rev. G. MICHAEL GRIBBLE, M.Div., St. Joseph Cathedral, 212 E. Broad St., Columbus, 43215. Tel: 614-224-1295.

Pontifical Mission Societies— The Society for the Propagation of Faith, Holy Childhood Association, The Society of St. Peter Apostle DENEEN LEONARD-SMITH, Dir., 197 E. Gay St., Columbus, 43215. Tel: 614-228-8603.

Printing Services—NANCY EYERMAN, Mgr., 197 E. Gay St., Columbus, 43215. Tel: 614-224-0261.

Real Estate—DONALD A. BORROR, Consultant, 5501 Frantz Rd., P.O. Box 7166, Dublin, 43017. Tel: 614-761-6000.

Department of Religious Education—BARBARA ROMANELLO-WICHTMAN, Dir., 197 E. Gay St., Columbus, 43215. Tel: 614-221-4633.

Retreats—MARY E. MURPHY, Dir., St. Therese's Retreat Center, 5277 E. Broad St., Columbus, 43213-1389. Tel: 614-866-1611; Deacon MICKEY HAWKINS, Dir., Ss. Peter and Paul Retreat Center, 2734 Seminary Rd., S.E., Newark, 43056-9339. Tel: 740-928-4246; Fax: 740-928-1512.

Rural Life Apostolate—JERALD FREEWALT, Dir., 197 E. Gay St., Columbus, 43215. Tel: 614-241-2540.

St. Stephen's Community House—Ms. JUDITH STATTMILLER, Dir., 1500 E. 17th Ave., Columbus, 43219. Tel: 614-294-6347; Fax: 614-294-0258.

St. Francis Evangelization Center—Sr. LINDA LEWANDOWSKI, O.S.F., 108 W. Mill St., McArthur, 45651-1229. Tel: 740-596-4316.

St. Vincent de Paul Society—BILL HAMMOND, Pres.; STEVE DEMERS, Exec. Dir., 197 E. Gay St., Columbus, 43215. Tel: 614-221-3554.

St. Vincent de Paul Store—424 E. Locust St., Lancaster, 43130. Tel: 740-653-6037.

Scout Chaplain—Deacon KLAUS FRICKE, St. Michael Church, 5750 N. High St., Worthington, 43085. Tel: 614-885-7814.

Department of Social Concerns—MARK H. HUDDY, J.D., Dir., 197 E. Gay St., Columbus, 43215. Tel: 614-241-2540.

Catholic Latino Center and Hispanic Ministry—ANGELA JOHNSTON, Dir., 143 E. Patterson Ave., Columbus, 43202. Tel: 614-262-7992; Fax: 614-263-6882. Email: cathlatinocntr@aol.com.

Victim Assistance Coordinator—Rev. Msgr. STEPHAN J. MOLONEY, M.A., M.Div., J.C.L. Tel: 614-224-2251. Email: smoloney@colsdioc.org.

Vocations Office—Rev. MATTHEW N. HOOVER, Dir., 197 E. Gay St., Columbus, 43215. Tel: 614-221-5565.

Youth and Young Adult Ministry—MARK BUTLER, Dir., 197 E. Gay St., Columbus, 43215. Tel: 614-241-2565.

CLERGY, PARISHES, MISSIONS AND PAROCHIAL SCHOOLS

CITY OF COLUMBUS
(FRANKLIN COUNTY)

1—ST. JOSEPH CATHEDRAL (1878), Revs. G. Michael Gribble, M.Div., Rector; David A. Poliafico; Ronald J. Atwood; Deacons Thomas Johnston; James Gorski. In Res., Rev. Frederick A. Loyd.
Res.: 212 E. Broad St., 43215. Tel: 614-224-1295; Fax: 614-224-1176.
Church: E. Broad St. & N. Fifth St., 43215.

2—ST. AGATHA (Upper Arlington) (1940), Rev. Msgr. David R. Funk, B.A., S.T.B.; Rev. John L. Bakle, S.M.; Deacon Kenneth L. Drummer; Sr. Mary Faith Geelan, O.P., Pastoral Min. In Res., Rev. Robert J. Schuer (Retired).
Res.: 1860 Northam Rd., 43221. Tel: 614-488-6149; Fax: 614-488-6596.
School—1880 Northam Rd., 43221. Tel: 614-488-9000; Fax: 614-488-5783. Mrs. Joan Mastell, Prin. Lay Teachers 25; Students 437.
Catechesis/Religious Program—Tel: 614-488-4975. Mrs. Jeanne Altiero, D.R.E. Students 485.

3—ST. AGNES (1954), Rev. William J. Metzger.
Res.: 2364 W. Mound St., 43204-2997. Tel: 614-276-5413; Fax: 614-276-5608.
Catechesis/Religious Program—Students 10.

4—ST. ALOYSIUS (1906), Rev. Dennis E. Stevenson, J.C.L., Admin. In Res., Rev. Msgr. Donald C. Schulz (Retired).
Res.: 32 Clarendon Ave., 43223. Tel: 614-276-6587; Fax: 614-276-1793.

Catechesis/Religious Program—2350 W. Mound St., 43204. Tel: 614-276-5413; Fax: 614-276-5608. Students 13.

5—ST. ANDREW (1955), Revs. Michael B. Watson, M.Div.; Anthony A. Dinovo Jr.; Deacon James F. Keating.
Res.: 1899 McCoy Rd., 43220. Tel: 614-451-4290; Fax: 614-451-8300.
School—4081 Reed Rd., 43220. Tel: 614-451-1626; Fax: 314-451-0272. Merrlyn Cahill, Prin.; Suzanne Emsweller, Asst. Prin. Lay Teachers 24; Students 491.
Catechesis/Religious Program—Tel: 614-451-2855; Fax: 614-451-8300. Kris Pellissier, Coord. Students 319.

6—SAINT ANTHONY (1963), Rev. Mark V. Ghiloni; Mrs. Colleen Buzenski, Pastoral Asst.
Res.: 4913 Atwater Dr., 43229. Tel: 614-885-4857.
School—(Grades K-8), 1300 Urban Dr., 43229. Tel: 614-888-4268; Fax: 614-888-4435. Chris Iaconis, Prin. Lay Teachers 8; Students 191.
Catechesis/Religious Program—(Grades 1-8) Tel: 614-888-8190. Judy McElwee, D.R.E. Students 72.

7—STS. AUGUSTINE AND GABRIEL (1984), Rev. Thomas G. Petry.
Office—1567 Loretta Ave., Ste. 111, 43211-1677. Tel: 614-268-3123; Fax: 614-268-8130.
Church: 1550 E. Hudson St., 43211.
Catechesis/Religious Program—Students 16.

8—ST. CATHARINE (1931), Rev. Msgr. David V. Sorohan, M.A., S.T.L., Ph.D.; Sr. Christella Ritchey, O.S.F., Pastoral Assoc.; James Kebe, Chap., Pastoral Care. Tel: 614-231-4509. In Res., Rev. Joseph N. Bay, M.A., M.Div., J.C.L.
Res.: 500 S. Gould Rd., 43209. Tel: 614-231-4509; Fax: 614-231-8366.
School—2865 Fair Ave., 43209. Tel: 614-235-1396; Fax: 614-235-9708. Mrs. Janet Weisner, Prin. Lay Teachers 20; Students 276.
Catechesis/Religious Program—Tel: 614-231-4500. Sr. Christella Ritchey, O.S.F., D.R.E.; Mrs. Chris Schleicher, D.R.E. Students 252.

9—ST. CECILIA (1882), Revs. Craig R. Eilerman; Shawn D. Corcoran.
Res.: 434 Norton Rd., 43228. Tel: 614-878-5353; Fax: 614-878-0459.
School—440 Norton Rd., 43228. Tel: 614-878-3555; Fax: 614-878-6852. Jeffrey Kanowsky, Prin. Lay Teachers 14; Students 251.
Catechesis/Religious Program—Tel: 614-878-0133. Richard Keyes, D.R.E. Students 311.

10—CHRIST THE KING (1946), Rev. Msgr. Edward F. Trenor, J.C.L.; Deacon Peter C. Labita. In Res., Rev. James W. Jones (Retired).
Res.: 2770 Dover Rd., 43209. Tel: 614-237-0401; Fax: 614-237-4689.
School—2855 E. Livingston Ave., 43209. Tel: 614-231-3391; Fax: 614-338-2170. Ms. Barb Davis, Prin. Lay Teachers 13; Students 163.
Catechesis/Religious Program—Tel: 614-231-8374. Karen Laihr, D.R.E. Students 80.

11—ST. CHRISTOPHER (1947), Rev. Arthur W. Wiles; John J. Dawson, Business Mgr.
Res.: 1420 Grandview Ave., 43212. Tel: 614-486-0457; Fax: 614-486-0433.
School—Trinity, 1381 Ida Ave., 43212. Tel: 614-488-7650; Fax: 614-488-4687. Mrs. Raenita Kownacki, Prin. Sisters 1; Lay Teachers 16; Students 195.
Catechesis/Religious Program—Mrs. Diane Hayhurst, D.R.E. Students 188.

12—COLUMBUS VIETNAMESE CATHOLIC COMMUNITY, Rev. Joseph N. Bay, M.A., M.Div., J.C.L., Chap.
500 S. Gould Rd., 43209. Tel: 614-235-4297. Email: josephbay@att.net.

13—COMMUNITY OF HOLY ROSARY AND ST. JOHN (1979), (African American), Rev. Dennis T. Dillon, S.J.
Res.: 648 S. Ohio Ave., 43205. Tel: 614-252-5926; Fax: 614-252-5933.
Catechesis/Religious Program—Tel: 314-252-5926, Ext. 226. Sr. Diane Kozlowski, O.P., D.R.E. Students 64.

14—CORPUS CHRISTI (1925), Rev. John E. Stattmiller; Deacon J. Jerry Butts. In Res., Rev. Paul O. Smith (Retired).
Parish Administrative Office: 277 Reeb Ave., 43207.
Res.: 1111 E. Stewart Ave., 43206. Tel: 614-444-9871; Fax: 614-444-1018.
Catechesis/Religious Program—Tel: 614-443-2828; Fax: 614-444-0523. Clustered with St. Ladislas, Columbus.

15—ST. DOMINIC (1889), (African American), Rev. James L. Colopy; Deacon Robert A. Neely. Tel: 740-382-5781, Ext. 2346.
Mailing Address & Res.: 453 N. 20th St., P.O. Box 83572, 43203-0572. Tel: 614-252-4913; Fax: 614-252-1655.
Catechesis/Religious Program—Students 25.

16—ST. ELIZABETH (1967), Rev. Charles E. Cotton; Deacons Frank X. Ball; John J. Rericha; Frank X. McDevitt.
Church: 6077 Sharon Woods Blvd., 43229. Tel: 614-891-0150; Fax: 614-891-3243.
Res.: 1682 Lynnhurst Rd., 43229. Tel: 614-882-1782.
Catechesis/Religious Program—Students 125.

17—ST. FRANCIS OF ASSISI (1892), Rev. Richard C. Weyls, M.A., M.Div., S.T.L.
Res.: 386 Buttles Ave., 43215. Tel: 614-299-5781; Fax: 614-299-1987.

18—ST. GABRIEL, Merged, with St. Augustine. See separate listing.

19—HOLY CROSS (1833), (German), Rev. Jerome D. Stluka. In Res., Rev. Msgr. Lawrence J. Corcoran, P.A. (Retired).
Res.: 204 S. Fifth St., 43215. Tel: 614-224-3416; Fax: 614-224-9916.

20—HOLY FAMILY (1877), Rev. Kevin F. Lutz; Deacons W. Earl McCurry; Frank A. Paniccia. In Res., Rev. Msgr. John K. Cody, B.A., M.Div., J.C.L.
Res.: 584 W. Broad St., 43215-2710. Tel: 614-221-4323; Fax: 614-221-9818.
Catechesis/Religious Program—Students 72.

21—HOLY NAME (1905), Rev. Msgr. James L.T. Ruef.
Res.: 154 E. Patterson Ave., 43202. Tel: 614-262-0390; Fax: 614-262-0390.
Catechesis/Religious Program—Students 9.

22—HOLY SPIRIT (Whitehall) (1947), Rev. Raymond Larussa.
Res.: 4383 E. Broad St., 43213. Tel: 614-861-1521; Fax: 614-861-3746.
School—4382 Duchene Ln., 43213. Tel: 614-861-0475; Fax: 614-861-8608. Linda Saelzler, Prin. Lay Teachers 14; Students 266.
Catechesis/Religious Program—Erin Arnett, Youth Min. Students 54.

23—IMMACULATE CONCEPTION (1917), Rev. Msgrs. Anthony N. Missimi; Thomas M. Bennett.
Res.: 414 E. North Broadway, 43214. Tel: 614-267-9241; Fax: 614-267-7720.
School—366 E. North Broadway, 43214 Tel: 614-267-6579. John Grossman, Prin. Lay Teachers 22; Students 480.
Catechesis/Religious Program—440 E. North Broadway, 43214. Tel: 614-267-0279. John Hoffman, D.R.E. Students 720.

24—ST. JAMES-THE-LESS (1947), Revs. Richard Nieberding, C.PP.S.; Patrick Patterson, C.PP.S.; Deacon Joseph P. Checca; Tim Feeney, Business Mgr.
Res.: 1652 Oakland Park Ave., 43224. Tel: 614-262-1179; 614-262-1170; Fax: 614-262-6798.
School—1628 Oakland Park Ave., 43224. Tel: 614-268-3311; Fax: 614-262-6798. Sandra Hay, Prin. Lay Teachers 15; Students 296.
Catechesis/Religious Program—Bev Cremeans, D.R.E. Students 30.

25—ST. JOHN THE BAPTIST (1896), (Italian), Rev. William A. Metzger, B.A.
Res.: 720 Hamlet St., 43215. Tel: 614-294-5319; Fax: 614-294-4303.
Catechesis/Religious Program—Students 11.

26—KOREAN CATHOLIC COMMUNITY (1978), (Asian), [CEM] Rev. Jong-Hyun Lee (Korea, South).
Mailing Address: 5500 Broadview Rd., Gahanna, 43230. Tel: 614-476-9974; Fax: 614-476-9974.
Catechesis/Religious Program—Tel: 614-527-9618; Fax: 614-527-1425. Students 45.

27—ST. LADISLAS (1908), (Hungarian), Rev. John E. Stattmiller.
Res.: 1111 E. Stewart Ave., 43206. Tel: 614-444-9871; Fax: 614-444-1018.
Catechesis/Religious Program—277 Reeb Ave., 43207. Tel: 614-443-2828; Fax: 614-444-0523. (Clustered with Corpus Christi.) Students 90.

28—ST. LEO (1903), (German), Closed., For inquiries for parish records please see St. Mary, Columbus.

29—ST. MARGARET OF CORTONA (1921), Rev. Msgr. Frank P. Lane, B.A., M.A., M.Th., M.Div.; Sr. Juliana D'Amato, O.P., Pastoral Assoc.
Res.: 1600 Hague Ave., 43204-1606. Tel: 614-279-1690; Fax: 614-279-2386.
Catechesis/Religious Program—Tel: 614-272-7571. Sharon Curtin, D.R.E. Students 380.

30—ST. MARY (1865), (German), Rev. Mark J. Hammond, J.C.L., S.T.L.; Jason Shanks, Pastoral Assoc.; Deacon Michael Ross, Ph.D. In Res., Rev. Joseph E. Stanton (Retired).
Res.: 684 S. Third St., 43206. Tel: 614-445-9668; Fax: 614-444-1688.
School—700 S. Third St., 43206. Tel: 614-444-8994; Fax: 614-445-2853. Kathleen McClernon, Prin. Lay Teachers 17; Students 281.
Catechesis/Religious Program—Students 20.

31—ST. MARY MAGDALENE (1928), Revs. Stanley Benecki; Carmen J. Arcuri.
Res.: 473 S. Roys Ave., 43204. Tel: 614-274-1121; Fax: 614-274-1122.
School—2940 Parkside Rd., 43204. Tel: 614-279-9935; Fax: 614-279-9575. Rocco Fumi, Prin. Lay Teachers 20; Students 318.
Catechesis/Religious Program—Tel: 614-875-0346. Students 38.

32—ST. MATTHIAS (1956), Rev. James T. Smith; Sr. Marie Shields, S.N.D.deN., Pastoral Assoc.
Res.: 1582 Ferris Rd., 43224. Tel: 614-267-3406.
School—1566 Ferris Rd., 43224. Tel: 614-268-3030; Fax: 614-268-4681. Mr. Daniel Kinley, Prin. Sisters 1; Lay Teachers 11; Students 301.
Catechesis/Religious Program—Nancy Mead, D.R.E. Students 87.

33—OUR LADY OF PEACE (1946), Rev. Msgr. Kenneth F. Grimes; Sisters Mary Agnes Jones, O.P., Pastoral Min.; Barbara Kolesar, O.P., Pastoral Min.; Deacon John D. Rankin.
Res.: 20 E. Dominion Blvd., 43214. Tel: 614-263-8824; Fax: 614-263-3383.
School—40 Dominion Blvd., 43214. Tel: 614-267-4535; Fax: 614-267-2333. Carol Folian, Prin. Lay Teachers 14; Students 284.
Catechesis/Religious Program—Tel: 614-263-4271. Andrea McAuliffe, D.R.E. Students 30.

34—OUR LADY OF THE MIRACULOUS MEDAL (1967), Rev. William H. DeVille; Deacons Joseph D. Poland (Poland); Stephen A. Venturini, Pastoral Assoc.
Res.: 5225 Refugee Rd., 43232. Tel: 614-861-1242; Fax: 614-861-1499.
Catechesis/Religious Program—Tel: 614-868-1414. Students 44.

35—OUR LADY OF VICTORY (1922), Rev. Msgr. Romano Ciotola; Deacon Richard L. Baumann.
Res.: 1559 Roxbury Rd., 43212. Tel: 614-488-2428; Fax: 614-488-0507.
School—Trinity, Tel: 614-488-7650; Fax: 614-488-4687. See St. Christopher, Columbus for details.
Catechesis/Religious Program—Tel: 614-486-7678; Fax: 614-488-0507. Sr. Patricia Rooks, S.N.D.deN., D.R.E. Students 257.

36—ST. PATRICK (1852), (Irish), Revs. Ambrose Eckinger, O.P.; Andre Joseph LaCasse, O.P. In Res., Revs. Luke Tancrell, O.P.; J. Jordan Lenaghan, O.P.
Res.: 280 N. Grant Ave., 43215. Tel: 614-224-9522; Fax: 614-240-5928.
Catechesis/Religious Program—Tel: 614-240-5925; Fax: 614-240-5928. Students 264.

37—ST. PETER (1970), Rev. Msgr. John G. Johnson, J.C.D.; Deacons Joseph E. Schermer; Philip M. Paulucci. In Res., Rev. Stephen G. Virginia.
Res.: 6899 Smoky Row Rd., 43235-1998. Tel: 614-889-2221; Fax: 614-889-6612.
Catechesis/Religious Program—Tel: 614-889-1407. Students 654.

38—ST. PHILIP THE APOSTLE (1956), Rev. Patrick W. Rogers; Deacon Joseph W. Farry.
Res.: 1573 Elaine Rd., 43227. Tel: 614-237-1671; Fax: 614-231-8416.
School—1555 Elaine Rd., 43227. Tel: 614-237-5278; Fax: 614-237-3021. Susan Donovan, Prin. Sisters of St. Francis 1; Lay Teachers 11; Students 151.
Catechesis/Religious Program—Tel: 614-237-6500. Students 25.

39—SACRED HEART (1875), Rev. Samuel E. Ritchey.
Res.: 893 Hamlet St., 43201. Tel: 614-299-4191; Fax: 614-299-4192.
Catechesis/Religious Program—Students 3.

40—SANTA CRUZ PARISH (1993), (Spanish), Rev. Jose Perez (Venezuela).
Mailing Address: P.O. Box 82205, 43202.
Church: 143-155 E. Patterson Ave., 43202. Tel: 614-784-9732; Fax: 614-784-9732.

41—SHRINE OF BLESSED MARGARET OF CASTELLO (1957),, Shrine dedicated to promoting the sanctity of life, and the cause of canonization of Blessed Margaret of Castello, Mailing Address: *c/o St. Patrick*, 262 N. Grant Ave., 43215. Tel: 614-240-5914; Fax: 614-240-5928.

42—SAINT STEPHEN THE MARTYR (1963), Sr. Anne McCarrick, S.N.D.deN., Pastoral Admin.; Rev. John L. Bakle, S.M.; Rev. Msgr. Stephan J. Moloney, M.A., M.Div., J.C.L.
Res.: 4031 Clime Rd., 43228. Tel: 614-272-5206; Fax: 614-272-5200.
Catechesis/Religious Program—Students 111.

43—ST. THOMAS THE APOSTLE (1900), Rev. Denis Kigozi.
Res.: 2692 E. Fifth Ave., 43219. Tel: 614-252-0976; Fax: 614-252-0977.
School—767 N. Cassady Ave., 43219. Tel: 614-252-7136; Fax: 614-252-7326. Gary Cross, Prin. Lay Teachers 6; Students 75.
Catechesis/Religious Program—Students 25.

44—ST. TIMOTHY (1961), Rev. Thomas Shonebarger. In Res., Rev. James Coleman.
Res.: 1088 Thomas Ln., 43220. Tel: 614-451-2671; Fax: 614-451-4181.
School—1070 Thomas Ln., 43220. Tel: 614-451-0739; Fax: 614-451-3108. Norma A. Horan, Prin. Lay Teachers 12; Students 265.
Catechesis/Religious Program—Tel: 614-451-3867; Fax: 614-451-3108. Rita Feige, D.R.E. Students 90.

OUTSIDE THE CITY OF COLUMBUS

ADA, HARDIN CO., OUR LADY OF LOURDES (1874), Rev. Daniel J. Millisor; Deacon John P. Stahl.

Res.: 222 E. Highland Ave., 45810. Tel: 419-634-2626; Fax: 419-634-6555.
Catechesis/Religious Program—Tel: 419-634-2445. Mr. David Savino, D.R.E. Students 104.

BREMEN, FAIRFIELD CO., ST. MARY (1917), [CEM] Rev. Msgr. Thomas G. Bender.
Res.: 602 Marietta St., 43107. Tel: 740-569-4272; Fax: 740-569-4272.
Catechesis/Religious Program—Tel: 740-569-7724. Patricia Davis, D.R.E. Students 52.

BUCKEYE LAKE, LICKING CO., OUR LADY OF MT. CARMEL (1929), Rev. Msgr. Frank J. Meagher; Deacons Joe Farmer, Pastoral Assoc. (Retired); Richard B. Busic; Betty Friend, Pastoral Assoc.
Res.: 5133 Walnut Rd., S.E., P.O. Box 45, 43008. Tel: 740-928-3266; Fax: 740-928-9536.
Catechesis/Religious Program—Tel: 740-928-3264. Silvia Zaboroski, D.R.E. Students 75.

CANAL WINCHESTER, FAIRFIELD CO., POPE JOHN XXIII (2000), Rev. Msgr. A. Anthony Frecker, M.Div., MTh; Deacon Roger Pry.
Res.: 7820 White Ash Ct., 43110. Tel: 614-920-1563; Fax: 614-920-1564.
Catechesis/Religious Program—Students 164.

CARDINGTON, MORROW CO., SACRED HEARTS (1868), Rev. Msgr. Charles J. Foeller.
Res.: 4680 U.S. Rte. 42, 43315. Tel: 419-946-3611. Email: foeller@bright.net.
Catechesis/Religious Program—Kevin Tebbe, D.R.E.; Sharon Tebbe, D.R.E. Students 91.

CHILLICOTHE, ROSS CO.
1—ST. MARY (1837), [CEM] [JC] Rev. Lawrence L. Hummer; Deacon George L. Lovensheimer.
Res.: 61 S. Paint St., 45601. Tel: 740-772-2061; Fax: 740-772-2061.
School—Tel: 740-774-2970; Fax: 740-774-2998. Ken Kessler, Prin. Lay Teachers 22.
Catechesis/Religious Program—570 Parsons Ave., 45601. Tel: 740-773-3455. Students 115.
2—ST. PETER (1845), (German), [CEM] [JC] Rev. James P. Black; Deacon Richard T. Krick. In Res., Rev. Charles R. Griffin (Retired).
Res.: 122 Church St., 45601. Tel: 740-774-1407.
School—Bishop Flaget Consolidated, (Grades PreK-8), 570 Parsons Ave., 45601. Tel: 740-774-2970; Fax: 740-774-2889. Mr. Kenneth Kessler, Prin. Lay Teachers 19; Students 208.
Catechesis/Religious Program—Tel: 740-773-3455. Students 142.

CIRCLEVILLE, PICKAWAY CO., ST. JOSEPH'S (1840), [CEM] Rev. Stephen L. Krile; Mary Kay Wood, Pastoral Assoc.
Res.: 134 W. Mound St., P.O. Box 659, 43113. Tel: 740-477-2549; Fax: 740-477-1453.
Catechesis/Religious Program—Theresa Jenkins, D.R.E. Students 341.

CORNING, PERRY CO., ST. BERNARD (1882), Rev. Robert E. Willmann, J.C.L. In Res., Sr. Diana Durling, S.C.
Res.: 425 Adams St., 43730. Tel: 740-347-4700.
Catechesis/Religious Program—Students 30.

COSHOCTON, COSHOCTON CO., SACRED HEART (1856), [CEM] Rev. Homer D. Blubaugh; Sr. Mary Emma Muckensturm, Pastoral Assoc.; Deacons Frank A. Duda; Douglas Mould.
Res.: 805 Main St., 43812. Tel: 740-622-8817.
School—39 Burt Ave., 43812. Tel: 740-622-3728; Fax: 740-622-9151. Deacon Frank A. Duda, Prin. Lay Teachers 11; Students (K-6) 90; Students (PreK) 37.
Catechesis/Religious Program—(Grades PreK-6), 128 Burt Ave., 43812. Tel: 740-622-8818. Deacon Douglas Mould, D.R.E. Students 72.

CROOKSVILLE, PERRY CO., CHURCH OF THE ATONEMENT (1896), [CEM] Rev. Francis M. Stanton.
Res.: 320 Winter St., 43731. Tel: 740-982-3816.
Catechesis/Religious Program—Tel: 740-982-2386. Mary King, D.R.E. Students 59.

DANVILLE, KNOX CO., ST. LUKE (1820), [CEM] Rev. F. Richard Snoke.
Res.: 307 S. Market St., P.O. Box P, 43014. Tel: 740-599-6362.
Catechesis/Religious Program—St. Luke Community Center, 7 W. Rambo, P.O. Box P, 43014-0616. Tel: 740-599-7367. Thomas Harrmann, D.R.E. Students 121.

DELAWARE, DELAWARE CO., ST. MARY (1835), [CEM] Revs. Kevin J. Kavanagh; David W. Sizemore; Sr. Cecilia Taphorn, C.PP.S., Pastoral Assoc.; Deacon Felix Azzola.
Res.: 82 E. William St., 43015. Tel: 740-363-4641; 740-369-9644; Fax: 740-363-9915.
School—66 E. William St., 43015. Tel: 740-362-8961; Fax: 740-362-3733. Becky Piela, Prin. (Grades PreK-8). Lay Teachers 19; Students 278.
Catechesis/Religious Program—Tel: 740-369-8228. Sandy Murray, D.R.E. Students 360.

DENNISON, TUSCARAWAS CO., IMMACULATE CONCEPTION (1871), [CEM] Rev. Martin J. Ralko.
Res.: 206 N. First St., 44621. Tel: 740-922-3533; Fax: 740-922-2486.
School—100 Sherman St., 44621. Tel: 740-922-3539; Fax: 740-922-2486. John Zucal, Prin. Lay Teachers 10; Students 130.
Catechesis/Religious Program—Richard Passio, D.R.E. Students 20.

DOVER, TUSCARAWAS CO., ST. JOSEPH (1849), (German—Italian), [CEM 2] Rev. William L. Arnold; Deacons Ronald H. Fondriest; Joseph James.
Res.: 613 N. Tuscarawas Ave., 44622. Tel: 330-364-6661; Fax: 330-602-7488.
School—600 N. Tuscarawas Ave., 44622. Tel: 330-343-9134; Fax: 330-343-3704. Sr. Valerie Shaul, O.P., Prin. Lay Teachers 14; Students 242.
Catechesis/Religious Program—Tel: 330-364-8257. Ms. Cindy Teynor, D.R.E. Students 202.

DRESDEN, MUSKINGUM CO., ST. ANN'S (1889), Rev. Jack G. Maynard.
Res.: 405 Chestnut St., Box 107, 43821. Tel: 740-754-2221.
Catechesis/Religious Program—Students 40.
Mission—St. Mary [CEM] Nashport. 6280 St. Mary's Rd., Mattingly Settlement, Muskingum Co. 43830.

DUBLIN, FRANKLIN CO., ST. BRIGID OF KILDARE (1987), Rev. Msgr. Joseph M. Hendricks; Rev. Jeffrey Coning; Deacon Frank A. Iannarino; Sr. Patricia McMahon, O.S.F., Pastoral Assoc.
Res.: 7179 Avery Rd., P.O. Box 3130, 43016-0062. Tel: 614-761-3734; Fax: 614-889-6638. Joseph Burger, Business Mgr.
School—7175 Avery Rd., 43017. Tel: 614-718-5825; Fax: 614-718-5831. Ms. Kathleen O'Reilly, Prin. Lay Teachers 30; Students 627.
Catechesis/Religious Program—Tel: 614-761-1176; Fax: 614-718-5831. Mary Fran Cassidy, D.R.E. Students 1,364.

GAHANNA, FRANKLIN CO., ST. MATTHEW (1959), Rev. Paul A. Noble, M.A., Ph.D. In Res., Rev. Msgr. Stephan J. Moloney, M.A., M.Div., J.C.L.; Rev. Matthew N. Hoover.
Res.: 807 Havens Corners Rd., 43230. Tel: 614-471-0212; Fax: 614-471-0247.
School—795 Havens Corners Rd., 43230. Tel: 614-471-4930; Fax: 614-471-1673. Carole G. Marsh, Prin. Lay Teachers 27; Students 599.
Catechesis/Religious Program—Tel: 614-471-2067; Fax: 614-471-1693. Julie Zarichny, D.R.E. Students 561.

GRANVILLE, LICKING CO., ST. EDWARD THE CONFESSOR (1946), Rev. Msgr. Paul P. Enke, Pastor; Michael Millisor, Pastoral Assoc.
Res.: 785 Newark Rd., 43023. Tel: 740-587-3254; Fax: 740-587-0149.
Catechesis/Religious Program—Tel: 740-587-4160. Students 352.

GROVE CITY, FRANKLIN CO., OUR LADY OF PERPETUAL HELP (1954), Revs. John L. Swickard; Joseph J. Trapp II.
Church & Mailing Address: 3730 Broadway, 43123. Tel: 614-875-3322; Fax: 614-875-6033.
School—3752 N. Broadway, 43123. Tel: 614-875-6779. Mrs. Jeanette Kam, Prin. Lay Teachers 21; Students 460.
Catechesis/Religious Program—Tel: 614-875-9345. Mrs. Camille Kopczewski, D.R.E. Students 334.

GROVEPORT, FRANKLIN CO., ST. MARY'S (1871), Rev. Richard Metzger; Deacon Frederick J. Schmitt.
Res.: 5684 Groveport Rd., 43125. Tel: 614-497-1324; Fax: 614-497-2706.
Catechesis/Religious Program—Tel: 614-497-1437. Alice Doran, D.R.E. Students 137.

HEATH, LICKING CO., ST. LEONARD (1962), Revs. Michael J. Reis; Ronald Boccali, P.I.M.E.
Res.: 57 Dorsey Mill Rd., 43056. Tel: 740-522-5270; Fax: 740-522-5261.
Catechesis/Religious Program—Tel: 740-522-6410. Steven Connor, D.R.E. Students 67.

HILLIARD, FRANKLIN CO., ST. BRENDAN (1957), Revs. Rodric J. DiPietro; Dean Mathewson; Deacons Patrick J. Wiggins; Gilbert L. Plummer.
Res.: 4475 Dublin Rd., 43026. Tel: 614-876-1272; Fax: 614-876-1482.
School—(Grades 1-8) Tel: 614-876-6132; Fax: 614-529-8929. Mary Lang, Prin. Lay Teachers 22; Students 431.
Catechesis/Religious Program—Tel: 614-876-9533. S. Joanne Fogarty, D.R.E. Students 1,280.

JACKSON, JACKSON CO., HOLY TRINITY (1875), [CEM] Rev. Msgr. Robert E. Metzger.
Res.: 215 Columbia St., 45640. Tel: 740-286-1428.
Catechesis/Religious Program—Donna Lyons, D.R.E. Students 66.

JOHNSTOWN, LICKING CO., CHURCH OF THE ASCENSION (1912), [CEM] Rev. J. Lawrence Reichert.
Res.: 276 S. Main St., 43031. Tel: 740-967-7871.
Catechesis/Religious Program—Tel: 740-967-1338. Anne Grossman, D.R.E. Students 143.

JUNCTION CITY, PERRY CO., ST. PATRICK (1820), [CEM] Rev. Robert E. Willmann, J.C.L.; Mr. Al Kunkler, Pastoral Assoc.
Res.: 1170 S.R. 668S, 43748. Tel: 740-987-2691.
Catechesis/Religious Program—Sr. Marie Tessmer, S.C., D.R.E. Students 46.

KENTON, HARDIN CO., IMMACULATE CONCEPTION (1836), [CEM] Rev. James Csaszar.
Res.: 215 E. North St., 43326. Tel: 419-675-1162.
Parish Center—220 E. North St., 44326. Tel: 419-675-9461.
Catechesis/Religious Program—Tel: 419-675-1162. Jean M. Bruner, D.R.E. Students 39.

LA RUE, MARION CO., ST. JOSEPH'S (1864), Rev. Joseph F. Losh.
Res.: 285 N. High St., P.O. Box 347, 43332-0347. Tel: 740-499-3614.
Catechesis/Religious Program—Students 12.

LANCASTER, FAIRFIELD CO.
1—ST. BERNADETTE (1963), Rev. Justin J. Reis; Deacons Paul Deshaies; Mark A. Scarpitti.
Res.: 1343 Wheeling Rd., 43130-8701. Tel: 740-654-1893; Fax: 740-687-5926.
School—1325 Wheeling Rd., 43130. Tel: 740-654-3137; Fax: 740-654-1602. Pam Eltringham, Prin. Lay Teachers 9; Students 159.
Catechesis/Religious Program—Tel: 740-654-1644. Ed Christ, Admin. Students 243.
2—ST. MARK (1960), [JC] Rev. Ronald L. Arter. In Res., Rev. Msgr. Robert L. Noon (Retired).
Res.: 324 Gay St., 43130. Tel: 740-654-2874; Fax: 740-653-8329.
Catechesis/Religious Program—331 Gay St., 43130. Tel: 740-654-7154; 740-653-1229. Jackie Moore, D.R.E. (K-6); Debbie Hibbard, D.R.E. (7-12). Students 150.
3—ST. MARY (1818), [CEM] Revs. Donald E. Franks; Jonathan F. Wilson; Sr. Mary Cecil Grandpre, O.P., Pastoral Assoc.; Deacon Frank K. Sullivan.
Res.: 132 S. High St., 43130. Tel: 740-653-0997; Fax: 740-653-0337.
School—309 E. Chestnut St., 43130. Tel: 740-654-1632; Fax: 740-654-0877. Carlton B. Rider, Prin. Lay Teachers 21; Students 418.
Catechesis/Religious Program—Tel: 740-653-5054; Fax: 740-653-0337. Sr. Louis Mary Passeri, O.P., D.R.E. Students 150.

LOGAN, HOCKING CO., ST. JOHN (1841), (German), [CEM] Rev. Msgr. William A. Dunn.
Res.: 351 N. Market St., 43138. Tel: 740-385-2549; Fax: 740-380-2837.
School—321 N. Market St., 43138. Tel: 740-385-2767; Fax: 740-385-9727. Joan M. Miller, Prin. Lay Teachers 5; Students 93.
Catechesis/Religious Program—Tel: 740-385-8608. Cathy Kerns, D.R.E. Students 40.

LONDON, MADISON CO., ST. PATRICK (1865), (German—Irish), [CEM] Rev. Theodore K. Sill, M.Div., M.Th.; Deacon Daniel W. Hann.
Res.: 61 S. Union St., 43140. Tel: 740-852-0942; Fax: 740-852-5008.
School—(Grades K-8), 226 Elm St., 43140. Tel: 740-852-0161; Fax: 740-852-0602. Dr. Jacob Froning, Prin. Lay Teachers 11; Students 169.
Catechesis/Religious Program—Students 125.

MARION, MARION CO., ST. MARY (1864), [CEM] Revs. Michael Nimocks, Pastor; Rodney M. Damico, Pastoral Assoc.
Res.: 251 N. Main St., 43302. Tel: 740-382-2118; Fax: 740-382-2110.
School—274 N. Prospect St., 44302. Tel: 740-382-1607. Bob Rush, Prin. Lay Teachers 11; Students 140.
High School—(Grades 7-12) Tel: 740-389-2381; Fax: 740-389-5243. Fran Voll, Prin. Lay Teachers 17; Students 117.
Catechesis/Religious Program—Tel: 740-382-2262. Students 315.

MARYSVILLE, UNION CO., OUR LADY OF LOURDES (1866), [CEM] Rev. John B. Bentz; Deacon Gordon T. Kunkler.
Res.: 1033 W. Fifth St., 43040. Tel: 937-644-6020; Fax: 937-644-6020.
Catechesis/Religious Program—Tel: 937-644-6030; Fax: 937-644-0423. Diane Campbell, D.R.E. Students 260.
Mission—Haiti Parish Twinning Program Aquin.

MILLERSBURG, HOLMES CO., ST. PETER (1877), [CEM] [JC] Rev. Ronald J. Aubry.
Res.: 379 S. Crawford St., 44654-1463. Tel: 330-674-1671.
Catechesis/Religious Program—Tel: 330-674-0333. Patricia A. Huebner, D.R.E. Students 20.
Mission—SS. Peter and Paul (1857), SR 520, Glenmont, Holmes Co. 44628. Tel: 330-674-1671.

MINERAL CITY, TUSCARAWAS CO., SAINT PATRICK, Closed., For sacramental records contact Holy Trinity, Bolivar.

MT. VERNON, KNOX CO., ST. VINCENT DE PAUL (1842), [CEM] Rev. Charles Theodore Thomas; Sr. Jean Welling, S.C., Pastoral Assoc.
Res.: 303 E. High St., 43050. Tel: 740-392-4711; Fax: 740-392-4714.
School—206 E. Chestnut St., 43050. Tel: 740-393-3611; Fax: 740-393-0236. Julie Kenney, Prin. Lay

Teachers 12; Students 171.
Catechesis/Religious Program—Shirley Lower, D.R.E. Students 280.

MURRAY CITY, HOCKING CO., ST. PHILIP NERI, Closed., For inquiries for sacramental records contact St. John, Logan.

NEW ALBANY, FRANKLIN CO., CHURCH OF THE RESURRECTION (1983), Rev. Jerome Rodenfels; Deacon Byron Phillips.
Res.: 6300 E. Dublin-Granville Rd., 43054. Tel: 614-855-1400; Fax: 614-855-0779.
Catechesis/Religious Program—(Grades K-6) Tel: 614-939-1794; Fax: 614-855-0779. Ms. Joan Lucius, D.R.E. Students 657.

NEW BOSTON, SCIOTO CO., ST. MONICA (1915), [CEM] Rev. Peter M. Gideon; Sr. Theresa Kehres, O.S.F., Pastoral Assoc.
Res.: 4252 Pine St., 45662. Tel: 740-456-5154; Fax: 740-456-5154.
Catechesis/Religious Program—Students 56.

NEW LEXINGTON, PERRY CO., ST. ROSE OF LIMA (1867), [JC] Rev. Robert E. Willmann, J.C.L.; Sr. Diana Durling, S.C., Pastoral Min.
Res.: 309 N. Main St., 43764. Tel: 740-342-1348.
School—119 W. Water St., 43764. Tel: 740-342-3043; Fax: 740-342-1082. Miss Martha Raines, Prin. Lay Teachers 9; Students 128.
Catechesis/Religious Program—Tel: 740-987-2691; 740-342-3043. Sr. Marie Tessmer, S.C., D.R.E. Students 79.

NEW PHILADELPHIA, TUSCARAWAS CO., SACRED HEART (1895), [CEM 2] Rev. Msgr. George J. Schlegel, B.A.
Res.: 139 3rd St., N.E., 44663-3900. Tel: 330-343-6976; Fax: 330-343-1406.
School—320 Fair Ave., N.E., 44663-3914. Tel: 330-343-1721; Fax: 330-364-4334. Scott Power, Prin. Lay Teachers 11; Students 169.
Catechesis/Religious Program—Students 134.

NEWARK, LICKING CO.
1—CHURCH OF THE BLESSED SACRAMENT (1904), [JC] Rev. Timothy M. Hayes, S.T.L.; Deacons Charles F. Stevens, (Retired); Robert W. Ghiloni.
Res.: 378 E. Main St., 43055. Tel: 740-345-4290; Fax: 740-345-3890.
School—15 Penny Ave., 43055. Tel: 740-345-4125; Fax: 740-345-6168. Mary Packham, Prin. Lay Teachers 12; Students 173.
Catechesis/Religious Program—Tel: 740-763-4304. Debbie Wills, D.R.E. Students 42.
2—ST. FRANCIS DE SALES (1842), [CEM 2] Revs. Robert Penhallurick; David Orians; Sr. Barbara Catalano, O.P., Pastoral Assoc.; Deacon Jack Elam.
Res.: 66 Granville St., 43055. Tel: 740-345-9874; Fax: 740-345-1585.
School—38 Granville St., 43055. Tel: 740-345-4049; Fax: 740-345-9768. Gretchen O'Neill, Prin. Lay Teachers 22; Students 515.
Catechesis/Religious Program—Tel: 740-345-9874, Ext. 222; Fax: 740-345-1585. Lori Mazone, D.R.E.; Joe Dunlevy, Youth Minister. Students 392.

NEWCOMERSTOWN, TUSCARAWAS CO., ST. FRANCIS DE SALES (1918), [JC] Rev. William J. Faustner.
Res.: 440 River St., 43832. Tel: 740-498-7368.
Catechesis/Religious Program—Tel: 740-498-5497. Victor Cardenzana, D.R.E. Students 59.

OTWAY, SCIOTO CO., OUR LADY OF LOURDES (1917), [CEM] Rev. David E. Young, B.A., M.Div.
Res.: 2215 Galena Pike, West Portsmouth, 45663. Tel: 740-858-4600; Fax: 740-858-4600.
Catechesis/Religious Program—Students 16.
Otway Community Service Center—P.O. Box 8, 45657. Tel: 740-372-2202.

PICKERINGTON, FAIRFIELD CO., SETON PARISH (1978), Rev. James Klima, Admin.; Deacon David J. Kruse.
Res.: 600 Hill Rd., 43147. Tel: 614-833-0482; Fax: 614-833-4154.
Catechesis/Religious Program—Tel: 614-833-0485. Mrs. Mary Houze, D.R.E. Students 1,015

PLAIN CITY, MADISON CO., ST. JOSEPH (1864), Rev. Patrick A. Toner; Deacon Anthony Bonacci.
Res.: 6604 Perry Park, 43064. Tel: 614-873-8850; Fax: 614-873-8850.
Catechesis/Religious Program—Tel: 614-873-8551. Heidi Kellett, D.R.E. Students 133.
Oratory—Sacred Heart Milford Center, Union Co.

PORTSMOUTH, SCIOTO CO.
1—HOLY REDEEMER (1852), (Irish), [CEM] [JC] Rev. Dwayne A. McNew; Ann Kempf, Pastoral Assoc. Tel: 740-353-4425.
Office—805 Offnere St., 45662. Tel: 740-353-4425.
Res.: 1325 Gallia St., 45662. Tel: 740-354-8691; Fax: 740-354-4586.
School—Notre Dame Elementary, (Grades PreK-6), 1401 Gallia St., 45662. Tel: 740-353-8510; Fax: 740-353-6769. Kay Kern, Prin. Serving all 7 parishes in Scioto County. Lay Teachers 15; Students 303.
Catechesis/Religious Program—Tel: 740-354-1171. Students 55.
2—ST. MARY (1841), (German), [CEM] Rev. Theodore F. Machnik; Deacon George E. Horsley.
Res.: 524 Sixth St., 45662. Tel: 740-354-4551; Fax: 740-354-5799.
Catechesis/Religious Program—Students 197.

POWELL, DELAWARE CO., ST. JOAN OF ARC (1987), Revs. Jeffrey J. Rimelspach; Jeffrey E. Tigyer; Deacons Thomas M. Berg Sr., B.A., M.J., M.P.S.; James A. Rouse.
Res.: 10700 Liberty Rd. S., 43065-9303. Tel: 614-761-0905; Fax: 614-761-0850.
Catechesis/Religious Program—Tel: 614-761-0903. Natalie Hutchison, D.R.E. Students 1,189.

REYNOLDSBURG, FRANKLIN CO., ST. PIUS X (1958), Revs. Daniel L. Ochs; Joseph A. Ehwald; Deacon John Velleni; Ms. Christin Jungers, Pastoral Assoc.; Ms. Regina Courey, Pastoral Assoc.
Res.: 1051 Waggoner Rd., 43068. Tel: 614-866-2859; Fax: 614-866-1499.
School—1061 Waggoner Rd., 43068. Tel 614-866-6050; Fax: 614-866-6187. Kathleen DeMatteo, Prin. Lay Teachers 30; Students 577.
Catechesis/Religious Program—Tel: 614-864-3505. Judy Cafmeyer, D.R.E. Students 295.

ROSWELL, TUSCARAWAS CO., ST. ELIZABETH Closed., For sacramental records contact Sacred Heart Parish, New Philadelphia.

SHAWNEE, PERRY CO., ST. MARY & ST. AUGUSTINE, Closed., For sacramental records contact St. Rose of Lima Parish, New Lexington.

SOMERSET, PERRY CO.
1—HOLY TRINITY (1827), [CEM] Rev. J.A. Breen, O.P.; Deacon Eugene O. Dawson, Pastoral Assoc.
Res.: 5757 State Rte. 383 N.E., P.O. Box 190, 43783. Tel 740-743-1317.
School—S. Columbus St., 43783. Tel: 740-743-1324; Fax: 740-743-1324. Mrs. Catherine Fields, Prin. Lay Teachers 8; Students 122.
Catechesis/Religious Program—Tel: 740-743-1855. Students 54.
2—ST. JOSEPH'S (1818), [CEM] Rev. J.A. Breen, O.P.; Deacon Eugene O. Dawson, Pastoral Assoc.
Res.: 5757 State Rte. 383 N.E., P.O. Box 190, 43783. Tel 740-743-1317.
Catechesis/Religious Program—Tel: 740-743-1855. Students 30.

STRASBURG, TUSCARAWAS CO., ST. ALOYSIUS (1911), Closed., For sacramental records contact Holy Trinity, Bolivar.

SUGAR GROVE, FAIRFIELD CO., ST. JOSEPH (1892), [CEM] [JC] Rev. Msgr. James A. Geiger.
Res.: 306 Elm St., 43155. Tel: 740-746-8302.
Catechesis/Religious Program—Tel: 740 746-8302. Barbara Uhl, D.R.E. Students 57.

SUNBURY, DELAWARE CO., ST. JOHN NEUMANN (1983), Rev. James A. Walter.
Res.: 275 Carters Corner Rd., 43074-9536. Tel: 740-965-1358; Fax: 740-965-1377.
Church: 9633 E. State Rte. 37, 43074-9593. Tel: 740-965-1358.
Social Hall—Tel: 740-965-4877.
Catechesis/Religious Program—Tel: 740 965-4877. Robert M. Steinbauer, D.R.E. Students 804.

UTICA, LICKING CO., CHURCH OF THE NATIVITY (1909), Rev. Stephen A. Metzger.
Res.: 271 Jefferson St., P.O. Box 506, 43080. Tel: 740-892-2321.
Catechesis/Religious Program—Rose Gorius, D.R.E. Students 72.

WAINWRIGHT, TUSCARAWAS CO., PARISH COMMUNITY OF ST. THERESE AND ST. PAUL, Closed., For St. Therese's sacramental records contact Immaculate Conception, Dennison. For St. Paul's sacramental records contact Sacred Heart, New Philadelphia.

WASHINGTON COURT HOUSE, FAYETTE CO., ST. COLMAN (1885), [CEM] Rev. Jan C. Sullivan.
Office—219 S. North St., 43160. Tel: 740-335-5000; Fax: 740-335-5066.
Res.: 223 E. East St., 43160. Tel: 740-335-3457.
Catechesis/Religious Program—Tel: 740-335-5005. Tracie Rush, D.R.E. (Grades PreK-12) Students 127.

WAVERLY, PIKE CO., ST. MARY, QUEEN OF THE MISSIONS (1878), [JC] Rev. James P. Black.
Res.: 407 S. Market St., 45690. Tel: 740-947-2436.
Catechesis/Religious Program—Students 27.

WELLSTON, JACKSON CO., SS. PETER AND PAUL (1881), [CEM] Rev. Donald M. Maroon.
Res.: 227 S. New York Ave., 45692. Tel: 740-384-2359; Fax: 740-384-2945.
School—229 S. New York Ave., 45692. Tel: 740-384-6354. Barbara Apsley, Prin. Lay Teachers 6; Students 92.
Catechesis/Religious Program—Students 92.

WEST JEFFERSON, MADISON CO., SS. SIMON AND JUDE (1866), (German—Irish), [CEM] Revs. Michael J. Devaney, O.M.I.; Ralph J. Karl, O.M.I (Retired); Deacon Ralph L. Parsons.
Res.: 95 W. Main St., 43162-1295. Tel: 614-879-8562; Fax: 614-879-7605.
Catechesis/Religious Program—Tel: 740-852-4305. Mary Wanner, D.R.E.; Kathy Maggred, RCIA Coordinator. Students 106.

WEST PORTSMOUTH, SCIOTO CO., OUR LADY OF SORROWS (1944), [CEM] Rev. David E. Young, B.A., M.Div.
Res.: 2215 Galena Pike, 45663. Tel: 740-858-4600; Fax: 740-858-4600.
New To You Service Center—Tel: 740-858-3176. Mary Horn, Dir.
Catechesis/Religious Program—P.O. Box 31, Otway, 45657. Tel: 740-372-7115; Fax: 740-372-7115. Students 10.
Mission—Holy Trinity 2215 Galena Pike, Pond Creek, Scioto Co. 45663.

WESTERVILLE, DELAWARE CO., ST. PAUL THE APOSTLE (1913), Revs. Charles Klinger; William A. Hritsko; Raymond E. Lavelle (Retired); Deacons Thomas Barford; Mickey B. Hawkins; Susan Bellotti. In Res., Rev. Alan M. Sprenger.
Res.: 313 N. State St., 43082. Tel: 614-882-2109; Fax: 614-891-7476.
School—61 Moss Rd., 43082. Tel: 614-882-2710; Fax: 614-882-5998. Anne O'Flynn, Prin.; Sharon Gillivan, Asst. Prin. Lay Teachers 36; Students 901.
Catechesis/Religious Program—Tel: 614-882-5045. Janet Brewer, D.R.E. Students 1,017.

WHEELERSBURG, SCIOTO CO., ST. PETER (1855), [CEM] Rev. Peter M. Gideon.
Res.: 2167 Lick Run Lyra Rd., 45694. Tel: 740-574-5486; Fax: 740-574-6641 (Call before sending).
Catechesis/Religious Program—Lisa Warner, D.R.E. Students 96.

WILLS CREEK, COSHOCTON CO., OUR LADY OF LOURDES, Closed., For sacramental records contact Sacred Heart, Coshocton.

WORTHINGTON, FRANKLIN CO., ST. MICHAEL (1946), Revs. Richard J. Pendolphi; Thomas J. Brosmer; Joseph C. Klee; Deacons John R. Crerand; Klaus Fricke.
Res.: 5750 N. High St., 43085. Tel: 614-885-7814; Fax: 614-885-3446.
School—64 E. Selby Blvd., 43085-3986. Tel: 614-885-3149; Fax: 614-885-1249. Miss Christine Armbrust, Prin. Lay Teachers 25; Students 591.
Catechesis/Religious Program—Tel: 614-888-5384. James Hahn, D.R.E. Students 763.

ZALESKI, VINTON CO., ST. SYLVESTER (1862), (Irish), [CEM] Rev. David E. Gwinner.
Res.: 119 N. Second St., P.O. Box 264, 45698-0264. Tel: 740-596-5474.
Catechesis/Religious Program—Students 30.

ZANESVILLE, MUSKINGUM CO.
1—ST. NICHOLAS (1842), (German), [CEM] Rev. Leo Connolly; James E. Cope, Pastoral Assoc.; Sr. Ruth Flynn, C.D.P., Pastoral Assoc.; Deacons B. N. Peterson Jr., Pastoral Assoc.; James P. Feerick, Pastoral Assoc.; Robert E. Staker, Pastoral Assoc.
Res.: 925 E. Main St., 43701. Tel: 740-453-0597; Fax: 740-453-0590.
School—1030 E. Main St., 43701. Tel: 740-453-2637; Fax: 740-454-0653. Mrs. Karen Robinson, Prin. Lay Teachers 17; Students 240.
Catechesis/Religious Program—Tel: 740-450-7461. Judy Schiele, D.R.E. Students 51.
2—ST. THOMAS AQUINAS (1820), [CEM 2] Revs. S. Jordan McConway, O.P.; Thomas V. DiFede, O.P.; Emmanuel Bertrand, O.P.; Louis Luke Turon, O.P.; Sr. Maureen Mahon, O.S.F., Pastoral Assoc.
Res.: 130 N. Fifth St., 43701. Tel: 740-453-3301; Fax: 740-453-0333.
School—139 N. Fifth St., 43701. Tel: 740-454-9731; Fax: 740-454-9732. Mr. Michael Sens, Prin. Lay Teachers 12; Students 197.
Catechesis/Religious Program—Tel: 740-453-3301, Ext. 15. Melanie Von Gunten, D.R.E.; Carol A. Luby, Business Mgr. Students 140.
Mission—St. Ann 79 Main St., Philo, Muskingum Co. 43771. Tel: 740-674-6448.

ZOAR, TUSCARAWAS CO., HOLY TRINITY (1995), [CEM 4] Rev. Edward Keck; Deacon Lyn Houze.
Res.: 141 Water St., S.W., Bolivar, 44612. Tel: 330-874-4716; Fax: 330-874-4461.

Chaplains of Public Institutions

COLUMBUS. *Children's Hospital*. Rev. Mark Hoying, C.PP.S.
Corrections Medical Center. Mrs. Rose Hamilton.
Grant Hospital. Rev. Jerome D. Stluka.
OSU Hospital East. Rev. James Colopy.
OSU Medical Center. Rev. Thomas G. Petry.
Regency Manor. Rev. Msgr. Edward F. Trenor, J.C.L.

CHILLICOTHE. *Chillicothe Correctional Institution*, P.O. Box 5500, 45601. Tel: 740-773-2616, Ext. 248. Rev. Charles R. Griffin (Retired).
Res.: 122 Church St., 45601. Tel: 740-773-4391.
Ross Correctional Institution, P.O. Box 7010, 45601. Tel: 740-774-4182, Ext. 2519. Rev. Charles R. Griffin (Retired).
Res.: 122 Church St., 45601. Tel: 740-773-4391.
Veteran's Affairs Medical Center, 17273 S.R. 104, 45601. Tel: 740-773-1141, Ext. 7203. Rev. Joseph O. Vazhupadickal, S.A.C.

LANCASTER. *Southeastern Correctional Institution*, Tel: 740-653-4324. Mrs. Martha Vanderbilt.
Res.: P.O. Box 264, Sugar Grove, 43155. Tel: 740-746-8007.

LONDON. *London Correctional Institution*. Rev. Patrick A. Toner. Tel: 740-852-2454, Ext. 451.
Madison Correctional Institution. Deacon Dan Hann.

LUCASVILLE. *Southern Ohio Correctional Facility*, Tel: 740-259-5544. (Vacant)

MARION. *Marion Correctional Institution*. Deacon Robert A. Neely. Tel: 740-382-5781, Ext. 2346.

MARYSVILLE. *Ohio Reformatory for Women*.
305 Acton Rd., 43214. Tel: 614-267-7500. Rev. John B. Bentz. Tel: 937-642-1065, Deacon Gregory L. Eiden.

MOUNT VERNON. *Mount Vernon Developmental Center*, St. Vincent de Paul Parish, 303 E. High St., 43050. Tel: 740-392-4711.

ORIENT. *Corrections Reception Center*. Rev. Shawn Corcoran, Sacramental Min.
Pickaway Correctional Institution, Tel: 614-877-4362. Deacon Larry Koebel.

On Duty Outside the Diocese:
Revs.—
Anderson, Kenneth A., St. Priscilla, Chicago, IL.
Ascencio, Joseph A., Chap., Federal Prison System, Florence, CO 81226.
Klein, Terrance W., St. Augustine, Brooklyn, NY.
Naughton, Patrick J. (Scranton), St. David, Davie, FL.
Schilder, David M., Chap., Ashland Federal Correctional Institution, Ashland, KY.

Military Services:
Rev.—
Everett, Willis E., CHC, USNR

Retired:
Rev. Msgrs.—
Borrelli, Anthony A., 3140 El Greco Dr., 43204.
Carroll, James J., 12915 Galaxy Dr., Sun City West, AZ.
Clagett, Carl P., 2601 Aspen Rd., Frazeysburg, 43822.
Corcoran, Lawrence J., P.A., Holy Cross, 204 S. 5th St., 43215.
Dittoe, John T., S.T.D., S.T.B., 2675 Trottersway Dr., 43235.
Dreese, John J., P.O. Box 39, New Straitsville, 43766.
Fairchild, Edward, 3306 Beachworth Dr., 43232.
Faistl, Clement F., Villas at St. Therese, 25 Noe Bixby Rd., Rm. 123, 43213.
Gallen, F. Thomas, B.A., C.G.M., The Villas at St. Therese Assisted Living, 25 Noe Bixby Rd., Room 107, 43213.
Griffin, Patrick J., 3881 Monterey Dr., Grove City, 43123.
Hanley, James P., 2492 Timberside Dr., 43235.
Healey, Edward F., Villas at St. Therese, 25 Noe Bixby Rd., Room 133, 43213.
Huntzinger, Ralph J., 8797 State Rte. 273 W., Belle Center, 43310-9580.
Kessler, Edward L., Logan Health Care Center, 300 Arlington Ave., Logan, 43138.
Maroon, William J., P.O. Box 285, New Straitsville, 43766.
McFarland, Edward J., 6818 Albany Woods Blvd., New Albany, 43054.
Noon, Robert L., St. Mark Church, 324 Gay St., Lancaster, 43130.
Nugent, Michael A., The Villas at St. Therese, 25 Noe Bixby Rd., Room 120, 43213.
Schmidt, Robert R., Seton Square E., 1235 Briarcliff Rd, #126, Reynoldsburg, 43068.
Schneider, Robert E., St. Therese, 5253 E. Broad St., # 108, 43213.
Schulz, Donald C., St. Aloysius Church, 32 Clarendon Ave., 43223.
Schweitzer, Francis X., Nazareth Towers, 300 E. Rich St., #410, 43215.
Serraglio, Mario, P.O. Box 703, Canal Winchester, 43110.
Spiers, Edward F., Villas at St. Theresa, 5253 E. Broad St. #119, 43313.
Wolf, John V., S.T.D., 104 N. Mulberry St., Fredericktown, 43019-1051. Tel: 614-694-2505

Revs.—
Bernans, Arvids, 4970 Deer Run. Pl., Westville, 43081.
Byrne, Patrick J., 4468 Beachwood Lake Dr., Naples, FL 34112.
Carter, Raymond J., Villas at St. Therese, 5253 E. Broad St., #204, 43213.
Connor, William J., 10248 W. Snead Cir. N., Sun City, AZ 85351.
Durbin, Clement B., Sharon Brook Inn, 920 Sharon Vally Rd., #219, Newark, 43055.
Engle, Richard F., 192 Grand Ave., Chillicothe, 45601.
Essman, Charles P., Thurber Towers, 645 Neil Ave. #409, 43215.
Fulcher, John M., P.O. Box 574, New Lexington, 43764.
Gamba, John J., P.O. Box 184, Doylestown, 44230.
Gately, Robert E., 702 Valley Forge Blvd., Sun City, FL 33573.
Griffin, Charles R., 122 Church St., Chillicothe, 45601.
Haluska, Charles A., Jennings Center for Older Adults, 10210 Granger Rd., Room 274, Cleveland, 44125.
Jerabeck, Joseph F., Villas at St. Therese, 25 Noe Bixby Rd., Room 124, 43213.
Jones, James W., 2770 Dover Rd., 43209.
Klee, Robert A., Arlington Court Nursing and Rehabilitation Center, 1605 Northwest Professional Plaza, #101, 43220.
Laurinaitis, Saulius P., P.O. Box 1417, Hilliard, 43026.
Lavelle, Raymond E., 6415 Pinehurst Pointe, Westerville, 43082.
Marzluf, George J., Altercare of Navarre, 514 Park St., Navarre, 44662.
McClory, Bernard J., 1288 S. 4th St., 43206.
McNulty, Edwin J., St. Rita Home, 880 Greenlawn Ave., 43223.
Metzger, John L., P.O. Box 55, New Lexington, 43764.
Miller, Frank P., The Villas at St. Therese, 25 Noe Bixby Rd., #109, 43213.
Reilly, Robert F., Nazareth Towers, 300 E. Rich St., #1203, 43215.
Schneider, Harold E., 913 Hartney Dr., Gahanna, 43230.
Schuer, Robert J., St. Agatha, 1860 Northam Rd., 43221.
Smith, Paul O., Corpus Christi Church, 1111 E. Stewart Ave., 43206.
Sprenger, Alan H., St. Paul Church, 313 N. State St., Westerville, 43082.
Stanton, Joseph E., St. Mary, 684 S. 3rd St., 43206.
Totten, Raymond F., 329 Carnegie Pl., Pittsburgh, PA 15208.
Wise, Kenneth F., Immaculate Conception Church, 206 N. First St., Dennison, 44621.

Permanent Deacons:
Allison, Mark D., Leave of Absence
Azzola, Feliz F., St. Mary, Delaware
Ball, Frank X., St. Elizabeth, Columbus
Barford, Thomas M., St. Paul, Westerville
Baumann, Richard L., Our Lady of Victory, Columbus
Belhorn, Paul C., Leave of Absence
Berg, Thomas M., Sr., B.A., M.J., M.P.S., St. Joan of Arc, Powell
Bonacci, Anthony C., St. Joseph, Plain City
Busic, Richard B., Our Lady of Mt. Carmel, Buckeye Lake
Butts, Jerome J., Corpus Christi, Columbus
Cain, Albert E.
Checca, Joseph P., St. James the Less, Columbus
Crerand, John R., St. Michael, Worthington
Davies, Martin, Office of Liturgy
Davis, James R., (Retired)
Davis, William J.F., St. Peter, Columbus
Dawson, Eugene O., St. Joseph, Somerset
Deshaies, Paul, St. Bernadette, Lancaster
Drummer, Kenneth I., St. Agatha, Columbus
Duda, Frank A., Sacred Heart, Coshocton
Eiden, Gregory L., Kairos Prison Ministry
Elam, Jack W., St. Francis de Sales, Newark
Farmer, Joseph A., (Retired)
Farry, Joseph W., St. Philip, Columbus
Feerick, James P., (Retired)
Fondriest, Ronald H., St. Joseph, Dover
Franks, Michael J., Sr., Leave of Absence
Fricke, Klaus, St. Michael, Worthington
Ghiloni, Robert W., Blessed Sacrament, Newark
Gorman, William J., Leave of Absence
Gornick, Thomas W., Leave of Absence
Gorski, James, St. Joseph Catherdral, Columbus
Hann, Daniel W., Chap., Madison Correctional Institution
Hawkins, Mickey, St. Paul, Westerville
Horsley, George E., St. Mary, Portsmouth
Houze, Lester, Holy Trinity, Zoar
Iannarino, Francis A., Dir. Diaconate Office, St. Brigid of Kildare, Dublin; Bishop Watterson High School, Columbus
James, Joseph St Joseph, Dover
Johnston, Thomas V., St. Joseph Cathedral, Columbus
Keating, James, Ph.D., St. Andrew, Columbus
Koebel, Lawrence F., Chap., Pickaway Correctional Institute
Krick, Richard T., St. Peter, Chillicothe
Kruse, David J., Seton, Pickerington
Kunkler, Gordon T., Our Lady of Lourdes, Marysville
Labita, Peter C., Christ the King, Columbus
Lampe, Elmer L., Unassigned
Larcomb, Dwight T., Leave of Absence
Lovensheimer, George L., St. Mary, Chillicothe
McCurry, William E., County Sheriff's Office, Marion; Holy Family, Columbus
McDevitt, Francis X., St. Elizabeth, Columbus
Mould, Douglas, Sacred Heart, Coshocton
Neely, Robert A., St. Dominic, Columbus; Chap., Marion Correctional Institute
Paniccia, Frank A., (Retired)
Parsons, Ralph L., Sts. Simon & Jude, West Jefferson
Paulucci, Philip M., St. Peter, Columbus
Peterson, Burdette N., St. Nicholas, Zanesville
Phillips, Byron, Church of the Resurrection, New Albany
Plummer, Gil L., Sr., St. Brendan, Hilliard
Poland, Joseph D. (Poland), Our Lady of Miraculous Medal, Columbus
Pry, Roger F., Pope John XXIII, Lancaster
Rankin, John, Our Lady of Peace, Columbus
Rericha, John J., St. Elizabeth, Columbus
Rouse, James A., Vice Chancellor, St. Joan of Arc, Powell
Rzewnicki, Phil E., Leave of Absence
Scarpitti, Mark A., St. Bernadette, Lancaster
Schermer, Joseph E., St. Peter, Columbus
Schmitt, Frederick J., St. Mary, Groveport
Spina, Philip V., Jr., Leave of Absence
Stahl, John P., Our Lady of Lourdes, Ada
Staker, Eugene R., St. Nicholas, Zanesville
Stevens, Charles F., (Retired)
Sullivan, Frank, St. Mary, Lancaster
Turner, Harry, St. Matthew, Gahanna
Vellani, Albert J., St. Pius X, Reynoldsburg
Venturini, Stephen A., Our Lady of the Miraculous Medal, Columbus
Wiggins, Patrick J., St. Brendan, Hilliard

INSTITUTIONS LOCATED IN THE DIOCESE

[A] SEMINARIES, PONTIFICAL COLLEGES

COLUMBUS. *Pontifical College Josephinum*, 7625 N. High St., 43235-1498. Tel: 614-885-5585; Fax: 614-885-2307. Web: www.pcj.edu. Faculty 21; Total Enrollment 136.
Chancellor & Vice Chancellor Most Revs. Gabriel Montalvo, Apostolic Nuncio to the United States, Chancellor; James A. Griffin, J.D., J.C.L., Bishop of Columbus & Vice Chancellor.
General Administration Rev. Msgr. Paul J. Langsfeld, S.T.D., Rector & Pres.; Rev. Robert A. Gonzales, Ph.D. (TUC), Vice Rector, College of Liberal Arts; Deacon Michael Ross, Ph.D., Acting Academic Dean; Frank Heil, C.P.A., Treas.
Administrative Officers Revs. Thomas Buffer, S.T.D. (Canada), Dean Men & Dir. Formation, School of Technology; W. Thomas Kessler, Ph.D., Dir. Pastoral Formation; Lawrence C. Landini, O.F.M., H.E.D., Dir. Spiritual Formation, College of Liberal Arts; Kevin Louis, Dean Men & Dir. Formation, College of Liberal Arts; W. Shawn McKnight, S.T.D. (WCH), Dir. Liturgy; Richard J. Tomasek, S.J., S.T.L., Dir. Spiritual Formation, School of Theology; Barbara Couts, Registar; John Heise, Dir. Plant Operations; Peter G. Veracka, Dir. Library.
School of Theology full-time faculty Revs. Thomas J. Buffer, S.T.D.; W. Thomas Kessler, Ph.D.; W. Shawn McKnight, S.T.D. (WCH); Joseph A. Murphy, S.J., S.T.D.; Richard J. Tomasek, S.J., S.T.L.
Resident Emeritus Professors Revs. William Dettling, O.P., S.T.D.; William D. Lynn, S.J., S.T.D.
Resident Adjunct Professors Rev. John Michael McDermott, S.J., S.T.D.
Other full-time faculty Sr. Carolyn Thomas, S.C.N., Ph.D.; Deacons James Keating, Ph.D.; Michael Ross, Ph.D.; Peter G. Veracka; James A. Yeager, D.M.A.
College of Liberal Arts-full-time faculty Revs. Robert A. Gonzales, Ph.D. (TUC); Charles A. Jackson, S.T.L.; Lawrence C. Landini, O.F.M., H.E.D.; Kevin C. Louis, S.T.L. (LC); Alma Amwell, Ph.D.; David J. De Leonardis, Ph.D.; Beverly Lane, M.L.S.; Carolyn Scott, Ph.D.

[B] COLLEGES AND UNIVERSITIES

COLUMBUS. *Ohio Dominican University*, 1216 Sunbury Rd., 43219. Tel: 614-253-2741; Fax: 614-252-0776. Email: admissions@ohiodominican.edu. Web: www.ohiodominican.edu. Dr. Jack P. Calareso, Ph.D., Pres.; Dr. Richard Farmer, Ed.D., Exec. Vice Pres. Finance & Admin.; David Archibald,

Vice Pres. Enrollment Mgmt. & Mktg.; Michael D. Bromberg, Vice Pres. Business Affairs; Thomas G. Hoffman II, Vice Pres. Univ. Advancement; Andrew Klein, Vice Pres. Student Devel.; Rev. C. Gregory Jones, C.S.V., Dir. Campus Min. Dominican Sisters of the Third Order of St. Dominic Sisters 9; Lay Teachers 145; Students 2,500.

[C] HIGH SCHOOLS, DIOCESAN OR INTERPAROCHIAL

COLUMBUS. *Bishop Hartley High School*, 1285 Zettler Rd., 43227. Tel: 614-237-5421; Fax: 614-237-3809. Email: hartley@cdeducation.org. Mike Winters, Prin.; Randy Kortokrax, Dean of Students; Dave Thompson, Athletic Dir. Lay Teachers 39; Students 590.

Bishop Ready High School, 707 Salisbury Rd., 43204. Tel: 614-276-5263; Fax: 614-276-5116. Email: cseamen@cdeducation.org. Web: www.brhs.org. Celene A. Seamen, Prin. Lay Teachers 34; Students 485.

Bishop Watterson High School, 99 E. Cooke Rd., 43214. Tel: 614-268-8671; Fax: 614-268-0551. Web: www.cd.education.org/schools/bw. Mrs. Marian Hutson, Prin.; Deacon Frank A. Iannarino, Chap. Deacons 1; Sisters 1; Lay Teachers 80; Students 1,140.

Development Office, 100 Indian Springs Dr., 43214. Tel: 614-268-3041; Fax: 614-268-4309.

St. Charles Preparatory School, 2010 E. Broad St., 43209. Tel: 614-252-6714; Fax: 614-251-6800. Email: dcavello@cdeducation.org. Web: www.stcharlesprep.org. Dominic J. Cavello, Prin.; Scott M. Pharion, Asst. Prin.; James Lower, Asst. Prin.; Rev. Msgr. Thomas M. Bennett; Sr. Margaret Hoffman, R.S.C.J. Priests 1; Sisters 1; Lay Teachers 27; Students 578.

St. Francis de Sales High School, 4212 Karl Rd., 43224. Tel: 614-267-7808; Fax: 614-265-3375. Email: prossett@cdeducation.org. Web: www.cdeducation.org/school/ds. Mr. Patrick D. Rossetti, Prin.; Mr. Dan Garrick, Asst. Prin.; Jackie Messerschmitt, Asst. Prin. Lay Teachers 57; Students 927.

LANCASTER. *William V. Fisher Catholic High School*, 1803 Granville Pike, 43130. Tel: 740-654-1231; Fax: 740-654-1233. Email: jcondron@cdeducation.org. Web: fishercatholic.org. Mr. James P. Condron, Prin.; Joe Holbrook, Campus Min. Lay Teachers 22; Students 327.

MARION. *Marion Catholic High School*, 1001 Mt. Vernon Ave., 43302. Tel: 740-389-2381; Fax: 740-389-5243. Email: mchs@cd.pvt.k12.oh.us. Web: www.marioncatholicschools.com. Fran Voll, Prin. Lay Teachers 16; Students 117.

NEW PHILADELPHIA. *Central Catholic High School*, 777 Third St., N.E., 44663. Tel: 330-343-3302; Fax: 330-343-6388. Email: afranz@cdeducation.org/webmail. Web: webl.tusco.net/tcc/. Dawn R. Franz, Prin. Brothers 1; Lay Teachers 13; Students 168.

NEWARK. *Newark Catholic High School*, 1 Green Wave Dr., 43055. Tel: 740-344-3594; Fax: 740-344-0421. Email: bhill@cdeducation.org. Web: www.newarkcatholic.org/newcath.htm. Beth Hill, Prin.; Susie Gribble, Campus Min. Lay Teachers 27; Students 310.

PORTSMOUTH. *Notre Dame High School*, (Grades 7-12), 2220 Sunrise Ave., 45662. Tel: 740-353-0719; Fax: 740-353-2526. Email: kmilliga@cdeducation.org. Kathleen Milligan, Prin. Sisters 1; Lay Teachers 15; Students 177.

ZANESVILLE. *Bishop Rosecrans High School*, 1040 E. Main St., 43701. Tel: 740-452-7504; Fax: 740-455-5080. Email: dmorland@cd.pvt.k12.oh.us. Web: www.cdeducation.org/schools/bro. Revs. Leo L. Connolly, Prin.; James C. Csaszar. Priests 1; Lay Teachers 16; Students 195.

[D] MONTESSORI SCHOOLS

COLUMBUS. *St. Joseph Montessori School*, 933 Hamlet St., 43201-3595. Tel: 614-291-8601; Fax: 614-291-7411. Email: dbarton@cd.pvt.k12.oh.us. Web: www.sjms.net. Donna Barton, Admin. Lay Teachers 35; Students 310.

[E] PRIVATE SCHOOLS

COLUMBUS. *Our Lady of Bethlehem School and Childcare*, 4567 Olentangy River Rd., 43214. Tel: 614-451-6631; Fax: 614-451-3706. Marilyn P. Dono, Prin. Preschool - 3rd grade childcare and latchkey program. Total Staff 32; Children 240.

[F] GENERAL HOSPITALS

COLUMBUS. *Mohun Health Care Center*, 2320 Airport Dr., 43219. Tel: 614-253-8517; Fax: 614-251-0338. Web: columbusdominicans.org. Alan Pauley, Admin. Total Staff 111; Bed Capacity 75; Patients Assisted Annually 98.

Mount Carmel Health System, 793 W. State St., 43222. Tel: 614-234-5423; Fax: 614-234-5985. Web: mountcarmelhealth.com. Joseph Calvaruso, Pres. & CEO. Bed Capacity 915; Staff 7,000 Patients Assisted Annually 966,081.

Legal Holdings:

Mount Carmel Health System Tel: 614-234-5423; Fax: 614-234-1359.

Mount Carmel West (General Hospital) Tel: 614-234-5000; Fax 614-234-5756.

Mount Carmel East (General Hospital) Tel: 614-234-6000; Fax 614-234-6408.

Mount Carmel Care Continuum Businesses Tel: 614-234-0224; Fax: 614-234-5756.

Mount Carmel College of Nursing Tel 614-234-5800; Fax 614-234-2875.

Mount Carmel St. Ann's (General Hospital), Westerville. Tel: 614-898-4000; Fax: 614-898-8668.

Mount Carmel Health System Foundation Tel: 614-234-5290; Fax: 614-234-1920.

ZANESVILLE. *Genesis Healthcare System*, 800 Forest Ave. & 2951 Maple Ave, 43701. Tel: 740-454-4638; Fax: 740-455-4914. Mr. Thomas L. Sieber, Pres. Franciscan Sisters of Christian Charity 4; Bed Capacity 398; Total Staff 2,702.

[G] HOMES FOR AGED AND HOUSING FOR ELDERLY

COLUMBUS. *Mother Angeline McCrory Manor, Inc.*, 5277 E. Broad St., 43213. Tel: 614-751-5700; Fax: 614-751-8311. Sr. Pauline Ross, Admin.

Nazareth Towers, 300 E. Rich St., 43215. Tel: 614-464-4780; Fax: 614-464-1733. Sally Haban, Admin. Total in Residence 208; Total Staff 5.

St. Raphael Home for the Aged, Inc., 1550 Roxbury Rd., 43212. Tel: 614-486-0436; Fax: 614-486-1640. Email: nsghomstraph@greenapple.com. Web: straphael strita.com. Sr. Kathleen Dominick, O.Carm., Admin. & Supr.; Rev. Larry Nolan, Chap. Carmelite Sisters for the Aged and Infirm Residents 78; Total Skilled / Intermediate 78; Total Staff 105.

St. Rita Home, 880 Greenlawn Ave., 43223. Tel: 614-443-9433; Fax: 614-443-1196. Sr. M. Jacqueline, O.Carm., Supr. & Admin.; Rev. Thomas J. Cadden, Chap. Carmelite Sisters for the Aged and Infirm 6. Total Staff 125; Guests 100; Total Assisted 190.

Seton Coshocton, Inc., 377 Clow Ln., Coshocton, 43812. Tel: 330-343-3611 Dover Tel.; 740-622-7664 Coshocton No.. Email: setonsquare@tusco.net Bob Campitelli, Mgr.; Mary Campitelli, Asst. Apartments 40; Total in Residence 36; Total Staff 2.

Seton South Columbus, Inc., 155 Highview Blvd., 43207. Tel: 614-492-9944; Fax: 614-492-9955. Suzanne Schulmeyer, Mgr. Total in Residence 40; Total Staff 2.

Seton Square Dover, II, Inc., 139 Filmore St., Dover, 44622. Tel: 330-343-3611; Fax: 330-602-7969. Email: setonsquare@tusco.net. Bob Campitelli, Mgr.; Mary Campitelli, Asst. Total in Residence 36; Total Staff 2.

Seton Square North, 1776 Drew Ave., 43235. Tel: 614-451-1995; Fax: 614-451-3798. Email: ssnaline@ameritech.net. Aline Taylor, Mgr. Total in Residence 225; Total Staff 5.

Seton Square, West, 3999 Clime Rd., 43228. Tel: 614-274-3550. Linda Hatmacher, Mgr. Staff 2; Total in Residence 51.

The Villas at St. Therese Assisted Living, Inc., 25 Noe-Bixby Rd., 43213-1461. Tel: 614-864-3576; Fax: 614-864-3577. Sr. Patricia Michael Sweeney, O.Carm. Admin.; Rev. Msgr. Joseph M. Hendricks, Contact Person.

The Villas at St. Therese Independent Living, Inc., 5253 E. Broad St., 43213. Tel: 614-864-3576; Fax: 614-864-3577. Rev. Msgr. Joseph M. Hendricks, Contact Person.

DOVER. *Seton Square Dover, I, Inc.*, 501 S. James St., 44622. Tel: 330-343-3611; Fax: 330-343-4473. Email: setondover@tusco.net. Bob Campitelli, Mgr.; Mary Campitelli, Asst. Total in Residence 50; Total Staff 3.

KENTON. *Seton Kenton, Inc.*, 699 Morningside Dr., 43326. Tel: 419-673-7202; Fax: 419-673-7202. Mary Lou Sweet, Mgr. Total in Residence 48; Total Staff 2.

LANCASTER. *Seton Lancaster, Inc.*, 232 Gay St., 43130. Tel: 740-681-1403; Fax: 740-681-9178. Roxanne Bailey, Mgr. Total in Residence 35; Total Staff 2.

LONDON. *Seton London, Inc.*, 350 Cambridge Dr., 43140. Tel: 740-852-4233. Linda Hatmacher, Mgr. Total in Residence 62; Total Staff 2.

MARION. *Seton Square Marion, Inc.*, 255 Richland Rd., 43302. Tel: 740-389-4746; Fax: 740-389-9780. Email: Seton504@aol.com. Debra J. Erwin, Mgr. Total in Residence 111; Total Staff 3.

REYNOLDSBURG. *Seton Square East, Inc.*, 1235 Briarcliff Rd., 43068. Tel: 614-861-4860; Fax: 614-861-8022. Email: ssejudyw@copper.net. Judy Warschauer, Mgr. Total in Residence 104; Total Staff 3.

WASHINGTON COURT HOUSE. *Seton Washington Court House, Inc.*, 400 N. Glenn Ave., 43160. Tel: 740-335-2292; Fax: 740-335-2291. Email: sproperties@In-Touch.net. Linda Hatmacher, Mgr. Total in Residence 40; Total Staff 3.

WELLSTON. *Seton Square Wellston, Inc.*, 570 W. First St., 45692. Tel: 740-384-6174; Fax: 740-384-1514. Tami Jolly, Mgr. Total in Residence 49; Total Staff 2.

ZANESVILLE. *Seton Housing, Inc.*, 516 Sheridan St., 43701. Tel: 740-453-4422; Fax: 740-453-4950. Penne Harvey, Mgr. Total in Residence 47; Total Staff 2.

[H] MONASTERIES AND RESIDENCES OF PRIESTS AND BROTHERS

COLUMBUS. *Salesian Residence*, 80 S. 6th St., 43215. Tel: 614-224-8000; Fax: 614-224-8000. Email: sdbcol1@aol.com. Web: www.sbgcc.org. Revs. John Puntino, S.D.B. (NY), Dir.; Dennis Donovan, S.D.B., Vice Dir. & Exec. Dir. Boys & Girls Club; Richard Cressman, S.D.B.; Joseph Tyminski, S.D.B.; Bros. Michael Brinkman, S.D.B.; Robert Metell, S.D..B. Brothers 2; Total Staff 6.

SOMERSET. *St. Joseph's Rectory*, 5757 State Rte. 383 N.E., P.O. Box 190, 43783. Tel: 740-743-1317. Email: anthonypo@angelfire.com. Rev. J.A. Breen, O.P.; Deacon Gene Dawson, Parish Admin. Total Staff 2; Total in Residence 1.

WEST JEFFERSON. *SS. Simon and Jude*, 95 W. Main St., 43162-1225. Tel: 614-879-8562; Fax: 614-879-7605. Email: fathermike@juno.com. Revs. Michael J. Devaney, O.M.I.; Ralph J. Karl, O.M.I. (Retired); Deacon Ralph L. Parsons.

[I] CONVENTS AND RESIDENCES FOR SISTERS

COLUMBUS. *Carmelite Sisters for Aged and Infirm*, Queen of Hope Residence, 5749 Willow Creek Cir., 43213. Tel: 614-501-8038; Fax: 614-501-8035. Carmelite Sisters operate the Villas at St. Therese.

St. Mary of the Springs, 2320 Airport Dr., 43219-2098. Tel: 614-416-1900; Fax: 614-252-7435. Email: jbaumop@yahoo.com. Web: www.columbusdominicans.org. Sisters 286; Novices 2; Total in Congregation 286.

Leadership Team: Sisters Jacqueline Baum, O.P., Councilor, Secretary-General; Anne Keenan, O.P., Vicaress; Anne Kilbride, O.P., Prioress; Helena Sanse, O.P., Councilor; Patricia Twohill, O.P., Councilor.

Sisters' Residence: Sr. Sheila Marie McIntyre, Coord.

Mohun Health Care Center Tel: 614-253-8517; Fax: 614-251-0338. Alan Pauley, Admin.; Sr. Mary Patricia Gallagher, O.P., Dir. of Resident Life; Rev. Benedict Joseph, O.P., Chap.

Sisters of the Good Shepherd, 2440 Dawnlight Ave., 43211-1934. Tel: 614-471-2626; Fax: 614-475-2264. Email: srrose3@juno.com. Good Shepherd International Missions buys from Good Shepherd Missions in the developing world for resale. Proceeds are sent back to the missions to better the lives of women in the developing world. Sisters of the Good Shepherd 3.

PORTSMOUTH. *St. Joseph Adoration Monastery, Poor Clares of Perpetual Adoration* , (Public Chapel) , 2311 Stockham Ln., 45662-3049. Tel: 740-353-4713. Sr. Delores Marie, P.C.P.A., Abbess; Rev. William C. Patterson, Chap. Professed Cloistered Nuns 6.

[J] NEWMAN CENTERS

COLUMBUS. *Campus Ministry Ohio State University*, 64 W. Lane Ave., 3201. Tel: 614-291-4674; Fax: 614-291-2065. Email: mailbox@thenewmancenter.net. Web: www.thenewmancenter.net. Revs. David W. O'Brien, C.S.P., Dir.; Vincent W. McKiernan, C.S.P.; Lawrence Rice, C.S.P.

[K] FOUNDATIONS

COLUMBUS. **The Foundation of the Catholic Diocese of Columbus*, 1071 S. High St., 43206. Tel: 614-443-8893; Fax: 614-443-8894. Email: kspencer@catholic-foundation.org. Kathy Spencer, Exec. Dir.

Legacy of Catholic Learning Endowment Program, 198 E. Broad St., 43215. Tel: 614-224-1221.

LANCASTER. **William V. Fisher Catholic High School Endowment Fund*, 1803 Granville Pike, 43130. Tel: 740-654-1231; Fax: 740-654-1233. Email: jcondron@cdeducation.org. Web: fishercatholic.org.

MARION. *Marion Catholic High School Endowment Fund*, 1001 Mount Vernon Ave., 43302. Tel: 740-389-2381; Fax: 740-389-5243. Email: mchs@cdeducation.org.

NEW PHILADELPHIA. *Tuscarawas Central Catholic*

High School Endowment Fund, 777 Third St. N.E., 44663. Tel: 330-343-3302; Fax: 330-343-6388. Email: dfranz@cdeducation.org.

NEWARK. **Newark Catholic High School Endowment Fund*, One Green Wave Dr., 43055. Tel: 740-344-5671; Fax: 740-344-0412. Email: kdellner@laca.org.

ZANESVILLE. *Bishop Rosecrans High School Foundation*, 1040 E. Main St., 43701. Tel: 740-450-7993; Fax: 740-450-7994. Email: gpellegr@cdeducation.org. Web: www.cdeducation.org/schools/bro.

[L] MISCELLANEOUS

COLUMBUS. *Blessed Margaret Guild, Inc. c/o St. Patrick Church*, 262 N. Grant Ave., 43215. Tel: 614-240-5910; Fax: 614-240-5928. Total Staff 1.

Catholic Alumni Club, P.O. Box 695, 43216. Email: peggyschano@insight.rr.com. Web: www.angelfire.com/oh/CatholicAlumniClub. Peggy Schano, Contact Person. Tel: 614-575-0518; Dan Doell, Contact Person. Tel: 614-846-7489.

The Christ Child Society of Columbus, Inc., P.O. Box 340091, 43234-0091. Tel: 614-279-9660; 614-451-2131. Email: mvisconti@columbus.rr.com. Web: www.rc.net/columbus/christchild. Shirley Powers, Pres.

Diocesan Retirement Community Corp., 198 E. Broad St., 43215. Tel: 614-224-2251; Fax: 614-224-6306. Rev. Msgr. Joseph M. Hendricks, Pres. & CEO.

St. Stephen's Community House, 1500 E. 17th Ave., 43219. Tel: 614-294-6347; Fax: 614-294-0258. Email: sschjs@aol.com. Ms. Judith Stattmiller, Exec. Dir. Total Assisted 22,000; Total Staff 131.

LANCASTER. **St. Mary of the Assumption Foundation*, 132 S. High St., 43130. Tel: 740-653-0997; Fax: 740-653-0337. Rev. Donald E. Franks, Contact Person.

ZANESVILLE. *St. Nicholas Foundation*, 925 E. Main St., 43701. Tel: 740-453-0597; Fax: 740-453-0590. Email: chapcop@rrohio.com.

RELIGIOUS INSTITUTES OF MEN REPRESENTED IN THE DIOCESE

For further details refer to the corresponding bracketed number in the Religious Institutes of Men or Women section.

[0350]—*Cistercians Order of the Strict Observance-Trappists*—O.C.S.O.
[1320]—*Clerics of St. Viator*—C.S.V.
[0520]—*Franciscan Friars, Province of St John the Baptist*—O.F.M.
[0690]—*Jesuit Fathers and Brothers* (Detroit and Maryland Provs.)—S.J.
[0910]—*Oblates of Mary Immaculate*—O.M.I.
[0430]—*Order of Preachers-Dominicans* (Prov. of St. Joseph)—O.P.
[1030]—*Paulist Fathers*—C.S.P.
[1050]—*Pontifical Institute for Foreign Missions*—P.I.M.E.
[1190]—*Salesians of St. John Bosco*—S.D.B.
[0760]—*Society of Mary*—S.M.
[0990]—*Society of the Catholic Apostolate*—S.A.C.
[1060]—*Society of the Precious Blood* (Cincinnati Prov.)—C.PP.S.

RELIGIOUS INSTITUTES OF WOMEN REPRESENTED IN THE DIOCESE

[0330]—*Carmelite Sisters for the Aged and Infirm*—O.Carm.
[1000]—*Congregation of Divine Providence, KY*—C.D.P.
[3710]—*Congregation of the Sisters of St. Agnes*—C.S.A.
[1920]—*Congregation of the Sisters of the Holy Cross*—C.S.C.
[1730]—*Congregation of the Sisters of the Third Order of St. Francis, Oldenburg, IN*—O.S.F.
[1710]—*Congregation of the Third Order of St. Francis of Mary Immaculate, Joliet, IL*—O.S.F.
[1070-02]—*Dominican Sisters* (Columbus, OH)—O.P.
[1070-25]—*Dominican Sisters* (Kenosha, WI)—O.P.
[1070-13]—*Dominican Sisters* (Adrian, MI)—O.P.
[1105]—*Dominican Sisters of Hope*—O.P.
[1180]—*Franciscan Sisters* (Allegany, NY)—O.S.F.
[1230]—*Franciscan Sisters of Christian Charity* (Manitowoc, WI)—O.S.F.
[1440]—*Franciscan Sisters of the Poor*—S.F.P.
[3210]—*Poor Clares of Perpetual Adoration*—P.C.P.A.
[1070-03]—*Sinsinawa Dominican Congregation of the Most Holy Rosary*—O.P.
[0440]—*Sisters of Charity of Cincinnati, Ohio*—S.C.
[0500]—*Sisters of Charity of Nazareth, Kentucky*—S.C.N.
[0990]—*Sisters of Divine Providence*—C.D.P.
[3000]—*Sisters of Notre Dame de Namur*—S.N.D.deN.
[1630]—*Sisters of St. Francis of Penance and Christian Charity* (Stella Niagara, NY)—O.S.F.
[1530]—*Sisters of St. Francis of the Congregation of Our Lady of Lourdes, Sylvania, OH*—O.S.F.
[3830-05]—*Sisters of St. Joseph* (Brentwood, NY)—C.S.J.
[3830-08]—*Sisters of St. Joseph* (Cleveland, OH)—C.S.J.
[3880]—*Sisters of St. Joseph of Medaille*—C.S.J.
[3220]—*Sisters of the Poor Child Jesus*—P.C.J.
[3260]—*Sisters of the Precious Blood* (Dayton, OH)—C.PP.S.
[3320]—*Sisters of the Presentation of the B.V.M.*—P.B.V.M.
[1760]—*Sisters of the Third Order of St. Francis of Penance and of Charity* (Tiffin, OH)—O.S.F.
[1720]—*Sisters of the Third Order Regular of St. Francis of the Congregation of Our Lady of Lourdes*—O.S.F.
[4120-04]—*The Ursuline Nuns of Cleveland*—O.S.U.

DIOCESAN CEMETERIES

COLUMBUS. *Mount Calvary*, 518 Mt. Calvary Ave., 43223-2217. Tel: 614-491-2751. Rich Finn, Dir. & Gen. Mgr.

LEWIS CENTER. *Resurrection*, 9571 N. High St., 43035-9413. Tel: 614-888-1805; Fax: 614-888-1810. Rich Finn, Dir. & Gen. Mgr.

LOCKBOURNE. *St. Joseph*, 6440 S. High St., 43137-9208. Tel: 614-491-2751; Fax: 614-491-4264. Rich Finn, Dir. & Gen. Mgr.

PATASKALA. *Holy Cross*, 11539 National Rd. S.W., 43062-8304. Tel: 740-927-4442; Fax: 740-927-4645. Rich Finn, Dir. & Gen. Mgr.

NECROLOGY

† Grimes, Rev. Msgr. J. Colby—Died April 18, 2003
† Dimond, Arthur J.—Died April 29, 2003
† Raiser, Jerome K.—Died June 5, 2003

Diocese of Corpus Christi

(Dioecesis Corporis Christi)

Most Reverend

EDMOND CARMODY, D.D.

Seventh Bishop of Corpus Christi; ordained June 8, 1957; appointed Auxiliary Bishop of the Archdiocese of San Antonio November 8, 1988; consecrated December 15, 1988; appointed Bishop of the Diocese of Tyler March 24, 1992; installed May 25, 1992; appointed Bishop of the Diocese of Corpus Christi February 3, 2000; installed March 17, 2000. *Mailing Address: P.O. Box 2620, Corpus Christi, TX 78403-2620.* Tel: 361-882-6191; Fax: 361-654-1270.

Most Reverend

RENE H. GRACIDA, D.D.

Bishop Emeritus of Corpus Christi; ordained May 23, 1959; appointed Titular Bishop of Masuccaba and Auxiliary of Miami December 6, 1971; consecrated January 25, 1972; appointed Bishop of Pensacola-Tallahassee October 1, 1975; Transferred to Corpus Christi May 19, 1983; installed July 11, 1983; retired April 1, 1997. *Res.: 4126 Ocean Dr., Corpus Christi, TX 78411-1224. Office: 620 Lipan St., P.O. Box 2620, Corpus Christi, TX 78403-2620.* Tel: 361-882-6191.

The Chancery Office: 620 Lipan St., P.O Box 2620, Corpus Christi, TX 78403-2620. Tel: 361-882-6191; Fax: 361-882-1018; 361-883-8850; 361-654-1270.

Web: www.diocesecc.org

Email: chancery@diocesecc.org

Square Miles 10,951.

Erected a Vicariate Apostolic in 1874; elevated to a Diocese March 23, 1912.

The territory embraced by the Diocese of Corpus Christi comprises the Counties of Aransas, Bee, Brooks, Duval, Jim Wells, Kleberg, Kenedy, Live Oak, Nueces, Refugio, San Patricio, and parts of McMullen in the State of Texas.

For legal titles of parishes and diocesan institutions, consult the Chancery Office.

STATISTICAL OVERVIEW

Personnel	
Bishop	1
Retired Bishops	1
Priests: Diocesan Active in Diocese	86
Priests: Diocesan Active Outside Diocese	6
Priests: Retired, Sick or Absent	25
Number of Diocesan Priests	117
Religious Priests in Diocese	42
Total Priests in Diocese	159
Extern Priests in Diocese	18
Ordinations:	
Diocesan Priests	4
Religious Priests	4
Transitional Deacons	1
Permanent Deacons in Diocese	67
Total Brothers	13
Total Sisters	182
Parishes	
Parishes	67
With Resident Pastor:	
Resident Diocesan Priests	55
Resident Religious Priests	12
Missions	32
Pastoral Centers	3
New Parishes Created	2
Professional Ministry Personnel:	
Brothers	1
Sisters	19
Lay Ministers	55
Welfare	
Catholic Hospitals	6
Total Assisted	586,779
Homes for the Aged	2
Total Assisted	105
Day Care Centers	2
Total Assisted	115
Specialized Homes	3
Total Assisted	979
Special Centers for Social Services	5
Total Assisted	44,826
Educational	
Diocesan Students in Other Seminaries	12
Students Religious	10
Total Seminarians	22
Colleges and Universities	1
Total Students	27
High Schools, Private	1
Total Students	234
Elementary Schools, Diocesan and Parish	14
Total Students	2,089
Elementary Schools, Private	2
Total Students	473
Catechesis/Religious Education:	
High School Students	3,247
Elementary Students	10,632
Total Students under Catholic Instruction	16,724
Teachers in the Diocese:	
Priests	6
Brothers	1
Sisters	29
Lay Teachers	217
Vital Statistics	
Receptions into the Church:	
Infant Baptism Totals	2,922
Adult Baptism Totals	170
Received into Full Communion	317
First Communions	2,674
Confirmations	705
Marriages:	
Catholic	589
Interfaith	117
Total Marriages	706
Deaths	1,761
Total Catholic Population	384,308
Total Population	549,012

Former Bishops—Rt. Revs. DOMINIC MANUCY, consecrated Dec. 8, 1874; transferred to Mobile March 9, 1884; reappointed to Vicariate Apostolic of Brownsville Feb. 1, 1885; died Dec. 4, 1885, before taking possession; PETER VERDAGUER, consecrated Nov. 9, 1890; died Oct. 26, 1911; PAUL JOSEPH NUSSBAUM, C.P., D.D., consecrated May 20, 1913; resigned March 26, 1920; Bishop of Marquette; appt. Nov. 14, 1922; died June 24, 1935; Most Revs. EMMANUEL B. LEDVINA, D.D., LL.D., appt. April 30, 1921; consecrated June 14, 1921; Assistant at Pontifical Throne May 30, 1931; resigned March 15, 1949; died Dec. 15, 1952; MARIANO S. GARRIGA, D.D., LL.D., Coadjutor cum jure successionis,; appt. June 20, 1936; consecrated Sept. 21, 1936; succeeded to See March 15, 1949; assistant at Pontifical Throne April 14, 1951; died Feb. 21, 1965; THOMAS J. DRURY, D.D., Fourth Bishop of Corpus Christi; Bishop of San Angelo; appt. Oct. 16, 1961; consecrated Jan. 24, 1962; fourth Bishop of Corpus Christi; appt. July 19, 1965; installed Sept. 1, 1965; retired Bishop of Corpus Christi; appt. May 19, 1983; died July 22, 1992; RENE H. GRACIDA, D.D. (Retired), Bishop Emeritus; Fifth Bishop of Corpus Christi; appt. Titular Bishop of Masuccaba and Auxiliary of Miami Dec. 6, 1971; consecrated Jan. 25, 1972; appt. Bishop of Pensacola-Tallahassee Oct. 1, 1975; transferred to Corpus Christi May 19, 1983; installed July 11, 1983; retired April 1, 1997; ROBERTO O. GONZALEZ, O.F.M., Sixth Bishop of Corpus Christi; appt. Titular Bishop of Ursona and Auxiliary Bishop of Boston July 19, 1988; ord. Oct. 3, 1988; appt. Coadjutor Bishop of Corpus Christi May 16, 1995; transferred to Corpus Christi June 26, 1995; succeeded to See April 1, 1997; appt. Apostolic Administrator to Corpus Christi and Archbishop of San Juan, March 26, 1999; installed Archbishop of San Juan, Puerto Rico May 8, 1999.

Diocesan Curia—620 Lipan St., P.O. Box 2620, Corpus Christi, 78403-2620.

Office of the Bishop—Most Rev. EDMOND CARMODY, D.D.; Rev. Msgr. RICHARD SHIRLEY, Vicar General; Revs. EMILO JIMENEZ, Chancellor; THOMAS P. FEENEY, J.C.L., Judicial Vicar.

Bishop's Office—620 Lipan St., P.O. Box 2620, Corpus Christi, 78403-2620. Tel: 361-882-6191; Fax: 361-654-1270. MARTY WIND, Dir. Communications; Sr. KATHLEEN MCDONAGH, I.W.B.S., Dir. Consecrated Life; Deacons STANLEY MILLSAP, Co Dir. Deacons & Dir. Human Resources; MICHAEL MANTZ, Co Dir. Deacons; Dr. FRANK LUCIDO, Diocesan Dir. Rel. Educ.; Rev. Msgrs. LEONARD PIVONKA, J.C.D., Health Care; TOM MCGETTRICK, Vicar for Priests; Revs. FRANCISCO XAVIER MARTINEZ, S.T.L., Dir. Pastoral Ministries; PAUL HESSE, Dir. Seminary Formation & Vocations.

Consultative Bodies—620 Lipan St., P.O. Box 2620, Corpus Christi, 78403-2620.

Council Of Religious—Sr. KATHLEEN MCDONAGH, I.W.B.S.

Deans—Rev. Msgr. LEONARD PIVONKA, J.C.D., Alice Deanery; Revs. PETER J. GAJDA, Beeville Deanery; MARK CHAMBERLIN, Corpus Christi Central Deanery; Rev. Msgr. LAWRENCE E. WHITE, Corpus Christi Westside Deanery; Rev. MATTHEW LYNG, Fivepoints Deanery; Rev. Msgr. TOM MCGETTRICK, Southside Deanery; Revs. JOHN C. OUELLETTE,

Kingsville Deanery; CELESTINE MURRAY, Refugio Deanery.

College of Consultors—Revs. MARK CHAMBERLIN; PIOTR J. GAJDA; EMILIO JIMENEZ, Chancellor; MATTHEW LYNG; Rev. Msgr. TOM MCGETTRICK; Revs. CELESTINE MURRAY; JOHN C. OUELLETTE; Rev. Msgrs. LEONARD PIVONKA, J.C.D.; RICHARD SHIRLEY; LAWRENCE E. WHITE.

Diaconal Screening Committee—Deacon MANNY MALDONADO; Sr. ANNETTE WAGNER, I.W.B.S.; Rev. MATTHEW J. STEPHAN; MARY COSTLEY; ELVA MANTZ; NINA JOINER; Deacons TONY BITONI; RICARDO E. COSTLEY; MICHAEL MANTZ, Co Dir. for Deacons; STANLEY MILLSAP, Co Dir. for Deacons; JOHN R. JOINER.

Finance Council—Most Rev. EDMOND CARMODY, D.D.; Rev. Msgrs. RICHARD SHIRLEY; LOUIS F. KIHNEMAN; Rev. GREGORY DEAN; Sr. AGNES MARIE TENGLER, I.W.B.S.; Mr. ADELFINO PALACIOS; Mrs. ROBIN PERRONE, C.P.A.; Mr. CECILE CARLISLE; Mrs. YOLANDA OLIVAREZ; Ms. NELDA MARTINEZ. Consultants: Mr. GREG SEAGRAVE; Mr. GARY A. RAMIREZ.

Personnel Board - Priests—Rev. Msgr. RICHARD SHIRLEY, Chm.; Revs. MATTHEW LYNG; PIOTR J. GAJDA; MARK CHAMBERLIN, Vice Chm.; Rev. Msgr. TOM MCGETTRICK; Revs. CELESTINE MURRAY; JOHN C. OUELLETTE; Rev. Msgrs. LEONARD PIVONKA, J.C.D.; LAWRENCE E. WHITE.

Presbyteral Council—Revs. ROGER SMITH, Chm.; MARK CHAMBERLIN, Vice Chm.; PIOTR J. GAJDA; Rev. Msgrs. MICHAEL J. ADAMS; MICHAEL HOWELL; Revs. EMILIO JIMENEZ, Chancellor; PRINCE KURUVILA; JOHN C. OUELLETTE; MATTHEW LYNG; Rev. Msgr. TOM MCGETTRICK; Rev. W. CELESTINE MURRAY; Rev. Msgrs. LEONARD PIVONKA, J.C.D.; RICHARD SHIRLEY; LAWRENCE E. WHITE; LOUIS F. KIHNEMAN; Revs. MORGAN ROWSOME; RODOLFO D. VASQUEZ, Sec.

Tribunal—Rev. THOMAS P. FEENEY, J.C.L., Judicial Vicar, 620 Lipan St., P.O. Box 2620, Corpus Christi, 78403-2620. Tel: 361-882-6191; Fax: 361-882-1018.

Judges—Rev. Msgr. THOMAS MEANY (Retired); Rev. THOMAS P. FEENEY, J.C.L.; Rev. Msgr. LEONARD PIVONKA, J.C.D.; Revs. JAMES HAMILTON (Retired); JOSEPH A. LOPEZ; Rev. Msgr. MICHAEL HOWELL; Revs. ROGER SMITH; MARK CHAMBERLIN.

Defenders of the Bond—Rev. Msgr. RICHARD SHIRLEY; Rev. ANGEL MONTANO.

Notaries-Secretaries—GRACIE RODRIGUEZ; BELINDA HARRIS.

Instructor—Rev. ANTONIO HERRERA FLOVER, J.C.L.

Villa Maria, Inc., Board—ROBERT BECQUET, Pres.; JOHN T. WRIGHT, Vice Pres.; VERNON SMITH, Treas.; Sr. AGNES MARIE TENGLER, I.W.B.S., Sec., 3146 Saratoga Blvd., Corpus Christi, 78413. Tel: 361-857-6171; Fax: 361-857-6173.

Administrative Offices

The Chancery Office—620 Lipan St., P.O. Box 2620, Corpus Christi, 78403-2620. Tel: 361-882-6191; Fax: 361-882-1018 (Admin.); 361-883-8850 (Fiscal Office); 361-654-1270 (Bishop's Office). Office Hours: Mon.-Fri., 8:30-5. Closed holy days and holidays.

Office of the Bishop—Most Rev. EDMOND CARMODY, D.D.

Office of the Bishop Emeritus—Most Rev. RENE H. GRACIDA, D.D.

Canonical Affairs—Rev. THOMAS P. FEENEY, J.C.L.

Administrative Assistant—MARY SEDBERRY.

Vicar General—Rev. Msgr. RICHARD SHIRLEY.

Judicial Vicar—Rev. THOMAS P. FEENEY, J.C.L.

Director for Pastoral Ministries—Rev. FRANCISCO XAVIER MARTINEZ, S.T.L.

Co Director for Deacons & Director Human Resources—Deacon STANLEY MILLSAP.

Director for Deacons—Deacon MICHAEL MANTZ.

Vicar for Priests—Rev. Msgr. TOM MCGETTRICK.

Chancellor—Rev. EMILIO JIMENEZ.

Family Life Office—Deacon BOB ALLEN.

Fiscal Officer—Mr. GREG SEAGRAVE.

Controller—PAUL A. DAMEROW, C.P.A.

Bishop's Annual Appeal—Mr. DALE BAIRD, Devel. Consultant.

Data Processing Office—CATHY LOPEZ, MIS Technical Dir.

Real Property Office—CY RICHARDS, Mgr.

Alliance for Human Life—Rev. FRANCISCO XAVIER MARTINEZ, S.T.L.

Operations Manager—SUSAN CAMPBELL.

Personnel Office—Deacon STANLEY MILLSAP.

Propagation of the Faith Office—Rev. RAYMOND YRLAS, P.O. Box 2620, Corpus Christi, 78403-2620.

Seminary Formation & Vocations—Rev. PAUL HESSE, Chancery Office, P.O. Box 2620, Corpus Christi, 78403-2620. Tel: 361-882-6191.

Archives—Mr. CY RICHARDS III, Archivist. Tel: 361-855-2345 Mon.-Thurs. 9-2.

Catholic Schools Office—Deacon RENE GONZALEZ, Supt., Chancery Office, P.O. Box 2620, Corpus Christi, 78403-2620. Tel: 361-882-6191; Fax: 361-814-1831.

Catholic Cemeteries—Mr. GREG SEAGRAVE, P.O. Box 2620, Corpus Christi, 78403-2620. Tel: 361-882-6191.

Office for Child Protection—GRACE S. RANK, R.N., B.S.N., P.O. Box 2620, Corpus Christi, 78403-2620. Tel: 361-882-6191.

Office of Communications—MARTY WIND, Dir. Communications, 1200 Lantana, Corpus Christi, 78407. Tel: 361-289-6437; Fax: 361-289-1420.

Education—Deacon RENE GONZALEZ, Supt., Chancery Office, P.O. Box 2620, Corpus Christi, 78403-2620. Tel: 361-882-6191; Fax: 361-814-1831.

Natural Family Planning - Understanding Sexuality—JANE TISDALE, Dir., 4455 S. Padre Island Dr. #28, Corpus Christi, 78411. Tel: 361-852-0222.

Newspaper "The South Texas Catholic"—Most Rev. EDMOND CARMODY, D.D., Publisher; PAULA GOLDAPP, Editor, P.O. Box 2620, Corpus Christi, 78403-2620. Tel: 361-882-6191; Fax: 361-883-2556.

Pastoral Institute for Ministry and Christian Service—Sr. ANNETTE WAGNER, I.W.B.S., Dir., Chancery Office, P.O. Box 2620, Corpus Christi, 78403-2620. Tel: 361-882-6191; Fax: 361-814-1831.

Office for Persons with Disabilities—Rev. DAVID WALSH, C.SS.R., Dir., 1322 Comanche, Corpus Christi, 78401. Tel: 361-814-2181; Fax: 361-654-2020.

Religious Education—Dr. FRANK LUCIDO, Diocesan Dir. Rel. Educ., Chancery Office, P.O. Box 2620, Corpus Christi, 78403-2620. Tel: 361-882-6191; Fax: 361-814-1831.

Office of Youth And Young Adult Ministry—Rev. PETE ELIZARDO, Dir., Chancery Office, P.O. Box 2620, Corpus Christi, 78403-2620. Tel: 361-882-6191; Fax: 361-882-1157.

Diocese of Corpus Christi Perpetual Benefit Endowment Fund, Inc.—P.O. Box 2620, Corpus Christi, 78403-2620. Tel: 361-882-6191.

Diocese of Corpus Christi Perpetual Deposit and Loan Fund, Inc.—P.O. Box 2620, Corpus Christi, 78403-2620. Tel: 361-882-6191.

Office of Worship—Rev. KEN ANDERSON, Dir., P.O. Box 2620, Corpus Christi, 78403-2620. Tel: 361-882-6191; Fax: 361-882-1018.

Juvenile Ministry—Deacon ISRAEL BLANCO, Dir., P.O. Box 2620, Corpus Christi, 78403-2620. Tel: 361-779-4416.

Hispanic Ministry—Deacon RUDY VASQUEZ, P.O. Box 2620, Corpus Christi, 78403-2620. Tel: 361-991-1866.

Other Offices and Organizations

Alhambra—Mr. KENNETH MORGAN JR., Grand Commander, 1013 Karnak, Corpus Christi, 78412. Tel: 361-992-2622; Mrs. PATRICIA MCLEMORE, Grand Sultana, 5641 Antigua, Corpus Christi, 78411. Tel: 361-855-0937.

Apostleship of the Sea—Rev. VINCENT M. PATRIZI, Dir., P.O. Box 1899, Corpus Christi, 78403. Tel: 361-883-4507.

Birthright Counseling—MILDRED HOFFER, Pres., 1422 Baldwin, Corpus Christi, 78404. Tel: 361-884-2662.

Blue Army (World Apostolate of Fatima)—Mrs. MARTHA MAJEK, Pres., 12126 Up River Rd., Corpus Christi, 78410. Tel: 361-242-1533.

Campus Ministries—Texas A&M University-Kingsville, St. Thomas Aquinas University Catholic Center, 1119 Santa Gertrudis, P.O. Box 2193, Kingsville, 78363. Tel: 361-592-7831; Fax: 362-592-8617. *Del Mark College, St. Thomas More, 2045 18th St., Corpus Christi, 78404.* Tel: 361-883-9308. *The Cardinal John Henry Newman Catholic Student Center, at Texas A&M Univ.-Corpus Christi, 7002 Ocean Dr., Corpus Christi, 78412.* Tel: 361-993-5898.

Catholic Daughters of the Americas—JULIE GUERRERO, Dist. 16, Corpus Christi. Tel: 361-528-3915; NATIVIDAD MARTINEZ, Dist. 23, Premont. Tel: 361-348-2058; DONNA NUNNELLY, Dist. 36, Three Rivers. Tel: 361-786-3158; DALIA SANCHEZ, Dist. 47, Portland. Tel: 361-643-3244; FRANCES SALAZAR, Dist. 41, Corpus Christi. Tel: 361-993-6654; ELIDA GARZA, Dist. 43, Hebbronville. Tel: 361-527-4185; EVE TREVINO, Dist. 48, Corpus Christi. Tel: 361-994-8553.

Catholic Charities—Sr. BARBARA NETEK, I.W.B.S., Admin., 1322 Comanche, Corpus Christi, 78401. Tel: 361-884-0651; Fax: 361-884-3956.

Catholic Charismatic Renewal—Rev. ROGER SMITH, Spiritual Dir.; CHRIS HOLLAND, Contact Person. Tel: 361-225-3449. Email: cmhdch@aol.com.

Corpus Christi Catholic Retreat Center, Inc.—Rev. Msgr. RICHARD SHIRLEY, Chm., P.O. Box 2620, Corpus Christi, 78403-2620. Tel: 361-882-6191; Fax: 361-882-1018.

Cursillo Movement (English)—JERRY FRANCO, Contact Person. Tel: 361-855-2621; Rev. Msgr. PATRICK HIGGINS, Spiritual Dir.

Cursillo Movement (Spanish)—RAY MUNOZ, Contact Person. Tel: 361-592-5990; Deacon MANNY MALDONADO, Spiritual Dir.

Diocesan Council Of Catholic Women—THERESA CHAVARRY, 2058 Jenica Dr., Ingleside, 78362. Tel: 361-960-3649.

Diocesan Telecommunications Corporation—MARTY WIND, Exec. Vice Pres. & Gen. Mgr., 1200 Lantana, Corpus Christi, 78407. Tel: 361-289-6437; Fax: 361-289-1420.

Disaster Relief—Sr. BARBARA NETEK, I.W.B.S., Admin., 1322 Comanche St., Corpus Christi, 78401. Tel: 361-884-0651.

Emergency Aid—Sr. BARBARA NETEK, I.W.B.S., Admin., 1322 Comanche, Corpus Christi, 78401. Tel: 361-884-0651.

Family Counseling—Sr. BARBARA NETEK, I.W.B.S., Admin., 1322 Comanche St., Corpus Christi, 78401. Tel: 361-884-0651.

Catholic Singles in Christ—Deacon BOB ALLEN, Dir.; Ms. LILY REYES, Pres., P.O. Box 2620, Corpus Christi, 78403-2620. Tel: 361-851-5019.

Catholic Engaged Encounter—Coordinators: ANGEL ESCOBAR; TULIS ESCOBAR. Email: tulises@swbell.net. Booking Couple: JESSE RODRIGUEZ; HOPIE RODRIGUEZ. Tel: 361-853-9850.

Guadalupanas—P.O. Box 2620, Corpus Christi, 78403-2620. Tel: 361-883-6015. Rev. FRANCISCO XAVIER MARTINEZ, S.T.L., Dir.; Mr. JOE DE LA GARZA, Contact Person.

Immigration Services—Sr. BARBARA NETEK, I.W.B.S., Admin., 1322 Comanche, Corpus Christi, 78401. Tel: 361-884-0651.

Jail Ministries—Deacon MARIO RIVERA, Dir. Tel: 361-664-9724; PEDRO COSTILLO, Coord. Tel: 361-960-4798.

Knights of Columbus—ADALBERTO PENA, Diocesan Deputy, 3601 Waterloo, Corpus Christi, 78415.

Lay Maryans—MANUEL GARCIA, Dir., 5310 Hitching Post Ln., Corpus Christi, 78415. Tel: 361-855-9288.

Legion of Mary—VIANN HERMANN, Pres., 610 Wilshire Pl., Corpus Christi, 78411. Tel: 361-855-8321.

Marriage Encounter—Coordinators: EDGAR VANGEEM; SANDRA VANGEEM. Tel: 361-882-7260.

Radio Stations - KLUX FM—RUSSEL WAYNE MARTIN, Dir. Broadcast Oper., 1200 Lantana St., Corpus Christi, 78407. Tel: 361-289-2487.

Serra International—JIM RIDDLEY, Pres., 3453 Aransas, Corpus Christi, 78411. Tel: 361-852-8367.

Theresians—DOROTHY SEERDER, Pres., 5050 Moultrie Dr., Corpus Christi, 78413. Tel: 361-992-4715.

Victim Assistance Coordinator—GRACE S. RANK, R.N., B.S.N. Tel: 361-882-6191, Ext. 388. Email: grank@diocesecc.org.

Villa Maria, Inc.—BARBARA A. MERLIN, Dir., Box 4, 3146 Saratoga Blvd., Corpus Christi, 78415. Tel: 361-857-6171; Fax: 361-857-6173.

CLERGY, PARISHES, MISSIONS AND PAROCHIAL SCHOOLS

CITY OF CORPUS CHRISTI
(NUECES COUNTY)

1—CORPUS CHRISTI CATHEDRAL (1853), [CEM] Rev. Msgr. Michael Howell, Rector; Rev. Pedro (Pete) T. Elizardo Jr.; Deacons Michael Mantz; Paul Moore.
Res.: 505 N. Upper Broadway, 78401. Tel: 361-883-4213; Fax: 361-883-1918.
Catechesis/Religious Program—Tel: 361-883-4213. Students 140.
Chapel—Emmanuel
Chapel—Blessed Sacrament
Chapel—Perpetual Eucharistic Adoration

2—SAINT ANDREW BY THE SEA PARISH (1986), Rev. Msgr. Tom McGettrick.
Res.: 14238 Encantada Ave., 78418-6432. Tel: 361-949-7193; Fax: 361-949-0717.
Catechesis/Religious Program—Tel: 361-949-8834. Students 73.

3—ST. ANSELM ANGLICAN USE COMMUNITY (1992), Rev. Eckley Macklin, S.O.L.T.
Catechesis/Religious Program—Students 2.
Church: 1200 Lantana St., 78407. Tel: 361-289-9160.

4—CHRIST THE KING (1946), (Mexican), Revs. Juan

Antonio Perez, O.SS.T.; Luke Mennella, O.SS.T.; Deacons Antonio M. Castillo; Israel Blanco.
Res.: 3423 Rojo, 78415. Tel: 361-883-2821; Fax: 361-888-7048.
Catechesis/Religious Program—Tel: 361-883-1404. Carol A. Enloe, D.R.E. Students 185.
Convent—1625 Arlington, 78415. Tel: 512-883-0212.

5—COLLEGIATE PARISH OF ST. THOMAS MORE (1990), Rev. Tomasz Kozub.
Church: 2045 18th St., 78404-3862. Tel: 361-888-9308; Fax: 361-888-6119.
Catechesis/Religious Program—Students 4.

6—SS. CYRIL AND METHODIUS (1947), (Hispanic), Rev. Msgr. Lawrence E. White, Pastor; Rev. P. R. Victor, Vicar; Deacon Ron Dubuque.
Res.: 3210 S. Padre Island Dr., 78415. Tel: 361-853-7371; Fax: 361-851-1438.
Catechesis/Religious Program—Tel: 361-852-1651. Mona Lucido, D.R.E. Students 500.

7—HOLY CROSS (1914), (African American), Rev. Msgr. Patrick Higgins.
Res.: 1109 N. Staples St., 78401. Tel: 361-888-4012; Fax: 361-888-5338.
Catechesis/Religious Program—Tel: 361-888-5259. Students 40.

8—HOLY FAMILY (1946), (Hispanic), Revs. Francisco Xavier Martinez, S.T.L., Pastor; Isaias Estepa; Deacon Manny Maldonado.
Res.: 2509 Nogales St., 78416. Tel: 361-832-3245; Fax: 361-882-4968.
Catechesis/Religious Program—Tel: 361-882-3245. Students 255.
Convent—1723 Frio St., 78417. Tel: 361-884-9142. Sisters of Mercy of the Blessed Sacrament 6.

9—SAINT JOHN THE BAPTIST (2001), Rev. Rafael Dopierala, Admin.; Deacon Stacy Millsap.
Mailing Address: P.O. Box 270143, 78427-0143. Tel: 361-991-4400; Fax: 361-991-4401.
Res.: 7522 Everhart, 78413.
Catechesis/Religious Program—Students 55.

10—ST. JOSEPH (1950), (Hispanic), Revs. Thomas L. Goodwin; Joseph Lawless, M.S.F.; Joseph A. Lopez; Deacon Reynaldo Rojas.
Res.: 710 S. 19th St., P.O. Box 5196, 78465-5196. Tel: 361-882-7912; Fax: 361-882-6853.
Catechesis/Religious Program—Mrs. Elizabeth Contreras, D.R.E. Students 80.
Convent—2100 Morris St., 78405. Tel: 361-888-4027. Sisters 3.

11—MARY, MOTHER OF THE CHURCH MISSION, Rev. Shaji Varghese.
Mailing Address: 1755 Frio St., 78417. Tel: 361-852-0249; Fax: 361-852-8463.

12—ST. MICHAEL THE ARCHANGEL LATIN MASS COMMUNITY (1995), Rev. Paul L. Roman, F.S.S.P.
Res.: 3036 Saratoga Blvd., 78415. Tel: 361-855-8244.
Catechesis/Religious Program—Students 10.

13—MOST PRECIOUS BLOOD (1966), Revs. Bob Dunn; Rodolfo D. Vasquez; Deacons Fernando G. Rodriguez; Garland Frazier; Ray Ahlers.
Res.: 3502 Saratoga Blvd., 78415. Tel: 361-854-3800; Fax: 361-854-9253.
Catechesis/Religious Program—Tel: 361-854-9219. Students 445.

14—OUR LADY OF GUADALUPE (1969), (Hispanic), Revs. Manuel Hernandez Jr.; Flover H. Osorio; Deacons Armando Cavada; Joaquin Ortiz.
Res.: 540 Hiawatha, 78405. Tel: 361-882-1951; Fax: 361-888-5813.
Catechesis/Religious Program—Tel: 361-882-8801. Mary Cabriales, D.R.E. Students 170.

15—OUR LADY OF MOUNT CARMEL (1969), Rev. Sebastian Pasupalety.
Res.: 1080 S. Clarkwood Rd., 78406. Tel: 361-265-0610; Fax: 361-265-0757.
Mission—St. Vivian 3516 FM 665 W., Robstown, 78380.

16—OUR LADY OF PERPETUAL HELP (1954), Rev. Msgr. Michael Heras; Revs. Ernesto Perez; James Farfaglia; Jose Angel Ortiz.
Mailing Address: 5830 Williams Dr., 78412. Tel: 361-991-7891; Fax: 361-993-1211.
Catechesis/Religious Program—Students 335.
Mission—St. Helena of the True Cross of Jesus (2001), Woolridge Rd., & Victoria Park Rd., Nueces Co. 78412.

17—OUR LADY OF THE PILLAR (1964), (Hispanic), Rev. Marcos Martinez; Deacon Armando M. Bolanos.
Res.: 1101 Bloomington St., 78416. Tel: 361-852-6327; Fax: 361-852-2614.
Catechesis/Religious Program—Tel: 361-852-6843. Students 219.

18—OUR LADY OF THE ROSARY (1967), (Hispanic), Rev. John V. Karumanchi, Admin. In Res., Rev. Mahendra Anandappa, S.S.S. (FTW).
Res.: 1123 Main Dr., 78409. Tel: 361-241-2004; 361-242-9571; Fax: 361-242-1099.
Catechesis/Religious Program—Tel: 361-241-6185. Students 37.

19—OUR LADY STAR OF THE SEA (1950), [CEM] Rev. Vincent M. Patrizi; Deacon M.M. Peter Horseman.
Res.: 3110 E. Causeway Blvd., P.O. Box 1899, 78403. Tel: 361-883-4507; Fax: 361-888-6411.
Catechesis/Religious Program—Students 80.

20—ST. PATRICK (1944), (Hispanic), Revs. Roger R. Smith; Edmund Benedetti, S.J.; Dennis P. Zerr.
Res.: 3350 S. Alameda St., 78411. Tel: 361-855-7391; Fax: 361-853-4790.
Catechesis/Religious Program—Tel: 361-855-7567. Students 330.

21—ST. PAUL THE APOSTLE (1967), Revs. Hubert Hosanna Anthony (India); James G. Stembler.
Res.: 2233 Waldron Rd., 78418. Tel: 361-937-3864; Fax: 361-939-7774.
Catechesis/Religious Program—Tel: 361-937-6908. Sr. M. Purificacion Palis, O.P., D.R.E. Students 281.

22—ST. PETER PRINCE OF APOSTLES (1957), Rev. Morgan Rowsome.
Res. & Mailing Address: 3901 Violet Rd., 78410-2924. Tel: 361-241-3249; Fax: 361-241-0533.
Catechesis/Religious Program—Tel: 361-241-3372. Sr. Jude Janecek, I.W.B.S., D.R.E. Students 626.
Mission—St. Mary 4849 Cynthia, Nueces Co. 78410. Tel: 361-241-3432.

23—ST. PHILIP THE APOSTLE (1982), Rev. Hanh Van Pham; Deacons Bob Allen; Gaspar Gomez.
Res.: 6329 N. Washam St., 78414. Tel: 361-993-9474; 361-315-0505.
Church: 3513 Cimarron Rd., 78414. Tel: 361-991-5146; Fax: 361-991-9135.
Catechesis/Religious Program—Tel: 361-993-1710; Fax: 361-993-1710. Sr. Esther Gerbermann, D.R.E. Students 521.

24—ST. PIUS X (1963), Rev. Msgr. Richard Shirley; Revs. Bradley A. Barber; William J. Marquis; Deacons Salvador Alvarado; George Phillips.
Res.: 5620 Gollihar Rd., 78412. Tel: 361-993-4053; Fax: 361-992-0352.
Catechesis/Religious Program—Tel: 361-993-9024. Students 257.

25—SACRED HEART (1916), (Hispanic), [CEM] Revs. Jose A. Almazan; John V. Karumanchi Deacon Rudy Ramirez.
Res.: 422 N Alameda St., 78401-2604. Tel: 361-883-6082; Fax: 361-883-6248.
Catechesis/Religious Program—Tel: 361-882-1472. Students 43.
Station—Nueces County Jail, Tel: 361-887-2300.
Station—Navarro Place, Tel: 361-882-492-.

26—ST. THERESA (1947), Rev. Richard Libby In Res., Rev. Msgr. Raymond F. Rau (BRK).
Res.: 1302 Lantana St., 78407. Tel: 361-289-2759; Fax: 361-289-2018.
Catechesis/Religious Program—Tel: 361-289-2238. Mrs. Josie Martinez, D.R.E. Students 40.

OUTSIDE THE CITY OF CORPUS CHRISTI

AGUA DULCE, NUECES CO., ST. FRANCES OF ROME (1934), (Czech—Hispanic), Rev. James A. Hayes, M.S.C.
Mailing Address: P.O. Box 598, 78330. Tel: 361-998-2216; Fax: 361-998-2149.
Catechesis/Religious Program—Students 119.
Mission—St. Michael the Archangel Banquete, Nueces Co.
Catechesis/Religious Program—Students 150.

ALICE, JIM WELLS CO.

1—ST. ELIZABETH (1918), Rev. Msgr. Leonard Pivonka, J.C.D.; Deacons James A. Carlisle; Alan K. Borse. 603 E. 5th St., 78333.
Res.: 518 N. Almond St., P.O. Box 1009, 78333. Tel: 361-664-6481; Fax: 361-664-7243.
Catechesis/Religious Program—Tel: 361-664-7719. Students 255.

2—ST. JOSEPH (1911), (Hispanic), Revs. Emilio B. Jimenez, Admin.; Glen Mullan; Jose Naul Ordonez; Deacon Mario Rivera.
Res.: 801 S. Reynolds St., 78332. Tel: 361-664-7551; Fax: 361-664-2388.
School—Tel 361-664-4642. Students 101.
Catechesis/Religious Program—311 Dewey St., 78332. Students 298.
Convent—808 S. Wright, P.O. Box 868, 78332. Tel: 361-664-6283. Sisters 3.
Mission—Sacred Heart, Jim Wells Co.
Chapel—Perpetual Eucharistic Adoration

3—OUR LADY OF GUADALUPE (1969), (Hispanic), Rev. Raynaldo Yrlas Jr.
Res.: 1318 Guerra St., P.O. Box 411, 78332. Tel: 361-664-2953; Fax: 361-664-4001.
Catechesis/Religious Program—Tel: 361-664-0437; Fax: 361-664-0437. Dora Rosales, D.R.E. Students 285.
Mission—Santo Nino De Atocha, Jim Wells Co. 78333. Fax: 361-664-2953.

4—ST. PETER MISSION, Rev. George Dobosz.
Mailing Address: P.O. Box 2150, 78333-2150. Tel: 361-664-3942.

ARANSAS PASS, SAN PATRICIO CO., ST. MARY, STAR OF THE SEA (1948), Rev. Michael Lenihan.
Res.: 342 S. Rife St., 78336. Tel: 361-758-2662; Fax: 361-758-3964.
Catechesis/Religious Program—Ginny Vega, D.R.E. & Sec. Students 307.

BANQUETE, NUECES CO., SAINT MICHAEL THE ARCHANGEL, Formerly Saint Michael the Archangel Mission (1857), (Hispanic), [JC] Rev. J. Patrick Serna.
Mailing Address: P.O. Box 9, 78339. Tel: 361-387-8371; Fax: 361-387-7607.
Catechesis/Religious Program—Students 225.

BEEVILLE, BEE CO.

1—ST. JAMES (Alta Vista) (1966), (Hispanic), Rev. Balaswamy Pasala; Deacon Jesus Vasquez.
Res.: 605 Alta Vista, 78102. Tel: 361-358-4825; Fax: 361-358-5150.
Catechesis/Religious Program—Miss Mary Elizabeth Garcia, D.R.E. Students 86.

2—ST. JOSEPH (Alta Vista) (1895), [CEM] Revs. Patrick K. Donohoe; Lowery Ross; Deacons Luis Trevino; Rolando R. Salazar.
Res.: 609 E. Gramman St., 78102. Tel: 361-358-3239; Fax: 361-358-4270.
Catechesis/Religious Program—Debra Olivares, (Elementary). Students 261.
Convent—610 E. Gramman St., 78102. Tel: 361-358-9405; Fax: 361-362-0973. Sisters 5.

3—OUR LADY OF VICTORY (1908), (Hispanic), Rev. Richard Gonzales.
Mailing Address: 707 North Ave. E., 78102. Tel: 361-358-3761; Fax: 361-358-2028.
Rectory—403 W. Carter St., 78102.
Catechesis/Religious Program—Tel: 361-358-4241. Sr. Julien Valdevieso, O.P., D.R.E. (Elementary); Iantha Richardson, D.R.E. (Junior High & High School). Students 200.

4—SACRED HEART MISSION (1966),, (Independent) Rev. Joseph V. Varghese, Admin.; Deacon Manuel G. Carranco.
Mailing Address: P.O. Box 414, Pettus, 78146-0414. Tel: 361-375-2512.
Catechesis/Religious Program—Guadalupe Aguirre, D.R.E. Students 14.

BENAVIDES, DUVAL CO., ST. ROSE OF LIMA (1941), (Hispanic), Rev. Andrew Hejdak.
Res.: 203 Santa Rosa de Lima St., P.O. Drawer W, 78341. Tel: 361-256-3427; Fax: 361-256-4780.
Catechesis/Religious Program—Tel: 361-256-3319. Gracie Garcia, D.R.E. Students 162.
Mission—St. Joseph P.O. Box W, San Jose Ranch, Duval Co. 78341.

BISHOP, NUECES CO., ST. JAMES (1938), [CEM] Rev. Patrick O'Connor, M.S.C.
Res.: 601 W. 3rd St., P.O. Box 843, 78343. Tel: 361-584-3250; Fax: 361-584-1046.
Catechesis/Religious Program—Students 98.
Mission—St. James 310 W. Ave. B, Driscoll, Nueces Co. 78351.

EDROY, SAN PATRICIO CO., OUR LADY OF GUADALUPE MISSION, Rev. Joseph Kallukalam.
Mailing Address: P.O. Box 127, 78352. Tel: 361-368-3097; Fax: 361-368-3105.

FALFURRIAS, BROOKS CO., SACRED HEART (1914), (Hispanic), [CEM] Rev. Matthew J. Stephan; Deacon Ricardo E. Costley.
Res.: 304 S. Caldwell St., 78355. Tel: 361-325-3455; Fax: 361-325-2486.
Catechesis/Religious Program—Tel: 361-325-5067. Joan Bostwick, D.R.E. Students 435.
Mission—St. Ann c/o Sacred Heart Parish, Encino, Brooks Co. 78355.

FREER, DUVAL CO., ST. MARY (1968), Rev. Angel Montano; Deacon Eluterio Bitoni.
Res.: 1500 Duval St., Box B, 78357. Tel: 361-394-6832; Fax: 361-394-6568.
Catechesis/Religious Program—Tel: 361-394-7244. Rosie Trevino. Students 220.

GEORGE WEST, LIVE OAK CO., ST. GEORGE (1924), Rev. Joseph Olikkara, M.S.T. (India).
Oratory— [CEM] [JC] 304 Crockett St., P.O. Box 580, Live Oak Co. 78022. Tel: 361-449-1893; Fax: 361-449-1886.
Catechesis/Religious Program—Tel: 361-449-1336. Debbie Brown, D.R.E. Students 175.
Mission—St. Joseph [CEM] [JC] Gussetville, Live Oak Co.

GREGORY, SAN PATRICIO CO., IMMACULATE CONCEPTION (1926), (Hispanic), Rev. Raju Thottankara; Deacon Juan Gomez.
Res.: 107 Church St., P.O. Box 108, 78359-0108. Tel: 361-643-4505; Fax: 361-643-1509.
Catechesis/Religious Program—Students 379.

INGLESIDE, SAN PATRICIO CO., OUR LADY OF THE ASSUMPTION (1970), Rev. Thomas Wellar.
Res.: 2414 Main, 78362. Tel: 361-776-2644; 361-776-2446; Fax: 361-776-3963.
Catechesis/Religious Program—Faith Repka, D.R.E. Students 185.
Our Lady of the Assumption Early Learning Center—Tel: 361-776-3643.

KINGSVILLE, KLEBERG CO.

1—ST. GERTRUDE (1908), (Hispanic), Rev. Piotr A. Koziel; Deacon John R. Joiner.

Office Address—605 Caesar Ave., 78363. Tel: 361-592-7351; Fax: 361-592-0028.
Res.: 1120 S. 8th St., 78363.
School—Tel: 361-592-6522; Fax: 361-592-0100. Students 121.
Catechesis/Religious Program—Tel: 361-592-2443. Sr. Colette Brehony, I.W.B.S., D.R.E. Students 180.
Mission—St. Thomas Aquinas Catholic Campus Center - Texas A & M P.O. Box 2193, Kleberg Co. 78363. Tel: 361-592-5781.

2—St. Joseph (1973), (Hispanic), Revs. Romeo Salinas, Admin.; Jairo Motta Castano (Colombia).
Res.: 1400 Brookshire, P.O. Box 1602, 78364-1602. Tel: 361-592-5689; Fax: 361-516-1397.
Catechesis/Religious Program— Sr. Maxie Cruz, D.R.E. Students 210.

3—St. Martin (1914), (Hispanic), Rev. James Foelker, O.M.I.; Deacons Tiburcio Garcia; Raul G. Rosales.
Res.: 715 N. Eighth St., 78363. Tel: 361-592-4602; Fax: 361-592-4602.
Catechesis/Religious Program—Tel: 361-592-0881. Gloria DeLeon, D.R.E. Students 143.
Convent—919 N. Ninth St., 78363. Tel: 361-595-1087. Sisters 10.
Mission—Christ the King King Ranch, Kleberg Co.

4—Our Lady of Good Counsel (1967), (Mexican), [CEM 3] [JC] Rev. Paul Puthenangady.
Res.: 1102 E. Kleberg, 78363. Tel: 361-592-3489; Fax: 361-592-3489.
Catechesis/Religious Program—Tel: 361-592-9546. Norma Hinojosa, D.R.E. Students 106.

5—St. Thomas Aquinas, University Catholic Center (1990), Rev. Piotr A. Koziel.
Res. & Mailing Address: 1120 S. 8th, 78363. Tel: 361-592-5781.
Church: 1119 W. Santa Gertrudis, 78363.

Mathis, San Patricio Co.

1—Saint Patrick Mission (1829), (Hispanic), [CEM] Rev. Francis Sebastian.
Res.: 20742 Magnolia, 78368. Tel: 361-547-5748; Fax: 361-547-8004.

2—Sacred Heart (1942), [JC] Rev. Jose Angel Salazar.
Res.: 114 S. Aransas, P.O. Box 608, 78368-0608. Tel: 361-547-9181; Fax: 361-547-6111.
Catechesis/Religious Program—Glenn Goldapp, D.R.E. Students 471.

Odem, San Patricio Co., Sacred Heart (1934), (Hispanic), Rev. Henry Heese.
Res.: 401 Willis St., P.O. Box 276, 78370. Tel: 361-368-9156.
Catechesis/Religious Program—Tel: 361-368-2746. Sr. Guadalupe Flores, C.M.S.T., D.R.E. Students 268.
Convent—402 Borden, 78370. Tel: 512-368-2560. Sisters 3.

Orange Grove, Jim Wells Co., St. John of the Cross (1925), [CEM] Rev. Prince Kuruvila, Admin.
Mailing Address: P.O. Box 329, 78372. Tel: 361-384-2795; Fax: 361-384-0056.
Catechesis/Religious Program—Tel: 361-384-2246. Students 232.

Port Aransas, Nueces Co., St. Joseph (1860), [JC] Rev. Msgr. Gregory S. Deane.
Mailing Address: 412 Lantana St., 78373. Tel: 512-749-5825; Fax: 512-749-5509.
Catechesis/Religious Program—Students 64.

Portland, San Patricio Co., Our Lady of Mount Carmel (1961), Revs. Mark Chamberlin; Jerome G. Zurovetz; Deacon John W. Sutherland.
Res.: 1008 Austin St., 78374. Tel: 361-643-7533; Fax: 361-643-5544.
Catechesis/Religious Program—Tel: 361-643-3548. Mrs. Melanee Warner, D.R.E. Students 422.

Premont, Jim Wells Co., St. Theresa of the Infant Jesus (1958), [JC] Revs. John C. Ouellette; Banda Showry; Deacon Raul Hinojosa.
Res.: 235 S.W. 4th St., P.O. Box 569, 78375. Tel: 361-348-2202; Fax: 361-348-3533.
Catechesis/Religious Program—Students 192.
Mission—Immaculate Conception Concepcion, Duval Co.
Mission—St. Francis of Assisi Rios, Duval Co.
Mission—Our Lady of Guadalupe Ramirez, Duval Co.

Refugio, Refugio Co.

1—St. James the Apostle (1886), (Hispanic), [CEM] [JC] Rev. Zenon Konowalek.
Mailing Address: 205 E. Santiago St., 78377.
Catechesis/Religious Program—Tel: 361-526-2714. Students 114.

2—Our Lady of Refuge (1795), [CEM] [JC] Rev. Gnana Prakash Chinnabathini (India).
Res.: 1008 S. Alamo St., 78377. Tel: 361-526-2083; Fax: 361-526-5653.
Catechesis/Religious Program—106 W. Roca, 78377. Tel: 361-526-2053. Students 56.

Robstown, Nueces Co.

1—St. Anthony (1914), (Hispanic), [CEM] Revs. Gerard J. Sheehan, S.O.L.T.; Isidore Usit Nyein, S.O.L.T.; Eduardo Montemayor, S.O.L.T.; Deacon Wayne Lickteig, S.O.L.T.
Res.: 204 Dunne St., P.O. Box 792, 78380-0792. Tel: 361-387-2772; 361-767-1705; Fax: 361-387-2774.
Catechesis/Religious Program—Tel: 361-387-9874. Eva Hernandez, D.R.E. Students 225.
Convent—612 Indiana, 78380. Tel: 512-387-3810.
Mission—St. Mary, Nueces Co. Tel: 361-387-1705.

2—St. John Nepomucene (1924), (Czech), [JC] In Res., Rev. Thomas Showalter, S.O.L.T.; Deacon John Demay.
Res.: 603 N. First St., 78380. Tel: 361-387-3705; Fax: 361-387-3681.
Catechesis/Religious Program—Tel: 361-387-3011. Melinda Youngblood, D.R.E. Students 94.

3—St. Thomas the Apostle (1980), Rev. Matthew Lyng; Deacon Bill Cleavelin.
Office—16602 F.M. 624, 78380. Tel: 361-387-1312; Fax: 512-387-9311.
Catechesis/Religious Program—Shirley Syamken, D.R.E. Students 282.

Rockport, Aransas Co.

1—St. Peter Indo-Chinese Parish (1989), (Vietnamese), [JC 2] Rev. Peter Nghi Duc Pham, S.O.L.T.
Mailing Address: P.O. Box 1060, 78382. Tel: 361-729-3008; Fax: 361-727-0191.
Catechesis/Religious Program—2761 FM 1781, 78382-1060. Tel: 361-549-7850. Students 45.

2—Sacred Heart (1838), Rev. Msgr. Louis F. Kihneman; Rev. Tung Tran; Deacons Jerre H. Ledbetter; George Joe Wiest.
Res.: 704 Cornwall St., 78382. Tel: 361-729-2174; Fax: 361-729-1989.
Catechesis/Religious Program—Tel: 361-729-8283. Students 380.
Convent—114 N. Church St., 78382. Tel: 361-729-5311.

San Diego, Duval Co., St. Francis de Paula (1866), Revs. Benito Retortillo, O.P.; Epifanio Rodriguez, O.P.; Deacons Abelardo Garza; Carlos Tamayo.
Res.: 401 S. Victoria St., P.O. Box 279, 78384. Tel: 361-279-3596; Fax: 361-279-8288.
Catechesis/Religious Program—411 S. Victoria St., 78384. Tel: 361-279-3586. Students 380.
Mission—St. Joseph Palito Blanco, Jim Wells Co. 78384.

Sarita, Kenedy Co., Our Lady of Guadalupe (1935), Rev. Adolph K. Kaler, O.M.I.
Mailing Address: P.O. Box 6, 78385. Tel: 361-294-5350; Fax: 361-294-5406.
Catechesis/Religious Program—Students 25.
Mission—Santa Elena Norias Ranch, Kenedy Co.

Sinton, San Patricio Co.

1—Our Lady of Guadalupe (1954), (Hispanic), [CEM] [JC] Rev. David Taurasi, Pastor.
Res.: 725 Sodville Ave., 78387. Tel: 361-364-2210; Fax: 361-364-5204.
Catechesis/Religious Program—Tel: 361-364-4542. Students 338.

2—Sacred Heart (1916), Revs. Paul Peter Antony (India); Efren B. Nano, Admin.
Res.: 906 E. Sinton St., P.O. Box 266, 78387. Tel: 361-364-1768; Fax: 361-364-5325.
Catechesis/Religious Program—Tel: 361-364-1772. Mary Connors, D.R.E.; Solomon T. Willis III, D.R.E. Students 257.
Mission—St. Paul P.O. Box 266, St. Paul, San Patricio Co. 78387.

Skidmore, Bee Co., Immaculate Conception (1915), [JC] Rev. Paul K. Rajareegam (India).
Res.: 600 First St., P.O. Box 189, 78389. Tel: 361-287-3256; Fax: 361-287-3696.
Catechesis/Religious Program—Students 58.
Mission—St. Francis Xavier Frio St., Tynan, Bee Co. 78384.

Taft, San Patricio Co.

1—Holy Family (1957), [JC] Rev. George Kunnath, M.C.B.S. (India).
Mailing Address: P.O. Box 173, 78390. Tel: 361-528-3132; Fax: 361-528-4941.
Res.: 646 McIntyre, 78390.
Catechesis/Religious Program—Students 68.

2—Immaculate Conception (1928), Rev. Jesus Francisco Lopez.
Res. & Mailing Address: 120 E. Escobedo, P.O. Box 868, 78390. Tel: 361-528-2626; 361-528-4842; Fax: 361-528-3907.
Catechesis/Religious Program—Tel: 361-528-5300. Students 503.

Three Rivers, Live Oak Co., Sacred Heart (1948), Rev. Piotr J. Gajda.
303 E. Alexandra, P.O. Box 729, 78071-0729. Tel: 361-786-3398; 361-786-1010; Fax: 361-786-1928.
Catechesis/Religious Program—Students 118.
Mission—Our Lady of Guadalupe P.O. Box 729, Pawnee, Bee Co. 78071.

Tivoli, Refugio Co., Our Lady of Guadalupe (1936),, Mailing Address: P.O. Drawer I, 77990-0001. Tel: 361-286-3349; Fax: 361-286-3665.
Catechesis/Religious Program—Students 65.
Mission—St. Anthony of Padua Austwell, Refugio Co.
Mission—St. Dennis O'Connor Ranch, Refugio Co.

Vattman, Kleberg Co., Our Lady of Consolation (1914), (German), [CEM] Rev. Brendan Michael Ashe.
Res.: 204 Palm Ave., 78379. Tel: 361-297-5255; Fax: 361-297-5155.
Catechesis/Religious Program—Students 45.
Mission—Our Lady of Guadalupe 111 S. Second St., Riviera, Kleberg Co.
Mission—Sacred Heart W. County Rd. 2160, Ricardo, Kleberg Co.

Violet, Nueces Co., St. Anthony (1910), [CEM] Rev. Richard W. Filice.
Res.: 3918 County Rd. 61, Robstown, 78380. Tel: 361-387-4434; Fax: 361-767-3881.
Catechesis/Religious Program—Students 25.

Woodsboro, Refugio Co., St. Therese, The Little Flower (1915), (Hispanic), [CEM] Rev. Celestine Murray.
Res.: 315 Pugh St., Drawer 1076, 78393-1140. Tel: 361-543-4166; Fax: 361-543-5922.
Catechesis/Religious Program—Tel: 361-543-5306. Students 165.
Mission—St. Mary Bayside, Refugio Co.

On Special Assignment:
Rev. Msgr.—
Flores, Daniel E., S.T.D.
Revs.—
Downey, Donald, Chap.
Gutirerrez, Jose, Chap.
Nesse, Paul, Dir. Vocations
Nwachukwu, Thomas Kizito, Chap.
Spencer, Robert
Walsh, David, C.SS.R., Dir., Office of Persons with Disabilities

---

On Duty Outside the Diocese:
Revs.—
Bauta, Krzysztof T., 5411 Vicksburg, Arlington, 76017.
Bergin, Paschal, P.O. Box 188, Runge, 78151.
McGerity, Francis X., Ave Maria University: Pre-theologcte, 1025 Commons Circle, Naples, FL 34119.

Military Chaplains:
Rev. Msgr.—
Chilen, Michael D., 18 Ripley Dr., Redstone Arsenal, AL 35808.
Rev.—
Shuley, Keith, C.C., LCDR CHC USN, USS Pelcliu (LHA-5), FPU, AP 96624-1620. U.S. Coast Guard, Active Duty

---

Retired:
Most Rev.—
Gracida, Rene H., P.O. Box 2620, 78403-2620.
Rev. Msgrs.—
Adams, Michael, Mount Carmel Home, 4130 S. Alameda, 78411.
Meany, Thomas, 3146 Saratoga #1, 78415.
Rau, Raymond, 1302 Lantana St., 78407.
Tengler, Alvin, 1011 7th St., 78404.
Thompson, William P.A., 4809 Fern Forest, 78413.
Revs.—
Boensch, Gregory A., 471 Englehart Rd., San Antonio, 78264.
Bradley, Robert, Mt. Carmel Home, 4130 S. Alameda, 78411. Tel: 361-855-3767
Brown, W.T. St. John, 1177 E. Mesquite Ave., Palm Springs, CA 92264-8416. Tel: 760-325-0354
Burke, Michael, c/o Immaculate Conception Rectory, P.O. Box 1670, Waterbury, CT 06721-1670.
Critchlow, Donald E., 10605 Grant Rd., Ste. 208, Houston, 77070.
De Llano, Domingo, 6106 Vance Jackson, #5, San Antonio, 78230.
Doherty, Charles, 127 Lakeview Rd., Rockport, 78382.
Feminelli, John, Villa Maria, 3146 Saratoga, 78415.
Fidalgo, Federico, 8326 N. Vandiver, #508, San Antonio, 78209.
Garcia, Eduardo, Villa Maria, 3146 Saratoga, Box 26, 78418.
Hamilton, James, c/o St. Mary Star of the Sea, P.O. Box 1541, Aransas Pass, 78335.
Iglesias, Luis Fernando, P.O. Box 1395, Freer, 78357.
Killeen, John P.
Masterson, Clyde, Pocasset Lodge #12, Old Pocasset Ln., Apt. 123, Johnston, RI 02919.
McGowan, Seamus, 132 Sabine, Portland, 78374.
McNomara, Peter, 184 Vista Linda, Zapata, 78706.
Mikolajczyk, Bruno, 1800 Fuller Wiser Rd. #706, Euless, 76039.
Noone, Sean, Villa Maria Apartments, 3146 Saratoga Blvd., Box 12, 78415. Tel: 361-853-4814;

361-855-5869 (Apartments)
O'Donovan, Thomas P., Villa Marie Apts., 3146 Saratoga # 46, 78415.
Walsh, Arthur, Mt. Carmel Home, 4130 Alameda, 78411.

Permanent Deacons:
Ahlers, Ray, Most Precious Blood, Corpus Christi
Allen, Robert J., Assoc. Dir. Pastoral Svcs., St. Philip the Apostle, Corpus Christi
Alvarado, Carlos
Alvarado, Salvador, St. Pius X, Corpus Christi
Benys, Victor, Our Lady of Perpetual Help, Corpus Christi
Bitoni, Eluterio, St. Mary Parish, Freer
Blanco, Israel, Christ the King, Corpus Christi
Bolanos, Armando M., Our Lady of Pillar, Corpus Christi
Borse, Alan T., St. Elizabeth, Alice
Botello, Armando, On Sabbatical
Breland, Walter N.
Carlisle, James A., St. Elizabeth, Alice
Carranco, Manuel G., Chap., Sacred Heart Mission
Carrizales, Alejandro, Holy Family, Corpus Christi
Castillo, Antonio M., Christ the King, Corpus Christi
Cavada, Armando, Our Lady of Guadalupe, Corpus Christi
Cleavelin, William, St. Thomas the Apostle, Robstown
Costley, Ricardo E., Dir. Formation & Deanery Rep., Sacred Heart, Falfurrias
de Anda, Candido, St. Francis of Rome, Agua Dulce
Dubuque, Roland, SS. Cyril & Methodius Parish, Corpus Christi
Flores, Arturo, Our Lady of Good Counsel, Kingsville
Frazier, Garland, Most Precious Blood, Corpus Christi
Garcia, Tiburcio, St. Martin, Kingsville
Garza, Abelardo, St. Francis de Paula, San Diego
Gomez, Gaspar, St. Phillip the Apostle, Corpus Christi
Gomez, Juan, Immaculate Conception, Taft
Grassedonio, Roy M., St. Andrew by the Sea, Corpus Christi
Hinojosa, Raul, Spiritual Dir. Cursillo Movement, Mission of St. Theresa of the Infant Jesus, Premont
Horseman, M.M. Peter, Our Lady Star of the Sea, Corpus Christi
Joiner, John R., Admin. Asst. Diaconate Formation, St. Gertrude, Kingsville
Kaizen, Joseph, (Retired), St. Paul the Apostle, Corpus Christi
Lara, Antonio S., Diocesan Dir. Charismatic Renewal, Immaculate Conception, Skidmore
Ledbetter, Jerre H., Deanery Representative, Sacred Heart, Rockport
Lickteig, Wayne, S.O.L.T., Dir., Lay Council of Society, St. Anthony, Robstown
Maldonado, Manny, Holy Family, Corpus Christi
Mantz, Michael, Dir. Deacons, Corpus Christi Cathedral, Corpus Christi
Millsap, Stacy, St. Phillip the Apostle Corpus Christi
Millsap, Stanley, Co-Dir. Deacons & Dir. Human Resources
Moore, Paul, Assoc. Dir. Deacons, Cathedral, Corpus Christi
Nartowicz, Edward, St. Paul the Apostle, Our Lady of Guadalupe Chapel, N.A.S., Corpus Christi
Oliver, Willard F., (Retired)
Ortiz, Joaquin
Ouellette, Roland, Sacred Heart, Three Rivers
Panas, George, (Retired)
Phillips, George, St. Pius X, Corpus Christi
Ramirez, Rudy, Sacred Heart, Corpus Christi
Rauen, Mike, Our Lady of Perpetual Help, Corpus Christi
Rivera, Gonzalo, (Retired)
Rivera, Mario, Area Coord. Cursillo Movement & Deanery Representative, St. Joseph, Alice
Rodriguez, Alonzo, (Retired)
Rodriguez, Fernando G., Most Precious Blood, Corpus Christi
Rodriguez, Reynaldo, Jr.
Rojas, Reynaldo, St. Joseph, Corpus Christi
Rosales, Raul G., St. Martin, Kingsville
Salazar, Rolando R., St. Joseph, Beeville
Sutherland, John W., Our Lady of Mount Carmel, Portland
Tamayo, Carlos, St. Francis de Paula, San Diego
Trevino, Luis, St. Joseph, Beeville
Vasquez, Guadalupe C.
Vasquez, Jesus, St. James, Beeville
Wiest, George Joe, Outreach Coord. for St. Vincent de Paul Society, Sacred Heart, Rockport, Chap. Prision Ministry
Ybarra, Pedro M., (Retired)

INSTITUTIONS LOCATED IN THE DIOCESE

[A] HIGH SCHOOLS

CORPUS CHRISTI. *Incarnate Word Academy High School* (Private) , 2910 S. Alameda, 78404. Tel: 361-883-0857; Fax: 361-883-2185. Email: lugaresi@iwacc.org. Web: www.iwacc.org. Mr. Gerald Lugaresi, Prin. Sisters 8; Lay Teachers 20; Students 234.

[B] JUNIOR HIGH AND ELEMENTARY SCHOOLS

CORPUS CHRISTI. *Bishop Garriga Middle School* (Diocesan) , 3114 Saratoga Blvd., 78415. Tel: 361-851-0853; Fax: 361-853-5145. Email: rdavila@bgms.org. Web: www.bgms.org. Rosario Davila, Prin. Lay Teachers 8; Students 85.

Central Catholic Elementary (Parochial) , 1218 Comanche St., 78401. Tel: 512-883-3873; Fax: 361-883-5879. Email: sisteranne@centralcatholic.us. Web: www.centralcatholic.us. Sr. Anne Brigid Schlegel, I.W.B.S., Prin. Sisters 2; Lay Teachers 6; Students 135.

Christ the King School (Parochial) , 1625 Arlington Dr., 78415. Tel: 361-883-5391; Fax: 361-888-9207. Email: dmuscarello@ctkcrusaders.org. Web: christthecatholicschool.org. Denise Muscarello, Prin. Priests 2; Lay Teachers 12; Students 80.

SS. Cyril and Methodius School (Parochial) , 5002 Kostoryz Rd., 78415. Tel: 361-853-9392; Fax: 361-853-0282. Email: princhatch@aol.com. Web: www.mahpro.com/sscm.html. Mrs. Nannette Hatch, Prin. Lay Teachers 8; Students 120.

Holy Family School (Parochial) , 2526 Soledad St., 78416. Tel: 361-884-9142; Fax: 361-884-1750. Email: holyfamilyschool@interconnet.net. Web: www.holyfamilyangles.com. Sr. Patricia Rodriguez, H.M.S.S., Prin.; Rev. Francisco Xavier Martinez, S.T.L., Pastor. Sisters 3; Lay Teachers 13; Students 247.

Incarnate Word Elementary (Private) , 450 Chamberlain, 78404. Tel: 361-883-0857; Fax: 361-883-2185. Email: sherlihy@iwaccel.org. Web: www.iwacc.org. Sr. Camelia Herlihy, Prin. Sisters 4; Lay Teachers 16; Students 268.

Incarnate Word Middle School (Private) , 2917 Austin St., 78404. Tel: 361-883-0857, Ext. 113; Fax: 361-882-9193. Email: agarza@iwacc.org. Web: www.iwacc.org. Mr. Aldolfo Garza, Prin. Priests 1; Sisters 1; Lay Teachers 19; Students 205.

Most Precious Blood School (Parochial) , 3502 Saratoga Blvd., 78415. Tel: 361-852-4800; Fax: 361-855-8707. Email: mpbschool@birch.net. Religious Teachers 2; Lay Teachers 11; Students 160.

Our Lady of Perpetual Help School (Parochial) , 5814 Williams Dr., 78412. Tel: 361-991-3305; 361-992-5951; Fax: 361-994-1806. Email: lindacantu@hotmail.com. Web: www.olphcctex.org. Ms. Linda Cantu, Prin. Sisters 1; Lay Teachers 14; Students 202.

St. Patrick School (Parochial) , 3340 S. Alameda St., 78411. Tel: 361-852-1211; Fax: 361-852-4855. Email: sps@stpatrickschoolcc.org. Web: www.stpatrickschoolcc.org. Julia Strubhart, Prin. Lay Teachers 22; Students 274.

St. Pius X School (Parochial) , 737 St. Pius Dr., 78412. Tel: 361-992-1343; Fax: 361-992-0329. Email: spxs@stpiusxschoolcc.org. Web: www.stpiusxcc.org. Kathy Clark, Prin. Lay Teachers 15; Students 181.

ALICE. *St. Elizabeth School* (Parochial) , 615 E. Fifth, 78332. Tel: 361-664-6271; Fax: 361-668-4250. Email: smgarcia@myctsonline.com. Web: www.stelizabeth.tx.schoolwebpages.com. Selina M. Rodriguez, Prin. Lay Teachers 9; Students 133.

St. Joseph School (Parochial) , 311 Dewey, 78332. Tel: 361-664-4642; Fax: 361-664-4642. Email: sjsaints@awesomenet.net. Mrs. Patricia C. Flores, Prin. Sisters 2; Lay Teachers 7; Students 101.

KINGSVILLE. *St. Gertrude School* (Parochial) , 400 E. Caesar St., 78363. Tel: 361-592-6522; Fax: 361-592-0100. Email: stgertrude@interconnect.net. Web: www.stgertrudeparish.com. Beverly Lanmon, Prin. Lay Teachers 11; Students 121.

ROBSTOWN. *St. Anthony School* (Parochial) , 203 Dunne St., 78380. Tel: 361-387-3814; Fax: 361-387-3814. Email: jeffeppler40@hotmail.com. Rev. Jeff Eppler, Prin. Priests 1; Brothers 1; Sisters 1; Lay Teachers 9; Students 120.

ROCKPORT. *Sacred Heart School* (Parochial) 111 N. Church St., 78382. Tel: 361-729-2672; Fax: 361-729-9382. Email: shsoff1@shsrockport.org. Web: www.shsrocksport.org. Katherine K. Barnes, Prin. Sisters 1; Lay Teachers 7; Students 130.

[C] DAY NURSERY, PRE-KINDER, KINDER

CORPUS CHRISTI. *Our Lady of the Rosary Learning Center,* 2237 Waldron Rd., 78418. Tel: 361-939-9847; Fax: 361-937-0890. Email: rosary7@swbell.net. Sr. Maria Paz Aribon, O.P., Dir. Sisters 8; Lay Teachers 1; Students 40.

INGLESIDE. *Our Lady of the Assumption Early Learning,* 2414 Main St., 78362. Tel: 361-776-3643. Enrollment 75.

ROBSTOWN. *St. Joseph's Dream,* 3660 Jack Dr., 78380. Tel: 361-387-9598. Lay Staff 10; Staff 2.

[D] GENERAL HOSPITALS

CORPUS CHRISTI. *CHRISTUS Spohn Health System,* 1702 Santa Fe, 78404. Tel: 361-881-3400; Fax: 361-885-0566. Email: jennifer.cochran@christushealth.org. Mailing Address:: 1702 Santa Fe, 78404. Bed Capacity 1,195; Total Staff 4,431; Total Annually Assisted 556,405.

CHRISTUS Spohn Hospital Shoreline, 1702 Santa Fe, 78404. Email: paul.trevino@christushealth.org. Mailing Address:: 1702 Santa Fe, 78404.
600 Elizabeth St., 78404. Tel: 361-881-3148; Fax: 361-881-3149. Email: andy_harris@iwhs.org. Paul Trevino, Vice Pres. & Admin.
Pastoral Staff: Revs. Angel Baldonado, S.D.B.; Lois Congdon; Donald Downey; Jose Guiterrez; David Saenz; Kay Holmes; Peter Muroko.

CHRISTUS Spohn Hospital Memorial, 1702 Santa Fe, 78404. Email: jennifer.cochran@christushealth.org. Mailing Address:: 1702 Santa Fe, 78404.
2606 Hospital Blvd., 78405. Tel: 361-902-4000; Fax: 361-902-4949. Email: reese_jackson@iwhs.org. Mr. Peter Banko, Vice Pres. & Admin.
Pastoral Staff: Lynne Blackler, Chap.; Revs. Yoke-Lye Lim, Dir.; Thomas Kizito Nwachukwu; Robert Rank.

CHRISTUS Spohn Hospital South, 1702 Santa Fe, 78404. Mailing Address:: 1702 Santa Fe, 78404. Sisters of Charity of the Incarnate Word (San Antonio, TX)
5950 Saratoga Blvd., 78414. Tel: 361-959-5000; Fax: 361-985-5109. Email: miket.johnson@christushealth.org. Mike T. Johnson, Vice Pres. & Admin.; Revs. Joe Alverson, Chap.; Eduardo Salazar, S.J. Total Staff 474; Bed Capacity 142; Patients Assisted Annually 58,423.

ALICE. *CHRISTUS Spohn Hospital Alice* Tel: 361-881-3400; Fax: 361-885-0566. Email: jennifer.cochran@christushealth.org. Web: www.christusspohn.org. Mailing Address:: 1702 Santa Fe, 78404. Email: margot.rios@christushealth.org.
700 N. Flournoy Rd., 78332. Tel: 361-661-8000; Fax: 361-661-8073. Margot Rios, Vice Pres. & Admin.; Sr. Carmen Avila, Pastoral Staff. Bed Capacity 73; Staff 255; Patients Assisted Annually 43,976.

BEEVILLE. *CHRISTUS Spohn Hospital Beeville* Tel: 361-881-3400; Fax: 361-885-0566. Email: jennifer.cochran@christushealth.org. Web: www.christusspohn.org. Mailing Address:: 1702 Santa Fe, 78404.
1500 E. Houston Hwy., 78102. Tel: 361-354-2000; Fax: 361-358-9322. Email: david.wagner@christushealth.org. David S. Wagner, Vice Pres. & Admin.; Sr. Delia Herrara, Pastoral Staff. Total Staff 283; Bed Capacity 69; Patients Assisted Annually 55,390.

KINGSVILLE. *CHRISTUS Spohn Hospital Kleberg,* Mailing Address:: 1702 Santa Fe, 78404. Email: buddyflores@iwhs.org. Operated by the Sisters of Charity of the Incarnate Word (San Antonio, TX).
1311 General Cavazos Blvd., 8363. Tel: 631-595-1661; Fax: 361-595-9888. Mr. Ernesto Flores, Vice Pres. & Admin.; Sr. Elizabeth Smith, Pastoral Care. Total Staff 418; Bed Capacity 100; Patients Assisted Annually 82,859.

[E] HOMES FOR THE AGED

CORPUS CHRISTI. *Mount Carmel Home,* 4130 S. Alameda St., 78411. Tel: 361-855-6243; Fax: 361-855-3690. Sr. M. Michelle, Admin.; Rev. Msgr. Arnold Anders, Chap. Sisters 9; Residents 50; Total Staff 20.

Villa Maria, Inc., 3146 Saratoga Blvd., 78415. Tel: 361-857-6171; Fax: 361-857-6173. Apartment complex for senior adults. Total Staff 4; Total in Residence 55.

[F] RETREAT HOUSE

SARITA. *Lebh Shomea House of Prayer,* La Parra Ranch, P.O. Box 9, 78385-0009. Tel: 361-294-5369; Fax: 361-294-5791. Email: admin@lebhshomea.org. Web: www.lebhshomea.org. Rev. Francis Kelly Nemeck, O.M.I. Total in Residence

5; Total Staff 4; Brothers 8; Priests 5; Novices 3.

[G] MONASTERIES AND RESIDENCES OF PRIESTS AND BROTHERS

HEBBRONVILLE. *Catholic Solitudes*, Rancho Maria, P.O. Box 748, 78361. Tel: 361-527-4636; Fax: 361-527-4482. Email: cathsol@aol.com. Web: www.catholicsolitudes.org. Rev. Patrick Meaney, Dir. Special Apostolate: A fraternal community stressing eremitical contemplative prayer, welcoming eremitical vocations and spiritual formational retreats for young people under directives of Diocesan Bishop. Total Staff 4; Total in Residence 8.

ROBSTOWN. *Society of Our Lady of the Most Holy Trinity*, P.O. Box 152, 78380-0152. Tel: 361-387-2754; Fax: 361-387-3818. Email: casasanjose@softhome.net. Web: www.solt3.org. Revs. Fred Alexander; Anthony Anderson, S.O.L.T.; Derek Anderson; John M. Ayang, S.O.L.T.; Alphonsus Bakyil; Anthony Blount; James Blount; Scott Braathan, S.O.L.T.; James Brady; Scott Brossart; Mark Byrne; George Carlin; Phillip Chavez; John Corapi; Dale Craig; Jacques Dolbec; Dennis Dolter; Steve Dougherty; Jeff Eppler; Dan Estes; John M. Fiala; James Flanagan, S.O.L.T.; Alfredo Gaytan, S.O.L.T.; Thomas Gier; Kevin Gillen, S.O.L.T.; Paul Graia; Joseph Hadgkiss; Paul Hu, S.O.L.T.; Paul Johnston; Ralph Jones; Michael Jordan, S.O.L.T.; James R. Kelleher, S.O.L.T.; Thaddeus Simon Kiwera; David Liptak; Brian List; Benjamin Lopez; Mario Lopez Garcia; William Mac Kinnon III; Clement Machado; Eckley Macklin, S.O.L.T. (KC); Guilbert Mariani; John McHugh, S.O.L.T.; Joseph Mc Manus; Glenn Meaux; Eduardo Montemayor, S.O.L.T.; Christopher Myers; Peter Hung Nguyen; Vincent Nicosia; Isidore Usit Nyein, S.O.L.T.; Joseph O'Connell, S.O.L.T.; Morty O'Shea; Frank Papa; John H. Patterson; John Mary Perez, S.O.L.T.; Peter Pham; Tan Pham; Santan Pinto; Jack Purtell; Val Radimecky; Edward Roche; Mark Ropel, S.O.L.T.; James Sanchez; Margarito Sanchez; Ramon Santa Cruz; Robert Shaldone; Gerard J. Sheehan, S.O.L.T.; Thomas Showalter, S.O.L.T.; Neal Stull; James Tambornino; Lawrence E. Tucker, S.O.L.T.; Isidore Usit; Gabriel Uzondu; Mark Wendling; Glenn Whewell, S.O.L.T.; Robert Wright; Dominic Zimmermann; Deacon Wayne Lickteig, S.O.L.T.

SAN DIEGO. *Vicariate of Holy Rosary*, St. Francis de Paul Church, P.O. Box 279, 78384. Tel: 361-279-3596; Fax: 361-279-8288. Email: berem@vsta.com. Rev. Benito Retortillo, O.P., Local Supr. Order of Preachers, U.S. Foundation of the Province of Spain

[H] CONVENTS AND RESIDENCES FOR SISTERS

CORPUS CHRISTI. *Bethany Convent*, 2962 Austin St., 78404. Tel: 512-888-7537. Email: smigonzalez@hotmail.com. Sisters of the Incarnate Word and Blessed Sacrament 3.

Blessed Sacrament Chapel, 4105 Ocean Dr., 78411-1223. Tel: 361-852-6212; Fax: 361-853-3811. Email: bscccm@msn.com. Web: www.mountgraceconvent.org. Sr. Mary Margaret Friedl, S.Sp.S. de A.P., Supr. Sister-Servants of the Holy Spirit of Perpetual Adoration (Motherhouse, Steyl, Holland) 9.

Casa de Matel Residence, 3030 S. Alameda, 78404. Tel: 361-887-5064. Email: mkuntscher@netscape.net. Sr. Olga Cardona, I.W.B.S., Local Supr. & Contact person. Sisters of the Incarnate Word and Blessed Sacrament Sisters 3.

Dominican of Santo Tomas de Aquino, Formerly Dominican Daughters of Santo Tomas de Aquino, 12217 Hearn Rd., 78410. Tel: 361-242-8829; Fax: 361-241-3621. Email: domstthomas@juno.com. Sr. Maria P. Vega, Local Supr. Sisters 3.

Incarnate Word Convent, 2930 S. Alameda, 78404. Tel: 361-882-5413; Fax: 361-880-4152. Email: smigonzalez@hotmail.com. Web: www.iwbscc.org. Sr. Maria Irma Gonzalez, I.W.B.S., Supr. Tel: 361-882-5413, Ext. 119.

Legal Title: *Convent Academy of the Incarnate Word.* Sisters of the Incarnate Word and Blessed Sacrament Sisters 41; Total Staff 16; Total in Residence 41.

Lawnview Residence, 2953 Lawnview, 78404. Tel: 361-887-6308. Email: wagsra@stx.rr.com. Sisters of the Incarnate Word and Blessed Sacrament Sisters 2.

Mercedarian Sisters of the Blessed Sacrament, 1723 Frio St., 78417. Tel: 361-854-2370; Fax: 361-854-2257. Sr. Guadalupe Barcena, H.M.S.S., Local Supr. Sisters 7.

Missionaries of the Rosary of Fatima, 2509 Nogales, 78416. Tel: 361-882-3245; Fax: 361-882-4946. Sr. Marysol Bacob Heredia, M.R.F., Local Supr.

Mount Carmel Home Convent, 4130 S. Alameda St., 78411. Tel: 361-855-6243; Fax: 361-854-8513. Carmelite Sisters of the Divine Heart of Jesus 9.

Mount Tabor Convent, 12940 Leopard St., 78410. Tel: 361-241-1955. Central Regional House of the Missionary Sisters of Jesus, Mary, and Joseph.

The Ark Assessment Center & Emergency Shelter for Youth, 12960 Leopard St., 78410.

Pax Christi Residence, 4601 Calallen Dr., 78410. Tel: 361-241-2833; Fax: 361-241-5479. Email: mary2034@aol.com. Sr. Teresa Santoyo, P.C.I., Supr. Gen. Pax Christi Institute. Sisters 16; Total Staff 16; Total Assisted 3,850.

Religious Missionaries of St. Dominic, Inc. (Congregacion de Religiosas Misioneras de Santo Domingo) 2237 Waldron Rd., 78418. Tel: 361-939-8102 (Office of Delegate); 361-937-5978 (Community); Fax: 361-939-8203 (Office of Delegate). Email: crmsdsis@swbell.net.

Our Lady of the Rosary Learning Center, 2237 Waldron Rd.. Tel: 361-939-9847; Fax: 361-937-0890. Sisters Maria Paz Aribon, O.P., Delegate of the Supr. Gen.; Maria Paz Aribon, O.P., Dir.

Sisters of Adoration of the Blessed Sacrament, 1601 Ocean Dr., Apt. 5, 78404. Tel: 361-884-7136; Fax: 361-884-7136. Email: shprovince@aol.com. Sr. Elizabeth Pathiparambil, Supr. Sisters 2.

Sisters of Our Lady of Charity Convent, 1201 Lantana St., 78407. Tel: 361-289-2611; Fax: 361-289-5162. Sisters of Our Lady of Charity

Spohn Hospital Convent, 1725 2nd St., 78404. Tel: 361-881-3000; 361-884-0702; Fax: 361-881-3149. Email: brideus@gateway.net. Congregation of Sisters of Charity of the Incarnate Word - San Antonio Sisters 3.

KINGSVILLE. *Missionary Daughters of the Most Pure Virgin Mary*, 919 N. Ninth St., 78363. Tel: 361-595-1087; Fax: 361-221-9763. Email: mdpvmkingssbc.com. Sr. Consuelo Ramirez, M.D.P.V.M., Supr. Sisters 9.

ROCKPORT. *Schoenstatt Sisters of Mary*, 130 Front St.,, 78382-7800. Tel: 361-729-1868; Fax: 361-729-1685. Email: marysch@pyramid3.net. Sr. M. Antoinette Buffler, I.S.S.M., Prov. Supr. Secular Institute of the Schoenstatt Sisters of Mary Sisters 37; Total in Residence 16.

SARITA. *Lebh Shomea House of Prayer*, La Parra Ranch, P.O. Box 9, 78385-0009. Tel: 361-294-5369; Fax: 361-294-5791. Email: admin@lebhshomea.org. Web: www.lebhshomea.org. Total Staff 4; Total in Residence 5.

[I] MISCELLANEOUS

CORPUS CHRISTI. *The Cathedral Concert Series*, 505 N. Upper Broadway, 78401. Tel: 361-888-6520; 361-888-7444 (Information); Fax: 361-883-1918. Email: lgccso@intcomm.net. Web: www.goccn.org/diocese/ccs/. Mr. Lee Gwozdz, Exec. Dir.

The Counseling Center, 1322 Comanche, 78401. Tel: 361-884-0651; Fax: 361-884-3956. Ms. Gloria Garcia, Lead Counselor. Total Staff 2; Patients Assisted Annually 500.

Cursillo Movement Eastern Vicariate, 3360 San Antonio, 78411. Tel: 361-855-3534; Fax: 361-855-3534. Dr. Michael Meaney, Pres.; Rev. Msgr. Patrick Higgins.

Fannie Bluntzer Nason Renewal Center, Inc., 2930 S. Alameda St., 78404. Tel: 361-882-5413; Fax: 361-880-4152. Email: smigonzalez@hotmail.com. Sr. Maria Irma Gonzalez, I.W.B.S., Contact Person.

Hope, Faith & Love, Inc., P.O. Box 2620, 78403. Tel: 361-882-6191; Fax: 361-882-1018.

Incarnate Word Academy Foundation, 2930 S. Alameda, 78404. Tel: 361-882-5413; Fax: 361-880-4152. Email: smigonzalez@hotmail.com. Web: www.iwacc.org. Sr. Maria Irma Gonzalez, I.W.B.S., Pres.

Journey to Damascus, Inc., 5620 Gollihar Rd., 78412. Tel: 888-546-7382; Fax: 361-992-0352. Email: j2damascus@yahoo.com. Web: www.journeytodamascus.org. Melissa Ricard, Pres.

Mother Teresa Shelter, Inc., 513 Sam Rankin, 78401. Tel: 361-883-7372. Email: bnetek@diocesecc.org. Web: goccn.org. Sr. Barbara Netek, I.W.B.S., Dir. A day shelter used as a homeless gathering facility; providing bath, laundry, limited eating facilities and counseling services. Total assisted annually 40,000.

Our Lady of Corpus Christi Catholic Undergraduate Liberal Arts, Tel: 361-289-9095; Fax: 361-289-0087. Email: colcc@juno.com. Web: www.colcc.com. P.O.Box 9785, 78469.

1200 Lantana, 78407. Tel: 361-289-9095; Fax: 361-289-0087. Email: colcc@juno.com. Web: colcc.com. Revs. James Sanchez, Chap.; Scott Braathan, S.O.L.T., Chap.; Paul Hu, S.O.L.T.; Eckley Macklin, S.O.L.T.; Dr. David Marzak, Pres.; Mr. Matthew Moore, Dean of Admissions. Priests 2; Lay Teachers 8; Total Staff 13; Students 27.

Search Retreats, P.O. Box 2620, 78415. Tel: 361-882-6191; Fax: 361-882-1157. Email: info@searchretreats.org. Web: searchretreats.org. Revs. Pete Elizardo, Prog. Dir.; Richard Libby, Spiritual Dir.; Miss Hillary Johnston, Prog. Asst.

Secular Institute of the Schoenstatt Fathers aka Schoenstatt Fathers, 4343 Gaines St., 78412-2541. Tel: 361-992-9841; Fax: 361-992-9842. Email: schtx@sbcglobal.net. Revs. Hector R. Vega, I.Sch., Supr. & Contact Person; Christian Christensen, I.Sch.

Teens Encounter Christ and Church "TECC", P.O. Box 2620, 78403-2620. Tel: 361-882-6191; Fax: 361-882-1157. Email: DCarranza@DioceseCC.org. Delia Carranza, Prog. Dir.

The Catholic Campaign for Human Development, Formerly The Catholic Campaign of America, Inc.P.O. Box 2620, 78403-2620. Tel: 361-882-6191; Fax: 361-882-1018. Sisters Michelle Marie Kuntschen, I.W.B.S.., Co-Dir.; Martha Ann Snapka, I.W.B.S., Co-Dir.

St. Vincent DePaul Society, 2302 Laredo St., 78405. Tel: 361-882-5101. Email: barbara.peterson10@gte.net. Barbara Peterson, Contact Person & District Council Pres. Tel: 361-991-4119.

KINGSVILLE. *FirePower Retreats*, P.O. Box 2620, 78403-2620. Tel: 361-882-6191. Revs. Paul Hesse, Spiritual Dir.; Pete Elizardo, Spiritual Dir.; Tim Etzler, Prog. Dir.

RELIGIOUS INSTITUTES OF MEN REPRESENTED IN THE DIOCESE

For further details refer to the corresponding bracketed number in the Religious Institutes of Men or Women section.

[0150]—*Augustinian Recollects*—O.A.R.
[0140]—*Augustinians*—O.S.A.
[0200]—*Benedictine Monks*—O.S.B.
[]—*Catholic Solitudes (Hermits)*
[0630]—*Congregation of the Missionaries of the Holy Family*—M.S.F.
[0430]—*Dominican, Order of Preachers* (Spain)—O.P.
[0520]—*Franciscan Friars*—O.F.M.
[]—*Missionaries of St. Joseph*—M.J.
[1110]—*Missionaries of the Sacred Heart*—M.S.C.
[]—*Missionary Congregation of the Blessed Sacrament* (India)—M.C.B.S.
[]—*Missionary Society of St. Thomas the Apostle* (India)
[0910]—*Oblates of Mary Immaculate*—O.M.I.
[1310]—*Order of the Holy Trinity* (Prov. of Baltimore)—O.SS.T.
[1065]—*Priestly Fraternity of St. Peter, Society of Apostolic Life*—F.S.S.P.
[1070]—*Redemptorists*—C.Ss.R.
[1190]—*Salesians of St. John Bosco*—S.D.B.
[]—*Schoenstatt Fathers*—I.Sch.
[]—*Secular Institute*
[0690]—*Society of Jesus*—S.J.
[0975]—*Society of Our Lady of the Most Holy Trinity, Society of Apostolic Life*—S.O.L.T.

RELIGIOUS INSTITUTES OF WOMEN REPRESENTED IN THE DIOCESE

[1810]—*Bernardine Sisters of the Third Order of St. Francis*—O.S.F.
[0360]—*Carmelite Sisters of the Divine Heart of Jesus*—Carmel.D.C
[]—*Catholic Solitudes (Women's Household)*
[0460]—*Congregation of the Sisters of Charity of the Incarnate Word* (San Antonio, TX)—C.C.V.I.
[1070-19]—*Dominican Sisters* (Houston, TX)—O.P.
[]—*Dominican Sisters of St. Thomas Aquinas*—O.P.
[2590]—*Mercedarian Sisters of the Blessed Sacrament*—H.M.S.S.
[0390]—*Missionary Carmelites of St. Teresa*—C.M.S.T.
[2690]—*Missionary Catechists of Divine Providence* (San Antonio, TX)—M.C.D.P.
[]—*Missionary Daughters of the Most Pure Virgin Mary* (U.S. Foundation-Mexico)—M.D.P.V.M.
[2770]—*Missionary Sisters of Jesus, Mary, and Joseph*—M.J.M.J.
[]—*Missionary Sisters of the Rosary of Fatima*—H.M.R.F.
[]—*Pax Christi Institute*—P.C.I.
[]—*Religious Missionaries of St. Dominic* (Spanish Prov.)—O.P.
[]—*Schoenstatt Sisters of Mary (Secular Institute)*—I.S.S.M.
[3540]—*Sister Servants of the Holy Spirit of Perpetual Adoration*—S.Sp.S.deA
[]—*Sisters of Adoration of the Blessed Sacrament* (India)—S.A.B.S.
[3070]—*Sisters of Our Lady of Charity* (Dallas, TX)—O.L.C.
[3360]—*Sisters of Providence of Saint Mary-of-the-Woods, IN*—S.P.

[3718]—*Sisters of St. Anne*—S.S.A.
[2040]—*Sisters of the Holy Spirit*—S.H.Sp.
[2205]—*Sisters of the Incarnate Word and Blessed Sacrament*—I.W.B.S.
[]—*Sisters of the Society of Our Lady of the Most Holy Trinity (Society of Apostolic Life)*—S.O.L.T.

NECROLOGY

† Clarke, Rev. Msgr. Hugh, (Retired)—Died Dec. 16, 2002
† Freeman, Rev. Msgr. Robert E., (Retired)—Died Sept. 16, 2003
† Kinast, Timothy J.—Died Nov. 6, 2003
† Kircher, Edward H., (Retired)—Died Jan. 25, 2003

Diocese of Covington

(Dioecesis Covingtonensis)

Most Reverend

ROGER J. FOYS, D.D.

Bishop of Covington; ordained May 16, 1973; appointed Bishop of Covington May 31, 2002; consecrated and installed July 15, 2002 *Mailing Address: P.O. Box 18548, Erlanger, KY 41018-0548*. Tel: 859-283-6212; Fax: 859-283-6239.

Most Reverend

WILLIAM A. HUGHES

Retired Bishop of Covington; ordained April 6, 1946; appointed Titular Bishop of Inis Cathaig and Auxiliary of Youngstown July 23, 1974; consecrated September 12, 1974; appointed Bishop of Covington April 13, 1979; transferred to Covington May 8, 1979; retired July 4, 1995. *Res.: Cathedral Basilica of the Assumption*, 1140 Madison Ave., Covington, KY 41011-3116.

ESTABLISHED JULY 29, 1853.

Square Miles 3,359.

Comprises 14 Counties of the Commonwealth of Kentucky in the north and east of the Commonwealth, including Bracken, Boone, Campbell, Carroll, Fleming, Gallatin, Grant, Harrison, Kenton, Lewis, Mason, Owen, Pendleton and Robertson Counties.

For legal titles of parishes and diocesan institutions, consult the Chancery Office.

The Catholic Center: P.O. Box 18548, Erlanger, KY 41018-0548. Tel: 859-283-6200; Fax: 859-283-6334.

Web: www.covingtondiocese.org

Email: swagner@covingtondiocese.org

STATISTICAL OVERVIEW

Personnel	
Bishop	1
Retired Bishops	1
Priests: Diocesan Active in Diocese	49
Priests: Retired, Sick or Absent	46
Number of Diocesan Priests	95
Religious Priests in Diocese	2
Total Priests in Diocese	97
Extern Priests in Diocese	1
Ordinations:	
Permanent Deacons	3
Permanent Deacons in Diocese	28
Total Brothers	8
Total Sisters	379
Parishes	
Parishes	46
With Resident Pastor:	
Resident Diocesan Priests	38
Without Resident Pastor:	
Administered by Priests	3
Administered by Deacons	2
Administered by Religious Women	3
Missions	6
Closed Parishes	1
Professional Ministry Personnel:	
Sisters	14
Lay Ministers	33
Welfare	
Catholic Hospitals	3
Total Assisted	418,683
Homes for the Aged	3
Total Assisted	896
Residential Care of Children	2
Total Assisted	165
Day Care Centers	1
Total Assisted	93
Special Centers for Social Services	3
Total Assisted	80,092
Other Institutions	1
Total Assisted	7,453
Educational	
Diocesan Students in Other Seminaries	10
Total Seminarians	10
High Schools, Diocesan and Parish	7
Total Students	2,393
High Schools, Private	2
Total Students	747
Elementary Schools, Diocesan and Parish	27
Total Students	8,309
Elementary Schools, Private	2
Total Students	461
Catechesis/Religious Education:	
High School Students	274
Elementary Students	3,660
Total Students under Catholic Instruction	15,854
Teachers in the Diocese:	
Priests	1
Brothers	1
Sisters	50
Lay Teachers	698
Vital Statistics	
Receptions into the Church:	
Infant Baptism Totals	1,434
Adult Baptism Totals	227
Received into Full Communion	189
First Communions	1,588
Confirmations	1,586
Marriages:	
Catholic	341
Interfaith	207
Total Marriages	548
Deaths	889
Total Catholic Population	88,154
Total Population	464,629

Former Bishops—Rt. Revs. GEORGE ALOYSIUS CARRELL, S.J., D.D., consecrated Nov. 1, 1853; died Sept. 25, 1868; AUGUSTUS MARIA TOEBBE, D.D., consecrated Jan. 9, 1870; died May 2, 1884; CAMILLUS PAUL MAES, D.D., consecrated Jan. 25, 1885; died May 11, 1915; FERDINAND BROSSART, D.D. (Retired), consecrated Jan. 25, 1916; retired March 14, 1923; died Aug. 6, 1930; Most Revs. FRANCIS WILLIAM HOWARD, D.D., consecrated July 15, 1923; died Jan. 18, 1944; WILLIAM THEODORE MULLOY, D.D., LL.D., consecrated Jan. 10, 1945; died June 1, 1959; RICHARD HENRY ACKERMAN, C.S.Sp., D.D. (Retired), consecrated May 22, 1956; transferred to Covington April 6, 1960; retired Nov. 28, 1978; died Nov. 18, 1992; WILLIAM ANTHONY HUGHES, D.D. (Retired), consecrated Sept. 12, 1974; appt. April 13, 1979; retired July 4, 1995; ROBERT W. MUENCH, D.D., consecrated June 29, 1990; appt. Bishop of Covington, Jan. 5, 1996; installed March 19, 1996; transferred to Baton Rouge, Dec. 15, 2001; installed Bishop of Baton Rouge March 14, 2002.

Vicar General and Episcopal Vicar for Administrative Services—Rev. GERALD L. REINERSMAN.

Episcopal Vicar for Pastoral Services—Very Rev. J. MICHAEL DUE, V.E.

Chancellor—Ms. MARGARET M. SCHACK.

Diocesan Tribunal—Very Rev. DONALD A. ENZWEILER, J.C.L., Judicial Vicar; Ms. KATHLEEN VITT, Case Promoter & Notary; Sr. MARTHA WALTHER, O.S.B., Sec. & Notary.

Judges—Very Revs. DONALD A. ENZWEILER, J.C.L.; JAMES M. RYAN, V.F.; Revs. ROBERT C. WEHAGE; BARRY M. WINDHOLTZ; Sr. MARY CATHERINE WENSTRUP, J.C.L.

Defenders of the Bond—Revs. GREGORY E. OSBURG; GERALD E. TWADELL; PAUL L. BERSCHIED; GILBERT J. RUTZ.

Diocesan Consultors—Revs. GERALD L. REINERSMAN; WILLIAM B. NEUHAUS; Very Revs. JOHN W. CAHILL, V.F.; JAMES M. RYAN, V.F.; GERALD E. TWADDELL, V.F.; Revs. JOSEPH N. BOSCHERT; JEROME C. BRITT; Rev. Msgr. DONALD F. HELLMANN (Retired); Very Rev. J. MICHAEL DUE, V.E.

Deans—Very Revs. JOHN W. CAHILL, V.F., Covington; GERALD E. TWADDELL, V.F., Northern Kenton County; JAMES M. RYAN, V.F., Southwest; Revs. RICHARD G. BOLTE, Newport, Bellevue, Dayton; WILLIAM B. NEUHAUS, Campbell County; Very Rev. WILLIAM H. HINDS, V.F., Southeast.

Diocesan Pastoral Council—Mr. EDWARD P. RAWE, Chm.

Presbyteral Council—Rev. WILLIAM B. NEUHAUS, Chm.; Very Rev. JAMES M. RYAN, V.F., Vice-Chm.; Rev. JEROME C. BRITT, Sec.

Due Process Board of Administrative Review—Mr. MICHAEL HAMMONS, J.D., Chm.; Mr. STEPHEN KOPLYAY, Sec.

Diocesan Offices and Directors

The Catholic Center—947 Donaldson Hwy., P.O. Box 18548, Erlanger, 41018-0548. Tel: 859-283-6200; Fax: 859-283-6334. Office Hours: Mon.-Fri. 8:30-4:30

Archives—Mr. THOMAS S. WARD, Archivist.

Board of Total Catholic Education—Dr. LAWRENCE W. BOWMAN, Ed.D.; Mr. ROGER F. KELLER, Chm.

Campus Ministry-Newman Center—Mr. AL CUCCHETTI, Parish Life Collaborator, Northern Kentucky Univ., 512 Johns Hill Rd., P.O. Box 76174, Highland Heights, 41076-1449. Tel: 859-781-3775.

Cathedral Foundation, Inc.—Mrs. JENNIFER WEBER, Exec. Dir., 1140 Madison Ave., Covington, 41011-3116. Tel: 859-431-2061; Fax: 859-431-8444.

Catholic Charities—Sr. JOAN MARIE BOBERG, C.D.P., Dir., 3629 Church St., Covington, 41015-1499. Tel: 859-581-8974; Fax: 859-581-9595.

Catholic Scouting—Rev. JEROME C. BRITT, Chap.; Mrs. BETH WORLAND, Chm.

Cemeteries—Mr. JOHN NIENABER, Dir.

Censor Librorum—Rev. JAMES E. QUILL, S.T.D. (Retired).

Charismatic Renewal—Contact Persons: Mr. HARRY HUMPERT; Mr. JOSEPH BESSLER.

Communication—Mr. TIMOTHY L. FITZGERALD, Dir.
Continuing Education of Priests—Rev. RONALD M. KETTELER, Dir.
Corpus Central Purchasing—Ms. SANDRA NARE, Gen. Mgr. Buyers: MIKE FREUDENBERG, Buyer; BOB MOELLMAN, Buyer, 845 Isabella St., Newport, 41071-1338. Tel: 859-491-8100; 800-955-2541; Fax: 859-491-6587. Email: sandien@corpuscentral.com. Web: www.corpuscentral.com.
Cursillo Movement—Ms. MARY KRAHE, Lay Dir.
Disabilities Committee—Mr. STEPHEN KOPLYAY, Chm.
Ecumenism—Rev. RONALD M. KETTELER, Thomas More College, 333 Thomas More Pkwy., Crestview Hills, 41017-3428. Tel: 859-344-3393.
Initiation—Rev. WILLIAM M. FITZGERALD, O.Praem., S.T.L., Dir.
Family Ministry—Mrs. SUSAN VOGT, Dir.
Finance—Mr. ANTHONY G. DEPENBROCK, Dir.
Hispanic Ministry—Mr. FERNANDO POPPE, Dir.
Justice and Peace/Inclusive Church—Sr. RUTH KETTMAN, C.S.J., Dir.
Legion of Mary—Rev. JOSEPH J. RUETER, Spiritual Dir. (Retired).
Liaison for Retired Priests—Rev. ROBERT L. VATER (Retired).
Ministry Development Program—Rev. GILBERT J. RUTZ, Dir.
Mission Services— See Stewardship and Missions.
Missions Among Black and Native Americans—Sr. JANET BUCHER, C.D.P. Tel: 859-491-5872; Fax: 859-431-8444.
Mustard Seed Community—Contact Persons: Mr. JOSEPH BESSLER; Mr. HARRY HUMPERT.
Newspaper "Messenger"—Mr. TIMOTHY L. FITZGERALD, Editor & Gen. Mgr.
Pastoral Ministry Formation—Rev. GILBERT J. RUTZ, Dir.
Pastoral Office for the Deaf—Sr. RITA ANN WIGGINTON, O.S.U., Dir.
Pastoral Planning and Research—Mrs. JAN VON HANDORF, Dir.
Permanent Diaconate Formation—Rev. GILBERT J. RUTZ, Dir.
Priest Personnel—Rev. Msgr. DONALD F. HELLMANN, Dir. (Retired).
Priests' Retirement Committee—Rev. JOSEPH C. BRINK, Chm.
Religious—Sr. M. CATHERINE HUNT, C.D.P., Dir.
Serra Club of Diocese of Covington—Rev. JOHN J. STERLING, Chap.
St. Vincent de Paul Salvage Bureau—Mrs. CATHY KLUG, Gen. Mgr.
St. Vincent de Paul Community Pharmacy, Inc.—Contacts: ROSANA AYDT; MARY BETH BEIMESCH.
Stewardship and Missions—Mrs. SUE GRETHEL, Dir., Includes Pontifical Aid Societies, Campaign for Human Development, Catholic Relief Fund, Holy Childhood Assoc., Inner City Missions.
Total Catholic Education—Dr. LAWRENCE M. BOWMAN, Ed.D., Dir. Catholic Education & Supt.; Mr. EUGENE A. KUEHNE, Assoc. Dir. Business Svcs.; Sr. STELLA MARIE GOUGH, O.S.B., Assoc. Dir. Catechetical Svcs.
Vocations Office—Rev. JOHN J. STERLING, Dir.
Vocation Council—Rev. JOHN J. STERLING, Dir.
Worship Commission—Rev. WILLIAM M. FITZGERALD, O.Praem., S.T.L.
Office of Worship, Evangelization & Initiation—Rev. WILLIAM M. FITZGERALD, O.Praem., S.T.L., Dir.
Office of Youth and Young Adult Ministry—Mrs. BETH WORLAND, Dir.
Victim Assistance Coordinator—Ms. MARGARET M. SCHACK. Tel: 859-283-6215. Email: mschack@covingtondiocese.org.

CLERGY, PARISHES, MISSIONS AND PAROCHIAL SCHOOLS

CITY OF COVINGTON
(KENTON COUNTY)

1—CATHEDRAL, BASILICA OF THE ASSUMPTION (1837), Very Rev. John W. Cahill, V.F.; Deacon Edward E. Stieritz. In Res., Most Rev. William A. Hughes (Retired); Rev. Robert C. Rosing (Retired).
Res.: 1140 Madison Ave., Covington, 41011-3116. Tel: 859-431-2060; Fax: 859-431-8444.

2—ST. AGNES (1930), Revs. Mark A. Keene; Brian K. Wigger; James E. Quill, S.T.D. (Retired); Deacons Joseph Cleves; David Flynn; Robert Stoeckle.
Res.: 1680 Dixie Hwy., Fort Wright, 41011-2779. Tel: 859-431-1802; Fax: 859-291-7017.
School—Tel: 859-261-0543; Fax: 859-261-9778. Lay Teachers 39; Students 499.
Catechesis/Religious Program—Students 92.

3—ST. AUGUSTINE (1870), Rev. Leo C. Schmidt. In Res., Rev. Robert J. Reinke (Retired).
Res.: 1839 Euclid Ave., Covington, 41014-1162. Tel: 859-431-3943; Fax: 859-431-4036.
School—Tel: 859-261-5564; Fax: 859-261-5402. Sisters of Notre Dame 3; Lay Teachers 7; Students 166.
Catechesis/Religious Program—Students 4.

4—ST. BENEDICT (1885), Rev. Douglas J. Lauer.
Res.: 338 E. 17th St., Covington, 41014-1315. Tel: 859-431-5607; Fax: 859-431-5847.
Catechesis/Religious Program—Students 60.

5—CHURCH OF OUR SAVIOR (1943), (African American), Sr. Janet Marie Bucher, C.D.P., Parish Life Coord.; Rev. Robert C. Rosing (Retired).
Res.: 246 E. 10th St., Covington, 41011-3026. Tel: 859-491-5872; Fax: 859-431-8444.
Catechesis/Religious Program—Students 120.

6—HOLY CROSS (1890), Rev. Thomas C. Barnes; Mrs. Bernie Whittle, Pastoral Assoc. In Res., Deacon Ralph Colatrella.
Res.: 3612 Church St., Covington, 41015-1431. Tel: 859-431-0636; Fax: 859-431-6917.
School—Tel: 859-581-6599; Fax: 859-581-3462. Religious 1; Lay Teachers 12; Students 196.
Catechesis/Religious Program—Students 40.

7—ST. JOHN (1854), Rev. Douglas F. Fortner; Deacon Robert J. Hermann.
Res.: 627 Pike St., Covington, 41011-2148. Tel: 859-431-5314; Fax: 859-431-8397.
Catechesis/Religious Program—Students 11.
Mission—St. Ann (1860), 1274 Parkway, Covington, Kenton Co. 41011-1060.

8—MOTHER OF GOD (1841), Rev. Raymond S. Hartman; Deacon Steven I. Durkee. In Res., Rev. John J. Sterling.
Res.: 119 W. 6th St., Covington, 41011-1409. Tel: 859-291-2288; Fax: 859-291-2065.
Catechesis/Religious Program—Students 25.

OUTSIDE THE CITY OF COVINGTON

ALEXANDRIA, CAMPBELL CO., ST. MARY OF THE ASSUMPTION (1860), [CEM] Rev. Joseph C. Brink; Deacon Dennis Lehmkuhl.
Res.: 121 W. Main St., 41001-1217. Tel: 859-635-4188; Fax: 859-635-4189.
School—9 S. Jefferson St., 41001-1398. Tel: 859-635-9539; Fax: 859-448-4824. Brothers 1; Sisters of Notre Dame 3; Lay Teachers 30; Students 544.
Catechesis/Religious Program—Students 149.

AUGUSTA, BRACKEN CO., ST. AUGUSTINE (1860), [JC] Rev. Daniel J. Saner; Deacon Frank Estill.
Res.: 215 E. Fourth St., 41002-1117. Tel: 606-756-2377; Fax: 606-756-2377.
School—Tel: 606-756-3229; Fax: 606-756-2377. Sisters of Notre Dame 3; Lay Teachers 5; Students 120.
Catechesis/Religious Program—Students 12.

BELLEVUE, CAMPBELL CO.
1—ST. ANTHONY (1889), Merged, with Sacred Heart, Bellevue to form Divine Mercy, Bellevue.
2—DIVINE MERCY (2003), Revs. Michael E. Comer; John H. Kroger (Retired); Sr. Marlene Rust, Pastoral Min.; Deacons Charles Dietz; David W. Klingenberg.
Res.: 318 Division St., 41073-1198. Tel: 859-261-8506; Fax: 859-581-7260.
3—SACRED HEART (1874), Merged, with St. Anthony, Bellevue to form Divine Mercy, Bellevue.

BROOKSVILLE, BRACKEN CO., ST. JAMES (1868) [CEM] Rev. Daniel J. Saner; Deborah Bartlett, Pastoral Assoc.
Res.: P.O. Box 27, 41004-0027. Tel: 606-735-2271; Fax: 606-735-2271.
Catechesis/Religious Program—Students 42.
Mission—St. James Kentucky Rd., Minerva, Mason Co. 41062. Tel: 606-735-2271.

BURLINGTON, BOONE CO., IMMACULATE HEART OF MARY (1954), Rev. Jerome C. Britt; Deacons Richard J. O'Donnell; James L. Bayne.
Church: 5876 Veterans Way, 41005-8824. Tel: 859-689-5010; Fax: 859-689-5636.
School—Tel: 859-689-4303; Fax: 859-689-5636. Sisters of Divine Providence of Kentucky 1; Lay Teachers 35; Students 666.
Catechesis/Religious Program—Students 400.

CALIFORNIA, CAMPBELL CO., STS. PETER AND PAUL (1854), [CEM 2] Rev. Joseph N. Boschert.
Res.: 2162 California Crossroads, 41007-9713. Tel: 859-635-2924; Fax: 859-635-9184.
School—Tel: 859-635-4382; Fax: 859-635-9184. Lay Teachers 10; Students 201.
Catechesis/Religious Program—Students 21.
Mission—Immaculate Conception Stepstone, Pendleton Co.

CAMP SPRINGS, CAMPBELL CO., ST. JOSEPH (1845), [CEM] Sr. Mary Kevan Seibert, S.N.D., Pastoral Admin.; Very Rev. Gerald E. Twaddell, V.F.
Mailing Address: 6833 Four Mile Rd., 41059-9746. Tel: 859-635-2491; Fax: 859-635-7336.
School—Tel: 859-635-5652; Fax: 859-635-7336. Lay Teachers 4; Students 73.
Catechesis/Religious Program—Students 30.

CARROLLTON, CARROLL CO., ST. JOHN THE EVANGELIST (1853), [CEM] Rev. Michael D. Barth.
Res.: 507 Fifth St., 41008-1203. Tel: 502-732-5776; Fax: 502-732-9062.
Catechesis/Religious Program—Students 120.
Mission—Transfiguration Perry Park, Owen Co.

COLD SPRING, CAMPBELL CO., ST. JOSEPH (1870), [CEM] Rev. Robert J. Henderson. In Res., Very Rev. Donald A. Enzweiler, J.C.L.; Rev. Joseph J. Rueter (Retired); Deacon Timothy Schabell.
Res.: 4011 Alexandria Pk., 41076-1895. Tel: 859-441-1604; Fax: 859-441-7681.
School—Tel: 859-441-2025; Fax: 859-441-2057. Sisters of Notre Dame 2; Lay Teachers 38; Students 655.
Catechesis/Religious Program—Students 77.

CRESCENT SPRINGS, KENTON CO., ST. JOSEPH (1916), Rev. Edward J. Brodnick; Deacons Marvin Holstein; Joseph Baker. In Res., Rev. Ronald M. Ketteler.
Res.: 2470 Lorraine Ct., 41017-1406. Tel: 859-341-6609; Fax: 859-578-2741.
School—Tel: 859-578-2742; Fax: 859-578-2754. Lay Teachers 34; Students 556.
Catechesis/Religious Program—Students 102.

CYNTHIANA, HARRISON CO., ST. EDWARD (1872), [CEM] Rev. Richard W. Frazier.
Res.: 107 N. Walnut St., 41031-1225. Tel: 859-234-5444; Fax: 859-234-9823.
School—Tel: 859-234-2731; Fax: 859-234-9597. Lay Teachers 5; Students 81.
Catechesis/Religious Program—Students 35.

DAYTON, CAMPBELL CO., ST. BERNARD (1853), Rev. Michael E. Comer; Deacons Charles Dietz; David W. Klingenberg.
Church: 701 Fifth St., 41074-1139. Tel: 859-261-8506; Fax: 859-581-7260.
Res.: 318 Division St., Bellevue, 41073-1198.
Catechesis/Religious Program—Students 18.

EDGEWOOD, KENTON CO., ST. PIUS X (1958), [CEM] Revs. Robert C. Wehage; David B. Gamm. In Res., Rev. John J. Riesenberg (Retired).
Res.: 340 Dudley Rd., 41017-2609. Tel: 859-341-4900, Ext. 2; Fax: 859-578-8597.
School—Tel: 859-341-4900; Fax: 859-578-8597. Priests 3; Lay Teachers 41; Students 649.
Catechesis/Religious Program—Students 191.

ELSMERE, KENTON CO., ST. HENRY (1890), Revs. James J. Ryan; George Syamala; Deacon Gerald R. Franzen; Jack Alexander, Pastoral Assoc.
Res.: 3813 Dixie Hwy., 41018-1809. Tel: 859-342-2540; Fax: 859-342-2542.
School—Tel: 859-342-2551; Fax: 859-342-2554. Religious 1; Lay Teachers 29; Students 520.
Catechesis/Religious Program—Students 236.

ERLANGER, BOONE CO., MARY, QUEEN OF HEAVEN (1955), Rev. Richard W. Wurth; Deacon Thomas Dushney.
Res.: 1150 Donaldson Hwy., 41018-1048. Tel: 859-525-6909; Fax: 859-525-7067.
School—Tel: 859-371-8100; Fax: 859-371-8100. Sisters 1; Lay Teachers 12; Students 202.
Catechesis/Religious Program—Students 57.

ERLANGER, KENTON CO., ST. BARBARA (1967), Rev. G. Michael Greer; Deacon Bernard J. Kaiser.
Res.: 4042 Turkeyfoot Rd., 41018-2921. Tel: 859-371-3100; Fax: 859-371-3101.
Catechesis/Religious Program—Students 213.

FALMOUTH, PENDLETON CO., ST. FRANCIS XAVIER (1880), [CEM] Rev. Gregory J. Bach.
Res.: 202 Second St., 41040-1118. Tel: 859-654-8241; Fax: 859-654-5203.
Catechesis/Religious Program—Students 73.

FLEMINGSBURG, FLEMING CO., ST. CHARLES (1859), Rev. Verne F. Hogan.
Res.: 211 Mt. Carmel Ave., 41041-1315. Tel: 859-845-4601.

FLORENCE, BOONE CO., ST. PAUL (1832), Revs. Thomas B. Sacksteder; William F. Cleves; Deacon Nicholas J. Schwartz. In Res., Rev. Msgr. Donald F. Hellmann (Retired).
Res.: 7301 Dixie Hwy., 41042-2126. Tel: 859-371-8051; Fax: 859-647-4073.
School—Tel: 859-647-4070; Fax: 859-647-0644. Lay Teachers 30; Students 594.
Catechesis/Religious Program—Students 324.

FORT MITCHELL, KENTON CO., BLESSED SACRAMENT (1920), Revs. Daniel J. Vogelpohl; Mark A. Steidle; Sr. Ann Middendorf, O.S.B., Pastoral Assoc.; Deacon David J. Meyer. In Res., Rev. Paul F. Tenhundfeld (Retired).
Res.: 2415 Dixie Hwy., 41017-2936. Tel: 859-331-4302; Fax: 859-578-4752.
School—Tel: 859-331-3062; Fax: 859-344-7323. Lay Teachers 35; Students 597.
Catechesis/Religious Program—Students 220.

FORT THOMAS, CAMPBELL CO.

1—ST. CATHERINE OF SIENA (1930), Rev. James B. Egbers.
Mailing Address: 1803 N. Ft. Thomas Ave., 41075-1170. Tel: 859-441-1352; Fax: 859-572-2686.
In Res., Rev. Robert L. Vater (Retired).
School—Tel: 859-572-2680; Fax: 859-572-2699. Lay Teachers 18; Students 225.
Catechesis/Religious Program—Students 160.
2—ST. THOMAS (1902), Rev. William B. Neuhaus.
Mailing Address: 26 E. Villa Pl., 41075-2223. Tel: 859-441-1282; Fax: 859-572-4640. In Res., Revs. Albert E. Ruschman (Retired); Louis B. Brinker (Retired); William M. Fitzgerald, O.Praem., S.T.L.
School—Tel: 859-572-4641; Fax: 859-572-4644. Lay Teachers 28; Students 235.
Catechesis/Religious Program—Students 118.
INDEPENDENCE, KENTON CO., ST. CECILIA (1880), [CEM] Rev. Paul L. Berschied.
Res.: 5313 Madison Pk., P.O. Box 186,, 41051-0186. Tel: 859-363-4311; Fax: 859-363-4312.
School—Tel: 859-363-4314; Fax: 859-363-4315. Lay Teachers 17; Grades K-8 349.
Catechesis/Religious Program—Students 125.
KENTON, KENTON CO., ST. MATTHEW (1909), [CEM] Rev. Gregory E. Osburg.
Res.: 13816 Decoursey Pk., P.O. Box 82, 41053-0082. Tel: 859-356-6530; Fax: 859-356-6530.
Catechesis/Religious Program—Students 67.
Mission—Assumption of the Blessed Virgin 3711 St. Mary Rd., Morning View, Kenton Co. 41063.
LUDLOW, KENTON CO., STS. BONIFACE AND JAMES (1872), Rev. Robert J. Reinke (Retired); Deacon James C. Auton, Parish Life Coord.
Res.: 304 Oak St., 41016-1417. Tel: 859-261-5340; Fax: 859-261-0939.
Catechesis/Religious Program—Students 30.
MAY'S LICK, MASON CO., ST. ROSE OF LIMA (1864), Rev. Verne F. Hogan.
Church: P.O. Box 100, 41055-0100. Tel: 606-763-6304.
MAYSVILLE, MASON CO., ST. PATRICK (1847), [CEM] Rev. William H. Hinds.
Res.: 110 E. Third St., 41056-0248. Tel: 606-564-9015; Fax: 606-564-6108.
School—Tel: 606-564-5949; Fax: 606-564-8795. Lay Teachers 14; Students 193.
High School—Lay Teachers 10; Students 88.
Catechesis/Religious Program—Students 41.
MELBOURNE, CAMPBELL CO., ST. PHILIP (1908), Rev. Msgr. Roger P. Cooney.
Res.: 1402 Mary Ingles Hwy., 41059-9701. Tel: 859-441-8949; Fax: 859-442-0290.
School—Tel: 859-441-3423; Fax: 859-441-2611. Sisters of Divine Providence of Kentucky 3; Lay Teachers 5; Students 89.
Catechesis/Religious Program—Students 10.
NEWPORT, CAMPBELL CO.
1—ST. FRANCIS DE SALES, Closed., For sacramental records contact Holy Spirit, Newport.
2—HOLY SPIRIT (1997), Rev. Richard G. Bolte.
Res.: 825 Washington Ave., 41071-1999. Tel: 859-431-2533; Fax: 859-431-3247.
Catechesis/Religious Program—Students 15.
Mission—Corpus Christi (1844),, Campbell Co.
Mission—St. Francis de Sales (1911),, Campbell Co.
Mission—St. Stephen (1854),, Campbell Co.
Mission—St. Vincent de Paul (1916),, Campbell Co.
3—ST. STEPHEN, Closed., For sacramental records contact Holy Spirit, Newport.
4—ST. VINCENT DE PAUL, Closed., For sacramental records contact Holy Spirit, Newport.
SOUTHGATE, CAMPBELL CO., ST. THERESE OF THE INFANT JESUS (1927), Revs. Clarence J. Heitzman; Stephen M. Bankemper. In Res., Rev. Msgr. Elmer J. Grosser (Retired).
Res.: 11 Temple Pl., 41071-3133. Tel: 859-441-1654; Fax: 859-441-2395.
School—Tel: 859-441-0449; Fax: 859-441-7988. Sisters of Notre Dame 2; Lay Teachers 19; Students 372.
Catechesis/Religious Program—Students 90.
TAYLOR MILL, KENTON CO.
1—ST. ANTHONY (1878), Rev. Thomas P. Robbins.
Res.: 485 Grand Ave., Covington, 41015-0219. Tel: 859-431-1773; Fax: 859-431-1773.
School—Tel: 859-431-5987; Fax: 859-431-7353. Lay Teachers 10; Students 168.
Catechesis/Religious Program—Students 60.
2—ST. PATRICK (1966), Rev. Jeffrey D. Von Lehmen.
Mailing Address: 3285 Mills Rd., Covington, 41015-2480. Tel: 859-356-2171; Fax: 859-356-2171.
Catechesis/Religious Program—Students 230.
UNION, BOONE CO., ST. TIMOTHY (1989), Rev. Mark G. Witte; Deacon Thomas Nolan.
Res.: 10272 Hwy. 42, P.O. Box 120, 41091-0120. Tel: 859-384-1100; Fax: 859-384-1709.
Catechesis/Religious Program—Students 486.
VANCEBURG, LEWIS CO., HOLY REDEEMER (1965), Sr. Joseph Fillenwarth, S.P., Parish Life Coord.; Rev. Bruce C. Brylinski, G.H.M.
Mailing Address: P.O. Box 8, 41179-0008. Tel: 606-796-3052; Fax: 606-796-2606.
Catechesis/Religious Program—Students 9.
WALTON, BOONE CO., ALL SAINTS (1951), [CEM 2] Rev. John R. Schulte; Deacon Paul V. Yancey.
Mailing Address: 62 Needmore St., 41094-1029.
Res.: 46 Needmore St., 41094-1029. Tel: 859-485-4476; Fax: 859-485-6476.
Catechesis/Religious Program—Students 116.
WARSAW, GALLATIN CO., ST. JOSEPH (1864), [CEM] Rev. B. Gerald Witzemann (Retired).
Mailing Address: P.O. Box 495, 41095-0495.
Res.: 602 Sparta Pike, 41095-0495. Tel: 859-567-2425; Fax: 859-567-2425.
Catechesis/Religious Program—Students 78.
Mission—St. Edward (1958), 1335 Hwy. 22 E., R.R. 4, Owenton, Owen Co. 40359-9003.
WILDER, CAMPBELL CO., ST. JOHN (1847), Rev. Richard H. McGrath (Retired); Ms. Margaret Quirk, Pastoral Assoc.
Res.: 1307 John's Hill Rd., 41076-9762. Tel: 859-781-2117; Fax: 859-781-4889.
WILLIAMSTOWN, GRANT CO., ST. WILLIAM (1912), [CEM 2] Deacon Phillip J. Racine, Parish Life Coord.; Rev. Msgr. Donald F. Hellmann, Sacramental Min. (Retired).
Res.: 6 Church Dr., 41097-9454. Tel: 859-824-5381; Fax: 859-824-5381.
Catechesis/Religious Program—Students 88.
Mission—St. John's (1956), Dividing Ridge, Pendleton Co.

Chaplains of Public Institutions

FORT THOMAS. *St. Luke Hospital East*. Rev. John A. Seiler.
Veterans Hospital. Rev. Emeka L. Odor, Archdiocese for Military Services.

Leave of Absence:
Revs.—
Delange, Maurice
Gallenstein, Joseph A.

Retired:
Most Rev.—
Hughes, William A., 1140 Madison Ave., Covington, 41011-3116.
Rev. Msgrs.—
Grosser, Elmer J., St. Therese Rectory, 11 Temple Pl., Southgate, 41071-3133.
Hellmann, Donald F., St. Paul Rectory, 7301 Dixie Hwy., Florence, 41042-2126.
Meier, Allen J., Notre Dame Academy, 1699 Hilton Dr., Covington, 41011-2705.
Revs.—
Bradley, Allan W., St. Henry Rectory, 3813 Dixie Hwy., Elsmere, 41018-1809.
Brinker, Louis B., St. Thomas Rectory, 26 E. Villa Pl., 41075-2223.
Brinker, Paul J., Carmel Manor, 100 Carmel Manor Rd., 41075-2300.
Broering, Joseph H., Regina Cleri, 100 Carmel Manor Rd., 41075-2300.
Broering, Raymond L., 2 Cypress Run, Apt. 21B, Homosassa, FL 34446-4228.
Dickmann, Louis H., 1754 Licking Pike, Cold Spring, 41076-9717.
Gerrety, James P., 626 Laurel St., Ludlow, 41016.
Hoffer, Charles J., Carmel Manor, 100 Carmel Manor Road, 41075-2300.
Holtz, Raymond C., 226 Covington Ave., Covington, 41011-1414.
Jasper, Louis H., 1400 Sleepy Hollow, Apt. 4, Covington, 41011-2757.
Krebs, Paul F., 14 Orchard St., Southgate, 41071-3126.
Kroger, John H., 320 Poplar St., Bellevue, 41073-1109.
McGrath, Richard H., 18 Woodland Hills, Apt. 5, Southgate, 41071-2969.
McHugh, James L., 209 E. Second St., Maysville, 41056-1307.
Mulhern, Raymond F., 18100 S. 66th Ct., #314, Tinley Park, IL 60477-6483.
Quill, James E., S.T.D., St. Agnes Rectory, 1680 Dixie Hwy., Covington, 41011-2779.
Reifsnyder, John A., Sacred Heart Rectory, 310 Shady Ave., Pittsburgh, PA 15206-4306.
Reinke, Robert J., St. Augustine Rectory, 1839 Euclid Ave., Covington, 41014-1162.
Riesenberg, John J., St. Pius X Rectory, 340 Dudley Rd., Edgewood, 41017-2609.
Robotnik, Lawrence R., Passionist Monastery, 1149 Donaldson Rd., 41018-1000.
Rooks, Charles W., 1601 Dixie Hwy., Covington, 41011-2798.
Rosing, Robert C., Cathedral Rectory, 1140 Madison Ave., Covington, 41011-3116.
Rueter, Joseph J., St. Joseph Rectory, 4011 Alexandria Pike, Cold Spring, 41076-1817.
Ruschman, Albert E., St. Thomas Rectory, 26 E. Villa Pl., 41075-2223.
Shockey, David P., P.O. Box 364, Walton, 41094-0364.
Smith, R. Leroy, 17425 Walking Dr., Hudson, FL 34667.
Tenhundfeld, Paul F., Blessed Sacrament Rectory, 2415 Dixie Hwy., Fort Mitchell, 4107--936.
Toner, Edward R., 5614 Long Commons Cir., Sarasota, FL 34235-2401.
Urlage, Robert J., P.O. Box 75254, 41075-0254.
Vater, Robert L., St. Catherine of Siena Rectory, 10 Wesley Hills Dr., 41075-1213.
Weber, Charles E., St. Charles Lodge, 600 Farrell Dr., #306, Covington, 41011-5165.
Werner, John P., 104 Highland Ave., Apt. 1, Fort Mitchell, 41017-2920.
Witt, G. Robert, P.O. Box 210455, Royal Palm Beach, FL 33414-0455.
Witzemann, B. Gerald, P.O. Box 495, Warsaw, 41095-0495.

Permanent Deacons:
Auton, James C., Sts. Boniface & James, Ludlow
Baker, Joseph, St. Joseph, Crescent Springs
Bayne, James L., Immaculate Heart of Mary, Burlington
Cleves, Joseph A., St. Agnes, Covington
Colatrella, Ralph, Holy Cross, Latonia
Dietz, Charles, St. Bernard, Dayton & Sacred Heart, Bellevue
Durkee, Steven I., Mother of God, Covington
Dushney, Thomas M., Mary, Queen of Heaven, Erlanger
Estill, Andrew (Frank), St. Augustine, Augusta
Flynn, David J., St. Agnes, Covington
Franzen, Gerald R., St. Henry, Elsmere
Hermann, Robert J., St. John, Covington
Hillenmeyer, Ernest B., (Retired)
Holstein, Marvin, St. Joseph, Crescent Springs
Kaiser, Bernard, St. Barbara, Erlanger
Klingenberg, David W., Divine Mercy, Bellevue and St. Bernard, Dayton
Lehmkuhl, Dennis N., St. Mary, Alexandria
Meyer, David J., Blessed Sacrament, Fort Mitchell
Nolan, Thomas L., St. Timothy, Union
Norris, Eugene F., (Retired)
O'Donnell, Richard J., Immaculate Heart of Mary, Burlington & Airport Chap.
Racine, Phillip J., St. William, Williamstown
Schabell, Timothy, St. Joseph, Cold Spring
Schwartz, Nicholas J., St. Paul, Florence
Stieritz, Edward E., Cathedral, Covington
Stoeckle, Robert A., St. Agnes, Fort Wright
Sweigart, James H., (Retired)
Yancey, Paul V., Marydale Retreat Center and All Saints, Walton

PILGRIMAGE SHRINES

COVINGTON. *Shrine of St. Ann.* Attached to St. Ann Mission.
SOUTHGATE. *Shrine of the Little Flower*. Attached to St. Therese Church.

INSTITUTIONS LOCATED IN THE DIOCESE

[A] COLLEGES AND UNIVERSITIES

COVINGTON. *Thomas More College* (Coed) , 333 Thomas More Pkwy. Crestview Hills, 41017-3495. Tel: 859-341-5800; Fax: 859-344-3649. Email: joseph.lee@thomasmore.edu. Web: www.thomasmore.edu. Dr. Joseph E. Lee II, Pres.; Mr. John R. Parker, Vice Pres. Inst. Advancement; Dr. Dale K. Myers, Vice Pres. Academic Affairs; Ms. Peg Bradner Hancock, Vice Pres. Finance; Ms. Judith Kinman, Dir. of Campus Ministry; Mr. James McKellogg, Dir. Library; Ms. Patsy Kenner, Registrar; Ms. Linda Hayes, Dir. Financial Aid; Ms. Barbara Davis, Dir. Student Support Svcs.; Ms. Genie Wambaugh, Dir. Institute Planning & Effectiveness; Mr. James Harter, Vice Pres. Enrollment Management & Marketing. Priests 2; Lay Teachers 71; Sisters 1; Administration: Lay People 24; Students 1,555.

[B] HIGH SCHOOLS, DIOCESAN

COVINGTON. *Covington Catholic High School*, 1600 Dixie Hwy., 41011-2797. Tel: 859-431-5351; Fax: 859-655-4325. Email: mclines@covcath.org. Web: www.covcath.org. Mr. Michael T. Clines, Prin.; Rev. John J. Sterling. Lay Teachers 31; Boys 481.
Covington Latin School, 21 E. 11th St., 41011-3196. Tel: 859-291-7044; Fax: 859-291-1939. Email: headmaster@covingtonlatin.org. Web:

www.covingtonlatin.org. Mr. Richard Stewart, Dean; Mr. Andrew J. Barczak, Headmaster; Rev. Raymond S. Hartman, Chap. Lay Teachers 18; Boys 132; Girls 69.

Holy Cross High School, 3617 Church St., 41015-1498. Tel: 859-431-1335; Fax: 859-655-2184. Email: hchs@fuse.net. Web: hchscov.com. Mr. Clay Eifert, Prin.; Rev. Thomas P. Robbins, Chap. Religious 5; Lay Teachers 35; Students 441.

ALEXANDRIA. *Bishop Brossart High School*, Jefferson St. & Grove St., 41001-1295. Tel: 859-635-2108; Fax: 859-635-2135. Email: brossart@juno.com. Web: www.bishopbrossart.org. Mr. Thomas H. Seither, Prin.; Rev. Gregory J. Bach, Chap. Sisters of Notre Dame 1; Lay Teachers 30; Students 413.

ERLANGER. *St. Henry District High School*, 3755 Scheben Dr., 41018-3597. Tel: 859-525-0255; Fax: 859-525-5855. Email: dmotte@SHDHS.org. Web: www.SHDHS.org. Mr. David M. Otte, Prin.; Rev. Richard W. Wurth, Chap. Lay Teachers 39; Religious 1; Students 494.

MAYSVILLE. *St. Patrick High School*, 318 Limestone St., 41056-1248. Tel: 859-564-5949; Fax: 859-564-8795. Email: stpats318@hotmail.com. Mr. Jay Jacobs, Prin.; Rev. William H. Hinds, Chap. Lay Teachers 11; Students 88.

NEWPORT. *Newport Central Catholic High School*, 13 Carothers Rd., 41071-2497. Tel: 859-292-0001; Fax: 859-292-0656. Email: ncchs.com. Web: www.ncchs.com. Mr. Robert Noll, Prin.; Revs. Richard G. Bolte, Chap.; Stephen M. Bankemper; Michael E. Comer, Chap.; Mrs. Shelley Wykle, Administrative Team; Mrs. Jenny Mertle, Administrative Team. Sisters 1; Lay Teachers 37; Students 441.

[C] HIGH SCHOOLS, PRIVATE

COVINGTON. *Villa Madonna High School*, 2500 Amsterdam Rd., Villa Hills, 41017-3798. Tel: 859-331-6333; Fax: 859-331-8615. Email: pmcqueen@villamadonna.net. Web: www.villamadonna.net. Mr. Michael A. Whelan, Pres.; Ms. Pamela McQueen, Prin.; Rev. Jeffrey D. Von Lehmen, Chap. Sisters 4; Lay Teachers 17; Students 161.

PARK HILLS. *Notre Dame Academy*, Formerly Academy of Notre Dame, 1699 Hilton Dr., 41011-2769. Tel: 859-261-4300; Fax: 859-292-7722. Email: NDA@NDA-cvg.org. Web: www.NDA-cvg.org. Sr. Elaine Marie Winter, S.N.D., Prin.; Rev. Msgr. Allen J. Meier, Chap. (Retired); Rev. Brian K. Wigger, Chap. Sisters of Notre Dame Sisters 7; Lay Teachers 39; Girls 587.

[D] ELEMENTARY SCHOOLS, INTERPAROCHIAL

COVINGTON. *Holy Family Catholic School*, 338 E. 16th St., 41014-1398. Tel: 859-581-0290; Fax: 859-581-0624. Email: holyfamilycath@aol.com. Mrs. Patricia Leonard, Prin. Lay Teachers 7; Students 128.

Prince of Peace School, 625 Pike St., 41011-2798. Tel: 859-431-5153; Fax: 859-431-5153. Email: srose@princeofpeaceschool.ws. Web: www.princeofpeaceschool.ws. Sr. M. Suzanne Rose, S.N.D., Prin. Sisters of Notre Dame 4; Lay Teachers 7; Students 99.

BELLEVUE. *Holy Trinity Elementary School*, 235 Division St., 41073-1101. Tel: 859-291-6937; Fax: 859-291-6970. Email: holytrinity@fuse.net. Web: holytrinity-school.org. Sr. Mary Luke Murphy, C.D.P., Prin. Sisters 2; Lay Teachers 14; Students 190.

NEWPORT. *Holy Trinity Junior High School and Child Development Center*, Grand & Chesapeake Ave., 41071-2485. Tel: 859-292-0487; Fax: 859-292-0487. Email: smrlubbers@fuse.net. Web: holytrinity-school.org. Sr. Mary Ruth Lubbers, S.N.D., Prin. Sisters 2; Lay Teachers 12; Students 103.

[E] ELEMENTARY SCHOOLS, DIOCESAN

FORT MITCHELL. *Guardian Angel*, P.O. Box 17007, Orphanage Rd., 41017-0007. Tel: 859-331-2040; Fax: 859-344-5022. Email: akathman@beechwood.k12.ky.us. Sr. M. Ann Christine Kathman, S.N.D., Prin. School for the Emotional Behavioral Disabled. Sisters 3; Lay Teachers 4; Students 30.

[F] ELEMENTARY SCHOOLS, PRIVATE

COVINGTON. *Villa Madonna Elementary School*, 2500 Amsterdam Rd., Villa Hills, 41017-3798. Tel: 859-331-6333; Fax: 859-331-8615. Email: vmaelemprincipal@hotmail.com. Web: www.villamadonna.net. Mr. Michael Whalen, Dir.; Mrs. Donna Brigger, Prin. Lay Teachers 26; Students 252.

WALTON. *St. Joseph Academy*, 48 Needmore St., 41094-1028. Tel: 859-485-6444; Fax: 859-485-4262. Email: stjoseph0@insightbb.com. Web: www.saintjosephacademy.net. Sr. Patricia Jean, S.J.W., Prin. Sisters of St. Joseph the Worker Sisters 4; Lay Teachers 15; Students 208

[G] MONTESSORI SCHOOLS (PRESCHOOL)

VILLA HILLS. *Villa Madonna Montessori*, 2402 Amsterdam Rd., 41017-5316. Tel: 859-341-5145; Fax: 859-331-2136. Sr. Mary Peter Youtsey, O.S.B., Admin. Sisters of St. Benedict 1; Lay Teachers 7 Students 61.

[H] PRESCHOOLS

COVINGTON. *Julie Learning Center*, 1601 Dixie Hwy., 41011-2798. Tel: 859-291-8555; Fax: 859-291-1774. Email: julielearningcenter@juno.com. Shirley Schmitz, Dir. Daycare with educational emphasis for ages 4-6. Sisters of Notre Dame 1; Lay Teachers 6; Students 61.

[I] GENERAL HOSPITALS

COVINGTON. *St. Elizabeth Medical Center, North*, 401 E. 20th St., 41014-1585. Tel: 859-292-4000; Fax: 859-292-4437. Email: rross@stelizabeth.com. Web: www.stelizabeth.com. Mr. Joseph W. Gross, Pres. & CEO; Mr. Marc A. Hoffman, Senior Vice Pres. & COO; Ms. Jane Swain, Vice Pres. Nursing; Mr. Garren Colvin, Vice Pres. Finance; Mr. Thomas Horton, Vice Pres. Human Resources; Mr. Len Puthoff, Vice Pres. Gen. Svcs.; Mr. Thomas E. Saalfield, Vice Pres. Professional Svcs.; Mr. Michael J. Walters, Vice Pres. Systems Devel.; Mr. Allen Zobay, M.D., Vice Pres. Medical Affairs; Rev. Robert J. Ross, S.J., Chap. & Dir. Pastoral Care. Res.: 2028 Mackoy St., 41014-1543. Rev. Robert C. Rosing, Chap. (Retired).

1140 Madison Ave., Alexandria, 41001-3116. Bed Capacity 91; Patients Assisted Annually 65,281.

St. Elizabeth Medical Center Foundation, Inc. Tel: 859-344-3920; Fax: 859-344-3968.

EDGEWOOD. *St. Elizabeth Medical Center, South*, 1 Medical Village Dr., 41017-3441. Tel: 859-344-2000; Fax: 859-344-5412. Email: rross@stelizabeth.com. Web: www.stelizabeth.com. Mr. Joseph Gross, Pres. & CEO; Mr. Marc A. Hoffman, Senior Vice Pres. & COO; Revs. Robert J. Ross, S.J., Chap. & Dir. Pastoral Care; John P. Werner, Chap. (Retired); Robert C. Rosing Chap. (Retired). Bed Capacity 362; Patients Assisted Annually 327,612.

WILLIAMSTOWN. *St. Elizabeth Medical Center, Grant County*, 238 Barnes Rd., 41097-9482. Tel: 859-824-8240; Fax: 859-824-8818. Web: stelizabeth.com. Mr. Joseph Gross, Pres. & CEO; Mr. Marc A. Hoffman, Senior Vice Pres. & COO; Mr. Chris Carle, Admin.; Rev. Robert J. Ross, S.J., Chap. & Dir. Pastoral Care. Bed Capacity 15; Patients Assisted Annually 22,876.

[J] NURSING HOMES

COVINGTON. *St. Charles Care Center, Inc.*, 500 Farrell Dr., 41011-3798. Tel: 859-331-3224; Fax: 859-578-2065. Email: smluann@zoomtown.com. Web: www.stcharlescare.org. Sr. Mary Luann Bender, S.N.D., Admin. Adult Day Health Program, Licensed Outpatient Physical Therapy Department, Case Management and Private Duty Nursing. Sisters of Notre Dame 6; Bed Capacity 105; Senior Living Apartments 72; Cottages 44; Total Assisted Annually 621.

Madonna Manor, Inc., 2344 Amsterdam Rd., Villa Hills, 41017-3712. Tel: 859-341-3981; Fax: 859-578-7475. Email: suem@madonnamanor.org. Mrs. Susan McConn, Admin. Patients Assisted Annually 60.

[K] PROTECTIVE INSTITUTIONS

COVINGTON. *Diocesan Catholic Children's Home*, Orphanage Rd., P.O. Box 17007, Fort Mitchell, 41017-2730 Tel: 859-331-2040; Fax: 859-344-5022. Email: jhoffman@dcchome.org. Web: www.dcchome.org. Sisters Jean Marie Hoffman, S.N.D., Exec. Dir.; M. Ann Christine Kathman, S.N.D., Prin. Sisters of Notre Dame 4; Lay Staff 67; Children in Residence 34; Students 30.

COLD SPRING. *Campbell Lodge Boys Home*, 150 Skyline Dr., 41076-2099. Tel: 859-781-1214; Fax: 859-442-3473. Email: mlschroth@aol.com. Web: www.campbelllodgeboyshome.org. Mr. Michael Schroth, M.S.W., Exec. Dir. Total Staff 17; Boys 60.

Campbell Lodge Boys' Home Foundation, 150 Skyline Dr., 41076-2099. Tel: 859-781-1214. Kenneth Dorger, Chm.

[L] HOMES FOR AGED

FORT THOMAS. *Carmel Manor*, 100 Carmel Manor Rd., 41075-2395 Tel: 859-781-5111; Fax: 859-781-2337. Email: carmelmanor@fuse.net. Web: carmelmanor.com. Rev. Joseph H. Broering (Retired); Sr. Teresa Kennedy, O.Carm., Admin. Carmelite Sisters for the Aged and Infirm Total Staff 140; Residents 145.

Regina Cleri Home for Retired Priests, 100 Carmel Manor Rd., 41075-2395. Tel: 859-781-5111; Fax: 859-781-2337. Sr. Teresa Kennedy, O.Carm., Admin. Carmelite Sisters for the Aged and Infirm Residents 2.

[M] MONASTERIES AND RESIDENCES OF PRIESTS AND BROTHERS

COVINGTON. *Brothers of the Poor of St. Francis*, Holy Family Friary, 239 W. Robbins St., 41011-3078. Tel: 859-291-2938; Fax: 859-581-5796. Email: bjcphelan@aol.com. Bro. Mark Gastel, C.F.P., Resident Min. Gen. International Office. In Res. Bros. William Anuszkiewicz; Blaise Betley, C.F.P.; Joseph LaPlante, C.F.P.; Rock Larsen, C.F.P.; James Phelan, C.F.P.; Robert Reinke, C.F.P.; John Walsh, C.F.P.

[N] CONVENTS AND RESIDENCES FOR SISTERS

COVINGTON. *St. Joseph Heights Provincialate and Novitiate of the Sisters of Notre Dame*, 1601 Dixie Hwy., 41011-2798. Tel: 859-291-2040; Fax: 859-291-1774. Email: smshauna@sndky.org. Web: www.sndky.org. Sr. Mary Shauna Bankemper, S.N.D., Prov. Supr.; Rev. Charles W. Rooks, Chap. (Retired). Sisters in Community 150; Sisters in Prov. House 69.

St. Walburg Monastery, 2500 Amsterdam Rd., 41017-5316. Tel: 859-331-6324; Fax: 859-331-2136. Web: www.stwalburg.org. Sr. Rita Brink, O.S.B., Prioress; Rev. Gerald L. Reinersman, Chap. Benedictine Sisters Professed Sisters 85.

ERLANGER. *Monastery of the Sacred Passion*, 1151 Donaldson Hwy., 41018-1000. Tel: 859-371-8568; Fax: 859-371-8568. Sr. Margaret Mary, C.P., Supr.; Rev. Lawrence R. Robotnik, Chap. (Retired). Passionist Nuns Professed 8.

FORT THOMAS. *Sisters of the Good Shepherd*, Pelletier Hall, 930 Highland Ave., 41075-1707. Tel: 859-441-5531; Fax: 859-441-7340. Email: vbiery@aol.com. Web: goodshepherdsisters.org. Sr. Mary Elise Kramer, Admin.; Rev. Richard H. McGrath, Chap. (Retired). Sisters of the Good Shepherd 13.

KENTON HILLS. *St. Vincent's Convent*, 630 Jerol Ave., 41011. Tel: 859-431-5388. Intercongregational Residence. Sisters 3.

MELBOURNE. *St. Anne Convent*, 1000 St. Anne Dr., 41059-9603. Tel: 859-441-0679; Fax: 859-441-1510. Email: sbaumann@cdpkentucky.org. Web: www.cdpkentucky.org. Sr. Lynn Stenken, C.D.P., Prov. Supr. Provincial House and Novitiate of the Sisters of Divine Providence of Kentucky Sisters in Community 159; Sisters in Provincial House 18; Sisters in Residence 57.

Holy Family Home, Rte. 8, 2000 St. Anne Dr., 41059-9604. Tel: 859-781-0712; Fax: 859-781-8854. Email: cosburg@juno.com. Sr. Claire Osburg, C.D.P., Admin. Sisters in Residence 52.

WALTON. *St. William Convent*, One St. Joseph Ln., 41094-1036. Tel: 859-485-4914; 859-485-4256; Fax: 859-485-9302. Sr. Celeste Marie Downes, S.J.W., Supr. Sisters of St. Joseph the Worker Sisters in Community 15; Sisters in Motherhouse 8.

13 Mulberry St., 41094-1036. Tel: 859-485-7053. Rev. David P. Shockey, Chap. (Retired).

[O] SECULAR INSTITUTES

COVINGTON. *Society of St. Vincent de Paul*, 2655 Crescent Springs Rd., 41017-1504. Tel: 859-341-6995; Fax: 859-341-1610. Email: shawnborchardt@juno.com. Web: svdpcovington.org. Linda Stambaugh, Pres.; Cathy Klug, Gen. Mgr. District Council of Northern Kentucky. Executive Offices and Thrift Stores. 27 Parish Conferences in Northern Kentucky Thrift Stores, including Dayton, Newport, Crescent Springs, and Falmouth.; A Catholic lay organization of over 875,000 members worldwide whose members meet in parish and district groups in order to help in a personal way those in need. Total Stores 4.

[P] SOCIAL SERVICES

COVINGTON. *Catholic Social Services*, 3629 Church St., 41015-1499. Tel: 859-581-8974; Fax: 859-581-9595. Email: info@cssnky.org. Web: www.cssnky.org. Sr. Joan Marie Boberg, C.D.P., Dir. Total Assisted Annually 11,492; Total Staff 45.

Parish Kitchen, Pike St. & Russell St., P.O. Box 1234, 41011-1234. Tel: 859-581-7745; Fax: 859-581-7749. Email: parishkitc@aol.com. Ms. Molly Navin, Dir. Total Assisted Annually 53,450.

[Q] DIOCESAN RETREAT HOUSES

ERLANGER. *Marydale Retreat Center*, 945 Donaldson Hwy., 41018-1093. Tel: 859-371-4224; Fax: 859-647-5682. Email: marydale@catholicweb.com.

Deacon Edward Stieritz, Dir.; Rev. Robert C. Rosing, Chap. (Retired). Total Assisted Annually 7,010; Total Staff 18.

[R] NEWMAN CENTERS

HIGHLAND HEIGHTS. *Catholic Newman Center - Northern Kentucky University* 512 Johns Hill Rd., P.O. Box 76174, 41076-1449. Tel: 859-781-3775. Mr. Al Cucchetti, Parish Life Coord.

[S] INTERFAITH CENTERS

COVINGTON. *Interfaith Commission of Northern Kentucky*, P.O. Box 72296, Newport, 41072-0296. Tel: 859-581-2237; Fax: 859-261-6041. Email: nkyinterfaith@iso.net. Web: nkyinterfaith.com. Jeffrey Queen, Exec. Dir. Purpose: A religious organization committed to understanding the various faith traditions of our member bodies, while working together in response to the spiritual and human needs of all people of the Northern Kentucky area.

[T] MISCELLANEOUS

FORT MITCHELL. *Mission Share*, P.O. Box 176356, 41017-6356. Tel: 606-564-9015; 859-341-8405; Fax: 606-564-6108. Email: whinds@maysvilleky.net. Rev. William H. Hinds, Pres. Purpose: A mission society whose principle activity is to construct Catholic churches, priest houses, parish centers and other buildings of church work, for the advancement of the Catholic faith among the poorest of the poor in Columbia, Latin America especially focused in Columbia, South America and Mexico.

RELIGIOUS INSTITUTES OF MEN REPRESENTED IN THE DIOCESE

For further details refer to the corresponding bracketed number in the Religious Institutes of Men or Women section.

[0460]—*Brothers of the Poor of St. Francis* (Aachen, Germany)—C.F.P.

[0570]—*Glenmary Home Missioners*—Glmy.

[0690]—*Jesuit Fathers and Brothers* (Chicago Prov.)—S.J.

[0900]—*Order of Canons Regular of Premontre*—O.Praem.

RELIGIOUS INSTITUTES OF WOMEN REPRESENTED IN THE DIOCESE

[0230]—*Benedictine Sisters of Pontifical Jurisdiction*—O.S.B.

[0330]—*Carmelite Sisters for the Aged and Infirm* (Germantown, NY)—O.Carm.

[3180]—*Congregation of the Passion of Jesus Christ*—C.P.

[0440]—*Sisters of Charity of Cincinnati, Ohio*—S.C.

[1000]—*Sisters of Divine Providence of Kentucky*—C.D.P.

[2990]—*Sisters of Notre Dame*—S.N.D.

[3360]—*Sisters of Providence of Saint Mary-of-the-Woods, IN*—S.P.

[1640]—*Sisters of St. Francis of Perpetual Adoration* (Colorado Springs, CO)—O.S.F.

[3880]—*Sisters of St. Joseph of Medaille* (Cincinnati, OH)—C.S.J.

[3920]—*Sisters of St. Joseph the Worker*—S.J.W.

[1830]—*Sisters of the Good Shepherd*—R.G.S.

[4120]—*Ursuline Nuns, of the Congregation of Paris* (Brown County, OH)—O.S.U.

[4120-03]—*Ursuline Nuns, of the Congregation of Paris* (Louisville, KY)—O.S.U.

DIOCESAN CEMETERIES

COLD SPRING. *St. Joseph*

FORT MITCHELL. *St. John*
St. Mary

FORT THOMAS. *St. Stephen*

WILDER. *St. Joseph*

NECROLOGY

† Fleming, Rev. Msgr. W. Stanley—Died Jan. 17, 2003
† Welp, Rev. Msgr. Harry J.—Died April 7, 2003
† Garvey, Charles J.—Died March 30, 2003
† Gruber, Robert L.—Died Feb. 3, 2003
† Mertes, William H.—Died April 22, 2003

Diocese of Crookston

(Dioecesis Crookstoniensis)

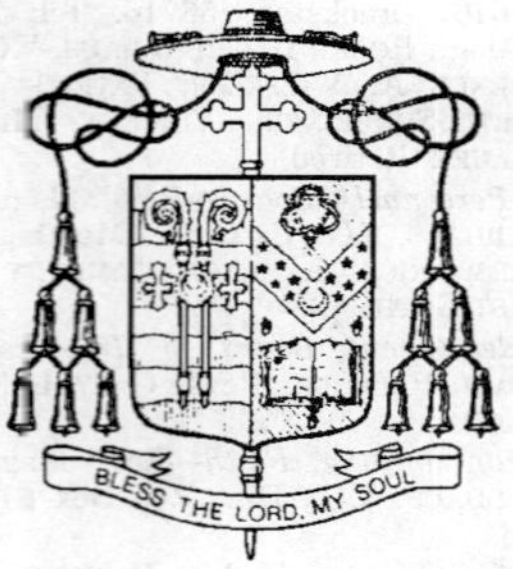

Most Reverend

VICTOR H. BALKE, D.D., PH.D.

Bishop of Crookston; ordained May 24, 1958; appointed July 7, 1976; Episcopal ordination September 2, 1976. *Res.: 1200 Memorial Dr., Crookston, MN 56716.* Tel: 218-281-4533.

Chancery Office: 1200 Memorial Dr., P.O. Box 610, Crookston, MN 56716. Tel: 218-281-4533; Fax: 218-281-3328.

Web: www.crookston.org

Email: rgrundhaus@crookston.org

ESTABLISHED BY HIS HOLINESS PIUS X, DECEMBER 31, 1909.

Square Miles 17,210.

Comprises the Counties of Becker, Beltrami, Clay, Clearwater, Hubbard, Kittson, Lake of the Woods, Marshall, Mahnomen, Norman, Pennington, Polk, Red Lake and Roseau in the State of Minnesota.

Patroness of the Diocese: The Immaculate Conception.

Legal Title: Diocese of Crookston.

For legal titles of parishes and diocesan institutions, consult the Chancery Office.

STATISTICAL OVERVIEW

Personnel	
Bishop	1
Priests: Diocesan Active in Diocese	29
Priests: Diocesan Active Outside Diocese	4
Priests: Retired, Sick or Absent	16
Number of Diocesan Priests	49
Religious Priests in Diocese	2
Total Priests in Diocese	51
Extern Priests in Diocese	2
Ordinations:	
Permanent Deacons	1
Permanent Deacons in Diocese	11
Total Brothers	1
Total Sisters	128
Parishes	
Parishes	68
With Resident Pastor:	
Resident Diocesan Priests	23
Resident Religious Priests	2
Without Resident Pastor:	
Administered by Priests	43
Administered by Deacons	3
Administered by Religious Women	2
Administered by Lay People	1
Closed Parishes	1
Professional Ministry Personnel:	
Brothers	1
Sisters	14
Lay Ministers	41
Welfare	
Catholic Hospitals	3
Total Assisted	53,954
Homes for the Aged	3
Total Assisted	304
Day Care Centers	1
Total Assisted	49
Educational	
Diocesan Students in Other Seminaries	5
Total Seminarians	5
High Schools, Diocesan and Parish	1
Total Students	174
Elementary Schools, Diocesan and Parish	9
Total Students	1,260
Catechesis/Religious Education:	
High School Students	2,226
Elementary Students	2,952
Total Students under Catholic Instruction	6,617
Teachers in the Diocese:	
Sisters	4
Lay Teachers	127
Vital Statistics	
Receptions into the Church:	
Infant Baptism Totals	644
Adult Baptism Totals	19
Received into Full Communion	75
First Communions	546
Confirmations	483
Marriages:	
Catholic	105
Interfaith	122
Total Marriages	227
Deaths	411
Total Catholic Population	36,263
Total Population	247,741

Former Bishops—Most Revs. TIMOTHY CORBETT, D.D., ord. June 12, 1886; consecrated May 19, 1910; resigned See Aug. 6, 1938; appt. Titular Bishop of Vita; died July 20, 1939; JOHN H. PESCHGES, D.D., ord. April 15, 1905; consecrated Nov. 9, 1938; died Oct. 30, 1944; FRANCIS J. SCHENK, D.D., ord. June 13, 1926; consecrated May 24, 1945; transferred to Duluth Jan. 27, 1960; died Oct. 28, 1969; LAURENCE A. GLENN, D.D. (Retired), ord. June 11, 1927; consecrated Sept. 12, 1956; appt. Bishop of Crookston Feb. 3, 1960; retired July 28, 1970; died Jan. 26, 1985; KENNETH J. POVISH, D.D., ord. June 3, 1950; appt. Bishop of Crookston July 28, 1970; consecrated Sept. 29, 1970; transferred to Lansing Oct. 21, 1975; died Sept. 5, 2003.

Vicar General—Rev. Msgr. ROGER L. GRUNDHAUS, V.G., 1200 Memorial Dr., P.O. Box 610, Crookston, 56716.

Chancery Office—1200 Memorial Dr., P.O. Box 610, Crookston, 56716. Tel: 218-281-4533; Fax: 218-281-3328.

Chancellor—Rev. DAVID J. SUPER.

Moderator of the Curia—Rev. Msgr. ROGER L. GRUNDHAUS, V.G.

Information Officer—Rev. Msgr. ROGER L. GRUNDHAUS, V.G.

Finance Manager—GEORGE NOEL.

Diocesan Tribunal—1200 Memorial Dr., P.O. Box 610, Crookston, 56716. Tel: 218-281-4533.

Judicial Vicar—Rev. MICHAEL SULLIVAN, J.C.L.

Defenders of the Bond—Revs. RICHARD BOYD; VIRGIL HELMIN, J.C.L.

Advocate—JOANNE TOLLEFSON.

Notary—KATHY MORVIG.

Psychological Consultant—ELIZABETH BARAGA SUPER, Ph.D.

Diocesan Offices And Directors

Diocesan Consultors—Rev. Msgr. ROGER L. GRUNDHAUS, V.G.; Revs. ROBERT SCHREINER; LAWRENCE A. WIESELER; VINCENT MILLER; JAMES BERNAUER (Retired); PATRICK A. SULLIVAN.

Finance Council—Most Rev. VICTOR H. BALKE, D.D.; Rev. Msgr. ROGER L. GRUNDHAUS, V.G.; Rev. DAVID J. SUPER; Rev. Msgr. MICHAEL PATNODE; Revs. MICHAEL H. FOLTZ, J.C.L.; DAVID BAUMGARTNER; KAY MACK; MARGEE KELLER; DAN RUST; GAYLE GUNNERSON; PETER ZAVORAL.

Adoption Referral/Post Adoption Search—BERNADETTE DUNN, P.O. Box 610, Crookston, 56716. Tel: 218-281-4533.

Beginning Experience—EVA PEARSON, Pres.; BERNADETTE DUNN, Bishop's Liaison P.O. Box 610, Crookston, 56716. Tel: 218-281-4533.

Boy Scouts—DON VOTAVA, Rte. 2, Box 172A, Warren, 56762. Tel: 218-745-5423; Rev. GARY LAMOINE, Chap.

Catholic Campaign for Human Development—BERNADETTE DUNN, P.O. Box 610, Crookston, 56716. Tel: 218-281-4533.

Catholic Relief Services—BERNADETTE DUNN, Dir., P.O. Box 610, Crookston, 56716. Tel: 218-281-4533.

Commission on Building and Planning—Rev. RICHARD D. LAMBERT; Sr. MARGUERITE STREIFEL, O.S.B.; RICHARD RUDE; JIM SHULIND; ROGER WINTER.

Commission on Catholic-Lutheran Rural Life—Rev. TIM LUNDEEN, Chm., P.O. Box 278, Lancaster, 56735. Tel: 218-762-1691.

Commission on Ecumenism—Deacon RANDY BAUER, Chm.; JOAN HARRINGTON; MARY CLAIRE SETHI; VIJAY SETHI; MICHAEL MCNEIL; FRANCIS DECOCK; AARON RONGEN, 1200 Memorial Dr., P.O. Box 610, Crookston, 56716. Tel: 218-281-4533.

Commission on Liturgy, Sacred Music and Art—Sisters MARGUERITE STREIFEL, O.S.B., Dir.; MARDELLE MOHS, O.S.B.; PATRICE EBLEN, O.S.B.; JULIE MAREK; JAN WOOD; BONNIE LEE; DEL KOHLSTORF; JULIE HARDMEYER; VIRGINIA MORGAN; JIM DOTTENWHY.

Commission on Respect Life—BERNADETTE DUNN, P.O. Box 610, Crookston, 56716. Tel: 218-281-4533.

Commission on Social Justice—BERNADETTE DUNN, P.O. Box 610, Crookston, 56716. Tel: 218-281-4533.

Commission on Women—BERNADETTE DUNN, P.O. Box 610, Crookston, 56716. Tel: 218-281-4533.

Cursillo—ROSE WEBER, Chm. of the Secretariat, Rte. 3, P.O. Box 116, Crookston, 56716.

Deans—Revs. GARY LAMOINE, Northwest; LAWRENCE A. WIESELER, Northeast; DAVID BAUMGARTNER, Western; Rev. Msgr. MICHAEL PATNODE, Eastern; Revs. JOE RICHARDS, Southwest; JERRY ROGERS, Southeast; JOHN KLEINWACHTER, Central.

Diaconate Office—Rev. ROBERT SCHREINER, Dir., 702 Summit Ave., Crookston, 56716. Tel: 218-281-1735.

Diocesan Board of Conciliation and Arbitration—Rev. Msgr. WILLIAM MEHRKENS (Retired), Red Lake, 56671; Sr. DOREEN CHAREST, C.S.J., Moorhead, 56560; Judge MICHAEL KRAKER, Mahnomen, 56557.

School Board, Diocesan—Ex Officio Members: Most Rev. VICTOR H. BALKE, D.D.; Sr. PAT MURPHY, C.S.J. Members: Revs. LARRY DELANEY; DAVID J. SUPER; MARY ANN GRIMM; ROBERT SCHOMER; STEVE WORMS; MARY YONKE; WANDA LYONS; TOM THOMPSON; TODD WOODS; DON JOHANNECK; JANEL KRESL.

Hispanic Ministry—Sr. LEONA ULEWICZ, C.D.P., Coord., P.O. Box 610, Crookston, 56716. Tel: 218-281-4533.

Holy Childhood Association—Rev. Msgr. ROGER L. GRUNDHAUS, V.G., Dir., P.O. Box 610, Crookston, 56716.

Native American Task Force—Rev. Msgr. WILLIAM MEHRKENS, Chm. (Retired), St. Mary's Mission Church, P.O. Box 189, Red Lake, 56671. Tel: 218-679-3614.

Natural Family Planning—SUE MODICH; STEVE MODICH, 2750 Ivy Ln., N.E., Bemidji, 56601. Tel: 218-751-6250.

Newspaper, "Our Northland Diocese"—CAROL EVENSON, Editor & Business Mgr., Diocese of Crookston, 1200 Memorial Dr., P.O. Box 610, Crookston, 56716-0610. Tel: 218-281-4533.

Pastoral Council—Most Rev. VICTOR H. BALKE, D.D., Chm. Coordinators: Sr. DOREEN CHAREST, C.S.J.; RICH VEIT; JIM DULKA, P.O. Box 610, Crookston, 56716. Tel: 218-281-4533.

Pastoral Office of Administration—GEORGE NOEL, Dir., 1200 Memorial Dr., P.O. Box 610, Crookston, 56716. Tel: 218-281-4533.

Pastoral Office of Christian Service—BERNADETTE DUNN, Dir., 1200 Memorial Dr., P.O. Box 610, Crookston, 56716. Tel: 218-281-4533.

Pastoral Office of the Word—Sr. PAT MURPHY, C.S.J., Dir., 1200 Memorial Dr., P.O. Box 610, Crookston, 56716. Tel: 218-281-4533.

Pastoral Office of Worship—Sr. MARGUERITE STREIFEL, O.S.B., Dir., 1200 Memorial Dr., P.O. Box 610, Crookston, 56716. Tel: 218-281-4533.

Priests' Council—Rev. ROBERT SCHREINER, Chm., P.O. Box 610, Crookston, 56716. Tel: 218-281-4533; Rev. Msgr. ROGER L. GRUNDHAUS, V.G., Sec.; Revs. LAWRENCE A. WIESELER; PATRICK A. SULLIVAN; ROBERT SCHREINER; VINCENT MILLER; JAMES BERNAUER (Retired).

Priests' Personnel Board—Rev. Msgr. ROGER L. GRUNDHAUS, V.G., Ex Officio Member; Revs. JERRY ROGERS; RICK LAMBERT; TIMOTHY H. MCGEE; AUGUST GOTHMAN.

Priests Retirement Board of Trustees—Rev. Msgr. MICHAEL PATNODE; Revs. GARY LAMOINE; LARRY DELANEY.

Propagation of the Faith—Rev. Msgr. ROGER L. GRUNDHAUS, V.G., Dir., P.O. Box 610, Crookston, 56716.

Faith Formation and Media—MICHAEL MCNEIL, Dir., 1200 Memorial Dr., P.O. Box 610, Crookston, 56716. Tel: 218-281-4533.

Schools—Sr. PAT MURPHY, C.S.J., Dir. Office of the Word, 1200 Memorial Dr., P.O. Box 610, Crookston, 56716. Tel: 218-281-4533.

TEC (Teens Encounter Christ)—Managers: Sr. EILEEN MOHS, O.S.B.; ELAINE RICARD, P.O. Box 610, Crookston, 56716. Tel: 218-281-4533.

Vocations—Rev. VINCENT MILLER, Dir. Associate Directors: RAY HOLLCRAFT; MITCH WALSKI, P.O. Box 610, Crookston, 56716. Tel: 218-281-4533.

Youth Ministry—RAY HOLLCRAFT, Dir., P.O. Box 610, Crookston, 56716. Tel: 218-281-4533.

Diocesan Sexual Misconduct Review Board—PAUL BIERMAIER, Chm.; Rev. Msgrs. ROGER L. GRUNDHAUS, V.G.; MICHAEL PATNODE; JOHN JEFFREY; CINDY HULST; MARJORIE BAUMGARTNER-HILL; MARK KREJCI, P.O. Box 610, Crookston, 56716. Tel: 218-281-4533.

Victim Assistance Coordinator—BERNADETTE DUNN. Tel: 218-281-4533. Email: bdunn@crookston.org.

CLERGY, PARISHES, MISSIONS AND PAROCHIAL SCHOOLS

CITY OF CROOKSTON
(POLK COUNTY)

1—CATHEDRAL OF THE IMMACULATE CONCEPTION, Revs. David J. Super; Robert Schreiner; Sr. Mardelle Mohs, O.S.B., Pastoral Assoc.; Deacon Dennis Bivens.
Church: 702 Summit Ave., 56716-2736. Tel: 218-281-1735; Fax: 218-281-4717.
School—The Cathedral School, (Grades K-6) Tel: 218-281-1835; Fax: 218-281-1747. Raymond Dusek, Prin. Lay Teachers 10; Students 112.
Mission—St. Mary Euclid, Polk Co.
Mission—St. Peter Gentilly, Polk Co.

2—ST. ANNE'S, Closed., For inquiries for parish records contact the Cathedral of the Immaculate Conception, Crookston.

OUTSIDE THE CITY OF CROOKSTON

ADA, NORMAN CO., ST. JOSEPH'S, [JC] Rev. David Baumgartner.
Res.: 405 E. Thorpe Ave., 56510. Tel: 218-784-4131.
Mission—Holy Family Halstad, Norman Co.
Mission—St. William Twin Valley, Norman Co.

AKELEY, HUBBARD CO.
1—ST. JOHN, Merged, with Immaculate Conception, Nevis to form Our Lady of the Pines, Akeley.
2—OUR LADY OF THE PINES, Rev. Duane Pribula.
Res.: 30 Chicago Ave., S.W., P.O. Box 219, 56433. Tel: 218-652-2785; Fax: 218-652-6801.
Mission—St. Theodore LaPorte, Hubbard Co. 56461.

ALMA, MARSHALL CO., ST. JOHN THE BAPTIST, Closed., For inquiries for parish records contact St. Stephen, Stephen. Tel: 218-478-2231.

ARGYLE, MARSHALL CO., ST. ROSE, [CEM], Served by SS. Peter and Paul, Warren. Rev. Gary LaMoine. P.O. Box 277, 56713. Tel: 218-437-6341.

BADGER, ROSEAU CO., ST. MARY'S, , Served by Sacred Heart, Roseau. Tel: 218-463-2441, Fax: 218-463-2443. , Mailing Address: 504 N. Main St., 56714.

BAGLEY, CLEARWATER CO., ST. JOSEPH, [CEM] Lois Jenkins, Pastoral Admin. Served by St. Mary's, Redlake.
Res.: P.O. Box 67, 56621. Tel: 218-694-6416.

BARNESVILLE, CLAY CO., ASSUMPTION, [CEM] Rev. Joseph Kieselbach.
Res.: 307 Front St. N., P.O. Box 339, 56514. Tel: 218-354-7320; Fax: 218-354-7659.
Mission—St. Cecilia Sabin, Clay Co.

BAUDETTE, LAKE OF THE WOODS CO., SACRED HEART, , Served by St. Mary's, Warroad. Deacon James Lukenbill, Pastoral Admin.
Res.: P.O. Box 738, 56623. Tel: 218-634-2689.
Mission—St. Joseph [CEM] Williams, Lake of the Woods Co.

BEAULIEU, MAHNOMEN CO., ST. JOSEPH, , Served by St. Michael, Mahnomen. Tel: 218-935-2503; Fax. 218-935-2503. , Mailing Address: 120 W. Jefferson, Mahnomen, 56557.

BEJOU, MAHNOMEN CO., IMMACULATE CONCEPTION, Closed., For inquiries for parish records contact St. Michael's, Mahnomen.

BEMIDJI, BELTRAMI CO., ST. PHILIP'S, [CEM] Rev. Msgr. Michael Patnode; Rev. Robert L. Stone; Deacons John Schuiling; Mike Tolin. In Res., Rev. Edward Nistler (Retired).
Res.: 710 Beltrami Ave. N.W., 56601-3046. Tel: 218-444-4262; Fax: 218-444-1381.
School—Tel: 218-444-4938; Fax: 218-444-1379. Mrs. Carol Rettinger, Prin. Lay Teachers 22; Students 314.
Mission—Sacred Heart Wilton, Beltrami Co.
Mission—St. Charles Pennington, Beltrami Co.
Mission—Holy Spirit Newman Center, Beltrami Co.

BENWOOD, ROSEAU CO., ST. JOSEPH THE WORKER, , Served by Sacred Heart, Roseau. Tel: 218-463-2441; Fax: 218-463-2443. , Mailing Address: P.O. Box 118, Roseau, 56751.

BIG ELBOW LAKE, BECKER CO., ST. FRANCIS CABRINI, , Served by St. Ann, Waubun. Tel: 218-473-2101. Rev. Robert Leising, O.M.I.
Mailing Address: 1112 3rd St., Waubun, 56589.

BLACKDUCK, BELTRAMI CO., ST. ANN'S, , Served by St. Patrick's, Kelliher. Tel: 218-647-8392. , Mailing Address: P.O. Box 330, 56630.

BROOKS, RED LAKE CO., ST. JOSEPH, , Mailing Address: P.O. Box 400, Red Lake Falls, 56750-0400. Served by St. Joseph's, Red Lake Falls. Tel: 218-253-2685; Fax. 218-253-2195.

CALLAWAY, BECKER CO., ASSUMPTION, [CEM], Served by Sacred Heart, Frazee Rev. Joseph DeCrans; Deacon Randy Bauer, Pastoral Assoc.
Res.: P.O. Box 67, 56521. Tel: 218-375-3571; Fax: 218-847-6367.

DETROIT LAKES, BECKER CO., HOLY ROSARY, [CEM] Revs. Jerry Rogers; Jan Klimek; Deacons Randall J. Bauer; James Thomas; Ole "Red" Elton.
Office—1043 Lake Ave., 56501-3499. Tel: 218-847-1393; Fax: 218-847-6367.
School—Tel: 218-847-5306; Fax: 218-847-6367. Kathleen Klindt, Prin. Lay Teachers 13; Students 141.
Mission—St. Andrew Hawley, Clay Co. 56549.
Mission—St. Francis Xavier Lake Park, Becker Co. 56554.

DILWORTH, CLAY CO., ST. ELIZABETH, , Served by St. Francis de Sales, Moorhead. 218-233-4780. Revs. Joseph D. Richards; Luis Segundo Buitron; Duane Koble, Pastoral Admin.
Mailing Address: P.O. Box 307, 56529-0307. Tel: 218-287-2705; Fax: 218-287-4587.

DOROTHY, RED LAKE CO., ST. DOROTHY, Closed., For inquiries for parish records contact St. Joseph's, Red Lake Falls.

EAST GRAND FORKS, POLK CO., SACRED HEART, [CEM] Revs. Larry Delaney; Gothman L. August.
Church: 200 Third St., N.W., 56721-1806. Tel: 218-773-0877; Fax: 218-773-8312.
School—Tel: 218-773-1579; Fax: 218-773-7042. Mr. David Andrys, Prin. Lay Teachers 15; Students 167.
High School—Tel: 218-773-0230; Fax: 218-773-0318. Mr. Phillip E. Meyer, Prin. Lay Teachers 20; Students 178.
Convent—Tel: 218-773-0563. Sr. Marguerite Streifel, O.S.B., Coord.
Mission—St. Francis Fisher, Polk Co.
Mission—Holy Trinity Tabor, Polk Co.

EUCLID, POLK CO., ST. MARY, , Served by the Cathedral of the Immaculate Conception, Crookston. Tel: 218-281-1735. , Mailing Address: P.O. Box 213, 56722.

FALUN, ROSEAU CO., ST. PHILIP, , Served by St. Mary's, Warroad. Tel: 218-386-1178. , Mailing Address: P.O. Box 33, Warroad, 56763.

FELTON, CLAY CO., ST. LAWRENCE, Closed., For inquiries for parish records contact St. Joseph's, Ada.

FERTILE, POLK CO., ST. JOSEPH, [CEM] Rev. Msgr. Roger L. Grundhaus, V.G.; Sr. Mary Jean Gust, O.S.B., Pastoral Assoc.
Mailing Address: 205 S.E. Elm St., 56540. Tel: 218-945-6649.
Res.: 1200 Memorial Dr., 56716. Tel: 218-281-4533; Fax: 218-281-3328.

FISHER, POLK CO., ST. FRANCIS, [CEM], Served by Sacred Heart, East Grand Forks. Tel: 218-773-0877. , Mailing Address: 304 Park Ave., 56723.

FLORIAN, MARSHALL CO., ASSUMPTION - FLORIAN, [CEM], Served by St. Stephen, Stephen. Rev. Vincent Miller; Deacon Courtney Abel.
Mailing Address: 26932 390th St. N.W., Strandquist, 56758. Tel: 218-478-3578.

FOSSTON, POLK CO., ST. MARY'S, [CEM], Served by St. Francis Xavier, Oklee. Rev. Richard Boyd; Sr. Debra Berry, S.M.P., Pastoral Admin.
Res. & Mailing Address: 725 6th St., N.E., 56542. Tel: 218-435-6484; Fax: 218-435-2549.

FRAZEE, BECKER CO., SACRED HEART, [CEM] Rev. Joseph DeCrans.
Res.: 202 W. Maple Ave., 56544. Tel: 218-334-4221.
Mission—Assumption Callaway, Becker Co. 56521.
Mission—St. Mary of the Lakes Lake Eunice Township, Becker Co.

GENTILLY, POLK CO., ST. PETER'S, [CEM], Mailing Address: 25823-185th Ave., S.W., 56716. Tel: 218-281-1735. Served by Cathedral of the Immaculate Conception, Crookston. Tel: 218-281-1735.

GEORGETOWN, CLAY CO., ST. JOHN, , Served by St. Francis de Sales, Moorhead. Tel: 218-233-4780. Revs. Joseph D. Richards; Luis Segundo Buitron.
Mailing Address: P.O. Box 248, 56546.

GOODRIDGE, PENNINGTON CO., ST. ANNE, , Served by St. Francis Xavier, Oklee. Tel: 218-435-6484.

GREENBUSH, ROSEAU CO., BLESSED SACRAMENT, [CEM] Rev. Donald Braukmann; Mitch & Lee Walski, Pastoral Ministers.
Res.: P.O. Box A, 56726. Tel: 218-782-2467.
Mission—St. Joseph Middle River, Marshall Co.
Mission—St. Edward Karlstad, Marshall Co.

GRYGLA, MARSHALL CO., ST. CLEMENT, , Served by St. Francis Xavier, Oklee. Tel: 218-435-6484.

HALLOCK, KITTSON CO., ST. PATRICK'S, Rev. Timothy T. Noah.
Res.: P.O. Box 519, 56728-0519. Tel: 218-843-2323.
Mission—Holy Rosary Lancaster, Kittson Co.

HALSTAD, NORMAN CO., HOLY FAMILY, , Served by St. Joseph, Ada. Tel: 218-784-4131. [JC] , Mailing Address: P.O. Box 51, 56548.

HAWLEY, CLAY CO., ST. ANDREW, , Served by Holy Rosary, Detroit Lakes. Tel: 218-847-1393; Fax: 218-238-6028. Revs. Jerry Rogers; Jan Klimek.
Mailing Address: 1418 Main St., P.O. Box 129, 56549. Tel: 218-483-4264; Fax: 218-483-4158.

KARLSTAD, KITTSON CO., ST. EDWARD THE CONFESSOR, , Served by Blessed Sacrament, Greenbush. Tel: 218-782-2467.

KELLIHER, BELTRAMI CO., ST. PATRICK, [JC] Rev. James Lyons.
Res.: P.O. Box 187, 56650. Tel: 218-647-8392.
Mission—St. Ann Blackduck, Beltrami Co.
Mission—St. Michael Northome, Koochiching Co.

LAKE EUNICE TOWNSHIP, BECKER CO., ST. MARY OF THE LAKES, , Served by Sacred Heart, Franzee. Tel: 218-238-6639. , Mailing Address: 20996 County Rd. #20, Detroit Lakes, 56501. Tel: 218-439-3938. In Res., Revs. Eugene L. Wesely (Retired); Joseph DeCrans.

LAKE ITASCA, CLEARWATER CO., ST. CATHERINE, Closed., For inquiries for parish records contact St. Peter's, Park Rapids.

LAKE PARK, BECKER CO., ST. FRANCIS XAVIER'S, [CEM] Revs. Jerry Rogers; Jan Klimek.
Res.: 2066 Second St., 56554-4402. Tel: 218-238-6639; Fax: 218-238-6028.

LANCASTER, KITTSON CO., HOLY ROSARY, , Mailing Address: *St. Patrick's*, P.O. Box 519, Hallock, 56728. Served by St. Patrick, Hallock. Tel: 218-843-2323.

LAPORTE, HUBBARD CO., ST. THEODORE - LAPORTE, , Served by Our Lady of the Pines, Akeley/Nevis. Tel: 218-652-2785. Rev. Duane Pribula.
Mailing Address: P.O. Box 219, Akeley, 56433.

LEO, ROSEAU CO., ST. ALOYSIUS, Closed., For inquiries for parish records contact Blessed Sacrament, Greenbush.

MAHNOMEN, MAHNOMEN CO., ST. MICHAEL'S, [CEM] Rev. Richard D. Lambert.

Res.: 120 W. Jefferson Ave., 56557. Tel: 218-935-2503; Fax: 218-935-2503.
School—Tel: 218-935-5222; Fax: 218-935-5222. Sr. Yvonne Schafer, O.S.B., Prin. Sisters of St. Benedict 2; Lay Teachers 7; Students 64.
Catechesis/Religious Program—Sr. Yvonne Schafer, O.S.B., D.R.E., (PreK-6); Vickie Anderson, D.R.E., (7-12). Students 264.
Mission—St. Joseph [CEM] Beaulieu, Mahnomen Co.

MENTOR, POLK CO., ST. LAWRENCE, Rev. Msgr. Roger L. Grundhaus, V.G.; Deacon John A. Bruggeman.
Mailing Address: P.O. Box 51, 56736. Tel: 218-637-8178.
Res.: 1200 Memorial Dr., 56716. Tel: 218-281-4533; Fax: 218-281-3328.

MIDDLE RIVER, MARSHALL CO., ST. JOSEPH, HUSBAND OF MARY, [CEM], Served by Blessed Sacrament, Greenbush. , Mailing Address: P. O. Box A, Greenbush, 56726. Tel: 218-782-2467.

MOORHEAD, CLAY CO.
1—ST. FRANCIS DE SALES, [JC] Revs. Joseph D. Richards; Luis Segundo Buitron.
Mailing Address: *Office*, 601 15th Ave. N , 56560. Tel: 218-233-4780; Fax: 218-233-0270.
Mission—St. John Georgetown, Clay Co. 56546.
Mission—St. Elizabeth Dilworth, Clay Co. 56529.
2—ST. JOSEPH'S, [JC] Revs. Michael H. Foltz, J.C.L.; Todd Arends.
Office—218 10th St. S., 56560. Tel: 218-236-5066; 218-236-9503 (Res.); Fax: 218-233-0717.
School—Tel: 218-233-0553. Valerie Ritland, Prin. Sisters 1; Lay Teachers 17; Students 205.
Catechesis/Religious Program—Tel: 218-236-1979. Joann Koble, D.R.E. Students 590.
Mission—St. Thomas Newman Center 707-11th St. S., Clay Co. Tel: 218-236-9596.

NAYTAHWAUSH, MAHNOMEN CO., ST. ANNE, , Served by St. Ann's, Waubun. Tel: 218-473-2101. Rev. Robert Leising, O.M.I.; Sr. Jean Schwartz, O.S.B., Pastoral Assoc.
Mailing Address: P.O. Box 157, 56566-0157. Tel: 218-935-5676; Fax: 218-473-2101.

NEBISH, BELTRAMI CO., ST. JOHN, , Served by St. Mary's Mission, Red Lake. Tel: 218-679-3614. , Mailing Address: *St. Mary's Mission*, P.O. Box 189, Red Lake, 56671.

NEVIS, HUBBARD CO., IMMACULATE CONCEPTION, Merged, with St. John's, Akeley to form Our Lady of the Pines, Akeley.

OGEMA, BECKER CO., MOST HOLY REDEEMER, [CEM] Rev. Mietek Bajek, O.M.I.
Res.: P.O. Box 57, 56569-0057. Tel: 218-983-3261; Fax: 218-473-2020.
Mission—St. Benedict White Earth, Becker Co. 56591.
Mission—St. Theodore Ponsford, Becker Co. 56575.

OKLEE, RED LAKE CO., ST. FRANCIS XAVIER'S, [CEM] Rev. John Kleinwachter.
P.O. Box 160, 56742. Tel: 218-796-5844.
Mission—St. Anne Goodridge, Pennington Co.
Mission—St. Clement Grygla, Marshall Co.
Mission—St. Mary Fosston, Polk Co. 56542.

OSLO, MARSHALL CO., ST. JOSEPH, [CEM], Served by SS. Peter and Paul, Warren. Tel: 218-745-4511. Lanette Sweeney, Pastoral Assoc.
Res.: P.O. Box 97, 56744. Tel: 218-695-2641.

PARK RAPIDS, HUBBARD CO., ST. PETER'S, [JC] Rev. Dennis J. Wieland.
Res.: P.O. Box 353, 56470-0353. Tel: 218-732-5142 (Office); 218-732-8852 (Res.); Fax: 218-732-2971.
Mission—St. Mary Two Inlets, Becker Co.

PENNINGTON, BELTRAMI CO., ST. CHARLES, , Served by St. Philip's, Bemidji. Tel: 218-444-4262 , Mailing Address: *St. Philip's*, 710 Beltrami Ave., N.W., Bemidji, 56601-3046.

PLUMMER, RED LAKE CO., ST. VINCENT DE PAUL, Closed., For inquiries for parish records contact St. Francis Xavier, Oklee.

PONSFORD, BECKER CO., ST. THEODORE, , Served by Most Holy Redeemer, Ogema. Tel: 218-983-3261. , Mailing Address: *Most Holy Redeemer*, P.O. Box 57, Ogema, 56569-0057.

RED LAKE FALLS, RED LAKE CO., ST. JOSEPH'S, [CEM] Rev. Timothy F. Bushy; Jan Wood, Pastoral Team Member.
Office & Res.: P.O. Box 400, 56750-0400. Tel: 218-253-2004 (Res.); 218-253-2685; Fax: 218-253-2195 (Office).
School—112 Edward Ave. N.W., P.O. Box 400, 56750-0400. Tel: 218-253-2188; Fax: 218-253-2195. Sr. Richarde Wolf, S.S.N.D., Prin. Lay Teachers 6; Students 64.
Mission—St. Joseph [CEM] Brooks, Red Lake Co. 56715.

RED LAKE, BELTRAMI CO., ST. MARY'S MISSION CHURCH, [CEM] Rev. Patrick A. Sullivan. In Res., Rev. Msgr. William Mehrkens (Retired).
Res.: P.O. Box 189, 56671-0189. Tel: 218-679-3614; Fax: 218-679-2212.
School—Tel: 218-679-3388. Sr. Sharon Sheridan, O.S.F., Prin. Sisters 3; Lay Teachers 8; Students 63.
Mission—St. John Nebish, Beltrami Co.
Mission—St. Joseph Bagley, Clearwater Co. 56621.

ROSEAU, ROSEAU CO., SACRED HEART, [CEM] Rev. Robert J. LaPlante.
Office: 403 Main Ave. N., 56751. Tel: 218-463-2441; Fax: 218-463-2443.
Mission—St. Mary's [CEM] Badger, Roseau Co.
Mission—St. Joseph, The Worker [CEM] Benwood, Roseau Co

SABIN, CLAY CO., ST. CECILIA, , Served by Assumption, Barnesville. Tel: 218-354-7320. Mailing Address: *Assumption*, P.O. Box 339, Barnesville, 56514-0339.

SHEVLIN, CLEARWATER CO., OUR LADY OF VICTORY, Closed., For inquiries for parish records contact St. Joseph's, Bagley.

STEPHEN, MARSHALL CO., ST. STEPHEN'S, [CEM] Rev. Vincent Miller.
Res.: P.O. Box 507, 56757. Tel: 218-478-2231; Fax: 218-478-2231.
Mission—Assumption Florian, Marshall Co.

TABOR, POLK CO., HOLY TRINITY CATHOLIC, , Served by Sacred Heart, East Grand Forks. Tel: 218-773-0877. , Mailing Address: 37639 140th St., N.W., Angus, 56762-8929.

TERREBONNE, RED LAKE CO., ST. ANTHONY Closed., For inquiries for parish records contact St. Joseph's, Red Lake Falls.

THIEF RIVER FALLS, PENNINGTON CO., ST. BERNARDS, [CEM] Rev. Timothy H. McGee.
Res.: 105 Knight Ave. N., 56701. Tel: 218 681-3571; Fax: 218-681-3560.
School—Tel: 218-681-1539; Fax: 218-681-2261. Sr. Kathy Kuchar, O.S.B., Prin. Lay Teachers 9; Students 128.

TWIN VALLEY, NORMAN CO., ST. WILLIAM, , Served by St. Joseph, Ada. Tel: 218-784-4131. , Mailing Address: P.O. Box 306, 56584.

TWO INLETS, BECKER CO., ST. MARY'S, , Served by St. Peter's, Park Rapids. Tel: 218-732-5142. Rev. Dennis J. Wieland; Sr. Janice Miller, C.S.J., Pastoral Assoc.
Mailing Address: 55744 Cty. Hwy. 44, Park Rapids, 56470. Tel: 218-732-4046; Fax: 218-732-4046.

WARREN, MARSHALL CO., SS. PETER AND PAUL, [CEM] Rev. Gary LaMoine.
Res.: 208 N. Seventh St., 56762. Tel: 218-745-4511; Fax: 218-745-5484.
Mission—St. Joseph P.O. Box 97, Oslo Marshall Co. 56744. Tel: 218-695-2641. Lanette Sweeney, Pastoral Assoc.
Mission—St. Rose of Lima Argyle, Marshall Co.

WARROAD, ROSEAU CO., ST. MARY'S, [CEM] Rev. Lawrence A. Wieseler.
Res.: P.O. Box 33, 56763. Tel: 218-386-1178; Fax: 218-386-3186.

Mission—St. Philip Falun, Roseau Co.

WAUBUN, MAHNOMEN CO., ST. ANN, [CEM] Rev. Robert Leising, O.M.I.
Res.: 1112 3rd St., 56589-9402. Tel: 218-473-2101; Fax: 218-473-2101.
Mission—St. Anne Naytahwaush, Mahnomen Co.
Mission—St. Francis Cabrini Big Elbow Lake, Becker Co.

WHITE EARTH, BECKER CO., ST. BENEDICT, [CEM], Served by Most Holy Redeemer, Ogema. Tel: 218-936-3261. Bro. William Lundberg, O.M.I., Pastoral Assoc.
Mailing Address: P.O. Box 57, Ogema, 56569-0057. Tel: 218-983-3519; Fax: 218-983-3261.

WILLIAMS, LAKE OF THE WOODS CO., ST. JOSEPH, , Served by Sacred Heart, Baudette. Tel: 218-634-2689. , Mailing Address: P.O. Box 738, Baudette, 56623.

WILTON, BELTRAMI CO., SACRED HEART, , Served by St. Philip, Bemidji. Tel: 218-751-4262. , Mailing Address: *St. Philip*, 710 Beltrami Ave., N.W., Bemidji, 56601-3046.

On Duty Outside the Diocese:
Revs.—
Bester, Robert (Retired)
Foley, Gerald K.
Freidl, Thomas A.
Silva, Luis
Sullivan, Michael

Leave of Absence:
Revs.—
Boyd, Richard
Skoczylas, Walter
Troska, Llewelyn J.

Retired:
Rev. Msgrs.—
Krebs, Donald H., 11659 Maple Lake Dr., S.E., Mentor, 56736.
Mehrkens, William, P.O. Box 189, Red Lake, 56671. Tel: 218-679-3614
Revs.—
Bernauer, James, P.O. Box 7, Dent, 56528. Tel: 218-758-3377
Bester, Robert
Felion, Jerome, 1171 FM 649, Rio Grande City, TX 78582. Tel: 956-486-2773
Kulhawik, Frank, P.O. Box 306, Twin Valley, 56584. Tel: 218-584-5200
Nistler, Edward, 710 Beltrami Ave., Bemidji, 56601. Tel: 218-444-4262
Noah, Daniel, 24344-265th St., S.W., 56716.
Noesen, Gerald, 14126 Salem Shore Rd., S.E., Mentor, 56736.
Palcisko, Raymond, 2769-28th St. N.W., Baudette, 56623.
Pryor, G. Robert, 286 Grantwood Dr., Henderson, NV 89014. U.S.A.F

Permanent Deacons:
Abel, Courtney, Assumption, Florian
Bauer, Randall J., Holy Rosary, Detroit Lakes; Assumption, Callaway
Bivens, Dennis, Cathedral of the Immaculate Conception, Crookston; St. Peter's, Gentilly; St. Mary's, Euclid
Bruggeman, John A., St. Lawrence, Mentor
Eisbrener, John, (Retired), Trail, MN; St. Bernard, Thief River Falls
Elton, Ole "Red", Holy Rosary, Detroit Lakes
Hannig, Daniel, Marshfield, WI
Lukenbill, James, Sacred Heart, Baudette
Schuiling, John, St. Philip, Bemidji
Thomas, James, Holy Rosary, Detroit Lakes
Tolin, Mike, St. Philip, Bemidji

INSTITUTIONS LOCATED IN THE DIOCESE

[A] ELEMENTARY SCHOOLS

RED LAKE. *St. Mary's Mission School*, P.O. Box 189, 56671-0189. Tel: 218-679-3388; Fax: 218-679-2212. Email: mission@paulbunyan.net. Rev. Patrick A. Sullivan. Benedictine Sisters (St. Joseph, MN) Sisters 3; Lay Teachers 5; Students 63.

[B] CONFRATERNITY OF CHRISTIAN DOCTRINE

CROOKSTON. *Cathedral - Religious Education/Faith Formation*, 702 Summit Ave., 56716. Tel: 218-281-1735; Fax: 218-281-1747. Email: cathedral@midconetwork.com. Raymond Dusek, D.R.E. (Grades PreK-6); Sr. Mardelle Mohs, O.S.B., Junior High Coord.; Michael Betting, Senior High Coord. Students (Grades K-8) 130; High School Students (Grades 9-11) 225.

ADA. *St. Joseph Parish, R.E. Program* 56510. Tel: 218-784-4131. Email: stjoseph@loretel.net. Students 130.

ARGYLE. *St. Rose Parish, R.E. Program*, Box 277, 56713. Tel: 218-437-6341; Fax: 218-437-6341. Email: straser@gvtel.com. Marilyn Kuznia, Dir. Students 113.

BEMIDJI. *St. Philips Parish, Religious Formation Program*, 620 Beltrami Ave., 56601. Tel: 218-444-5849; Fax: 218-444-4262. Kris Jensen, D.R.E. (Grades PreK-8); Mary Auger, D.R.E. (Grades 9-12). Students (Grades PreK-5) 110; Students (Grades 6-12) 200.

DETROIT LAKES. *Holy Rosary Parish, R.E. Program*, 1043 Lake Ave., 56501. Tel: 218-847-8970; Fax: 218-847-6367. JoAnne Knuttila, Coord. Students 300.

EAST GRAND FORKS. *Sacred Heart Parish, R.E. Program* 200 Third St. N.W., 56721. Tel: 218-773-0531; Fax: 218-773-8312. Web: www.sacredheartegf.net. Ginny Osowski, D.R.E. (Grades PreK-6); Sr. Mary Jean Gust, O.S.B., D.R.E. (Grades 7-10). Students 420.

GREENBUSH. *Religious Education Program*, P.O. Box A, 56726. Tel: 218-782-2263. Becka Nubson, Coord. Students 140.

THIEF RIVER FALLS. *Religious Education Program*, 105 Knight Ave. N., 56701. Tel: 218-681-3571; Fax: 218-681-3560. Email: thmcgee@mncable.net. Web: www.stbernardstrf.org. Margaret Rasmussen, Coord. Students 253; High School Students 101.

[C] GENERAL HOSPITALS

BAUDETTE. *Lakewood Health Center*, 600 South Main, 56623. Tel: 218-634-2120; Fax: 218-634-3416. Email: sharraypalm@catholichealth.net. Web: www.lakewood-baudette.org. SharRay Palm, Pres. & CEO. Affiliate of Catholic Health Initiatives. Bed Capacity: Acute 15; Long term care 50; Staff 164; Patients assisted annually 17,220.

Lakewood Care Center, 600 Main Ave. S., 56623. Tel: 218-634-1588; Fax: 218-634-3489. Affiliate of Catholic Health Initiatives. Sisters 1; Bed Capacity 50; Residents assisted annually 115.

DETROIT LAKES. **St. Mary's Regional Health Center* (Sub. of Benedictine Health System) , 1027 Washington Ave., 56501. Tel: 218-847-5611; Fax: 218-847-7674. Web: www.smrhc.com. Thomas R. Thompson, CEO; Tim Cook, Chap.; Sr. Lenore Paschke, O.S.B., Chap.

St. Mary's EMS, 1240 Washington Ave., P.O. Box 1410, 56501. Tel: 218-847-0817; Fax: 218-847-0842. Thomas R. Thompson, CEO. (Sub. of St. Mary's Regional Health Center) Beds Acute 87; Long Term Care 100; Patients Assisted Annually 21,559.

PARK RAPIDS. *St. Joseph Area Health Services*, 600 Pleasant Ave., 56470. Tel: 218-732-3311; Fax: 218-732-1368. Email: kathydickinson@catholichealth.net. Mr. Peter Jacobson, Pres. & CEO. Affiliate of Catholic Health Initiatives. Sisters 3; Bed Capacity 50; Patients assisted annually 18,000.

[D] HOMES FOR THE AGED

CROOKSTON. *Villa St. Vincent*, 516 Walsh St., 56716. Tel: 218-281-3424; Fax: 218-281-4755. Mr. Michael Siekas, Admin. Co-sponsored by the Benedictine Sisters of Crookston, Mt. St. Benedict Monastery and the Benectine Health System. Sisters of St. Benedict 2; 34; Assisted Living Beds 73; Skilled Nursing Beds 80; Alzheimer's Beds 24; Residents 159.

DETROIT LAKES. *St. Mary's Nursing Center* 56501. Thomas R. Thompson, Admin. Attended by Staff of St. Mary's Regional Health Center. Assisted Living 30; Independent Living 58.

[E] CONVENTS AND RESIDENCES FOR SISTERS

CROOKSTON. *Marywood Residential Community* (Retirement Residence) , 23616 U.S. Hwy. 2, S.W., 56716-9603.

23616 US Hwy. 2, S.W., 56716-9603. Tel: 218-281-3093; Fax: 218-281-6123. Web: www.sistersofstjoseph.org. Sr. Vivian Miron, C.S.J., Community Coord.; Thomas Lenertz, Admin.; Rev. Msgr. Roger L. Grundhaus, V.G.; Sr. Cecelia Forcier, C.S.J., Archivist. Congregation of the Sisters of St. Joseph of Medaille (Pontifical Jurisdiction) Marywood Residential Community 14; Crookston Regional Community 26.

Mount St. Benedict Monastery, 620 Summit Ave. E., 56716-2799. Tel: 218-281-3441; Fax: 218-281-6966. Email: sisters@msb.net. Web: www.msb.net. Sisters Catherine Merck, O.S.B., Prioress; Mary Ann Welsch, Subprioress. Motherhouse of the Order of the Sisters of St. Benedict of Pontifical Jurisdiction-The Federation of St. Gertrude. Sisters in Community 114.

Sisters of St. Benedict Initial Formation Tel: 218-281-3441; Fax: 218-281-6966. Sr. Lois Spors, O.S.B.

Sunrise Center for Children and Families Tel: 218-281-6540; Fax: 218-281-6966. Sr. Judith Moen, O.S.B., Dir.

[F] NEWMAN CENTERS

CROOKSTON. *University of Minnesota Cooperative Campus Ministry* 56716. Tel: 218-281-8516; Fax: 218-281-8504. Email: cboike@mail.crk.umn.edu. Web: www.crk.umn.edu. Chris Boike, Dir. Coop. Campus Ministry.

BEMIDJI. *Holy Spirit Newman Center* 1701 Birch Ln. N.E., 56601-2607. Tel: 218-444-4762; Fax: 218-444-7244. Email: ncenter@paulbunyan.net. Web: www.bemidjistate.edu/newmancenter. Rev. Msgr. Michael Patnode; Rev. Robert L. Stone; Lois Jenkins, Pastoral Assoc.

MOORHEAD. *St. Thomas Aquinas Newman Center* 707 11th St. S., 56560. Tel: 218-236-9596. Email: newman@mnstate.edu. Web: www.mnstate.edu/newman. Chris Yarnal, Campus Min.

[G] MISCELLANEOUS

CROOKSTON. **The Diocese of Crookston Catholic Community Foundation*, 1200 Memorial Dr., 56716. Tel: 218-281-4533; Fax: 218-281-3328. Email: ccf@crookston.org. Web: www.crookston.org/ccf.

**Mount Saint Benedict Foundation*, 620 Summit Ave., 56716-2799. Tel: 218-281-3441; Fax: 218-281-6966.

RELIGIOUS INSTITUTES OF MEN REPRESENTED IN THE DIOCESE

For further details refer to the corresponding bracketed number in the Religious Institutes of Men or Women section.

[0910]—*Oblates of Mary Immaculate*—O.M.I.

RELIGIOUS INSTITUTES OF WOMEN REPRESENTED IN THE DIOCESE

[0230]—*Benedictine Sisters of Pontifical Jurisdiction* (Congregation of St. Gertrude)—O.S.B.

[0230]—*Benedictine Sisters of Pontifical Jurisdiction (Federation of St. Benedict)*—O.S.B.

[]—*Congregation of the Blessed Virgin Mary of the Angels*—O.S.F.

[]—*Congregation of the Sisters of the Third Order of St. Francis*—O.S.F.

[2970]—*School Sisters of Notre Dame* (Mankato Province)—S.S.N.D.

[]—*Sisters of Divine Providence* (Pittsburgh, PA)—C.D.P.

[2450]—*Sisters of Mary of the Presentation* (Valley City, ND)—S.M.P.

[3880]—*Sisters of St. Joseph of Medaille*—C.S.J.

NECROLOGY

† Carriere, Henry G., (Retired)—Died Nov. 3, 2003

† Lemen, William F., Bemdiji, MN St. Philip—Died March 22, 2003

Diocese of Dallas

(Dioecesis Dallasensis)

Most Reverend

CHARLES V. GRAHMANN, D.D.

Bishop of Dallas; ordained March 17, 1956; appointed Titular Bishop of Equilio and Auxiliary of San Antonio June 30, 1981; consecrated August 29, 1981; appointed First Bishop of Victoria April 14, 1982; installed May 29, 1982; appointed Coadjutor of Dallas December 18, 1989; Reception as Coadjutor of Dallas February 21, 1990; appointed Bishop of Dallas July 14, 1990.

Chancery Office: 3725 Blackburn, P.O. Box 190507, Dallas, TX 75219. Tel: 214-528-2240; Fax: 214-526-1743.

Web: www.cathdal.org

Email: ccfcdal@cathdal.org

Most Reverend

THOMAS TSCHOEPE

Retired Bishop of Dallas; ordained May 30, 1943; appointed Bishop of San Angelo January 12, 1966; consecrated March 9, 1966; Transferred to Dallas August 27, 1969; Resigned July 14, 1990. *Res.: St. Joseph Residence, Inc.*, 330 W. Pembroke, Dallas, TX 75208.

ESTABLISHED DIOCESE OF DALLAS ON JULY 15, 1890.

Square Miles 7,523.

Redesignated Diocese of Dallas-Fort Worth on October 20, 1953.

Redesignated Diocese of Dallas on August 27, 1969.

Comprises the following nine Counties in the State of Texas: Collin, Dallas, Ellis, Fannin, Grayson, Hunt, Kaufman, Navarro and Rockwall.

For legal titles of parishes and diocesan institutions, consult the Chancery Office.

STATISTICAL OVERVIEW

Personnel	
Bishop	2
Retired Bishops	1
Abbots	1
Priests: Diocesan Active in Diocese	66
Priests: Diocesan Active Outside Diocese	4
Priests: Retired, Sick or Absent	27
Number of Diocesan Priests	97
Religious Priests in Diocese	76
Total Priests in Diocese	173
Extern Priests in Diocese	33
Permanent Deacons in Diocese	145
Total Brothers	7
Total Sisters	142
Parishes	
Parishes	67
With Resident Pastor:	
Resident Diocesan Priests	47
Resident Religious Priests	9
Without Resident Pastor:	
Administered by Priests	9
Administered by Deacons	2
Missions	8
Professional Ministry Personnel:	
Brothers	3
Sisters	44
Lay Ministers	276
Welfare	
Catholic Hospitals	1
Total Assisted	118,744
Homes for the Aged	1
Total Assisted	49
Day Care Centers	8
Total Assisted	279
Special Centers for Social Services	15
Total Assisted	36,087
Educational	
Seminaries, Diocesan	1
Students from This Diocese	6
Students from Other Diocese	36
Diocesan Students in Other Seminaries	9
Total Seminarians	15
Colleges and Universities	1
Total Students	3,170
High Schools, Diocesan and Parish	3
Total Students	1,733
High Schools, Private	4
Total Students	2,620
Elementary Schools, Diocesan and Parish	33
Total Students	10,605
Elementary Schools, Private	1
Total Students	174
Non-residential Schools for the Disabled	1
Total Students	122
Catechesis/Religious Education:	
High School Students	5,041
Elementary Students	35,527
Total Students under Catholic Instruction	59,007
Teachers in the Diocese:	
Priests	14
Scholastics	1
Brothers	4
Sisters	142
Lay Teachers	885
Vital Statistics	
Receptions into the Church:	
Infant Baptism Totals	15,794
Adult Baptism Totals	818
Received into Full Communion	574
First Communions	10,033
Confirmations	6,465
Marriages:	
Catholic	1,595
Interfaith	521
Total Marriages	2,116
Deaths	1,372
Total Catholic Population	930,352
Total Population	3,371,300

Former Bishops—Rt. Revs. THOMAS F. BRENNAN, D.D., consecrated April 5, 1891; resigned Nov. 17, 1892; died March 21, 1916; EDWARD JOSEPH DUNNE, D.D., consecrated Nov. 30. 1893; died Aug. 5, 1910; Most Revs. JOSEPH PATRICK LYNCH, D.D., LL.D., appt. June 8, 1911; consecrated July 12, 1911; Assistant at Pontifical Throne, May 13, 1936; died Aug. 19, 1954; THOMAS K. GORMAN, D.D., D.Sc.Hist., ord. June 23, 1917; Bishop of Reno; appt. April 24, 1931; consecrated July 22, 1931; Assistant at the Pontifical Throne, May 4, 1942; appt. Titular Bishop of Rhasus and Coadjutor to the Bishop of Dallas, Feb. 8, 1952; succeeded to Aug. 19, 1954; resigned and appointed Titular Bishop of Pinhel, Aug. 27, 1969. (Title rescinded); died Aug. 16, 1980; THOMAS TSCHOEPE (Retired), ord. May 30, 1943; appt. Bishop of San Angelo, Jan. 12, 1966; consecrated March 9, 1966; appt. Bishop of Dallas, Aug. 27, 1969; installed Oct. 29, 1969; retired July 14, 1990.

Vicar General—Rev. Msgr. GLENN D. GARDNER, V.G., J.C.D.

Chancery Office—3725 Blackburn, P.O Box 190507, Dallas, 75219. Tel: 214-528-2240; Fax: 214-526-1743. Office Hours: 9-5

Chancellor—MARY E. EDLUND.

Diocesan Tribunal—P.O. Box 190507, Dallas, 75219. Tel: 214-528-9970; Fax: 214-523-2437.

Judicial Vicar—Rev. Msgr. JOHN P. BELL.

Director of the Tribunal—WILLIAM C. HARE III, J.C.L.

Secretary to the Tribunal—MARGARET GILLETT.

Defenser Vinculi—JOHN P. GARGAN, J.C.D.; Rev. RONNY E. JENKINS, J.C.D.; Very Rev. RAMON ALVAREZ, V.F.; MARY E. EDLUND.

Assistant Judicial Vicars—Rev. Msgr. GLENN D. GARDNER, V.G., J.C.D.; Revs. DAVID L. COLELLA, O.SS.T.; JOHN LIBONE; Very Revs. MICHAEL DUCA; RAMON ALVAREZ, V.F.; MICHAEL DUCA; MARY E. EDLUND.

Notaries—MARGARET GILLETT; JANE HOFMEISTER; ALICE R. DAHL; BRENDA M. SMITH; NORA SMITH; ELSA BUENDIA.

Diocesan Judges—WILLIAM C. HARE III, J.C.L.; LYNDA ROBITAILLE, J.C.D.; DIANE L. BARR, J.C.D.; Sr. MARIE BREITENBECK, O.P., J.C.D.

Procurator-Advocates—Deacon LOUIS F. ADELMANN; LARRIE W. ARNOLD, M.D.; Sr. KATHLEEN BARNES, O.S.U.; DOUGLAS A. BOYD JR.; SUSAN C. BOYD; BEBE CANTU; JUDY CLARK; TRUDY COSTA; THOMAS L. DAHL SR.; DIANE DANIELS; KATHLEEN DAY; Rev. JOHN F. DEEVES, S.J.; ANTHONY R. FLEO; Deacon DON FORBRICH; DEBBIE FOWLER; Deacon ROBERT GARCIA; JEANNE MARIE GIRSCH; SANDRA WARNE GIST; Rev. MICHAEL GUADAGNOLI; MARY CATHERINE HARE; LANNAY N. HARTMANN; JOAN HEITING; LEO HEITING; Deacon JUAN IBARRA; MICHELLE JUNGWIRTH; Rev. GREGORY KELLY; Deacon JOHN PAUL KELLY; CECILIA A. LADDA; RONALD C. LAMPING; BARBARA LANDREGAN; Deacon JOHN LEBLANC; Rev. JOSEPH A. MEHAN JR.; PRISCILLA MAHAFFEY; LINDA MOSES; YOLANDA ORTIZ; DENISE G. PHILLIPS; MARY A. RASINS; Deacons MICHAEL S. RASINS; KENNETH REISOR; PAUL W. REITTINGER; MARY KAY RITCHIE; MARY ROBINSON; LILY SALVATO; Deacons JOSEPH L. SALVO; ROBERT SANCHEZ; Rev. MARK J. SEITZ; MONICA SPARKMAN; Deacon CARL H. THELIN; FRANCIS XAVIER THUONG ANH VUONG; Deacon GARY M. VOGEL.

Consultors of Pastors—Rev. Msgrs. RICHARD E. JOHNSON; JOHN MEYERS, V.F.; Revs. HENRY V. PETTER; TIMOTHY GOLLOB.

Diocesan Consultors—Very Rev. RAMON ALVAREZ, V.F.; Rev. Msgr. JOHN P. BELL; Very Rev. MICHAEL DUCA; Rev. Msgrs. G. DUFF GARDNER, V.G.; LARRY PICHARD; Rev. MARK J. SEITZ.

Presbyteral Council—Rev. Msgr. GLENN D. GARDNER, V.G., J.C.D., Ex Officio; Very Rev. RAMON ALVAREZ, V.F.; Rev. Msgr. JOHN P. BELL; Very Rev. J. DOUGLAS DESHOTEL, V.F.; Rev. Msgr. LEON DUESMAN; Very Rev. MICHAEL DUCA; Rev. Msgr. DON L. FISCHER; Revs. TIMOTHY GOLLOB; EDUARDO GONZALEZ, S.D.B.; Rev. Msgr. RICHARD E. JOHNSON; Revs. GREGORY KELLY; STEPHEN SANCHEZ, O.C.D.; Rev. Msgr. JOHN MEYERS, V.F.; Revs. HENRY V. PETTER; WILLIAM RICHARD; Rev. Msgr. LARRY PICHARD; Rev. MARK J. SEITZ; Rev. Msgr. DONALD F. ZIMMERMAN; Very Rev. ERNESTO TORRES.

Censor Librorum—Rev. Msgr. GLENN D. GARDNER, V.G., J.C.D.; Rev. ROBERT M. COERVER.

Diocesan Offices and Directors

Finance Council—Rev. DAVID J. FLORI; EUGENE VILFORDI; LOUIS G. MUNIN; J. OLIVER MCGONIGLE; MICHAEL T. WEIS; TOM DORAN; Rev. Msgr. GLENN D. GARNER.

Building Commission—Rev. Msgrs. JEROME P. DUESMAN; LARRY PICHARD; AL SALEM; MICHAEL T. WEIS; STEVE MALONE; JIM TUSKAN.

Pastoral Concerns Board—Rev. Msgr. GLENN D. GARDNER, V.G., J.C.D.; MARY E. EDLUND, Chancellor & Chm.; Mr. BRONSON HAVARD; ELLEN STELMAR; AURORA MADRIGAL.

Personnel Board—Rev. Msgrs. GLENN D. GARDNER, V.G., J.C.D.; DONALD F. ZIMMERMAN; Very Rev. RAMON ALVAREZ, V.F.; Rev. HENRY V. PETTER; Deacon GONZALO GONZALES; VICKI DI MARIA BURKE; Mr. WILLIAM KEFFLER; Most Revs. CHARLES GRAHMANN; JOSEPH A. GALANTE, D.D., J.C.D.; MARY E. EDLUND.

Ordination & Accreditation Board—Rev. BRUCE BRADLEY; Sr. ESTHER GUERRERO, M.C.D.P.; Deacon JESSE OLIVARES; MARY E. EDLUND.

Teaching Division

I. Catholic Education—Dr. CHARLES LEBLANC, Dir. Catholic Schools, P.O. Box 190507, Dallas, 75219. Tel: 214-528-2360.

Catechetical Services—SHIRLEY LANGE, Dir., P.O. Box 190507, Dallas, 75219. Tel: 214-528-2360.

Youth Ministry—SUSAN DORFMEISTER, Dir., P.O. Box 190507, Dallas, 75219. Tel: 214-528-2360.

II. Media—

Media Division Head—Rev. Msgr. JOHN P. BELL, P.O. Box 190507, Dallas, 75219. Tel: 214-528-2240.

Newspaper— "The Texas Catholic", Official Catholic Newspaper for the Diocese of Dallas Most Rev. CHARLES V. GRAHMANN, D.D., Publisher; Mr. BRONSON HAVARD, Exec. Editor; MARTY PERRY, Asst. Editor; ANTONIO RAMIREZ JR., Business Mgr. Tel: 214-528-8792; Fax: 214-528-3411.

"El Catolico de Texas"— Spanish Paper

Communications Office—MICHAEL MCGEE, Dir. Tel: 214-528-2240.

Sanctifying Division

Worship Office—Rev. T. MICHAEL DUGAN, Dir. Tel: 214-528-2360.

Cathedral Santuario de Guadalupe—Very Rev. RAMON ALVAREZ, V.F., Rector. Tel: 214-871-1362.

Catholic Conference and Formation Center—BARBARA LANDREGAN, Dir., 901 S. Madison Ave., Dallas, 75208. Mailing Address, P.O. Box 190507, Dallas, 75219. Tel: 214-943-6585; Fax: 214-943-6587.

Priestly Life and Ministry Office—Rev. ROBERT M. COERVER, Dir. Tel: 214-582-2360.

Sacraments of Initiation & Healing—MARTY NOEL, St. Patrick, 9643 Ferndale, Dallas, 75238. Tel: 214-348-7380.

Sacrament of Orders—

Seminary—Very Rev. MICHAEL DUCA, Rector, Holy Trinity Seminary, P.O. Box 140309, Irving, 75014-0309. Tel: 972-438-2212.

Vocations—Rev. JOSEF VOLLMER-KONIG, Dir.

Diaconal Ministry—Deacon ARNOLD PICON, Dir., 901 S. Madison Ave., Dallas, 75208. Mailing Address, P.O. Box 190507, Dallas, 75219. Tel: 214-943-6585.

Sacrament of Marriage—DIANE DANIELS, Dir. Tel: 214-528-2360.

Governing Division

Division Head—MICHAEL T. WEIS, P.O. Box 190507, Dallas, 75219. Tel: 214-528-2240.

Business Office—MICHAEL T. WEIS, Dir. Tel: 214-528-2240.

Catholic Community Appeal—PAUL VITANZA, Dir. Tel: 214-528-2240.

Pastoral Planning and Research—LYNN ROSSOL, Dir. Tel: 214-528-2240.

Tribunal—WILLIAM C. HARE III, J.C.L., Dir. Tel: 214-528-2240.

Archives—STEVE LANDREGAN, Archivist. Tel: 214-528-2240.

Mission Division

Division Head—Sr. MARY ANNE OWENS, S.S.N.D.

Catholic Charities—Sr. MARY ANNE OWENS, S.S.N.D., Dir. Tel: 214-520-6590.

Mission Awareness/Justice and Peace—Sr. NANCY SULLIVAN, D.C., Dir. Tel: 214-528-2240.

CHD Coordinator—Sr. NANCY SULLIVAN, D.C., Dir. Tel: 214-528-2240.

Propagation of Faith and Holy Childhood—Sr. NANCY SULLIVAN, D.C., Dir. Tel: 214-528-2240.

Pastoral Care Ministries—Deacon CHARLES STUMP JR., Dir. Tel: 214-528-2240.

Addictions Ministry—PHIL PASCHKE. Tel: 972-960-2166.

Ministries to People with Disabilities—Rev. AUSTIN E. GREEN, O.P. Tel: 214-528-2240.

Hospital Ministry—Deacon CHARLES STUMP JR. Tel: 214-528-2240.

Prison Ministry—Rev. PAUL GRAY, All Saints Parish, 5231 Meadowcreek, Dallas, 75248. Tel: 972-778-0307.

Victim Assistance Coordinator—MARY E. EDLUND. Tel: 214-528-2240. Email: medlund@cathdal.org.

Networks

Networks—LYNN ROSSOL, Chm., P.O. Box 190507, Dallas, 75219. Tel: 214-528-2240.

Family Life Network—BARBARA LANDREGAN, Chm.

Asian Network—VIVIEN RIVERA, Chm.

Black Network—Chairmen: SHERBIE MATHEWS; LOIS JENKINS.

Hispanic Network—RITA GRACIA-RIVERA.

Youth Network—SUSAN DORFMEISTER, Dir. Tel: 214-528-2360.

CLERGY, PARISHES, MISSIONS AND PAROCHIAL SCHOOLS

CITY OF DALLAS
(DALLAS COUNTY)

1—CATHEDRAL-SANTUARIO DE GUADALUPE (1869), Revs. Ramon Alvarez; Salvador Guzman; Eugene Azorji; Deacons Benito Garcia; Charles Stump; Larry Harmon; Leopoldo Cortinas III. In Res., Rev. Jose I. Figueroa.
Res.: 2215 Ross Ave., 75201. Tel: 214-871-1362; Fax: 214-954-1557.
Catechesis/Religious Program—Lourdes Mayer, D.R.E. Students 1,554.

2—ALL SAINTS (1976), Revs. Remigio Arcilla; Thomas Cloherty; Paul Gray; Richard Weaver; Deacons Denis Simon; Vincent Bathea; John R. Costello.
Res.: 5231 Meadowcreek, 75248. Tel: 972-661-9282; Fax: 972-233-5401.
School—Tel: 972-778-0333; Fax: 972-661-3963. Martha M. Owan, Prin.
Catechesis/Religious Program—Students 416.

3—ST. ANDREW KIM (1977), (Korean), Rev. Joseph C. Lee; Deacon Moses Chung.
Res.: 2712 Swiss Ave., 75204. Tel: 214-651-9150; Fax: 214-826-9099.
Catechesis/Religious Program—Paul Kim, D.R.E. Students 190.

4—ST. ANTHONY (1938), (African American), Rev. Timothy Gollob.
Res.: 2711 Romine St., 75215. Tel: 214-428-6926.

5—ST. AUGUSTINE CATHOLIC CHURCH (1937), Revs. Felix Vistal; Aristotle Aban; Deacons Robert Sanchez; Craig McAlister. In Res., Revs. Solh Saez; Wilson Blas.
Res.: 1054 N. St. Augustine Dr., 75217. Tel: 214-391-1513; Fax: 214-398-2580.
School—1064 N. St. Augustine Dr., 75217. Tel: 214-391-1381; Fax: 214-391-8781. Sisters 1; Lay Teachers 12; Students 180.
Catechesis/Religious Program—Ms. Irma Arce, D.R.E. Students 1,518.

6—ST. BERNARD OF CLAIRVAUX (1947), (Hispanic), Rev. August A. Melito; Deacons John Kelly; Armando Murillo.
Res.: 1404 Old Gate Ln., 75218. Tel: 214-321-0454; Fax: 214-320-0119.
School—1420 Old Gate Ln., 75218. Tel: 214-321-2897; Fax: 214-321-4060. Lay Teachers 21; Students 301.
Catechesis/Religious Program—Juanita Mitchell, D.R.E. Students 612.

7—BLESSED SACRAMENT (1901), Rev. Paul L. Weinberger; Deacon Ismael A. Guerra.
Res.: 231 N. Marsalis Ave., 75203. Tel: 214-948-6535; Fax: 214-948-1660.
Catechesis/Religious Program—Students 679.

8—ST. CECILIA (1933), (Hispanic), Revs. Antonio Salvador Rodriguez; Edmundo Paredes; Deacons Gonzalo Gonzales; Onesimo Martinez.
Res.: 1809 W. Davis St., 75208. Tel: 214-941-5821; Fax: 214-946-4466.
School—635 Marycliff Rd., 75208. Tel: 214-948-8628. Sisters of St. Mary of Namur 1; Lay Teachers 14; Students 216.
Catechesis/Religious Program—Students 1,020.

9—CHRIST THE KING (1941), Rev. Msgr. Donald F. Zimmerman; Mary Catherine Hare, Pastoral Assoc.; William C. Hare III, J.C.L., Pastoral Assoc.; Deacon Sam Franklin, Pastoral Assoc.
Res.: 8017 Preston Rd., 75225. Tel: 214-365-1200; Fax: 214-365-1205.
School—4100 Colgate St., 75225. Tel: 214-365-1234; Fax: 214-365-1236. Lay Teachers 47; Students 424.
Catechesis/Religious Program—Students 319.

10—ST. EDWARD (1903), Revs. Eduardo Gonzalez, S.D.B.; Jorge Laguna; Deacons Guadalupe A. Carreon; Juan G. Gonzalez; Timothy Dorsey.
Res.: 4014 Simpson St., 75246. Tel: 214-823-1291; Fax: 214-823-7535.
Catechesis/Religious Program—Claudio Mora, D.R.E. Students 1,050.

11—ST. ELIZABETH (1956), Revs. T. Michael Dugan; Fred Sidler; Alex Buitrago; Deacons Edward S. Jones; Denis Simon; Frank Kozarevich; Douglas Boyd Sr.
Res.: 4015 S. Hampton Rd., 75224. Tel: 214-331-4328; Fax: 214-331-2464.
School—4019 S. Hampton Rd., 75224. Tel: 214-331-5139; Fax: 214-467-4346. Lay Teachers 27; Students 365.
Catechesis/Religious Program—Douglas A. Boyd Jr., D.R.E. Students 187.

12—HOLY CROSS (1956), Rev. Timothy A. Gollob; Deacons Antonio D. Trevino; Henry Vault. In Res., Rev. James George McKenna.
Res.: 2926 E. Ledbetter Dr., 75216. Tel: 214-374-7952; Fax: 214-375-7457.
Catechesis/Religious Program—Students 406.

13—HOLY TRINITY (1907), Revs. John P. Cawley, C.M.; Ray Hays, C.M.; Deacons Don Forbrich; Edward Putonti.
Mailing Address: 3826 Gilbert Ave., 75219.
Res.: 3811 Oak Lawn Ave., 75219. Tel: 214-526-8555; Fax: 214-526-3477.
School—3815 Oak Lawn Ave., 75219. Lay Teachers 17; Students 202.
Catechesis/Religious Program—Students 359.

14—ST. JAMES (1934), Rev. Msgr. Mario Magbanua; Deacons Vincent F. Jimenez; Isidro Olvera.
Mailing Address: P.O. Box 763338, 75376.
Res.: 1002 E. Saner Ave., 75216. Tel: 214-371-9209; Fax: 214-371-0226.
Catechesis/Religious Program—Students 700.

15—ST. JUDE CHAPEL AND INFORMATION CENTER (Downtown Dallas) (1968), Rev. Victor Celio, O.P., Admin.
Res.: 1521 Main St., 75201. Tel: 214-742-2508; Fax: 214-748-5282.

16—MARY IMMACULATE (1956), Revs. Bruce Bradley; Benito Tamez; Deacons Gerard L. Bauwens; Patrick Hayes; J. Michael Weston. In Res., Rev. John Alphonso.
Res.: 14032 Dennis Ln., 75234. Tel: 972-243-7104; Fax: 972-406-1254.
School—Tel: 972-243-7105; Fax: 972-241-7678. Lay Teachers 36; Students 525.
Catechesis/Religious Program—Jo Ann Webb, D.R.E. Students 1,437.

17—ST. MARY OF CARMEL (1944), Rev. Jesus Sancho, O.C.D.
Res.: 2900 Vilbig Rd., 75212. Tel: 214-747-1433; Fax: 214-748-7481.
School—1716 Singleton Blvd., 75212. Tel: 214-748-2934; Fax: 214-760-9052. Sisters of the Holy Spirit 4; Lay Teachers 11; Students 162.
Catechesis/Religious Program—Students 172.

18—ST. MONICA (1954), Revs. John F. Meyers; Brindley Mills; John Hopka; Anibal Adorno; Deacons Larry Lucido; Bob Marrinan; Brian Mitchell; Abel Cortes.
Res.: 9933 Midway Rd., 75220. Tel: 214-358-1453; Fax: 214-351-1887.
School—4140 Walnut Hill Ln., 75229. Tel: 214-351-5688; Fax: 214-352-2608. Lay Teachers 57; Students 891.
Catechesis/Religious Program—Ms. Patricia Foley, D.R.E. Students 1,039.
Mission—Blessed Juan Diego

19—NUESTRA SENORA DEL PILAR, (Hispanic), Rev. Wilmer de Jesus Daza.
4455 W. Illinois Ave., 75211. Tel: 214-467-9116; Fax: 214-339-7249.

20—OUR LADY OF LOURDES (1954), Revs. Mario

Garcia, O.F.M.Cap. (Spain); Ignacio Cizur, O.F.M-.Cap. (Spain); Deacon Pete Rodriguez. In Res., Rev. Luis Gerardo Arraiza, O.F.M.Cap. (Spain).
Res.: 5605 Bernal Dr., 75212. Tel: 214-637-6673.
Catechesis/Religious Program—Amy Rodriguez, D.R.E. Students 775.

21—Our Lady of Perpetual Help (1942), (Hispanic), Revs. Juan Cruz Gaston, O.F.M.Cap. (Spain); Sabino Erro, O.F.M. (Spain); Deacons Albert Montes; Adolph Orozco Jr. In Res., Rev. Eric Azcona, O.F.M.Cap.
Res.: 7617 Cortland Ave., 75235. Tel: 214-352-6012; Fax: 214-351-9883.
School—7625 Cortland Ave., 75235. Tel: 214-351-3396; Fax: 214-351-9889. Lay Teachers 13; Students 163.
Catechesis/Religious Program—Olivia Valenzuela, D.R.E. Students 650.

22—Our Lady of San Juan De Los Lagos and St. Theresa (1928), Rev. Eric Azcona, O.F.M.Cap.
Res.: 2601 Singleton Blvd., 75212. Tel: 214-631-9627; Fax: 214-631-6267.
Catechesis/Religious Program—Tel: 214-688-0942. Students 200.

23—St. Patrick (1963), Rev. Msgr. Richard E. Johnson; Rev. Albert B. Becher; Deacon John C. Nordick.
Res.: 9643 Ferndale Rd., 75238. Tel: 214-348-7380; Fax: 214-340-5956.
School—9635 Ferndale Rd., 75238. Tel: 214-348-8070; Fax: 214-503-7230. Sisters of the Incarnate Word and Blessed Sacrament 2; Lay Teachers 32; Students 546.
Catechesis/Religious Program—Mrs. Martha Noel, D.R.E. Students 342.

24—St. Peter (1905), Rev. Stanislaw Michalek, S.Ch.
Res.: 2907 Woodall Rodgers Fwy., 75204. Tel: 214-855-1384; Fax: 214-855-1309.
Catechesis/Religious Program—Mercy Hamilton, D.R.E.; Sr. Marietta, D.R.E. Students 94.

25—St. Peter Vietnamese Catholic Community (1996), Rev. Nguyen Tam, Admin.
10123 Garland Rd., 75218. Tel: 214-320-9493; Fax: 214-320-9493.
Catechesis/Religious Program—Students 86.

26—St. Philip (1954), Rev. Stephen J. Mocio.
Res.: 8131 Military Pkwy., 75227. Tel: 214-388-5464; Fax: 214-388-2839.
School—8151 Military Pkwy., 75227. Tel: 214-381-4973; Fax: 214-381-0466. Sisters of the Holy Spirit 1; Lay Teachers 13; Students 195.
Catechesis/Religious Program—Ginna Curts, D.R.E. Students 176.

27—St. Pius X (1954), Rev. Msgr. Larry Pichard; Rev. Don Zeiler; Deacons Juan Ibarra; David Leerssen; Michael Shaw; John A. Schell.
Res.: 3030 Gus Thomasson Rd., 75228. Tel: 972-279-6155; Fax: 972-686-7510.
School—Tel: 972-279-2339; Fax: 972-613-2059. Lay Teachers 27; Students 520.
Catechesis/Religious Program—Tel: 972-279-2558. Kassie Andries, D.R.E. Students 1,280.

28—St. Rita (1961), Revs. Mark J. Seitz; John J. Heaney, S.J.; Patrick H. Koch, S.J.; Deacons William Schuster; Charles T. Sylvester; Tim Muldoon.
Office—12521 Inwood Rd., 75244. Tel: 972-934-8388; Fax: 972-934-8965.
Res.: 12626 Planters Glen, 75244. Tel: 972-239-5205.
School—12525 Inwood Rd., 75244. Tel: 972-239-3203; Fax: 972-934-3657. Lay Teachers 54; Students 658.
Catechesis/Religious Program—Pat Matula, D.R.E. Students 423.

29—Santa Clara (1993), (Hispanic), Revs. David L. Colella, O.SS.T.; Luis E. Hernandez (Colombia); Deacon Alberto Villarreal.
Res.: 321 Calumet St., 75211. Tel: 214-337-3936; Fax: 214-333-9148.
School—Santa Clara of Assisi Catholic Academy, Tel: 214-333-9423; Fax: 214-333-2556. Ms. Elizabeth Lopez, Prin.
Catechesis/Religious Program—Students 1,540.

30—St. Thomas Aquinas (1952), Rev. John Libone; Deacons Kenneth Reisor; Richard Harrington.
Res.: 6306 Kenwood Ave., 75214. Tel: 214-821-3360; Fax: 214-821-5395.
School—3741 Abrams Rd., 75214. Tel: 214-826-0566; Fax: 214-826-0251. Lay Teachers 51; Students 648.
Catechesis/Religious Program—Mrs. Mary Xuereb, D.R.E. Students 198.

OUTSIDE THE CITY OF DALLAS

Allen, Collin Co., St. Jude (1981), Revs. Timothy A. Church, Admin.; George Monaghan; Deacons Ronald Fejeran; George Polcer.
Mailing Address: P.O. Box 869, 75013.
Res.: 1515 N. Greenville, 75002. Tel: 972-727-1177; Fax: 972-727-1401.
Catechesis/Religious Program—Tel: 972-727-9998. Carole Anne Horstman, D.R.E. Students 1,105.

Bonham, Fannin Co., St. Elizabeth, Rev. Aristotle Aban; Deacons Joseph Culling; William B. Beste.
Res.: 409 W. 10th St., 75418. Tel: 903-583-7734; Fax: 903-583-7359.

Carrollton, Dallas Co., Sacred Heart of Jesus Christ (1999), Rev. Joseph Son Nguyen.
2121 N. Denton, 75006. Tel: 972-446-3461; Fax: 972-446-9551.

Commerce, Hunt Co., St. Joseph (1895), Rev. D. Stanley Corcoran.
Res.: 3695 Hwy. 50, Campbell, 75422. Tel: 903-886-7135.
Catechesis/Religious Program—Students 124.

Coppell, Dallas Co., St. Ann (1985), Rev. Msgr. Kilian J. Broderick; Deacons Ed Scarbrough; Joseph L. Salvo; Pedro Herran; Pete Markwood.
Church: 180 Samuel Blvd., 75019. Tel 972-393-5544; 972-393-7951 (Res.); Fax: 972-462-1617.
Catechesis/Religious Program—Sr. Ruth Ellen Dean, D.R.E. Students 2,075.

Corsicana, Navarro Co., Immaculate Conception (1871), Rev. Robert Williams; Deacon Lewis J. Palos.
Res.: 3000 Hwy. 22 W., P.O. Box 798, 75151. Tel: 903-874-4473; Fax: 903-874-2619.
School—James L. Collins Catholic School, Tel: 903-872-1751. Lay Teachers 13; Students 180.
Catechesis/Religious Program—Deacon Gerardo Alvarado D.R.E. Students 318.

Denison, Grayson Co., St. Patrick (1872), Rev. John Dick.
Res.: 314 N. Rusk Ave., 75020. Tel: 903-463-3275; Fax: 903 463-3447.
Catechesis/Religious Program—Catherine L. Haraldsen, D.R.E. Students 159.

Duncanville, Dallas Co., Holy Spirit (1974), Rev. Timothy Heines; Deacons Al Evans; Les Alt.
Res.: 1111 W. Danieldale Rd., 75137-3719. Tel: 972-298-4971; Fax: 972-709-1443.
Catechesis/Religious Program—Nanette Corbitt, D.R.E. Students 511.

Ennis, Ellis Co., St. John Nepomucene (1902), [CEM] Rev. Fred Caldwell; Deacons Dean Darnall; Don Griffith; Frutos Vega.
Res.: 401 E. Lampasas St., 75119. Tel: 972-878-2834; Fax: 972-875-2452.
School—701 S. Paris St., 75119. Tel: 972-878-5411; Fax: 972-878-2226. Sisters of Divine Providence 4; Lay Teachers 15; Students 171.
High School—Lay Teachers 9; Students 50.
Catechesis/Religious Program—Students 454.

Ferris, Ellis Co., Corpus Christi (1977), (Hispanic), Rev. Msgr. Oscar Gales, P.A.
Res.: 117 N. Wood, 75125. Tel: 972-842-2288; Fax: 972-842-2288.
Catechesis/Religious Program—Students 170.

Forney, Kaufman Co., St. Martin (1891), Rev. Msgr. Albert Cuschieri.
Res.: P.O. Box 2347, 75126. Tel: 972-564-9114; Fax: 972-564-9138.
Catechesis/Religious Program—Students 155.

Frisco, Collin Co., St. Francis of Assisi (1966), Rev. Msgr. Leon Duesman; Rev. Antonio Ortiz; Deacon Frank Reyna.
Res.: 3000 El Dorado Pkwy., 75034 Tel: 972-712-2645; Fax: 972-712-1087.
Catechesis/Religious Program—Students 1,100.

Garland, Dallas Co.

1—Good Shepherd (1944), Revs. Danilo Ramos; Antonio Ormaza, S.C.S.; Cherian E. Thomas (India); Deacon LeRoy J. Berens.
Res.: 1224 Main St., 75040. Tel: 972 276-8587; Fax: 972-494-3653.
School—214 S. Garland Ave., 75040. Tel: 972-272-6533 Fax: 972-272-0512. Brothers 1; Lay Teachers 24; Students 276.
Catechesis/Religious Program—Alex Sandoval, D.R.E. Students 895.

2—St. Mary Malankara (1996), Rev. Thomas Kottayil Cherian.
116 E. Ave. D, 75040. Tel: 972-494-5356.
c/o Good Shepherd Church: 201 S. 13th St., 75040. Tel: 972-272-4641; Fax: 972-494-3653.
Catechesis/Religious Program—Students 36.

3—St. Michael the Archangel (1980), Rev. James R. Sharp, Ph.D., Admin.; Deacons Joe Perez; Jim Harris. In Res., Rev. Marcus Chidozie.
Res.: 950 Trails Pkwy., 75043. Tel: 972-279-6581; 972-681-8026 (Rectory); Fax: 972-279-6647.
Catechesis/Religious Program—Carmen Villasana, D.R.E. Students 702.

4—Mother of Perpetual Help, (Vietnamese), Revs. Dominic Hai Dinh, C.SS.R.; Thong Nguyen, C.SS.R.
Res.: 2121 Apollo Rd., 75044. Tel: 972-414-7073.
Catechesis/Religious Program—Bro. Phong Lee, D.R.E. Students 320.

5—St. Thomas the Apostle (1992), Rev. John Melepuram.
Res.: 1210 Columbine, 75043. Tel: 972-303-5404; Fax: 469-366-5204.
Catechesis/Religious Program—Students 265.

Grand Prairie, Dallas Co.

1—Immaculate Conception (1916), Rev. Matthew Bagert; Deacons Jesus Belmontes; Michael S. Rasins; David Maida.
Res.: 610 N.E. 17th St., 75050. Tel: 972-262-5137; Fax: 972-264-7657.
School—400 N.E. 17th St., 75050. Tel: 972-264-8777; Fax: 972-264-7742. Sisters of the Holy Family of Nazareth 2; Sisters of Notre Dame 1; Daughters of Charity 1; Lay Teachers 19; Students 212.
Catechesis/Religious Program—Diane Gutierrez, D.R.E. Students 850.

2—St. Joseph Vietnamese Catholic Community (1993), Rev. Peter Phong Nguyen.
Res.: 802 E. Coral Way, 75051. Tel: 972-264-9441.
Catechesis/Religious Program—Students 246.

3—St. Michael the Archangel (1985), Rev. Clifford G. Smith, Admin.; Deacon Dennis Phillip Bryant.
2910 Corn Valley, 75052.
Res.: 2925 Lake Park Dr., 75051. Tel: 972-262-0552; Fax: 972-642-5429.
Catechesis/Religious Program—Tel: 972-262-6590. Students 519.

Greenville, Hunt Co., St. William (1892), Rev. Antonio Oscar Diez; Deacon Lee B. Davis.
Res.: 4300 Stuart St., 75401. Tel: 903-450-1177; Fax: 903-455-7134.
Catechesis/Religious Program—Tel: 903-455-8201. Carolyn Dorman, D.R.E. Students 258.
Mission—Our Lady of Fatima 1979 E. Quinlan Pkwy., Quinlan, Hunt Co. 57474.

Irving, Dallas Co.

1—Church of the Incarnation (1973), Rev. Msgr. Milam J. Joseph.
University of Dallas: 1845 E. Northgate Dr., 75062. Tel: 972-721-5375; Fax: 972-721-5351.

2—Holy Family of Nazareth (1964), Rev. Msgr. Jerome P. Duesman; Deacons Kenneth Hale; Kory Killgo; Robert Miller; Lee Stieber.
Res.: 2330 Cheyenne St., 75062. Tel: 972-252-5521; Fax: 972-252-5523.
School—2323 Cheyenne St., 75062. Tel: 972-255-0205; Fax: 972-252-4167. Sisters of the Holy Family of Nazareth 2; Lay Teachers 22; Students 289.
Catechesis/Religious Program—Kay Lehrberger, D.R.E. Students 445.

3—St. Luke (1902), Revs. Aidan O'Donovan, M.S.C.; Francisco Orozco, O.C.D.; Deacons Louis F. Adelmann; Jose Trevino; Daniel D. Segovia.
Res.: 1015 Schulze Dr., 75060. Tel: 972-259-3222; Fax: 972-259-3339.
School—1023 Schulze Dr., 75060. Tel: 972-253-8285. Lay Teachers 16; Students 196.
Catechesis/Religious Program—Jo Ann Dreyer, D.R.E. Students 1,298.

Kaufman, Kaufman Co., St. Ann (1935), Rev. Joseph A. Mehan Jr.; Deacons James Burkel; Sergio Morales.
Res.: 806 N. Washington St., 75142. Tel: 972-962-3247.
Catechesis/Religious Program—Jan Reznick, D.R.E. Students 216.

Lancaster, Dallas Co., St. Francis of Assisi (1973), Rev. Arthur D. Mallinson; Deacons Jose F. Hernandez; Ed Armstead.
Res.: 1537 Rogers Ln., 75134. Tel: 972-227-4124; Fax: 972-227-2882.
Catechesis/Religious Program—Tel: 972-227-0770. Sherry Granello, D.R.E. Students 326.

McKinney, Collin Co.

1—St. Gabriel the Archangel (1996), Rev. Gregory Kelly; Deacon Vic Machiano.
Mailing Address: 110 St. Gabriel Way, 75071. Tel: 972-562-0638; Fax: 214-544-1488.
Catechesis/Religious Program—Students 585.

2—St. Michael (1892), Rev. Stephen W. Bierschenk.
Res.: 411 Paula Rd., 75069. Tel: 972-562-4444; Fax: 972-562-0752.
Catechesis/Religious Program—Jay Semon, D.R.E. Students 440.
Mission—Holy Family P.O. Box 482, Van Alstyne, Grayson Co. 75495.

Mesquite, Dallas Co., Divine Mercy of Our Lord, Very Rev. Ernesto Torres.
Res.: 1819 N. Galloway, 75149. Tel: 972-289-7400; Fax: 972-289-7445.

Plano, Collin Co.

1—St. Elizabeth Ann Seton (1976), Revs. Henry V. Petter; Andrew V. Semler; Deacons Ted Perez; Thomas Roche; Bill Flynn; Roger David.
Res.: 2800 Piedra Ln., 75023. Tel: 972-596-5505; Fax: 972-985-7573.
Catechesis/Religious Program—Tel: 972-596-1923; Fax: 972-985-0431. Mary Frazier, D.R.E.; Bruce Baumann, D.R.E. Students 2,527.

2—St. Mark the Evangelist (1966), Rev. Msgr. Glenn D. Gardner, V.G., J.C.D.; Rev. Rodolfo Garcia; Most Rev. Jack W. Hopka; Rev. Dean Pratt;

Deacons Bob Scoggins; Michael A. Carrell; Shawn Patrick French; Arnold Picon.
Res.: 1201 Alma Dr., 75075. Tel: 972-423-5600; Fax: 972-423-5024.
School—Tel: 972-578-0610; Fax: 972-423-3299. Lay Teachers 33; Students 643.
Catechesis/Religious Program—Deacon Mike Carrell, D.R.E. Students 1,618.

3—OUR LADY OF ANGELS (2000), Rev. Msgr. John P. Bell.
Mailing Address: 7300 Alma Dr., #400, 75025. Tel: 469-467-9669; Fax: 469-467-0111.

4—PRINCE OF PEACE (1991), Revs. R. James Balint; Lawrence A. Beyer (Retired); Deacons Robert L. Staib; Louis L. Munoz; David E. Tompsett.
Res.: 5100 W. Plano Pkwy., 75093. Tel: 972-380-2100; Fax: 972-380-5162.
School—Tel: 972-380-5505; Fax: 972-380-2570. Lay Teachers 46; Students 641.
Catechesis/Religious Program—Students 432.

RICHARDSON, DALLAS CO.

1—ST. JOSEPH (1976), Rev. Msgr. Don L. Fischer. In Res., Rev. Thomas M. Speiser; Deacon Randall L. Engel.
Res.: 600 S. Jupiter Rd., 75081. Tel: 972-231-2951; Fax: 972-231-2875.
School—Tel: 972-234-4679; Fax: 972-692-4594. David M. Ross, Prin.
Catechesis/Religious Program—Tel: 972-690-5588. Students 902.

2—MISSION OF THE SACRED HEART OF JESUS (1993), (Chinese), Rev. Peter Chen.
Res.: Tel: 972-716-0077; Fax: 972-789-9537.
Church: 812 S. Sherman, 75081. Tel: 972-480-8472.
Catechesis/Religious Program—Ronald Chu, D.R.E. Students 66.

3—ST. PAUL THE APOSTLE (1956), Revs. David J. Flori; Jose L. Azcona-Weber; Deacons Carl H. Thelin; Paul W. Reittinger; Jesse Olivares.
Res.: 709 James Dr., 75080. Tel: 972-235-6105; Fax: 972-480-8528.
School—720 S. Floyd Rd., 75080. Tel: 972-235-3263; Fax: 972-690-1542. Lay Teachers 25; Students 439.
Catechesis/Religious Program—Tel: 972-235-2598; Fax: 972-664-9993. Jeremy (Jerri) Brandenburg, D.R.E. Students 765.

ROCKWALL, ROCKWALL CO., OUR LADY OF THE LAKE (1978), Rev. William Richard; Deacons Jesus Cerrato; Clifford H. Kopinski; Bronson Havard; Paul Husting; Jim Daniels.
Res.: P.O. Box 191, 75087. Tel: 972-771-6671 (Office); Fax: 972-771-7283.
Catechesis/Religious Program—Tel: 972-771-4253. Aline Kindle, D.R.E. Students 554.

ROWLETT, DALLAS CO., SACRED HEART (1899), Rev. Robert R. Crisp; Deacons Frank W. Dunlop Sr.; Kenneth Melston.
Res.: 3905 Hickox Rd., 75088. Tel: 972-475-4405; Fax: 972-475-6658.
Catechesis/Religious Program—Shelly Jungwirth, D.R.E. Students 321.

SHERMAN, GRAYSON CO., ST. MARY (1872), Revs. Jeremy Myers; Antonio Aureus; Deacons John Le Blanc; Tomas Avila.
Res.: 727 S. Travis, 75090. Tel: 903-893-5148; Fax: 903-813-5489.
School—713 Travis St., 75090. Tel: 903-893-2127. Lay Teachers 15; Students 135.
Catechesis/Religious Program—Annie Kremer, D.R.E. Students 365.
Mission—St. Francis of Assisi Whitesboro, Grayson Co.

TERRELL, KAUFMAN CO., ST. JOHN (1876), Rev. Jonathan Austin, Admin.; Deacons Leo Rener; Fermin Rodriquez.
Res.: 701 N. Frances St., 75160. Tel: 972-563-3643; Fax: 972-563-9718.
Catechesis/Religious Program—Susan Warner, D.R.E. Students 244.

WAXAHACHIE, ELLIS CO., ST. JOSEPH (1875), Rev. Michael Guadagnoli; Deacons Denver Crawley; Hugo Monsanto; Larry G. Hatch; Denis D. Corbin.
Office—512 E. Marvin St., 75165.
Res.: 504 E. Marvin St., 75165. Tel: 972-938-1953; Fax: 972-938-1956.
School—St. Joseph Catholic School, 506 E. Marvin St., 75165. Tel: 972-938-2652. Mary Kay Volker, Prin. Lay Teachers 18; Students 105.
Catechesis/Religious Program—Tel: 972-938-2858. Cheryl Bain, D.R.E. Students 351.
Mission—Epiphany 434 S. Ward, Italy, Ellis Co. 76651.

WYLIE, COLLIN CO., ST. ANTHONY (1900), [CEM] Rev. Loyd Morris, Admin.; Deacon Walter Gove.
Res.: 404 N. Ballard, 75098. Tel: 972-442-2765; Fax: 972-429-9215.
Catechesis/Religious Program—Students 544.

Chaplains of Public Institutions

DALLAS. *Baylor University Medical Center*, 3500 Gaston Ave., 75246. Tel: 214-820-2558. Rev. Eugene Azorji, Deacon Joe Perez.
Childrens Medical Center of Dallas, 1935 Motor St., 75235. Tel: 214-456-2822. Deacon Jose Trevino.
Dallas/Fort Worth Airport Catholic Chaplain, P.O. Box 190507, 75219. Tel: 214-528-2240, Ext. 318. Deacon Ed Scarbrough.
Doctors Hospital, Tel: 214-321-0454. Rev. August A. Melito.
Medical City Dallas Hospital, 7777 Forest Ln., 75230. Tel: 214-759-3064. Deacon Carl H. Thelin.
Methodist Charlton Medical Center, 3500 W. Wheatland Rd., 75237. Tel: 214-947-2470. Rev. Daniel Clayton.
Methodist Dallas Medical Center, 1441 N. Beckley Ave., 75265. Tel: 214-947-2470. Rev. Daniel Clayton.
Parkland Health & Hospital System, 5201 Harry Hines Blvd., 75235. Tel: 214-590-8512. Rev. Luis Buitrago, Sr. Irene Arredondo, S.H.Sp., Deacon Vic Machiano.
St. Paul Medical Center, 5909 Harry Hines Blvd., 75234. Tel: 214-879-3870. Revs. Patrick F. Hanser, John Alphonso.
Presbyterian Hospital of Dallas, 8200 Walnut Hill Ln., 75231. Tel: 214-759-3064. Deacon Paul Husting.
Veterans Administration Hospital, 2926 E. Ledbetter Dr., 75216. Tel: 214-374-7952. Rev. Timothy Gollob.
Zale/Lipshy University Hospital, 5151 Harry Hines Blvd., 75235. Tel: 214-490-3408. Rev. Patrick F. Hanser.

BONHAM. *Sam Rayburn Veterans Hospital*, 404 W. 10th St., 75418. Tel: 903-583-2111. Rev. Aristotle Aban.

HUTCHINS. *Texas Department of Criminal Justice*, 1500 E. Langdon Rd., 75241. Tel: 972-225-1304. Deacon Craig McAlister, Contact Person.

SEAGOVILLE. *Federal Correctional Institution*, 2113 N. Hwy. 75, 75159. Deacon Ismael A. Guerra.

TERRELL. *State Hospital*, 702 N. Frances St., 75160. Tel: 972-563-3643. Rev. Jonathan Austin.

On Duty Outside the Diocese:
Revs.—
Martin, Sean, Aquinas Institute of Theology, 3642 Lindell Blvd., St. Louis, MO 63108.
McKenna, James George, P.O. Box 190507, 75219.
Phan, Cho Dink Peter

Absent on Leave:
Revs.—
Diez, Oscar
Mallinson, Arthur D.

On Leave:
Rev.—
Villaroya, Ernesto

Retired:
Rev. Msgrs.—
Gulczynski, John T., 3700 Abrams Rd., 75214.
Johnson, Robert, 14 Greccio Ct., Crowley, 76036.
McCallum, John V., 3406 Tipps Dr., Greenville, 75401.
Rehkemper, Robert C., Our Lady of Good Hope, P.O. Box 517, Hope, AR 71801.
Weinzapfel, Thomas, 321 Crooket Creek, Garland, 75043.
Revs.—
Beyer, Lawrence A., Prince of Peace Parish, 5100 W. Plano Pkwy., Plano, 75093.
Drozd, Henry J., P.O. Box 42063, Savannah, GA 31409-0001.
Fernandez, Edward P., 5392 Bramble Ln., Las Vegas, NV 89120.
Fowler, John W., 1444 Rodando, Garland, 75042. Tel: 972-205-9307
Haugh, John, 1139 E. Sandy Lake Rd., Coppell, 75019.
Jayasuria, Jerome, 305 Blake Ln., Midlothian, 76039.
O'Rourke, John G., 1121 Nolte Dr., 75208.
Ortega, Efren
Schumacher, William
Scott, Raymond, 1147 E. Sandy Lake Rd., Coppell, 75019.
Slovacek, Emil C., 1815 Hamlet, 75203.
Vogel, Carl J., 216 James Dr., Heath, 75032.
White, Gale, 4306 Walnut Hill Ln., 75229. Tel: 214-357-4312

Permanent Deacons:
Adelman, Louis
Alt, Les
Argumaniz, Fernando L., (Retired)
Arredondo, Pastor G., (Retired)
Avila, Tomas
Bathea, Val Vincent
Bauwens, Gerard L.
Berens, LeRoy J.
Beste, William B.
Bourland, Fred, (On Duty Outside the Diocese)
Boyd, Douglas
Bryant, Dennis Phillip
Burkel, James
Carrell, Michael A.
Carreon, Guadalupe A., (Retired)
Catsoris, John A.
Cerrato, Jesus, Jr.
Chung, Hoan Moses
Coffey, Thomas, (On Duty Outside the Diocese)
Corbin, Denis D.
Cortes, Abel
Cortinas, Leopoldo, III
Costello, John R.
Crawley, Denver
Culling, Joseph
Daniels, James
Darnall, Dean
Davis, Lee B.
Davis, Roger
De La Garza, John, (On Duty Outside the Diocese)
Delin, Fred O.
Dorsey, Timothy, (On Duty Outside the Diocese)
Dunlop, Frank W., Sr.
Ellerbrock, Michael, (On Duty Outside the Diocese)
Elsberg, Alick, (On Duty Outside the Diocese)
Engel, Randall L.
Evans, Al
Fejeran, Ronald
Flynn, Bill
Forbrich, Don
Franklin, Sam
French, Shawn Patrick
Friedman, William L., (On Duty Outside the Diocese)
Garcia, Benito
Gonzales, Gonzalo
Gonzales, Jesse, (On Duty Outside the Diocese)
Gonzales, Juan G.
Gonzalez, Ronald, (On Duty Outside the Diocese)
Gordon, Ralph R., (Retired)
Gove, Walter
Granado, Eliseo
Griffith, Don
Guerra, Ismael A.
Guerrero, Joe, (Inactive)
Gutting, Justin
Gutting, Paul, (On Duty Outside the Diocese)
Hale, Kenneth
Hancock, John, (On Duty Outside the Diocese)
Harmon, Larry
Harrington, Richard
Harris, Jim
Hatch, Larry G.
Havard, Bronson
Hayes, Patrick
Henvey, Thomas, (On Duty Outside the Diocese)
Hernandez, Jose F.
Herran, Pedro
Husting, Paul
Ibarra, Juan
Jimenez, Vincent F.
Jones, Edward S.
Kelly, John Paul
Killgo, Kory
Kopinski, Clifford H.
Kozarevich, Frank
LeBlanc, John D.
Leerssen, David
Leicht, Robert R., Jr., (On Duty Outside the Diocese)
Lopez, Al
Lucido, Larry
Macero, Carl, Sr.
Machiano, Vic
Maida, David
Markwood, Pete
Marrinan, Robert, Sr.
Martinez, Onesimo
McAlister, Craig
McLean, Michael J., (On Duty Outside the Diocese)
McQuade, Joseph
Melston, Kenneth
Miller, Carl V., (On Duty Outside the Diocese)
Miller, J. Robert
Milliken, Frank M., (Retired)
Mitchell, Brian
Monsanto, Hugo
Montes, Jesus Alberto
Morales, Sergio
Muldoon, Tim
Munoz, Louis L.
Murillo, Armando
Nordick, John C.
O'Leary, John
Olivares, Jesse
Olvera, Isidro
Orozco, Adolph, Jr.
Palms, Howard

Palos, Lewis J.
Pena, Hector B.
Perez, Joe R.
Perez, Ted, Jr., (Retired)
Picard, Michael
Picon, Arnold
Polcer, George
Putonti, Edward
Rasins, Michael S.
Reisor, Kenneth
Reittinger, Paul W.
Rener, Bonnie Leo
Reyna, Frank
Roche, Thomas
Rodriguez, Fermin
Rodriguez, Pete
Salerno, John, (Retired)
Salinas, Hugo A., (On Duty Outside the Diocese)
Salvo, Joseph L.
Sanchez, Robert
Scarbrough, Ed
Schell, John A.
Schlebach, Eugene M., (Inactive)
Schnurr, Don, (Retired)
Schuster, William
Scoggins, Robert C., Jr.
Segovia, Daniel D.
Shaw, Michael
Simon, Denis
Staib, Bob
Stieber, Lee
Stump, Charles, Jr.
Sykora, Richard, (On Duty Outside the Diocese)
Sylvester, Charles T.
Thelin, Carl H.
Tompsett, David E.
Trevino, Antonio D.
Trevino, Jose
Van Scoy, Donald G.
Vara, Rudolph R., (Retired)
Vault, Henry, Jr.
Vega, Frutos
Veyna, Manuel, (Retired)
Villarreal, Alberto
Vogel, Gary M.
Washington, Warner
Webb, Philip E., (On Duty Outside the Diocese)
Weithman, James C., (Retired)
Welsh, James L.
Weston, Michael
Wong, Peter
Zacek, George E., (On Duty Outside the Diocese)
Zoeller, William C., (On Duty Outside the Diocese)

INSTITUTIONS LOCATED IN THE DIOCESE

[A] SEMINARIES, DIOCESAN

IRVING. *Holy Trinity Seminary* Diocesan College and Pre-Theology Seminary. , P.O. Box 140309, 75014-0309. Tel: 972-438-2212; Fax: 972-438-6530. Email: mduca@holytrinityseminary.com. Web: www.holytrinityseminary.com. Very Rev. Michael Duca, Rector; Revs. Douglas Deshotel, Vice Rector; James Orosco, Spiritual Dir.; Aaron Arce, O.P., Spiritual Dir.; Dr. Kathleen Burk, Academic Dean; Mr. Henry McDowell, Dir. Music; Mr. Eric Hendry, Formation. Priests 4; Seminarians 42; Lay Faculty 2; Total Staff 7. In Res Most Rev. Joseph Galante.

[B] COLLEGES AND UNIVERSITIES

IRVING. *University of Dallas*, President's Office, 1845 E. Northgate, 75062. Tel: 972-721-5203; Fax: 972-721-4040.
Administrative Officers: Most Rev. Charles V. Grahmann, D.D., Grand Chancellor Rev. Msgr. Milam J. Joseph, Pres.; Mr. Robert Galecke, Senior Vice Pres. Admin. & Finance; Dr. Thomas Lindsay, Provost & Vice Pres. Academic Affairs; Dr. Fred Zuker, Alumni & Studied Svcs.; Bob Lynch, Funding Dean; Most Rev. Joseph Galante.
Diocesan Priests: Revs. John Collet; Mitchell Pacwa, S.J.
Cistercian Priests: Revs. David Balas, O.Cist., Ph.D., S.T.D.; Ralph March, O. Cist., Ph.D.; Roch Keresz Ty; James Lehrberger, O.Cist., Ph.D.; Robert Maguire, O.Cist., Ph.D.

[C] HIGH SCHOOLS, DIOCESAN

DALLAS. *Bishop Dunne Catholic School, Inc.*, (Grades 7-12) , (Coed) , 3900 Rugged Dr., 75224. Tel: 214-339-6561; Fax: 214-339-1438. Email: kdailey@bdhs.org. Web: www.bdhs.org. Kate C. Collins Dailey, Prin. Lay Teachers 45; Administrators 8; Students 586.

Bishop Lynch High School, Inc., 9750 Ferguson Rd., 75228. Tel: 214-324-3607; Fax: 214-324-3600. Email: edleyden@bishoplynch.org. Web: www.bishoplynch.org. Mr. Edward E. Leyden, Pres.; Carol Olsen, Academic Dean; Rev. Victor Bartolotta. Priests 1; Sisters 1; Lay Teachers 81; Total Staff 84; Students 1,147.

[D] HIGH SCHOOLS, PRIVATE

DALLAS. *Jesuit College Preparatory School* (Boys) , 12345 Inwood Rd., 75244. Tel: 972-387-8700; Fax: 972-661-9349. Email: Ppostell@Jesuitcp.org. Web: www.jesuitcp.org. Mr. Michael A. Earsing, Prin.; Revs. Raymond Fitzgerald, S.J., Rector; Philip S. Postell, S.J., Pres.; Michael Chesney, S.J.; John F. Deeves, S.J.; Charles A. Leininger, S.J.; Gene Sessa, S.J.; John G. Stack, S.J.; Bro. Gerald J. Landry, S.J. Society of Jesus Priests 4; Lay Teachers 94; Students 1,002; Total Staff 99.

Ursuline Academy (Girls) , 4900 Walnut Hill Ln., 75229. Tel: 469-232-1800; Fax: 469-232-1836. Email: ebourgeois@ursuline.pvt.k12tx.us. Web: www.ursuline.pvt.k12.tx.us. Sr. Margaret Ann Moser, O.S.U., Pres.; Elizabeth C. Bourgeois, Prin. Faculty 73; Students 800.

IRVING. *Cistercian Preparatory School*, 3660 Cistercian Rd., 75039-4599. Tel: 469-499-5400; Fax: 469-499-5440. Email: pverhalen@cistercian.org. Web: www.infocistercian.org. Rev. Peter Verhalen, O.Cist., Headmaster. Cistercian Fathers of Our Lady of Dallas Abbey, (Boys) Priests 9; Lay Teachers 30; Students 345.

The Highlands School, 1451 E. Northgate Dr., 75062. Tel: 972-554-1980; Fax: 972-721-1691. Email: highlands@thehighlandsschool.org. Web: www.TheHighlandsSchool.org. Mr. David Maggio, Pres.; Ted O'Connor, Headmaster; Revs. Eugene Gormley, L.C., Chap.; Cliff Ermatinger, L.C., Supr. Lay Teachers 45; High School Students 113; Elementary 238; Middle 122; Students 473.

[E] ELEMENTARY SCHOOLS, PRIVATE

DALLAS. *Prince of Peace - Dallas*, 4500 W. Davis St., 75211. Tel: 214-337-0244; Fax: 214-339-1702. Email: popcs@lumen2000.com. Web: lumen2000.com/popweb. Gretchen Montgomery, MCSL & Prin. Lay Teachers 12; Students 142; Total Staff 25.

IRVING. *Cistercian Preparatory School* (Boys) , 3660 Cistercian Rd., 75039. Tel: 469-499-5400; Fax: 469-499-5440. Email: info@cistercian.org. Web: www.cistercian.org. Rev. Peter Verhalen, O.Cist., Headmaster. Cistercian Fathers of Our Lady of Dallas Abbey Priests 9; Lay Teachers 30; Students 345.

The Highland School, 1451 E. Northgate Dr., 75062. Tel: 972-554-1980; Fax: 972-721-1691. Email: highlands@thehighlandsschool.org. Web: www.thehighlandsschool.org. Rev. Cliff Ermatinger, L.C., Supr.; Mr. David Maggio, Pres.; Ted O'Connor, Headmaster; Rev. Eugene Gormley, L.C., Chap. Priests 2; Brothers 2; Lay Teachers 45; Students 473; Total Staff 29.

[F] SPECIAL SCHOOLS, PRIVATE

DALLAS. *Notre Dame of Dallas Schools, Inc.*, 2018 Allen St., 75204. Tel: 214-720-3911; Fax: 214-720-3913. Email: notredm@swbell.net. Web: www.notredameschool.org. Ms. Theresa Francis, Prin. Day School: Provides instructional education for mentally retarded children, ages 6-15.; Vocational Center: Provides vocational training for young adults, ages 16-21. Students 122; Sisters 2; Lay Staff 30.

[G] GENERAL HOSPITALS

DALLAS. *St. Paul Foundation*, 5909 Harry Hines Blvd., 75235. Tel: 214-879-2000; Fax: 214-879-2019. Email: john.hyde@swmcdallas.org. John Hyde, Vice Pres. (Texas Non-Profit Corp.); Support Organization for St. Paul University Hospital.

St. Paul University Hospital, 5909 Harry Hines Blvd., 75235. Tel: 214-879-1000; Fax: 214-879-8934. Web: www.stpauldallas.com. Mr. Bill McDonald, CEO & Pres.(Interim).
Department of Chaplain Services: Revs. F. Patrick Hanser, C.M., Dir., Vice Pres., Mission Affair & Ethics; John Alphonso (India); Royce Taylor, Baptist Chap.; Sisters Edith Thompson, D.C., Volunteer; Michael Friebe, D.C., Volunteer.

IRVING. *CHRISTUS Health*, 6363 N. Hwy. 161, Ste. 450, 75038. Tel: 877-980-0100; Fax: 214-492-8550. Email: john.zipprich@christushealth.org. Web: www.Christushealth.org. Thomas C. Royer, M.D., Pres. & CEO.

[H] CATHOLIC CHARITIES

DALLAS. *Brady Center*, 4009 Elm St., 75226. Tel: 214-826-8330; Fax: 214-826-8579. Email: mbrown@bradyctr.org. Web: www.catholiccharitiesdal.org. Mary N. Brown, Admin.

Catholic Charities of Dallas, Inc, 3725 Blackburn St., P.O. Box 190507, 75219. Tel: 214-520-6590; Fax: 214-520-6595. Email: mowens@cathdal.org. Web: catholiccharitiesdal.org. Sr. Mary Anne Owens, S.S.N.D.

Catholic Counseling Services, 3725 Blackburn St., P.O. Box 190507, 75219. Tel: 214-526-2772; Fax: 214-526-2941. Email: mwallace@cathdal.org. Mary Wallace, L.C.S.W., A.C.S.W, Admin.

Charities Home Center, 9850 Kingsley Rd., #405, 75238. Tel: 214-342-8231; Fax: 214-343-1533. Email: ershebet@aol.com. Liz Shearer, Admin.

Cross Family Center, 4906 Bonnie View Rd., 75241. Tel: 214-375-0133; Fax: 214-375-2511. Email: demgilb@aol.com. Web: www.catholiccharitiesdal.org. Demetrius Gilbert, M.S., Admin.

Immigration Counseling Services, 5415 Maple Ave., Ste. 400, 75235. Tel: 214-634-7182; Fax: 214-634-2531. Email: vanna@veriomail.com. Web: www.catholiccharitiesdal.org. Vanna Slaughter, L.M.S.W., A.C.P., Admin.

St. Joseph Adolescent and Family Services, 5415 Maple Ave., Ste. 320, 75235. Tel: 214-631-8336; Fax: 214-631-1506. Email: stjosepha-f@msn.com. Web: www.catholiccharitiesdal.org. Jennifer Peppe, L.M.F.T.A., L.P.C., Dir. Treatment Center for adolescent boys and girls ages 13-17.

Marillac Social Center, 2827 Lapsley, 75212. Tel: 214-638-4997; Fax: 214-638-1782. Email: mjdorn@ev1.net. Web: www.mjdornev1.net. Mary Jo Dorn, Admin.

St. Martin Family Service Center, Inc., 3725 Blackburn St., 75219. Tel: 214-520-6590; Fax: 214-520-6595. Purpose: To operate facilities in which social services are provided to assist the poor and indigent families of Dallas to become self-reliant.

Migration and Refugee Services; Refugee Resettlement; Refugee Job Placement, 9850 Kingsley Rd., Ste. 228, 75238. Tel: 214-553-9909; Fax: 214-553-8116. Email: admin@mrs-ccdallas.org. Diane Davis, Admin.

Parish and Community Services, 2827 Lapsley St., 75212. Tel: 214-638-4997; Fax: 214-638-1782. Sheryl Farrell, Dir.

COPPELL. *St. Joseph Village, Inc.*, 1201 E. Sandy Lake, 75019. Tel: 972-304-0300; Fax: 972-462-1099. Email: jwd@stjosephvillage.org.

[I] EDUCATION CENTERS

DALLAS. *Mount Carmel Center*, 4600 W. Davis St., 75211-3498. Tel: 214-331-6224; Fax: 214-330-0844. Web: www.mtcarmeldallas.org. Revs. Stephen Sanchez, O.C.D., Supr.; Francis de Sales Majors, O.C.D., Prog. Dir.; Jerome Earley, O.C.D. Discalced Carmelite Fathers of the Southwestern Province

Mount St. Michael Spiritual Life Center, 4500 W. Davis St., 75211. Tel: 214-331-1754; Fax: 214-333-1659. Email: mmc4500@airmail.net. Sr. Therese Blanchette, Supr. Sisters of Our Lady of Charity of Refuge 11.

[J] PERSONAL PRELATURES

IRVING. *Opus Dei* Prelature of the Holy Cross and Opus Dei , 3610 Wingren, 75062. Tel: 972-650-0064; Fax: 972-717-3580. Email: info@opusdei.org. Web: www.opusdei.org. Revs. Michael Manz; Victor Cortes.

[K] MONASTERIES AND RESIDENCES OF PRIESTS

DALLAS. *Capuchin Franciscan Friars, Vice Province of Texas*, 5605 Bernal Dr., 75212. Tel: 214-631-1937; Fax: 214-631-6276. Email: vicetexas@yahoo.com. Revs. Ignacio Cizur, O.F.M.Cap. (Spain); Mario Garcia, O.F.M.Cap. (Spain); Luis Gerardo Arraiza, O.F.M.Cap. (Spain); Sabino Erro, O.F.M. (Spain); Eric Azcona, O.F.M.Cap.; Juan Cizur Gaston, O.F.M.Cap. Priests 6.

Congregation of the Mission, Southern Province, 3826 Gilbert Ave., 75219. Tel: 214-526-0234; Fax: 214-526-3477. Email: CongMissSP@aol.com. Web: www.CMsouth.org. Rev. Dan Paul Borlik, C.M. Priests 25; Brothers 1.

IRVING. *Cistercian Abbey of Our Lady of Dallas*, 3550 Cistercian Rd., 75039. Tel: 972-438-2044; Fax: 972-579-7637. Email: DMFDenis@aol.com. Web: www.cistercian.org. Rt. Rev. Denis M. Farkasfalvy, O.Cist., S.S.L., M.S., S.T.D., Abbot, Vicar of the Abbot Pres. of Zirc; Revs. Peter Verhalen, O.Cist., Prior; Ralph March, O. Cist., Ph.D.; Bernard Marton, O.Cist., S.T.D., Subprior; Benedict Monostori, O.Cist., Ph.D.; Bede Lackner, O.Cist., Ph.D.; Pascal Kis-Horvath, O.Cist.; Aloysius Kimecz, O.Cist., M.A.; David Balas, O.Cist., Ph.D., S.T.D.; Matthew Kovacs, O.Cist., M.A.; Melchior Chladek, O.Cist., M.A.; Rochus Kereszty, O.Cist., S.T.D.; Julius Leloczky, O.Cist., S.T.D.; Henry Marton, O.Cist., S.T.D.; James Lehrberger, O.Cist., Ph.D.; Robert Maguire, O.Cist., Ph.D.; Gregory Schweers, O.Cist., M.A.; Mark Ripperger,

O.Cist., M.A.; Paul McCormick, O.Cist., M.A. (SLT); Bros. Abraham Frei, O.Cist., B.A.; Athanasius Rodriguez, O.Cist., B.S., M.Th.; Joseph Van House, O.Cist., B.A. Priests 19; Scholastics 2.

Dominican Priory of St. Albert the Great, Prior of Dominican Community, University of Dallas,, 3150 Vince Hagan Dr., 75062-4799. Tel: 972-438-1626; Fax: 972-438-6948. Very Rev. John Lydon, O.P., Prior; Revs. Aaron Arce, O.P.; James Burke, O.P.; Victor Celio, O.P.; Austin E. Green, O.P.; Charles Latour, O.P.; W. John Logan, O.P.; Edward M. Robinson, O.P., Subprior; Marcelo Solorzano, O.P.; Angel Vizcarra.

St. John Neumann Formation House, 1907 E. Grauwyler Rd., 75061. Tel: 972-438-4082; Fax: 972-438-4082. Email: longphi@hotmail.com. Revs. Dominic Long Nguyen, C.SS.R., Contact Person; Peter Phan Nguyen, C.SS.R.; John Mary Thong Nguyen, C.SS.R.; Peter Tuan Quang Bui, C.SS.R, Supr.

Legionaries of Christ, 1451 E. Northgate Dr., 75062. Tel: 972-554-1980; Fax: 972-554-8729. Email: highlands@thehighlandsschool.org. Web: www.thehighlandschool.org. Revs. Ned Brown; Cliff Ermatinger, L.C., Supr.; Eugene Gormley, L.C.; Frank Formolo; Bros. Michael Gross, L.C.; Nathan Miller, L.C.; Thong Nguyen, L.C.; Daniel Pajerski, L.C.

[L] CONVENTS AND RESIDENCES FOR SISTERS

DALLAS. *Bethany House*, 3017 Mallory, 75216. Tel: 214-371-4867. Email: mkldallas@aol.com. Web: www.web2.airmail.net/ssmn. Sr. Patricia Ann Ridgley, S.S.M.N., Contact Person. Sisters of St. Mary of Namur

Daughters of Charity Residence, 2911 Lapsley St., 75212. Tel: 214-631-6757. Email: laptex@juno.com. Sr. Marta Goski, D.C., Supr. Daughters of Charity of St. Vincent de Paul 5.

Missionaries of Charity, 2704 Harlandale, 75216. Tel: 214-374-3351. Sr. Mary Justus, M.C., Supr. Sisters 4.

Missionary Catechist of the Poor, 950 N. Montclair Ave., 75208. Tel: 214-942-6243; Fax: 214-942-6243. Email: mcpdallas@worlnet.att.net. Sr. Norma Edith Munoz, M.C.P., Supr. Sisters 9.

Monastery of Discalced Carmelites, 600 Flowers Ave., 75211. Tel: 214-330-7440; Fax: 214-339-3146. Sr. Mary Regina, O.C.D., Prioress. Professed Sisters 9.

School Sisters of Notre Dame, P.O. Box 227275, 75222. Tel: 214-330-9152; Fax: 214-330-9197. Email: jdaigle@ssndallas.org. Web: www.ssnd.org.

Provincial House of the Dallas Province, 4500 W. Davis, 75211. Tel: 214-330-9152; Fax: 214-330-9197. Prov. Sisters 155.

Other Addresses:

2930 Storey Ln., Apt. 101, 75220. Tel: 214-904-9547.

2810 Storey Ln., Apt. 101, 75220. Tel: 214-350-2863; Fax: 214-352-6513.

4401 Highview, 75211. Tel: 214-330-6623.

2826 Storey Ln., Apt. 101, 75220. Tel: 214-350-1534; Fax: 214-350-9033.

7550 S. Westmoreland, #118, 75234. Tel: 972-709-8374.

Ursuline Convent, 9905 Inwood Rd., 75220. Tel: 214-369-8159; Fax: 214-369-4004. Email: convent@ursuline.pvt.k12.tx.us. Web: www.osucentral.org.

Ursuline Academy, 4900 Walnut Hill Ln., 75229. Tel: 469-232-1800; Fax: 469-232-1836. Sisters Chabanel Mathison, O.S.U., Prioress; Margaret Ann Moser, O.S.U., Pres. Nuns 11.

GRAND PRAIRIE. *Sisters of the Holy Family of Nazareth* (Blessed Frances Siedliska Province) , 1814 Egyptian Way, P.O. Box 530959, 75053. Tel: 972-641-4496; Fax: 972-641-1668. Sr. M. Janice Kobierowski, C.S.F.N., Prov. Supr. Sisters 41.

IRVING. *Congregation of Mary, Queen-American Region (CMR)*, 723 Sunset Ave., 75061. Tel: 469-417-0123. Email: vocation@trinhvuong.org. Web: www.trinhvuong.org. Sr. Jacinta Tran, C.M.R., Contact Person.

[M] CAMPUS MINISTRY

IRVING. *Diocese of Dallas Campus Ministry* University of Dallas, 1845 E. Northgate Dr., 75062. Tel: 972-721-5375; Fax: 972-721-5351. Deacon Tim Muldoon, Office Mgr.; Denise G. Phillips, Dir. of Campus Ministry (Liturgy & Catechesis).

Southern Methodist University, Neuhoff Catholic Cntr., 3057 University Blvd., 75205. Tel: 214-987-0044; Fax: 214-987-3731. Michelle Freeman, Campus Min.

East Texas State University, St. Joseph Church, 2904 Melmar Pk., Commerce, 75428. Tel: 903-886-7135. Rev. D. Stanley Corcoran.

[N] MISCELLANEOUS LISTINGS

DALLAS. *Bishop Dunne Catholic School Building and Endowment Fund*, P.O. Box 190507, 75219. Tel: 214-528-2240; Fax: 214-523-2422. Most Rev. Charles V. Grahmann, Contact Person.

Bishop Grahmann Education Endowment Fund, P.O. Box 190507, 75219. Tel: 214-528-2240; Fax: 214-523-2422. Most Rev. Charles V. Grahmann, Trustee. Trust Fund for education of seminarians for Diocese of Dallas

Bishop Lynch High School Building and Endowment Trust, 9750 Ferguson Rd., 75228. Tel: 214-324-3607; Fax: 214-324-3600. Email: leyde@mail.bishoplynch.org. Web: www.ed.leyden@bishoplynch.org. Mr. Edward E. Leyden, Pres.

Carmelite Nuns Foundation, 600 Flowers Ave., 75211. Tel: 214-939-5503; Fax: 214-939-5503. Sr. Regina Parrish, Prioress.

Cathedral Restoration and Preservation Fund, Inc., 2215 Ross Ave., 75201. Tel: 214-361-8941; Fax: 214-954-1557. Email: rector@cathedralguadalupe.org. Web: www.cathedralguadalupe.org. Rev. Ramon Alvarez, Contact Person; Christy L. Frazer, Dir. of Devel.

Catholic Charities Endowment Trust, 3725 Blackburn St., 75219. Tel: 214-520-6590; Fax: 214-520-6595. Sr. Mary Anne Owens, S.S.N.D.

Catholic Community Appeal, Inc., 3725 Blackburn St., P.O. Box 190507, 75219. Tel: 214-528-2240; Fax: 214-526-1743. Email: pvitanza@cathdal.org. Web: www.cathdal.org. Paul Vitanza, Dir.

The Catholic Pro-Life Committee of North Texas, Inc., P.O. Box 703929, 75370. Tel: 972-267-LIFE; Fax: 972-267-0405. Email: cplc@prolifedallas.org. Web: www.prolifedallas.org. Karen Garnett, Exec. Dir.

Christian Community of God's Delight, 4500 W. Davis-Keating Hall, P.O. Box 225008, 75211. Tel: 214-333-2337; Fax: 214-333-2595. Email: vibezner@lumen2000.com.

Commission on Ecumenism, P.O. Box 190507, 75219. Tel: 214-528-2240; Fax: 214-523-2429. Revs. Robert R. Crisp, Member; Robert Williams, Chm.; Margie Medlund, Member; Lynn Rossol, Member.

Consecrated Virgins, 3725 Blackburn St., P.O. Box 190507, 75219. Tel: 214-528-2240; Fax: 214-526-1743. Most Rev. Joseph A. Galante, Coadjutor.

Dallas Vocation Guild, P.O. Box 12153, 75225. Tel: 972-991-9049. Bonni Castellaw Brophy, Pres.

Dave Fox Inner City Education Fund, P.O. Box 190507, 75219. Tel: 214-528-2240; Fax: 214-523-2422. Most Rev. Charles V. Grahmann, Trustee.

Diocesan Charitable Trust, P.O. Box 190507, 75219. Tel: 214-528-2240; Fax: 214-523-2422. Steve Malone, Contact Person. Owner/Operator of Subsidized Housing, Colonia Tepeyeac Apartments.

Diocesan Seminary Burse Endowment Fund Trust, P.O. Box 190507, 75219. Tel: 214-528-2240; Fax: 214-523-2422. Most Rev. Charles V. Grahmann, Trustee. Trust Fund for education of seminarians for Diocese of Dallas.

John Paul II High School Building and Endowment Fund, P.O. Box 190507, 75219. Tel: 214-528-2240; Fax: 214-523-2422. Email: mweis@cathdal.org. Michael T. Weis, Contact Person.

John Paul II High School, Inc., P.O. Box 190507, 75219. Tel: 214-528-2240; Fax: 214-523-2422. Web: www.jpiihs.org. Michael T. Weis, Treas. New Diocesan high school in developmental stage.

St. Joseph Residence, Inc., 330 W. Pembroke, 75208. Tel: 214-948-3597; Fax: 214-948-1209. Email: sisterabo1@aol.com. Sr. Adelaide Bocanegra, Bethl., Admin. For elderly ladies, gentlemen, and couples. Conducted by Daughters of the Sacred Heart of Jesus (Bethlemitas). Sisters 6; Residents 49.

Ladies of Charity of Dallas, P.O. Box 595666, 75359-0666. Tel: 214-821-5713.

Mary Benavides Education Fund, Formerly Mary Benavides TrustP.O. Box 190507, 75219. Tel: 214-528-2240; Fax: 214-523-2422. Most Rev. Charles V. Grahmann, Trustee. Trust Fund for the education of Hispanics.

St. Mary of Carmel Building Trust, 2900 Vilbig Rd., 75212. Tel: 214-747-1433. Email: C277372@aol.com.

The National Cursillo Center and Office of the National Secretariat, 4500 W. Davis, 75211. Tel: 214-339-6321; Fax: 214-339-6322. Email: nationalcursillo.center@verizon.net. Web: www.cursillo.org. P.O. Box 210226, 75211. Tel: 214-339-6321; Fax: 214-339-6322. Victor Lugo, English Coord.; Joachim Thong Le, Vietnamese Coord.; Jorge Barcelo, Hispanic Coord.

Dallas Cursillo Center, 5605 Bernal Dr., 75212. Tel: 214-631-7775. Rev. Fray Luis Arraiza, O.F.M.Cap., Spiritual Dir.

Nuestra Senora del Pilar Land & Development Trust, 4455W. Illinois Ave., 75211. Tel: 214-467-9116; Fax: 214-339-7249. Email: nspilarcathchurch@juno.com. Rev. Wilmer de Jesus Daza.

Santa Clara Endowment Fund Trust, P.O. Box 190507, 75219. Tel: 214-528-2240; Fax: 214-526-1743. Most Rev. Charles V. Grahmann, Trustee. Trust Fund to support Santa Clara School.

School Sisters of Notre Dame of Dallas Charitable Trust, 4500 W. Davis, 75211. Tel: 214-330-9152; Fax: 214-330-9197. Web: www.ssnd.org. P.O. Box 227275, 75222-7275.

Society of St. Vincent de Paul, 3826 Gilbert St., 75219. Tel: 214-641-5016, Ext. 146. Email: hhermann@sbcglobal.net. Robert Keim, Pres.; Henry Hermann, Pres. Central Office for all society activities in the Diocese of Dallas.

Southwestern Lieutenancy, Equestrian Order of the Holy Sepulchre of Jerusalem, 7303 Lane Park Ct., 75225. Tel: 214-369-5705; Fax: 214-239-2202. Email: jkacpa@flash.net. Jim Abney, Dallas Area Representative.

Ursuline Academy of Dallas Foundation, Inc., 4900 Walnut Hill, 75229. Tel: 469-232-3584; Fax: 462-232-3593. Email: mfrazier@ursuline.pvt.k12.tx_us. Web: www.ursuline.pvt.k12.tx..us. Sr. Margaret Ann Moser, O.S.U., Pres.

ALLEN. *St. Jude Parish Building Trust*, P.O. Box 869, 75013. Tel: 972-727-1177; Fax: 972-727-1177. Email: sjpall@cathdal.org. Rev. Timothy A. Church, Contact Person.

COPPELL. **St. Catherine of Siena, Inc.*, 180 Samuel Blvd., 75019. Tel: 972-393-5544; Fax: 972-393-5544. Email: msgrbroderick@stannparish.org. Rev. Msgr. Kilian J. Broderick, Contact Person.

**St. Martin de Porres, Inc.*, 180 Samuel Blvd., 75019. Tel: 972-462-1907; Fax: 972-304-8066.

St. Stephen, Inc., 180 Samuel Blvd., 75019. Tel: 972-288-7424; Fax: 972-288-3523. Email: msgrbroderick@stannparish.org. Rev. Msgr. Kilian J. Broderick, Contact Person.

Villa Santa Maria, Inc., 180 Samuel Blvd., 75019. Tel: 214-826-7863; Fax: 214-826-1567.

GRAND PRAIRIE. *Dallas Deanery Council of Catholic Women*, 1601 Ernie Ln., 75052. Tel: 972-647-8119. Email: swgist@aol.com. Paula Rogers, Pres.

Sisters of the Holy Family of Nazareth - Blessed Frances Siedliska Province Charitable Trust, 1814 Egyptian Way, P.O. Box 530959, 75053-0959. Tel: 972-641-4496; Fax: 972-641-1668. Sisters 41.

PLANO. *Dallas Diocesan Council of Catholic Women*, 3840 Dutton Dr., 75023. Tel: 972-618-1711. Email: Marilyn1@ont.com. Marilyn Ramsey, Pres.

St. Elizabeth Ann Seton Parish Building Trust, 2701 Piedra Dr., 75023. Tel: 972-596-5505; Fax: 972-985-7573. Email: twoolisc@eseton.org. Web: www.setonparish.org. Terry Wooliscroft, Business Mgr.

Our Lady of the Angels Building Trust, Formerly Our Lady of Angels Building Trust7300 Alma Dr., #400, 75023. Tel: 469-467-9669; Fax: 469-467-9669. Email: kcollom@ourladyofangelstx.org. Web: www.ourladyofangels.com. Karen Collom, Contact Person.

RELIGIOUS INSTITUTES OF MEN REPRESENTED IN THE DIOCESE

For further details refer to the corresponding bracketed number in the Religious Institutes of Men or Women section.

[0470]—*The Capuchin Friars*—O.F.M.Cap.
[0340]—*Cistercian Fathers*—O.Cist.
[0260]—*Discalced Carmelite Friars* (Oklahoma Prov.)—O.C.D.
[0690]—*Jesuit Fathers and Brothers* (New Orleans Prov.)—S.J.
[0730]—*Legionaries of Christ*—L.C.
[]—*Marian Servants of the Holy Spirit*—M.S.H.S.
[0800]—*Maryknoll*—M.M.
[1110]—*Missionaries of Sacred Heart*—M.S.C.
[0430]—*Order of Preachers (Dominicans)* (Southern Dominican Prov.)—O.P.
[1310]—*Order of the Holy Trinity*—O.SS.T.
[1065]—*Priestly Fraternity of St Peter*—F.S.S.P.
[]—*Redemptorists, Congregation of Most Holy Redeemer*—C.SS.R.
[1190]—*Salesians of St. John Bosco*—S.D.B.
[]—*Servant of Christ the Priest*
[1260]—*Society of Christ*—S.Ch.
[1330]—*Vincentian Fathers* (Southern Prov.)—C.M.

RELIGIOUS INSTITUTES OF WOMEN REPRESENTED IN THE DIOCESE

[0370]—*Carmelite Sisters of the Sacred Heart*—O.C.D.
[]—*Congregation of Mary Queen*—C.M.R.
[0760]—*Daughters of Charity of St. Vincent de Paul* (St. Louis Prov.)—D.C.
[0420]—*Discalced Carmelite Nuns*—O.C.D.
[1070-03]—*Dominican Sisters*—O.P.

[2710]—*Missionaries of Charity*—M.C.
[2690]—*Missionary Catechists of Divine Providence* (San Antonio, TX)—M.C.D.P.
[]—*Missionary Catechists of the Poor* (Mexico)—M.C.P.
[2970]—*School Sisters of Notre Dame*—S.S.N.D.
[]—*Sisters of Blessed Korean Martyrs*
[1010]—*Sisters of Divine Providence of San Antonio, Texas*—C.D.P.
[3071]—*Sisters of Our Lady of Charity*—O.L.C.
[3950]—*Sisters of Saint Mary of Namur* (Western Prov.)—S.S.M.N.
[1970]—*Sisters of the Holy Family of Nazareth* (Sacred Heart Vice Prov.)—C.S.F.N.
[2050]—*Sisters of the Holy Spirit and Mary Immaculate*—S.H.Sp.
[2205]—*Sisters of the Incarnate Word and Blessed Sacrament*—I.W.B.S.
[4110]—*Ursuline Nuns (Roman Union)* (Central Prov.)—O.S.U.

DIOCESAN CEMETERIES

DALLAS. *Calvary Hill Cemetary* A corporation owns and operates Diocesan cemeteries

Calvary Hill Cemetary, Old Calvary Hill.
Holy Redeemer Cemetary, Desoto.
Sacred Heart Cemetary, Rowlett.

PARISH CEMETERIES

ENNIS. *St. Joseph Cemetery*, St. John Nepomucene Parish.

WYLIE. *St. Paul Cemetery*, St. Anthony Parish.

NECROLOGY

(No Deaths)

Diocese of Davenport

(Dioecesis Davenportensis)

Most Reverend

WILLIAM E. FRANKLIN, D.D.

Bishop of Davenport *Res.: 2761 Scott St., Davenport, IA 52803*. Tel: 563-324-4774. *Office: St. Vincent Center,* 2706 N. Gaines St., Davenport, IA 52804-1998. Tel: 563-324-1911.

Chancery: St. Vincent Center, 2706 N. Gaines St., Davenport, IA 52804-1998. Tel: 563-324-1911; Fax: 563-324-5842.

Web: davenportdiocese.org

ERECTED MAY 8, 1881.

Square Miles 11,438.

Comprises that part of the State of Iowa bounded on the east by the Mississippi River; on the west by the western boundaries of the counties of Jasper, Marion, Monroe and Appanoose; on the south by the State of Missouri; on the north by the northern boundaries of the Counties of Jasper, Poweshiek, Iowa, Johnson, Cedar and Clinton.

Legal Title: For legal titles of parishes and diocesan institutions, consult the Chancery.

STATISTICAL OVERVIEW

Personnel	
Bishop	1
Priests: Diocesan Active in Diocese	79
Priests: Diocesan Active Outside Diocese	7
Priests: Retired, Sick or Absent	29
Number of Diocesan Priests	115
Religious Priests in Diocese	3
Total Priests in Diocese	118
Extern Priests in Diocese	4
Ordinations:	
Diocesan Priests	3
Permanent Deacons in Diocese	47
Total Brothers	1
Total Sisters	200
Parishes	
Parishes	85
With Resident Pastor:	
Resident Diocesan Priests	58
Resident Religious Priests	2
Without Resident Pastor:	
Administered by Priests	23
Administered by Lay People	2
Missions	1
Pastoral Centers	1
Professional Ministry Personnel:	
Sisters	14
Lay Ministers	46
Welfare	
Catholic Hospitals	3
Total Assisted	455,500
Homes for the Aged	2
Total Assisted	346
Special Centers for Social Services	1
Total Assisted	5,300
Educational	
Seminaries, Diocesan	1
Students from This Diocese	4
Diocesan Students in Other Seminaries	7
Total Seminarians	11
Colleges and Universities	2
Total Students	3,875
High Schools, Diocesan and Parish	7
Total Students	1,441
Elementary Schools, Diocesan and Parish	18
Total Students	3,844
Catechesis/Religious Education:	
High School Students	2,767
Elementary Students	9,393
Total Students under Catholic Instruction	21,331
Teachers in the Diocese:	
Priests	2
Sisters	5
Lay Teachers	387
Vital Statistics	
Receptions into the Church:	
Infant Baptism Totals	254
Adult Baptism Totals	256
Received into Full Communion	204
First Communions	1,977
Confirmations	1,733
Marriages:	
Catholic	351
Interfaith	273
Total Marriages	624
Deaths	1,061
Total Catholic Population	103,037
Total Population	728,048

Former Bishops—Rt. Revs. JOHN MCMULLEN, D.D., consecrated July 25, 1881; died July 4, 1883; HENRY COSGROVE, D.D., consecrated Sept. 14, 1884; died Dec. 22, 1906; JAMES DAVIS, D.D., consecrated Nov. 30, 1904; died Dec. 2, 1926; Most Revs. HENRY P. ROHLMAN, D.D., consecrated July 25, 1927; appt. Coadjutor-Archbishop of Dubuque and Titular Archbishop of Macra in Rhodope, June 15, 1944; Archbishop of Dubuque, Nov. 18, 1946; appt. Titular Archbishop of Cotrada, Dec. 2, 1954; died Sept. 13, 1957; RALPH LEO HAYES, D.D. (Retired), ord. Sept. 19, 1909; appt. Bishop of Helena June 23, 1933; consecrated Sept. 21, 1933; appt. Rector of North American College in Rome in Sept. 1935; transferred to Titular See of Hierapolis Oct. 26, 1935; transferred to Davenport Nov. 16, 1944; appt. Assistant at the Pontifical Throne April 30, 1958; transferred to Titular See of Naraggara; retired Oct. 20, 1966; died July 4, 1970; GERALD FRANCIS O'KEEFE, D.D. (Retired), ord. Jan. 29, 1944; appt. Auxiliary Bishop of St. Paul and Titular Bishop of Candyba May 5, 1961; consecrated July 2, 1961; transferred to Davenport Oct. 20, 1966; installed Jan 4, 1967; retired Nov. 12, 1993; died April 12, 2000.

Pastoral Center—2706 N. Gaines St., Davenport, 52804-1998. Tel: 563-324-1911; Fax: 563-324-5842. Email: communication@davenportdiocese.org. Web: www.davenportdiocese.org.

Vicar General and Moderator of the Curia—Rev. Msgrs. JOHN M. HYLAND, V.G., V.F.; MICHAEL MORRISSEY, M.A., J.C.L., V.G., V.F.

Chancellor—IRENE PRIOR LOFTUS, J.D., Send marriage matters to Tribunal.

Vice-Chancellors—CHARLENE MAASKE, C.P.A.; Revs. JOSEPH M. WOLF, J.C.L.; GEORGE W. MCDANIEL, Ph.D.

Diocesan Tribunal—Pastoral Center, 2706 N. Gaines St., Davenport, 52804-1998. Tel: 563-324-1911.

Judicial Vicar—Rev. JOSEPH M. WOLF, J.C.L.

Adjutant Judicial Vicar—Rev. Msgr. MICHAEL J. MORRISSEY, M.A., J.C.L., V.G., V.F.

Tribunal Auditor—THERESA M. DORAN.

Promoter of Justice—Rev. Msgrs. FRANCIS C. HENRICKSEN, E.V. (Retired); JAMES PARIZEK, J.C.L.

Defenders of the Bond—Rev. Msgr. LEO J. FEENEY; Revs. JOHN M. GALLAGHER, O.F.M.Cap., J.C.L.; WILLIAM E. REYNOLDS, J.C.L.

Notaries—THERESA M. DORAN; BARBARA VOSS; JUDITH JOHNSON; MARY FRICK; IRENE PRIOR LOFTUS, J.D.

Judges—Rev. JOHN P. BOYLE, Ph.D. (Retired); Very Rev. ROBERT J. BUSHER, V.F.; Rev. JOSEPH B. DENNING; Very Revs. EDWARD J. FITZPATRICK, V.F.; RUDOLPH T. JUAREZ, J.C.L., E.V.; Revs. ROBERT T. MCALEER; GEORGE W. MCDANIEL, Ph.D.; Rev. Msgrs. MICHAEL J. MORRISSEY, M.A., J.C.L., V.G., V.F.; JAMES PARIZEK, J.C.L.

Diocesan Consultors—Rev. NICHOLAS ADAM; Rev. Msgr. JOHN M. HYLAND, V.G., V.F.; Revs. PAUL CONNOLLY; KEN KUNTZ; Very Rev. RUDOLPH JUAREZ, E.V., J.C.L.; Rev. DAVID G. STEINLE.

Deans—Rev. Msgr. MICHAEL J. MORRISSEY, M.A., J.C.L., V.G., V.F., Davenport; Very Revs. H. ROBERT HARNESS, V.F., Clinton; EDWARD J. FITZPATRICK, V.F., Iowa City; Rev. Msgr. JOHN M. HYLAND, V.G., V.F., Keokuk; Rev. JOSEPH MILLER, C.PP.S., Ottumwa; Very Rev. ROBERT BUSHER, V.F., Grinnell.

Diocesan Corporate Board—Most Rev. WILLIAM E. FRANKLIN, D.D.; Rev. Msgrs. JOHN M. HYLAND, V.G., V.F.; MICHAEL MORRISSEY, M.A., J.C.L., V.G., V.F.; IRENE PRIOR LOFTUS, J.D.; ROBERT VAN VOOREN, J.D.; KATHY BUSH, C.P.A. Tel: 563-324-1911.

Finance Officer—CHARLENE MAASKE, C.P.A.

Finance Council—Most Rev. WILLIAM E. FRANKLIN, D.D.; IRENE PRIOR LOFTUS, J.D.; Rev. Msgr. MICHAEL J. MORRISSEY, M.A., J.C.L., V.G., V.F.; TERRY KILBURG, C.P.A.; MICHAEL BAUER; ROBERT VAN VOOREN, J.D.; RITA BAWDEN; KATHY BUSH, C.P.A.; JEFF HYLAND, C.P.A.

Vicar for Hispanics—Very Rev. RUDOLPH T. JUAREZ, J.C.L., E.V., 516 Fillmore St., Davenport, 52802.

Diocesan Offices

Pastoral Center—2706 N. Gaines St., Davenport, 52804-1998. Tel: 563-324-1911.

Finance and Administration—CHARLENE MAASKE, C.P.A.

Stewardship Coordinator—JUDY JOHNSON.

Database Coordinator—CHERYL CAREY.

Controller—KATIE MCCLEARY.

Accounting Coordinator—MICHELE TRAVER.

Planning, Publications and Communications—IRENE PRIOR LOFTUS, J.D.

Associate Director of Communication—DAVID MONTGOMERY.

Associate Director of Technology—ROBERT BUTTERWORTH.

Archivist—ARNOLD WIESER.

Pastoral Services—Rev. Msgr. JOHN M. HYLAND, V.G., V.F.

Director of Faith Formation and Education/ Superintendent of Schools—MARY M. WIESER.

Adult & Family Formation Lay Ministry Coordinator—ILAMAE HANISCH.

Youth Ministry Coordinator—JOE DVORAK.

Faith Formation Coordinator—PAT FINAN.

Curriculum & Media Educational Leadership Coordinator—Dr. BOB PILCHER.

Director of Social Action—Mr. DAN R. EBENER.

Coordinator of Intercultural Ministry—VACANT.

Immigration Program Coordinator—LAURA RAYA.

Director of Clergy Formation—Rev. CHARLES A. ADAM.

Director of Liturgy—VACANT.

Scouting—JOE DVORAK, Pastoral Center, 2706 N. Gaines St., Davenport, 52804-1998. Tel: 563-324-1911.

Catholic Relief Services—Mr. DAN R. EBENER, Dir., Pastoral Center, 2706 N. Gaines St., Davenport, 52804-1998. Tel: 563-324-1911.

Cemetery Committee—ROBERT MCCABE, Sec., 614 Main St., Davenport, 52801. Tel: 563-322-4438.

Campaign for Human Development—Mr. DAN R. EBENER, Pastoral Center, 2706 N. Gaines St., Davenport, 52804-1998. Tel: 563-324-1911.

Liturgical Commission—Rev. JAMES J. URBA, 2706 N. Gaines, Davenport, 52804. Tel: 563-678-2200.

D.C.C.W.—Rev. TIMOTHY J. REGAN, Dir., Pastoral Center, 2706 N. Gaines St., Davenport, 52804-1998. Tel: 563-324-1911.

Holy Childhood, Pontifical Association—Rev. Msgr. W. ROBERT SCHMIDT, Dir., Pastoral Center, 2706 N. Gaines St., Davenport, 52804-1998. Tel: 563-324-1911.

Newspaper—BARB ARLAND-FYE, Mng. Editor, P.O. Box 460, Davenport, 52805. Tel: 563-323-9959; Fax: 563-323-6612. Email: messenger@davenportdiocese.org. "The Catholic Messenger"

Pastoral Council—Most Rev. WILLIAM E. FRANKLIN, D.D., Pastoral Center, 2706 N. Gaines St., Davenport, 52804-1998. Tel: 563-324-1911.

Permanent Diaconate—Deacon ROBERT MCCOY, Pastoral Center, 2706 N. Gaines St., Davenport, 52804-1998. Tel: 563-324-1911.

Personnel Board—Pastoral Center, 2706 N. Gaines St., Davenport, 52804-1998. Tel: 563-324-1911.

Presbyteral Council—Rev. ROBERT T. MCALEER, St. John Vianney Rectory, 4097 18th St., Bettendorf, 52722-2120. Tel: 563-332-7910.

Priests' Aid Society—Rev. WILLIAM E. REYNOLDS, J.C.L., St. Mary Rectory, P.O. Box 628, Grinnell, 50112-0628. Tel: 641-236-5289; ANN RATLIFF, Contact, P.O. Box 1478, Newton, 50208-1478.

Priests Eucharistic League—Rev. MICHAEL T. PHILLIPS, Dir., St. Wenceslaus, 623 Fairchild St. Iowa City, 52245-2829. Tel: 319-337-4975; Fax: 319-337-5822. Email: stwenceslausic@compuserve.com.

Propagation of the Faith—IRENE PRIOR LOFTUS, J.D., Dir., Pastoral Center, 2706 N. Gaines St., Davenport, 52804-1998. Tel: 563-324-1911.

Social Action Commission—Mr. DAN R. EBENER, Pastoral Center, 2706 N. Gaines St., Davenport, 52804-1998. Tel: 563-324-1911.

Serra Club—Deacon RICK RASMUSSEN, 3236 Somerset Dr., Bettendorf, 52722. Tel: 563-332-7558.

Sisters' Council—Sr. PHYLLIS KERNZ, S.S.N.D., 512 E. Locust St., #1, Davenport, 52803-4365. Tel: 563-323-1584.

Vicar for Religious—Rev. Msgr. FRANCIS C. HENRICKSEN, E.V. (Retired), 1113 First St., Tipton, 52772-9289. Tel: 563-886-6285.

Victim Assistance Coordinator—THOMAS CROWLEY, P.O. Box, Bettendorf, 52722-0004. Tel: 563-349-5002. Email: vacdav@attglobal.net.

Vocations—Rev. CHARLES ADAM, Dir., St. Ambrose University, 518 W. Locust, Davenport, 52803. Tel: 563-333-6151.

Davenport Deanery—Rev. Msgr. MICHAEL J. MORRISSEY, M.A., J.C.L., V.G., V.F., 1315 W. Pleasant St., Davenport, 52804-2198. Tel: 563-324-0902.

CLERGY, PARISHES, MISSIONS AND PAROCHIAL SCHOOLS

CITY OF DAVENPORT
(SCOTT COUNTY)

1—SACRED HEART CATHEDRAL (1856), [JC] Rev. Msgr. Marvin A. Mottet; Rev. Joseph Khan V. Nguyen; Sr. Charla Bulko, S.S.S.F., Pastoral Assoc. In Res., Rev. Thomas F. Stratman (Retired).
Res.: 422 E. 10th St., 52803-5499. Tel: 563-324-3257; Fax: 563-326-6014.
School—Tel: 563-326-6278; Fax: 563-322-0889. Denise Tatoian, Prin. Lay Teachers 15; Students 110.
Catechesis/Religious Program—Sr. Mary Schmidt, O.S.B., D.R.E. Students 107.

2—ST. ALPHONSUS (1903), Rev. David G. Steinle.
Res.: 2618 Boies Ave., 52802. Tel: 563-322-0987; Fax: 563-323-1458.
School—Tel: 563-323-3204. Mr. Lewis Betts, Prin. Lay Teachers 11; Students 123.
Catechesis/Religious Program—Mary Ann Hagemann, D.R.E. Students 59.

3—ST. ANTHONY'S (1837), (Irish), Rev. Msgr. W. Robert Schmidt.
Res.: 417 N. Main St., 52801. Tel: 563-322-3303; Fax: 563-326-5136.
Catechesis/Religious Program—Students 178.

4—HOLY FAMILY (1897), Rev. Msgr. Michael Morrissey, M.A., J.C.L., V.G., V.F.; Rev. Robert M. Striegel; Deacons Gerald Timmerman, Pastoral Assoc.; Joseph Rosenthal.
Res.: 1923 Fillmore St., 52804. Tel: 563-322-0902 (Rectory); 563-322-0901; 563-326-3836 (Office); Fax: 563-884-4965.
School—1926 Marquette St., 52804. Tel: 563-324-3205; Fax: 563-324-9331. Lay Teachers 26; Students 281.
Catechesis/Religious Program—Sharon Weiland, (Grades K-8); Monica Hayz. Students 125.

5—ST. JOSEPH'S (1855), Closed., For inquiries for parish records contact Pastoral Center.

6—ST. MARY'S (1867), (Irish), Very Rev. Rudolph T. Juarez, J.C.L., E.V.; Deacons George D. Strader; Julian Gutierrez.
Res.: 516 Fillmore St., 52802. Tel: 563-322-3383; Fax: 563-322-3383.
Catechesis/Religious Program—Students 144.

7—OUR LADY OF VICTORY (1962), [JC] Rev. Msgr. James F. Parizek; Rev. Robert A. Lathrop; Deacons Paul Hittner; Marcel Mosse; Al Boboth.
Res.: 4105 No. Division, 52806. Tel: 319-391-4245; Fax: 319-445-1003. Email: olvdav@revealed.net.
School—John F. Kennedy Catholic, Tel: 319-391-3030; Fax: 319-388-5206. Chad Steimle, Prin. Lay Teachers 23; Students 263.
Catechesis/Religious Program—Tel: 319-391-8384. Patricia Gallagher, D.R.E.; Monica Hayz, D.R.E. Students 254.

8—ST. PAUL THE APOSTLE (1909), Revs. Michael Spiekermeier; Paul Appel; Deacon Robert McCoy.
Res.: 916 E. Rusholme St., 52803. Tel: 563-322-7994; Fax: 563-322-7995.
School—Tel: 563-322-2923; Fax: 563-322-9359. Sisters of Charity of the Blessed Virgin Mary 1; Lay Teachers 27; Students 481.
Catechesis/Religious Program—Tel: 319-322-3768. Rosie Megraw, D.R.E. Students 170.

OUTSIDE THE CITY OF DAVENPORT

ALBIA, MONROE CO., ST. MARY'S (1874), [CEM] Rev. William P. Walter, C.PP.S.
Res.: P.O. Box 365, 52531. Tel: 641-932-5130.
Catechesis/Religious Program—Tel: 641-932-5589. Jackie Maddy, D.R.E. Students 267.

ARDON, MUSCATINE CO., ST. MALACHY, Closed., For sacramental records, inquiries should be addressed to St. Joseph Parish, Columbus Junction

AUGUSTA, DES MOINES CO., ST. MARY'S (1881), Closed., For inquiries for parish records contact Pastoral Center.

BAUER, MARION CO., ST. JOSEPH, Closed., For inquiries for parish records contact Pastoral Center.

BETTENDORF, SCOTT CO.

1—ST. JOHN VIANNEY (1967), [JC] Rev. Robert T. McAleer; Deacons William Donnelly; Daryl Fortin.
Res.: 4097 18th St., 52722. Tel: 563-332-7910; Fax: 563-332-0833.
Catechesis/Religious Program—Tel: 563-332-7564. Students 815.

2—OUR LADY OF LOURDES (1903), Rev. Thomas J. Spiegel; Sr. Rita Lenaghan, C.H.M., Pastoral Assoc.; Deacons Dennis Duff; Charles Metzger; John D. Weber.
Res.: 1506 Brown St., 52722. Tel: 563-359-0345; Fax: 563-344-6017.
School—Tel: 563-359-3466. Mrs. Barbara Herter, Prin. Lay Teachers 28; Students 390.
Catechesis/Religious Program—Tel 563-359-1869. Students 425.

BLOOMFIELD, DAVIS CO., ST. MARY MAGDALEN (1953), Attended by, St. Patrick's, Ottumwa.

BLUE GRASS, SCOTT CO., ST. ANDREW (1976), [JC] Rev. Brian J. Shepley; Deacon Donald Frericks.
Res.: 333 W. Lotte St., 52726. Tel: 563-381-1363; Fax 563-381-1363.
Catechesis/Religious Program—Dorothy Spiess, D.R.E. Students 150.

BROOKLYN, POWESHIEK CO., ST. PATRICK, [CEM] Rev. Richard U. Okumu.
Mailing Address: P.O. Box 512, 52211-0512. Tel: 641-522-4323.
Catechesis/Religious Program—Students 132.

BRYANT, CLINTON CO., ST. MARY, Consolidated, with St. Joseph, Sugar Creek to form Sts. Mary and Joseph, Sugar Creek.

BUFFALO, SCOTT CO., ST. PETER'S (1912), [CEM] Attended by, St. Alphonsus, Davenport. Rev. David G. Steinle; Deacon Larry Dankert.
Mailing Address: 406 Fourth St., P.O. Box 488, 52728. Tel: 563-381-2865; 563-322-0987; Fax: 563-323-1458.
Catechesis/Religious Program—Students 41.

BURLINGTON, DES MOINES CO.

1—SS. JOHN & PAUL (1855), [JC] Rev. Msgr. John M. Hyland, V.G., V.F.; Rev. Patrick Hilgendorf; Sisters Nadine Meyer, S.S.N.D., Pastoral Assoc.; Kathy Braun, S.S.N.D., Pastoral Assoc.
Res.: 700 Division St., 52601-5415. Tel: 319-752-6733; Fax: 319-753-5211.
Catechesis/Religious Program—Tel: 319-753-0277. Sr. Virginia Klesner, S.S.N.D., D.R.E. Students 348.

2—ST. JOHN'S (1855), Merged, with St. Paul's, Burlington, to form SS. John & Paul, Burlington.

3—ST. PATRICK'S (1870), Merged with St. Mary, West Burlington to form SS. Mary and Patrick, West Burlington.

CAMANCHE, CLINTON CO., CHURCH OF THE VISITATION (1966), Rev. Joseph B. Denning; Deacon John H. Schmitt.
1032 Middle Rd., 52730-1032. Tel: 563-259-1188; Fax: 563-259-4462.
Catechesis/Religious Program—Tel: 563-259-1315; 563-259-8646. Barb Foster D.R.E.; Pat Haley, D.R.E. Students 95.

CENTERVILLE, APPANOOSE CO., ST. MARY'S (1870), Rev. Joseph Miller, C.PP.S.
Res.: 828 S. 18th St., 52544 Tel: 641-437-1984.
School—Lisa Hermsen, Prin Sisters 1; Lay Teachers 5; Students 56.
Catechesis/Religious Program—Students 150.

CHARLOTTE, CLINTON CO.

1—ASSUMPTION AND ST. PATRICK'S (1993), [CEM 2] Rev. Gary L. Beckman.
Res.: 147 Broadway St., 52731. Tel: 563-677-2758; Fax: 563-677-2739.
Catechesis/Religious Program—Students 70.

2—ASSUMPTION OF THE BLESSED MARY, Consolidated, with St. Patrick's, Villa Nova to form Assumption and St. Patrick's, Charlotte.

CLEAR CREEK, KEOKUK CO., SS. PETER & PAUL,, , See Holy Trinity, Keota.

CLINTON, CLINTON CO., JESUS CHRIST, PRINCE OF PEACE (1990), [CEM 2] Revs. Anthony Herold; Jeffry Belger; Deacons Jeffrey Schuetzle; Ramon Hilgendorf; Patrick Lennon; Arthur C. Donart; David Schnier, Business Mgr.; Phil O'Gara, Devel. Dir.
Parish Office—505 Ninth Ave. S., 52732. Tel: 563-242-3311; Fax: 563-242-3323. (Maintained for all four churches in Clinton.)
St. Mary's: 520 Ninth Ave. S., 52732.
Sacred Heart: 316 S. Fourth Ave., 52732.
St. Boniface: 2500 N. Pershing Blvd., 52732.
St. Irenaeus: 2811 N. Second St., 52732.
School—Tel: 563-242-1663; Fax: 563-243-8272. Nancy Peart, Prin. Students 287.
Catechesis/Religious Program—Tel: 563-243-8269. Betty Mantsch, D.R.E. Students 224.

COLFAX, JASPER CO., IMMACULATE CONCEPTION (1898), Rev. Philip A. Cardenzana; Deacon Joe Dvorak.
Mailing Address: 305 East Howard, 50054-1025. Tel: 515-674-3711; Fax: 515-674-4532.
Catechesis/Religious Program—Tel: 515-674-3358. Students 100.
Oratory—Sacred Heart Valeria, Jasper Co.

COLUMBUS JUNCTION, LOUISA CO., ST. JOSEPH (1853), Rev. Patrick L. Lumsden.
Mailing Address: 815 Second St., 52738. Tel: 319-728-8210.
Catechesis/Religious Program—Students 68.

COSGROVE, JOHNSON CO., ST. PETER'S (1878), Attended by, St. Mary, Oxford. Rev. Edmond J. Dunn; Deacon David Montgomery.
4022 Cosgrove Rd. S.W., Oxford, 52322. Tel: 319-828-4180; 319-545-2077.
Catechesis/Religious Program—Students 62.

DEWITT, CLINTON CO., ST. JOSEPH'S (1880), [CEM] Very Rev. H. Robert Harness, V.F.; Sr. Theresa Ann Spitz, R.S.M., Pastoral Assoc.; Deacon Mike Sheil.
Res.: 417 Sixth Ave., 52742. Tel: 563-659-3514; Fax: 563-659-2599.
School—Tel: 319-659-3812. Patrick Meade, Prin. Sisters of Mercy 1; Lay Teachers 12; Students 223.
Catechesis/Religious Program—Joyce Barnes, D.R.E. Students 222.

DELMAR, CLINTON CO., ST. PATRICK'S (1882), [CEM] Rev. Edward A. Botkin.
Res.: P.O. Box 293, 52037-0293. Tel: 563-674-4240.
Catechesis/Religious Program—Students 57.

DODGEVILLE, DES MOINES CO., ST. MARY'S (1850), [CEM] Rev. Patrick Lumsden; Deacon Clifford Beckman.
Res.: 13204 Dodgeville Rd., Sperry, 52650-9875. Tel: 319-985-2122.
Catechesis/Religious Program—Tel: 319-394-9379. Carol Abel, D.R.E.; Kim Hedges, D.R.E. Students 77.

EAST PLEASANT PLAIN, JEFFERSON CO., ST. JOSEPH'S (1902), [CEM] Attended by, St. Francis Xavier Cabrini, Richland. Rev. Charles J. Fladung.
Mailing Address: P.O. Box 130, Richland, 52585. Tel: 319-456-3161; Fax: 319-456-6408.
Catechesis/Religious Program—Students 45.

EDDYVILLE, MAHASKA CO., ST. MARY'S, Closed. For

inquiries for parish records contact the chancery.

ELDON, WAPELLO CO., ST. ALOYSIUS, Closed. For inquiries for parish records contact the chancery.

FAIRFIELD, JEFFERSON CO., ST. MARY'S (1864), Rev. Stephen C. Page.
Res.: 402 N. Third, 52556-2466. Tel: 641-472-3179; Fax: 641-472-6137.
Catechesis/Religious Program—Tel: 641-472-5991. Students 162.

FARMINGTON, VAN BUREN CO., ST. BONIFACE (1862), (German—English), [CEM] Rev. Apo T. Mpanda, Admin.
Church: 609 Washington St., 52626. Tel: 319-837-6808; Fax: 319-837-8112.
Res.: 311 Ave. C, P.O. Box 68, West Point, 52656.
Catechesis/Religious Program—Tel: 319-837-8905. Students 43.

FORT MADISON, LEE CO.

1—ST. JOSEPH'S, Consolidated, with St. Mary's to form SS. Mary & Joseph Parish.

2—SS. MARY & JOSEPH (1871), [CEM] Rev. Thomas L. Parlette; Sr. Mary Helen Hotze, S.S.N.D., Pastoral Assoc.; Donna Gengenbacher, Pastoral Assoc.
Res.: 1013 Ave. E, 52627. Tel: 319-372-3139; Fax: 319-372-7087.
Catechesis/Religious Program—Tel: 319-372-3970. Students 274.

3—ST. MARY'S, Consolidated, with St. Joseph's to form SS. Mary & Joseph Parish.

4—SACRED HEART (1893), Rev. Timothy J. Sheedy; Deacons Ronald Stein; Robert Gengenbacher.
Res.: 2204 Ave. I, 52627-4015. Tel: 319-372-3179; Fax: 319-372-3321.
Catechesis/Religious Program—Tel: 319-372-2486; 319-372-3970; Fax: 319-372-9574; 319-372-5013. Students 259.

GEORGETOWN, MONROE CO., ST. PATRICK'S (1851), (Irish), [CEM] Attended by, St. Peter's, Lovilia. Rev. Scott Lemaster.
Mailing Address: P.O. Box 183, Albia, 52531. Tel: 641-726-3529.
Catechesis/Religious Program—Tel: 641-932-5589. Clustered with St. Mary, Albia. Students 30.

GRAND MOUND, CLINTON CO., CHURCH OF ST. PHILIP AND JAMES (1876), [CEM] Very Rev. H. Robert Harness, V.F.
Res.: 606 Fulton St., P.O. Box 7, 52751-0007. Tel: 563-847-2271; Fax: 563-659-2599.
Catechesis/Religious Program—Students 72.

GRINNELL, POWESHIEK CO., ST. MARY'S (1924), [CEM] Rev. William E. Reynolds, J.C.L.
Res.: 1018 Broad St., P.O. Box 623, 50112. Tel: 641-236-5289; Fax: 641-236-7488.
Catechesis/Religious Program—Tel: 641-236-8838. Students 228.

HARPER, KEOKUK CO., ST. ELIZABETH'S, , See Holy Trinity, Keota.

HILLS, JOHNSON CO., ST. JOSEPH'S (1902), Rev. Louis J. Leonhardt.
Res.: 208 Iowa St., 52235. Tel: 319-679-2271; Fax: 319-679-2272.
Catechesis/Religious Program—Students 69.

HOLBROOK, IOWA CO., ST. MICHAEL, Closed., For inquiries for parish records contact the Pastoral Center.

HOUGHTON, LEE CO., ST. JOHN'S (1895), (German), [CEM] Rev. Dennis L. Hoffman.
Res.: Box 100, 52631. Tel: 319-469-2001.
School—(Grades PreK-6) Tel: 319-469-3581. Tammy Conrad, Prin. Lay Teachers 12; Students 188.
High School—Tel: 319-837-6131. Mr. Dan Kieler, Prin. Lay Teachers 15; Students 154.
Catechesis/Religious Program—Tel: 319-837-8905. Dixie Booten, D.R.E. Students 59.

IOWA CITY, JOHNSON CO.

1—ST. MARY (1840), [CEM 2] [JC] Revs. Kenneth E. Kuntz; Joseph Van Phung; Sr. Mary Agnes Giblin, B.V.M., Pastoral Assoc.
Mailing Address: 302 E. Jefferson, 52245-2137.
Res.: 228 E. Jefferson St., 52245-2137. Tel: 319-337-4314; Fax: 319-337-8551.
Catechesis/Religious Program—Regina Catholic School, Tel: 319-351-7638; Fax: 319-337-4109. Students 875.

2—ST. PATRICK'S (1872), (Irish), [JC] Rev. James J. Vrba.
Res.: 228 E. Court St., 52240-4998. Tel: 319-337-2856; Fax: 319-354-5590.
Catechesis/Religious Program—2150 Rochester Ave., 52245. Tel: 319-351-7638; Fax: 319-337-4109. Sr. Mary Frances Michalec, D.R.E. Students 326.

3—ST. THOMAS MORE (1944), [JC] Rev. Walter Helms.
Res.: 108 McLean St., 52246. Tel: 319-337-2173; Fax: 319-337-2174.
Catechesis/Religious Program—405 N. Riverside Dr., 52246. Tel: 319-337-4231. Michele Petersen, D.R.E. Students 200.

4—ST. WENCESLAUS (1893), (Bohemian), [JC] Rev. Michael T. Phillips.
Res.: 623 Fairchild St., 52245. Tel: 319-337-4957; Fax: 319-337-5822.

KEOKUK, LEE CO., ALL SAINTS (1982), Revs. Paul E. Connolly; Christopher J. David; Deacon William Cosgrove.
Res.: 310 S. Ninth St., 52632. Tel: 319-524-8334.
Catechesis/Religious Program—Students 246.

KEOTA, KEOKUK CO.

1—HOLY TRINITY (1992), [CEM 3] Rev. Martin G. Goetz.
Res.: 109 N. Lincoln St., 52248-9757. Tel: 641-636-3883; Fax: 641-636-3198.
St. Mary's: 109 N. Lincoln St., 52248-9757.
St. Elizabeth's: 20486 285th Ave., Harper, 52231.
SS. Peter & Paul: 30832 242nd St., Harper, 52231.
Catechesis/Religious Program—Tel: 515-636-3731. Students 150.

2—ST. MARY'S,, , See Holy Trinity, Keota.

KESWICK, KEOKUK CO., OUR LADY OF LOURDES (1914), (Irish—German), Attended by, St. Mary's, Sigourney. Rev. Philip R. Ryan; Deacon James Striegel.
Mailing Address: 415 E. Pleasant Valley St., Sigourney, 52591-1730. Tel: 641-622-3426.
Church: 50136. Tel: 641-622-2316.
Catechesis/Religious Program—Carole Olson, D.R.E. Students 24.

KINROSS, KEOKUK CO., SACRED HEART, Closed. For inquiries for parish records contact the chancery.

KNOXVILLE, MARION CO., ST. ANTHONY'S (1870), [CEM] Rev. Mark P. Spring.
Res.: 1202 Woodland St., 50138. Tel: 641-828-7050; Fax: 641-842-6249.
Catechesis/Religious Program—Tel: 641-842-3152. Martha Popson, D.R.E. Students 140.

LE CLAIRE-PRINCETON, SCOTT CO., OUR LADY OF THE RIVER (1969), Rev. Msgr. Leo J. Feeney.
Res.: 28200 226th St. Pl., P.O. Box 32, LeClaire, 52753. Tel: 563-289-5736.
Catechesis/Religious Program—Cheryl O'Klock, D.R.E. Students 131.

LONE TREE, JOHNSON CO., ST. MARY'S (1853), [CEM] [JC] Rev. Louis J. Leonhardt; Mrs. Carol Kaalberg, Parish Life Coord.
Mailing Address: Box 416, 52755.
Res.: 214 W. Jayne St., 52755. Tel: 319-629-4225; Fax: 319-629-4944.
Catechesis/Religious Program—Students 71.

LONG GROVE, SCOTT CO., ST. ANN'S (1853), [CEM] Rev. Stephen P. Ebel; Deacon Brian Krebs.
Res.: 16550 290th St., 52756. Tel: 563-285-4596; Fax: 563-285-4897.
Catechesis/Religious Program—Tel: 563-285-4020. Judy Shipman, D.R.E.; Margaret Liske, D.R.E.; Ann Mohr, D.R.E.; Chris Behnke, D.R.E. Students 610.

LOST NATION, CLINTON CO., SACRED HEART (1895), [CEM] Rev. John K. Sterling.
Res.: P.O. Box 127, 52254. Tel: 563-678-2200; Fax: 563-678-2389.

LOVILIA, MONROE CO., ST. PETER'S (1904), [CEM] Rev. Scott Lemaster.
Mailing Address: P.O. Box 8, 50150. Tel: 641-946-8298.
Catechesis/Religious Program—(Grades 6-12) Tel: 641-932-5589. Clustered with St. Mary, Albia and St. Patrick, Georgetown. Students 39.

MARENGO, IOWA CO., ST. PATRICK'S (1878), (Irish), [CEM] Rev. Joseph F. Roost.
Mailing Address: P.O. Box 183, 52301. Tel: 319-642-5438; Fax: 319-642-5648.
Catechesis/Religious Program—1661 P. Ave., 52301. Tel: 319-642-5628. Doris Jacobs, D.R.E. Students 118.

MECHANICSVILLE, CEDAR CO., ST. MARY'S (1872), Rev. Thomas Doyle.
Res.: P.O. Box 457, 52306-0457. Tel: 563-432-6236.
Catechesis/Religious Program—Tel: 319-432-6678. Joan Garner, D.R.E.; Ann Saver, D.R.E. Students 68.

MELCHER, MARION CO., SACRED HEART (1912), [CEM] [JC] Rev. Mark P. Spring.
315 S. Main, Box 277, 50163. Tel: 641-947-4981.
Catechesis/Religious Program—Tel: 641-947-2902. Lisa Alexander, D.R.E.; Phyllis Dittmer, D.R.E. Students 63.

MELROSE, MONROE CO., ST. PATRICK'S (1870), (Irish), [CEM] Rev. Scott Lemaster.
Res.: 200 Trinity St., P.O. Box 154, 52569-0154. Tel: 641-726-3531.
Catechesis/Religious Program—Joan Brubaker, D.R.E. Students 24.

MONTROSE, LEE CO., ST. JOSEPH'S (1860), [JC] Revs. Paul Connolly; Christopher J. David. In Res., Rev. Gerald A. Hoenig (Retired).
Res.: Box 206, 52639. Tel: 319-463-5443.
Catechesis/Religious Program—Tel: 319-463-5571. Students 19.

MOUNT PLEASANT, HENRY CO., ST. ALPHONSUS (1862), (Irish), [CEM] Rev. Nicholas Adam; Deacon Joe Demeter.
Res.: 607 S. Jackson St., 52641-2696. Tel: 319-385-8410; Fax: 319-385-0545.
Catechesis/Religious Program—Tel: 319-385-4937. Mary Hassenfritz, D.R.E. (Grades PreK-8); Sr. Ann Marie Dunn, O.S.F., D.R.E. Students 316.

MUSCATINE, MUSCATINE CO.

1—SS. MARY AND MATHIAS OF MUSCATINE, [CEM] Revs. John P. Gallagher; Jason Crossen; Bernard E. Weir; Deacon James Becker.
Res.: 215 W. Eighth St., 52761. Tel: 563-263-1878; 563-263-1416 (Parish Office); Fax: 563-263-2782.
Catechesis/Religious Program—Tel: 563-263-3264; 563-363-3848; Fax: 563-263-6700. Sr. Mary Cheryl Demmer, P.B.V.M., D.R.E. Students 322.

2—ST. MARY'S (1876), Merged, with St. Mathias to form SS. Mary and Mathias of Muscatine.

3—ST. MATHIAS (1842), Merged, with St. Mary to form SS. Mary and Mathias of Muscatine.

4—OUR LADY OF GUADALUPE CATHOLIC MISSION (1976), (Hispanic), Rev. Bernard E. Weir.
Res.: 417 Green St., 52761. Tel: 563-263-7788.

MYSTIC, APPANOOSE CO., ST. FRANCIS, Closed. For inquiries for parish records contact the chancery.

NEWPORT, JOHNSON CO., ST. MARY, Closed. For inquiries for parish records contact the chancery.

NEWTON, JASPER CO., SACRED HEART (1867), [CEM] Rev. Ernest E. Braida; Tammy Norcross, Pastoral Min.
Mailing Address: P.O. Box 1478, 50208-1478. Tel: 641-792-4625 (Rectory); Fax: 641-792-8639.
McCann Center—1115 S. Eighth Ave. E., P.O. Box 1478, 50208. Tel: 641-792-2050. (Parish Office and Religious Education Center)
Catechesis/Religious Program—Valerie Steinbach, D.R.E. (Grades K-12). Students 500.

NICHOLS, MUSCATINE CO., ST. MARY'S (1874), [CEM] [JC] Rev. Louis J. Leonhardt; Mrs. Carol Kaalberg, Parish Life Coord.
201 Short St., Box B, 52766. Tel: 319-723-4566; Fax: 319-629-4944.
Catechesis/Religious Program—Students 29.

NOLAN SETTLEMENT, JOHNSON CO., ST. BRIDGET'S, Closed. For inquiries for parish records contact the chancery.

NORTH ENGLISH, IOWA CO., ST. JOSEPH'S (1963), [JC] Rev. David Hitch.
Res.: 52316. Tel: 319-664-3325; Fax: 319-668-2582.
Catechesis/Religious Program—Tel: 319-668-2241. Students 95.

OSKALOOSA, MAHASKA CO., ST. MARY'S (1871), [CEM] Very Rev. Robert J. Busher, V.F.
Res.: 311 First Ave. E., 52577. Tel: 641-673-6680; Fax: 641-672-2211.
Catechesis/Religious Program—Tel: 641-673-0659. Mrs. Richelle Holle, D.R.E. Students 160.

OTTUMWA, WAPELLO CO.

1—ST. MARY OF THE VISITATION (1851), (German), Revs. John D. Spiegel; Troy Richmond.
Res.: 222 N. Ward St., 52501-4398. Tel: 641-682-4559; Fax: 641-682-4433.
Catechesis/Religious Program—Tel: 641-682-4496. Students 339.

2—ST. PATRICK'S (1880), Revs. John D. Spiegel; Troy Richmond.
Res.: 222 N. Ward St., 52501. Tel: 641-682-4212; Fax: 641-682-7915.
Catechesis/Religious Program—Ottumwa Regional Catholic Religious Education, Tel: 641-682-0320. Anna Hanson, D.R.E.; Gail Bates, D.R.E.; Mary Ryan, D.R.E. Students 339.

3—SACRED HEART, Merged, with St. Mary of the Visitation, Ottumwa.

OXFORD, JOHNSON CO., ST. MARY'S (1860), [CEM] Rev. Edmond J. Dunn.
Mailing Address: Box 80, 52322-0080. Tel: 319-828-4180; Fax: 319-828-4059.
Catechesis/Religious Program—Tel: 319-628-4466. Students 145.

PARNELL, IOWA CO., ST. JOSEPH'S (1880), (Irish), [CEM] Attended by, St. Joseph, North English. Rev. David Hitch.
862 F52 Trl., P.O. Box 17, 52325-0017. Tel: 319-668-2366.
Catechesis/Religious Program—F52 Trail. Tel: 319-668-2644. Students 50.

PELLA, MARION CO., ST. MARY'S (1869), [CEM] Rev. Robert Gruss.
Res.: 1203 Peace St., P.O. Box 144, 50219-0144. Tel: 641-628-4262; Fax: 641-628-3165.
Catechesis/Religious Program—Tel: 641-628-3078. Students 239.

PETERSVILLE, CLINTON CO., IMMACULATE CONCEPTION (1853), (Irish), [CEM] Rev. Edward A. Botkin.
Church: 1302 250th Ave., P.O. Box 293, Delmar, 52037-0293. Tel: 563-674-4240.
Catechesis/Religious Program—Tel: 563-652-6971. Students 8.

RATHBUN, APPANOOSE CO., ST. ANTHONY (1895), Closed. For inquiries for parish records contact the chancery.

RICHLAND, KEOKUK CO., ST. FRANCES XAVIER CABRINI (1946), (German), Rev. Charles J. Fladung.
Res.: 308 W. Main St., P.O. Box 130, 52585-0130. Tel: 319-456-3161; Fax: 319-456-6408.

Catechesis/Religious Program—Students 45.

RICHMOND, WASHINGTON CO., HOLY TRINITY (1854), (Bohemian), [CEM] Rev. Richard Adam.
Res.: 580 Howard St., Kalona, 52247-9558. Tel: 319-656-2802.
Catechesis/Religious Program—Tel: 319-656-2401. Students 118.

RIVERSIDE, WASHINGTON CO., ST. MARY OF THE ASSUMPTION (1877), (German), [CEM] Rev. Rich Adam; Deacon David Reha.
Res.: 51 St. Mary's St., P.O. Box C, 52327-0482. Tel: 319-648-2331; Fax: 319-648-5024.
Catechesis/Religious Program—Tel: 319-648-3017. Students 95.

ST. PAUL, LEE CO., ST. JAMES (1838), (German), [CEM] Attended by, St. John, Houghton. Rev. Dennis L. Hoffman.
Mailing Address: P.O. Box 100, Houghton, 52631-0100. Tel: 319-469-2001.
Catechesis/Religious Program—Tel: 319-837-8905. Dixie Booten, D.R.E. Students 381.

SIGOURNEY, KEOKUK CO., ST. MARY'S (1873), (N. European), [CEM] [JC] Rev. Philip R. Ryan; Deacon James Striegel.
Res.: 415 E. Pleasant Valley St., 52591. Tel: 641-622-3426 (Rectory); 641-622-2316 (Business).
Catechesis/Religious Program—Fax: 641-622-2706. Carole Olson, D.R.E. Students 85.
Mission—Our Lady of Lourdes 107 N. L St., Keswick, Keokuk Co. 50163. Tel: 319-738-3731.

SOLON, JOHNSON CO.
1—ST. MARY'S (1858), (Czech), [CEM] Rev. D. F. Wilkening.
Res.: 1749 Racine Ave., 52333-0069. Tel: 319-624-2228; Fax: 319-624-3564.
Catechesis/Religious Program—Tel: 319-624-3455. Julie Agne, D.R.E. Students 325.
2—SS. PETER & PAUL, Closed. For inquiries for parish records contact the chancery.

STRING PRAIRIE, LEE CO., ST. MARY, Closed. For inquiries for parish records contact the chancery.

SUGAR CREEK, CLINTON CO.
1—ST. JOSEPH'S, Consolidated, with St. Mary, Bryant, to form Sts. Mary and Joseph, Sugar Creek.
2—SS. MARY AND JOSEPH (1993), (Irish—German), [CEM 2] Rev. Gary L. Beckman.
3218 110th St., P.O. Box 428, Preston, 52069-0428. Tel: 563-677-2758; Fax: 563-689-6422.
Res.: 147 Broadway St., Charlotte, 52731-9686. Fax: 563-677-2739.
Catechesis/Religious Program—Jackie Winkler, D.R.E. Tel: 563-677-2251; Kathy Sellnau, D.R.E. Tel: 563-682-7372. Students 73.

TIPTON, CEDAR CO., ST. MARY'S (1856), [CEM] Rev. M. Eugene Benda; Deacons Adrian Panther; Robert Snavely.
Res.: P.O. Box 309, 52772-0309. Tel: 563-886-2506; Fax: 563-886-6326.
Catechesis/Religious Program—Tel: 319-886-2506. Mary Barnum, D.R.E. Students 266.

TORONTO, CLINTON CO., ST. JAMES (1855), [CEM] Attended by, Sacred Heart, Lost Nation. Rev. John K. Sterling.
Mailing Address: P.O. Box 127, Lost Nation, 52254. Tel: 563-678-2200; Fax: 563-678-2389.
Catechesis/Religious Program—Mary Stevenson, D.R.E. Students 43.

VALERIA, JASPER CO., SACRED HEART (1892), Closed. For inquiries for parish records contact the chancery.

VICTOR, IOWA CO., ST. BRIDGET'S (1886), (Belgian), [CEM] [JC] Rev. Richard U. Okumu.
Res.: 104 Third St., P.O. Box 266, 52347. Tel: 319-647-2220; Fax: 319-647-3231.
Catechesis/Religious Program—Tel: 319-647-2294. Students 116.

VILLA NOVA, CLINTON CO., ST. PATRICK, Consolidated, with Assumption of the Blessed Virgin Mary, Charlotte, to form Assumption and St. Patrick's, Charlotte.

WAPELLO, LOUISA CO., ST. MARY'S (1867), Attended by, St. Joseph, Columbus Junction. Rev. Patrick L. Lumsden.
Mailing Address: P.O. Box 214, 52653. Tel: 319-728-8210.

WASHINGTON, WASHINGTON CO., ST. JAMES (1860), [JC] Rev. Edward A. O'Melia.
Res.: 602 W. Second St., 52353-1994. Tel: 319-653-4504; Fax: 319-653-4504.
School—Tel: 319-653-3631; Fax: 319-653-3631. Ms. BethAnn McBride, Prin. Lay Teachers 10; Students 130.
Catechesis/Religious Program—Tel: 319-653-6213. Sr. Jane McCarthy, O.S.F., D.R.E. Students 145.

WELLER, MONROE CO., ST. MARY, Closed. For inquiries for parish records contact the chancery.

WELLMAN, WASHINGTON CO., ST. JOSEPH (1969), (German), [CEM] Rev. Richard A. Adam; Deacon David Reha.
Mailing Address: 235 11th St., P.O. Box C, Riverside, 52327-0482. Tel: 319-648-2331; Fax: 319-648-5024.
Catechesis/Religious Program—Tel: 319-646-2807. Donna Reha, D.R.E. Students 38.

WELTON, CLINTON CO., ST. ANNE (1910), Attended by, St. Patrick Delmar. Rev. Edward A. Botkin.
Mailing Address: P.O. Box 293, Delmar, 52037-0293. Tel: 563-674-4240.
Catechesis/Religious Program—Students 27.

WEST BRANCH, CEDAR CO., ST. BERNADETTE (1960), Attended by, St. Joseph, West Liberty. Rev. Edward A O'Melia.
507 E. Orange, Box 103, 52358-0103.
Church & Mailing Address: 507 E. Orange, Box 103, 52358-0103. Tel: 319-643-2095; 319-627-2229 (Pastor Only).
Catechesis/Religious Program—1720 Madison St., Tipton, 52772. Tel: 319-946-2162. Martha Freeman, D.R.E. Students 150.

WEST BURLINGTON, DES MOINES CO., SS. MARY AND PATRICK (1870), [CEM] Rev. Gerald E. Stouvenel.
Res.: 420 W. Mt. Pleasant St., P.O Box 415, 52655-0415. Tel: 319-752-8771.
Catechesis/Religious Program—700 S Roosevelt, Burlington, 52601. Tel: 319-753-0277. Sr. Virginia Klesner, S.S.N.D., D.R.E. Students 270.

WEST LIBERTY, MUSCATINE CO., ST. JOSEPH'S (1892), (Hispanic), [CEM] Rev. Dennis C. Martin.
Res.: 107 W. Sixth St., 52776-1246. Tel: 319-627-2229; Fax: 319-627-2552.
Catechesis/Religious Program—Students 143.

WEST POINT, LEE CO., ASSUMPTION OF THE BLESSED VIRGIN MARY, (German), [CEM] Rev. Apo T. Mpanda, Admin.
Res.: 311 Ave. C, P.O. Box 68, 52656. Tel: 319-837-6808.

WHAT CHEER, KEOKUK CO., ST. JOSEPH'S, Closed. For inquiries for parish records contact the chancery.

WILLIAMSBURG, IOWA CO., ST. MARY'S (1891), [CEM] Rev. Joseph F. Roost.
Res.: 102 E. Penn, Box 119, 52361. Tel: 319-668-1397; Fax: 319-668-2487.
Catechesis/Religious Program—Tel: 319-668-2757. Students 245.

WILTON, MUSCATINE CO., ST. MARY'S (1857), [CEM] Rev. Brian J. Shepley.
Res.: 701 E. 3rd St., P.O. Box 477, 52778. Tel: 563-732-2271.
Catechesis/Religious Program—Tel: 563-732-2269. Students 84.

Chaplains of Public Institutions

IOWA CITY. *State University of Iowa Hospital*. Revs. Vitolds Valainis, William Kneemiller.
Veteran's Administration Hospital. Rev. Rudolph C. Berndt. Attended from Mercy Hospital, Iowa City.

KNOXVILLE. *Veteran's Administration Hospital*.

Special Assignment:
Revs.—
Regan, Timothy J., Genesis Medical Center, c/o 2706 N. Gaines St., 52804.
Whalen, John J., 2706 N. Gaines St., 52804.

On Duty Outside the Diocese:
Revs.—
Beyer, Richard J., 1315 Chapelwood Dr., Waco, TX 76712.
Burnett, James E., 8505 Hemlock Ln., Darien, IL 60561.
Steckel, Gregory A., 2601 Olde Creek Ct., Leavenworth, KS 66048.
Young, Ronald E., 3660 W. San Jose, #218, Fresno, CA 93711.

Military Chaplains:
Rev. Msgr.—
Spiegel, Robert H., UNC/CFC/USFK/EUSA, CMR 415 Box 4772, APO, AE 09114.
Rev.—
Kneemiller, William, HSC 339th EN BN, 1st Armored Div, Apo, AE 09114

Absent on Leave:
Revs.—
Lasley, Jerry D.
Leu, James E.

Retired:
Rev. Msgrs.—
Henricksen, Francis C., E.V., 1113 First St., Tipton, 5277--289.
Walter, Robert J., 3406 Spring St., #3, 52807-2117.
Revs.—
Bevenour, Richard F., 622 W. Escalon St., Fresno, CA 93704.
Borger, Theodore R., 3694 33rd St., San Diego, CA 92104-4317.
Boyle, John P., Ph.D., The Devonshire, 1700 Robin Ln., Apt. 475, Lisle, IL 60532.
Brothersen, Maynard J., Pastoral Center, 2706 N. Gaines St., 52804.
Brownfield, Robert L., Pastoral Center, 2706 N. Gaines St., 52804.
Conrad, Anthony J., Kahl, 1101 W. Ninth St., 52804.
Conroy, James P., 103 Valley Heights Dr., P.O. Box 372, Buffalo, 52728.
Cross, Peter, 2220 10th St., Coralville, 52241.
Durkin, John R., 7402 Crestway Dr., #113, San Antonio, TX 78239-3120.
Egert, Clifford A., Kahl Home, 1101 W. Ninth St., 52804.
Farrell, Anthony G., 324 N. Main St., 52801-1427.
Grubb, James E., 514 Fahrney Blvd., Ottumwa, 52501-3254.
Hoening, Gerald, St. Joseph Rectory, P.O. Box 206, Montrose, 52639.
Hynes, John F., 3051 Holiday Ct., Bettendorf, 52722-3463.
Kokjohn, Joseph E., St. Ambrose University, 518 W. Locust St., 52803.
Lawrence, James T., Pastoral Center, 2706 N. Gaines St., 52804.
Linnenbrink, Harry H., Cottage Gove Place, 2115 1st Ave., S.E., Apt. 304, Cedar Rapids, 52402.
Manning, Martin B., 2617 Maplecrest #102, Bettendorf, 52722.
Meyer, William O., Pastoral Center, 2706 N. Gaines St., 52804.
Mohr, Thomas H., 2122 E. Elm St., 52803.
Mulligan, Louis J., Fort Armstrong Senior Residence, 1900 3rd Ave., #608, Rock Island, IL 61201-8028.
Reilman, Thomas J., 2301 Agency St., #59, Burlington, 52601.
Rogers, Joseph, Kahl Home, 1101 W. Ninth St., 52804.
Ruppenkamp, Raymond, 4233 180th St., Clinton, 52732-8818.
Shepler, Charles C., 21412 River Rd. N.,, Cordova, IL 61242-9743.
Stratman, Thomas F., 422 E. 10th St., 52803.
Von Ah, Richard J., Kahl Home, 1101 W. 9th St., 52804.

Permanent Deacons:
Anderson, Arthur, Davenport
Becker, James L., Muscatine
Beckman, Clifford C., Sperry
Boboth, Albert G., Davenport
Carl, Robert L., Muscatine
Cosgrove, William T., Keokuk
Dankert, Larry F., Davenport
Demeter, M. Joseph W., Mount Pleasant
Donart, Arthur C., Thomson, IL
Donnelly, William G., Bettendorf
Duff, Dennis L., Bettendorf
Dvorak, Joseph F., Colfax
Fortin, Daryl G., Le Claire
Frericks, Donald E., Blue Grass
Gengenbacher, Robert, Fort Madison
Gutierrez, Julian, Davenport
Hammer, Richard D., Burlington
Haut, Allen A., Bettendorf
Hilgendorf, Ramon C., Clinton
Hittner, Paul F., East Moline, IL
Krebs, Brian, Eldridge
Lennon, Patrick, Clinton
McCoy, Robert C., Davenport
Metzger, Charles A., Bettendorf
Miller, Jerome A., Iowa City
Montgomery, David, Oxford
Mosse, Marcel G., Davenport
Mueller, Aloysius P., Clinton
O'Connor, Arthur, Olatha, KS
Olson, William D., Grinnell
Panther, Adrian B., Tipton
Rasmussen, Richard J., Bettendorf
Reha, David, Wellman
Rosenthal, Joseph I., Davenport
Schmitt, John H., Low Moor
Schroeder, William E., Carroll
Schuetzle, Jeffrey C., Clinton
Sheil, Michael D., DeWitt
Snavely, Robert E., Tipton
Stein, Ronald K., Donnellson
Strader, George D., Davenport
Striegel, James L., Delta
Timmerman, Gerald L., Davenport
Tometich, Anton I., Muscatine
Vonderhaar, James J., West Point
Weber, John R., Bettendorf
Wiegand, William R., Oskaloosa
Witt, Stephen J., Grinnell

INSTITUTIONS LOCATED IN THE DIOCESE

[A] SEMINARIES, DIOCESAN

DAVENPORT. *St. Ambrose University Seminary* 52803. Tel: 563-333-6151; Fax: 563-333-6243. Email: adamcharlesa@sau.edu. Web: www.davenportdiocese.org. Revs. Charles A. Adam, Rector; George W. McDaniel, Ph.D., Spiritual Dir. Priests 2; Students 4.

[B] COLLEGES AND UNIVERSITIES

DAVENPORT. *St. Ambrose University* 52803-2898. Tel: 563-333-6300; Fax: 563-333-6243. Email: admit@sau.edu. Web: www.sau.edu/. Edward Rogalski, Ph.D., Pres.; Lori Rodrigues-Fisher, Ph.D., Vice Pres. Academic Affairs; Edward Henkhaus, Vice Pres. Finance; Dr. Edward G. Littig, Vice Pres. for Advancement; Dr. James P. Loftus, Ph.D., Vice Pres. Enrollment Mgmt.; Revs. Charles A. Adam, Campus Chap.; Robert L. Grant, Campus Min.; Sr. Audrey Cleary, O.S.B., Dir., Prayer & Spirituality Center; P. J. Foley, Coord. Service Learning & Justice Ministry; Sheila Deluhery, Campus Min. & Dir.; Deborah Sanborne, Chapel Music Dir. Priests 9; Sisters 1; Total Faculty & Staff 407; Lay Teachers 140; Students 3,874.

Priest Faculty: Revs. Charles A. Adam; Edward A. Botkin; William F. Dawson, Ph.D.; Joseph De Francisco, Ph.D. (BEA); Edmond J. Dunn; Robert L. Grant; Joseph E. Kokjohn (Retired); George McDaniel, Ph.D.; Brian Miclot, Ph.D.

CLINTON. *The Franciscan University*, Formerly Mt. St. Clare College (Coed) , 400 Bluff Blvd., P.O. Box 2967, 52733-2937. Tel: 563-242-4023; 800-242-4153; Fax: 563-242-8684. Email: admissns@tfu.edu. Web: www.tfu.edu. Dr. Michael E. Kaelke, Pres. Sisters of St. Francis, Clinton, IA Sisters 6; Lay Teachers 52; Total Staff 112; Students 520.

[C] SECULAR CAMPUSES

IOWA CITY. *Catholic Chair of Religion*, School of Religion, 314 Gilmore Hall, University of Iowa, 52242-1376. Tel: 319-335-2164.

[D] ADULT RELIGIOUS EDUCATION

DAVENPORT. *New Horizons of Faith, Inc.*, 820 W. Central Park Ave., 52804. Tel: 563-336-8415; Fax: 563-323-5209. Email: joannkk@msn.com. Web: www.chmiowa.org. Sr. Joann K. Kuebrich, C.H.M.

[E] HIGH SCHOOLS, INTERPAROCHIAL

DAVENPORT. *Assumption High School*, 1020 W. Central Park Ave., 52804-1899. Tel: 563-326-5313; Fax: 563-326-3510. Email: whitel@mail.assumption.pvt.k12.ia.us. Web: www.assumptionhigh.org. Mrs. Carmine Draude, Prin.; Mrs. Linda Duffy, Pres.; Stacey Clarquist, Campus Min. Lay Teachers 30; Students 416.

BURLINGTON. *Notre Dame High School*, 702 S. Roosevelt Ave., 52601-1602. Tel: 319-754-8431; Fax: 319-752-8690. Email: mcferren@nd-burl.pvt.k12.ia.us. David Edwards, Prin. Sisters 1; Lay Teachers 15; Students 153.

CLINTON. *Prince of Peace Catholic Academy & College Preparatory*, (Grades PreK-12), 312 S. 4th St., 52732-4499. Tel: 319-242-8929; 319-242-1663; Fax: 319-243-8272. Email: npeart@mail.prince.pvt.k12.ia.us. Web: www.prince.put.k12.ia.us. Mrs. Nancy Peart, Prin. Sisters of Charity B.V.M. 1; Lay Teachers 29; Students 329.

FORT MADISON. *Aquinas Junior-Senior High School*, 2600 Ave. A, 52627. Tel: 319-372-2486; Fax: 319-372-6310. Email: aquinasprincipal@hotmail.com. Web: aquinas.pvt.k12.ia.us. Mrs. Doris Turner, Prin. Lay Teachers 30; Students 331.

WEST POINT. *Marquette School, Inc.* Tel: 319-837-6131; Fax: 319-837-8112. (Marquette School System); See separate listing under Elementary Schools in the Institution section.

[F] EDUCATION CENTERS

CLINTON. *Prince of Peace Early Learning*, (Grades PreK-PreK), 314 S. 4th St., 52732. Tel: 563-242-9258. Nancy Peart, Prin. Lay Teachers 1; Students 57.

Prince of Peace Academy (Grades K-8), 312 S. Fourth St., 52732. Tel: 563-242-8929. Nancy Peart, Prin. Teachers 11; Students 162.

IOWA CITY. *The Regina Catholic Education Center*, 2140 Rochester Ave., 52245. Tel: 319-337-2580; Fax: 319-337-4109. Web: www.regina.pvt.k12.ia.us.

Regina Junior Senior High School, 2150 Rochester Ave., 52245. Tel: 319-338-5436; Fax: 319-887-3817. Email: rpechous@regina.pvt.k12.ia.us. Mr. Raymond Pechous, Prin. Lay Teachers 27; Students 372.

Regina Elementary School, 2120 Rochester Ave., 52245-3527. Tel: 319-337-5739; Fax: 319-337-4109. Email: cvincent@regina.pvt.k12.ia.us. Ms. Celeste Vincent, Prin. Lay Teachers 31; Students 501.

Regina Religious Education, 2140 Rochester Ave., 52245. Tel: 319-351-7638; Fax: 319-337-4109. Sr. Mary Frances Michalec.

Regina Fundraising Office, 2140 Rochester Ave., 52245. Tel: 319-358-2455; Fax: 319-337-4109.

Regina Preschool-Daycare, 2140 Rochester Ave., 52245. Tel: 319-337-6198; Fax: 319-337-4109. Ms. Mary Pechous.

Catholic Community Foundation, P.O. Box 1581, 52244. Tel: 319-354-5866; Fax: 319-354-1911. Ms. April Rouner.

KEOKUK. *Keokuk Catholic Schools, Inc.*, 2981 Plank Rd., 52632-2399. Tel: 319-524-5450; Fax: 319-524-5450. Jack Turner, Chief Admin.

St. Vincent's Elementary School (Grades K-6), 610 Timea St., 53632-5452. Tel: 319-524-6375; Fax: 319-524-5450. Email: jwturner5@hotmail.com. Robert Clifton, Admin. (Keokuk Catholic Schools, Inc.) Lay Teachers 13; Students 125.

St. Vincent's Extended Day Care Program, 610 Timea St., 52632-5452. Tel: 319-524-6375. Jack Turner, Prin. Lay Teachers 2; Students 60.

Cardinal Stritch Junior Senior High School (Grades 7-12), 2981 Plank Rd., 52632-5452. Tel: 319-524-5450; Fax: 319-524-5450. Jack Turner, Bldg. Coord. Lay Teachers 16; Students 90.

[G] ELEMENTARY SCHOOLS, INTERPAROCHIAL

BURLINGTON. *Burlington Area Catholic School System*, (Grades PreK-6), Notre Dame Elementary School, 700 S. Roosevelt Ave., 52601-1602. Tel: 319-752-3776; 319-754-4417; Fax: 319-752-8690. Email: kgavin@nd-burl.pvt.k12.ia.us. Katie Gavin, Prin. Lay Teachers 16; Students 296.

FORT MADISON. *Aquinas dba Fort Madison Catholic Schools* (Elem. Grades 1-6) , 509 Avenue F, 52627-2994. Tel: 319-372-5013; Fax: 319-372-5015. Total Staff 17; Students 138.

Aquinas Early Childhood Center, 2213 Avenue J, 52627-4004. Tel: 319-372-6428; Fax: 319-372-2443. Mr. Dennis Heth, Prin., Elementary & E.C.C. (PreK-K) Lay Teachers 3; Students 32.

MUSCATINE. *Bishop Hayes Catholic School*, 2407 Cedar St., 52761-2696. Tel: 563-263-3264; Fax: 563-263-6700. Email: jmosher@mail.mushayes.pvt.k12.ia.us. Web: www.bishophayes.com. Sr. Cheryl Demmer, Prin. Sisters 1; Lay Teachers 11; Students 161.

OTTUMWA. *Seton Catholic School*, 117 E. Fourth St., 52501-2992. Tel: 641-682-8826; Fax: 641-682-6202. Tim La Fleur, Prin. Lay Teachers 11; Students 104.

WEST POINT. *Marquette School, Inc.* (Marquette School System) , 52656. Tel: 319-837-6131; Fax: 319-837-8112.

Marquette School System: Marquette Primary (Grades K-3), 206 Main St., P.O. Box 134, Houghton, 52631-0134. Tel: 319-469-3581. Mrs. Tammy Conrad, Prin. (Houghton Center) Students 74.

Marquette School System: Marquette Intermediate (Grades PreK-6), 2040 Locust St., P.O. Box 71, St. Paul, 52657-0071. Tel: 319-469-3881; Fax: 319-837-8112. Mrs. Tammy Conrad, Prin. (St. Paul Center) Students 58.

Marquette School System: Marquette Jr./Sr. High (Grades 7-12), 413 Avenue C, P.O. Box 39, 52656-0039. Tel: 319-837-6131; Fax: 319-837-8112. Email: djkieler@hotmail.com. Mr. Daniel J. Kieler, Prin. (West Point) Lay Teachers 28; Students 144.

[H] CATHOLIC STUDENT CENTERS

IOWA CITY. *Newman Catholic Student Center*, 104 E. Jefferson St., 52245. Tel: 319-337-3106; Fax: 319-337-6858. Email: newman-center@uiowa.edu. Web: www.newman-ic.org. Very Rev. Edward J. Fitzpatrick, V.F., Dir.; Rev. John E. Stecher.

[I] RESIDENTIAL ADOLESCENT CARE CENTERS

BURLINGTON. *Act Day Treatment*, 4717 Sullivan Slough, 52601. Tel: 319-752-8095. Email: burlingtondaydx@younghouse.org. Rev. Lorie Bray, Dir.

Woodlands Treatment Center, 4715 Sullivan Slough Rd., 52601. Tel: 319-753-0700. John Korb, Coord.

CLINTON. *Arch, L'Arche in Clinton*, Box 278, 52733-0278. Tel: 563-243-9035; Fax: 563-243-9035. Email: larchia@clinton.net. Sr. Maria Zeimen, O.S.F., Exec. Dir. Total Assisted 19; Total Staff 11.

Arch I, 402 S. Fourth St., 52732. Tel: 563-243-3980.

Arch II, 734 Fifth Ave. S., 52732. Tel: 563-242-5082.

Arch III, 505 7th Ave. S., 52732. Tel: 563-242-8740.

MOUNT PLEASANT. *Christamore Family Treatment Center*, 905 S. Iris, 52641. Tel: 319-385-2906. Email: eford@younghouse.org. Eva Ford, Dir.

[J] GENERAL HOSPITALS

CENTERVILLE. *Mercy Medical Center - Centerville*, One St. Joseph's Dr., 52544. Tel: 641-437-4111; Fax: 641-437-3304. Email: wassell@mercydesmoines.org. Web: www.mercycenterville.org. William C. Assell, Pres. Owned by Mercy Medical Center, Des Moines.; Attended from St. Mary's, Centerville. Bed Capacity 54; Patients Assisted Annually 72,985; Total Staff 260.

Legacies, The Foundation of Mercy Medical Center Tel: 614-437-3434; Fax: 641-437-3304.

CLINTON. *Mercy Medical Center - Clinton* A subsidiary of Trinity Health. , 1410 N. Fourth St., 52732. Tel: 563-244-5555; Fax: 563-244-5592. Web: www.mercyclinton.com. Thomas J. Hesselmann, Pres.; Rev. John J. Stack. Bed Capacity 177; Staff 1,020; Annually Assisted 164,000.

Mercy Services for Aging, Bluff Terrace Nursing Home, 638 S. Bluff Blvd., 52732. Tel: 563-244-3888; Fax: 563-244-3882. Bed Capacity 87.

Wyndcrest Nursing Home, 600 14th Ave. N., 52732. Tel: 563-244-3888; Fax: 563-244-3882. Bed Capacity 86.

IOWA CITY. *Mercy Hospital*, 500 E. Market St., 52245-2633. Tel: 319-339-0300; Fax: 319-339-3788. Email: mercyoncall@mercyic.org. Web: www.mercyiowacity.org. Ronald R. Reed, Pres. & CEO; Michael Hensch, Dir., Pastoral Care. Tel: 319-358-2725; Revs. Andrew E. Kelly, Chap.; Rudolph C. Berndt, Chap.; Sisters Nora Welter, P.B.V.M., Chap.; Mary Josephus Lamansky, R.S.M., Chap.; Theresa Kruml, O.S.U., Chap.; David Oakland, Chap.; Tim Bernemann, Chap. Sisters 3; Bed Capacity 234; Total Staff 1,219; Patients Assisted Annually 298,504.

[K] SOCIAL ACTION DEPARTMENTS

DAVENPORT. *East Davenport Development Corporation*, 422 East 10th St., 52803-5499. Tel: 563-324-3257; Fax: 563-326-6014. Email: shcathedra@aol.com. Rev. Msgr. Marvin A. Mottet, Dir.

Interfaith Housing, Ltd., 422 E. 10th St., 52803-5499. Tel: 563-324-1483; Fax: 563-324-1485. Email: trtheis_interfaithhousing@emailmsn.com. Rev. Msgr. Marvin A. Mottet, Contact Person.

John Lewis Coffee Shop/Miriam House, 1202 W. 3rd St., P.O. Box 3245, 52808-3245. Tel: 563-322-0518; Fax: 563-323-3782. Email: jlcsiowa@aol.com. Web: www.jlcs.org. Kate Ridge, Agent. Total Assisted 6,000; Total Staff 52.

Project Renewal of Davenport, Inc., Nazarath House, 906 W. Fifth St., 52802. Tel: 563-324-0800. Email: projectrenewal@revealed.net. Ann Schwickerath, (In Res.); Carl Callaway, (In Res.).

Thomas Merton House, Inc., c/o 422 E. 10th St., 52803. Tel: 563-324-3257; Fax: 563-326-6014. Email: shcathedra@aol.com. Rev. Msgr. Marvin A. Mottet.

St. Vincent Center, 2706 N. Gaines St., 52804-1998. Tel: 563-324-1911; Fax: 563-324-5842. Email: shafer@davenportdiocese.org. Web: www.davenportdiocese.org. Rev. Msgr. Drake R. Shafer, V.G.

[L] HOMES FOR AGED

DAVENPORT. *Kahl Home for the Aged and Infirm*, 1101 W. Ninth St., 52804. Tel: 563-324-1621; Fax: 563-324-1723. Sisters M. Paul Anthony, O.Carm., Admin.; Deirdre Mary Ferguson, Supr.; Revs. Joseph Rogers, Chap. (Retired); Richard J. Von Ah (Retired); Clifford A. Egert (Retired); Anthony J. Conrad (Retired). Carmelite Sisters for the Aged and Infirm Sisters 4; Bed Capacity 134; Total Assisted 134; Total Staff 165.

CLINTON. *The Alverno Health Care Facility* 52732. Tel: 563-242-1521; Fax: 563-243-3016. Email: sdrobot@thealoerno.com. Web: www.alvernohealthcare.com. Steve Drobot, Pres. & CEO. Sisters of St. Francis, Clinton, IA 2; Bed Capacity 135; Total Assisted 174; Total Staff 219.

[M] MONASTERIES AND RESIDENCES FOR PRIESTS AND BROTHERS

DAVENPORT. *St. Vincent Center*, 2706 N. Gaines St., 52804. Tel: 563-324-1911; Fax: 563-324-5842. Email: loftus@davenportdiocese.org. Web: www.davenportdiocese.org. Revs. Francis E. Bass (Retired); Robert Shortall; Maynard J. Brothersen (Retired); Timothy J. Regan; Robert L. Brownfield (Retired); James M. Janssen (Retired); James T. Lawrence (Retired); Daniel C. Mannhardt (Retired); William O. Meyer (Retired); Most Rev. John J. Whalen; Rev. Joseph M. Wolf, J.C.L.

IOWA CITY. *O'Keefe Hall*, #104 E. Jefferson St., 52245. Tel: 319-337-3106; Fax: 319-337-6858. Email: newman-center@uiowa.edu. Web: www.newman-ic.org. Very Rev. Edward J. Fitzpatrick, V.F. In

Res. Revs. Rudolph C. Berndt; E. William Kaska; John E. Stecher; Vitalis Torwel (Nigeria).

WEVER. *Generalate of the Brothers of the Poor of Saint Francis*, 3405 190th St., 52658. Tel: 319-372-9543; Fax: 319-372-9543. Email: markgast@interl.net. Web: www.brothersofthepoorofstfrancis.org.

[N] CONVENTS AND RESIDENCES FOR SISTERS

DAVENPORT. *Franciscan Sisters of Christ the Divine Teacher*, 2605 Boies Ave., 52802. Tel: 563-323-1502. Sr. Bernadette Counihan, O.S.F., Supr. Sisters 7.

Humility Convent, 1310 W. Pleasant St., 52804. Tel: 563-326-3257. Sr. Rosalia Riedel, Contact Person.

Humility of Mary Center - Motherhouse of the congregation of the Humility of Mary, 820 W. Central Park Ave., 52804. Tel: 563-323-9466; Fax: 563-323-5209. Email: sisters@chmiowa.org. Web: chmiowa.org. Sr. Jude Fitzpatrick, C.H.M., Pres. Total in Residence 42; Total Staff 14.

Humility of Mary Novitiate, 820 W. Central Park Ave., 52804. Tel: 563-323-8533; Fax: 563-323-5209. Email: sisters@chmiowa.org. Web: chmiowa.org. Sr. Roberta Brich, C.H.M., Contact Person.

CLINTON. *The Canticle*, 841-13th Ave. N., 52732-5162. Tel: 563-242-7903; Fax: 563-242-8024. Sr. Marilyn Huegerich, O.S.F., Pres. Residence of the Sisters of St. Francis, Clinton, Iowa Total in Res. 35.

The Sisters of St. Francis, Clinton, Iowa, Administrative Center, 588 N. Bluff Blvd., 52732-3953. Tel: 563-242-7611; Fax: 563-243-0007. Email: sisters@clintonfranciscans.com. Web: www.clintonfranciscans.com. Sisters 90; Novices 2.

ELDRIDGE. *Carmel of the Queen of Heaven Discalced Carmelite Nuns*, 17937 250th St., 52748. Tel: 563-285-8387; Fax: 563-285-7467. Email: solitude@netins.net. Web: www.netins.net/showcase/solitude. Sr. Mary Joan Loebig, Prioress & Contact Person. Professed Sisters 11.

IOWA CITY. *Dominican Sisters*, 304 Oberlin St., 52245. Tel: 319-339-0993; Fax: 319-338-7475. Email: yahoeh@earthlink.net. Web: www.op.org/roman. Sr. Monique Be'langer, O.P., Major Supr. Tel: 207-782-3535. Sisters 3.

[O] RETREAT PROGRAMS-CENTERS

DAVENPORT. *Prayer and Spirituality Center*, 518 W. Locust St., 52803. Tel: 563-333-6189; Fax: 563-333-6234. Email: psc@saunix.sau.edu. Sr. Audrey Cleary, O.S.B., Dir.

BURLINGTON. *Beacon House, House of Prayer*, 915 N. Third, 52601. Tel: 319-752-2121. Bro. Mark Gastel, C.F.P., Dir. Total Staff 1.

WHEATLAND. *Our Lady of the Prairie Retreat*, 2664 145th Ave., 52777. Tel: 563-374-1092; Fax: 563-323-5209. Email: joannk@chmiowa.org.

[P] MISCELLANEOUS

DAVENPORT. *Assumption High School Foundation*, 1020 W. Central Park Ave., 52804. Tel: 563-326-5313; Fax: 563-326-3510. Email: duffy1@mail.assumption.pvt.k12.ia.us. Web: www.assumptionhigh.org.

Catholic Service Board, St. Vincent Center, 2706 N. Gaines St., 52804. Tel: 563-324-1911.

Commitment, St. Vincent Center, 2706 N. Gaines St., 52804-1998. Tel: 563-324-1911. Sandy Carlson, Assoc. Dir.

Congregation of the Humility of Mary Charitable Trust, 820 W. Central Park Ave., 52804. Tel: 563-323-9466; Fax: 563-323-5209. Email: sisters@chmiowa.org. Web: www.chmiowa.org. Sr. Jude Fitzpatrick C.H.M., Contact Person.

Humility of Mary Housing, Inc., 820 W Central Park Ave., 52804. Tel: 563-323-9466; Fax: 563-323-5209. Email: sisters@chmiowa.org. Web: www.chmiowa.org. Sr. Jude Fitzpatrick C.H.M., Contact Person. Total Assisted 302; Total Staff 10; Total in Residence 159.

Kingdom Co., 2706 N. Gaines St., 52804-1998. Tel: 563-324-1911; Fax: 563-324-5842. Email maaske@davenportdiocese.org. Web: www.davenportdiocese.org. Charlene Maaske, C.P.A., Contact Person.

New Horizons of Faith, Inc.: Our Lady of the Prairie Retreat, 820 W. Central Park Ave., 52804. Tel: 563-323-9466; Fax: 563-323-5209 Email: joannk@msn.com. Web: www.chmiowa.org.

Quad Cities Catholic Deaf Ministry, 4105 N. Division St., 52806-4741. Tel: 563-391-4245; Fax: 563-445-1003. Email: parizek@revealed.net. Rev. Msgr. James F. Parizek, Contact Person.

Spirit, Inc, 2214 Harrison St., 52804. Tel: 563-324-1776. Email: spiritinc@netzero.net. Paul Roe, Contact.

Vietnamese Catholic Community of the Quad Cities, 421 E. 10th St., 52803. Tel: 563-323-5994. Rev. Joseph Khan V. Nguyen.

St. Vincent Home Corporation, 2706 N Gaines St., 52804. Tel: 563-324-1911; Fax: 563-324-5842. Email: maaske@davenportdiocese.org. Web: www.davenportdiocese.org. Charlene Maaske, C.P.A., Contact Person.

BROOKLYN. *St. Patrick Parish Foundation*, 215 Jackson St., 52211-0512. Tel: 641-522-7714.

BURLINGTON. *Burlington Notre Dame Foundation*, 702 S. Roosevelt Ave., 52601. Tel: 319-752-8690; Fax: 319-752-8690. Deb Trine, Contact Person.

St. Vincent De Paul Society, St. John the Baptist Church Conference, 700 Division St., 52601. Tel: 319-752-9332. Tom Stevens, Contact Person.

R.E.B.A (Religious Education Burlington Area) Trust Fund, 700 Division St., 52601. Tel: 319-752-6733; Fax: 319-753-5221. Email: stjohnbu@inter.net.

CENTERVILLE. *St. Mary's Foundation of Centerville*, 828 S. 18th St., 52544. Tel: 641-437-1984. Rev. Joseph Miller, C.PP.S., Contact Person.

CLINTON. *Mercy Home Care and Hospice*, 638 S. Bluff, 52732. Tel: 563-244-3766; Fax: 563-244-3719. Email: noej@mercyhealth.com. Web: www.mercyclinton.com. Joan Noe, Admin.; Tom Hesselmann, CEO.

Mount St. Clare Speech & Hearing Center, Inc., 562 N. Bluff Blvd., 52732. Tel: 563-242-4070; Fax: 563-242-2426. Email: marnar@tfu.edu. Web: www.clintonfranciscans.com. Sr. Marcella Marie Narlock, Dir. Sisters of St. Francis

Sisters of St. Francis, Clinton, Iowa, Charitable Trust, 588 N. Bluff Blvd., 52732. Tel: 563-242-7611; Fax: 563-243-0007. Email: sisters@clintonfranciscans.com. Web: www.clintonfranciscans.com. Sr. Marilyn Huegerich, O.S.F., Pres.

IOWA CITY. *Catholic Community Foundation*, 1222 Rochester Ave., P.O. Box 1581, 52244. Tel: 319-354-5866; Fax: 319-354-1911. Email: cff@piano.inav.net. April E. Rouner, Dir.

Mercy Hospital Foundation, 500 E. Market St., 52245-2689. Tel: 319-339-3657; Fax: 319-358-2624. Mary DuCharme, Pres.

Mercy Hospital Guild of Iowa City, Iowa, 500 E. Market St., 52245. Carol Ebinger.

Mercy Outreach Iowa City, Inc., 500 E. Market St., 52245.

Mercy Hospital, Iowa City, Iowa, 500 E. Market St., 52245.

Roman Catholic Ministries of Iowa City, Iowa, 2710 E. Court St., 52242. Tel: 319-341-9629. Robert Dotzel, Contact Person.

KEOKUK. *Ladies of Charity of Keokuk*, 1524 High St., 52632. Tel: 319-524-7517. Lois Waldron, Pres.

WEST POINT. *Marquette Foundation*, Tel: 319-837-6379. Box 105, 52656. Tel: 319-837-6379. Mike Anderson, Contact Person; Sue Anderson, Contact Person.

RELIGIOUS INSTITUTES OF MEN REPRESENTED IN THE DIOCESE

For further details refer to the corresponding bracketed number in the Religious Institutes of Men or Women section.

[0460]—*Brothers of the Poor of St. Francis*—C.F.P.

[1060]—*Society of the Precious Blood*—C.PP.S.

[0560]—*Third Order Regular of Saint Francis*—T.O.R.

RELIGIOUS INSTITUTES OF WOMEN REPRESENTED IN THE DIOCESE

[0230]—*Benedictine Sisters of Pontifical Jurisdiction*—O.S.B.

[0330]—*Carmelite Sisters for the Aged and Infirm*—O.Carm.

[2100]—*Congregation of the Humility of Mary*—C.H.M.

[1780]—*Congregation of the Sisters of the Third Order of St. Francis of Perpetual Adoration*—F.S.P.A.

[1710]—*Congregation of the Third Order of St. Francis of Mary Immaculate, Joliet, IL*—O.S.F.

[0420]—*Discalced Carmelite Nuns*—O.C.D.

[1070-03]—*Dominican Sisters*—O.P.

[1120]—*Dominican Sisters of the Roman Congregation*—O.P.

[]—*Franciscan Sisters of Christ the Divine Teacher*—O.S.F.

[2575]—*Institute of the Sisters of Mercy of the Americas* (Chicago)—R.S.M.

[2970]—*School Sisters of Notre Dame*—S.S.N.D.

[1680]—*School Sisters of St. Francis*—O.S.F.

[0430]—*Sisters of Charity of the Blessed Virgin Mary*—B.V.M.

[1540]—*Sisters of Saint Francis, Clinton, Iowa*—O.S.F.

[1570]—*Sisters of St. Francis of the Holy Family*—O.S.F.

[3320]—*Sisters of the Presentation of the B.V.M.*—P.B.V.M.

[1770]—*Sisters of the Third Order of St. Francis* (Peoria, Illinois)—O.S.F.

[1705]—*Sisters of the Third Order of St. Francis of Assisi*—O.S.F.

[1760]—*Sisters of the Third Order of St. Francis of Penance and of Charity* (Tiffin, Ohio)—O.S.F.

NECROLOGY

† Colonnese, Louis M., (Retired)—Died Dec. 12, 2002
† Conrad, Sylvester A.—Died Oct. 29, 2003
† Donahue, Paul H., (Retired)—Died May 4, 2003
† Gannon, Charles E., (Retired)—Died March 18, 2003
† Lenoch, Francis J., (Retired)—Died Jan. 17, 2003
† Morrissey, John J., (Retired)—Died April 1, 2003
† Waldschmidt, Donald L., (Retired)—Died Sept. 28, 2003
† Wilson, James E., (Retired)—Died July 20, 2003

Archdiocese of Denver

Archidioecesis Denveriensis

Most Reverend

CHARLES J. CHAPUT, O.F.M.CAP., D.D.

Archbishop of Denver; ordained August 29, 1970; Episcopal ordination July 26, 1988; appointed Bishop of Rapid City April 11, 1988; appointed Archbishop of Denver February 18, 1997.

Most Reverend

JOSE H. GOMEZ, S.T.D.

Auxiliary Bishop of Denver; ordained August 15, 1978; appointed Auxiliary Bishop of Denver and Titular See of Belali January 23, 2001; ordained March 26, 2001.

ESTABLISHED A VICARIATE-APOSTOLIC IN 1868.

Square Miles 40,154.

Erected a Diocese August 16, 1887; created an Archdiocese November 15, 1941.

Comprises the northern part of the State of Colorado, including the 24 Counties of Adams, Arapahoe, Boulder, Clear Creek, Denver, Eagle, Garfield, Gilpin, Grand, Jackson, Jefferson, Larimer, Logan, Moffat, Morgan, Phillips, Pitkin, Rio Blanco, Routt, Sedgwick, Summit, Washington, Weld and Yuma.

For legal titles of parishes and archdiocesan institutions, consult the Chancery.

Pastoral Center: 1300 S. Steele St., Denver, CO 80210. Tel: 303-715-2000; Fax: 303-715-2041.

Web: www.archden.org/archden

Email: dcr@archden.org

STATISTICAL OVERVIEW

Personnel	
Cardinals	1
Archbishops	1
Retired Archbishops	1
Auxiliary Bishops	1
Abbots	1
Priests: Diocesan Active in Diocese	110
Priests: Diocesan Active Outside Diocese	4
Priests: Retired, Sick or Absent	48
Number of Diocesan Priests	162
Religious Priests in Diocese	119
Total Priests in Diocese	281
Extern Priests in Diocese	32
Ordinations:	
Diocesan Priests	4
Transitional Deacons	3
Permanent Deacons in Diocese	153
Total Brothers	14
Total Sisters	339
Parishes	
Parishes	120
With Resident Pastor:	
Resident Diocesan Priests	98
Resident Religious Priests	16
Without Resident Pastor:	
Administered by Priests	5
Administered by Deacons	1
Missions	29
Professional Ministry Personnel:	
Brothers	2
Sisters	18
Lay Ministers	200
Welfare	
Catholic Hospitals	3
Total Assisted	370,000
Health Care Centers	8
Total Assisted	5,000
Homes for the Aged	16
Total Assisted	1,200
Residential Care of Children	2
Total Assisted	100
Day Care Centers	5
Total Assisted	1,100
Specialized Homes	1
Total Assisted	30
Special Centers for Social Services	15
Total Assisted	100,000
Residential Care of Disabled	2
Total Assisted	14
Educational	
Seminaries, Diocesan	1
Students from This Diocese	35
Students from Other Diocese	14
Diocesan Students in Other Seminaries	1
Students Religious	41
Total Seminarians	77
High Schools, Diocesan and Parish	2
Total Students	1,000
High Schools, Private	5
Total Students	2,354
Elementary Schools, Diocesan and Parish	37
Total Students	9,656
Elementary Schools, Private	2
Total Students	593
Catechesis/Religious Education:	
High School Students	5,471
Elementary Students	26,858
Total Students under Catholic Instruction	46,009
Teachers in the Diocese:	
Brothers	2
Sisters	21
Lay Teachers	869
Vital Statistics	
Receptions into the Church:	
Infant Baptism Totals	11,501
Adult Baptism Totals	746
Received into Full Communion	1,291
First Communions	8,464
Confirmations	5,020
Marriages:	
Catholic	2,094
Interfaith	819
Total Marriages	2,913
Deaths	2,836
Total Catholic Population	380,739
Total Population	2,996,708

Former Bishops—Most Revs. JOSEPH PROJECTUS MACHEBEUF, D.D., consecrated Titular Bishop of Epiphania and Vicar Apostolic of Colorado and Utah, Aug. 16, 1868; first Bishop of Denver in 1887; died July 10, 1889; NICHOLAS CHRYSOSTOM MATZ, D.D., consecrated Titular Bishop of Telmessa and Coadjutor of Denver cum jure successionis, Oct. 28, 1887; succeeded to the See of Denver, July 10, 1889; died Aug. 9, 1917; J. HENRY TIHEN, D.D., ord. April 26, 1886; consecrated Bishop of Lincoln, July 6, 1911; transferred to the See of Denver, Sept. 21, 1917; resigned Jan. 6, 1931; Apostolic Admin. until July 16, 1931; died Jan. 14, 1940; URBAN J. VEHR, D.D., ord. May 29, 1915; Bishop of Denver; appt. April 17, 1931; consecrated June 10, 1931; installed July 16, 1931; elevated to Archiepiscopal dignity, Nov. 15, 1941; appt. Jan. 6, 1942; installed as Archbishop of Denver; resigned Feb. 22, 1967; died Sept. 19, 1973; JAMES V. CASEY, D.D., J.C.D., ord. Dec. 8, 1939; Titular Bishop of Citium and Auxiliary of Lincoln; appt. April 5, 1957; consecrated April 24, 1957; promoted to Archbishop of Denver, Feb. 22, 1967; died March 14, 1986; J. FRANCIS CARDINAL STAFFORD, D.D., ord. Dec. 15, 1957; consecrated Auxiliary Bishop of Baltimore, Feb. 29, 1976; installed Bishop of Memphis January 18, 1983; appt. Nov. 16, 1982; installed Archbishop of Denver July 31, 1986; appt. June 3, 1986; appt. President of the Pontifical Council for the Laity in Rome, Aug. 1996; elevated to Cardinal Feb. 21, 1998.

The Pastoral Center—1300 S. Steele St., Denver, 80210-2599. Tel: 303-715-2000; Fax: 303-715-2041.

Vicars General—Rev. Msgrs. RAYMOND N. JONES, V.G., P.A.; R. WALKER NICKLESS.

Moderator of the Curia—Rev. Msgr. JOSE H. GOMEZ, S.T.D., V.G.

Chancellor—FRANCIS X. MAIER.

Vice Chancellor—Mr. TIMOTHY J. MCCARTHY, J.C.L.

Executive Assistant to the Archbishop—PATRICIA J. MCDONALD.

Special Advisor to the Archbishop—NANCY WALLA.

Office of Deacons—Deacon ALFONSO M. SANDOVAL.

Office of Finance Administration and Planning—Mr. DAVID A. HOLDEN, CFO.

Vicar for Clergy and Seminarians—Rev. Msgr. THOMAS S. FRYAR.

Office of Religious—Sr. SHARON FORD, R.S.M.

Office of Catholic Education—RICHARD L. THOMPSON, Dir.

Office of Hispanic Ministry—MAR MUNOZ-VISOSO.

Presbyteral Council—Very Rev. ROBERT AMUNDSEN, V.F., Chm.; Rev. Msgr. THOMAS S. FRYAR, Sec.

Priests' Continuing Education Committee—Rev. Msgr. THOMAS S. FRYAR.

College of Consultors—Most Rev. JOSE H. GOMEZ, S.T.D., D.D.; Rev. Msgrs. EDWARD BUELT; EDWARD M. HOFFMANN, V.F.; RAYMOND N. JONES, V.G., P.A.; GEORGE SCHROEDER, V.F.; R. WALKER NICKLESS; Rev. ROBERT KINKEL, V.F.; Rev. Msgr. THOMAS S. FRYAR.

Archdiocesan Finance Council—Most Revs. CHARLES J. CHAPUT, O.F.M.Cap., D.D.; JOSE H. GOMEZ, S.T.D., S.T.D.; Rev. Msgr. R. WALKER NICKLESS; Mr. DAVID A. HOLDEN; Mr. JOHN P. BOX; Dr. LAWRENCE F. JOHNSTON; Mr. WILLIAM E. KEEFE; Mr. GERALD J. LABER; Honorable Judge LEONARD P. PLANK; Ms. KATHLEEN M. SPURCK; Ms. CAROL A. THURSTIN; Mr. NICK ZIESER; GERALD J. PICORNO; JOHN DOLAN.

Council for Religious—Sisters SHARON FORD, R.S.M.; JOSETTE KELLY, B.V.M.; Bro. LAURENCE LUJAN, C.SS.R; Sr. JEAN ANNE PANISKO, S.C.L.; Rev. ROBERT F. STAES, O.P.

Chairman of Deans—Very Rev. ROBERT AMUNDSEN, V.F.

Secretary of Deans—Rev. Msgr. THOMAS S. FRYAR.

Deaneries—Very Rev. KENNETH LIUZZI, V.F., East Denver; Rev. JAMES R. FOX, V.F., North Denver; Very Rev. CHRISTOPHER RENNER, V.F., West Denver; Rev. Msgr. EDWARD M. HOFFMANN, V.F., Southeast Denver; Very Rev. KENNETH LEONE, V.F., Southwest Denver; Rev. JAMES E. FOX, V.F., Aurora; Very Revs. ROBERT AMUNDSEN, V.F., Boulder; JOSEPH A. HARTMANN, V.F., Fort Collins; Rev. Msgr. MICHAEL J. CHAMBERLAIN, J.C.L., V.F., Eastern Plains; Very Revs. REINHOLD WEISSBECK, V.F., Greeley; FRANK MARONEY, V.F., Western Slope; PATRICK DOLAN, V.F., West Central Denver; Most Rev. JOSE H. GOMEZ, S.T.D., S.T.D., East Central Denver.

Metropolitan Tribunal

Judicial Vicar—Very Rev. JAMES S. MORENO, J.C.D.

Executive Director—Mr. TIMOTHY J. MCCARTHY, J.C.L.

Clerk of Due Process—Mr. TIMOTHY J. MCCARTHY, J.C.L.

Promoter of Justice—VACANT.

Judges—Very Rev. JAMES S. MORENO, J.C.D.; Rev. Msgr. MICHAEL J. CHAMBERLAIN, J.C.L., V.F.; Rev. ROBERT P. HUNDT, J.C.L.; Mr. TIMOTHY J. MCCARTHY, J.C.L.

Defenders of the Bond—Sr. MARY JUDITH O'BRIEN, J.C.D.; Rev. Msgr. THOMAS S. FRYAR.

Judicial Auditors—CHRISTOPHER BRUST; MARY BETH PAGE.

Canonical Advisor—VACANT.

Advocates— Advocates appointed individually for particular cases.

Ecclesiastical Notary—RONDA WHITEHURST.

Coordinator of Second Instance—RONDA WHITEHURST.

The Metropolitan Tribunal— Handles all marriage permissions and dispensations by delegation.

Archdiocesan Offices and Directors

The Archdiocese of Denver, a corporation sole—Most Rev. CHARLES J. CHAPUT, O.F.M.Cap., D.D., Archbishop of Denver, 1300 S. Steele St., Denver, 80210. Tel: 303-715-3129.

Archdiocese of Denver Archives—Ms. SYLVIA RAEL, Archivist. Tel: 303-715-3146; Fax: 303-282-3453.

Archdiocesan Campaign for Human Development—AL HOOPER, Dir. Tel: 303-715-3165.

The Archbishop's Guild—JULIA MARTINEZ, Pres., 9160 Vine St., Thornton, 80229. Tel: 303-287-3080.

Office of Finance, Administration and Planning—Mr. DAVID A. HOLDEN, CFO. Tel: 303-715-3258.

Director of Annual Giving—TODD J. SMITH. Tel: 303-715-3111.

Director of Construction and Engineering—WALTER E. WOSTENBERG.

Director of Property and Real Estate—LOU BISHOP.

Director of Cemetery & Mortuary—MICHAEL WRIGHT.

Director of Parish Accounting—ERNEST ARMSTRONG, C.P.A.

Director of Seminary Development—Deacon JOHN NEAL. Tel: 303-715-3119.

Director of Human Resources—BARBARA BUCHANAN.

Director of Information Services—MICHAEL MCKEE.

Director of Insurance & Risk—ROSE MARY NELSON.

Controller—JOYCE TALBURT, C.P.A.

C.C.W.A.D.—ALBERTA LOPEZ, Pres., 1300 S. Steele St., Denver, 80210. Tel: 303-715-3187.

AIDS Ministry—AL HOOPER, Dir.

Archdiocese of Denver Mortuary—12801 W. 44th Ave., Wheat Ridge, 80033. Tel: 303-425-9511; Fax: 303-425-0242. MICHAEL WRIGHT, Dir.

Archdiocesan Housing Committee, Inc.—Ms. MARY BOLAND, Exec. Dir., 1544 Pearl St., Denver, 80203. Tel: 303-830-0215.

Housing Management Services, Inc.—1544 Pearl St., Denver, 80203. Tel: 303-830-0215; Fax: 303-830-2885.

Boy and Girl Scouts—JAY ZOLITOR, 2071 S. Gray Dr., Denver, 80227. Tel: 303-987-2306.

Building Commission—RAYMOND L. CRITES; RICHARD G. DUCEY; PETER J. FURSTENBERG Sr. MOIRA DEBONO; RUTH GONZALES; JOHN F. MCGUIRE; GERHARD R. MUELLER; Rev. Msgr. JAMES W. RASBY (Retired); ROBERT C. GEIST; PHILLIP J. CRISTE; MICHAEL D. VANEK; WALTER E. WOSTENBERG.

Office of Catholic Schools—RICHARD L. THOMPSON, Dir.

Our Lady of the New Advent Theological Institute—Offers programs of study in philosophy and theology in its three divisions: St. John Vianney Theological Seminary, the Diaconate Formation Program and the Division of Lay Formation. Rev. KENT DROTAR, Assoc. Rector; Very Rev. MICHAEL GLENN, Pres.

St. John Vianney Theological Seminary— (See section A, Seminaries, Religious or Scholasticates)

Spirituality Year—Tel: 303-282-3429. Rev. CHRISTOPHER HELLSTROM, Dir., Two-year Philosophy Cycle and Four-year Theology Cycle.

Archbishop Vehr Theological Library—Tel: 303-715-3146; Fax: 303-282-3453. Ms. SYLVIA RAEL, Dir.

Office of Liturgy—Sr. MOIRA DEBONO, Dir.

Diaconate Formation Program—Tel. 303-715-3198. Deacon ALFONSO M. SANDOVAL, Dir., Aspirancy Year, Three Year Study and Continuing Education for Deacons.

Division of Lay Formation—Tel: 303-715-3195; 303-715-3101.

Catechetical School—JOE BURNS, Dir.

Catholic Biblical School—TIM GRAY, Dir. Tel: 303-715-3195.

Office of Marriage of Family—STEVE WEIDENKOPF. Tel: 303-715-3259; Fax: 303-715-2042.

Regional Catechetical Coordinators—DON SCHNEIDER; Sr. MARY REGIS LEAHY, R.S.M., Northern & East Plains, 336 Emery St., Longmont, 80501. Tel: 303-678-0900; Fax: 303-772-5636.

Youth/Young Adult and Campus Ministry—SEAN DALTON. Tel: 303-715-3203; Fax: 303-715-2042.

Respect Life Office—MIMI ECKSTEIN, Dir. Tel: 303-715-3205; Fax: 303-715-2040.

Mt. Olivet Cemetery Association—MICHAEL WRIGHT, Dir., 12801 W. 44th Ave., Wheat Ridge, 80033. Tel: 303-424-7785.

Catholic Charities and Community Services of the Archdiocese of Denver, Inc.—JAMES H. MAUCK, Pres., 2525 W. Alameda Ave., P.O. Box 19020, Denver, 80219. Tel: 303-742-0828; Fax: 303-742-0774. Catholic Charities Northern Services, 460 Linden Center Dr., Fort Collins, 80524. Tel: 303-484-5010 (For further details see Catholic Community Services-Northern, Inc. under Institutions located in the Archdiocese).

Office of Missions and Ministry—AL HOOPER. Tel: 303-715-3171 Missions: Campaign for Human Development; Catholic Relief Services; Society for Propagation of the Faith; Holy Childhood Association; Rural Life Ministry; Archdiocesan Aids Ministry; Catholic Deaf Community; Hmong Community; Korean Community; Vietnamese Community.

Colorado Catholic Conference 501(c)(4)—TIM DORE, 1535 Logan St., Denver, 80203. Tel: 303-894-8808.

Office of Communications—SERGIO GUTIERREZ, 1300 S. Steele St., Denver, 80210. Tel: 303-715-3123; Fax: 303-715-2045. Email: editor@archden.org.

John Paul II Center for the New Evangelization—MICHAEL MCKEE, 1300 S. Steele St., Denver, 80210. Tel: 303-715-2007.

Centro San Juan Diego—MAR MUNOZ-VISOSO, Exec. Dir.; Rev. JORGE DE LOS SANTOS, Dir. Formation; LUIS SOTO, Hispanic Youth Minister; Sisters MARIA LUISA MUNOZ, Migrant Ministry; MAGDALENA CONTRERAS, Comunidades de Base; ERLINDA MOSCOSO, Facility Coord., 2830 Lawrence St., Denver, 80205. Tel: 303-295-9470.

Office of Liturgy—Sr. MOIRA DEBONO, Dir. Liturgy. Tel: 303-715-3156.

Diaconate Program—Deacon ALFONSO M. SANDOVAL, Dir.

Religious—Sr. SHARON FORD, R.S.M. Tel: 303-364-1056.

Rural Life Conference—RITA MAILANDER, 3990 S. Syracuse Way, Denver, 80237. Tel: 303-741-2133.

Victim Assistance Coordinator—NANCY A. WALLA. Tel: 303-715-3226. Email: nancy.walla@archden.org.

Vocation Office—Rev. JEFFERY WILBORN, Dir. Tel: 303-282-3429; Fax: 303-282-3453.

CLERGY, PARISHES, MISSIONS AND PAROCHIAL SCHOOLS

CITY OF DENVER

(COUNTY OF DENVER)

1—CATHEDRAL OF THE IMMACULATE CONCEPTION (1860), Most Rev. Jose Gomez; Revs. Felix Zermeno-Martin, P.V.; Krzysztof Misiura. In Res., Rev. Andreas Hoeck; Deacons Joe Babish; Mark Salvato.
Res.: 1530 Logan St., 80203. Tel: 303-831-7010; Fax: 303-831-9514.
Catechesis/Religious Program—Students 104.

2—ALL SAINTS (1950), Rev. James F. Purfield; Deacon Arthur A. Vigil.
Res.: 2559 S. Federal Blvd., 80219. Tel: 303-922-3758; Fax: 303-922-3750.
Parish Center—2560 S. Grove St., 80219.
Catechesis/Religious Program—Tel: 303-922-7690. Students 309.

3—ANNUNCIATION (1883), Revs. John Toepfer, O.F.M-.Cap.; Cyrus Gallagher, O.F.M.Cap.
Office—3621 Humboldt St., 80205. Tel: 303-296-1024.
Res.: 3554 Humboldt St., 80205. Tel: 303-292-5110; Fax: 303-296-1026.
School—3536 Lafayette St., 80205. Tel: 303-296-2515. Sr. Jean Anne Panisko, S.C.L., Prin. Sisters of Charity of Leavenworth 5; Lay Teachers 9; Students 180.
Catechesis/Religious Program—Students 148.

4—ST. ANTHONY OF PADUA (1947), Rev. Daniel J. Norick.
Res.: 3801 W. Ohio Ave., 80219. Tel: 303-935-2431; Fax: 303-935-8969.
Parish Center—775 S. Newton St., 80219. Tel: 303-934-3763.
Catechesis/Religious Program—Tel: 303-936-5386; Fax: 303-935-8969. Students 425.

5—ASSUMPTION (1912), Rev. Peter Dinh; Deacon Harold DelReal. In Res., Rev Shane Wasinger.
Church: 2361 E. 78th Ave., 80229. Tel: 303-288-2159; Fax: 303-288-4716.
School—2341 E. 78th Ave., 80229. Tel: 303-288-2442. Colleen McManamon, Prin. Lay Teachers 13; Students 178.
Catechesis/Religious Program—Tel: 303-289-2713; Fax: 303-289-2713. Students 167.

6—BLESSED SACRAMENT (1912), Rev. Kenneth Liuzzi; Deacon Nathan Coursey.
Mailing Address & Office: 1912 Eudora St., 80220-1253.
Res.: 4930 Montview Blvd., 80207. Tel: 303-355-7361; Fax: 303-355-0894.
School—1973 Elm St., 80220. Tel: 303-377-8835; Fax: 303-321-7765. Lay Teachers 17; Students 150.
Catechesis/Religious Program—Students 66.

7—ST. CAJETAN (1922), (Hispanic), Revs. James Brohens, C.R.; Tomas Fraile, C.R.; Deacon Alfonso Sandoval.
Res.: 299 S. Stuart, 80219. Tel: 303-922-6306; Fax: 303-936-8285.
Church: 299 S. Raleigh, 80219 Tel: 303-935-4483.
Catechesis/Religious Program—Students 410.

8—ST. CATHERINE OF SIENA (1912), Revs. Jose Sanchez (Argentina); Damien Lucas (France).
Res.: 4200 Federal Blvd., 80211. Tel: 303-455-9090; Fax: 303-455-6651.
School—4280 Federal Blvd., 80211. Tel: 303-477-8035; Fax: 303-477-0110. Dilia Mapelli Taylor, Prin. Lay Teachers 13; Students 189.
Catechesis/Religious Program—Students 90.

9—CHRIST THE KING (1947), Rev. J. Darrell Schaffer. In Res., Rev. John Krenzke (Retired); Deacon Jack Sutton.
Res.: 845 Fairfax St., 80220. Tel: 303-388-1643; Fax: 303-355-0141.
School—860 Elm St., 80220. Tel: 303-321-2123; Fax: 303-321-2191. James Feldewerth, Prin. Nuns 3; Lay Teachers 15; Students 255.
Catechesis/Religious Program—Students 64.

10—CHURCH OF THE GOOD SHEPHERD (1981), Rev. Neal A. Pfister; Deacons Dominic Deprofio; George Morin.
Church and Res.: 2626 E. Seventh Ave. Pkwy., 80206-3809. Tel: 303-322-7706; Fax: 303-399-1382.
Business and D.R.E. Offices—2626 E. Seventh Ave. Pkwy., 80206.
School—620 Elizabeth St., 80206. Tel: 303-321-6231; Fax: 303-261-1059. Students 271.
Catechesis/Religious Program—Students 35.

11—CHURCH OF THE RISEN CHRIST (1967), Rev. Msgr. Edward M. Hoffmann, V.F.; Rev. Shabas Crasta.
Church: 3060 S. Monaco Pkwy., 80222. Tel: 303-758-8826; Fax: 303-782-9667.
Catechesis/Religious Program—Students 656.

12—CURE D'ARS (1952), Rev. Simon Kalonga (Congo); Deacon Clarence G. McDavid.
Office—3050 Dahlia St., 80207. Tel: 303-322-1119; Fax: 303-322-9335.
Church: 3201 Dahlia St., 80207. Tel: 303-322-7709.
Catechesis/Religious Program—Students 105.

13—ST. DOMINIC (1889), Revs. Dennis C. Woerter, O.P.; Brian Bricker, O.P. In Res., Revs. Giles R. Klapperich, O.P.; Michael G. Kyte, O.P.; Louis S. Morrone, O.P. (CHI), Novice Master; James A. Spahn, O.P.; Robert F. Staes, O.P.; Bros. Michael T. McGovern, O.P.; Jordan Coonan, O.P.
Res.: 3005 W. 29th Ave., 80211. Tel: 303-455-3613; Fax: 303-455-3087.
Catechesis/Religious Program—Students 235.

14—ST. ELIZABETH OF HUNGARY (1878), Rev. Chrysostom Frank.
Res. & Mailing Address: 1060 St. Francis Way, 80204. Tel: 303-534-4014; Fax: 303-534-4140.
Catechesis/Religious Program—Students 30.

15—ST. FRANCIS DE SALES (1892), Rev. Msgr. Frank G. Morfeld.
Res.: 301 S. Sherman St., 80209. Tel: 303-744-7211; Fax: 303-744-7211.
School—235 S. Sherman St., 80209. Tel: 303-744-7231. Sr. Eleanor O'Hearn, C.S.J., Prin. Sisters of St. Joseph 2; Lay Teachers 11; Students 230.

16—GUARDIAN ANGELS (1954), Rev. Sean McGrath; Deacon Richard Borda.

Res.: 1843 W. 52nd Ave., 80221. Tel: 303-433-8361; Fax: 303-477-2066.
School—Tel: 303-480-9005. Mary Gold, Prin. Lay Teachers 12; Students 174.
Catechesis/Religious Program—Students 145.

17—HOLY CROSS (Thornton) (1957), Rev. Thomas Coyte; Deacons Russell Halpine; Joe Benedetto; Nehemias Ruiz.
Res.: 9371 Wigham St., 80229. Tel: 303-289-2258 (Voice TDD); Fax: 303-289-2259.
Catechesis/Religious Program—Students 375.

18—HOLY FAMILY (1889), Rev. Msgr. Walker Nickless, V.G., Admin.; Rev. Stephen Siebert. In Res., Very Rev. James Moreno.
Res.: 4377 Utica St., 80212. Tel: 303-455-1664; Fax: 303-455-7732.
Church: W. 44th Ave. & Utica St., 80212.
Catechesis/Religious Program—4377 Utica St., 80212. Tel: 303-433-9781. Students 86.

19—HOLY GHOST (1905), Revs. William V. Mullen, O.M.V.; Daniel P. Barron, O.M.V., P.V.; James B. Doran, O.M.V., P.V.; Deacon Vernon L. Rompot.
Res.: 1900 California St., 80202. Tel: 303-292-1556; Fax: 303-292-5378.
Catechesis/Religious Program—Students 58.

20—HOLY PROTECTION OF THE MOTHER OF GOD (1974), (Byzantine),, Church: 1074 S. Coor St., 80209. For details, refer to Byzantine Eparchy of Van Nuys.

21—HOLY ROSARY (1918), Rev. Joseph A. Meznar.
Mailing Address: P.O. Box 8685, 80201-8685.
Res.: 4695 Pearl St., 80216. Tel: 303-296-3283.
Catechesis/Religious Program—Students 225.

22—ST. IGNATIUS LOYOLA (1924), Revs. C. Thomas Jost, S.J.; John F. Brady, S.J.; Deacon Guffie Menogan. In Res., Revs. Joseph Tuoc Nguyen, S.J.; Stephen W. Planning, S.J.
Res.: 2309 Gaylord St., 80205. Tel: 303-322-8042; Fax: 303-322-2927.
School—2350 Gaylord, 80205. Tel: 303-355-9900; Fax: 303-355-9911. Sisters of Charity of Cincinnati 3; Lay Teachers 8; Students 102.
Catechesis/Religious Program—Students 227.

23—ST. JAMES (1904), Rev. David Allen. In Res., Rev. Bill Brock.
Res.: 1336 Newport St., 80220. Tel: 303-322-7449; Fax: 303-399-2850.
School—Tel: 303-333-8275; Fax: 303-780-0137. Theresa Loiselle, Prin. Lay Teachers 18; Students 200.
Catechesis/Religious Program—Tel: 303-333-5189. Students 81.

24—ST. JOSEPH (1882), (Hispanic), Revs. Kyle Fisher, C.SS.R.; Timothy Watson, C.SS.R. In Res., Revs. Steve J. Nyl, C.SS.R.; Albert Castellino, C.SS.R.; Bro. Lawrence Lujan.
Res.: 605 W. 6th Ave., 80204. Tel: 303-534-4408; Fax: 303-534-4412.
Catechesis/Religious Program—Tel: 303-534-0884. Students 155.
Centro Bienstar de San Jose Social Ministry—623 Fox St., 80201. Tel: 720-904-2099; Fax: 720-904-2099. Sr. Alicia Cuaron, O.S.F., Contact Person.

25—ST. JOSEPH (1902), (Polish), Rev. Jan Mucha.
Res.: 517 E. 46th Ave., 80216. Tel: 303-296-3217.
Catechesis/Religious Program—Students 18.

26—ST. MARY MAGDALENE (1907), Rev. Msgr. Walker Nickless, V.G.; Deacons Richard Vieira, Pastoral Admin.; Gary Miller. In Res., Revs. Gerard Beigel; Jeffrey Willborn.
Res.: 2771 Zenobia St., 80212. Tel: 303-477-4533; Fax: 303-477-2049.
Catechesis/Religious Program—Tel: 303-455-1968. Students 70.

27—MONTBELLO CATHOLIC PARISH-CHURCH OF THE ASCENSION (1972), Rev. Mauricio Moreno, Admin.; Deacon William J. Stow.
Church: 14050 Maxwell Pl., 80239. Tel: 303-371-0786; 303-373-4950 (Church); Fax: 303-373-4954.
Rectory—13190 E. 48th Ave., 80239.

28—MOST PRECIOUS BLOOD (1952), Rev. Kenneth Koehler; Deacons Lewis Barbato, (Retired); Sam Lopez.
Res.: 2250 S. Harrison, 80210. Tel: 303-756-3083; Fax: 303-756-5628.
School—3959 E. Iliff, 80210. Tel: 303-757-1279; Fax: 303-757-1270. Jerry Ann Walker, Prin. Lay Teachers 26; Students 300.
Catechesis/Religious Program—Students 185.

29—MOTHER OF GOD (1949), Rev. Msgr. Raymond N. Jones, V.G., P.A.
Res.: 475 Logan St., 80203. Tel: 303-744-1715; Fax: 303-744-1716.

30—NOTRE DAME (1957), Rev. Msgr. Leo R. Horrigan; Rev. William Jungmann; Deacons Charles J. Parker Jr.; Kevin Leiner.
Mailing Address: 5100 W. Evans Ave., 80219.
Church: 2190 S. Sheridan Blvd., 80227.
Parish Center—Tel: 303-935-3900; Fax: 303-937-6699.
School—2165 S. Zenobia St., 80219. Tel: 303-935-3549; Fax: 303-937-4868. Stephen Furches, Prin. Lay Teachers 21; Students 471.
Catechesis/Religious Program—2160 S. Zenobia St., 80219. Tel: 303-922-9875; Fax: 303-937-6699. Students 387.

31—OUR LADY OF GRACE (1951), Rev. Patrick Kennedy.
Res.: 2645 E. 48th Ave., 80216. Tel: 303-297-3440; Fax: 303-297-3430.
Catechesis/Religious Program—Tel: 303-297-3440; Fax: 303-296-3486. Students 75.

32—OUR LADY OF GUADALUPE (1936), (Hispanic), Rev. Franco Plascencia.
Res.: 1209 W. 36th Ave., 80211. Tel: 303-477-1402; 303-477-8113; Fax: 303-477-4013.

33—OUR LADY OF LOURDES (1947), Rev. Robert D. Fisher; Deacons Philip Harrington; John Driesbach.
Res.: 2200 S. Logan St., 80210. Tel: 303-722-6861; Fax: 303-722-4810.
School—2256 S. Logan St., 80210. Tel: 303-722-7525. Joan Sheehan, Prin. Lay Teachers 13; Students 170.
Catechesis/Religious Program—Students 66.

34—OUR LADY OF MT. CARMEL (1894), (Italian), Revs. Joseph M. Carbone, O.S.M.; Mark Franceshini; Lawrence E. Walling, O.S.M.; Gabriel M. Weber, O.S.M. In Res., Rev. Gabriel M. Ramacciotti, O.S.M.
Res.: 3549 Navajo St., 80211. Tel: 303-455-0447; Fax: 303-455-5487.
Catechesis/Religious Program—Students 30.

35—PRESENTATION OF OUR LADY (1913), (Hispanic), Rev. Vincent Phung.
Res.: 665 Irving St., 80204. Tel: 303-534-4882; Fax: 303-893-5056.
School—660 Julian St., 80204. Tel: 303-629-6562. Lay Teachers 14; Students 141.
Catechesis/Religious Program—Students 65.

36—ST. ROSE OF LIMA (1924), Very Rev. Patrick Dolan, V.F.
Res.: 1320 W. Nevada Pl., 80223. Tel: 303-778-7673; Fax: 303-778-6601.
School—1345 W. Dakota Ave., 80223. Tel: 303-733-5806; Fax: 303-733-0125. Lay Teachers 11; Students 149.
Catechesis/Religious Program—Tel: 303-778-1397. Students 100.

37—SACRED HEART (1879), (Hispanic), Rev. Marcus Medrano.
Res.: 2760 Larimer St., 80205. Tel: 303-294-9830; Fax: 303-296-0171.
Catechesis/Religious Program—Students 75.

38—TRANSFIGURATION OF OUR LORD (1954), (Ukranian), Rev. Peter A. Bohdanowycz.
Res.: 4118 Shoshone St., 80211. Tel: 303-433-2347.

39—ST. VINCENT DE PAUL (1926), Rev. Michael Walsh; Deacons Marvin A. Hegarty; Bob Finan; Bill Ward.
Res.: 2375 E. Arizona Ave., 80210. Tel: 303-744-6119; Fax: 303-744-6124.
School—1164 S. Josephine St., 80210. Tel: 303-777-3812; Fax: 303-773-9528. Sr. Mary Reginald, O.P., Prin. Sisters 5; Lay Teachers 35; Students 484.
Catechesis/Religious Program—Tel: 303-744-6119, Ext. 17; Fax: 303-744-0124. Students 125.

OUTSIDE THE CITY OF DENVER

AKRON, WASHINGTON CO., ST. JOSEPH (1917), [CEM] Rev. Joseph Blanco.
Res.: 551 W. 6th St., 80720. Tel: 970-345-6996; Fax: 970-345-6504.
Catechesis/Religious Program—Students 98.

ARVADA, JEFFERSON CO.

1—ST. JOAN OF ARC (1967), Rev. Joseph T. Cao. In Res., Rev. Walter Watson, S.J.; Deacons Buddy Fricke; Rex Pilger.
Res.: 12735 W. 58th Ave., 80002. Tel: 303-420-1232; Fax: 303-420-0126.
Catechesis/Religious Program—Sally Carrera, D.R.E.; Dana Rotkovich, Youth Min. Students 407.
Mission—Coal Creek Catholic Community 80403. P.O. Box 7302, Golden, Jefferson Co. 80403.

2—OUR LADY OF MOUNT CARMEL TRIDENTINE LATIN MASS COMMUNITY, Rev. Jose Salgado, F.S.S.P.
Res.: 6985 Sheridan Blvd., 80003. Tel: 303-703-8538; Fax: 303-795-5411.
Catechesis/Religious Program—Students 90.

3—SHRINE OF ST. ANNE (1920), [CEM] Rev. David P. Croak; Deacons Michael Ritz, (Retired); Rodger Creel; Ken Hawkins, (Retired).
Res.: 7555 Grant Pl., 80002. Tel: 303-420-1280; Fax: 303-420-1341.
School—Tel: 303-422-1800; Fax: 303-422-1011. Kathie Kuehl, Prin. Lay Teachers 22; Students 478.
Catechesis/Religious Program—Loretta Flom, D.R.E. Students 462.

4—SPIRIT OF CHRIST PARISH (1974), Revs. Robert J. Kinkel; Gaston Muyombo; Deacons Michael Howard; Richard Baker; Hugh Downey; Earl Webster; Mel Corley.
Res.: 7400 W. 80th Ave., 80003. Tel: 303-422-9173; Fax: 303-422-8251.
Catechesis/Religious Program—Students 895.

ASPEN, PITKIN CO., ST. MARY (1892), Rev. Michael J. O'Brien.
Mailing Address: 533 E. Main St., 81611.
Res.: 104 S. Galena St., 81611. Tel: 970-925-7339; Fax: 970-925-1889.
Catechesis/Religious Program—Tel: 970-429-2137; Fax: 970-920-4274. Students 125.
Mission—Snowmass in Snowmass Village Snowmass Village. 5307 Owl Creek Rd., Pitkin Co. 81615.

AULT, WELD CO.

1—ST. MARY, , See Our Lady of Peace, Greeley.

2—ST. MARY (1953), Rev. James Spahn.
Mailing Address: P.O. Box 1373, 80610.
Res.: 267 E. 4th St., 80610. Tel: 970-834-1609; Fax: 970-686-9169.
Catechesis/Religious Program—Students 105.

AURORA, ARAPAHOE CO.

1—ST. LAWRENCE KOREAN CATHOLIC CHURCH (1981), Rev. In-Kyun Hwang.
Res.: 4310 S. Pitkin St., 80015-1974. Tel: 303-617-7555; Fax: 303-617-8265.
Catechesis/Religious Program—Students 16.

2—ST. MICHAEL THE ARCHANGEL (1978), Rev. James E. Fox, V.F. In Res., Rev. James H. Crisman; Deacon Marty Wilhelm.
Res.: 3320 S. Cathay St., 80013. Tel: 303-617-6226.
Parish Center, Office & Mailing Address: 19099 E. Floyd Ave., 80013. Tel: 303-690-6797; Fax: 303-690-6932.
Catechesis/Religious Program—Tel: 303-690-7697. Students 754.

3—ST. PIUS X (1956), Rev. Stephen Adams.
Res.: 13670 E. 13th Pl., 80011. Tel: 303-364-7435; Fax: 303-340-0122.
School—13680 E. 14th Pl., 80011. Tel: 303-364-6515; Fax: 303-364-1822. Mrs. Debra Roberts. Lay Teachers 23; Students 497.
Catechesis/Religious Program—Students 196.

4—QUEEN OF PEACE (1968), Revs. Martin Lally; Malachy R. McBride, O.F.M.Cap.; Noe Carreon; Deacon John Thunblom.
Res.: 13120 E. Kentucky Ave., 80012. Tel: 303-364-1056; Fax: 303-364-3944.
Catechesis/Religious Program—Students 677.

5—ST. THERESE (1926), Revs. Elbert Chilson; Jorge I. Rodriguez; Deacon Alfredo Sanchez.
Res.: 1243 Kingston St., 80010. Tel: 303-344-0132; Fax: 303-344-0133.
School—Tel: 303-364-7494; Fax: 303-364-1340. Laura Berger, Prin. Sisters 3; Lay Teachers 16; Students 200.
Catechesis/Religious Program—Students 390.

BASALT, EAGLE CO., ST. VINCENT (1970), Revs. Thomas Bradtke; Thomas McCormick.
Res.: 0397 White Hill Rd., Carbondale, 81623. Tel: 970-704-0820; Fax: 970-704-0830.
Catechesis/Religious Program—Students 225.
Mission—St. Mary of the Crown Carbondale, Garfield Co. 81623. Tel: 970-963-1270.

BOULDER, BOULDER CO.

1—ST. MARTIN DE PORRES (1968), Rev. Hermanagild Jayachandra; Deacon Karl T. Matz.
Res.: 3300 Table Mesa Dr., 80303. Tel: 303-499-7744; Fax: 303-494-8754.
Catechesis/Religious Program—Tel: 303-449-4061. Students 35.

2—SACRED HEART OF JESUS (1875), [JC] Revs. William E. Breslin; Donald Leonard; Deacon Richard Pelis.
Res.: 2312 14th St., 80302. Tel: 303-442-6158; Fax: 303-442-7905.
School—(Grades PreK-8) Tel: 303-447-2362; Fax: 303-443-2466. Jan Altevogt, Prin. Lay Teachers 30; Students 386.
Catechesis/Religious Program—Students 235.
Mission—St. Rita P.O. Box 901, Nederland, Boulder Co. 80466. Tel: 303-642-7348; Fax: 303-642-7348. Deacon Francis Boselli, Admin.

3—SACRED HEART OF MARY (1873), [CEM] Rev. Dorino DeLazzer.
Res.: 6739 S. Boulder Rd., 80303. Tel: 303-494-7572; Fax: 303-494-7581.
Rectory—Tel: 303-494-1266.
Catechesis/Religious Program—Students 803.

4—ST. THOMAS AQUINAS UNIVERSITY PARISH (1950),, (Campus Ministry), University of Colorado. Revs. Paul D. Huesing, C.S.P.; David P. Dwyer, C.S.P.; Thomas J. Holahan, C.S.P.
Pastoral Center—904 14th St., 80302. Tel: 303-443-8383; Fax: 303-443-8399.
Catechesis/Religious Program—Students 371.

BRECKENRIDGE, SUMMIT CO., ST. MARY (1875), Revs. John Kauffman; Robert Zuncan.
Mailing Address: No. 2 W. Miner's Cr. Rd., P.O. Box 2670, Frisco, 80443. Tel: 970-668-8700; Fax: 970-668-3213.
Catechesis/Religious Program—Tel: 970-453-0982. Students 230.
Mission—Our Lady of Peace Frisco. Straight Creek

Rd. & Little Beaver Trail, Dillon Valley, Summit Co. 80443.
BRIGHTON, ADAMS CO., ST. AUGUSTINE (1887), Rev. Reinhold B. Weissbeck. In Res., Rev. Robert L. Wedow; Deacon Antonio A. Sandoval.
Res.: 675 E. Egbert St., 80601. Tel: 303-659-1410; Fax: 303-659-6449.
Catechesis/Religious Program—Tel: 303-659-1414. Students 542.
BROOMFIELD, BOULDER CO., NATIVITY OF OUR LORD (1958), Rev. John D. McCormick; Deacons Richard Medenwaldt; Leonard "Buz" Onesky.
Office & Church: 900 W. Midway Blvd., 80020. Tel: 303-469-5171; Fax: 303-469-5172.
School—Tel: 303-466-4177. Ms. Winnie Aiton, Prin. Lay Teachers 23; Students 506.
Catechesis/Religious Program—Tel: 303-469-5171, Ext. 104. Students 650.
BRUSH, MORGAN CO., ST. MARY (1911), Rev. David A. Stahl.
Res.: 340 Stanford St., 80723. Tel: 970-842-2216; Fax: 970-842-4461.
Catechesis/Religious Program—Students 173.
Mission—St. John 340 Stanford, Stoneham, Morgan Co. 80723.
BYERS, ARAPAHOE CO., OUR LADY OF THE PLAINS (1972), Rev. Msgr. Edward T. Madden.
Res.: 186 N. McDonnell St., 80103. Tel: 303-822-5880; Fax: 303-822-5780.
Catechesis/Religious Program—Students 137.
CENTENNIAL, ARAPAHOE CO., ST. THOMAS MORE (1972), Revs. Andrew Kemberling, O.S.B.; John Paul Leyba; James S. Spahn; Deacons Gary Rogge; Steven Stemper.
Res.: 8035 S. Quebec St., 80112. Tel: 303-770-1155; Fax: 303-220-3399.
School—7071 E. Otero Ave., 80112. Tel: 303-770-0441; Fax: 303-267-1899. Paul Mott, Prin. Lay Teachers 39; Students 645.
Catechesis/Religious Program—Students 1,772.
COMMERCE CITY, ADAMS CO., OUR LADY MOTHER OF THE CHURCH (1946), Rev. Terrence Kissell.
Res.: 6690 E. 72nd Ave., 80022. Tel: 303-289-6489; Fax: 303-289-6480.
Catechesis/Religious Program—Tel: 303-288-2966. Students 398.
CONIFER, JEFFERSON CO., OUR LADY OF THE PINES (1979), Rev. Reuben Payo; Deacon Gerald F. Kotas.
Mailing Address: 9444 Eagle Cliff Rd., 80433. Tel: 303-838-0338; Fax: 303-838-1663.
Catechesis/Religious Program—Students 222.
Mission—St. Elizabeth 9444 Eagle Cliff, Buffalo Creek, Jefferson Co. 80433. Deacon Norman Beabout.
CRAIG, MOFFAT CO., SAINT MICHAEL, Formerly St. Michael (1920), Revs. Roger L. Lascelle; Ernest H. Bayer.
Office and Mailing Address: 678 School St., 81625. Tel: 970-824-5330; Fax: 970-824-7870. Email: stmich@itiworks.com.
Catechesis/Religious Program—Students 75.
EAGLE, EAGLE CO., ST. MARY, , See St. Clare of Assisi, Edwards.
EDWARDS, EAGLE CO., ST. CLARE OF ASSISI (1993), Rev. Edward J. Poehlmann.
Mailing Address: P.O. Box 1390, 81632. Tel: 970-926-2821; Fax: 970-926-5350.
Res.: 53 Old County Ln., 81631.
Catechesis/Religious Program—Students 578.
Mission—St. Mary Chapel 215 Capitol, Eagle, Eagle Co. 81631.
Mission—Beaver Creek Chapel 33 Elk Track Rd., Beaver Creek, Eagle Co. 81620.
ENGLEWOOD, ARAPAHOE CO.
1—ALL SOULS (1954), Rev. Philip S. Meredith; Deacons Kevin Brath; Russ Barrows.
Church: 4950 S. Logan, 80110. Tel: 303-789-0007; Fax: 303-789-0491.
School—4951 S. Pennsylvania, 80110. Tel: 303-789-2155; Fax: 303-789-0491. William Moore, Prin. Lay Teachers 22; Students 438.
Catechesis/Religious Program—Students 255.
2—HOLY NAME (1894), Rev. William P. Murphy.
Res.: 3290 W. Milan Ave., 80110. Tel: 303-781-6093; Fax: 303-781-6398.
Catechesis/Religious Program—Students 142.
3—ST. LOUIS (1911), Rev. Robert J. Reycraft; Deacon Marty Wager.
Res.: 3310 S. Sherman St., 80110. Tel: 303-761-3940; Fax: 303-806-5394.
School—3301 S. Sherman St., 80110. Tel: 303-762-8307; Fax: 303-762-0156. Lay Teachers 11; Students 117.
Catechesis/Religious Program—Tel: 303-978-0242. Students 108.
ERIE, WELD CO., ST. SCHOLASTICA (1899), Rev. Robert Whipkey.
Office—575 Wells, P.O. Box 402, 80516. Tel: 303-828-4221; Fax: 303-833-3000.
Church: 615 Main St., 80516.
Catechesis/Religious Program—Students 100.
ESTES PARK, LARIMER CO., OUR LADY OF THE MOUNTAINS (1947), Rev. Gregory Cioch.
Res.: P.O. Box 1706, 80517. Tel: 970-586-8111; Fax: 970-586-8112.
Catechesis/Religious Program—Students 62.
EVERGREEN, JEFFERSON CO., CHRIST THE KING (1932), Rev. Christopher A. Renner; Deacons George Fitterer, (Retired); Tom Quinlan; Brian Kerby; Ronald Roderick.
Res.: 4291 Evergreen Pkwy., 80439-7723. Tel: 303-674-3155; Fax: 303-674-3285.
Catechesis/Religious Program—Tel: 303-674-5282. Students 407.
FORT COLLINS, LARIMER CO.
1—ST. ELIZABETH ANN SETON (1981), Rev. Lawrence P. Christensen, C.M., P.V., Admin.; Deacons William Trewartha; James "Jim" Devlin.
Res.: 5450 S. Lemay Ave., 80525. Tel: 970-226-1303; Fax: 970-226-5780.
Catechesis/Religious Program—Tel: 970-226-6549. Students 805.
2—HOLY FAMILY (1924), (Hispanic), Rev. Douglas Hunt, C.R.
Res.: 326 N. Whitcomb St., 80521. Tel: 970-482-6599; Fax: 970-482-8045; 970-482-8045.
Catechesis/Religious Program—Students 146.
3—JOHN XXIII UNIVERSITY PARISH (1967) Rev. Donald Willette; Deacons Leonard Benzel; William McClellan.
Res.: 1220 University Ave., 80521. Tel: 970-484-3356; Fax: 970-484-3434.
Catechesis/Religious Program—Students 351.
4—ST. JOSEPH (1879), Revs. Dennis K. Ryan; Michael V. Delaney, S.J.; Deacons Warren G. Lybarger; Rick Grimler.
Res.: 308 W. Mountain Ave., P.O. Box 502, 80522. Tel: 970-482-4148; Fax: 970-221-0635.
School—127 N. Howes St., 80522. Tel: 970-484-1171; Fax: 970-221-0635. Barbara Bullock, Prin. Lay Teachers 25; Students 332.
Catechesis/Religious Program—Students 130.
Mission—Our Lady of the Lakes P.O. Box 502, Red Feather Lakes, Larimer Co. 80522.
FORT LUPTON, WELD CO., ST. WILLIAM (1909), Rev. Gregorio L. Mirto.
Res.: 1025 Fulton Ave., 80621. Tel: 303-857-0171; Fax: 303-857-6643.
Catechesis/Religious Program—Tel: 303-857-4754. Students 192.
FORT MORGAN, MORGAN CO., ST. HELENA (1910), Rev. Lawrence B. Kaiser.
Res. 917 W. 7th Ave., 80701. Tel: 970-867-2885.
Catechesis/Religious Program—923 Pawnee, 80701. Tel: 970-867-5768. Students 400.
Mission—St. Francis of Assisi Weldona, Morgan Co. 80701. Attended by St. Mary, Brush.
FOXFIELD, ARAPAHOE CO., OUR LADY OF LORETO (1998), Rev. Msgr. Edward Buelt. In Res., Deacon George Brown.
Res.: 18000E. Arapahoe Rd., 80016. Tel: 303-766-3800; Fax: 303-766-3700.
FREDERICK, WELD CO., ST. THERESA (1923), Rev. Robert Whipkey.
Res.: 436 Fifth St., P.O. Box 418, 80530. Tel: 303-833-2966; Fax: 303-833-3000.
Catechesis/Religious Program—Students 117.
GILCREST, WELD CO., SACRED HEART (2002), Rev. William L. Smith, C.S.Sp.
Mailing Address: 809 Charlotte St., Johnstown, 80535.
Res.: 4th St. & Starbird Rd.. Tel: 970-587-2879; Fax: 970-587-2879.
GLENWOOD SPRINGS, GARFIELD CO., ST. STEPHEN (1885), Rev. Cliff J. McMillan; Deacons Victor Fimminau; Charles Sprick, (Retired).
Res.: 1010 Grand Ave., 81601. Tel: 970-945-6673; Fax: 970-945-1208.
School—414 S. Hyland Park Dr., 81601. Tel: 970-945-7746. Dr. Tom Alby, Prin. Lay Teachers 9; Students 75.
Catechesis/Religious Program—Tel: 970-945-6673. Students 150.
GOLDEN, JEFFERSON CO., ST. JOSEPH (1867), Rev. Joseph E. Monahan; Deacon Dennis Kelly.
Res.: 969 Ulysses St., 80401. Tel: 303-279-4464; Fax: 303-273-9811.
Catechesis/Religious Program—Students 380.
GRAND LAKE, GRAND CO., ST. ANNE (1944), Rev. Francis J. Gerber Jr.; Deacon James R. Moat.
Res.: 219 Hancock St., P.O. Box 2029, Granby, 80446. Tel: 970-627-3450; 970-887-0032 (Office); Fax: 970-627-3064; 970-887-9662 (Office).
Catechesis/Religious Program—Students 24.
Mission—Our Lady of the Snow P.O. Box 2029, Granby, Grand Co. 80446.
Mission—St. Bernard P.O. Box 510, Winter Park, Grand Co. 80447.
GREELEY, WELD CO.
1—ST. MARY (1965), Rev. Peter Quang Nguyen; Deacon Joseph H. Meilinger.
Res.: 2222 23rd Ave., 80634. Tel: 970-352-1724; Fax: 970-352-1729.
School—Tel: 970-353-8100; Fax: 970-353-8102. Lay Teachers 14; Students 204.
Catechesis/Religious Program—Tel: 970-352-1722. Students 430.
2—OUR LADY OF PEACE (1948), Rev. Bernard A. Schmitz.
Res.: 1311 3rd St., 80631. Tel: 970-353-1747; Fax: 970-353-4830.
Catechesis/Religious Program—1303 3rd St., 80631. Tel: 970-351-6473; Fax: 970-353-4830. Students 455.
3—ST. PETER (1995), Rev. Rocco Porter. In Res., Rev. Isaac Raney, M.Ss.A.
Office—915 12th St., 80631. Tel: 970-352-1060; Fax: 970-352-1062.
Catechesis/Religious Program—Tel: 970-346-9777. Students 463.
HOLYOKE, PHILLIPS CO., ST. PATRICK (1893), Rev. Daniel Zimmerschied.
Res.: 519 S. Interocean, 80734. Tel: 970-854-2762; 970-859-2866 (Hall); Fax: 970-854-2781.
Catechesis/Religious Program—Students 44.
Mission—Christ the King 306 N. Iris, Haxtun, Phillips Co. 80731. Tel: 970-774-7640.
Mission—St. Peter the Apostle [CEM] 40027 CR 18, Rt. 1, Fleming, Logan Co. 80728. Tel: 970-265-2792.
IDAHO SPRINGS, CLEAR CREEK CO., ST. PAUL (1881), Rev. Michael F. Kerrigan.
Res.: P.O. Box 848, 1632 Colorado Blvd., 80452. Tel: 303-567-4662; Fax: 303-567-4662.
Catechesis/Religious Program—Tel: 303-567-4138. Students 64.
Mission—St. Mary of the Assumption P.O. Box 848, Central City, Gilpin Co. 80452.
Mission—Our Lady of Lourdes [CEM] P.O. Box 848, Georgetown, Clear Creek Co. 80452.
ILIFF, LOGAN CO., ST. CATHERINE OF SIENA (1927), Rev. James Baird.
Res.: 111 S. Fifth St., P.O. Box 221, 80736. Tel: 970-522-8040; Fax: 970-334-2227.
JOHNSTOWN, WELD CO., ST. JOHN THE BAPTIST (1937), Rev. William Smith, C.S.Sp.
Res.: 809 Charlotte St., 80534. Tel: 970-587-2879; Fax: 970-587-2879.
Catechesis/Religious Program—Students 130.
JULESBURG, SEDGWICK CO., ST. ANTHONY (1907), Rev. Msgr. Michael Chamberlian.
Res.: 606 W. 3rd St., 80737. Tel: 970-474-2655; Fax: 970-474-2655.
Catechesis/Religious Program—Students 109.
Mission—St. Peters 612 E. 3rd, Crook, Logan Co. 80726.
KREMMLING, GRAND CO., ST. PETER (1944), Rev. John J. Murphy.
Church and Office: 106 S. 5th St., P.O. Box 428, 80459. Tel: 970-724-3428.
Mission—St. Ignatius Walden, Jackson Co. 80459. Tel: 970-724-3428.
Catechesis/Religious Program—Students 17.
LAFAYETTE, BOULDER CO., IMMACULATE CONCEPTION (1907), Very Rev. Robert L. Amundsen. In Res., Rev. Peter Urban.
Res.: 110 W. Simpson, 80026. Tel: 303-665-5103; Fax: 303-604-9077.
Catechesis/Religious Program—Students 187.
LAKEWOOD, JEFFERSON CO.
1—ST. BERNADETTE (1947), Rev. Donald Romero; Deacons L. Kenneth Dreiling; Jim Wall.
Res.: 7240 W. 12th Ave., 80215. Tel: 303-233-1523; Fax: 303-233-7285.
Church: W. 12th Ave. & Teller St., 80215.
School—1100 Upham St., 80215. Tel: 303-237-0401. Henrietta Linenbrink, Prin. Lay Teachers 11; Students 142.
Catechesis/Religious Program—Deacon Ken Dreiling, D.R.E. Students 90.
2—CHRIST ON THE MOUNTAIN PARISH (1975), Rev. John Grabrian.
Church: 13922 W. Utah Ave., 80228-4110. Tel: 303-988-2222; Fax: 303-986-6956.
Catechesis/Religious Program—Students 233.
3—ST. JUDE (1967), Rev. Michael W. Gass; Deacons Joel J. Paulson; Alan C. Spears.
Office: 9405 W. Florida Ave., 80232-5111. Tel: 303-988-6435; Fax: 303-988-6438.
Res.: 1666 S. Jellison St., 80226.
Catechesis/Religious Program—Tom Zupancich, D.R.E. Students 547.
4—OUR LADY OF FATIMA (1958), Rev. Msgr. Walker Nickless, V.G.; Rev. Gary Selin; Deacon Joseph W. Hawley.
Res.: 1985 Miller St., 80215. Tel: 303-233-6236; Fax: 303-237-6097.
School—Tel: 303-233-2500; Fax: 303-205-1567. Mrs. Erlene Madsen, Prin. Lay Teachers 23; Students 300.
Catechesis/Religious Program—Students 379.
LITTLETON, ARAPAHOE CO., ST. MARY (1901), [JC] Revs. David Blue Jacket; Frank Lomica; Deacons Edward Clements; Craig Fucci. In Res., Rev.

Msgrs. Thomas S. Fryar; Richard Malone (PH).
Res.: 6853 S. Prince, 80120. Tel: 303-798-8506; Fax: 303-347-2270.
School—(Grades K-8) Tel: 303-794-4757 (Grades K-3); 303-798-2375 (Grades 4-8). Mary Cohen, Prin. Lay Teachers 40; Students 659.
Catechesis/Religious Program—Tel: 720-283-4728. Students 840.

LITTLETON, JEFFERSON CO.
1—ST. FRANCES CABRINI PARISH (1972), Rev. Kenneth Leone. In Res., Rev. Michael Pavlakovick; Deacon Paul Grimm.
Res.: 6673 W. Chatfield Ave., 80128. Tel: 303-979-7688; Fax: 303-972-8566.
Catechesis/Religious Program—Students 1,710.
2—LIGHT OF THE WORLD PARISH (1979), Rev. Jerome M. Rohr; Deacons Eugene Mooneyham; Joe Donohoe.
Mailing Address: 10316 W. Bowles Ave., 80127. Tel: 303-973-3969; Fax: 303-973-2122.
Catechesis/Religious Program—Eileen Love, D.R.E. Students 793.

LONGMONT, BOULDER CO.
1—ST. JOHN THE BAPTIST (1882), [JC] Rev. Brian Morrow; Deacons Bob Howard; Mike Berens.
323 Collyer St., 80501. Tel: 303-776-0737; Fax: 303-772-5636. In Res., Revs. Mickey Flaska; Stephen Siebert.
School—350 Emery St., 80501. Tel: 303-776-8760. Ms. Mary Cronley, Prin. Lay Teachers 26; Students 413.
Catechesis/Religious Program—Tel: 303-772-5637. Students 580.
2—SPIRIT OF PEACE PARISH (1982), [JC] Rev. Brian Morrow; Mary Franch, Pastoral Team; Christine Hersey, Pastoral Team; Mitzi Wimer, Pastoral Team.
Church and Office: 1500 Hover Rd., 80501. Tel: 303-772-6322; Fax: 303-772-9415.
Catechesis/Religious Program—Students 392.

LOUISVILLE, BOULDER CO., ST. LOUIS (1884), Revs. G. Timothy Gaines; Henri Tshibambe, P.V.; Daniel Flaherty (Retired); Deacons R. Taylor Elder; Steven J. Vallero.
Office—902 Grant Ave., 80027. Tel: 303-666-6401; Fax: 303-666-0826.
School—925 Grant Ave., 80027. Tel: 303-666-6220. Lay Teachers 24; Students 245.
School—Preschool, 901 Grant Ave., 80027. Tel: 303-665-0606.
Catechesis/Religious Program—902 Grant Ave., 80027. Tel: 303-604-6055. Students 350.

LOVELAND, LARIMER CO., ST. JOHN THE EVANGELIST (1902), Very Rev. Joseph A. Hartmann, V.F.; Rev. Jason M. Thuerauf; Deacons Robert Haigh, (Retired); John McKeown, (Retired); Daniel Marthe, (Retired); John Kunsemiller, (Retired).
Office—1515 Hilltop Dr., 80537. Tel: 970-669-2720; Fax: 970-669-5743.
Res.: 1523 Hilltop Dr., 80537. Tel: 970-663-3457.
School—1730 W. 12th St.. Tel: 970-667-6846. Students 331.
Catechesis/Religious Program—Elizabeth Miller, D.R.E. Students 310.

MEEKER, RIO BLANCO CO., HOLY FAMILY (1905), Attended by, Saint Michael, Craig. Revs. Roger L. Lascelle; Ernest Bayer.
Mailing Address: P.O. Box 866, 81641. Tel: 970-878-3300; Fax: 970-878-3300. Email: stmich@itiworks.com.
Catechesis/Religious Program—Students 30.

MINTURN, EAGLE CO., ST. PATRICK'S (1913), Very Rev. Frank Maroney, V.F.; Rev. George R. Fitzgerald, C.S.P. Tel: 970-827-5784, Ext. 20.
Admin. & Mailing Address: 19 Vail Rd., Vail, 81657.
Res.: 476 Pine St., 81645. Tel: 970-477-0378; Fax: 970-476-3347.
Catechesis/Religious Program—Tel: 970-827-5784; Fax: 970-827-9454. Students 100.
Mission—The Interfaith Chapel Vail, Eagle Co.

NORTHGLENN, ADAMS CO., IMMACULATE HEART OF MARY (1967), Revs. Gregory Ames; James Abosike; Deacons Leo Oehrle; Lynn Waring; James Gollhofer.
Offices & Mailing Adress: 11385 Grant Dr., 80233. Tel: 303-452-2041; Fax: 303-452-7546.
Res.: 335 E. 112th Dr., 80233. Tel: 303-452-9104.
Catechesis/Religious Program—Students 600.

OAK CREEK, ROUTT CO., ST. MARTIN OF TOURS, Attended by, Holy Name, Steamboat Springs.

PEETZ, LOGAN CO., SACRED HEART, [CEM] Rev. James Baird.
Res.: 621 Logan, P.O. Box D, 80747. Tel: 970-334-2227; Fax: 970-334-2227.
Catechesis/Religious Program—Students 52.

PLATTEVILLE, WELD CO.
1—ST. NICHOLAS (2002), Attended by, St. John the Baptist, Johnston. Rev. William Smith, C.S.Sp.
Mailing Address: 809 Charlotte St., Johnstown, 80535. Tel: 970-587-2879; Fax: 970-587-2879.
514 Marion St., 80651. Tel: 970-785-2143; Fax: 303-857-6643.

RANGELY, RIO BLANCO CO., ST. IGNATIUS (1931), Revs. Roger L. Lascelle; Ernest Bayer; Deacon George Fortunato.
Mailing Address: 109 S. Stanolind Ave., 81648. Tel: 970-675-8935; Fax: 970-675-8935. Email: stmich@itiworks.com.
Catechesis/Religious Program—Students 15.

RED FEATHERS LAKES, LARIMER CO., OUR LADY OF THE LAKES, , See St. Joseph, Fort Collins.

RIFLE, GARFIELD CO., ST. MARY'S (1910), Rev. Robert E. Hehn.
Res.: 790 E. 7th St., 81650. Tel: 970-625-2547; Fax: 970-625-9025.
Catechesis/Religious Program—761 Birch Ave., 81650. Tel: 970-625-1800. Students 261.
Mission—Sacred Heart P.O. Box 191, Silt, Garfield Co. 81650.
Mission—St. Brendan P.O. Box 191, Parachute, Garfield Co. 81650.

ROGGEN, WELD CO., SACRED HEART (1924), Rev. Robert L. Wedow, Admin.
Res.: 38044 Weld County Rd. 16, 80652. Tel: 303-849-5313; Fax: 303-849-5674.
Catechesis/Religious Program—Students 133.
Mission—Holy Family 38044 Weld County Rd. 16, Keenesburg, Weld Co. 80652.
Mission—Our Lady of Lourdes 38044 Weld County Rd. 16, Wiggins, Morgan Co. 80652.

STEAMBOAT SPRINGS, ROUTT CO., HOLY NAME (1907), Rev. Msgr. George M. Schroeder.
Res.: 504 Oak St., P.O. Box 774198, 80477-4198. Tel: 970-879-0671; Fax: 970-879-7406.
Catechesis/Religious Program—Tel: 970-879-1225. Students 224.
Mission—St. Martin of Tours 301 S. Sharp Ave., Oak Creek, Routt Co. 80467.

STERLING, LOGAN CO., ST. ANTHONY (1888), Very Rev. James R. Baird, V.F.
Res.: 327 S. 3rd St., 80751. Tel: 970-522-6422; Fax: 970-522-6442.
School—Tel: 970-522-7567. Lay Teachers 12; Students 160.
Catechesis/Religious Program—326 S. 3rd St., 80751. Tel: 970-522-7568. Students 260.

STONEHAM, WELD CO., ST. JOHN, , See St. Mary, Brush.

VAIL, EAGLE CO., THE INTERFAITH CHAPEL, , See St. Patrick's, Minturn.

WALDEN, JACKSON CO., ST. IGNATIUS, , See St. Peter, Kremmling.

WATTENBERG, FORT LUPTON CO., OUR LADY OF GRACE, , See St. William, Fort Lupton.

WELDONA, MORGAN CO., ST. FRANCIS OF ASSISI, , See St. Helena, Fort Morgan.

WESTMINSTER, ADAMS CO.
1—HOLY TRINITY (1956), Revs. John L. Hilton; Giovanni Capucci; Deacon Lloyd Quintana.
Res.: 7595 N. Federal, 80030. Tel: 303-428-3594; Fax: 303-427-4125.
School—Tel: 303-427-5632. Mr. Don Baker, Prin. Lay Teachers 15; Students 202.
Catechesis/Religious Program—Tel: 303-427-3594, Ext. 12. Students 165.
Mission—Our Lady of Visitation 2531 W. 65th Pl., Adams Co. 80221. Tel: 303-429-7947.
2—ST. MARK (1973), Rev. James R. Fox, V.F.; Deacon Anthony Ronco.
Res.: 3141 W. 96th Ave., 80031. Tel: 303-466-8720; Fax: 303-466-0998.
Catechesis/Religious Program—Students 246.

WHEAT RIDGE, JEFFERSON CO.
1—SS. PETER AND PAUL (1949), Rev. James K. Goggins; Deacon John Pontillo.
Res.: 3900 Pierce St., 80033. Tel: 303-424-3706; Fax: 303-424-0819.
School—Tel: 303-420-0402; Fax: 303-456-1888. Kathy Byrnes, Prin. Religious 4; Lay Teachers 23; Students 417.
Catechesis/Religious Program—Students 133.
2—QUEEN OF VIETNAMESE MARTYRS (1976), (Asian), Revs. Hilary Hai Khanh Nguyen, C.M.C.; Leo Dinh Huyen Vu, C.M.C.; Deacons Joseph Van Le Tam; Peter Hung Phi Dang.
Res.: 4655 Harlan St., 80033. Tel: 303-431-0382; Fax: 303-431-1876.

WIGGINS, MORGAN CO., OUR LADY OF LOURDES, , See Sacred Heart, Roggen.

WINDSOR, WELD CO., OUR LADY OF THE VALLEY, Rev. James Spahn, Admin.; Deacon Harold Kimble.
Office—P.O. Box 1018, 80550. Tel: 970-686-5084; Fax: 970-686-9169.
Res.: 809 Charlotte St., Johnstown, 80534. Tel: 303-587-2879.

WINTER PARK, GRAND CO., ST. BERNARD OF MONTJOUX, , See St. Anne, Grand Lake.

WRAY, YUMA CO., ST. ANDREW (1891), Rev. Gerald A. Young, Admin.
Res.: 412 Dexter St., 80758. Tel: 970-332-5858.
Catechesis/Religious Program—Students 120.

YUMA, YUMA CO., ST. JOHN (1888), Rev. Adelberto De Gante.
Res.: 508 S. Ash St., 80759. Tel: 970-848-5973; Fax: 970-848-2817.
Catechesis/Religious Program—Students 130.

On Duty Outside the Archdiocese:
Rev. Msgr.—
McDaid, J. Anthony, Congregation for the Clergy, 00120, Vatican City State.
Revs.—
Denig, Philip P., Chap. (Capt.), 1200 Varnum St., Washington, DC 20017.
Kelly, Thomas D., 2315 Alma Ave., Manhattan Beach, CA 90266.

Absent on Leave:
Rev.—
Simko, James

Retired:
Rev. Msgrs.—
Dentici, Thomas, St. Mary of the Crown, 0397 White Hill Rd., Carbondale, 81623.
Jones, William H., Mullen Home, 3629 W. 29th Ave, 80211.
Rasby, James W., 1011 S. Valencia, Villa 3, 80231.
Very Rev.—
Kleiner, James, P.V., V.F., P.O. Box 300545, 80203.
Revs.—
Banigan, Herbert, 1256 W. Canfield Ave., Coeur D Alene, ID 83815.
Blach, Leo M., Gardens St. Elizabeth, 2835 W. 32nd Ave. #12, 80211.
Breunig, Robert L., Mullen Home, 3629 W. 29th Ave, 80211.
Canjar, John A., 6780 E. Cedar Ave., Apt. 706A, Denver 80224.
Cuneo, James J., 6991 Nile Ct., Arvada, 80007.
Deml, Francis S., 625 S. Alton Way # 7C, 80231.
Dona, Thomas M., Gardens at St. Elizabeth, 2835 W. 32nd Ave. # 34, 80211.
Flaherty, Daniel J., 902 Grant St., Louisville, 80027.
Gibbons, John, Mullen Home, 3629 W 29th Ave, 80211.
Jones, Charles, 1129 Fillmore, 80206. Tel: 303-322-0624
Kane, James E., 2397 S. Xanadu Way, Bldg. 9 #402, Aurora, 80014.
Longwill, Carl, 415 N.E. 105th St., Miami, FL 33138-2000.
Meznar, Robert P., 4330 Thompson Ct., 80216.
Nevans, Robert V., 1575 Pennsylvania St. #105, 80203.
O'Malley, Joseph M., 1542 E. Nicholas Dr., Littleton, 80122-2945.
Ossino, Angelo, 13800 E. Marina Dr. # 312, Aurora, 80014.
Puhl, Albert E., Gardens St. Elizabeth, 2835 W. 32nd Ave. #105, 80211.
Salmon, Charles P., Gardens St. Elizabeth, 2835 W. 32nd Ave. #128, 80211.
Sanger, Charles P., Gardens St. Elizabeth, 2835 W. 32nd Ave., 80211.
Smith, Vincent Leo, P.O. Box 82, Fairplay, 80440.
Sullivan, Joseph, 601 W. 11th Ave. Bldg. 1 #908, 80204.
Sullivan, Patrick, Box 274, 8962 E. Hampden Ave., 80231-4996.
Urban, Peter, 110 W. Simpson St., Lafayette, 80026.
Weibel, George L., 13902 E. Marina Dr. #207, Aurora, 80014.

Permanent Deacons:
Anderson, Ernest J., (Retired)
Ansay, Ronald J., (Retired)
Atencio, Sidney, St. Cajetan, Denver
Babish, Joseph T., Immaculate Conception Cathedral, Denver
Baker, Richard L., Spirit of Christ, Arvada
Ball, James J., Sr., (Leave of Absence)
Barbato, Lewis, M.D., (Retired)
Barrows, Russell, All Souls, Englewood
Beabout, Norman, St. Elizabeth, Buffalo Creek
Benedetto, Joseph, Hearing Impaired Ministry
Benzel, Leonard, (Retired)
Borda, Richard S., Assoc. Dir. Deacons, Guardian Angels, Arvada
Boselli, Francis "Bud", Admin., St. Rita's Mission, Nederland
Bowles, Richard J., Colorado Springs Diocese
Brady, Richard A., (Retired)
Brown, James, Queen of Peace, Aurora
Clements, Edward R., St. Mary, Littleton
Combs, Richard, Archdiocese, Seattle
Corley, Melvin G., Spirit of Christ, Arvada
Coursey, Nathan D., Blessed Sacrament Parish, Denver
Creel, Rodger L., Shrine of St. Anne, Arvada

Dang, Peter Hung Phi, Queen of Vietnamese Martyrs, Wheat Ridge
Del Real, Harold, Assumption, Denver
DeProfio, Dominic, Church of the Good Shepherd, Denver
DiPentino, John L., Mt. Carmel, Denver
Dolan, L. Stephen, (Retired)
Donohoe, Joseph H., Light of the World, Littleton
Dorwart, Jason, (Retired)
Downey, Hugh, Spirit of Christ, Arvada
Dreiling, L. Kenneth, St. Bernadette, Lakewood
Dunn, Darryl, (Retired)
Elder, R. Taylor, St. Louis, Louisville
Finan, Robert E., Assoc. Dir. Deacons, St. Vincent de Paul, Denver
Fitterer, George, (Retired)
Fortunato, George R., (On Leave of Absence)
Franklin, John, Holy Name, Steamboat Springs
Frisinger, Howard, (Retired)
Fucci, Craig, St. Mary, Littleton
Gallagher, Michael, St. Patrick, Minturn
Gollhofer, James D., Immaculate Heart of Mary, Northglenn
Grimler, Richard, St. Joseph, Fort Collins
Grimm, R. Paul, St. Francis Cabrini, Littleton
Haigh, Robert, (Retired)
Halpine, Russell, Holy Cross, Thornton
Harrington, Philip, Our Lady of Lourdes, Denver
Hastings, William O., St. Mary, Greeley
Hawkins, Kenneth I., Jr., (Retired)
Hawley, Joseph W., Our Lady of Fatima, Lakewood
Hegarty, Marvin A., St. Vincent de Paul, Denver
Howard, Michael J., (Retired)
Howard, Robert J., St. John the Baptist, Longmont
Hudec, Gordon D., Christ on the Mountain, Lakewood
Jordan, Bill, St. Augustine, Brighton
Kelly, Dennis M., St. Joseph, Golden
Kenny, Timothy M., St. Thomas More, Centennial
Kerby, Brian J., Mt. Evans Hospice & Christ the King, Evergreen
Kilbarger, Timothy M., Holy Name Parish, Englewood
Kimble, Harold, Our Lady of the Valley, Windsor
Kimminau, Victor H., St. Stephen, Glenwood Springs
Kulinski, Jerome N., (Retired)
Kunsemiller, John, (Retired)
Lamar, Charles, St. Mary, Breckenridge
Le, Joseph Tam Van, (Retired)
Lee, William S., (Retired)
Lenzo, Carl, St. James, Denver
Lopez, Samuel, Most Precious Blood, Denver
Loushin, Albert J., St. Vincent, Basalt
Lujan, Edward, (Retired)
Lybarger, Warren G., St. Joseph, Ft. Collins
Marthe, Daniel M., (Retired)
Martin, Gregory "Dusty", St. Pius X, Aurora
Matz, Karl T., (Retired)
McClellan, William, St. John XXIII, Ft. Collins
McDavid, Clarence G., Cure D'Ars, Denver
McKeown, John, (Retired)
Medenwaldt, Richard A., Nativity of Our Lord, Broomfield
Meilinger, Joseph H., St. Mary, Greeley
Menogan, Guffie E., St. Ignatius Loyola, Denver
Mich, Lawrence E., (Retired)
Miller, Gary E., St. Mary Magdalene, Denver
Moat, James, St. Anne, Grand Lake
Mooneyham, Eugene, Light of the World, Littleton
Morin, George C., Church of the Good Shepherd, Denver
Neal, John R., Church of Risen Christ Denver
Oehrle, Leo A., (Retired)
Onesky, Leonard "Buz", Nativity of Our Lord, Broomfield
Padilla, Carlos L., (Retired)
Parker, Charles J., Jr., Notre Dame, Denver
Paulson, Joel J., St. Jude, Lakewood
Pelis, Richard F., Sacred Heart of Jesus, Boulder
Pilger, Rex H., Jr., Assoc. Dir. Deacons, St. Joan of Arc
Polak, Leonard E., St. Catherine of Siena, Denver
Pontillo, John E., Sts. Peter & Paul, Wheat Ridge
Quinlan, Thomas, Christ the King, Evergreen
Quintana, Lloyd, Holy Trinity, Westminster
Rael, Gilbert E., (Leave of Absence)
Reinert, George J., (Retired)
Ritchey, Ronald T., St. Rose of Lima, Denver
Ritz, Michael P., Jr., (Retired)
Rogge, Gary, St. Thomas More, Centennial
Rompot, Vernon L., Holy Ghost Church, Denver
Roucc, Anthony F., St. Mark's, Westminster
Ruiz, Nehemias, Holy Cross, Thornton
Runck, Merle, Pueblo Diocese
Salvato, Mark, Cathedral of the Immaculate Conception, Denver
Sanchez, Alfredo, St. Therese, Aurora
Sanchez, Maclovio, (Retired)
Sanchez, Wilfred G., Presentation of Our lady Parish, Denver
Sandoval, Alfonso M., Sec. for Deacons & Dir. Formation
Sandoval, Antonio A., Our Lady Mother of the Church
Sandoval, Henry, (Retired)
Smith, John L., Assoc. Sec. Deacons, Holy Family, Denver
Sorber, William M., (Retired)
Spears, Alan C., St. Jude, Lakewood
Spellman, William, (Retired)
Sprick, Charles B., (Retired)
Stemper, Steven, St. Thomas More, Englewood
Stephenson, Billy C., (Retired)
Stow, William J., Ascension Parish, Denver
Sutton, Jack, Christ the King, Denver
Thunblom, John, Queen of Peace, Aurora
Tirgrath, Howard L., (Retired)
Torrez, Frederick L., Our Lady of Peace, Greeley
Trewartha, William D.P.M., St. Elizabeth Ann Seton, Fort Collins
Trujillo, Samuel R., Our Lady of Grace, Denver
Ubowski, Chester W., St. Frances Cabrini, Littleton
Vallero, Steven J., St. Louis Parish, Louisville
Vieria, Richard, Admin., St. Mary Magdalene, Denver
Vigil, Arthur A., All Saints, Denver
Vlchek, Douglas, Cheyenne Diocese
Wager, Martin A., St. Louis, Englewood
Wall, James R., St. Bernadette, Lakewood
Ward, William, St. Vincent de Paul, Denver
Waring, Lynn E., (On Leave of Absence)
Webster, Earl, Spirit of Christ, Arvada
Whaley, Patrick, Our Lady of Guadalupe, Denver
Wilhelm, Martin A., St. Michael the Archangel, Aurora
Young, John Joseph, (Retired)

INSTITUTIONS LOCATED IN THE ARCHDIOCESE

[A] SEMINARIES, RELIGIOUS OR SCHOLASTICATES

DENVER. *St. Andrew's Theatine Religious House*, 1050 S. Birch St., 80246. Tel: 303-756-5522; Fax: 303-691-2969. Very Rev. Patrick Valdez, C.R., Prov. Supr.; Rev. Bart Nadal, C.R., Rector. Theatine Fathers Priests 3. In Res. Revs. Anselmo (Bud) Jaramillo, C.R.; Angelo Urdiain, C.R.

St. Dominic Priory, 3005 W. 29th Ave., 80211. Tel: 303-455-3614; Fax: 303-455-3087. Email: jspahn@dominicans.org. Revs. James Anthony Spahn, O.P., Prior; Giles R. Klapperich, O.P., Sub-prior; Bros. Jordan Coonen, O.P.; Michael T. McGovern, O.P.; Revs. Michael G. Kyte, O.P., Brian Bricker, O.P., Assoc. Pastor; Robert F. Staes, O.P.; Louis S. Morrone, O.P. (CHI), Novice Master; Dennis C. Woerter, O.P. Province of St. Albert the Great Priests 7; Brothers 2; Novices 11.

Assigned but living elsewhere: Revs. Herbert Hayek, O.P. (COS); George Reynolds, O.P. (COS).

Novices: Bros. Timothy Combs; DePorres Durham; Martin Farrell; Michail Ford; John Iffert; Jonah Lewis; Andrew McAlpin; Athansius Richied; Michael Spretnjak; Vito Tinaburri; Patrick Tobin.

St. John Vianney Theological Seminary, 1300 S. Steele St., 80210. Tel: 303-282-3427; Fax: 303-282-3453. Very Rev. Michael Glenn, Rector; Rev. Kent Drator, Vice Rector. A division of Our Lady of the New Advent Theological Institute.

Redemptoris Mater House of Formation, 3434 E. Arizona Ave., 80210. Tel: 303-733-2220; Fax: 303-733-2223. Email: rematerden@juno.com. Very Rev. Florian Martin-Calama, Rector for Redemptoris Mater Archdiocesan Missionary Seminary; Revs. Federico Colautti, Vice Rector; Jose Maria Fuenmayor, Spiritual Dir. Priests 3; Diocesan Seminarians 36; Total Staff 5.

[B] COLLEGES AND UNIVERSITIES

DENVER. *Regis University* A university conducted under the auspices of the Society of Jesus. , 3333 Regis Blvd., 80221-1099. Tel: 303-458-4100; Fax: 303-458-4921. Web: www.regis.edu. Martin T. Hart, Chm. Bd. of Trustees. Revs. Michael J. Sheeran, S.J., Pres.; David M. Clarke, S.J., Chancellor; Dr. Allan L. Service, Provost & Vice Pres. Academic Affairs; Ms. Karen Webber, Vice Pres. Univ. Svcs.; Dr. Thomas E. Reynolds, Vice Pres. Mission & Student Devel.; Ms. Julia Crockett, Vice Pres. Univ. Relations; Dr. Paul Ewald, Dean Regis College; Dr. William J. Husson, Vice Pres. & Academic Dean School for Professional Studies; Dr. Patricia A. Ladewig, Dean School for Health Care Professions; Mr. Ivan Gaetz, Dean Libraries; Ms Kathleen M. Schaefer, Dir. Campus Ministry; Dr. Joseph C. Weber, Vice Provost Fin. & Budget; Mr. Dwight Greer, Assoc. Provost Diversity; Dr. Robert Kaffer, Exec. Asst. to the Pres. Priests 12; Sisters 1; Lay Teachers 500; Students 16,157.

[C] INTER-PAROCHIAL HIGH SCHOOLS

DENVER. *Bishop Machebeuf Catholic High School*, 458 Uinta Way, 80230-6934. Tel: 303-344-0082; Fax: 303-344-1582. Web: www.machebeuf.org. Lisa Switzer, Prin. Sisters 2; Lay Teachers 38; Students 490.

BROOMFIELD. *Holy Family High School*, 5195 W. 144th Ave., 80020. Tel: 303-440-1411; Fax: 303-466-1935. Web: www.holyfamilyhs.com. Sr. Mary Rose Lieb, O.S.F., Prin. Sisters 5; Lay Teachers 40; Students 512.

[D] HIGH SCHOOLS, PRIVATE

DENVER. *Arrupe Corporate Work-Study Program*, 4343 Utica, 80212. Tel: 303-455-7449; Fax: 303-455-7453. Email: dobrien@arrupejesuit.com. Web: www.arrupejesuit.com. Daniel F. O'Brien, Pres. & Contact Person. Jesuit 1; Lay Staff 4; Total Staff 14; Total Enrollment 65.

Arrupe Jesuit High School, 4343 Utica St., 80212. Tel: 303-455-7449; Fax: 303-455-7453. Email: planningsj@juno.com. Web: www.arrupejesuit.com. Rev. Stephen W. Planning, S.J., Pres. Priests 2; Lay Teachers 4; Volunteers 2; Administrators 6; Volunteers 65.

J.K. Mullen High School, Corp., 3601 S. Lowell Blvd., 80236. Tel: 303-761-1764; Fax: 303-761-0502. Email: schwall@mullen.pvt.k.12.co.us. Linda Brady, Prin.

Legal Title: *The Christian Brothers of J.K. Mullen High School.* Brothers of the Christian Schools, Coed Day School. Brothers 1; Sisters 1; Lay Teachers 61; Students 1,010.

AURORA. *Regis Jesuit High School* Co-Institutional , 16300 E. Weaver Pl., 80016. Tel: 303-269-8000; Fax: 303-766-2240; Tel: 303-221-1048 Girls Div.; Fax: 303-221-4772 Girls Div. Web: www.regisjesuit.comFax: 303-766-2240. Revs. Walter T. Sidney, S.J., Pres. Boys & Girls Division; Carl J. Heumann, S.J., Theology Teacher; John A. Apel, S.J., Supr. of Community; Leo F. Weber, S.J., Asst. to Pres. for Devel.; David A. Wayne, S.J., Dir. of Facilities; Thomas Valliquette, S.J., Faculty Chap.; Mr. Charlie Saulino, Prin., Boys Div.; Friar Leo Weber, Chap. Girls Div.; Ms. Gretchen Kessler, Prin. Girls Div. Day School for Boys.; Day School for Girls. Boys Division: Priests 6; Lay Teachers 58; Students 816; Girls Division: Priests 2; Lay Teachers 19; Students 170.

ENGLEWOOD. *St. Mary's Academy High School*, 4545 S. University Blvd., 80110. Tel: 303-762-8300; Fax: 303-783-6201. Web: www.smanet.org. Judith Baenen, Pres.; Kathryn McNamee, Prin. Sisters of Loretto at the Foot of the Cross Lay Teachers 27; Girls 302.

[E] ELEMENTARY SCHOOLS, PRIVATE

DENVER. *Escuela De Guadalupe Elementary School*, (Grades K-6), 3401 Pecos St., 80211. Tel: 303-964-8456; Fax: 303-964-0755. Email: tonyvigil@escuelaguadalupe.org. Dr. Anthony Vigil, Prin. Lay Teachers 6; Total Staff 9; Students 110.

St. Mary's Academy Lower School, (Grades K-5), 4545 S. University Blvd., 80110. Tel: 303-762-8300; Fax: 303-783-6201. Web: www.smanet.org. Judith Baenen, Pres.; Mary Jane Frederick, Prin.; Jane Hoogerwerf, Asst. Prin. Sisters of Loretto at the Foot of the Cross Sisters 1; Lay Teachers 24; Students 286.

ENGLEWOOD. *St. Mary's Academy, Middle School*, (Grades 6-8), 4545 S. University Blvd., 80110. Tel: 303-762-8300; Fax: 303-783-6201. Web: www.smanet.org. Sr. Denise Ann Clifford, S.L., Prin.; Judith Baenen, Pres. Lay Teachers 14; Students 209.

[F] SPECIAL EDUCATION

DENVER. *The Bridge Community, Inc.*, 3101 W. Hillside Pl., 80219. Tel: 303-935-4740; Fax: 303-935-7795. Email: bridge@myexcel.com. Risha Dimas, Contact Person. Sisters 1; Priests 1; Lay Staff 6; Bed Group Home 8.

Mt. St. Vincent's Home, 4159 Lowell Blvd., 80211. Tel: 303-458-7220; Fax: 303-477-7559. Email: kidsfirst@msvhome.org. Web: www.msvhome.org. Dallas L. Rychener, Exec. Dir. Sisters of Charity of Leavenworth 8; Lay Teachers 5; Students 65; Total Staff 12.

LITTLETON. *Havern Center, Inc.*, 4000 S. Wadsworth Blvd., 80123. Tel: 303-986-4587; Fax: 303-986-0590. Email: cpasquariello@haverncenter.org. Web: www.haverncenter.org. Sr. Barbara Schulte, S.L., Contact Person. Sisters 2; Teachers 26; Students 82.

[G] MINISTRY TO THE HANDICAPPED

DENVER. *The Carron Center*, 1050 S. Birch St., 80222. Tel: 303-759-5150; Fax: 303-759-5694. Email: carycarron@hotmail.com. Mrs. Cary Carron, Supvr.

Special Religious Education-Pastoral Care of Developmentally Disabled Persons, 3101 W. Hillside Pl., 80219. Tel: 303-934-1999; Fax: 303-935-7795. Rev. Roland P. Freeman, Dir.; Sr. Mary Catherine Widger, S.L., Assoc. Dir.; Risha Dimas, Dir. Bridge Community Group Home. Religious education of approximately 400 mentally retarded children and adults; One 8 bed group home

[H] GENERAL HOSPITALS

DENVER. **Centura Health*, 1601 Lowell Blvd., 80204. Tel: 303-825-2190; Fax: 303-899-5160.

Gardens at St. Elizabeth An operating unit of Sisters of Charity Health Services Colorado. , 2835 W. 32nd Ave., 80211. Tel: 303-477-4442; Fax: 303-964-2340.

Centura Senior Life Center, 1601 Lowell Blvd., 80204. Tel: 303-825-2190; Fax: 303-899-5059. An operating unit of Sisters of Charity Health Services Colorado.

Centura Adult Day Care, 4165 Eaton St., 80033. Tel: 303-422-9000. Kris Ordelheide, Senior Vice Pres. General Counsel. An operating unit of Catholic Health Initiatives Mountain Region.

Centura Health St. Anthony Central Hospital, 4231 W. 16th Ave., 80204. Tel: 303-629-4224; Fax: 303-595-6909. Email: bevlilly@centura.org. Beverly Lilly, Contact. An operating unit of Catholic Health Initiatives Mountain Region.

Centura Health St. Anthony Hospital North, 2551 W. 84th Ave., 80030. An operating unit of Catholic Health Initiatives Mountain Region.

Centura Senior Life Center, 1601 Lowell Blvd., 80204. Tel: 303-899-5411; Fax: 303-899-5160. Kris Ordelheide, Senior Vice Pres. General Counsel. An operating unit of Catholic Health Initiatives Mountain Region. Bed Capacity 66.

St. Joseph Hospital, 1835 Franklin St., 80218. Tel: 303-837-7111. Leslie D. Hirsch, Pres. & CEO; Very Rev. James Kleiner, P.V., V.F., Chap.; Revs. Philip Negele, O.C.S.O., Chap.; John Waters, Chap.; Thomas Woerth, Chap. Sisters of Charity of Leavenworth 13; Bed Capacity 565; Patients Assisted Annually 118,000; Outpatients assisted annually 93,300.

Provenant Home Health and Eldercare Services, 1560 Meade St., 80204. Affiliate of Catholic Health Initiatives Mountain Region.

The Villas at Sunny Acres An operating unit of Catholic Health Initiatives Mountain Region. , 2501 E. 104th Ave., 80233. Tel: 303-452-4181; Fax: 303-457-9885. Web: www.centura.org. Independent, Assisted & Nursing Home Total Apartments 283; Bed Capacity 104; Assisted Living 45.

[I] HOMES FOR AGED

DENVER. *St. Andrew's Village at Heather Gardens*, 3300 S. Parker Rd., Ste. 204, Aurora, 80014. Tel: 303-695-8100. Web: www.standrewsccrc.com. Richard O. Campbell Esq., Contact Person. Total Assisted Annually 60; Total Staff 5.

Francis Heights, Inc., 2626 Osceola St., 80212. Tel: 303-433-6268; Fax: 303-455-5359. Web: www.wfs-inc.org. Rev. Declan A. Madden, O.F.M., Chap.; Barry Weaver, Property Mgr. Franciscan Sisters, Daughters of the Sacred Hearts of Jesus and Mary, (Wheaton, IL)., Housing Ministry and Senior Citizens. Housing Units 383; Residents 387.

**Gardens at St. Elizabeth*, 2835 W. 32nd Ave., 80211. Tel: 303-964-2005; Fax: 303-964-2340. Email: jackieleech@centura.org. Web: www.centura.org. Beth Breen, Admin.; Sr. Jacqueline Leech, Chap. Sisters of St. Francis of Colorado Springs (O.S.F.), (Men and Women); An operating unit of Catholic Health Initiatives Mountain Region. Sisters 8; Independent Living 180; Total Assisted Annually 92; Total Staff 100.

Little Sisters of the Poor Mullen Home for the Aged, 3629 W. 29th Ave., 80211. Tel: 303-433-7221; Fax: 303-455-9184. Sr. Mary Michael Nickles, L.S.P., Admin.; Rev. John Murphy, Chap. Little Sisters of the Poor 11; Aged Residents 70; Total Assisted Annually 6; Total Staff 85.

Marycrest Assisted Living, 2850 Columbine Rd., 80221. Tel: 303-433-2276. Email: ppmarycrest@aol.com. Web: www.marycrest.org. Paula Padilla, Contact. Patients Assisted Annually 162.

AURORA. *Congregation of Sisters of Charity of St. Vincent de Paul, Colorado Chapter Inc.*, 3147 S. Pagosa St., 80013. Tel: 303-627-2986; Fax: 303-627-2986. Email: annahome726@hotmail.com. Sr. Julietta Cha, Pres. Total Assisted Annually 4; Total Staff 4.

[J] HOMES AND SERVICES FOR AGED AND INFIRM

DENVER. *Hospice of Peace*, 2420 W. 26th Ave., 200-D, 80211. Tel: 303-561-5100; Fax: 303-561-5050. Email: susietomes@centura.org. Teri Morrison, Dir. Home Hospice Care.

St. Raphael Catholic Center, Inc., 1300 S. Steele St., 80210. Tel: 303-715-2000; Fax: 303-715-2046. David Holden, Sec. of Finance, Administration & Planning. To acquire, develop, maintain, operate and dispose of real and personal property for the purpose of providing retirement, assisted living and long term care facilities for retired priests of the Archdiocese of Denver and other persons.

[K] SPECIAL CARE FACILITIES

DENVER. *Marycrest Assisted Living*, 2850 Columbine Rd., 80221. Tel: 303-433-0282. Email: ppmarycrest@aol.com. Web: www.marycrest.org. Paula Padilla, Contact. Residents 162.

BOULDER. *The Sacred Heart of Jesus Housing Foundation - Dunn Memorial Senior Housing*, 1300 S. Steele St., 80210. Tel: 303-722-4687.

[L] HOUSING FOR THE ELDERLY AND FOR FAMILIES (LOW INCOME)

DENVER. *Archdiocesan Housing Committee*, 1544 Pearl St., 80203. Tel: 303-830-0215; Fax: 303-830-2885. Email: HMSAHCI@qwest.net. Web: www.archdiocesanhousing.org.

Archdiocesan Family Housing, Inc., 1544 Pearl St., 80203. Angela Fletcher, Contact Person. Housing for Low-Income Families.
3700 Humboldt, 80205.
1900 S. Raritan, 80223.
1300 S. Irving, 80219.
800 S. Monaco, 80224.

Cathedral Plaza Inc., 1544 Pearl St., 80203. Tel: 303-837-1424.
Housing for Low-Income Elderly:

Holy Family Plaza, Inc., 1544 Pearl St., 80212. Tel: 303-455-4433.

Marian Plaza, Inc., 1544 Pearl St., 80203. Tel: 303-837-1818.

Higgins Plaza, Inc., 1380 Detroit St., 80206. Tel: 303-320-4990.

Madonna Plaza, Inc., 6275 Kearney St., Commerce City, 80022. Tel: 303-289-2626.

St. Martin Plaza, Inc., 1300 Bruce Randolph Ave., 80205. Tel: 303-297-1414.

Colorado Affordable Catholic Housing Corp., 1544 Pearl St., 80203. Tel: 303-830-0215; Fax: 303-830-2885.

Clare Gardens, Inc., 2626 Osceola St., 80212. Tel: 303-433-6268; Fax: 303-455-5359. Web: www.wfs-inc.org. Rev. Declan A. Madden, O.F.M., Chap.; Sheila Harris, Property Mgr. Franciscan Sisters, Daughters of the Sacred Hearts of Jesus and Mary (Wheaton, IL), Housing Ministry, low-income family units. Housing Units 128; Residents 600.

Damen Project, c/o Sisters of St. Francis, 2851 W. 52nd Ave., 80221-7636. Tel: 303-433-4280; Fax: 303-433-8225. Web: www.damenhouse.org. Shelter and Safehouse for Homeless Women and Children and Day Care Services. Total Staff 12; Total Assisted 125.

Dayspring Villa, Inc., 3777 W. 26th Ave., 80211. Tel: 303-455-5066; Fax: 303-455-8966. Barry Weaver, Admin. Total Assisted 71; Total Staff 34.

Housing Management Services, Inc., 1544 Pearl St., 80203. Tel: 303-830-0215; Fax: 303-830-2885. Email: hmsahci@qwest.net. Anna Strobl, Contact Person.

WESTMINSTER. *Clare of Assisi Homes - Westminster, Inc.*, 2451 W. 82 Pl., 80003. Tel: 303-427-4406; 303-462-9271 (Corporate). Total Staff 5.

Villa Maria, Inc., 2461 W. 82nd Pl., 80031-4065. Tel: 303-427-4406; Fax: 303-412-5771. Total Assisted 40; Total Staff 5.

[M] CATHOLIC CHARITIES & COMMUNITY SERVICES

DENVER. *The Associated Catholic Charities of Colorado*, 2525 W. Alameda Ave., P.O. Box 19020, 80219. Tel: 303-742-0828; Fax: 303-742-0774. Email: mboland@catholiccharitiesden.com. Ms. Mary Boland, Exec. Dir.

The Associated Catholic Charities of Colorado, 2525 W. Alameda Ave., P.O. Box 19020, 80219. Tel: 303-742-0828; Fax: 303-742-0774. Email: mboland@catholiccharitiesden.com. Ms. Mary Boland, Exec. Dir.

Catholic Charities and Community Services of the Archdiocese of Denver, Inc., 2525 W. Alameda Ave., 80219. Tel: 303-742-0828; Fax: 303-742-0774. Email: info@catholiccharitiesden.com. Web: www.catholiccharitiesdenver.org. James H. Mauck, Pres., Admin. Day Care Centers 11; Total Assisted 750; Special Centers for Social Services 22; Total Assisted 124,000.

Samaritan House Shelter for Homeless , 2301 Lawrence St., 80205. Tel: 303-294-0241; Fax: 303-294-9523.
Transitional Housing

Courtyard Commons, 1122 Pearl St., #1-A, 80203. Tel: 303-860-9098; Fax: 303-832-1790.

Lowry Housing, 1445 Emporia St., Aurora, 80010. Tel: 303-360-9686; Fax: 303-742-0774.

The Carron Center, For persons with disabilities. 3801 Florida Ave., # 208, 80210. Tel: 303-759-5150. Services for Developmentally Disabled Adults and Ministry to deaf persons.
Child Care Centers:

Early Learning Center, 4440 Navajo St., 80211. Tel: 303-477-7610; Fax: 303-477-7664.

Catholic Charities Margery Reed Mayo Child Care Center, 1128 28th St., 80205. Tel: 303-308-1420; Fax: 303-308-1421.

Catholic Charities Child Development Center, 1155 Decatur St., 80204. Tel: 303-629-5466; Fax: 303-629-6710.

Garfield Child Care, 872 S. Knox Ct., 80219. Tel: 303-922-9453.

Carino Child Care, 1580 Julian St., 80204. Tel: 303-742-0828.

Family Services Center, 2525 W. Alameda Ave., 80219. Tel: 303-742-0828; Fax: 303-742-4373. Counseling, Adoption, Foster Care & Senior Services.

Camp Santa Maria, 2525 W. Alameda Ave., 80219. Tel: 303-742-0828; Fax: 303-742-4410. Camping for Children, Youth & Seniors.

Catholic Charities Head Start Services Shelter for Homeless , 2525 W. Alameda Ave., 80219. Tel: 303-742-0828; Fax: 303-742-4410.

Plaza del Milagro Child Care Migrant Farm Workers Child Care. , 2500 1st Ave., Bldg. CC, Greeley, 80631. Tel: 970-346-2897.

Immigration Services, 2525 W. Alameda Ave., 80219. Tel: 303-742-0828; Fax: 303-742-4410.

Immigration Services, Western Slope, 1010 Grand Ave., Glenwood Springs, 81601. Tel: 970-384-2060.

Immigration Services, Northern, 2500 1st Ave., Bldg. CB, Greeley, 80631. Tel: 970-353-6433.

Employment Resource Center, 2301 Lawrence St., 80205. Tel: 303-294-0241; Fax: 303-742-4410.

SHARE Colorado, 9360 Federal Blvd., Federal Heights, 80221. Tel: 303-428-0400; Fax: 303-427-4440.

Food Bank Partners, 9360 Federal Blvd., Federal Heights, 80221. Tel: 303-303-0400; Fax: 303-427-4440.

Homeless Prevention Services, 2525 W. Alameda Ave., 80219. Tel: 303-742-0828; Fax: 303-742-1181.

Catholic Charities Northern-Fort Collins, 460 Linden Center Dr., Fort Collins, 80524. Tel: 970-484-5010; Fax: 970-484-0259. Shelter for Homeless, Job Bank, Emergency Assistance, Senior Services & Farm Labor Housing Corp.

Catholic Charities Northern - Greeley, 1311 11th St., Greeley, 80631. Tel: 970-353-6433; Fax: 970-353-3861. Shelter for the Homeless & Senior Services.

Plaza del Milagro, Child Care Center, 2500 1st Ave., #CB, Greeley, 80631. Tel: 970-353-6433; Fax: 970-353-3861.

Catholic Charities - Western Slope, 1010 Grand Ave., Glenwood Springs, 81601. Tel: 970-384-2060; Fax: 970-945-2089.

Aurora Family Assistance Center, 1468 Iola St., Aurora, 80010. Tel: 303-363-9543; Fax: 303-363-9544.

North Area Cares Emergency Assistance, 7280-A Irving, #106-A, Westminster, 80030. Tel: 303-427-6256; Fax: 303-650-9551.

Northeast E.A. Center, 6621 E.72nd Ave., Commerce City, 80022. Tel: 303-287-1127; Fax: 303-287-1153.

Central Emergency Assistance Center, 1440 Poplar St., 80220. Tel: 303-399-1558; Fax: 303-393-1560.

Southwest Emergency Assistance Center, 902 S. Sheridan Blvd., 80601. Tel: 303-922-5205; Fax: 303-922-5048.

Plaza del Milagro, Farm Labor Housing, 2500 1st Ave., #CC, Greeley, 80631. Tel: 970-353-6433.

Brighton Emergency Assistance Center, 178 S. Sixth St., Brighton, 80601. Tel: 303-654-1040; Fax: 303-654-1003.

[N] MONASTERIES AND RESIDENCES OF PRIESTS AND BROTHERS

DENVER. *Annunciation Friary*, 3621 Humboldt St., 80205. Tel: 303-296-1024.

The Community of the Beatitudes, 2924 W. 43rd Ave., 80211. Tel: 720-855-9412; Fax: 509-275-1658. Email: info@beatitudes.us. Web: beatitudes.us. Christian Meert, Dir.; Friars Jose Sanchez; Seraphim; Agnieszka.

Congregation of the Mission Midwest Province: De Paul House, 2340 S. University Blvd., 80210. Tel: 303-705-9123; Fax: 303-777-0468. Revs. Paul L. Golden, C.M.; John H. Karssen, C.M.; Richard R. Ryan, C.M.; E. Hartrick Sullivan, C.M.; Thomas J. Nelson, C.M.; Prudencio Rodriguez de Yurre,

C.M.; Robert A. Schwane, C.M., Supr.

St. Francis of Assisi Friary, 3553 Wyandot St., 80211-2948. Tel: 303-477-5542; Fax: 303-477-6925. Email: stfrancis@midamcaps.org. Total in Residence 7; Total Staff 1. In Res. Revs. Harvey P. Dinkel, O.F.M.Cap., Vicar, Exec. Sec. & Treas.; Thomas More Janeck, O.F.M.Cap.; John Lager, O.F.M.Cap., Dir. Devel.; Regis Scanlon, O.F.M.Cap.; Very Rev. Michael Scully, O.F.M.Cap., Prov. Min.; Bros. Eugene Pellegrino, O.F.M.Cap.; Mark Schenk, O.F.M.Cap., Guardian.

Fraternidad San Antonio, 3554 Humboldt St., 80205-3940. Tel: 303-292-5110; Fax: 303-292-5148. In Res. Revs. Cyrus Gallagher, O.F.M.Cap.; Malachy McBride, O.F.M.Cap.; David Songy, O.F.M.Cap., Guardian; Michael Suchnicki, O.F.M.Cap.; John Toepfer, O.F.M.Cap., Vicar.

Loyola Parish - Jesuit Community, 2309 Gaylord St., 80205-5627. Tel: 303-322-8042; Fax: 303-322-2927. Revs. C. Thomas Jost, S.J.; John F. Brady, S.J.; Frank J. Schmitt, S.J.; Kevin L. Cullen, S.J.; Joseph Tuoc Nguyen, S.J.

Maryknoll Fathers and Brothers, 4460 Federal Blvd., 80211. Tel: 303-455-5669; Fax: 303-455-5753. Email: mkldenver@aol.org. Web: www.maryknoll.org. Revs. Charles J. McPadden, M.M. (NY); Thomas J. Marti, M.M. (NY), Dir.
Legal Title: *Catholic Foreign Mission Society of America*

The Redemptorists/Denver Province (1996), Provincial Residence, Box 300399, 80203-0399. Tel: 303-370-0035; Fax: 303-370-0036. Web: www.redemptorists-denver.org.
Res.: 2130 E. Fourteenth Ave., 80206. Very Rev. Richard Thibodeau, C.SS.R., Prov. Supr.; Revs. Peter Connolly, C.SS.R., Prov. Vicar; Paul Coury, C.SS.R., Prov. Consultor; Lawrence Sanders, C.SS.R., Office Fin. Svcs.; Bro. Thomas Wright, C.SS.R., Office Fin. Svcs. Total in Community: Priests 150; Deacons 2; Brothers 26.
Serving abroad:
Residencia do Bispro C.P.531 83203-970, PR, Brazil. Tel: 55-41-422-7717; Fax: 55-41-422-7717. Most Rev. Alfred Novak, C.SS.R.
Casa Sant'Alfonso, C.P. 2458, 00100 Rome, Italy. Tel: 39-06-49490-1; Fax: 39-06-44660-12. Very Rev. Joseph W. Tobin, C.SS.R., Supr. Gen.
Klm 8 Ifc Rd., P.O. Box 29585 Secretariat, Kolodi Village, Ibadan, Oyo State, Nigeria. Tel: 234-2-241-3040; Fax: 234-2-810-1401. Revs. William Cleary, C.SS.R.; William A. Peterson, C.SS.R.; Richard Thiele, C.SS.R.; Robert Wirth, C.SS.R.
C.P. 400, 48900 Juazeiro, Bahia Brazil. Rev. William Fitzgerald, C.SS.R.
Serving elsewhere, not listed:
Nazareth House, 2121 N. 1st St., Fresno, CA 93703. Rev. Pascal Drieci.
Loyalton #39, 205 E. Anton, Coeur D Alene, ID 83815. Tel: 208-659-8511. Rev. George Rassley, C.SS.R.
P.O. Box 1209, Coeur D Alene, ID 83816. Tel: 208-765-1894; Fax: 208-666-1593. Bro. William Green, C.SS.R.
3662 S. 7th Ave., Tucson, AZ 85713-6115. Tel: 520-206-9772. Rev. Ricardo Elford, C.SS.R.
C.P. 2458, Roma 1-00100 Italy. Tel 011 39 06 49 490 1. Rev. Joseph Dorcey, C.SS.R.
Gubernium Generale C.SS.R., C.P. 2458, Roma 1-00100 Italy. Tel: 011 39 06 49 490 1.
The Redemptorists of Denver, Colorado, 605 W. 6th Ave., 80204. Tel: 303-825-8371; Fax: 303-534-4412. Revs. Kyle Fisher, C.SS.R., Supr.; Albert Castellino, C.SS.R.; Steven Nyl, C.SS.R.; Timothy Watson, C.SS.R.; Bro. Laurence Lujan, C.SS.R.

Regis Jesuit Community (The Jesuits at Regis University), Jesuit House M12, 3333 Regis Blvd., 80221-1099. Tel: 303-458-4100; Fax: 303-964-5525. Revs. James B. Guyer, S.J., Rector; David M. Clarke, S.J.; J. Daniel Daly, S.J.; Donald E. Highberger, S.J.; Edward L. Maginnis, S.J.; Edward T. Oakes, S.J.; John K. Ridgway, S.J.; Michael J. Sheeran, S.J.; Charles M. Shelton, S.J.; John P. Teeling, S.J.

Xavier Jesuit Center, 3450 W. 53rd, 80221-6568. Tel: 303-480-3900; Fax: 303-480-3919. Revs. John J. Waters, S.J., Supr.; Richard F. Bocklage, S.J.; Joseph F. Bona, S.J.; John J. Campbell, S.J.; John R. Daly, S.J.; Robert R. DeRouen, S.J.; Edward F. Flaherty, S.J.; John C. Futrell, S.J.; Harry E. Hoewischer, S.J.; J. Timothy Lawless, S.J.; Tuan Q. Le, S.J.; William T. Miller, S.J.; Anthony J. Short, S.J.; James C. Sunderland, S.J.; William S. Udick, S.J.; James P. Walsh, S.J.; William W. Williams, S.J., Min.

CENTENNIAL. *Regis High Jesuit Community*, 16810 E. Caley Ave., 80016-1005. Tel: 303-690-4782; Fax: 303-680-7662. Revs. John Apel, S.J.; Walter T. Sidney, S.J.; David A. Wayne, S.J.; Thomas M. Valiquette, S.J.; Leo F. Weber, S.J.; Carl J. Heumann, S.J.

SNOWMASS. *St. Benedict's Monastery*, 1012 Monastery Rd., 81654. Tel: 970-927-3311; Fax: 970-927-3399. Email: retreat@rof.net. Web: www.snowmass.org. Rt. Rev. Joseph Boyle, O.C.S.O.; Revs. Thomas Keating, O.C.S.O.; Theophane Boyd, O.C.S.O.; William Meninger, O.C.S.O. The Order of Cistercians of the Strict Observance (Trappists) Professed Monks 11; Novices 1.

[O] CONVENTS AND RESIDENCES FOR SISTERS

DENVER. *Dominican Sisters of Hope*, 2501 Gaylord St., 80205. Tel: 303-322-1413, Ext. 11; Fax 303-322-2702. Web: www.dominicansisters.org. Sr. Marie Therese McGath, O.P., Contact. Dominican Sisters Home Health Agency of Denver, Inc. Served 105 patients. Sisters 3.

**Hermanas Josefinas, O.D.C.*, Provincial House, 4358 Utica St., 80212. Sisters Maria C. Barba, Prov. Supr.; Genoveva Romero Martinez, H.J., Contact Person. (Josephine Sisters)

Marycrest Convent Franciscan Sisters, 2851 W. 52nd Ave., 80221. Tel: 303-458-6270; Fax: 303-477-4105. Email: sartfri@marycrest.org. Web: www.marycrest.org. Sisters Karen Crouse, Prov. Min.; Alicia Cuaron, Min. Special Center for Social Assistance.; Retreat and Conference Center. Sisters in the Province 63; Total in Res. 6; Total Assisted 2,970; Total Staff 2; Total Serviced 2,700.

Missionaries of Charity, 1840 Grant St., 80203. Tel: 303-860-8040. Sr. M. Vincenta, M.C., Supr. & Contact. AIDS Home for 15 People. Total Assisted 37.

Monastery of Our Lady of Light (Capuchin Poor Clares) (Strict Enclosure) , 3325 Pecos, 80211. Tel: 303-458-6339; Fax: 303-477-4924. Email: capclares1@aol.com. Sr. Maria De Jesus Armadillo, Abbess; Rev. Thomas More Janeck, O.F.M.Cap., Chap.
Legal Title: *Capuchin Poor Clares of Denver, Inc.* Sisters 9.

Our Lady of Mercy Convent, Religious Sisters of Mercy, 1330 S. Steele St., 80210. Tel: 303-765-4592; Fax: 303-765-4595. Email: vocation@rsmofalma.org. Web: rsmofalma.org. Sr. Mary Judith O'Brien, R.S.M., Local Supr. Religious Sisters of Mercy (Alma, Michigan) Sisters 6.

Queen of Peace Convent, 5360 Columbine Rd., 80221-1277. Tel: 303-477-9139. Web: www.marycrest.org. Sisters of St. Francis of Penance and Christian Charity Sisters 5.

GOLDEN. *Mother Cabrini Shrine*, 20189 Cabrini Blvd., 80401. Tel: 303-526-0758; Fax: 303-526-9795. Email: mcshrine@den-cabrini-shrine.org. Web: www.den-cabrini-shrine.org. Sr. Bernadette Casciano, M.S.C., Contact; Thomas M. James, Registered Agent. Missionary Sisters of the Sacred Heart of Jesus(M.S.C.) 4.

LITTLETON. *Carmel of Holy Spirit*, 6138 S. Gallup St., 80120-2702. Tel: 303-798-4176. Sr. Judith of the Immaculate Heart, D.C., Prioress. Discalced Carmelites (O.C.D.) Sisters 10.

Loretto Center, 4000 S. Wadsworth 80123-1309. Tel: 303-986-1541; Fax: 303-795-2378. Email: judiosb@aol.com. Sr. Ann Lucille Ryan, S.L., Coord. Sisters 31.

Sisters of Benedict of Colorado, Inc., 4264 W. Ponds View Dr., 80123. Tel: 303-795-2378. Email: judiosb@aol.com. Sr. Judith Elms, O.S.B., Supr.

VIRGINIA DALE. *Abbey of St. Walburga*, 32109 N. U.S. Hwy. 287, 80536-8942. Tel: 970-472-0612; Fax: 970-484-4342. Email: abbey@walburga.org. Web: www.walburga.org. Sr. Maria Michael, O.S.B., Abbess. Benedictine Nuns 17; Novices 2.

[P] RETREAT CENTERS

ALLENSPARK. *Camp St. Malo Religious Retreat and Conference Center*, 10758 Hwy 7, 80510. Tel: 303-747-0201; Fax: 303-747-2892. Email: malo@webaccess.net. Web: www.saintmalo.org. Jose Ambrozic, Dir.

LITTLETON. *Jesus Our Hope Hermitage*, 10519 S. Deer Creek Rd., 80127. Tel: 303-697-7539; Fax: 303-697-7539. Email: jesus_our_hope@att.net. Sr. Marie Joann Rekart, S.L., Contact.

[Q] CAMPUS MINISTRY

DENVER. *Christian Life Movement, Inc.* 1060 St. Francis Way, 80204. Tel: 303-629-5100; Fax: 303-629-5101. Email: denverclm@aol.com. Daniela Neuenschwander, Contact Person.

Director of Campus Ministry 1300 S. Steele St., 80210. Tel: 303-715-3203; Fax: 303-715-2042. Email: onfire@archden.org. Web: www.archden.org.

Regis University (Denver) 3333 Regis Blvd., Ste. 200, 80221. Tel: 303-458-4153; Fax: 303-964-5530. Email: mschaefe@regis.edu. Mrs. Kathleen Schaefer, Dir.; Mr. Ken Phillips, Dir.

University of Denver Catholic Campus Ministry House, 1795 S. Williams St., 80210. Tel: 303-778-7657. Sr. Maria Regis, S.C.J.

BOULDER. *University of Colorado (Boulder)* St. Thomas Aquinas Parish, 904 Fourteenth St., 80302. Tel: 303-443-8383; Fax: 303-443-8399. Web: www.sttoms.org. Revs. Thomas J. Holahan, C.S.P.; Paul D. Huesing, C.S.P.; David P. Dwyer, C.S.P.; Ms. Diana Ahroush, Campus Ministry Coord.; Ms. Kathleen Ahl, Liturgy Coordinator; Ms. Myrna Deemy, Music Dir.; Sr. Carole Frances Miller, S.S.N.D., Faith Formation Dir.

FORT COLLINS. *Colorado State University (Fort Collins)* John XXIII University Center, 1220 University Ave., 80521-4555. Tel: 303-484-3356; Fax: 303-484-3434. Email: john23@webaccess.net. Web: www.john23.com. Rev. Donald C. Willette; Ms. Rachel Hoch; Ms. Pegge Bernecker; Dr. Joachim Viens, S.T.D.

Resident Catholic Theologian Program John XXIII University Ctr., 1200 University Ave., 80521. Tel: 970-493-8984; Fax: 970-484-3434. Email: jviens@lamar.colostate.edu. Web: www.john23.com. Dr. Joachim Viens, S.T.L., Ed.D., Dir.

GOLDEN. *Colorado School of Mines (Golden)* 15755 W. 3rd Ave., 80401. Tel: 303-273-3460. Mr. Edward Mantz.

GREELEY. *Fellowship of Catholic University Students (FOCUS)* P.O. Box 1210, 80632. Tel: 970-336-9881; Fax: 970-336-1167. Email: info@focusonline.org. Web: www.focusonline.org. Katherine Manak, CFO.

University of Northern Colorado (Greeley) St. Peter's Parish, 915 12th St., 80631. Tel: 970-352-1060; Fax: 970-352-1062. Rev. Roco Portor.

RANGELY. *Colorado Northwestern Community College (Rangely)* 109 S. Stanolind Ave., P.O. Box 370, 81648. Tel: 303-675-8935; Fax: 303-878-5736 (Meeker). Rev. Roger L. Lascelle; Deacon George G. Fortunato.

STEAMBOAT SPRINGS. *Colorado Mountain College* . Tel: 970-879-0671; Fax: 970-879-7406. Email: holyname@holynamecc.org. Web: www.holynamecc.org. Rev. Msgr. George M. Schroeder.

STERLING. *Northeastern Junior College (Sterling)* St. Anthony Church, 326 S. Third St., 80751. Tel: 970-522-6422. Very Rev. James R. Baird, V.F.

WESTMINSTER. *Front Range Community College* c/o Mr. Frank Sullivan, 3645 W. 112 Ave., 80030. Tel: 303-404-5282; Fax: 303-404-2178. Email: fsulliva@ophir.frcc.cccoes.edu. Web: frcc.cc.co.us.

[R] ASSOCIATIONS OF CONSECRATED LIFE

WHEAT RIDGE. *Marian Community of Reconciliation*, 1060 St. Francis Way, 80204. Tel: 303-629-0500; Fax: 303-629-5101. Email: mcrdenver@aol.com. Rossana Goni, Contact Person.

[S] MISCELLANEOUS LISTINGS

DENVER. *St. Anthony Health Foundation*, 4231 W. 16th Ave., 80204. Tel: 303-629-4446. Paul Brewster, Exec. Dir. An operating unit of Catholic Health Initiatives Colorado Foundation.

Archdiocesan of Denver Management Co., 1300 S. Steele St., 80210. Tel: 303-715-3258; Fax: 303-715-2046.

The Archdiocese of Denver Cemeteries Perpetual Care Trust, 1300 S. Steele St., 80210. Tel: 303-715-3258; Fax: 303-715-2046. David Holden, Contact Person.

The Archdiocese of Denver Irrevocable Revolving Trust Agreement, 1300 S. Steele St., 80210. Tel: 303-715-3258; Fax: 303-715-2046.

The Archdiocese of Denver Risk Management Property/Casualty Insurance Trust, 1300 S. Steele St., 80210. Tel: 303-715-3150; Fax: 303-715-2041. Email: rosemary.nelson@arch.den.org.

The Archdiocese of Denver Welfare Benefits Trust, 1300 S. Steele St., 80210. Tel: 303-715-3133; Fax: 303-715-2041.

Association for Catholic Information, 1060 St. Francis Way, 80204. Tel: 303-747-0209. Email: jorgeluna@multimedios.org. Web: www.catholicnewsagency.com. Bro. Jorge S. Luna Diaz del Olmo.

Bishop Machebeuf High School, Inc., 1300 S. Steele St., 80210. Tel: 303-715-3263; Fax: 303-715-2043. Email: Vicargen@archden.org.

Blessed Sacrament Catholic Educational Foundation, 4930 Montview Blvd., 80207. Tel: 303-355-7361; Fax: 303-355-0894. Rev. Kenneth Liuzzi, Exec. Officer & Contact Person.

Camp St. Malo Religious Retreat and Conference Center, Inc., 1300 S. Steele St., 80210. Tel: 303-747-0201; Fax: 303-747-2892. Web: www.saintmalo.org.

Catholic Alumni Club of Colorado, P.O. Box 6111, Cherry Creek Station, 80206. Tel: 303-477-3572. Email: cacofco@hotmail.com.

The Catholic Foundation for the Archdiocese of Denver, 1300 S. Steele St., 80210. Tel: 303-722-4687; Fax: 303-715-2046. Email:

catholic.foundation@archden.org. John F. Dolan, Pres.

Catholic Health Initiatives, 1999 Broadway, Ste. 2600, 80202. Tel: 303-298-9100; Fax: 303-298-9690. Email: peggymartin@catholichealth.net. Web: www.catholichealthinit.org. Kevin E. Lofton, Pres. & CEO; Sr. Peggy Ann Martin, O.P., J.C.L., Contact.

**Colorado Vincentian Volunteers*, 1732 Pearl St., 80203. Tel: 303-863-8141; Fax: 303-863-8141. Email: cvv@covivo.org. Web: www.covivo.org. Bill or Mary Frances Jaster, Dir.

Decatur Place, 601 E. 18th Ave., Ste. 150, 80203. Tel: 303-830-3300; Fax: 303-830-3301. Web: www.mercyhousing.org. Brendalee Connors, Contact; Lillian Murphy, R.S.M., Pres.

Denver Catholic Register, Archdiocesan Religious Newspaper, 1300 S. Steele St., 80210. Tel: 303-715-3123. Sergio Gutierrez, Gen. Mgr.

ENDOW, 1300 S. Steele St., 80210. Tel: 303-715-3233. Email: terry.polakovic@archden.org. Ms. Therese A. Polakovic, Exec. Dir.

Family of Nazareth, Inc., 3434 E. Arizona Ave., 80210. Tel: 303-758-1280; Fax: 303-758-1380. Email: steve.waymel@trippak.com. Donald McCleod, Contact Person.

Franciscan Sisters Charitable Fund of Colorado, Inc., 2626 Osceola St., 80212. Tel: 303-433-6268; Fax: 303-455-5359. Email: theresalan@cmconline.com. Sr. Theresa Langfield, O.S.F., Pres. & Admin. Franciscan Sisters, Daughters of the Sacred Heart of Jesus and Mary, (Wheaton, IL)

Health S.E.T., Raleigh Bldg., 4200 N. Conejos #436, 80204-1312. Tel: 303-595-6633; Fax: 303-595-6645. Web: www.healthset.org. Total Staff 13; Total Volunteers 130; Total Assisted 6,000.

Hmong Catholic Community, All Saints Parish, 2559 S. Federal Blvd., 80219. Tel: 303-922-3758; 303-429-6427; Fax: 303-922-3750. Lo Fong Chang, Contact.

Holy Family High School, Inc., 1300 S. Steele St., 80210. Tel: 303-715-3263; Fax: 303-715-2043. Email: Vicargen@archden.org.

Saint Joseph Hospital Foundation, 1835 Franklin St., 80218. Tel: 303-837-7043; Fax: 303-837-7115. Email: unrein@exempla.org. Web: www.sjhfdenver.org. Carl Unrein, Pres. & CEO.

Kateri Catholic Indian Community of Colorado, 2340 S. University Blvd #32, 80210. Tel: 303-778-5966. Email: quentin@priest.com. Rev. John Q. O'Connell, C.M.

Marycrest Franciscan Ministries, Formerly Marycrest Health System2861 W. 52nd Ave., 80221-7636. Tel: 303-458-6270; Fax: 303-477-4105. Sisters Gloria Shuffer, O.S.F., Pres.; Susan Artone-Fricke, Contact Person.

Mercy Housing, Inc., 601 E. 18th Ave., Ste. 150, 80203. Tel: 303-830-3300; Fax: 303-830-3301. Email: mail@mercyhousing.org. Web: BHConline.org/mercyhousing. Sr. Lillian Murphy, Pres. Affordable Housing Properties. Units 570; Total Served 1,378; Day Care Centers 3; Total Served 334.

Mercy Services Corp., 601 E. 18th Ave., Ste. 150, 80203. Tel: 303-830-3300; Fax: 303-830-3301. Charles Hoag, Pres.

Homes Again Program, 601 E. 18th Ave., Ste. 150, 80203. Tel: 303-830-3300; Fax: 303-830-3301. Chuck Wehrwein, Vice Pres. Gen. Partner.

Mercy Housing Colorado, 601 E. 18th Ave., Ste. 150, 80203. Tel: 303-830-3300; Fax: 303-830-3301. Chuck Wehrwein, Vice Pres.

Mercy Properties, Inc., 601 E. 18th Ave., Ste. 150, 80203. Tel: 303-830-3397; Fax: 303-830-3301. Lillian Murphy, R.S.M., Pres.

Willow Street Apartments, 601 E. 18th Ave., Ste. 150, 80203. Tel: 303-830-3397. Chuck Wehrwein, Contact.

Mercy Holly Park East, 601 E. 18th Ave., Ste. 150, 80203. Tel: 303-830-3397; Fax: 303-830-3301. Chuck Wehrwein, Contact.

Mercy Holly Park West, 601 E. 18th Ave., Ste. 150, 80203. Tel: 303-830-3397; Fax: 303-830-3301. Chuck Wehrwein, Contact.

Our Lady of the New Advent Theological Institute, 1300 S. Steele St., 80210. Tel: 303-282-3427; Fax: 303-282-3453. Email: menagallegos@archden.org. Mena Gallegos, Contact.

Redemptorist Fathers (Idaho), *c/o The Redemptorists/Denver Province*, P.O. Box 300399, 80203-0399. Tel: 303-370-0035; Fax: 303-370-0036. Rev. Peter Connolly, Prov. Vicar.

Redemptorist Fathers (Idaho), P.O. Box 300399, 80203-0399. Tel: 303-370-0035; Fax: 303-370-0036. Rev. Peter Connolly, Prov. Vicar.

The Redemptorist of Greeley, Colorado, Inc., c/o The Redemptorist, Denver Province, P.O. Box 300 399, 80203-0399. Tel: 303-370-0035; Fax: 303-370-0036.

Redemptorist Society of Alaska, c/o The Redemptorist/Denver Province, P.O. Box 300 399, 80203-0399. Tel: 303-370-0035; Fax: 303-370-0036.

Redemptorist Society of Iowa, c/o The Redemptorists/Denver Province, P.O. Box 300399, 80203-0399. Tel: 303-370-0035; Fax: 303-370-0036. Rev. Peter Connolly, Prov. Vicar.

Redemptorist Society of Oregon, c/o The Redemptorists/Denver Province, P.O. Box 300399, 80203-0399. Tel: 303-370-0035; Fax: 303-370-0036.

Sacred Heart House of Denver, 2844 Lawrence St., 80205. Tel: 303-296-6686; Fax: 303-296-2903. Web: sacredhearthouse.org. Ms. Janet L. Morris, Exec. Dir.

Seeds of Hope Charitable Trust, 1300 S. Steele St., 80210. Tel: 303-715-3127; Fax: 303-715-2042. Email: seeds@archden.org. Web: www.seedsofhopetrust.org. Laurie A. Vieira, Exec. Dir.; Debbie Lovill, Contact Person.

St. Vincent de Paul Stores, Inc., Administration: 2525 W. Alameda Ave., 80219. Tel: 303-742-0828; Fax: 303-742-0774. . Tel: 303-388-3315. . Tel: 303-750-2604. . Tel: 303-781-5819. Mr. James Mauck, CEO.

7100 E. Colfax Ave.. Tel: 303-388-3315.

10015 E. Hampton Ave.. Tel: 303-750-2604.

2795 S. Broadway. Tel: 303-781-5819.

St. Vincent DePaul Society Denver-Metro Council, 2560 S. Grove St., 80219-5814. Tel: 303-922-4430; Fax: 303-922-3750. Chance Christie, Pres.; Robert S. Huff, Exec. Sec.

ARVADA. **Buena Vista, Inc.*, P.O. Box 745475, 80006-5475. Tel: 303-477-0180. Email: br@buenavista.org. Web: www.buenavista.org. Amy Sheber Howard, Natl. Coord.; William Breay, Admin. Asst. to the Board.

BOULDER. *Sacred Heart School Foundation*, 2312 14th St., 80304. Tel: 303-444-3478; Fax: 303-444-3057. Email: timeileen@msn.com. Mr. Tim Mullen, Contact.

CENTENNIAL. *LC Pastoral Services Inc.*, 8077 S. Quince Cir., 80122. Tel: 303-689-9932; Fax: 303-689-9932. Rev. Daniel Polzer, L.C., Dir.

The Padre, Inc., 8035 S. Quebec St., 80112. Tel: 303-770-1155. Mary Hendricks, Contact.

ENGLEWOOD. *Catholic Health Initiatives Colorado*, 5570 DTC Pkwy., 80111. Tel: 303-290-6500; Fax: 303-290-6699. Mr. Joseph R. Swedish, Pres. & CEO; Susan Lindsay, Contact.

Queen of the Apostles Mission Association, Inc., 2375 E. Arizona Ave., 80210Web: www.qama.org. Matt Werner, Pres.

ESTES PARK. **Our Lady of Tenderness, Poustinia*, Box 4311, 80517. Tel: 970-577-1383. Web: www.ourladyoftenderness.org. Lucille Dupuis, Dir.

FORT COLLINS. *West African Development Support Organization*, 3124 Appaloosa Ct., 80526. Email: steveh@webaccess.net. Rev. Donald Willette; Cindy Lloyd, Pres.; Steve Henry, Contact Person.

GREELEY. *Catholic Educators Resource Center, U.S.A.*, 2414 W. 15th St., 80634-6413. Tel: 604-485-0561. Email: info@catholiceducation.org. John Helecek, Contact; J. Fraser Field, Exec. Officer.

St. Mary's Catholic Education Foundation Greeley, 2222 23rd Ave., 80634. Tel: 970-352-1724; Fax: 970-352-1729. Email: benke99714@yahoo.com. Susan Benke, Contact.

RELIGIOUS INSTITUTES OF MEN REPRESENTED IN THE ARCHDIOCESE

For further details refer to the corresponding bracketed number in the Religious Institutes of Men or Women section.

[0200]—*Benedictine Monks* (Canon City, CO)—O.S.B.
[]—*Bethlehem Fathers*—S.M.B.
[0330]—*Brothers of the Christian Schools*—F.S.C.
[0460]—*Brothers of the Poor of St. Francis*—C.F.P.
[0470]—*The Capuchin Friars* (Denver, CO)—O.F.M.Cap.
[0350]—*Cistercians of the Strict Observance-Trappists* (St. Benedict Abbey)—O.C.S.O.
[]—*Congregation of Mother Coredemptrix* (Carthage, MO)—C.M.C.
[1330]—*Congregation of the Mission* (Western Prov.)—C.M.
[]—*Cor Jesu (Societas Cordis Jesu, Fontis Vitae et Sanctitatis)*
[0520]—*Franciscan Friars* (Provs. of the Most Holy Name of Jesus & Our Lady of Guadalupe)—O.F.M.
[0690]—*Jesuit Fathers and Brothers* (Missouri, Milwaukee, Oregon, Maryland Provs.)—S.J.
[0800]—*Maryknoll* (Denver)—M.M.
[0430]—*Order of Preachers-Dominicans* (Prov. of St. Albert the Great)—O.P.
[1030]—*Paulist Fathers*—C.S.P.
[1070]—*Redemptorist Fathers* (St. Louis Prov.)—C.SS.R.
[1240]—*Servites* (Western Prov.)—O.S.M.
[1300]—*Theatine Fathers* (Rome, Italy)—C.R.

RELIGIOUS INSTITUTES OF WOMEN REPRESENTED IN THE ARCHDIOCESE

[0190]—*Benedictine Nuns*—O.S.B.
[0230]—*Benedictine Sisters of Pontifical Jurisdiction* (Colorado Springs, CO; Boulder, CO; Denver, CO; Oklahoma City, OK)—O.S.B.
[]—*Capuchin Poor Clares*—O.S.C.Cap.
[3110]—*Congregation of Our Lady of the Retreat in the Cenacle*—R.C.
[2100]—*Congregation of the Humility of Mary* (Davenport, IA)—C.H.M.
[1780]—*Congregation of the Sisters of the Third Order of St. Francis of Perpetual Adoration* (La Crosse, WI)—F.S.P.A.
[0760]—*Daughters of Charity of St. Vincent de Paul*—D.C.
[0960]—*Daughters of Wisdom*—D.W.
[0420]—*Discalced Carmelite Nuns*—O.C.D.
[1070-14]—*Dominican Sisters*—O.P.
[1070-24]—*Dominican Sisters*—O.P.
[1070-28]—*Dominican Sisters*—O.P.
[1070-18]—*Dominican Sisters*—O.P.
[1070-03]—*Dominican Sisters* (Sinsinawa)—O.P.
[1070-16]—*Dominican Sisters*—O.P.
[]—*Dominican Sisters of the Congregation of St. Cecilia* (Nashville)
[1240]—*Franciscan Sisters, Daughters of the Sacred Hearts of Jesus and Mary* (Wheaton, IL)—O.S.F.
[2575]—*Institute of the Sisters of Mercy of the Americas*—R.S.M.
[2340]—*Little Sisters of the Poor*—L.S.P.
[2710]—*Missionaries of Charity*—M.C.
[]—*Missionaries of Charity of Mary Immaculate*—M.C.M.I.
[2860]—*Missionary Sisters of the Sacred Heart*—M.S.C.
[3130]—*Our Lady of Victory Missionary Sisters*—O.L.V.M.
[1680]—*School Sisters of St. Francis* (Milwaukee, WI)—O.S.F.
[0440]—*Sisters of Charity of Cincinnati, Ohio*—S.C.
[0480]—*Sisters of Charity of Leavenworth, Kansas*—S.C.L.
[0430]—*Sisters of Charity of the Blessed Virgin Mary*—B.V.M.
[2360]—*Sisters of Loretto at the Foot of the Cross* (Nerinx, KY)—S.L.
[2990]—*Sisters of Notre Dame*—S.N.D.
[1705]—*Sisters of St. Francis of Assisi* (Milwaukee, WI)—O.S.F.
[1630]—*Sisters of St. Francis of Penance and Christian Charity*—O.S.F.
[1640]—*Sisters of St. Francis of Perpetual Adoration* (Colorado Springs, CO)—O.S.F.
[3830-05]—*Sisters of St. Joseph*—C.S.J.
[3830-15]—*Sisters of St. Joseph*—C.S.J.
[3840]—*Sisters of St. Joseph of Carondelet*—C.S.J.
[3930]—*Sisters of St. Joseph of the Third Order of St. Francis* (Immaculate Conception Prov.)—S.S.J.-T.O
[1830]—*Sisters of the Good Shepherd*—R.G.S.
[]—*Sisters of the New Covenant*—S.N.C.
[3260]—*Sisters of the Precious Blood* (Dayton, OH)—C.PP.S.
[1720]—*Sisters of the Third Order Regular of St. Francis of the Congregation of Our Lady of Lourdes* (Rochester, MN)—O.S.F.

ARCHDIOCESAN CEMETERIES

DENVER. *St. Simeon Cemetary Association*, 1300 S. Steele St., 80210. Tel: 303-715-3258; Fax: 303-715-2041.

WHEAT RIDGE. *Archdiocese of Denver Mortuary at Mt. Olivet, Inc.*, 12801 W. 44th Ave., 80033. Tel: 303-425-9511; Fax: 303-425-0242.

Mount Olivet Cemetery, 12801 W. 44th Ave., 80033. Tel: 303-424-7785; Fax: 303-424-5263.

NECROLOGY

† Barry, Rev. Msgr. Thomas P.—Died April 1, 2003
† Schmitt, Rev. Msgr. J. Harley, Chap., Denver, CO Mullen Home—Died June 25, 2003
† St. Peter, Rev. Msgr. Lawrence—Died Aug. 18, 2003
† Kearney, George W., (Retired)—Died Jan. 30, 2003
† O'Shea, John L., Denver, CO Cathedral of the Immaculate Conception—Died Oct. 2, 2003

Diocese of Des Moines

(Dioecesis Desmoinensis)

ERECTED BY POPE ST. PIUS X, AUGUST 12, 1911.

Square Miles 12,446.

Comprises that part of the State of Iowa which is bounded on the east by the eastern boundaries of the Counties of Polk, Warren, Lucas and Wayne; on the south by the State of Missouri; on the west by the Missouri River; and on the north by the northern boundaries of the Counties of Harrison, Shelby, Audubon, Guthrie, Dallas and Polk.

Patrons of the Diocese: I. Blessed Virgin Mary Queen; II. Pope Saint Pius X. Diocese solemnly consecrated to the Immaculate Heart of Mary on May 16, 1948.

Legal Title: "The Roman Catholic Diocese of Des Moines."

For legal titles of parishes and diocesan institutions, consult the Chancery Office.

Most Reverend

JOSEPH L. CHARRON, C.PP.S., S.T.D.

Bishop of Des Moines; ordained June 3, 1967; appointed Titular Bishop of Bencenna and Auxiliary Bishop of Saint Paul and Minneapolis November 6, 1989; consecrated January 25, 1990; appointed Bishop of Des Moines November 12, 1993; installed January 21, 1994.

Chancery 601 Grand Ave., Des Moines IA 50309. Tel: 515-243-7653; Fax: 515-237-5070.

Web: www.dmdiocese.org

Email: bishop@dmdiocese.org

STATISTICAL OVERVIEW

Personnel	
Bishop	1
Priests: Diocesan Active in Diocese	63
Priests: Diocesan Active Outside Diocese	3
Priests: Diocesan in Foreign Missions	1
Priests: Retired, Sick or Absent	25
Number of Diocesan Priests	92
Religious Priests in Diocese	11
Total Priests in Diocese	103
Ordinations:	
Diocesan Priests	1
Transitional Deacons	2
Permanent Deacons in Diocese	70
Total Brothers	5
Total Sisters	91
Parishes	
Parishes	84
With Resident Pastor:	
Resident Diocesan Priests	53
Resident Religious Priests	5
Without Resident Pastor:	
Administered by Priests	24
Administered by Deacons	2
Professional Ministry Personnel:	
Sisters	10
Lay Ministers	49
Welfare	
Catholic Hospitals	3
Total Assisted	711,329
Homes for the Aged	1
Total Assisted	294
Specialized Homes	1
Total Assisted	986
Special Centers for Social Services	4
Total Assisted	76,744
Educational	
Students from Other Diocese	15
Total Seminarians	15
Colleges and Universities	1
Total Students	616
High Schools, Diocesan and Parish	2
Total Students	1,367
Elementary Schools, Diocesan and Parish	16
Total Students	4,869
Catechesis/Religious Education:	
High School Students	1,878
Elementary Students	10,553
Total Students under Catholic Instruction	19,298
Teachers in the Diocese:	
Priests	2
Brothers	1
Sisters	7
Lay Teachers	376
Vital Statistics	
Receptions into the Church:	
Infant Baptism Totals	2,042
Adult Baptism Totals	202
Received into Full Communion	330
First Communions	1,940
Confirmations	1,816
Marriages:	
Catholic	291
Interfaith	302
Total Marriages	593
Deaths	805
Total Catholic Population	97,628
Total Population	748,153

Former Bishops—Most Revs. AUSTIN DOWLING, D.D., first Bishop of Des Moines; ord. June 24, 1891; appt. Bishop Jan. 31, 1912; consecrated April 25, 1912; promoted to the See of St. Paul, Jan., 1919; THOMAS W. DRUMM, D.D., Bishop of Des Moines; ord. Dec. 21, 1901; consecrated May 21, 1919; died Oct. 24, 1933; GERALD T. BERGAN, D.D., ord. Oct. 28, 1915; appt. March 24, 1934; consecrated June 13, 1934; Enthroned June 21, 1934; elevated to Archiepiscopal dignity and promoted to Omaha Feb. 9, 1948; EDWARD C. DALY, O.P., S.T.M., Bishop of Des Moines; ord. June 12, 1921; appt. March 13, 1948; consecrated May 13, 1948; named Asst. at Papal Throne, May 23, 1958; died Nov. 23, 1964; GEORGE J. BISKUP, D.D., ord. March 19, 1937; appt. Auxiliary Bishop of Dubuque, March 9, 1957; consecrated April 24, 1957; appt. Bishop of Des Moines, Feb. 3, 1965; appt. Coadjutor Archbishop of Indianapolis, July 26, 1967; succeeded to See Jan. 14, 1970; MAURICE J. DINGMAN, D.D. (Retired), Bishop of Des Moines; ord. Dec. 8, 1939; appt. Bishop of Des Moines April 2, 1968; consecrated June 19, 1968; installed July 7, 1968; retired Oct. 14, 1986; died Feb. 1, 1992; WILLIAM H. BULLOCK, ord. June 7, 1952; appt. Auxiliary Bishop of St. Paul and Minneapolis and Titular Bishop of Natchez June 3, 1980; consecrated Aug. 12, 1980; appt. Bishop of Des Moines Feb. 10, 1987; installed April 2, 1987; appt. to Diocese of Madison April 13, 1993.

Vicar General and Moderator of the Curia—Rev. Msgr. STEPHEN ORR, 601 Grand Ave., Des Moines, 50309. Tel: 515-237-5044; 515-222-9577 (Res.).

Chancery—601 Grand Ave., Des Moines, 50309. Tel: 515-243-7653; Fax: 515-237-5070. Office Hours: Mon.-Fri. 8:30-4:30

Chancellor—THOMAS K. CHAPMAN, All Matrimonial Correspondence to Tribunal.

Secretary to the Bishop—MARY BARNUM, 601 Grand Ave., Des Moines, 50309. Tel: 515-237-5039; Fax: 515-237-5071.

Finance Officer—TAMERA MASON, 601 Grand Ave., Des Moines, 50309. Tel: 515-237-5012.

Vicar for Finance—Rev. Msgr. EDWARD HURLEY, 601 Grand Ave., Des Moines, 50309. Tel: 515-237-5030.

Judicial Vicar—Rev. CHRISTOPHER HARTSHORN, J.C.L.

Director of Tribunal—Deacon MICHAEL E. RILEY, J.C.L.

Defenders of the Bond—Revs. MICHAEL AMADEO; LAWRENCE R. HOFFMANN; SAMUEL PALMER, J.C.L.; DAVID J. POLICH; Deacon ROBERT L. HOWE.

Judges—Rev. Msgr. LAWRENCE A. BEESON, J.C.D.; Revs. CHRISTOPHER HARTSHORN, J.C.L.; DANIEL F. KRETTEK, J.C.L.; Deacon MICHAEL E. RILEY, J.C.L.; Rev. Msgrs. STEPHEN L. ORR, Vicar Gen.; EDWARD B. PFEFFER, J.C.L. (Retired); Rev. THOMAS J. PFEFFER (Retired).

Notary—DORIS KLANG.

Advocates—Revs. EUGENE R. KOCH; JOHN P. LUDWIG; VINCE G. ROSONKE; JOHN DORTON; HOWARD FITZGERALD; Mrs. JOYCE RILEY; Mrs. PHYLLIS CACCIATORE; Mrs. SARAH LUFT.

Diocesan Consultors—Rev. Msgr. STEPHEN ORR; Revs. RICHARD BERGMAN; KENNETH GROSS; ROBERT HOEFLER; VINCENT ROSONKE; DANIEL SIEPKER.

Diocesan Corporation Board—Most Rev. JOSEPH L. CHARRON, C.PP.S., S.T.D.; Rev. Msgr. STEPHEN ORR; THOMAS CHAPMAN; CYNTHIA EISENHAUER; TAMERA MASON; Deacon MICHAEL E. RILEY, J.C.L.

Diocesan Offices and Directors

Catholic Charities—NANCY GALEAZZI, 601 Grand Ave., Des Moines, 50309. Tel: 515-237-5055.

Social Service Division—Des Moines Office, 601 Grand Ave., Des Moines, 50309. Tel: 515-237-5055.

Council Bluffs Office—411 E. Broadway, Council Bluffs, 51503. Tel: 712-328-3086; Fax: 712-328-1348.

Charismatic Renewal Liaison—Rev. DANIEL KRETTEK, 1521 Center St., Des Moines, 50314. Tel: 515-282-4839.

Communications, Office of—ANNE MARIE COX, Dir., 601 Grand Ave., Des Moines, 50309. Tel: 515-237-5057; Fax: 515-237-5070.

Continuing Education for Clergy—Rev. LYLE PETERS, St. Bernard's Church, 222 E. Pearl St., Osceola, 50213. Tel: 641-342-2850.

Deaf-Handicapped, Office of—Sr. HELEN SEIVERT, O.S.F., Dir., 411 E. Broadway, Council Bluffs, 51503. Tel: 712-328-3086.

Stewardship and Development Office—JOSH FABER, Dir. Devel. Tel: 515-237-5079. 601 Grand Ave., Des Moines, 50309.

Diocesan Council of Catholic Women—LIZ SCHMID, Pres., 1503 Birchwood Dr., Red Oak, 51566. Tel: 712-623-3209.

Diaconate (Permanent)—Deacon JEFFREY BOEHLERT, Dir., 313 N.E. 31st St., Ankeny, 50021.

Diaconate Formation—Directors: Deacon RON MYERS; TAMMY MYERS, 601 Grand Ave., Des Moines, 50309. Tel: 515-237-5037.

Evangelization, Office of—JIM BOND, Dir., 601 Grand Ave., Des Moines, 50309. Tel: 515-237-5046.

Holy Childhood, Pontifical Association—Dr. LUVERN GUBBELS, 601 Grand Ave., Des Moines, 50309. Tel: 515-237-5013.

Legislative Activities, Office of—601 Grand Ave., Des Moines, 50309. Tel: 515-237-5047.

Newspaper—ANNE MARIE COX, Editor, 601 Grand Ave., Des Moines, 50309. Tel: 515-237-5041. "The Catholic Mirror"

Priests' Pension Fund Society—Most Rev. JOSEPH L. CHARRON, C.PP.S., S.T.D.; Rev. Msgrs. MICHAEL HESS; EDWARD HURLEY; Rev. ROBERT SCHOEMANN; Rev. Msgr. EDWARD PFEFFER.

Propagation of the Faith—Rev. PAUL BIANCHI, Dir., 601 Grand Ave., Des Moines, 50309. Tel: 515-237-5029.

Office of Catechetical Services—JOANNE DALHOFF, Dir., 601 Grand Ave., Des Moines, 50309. Tel: 515-237-5052.

St. Vincent de Paul Society—Deacon JOE COAN, Spiritual Dir., 1800 Grand Ave. #392, West Des Moines, 50265. Tel: 515-267-8128.

Schools—Dr. LUVERN GUBBELS, Supt. & Dir. Educ.; REBECCA LINDAHL, School Improvement Coord.; JACQUELINE KRESAL, Educational Svcs. Coord., 601 Grand Ave., Des Moines, 50309. Tel: 515-237-5013.

Office of Social Justice—VACANT, 601 Grand Ave., Des Moines, 50309. Tel: 515-237-5047.

Vocations—Rev. JOHN ACREA, Coord., 601 Grand Ave., Des Moines, 50309. Tel: 515-237-5014.

Office of Worship (Liturgy, Music, Art and Architecture)—JIM BOND, Dir., 601 Grand Ave., Des Moines, 50309. Tel: 515-237-5046.

Youth Ministry, Office of—BOB PERRON, Dir., St. Thomas More Center, 6177 Panorama Rd., Panora, 50216. Tel: 515-755-3164.

Office of Adult Faith Formation—Rev. P. TIMOTHY FITZGERALD, 601 Grand Ave., Des Moines, 50309. Tel: 515-237-5026.

Office of Marriage Ministry—Deacon DENNIS LUFT; Mrs. SARAH LUFT, 601 Grand Ave., Des Moines, 50309. Tel: 515-237-5056.

Victim Assistance Coordinator—JO MULVIHILL. Tel: 515-286-2031. Email: advocate@dmdiocese.org.

CLERGY, PARISHES, MISSIONS AND PAROCHIAL SCHOOLS

CITY OF DES MOINES
(POLK COUNTY)

1—ST. AMBROSE CATHEDRAL (1856), [JC] Revs. James W. Kiernan, Rector; Joseph Ly Quy Chu; Sr. Patricia Scherer, Pastoral Min.; Deacons Lee Pao Yang; Dave Garza; Jack Inman; Chris Rohwer.
Res.: 607 High St., 50309. Tel: 515-288-7411; Fax: 515-288-3969.
Catechesis/Religious Program—Sr. Virginia Jennings, O.S.F., D.R.E. Students 162.

2—ALL SAINTS (1914), [JC] Rev. Robert L. Schoemann.
650 N.E. 52nd Ave., 50313. Tel: 515-265-5001; Fax: 515-265-5636.
Catechesis/Religious Program—Students 135.

3—ST. ANTHONY'S (1905), Rev. Raymond Higgins; Deacons William Smith; Tony Romeo.
Res.: 15 Indianola Rd., 50315. Tel: 515-244-4709; Fax: 515-280-6959.
School—16 Columbus Ave., 50315. Tel: 515-243-1874; Fax: 515-243-4467. Sisters 2; Lay Teachers 23; Students 387.
Catechesis/Religious Program—Tel: 515-244-1119. Students 183.

4—ST. AUGUSTIN'S (1923), Revs. James C. Polich; Vincent Nnatuanya, C.S.Sp.; Deacon Fred Pins.
Res.: 545 42nd St., 50312. Tel: 515-255-1175; Fax: 515-255-7969.
School—4320 Grand Ave., 50312. Tel: 515-279-5947; Fax: 515-279-8049. Lay Teachers 22; Students 236.
Catechesis/Religious Program—Students 121.

5—BASILICA OF SAINT JOHN (1905), Rev. Aquinas Nichols, O.S.B., Admin.; Deacon Patrick Kirkman.
Res.: 1915 University Ave., 50314. Tel: 515-244-3101; Fax: 515-244-3165.
Catechesis/Religious Program—Students 59.

6—ST. CATHERINE OF SIENA CATHOLIC STUDENT CENTER (1969),, (Non-Territorial University Parish) Rev. James Laurenzo.
Church: 1150-28th St., 50311-4142. Tel: 515-271-4747; Fax: 515-271-1918.
Catechesis/Religious Program—Students 64.

7—CHRIST THE KING (1939), Rev. Msgr. Frank E. Bognanno; Deacon Charles Putbrese, Pastoral Assoc.
Res.: 5711 S.W. 9th St., 50315. Tel: 515-285-2888; Fax: 515-285-8182.
School—701 Wall St., 50315. Tel: 515-285-3349; Fax: 515-285-0381. Lay Teachers 15; Students 199.
Catechesis/Religious Program—Students 208.

8—HOLY TRINITY (1920), Rev. Anthony Aiello; Deacon Robert Howe.
Res.: 2926 Beaver Ave., 50310-4040. Tel: 515-255-3162; Fax: 515-255-1381.
School—Lay Teachers 32; Students 455.
Catechesis/Religious Program—Students 170.

9—ST. JOSEPH'S (1924), Rev. Msgr. Robert J. Chamberlain; Deacon Marvin Brewer.
Res.: 3300 Easton Blvd., 50317. Tel: 515-266-2226.
School—Tel: 515-266-3433; Fax: 515-266-2860. Lay Teachers 14; Students 193.
Catechesis/Religious Program—Students 86.

10—ST. MARY OF NAZARETH (1964), Rev. Msgr. Gerald E. Ryan; Rev. David J. Santoro, O.P. (CHI); Deacon George Catanzano.
Res.: 4605 N.W. 47th Ct., P.O. Box 13170, 50310. Tel: 515-276-4042; Fax: 515-252-1995.
Catechesis/Religious Program—Tel: 515-276-7589. Students 460.

11—OUR LADY OF THE AMERICAS (2003), Rev. Kevin Cameron.

Worship Centers:
St. Peter: 607 E. 18th St., 50316. Tel: 515-266-4265; Fax: 515-266-3945.
Visitation: 1271 E. 9th St., 50316. Tel: 515-266-6695; Fax: 515-266-9803.
School—Holy Family, (Grades PreK-8) , (Consolidated) Tel: 515-262-8025; Fax: 515-280-5482. Lay Teachers 21; Students 215.

12—ST. PETER'S (1915), Merged, with Visitation, Des Moines to form Our Lady of the Americas, Des Moines.

13—ST. THERESA OF THE CHILD JESUS (1951), [JC] Revs. Lawrence Hoffmann; Robert A. Hoefler; Deacons Joe Cortese II; Earl Weisenhorn.
Res.: 1230 Merle Hay Rd., 50311-2098. Tel: 515-279-4654; Fax: 515-277-0838.
School—5810 Cara Carpenter, 50311. Tel: 515-277-0178; Fax: 515-255-2415. Lay Teachers 24; Students 430.
Catechesis/Religious Program—Students 118.

14—VISITATION (1882), Merged, with St. Peter's, Des Moines to form Our Lady of the Americas, Des Moines.

OUTSIDE THE CITY OF DES MOINES

ADAIR, ADAIR CO., ST. JOHN (1879), Attended by, St. Mary, Anita.
Res.: P.O. Box 277, Anita, 50020. Tel: 712-762-3484; 712-762-3773 (Office); Fax: 712-762-3484.
Catechesis/Religious Program—Students 24.

ADEL, DALLAS CO., ST. JOHN (1917), Rev. Albert Sherbo.
Mailing Address: P.O. Box 185, 50003-0185. Tel: 515-993-4482.
Catechesis/Religious Program—Tel: 515-993-4590. Students 185.

AFTON, UNION CO., ST. EDWARD (1878), Attended by, Paul VI Pastoral Ministry from Creston. , Mailing Address: 406 W. Clark, Creston, 50801. Tel: 641-782-5278; Fax: 641-782-5924.
Church: 104 W. Union, 50830. Tel: 641-347-8452.
Catechesis/Religious Program—Students 34.

ALTOONA, POLK CO., SS. JOHN AND PAUL (1983), Rev. Howard E. Fitzgerald; Deacon Tom Maly.
Res.: 1401 First Ave., S., 50009. Tel: 515-967-3796; Fax: 515-967-7197.
Catechesis/Religious Program—Students 528.

ANITA, CASS CO., ST. MARY (1924), Deacon Fred Cornwell.
Church: P.O. Box 277, 50020. Tel: 712-762-3484; 712-762-3773 (Office); Fax: 712-762-3484.
Catechesis/Religious Program—Students 47.

ANKENY, POLK CO., OUR LADY'S IMMACULATE HEART (1961), Rev. Gregory Leach.
Res.: 510 E. First St., 50021. Tel: 515-964-3038; Fax: 515-964-5997.
Catechesis/Religious Program—Tel: 515-964-3545. Students 1,250.

ATLANTIC, CASS CO., SS. PETER AND PAUL (1871), Rev. Msgr. Lawrence A. Beeson, J.C.D.
Res.: 106 W. 6th St., 50022. Tel: 712-243-4721.
Catechesis/Religious Program—Tel: 712-243-2144. Students 190.

AUDUBON, AUDUBON CO., ST. PATRICK (1918), [CEM] Rev. Wayne Gubbels.
Res.: 116 E. Division St., 50025. Tel: 712-563-2283; Fax: 712-563-3238.
Catechesis/Religious Program—Students 145.

AVOCA, POTTAWATTAMIE CO., ST. MARY, MEDIATRIX OF ALL GRACES (1882), Rev. John M. Frost.
Res.: 109 N. Maple St., P.O. Box 38, 51521. Tel: 712-343-6948.
Catechesis/Religious Program—Students 86.

BAYARD, GUTHRIE CO., ST. PATRICK (1882), Rev. Tan Van Tran.
Res.: 214 Prairie St., P.O. Box 274, 50029. Tel: 712-651-2676.
Catechesis/Religious Program—Students 29.

BEDFORD, TAYLOR CO., SACRED HEART, Attended by, St. Clare, Clarinda. Rev. Thomas Coenen.
Mailing Address: 300 E. Lincoln Blvd., Clarinda, 51632.
Catechesis/Religious Program—Students 14.

CARLISLE, WARREN CO., ST. ELIZABETH SETON (1979), Rev. Wayne Gubbels.
Mailing Address: 2566 Scotch Ridge Rd., P.O. Box 35, 50047. Tel: 515-989-0659; Fax: 515-989-4525.
Catechesis/Religious Program—Students 126.

CARTER LAKE, POTTAWATTAMIE CO., OUR LADY OF CARTER LAKE (1970), Revs. Daniel Kirby; Raymond McHenry. Attended by Our Lady, Queen of Apostles, Council Bluffs.
Church: 3501 N. 9th St., 51510. Tel: 712-347-6631; Fax: 712-325-2411.

CASEY, GUTHRIE CO., ST. JOSEPH (1898), Closed. For inquiries for parish records contact the chancery.

CHARITON, LUCAS CO., SACRED HEART (1869), Rev. William Miller, C.PP.S.
Res.: 407 N. Main, 50049. Tel: 681-774-4978.
Catechesis/Religious Program—Students 132.

CHURCHVILLE, WARREN CO., ASSUMPTION OF THE BLESSED VIRGIN MARY (1855), Rev. Daniel Krettek.
Res.: P.O. Box 88, St. Mary's, 50241. Tel: 515-297-2267.
Catechesis/Religious Program—Students 15.

CLARINDA, PAGE CO., ST. CLARE (1942), Rev. Thomas Coenen.
Res.: 300 E. Lincoln Blvd., 51632. Tel: 712-542-2030.
Catechesis/Religious Program—Students 35.

CORNING, ADAMS CO., ST. PATRICK'S (1869), [CEM] Rev. Daniel E. Siepker.
Res.: 504 Grove Ave., 50841. Tel: 515-322-3363; Fax: 515-322-4370.
Catechesis/Religious Program—Students 92.

CORYDON, WAYNE CO., ST. FRANCIS (1969), Attended by, Chariton of the South Central Catholic Ministry Team. , Mailing Address: 213 W. Jackson, 50060. Tel: 515-774-4978.
Catechesis/Religious Program—Students 24.

COUNCIL BLUFFS, POTTAWATTAMIE CO.

1—HOLY FAMILY (1908), Revs. Daniel J. Kirby; Raymond McHenry.
Res.: 2217 Ave. B, 51501. Tel: 712-328-3869.
Catechesis/Religious Program—Students 85.

2—OUR LADY, QUEEN OF APOSTLES (1957), Revs. Daniel J. Kirby; Raymond McHenry; Deacon Monty Montagne.
Res.: 3304 4th Ave., 51501. Tel: 712-323-2916; Fax: 712-323-4716.
Catechesis/Religious Program—Students 156.

3—ST. PATRICK (1924), Rev. John Bertogli; Deacons Charles Hannan; James Webering; James Mason.
Res.: 223 Harmony St., 51503. Tel: 712-323-1484.
Catechesis/Religious Program—Students 230.

4—ST. PETER (1887), (German), Rev. Charles Kottas.
Res.: One Bluff St., 51503. Tel: 712-322-8889; Fax: 712-323-1442.
Catechesis/Religious Program—Students 477.
St. Francis Worship Center—238 6th St., 51501. Tel: 712-328-7272.

CRESTON, UNION CO., HOLY SPIRIT (1975), Rev. Leonard A. Kenkel.
Res.: 406 W. Clark, 50801. Tel: 641-782-5278; Fax: 641-782-7628.
Church: 104 W. Union St., Afton, 50801. Also serving the parish of St. Edward, Afton.
School—St. Malachy, Tel: 641-782-7125; Fax: 641-782-5924. Lay Teachers 11; Students 133.
Catechesis/Religious Program—Students 72.

CUMBERLAND, CASS CO., ST. TIMOTHY (Reno) (1883), Rev. Paul Mahowald, S.J.
Mailing Address: P.O. Box 605, Griswold, 51535-0605. Tel: 712-778-4540.
Catechesis/Religious Program—Students 34.

CUMMING, WARREN CO., ST. JOHN (1892), Rev. John P. Ludwig.
Res.: 224 N. 43rd St., P.O. Box 5, 50061. Tel: 515-981-4855; Fax: 515-981-9188.
Catechesis/Religious Program—Students 215.

DEFIANCE, SHELBY CO., ST. PETER (1882),, Served from Earling. Rev. Michael Berner.
Res.: P.O. Box 127, 51527. Tel: 712-748-3501; Fax: 712-748-3500.
Catechesis/Religious Program—Students 98.

DUNLAP, HARRISON CO., ST. PATRICK, Rev. Paul J. Strittmatter, S.J.
Res.: 509 S. 3rd St., 51529. Tel: 712-643-5808.
Catechesis/Religious Program—Students 145.

EARLING, SHELBY CO., ST. JOSEPH (1882), (German), Rev. Michael Berner.
Res.: P.O. Box 225, 51530. Tel: 712-747-2091; Fax: 712-747-9501.
School—Tel: 712-747-3081. See Shelby County Board of Catholic Education under Education Centers in the Institution section.
Catechesis/Religious Program—Students 36.

ELKHART, POLK CO., ST. MARY/HOLY CROSS (1885), Rev. Michael A. Amadeo; Deacon Jerry Barnwell.
Res.: 214 N. Washington, P.O. Box 110, 50073. Tel: 515-367-2685; Fax: 515-367-2685.
Catechesis/Religious Program—Students 170.

EXIRA, AUDUBON CO., HOLY TRINITY, Attended by, St. Patrick. Revs. Christopher Fontanini; Wayne

Gubbels.
116 E. Division St., Audubon, 50025. Tel: 712-563-2283; Fax: 712-268-3238.
Catechesis/Religious Program—Students 30.

GLENWOOD, MILLS CO., OUR LADY OF THE HOLY ROSARY (1955), Rev. Paul Monahan; Deacons Joseph Blankenship; Ronald Kohn; Richard Maiers.
Res.: 24116 Marian Ave., 51534-5291. Tel: 712-527-5211; Fax: 712-527-3829.
Catechesis/Religious Program—Students 318.

GRAND RIVER, DECATUR CO., ST. PATRICK, , Served from St. Bernard, Osceola
Res.: 222 E. Pearl, Osceola, 50213. Tel: 641-342-2850.

GRANGER, DALLAS CO., ASSUMPTION OF THE BLESSED VIRGIN MARY (1871), Rev. Eugene R. Koch.
Res.: 1906 Sycamore, P.O. Box 159, 50109. Tel: 515-999-2239; Fax: 515-999-2208.
School—Tel: 515-999-2211. Lay Teachers 9; Students 109.
Catechesis/Religious Program—Students 159.

GREENFIELD, ADAIR CO., ST. JOHN (1907), Revs. Michael McLaughlin, Admin.; Dean Nimerichter.
Res.: 303 N.E. Elm St., 50849. Tel: 515-743-2641; Fax: 515-343-7065.
Catechesis/Religious Program—Students 112.

GRISWOLD, CASS CO., OUR LADY OF GRACE (1911), Rev. Paul Mahowald, S.J.
Mailing Address: P.O. Box 605, 51535-0605. Tel: 712-778-4540.
Catechesis/Religious Program—Students 50.

GUTHRIE CENTER, GUTHRIE CO., ST. MARY (1906), Rev. Christ Fontanini; Deacons Richard Ziller; Hans Seeman.
Res.: 603 Main St., 50115. Tel: 515-747-2569.
Catechesis/Religious Program—Students 94.

HAMBURG, FREMONT CO., ST. MARY (1874), Attended by, St. Mary, Shenandoah. Rev. Donald Bruck.
Res.: 1306 Washington St., 51640. Tel: 712-382-2871.
Catechesis/Religious Program—Students 42.

HARLAN, SHELBY CO., ST. MICHAEL (1888), Revs. Jack H. McClure, C.PP.S.; Robert A. Hoefler; Deacon Patrick Davitt.
Res.: 1912-18th St., 51537. Tel: 712-755-5244; Fax: 712-755-2604.
School— See Shelby County Board of Catholic Education under Education Centers in the Institution section.
Catechesis/Religious Program—Tel: 712-755-5366. Students 280.

INDIANOLA, WARREN CO., ST. THOMAS AQUINAS (1958), Rev. Frank S. Palmer.
Res.: 1202 W. Iowa Ave., 50125. Tel: 515-961-3026; Fax: 515-961-3458.
Catechesis/Religious Program—Tel: 515-961-0447. Students 290.

IRISH SETTLEMENT, MADISON CO., ST. PATRICK (1852), Rev. Daniel Krettek.
Res.: P.O. Box 88, St. Marys, 50241. Tel: 641-297-2267.
Catechesis/Religious Program—Students 32.

JAMAICA, GUTHRIE CO., ST. JOSEPH (1903), Attended by, St. Patrick, Bayard. , 214 Prairie, P.O. Box 274, Bayard, 50029. Tel: 712-651-2676.
Catechesis/Religious Program—Students 6.

LACONA, WARREN CO., HOLY TRINITY CHURCH OF SOUTHEAST WARREN COUNTY (1978), Rev. Felix A. Onuora, C.S.Sp.
Res.: 304 N. Washington Ave., P.O. Box 145, 50139-0145. Tel: 641-534-4691; Fax: 641-534-4691.
Worship Centers— St. Mary of the Assumption Church, Lacona (Tel: 641-534-4871); St. Augustine Church, Milo (Tel: 641-942-6395); St. Mary of Perpetual Help Church, Rosemount (Tel: 641-534-3145).
Catechesis/Religious Program—Students 84.

LENOX, TAYLOR CO., ST. PATRICK (1872), Attended by, St. Patrick, Corning.
Church: 600 W. Michigan, 50851. Tel: 641-336-2893.
Catechesis/Religious Program—Students 40.

LEON, DECATUR CO., ST. BRENDAN (1856), (Irish), Rev. Thomas V. Dooley.
Res.: 1001 N.W. Church St., 50144. Tel: 515-446-4789.
Catechesis/Religious Program—Students 59.

LOGAN, HARRISON CO., ST. ANNE (1920), Rev. John Harmon.
Res.: 112 W. 3rd St., 51546. Tel: 712-644-2535.
Catechesis/Religious Program—Students 135.

MALOY, RINGGOLD CO., IMMACULATE CONCEPTION (1874), [CEM] Rev. Thomas V. Dooley.
Res.: 103 Shay St., 50836. Tel: 515-446-4789.
Catechesis/Religious Program—Students 12.

MASSENA, CASS CO., ST. PATRICK (1888),, Served from Greenfield. Rev. Michael McLaughlin, Admin.; Deacon Eugene Krawczyk.
Res.: 303 N.E. Elm St., Greenfield, 50849.
Church: 503 Main St., 50853.
Catechesis/Religious Program—Students 27.

MISSOURI VALLEY, HARRISON CO., ST. PATRICK (1877), Rev. Robert Harris.
Res.: 215 N. Seventh St., 51555. Tel: 712-642-3124; Fax: 712-642-2518.
School—219 N. Seventh St., 51555. Tel: 712-642-3155; Fax: 712-642-2518. Lay Teachers 4; Students 46.
Catechesis/Religious Program—Students 105.

MONDAMIN, HARRISON CO., HOLY FAMILY (1970), Attended by, St. Anne. , 112 W. 3rd St., Logan, 51546. Tel: 712-644-2535.
Catechesis/Religious Program—Students 6.

MT. AYR, RINGGOLD CO., ST. JOSEPH (1913), Attended by, St. Brendan.
Church: 100 N. Polk, 50854. Tel: 641-464-2826.
Catechesis/Religious Program—Students 29.

NEOLA, POTTAWATTAMIE CO., ST. PATRICK (1882), Rev. Raphael Masabakhwa.
Res.: P.O. Box 127, 51559. Tel: 712-485-2124; Fax: 712-485-2124.
Catechesis/Religious Program—Students 217.

ORIENT, ADAIR CO., ST. MARK, Closed. For inquiries for parish records contact the chancery.

OSCEOLA, CLARKE CO., ST. BERNARD (1885), Rev. Lyle Peters.
Res.: 222 E. Pearl, 50213. Tel: 641-342-2850.
Catechesis/Religious Program—Students 70.

PANAMA, SHELBY CO., ST. MARY OF THE ASSUMPTION (1899), Rev Michael G. Peters.
Res.: Box 203, 51562. Tel: 712-489-2030.
School— See Shelby County Board of Catholic Education under Education Centers in the Institution section.
Catechesis/Religious Program—Students 41.

PANORA, GUTHRIE CO., ST. CECILIA (1907), Attended by, St. Mary, Guthrie Center Tel: 515-747-2569. Rev. Chris Fontanini; Deacons Richard Ziller; Hans Seeman.
Church: 220 N. First St., 50216. Tel: 515-755-2658.
Catechesis/Religious Program—Students 55.

PERRY, DALLAS CO., ST. PATRICK (1881), Rev. David Polich.
Res.: 1312 3rd St., 50220. Tel: 515-465-4387; Fax: 515-465-4387.
School—1302 5th St., 50220. Tel: 515-465-4186; Fax: 515-465-9808. Lay Teachers 12; Students 105.
Catechesis/Religious Program—Students 125.

PORTSMOUTH, SHELBY CO., ST. MARY (1885), Rev. Paul Bianchi.
Res.: P.O. Box 98, 51565. Tel: 712-743-2625; Fax: 712-743-2010.
Catechesis/Religious Program—Students 104.

RED OAK, MONTGOMERY CO.
1—ST. MARY (1902), Rev. Kenneth Gross.
Res.: 1510 Highland Ave., 51566. Tel: 712-623-2744.
Catechesis/Religious Program—Students 129.
2—ST. PATRICK (1880), (Irish), Rev. Kenneth Gross.
Res.: 1510 Highland, 51566. Tel: 712-386-2123.
Catechesis/Religious Program—Tel: 712-386-2200. Students 68.

ST. MARYS, WARREN CO., IMMACULATE CONCEPTION (1871), Rev. Daniel Krettek.
Res.: P.O. Box 88, 50241. Tel: 641-297-2267.
Catechesis/Religious Program—Students 30.

SHENANDOAH, PAGE CO., ST. MARY, Rev. Donald Bruck; Deacon Ed Miller.
Res.: 512 W. Thomas Ave., 51601. Tel: 712-246-1718.
Catechesis/Religious Program—Students 128.

STUART, GUTHRIE CO., ALL SAINTS (1876), Rev. David Fleming.
Res.: P.O. Box 605, 50250. Tel: 515-523-1497.
Catechesis/Religious Program—Tel: 515-523-1943. Students 108.

URBANDALE, POLK CO., ST. PIUS X (1955), Rev. Msgr. Joseph McDonnell; Rev. Anthony Adibe; Deacons Dave Bartemes; Rick Condon; Mary Sue Lone, Pastoral Min.; Barbara Mease, Pastoral Min.; Jane Morgan, Pastoral Min.
3663 66th St., 50322. Tel: 515-276-2059; Fax: 515-276-8351.
School—3601 66th St., 50322. Tel: 515-276-1061; Fax: 515-273-0350. Lawrence Zahm, Prin. Sisters 1; Lay Teachers 26; Students 388.
Catechesis/Religious Program—Tel: 515-278-5684. Mary Heinrich, D.R.E.; Alyssa Englund D.R.E. Students 400.

VILLISCA, MONTGOMERY CO., ST. JOSEPH (1947), Attended by, St. Clare, Clarinda. Rev. Thomas Coenen.
304 E. Lincoln St., Clarinda, 51632. Tel: 712-826-8841.
Catechesis/Religious Program—Students 14.

WALNUT, POTTAWATTAMIE CO., ST. PATRICK (1882), Attended by, St. Mary, Mediatrix of All Graces, Avoca. Rev. John M. Frost.
Mailing Address: 109 N. Maple St., P.O. Box 38, Avoca, 51521. Tel: 712-343-6948.
Catechesis/Religious Program—Students 33.

WAUKEE, DALLAS CO., ST. BONIFACE (1880), Rev. Vince Rosonke; Rebecca Burrows, Pastoral Min.
Res.: 1200 Warrior Ln., 50263-9587. Tel: 515-987-4597; Fax: 515-987-5272.
Catechesis/Religious Program—Students 410.

WEST DES MOINES, POLK CO.
1—ST. FRANCIS OF ASSISI (1991), Rev. Msgr. Edward Hurley; Rev. Christopher Pisut; Deacon David O'Brien.
7075 Ashworth Rd., 50266. Tel: 515-223-4577; Fax: 515-223-4768.
School—Tel: 515-457-7167. Lay Teachers 26; Students 424.
Catechesis/Religious Program—Students 728.
2—SACRED HEART (1892), Revs. Michael N. Hess; Remi C. Okere, C.S.Sp.; Sr. Mary Margaret O'Toole, Pastoral Assoc.; Deacon Ron Myers.
1627 Grand Ave., 50265. Tel: 515-225-6414; Fax: 515-225-0286.
School—1601 Grand Ave., 50265. Tel: 515-223-1284; Fax: 515-223-9413. Sisters 2; Lay Teachers 27; Students 458.
Catechesis/Religious Program—Tel: 515-225-1641; Fax: 515-225-0286. Students 530.

WESTON, POTTAWATTAMIE CO., ST. COLUMBANUS (1883), Attended by, St. Patrick, Neola. Rev. Raphael Masabakhwa.
St. Patrick's Church: P.O. Box 127, Neola, 51559. Tel: 712-485-2124.
Catechesis/Religious Program—Students 40.

WESTPHALIA, SHELBY CO., ST. BONIFACE (1873), Rev. Michael G. Peters.
Church: 207 Duren Strasse, P.O. Box 86, 51578. Tel: 712-489-2030; Fax: 712-489-2030.
Catechesis/Religious Program—Students 57.

WINTERSET, MADISON CO., ST. JOSEPH (1893), Rev. Christopher Hartshorn.
Res.: 607 W. Green St., 50273. Tel: 515-462-1083; Fax: 515-462-2378.
Catechesis/Religious Program—Students 175.

WOODBINE, HARRISON CO., SACRED HEART (1902), Attended by, St. Patrick's, Dunlap. Rev. Paul J. Strittmatter, S.J.
33 Seventh St., 51579. Tel: 712-647-2871.
Catechesis/Religious Program—Students 75.

WOODWARD, DALLAS CO., ST. ANN (1934), Closed., For inquiries for parish records contact Assumption Church, Granger.

Chaplains of Public Institutions

DES MOINES. *United States Veterans Hospital*, 3600 30th St., 50310. Rev. Paul Holt.

CLARINDA. *State Hospital*. Served from St. Clare Church, Clarinda.

COUNCIL BLUFFS. *Iowa School for the Deaf*, 411 E. Broadway, 51503. Tel: 712-322-2449. Sr. Helen Seivert, Chap. & D.R.E.

DEXTER. *City Chaplaincy Program*, P.O. Box 371, 50070. Rev. Robert J. Aubrey.

GLENWOOD. *Glenwood State School*. Vacant.

MITCHELLVILLE. *Iowa Correctional Institution for Women*. Kay Kopatich, Chap. & Coord., Svcs. to Catholic Residents.

On Special Assignment:
Rev. Msgr.—
Orr, Stephen, Vicar Gen.
Revs.—
Acrea, John, Vocations
Amadeo, Michael A., Diocesan Tribunal Office
Fitzgerald, P. Timothy, Office of Adult Faith Formation

On Duty Outside the Diocese:
Rev. Msgr.—
Chiodo, Frank, St. Thomas More Church, 4804 Grover St., Omaha, NE 68106.
Revs.—
Freeman, James, St. Joseph, 215 Craycraft Rd., Tucson, AZ 85711.
Grant, Robert, St. Ambrose University, Davenport, 52803.
Koch, Paul M., Casilla 919, Santa Cruz, Bolivia.

On Sabbatical:
Rev.—
Dorton, John

Leave of Absence:
Revs.—
Chevalier, Martin
Cordaro, Frank
Crowley, Thomas

Absent on Sick Leave:
Rev.—
Gittins, Gordon

Retired:
Rev. Msgrs.—
Conley, Raymond J., 1390 Buffalo Rd., West Des Moines, 50265.
Connelly, Paul J., 615 Park St., #1501, 50309.
McIlhon, John J., 1390 Buffalo Rd., West Des

Moines, 50265.
Pfeffer, Edward B., J.C.L., 1390 Buffalo Rd., West Des Moines, 50265.
Schwarte, Michael W., P.O. Box 288, Earling, 51530.
Stessman, Gerald, 1390 Buffalo Rd., West Des Moines, 50265.

Revs.—
Bergman, Richard, 1390 Buffalo Rd., West Des Moines, 50265.
Clarke, John, 300 W. 6th St., Apt 1, Atlantic, 50022.
Culver, Garry, 1050 Capri Isle Blvd. # H 106, Venice, FL 34292.
Cunningham, John E., 1390 Buffalo Rd., West Des Moines, 50265.
Elias, Woodrow, 7327 Sawgrass, San Antonio, TX 78244.
Fenelon, David, 934 Lincoln St., Waterloo, 50703.
Kenkel, Benedict J., St. Francis Rectory, 238 S. 6th St., #3, Council Bluffs, 51501.
Kleffman, James, 4624 Navajo St., #17, Council Bluffs, 51501.
Leto, Nelo A., 710 Davis, 50315.
Lorenz, John F., 1390 Buffalo Rd., West Des Moines, 50265.
Maier, John, 8440 Silver Way, Tampa, FL 33615.
McCann, Arthur L., 1610 60th St., 50322.
Palmer, Samuel I., 3105 67th St., Urbandale, 50322.
Pfeffer, Thomas J., 3422 E. 12th St., 50316.
Reischl, Fred P., St. Francis Rectory, 238 S. 6th St., Council Bluffs, 51503.

Permanent Deacons:
Ayers, John, (Dubuque)
Barnwell, Jerry
Bartemes, David
Blankenship, Joseph, (Retired)
Blouin, Mike, (Dubuque)
Boehlert, Jeffrey
Bray, Robert, (Retired)
Brewer, Marvin
Catanzano, George
Coan, Joseph II
Condon, Rick
Cord, Michael
Cornwell, Fred
Cortese, Joseph
Critelli, Anthony, (Retired)
Davitt, Patrick
Doyle, James, (Retired)
Erickson, Gregg
Garza, David
Gaul, Leo, (Retired)
Hannan, Charles
Herman, James
Howe, Robert
Huynh, Joseph, (Retired)
Inman, Jack
Jacobi, Donald, (Retired)
Jager, Gene
Kirkman, Patrick
Kirlin, Dennis, (Retired)
Klein, Marvin
Knotek, Lawrence, (Retired)
Kohn, Ronald
Krawczyk, Gene
Leininger, Jerry, (Retired)
Lovell, David
Lovell, Dennis
Luft, Dennis M.
Maiers, Richard, (Retired)
Mason, James
McCarthy, Michael
McGuire, Dan
Miller, Edward, (On Leave)
Montagne, Monty
Myers, Ron
O'Brien, David
Parr, James, (On Leave)
Pins, Fred
Putbrese, Charles
Rallis, Stephen
Richardson, Alan, (Retired)
Riley, Mike
Rohwer, Chris
Romeo, Tony
Scurlock, Joseph, (Retired)
Seeman, Hans
Smith, William
Spinler, Gene
Stageman, Mark, (Retired)
Starbuck, Tom
Stessman, Gail
Stessman, John, (Retired)
Sullivan, Robert, (Retired)
Von Behren, Lyle
Webering, James
Weisenhorn, Earl
Wolford, Charles
Woltanski, Mike
Yang, LyPao
Ziller, Richard

INSTITUTIONS LOCATED IN THE DIOCESE

[A] EDUCATION CENTERS

COUNCIL BLUFFS. *Council Bluffs Area Catholic Education Systems, Inc.*, 400 Gleason Ave., 51503. Tel: 712-329-9000; Fax: 712-328-0228. Web: www.saintalbertschools.org. Priests 1; Total Lay Teachers 56; Total Staff 100; Total Enrollment (K-12) 763.

St. Albert Junior High School (Grades 7-8), 400 Gleason Ave., 51503. Tel: 712-328-2316; Fax: 712-328-8316. Lay Teachers 8; Students 146.

St. Albert Intermediate School (Grades 4-6), 400 Gleason Ave., 51503. Tel: 712-322-7004; Fax: 712-322-0399. Lay Teachers 13; Students 159.

St. Albert Primary School (Grades PreK-3), 2912 9th Ave., 51501. Tel: 712-323-3703; Fax: 712-323-6132. Lay Teachers 17; Students 287.

Religious Education Center, 424 Gleason Ave., 51503. Tel: 712-322-4339; Fax: 712-328-0228. Mary B. Fisher, Dir.

PANAMA. *Shelby County Board of Catholic Education*, 208 St. Mary's Ave., 51562-0183. Tel: 712-489-2727; Fax: 712-489-2727. Email: kteno@shelcocath.pvt.k12.ia.us. Web: www.shelcocath.pvt.k12.ia.us.

Elementary Schools: Shelby County Catholic Schools Tel: 712-489-2727; Fax: 712-489-2727. Total Lay Teachers 21; Total Staff 23; Total Enrollment 288. Attendance Centers:

St. Mary's Center, 208 St. Mary's Ave., 51562-0183. Tel: 712-489-2727; Fax: 712-489-2727. Lay Teachers 4; Students 59.

St. Joseph's Center, 208 Main St., Earling, 51530-0227. Tel: 712-747-3081; Fax: 712-747-3081. Lay Teachers 5; Students 77.

St. Michael's Center, 205 College Blvd., Harlan, 51537. Tel: 712-755-5634; Fax: 712-755-3332. Lay Teachers 8; Students 148.

WEST DES MOINES. *St. Joseph Educational Center*, 1400 Buffalo Rd., 50265. Tel: 515-225-3000; Fax: 515-222-1056. Dr. Jerry Deegan, Pres.

Religious Education Tel: 515-222-1044; Fax: 515-222-1056. Mr. Andrea Molinaro, Ph.D., Dir. Adult and Youth Ministries.

[B] COLLEGES AND UNIVERSITIES

DES MOINES. *Mercy College of Health Sciences*, 928-6th Ave., 50309-1239. Tel: 515-643-3180; Fax: 515-643-6698. Email: admissions@mchs.edu. Web: www.mchs.edu. Deanne M. Remer, Ph.D., Pres.; Susan Rhoades, M.S.Ed., Dir. Enrollment & Student Svcs.; Hugh B. Hansen, M.S., Dean of Institutional Research, Planning and Assessment; Lucinda Green, Ed.D., Dean of Academic Affairs and Allied Health; Warren Towles, B.S., CFO; Brian Tingleff, B.A., Dir. Institute Advancement. Member of Mercy Health Network; Sponsored by Catholic Health Initiatives. Lay Teachers 24; Students 616.

[C] HIGH SCHOOLS, INTERPAROCHIAL

COUNCIL BLUFFS. *Saint Albert Catholic Schools*, (Grades 9-12), 400 Gleason Ave., 51503. Tel: 712-328-2316; Fax: 712-328-8316. Email: tragerb@stalbert.pvt.k12.ia.us kochj@stalbert.pvt.k12.ia.us. Web: www.saintalbertschools.org. Jonna Anderson, Prin.; Rev. Phillip Hobt. Serving all parishes in Council Bluffs; St. Patrick, Missouri Valley; St. Patrick, Neola; Holy Rosary, Glenwood; St. Columbanus, Weston. Priests 1; Lay Teachers 29; Total Staff 52; Students 222.

WEST DES MOINES. *Dowling Catholic High School*, 1400 Buffalo Rd., 50265. Tel: 515-225-3000; Fax: 515-222-1056. Email: Jdeegan@dowling.pvt.k12.ia.us. Web: www.dowlinghighschool.org. Dr. Jerry Deegan, Pres.; James Dowdle, Prin.; Carol McConnell, Registrar; Rev. Jim Kirby. Serving all parishes in Des Moines; Sacred Heart, West Des Moines; St. Francis of Assisi, West Des Moines; St. Boniface, Waukee; Assumption, Granger; St. John, Cumming; St. Mary, Elkhart; Holy Cross, Elkhart; SS. John and Paul, Atoona; Immaculate Heart, Ankeny. Priests 1; Lay Teachers 84; Students 1,168.

[D] GENERAL HOSPITALS

DES MOINES. *Mercy Medical Center*, 1111 Sixth Ave., 50314. Tel: 515-247-3121; Fax: 515-247-4259. Web: www.mercydesmoines.org. Dave Vellinga, Pres. & CEO; Rose Mary Boyd, M.Div., M.A., Dir., Pastoral Care. Catholic Health Initiatives Denver, CO. Patients Assisted Annually 754,514.

Mercy Clinics, Inc.

Mercy Court

Mercy College of Health Sciences

Clark Street House of Mercy

CORNING. *Mercy Midlands: Mercy Hospital*, Rosary Dr., P.O. Box 368, 50841. Tel: 641-322-3121; Fax: 641-322-4872 3389. James C. Ruppert, Admin.; Rev. Daniel E. Siepker, Chap. Patients assisted annually: Inpatient 565; Outpatient 11,400.

COUNCIL BLUFFS. *Alegent Health: Mercy Hospital*, Formerly Bergan Mercy Alegent Health System: Mercy Hospital, 800 Mercy Dr., 51503. Tel: 712-328-5000; Fax: 712-325-2432. Web: www.alegent.org. Sheila Burke, Chap. Bed Capacity 284; Patients Assisted Annually 43,229.

Psychiatric Associates, Formerly The Mercy Center 801 Harmony St., Ste. 302, 51503. Tel: 712-328-2609; Fax: 712-325-9247. Cindy Sickler, Chap.

[E] HOMES FOR AGED

JOHNSTON. *Bishop Drumm Retirement Center* (Affiliate of Catholic Health Initiatives, Mercy Health Network & Mercy Medical Center-Des Moines), 5837 Winwood Dr., 50131-1651. Tel: 515-270-1100; Fax: 515-276-1714. Mr. Brian E. Farrell, Pres. & CEO; Mr. Matthew F. Garcia, Admin. Sisters of Mercy of the Americas (Omaha Province) 10; Care Center Residents 150; Apartment Residents 80. In Res. Rev. Thomas M. DeCarlo, Resident Chap.

McAuley Terrace Apts., 5921 Winwood Dr., 50131-1689. Tel: 515-270-6640. Mrs. Dawn Statton, Mgr.

Martina Place Assisted Living Residence, 5815 Winwood Dr., 50131-1666. Tel: 515-251-7999; Fax: 515-331-8860. Mrs. Sharon Brown, Mgr. Residents 64.

[F] SPECIAL CARE FACILITIES

DES MOINES. *House of Mercy*, 1409 Clark St., 50314-1964. Tel: 515-643-6500; Fax: 515-643-6598. Email: tbeveridge@mercydesmoines.org. Mr. Todd Beveridge, Dir.

[G] SECULAR INSTITUTES

DES MOINES. *Institute of the Heart of Jesus*, P.O. Box 4634, 50306. Tel: 515-222-1089; Fax: 515-222-1056. Email: fatherjfl@aol.com. Web: www.secularinstitutes.org. Rev. John F. Lorenz (Retired). Secular Priests and Lay People.

[H] SPIRITUAL MINISTRY TO THE DIOCESE

DES MOINES. *Emmaus House*, 1521 Center St., 50314. Tel: 515-282-4839. Email: emmausdm@aol.com. Rev. Daniel Krettek, Co-Dir.; Sr. Charlotte Huetteman, O.S.M, Co-Dir.

[I] NEWMAN CENTERS

DES MOINES. *St. Catherine of Siena Catholic Student Center*, (Drake Newman Community), 1150-28th St., 50311-4142. Tel: 515-271-4747; Fax: 515-271-1918. Email: saint.catherine@drake.edu. Rev. Jim Laurenzo. Students 160; Non-Students 250.

[J] MISCELLANEOUS LISTINGS

DES MOINES. *Bishop's Endowment Fund Foundation*, 601 Grand Ave., 50309.

Dowling-St. Joseph Alumni Foundation, 1400 Buffalo Rd., 50265. Tel: 515-225-3000; Fax: 515-222-1056. Email: jdeegan@dowling.pvt.k12.ia.us. Web: www.dowlinghighschool.org. Tom Mahoney, Pres.; Dr. Jerry Deegan, Sec.

St. Gabriel Benedictine Priory, 1913 University Ave., 50314. Tel: 515-244-3101; Fax: 515-244-3165. Email: anicholsosb@msn.com. Web: www.stgabrielspriory.org. Rev. Aquinas Nichols, O.S.B., Prior. Priests 1; Brothers 3.

Holy Family School Inner-City Youth Foundation, P.O. Box 8437, 50301. Tel: 515-262-7466; Fax: 515-266-9665. Email: hfsfoundation@qwest.net. Web: www.hfsdm.org. Jean Fitzpatrick, Foundation Admin.

St. Joseph Emergency Shelter, 1535 - 11th St., 50314. Tel: 515-282-1235. Email: jshelter@dmdiocese.org.

Life in the Spirit Community, Inc., 5419 S.E. 32nd St., 50315. Tel: 515-287-4480. Eric Zingler, Contact Person.

St. Mary Family Center, 1815 Hubbell Ave., 50316. Tel: 515-262-7290; Fax: 515-262-4036. Email: stmarys@dmdiocese.org.

Mercy Child Development Center, 6th & University, 50314. Tel: 515-243-6232. Diane Engelking, Dir.

Mercy Foundation of Des Moines - Affiliate of Catholic Health Initiatives, 921 Sixth Ave., Ste. A, 50314-1200. Tel: 515-247-3248. Timothy J. Acton, CFRE, Pres.

National Catholic Rural Life Conference, 4625 Beaver Ave., 50310. Tel: 515-270-2634; Fax: 515-270-9447. Email: ncrlc@aol.com. Web: www.ncrlc.com. Most Rev. David L. Ricken, Pres., (Bishop of Cheyenne); Bro. David G. Andrews, C.S.C., Exec. Dir.

Roman Catholic Pastoral Center Foundation, 601 Grand Ave., 50309. Tel: 515-237-5044; Fax: 515-237-5070. Email: finance@dmdiocese.org. Web: www.dmdiocese.org. Rev. Msgr. Stephen Orr, Vicar Gen.

Roman Catholic Priests' Medical Fund Foundation, 601 Grand Ave., 50309.

Roman Catholic Seminary Fund Foundation, 601 Grand Ave., 50309. Email: tmason@dmdiocese.org. Tamera Mason, Contact Person.

Society of Saint Vincent de Paul, 1426 6th Ave., 50314. Tel: 515-282-8327. Virginia Klemm, Pres.

TEC Conference Teens Encounter Christ, Formerly Teens Encounter Christ (TEC) Conference618 E. 18th St., 50316-3625. Tel: 515-266-3893; Fax: 515-266-3998. Email: natecconf@netins.net. Web: www.tecconference.org. Janet Drey, Dir.

COUNCIL BLUFFS. *St. Albert Educational Foundation*, 400 Gleason Ave., 51503. Tel: 712-329-9000; Fax: 712-328-0228. Email: kochj@stalbert.pvt.k12.ia.us. Web: www.saintalbertschools.org.

St. Joseph Catholic Cemetery Association, 17510 Sunnydale Rd., 51503. Tel: 712-322-7963. John E. O'Connor, Mgr.

Mercy Hospital Foundation, Council Bluffs, 800 Mercy Dr., P.O. Box 1C, 51502. Tel: 712-328-5372; Fax: 712-325-2425. Richard A. Hachten II, Pres.

DEXTER. *City Hospital Chaplaincy Service*. 8229 Lakeshore Dr., P.O. Box 371, 50070-0371. Tel: 515-523-1080. Email: baubrey@infinionline.net. Rev. Robert J. Aubrey. Serving all non-Catholic hospitals in Des Moines.

GRISWOLD. *Creighton University Retreat Center*, 16493 Contrail Ave., 51535. Tel: 712-778-2466; Fax: 712-779-2467. Email: curc@netins.net. Web: www.creighton.edu/CURC/curc.html. Revs. David L. Smith, S.J., Dir. & Contact Person; James H. Ryan, S.J.

HARLAN. *Shelby County Catholic Education Foundation* 2005 College Pl., 51537. Tel: 712-755-5634; Fax: 712-755-3332. Email: kteno@shelcocath.pvt.k12.ia.us. Web: shelco.pvt.k12.ia.us. Kevin Teno, Contact Person.

JOHNSTON. *Bishop Drumm Development Office* A division of Mercy Foundation - Affiliate of Catholic Health Initiatives and Mercy Health Network. , 5921 Winwood Dr., 50131. Tel: 515-331-8890; Fax: 515-331-8875. Email: ahansen@mercydesmoines.org.

PANORA. *St. Thomas More Center*, 6177 Panorama Rd., 50216. Tel: 641-755-3164; Fax: 641-755-4157. Email: stmg@netins.net. Web: www.netins.net/showcase/stmore. Rev. Christopher Fontanini.

RELIGIOUS INSTITUTES OF MEN REPRESENTED IN THE DIOCESE

For further details refer to the corresponding bracketed number in the Religious Institutes of Men or Women section.

[0600]—*Brothers of the Congregation of the Holy Cross*—C.S.C.

[]—*Congregation of the Holy Ghost* (Nigeria)

[0690]—*Jesuit Fathers and Brothers* (Wisconsin Prov.)—S.J.

[0430]—*Order of Preachers-Dominicans*—O.P.

[0200]—*Order of St. Benedict* (Conception, MO)—O.S.B.

RELIGIOUS INSTITUTES OF WOMEN REPRESENTED IN THE DIOCESE

[0230]—*Benedictine Sisters of Pontifical Jurisdiction*—O.S.B.

[2100]—*Congregation of the Holy Humility of Mary*—C.H.M.

[1920]—*Congregation of the Sisters of the Holy Cross*—C.S.C.

[1070-14]—*Dominican Sisters*—O.P.

[1070-03]—*Dominican Sisters*—O.P.

[1070-13]—*Dominican Sisters*—O.P.

[1120]—*Dominican Sisters of the Roman Congregation*—O.P.

[1310]—*The Franciscan Sisters of Little Falls, MN*—F.S.M.

[2575]—*Institute of the Sisters of Mercy of the Americas* (Cedar Rapids, IA; Omaha, NE; Chicago, IL)—R.S.M.

[2960]—*Notre Dame Sisters* (Omaha, NE)—N.D.

[1680]—*School Sisters of St. Francis*—O.S.F.

[3580]—*Servants of Mary*—O.S.M.

[0480]—*Sisters of Charity of Leavenworth, Kansas*—S.C.L.

[0430]—*Sisters of Charity of the Blessed Virgin Mary*—B.V.M.

[2630]—*Sisters of Mercy of the Holy Cross*—S.C.S.C.

[3000]—*Sisters of Notre Dame de Namur*—S.N.D.de.N

[3320]—*Sisters of Presentation of the Blessed Virgin Mary*—P.B.V.M.

[1540]—*Sisters of Saint Francis, Clinton, Iowa*—O.S.F.

[1705]—*The Sisters of St. Francis of Assisi*—O.S.F.

[1570]—*Sisters of St. Francis of the Holy Family*—O.S.F.

NECROLOGY

† Daleke, Don, (Retired)—Died Dec. 18, 2002
† Gaul, Cornelius, (Retired)—Died June 22, 2003
† Reisz, Adam, (Retired)—Died Jan. 30, 2003

Archdiocese of Detroit

(Archidioecesis Detroitensis)

His Eminence

ADAM CARDINAL MAIDA, J.C.L., J.D., S.T.L.

Archbishop of Detroit; ordained May 26, 1956; appointed to Green Bay November 8, 1983; consecrated January 25, 1984; installed as Archbishop of Detroit June 12, 1990; created Cardinal on November 26, 1994.

Cardinal's Office: 1234 Washington Blvd., Detroit, MI 48226. Fax: 313-237-4642.

Most Reverend

THOMAS J. GUMBLETON, D.D.

Auxiliary Bishop of Detroit; ordained June 2, 1956; appointed Auxiliary Bishop of Detroit and Titular Bishop of Ululi March 8, 1968; consecrated May 1, 1968. *Office: 1234 Washington Blvd., Detroit, MI 48226.*

Most Reverend

WALTER J. SCHOENHERR, D.D.

Retired Auxiliary Bishop of Detroit; ordained October 27, 1945; appointed Auxiliary Bishop of Detroit and Titular Bishop of Timidana March 8, 1968; consecrated May 1, 1968; retired March 7, 1995. *Office: 1234 Washington Blvd., Detroit, MI 48226.*

Most Reverend

MOSES B. ANDERSON, S.S.E., D.D.

Retired Auxiliary Bishop of Detroit; ordained May 30, 1958; appointed Auxiliary Bishop of Detroit and Titular Bishop of Vatarba December 3, 1982; consecrated January 27, 1983; retired October 24, 2003. *650 Waverly, Dearborn, MI 48128-1628.*

Most Reverend

JOHN M. QUINN

Auxiliary Bishop of Detroit; ordained March 17, 1972; appointed Auxiliary Bishop of Detroit July 7, 2003; consecrated August 12, 2003.

Most Reverend

FRANCIS R. REISS

Auxiliary Bishop of Detroit; ordained June 4, 1966; appointed Auxiliary Bishop of Detroit July 7, 2003; consecrated August 12, 2003. *Office: 1234 Washington Blvd., Detroit, MI 48226.*

Most Reverend

EARL A. BOYEA

Auxiliary Bishop of Detroit; ordained May 20, 1978; appointed Auxiliary Bishop of Detroit and Titular Bishop of Siccenna July 22, 2002; consecrated September 13, 2002. *Office: 1234 Washington Blvd., Detroit, MI 48226.*

Most Reverend

WALTER A. HURLEY

Auxiliary Bishop of Detroit; ordained June 5, 1965; appointed Auxiliary Bishop of Detroit July 7, 2003; consecrated August 12, 2003. *Office: 1234 Washington Blvd., Detroit, MI 48226.*

Square Miles 3,901.

Established March 8, 1833; Created An Archbishopric August 3, 1937.

Comprises the Counties of Lapeer, Macomb, Monroe, Oakland, St. Clair and Wayne.

Legal Title: For legal titles of parishes and archdiocesan institutions, consult the Cardinal's Office.

STATISTICAL OVERVIEW

Personnel	
Cardinals	1
Auxiliary Bishops	5
Retired Bishops	2
Priests: Diocesan Active in Diocese	292
Priests: Diocesan Active Outside Diocese	9
Priests: Diocesan in Foreign Missions	2
Priests: Retired, Sick or Absent	166
Number of Diocesan Priests	469
Religious Priests in Diocese	233
Total Priests in Diocese	702
Extern Priests in Diocese	47
Ordinations:	
Diocesan Priests	6
Religious Priests	1
Transitional Deacons	8
Permanent Deacons	12
Permanent Deacons in Diocese	140
Total Brothers	112
Total Sisters	1,897
Parishes	
Parishes	309
With Resident Pastor:	
Resident Diocesan Priests	252
Resident Religious Priests	27
Without Resident Pastor:	
Administered by Priests	25
Administered by Deacons	5
Missions	6
Welfare	
Catholic Hospitals	12
Total Assisted	1,601,237
Health Care Centers	8
Total Assisted	13,416
Homes for the Aged	12
Total Assisted	2,368
Residential Care of Children	8
Total Assisted	1,612
Day Care Centers	2
Total Assisted	711
Specialized Homes	8
Total Assisted	2,819
Special Centers for Social Services	13
Total Assisted	24,188
Residential Care of Disabled	1
Total Assisted	84
Educational	
Seminaries, Diocesan	2
Students from This Diocese	33
Students from Other Diocese	70
Diocesan Students in Other Seminaries	2
Seminaries, Religious	2
Students Religious	14
Total Seminarians	49
Colleges and Universities	4
Total Students	19,922
High Schools, Diocesan and Parish	16
Total Students	4,468
High Schools, Private	16
Total Students	8,701
Elementary Schools, Diocesan and Parish	110
Total Students	38,875
Elementary Schools, Private	7
Total Students	1,822
Catechesis/Religious Education:	
High School Students	6,340
Elementary Students	66,269
Total Students under Catholic Instruction	146,446
Teachers in the Diocese:	
Priests	12
Brothers	29
Sisters	112
Lay Teachers	2,680
Vital Statistics	
Receptions into the Church:	
Infant Baptism Totals	13,949
Adult Baptism Totals	1,158
Received into Full Communion	1,619
First Communions	13,817
Confirmations	11,227
Marriages:	
Catholic	2,674
Interfaith	1,222
Total Marriages	3,896
Deaths	10,257
Total Catholic Population	1,481,866
Total Population	4,441,551

Former Bishops—Rt. Revs. FREDERIC RESE, D.D., consecrated Oct. 6, 1833; resigned Aug. 19, 1840; died Dec. 30, 1871; PETER PAUL LEFEVERE, D.D., consecrated Nov. 22, 1841; Bishop of Zela, coadjutor and admin. of Detroit; died March 4, 1869; CASPAR HENRY BORGESS, D.D., consecrated April 24, 1870; Bishop of Calydon, coadjutor and admin. of Detroit; became Bishop of Detroit Dec. 30, 1871; resigned April 16, 1887; died May 3, 1890; JOHN SAMUEL FOLEY, D.D., consecrated Nov. 4, 1888; died Jan. 5, 1918; Most Rev. MICHAEL JAMES GALLAGHER, D.D., consecrated Sept. 8, 1915; Bishop of Tipasa, coadjutor of Grand Rapids; became Bishop of Grand Rapids Dec. 26, 1916; transferred to Detroit July 18, 1918; died Jan. 20, 1937; His Eminence EDWARD CARDINAL MOONEY, D.D., appt. Apostolic Delegate in India Jan. 8, 1926; appt. Titular Archbishop of Irenopolis Jan. 18, 1926; consecrated Jan. 31, 1926; appt. Apostolic Delegate in Japan Feb. 25, 1931; transferred to the Diocese of Rochester Aug. 28, 1933; transferred to the Archdiocese of Detroit Aug. 3, 1937; created Cardinal Priest of the title of S. Susanna Feb. 18, 1946; died Oct. 25, 1958; JOHN CARDINAL DEARDEN, D.D., ord. Dec. 8, 1932; consecrated Titular Bishop of Sarepta and coadjutor Bishop of Pittsburgh Dec. 22, 1950; installed Archbishop of Detroit Jan. 29, 1959; created Cardinal April 28, 1969; resigned as Archbishop July 15, 1980; died Aug. 1, 1988; EDMUND CARDINAL SZOKA, J.C.L., D.D., Archbishop Emeritus of Detroit; ord. June 5, 1954; appt. Bishop of Gaylord June 15, 1971; consecrated July 20, 1971; installed July 20, 1971; promoted to See of Detroit March 28, 1981; installed May 17, 1981; created Cardinal June 28, 1988; appt. Pres., Prefacture for Economic Affairs of the Holy See June 25, 1990.

Archdiocesan Departments and Divisions

Information and Reference—Tel: 313-237-5800.

Cardinal's Office—1234 Washington Blvd., Detroit, 48226. Fax: 313-237-4642. Revs. JEFFREY M. MONFORTON, Cardinal's Personal Sec. Tel: 313-237-5816; ROBERT MCCLORY, Chancellor. Tel: 313-237-5816; Fax: 313-237-4643; Rev. Msgr. JOHN P. ZENZ, Moderator of the Curia. Tel: 313-237-5783. All official mail should be directed to this office.

Auxiliary Bishops—Most Revs. LEONARD P. BLAIR, D.D., Region 1. Tel: 313-237-5859; ALLEN J. VIGNERON, D.D., Region 2. Tel: 313-883-8501; KEVIN M. BRITT, D.D., Region 3. Tel: 313-237-5848.

College of Consultors—Rev. Msgrs. RICARDO E. BASS, J.C.L.; ROBERT S. HUMITZ; Rev. TIMOTHY F. BABCOCK; Rev. Msgr. JAMES A. MOLONEY; Revs. THOMAS J. SUTHERLAND; FREDERICK J. SCHWEIHOFER; Rev. Msgrs. ANTHONY M. TOCCO; JOHN P. ZENZ.

Presbyteral Council—Rev. Msgrs. EDWARD J. BALDWIN (Retired); RICARDO E. BASS, J.C.L.; Revs. ROBERT FISHER, S.V.D.; GERARD W. BATTERSBY; JAMES L. BJORUM, J.C.L.; GEORGE BROWNE (Retired); JOHN G. BUDDE; BRIAN K. COKONOUGHER; JESSE DEPORRES COX; Rev. Msgr. JOHN P. ZENZ; Revs. THOMAS A. BELCZAK; DAVID A. BUERSMEYER; RAYMOND H. LEWANDOWSKI; ROBERT S. LIBERTY; ROBERT MCCABE; GERALD A. MCENHILL; EZEQUIEL

MONDRAGON; THOMAS J. SUTHERLAND; Rev. Msgr. ROBERT S. HUMITZ; Revs. JOHN RICCARDO; MARK SOEHNER, O.F.M.; SEAN SYLVESTER; WILLIAM TINDALL; GEORGE WILLIAMS; MICHAEL VERSCHAEVE; DANIEL J. TRAPP; GERARD LEBOEUF; CARL A. BONK, S.J.; RICHARD A. HARTMANN; Mr. ANTHONY CAMILLERI.

Archdiocesan Vicars—Revs. JEROME A. BRZEZINSKI, Pontiac Area (3); P. LARRY SIROSKEY, Downriver (4); THOMAS H. CUSICK, Western Wayne (4); JAMES M. PROFOTA, Serf (1); WILLIAM J. PROMESSO, West Detroit (3); DAVID G. BURGARD, Belle River (2); THEODORE K. PARKER, O.S.C., Northwest Detroit (3); JOSEPH M. ESPER, Port Huron (2); JAMES F. KEAN, Southland (4); STEPHEN ROONEY, Monroe (4); JEROME C. SINGER, East Side (1); MICHAEL G. SAVICKAS, Vicariate of the Lakes (3); THOMAS J. KRAMER, Dearborn (4); STANLEY A. ULMAN, North Central (2); KENNETH R. KAUCHECK, J.C.D., Birmingham-Bloomfield-Troy (3); WILLIAM D. SINATRA, Farmington-Southfield (3); PATRICK P. CASEY, The Hub (4); THOMAS JOHNSON, North Macomb (2); GARY SCHULTE, Warren-Centerline (1); DAVID J. BLAZEK, Detroit-Grosse Pointe (1); JOSEPH MALLIA, Northwest Wayne (4); MICHAEL N. COONEY, East Macomb (1); WAYNE G. UREEL, Thumb (3); EDWARD F. ZAORSKI, Southwest (4); STEVEN C. KOEHLER, Southeast Oakland (3); VACANT, Sterling Heights (2).

Archdiocesan Pastoral Council—Ms. PAMELA BEECH.

The Metropolitan Tribunal—305 Michigan Ave., Detroit, 48226. Tel: 313-237-5865; Fax: 313-237-5872. Office Hours: Mon.-Fri. 8:30-4:30

Judicial Vicar—Very Rev. GEORGE P. MILLER, J.C.L.

Adjutant Judicial Vicars—Revs. JEROME SLOWINSKI, J.C.L.; ROBERT H. WILLIAMS, J.C.L.

Administrator—ANDREA M. PINTO.

Second Instance Coordinator—JACQUELINE L. LOVE.

Judges—Most Rev. WALTER A. HURLEY, J.C.L.; Rev. Msgr. MICHAEL LEFEVRE, J.C.L.; Revs. TIMOTHY F. BABCOCK; JAMES L. BJORUM, J.C.L.; JOACHIM CULOTTA, O.P., J.C.D.; JOHN GAGALA, J.C.L.; RONALD J. JOZWIAK, J.C.L.; KENNETH R. KAUCHECK, J.C.D.; ROBERT MCCLORY; GARY M. TIERNEY, J.C.L.; Mr. MICHAEL TRUEMAN, J.C.L.; Rev. ROBERT H. WILLIAMS, J.C.L.

Defenders of Bond—Most Rev. FRANCIS REISS, J.C.L.; Rev. Msgr. RICARDO E. BASS, J.C.L.; Revs. RICHARD CAVELLIER, J.C.L.; NORMAN D. NAWROCKI, J.C.L.; FRANCIS SYLVESTER.

Promoter of Justice—Rev. RONALD T. BROWNE, J.C.L.

Notaries—GLORIA ANFIELD; IRENE S. KRAWCZYK; PATRICIA MKRTUMIAN; PATRICIA SAMSON; ESTHER SMITH.

Auditors—Mr. ROBERT CADOTTE; Rev. MICHAEL LOYSON.

Court Expert—Sr. JUDITH MCMANUS, O.P., L.M.F.T., A.C.S.W.

Office of Human Services and Pastoral Care—KRISTA BAJOKA. Tel: 313-237-4687.

Department of Communications—NED MCGRATH, Dir., 305 Michigan Ave., Detroit, 48226. Tel: 313-237-5943; Fax: 313-237-4644.

Office of Public Relations—NED MCGRATH. Tel: 313-237-5943; Fax: 313-237-4644.

Office of Printing and Mailing—DENNIS MILLIGAN, 1501 Sixth St., Detroit, 48226. Tel: 313-237-5967; Fax: 313-965-8471.

Office of Television—KEN KOLB. Tel: 313-237-5938; Fax: 313-237-5928.

Department of Education—Sr. FRANCES MADOLNY, O.P., Ph.D., Dir., 305 Michigan Ave., Detroit, 48226. Tel: 313-237-4675; Fax: 313-237-5867.

Catholic Schools—Sr. MARY GEHRINGER, Supt. Tel: 313-237-5775.

Office of Catechetics/Religious Education—MAUREEN O'REILLY. Tel: 313-237-4670.

Office of Family Life/Youth Ministry—Deacon ROBERT OWIES. Tel: 313-237-5892.

St. John Center for Family and Youth—Deacon JOHN H. BALL, Dir., 44011 Five Mile Rd., Plymouth, 48170. Tel: 734-414-1111; Fax: 734-414-1150.

Department of Development—MICHAEL E. MURPHY, Dir., 2701 Chicago Blvd., Detroit, 48206. Tel: 313-883-8657; Fax: 313-883-8681.

Catholic Services Appeal—THERESA J. KACH. Tel: 313-883-8656.

Planned Giving—THOMAS P. SCHOLLER. Tel: 313-883-8657.

Donor Relations—SARAH C. ABATE; JESSICA I. ORZECHOWSKI. Tel: 313-883-8657.

Pathways of Hope—Tel: 313-883-8658.

Stewardship Education—DAVID P. CASNOVSKY. Tel: 313-883-8567.

Department of Finance and Administrative Services—Mr. MICHAEL H. GORMAN, Dir., 1234 Washington Blvd., Detroit, 48226. Tel: 313-237-5834; Fax: 313-237-5868.

Archdiocesan Buildings—FRANK MACDONELL. Tel: 313-237-5845.

Archdiocesan Properties—C. MARY CARLISLE. Tel: 313-237-5820.

Financial Services—ABELARDO B. BUSQUE. Tel: 313-237-5828.

Information Technology—VINCENT CHRISMAN. Tel: 313-237-5797; Fax: 313-237-5979.

Sacred Heart Building Administration—JOHN DUNCAN. Tel: 313-883-8599.

Archdiocese of Detroit Endowment Foundation—1234 Washington Blvd., Detroit, 48226.

Administration—Mr. MICHAEL H. GORMAN, Dir. Tel: 313-237-5834; Fax: 313-237-5868.

Development—MICHAEL E. MURPHY, Dir. Tel: 313-883-8657; Fax: 313-883-8681.

Department of Parish Life—CATHERINE WAGNER, Dir.; LORY MCGLINNEN, Assoc. Dir., 305 Michigan Ave., Detroit, 48226. Tel: 313-237-5934; Fax: 313-237-5869.

Evangelization—Rev. DANIEL HAVRON, O.F.M. Tel: 313-237-4686.

Office of Christian Worship—DANIEL MCAFEE. Tel: 313-237-5932.

Council of Catholic Women—JULIE RACINE, Pres. Tel: 313-237-5896.

Hispanic Catholic Ministries—Tel: 313-237-5761.

Black Catholic Ministries—Rev. CLARENCE E. WILLIAMS, C.PP.S. Tel: 313-237-5934.

Office of Leadership Formation—Ms. PAMELA BEECH. Tel: 313-237-5887.

Office of Pastoral Ministers and Permanent Diaconate—Deacon RONALD L. MCINTYRE. Tel: 313-237-5778.

Delegate for Religious—Tel: 313-237-4682.

Pastoral Resources—Dr. MICHAEL MCCALLION. Tel: 313-237-5760.

"The Michigan Catholic" Newspaper—Rev. THOMAS G. RICE, Editor in Chief, 305 Michigan Ave., Detroit, 48226. Tel: 313-224-8000.

Archivist—ROMAN P. GODZAK, 1234 Washington Blvd., Detroit, 48226. Tel: 313-237-5846; Fax: 313-237-4643.

Human Resources—RONALD MCGUIRE. Tel: 313-237-5947; Fax: 313-237-5791.

Propagation of the Faith (Missions)—Rev. Msgr. JAMES A. MOLONEY, 17650 W. Outer Dr., Dearborn Heights, 48127.

Holy Childhood Association—1230 Washington Blvd., Detroit, 48226. Tel: 313-237-5807.

Catholic Youth Organization—SUZANNE HEATH, Dir., Gabriel Richard Bldg., 305 Michigan Ave., Detroit, 48226. Tel: 313-963-7172.

Archdiocesan Theological Commission—Rev. Msgr. JOHN P. ZENZ. Tel: 313-237-5783.

Vocation Office—Rev. JAMES D. BILOT, Dir. Tel: 313-237-5875; Sr. ANGELA CERNA-PLATA, I.H.M., Asst. Dir. Fax: 313-237-6070.

Priests Conference for Parish Affairs of the Archdiocese of Detroit—Rev. WALTER J. PTAK, Pres.

Victim Assistance Coordinator—Sr. BEVERLY HINDSON, I.H.M. Tel: 866-343-8055.

CLERGY, PARISHES, MISSIONS AND PAROCHIAL SCHOOLS

CITY OF DETROIT
(WAYNE COUNTY)

1—CATHEDRAL, CHURCH OF THE MOST BLESSED SACRAMENT, Rev. Msgrs. Michael LeFevre, J.C.L., Rector; James P. Robinson, S.S.E., Rector Emeritus; Rev. Okeychukwu Iwuji.
Res.: 9844 Woodward Ave., 48202. Tel: 313-865-6300; Fax: 313-867-4613.

2—ALL SAINTS, Rev. Edward F. Zaorski.
Res.: 2430 S. Beatrice St., 48217. Tel: 313-841-1428; Fax: 313-841-3009.

3—ST. ALOYSIUS, Revs. Mark Soehner, O.F.M ; Mel P. Brady, O.F.M.; Sr. Kathleen Gaynor, O.P., Pastoral Assoc. In Res., Rev. Tod Laverty, O.F.M.
Chancery Bldg.: 1234 Washington Blvd., 48226. Tel: 313-237-5810; Fax: 313-963-9076.

4—ST. ANDREW, (Polish), Rev. Julian Chmura.
Res.: 7060 McGraw Ave., 48210. Tel: 313-361-1717; Fax: 313-361-9816.

5—SS. ANDREW AND BENEDICT, (Slovak), Rev. Edward F. Zaorski; Deacon Norbert Motowski.
Res.: 2430 S. Beatrice St., 48217. Tel: 313-381-1184; Fax: 313-831-0416.

6—ANNUNCIATION, Merged, with Our Lady of Sorrows, Detroit to form Annunciation/Our Lady of Sorrow, Detroit.

7—ANNUNCIATION/OUR LADY OF SORROWS, Rev. Michael C. Nkachukwu; Deacon Allen F. Love, Pastoral Assoc.
Res.: 1265 Parkview Ave., 48214. Tel: 313-822-1262; Fax: 313-822-8988.
Stapleton Center—9341 Agnes, 48214. Tel: 313-822-0397; Fax: 313-822-3994.
St. Rose Senior Citizen Center—5555 Conner, Ste. 1052, 48213. Tel: 313-921-9277; Fax: 313-921-9145. Sr. Rose Bernadette, Dir.

8—ST. ANTHONY, Rev. Michael C. Nkachukwu.
Office—5247 Sheridan Ave., 48213. Tel: 313-921-0263; Fax: 313-924-4040.

9—ST. ANTHONY, (Lithuanian), Rev. Alphonse Babonas.
Res.: 1750 25th St., 48216. Tel: 313-554-1284.

10—ASSUMPTION GROTTO, [CEM] Rev. Eduard Perrone. In Res., Rev. Boleslaus Lipczewski (Retired).
Res.: 13770 Gratiot Ave., 48205. Tel: 313-372-0762; Fax: 313-372-2064.

11—ST. AUGUSTINE AND ST. MONICA, Rev. Daniel J. Trapp.
Res.: 4151 Seminole St., 48214. Tel: 313-921-4107; Fax: 313-921-1115.

12—ST. BARTHOLOMEW, Rev. Boleslaus Krol.
Res.: 2291 E. Outer Dr., 48234. Tel: 313-892-1446; Fax: 313-892-1149.
School—Tel: 313-366-3640; Fax: 313-366-0257. Ms. Sharon Perko, Prin. Lay Teachers 9; Students 135.
Convent—2251 E. Outer Dr., 48234. Tel: 313-366-0525. Sisters 3.

13—ST. BRENDAN, Rev. Louis Resma, Admin.
Res.: 11433 Beaconsfield, 48224. Tel: 313-372-1644; Fax: 313-372-7195.

14—ST. CECILIA, Rev. Theodore K. Parker, O.S.C.
Res.: Box 04209, 10400 Stoepel Ave., 48204. Tel: 313-933-6788; Fax: 313-933-1439.
Church: Livernois at Stearns, 48204.
School—Tel: 313-933-2400; Fax: 313-933-9332. Sr. Margaret Sweeney, I.H.M., Prin. Sisters-Servants of the Immaculate Heart of Mary 2; Lay Teachers 10; Students 210.
High School—St. Martin de Porres, Tel: 313-864-3330; Fax: 313-864-3648. Ms. Sunbeam Hughes, Prin. Priests 1; Sisters 3; Lay Teachers 24.

15—ST. CHARLES BORROMEO, Rev. David Preuss, O.F.M.Cap. In Res., Rev. Augustine Cops, O.F.M.Cap.
Res.: 1491 Baldwin Ave., 48214. Tel: 313-331-0253; Fax: 313-331-4834.

16—CHRIST THE KING, Rev. Victor Clore; Sr. Fiorentina D'Amore, H.V.M, Pastoral Assoc.
Res.: 16805 Pierson, 48219. Tel: 313-532-1211; Fax: 313-532-1216.
Church: 20300 Grand River & Burt Rd., 48219.
School—Tel: 313-532-1213; Fax: 313-532-1050. Mrs. Rosanne Jodway, Prin. Lay Teachers 20; Students 190.

17—ST. CHRISTINE, Rev. Mark S. Brauer.
Office—15317 Dacosta, Box 231209, 48223. Tel: 313-535-7272; Fax: 313-535-3439.
Res.: 23450 W. Davison, 48223. Tel: 313-255-3666; Fax: 313-537-0598.

18—ST. CHRISTOPHER, Rev. Gerard W. Battersby; Deacon John Marku.
Res.: 7800 Woodmont Ave., 48228. Tel: 313-584-7460; Fax: 313-584-6361.
School—Tel: 313-846-1430; Fax: 313-846-5080. Cynthia Szweda, Prin. Sisters of the Holy Family of Nazareth 4; Lay Teachers 4; Students 65.
Convent—7800 Woodmont Ave., 48228. Tel: 313-584-7579.

19—ST. CUNEGUNDA, Rev. Zbigniew Grankowski.
Res.: 5900 St. Lawrence Ave., 48210. Tel: 313-843-4717; Fax: 313-841-4255.
School—Tel: 313-843-0004; Fax: 313-843-8812. Sr. Mary Alexander, C.S.S.F., Prin. Lay Teachers 5; Religious 4; Students 185.

20—ST. DOMINIC, Rev. Patrick Casey.
Res.: 4844 Trumbull Ave., 48208. Tel: 313-831-8790; Fax: 313-831-2965.

21—ST. ELIZABETH, Rev. John W. Markham (Retired).
Res.: 3138 E. Canfield Ave., 48207. Tel: 313-921-9225; Fax: 313-921-9475.

22—ST. FRANCIS D'ASSISI, Rev. Robert J. Wojciechowski.
Res.: 4500 Wesson St., 48210. Tel: 313-897-7229; Fax: 313-897-7485.

23—ST. FRANCIS DE SALES, Rev. James E. O'Reilly, S.J. In Res., Revs. Justin J. Kelly, S.J.; David F. Mastrangelo, S.J.; Bro. Michael Baranek, S.J.; Deacon Paul O'Connor.
Res.: 10600 Fenkell Ave., 48238. Tel: 313-861-4020; Fax: 313-861-4718.

24—ST. GABRIEL, Deacon Raul Feliciano, Temp. Admin.
Res.: 8118 W. Vernor Hwy., 48209-1524. Tel: 313-841-0753; Fax: 313-841-0916.
Catechesis/Religious Program—Tel: 313-841-0419. Students 511.

25—ST. GEMMA GALGANI, Rev. Mark S. Brauer.
Res.: 23450 W. Davison, 48223. Tel: 313-255-3666; Fax: 313-537-0598.

26—ST. GERARD, Rev. Donald Archambault; Deacons Alfons Hogrebe; Hubert Sanders; Lester Arquette.
Res.: 19800 Pembroke, 48219. Tel: 313-537-5770;

Fax: 313-537-5773.
School—19900 Evergreen Rd., 48219. Tel: 313-533-4353; Fax: 313-533-2190. Lay Teachers 12; Students 198.
Catechesis/Religious Program—Tel: 313-533-0197. Christine Laing, D.R.E. Students 242.
Convent—19910 Evergreen Rd., 48219.
27—GESU, Rev. Norman J. Dickson, S.J.
Res.: 17204 Oak Dr., 48221. Tel: 313-862-4400; Fax: 313-862-1083.
School—Mr. John Champion, Prin. Tel: 313-863-4677. Lay Teachers 10; Students 220.
28—ST. GREGORY, Deacon Benjamin Prince.
Res.: 15031 Dexter, 48238. Tel: 313-861-0363; Fax: 313-862-6805.
29—GUARDIAN ANGELS, Rev. Louis Resma, Admin.
Res.: 12545 Kelly Rd., 48224. Tel: 313-526-0735; Fax: 313-526-7382.
30—ST. HEDWIG, Rev. Christopher P. Maus.
Res.: 3245 Junction Ave., 48210. Tel: 313-894-5409; Fax: 313-894-4730.
31—HOLY CROSS, (Hungarian), Revs. Barnabas G. Kiss, O.F.M.; Angelus Ligeti, O.F.M.
Res.: 8423 South St., 48209. Tel: 313-842-1133; Fax: 313-842-2773.
32—HOLY FAMILY, (Italian), Rev. John Stopponi, O.S.B., Admin.
Res.: 641 Walter P. Chrysler Expwy., 48226. Tel: 313-963-2046; Fax: 313-961-0065.
33—HOLY REDEEMER, Revs. Donald F. Hanchon; Jaime Hinojos-Ortega; Jean Louis Rattier; Deacon Ronald L. McIntyre.
Res.: 1721 Junction Ave., 48209. Tel: 313-842-3450; Fax: 313-849-0539.
School—Tel: 313-841-5230; Fax: 313-841-3640. Sr. Elizabeth Fleckenstein, I.H.M., Prin. Sisters Servants of the Immaculate Heart of Mary 2; Sisters of St. Joseph 1; Lay Teachers 11; Students 251.
High School—Tel: 313-841-4433; Fax: 313-841-2116. Joseph Redican, C.S.B., Pres.; Rev. Dennis Noelke, C.S.B., Prin.; Bill May, Chap. Priests 4; Sisters 1; Lay Teachers 17; Students 192.
Convent—5678 Eldred Ave., 48209. Tel: 313-841-8420.
34—ST. HYACINTH, (Polish), Rev. Francis S. Skalski.
Res.: 3151 Farnsworth Ave., 48211. Tel: 313-922-1507; Fax: 313-922-2459.
35—IMMACULATE HEART OF MARY, Rev. Donald Archambault; Sr. Stephanie Holub, R.S.M., Pastoral Assoc.
Res.: 16000 Pembroke Ave., 48235. Tel: 313-272-0990; Fax: 313-272-9772.
Convent—19960 Mansfield Ave., 48235. Tel: 313-836-4641.
36—ST. JEROME, Closed. For inquiries for parish records contact the chancery.
37—ST. JOHN BERCHMANS-ST. JULIANA, Rev. David Preuss, O.F.M.Cap., Admin.; Ms. Jacqueline Palmer, Pastoral Assoc.
Res.: 9801 Chalmers, 48213. Tel: 313-526-7254; Fax: 313-526-7553.
School—St. Juliana, 9755 Chalmers, 48213. Tel: 313-526-0062; Fax: 313-526-2988. Servite Sisters 1; Lay Teachers 10; Students 190.
38—ST. JOHN CANTIUS, (Polish), Rev. Edward F. Zaorski.
Res.: 844 Harbaugh Ave., 48209. Tel: 313-842-2276; Fax: 313-842-2268.
39—ST. JOSAPHAT, (Polish), Rev. Mark Borkowski.
Res.: 691 E. Canfield Ave., 48201. Tel: 313-831-1072; Fax: 313-831-8522.
40—ST. JOSEPH, Rev. Msgr. John F. Schweder. In Res., Rev. Felix S. Alsola (Philippines).
Res.: 1828 Jay St., 48207. Tel: 313-393-8212; Fax: 313-393-8294.
41—ST. JUDE, Rev. Brian K. Cokonougher; Sr. Jacquelyn Laster, R.S.M., Pastoral Assoc.; Deacon Valere Buyle.
Res.: 15889 E. Seven Mile Rd., 48205. Tel: 313-527-0380; Fax: 313-527-3511.
School—15865 E. Seven Mile, 48205. Tel: 313-839-6792; Fax: 313-527-2093. Sisters 4; Lay Teachers 10; Students 130.
Catechesis/Religious Program—Students 30.
42—ST. LEO, Most Rev. Thomas J. Gumbleton; Angela Thomas-Weldon, Pastoral Assoc.
Church & Res.: 4860 15th St., 48208. Tel: 313-894-0357; Fax: 313-894-1172.
43—ST. LOUIS THE KING, Revs. Boleslaus Krol; Ron Borg, C.S.B.
Res.: 18891 St. Louis Ave., 48234. Tel: 313-891-1766; Fax: 313-891-7959.
44—ST. LUKE, Rev. John M. Currin; Sr. Marie Roy, S.S.J., Pastoral Assoc.
Res.: 8017 Ohio Ave., 48204. Tel: 313-935-6161; Fax: 313-935-0788.
School—St. Luke & St. Brigid Elementary School, St. Brigid Montessori Preschool, 8091 Ohio, 48204. Tel: 313-933-9611; Fax: 313-933-9522. Mrs. Clima Fields, Prin. Lay Teachers 13; Students 141.
45—MADONNA, Deacon Benjamin Prince.
Res.: 1125 Oakman Blvd., 48238. Tel: 313-868-4308; Fax: 313-868-9771.
46—MARTYRS OF UGANDA, Rev. Tyrone Robinson; Deacon Douglas Jackson.
Res.: 7601 Rosa Parks Blvd., 48206. Tel: 313-896-2335; Fax: 313-896-0925.
Catechesis/Religious Program—Mr. Mesfid Bely, D.R.E. Students 35.
47—ST. MARY, Rev. Edward J. Vilkauskas, C.S.Sp.
Res.: 646 Monroe Ave., 48226. Tel: 313-961-8711; Fax: 313-961-4994.
48—ST. MARY'S OF REDFORD, Rev. Robert McCabe.
Mailing Address: 14750 St. Mary's, 48227. Tel: 313-273-1100; Fax: 313-273-2002.
School—St. Mary of Redford Grade School, 14751 Mansfield, 48227. Tel: 313-835-6834; Fax: 313-836-4184. Sr. Loretta Schroeder, I.H.M., Prin. Religious 4; Lay Teachers 12; Students 190.
Convent—14601 Mansfield, 48227. Tel: 313-272-2727. Sisters 4.
49—ST. MATTHEW, Rev. Duane R. Novelly; Sr. Karen Eklund, I.H.M., Pastoral Min.
Res.: 6021 Whittier Ave., 48224. Tel: 313-884-4470; Fax: 313-884-4276.
50—MOST HOLY TRINITY, Rev. Russell E. Kohler.
Res.: 1050 Porter St., 48226. Tel: 313-965-4450; Fax: 313-965-4453.
Convent—Center: 1234 Porter St., 48226.
51—NATIVITY OF OUR LORD, Rev. Jerome C. Singer.
Res.: 5900 McClellan Ave., 48213. Tel: 313-922-0033; Fax: 313-922-0033.
52—OUR LADY GATE OF HEAVEN, Closed., for inquiries for parish records please see St. Suzanne/Our Lady Gate of Heaven, Detroit.
53—OUR LADY HELP OF CHRISTIANS, (Polish), Rev. George A. Rutkowski.
Res.: 12635 McDougall Ave., 48212. Tel: 313-892-6116.
Convent—12541 McDougall Ave., 48212. Tel: 313-891-5280.
54—OUR LADY OF GOOD COUNSEL, Rev. Robert J. Kotlarz; Deacon Donald Sandstrom, Pastoral Assoc.
Res.: 17142 Rowe Ave., 48205. Tel: 313-372-1698; Fax: 313-372-1211.
55—OUR LADY OF MT. CARMEL, Rev. Robert Cini, M.S.S.P.
Res.: 555 Oakwood Blvd., 48217. Tel: 313-841-8478; Fax: 313-841-0209.
56—OUR LADY OF SORROWS, Merged, with Annunciation, Detroit to form Annunciation/Our Lady of Sorrows, Detroit.
57—OUR LADY OF THE ROSARY, Rev. Robert Morand.
Res.: 5930 Woodward Ave., 48202. Tel: 313-875-6011; Fax: 313-872-0758.
58—OUR LADY QUEEN OF ANGELS, Rev. James Henning, O.F.M.Conv.
Res.: 4200 Martin Ave., 48210. Tel: 313-897-8160; Fax: 313-897-8126.
School—Tel: 313-894-6266; Fax: 313-897-3397. Ms. Margaret Schefke, Prin. Franciscan Sisters of St. Joseph 2; Lay Teachers 5; Students 87.
Convent—4108 Martin Ave., 48210. Tel: 313-894-3462.
59—OUR LADY QUEEN OF HEAVEN, Rev. Donald A. Sopiak.
Res.: 8200 Rolyat Ave., 48234. Tel: 313-891-4553; Fax: 313-891-5782.
60—ST. PATRICK, Rev. Patrick Casey; Floria Ellison, Pastoral Assoc. In Res., Rev. Thomas J. Duffey (Retired).
Church: 58 Parsons, 48201. Tel: 313-833-0857; Fax: 313-831-1619.
St. Patrick Senior Center, Inc.—Tel: 313-833-7080; Fax: 313-833-0128. Sr. Mary Watson, O.P., Pres.
61—SS. PETER AND PAUL (West Side), Rev. Stanley Tokarski. In Res., Rev. Mitchell Szarek.
Res.: 7685 Grandville Ave., 48228. Tel: 313-846-2222; Fax: 313-584-1484.
62—SS. PETER AND PAUL JESUIT, Rev. Carl A. Bonk, S.J.; Bro. James T. Horgan, S.J.
Res.: 438 St. Antoine St., 48226. Tel: 313-961-8077; Fax: 313-963-5134.
63—ST. PHILOMENA, Rev. Peter S. Lentine.
Res.: 4281 Marseilles Ave., 48224. Tel: 313-882-4300; Fax: 313-882-1661.
Catechesis/Religious Program—Kathleen McKenzie, D.R.E. Tel: 313-884-2422. Students 204.
64—PRECIOUS BLOOD, Deacons Wyatt L. Jones, Pastoral Admin.; Bill Stimpson. In Res., Rev. Vincent Odikanoro (Nigeria).
Res.: 13305 Grove Ave., 48235. Tel: 313-342-5292; Fax: 313-342-3513.
65—PRESENTATION-OUR LADY OF VICTORY, Rev. Hubert Sanders, Admin.
Res.: 19760 Meyers Rd., 48235. Tel: 313-342-1333; Fax: 313-342-4182.
66—ST. RAYMOND, Rev. Robert J. Kotlarz.
Res.: 20103 Joann Ave., 48205. Tel: 313-527-0525; Fax: 313-527-9776.
Community Center—20055 Joann Ave., 48205. Tel: 313-372-0437.
67—ST. RITA, Rev. Timothy Kane.
Res.: 1000 E. State Fair, 48203. Tel: 313-366-2340; Fax: 313-891-0677.
68—SACRED HEART OF JESUS, Rev. Norman P. Thomas.
Res.: 1000 Eliot St., 48207. Tel: 313-831-1356; Fax: 313-831-8603.
Catechesis/Religious Program—Barbara Hunt, D.R.E. Students 155.
69—SACRED HEART-CHALDEAN PARISH, Rev. Jacob O. Yasso.
Res.: 310 W. Seven Mile Rd., 48203. Tel: 313-368-6214; Fax: 313-891-0132.
70—ST. SCHOLASTICA, Rev. Livius Paoli, O.S.B.
Res.: 17320 Rosemont Rd., 48219. Tel: 313-531-0140; Fax: 313-531-0739.
Church: Southfield Rd. & West Outer Dr., 48219.
School—Tel: 313-532-1916; Fax: 313-532-0140. Faye Vaughn, Elementary Prin. Sisters of St. Dominic (Adrian) 1; Lay Teachers 14; Students 205.
High School—Benedictine High School, Tel: 313-532-1274; Fax: 313-532-5767. David Suttner, High School Prin. Sisters 1; Lay Teachers 13; Students 130.
Convent—17305 Ashton, 48219. Tel: 313-541-4368.
71—STE. ANNE, Rev. Thomas W. Sepulveda, C.S.B. In Res., Revs. L. Leo Reilly, C.S.B.; Manuel J. Chircop, C.S.B.
Res.: 1000 Ste. Anne St., 48216. Tel: 313-496-1701; Fax: 313-496-0429.
72—ST. STEPHEN-MARY MOTHER OF THE CHURCH, Revs. Francisco Restrepo; Rafael Jimenez.
Res.: 4311 Central Ave., 48210. Tel: 313-841-0783; Fax: 313-841-4868.
Catechesis/Religious Program—4330 Central Ave., 48210. Tel: 313-841-9103.
73—ST. SUZANNE/OUR LADY GATE OF HEAVEN, Rev. Robert McCabe; Sr. Lucy Abbey, I.H.M., Pastoral Assoc.
Res.: 9357 Westwood Ave., 48228. Tel: 313-838-6780; Fax: 313-838-1063.
74—SWEETEST HEART OF MARY, (Polish), [CEM] Rev. Mark Borkowski.
Res.: 4440 Russell St., 48207. Tel: 313-831-6659; Fax: 313-831-8522.
75—ST. THOMAS AQUINAS, Rev. William J. Promesso; Deacon John Santeramo; Catherine Odom Prowse, Pastoral Assoc.; Micheleen Troutman, Pastoral Assoc.
Parish Center—5780 Evergreen Rd., 48228. Tel: 313-271-4170; Fax: 313-271-8773.
Catechesis/Religious Program—Tel: 313-271-0813. Nikki Zakrzewski, D.R.E. Students 88.
76—TRANSFIGURATION, Rev. Andrew Wesley.
Res.: 5830 Simon K. St., 48212. Tel: 313-892-1310; Fax: 313-893-2478.
School—Tel: 313-366-3810. Sr. Angelica Zajkowski, Prin. Sisters of the Holy Family of Nazareth 2; Lay Teachers 8; Students 150.
Convent—5821 Rupert, 48212. Tel: 313-891-9273.

OUTSIDE THE CITY OF DETROIT

ALGONAC, ST. CLAIR CO., ST. CATHERINE, [CEM] Rev. Douglas J. Bignall.
Res.: 1103 Washington, 48001. Tel: 810-794-3301; Fax: 810-794-1849.
Catechesis/Religious Program—Tel: 810-794-3843. William Terrien, D.R.E. Students 127.
ALLEN PARK, WAYNE CO., ST. FRANCES CABRINI, Revs. Joseph Mallia; John Christopher Bustamante.
Res.: 9000 Laurence Ave., 48101. Tel: 313-381-5601; Fax: 313-381-7837.
School—Tel: 313-928-6610; Fax: 313-928-8502. Ted Behn, Prin. Lay Teachers 30; Students 335.
High School—Tel: 313-388-0110; Fax: 313-388-1876. Ted Behn, Prin. Lay Teachers 19; Students 97.
Catechesis/Religious Program—Ed McLeod, D.R.E. Students 405.
ALLENTON, ST. CLAIR CO., ST. JOHN THE EVANGELIST, Rev. Gerard Frawley, S.C.A.
Res.: 872 Capac Rd., 48002. Tel: 810-395-7074; Fax: 810-395-7718.
Catechesis/Religious Program—Tel: 810-395-2301.
ANCHORVILLE, ST. CLAIR CO., IMMACULATE CONCEPTION, [CEM] Rev. David G. Burgard.
Mailing Address: P.O. Box 106, 48004. Tel: 586-725-3051; Fax: 586-725-2474.
School—7403 Church Rd., 48004. Tel: 586-725-0078; Fax: 586-725-2474. Kathleen Steele, Prin. Lay Teachers 12; Students 250.
Catechesis/Religious Program—Jane Petitpren, D.R.E. Tel: 586-725-1762. Students 330.
ARMADA, MACOMB CO., ST. MARY MYSTICAL ROSE, Rev. Bradley Forintos.
Res.: 24040 Armada Ridge, 48005. Tel: 586-784-5966; Fax: 586-784-9330.
Catechesis/Religious Program—Tel: 586-784-4157. Students 302.
AUBURN HILLS, OAKLAND CO.
1—ST. JOHN FISHER CHAPEL UNIVERSITY PARISH, Rev. Jerome A. Brzezinski; Sisters Mary Van Gilder, Pastoral Assoc.; Mary Ann Dixon, Pastoral Assoc.;

Ms. Lisa Brown, Pastoral Assoc.; Mr. Paul Borucki, Pastoral Assoc.; Mrs. Susan Buratto, Pastoral Assoc.; Ms. Nancy Mason Bordley, Pastoral Assoc.
Res.: 3665 Walton Blvd., 48326. Tel: 248-373-6457; Fax: 248-373-5479.
Catechesis/Religious Program—Tel: 248-373-3130. Sr. Mary Ann Dixon, D.R.E. Students 350.

2—SACRED HEART OF THE HILLS, Rev. James A. Mayworm.
Res.: 3400 Adams Rd., 48326. Tel: 248-852-4170; Fax: 248-852-5745.
Catechesis/Religious Program—Tel: 248-852-3620. Students 245.

BELLEVILLE, WAYNE CO., ST. ANTHONY, Rev. Thomas H. Cusick; Terrence D. Taylor, Pastoral Assoc.; Deacon Peter Cornell.
Res.: 409 W. Columbia Ave., 48111. Tel: 734-697-1211; Fax: 734-697-6217.
School—Tel: 734-699-4313; Fax: 734-699-0824. Mrs. Stephanie Tozer, Prin. Sisters of St. Joseph of the Third Order of St. Francis 2; Lay Teachers 10; Students 169.
Catechesis/Religious Program—373 W. Columbia. Students 207.
Convent—371 W. Columbia Ave., 48111. Tel: 734-697-6661.

BERKLEY, OAKLAND CO., OUR LADY OF LA SALETTE, Rev. Patrick J. Connell; Deacons Daniel M. Darga, Pastoral Assoc.; Brian Carroll, Pastoral Assoc.
Res.: 2600 Harvard Rd., 48072. Tel: 248-541-3762; Fax: 248-541-4250.
School—Tel: 248-542-3757; Fax: 248-541-6559. Mrs. Carol Smith, Prin. Lay Teachers 10; Students 183.
Catechesis/Religious Program—Students 258.

BEVERLY HILLS, FRANKLIN CO., OUR LADY OF ALBANIANS, Rev. Nue Gjergji.
Res.: 20855 W. Thirteen Mile Rd., 48025. Tel: 248-642-0816; Fax: 248-642-0251.

BEVERLY HILLS, OAKLAND CO., OUR LADY QUEEN OF MARTYRS, Rev. Michael J. Heppen, C.S.C., Admin. In Res., Rev. Edward J. Mitchell (Retired).
Res.: 32340 Pierce Ave., 48025. Tel: 248-644-8620; Fax: 248-644-8623.
School—32460 Pierce Ave., 48025. Tel: 248-642-2616; Fax: 248-642-3671. Peter J. Ferguson, Prin. Lay Teachers 31; Students 461.
Catechesis/Religious Program—Tel: 248-647-6068. Philippa Monteleon, D.R.E. Students 189.

BIRMINGHAM, OAKLAND CO.

1—ST. COLUMBAN, Rev. Sylvester Taube; Patricia Costigan, Pastoral Assoc.; Deacon Robert Ovies.
Res.: 2200 Dunstable, 48009. Tel: 248-642-1148; Fax: 248-642-4636.
Church: 1775 Melton, 48009. Tel: 248-646-5224; Fax: 248-646-9376.
Catechesis/Religious Program—Tel: 248-646-5225. Nancy Sullivan, D.R.E. Students 230.

2—HOLY NAME, Rev. Raymond J. Sayers; Sr. Shirlee Hoski, S.S.J.-T.O.S.F., Pastoral Assoc.; Deacon Michael J. McKale, Pastoral Assoc.; Donna M. Hansen, Pastoral Assoc.; Mary A. Pineau, Pastoral Assoc.
Parish Office—630 Harmon St., 48009. Tel: 248-646-2244; Fax: 248-646-2286.
Res.: 645 Woodland Ave., 48009.
School—Tel: 248-644-2722; Fax: 248-644-1191. Sr. Annice Mordenski, O.P., Prin. Sisters 2; Lay Teachers 27; Students 462.
Catechesis/Religious Program—Tel: 248-642-4130. Mary Morian, D.R.E. Students 558.

BLOOMFIELD HILLS, OAKLAND CO.

1—ST. HUGO OF THE HILLS, Rev. Msgr. Anthony M. Tocco; Rev. James R. Rafferty; Deacon Michael T. Smith.
Res.: 2215 Opdyke Rd., 48304. Tel: 248-644-5460; Fax: 248-644-1758.
School—380 E. Hickory Grove, 48304. Tel: 248-642-6131; Fax: 248-642-4457. Sr. Margaret Van Velzen, I.H.M., Prin. Sisters, Servants of the Immaculate Heart of Mary 5; Lay Teachers 37; Students 806.
Catechesis/Religious Program—Tel: 248-642-6062. Students 420.

2—ST. OWEN, Rev. Clifford F. Ruskowski; Sisters Carolyn Nelson, Pastoral Min.; Susanne Hofweber, O.P., Pastoral Min.; Mrs. Laura Broyles, Pastoral Min.; Mrs. Judy Thibodeau, Pastoral Min.
Res.: 6869 Franklin Rd., 48301. Tel: 248-626-0840; Fax: 248-626-0345.
Catechesis/Religious Program—Tel: 248-626-2300. Sue Fredenberg, D.R.E.; Karen Heuer, D.R.E. Students 538.

3—ST. REGIS, Rev. Norman D. Nawrocki, J.C.L. In Res., Rev. Janvier Wopoule.
Res.: 3695 Lincoln, 48301. Tel: 248-646-2686; Fax: 248-646-4643.
School—Tel: 248-646-2686, Ext. 301; Fax: 248-644-0944. Suzanne M. Pientak, Prin. Lay Teachers 18; Students 430.
Catechesis/Religious Program—Tel: 248-646-2686, Ext. 307. Robert Metz, D.R.E. Students 265.

CANTON, WAYNE CO.

1—SAINT JOHN NEUMANN, Revs. George Williams; Anthony Charles Richter; Eugene Kijek Pastoral Min. In Res., Rev. Tony Richter.
Res.: 44800 Warren Rd., 48187. Tel: 734-455-5910; Fax: 734-455-6779.
Catechesis/Religious Program—Ms. Beverly Thompson, D.R.E. Students 1,100.

2—RESURRECTION, Rev. Richard A. Perfetto
48755 Warren Rd., 48187-1216. Tel: 734-451-0444; Fax: 734-451-0454.
Catechesis/Religious Program—Students 245.

3—ST. THOMAS A BECKET, Rev. C. Richard Kelly.
Res.: 555 S. Lilley Rd., 48188. Tel: 734-981-1333; Fax: 734-981-1481.
Catechesis/Religious Program—Tel: 734-981-6680. Students 1,156.

CAPAC, ST. CLAIR CO., ST. NICHOLAS, Rev. Gerard Frawley, S.C.A.
Church: 4231 Capac Rd., Box 129, 48014. Tel: 810-395-7572; Fax: 810-395-7572.

CARLETON, MONROE CO., ST. PATRICK, [CEM 3] Rev. Robert A. Bauer.
Res.: 2996 W. Labo Rd., 48117. Tel: 734-654-2500; Fax: 734-654-6594.
School—Tel: 734-654-2522; Fax: 734-654-8120. Ms. Ruth Meiring, Prin. Lay Teachers 11; Students 130.
Catechesis/Religious Program—Tel: 734-654-6444. Diane Janssens, D.R.E. Students 202.
Convent—2970 Labo Rd., 48117. Tel: 734-654-2904.

CENTERLINE, MACOMB CO., ST. CLEMENT, [CEM] Revs. Alberto P. Bondy; Mathew Charthakuzhiyil.
Res.: 8075 Ritter Ave., 48015-1499. Tel: 810-757-3306; Fax: 810-757-5390.
School—Tel: 810-757-7500; Fax: 810-757-4724. Christopher Ciagne, Prin. Lay Teachers 20; Students 297.
High School—Tel: 810-757-1739; Fax: 810-757-1797. Christopher Ciagne, Prin. Lay Teachers 20; Students 135.
Catechesis/Religious Program—Tel: 810-757-3306; Fax: 810-757-5390. Terri Robinson, D.R.E. Students 118.

CLARKSTON, OAKLAND CO., ST. DANIEL, Rev. Msgr. Robert S. Humitz.
Res.: 7010 Valley Park Dr., 48346. Tel: 248-625-4580; Fax: 248-620-9839.
Catechesis/Religious Program—Tel: 248-625-1750. Frieda Arpsika, D.R.E.; Betty Haran, D.R.E. Students 1,050.

CLAWSON, OAKLAND CO., GUARDIAN ANGELS, Revs. Charles Kosanke; Pawel Kaczmarczyk; Deacons Eugene Tombler; Kenneth Fry.
Res.: 581 E. 14 Mile Rd., 48017. Tel: 248-588-1222; Fax: 248-588-8767.
School—Tel: 248-588-5545. Mrs. Susan Leslie, Prin. Dominican Sisters (Adrian) 1; Lay Teachers 24; Students 366.
Catechesis/Religious Program—Denise Ficorelli, D.R.E. Students 224.

CLINTON TWP., MACOMB CO.

1—ST. CLAUDE, Revs. Gary T. Smetanka, Admin.; Michael Gawlowski.
Res.: 33826 Beaconsfield, 48035. Tel: 586-791-6630; Fax: 586-791-0017.
Catechesis/Religious Program—Brenda Manzo, D.R.E. Students 9.

2—ST. LOUIS, Rev. Anthony P. Sulkowski; Deacon Donald C. Junak, Pastoral Assoc.
Res.: 24415 Crocker Blvd., 48036. Tel: 586-468-8734; Fax: 586-468-9647.
Catechesis/Religious Program—Tel: 586-468-4332. Joyce Appelt, D.R.E. Students 200.

3—ST. PAUL OF TARSUS, Rev. Ronald Essman; Rev. Msgr. Eugene Edyk; Rev. Gary Morelli; Deacon Edward C. Wilson Jr.
Res.: 41300 Romeo Plank Rd., 48038. Tel: 810-228-1210; Fax: 810-228-8935.
Catechesis/Religious Program—Tel: 810-228-0047. Claudia Dombrowski, D.R.E. Students 1,207.

4—ST. RONALD, Rev. James Andres, O.F.M.Cap.
Res.: 17701 15 Mile Rd., 48035-2401. Tel: 586-792-1190; Fax: 586-792-0765.
Catechesis/Religious Program—Tel: 586-792-1276. Students 202

5—SAN FRANCESCO COMMUNITY, Rev. Giulio Schiavi, P.I.M.E.
Res.: 22870 S. Nunneley Rd., 48035. Tel: 586-792-5346; Fax: 586-792-5119.
Catechesis/Religious Program—Students 140.

6—ST. THECLA, Revs. Gary T. Smetanka; Michael Gawlowski.
Res.: 20740 Nunneley Rd., 48035-1628. Tel: 586-791-3930; Fax: 586-791-3890.
School—Tel: 586-791-2170; Fax: 586-791-2356. Felician Sisters 4; Lay Teachers 23; Students 512.
Catechesis/Religious Program—Tel: 586-792-0550. Students 485.

7—ST. VALERIE OF RAVENNA, Rev. Richard Cavellier, J.C.L.
Res.: 23300 King Dr., 48035. Tel: 586-791-5450; Fax: 586-791-3876.

COLUMBUS, ST. CLAIR CO., ST. PHILIP NERI, [CEM] Revs. Erwin J. Bauer (Retired); Leo P. Broderick (Retired).
Res.: 9735 Dolan Rd., 48063. Tel: 586-727-7263; Fax: 586-727-7247.
Mission—Holy Rosary 7093 Main St., Smiths Creek, St. Clair Co. 48074.

DEARBORN HEIGHTS, WAYNE CO.

1—ST. ALBERT THE GREAT, Rev. Daniel Zaleski; Sr. Barbara Ennis, S.S.J.-T.O.S.F., Pastoral Assoc.; Deacon Raymond Gabel.
Res.: 4855 Parker, 48125. Tel: 313-292-0430; Fax: 313-292-8565.
School—Tel: 313-292-1144. Marist Sisters 1; Lay Teachers 9; Students 154.
Catechesis/Religious Program—Tel: 313-292-9370. Students 140.
Convent—4864 Parker, 48127. Tel: 313-292-0493.

2—ST. ANSELM, Rev. Msgr. James A. Moloney, Pastor & Dir., Society for The Propagation of The Faith.
Res.: 17650 W. Outer Dr., 48127. Tel: 313-565-4808; Fax: 313-565-7514.
School—Tel: 313-563-3430. John Paul Palgut, Prin. Sisters 1; Lay Teachers 10; Students 220.
Catechesis/Religious Program—Tel: 313-561-0512. Maryanne Walkuski, D.R.E. Students 140.

3—ST. JOHN THE BAPTIST, Rev. Edwin W. Balazy.
Res.: 26123 McDonald Ave., 48125. Tel: 313-292-9693; Fax: 313-292-1755.

4—ST. LINUS, Rev. Robert A. LaCroix.
Parish Office—6466 Evangeline, 48127-2086. Tel: 313-274-4500; Fax: 313-562-2821.
School—Tel: 313-274-5320. Dena Jayson, Prin. Lay Teachers 9; Students 146.
Catechesis/Religious Program—Tel: 313-274-5778. Students 85.
Convent—25450 Hass, 48127.

5—ST. MEL, Rev. Thomas J. Kramer.
Church: 7506 Inkster Rd., 48127. Tel: 313-274-0684; Fax: 313-274-4248.
School—Tel: 313-274-6270; Fax: 313-274-9080. Mrs. Georgene Wojciechowski, Prin. Lay Teachers 12; Students 148.
Catechesis/Religious Program—Tel: 313-274-3977. Donna Trudell, D.R.E. Students 173.

6—OUR LADY OF GRACE, Rev. Ronald Cyprys; Deacon Robert DeWitt. In Res., Rev. Charles F. O'Neill (Retired).
Res.: 8679 Riverview, 48127. Tel: 313-561-6373; Fax: 313-359-2727.
Church: 23700 Joy Rd., 48127.

7—ST. SABINA, Rev. Joseph L. Romano.
Res.: 25605 Ann Arbor Tr., 48127. Tel: 313-561-1977; Fax: 313-561-7898.
School—Tel: 313-274-5628. Sisters 3; Lay Teachers 7; Students 183.
Catechesis/Religious Program—Tel: 313-274-5635. Students 80.

8—ST. SEBASTIAN, Rev. Jeffrey Day; Deacon Lawrence Girard.
Res.: 22710 Colgate, 48125. Tel: 313-562-5356; Fax: 313-562-0058.
School—Tel: 313-563-6640. Franciscan Sisters of St. Joseph 3; Lay Teachers 18; Students 336.
Catechesis/Religious Program—Tel: 313-563-0960. Susan Campbell, D.R.E. Students 319.
Convent—20700 Colgate Ave., 48125. Tel: 313-562-7733.

DEARBORN, WAYNE CO.

1—ST. ALPHONSUS, Rev. Michael W. Quaine; Sr. Margaret Urban, O.P., Pastoral Assoc.
Res.: 7455 Calhoun Ave., 48126. Tel: 313-581-5218; Fax: 313-584-9560.
School—Tel: 313-581-1886; Fax: 313-582-5224. Mrs. Michelle Pazur, Grade School Prin. Lay Teachers 10; Students 150.
Catechesis/Religious Program—Tel: 313-581-5218. Raymond Berry, D.R.E. Students 150.
Convent—13541 Gould Ave., 48126. Tel: 313-584-4350.

2—ST. BARBARA, Rev. Zbigniew Grankowski.
Res.: 13534 Colson Ave., 48126. Tel: 313-582-8383; Fax: 313-582-1581.

3—ST. BERNADETTE, Closed. For inquiries for parish records contact the chancery.

4—ST. CLEMENT, Rev. Arnold V. Dachille; Rev. Msgr. Vincent J. Horkan (Retired); Rev. John Sarosiek; Sisters Ann Dineen, S.M., Pastoral Assoc.; Mary Downey, I.H.M.
Res.: 5275 Kenilworth Ave., 48126. Tel: 313-581-7495; Fax: 313-581-4233.
Catechesis/Religious Program—Tel: 313-846-2443. Cristena Flores, D.R.E. Students 67.

5—DIVINE CHILD, Rev. Msgr. Herman W. Kucyk; Revs. Brian Hurley; Dariusz Strzalkowski.
Res.: 25001 Hollander, 48128. Tel: 313-277-3110; Fax: 313-277-3211.
School—Tel: 313-562-1090; Fax: 313-562-2045. Sr. Cecilia Bondy, Elementary Prin. Bernardine Sisters 4; Lay Teachers 32; Students 796.

High School—Tel: 313-562-1990; Fax: 313-562-9361. Rev. John Kiselica, High School Prin. Priests 1; Bernardine Sisters 8; Lay Teachers 63; Students 926.
Catechesis/Religious Program—Diana Kinaschuk, D.R.E.; Karen Mitchell, D.R.E. Students 283.
Convent—1045 N. Silvery Ln., 48128. Tel: 313-561-5455.
6—ST. JOSEPH, Rev. Adolph Redwick.
Res.: 16101 Rotunda Dr., 48120. Tel: 313-336-3227; Fax: 313-441-6769.
7—ST. MARTHA, Rev. Donald L. Walker.
Res.: 18200 Oakwood Blvd., 48124. Tel: 313-336-4090; Fax: 313-336-3318.
8—SACRED HEART, [CEM] Rev. Lawrence H. Kaiser; Fran Helner. In Res., Rev. John F. Child (Retired).
Res.: 22430 W. Michigan Ave., 48124. Tel: 313-278-5555; Fax: 313-278-8582.
School—22513 Garrison, 48124. Tel: 313-561-9192; Fax: 313-561-1598. Lorelei Darga, Prin. Sisters 1; Lay Teachers 19; Students 359.
Catechesis/Religious Program—Julie Wieleba-Milkie, D.R.E. Students 322.
DRYDEN, LAPEER CO., ST. CORNELIUS, Rev. Wayne G. Ureel.
Res.: 3834 Mill St., P.O. Box 208, 48428. Tel: 810-796-2926; Fax: 810-796-9713.
DUNDEE, MONROE CO., ST. IRENE, Rev. Michael A. Woroniewicz.
Res.: 576 Main St., 48131. Tel: 734-529-2160.
EASTPOINTE, MACOMB CO.
1—ST. BARNABAS, Rev. Robert Schuster; Deacon Tom Thomas.
Res.: 24800 Phlox Ave., 48021. Tel: 586-775-2284; Fax: 586-775-6933.
Catechesis/Religious Program—Tel: 586-775-4650. Geraldine Combetta, D.R.E. Students 140.
2—ST. BASIL, Rev. James H. Profota.
Parish Center—22851 Lexington Ave., 48021. Tel: 586-777-5610; Fax: 586-779-3341.
Catechesis/Religious Program—Tel: 586-772-5434. Students 79.
3—OUR LADY OF GRACE VIETNAMESE PARISH (1999), Rev. Vincent Nguyen An Ninh.
Res.: 19300 Stephens, 48021. Tel: 810-447-0504; Fax: 810-447-0508.
4—ST. VERONICA, Revs. Stanley L. Pachla Jr.; Kulan-Daisamy Arokiasamy (India).
Res.: 21440 Universal Dr., 48021. Tel: 586-777-0331; Fax: 586-777-0615.
School—Tel: 586-775-8333. Sr. Rochelle Holly, C.D.P., Prin. Adrian Dominican 1; Sisters of Divine Providence 1; Sisters of St. Joseph 1; Lay Teachers 9; Students 145.
Catechesis/Religious Program—Tel: 586-777-5810. Sisters Mary Ann Ankoviak, S.S.J., D.R.E.; Geraldine Arnold, S.S.J., D.R.E. Students 176.
Convent—21357 Redmond, 48021. Tel: 586-777-0321.
ECORSE, WAYNE CO., ST. FRANCIS XAVIER, [CEM] Rev. Victor Roman.
Res.: 4250 W. Jefferson Ave., 48229. Tel: 313-383-8514; Fax: 313-383-7508.
Catechesis/Religious Program—Joan Morrison, D.R.E. Students 104.
EMMETT, ST. CLAIR CO., OUR LADY OF MOUNT CARMEL, Rev. Jasper F. Sirianni (Retired).
Res.: 10828 Brandon Rd., 48022. Tel: 810-384-1338; Fax: 810-384-1338.
Catechesis/Religious Program—10832 Brandon Rd., 48022. Tel: 810-384-6925. Students 234.
ERIE, MONROE CO., ST. JOSEPH, [CEM] Rev. Joseph Plawecki.
Res.: 2214 Manhattan Ave., 48133. Tel: 734-848-6125; Fax: 734-848-2784.
School—Tel: 734-848-6985. Sisters 2; Lay Teachers 10; Students 178.
Convent—2238 Manhattan Ave., 48133. Tel: 734-848-8754.
FARMINGTON HILLS, OAKLAND CO.
1—ST. ALEXANDER, Rev. James B. Wright; Deacon Mark Springer.
Res.: 27835 Shiawassee, 48336. Tel: 248-474-5748; Fax: 248-427-0883.
Catechesis/Religious Program—Tel: 248-474-8126; Fax: 248-474-8231. Students 233.
2—ST. CLARE OF ASSISI, Rev. Frederick J. Klettner.
Res.: 29200 W. Ten Mile, 48336. Tel: 248-477-9870; Fax: 248-477-4785.
3—ST. FABIAN, Rev. Brian J. Chabala.
Church: 32200 W. 12 Mile Rd., 48334. Tel: 248-553-4610; Fax: 248-553-6296.
School—Tel: 248-553-2750; Fax: 248-848-3035. Karen Stoller, Prin. Lay Teachers 25; Students 487.
Catechesis/Religious Program—Tel: 248-553-4860; Fax: 248-553-2041. Gina Karl, D.R.E.; Nancy Pawlukiewicz, D.R.E. Students 669.
Convent—32170 Twelve Mile Rd., 48334. Tel: 248-553-4186.
FARMINGTON, OAKLAND CO.
1—ST. COLMAN, Rev. Norbert V. Kendzierski; Mrs. Kathleen O. Daray, Pastoral Assoc.
Res.: 32500 Middlebelt Rd., Farmington Hills, 48334. Tel: 248-626-0285; Fax: 248-626-5420.
Catechesis/Religious Program—Tel: 248-626-0287. Students 70.
2—ST. GERALD, Rev. Gerald A. McEnhill.
Res.: 21300 Farmington Rd., 48336. Tel: 248-477-7470; Fax: 248-477-3878.
Catechesis/Religious Program—Tel: 248-476-7677. Mary Taylor, D.R.E. Students 295.
3—OUR LADY OF SORROWS, Revs. John H. West; Ronald T. Browne, J.C.L.; Sr. Christine Mihelcic, S.J., Dir. Pastoral Svcs. In Res., Rev. Loren F. O'Dea (Retired); Deacon Don F. Sobolewski.
Res.: 23815 Power Rd., 48336. Tel: 248-474-5720; Fax: 248-474-1340.
School—(Grades PreK-8) Tel: 248-476-0977; Fax: 248-615-5567. James Watson, Prin. (Grades PreK-8). Lay Teachers 46; Students 1,023.
Catechesis/Religious Program—Tel: 248-474-6480. Katherine D. Kelly, D.R.E. Students 412.
FERNDALE, OAKLAND CO., ST. JAMES, Rev. Robert L. Wurm; Sr. Eveleen Forkin, Pastoral Min.; W. Michael O'Neill, Pastoral Assoc.
Res.: 241 W. Pearson Ave., 48220-1824. Tel: 248-542-8835; Fax: 248-542-0267.
Catechesis/Religious Program—W. Michael O'Neill, D.R.E. Students 147.
FLAT ROCK, WAYNE CO., ST. ROCH, Rev. Richard A. Hartmann; Deacon Harold Goodhue.
Res.: 25022 Gibraltar Rd., 48134. Tel: 734-782-4471; Fax: 734-782-5450.
FRASER, MACOMB CO., OUR LADY QUEEN OF ALL SAINTS, Rev. Ronald J. Babich; Sr. Nancy Zajac, O.P., Pastoral Assoc.
Res.: 31740 Cyril Dr., 48026. Tel: 586-293-4050; Fax: 586-293-1041.
Catechesis/Religious Program—Tel: 810-294-6180. Students 363.
GARDEN CITY, WAYNE CO.
1—ST. DUNSTAN, Rev. Donald Demmer; Deacon Michael J. Markulike.
Res.: 1646 Belton Ave., 48135. Tel: 734-425-6720; Fax: 734-425-8411.
School—1615 Belton Ave., 48135. Tel: 734-425-4380. Sr. Mariella Chrusciel, Prin. Sisters 1; Lay Teachers 9; Students 180.
Catechesis/Religious Program—Tel: 734-425-4396. Trichia O'Keefe, D.R.E. Students 150.
2—ST. RAPHAEL THE ARCHANGEL, Rev. Scott Thibodeau; Sr. Ritamary Pyzick, Pastoral Min.
Parish Center—31530 Beechwood, 48135. Tel: 734-427-1533; Fax: 734-427-8594.
Parish Hall—5875 Merriman, 48135. Tel: 734-422-9617.
School—Tel: 734-425-9771. Miss Judith McBride, Prin. Lay Teachers 20; Students 338.
Catechesis/Religious Program—Tel: 734-425-5550. Sr. Diann Cousino, I.H.M., D.R.E. Students 335.
GIBRALTAR, WAYNE CO., ST. VICTOR, Rev. Roger A. Knapp.
Res.: 14100 Navarre, 48173. Tel: 734-675-0100; Fax: 734-675-6952.
GROSSE ILE, WAYNE CO., SACRED HEART, [CEM] Rev. James C. Scheick; Deacon Robert Tremmel.
Parish Center—21599 Parke Ln., 48138. Tel: 734-676-1378; Fax: 734-676-3623.
Catechesis/Religious Program—Students 550.
GROSSE POINTE FARMS, WAYNE CO., ST. PAUL CATHOLIC CHURCH, [CEM] Revs. Thomas Urban; John Wynnycky; Sr. Ruthanne Reed, O.P., Pastoral Assoc.; Deacon Richard Shubik, Pastoral Assoc.
Res.: 157 Lake Shore Rd., 48236. Tel: 313-885-8855; Fax: 313-886-6467.
School—170 Grosse Pointe Blvd., 48236. Tel: 313-885-3430; Fax: 313-885-9357. Cynthia J. Leaman, Prin. Sisters 3; Lay Teachers 25; Students 471.
Catechesis/Religious Program—Tel: 313-885-7022; Fax: 313-885-9316. Mrs. Judith Jones, D.R.E. Students 471.
GROSSE POINTE PARK, WAYNE CO.
1—ST. AMBROSE, Rev. Timothy R. Pelc; Mr. Charles J. Dropiewski, Pastoral Assoc.
Res.: 15020 Hampton, 48230. Tel: 313-822-2814; Fax: 313-822-9838.
Catechesis/Religious Program—Bernadette Gutowski, D.R.E. Students 222.
2—ST. CLARE OF MONTEFALCO, Most Rev. John C. McNabb, O.S.A.; Rev. W. Timothy Cuny, O.S.A. In Res., Rev. Joseph F. Hartman, O.S.A.
Res.: 1401 Whittier Rd., 48230. Tel: 313-647-5000; Fax: 313-647-5005.
School—16231 Charlevoix, 48230. Tel: 313-647-5100; Fax: 313-647-5105. Henry Burakowski, Prin.
Catechesis/Religious Program—Tel: 313-647-5050; Fax: 313-647-5055. Paula Miller, D.R.E. Students 382.
GROSSE POINTE, WAYNE CO., OUR LADY STAR OF THE SEA, Rev. Msgr. Dennis Harrity; Rev. Roger Lumbre (Philippines); Deacon William E. Jamieson. In Res., Rev. William J. McGoldrick (Retired); Rev. Msgr. John F. Schweder.
Church: 467 Fairford, 48236. Tel: 313-884-5554; Fax: 313-885-5591.
School—Tel: 313-884-1070; Fax: 313-884-0406. Patricia Stumb, Prin. Lay Teachers 31; Students 496.
Catechesis/Religious Program—Tel: 313-884-7407. Helen L. Goettl, D.R.E. Students 526.
Convent—19950 Morningside Dr., 48236. Tel: 313-884-4074.
HAMTRAMCK, WAYNE CO.
1—ST. FLORIAN, Rev. Thomas Sielicki, S.Ch. In Res., Rev. Stanislaw Kuczaik, S.Ch.
Res.: 2626 Poland Ave., 48212. Tel: 313-871-2778; Fax: 313-871-5947.
Church: Florian and Latham Aves., 48212.
School—Tel: 313-875-3040; Fax: 313-872-1242. Sr. Mary Thaddea, C.S.S.F., Prin. Felician Sisters 2; Lay Teachers 10; Students 127.
Convent—2622 Florian Ave., 48212. Tel: 313-872-5775.
2—ST. LADISLAUS, (Polish), Rev. Stanley A. Ulman. In Res., Rev. Stanislaus Czapiewski, S.J.
Res.: 2730 Caniff Ave., 48212. Tel: 313-872-0709; Fax: 313-872-5906.
3—OUR LADY QUEEN OF APOSTLES, (Polish), Rev. Bogdan Milosz.
Res.: 3851 Prescott Ave., 48212-3115. Tel: 313-891-1520; 313-891-1521; Fax: 313-891-3552.
HARPER WOODS, WAYNE CO.
1—OUR LADY QUEEN OF PEACE, Rev. David J. Blazek. In Res., Rev. John M. Fee, SS.CC.
Res.: 20955 Bournemouth Ave., 48225. Tel: 313-881-5212; Fax: 313-881-7813.
School—Tel: 313-881-3629; Fax: 313-881-4198. Judy Meerschaert, Prin. Lay Teachers 13; Students 100.
Catechesis/Religious Program—Tel: 313-884-8744. Students 150.
2—ST. PETER THE APOSTLE, Rev. Robert J. Keller.
Res.: 19851 Anita St., 48225. Tel: 313-886-1771; Fax: 313-886-1489.
HARRISON TWP., MACOMB CO., ST. HUBERT, Rev. James J. O'Leary.
Res.: 38775 Prentiss, 48045. Tel: 810-463-5877; 810-463-7796; Fax: 810-463-1734.
Catechesis/Religious Program—Tel: 810-463-5875; Fax: 810-463-5875. Mr. Allan Ranusch, D.R.E. Students 729.
HARSENS ISLAND, ST. CLAIR CO., ST. MARK, Rev. James R. Wysocki, Admin.
Church and Rectory: P.O. Box 70, Harsen's Island, 48028. Tel: 810-748-3828; Fax: 810-748-9148.
HAZEL PARK, OAKLAND CO.
1—ST. JUSTIN, Rev. Robert Hayes Williams.
Res.: 1631 E. Elza St., 48030. Tel: 248-542-2129; Fax: 248-542-2715.
2—ST. MARY MAGDALEN, Rev. Bede Louzon, O.F.M.Cap.
Res.: 50 E. Annabelle, 48030. Tel: 248-542-8060; Fax: 248-542-4563.
School—Tel: 248-547-3363; Fax: 248-547-1610. Suzanne Kisseberth, Prin. Lay Teachers 9; Students 150.
Catechesis/Religious Program—Tel: 248-547-0323. David Troiano, D.R.E. Students 100.
HIGHLAND PARK, WAYNE CO., ST. BENEDICT, Rev. Robert B. McGrath.
Res.: 60 Church Ave., 48203. Tel: 313-868-3876; Fax: 313-868-0110.
School—53 Candler, 48203. Tel: 313-868-7502. Sharon Taylor, Prin. Lay Teachers 15; Students 180.
HIGHLAND, OAKLAND CO., CHURCH OF THE HOLY SPIRIT, Rev. Leo T. Lulko; Deacon Arthur Van Brook.
Church: 3700 Harvey Lake Rd., 48356. Tel: 248-887-5364; Fax: 248-889-1374.
Catechesis/Religious Program—Tel: 248-887-1634. Joann Dalton, D.R.E. Students 598.
HOLLY, OAKLAND CO., ST. RITA, Rev. Alberto C. Seson.
Res.: 309 E. Maple, 48442. Tel: 248-634-4841; Fax: 248-634-4858.
Catechesis/Religious Program—Tel: 248-634-1658; Fax: 248-634-4863. Maryann Rudelic, D.R.E. Students 275.
IDA, MONROE CO., ST. JOSEPH, [CEM] Rev. John P. LaCasse, Admin.
Res.: 8295 Van Akin St., 48140. Tel: 734-269-3895.
Catechesis/Religious Program—Tel: 734-269-3414. Linda Wilson, D.R.E. Students 209.
IMLAY CITY, LAPEER CO., SACRED HEART, [CEM] Rev. Ezequiel Mondragon.
Res.: 700 Maple Vista, 48444. Tel: 810-724-1135; Fax: 810-724-0870.
Catechesis/Religious Program—Tel: 810-724-1145. Students 120.
INKSTER, WAYNE CO.
1—HOLY FAMILY PARISH, Rev. Jack H. Baker, Admin.
Res.: 27800 Annapolis Rd., 48141. Tel: 313-563-8242; Fax: 313-563-0696.
2—SS. KEVIN AND NORBERT, Rev. Jack H. Baker, Admin.

Office—27355 Woodsfield, 48141. Tel: 313-563-0993; Fax: 313-563-3148.
Res.: 604 Sherbourne Dr., 48141.
Catechesis/Religious Program—Tel: 313-278-4924; Fax: 313-563-3148. Students 60.

LAKE ORION, OAKLAND CO., ST. JOSEPH, Revs. C. Michael Verschaeve; Stanislaw Obloj; Deacon Joseph A. Hulway; Ms. Mary Martin, M.A., Pastoral Assoc.; Peggy Bartz-Vieaux, Pastoral Assoc.
Res.: 715 N. Lapeer Rd., 48362. Tel: 248-693-0440; Fax: 248-693-3724.
School—Tel: 248-693-6215; Fax: 248-693-0958. Sr. Theresa Darga, O.S.F., Prin. Lay Teachers 19; Students 399.
Catechesis/Religious Program—Tel: 248-693-9555; Fax: 248-693-9555. Regina Moskal, D.R.E. Students 1,047.

LAKEPORT, ST. CLAIR CO., ST. EDWARD'S ON THE LAKE, [CEM] Rev. Joseph M. Esper.
Res.: 6945 Lakeshore Rd., 48059. Tel: 810-385-4340; Fax: 810-385-6972.
School—(Grades K-5) Tel: 810-385-4461; Fax: 810-385-6070. For grades 6-8 please refer to McCormick Consolidated Academy, Port Huron, under Elementary Schools, Inter-Parochial in the Institutions Located in the Archdiocese section. Students 113.
Convent—6975 Lakeshore Rd., 48059.

LAPEER, LAPEER CO., IMMACULATE CONCEPTION OF THE BLESSED VIRGIN MARY, [CEM] Revs. Douglas J. Terrien; Janusz Iwan; Deacon Gerald Deshaw.
Res.: 814 Nepessing, 48446. Tel: 810-664-8594; Fax: 810-664-4564.
School—*Bishop Kelley School*, Tel: 810-664-5011; Fax: 810-664-5606. Lay Teachers 9; Students 284.

LINCOLN PARK, WAYNE CO.
1—CHRIST THE GOOD SHEPHERD, Rev. Kevin Thomas.
Res.: 1540 Riverbank Ave., 48146. Tel: 313-928-1324; Fax: 313-928-1326.
School—Tel: 313-386-0633. Thomas Caruso, Prin. Lay Teachers 19; Students 380.
2—ST. HENRY, Rev. Gerard J. Cupple.
Res.: 1358 Council Ave., 48146. Tel: 313-381-0711; 313-381-0712; Fax: 313-381-6746.
Catechesis/Religious Program—Christine Brennan, D.R.E. Students 75.

LIVONIA, WAYNE CO.
1—ST. AIDAN, Rev. Ronald Kurzawa; Deacon William Meahan.
Res.: 17500 Farmington Rd., 48152. Tel: 734-425-5950; Fax: 734-425-3687.
Catechesis/Religious Program—Tel: 734-425-9333. David Concrad, D.R.E. Students 677.
2—ST. COLETTE, Rev. Henry W. Roodbeen; Deacons Alfred J. Morad; Leo D'Argis.
Res.: 17600 Newburgh, 48152-2699. Tel: 734-464-4433; Fax: 734-464-1694.
Catechesis/Religious Program—Tel: 734-464-4435; Fax: 734-464-7817. Mary Ellen Skene D.R.E. Students 529.
3—ST. EDITH, Rev. Timothy J. Murray; Deacons John Kenny; Ric Misiak.
Res.: 15089 Newburgh, 48154. Tel: 734-464-1222; Fax: 734-464-7582.
School—Tel: 734-464-1250; Fax: 734-464-6765. Sr. Margaret Kijek, C.S.S.F., Prin. Felician Sisters 1; Lay Teachers 9; Students 257.
Catechesis/Religious Program—Tel: 734-464-2020. Elizabeth Nowak, D.R.E. Students 550.
4—ST. GENEVIEVE, Rev. Howard L. Vogan.
Res.: 29015 Jamison, 48154. Tel: 734-427-5220; Fax: 734-422-1763.
School—Tel: 734-425-4420; Fax: 734-458-3915. Mrs. Rita Gray, Prin. Lay Teachers 12; Students 234.
Catechesis/Religious Program—Tel: 734-261-5920. Diana Tarnacki, D.R.E. Students 259.
5—ST. MAURICE, Rev. Sidney J. Eckert; Darlene Bellmore, Pastoral Assoc.
Res.: 32765 Lyndon Ave., 48154. Tel: 734-522-1616; Fax: 734-522-5092.
Catechesis/Religious Program—Tel: 734-421-5240. Mrs. Mary Rice, D.R.E. Students 160.
6—ST. MICHAEL, Rev. William Tindall.
Res.: 11441 Hubbard Ave., 48150. Tel: 734-261-1455; Fax: 734-522-1123.
School—Tel: 734-421-7360; Fax: 734-466-9713. Sr. M. Carolyn Ratkowski, C.S.S.F., Prin. Felician Sisters 5; Lay Teachers 25; Students 820.
Catechesis/Religious Program—Tel: 734-261-1790. Students 158.
Convent—11400 Fairfield. Tel: 734-421-7522.
7—ST. PRISCILLA, Rev. Raymond H. Bucon; Deacon Raymond L. Kunik.
19120 Purling Brook Rd., 48152. Tel: 248-476-4700; Fax: 248-476-7831.
Catechesis/Religious Program—Tel: 248-476-4702. Students 198.

MACOMB, MACOMB CO.
1—ST. ISIDORE, Revs. Michael Hrydziuszko; John Ortman; Deacon Anthony Kendzierski.
Res.: 18201 Twenty-three Mile Rd., 48042. Tel: 586-286-1700; Fax: 586-286-8753.
Catechesis/Religious Program—Tel: 586-286-4433. Diane Bucko, D.R.E. Students 1,300.
2—ST. MAXIMILIAN KOLBE, Rev. Robert H. Blondell; Sr. Lois Berror, S.S.J., Pastoral Assoc.
23965 23 Mile Rd., Macomb Township, 48042. Tel: 586-598-3314; Fax: 586-598-3346.

MADISON HEIGHTS, OAKLAND CO., ST. VINCENT FERRER, Rev. Steven C. Koehler; Deacons John H. Ball; Andrew Fairbanks.
Res.: 1087 E. Gardenia Ave., 48071. Tel: 248-542-8720; Fax: 248-542-8721.
School—1075 E. Gardenia, 48071. Tel: 248-398-4190; Fax: 248-398-4191. Mr. Raymond Dudus, Prin. Lay Teachers 14; Students 110.
Catechesis/Religious Program—Michael Novak, D.R.E. Students 160.

MARINE CITY ST. CLAIR CO., HOLY CROSS, [CEM] Rev. Timothy F. Birney; Deacon Gary R. Krueger. In Res., Revs. Alfred H. Sadler (Retired); George Browne (Retired); Frederick A. Bodde (Retired).
Res.: 610 S. Water St., 48039. Tel: 810-765-3568; Fax: 810-765-2974.
School—*Holy Cross Elementary*, 618 S. Water St., 48039. Tel: 810-765-3591; Fax: 810-765-9074. Mrs. Dianne Lovette, Prin. Dominican Sisters 1; Lay Teachers 11; Students 178.
High School—*Cardinal Mooney Catholic*, Tel: 810-765-8825; Fax: 810-765-7164. Sr. Karen Leitz, Prin. Sisters 2; Lay Teachers 17; Students 205
Catechesis/Religious Program—Tel: 810-765-8300. Sr. Kathleen Mulso, O.S.F., D.R.E. Students 330.

MARYSVILLE, ST. CLAIR CO., ST. CHRISTOPHER, Rev. Arthur R. Baranowski; Sr. Lynn Pascoe, O.S.F., Pastoral Min.
Res.: 1000 Michigan Ave., 48040. Tel: 810-364-4100; Fax: 810-364-5947.
Catechesis/Religious Program—Tel: 810-364-7080. Theresa Doyle, D.R.E. Students 450.

MAYBEE, MONROE CO., ST. JOSEPH, [CEM] Rev. Michael D. Malawy.
Res.: 9207 Joseph St., Box 125, 48159. Tel: 734-587-8835; Fax: 734-587-3490.
Convent—9147 Joseph St., Box 118, 48159. Tel: 734-587-8785.

MELVINDALE, WAYNE CO.
1—ST. CONRAD, Rev. Joseph A. Gagnon.
Res.: 3320 Melwood, 48122. Tel: 313-383-0303; Fax: 313-383-5704.
2—ST. MARY MAGDALEN, Rev. Jeffrey Anifer.
Res.: 19624 Wood St., 48122. Tel: 313-381-8566; Fax: 313-381-1319.
School—Tel: 313-381-8566, Ext. 11. Dwayne Dorey, Prin. Lay Teachers 12; Students 178.
Catechesis/Religious Program—Tel: 313-381-8566, Ext. 115. Mary Whalen, D.R.E. Students 118.

MEMPHIS, MACOMB CO., ALL SAINTS, Rev. Joseph R. Horn.
Church: 79780 Main St., 48041. Tel: 810-392-2056; 810-392-3232; Fax: 810-392-2043.
Catechesis/Religious Program—Toni Zweng, D.R.E. Students 251.

MILFORD, OAKLAND CO., ST. MARY, OUR LADY OF THE SNOWS, [CEM] Rev. Ronald Anderson; Kathryn Michalik, Pastoral Assoc.
Res.: 1955 E. Commerce, 48381. Tel: 248-685-1482; Fax: 248-684-5642.
Catechesis/Religious Program—Tel: 248-685-2702. Judith Ulbrich, D.R.E. Students 1,228.

MONROE, MONROE CO.
1—ST. ANNE, Revs. William F. Fisher, O.S.F.S.; Robert C. Mossett, O.S.F.S.
Res.: 2420 N. Dixie Hwy., 48162. Tel: 734-289-2910; Fax: 734-289-1098.
Catechesis/Religious Program—Students 131.
2—ST. JOHN THE BAPTIST, Rev. Jack Quinlan.
Res.: 511 S. Monroe St. S., 48161. Tel: 734-241-8910; Fax: 734-241-1943.
School—Tel: 734-241-1670; Fax: 734-241-8782. Patricia Cousino, Prin. Lay Teachers 10; Students 257.
Catechesis/Religious Program—Sharon DuVall, D.R.E.; Karon Kinsey, D.R.E. Students 131.
3—ST. JOSEPH'S, [JC] Rev. William F. Fisher, O.S.F.S.
Res.: 924 E. Second St., 48161. Tel: 734-241-9590; Fax: 734-241-5296.
Catechesis/Religious Program—Mrs. Joan Allor, D.R.E. Students 130.
4—ST. MARY'S, [JC] Rev. Timothy F. Babcock; Sr. Carmela Whitlon, Pastoral Assoc.; Deacon Michael M. Ingels; Scott Aunastasia, Pastoral Assoc.
Res.: 127 N. Monroe St., 48162. Tel: 734-241-1644; Fax: 734-241-3077.
School—Tel: 734-241-3377; Fax: 734-241-0497. Mary Ann Lapinski, Prin. Lay Teachers 13; Students 270.
Catechesis/Religious Program—Tel: 734-241-6097. Doreen Schultz, D.R.E. Students 190.
5—ST. MICHAEL, [JC] Rev. Stephen Rooney.
Res.: 502 W. Front St., 48161. Tel: 734-241-8645; Fax: 734-241-6132.
School—Tel: 734-241-3923; Fax: 734-241-3924. Karen Pilon, Prin. Lay Teachers 10; Students 230.
Catechesis/Religious Program—Tel: 734-241-8663. Mrs. Kathleen Dubay, D.R.E. Students 145.

MOUNT CLEMENS, MACOMB CO., ST. PETER, [CEM] Rev. Michael N. Cooney; Sheila Roy, Pastoral Min.; Molra Shaum, Admin.
Admin. Bldg.—98 New St., 48043. Tel: 586-468-4578; Fax: 586-468-3199.
School—*St. Mary*, Tel: 586-468-4570. Carol Budchuk, Prin. Lay Teachers 29; Students 660.
Catechesis/Religious Program—Judy Coll, D.R.E. Students 415.

NEW BALTIMORE, MACOMB CO., ST. MARY QUEEN OF CREATION, [CEM] Rev. Nicholas Zukowski; Glorianne Gauveau, Parish Nurse Coord.; Deacons Anthony Lewandoski, (Retired); Richard Damaske.
Res.: 50931 Maria St., 48047. Tel: 586-725-2441; Fax: 586-725-3647.
Catechesis/Religious Program—Tel: 586-725-7579; Fax: 586-725-0838. Carolyn Bissett, D.R.E. Students 1,068.

NEW BOSTON, WAYNE CO., ST. STEPHEN, [CEM] Revs. Alexander J. Wytrwal; Joseph Szewczyk.
Res.: 18858 Huron River Dr., 48164-9599. Tel: 734-753-4305; Fax: 734-753-5828.
School—Tel: 734-753-4175. Sr. M. Virginia Gola, C.S.S.F., Prin. Felician Sisters 3; Lay Teachers 9; Students 183.
Catechesis/Religious Program—Tel: 734-753-4722. Sr. M. Pauline Winowiecki, C.S.S.F., D.R.E. Students 189.
Convent—Tel: 734-753-9937.

NEWPORT, MONROE CO., ST. CHARLES BORROMEO, [CEM] Rev. Frederick Misiolek; Sr. Pamela J. Nosbusch, O.S.F., Pastoral Assoc.
Res.: 8109 Swan Creek Rd., 48166. Tel: 734-586-2531; Fax: 734-586-3900.
School—Tel: 734-586-2531, Ext. 3. Charlene Jenkins, Prin. Lay Teachers 9; Students 194.
Catechesis/Religious Program—Tel: 734-586-2531, Ext. 4. Mrs. Michaelene Kowalczik, D.R.E. Students 176.

NORTH BRANCH, LAPEER CO.
1—ST. MARY'S BURNSIDE, [CEM] Rev. Richard L. Treml.
Res.: 5622 Summers Rd., P.O. Box 268, 48461. Tel: 810-688-3648; Fax: 810-688-3588.
Mission—*Sacred Heart* [CEM] Brown City, Sanilac Co.
2—SS. PETER AND PAUL, [CEM] Rev. Richard L. Treml.
Res.: Box 208, 6645 Washington, 48461. Tel: 810-688-3797; Fax: 810-688-2969.
Catechesis/Religious Program—Tel: 810-688-9019. Barbara Sinka, D.R.E. Students 220.
Mission—*St. Patrick's* [CEM] Clifford, Lapeer Co.

NORTHVILLE, WAYNE CO.
1—ST. ANDREW KIM KOREAN CATHOLIC CHURCH, Rev. John N.K. Baek.
Res.: 21177 Halsted Rd., 48167. Tel: 248-442-9026; Fax: 248-442-9020.
2—OUR LADY OF VICTORY, Revs. Terrence D. Kerner; Paul Czarnota; Deacon Donald Quigley.
Res.: 770 Thayer, 48167. Tel: 248-349-2621; Fax: 248-349-7329.
School—Tel: 248-349-3610; Fax: 248-380-7247. Lay Teachers 18; Students 339.
Catechesis/Religious Program—Tel: 248-349-2559. Ms. Eileen Moss, D.R.E. Students 586.
Convent—Center: 103 Orchard Dr., 48167. Tel: 248-348-8650.

NOVI, OAKLAND CO.
1—HOLY FAMILY, Revs. John G. Budde; Paul Ballien; Deacon William L. Waldmann.
Res.: 24505 Meadowbrook, 48375. Tel: 248-349-8847; Fax: 248-349-3711.
Catechesis/Religious Program—Tel: 248-349-8837. Maria Koncius, D.R.E. Students 1,108.
2—ST. JAMES, Rev. George Charnley.
Church: 46325 Ten Mile Road, 48374-3007. Tel: 248-347-7778; Fax: 248-347-9625.
Catechesis/Religious Program—Sylvia Shorter, D.R.E. Students 1,180.

OAK PARK, OAKLAND CO., OUR LADY OF FATIMA, Rev. Paul F. Chateau; Sr. Jane Zoltek, S.S.J., Pastoral Assoc. In Res., Rev. Nicholas H. Amico (Ecuador).
Res.: 13500 Oak Park Blvd., 48237. Tel: 248-545-2310; Fax: 248-545-2312.

ORCHARD LAKE, OAKLAND CO., OUR LADY OF REFUGE, Rev. William J. Murphy.
Res.: 3663 Erie Dr., 48324. Tel: 248-682-0920; Fax: 248-682-3794.
School—Tel: 248-682-3422; Fax: 248-683-2265. Sr. Mary Ruth Koralewski, C.S.S.F., Prin. Sisters 2; Lay Teachers 22; Students 464.
Catechesis/Religious Program—Tel: 248-682-6381. Barbara Brown, D.R.E. Students 285.
Convent—3725 Erie Dr., 48324. Tel: 248-682-1876.

ORION TOWNSHIP, OAKLAND CO., CHRIST THE REDEEMER, Rev. Joseph E. Dailey; Deacon Alex

Jablonowski.
Res.: 2700 Waldon Rd., Lake Orion, 48360. Tel: 248-391-1621; Fax: 248-391-3412.
Catechesis/Religious Program—Tel: 248-391-4074. Henry Mucha, D.R.E. Students 711.

ORTONVILLE, OAKLAND CO., ST. ANNE, Rev. Bernard J. Mullen.
Res.: 825 S. Ortonville Rd., 48462. Tel: 248-627-3965; Fax: 248-627-5153.
Catechesis/Religious Program—Elaine Young, D.R.E. Students 392.

PLYMOUTH, WAYNE CO.

1—ST. KENNETH, Rev. William J. Pettit (Retired).
Res.: 14951 Haggerty Rd., 48170. Tel: 734-420-0288; Fax: 734-420-2921.
Catechesis/Religious Program—Tel: 734-420-3031. Mrs. Laurel McGrane, D.R.E. Students 713.

2—OUR LADY OF GOOD COUNSEL, Revs. John J. Sullivan; Edward McNulty (SD); Elias Salomon, S.S.J.V. (Philippines); Deacons Timothy Sullivan; Donald Leach, Pastoral Assoc.
Res.: 1062 Church St., 48170. Tel: 734-453-0326; Fax: 734-416-9257.
School—Tel: 734-453-3053; Fax: 734-453-3620. Kay Reilly, Prin. Lay Teachers 33; Students 603.
Catechesis/Religious Program—Tel: 734-455-0242. Students 625.

PONTIAC, OAKLAND CO.

1—ST. JOSEPH, Revs. Timothy A. Laboe; Sean Sylvester; Sr. M. Patricia Malone, R.S.M., Pastoral Assoc.; Deacon John M. Fleming; Revs. Fabian B. Slominski, Liturgical Presiders (Retired); Thomas R. Physician, Liturgical Presiders (Retired).
400 South Blvd. W., 48341-2465. Tel: 248-332-9872; Fax: 248-334-0528.
Res.: 46408 Woodward Ave., 48342. Tel: 248-332-0283.
Mission—St. Vincent de Paul, Oakland Co.

2—ST. MICHAEL, Revs. Timothy A. Laboe; Sean Sylvester; Deacon Brian S. White.
Res.: 120 Lewis, 48342. Tel: 248-332-9167; Fax: 248-332-3901.

3—ST. VINCENT DE PAUL, Revs. Timothy A. Laboe; Sean Sylvester; Deacons Fernando Valdez, Pastoral Assoc.; Jesus Vasquez, Pastoral Assoc.; Brigido Rodriguez, Pastoral Assoc.; Brian S. White, Pastoral Assoc.; Maria Jimenez, Pastoral Assoc.; Willie McCray, Min. of Service.
Res.: 46408 Woodward Ave., 48342. Tel: 248-332-0283; Fax: 248-332-7041.

PORT HURON, ST. CLAIR CO.

1—ST. JOSEPH, [JC] Rev. Rene L. Desmarais; Deacon John J. Connors. In Res., Rev. Simeon T. Iber.
Res.: 1317 7th St., 48060. Tel: 810-985-9616; Fax: 810-985-9807.
Catechesis/Religious Program—Tel: 810-982-2343. Lucy Sebastian, D.R.E. Students 55.

2—ST. MARY, Rev. Stanley Wyczawski.
Res.: 1505 Ballentine St., 48060. Tel: 810-982-7906; Fax: 810-987-8255.
School—Mr. Tim Toepel. Lay Teachers 8; Students 128.
Catechesis/Religious Program—Patricia Isaacson, D.R.E. Students 315.

3—ST. STEPHEN, Rev. David Lesniak.
Res.: 325 32nd St., 48060. Tel: 810-984-2689; Fax: 810-984-8559.
Parish Center—2865 Henry, 48060. Tel: 810-984-2689.
Catechesis/Religious Program—Tel: 810-985-9069. Karen Clor, D.R.E. Students 102.

PORT HURON, ST. CLAIRE CO., ST. JOSEPH MALANKARA CATHOLIC MISSION, Rev. Mathew Charthakuzhiyil, Admin.
Church: 1505 Ballentine W., 48060. Tel: 810-982-7906; Fax: 810-987-8255.

RAY TOWNSHIP, MACOMB CO., ST. FRANCIS OF ASSISI, Rev. Robert H. Blondell.
Res.: 62811 New Haven Rd., Ray Twp., 48096. Tel: 586-749-9584; Fax: 586-749-6021.

REDFORD TOWNSHIP, WAYNE CO.

1—ST. HILARY, Rev. John T. Nowlan; Sr. Marie Miller, I.H.M.
Res.: 23901 Elmira, 48239. Tel: 313-533-1560; Fax: 313-533-1735.

2—ST. ROBERT BELLARMINE, Rev. Denis B. Theroux; Faith Offman, Pastoral Assoc.
Res.: 27101 W. Chicago, 48239. Tel: 313-937-1500; Fax: 313-937-1185.
School—Tel: 313-937-1655; Fax: 313-937-9755. Nancy Kuszczak, Prin. Lay Teachers 25; Students 320.
Catechesis/Religious Program—Tel: 313-937-1531; Fax: 313-937-5060. Paula Nemeth, Pastoral Min. of Faith Formation. Students 300.

REDFORD, WAYNE CO.

1—ST. AGATHA, Rev. James Livingston.
Parish Office—19750 Beech Daly Rd., 48240. Tel: 313-531-0371; Fax: 313-531-1805.
Res.: 19650 Beech Daly Rd., 48240.
School—Tel: 313-532-6940. Daniel Parent, Prin. Lay Teachers 9; Students 161.
High School—St. Katharine Drexel Vicariate, Tel: 313-532-3317; Fax: 313-532-2277. Timothy Scanlon, Prin. Lay Teachers 10; Students 73.
Catechesis/Religious Program—Students 80.

2—ST. JOHN BOSCO, Rev. Richard A. Osebold.
Res.: 12100 Beech-Daly Rd., 48239. Tel: 313-937-9690; Fax: 313-937-2927.

3—OUR LADY OF LORETTO, Rev. John J. Mech; Sr. Margretta Wojcik, O.S.F., Pastoral Assoc.; Deacon Gary Pardo.
Res.: 17116 Olympia Ave., 48240. Tel: 313-534-9000; Fax: 313-534-6744.
School—Tel: 313-532-4764; Fax: 313-794-1506. Lay Teachers 13; Students 210.
Catechesis/Religious Program—Tel: 313-532-3707. Rosemary Demeyer, D.R.E. Students 211.

4—ST. VALENTINE, Rev. Thomas A. Belczak.
Res.: 25881 Dow, 48239. Tel: 313-532-4394; Fax: 313-537-2237.
School—25875 Hope St., 48239. Tel: 313-533-7149; Fax: 313-533-3060. Laura McClure, Prin. Lay Teachers 21; Students 308.
Catechesis/Religious Program—Tel: 313-538-9161. Sharon Larkin, D.R.E. Students 230.
Convent—25900 Dow St., 48239. Tel: 313-533-7828.

RICHMOND, MACOMB CO., ST. AUGUSTINE, [CEM] Rev. James E. Commyn.
Res.: 68035 Main St., 48062. Tel: 586-727-5215; Fax: 586-727-3760.
School—Tel: 586-727-9365. Lay Teachers 14; Students 275.
Catechesis/Religious Program—Tel: 586-727-9290. Students 235.

RIVER ROUGE, WAYNE CO., OUR LADY OF LOURDES, Rev. James F. Wieging; Dr. Paul D. Bodrie, Pastoral Assoc.
Res.: 1440 Coolidge Highway, 48218. Tel: 313-842-3320; 313-842-3321; Fax: 313-842-4507.

RIVERVIEW, WAYNE CO., ST. CYPRIAN, Very Rev. Jude Verley, O.S.C.; Rev. Dale Ettel, O.S.C. In Res., Revs. Francis K. Scheets, O.S.C.; John G. Hawkins, O.S.C.; Dale H. Redwanski, O.S.C.; Richard M. Leliaert, O.S.C.; Gordon Van Hoof, O.S.C.
Res.: 13249 Pennsylvania, 48192. Tel: 734-283-0112; 734-283-1366; Fax: 734-283-2809.
School—Tel: 734-283-9442. Ken Kosowski, Prin. Lay Teachers 14; Students 176.
Catechesis/Religious Program—Tel: 734-283-2239; Fax: 734-283-2239. Ms. Denise LaPorte, D.R.E. Students 462.

ROCHESTER HILLS, OAKLAND CO.

1—ST. MARY'S OF THE HILLS, Rev. Eugene Strain.
Res.: 2675 John R, 48307-4652. Tel: 248-853-5390; Fax: 248-853-7989.
Catechesis/Religious Program—Tel: 248-844-8662. Peggy Casing, D.R.E. Students 605.

2—ST. PAUL ALBANIAN CATHOLIC COMMUNITY, Rev. Anton Kcira, Admin.
Office—525 Auburn Rd., 48307. Tel: 248-844-8201; Fax: 248-844-8092.

ROCHESTER, OAKLAND CO.

1—ST. ANDREW, Revs. Thomas Slowinski; Stephen Burr; Sr. Rebecca Hodge, O.P., Pastoral Assoc.
Res.: 1400 Inglewood, 48307. Tel: 248-651-7486; Fax: 248-651-3950.
Catechesis/Religious Program—Tel: 248-651-6401; Fax: 248-651-2844. Nancy Clancy, D.R.E. Students 1,817.

2—ST. IRENAEUS, Rev. A. Frank Pollie.
Res.: 771 Old Perch Rd., Rochester Hills, 48309. Tel: 248-651-9595; Fax: 248-651-1504.
Catechesis/Religious Program—Tel: 248-651-2443; Fax: 248-651-8767. Patricia Egan-Myers, D.R.E. Students 702.

ROCKWOOD, WAYNE CO., ST. MARY, [CEM] Rev. Marc A. Gawronski.
Res.: 32451 Church, 48173. Tel: 734-379-9248; Fax: 734-379-6548.
School—Tel: 734-379-9285; Fax: 734-379-9088. Michelle E. Seward, Prin. Lay Teachers 11; Students 184.
Catechesis/Religious Program—Tel: 734-379-9406. Maryjo Heitzman, D.R.E. Students 200.

ROMEO, MACOMB CO., ST. CLEMENT OF ROME, Rev. Stephen C. Reckker.
Res.: 343 S. Main St., 48065. Tel: 586-752-9611; Fax: 586-752-1601.
Catechesis/Religious Program—Tel: 586-752-6951; Fax: 586-752-7093. Deborah Knoblock, D.R.E. Students 782.

ROMULUS, WAYNE CO., ST. ALOYSIUS, Rev. Festus Ejimadu.
Res.: 11280 Ozga Rd., 48174. Tel: 734-941-5056; Fax: 734-941-6018.
School—Tel: 734-941-3340. Mary Confer, Prin. Lay Teachers 5; Students 56.

ROSEVILLE, MACOMB CO.

1—ST. ANGELA, Revs. Robert J. Schafer; Joy Chakian. In Res., Deacon Lee Smith.
Res.: 25001 Chippendale, 48066.
Church: Ten Mile Rd. and Chippendale, 48066. Tel: 586-445-6360; Fax: 586-445-6366.
School—Tel: 586-445-6375; Fax: 586-445-6382. Sr. M. LaVerne, C.S.B., Prin. Sisters 4; Lay Teachers 13; Students 354.
Catechesis/Religious Program—Tel: 586-445-6377. Elizabeth Hermes, D.R.E. Students 153.
Convent—25165 Chippendale, 48066. Tel: 586-445-6370.

2—ST. ATHANASIUS, Rev. William P. Siebert; Deacon Michael O'Keefe.
Res.: 18720 Thirteen Mile Rd., 48066. Tel: 586-772-1170; Fax: 586-776-2945.
Catechesis/Religious Program—Carol Buboi, D.R.E. Students 202.

3—ST. DONALD, Rev. Michael A. Donovan.
Res.: 16330 Twelve Mile Rd., 48066. Tel: 586-773-3440; Fax: 586-773-1235.

4—HOLY INNOCENTS, Rev. Robert Schuster.
Res.: 26100 Ridgemont Rd., 48066. Tel: 586-777-7543; Fax: 586-777-1536.
Catechesis/Religious Program—Geraldine Combetta, D.R.E. Students 87.

5—SACRED HEART, Rev. William Bonnici; Sr. Anne Mamienski, Pastoral Assoc.
Res.: 18430 Utica Rd., 48066. Tel: 586-777-9116; Fax: 586-777-7958.
Catechesis/Religious Program—Tel: 810-777-8150; Fax: 586-777-3288. LaJoy Smith, D.R.E. Students 70.

ROYAL OAK, OAKLAND CO.

1—ST. DENNIS, Revs. John P. Christ, O.S.C.; Tony Ong.
Res.: 2200 E. 12 Mile Rd., 48067-1504. Tel: 248-544-2181; Fax: 248-544-9443.
School—1415 N. Stephenson, 48067-1504. Tel: 248-398-6555; Fax: 248-398-2878. Michael Reece, Prin. Lay Teachers 17; Students 238.
Catechesis/Religious Program—Tel: 248-545-1926. Christine Wagberg, D.R.E. Students 129.

2—ST. MARY, [CEM] Rev. Andrew J. Tomasko; Rev. Msgr. Thomas H. Villerot (Retired); Deacon Timothy P. Renaud; Sr. Therese Allgeyer, O.P.
Res.: 730 Lafayette Ave. S., 48067. Tel: 248-547-1818; Fax: 248-547-4577.
School—628 Lafayette Ave. S., 48067. Tel: 248-545-2140; Fax: 248-545-2303. Greg Carnacchi, Prin. Lay Teachers 12; Students 147.
Catechesis/Religious Program—Tel: 248-547-1810. Ms. Bridget Nemzek, D.R.E. Students 80.

3—NATIONAL SHRINE OF THE LITTLE FLOWER, Rev. Msgr. William M. Easton; Revs. Michael J. Heppen, C.S.C.; Robert S. Liberty; Deacon Lynn Henning. In Res., Rev. Lambert H. Smits.
Res.: 2123 Roseland Ave., 48073. Tel: 248-541-4122 (Office); Fax: 248-541-2838.
Church: 2123 Roseland, 48067.
School—1621 Linwood, 48067. Tel: 248-541-4622; Fax: 248-541-6969. Sharon Dixon, Prin. Lay Teachers 30; Students 651.
Academy—Tel: 248-549-2928; Fax: 248-546-2953. Gabrielle Erken, Prin. Lay Teachers 8; Students 174.
High School—3500 W. Thirteen Mile Rd., 48073. Tel: 248-549-2925; Fax: 248-549-2953. Mr. Thomas P. Kirkwood, Prin. Lay Teachers 25; Students 305.
Catechesis/Religious Program—Tel: 248-541-5133. Judy Maten, D.R.E. Students 625.

ST. CLAIR SHORES, MACOMB CO.

1—ST. GERMAINE, Rev. James L. Bjorum, J.C.L.; Deacon Terrance E. Downey, Pastoral Assoc.
Office—28301 Little Mack, 48081. Tel: 810-771-1750; Fax: 810-771-7634.
School—Tel: 810-771-0890. Mr. Alvin C. Rader, Prin. Lay Teachers 13; Students 308.
Catechesis/Religious Program—Deacon Edwin McLeod, D.R.E. Students 130.

2—ST. GERTRUDE, [CEM] Rev. John G. McGreevy, O.P. In Res., Rev. Gregory Moore, O.P.
Res.: 28839 Jefferson Ave., 48081. Tel: 586-777-9120; Fax: 586-777-8390.
Catechesis/Religious Program—Tel: 586-775-5820; Fax: 586-447-4729. Paul Lippard, D.R.E. Students 202.

3—ST. ISAAC JOGUES, Rev. Timothy P. Mazur.
Parish Center—21120 Benjamin Dr., 48081. Tel: 586-778-5100; Fax: 586-778-4458.
School—Tel: 586-771-3525; Fax: 586-778-8183. Lay Teachers 20; Students 400.
Catechesis/Religious Program—Jean Hartman, D.R.E. Students 420.

4—ST. JOAN OF ARC, Rev. Msgr. Ricardo E. Bass; Rev. Joseph A. Gerardi; Deacon Robert F. Busch.
Parish Center—22412 Overlake, 48080. Tel: 586-777-3670; Fax: 586-774-5528.
School—22415 Overlake, 48080. Tel: 586-777-8370; Fax: 586-447-3574. Mr. Don Ancypa, Prin. Lay Teachers 35; Students 749.
Catechesis/Religious Program—Tel: 586-772-1282. Suzanne Cornelius, D.R.E. Students 749.

5—ST. LUCY, Rev. John C. Esper; Deacon Robert

Herta. In Res., Rev. Michael Loyson.
Res.: 23401 Jefferson, 48080. Tel: 586-771-8300; Fax: 586-447-4220.
Catechesis/Religious Program—Tel: 810-447-4222. Ms. Betty Frei-Sheehan, D.R.E. Students 292.
6—ST. MARGARET OF SCOTLAND, Rev. Ronald DeHondt; Deacon Ronald Channell.
Res.: 21201 Thirteen Mile Rd., 48082. Tel: 586-293-2240; Fax: 586-293-0116.
Catechesis/Religious Program—Tel: 586-293-3280. Students 420.

ST. CLAIR, ST. CLAIR CO., ST. MARY, [CEM] Rev. Ronald J. Victor; Deacon Robert E. McLeod, Pastoral Assoc.
Res.: 415 N. 6th St., 48079. Tel: 810-329-2255; Fax: 810-329-5997.
School—Tel: 810-329-4150; Fax: 810-329-5705. Mrs. Marilynn Pavlov, Prin. Lay Teachers 16; Students 297.
Catechesis/Religious Program—Tel: 810-329-7801. Mrs. Sue Karas, D.R.E. Students 479.
Convent—811 Orchard St., 48079. Tel: 810-329-2400.

SHELBY TWP.
1—ST. JOHN VIANNEY CHURCH, Rev. Jerome J. Machlik.
Res.: 54045 Schoenherr Rd., 48315. Tel: 586-781-6525; Fax: 586-781-6527.
Catechesis/Religious Program—Tel: 586-781-2627. Fritzi Bohlmann, D.R.E.; Mary Lundgaard, D.R.E.; Ida Johns, D.R.E.; Barbara Bakotich, D.R.E. Students 1,590.
2—ST. KIERAN, Rev. H. Thomas Johnson; Deacons James A. Cron; Stephen Marks.
Res.: 53600 Mound Rd., 48316. Tel: 586-781-4901; Fax: 586-781-6516.
Catechesis/Religious Program—Tel: 586-781-6515. Patricia Radacsy, D.R.E. Students 1,418.
3—ST. THERESE OF LISIEUX, Revs. Thomas J. Sutherland; Meyrl E. Schmit (JKS).
Church: 48115 Schoenherr Rd., 48315-4225. Tel: 586-254-4433; Fax: 586-254-5463.
Catechesis/Religious Program—Students 857.

SOUTH LYON, OAKLAND CO., ST. JOSEPH, Rev. Kenneth M. Chase; Sr. Eleanor Furman, O.S.F., Pastoral Assoc.; Deacon William Otto, Pastoral Assoc.
Res.: 830 S. Lafayette, 48178. Tel: 248-446-8700; Fax: 248-446-8746.
Catechesis/Religious Program—Tel: 248-446-8728. Mary Ann Sikorski, D.R.E. Students 1,397.

SOUTHFIELD, OAKLAND CO.
1—ST. BEATRICE, Rev. John Gagala, J.C.L.
Res.: 17235 Mt. Vernon, 48075. Tel: 248-557-3342; Fax: 248-557-3427.
2—ST. BEDE, Rev. Lawrence A. Pettke.
Res.: 18290 W. Twelve Mile Rd., 48076. Tel: 248-559-0577; Fax: 248-559-0752.
Church: Twelve Mile and Southfield Rds., 48076.
School—Tel: 248-559-0572. Beth Kascheres, Prin. Lay Teachers 9; Students 179.
Catechesis/Religious Program—Tel: 248-559-0578. Pat Metz, D.R.E. Students 23.
3—DIVINE PROVIDENCE, (Lithuanian), Rev. Aloyzas Volskis.
Res.: 25335 W. 9 Mile Rd., 48034. Tel: 248-354-3429; Fax: 248-354-1773.
4—ST. IVES, Rev. William D. Sinatra; Deacon Ronald E. Rohlman.
Res.: 29350 Lahser, 48034. Tel: 248-353-3410; Fax: 248-353-5412.
Catechesis/Religious Program—Tel: 248-353-4550. Students 63.
5—ST. MICHAEL, Revs. Robert Weakley, O.F.M.; David Kobak, O.F.M.; Roch Farland, O.F.M. (Retired); Bros. Michael Schebeci, O.F.M., Pastoral Assoc.; Luke Simon, O.F.M., Pastoral Assoc.
Res.: 25225 Code Rd., 48034. Tel: 248-356-8787; Fax: 248-356-1240.

SOUTHGATE, WAYNE CO.
1—ST. HUGH, Rev. Eugene E. Wojtewicz.
Res.: 11300 Reeck Rd., 48195. Tel: 734-287-6990; Fax: 734-287-8109.
2—ST. PIUS X, Rev. Peter Petroske.
Office—14101 Superior Ave., 48195. Tel: 734-285-1100; Fax: 734-285-5310.
Res.: 14160 Longtin Ave., 48195.
School—Tel: 734-284-6500; Fax: 734-285-6525. Ann Hall, Elementary Prin. Lay Teachers 15; Students 253.
Catechesis/Religious Program—Liela Abass D.R.E. Students 188.

STERLING HEIGHTS, MACOMB CO.
1—ST. BLASE, Rev. Randall Phillips; Mary Dumm, Pastoral Assoc.
Res.: 12151 E. 15 Mile Rd., 48312-5120. Tel: 586-268-2244; Fax: 586-268-1174.
Catechesis/Religious Program—Tel: 586-268-3050. Students 625.
2—SS. CYRIL AND METHODIUS, Rev. Benjamin Kosnac (Slovakia); Deacon Gerald Smigel.
Res.: 41233 Ryan Rd., 48314. Tel: 586-726-6911; Fax: 586-726-5913.
3—ST. EPHREM, Rev. Ronald Milligan.
Res.: 38900 Dodge Rd., 48312. Tel: 586-264-1230; Fax: 586-264-2757.
Catechesis/Religious Program—Tel: 586-264-2777. Students 241.
4—ST. JANE FRANCES DE CHANTAL, Rev. Gerard LeBoeuf.
Res.: 38750 Ryan Rd., 48310. Tel: 586-977-8080; Fax: 586-977-9305.
Catechesis/Religious Program—Tel: 586-977-0310. Students 404.
5—ST. MALACHY, Rev. Joseph J. Gembala; Deacon Eugene Mignacca.
Res.: 14115 14 Mile Rd., 48312-6506. Tel: 586-264-1220; Fax: 586-264-1656.
Catechesis/Religious Program—Tel: 586-268-4430. Ms. Patricia Whelan, D.R.E. Students 385.
6—ST. MATTHIAS, Rev. Richard E. Cyr.
Res.: 12509 Nineteen Mile Rd., 48313. Tel: 586-731-1300; Fax: 586-731-2576.
Catechesis/Religious Program—Tel: 586-731-0650. Donna Latimer, D.R.E. Students 380.
7—ST. MICHAEL, Revs. Lawrence J. Jackson; Jacek Brewczynski; Deacon Lawrence Healy; Carrie Orlando, Pastoral Assoc.
Church: 40501 Hayes Rd., 48313. Tel: 586-247-0020; Fax: 586-247-4081.
Res.: 39443 Heatherheath, Clinton Twp., 48038. Tel: 586-286-3322.
Catechesis/Religious Program—Tel: 586-247-0098. Emily Gordon, D.R.E.; Catherine McInerney, D.R.E. Students 813.
8—OUR LADY OF CZESTOCHOWA, Revs. Stanislaw Kowalski, S.Ch.; Marek Ciesielski, S.Ch.; Konrad Urbanowski, S.Ch.
Res.: 3100 18 Mile Rd., 48314-3810. Tel: 586-977-7267; Fax: 586-977-2074.
Catechesis/Religious Program—Sr. Margaret Romanowska, M.Chr., D.R.E. Students 350.
9—ST. RENE GOUPIL, Rev. Frederick J. Schweihofer; Sr. Mary Schmidlin, O.S.F., Pastoral Assoc.; Deacon Robert Ovies.
Res.: 35955 Ryan Rd., 48310. Tel: 586-939-7500; Fax: 586-939-7839.
Catechesis/Religious Program—Tel: 586-939-7688. Sandra Mals, D.R.E. Students 495.

TAYLOR, WAYNE CO.
1—ST. ALFRED, Revs. James F. Kean, Admin.; John G. Hawkins, O.S.C.
Res.: 9500 Banner, 48180. Tel: 313-291-6464; Fax: 313-291-2733.
Catechesis/Religious Program—Tel: 313-291-3210. Beth A. Oley, D.R.E. Students 205.
2—ST. CONSTANCE, Rev. Leo F. Sabourin; Deacon Joseph Mouro.
Res.: 21555 Kinyon Rd., 48180. Tel: 313-291-4050; Fax: 313-291-5655.
3—ST. CYRIL OF JERUSALEM, Rev. Bernard Fraser; Deacons Daniel J. Hurley; William A. Thome.
Res.: 6442 Pelham Rd., 48180. Tel: 313-381-3000; Fax: 313-381-5528.
School—Taylor Catholic, Tel: 313-383-8585. Marcia Guerra, Prin.
Catechesis/Religious Program—Tel: 313-383-5663. Michael Grube, D.R.E. Students 228.
4—ST. PASCHAL, Rev. Robert Cislo.
Res.: 22210 Champaign St., 48180. Tel: 313-291-4880; Fax: 313-291-7514.
School—Tel: 313-291-6650; Fax: 313-291-2657. Marcia Guerra, Prin. Lay Teachers 9; Students 113.

TEMPERANCE, MONROE CO.
1—ST. ANTHONY, [CEM] Rev. Gregory J. Deters.
Res.: 4605 St. Anthony Rd., 48182. Tel: 734-854-1143; Fax: 734-854-4622.
School—Tel: 734-854-1160. Linda Schulte, Prin. Sisters of Notre Dame 4; Dominican Sisters 1; Lay Teachers 11 Students 188.
Catechesis/Religious Program—Students 172.
Convent—4607 St. Anthony Rd., 48182. Tel: 734-854-2779.
2—OUR LADY OF MT. CARMEL, Rev. Stephen L. Vileo, Admin.; Sr. Aloise Paluszak, O.S.F.; Hazel Destatte, Pastoral Assoc.
Res.: 810 Donna Dr., 48182. Tel: 734-847-2805; Fax: 734-847-8970.
Catechesis/Religious Program—Tel: 734-847-1725. Students 469.

TRENTON, WAYNE CO.
1—ST. JOSEPH, [JC] Rev. Steven A. Wertenen; Sr. Helen Sohn O.P., Pastoral Assoc.
Parish Center—2565 Third St., 48183. Tel: 734-676-9082; Fax: 734-676-6255.
School—Tel 734-676-2565; Fax: 734-676-9744. Wanda Rovenskie, Prin. Lay Teachers 10; Students 197.
Catechesis/Religious Program—Tel: 734-676-7115. Fran Dawson, D.R.E. Students 335.
2—ST. TIMOTHY, Rev. Charles S. Fontana.
Parish Office—2901 Manning Dr., 48183. Tel: 734-676-5115; Fax: 734-676-6863.
Catechesis/Religious Program—Tel: 734-676-5616. Fritzi Bohlmann, D.R.E.; Fran Dawson, D.R.E. Students 223.

TROY, OAKLAND CO.
1—ST. ALAN, Rev. Gary M. Tierney, J.C.L.; Sr. Mary Choiniere, S.S.J., Pastoral Assoc.; Frank W. Spencer, Pastoral Assoc. In Res., Rev. John A. Blaska (Retired).
Church: 3077 Gloucester, 48084. Tel: 248-649-5510; Fax: 248-649-6729.
Res.: 2345 Coolidge Rd., 48084. Tel: 248-649-5511.
2—ST. ANASTASIA, Revs. Kenneth R. Kaucheck, J.C.D.; Francis A. Hanudel, O.F.M.; Sr. Kay Allberry, O.P., Pastoral Assoc.; Deacon Ronald W. Cook, Pastoral Assoc.
Res.: 4571 John R. Rd., 48085. Tel: 248-689-8380; Fax: 248-689-7489.
Catechesis/Religious Program—Tel: 248-689-1431. Regina Simony, D.R.E.; Nancy Lanzon, D.R.E. Students 1,206.
3—ST. ELIZABETH ANN SETON, Rev. Ronald J. Jozwiak, J.C.L.
Res.: 280 E. Square Lake Rd., 48085. Tel: 248-879-1310; Fax: 248-879-2886.
Catechesis/Religious Program—Tel: 248-879-1314. Students 280.
4—ST. LUCY, (Croatian), Rev. Nikola Pasalic, O.F.M.
Res.: 200 E. Wattles Rd., 48085. Tel: 248-619-9910; Fax: 248-619-9912.
5—ST. THOMAS MORE, Rev. Edward A. Belczak; Deacon John Vanneste.
Res.: 4580 Adams Rd., 48098. Tel: 248-647-2222; Fax: 248-647-8192.
Catechesis/Religious Program—Tel: 248-647-4680. Students 960.

UTICA, MACOMB CO., ST. LAWRENCE, Revs. Robert J. Fisher; William J. Herman; Sr. Janet Sullivan, I.H.M., Pastoral Assoc.
Res.: 44633 Utica Rd., 48317. Tel: 586-731-5347; Fax: 586-731-5393.
School—Tel: 810-731-0135. Karen Pawlak, Prin. Lay Teachers 30; Students 758.
Catechesis/Religious Program—Tel: 586-731-5072. Mary Paonessa, D.R.E. Students 736.

WALLED LAKE, OAKLAND CO., ST. WILLIAM, Rev. Michael G. Savickas; Deacon Richard T. Smith.
Res.: 531 Common St., 48390. Tel: 248-624-1421; Fax: 248-624-5273.
School—135 O'Flaherty, 48390. Tel: 248-669-4440; Fax: 248-669-2245. Linda Jackson, M.A., Prin. Lay Teachers 16; Students 238.
Catechesis/Religious Program—Tel: 248-624-1371. Claudia Givinsky, D.R.E. Students 590.

WARREN, MACOMB CO.
1—ST. ANNE'S, Revs. Michael Kazer; Jerome Slowinski, J.C.L.; Sr. Alice Miller, I.H.M., Pastoral Assoc.; Deacon Marvin Strzyzewski. In Res., Rev. Francis A. Weingartz (Retired).
Res.: 32000 Mound Rd., 48092. Tel: 586-268-3434; Fax: 586-268-4142.
School—Tel: 586-264-2911; Fax: 586-264-4533. Dr. Thom Engel, Prin. Intercommunity Sisters 1; Lay Teachers 29; Students 778.
Catechesis/Religious Program—Clare Cooper, D.R.E. Students 241.
2—ASCENSION, Rev. Norbert Maciejewski.
Res.: 21050 Ascension St., 48089. Tel: 586-754-4000; Fax: 586-757-2342.
Catechesis/Religious Program—Tel: 586-754-6741. Students 57.
3—ST. CLETUS, Rev. Philip Briffa; Rose Marie Miller, Pastoral Assoc.
Office—26256 Ryan Rd., 48091. Tel: 586-755-1313; Fax: 586-756-0724.
Res.: 26262 Ryan Rd., 48091.
Catechesis/Religious Program—Tel: 586-755-1350. Students 88.
4—ST. DOROTHY, Revs. Richard Welsh; Thomas Puzio; Cathy Gasowski, Pastoral Assoc.
Res.: 12255 Frazho, 48089. Tel: 586-754-3232; Fax: 586-754-3152.
Catechesis/Religious Program—Tel: 586-759-1040. Students 185.
5—ST. EDMUND, Revs. Robert J. Witkowski; Wojciech Wojcicki; Deacon Larry Sullivan.
Res.: 14025 Twelve Mile Rd., 48088. Tel: 586-772-2720; Fax: 586-772-5576.
Catechesis/Religious Program—Tel: 586-773-9220; Fax: 586-772-5021. Students 278.
6—ST. LEONARD OF PORT MAURICE, [CEM] Rev. Norbert Maciejewski; Deacon Edward Swartz.
Res.: 14057 E. Nine Mile, 48089. Tel: 586-777-1350; Fax: 586-777-1247.
7—ST. LOUISE, Rev. Thomas G. Rice; Sr. Carmen Coccimiglio, S.L.W.; Deacons Wilhelm Kessler; Art Majewski.
Res.: 2500 Twelve Mile Rd., 48092. Tel: 586-751-3340; Fax: 586-751-0603.
Catechesis/Religious Program—Tel: 586-751-3486. Mrs. Irmgard Kovacs, D.R.E. Students 220.
8—ST. MARK, Rev. Robert A. Ruedisueli; Deacon George R. Posavetz; Joann Loria, Pastoral Assoc.

Res.: 4257 Bart, 48091. Tel: 586-759-3020; Fax: 586-759-3024.
Catechesis/Religious Program—Tel: 586-759-3022. Students 255.

9—ST. MARTIN DE PORRES, Rev. Roman Pasieczny.
Res.: 31555 Hoover Rd., 48093. Tel: 586-264-7515; Fax: 586-264-4013.
Catechesis/Religious Program—Tel: 586-264-7970. Mrs. Christine Cabe, D.R.E. Students 375.

10—ST. SYLVESTER, Revs. Gary Schulte; Artemio Galos; Sr. Ann Glombowski, O.P., Pastoral Assoc.; Deacon John L. Skladanowski, Pastoral Assoc.
Res.: 11200 Twelve Mile Rd., 48093. Tel: 810-751-3636; Fax: 810-751-1766.
Catechesis/Religious Program—Tel: 810-751-3510; Fax: 810-751-2208. Students 352.

WASHINGTON, MACOMB CO., SS. JOHN AND PAUL, Rev. David A. Buersmeyer; JoAnne Owens, Pastoral Assoc.
Res.: 7777 W. 28 Mile Rd., 48094. Tel: 586-781-9010; Fax: 586-781-7061.
Catechesis/Religious Program—Tel: 586-781-9488. Students 424.

WATERFORD, OAKLAND CO.

1—ST. BENEDICT, Rev. H. Thomas Kuehnemund; Maria Geryk, Pastoral Assoc.
Parish Office—80 S. Lynn, 48328. Tel: 248-681-1534; Fax: 248-681-4501.
Catechesis/Religious Program—Tel: 248-682-5580, Ext. 217. Students 134.

2—OUR LADY OF THE LAKES, Revs. Lawrence Delonnay; Robert McClory.
Res.: 5481 Dixie Hwy., 48329. Tel: 248-623-0274; Fax: 248-623-2723.
School—Tel: 248-623-0250; Fax: 248-623-2274. Carl Uberti, Elementary Prin. Lay Teachers 26; Students 492.
High School—Tel: 248-623-0340; Fax: 248-623-7536. Carl Uberti, Prin. Sisters 1; Lay Teachers 19; Students 224.
Catechesis/Religious Program—Tel: 248-623-0291; Fax: 248-623-1280. Patricia Tola, D.R.E. Students 360.

3—ST. PERPETUA, Rev. Richard S. Rakoczy.
Res.: 134 Airport Rd., 48327. Tel: 248-682-6431; Fax: 248-682-7088.
Catechesis/Religious Program—Bonnie Banaszek, D.R.E. Students 302.

WAYNE, WAYNE CO., ST. MARY, Rev. Jack H. Baker; Sr. Patricia Hergenroether, S.S.J., Pastoral Assoc.
34530 Michigan Ave., 48184. Tel: 734-721-8745; Fax: 734-721-0260.
School—34516 Michigan Ave., 48184. Tel: 734-721-1240; Fax: 734-467-7381. Ms. Catherine Myszka, Prin. Lay Teachers 13; Students 273.
Catechesis/Religious Program—Tel: 734-326-8180. Students 274.

WEST BLOOMFIELD, OAKLAND CO., PRINCE OF PEACE, Rev. Arnold J. Kosco; Deacon Edward Hilger.
Res.: 4300 Walnut Lake Rd., 48323. Tel: 248-681-9424; Fax: 248-681-5543.
Catechesis/Religious Program—Tel: 248-681-5070. Carol Wojciak, D.R.E. Students 400.

WESTLAND, WAYNE CO.

1—ST. BERNARDINE, Rev. Salvino Briffa; Sharon Williams, Pastoral Assoc. & D.R.E.
Res.: 31463 Ann Arbor Trail, 48185. Tel: 734-427-5150; Fax: 734-427-3319.
Catechesis/Religious Program—Tel: 313-261-3050. Students 135.

2—CHURCH OF THE DIVINE SAVIOR, Rev. Alexander A. Kuras; Deacons Paul F. Pelchat; Eugene B. Desjarlais.
Church: 39375 Joy Rd., 48185. Tel: 734-455-3620; Fax: 734-455-7998.
Res.: 9249 Caprice, Plymouth, 48170. Tel: 734-455-6964.
Catechesis/Religious Program—Stephen Reyes, D.R.E. Students 200.

3—ST. DAMIAN, Rev. Lawrence Zurawski.
Res.: 30055 Joy Rd., 48185. Tel: 734-421-6130; Fax: 734-513-4916.
School—Tel: 734-427-1680. Mrs. Susan Perna, Prin. Felician Sisters 2; Lay Teachers 13; Students 240.
Catechesis/Religious Program—Tel: 734-522-5383. Sr. M. Patricia, C.S.S.F., D.R.E. Students 163.

4—ST. RICHARD, Rev. Terence Treppa.
Res.: 35637 Cherry Hill, 48186. Tel: 734-729-2240; Fax: 734-729-3132.
Church Office: 35637 Cherry Hill Rd., 48186. Tel: 734-729-4420.
Catechesis/Religious Program—Tel: 734-729-4411. Jeanne Martin, D.R.E. Students 175.

5—SS. SIMON AND JUDE, Rev. Gerard V. Bechard.
Office—32500 Palmer Rd., 48186. Tel: 734-722-1343; Fax: 734-326-5466.
Catechesis/Religious Program—Mary Ann Kocsis, D.R.E.; Margaret Reyez, D.R.E. Students 164.

6—ST. THEODORE OF CANTERBURY, Rev. Gary Michalik; Deacons John Kenny; Joseph Sullivan, (Retired); James L. Hensel, (Retired).
Res.: 8200 Wayne Rd., 48185. Tel: 734-425-4421; Fax: 734-425-0650.
Catechesis/Religious Program—Tel: 734-425-7310. Students 270.

WHITE LAKE, OAKLAND CO., ST. PATRICK, Revs. Thomas L. Meagher; Frederick Kalaj.
Res.: 9086 Hutchins Rd., 48386. Tel: 248-698-3100; Fax: 248-698-2350.
School—9040 Hutchins Rd., 48386. Tel: 248-698-2340. Mrs. Linda Meese, Prin. Lay Teachers 23; Students 433.
Catechesis/Religious Program—Students 1,183.

WOODHAVEN, WAYNE CO., OUR LADY OF THE WOODS, Rev. Richard Macey.
Res.: 21892 Gudith Rd., 48183. Tel: 734-671-5102; Fax: 734-671-2901.
Catechesis/Religious Program—Tel: 734-671-0525. Patricia Butler, D.R.E. Students 1,013.

WYANDOTTE, WAYNE CO.

1—ST. ELIZABETH, Rev. Charles M. Morris.
Res.: 138 Goodell St., 48192. Tel: 734-284-7727; Fax: 734-284-7891.

2—ST. HELENA, Rev. P. Larry Siroskey.
Res.: 753 Forest St., 48192. Tel: 734-284-4988; Fax: 734-282-0710.

3—ST. JOSEPH, Rev. Thomas J. Moloney, S.C.A.
Res.: 353 Elm St., 48192. Tel: 734-285-9840; Fax: 734-285-9745.
School—Tel: 734-285-2030; Fax: 734-285-0327. Mary Swinkey, Prin. Lay Teachers 13; Students 150.
Catechesis/Religious Program—Tel: 734-285-6453. Laurie Spano, D.R.E. Students 187.

4—OUR LADY OF MT. CARMEL, (Polish), [CEM] Rev. Walter J. Ptak.
Res.: 976 Pope John Paul II Ave., 48192. Tel: 734-284-9135; Fax: 734-284-1367.
School—2609 Tenth St., 48192. Tel: 734-285-5520; Fax: 734-285-9245. Miss Millie Bardoni, Elementary Prin. Felician Sisters 2; Lay Teachers 9; Students 160.
High School—Tel: 734-284-7311; Fax: 734-284-6235. Sr. Mary Joseph VanCamp, C.S.S.F., High School Prin. Felician Sisters 1; Lay Teachers 12; Students 80.
Catechesis/Religious Program—Tel: 734-284-6145. Sr. Mary Sophie Straksys, C.S.S.F., D.R.E. Students 162.
Convent—2609 Tenth St., 48192. Tel: 313-284-7253.

5—ST. PATRICK, [JC] Rev. Raymond H. Lewandowski.
Office—135 Superior Blvd., 48192. Tel: 734-285-9470; Fax: 734-285-1623.
Res.: 105 Superior Blvd., 48192. Tel: 734-285-9472.
School—Wyandotte Catholic Consolidated School, Tel: 734-285-2030; Fax: 734-285-0327. Mary Swinkey, Elementary Prin. Lay Teachers 9; Students 150.
High School—Gabriel Richard H.S., Tel: 734-284-1875. Bro. James Rottenbucher, C.S.C., Prin. Students 440.

6—ST. STANISLAUS KOSTKA, (Polish), Rev. John P. Hedges; Deacons Patrick T. Bruen; Kenneth Trabbic.
Res.: 266 Antoine St., 48192. Tel: 734-285-9509; Fax: 734-285-0124.
School—240 Antoine St., 48192. Tel: 734-282-3105; Fax: 734-282-7425. Lay Teachers 8; Students 99.

YALE, ST. CLAIR CO., SACRED HEART, [CEM] Rev. Gene Katcher.
Res.: 310 N. Main St., 48097. Tel: 810-387-2998.
Catechesis/Religious Program—Tel: 810-387-3361. Mark Ladd, D.R.E. Students 120.

Chaplains of Public Institutions

DETROIT. *Alexander Blaine Memorial*, Tel: 313-961-8077. Attended from St. Peter and Paul.
Annapolis. Rev. Bernard Pilarski.
Art Centre Hospital, Tel: 313-875-6011. Attended from Lady of the Rosary.
Beaumont Hospital. Revs. Christopher Welch, Lloyd Thiel, O.F.M. Cap.
Bi-County Osteopathic. Rev. Luke Krotkiewicz.
Bon Secours. Sr. Therese Tighe, O.P., Chap., Rita McEachen Neal, Chap.
Children's Hospital, Tel: 313-745-5917. Sisters Janet Ryan, I.H.M., Dir., Beverly Hindson, I.H.M., Chap.
Cottage Hospital, Tel: 810-785-8855. Attended from St. Paul's.
Crittendon Hospital. Rev. Walter Lezochowski.
Detroit General Hospital 48226. Tel: 313-224-0541. Sr. Adelaide Eiden, Chap.
Detroit Osteopathic Hospital 48226. Tel: 313-865-6300. Attended from Cathedral of the Most Blessed Sacrament.
Detroit Psychiatric Institute 48226. Tel: 313-427-1533. Rev. Daniel O'Sullivan (Retired).
Detroit Receiving Hospital 48226. Rev. Gabriel Comelo, Sr. Janet Hudspeth, Chap.
Detroit Riverview Hospital. Attended from St. Charles.
Doctor's Hospital, St. Peter and Paul, 48226. Tel: 313-961-8077. Vacant.
Garden City Osteopathic Hospital. Rev. Bernard Pilarski.
Glen Eden Hospital. Attended from the Capuchin Community.
Grace Hospital-Northwest University. Mary Bartnik, Chap.
Harper Hospital and Rehabilitation Center. Revs. Gabriel Cohelo, O.F.M.Cap., Anthony Abgali.
Henry Ford Hospital. Rev. Emiliano Auwen Diere, Sr. Fran Pokreifka, I.H.M., Chap., Mrs. Marie Handley, Chap.
Heritage Hospital, Tel: 810-295-6700. Sherri Christ.
Hutzel Hospital, Tel: 313-831-3139. Rev. Gabriel Comelo, (Emergencies).
Kirkwood Hospital, Tel: 313-861-0363. Attended from St. Gregory.
Lapeer Regional, Tel: 810-664-8594. Attended from Immaculate Conception.
Lincoln Hospital, Tel: 313-842-3450. Attended from Holy Redeemer.
Macomb Hospital Center. Mrs. Katherine Breslin, Chap. (St. John's Health System)
Martin Place East Hospital, Tel: 810-542-8720. Attended from St. Vincent Ferrer.
McNamara Hospital, Tel: 810-751-0410. Attended from the Capuchin Community.
Mercy Hospital Detroit 48226. Sr. Rose Petrozzo, O.P., Chap.
Michigan Health Care Corporation. Vacant.
North Woodward Hospital, Tel: 313-865-6300. Attended from Blessed Sacrament Cathedral.
Northville State Hospital, Tel: 810-349-1800. Rev. Stanislaus C. Kukulski (Retired).
Oakland General Osteopathic. Sr. Stephanie Thompson, Chap. (St. John's Health System)
Oakwood Hospital. Revs. Michael Gormley, S.A.C., Richard Lileart, Sr. Ann Foley, Chap.
Palmer Osteopathic Hospital, Tel: 313-868-3876. Attended from St. Benedict.
Palmer Osteopathic Hospital-East, Tel: 313-881-4049. Attended from St. Matthew.
Pontiac Correction Camp, Tel: 810-363-2441. Attended from St. Patrick, Union Lake.
Pontiac General Hospital. Diane Guappone, Chap.
Pontiac Osteopathic Hospital. Diane Guappone, Chap.
Redford Community Hospital, Tel: 313-531-0371. Attended from St. Agatha.
Rehabilitation Institute. Sisters Therese LeBlanc, Dir., Leslie Hartway, Chap.
Riverside Osteopathic Hospital, Tel: 313-676-9082. Attended from St. Joseph.
Saratoga General Hospital. Rev. Louis Resma.
Sinai Hospital. Rev. Kenneth J. Noetzel, S.J.
Southwest Detroit Hospital 48226. Tel: 313-963-4539. Rev. Thomas Lumpkin.
Veterans Administration Hospital. Rev. Joseph Duc Vu.
Warren Memorial Hospital. Vacant.
Wayne and Monroe County-Adults, 305 Michigan Ave., 48226. Tel: 313-237-4684. John Humphrey, Chap.
Wayne Co., 305 Michigan Ave., 48226. Tel: 313-237-4684. Abdulami Osman, Outreach Coord.
Wayne County Juvenile Justice, c/o Team for Justice, 1035 St. Antoine, 48226. Tel: 313-965-3242. Bill Kresse, Chap.
Wayne County Youth Home, 305 Michigan Ave., 48226. Tel: 313-237-5900. Thomas Carlier, Chap.
Wyandotte General Hospital, Tel: 313-284-4988. Attended from St. Helena.
Yale Community Hospital, Tel: 810-387-2998. Attended from Sacred Heart.
Zieger Osteopathic Hospital, Tel: 313-825-4696. Attended from Our Lady Queen of Angels.

CLINTON TOWNSHIP. *State Prisons*, 24415 Crocker Blvd., 48036. Tel: 810-755-9359. Rev. Thomas R. Physician (Retired).

FARMINGTON. *Botsford General Hospital*, St. Alexander's. Tel: 810-474-5748. Rev. Louis Resma.

MOUNT CLEMENS. *Macomb County Adults & Macomb County Jail*, c/o Macomb County Jail, 43565 Elizabeth Rd., 48043. Tel: 810-307-9326. Jo Kudela, Chap.
Macomb County Youth Home, Tel: 313-237-5962. Attended from St. Peter's, Mount Clemens.
Monroe County Jail, Tel: 313-237-5900. Vacant.
Mount Clemens General Hospital. Rev. John P. Hedges.

PONTIAC. *Oakland and Lapeer County-Adults*, 14 Judson St., 3rd Floor, P.O. Box 431366, 48343-1366. Tel: 810-338-9310. Peggy Devaney, Chap.
Oakland, Lapeer, and St. Clair County, 14 Judson St., 3rd Floor, P.O. Box 431366, 48343-1366. Tel: 810-338-9310. Betty Clark, Chap., Miguel Rivera, Chap.
Oakland, Lapeer, Macomb, and St. Clair Counties-Juveniles, 14 Judson St., 3rd Floor, P.O. Box 431366, 48343-1366. Tel: 810-338-9310. Carleen Ward, Chap.

PORT HURON. *Mercy Hospital Port Huron* 48060.

Sisters Margaret Weber, R.S.M., Chap., M. Frances Villerot, R.S.M., Chap.

Port Huron Hospital 48060. Tel: 810-985-7750. Attended from St. Joseph.

Special Assignment:

Rev. Msgrs.—

Dylag, Michael R., Pope John Paul II Cultural Center

Sable, Robert M., Prelate Auditor of the Roman Rota, Vatican

Zenz, John P., Moderator of the Curia

Revs.—

Banazak, Gregory, Faculty, Orchard Lake

Bilot, James D., Vocations Office

Bugarin, Michael, Catholic Univ., Washington, D.C.

Byrnes, Michael J., Sacred Heart, Major Seminary

DePorres-Cox, Jesse, O.P., St. Augustine/ St. Monica; Evangelization Office at Annunciation/Our Lady of Sorrows Parish

Fabian, John, Companions of Christ the Lamb, Paradise.

Halfpenny, Patrick F., Vice-Rector, SHMS

Havron, Daniel, O.F.M., Office of Evangelization

Kasza, John, Asst. Chancellor, Faculty SHMS, Office of Christian Worship, St. Aidon, Livonia

Kohler, Russell E., Chap., Apostleship of the Sea

Kreimes, Paul, SHMS Faculty

Lajiness, Todd, Faculty, SHMS, St. Mary Queen of Creation, New Baltimore

Malawy, Michael D., Airport Chap.

McClory, Robert O., Chancellor, facculty S.H.M.S., Our Lady of the Lakes, Waterford

Monforton, Jeffrey M., Personal Sec. to Cardinal Maida, 1234 Washington Blvd., 48226-1808. St. Jane Francis de Chantal, Sterling Heights

Riccardo, John, St. John's Center for Youth & Family

Rice, Thomas G., ASSO. Publisher/Editor in Chief, Michigan, Catholic

Slowinski, Jerome, J.C.L., Tribunal, Assoc. Pastor, St. Anne, Warren, MI

Spezia, Robert R., Faculty, SHMS, St. Margaret of Scotland, St. Clair Shores

Williams, Clarence E., C.PP.S., African American Catholic Ministries Office

Williams, Robert Hayes, Tribunal & Pastor, St. Justin, Hazel Park

On Duty Outside the Archdiocese:

Revs.—

Cassidy, Richard, Ph.D. (BUF), East Aurora, NY

Molnar, Michael, Pastoral Care, Cayman Islands

Prince, Michael, Sec. to Cardinal Edmund Szoka, Full-time Studies, Pontifical Univ. of St. Thomas Aquinas

Singelyn, Robert K., Recife, Brazil

Trent, James F., Admin., St. Joseph Parish, Fortuna, CA

Walsh, Jerome, Univ. of Dallas, TX

Military Chaplains:

Revs.—

Bucon, Raymond H., U.S. Army Reserve

Hogan, Timothy D., U.S. Navy

Kaul, John, U.S. Naval Reserves

Graduate Studies:

Revs.—

Byrnes, Michael J., Pontifical Gregorian University, Rome

Jones, Daniel J., Pontifical North American College, Rome

Prince, Michael, Sec. to Cardinal Edmund Szoka, Full-Time Studies, Pontifical Univ. of St. Thomas Aquinas

Absent on Leave:

Revs.—

Brady, Reginald

Carnago, William J.

Currin, John M.

Ellis, Matthew

Farrar, Charles

Hogan, Richard

Stochmal, Marek

Webster, Andrew

Absent on Sick Leave:

Revs.—

Kirwan, Thomas

MacLennan, Donald

Retired:

Rev. Msgrs.—

Baldwin, Edward J., Sacred Heart Seminary, 2701 Chicago Blvd., 48206.

DeCneudt, Ferdinand, Father Tallieu Senior Citizen Residence, Apt. B105, 18740 Thirteen Mile Rd., Roseville, 48066-1378.

Flanigan, Gerald A., 14469-B Levan Rd., Livonia, 48154-5094.

Horkan, Vincent J., 15181 Ford Rd., Apt. 119, Chapel Ct., Dearborn, 48126.

Milewski, Stanley E., SS. Cyril & Methodius Seminary, 3535 Indian Trail, Orchard Lake, 48324.

Monticello, Robert V., 14469 Levan Rd., Apt. C, Livonia, 48154-5094.

Sherzer, William J., St. Priscilla Parish, 19120 Purlingbrook Rd., Livonia, 48152-1986.

Trese, John A., 470 E. Drayton, Ferndale, 48220.

Villerot, Thomas H., 14453 Levan Rd., Apt. A, Livonia, 48154-5090.

Weier, John A., Maryhaven, 11350 Reeck Rd., Rm. 73, Southgate, 48195-2278.

Revs.—

Alder, Ronald, 16333 Allen Rd., Apt. 107, Southgate, 48195.

Bauer, Erwin J., 4190 Green Dr., Harsens Island, 48028-9557.

Berg, Paul, Sacred Heart Major Seminary, 2701 Chicago Blvd., 48206-1799.

Blaska, John A., St. Alan Parish, 2345 Coolidge Hwy., Troy, 48084-3665.

Blaszczyk, Thaddeus J., 8852 W. McNab Rd., Bldg. 10, Apt. 305, Tamarac, FL 33321-3651.

Bodde, Frederick A., 6116 River Rd., East China, 48054-4781.

Bologna, Anthony F., The Arbor Inn, 14030 E. Fourteen Mile Rd., #716, Warren, 48088.

Britz, Gerald F., 8781 Lakeshore, Lexington, 48450-9600.

Brock, David F., 41464 Whitetail Ln., Canton, 48188-2073.

Broderick, Leo P., St. Philip Neri Parish, 9735 Dolan Rd., Columbus, 48063-1105.

Browne, George, 165 S. Water St., #204 Marine City, 48039.

Burke, Walter E., 17582 N. Whitefish Point Rd., Paradise, 49768-9615.

Byrne, Thomas, P.O. Box 375, Flat Rock, 48134-0375.

Canavan, John D., 11395 Oakwood Dr., Jerome, 49249-9516.

Child, John F., Sacred Heart Parish, 22430 Michigan Ave., Dearborn, 48124.

Ciesniewski, Richard P., Casa Del Rio Apts., 12751 Plaza Del Rio Blvd., #3107, Peoria, AZ 85381.

Complo, Daniel C., 38 E. Willow, Apt. C, Monroe, 48162-2644.

Curtin, James E., 14465 Levon Rd., Apt. C., Livonia, 48154.

Dacey, Donald, Fairlane Meadows, 5148 Heather Dr., #116, Dearborn, 48126-2884.

Decker, Maurice C., Rapalo North Condominiums, 306, 1701 S. Flagler, West Palm Beach, FL 33401-7344.

Dietz, Francis, 14453 Levan Rd., Apt. C, Livonia, 48154-5090.

Dorr, Richard J., 38110 John P. St., Clinton Twp., 48036-1218.

Dowell, William J., 14467 Levan Rd., Apt. A, Livonia, 48154-5093.

Duffey, Thomas J., 415 Withington, Apt. 511, Ferndale 48220.

Dunn, John, Lourdes Nursing Home, 2300 Watkins Lake Rd. Waterford, 48328-1439.

Dunn, Lawrence E., P.O. Box 115, Jonannesburg, 49751.

Esper, Thomas, 164 Shoreline Dr., East Port Sanilac, 48469-9769.

Fares, Lawrence, 36773 Kelly Rd., Clinton Township, 48035-1325.

Farrell, Edward, S.H.M.S., 2701 Chicago Blvd., 48206.

Fauser, Arthur W., 2000 E. Park Dr., A, Algonac, 48001.

Ferens, Joseph F., 1870 Lakesview Blvd., Oxford, 48371-4548.

Ferrero, Bartholomew 10060 Pancalieri Instituto Figlie S. Gaetano Casa Boccardo, Via Roma n. 9, Torino, Italy.

Flynn, Thomas P., 22034 Sunnyside, St. Clair Shores, 48080.

Forish, Andrew, 19450 Mayfield, Apt. 104, Livonia, 48152-1389.

Gattari, Valentine A., St. Matthias Parish, 12509 19 Mile Rd., Sterling Heights, 48313.

Goodrow, Robert A., Chap., 17413 S.E. 77th Helmsdale Ct., The Villages, FL 32162. USNR, (Retired)

Hadad, Gerard A., 57 Seabeeze Ln., Bristol, RI 02809.

Hall, John F., St. Lawrence Parish, 44333 Utica Rd., Utica, 48317-5468.

Hayes, James L., Villa Maria, Apt. 1, 15237 Newburg Rd., Livonia, 48154-5035.

Heidelberger, Ronald, 555 Brush St., Apt. 2214, 48226.

Herman, Jerome A., 1604 S.E. 9th St., Stuart, FL 34996-3233.

Higdon, C. Paul, 3900 Aspen Dr., #345, 48060-8622.

Hoffmaster, Harry, 2500 River Rd. #41, Marysville, 48040-1949.

Hubble, Karl D., 1593 River Rd., Apt. 1-D, St. Clair, 48079-3543.

Immel, William A., 616 Schock Rd., Apt. 113, Habor Beach, 48441.

Janiga, Joseph, 7039 Sarena, 48210-1549.

Kaznowski, Valentine J.

Keveney, William

Killeen, Joseph P., 5126 Sandalwood Cir., Grand Blank, 48439.

Koltuniak, Michael P., Marybrook Manor, 36975 Five Mile Rd., C-108, Livonia, 48154.

Konopka, Edward F., 7950 N. McNab, Apt. 210, Tamarac, FL 33321-8436.

Kosicki, Bohdan W., 5630 Klettner, St. Clair, 48079-1918.

Kowalczyk, Sigismund C., 879 N. Channel Dr., Harsens Island, 48028.

Kowalski, George, 12765 Walnut St., Southgate, 48195-1161.

Kowalski, Ralph E., 14467-D Levan Rd., Livonia, 48154-5093.

Kreft, Henry S., 3621 Port Austin Rd., Port Austin, 48467-9624.

Krieg, Jerome L., 2450 Watkins Lake Rd., Apt. 219, Waterford, 48328-1439.

Krisciunevicius, Victor, 11427 Irene Ave., Warren, 48093-6545.

Kubik, John M., 34680 Huntley Dr., Apt. K-27, Sterling Hts., 48312.

Kukulski, Stanislaus C., 3021 Evaline, Hamtramck, 48212.

Kuntz, Donald B., 9245 North River Rd., Algonac, 48001-4007.

Lipczewski, Boleslaus, Our Lady of Christians Parish, 12635 McDougall, 48212.

LoGrosso, Pasquale, 14560 Lakeside Cir., Sterling Hts., 48313.

Lombardi, Albert U., 14465 Levan Rd., Apt. B, Livonia, 48154-5092.

Maloney, Richard E.

Markham, John W., St. Elizabeth Parish, 3138 E. Canfield St., 48207-1597.

McGoldrick, William J., Our Lady Star of the Sea Parish, 467 Fairford Rd., Grosse Pointe, 48236-2410.

Mikus, Elemir, 90863 Oreske 5, Skalica, Slovakia.

Mitchell, Edward J., 14467 Levan Rd., Apt. C, Livonia, 48154.

Muir, Edmund D., 443 Cerromar Ln., Apt. 300, Venice, FL 34293-4408.

Murphy, Daniel J., 14455 Levan Rd., Apt. A, Livonia, 48154.

Ndrevashay, Primus P., 20802 N. Cave Creek Rd., Apt. 35, Phoenix, AZ 85024.

Neffy, Arthur, 2115 N.E. 37th Dr., Apt. 238, Fort Lauderdale, FL 33308.

O'Brien, Kevin, 32090 Grand River Ave., #94, Farmington, 48336-4172.

O'Dea, Loren F., Our Lady of Sorrows Parish, 23815 Power, Farmington, 48336-2461.

O'Hagan, James P., Lourdes Nursing Home, 2300 Watkins Lake Rd., Waterford, 48328.

O'Neill, Charles F., Our Lady of Grace Parish, 8679 Riverview, Dearborn Heights, 48127-1482.

O'Sullivan, Daniel, 3941 Crooks Rd., Troy, 48084.

Osmialowski, Sigmund, 16590 Kyla Dr., Clinton Township, 48038.

Page, Leon J., 12109 Avondale, Warren, 48089-3922.

Partensky, Leonard J., 6747 N. Wayne Rd., 440 Bldg. A-3, Westland, 48185-2798.

Petron, William G., 15745 Charleston Dr., Clinton Township, 48038-1016.

Pettit, William J., St. Kenneth Parish, 14951 Haggerty Rd., Plymouth, 48170.

Phalen, John L., 10000 US Hwy. 98 N., LOT 643, Lakeland, FL 33809.

Physician, Thomas R., St. Barnabus Parish, 24800 Phlox, Eastpointe, 48021.

Prus, Edward J., St. James Parish, 241 Pearson, Ferndale, 48220-1896.

Reckinger, Robert A., 14455 Levan Rd., Apt. C, Livonia, 48154-5091.

Reyesmedina, Carlos, St. Mary Magdalen Parish, 19624 Wood, Melvindale, 48122.

Ritter, Edward, 5325 Pointe Dr., East China, 48054.

Ryder, Joseph F., 3015 Moonlake Dr., West Bloomfield, 48323-1844.

Sadler, Alfred H., 5571 Pointe Dr., East China, 48054-4163.

Samonie, Jacob, 34644 Spring Valley Dr., Westland, 48185-9457.

Sauter, Thomas M., 20300 Fort St., Apt. 229, Riverview, 48192.

Sayes, Ronald, Andover Heights, 8401 Eighteen Mile Rd., #217, Sterling Heights, 48313.

Scheuerman, Edward L.

Schmidberger, Richard, 4171 Fourth St., P.O. Box

535, Brown City, 48416.
Sirianni, Jasper F., Our Lady of Mt. Carmel Parish, 10828 Brandon Rd., Emmett, 48022-4504.
Slominski, Fabian B., 5405 Christi Dr., Warren, 48091-4196.
Stanievich, J. Walter, 16531 Rotunda Dr., Dearborn, 48120.
Szarek, Mitchell, SS. Peter & Paul Parish (Westside), 7685 Grandville, 48228.
Tucci, Italo, Fr. Taillieu Sr. Citizens Apt. B-108, 18740-13 Mile Rd., Roseville, 48066-1382.
Ugolik, Richard, 57088 Copper Creek Dr., Washington Township, 48094-2822.
Villerot, Henry E., De Serrano Residence, 17255 Common Rd. B-200, Roseville, 48066-1954.
Weingartz, Francis A., St. Anne Parish, 32000 Mound Rd., Warren, 48092-1200.
Wolber, Ferdinand A., Woodlore Condominiums, 33399 Fargo, Livonia, 48152-1453.
Worthy, Donald, St. Philomena Parish, 4281 Marseilles, 48224.
Xuereb, Paul, St. Isaac Jogues Parish, 21120 Benjamin, St. Clair Shores, 48081.
Zdrodowski, Francis, Marywood Nursing Home, 36975 W. Five Mile Rd., Livonia, 48154.
Zeeb, Charles, 18569 Manorwood West, Clinton Township, 48038-1266.
Zielinski, Francis, 2477 Yordy Rd., Mio, 48647.
Ziemba, Walter J., SS. Cyril & Methodius Seminary, 3535 Indian Trail, Orchard Lake, 48324-1623.
Zwers, John B., 14461 Levan Rd., Apt. D, Livonia, 48154.

Permanent Deacons:
Abler, Donald, Senior Status
Arquette, Lester, St. Gerard, Detroit
Ball, John H., St. Vincent Ferrer, Madison Heights
Barbera, John, St. Claude/St. Thecla, Clinton Twp.
Belanger, Stan, Senior Status
Berch, James, St. Isaac Joghes, St. Clair Shores
Bloomfield, Richard, Our Lady of Mt. Carmel, Wyandotte
Bovitz, Robert, St. Pius X, Southgate
Braun, Bernard, Senior Status
Bruen, Patrick T., St. Stanislaus Kostka, Wyandotte
Busch, Robert F., St. Joan of Arc, St. Clair Shores
Buyle, Valere, St. Jude, Detroit
Carroll, Brian, Our Lady of La Salette, Berkley
Channell, Ronald, St. Margaret of Scotland, St. Clair Shores
Chaudoan, Francis X., Our Lady of Grace, Dearborn Heights
Conlen, Patrick, St. Joan Neumann, Canton; St. Paul of the Cross Retreat House, Detroit
Conlin, Richard R., Senior Status
Connors, John J., St. Joseph, Port Huron
Cook, Ronald W., St. Anastasia, Troy
Cornell, Peter, St. Anthony, Belleville & St. Paul of the Cross Retreat Center, Detroit
Cousino, Wesley, St. Joseph, Erie
Cox, Donald J., St. Cornelius, Dryden
Cron, James A., St. Kieran, Shelby Twp.
D'Argis, Leo, St. Colette, Livonia
Damaske, Richard, St. Mary Queen of Creation, New Baltimore
Daratony, Joseph J., Resurrection, Canton
Darga, Daniel M., Our Lady of La Salette, Berkley
Delbeke, Robert G., St. Aidan, Livonia
Deshaw, Gerald, Immaculate Conception, Lapeer
Desjarlais, Eugene B., Divine Savior, Westland
Desmedt, Frank, Senior Status
DiCresce, Eugene, St. Joan of Arc, St. Clair Shores
Downey, Terrance E., St. Germaine, St. Clair Shores
Ervin, Robert, St. Michael, Sterling Hts.
Fairbanks, Andrew, St. Vincent Ferrer, Madison Heights
Feliciano, Raul, St. Gabriel, Detroit
Fitzgerald, Robert C., St. Michael, Livonia
Fleming, Michael J., St. Joseph, Pontiac
Flores, Luis, St. Frances Cabrini, Allen Park
Fosmire, Charles, Senior Status
Fry, Kenneth, Guardian Angels, Clawson
Gabel, Raymond, St. Albert the Great, Dearborn Heights
Gemellaro, Marc, St. Andrew, Rochester
Gennette, James, Assumption Grotto, Detroit
Girard, Lawrence, St. Sebastian, Dearborn Heights
Goodhue, Harold, Senior Status
Hardwick, Ralph, Senior Status
Healy, Lawrence, St. Michael, Sterling Heights
Henning, Lynn, National Shrine of the Little Flower, Royal Oak
Hensel, James L., Senior Status
Herta, Robert, St. Lucy, St. Clair Shores
Hilger, Edward, Prince of Peace, West Bloomfield
Hogrebe, Alfons, Senior Status
Hulan, Richard, St. Irenaeus, Rochester Hills
Hulway, Joseph A., St. Joseph, Lake Orion
Hurley, Daniel J., St. Cyril, Taylor
Igoe, James, St. Richard, Westland
Ingels, Michael M., St. Mary, Monroe
Iskra, Joseph, St. Raymond, Detroit
Jablonowski, Alexander, Christ the Redeemer, Lake Orion
Jackson, Douglas, Martyrs of Uganda, Detroit
Jamieson, William E., Our Lady Star of the Sea, Grosse Pointe
Jimenez, Rafael, St. Stephen, Mary Mother of the Church
Johnson, Charles, Senior Status
Johr, William H., Senior Status
Jones, Wyatt L., Precious Blood, Detroit
Junak, Donald C., St. Louis, Mount Clemens
Jurewicz, Marion, St. Martin de Porres, Warren
Kendzierski, Anthony, St. Isidore, Macomb
Kenny, John, St. Edith, Livonia
Kessler, Wilhelm, St. Louise, Warren
Kownlski, Eugene, St. Mary of the Hills, Rochester Hills
Krueger, Gary R., Holy Cross, Marine City
Krzeminski, Eugene, St. Joseph, South Lyon
Kunik, Raymond L., St. Priscilla, Livonia
Lalone, Norman, Senior Status
Lang, Joseph, St. Michael, Southfield
Leach, Donald, Resurrection, Canton
Lewandoski, Anthony, Senior Status
Liddle, John, St. Beatrice, Southfield
Lubien, Raymond J., St. Bartholomew, Detroit
Maiuri, Rocco, St. Isaac Joques, St. Clair Shores
Marks, Stephen, St. Kieran, Shelby Twp.
Marku, John, St. Christopher, Detroit
Markulike, Michael J., Senior Status
McIntyre, Ronald L., Holy Redeemer, Detroit
McKale, Michael J., Holy Name, Birmingham
McLeod, Edwin, St. Ephrem, Sterling Heights
McLeod, Robert E., St. Mary, St. Clair
Meahan, William, St. Aidan, Livonia
Meerschart, Gary, St. Louise, Warren
Mignacca, Egidio, St. Malachy, Sterling Heights
Misiak, Richard, St. Edith, Livonia
Mitchell, Steven, Sacred Heart, Auburn Hills
Modes, Robert, St. John Bosco, Redford
Morad, Alfred J., Senior Status
Morello, Steven, Holy Family, Novi
Morici, Anthony, St. Lawrence, Utica
Motowski, Norbert, All Saints, St. John Cantius, and SS. Andrew & Benedict, Detroit
Mouro, Joseph, Senior Status
Murphy, Thomas, Our Lady of the Woods, Woodhaven
Noon, Archie J., Senior Status
Nowicki, Kenneth, Immaculate Conception, Anchorville
O'Brien, Michael, St. Fabian, Farmington Hills
O'Donnell, Charles, Divine Child, Dearborn
O'Keefe, Michael, St. Athanasius, Roseville
Otto, William, St. Joseph, South Lyon
Ovies, Robert, St. Rene Goupil, Sterling Heights
Pardo, Gary, Our Lady of Loretto, Redford
Pelchat, Paul F., Senior Status
Pickett, Brock, St. Irene, Dundee
Pilon, Timothy, St. William, Walled Lake
Piro, Rudolph P., St. Genevieve, Livonia
Posavetz, George R., St. Mark, Warren
Prince, Benjamin, St. Gregory the Great, Detroit
Quigley, Donald, Our Lady of Victory, Northville
Redwine, Mark, Our Lady of the Woods, Woodhaven
Renaud, Timothy P., St. Mary, Royal Oak
Riopelle, Ernest, Senior Status, St. Conrad, Melvindale
Rivera, Rafael, Senior Status
Rodriguez, Brigido, Senior Status
Rohlman, Ronald E., St. Ives, Southfield
Sanders, Hubert, Presentation/Our Lady of Victory, Detroit
Sandstrom, Donald, Our Lady of Good Counsel, Detroit
Santeramo, John, St. Thomas Aquinas, Detroit
Schwartz, Robert, St. Jane Frances de Chantal, Sterling Heights
Shubik, Richard, St. Paul, Grosse Pointe Farms
Skladanowski, John L., St. Sylvester, Warren
Skubick, Charles G., St. Andrew, Rochester
Smigel, Gerald, SS. Cyril & Methodius, Sterling Heights
Smith, Lee, St. Angela, Roseville
Smith, Michael T., St. Hugo of the Hills, Bloomfield Hills
Smith, Richard, St. William, Walled Lake
Sobolewski, Don F., Our Lady of Sorrows, Farmington
Solomon, James, Redemption, Melkite, Warren
Springer, Mark, St. Alexander, Farmington Hills
Stankiewicz, Clement, St. Christine/St. Gemma/St. Paul of the Cross Retreat Center, Detroit
Stevens, Truman, St. Clare of Montefalco, Grosse Pointe
Stimpson, Bill, Precious Blood, Detroit
Strye, Edward, St. William, Walled Lake
Strzyzewski, Marvin, St. Anne, Warren
Sullivan, Joseph, Senior Status, St. Theodore, Westland
Sullivan, Lawrence, St. Edmund, Warren
Sullivan, Timothy, Our Lady of Good Counsel, Plymouth
Swartz, Edward, St. Leonard/Ascension, Warren
Sweeney, Daniel, St. Dominic, Detroit
Szwarc, John, Christ the Good Shepherd, Lincoln Park
Thomas, Thomas, Leave of Absence
Thome, William A., St. Cyril of Jerusalem, Taylor
Thompson, John, St. Basil, Eastpointe
Tombler, Eugene, Guardian Angels, Clawson
Trabbic, Kenneth, St. Stanislaus Kostka, Wyandotte
Tremmel, Robert, Sacred Heart, Grosse Ile
Valdez, Fernando, St. Vincent de Paul, Pontiac
Van Brook, Arthur, Holy Spirit, Highland
Vanneste, John, St. Thomas More, Troy
Vasquez, Jesus, Senior Status
Vestuto, Richard, St. Michael, St. Joseph & St. Vincent de Paul, Pontiac
Waldmann, William L., Holy Family, Novi
Ward, James, St. Thomas a Becket, Canton
White, Brian S., St. Joseph/St. Michael/St. Vincent de Paul, Pontiac
Wilson, Edward C., Jr., St. Paul of Tarsus, Clinton Township
Wright, Richard, Senior Status
Yezak, Thomas, St. Cornelius, Dryden

INSTITUTIONS LOCATED IN THE DIOCESE

[A] SEMINARIES, ARCHDIOCESAN

DETROIT. *Sacred Heart Major Seminary, Inc.*, 2701 Chicago Blvd., 48206. Tel: 313-883-8500. Very Rev. Steven Boguslawski, O.P., Rector & Pres.; Revs. Patrick F. Halfpenny, Vice Rector & Dean of Seminarians; Todd Lajiness, Dean of Studies; Ms. Jane Jeffrey, Asst. Dean; Ms. Michelle Szczepanski, Asst. Dean; Mrs. Anne Marie Fry, Dean Admin. & Advancement; Ms. Janet Galea, Registrar.

The College of Liberal Arts Revs. Todd Lajiness, Dir. Undergraduate Seminarians; Robert Spezia, Spiritual Dir. Undergraduate Seminarians; Gerard Bolduc, O.M.I., Pastoral Formation Dir.; Sr. Mary Finn, H.V.M., Dir. The Apostolic Experience Prog.; Mrs. Karen Mehaffey, Dir. of Libraries; Mr. Calvin Shenk, Dir. Music; Dr. Ronald Kolito, Dir. Learning Center.

The School of Theology Robert Fastiggi, Division Dir.; Revs. Daniel J. Trapp, Spiritual Dir.; Gerard Bolduc, O.M.I.

The Institute for Pastoral Ministry Mrs. Patricia A. Rennie, Dean of The Institute for Ministry; Dr. Peter Williamson, Asst. Dean, Institute of Ministry. Priests 13; Sisters 2; Lay Faculty 10; Students 425.

ORCHARD LAKE. *SS. Cyril and Methodius Seminary*, 3535 Indian Trail, 48324. Tel: 248-683-0311; 313-963-8075; Fax: 248-738-6735. Rev. Jaroslaw Zaniewski, Rector; Sr. Karen Shirilla, S.J., Ph.D., Academic Dean; Mrs. Carol Boulanger, Dir. Lay Ministry; Rev. Darius Z. Dudzik, J.C.L. (NOR), Dean of Formation; Gary Lovio, Comptroller; Mrs. Mary Jo Wagener, Registrar; Revs. Stanislaw Flis, S.T.D. (Poland), Dir. Admissions & Recruitment; James K. Mazurek, M.Div. (PIT), Vice Chancellor; Roman Nir (Poland), Archivist; Sr. Mary McDevitt, I.H.M., D.Min., Dir. Field Education; Raymond Myslakowski, Dir. Liturgical Music; Mrs. Pat Higo, Librarian; Revs. Timothy F. Whalen, M.Div. (PIT), Chancellor of Orchard Lake Schools; Gregory Banazak; Janusz Kukulka, M.A. (Poland). Students 95.

[B] SEMINARIES, RELIGIOUS OR SCHOLASTICATES

BERKLEY. *Loyola House* (Novitiate of the Chicago-Detroit Provinces of the Society of Jesus), , 2599 Harvard Rd., 48072. Tel: 248-399-8132; Fax: 248-399-0910. Revs. William L. Verbryke, S.J., Dir. Novices & House Supr.; Walter L. Farrell, S.J., Dir. Novices; Brian J. Lchane, S.J., Asst. Dir. Novices; Bro. James J. Boynton, S.J., Min. Priests 3; Brothers 1; Novices 13.

OXFORD. *St. Benedict Monastery*, 2711 E. Drahner Rd., 48370. Tel: 248-628-2249; Fax: 248-628-4658. Revs. Daniel J. Homan, O.S.B., Conventual Prior & Retreat Dir.; Michael R. Green, O.S.B., Subprior. Headquarters Novitiate House of

Sylvestrine Benedictine Monks in the United States. Priests 3; Brothers 7; Chapels 2.

[C] COLLEGES AND UNIVERSITIES

DETROIT. *Marygrove College* (Coed) ; Incorporated. , 8425 W. McNichols Rd., 48221. Tel: 313-927-1200. Dr. Glenda Price, Pres.; Dr. Joan Connell, Interim Vice Pres., Academic Affairs & Dean of Faculty; Dr. Lisa Jones Brown, Vice Pres., Student Affairs; Mr. James McKinney, Vice Pres., Finance & Admin.; Sr. Jacqueline Wetherholf, S.S.J., Vice Pres., Institutional Advancement. Sisters, Servants of the Immaculate Heart of Mary I.H.M. Sisters 5; Sisters 1; Priests 1; Lay 250; Students 6,459.

University of Detroit Mercy, McNichols Campus, 4001 W. McNichols Rd. at Livernois, 48219-0900. Tel: 313-993-1000; Fax: 313-993-1534.

Outer Drive Campus, 8200 W. Outer Dr., 48219-0900.

Law School, 851 E. Jefferson, 48226. Tel: 313-596-0210; Fax: 313-596-0280.

Dental School, 8200 E. Outer Dr., 48219-0900. Tel: 313-494-6621; Fax: 313-494-6627. Sr. Maureen Fay, O.P., Pres.; Rev. Gerard L. Stockhausen, S.J., Vice Pres. Academic Affairs & Provost; Mr Michael Joseph, Vice Pres. for Enrollment; Mr. Dale Tucker, Vice Pres. Business & Finance; Mr. Adrian Kerrigan, Vice Pres.; Dr. Susan Yowell, Vice Pres. Student Affairs. Priests 14; Sisters 19; Lay Staff 518; Students 3,979.

LIVONIA. *Madonna University*, 36600 Schoolcraft Rd., 48150. Tel: 734-432-5300; Fax: 734-432-5393. Sr. Rose Marie Kujawa, C.S.S.F., Pres.; Ms. Andrea R. Nodge, Vice Pres. Univ. Advancement; Dr. Ernest Nolan, Vice Pres. Academic Affairs; Sr. Nancy Marie Jamroz, C.S.S.F., Vice Pres Student Svcs.; Ms. Kathleen Grenda, Registrar; Mr. Leonard Wilhelm, Vice Pres. Finance; Mr. Frank Hribar, Vice Pres. Planning & Enrollment Mgmt.; Sr. Serafina Dixon, C.S.S.F., Dir. Information Systems; Mr. Chris Ziegler, Dir. Financial Aid; Rev. Xavier Ray, Dir. Campus Ministry. Coeducational, resident and non-resident.; Conducted by the Felician Sisters. Priests 8; Sisters 19; Lay Staff 518; Students 3,979.

[D] HIGH SCHOOLS, INTER-PAROCHIAL

DETROIT. *East Catholic High School*, 7320 St. Anthony Pl., 48213. Tel: 313-921-9650; Fax: 313-921-8905. Sr. Jolene Van Handel, O.P., Prin. Sisters 3; Lay Teachers 14; Students 122.

St. Martin de Porres High, 13436 Grove, 48235. Tel: 313-864-3330; Fax: 313-864-3648. Ms. Sunbeam Hughes, Prin. Priests 1; Sisters 2; Lay Teachers 17; Students 206.

HARPER WOODS. *Trinity Catholic High School*, 19360 Harper, 48225. Tel: 313-886-0855; Fax: 313-886-6398. James J. Wasukanis, Co-Prin.; Paricia Domagala, Co-Prin. Sisters 4; Lay Teachers 15; Students 200.

MADISON HEIGHTS. *Bishop Foley Catholic High School*, 32000 Campbell Rd., 48071. Tel: 248-585-1210; Fax: 248-585-3667. Deacon Charles Kosanke, Pres., Board of Pastors; Alex M. Gajewski, Prin. Sisters 1; Lay Teachers 35; Students 455.

Bishop Foley Venture Fund, 32000 Campbell Rd., 48071. Tel: 248-585-1210; Fax: 248-585-3667. Tim Lata, Pres.

MARINE CITY. *Cardinal Mooney Catholic School*, 660 S. Water St., 48039. Tel: 810-765-8825; Fax: 810-765-7164. Sr. Karen Lietz, O.P., Prin. Sisters 2; Lay Teachers 18; Students 171.

MONROE. *St. Mary Catholic Central High School* (Coed) , 108 W. Elm Ave., 48162. Tel: 734-241-0663; Fax: 734-241-9042. Ms. Beth A. Dusseau, Prin. Sisters 1; Lay Teachers 29; Students 442.

PONTIAC. *Notre Dame Preparatory High School and Marist Academy*, 1300 Giddings Rd., 48340-2108. Tel: 248-373-5300; Fax: 248-373-8024. Revs. Leon M. Olszamowski, S.M., Pres.; Joseph C. Hindelang, S.M., Prin.; Michael Flynn, S.M.; Deacons Anthony Morici; Wilhelm Kessler. Priests 3; Brothers 1; Deacons 2; Lay Teachers 82; Students 1,093.

REDFORD. *Bishop Borgess High School*, 11685 Appleton, 48239. Tel: 313-255-1100; Fax: 313-255-1102. Sr. Joan Charnley, I.H.M., Prin.; Ms. Patrice Evans, Youth Min. Sisters 2; Lay Teachers 18; Lay Admin. & Personnel 2; Students 200.

RIVERVIEW. *Gabriel Richard High School*, 15325 Pennsylvania Rd., 48192. Tel: 734-284-1875; Fax: 734-284-9304. Bro. James Rottenbucher, C.S.C., Prin. Brothers 1; Sisters 2; Lay Teachers 28; Students 440.

ROYAL OAK. *Shrine High School*, 3500 W. 13 Mile Rd., 48073. Tel: 248-549-2925; Fax: 248-549-2953. Mr. Thomas P. Kirkwood, Prin. Lay Teachers 32; Students 302.

[E] HIGH SCHOOLS, PRIVATE

DETROIT. *Dominican High School and Academy*, 9740 McKinney Ave., 48224. Tel: 313-882-8500 (High School & Academy); Fax: 313-882-9409. Adrian Dominican Sisters Sisters 3; Lay Teachers 22; Students 242.

Admin. Team: Sr. Tarianne DeYonker, O.P., Pres.; Mrs. Rosalie Cohen, Prin.; Mrs. Patricia Hojnacki, Business Mgr.

Loyola High School, 15325 Pinehurst, 48238-1633. Tel: 313-861-2407; Fax: 313-861-4718. Revs. David F. Mastrangelo, S.J., Pres. & Prin.; Justin J. Kelly, S.J.; James E. O'Reilly, S.J. Deacons 1; Priests 3; Brothers 1; Sisters 1; Lay Teachers 14; Students 130.

University of Detroit Jesuit High School and Academy, 8400 S. Cambridge, 48221. Tel 313-862-5400; Fax 313-862-3299. Rev. Karl Kiser, S.J., Pres.; Bro John Moriconi, S.J.; Rev. Patrick J. Rice, S.J.; Very Rev. Robert J. Scullin, S.J.; Revs. Richard H. Twohig, S.J.; Thomas M. Ryan, S.J.; Bro. James J. Boynton, S.J.; Rev. Leo P. Cachat, S.J.; Bros Richrd C. Conroy, S.J.; James T. Horgan, S.J.; Revs. Donald J. Petkash, S.J.; James F. Riley, S.J. Priests 8; Lay Teachers 66; Students 843; Chapels 1.

BLOOMFIELD HILLS. *Academy of the Sacred Heart*, 1250 Kensington Rd., 48304-3029. Tel: 248-646-8900; Fax: 248-646-4143. Sr. Bridget Bearss, R.S.C.J., Headmistress. Religious of the Sacred Heart Sisters 2; Lay Teachers 59; Students 470.

Brother Rice Endowment Fund (The "Foundation") , 7101 Lahser Rd., 48301-4045. Tel: 248-647-2526; Fax: 248-647-2532. Edward M. Kowalchick, School Dir.; Margie Clugston, Dir. Advancement & Contact Person.

Brother Rice High School, 7101 Lahser Rd., 48301-4045. Tel: 248-647-2526; Fax: 248 647-8170. Edward M. Kowalchick, School Dir. Congregation of Christian Brothers Brothers 3; Sisters 1; Lay Teachers 44; Students 657.

Marian High School for Young Women, 7225 Lahser Rd., 48301. Tel: 248-644-1750; Fax: 248-644-6107. Sr. Lenore Pochelski, I.H.M., Prin. Sisters 2; Lay Teachers 36; Students 575.

FARMINGTON HILLS. *Mercy High School for Girls*, 29300 Eleven Mile Rd., 48336. Tel: 248-476-8020; Fax: 248-476-3691. Sr. Carolyn R. Witte, Prin. Sisters of Mercy Faculty 59; Students 904.

HARPER WOODS. *Notre Dame High School*, 20254 Kelly Rd., 48225-1287. Tel: 313-371-8965; Fax: 313-371-7690. Revs. John Sajdak, S.M., Prin.; John Bryson, S.M.; Juan Gonzalez, S.M.; Bro. Maciej Pawlowski, S.M. Marist Fathers Priests 3; Sisters 2; Lay Teachers 28; Students 400.

Regina High School for Girls, 20200 Kelly Rd., 48225-1284. Tel: 313-526-0220; Fax: 313-526-5850. Deacon James F. Leap, Prin. Sisters of St. Joseph of the Third Order of St. Francis 6; Dominican Sisters 3; Lay Teachers 36; Students 610.

LIVONIA. *Ladywood High School*, 14680 Newburgh Rd., 48154. Tel: 734-591-1544; Fax: 734-591-4214. Sr. Mary Ann Smith, C.S.S.F., Prin. (Private School for Girls) Students 469.

ORCHARD LAKE. *St. Mary's Preparatory*, 3535 Indian Trail, 48324. Tel: 248-683-0530. Mr. James Glowacki Headmaster; Rev. Timothy Whalen, Chancellor; Mr. Joseph Whalen, Dir., Admissions; Mr. Leonard Karschnia, Academic Dean. Priests 1; Lay Teachers 42; Students 416.

REDFORD. *The Catholic Central Endowment Trust*, 14200 Breakfast Dr., 48239-2999. Tel: 313-534-0660. Gregory Grabowski, Dir.

Catholic Central High School, 14200 Breakfast Dr., 48239. Tel: 313-534-0660; 313-261-3387 (Res); Fax: 313-534-2683. Revs. Michael A. Buentello, C.S.B.; Richard J. Elmer, C.S.B., Pres.; John J. Ward, C.S.B.; Edward W. Donoher, C.S.B.; Kenneth B. McKernan, C.S.B.; John H. Menner, C.S.B.; Raymond Paramo, C.S.B.; Richard A. Ranalletti, C.S.B., Prin.; Charles C. Smith, C.S.B.; Joseph A. Miller, C.S.B.; John P. Wheeler, C.S.B.; Edwin J. Kline, C.S.B.; Marivn W. Labute, C.S.B., Supr. Basilian Fathers Priests 1; Lay Teachers 52; Students 960.

WARREN. *De La Salle Collegiate*, 14600 Common Rd., 48088-3387. Tel: 586-778-2207; Fax: 586-778-5118. Bro. Norbert Carnaghi, F.S.C., Pres.; Mr. Terrence George, Prin. High School Brothers of the Christian Schools Brothers 6; Sisters 1; Lay Teachers 50; Students 701.

La Salle Warren, Inc., 14600 Common Rd., 48093. Tel: 908-842-7420. Bro. Kevin Gilhooly, F.S.C., Contact Person.

[F] ELEMENTARY SCHOOLS, INTER-PAROCHIAL

DETROIT. *St Casimir Elementary School* 3361 23rd St., 48208. Tel: 313-894-0880; Fax: 313-494-2098. Sr. M. Leonard Bartkowiak, S.F.C.C., Prin. Sisters 1; Lay Teachers 4; Total Enrollment 130.

Eastside Vicariate School, 4230 McDougall, 48207. Tel: 313-921-0023; Fax: 313-921-0009. Ms. Gayle Koyton, Prin. Sisters 2; Lay Teachers 10; Total Enrollment 111.

Our Lady of Guadalupe Middle School, 4330 Central Ave., 48210. Tel: 313-849-2965; Fax: 313-849-3144. Email: olgperrone@aol.com. Ms. Mary Anne Perrone, Contact Person.

CANTON. *All Saints Regional School*, 48735 Warren Rd., 48187-1233. Tel: 734-459-2490; Fax: 734-459-0981. Ms. Jacqueline Brown, Prin. Total Enrollment 514.

PORT HURON. *McCormick Catholic Academy*, (Grades 6-8), 2865 Henry, 48060. Tel: 810-985-9599; Fax: 810-985-9686. Mrs. Deborah A. Krueger, Prin. Lay Teachers 4; Students 78.

ROCHESTER. *Holy Family Regional School - North Campus*, (Grades K-3), 1240 Inglewood, 48307. Tel: 248-656-1234; Fax: 248-656-3494. Sr. Karen Hawver, S.C., Prin.

Holy Family Regional School - South Campus (Grades 4-8), 2633 John R. Rd., Rochester Hills, 48307. Tel: 248-299-3798; Fax: 248-299-3843. Sr. Karen Hawver, S.C., Prin. Total Students 1,127.

[G] ELEMENTARY, PRIVATE

BLOOMFIELD HILLS. *Academy of the Sacred Heart*, 1250 Kensington Rd., 48304-3029. Tel: 248-646-8900; Fax: 248-646-4143. Sr. Bridget Bearss, R.S.C.J., Headmistress. Religious of the Sacred Heart Sisters 2; Lay Teachers 59; Students 470.

[H] GENERAL HOSPITALS

DETROIT. *St. John Hospital and Medical Center* (Subsidiary of St. John Health System) , 22101 Moross Rd., 48236. Tel: 313-343-4000. Dr. Anthony R. Tersigni, Ed.D., Pres. & CEO; Sr. Suzanne Zieske, S.S.J., Vice Pres. Sponsorship. Sisters of Saint Joseph (Nazareth, Michigan) 12; Bed Capacity 607; Patients Assisted Annually 154,939; Outpatients 66,007.

Affiliates:

Eastwood Community Clinics, Eastpointe.

Affiliated Health Services, Inc.

St. John Senior Community

St. John Northeast Community Hospital, 4777 E. Outer Dr., 48234.

St. John Oakland Hospital

St. John River District Hospital

CLINTON TOWNSHIP. *Mercy Mount Clemens Corporation* (Acting under the assumed name of St. Joseph's Mercy of Macomb or St. Joseph's Mercy Hospitals and Health Services). A subsidiary of Trinity Health-Michigan. , 15855 Nineteen Mile Rd., 48038. Tel: 810-263-2300; Fax: 810-263-2614. Jack Weiner, Pres. & CEO; Debora Murray, Dir., Spiritual Care Svcs. Provides acute care hospital services, home health care services, outpatient medical center services, hospice care services, long term service and fund-raising services. Bed Capacity 512.

St. Joseph's Mercy - West, 15855 Nineteen Mile Rd., 48038. Tel: 810-263-2300; 810-263-2330; Fax: 810-263-2614.

St. Joseph's Mercy - East, 215 North Ave., Mt. Clemens, 48043. Tel: 810-466-9300.

St. Joseph's Mercy - North, 80650 Van Dyke, Romeo, 48065. Tel: 810-752-3551.

Additional divisional operations:

St. Joseph's HomeCare

St. Joseph's Medical Centers

St. Joseph's Mercy Foundation

St. Joseph's Mercy Healthier Image

GROSSE POINTE. **Bon Secours Cottage Health Services*, 468 Cadieux Rd., 48230. Tel: 313-343-1900; Fax: 313-884-8927.

Bon Secours Cottage Health Services Foundation, 468 Cadieux, 48230. Tel: 313-640-2528. Email: john_danaher@bshsi.com. John E. Danaher, Contact Person.

Bon Secours Hospital, 468 Cadieux Rd., 48230. Tel: 313-343-1000; Fax: 313-884-8927. Richard Van Lith, CEO; Nickolas Vitale, CFO; Sr. Patricia Hedth, Vice Pres. Mission; Rev. Michael Rumble, Dir. of Spiritual Care. Sisters of Bon Secours 1; Sisters 3; Registered Nurses 480; Practical Nurses 61; Bed Capacity 290; Bassinets 28; Patients Assisted Annually 175,000.

**Bon Secours Cottage Health Services*

Bon Secours of Michigan Foundation Jeffrey Collins, Vice Pres. Operation.

LIVONIA. *Marian Village Corporation*, 36800 Schoolcraft, 48150. Tel: 734-591-1730; Fax: 734-591-1710. Sr. Mary Renetta Rumpz, C.S.S.F., Pres. & CEO.

Marybrook Manor, 36975 W. Five Mile Rd., 48154. Tel: 734-464-9667; Fax: 734-464-4846. Sr. Elizabeth Ann Marie Schilling, C.S.S.F., Admin. (Assisted Living)

Marywood Nursing Care Center, 36975 W. Five Mile Rd., 48154. Tel: 734-464-0600; Fax: 734-464-4846.

St. Mary Hospital, 36475 W. Five Mile Rd., 48154.

Tel: 734-655-4800; Fax: 734-655-1620. Mr. David Spivey, Pres.; Revs. Louis Tuffour; Jude Inweregbu. Sisters 10; Bed Capacity 304; Patients Assisted Annually 181,416; RN's 414; LPN's 15.

Congregation of the Sisters of St. Felix, 36800 Schoolcraft, 48150. Felician Sisters

PONTIAC. *St. Joseph Mercy - Oakland* (Div. of Trinity Health-Michigan) , 44405 Woodward Ave., 48341-2985. Tel: 248-858-3000; Fax: 248-858-3299. Deborah VandenBroek, Pres. & CEO; Sr. Jane Fox, R.S.M., Dir. Mission, Values & Ethics; Linda Thompson, Chap.; Rev. Donald Worthy, Chap. (Retired); Alice Murphy, Chap.; Rev. Frederick B. Moore, Chap. Sponsored Work of the Health Ministeries of Detroit.; A community healthcare system comprised of: Mercy Bellbrook Living Center, Rochester Hills; Alexander Living Center, Royal Oak; Seven Clinics & St. Joseph Mercy Hospital, Pontiac, MI.

PORT HURON. *Mercy Hospital of Port Huron* (Div. of Trinity Health-Michigan) , 2601 Electric, 48060-6518. Tel: 810-985-1500; Fax: 810-985-1508. Mary R. Trimmer, Pres. & CEO; Rev. C. Paul Higdon, Chap. (Retired); Sisters Mary Mercita Logan, R.S.M., Chap.; Helen Ruhl, R.S.M., Chap.; Susan Stockwell, Chap. Bed Capacity 119; Patients Assisted Annually 151,818.

SOUTHFIELD. *Providence Hospital* (A unit of Ascension Health/St. John Health System) , 16001 W. Nine Mile Rd., P.O. Box 2043, 48037. Tel: 248-849-3000; Fax: 248-849-3035. Mr. Robert Casalou, Pres.; Sr. Theresa Sullivan, Dir. Community Svcs. & Mission Integration; Revs. John Gagala, J.C.L., Chap.; Felix Alsola, Chap.; Mrs. Rita McEachen-Neal, Chap.; Ms. Carol Crowley, Chap. Medical and Surgical Residences. Daughters of Charity of St. Vincent de Paul 6; Bed Capacity 459; Bassinets 65; Lay Staff 3,160; Patients Assisted Annually 651,616.

[I] SPECIAL HOSPITALS AND SANATORIA FOR INVALIDS

LAKE ORION. *Guest House for Women Religious*, 1840 W. Scripps Rd., Box 68, 48360. Tel: 248-391-3100; Fax: 248-391-1553. Sr. Lee Anne Farrell, S.S.N.D., V.P. Women's Prog. A state licensed and JCAHO accredited endorsed residential treatment center for Catholic sisters and women in formation.; Central Admissions Office, from U.S. & Canada call: 800-626-6910. Bed Capacity 20.

Guest House Recovery Residence, 444 Nakomis Rd., 48362. Tel: 248-693-8973.

Office of Guest House, Inc., 1601 Joslyn Rd., P.O. Box 420, 48361. Tel: 248-391-4445; Fax: 248-391-0210. Mr. Daniel A. Kidd, Pres. & CEO. Management Services Offices.

LIVONIA. *Marycrest Manor*, 15475 Middlebelt Rd., 48154. Tel: 734-427-9175; Fax: 734-427-5044. Sr. M. Innocent, F.S.S.J., Admin. Skilled nursing facility. Served by Marianhill Fathers., Ownership: Franciscan Sisters of St. Joseph. Sisters 2; Residents 55.

Marywood Nursing Care Center, 36975 W. Five Mile Rd., 48154. Tel: 734-464-0600; Fax: 734-464-4846. Sr. Elizabeth Ann, C.S.S.F., N.H.A., Admin. Long-term care Facility. Sisters 4; Capacity 91.

MOUNT CLEMENS. *St. Joseph Mercy Living Care Center* A Division of Mercy Mt. Clemens Corp. , 37700 Harper, 48043. Tel: 810-468-0827. Robert L. Beyer, Pres. Bed Capacity 264.

WATERFORD. *Lourdes Nursing Home* Dominican Sisters of Oxford, MI , 2300 Watkins Lake Rd., 48328. Tel: 248-674-2241; Fax: 248-674-1211. Ms. Jeanette Reichner, Admin.; Rev. James P. O'Hagan, Resident Chap. (Retired). Skilled & basic nursing facility for men and women rehabilitation and 24 hour nursing care. Residents 108.

[J] HOUSING AND/OR COMMUNITY FACILITIES FOR THE AGING

DETROIT. *St. Catherine's House*, 1641 Webb Ave., 48206. Tel: 313-868-4505. Mary Connors, Mgr. For elderly-ambulatory & younger disabled ambulatory women. Capacity 12.

St. Joseph's Home, 4800 Cadieux Rd., 48224. Tel: 313-882-3800; Fax: 313-882-6944. Sr. Mary Magdalene, Admin. Carmelite Sisters of the Divine Heart of Jesus Sisters 5; Lay Staff 68; Aged Residents 104.

BLOOMFIELD HILLS. *St. Elizabeth Briarbank Home for the Aged*, 39315 Woodward Ave., 48304. Tel: 248-644-1011; Fax: 248-644-1596. Sr. M. Celeste, Admin. Daughters of Divine Charity Sisters 14; Aged Residents 42.

CLINTON TWP.. *A Friend's House Adult Day Services*, 16931 19 Mile Rd., Ste. 140, 48038. Tel: 586-412-8494; Fax: 586-412-8084. Daytime care for older adults. Support services for care giving families. A service of Catholic Services of Macomb.

14200 Eleven Mile Rd., Warren, 48089. Tel: 586-777-8700; Fax: 586-777-8740. Suzanne Szczepanski-White, Dir. of Senior Svcs.

FARMINGTON HILLS. *Trinity Continuing Care Services*, P.O. Box 9185, 48331-9185. Tel: 248-305-7600; Fax: 248-305-7933. Jaclyn Harris, Pres. & CEO.

LIVONIA. *Marybrook Manor*, 36975 W. Five Mile Rd., 48154. Tel: 734-464-9667; Fax: 734-464-4846. Sr. Elizabeth Ann, C.S.S.F., N.H.A., Admin. Residents 29.

Ryan Senior Residences of the Archdiocese of Detroit, Inc., Central Office, 36800 Schdolcraft, 48150. Tel: 313-953-5873. Edel Dunne O'Toole, Exec. Dir.

Madonna Villa, 17825 Fifteen Mile Rd., Clinton Township, 48035. Tel: 810-792-0358. Suzanne Szczepanski-White, Admin. Total Staff 14; Units 86; Total Assisted Annually 1,032.

Casa Maria, 600 Maple Vista, Imlay City, 48444. Tel: 810-724-6300. Paul Walker, Admin. Total Staff 19; Units 84; Total Assisted Annually 1,080.

Villa Marie, 15131 Newburgh, 48154. Tel: 734-464-9494. Sr. Lucille Blizman, O.P., Admin. Total Staff 15; Units 86; Total Assisted Annually 1,080.

Marian Place, 408 W. Front St., Monroe, 48161. Tel: 734-241-2414. Karen Morrin, Admin. Total Staff 11; Units 53; Total Assisted Annually 636.

Kundig Center, 3300 Jeffries Fwy., 48208. Tel: 313-894-0555. Pamela Alexander, Admin. Total Staff 18; Units 160; Total Assisted Annually 1,680.

Stapleton Center, 9341 Agnes, 48214. Tel: 313-822-0397. Jennie Boyd, Admin. Total Staff 11; Units 59; Total Assisted Annually 1,108.

Marian Oakland-West, 29250 W. Ten Mile Rd., Farmington Hills, 48336. Tel: 248-474-7204. Elaine McDermott, Admin. Total Staff 14; Units 87; Total Assisted Annually 1,080.

Marydale Center, 3147 Tenth Ave., Port Huron, 48060. Tel: 810-985-9683. Sr. Ann Christine Charron, Admin. Total Staff 20; Units 56; Total Assisted Annually 672.

Maryhaven, 11350 Reeck Road, Southgate, 48195. Tel: 734-287-2111. Sr. Paula Cooney, I.H.M., Admin. Total Staff 20; Units 90; Total Assisted Annually 700.

ST. CLAIR SHORES. *Sisters of Bon Secours Nursing Care Center*, 26001 E. Jefferson, 48081. Tel: 810-779-7000. Anne Sadler, Admin. A member of the Bon Secours of Michigan Healthcare Systems, Inc. operated by the Sisters of Bon Secours. The center provides short and long term nursing, residential care and rehabilitative services for older adults. Bed Capacity 200.

SOUTHFIELD. *Sheltering Arms*, 18310 W. 12 Mile, 48076. Tel: 248-557-7373; Fax: 248-559-1140. Adult day care for the elderly. A service of Catholic Social Services of Oakland County.

2177 Orchard Lake Rd., Sylvan Lake, 48320. Tel: 248-334-9680; Fax: 248-334-9690. Lay Staff 15; Volunteers 35; Patients Assisted Annually 90.

WATERFORD. *Fox Manor, Inc.*, 2350 Watkins Lake Rd., 48328. Tel: 248-674-9590; Fax: 248-674-1211. Sr. Frances Mary Kernasovich, Senior Campus Admin. Dominican Sisters, Residential facility for independent senior citizens of moderate or limited means.

Lourdes Assisted Living Corporation, 2300 Watkins Lake Rd., 48328. Tel: 248-674-2241; Fax: 248-674-1211. Sr. Frances Mary Kernasovich, Admin.

[K] MONASTERIES AND RESIDENCES OF PRIESTS AND BROTHERS

DETROIT. *St. Bonaventure Friary*, 1740 Mt. Elliott Ave., 48207-3496. Tel: 313-579-2100; Fax: 313-579-2275.

Legal Title: *Province of St. Joseph of the Capuchin Order, Inc.*

Provincialate, 1820 Mt. Elliott Ave., 48207. Tel: 313-579-2100; Fax: 313-579-2275. Rev. Daniel Anholzer, O.F.M.Cap., Prov. Min.; Bro. Robert Smith, Prov. Vicar; Revs. Randolph Graczyk, O.F.M.Cap., Sec. Religious Affairs; Lloyd Thiel, O.F.M. Cap., Public Rels. & Devel. Tel: 313-579-2100, Ext. 151; William Hugo, O.F.M.Cap., Dir. Personnel & Mission Effectiveness; Campion Baer, O.F.M.Cap., Mission Secretariat; Patrick McSherry, O.F.M.Cap., Archivist.

Priests of the Province Assigned Outside the U.S.:

St. Lawrence Community, 545 Tingal Rd., Wynnum North, Qld. 4178, Australia. Fax: 011-61-7-3348-5141. Rev. Carmel Flora, O.F.M.Cap.

59 Newton Rd., Newton Adelaide SA 5074 Australia. Rev. John Myers, O.F.M.Cap.

In Residence in the Archdiocese of Detroit (excluding parishes):

Canterbury Woods, 700 Tobin Dr., Apt. 15, Inkster, 48141. Bro. Sam Ciraulo, O.F.M.Cap.

Assigned to St. Bonaventure Friary: Bro. Larry LaCross, O.F.M.Cap., Local Min.; Revs. Philip Naessens, O.F.M.Cap., Vicar; Daniel Fox, O.F.M-.Cap.; Charles Hart, O.F.M.; Joseph Maloney, O.F.M.Cap.; Albert Sandor, O.F.M.Cap.; Lloyd Thiel, O.F.M. Cap.; James Wolf, O.F.M.Cap.; Bros. Michael Drobnicki, O.F.M.Cap.; David Heffron, O.F.M.Cap.; Thomas Kroll, O.F.M.Cap.; Steven Kropp, O.F.M-.Cap.; Richard Merling, O.F.M.Cap.; Joseph Monachino, O.F.M.Cap.; Leo Wollenweber, O.F.M-.Cap.

Jesuit Community at the University of Detroit Mercy, Lansing-Reilly Hall, 4001 W. McNichols Rd., 48221. Tel: 313-993-1000. P.O. Box 19900, 48219. Revs. Gary R. Wright, S.J., Rector; R. Gerard Albright, S.J.; Carl A. Bonk, S.J.; Gerald F. Cavanagh, S.J.; Norman J. Dickson, S.J.; Brian P. O'Donnell, S.J.; Oswald A. Mascarenhas, S.J. (India); Herman J. Muller, S.J.; John D. O'Neill, S.J.; John A. Saliba, S.J. (Malta); Raphael Shen, S.J. (China); John M. Staudenmaier, S.J.; Gerard L. Stockhausen, S.J.; Bros. Henry C. Kuhn, S.J., Min.; Richard D. Hittle, S.J.; Michael R. Simone, S.J. (Corporate Title: The Jesuit Community Corporation at the University of Detroit Mercy).

Jesuit Provincial Office-Detroit Province of the Society of Jesus, 7303 W. Seven Mile Rd., 48221-2198. Tel: 313-861-7500; Fax: 313-861-4230. Very Rev. Robert J. Scullin, S.J., Prov.; Revs. James F. Riley, S.J., Exec. Asst.; John E. Dister, S.J., Asst. for Social Min. & Dir. of Ignatian Lay Volunteer Corps.; Walter L. Farrell, S.J., Treas.; David E. Watson, S.J., Asst. for Parish Ministry; Dennis T. Dillon, S.J., Asst. for Formation; Richard H. Twohig, S.J., Asst., Secondary Educ. & Intl. Missions; M. Joseph Casey, S.J., Asst. for Health Care. Priests 147; Brothers 16; Scholastics 12.

Priests assigned outside the U.S.:

Piazza S. Maria Maggiore 7, Rome 00185 Italy. Tel: 447-417140 (39-06); Fax: 446-5576 (39-06). Rev. Richard M. Mackowski, S.J.

Piazza della Pilotta 4, Rome 00187 Italy. Tel: 39667015454; Fax: 39667015413. Rev. W. Jared Wicks, S.J.

Loyola House, Ngong Rd., P.O. Box 21399, Nairobi 00505 Kenya. Tel: 254-20569-494; Fax: 254-20566-873. Rev. Michael A. Evans, S.J.

St. Augustine University of Tanzania, P.O. Box 307, Mwanza, Tanzania. Tel: 255-28-2550560; Fax: 255-28-2550167. Rev. Theodore W. Walters, S.J.

Canisius College, 102 Mona Vale Rd., P.O. Box 136, Pymble NSW 2073 Australia. Tel: 02-9488-4500; Fax: 02-9488-4519. Rev. Gregory J. Hyde, S.J.

Pontificia Universita Gregoriana, Piazza Della Pilotta 4, 00187 Rome, Italy. Tel: 39-6-6701-5213; Fax: 39-6-6701-5413. Rev. Kevin L. Flannery, S.J.

Isiklar Caddesi, Kardesler Sokak 15 TR 06250 ULUS, Ankara, Turkey. Tel: 90-312-309-8285; Fax: 90-312-309-8014. John A. Lucal, S.J.

Colegio Centroamericano, Apdo. 2419, Managua, Nicaragua. Tel: 505-278-6965. Revs. Joseph E. Mulligan, S.J.; Timothy T. Shannon, S.J.

Members in the U.S. residing outside the Province: Revs. Steven J. Abostino, S.J.; Thomas S. Acker, S.J.; David C. Bayne, S.J.; Mark R. Bandsuch, S.J.; Frederick J. Benda, S.J.; Peter J. Bernardi, S.J.; Martin J. Calkins, S.J.; Martin L. Chase, S.J.; Martin T. Connell, S.J.; Joseph P. Daoust, S.J.; J. Peter Deane, S.J.

606 W. Sterns Rd., Apt. F, Temperance, 48182. Tel: 734-847-3738. Revs. Joseph F. Downey, S.J.; Francis T. Gignac, S.J.; Dennis T. Glasgow, S.J.; Fred M. Henley, S.J.; Francis J. Houdek, S.J.; Joseph B. Kappes, S.J.; Patrick M. Kelly, S.J.; John L. Kieffer, S.J.; William F. King, S.J.; R. James Kurtz, S.J.; John P. Langan, S.J.; John F. Libens, S.J.; Daniel P. Liderbach, S.J.; Edward J. Mattimoe, S.J.; J. Thomas McClain, S.J.; John M. McManamon, S.J.; Timothy J. Meier, S.J.; Joseph G. Mueller, S.J.; George B. Murray, S.J.; John W. O'Malley, S.J.; Daniel T. Reim, S.J.; Philip C. Rule, S.J.; Richard D. Salmi, S.J.; Donald M. Serva, S.J.; Edward J. Siebert, S.J.; Michael F. Steltenkamp, S.J.; Michael J. Vjecha, S.J.; Earl A. Weis, S.J.; Eric A. Zimmer, S.J.

St. Mary's Friary, 5275 Kensington, 48224. Tel: 313-884-5303; Fax: 313-884-7370. Revs. William Hugo, O.F.M.Cap.; James Zelinski, O.F.M.Cap.; Michael Gaffney, O.F.M.Cap.

P.I.M.E. Missionaries (Pontifical Institute for Foreign Missions)

P.I.M.E. Motherhouse in Detroit, 17330 Quincy, 48221. Tel: 313-342-4066; Fax: 313-342-6816. Revs. Bruno Piccolo, P.I.M.E., Prov. Supr.; George Berendt, P.I.M.E.; Dominic Rossi, P.I.M.E.; Edward Miley, P.I.M.E.; Adriano Cadei, P.I.M.E.; Timothy Sattler, P.I.M.E.; Dino Vanin, P.I.M.E.; Bro. Anthony Testori. Franciscan Sisters of St. Joseph (Mexico City) 4.

St. Paul of the Cross Community, Congregation of the Passion, 23335 Schoolcraft, 48223. Tel: 313-531-0562; Fax: 313-535-8468. Revs. Arthur Carrilo, C.P.; Sebastian MacDonald, C.P., Supr.; Rene Champagne, C.P.; John Devany, C.P.; James Thoman, C.P., Dir. Retreat Center; Randal Joyce,

C.P.; Paul Kim, C.P.; Robert Weiss, C.P.; Bros. William Baalman, C.P.; Kevin O'Malley, C.P. A center for the Passionist Fathers & Brothers in mid-western & north central United States. Members of this community conduct parish missions, renewals & retreats for laity, clergy & religious, Forty Hours Devotion & other ministries. Priests 7; Brothers 2.

St. Sylvester Monastery, 17320 Rosemont Rd., 48219. Tel: 313-532-6064; Fax: 313-531-0739. Revs. Livius Paoli, O.S.B., Prior; Bartholomew Kraemer, O.S.B.; John Stopponi, O.S.B.; Leo Cornelli, O.S.B.; John Colautti, O.S.B.

Holy Family Church: 641 Chrysler Express Way. Tel: 313-963-2046; Fax: 313-961-0065. Rev. John Stopponi, O.S.B.

BLOOMFIELD HILLS. *Congregation of Christian Brothers, Brother Rice Community*, Carroll Hall, 3575 Lincoln Dr., 48301-4001. Tel: 248-647-1547; Fax: 248-647-8170. Bro. David A. MacIntyre, C.F.C., Supr. Brothers 5. In Res. Bros. Arthur M. Arndt, C.F.C.; Benjamin L. Favero, C.F.C.; Norbert B. Hueller, C.F.C.; David A. MacIntyre, C.F.C.; W. Rudolph Younghans, C.F.C.

DEARBORN. *Society of St. Paul*, 7050 Pinehurst, 48126. Tel: 313-582-2033; Fax: 313-582-2970. Revs. Anthony Cheveney, S.S.P.; Joseph A Triano, S.S.P., Supr.; Bros. Gerard T. Roche, S.S.P.; Emmanuel Cana, S.S.P.; Aloysius Milella, S.S.P.; John Naranjo, S.S.P. Priests 2; Brothers 4.

DEARBORN HEIGHTS. *Our Lady of Grace Monastery*, Mariannhill Mission Society, 23715 Ann Arbor Trail, 48127. Tel: 313-561-7140; 313-561-8888; Fax: 313-561-9486.

Vocation Office Tel: 313-561-7140, Ext. 25. Revs. Francis Claerr, C.M.M.; Anthony Kirschner, C.M.M. (Retired); Raymond Lucasinsky, C.M.M., Supr. of House; Timothy Mock, C.M.M., Asst. Prov. Treas.; Thomas Szura, C.M.M., Prov. Treas.; Aloysius Blonigen, C.M.M., Retreat Dir. & Mission Procurator; Reinhold Schmitt, C.M.M.; Thomas Heier, C.M.M., Editor of LEAVES; Vergil Heier, C.M.M., Vocation Dir.; Lambert Kempkes, C.M.M. Priests 10; Brothers 3. In Res. Bros. Francis Berridge, C.M.M.; Jamie Miller, C.M.M.; Otto Waldmueller, C.M.M.

GROSSE POINTE. *Order of Canons Regular of the Holy Cross*, 576 Neff Rd., 48230. Tel: 313-884-1121; Fax: 313-882-1763. Rev. Basil Nortz, O.R.C.

HAMTRAMCK. *Redemptorists of Hamtramck*, 2697 Caniff Ave., 48212. Tel: 313-365-8813; Fax: 313-365-8796. Rev. Richard Mevissen, C.SS.R., Pres.

LIVONIA. *Marist Fathers & Brothers Community*, 32509 Scone, 48154-4165. Tel: 734-266-1475; Fax: 734-266-1575. Revs. Ronald DesRosiers, S.M., Local Supr. & Madonna Univ.; Frank Grispino, S.M., Madonna Univ.

RIVERVIEW. *Crosier Community of Riverview*, 13249 Pennsylvania Rd., 48192. Tel: 313-283-0112; Fax: 313-283-2809. Very Rev. Jude Verley, O.S.C., Supr.; Revs. John P. Christ, O.S.C.; Dale Ettel, O.S.C.; John G. Hawkins, O.S.C.; Richard M. Leliaert, O.S.C.; Bruce Maxwell, O.S.C.; Theodore K. Parker, O.S.C.; Dale H. Redwanski, O.S.C.; Francis K. Scheets, O.S.C.; Gordon Van Hoof, O.S.C.; James Vedro, O.S.C. Priests 10.

STERLING HEIGHTS. *Society of Christ Provincial Home*, Provincial Home, 3000 18 Mile Rd., 48314. Tel: 586-939-5022; Fax: 586-939-0195. Revs. Andrzej Maslejak, S.Ch., Prov.; Pawel Bandurski, S.Ch., Asst. Prov.; Stanislaw Hajkowski, S.Ch., Treas.

WYANDOTTE. *Pallottine Missionary Center (Irish Province)*, 3352 Fourth St., P.O. Box 249, 48192. Tel: 734-285-2966; Fax: 734-285-1059. Revs. Hubert Flanagan, S.A.C., Pres., Rector & Mission Promotion Dir.; Michael Cremin, S.A.C., Vice Rector & Mission Promotions Associate.; John Kelly, S.A.C., Sec. & Treas.; Bro. Faustino Paez, S.A.C., Mission Promotion Associate.

Pallotine Missionary Center (Irish Province), 424 Orange St., 48192. Tel: 734-285-2966; Fax: 734-285-2966.

[L] CONVENTS AND RESIDENCES FOR SISTERS

DETROIT. *Missionaries of Charity*, 8901 W. Vernor Hwy., P.O. Box 9260, 48209. Sr. M. Carolina Navarrete, M.C., Supr.

Sisters of Jesus the Savior (1985), (Founded in Elele, Nigeria) , St. Scholastica Convent, 17305 Ashton Rd., 48219. Tel: 313-541-4368. Ministry in Education and Social Assistance. Sisters 10.

Sisters, Home Visitors of Mary Convent, 121 E. Boston, 48202. Tel: 313-869-2160; Fax: 313-869-2161. Sr. Rosemarie Abate, H.V.M., Admin.

BLOOMFIELD HILLS. *Daughters of Divine Charity - Holy Trinity Province* (1972), Holy Trinity Provincialate, 39315 N. Woodward Ave., 48304. Tel: 248-644-1011; Fax: 248-644-1596. Sr. Hyacinth Vamos, F.D.C., Prov. Supr. Sisters in Community 26.

CLARKSTON. *Servants of Jesus*, 2600 Harvard Rd., Berkley, 48072. Tel: 248-548-6337; Fax: 248-548-8332.

Leadership Team: Sisters Barbara Celeskey, S.J., Pres.; Roberta Kolasa, S.J.; Betty Cldr, S.J.

S.J. Charitable Trust (Retired & Infirm Sisters), Servants of Jesus Community Support Trust, 2600 Harvard Rd., Berkley, 48072.

CLINTON TWP.. *Monastery of St. Therese of the Child Jesus*, 35750 Moravian Dr., 48035-2138. Tel: 586-790-7255; Fax: 586-790-7271. Sr. Mary Elizabeth, O.C.D., Prioress. Discalced Carmelite Nuns Professed Nuns 9; Extern Sisters 1.

DEARBORN HEIGHTS. *Contemplative Sisters of the Good Shepherd (CGS)*, 20651 W. Warren Ave., 48127-2693. Tel: 313-271-4150; Fax: 313-271-4151. Sr. Dorothy John Bosco Wolf, Contact Person.

Sisters of the Good Shepherd (RGS), 20651 W. Warren Ave., 48127-2698. Tel: 313-271-4150; Fax: 313-271-4151. Sr. Marie Belanger, Contact Person.

EASTPOINTE. *Marist Sisters, Inc.*, 16057 Hauss, 48021. Sr. Eleanor Keaney, S.M., Contact Person.

FARMINGTON HILLS. *Bernardine Franciscan Sisters of Michigan*, Our Lady of the Rosary Convent, 27405 W. 10 Mile Rd., 48336-1502. Tel: 248-476-4111; Fax: 248-476-6950. Sr. Mary Elena Sabalausky, O.S.F., Province Min. Bernardine Sisters of the Third Order of St. Francis Sisters in Area 48.

Monastery of the Blessed Sacrament, 29575 Middlebelt Rd., 48334-2311. Tel: 248-626-8253; Fax: 248-626-8724. Sr. Mary Rose, O.P., Prioress; Rev. Martin F. McCormick, O.P., Chap. Nuns of the Order of Preachers (Cloistered Dominican Nuns, Perpetual Adoration) Cloistered Sisters 34; Extern Sister 3.

Sisters of Mercy-Regional Community of Detroit, Inc., 29000 Eleven Mile Rd., 48336. Tel: 248-476-8000; Fax: 248-476-4222. Sr. Linda Werthman, R.S.M., Pres. Sisters 242; U.S. Professed 215; In Argentine-Professed 28; Candidates 1.

Sisters of Mercy of the Americas Regional Community of Detroit, Charitable Trusts 1 & 2

LIVONIA. *Provincial House and Novitiate of the Sisters of St. Felix*, 36800 Schoolcraft Rd., 48150. Tel: 734-591-1730; Fax: 734-591-1710. Sr. Mary Renetta Rumpz, C.S.S.F., Prov. Min.

Legal Title: *Provincial House and Novitiate of the Congregation of the Sisters of St. Felix, C.S.S.F., Felician Sisters* Professed Sisters 206; Novices 3.

MONROE. *Sisters, Servants of the Immaculate Heart of Mary, Leadership Council*, 610 W. Elm Ave., 48162-7909. Tel: 734-240-9700; Fax: 734-240-9784. Sisters Virginia Pfau, I.H.M., Pres.; Mary Katherine Hamilton, I.H.M., Vice Pres.; Frances Mlocek, I.H.M., CFO; Carolyn Campbell, I.H.M., Leadership Council; Paula Cooney, I.H.M., Leadership Council; Anne Crimmins, I.H.M., Leadership Council; Janet Ryan, I.H.M., Leadership Council; Barbara Weigand, I.H.M., Leadership Council.

ORTONVILLE. *Our Lady of Mt. Thabor Monastery*, 1295 Bald Eagle Lake Rd., 48462. Tel: 248-627-4355. Sr. Anne Mary, Prioress. Dominican Nuns of Mt. Thabor

OXFORD. *Dominican Sisters, Congregation of St. Rose of Lima, St. Joseph Convent*, 775 W. Drahner Rd., 48371. Tel: 248-628-2872; Fax: 248-628-1725. Sisters Gene Poore, O.P., Councilor; Teresita Lipar, O.P., Prioress; Sue McMahon, O.P., Vicaress. General Mother House and Novitiate of the Dominican Sisters; St. Mary Retreat House; Dominican Center; St. Raphael's Dominican Sisters of Oxford Charitable Trust. Professed Sisters 42.

RIVERVIEW *Sisters of Mary Reparatrix*, 17320 Grange Rd., 48192. Tel: 734-285-4510; Fax: 734-285-8147. Sisters 10.

[M] HOMES FOR MEN AND WOMEN

DETROIT. *St. Mary's Residence Adult Foster Care*, 2120 Orleans St., 48207. Tel: 313-259-6874; 313-259-0459. Sr. M. Fidelis, F.D.C., Admin. Rev. William Lunnon. Daughters of Divine Charity, A residence for women desiring home-like surroundings. Sisters 6; Residents 60.

[N] CATHOLIC SOCIAL SERVICE AGENCIES

DETROIT. *Catholic Social Services of Wayne County*, 9851 Hamilton Ave., 48202. Tel: 313-883-2339; Fax: 313-883-3957. Patrick J. Heron, Pres. & CEO. Family service, marriage counseling, adoption services, services to unwed mothers, planned respite care, substance abuse counseling, foster family care & services to youth & older persons including Foster Grandparent, Senior Companion & Retired Senior Volunteer Programs.

Branches:

20385 Van Born Rd., Dearborn Heights, 48125. Tel: 313-792-9286; Fax: 313-792-0444.

17316 Farmington Rd., Livonia, 48152. Tel: 734-421-3730; Fax: 734-421-3733.

15200 E. Jefferson, Ste. 105, Grosse Pointe Park, 48230. Tel: 313-821-2590; Fax: 313-821-1046.

Teen Empowerment Program, 5247 Sheridan, 48213. Tel: 313-922-0094; Fax: 313-922-0514.

CLINTON TOWNSHIP. *Catholic Services of Macomb*, 15945 Canal Rd., 48038. Tel: 586-416-2300; Fax: 586-416-2311. Mr. Thomas Reed, Pres. & CEO.

Branch Offices:

12434 Twelve Mile Rd., Ste. 202, Warren, 48093. Tel: 586-558-7551; Fax: 586-573-8016.

18720 Thirteen Mile Rd., Roseville, 48066. Tel: 586-558-7551; Fax: 586-573-8016.

347 S.Main, Romeo, 48065. Tel: 586-336-6844; Fax: 586-336-6843.

14200 Eleven Mile Rd., Warren, 48089. Tel: 586-777-8700; Fax: 586-777-8740.

LAPEER. *Christian Family Services of Lapeer County, Inc.*, 441 Clay St., 48446. Tel: 810-664-4557; Fax: 810-664-5181.

MONROE. *Catholic Social Services of Monroe County*, 16 E. Fifth St., 48161. Tel: 734-242-3800; Fax: 734-242-6203. Candy S. Salazar, Pres. & CEO.

South County Office, 8330 Lewis Ave., P.O. Box 10, Temperance, 48182. Tel: 734-847-1523; Fax: 734-847-1523.

Head Start Office, 502 W. Elm St., 48162. Tel: 734-241-8727; Fax: 734-241-6125.

PONTIAC. *Catholic Social Services of Oakland County*, 50 Wayne St., 3rd Floor, 48342. Tel: 248-333-3700; Fax: 248-333-3718. Margaret A. Huggard, M.S.W., Pres.

Branches:

53 Franklin Blvd., 48341. Tel: 248-334-3595; Fax: 248-334-3781.

6637 Highland Rd., Waterford, 48327. Tel: 248-666-8870; Fax: 248-666-5023.

29475 Inkster Rd., Farmington Hills, 48334. Tel: 248-539-3592.

1424 E. Eleven Mile Rd., Royal Oak, 48067. Tel: 248-548-4044.

Sheltering Arms Adult Day Center, 18310 W. 12 Mile Rd., Southfield, 48076. Tel: 248-557-7373; Fax: 248-559-1140.

2177 Orchard Lake Rd., Sylvan Lake, 48320. Tel: 248-334-9680; Fax: 248-334-9690.

Older Adult Services, 18310 W. 12 Mile Rd., Southfield, 48076. Tel: 248-557-7373; Fax: 248-559-1140.

Hispanic Outreach, 295 W. Huron, 48342. Tel: 248-338-4250.

PORT HURON. *Catholic Social Services of St. Clair County, Inc.*, 2601 Thirteenth St., 48060. Tel: 810-987-9100; Fax: 810-987-9100. Patrick L. Cogley, M.A., Pres.

[O] SPECIALIZED CHILD CARE FACILITIES AND SCHOOLS

DETROIT. *Christ Child House*, 15751 Joy Rd., 48228. Tel: 313-584-6077; Fax: 313-584-1148. John Yablonky, A.C.S.W, Exec. Dir.

Don Bosco Hall, Inc., 2340 Calvert, 48206. Tel: 313-869-2200; Fax: 313-869-8220. Charles Small, Dir. Residential treatment center for boys, ages 12-17, in need of care, guidance and therapy. Lay Staff 75; Residents 41; Emergency Shelter Program 20; Transitional Services 180; Mentoring Program 155.

Holy Cross Children's Services, 5555 Conner, 48213. Tel: 313-579-4400; Fax: 313-267-1185. Bro. Francis Boylan, C.S.C., Pres.; Paul S. Neitman, Vice Pres.; William D. Brazier, Dir. of Devel.; Loren Brown, Vice Pres. Residential and communtiy based treatment programs for troubled youth and families with facilities located throughout the state of Michigan and one in the state of Ohio under the auspices of the Brothers of Holy Cross at Notre Dame.

Andre House, 7001 Burlingame, 48204. Tel: 313-935-0769; Fax: 313-935-7930.

Bowman House/Holy Cross Children's Services, 17200 Rowe St., 48205. Tel: 313-372-7320; Fax: 313-372-8623.

Boysville's Family & Community Support Program, 19403 W. Chicago, 48228. Tel: 313-838-7500; Fax: 313-838-7584. Bro. Francis Boylan, C.S.C., Pres.; Lynne Alexander, Regl. Dir. Includes specialized foster care, supervised independent living, in-home family treatment.

Cabrini Center/Holy Cross Children's Services, 23915 Elmira, Redford, 48239. Tel: 313-537-7868; Fax: 313-838-7584. Girls 16.

Hitchcock Center/Holy Cross Children's Services, 5675 Larkins, 48210. Tel: 313-895-5119; Fax: 313-895-5135. Boys 13.

Holy Cross Center/Holy Cross Children's Services, 5690 Cecil, 48210. Tel: 313-895-2200; Fax: 313-895-4010. Day treatment, education, recreation program for Detroit region.

Johnson House/Holy Cross Children's Services, 7798 W. Fort St., 48209. Tel: 313-554-1700; Fax: 313-554-1748. Boys 111.

King House/Holy Cross Children's Services, 24455 Crocker Blvd., Mt. Clemens, 48043. Tel: 810-463-7130; Fax: 810-962-3426. Boys 22.

Moreau Center/Holy Cross Children's Services, 3500 Comboni Way, Monroe, 48162. Tel: 734-242-5898; Fax: 734-242-6828. George Birkam, Regl. Dir. Boys 65.

Kennedy House/Holy Cross Children's Services, 7001 Burlingame St., 48204. Tel: 313-372-7320; Fax: 313-935-0605. Boys 17.

St. Thomas Center, 8333 Townsend, 48213. Tel: 313-924-9515.

Xavier Center/Holy Cross Children's Services, 27652 W. Outer Dr., Ecorse, 48229. Tel: 313-381-5845; Fax: 313-381-0197. Boys 23.

DEARBORN HEIGHTS. *Vista Maria*, 20651 W. Warren Ave., 48127. Tel: 313-271-3050; Fax: 313-271-6250. Mr. Cameron Hosner, Exec. Dir. Residential and community-based treatment programs for adolescent girls involved in The Juvenile Justice & Child Welfare Systems. Sponsored by the Sisters of the Good Shepherd. Sisters 2; Girls Residential 168; Lay Staff 243; S.F.C. 38; Independent Living 6.

FARMINGTON HILLS. *Marillac Programs* A Division of St. Vincent and Sarah Fisher Center, Outreach case management and counseling services for pregnant and parenting teens and young families in the tri-county area. Nine beds for the transitional housing of teen mothers 16-18 years of age who are wards of the state and nine homeless babies 0-18 months of age.

22255 Greenfield, Ste. 330, Southfield, 48334. Tel: 248-559-2272; Fax: 248-559-2226. Jean Vickers, Exec. Dir.; Jackie Dunn Bell, Prog. Mgr.; Sr. Wanda Sheber, D.C., Division Dir., Residential Svcs.

Seton Nursery School and Infant-Toddler Child Care Center, 29475 Inkster Rd., 48018. Tel: 810-626-6990. Ann Coyle, Dir.

Legal Title: *Seton Nursery School and Infant-Toddler Child Care Center - St. Vincent Sara Fisher Center*, Center licensed for 80 children, 8 weeks-5.5 years. In Day Care 19.

St. Vincent and Sarah Fisher Center, 27400 W. Twelve Mile Rd., 48334. Tel: 248-626-7527; 888-577-7271; Fax: 248-626-0865. Paulo J. Herbert, Pres. Licensed capacity for: Residential care 60 (ages 4-15), Specialized Foster Care 120 (ages 0-17).; Pregnancy and Parenting For Teen Parents (Ages 16-19) Outreach Program. Residential 41.

SOUTHFIELD. *St. Francis Family Services*, 17500 W. Eight Mile Rd., 48075. Tel: 248-552-0750; Fax: 248-552-9019. James P. Lewis, Exec. Dir. Foster home respite & adoption services for infants through 17 years.

[P] RETREAT HOUSES

DETROIT. *St. Paul of the Cross Retreat Center* Conducted by the Passionist Community. , 23333 Schoolcraft, 48223-2499. Tel: 313-535-9563; Fax: 313-535-9207. Revs. James Thoman, C.P., Retreat Dir.; Tu-Jin Paul Kim, C.P., Asst. Retreat Dir. & Team Member; Deacons Patrick Conlen, Team Member; Peter Cornell, Team Member; Clement Stankiewicz, Team Member; Mrs. Cathy Anthony, Team Member.

BLOOMFIELD HILLS. *Manresa Jesuit Retreat House*, 1390 Quarton Rd., 48304-3554. Tel: 313-564-6455; 248-644-4933; Fax: 248-644-8291. Revs. James K. Serrick, S.J., Dir. Supr.; Peter J. Fennessy, S.J., Retreat Dir.; Bernard J. Owens, S.J., Retreat Dir.; Kenneth M. Kunert, S.J., Retreat Dir.; Daniel D. Dunnigan, S.J., Retreat Dir.; Bro. Joseph A. Subitowski, S.J., Maintenance. Priests 5; Brothers 1.

CLARKSTON. *Colombiere Center*, 9075 Big Lake Rd., Box 139, 48347. Tel: 248-625-5611; Fax: 248-625-3526. Revs. M. Joseph Casey, S.J., Supr. & Dir.; Jerome K. Odbert, S.J., Asst. Supr.; Thomas F. Ankenbrandt, S.J.; John D. Baggarly, S.J.; Thomas J. Bain, S.J.; John E. Beez, S.J.; James N. Brichetto, S.J.; Francis X. Budovic, S.J.; Malcolm Carron, S.J.; Edward E. Cincoski, S.J.; Paul J. Clifford, S.J.; Paul F. Conen; Cornelius L. Curtin, S.J.; Stanislaus Czapiewski, S.J. Spirituality Conference Center and Jesuit Health Care Community for the Detroit Province and Chicago Province.

St. Ladislaus, 2730 Caniff, Hamtramck, 48212. Tel: 313-872-0709. Revs. William A. Dehler, S.J.; Joseph F. Downey, S.J.; George R. Follen, S.J.; Reynaldo A. Garcia, S.J.; Henry C. Gelin, S.J.; Francis X. Grollig, S.J.; Fred M. Henley, S.J.; Robert G. Humbert, S.J.; John C. Kehres, S.J.; Kenneth M. Kunert, S.J.; Lester A. Linz, S.J.; Stephen A. Meder, S.J.; Harold R. Meirose, S.J., Pastoral Care, Asst. Dir.; Benjamin R. Morin, S.J.; Robert J. Murphy, S.J.; Edward M. Nemeth, S.J.; Joseph P. Owens, S.J.; Robert A. Pollauf, S.J.; John J. Powell, S.J.; Francis D. Rabaut, S.J.; L. Harold Sanford, S.J.; John T. Schuett, S.J.; George T. Tolbert, S.J.; William G. Topmoeller; Jerome F. Treacy; Stanley T. Wisniewski, S.J.; Bros. Robert G. Cardosi, S.J.; Herman F. Elsaesser, S.J.; John E. Foy, S.J.; James F. Gates; Bruno W. Karpinski, S.J.; Joseph A. LaMielle, S.J.; Daniel J. McCullough, S.J.; John J. Petrus, S.J.; Bernard L. Polinak, S.J.; George A. Prickril, S.J.; Jerome Pryor; Robert W. Schneider, S.J. Priests 40; Brothers 12.

MONROE. *Visitation Spirituality Center*, 529 Stewart Rd., 48162. Tel: 734-242-5520; Fax: 734-242-5530. Sponsorship of I.H.M. Congregation. Sisters 5.

PLYMOUTH. *St. John Center for Youth and Family*, 44011 Five Mile Rd., 48170-2555. Tel: 734-414-1111; Fax: 734-414-1150. Deacon John H. Ball, Exec. Dir.

Cardinal Maida Institute for Leadership Formation Rev. John Riccardo, Dir. Tel: 734-414-1245.

WASHINGTON. *Capuchin Retreat*, 62460 Mt. Vernon Rd., P.O. Box 396, 48094. Tel: 248-651-4826; Fax: 248-650-4910. Revs. Jogues Constance, O.F.M.Cap.; Randall Knauf, O.F.M.Cap.

[Q] SPECIAL SERVICES

DETROIT. *Capuchin Soup Kitchen*, 1820 Mt. Elliott, 48207. Tel: 313-579-2100; Fax: 313-571-1822. W. DeWayne Wells, Exec. Dir.; Bro. Vincent Reyes, O.F.M.Cap., Pastoral Dir.

Jefferson House, 8311 E. Jefferson, 48214. Tel: 313-331-8900; Fax: 313-331-2322. Mr. James Fleming, Site Dir. Transitional alcohol-drug residence.

Catholic Community Services of the Archdiocese of Detroit, Inc., 1234 Washington Blvd., 48226. Tel: 313-237-5885; Fax: 313-237-4642. His Eminence Adam J. Maida, Pres.; Rev. Msgr. John P. Zenz, Sec.; Mr. Michael H. Gorman, Treas.

Manna Community Meal (Soup Kitchen) , 1950 Trumbull, 48226. Tel: 313-963-8708.

St. Patrick's Senior Center, Inc., 58 Parsons, 48201. Tel: 313-833-7080; Fax: 313-833-0128. Sr. Mary Watson, O.P., Pres. Lay Staff 10; Patients Assisted Annually 1,400.

Pope John XXIII Hospitality House, 3977 2nd Ave., 48201. Tel: 313-832-4357; Fax: 313-965-4453. Rev. Russell E. Kohler. Cancer outpatient-residents, Transportation for Area Pediatric Cancer Patients.

St. Vincent de Paul Society, Archdiocesan Council, 2929 E. Grand Blvd., 48202. Tel: 313-972-3100; Fax: 313-972-3147. Bat Seymour III, Pres.; Thomas P. Moore III, Exec. Dir.; Rev. John H. West, Spiritual Dir.

HARRISVILLE. *The Oratory*, 407 N. Lake St., 48740. Tel: 313-965-4450; Fax: 313-965-4453.

MEMPHIS. *Sacred Heart Rehabilitation Center, Inc.*, 400 Stoddard Rd., Box 41038, 48041-1038. Tel: 810-392-2167; Fax: 810-392-3385. John Sass Jr., Pres. Treatment for alcoholism and drug dependency to adult men and women. Detox and residential services. Bed Capacity 112.

ONSTED. *St. Patrick's Retreat*, 11528 Killarney Hwy., 49265. Tel: 313-965-4450; Fax: 313-965-4453. Rev. Russell E. Kohler, Dir. Tel: 313-832-4357. Retreats for Family with cancer outpatient; small groups of handicapped-developmentally disabled; small parish team meetings; hospice & chaplain's meetings and offers assistance for patient visits to world shrines.

TROY. *Gabriel Richard Institute*, 3641 Estates Dr., 48084. Tel: 248-643-8887; Fax: 248-643-8887. Dolores Ammar, Exec. Dir. Adult and youth Christopher Leadership training for Catholic laymen, women, clergy & religious.

WARREN. *St. John's Deaf Center*, 8245 Fisher, 48089. Tel: 586-758-0710 (TDD); 586-758-0714 (Voice); Fax: 586-758-0714. Rev. Richard J. Yost, O.S.F.S., Dir.

WATERFORD. *Lourdes Alzheimers Special Care Center*, 2300 Watkins Lake Rd., 48328. Tel: 248-674-2241; Fax: 248-674-1211. Sr. Sue McMahon, O.P., Contact Person.

[R] CAMPS AND COMMUNITY CENTERS

DETROIT. *C.Y.O. Boys Camp*, CYO Camps, Catholic Youth Organization, 305 Michigan Ave., 48226. Tel: 313-963-7172; Fax: 313-963-7179.

C.Y.O. Girls Camp, CYO Camps, Catholic Youth Organization, 305 Michigan Ave., 48226. Tel: 313-963-7172; Fax: 313-963-7179.

Camp Ozanam, Central Office-St. Vincent de Paul Society, 2929 E. Grand Blvd., 48202-0518. Tel: 313-972-3100; Fax: 313-972-3147. A free week long Christian camping experience for boys 8-12. Recruitment through Parish Conferences of the Society of St. Vincent de Paul.

Camp Stapleton-St. Vincent de Paul Society, Central Office, 2929 E. Grand Blvd., 48202. Tel: 313-972-3100; Fax: 313-972-3147. A free week long Christian camping experience for girls 8-12. Recruitment through Parish Conferences of the Society of St. Vincent de Paul.

[S] CAMPUS MINISTRIES

DETROIT. *Marygrove College Campus Ministry* 8425 West McNichols Rd., 48221. Tel: 313-927-1404; Fax: 313-927-1345. Sisters Marie Sweeney, I.H.M., Campus Ministry; Kathleen O'Brien, I.H.M., Campus Ministry.

University of Detroit Mercy University Ministry P.O. Box 19900, 48219-0900.

McNichols Campus Tel: 313-993-1560. Rev. Gary R. Wright, S.J., Dir.; Sisters Beth Ann Finster, S.S.J., Asst. Dir.; Jacquelyn Laster, R.S.M.; Mr. Michael Simone, S.J.

College of Health Professions & School of Dentistry Tel: 313-993-6216. Bridget Deagan Krause, M.Div.

Wayne State University, Newman Center 761 Student Center, 48202. Tel: 313-577-3462. Ms. Jean Murphy, Chap.

AUBURN HILLS. *St. John Fisher Chapel University Parish* 3665 Walton Blvd., 48326. Tel: 248-373-6457; Fax: 248-373-5479. Rev. Jerome A. Brzezinski; Ms. Lisa Brown; Ms. Nancy Mason Bordley; Mrs. Susan Buratto; Sisters Mary Ann Dixon; Mary Van Gilder; Mr. Paul Borucki. Campus Ministry for Oakland University.

DEARBORN. *Univ. of Michigan, Dearborn, Henry Ford Community College Newman Center* , Gabriel Richard Campus Ministry Center , 5001 Evergreen Rd., 48128. Tel: 313-271-6000. Shannon Dyer, Campus Min.

LIVONIA. *Madonna University Campus Ministry* 36600 Schoolcraft, 48150. Tel: 734-432-5419; Fax: 734-432-5393. Rev. Xavier Ray, Dir. Campus Min.

Schoolcraft College, Newman Center , (Campus Ministry) , 17600 Haggerty Rd., 48152. Tel: 734-464-2160; Fax: 734-464-1694.

PORT HURON. *John Courtney Murray Newman Center* 505 Huron Ave., 48060. Tel: 810-948-5195; Fax: 810-984-8814. Revs. Rene L. Desmarais; Simeon T. Iber; Sr. Margaret Dowd, Co-Dir.

WARREN. *Macomb Community College Campus Ministry* 14500 Twelve Mile Rd., 48088. Tel: 586-445-7378; Fax: 586-445-7172. Sr. Joyce Campbell, I.H.M., Campus Min.; Mr. Thomas Salas, Campus Min.; Ms. Paula Makowski, Asst.

[T] MISCELLANEOUS LISTINGS

DETROIT. *The Black Catholic Televangelization Network*, P.O. Box 13559, 48213-0559. Tel: 313-521-7777; Fax: 313-521-7766. Rev. Clarence E. Williams, C.PP.S., Pres. Search, Black and Catholic (TV), the Catholic African World Network, and the Institute for Recovery from Racisms.

Christ Child Society, 15751 Joy Rd., 48228. Tel: 313-584-6077; Fax: 313-584-1148. Rev. Msgr. John P. Zenz, Spiritual Dir.; Madelon Ward, Pres.

Clergy Health Plan, Chancery Building, 1234 Washington Blvd., 48226. Rev. Jack Fabian, Dir.

Council of Catholic Women, 305 Michigan Ave., 48226. Tel: 313-237-5896; Fax: 313-237-5869. Julie Racine, Pres.

Dominican Literacy Center, 9400 Courville, 48224. Tel: 313-882-4853; Fax: 313-882-0436. Sr. Marie Schoenlein, O.P., Dir.

Foster Parents Mission Club, 17330 Quincy Ave., 48221. Tel: 313-342-4066; Fax: 313-342-6816. Rev. Bruno Piccolo, P.I.M.E., Dir.; Maria Biernacki, Exec. Sec. An agency of the P.I.M.E. Missionaries.

The Franciscan Project, Inc., 4603 Vinewood, 48208-1879. Tel: 313-896-7103; Fax: 313-896-7103. P.O. Box 310633, 48231-0633. Sr. Patricia Mary Hackett, S.A., Pres.

Gabriel Richard Historical Society, 1000 St. Dnove St., 48216. Tel: 313-963-1888; Fax: 313-496-0429. Rev. Manual Cnircop, C.S.B., Contact Person.

Institute for Communal Contemplation and Dialogue, 8531 W. McNichols, 48221. Tel: 313-341-7208; Fax: 313-801-1764. Sr. Nancy Sylvester, I.H.M., Exec. Dir.

Jesuit Seminary Association, 7303 W. Seven Mile Rd., 48221. Tel: 313-861-7500; Fax: 313-861-4230. Rachel M. Brennan, Dir. of Development & of Jesuit Seminary Assoc.

Jesuit International Missions Tel: 313-861-7500; Fax: 313-861-4230. Rev. Richard H. Twohig, S.J.

Jesuit Volunteer Corps. Midwest, Inc., 7333 W. Seven Mile Rd., 48221. Tel: 313-345-3480; Fax: 313-345-5410. P.O. Box 21936, 48221-0936. Timothy McCabe, Exec. Dir.

Latino Cultural Pastoral Center, 2020 14th St., 48216. Tel: 313-962-8491; Fax: 313-962-8493. Deacon Raul Feliciano, Dir.

Leprosy Relief Society, 17330 Quincy Ave., 48221. Tel: 313-342-4066; Fax: 313-342-6816. Barbara J. Rubaie, Dir. An agency of the P.I.M.E. Missionaries

Midwest Cultural Institute of Leadership (ICLM), 438 St. Antoine, 48226. Tel: 313-961-7213; Fax: 313-961-7236. Rev. Thomas W. Florek, S.J., Coord.

Pontiac Vision 2000 Schools, Inc., 1234 Washington Blvd., 48226. Tel: 313-237-5803. Mr. Michael H. Gorman, Sec. & Treas.

*Pope John Paul II Cultural Foundation, Inc.*Web: www.jp2cc.org.

Foundation Office, 1234 Washington Blvd., 48226. Tel: 313-237-5816; Fax: 313-237-4642.

Operations Office, Pope John Paul II Cultural Center, 3900 Harewood Rd., N.E., Washington, DC 20017-1555. Tel: 202-635-5400; Fax: 202-635-5411. His Eminence Adam Cardinal Maida, Pres.; Most Revs. John J. Myers, J.C.D., First Vice Pres.; Donald W. Wuerl, S.T.D., Vice Pres.; Bernard J. Harrington, Sec.; Mr. Michael H. Gorman, Treas.; Rev. G. Michael Bugarin, Exec. Dir.; Penelope C. Fletcher, Deputy Dir.; Steven A. Wright, Dir. of Finance & Admin.

West Detroit Catholic Schools Alliance, 23450 W. Davison, 48223. Tel: 313-255-3666; Fax: 313-537-0598. Sr. Diane Odette, O.P., Dir.; Rev. Mark S. Brauer, Vicar. Purpose: an alliance of the following Catholic Schools-Bishop Borgess Academy, Bishop Borgess High School, and St. Christopher Elementary.

BLOOMFIELD HILLS. *Amicare Home Health Care - Metro Detroit*, 281 Enterprise Dr., Ste. 200, 48302. Tel: 248-858-7735. Karen Struve, Pres.

Chinese Catholic Society of Michigan, Inc., 1000 Bretton Ln., 48304. Tel: 248-647-5464; Fax: 248-647-7736. Elizabeth V. King, Pres.; Thomas McGuire, Spiritual Dir.

**Cranbrook Hospice Care*, 281 Enterprise Ct., Ste. 300, 48302. 27870 Cabot Dr., Novi, 48377-2920. Tel: 248-452-5300; Fax: 248-334-7064. Agnes Haggerty, Assoc. Gen. Counsel, Trinity Health.

Logos, Inc. (Michigan), 2460 Opdyke Rd., 48304. Tel: 248-922-2084; Fax: 248-642-4668. Rev. Lorenzo Gomez, L.C., Rector; Bro. Joseph Brickner, L.C., Vice Rector; Rev. Juan Gabriel Guerra, L.C.; Bro. Brendan Jaldway.

**Mercy Amicare Home Healthcare, Oakland*, 281 Enterprise Ct., Ste. 200, 48302. 27870 Cabot Dr., Novi, 48377-2920. Tel: 248-489-6764. Agnes Haggerty, Assoc. Gen. Counsel, Trinity Health.

Opdyke, Inc., 2460 Opdyke Rd., 48304. Tel: 248-644-2954; Fax: 248-642-4668. Rev. Lorenzo Gomez, L.C., Contact.

WCVA, Inc. - Michigan Catholic Radio, 38500 N. Woodward, Ste. 350, 48304-2964. Tel: 248-642-6226; Fax: 248-642-6027. John F.X. Browne, Pres.; John G. Kruse, Devel. Dir.

CLARKSTON. *The Legion of Christ, Inc.*, 5935 Clarkson Rd., 48348. Tel: 248-922-2084; Fax: 248-922-2087. Revs. Juan Gabriel Guerrs, L.C.; Ernst Daly, L.C.; Alfonse Nozorro, L.C.; Bros. Joseph Brickner, L.C.; Brendan Jaldway.

CLAWSON. *American Friends of the Vatican Library*, 581 E. 14 Mile Rd., 48017-2175. Tel: 248-589-7305; Fax: 248-588-8767. Rev. Charles Kosanke, Pres.

CLINTON TOWNSHIP. *St. Mary Magdalen Catholic Community*, Ryan Correctional Facility, 24415 Crocker, 48036. Tel: 810-755-9359. Rev. Thomas R. Physician, Chaplaincy Coord. (Retired).

DEARBORN. *Archdiocesan Catholic Campus Ministry Association, Gabriel Richards Campus Ministry*, University of Michigan-Dearborn, 5001 Evergreen, 48128. Tel: 313-271-6000. Shannon Dyer, Leadership Team; Michael Laughlin, Leadership Team; Silvia Shorter, Leadership Team; Kathy Eubanks, Leadership Team.

Leo XIII Society, 1840 N. Melborn, 48128. Tel: 313-359-1499; Fax: 313-359-1767. Ernie Scarano, Pres.

DEARBORN HEIGHTS. *Dominican Center for Religious Development*, 7430 N. Inkster Rd. 48127. Tel: 313-730-8759; Fax: 313-791-0319. Sr. Rosemarie Kieffer, O.P.

EASTPOINTE. *Detroit Catholic Charismatic Renewal Center*, 22851 Lexington, 48021. Tel: 586-777-7780; Fax: 586-777-5171.

D.C.C.R. Assembly: Rev. John C. Esper, Liaison; Arlene Apone, Assoc. Liaison; Ann Bonenfant; Clare Cooper; Steve Cooper; Rosa Curry; Darlene Czop; Gene Kempski; Dick Lajiness; Jim Lovelock; Sylvia Murphy; Tom Murphy; Frank Potter; Judy Siekierski; Ben Stapel.

FARMINGTON HILLS. **Amicare Home Health Services, Inc.*, P.O. Box 9185, 48333-9185. Tel: 248-305-7921; Fax: 248-305-7632. Karen Struve, Pres.

**Amicare Hospice Services, Inc.*, 34605 Twelve Mile Rd., 48331. Fax: 248-489-6204. Karen Struve, Pres.

Dominican Consultation Center, 31487 Northwestern Hwy., Ste. A, 48334-2526. Tel: 248-855-1695.

St. Clair Shores Office, 22811 Greater Mack, Ste. L-9, St. Clair Shores, 48080. Tel: 586-775-5620. Sr. Diane Burgermeister, O.P.

Mercy Services for Aging, Non-profit Housing Corporation Wholly owned subsidiary of Mercy Services for Aging , 34605 Twelve Mile Rd., 48331. Tel: 248-305-7600; Fax: 248-305-7632. Joclyn Harris, Pres. & CEO.

Trinity Health International, 34605 Twelve Mile Rd., 48331. Tel: 248-489-6100; Fax: 248-489-6102. David Velinga, Pres.; Patricia Williams, Dir.

GROSSE POINTE. *John Paul II Foundation of Michigan, Inc.*, 35 Warner Rd., 48236. Tel: 313-882-2140; Fax: 313-882-1292. Mrs. Frank A. Germack Jr., Pres. Conducts religious, cultural, educational, humanitarian and fund raising activities in Michigan in liaison with the John Paul Foundation in Rome. Regular, supporting and life memberships.

LIVONIA. **Angela Hospice Home Care, Inc.*, 14100 Newburgh Rd., 48154-5010. Tel: 734-464-7810.

Felician Sisters of Livonia Foundation, 36800 Schoolcraft, 48150. Tel: 734-591-1730; Fax: 734-591-1710 Sr. Mary Renetta Rumpz, C.S.S.F., Pres.

MONROE. *SSIHM Charitable Trust (Retired and Infirm Sisters)*, 610 W. Elm Ave., 48162-7909. Tel: 734-241-0092; Fax: 734-241-9114. Sr. Frances Mlocek, I.H.M., Trustee.

NOVI. *Trinity Continuing Care Services - Indiana, Inc.*, 39500 Orchard Hill Place Dr. Ste. 400, 48375. Tel: 248-305-7600; Fax: 248-305-7933. Karen Struve, Pres. & CEO.

Trinity Health Corporation, 27870 Cabot Dr., 48377-2920. Tel: 248-489-6000; Fax: 248-489-6775. Email: HaleD@Trinity-Health.org. Judith M. Pelham, Pres. & CEO.

Trinity Health-Michigan, 27870 Cabot Dr., 48377-2920. Tel: 248-489-6000; Fax: 248-489-6775. Judith C. Pelham, Pres. Organization owns & operates 9 hospital divisions in Michigan. In addition to acute care facilities, Trinity Health - Michigan operates other related health care programs and facilities. Trinity Health - Michigan is part of Trinity Health, a multi-state health care organization.

OXFORD. *Queen of the Family Retreat Center*, 751Drahner Rd., 48371. Tel: 248-625-5560; Fax: 248-628-4898. Rev. Lorenzo Gomez, L.C., Dir.

PARADISE. *Companions of Christ the Lamb*, P.O. Box 12, 49768. Tel: 906-492-3647; Fax: 906-492-3648. Rev. Jack Fabian, Dir.

PLYMOUTH. *Miles Christi*, P.O. Box 701200, 48170. Tel: 248-596-9677; Fax: 248-596-9678. Email: infousa@ mileschristi.org. Rev. Caesar Bertolacci, M.C.

Widowed Friends, St. John Center for Youth and Family 44011 Five Mile Rd., 48170-2555. Tel: 734-414-1235. Deacon Robert Oves, Contact Person.

PONTIAC. *Mt. Hope Catholic Cemetery Association*, 727 Orchard Lake Rd., 48341-2076. Tel: 248-332-1079; Fax: 248-332-1079. Rev. Timothy A. Laboe, Admin.; Joseph E. Alessi, Supt.

REDFORD. *Siena Literacy Center*, 11635 Appleton, 48239. Tel: 313-532-8404; Fax: 313-532-8409. Sr. Mary Hemmen, O.P., Dir.

ROMEO. **EVM Foundation*, 11070 West Gates, 48065. Tel: 248-656-3890; Fax: 810-752-5077. Brian Palmer, Pres.

ROSEVILLE. *Cursillos in Christianity Movement of the Archdiocese of Detroit*, 18430 Utica Rd., 48066. Tel: 810-776-4533. Rev. Charles M. Morris, Spiritual Advisor; Mr. William Pfarnes, Lay Dir. Tel: 810-524-1951.

Servants of Jesus of Divine Mercy, P.O. Box 66236, 48066 Tel: 586-792-0309; Fax: 586-792-0006. Catherine M. Lanni, Chairperson.

ST. CLAIR SHORES. *Catholic Kolping Society of America, Detroit Branch, Inc.*, 24409 Jefferson, 48080. Tel: 586-775-9159. Roz Seubert, Pres. Tel: 248-435-2979; Thekla Abels, Contact Person. Tel: 313-885-1189; Rev. Daniel Fox, O.F.M.Cap.

**Celebrate Life Ministries*, 28111 Jefferson, A6, 48081. Tel: 586-778-4446. Ms. Patricia Haas, Coord.

WARREN. *St. John Health System* Holding Company sponsored by Sisters of St. Joseph and the Daughters of Charity of St. Vincent de Paul which operates: St. John Hospital & Medical Center; St. John Ambulatory Corp.; Affiliated Health Services; St. John Senior Community; Eastwood Community Clinics; St. John Northeast Community Hospital; St. John Oakland Hospital; St. John-North Shores; St. John River District Hospital; St. John Riverview Hospital; St. John Macomb Hospital; Father Murray Nursing Home; St. John Health System Home Services; St. John Health System Foundation; Providence Hospital and Medical Centers; Seiton Health Corporation of Southeast Michigan. , 28000 Dequindre Rd., 48092. Tel: 810-753-0911. Dr. Anthony R. Tersigni, Ed.D., Pres. & CEO.

WATERFORD. *Dominican Health Care Corporation*, 2300 Walkins Lake Rd., 48328. Tel: 248-674-2241; Fax: 248-674-1211. Sr. Frances Mary Kernasovich, Contact Person.

Lourdes Campus Fund, 2300 Watkins Lake Rd., 48328. Tel: 248-674-2241; Fax: 248-674-1211. Sr. Frances Mary Kernasovich, Contact Person.

[U] CLOSED INSTITUTIONS

DETROIT. *Archdiocesan Archives* The following institutional sacramental records can be found at the following address unless otherwise indicated. , 1234 Washington Blvd., 48226. Tel: 313-237-5846; Fax: 313-237-4643.

St. Agnes
St. Albertus
Anawim Community
Assumption of the Blessed Virgin Mary
St. Augustine
St. Benedict the Moor
St. Bernadette
St. Bernadette Chapel
St. Bernard
St. Boniface
St. Brigid
St. Camillus
Cardinal Leger Community
St. Catherine
St. Casimir
Corpus Christi
St. David
St. Edward
Emmaus Community
Epiphany
St. Eugene
St. Francis Hospital
St. George (Lithuanian)
Holy Ghost
Holy Name of Jesus
St. Ignatius of Antioch
Immaculate Conception
St. Joachim
St. John the Evangelist
St. John Nepomucene
St. John Vianney
St. Joseph Mercy Hospital
St. Lawrence
St. Margaret Mary
St. Martin
St. Mary Hospital - Detroit Memorial Hospital
St. Monica
Mother of Consolation
Mother of Our Savior
Mount Carmel Mercy Hospital
Our Lady of Guadalupe
Our Lady of Help
Our Lady of the Hills
Our Lady Queen of Hope
St. Paul Maltese
Patronage of St. Joseph
St. Peter (Lithuanian)
St. Philip Neri
Resurrection
St. Rose of Lima
St. Stanislaus Bishop and Martyr
St. Theresa
St. Thomas the Apostle
St. Vincent de Paul
Santa Maria
Vida Nueva Community
Visitation
St. Wenceslaus

RELIGIOUS INSTITUTES OF MEN REPRESENTED IN THE ARCHDIOCESE

For further details refer to the corresponding bracketed number in the Religious Institutes of Men or Women section.

[0140]—*The Augustinians* (Chicago)—O.S.A.
[0170]—*Basilian Fathers* (Toronto, Ont.)—C.S.B.
[0200]—*Benedictine Monks* (Detroit Prov.)—O.S.B.
[0330]—*Brothers of the Christian Schools* (New York Prov., Chicago, IL)—F.S.C.
[0600]—*Brothers of the Congregation of Holy Cross* (Midwest Prov.)—C.S.C.
[]—*Canons Regular of the Holy Cross*—O.R.C.
[0400]—*Canons Regular of the Order of the Holy Cross* (Prov. of St. Odilia)—O.S.C.
[0470]—*The Capuchin Friars* (St. Joseph Prov.)—O.F.M.Cap.
[0310]—*Congregation of Christian Brothers* (American Prov.)—C.F.C.
[0750]—*Congregation of Marianhill Missionaries*—C.M.M.
[1000]—*Congregation of the Passion* (Western Prov.)—C.P.
[1140]—*Congregation of the Sacred Hearts of Jesus and Mary*—SS.CC.
[0480]—*Conventual Franciscans*—O.F.M.Conv
[0520]—*Franciscan Friars (Custody of the Holy*

Family/Croatian; Prov. of St. John the Baptist)—O.F.M.
[]—*Franciscan Missionories of Jesus Crucified*—F.M.J.C.
[0690]—*Jesuit Fathers and Brothers* (Detroit Prov.)—S.J.
[0730]—*Legionaries of Christ*—L.C.
[]—*Little Brothers of Jesus*
[0780]—*Marist Fathers* (Northeastern Prov.)—S.M.
[]—*Miles Christi Institute*—M.C.
[]—*Missionary Society of St. Paul*—M.S.S.P.
[]—*Missionary Yarcumal*—M.X.Y.
[0860]—*Missionhurst Congregation of the Immaculate Heart of Mary*—C.I.C.M.
[0910]—*Missonary Oblates of Mary Immaculate*—O.M.I.
[0920]—*Oblates of St. Francis De Sales*—O.S.F.S.
[0430]—*Order of Preachers-Dominicans* (Prov. of St. Albert the Great)—O.P.
[1020]—*Pauline Fathers and Brothers*—S.S.P.
[1050]—*Pontifical Institute for Foreign Missions*—P.I.M.E.
[1070]—*Redemptorist Fathers* (Denver Prov.)—C.SS.R.
[1240]—*Servites*—O.S.M.
[1260]—*Society of Christ* (American-Canadian Prov.)—S.Ch.
[0440]—*Society of Saint Edmund*—S.S.E.
[0990]—*Society of the Catholic Apostolate*—S.A.C.
[1060]—*Society of the Precious Blood* (Cincinnati Prov.)—C.PP.S.
[0650]—*Spiritans* (Eastern Prov.)—C.S.Sp.

RELIGIOUS INSTITUTES OF WOMEN REPRESENTED IN THE ARCHDIOCESE

[]—*Assumption Sisters of Kenya, Africa*—A.S.N.
[1810]—*Bernardine Sisters of the Third Order of St. Francis*—O.S.F.
[0360]—*Carmelite Sisters of the Divine Heart of Jesus Carmel*—D.C.J.
[3810]—*Catholic Mission Sisters of St. Francis Xavier*—X.S.
[0270]—*Congregation of Bon Secours*—C.B.S.
[1730]—*Congregation of the Sisters of the Third Order of St. Francis Oldenburg, IN*—O.S.F.
[1830]—*Contemplative Sisters of the Good Shepherd*—C.G.S.
[0760]—*Daughters of Charity of St. Vincent de Paul*—D.C.
[0790]—*Daughters of Divine Charity*—F.D.C.
[]—*Daughters of Mary Immaculate (Chaldean)*—D.M.I.
[]—*Daughters of Mary, Mother of Mercy*—D.M.M.M.
[0940]—*Daughters of St. Mary of Providence*—D.S.M.P.
[0810]—*Daughters of the Heart of Mary*—D.H.M.
[0420]—*Discalced Carmelite Nuns*—O.C.D.
[1050]—*Dominican Contemplative Nuns*—O.P.
[1070-13]—*Dominican Sisters (Adrian, MI)*—O.P.
[1070-02]—*Dominican Sisters (Columbus,OH)*—O.P.
[1070-17]—*Dominican Sisters (Elkin Park)*—O.P.
[1070-14]—*Dominican Sisters (Grand Rapids, MI)*—O.P.
[1070-16]—*Dominican Sisters (Hope)*—O.P.
[]—*Dominican Sisters of Mt. Thabor*—O.P.
[1070-26]—*Dominican Sisters (Oxford, MI)*—O.P.
[1070-09]—*Dominican Sisters (Racine, WI)*—O.P.
[1170]—*Felician Sisters*—C.S.S.F.
[]—*Franciscan Missionaries of Jesus Crucified*—F.M.J.C.
[1470]—*Franciscan Sisters of St. Joseph*—F.S.S.J.
[1480]—*Franciscan Sisters of St. Joseph* (Mexico)—F.S.S.J.
[1190]—*Franciscan Sisters of the Atonement*—S.A.
[1440]—*Franciscan Sisters of the Poor*—S.F.P.
[2430]—*Marist Sisters Congregation of Mary*—S.M.
[2480]—*Medical Missionary of Mary*—M.M.M.
[2720]—*Mission Helpers of the Sacred Heart*—M.H.S.H.
[2710]—*Missionaries of Charity*—M.C.
[]—*Missionaries of the Kingship of Christ*—S.I.M.
[]—*Missionary Sisters of Christ the King for Polonia*—M.Chr.
[3130]—*Our Lady of Victory Missionary Sisters*—O.L.V.M.
[2970]—*School Sisters of Notre Dame*—S.S.N.D.
[3560]—*Servants of Jesus*—S.J.
[3590]—*Servants of Mary (Servite Sisters)*—O.S.M.
[0440]—*Sisters of Charity of Cincinnati, Ohio*—S.C.
[0520]—*Sisters of Charity of Our Lady, Mother of Mercy*—S.C.M.M.
[0990]—*Sisters of Divine Providence*—C.D.P.
[2245]—*Sisters of Jesus the Savior*—S.J.S.
[2575]—*Sisters of Mercy of the Americas*—R.S.M
[2990]—*Sisters of Notre Dame*—S.N.D.
[]—*Sisters of SS. Cyril & Methodius*—S.S.C.M.
[1630]—*Sisters of St. Frances of Penance & Christian Charity*—O.S.F.
[1530]—*Sisters of St. Francis of the Congregation of Our Lady of Lourdes* (Sylvania, OH & Tiffin, OH)—O.S.F.
[3830-11]—*Sisters of St. Joseph*—S.S.J.
[3930]—*Sisters of St. Joseph of the Third Order of St. Francis*—S.S.J.-T.O.S.F.
[1830]—*Sisters of the Good Shepherd*—R.G.S.
[]—*Sisters of the Holy Cross*
[1970]—*Sisters of the Holy Family of Nazareth*—C.S.F.N.
[1990]—*Sisters of the Holy Names of Jesus and Mary*—S.N.J.M.
[2350]—*Sisters of the Living Word*—S.L.W.
[3730]—*Sisters of the Order of St. Basil the Great*—O.S.B.M.
[3260]—*Sisters of the Precious Blood (Dayton, Ohio)*—C.PP.S.
[2090]—*Sisters, Home Visitors of Mary*—H.V.M.
[2150]—*Sisters, Servants of the Immaculate Heart of Mary*—I.H.M.
[2460]—*Society of Mary Reparatrix*—S.M.R.
[4070]—*Society of the Sacred Heart*—R.S.C.J.
[]—*Vestiarski Sisters of Jesus*—V.S.

ARCHDIOCESAN CEMETERIES

DETROIT. *Owned and Operated by the Archdiocese of Detroit*
Holy Cross
Holy Sepulchre, Southfield.
Our Lady of Hope, Southgate.
Owned and Operated by the Mt. Elliott Cemetery Association
Mt. Elliott
Mt. Olivet
Resurrection, Clinton Township.
All Saints, Waterford.
Owned and Operated by the Conventual Franciscan Friars
St. Hedwig, Dearborn Heights.

NECROLOGY

† Bartone, Donald Edmund, Marine City, MI Holy Cross—Died Dec. 11, 2002
† Borowski, Ladislaus—Died Sept. 5, 2003
† Bresnahan, Thomas James, (Retired)—Died June 7, 2003
† Burke, Robert Emmett, Birmingham, MI Holy Name—Died March 8, 2003
† Burns, Francis Henry, (Retired)—Died April 21, 2003
† Erpelding, Martin Bernard, (Retired)—Died Nov. 3, 2002
† Goentges, Charles Joseph, (Retired)—Died Dec. 26, 2002
† O'Leary, Michael George, Grosse Pointe, MI Bon Secours Hospital—Died Feb. 10, 2003
† Schweihoffer, Walter John, (Retired)—Died Nov. 17, 2002
† Wittstock, John Joseph, (Retired)—Died Nov. 15, 2002

Diocese of Dodge City

(Dioecesis Dodgepolis)

Most Reverend

RONALD M. GILMORE, S.T.L., D.D.

Bishop of Dodge City; ordained June 7, 1969; appointed Bishop of Dodge City May 12, 1998; installed July 16, 1998 *Office: 910 Central Ave., Box 137, Dodge City, KS 67801.*

Most Reverend

STANLEY G. SCHLARMAN, D.D.

Bishop Emeritus of Dodge City; ordained July 13, 1958; appointed to the Titular See of Capri and Auxiliary Bishop of Belleville, March 13, 1979; consecrated May 14, 1979; appointed Bishop of Dodge City March 1, 1983; installed May 4, 1983; retired May 12, 1998 *Res.: 16 S. Illinois St., Belleville, IL 62220-2104.*

Catholic Church Offices: 910 Central Ave., P.O. Box 137, Dodge City, KS 67801-0137. Tel: 620-227-1500; Fax: 620-227-1570.

Web: www.dcdiocese.org

Email: dcdiocese@dcdiocese.org

ESTABLISHED MAY 19, 1951.

Square Miles 23,000.

Comprises the following Counties in the State of Kansas: Barton, Stafford, Pratt, Barber, Rush, Ness, Lane, Scott, Wichita, Greeley, Hamilton, Kearny, Finney, Hodgeman, Pawnee, Edwards, Ford, Gray, Haskell, Grant, Stanton, Morton, Stevens, Seward, Meade, Clark, Kiowa and Comanche.

Principal Patron: Our Lady of Guadalupe.

Secondary Patron: St. John the Baptist.

Legal Title: For legal titles of parishes and diocesan institutions, consult the Chancery Office.

STATISTICAL OVERVIEW

Personnel	
Bishop	1
Priests: Diocesan Active in Diocese	19
Priests: Diocesan Active Outside Diocese	2
Priests: Retired, Sick or Absent	15
Number of Diocesan Priests	36
Religious Priests in Diocese	10
Total Priests in Diocese	46
Extern Priests in Diocese	15
Ordinations:	
Transitional Deacons	2
Permanent Deacons in Diocese	8
Total Sisters	96
Parishes	
Parishes	49
With Resident Pastor:	
Resident Diocesan Priests	20
Resident Religious Priests	4
Without Resident Pastor:	
Administered by Priests	20
Administered by Professed Religious Men	5
Professional Ministry Personnel:	
Sisters	15
Lay Ministers	5
Welfare	
Catholic Hospitals	3
Total Assisted	97,618
Special Centers for Social Services	4
Total Assisted	257,775
Educational	
Diocesan Students in Other Seminaries	1
Total Seminarians	1
Elementary Schools, Diocesan and Parish	9
Total Students	1,138
Catechesis/Religious Education:	
High School Students	1,728
Elementary Students	3,860
Total Students under Catholic Instruction	6,727
Teachers in the Diocese:	
Lay Teachers	90
Vital Statistics	
Receptions into the Church:	
Infant Baptism Totals	1,001
Adult Baptism Totals	70
Received into Full Communion	66
First Communions	1,092
Confirmations	684
Marriages:	
Catholic	175
Interfaith	80
Total Marriages	255
Deaths	362
Total Catholic Population	55,053
Total Population	222,502

Former Bishops—Most Revs. JOHN BAPTIST FRANZ, D.D., consecrated Aug. 29, 1951; transferred to the See of Peoria Aug. 8, 1959; MARION F. FORST, D.D. (Retired), consecrated March 24, 1960; transferred to See of Kansas City, KS as Auxiliary Oct. 16, 1976; retired as Auxiliary Bishop Dec. 23, 1986; EUGENE J. GERBER, D.D., consecrated Dec. 14, 1976; transferred to See of Wichita, KS Nov. 23, 1982; STANLEY G. SCHLARMAN D.D. (Retired), consecrated May 14, 1979; appt. Bishop of Dodge City March 1, 1983; installed May 4, 1983; retired May 12, 1998.

Vicar General and Moderator of the Curia—Rev. ROBERT A. SCHREMMER, V.G.

Catholic Church Offices—910 Central Ave., P.O. Box 137, Dodge City, 67801-0137. Tel: 620-227-1500; Fax: 620-227-1545. Office Hours: Mon.-Fri. 9-4:30

Chancellor—Sr. JANICE GROCHOWSKY, C.S.J.

Diocesan Archivist—Mr. TIMOTHY F. WENZL.

Finance Director—Mr. DANIEL M. STREMEL, C.P.A.

Presbyteral Council—Most Rev. RONALD M. GILMORE, S.T.L., D.D.; Revs. MICHAEL L. HELMS; ROBERT A. SCHREMMER, V.G., Chm.; TED A. SKALSKY, V.F.; JOHN R. STRASSER, V.F., Vice Chm.; GILBERT P. HERRMANN; TED D. STOECKLEIN; BRIAN R. MOORE, Ph.D., Sec.

College of Consultors—Revs. BRIAN R. MOORE, Ph.D.; TED A. SKALSKY, V.F.; ROBERT A. SCHREMMER, V.G.; TED D. STOECKLEIN; JOHN R. STRASSER, V.F.; JOHN J. MAES.

Deans—Revs. JAMES E. BAKER, J.C.L., V.F., Garden City; JOHN R. STRASSER, V.F., Great Bend; TED A. SKALSKY, V.F., Dodge City.

Matrimonial Tribunal—910 Central Ave., P.O. Box 137, Dodge City, 67801-0137. All matrimonial correspondence is to be sent to the attention of: Director of the Tribunal, Sr. Janice Grochowsky, C.S.J.

Judicial Vicar—Rev. JAMES E. BAKER, J.C.L., V.F.

Synodal Judge—Rev. JAMES E. BAKER, J.C.L., V.F.

Promoter of Justice—Rev. DAVID H. KRAUS, J.C.L.

Defender of the Bond—Rev. DAVID H. KRAUS, J.C.L.

Advocates—Revs. TED A. SKALSKY, V.F.; ROBERT A. SCHREMMER, V.G.; Deacon ERASMO RODRIGUEZ; Sr. CATHERINE THERESE PAULIE, C.S.J.

Notaries—Sr. JANICE GROCHOWSKY, C.S.J.; PAMELA POLLEY.

Diocesan Offices and Directors

Superintendent of Schools - Elementary School Religious Education—Mrs. ANN DEPPERSCHMIDT.

Catholic Social Service Offices—Rev. TED A. SKALSKY, V.F., Exec. Dir., P.O. Box 670, Dodge City, 67801. Tel: 620-225-4802; DEBBIE SNAPP, Prog. Dir.

Priestly Life and Ministry—Revs. BRIAN R. MOORE, Ph.D., Chm.; GREGORY LEBLANC; JOHN R. STRASSER, V.F.

Commission for Ministry to Priests—Revs. CHARLES MAZOUCH; TED SKALSKY.

Cursillo—805 Ave. J, Dodge City, 67801.

Diocesan Attorney— Foulston & Siefkin, L.L.P., *810 Frontview, Dodge City, 67801.* Tel: 620-227-8126. TAMARA L. DAVIS, P.A., 100 Military Plaza, Ste. 208, Dodge City, 67801. Tel: 620-225-1674; Fax: 620-227-2770.

Diocesan Finance Council—Most Rev. RONALD M. GILMORE, S.T.L., D.D., Ex Officio; Mr. DANIEL M. STREMEL, C.P.A., Ex Officio, Sec. & Treas.; JOHN ACKERMAN, Ex Officio; CLARINE HEIMAN; EUGENE HEIMAN; CARL HELFRICH, C.P.A.; Rev. WARREN STECKLEIN; RON VRATIL, C.P.A.

Diocesan Fitness Review Board—DAVID H. SNAPP, Admin. Tel: 620-225-5051 (Office); 620-225-2412 (Home).

Diocesan Pastoral Council—Most Rev. RONALD M. GILMORE, S.T.L., D.D., Ex Officio; Rev. JOHN R. STRASSER, V.F.; TOM GIESSEL; ELEANOR STRECKER; JERRY ESFELD; Revs. JAMES E. BAKER, J.C.L., V.F.; TED A. SKALSKY, V.F.; GENE JUNO; ELLEN PETERS; MYREL RICH; ADALBERTO SEPULVEDA.

Priests' Trust Fund—Revs. ROBERT A. SCHREMMER, V.G., Chm.; GERALD A. HAMMEKE; JOSEPH E. BAHR; CHARLES MAZOUCH; TED D. STOECKLEIN.

Diocesan School Council—ANN DEPPERSCHMIDT, Supt. Schools, 910 Central Ave., Dodge City, 67801. Tel: 620-227-1514; STEPHANIE GROTH, Sacred Heart School, 1912 Burr Pkwy., Dodge City, 67801. Tel: 620-225-5499; LANCE FELLHOELTER, Sacred Heart School, 1003 S. Pearl, Pratt, 67124. Tel: 620-672-3335; THOMAS SNELL, St. Joseph School, 509 W. 6th, Ellinwood, 67526. Tel: 620-564-3312; Revs. JAMES E. BAKER, J.C.L., V.F., St. Mary School, 509 St. John St., Garden City, 67846-5294. Tel: 620-275-4204; REGINALD URBAN, Holy Family School, 4100 Broadway, Great Bend, 67530. Tel: 620-792-1396; NICANOR FERANGCO, St. Nicholas School, 706 E Sixth St., Kinsley, 67547. Tel: 620-659-2692; DENNIS REED, Sacred Heart School, 527 W. 12th St., Larned, 67550. Tel: 620-285-3025; GREGORY S. LEBLANC, Sacred Heart School, 606 S. School St., Ness City, 67560. Tel: 785-798-3195; JOSEPH E. BAHR, St. Dominic School, 806 Labrador Blvd.,

Garden City, 67846. Tel: 620-276-6422.

Interactive Television Network—Mrs. COLEEN STEIN, Coord., Office at Hennessy Hall, 236 San Jose, Ste. 42, Dodge City, 67801. Tel: 620-227-1531.

Diocesan Newspaper Office—DAVID MYERS, Editor. "The Southwest Kansas Register", Diocesan Bimonthly,

Office of Family Ministries—STEVEN POLLEY, Dir.

Office of Hispanic Ministry—Revs. JOHN FAHEY-GUERRA, C.SS.R.; TONY JUDGE, C.SS.R.; MIKE MCANDREW, 419 W. First St., Liberal, 67901. Tel: 620-624-7846; Fax: 620-624-4193.

Office of Liturgy and Worship (R.C.I.A.)—Rev. Msgr. BRIAN MOORE, Dir. Liturgy, 910 Central, P.O. Box 137, Dodge City, 67801. Tel: 620-227-1533.

Catholic Agency - Migration and Refugee Services—LEVITA ROHLMAN, Exec. Dir., 1510 Taylor Plaza E., Garden City, 67846. Tel: 620-276-7610; Fax: 620-276-9228.

Catechist Formation/Certification—Coordinators, Spanish: Rev. TONY JUDGE, C.SS.R., 419 W. First St., Liberal, 67901. Tel: 620-624-7846; Fax: 620-624-4193; Sr. MARIE ELENA MARTINEZ-SIFUENTES, M.C.M.I., 509 St. John St., Garden City, 67846-5294. Tel: 620-275-4204. Coordinator, English:: Mr. MICHAEL DORSEY, 615 J.C. St., Garden City, 67846-6334. Tel: 620-276-3500.

Diocesan Ecumenical and Interfaith Officer—Mr. MICHAEL DORSEY, 615 J.C. St., Garden City, 67846-6334. Tel: 620-276-3500.

Diaconate Office—Revs. ROBERT A. SCHREMMER, V.G., Diaconate Formation Dir.; TED A. SKALSKY, V.F., Dir. Deacon Personnel.

Pastoral Ministry Formation—Rev. Msgr. BRIAN R. MOORE, Dir. Tel: 620-227-1533; Mrs. COLEEN STEIN, Coord. Tel: 620-227-1531. 236 San Jose, Ste. 42, Dodge City, 67801.

Propagation of the Faith and Pontifical Association of the Holy Childhood—Sr. KAREN ACKERMAN, A.S.C., St. Lawrence Parish, P.O. Box 278, Jetmore, 67854-0278. Tel: 620-357-8791.

Office of Religious Formation, Youth Ministry—STEVEN D. POLLEY, Dir.

Scouting—Rev. JAMES E. BAKER, J.C.L., V.F., 509 St. John St., Garden City, 67846-5294. Tel: 620-275-4204.

Technical Services—Rev. HENRY HILDEBRANDT, Dir., 910 Central, P.O. Box 137, Dodge City, 67801. Tel: 620-227-1586.

Victim Assistance Coordinator—Mrs. DONNA STAAB, M.S.N., R.N., B.C. Tel: 620-793-1960. Email: donna@cpcis.net.

Vocation Office—VACANT.

CLERGY, PARISHES, MISSIONS AND PAROCHIAL SCHOOLS

CITY OF DODGE CITY
(FORD COUNTY)

1—THE CATHEDRAL OF OUR LADY OF GUADALUPE (2001), [JC] Rev. Msgr. Brian R. Moore, Dir.; Revs. Ted A. Skalsky, V.F., Moderator; Angel Dy; Deacon Erasmo Rodriguez.
Mailing Address: P.O. Box 670, 67801. Tel: 620-225-4802; 620-227-3442 (Spanish line); Fax: 620-338-8268.
School—905 Central Ave., 67801. Tel: 620-227-6532; Fax: 620-227-3221. Wayne Winkler, Prin. Lay Teachers 27; Students 326.
Catechesis/Religious Program— Sr. Catalina Fresquez, D.R.E., (Elementary); Dave Geist, D.R.E., (High School). Students 878.

2—CHURCH OF THE SACRED HEART, Closed., For inquiries for sacramental records, please contact The Cathedral of Our Lady of Guadalupe, Dodge City.

OUTSIDE THE CITY OF DODGE CITY

ASHLAND, CLARK CO., ST. JOSEPH (1886), (German), [JC] Rev. Maurice H. Cummings, O.Carm.
Res.: 514 Main St., P.O. Box 577, 67831-0577. Tel: 620-635-2338; 620-635-2240 (office).
Catechesis/Religious Program—Tel: 620-635-2679. Becky Luerman, D.R.E. Students 38.

BEAVER, BARTON CO., ST. JOSEPH, Closed., Sacramental records can be found at St. John, Hoisington.

BELPRE, EDWARDS CO., ST. BERNARD (1901), Rev. Dennis L. Reed.
Res.: 203 Hudson St., P.O. Box 188, 67519-0188. Tel: 620-995-4305.
Catechesis/Religious Program—Tel: 620-348-4725. Karen Vosburgh, D.R.E. Students 42.

BUCKLIN, FORD CO., ST. GEORGE, Closed., Sacramental records can be found at Our Lady of Guadalupe, Dodge City.

BURDETT, PAWNEE CO., HOLY ROSARY, Closed., Sacramental records can be found at Sacred Heart, Larned.

CLAFLIN, BARTON CO., IMMACULATE CONCEPTION (1904), [JC] Rev. John J. Maes; Sr. Renee Kirmer, A.S.C., Pastoral Assoc.
Mailing Address: P.O. Box 197, 67525. Tel: 620-587-3628; Fax: 620-587-3204.
Catechesis/Religious Program—Students 105.

COLDWATER, COMANCHE CO.
1—HOLY SPIRIT, Closed., Sacramental records can be found at St. Joseph, Ashland.
2—HOLY SPIRIT STATION (1984), (German), [JC] Attended by, St. Joseph, Ashland. Rev. Maurice H. Cummings, O.Carm.
Mailing Address: *c/o Holy Spirit Catholic School*, Box 417, 67029. Tel: 620-582-2154.
Catechesis/Religious Program—P.O. Box 352, 67029. Tel: 620-582-2106. Kim Alexander, D.R.E. Students 12.

DEERFIELD, KEARNEY CO., CHRIST THE KING (1937), (Hispanic), Rev. Michael L. Helms.
Mailing Address: P.O. Box 455, 67838. Tel: 620-355-6405.
Catechesis/Religious Program—Tel: 620-277-0309. Cynde Pfeifer, D.R.E. Students 50.

DIGHTON, LANE CO., ST. THERESA (1927), [JC] Attended by, St. Joseph, Scott City. Rev. David H. Kraus, J.C.L.
Res.: 322 S. First St., P.O. Box 787, 67839. Tel: 620-397-5357.
Catechesis/Religious Program—Tel: 620-397-5711. Annette Wilson, D.R.E. Students 55.

DUBUQUE, BARTON CO., ST. CATHERINE, Closed., Sacramental records can be found at St. John the Evangelist, Hoisington.

ELKHART, MORTON CO., ST. JOAN OF ARC (1921), (Hispanic), [JC] Rev. Francis Khoi Nguyen.
Res.: 723 S. Baca Ave., P.O. Box 570, 67950-0570. Tel: 620-697-4622.
Catechesis/Religious Program—Tel: 620-697-4587. Traci O'Hanlon, D.R.E. Students 60.

ELLINWOOD, BARTON CO., ST. JOSEPH (1876), (German), Rev. John J. Maes.
Res.: 214 N. Main St., 67526. Tel: 620-564-2534; Fax: 620-564-2613.
School—111 W. Third, 67526. Tel: 620-564-2721; Fax: 620-564-2714. Adorers of the Blood of Christ 2; Lay Teachers 6; Students 62.
Catechesis/Religious Program—Students 50.

FOWLER, MEADE CO., ST. ANTHONY (1910), [JC] Attended by, St. John the Baptist, Meade. Rev. Francis Stuart, O.S.B., Admin.; Judy Dewell, Pastoral Assoc.; Steve Dewell, Pastoral Assoc.
Res.: 411 Fourth St., P.O. Box 80, 67844. Tel: 620-646-5297; Fax: 620-646-5207.
Catechesis/Religious Program—Brenda Harris, D.R.E. Students 90.

GARDEN CITY, FINNEY CO.
1—ST. DOMINIC (1965), Rev. Joseph E. Bahr; Sr. Catherine Therese Paulie, C.S.J., Pastoral Min.; Mike Dorsey, Ecumenical/Interfaith Officer.
Office—615 J. C. St., 67846. Tel: 620-276-2024; Fax: 620-276-2086.
School—617 J. C. St., 67846. Tel: 620-276-8981. Lay Teachers 10; Students 199.
Catechesis/Religious Program—Tel: 620-276-3500. Michael Dorsey, D.R.E. Students 246.
2—ST. MARY (1898), [CEM 2] [JC 2] Revs. James E. Baker, J.C.L., V.F.; Carlos Garcia-Pena.
Res.: 509 St. John St., 67846. Tel: 620-275-4204; Fax: 620-272-9971.
School—503 W. St. John St., 67846. Tel: 620-276-2241; Fax: 620-276-7067. Trina Delgado, Prin. Lay Teachers 10; Students 146.
Catechesis/Religious Program—Tel: 620-276-2716. Patricia Nieman, D.R.E. Students 418.

GREAT BEND, BARTON CO.
1—ST. PATRICK (1960), [JC] Revs. Ted D. Stoecklein; Reginald Urban.
Mailing Address: P.O. Box 87, 67530.
Res.: 4100 Broadway, 67530. Tel: 620-792-1396; Fax: 620-792-3642.
Catechesis/Religious Program— Raechel Manley, D.R.E. Merged with St. Rose of Lima, Great Bend. Students 289.
2—ST. ROSE OF LIMA (1878), [JC] In Res., Revs. Ted D. Stoecklein; Reginald Urban.
Res.: 1423 Holland St., P.O. Box 1007, 67530. Tel: 620-792-3641; Fax: 620-792-3642.
Catechesis/Religious Program—Tel: 620-792-1396. Raechel Manley, D.R.E. Students 289.

GREENSBURG, KIOWA CO., ST. JOSEPH (1952), Attended by, Sacred Heart, Pratt. Rev. Warren L. Stecklein.
Res.: c/o 332 N. Oak, Pratt, 67124. Tel: 620-672-6352; Fax: 620-672-3748.
Catechesis/Religious Program—Tel: 620-723-2534; Fax: 620-723-2534. Students 45.

HANSTON, HODGEMAN CO., ST. ANTHONY (1908), [CEM] Attended by, St. Laurence, Jetmore. Rev. Henry F. Hildebrandt.
Mailing Address: *c/o St. Lawrence Church*, P.O. Box 278, Jetmore, 67854. Tel: 620-357-8791; Fax: 620-357-8828.
Catechesis/Religious Program—Students 34.

HOISINGTON, BARTON CO., ST. JOHN THE EVANGELIST (1892), [CEM] Rev. Pascal L. Klein; Sr. Kathy Goetz, Pastoral Min.
Office—122 E. 5th St., 67544. Tel: 620-653-2963; Fax: 620-653-2934.
Rectory—108 E. 5th St., 67544. Tel: 620-653-2695.
Catechesis/Religious Program— Pam Willis, D.R.E. Students 172.

HUGOTON, STEVENS CO., ST. HELEN (1948), (Hispanic), Rev. Francis Khoi Nguyen.
Parish Office—1011 S. Jefferson St., 67951-2823. Tel: 620-544-2551.
Catechesis/Religious Program—Tel: 316-544-7544. Phillys Mendes, D.R.E. Students 70.

INGALLS, GRAY CO., ST. STANISLAUS (1909), [JC] Revs. Joseph E. Bahr; Francis G. Jordan (Retired).
Mailing Address: P.O. Box 175, 67853. Tel: 620-335-5202; Fax: 620-335-5865.
Catechesis/Religious Program—Kathy Hornung, D.R.E. Students 142.

JETMORE, HODGEMAN CO., ST. LAWRENCE (1923), Attended by, St. John the Baptist, Spearville. Rev. Henry F. Hildebrandt.
Mailing Address: P.O. Box 278, 67854. Tel: 620-357-8791; Fax: 620-357-8828.
Catechesis/Religious Program—P.O. Box 278, 67854. Students 39.

JOHNSON, STANTON CO., ST. BERNADETTE (1949), (Hispanic), Attended by, Mary Queen of Peace, Ulysses. Rev. James P. Dieker.
Mailing Address: *c/o Mary, Queen of Peace Church*, 804 Colorado, Ulysses, 67880. Tel: 620-356-1532; Fax: 620-424-1065.
Catechesis/Religious Program—Tel: 620-492-1554. Kim Gerard, D.R.E. Students 75.

KINSLEY, EDWARDS CO., ST. NICHOLAS (1883), (Irish—German), [CEM] Rev. Nicanor Ferangco (Philippines). In Res., Rev. Austin Herrmann, C.PP.S.
Res.: 706 E. Sixth St., 67547. Tel: 620-659-2692; Fax: 620-659-2049.
School—720 E. Sixth St., 67547. Tel: 620-659-2521. Mrs. Cynthia Baker, Prin. Lay Teachers 4; Students 50.
Catechesis/Religious Program—Students 30.

KIOWA, BARBER CO., ST. JOHN THE APOSTLE (1885), Attended by, Holy Rosary, Medicine Lodge and St. Boniface, Sharon. Rev. John R. Strasser, V.F.
Res.: 920 E. Main St., 67070. Tel: 620-825-4361; 877-886-1255.
Catechesis/Religious Program—Tel: 620-825-4836. Linda Forester, D.R.E. Students 40.

LACROSSE, RUSH CO., ST. MICHAEL (1911), (German), [JC] Rev. Charles Mazouch.
Res.: 918 Lincoln St., P.O. Box 309, 67548. Tel: 785-222-2561.
Catechesis/Religious Program—Tel: 913-222-3202. Ruth Baalmann, D.R.E. Students 79.

LAKIN, KEARNY CO., ST. ANTHONY (1909), [JC] Rev. Michael L. Helms.
Res.: 600 Soderberg St., P.O. Box 983, 67860. Tel: 620-355-6405; Fax: 620-355-6406.
Catechesis/Religious Program—Tel: 620-355-7119. Delia Stahlecker, D.R.E. Students 199.
Mission—Christ the King 812 Main St., Deerfield, Kearny Co. 67838. Tel: 620-426-6996.

LARNED, PAWNEE CO., SACRED HEART (1912), [CEM] [JC] Rev. Dennis L. Reed.
Res.: 1111 State St., 67550. Tel: 620-285-2035; Fax: 620-285-0097.
School—527 W. 12th St., 67550. Tel: 620-285-3025. Lay Teachers 4; Students 41.
Catechesis/Religious Program—Students 125.

LEOTI, WICHITA CO., ST. ANTHONY OF PADUA (1887), [JC] Rev. Benjamin Martin.
Res.: P.O. Box D, 67861. Tel: 620-379-4431; Fax: 620-379-4479.
Catechesis/Religious Program—Tel: 620-379-4427. Students 48.

LIBERAL, SEWARD CO., ST. ANTHONY (1916), Rev. Patrick A. Keyes, C.SS.R.; Deacons Victor Mencos; Ruben Sigala; Rev. Brian Gilles, C.S.S.R.; Deacon Oscar Rodriguez.
Res.: 1510 N. Calhoun, 67901. Tel: 620-624-4135; Fax: 620-624-3553.
Catechesis/Religious Program—Mindee Limon, D.R.E. Students 450.

LIEBENTHAL, RUSH CO., ST. JOSEPH (1876), (German), [CEM] Attended by, St. Michael, LaCrosse. Rev. Charles Mazouch.
Mailing Address: P.O. Box 173, 67553. Tel: 785-222-3160.
Catechesis/Religious Program—Tel: 785-222-2561.

Twinned with St. Michaels, LaCrosse.

LORETTO, ST. MARY, HELP OF CHRISTIANS, Closed., Sacramental records can be found at St. Joseph, Liebenthal.

MARIENTHAL, WICHITA CO., ST. MARY (1886), [CEM] Rev. Benjamin Martin.
Mailing Address: P.O. Box 7, 67863. Tel: 620-379-4427; Fax: 620-379-4479.
Catechesis/Religious Program—Tel: 620-379-4429. Jenny Winter, D.R.E. Students 64.

MCCRACKEN, RUSH CO., ST. MARY (1886), Closed. For inquiries for parish records contact the chancery.

MEADE, MEADE CO., ST. JOHN THE BAPTIST (1889), [JC] Rev. Francis Stuart, O.S.B.
Res.: 412 W. Carthage St., P.O. Box 1207, 67864. Tel: 620-873-2003.
Catechesis/Religious Program—Tel: 620-873-2654. Audrey Flowers, D.R.E. Students 43.

MEDICINE LODGE, BARBER CO., HOLY ROSARY (1952), Attended by, St. John the Apostle, Kiowa and St. Boniface, Sharon. Rev. John R. Strasser, V.F.
Mailing Address: 300 Curry Lane, 67104. Tel: 620-886-3596; 887-886-1255.
Catechesis/Religious Program—Tel: 316-886-3242. Rob Stickney, D.R.E. Students 50.

NESS CITY, NESS CO., SACRED HEART (1912), [CEM] Rev. Gregory LeBlanc.
Res.: 606 S. School St., P.O. Box 310, 67560. Tel: 785-798-3195.
School—510 S. School St., 67560. Tel: 785-798-3530; Fax: 785-798-3004. Ann Depperschmidt, Prin. Adorers of the Blood of Christ 2; Lay Teachers 6; Students 68.
Catechesis/Religious Program—Joby Henning, D.R.E. Students 68.

NORTH ELLINWOOD, BARTON CO., STS. PETER & PAUL, Closed., Sacramental records can be found at St. Joseph, Ellinwood.

NORTH KINSLEY, EDWARDS CO., SS. PETER AND PAUL, Closed., Sacramental records can be found at St. Nicholas, Kinsley.

ODIN, BARTON CO., HOLY FAMILY (1879), [CEM] Rev. Pascal L. Klein.
Mailing Address: *c/o St. John the Evangelist Parish*, 122 E. 5th St., Hoisington, 67544. Tel: 620-653-2963; Fax: 620-653-2934.
Catechesis/Religious Program— Teresa Hickel, D.R.E. Students 58.

OFFERLE, EDWARDS CO., ST. JOSEPH (1876), (Irish—German), [CEM 2] Unassigned.
Res.: c/o 706 E. Sixth St., Kinsley, 67547. Tel: 620-659-2692.
Catechesis/Religious Program—Students 15.

OLMITZ, BARTON CO., ST. ANN (1889), (Austrian—German), [CEM] Rev. Ultan P. Murphy, Admin.
Res.: 115 Cleveland St., P.O. Box 8, 67564. Tel: 620-586-3306.
Catechesis/Religious Program—Tel: 620-586-3282. Terese Frieb, D.R.E. Students 90.

PLAINS, MEADE CO., ST. PATRICK (1916), [JC] Attended by, St. John the Baptist, Meade. Rev. Francis Stuart, O.S.B.
Res.: *c/o St. John the Baptist*, 412 W. Carthage, P.O. Box 1207, Meade, 67864. Tel: 620-873-2003.
Church: 601 Superior, P.O. Box 247, 67869. Tel: 620-563-7663.
Catechesis/Religious Program—P.O. Box 102, 67869. Tel: 620-563-7874. Jenny Amerin, D.R.E. Students 75.

PRATT, PRATT CO., SACRED HEART (1887), In Res., Rev. Warren L. Stecklein.
Res.: 332 N. Oak St., 67124. Tel: 620-672-6352; Fax: 620-672-3748.
School—(Grades PreK-5), 330 N. Oak St., 67124. Tel: 620-672-3687. Don Ruda, Prin. Lay Teachers 7; Students 108.
Catechesis/Religious Program—Students 127.

RANSOM, NESS CO., ST. ALOYSIUS (1903), [CEM] Attended by, Sacred Heart, Ness City. Rev. Gregory LeBlanc.
Mailing Address: P.O. Box 96, 67572. Tel: 785-731-2497.
Catechesis/Religious Program—Students 41.

ST. JOHN, STAFFORD CO., ST. JOHN THE APOSTLE (1949), Attended by, St. Francis Xavier, Steward. Rev. Rene Guesnier, O.S.B.
Res.: 609 E. Fourth St., Rte. 2, Box 100, 67576. Tel: 620-549-3538.
Catechesis/Religious Program—Tel: 620-549-3424; Fax: 620-549-6188. Linda Gleason, D.R.E. Students 31.

ST. MARY, HODGEMAN CO., ST. MARY, Closed., Sacramental records can be found at St. John the Baptist, Spearville.

SATANTA, HASKELL CO., ST. ALPHONSUS (1946), (Hispanic), Sr. Matilde Monterrosso, Parish Life Coord.
Res.: 603 Tecumseh, Box 65, 67870. Tel: 620-649-2692; Fax: 620-649-2550.
Church: 601 Tecumseh, 67870.
Catechesis/Religious Program—Tel: 620-649-3508. Students 72.

SCOTT CITY, SCOTT CO., ST. JOSEPH (1911), [JC] Rev. David H Kraus, J.C.L.
Res.: 1004S. Main St., P.O. Box 228, 67871-0228. Tel: 620-872-7388; 620-872-3644 (Sec.)
Rectory—1004 S. Main St., 67871. Tel: 620-872-7388.
Catechesis/Religious Program—Tel: 620-872-5405. Jennifer Gerber, D.R.E.; Jeff Schmitt, D.R.E. Students 200.

SEWARD, STAFFORD CO., ST. FRANCIS XAVIER (1886), Rev. Rene Guesnier, O.S.B.
Mailing Address: 504 Main St., 67576. Tel: 620-458-5691; Fax: 620-458-3167.
Catechesis/Religious Program—Students 4.

SHARON, BARBER CO., ST. BONIFACE (1904), [CEM] Attended by, Holy Rosary, Medicine Lodge and St. John the Apostle, Kiowa. Rev. John R. Strasser, V.F.
Res.: 410 N. Main St., P.O. Box 118, 67138. Tel: 620-294-5526; Fax: 877-886-1255 (Voice Mail).
Catechesis/Religious Program—Tel: 620-294-5258. Michelle Eck, D.R.E. Students 69.

SPEARVILLE, FORD CO., ST. JOHN THE BAPTIST (1904), [CEM] [JC 2] In Res., Rev. Henry F. Hildebrandt.
Res.: 100 S. Main St., P.O. Box 187, 67876. Tel: 620-385-2212; Fax: 620-385-2396.
Catechesis/Religious Program—Tel: 620-385-2674. Carol Durler, D.R.E. Students 170.

SYRACUSE, HAMILTON CO., ST. RAPHAEL (1906), [CEM] [JC] Rev. Michael L. Helms.
Mailing Address: P.O. Box 731, 67878. Tel: 620-384-7357; Fax: 620-384-5946.
Catechesis/Religious Program—Tel: 620-384-5582. Roxane Guererro, D.R.E. Students 82.

TIMKEN, RUSH CO., HOLY TRINITY (1904), (Czech), [CEM] [JC] Attended by, St. Michael, LaCrosse. Rev. Charles Mazouch.
Mailing Address: *c/o St. Michael Church*, P.O. Box 309, Lacrosse, 67548. Tel: 785-222-2561.
Catechesis/Religious Program—Tel: 913-387-2552. Marie Stremel D.R.E. Students 35.

TRIBUNE, GREELEY CO., ST. JOSEPH (1950), [JC] Attended by, St. Francis Xavier, Steward. Rev. Benjamin Martin.
Mailing Address: Box 67, 67879. Tel: 620-376-2292; Fax: 620-376-2297.
Catechesis/Religious Program—Tel: 620-376-2490; Fax: 620-376-2792. Lisha Bauck, D.R.E. Students 40.

ULYSSES, GRANT CO., MARY QUEEN OF PEACE (1948), (Hispanic), Deacon Apolonio Rodriguez. In Res., Rev. James P. Dieker.
Res.: 804 N. Colorado, 67880. Tel: 620-356-1532; Fax: 620-424-1065.
Catechesis/Religious Program—Tel: 620-356-1532; Fax: 620-424-1065. Toney Hernandez, D.R.E.; Socorro Martinez, D.R.E. Students 390.

WINDTHORST, FORD CO., IMMACULATE HEART OF MARY, Closed., Sacramental records can be found at St. John the Baptist, Spearville.

WRIGHT, FORD CO., ST. ANDREW (1909), [CEM] Rev. Robert A. Schremmer, V.G.
Mailing Address: 10893 St. Andrew Rd., P.O. Box 125, 67882. Tel: 620-227-3363; Fax: 620-227-3501.
Parish Center—11792 Jewel Rd., 67882. Tel: 620-225-7345.
Catechesis/Religious Program—Tel: 620-225-1299. Regina Lix, D.R.E. Students 45.

On Duty Outside the Diocese:
Revs.—
Suellentrop, Anthony J.
Trong Dinh Hoang, Louis, Diocese of Honolulu

On Leave of Absence:
Rev.—
Flagor, David A.

Retired:
Rev. Msgrs.—
Leahy, Patrick J., 6900 E. 45th St. N., Wichita, 67226.
Preisner, A. F., 105 Kent, 67801.
Revs.—
Dreher, Jacob J., 3706 Meadowlark, Great Bend, 67530.
Fiedler, Donald J.
Kelly, James, 6900 E. 45th St. N., Apt. D-4, Wichita, 67226.
Kenny, Eugene, 1301 Warner Rd., Great Bend, 67530.
Lavrih, John, 6900 E. 45th St. N., Apt. D-2, Wichita, 67226.
Pottorff, Lisle J., Rte. 2, Box 247, Douglass, 67039.
van Sloun, Eugene G., Rijksweg C.10, 6161EE, Geleen, The Netherlands.

Permanent Deacons:
Hermocillo, Martin, Garden City
Lampe, Dwaine, (Retired), St. Anthony, Fowler
Mencos, Victor A., St. Anthony, Liberal
Rodriguez, Apolonio, Mary Queen of Peace, Ulysses
Rodriguez, Erasmo, St. Anthony, Liberal
Rodriguez, Oscar, St. Anthony, Liberal
Rondeau, Richard, (Retired)
Sigala, Ruben, St. Anthony, Liberal

INSTITUTIONS LOCATED IN THE DIOCESE

[A] GENERAL HOSPITALS

GARDEN CITY. *St. Catherine Hospital*, 401 E. Spruce, 67846-5679. Tel: 620-272-2222; Fax: 620-272-2566. Web: www.stcath-hosp.org. Mark Steadham, Pres. & CEO; Leanne Irsik, Senior Vice Pres.; Bonnie Peters, Vice Pres. Patient Svcs.; Susan Rutter, Chap. & Exec. Dir. Missions Min.; Carolyn Allen, CFO; Victor Hawkins, Exec. Dir. & Mktg.; Nicole Tefft, Exec. Dir. Human Resources; Doug Williams, Chap.; Jonathon Galia, Chap.; Remigius Ekweafiri, Chap. Affiliated with Catholic Health Initiatives. Bed Capacity 100; Patients Assisted Annually 46,183; Total Staff 600.

GREAT BEND. *Central Kansas Medical Center*, 3515 Broadway, 67530. Tel: 620-792-2511; Fax: 620-786-6298. Email: ckmc@greatbend.com. Web: www.ckmc.org. Tom Sommers, Pres. & CEO; Judy Scott, Vice Pres. Fiscal Svcs.; Lucy Flannagan, Dir. Human Resources; Sr. Jean Marie Lehtinen, O.P., Dir. Mission Effectiveness. Sisters of the Third Order of St. Dominic, Member-Catholic Health Initiatives. Sisters 5; Bed Capacity 117; Total Staff 549; Patients Assisted Annually 42,264.

LARNED. *St. Joseph Memorial Hospital, Inc.*, 923 Carroll St., 67550. Tel: 620-285-3161; Fax: 620-285-8883. Judy Scott, Contact. Bed Capacity 55; Total Staff 87; Total Assisted Annually 10,476.

[B] RETREAT CENTERS

GREAT BEND. *Heartland Center for Spirituality*, 3600 Broadway, 67530-3692. Tel: 620-792-1232; Fax: 620-792-1746. Email: office@heartlandspirituality.org. Web: www.heartlandspirituality.org. Sisters Louise Hageman, O.P., Co-Dir.; Renee Dreiling, O.P., Co-Dir. Retreat Center. Total Staff 6.

PAWNEE ROCK. *Heartland Farm*, R.R. 1, Box 37, 67567-9602. Tel: 620-923-4585. Email: hfarm@gbta.net. Sr. Mary Terence Wasinger, O.P., Contact Person. A Ministry of the Dominican Sisters of Great Bend, KS., Organic sustainable agriculture, body massage, retreat opportunities in rural setting. Total Staff 7.

[C] EDUCATIONAL ENDOWMENT FUNDS

DODGE CITY. *The Sacred Heart School Endowment*, 905 Central, 67801. Tel: 620-225-4802; Fax: 620-338-8268. Email: shcsclc@hotmail.com.

ELLINWOOD. *St. Joseph School Education Endowment Fund*, 214 N. Main St., 67526. Tel: 620-564-2534; Fax: 620-564-2613. Email: stjosephschurch@earthlink.net.

GARDEN CITY. *St. Dominic Grade School Endowment Fund*, 615 J.C. St., 67846. Tel: 620-276-2024; Fax: 620-276-2086.
The St. Mary Catholic Education Endowment Fund, 509 St. John St., 67846. Tel: 620-275-4204; Fax: 620-272-9971. Email: jimbaker@gcnet.com.

GREAT BEND. *Catholic Social Service Endowment Fund*, 2546 20th St., 67530. Tel: 620-792-1393; Fax: 620-792-1399. Email: slytle@cpcis.net.
Holy Family School, 4200 Broadway, 67530. Tel: 620-793-3265; Fax: 620-792-2798. Email: office@gbfamilycommunity.com. Mrs. Karen Moeder, Prin.

KINSLEY. *St. Nicholas School Endowment*, 720 E. 6th St., 67547. Tel: 620-659-2521; Fax: 620-659-2049. Email: stnick@midway.net. Maurice Gleason, Contact Person. Tel: 620-659-2919.

LARNED. *The Sacred Heart Grade School of Larned Education Endowment Fund*, 527 W. 12th St., 67550. Tel: 620-285-3025; Fax: 620-285-0097. Email: heartlarned@yahoo.com.

LIBERAL. *St. Anthony School Endowment Fund*, 1510 N. Calhoun St., 67901. Tel: 620-624-4135; Fax: 620-624-3553. Email: theroths@ptsi.net. Mark Roth, Contact Person.

PRATT. *The Sacred Heart School Education Endowment, Inc.*, 332 N. Oak St., 67124. Tel: 620-672-6352; Fax: 620-672-3748.

[D] CONVENTS AND RESIDENCES FOR SISTERS

GREAT BEND. *Immaculate Conception Convent*, 3600

Broadway, 67530-3692. Tel: 620-792-1232; Fax: 620-792-1746. Email: sisters@ksdom.org. Web: www.ksdom.org. Sisters Gemma Doll, O.P., Prioress; Lorena Bolte, O.P., Asst. Prioress; Renee Dreiling, O.P., Council Member; Amy McFrederick, O.P., Council Member; Eloise Hertel, O.P., Council Member.

Legal Title: *The Nuns of the Third Order of St. Dominic* Dominican Sisters of Great Bend Final Professed Sisters 115; Lay Associates 73.

Great Bend Dominican Sisters Office of Mission and Ministry 3600 Broadway, 67530-3692. Tel: 620-792-1232; Fax: 620-792-1746. Retreat Center. Total in Residence 45.

[E] SERVICES FOR THE ELDERLY

GREAT BEND. *Cedar Park Place, Inc.*, 3910 Cedar Park Pl., 67530-3692. Tel: 620-793-8115; Fax: 620-792-1746. Email: cedarpark.@ckan.com. Low and Middle Income Housing for Elderly and Handicapped.

[F] MISCELLANEOUS

DODGE CITY. *Manna House*, 1012 First, 67801. Tel: 620-227-6707. Laura Koehn, Exec. Dir. Short-term housing and food distrubution need. Total Staff 2; Total Assisted 2,964.

GARDEN CITY. *Catholic Agency-Migration & Refugee Service*, 1510 Taylor Plaza E., 67846. Tel: 620-276-7610; Fax: 620-276-9228. Email: mrs@gcnet.com. Ms. Levita Rohlman, Exec. Dir. Total Staff 1; Assisted 3,000.

GREAT BEND. *Family Crisis Center*, 1806 12th, P.O. Box 1543, 67530. Tel: 620-793-1965; 620-793-1966; 620-792-1885 (Crisis Line); Fax: 620-793-1964. Email: family.crisis@greatbend.com. Patty Henry, Contact Person. Total Staff 10; Total Assisted 690.

Heartland Center for Wholistic Health, 1005 Williams, 67530. Tel: 620-793-9067; Fax: 620-793-5817. Email: hcwh@ckan.com. Web: www.ckan.com/hcwh. Sr. Anita Schugart, O.P., Contact Person. A Ministry of the Dominican Sisters of Great Bend, KS., Reflexology, body massage, herbals. Total Staff 4.

St. Rose - Dominican Nurses Alumnae Association, 3600 Broadway, 67530. Tel: 620-792-1232; Fax: 620-792-1746. Email: sisters@ksdom.org. Sr. M. Terence Wasinger, Sec. & Contact Person.

Sommerset Place, 5803 16th Terrace, 67530. Tel: 620-793-8075; Fax: 620-793-7417. Email: bernie@somerset.kscoxmail.com. 60 Unit Apartment Complex.

LIBERAL. *Liberal Redemptorist Hispanic House Ministry, Inc.*, 419 W. First St., 67901-3601. Tel: 620-624-7846; Fax: 620-624-4193. Email: tjcssr@juno.com. Revs. Anthony Judge, C.Ss.R., Local Supr.; Michael McAndrew, C.Ss.R.; John Fahey, C.Ss.R.; Patrick A. Keyes, C.SS.R.; Brian Gilles, C.S.S.R.

RELIGIOUS INSTITUTES OF MEN REPRESENTED IN THE DIOCESE

For further details refer to the corresponding bracketed number in the Religious Institutes of Men or Women section.

[0200]—*Benedictine Monks*—O.S.B.
[0690]—*Jesuit Fathers and Brothers*—S.J.
[0270]—*Order of Carmelites*—O.Carm.
[1070]—*Redemptorist Fathers*—C.SS.R.
[1060]—*Society of the Precious Blood*—C.PP.S.

RELIGIOUS INSTITUTES OF WOMEN REPRESENTED IN THE DIOCESE

[0100]—*Adorers of the Blood of Christ*—A.S.C.
[]—*Mexican Passionist Srs.*—C.F.P.
[]—*Missionaries of the Charity of Mary Immaculate*—M.C.M.I.
[1070-24]—*Nuns of the Third Order of St. Dominic*—O.P.
[3830-18]—*Sisters of St. Joseph*—C.S.J.

NECROLOGY

† Birzer, Wenzel Leonard (Retired)—Died June 3, 2003

Archdiocese of Dubuque

(Archidioecesis Dubuquensis)

Most Reverend

JEROME HANUS, O.S.B., D.D.

Archbishop of Dubuque; ordained July 30, 1966; appointed Bishop of St. Cloud July 6, 1987; ordained and installed August 24, 1987; appointed Coadjutor Archbishop of Dubuque August 23, 1994; welcomed October 27, 1994; succeeded to the See October 16, 1995.

Most Reverend

DANIEL W. KUCERA, O.S.B., PH.D., D.D.

Retired Archbishop of Dubuque; ordained May 26, 1949; appointed Titular Bishop of Natchez and Auxiliary Bishop of Joliet June 6, 1977; ordained Bishop July 21, 1977; appointed Bishop of Salina March 11, 1980; installed May 7, 1980; appointed Archbishop of Dubuque December 20, 1983; installed February 23, 1984; retired October 16, 1995. *13952 E. Marina Dr., #612, Aurora, CO 80014.*

Chancery-Archdiocesan Center: P.O. Box 479, Dubuque, IA 52004-0479. Tel: 563-556-2580; Fax: 563-556-5464.

Web: www.arch.pvt.k12.ia.us

Email: dbqcco@arch.pvt.k12.ia.us

Square Miles 17,403.

Established July 28, 1837; Created an Archdiocese June 15, 1893.

Patrons of the Archdiocese: Primary: St. Raphael, the Archangel; Secondary: St. John Mary Vianney, Cure of Ars.

Corporate Title: The Archdiocese of Dubuque.

Comprises 30 Counties, that part of the State of Iowa north of the Counties of Polk, Jasper, Poweshiek, Iowa, Johnson, Cedar and Clinton and east of the Counties of Kossuth, Humboldt, Webster and Boone.

For legal titles of parishes and archdiocesan institutions, consult the Chancery.

STATISTICAL OVERVIEW

Personnel	
Archbishops	1
Retired Archbishops	1
Abbots	1
Retired Abbots	2
Priests: Diocesan Active in Diocese	123
Priests: Diocesan Active Outside Diocese	9
Priests: Retired, Sick or Absent	92
Number of Diocesan Priests	224
Religious Priests in Diocese	29
Total Priests in Diocese	253
Extern Priests in Diocese	2
Ordinations:	
Diocesan Priests	2
Transitional Deacons	3
Permanent Deacons	8
Permanent Deacons in Diocese	76
Total Brothers	26
Total Sisters	837
Parishes	
Parishes	199
With Resident Pastor:	
Resident Diocesan Priests	90
Resident Religious Priests	1
Without Resident Pastor:	
Administered by Priests	84
Administered by Deacons	7
Administered by Professed Religious Men	5
Administered by Religious Women	9
Administered by Lay People	3
Missions	1
Pastoral Centers	1
Closed Parishes	2
Professional Ministry Personnel:	
Brothers	2
Sisters	60
Lay Ministers	400
Welfare	
Catholic Hospitals	7
Total Assisted	1,398,575
Health Care Centers	3
Total Assisted	257
Homes for the Aged	6
Total Assisted	459
Day Care Centers	1
Total Assisted	24
Special Centers for Social Services	2
Total Assisted	419
Educational	
Seminaries, Diocesan	1
Students from This Diocese	2
Students from Other Diocese	1
Diocesan Students in Other Seminaries	9
Seminaries, Religious	1
Students Religious	95
Total Seminarians	106
Colleges and Universities	3
Total Students	4,392
High Schools, Diocesan and Parish	7
Total Students	2,666
Elementary Schools, Diocesan and Parish	52
Total Students	12,680
Catechesis/Religious Education:	
High School Students	6,114
Elementary Students	13,183
Total Students under Catholic Instruction	39,141
Teachers in the Diocese:	
Priests	3
Sisters	21
Lay Teachers	994
Vital Statistics	
Receptions into the Church:	
Infant Baptism Totals	2,983
Adult Baptism Totals	145
Received into Full Communion	337
First Communions	3,390
Confirmations	2,631
Marriages:	
Catholic	779
Interfaith	540
Total Marriages	1,319
Deaths	2,092
Total Catholic Population	211,847
Total Population	927,161

Former Bishops—Most Revs. MATHIAS LORAS, D.D., consecrated Dec. 10, 1837; died Feb. 19, 1858; CLEMENT SMYTH, O.C.S.O., D.D., consecrated May 3, 1857; died Sept. 22, 1865; JOHN HENNESSY, D.D., First Archbishop; consecrated Sept. 30, 1866; raised to the Archiepiscopal Dignity, June 16, 1893; died March 4, 1900; JOHN J. KEANE, D.D., consecrated Bishop of Richmond, Aug. 25, 1878; transferred to the Titular See of Jasso, Aug. 12, 1888; elevated to the Archiepiscopal Dignity with the title of Archbishop of Damascus, Jan. 29, 1897; transferred to the See of Dubuque, July 24, 1900; resigned April 3, 1911; appt. Titular Archbishop of Cios, April 28, 1911; died June 22, 1918; JAMES JOHN KEANE, D.D., ord. Dec. 23, 1882; consecrated Bishop of Cheyenne, Oct. 28, 1902; elevated to the Archiepiscopal Dignity and transferred to Dubuque, Aug. 11, 1911; died Aug. 2, 1929; FRANCIS J. L. BECKMAN, S.T.D., Titular Archbishop of Phulli; ord. June 20, 1902; appt. Bishop of Lincoln, Dec. 23, 1923; consecrated Bishop of Lincoln, May 1, 1924; Apostolic Administrator of Omaha, June 1, 1926 to July 4, 1928; elevated to Archiepiscopal Dignity and transferred to Dubuque, Jan. 17, 1930; appt. Assistant at the Pontifical Throne, April 21, 1928; resigned Nov. 11, 1946; died Oct 17, 1948; HENRY P. ROHLMAN, D.D., appt. Bishop of Davenport, May 20, 1927; consecrated July 25, 1927; appt. Coadjutor Archbishop of Dubuque "cum jure successionis" and Apostolic Administrator, June 15, 1944; installed Sept. 12, 1944; succeeded to Nov. 11, 1946; named Assistant at Pontifical Throne, Sept. 2, 1950; resigned and named Titular Archbishop of Cotrada, Dec. 2, 1954; died Sept. 13, 1957; LEO BINZ, D.D. (Retired), ord. March 15, 1924; appt. Titular Bishop of Pinara, Coadjutor Bishop and Apostolic Administrator of Winona, Nov. 21, 1942; consecrated Dec. 21, 1942; named Titular Archbishop of Silyum and Coadjutor to the Archbishop of Dubuque "cum jure successionis," Oct. 15, 1949; named Assistant at the Pontifical Throne, June 11, 1954; Archbishop of Dubuque, Dec. 2, 1954; Pallium conferred, June 12, 1958;; appt. Archbishop of St. Paul, Dec. 16, 1961; retired July, 1975; died Oct. 9, 1979; JAMES J. BYRNE, S.T.D. (Retired), appt. Titular Bishop of Etenna and Auxiliary Bishop of St. Paul, May 10, 1947; ord. Bishop, July 2, 1947; transferred to Boise, ID, June 16, 1956; appt. Archbishop of Dubuque, March 19, 1962; retired Aug. 23, 1983; named Apostolic Administrator; died Aug. 2, 1996; DANIEL W. KUCERA, O.S.B., Ph.D., D.D. (Retired), ord. May 26, 1949; appt. Titular Bishop of Natchez and Auxiliary Bishop of Joliet, June 6, 1977; ord. Bishop, July 21, 1977; appt. Bishop of Salina, KS, March 11, 1980; installed May 7, 1980; named Archbishop of Dubuque, Dec. 20, 1983; installed Feb. 23, 1984; retired Oct. 16, 1995.

Archbishop—Most Rev. JEROME HANUS, O.S.B., Archdiocesan Center, 1229 Mt. Loretta Ave., P.O. Box 479, Dubuque, 52004-0479. Tel: 563-556-2580.

Vicar General and Episcopal Vicar for Dubuque Region—Rev. Msgr. JAMES O. BARTA, Archdiocesan Center, 1229 Mt. Loretta Ave., P.O. Box 479, Dubuque, 52004-0479. Tel: 563-556-2580.

Episcopal Vicar for Cedar Rapids Region—Rev. Msgr. RUSSELL M. BLEICH, P.O. Box 2307, Cedar Rapids, 52406-2307. Tel: 319-366-1647; Fax: 319-366-0426.

Episcopal Vicar for Waterloo Region—Rev. Msgr. W.

DEAN WALZ, 320 Mulberry St., Waterloo, 50703. Tel: 319-235-5566; Fax: 319-235-5567.

Vicar for Hispanic Ministry—Rev. Msgr. LEON L. CONNOLLY, 320 Mulberry St., Waterloo, 50703-3598. Tel: 319-287-6414.

Vicar for Education—Rev. Msgr. THOMAS E. TOALE, Archdiocesan Center, 1229 Mt. Loretta Ave., P.O. Box 479, Dubuque, 52004-0479. Tel: 563-556-2580.

Judicial Vicar—Rev. THOMAS R. ZINKULA, Archdiocesan Center, 1229 Mt. Loretta Ave., P.O. Box 479, Dubuque, 52004-0479. Tel: 563-556-2580.

Chancellor—Sr. MARY LIANA GLYNN, O.P., J.C.L., Archdiocesan Center, 1229 Mt. Loretta Ave., P.O. Box 479, Dubuque, 52004-0479. Tel: 563-556-2580.

Archdiocesan Pastoral Center—Co-Directors: Rev. Msgr. JAMES O. BARTA; Sr. MARY LIANA GLYNN, O.P., J.C.L.; MADONNA WHITAKER, Sec., Archdiocesan Center, 1229 Mt. Loretta Ave., P.O. Box 479, Dubuque, 52004-0479. Tel: 563-556-2580.

Finance Officer—RICHARD L. RUNDE, Archdiocesan Center, 1229 Mt. Loretta Ave., P.O. Box 479, Dubuque, 52004-0479. Tel: 563-556-2580.

College of Consultors—Most Rev. JEROME HANUS, O.S.B.; Rev. Msgrs. W. DEAN WALZ; RUSSELL M. BLEICH; JAMES O. BARTA; Revs. RICHARD J. AMENT; CARL A. RIES; Rev. Msgr. RALPH P. SIMINGTON; Very Rev. LYLE L. WILGENBUSCH.

Deans—Very Revs. DONALD J. PLAMONDON, Bellevue; DONALD L. KLEIN, Cedar Rapids; GARY KRAPFL, Decorah; LYLE L. WILGENBUSCH, Dubuque; Rev. Msgr. EDWARD C. PETTY, Dyersville; Very Rev. FREDERICK C. FANGMANN, Elkader; Rev. Msgr. RALPH P. SIMINGTON, Independence; Very Revs. EVERETT HEMANN, Marshalltown; KENNETH B. GEHLING, Mason City; Rev. Msgr. JOHN W. HEMANN, New Hampton; Very Revs. DENNIS D. JUHL, Waterloo; JAMES L. MILLER, Webster City.

Archdiocesan Central Offices

Archdiocesan Pastoral Center—1229 Mt. Loretta Ave., Dubuque, 52003-8787. Tel: 563-556-2580; Fax: 563-556-5464. *P.O. Box 479, Dubuque, Office Hours: Mon.-Fri. 8:30-4:30 52004-0479.* Most Rev. JEROME HANUS, O.S.B., D.D.; Rev. Msgr. JAMES O. BARTA, Vicar Gen. & Co-Dir. Pastoral Center; Sr. MARY LIANA GLYNN, O.P., J.C.L., Chancellor & Co-Dir. Pastoral Center. Secretaries: BETTY SCHUELLER; BEV RECH.

Archives—Rev. LORAS C. OTTING, Dir. (Retired); Rev. Msgr. EDGAR J. KURT, Archivist Emeritus (Retired).

Campaign for Human Development—JAMES L. YEAST, Dir., 1229 Mt. Loretta Ave., P.O. Box 1309, Dubuque, 52004-1309. Tel: 563-556-2580; ED HABERKORN, Admin. Asst.

Campus Ministry—Rev. JOHN S. HAUGEN, Dir., Loras College, P.O. Box 178, Dubuque, 52004-0178. Tel: 563-588-7108.

Catholic Cemeteries of the Archdiocese of Dubuque—RICHARD L. RUNDE, Dir., Finance Office, 1229 Mt. Loretta Ave., Dubuque, 52003-8787. Tel: 563-556-2580.

Catholic Charities—

Administrative Offices—JAMES L. YEAST, Dir.; JOSEPH FEATHERSTON, Assoc. Dir. Catholic Charities; ED HABERKORN, Admin. Asst.; DEBRA JASPER, Office Mgr.; MARTHA DEVEAUX, Sec.; CAROL CALLAHAN, Business Mgr., Business Office, 1229 Mt. Loretta Ave., P.O. Box 1309, Dubuque, 52004-1309. Tel: 563-556-2580.

Branch Offices—

Ames—MARY JO PFEIFER, 2210 Lincoln Way, Ames, 50014. Tel: 515-296-2759.

Cedar Rapids—GARY STEJSKAL, Supvr.; LYN PIOTROWSKI, Office Mgr.; JENNIFER BARRY; MARIA GARLIE, 1430 Second Ave. S.E., Cedar Rapids, 52403. Tel: 319-364-7121.

Decorah—CHARLES DOPKE, P.O. Box 1309, Dubuque, 52004-1309. Tel: 800-772-2758.

Dubuque—JOSEPH FEATHERSTON, Supvr.; ERIN LANGE; TOM SHEA; ANGELLA LINK, P.O. Box 1309, Dubuque, 52004-1309. Tel: 563-556-2580.

Mason City—THOMAS FLAHERTY, Will F. Muse Center, 600 First St. N.W., Ste. 105, Mason City, 50401. Tel: 641-424-9683.

Waterloo—THOMAS FLAHERTY, Supvr.; DENISE MAAS-ROUS; ORLYN WATHIER; Rev. KENNETH C. STECHER; MICHELLE SPRIO, Office Mgr., Kimball Ridge Center, 2101 Kimball Ave., Waterloo, 50702. Tel: 319-272-2080.

Special Programs—

Adoption—JOYCE CONNORS, Dubuque Office.

Hispanic Counselor—Sr. EILEEN MCGOVERN, B.V.M.

Refugee Resettlement and Immigration—Dubuque Office: JOSEPH FEATHERSTON; MARCIA SOLA.

Social Concerns/Iowa Catholic Conference—JAMES L. YEAST, Dubuque Office.

Catholic Committee on Scouting—Very Rev. LYLE L. WILGENBUSCH, Archdiocesan Chap., St. Joseph the Worker, 60 S. Algona St., Dubuque, 52001-5605. Tel: 563-588-1433; G. J. (JERRY) HOLBACH, Chm., Box 1977, Waterloo, 50704-1977. Tel: 319-296-2950 (office).

Continuing Formation of Clergy—Rev. Msgrs. JAMES O. BARTA, Dir., Sabbaticals & Priests' Graduate Studies; W. DEAN WALZ, Dir. Continuing Educ. & Priests' Convocation; BEV RECH, Sec., Archdiocesan Center, 1229 Mt. Loretta Ave., Dubuque, 52003-8787. Tel: 563-556-2580.

Council of Catholic Women—Rev. Msgr. W. DEAN WALZ, Moderator; EDNA BRUNKHORST, 104 Willow Circle, Waverly, 50677. Tel: 319-352-3486; MARGARET KOLASH, Sec. & Public Rels., Office, 1229 Mt. Loretta Ave., Dubuque, 52003-8787. Tel: 563-556-2580; 319-479-2214.

Bellevue Deanery—HELEN ZEIMET, Springbrook. Tel: 563-689-4466.

Cedar Rapids Deanery—LILLIAN MCGIVERN, Keystone. Tel: 319-442-3486.

Decorah Deanery—MARY RAUSCH, Fort Atkinson. Tel: 563-586-2150.

Dubuque Deanery—MARY DUNNE, Dubuque. Tel: 563-556-7997.

Dyersville Deanery—ANN DIETRICH, Earlville. Tel: 563-923-5415.

Elkader Deanery—NEVA FISCHER, Strawberry Point. Tel: 563-933-4957.

Independence Deanery—CONNIE MAHONEY, Independence. Tel: 319-334-4679.

Marshalltown Deanery—ELAINE UPAH, Garwin. Tel: 641-752-2165.

Mason City Deanery—CINDY MARY, Forest City. Tel: 641-585-2082.

New Hampton Deanery—FLORENCE THRONDSON, New Hampton. Tel: 641-394-4873.

Waterloo Deanery—MARY ELLEN HELLMAN, Waterloo. Tel: 319-233-7084.

Webster City Deanery—MARY ANN SPITLER, Belmond. Tel: 641-444-3174.

Development Office—PAUL J. FROMMELT, Dir., P.O. Box 479, Dubuque, 52004-0479. Tel: 563-556-2580; LOIS THILMANY, Office Mgr.; DENISE AIRD, Sec.

Educational System—

Vicar for Educational Services and Superintendent of Schools—Rev. Msgr. THOMAS E. TOALE, Vicar, Educational & Supt. of Schools; JAMES OSTERBERGER, Dir., Educational Planning & Technology; CHERIE CASEY, Curriculum Dir.; ITZA HEIM, Sec.

Catholic Schools (in addition to the above)—DEB FLECKENSTEIN, Special Projects Coord.; Sr. JEAN MARIE BRADY, B.V.M., Cedar Rapids Regl. Dir. Educational Svcs.; JULIE KAPSCH, Sec.; ALICE CONLON, Waterloo Regl. Dir. Educational Svcs.

Catechetical Services (in addition to the above)—LORETTA RYAN, Dir. Catechetical Svcs. Assoc. Directors Catechetical Services: MARGE KRAWCZUK, Dubuque; JULIE JOHNSON, Cedar Rapids; BETH DERR, Dyersville; Sr. MARGARET ANN KRAMER, P.B.V.M., Dubuque; PHYLLIS BERTHEL, Sec.

Persons With Disabilities—Sr. MARCI BLUM, O.S.F., Dir.; PATRICIA NEISES, Sec.

Family Life and Adult Faith Office—Sr. MARCI BLUM, O.S.F., Dir.; GINNY NEUWOEHNER, Sec., Archdiocesan Center, 1229 Mt. Loretta Ave., Dubuque, 52003-8787. Tel: 563-556-2580.

Engaged Encounter—Rev. PHILLIP E. SCHMITT, Spiritual Advisor (Retired), 212 1/2 7th St., S.E., Mt. Vernon, 52314-1518. Tel: 319-895-0404.

For Registration—Family Life Office, 1229 Mt. Loretta Ave., Dubuque, 52003-8787. Tel: 563-556-2580.

Marriage Encounter—Family Life Office, 1229 Mt. Loretta Ave., Dubuque, 52003-8787. Tel: 563-556-2580.

Worldwide Marriage Encounter—Tel: 800-795-LOVE.

Marriage Retorno—Directors: Deacon MICHAEL OATES; MAUREEN OATES, 127 Kaspend Pl., Cedar Falls, 50613. Tel: 319-268-0202.

Natural Family Planning—JERRY GREBASCH; DIANA GREBASCH. Tel: 515-387-1378.

Pre-Cana—Family Life Office, 1229 Mt. Loretta Ave., Dubuque, 52003-8787. Tel: 563-556-2580. Dubuque Area: SANDY ERNSDORFF, 2085 Hale St., Dubuque, 52001. Tel: 563-556-2859; TOM DANNER; MARY JO DANNER, 16247 Country Club Dr., Peosta, 52068. Tel: 563-588-4069. Dyersville Area, Directors: JUDD GROVER; MICHELLE GROVER, 803 1st Ave. W., Dyersville, 52040. Tel: 563-875-8434. Decorah, Elkader, New Hampton Areas: VACANT, For registration contact: Family Life Office, 1229 Mt. Loretta Ave., Dubuque, 52003-8787. Tel: 563-556-2580. Independence & Waterloo Areas: VACANT, Family Life Office, 1229 Mt. Loretta Ave., Dubuque, 52003-8787. Tel: 563-556-2580. Cedar Rapids Area: MARY MCDOWELL, Contact Person, 4107 Lark Ct., N.E., Cedar Rapids, 52403. Tel: 319-393-9126; PAT MURPHY, Co. Dir.; SANDY MURPHY, Co. Dir., 1130 33rd St. S.E., Cedar Rapids, 52403. Tel: 319-365-9839. Marshalltown & Webster City Areas: TIM SIMODYNES; TERRI SIMODYNES, 1510 Jackson Dr., Ames, 50010. Tel: 515-663-0715. Mason City Area, Directors: DENNIS POPOWSKI; CHAR POPOWSKI, 560 Center Ave., Garner, 50438. Tel: 641-923-6045.

Retrouvaille—Contacts: GEORGE CRUM; DEE CRUM, Box 448, Le Grand, 50142. Tel: 641-479-2650; DICK SMITH; JOYCE SMITH, 420 10th Ave., S.E., Dyersville, 52040. Tel: 563-875-8791.

Sponsor Couple— Contact parish.

Re-marriage Preparation—Family Life Office, 1229 Mt. Loretta Ave., Dubuque, 52003-8787. Tel: 563-556-2580.

Finance Office—RICHARD L. RUNDE, Finance Officer; PENNY CARPENTER, Auditor; PAULA MONTAG, Controller; KEN RAHE, Business Mgr.; JANICE TUEGEL, Accounting Clerk; ELAINE HILDEBRAND, Bookkeeper/Sec., P.O. Box 479, Dubuque, 52004-0479. Tel: 563-556-2580.

Health Care—JANINE MARIE IDZIAK, Ph.D., Consultant, P.O. Box 479, Dubuque, 52004-0479. Tel: 563-556-2580; PHYLLIS BERTHEL, Sec.

Hispanic Ministry—Cedar Rapids Office: MONICA PAULINA VALLEJO, 857 3rd Ave. S.E., Cedar Rapids, 52403. Tel: 319-362-8689; Fax: 319-362-4826. Dubuque Office: Sr. JEANETTE MCCARTHY, P.B.V.M., 1425 Iowa St., Dubuque, 52001-4890. Tel: 563-584-0640; Fax: 563-584-0093. Hampton Office: HECTOR HERNANDEZ, 1405 N. Federal St., Hampton, 50441. Tel: 641-456-2797. Marshalltown Office: Sr. CHRISTINE FEAGAN, O.P., 12 W. Linn, P.O. Box 642, Marshalltown, 50158-0642. Tel: 641-753-7815; Fax: 641-752-6277. Postville Office: PAUL RAEL, P.O. Box 369, Postville, 52162-0369. Tel: 563-864-3142. Waterloo Office: Sr. KATHLEEN GRACE, O.S.F., 320 Mulberry St., Waterloo, 50703-3598. Tel: 319-234-6744.

Hispanic Pastoral Outreach—JAMES L. YEAST, Archdiocesan Dir.

Priests Assigned to Hispanic Ministry—Rev. Msgr. LEON L. CONNOLLY; Revs. BERNARD C. GRADY; RICARDO CORONADO ARRASCUE; Very Rev. JAMES L. MILLER.

Parish Hispanic Ministry—New Hampton: Sr. JEANNE TRANEL, O.P., 239 S. Walnut, New Hampton, 50659. Tel: 641-394-2105. Tama: TOM CHRISTOFFER; ANNE CHRISTOFFER, 900 Park St., Tama, 52339. Tel: 641-484-2306.

Holy Childhood, Pontifical Association—Rev. Msgr. ROBERT L. FERRING, Dir. (Retired), Archdiocesan Center, 1229 Mt. Loretta Ave., Dubuque, 52003-8787. Tel: 563-556-2580; NANCY EISBACH, Sec.

Human Resources—PAM GEHL, Dir.; TERRY DUVALL-GELMS, Sec., 1229 Mt. Loretta Ave., Dubuque, 52003-8787. Tel: 563-556-2580.

Insurance: Property and Liability (Dubuque Archdiocesan Protection Program)—RICH EARLES, Field Representative, Archdiocesan Center, 1229 Mt. Loretta Ave., Dubuque, 52003-8787. Tel: 563-556-2580; PATRICIA NEISES, Sec.

Jail and Prison Ministry—Deacon ED WEBER, Coord., 1158 Independence Ave., Waterloo, 50703. Tel: 319-232-1584.

Lay Formation—Sr. CARLA POPES, P.B.V.M., Dir. Secretaries: JANE MOURING; JUDY ARLEN, Archdiocesan Center, 1229 Mt. Loretta Ave., P.O. Box 479, Dubuque, 52004-0479. Tel: 563-556-2580.

Legion of Mary—Rev. JOHN R. HUSSMANN (Retired), P.O. Box 479, Dubuque, 52004-0479. Tel: 563-556-2580.

Management Information Services—JOHN NIGG, Dir.; MARY DOLAN, Email Admin.; PEG HENNAGIR, Sec.

Media Services—KIM FELDMAN, Dir.; Sr. CAROL HOVERMAN, O.S.F., Dir. Communications; LARRY GAUL, Media Technician, 1229 Mt. Loretta Ave., Dubuque, 52003-8787. Tel: 563-556-2580; 800-876-3546; BARBARA TUCKER, Media Center Specialist; BARBARA GLEASON, Media Clerk.

Metropolitan Tribunal—P.O. Box 479, Dubuque, 52004-0479. Tel: 563-556-2580. (Please send all dispensation requests to the Tribunal.)

Judicial Vicar—Rev. THOMAS R. ZINKULA.

Defenders of the Bond—Rev. Msgr. RICHARD P. FUNKE; Sr. MARY LIANA GLYNN, O.P., J.C.L.; Very Rev. DONALD J. PLAMONDON; Rev. Msgr. DAVID A. WHEELER (Retired).

Judges—Revs. SCOTT E. BULLOCK; JOSEPH L. HAUER; Deacon GERALD JORGENSEN, Ph.D., J.C.L.; Revs. DOUGLAS J. LOECKE; MARK R. NEMMERS; Sr. FRANCINE QUILLIN, P.B.V.M., J.C.L.; Rev. Msgr. W. DEAN WALZ; Rev. THOMAS R. ZINKULA.

Ecclesiastical Attorneys—Rev. Msgrs. RICHARD P. FUNKE; W. DEAN WALZ.

Promoter of Justice—Rev. Msgr. DAVID A. WHEELER (Retired).

Notary and Office Secretaries—THERESA HOUSELOG; CHARLOTTE NEISES.

Newly Ordained Program—Rev. SCOTT E. BULLOCK,

Dir.; BEV RECH, Sec., 1229 Mt. Loretta Ave., Dubuque, 52003-8787. Tel: 563-556-2580.

Newspaper "The Witness"—Sr. CAROL HOVERMAN, O.S.F., Editor, Archdiocesan Center, 1229 Mt. Loretta Ave., P.O. Box 917, Dubuque, 52004-0917. Tel: 563-588-0556. Staff: JUDY BANDY, Advertising & Staff Writer; BRET FEAR, Production & Design; CAROLE WELU, Circulation & Sec.; STEVE MCMAHON, Staff Writer.

Pastoral Planning Office—Sr. MARY MONTGOMERY, O.P., Dir.; MADONNA WHITAKER, Sec., P.O. Box 479, Dubuque, 52004-0479. Tel: 563-556-2580.

Permanent Diaconate Program—Deacon TOM LANG, Dir., 1229 Mt. Loretta Ave., P.O. Box 479, Dubuque, 52004-0479. Tel: 563-556-2580. Asst. Directors: Deacons JOHN BAKER; LEONARD FROYEN; GERALD JORGENSEN, Ph.D., J.C.L.

Print Shop—ROBERT GOLDTHORPE, Mgr., P.O. Box 479, Dubuque, 52004-0479. Tel: 563-556-2580.

Propagation of the Faith—Rev. Msgr. ROBERT L. FERRING (Retired); NANCY EISBACH, Sec., Archdiocesan Center, 1229 Mt. Loretta Ave., Dubuque, 52003-8787. Tel: 563-556-2580.

Respect Life Office—JAMES L. YEAST, Dir., Catholic Charities; ED HABERKORN, Admin. Asst., P.O. Box 1309, Dubuque, 52004-1309. Tel: 563-556-2580; 800-772-2758.

Rural Life Office—DONALD KLAUKE, Archdiocesan Dir.; MARY THERESE KLAUKE, Sec., 511 Bear Creek Dr., Dorchester, 52140-7505. Tel: 800-772-2758.

Saint Mary's Home, Inc.—JAMES L. YEAST, Dir., P.O. Box 1309, Dubuque, 52004. Tel: 563-556-2580; PAUL SCHROEDER, Housing Admin. Tel: 563-556-5125.

Seminarians—Rev. SCOTT E. BULLOCK, Dir.; BEV RECH, Sec., 1229 Mt. Loretta Ave., Dubuque, 52003-8787. Tel: 563-556-2580.

Stewardship—Ms. LINDA MANTERNACH, Dir.; LOIS THILMANY, Office Mgr. Tel: 563-556-2530.

Vocation Awareness—Revs. PHILLIP G. GIBBS, Dir.; DAVID M. BECKMAN, Assoc. Dir., Waterloo Region; JON M. SEDA, Assoc. Dir., Cedar Rapids Region; HENRY P. HUBER, Assoc. Dir., Dubuque Region; BEV RECH, Sec., Archdiocesan Center, 1229 Mt. Loretta Ave., Dubuque, 52003-8787. Tel: 563-556-2580.

Worship Office—THERESA HARVEY, Dir. Secretaries: JANE MOURING; GINNY NEUWOEHNER, 1229 Mt. Loretta Ave., P.O. Box 479, Dubuque, 52004-0479. Tel: 563-556-2580.

Youth Formation/Young Adult Ministry—DIANE FLAHERTY, Dir.; JUDY ARLEN, Sec., Archdiocesan Center, 1229 Mt. Loretta Ave., Dubuque, 52003-8787. Tel: 563-556-2580.

Archdiocesan Boards, Commissions and Councils

Administrative Board—Most Rev. JEROME HANUS, O.S.B.; Rev. Msgr. JAMES O. BARTA; Sisters MARY LIANA GLYNN, O.P., J.C.L.; MARY MONTGOMERY, O.P.; RICHARD L. RUNDE.

Adult Formation Committee—JULIE BLOOME; Sisters MARCI BLUM, O.S.F.; DONNA BURKE, O.S.F.; DAVE CUSHING; BARBARA DUGGAN; Sisters LOIS ERPELDING, O.S.F.; MADONNA M. FRIEDMAN, O.S.F.; BARBARA GATCH; Sisters MARYANN GREENWALD, S.S.N.D.; MARY HARGRAFEN, O.S.F.; MARY L. LECHTENBERG, O.S.F.; DENNIS MCDERMOTT; CINDY PFIFFNER; CATHY SCHMITZ; Deacon TOM SINK.

Advisory Committee of Persons with Disabilities—MITZI BAKER; WILMA BILLHORN; Sr. MARCI BLUM, O.S.F.; BOB BRUNKAN; FRANCES BRUNKAN; DONNA FELD; D. J. JAEGER; Rev. JERRY KOPACEK; Deacon STEPHEN MACDONALD; KIM MAJERUS; CATHY MURPHY; STEVEN SCHRADER; NANCY THOMPSON; KEVIN WILLE.

American Martyrs Retreat House Advisory Board—Sr. M. JEANINE KUHN, P.B.V.M, Dir.; JANINE WHIPPS, Chm.; JOAN GLAZA, Sec.; MARGUERITE BERTELSEN; EDWARD J. GALLAGHER JR.; Sr. MARY MICHELLE GALLAGHER, P.B.V.M.; ROGER UETER; RON LEIBOLD; Rev. Msgr. W. DEAN WALZ, Ex Officio.

Board of Education—JIM BOWES, Pres., Appointed; BILL BROWN, Vice Pres., Dyersville Deanery; JEAN T. JOHNSON, Sec., Marshalltown Deanery, Members:. Sister Representatives: Sisters BENJAMIN DUSCHNER, P.B.V.M.; MARIE GEMAR, O.S.F. Priest Representatives: Revs. KENNETH J. GLASER; DWAYNE J. THOMAN. Appointed by Archbishop: MARTHA GARCIA; JOHN WALDMEIER; KAREN A. VOLZ; RON THIELEN, Bellevue Deanery; JULIE BELLENDIER, Cedar Rapids Deanery; MARY KOOPMAN, Decorah Deanery; NORMA "PEGGY" SWIFT, Dubuque Deanery; JOHN KALB, Elkader Deanery; VACANT, Independence Deanery; JUDY KRAMER, Mason City Deanery; KENDRA GILBERT, New Hampton Deanery; RICHARD KLEIN, Waterloo Deanery; RICHARD PEED, Webster City Deanery. Liaisons: CATHY SCHMITZ, Adult Formation Committee; Rev. JERRY F. KOPACEK, Archdiocesan Advisory Committee on Persons with Disabilities. Ex Officio Members: Most Rev. JEROME G. HANUS, O.S.B., Archbishop of Dubuque; Rev. Msgrs. JAMES O. BARTA; RUSSELL M. BLEICH; W. DEAN WALZ; THOMAS E. TOALE, Vicar Education & Supt. Schools; LORETTA RYAN, Dir. Catechetical Svcs.

Building Commission—Rev. Msgr. RUSSELL M. BLEICH, Chair; CHUCK DEKOVIC; RALPH EMERSON; Deacon LAVERNE FLAGEL; THERESA HARVEY; Rev. Msgr. STANLEY J. HAYEK (Retired); JAMES HYNES; RAY LARSEN; Rev. NEIL J. MANTERNACH; JAMES OSTERBERGER; KEN RAHE, Recording Sec.; RICHARD L. RUNDE Exec. Sec.; Rev. Msgr. CARL L. SCHMITT; WAYNE SNYDER; LEO THEISEN; Rev. Msgr. NEIL W. TOBIN (Retired); ED WINEINGER.

Catholic Charities and St. Mary's Home Boards of Directors—Most Rev. JEROME HANUS, O.S.B., Pres.; Rev. Msgr. JAMES O. BARTA, Vice Pres.; JAMES L. YEAST, Treas.; ALFRED HUGHES, Sec.

Deanery Representatives—MARCI CAPESIUS, Bellevue; MARY JO RATER, Cedar Rapids; VACANT, Decorah; FRITZ GANSHIRT, Dubuque; ROBERT BRUNKAN, Dyersville; LARRY MURPHY, Elkader; CATHY NEWTON, Independence; JUDY MCGEE, Marshalltown; SUE FOY, Mason City; WILLIAM FELLER, New Hampton; JEFFREY FITZPATRICK, Waterloo; TERRY ANDERSON, Webster City; ELDON HERRIG, At Large; Deacon TOM WALSH, At Large.

Church Design/Renovation Commission—THERESA HARVEY, Exec. Sec.; PAM JOHNSTON, Chm.; Very Rev. DENNIS D. JUHL; Rev. NEIL J. MANTERNACH; Sr. RUTH JACKSON, S.V.M.

Diaconal Council—Most Rev. JEROME HANUS, O.S.B., Pres.; Deacons JIM FREET, Chm.; TOM LANG, Exec. Sec.

Ames Region—Deacon ROGER FOLT; CHAR VANKERCKVOORDE.

Cedar Rapids Region—Deacons LAVERNE FLAGEL; TOM WALSH.

Dubuque Region—Deacons JAMES KEAN; PAUL PECKOSH.

Mason City Region—Deacon DENNIS POPOWSKI; JEAN CASEY.

Waterloo Region—LORI FREET; Deacon NORMAN SCHAULS.

Appointed—Deacons JOHN BAKER; JOHN HERMAN; JIM FREET, APC Liaison.

Iowa Catholic Conference Liaison—Deacon MICHAEL OATES.

Due Process Board—ALFRED HUGHES, Chair, Dubuque. Tel: 563-557-7360 (Office); 563-583-7541 (Home); Sr. SHEILA GERAGHTY, R.S.M.; BEV KIRBY; PATRICK LENANE; Sr. JOAN LINGEN, B.V.M.; JEANINE MATT; Deacon MICHAEL OATES; Rev. STEVEN J. ROSONKE; JOSEPH STAUDT; Rev. CRAIG E. STEIMEL.

Family Life Advisory Board—JAYNE ROUSE, Chm.; DICK HENNEBERRY, Vice Chm.; Rev. PHILLIP G. GIBBS; ARLENE HENNEBERRY; TROY MUNDT; GINNY NEUWOEHNER; ALICE NOETHE, O.S.F.; Sr. MARCI BLUM, O.S.F.; JAYNE ROUSE; DAN ROUSE; Rev. KENNETH C. STECHER; SAL WEBER.

Finance Council—Most Rev. JEROME HANUS, O.S.B., Chm.; RICHARD L. RUNDE, Exec. Sec.; KEN RAHE, Recording Sec.; Rev. Msgr. JAMES O. BARTA; DONALD BERGAN; Rev. Msgrs. RICHARD P. FUNKE; ROBERT G. HOGAN; Deacon MATTHEW F. BERRY; Sr. MARGARET COSGROVE, B.V.M.; PAUL J. FROMMELT; ANN OSTERHAUS; KAREN STUEM; Rev. Msgr. THOMAS E. TOALE; DAN WELU.

Human Resources Advisory Committee—PAM GEHL, Chm.; Sr. JEAN GORDON, B.V.M.; DAVID HEIAR; JERRY KOPPES; Very Rev. GARY KRAPFL; KATHY KRUSIE; JULIE NEIMEYER.

Lay Formation Advisory Board—Rev. Msgr. JAMES O. BARTA; Rev. JAMES P. BROKMAN; DAVE CUSHING; ANDREW CONRAD; Very Rev. DENNIS D. JUHL; PAT NIXON; JANET O'MEARA; Sr. CARLA POPES, P.B.V.M.; SUSAN M. SCHLETTER CATHY SCHMITZ; MARTHA SIMMONS.

Medical-Moral Commission—JANINE MARIE IDZIAK, Ph.D., Chm.; Rev. DAVID M. BECKMAN; Sr. JAMES MARIE DONAHUE, R.S.M., Ph.D.; KEVIN HEALY, M.D.; STEPHEN HOY, M.D.; Revs. WILLIAM M. JOENSEN; STEPHEN A. LUNDGREN; CAROL SCHMIDT, R.N.C., M.S.H.; Sr. DOLORES ULLRICH, O.S.F.; RICHARD WHITTY, J.D.

PAMAD (Pastoral Associates/Ministers of the Archdiocese of Dubuque)—Sr. MARLENE MCDOWELL, S.F.C.C., Pres. Tel: 563-852-5104; ROSEANN WILEY-HAYEK, Vice Pres. Tel: 319-363-5238; BARBARA GATCH, Sec. Tel: 563-582-7646; PEG MCGARVEY, Treas. Tel: 319-233-8060.

Pastoral Council—Most Rev. JEROME HANUS, O.S.B., Pres.; Sr. MARY HARGRAFEN, O.S.F., Chm.; DAVID HEIAR, Vice Chm.; JUDY SHEPARD, Sec.; Sr. MARY MONTGOMERY, O.P., Exec. Sec. JOHN BALONG; Rev. Msgrs. JAMES O. BARTA; RUSSELL M. BLEICH; Sr. DONNA BURKE, O.S.F.; JOE DAVIS; ROSA MARIA DE FINDLAY; GARY DELLAERT; Deacon JIM FLEET; Sr. MARY CORITA HEID, R.S.M.; JOAN HOFFMANN; DAN KOCH; PATRICK LENANE; Sr. JOANN O'CONNELL, B.V.M.; J. PATRICK MCDONNELL; BARBARA MILLS; MARGARET MOHR; MARY O'NEILL; JOSEPH STAUDT; Rev. Msgr. W. DEAN WALZ; DIANE ZINKULA.

Permanent Diaconate Formation Board—Deacon TOM LANG, Chm.; CLARICE FLAGEL; Deacon LEONARD FROYEN; Rev. JOHN S. HAUGEN; Deacon DANIEL HOEGER; MARY JENNEY; Deacons GERALD JORGENSEN, Ph.D., J.C.L.; MICHAEL WHITTERS.

Personnel Advisory Board—Revs. PHILIP E. THOMPSON, Chm., At Large; DENNIS J. COLTER, Sec., Age Group II; ALOYSIUS J. VORWALD, Age Group I; MICHAEL J. MESCHER, Age Group III; THOMAS J. MCDERMOTT, Age Group IV.

Priests' Council—Most Rev. JEROME HANUS, O.S.B., Pres.; Rev. SCOTT E. BULLOCK, Chm. Ex Officio Members: Rev. Msgrs. JAMES O. BARTA; RUSSELL M. BLEICH; W. DEAN WALZ; THOMAS E. TOALE; LEON L. CONNOLLY.

Retired Priests' Representatives—Rev. GERALD A. CONDON (Retired); Rev. Msgr. DAVID A. WHEELER (Retired).

Religious Priests Representative—Rev. XAVIER L. DIETER, O.C.S.O.

Deanery Representatives—Revs. ROBERT F. DAVIES, Bellevue Deanery; DAVID H. O'CONNOR, Cedar Rapids Deanery; THOMAS J. MCDERMOTT, Cedar Rapids Deanery; JOHN A. MOSER, Decorah Deanery; DANIEL J. KNEPPER, Dubuque Deanery; MICHAEL J. MESCHER, Dubuque Deanery; RAYMOND A. BURKLE, Dyersville Deanery; MARVIN J. BRIES, Elkader Deanery; GABRIEL C. ANDERSON, Independence Deanery; SCOTT F. BOONE, Marshalltown Deanery; JERRY W. BLAKE, Mason City Deanery; Rev. Msgr. CARL L. SCHMITT, New Hampton Deanery; Revs. CLAYTON LANDHERR, Waterloo Deanery; JACK R. FLAHERTY, Webster City Deanery.

Review Board for Sexual Abuse of Minors by Clergy and Other Church Personnel—F. JAMES BRADLEY, Cedar Rapids; CHRIS CORKEN, Dubuque; KATHY LOCH KLEIN, Dubuque; JANET MEAD, Marshalltown; MARY NAUMAN, Dubuque; Rev. JAMES NIEMAN, Dubuque; Sr. SUSAN O'CONNOR, R.S.M., Cedar Rapids; Rev. Msgrs. THOMAS E. TOALE, Dubuque; DAVID A. WHEELER, Dubuque (Retired); Dr. BARBARA SULLIVAN WOODWARD, Dubuque.

Saint Raphael Priest Fund Society—

Board of Directors/Priest Pension Plan Board of Trustees—Most Rev. JEROME HANUS, O.S.B., Pres.; Rev. Msgr. JAMES O. BARTA, Vice Pres.; Rev. EUGENE C. KUTSCH, Sec. & Treas. (Retired); RICHARD L. RUNDE, Plan Admin. Directors: Rev. Msgr. WALTER L. BRUNKAN; Revs. GERALD A. CONDON (Retired); PATRICK G. GEARY (Retired); Rev. Msgrs. KARL L. GLOVIK; STANLEY J. HAYEK (Retired); ROBERT G. HOGAN; Revs. JERRY F. KOPACEK; THOMAS J. MCDERMOTT; MICHAEL J. MESCHER; Rev. Msgrs. RALPH P. SIMINGTON; NEIL W. TOBIN (Retired); Rev. THOMAS R. ZINKULA.

Seminary Board—Rev. SCOTT E. BULLOCK, Chm.; ANN M. BECKMAN; Revs. JERRY F. KOPACEK; DAVID A. SCHATZ; LOUIS M. JAEGER.

Stewardship and Development Committee—DONALD BERGAN; JIM BOWES; MATT BRANDES; BARBARA DUGGAN; FAYE FINNEGAN; Revs. JOHN A. GOSSMAN; BERNARD C. GRADY; MICHAEL G. SCHUELLER; SEAN SMITH; KAREN A. VOLZ; Very Rev. LYLE L. WILGENBUSCH; SANDY WILGENBUSCH. Ex Officio: PAUL J. FROMMELT; Rev. Msgr. ROBERT G. HOGAN; Ms. LINDA MANTERNACH; RICHARD L. RUNDE; Rev. Msgr. THOMAS E. TOALE.

Victim Assistance Coordinator—Dr. THOMAS ANDEREGG. Tel: 563-556-1225; JOAN HOFFMANN. Tel: 866-319-4636; MAUREEN OATES. Tel: 800-803-6758.

Worship Commission—Sr. ROSEMARY RIESBURG, F.S.P.A., Chm.; CHRISTINE CARRIER, Vice Chm.; THERESA HARVEY, Exec. Sec.; BOB BURKE, Recording Sec.; Very Rev. EVERETT HEMANN; Deacon TIMOTHY LOBIANCO; Rev. CLAYTON LANDHERR; Sr. MILDRED LEUENBERGER, O.S.F.; JEAN LEUTE; Sr. JULIE MARSH, P.B.V.M.; Rev. DENNIS J. QUINT; Ms. BECKY SEARCY; Rev. JAMES L. SECORA.

Youth Commission—DIANE FLAHERTY, Exec. Dir. Adult Members: BETH DERR; BOB GARDNER; Rev. KENNETH J. GLASER; ANN NICKLAUS-SCHMELZER. Youth Members: RICK ADAMS; CATHERINE BOUSKA; MICHAEL DALY; AMY FUNKE; LIZ GEISTKEMPER; MONICA GREEN; RENEE HARPER; ASHLEIGH HEINRICH; LAUREN HENSON; BEN KAYSER; SAM KELLY; CHELSEA KLOCKE; KATIE LARSEN; KATE LIEVENS; NICK LOMBARDI; MATT MALONEY; MICHELLE MAUBACH; CHRIS PEIFFER; LIA PLAKKE; HEATHER PRICE; LEIGH SCHLICHTE; JANAE SMITH; ALYSON SPORE; LAUREN SQUIRES; MATT VENDITTI; SARA VOSS; CHAD WEBER; ANTHONY WULFEKUHLE.

CLERGY, PARISHES, MISSIONS AND PAROCHIAL SCHOOLS

CITY OF DUBUQUE
(DUBUQUE COUNTY)

1—ST. RAPHAEL CATHEDRAL (1833), [JC] Rev. Msgr. Wayne A. Ressler, Rector; Barbara Gatch, Pastoral Assoc.; Sr. Ruth Jackson, S.V.M., Music Dir. & Liturgist. In Res., Rev. Dwayne J. Thoman; Deacon Paul Peckosh.
Church, Res. & Office: 231 Bluff St., 52001-6918. Tel: 563-582-7646; Fax: 563-556-6796.
Catechesis/Religious Program—Jean Leute, D.R.E. Students 92.

2—ST. ANTHONY (1867), [JC] Rev. Daniel J. Knepper; Sr. Margaret Ann Kramer, P.B.V.M., Pastoral Assoc.; Deacon William Mauss.
Res. & Office: 1870 St. Ambrose St., 52001-4196. Tel: 563-588-0571; Fax: 563-588-0572.
Church: 1880 St. Ambrose St., 52001.
School—2175 Rosedale, 52001-4147. Tel: 563-556-2820; Fax: 563-556-2131. Robert Burke, Prin. Lay Teachers 21; Students 338.
Catechesis/Religious Program—Carol A. Witry, D.R.E. Students 158.

3—CHURCH OF THE RESURRECTION (1857), [CEM] Revs. Joseph L. Hauer; Thomas P. Rastrelli; Deacon Gerald Jorgensen, Ph.D., J.C.L.; Sr. Francine Quillin, P.B.V.M., J.C.L., Pastoral Assoc.
Church, Res., & Office: 4300 Asbury Rd., 52002-0499. Tel: 563-556-7511; Fax: 563-556-7419.
School—Rev. Joseph Maloney, O.F.M.Cap. (DET), Prin. Sisters of the Presentation 1; Lay Teachers 22; Students 489.
Catechesis/Religious Program—Cathy Stierman, D.R.E. Students 405.

4—ST. COLUMBKILLE (1887), [JC] Rev. Phillip F. Kruse; Deacons William Biver; Frank Dunn. In Res., Revs. Ronald G.. Friedell; Ardel H. Barta.
Res. & Office: 1240 Rush St., 52003-7598. Tel: 563-583-9117; Fax: 563-583-5909.
School—1198 Rush St., 52003-7598. Tel: 563-582-3532; Fax: 563-583-4884. Barb Roling, Prin. Lay Teachers 22; Students 346.
Catechesis/Religious Program—Students 62.

5—HOLY GHOST (1896), [JC] Revs. Paul J. Otting; Henry P. Huber; Sr. Dolores Banowetz, O.S.F., Pastoral Assoc.
Office & Res.: 2917 Central Ave., 52001-1999. Tel: 563-582-5443; Fax: 563-557-0844.
Church: 2921 Central Ave., 52001.
School—Mary Smock, Prin. Lay Teachers 19; Students 242.
Catechesis/Religious Program—Peggy Swift, D.R.E. Students 116.

6—HOLY TRINITY (1910), [JC] Rev. Mark R. Nemmers.
Office & Res.: 1700 Lincoln Ave., 52001-2104. Tel: 563-556-0733.
Church: 1701 Rhomberg, 52001.
School—St. Francis Consolidated, 2222 Queen St., 52001. See separate listing under Institutions located in the Archdiocese for details.
Catechesis/Religious Program—Sr. Mary Kivlahan, O.S.F., D.R.E. Students 80.

7—ST. JOSEPH THE WORKER (1949), [JC] Very Rev. Lyle L. Wilgenbusch; Deacon Stephen MacDonald.
Res.: 90 S. Algona St., 52001-5605. Tel: 563-588-2934.
Office—60 S. Algona, 52001-5605. Tel: 563-588-1433; Fax: 563-588-4108.
Church: 2001 St. Joseph St., 52001.
School—2105 St. Joseph St., 52001. Tel: 563-588-4194. Kimberly Hermsen, Prin. Sisters 1; Lay Teachers 23; Students 352.
Catechesis/Religious Program—Sr. Marilyn Breen, P.B.V.M., D.R.E. Students 183.

8—ST. MARY, Formerly St. Mary's (1850), [JC] Deacon Timothy LoBianco, Pastoral Admin.; Very Rev. Lyle L. Wilgengbusch, Priest Supvr.; Rev. Ardel H. Barta, Sacramental Priest. In Res., Rev. Msgr. David A. Wheeler (Retired).
Church, Res., & Office: 1584 White St., 52001-4905. Tel: 563-582-5469.
School—St. Francis Consolidation, 2222 Queen St., 52001. See separate listing under Institutions located in the Archdiocese for details.
Catechesis/Religious Program— Twinned with St. Patrick, Dubuque. Ann Wertz, D.R.E. Students 71.

9—NATIVITY (1923), [JC] Rev. Michael J. Mescher; Deacon David McGhee, Pastoral Assoc.
Church & Office: 1225 Alta Vista St., 52001-4398. Tel: 563-582-1839; Fax: 563-582-1830.
Res.: 1075 University, 52001. Tel: 563-582-0703.
School—1001 Alta Vista St.. Tel: 563-582-7236. Melissa O'Brien, Prin. Lay Teachers 19; Students 274.
Catechesis/Religious Program—Sr. Beth Kress, P.B.V.M., D.R.E. Students 103.

10—ST. PATRICK, Formerly St. Patrick's (1862), [JC] Deacon Timothy LoBianco, Pastoral Admin.; Very Rev. Lyle L. Wilgenbusch, Priest Supvr.; Rev. Ardel H. Barta, Sacramental Priest.
Church & Parish Office: 1425 Iowa St., 52001-4890. Tel: 563-583-9749.
School—St. Francis Consolidated, 2222 Queen St., 52001. See separate listing under Institutions located in the Archdiocese for details.
Catechesis/Religious Program—Ann Wertz, D.R.E. Twinned with St. Mary, Dubuque. Students 24.

11—SACRED HEART (1879), [JC] Rev. James T. Chappell. In Res., Rev. Harold J. Drexler (Retired).
Church, Res., & Office: 2215 Windsor Ave., 52001-0698. Tel: 563-583-1709.
School—St. Francis Consolidated, 2222 Queen St., 52001. See separate listing under Institutions located in the Archdiocese for details.
Catechesis/Religious Program—Ann Kirk, D.R.E. Students 91.

OUTSIDE THE CITY OF DUBUQUE

ACKLEY, FRANKLIN CO., ST. MARY (1891), [CEM] Very Rev. James L. Miller; Deacon David David Jones.
Mailing Address: 1405 N. Federal, Hampton, 50441-1005. Tel: 641-456-4857; Fax: 641-456-2426.
Church: 611 Sherman Ave, 50601.
Catechesis/Religious Program—Jennifer Pfaltzgraff, D.R.E. Students 96.

ALLISON, BUTLER CO., IMMACULATE CONCEPTION, Closed., For inquiries for parish records contact St. Mary, Greene.

ALTA VISTA, CHICKASAW CO., ST. BERNARD (1897), [CEM] Rev. Msgr. John W. Hemann; Sr. Mildred Leuenberger, O.S.F., Pastoral Assoc.
Office: 207 Seventh St., P.O. Box 38, Elma, 50628-0038. Tel: 641-393-2520.
Church: 116 E. Washington, 50603.
Catechesis/Religious Program—Coleen Marvin, D.R.E. Students 58.

AMES, STORY CO.

1—ST. CECILIA (1899), Rev. Terrence Rassmussen, O.F.M.Conv.; Deacons Gary Aitchison; John McCully; Richard Tondra.
Church, Res., & Office: 2900 Hoover Ave., 50010-4498. Tel: 515-233-3092; Fax: 515-233-6423.
School—(Grades K-6) Tel: 515-232-5290. Duane Siepker, Prin. Lay Teachers 9; Students 180.
Catechesis/Religious Program—Tel: 515-232-3514. William Monosmith, D.R.E. Students 483.

2—ST. THOMAS AQUINAS CHURCH (AND CATHOLIC STUDENT CENTER) (1947), Very Rev. Everett Hemann; Rev. Scott F. Boone. Tel: 515-292-3029; Bobby LeBlanc, Business Mgr.; Crystal Caruana Sullivan, Campus Ministry.
Church & Office: 2210 Lincoln Ave., 50014-7184. Tel: 515-292-3810; Fax: 515-292-3841.
Res.: 129 Ash, 50014. Tel: 515-292-1192.
Catechesis/Religious Program—Sr. Mary Ann Aman, C.H.M., D.R.E. Students 214.

ANAMOSA, JONES CO., ST. PATRICK (1861), [CEM] Sr. Susan Dunnwald, R.S.M., Pastoral Admin.; Very Rev. Donald L. Klein, Priest Supvr.; Rev. Carl J. Manternach, Sacramental Priest (Retired).
Res. & Office: 215 N. Garnavillo St., 52205-1121. Tel: 319-462-2141.
Church: 217 N. Garnavillo St., 52205.
School—(Grades PreK-6) Tel: 319-462-2688. Charlotte Scheckel, Prin. Lay Teachers 8; Students 98.
Catechesis/Religious Program—Marlene Bartlett, D.R.E. Students 122.

ANDREW, JACKSON CO., ST. JOHN (1914), [CEM] Sr. Virginia Crilly, B.V.M., Pastoral Admin.; Very Rev. Donald J. Plamondon, Supr.; Rev. Paul E. Lippstock, Sacramental Priest.
Res. and Mailing Address: St. John Rectory, 507 Elm St., P.O. Box 26, La Motte, 52054-0026. Tel: 563-773-2323.
Church: 204 Main St., 52030.
Catechesis/Religious Program—Phyllis Gerlach, D.R.E. Students 58.

BALDWIN, JACKSON CO., HOLY TRINITY ORATORY, Closed., Sacramental Records are located at Sacred Heart, Maquoketa

BALLTOWN, DUBUQUE CO., ST. FRANCIS OF ASSISI (1891), [CEM] Bro. Stephen W. Markham, F.S.C., Pastoral Admin.; Rev. Msgr. James O. Barta, Supr.; Rev. Henry P. Huber, Sacramental Priest; Sr. Mildred Leuenberger, O.S.F., Pastoral Admin.
Parish Office & Mailing Address: P.O. Box 398, Holy Cross, 52053. Tel: 563-870-4041.
Church: 468 Balltown Rd., Sherrill, 52073.
School—Balltown-Sherrill Consolidated School See separate listing under the Institutions Located in the Archdiocese for details.
Catechesis/Religious Program—Mary Anne Manternach, D.R.E. Twinned with Holycross, Luxemberg, Rickardsville. Students 22.

BANKSTON, DUBUQUE CO., ST. CLEMENT (1859), [CEM] Rev. Dennis R. Cain; Betty Pins, Pastoral Assoc.
Church & Office: 24287 New Vienna Rd., Epworth, 52045-9732. Tel: 563-744-3314.
School—Seton Catholic Elementary School, Epworth See separate listing under the Institutions Located in the Archdiocese for details.
Catechesis/Religious Program—Betty Pins, D.R.E. Students 55.

BARCLAY, BLACKHAWK CO., ST. FRANCIS (1862), [CEM] Rev. Donald R. Bruggeman.
Office: 7837 E. Airline Hwy., Dunkerton, 50626-9715. Tel: 319-822-7477.
Church: 7838 E. Airline Hwy., Dunkerton, 50626.
Catechesis/Religious Program—Arlene Widdel, D.R.E. Students 82.

BELLE PLAINE, BENTON CO., ST. MICHAEL (1885), Deacon J.C. Otto, Pastoral Admin.; Very Rev. Donald L. Klein, Priest Supvr.; Rev. Steven G. O'Brien, Sacramental Priest.
Church & Mailing Address: 1304 Ninth Ave., 52208-1614. Tel: 319-444-3106; Fax: 319-444-3737.
Catechesis/Religious Program—Lisa Daily, D.R.E. Students 109.

BELLEVUE, JACKSON CO., ST. JOSEPH (1841), [CEM] Revs. Stephen L. Meyer; Scott E. Bullock.
Church, Res., & Office: 405 Franklin St., 52031-1596. Tel: 563-872-3234; 563-872-5938.
School—Bellevue Area Catholic Elementary School See separate listing under the Institutions Located in the Archdiocese for details.
Catechesis/Religious Program—Sr. Linda Bechen, R.S.M., D.R.E. Students 144.

BELMOND, WRIGHT CO., ST. FRANCIS XAVIER (1870), [CEM] Rev. David M. Beckman; Regina Lamoureux, Pastoral Assoc.
Church, Parish Office & Mailing Address: 1207 Third St. N.E., 50421-1608. Tel: 641-444-3249.
Catechesis/Religious Program—Deborah Sloth, D.R.E. Students 90.

BLAIRSTOWN, BENTON CO., ST. JOHN (1948), Rev. Paul C. Baldwin; Sr. Nora Rochford, O.S.F., Pastoral Assoc.; Deacon Robert F. Hurych.
Church & Mailing Address: 105 West St. N.W., 52209-0170.
Res.: 405 4th Ave., P.O. Box 250, Van Horne, 52346-0250. Tel: 319-228-8131.
Catechesis/Religious Program—Patricia Angerman, D.R.E. Students 59.

BLESSING, BLACKHAWK CO., IMMACULATE CONCEPTION (1875), [CEM] Deacon Carl Adams, Pastoral Admin.; Very Rev. Dennis D. Juhl; Revs. Paul C. McManus, Sacramental Min.; Christopher R. Podhajsky, Sacramental Min.
Office & Mailing Address: 1435 E. Eagle Rd., Waterloo, 50701-9545. Tel: 319-342-3491.
Church: 14004 S. Hudson Rd., Hudson, 50643.
Catechesis/Religious Program—Leslie Selenke, D.R.E. Students 56.

BLUFFTON, WINNESHIEK CO., ST. BRIDGET (1858), [CEM] Rev. Henry W. Charipar; Sr. Mary Hargrafen, O.S.F., Pastoral Assoc.
Office & Mailing Address: 116 Third St. E., Cresco, 52136. Tel: 563-547-3565.
Church: 3094 253rd Ave., Ridgeway, 52165.
Catechesis/Religious Program—Wade Marlow, D.R.E. Students 29.

BRITT, HANCOCK CO., ST. PATRICK (1880), [CEM] Revs. Michael G. Schueller; Jerry W. Blake.
Office & Mailing Address: 139 Third St. S.E., 50423-1726. Tel: 641-843-3215; Fax: 641-843-3557.
Church: 335 First Ave. S.E., 50423.
Catechesis/Religious Program—Kathryn Smith, D.R.E. Students 136.

BUFFALO CENTER, WINNEBAGO CO., ST. PATRICK, Formerly St. Patrick's (1899), Revs. Michael G. Schueller; Jerry W. Blake.
Office & Mailing Address: St. James Rectory, 906 W. O St., Box 310, Forest City, 50436. Tel: 641-585-4856.
Church: 115 5th Ave. N.W., 50424.
Catechesis/Religious Program—Jody Smith, D.R.E. Students 36.

CALMAR, WINNESHIEK CO., ST. ALOYSIUS (1875), [CEM] Rev. Donald J. Hawes.
Church & Res.: 304 S. Maryville, P.O. Box 819, 52132-0819. Tel: 563-562-3603.
School—Calmar-Festina-Spillville (CFS) Catholic Elementary School See separate listing under the Institutions Located in the Archdiocese for details.
Catechesis/Religious Program—Patty Smith, D.R.E.; Kris Smith, D.R.E. Combined with Our Lady of Seven Dolors, Festina and St. Wenceslaus, Spillville. Students 101.

CARROLL TOWNSHIP, CARROLL CO., ST. WENCESLAUS ORATORY, , Sacramental Records are located at Immaculate Conception, Clutier.

CARTERSVILLE, CERRO GORDO CO., ST. JOHN ORATORY, Closed., Sacramental Records located at Sacred Heart, Rockwell.

CASCADE, DUBUQUE CO., ST. MATTHIAS, [CEM] Rev. Daniel J. Krapfl; Sr. Marlene McDonnell, S.F.C.C., Pastoral Assoc.
Mailing & Parish Office Address: 411 4th Ave., P.O. Box 699, 52033. Tel: 563-852-3524.
School—Aquin Educational System See separate

listing under the Institutions Located in the Archdiocese for details.
Catechesis/Religious Program—Rebecca Smith, D.R.E. Clustered with Sacred Heart, Fillmore; St. Patrick's, Garryowen; and St. Peter's, Temple Hill. Students 192.

CASTLE GROVE, JONES CO., IMMACULATE CONCEPTION (1877), Closed., For inquiries for sacramental records, please see Sacred Heart, Monticello.

CEDAR FALLS, BLACKHAWK CO., ST. PATRICK (1855), Rev. James L. Secora; Deacons Tom Sink, Pastoral Assoc.; Michael Oates; Michael Moetsch.
Mailing & Parish Office Address: 705 Main St., 50613-2950. Tel: 319-266-3523; Fax: 319-266-2179.
Church: 8th & Washington St., 50613.
School—Tel: 319-277-6781. Sr. Marilou Irons, P.B.V.M., Prin. Sisters 1; Lay Teachers 21; Students 292.
Catechesis/Religious Program—Amy Hoyer, D.R.E.; Nancy Meyer, D.R.E. Students 396.

CEDAR RAPIDS, LINN CO.

1—ALL SAINTS (1947), [JC] Rev. David H. O'Connor; Deacon LaVerne Flagel.
Church, Parish Office & Mailing Address: 720 29th St., S.E., 52403-3099. Tel: 319-363-6130; Fax: 319-861-2240.
Res.: 830 Beaver Ridge Ct. S.E., 52403. Tel: 319-362-1691.
School—Tel: 319-363-4110; Fax: 319-363-9547. Marlene Bartlett, Prin. Lay Teachers 19; Students 278.
Catechesis/Religious Program—Elaine Collins, D.R.E.; Sharon Harschnek, D.R.E. Students 172.

2—IMMACULATE CONCEPTION (1858), [JC] Rev. Msgr. Karl L. Glovik; Sr. Francesca Oldham, R.S.M., Pastoral Assoc.; Deacon Gerald D. Pettit, Pastoral Assoc.; Mary Ann McEniry, Pastoral Assoc.
Mailing Address: P.O. Box 1247, 52406. In Res., Revs. James P. Brokman; David J. Ambrosy; Richard J. Hess (Retired).
Res.: 857 Third Ave. S.E., 52403. Tel: 319-362-7181.
Church: 3rd Ave. & 10th St. S.E., 52401.
Catechesis/Religious Program—Mary Ann McEniry, D.R.E. Students 129.

3—JOHN XXIII, Rev. Philip E. Thompson.
Mailing Address: 3104 80th St. S.W., 52404. Tel: 319-846-3139; Fax: 319-846-3159.
Church: 5200 E. Ave., N.W., 52405.
Catechesis/Religious Program—Mary Beth Siemann, D.R.E. Students 73.

4—ST. JUDE (1962), [JC] Revs. Richard J. Ament; Donald J. Czapla; Mark McDermott, Pastoral Assoc.; Deacon Tom Walsh.
Res.: 3601 First Ave. S.W., 52405. Tel: 319-396-8827.
Church & Office Address: 50 Edgewood Rd., N.W., 52405-4598. Tel: 319-390-3520.
School—Holy Family Consolidated Catholic School See separate listing under the Institutions Located in the Archdiocese for details.
Catechesis/Religious Program—Mary Beth Siemann, D.R.E.; Diann Morse, D.R.E. Students 465.

5—ST. LUDMILA (1922), [JC] Rev. Thomas J. McDermott; Sr. Mary L. Lechtenberg, O.S.F., Pastoral Assoc.; Deacons Richard Manning; James Berger.
Office & Res.: 2107 J St., S.W., 52404-3615. Tel: 319-362-7282.
Church: 211 21st Ave., S.W., 52404.
School—Holy Family Consolidated Catholic School See separate listing under Institutions located in the Archdiocese for details.
Catechesis/Religious Program—Sue Berger, D.R.E. Students 216.

6—ST. MATTHEW (1922), [JC] Revs. Mark Osterhaus; Ricardo Coronado; Deacon Phil Saunders; Roseann Wiley-Hayek, Pastoral Assoc. In Res., Rev. Steven G. O'Brien.
Church, Res. & Office: 2310 First Ave. N.E., 52402-4999. Tel: 319-363-8269; Fax: 319-363-8260.
School—Tel: 319-362-3021. Joe Wolf, Prin. Sisters 1; Lay Teachers 16; Students 253.
Catechesis/Religious Program—Betsy Schmuck, D.R.E. Students 279.

7—ST. PATRICK (1886), [JC] Rev. Steven J. Rosonke; Sr. Mary Klisart, O.S.F., Pastoral Assoc.; Deacon Daniel Hoeger.
Parish Office: 516 A Ave. N.W., 52405-3935. Tel: 319-362-7966; 319-366-5369.
Church: 500 First Ave. N.W., 52405.
Catechesis/Religious Program—Penny Ackerman, D.R.E. Students 106.

8—ST. PIUS X (1959), [JC] Very Rev. Donald L. Klein; Rev. David A. Schatz; Deacons Albert Scharosch; Paul Zimmerman; Anne Johnson, Pastoral Assoc.; Liz Pollard, Pastoral Assoc.
Church and Office: 4949 Council St. N.E., 52402-2492. Tel: 319-393-4445; Fax: 319-393-9424.
Rectory: 1500 48th St. N.E., 52402. Tel: 319-393-0452.
School—(Grades K-8) Tel: 319-393-4507. Candace Hurley, Prin. Lay Teachers 23; Students 449.
Catechesis/Religious Program—Sara Kane, D.R.E. Students 411.

9—ST. WENCESLAUS (1874), [JC] Rev. Msgr. Karl L. Glovik; Deacon William Cisler.
Mailing Address: 510 16th Ave. S.E., 52401-2612. Tel: 319-362-8061.
Church: 1224 Fifth St. S.E., 52401.
Catechesis/Religious Program—Students 26.

CENTRAL CITY, LINN CO., ST. STEPHEN (1932), Rev. Wayne J. Droessler; Sr. Anne Kisting, O.S.F., Pastoral Assoc.
Res. & Mailing Address: 410 Terrace Dr., P.O. Box S, 52214-0420. Tel: 319-438-6625.
Parish Office Address—211 3rd St. N., P.O. Box 47, 52218-0047.
Church: 4700 Valley Farm Rd., 52214.
Catechesis/Religious Program—Marci Luedeman, D.R.E. Students 84.

CHARLES CITY, FLOYD CO., IMMACULATE CONCEPTION (1857), [CEM] Rev. Carl A. Ries; Sr. M. Jennifer Rausch, P.B.V.M., Pastoral Assoc.
Church & Office: 106 Chapel Ln., 50616-2810. Tel: 641-228-1071; Fax: 641-228-1072.
School—Tel: 641-228-1225; Fax: 641-228-7692. Barbara Emerson, Prin. Lay Teachers 17; Students 224.
Catechesis/Religious Program—Patricia Rottinghaus, D.R.E. Students 213.

CHELSEA, TAMA CO., ST. JOSEPH (1867), [CEM] Deacon J.C. Otto, Pastoral Admin.; Very Rev. Donald L. Klein, Priest Supvr.; Rev. Steven G. O'Brien, Sacramental Priest.
Mailing Address: 1304 9th Ave., Belle Plaine, 52208-1504. Tel: 319-444-3106.
Church 307 Station St., 52215.
Catechesis/Religious Program—Beth Henning, D.R.E. Students 47.

CHERRY MOUND, ALLAMAKEE CO., ST. PIUS (1863), [CEM] Rev. Louis J. Trzil.
Mailing Address: 1416 Great River Rd., Lansing, 52151. Tel: 563-586-2150.
Church & Religious Education Office: 699 State Forest Rd., Harper's Ferry, 52151. Tel: 563-535-7143.
Catechesis/Religious Program—Lisa Ashbacker, D.R.E. Students 42.

CHESTER HOWARD CO., ST. STEPHEN (1916), Rev. Ray E. Atwood.
Mailing & Office Address: 209 E. Main St., P.O. Box 146, Riceville, 50466-0146. Tel: 641-985-2028.
Church: 408 Main St., 52134.
Catechesis/Religious Program—Mary Ann Kelly, D.R.E. Students 34.

CLARION, WRIGHT CO., ST. JOHN (1885), [CEM] Rev. David M. Beckman; Deacon Michael Whitters; Sr. Mary K. Doughan, R.S.M., Pastoral Assoc.
Church and Mailing Address: 608 Second Ave. N.E., P.O. Box 26, 50525-0026. Tel: 515-532-3586; Fax: 515-532-2478.
Catechesis/Religious Program—Cathy Wendel, D.R.E.; Gloria Kisor, D.R.E. Students 144.

CLEAR LAKE, CERRO GORDO CO., ST. PATRICK (1901), Rev. Msgr. Robert G. Hogan.
Church, Res. & Office: 1001 Ninth Ave. S., 50428-2615. Tel: 641-357-3214; Fax 641-357-2091.
Catechesis/Religious Program—Jennifer Clancy, D.R.E. Students 204.

CLERMONT, FAYETTE CO., ST. PETER (1855), Rev. Dale J. Rausch.
Church and Mailing Address: 608 Larrabee, 52135-0025. Tel: 563-423-7293.
Catechesis/Religious Program—Mary Olson, D.R.E. Students 136.

CLUTIER, TAMA CO., IMMACULATE CONCEPTION (1900), [CEM] Rev. John R. Tilp.
Res & Mailing Address: 1102 Walnut St., Traer, 50675. Tel: 319-478-2222.
Church: 501 5th St., 52217.
Catechesis/Religious Program—Lynne McGivern, D.R.E. Students 38.

COGGON, LINN CO., ST. JOHN THE EVANGELIST (1912), [CEM] Rev. Wayne J. Droessler; Sr. Anne Kisting, O.S.F., Pastoral Assoc.
Mailing Address: 211 Third St. N., P.O. Box 47, 52218-0047. Tel: 319-435-2236.
Church: 211 Third St. N., 52218.
Catechesis/Religious Program—Pamela Klima, D.R.E. Students 55.

COLESBURG, DELAWARE CO., ST. PATRICK (1862), [CEM] Rev. John J. Friederick.
Office & Res.: St. Mark Rectory, 205 S. Locust, P.O. Box 365, Edgewood, 52042-0365. Tel: 563-856-2265.
Church: Delaware St., 52035.
Catechesis/Religious Program—Gene Kruse, D.R.E.; Ramona Engelken, D.R.E. Students 61.

COLO, STORY CO., ST. MARY, [CEM] Rev. Jon M. Seda; Sr. Jeanne Marie Roche, R.S.M., Pastoral Assoc.; Deacon Steven Van Kerchvoorde.
Rectory & Mailing Address: 410 Bailey, P.O. Box 236, 50056-0236. Tel: 641-377-2710.
Church: 422 Fourth St., 50056.
Catechesis/Religious Program—Sarah Grover, D.R.E. Students 48.

CORWITH, HANCOCK CO., ST. MARY (1912), Closed., For inquiries for sacramental records, please contact St. Patrick, Britt.

CRESCO, HOWARD CO.

1—ASSUMPTION OF THE BLESSED VIRGIN MARY (1858), Merged, with St. Joseph's, Cresco to form Notre Dame, Cresco.

2—ST. JOSEPH (1870), Merged, with Assumption of the Blessed Virgin Mary, Cresco to form Notre Dame, Cresco.

3—NOTRE DAME (1999), [JC] Rev. Henry W. Charipar; Sr. Mary Hargrafen, O.S.F., Pastoral Assoc.
Mailing Address & Parish Office: 116 Third St. E., 52136. Tel: 563-547-3565; Fax: 563-547-3835.
Rectory: 221 Third Ave. W., 52136. Tel: 563-547-5826.
Assumption Worship Center: 229 3rd Ave. W., 52136.
St. Joseph Worship Center: 223 2nd Ave. E., 52136.
School—221 Second Ave. E., 52136. Tel: 563-547-4513. Wendy Schatz, Prin. Teachers 14; Students 206.
Catechesis/Religious Program—Tel: 563-547-3760. Wade Marlow, D.R.E. Students 226.
Convent—221 Second Ave. E., 52136. Tel: 563-547-4023.

DECORAH, WINNESHIEK CO., ST. BENEDICT (1864), [CEM] Very Rev. Gary Krapfl.
Church, Res. & Office: 307 W. Main St., 52101-1778. Tel: 563-382-9631; Fax: 563-382-6436.
School—Tel: 563-382-4668. Ruth Palmer, Prin. Lay Teachers 16; Students 208.
Catechesis/Religious Program—Jill Brusse, D.R.E. Students 304.

DELHI, DELAWARE CO., ST. JOHN (1872), [CEM] Rev. John R. Kremer.
Church & Res.: 307 South St., P.O. Box 187, 52223-0187. Tel: 563-922-2251.
Catechesis/Religious Program—JoLynn Heims, D.R.E.; Janet Hoeger, D.R.E. Students 169.

DIKE, GRUNDY CO., ST. MARY (1880), [CEM] Rev. Dennis J. Quint.
Office & Mailing Address: 204 G Ave., Grundy Center, 50638-1939. Tel: 319-824-3572; Fax: 319-824-3827.
Church: 680 Main St., 50624.
Catechesis/Religious Program—Ann Nicklaus-Schmelzer, D.R.E. Students 67.

DORCHESTER, ALLAMAKEE CO., ST. MARY (1865), [CEM] Rev. Joseph M. Schneider.
Mailing Address: 109 2nd St., P.O. Box 146, Waukon, 52172-0146. Tel: 563-568-3671; Fax: 563-568-2170.
Church: 590 Waterloo Creek Rd., 52140.
Catechesis/Religious Program—Kathy Kruse, D.R.E.

DOUGHERTY, CERRO GORDO CO., ST. PATRICK (1870), [CEM] Rev. Craig E. Steimel.
Mailing Address: 410 Patrick St., P.O. Box 208, 50433-0208.
Church: 410 Patrick St., 50433.
Sacred Heart Rectory: 305 Elm St., P.O. Box 30, Rockwell, 50469-0030. Tel: 641-822-4957.
Catechesis/Religious Program—Dolores Marzen, D.R.E. Students 27.

DUMONT, BUTLER CO., ST. FRANCIS (1890), Closed., For inquiries for parish records please see St. Patrick, Hampton.

DUNCAN, HANCOCK CO., ST. WENCESLAUS (1900), [CEM] Revs. Michael G. Schueller; Jerry W. Blake.
Res. & Mailing Address: St. Boniface Rectory, 660 Bush Ave., Garner, 50438-1513. Tel: 641-923-2329; Fax: 641-923-2480.
Church: 2343 Navy Ave., Britt, 50423.
Catechesis/Religious Program—Rebecca Rolling, D.R.E. Students 49.

DYERSVILLE, DUBUQUE CO.

1—BASILICA OF ST. FRANCIS XAVIER (1859), [CEM] Rev. Msgr. Edward C. Petty; Rev. Mark J. McGovern; Sr. Marian Einck, O.S.F., Pastoral Assoc.
Res.: 104 Third St. S.W., 52040-1696. Tel: 563-875-7325; Fax: 563-875-8716.
Church: Second St. S.W., 52040.
School—(Grades 1-6) Tel: 563-875-7376; Fax: 563-875-7037. Ralph Pauly, Prin. Sisters of St. Francis of the Holy Family 1; Lay Teachers 23; Students 320.
Catechesis/Religious Program—Nancy Drees, D.R.E.; Ruth Jacque, D.R.E. Students 171.
Convent—120 Third St. S.W., 52040-1697. Tel: 563-875-8226.

2—SS. PETER AND PAUL (1867), [CEM] Rev. John J. O'Connor.
Church, Res. & Mailing Address: 1625 300th Ave., 52040. Tel: 563-875-7992.
School—Archbishop Hennessy Catholic, New Vienna See separate listing under the Institutions Located in the Archdiocese for details.

DYSART, TAMA CO., ST. JOSEPH (1878), [CEM] Rev. John R. Tilp.
Mailing Address: 1102 Walnut St., Traer, 50675-1440. Tel: 319-472-2222.

Church: 101 Clark St., 52224.
Catechesis/Religious Program—Lynne McGivern, D.R.E. Students 60.

EAGLE CENTER, BLACKHAWK CO., ST. MARY OF MT. CARMEL (1859), [CEM] Deacon Carl Adams, Pastoral Admin.; Very Rev. Dennis D. Juhl, Priest Supvr.; Revs. Paul C. McManus, Sacramental Min.; Christopher R. Podhajsky, Sacramental Min.
Church & Mailing Address: 1435 E. Eagle Rd., Waterloo, 50701-9545. Tel: 319-342-3491.
Catechesis/Religious Program—Students 114.

EAGLE GROVE, WRIGHT CO., SACRED HEART (1882), [CEM] Rev. David M. Beckman.
Mailing Address: 221 S. Jackson Ave., 50533-2311. Tel: 515-603-4765; Fax: 515-603-4765.
Church: 201 S. Jackson Ave., 50533.
Catechesis/Religious Program—Michele Choquette, D.R.E. Students 106.

EARLVILLE, DELAWARE CO., ST. JOSEPH (1887), [CEM] Rev. Herbert L. Tegeler; Deacon James Steger.
Res. & Mailing Address: 307 Mary St., P.O. Box 187, 52041-0187. Tel: 563-923-3135; Fax: 563-923-2895.
Church: 303 Mary St., 52041.
School—(Grades K-6) Julie Orris, Prin. Lay Teachers 5; Students 40.
Catechesis/Religious Program—Joan Steger, D.R.E. Students 103.

EDGEWOOD, DELAWARE CO., ST. MARK (1916), [CEM] Rev. John J. Friederick.
Church & Office: 207 S. Locust St., P.O. Box 365, 52042-0365. Tel: 563-928-6938; 563-928-7200.
Catechesis/Religious Program—Jody Kerns, D.R.E. Students 178.

ELDORA, HARDIN CO., ST. MARY (1868), [CEM] Rev. James W. Dubert; Sr. Connie Howe, R.S.M., Pastoral Assoc.
Church & Parish Office: 614 Washington, 50627-1257. Tel: 641-939-5545.
Catechesis/Religious Program—Sarah Harper, D.R.E. Students 71.

ELKADER, CLAYTON CO., ST. JOSEPH (1844), [CEM] Rev. Paul R. Peters.
Church, Res. & Office: 330 First St., P.O. Box 626, 52043-0626. Tel: 563-245-2548.
Catechesis/Religious Program—Nancy Schroeder, D.R.E.; Kathy Schutte, D.R.E. Students 135.

ELMA, HOWARD CO., IMMACULATE CONCEPTION (1887), [CEM] Rev. Msgr. John W. Hemann; Sr. Mildred Leuenberger, O.S.F., Pastoral Assoc.
Office & Res.: 207 Seventh St., P.O. Box 38, 50628-0038. Tel: 641-393-2520.
Church: 203 Seventh St., 50628.
Catechesis/Religious Program—Eleanor Burke, D.R.E. Students 65.

EPWORTH, DUBUQUE CO., ST. PATRICK (1879), [CEM] Rev. Raymond A. Burkle; Deacon James Kean.
Mailing Address & Parish Office: 104 First St. S.E., P.O. Box 286, 52045-0286. Tel: 563-876-5540.
Res.: 22453 E. Pleasant Grove Rd., Placid. Tel: 563-876-5501.
Church: 102 1st St. S.E., 52045.
School—Seton Catholic Elementary School, Epworth See separate listing under the Institutions Located in the Archdiocese for details.
Catechesis/Religious Program—Robin Flick, D.R.E. Students 107.

EVANSDALE, BLACKHAWK CO., ST. NICHOLAS (1951), Merged, with St. Mary's, St. John's & St. Joseph, Waterloo to form Queen of Peace, Waterloo. Sacramental records are located at Queen of Peace.

FAIRBANK, BUCHANAN CO., IMMACULATE CONCEPTION (1858), [CEM] Rev. Kenneth C. Stecher.
Church, Res. & Office: 302 W. Main St., P.O. Box 505, 50629-0505. Tel: 319-635-2211.
Catechesis/Religious Program—Dan Cutsforth, D.R.E. Students 174.

FAIRFAX, LINN CO., ST. PATRICK'S (1875), [CEM] Rev. Philip E. Thompson, Admin.; Sr. Maryann Greenwald, S.S.N.D., Pastoral Assoc.; Deacon John Malone.
Parish Office: 620 Church St., P.O. Box 219, 52228-0219. Tel: 319-846-2025; Fax: 319-846-3472.
Church: 324 Church St., 52228.
Catechesis/Religious Program—Kelly Giese, D.R.E. Students 167.

FARLEY, DUBUQUE CO., ST. JOSEPH'S (1914), [CEM] Rev. Dennis R. Cain; Sr. Evelyn Menster, B.V.M., Pastoral Min.
Church, Res. & Office: 204 Second Ave. S.E., P.O. Box 67, 52046. Tel: 563-744-3865.
School—Seton Catholic Elementary School, Epworth See separate listing under the Institutions Located in the Archdiocese for details.
Catechesis/Religious Program—Monica Lynch, D.R.E. Students 161.

FESTINA, WINNESHIEK CO., OUR LADY OF SEVEN DOLORS (1843), [CEM] Rev. Msgr. Cletus J. Hawes.
Church & Mailing Address: 2348 County Rd. B 32, 52144-7701. Tel: 563-532-9366.
School—Calmar-Festina-Spillville (CFS) Elementary See separate listing under the Institutions Located in the Archdiocese for details.
Catechesis/Religious Program—Patty Frana, D.R.E. Combined with St. Aloysius, Calmar and St. Wenceslaus, Spillville. Students 29.

FILLMORE, DUBUQUE CO., SACRED HEART (1890), [CEM] Rev. Daniel A. Krapfl; Deacon Marvin Recker.
Church & Mailing Address: 19661 Sacred Heart Ln., Bernard, 52032-9722. Tel: 563-879-3103.
School—Aquin Elementary School See separate listing under the Institutions Located in the Archdiocese for details.
Catechesis/Religious Program—Rebecca Smith, D.R.E. Clustered with St. Matthias, Cascade; St. Patrick's, Garryowen; and St. Peter's, Temple Hill. Students 25.

FOREST CITY, WINNEBAGO CO., ST. JAMES (1870), [CEM] Revs. Michael G. Schueller; Jerry W. Blake.
Mailing & Parish Office Address: 906 W. O St., 50436. Tel: 641-585-4856.
Catechesis/Religious Program—Rita Kleemeier, D.R.E. Students 112.

FORT ATKINSON, WINNESHIEK CO., ST. JOHN NEPOMUCENE (1875), [CEM] Rev. John A. Moser. In Res., Rev. Raphael A. Ludwig (Retired).
Office & Res.: 202 Second St. S.E., P.O. Box 157, 52144-0157. Tel: 563-534-7298.
Church: 201 Oak St., 52144.
School—Trinity Catholic School, Protivin See separate listing under the Institutions Located in the Archdiocese for details.
Catechesis/Religious Program—Mary Schwamman, D.R.E. Students 98.

GARBER, CLAYTON CO., ST. MICHAEL (1917), [CEM] Closed., For inquiries for parish records please see St. Joseph, Garnavillo.
Church: 800 Main St., 52048.

GARNAVILLO, CLAYTON CO., ST. JOSEPH (1846), [CEM] Rev. Richard G. Gaul.
Office & Res.: 402 S. Washington St., P.O. Box 7, 52049-0007. Tel: 563-964-2168.
Church: 204 W. Oak St., 52049.
Catechesis/Religious Program—Darlene Wille, D.R.E. Students 74.

GARNER, HANCOCK CO., ST. BONIFACE (1883), [CEM] Revs. Michael G. Schueller; Jerry W. Blake; Deacon Dennis Popowski.
Office & Res.: 660 Bush Ave., 50438-1513. Tel: 641-923-2329; Fax: 641-923-2480.
Church: 600 Bush Ave., 50438.
Catechesis/Religious Program—Rebecca Rolling, D.R.E. Students 188.

GARRYOWEN, JACKSON CO., ST. PATRICK (1840), [CEM] Rev. Thomas R. Bisenius.
Church, Res. & Office: 28914 46th Ave., Bernard, 52032-9289. Tel: 563-879-3303; Fax: 563-879-3363.
School—Aquin Elementary School See separate listing under the Institutions Located in the Archdiocese for details.
Catechesis/Religious Program—Joann Harry, D.R.E. Clustered with St. Matthias, Cascade; Sacred Heart, Fillmore; and St. Peter's, Temple Hill. Students 57.

GARWIN, TAMA CO., ST. BONIFACE (1884), [JC] Rev. Keith L. Birch.
Office & Mailing Address: 900 Park St., Tama, 52339-1238. Tel: 641-484-3039; Fax: 641-484-8039.
Church: 306 4th St., 50632.
Catechesis/Religious Program—Beverly Stanley, D.R.E. Students 40.

GENEVA, FRANKLIN CO., ST. PAUL, Closed., Sacramental records are located at St. Mary, Ackley.

GILBERT, STORY CO., SS. PETER AND PAUL (1882), [CEM] Very Rev. Everett Hemann; Rev. Scott F. Boone.
Mailing Address: 2210 Lincoln Way, Ames, 50010. Tel: 515-292-3810; 515-292-3841.
Church: 14238 500th Ave., 50105.
Catechesis/Religious Program—Jean T. Johnson, D.R.E.; Peg Stowell, D.R.E. Students 64.

GILBERTVILLE, BLACKHAWK CO., IMMACULATE CONCEPTION (1875), [CEM] Rev. Rick D. Dagit.
Office & Res.: 311 15th Ave., P.O. Box 136, 50634. Tel: 319-296-1092; Fax: 319-296-2087.
Church: 325 15th Ave., 50634-0136.
School—Immaculate Conception-St. Joseph (Gilbertville-Raymond Consolidated). See separate listing under the Institutions Located in the Archdiocese for details.
Catechesis/Religious Program—Teresa Mangrich, D.R.E. Students 32.

GREELEY, DELAWARE CO., ST. JOSEPH (1870), [CEM] Rev. Msgr. Ralph P. Simington; Rev. Dennis W. Miller.
Mailing & Parish Address, 208 E. Second St., P.O. Box 98, 52050-0098. Tel: 563-925-2491.
Church: 202 E. 2nd Ave., 52050.
Catechesis/Religious Program—Students 25.

GREEN ISLAND, JACKSON CO., SACRED HEART, Closed., For inquiries for sacramental records, please see St. Joseph, Preston.

GREENE, BUTLER CO., ST. MARY (1872), [CEM] Rev. Msgr. Walter L. Brunkan.
Church & Res.: 105 N. Main, P.O. Box 480, 50636-0480. Tel: 641-823-4146.
Catechesis/Religious Program—Sherilyn Backer, D.R.E. Students 117.

GRUNDY CENTER, GRUNDY CO., SACRED HEART (1885), [CEM] Rev. Dennis J. Quint.
Office & Res.: 204 G Ave., 50638-1939. Tel: 319-824-3572; Fax: 319-824-3857.
Church: G Ave. & Second St., 50638.
Catechesis/Religious Program—Ann Nicklaus Schmelzer, D.R.E. Students 73.

GUTTENBERG, CLAYTON CO., ST. MARY, Formerly St. Mary's (1851), [CEM] Rev. Marvin J. Bries; Deacon James Pfaffly.
Res. & Office: 502 S. Second, P.O. Box 847, 52052-0847. Tel: 563-252-1247; Fax: 563-252-1363.
Church: 520 S. 2nd, 52052.
School—Guttenberg-North Buena Vista Consolidated See separate listing under the Institutions Located in the Archdiocese for details.
Catechesis/Religious Program—Becky Pfaffly, D.R.E. Students 147.

HAMPTON, FRANKLIN CO., ST. PATRICK, Formerly St. Patrick's (1870), Very Rev. James L. Miller; Hector Hernandez, Hispanic Min.
Office: 1405 N. Federal, P.O. Box 514, 50441-1005. Tel: 641-456-4857.
Res.: 2 19th Ave. N.E., 50441. Tel: 641-456-3406.
Catechesis/Religious Program—Judy Nelson, D.R.E. Students 196.

HANOVER, ALLAMAKEE CO., ST. MARY (1875), Rev. Joseph M. Schneider.
Mailing Address: c/o St. Patrick Parish, 109 Second St. S.W., Waukon, 52172-0146. Tel: 563-568-3671; Fax: 563-568-2170.
Church: 2096 Hwy. 76, Waukon, 52172.
Catechesis/Religious Program—Mary Therese Klauke, D.R.E. Students 13.

HARPERS FERRY, ALLAMAKEE CO., ST. ANN-ST. JOSEPH (1855), [CEM] Rev. Louis J. Trzil.
Res. & Mailing Address: Immaculate Conception (Wexford), 1416 Great River Rd., Lansing, 52151-7519. Tel: 563-586-2150.
Church: 307 W. Orange, Harper's Ferry, 52146.
Catechesis/Religious Program—Brigid Cota, D.R.E. Students 40.

HAVERHILL, MARSHALL CO., IMMACULATE CONCEPTION (1877), [CEM] Rev. Louis M. Jaeger; Debra Heil, Pastoral Assoc.
Parish Office & Mailing Address: 221 Olive St., Marshalltown, 50158-4248. Tel: 641-753-7374.
Church: 101 Second St., 50120.
School—Marshalltown Area Consolidated Catholic See separate listing under the Institutions Located in the Archdiocese for details.
Catechesis/Religious Program—Students 22.

HAWKEYE, FAYETTE CO., ST. FRANCIS XAVIER (1891), Rev. John J. Purtell.
Office & Mailing Address: Immaculate Conception, 413 W. First St., Sumner, 50674-1313. Tel: 563-578-5366.
Church: 304 E. Main, 52147.
Catechesis/Religious Program—Donna Scholbrock, D.R.E. Students 3.

HAZLETON, BUCHANAN CO., ST. MARY (1881), [CEM] Rev. John C. Paisley; Deacon Richard Gehrke; Linnea K. Kjar, Pastoral Assoc.
Mailing Address & Parish Office: 305 Worth St., P.O. Box 180, Lamont, 50650-0180. Tel: 319-924-2691.
Church: 209 Benton, 50641.
Catechesis/Religious Program—Students 2.

HIAWATHA, LINN CO., ST. ELIZABETH ANN SETON PARISH (1989), [JC] Rev. Neil J. Manternach; Marlene Myers, Pastoral Min.; Dennis McDermoth, Pastoral Assoc.
Church & Office: 1350 Lyndhurst Dr., 52233. Tel: 319-393-3778; Fax: 319-393-7165.
Res.: 1385 Lyndhurst, 52233. Tel: 319-393-2646.
Catechesis/Religious Program—Sara Kane, D.R.E. Students 415.

HOLY CROSS, DUBUQUE CO., HOLY CROSS (1845), [CEM] Bro. Stephen W. Markham, F.S.C., Pastoral Admin.; Rev. Msgr. James O. Barta, Supr.; Revs. Thomas R. Zinkula, Sacramental Priest; Henry P. Huber, Sacramental Priest.
Office: 835 Church St., P.O. Box 398, 52053. Tel: 563-870-4041.
Church: 875 Church St., 52053.
School—Rickardsville-Holy Cross-Luxemburg (RHCL) Catholic See separate listing under the Institutions Located in the Archdiocese for details.
Catechesis/Religious Program—Mary Anne Manternach, D.R.E. Students 16.

HOPKINTON, DELAWARE CO., ST. LUKE (1922), Rev. John R. Kremer; Patricia Hucker, Pastoral Assoc.
Office & Mailing Address: 206 First St., S.E., 52237-0159. Tel: 563-926-2613.

Church: 206 First St. S.E., 52237.
Catechesis/Religious Program—Patricia Hucker, D.R.E. Students 101.
Oratory—Immaculate Conception Sand Springs. Closed. Sacramental Records at St John's, Delhi.

INDEPENDENCE, BUCHANAN CO., ST. JOHN THE EVANGELIST (1856), [CEM] Rev. Aloysius J. Vorwald.
Church, Res. & Office: 209 Fifth Ave. N.E., 50644-1998. Tel: 319-334-7191; Fax: 319-334-7192.
School—Anita Benna, Prin. Lay Teachers 10; Students 143.
Catechesis/Religious Program—Anita Benna, D.R.E. Students 243.

IONIA, CHICKASHAW CO., ST. BONIFACE (1899), [CEM] Rev. Msgr. John W. Hemann; Sr. Mildred Leuenberger, O.S.F., Pastoral Assoc.
Parish Office & Mailing Address: 612 Cedar St., P.O. Box 308, Nashua, 50658-0308. Tel: 641-435-2070.
Church: 204 E. Prairie, 50645.
Catechesis/Religious Program—Delilah Hughes, D.R.E. Students 40.

IOWA FALLS, HARDIN CO., ST. MARK (1855), [CEM] Rev. James W. Dubert; Sr. Connie Howie, R.S.M., Pastoral Assoc.
Church, Res. & Office: 415 Main St., P.O. Box 368, 50126-0368. Tel: 641-648-9547; Fax: 641-648-9562.
Catechesis/Religious Program—Judith Connell, D.R.E. Students 133.

JESUP, BUCHANAN CO., ST. ATHANASIUS (1880), [CEM] Rev. Donald R. Bruggeman; Sr. Donna Burke, O.S.F., Pastoral Assoc.
Office & Res.: 634 Stevens St., P.O. Box 316, 50648-0316. Tel: 319-827-6682; Fax: 319-827-1124.
Church: 623 Stevens St., 50648.
School—(Grades K-8) Steve Bradley, Prin. Lay Teachers 10; Students 116.
Catechesis/Religious Program—Alice Weber, D.R.E. Students 107.

JEWELL, HAMILTON CO., GOOD SHEPHERD (1915), Closed., For inquiries for parish records please see St. Cecelia, Ames

KEY WEST, DUBUQUE CO., ST. JOSEPH'S (1872), Rev. Donald V. Bakewell; Deacon Tom Lang.
Office & Res.: 10234 Key West Dr., 52003-8936. Tel: 563-582-7392.
Church: 10334 Key West Dr., 52003.
School—10244 Key West Dr., 52003. Tel: 563-582-2866. Connie Kessler, Prin. Lay Teachers 14; Students 205.
Catechesis/Religious Program—Linda Cravens, D.R.E. Students 106.

LA MOTTE, JACKSON CO., HOLY ROSARY (1893), [CEM] Sr. Virginia Crilly, B.V.M., Pastoral Admin.; Very Rev. Donald J. Plamondon, Supr.; Rev. Paul E. Lippstock.
Church, Res. & Office: 507 Elm St., P.O. Box 26, 52054-0026. Tel: 563-773-2323.
School—Bellevue Area Catholic Elementary See separate listing under the Institutions Located in the Archdiocese for details.
Catechesis/Religious Program—Sandy Koos, D.R.E. Students 24.

LA PORTE CITY, BLACKHAWK CO., SACRED HEART (1887), Deacon Carl Adams, Pastoral Admin.; Very Rev. Dennis D. Juhl, Priest Supvr.; Revs. Paul C. McManus, Sacramental Min.; Christopher R. Podhajsky, Sacramental Min.
Office Address: 1435 E. Eagle Rd., Waterloo, 50701. Tel: 319-342-3491.
Church: 1019 Poplar St., 50651.
Catechesis/Religious Program—Deborah Appleton, D.R.E. Students 133.

LAKE MILLS, WINNEBAGO CO., ST. PATRICK (1870), [CEM] Revs. Michael G. Schueller; Jerry W. Blake.
Res. & Mailing Address: 906 West St., Forest City, 50436-0310. Tel: 641-585-4856.
Church: 406 S. Grant St., 50450.
Catechesis/Religious Program—Carla Langfald, D.R.E. Students 46.

LAMONT, BUCHANAN CO., ST. MARY'S (1894), [CEM] Rev. John C. Paisley; Linnea K. Kjar, Pastoral Assoc.
Res. & Mailing Address: 305 Worth St., P.O. Box 180, 50650-0180. Tel: 563-924-2691.
Church: 845 Pearl St., 50650.
Catechesis/Religious Program—Deb Carpenter, D.R.E. Students 72.

LANSING, ALLAMAKEE CO., IMMACULATE CONCEPTION (1855), [CEM] Rev. Daniel J. Knipper.
Church, Res. & Office: 648 Main St., 52151-9685. Tel: 563-538-3933.
Catechesis/Religious Program—Karen Weber, D.R.E. Students 106.

LATTNERVILLE, DUBUQUE CO., ST. WENCESLAUS ORATORY, Closed., For inquiries for parish records please see St. John, Peosta.

LAWLER, CHICKASAW CO., OUR LADY OF MT. CARMEL (1869), [CEM] Rev. Marvin C. Salz; Sr. LouAnn Doering, P.B.V.M., Pastoral Assoc.
Church, Mailing Address & Parish Office: 2940 Hwy. 24, P.O. Box 119, 52150. Tel: 563-238-3444.
Catechesis/Religious Program—Gail Stammeyer, D.R.E.; Karen Franzen, D.R.E. Students 56.

LITTLE TURKEY, CHICKASAW CO., ASSUMPTION OF THE B. V. M. (1902), [CEM] Rev. John A. Moser.
Office & Mailing Address: 110 Commercial Ave., P.O. Box 205, Protivin, 52163. Tel: 563-569-8259.
Church: 3303 160th St., Lawler, 52154.
Catechesis/Religious Program—Missy Reicks, D.R.E. Students 71.

LITTLEPORT, CLAYTON CO., SACRED HEART Closed., For inqueries for sacramental records, please see St. Joseph, Garnavillo, IA.

LOURDES, HOWARD CO., OUR LADY OF LOURDES (1875), [CEM] Rev. Msgr. John W. Hemann, Admin.; Sr. Mildred Leuenberger, O.S.F., Pastoral Assoc.
Res. & Mailing Address: 207 7th St., P.O. Box 38, Elma, 50628-0038. Tel: 641-393-2520.
Church: 14068 175th St., Elma, 50628.
Catechesis/Religious Program—Julie Loftus, D.R.E. Students 10.

LUXEMBURG, DUBUQUE CO., HOLY TRINITY (1865), [CEM] Bro. Stephen W. Markham, F.S.C., Pastoral Admin.; Rev. Msgr. James O. Barta, Supvr.; Revs. Thomas E. Zuikula; Henry P. Hober, Sacramental Min.
Office & Mailing Address: 835 Church St., P.O. Box 398, Holy Cross, 52053. Tel: 563-870-4041.
Church: 103 S. Andres St., 52056.
School—Rickardsville-Holy Cross-Luxemburg (RHCL) Catholic See separate listing under the Institutions Located in the Archdiocese for details.

LYCURGUS, ALLAMAKEE CO., ST. MARY (1859), [CEM] Rev. Daniel J. Knipper.
Office & Mailing Address: 648 Main St., Lansing, 52151. Tel: 563-538-4171.
Church: 1831 Lycurgus Rd., Waukon, 52172.
Catechesis/Religious Program—Rita Whalen, D.R.E. Students 36.

MANCHESTER, DELAWARE CO., ST. MARY (1872), [CEM] Rev. Msgr. Ralph P. Simington; Rev. Dennis W. Miller.
Church, Res. & Office: 119 W. Fayette St., 52057-1596. Tel: 563-927-4710; Fax: 563-927-9949.
School—(Grades K-6) Joseph Bearns, Prin. Lay Teachers 16; Students 219.
Catechesis/Religious Program—Joan Rowland, D.R.E. Students 391.

MANLY, WORTH CO., SACRED HEART (1883), [CEM] Rev. David G. Kucera; Deacon Robert Mega.
Church, Res. & Office: 120 E. North, P.O. Box 160, 50456-0160. Tel: 641-454-2586.
Catechesis/Religious Program—Lori Johnson, D.R.E. Students 96.

MAQUOKETA, JACKSON CO., SACRED HEART (1873), [CEM] Rev. Robert F. Davies; Sr. Romaine Pickart, O.S.F., Pastoral Min.; Deacon Robert Head.
Church, Res. & Office: 200 S. Vermont St., P.O. Box 635, 52060-0635. Tel: 563-652-5931; Fax: 563-652-7077.
School—Sr. Rita Green, O.S.F., Prin. Sisters 1; Lay Teachers 9; Students 134.
Catechesis/Religious Program—Cary Broch, D.R.E. Students 129.

MARION, LINN CO., ST. JOSEPH (1890), [JC] Rev. John A. Gossman; Deacon Ed Pantaloni; Rodney Bluml, Pastoral Assoc.
Church, Res. & Office: 1790 14th St., 52302-2267. Tel: 319-377-4869; Fax: 319-377-9043.
School—Marie Pishko, Prin. Lay Teachers 24; Students 300.
Catechesis/Religious Program—Ruth Ard, D.R.E.; Mary Hauschildt, D.R.E. Students 632.

MARSHALLTOWN, MARSHALL CO.

1—ST. HENRY (1959), [JC] Rev. Louis M. Jaeger; Deacons Irvin Vaske; Roger Polt; Karen Mroz, Pastoral Assoc.
Church & Parish Office: 221 W. Olive St., 50158-4248. Tel: 641-753-7374; Fax: 641-753-1499.
Rectory: 1610 Crestview Dr., 50158. Tel: 641-752-2043.
School—Marshalltown Area Consolidated Catholic See separate listing under the Institutions Located in the Archdiocese for details.
Catechesis/Religious Program—Mark Dolash, D.R.E.; Shelby Dolash, D.R.E. Students 219.

2—ST. MARY (1869), [JC] Rev. Bernard C. Grady; Deacon Edward J. Mead; Sisters Diana Blong, P.B.V.M., Pastoral Assoc.; Christine Feagan, O.P., Hispanic Min.
Office & Res.: 9 W. Linn St., P.O. Box 642, 50158-0642. Tel: 641-753-6278; Fax: 641-753-1279.
Church: 11 W. Linn St., 50158.
School—Marshalltown Area Consolidated Catholic See separate listing under the Institutions Located in the Archdiocese for details.
Catechesis/Religious Program—Jeannine Grady, D.R.E. Students 163.

MASON CITY, CERRO GORDO CO.

1—HOLY FAMILY (1908), [JC] Rev. Dennis H. Cahill; Deacons Matthew F. Berry; Charles Cooper; Debbie Cahalan, Pastoral Assoc.; Pat Dixon, Pastoral Assoc. In Res., Very Rev. Kenneth B. Gehling.
Church, Res. & Office: 714 N. Adams St., 50401-2199. Tel: 641-423-7301; Fax: 641-428-7663.
School—Newman Catholic See separate listing under the Institutions Located in the Archdiocese for details.
Catechesis/Religious Program—Ginny Verstegen, D.R.E. Clustered with St. Joseph's, Mason City. Students 115.

2—ST. JOSEPH (1873), Revs. Harry H. Koelker; Michael J. Podhajsky; Sr. Lois Erpelding, O.S.I., Pastoral Assoc.
Church, Parish Office & Res.: 302 Fifth St. S.E., 50401-4005. Tel: 641-423-5001; Fax: 641-423-8553.
School—Newman Catholic See separate listing under the Institutions Located in the Archdiocese for details.
Catechesis/Religious Program—Ginny Verstegen, D.R.E. Clustered with Holy Family, Mason City. Students 249.

MASONVILLE, DELAWARE CO., IMMACULATE CONCEPTION (1883), [CEM] Rev. Ivan R. Nienhaus; Sr. Mary Valentine Smith, O.S.F., Pastoral Assoc.
Res. and Mailing Address: 555 First St., P.O. Box 236, Winthrop, 50682. Tel: 319-935-3523.
Church: Bernhart St., 50654.
Catechesis/Religious Program—Julie Francois, D.R.E. Students 48.

MCGREGOR, CLAYTON CO., ST. MARY (1873), [CEM] Sr. Mary McCauley, B.V.M., Pastoral Admin.; Very Rev. Frederick C. Fangmann, Supvr.; Revs. Robert M. Hirsch (Retired); Robert J. Levenhagen, Sacramental Min. (Retired).
Office: 403 S. East St., P.O. Box U, Monona, 52159. Tel: 563-539-4442; Fax: 563-539-4383.
Church: 311 Seventh St., 52157. Tel: 563-539-4442; Fax: 563-539-4383.
Catechesis/Religious Program—John Kohlstedt, D.R.E. Students 51.

MCINTIRE, MITCHELL CO., ST. MEL, Closed., For inquiries for sacramental records, please see Visitation, Stacyville.

MEYER, MITCHELL CO., SACRED HEART (1900), [CEM] Rev. Mark J. Reasoner; Alice Noethe, O.S.F., Pastoral Assoc.
Mailing Address: 1209 State St., Osage, 50461. Tel: 641-732-4342.
Parish Office: 704 Fourth St., P.O. Box 396, St. Ansgar, 50472-0396. Tel: 641-737-2262.
Church: 2695 480th St. W., McIntire, 50455.
Catechesis/Religious Program—Barbara Brumm, D.R.E. Students 52.

MONONA, CLAYTON CO., ST. PATRICK (1856), [CEM] Sr. Mary McCauley, B.V.M., Pastoral Admin.; Very Rev. Frederick C. Fangmann, Supvr.; Rev. John W. Moran, Sacramental Min. (Retired).
Church & Res.: 403 East St. S., P.O. Box U, 52159-0557. Tel: 563-539-4442.
Catechesis/Religious Program—Marilyn Ryan, D.R.E. Students 188.

MONTI, BUCHANAN CO., ST. PATRICK (1855), [CEM] Rev. Ivan R. Nienhaus; Sr. Mary Valentine Smith, O.S.F., Pastoral Assoc.
Mailing Address: 555 1st St., P.O. Box 236, Winthrop, 50682. Tel: 319-935-3523.
Church: 2856 Washington Ave., 52218.
Catechesis/Religious Program—Linda Dolan, D.R.E. Students 60.

MONTICELLO, JONES CO., SACRED HEART (1868), [CEM] Rev. Donald P. Schmitt.
Office & Res.: 328 N. Sycamore, 52310-1213. Tel: 319-465-5944.
Church: 302 N. Sycamore, 52310.
School—William Sadler, Prin. Lay Teachers 9; Students 149.
Catechesis/Religious Program—Linda Becker, D.R.E. Students 242.

MOUNT VERNON, LINN CO., ST. JOHN THE BAPTIST (1843), [CEM] Susan M. Schettler, Pastoral Admin.; Very Rev. Donald L. Klein, Admin & Supvr.; Rev. David J. Ambrosy, Sacramental Min. In Res., Rev. Ernest J. Engler (Retired).
Church, Res. & Office: 212 7th St. S.E., P.O. Box 169, 52314-0169. Tel: 319-895-6246; Fax: 319-895-0973.
Catechesis/Religious Program—Michelle Gcieszinski, D.R.E. Students 310.

NASHUA, CHICKASAW CO., ST. MICHAEL (1870), [CEM] Rev. Msgr. John W. Hemann; Sr. Mildred Leuenberger, O.S.F., Pastoral Assoc.
Res.: 612 Cedar St., P.O. Box 308, 50658-0308. Tel: 641-435-2070.
Church: 602 Cedar St., 50658.
Catechesis/Religious Program—Leslie Bonzer, D.R.E. Students 100.

NEVADA, STORY CO., ST. PATRICK (1870), [CEM] Rev. Jon M. Seda; Deacon Steven Vankerckvoorde.
Res. and Mailing Address: 410 Bailey St., P.O. Box 236, Colo, 50056-0236. Tel: 641-377-2710.
Church: 1127 Tenth St., 50201.

Catechesis/Religious Program—Barb Kuebler, D.R.E. Students 142.

NEW ALBIN, ALLAMAKEE CO., ST. JOSEPH'S (1910), [CEM] Rev. Daniel J. Knipper.
Office: 648 Main St., Lansing, 52151. Tel: 563-538-4171.
Church: 154 Third St. N.E., Lansing, 52151.
Catechesis/Religious Program—Karen Weber, D.R.E. Students 55.

NEW HAMPTON, CHICKASAW CO.

1—HOLY FAMILY, [CEM] Rev. Msgr. Carl L. Schmitt; Christine Carrier, Pastoral Assoc.; Sr. Jeanne Tranel, O.P., Pastoral Assoc.; Deacon Robert Baltes, Pastoral Assoc.
Parish Office & Mailing Address: 202 N. Broadway, 50659-1111. Tel: 641-394-2105; Fax: 641-394-5154.
Churches:—St. Joseph Worship Center; St. Mary Worship Center: 239 S. Walnut Ave., 50659-0066.
School—Kathleen Butler, Prin. Sisters 1; Lay Teachers 14; Students 220.
Catechesis/Religious Program—Marge Zipse, D.R.E. Students 258.

2—ST. JOSEPH (1870), Merged, with St. Mary, New Hampton, to form Holy Family, New Hampton.

3—ST. MARY (1894), Merged, with St. Joseph, New Hampton to form Holy Family, New Hampton.

NEW HARTFORD, BUTLER CO., ST. JOSEPH, Closed., For inquiries for sacramental records please see St. Patrick, Parkersburg.

NEW HAVEN, MITCHELL CO., ST. PETER (1876), [CEM] Rev. Ray E. Atwood.
Office: 209 E. Main St., P.O. Box 146, Riceville, 50461-0146. Tel: 641-985-2028.
Church: 2985 360th St., Osage, 50461.
Catechesis/Religious Program—Diane Sullivan, D.R.E. Students 34.

NEW MELLERAY, DUBUQUE CO., HOLY FAMILY (1850), [CEM] Rev. Richard W. Kuhn.
Res. & Office: St. John the Baptist, 241 Peosta Rd., Peosta, 52068-9507. Tel: 563-582-4217; Fax: 563-582-4217.
Church: 16500 Holy Family Ln., Peosta, 52068.
Catechesis/Religious Program—Kay Goedken, D.R.E. Students 86.

NEW VIENNA, DUBUQUE CO, ST. BONIFACE (1845), [CEM] Rev. John J. O'Connor.
Mailing Address: 7401 Columbus St., P.O. Box 215, 52065-0215. Tel: 563-921-2465.
Church: 7401 Columbus St., 52065.
School—Archbishop Hennessy Catholic See separate listing under the Institutions Located in the Archdiocese for details.
Catechesis/Religious Program—Students 8.

NEWHALL, BENTON CO., ST. PAUL (1914), Rev. Paul C. Baldwin; Sr. Nora Rochford, O.S.F., Pastoral Assoc.; Deacon Robert F. Hurych.
Mailing Address & Office: 405 Fourth Ave., P.O. Box 250, Van Horne, 52346-0250. Tel: 319-228-8131.
Church: 303 Third St. E., 52315.
Catechesis/Religious Program—Tina Becker, D.R.E. Students 121.

NORTH BUENA VISTA, CLAYTON CO., IMMACULATE CONCEPTION (1898), [CEM] Rev. Marvin J. Bries.
Mailing Address: 520 Second St., P.O. Box 847, Guttenberg, 52052-0847. Tel: 563-252-1247; 563-252-1577; Fax: 563-253-1363.
Church: 218 Main St., 52066.
Catechesis/Religious Program—Students 18.

NORTH WASHINGTON, CHICKASAW CO., IMMACULATE CONCEPTION (1868), Rev. Msgr. John W. Hemann; Sr. Mildred Leuenberger, O.S.F., Pastoral Assoc.
Mailing & Office Address: 612 Cedar St., P.O. Box 308, Nashua, 50658. Tel: 641-435-2070.
Church: 114 N. Wapsi St., 50661.
Catechesis/Religious Program—Mary Roethler, D.R.E. Students 37.

NORWAY, BENTON CO., ST. MICHAEL (1867), [CEM] Rev. Paul C. Baldwin.
Office: 405 Fourth Ave., P.O. Box 250, Van Horne, 52346-0250. Tel: 319-288-8131.
Church: 512 Evergreen, 52318.
Catechesis/Religious Program—Andrea Berger, D.R.E. Students 132.

OELWEIN, FAYETTE CO., SACRED HEART (1876), [CEM] Very Rev. Frederick C. Fangmann; Carol Hamilton, Pastoral Assoc.
Church & Res.: 628 S. Frederick Ave., 50662. Tel: 319-283-3743.
School—Sr. Benjamin Duschner, P.B.V.M., Prin. Sisters of Mercy 2; Lay Teachers 11; Students 177.
Catechesis/Religious Program—Michael Meyer, D.R.E. Students 199.

OSAGE, MITCHELL CO., SACRED HEART (1878), [CEM] Rev. Mark J. Reasoner.
Office: 1209 State St., 50461. Tel: 641-732-4342.
Church: 1204 State St., 50461.
School—Cathy Walz, Prin. Lay Teachers 8; Students 95.
Catechesis/Religious Program—Deb Angell, D.R.E.; Ann Michels, D.R.E. Students 224.

OSSIAN, WINNESHIEK CO., ST. FRANCIS DE SALES (1876), [CEM] Rev. Msgr. Cletus J. Hawes; Rev. Donald J. Hawes.
Res. & Office: 418 E. Main St., 52161-9998. Tel: 563-532-9366.
Church: 420 E. Main St., 52161.
School—Mae Becker, Prin. Lay Teachers 9; Students 124.
Catechesis/Religious Program—Patricia Frana, D.R.E. Students 92.

OTTER CREEK, JACKSON CO., ST. LAWRENCE (1854), Sr. Virginia Crilly, B.V.M., Pastoral Admin.; Very Rev. Donald J. Plamondon, Supvr.; Rev. Paul E. Lippstock, Sacramental Min.
Mailing & Parish Office Address: 507 Elm St., P.O. Box 26, La Motte, 52054-0026. Tel: 319-773-2323.
Church: 17434 Bellevue-Cascade Rd., Zwingle, 52079.
Catechesis/Religious Program—Kelly McMahon, D.R.E. Students 30.

OXFORD JUNCTION, JONES CO., SACRED HEART (1890), Rev. John K. Sterling.
Mailing Address: 301 Hwy. 136, P.O. Box 127, Lost Nation, 52254-0127. Tel: 563-678-2200; Fax: 563-678-2389.
Church: 309 Church St., 52323.

PARKERSBURG, BUTLER CO., ST. PATRICK (1889), [CEM] Rev. Dennis J. Quint.
Parish Office: 204 G. Avenue, Grundy Center, 50638. Tel: 319-824-3572; Fax: 319-824-3857.
Church: 304 Second St., 50665.
Catechesis/Religious Program—Ann Nicklaus-Schmelzer, D.R.E. Students 52.

PEOSTA, DUBUQUE CO., ST. JOHN THE BAPTIST (1874), [CEM] Rev. Richard W. Kuhn; Sr. Mary Kent Pearson, O.P., Pastoral Assoc.
Res. & Office: 241 Peosta St., 52068-9507. Tel: 563-582-4217; Fax: 563-582-4217.
Church: 235 Peosta St., 52068.
School—Seton Catholic Elementary Consolidation, Epworth See separate listing under the Institutions Located in the Archdiocese for details.
Catechesis/Religious Program—Sr. Mary Kent Pearson, O.P., D.R.E. Students 123.

PINHOOK, ST. BRIDGET ORATORY, Closed., Sacramental Records located at Immaculate Conception, Sumner.

PLACID, DUBUQUE CO., ST. JOHN'S (1874), [CEM] Rev. Raymond A. Burkle; Deacon Gerald Koopmann.
Office—104 First St. S.E., P.O. Box 286, Epworth, 52045.
Res.: 22453 E. Pleasant Grove Rd., Epworth, 52045. Tel: 563-876-5501.
School—Seton Catholic Elementary School, Epworth See separate listing under the Institutions Located in the Archdiocese for details.
Catechesis/Religious Program—Robin Flick, D.R.E. Students 34.

PLYMOUTH ROCK, WINNESHIEK CO., ST. AGNES (1857), Closed., Sacramental records are located at Notre Dame, Cresco.

PLYMOUTH, CERRO GORDO CO., ST. MICHAEL (1872), Rev. David G. Kucera.
Office—Sacred Heart Parish, 120 E. North, P.O. Box 160, Manly, 50456-0160. Tel: 641-454-2586.
Church: 901 Rock St., 50464.

POSTVILLE, ALLAMAKEE CO., ST. BRIDGET'S (1872), Very Rev. Frederick C. Fangmann; Revs. Lloyd Paul Ouderkirk (Retired); Richard G. Goul; Sr. Mary McCauley, B.V.M., Pastoral Admin.
Office: 403 East St., P.O. Box U, Monona, 52159-0557. Tel: 563-539-4442; Fax: 563-539-4383.
Church: 141 W. Williams St., 52162.
Catechesis/Religious Program—Ann Erickson, D.R.E.; Michael Erickson, D.R.E. Students 87.

PRAIRIE, JASPER CO., ST. JOSEPH, Closed., For inquiries for parish records, please see St. John the Baptist, Peosta.

PRAIRIEBURG, LINN CO., ST. JOSEPH (1874), [CEM] Rev. Wayne J. Droessler; Sr. Anne Kisting, O.S.F., Pastoral Assoc.
Mailing Address: P.O. Box 4248, 52219-4248.
Parish Office—211 3rd St. N., P.O. Box 47, Coggon, 52218. Tel: 319-435-2236.
Church: 300 West Ave., 52219.
Catechesis/Religious Program—Marci Luedeman, D.R.E. Students 25.

PRESTON, JACKSON CO., ST. JOSEPH (1881), [CEM] Very Rev. Donald J. Plamondon.
Church, Res. & Mailing Address: 250 S. Faith St., P.O. Box 309, 52069-0309. Tel: 563-689-5161.
Catechesis/Religious Program—Irene Entsminger, D.R.E.; Rosemary Sievers, D.R.E. Students 192.

PROTIVIN, HOWARD CO., HOLY TRINITY (1878), [CEM] Rev. John A. Moser.
Res. & Mailing Address: 110 Commercial Ave., P.O. Box 205, 52163-0205. Tel: 563-569-8259; Fax: 563-569-8272.
Church: 124 N. Main St., 52163.
School—Dana Spry, Prin. Lay Teachers 10; Students 83.
Catechesis/Religious Program—Sheila Rassman, D.R.E. Students 67.

RAYMOND, BLACKHAWK CO., ST. JOSEPH (1905), [CEM] Rev. Rick D. Dagit.
Res. & Mailing Address: 311 15th Ave., P.O. Box 136, Gilbertville, 50634. Tel: 319-296-1092.
Church: 313 E. Central St.., 50667.
School—Immaculate Conception-St. Joseph (Gilbertville-Raymond Consolidated Elementary) See separate listing under the Institutions Located in the Archdiocese for details.

REILLY SETTLEMENT, CHICKASAW, CO., SACRED HEART, Closed., For inquiries for parish records, please see Assumption, Little Turkey.

REINBECK, GRUNDY CO., QUEEN OF HEAVEN (1958), [CEM] Rev. Dennis J. Quint.
Office & Res.: 204 G Ave., Grundy Center, 50638. Tel: 319-824-3572; Fax: 319-824-3857.
Church: 1006 Blackhawk St., 50669.
Catechesis/Religious Program—Ann Nicklaus Schmelzer, D.R.E. Students 75.

RICEVILLE, HOWARD CO., IMMACULATE CONCEPTION (1879), [CEM] Rev. Ray E. Atwood.
Res. and Mailing Address: 209 E. Main St., Box 146, 50466-0146. Tel: 641-985-2028.
Church: 211 Main St., 50466.
Catechesis/Religious Program—Deborah Oulman, D.R.E. Students 114.

RICKARDSVILLE, DUBUQUE CO., ST. JOSEPH (1840), [CEM] Bro. Stephen W. Markham, F.S.C., Pastoral Admin.; Rev. Msgr. James O. Barta, Supvr.; Revs. Thomas R. Zinkula; Henry P. Huber, Sacramental Min.
Res.: 835 Church St., P.O. Box 398, Holy Cross, 52053. Tel: 563-870-4041.
Church: 20249 St. Joseph Dr., 52039-9757.
School—Rickardsville-Holy Cross-Luxemburg (RHCL) Catholic See separate listing under the Institutions Located in the Archdiocese for details.
Catechesis/Religious Program—Mary Anne Manternach, D.R.E. Students 33.

ROCKFORD, FLOYD CO., HOLY NAME (1910), Rev. Craig E. Steimel.
Church & Parish Office: 507 First Ave. N.W., 50468. Tel: 641-756-3569.
Catechesis/Religious Program—Mabel Zeran, D.R.E. Students 107.

ROCKWELL, CERRO GORDO CO., SACRED HEART (1878), [CEM] Rev. Craig E. Steimel.
Church, Res. & Mailing Address: 305 Elm St. E., P.O. Box 30, 50469. Tel: 641-822-4957.
Catechesis/Religious Program—Students 88.

ROSEVILLE, FLOYD CO., ST. MARY (1867), [CEM] Rev. Msgr. Walter L. Brunkan.
Office & Res.: 105 N. Main, P.O. Box 480, Greene, 50636-0480. Tel: 641-823-4146.
Church: 2397 Hwy. 14, Marble Rock, 50653.
Catechesis/Religious Program—Janet Willert, D.R.E. Students 61.

ROWLEY, BUCHANAN CO., ALL SAINTS (1896), Rev. Aloysius J. Vorwald.
Mailing Address: 3103 Michael, 52329-0206.
Office & Res.: 209 Fifth Ave. E., Independence, 50644. Tel: 319-334-7191.
Church: 219 Park Ave., 52329.
Catechesis/Religious Program—Students 23.

RYAN, DELAWARE CO., ST. PATRICK (1882), [CEM] Rev. Msgr. Ralph P. Simington; Rev. Dennis W. Miller.
Mailing Address & Res.: 615 Howard St., P.O. Box 219, 52330-0219. Tel: 563-932-2151.
Church: 606 Franklin St., 52330.
Catechesis/Religious Program—Kathy Oberreuter, D.R.E. Students 78.

ST. ANSGAR, MITCHELL CO., ST. ANSGAR (1951), Rev. Mark J. Reasoner; Alice Noethe, O.S.F., Pastoral Assoc.
Mailing Address: 1209 State St., Osage, 50461.
Catechesis/Religious Program—Diane Mayer, D.R.E.; Lisa Heimer, D.R.E. Students 76.

ST. ANTHONY, MARSHALL CO., SACRED HEART (1878), [CEM] Rev. Jon M. Seda; Deacon Steven Van Kerchvoorde.
410 Bailey St., P.O. Box 236, Colo, 50056.
Parish Office: 1110 11th St., Nevada, 50201. Tel: 515-382-2974; Fax: 515-382-5966.
Church: 416 Main St., 50239.
Catechesis/Religious Program—Students 3.

ST. CATHERINE, DUBUQUE CO., ST. CATHERINE (1887), [CEM] Revs. Stephen L. Meyer; Scott E. Bullock; Sr. Linda Bechen, R.S.M., Pastoral Assoc.
Church & Mailing Address: 5189 St. Catherine Rd., 52003. Tel: 563-583-0092.
School—Bellevue Area Catholic Elementary See separate listing under the Institutions Located in the Archdiocese for details.
Catechesis/Religious Program—Sr. Linda Bechen, R.S.M., D.R.E. Students 22.

ST. CECILIA, HOWARD CO., ST. PATRICK'S, Closed., Sacramental records are located at Immaculate Conception, Elma.

ST. DONATUS, JACKSON CO., ST. DONATUS (1853), [CEM] Revs. Stephen L. Meyer; Scott E. Bullock,

Sacramental Priest.
Res. and Mailing Address: 5189 St. Catherine Rd., 52003. Tel: 563-583-0092.
Church: E. First St., 52071.
School—Bellevue Area Catholic Elementary See separate listing under the Institutions Located in the Archdiocese for details.
Catechesis/Religious Program—Sr. Linda Bechen, R.S.M., D.R.E. Students 25.

ST. LUCAS, FAYETTE CO., ST. LUKE, Formerly St. Luke's (1855), [CEM] Rev. Marvin C. Salz; Sr. LouAnn Doering, P.B.V.M., Pastoral Assoc.
Church & Res.: 207 E. Main St., P.O. Box 187, 52166-0187. Tel: 563-778-2370.
School—Trinity Catholic School, Protovin See separate listing under the Institutions Located in the Archdiocese for details.
Catechesis/Religious Program—Kathleen Drilling, D.R.E. Students 66.

ST. THERESA, JACKSON CO., ST. THERESA, Formerly St. Theresa's (1853), [CEM] Sr. Virginia Crilly, B.V.M., Pastoral Admin.; Very Rev. Donald J. Plamondon; Rev. Paul E. Lippstock.
Mailing Address: 507 Elm St., P.O. Box 26, LaMotte, 52054-0026. Tel: 563-773-2341.
Catechesis/Religious Program—Mary Kay Kane, D.R.E. Students 31.

SABULA, JACKSON CO., ST. PETER (1840), [CEM] Joan M. Head, Pastoral Admin.; Very Rev. Donald J. Plamondon, Priest Supr. & Sacramental Priest.
Church & Parish Office: 504 Elk St., P.O. Box 429, 52070. Tel: 563-687-2525.
Catechesis/Religious Program—Joan M. Head, D.R.E. Students 29.

SAND SPRINGS, DELAWARE CO., IMMACULATE CONCEPTION, Closed., For inquiries for sacramental records, please see St. Luke, Hopkinton.

SCHLEY, HOWARD CO., HOLY CROSS ORATORY, Closed., For inquiries for sacramental records, please see Holy Trinity, Protivin.

SHELL ROCK, BUTLER CO., HOLY NAME, Closed., Sacramental records are located at St. Mary, Waverly.

SHERRILL, DUBUQUE CO., SS. PETER AND PAUL (1852), [CEM] Bro. Stephen W. Markham, F.S.C.; Rev. Msgr. James O. Barta, Priest Supvr.; Revs. Thomas R. Zinkula, Sacramental Priest; Henry Huber, Sacramental Priest.
Office & Res. Address: 835 Church St., P.O. Box 398, Holy Cross, 52053. Tel: 563-870-4041.
Church: 5131 Sherrill Rd., 52073-9612.
School—Balltown-Sherrill Catholic See separate listing under the Institutions Located in the Archdiocese for details.
Catechesis/Religious Program—Mary Anne Manternach, D.R.E. Students 84.

SOUTH GARRYOWEN, ST. ALOYSIUS, Closed., For sacramental records please contact St. Patrick, Garryowen, Bernard.

SPILLVILLE, WINNESHIEK CO., ST. WENCESLAUS (1860), [CEM] Rev. Donald J. Hawes.
Church & Res.: 207 Church St., Box 128, 52168-0128. Tel: 563-562-3637.
School—Calmar-Festina-Spillville (CFS) Catholic Elementary See separate listing under the Institutions Located in the Archdiocese for details.
Catechesis/Religious Program—Helen Pinter, D.R.E. Combined with St. Aloysius, Calmar, and Our Lady of Seven Dolors, Festina. Students 73.

SPRINGBROOK, JACKSON CO., SS. PETER AND PAUL (1864), [CEM] Very Rev. Donald J. Plamondon.
Mailing Address: 105 E. Main St., P.O Box 97, 52075. Tel: 563-872-3875.
Church: 107 E. Main St., 52075.
School—Bellevue Area Catholic Elementary See separate listing under the Institutions Located in the Archdiocese for details.
Catechesis/Religious Program—Sr. Linda Bechen, R.S.M., D.R.E. Students 30.

SPRINGVILLE, LINN CO., ST. ISIDORE (1961), Susan M. Schettler, Pastoral Admin.; Very Rev. Donald L. Klein, Supvr.; Rev. David J. Ambrosy, Sacramental Min.
Mailing Address: 603 6th St., P.O. Box 318, 52336. Tel: 319-854-6141; Fax: 319-854-7414.
Church: 603 6th St. S., 52336.
Catechesis/Religious Program—Dee Heinrich, D.R.E. Students 83.

STACYVILLE, MITCHELL CO., CHURCH OF THE VISITATION (1894), [CEM] Rev. Mark J. Reasoner; Alice Noethe, O.S.F., Pastoral Assoc.
Parish Office & Mailing Address: 1209 State St., Osage, 50461. Tel: 641-732-4342.
Church: 604 N. Broad St., 50476.
Catechesis/Religious Program—Denise Mayer, D.R.E. Students 79.

STATE CENTER, MARSHALL CO., ST. JOSEPH (1870), [CEM] Rev. Jon M. Seda; Deacon Steven Van Kerchvoorde.
Mailing Address: 410 Bailey St., P.O. Box 236, Colo, 50056. Tel: 641-377-2710.
Church: 610 Third St. S.W., 50247.
Catechesis/Religious Program—Judy Goodman, D.R.E. Students 99.

STONE CITY JONES CO., ST. JOSEPH ORATORY, Closed., Sacramental records are located at St. Patrick, Anamosa

STRAWBERRY POINT, CLAYTON CO., ST. MARY (1876), [CEM] Rev. John C. Paisley.
Church & Mailing Address: 314 W. Mission St., 52076-9432. Tel: 563-933-6090.
Catechesis/Religious Program—Patty Hilton, D.R.E.; Mary Hamblin, D.R.E. Students 108.

SUMNER, BREMER CO.

1—ST. FRANCIS OF ASSISI (1879), [CEM] Rev. John J. Purtell.
Mailing Address: 413 W. First St., 50674. Tel: 563-578-5366.
Church: 205 Lovers Ln., Fayette, 52142.
Catechesis/Religious Program—Holly Streeter, D.R.E. Students 81.

2—IMMACULATE CONCEPTION (1894), [CEM] Rev. John J. Purtell.
Church, Res. & Office: 413 W. First St., 50674-1313. Tel: 563-578-5366.
Catechesis/Religious Program—Kyle Flynn, D.R.E. Students 123.

SWALEDALE, CERRO GORDO CO., ST. LAWRENCE, Closed., For sacramental records please contact Sacred Heart, Rockwell.

SYLVIA, DUBUQUE CO., ASSUMPTION (1896), Very Rev. Donald J. Plamondon, Supvr.; Rev. Paul E. Lippstock; Sr. Virginia Crilly, B.V.M., Pastoral Admin.
Mailing Address: 507 Elm St., P.O. Box 26, La Motte, 52054. Tel: 563-773-2323.
Church: Washington-Mills Rd., Zwingle, 52079.
Catechesis/Religious Program—Mary Kay Kane, D.R.E. Students 17.

TAMA, TAMA CO., ST. PATRICK (1864), [CEM] Rev. Keith L. Birch; Tom Christoffer, Pastoral Assoc.
Res. & Office: 900 Park St., 52339. Tel: 641-484-3039; 641-484-4242.
Church: 600 Oswego, 52339.
Catechesis/Religious Program—Anne Christoffer, D.R.E. Students 168.

TEMPLE HILL, JONES CO., ST. PETER (1852), [CEM] Rev. Msgr. Thomas E. Toale.
Res. & Office: 20189 Temple Hill Rd., Cascade, 52033. Tel: 563-852-3448.
Church: 20123 Temple Hill Rd., Cascade, 52033.
School—Aquin Elementary School See separate listing under the Institutions Located in the Archdiocese for details.
Catechesis/Religious Program—Julie Orris, D.R.E. Clustered with St. Matthias, Cascade; Sacred Heart, Fillmore; and St. Patrick, Garryowen. Students 30.

TRAER, TAMA CO., ST. PAUL (1912), [CEM] Rev. John R. Tilp.
Church, Res. & Office: 1102 Walnut St., 50675-1440. Tel: 319-478-2222.
Catechesis/Religious Program—Lynne McGivern, D.R.E. Students 70.

URBANA, BENTON CO., ST. MARY (1872), [CEM] Rev. Gabriel C Anderson.
Mailing Address: 516 Rowley St., P.O. Box 116, Walker, 52352-0116. Tel: 319-448-4316.
Church: 401 Ash Ave., 52345.
Catechesis/Religious Program—Cheryl Becker, D.R.E.; Tom Dricken, D.R.E. Students 137.

VAN HORNE BENTON CO., IMMACULATE CONCEPTION (1869), [CEM] Rev. Paul C. Baldwin; Sr. Nora Rochford, O.S.F., Pastoral Assoc.; Deacon Robert F. Hurych.
Church & Res.: 405 Fourth Ave., P.O. Box 250, 52346-0250. Tel: 319-228-8131.
Catechesis/Religious Program—Angie Hagen, D.R.E. Students 93.

VINING, TAMA CO., ST. MARY (1874),, Oratory. For sacramental records, please see St. Paul, Traer.

VINTON, BENTON CO., ST. MARY (1878), [CEM] Rev. Joseph E. McGuire.
Church, Res. & Office: 2200 S. Second Ave., 52349. Tel: 319-472-4448.
Catechesis/Religious Program—Diane Walston, D.R.E. Students 190.

VOLGA, CLAYTON CO., SACRED HEART (1859), [CEM] Rev. Paul R. Peters.
Mailing Address: P.O. Box 135, 52077-0135. Tel: 563-245-2548.
Parish Office Address—330 1st St. S.W., P.O. Box 626, Elkader, 52043-0626.
Church: 304 White St., 52077.
Catechesis/Religious Program—Jennifer Dillon, D.R.E. Students 47.

WADENA, FAYETTE CO., ST. JOSEPH ORATORY, Closed., Sacramental Records located at St. Joseph, Elkader.

WALFORD, LINN CO., HOLY TRINITY (1890), Closed., For sacramental records, please see John XIII, Cedar Rapids.

WALKER, LINN CO., SACRED HEART (1885), CEM] Rev. Gabriel C. Anderson.
Res.: 516 Rowley St., P.O. Box 116, 52352-0116. Tel: 319-448-4316.
Church: 518 Rowley St., 52352.
Catechesis/Religious Program—Bonnie Morris, D.R.E.; Cheryl Becker, D.R.E. Students 111.

WATERLOO, BLACKHAWK CO.

1—BLESSED SACRAMENT (1947), [JC] Very Rev. Dennis D. Juhl; Sr. Madonna M. Friedman, O.S.F., Pastoral Assoc.; Deacons John Herman; James Freet; Norman Schauls.
Church, Res. & Office: 650 Stephan Ave., 50701-2099. Tel: 319-233-6179; Fax: 319-233-6051.
School—Tel: 319-233-7863. Nancy Stirm, Prin. Lay Teachers 12; Students 198.
Catechesis/Religious Program—Barbara Duggan, D.R.E. Students 202.

2—ST. EDWARD (1945), [JC] Revs. Jerry Kopacek; Christopher R. Podhajsky; Deacon John Baker; Karol Rae Hoth, Pastoral Assoc.
Church, Res. & Office: 1423 Kimball Ave., 50702-3837. Tel: 319-233-8060.
School—Chris Mitchell, Prin. (Elementary). Sisters 1; Lay Teachers 23; Students 404.
Catechesis/Religious Program—Mary Pedersen, D.R.E. Students 149.

3—ST. JOHN (1923), Merged, with St. Mary & St. Joseph, Waterloo and St. Nicholas, Evansdale to form Queen of Peace, Waterloo.

4—ST. JOSEPH, Merged, with St. Mary & St. John, Waterloo and St. Nicholas, Evansdale to form Queen of Peace, Waterloo.

5—ST. MARY (1898), Merged, with St. John & St. Joseph, Waterloo and St. Nicholas, Evansdale to form Queen of Peace, Waterloo.

6—QUEEN OF PEACE (1868), Revs. Dennis J. Colter; Kenneth J. Glaser; Sr. JoAnn O'Connell, B.V.M., Pastoral Assoc.; Deacons Larry Gram; William Jenney; Ed Weber.
Mailing, Parish Office & Rectory Address: 2127 E. 4th St., 50703-2699. Tel: 319-226-3655. Email: dbq213@arch.pvt.k12.ia.us.
School—Beth Wright, Prin. Sisters 1; Lay Teachers 12; Students 130.
Catechesis/Religious Program—Martha Real, D.R.E.; Bev Byford, D.R.E. Students 142.

7—SACRED HEART (1909), [JC] Rev. Clayton Landherr; Nancy Rigel, Pastoral Assoc.
Church, Res. & Office: 627 W. Fourth St., 50702-1501. Tel: 319-234-4996.
School—Julie Niemeyer, Prin. Sisters 1; Lay Teachers 18; Students 304.
Catechesis/Religious Program—Pam Johnston, D.R.E. Students 105.

WATKINS, BENTON CO., ST. PATRICK (1880), [CEM] Rev. Paul C. Baldwin.
Mailing Address: 405 Fourth Ave., P.O. Box 250, Van Horne, 52346. Tel: 319-227-8131.
Church: 2nd St., 52354.
Catechesis/Religious Program—Yvonne Brecht, D.R.E. Students 37.

WAUCOMA, FAYETTE CO., ST. MARY (1898), [CEM] Rev. Marvin C. Salz.
Mailing Address & Church: 218 3rd St. N.W., P.O. Box 215, 52171. Tel: 563-776-6364.
Catechesis/Religious Program—Maxine Balk, D.R.E.; Cathy Humpal, D.R.E. Students 81.

WAUKON, ALLAMAKEE CO., ST. PATRICK (1851), [CEM] Rev. Joseph M. Schneider.
Res.: 109 Second St. S.W., Box 146, 52172. Tel: 563-568-3671; Fax: 563-568-2170.
School—Tel: 563-568-2415. Marcia Kruse, Prin. Lay Teachers 12; Students 130.
Catechesis/Religious Program—Kris Ward, D.R.E. Students 298.

WAVERLY, BREMER CO., ST. MARY (1856), [CEM] Rev. Michael L. Tauke.
Res.: 112 Second Ave. S.E., 50677-3404. Tel: 319-352-2493; Fax: 319-352-0204.
Church: 120 Second Ave., S.E., 50677.
Catechesis/Religious Program—Katie Pfiffner, D.R.E. Students 408.

WEBSTER CITY, HAMILTON CO., ST. THOMAS AQUINAS (1870), [CEM] Rev. John R. Flaherty.
Res. & Office: 1000 Des Moines St., 50595-2147. Tel: 515-832-1190; Fax: 515-832-1304.
Church: 1010 Des Moines St., 50595-2147.
School—Tel: 515-832-1346. Michael Pavik, Prin. Lay Teachers 10; Students 142.
Catechesis/Religious Program—(Grades K-6) Jennifer Maharry, D.R.E. Students 135.

WEST RIDGE, ALLAMAKEE CO., ST. JOHN THE BAPTIST ORATORY, Closed., Sacramental Records are located at St. Patrick, Waukon.

WEST UNION, FAYETTE CO., HOLY NAME (1870), [CEM] Rev. Dale J. Rausch.
Church, Res. & Office: 128 N. Walnut St., 52175. Tel: 563-422-3184.
Catechesis/Religious Program—Marion Broghammer, D.R.E.; Sue McDonough, D.R.E. Students 213.

WEXFORD, ALLAMAKEE CO., IMMACULATE CONCEPTION

(1851), [CEM] Rev. Louis J. Trzil.
Church, Res. & Mailing Address: 1416 Great River Rd., Lansing, 52151. Tel: 563-586-2150.
Catechesis/Religious Program—Regina Manning, D.R.E. Students 36.

WILLIAMS, HAMILTON CO., ST. MARY (1875), [CEM] Rev. John R. Flaherty.
Mailing Address: 1010 Des Moines St., Webster City, 50595-2147. Tel: 515-854-2241; Fax: 515-854-2343.
Parish Office Address—404 4th St., P.O. Box 157, 50271-0157. Tel: 515-854-2241.
Church: 404 Fourth St., 50271.
Catechesis/Religious Program—Students 13.

WINTHROP, BUCHANAN CO., ST. PATRICK (1894), [CEM] Rev. Ivan R. Nienhaus; Sr. Mary Valentine Smith, O.S.F., Pastoral Assoc.
Church & Res.: 555 First St., P.O. Box 236, 50682-0236. Tel: 319-935-3523.
Catechesis/Religious Program—Deb Steffen, D.R.E. Students 149.

WODEN, HANCOCK CO., SACRED HEART (1900), Closed., For sacramental records, please see St. Patrick, Britt.

WORTHINGTON, DUBUQUE CO., ST. PAUL'S (1875), [CEM] Rev. Msgr. Edward C. Petty. In Res., Rev. Douglas J. Loecke.
Office—314 Third Ave. S.W., P.O. Box 38, 52078-0038. Tel: 563-855-2405.
Church: 301 S. 2nd Ave. S.W., 52078.
School—Vicki Palmer, Prin. Lay Teachers 5; Students 64.
Catechesis/Religious Program—Julie Bries, D.R.E. Students 46.

ZEARING, STORY CO., ST. GABRIEL (1904), Rev. Jon M. Seda; Deacon Steven Van Kerchvoorde.
Mailing Address: 410 Bailey St., P.O. Box 236, Colo, 50056-0236. Tel: 641-377-2710.
Church: 302 N. Center, 50278.
Catechesis/Religious Program—Students 12.

Chaplains of Public Institutions

ANAMOSA. *Iowa State Men's Reformatory*. Sacramental Services: (Vacant).
INDEPENDENCE. *Mental Health Institute Sacramental Services*. (Vacant)
MARSHALLTOWN. *Veterans' Home*. Sr. Rosemary Vaske, O.S.F., Chap., Rev. Jon M. Seda, Sacramental Priest.

On Special or Other Archdiocesan Assignment:
Rev. Msgrs.—
Barta, James O., Vicar General & Dubuque Region Episcopal Vicar
Bleich, Russell M., Episcopal Vicar, Cedar Rapids Region
Connolly, Leon L., Vicar for Hispanic Min.
Walz, W. Dean, Episcopal Vicar, Waterloo Region
Revs.—
Gibbs, Phillip G. Tel: 563-556-2580 Dir. of Vocation Awareness
Haugen, John S., 1450 Alta Vista St., 52001. Spiritual Dir. & Advocate for Catholic Mission & Identity at Loras College, Dubuque
Ressler, Mark A., 1019 W. 23rd St., Cedar Falls, 50613. Dir. of St. Stephen the Witness Student Center

On Duty Outside the Archdiocese:
Rev. Msgr.—
Funke, Richard P., 7974 Sailboat Key Blvd., Box 602, South Pasadena, FL 33707. Tel: 727-363-1754
Revs.—
Flanagan, James W., Dept. of Religion, Mather House, Case Western Reserve Univ., Cleveland, OH 44106. Tel: 216-791-3030; 216-368-4129
Lundgren, Stephen A., St. Agnes Medical Center, 1303 E. Herndon Ave., Fresno, CA 93720. Tel: 559-323-8059
Riley, Leo P., St. Charles Borromeo, 21505 Augusta Ave., Ste. 4, Port Charlotte, FL 33952. Tel: 941-625-4754
Wild, Alexander, P.O. Box 479, 52004-0479.

Military Chaplains:
Revs.—
Lawrence, Andrew Ch. (Cpt..) 95/033 Kahoea St., #212, Mililani, HI 96789. Tel: 808-625-3852
Lippstock, Paul E. Ch. (Maj.) South Cargo, TF-1-133 IN (AASLT) Headquarters Co., Unit 31530, Apo, AE 09833.
Remy, David P., CDR,CHC, USN, 3101 Marcus Pointe Blvd., Pensacola, FL 32505. Tel: 850-473-9426
Schueller, La Verne L. Ch. Col. 504 Greenwood Cove S., Niceville, FL 32578. Tel: 850-897-0155

Retired:
Rev. Msgrs.—
Chihak, John P., 420 W. Lyon St., Garner, 50438. Tel: 641-923-3365
Connolly, Leon L., 320 Mulberry St., Waterloo, 50703-3598. Tel: 319-287-6414
Dalton, John W., 1301 Rhodes, Naperville, IL 60540. Tel: 630-355-2664
Ferring, Robert L., Villa Raphael, 1155 Mt. Loretta Ave., 52003. Tel: 563-556-8942
Friedl, Francis P., Villa Raphael, 1155 Mt. Loretta Ave., 52003. Tel: 563-588-8018
Hayek, Stanley J., 210 Park Ave., Charles City, 50616. Tel: 641-228-1664
Heineman, Donald P., 108 3rd St. S.E., P.O. Box 187, Fort Atkinson, 52144-0187. Tel: 563-534-3052
Heles, Frederic G., P.O. Box 1435, Venice, FL 34284-1435. Tel: 941-488-6401
Heuring, Alvan P., 3458 Edison St., San Mateo, CA 94403-3401. Tel: 650-341-1645
Kurt, Edgar J., Villa Raphael, 1155 Mt. Loretta Ave., 52003. Tel: 563-583-1658
Lang, Charles E., 8359 W. Addison, #404, Chicago, IL 60634. Tel: 773-589-2660
Lechtenberg, Edward W., 321 Diagonal St., Lansing, 52151. Tel: 563-538-4773
Leonard, William P., 971 Mt. Loretta Ave., 52003. Tel: 563-583-9003
Manternach, Albert V., 617 1st Ave. W., P.O. Box 728, Cascade, 52033. Tel: 563-852-3696
McAvoy, Ambrose A., Stonehill Care Center, 3485 Windsor Ave., 52001-1312. Tel: 563-588-4617
McClean, John R., 1538 Kehl Ct., 52003. Tel: 563-556-1922
Norton, Claude B., Stonehill Care Center, 3485 Windsor Ave., 52001-1312.
Ralph, Thomas J., 400 Woodland Ridge, 52003. Tel: 563-587-1977
Reicks, Leander H., Colonial Manor, 9th & Maple, Elma, 50628. Tel: 641-393-2094
Slepicka, Joseph J., 313 N. 13th St., Clear Lake, 50428. Tel: 641-357-2448
Steimel, Paul T., 3709 W. 9th St., Apt. 8, Waterloo, 50702. Tel: 319-233-5287
Tobin, Neil W., 3580 Pennsylvania Ave., Unit 5, 52002-5181. Tel: 563-567-7030
Vogl, Robert R., Villa Raphael, 1155 Mt. Loretta Ave, 52003. Tel: 563-556-4997
Wheeler, David A., St. Mary Rectory, 1584 White St., 52001-4905. Tel: 563-556-9251
Revs.—
Ament, Robert J., 1375 273rd Ave., Fort Atkinson, 52144-7405. Tel: 563-534-3023
Auer, Robert F., 1027 N. Third St., Guttenberg, 52052. Tel: 563-252-2109
Barnes, John G., 114 Sheakley, New Hampton, 50659. Tel: 641-394-2394
Bodensteiner, Peter C., 108 W. Spring St., Apt. A-1, Lawler, 52154. Tel: 563-238-8751
Braak, Thomas E., 205 W. Ingledue St., 50158. Tel: 641-752-3846
Burke, Clement J., 2321 Aldrich Ave. S., #315, Minneapolis, MN 55405. Tel: 612-377-0991
Carpender, John W., 720 Duggan Dr., #1, 52003-0250. Tel: 563-582-6993
Carpender, Thomas J., Brookwood, Apt. 413, 1320 E. 48th Pl., Tulsa, OK 74105. Tel: 918-745-0732
Condon, Gerald A., 1320 Wenig Rd. N.E., #10, Cedar Rapids, 52402. Tel: 319-366-1287
Devine, William P., 22623 V Ave., Eldora, 50627-8012. Tel: 641-858-2222
Drexler, Harold J., Sacred Heart Rectory, 2215 Windsor Ave., 52001-1698. Tel: 563-583-1709
Engler, Ernest J., 1875 Pinehurst Ct., Waterloo, 50701. Tel: 319-232-8733
Evans, Paul J., 400 Blunt St., Charles City, 50616. Tel: 641-228-9835
Friedell, John C., 1920 Cox St., Apt. #3, 52001. Tel: 563-556-9176
Gallagher, John R., Mercy Medical-Hallmar, 701 Tenth St. S.E., Cedar Rapids, 52403. Tel: 319-398-6011
Geary, Patrick G., 443 S. Roosevelt Rd., Evansdale, 50707-1269. Tel: 319-236-2869
Hamilton, Philip A., 12 Padgett Ct., Bluffton, SC 29909.
Heimerman, Francis D., 151 Main St., P.O. Box 623, Nashua, 50658. Tel: 641-435-2261
Hemann, Melvin D., 127 Kaspend Pl., Cedar Falls, 50613-1683. Tel: 319-266-3889
Herzog, John M., 1004 Mesa Verde Pl., Ames, 50014. Tel: 515-292-0558
Hess, Richard J., Immaculate Conception Rectory, 857 3rd Ave. S.E., P.O. Box 1247, Cedar Rapids, 52406. Tel: 319-362-7181
Hilmer, Robert E., 320 Mulberry St., Waterloo, 50703-3598. Tel: 319-287-6411
Hirsch, Robert M., 411 N. Jefferson St., P.O. Box 609, Calmar, 52132-0609. Tel: 563-562-4062
Hussmann, John R., Villa Raphael, 1155 Mt. Loretta Ave., 52003. Tel: 563-582-4339
Karal, John W., 308 W. Nevada, 50158-2751. Tel: 641-753-8345
Karnik, George W., 750 River Forest Rd., #35, Evansdale, 50707. Tel: 319-226-5412
Katz, Roger L., 400 17th St. W., Clear Lake, 50428. Tel: 641-357-2003
Keppler, Daniel J., 1524 Riverview Dr., Lansing, 52151. Tel: 563-586-2828
Kissling, John M., P.O. Box 356, Chetek, WI 54728. Tel: 715-924-4563
Kleinfehn, Walter J., 4850 16th Ave., S.W., Apt.103, Cedar Rapids, IL 52404. Tel: 319-390-0643
Kurt, Allan J., P.O. Box 479, 52004-0479.
Kutsch, Eugene C., 2622 New Haven St., 52001. Tel: 563-583-1638
LaBarge, Charles F., 1235 Mt. Loretta Ave., 52003-7826. Tel: 563-556-6936
Laughlin, Martin T., Holy Family Church, 24 Pope Ave., Hilton Head Island, SC 29938. Tel: 843-785-2895
Levenhagen, Robert J., 283 Harbor Lights Dr., Brownsville, MN 55919. Tel: 507-482-6602
Ludwig, Raphael A., St. John Nepomucene Rectory, 202 Second St. S.E., Fort Atkinson, 52144-0157. Tel: 563-534-7663
Maichen, Richard F., 1009 New St., Manchester, 52057. Tel: 563-927-8137
Manternach, Carl J., 420 N. Maple, Monticello, 52310. Tel: 319-465-6348
McAndrew, Thomas F., 14258 Dietz Dr., 52002. Tel: 563-588-3389
McDonald, Paul F., 8915 Willmon Way, San Antonio, TX 78239. Tel: 210-637-1990 U.S.A.F.
Menster, William J., Villa Raphael, 1155 Mt. Loretta Ave, 52003. Tel: 563-556-6718
Merfeld, Vincent C., 751 S. Windsor Blvd., Los Angeles, CA 90005. Tel: 213-938-3577
Moran, John W., 507 Cherry Dr., P.O. Box 970, Monona, 52159. Tel: 563-539-2927
O'Brien, Joseph V., Villa Raphael, 1155 Mt. Loretta Ave., 52003. Tel: 563-556-4326
O'Brien, William D., Villa Raphael, 1155 Mt. Loretta Ave., 52003. Tel: 563-582-9933
Otting, Loras C., Villa Raphael, 1155 Mt. Loretta Ave., 52003. Tel: 563-583-3866
Ouderkirk, Lloyd Paul, 24876 Mississippi Rd., Garnavillo, 52409. Tel: 563-252-1248
Pepper, David J., 102 W. Spring, Box 120, Lawler, 52154. Tel: 563-238-2701
Perry, Francis J., Villa Raphael, 1155 Mt. Loretta Ave., 52003. Tel: 563-583-2452
Pitzen, John J., 215 Vanderbilt St., Fairfax, 52228. Tel: 319-846-2206
Ptacek, John P., 206 7th St. S.E., Farley, 52046. Tel: 563-744-9105
Purtell, Thomas W., 615 W. Prospect St, New Hampton, 50659. Tel: 641-394-4504
Rasing, Linus E., 615 W. Prospect St., New Hampton, 50659. Tel: 641-394-4504
Recker, Philip F., 1849 Doral Park Rd., S.E.,, Rio Rancho, NM 87124-7118. Tel: 505-896-9449
Reuter, Lloyd E., 1905 5th St., P.O. Box 114, Gilbertville, 50634. Tel: 319-296-0848
Rhomberg, Thomas W., 1510 Kehl Ct., Apt. 6, 52003. Tel: 563-582-3545
Rogers, Daniel J., 7678 Moonlight Ln., Bellevue, 52031. Tel: 563-582-6605
Ruhland, Carl J., Shady Rest Care Center, 701 Johnson St., N.W., Cascade, 52033.
Schmidt, Florian J., 2160 Woodland Dr. E6, 52002. Tel: 563-582-4066
Schmitt, Phillip E., 212-1/2 7th St. S.E.,, Mt. Vernon, 52314-1518. Tel: 319-895-0404
Schwinn, Thomas J., 56858 McMichael St., Victory DeSoto, WI 54624. Tel: 608-648-3702
Simon, Vincent J., 100 South St., Ossian, 52161. Tel: 563-532-9227
Smith, John P., Stonehill Care Center, 3485 Windsor Ave., Dubuque 52001-1312.
Walsh, John J., Villa Raphael, 1155 Mt. Loretta Ave., 52003. Tel: 563-556-4897
Weydert, Donald D., 2249 Del Monaco Dr., 52002. Tel: 563-556-2562
Whalen, Charles W., 2245 Chaney Rd., #4, 52001-2939. Tel: 563-556-5508
Wilkie, William E., Ph.D., 1920 Cox St., #4, 52001. Tel: 563-588-7100
Zee, Louis C., 4605 Jetty Lane, Houston, TX 7707. Tel: 281-575-8855

Permanent Deacons:
Aitchison, Gary, St. Cecilia, Ames
Ayers, John, Des Moines, IA
Baker, John, St. Edward, Waterloo
Baltes, Robert, Holy Family, New Hampton
Bassler, Eugene, (Retired), Dubuque
Behounek, Joseph, St. Joseph, Chelsea & St. Michael, Belle Plaine
Berger, James, St. Ludmila, Cedar Rapids
Berry, Matthew F., Holy Family, Mason City
Biver, William, St. Columbkille, Dubuque
Blouin, Mike, (Leave of Absence), Des Moines

Brustkern, Leo J., (Retired), La Porte City
Cashatt, Wayne, (Retired), Eldora
Cisler, William, St. Wenceslaus, Cedar Rapids
Cooper, Charles, Holy Family, Mason City
DiPietre, Dennis, Columbia, MO
Fessler, Ray, (Retired), Dubuque
Flagel, LaVerne, All Saints, Cedar Rapids
Fortin, Daryl, LeClaire
Freet, James, Blessed Sacrament, Waterloo
Frost, Irwin, (Retired), Waterloo
Froyen, Leonard, St. Stephen the Witness Student Center, Cedar Falls
Gehrke, Richard, St. Mary, Hazleton
Gram, Clarence, Queen of Peace, Waterloo
Groh, Victor, (Retired), Thornton
Harris, Jeff, St. Mary, Marshalltown
Hayes, Joseph, (Retired), Cascade
Head, Robert, Sacred Heart, Maquoketa
Herman, John, Blessed Sacrament, Waterloo
Hoeger, Daniel, St. Patrick, Cedar Rapids
Hurych, Robert F., St. Paul, Newhall; Immaculate Conception, Van Horne; St. John, Blairstown
Jenney, William, Queen of Peace, Waterloo
Jones, David, St. Mary, Ackley
Jorgensen, Gerald, Ph.D., J.C.L., Resurrection, Dubuque
Kean, James, St. Patrick, Epworth
Koopmann, Gerald, St. John, Placid
Lang, Tom, St. Joseph, Key West
Larsen, Raymond, St. Edward, Waterloo
LoBianco, Timothy, St. Patrick & St. Mary, Dubuque
Lynch, Richard, St. Edward, Waterloo
MacDonald, Stephen, St. Joseph the Worker, Dubuque
Malone, John, St. Patrick, Fairfax
Manning, Richard, St. Ludmila, Cedar Rapids
Mauss, William, St. Anthony, Dubuque
McCully, John, St. Cecilia, Ames
McGhee, David, Nativity, Dubuque
Mead, Edward J., St. Mary, Marshalltown
Mega, Robert, Sacred Heart, Manly
Moetsch, Michael, St. Patrick, Cedar Falls
Oates, Michael, St. Patrick, Cedar Falls
Otto, J. C., St. Michael, Belle Plaine; St. Joseph, Chelsea
Pantaloni, Ed, St. Joseph, Marion
Peckosh, Paul, St. Raphael Cathedral, Dubuque
Peterson, Lanny, St. Pius X, Cedar Rapids
Pettit, Gerald D., Immaculate Conception, Cedar Rapids
Pfaffly, James, St. Mary, Guttenberg
Popowski, Dennis, St. Boniface, Garner
Pusillo, Gary, St. Henry, Marshalltown
Recker, Marvin, Sacred Heart, Fillmore
Saunders, Phil, St. Matthew, Cedar Rapids
Scharosch, Albert, St. Pius X, Cedar Rapids
Schauls, Norman, Blessed Sacrament, Waterloo
Schmall, Leo, (Retired), Marion
Schmit, Nick, (Retired), Belmond
Sinnwell, James E., (Retired), Charles City
Smith, Sean, St. Joseph, Marion
Steger, James, St. Joseph, Earlville
Tondra, Richard, St. Cecilia, Ames
Van Kerchvoorde, Steven, St. Mary, Colorado; St. Patrick, Nevada; Sacred Heart, St. Anthony, St. Joseph, State Center, St. Gabriel, Zearing
Vaske, Irvin, St. Henry, Marshalltown
Wallace, Richard, St. Matthew, Cedar Rapids
Walsh, Tom, St. Jude, Cedar Rapids
Weber, Ed, Queen of Peace, Waterloo
Whitters, Michael, St. John, Clarion
Wilson, James, (Retired), Waterloo
Zimmerman, Paul, St. Pius X, Cedar Rapids

INSTITUTIONS LOCATED IN THE DIOCESE

[A] SEMINARIES, ARCHDIOCESAN

DUBUQUE. *Seminary of St. Pius X*, Loras College, 1450 Alta Vista St., P.O. Box 178, 52004-0178. Tel: 563-588-7661. Revs. Scott E. Bullock, Rector & Dir. Pre-Theology Formation; Phillip G. Gibbs, Vice Rector; William M. Joensen, Spiritual Dir. Students for Archdiocese of Dubuque 3.

[B] SEMINARIES, RELIGIOUS OR SCHOLASTICATES

EPWORTH. *Divine Word College*, 102 Jacoby Dr. S.W., P.O. Box 380, 52045-0380. Tel: 563-876-3353; Fax: 563-876-3407. Email: hutchins@dwci.edu. Web: www.dwci.edu. Revs. William Shea, S.V.D.; Michael Hutchins, S.V.D., Pres.; Kenneth Anich, S.V.D.; Gus Wall, S.V.D., Vice Pres. Formation & Dean of Students; Joseph McDermott, S.V.D.; John Tra, S.V.D.; Bros. Rodney Bowers, S.V.D., Rector; Michael Decker, S.V.D.; Kevin Diederich, S.V.D.; Tony Kreinus, S.V.D.; Wayne Till, S.V.D.; James Zabransky, S.V.D.; Revs. Walter Binofsky, S.V.D.; James Heiar, S.V.D., Assoc. Devel. Dir.; Paul LaForge, S.V.D.; Binh Nguyen, S.V.D.; Son Van Nguyen, S.V.D.; Michael Quang Nguyen, S.V.D.; Vinh Duc Nguyen, S.V.D.; Thu Pham, S.V.D., Assoc. Devel. Dir.; Darius Piwowarezyk, S.V.D. Society of the Divine Word (S.V.D.) Priests 15; Brothers 6; Sisters 2; Lay Teachers 15; Students 84.

[C] COLLEGES AND UNIVERSITIES

DUBUQUE. *Clarke College*, 1550 Clarke Dr., 52001. Tel: 563-588-6300; Fax: 563-588-6789. Email: clarke-info@clarke.edu. Web: www.clarke.edu. Sr. Catherine Dunn, B.V.M., Ph.D., Pres.; Kristi Droessler, Registrar; Sr. Margaret Feldner, O.S.F., Vice Pres. Academic Affairs; Louise Ottavi, Assoc. Academic Dean; Kate Zanger, Vice Pres. Student Life; Eugene Kirschbaum, M.B.A., Vice Pres. Business & Finance; Mary Russell, Dir. Career Svcs. & Campus Ministry; Omar Correa, Exec. Dir. Admissions & Financial Aid. Liberal Arts College. (Coed); Conducted by Sisters of Charity, B.V.M. Sisters 13; Lay Teachers 69; Students 1,116.

Loras College, 1450 Alta Vista St., P.O. Box 178, 52004-0178. Tel: 563-588-7100; Fax: 563-588-7964. Email: kerrigan@loras.edu. Dr. John Kerrigan, Interim Pres.; Mary K. Week, Ed.D., Vice Pres. Enrollment Mgmt.; Jeanne L. Skiil, Vice Pres. Information Technology; James Collins, Senior Vice Pres. Institute Advancement; Stephen J. Schmall, C.P.A., Vice Pres. Finance & Admin. Svcs.; Rev. John S. Haugen, Spiritual Dir., Advocate Catholic Mission & Identity; Cheryl Jacobsen, Ph.D., Vice Pres. Academic Affairs; Michael J. Boyd, Ph.D., Dir. Campus Ministry. (Accredited by the North Central Assoc. of Colleges and Secondary Schools) Priests 3; Sisters 1.

College Faculty: Revs. Robert R. Beck; Douglas O. Wathier, S.T.D.; William M. Joensen In Res. Revs. John C. Friedell (Retired); William E. Wilkie, Ph.D. (Retired).

CEDAR RAPIDS. *Mount Mercy College*, 1330 Elmhurst Dr., N.E., 52402-4797. Tel: 319-363-8213; Fax: 319-368-6496. Email: admission@mmc.mtmercy.edu. Web: www.mtmercy.edu. Dr. Robert W. Pearce, Pres.; Lori Heying, Registrar; Dr. Susan E. Pauly, Vice Pres. Academic Affairs. Sisters 1; Lay Teachers 71; Students 1,473.

[D] HIGH SCHOOLS, INTERPAROCHIAL

DUBUQUE. *Wahlert High School dba Holy Family Catholic Schools*, 2005 Kane St., 52001. Tel: 563-583-9771; Fax: 563-583-9775. Email: dbqh04@arch.pvt.k12.ia.us. Mr. Donald Sisler, Prin.; Rev. Dwayne J. Thoman, Spiritual Dir. Serving all Parishes in Dubuque; Holy Family, New Melleray; St. Joseph's, Key West; SS. Peter and Paul, Sherrill. Priests 1; Sisters 1; Lay Teachers 48; Students 687.

BELLEVUE. *Marquette High School*, 502 Franklin St., 52031. Tel: 563-872-3356; Fax: 563-872-3285. Email: DBQE04@arch.pvt.k12.i.a.u.s. Very Rev. Donald J. Plamondon, Pastoral Coord.; Rev. Paul E. Lippstock, Chap.; Jim Squiers, Prin.; Karen Timmerman, Asst. Admin. Serving St. John, Andrew; St. Joseph, Bellevue; St. Catherine, St. Catherine; St. Donatus, St. Donatus; Holy Rosary, LaMotte; St. Peter, Sabula; SS. Peter and Paul, Springbrook. Priests 1; Sisters 1; Lay Teachers 7; Students 115.

CEDAR RAPIDS. *Metropolitan Office of Catholic Education*, Cedar Rapids Metro Office, 516 A Ave. N.W., P.O. Box 2307, 52406-2307. Tel: 319-366-2517; Fax: 319-366-0426. Email: dbqcrm@arch.pvt.k12.ia.us. Web: www.cr-cath.pvt.k12.ia.us. Sr. Jean Marie Brady, B.V.M., Assoc. Dir. Educational Svcs.

Xavier High School, 6300 42nd St., N.E., 52411. Tel: 319-294-6635; Fax: 319-294-6712. Email: DBQH02@arch-pvt.k12.ia.us. Rev. John A. Gossman, Pastoral Coord.; Jeff Henderson, Prin. & Contact Person; Rev. Steven G. O'Brien, Spiritual Dir. Serving St. Patrick, Fairfax; John XXIII; St. Jude, St. Ludmila, St. Patrick, Immaculate Conception, St. Wenceslaus, St. Matthew, All Saints, St. Pius X, Cedar Rapids; St. Joseph, Marion; St. Elizabeth Ann Seton, Hiawatha. Priests 1; Lay Teachers 46; Students 682.

Xavier High School Foundation, 6300 42nd St. N.E., P.O. Box 1394, 52406. Tel: 319-378-4571; Fax: 319-378-2953. Email: acunningham@xavierfoundation.org. Anne Cunningham, Exec. Dir.; Rev. Philip E. Thompson, Pastoral Coord.

DYERSVILLE. *Beckman High School*, (Grades 7-12), (Coed), 1325 Ninth St. S.E., 52040. Tel: 563-875-7188; Fax: 563-875-7242. Email: dbqh05@arch.pvt.k12.ia.us. Michael Cooper, Prin.; Rev. Msgr. Edward C. Petty, Pastoral Coord. Serving the following Parishes: St. Francis Xavier, Dyersville; St. Joseph, Earlville; St. Boniface, New Vienna; Ss. Peter and Paul, Petersburg; St. Paul, Worthington. Lay Teachers 33; Students 503.

GILBERTVILLE. *Don Bosco High School*, 405 13th Ave., 50634. Tel: 319-296-1692; Fax: 319-296-1693. Email: dbqH06@arch.pvt.k12.ia.us. Rev. Donald R. Bruggeman, Pastoral Coord.; James Hrabe, Prin.; Deacon Carl J. Adams Jr., Spiritual Dir.; Kara Thompson, Guidance Counselor. Serving St. Francis, Barclay, Dunkerton; Immaculate Conception, Gilbertville; St. Athanasius, Jesup; Sacred Heart, LaPorte City; St. Joseph, Raymond; St. Mary of Mt. Carmel, Eagle Center. Lay Teachers 17; Students 172.

WATERLOO. *Columbus High School dba Cedar Valley Catholic Schools*, 3231 W. Ninth St., 50702. Tel: 319-233-3358; Fax: 319-235-0733. Email: dbqH08@arch.pvt.k12.ia.us. Rev. Jerry Kopacek, Pastoral Coord.; Mr. Todd Dirth, Prin. Serving all parishes in Waterloo; St. Nicholas, Evansdale; St. Patrick's, Cedar Falls. Priests 1; Sisters 1; Lay Teachers 3; Students 35.

[E] SCHOOLS OF RELIGION

CALMAR. *Christian Family School & Religion*, Formerly Christian Family School, P.O. Box 821, 52312. Tel: 563-562-3045; Fax: 563-562-3292. Email: dbqrT1@arch.pvt.k12.ia.us. Rev. Msgr. Cletus J. Hawes, Exec. Coord.; Patty Frana, D.R.E. Priests 1; Lay Teachers 1; Students 195.

CASCADE. *Aquin Religious Education Center*, 608 Third Ave. N.W., P.O. Box 460, 52033. Tel: 563-852-7875; Fax: 563-852-5269. Email: dbq023RE@arch.pvt.k12.ia.us. Rev. Daniel A. Krapfl, Pastoral Coord.; Rebecca Smith, D.R.E. Lay Teachers 24; Students 284.

LANSING. *Lansing School of Religion*, 660 Main St., 52151. Tel: 563-538-3933; 563-538-4360. Rev. Daniel J. Knipper; Karen Weber, D.R.E. Priests 1; Lay Teachers 15; Students 114.

MANCHESTER. *St. Paul's School of Religion*, 408 Clara Ave., 52057. Tel: 563-927-2900; Fax: 563-927-6506. Email: dbqrt3@arch.pvt.k12.ia.us. Rev. Msgr. Ralph P. Simington, Pastoral Coord.; Wilma Billhorn, Dir. Priests 1; Lay Teachers 7; Students 390.

NEW HAMPTON. *St. John's School*, 823 W. Main St., Box 108, 50659. Tel: 641-394-3171. Email: dbqrt4@arch.pvt.k12.ia.us. Rev. Msgr. Carl L. Schmitt, Pastoral Coord.; Marjorie Zipse, Dir. Lay Teachers 3; Students 159.

[F] CONSOLIDATED PARISH SCHOOLS

DUBUQUE. *St. Francis Consolidation, Primary*, (Grades Day Care-8), 2222 Queen St., 52001-0608. Tel: 563-588-4657; Fax: 563-584-0115. Email: dbqe25@arch.pvt.k12.ia.us. Lori Apel, Prin. Lay Teachers 18; Students 173; Preschool Students 31; Day Care Students 364.

Intermediate, 180 W. 15th St., 52001. Tel: 563-582-2127; Fax: 563-585-0082. Lori Apel, Prin.

Holy Family Schools, 2005 Kane St., 52001. Tel: 563-582-5456; Fax: 563-583-3885. Rev. Msgr. Wayne A. Ressler, Pastoral Coord.; Donald Miller, Chief Admin. Serving the parishes of Dubuque, Key West and St. Catherine. Sisters 1; Lay Teachers 22; Students 452.

BELLEVUE. *Bellevue Area Catholic Elementary School*, (Grades PreK-8), 403 Park St., 52031. Tel: 563-872-3284; Fax: 563-872-3285. Email: dbqe04@arch.pvt.k12.ia.us. Jim Squiers, Prin.; Very Rev. Donald J. Plamondon, Pastoral Coord. Consolidation of the following parishes: St. Donatus, St. Donatus; SS. Peter & Paul, Springbrook; St. Joseph, Bellevue (School location); Holy Rosary, LaMotte. Lay Teachers 17; Day Care 10; Students 218.

CALMAR. *Calmar-Festina-Spillville (CFS) Catholic Elementary School*, (Grades PreK-8), 300 S. Maryville, Box 815, 52132. Tel: 563-562-3291; Fax: 563-562-3292. Email: dbqe05@arch.pvt.k12.ia.us. Katie Schmitt, Prin.; Rev. Donald J. Hawes, Pastoral Coord. Consolidation of the following parishes: Our Lady of Seven Dolors (St. Mary), Festina; St. Wenceslaus, Spillville; St. Aloysius, Calmar; St. Wenceslaus (Grades 1-4); St. Aloysius (Grades K-8). Lay Teachers 12; Pre-School 24; Students 155.

CASCADE. *Aquin Elementary School*, (Grades PreK-8), 608 Third Ave. N.W., P.O. Box 460, 52033-0460. Tel: 563-852-7875; Fax: 563-852-5269. Email: dbqe06@arch.pvtk12.ia.us. Peter Smith, Prin.

Consolidation of the following parishes: St. Matthias, Cascade; Sacred Heart, Fillmore; St. Patrick, North Garryowen; St. Peter, Temple Hill. Lay Teachers 20; Pre-School 34; Students 259.

CEDAR RAPIDS. *Holy Family Catholic Consolidated School*

LaSalle Middle School (Grades 5-8), 3700 First Ave. N.W., 52405. Tel: 319-396-7792; Fax: 319-390-6527. Email: dbqe12@arch.pvt.k12.ia.us. Rev. Steven J. Rosonke, Pastoral Coord.; Fred Althoff, Prin. Lay Teachers 48; Day Care 88; Pre-School 97; Students 624.

St. Ludmila Center, 215 21st Ave. S.W., 52404. Tel: 319-362-1943; Fax: 319-364-4149. Email: dbqe10@arch.pvt.k12.ia.us. Janet Whitney, Admin. Assoc.

St. Jude Center, 3700 First Ave. N.W., 52405. Tel: 319-396-7818; Fax: 319-390-0952. Email: dbqe09@arch.pvt.k12.ia.us. Jim Clancy, Admin. Assoc.

Regis Middle School, (Grades 6-8), 735 Prairie Dr. N.E., 52402. Tel: 319-363-1968; Fax: 319-247-6099. Email: dbqm02A@arch.pvt.k12.ia.us. Very Rev. Donald L. Klein, Pastoral Coord.; Rick Blackwell, Prin. Lay Teachers 24; Students 409.

CRESCO. *Notre Dame System of Education*, (Grades PreK-6), 221 Second Ave. E., 52136. Tel: 563-547-4513; Fax: 563-547-3835. Email: dbqe15@arch.pvt.k12.ia.us. Wendy Schatz, Prin. Lay Teachers 14; Pre-School 48; Students 180.

FARLEY. *Seton Catholic Elementary School*, (Grades PreK-8), 210 Second St. S.E., 52046. Tel: 563-744-3290; Fax: 563-744-3450. Email: dbqe28@arch.pvt.k12.ia.us. Steven Cornelius, Prin.; Rev. Richard W. Kuhn, Pastoral Coord. Consolidation of the following parishes: St. Patrick, Epworth; St. John, Peosta; St. John, Placid; St. Joseph, Farley; St. Clement, Bankston. Sisters of the Presentation 1; Lay Teachers 22; Pre-School 115; Students 337.

GILBERTVILLE. *Immaculate Conception-St. Joseph School*, (Grades K-8) , Gilbertville-Raymond Consolidated Elementary School , 311 16th Ave., 50634-0256. Tel: 319-296-1089; Fax: 319-296-3847. Email: dbqe31@arch.pvt.k12.ia.us. Matthew O'Loughlin, Prin.; Rev. Rick A. Dagit, Pastoral Coord. Consolidation of the following parishes: St. Joseph, Raymond; Immaculate Conception, Gilbertville; St. Joseph (Grades K-2); Immaculate Conception (Grades 3-8). Lay Teachers 22; Day Care 15; Students 295.

GUTTENBERG. *Guttenberg-North Buena Vista Consolidated School*, (Grades K-8), 502 S. Second St., S., P.O. Box 100, 52052. Tel: 563-252-1577; Fax: 563-252-1363. Email: dbqe32@arch.pvt.k12.ia.us. Sr. Suzanne Gallagher, P.B.V.M., Prin.; Rev. Marvin J. Bries, Pastoral Coord. Consolidation of the following parishes: St. Mary, Guttenberg; Immaculate Conception, North Buena Vista. Sisters 1; Lay Teachers 9; Students 139.

HOLY CROSS. *Rickardsville-Holy Cross-Luxemburg (RHCL) Catholic School*, (Grades PreK-8), 835 Church St., P.O. Box 368, 52053-0368. Tel: 563-870-2405; Fax: 563-870-4101. Email: dbqe34@arch.pvt.k12.ia.us. Bro. Stephen W. Markham, F.S.C., Pastoral Coord.; Dennis Rima, Prin. Consolidation of the following parishes: St. Joseph, Rickardsville; Holy Cross, Holy Cross; Holy Trinity, Luxemburg (Grades K-3); Holy Cross (Grades 4-8). Lay Teachers 10; Pre-School 18; Students 164.

MARSHALLTOWN. *Marshalltown Area Consolidated Catholic School*, (Grades PreK-6), 10 W. Linn St., 50158. Tel: 641-753-7977; Fax: 641-753-0337. Email: dbqe40@arch.pvt.k12.ia.us. Rebecca Jacobson, Prin.; Rev. Louis M. Jaeger, Pastoral Coord. Consolidation of the following parishes: St. Mary, Marshalltown (Grades 3-6); St. Henry, Marshalltown; Immaculate Conception, Haverhill. Lay Teachers 20; Day Care 18; Pre-School 60; Students 234.

NEW VIENNA. *Archbishop Hennessy Catholic School*, (Grades PreK-6), 7420 Columbus, Box 170, 52065. Tel: 563-921-2635; Fax: 563-921-3003. Email: dbqe33@arch.pvt.k12.ia.us. Carrie Manternach, Prin.; Rev. John J. O'Connor, Pastoral Coord. Consolidation of the following parishes: St. Boniface Center (Grades K-3), New Vienna; SS. Peter & Paul (Grades 4-6), Petersburg. Sisters 1; Lay Teachers 6; Pre-School 11; Students 101.

PROTIVIN. *Trinity Catholic School*, (Grades PreK-6), 116 N. Main St., 52163-0205. Tel: 563-569-8556; Fax: 563-569-8477. Email: dbqe47@arch.pvt.k12.ia.us. Dana Spry, Prin. Consolidation of the following parishes: Holy Trinity, Protovin; St. Luke, St. Lucas; St. John, Fort Atkinson. Lay Teachers 11; Preschool 12; Students 77.

SHERRILL. *Balltown-Sherrill Catholic School*, (Grades PreK-6), 5135 Sherrill Rd., Box 49, 52073. Tel: 563-552-2166; Fax: 563-552-2166. Email: dbqe03@arch.pvt.k12.ia.us. Carol Gebhart, Prin.; Bro. Stephen W. Markham, F.S.C., Pastoral Coord. Consolidation of the following parishes: St. Francis, Balltown; SS. Peter & Paul, Sherrill. Lay Teachers 5; Pre-School 11; Students 49.

WATERLOO. *Cedar Valley Catholic Schools Office*, 123 E. Parker St., 50703. Tel: 319-232-1422; Fax: 319-232-3977. John Carlucci, System Admin.; Rev. Jerry Kopacek, Pastoral Coord.; Alice Conlon, Assoc. Dir. Educ.Svcs.

[G] CONSOLIDATED K-12 SYSTEMS

MASON CITY. *Newman Catholic* Parishes served: Holy Family, St. Joseph, Mason City: St. Patrick, Clear Lake; Sacred Heart, Manly; St. Michael, Plymouth; Sacred Heart, Rockwell.

Newman High and Middle School (Grades PreK-12), 2445 19th St. S.W., 50401. Tel: 641-423-6939; Fax: 641-423-6653. Email: dbqe41@arch.pvt.k12.ia.us.

Newman Catholic System, 2000 S. McKinley Ave., 50401. Tel: 641-423-3101; Fax: 641-422-1181.

Newman Catholic Child Care, 713 N. Adams, 50401. Tel: 641-423-0168; Fax: 641-423-3521. Revs. Dennis H. Cahill, Pastoral Coord.; Michael G. Schueller, Spiritual Dir.; Michael Kavars, Secondary Prin.; Kathy Lloyd, Early Childhood Dir.; Janet Avery, Admin. Priests 1; Sisters 3; Lay Teachers 43; Infant Care 34; Day Care 213; Pre-School 78; Elementary 465; High School 203.

[H] GENERAL HOSPITALS

DUBUQUE. *Mercy Medical Center-Dubuque* (A Division of Mercy Health Services-Iowa) , 250 Mercy Dr., 52001. Tel: 563-589-8000; Fax: 563-589-8073. Russell Knight, Pres.; Patrick Conlon, Dir. Pastoral Care Dept.; Sisters Rosalyn Ulfers, P.B.V.M., Chap.; Gabrielle Hoefer, R.S.M., Chap.; MaryAnn Dunn, Chap.; Joan Haug, Chap. Bed Capacity 402; Total Staff 1,109; Patients Assisted Annually 43,645.

CEDAR FALLS. **Sartori Health Care Foundation, Inc.*, 515 College St., 50613. Tel: 319-268-3025; Fax: 319-268-3270. David Swinehart, Devel. Dir.

Sartori Memorial Hospital, Inc., Formerly Sartori Memorial Hospital (Formerly known as S.F.H., Inc.) , 515 College St., 50613. Tel: 319-268-3000; Fax: 319-268-3270. Email: schruppd@covhealth.com. Richard A. Schrupp, Pres. Total Staff 302; Bed Capacity 101; Patients Assisted Annually 40,893.

CEDAR RAPIDS. *Mercy Medical Center, Endowment Foundation, Inc., Cedar Rapids, IA*, Formerly Mercy Medical Center, Cedar Rapids, Iowa, Endowment Foundation, Inc., 701 Tenth St. S.E., 52403. Tel: 319-398-6278. Cathy Gullickson, Pres.; Sr. James Marie Donahue, R.S.M., Ph.D., Chairwoman of the Bd.

Mercy Medical Center-Cedar Rapids (Sisters of Mercy-Regional Community of Cedar Rapids) , 701 Tenth St. S.E., 52403. Tel: 319-398-6011. Email: mercylib@crpl.cedar-rapids.lib.ia.us. Web: www.mercycare.org. A. James Tinker, CEO; Revs. James L. Blocklinger, Resident Chap.; Kerry Egan, Chap.; Ken Glandorf, Chap.; Sisters Margaret Murphy, R.S.M., Dir. Pastoral Care Office; Maureen Fiery, R.S.M., Chap.; Bernice Kurt, R.S.M., Chap. Sponsored by the Sisters of Mercy, Cedar Rapids Regional Community. Staff 1,326; Bed Capacity Acute 355; Skilled Nursing 29; Patients Assisted Annually 201,292.

Mercycare Service Corporation (Parent Corp.) , 701 10th St. S.E., 52403. Tel: 319-398-6011. A. James Tinker, CEO. Sponsored by the Sisters of Mercy, Cedar Rapids Regional Community.

DYERSVILLE. *Mercy Medical Center-Dubuque (Dyersville)* (A Division of Mercy Health Services Iowa) , 1111 Third St. S.W., 52040. Tel: 563-875-7101; Fax: 563-875-2957. Russell Knight, Pres. Bed Capacity 49; Total Staff 54; Patients Assisted Annually 5,885.

MASON CITY. *Mercy Medical Center-North Iowa* (Member of Mercy Health Network) , 1000 4th St. S.W., 50401. Tel: 641-422-7000; Fax: 641-422-7827. James G. Fitzpatrick, Pres. & CEO; Very Rev. Kenneth B. Gehling, Chap.; Sr. Emily Devine, R.S.M., Chap.; Rose Schlueter, Lay Chap.; Revs. Barbara Stewart, Chap. (Episcopal); Ron Stein, Chap. (Baptist); William Peake, Chap. Reformed (RCA). Bed Capacity 346; Staff 2,760; Patients Assisted Annually 750,510.

NEW HAMPTON. *Mercy Medical Center-New Hampton* (Member of Mercy Health Network) , 308 N. Maple Ave., 50659. Tel: 641-394-4121; Fax: 641-394-1695. Carolyn Martin-Shaw, Pres. & CEO; Doug Schueth, Bd. Chm., Member Organization Board; Rev. John Harpel, S.V.D., Chap. Staff 146; Bed Capacity 43; Patients Assisted Annually 17,790.

OELWEIN. *Mercy Hospital of Franciscan Sisters*, 201 8th Ave. S.E., 50662. Tel: 319-283-6000; Fax: 319-283-6004. Richard A. Schrupp, Pres.; Rev. Frederick Fangman, Chap. Franciscan Sisters. Daughters of the Sacred Hearts of Jesus and Mary, Wheaton, IL Bed Capacity 64; Patients Assisted Annually 25,251; Staff 189.

WATERLOO. *Covenant Health System, Inc.*, 3421 W. Ninth St., 50702. Tel: 319-272-7302; Fax: 319-272-7313. Mr. Jack Dusenbery, Pres.

Covenant Medical Center, Inc., 3421 W. Ninth St., 50702. Tel: 319-272-8000; Fax: 319-272-7313. Mr. Jack Dusenbery, Pres. Franciscan Sisters. Daughters of the Sacred Hearts of Jesus and Mary, Wheaton, IL Staff 2,622; Bed Capacity 346; Patients Assisted Annually 313,309.

Covenant Foundation, Inc., 3421 W. Ninth St., 50702. Tel: 319-272-7676; Fax: 319-272-7313. Allen Ricks, Exec. Dir.

[I] SPECIAL HEALTH CENTERS

DUBUQUE. *Holy Family Hall Infirmary*, 3340 Windsor Ave., 52001-1300. Tel: 563-583-9786; Fax: 563-583-6080. Email: info@osfdbq.org. Web: www.osfdbq.org. Rev. Ronald G.. Friedell, Chap.; Sr. Eileen Miller, O.S.F., Dir. Sister Support Svcs. Sisters of St. Francis, Dubuque Bed Capacity 95; Professed Sisters 81; Patients Assisted Annually 100.

Marian Hall Infirmary, 1050 Carmel Dr., 52003. Tel: 563-556-5474; Fax: 563-588-1975. Email: mhall@bvmcong.org. Web: www.bvmcong.org. Rev. Msgr. Robert R. Vogl, Chap. (Retired). Professed Sisters 96; Bed Capacity 104; Staff 168.

Caritas Center, 1130 Carmel Dr., 52003-7911. Tel: 563-556-3240; Fax: 563-557-1349. Email: mhouse@bvmcong.org. Susan M. Hostert, Central Admin. Mount Carmel Continuing Care Retirement Community. Professed Sisters 48; Bed Capacity 53; Staff 105.

[J] HOMES FOR AGED

DUBUQUE. *Stonehill Franciscan Services, Inc.*, 3485 Windsor Ave., 52001-1312. Tel: 563-557-7180; Fax: 563-584-9282. Email: dullrich@stonehilldbg.com. Dennis Ryan, Chm. Svcs. Bd.; Sr. Dolores Ullrich, O.S.F., Pres. & CEO. Sisters of St. Francis of the Holy Family 8; Staff 286; Residents-Nursing Home 250; Residents-Retirement Units 51; Adult Day Care Program 24.

Stonehill Benevolent Foundation Tel: 563-557-7180; Fax: 563-584-9282. Sr. Mary Clare O'Toole, O.S.F., Chair, Stonehill Benevolent Foundation Board. Sponsored by Sisters of St. Francis of the Holy Family.

Villa Raphael, 1155 Mt. Loretta Ave., 52003. Tel: 563-588-2049. Email: dbqvilla@arch.pvt.k12.ia.us. Patricia Flores, Dir. Administered by the Archdiocese of Dubuque.; Accommodations for 16 priests. Total Staff 5; Total in Residence 13.

CEDAR RAPIDS. *Hallmar-Mercy Medical Center*, 701 Tenth St. S.E., 52403. Tel: 319-398-6241. A. James Tinker, CEO. Sisters of Mercy, Cedar Rapids Regional, owned and operated by Mercy Medical Center. Home for Aged. Total Assisted 64; Total Staff 32; Residents 51.

CRESCO. *Elder Hospitality of Iowa, Inc.* (Village Apartments) , Franciscan SKEMP Healthcare, 301 First Ave., 52136. Tel: 563-547-3325; 608-785-0940; 608-791-9749; Fax: 608-791-9780. Richard Berendes, Admin., Extended Care. Franciscan Sisters of Perpetual Adoration, La Crosse, Wisconsin and Mayo Foundation, Rochester, MN, Elderly housing for low income. HUD section 202. Units 12.

Elder Hospitality of Iowa II, Inc., Franciscan SKEMP Healthcare, 509 Goose Island Dr., Decorah, 52101. Tel: 563-382-2863; 608-785-0940; 608-791-9749; Fax: 608-791-9780. Richard Berendes, Admin., Extended Care. Franciscan Sisters of Perpetual Adoration, La Crosse, Wisconsin and Mayo Foundation, Rochester, MN., (Village Apartments); Elderly housing for low income. HUD section 202. Units 24.

DYERSVILLE. *Mercy Medical Center-Dubuque-Dyersville-Oakcrest Manor* (A Division of Mercy Health Services - Iowa) , 1111 Third St. S.W., 52040. Tel: 563-875-7101; Fax: 563-875-2957. Web: www.mercydubuque.com. Russell Knight, Pres. Bed Capacity 40; Total Staff 27; Patients Assisted Annually 63.

[K] MONASTERIES AND RESIDENCES OF PRIESTS AND BROTHERS

PEOSTA. *New Melleray Abbey, Order of Cistercians of the Strict Observance*, 6500 Melleray Cir., 52068. Tel: 563-588-2319; Fax: 563-588-4117. Email: monks@newmelleray.org. Web: www.newmelleray.org. Rt. Rev. David R. Bock, O.C.S.O., Retired Abbot (Retired); Revs. Bernard J. Cullen, O.C.S.O.; Xavier L. Dieter, O.C.S.O.; Alberic R. Farbolin, O.C.S.O.; Rt. Rev. Brendan J. Freeman, O.C.S.O., Abbot; Revs. James B. Henderson, O.C.S.O.; Thaddeus J. Kennedy,

O.C.S.O.; Rt. Rev. James J. Kerndt, O.C.S.O., Retired Abbot; Revs. Daniel F. Lenihan, O.C.S.O.; Thomas J. McCarty, O.C.S.O.; Thomas A. MacMaster, O.C.S.O., Prior; James E. O'Connor, O.C.S.O.; Neil Paquette, O.C.S.O.; Kenneth F. Tietjen, O.C.S.O.; Stephen Verbest, O.C.S.O.; Timothy L. Welsh, O.C.S.O.; Bros. Benedict Babor, O.C.S.O.; Albert Bracket, O.C.S.O.; Paul Halaburt, O.C.S.O.; Michael Isenhart, O.C.S.O.; Kevin Knox, O.C.S.O.; Felix Leja, O.C.S.O.; Augustine Nave, O.C.S.O.; John O'Driscoll, O.C.S.O.; Ephrem Poppish, O.C.S.O.; Aidan Rachford, O.C.S.O.; Walter Schoenberg, O.C.S.O.; Tobia Shanahan, O.C.S.O.; Robert Simon, O.C.S.O.; Raymond Sullivan, O.C.S.O.; Paul Andrew Tanner, O.C.S.O.; Dennis Vavra, O.C.S.O.; Jonah Wharf, O.C.S.O.; Placid Zilka, O.C.S.O.

Legal Title: *Corporation of New Melleray* Total Residents 34; Priests 17; Brothers 17.

[L] CONVENTS AND RESIDENCES FOR SISTERS

DUBUQUE. *St. Joseph's Convent, Mount Carmel*, 1150 Carmel Dr., 52003. Tel: 563-556-3240; Fax: 563-557-1349. Email: bvmcenter@bvmcong.org. Web: www.bvmcong.org. Sr. Carol Marie Baum, B.V.M., Admin.; Rev. Msgr. James O. Barta, Chap. Motherhouse of the Sisters of Charity of the Blessed Virgin Mary. Professed Sisters 95; Staff 25.

Mt. Loretto Convent Motherhouse and Novitiate of the Sisters of the Presentation of the B.V.M. , 2360 Carter Rd., 52001-2997. Tel: 563-588-2008; Fax: 563-588-4463. Email: joyp@yousq.net. Sisters Joy Peterson, P.B.V.M., Pres.; Ruth Ann Takes, P.B.V.M., Dir.; Rev. Douglas O. Wathier, S.T.D., Chap. Professed Sisters 66.

International Presentation Association Tel: 212-629-4258; Fax: 212-629-4259.

Mt. St. Francis, 3390 Windsor Ave., 52001-1311. Tel: 563-583-9786; Fax: 563-583-3250. Email: info@osfdbq.org. Web: www.osfdbq.org. Sisters Marie Cigrand, O.S.F., Contact Person; Dorothy Heiderscheit, O.S.F., Pres.; Eileen Miller, O.S.F., Dir. Sister Support Svcs.; Rev. Robert R. Beck, Chap. Sisters of St. Francis of the Holy Family Charitable Trust, Motherhouse and Novitiate of the Sisters of St. Francis of the Holy Family. Professed Sisters 118.

Our Lady of the Mississippi Abbey, 8400 Abbey Hill, 52003. Tel: 563-582-2595; Fax: 563-582-5511. Email: sisters@mississippiabbey.org. Sr. Gail Marie Fitzpatrick, O.C.S.O., Abbess; Rev. Thomas J. McCarty, O.C.S.O., Chap. The Cistercian Nuns of the Strict Observance, (Monastery of Trappistine Nuns). Professed Nuns 23.

Sisters of Charity of the Blessed Virgin Mary, BVM Center, Mount Carmel, 1100 Carmel Dr., 52003-7991. Tel: 563-588-2351; Fax: 563-588-4832. Email: bvmcenter@bvmcong.org. Web: www.bvmcong.org. Sisters Joellen McCarthy, B.V.M., Pres. Congregation; Margaret Nolan, B.V.M., 1st Vice Pres.; Mary Ann Zollmann, B.V.M., 2nd Vice Pres. Sisters of Charity of the Blessed Virgin Mary: Retirement Trust Plan and Charitable Trust Total Staff 33.

Sisters of the Visitation, 2950 Kaufmann Ave., 52001-1631. Tel: 563-556-2440. Email: dbqsvm@arch.pvt.k12.ia.us. Sr. Bernadine Curoe, S.V.M., Pres. Sisters of the Visitation of the Congregation of the Immaculate Heart of Mary Professed Sisters 7.

CEDAR RAPIDS. *Sacred Heart Convent*, 1125 Prairie Dr., N.E., 52402-4737. Tel: 319-364-5196; Fax: 319-364-7383. Sisters Kathy Thornton, R.S.M., Pres.; Shari Sutherland, R.S.M., Vice Pres.; Marianne Arndorfer, Admin. Sacred Heart Convent. Sisters of Mercy, Cedar Rapids, Motherhouse of the Sisters of Mercy (Cedar Rapids Regional Community). Professed Sisters 85; Total Staff 30.

Sisters of Mercy Charitable Trust Tel: 319-364-5196; Fax: 319-364-7383.

Catherine McAuley Center for Women, Cedar Rapids Tel: 319-363-4993; Fax: 319-363-8332.

Mount Mercy College, Cedar Rapids Tel: 319-363-8213; Fax: 319-363-5270.

Mercy Medical Center, Cedar Rapids Tel: 319-398-6011; Fax: 319-398-6912.

[M] RETREAT HOUSES

DUBUQUE. *New Melleray Guest House*, 6500 Melleray Cir., 52068. Tel: 563-588-2319; Fax: 563-588-4117. Email: melleray@mwci.net. Web: www.osb.org/cist/melleray.

Shalom Retreat Center, 1001 Davis St., 52001-1398. Tel: 563-582-3592; Fax: 563-582-5872. Email: dbqshalom@aol.com. Sr. Margaret Jungers, O.S.F., Dir. Total Staff 11; Retreatants 8,500.

CEDAR FALLS. *American Martyrs Retreat House*, 2209 North Union Rd., P.O. Box 605, 50613-0605. Tel: 319-266-3543; Fax: 319-266-3543. Email: dbqamrh@arch.pvt.k12.ia.us. Sr. Jeanine Kuhn, P.B.V.M., Dir. 0; Total Staff 22.

HIAWATHA. *Prairiewoods Franciscan Spirituality Center*, 120 E. Boyson Rd., 52233-1277. Tel: 319-395-6700; Fax: 319-395-6703. Email: ecospirit@prairiewoods.org. Web: www.prairiewoods.org.

[N] NEWMAN CENTERS

AMES. *St. Thomas Aquinas Church and Catholic Student Center (Iowa State University)* 2210 Lincoln Way, 50014-7184. Tel: 515-292-3810; Fax: 515-292-3841. Email: dbq004@arch.pvt.k12.ia.ua. Web: www.staparish.net. Very Rev. Everett Hemann; Sr. Lorraine Schmaltz, Parish Family Life & RCIA Coord.; John Donaghy, Dir Campus Ministry & Charity, Justice & Peace Coord.; Robert LeBlanc, Church Business Admin & Contact Person; Crystal Caruana Sullivan, Campus Min.; Sr. Mary Ann Aman, C.H.M., D.R.E.; Jenifer Fliehler, Devel. Coord.; Jeremy Tevis, Youth Min.; Rev. Scott F. Boone Campus Min.; Marty Doerning, Liturgist & Music Coord.

CEDAR FALLS. *St. Stephen the Witness Catholic Student Center, University of Northern Iowa* 1019 W. 23rd St., 50613-3550. Tel: 319-266-9863; Fax: 319-266-3706. Email: frjsh@stephenuni.org. Web: www.ststephenuni.org. Rev. Mark A. Ressler, Dir. & Campus Pastor; Deacon Leonard Froyen; Sisters Mary Lou Specha, P.B.V.M., Campus Min.; Julie Marsh, P.B.V.M., Dir. of Liturgy; Regena Huffman, Business Mgr.; Lisa Geisler, Admin. Asst. Staff 10.

FAYETTE. *Upper Iowa University* 605 Washington St., 52142. Tel: 563-425-5310.

O] MISCELLANEOUS

DUBUQUE. *Archdiocese of Dubuque Deposit and Loan Fund*, 1229 Mt. Loretta, 52003-7800. Tel 563-556-2580; Fax: 563-556-5464. Email: DBQCFO@arch.pvt.k12.ia.us. Richard L. Runde, Finance Officer.

Archdiocese of Dubuque Education Fund, 1229 Mt. Loretta, 52003-7800. Tel: 563-556-2580; Fax: 563-556-5464. Email: DBQCFO@arch.pvt.12.ia.us. Richard L. Runde, Finance Officer.

Archdiocese of Dubuque Perpetual Care Fund, 1229 Mt. Loretta, 52003-7800. Tel: 563-556-2580; Fax: 563-556-5464. Email: DBQCFO@arch.pvt.k12.ia.us. Richard L. Runde, Finance Officer.

Archdiocese of Dubuque Seminarian Education Fund, 1229 Mt. Loretta, 52003-7800. Tel: 563-556-2580; Fax: 563-556-5464. Email: DBQCFO@arch.pvt.k12.ia.us. Richard L. Runde, Finance Officer.

Cistercian Studies Quarterly, Inc., Mississippi Abbey, 8400 Abbey Hill, 52003. Tel: 563-582-2595; Fax: 563-582-5511. Email: csq@mississippiabbey.org. Sr. Sheryl Frances Chen, O.C.S.O., Contact Person. Sponsor: Cistercian Order of the Strict Observance of the USA Region.

Heartland Housing Initiative, 90 Main St., 52001. Tel: 563-583-9653; Fax: 563-583-6490. Email: jschmidt@mercyhousing.org. Julie Schmidt, Asst. Mgr., Sponsored by the Wheaton Franciscan Sisters, Wheaton, IL and a corporation of Wheaton Franciscan System. (A member of the Mercy Housing System, Mercy Housing Corp.) Total Staff 3; Total Assisted 282.

Hennessy Charitable Trust, 2360 Carter Rd., 52001-2297. Tel: 563-588-2008; Fax: 563-588-4463. Email: lfang@yousq.net. Web: www.dubuquepresentations.org. Sisters Mary Joy Peterson, Pres.; Lynn Fangman, P.B.V.M., Contact Person. Sponsored by the Sisters of the Presentation

Opening Doors, 1561 Jackson St., 52001 Tel: 563-582-7480; Fax: 563-582-7467. Email: michellebrown5@mchsi.com. Carol Walsh, Pres. Sponsors: Sinsinawa Dominicans, Sisters of the Presentation, Sisters of Charity, B.V.M., Sisters of the Visitation, Dubuque Franciscan Sisters, Sisters of Mercy Regional Community of Detroit., Purpose: to provide emergency housing, related support services, shelter and temporary transitional housing for women who are alone or with children. Patients Assisted Annually 69.

Presentation Lantern, 1501 Jackson St., Ste. B, 52001. Tel: 563-557-7134. Email: corinemurray@aol.com. Sr. Corine Murray, P.B.V.M., Contact Person.

St. Vincent de Paul Society of the Archdiocese of Dubuque

Dubuque Council, 1351 Iowa St., 52001. Tel: 563-582-3733; Fax: 563-584-2225. Paul Hoppman, Natl. Trustee & Pres.

Waterloo Council, 4114 Heritage Rd., Cedar Falls, 50613. Tel: 319-232-8662. Richard McGrane, Pres.

Cedar Rapids Council, 339 22nd Ave. S.W., Cedar Rapids, 52404. Tel: 319-364-0748. Robert Crawford, Pres.

CEDAR RAPIDS. *Sisters of Mercy of the Americas. Regional Community of Cedar Rapids, Iowa Charitable Trust*, 1125 Prairie Dr., N.E., 52402-4730. Tel: 319-364-5196; Fax: 319-364-7383. Sr. Kathy Thornton, R.S.M., Regl. Community Pres.; Marie Schulte, Contact Person. Sisters of Mercy of the Americas, Regional Community of Cedar Rapids.

WATERLOO. *Ridgeway Place, Inc.* 155 E. Ridgeway Ave., 50702. Tel: 319-272-2622; Fax: 319-272-2633. Assisted Living Housing Units 96; Patients Assisted Annually 105; Staff 32.

WEBSTER CITY. *St. Thomas Aquinas Foundation*, 1000 Des Moines St., 50595-2147. Tel: 515-832-1190. Rev. John R. Flaherty, Contact Person. St. Thomas Aquinas Parish

RELIGIOUS INSTITUTES OF MEN REPRESENTED IN THE ARCHDIOCESE

For further details refer to the corresponding bracketed number in the Religious Institutes of Men or Women section.

[1180]—*Brothers of Saint Pius X*—C.S.P.X.

[0330]—*Brothers of the Christian Schools* (Midwest Prov.)—F.S.C.

[0350]—*Cistercians Order of the Strict Observance-Trappists* (Our Lady of New Melleray)—O.C.S.O.

[0420]—*Society of the Divine Word* (Northern Prov.)—S.V.D.

RELIGIOUS INSTITUTES OF WOMEN REPRESENTED IN THE ARCHDIOCESE

[0670]—*Cistercian Nuns of the Strict Observance*—O.C.S.O.

[2100]—*Congregation of the Humility of Mary* (Davenport, IA)—C.H.M.

[1780]—*Congregation of the Sisters of the Third Order of St. Francis of Perpetual Adoration*—F.S.P.A.

[1070-03]—*Dominican Sisters Congregation of the Most Holy Rosary* (Sinsinawa, WI)—O.P.

[1820]—*Hospital Sisters of the Third Order of St. Francis*—O.S.F.

[2960]—*Notre Dame Sisters* (Omaha, NE)—N.D.

[3130]—*Our Lady of Victory Missionary Sisters*—O.L.V.M.

[2970]—*School Sisters of Notre Dame* (Mankato, MN; St. Louis Prov.)—S.S.N.D.

[1680]—*School Sisters of St. Francis* (Milwaukee, WI)—O.S.F.

[]—*Sisters for Christian Communities* (Cincinnati, OH)

[0430]—*Sisters of Charity of the Blessed Virgin Mary*—B.V.M.

[2575]—*Sisters of Mercy of the Americas* (Cedar Rapids, IA)—R.S.M.

[2575.2]—*Sisters of Mercy of the Americas* (Detroit, MI)—R.S.M.

[1540]—*Sisters of St. Francis* (Clinton, IA)—O.S.F.

[1570]—*The Sisters of St. Francis of the Holy Family*—O.S.F.

[3320]—*Sisters of the Presentation of the B.V.M.* (Dubuque, IA; Fargo, SD)—P.B.V.M.

[1720]—*Sisters of the Third Order Regular of St. Francis of the Congregation of Our Lady of Lourdes*—O.S.F.

[4200]—*Sisters of the Visitation of the Congregation of the Immaculate Heart of Mary* (Dubuque, IA)—S.V.M.

CEMETERIES

DUBUQUE. *Mount Calvary*
Mount Olivet

CEDAR RAPIDS. *St. John*
St. Joseph
Mount Calvary

CRESCO. *Calvary*

LITTLEPORT. *Sacred Heart*

MARSHALLTOWN. *St. Mary*

MCINTIRE. *St. Mel & St. Patrick*

PRAIRIE. *St. Joseph*

RHODES. *St. Joseph*

SOUTH GARRYOWEN. *St. Aloysius*

SPRUCE CREEK. *St. Nicholas*

WATERLOO. *Catholic Cemeteries, Inc.*

NECROLOGY

† Collins, Rev. Msgr. Bernard G., (Retired)—Died Oct. 16, 2003

† Spaight, Rev. Msgr. Robert L., (Retired)—Died Jan. 20, 2003

† Supple, Rev. Msgr. James A., (Retired)—Died Aug. 31, 2003

† Axen, Ronald J., (Retired)—Died Feb. 22, 2003

† Benda, Frank M., (Retired)—Died May 5, 2003

† Goedken, James J., Waterloo, IA Queen of Peace—Died June 3, 2003

† Graham, John E., (Retired)—Died Feb. 15, 2003

† Kane, Justin A., (Retired)—Died May 15, 2003

Diocese of Duluth

(Dioecesis Duluthensis)

Most Reverend

DENNIS M. SCHNURR

Bishop of Duluth; ordained July 20, 1974; appointed Bishop of Duluth January 18, 2001; ordained April 2, 2001

Pastoral Center: 2830 E. Fourth St., Duluth, MN 55812. Tel: 218-724-9111; Fax: 218-724-1056.

Web: www.dioceseduluth.org

Email: duluth@dioceseduluth.org

ESTABLISHED OCTOBER 3, 1889.

Square Miles 22,354.

Corporate Title: Diocese of Duluth.

Comprises the counties of Aitkin, Carlton, Cass, Cook, Crow Wing, Itasca, Koochiching, Lake, Pine and St. Louis in the State of Minnesota.

Legal Title: For legal titles of parishes and diocesan institutions, consult the Chancery Office.

STATISTICAL OVERVIEW

Personnel	
Bishop	1
Priests: Diocesan Active in Diocese	50
Priests: Diocesan Active Outside Diocese	5
Priests: Retired, Sick or Absent	19
Number of Diocesan Priests	74
Religious Priests in Diocese	9
Total Priests in Diocese	83
Extern Priests in Diocese	3
Ordinations:	
Diocesan Priests	1
Permanent Deacons in Diocese	33
Total Brothers	1
Total Sisters	155
Parishes	
Parishes	93
With Resident Pastor:	
Resident Diocesan Priests	43
Without Resident Pastor:	
Administered by Priests	42
Administered by Deacons	3
Professional Ministry Personnel:	
Brothers	1
Sisters	2
Lay Ministers	45
Welfare	
Catholic Hospitals	2
Total Assisted	403,750
Homes for the Aged	2
Total Assisted	305
Day Care Centers	1
Total Assisted	146
Educational	
Diocesan Students in Other Seminaries	14
Total Seminarians	14
Colleges and Universities	1
Total Students	2,750
Elementary Schools, Diocesan and Parish	12
Total Students	1,868
Catechesis/Religious Education:	
High School Students	4,150
Elementary Students	4,310
Total Students under Catholic Instruction	13,092
Teachers in the Diocese:	
Sisters	10
Lay Teachers	149
Vital Statistics	
Receptions into the Church:	
Infant Baptism Totals	912
Adult Baptism Totals	51
Received into Full Communion	123
First Communions	978
Confirmations	810
Marriages:	
Catholic	198
Interfaith	175
Total Marriages	373
Deaths	1,070
Total Catholic Population	70,950
Total Population	431,000

Former Bishops—Rt. Revs. JAMES MCGOLRICK, D.D., consecrated Dec. 27, 1889; died Jan. 23, 1918; JOHN T. MCNICHOLAS, O.P., S.T.D., consecrated Sept. 8, 1918; appt. Archbishop of Cincinnati July 8, 1925; died April 22, 1950; Most Revs. THOMAS A. WELCH, D.D., consecrated Feb. 3, 1926; died Sept. 9, 1959; FRANCIS J. SCHENK, D.D., consecrated May 24, 1945; appt. to Duluth Jan. 19, 1960; resigned April 30, 1969; died Oct. 28, 1969; PAUL F. ANDERSON, D.D., appt. Titular Bishop of Polignando and Coadjutor Bishop with right of succession July 19, 1968; consecrated Oct. 17, 1968; succeeded to See April 10, 1969; resigned Aug. 7, 1982; appt. Apostolic Administrator Aug. 7, 1982; appt. Auxiliary Bishop of Sioux Falls, SD March 25, 1983; died Jan. 4, 1987; ROBERT H. BROM, D.D., consecrated May 23, 1983; appt. Coadjutor Bishop of San Diego, CA, May 9, 1989; ROGER SCHWIETZ, O.M.I., D.D., ord. Dec. 20, 1967; appt. Bishop of Duluth Dec. 12, 1989; consecrated Feb. 2, 1990; appt. Coadjutor Archbishop of Anchorage, Jan. 18, 2000; installed March 24, 2000; succeeded to See March 3, 2001.

Vicar General—Rev. DALE NAU, J.C.L.

Chancellor—Rev. DALE NAU, J.C.L.

Pastoral Center—2830 E. Fourth St., Duluth, 55812. Tel: 218-724-9111; Fax: 218-724-1056. Office Hours: Mon.-Fri. 8:30-12 & 1-4:30

Deans—Revs. PAUL FRUTH, Brainerd; CORNELIUS KELLEHER, Cloquet; JEROME WEISS, Duluth; RONALD GAGNE, Hibbing; JAMES SCHEUER, Virginia.

Diocesan Tribunal—2830 E. Fourth St., Duluth, 55812. Tel: 218-724-9111.

Judicial Vicar—Rev. JAMES BISSONETTE, J.C.L.

Vicar for Canonical Affairs—Rev. DALE NAU, J.C.L.

Defender of the Bond—Rev. DALE NAU, J.C.L.

Advocate—BETTE DAMBERG.

Notary—ROSE MARIE EICHMUELLER.

Priests' Pension Board—Mr. JAY STOFFEL; Revs. WILLIAM FIDER; FREDRICK METHOD; DALE NAU, J.C.L.; DAVID TUSHAR; JERRY WEISS; Mr. ROBERT HOWE.

Presbyteral Council—Rev. TONY WROBLEWSKI, O.M.I., Chm.

Corporate Board—Most Rev. DENNIS M. SCHNURR; Revs. DALE NAU, J.C.L.; JAMES BISSONETTE; Mrs. MARILYN GRATTO.

Finance Council—Most Rev. DENNIS SCHNURR; Revs. DALE NAU, J.C.L.; LAWRENCE O'SHEA; GARY BUBALO; Mrs. MARILYN GRATTO; DOUG HILDENBRAND; RONALD KARLEN; JIM JAROCKI; DARRYL LISOWSKI.

Diocesan Offices and Directors

Archivist—Mrs. ROSIE KNUDSEN, 2830 E. Fourth St., Duluth, 55812. Tel: 218-724-9111.

Boy Scouts—Rev. LLOYD MUDRAK, P.O. Box 290, Coleraine, 55722. Tel: 218-245-1684.

Campus Ministry—Rev. DALE NAU, J.C.L., Dir., 2830 E. 4th St., Duluth, 55812. Tel: 218-728-3646.

Cemeteries—Rev. DALE NAU, J.C.L., Dir., 2830 E. Fourth St., Duluth, 55812. Tel: 218-724-9111.

Censor of Books—VACANT.

Continuing Formation of Priests—Rev. DALE NAU, J.C.L., 2830 E. Fourth St., Duluth, 55812. Tel: 218-724-9111.

Director of Catechesis—DENICE MACIEJ, 2830 E. Fourth St., Duluth, 55812. Tel: 218-724-9111.

Director of Youth Ministry—VACANT, Dir.; GRACE ROMANEK, Contact Person, 2830 E. Fourth St., Duluth, 55812. Tel: 218-724-9111.

Council of Catholic Women—Rev. PAUL FRUTH, Moderator, 309 2nd St., N.W., Aitkin, 56431. Tel: 218-927-6581.

Cursillo Movement—Rev. ROMAN SPORS, Spiritual Advisor, Box 266, Emily, 56477. Tel: 218-763-2101; BRYON HARKER, Lay Dir., Rte. 1, Box 245, Longville, 56655. Tel: 218-363-2567.

Ecumenical and Inter-faith Affairs—Rev. DALE NAU, J.C.L., 2830 E. Fourth St., Duluth, 55812. Tel: 218-724-9111.

Finance Officer—Rev. LAWRENCE O'SHEA, 2830 E. Fourth St., Duluth, 55812. Tel: 218-724-9111.

Department of Liturgy—Rev. JOEL HASTINGS, S.T.L., Coord., 2830 E. Fourth St., Duluth, 55812. Tel: 218-724-9111.

Mission Outreach and Propagation of the Faith—Rev. LAWRENCE O'SHEA, Dir., 2830 E. Fourth St., Duluth, 55812. Tel: 218-724-9111.

Newspaper "Catholic Outlook"—Rev. DALE NAU, J.C.L., Editor, 2830 E. Fourth St., Duluth, 55812. Tel: 218-724-9111.

Department of Indian Ministry—Sr. MARIE ROSE MESSINGSCHLAGER, C.D.P., Dir., 2830 E. Fourth St., Duluth, 55812. Tel: 218-724-9111.

Department of Ministry Formation—

Vocations and Priestly Formation—Most Rev. DENNIS SCHNURR, Dir. Assistant Directors: Rev. RICHARD KUNST; Deacon MIKE KNUTH, 2830 E. 4th St., Duluth, 55812. Tel: 218-724-9111.

Director of Permanent Diaconate—Deacon DAVID CRAIG, 2830 E. 4th St., Duluth, 55812. Tel: 218-724-9111.

Department of Communications—Rev. DALE NAU, J.C.L., Coord., 2830 E. Fourth St., Duluth, 55812. Tel: 218-724-9111.

Director of Schools—Ms. CYNTHIA ZOOK, 2830 E. Fourth St., Duluth, 55812. Tel: 218-724-9111.

Department of Development—MIKE BILDEN, Dir., 2830 E. Fourth St., Duluth, 55812. Tel: 218-724-9111.

Director of Family Life—Mr. DICK FROST, 2830 E. Fourth St., Duluth, 55812. Tel: 218-724-9111.

Rural Life—VACANT.

Director of the Social Apostolate—PATRICE CRITCHLEY-MENOR, 2830 E. Fourth St., Duluth, 55812. Tel:

218-724-9111.

Victim Assistance Coordinator—ESTHER REAGAN. Tel: 218-820-9220.

CLERGY, PARISHES, MISSIONS AND PAROCHIAL SCHOOLS

CITY OF DULUTH
(ST. LOUIS COUNTY)

1—CATHEDRAL OF OUR LADY OF THE ROSARY, Rev. Dale Nau, Rector. In Res., Rev. James Crossman; Deacon Roger Brannan.
Res.: 2801 E. 4th St., 55812. Tel: 218-728-3646; Fax: 218-728-3647.
School—Holy Rosary, Tel: 218-724-8565. Sr. Karen Kvidera, O.P. Sisters 2; Lay Teachers 18; Students 289.
Catechesis/Religious Program—Tel: 218-728-6985. Tisha Greenslade, D.R.E. Students 227.
Convent—Sisters of the Third Order of St. Dominic (Springfield, IL), 443 Lakeview Ave., 55812. Tel: 218-724-4370.

2—ST. ANTHONY, Closed. For inquiries for parish records contact the chancery.

3—ST. BENEDICT'S, Rev. Richard Kunst; Deacon Dennis Anderson.
Parish Office—1419 St. Benedict St., 55811. Tel: 218-724-4828; Fax: 218-728-2683.
Res.: 1419 Arrowhead Rd., 55811. Tel: 218-724-8926.
Catechesis/Religious Program—Brandon Moravitz, D.R.E. Students 407.

4—ST. ELIZABETH'S, Rev. Noel Stretton.
Res.: 610 99th Ave. W., 55808. Tel: 218-626-2283.
Catechesis/Religious Program—Mrs. Ann Menart, D.R.E. Students 85.

5—GOOD SHEPHERD, Closed. For inquiries for parish records contact the chancery.

6—HOLY FAMILY, Rev. Anthony Wroblewski, O.M.I. In Res., Rev. James Datko, O.M.I.
Parish Office—2430 W. 3rd St., 55806-1801. Tel: 218-722-4445; Fax: 218-722-8979.
Res.: Tel: 218-722-0730.
Catechesis/Religious Program—Desiree Taylor, D.R.E. Students 100.

7—ST. JAMES, Rev. Charles Flynn; Deacon Ted Windus.
Res.: 721 N. 57th Ave. W., 55807. Tel: 218-624-0125; Fax: 218-624-3750.
School—Tel: 218-624-1511. Sharon Pristash, Prin. Lay Teachers 12; Students 159.
Catechesis/Religious Program—Richard A. Witikko, D.R.E. Students 124.

8—ST. JOHN'S (Woodland), Rev. Jerome P. Weiss; Deacon Walt Beier.
Res.: 4230 St. John's Ave., 55803. Tel: 218-724-6332.
School—Tel: 218-724-9392; Fax: 218-724-9368. Peggy Frederickson, Prin. Lay Teachers 8; Students 175.
Catechesis/Religious Program—Students 227.

9—ST. JOSEPH'S (Duluth Heights), Rev. William Fournier.
Res.: 2404 Morris Thomas Rd., 55811. Tel: 218-722-2259; Fax: 218-733-0414.
Catechesis/Religious Program—Vicky Schweiger, D.R.E. Students 57.

10—ST. LAWRENCE'S, Rev. William Fournier.
Res.: 2410 Morris Thomas Rd., 55811. Tel: 218-722-1900; 218-722-2259; Fax: 218-733-0414.
Catechesis/Religious Program—Tel: 218-722-6965. Shawna Hansen, D.R.E. Students 287.

11—ST. MARGARET MARY, , (Morgan Park) Rev. John Petrich.
Res.: 1467 88th Ave. W., 55808. Tel: 218-626-2379; 218-626-4724.
Catechesis/Religious Program—Students 65.

12—ST. MARY STAR OF THE SEA, Deacon Roger Birkland.
Res.: 325 E. Third St., 55805. Tel: 218-722-3078; Fax: 218-279-5070.
Catechesis/Religious Program—Tel: 218-722-3078. Shirley Baker, D.R.E. Students 67.

13—ST. MICHAEL'S, Rev. William P. Fider. Tel: 218-525-7513; Deacons Richard Laumeyer; Chico Anderson.
Office—4901 E. Superior St., 55804. Tel: 218-525-1902; Fax: 218-525-1904.
School—St. Michael Lakeside School, 4628 Pitt St., 55804. Tel: 218-525-1931; Fax: 218-525-0296. Amy Flaig, Prin. Teachers 13; Students 158.
Catechesis/Religious Program—Debra Lieberg, D.R.E. Students 178.

14—OUR LADY OF MERCY, Unassigned., Mailing Address: 325 E. Third St., 55805. Tel: 218-722-3078; Fax: 218-279-5070. In Res., Rev. Msgr. Patrick McDowell. Tel: 218-726-1362.
Church: 2002 Minnesota Ave., 55805.

15—SS. PETER AND PAUL, Closed. For inquiries for parish records contact the chancery.

16—ST. PETER'S, Deacon Roger Birkland.
Mailing Address: 325 E. Third St., 55805. Tel: 218-722-3078; Fax: 218-279-5070.
Church: 3rd & 8th Ave. W., 55805.

17—ST. RAPHAEL'S, Rev. Lawrence O'Shea.
Parish Office—5779 Seville Rd., 55811. Tel: 218-729-7537.
Catechesis/Religious Program—Tel: 218-729-7537. Georgiann Kuberra, D.R.E. Students 205.

18—WEST END CATHOLIC PARISH OF SS. CLEMENT AND JEAN, Closed. For inquiries for parish records contact the chancery.

OUTSIDE THE CITY OF DULUTH

AITKIN, AITKIN CO., ST. JAMES, [CEM] Rev. Paul Fruth.
Res.: 309 Second St., N.W., 56431. Tel: 218-927-6581; Fax: 218-927-3918.
Catechesis/Religious Program—Students 170.

AURORA, ST. LOUIS CO., HOLY ROSARY, Rev. David Forsman.
Res.: 16 W. Fifth Ave. N., 55705. Tel: 218-229-3210; Fax: 218-229-3434.
Catechesis/Religious Program—Tel: 218-229-3434. Students 43.

BABBITT, ST. LOUIS CO., ST. PIUS X, Rev. James Scheuer; Deacon Gregory Hutar, Pastoral Admin.
Parish Office—15 Ash Blvd., 55706. Tel: 218-827-2291.
Res.: 231 E. Camp St., Ely, 55731. Tel: 218-365-4017.
Catechesis/Religious Program—Students 53.

BALL CLUB, ITASCA CO., ST. JOSEPH'S, [CEM] Rev. Stephen Solors.
Res.: 51061 Wolf Dr., Deer River, 56636. Tel: 218-246-8105.
Catechesis/Religious Program—Students 50.

BENA, CASS CO., ST. ANNE, [CEM] Rev. Stephen Solors.
Res.: 51061 Wolf Dr., Deer River, 56636.
Church: 56626. Tel: 218-246-8105.

BEROUN, PINE CO., ST. JOSEPH'S, [CEM] Rev. Cornelius Kelleher.
Parish Office—19390 Praha Ave., 55063. Tel: 320-384-6313.
Res.: 203 Lawler Ave., S., Hinckley, 55037. Tel: 320-384-6313.
Catechesis/Religious Program—Students 4.

BIGFORK, ITASCA CO., OUR LADY OF THE SNOWS, Rev. Steven Daigle.
Parish Office—P.O. Box 11, 56628. Tel: 218-743-3255; Fax: 218-743-3257.
Catechesis/Religious Program—Students 35.

BIWABIK, ST. LOUIS CO., ST. JOHN'S, Rev. Frank Perkovich.
Parish Office—Box 569, 55708. Tel: 218-865-6774.
Res.: Box 788, Gilbert, 55741. Tel: 218-741-9551.
Catechesis/Religious Program—Students 49.

BRAINERD, CROW WING CO.

1—ST. ANDREW'S, Revs. Seamus Walsh; William Skarich; Deacons Roger Marks; Mike Koecheler.
1108 Willow St., 56401. Tel: 218-822-4040; Fax: 218-829-1340.
Catechesis/Religious Program—Laura Bielke, D.R.E.; Pam Nelson, D.R.E.; Celeste Badger, D.R.E.; Kim Koning-Roth, D.R.E. Students 415.

2—ST. FRANCIS, [CEM] Revs. Seamus Walsh; William Skarich; Deacons John Reed; David Brown.
Res.: 422 N. 3rd St., 56401. Tel: 218-829-3833.
Church: 412 N. 8th St., 56401. Tel: 218-822-4040; Fax: 218-829-1340.
School—Tel: 218-829-2344. Debra Euteneuer, Prin. Lay Teachers 13; Students 226.
Catechesis/Religious Program—Kim Koning, D.R.E.; Celeste Badger, D.R.E.; Laura Bielke, D.R.E.; Pam Nelson, D.R.E. Students 556.

BRUNO, PINE CO., SACRED HEART, [CEM] Rev. Alcuin Henger, O.M.I.
Res.: Box 644, Sandstone, 55072. Tel: 320-245-5175.

BUHL, ST. LOUIS CO., OUR LADY OF THE SACRED HEART, Rev. Jon Wild.
Parish Office—Box 27, 55713. Tel: 218-254-5703; Fax: 218-254-3636.
Res.: 113 S.W. 4th St., Chisholm, 55719. Tel: 218-254-4744; Fax: 218-254-3636.

CARLTON, CARLTON CO., ST. FRANCIS, [CEM] Rev. David Tushar.
Parish Office & Res., 509 Sunrise Dr., 55718. Tel: 218-384-4563; 218-879-6958 Res..
Catechesis/Religious Program—Students 120.

CASS LAKE, CASS CO., ST. CHARLES, Rev. Anselm Thevarkunnel.
Res.: Box 368, 56633. Tel: 218-335-2359; Fax: 218-335-2618.
Catechesis/Religious Program—Students 34.

CHISHOLM, ST. LOUIS CO., ST. JOSEPH, [CEM] Rev. Jon Wild.
Res.: 113 S.W. Fourth St., 55719. Tel: 218-254-5703; 218-254-4744; Fax: 218-254-3636.
Catechesis/Religious Program—Students 220.

CLOQUET, CARLTON CO.

1—HOLY FAMILY, [CEM] Rev. Joseph Sirba; Deacon Terry Twomey.
Res.: 45 5th St., 55720. Tel: 218-879-6958.
Church: 280 Reservation Rd., 55720. Tel: 218-879-9047.
Convent—Maryknoll Sisters 55720.

2—QUEEN OF PEACE, [CEM 2] Rev. Joseph Sirba; Deacon Terry Twomey.
Res.: 45 5th St., 55720. Tel: 218-879-6958; Fax: 218-879-2654.
Church: 102 4th St., 55720. Tel: 218-879-6793.
School—Tel: 218-879-8516. Gerald Carr, Prin. Lay Teachers 9; Students 98.
Catechesis/Religious Program—Irene McKay, D.R.E. Students 70.
Convent—Franciscan Sisters of the Eucharist, 5613 Lilac Hill Rd., 55810. Tel: 218-624-9038.

COHASSET, ITASCA CO., ST. AUGUSTINE, Rev. Paul Larson.
Church & Res.: P.O. Box 98, Deer River, 56636. Tel: 218-246-8582.

COLERAINE, ITASCA CO., MARY IMMACULATE, Rev. Lloyd Mudrak.
Res.: Box 290, 55722. Tel: 218-245-1684.
Catechesis/Religious Program—Students 77.

COOK, ST. LOUIS CO., ST. MARY'S, [CEM] Rev. Lawrence T. Antus, O.M.I.
Res.: Box 609, 55723. Tel: 218-666-5334.
Catechesis/Religious Program—Students 57.

CROMWELL, CARLTON CO., IMMACULATE CONCEPTION, Rev. Michael Thomas Patullo.
Res.: Box 378, Floodwood, 55736. Tel: 218-476-1617.
Church: Tel: 218-476-2367.

CROSBY, CROW WING CO., ST. JOSEPH'S, Rev. Howard P. Eisel, S.S.C.; Deacon Philip Mayer.
Res.: P.O. Box 69, 56441. Tel: 218-546-6559; Fax: 218-545-1548.
Catechesis/Religious Program—Students 113.

CROSSLAKE, CROW WING CO., IMMACULATE HEART, Rev. Dennis Hoffman; Deacon James Baskfield.
Res.: Box 155, 56442. Tel: 218-692-3731; Fax: 218-692-3732.
Catechesis/Religious Program—Students 123.
Chapel—Our Lady of Snows, Fax: 218-692-3731.

DEER RIVER, ITASCA CO., ST. MARY, Rev. Paul Larson.
Res.: P.O. Box 98, 56636. Tel: 218-246-8582; Fax: 218-246-4017.
Catechesis/Religious Program—Students 79.

DEERWOOD, CROW WING CO., ST. JOSEPH, Rev. Howard Eisel, S.S.C.
Res.: P.O. Box 69, Crosby, 56441. Tel: 218-546-6559; 218-534-3182 (Church).
Catechesis/Religious Program—Students 30.

ELY, ST. LOUIS CO., ST. ANTHONY, Rev. James Scheuer; Deacon Gregory Hutar.
Res.: 231 E. Camp St., 55731. Tel: 218-365-4017; Fax: 218-365-3296.
Catechesis/Religious Program—Nancy Weisinger, D.R.E.; Patricia Zupancich, D.R.E. Students 183.

EMILY, CROW WING CO., ST. EMILY, Rev. Roman Spors; Deacon Barry Olson.
Res.: Box 25, 56447. Tel: 218-763-2101; Fax: 218-763-2301.
Catechesis/Religious Program—Students 21.

EVELETH, ST. LOUIS CO., RESURRECTION, Rev. Joel Hastings; Deacon Herb Riley.
Res.: Box 586, 55734. Tel: 218-744-3277; Fax: 218-744-1723.
Catechesis/Religious Program—Tel: 218-744-3305. Pam Rapacz, D.R.E., (Grades K-6); Jill Piette, D.R.E., (Grades 7-12). Students 252.

FEDERAL DAM, CASS CO., SACRED HEART, Rev. Stephen Solors.
Res.: 51061 Wolf Dr., Deer River, 56636.
Church: Tel: 218-246-8105.

FINLAYSON, PINE CO., ST. JOSEPH, [CEM] Rev. Alcuin Henger, O.M.I.
Res.: Box 644, Sandstone, 55702. Tel: 320-245-5175.

FLOODWOOD, ST. LOUIS CO., ST. LOUIS, [CEM] Rev. Michael Thomas Patullo.
Res.: Box 378, 55736. Tel: 218-476-2367; 218-476-1617; Fax: 218-476-2376.
Catechesis/Religious Program—Students 56.

FORT RIPLEY, CROW WING CO., ST. MATHIAS, [CEM] Revs. Seamus Walsh; William Skarich.
Church: 4529 County Rd. 121, 56449. Tel: 218-822-4040; 218-829-1340.
Res.: 1108 Willow St., S.E., Brainerd, 56401.
Catechesis/Religious Program—Students 125.

GARRISON, CROW WING CO., OUR LADY OF FATIMA, Rev. Paul Fruth. In Res, Rev. Gabriel Binye.
Res.: 9490 Tower Rd., 56450. Tel: 320-692-4466; 320-692-5705.
Catechesis/Religious Program—Students 5.

GILBERT, ST. LOUIS CO., ST. JOSEPH'S, Rev. Frank Perkovich.
Res.: Box 788, 55741. Tel: 218-741-9551.
Catechesis/Religious Program—Tel: 218-741-1624. Students 81.

GNESEN, ST. LOUIS CO., ST. JOSEPH, [CEM] Rev. Jerome P. Weiss; Deacon Walt Beier.
Res.: 4230 St. John's Ave., 55803. Tel: 218-724-6332.

GRAND MARAIS, COOK CO., ST. JOHN'S, [CEM] Rev. Stephen White.
Res.: 10 E. 5th St., Box 549, 55604. Tel: 218-387-1409.
Catechesis/Religious Program—Students 35.

GRAND PORTAGE, COOK CO., HOLY ROSARY, [CEM] Rev. Stephen White.
Res.: 10 E. St., Grand Marais, 55604. Tel: 218-387-1409.

GRAND RAPIDS, ITASCA CO., ST. JOSEPH, Rev. Thomas Radaich; Deacon Jerome Sura.
Parish Center—P.O. Box 110, 55744. Tel: 218-326-2843; 218-326-3959; Fax: 218-326-9115.
School—Tel: 218-326-6232; Fax: 218-326-6034. Teresa Matetich, Prin. Lay Teachers 9; Students 131.
Catechesis/Religious Program—Tel: 218-326-3720. Lori Dowling, D.R.E. Students 450.

HACKENSACK, CASS CO., SACRED HEART, Rev. Fredrick Method.
Res.: Box 874, Walker, 56484. Tel: 218-547-1054.

HIBBING, ST. LOUIS CO.
1—BLESSED SACRAMENT, Revs. Peter Muhich; Michael Schmitz; Clem Gustin, O.S.C. In Res., Deacons James Griffiths; Ray Sampson.
Office—218 E. 39th St., 55746. Tel: 218-262-5541; Fax: 218-263-3682.
Res.: 2328 Seventh Ave. E., 55746. Tel: 218-263-3681.
School—*Hibbing Catholic*, Tel: 218-263-3054; Fax: 218-263-3058. Claudia Mescher, Prin. Lay Teachers 14; Students 197.
Catechesis/Religious Program—Dan Turnbloom, D.R.E. Students 550.
Chapel—*Side Lake, Blessed Sacrament Chapel*
2—IMMACULATE CONCEPTION, Consolidated, with Blessed Sacrament, Hibbing.
3—ST. LEO'S, Consolidated, with Blessed Sacrament, Hibbing.

HILL CITY, AITKIN CO., ST. JOHN, Rev Edward Buczynski.
Res.: Box 156, 55748. Tel: 218-697-2465.

HILLMAN, CROW WING CO., HOLY FAMILY, [CEM] Rev. Paul Fruth.
Res.: 309 2nd St. N.W., Aitkin, 56431. Tel: 218-927-6581.
Church: 1182 County Rd. 8, 56338. Tel: 320-277-3386.
Catechesis/Religious Program—Students 11.

HINCKLEY, PINE CO., ST. PATRICK'S, [CEM] Rev. Cornelius Kelleher.
Res.: Box 490, 55037-0490. Tel: 320-384-6313; Fax: 320-384-6357.
Catechesis/Religious Program—Students 87.

HOYT LAKES, ST. LOUIS CO., QUEEN OF PEACE, Rev. David Forsman.
Res.: 513 Hampshire Dr., P.O. Box 211, 55750. Tel: 218-225-2867.
Catechesis/Religious Program—Tel: 218-229-3434. Students 58.

INTERNATIONAL FALLS, KOOCHICHING CO., ST. THOMAS AQUINAS, [CEM] Revs. Roger Bergkamp, O.M.I.; Thomas Meyer, O.M.I.; Norman Pahl, O.M.I.; Bro. Thomas Ruhmann, O.M.I.; Deacon Francis Zaren.
Res.: 810 Fifth St., 56649. Tel: 218-283-3293; Fax: 218-283-3553.
School—Tel: 218-283-3430. Mrs. Lynn Naeckel, Prin. Lay Teachers 12; Students 114.
Catechesis/Religious Program—Patricia Bjorum, D.R.E. Students 225.

KEEWATIN, ITASCA CO., ST. MARY'S, Rev. Ronald Gagne.
Res.: 326 2nd St., Nashwauk, 55769. Tel: 218-885-1126.
Church: Box 219, 55753. Tel: 218-778-6379.

LITTLEFORK, KOOCHICHING CO., ST. COLUMBAN, Rev. Roger Bergkamp, O.M.I.
Res.: 810 5th St., International Falls. Tel: 218-283-3293; Fax: 218-283-3553.
Church: Box 44, 56653. Tel: 218-278-6638.

LONGVILLE, CASS CO., ST. EDWARD'S, Rev. Roland Antus.
Res.: P.O. Box 38, 56655-0038. Tel: 218-363-2799.
Catechesis/Religious Program—Students 25.

MARBLE, ITASCA CO., ST. MARY, Rev. Lloyd Mudrak.
Res.: Box 290, Coleraine, 55722. Tel: 218-245-1684.
Church: Box 411, 55764. Tel: 218-247-7368.
Catechesis/Religious Program—Students 35.

MCGRATH, AITKIN CO., OUR LADY OF FATIMA, [CEM] Rev. John Fleischhacker, O.S.C.
Res.: Box 156, McGregor, 55760. Tel: 218-768-2702.

MCGREGOR, AITKIN CO., HOLY FAMILY, Rev. John J. Fleischhacker, O.S.C.
Res.: Box 156, 55760. Tel: 218-768-2702; Fax: 218-768-2131.
Catechesis/Religious Program—Students 75.

MEADOWLANDS, ST. LOUIS CO., ST. MARY, Rev. Michael Thomas Patullo.
Res.: Box 378, Floodwood, 55736. Tel: 218-476-1617.
Church: Box 184, 55765. Tel: 218-427-2625.
Catechesis/Religious Program—Students 35.

MOOSE LAKE CARLTON CO., HOLY ANGELS [CEM] Rev. Eamonn Boland.
Res.: P.O. Box 487, 55767. Tel: 218-485-4909.
Catechesis/Religious Program—Tel: 218-485-8214. Peggy Rosera, D.R.E.; Mary Rose Rose, D.R.E. Students 145.

MOUNTAIN IRON, ST. LOUIS CO., SACRED HEART, Revs. John O'Donnell; John Doyle; Joseph Valliyamtha Dathil.
Res.: 306 S. 2nd St., Virginia, 55792. Tel: 218-741-6344.
Church: 8861 Main St., 55768. Tel: 218-735-8248.

NASHWAUK, ITASCA CO., ST. CECILIA'S, Rev. Ronald Gagne; Deacon Richard Johnston.
Res.: 326 Second St., 55769. Tel: 218-885-1126; Fax: 218-885-1145.
Catechesis/Religious Program—Students 105.

NISSWA, CROW WING CO., ST. CHRISTOPHER, Rev. George Zeck.
Church: P.O. Box 12, 56468. Tel: 218-568-6707; Fax: 218-568-6707. Students 145.

NORTHOME, KOOCHICHING CO., ST. MICHAEL'S, , (Under the jurisdiction of the Duluth Diocese; administered by the Crookston Diocese) Rev. James Lyons.
Res.: P.O. Box 187, Kelliher, 56650. Tel: 218-647-8392.

ORR, ST. LOUIS CO., HOLY CROSS, Rev. Lawrence T. Antus, O.M.I.
Res.: P.O. Box 609, Cook, 55723. Tel: 218-666-5334.
Church: Box 218, 55771. Tel: 218-757-3273.
Catechesis/Religious Program—Students 29.
Chapel—*Buyck, St. Joseph's*

PENGILLY, ITASCA CO., ST. KEVIN, Rev. Ronald Gagne; Deacon Richard Johnston.
Res.: 326 2nd St., Nashwauk, 55769. Tel: 218-885-1126.

PEQUOT LAKES, CROW WING CO., ST. ALICE'S, Rev. George Zeck; Deacons David Craig; Richard Paine.
Res.: Box 159, 56472. Tel: 218-568-4760; Fax: 218-568-6707.
Catechesis/Religious Program—Students 157.

PINE BEACH, CROW WING CO., ST. THOMAS, [CEM] Rev. Seamus Walsh.
Parish Office—1108 Willow St., Brainerd, 56401. Tel: 218-829-3833.
Church: Tel: 218-822-4040.

PINE CITY, PINE CO., IMMACULATE CONCEPTION, [CEM] Rev. Michael J. Lyons; Deacon Eugene Biever.
Res.: 535 8th St. S.W., 55063. Tel: 320-629-2935; Fax: 320-629-1438.
School—*St. Mary's*, 815 Sixth Ave., S.W., 55063. Tel: 320-629-3953. Sr. Helen Giesen, C.S.B., Prin. Lay Teachers 5; Students 78.
Catechesis/Religious Program—Tel: 320-629-3911. Students 158.

PINE RIVER, CASS CO., OUR LADY OF LOURDES, Rev. George Zeck. In Res., Rev. Bruce Engen.
Res.: Box 44, 56474. Tel: 218-587-4163; Fax: 218-568-6707.
Catechesis/Religious Program—Tel: 218-587-4163. Students 60.

PROCTOR, ST. LOUIS CO., ST. ROSE CATHOLIC CHURCH, Rev. James Bissonette.
Res.: 3 Sixth Ave., 55810. Tel: 218-624-0007; Fax: 218-628-1462.
School—Tel: 218-624-0818; Fax: 218-624-0984. Timothy Johnson, Prin. Lay Teachers 7; Students 85.
Catechesis/Religious Program—Tel: 218-624-9580. Becky Kubat, D.R.E. Students 103.

REMER, CASS CO., ST. PAUL, Rev. Roland Antus.
Res.: P.O. Box 38, Longville, 56655. Tel: 218-363-3498.
Church Box 38, 56672. Tel: 218-566-2954.

ST. MATHIAS, CROW WING CO., ST. MATHIAS, Rev. Seamus Walsh.
Res.: 4529 Co. Rd. 121, Fort Ripley 56449. Tel: 218-829-4061; Fax: 218-829-4061.
Catechesis/Religious Program—Students 125.
Station—*Crow Wing State Park*

SAGINAW, ST. LOUIS CO., ST. PHILIP NERI, Rev. James Bissonette.
Res.: 3 Sixth Ave., Proctor, 55810. Tel: 218-624-0007; Fax: 218-628-1462.
Church: P.O. Box 83, 55779.
Catechesis/Religious Program—Students 23.

SANDSTONE, PINE CO., ST. LUKE, [CEM] Rev. Alcuin Henger, O.M.I.
Res.: Box 644, 55072. Tel: 320-245-5175; Fax: 320-245-0411.
Catechesis/Religious Program—Tel: 320-245-0061. Students 65.

SAWYER, CARLTON CO., SS. MARY & JOSEPH, Rev. David Tushar.
Res.: 509 Sunrise Dr., Carlton, 55718. Tel: 218-879-6958.
Church: Tel: 218-384-4563.

SILVER BAY, LAKE CO., ST. MARY, Revs. Mark Coen; Francis Paquette. In Res., Deacons Fred Wright; Jack Ferris.
Res.: 57 Horn Blvd., 55614. Tel: 218-226-3100; Fax: 218-226-3116.
Catechesis/Religious Program—Students 65.

SQUAW LAKE, ITASCA CO., ST. CATHERINE, Rev. Steven Daigle.
Parish Office: P.O. Box 379, 56681. Tel: 218-743-3255.
Church: Tel: 218-659-4353.

STURGEON LAKE, PINE CO., ST. ISIDORE, [CEM] Rev. Timothy Deutsch.
Church: Tel: 218-372-3446.

TACONITE, ITASCA CO., ST. JOSEPH, Rev. Lloyd Mudrak.
Res.: Box 290, Coleraine, 55722. Tel: 218-245-1684.

TOWER, ST. LOUIS CO., ST. MARTIN'S, Rev. Rudolph Pakiz.
Res.: Box 757, 55790. Tel: 218-753-4310.
Catechesis/Religious Program—Students 58.

TWO HARBORS, LAKE CO., HOLY SPIRIT, [CEM] Rev. Mark Coen.
Res.: 227 Third St., 55616. Tel: 218-834-4313; Fax: 218-834-7082.
Catechesis/Religious Program—Students 191.

VIRGINIA, ST. LOUIS CO.
1—HOLY SPIRIT, Rev. John O'Donnell.
Res.: 306 S. Second St., 55792. Tel: 218-741-6344; Fax: 218-749-3496.
Catechesis/Religious Program—Tel: 218-741-6345. Linda Strukel, D.R.E. Students 310.
2—SACRED HEART, Rev. John O'Donnell. In Res., Rev. John Doyle.
Res.: 603 12th St. N., 55792. Tel: 218-741-2322.

WALKER, CASS CO., ST. AGNES, Rev. Fredrick Method.
Res.: Box 874, 56484. Tel: 218-547-1054; Fax: 218-547-1376.
Catechesis/Religious Program—Students 115.
Station—*Ah-Gwah Ching State Nursing Home* , SD.

WARBA, ITASCA CO., ST. PAUL, Rev. Edward Bucyznski.
Res.: Box 156, Hill City, 55748. Tel: 218-697-2465.

WILLOW RIVER, PINE CO., ST. MARY'S, [CEM] Rev. Timothy Deutsch.
Res.: Box 97, 55795. Tel: 218-372-3446.
Catechesis/Religious Program—Students 45.

INDIAN MISSIONS

DULUTH, ST. LOUIS CO., INDIAN MISSIONS, Sr. Marie Rose Messingschlager, C.D.P.
c/o Chancery Office, 2830 E. Fourth St., 55812. Tel: 218-724-9111; Fax: 218-724-1056.

Chaplains of Public Institutions

Hospitals

DULUTH. *St. Luke's Hospital*, 1467 88th Ave. W., 55808. Tel: 218-626-4724. Rev. John C. Petrich, Chap.
Miller Dwan Hospital. Mrs. Jan Rohweder, Dir. of Chaplains. Tel: 218-727-1089.

MOOSE LAKE. *Moose Lake State Hospital*, 112 Cedar, 55767. Tel: 218-485-4909. Rev. Eamonn Boland, Chap.

Correctional Institutions

DULUTH. *Duluth Federal Prison*. Rev. Noel Stretton. Tel: 218-722-1021.

SAGINAW. *Northeast Regional Correctional Institution*. Rev. John C. Petrich, Chap. Tel: 218-626-4724.

WILLOW RIVER. *Youth Conservation Camp*. Rev. Timothy Deutsch, Chap. Tel: 218-372-3446.

On Duty Outside the Diocese:
Revs.—
Graham, William C., 5119 N. Kenmore St., 1 W., Chicago, IL 60640.
Hauver, James, Church of St. Patrick, 137 Moseman Rd., Yorktown Heights, NY 10598.
Johnson, Lawrence P., 1820 Froude St., San Diego, CA 92107.
Kaster, Alfred D., 6716 Woodland Dr., Paradise, CA 95969.

Military Chaplains:
Rev.—
Lambert, Peter S., PSC 5, Box 711, APO, AE 09050.

Absent on Sick Leave:
Revs.—
Kisting, Thomas, 2238 Abbe Court, S.W., Pine River, 56474.
Moran, Patrick, Strokestown Rd., Ballyleague, Ireland.

On Leave:
Rev.—
Sailstad, Kenton, Lanesboro, Co. Longford, Ireland.

Retired:
Rev. Msgr.—
Popesh, Bernard, 1181 Ring Rock Rd., Ely, 55731.

Tel: 218-365-6085

Revs.—

Arimond, Vincent, 330 E. 3rd St., #104, 55805. Tel: 218-727-4184

Blanchard, Kirby, Bethany Good Samaritan Home, Brainerd, 56401. Tel: 218-825-9062

Bouchard, Thomas, 20 6th St., S.W., Chisholm, 55712. Tel: 218-254-4529

Cossette, Raymond, 12788 County Rd. 8 S.E., Brainerd, 56401. Tel: 218-764-2941

Coyle, Patrick, 4300 W. River Parkway, #314, Minneapolis, 55406. Tel: 612-724-1475

Dolsina, Stanley, 2423 Morris Thomas Rd., 55811. Tel: 218-727-3271

Faith, Rudolph, 935 Kenwood Ave., #311, 55811.

Foster, Edward

Gaber, Francis, 129 E. 6th Ave., Pine City, 55063. Tel: 612-629-3342

Golden, James, 204-4th Ave., Keewatin, 55753. Tel: 218-778-6949

Golobich, John, 524 N. Oak Bend Drive, #102, 55811. Tel: 218-723-1566

La Patka, Gerald, 4202 E. Broadway Rd., #75, Mesa, AZ 85206. Tel: 480-325-5103

Lyttle, Eugene, 1115 S. Lake Ave., 55802. Tel: 218-726-0602

Paquette, Francis, 57 Horn Blvd., Silver Bay, 55614. Tel: 218-220-0122

Partika, Richard, 925 Kenwood Ave., #1157, 55811. Tel: 218-728-3498

Sustarsic, John, 330 E. 3rd St., #524, 55805. Tel: 218-279-4001

Permanent Deacons:

Anderson, Dennis, St. Benedict, Duluth

Anderson, H. L., St. Michael, Duluth

Anderson, Laverne

Baskfield, Jim, Immaculate Conception, Crosslake

Beier, Walter, St. John's, Duluth

Biever, Eugene, Immaculate Conception Church, Pine City

Birkland, Roger, St. Mary Star of the Sea, Duluth

Brannan, Roger, Cathedral, Duluth

Brown, David, Brainerd Area Catholic Churches

Christensen, Robert, (Retired)

Craig, David, St. Alice, Pequot Lakes

Ferris, Jack, St. Mary's, Silver Bay

Griffiths, James, Blessed Sacrament Hibbing

Hutar, Gregory, St. Anthony, Ely

Johnston, Richard, Nashwauk Keewatin, Pengilly

Kittelson, Timothy, Holy Family, Duluth

Knuth, Michael, St. Alice, Pequot Lakes

Koecheler, Michael, St. Francis, Brainerd

Kubat, Thomas, St. Rose, Proctor

Laumeyer, Richard, St. Michael's, Duluth

Marks, Roger, Holy Family, Hillman

Mayer, Philip, St. Joseph's, Crosby

Olson, Barry, Immaculate Heart, Cross Lake

Paine, Richard, St. Alice, Pequot Lakes

Reed, John, St. Francis, Brainerd

Riley, Herbert, Resurrection, Eveleth

Sampson, Ray, Blessed Sacrament, Hibbing

Sura, Jerome, St. Joseph, Grand Rapids

Szyman, Robert, (Retired)

Twomey, Terence, Queen of Peace, Cloquet

Windus, Theodore, Sr., St. James, Duluth

Wright, Fred, St. Mary's, Silver Bay

Zaren, Francis

INSTITUTIONS LOCATED IN THE DIOCESE

[A] COLLEGES AND UNIVERSITIES

DULUTH. *College of St. Scholastica*, 1200 Kenwood Ave., 55811. Tel: 218-723-6000; Fax: 218-723-6290. Web: www.css.edu. Dr. Larry Goodwin, Pres.; Sr. Mary Odile Cahoon, O.S.B., Senior Vice Pres.; Steve Lyons, Dean of Student Affairs. A coed Benedictine college for resident and day students. Sisters 9; Lay Faculty 118; Students 2,750.

[B] ELEMENTARY SCHOOLS, INTERPAROCHIAL

VIRGINIA. *Marquette Catholic School*, 311 Third St. S., 55792. Tel: 218-741-6811; Fax: 218-741-2158. Email: mcs@cpinternet.com. Marianne Runkle, Prin. Serving the parishes of Holy Spirit & Sacred Heart. Lay Teachers 7; Students 100.

[C] GENERAL HOSPITALS

DULUTH. *St. Mary's Medical Center*, 407 E. Third St., 55805. Tel: 218-786-4000; Fax: 218-786-4383. Email: shofer@smdc.org. Web: www.smdc.org. Sr. Kathleen Hofer, O.S.B., Pres.; John Gibbs, M.Div., Dir. of Chap. Svcs. Sisters 5; Nurses 825; Patients Assisted Annually 283,955; Bed Capacity 325; Bassinets 43; Total Staff 2,607.

BRAINERD. *St. Joseph's Medical Center*, 523 N. Third St., 56401. Tel: 218-829-2861; Fax: 218-828-3103. Email: sjmc@sjmcmn.org. Web: www.sjmcmn.org. Sr. Jani Wiebolt, Vice Pres. Operations; Karen DuBord, Dir. Spiritual Care. Nurses 277; Patients Assisted Annually 127,600; Bed Capacity 162; Total Staff 950.

[D] HOMES FOR AGED

DULUTH. *St. Ann's Senior Residence*, 330 E. Third St., 55805. Tel: 218-727-8831; Fax: 218-727-8833. Web: www.stanns.com. Sisters of St. Benedict 2; Residents 185.

Arrowhead Senior Living Community, 503 E. 3rd St., Ste. 400, 55805. Tel: 218-786-2370. Subsidiaries: St. Michael's Health and Rehab Center, Virginia, MN; Arrowhead Senior Living Community, Eveleth, MN

Benedictine Health Center, 935 Kenwood Ave., 55811. Tel: 218-723-6408; Fax: 218-723-6449. Marianne Snyder, Dir. of Spiritual Care; Sr. Mary Susan DeWitt, O.S.B., Chap.; Joan Mork, Chap. (Sub. of Benedictine Health System); Rehabilitation services and respite care, Senior Housing and Assisted Living, post acute, Alzheimer Care Senior Housing Apts. 45; Assisted Living Apts. 35; Permanent Guests 120; Day Care: Adults 25; Children 70.

[E] CONVENTS AND RESIDENCES FOR SISTERS

DULUTH. *Motherhouse and Novitiate of the Sisters of Saint Benedict*, St. Scholastica Monastery, 1001 Kenwood Ave., 55811. Tel: 218-723-6555; Fax: 218-723-5902. Email: khoferosb@aol.com. Web: www.duluthbenedictines.org. Sr. Aelred Roehl, O.S.B., Archivist. Professed Sisters 136.

[F] NEWMAN CENTERS

DULUTH. *University of MN-Duluth* 421 W. Marie St., 55811. Tel: 218-728-3757. Leah Jacobson, Coord.

[G] MISCELLANEOUS LISTINGS

DULUTH. *Benedictine Sisters Benevolent Association* (Parent Co.) , 1001 Kenwood Ave., 55811-2300. Tel: 218-728-1817; Fax: 218-723-5902. Email: khoferosb@aol.com. Web: www.duluthbenedictines.org. Sr. Kathleen Hofer, O.S.B., Pres.

Benedictine Health System, 503 E. Third St., Ste. 400, 55805. Tel: 218-786-2370; Fax: 218-786-2373. Dale M. Thompson, Pres. & CEO. (Sub. of Benedictine Sisters Benevolent Association); Benedictine Health System Subsidiaries Not Located In The Diocese: Benedictine Care Centers; Benedictine Health Dimensions; Good Shepherd Care Center; Madonna Towers of Rochester, Inc.; Mount Carmel Health & Rehabilitation Center; St. Anne of Winona; St. Francis Regional Medical Center; St. Gertrude's Health Center; St. Mary's Care Center; St. Mary's Hospital; St. Mary's Regional Health Center; Tekakwitha Nursing Center, Inc.; Trinity; Villa St. Benedict; Villa St. Vincent; City of Lakes Care Center; Maddona Meadows; Preferred Choice Pharmacy; Living Community of St. Joseph; St. Anthony Continuing Care Center, Steeple Pointe Senior Living Community.

St. Mary's Medical Center, 407 E. Third St., 55805. Tel: 218-786-4000; Fax: 218-786-4383. Sr. Kathleen Hofer, O.S.B., Pres. & Chm. Bd.; Peter Person, M.D., CEO. Affiliate: St. Mary's Hospital of Superior.

St. Joseph's Medical Center, Brainerd, 523 N. Third St., Brainerd, 56401. Tel: 218-829-2861; Fax: 218-828-3103. Thomas Prusak, Pres. & CEO. (Sub. of Benedictine Health System)

Benedictine Health System Foundation, Inc., 503 E. Third St., 55805. Tel: 218-786-2370; Fax: 218-786-2373. Dale M. Thompson, Exec. Dir. (Sub. of Benedictine Health System)

Benedictine Health Center (Sub. of Benedictine Health System) , 935 Kenwood Ave., 55811. Tel: 218-723-6408; Fax: 218-723-6449. Mark Broman, Admin. & CEO.

Polinsky Medical Rehabilitation Center,, 530 E. Second St., 55805. Tel: 218-786-5360; Fax: 218-786-5340. Ann Bussey, Dir. (Sub. of St. Mary's Medical Center)

St. Mary's/Polinsky Center for Personal Fitness, 5th Ave. E. & 2nd St., 55805. Tel: 218-786-5410; Fax: 218-786-5435. (Sub. of St. Mary's Medical Center)

Benedictine Living Communities, 503 E. Third St., Ste. 400, 55805. Tel: 218-786-2370; Fax: 218-786-2373. Kevin Greff, Pres. & CEO. (Sub. of Benedictine Health System)

The Blessed Nuno Society, P.O. Box 3484, 55803. Tel: 218-728-0447. Email: director@blessednuno.org. Web: www.blessednuno.org. Tim Heinan, Dir.

Holy Rosary Parish Endowment Fund, 2801 E. Fourth St., 55812. Tel: 218-728-3646. Email: cathdulth@aol.com.

The Human Life and Development Fund of the Diocese of Duluth, 2830 E. Fourth St., 55812. Tel: 218-724-9111; Fax: 218-724-1056.

John S. Duss Memorial Music Conservatory, 2211 Greysolon Rd., 55812. Tel: 218-724-2052; Fax: 218-724-3318. Franciscan Sisters of the Eucharist, Part of Franciscan Life Center Network, Inc.

The Seminary Endowment Fund of the Diocese of Duluth, 2830 E. 4th St., 55812. Tel: 218-724-9111; Fax: 218-724-1056. Mike Bilden, Devel. Dir.

The Catholic Religious Education Endowment Fund of the Diocese of Duluth, 2830 E. 4th St., 55812. Tel: 218-724-9111; Fax: 218-724-1056. Mike Bilden, Devel. Dir.

St. Vincent de Paul Society, 109 W. Fourth St., 55806. Tel: 218-727-9145. Email: svdpkul@aol.com. Joseph Jodouin, Pres.

CLOQUET. *Queen of Peace Cloquet Educational Endowment Trust*, 102 4th St., 55720. Tel: 218-879-6793. Rev. Joseph Sirba, Contact Person.

HACKENSACK. *S.W. Deanery Chapter of Magnificat of the Diocese of Duluth*, P.O. Box 100, 56452. Tel: 218-675-6180. Email: garoutte@uslink.net.

HIBBING. *Hibbing Catholic Schools Endowment Fund*, 218 E. 39th St., 55746. Tel: 218-262-5541. Rev. Peter Muhich, Contact Person.

**Sister Thea Bowman Black Catholic Educational Foundation*, 627 E. 39 St., 55746. Tel: 216-263-4865. Email: maryloujll@aol.com. Mrs. Mary Lou Jennings, Exec. Dir.

RELIGIOUS INSTITUTES OF MEN REPRESENTED IN THE DIOCESE

For further details refer to the corresponding bracketed number in the Religious Institutes of Men or Women section.

[0400]—*Canons Regular of the Order of Holy Cross*—O.S.C.

[0910]—*Oblates of Mary Immaculate* (Central Prov.)—O.M.I.

[0370]—*Society of St. Columban*—S.S.C.

RELIGIOUS INSTITUTES OF WOMEN REPRESENTED IN THE DIOCESE

[0230]—*Benedictine Sisters of Pontifical Jurisdiction* (St. Joseph, MN; Watertown, SD; St. Paul, MN; Duluth, MN)—O.S.B.

[1000]—*Congregation of Divine Providence of Kentucky*—C.D.P.

[1070-10]—*Dominican Sisters*—O.P.

[1250]—*The Institute of the Franciscan Sisters of the Eucharist* (Meriden, CT)—F.S.E.

[2470]—*Maryknoll Sisters of St. Dominic*—M.M.

[2970]—*School Sisters of Notre Dame* (Mankato Prov.)—S.S.N.D.

[3840]—*Sisters of St. Joseph of Carondelet*—C.S.J.

[2150]—*Sisters Servants of the Immaculate Heart of Mary*—I.H.M.

DIOCESAN CEMETERIES

DULUTH. *Calvary Cemetery*, 1312 Howard Gnesen Rd., 55803. Tel: 218-724-3376. Rev. Dale Nau, Dir.; Mr. Tim Stresow, Supt.

NECROLOGY

† Hayes, Michael T., Moose Lake, MN Holy Angels Church—Died Aug. 4, 2003

† Kottiry, Alphonsus, (On Duty Outside the Diocese)—Died Oct. 12, 2003

Diocese of El Paso

(Dioecesis Elpasensis)

Most Reverend

ARMANDO X. OCHOA, D.D.

Bishop of El Paso; ordained May 23, 1970; appointed Titular Bishop of Sitifi and Auxiliary of the Archdiocese of Los Angeles December 29, 1986; ordained Bishop February 23, 1987; appointed Bishop of El Paso April 1, 1996; installed June 26, 1996

Chancery Office: 499 St. Matthews St., El Paso, TX 79907. Tel: 915-872-8407; Fax: 915-872-8413.

Web: www.elpasodiocese.org

ERECTED MARCH 3, 1914.

Square Miles 26,686.

Comprises in Texas, the Counties of El Paso, Brewster, Culberson, Hudspeth, Jeff Davis, Loving, Presidio, Reeves, Ward and Winkler.

Legal Title: For legal titles of parishes and diocesan institutions, consult the Chancery Office.

STATISTICAL OVERVIEW

Statistical report was not submitted for 2004.

Personnel	
Bishop	1
Priests: Diocesan Active in Diocese	55
Priests: Diocesan Active Outside Diocese	2
Priests: Retired, Sick or Absent	23
Number of Diocesan Priests	80
Religious Priests in Diocese	36
Total Priests in Diocese	116
Extern Priests in Diocese	3
Permanent Deacons in Diocese	10
Total Brothers	13
Total Sisters	254
Parishes	
Parishes	58
With Resident Pastor:	
Resident Diocesan Priests	38
Resident Religious Priests	15
Without Resident Pastor:	
Administered by Priests	2
Administered by Deacons	3
Missions	22
Professional Ministry Personnel:	
Sisters	20
Lay Ministers	32
Welfare	
Homes for the Aged	1
Total Assisted	90
Educational	
Seminaries, Diocesan	1
Students from This Diocese	5
Students from Other Diocese	7
Diocesan Students in Other Seminaries	3
Seminaries, Religious	2
Students Religious	24
Total Seminarians	32
High Schools, Diocesan and Parish	1
Total Students	568
High Schools, Private	2
Total Students	353
Elementary Schools, Diocesan and Parish	9
Total Students	3,571
Elementary Schools, Private	3
Total Students	857
Catechesis/Religious Education:	
High School Students	5,671
Elementary Students	13,740
Total Students under Catholic Instruction	24,792
Teachers in the Diocese:	
Priests	4
Brothers	5
Sisters	32
Lay Teachers	316
Vital Statistics	
Receptions into the Church:	
Infant Baptism Totals	9,538
Adult Baptism Totals	144
Received into Full Communion	288
First Communions	6,062
Confirmations	3,957
Marriages:	
Catholic	1,298
Interfaith	130
Total Marriages	1,428
Deaths	2,064
Total Catholic Population	656,035
Total Population	811,739

Former Bishops—Most Revs. JOHN J. BROWN, S.J., preconized Bishop of El Paso, Jan. 22, 1915; resigned June 16, 1915; ANTHONY J. SCHULER, S.J., D.D., consecrated Oct. 28, 1915; died June 3, 1944; SIDNEY M. METZGER, S.T.D., J.C.D. (Retired), consecrated April 10, 1940; succeeded to See, Nov. 29, 1942; retired May 29, 1978; died April 12, 1986; PATRICK F. FLORES, D.D., consecrated May 5, 1970; installed Bishop of El Paso, May 29, 1978; appt. Archbishop of San Antonio, Aug. 28, 1979; RAYMUNDO J. PENA, D.D., consecrated Dec. 13, 1976; appt. Bishop of El Paso, April 29, 1980; appt. Bishop of Brownsville, May 23, 1995.

Vicars General—Rev. Msgr. FRANCIS J. SMITH, P.A.; Rev. JOHN STOWE, O.F.M.Conv.

Vicar for Clergy—Rev. JOHN TELLES.

Moderator of the Curia—Rev. JOHN STOWE, O.F.M.Conv.

Chancellor—Mrs. SUSAN MARTINEZ, L.M.S.W.-A.C.P.

Diocesan Pastoral Staff—Revs. JOHN STOWE, O.F.M.Conv., Moderator of the Curia; JOHN TELLES, Vicar for Clergy; Mrs. SUSAN MARTINEZ, L.M.S.W.-A.C.P., Chancellor.

Liaison for Women Religious—VACANT, 499 St. Matthews St., El Paso, 79907. Tel: 915-872-8407.

Diocesan Pastoral Center—499 St. Matthews St., El Paso, 79907. Tel: 915-872-8400; Fax: 915-872-8423. Refer all official business to this address.

Diocesan Tribunal—499 St. Matthews St., El Paso, 79907. Tel: 915-872-8402. Revs. ANTHONY CELINO, J.C.L., Judicial Vicar; STEPHEN PETERS, Adjutant Vicar.

Presbyteral Council—Rev. FRANCISCO HERRERA (Retired); Rev. Msgr. JOHN PETERS; Revs. EMANUEL ALCAZAR; BENJAMIN FLORES-RUIZ; KEN DUCRE; JUAN NAREZ; LEONIDES RIVERO; RICARDO RUIZ. Ex Officio Members: Rev. Msgr. FRANCIS J. SMITH, P.A.; Revs. JOHN STOWE, O.F.M.Conv.; JOHN TELLES.

Judges—Revs. STEPHEN PETERS; ROBERT S. KOBE; JAMES W. HALL; GILES CARIE, O.F.M.Conv.

Defenders of the Bond—Rev. Msgr. DAVID G. FIERRO; Rev. TRINI FUENTEZ; Deacon GEORGE LEVY; Sr. DIANE MASSON, C.S.S.F., J.C.L.

Advocates—Rev. Msgr. FRANCIS J. SMITH, P.A.; Rev. FRANCISCO LOPEZ.

Lay Advocates—OUISA DAVIS; CARMEN RODRIGUEZ; SUE KURITA; RUDY VILLALOBOS.

Tribunal Ecclesiastical Notary—YOLANDA RUIZ.

Peritus—VACANT.

Vicar for Clergy—Rev. JOHN TELLES.

Vicars-Vicariates—St. Peter: Rev. TRINIDAD FUENTEZ, Queen of Peace Parish, 1551 Belvidere, El Paso, 79912. Tel: 915-584-5817. St. Paul Rev. RAFAEL GARCIA, S.J., Sacred Heart Church, 602 S. Oregon, El Paso, 79901. Tel: 915-532-5447. St. John: Rev. RICHARD WEISS, Our Lady of Assumption Church, 4800 Byron, El Paso, 79930. Tel: 915-566-4040. St. Mark and St. Luke: Rev. JOHN LUCIDO, St. John the Apostle Church, 5th & Ike St., Monahans, 79756. Tel: 915-943-5114. St. Matthew: Rev. RAUL TRIGUEROS, Cristo Rey Parish, 8011 Williamette, El Paso, 79907. Tel: 915-591-0688. Our Lady of Guadalupe: Rev. Msgr. FRANCIS J. SMITH, P.A., St. Raphael Parish, 2301 Zanzibar, El Paso, 79925. Tel: 915-598-3431.

Diocesan Master of Ceremonies—Rev. MARCUS MCFADIN.

Peace & Justice Office—VACANT, Dir., 499 St. Matthews, El Paso, 79907. Tel: 915 872-8422.

Finance Council—Most Rev. ARMANDO X. OCHOA, D.D.; Rev. Msgrs. FRANCIS J. SMITH, P.A.; DAVID FIERRO; E. H. BAEZA; FRANK GORMAN; MARIA ELENA FLOOD; PHILLIP MULLIN.

Diocesan Building Committee—Most Rev. ARMANDO X. OCHOA, D.D.; Rev. RAFAEL GARCIA, S.J.; FRANK ALDERETE; RICARDO BACA; ROSIE TORRES.

Priests' Personnel Advisory Committee—Rev. Msgr. FRANCIS J. SMITH, P.A.; Revs. TRINI FUENTEZ; RAFAEL GARCIA, S.J.; RICHARD WEISS; JOHN LUCIDO; RAUL TRIGUEROS; JOHN STOWE, O.F.M.Conv.

Catholic Ministry in Hospitals—VACANT, 499 St. Matthews, El Paso, 79907. Tel: 915-872-8427.

Laity, Office of the—Rev. Msgr. ARTURO BANUELAS; Mr. MARCOS MARTINEZ, Youth Ministry, 499 St. Matthews, El Paso, 79907. Tel: 915-872-8410 The following associations are under the direction of the Office of the Laity:.

Adoracion Nocturna (Nocturnal Adoration)—

Apostolado de la Cruz (Apostolate of the Cross)—

Blue Army—

Catholic Daughters of America—

Catholic Knights of America—

Cursillos de Cristianidad—

Franciscans, Secular Order of Franciscans—VACANT.

Knights of Columbus—Rev. Msgr. FRANCIS J. SMITH, P.A.

Knights of the Holy Sepulchre—Rev. Msgr. FRANCIS J. SMITH, P.A.

Knights of St. Gregory—VACANT.

Ladies of Charity; Daughters of Charity; Ladies of the Holy Sepulchre—Rev. Msgr. FRANCIS J. SMITH, P.A.

Legion of Mary—VACANT.

Serra Club—FRANCIS FLOOD.

St. Vincent de Paul Society—CARLOS RUBIO.

Young Adults—VACANT, 499 St. Matthews, El Paso, 79907. Tel: 915-872-8438.

Catholic Communications Ministry—Rev. RAUL TRIGUEROS, 499 St. Matthews St., El Paso, 79907. Tel: 915-872-8414.

Diocesan Newspaper—ANDY SPARKE, Editor, 499 St. Matthews St., El Paso, 79907. Tel: 915-872-8414. "Rio Grande Catholic"

Persons with Disabilities—VACANT.

Campaign for Human Development—VACANT, 499 St.

Matthews St., El Paso, 79907. Tel: 915-872-8422.

Office of Marriage and Family Life—Mr. LUIS ROBLES, 499 St. Matthews St., El Paso, 79907. Tel: 915-872-8401.

Historical Archives & Diocesan Museum—Mrs. SUSAN MARTINEZ, L.M.S.W.-A.C.P., 499 St. Matthews St., El Paso, 79907. Tel: 915-872-8407.

Permanent Diaconate Office—Deacon PETE VELOTT, 499 St. Matthews St., El Paso, 79907. Tel: 915-872-8400.

Priests' Retirement and Disability Plan—Rev. Msgrs. JOHN PETERS; FRANCIS J. SMITH, P.A., Pres.; WILLIAM RYAN; Mr. YAZBIK DAW.

Missions Office—Rev. JOHN STOWE, O.F.M.Conv., 499 St. Matthews St., El Paso, 79907. Tel: 915-872-8407.

Office of Education—Sr. ELIZABETH SWARTZ, S.S.N.D., Supt., 499 St. Matthews St., El Paso, 79907. Tel: 915-872-8426.

Tepeyac Institute—Rev. Msgr. ARTURO BANUELAS, S.T.D., Dir.; Sr. ESTHER ORTEGA, O.P., Assoc. Dir., 499 St. Matthews St., El Paso, 79907. Tel: 915-872-8420.

Reverence for Life Ministry—MARIA ACOSTA, 499 St. Matthews St., El Paso, 79907. Tel: 915-872-8401.

Vocations & Seminarians—Revs. JOHN TELLES; JOE MOLINE, 499 St. Matthews St., El Paso, 79907. Tel: 915-872-8403.

Religious Formation—Sr. GLORIA RODRIGUEZ, M.J.M.J., 499 St. Matthews, El Paso, 79907. Tel: 915-872-8432.

Jail Ministry—VACANT, 499 St. Matthews St., El Paso, 79907. Tel: 915-872-8427.

Cursillo—Rev. PABLO MATTA, 104 Fewel, El Paso, 79902. Tel: 915-532-8462.

Movimiento Familiar Cristiano—Rev. Msgr. JOSE GOMEZ, Dir.

Victim Assistance Coordinator—Mrs. SUSAN MARTINEZ, L.M.S.W.-A.C.P. Tel: 915-872-8407. Email: susanm@elpasodiocese.org.

CLERGY, PARISHES, MISSIONS AND PAROCHIAL SCHOOLS

CITY OF EL PASO
(EL PASO COUNTY)

1—ST. PATRICK'S CATHEDRAL, Rev. Richard A. Matty, Rector; Sr. Maureen Serkowski, Pastoral Assoc.; Deacon Ken Flynn.
Res.: 1118 N. Mesa St., 79902. Tel: 915-533-4451; Fax: 915-532-8761.
School—(Grades K-8), 1111 N. Stanton St., 79902. Tel: 915-532-4142. Lay Teachers 22; Students 460.
Catechesis/Religious Program—Students 547.

2—OUR LADY OF MT. CARMEL, [CEM] Revs. Charles McCarthy; John Stowe, O.F.M.Conv.; Giles Carie, O.F.M.Conv.; Vincent Petersen, O.F.M.Conv.
Res.: 131 S. Zaragoza, 79907. Tel: 915-859-9848; Fax: 915-860-9340.
School—(Grades K-8), 9101 Socorro Rd., 79907. Tel: 915-859-9812; Fax: 915-859-2386. Roger Parks, Prin. Sisters 3; Lay Teachers 9; Students 157.

3—ALL SAINTS, Rev. Kennon Y. Ducre, S.T.L.
Res.: 1415 Dakota St., 79930. Tel: 915-566-9711; Fax: 915-566-9737.

4—BLESSED SACRAMENT, Rev. Stephen Peters.
Res.: 9025 Diana Dr., 79924. Tel: 915-755-7658.
School—(Grades PreK-8) Tel: 915-755-2711; Fax: 915-755-0434. Lay Teachers 15; Students 150.
Catechesis/Religious Program—Tel: 915-755-7658, Ext. 15. Teri Valdez, D.R.E. Students 650.

5—CHRIST THE SAVIOR, Rev. Robert S. Kobe; Deacon Tom Wauson.
Res.: 5301 Wadsworth Ave., 79924. Tel: 915-821-3766.

6—CORPUS CHRISTI, Rev. Wilson Cuevas.
Res.: 9205 N. Loop Dr., 79907. Tel: 915-858-0488; Fax: 915-858-0812.
Catechesis/Religious Program—Students 789.

7—CRISTO REY CHURCH, Rev. Raul Trigueros.
Res.: 8011 Williamette, 79907. Tel: 915-591-0688; Fax: 915-593-0470.

8—ST. FRANCES XAVIER CABRINI PARISH, Rev. Frank Lopez.
Church: 12200 Vista del Sol, 79936. Tel: 915-857-1263; Fax: 915-921-1709.

9—ST. FRANCIS XAVIER, Rev. Esteban Sescon.
Res.: 519 S. Latta St., 79905. Tel: 915-532-2761; Fax: 915-544-5103.

10—GUARDIAN ANGEL, Revs. Jesus Perez Recio, O.A.R.; Antonio Lasheras, O.A.R. (Spain) (NEW).
Res.: 3021 Frutas Ave., 79905. Tel: 915-533-2077; Fax: 915-533-3649.

11—HOLY FAMILY, Rev. Msgr. Jose A. Gomez.
Res.: 104 Fewel St., 79902. Tel: 915-532-8462.

12—ST. IGNATIUS OF LOYOLA, Revs. Jeronimo Melendez, O.S.M.; Ernesto Ruoalcala, O.S.M.; Francisco DiTomasi, O.S.M.; Miguel Flores, O.S.M., J.C.L.
Res.: 408 Park St., 79901. Tel: 915-532-9534; Fax: 915-577-0433.

13—IMMACULATE CONCEPTION, Rev. Msgr. William H. Ryan.
Res.: 118 N. Campbell St., 79901-2404. Tel: 915-533-3427; Fax: 915-533-3228.

14—ST. JOSEPH'S, Rev. Joseph Hermoso.
Res.: 1315 Travis St., 79903. Tel: 915-566-9396; Fax: 915-566-5606.
School—(Grades K-8), 1300 Lamar, 79903. Tel: 915-566-1661; Fax: 915-566-2006. Bro. Edwin Gallagher, Prin. Brothers 3; Lay Teachers 25; Students 500.

15—LA PURISIMA, Rev. Juan Narez.
Res.: 328 S. Nevarez St., 79927. Tel: 915-859-7718.

16—ST. LUKE, Rev. Msgr. John Peters; Deacon Pete Velott.
Res.: 930 E. Redd Rd., 79912. Tel: 915-585-0255.

17—ST. MARK, Rev. Leonides Rivero.
Church: 11700 Pebble Hills, 79936. Tel: 915-857-2955; Fax: 915-857-7133.

18—ST. MATTHEW, Rev. Msgr. David G. Fierro, Admin.
Res.: 400 W. Sunset Rd., 79922. Tel: 915-584-3461; Fax: 915-584-2107.
Catechesis/Religious Program—Mrs. Bea Chavez, D.R.E.; Mrs. Isabel Cortez, D.R.E. Students 455.

19—MOST HOLY TRINITY, Rev. Msgr. Robert S. Calles.
Res.: 10000 Pheasant Rd., 79924. Tel: 915-751-6416; Fax: 915-751-5440.
School—(Grades K-8) Tel: 915-751-2566; Fax: 915-751-2596. Celia Campos, Prin. Lay Teachers 25; Students 165.

20—OUR LADY OF ASSUMPTION, Revs. Richard Weiss; Miguel Luna.
Res.: 4800 Byron St., 79930. Tel: 915-566-4040; Fax: 915-566-4049.
School—(Grades PreK-8) Tel: 915-565-3411; Fax: 915-565-3411. Sisters 2; Lay Teachers 10; Students 138.

21—OUR LADY OF GUADALUPE, Revs. Martin Arriaga; Hugo Cordova, O.F.M.; Fernando Mendoza, O.F.M.
Res.: 2709 Alabama St., 79930. Tel: 915-562-4304; Fax: 915-562-3509.
Catechesis/Religious Program—Fax: 915-566-3307. Mrs. Zenaida Servin, D.R.E. Students 457.

22—OUR LADY OF SORROWS, Revs. Arturo Gonzalez, O.S.M.; Andres Ponso, O.S.M.; Tobias Maceas, O.S.M.; Perry McCoy, O.S.M.
Res.: 7712 Rosedale St., 79915. Tel: 915-772-4834; Fax: 915-772-9078.

23—OUR LADY OF THE LIGHT, Rev. Alfred Villanueva; Sr. Maria Teresa Alcantara, Pastoral Assoc.
Res.: 4700 Delta Dr., 79905. Tel: 915-532-1757.

24—OUR LADY OF THE VALLEY, Rev. John Rini.
Res.: 8600 Winchester, 79907. Tel: 915-859-7939.
School—Tel: 915-859-6448; Fax: 915-859-3908. Sr. Caroline Vasquez, O.S.F., Prin. Lay Teachers 14; Students 265.

25—ST. PAUL THE APOSTLE, Rev. Emanuel Alcazar; Deacon Vicente Aguirre.
Res.: 7424 Mimosa, 79915. Tel: 915-778-5304; Fax: 915-778-5398.

26—STS. PETER AND PAUL, Rev. Saul de Jesus Uribe. In Res., Rev. Celimo Osorio.
Res.: 673 Old Hueco Tanks Rd., 79927. Tel: 915-859-3758; Fax: 915-858-1501.

27—ST. PIUS X, Rev. Msgr. Arturo Banuelas; Rev. Rolando Fonseca; Deacon Jim Szostek.
Res.: 1050 N. Clark Rd., 79905. Tel: 915-772-3226; Fax: 915-771-6665.
School—(Grades PreK-8) Tel: 915-772-6598. Sisters 3; Lay Teachers 35; Students 535.
Catechesis/Religious Program—Tel: 915-772-0224; Fax: 915-771-6665. Students 532.

28—QUEEN OF PEACE, Rev. Trinidad Fuentez.
Res.: 1551 Belvidere, 79912. Tel: 915-584-5817; Fax: 915-584-7761.
Catechesis/Religious Program—Pat Fowler, D.R.E. Students 586.

29—ST. RAPHAEL, Rev. Msgr. Francis J. Smith, P.A.; Revs. Vicente Calderon Jr.; Roberto Alvarado; Deacons George Levy; Frank Mares.
Res.: 2301 Zanzibar Rd., 79925. Tel: 915-598-3431; 915-598-3432; Fax: 915-598-0944.
School—(Grades PreK-8), 2310 Woodside, 79925. Tel: 915-598-2241; Fax: 915-598-3002. Elizabeth Wiehe, Prin. Lay Teachers 50; Students 589.
Catechesis/Religious Program—Students 1,006.

30—SACRED HEART, Revs. Rafael Garcia, S.J.; John Paul, S.J.; Bro. Manuel Cabral, S.J. In Res., Revs. Antonio Concha, S.J.; Frank Renfroe, S.J.; Robert M. McCown, S.J.; James Marshall, S.J.
Res.: 602 S. Oregon St., 79901. Tel: 915-532-5447; Fax: 915-533-0013.

31—SAN ANTONIO, Rev. Benjamin Flores.
Res.: 503 Hunter, 79915. Tel: 915-598-1457; Fax: 915-590-1312.

32—SAN JOSE, Rev. Jose Alcocer.
Res.: 8100 San Jose Rd., 79907. Tel: 915-598-6285.

33—SAN JUAN BAUTISTA, Rev. Michael Rodriguez.
Res.: 5649 Dailey Ave., 79905. Tel: 915-779-1583; Fax: 915-778-7127.

34—SAN JUAN DIEGO PARISH, Rev. Edward Roden-Lucero.
Res.: 14520 E. Montana, 79938. Tel: 915-855-2217; Fax: 915-855-7716.

35—SAN JUDAS TADEO, Rev. Pablo Matta.
Res.: 4006 Hidden Way, 79922. Tel: 915-584-1095.
Mission—Santa Teresita 3400 Zapal St., El Paso Co. 79922.

36—SANTA LUCIA, Rev. Anthony Celino, J.C.L., Admin.
Res.: 518 Gallagher St., 79915. Tel: 915-592-5245; Fax: 915-592-5336.

37—SANTO NINO DE ATOCHA, Rev. Joe Molina.
Res.: 210 S. Clark, 79905. Tel: 915-779-3164; Fax: 915-779-1811.

38—ST. STEPHEN, DEACON AND MARTYR, Rev. Marcus McFadin; Deacon Gus Rodriguez Sr.
Church: 1700 George Dieter, 79936. Tel: 915-855-1661; Fax: 915-857-5800.

39—SAINT THERESE OF THE LITTLE FLOWER PARISH, Rev. Jose Luis Garayoa, O.A.R.
Church: 171 Polo Inn, 79915. Tel: 915-772-1285.

40—ST. THOMAS AQUINAS, Rev. James W. Hall.
Church: 10970 Bywood, 79936. Tel: 915-592-1313; Fax: 915-592-9733.
Catechesis/Religious Program—Students 640.

OUTSIDE THE CITY OF EL PASO

ALPINE, BREWSTER CO., OUR LADY OF PEACE, [CEM] Revs. Ricardo Ruiz; Mike Alcuino.
Mailing Address: 406 S. Sixth, 79830. Tel: 432-837-3304; Fax: 432-837-1752.
Mission—St. Mary Marathon. P.O. Box 268, Terlingua, Brewster Co. 79842.

BALMORHEA, REEVES CO., CHRIST THE KING, Unassigned.
Res.: Rte. 1, Box 3, 79718. Tel: 432-375-2347.
Mission—Our Lady of Guadalupe Saragosa, Reeves Co. Tel: 432-375-2636.

CANUTILLO, EL PASO CO., ST. PATRICK, Rev. Jose Velasquez.
Res.: 7065 Second St., P.O. Box 10, 79835. Tel: 915-877-3997.
Mission—Immaculate Heart of Mary 8701 Joplin Rd., Westway, El Paso Co. 79835. Tel: 915-886-3539. Rev. Miguel Meneses.

CLINT, EL PASO CO., SAN LORENZO, Rev. Edilberto Lopez; Sr. Rita Bujold, C.S.J., Pastoral Assoc.
Res.: P.O. Box 215, 79836. Tel: 915-851-2255; Fax: 915-851-5251.

FABENS, EL PASO CO., OUR LADY OF GUADALUPE, [CEM] Rev. Antonio Mena.
Res.: P.O. Box 356, 127 W. Main St., 79838. Tel: 915-764-3942.
Mission—San Jose Cuadrilla, El Paso Co.
Mission—Santa Rita Tornillo, El Paso Co.
Mission—San Luis La Isla, El Paso Co.

FORT DAVIS, JEFF DAVIS CO., ST. JOSEPH, [CEM] Sr. Margie Silguero, M.J.M.J., Pastoral Coord.
Res.: P.O. Box 787, 79734. Tel: 432-426-3284.

FORT HANCOCK, HUDSPETH CO., SANTA TERESA, Rev. John Telles. Tel: 915-769-3711.
Res.: P.O. Box 215, 79839.

HORIZON CITY, EL PASO CO., HOLY SPIRIT, , (Independent Mission) Rev. Ralph Solis Jr.
Res.: 14132 McMahon St., 79927. Tel: 915-852-3582.

KERMIT, WINKLER CO.
1—ST. JOSEPH THE WORKER, Consolidated, with St. Thomas in 1990.
2—ST. THOMAS & ST. JOSEPH, Revs. John Lucido, Admin.; Rodolfo Lacerna.
Res.: 838 Bellaire Rd., 79745. Tel: 432-586-3922.

MARFA, PRESIDIO CO., ST. MARY'S, [CEM] Sr. Margie Silguero, M.J.M.J., Pastoral Coord.
Res.: Box 356, 79843. Tel: 432-729-4694.

MONAHANS, WARD CO., ST. JOHN THE APOSTLE AND EVANGELIST, [JC] Revs. John Lucido; Richard Waiwood.
Res.: 5th & S. Ike St., 79756. Tel: 432-943-5114.
Mission—St. Gertrude P.O. Box 181, Grandfalls, Ward Co. 79742. Tel: 432-547-2484.

PECOS, REEVES CO.
1—ST. CATHERINE, Revs. Manuel Munoz; Gustavo Lopez; Deacon George Vasquez.
Res.: P.O. Box 670, 79772. Tel: 432-447-9231.
Mission—St. Emily Toyah, Reeves Co.
2—SANTA ROSA CHURCH, [CEM] Revs. Benjamin Flores; Miguel Angel Sanehez.
Res.: 620 E. 4th St., Box 686, 79772. Tel: 915-445-2309; Fax: 915-445-2977.
Mission—Our Lady of Refuge Barstow, Ward Co.

PRESIDIO, PRESIDIO CO., SANTA TERESA DE JESUS, [CEM] Revs. Lazaro Gonzalez, O.F.M.; Armando Vasquez, O.F.M.

Res.: P.O. Box 2049, 79845. Tel: 432-229-3235.
Mission—Sgdo. Corazon de Jesus Shafter, Presidio Co.
Mission—San Jose Redford, Presidio Co.
Mission—Our Lady of Peace Candelaria, Presidio Co.
Mission—Lajitas Mission Lajitas, Brewster Co.
SAN ELIZARIO, EL PASO CO.
1—SAN ELCEARIO, [JC] Rev. Edward C. Carpenter.
Res.: P.O. Box 910, 79849. Tel: 915-851-2333.
2—SAN FELIPE DE JESUS, Rev. Celimo Osorio.
Res.: P.O. Box 1070, 79849. Tel: 915-851-3039.
VAN HORN, CULBERSON CO., OUR LADY OF FATIMA, Rev. Miguel Angel Sanchez.
Res.: 308 Almond St., P.O. Box 398, 79855. Tel: 432-283-2042.
Mission—Our Lady of Miracles P.O. Box 15, Sierra Blanca, Hudspeth Co. 79851.
Mission—San Isidro Dell City, Hudspeth Co.
Mission—Sacred Heart General Delivery, Valentine, Jeff Davis Co. 79854.

Chaplains of Public Institutions

EL PASO. *El Paso County Jail.* Vacant.
El Paso Juvenile Detention Center. Vacant.
ANTHONY. *La Tuna Federal.* Vacant.

7045 Second St., P.O. Box 10, Canutillo, 79835.

On Duty Outside of Diocese:
Revs.—
Aguilera, Salvador, U.S. Naval Academy, Annapolis, MD 21402. U.S. Navy
Rowland, Thomas, Madonna House, Combermere ON K0J 1L0 Canada.

Absent on Leave:
Revs.—
Celino, Juventino
Kleinworth, Robert
Knopp, John
Madrid, Jaime
Maraya, Felipe
Marin, Miguel
Ramirez, Jose Nieves
Zamarano, Richard

Retired:
Rev. Msgr.—
Hartford, A. Dixon
Revs.—
Acevedo, Luis H.
Bertasius, Anthony
Burkus, John
Cervantes, Fidel
Herrera, Francisco
Lafrenz, James
Lucero, Lorenzo
Perera, Paul
Saez, Jose
Stegman, Leonard F.

Permanent Deacons:
Aguirre, Vicente G., St. Paul, El Paso
Flynn, Ken, St. Patrick's Cathedral, El Paso
Grijalva, Pilar, San Elceario, El Paso
Guerrero, Teofilo, Prison Ministry
Levy, George, St. Raphael, El Paso
Mares, Frank J., St. Raphael, El Paso
Montes, Louis A., St. Francis Xavier, El Paso
Rodriguez, Gus J., St. Stephen, El Paso
Schuffer, George M., Jr., William Beaumont Army Medical Center, El Paso
Solis, Ralph, Our Lady of Assumption, El Paso
Szostek, James T., St. Pius X, El Paso
Vasquez, George, St. Catherine, Pecos
Velott, Pete, St. Luke
Wauson, Thomas J., Christ the Saviour, El Paso

INSTITUTIONS LOCATED IN THE DIOCESE

[A] SEMINARIES, DIOCESAN

EL PASO. *St. Charles Seminary College Program*, P.O. Box 17548, 79917. Tel: 915-872-8460; Fax: 915-872-8468. Rev. John Telles; Sr. Darlene Stocklein, A.S.C., Librarian/Formation Staff.

[B] SEMINARIES, RELIGIOUS OR SCHOLASTICATES

EL PASO. *St. Anthony's School of Theology*, Hastings St. and Crescent Dr., 79903. Tel: 915-566-2261. Revs. Joaquin Acevedo, O.F.M.; Alfonso Resendiz; Eduardo Lopez; Jorge Frausto; Mauro Munoz. Franciscan Fathers of St. Peter and St. Paul Province, Michoacan, Mexico Priests 9; Scholastics 34; Brothers 4.
Roger Bacon College (1940), 2400 Marr St., 79903. Tel: 915-565-2921. Revs. Raul Vasquez, O.F.M.; Francisco Javier Canargo, O.F.M.; Romauldo Rangel, O.F.M. Minor Seminary of the Franciscan Fathers, Province of the Holy Gospel. Priests 3; Brothers 1.

[C] HIGH SCHOOLS, DIOCESAN

EL PASO. *Cathedral High School* (Boys) , 1309 N. Stanton St., 79902. Tel: 915-532-3238; Fax: 915-533-8248. Email: chsirish@elp.rr.com Mr. Sam Govea, Prin. Sisters 1; Brothers 4; Lay Teachers 35; Students 625.

[D] HIGH SCHOOLS, PRIVATE

EL PASO. 1300 Hardaway, 79903. Tel: 915-566-8400; Fax: 915-566-0636. Sisters of Loretto at the Foot of the Cross Sisters 4; Lay Teachers 50; Students 660; Priests 1.
Father Yermo High School, 250 Washington St., 79905. Tel: 915-533-3185; Fax: 915-544-0738. Servants of the Sacred Heart of Jesus and of the Poor Sisters 6; Lay Teachers 14; Students 177.

[E] ELEMENTARY SCHOOLS, PRIVATE

EL PASO. *Father Yermo Elementary School*, (Grades K-8), 237 Tobin Pl., 79905. Tel: 915-533-4693. Servants of the Sacred Heart and of the Poor Sisters 4; Lay Teachers 12; Students 330.
Loretto Academy Middle School, 1300 Hardaway, 79903. Tel: 915-566-8400, Ext. 30; Fax: 915-564-0563. Mr. Abe Ramirez, Dir. Sisters of Loretto at the Foot of the Cross Sisters 1; Lay Teachers 7; Students 88.
Loretto Elementary School-Loretto Academy, (Grades PreK-5), 1300 Hardaway, 79903. Tel: 915-566-8400; Fax: 915-562-0567. Jane Gorman, Dir. Sisters of Loretto at the Foot of the Cross Priests 1; Lay Teachers 15; Students 208.
St. Michael School, 616 S. Virginia, 79901. Tel: 915-542-1253; Fax: 915-532-1121. Sr. Teresa Escamilla, S.S.H.J.P. Servants of the Sacred Heart of Jesus and of the Poor: Father Yermo delegation Sisters 4; Lay Teachers 5; Students 80.

[F] CLINICS

EL PASO. *Centro San Vicente* (Affiliated with Daughters of Charity National Health System) , 8061 Alameda, 79915. Tel: 915-859-7545. Jim C. Parker, Exec. Dir.
Legal Title: *Centro San Vicente*, Community Oriented Primary Health Care Center (Medical Care). Total Assisted 32,000.
La Clinica Guadalupana, Inc., 901 Ascencion, 79928. Tel: 915-852-3328; Fax: 915-852-4246. Email: guadalupana1@juno.com. Sisters Peggy Deneweth, Contact Person; Janet Gildea, M.D., Staff Physician & Medical Dir.

[G] AGENCIES AND INSTITUTIONS OF THE CHARITIES OF THE DIOCESE

EL PASO. *Catholic Emergency Assistance*, 1013 E. San Antonio St., 79901. Tel: 915-532-9532. Sr. Marian Kluesner, F.S.P.A., Dir.

[H] DAY CARE CENTERS

EL PASO. *St. Joseph of the Valley*, 7681 Barton, 79915. Tel: 915-778-3407; Fax: 915-778-3407. Sisters 3; Lay Teachers 10; Students 100.

[I] HOMES FOR AGED

EL PASO. *Nazareth Hall*, 4614 Trowbridge 79903. Tel: 915-565-4677; Fax: 915-566-7530.

[J] MONASTERIES & RESIDENCES FOR PRIESTS & BROTHERS

EL PASO. *Christian Brothers*, 1204 N. Mesa, 79902-4012. Tel: 915-532-9314. Email: brothernick@juno.com.

[K] CONVENTS AND RESIDENCES FOR WOMEN

EL PASO. *Adorers of the Blood of Christ (A.S.C.)*, 2209 Pittsburg, 79930. Tel: 915-566-5855. Email: micasa-@juno.com. Sr. Darlene Stoecklein, A.S.C., Contact Person. Sisters 2.
Association of Mary Immaculate (A.I.M.), 3900 La Luz St., 79903. Tel: 915-566-0467. Sr. Sue Castaneda, A.I.M., Contact Person.
Daughters of Charity of St. Vincent De Paul (D.C.), 1020 N. Campbell St., 79902. Tel: 915-533-9013; Fax: 915-859-9862. Sisters 5.
Hermanas Contemplativas del Buen Pastor (H.B.P.) (Cloistered) , Good Shepherd Convent, 8824 Old County Rd., P.O. Box 17254, 79917. Tel: 915-859-3683. Sr. Ernestina Estrada, Supr. Sisters 11.
Hermanas del Servicio Social, 6372 Saint Lo Dr., 79925-1807. Tel: 915-771-0780; Fax: 915-771-0780.
Hermanas Dominicas de la Doctrina Cristiana (O.P.), San Alberto Magno Convent, P.O. Box 17391, 79917. Tel: 915-590-3107; Fax: 915-590-6169. Sisters Herminia Medina, Prov. Supr.; Herminia Morfin, Local Supr. Sisters 22.
Missionary Sisters of Jesus, Mary & Joseph (M.J.M.J.), 7681 Barton Dr., 79915. Tel: 915-778-3407. Sr. Gloria Rodriquez, Supr. Sisters 6.
North American Union Sisters of Our Lady of Charity, 415 N. Glenwood Dr., 79905. Tel: 915-772-0737; Fax: 915-779-2664. Sr. Yolanda Martinez, Supr. Sisters 12.
School Sisters of St. Francis (O.S.F.) 124 Bauxite, 79932. Tel: 915-581-2776. Email: romel3@juno.com. Sr. Imelda Kaufman, Contact Person. Sisters 2.
Servants of the Sacred Heart of Jesus and of the Poor (S.S.H.J.P.), Father Yermo Convent, 237 Tobin Pl., 79905. Tel: 915-533-3338 Fax: 915-532-7511. Sr. Angelica Omana, S.S.H.J.P., Supr. Sisters 13.
Queen of Peace Convent, 3119 Pera Ave., 79905. Tel: 915-533-0590. Sr. Gloria Margarita Rodriguez, Supr. Sisters 11.
Sisters of Loretto at the Foot of the Cross (S.L.), 1400 Hardaway St., 79903. Tel: 915-566-1628; Fax: 915-566-5127. Sisters 8.
Sisters of Our Lady of Charity of the Good Shepherd (R.G.S.), Good Shepherd Convent, 8824 Old County Rd., P.O. Box 17635, 79917. Tel: 915-859-6004. Sr. Ma. Emanuel Galvan, Supr. Sisters 10.
Sisters of Perpetual Adoration (A.P.), Corpus Christi Monastery, 451 Mockingbird Ln., 79907. Tel: 915-591-5662; Fax: 915-598-6203. Email: ccmonast@aol.com. Sr. Maria Gema Valencia, Supr. (Cloistered) Sisters 11; Novices 1.
Cristo Rey Monastery of Perpetual Adoration, 145 Cotton St., 79901. Tel: 915-533-5323. Sisters 17; Novices 1.
Sisters of St. Joseph of Carondelet (C.S.J.), 2200 Hubbert Pl., 79903. Tel: 915-566-7635. Sisters 2.
MARFA. *Missionary Sisters of Jesus, Mary & Joseph*, P.O. Box 1118, 79843. Tel: 432-729-3385. Sisters 2.
PRESIDIO. *Sisters of the Most Precious Blood of O'Fallen, Missouri*, P.O. Box 893, 79845. Tel: 915-229-3409 (Residence). Email: calo@brooksdata.net.
SIERRA BLANCA. *School Sisters of St. Francis, (S.S.S.F.)*, P.O. Box 303, 79851. Tel: 915-369-2062; 915-369-2651.

[L] NEWMAN CENTERS

ALPINE. *Sul Ross State University Newman Center* P.O. Box C 78, 79832. Tel: 915-837-2905; Fax: 915-837-8714. Email: plister@sulross.edu. Dr. Paul Lister.

[M] MISCELLANEOUS LISTINGS

EL PASO. *Annunciation House*, 1003 E. San Antonio, 79901. Tel: 915-545-4509. Mr. Ruben Garcia, Dir.
Casa Vides (Shelter for Refugees) , 325 Leon St., 79901. Mr. Ruben Garcia, Dir.
Catholic Counseling Services, Inc., 499 St. Matthews St., 79907. Tel: 915-872-8496. Mr. Jose Castrellon, Exec. Dir.
Catholic Legal Immigration Network, Inc. (CLINIC) Subsidiary of the USCCB Southwest Regional Office. , 1205 N. Oregon, 79902. Tel: 915-533-3971; Fax: 915-533-3974. Email: clinictx@aol.com. Services: National immigration support network to the Catholic Dioceses throughout the U.S. Southwest regional CLINIC office provides technical assistance, basic organizational program services, management assessments, and immigration law training for its diocesan affiliates. CLINIC assists dioceses in applying for agency recognition and staff accreditation before the Immigration Board of Appeals. CLINIC assists dioceses and religious congregations in obtaining legal status for foreign clergy as non-immigrant and legal permanent residents.
Catholic Properties of El Paso, Inc., 499 St. Matthews St., 79907. Tel: 915-872-8406. Mr. Jorge Vergen, Exec. Dir.
Christ Child Society, 2353 Anise, 79925.
Diocesan Migrant and Refugee Services, Inc., 2400-A E. Yandell, 79903. Tel: 915-532-3975; 915-532-3976; Fax: 915-532-4071. Web: www.elpasodiocese.org/dmrs.htm. Ouisa Davis, Exec. Dir.
Diocese of El Paso Catholic Scholarship Trust, 499 St. Matthews St., 79907. Tel: 915-872-8400.
Diocese of El Paso Charity Trust, 499 St. Matthews St., 79907. Tel: 915-872-8400.
Diocese of El Paso Clergy Continuing Education Trust, 499 St. Matthews St., 79907.
Diocese of El Paso Historic Missions Restoration

Trust, 499 St. Matthews St., 79907.
Diocese of El Paso Insurance Trust, 499 St. Matthews St., 79907.
Diocese of El Paso Investment Trust, 499 St. Matthews St., 79907.
Diocese of El Paso Seminarian Education Trust, 499 St. Matthews St., 79907.
Foundation for the Diocese of El Paso (Vacant) , 499 St. Matthews, 79907.
Historic Missions Restoration, Inc., 499 St. Matthews St., 79907.
La Posada Home, 248 Francis St., 79905-4416. Tel: 915-544-4595. Email: monyalmuina@hotmail.com. Shelter for Displaced Women.
Mount Carmel Cemetery Perpetual Care Trust, 499 St. Matthews St., 79907. Tel: 915-872-8400.
Open Arms Community, Centro Santa Fe, 8210 N. Loop Dr., 79907. Tel: 915-595-0589. Joanne D. Ivey, Dir.
Our Lady's Youth Center, 501 E. Paisano, P.O. Box 1422, 79948. Tel: 915-533-5260; 915-533-9122; Fax: 505-233-3725. Email: ourlady@cs.com. Rev. Richard M. Thomas, S.J., Dir. The Lord's Ranch & The Lord's Food Bank.
Progress for the Diocese of El Paso, 499 St. Matthews St., 79907. Email: gmorales@whc.net. Mr. Gilberto Morales, Dir.
Zaragosa, Texas Catholic Relief Trust, 499 St. Matthews St., 79907. Tel: 915-872-8407.

RELIGIOUS INSTITUTES OF MEN REPRESENTED IN THE DIOCESE

For further details refer to the corresponding bracketed number in the Religious Institutes of Men or Women section.
[0330]—*Brothers of the Christian Schools* (New Orleans and Santa Fe Provs.)—F.S.C.
[0460]—*Brothers of the Poor of St. Francis*—C.F.P.
[0480]—*Conventual Franciscan Friars* (Province of Our Lady of Consolation)—O.F.M.Conv
[0520]—*Franciscan Friars* (Holy Gospel Prov. and St. Peter & Paul Prov.)—O.F.M.
[0690]—*Jesuit Fathers and Brothers* (Prov. of New Orleans)—S.J.
[]—*Order of Preachers*—O.P.
[0150]—*Order of the Augustinian Recollects* (Prov. of San Nicolas of Tolentino, Italy)—O.A.R.
[1240]—*Servites* (Province of Mexico)—O.S.M.

RELIGIOUS INSTITUTES OF WOMEN REPRESENTED IN THE DIOCESE

[0100]—*Adorers of the Blood of Christ*—A.S.C.
[]—*Adrian Dominican Sisters*—O.P.
[]—*Association of Mary Immaculate*—A.I.M.
[1010]—*Congregation of Divine Providence of San Antonio, Texas*—C.D.P.
[1780]—*Congregation of the Sisters of the Third Order of St. Francis of Perpetual Adoration* (Central Region)—F.S.P.A.
[0760]—*Daughters of Charity of St. Vincent de Paul*—D.C.
[1070-13]—*Dominican Sisters*—O.P.
[1070-14]—*Dominican Sisters*—O.P.
[]—*Dominican Sisters of St. Thomas Aquinas*—O.P.
[1370]—*Franciscan Missionaries of Mary*—F.M.M.
[1430]—*Franciscan Sisters of Our Lady of Perpetual Help*—O.S.F.
[]—*Franciscan Sisters of Perpetual Adoration*—F.S.P.A.
[]—*Hermanas Contemplativas del Buen Pastor*—H.B.S.
[]—*Hermanas de San Jose de Lyon*—Prov.Mex
[]—*Hermanas del Buen Pastor*—S.G.S.
[]—*Hermanas del Servico Social*—H.S.S.
[]—*Hermanas Dominicanas de la Doctrina Cristiana*—O.P.
[2490]—*Medical Mission Sisters*—M.M.S.
[2770]—*Missionaries of Jesus, Mary and Joseph*—M.J.M.J.
[2770]—*Missionary Sisters of Jesus, Mary and Joseph*—M.J.M.J.
[2760]—*Missionary Srs of the Immaculate Conception*—S.M.I.C.
[3070]—*North American Union of the Sisters of Our Lady of Charity*—N.A.U.-O.L
[3190]—*Nuns of the Perpetual Adoration of the Blessed Sacrament*—A.P.
[3450]—*Religious of Jesus & Mary*—R.J.M.
[3450]—*Religious of Jesus and Mary*—R.J.M.
[2970]—*School Sisters of Notre Dame*—S.S.N.D.
[1680]—*School Sisters of St. Francis*—S.S.S.F.
[3660]—*Servants of the Sacred Heart of Jesus and of the Poor*—S.S.H.J.P.
[]—*Sisters of Charity of Cincinnati*—S.F.C.C.
[0460]—*Sisters of Charity of Incarnate Word*—C.C.V.I.
[]—*Sisters of Charity of New Jersey*—S.C.
[1010]—*Sisters of Divine Providence*—C.D.P.
[2360]—*Sisters of Loretto at the Foot of the Cross*—S.L.
[]—*Sisters of Mercy*—R.S.M.
[]—*Sisters of St. Francis of Philadelphia*—O.S.F.
[3830-15]—*Sisters of St. Joseph*—C.S.J.
[3840]—*Sisters of St. Joseph of Carondelet* (Prov. of St. Paul)—C.S.J.
[3850]—*Sisters of St. Joseph of Chambery, Conn.*—C.S.J.
[]—*Sisters of St. Joseph of Concordia, Kansas*—C.S.J.
[]—*Sisters of St. Joseph of Lyon, Maine*—C.S.J.
[]—*Sisters of St. Joseph of Medaille, N. Orleans*—C.S.J.
[1830]—*The Sisters of the Good Shepherd* (St. Louis Province)—R.G.S.

DIOCESAN CEMETERY

EL PASO. *Mount Carmel*, Box 17655, 79917. Tel: 915-860-0605.

NECROLOGY

† Ascherl, Vincent, (Retired)—Died Oct. 1, 2003

Diocese of Erie

(Dioecesis Eriensis)

Most Reverend

DONALD W. TRAUTMAN, S.T.D., S.S.L.

Bishop of Erie; ordained April 7, 1962; appointed Titular Bishop of Sassura and Auxiliary Bishop of Buffalo February 27, 1985; consecrated April 16, 1985; appointed to Erie June 12, 1990; installed July 16, 1990. *Res.: 205 West 9th St., Erie, PA 16501.* Tel: 814-824-1120; Fax: 814-824-1124.

Most Reverend

MICHAEL J. MURPHY, D.D., S.T.L.

Retired Bishop of Erie; ordained February 28, 1942; appointed Titular Bishop of Arindela and Auxiliary Bishop of Cleveland April 20, 1976; consecrated June 11, 1976; appointed Coadjutor Bishop of Erie November 28, 1978; succeeded to See July 16, 1982; retired July 16, 1990. *Mailing Address: St. Patrick/St. Hedwig Parish Cluster,* 130 East 4th St., Erie, PA 16507. Tel: 814-454-8085.

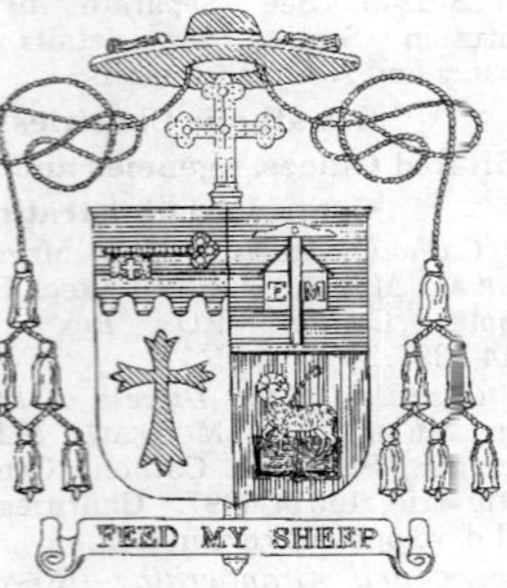

Chancery: St. Mark Catholic Center, P.O. Box 10397, Erie, PA 16514. Tel: 814-824-1111; Fax: 814-824-1128.

Web: www.eriercd.org

ESTABLISHED 1853.

Square Miles 9,936.

Comprises the following Counties in Northwestern Pennsylvania: Erie, Crawford, Mercer, Venango, Forest, Clarion, Jefferson, Clearfield, Cameron, Elk, McKean, Potter and Warren.

For legal titles of parishes and diocesan institutions, consult the Chancery.

STATISTICAL OVERVIEW

Personnel	
Bishop	1
Retired Bishops	1
Priests: Diocesan Active in Diocese	163
Priests: Diocesan Active Outside Diocese	7
Priests: Retired, Sick or Absent	48
Number of Diocesan Priests	218
Religious Priests in Diocese	8
Total Priests in Diocese	226
Extern Priests in Diocese	4
Ordinations:	
Diocesan Priests	2
Permanent Deacons	8
Permanent Deacons in Diocese	31
Total Sisters	425
Parishes	
Parishes	126
With Resident Pastor:	
Resident Diocesan Priests	96
Resident Religious Priests	4
Without Resident Pastor:	
Administered by Priests	26
Missions	19
Professional Ministry Personnel:	
Sisters	19
Lay Ministers	12
Welfare	
Catholic Hospitals	1
Total Assisted	147,109
Homes for the Aged	4
Total Assisted	1,569
Day Care Centers	2
Total Assisted	337
Specialized Homes	2
Total Assisted	169
Special Centers for Social Services	9
Total Assisted	149,059
Other Institutions	1
Total Assisted	451
Educational	
Seminaries, Diocesan	1
Students from This Diocese	15
Diocesan Students in Other Seminaries	10
Total Seminarians	25
Colleges and Universities	2
Total Students	6,819
High Schools, Diocesan and Parish	5
Total Students	1,676
High Schools, Private	2
Total Students	1,217
Elementary Schools, Diocesan and Parish	39
Total Students	8,183
Elementary Schools, Private	1
Total Students	398
Catechesis/Religious Education:	
High School Students	5,794
Elementary Students	9,985
Total Students under Catholic Instruction	34,097
Teachers in the Diocese:	
Priests	22
Sisters	39
Lay Teachers	741
Vital Statistics	
Receptions into the Church:	
Infant Baptism Totals	1,817
Adult Baptism Totals	461
Received into Full Communion	201
First Communions	2,291
Confirmations	2,245
Marriages:	
Catholic	497
Interfaith	375
Total Marriages	872
Deaths	2,609
Total Catholic Population	225,607
Total Population	874,057

Former Bishops—Most Revs. MICHAEL O'CONNOR, consecrated Bishop of Pittsburgh, Aug. 15, 1843; transferred from Pittsburgh as first Bishop of Erie in 1853; transferred back to Pittsburgh in 1854; died Oct. 18, 1872; JOSUE M. YOUNG, consecrated April 23, 1854; died Sept. 18, 1866; TOBIAS MULLEN, D.D., consecrated Aug. 2, 1868, Bishop of Erie; resigned Aug. 10, 1899, and appt. to Titular See of Germanicopolis; died April 22, 1900; JOHN E. FITZMAURICE, D.D., consecrated Feb. 24, 1898; died June 18, 1920; EDWARD P. MCMANAMAN, S.T.D., Titular Bishop of Floriana and Auxiliary Bishop of Erie; consecrated Oct. 28, 1948; died July 18, 1964; JOHN MARK GANNON, D.D., Archbishop-Bishop of Erie; ord. Dec. 21, 1901; appt. Titular Bishop of Nilopolis, Nov. 13, 1917; consecrated Feb. 6, 1918; transferred to Erie, Aug. 26, 1920; installed Dec. 16, 1920; appt. Assistant at the Pontifical Throne Nov. 4, 1944; appt. Archbishop "ad personam" Nov. 25, 1953; resigned Sept. 21, 1966 and transferred to Titular See of Tacarata, Dec. 14, 1966; died Sept. 5, 1968; JOHN F. WHEALON, D.D., appt. Titular Bishop of Andrapa and Auxiliary Bishop of Cleveland, June 2, 1961; consecrated July 6, 1961; transferred to the See of Erie, Dec. 14, 1966; transferred to the Archdiocese of Hartford; died Aug. 2, 1991; ALFRED M. WATSON, D.D. (Retired), Bishop of Erie; ord. May 10, 1934; Titular Bishop of Nationa and Auxiliary Bishop of Erie; appt. May 17, 1965; consecrated June 29, 1965; succeeded to See, March 19, 1969; retired July 16 1982; died Jan. 4, 1990 Cleveland; MICHAEL J MURPHY, D.D., S.T.L. (Retired), Titular Bishop of Arindela and Auxiliary Bishop of Cleveland; appt. April 20, 1976; consecrated June 11, 1976; Coadjutor Bishop of Erie; appt. Nov. 28, 1978; succeeded to See, July 16, 1982; retired July 16, 1990.

Vicar General—Rev. Msgr. ROBERT J. SMITH, J.C.L., V.G., St. Mark Catholic Center P.O. Box 10397, Erie, 16514-0397. Tel: 814-824-1130.

Office of the Bishop—ROBERTA PALMISANO, Sec. to the Bishop, St. Mark Catholic Center, P.O. Box 10397, Erie, 16514. Tel: 814-824-1120.

Chancery—St. Mark Catholic Center, P.O. Box 10397, Erie, 16514. Tel: 814-824-1135; Fax: 814-824-1124.

Chancellor—VACANT.

Vice Chancellor—Rev. EDWARD M. LOHSE, S.T.D., J.C.L.

Diocesan Archivist and Historian—Rev. Msgr. ROBERT G. BARCIO, Ph.D. (Retired) Unless otherwise indicated all diocesan offices and personnel listed in directory can be reached at: St. Mark Catholic Center, 429 E. Grandview Blvd., P.O. Box 10397, Erie, 16514-0397. Tel: 814-824-1111.

Episcopal Vicars—

Northern Vicariate—Rev. Msgr. ROBERT J. SMITH, J.C.L., V.G., St. Mark Catholic Center, P.O. Box 10397, Erie, 16514. Tel: 814-824-1130.

Eastern Vicariate—Rev. Msgr. CHARLES A. KAZA, E.V., 1100 Hewett St., Brockway, 15824. Tel: 814-265-1374.

Western Vicariate—Rev. Msgr. MICHAEL T. GAINES, E.V., St. Mark Catholic Center, P.O. Box 10397, Erie, 16514. Tel: 814-824-1195.

Vicar for Religious—Sr. MARY RITA KUHN, S.S.J., St. Mark Catholic Center, P.O. Box 10397, Erie, 16514-0397. Tel: 814-824-1125.

Office for the Protection of Children and Youth—KAREN STREETT, Coord., St. Mark Catholic Center, P.O. Box 10397, Erie, 16514-0397. Tel: 814-824-1222.

Advisory To Bishop

Administrative Cabinet—Rev. Msgrs. ROBERT J. SMITH, J.C.L., V.G.; CHARLES A. KAZA, E.V.; Sr. MARY RITA KUHN, S.S.J.; Rev. JOHN SCHULTZ; Rev. Msgrs. MICHAEL D. MCGRAW, M.Ss.A., L.S.W.; CONRAD KRAUS; DAVID MURPHY; Rev. Msgrs. MICHAEL T. GAINES, E.V.; THOMAS J. MCSWEENEY. Special Consultant:: GARY LONCKI.

College of Consultors—Rev. Msgrs. MICHAEL T. GAINES, E.V.; CHARLES A. KAZA, E.V.; RICHARD G. MAYER; ROBERT J. SMITH, J.C.L., V.G.; RICHARD J. SULLIVAN; JOHN SWOGER, V.F.

Finance Council—Most Rev. DONALD W. TRAUTMAN, S.T.D., S.S.L.; Very Rev. JOSEPH P. STASZEWSKI, V.F.; THOMAS C. GUELCHER; HAROLD LANZEL; PATRICIA LIEBEL; JAMES F. TOOHEY, Esq.; Sr. CATHERINE MANNING, S.S.J.; PETER J. BUCHEIT; Rev. Msgrs. ROBERT L. BRUGGER; CHARLES A. KAZA, E.V. Ex Officios: Rev. Msgr. ROBERT J. SMITH, J.C.L., V.G.; DAVID J. MURPHY.

Deans—Very Rev. RICHARD C. TOMASONE, V.F., Erie East; Rev. Msgr. WILLIAM E. BIEBEL, V.F., Erie West; Very Rev. JOSEPH C. GREGOREK, V.F., Gannon University; Rev. Msgrs. EDWARD J. ZEITLER, V.F., Sharon; JOHN W. SWOGER, V.F., Oil City; Very Rev. PHILLIP A. PINCZEWSKI, V.F., Bradford; Rev. Msgr. H. DESMOND MCGEE, V.F., Clearfield; Rev. PATRICK J. SPEER, Meadville (Retired); Very Revs. JOSEPH P. STASZEWSKI, V.F., Dubois; THEODORE B. MARCONI, St. Marys; Rev. Msgr. JOHN J. LUCAS, V.F., Warren.

Presbyteral Council—Most Rev. DONALD W. TRAUTMAN, S.T.D., S.S.L., Pres.; Rev. Msgr. H. DESMOND MCGEE, V.F., Chm.; Rev. JOHN B. JACQUEL, Sec.

Priest Personnel Board—Rev. Msgrs. MICHAEL T. GAINES, E.V., Chm.; RICHARD G. MAYER, Vice Chm.; Rev. SCOTT E. KATREN, J.C.L., Sec.

Priest Retirement Board—Most Rev. DONALD W. TRAUTMAN, S.T.D., S.S.L., Chm. Members: Sr. JEAN BAPTISTE DILUZIO, S.S.J.; JAMES HOLLAND; JAMES TOOHEY, Attorney; Deacon MARTIN EISERT; Rev. Msgrs. JOHN R. SNYDER (Retired); ROBERT J. SMITH, J.C.L., V.G. Staff: DAVID J. MURPHY; Rev. Msgr. MICHAEL T. GAINES, E.V.

Episcopal Delegate for Retired Priests—Rev. Msgr. JOHN R. SNYDER (Retired).

Pennsylvania Catholic Conference—VACANT, Personal Rep. of the Bishop, St. Mark Catholic Center, P.O. Box 10397, Erie, 16514.

The Bishop's Theological Advisory Committee—Rev. Msgr. GERALD L. ORBANEK, M.A., Chm.; Revs. EDWARD KRAUSE, Ph.D.; CASIMIR J. WOZNIAK; Very Rev. MICHAEL T. KESICKI, S.S.L.; Mr. PATRICK O'CONNELL, Ph.D.; Sr. MICHELLE HEALY, S.S.J., M.A.

Lake Shore Visitor Advisory Board—Most Rev. DONALD W. TRAUTMAN, S.T.D., S.S.L.; LISA GINN; GARY LONCKI, Editor; Rev. Msgrs. WILLIAM E. BIEBEL, V.F.; GERALD L. ORBANEK, M.A.; Rev. EDWARD KRAUSE, C.S.C.; PAUL CORBRAN; JAMES BOGNIAK; DAVID SLOMSKI; VACANT, Chancellor; Sr. MARY LOUIS EICHENLAUB, O.S.B.; TOM BRENNAN; KEVIN EGAN, Advertising.

Matrimonial Concerns

All requests for marriage dispensations, permissions, and rogatory commissions should be sent to this office

Diocesan Tribunal—St. Mark Catholic Center, P.O. Box 10397, Erie, 16514. Tel: 814-824-1140; Fax: 814-824-1128.

Bishop's Delegate for Dispensations—Rev. SCOTT E. KATREN, J.C.L.

Judicial Vicar—Rev. Msgr. MARK L. BARTCHAK, J.C.D.

Adjutant Judicial Vicar—Rev. SCOTT E. KATREN, J.C.L.

Promoter of Justice—VACANT.

Defender of the Bond—Rev. GREGORY A. KIRSCH, J.C.L.

Matrimonial Judges—Rev. Msgrs. ROBERT J. SMITH, J.C.L., V.G.; RICHARD J. STACK, J.C.L.; MARK L. BARTCHAK, J.C.D.; Revs. JOHN P. BEAL, J.C.D.; SCOTT E. KATREN, J.C.L.; Deacon RICHARD D. SHEWMAN, J.C.L.; BARBARA A. BETTWY, J.C.L.

Auditors—Sisters REBECCA ANN COSTA, S.S.J.; JEAN BAPTISTE DILUZIO, S.S.J.

Secretary/Notary—CAROL GRYGIER; CINDY MANGIARACINA.

Office of Conciliation & Arbitration—St. Mark Catholic Center, P.O. Box 10397, Erie, 16514. Tel: 814-824-1140. Rev. Msgr. MARK L. BARTCHAK, J.C.D., Dir.

Catholic Education

Vicar for Catholic Education—Rev. JOHN M. SCHULTZ, St. Mark Catholic Center, P.O. Box 10397, Erie, 16514-0397.

Associate Vicar for Catholic Education—Sr. MARY ARNOLD TANN, S.S.J., St. Mark Catholic Center, P.O. Box 10397, Erie, 16514-0397.

Elementary Education—Mrs. DARLENE KOVACS, Coord.

Government Programs—ROBERTA BUCCI, Coord.

Teacher Personnel—Ms. PATRICIA MCLAUGHLIN, Supvr.

Elementary Athletic Programs—DOUGLAS CHUZIE, Coord., St. Mark Catholic Center, P.O. Box 10397, Erie, 16514-0397.

Diocesan Athletic Director—DOUGLAS CHUZIE, St. Mark's Catholic Center, P.O. Box 10397, Erie, 16514-0397. Tel: 814-824-1245.

Religious Education—Mr. JOSEPH STREETT, Supvr.; Sr. NANCY FISCHER, S.S.J., Supvr., Community Formation & Lay Ministry Formation; GREGORY SCHLUETER, Supvr., Office of Youth & Young Adults; BARBARA BURKETT, B.S., Coord., NFP, Heart & Soul, & Chastity Programs, St. Mark Catholic Center, P.O. Box 10397, Erie, 16514-0397; KAREN STREETT, Coord., Media Resources, St. Mark Catholic Center, P.O. Box 10397, Erie, 16514-0397.

Campus Ministry—Sr. MARY DREXLER, S.S.J., Diocesan Coord., Penn State Erie, The Behrend College, Station Rd., Erie, 16563. Tel: 814-898-6245 See Separate listing in the Institution Section for details on Campus Ministry and Newman Centers.

Catholic Charities

Affiliated Offices, Agencies and Institutions

Central Administration

Office of Catholic Charities—Rev. Msgr. MICHAEL D. MCGRAW, M.Ss.A., L.S.W., Exec. Dir., St. Mark Catholic Center, P.O. Box 10397, Erie, 16514-0397.

Catholic Charities of the Diocese of Erie, Inc.—Rev. Msgr. MICHAEL D. MCGRAW, M.Ss.A., L.S.W., Exec. Dir., St. Mark Catholic Center, P.O. Box 10397, Erie, 16514-0397. Charities program and fiscal development corporation.

Development and Grantwriting—ROSMARI GRAHAM, Supvr., St. Mark Catholic Center, P.O. Box 10397, Erie, 16514-0397.

Pastoral Social Services

Family Ministries—MARY MAXWELL, M.A., Supvr., St. Mark Catholic Center, P.O. Box 10397, Erie, 16514-0397. Office includes Marriage Preparation and Enrichment Programs, Rainbows, Separated and Divorced, Retrouvaille, Elizabeth Ministry.

Parish Social Ministry/Respect Life—JEAN KECK, M.S., Supvr., St. Mark Catholic Center, P.O. Box 10397, Erie, 16514-0397. Consultant for Parish Care and Concern model and Social Justice & Respect Life Programs.

Office of Diocesan and International Mission Activities—PAT MARSHALL, Supvr., St. Mark Catholic Center, P.O. Box 10397, Erie, 16514-0397.

Healing Ministries and Office of Disabilites—JACKLYN JOHNSON, R.N., Supvr., Ministry on spiritual enrichment and inclusion of persons with disabilities into the life of the parish.

Victim Assistance Coordinator—Dr. ROBERT NELSEN. Tel: 814-871-7723. Email: nelsen001@gannon.edu.

Community Counseling Services

Catholic Charities Counseling and Adoption Services—ROBERT F. MCCRARY, A.C.S.W., L.S.W., Agency Dir.; ROSE MARIE RADOMSKI, M.A., M.S., Clinical Dir.

Northern Vicariate - Erie Office—329 W. Tenth St., Erie, 16502. Tel: 814-456-2091.

Western Vicariate - Sharon Office—JILL ZIKMUND, M.A., Area Supvr., 786 E. State St., Sharon, 16146. Tel: 412-346-4142.

Eastern Vicariate - DuBois Office—NANCI MATTISON, M.A., Area Supvr., Ste. 119 D, Box 2, 90 Beaver Dr., DuBois, 15801.

Residential Services for Older Persons

John XXIII Home—KIRK HAWTHORNE, Admin., 2250 Shenango Fwy., Hermitage, 16148. Tel: 814-981-3200.

Christ the King Manor—Rev. Msgr. JOHN W. MIGNOT, Admin., 1100 W. Long Ave., Du Bois, 15801. Tel: 814-371-3180.

Community Social Services

* *St. Martin Center*—CHERYL WEBER, M.A., Dir., 1701 Parade St., Erie, 16503. Tel: 814-452-6113.

Harborcreek Youth Services—Mr. JOHN D. PETULLA, A.C.S.W., L.S.W., 5712 Iroquois Ave., Harborcreek, 16421. Tel: 814-899-7664.

Prince of Peace Center—Sr. CLARE MARIE BEICHNER, S.S.J., L.S.W., Dir., 502 Darr Ave., Box 89, Farrell, 16121. Tel: 412-346-5777.

Better Housing for Erie, c/o H.A.N.D.S.—CHARLES G. SCALISE, Dir., 139 E. 12th St., Erie, 16501. Tel: 814-459-1047.

Good Samaritan Center—ANTHONY INDELICATO, Dir., 1 E. Locust St., Clearfield, 16830. Tel: 814-236-1896; 814-768-7229.

Other Charitable/Social Agencies and Institutions

Gannondale Residential Center for Girls—NANCY SABOL, Exec. Dir., 4635 E. Lake Rd., Erie, 16511. Tel: 814-899-7659.

St. Mary's Home—Sr. PHYLLIS MCCRACKEN, Pres. & C.E.O., 607 E. 26th St., Erie, 16504. Tel: 814-459-0621.

St. Mary's Home at Asbury Ridge—4855 W. Ridge Rd., Erie, 16506.

Mercy Center For Women—CHRISTINE TOMBAUGH, Dir., 1039 E. 27th St., Erie, 16507. Tel: 814-455-4577.

Young People Who Care—Sr. THERESE DUSH, C.A., Dir., Frenchville, 16836. Tel: 814-263-4177.

Maria House Projects—Rev. Msgr. JAMES PETERSON, Dir., P.O. Box 10682, Erie, 16514. Tel: 814-454-0891.

Emmaus Ministries—Sr. MARY MILLER, O.S.B., Dir., 218 E. 11th St., Erie, 16501. Tel: 814-459-8754.

St. Patrick Haven—Sr. MARY EILEEN MOYER, S.S.J., Dir., 147 E. 12th St., Erie, 16501. Tel: 814-454-7219.

Parish Services

Office of Evangelization—Co Directors: Rev. Msgrs. CONRAD KRAUS; THOMAS J. MCSWEENEY.

Office of Worship and Worship Outreach—Rev. Msgr. CONRAD KRAUS, Dir.; MATTHEW CLARK, Assoc. Dir., St. Mark Catholic Center, P.O. Box 10397, Erie, 16514-0397.

R.C.I.A.—Sr. NANCY FISCHER, S.S.J., Coord., St. Mark Catholic Center, P.O. Box 10397, Erie, 16514-0397.

Office of Communications and Public Relations—Rev. Msgr. THOMAS J. MCSWEENEY, Dir.

Communications Consultant—GARY LONCKI.

"Lake Shore Visitor" - Diocesan Newspaper—GARY LONCKI, Editor; ANDREA BARAN, Asst. Editor, P.O. Box 10668, Erie, 16514-0668. Tel: 814-824-1160; Fax: 814-824-1128.

Finance and Development

Chief Financial Officer—DAVID J. MURPHY, St. Mark Catholic Center, P.O. Box 10397, Erie, 16514-0397.

Financial Services Office—DAVID J. MURPHY, Dir.; JAMES L. BOGNIAK, Mgr., Accounting & Budgeting; THOMAS E. BURIK, C.P.A., Mgr., Parish Financial Svcs.; CHARLES BANDUCCI, Mgr., School Financial Svcs. Tel: 814-824-1188. St. Mark Catholic Center, P.O. Box 10397, Erie, 16514-0397. Tel: 814-824-1180.

Stewardship and Development Office—JOSEPH W. HOAG, Dir., St. Mark Catholic Center, P.O. Box 10397, Erie, 16514-0397.

Diocesan Attorney—FRANK L. KROTO JR., Esq., Quinn, Buseck, Leemhuis, Toohey & Kroto, Inc., 2222 W. Grandview Blvd., Erie, 16506. Tel: 814-833-2222.

Erie Diocesan Cemeteries—Board of Members: Most Rev. DONALD W. TRAUTMAN, S.T.D., S.S.L.; Rev. Msgr. ROBERT J. SMITH, J.C.L., V.G.; Rev. THOMAS M. FIALKOWSKI, Bishop's Liaison; DAVID J. MURPHY; JOHN HROMYAK, Dir., 3325 West Lake Rd., Erie, 16505. Tel: 814-838-7724.

Clergy Formation

Clergy Personnel—Rev. Msgr. MICHAEL T. GAINES, E.V., Dir., St. Mark Catholic Center, P.O. Box 10397, Erie, 16514-0397.

Clergy Continuing Education and Formation—Rev. RICHARD R. SIEFER, Coord., St. Catherine Parish, 116 S. State St., DuBois, 15801. Tel: 814-371-8556. St. Mark Catholic Center, P.O. Box 10397, Erie, 16514-0397. Tel: 814-824-1195.

Vocation Office—Rev. EDWARD M. LOHSE, S.T.D., J.C.L., St. Mark Catholic Center, P.O. Box 10397, Erie, 16514-0397.

St. Mark Seminary—Very Rev. MICHAEL T. KESICKI, S.S.L., Rector & Dir. Seminarians; Rev. NICHOLAS J. ROUCH, S.T.D., Vice Rector & Assoc. Dir. Seminarians; Sr. MARY ANDREW HIMES, R.S.M., Dir. Liturgical Music, St. Mark Catholic Center, P.O. Box 10397, Erie, 16514-0397.

Special Apostolates

Spiritual Apostolates—Rev. Msgr. JOHN T. CARTER, Dir., 5145 Peach St., Erie, 16509. Tel: 814-864-0622.

Black Apostolate—Rev. EDWARD C. KRAUSE, C.S.C., 233 E. 16th St., Erie, 16503. Tel: 814-454-1615.

Hispanic Apostolate—Rev. JORGE VILLEGAS, Dir., 1237 W. 21st St., Erie, 16502. Tel: 814-459-0543.

Apostleship of the Sea and Chaplain to the Port of Erie—Rev. Msgr. L. THOMAS SNYDERWINE, Dir., c/o St. Luke Church, 421 E. 38th St., Erie, 16504-1699. Tel: 814-825-6920.

World Apostolate of Fatima (Blue Army)—Rev. DAVID L.. POULSON, Dir., 502 Peach St., Erie, 16501-1104. Tel: 814-454-6494.

Cursillo Movement—Rev. JOHN J. HILBERT, Dir., 1611 Peach St., Ste. 450, Erie, 16501. Tel: 814-456-2948.

Legion of Mary—Rev. Msgr. JAMES E. SPERRY, Dir. (Retired), 5145 Peach St., Erie, 16509. Tel: 814-864-0622.

Charismatic Movement—MICHAEL VEHEC, Diocesan Liaison, St. Mark Catholic Center, P.O. Box 10397, Erie, 16514-0397.

Bread of Life Community—Rev. LAWRENCE RICHARDS,

Moderator, St. Joseph Parish, 147 W. 24th St., Erie, 16502-2897. Tel: 814-452-2982.

Word of Life Charismatic Renewal—St. Mark Catholic Center, 429 E. Grandview Blvd., P.O. Box 10397, Erie, 16514-0397. Tel: 814-824-1286.

Ecumenism

Pennsylvania Conference on Inter-Church Cooperation—VACANT, Diocesan Rep.

Ecumenical Officers—

Eastern Vicariate—Very Rev. PHILLIP PINCZEWSKI, V.F.

Western Vicariate—Rev. CHRISTOPHER MERRY, St. Joseph, 79 Case Ave., Sharon, 16146. Tel: 412-981-3232.

Northern Vicariate—Rev. Msgr. WILLIAM E. BIEBEL, V.F., St. Peter Cathedral, 230 W. 10th St., Erie, 16501. Tel: 814-453-6677.

CLERGY, PARISHES, MISSIONS AND PAROCHIAL SCHOOLS

CITY OF ERIE

(ERIE COUNTY)

ERIE

1—ST. PETER CATHEDRAL (1893), Rev. Msgr. William E. Biebel, V.F., Rector; Rev. David A. Perry; Sisters Mary McCarthy, R.S.M., D.R.E.; Martha Howick, S.S.J., Pastoral Min. In Res., Rev. Msgrs. Michael T. Gaines, E.V.; Robert G. Barcio, Ph.D., Archivist (Retired).
Res.: 230 W. 10th St., 16501. Tel: 814-453-6677; Fax: 814-456-1351.
Church: 10th St. & Sassafras St., 16501.
School—Tel: 814-452-4276; Fax: 814-452-0479. Lay Teachers 22; Students 344.

2—ST. ANDREW (1871), Rev. Msgr. Richard J. Sullivan; Sr. Nancy Sonnenfeld, S.S.J., Computer Svcs. In Res., Rev. Christopher M. Hamlett.
Res.: 1116 W. Seventh St., 16502. Tel: 814-454-2486; Fax: 814-456-4443.
School—Tel: 814-454-2454; Fax: 814-456-3737. Sisters 1; Lay Teachers 11; Students 152

3—ST. ANN (1887),, (See Holy Family for Ministry Team.) Rev. James T. O'Hara. In Res., Rev. Msgr. Gerald J. Koos.
Church: 921 East Ave., 16503. Tel: 814-453-4681.

4—BLESSED SACRAMENT (1938), Revs. Daniel E. Magraw; Michael G. DeMartinis; William M. Calabrese; Deacon Dennis Kudlak; Sr. Mary Andrew Himes, R.S.M.
Res.: 1626 W. 26th St., 16508. Tel: 814-454-0171; Fax: 814-459-6832.
School—Tel: 814-455-1387; Fax: 814-455-1388. Sisters of St. Joseph 1; Lay Teachers 25; Students 344.

5—ST. BONIFACE (1857), [CEM] Rev. Msgr. Daniel K. Arnold. In Res., Rev. Raymond W. Hahn.
Res.: 7615 Wattsburg Rd., 16509. Tel: 814-825-4439; Fax: 814-825-4430.
School—Tel: 814-825-4238; Fax: 814-825-8101. Lay Teachers 10; Students 149.

6—ST. CASIMIR (1914), (Polish), Rev. James T. O'Hara. In Res., Rev. John E. Santor.
Church: 629 Hess Ave., 16503. Tel: 814-459-7361.

7—ST. GEORGE (1922), Rev. Msgrs. Richard G. Mayer; John T. Carter; Rev. Christopher J. Singer; Sr. Maria O'Connor, R.M.S., Pastoral Min.; Deacons Dalhart Dobbs; Norbert Smith.
Res.: 5145 Peach St., 16509. Tel: 814-864-0622; Fax: 814-866-7532.
School—Tel: 814-864-4821; Fax: 814-866-7532. Sisters 2; Lay Teachers 30; Students 623.

8—ST. HEDWIG/ST. PATRICK (1910), Rev. Msgr. William E. Sutherland. In Res., Rev. Msgr. Lawrence E. Brandt.
Res.: 521 E. 3rd St., 16507. Tel: 814-454-8096.

9—HOLY FAMILY/ST. ANN/ST. CASIMIR (1902), (Slovak), Rev. James T. O'Hara.
Office—913 Fulton St., 16503. Tel: 814-452-4832.
School—Tel: 814-452-4720. Sisters 1; Lay Teachers 9; Students 133.

10—HOLY ROSARY (1927), Revs. James G. Gutting; Michael P. Allison.
Res.: 2701 East Ave., 16504. Tel: 814-456-4254; Fax: 814-456-4255.
School—Tel: 814-456-7212; Fax: 814-454-5467. Sisters 1; Lay Teachers 10; Students 131.

11—HOLY TRINITY (1903), (Polish), Rev. Msgr. Thomas J. McSweeney; Deacon Martin Eisert.
Res.: 2220 Reed St., 16503. Tel: 814-456-0671; Fax: 814-461-1150.

12—IMMACULATE CONCEPTION (1946), (African American), Rev. Edward C. Krause, C.S.C. Admin.
Res.: 109 University Square, 16541. Tel: 814-871-7545.
Church: 233 E. 16th St., 16503. Tel: 814-454-1615.

13—ST. JAMES (1921), Rev. Dennis C. Hadberg. In Res., Rev. James McCormick; Sisters Susan Freitag, O.S.B., Sec.; Colette Hilow, C.D.S.
Res.: 2635 Buffalo Rd., 16510. Tel: 814-899-6178; Fax: 814-899-7681.
School—Tel: 814-899-3429; Fax: 814-898-8285. Sr. Colette Hilow, C.D.S., D.R.E. Sisters of the Congregation of the Divine Spirit 4; Lay Teachers 14; Students 283.

14—ST. JOHN THE BAPTIST (1870), Very Rev. Richard C. Tomasone, V.F.
Res.: 509 E. 26th St., 16504. Tel 814-454-2873; Fax: 814-456-7073.
School—Tel: 814-452-6874; Fax: 814-456-7033. Lay Teachers 11; Students 174.

15—ST. JOSEPH (1867), (German), Rev. Lawrence R. Richards. In Res., Revs. Gerard H. Krebs; Richard Toohey; Deacon Andrew Froberg.
Res.: 147 W. 24th St., 16502. Tel: 814-452-2982; Fax: 814-452-4400.

16—ST. JUDE THE APOSTLE (1955), Rev. Msgr. Robert L. Brugger. In Res., Rev. Msgr. Ernest J. Daley; Rev. Michael P. Ferrick; Deacons David Pratt; James McGuinness.
Res.: 2801 W. 6th St., P.O. Box 8408, 16505. Tel: 814-833-0927; Fax: 814-833-9692.
School—Our Lady's Christian, Tel: 814-838-7676; Fax: 814-838-6860. Lay Teachers 23; Students 402.

17—ST. JULIA (1938), Rev. Msgr. Richard J. McGuire.
Res.: 638 Roslyn Ave., 16505. Tel: 814 833-4347; Fax: 814-833-4347.
School—Our Lady's Christian (See St. Jude the Apostle for details.)

18—ST. LUKE (1954), Rev. Msgr. L. Thomas Snyderwine; Deacons Richard Shewman; Glen Kuzma. In Res., Rev. Msgr. Robert D. Goodill (Retired); Rev. Richard J. Allen.
Res.: 421 East 38th St., 16504. Tel: 814-825-6920; Fax: 814-825-6920.
School—Tel: 814-825-7105. Lay Teachers 25; Students 415.

19—ST. MARK THE EVANGELIST (Lawrence Park) (1938), Rev. Joseph F. Finucane (Retired); Deacon Drew DeCrease.
Res.: 695 Smithson Ave., 16511. Tel: 814-899-3000; Fax: 814-899-5212.

20—ST. MARY (1840), (German), Rev. Msgr. Robert J. Reilly (Retired).
Res.: 315 E. 9th St., 16503. Tel: 814-452-2410; Fax: 814-455-7992.

21—ST. MATTHEW IN THE WOODS (1966), Rev. Thomas J. Whitman.
Res.: 1290 Townhall Rd. West, 16509. Tel: 814-866-6248.

22—MOUNT CALVARY (1951), Rev. Phillip M. Oriole.
Res.: 2004 East Lake Rd., 16511. Tel: 814-454-0061; Fax: 814-454-7177.
School—Tel: 814-455-1268. Lay Teachers 8; Students 110.

23—OUR LADY OF MERCY (1946), Rev. Gerald T. Ritchie; Sr. Mary Rose Romeo, S.J., Liturgical Min.; Deacon John Brophy.
Res.: 837 Bartlett Rd., Harborcreek, 16421. Tel: 814-899-5342; Fax: 814-898-3306.

24—OUR LADY OF MT. CARMEL (1960), Rev. Msgr. Bruce R. Allison; Rev. James A. Reardon; Deacon Frank Pregler.
Res.: 1553 E. Grandview Blvd., 16510. Tel: 814-825-7313; Fax: 814-825-4190.
School—Tel: 814-825-2822; Fax: 814-825-4190. Lay Teachers 19; Students 310.

25—OUR LADY OF PEACE (1955), Revs. Thomas M. Brooks; Matthew J. Kujawinski; Sr. Elizabeth Bauer, O.S.F., Pastoral Assoc.; Deacons Ralph DeCecco; Anthony Alleruzzo. In Res., Very Rev. John M. Shultz; Rev. Msgr. Michael D. McGraw, M.Ss.A., L.S.W.
Res.: 2401 W. 38th St., 16506. Tel: 814-833-7701; Fax: 814-833-7702.
School—Tel: 814-838-3548. Sr. Claudia Dombrowski, S.S.J. Prin. Sisters 1; Lay Teachers 31; Students 621.

26—ST. PATRICK/ST. HEDWIG (1834), Rev. Msgr. William E. Sutherland, Admin.; Sr. Marie Stephen Kebort, S.S.J., D.R.E.; Deacon Jerome Peterson. In Res., Most Rev. Michael J. Murphy; Rev. Msgr. Joseph V. Wardanski.
Res.: 130 E. 4th St., 16507. Tel: 814-454-8085; Fax: 814-459-8685.

27—ST PAUL (1891), (Italian), Rev. Msgr. Richard J. Stack, J.C.L. In Res., Rev. Ronald E. Gmerek.
Res.: 1617 Walnut St., 16502. Tel 814-459-3173; Fax: 814-459-3173.

28—SACRED HEART (1894), Revs. John J. Detisch; Scott E. Katren, J.C.L.; Deacon Robert Walker. In Res., Revs. Jerome S. Simmons; Daniel J. Dymski.
Res. 816 W. 26th St., 16508. Tel: 814-456-6256.
School—Tel: 814-459-7247; Fax: 814-459-8838. Sisters 2; Lay Teachers 14; Students 220.

29—ST. STANISLAUS (1885), (Polish), [CEM] Rev. Msgr. Bernard J. Urbaniak; Sisters Elizabeth Oettel, O.S.B., D.R.E.; Mary Ann White, C.S.F.N., Pastoral Min.; M. Elizabeth Dettel, O.S.B.
Res.: 516 E. 13th St., 16503. Tel: 814-452-6606; Fax 814-452-6606.

30—ST. STEPHEN (1917), Rev. Jorge C. Villegas; Deacon Miguel Alvarez.
Res.: 1237 W. 21 St., 16502. Tel: 814-459-0543.

OUTSIDE THE CITY OF ERIE

ALBION, ERIE CO., ST. LAWRENCE (1914), Rev. John M. Fischer.
Res.: 180 E. State St., 16401. Tel: 814-756-3623; Fax: 814-756-3623.
St. Lawrence Catechetical Center—129 E. Pearl St., 16401. Tel: 814-756-4840.

ANITA, JEFFERSON CO., ST. JOSEPH (1898), [CEM] Rev. James F. Bird, Admin.
Res.: Box 24, Walston, 15781. Tel: 814-938-9687.

BRADFORD, MCKEAN CO.

1—ST. BERNARD (1880), [CEM] Revs. Leo J. Gallina; Daniel J. Prez. In Res., Rev. Msgr. Jan C. Olowin.
Res.: P.O. Box 2394, 16701-5394. Tel: 814-362-6825; Fax: 814-362-1479.
School—Tel: 814-368-5891; Fax: 814-368-1464. Lay Teachers 13; Students 163.

2—ST. FRANCIS OF ASSISI (1846), [JC] Rev. Samuel Slocum.
Res.: 574 E. Main St., 16701. Tel: 814-368-6959; Fax: 814-368-6959.

BRANDY CAMP, ELK CO., HOLY CROSS (1908), (Italian), [CEM] Rev. Robert Horgas, Admin.
Mailing Address: P.O. Box 65, 15822. Tel: 814-265-4331.
Res.: 287 Treasure Lake, Du Bois, 15821. Tel: 814-371-2899.

BROCKWAY, JEFFERSON CO., ST. TOBIAS (1898), [CEM] Rev. Msgr. Charles A. Kaza, E.V.; Deacons Edward Ward; Robert De Noon.
Res.: 1100 Hewett St., 15824. Tel: 814-268-3655; Fax: 814-268-1147.

BROOKVILLE, JEFFERSON CO., IMMACULATE CONCEPTION (1852), [CEM] Very Rev. Joseph P. Staszewski, V.F.
Res.: 129 Graham Ave., 15825. Tel: 814-849-8697.
Mission—St. Dominic [CEM] Sigel, Jefferson Co.

CAMBRIDGE SPRINGS, CRAWFORD CO., ST. ANTHONY (1899), Rev. Patrick J. Speer (HRT) (Retired).
Res.: 165 Beach Ave., 16403. Tel: 814-398-4234; Fax: 814-734-2868.

CLARION, CLARION CO., IMMACULATE CONCEPTION (1855), [CEM] Rev. Msgr. Joseph J. Riccardo; Rev. James G. Faluszczak; Sr. Bernadine Gehinger, S.S.J., Pastoral Min.
Res.: 720 Liberty St., 16214. Tel: 814-226-8433; Fax: 814-226-1090.
School—Tel: 814-226-9690. Lay Teachers 10; Students 123.
Catechesis/Religious Program—Students 395.

CLEARFIELD, CLEARFIELD CO., ST. FRANCIS (1830), [CEM] Rev. Msgr. H. Desmond McGee, V.F. In Res., Rev. Msgr. Henry L. Krebs, V.F.; Rev. John G. Chapin; Deacon Eugene Miller Jr.
Res.: 212 S. Front St., 16830. Tel: 814-765-9671; Fax: 814-765-9489.
School—Tel: 814-765-2618; Fax: 814-765-6704. Lay Teachers 11; Students 142.

COALPORT, CLEARFIELD CO., ST. BASIL THE GREAT (1887), [CEM] Rev. Alexander D. Amico.
Res.: Box 395, 16627. Tel: 814-672-5561; Fax: 814-672-5954.

CONNEAUT LAKE, CRAWFORD CO., OUR LADY QUEEN OF THE AMERICAS (1958), [CEM] Rev. Stephen A. Anderson.
Res.: 9th & Water Sts., Box 110, 16316. Tel: 814-382-7252; Fax: 814-382-9575.

CONNEAUTVILLE, CRAWFORD CO., ST. PETER (1853), (Irish), [CEM] In Res., Rev. John A. Walsh.
Res.: 626 Washington St., P.O. Box F, 16406. Tel: 814-587-3435.
Convent—Sacred Heart, High St., P.O. Box 305, 16406. Tel: 814-587-2011.

CORRY, ERIE CO.

1—ST. ELIZABETH (1876), [CEM] Rev. Thomas E. Brown.
Res.: 26 W. Pleasant St., 16407. Tel: 814-664-7105.
Oratory—Our Lady of Victory Spartansburg, Crawford Co. 16434. Tel: 814-664-7105. Spartansburg, PA

2—ST. THOMAS THE APOSTLE (1856), [CEM] Rev. Thomas E. Brown.
Res.: 203 W. Washington St., 16407. Tel: 814-663-3041; Fax: 814-663-0505.
School—Tel: 814-665-7375; Fax: 814-663-0505. Lay Teachers 11; Students 111.

COUDERSPORT, POTTER CO., ST. EULALIA (1891), [CEM] Rev. John F. Weibel.
Res.: 16915. Tel: 814-274-8646.
Mission—St. Augustine [CEM] Austin, Potter Co.

CROSSINGSVILLE, CRAWFORD CO., ST. PHILIP (1840), [CEM] Rev. Thaddeus T. Kondzielski.
Res.: Crossingville, R.D. 2, Edinboro, 16412. Tel:

814-734-7395.
CROWN, CLARION CO., ST. MARY (1848), [CEM 2] Rev. Dennis J. Veltri.
Res.: 16220. Tel: 814-744-9919; Fax: 814-744-8624.
Mission—St. Anne Marienville, Forest Co.
CURWENSVILLE, CLEARFIELD CO., ST. TIMOTHY (1915), [CEM] Rev. Msgr. Joseph K. Bobal, V.F.
Res.: 306 Walnut St., 16833. Tel: 814-236-1845; Fax: 814-236-1845.
DAGUSCAHONDA, ELK CO., ST. BENEDICT, Closed., Effective April 30, 1995, St. Benedict in Daguscahonda became a Public Oratory (Cannon 1223).
DELANCEY, JEFFERSON CO., ST. ADRIAN, Rev. James F. Bird, Admin.
Res.: Box 24, Walston, 15781. Tel: 814-938-9687.
DU BOIS, CLEARFIELD CO.
1—ST. CATHERINE (1877), [CEM] Revs. Richard R. Siefer; Edward J. Walk; Zab Amar; Deacons Robert Kuntz; William Wright.
Res.: 116 S. State St., 15801. Tel: 814-371-8556; Fax: 814-371-0592.
School—Tel: 814-371-2570; Fax: 814-371-1551. Joseph Ryan, Prin. Lay Teachers 16; Students 242.
2—ST. JOSEPH (1893), (Lithuanian), [CEM] Rev. Richard R. Siefer.
Res.: 15 South Ave., 15801. Tel: 814-371-7956; 814-371-7604; Fax: 814-371-6687.
3—ST. MICHAEL (1912), [CEM] Rev. Thomas S. Hoderny. In Res., Rev. Mark S. Swoger.
Res.: 15 Robinson St., 15801. Tel: 814-371-5773; Fax: 814-371-5794.
EAST BRADY, CLARION CO., ST. EUSEBIUS (1877), [CEM] Rev. William M. Kuba.
Res.: R.D. 1, Box 747, 16028. Tel: 412-526-3366.
Mission—St. Richard Rimersburg, Clarion Co.
EDINBORO, ERIE CO., OUR LADY OF THE LAKE (1950), Rev. John B. Jacquel.
Res.: Box 838, 128 Sunset Dr., 16412. Tel: 814-734-3113; Fax: 814-734-3085.
ELDRED, MCKEAN CO., ST. RAPHAEL (1847), [CEM 2] Rev. Daniel J. Kresinski.
Res.: 16 First St., Box No. 252, 16731. Tel: 814-225-4231; Fax: 814-225-4298.
Mission—St. Mary [CEM] Sartwell, McKean Co.
EMLENTON, VENANGO CO., ST. MICHAEL (1867), [CEM] Rev. Msgr. Conrad L. Kraus.
Res.: Chestnut St., P.O. Box 177, 16373. Tel: 724-867-2422; Fax: 724-867-6815.
EMPORIUM, CAMERON CO., ST. MARK (1888), [CEM] Rev. Paul S. Siebert; Sr. Mercedes Muskovish, O.S.B., Parish Min.
Res.: 235 E. 4th St., 15834. Tel: 814-486-0569; Fax: 814-486-3298.
Mission—St. James Driftwood, Cameron Co.
FAIRVIEW, ERIE CO., HOLY CROSS (1963), Rev. J. Thomas Dugan.
Res.: 3627 Shauna Ave., P.O. Box 10, 16415. Tel: 814-474-2605; Fax: 814-474-1256.
FALLS CREEK, JEFFERSON CO., ST. BERNARD (1952), Rev. Robert Horgas.
Res.: 205 Taylor Ave., 15840. Tel: 814-371-7419.
FARRELL, MERCER CO.
1—ST. ADALBERT (1913), [CEM] Rev. John R. Boeckman.
Res.: 1035 Fruit Ave., 16121. Tel: 724-346-5379; Fax: 724-342-0831.
2—ST. ANN (1904), (Slovak), [CEM] In Res., Rev. Stephen J. Schreiber.
Res.: 1035 Fruit Ave., 16121. Tel: 724-346-5979; Fax: 724-347-5553.
3—HOLY TRINITY (1915), (Hungarian), [CEM] Rev. John R. Boeckman.
Res.: 601 Fruit Ave., 16121. Tel: 412-342-0794; Fax: 412-342-0831.
4—OUR LADY OF FATIMA (1952), [CEM 2] Revs. Donald E. Berdis; Joseph A. Ciaiola (Retired); Deacon Joseph Messina.
Res.: 601 Roemer Blvd., 16121. Tel: 724-346-3359.
School—Monsignor Geno Monti School, Tel: 724-347-1440. Sisters 1; Lay Teachers 9; Students 146.
FORCE, ELK CO., ST. JOSEPH (1906), [CEM] Rev. Regis J. Meenihan.
Res.: 15841. Tel: 814-787-4151; Fax: 814-787-4151.
FRANKLIN, VENANGO CO., ST. PATRICK (1867), [CEM] Rev. Msgr. John J. Herbein; Rev. Robert A. Manning.
Res.: 949 Liberty St., 16323. Tel: 814-437-5763; Fax: 814-437-6326.
School—Tel: 814-432-8689. Lay Teachers 9; Students 147.
FRENCHTOWN, CRAWFORD CO., ST. HIPPOLYTE (1838), [CEM] Rev. Monty Sayers.
Res.: R.D. 2, Guys Mills, 16327. Tel: 814-789-2022; Fax: 814-789-2025.
Mission—Our Lady of Lourdes Cochranton, Crawford Co.
Chapel— Sts. Peter & Paul, Pettis. (Devotional Chapel)
FRENCHVILLE, CLEARFIELD CO., ST. MARY OF THE ASSUMPTION (1840), [CEM] Rev. Samuel Bungo; Deacon Joseph Lyncha.
Res.: P.O. Box 159, 16836. Tel: 814-263-4354; Fax: 814-263-4219.
Mission—SS. Peter & Paul [CEM] Grass Flats, Clearfield Co.
Mission—St. Severin [CEM] Drifting, Clearfield Co.
Chapel— Sts. John & Paul, Karthaus. (Devotional Chapel)
FRYBURG, CLARION CO., ST. MICHAEL (1846), [CEM] Rev. David L.. Poulson.
Res.: P.O. Box 46, Main St., Rte. 208, 16326. Tel: 814-354-2467.
School—Tel: 814-354-2523. Sisters 1; Lay Teachers 5; Students 44.
GALETON, POTTER CO., ST. BIBIANA (1888), (Italian), [CEM] Rev. Brian E. Vossler.
Res.: 111 Germania, 16922. Tel: 814-435-2303.
Mission—Sacred Heart Genesee, Potter Co.
Chapel— St. Germain, Germania. (Devotional Chapel)
GIRARD, ERIE CO., ST. JOHN THE EVANGELIST (1853), [CEM] Rev. Glenn R. Whitman; Sr. Geraldine Kasper, O.S.F., D.R.E.
Res.: 142 E. Main St., Box 336, 16417. Tel: 814-774-4108.
School—Tel: 814-774-8865; Fax: 814-774-0604. Lay Teachers 11; Students 121.
GRAMPIAN, CLEARFIELD CO., ST. BONAVENTURE (1833), [CEM] Rev. James Mckee, S.J., Admin.
Res.: P.O. Box 127, 16838. Tel: 814-236-0364.
GREENVILLE, MERCER CO., ST. MICHAEL (1850), [CEM] Rev. Msgr. Andrew H. Karg; Rev. Mark O'Hern; Sr. Mary Gertrude McElhinny, S.C., Pastoral Min.; Deacon William Brown. In Res., Rev. Paul A. Schill.
Res.: 85 N. High St., 16125. Tel: 412-588-9800; Fax: 412-588-7053.
School—Tel: 724-588-7050; Fax: 724-588-7053. Lay Teachers 15; Students 185.
Mission—St. Margaret Jamestown, Mercer Co.
GROVE CITY, MERCER CO., BELOVED DISCIPLE (1925), [CEM] Rev. Msgr. Edward J. Zeitler, V.F.
Res.: 321 N. Broad St., 16127. Tel: 724-458-7145.
HERMITAGE, MERCER CO., CHURCH OF NOTRE DAME (1960), Rev. Msgr. John B. Hagerty; Rev. Jason Glover; Deacon W. Jack Tupper.
Res.: 2325 Highland Rd., 16148. Tel: 724-981-5566; Fax: 724-981-3215.
School—Tel: 724-342-2205. Lay Teachers 17; Students 265.
HOUTZDALE, CLEARFIELD CO., CHRIST THE KING (1970), [CEM] Rev. Msgr. Donald J. Cooper.
Res.: 123 Good St., 16651. Tel: 814-378-7653.
Mission—Immaculate Conception Madera, Clearfield Co.
JOHNSONBURG, ELK CO., HOLY ROSARY (1896), [CEM] Rev. David J. Wilson.
Res.: 606 Penn St., 15845. Tel: 814-965-2819; Fax: 814-965-5528.
KANE, MCKEAN CO., ST. CALLISTUS (1878), [CEM] Very Rev. Phillip A. Pinczewski, V.F.; Sr. Francis Therese Matia, S.S.J., D.R.E.
Res.: 342 Chase St., 16735. Tel: 814-837-6694; Fax: 814-837-6694.
Convent—116 Haines St., 16735.
Chapel— Sts. John & Stephen, James City. (Devotional Chapel)
KERSEY, ELK CO., ST. BONIFACE (1832), [CEM] Rev. John A. Kuzilla.
Res.: 355 Main St., 15846. Tel: 814-885-8941.
School—Tel: 814-885-8093; Fax: 814-885-8931. Sr. Laura Vallimont, O.S.B., Prin. Lay Teachers 9; Students 78.
LEWIS RUN, MCKEAN CO., OUR MOTHER OF PERPETUAL HELP (1946), Rev. Samuel B. Slocum.
Res.: 31 Lafayette, 16738. Tel: 814-368-6355.
LINESVILLE, CRAWFORD CO., ST. PHILIP (1957), [CEM] Rev. John G. Barwin.
Res.: R.D. 1, Box 1C, 16424. Tel: 814-683-5313.
LUCINDA, CLARION CO., ST. JOSEPH (1840), [CEM] Rev. Joseph R. Czarkowski.
Res.: 16235. Tel: 814-226-7288; Fax: 814-226-5225.
School—Tel: 814-226-8018. Sr. Monica Steiner, O.S.B., Prin., D.R.E. Sisters 1; Lay Teachers 4; Students 77.
MCKEAN, ERIE CO., ST. FRANCIS XAVIER (1838), [CEM] Rev. Msgr. A. Joseph Book. In Res., Rev. Mark A. Nowak.
Res.: 16426. Tel: 814-476-7657; Fax: 814-476-7657.
MEADVILLE, CRAWFORD CO.
1—ST. AGATHA (1849), [CEM] Rev. Gregory P. Passauer.
Res.: 353 Pine St., 16335. Tel: 814-336-1112.
School—Seton School, Tel: 814-336-2320; Fax: 814-336-2328. Consolidation of St. Agatha Elementary and St. Brigid Elementary. Sisters 1; Lay Teachers 10; Students 190.
Mission—St. Bernadette 222 Renner Ln., Saegertown, Crawford Co. 16433. Tel: 814-763-2831. Rev. Mark A. Nowak.
2—ST. BRIGID (1865), [CEM] Revs. David Findlay; Rocco A. Tito.
Res.: 967 Chancery Ln., 16335. Tel: 814-336-4459; Fax: 814-724-2996.
3—ST. MARY (1909), Rev. Mark A. Hoffman.
Res.: 1085 Water St., 16335. Tel: 814-333-6161.
MERCER, MERCER CO., IMMACULATE HEART (1838), [CEM] Rev. James J. Kennelley.
Res.: 16137. Tel: 724-662-2999.
Chapel— St. Hermenegild, Pardoe. (Devotional Chapel)
MORRISDALE, CLEARFIELD CO., ST. AGNES (1891), [CEM] Rev. Gregory A. Kirsch, J.C.L.; Deacon Robert Hoover.
Res.: 16858. Tel: 814-342-2583; Fax: 814-342-6377.
Mission—SS. Peter & Paul [CEM] Hawk Run, Clearfield Co.
Chapel— Sts. Cyril & Methodius, Winburne. (Devotional Chapel)
MOUNT JEWETT, MCKEAN CO., ST. JOSEPH (1898), Rev. David E. Prenatt.
Res.: P.O. Box 520, 17 Division St., 16740. Tel: 814-778-5520.
NEW BETHLEHEM, CLARION CO., ST. CHARLES (1872), [CEM] Rev. William M. Laska.
Res.: 201 Washington St., 16242. Tel: 814-275-3446.
Mission—St. Nicholas [CEM] Crates, Clarion Co.
NORTH EAST, ERIE CO., ST. GREGORY THAUMATURGUS (1875), [CEM] Rev. Thomas L. Tyler.
Res.: 136 W. Main St., 16428. Tel: 814-725-9691; Fax: 814-725-1225.
School—140 W. Main St., 16428. Tel: 814-725-4571. Sisters of St. Benedict 1; Lay Teachers 10; Students 105.
OIL CITY, VENANGO CO.
1—ASSUMPTION OF THE BLESSED VIRGIN MARY (1899), (Polish), In Res., Rev. John Neff.
Res.: 210 Emerald St., 16301. Tel: 814-677-2032.
Mission—St. Venantius Rouseville, Venango Co.
2—ST. JOSEPH (1865), [CEM 2] Rev. John W. Swoger.
Res.: 35 Pearl Ave., 16301. Tel: 814-677-4004; Fax: 814-677-5977.
3—OUR LADY HELP OF CHRISTIANS (1914), Rev. John P. Mathaner.
Res.: 69 Willow St., 16301. Tel: 814-677-3078.
4—ST. STEPHEN (1898), Rev. Jeffrey J. Noble; Rev. Msgr. William C. Karg.
Res.: 210 Reed St., 16301. Tel: 814-677-3020; Fax: 814-678-8841.
School—Tel: 814-677-2053; Fax: 814-677-2053. Lay Teachers 12; Students 200.
PORT ALLEGANY, MCKEAN CO., ST. GABRIEL THE ARCHANGEL (1876), [CEM] Rev. Charles R. Schmitt.
Res.: 203 Arnold Ave., 16743. Tel: 814-642-2847.
Mission—St. Mary Roulette, Potter Co.
PUNXSUTAWNEY, JEFFERSON CO., SS. COSMAS AND DAMIAN (1885), [CEM] Rev. John F. Bauer. In Res., Rev. James F. Bird.
Res.: 616 W. Mahoning St., 15767. Tel: 814-938-6540; Fax: 814-938-7439.
School—Tel: 814-938-4224; Fax: 814-939-3759. Lay Teachers 12; Students 158.
RAMEY, CLEARFIELD CO., HOLY TRINITY (1937), [CEM] Rev. Donald L. Cooper.
Res.: Box 196, 16671. Tel: 814-378-7193.
REYNOLDSVILLE, JEFFERSON CO., ST. MARY (1872), [CEM] Rev. Msgr. John W. Mignot.
Res.: 607 Main St., 15851. Tel: 814-653-8586.
RIDGWAY, ELK CO., ST. LEO THE GREAT (1874), [CEM] Very Rev. Theodore B. Marconi; Rev. D.G. "Skip" Davis. In Res., Rev. Joseph P. Reigel.
Res.: 111 Depot St., 15853. Tel: 814-772-3135; Fax: 814-772-3225.
School—Tel: 814-772-9775. Sr. Mary Joan Beauseigneur, S.S.J., Prin. Lay Teachers 12; Students 142.
Convent—117 Depot St., 15853.
Chapel— St. Leo, Daguscahonda. (Devotional Chapel)
ROUSEVILLE, VENANGO CO., ST. VENANTIUS (1870), Rev. John Neff.
Res.: 210 Emerald St., Oil City, 16301. Tel: 814-677-2032.
Church: 403 Main St., 16344.
ST. MARYS, ELK CO.
1—ST. MARY (1842), (German), [CEM] Revs. Frank Ziemkiewicz, O.S.B.; James H. Loew, O.S.B.
Res.: 144 Church St., 15857. Tel: 814-781-1019; Fax: 814-834-6795.
School—Tel: 814-834-2665; Fax: 814-834-5339. Lay Teachers 34; Students 406.
School—St. Mary's Catholic Elementary School System, 303 Church St., St. Mary's. Tel: 814-834-9493. Ms. Mary Agnes Marshall, Prin.
2—QUEEN OF THE WORLD (1954), Revs. Daniel C. Wolfel, O.S.B. (GBG); Matthew T. Laffey, O.S.B.; Sr. Josephine DiPetro, S.S.J., Coord. Inter-Parish Svcs.
Res.: 134 Queens Rd., 15857. Tel: 814-834-4701; Fax: 814-834-3422.
3—SACRED HEART OF JESUS (1876), [JC] Revs. Eric Vogt, O.S.B.; Jeremy Loew; Deacon William Gibson.
Res.: 323 Center St., 15857. Tel: 814-834-7861; Fax: 814-834-1376.
School—Tel: 814-834-4017. Lay Teachers 17; Students 252.

SHARON, MERCER CO.
1—ST. ANTHONY (1924), (Croatian), [CEM] Rev. Matthew Ruyechan, O.F.M.
Res.: 804 Idaho St., 16146. Tel: 724-342-7391; Fax: 724-342-7981.
2—ST. JOSEPH (1892), [CEM] [JC] Revs. Christopher C. Morry; Marc Stockton; Sr. Sandy Pedone, H.M., D.R.E.
Res.: 79 Case Ave., 16146. Tel: 724-981-3232; Fax: 724-981-4174.
School—Tel: 412-938-8382. Lay Teachers 13; Students 238.
3—SACRED HEART (1864), [CEM] Rev. Stanley J. Swacha.
Res.: 40 S. Irvine Ave., 16146. Tel: 724-346-3567; Fax: 724-346-3567.
4—ST. STANISLAUS KOSTKA (1931), (Polish), [CEM] Rev. Jeffery J. Lucas.
Res.: 370 Spruce Ave., 16146. Tel: 412-347-7526; Fax: 412-347-1760.
Catechesis/Religious Program—Rose DeSantis, D.R.E. Students 180.
SHARPSVILLE, MERCER CO., ST. BARTHOLOMEW (1874), Rev. John S. Lynch.
Res.: 311 W. Ridge Ave., 16150. Tel: 724-962-7130; Fax: 724-962-1771.
SHEFFIELD, WARREN CO., ST. ANTHONY (1878), Rev. Raymond Gramata.
Res.: P.O. Box 518, Four Mile Rd., 16347. Tel: 814-968-5915.
SHINGLEHOUSE, POTTER CO., ST. THERESA (1901), [CEM] Rev. Daniel J. Kresinski.
Res.: P.O. Box 277, 16748. Tel: 814-697-6900.
SMETHPORT, MCKEAN CO., ST. ELIZABETH (1875), [CEM] Rev. David E. Prenatt.
Res.: 307 Franklin St., 16749. Tel: 814-887-9254; Fax: 814-887-1930.
STONEBORO, MERCER CO., ST. COLUMBKILLE (1874), [CEM] Rev. Henry C. Andrae, Admin.
Res.: Franklin St., P.O. Box 206, 16153. Tel: 724-376-3393; Fax: 724-376-3396.
SYKESVILLE, JEFFERSON CO., ASSUMPTION OF BLESSED VIRGIN MARY (1923), [CEM] Rev. Mark J. Mastrain.
Res.: 20 Shaffer St., 15865. Tel: 814-894-2772; Fax: 814-894-7981.
TIDIOUTE, WARREN CO., ST. JOHN (1866), [CEM] Rev. Thomas M. Aleksa.
Res.: 25 First St., 16351. Tel: 814-484-7747; Fax: 814-484-7231.
Mission—St. Anthony Tionesta, Forest Co.
TITUSVILLE, CRAWFORD CO.
1—ST. TITUS (1962), [CEM] [JC] Rev. V. David Foradori; Sr. Edith Hirsch, R.M.S., Pastoral Min.
Res.: 513 W. Main St., 16354. Tel: 814-827-4636; Fax: 814-827-4637.
School—Tel: 814-827-3312. Sisters 1; Lay Teachers 1; Students 61.
Christian Activities Center—505 W. Walnut St., 16354. Tel: 814-827-7223; Fax: 814-827-8711.
Mission—Immaculate Conception Mageetown, Crawford Co. Tel: 814-827-2075.
2—ST. WALBURGA (1872), (German), [CEM] Unassigned. In Res., Rev. William J. O'Brien.
Res.: 120 Brook St., 16354. Tel: 814-827-3958.
UNION CITY, ERIE CO., ST. TERESA OF AVILA (1906), [CEM] Rev. F. Thomas Suppa.
Res.: 9 Third Ave., 16438. Tel: 814-438-2924.
Mission—Our Lady of Fatima Canadohta Lake, Crawford Co.
WALSTON, JEFFERSON CO., ST. ANTHONY (1898), Rev. James F. Bird, Admin.
Res.: Box 24, 15781. Tel: 814-938-9687.
WARREN, WARREN CO.
1—HOLY REDEEMER (1912), Rev. Msgr. John L. Lucas, V.F.; Deacons Joseph Lucia Jr.; Raymond Wiehagen.
Res.: 11 Russell St., 16365. Tel: 814-726-3360; Fax: 814-726-3351.
2—ST. JOSEPH (1858), [CEM] [JC] Rev. Walter E. Packard; Rev. Msgr. Thomas J. McSweeney; Deacon Joseph Lucia Jr.
Res.: 600 Penna. Ave. W., 16365. Tel: 814-723-2090; Fax: 814-723-6042.
School—Tel: 814-723-2030. Sisters 1; Lay Teachers 12; Students 139.
WATERFORD, ERIE CO., ST. CYPRIAN (1878), Rev. Thomas J. Whitman.
Church: 12775 Donation Rd., Box 535, 16441. Tel: 814-796-4329.
WEST MIDDLESEX, MERCER CO., GOOD SHEPHERD (1955), [JC] Rev. Howard J. King.
Res.: P.O. Box 226, 16159. Tel: 724-528-2539.
WILCOX, ELK CO., ST. ANNE (1890), [JC] Rev. David Willson.
Res.: P.O. Box 65, Clarion St., 15870. Tel: 814-929-5577.
WINBURNE, CLEARFIELD CO., SS. CYRIL AND METHODIUS (1904), (Slovak—Hungarian), Closed. For inquiries for parish records contact the chancery.
YOUNGSVILLE, WARREN CO., ST. LUKE (1958), Rev. William C. Miller; Deacons William Sproweri; Phillip Sekerda.
Res.: 420 N. Main St., 16371. Tel: 814-563-4432.

Chaplains of Public Institutions

ERIE. *Erie County Prison*. Rev. Robert P. Fedor.
Hamot Medical Center, 201 State St., 16550. Rev. Msgr. Gerald J. Koos.
Pleasant Ridge Manor East. Rev. John E. Santor.
Pleasant Ridge Manor West. Rev. J. Daniel Dymski.
Shriners Hospital for Crippled Children, 1116 W. 7th St., 16550. Vacant.
Soldiers and Sailors Home. Rev. Jerry E. Priscaro.
Veterans Administration Hospital. Rev. Thomas M. Fialkowski, Chap.
St. Vincent's Health Center, 232 W. 25th St., 16544. Rev. Dennis A. Martin, Chap.
ALBION. *Albion State Correctional Facility*. Deacon Ralph DeCecco.
BRADFORD. *Federal Correction Institution*, P.O. Box 5000, 16701-0950. Rev. Msgr. Jan C. Dlowin.
CAMBRIDGE SPRINGS. *Cambridge Springs Correction Institution*. Rev. J. Daniel Dymski.
DU BOIS. *Du Bois Regional Hospital*, 100 Hospital Ave., 15801. Sr. Jude McCluskey, R.S.M., Chap.
MEADVILLE. *Crawford County Care Center*, 967 Chancery Ln., 16335. Rev. David Findlay, Chap.
MERCER. *State Correctional Facility*, Box 530, 16137. Rev. Msgr. Charles S. Murcko, Chap. (Retired).
POLK. *Polk Center*, Box 94, 16342. Rev. John Neff.
WARREN. *Warren State Hospital*. Rev. Raymond Gramata.

Special or Diocesan Assignment:
Rev.—
Fischer, G. William, O.S.F.S., 10018 Seeley St., Lake City, 16423-1546. Tel: 814-774-9655

On Duty Outside Diocese:
Revs.—
Beal, John P., J.C.D., Washington, DC
Detisch, Scott P., Ph.D.
Jeselnick, Stephen E., AFB
Malene, Robert, AZ

On Leave of Absence:
Rev. Msgr.—
Kriegel, Henry A.
Rev.—
Gmerek, Ronald E.

Retired:
Rev. Msgrs.—
Adams, George
Barcio, Robert G., Ph.D.
Bogniak, Casimir
Daniszewski, John D.
DeWalt, Homer C.
Dollinger, John M.
Enright, Vincent L.
Geddes, Thomas C.
Goodill, Robert D.
Heberlein, Louis J.
Lohse, Walter H.
Martin, Daniel J.
Meier, Raymond O.
Mitchell, Salvatore P.
Murcko, Charles S.
Peterson, James W.
Reilly, Robert J.
Sanner, James E.
Schauerman, Henry J.
Schriefer, Robert F.
Slater, John J.
Snyder, John R.
Sperry, James E.
Revs.—
Andersen, Emil
Bicsey, John
Burke, John R.
Buzga, John P.
Ciaiola, Joseph A.
Collins, Stephen L.
Craig, Robert G.
Dipre, Gilio L., Ph.D.
Driscoll, William J.
Fin, Robert G., Ph.D.
Finucane, Joseph F.
Groucutt, George L.
Kacprowicz, Joseph A.
Levis, Robert J., Ph.D.
Maloney, William J.
Maryland, Joseph A.
Matuszak, Edward S.
Powers, Richard E.
Ruhling, James P.
Skinner, Charles D.
Somers, Eldon K.
Stutz, Edward J.
Weber, James H.
Wolf, Norbert G.

INSTITUTIONS LOCATED IN THE DIOCESE

[A] SEMINARIES, DIOCESAN

ERIE. *St. Mark's Seminary*, 429 E. Grandview Blvd., P.O. Box 10397, 16514. Tel: 814-824-1200. Very Rev. Michael T. Kesicki, S.S.L., Rector; Rev. Edward M. Lohse, S.T.D., J.C.L., Vice Rector.

[B] COLLEGES AND UNIVERSITIES

ERIE. *Gannon University*, University Square, 16541. Tel: 814-871-7000. Web: www.gannon.edu. Antoine M. Garibaldi, Ph.D., Pres.; Rev. Msgrs. Addison Yehl, M.S.; Gerald L. Orbanek, M.A.; Very Rev. Joseph C. Gregorek, V.F.; Revs. Gilio L. Dipre, Ph.D. (Retired); Robert G. Fin, Ph.D. (Retired); Edward C. Krause, C.S.C.; Robert J. Levis, Ph.D. (Retired); Nicholas J. Rouch, S.T.D.; Robert P. Susa, M.A.; Casimir J. Wozniak; Very Rev. Michael T. Kesicki, S.S.L.; Revs. Christopher M. Hamlett; George E. Strohmeyer, M.A. Priests 7; Sisters 1; Lay Teachers 161; Students 3,415.
Mercyhurst College, 501 E. 38th St., 16546. Tel: 814-824-2000; Fax: 814-824-2098. Email: aroth@mercyhurst.edu. Web: www.mercyhurst.edu. Dr. William P. Garvey, Pres.; Andrew P. Roth, Ph.D., Dean & Vice Pres., Academic Affairs & Dean, Mercyhurst College; Rev. James Piszker, Chap.; Pat Wieser, Contact Person. Priests 2; Sisters 10; Lay Teachers 120; Students 3,404.

[C] HIGH SCHOOLS, DIOCESAN

ERIE. *Cathedral Preparatory School*, 225 W. Ninth St., 16501. Tel: 814-453-7737; Fax: 814-455-5462. Rev. Scott W. Jabo, Headmaster. Priests 7; Sisters 1; Laymen 42; Laywomen 32; Students 557.
Faculty: Revs. Bruce Allison; William Fischer; Raymond W. Hahn; James McCormick; Richard Toohey; Sr. James Francis Mulligan.
DU BOIS. *DuBois Area Catholic School*, P.O. Box 567, 15801. Tel: 814-371-3060; Fax: 814-371-3215. Email: central@cchs.pvt.k12.pd.us. Revs. Mark S. Swoger, Headmaster; Edward J. Walk, Asst. Headmaster. Priests 2; Lay Teachers 52; Students 675.
Central Catholic High School
Central Catholic Middle School
HERMITAGE. *Kennedy Catholic High School*, 2120 Fwy., 16148. Tel: 724-346-5531 Fax: 724-346-3011. Email: kchs@kennedy-catholic.org. Mr. Peter Iacono, Pres.; Mrs. Christine Perry, Prin. Priests 3; Sisters 1; Lay Teachers 24; Students 320.
OIL CITY. *Venango Catholic High School*, 1505 W. 1st St. 16301-3298. Tel: 814-677-3098; Fax: 814-676-4453. Email: jpsm5.vchs@choicecnemail.com. Rev. John P. Malthaner, Headmaster. Lay Teachers 13; Students 95.
SAINT MARYS. *Elk County Catholic High School*, 600 Maurus St., St. Marys, 15857. Tel: 814-834-7800; Fax: 814-781-3441; 814-774-4893 (Schlimm). Email: ecchs@ncentral.com. Mr. John W. Kowach, Headmaster; Jen Meyer, Campus Ministry Coord. Lay Teachers 27; Students 358.

[D] HIGH SCHOOLS, PRIVATE

ERIE. *Mercyhurst Preparatory School*, 538 E. Grandview Blvd., 16504. Tel: 814-824-2210; Fax: 814-824-2116. Email: maste@mpslakers.com. Sr. Mary Ann Bader, R.S.M., Pres.; Margaret Aste, Prin.; Marcia DiTullio, Contact Person. Sisters 5; Lay Teachers 58; Students 766.
Villa Maria Academy, 2403 W. 8th St., 16505. Tel: 814-838-2061; Fax: 814-838-0376. Email: villa@villamaria.com. Web: www.villamaria.com. Ms. Geri Cicchetti, Pres.; Sr. Ann Marie Joint, S.S.J., Prin.; Mrs. Kathleen DiNicola, Asst. Admin. Sisters 5; Lay Teachers 41; Students 456.

[E] ELEMENTARY SCHOOLS, PRIVATE

ERIE. *Villa Maria Elementary School*, 2551 W. 8th St., 16505. Tel: 814-838-5451; Fax: 814-833-3315. Sr. Margaret Frank, S.S.J., Prin. Sisters of St. Joseph 2; Lay Teachers 27; Students 398.

[F] SPECIAL MINISTRIES

ERIE. *St. Benedict Child Development Center*, 345 E. 9th St., 16503. Tel: 814-454-4514; Fax: 814-452-1905. Email: stbens@erie.net. Sr. Diane Rabe, O.S.B., Admin. Students 105.
St. Benedict Education Center, 330 E. 10th St., 16503. Tel: 814-452-4072; Fax: 814-454-2686. Email: mmashank@stben.org. Sr. Miriam Mashank, O.S.B., Dir. Students 800.
Erie East Coast Migrant Programs, 345 E. 9th St.,

16503. Tel: 814-454-4514; Fax: 814-452-1905. Email: admin@stbenedictctr.com. Sr. Diane Rabe, O.S.B., Dir. Benedictine Sisters of Erie Students 46.

L'Arche Erie, 1101 Peach St., 2nd Fl., 16501. Tel: 814-452-2065; Fax: 814-452-4188. Email: office@larcheerie.org.

Mercy Center of the Arts, 444 E. Grandview Blvd., 16504. Tel: 814-824-2519; Fax: 814-824-2127. Email: rsmarts@velocity.net.

Word of Life Catholic Charismatic Renewal, St. Mark Catholic Center, 429 E. Grandview Blvd., P.O. Box 10397, 16514-0397. Tel: 814-824-1286; Fax: 814-824-1128. Email: wolccrc@aol.com.

FAIRVIEW. *Camp Notre Dame*, 400 Eaton Rd., P.O. Box 74, 16415. Tel: 814-474-5001; Fax: 814-474-4818. Email: cnd@erie.net. Web: www.campnotredame.com. Kathleen Baston, Pres.; Rev. Msgr. Lawrence T. Spiece, Vice Pres.

ROULETTE. *Catholic Rural Ministry*, P.O. Box 11, 16746-0011. Tel: 814-544-8017. Email: crm@adelpia.net. Sr. Phyllis Schleicher, O.S.B., Contact Person.

[G] GENERAL HOSPITALS

ERIE. **Saint Vincent Health Center*, 232 W. 25th St., 16544. Tel: 814-452-5000; Fax: 814-452-5102; 814-452-7611 (Surkala). Ms. Angela Bontempo, Pres. & CEO; Revs. Raymond Gramata, Chap.; Dennis A. Martin, Chap.; Kelly Kidd, Contact Person.

Saint Vincent Health System Ms. Angela Bontempo, Pres. & CEO, St. Vincent Health System.

[H] PROTECTIVE INSTITUTIONS

ERIE. *Gannondale, Inc.*, 4635 E. Lake Rd., 16511. Tel: 814-899-7659; Fax: 814-898-4266. Email: gannondale@aol.com. Sr. Severiana Morales, Coord.; Nancy Sabol, Exec. Dir. North American Union of Sisters of Our Lady of Charity-Erie Residents 45.

HARBORCREEK. *Harborcreek Youth Services*, 5712 Iroquois Ave., 16421. Tel: 814-899-7664; Fax: 814-899-3075. Email: jpetulla@hys-erie.org. Mr. John D. Petulla, A.C.S.W., L.S.W., C.E.O. Children 124.

[I] APARTMENTS FOR SENIOR CITIZENS

ERIE. *Mercy Terrace Apartments*, 430 E. Grandview Blvd., 16504. Tel: 814-825-6791; Fax: 814-824-2127. Email: mta@erie.net. Sr. M. Felice Duska, R.S.M., Mgr. Sisters of Mercy of Erie

HARBORCREEK. **Benetwood Apartments for Persons Elderly and Handicapped*, 641 Troupe Rd., 16421-1048. Tel: 814-899-0088; Fax: 814-898-2513. Email: benetwood@adelphia.net. Sr. Patricia Hause, O.S.B., Admin. Benedictine Sisters of Erie Residents 80.

[J] RESIDENCES FOR RETIRED PRIESTS

ERIE. *Bishop Michael J. Murphy Residence for Retired Priests*, 400 E. Gore Rd., 16509. Tel: 814-825-0680; Fax: 814-825-9761. Rev. Msgr. Robert J. Smith, J.C.L., V.G., Dir.

[K] NURSING HOMES

ERIE. *Saint Mary's Home at Asbury Ridge*, 4855 W. Ridge Rd., 16506. Tel: 814-836-5300. Rev. William M. Calabrese.

St. Mary's Home of Erie, 607 E. 26th St., 16504. Tel: 814-459-0621; Fax: 814-454-0909. Email: pmccracken@stmaryshome.org. Web: www.stmaryshome.org. Sr. Phyllis McCracken, S.S.J., N.H.A., Pres., CEO & Contact Person; Rev. Msgr. Joseph V. Wardanski, Chap. Sisters 16; Residents 131; Patients-Nursing Home 139.

DU BOIS. *Christ the King Manor, Inc.*, 1100 W. Long Ave., 15801. Tel: 814-371-3180; Fax: 814-371-4101. Email: etkm@penn.com. Rev. Mark S. Swoger, Chap. Residents 160.

HERMITAGE. *John XXIII Home*, 2250 Shenango Fwy., 16148. Tel: 724-981-3200; Fax: 724-981-1677. Email: khawthorne@johnxxIIIhome.org. Web: www.johnXXIIIhome.org. Kirk L. Hawthorne, Admin.; Rev. James A. Wiley. Residents 173.

[L] SHELTERS FOR MEN AND WOMEN

ERIE. *Mercy Center for Women*, 1039 E. 27th St., 16504. Tel: 814-455-4577; Fax: 814-459-7012. Email: ctombaugh@mcwerie.org. Web: mcwerie.org. Christine Tombaugh, Exec. Dir.

St. Patrick Haven, Inc., 147 E. 12th St., 16501. Tel: 814-454-7219; 814-836-5301; Fax: 814-454-7219. Sr. Marie Eileen Moyer, Admin.

[M] CONVENTS AND RESIDENCES FOR SISTERS

ERIE. *Benet Priory*, 330 E. 10th St., 16503. Tel: 814-459-5103. Benedictine Sisters of Erie 2.

Congregation of the Divine Spirit, 409 W. 6th St., 16507. Tel: 814-455-3590; Fax: 814-454-8899. Email: keltymarty@aol.com. Sr. Patricia O'Connor, C.D.S., Supr. Gen.; Rev. Richard Powers. Members 41.

Holy Family Monastery, 510 E. Gore Rd., 16509-3799. Sr. Emmanuel of the Mother of God, O.C.D., Prioress; Very Rev. Michael T. Kesicki, S.S.L., Chap.; Rev. Nicholas J. Rouch, S.T.D., Chap. Discalced Carmelites 8.

Kraus House Priory, 436 E. 9th St., 16503. Tel: 814-454-4846. Benedictine Sisters of Erie Sisters 4.

Mount Saint Benedict Monastery, 6101 E. Lake Rd., 16511. Tel: 814-899-0614; Fax: 814-898-4004. Email: prioress@mtstbenedict.org. Web: www.eriebenedictines.org. Sr. Christine Vladimiroff, O.S.B., Prioress; Patricia McGreevy, Contact Name. Benedictine Sisters of Erie Professed Sisters in Community 118; Sisters in Formation 3.

North American Union Sisters of Our Lady of Charity, 4635 E. Lake Rd., 16511. Tel: 814-899-1052; Fax: 814-899-1573. Email: olcsup@aol.com. Sr. Severiana Morales, Local Supr.

Om Shanti, 1239 W. 7th St., 16502. Tel: 814-459-3215. Email: marycook@erie.net. Web: www.eriebenedictine.org. Benedictine Sisters of Erie 2.

Sophia House, 1245 W. 10th St., 16502. Tel: 814-454-1212. Benedictine Sisters of Erie 3.

Bethany House, 218 E. 11th St., 16503. Tel: 814-455-4574. Benedictine Sisters of Erie 3.

Peace House, 103 E. 35th St., 16504. Tel: 814-455-6066. Benedictine Sisters of Erie 2.

Benedicta Riepp Priory, 3904 Tuttle Ave., 16504. Tel: 814-825-2767. Benedictine Sisters of Erie 2.

Pax Priory, 345 E. Ninth St., 16503. Tel: 814-452-6318; Fax: 814-459-8066. Email: paxprior@erie.net. Web: www.eriebenedictine.org. Benedictine Sisters of Erie 5.

St. Scholastica Priory, 355 E. 9th St., 16503. Tel: 814-454-4052; Fax: 814-459-8066. Email: schlstca@erie.net. Web: eriebenedictines.org. Benedictine Sisters of Erie 4.

Sisters of Mercy Motherhouse, 444 E. Grandview Blvd., 16504. Tel: 814-824-2516; Fax: 814-824-2127. Email: rsmpres@mercyerie.org. Web: www.mercyerie.org. Sr. JoAnne Courneen, R.S.M., Pres. Professed Sisters 63.

Villa Maria, 5031 W. Ridge Rd., 16506-1249. Tel: 814-836-4100; Fax: 814-836-4278. Email: s.rvincent@ssjerie.org. Web: www.ssjerie.org. Sr. Ricarda Vincent, S.S.J., Pres.; Rev. Msgr. Gerald L. Orbanek, M.A., Chap. The Sisters of St. Joseph of Northwestern PA Professed Sisters in Community 155.

St. Walburga Priory, 302 E. 10th St., 16503. Tel: 814-454-3706. Email: walburga@stargate.net. Web: www.eriebenedictines.org. Benedictine Sisters of Erie 2.

ST. MARYS. *Benedictine Sisters of Elk County St. Joseph Monastery*, Formerly Benedictine Sisters of Elk County O.S.B. St. Joseph Monastery, 303 Church St., 15857. Tel: 814-834-2267; Fax: 814-834-3270. Email: svallimont@alltell.net. Sr. Laura Vallimont, O.S.B., Prioress. Professed Sisters 26; Novices 2.

[N] SOCIOLOGICAL

ERIE. *Saint Benedict Community Center*, 320 E. 10th St., 16503. Tel: 814-459-2406. Email: iluv2kayak@hotmail.com. Sr. Dianne Sabol, O.S.B., Dir.

Emmaus Ministries, 345 E. 9th St., 16503. Tel: 814-459-8349. Sr. Mary Miller, O.S.B., Dir.

ERIE DAWN, 330 E. Tenth St., 16503. Tel: 814-453-5921; Fax: 814-453-5831. Email: srphyllis@eriedawn.org. Web: www.eriedawn.org. Sr. Phyllis Hilbert, S.S.J., Admin.

Mercy Center for Women, 1039 E. 27th St., 16504. Tel: 814-455-4577; Fax: 814-459-7012. Email: mcw@erie.org. Web: www.mcwerie.org. Christine Tombaugh, Exec. Dir.

Mercy Center on Aging, 444 E. Grandview Blvd., 16504-2604. Tel: 814-824-2214; Fax: 814-824-2127. Email: smdrsm@erie.net. Web: mercycenteronaging.com. Sr. Mary Dolores, R.S.M., Exec. Dir.

Sisters of St. Joseph Neighborhood Network, Inc., 425 W. 18th St., 16502. Tel: 814-454-7814; Fax: 814-454-7913. Email: ssjnn@svhs.org. Sr. Mary Herrmann, S.S.J., Exec. Dir.

[O] RETREAT & RENEWAL CENTERS

ERIE. *Ecclesia Center/Renewal Center*, 9101 Ridge Rd., 16417-9625. Tel: 814-774-9691; Fax: 814-774-4893. Email: ecclesia@erie.net. Web: www.ecclesiacenter.org. Rev. Jerome S. Simmons; Kathleen Kutz, Contact Person.

Glinodo Center, 6270 E. Lake Rd., 16511. Tel: 814-899-0614; Fax: 814-898-4004. Email: physical@mstbenedict.org. Web: www.eriebenedictines.org. Sr. Charles Marie Holze, O.S.B., Dir. Benedictine Sisters of Erie

Special Ministries, P.O. Box 10682, 16514. Tel: 814-456-0891. Rev. Msgr. James W. Peterson, Dir. (Retired).

FRENCHVILLE. *Young People Who Care Center, Caritas Mission*, P.O. Box 129, 16836. Tel: 814-263-4177. Email: bethanyyouth@pennswoods.net. Web: www.vicon.net/~caritasm. Sr. Suzanne Thiballt, C.A., Dir.

UNION CITY. *Avila Retreat Center*, 61 E. High St., 16438. Tel: 814-438-7020. Mr. Steve Viera, Pres.

[P] CAMPUS MINISTRY

ERIE. *Newman Centers and Campus Ministry* c/o Penn State Erie, The Behrend College, 5091 Station Rd., 16563-0901. Tel: 814-898-6245; Fax: 814-898-6608. Email: mcd24@psu.edu. Sr. Mary Drexler, S.S.J., Diocesan Dir. Campus Ministry.

Allegheny College, 520 N. Main St., P.O. Box 101, Meadville, 16335. Tel: 814-332-2800; Fax: 814-332-2340. Rev. Mark A. Hoffman.

St. Bernard Parish, P.O. Box 2394, Bradford, 16701. Tel: 814-362-6825; Fax: 814-362-1497. Rev. Daniel J. Prez. University of Pittsburgh-Bradford Campus

Clarion University of Pennsylvania, 60 Greenville Ave., Clarion, 16214. Tel: 814-226-6869; Fax: 814-226-8442. Rev. James Faluszczak.

St. Francis Parish, 212 S. Front St., 16830. Tel: 814-765-9671; Fax: 814-226-1090. Lockhaven University-Clearfield Campus

St. Catherine Parish, 116 State St., DuBois, 15801. Tel: 814-371-8556. Penn State University-DuBois Campus

Edinboro University of PA, Newman Center, 300 Darrow Rd., P.O. Box 820, Edinboro, 16412. Tel: 814-734-1651; Fax: 814-734-3085. Rev. Mark A. Nowak, Campus Min.

Gannon University, University Sq., 16541. Tel: 814-871-7435. Mr. Stephen Washek, Campus Min.; Rev. George E. Strohmeyer, M.A., Chap.

Grove City College, Beloved Disciple Parish, 321 N. Broad St., Grove City, 16127. Tel: 412-458-7145.

Mercyhurst College, 501 E. 38th St., 16546. Tel: 814-824-2301. Sr. Geri Rosinski, R.S.M., Campus Min. Tel: 814-824-2430; Rev. James Piszker, Chap. & Dir. Tel: 814-824-2467; Daniel Cabanillas, Campus Min. Tel: 814-824-2430.

Mercyhurst College, North East, 1611 Peach St., Ste. 450, 16501. Tel: 814-456-6189. Rev. John J. Hilbert.

St. Stephen Parish, 210 Reed St., Oil City, 16301. Tel: 814-677-3020. Clarion State University of PA-Venango Campus

Penn State Erie, The Behrend College, Formerly Penn State University, The Behrend College 5091 Station Rd., 16563-0901. Tel: 814-898-6245; Fax: 814-898-6608. Sr. Mary Drexler, S.S.J., Campus Min.

S.S. Cosmos & Damian Parish, 616 W. Mahoning St., Punxsutawney, 15767. Tel: 814-938-6540. Indiana University of PA-Punxsutawney Campus

St. Joseph Parish, 74 Case Ave., Sharon, 16146. Tel: 412-981-3232. Penn State University-Shenano Valley Campus

Thiel College Rev. Msgr. Andrew H. Karg.

St. Michael Parish, 85 N. High St., Greenville, 16125. Tel: 724-588-9800. Joanne Schell, Dir. of Career Center. Tel: 724-589-2014.

St. Titus Parish, 513 W. Main St., Titusville, 16354. Tel: 814-827-4636. Deacon William Brown, Campus Min. University of Pittsburgh-Titusville Campus

[Q] MISCELLANEOUS

ERIE. *Alliance for International Monasticism (AIM)*, 345 E. 9th St., 16503. Tel: 814-453-4724; Fax: 814-459-8066. Email: aim@erie.net. Web: www.aim-usa.org. Sr. Susan Doubet, O.S.B., Exec. Dir. AIM is an organization founded to assist Benedictine and Cistercian monasteries in the Third World.

Star Foundation, c/o St. Mark Catholic Center, 429 E. Grandview Blvd., P.O. Box 10397, 16514-0397. Tel: 814-824-1240; Fax: 814-824-1128. Email: nsmith@eriercd.org. Ned Smith, Coord.

St. Thomas More Society, 429 E. Grandview Blvd., 16514.

FRENCHVILLE. *Anawim Community of Frenchville*, P.O. Box 186, 16836. Tel: 814-263-4518; Fax: 814-263-7106. Email: anawim@pennswoods.net. Web: www.ypwc.org. Sr. Therese Dush, C.A., Dir.

ST. MARYS. *Opportunity for Parochial Education Network (OPEN)*, 575 Charles St., 15857. Tel: 814-834-6181. Richard J. Reuscher, Trustee.

RELIGIOUS INSTITUTES OF MEN REPRESENTED IN THE DIOCESE

For further details refer to the corresponding bracketed number in the Religious Institutes of Men or Women section.

[0200]—*Benedictine Monks (St. Vincent's Archabbey)*—O.S.B.
[0520]—*Franciscan Friars*—O.F.M.
[0290]—*Oblates of St. Francis de Sales*
[0610]—*Priests of the Congregation of Holy Cross*—C.S.C.

RELIGIOUS INSTITUTES OF WOMEN REPRESENTED IN THE DIOCESE

[0230]—*Benedictine Sisters of Elk Co.*—O.S.B
[0160]—*Benedictine Sisters of Erie*—O.S.B.
[]—*Congregation of Divine Providence* (Pittsburgh)—C.D.P.
[]—*Congregation of the Divine Spirit*—C.D.S.
[]—*Congregation of the Sisters of St. Joseph* Pittsburgh—C.S.J.
[0420]—*Discalced Carmelite Nuns*—O.C.D.
[1840]—*Gray Nuns of the Sacred Heart*—G.N.S.H.
[2720]—*Mission Helpers of the Sacred Heart*—M.H.S.H.
[2820]—*Missionary Sisters of Our Lady of Africa*—M.S.O.L.A.
[3070]—*North American Union of Sisters of Our Lady of Charity*—N.A.U.-O.L
[1690]—*School Sisters of the Third Order of St. Francis*—C.S.F.
[0507]—*Sisters of Charity of Seton Hill, Greenburg, PA*—S.C.
[2570]—*Sisters of Mercy*—R.S.M.
[1620]—*Sisters of St. Francis of Millvale, PA*—O.S.F.
[3830]—*Sisters of St. Joseph*—S.S.J.
[2110]—*Sisters of the Humility of Mary*—H.M.

DIOCESAN CEMETERIES

ERIE. *Queen of Peace*
Trinity, Calvary & Gate of Heaven

NECROLOGY

† Cohan, Rev. Msgr. Robert W., Erie, PA St. James—Died May 30, 2003
† Donovan, Rev. Msgr. Edmund J., (Retired)—Died Oct. 25, 2003
† Feeney, Rev. Msgr. Edward J., Erie, PA Holy Family—Died May 4, 2003
† Reszkowski, Rev. Msgr. Joseph V., (Retired)—Died Sept. 4, 2003
† Ritchie, Rev. Msgr. G. Carlton, (Retired)—Died April 25, 2003
† Pisoni, Otto B., (Retired)
† Wilson, Edward M., (Retired)—Died Nov. 19, 2003

Diocese of Evansville

(Dioecesis Evansvicensis)

Most Reverend

GERALD ANDREW GETTELFINGER

Bishop of Evansville; ordained May 7, 1961; appointed Fourth Bishop of Evansville March 11, 1989; ordained and installed April 11, 1989 *Res.: 3980 Woodcastle, Evansville, IN 47711. Catholic Center*, 4200 N. Kentucky Ave., P.O. Box 4169, Evansville, IN 47724-0169. Fax: 812-436-7450.

Catholic Center: 4200 N. Kentucky Ave., P.O. Box 4169, Evansville, IN 47724-0169. Tel: 812-424-5536; Fax: 812-421-1334.

Web: www.evansville-diocese.org

ESTABLISHED NOVEMBER 11, 1944.

Square Miles 5,010.

Comprises twelve Counties in the Southwestern part of Indiana: Daviess, Dubois, Gibson, Greene, Knox, Martin, Pike, Posey, Spencer (except township of Harrison), Sullivan, Vanderburgh, Warrick.

The Diocese of Evansville was established by decree of Pope Pius XII, November 11, 1944, and the See was fixed at Evansville.

Legal Title: For legal titles of parishes and diocesan institutions, consult the Chancery.

STATISTICAL OVERVIEW

Personnel	
Bishop	1
Priests: Diocesan Active in Diocese	58
Priests: Diocesan Active Outside Diocese	2
Priests: Retired, Sick or Absent	28
Number of Diocesan Priests	88
Religious Priests in Diocese	6
Total Priests in Diocese	94
Ordinations:	
Transitional Deacons	3
Permanent Deacons	1
Permanent Deacons in Diocese	21
Total Brothers	2
Total Sisters	277
Parishes	
Parishes	70
With Resident Pastor:	
Resident Diocesan Priests	47
Resident Religious Priests	3
Without Resident Pastor:	
Administered by Priests	18
Administered by Deacons	1
Administered by Religious Women	1
Pastoral Centers	5
Professional Ministry Personnel:	
Sisters	18
Lay Ministers	55
Welfare	
Catholic Hospitals	2
Total Assisted	448,620
Health Care Centers	1
Total Assisted	58
Homes for the Aged	2
Total Assisted	105
Day Care Centers	1
Total Assisted	272
Special Centers for Social Services	9
Total Assisted	134,000
Educational	
Diocesan Students in Other Seminaries	11
Total Seminarians	11
High Schools, Diocesan and Parish	4
Total Students	1,553
Elementary Schools, Diocesan and Parish	24
Total Students	6,376
Non-residential Schools for the Disabled	1
Total Students	37
Catechesis/Religious Education:	
High School Students	2,259
Elementary Students	6,386
Total Students under Catholic Instruction	16,622
Teachers in the Diocese:	
Priests	1
Brothers	2
Sisters	14
Lay Teachers	461
Vital Statistics	
Receptions into the Church:	
Infant Baptism Totals	1,267
Adult Baptism Totals	115
Received into Full Communion	145
First Communions	1,393
Confirmations	860
Marriages:	
Catholic	317
Interfaith	231
Total Marriages	548
Deaths	849
Total Catholic Population	89,015
Total Population	491,956

Former Bishops—Most Revs. HENRY JOSEPH GRIMMELSMAN, D.D. (Retired), appt. Nov. 11, 1944; consecrated Dec. 21, 1944; retired and named Titular Bishop of Tabla Oct. 20, 1965; died June 26, 1972; PAUL F. LEIBOLD, D.D., appt. Titular Bishop of Trebenna and Auxiliary of Cincinnati April 10, 1958; consecrated June 17, 1958; appt. to Evansville April 6, 1966; translated to Archbishop of Cincinnati July 23, 1969;; died June 1, 1972; FRANCIS R. SHEA (Retired), appt. Dec. 10, 1969; retired April 11, 1989; died Aug. 18, 1994.

Catholic Center—4200 N. Kentucky Ave., P.O. Box 4169, Evansville, 47724-0169. Tel: 812-424-5536; Fax: 812-421-1334. Office Hours: Mon.-Thurs. 8-5, Fri. 8-4:30

Vicar General—Rev. Msgr. KENNETH R. KNAPP, A.C.S.W., M.S.

Chancellor—JUDITH A. NEFF.

Secretary to the Bishop—DEANNA RUSTON.

Treasurer—ROBERT J. COX.

Associate Treasurer—SCOTT BRITT.

Assistant Treasurer—PHYLLIS HIGGINS.

Diocesan Tribunal—P.O. Box 4169, Evansville, 47724-0169.

Judicial Vicar—Rev. J. KENNETH WALKER, J.C.L., B.A., M.Div., M.C.L.

Defenders of the Bond—Rev. Msgr. CLINTON F. HIRSCH, J.C.L. (Retired); Revs. JAMES ENDRESS, S.T.L., M.S., M.A.; JOSEPH ERBACHER.

Judges—Revs. RAYMOND L. KUPER; STEPHEN P. LINTZENICH; MARY GEN BLITTSCHAU, M.A., M.C.L., J.C.L.; Rev. Msgr. CHARLES J. KOCH, S.T.L., J.C.L.

Advocates—Revs. JOHN H. SCHIPP; MICHAEL MADDEN.

Secretary and Notary—CHARLEEN HEBERT.

Archivist—JUDITH A. NEFF.

Diocesan Consultors—Rev. Msgr. KENNETH R. KNAPP, A.C.S.W., M.S.; Revs. J. KENNETH WALKER, J.C.L., B.A., M.Div., M.C.L.; DAVID NUNNING; JOSEPH ZILIAK, S.T.L.; JAMES ENDRESS; DAVID FLECK; FRANCIS SCHROERING.

Diocesan Council of Priests—Rev. Msgr. KENNETH R. KNAPP, A.C.S.W., M.S.; Revs. J. KENNETH WALKER, J.C.L., B.A., M.Div., M.C.L.; JACK J. DURCHHOLZ; WILLIAM WARGEL; GREGORY CHAMBERLIN, O.S.B.; DAVID FLECK; JOHN BREIDENBACH; GORDON MANN; STEPHEN P. LINTZENICH; JAMES KORESSEL; JOHN SCHIPP; ANTHONY ERNST.

Personnel Board—Rev. Msgr. KENNETH KNAPP; Revs. JAMES ENDRESS; RAYMOND BRENNER; GORDON MANN; TIMOTHY TENBARGE; JOHN DAVIDSON; WILLIAM TRAYLOR.

Deans—Rev. Msgr. KENNETH R. KNAPP, A.C.S.W., M.S., Evansville, East; Revs. DAVID NUNNING, Evansville, West; DONALD ACKERMAN, Jasper; JOSEPH ZILIAK, S.T.L., Newburgh; FRANCIS SCHROERING, Princeton; ROBERT BULTMAN, Vincennes; JAMES KORESSEL, Washington.

Censors Of Books—Rev. Msgr. CHARLES J. KOCH, S.T.L., J.C.L.; Rev. JOSEPH ZILIAK, S.T.L.

Diocesan Offices And Directors

Boy Scouts—JACK THOMPSON, Chap.

Campus Ministry—CHRISTINE HOEHN, Coord.

Catholic Charities—JAMES F. COLLINS, Exec. Dir., Court Building, Ste. 603, 123 N.W. Fourth St., Evansville, 47708. Tel: 812-423-5456.

Catholic Diocese of Evansville, Inc.—Most Rev. GERALD A. GETTELFINGER.

Catholic Education Endowment, Inc. (Washington)—BONNIE GRAHAM, Pres.

Catholic Education Foundation, Inc. (Evansville)—MARGARET ANGERMEIER, Exec. Dir.

The Catholic Foundation of Southwestern Indiana, Inc.—DONNA LEADER, Exec. Dir., P.O. Box 4169, Evansville, 47724-0169.

Holy Family Catholic School Foundation, Inc.—WILFRED WEINZAPFEL, Pres., 950 Church Ave., Jasper, 47546.

Catholic Education, Office of—PHYLLIS BUSSING, Dir. Schools; DONNA HALVERSON, Asst. Dir.; RUTH SAALWEACHTER, Sec.; MARY GARRETT, Media Clerk & Sec.; STEVE BAGBEY, Safety & Security Coord.

Catholic Communication Office—PAUL LEINGANG, Dir., P.O. Box 4169, Evansville, 47724-0169.

Catholic Hospitals, Diocesan Representative—VACANT, St. Mary's Medical Center, 3700 Washington Ave., Evansville, 47750.

Catholic Relief Services—JAMES F. COLLINS, Court Building, Ste. 603, 123 N.W. Fourth St., Evansville, 47708. Tel: 812-423-5456.

Cemeteries—Rev. EUGENE SCHROEDER, Dir., 6202 W. St. Joseph Rd., Evansville, 47720. Tel: 812-963-3273.

Christian Educational Foundation of Vincennes, Inc.—MIKE RUSCH, Pres.

Continuing Education of Clergy—Rev. JAMES SAUER, P.O. Box 4169, Evansville, 47724-0169.

Cursillos in Christianity—BRUCE BONENBERGER, Lay Dir.

Deaf Ministry—Rev. HENRY KUYKENDALL, 3635 Pollack, Evansville, 47714. Tel: 812-476-4646.

Diocesan Finance Council—Ex Officio: Most Rev. GERALD A. GETTELFINGER; Rev. Msgr. KENNETH R. KNAPP, A.C.S.W., M.S.; ROBERT COX; GARY BECKMAN; ALAN HOFFMAN; CHRIS MELTON; STEVE WITTING; JAMES ROACH; DEAN HAPPE; WILLIAM KAISER.

Diocese of Evansville Retirement Trust Agreement and Plan for Priests—Office of the Bishop: 4200 N.

Kentucky Ave., P.O. Box 4169, Evansville, 47724-0169. Tel: 812-424-5536.

Ecumenism—4200 N. Kentucky Ave., P.O. Box 4169, Evansville, 47724-0169. Tel: 812-424-5536.

Evangelization, Office of—4200 N. Kentucky Ave., P.O. Box 4169, Evansville, 47724-0169. Tel: 812-424-5536.

Girl Scouts—JACK THOMPSON, Chap.

Spanish Speaking Ministry—Rev. EUGENE HEERDINK, Dir.; Sr. KAREN DURLIAT, O.S.B., Assoc. Dir., Guadalupe Center, 317 N. Washington, Huntingburg, 47542. Tel: 812-683-5212.

Propagation of the Faith and Holy Childhood Association—C. JUSTIN CLEMENTS, Dir., 4200 N. Kentucky Ave., P.O. Box 4169, Evansville, 47724-0169. Tel: 812-424-5536.

Justice and Peace— (Please refer to Catholic Charities for further information).

Legion of Mary—Rev. RAY REISING, Evansville; Deacon DONALD HAAG, Washington.

Message, The— Catholic Press of Evansville; Publisher, Most Rev. GERALD A. GETTELFINGER; PAUL LEINGANG, Editor.

Permanent Diaconate Program—Rev. JEAN VOGLER, Dir., 219 N.W. Third St., Evansville, 47708; Deacon THOMAS HOLSWORTH, Coord. Deacons, 1066 W. Tenth, Jasper, 47546.

Adult Formation/RCIA—Sr. GERALDINE HEDINGER, O.S.B., Dir.; DONNA GISH, Asst. Dir.

Rural Life Conference—Rev. JOHN BOEGLIN, Dir., Holy Family Church, 950 E. Church Ave., Jasper, 47546-3797.

St. Vincent De Paul Society—Deacons ROBERT HAYDEN, Diocesan Chap.; CHARLES SEIFERT, Spiritual Dir., Jasper District Council; Rev. ROBERT BULTMAN, Spiritual Dir., Vincennes District Council.

Sarto Retreat House—GEORGE ANNE RYDER, Dir.; JULIE YOUNG, Sec.

Secretariat for Charismatic Renewal—Rev. WILLIAM TRAYLOR.

Stewardship/Development, Office of—C. JUSTIN CLEMENTS, Dir., P.O. Box 4169, Evansville, 47724-0169. Tel: 812-424-5536.

Victim Assistance Coordinator—MARTHA HALTERMAN. Tel: 812-423-5456. Email: mhalterman@evansville-diocese.org.

Vocation Office—Rev. BERNARD ETIENNE, Vocation Dir., P.O. Box 4169, Evansville, 47724-0169. Tel: 812-424-5536.

Worship—VACANT, 4200 N. Kentucky, P.O. Box 4169, Evansville, 47724-0169. Tel: 812-424-5536.

Youth and Young Adult Ministry—MICHAEL H. EPPLER, Dir., 4200 N. Kentucky, P.O. Box 4169, Evansville, 47724-0169. Tel: 812-424-5536.

CLERGY, PARISHES, MISSIONS AND PAROCHIAL SCHOOLS

CITY OF EVANSVILLE
(VANDERBURGH COUNTY)

1—ST. BENEDICT CATHEDRAL, Rev. Gregory D. Chamberlin, O.S.B.; Sr. Mary Agnes Sermersheim, Pastoral Assoc.
Parish Center—1328 Lincoln Ave., 47714-1598. Tel: 812-425-3369; Fax: 812-425-3378.
Res.: 1312 Lincoln Ave., 47714.
School—530 S. Harlan Ave., 47714-1598. Tel: 812-425-4596. Sisters of St. Benedict 2; Lay Teachers 23; Students 357.
Catechesis/Religious Program—Marty Horning, D.R.E. Students 94.

2—ST. AGNES, [CEM] Rev. David H. Nunning; Deacon Richard Grannan.
Res.: 1600 Glendale Ave., 47712. Tel: 812-425-9140; Fax: 812-423-4240.
School—Westside Catholic Consolidated, (Grades 1-4) Lay Teachers 10; Students 110.
Catechesis/Religious Program—Mary Jo Werner, D.R.E. Students 21.

3—ST. ANTHONY, Rev. John Davidson; Sisters Joan Miller, O.S.F., Pastoral Assoc.; Jackie Kissel, O.S.B., Pastoral Assoc.
Res.: 704 First Ave., 47710. Tel: 812-423-5209; Fax: 812-424-5498.
Catechesis/Religious Program—Sr. Jackie Kissel, O.S.B., D.R.E. Students 55.

4—ASSUMPTION CATHEDRAL, Closed., For inquiries for parish records contact Holy Trinity.

5—ST. BONIFACE, Rev. Jack Durchholz; Deacon Richard Preske.
Res.: 418 N. Wabash Ave., 47712. Tel: 812-425-8375; Fax: 812-401-7690.
School—Westside Catholic Consolidated, (Grades 5-8), 2031 W. Michigan St., 47712. Serves St Agnes, St. Boniface and Sacred Heart Parishes. Lay Teachers 9; Students 109.

6—CHRIST THE KING, Rev. Msgr. Kenneth R. Knapp, A.C.S.W., M.S.; Deacon Francis Hillenbrand.
Res.: 3109 Bayard Park Dr., 47714-2602. Tel: 812-476-3061; Fax: 812-476-3062.
School—Lay Teachers 16; Students 229.
Catechesis/Religious Program—Robert Henson, D.R.E. Students 8.

7—CORPUS CHRISTI, Rev. James Blessinger.
Res.: 5528 Hogue Rd., 47712-3218. Tel: 812-422-2027; Fax: 812-421-8316.
School—Lay Teachers 14; Students 223.
Catechesis/Religious Program—Kathryn Curtis, D.R.E. Students 45.

8—GOOD SHEPHERD, Rev. Joseph Kane; Deacons Edward Wilkerson; Cyril Will.
Res.: 2301 N. Stockwell, 47715. Tel: 812-477-5405; Fax: 812-469-2907.
School—Lay Teachers 24; Students 381.
Catechesis/Religious Program—Deacon Ed Wilkerson, D.R.E. Students 45.

9—HOLY REDEEMER, Revs. Ronald Zgunda; Paul Anthony Ferguson; Deacon Robert Hayden.
Res.: 918-A W. Mill Rd., 47710. Tel: 812-424-8344; Fax: 812-424-7166.
School—Lay Teachers 23; Students 334.
Catechesis/Religious Program—Doug Rasler, D.R.E. Students 126.

10—HOLY ROSARY, Rev. Raymond L Kuper; Rev. Msgr. Maurilius Bilskie, Pastor Emeritus; Rev. Attila Frohlich.
Res.: 1301 S. Green River Rd., 47715. Tel: 812-477-8923; Fax: 812-471-7226.
School—Lay Teachers 23; Students 438.
Catechesis/Religious Program—Carol Ann Gaddis, D.R.E. Students 58.

11—HOLY SPIRIT, Rev. Henry Kuykendall; Mary Ruth Krack, Pastoral Assoc.
Church: 1800 S. Lodge Ave., 47714. Tel: 812-477-1738; Fax: 812-469-6633.
School—Lay Teachers 13; Students 184.
Catechesis/Religious Program—Leah Parker, D.R.E. Students 18.
Convent—Sisters of St. Benedict Sisters 3.

12—HOLY TRINITY, Revs. Jean Vogler; Gregory D. Chamberlin, O.S.B., Admin.
219 N.W. Third St., 47708-1233. Tel: 812-422-5150.

13—ST. JOHN THE APOSTLE, Sr. Jane Nesmith, S.B.S., Pastoral Life Coord.; Rev. Stephen P. Lintzenich, Pastoral Moderator.
Church: 617 Bellemeade Ave., 47713-1707. Tel: 812-424-9261; Fax: 812-424-5933.
Catechesis/Religious Program—Sr. Jane Nesmith, S.B.S., D.R.E. Students 17.

14—ST. JOHN THE EVANGELIST, [CEM] Rev. Robert A. Deig; Robert Vollmer, Pastoral Assoc.; Deacon Cyril Will.
Church: 5301 Daylight Dr., 47725-7636. Tel: 812-867-3718.
Res.: 4020 E. Boonville-New Harmony Rd., 47725. Tel: 812-867-3987.
Catechesis/Religious Program—Bob Vollmer, D.R.E. Students 126.

15—ST. JOSEPH, Rev. William Traylor.
Office—607 E. Iowa, 47711.
Res.: 600 E. Virginia St., 47711. Tel: 812-422-5668; Fax: 812-425-2730.
Catechesis/Religious Program—Sr. Jennifer Miller, O.S.B., D.R.E. Students 29.

16—ST. JOSEPH, [CEM] Rev. Eugene A. Schroeder.
Res.: 5202 W. St. Joseph Rd., 47720. Tel: 812-963-3273; Fax: 812-963-6254.
School—Sisters 2; Lay Teachers 10; Students 162.
Catechesis/Religious Program—Sharon Vogler, D.R.E. Students 49.
Convent—Sisters of St. Benedict Sisters 4.

17—ST. MARY, Rev. Stephen P. Lintzenich; Sisters Jenny Schmitt, O.S.B., Pastoral Assoc.; Barbara L. Schmitz, O.S.B., Pastoral Assoc.; Deacon James Cavera.
Parish Office—613 Cherry St., 47713.
Res.: 609 Cherry St., 47713. Tel: 812-425-1577; Fax: 812-426-1416.
Catechesis/Religious Program—Ann Cavera, D.R.E. Students 54.

18—NATIVITY, Rev. Henry Kuykendall.
Res.: 3635 Pollack, 47714. Tel: 812-476-7186; Fax: 812-476-7956.
Catholic Ministry of the Deaf Office—Tel: 812-476-4646.
Catechesis/Religious Program—Leah Parker, D.R.E. Students 44.

19—RESURRECTION, Rev. Philip Kreilein; Sr. Jolinda Naas, O.S.B., Pastoral Assoc.; Deacon Joseph Schapker.
Res.: 5301 New Harmony Rd., 47720-1774. Tel: 812-963-3121; Fax: 812-963-1141
School—Sisters of St. Benedict 2; Lay Teachers 21; Students 370.
Catechesis/Religious Program—Sr. Jolinda Naas, O.S.B., D.R.E. Students 83.
Convent—Sisters of St. St. Benedict Sisters 3.

20—SACRED HEART, Rev. David Nunning.
Office: 2701 W. Franklin St., 47712. Tel: 812-425-5505; Fax: 812-425-8443.
School—Westside Catholic Consolidated, (Grades PreK-K) Lay Teachers 9; Students 130.
Catechesis/Religious Program—Mary Kae Lehman, D.R.E. Students 25.

21—ST. THERESA, Rev. William Traylor; Sr. Annette Langenderfer, O.S.F., Pastoral Assoc.
Mailing Address: 600 Herndon Dr., 47711-3830.
Res.: Tel: 812-422-8211; Fax: 812-422-5345.
School—Lay Teachers 12; Students 216.
Catechesis/Religious Program—Students 34.
Convent—Sisters of St. Benedict Sisters 4.

22—ST. WENDEL, [CEM] Rev. Gordon Mann.
Parish Office—10542 W. Boonville-New Harmony Rd., 47720-7901. Tel: 812-963-3733; Fax: 812-963-3835.
School—Lay Teachers 11; Students 166.
Catechesis/Religious Program—Elaine Michl, D.R.E. Students 28.
Convent—Sisters of St. Francis Sisters 2.

OUTSIDE CITY OF EVANSVILLE

BICKNELL, KNOX CO., ST. PHILIP NERI, Rev. Frank G. Renner.
Res.: 605 W. Fourth St., 47512. Tel: 812-735-4069.
Catechesis/Religious Program—Carol Wampler, D.R.E. Students 39.

BLOOMFIELD, GREENE CO., HOLY NAME, [CEM] Rev. Michael Madden.
Res.: 700 Lincoln Dr., 47424-0124. Tel: 812-384-8415.
Catechesis/Religious Program—Lora Burris, D.R.E. Students 52.

BOONVILLE, WARRICK CO., ST. CLEMENT, Rev. Lowell Will; Deacon Tom Lambert.
Res.: 422 E. Sycamore, 47601. Tel: 812-897-4653; Fax: 812-897-4653.
Catechesis/Religious Program—Sr. Jayn Lein, O.S.B., D.R.E. Students 130.

CANNELBURG, DAVIESS CO., ALL SAINTS, Attended by, St. Peter, Montgomery. Rev. James Koressel.
Tel: 812-486-3149.
Catechesis/Religious Program— (Twinned with St. Peter Montgomery) Mary Sue Wiscaver, D.R.E.; Karen Kane, D.R.E. Students 118.

CELESTINE, DUBOIS CO., ST. PETER CELESTINE, [CEM] Rev. Wilfred Englert; Sr. Brenda Engleman, O.S.B., Pastoral Assoc.
Res.: 6864 E. State Rd. 164, P.O. Box 1, 47521-0001. Tel: 812-634-1875; Fax: 812-634-1875.
Catechesis/Religious Program—Glenda Burke, D.R.E. Students 286.

CHRISNEY, SPENCER CO., ST. MARTIN, [CEM] Rev. Edward Schnur; Mary Jo Ressel, Pastoral Assoc.
Office:—58 S. Church St., 47611-0147. Tel: 812-362-7313; Fax: 812-362-7390.
Catechesis/Religious Program—Mary Jo Ressel, D.R.E. Students 43.

DALE, SPENCER CO., ST. JOSEPH, [CEM] Rev. James Sauer.
Res.: 8 E. Maple St., R.R. 1, Box 308, 47523. Tel: 812-937-2200; Fax: 812-937-4349.
Catechesis/Religious Program—Nora Weber, D.R.E. Students 109.

DUBOIS, DUBOIS CO., ST. RAPHAEL, [CEM] Rev. Wilfred Englert; Sr. Brenda Engleman, O.S.B., Pastoral Assoc.
Res.: 5564 E. St. Raphael St., 47527. Tel: 812-678-2011; Fax: 812-678-5096.
Catechesis/Religious Program—Teresa Hopf, D.R.E. Students 230.

FERDINAND, DUBOIS CO.

1—ST. FERDINAND, [CEM] Rev. William J. Wargel.
Res.: 840 Maryland, P.O. Box 156, 47532. Tel: 812-367-1212; Fax: 812-367-1066.
Spiritual Life Center—Tel: 812-367-1092.
Catechesis/Religious Program—Sheila Hurst, D.R.E. Students 616.

2—ST. HENRY, [CEM] Rev. Damian Schmelz, O.S.B.
Res.: 1311 W. 1100 S., 47532-9710. Tel: 812-367-2731.
Catechesis/Religious Program—Jeanne Rush, D.R.E. Students 119.

FORT BRANCH, GIBSON CO.

1—ST. BERNARD, [CEM] Revs. Anthony Ernst; William Deering, Pastor Emeritus; Deacon Sandy Hall.
Res.: R.R. 2, Box 115, 47648. Tel: 812-753-4568.
Catechesis/Religious Program—Rose Obert, D.R.E.; Jeanne Vieke, D.R.E. Students 68.

2—HOLY CROSS, [CEM] Rev. Anthony Ernst; Deacon Sandy Hall.
Res.: 305 E. Walnut St., 47648. Tel: 812-753-3548.
School—Sisters 2; Lay Teachers 9; Students 118.
Catechesis/Religious Program—Bonnie Wink, D.R.E. Students 127.

HAUBSTADT, GIBSON CO.

1—ST. JAMES, [CEM] Rev. Kenneth Betz.

Res.: R.R. 1, Box 280, 47639. Tel: 812-867-5175; Fax: 812-867-5589.
School—Lay Teachers 12; Students 167.
Catechesis/Religious Program—Connie Baehl, D.R.E. Students 254.
2—SS. PETER AND PAUL, [CEM] Rev. Anthony Ernst. In Res., Rev. Francis A. Schroering.
Res.: 201 Vine St., 47639. Tel: 812-768-6457; Fax: 812-768-6521.
School—(Grades PreK-5) Sisters of Benedict 1; Lay Teachers 11; Students 185.
Catechesis/Religious Program—Bonnie Wink, D.R.E. Students 201.
HUNTINGBURG, DUBOIS CO., VISITATION OF THE BLESSED VIRGIN MARY, [CEM] Rev. Pius Klein, O.S.B.
Res.: 313 Washington St., 47542. Tel: 812-683-4903; Fax: 812-683-2747.
Catechesis/Religious Program—Michelle Fischer, D.R.E. Students 476.
IRELAND, DUBOIS CO., ANNUNCIATION OF THE BLESSED VIRGIN MARY, [CEM], (St. Mary's) Rev. Donald K. Ackerman.
Res.: P.O. Box 67, 47545. Tel: 812-482-7041; Fax: 812-482-3699.
Catechesis/Religious Program—Marilyn Mundy, D.R.E. Students 506.
JASONVILLE, GREENE CO., ST. JOAN OF ARC, Attended by, St. Mary, Sullivan, Tel: 812-268-4088.
JASPER, DUBOIS CO.
1—HOLY FAMILY, [JC] Rev. John Boeglin; Deacon Charles Seifert.
Res.: 950 E. Church Ave., 47546-3797. Tel: 812-482-3076; Fax: 812-634-6998.
School—Sisters of St. Benedict 1; Lay Teachers 22; Students 323.
Catechesis/Religious Program—Donna Mundy, D.R.E. Students 118.
Convent—Sisters of St. Benedict Sisters 2.
2—ST. JOSEPH, [JC] Revs. Raymond Brenner; Claude Thomas Burns.
Res.: 1020 Kundek St., 47546. Tel: 812-482-1805; Fax: 812-482-1814.
Catechesis/Religious Program—Phil Coit, D.R.E. Students 637.
3—PRECIOUS BLOOD, [JC] Rev. Joseph Erbacher; Sr. Betty Koressel, S.P., Pastoral Assoc.
Res.: 1517 Gregory Ln., 47546.
Church: 1385 W. Sixth St., 47546. Tel: 812-482-3589; Fax: 812-482-3589.
School—(Grades PreK-5) Lay Teachers 15; Students 252.
Catechesis/Religious Program—Pam Schneider, D.R.E. Students 377.
Convent—Sisters of Providence Sisters 2.
LINTON, GREENE CO., ST. PETER, [CEM] Rev. Hilary F. Vieck.
Res.: 489 E St. N.E., 47441. Tel: 812-847-7821; Fax: 812-847-8892.
Catechesis/Religious Program—Deborah Wright, D.R.E. Students 71.
LOOGOOTEE, MARTIN CO.
1—ST. JOHN, [CEM] Rev. Thomas Kessler.
Office: 408 Church St., 47553. Tel: 812-295-2225; Fax: 812-295-2031.
Catechesis/Religious Program—Alice Weisheit, D.R.E. Students 280.
2—ST. MARTIN'S, [CEM] Rev. Thomas Kessler.
Mailing Address: 408 Church St., 47553. Tel: 812-295-2225; Fax: 812-295-3445.
Catechesis/Religious Program—Roberta Burch, D.R.E.; Dennis Craney, D.R.E. Students 28.
MARIAH HILL, SPENCER CO., MARY, HELP OF CHRISTIANS, [CEM] Rev. Paul Roos.
Church: P.O. Box 170, 47556. Tel: 812-937-4326.
Catechesis/Religious Program—Students 139.
MONTGOMERY, DAVIESS CO., ST. PETER, [CEM] Rev. James Koressel.
Res.: P.O. Box 10, 47558. Tel: 812-486-3149; Fax: 812-486-2571.
Catechesis/Religious Program— (Twinned with All Saints Cannelburg) Mary Sue Wiscaver, D.R.E.; Karen Kane, D.R.E. Students 118.
Chapel—Corning, St. Patrick's
MOUNT VERNON, POSEY CO.
1—ST. MATTHEW, [CEM] Rev. Kenneth Steckler.
Res.: 421 Mulberry St., 47620. Tel: 812-838-2535.
School—Sisters 1; Lay Teachers 9; Students 76.
Catechesis/Religious Program—Irene Evans, D.R.E. Students 120.
Convent—
2—ST. PHILIP'S, [CEM] Rev. David Fleck.
Res.: 3500 St. Philip Rd. S., Mt. Vernon, 47620. Tel: 812-985-2275; Fax: 812-985-2590.
School—Lay Teachers 15; Students 285.
Catechesis/Religious Program—Students 66.
NEW BOSTON, SPENCER CO., ST. JOHN CHRYSOSTOM, [CEM] Rev. Paul Roos.
Mailing Address: R.R. 1, Box 156, Evanston, 47531. Tel: 812-357-6531.
Catechesis/Religious Program—Sharon Hedinger, D.R.E. Students 16.
NEW HARMONY, POSEY CO., HOLY ANGELS, Rev. William Dietsch; Sr. Leta Zeller, O.S.B., Pastoral Assoc.
Mailing Address: 423 South St., P.O. Box 548, 47631. Tel: 812-682-4224.
Catechesis/Religious Program—Sr. Leta Zeller, O.S.B., D.R.E. Students 28.
NEWBURGH, WARRICK CO., ST. JOHN THE BAPTIST, [CEM] Revs. Joseph L. Ziliak; John Breidenbach; Sr. Jeanne Voges, O.S.B., Pastoral Assoc.; Lynda Provence, Pastoral Assoc.; Marty Brown, Pastoral Assoc.; Deacon Joseph Seibert.
Res.: 625 Frame Rd., 47630. Tel: 812-853-6181; Fax: 812-853-6182.
School—Lay Teachers 22; Students 492.
Catechesis/Religious Program—Connie Schnapf, D.R.E.; Cindy Shoulders, D.R.E. Students 337.
OAKLAND CITY, GIBSON CO., BLESSED SACRAMENT, Rev. Bernard Etienne.
Res.: Rte. 1, Box 72-A, 47660. Tel: 812-749-4474.
Catechesis/Religious Program—Doris Stolz, D.R.E.; Lynn Hook, D.R.E. Students 36.
PETERSBURG, PIKE CO., SS. PETER AND PAUL, Rev. Edward Schneider; Deacon Donald Haag.
Res.: 711 Walnut St., 47567. Tel: 812-354-6942.
Catechesis/Religious Program—Sandy Ficklin, D.R.E. Students 34.
POSEYVILLE, POSEY CO., ST. FRANCIS XAVIER, [CEM] Rev. William Dietsch; Sr. Leta Zeller, O.S.B., Pastoral Assoc.
Res.: 10 N. St. Francis Ave., 47633. Tel: 812-874-2258; Fax: 812-874-2639.
Catechesis/Religious Program—Sr. Leta Zeller, O.S.B., D.R.E. Students 171.
PRINCETON, GIBSON CO., ST. JOSEPH, [CEM] Rev. Bernard Etienne.
Res.: 410 S. Race St., 47670. Tel: 812-385-2617; Fax: 812-385-2603.
School—Lay Teachers 10; Students 160.
Catechesis/Religious Program—Andrea Gunter, D.R.E. Students 95.
RED BRUSH, WARRICK CO., ST. RUPERT, [CEM] Rev. Sylvester Loehrlein.
Church: 1244 Red Brush Rd., Newburgh, 47630. Tel: 812-853-3040.
Catechesis/Religious Program—Robert Hildenbrand, D.R.E. Students 28.
ROCKPORT, SPENCER CO., ST. BERNARD, [CEM] Rev. Edward C. Schnur; Mary Jo Ressel, Pastoral Assoc.
Res.: 547 Elm St., 47635. Tel: 812-649-4811; Fax: 812-649-4176.
School—Sisters of St. Benedict 1; Lay Teachers 9; Students 177.
ST. ANTHONY, DUBOIS CO., ST. ANTHONY, [CEM] Rev. Timothy Tenbarge.
Res.: 4444 S. Ohio St., P.O. Box 98, 47575-0098. Tel: 812-326-2777; Fax: 812-326-9028.
Catechesis/Religious Program—Janie Kempf, D.R.E. Students 263.
ST. JOSEPH, MARTIN CO., ST. JOSEPH'S, [CEM] Rev. Thomas Kessler.
Mailing Address: 408 Church St., Loogootee, 47553. Tel: 812-295-2225.
Catechesis/Religious Program—Peggy Padgett, D.R.E. Students 40.
Chapel—Barr Township, St. Mary
SANTA CLAUS, SPENCER CO., ST. NICHOLAS, Rev. James Sauer.
Office—181 Balthazar, P.O. Box 351, 47579. Tel: 812-937-2380; Fax: 812-937-2385.
Catechesis/Religious Program—Michele Paulin, D.R.E. Students 140.
SCHNELLVILLE, DUBOIS CO., SACRED HEART, [CEM] Rev. Ralph Schipp.
Res.: 2504 Walnut St., 47580. Tel: 812-389-2535.
Catechesis/Religious Program—Bernadette Heeke, D.R.E. Students 129.
SHOALS, MARTIN CO., ST. MARY'S, [CEM] Attended by, St. John, Loogootee, Tel: 812-295-2225. Rev. Thomas Kessler.
Catechesis/Religious Program—Alice Boyd, D.R.E. Students 26.
SULLIVAN, SULLIVAN CO., ST. MARY, Rev. Eugene Schmitt.
Res.: 105 E. Jackson St., P.O. Box 506, 47882. Tel: 812-268-4088.
Catechesis/Religious Program—Students 63.
VINCENNES, KNOX CO.
1—BASILICA OF ST. FRANCIS XAVIER, [JC] Rev. John H. Schipp.
Res.: 205 Church St., 47591. Tel: 812-882-5638; Fax: 812-882-4042.
School—Vincennes Schools Consolidated See St. John the Baptist for details.
Catechesis/Religious Program—Students 53.
2—ST. JOHN THE BAPTIST, [JC] Rev. Robert Bultman.
Res.: 803 Main St., 47591. Tel: 812-882-1762; Fax: 812-886-9151.
Parish Center—828 Vigo St., 47591.
School—Vincennes Schools Consolidated Lay Teachers 16; Students 313.
Catechesis/Religious Program—Lynn Carie, D.R.E. Students 128.
3—SACRED HEART, [JC] Rev. Joseph M. Swartz.
Res.: 2004 N. Second St., 47591. Tel: 812-882-8382; Fax: 812-886-4676.
School—Vincennes Schools Consolidated See St. John the Baptist for details.
Catechesis/Religious Program—Lucille Pierpont, D.R.E. Students 73.
4—ST. THOMAS THE APOSTLE, [CEM] Rev. Robert Bultman, Pastoral Moderator; Deacon Joseph Sturgis, Pastoral Life Coord.
Res.: 6268 S. St. Thomas Rd., 47591. Tel: 812-882-2478.
Catechesis/Religious Program—Deacon Joe Sturgis, D.R.E. Students 62.
5—ST. VINCENT DE PAUL, [CEM] Rev. Albert J. Scheller.
Res.: 1837 S. Hart St. Rd., 47591. Tel: 812-882-8968.
Catechesis/Religious Program—Pat West, D.R.E. Students 20.
WASHINGTON, DAVIESS CO.
1—IMMACULATE CONCEPTION, [JC] Rev. David A. Martin; Yvonne Evans, Pastoral Assoc.; Deanna Youngs, Pastoral Assoc.
Res.: 114 W. Van Trees St., 47501. Tel: 812-254-3187; Fax: 812-257-1133.
School—Elementary & Middle - Washington Catholic Interparochial Schools See St. Simon Parish for details.
High School—Washington Catholic Interparochial Schools See High Schools, Diocesan under Institutions Located in the Diocese for details.
Catechesis/Religious Program—Mary Smith, D.R.E. (Combined with St. Simon) 80.
2—ST. SIMON, [JC] Rev. David A. Martin; Yvonne Evans, Pastoral Assoc.; Deanna Youngs, Pastoral Assoc.
Res.: 315 N.E. Third St., 47501. Tel: 812-254-2883; Fax: 812-254-2884.
School—310 N.E. Second St., 47501. Dennis Bradley, M.S., Prin. Schools Operated jointly by St. Mary & St. Simon Parishes. Washington Catholic Interparochial Schools Elementary. Lay Teachers 14; Students 266; Sisters of St. Benedict 1.
School—Washington Catholic Interparochial Schools Middle, (Grades 6-8), 200 W. Main St., 47501. Sisters 1; Lay Teachers 8; Students 81.
High School— See High Schools, Diocesan under Institutions Located in the Diocese for details.
Catechesis/Religious Program— (Twinned with Immaculate Conception) Mary Smith, D.R.E. Students 80.

Special Assignment:
Rev. Msgrs.—
Knapp, Kenneth R., A.C.S.W., M.S., Vicar Gen., 3109 Bayard Pk. Dr., 47714.
Koch, Charles J., S.T.L., J.C.L., P.O. Box 4169, 47724-0169.
Revs.—
Endress, James R., 600 Cullen Ave., Apt. 510, 47715.
Etienne, Bernard, 410 Race St., Princeton, 47670.
Herr, Kenneth, Faculty Residence, 1500 Lincoln Ave., 47714.
Nemergut, Robert S., P.O. Box 432, Carlisle, 47838.
Sauer, James, R.R. 1, Box 308, Dale, 47523.
Steckler, Kenneth, 421 Mulberry, Mount Vernon, 47620.
Walker, J. Kenneth, J.C.L., B.A., M.Div., M.C.L., Judicial Vicar, P.O. Box 4169, 47724-0169.

On Duty Outside the Diocese:
Revs.—
Kissel, Anthony, 14235 21st St., Dade City, FL 33523.
Kress, Robert, 2845 Hikes Ln., Apt. 102, Louisville, KY 40218.

On Leave of Absence:
Revs.—
Lamkin, Donald
Verkamp, Bernard J.

Retired:
Rev. Msgrs.—
Bilskie, Maurilius, 1211 Spring, 47714.
Hirsch, Clinton F., J.C.L., Villa Maria, 1640 Lincoln Ave., Apt. 102, 47714.
Shetler, Carl A., 407 Rumbach Ave., Jasper, 47546.
Revs.—
Brune, James, Villa Maria, 1640 Lincoln Ave., Apt. 101, 47714.
Busch, August, 5221 New Harmony Rd., 47720.
Deering, William, St. Bernard, R.R. 2, Box 115, Fort Branch, 47648.
Dick, Firmus, 3203 E. 1160S, Ferdinand, 47532.
Dilger, Donald, 6621 Smith Diamond Rd., 47712.

Egloff, Adolph, 2017 N. Second St., Vincennes, 47591.
Emge, John P., St. John's Home, 1236 Lincoln Ave., 47714.
Foster, Patrick, 962 Forder Crossing Dr., St. Louis, MO 63129.
Graehler, Kenneth, 104 Southside Ave., 47501.
Hoffman, Richard L., 5601 Flagstone Dr., 47711.
Hut, Clemens, 1711 E. Grandview, Mesa, AZ 85203.
Lefler, John, 7788 Taylorville Rd., Tennyson, 47637.
Lutz, Bernard, 200 Hill Dr., St. Meinrad, 47577.
O'Brien, Christopher, 3904 Park Blvd., Silver Hill, MD 20746.
Reising, Raymond, 7206 Bayard Park Dr., 47715.
Rogers, James, 801 N. Shortridge Rd., Apt. F4, Indianapolis, 46219.
Rohleder, Earl, 2 Corte Patricia, Santa Fe, NM 87508.
Schroering Raymond A., Villa Maria, 1640 Lincoln Ave., Apt. 201, 47714.
Spaulding, Donald E., 112 W. Third St., Cannelburg, 47519.
Tempel, Theodore, 1236 Lincoln Ave., 47714.
Wannemuehler, Robert, 1611 S. Bosse, 47712.

Permanent Deacons:
Blankenberger, Joseph V., (Retired)
Cavera, James, St. Mary Parish, Evansville
Dow, Lancaster, Jr., Unassigned
Franklin, David, Unassigned
Grannan, Richard, St. Agnes Parish, Evansville
Haag, Donald, SS. Peter & Paul Parish, Petersburg
Hall, Sandy, St. Bernard Parish & Holy Cross, Fort Branch
Hayden, Robert, Holy Redeemer, Evansville
Hillenbrand, Francis, Christ the King, Evansville
Holsworth, Thomas, Permanent Deacon Coord.
Jones, Michael R., Martin County Catholic Churches
Lambert, Thomas, St. Clement, Boonville
Morris, Michael, Prison Ministry
Preske, Richard, (Retired)
Schapker, Joseph, Resurrection Parish, Evansville
Seibert, Joseph S., St. John, Newburgh
Seifert, Charles, Holy Family Parish, Jasper
Sturgis, Joseph V., St. Thomas Parish, Vincennes
Thurgood, Robert, (Retired)
Wilkerson, Edward, Good Shepherd, Evansville
Will, Cyril, Good Shepherd, Evansville; St. John, Daylight

INSTITUTIONS LOCATED IN THE DIOCESE

[A] HIGH SCHOOLS, DIOCESAN

EVANSVILLE. *Mater Dei High School*, 1300 Harmony Way, 47712. Tel: 812-426-2258; Fax: 812-421-5717. Web: www.materdeiwildcats.com. Marie Williams, Prin.; Rev. Kenneth Steckler, Chap. Priests 1; Sisters 2; Lay Teachers 39; Students 571.

Reitz Memorial High School, 1500 Lincoln Ave., 47714. Tel: 812-476-4973; Fax: 812-474-2942. Web: www.memorial.evansville.net. Mr. Gerry Adams, M.A., Ed.S., Prin.; Del Schiavone, Asst. Prin., Student Svcs.; Rev. Kenneth Herr, Chap.; Mrs. Lisa Popham, Asst. Prin., Curriculum & Instruction. Brothers 2; Clergy 2; Lay Teachers 52; Students 824.

VINCENNES. *Jean Francois Rivet High School* (Vincennes Area) , 210 Barnett St., 47591. Tel: 812-882-6215; Fax: 812-886-1939. Web: www.rivet.wvc.net. Mary Traylor, Prin. Lay Teachers 14; Students 141.

WASHINGTON. *Washington Catholic Interparochial Schools*, 201 N.E. Second St., 47501. Tel: 812-254-2050; Fax: 812-254-2050. Web: www.dmrtc.net/~wchsb/index.html. Chad Ballengee, Prin.; Dennis Bradley, M.S., Supt. Sisters 1; Lay Teachers 12; Students 92.

[B] SCHOOLS OF SPECIAL EDUCATION

EVANSVILLE. *Marian Day School*, 700 Herndon Dr., 47711. Tel: 812-422-5346; Fax: 812-422-5345. Web: www.mariandayschool.com. Bev Williamson, Dir. Lay Teachers 3; Students 37.

[C] DAY CARE CENTERS

EVANSVILLE. *St. Vincent Day Care Center*, 730 W. Delaware, 47710. Tel: 812-424-4780. Sr. Catherine Marie Lowe, D.C., Admin. Daughters of Charity of St. Vincent de Paul 3; Children 272.

[D] GENERAL HOSPITALS

EVANSVILLE. *St. Mary's Medical Center of Evansville, Inc.*, 3700 Washington Ave., 47750. Tel: 812-485-4000; Fax: 812-485-4927. Web: www.stmarys.org. Kathleen Korbelak, Pres.; Frank Tiedemann, Pres. & CEO St. Mary's Health System; Sr. Jane Burger, D.C., Sr. Vice Pres., Mission Integration. Daughters of Charity of St. Vincent de Paul 7; Bed Capacity 498; Patients Assisted Annually 318,100.

JASPER. *Memorial Hospital and Health Care Center, Little Company of Mary Hospital of Indiana, Inc.*, 800 W. Ninth St., 47546. Tel: 812-482-2345; Fax: 812-482-0319. Ray Snowden, Pres. & CEO; Sisters M. Adrian Davis, L.C.M., Bd. Chairperson; Maura Beckman, O.S.B., Chap. Sisters of the Little Company of Mary 2; Bed Capacity 124; Patients Assisted Annually 130,520; Palliative Care Patients 53.

Memorial Hospital Foundation, Inc. 47546. Tel: 812-481-8423; Fax: 812-481-8424. William Rubino, Pres.; Michael A. Jones, Exec. Dir.

[E] HOMES FOR AGED

EVANSVILLE. *St. John's Home for the Aged*, 1236 Lincoln Ave., 47714. Tel: 812-464-3607; Fax: 812-464-2141. Sr. Rose Marie Mayock, L.S.P., Admin.; Rev. Theodore Tempel, Chap. (Retired). Little Sisters of the Poor 11; Residents 44; Apartments 22.

Seton Residence, 9200 New Harmony Rd., 47720-8918. Tel: 812-963-7600; Fax: 812-963-7654. Sisters Anthony Prugger, Admin.; Dorothea Huber, Supr. Home for the Senior Sisters of the Daughters of Charity of St. Vincent de Paul. Senior Sisters 61; Sisters on Staff 8.

JASPER. *Providence Home, Nursing Home for the Needy*, 520 W. Ninth St., 47546. Tel: 812-482-6603; Fax: 812-481-1778. David McDaniel, Admin.; Rev. Angelo Quadrini, Supr. Conducted by the Sons of Divine Providence. Priests 2; Residents 58; Staff 72.

[F] RETREAT HOUSES

EVANSVILLE. *Sarto Retreat House*, 4200 N. Kentucky Ave., P.O. Box 4169, 47724-0169. Tel: 812-424-5536; Fax: 812-421-1334. Mrs. George-Anne Ryder, Dir.; Julie Young, Sec.

FERDINAND. *Kordes Enrichment Center*, 841 E. 14th St., 47532-9216. Tel: 812-367-2777. Email: kordes@thedome.org. Web: www.thedome.org/kordes Sr. Barbara L. Schmitz, O.S.B., Dir.

[G] CONVENTS AND RESIDENCES FOR SISTERS

EVANSVILLE. *Daughters of Charity of St. Vincent de Paul of Indiana, Inc.*, 9400 New Harmony Rd., 47720 Tel: 812-963-3341; Fax: 812-963-7589. Sr. Catherine Madigan, D.C., Visitatrix; Rev. Patrick Harrity, C.M., Prov. Dir.

Legal Title: *Daughters of Charity of St. Vincent de Paul of Indiana, Inc., Mater Dei Provincialate, Inc.* Sisters in Residence 6.

Monastery of St. Clare, 6825 Nurrenbern Rd., 47712. Tel: 812-425-4396; Fax: 812-425-0089. Sr. Jane De Land, O.S.C., Supr. Franciscan Poor Clare Nuns Solemnly Professed Cloistered Nuns 12.

FERDINAND. *Sisters of St. Benedict of Ferdinand, IN, Inc., Monastery Immaculate Conception*, 802 E. Tenth St., 47532. Tel: 812-367-1411; Fax: 812-367-2313. Web: www.thedome.org. Sr. Kristine Harpenau, O.S.B., Prioress; Rev. Tobias Colgan, O.S.B., Chap., St. Meinrad Chaplain Team Coord. Sisters of St. Benedict Professed Sisters in Community 196; Temporary Commitment 12; Novices 6; Postulants 3.

[H] NEWMAN CENTERS & CAMPUS MINISTRY

EVANSVILLE. *Newman Center for the University of Evansville* 1901 Lincoln Ave., 47714. Tel: 812-477-6446. Kristel Riffert, Dir.

University of Southern Indiana Newman Center 8133-A O'Daniel Ln., 47712. Tel: 812-465-7095. Christine Hoehn, Dir.

OAKLAND CITY. *Oakland City College Newman Center* Blessed Sacrament Church, R.R. 1, Box 72-A, 47660. Tel: 812-749-4474.

VINCENNES. *Vincennes University-Newman Center* Vigo Hall, 47591. Tel: 812-888-4572. Ronald Campbell, Dir.

[I] MISCELLANEOUS

EVANSVILLE. *Catholic Education Foundation, Inc.*, P.O. Box 4169, 47724-0169. Margaret Angermeier, Dir.

Mission and Ministry, Inc., 9400 New Harmony Rd., 47720. Tel: 812-963-3341; Fax: 812-963-7589. Mary Wildeman, Exec. Dir.

Seton Health Corporation of Southern Indiana, 25 N.W. Riverside, Ste. 100, 47708. Tel: 812-434-1530; Fax: 812-434-1501. Marc Chivcop, Senior Vice Pres.

LOOGOOTEE. *American-Innsbruck Alumni Association*, 315 Doyle Ave., 47553. Tel: 812-295-3214. Rev. Leo C. Kiesel, Contact Person.

SANTA CLAUS. *The Outpost*, P.O. Box 64, 47579. Tel: 812-937-2723. Michael H. Eppler.

VINCENNES. *Old Cathedral Library & Museum, Inc.*, 205 Church St., 47591. Tel: 812-882-7016. Web: birch.palni.edu/~oldcath/oldcath.htm. Rev. John H. Schipp, Registered Agent.

WASHINGTON. *St. Vincent de Paul Society of Washington, IN, Inc.*, 815 E. Main St., 47501. Tel: 812-254-0900. Email: carann@charter.net. Rev. David Martin, Spiritual Dir.; Richard Risch, Vice. Pres. Store Operations.

RELIGIOUS INSTITUTES OF MEN REPRESENTED IN THE DIOCESE

For further details refer to the corresponding bracketed number in the Religious Institutes of Men or Women section.

[0200]—*Benedictine Monks*—O.S.B.
[0600]—*Brothers of the Congregation of Holy Cross* (Midwest Prov.)—C.S.C.
[1330]—*Congregation of the Mission*—C.M.
[0410]—*Sons of Divine Providence*—F.D.P.

RELIGIOUS INSTITUTES OF WOMEN REPRESENTED IN THE DIOCESE

[0230]—*Benedictine Sisters of Pontifical Jurisdiction*—O.S.B.
[1730]—*Congregation of the Third Order of St. Francis*—O.S.F.
[0760]—*Daughters of Charity of St. Vincent de Paul*—D.C.
[2340]—*Little Sisters of the Poor*—L.S.P.
[3760]—*Order of St. Clare*—O.S.C.
[]—*Sisters for Christian Community*—S.F.C.C.
[3360]—*Sisters of Providence of Saint Mary-of-the-Woods, Indiana*—S.P.
[0260]—*Sisters of the Blessed Sacrament*—S.B.S.
[2270]—*Sisters of the Little Company of Mary*—L.C.M.
[1760]—*Sisters of the Third Order of St. Francis, of Penance and Charity*—O.S.F.

JOINT CEMETERIES

EVANSVILLE. *St. Joseph*, 2500 Mesker Park Dr., 47712.
JASPER. *Fairview*, 1215 Newton St., 47546.
VINCENNES. *Calvary*, P.O. Box 4, 47591.
WASHINGTON. *St. John*, 101 N. Meridian St., 47501-2931.

NECROLOGY

† Conti, Rev. Msgr. Leo J., (Retired)—Died Dec. 11, 2002
† Kilfoil, Rev. Msgr. J. Patrick, (Retired)—Died June 6, 2003
† Schoettelkotte, Rev. Msgr. Charles T., (Retired)—Died Nov. 22, 2002
† Clauss, Joseph, (Retired)—Died Oct. 11, 2003
† Finis, John J., (Retired)—Died Nov. 18, 2002

Diocese of Fairbanks

Most Reverend

DONALD J. KETTLER

Bishop of Fairbanks; ordained May 29, 1970; appointed Bishop of Fairbanks June 7, 2002; installed August 22, 2002. *Office: 1316 Peger Rd., Fairbanks, AK 99709.*

Chancery Office: 1316 Peger Rd., Fairbanks, AK 99709. Tel: 907-374-9500; Fax: 907-374-9580.

Web: www.ptialaska.net / ~cbna

Email: bishop@cbna.org

Square Miles 409,849.

Corporate Title: "Catholic Bishop of Northern Alaska."

Established as the Prefecture Apostolic of Alaska, July 27, 1894.

Erected into the Vicariate of Alaska, Dec. 22, 1916; elevated to a Diocese, Aug. 8, 1962.

Comprises all of the State of Alaska, north of the old Territorial Third Judicial Division whose boundary extended in a northwesterly direction from the Canadian Border along the crest of the Alaska range to Mount McKinley, thence southwesterly to Cape Newenham and west along the 58 parallel north of the Pribilof Islands.

For legal titles of parishes and diocesan institutions, consult the Chancery Office.

STATISTICAL OVERVIEW

Personnel	
Bishop	1
Priests: Diocesan Active in Diocese	6
Priests: Diocesan Active Outside Diocese	1
Priests: Retired, Sick or Absent	1
Number of Diocesan Priests	8
Religious Priests in Diocese	15
Total Priests in Diocese	23
Extern Priests in Diocese	3
Ordinations:	
Permanent Deacons	1
Permanent Deacons in Diocese	39
Total Brothers	3
Total Sisters	20
Parishes	
Parishes	47
With Resident Pastor:	
Resident Diocesan Priests	8
Resident Religious Priests	10
Without Resident Pastor:	
Administered by Priests	17
Administered by Professed Religious Men	4
Administered by Religious Women	4
Administered by Lay People	3
Administered by Pastoral Teams, etc.	1
Pastoral Centers	2
Professional Ministry Personnel:	
Brothers	3
Sisters	20
Lay Ministers	11
Welfare	
Special Centers for Social Services	1
Total Assisted	2,033
Educational	
Diocesan Students in Other Seminaries	3
Total Seminarians	3
High Schools, Diocesan and Parish	1
Total Students	234
Elementary Schools, Diocesan and Parish	1
Total Students	301
Catechesis/Religious Education:	
High School Students	594
Elementary Students	1,630
Total Students under Catholic Instruction	2,762
Teachers in the Diocese:	
Sisters	1
Lay Teachers	29
Vital Statistics	
Receptions into the Church:	
Infant Baptism Totals	353
Adult Baptism Totals	19
Received into Full Communion	12
First Communions	362
Confirmations	124
Marriages:	
Catholic	22
Interfaith	27
Total Marriages	49
Deaths	102
Total Catholic Population	17,833
Total Population	157,000

Former Bishops—Most Revs. JOSEPH RAPHAEL CRIMONT, S.J., D.D., Vicar-Apostolic of Alaska; ord. Aug. 26, 1888; appt. Prefect-Apostolic March 28, 1904; appt. Vicar-Apostolic of Alaska Feb. 15, 1917; preconized Titular Bishop of Ammaedera, March 22, 1917; consecrated July 25, 1917; died May 20, 1945; WALTER J. FITZGERALD, S.J., D.D., Vicar-Apostolic of Alaska; ord. May 16, 1918; appt. Coadjutor Vicar-Apostolic of Alaska cum jure successionis, Dec. 14, 1938; consecrated Titular Bishop of Tymbrias, Feb. 24, 1939; succeeded to as Vicar-Apostolic of Alaska, May 20, 1945;; died July 19, 1947; GEORGE T. BOILEAU, S.J., D.D., appt. Coadjutor Bishop cum jure successionis, April 21, 1964; consecrated Titular Bishop of Ausuccura, July 31, 1964; died Feb. 25, 1965; FRANCIS D. GLEESON, S.J., D.D. (Retired), ord. July 29, 1926; appt. Titular Bishop of Cotenna and Vicar-Apostolic of Alaska Jan. 8, 1948; consecrated April 5, 1948; appt. First Bishop of Fairbanks Aug. 8, 1962; retired Nov. 30, 1968; transferred to Titular See of Cuicul in Numidia and Assistant at the Pontifical Throne by Pope Paul VI, Feb. 3, 1969; died April 30, 1983; ROBERT LOUIS WHELAN, S.J., D.D. (Retired), retired Bishop of Fairbanks; ord. June 17, 1944; appt. Titular Bishop of Sicilibba and Coadjutor Bishop of Fairbanks, cum jure successionis Dec. 6, 1967; consecrated Feb. 22, 1968; succeeded to Nov. 30, 1968;; retired July 28, 1985; died Sept. 15, 2001; MICHAEL J. KANIECKI, S.J., D.D., ord. June 5, 1965; appt. Coadjutor Bishop cumjure successionis, March 8, 1984; consecrated May 1, 1984; succeeded to July 28, 1985; died Aug. 6, 2000.

Vicar General—VACANT.

Superior Regular—Rev. MARK A. HOELSKEN, S.J., Bro. Joe Prince Jesuit Community, St. Mary's Mission Center, P.O. Box 49, St. Marys, 99658.

Chancery Office—1316 Peger Rd., Fairbanks, 99709. Tel: 907-474-0753; Fax: 907-474-8009.

Chancellor—Rev. RICHARD D. CASE, S.J.

Secretary to Bishop—GERALDINE JAUHOLA.

Treasurer—GEORGE W. BOWDER.

Tribunal—Rev. PATRICK TRAVERS, J.C.L., J.D.

Adjutant Judicial Vicar—Rev. PATRICK TRAVERS, J.C.L., J.D.

Defender of the Bond—Rev. JOSEPH E. LAUDWEIN, S.J.

Promoter of Justice—Sr. CAROLYN A. ROEBER, O.P.

Auditor—BARBARA THIEME TOLLIVER.

Notaries—BARBARA THIEME TOLLIVER; Rev. RICHARD D. CASE, S.J.; GERALDINE JAUHOLA.

Presbyteral Council—Revs. PATRICK BERGQUIST; PAUL COCHRAN, S.J.; EDWARD HARTMANN; JOHN HINSVARK; MARK A. HOELSKEN, S.J.; AL LEVITRE; RICHARD MCCAFFREY, S.J.; MACIEJ NAPIERALSKI; ROSS TOZZI.

Consultors—Revs. PATRICK BERGQUIST; PAUL COCHRAN, S.J.; EDWARD HARTMANN; JOHN HINSVARK; MARK A. HOELSKEN, S.J.; AL LEVITRE; RICHARD MCCAFFREY, S.J.; MACIEJ NAPIERALSKI; ROSS TOZZI.

Diocesan Archivist—Rev. RICHARD D. CASE, S.J.; DAVID SCHIENLE, Sec.

Diocesan Offices and Directors

Apostleship of Prayer—Rev. J. ALBERT LEVITRE JR., Dir.

"Alaskan Shepherd" Office—Mrs. PATTY WALTER, Editor, 1312 Peger Rd., Fairbanks, 99709. Tel: 907-474-0753.

Catholic Campaign for Human Development—Mr. THOMAS BUZEK.

Campus Ministry—Rev. GERALD ORNOWSKI, M.I.C., 514 Copper Ln. - UAF, P.O. Box 750166, Fairbanks, 99775. Tel: 907-474-6776.

Catholic Community Resources—VACANT, 1316 Peger Rd., Fairbanks, 99709. Tel: 907-474-0656.

Fairbanks Counseling and Adoption—RITA COOPER, Exec. Dir., 912 Barnette, P.O. Box 1544, Fairbanks, 99707. Tel: 907-456-4729.

Holy Angels Thrift Shop—MARK CLINE, Dir.; DOREEN FITZGERALD, Mgr., 401 Driveway St., Fairbanks, 99701. Tel: 907-456-4918.

Beginning Experience—Rev. TIMOTHY SANDER, O.S.B., Dir., Box 74401, Fairbanks, 99707. Tel: 907-452-1215.

Ecumenical Commission—VACANT.

Communications, Radio and TV—THOMAS BUSCH, Dir., KNOM Radio Station, P.O. Box 988, Nome, 99762. Tel: 907-443-5221.

Cursillo Movement—PEGGY MANTEI, Lay Dir.; Rev. J. ALBERT LEVITRE JR., Spiritual Dir.

The Children and Family Life Center—MADELINE NANCE.

Construction Committee—GEORGE W. BOWDER; Deacon PAUL PERREAULT, Chm.; GEORGE SUNDBORG JR.

Engaged Encounter—VACANT.

Finance Advisory Board—Rev. RICHARD D. CASE, S.J., Chm.; DONALD HOOVER; MICHAEL KELLIHER; JAMES LYNCH; Mr. NOLI ALCANTARA; JOSEPH PASKVAN; Sr. KATHLEEN RADICH, O.S.F.

Hispanic Ministry—Rev. NORMAND PEPIN, S.J.

Native Alaskan Ministries Coordinators—Sr. KATHLEEN RADICH, O.S.F., St. Mary's Conf. Ctr., P.O. Box 29, St. Marys, 99658; Bro. ROBERT RUZICKI, O.F.M., Our Lady of the Snows, P.O. Box 89, Nulato, 99765.

Marriage Encounter—VACANT.

Ministry of Sick, Aged and Imprisoned—Rev. JOSEPH LAUDWEIN, S.J.

Office of Religious Education—VACANT, 1316 Peger Rd., Fairbanks, 99709. Tel: 907-474-0753.

Office of Native Permanent Diaconate—Rev. MARK A. HOELSKEN, S.J., Dir., Jesuit Community, P.O. Box 49, St. Marys, 99658. Tel: 907-438-2536; Fax: 907-438-2536.

Office of Urban Permanent Diaconate—VACANT, 1316 Peger Rd., Fairbanks, 99709. Tel: 907-474-0753; Fax: 907-474-8009.

Office of Worship—BETTY JOHNSON, Dir., 1316 Peger Rd., Fairbanks, 99709. Tel: 907-474-0753.

Personnel—Rev. RICHARD D. CASE, S.J., Dir.; RONNIE ROSENBERG, Assoc.

Pontifical Association of the Holy Childhood—Chancery Office.

Pontifical Society for Propagation of the Faith—THOMAS BUZEK, Chancery Office.

Schools—VACANT, Dir., 615 Monroe St., Fairbanks, 99701. Tel: 907-456-7114.

Victim Assistance Coordinator—COLEEN TURNER, Exec. Dir. Tel: 907-456-2866, Ext. 107; 800-969-7272. Email: cturner@rcpcfairbanks.org.

Vocations—Ordained Ministries Formation Board: VACANT.

Vocation Director—Rev. JOHN HINSVARK.

CLERGY, PARISHES, MISSIONS AND PAROCHIAL SCHOOLS

CITY OF FAIRBANKS NORTH STAR BOROUGH

1—SACRED HEART CATHEDRAL (1966), Rev. Edward J. Hartmann; Deacon Bill Dourte.
Res.: 1316 Peger Rd., 99709. Tel: 907-474-0836; Fax: 907-479-3327.
Church: 2501 Airport Way, 99709. Tel: 907-474-9032.
Catechesis/Religious Program—Tel: 907-474-3327. Gigi Martinez, D.R.E. Students 233.

2—IMMACULATE CONCEPTION (1904), [JC] Rev. Richard L. McCaffrey, S.J.; Deacons Robert Mantei; Sean Stack.
Res.: 115 N. Cushman St., 99701. Tel: 907-452-3533; Fax: 907-456-3336.
Catechesis/Religious Program—Deacon Robert Bernard, D.R.E. Students 120.

3—ST. MARK UNIVERSITY PARISH (1977), Rev. Gerald Ornowski, M.I.C.
Res.: Box 750166, 99775. Tel: 907-474-6776.
Catechesis/Religious Program—Students 8.

4—ST. RAPHAEL'S (1991), Rev. Patrick D. Bergquist.
Res.: P.O. Box 10508, 99710. Tel: 907-457-6603; Fax: 907-457-4461.
Catechesis/Religious Program—Gloria Slagle, D.R.E., (Grades K-12). Students 80.

OUTSIDE CITY OF FAIRBANKS

ALAKANUK, ST. IGNATIUS (1954), (Yup'ik), [CEM] [JC] Rev. Thomas G. Provinsal, S.J.; Sr. Mary Ann Kollmer, O.P., Parish Admin.; Deacons Joseph Phillip, (Retired); Emmanuel Stanislaus; Revs. Denis Shelden; Charles Clyde Smith.
Res.: P.O. Box 53, 99554. Tel: 907-238-3914.
Mission—St. Peter's P.O. Box 45, Nunam Iqua, 99666. Tel: 907-498-4246.

ANIAK, ST. THERESA (1935), (Yup'ik), [CEM] Rev. Maciej Napieralski.
Res.: P.O. Box 308, 99557. Tel: 907-675-4448.
Mission— Box 11, Kalskag, 99607. Tel: 907-471-2298.

BARROW, NORTH SLOPE BOROUGH, ST. PATRICK (1954), [JC] Unassigned., Mailing Address: P.O. Box 389, 99723. Tel: 907-852-3515.
Catechesis/Religious Program—Students 18.

BETHEL, IMMACULATE CONCEPTION (1942), Rev. Eugene P. Delmore, S.J.; Deacons Peter Aluska; Louie Andrew; Brian McCaffery.
Res.: 790 River St., P.O. Box 428, 99559. Tel: 907-543-2464.
Catechesis/Religious Program—Susan Murphy, D.R.E. Students 140.

CHEFORNAK, ST. CATHERINE (1937), (Yup'ik), [CEM] Rev. Paul Cochran, S.J.; Agnes Kairaiuak, Acting Parish Admin.; Deacons David Parruk; Joe Avugiak; Cyril Alexie, (Retired); David Erik, (Retired).
Res.: P.O. Box 90, 99561. Tel: 907-867-8702.
Catechesis/Religious Program—Students 153.

CHEVAK, SACRED HEART (1952), (Cup'ik), [CEM] Rev. Gregg D. Wood, S.J.; Deacons Frank Smart; David Boyscout, (Retired); Mary Agimuk, Acting Parish Admin.
Res.: P.O. Box 249, 99563. Tel: 907-858-7826.
Catechesis/Religious Program—Students 63.

DELTA JUNCTION, OUR LADY OF SORROWS (1959), Rev. John Martinek.
Res.: 2565 Deborah St., Box 446, 99737. Tel: 907-895-5232.
Catechesis/Religious Program—Students 27.
Station—St. Ann Northway.
Station—St. Francis Xavier Eagle.

EMMONAK, SACRED HEART (1953), (Yup'ik), [JC] Rev. Thomas G. Provinsal, S.J.; Deacon Bart Agathluk Sr.; Rev. Raymond Waska.
Res.: P.O. Box 190, 99581. Tel: 907-949-1012.
Catechesis/Religious Program—Matrona Kozevenikoff, D.R.E. Students 230.

GALENA, ST. JOHN BERCHMAN (1923), (Athabascan), Bro. Justin Huber, O.F.M.
Res.: P.O. Box 131, 99741. Tel: 907-656-1240; Fax: 907-656-1240.
Catechesis/Religious Program—Students 16.
Station—St. Francis Regis Huslia. Tel: 907-829-2234.

HEALY, DENALI BOROUGH, HOLY MARY OF GUADALUPE (1984), Rev. Jack de Verteuil; Barbara Walters, Pastoral Min.
Mailing Address: P.O. Box 32, 99743.
Church: P.O. Box 32, 99743. Tel: 907-683-2535; 907-683-1018 (Rectory).
Catechesis/Religious Program—Students 47.
Mission— [JC] Cantwell.

HOLY CROSS, HOLY FAMILY (1888), Rev. Maciej Napieralski.
Res.: P.O. Box 101, 99602. Tel: 907-476-7144; Fax: 907-476-7144.

HOOPER BAY LITTLE FLOWER OF JESUS (1928), (Yup'ik), [JC] Rev. Gregg D. Wood, S.J.; Deacon James Gump, (Retired).
Res.: P.O. Box 9, 99604. Tel: 907-758-4620; Fax: 907-758-4520.

KALTAG, ST. TERESAS, (Athabascan), [JC] Rev. Joseph Hemmer, O.F.M.; Sisters Rose Beck, S.S.N.D., Pastoral Min.; Cynthia Borman, S.S.N.D., Asst. Pastoral Min.
Res.: P.O Box 69, 99748. Tel: 907-534-2218.
Catechesis/Religious Program—Students 22.

KOTLIK, ST. JOSEPH (1949), (Yup'ik), Rev. Thomas Provinsal, S.J.; Deacon Aloysius Wasuli.
Church: P.O. Box 20228, 99620. Tel: 907-899-4715.
Catechesis/Religious Program—Students 35.

KOTZEBUE, NORTHWEST ARCTIC BOROUGH, ST. FRANCIS XAVIER (1929), [CEM] [JC] Rev. John Hinsvark.
Res.: Box 358, 99752. Tel: 907-442-3239; Fax: 907-442-3239.

KOYUKUK, ST. PATRICK, (Athabascan), Rev. Albert Levitre.
Res.: P.O. Box 54101, 99754. Tel: 907-927-2240.

MARSHALL, WADE HAMPTON (CA) CO., IMMACULATE HEART OF MARY (1930), (Yup'ik), Unassigned. Ms. Clara Shorty, Parish Admin.
Mailing Address: P.O. Box 69, 99585. Tel: 907-679-6639; Fax: 907-679-6639.
Mission—Our Lady of Guadalupe Russian Mission P.O. Box 56, Russian Mission, Wade Hampton Co. 99657. Tel: 907-584-5173.

MCGRATH, ST. MICHAEL (1960), Bro. Kirby Boone, C.F.X., Pastoral Admin.
Res.: P.O. Box 141, 99627. Tel: 907-524-3928.
Station— Takotna. Tel: 907-298-2328.

MOUNTAIN VILLAGE, NORTHWEST ARCTIC BOROUGH, ST. LAWRENCE, (Yup'ik), Rev. Elmer Beans; Sr. Dorothy Giloley, S.S.J., Parish Admin.
Res. & Mailing Address: P.O. Box 32205, 99632. Tel: 907-591-2348; Fax: 907-591-2348 Prior Arrangement).

NENANA, DENALI BOROUGH, ST. THERESA (1922), [JC], Served out of Healy, AK. Penelope A. Forness, Parish Admin.; Rev. Jack deVerteuil, Visiting Priest.
Mailing Address: P.O. Box 312, 99760. Tel: 907-832-5617.
Catechesis/Religious Program—Students 15.

NEWTOK, HOLY FAMILY (1950), (Yup'ik), [CEM] Rev. Paul Cochran, S.J.; Deacons Larry Charles; Mark Tom; Ignatius Tommy, Parish Admin.
Res.: P.O. Box WWT, 99559. Tel: 907-237-2427.
Catechesis/Religious Program—Sophie John, D.R.E. Students 110.

NIGHTMUTE, OUR LADY OF PERPETUAL HELP (1950), (Yup'ik), [CEM] Rev. David Anderson, S.J.; Jane Tulik, Acting Parish Admin.; Deacons Thomas Jumbo; Camillus Tulik, (Retired); Ignatius Matthias.
Res.: 99690. Tel: 907-647-6428.
Catechesis/Religious Program—Students 65.

NOME, ST. JOSEPH (1901), [CEM] Rev. John Hinsvark.
Res.: P.O. Box 1010, 99762. Tel: 907-443-5527; Fax: 907-443-5757.
Catechesis/Religious Program—Students 31.
Mission—St. Jude P.O. Box 7999, Diomede, 99762.

NORTH POLE, NORTH STAR BOROUGH, ST. NICHOLAS (1975), Rev. Ross Tozzi; Deacon Walt Gelinas.
Res.: 707 St. Nicholas Dr., 99705. Tel: 907-488-2595; Fax: 907-488-9625.
Catechesis/Religious Program—Christina Fortenberry, D.R.E. Students 117.
Station— Manley Hot Springs.

NULATO, OUR LADY OF THE SNOWS (1877), (Athabascan), Bro. Robert Ruzicka, O.F.M., Pastoral Admin.
Res.: P.O. Box 89, 99765. Tel: 907-898-2242.
Catechesis/Religious Program—Students 55.

PILOT STATION, WADE HAMPTON (CA) CO., ST. CHARLES SPINOLA (1914), (Yup'ik), [JC] Sr. Dorothy Giloley, S.S.J., Parish Admin.
Mailing Address: P.O. Box 5120, 99650. Tel: 907-549-3231; Fax: 907-549-3231.
Catechesis/Religious Program—Students 75.

RUBY, ST. PETER-IN-CHAINS (1912), (Athabascan), [JC] Rev. Joseph Hemmer, O.F.M.
Res.: P.O. Box 207, 99768. Tel: 907-468-4482; 907-468-4413.

ST. MARYS, CHURCH OF THE NATIVITY, [CEM] Rev. Theodore E. Kestler, S.J.; Deacon Patrick L. Beans Sr., (Retired).
Res.: P.O. Box 109, 99658. Tel: 907-438-2133; Fax: 907-438-2146.
Catechesis/Religious Program—Students 62.

ST. MICHAEL, ST. MICHAEL (1895), (Yup'ik), [JC] Rev. Stanislaw Jaszek.
Res.: P.O. Box 29, 99659. Tel: 907-923-3151.

SCAMMON BAY, BLESSED SACRAMENT (1930), (Yup'ik), [JC] Darlene Cholok, Admin.; Rev. Gregg D. Wood, S.J., Itinerant Min.; Deacon Francis Charlie.
Res.: P.O. Box 133, 99662. Tel: 907-558-5229.

STEBBINS, ST. BERNARD (1908), (Yup'ik), [JC] Rev. Stanislaw Jaszek; Margaret Marlin, Acting Admin.
Res.: 99671. Tel: 907-934-3151.

TANANA, ST. ALOYSIUS (1887), (Athabascan), [JC] Bro. Kirby Boone, C.F.X., Pastoral Admin.; Rev. Joseph Laudwein, S.J., Visiting Priest.
Res.: P.O. Box 6, 99777. Tel: 907-366-7238.

TELLER, NOME (CA) CO., ST. ANN (1909), Rev. John Hinsvark.
Res.: P.O. Box 529, 99778. Tel: 907-642-3831.

TOK, SOUTHEAST FAIRBANKS (CA) CO., HOLY ROSARY (1949), Rev. John Martinek.
Res.: P.O. Box 369, 99780. Tel: 907-883-4111; Fax: 907-883-4111.
Catechesis/Religious Program—Students 15.

TOKSOOK BAY, ST. PETER THE FISHERMAN (1964), (Central Yup'ik), [CEM] Deacon James Charlie; Rev. David J. Anderson, S.J.; Deacons Joseph Asuluk Sr.; Nick Therchik Sr.; Gregory Charlie; Maggie John, Parish Admin.
Mailing Address: P.O. Box 37046, 99637. Tel: 907-427-7813; Fax: 907-427-7813.
Catechesis/Religious Program—Tel: 907-427-7826; Fax: 907-427-7820. Laura Therchik, D.R.E. Students 229.
Station— Umkumute.

TUNUNAK, NORTHWEST ARCTIC BOROUGH, ST. JOSEPH (1889), (Yup'ik), [CEM] Rev. David J. Anderson, S.J.; Josephine Link, Acting Admin.; Deacon Dick Lincoln, (Retired).
Res.: P.O. Box 09, 99681. Tel: 907-652-6214; Fax: 907-652-6214.
Catechesis/Religious Program—Tel: 907-652-6237. Students 99.

UNALAKLEET, NORTHWEST, CHURCH OF THE HOLY ANGELS (1952), Rev. Stanislaw Jaszek.
Res.: P.O. Box 152, 99684. Tel: 907-624-3711.
Catechesis/Religious Program—Students 12.

Leave of Absence:
Rev.—
Wallner, Gerhard

Permanent Deacons:
Agathluk, Bart, Sacred Heart, Emmonak
Alexie, Cyril, St. Catherine's, Chefornak
Aluska, Peter, Sr., Immaculate Conception, Bethel
Asuluk, Joe, St. Peter Fisherman, Toksook Bay
Avugiak, Joe, St. Catherine, Chefornak
Barnard, Robert, Fairbanks - Fort Wainwright
Beans, Elmer, St. Lawrence Church, Mountain Village
Beans, Patrick L., Sr., Church of the Nativity, St. Mary
Bowder, George
Boyscout, David, Sacred Heart Church, Chevak
Charles, Larry, Holy Family Church, Newtok
Charlie, Francis, Blessed Sacrament, Scammon Bay
Charlie, Gregory, St. Peter the Fisherman, Toksook Bay
Charlie, James, St. Peter the Fisherman, Toksook Bay
Dourte, William, Sacred Heart Cathedral, Fairbanks
Edwards, Patrick, St. Charles Spinola, Pilot Station
Eric, David, St. Catherine's, Chefornak
Gelinas, Walt, St. Nicholas, North Pole
Gump, James, Little Flower Mission, Hooper Bay
Jumbo, Thomas, Our Lady of Perpetual Help, Nightmute
Lincoln, Dick, St. Joseph's, Tununak

Louie, Andrew Ignatius
Mantei, Robert, Immaculate Conception, Fairbanks
Matthias, Ignatius
McCaffrey, Brian
Panruk, David, St. Catherine, Chefornak
Perreault, Paul, Sacred Heart Cathedral, Fairbanks
Phillip, Joseph, St. Ignatius, Alakanuk
Shelden, Denis, St. Ignatius, Alakanuk
Smart, Frank, Sacred Heart Church, Chevak
Smith, Clyde, St. Ignatius, Alakanuk
Stack, Sean, Immaculate Conception, Fairbanks
Stanislaus, Emmanuel, St. Ignatius, Alakanuk
Teeluk, Henry, St. Joseph Church, Kotlik
Therchik, Nick, St. Peter the Fisherman, Toksook Bay
Tom, Mark, Holy Family, Newtok
Tulik, Camillus, Our Lady of Perpetual Help, Nightmute
Waska, Ray, Sacred Heart, Emmonak
Wasuli, Aloysius, St. Joseph, Kotlik

INSTITUTIONS LOCATED IN THE DIOCESE

[A] HIGH SCHOOLS, DIOCESAN

FAIRBANKS. *Monroe Catholic Junior-Senior High School*, 615 Monroe St., 99701. Tel: 907-452-2044; Fax: 907-452-5978. Email: monroehs@polarnet.com. Web: www.catholic-schools.org. Douglas J. Wasko, Prin.; Rev. Normand A. Pepin, S.J. Priests 1; Lay Teachers 23; Religious 1; Students 234.

[B] GRADE SCHOOLS, DIOCESAN

FAIRBANKS. *Immaculate Conception Grade School*, 715 Monroe St., 99701. Tel: 907-456-4574; Fax: 907-452-5978. Email: monroehs@polarnet.com. Amanda Angaiak, Prin. Sisters 1; Lay Teachers 4; Students 301.

[C] RESIDENCES FOR PRIESTS AND BROTHERS

FAIRBANKS. *Jesuit Residence*, 1318 Peger Rd., 99709. Tel: 907-474-9320; Fax: 907-479-9073. Email: jelaudwein@nwjesuits.org. Revs. Joseph Laudwein, S.J., Supr.; Richard D. Case, S.J.; Thomas N. Gallagher, S.J.; Normand A. Pepin, S.J.; Richard L. McCaffrey, S.J. Regional Offices of the Society of Jesus, Alaska

[D] CONVENTS AND RESIDENCES OF SISTERS

FAIRBANKS. *Immaculate Conception Convent*, 615 Betty St., 99701. Tel: 907-452-2750. Sisters Felicitas Farrell, O.P.. Email: ffarrellop@hotmail.com; Michele Kaelin, C.S.J.. Email: michcsj@hotmail.com; Patricia Mayer, S.C.. Email: sisterpatmayer@hotmail.com. Sisters 3.

NOME. *Little Sisters of Jesus*, Box 845, 99762. Tel: 907-443-2094. Sisters Alice Ann; Damiene; Odette. Sisters 3.

[E] MISCELLANEOUS LISTINGS

FAIRBANKS. *House of Prayer*, 1316 Peger Rd., 99709. Tel: 907-474-9379. Rev. Normand A. Pepin, S.J., Dir.; Sr. Ann Sabol, C.S.J.

**Monroe Foundation, Inc.*, 718 Betty St., 99707. Tel: 907-456-7114; Fax: 907-456-7481. Email: director@catholic_schools.org. Web: www.catholic_schools.org. Rose Anne Sample, Exec. Dir.

Voice in the Wilderness Prayer Community, 4028 Birch Ln., 99709. Tel: 907-479-8512. Email: spiritfilled@gci.net. Gail Riedman, Dir.

GALENA. *Kateri Tekakwitha Center*, P.O. Box 297, 99741. Tel: 907-656-4570. Email: mmarx@cbna.org. Sisters Marilyn Marx, S.N.J.M., Dir. Ministry Training; Marita Soucy, C.S.J., Dir. Pastoral Outreach Training.

NOME. *Alaska Radio Mission, Station KNOM*, Box 988, 99762. Tel: 907-443-5221; Fax: 907-443-5757. Email: Tbusch@knom.org. Web: www.knom.org. Thomas Busch, Gen. Mgr. Total Staff 11; Total in Residence 5.

ST. MARYS. *Brother Joe Prince Jesuit Community*, P.O. Box 49, 99658. Tel: 907-438-2536; Fax: 907-438-2146. Email: mhoelsken@juno.com. Revs. Mark A. Hoelsken, S.J., Supr., Pastoral Ministry & Dir. Native Deacon Prog.; David J. Anderson, S.J., Pastoral Ministry, Toksook Bay, Tununak & Nightmute, AK; Paul Cochran, S.J., Pastoral Ministry, Chefornak & Newtok; Eugene P. Delmore, S.J., Pastor, Immaculate Conception, Bethel, AK; Theodore E. Kestler, S.J., Asst. in Native Ministry Training Program, Pastoral Ministry, St. Mary's, AK; Thomas G. Provinsal, S.J., Pastoral Ministry, Alakunak, Emmonak & Kotlik, AK; Gregg D. Wood, S.J., Pastoral Ministry, Hooper Bay, Scammon Bay, & Chevak, AK.

Native Ministry Training Program, P.O. Box 29, 99658-0029. Tel: 907-438-2832; Fax: 907-438-2832. Email: nmtp@juno.com. Sr. Ellen Callaghan, O.S.F., Dir.; Revs. Paul M. Cochran, S.J.; Theodore E. Kestler, S.J.; Sr. Rose Monica Katusz, O.S.F.; Ms. Theresa E. Kelly. Total Staff 5; Total in Residence 5.

RELIGIOUS INSTITUTES OF MEN REPRESENTED IN THE DIOCESE

For further details refer to the corresponding bracketed number in the Religious Institutes of Men or Women section.

[0200]—*Benedictine Monks*—O.S.B.
[0520]—*Franciscan Friars and Brothers*—O.F.M.
[0690]—*Jesuit Fathers and Brothers*—S.J.
[0740]—*Marian Fathers*—M.I.C.
[1350]—*Xaverian Brothers*—C.F.X.

RELIGIOUS INSTITUTES OF WOMEN REPRESENTED IN THE DIOCESE

[1070-03]—*Dominican Sisters*—O.P.
[1070-05]—*Dominican Sisters*—O.P.
[2330]—*Little Sisters of Jesus*—L.S.J.
[2970]—*School Sisters of Notre Dame*—S.S.N.D.
[0590]—*Sisters of Charity of Saint Elizabeth, Convent Station* (Northern Prov.)—S.C.
[1650]—*The Sisters of St. Francis of Philadelphia*—O.S.F.
[3830-12]—*Sisters of St. Joseph* Ogdensburg—S.S.J.
[3850]—*Sisters of St. Joseph of Chambery*—C.S.J.
[1990]—*Sisters of the Holy Names of Jesus and Mary*—S.N.J.M.
[4110]—*Ursuline Nuns*—O.S.U.

NECROLOGY

(No Deaths)

Diocese of Fall River

(Dioecesis Riverormensis)

Most Reverend

GEORGE W. COLEMAN

Bishop of Fall River; *ordained December 16, 1964; appointed Bishop of Fall River April 30, 2003; consecrated July 22, 2003. Office: P.O. Box 2577, Fall River, MA 02722.*

The Chancery: P.O. Box 2577, Fall River, MA 02722. Tel: 508-675-1311; Fax: 508-730-2447.

Email: chancery@dioc-fr.org

ESTABLISHED MARCH 12, 1904.

Square Miles 1,194.

Comprises Bristol, Barnstable, Dukes and Nantucket Counties, and the Towns of Marion, Mattapoisett and Wareham in Plymouth County, Massachusetts.

Legal Title: For legal titles of parishes and diocesan institutions, consult the Chancery Office.

STATISTICAL OVERVIEW

Statistical report was not submitted for 2004.	
Personnel	
Priests: Diocesan Active in Diocese	133
Priests: Diocesan Active Outside Diocese	4
Priests: Diocesan in Foreign Missions	2
Priests: Retired, Sick or Absent	34
Number of Diocesan Priests	173
Religious Priests in Diocese	141
Total Priests in Diocese	314
Extern Priests in Diocese	2
Ordinations:	
Diocesan Priests	1
Transitional Deacons	1
Permanent Deacons	17
Permanent Deacons in Diocese	90
Total Brothers	16
Total Sisters	295
Parishes	
Parishes	101
With Resident Pastor:	
Resident Diocesan Priests	87
Resident Religious Priests	11
Without Resident Pastor:	
Administered by Priests	3
Missions	11
New Parishes Created	1
Closed Parishes	3
Professional Ministry Personnel:	
Sisters	13
Lay Ministers	61
Welfare	
Catholic Hospitals	1
Total Assisted	140,303
Health Care Centers	1
Total Assisted	62
Homes for the Aged	4
Total Assisted	938
Residential Care of Children	1
Total Assisted	60
Specialized Homes	6
Total Assisted	45,782
Educational	
Diocesan Students in Other Seminaries	15
Total Seminarians	15
Colleges and Universities	1
Total Students	2,550
High Schools, Diocesan and Parish	4
Total Students	2,871
Elementary Schools, Diocesan and Parish	24
Total Students	5,864
Catechesis/Religious Education:	
High School Students	6,134
Elementary Students	28,996
Total Students under Catholic Instruction	46,430
Teachers in the Diocese:	
Priests	14
Brothers	5
Sisters	17
Lay Teachers	647
Vital Statistics	
Receptions into the Church:	
Infant Baptism Totals	4,585
Adult Baptism Totals	90
Received into Full Communion	168
First Communions	4,833
Confirmations	4,012
Marriages:	
Catholic	1,280
Interfaith	322
Total Marriages	1,602
Deaths	4,084
Total Catholic Population	346,054
Total Population	824,235

Former Bishops—Most Revs. WILLIAM STANG, D.D., ord. June 15, 1878; appt. March 12, 1904; consecrated May 1, 1904; died Feb. 2, 1907; DANIEL F. FEEHAN, D.D., ord. Dec. 20, 1879; appt. July 2, 1907; consecrated Sept. 19, 1907; died July 19, 1934; JAMES E. CASSIDY, D.D., ord. Sept. 8, 1898; appt. Titular Bishop of Ibora and Auxiliary, March 21, 1930; consecrated May 27, 1930; succeeded to the See, July 28, 1934; died May 17, 1951; JAMES L. CONNOLLY, D.D., D.Sc.H. (Retired), ord. Dec. 21, 1923; appt. Titular Bishop of Mylasa and Coadjutor "cum jure successionis," April 18, 1945; consecrated May 24, 1945; succeeded to See, May 17, 1951; retired Oct. 30, 1970; died Sept. 12, 1986; DANIEL A. CRONIN, D.D., S.T.D., ord. Dec. 20, 1952; appt. Titular Bishop of Egnatia and Auxiliary Bishop of Boston, June 10, 1968; consecrated Sept. 12, 1968; transferred to Fall River, Oct. 30, 1970; installed Dec. 16, 1970; transferred to Hartford, Dec. 9, 1991; SEAN O'MALLEY, O.F.M.Cap., Ph.D., ord. Aug. 29, 1970; appt. Coadjutor Bishop of St. Thomas, Virgin Islands May 30, 1984; ord. Aug. 2, 1984; succeeded to See Oct. 16, 1985; appt. Bishop of Fall River June 16, 1992; installed Aug. 11, 1992; transferred to Palm Beach Sept. 3, 2002; installed Oct. 19, 2002; transferred to Boston July 1, 2003; installed July 30, 2003.

Vicar General—Rev. Msgr. JOHN A. PERRY, V.G., P.O. Box 2577, Fall River, 02722.

The Chancery—450 Highland Ave., Fall River, 02720. Mailing Address, P.O. Box 2577, Fall River, 02722-2577. Tel: 508-675-1311; Fax: 508-730-2447.

Chancellor—Rev. MICHAEL K. MCMANUS.

Secretary to the Bishop—Rev. RICHARD D. WILSON, J.C.L., 47 Underwood St., Fall River, 02720.

Diocesan Tribunal—887 Highland Ave., Fall River, 02720. Tel: 508-675-7150; Fax: 508-675-7295.

Judicial Vicar—Rev. PAUL F. ROBINSON, O.Carm.

Promoter Justitiae—Rev. Msgr. DANIEL F. HOYE, J.C.L.

Judges—Revs. PAUL F. ROBINSON, O.Carm.; THOMAS L. RITA; JAY T. MADDOCK, J.C.L.; MARK R. HESSION, J.C.L.; Deacon VICTOR HADDAD.

Defenders of the Bond—Rev. Msgrs. THOMAS J. HARRINGTON, J.C.L.; DANIEL F. HOYE, J.C.L.; Revs. GERARD A. HEBERT, J.C.L.; THOMAS E. MCGLYNN, J.C.L.

Procurator-Advocates—Revs. MARC H. BERGERON; DAVID M. ANDRADE; BRUCE M. NEYLON.

Auditors—Revs. DANIEL W. LACROIX; JOHN J. PERRY; HENRY J. DAHL; DAVID M. ANDRADE; THOMAS E. MCGLYNN, J.C.L.; DERMOT RODGERS; RICHARD D. WILSON, J.C.L.; Deacon ROBERT SURPRENANT.

Office Manager—Mrs. DENISE D. BERUBE.

Notaries—Mrs. DENISE D. BERUBE; Mrs. HELENE P. BEAUDOIN.

Diocesan Consultors—Rev. PAUL E. CANUEL; Rev. Msgr. EDMUND J. FITZGERALD, V.F.; Revs. EDWARD J. HEALEY; MICHAEL K. MCMANUS; JOHN J. OLIVEIRA; Rev. Msgr. JOHN A. PERRY, V.G.

Deans—Fall River Deanery: Rev. Msgr. EDMUND J. FITZGERALD, V.F., 945 Main Rd., P.O. Box 3328, Westport, 02790. Taunton Deanery: Very Rev. BENTO R. FRAGA, V.F., 261 Tremont St., Taunton, 02780. Attleboro Deanery: Very Rev. GEORGE C. BELLENOIT, V.F., St. Mary's Rectory, 330 Pratt St., Mansfield, 02048. Cape Cod Deanery: Very Rev. MARCEL H. BOUCHARD, V.F., Corpus Christis Rectory, P.O. Box 1170, East Sandwich, 02537. New Bedford Deanery: Very Rev. EDWARD E. CORREIA, V.F., 233 County St., New Bedford, 02740.

Diocesan Offices and Directors

Apostolate for Persons with Disabilities—MATTHEW DANSEREAU, Coord., 1600 Bay St., Fall River, 02724. Tel: 508-997-7337; 508-679-8373.

Campus Ministry—

Bristol Community College—777 Elsbree Street, Fall River, 02720. Tel: 508-678-2811, Ext. 301. Rev. SCOTT A. CIOSEK, 777 Elsbree St., Fall River, 02720. Tel: 508-678-2811, Ext. 301; Sr. FAYE MEDINA, O.P., 777 Elsbree St., Fall River, 02720. Tel: 508-678-2811, Ext. 301.

University of Massachusetts Dartmouth—285 Old Westport Rd., North Dartmouth, 02747. Tel: 508-999-8872. Rev. CRAIG A. PREGANA; Sr. MADELEINE TACY, O.P., 285 Old Westport Rd., North Dartmouth, 02747. Tel: 508-999-8872.

Wheaton College—Rev. CRAIG A. PREGANA, Norton.

Massachusetts Maritime Academy—VACANT.

Cape Cod Community College—VACANT.

Catholic Youth Organization—Rev. JAY T. MADDOCK, J.C.L., Dir., 403 Anawan St., Fall River, 02720.

Catholic Charities Appeal—Rev. Msgr. THOMAS J. HARRINGTON, J.C.L., Dir., Office, 450 Highland Ave., Fall River, 02720.

Diocesan Apostolate to Hispanics—Rev. RICHARD D. WILSON, J.C.L., Diocesan Dir.; Sr. AIDA SANSOR, M.G.Sp.S., P.O. Box 2577, Fall River, 02722. Tel: 508-675-1311; Fax: 508-679-9220. Area Offices:: Fall River: Rev. RICHARD D. WILSON, J.C.L., Dir.; Sr. AIDA SANSOR, M.G.Sp.S., Pastoral Assoc., Saint Mary's Cathedral, 327 Second St., Fall River, 02721. Tel: 508-672-9303. Attleboro: Rev. MICHAEL CARVILL, F.S.C.B., Dir., Saint Joseph's Church, 208 S. Main St., Attleboro, 02702. Tel: 508-222-1730; Sr. ALICIA LOPEZ, M.G.Sp.S., Pastoral Assoc. Tel: 508-997-8729; 508-226-0234. Taunton: Rev. FRANCIS T. ZLOTKOWSKI, C.S.C., Dir. Tel: 508-822-7116; Fax: 508-822-7117; Sr. ALICIA LOPEZ, M.G.Sp.S., St. Mary's Church, 14 St. Mary's Square, Taunton, 02780. Tel: 508-997-8729; 508-880-0410. New Bedford: Rev. RAMON DOMINGUEZ,

Dir. Tel: 508-996-5862; Fax: 508-992-2208; Sr. MARGARITA OCANA, M.G.Sp.S, Pastoral Assoc. Tel: 508-997-8729; Fax: 508-997-4537. Nuestra Senora de Guadalupe Parish, P.O. Box 40605, New Bedford, 02744. Tel: 508-996-5862; Fax: 508-992-2208; Rev. PABLO RUANI, I.V.E., Dir., Mailing Address, 306 Ashley Blvd., New Bedford, 02746. Tel: 508-992-7587; Fax: 508-994-0281. Nantucket: Sr. MARTA ELENA PEREZ, M.G.Sp.S., Pastoral Assoc. Tel: 508-997-8729; Cell: 508-965-0863; NOE PINEDA, Contact Person, Mailing Address, P.O. Box 2067, Nantucket, 02584. Tel: 508-843-5873; Fax: 508-997-4537. Cape Cod: Rev. WILLIAM RODRIGUES, Dir., 21 Cross St., Hyannis, 02601. Tel: 508-775-0818; Fax: 508-771-5940; Sr. OBDULIA OLIVAR, M.G.Sp.S., Pastoral Assoc., St. Francis Xavier Church, 21 Cross St., Hyannis, 02601. Tel: 508-771-2658; 508-997-8729.

Director of Portuguese Ministry—Rev. JOHN J. OLIVEIRA, 230 Bonney St., New Bedford, 02744.

Diocesan Archives—Rev. BARRY W. WALL, P.O. Box 2577, Fall River, 02722.

Diocesan Office of Communications—Rev. Msgr. JOHN F. MOORE, Dir.; JOHN E. KEARNS JR., Assoc. Dir., 887 Highland Ave., Fall River, 02720. Tel: 508-675-7151. Mailing Address, P.O. Box 7, Fall River, 02722.

Diocesan Director of Cemeteries—Rev. JOHN J. PERRY, 1335 N. Main St., Fall River, 02720.

Diocesan Education Center—Mr. GEORGE A. MILOT, Supt. Schools; Dr. DONNA BOYLE, Asst. Supt. Curriculum; KATHLEEN A. SIMPSON, Asst. Supt. Personnel; Deacon BRUCE J. BONNEAU, Dir. Rel. Educ.; LISA M. GULINO, Dir. Adult Educ., Office, 423 Highland Ave., Fall River, 02720. Tel: 508-678-2828; Fax: 508-674-4218.

Diocesan Department of Pastoral Care for the Sick—Rev. EDWARD J. HEALEY, Dir., Office: 327 Second St., Fall River, 02721. Tel: 508-673-2833; Fax: 508-672-0667; Sr. CAROLE MELLO, O.P.; Revs. JOHN DIAS, C.S.C.; PATRICK MCGEE; Sr. MARIE THERESE DYER, F.C.J.; Mr. CHARLES FOLEY; Sr. LORNA RIORDAN, O.P., St. Anne's Hospital, 795 Middle St., Fall River, 02721; Revs. MAREK S. TUPTYNSKI; BRIAN ALBINO; Deacon JOAO MONIZ; Sisters JACQUELINE DUBOIS, S.S.A.; LUCILLE SOCCIARELLI, R.S.M., Charlton Memorial Hospital, Fall River, 02721; Revs. VINCENT NAGLE, F.S.C.B.; ROBERT J. POWELL, O.S.B.Cam.; Sr. ANNETTE LANGLOIS, S.A.S.V., Sturdy Memorial Hospital, Attleboro, 02703; Rev. JOHN M. MURRAY; Mrs. KATHERINE SULLIVAN, Cape Cod Hospital, Hyannis, 02601; Revs. MICHAEL S. RACINE; WILLIAM RODRIGUES; Sisters ROBERTA O'CONNELL, F.C.J.; KATHLEEN SCHMITH, R.S.M.; M. HOPE HUGHES, R.S.M., St. Luke's Hospital, New Bedford, 02745; Rev. EDWARD A. MURPHY; Sr. NOELLA LUSSIER, P.M., Morton Hospital, Taunton, 02780; Ms. LEONA LEONARD, Tobey Hospital, Wareham, 02571. Rehabilitation Hospital of the Cape and Islands, East Sandwich, 02537; Rev. JOSEPH MAURITZEN, Falmouth Hospital, Falmouth, 02540.

Diocesan Department of Catholic Social Services and Special Apostolates—ARLENE A. MCNAMEE, L.C.S.W., Exec. Dir., Office, 1600 Bay St., Box M, S. Station, Fall River, 02724. Tel: 508-674-4681; Fax: 508-675-2224.

Diocesan Finance Council—Members: Rev. Msgr. JOHN A. PERRY, V.G.; Mr. OWEN GAFFNEY; Mr. PAUL KAWA; FREDERIC J. TORPHY, Esq.; Mr. WILLIAM N. WHELAN; Rev. MICHAEL K. MCMANUS, Finance Officer, P.O. Box 2577, Fall River, 02722. Tel: 508-675-1311.

Diocesan Guild for the Blind—Rev. BRUCE M. NEYLON, 36 Rockland St., P.O. Box 111, Fall River, 02724. Tel: 508-672-0423.

Diocesan Health Facilities—Rev. Msgr. EDMUND J. FITZGERALD, V.F., Dir., Office, 368 N. Main St., Fall River, 02720. Tel: 508-679-8154; Fax: 508-679-1422.

Diocesan Insurance Department—JOSEPH A. FIGLOCK, Benefits Mgr. & Insurance Coord.; SHAUN P. KERRIGAN, Asst. Benefits Mgr., P.O. Box 2577, Fall River, 02722. Tel: 508-675-1311; Fax: 508-672-3802.

Diocesan Newspaper—Rev. Msgr. JOHN F. MOORE, Exec. Editor; Mr. DAVID B. JOLIVET, Editor, Office, 887 Highland Ave., Fall River, 02722. Tel: 508-675-7151. Mailing Address, P.O. Box 7, Fall River, 02722. "The Anchor"

Ecumenical Officer—Rev. MARC H. BERGERON, 818 Middle St., Fall River, 02721. Tel: 508-674-5651.

Episcopal Representative for Religious—Sr. ELAINE HEFFERNAN, R.S.M., 500 Slocum Rd., North Dartmouth, 02747. Tel: 508-992-9921.

Family Ministry—Rev. THOMAS A. FRECHETTE, Dir., Family Life Center, 500 Slocum Rd., North Dartmouth, 02747. Tel: 508-999-6420.

Holy Childhood Association, The—Rev. Msgr. JOHN J. OLIVEIRA, P.A., Dir., 106 Illinois St., New Bedford, 02745. Tel: 508-995-3593.

In Support of Life Program—Sr. ELAINE HEFFERNAN, R.S.M., Contact Person, Family Life Center, 500 Slocum Rd., North Dartmouth, 02747. Tel: 508-999-6420.

Missionary Cooperative Plan—Rev. Msgr. JOHN J. OLIVEIRA, P.A., Dir., 106 Illinois St., New Bedford, 02745. Tel: 508-995-3593.

Office for Divine Worship—Rev. Msgr. STEPHEN J. AVILA, 157 Middleboro Rd., P.O. Box 718, East Freetown, 02717. Tel: 508-763-2240; Fax: 508-763-3040.

Office of AIDS Ministry, Inc.—KRYSTEN WINTER-GREEN, Ph.D., Exec. Dir., 243 Forest St., Clemence Hall, Rm. 225, Fall River, 02721. Tel: 508-674-5600, Ext. 2295.

Office of Pastoral Planning—Rev. Msgr. RONALD A. TOSTI, Dir.; ROSE SIMPSON, Assoc., 4451 Old Falmouth Rd., Rte.28, Cotuit, 02635. Mailing Address, P.O. Box 1800, Mashpee, 02649. Tel: 508-428-9557; 508-428-9157; Fax: 508-428-9526.

Permanent Diaconate Program—Rev. Msgr. JOHN J. OLIVEIRA, P.A., Dir.; Rev. CRAIG A. PREGANA, Assoc. Dir., 500 Slocum Rd., North Dartmouth, 02747. Tel: 508-993-9935; 508-993-9938; Fax: 508-993-9950.

Pro-Life Apostolate—Rev. STEPHEN A. FERNANDES, Dir.; Mrs. MARIAN DESROSIERS, Asst., 500 Slocum Rd., North Dartmouth, 02747. Tel: 508-997-2290; Fax: 508-997-2923.

Propagation of the Faith—Rev. Msgr. JOHN J. OLIVEIRA, P.A., Dir., Office, 106 Illinois St., New Bedford, 02745. Tel: 508-995-3593; Fax: 508-995-2453.

St. Vincent De Paul Society—Rev. DAVID A. COSTA, 58 Church St., P.O. Box 470, North Attleboro, 02761-0470. Tel: 508-699-8383; Fax: 508-699-7016.

Television Apostolate—Rev. Msgr. STEPHEN J. AVILA, Coord., 157 Middleboro Rd., P.O. Box 718, East Freetown, 02717. Tel: 508-763-2240; Fax: 508-763-3040.

Victim Assistance Coordinator—ARLENE A. MCNAMEE, L.C.S.W. Tel: 508-674-4681. Email: aam@cssdioc.org.

Vocations—Rev. CRAIG A. PREGANA, Dir., 47 Underwood St., Fall River, 02720. Tel: 508-675-1311; Fax: 508-679-9220.

Youth-Office of Youth Ministry—VACANT, Dir., P.O. Box 1167, Fall River, 02722. Tel: 508-675-3847; 508-675-3867.

Commissions and Councils

Campaign for Human Development—ARLENE A. MCNAMEE, L.C.S.W., P.O. Box M, S. Station, Fall River, 02724. Tel: 508-674-4681; Fax: 508-675-2224.

Catholic Scouting Program—Rev. STEPHEN B. SALVADOR, Dir., 250 Snell St., Fall River, 02721. Tel: 508-676-8463; Fax: 508-678-8070.

Continuing Education of the Clergy—Rev. MARK R. HESSION, J.C.L., Dir., 230 S. Main St., Centerville, 02632. Tel: 508-775-5744; Fax: 508-771-0170.

Mentoring Program for Priests—Rev. JOHN J. OLIVEIRA, Dir., 230 Bonney St., New Bedford, 02744. Tel: 508-993-4704; Fax: 508-991-5536.

Diocesan Council of Catholic Nurses—Rev. MARK R. HESSION, J.C.L., Moderator, 230 S. Main St., Centerville, 02632. Tel: 508-775-5744; Fax: 508-771-0170.

Diocesan Council of Catholic Women—Sr. EUGENIA BRADY, S.J.C., Moderator, Cluny Convent, 90 Brenton Rd., Newport, RI 02840. Tel: 401-924-0953.

Diocesan Liaison with Charismatic Groups—Rev. EDWARD A. MURPHY, Dir., 709 Hanover St., Fall River, 02720. Tel: 508-679-6732.

Diocesan Liaison with Portuguese Charismatic Groups—Rev. HENRY S. ARRUDA, St. Anthony's Rectory, 126 School St., Taunton, 02780. Tel: 508-822-0714.

Diocesan Liaison with Cursillo—Rev. BRUCE M. NEYLON, 36 Rockland St., P.O. Box 111, Fall River, 02724. Tel: 508-672-0423.

Diocesan Pastoral Council—Rev. Msgr. JOHN A. PERRY, V.G., P.O. Box 2577, Fall River, 02722.

Legion of Mary—Rev. BARRY W. WALL, 120 Beattie St., Fall River, 02723. Tel: 508-672-7232.

CLERGY, PARISHES, MISSIONS AND PAROCHIAL SCHOOLS

CITY OF FALL RIVER
(BRISTOL COUNTY)

1—CATHEDRAL OF ST. MARY OF THE ASSUMPTION (1838), Revs. Edward J. Healey, Rector; Edson S. Shiramizu. In Res., Rev. Thomas E. McGlynn, J.C.L.
Res.: 327 Second St., 02721. Tel: 508-673-2833; Fax: 508-672-0667.
Catechesis/Religious Program—467 Spring St., 02721. Tel: 508-672-5531. Students 71.

2—ST. ANNE'S (1869), (French), Revs. Marc H. Bergeron; Christopher Stanibula.
Res.: 818 Middle St., 02721. Tel: 508-674-5651; 508-678-5322; Fax: 508-672-0939.
School—Tel: 508-678-2152; Fax: 508-674-5190. Mr. Felipe M. Felipe, Prin. Lay Teachers 24; Students 371.
Catechesis/Religious Program—Tel: 508-678-1510. Susan Chapdelaine, D.R.E. Students 332.

3—ST. ANTHONY OF PADUA (1911), (Portuguese), Rev. John C. Martins.
Res.: 48 Sixteenth St., 02723. Tel: 508-673-2402; Fax: 508-730-2519.
Catechesis/Religious Program—Tel: 508-674-1986. Deborah Polselli, D.R.E. (1st & 2nd grades); John Janeiro, D.R.E. (3rd - 9th grades). Students 290.

4—BLESSED SACRAMENT (1902), (French), Merged, with Our Lady of the Angels and St. Patrick's, Fall River to form the Parish of the Good Shepherd, Fall River.

5—ST. ELIZABETH'S (1915), Merged, with St. Jean Baptiste and St. William to form Holy Trinity.

6—ESPIRITO SANTO (1904), (Portuguese), Rev. James Ferry; Deacons John de Amaral Moniz; Thomas Souza.
Res.: 311 Alden St., 02723. Tel: 508-672-3352; Fax: 508-646-1787.
School—143 Everett St., 02723. Tel: 508-672-3362; Fax: 508-672-7724. Mary Bolton, Prin. Lay Teachers 13; Students 269.
Catechesis/Religious Program—Beverly Tavares, D.R.E. Students 325.

7—HOLY CROSS (1916), (Polish), Merged, with SS. Peter & Paul, Fall River.

8—HOLY NAME (1923), Revs. Francis L. Mahoney; Michael A. Ciryak, O.F.M.
Res.: 709 Hanover St., 02720. Tel: 508-679-6732; Fax: 508-675-4755.
School—850 Pearce St., 02720. Tel: 508-674-9131; Fax: 508-675-4755. Religious Sisters of Mercy 1; Lay Teachers 12; Students 228.
Catechesis/Religious Program—Tel: 508-679-3127. Students 500.

9—HOLY TRINITY (2000), Rev. David M. Andrade.
Res.: 951 Stafford Rd., 02721. Tel: 508-672-3200; Fax: 580-673-5518.
School—64 Lamphor St., 02721. Tel: 508-673-6772; Fax: 508-730-1864. Kathleen Barboza, Prin. Lay Teachers 19; Students 244.
Catechesis/Religious Program—Tel: 508-672-8340; Fax: 508-673-0512. Patricia Pasternak, D.R.E. Students 271.

10—ST. JEAN BAPTISTE (1901), Merged, with St. Elizabeth and St. William to form Holy Trinity Parish.

11—ST. JOSEPH'S (1873), Rev. Msgr. John A. Perry, V.G.
Res.: 1335 N. Main St., 02720. Tel: 508-673-1123; Fax: 508-673-7230.
Catechesis/Religious Program—Students 250.

12—ST. LOUIS (1885), Closed., Sacramental records can be found at St. Mary's Cathedral.

13—ST. MICHAEL (1902), (Portuguese), Revs. Luis A. Cardoso; Scott A. Ciosek.
Res.: 189 Essex St., 02720. Tel: 508-672-6713; Fax: 508-679-1841.
School—Tel: 508-678-0266; Fax: 508-324-4433. Religious of the Holy Union of the Sacred Hearts 1; Lay Teachers 10; Students 180.
Catechesis/Religious Program—Tel: 508-678-0266; Fax: 508-679-1841. Students 245.

14—NOTRE DAME DE LOURDES (1874), (French), Rev. Richard L. Chretien. In Res., Revs. Leonard Hindsley, O.P.; Marek S. Tuptynski; Kenneth R. Gumbert, O.P. (Oakland Prov.).
Res.: 529 Eastern Ave., 02723. Tel: 508-679-1991; Fax: 508-676-5276.
School—34 St. Joseph St., 02723. Tel: 508-672-5461; Fax: 508-673-8430. Lay Teachers 11; Students 175.
Catechesis/Religious Program—Students 137.

15—OUR LADY OF HEALTH (1924), (Portuguese), Rev. Michael M. Camara; Deacon Robert A. Faria.
Res.: 642 Cambridge St., 02721. Tel: 508-672-0819.
Catechesis/Religious Program—49 Somerset St., 02721. Tel: 508-673-8987. Students 180.

16—OUR LADY OF THE ANGELS (1915), (Portuguese), Merged, with Blessed Sacrament and St. Patrick's, Fall River to form the Parish of the Good Shepherd, Fall River.

17—OUR LADY OF THE HOLY ROSARY (1904), (Italian), Rev. Barry W. Wall.
Res.: 120 Beattie St., 02723. Tel: 508-672-7232; Fax: 508-672-1506.
Catechesis/Religious Program—84 Beattie St.,

02723. Tel: 508-672-7262; Fax: 508-672-1506. Robert T. Houghton, D.R.E. Students 57.

18—OUR LADY OF THE IMMACULATE CONCEPTION (1882), Rev. Richard L. Chretien, Admin.
Res.: 15 Thomas St., P.O. Box 4127, 02723. Tel: 508-673-2122; Fax: 508-730-1694.
Catechesis/Religious Program—Tel: 508-672-3254. Mrs. Colleen Laliberte, D.R.E. Students 130.

19—PARISH OF THE GOOD SHEPHERD (2002), Rev. Fred Babiczuk; Deacon John F. Branco.
Res.: 1598 S. Main St., 02724-2586. Tel: 508-678-7412; Fax: 508-673-1280.
Catechesis/Religious Program—Tel: 508-677-4702. Students 350.

20—ST. PATRICK'S (1873), Merged, with Blessed Sacrament and Our Lady of the Angels, Fall River to form the Parish of the Good Shepherd, Fall River.

21—SS. PETER AND PAUL (1882), Rev. Stephen B. Salvador.
Res.: 250 Snell St., 02721. Tel: 508-676-8463; Fax: 508-678-8070.
Worship Site—Holy Cross Church, 47 Pulaski St., 02721.
School—(Grades PreK-8), 240 Dover St., 02721. Tel: 508-672-7258; Fax: 508-674-6042. Lay Teachers 11; Students 196.
Catechesis/Religious Program—(Grades K-8) Tel: 508-672-3720. Students 140.

22—SACRED HEART (1872), Rev. Raymond Cambra. In Res., Rev. Craig A. Pregana.
Res.: 160 Seabury St., 02720. Tel: 508-673-0852; Fax: 508-678-0873. Email: sacred_heart_church@msn.com.
Catechesis/Religious Program—Tel: 508-730-1481. Mrs. Maureen Costa, D.R.E. Students 100.

23—SANTO CHRISTO (1891), (Portuguese), Revs. Gastao A. Oliveira; Brian Albino.
Res.: 185 Canal St., 02721. Tel: 508-676-1184; Fax: 508-676-9701.
Catechesis/Religious Program—Tel: 508-675-3007. Mr. Osvaldo Pacheco, D.R.E. Students 493.

24—ST. STANISLAUS (1898), (Polish), Rev. Bruce M. Neylon; Deacon Franciszek W. Mis.
Res.: 36 Rockland St., P.O. Box 111, 02724. Tel: 508-672-0423; Fax: 508-677-1378.
School—37 Rockland St., 02724. Tel: 508-674-6771; Fax: 508-677-1622. Miss Jean Willis, Prin. Lay Teachers 11; Students 167.
Catechesis/Religious Program—Students 31.

25—ST. WILLIAM'S (1905), Merged, with St. Elizabeth and St. Jean Baptiste to form Holy Trinity Parish.

OUTSIDE THE CITY OF FALL RIVER

ACUSHNET, BRISTOL CO., ST. FRANCIS XAVIER'S (1915), Rev. Daniel W. Lacroix; Deacon Michael P. Guy.
Res.: 125 Main St., 02743. Tel: 508-995-7600; Fax: 508-995-1794.
School—223 Main St., 02743. Tel: 508-995-4313; Fax: 508-995-0456. Donald A. Pelletier, Prin. Religious 2; Lay Teachers 14; Students 244.
Catechesis/Religious Program—Tel: 508-998-7445. Students 350.

ASSONET, BRISTOL CO., ST. BERNARD'S (1978), Rev. Timothy J. Goldrick.
Res.: 32 S. Main St., P.O. Box 370, 02702. Tel: 508-644-5585; Fax: 508-644-2136. Email: stbernardassonet@aol.com. Web: www.stbernardassonet.org.
Catechesis/Religious Program—Tel: 508-644-2032. Brian Correia, D.R.E.; Marlene Correia, D.R.E. Students 497.

ATTLEBORO FALLS, BRISTOL CO., ST. MARK'S (1967), Rev. Peter N. Graziano, S.T.L., M.A., M.S.W.; Deacon Richard J. Gundlach.
Res.: 105 Stanley St., Box 1240, 02763-0240. Tel: 508-699-7566; Fax: 508-643-0103. Email: stmarkoffice@comcast.net. Web: www.stmarks-attleborofalls.org.
Catechesis/Religious Program—Tel: 508-695-7773. Mrs. Elaine Corvese, D.R.E. Students 875.

ATTLEBORO, BRISTOL CO.

1—HOLY GHOST (1921), Rev. John A. Raposo.
Res.: 71 Linden St., 02703. Tel: 508-222-3266; Fax: 508-222-3292.
Catechesis/Religious Program—Tel: 508-222-6756. Pedro Teixeira, Coord. Students 90.

2—ST. JOHN THE EVANGELIST (1883), [CEM] Rev. Msgr. Daniel F. Hoye, J.C.L.
Res.: One St. John Pl., 02703-2251. Tel: 508-222-1206; Fax: 508-226-6461.
School—13 Hodges St., 02703. Tel: 508-222-5062; Fax: 508-223-1737. Mrs. Claire Powers, Prin. Lay Teachers 12; Students 270.
Catechesis/Religious Program—Tel: 508-222-0707; Fax: 508-222-0701. Students 840.

3—ST. JOSEPH'S (1905), Rev. Michael Carvill, F.S.C.B. In Res., Revs. Vincent Nagle, F.S.C.B.; Luca Brancolini, F.S.C.B.
Res.: 208 S. Main St., 02703. Tel 508-226-1115; Fax: 508-226-0234.
Catechesis/Religious Program—10 Maple St.. Tel: 508-222-1780. Students 185.

4—ST. STEPHEN'S (1875), [CEM] Rev. James H. Morse.
Res.: 683 S. Main St., 02703-6397. Tel: 508-222-0641; Fax: 508-222-1855.
Catechesis/Religious Program— Chris Adams; Patty Adams. Students 245.

5—ST. THERESA OF THE CHILD JESUS (1925), Rev. James W. Fahey.
Res.: 18 Baltic St., South Attleboro, 02703. Tel: 508-761-8111; Fax: 508-761-5475.
Catechesis/Religious Program—Tel: 508-761-5367. Mrs. Theresa Paquette, D.R.E. Students 320.

BREWSTER, BARNSTABLE CO., OUR LADY OF THE CAPE (1961), Revs. Bernard Baris, M.S.; William Kaliyadan, M.S.; Henry Brodeur, M.S.; Deacons R. Donald Bibon; James Leavitt.
Res.: Stony Brook Rd., P.O. Box 1799, 02631. Tel: 508-385-3252; Fax: 508-385-6864.
Catechesis/Religious Program—Tel: 508-385-2115. Elizabeth M. McCullough, D.R.E. Students 386.
Mission—Immaculate Conception Rte. 6A, East Brewster, Barnstable Co. 02631.

BUZZARDS BAY, BARNSTABLE CO., ST. MARGARET (1915), [JC] Rev. Gilbert J. Silverio, O.F.M.
Res.: 141 Main St., 02532. Tel: 508-759-7777; Fax: 508-759-3920.
School—Tel: 508-759-2213; Fax: 508-759-8776. Lay Teachers 14; Students 247.
Catechesis/Religious Program—Tel: 508-743-4604. Manuel Sabda, D.R.E. Students 381.
Mission—St. Mary Star of the Sea Onset, Plymouth Co.

CENTERVILLE, BARNSTABLE CO., OUR LADY OF VICTORY (1957), Revs. Mark R. Hession, J.C.L.; David C. Frederici Deacons Joseph P. Stanley; James M. Barrett; Theodore Lukac.
In Res—Rev. John M. Murray.
Res.: 230 S. Main St., 02632. Tel: 508-775-5744; Fax: 508-771-0170.
Catechesis/Religious Program—Tel: 508-771-1614. Elide Rodrigues, D.R.E. Students 1,188.
Mission—Our Lady of Hope Rte. 6A, West Barnstable, Barnstable Co. 02668.

CHATHAM, BARNSTABLE CO., HOLY REDEEMER (1955), [JC] Rev. Jon-Paul Gallant; Deacons Joseph F. Mador; Gabriel M. Liegey Jr.; Richard B. Stenberg.
Res.: 57 Highland Ave., Box 687, 02633. Tel: 508-945-0677; Fax: 508-945-3186.
Catechesis/Religious Program—Students 100.
Mission—Our Lady of Grace P.O. Box 687, South Chatham, Barnstable Co. 02633.

DIGHTON, BRISTOL CO., ST. PETER'S 1904), Rev. Gerald P. Barnwell.
Res.: 2039 County St., 02715. Tel: 508-669-6463; Fax: 508-669-6463.
Catechesis/Religious Program—Tel: 508-669-6925; Fax: 508-669-6925. Students 155.

EAST FALMOUTH, BARNSTABLE CO., ST. ANTHONY'S (1923), [CEM] Rev. William M. Costello.
Res.: 167 E. Falmouth Hwy., 02536. Tel: 508-548-0108; Fax: 508-457-1723.
Catechesis/Religious Program—Tel: 508-548-3515; Fax: 508-548-3515. Students 435.

EAST FREETOWN, BRISTOL CO., ST. JOHN NEUMANN (1984), Rev. Msgr. Stephen J. Avila, Pastor; Deacon Bruce J. Bonneau.
Res.: 157 Middleboro Rd., Box 718, 02717. Tel: 508-763-2240; Fax: 508-763-3040. Web: www.sjn.freetown.org.
Catechesis/Religious Program—Tel: 508-763-8122. Dr. Doris Thibault, D.R.E.; Mrs. Madeleine Oliver, D.R.E.; Mrs. Suzanne Medeiros, D.R.E. Students 618.

EAST TAUNTON, BRISTOL CO., HOLY FAMILY (1900), Rev. Jay T. Maddock, J.C.L.; Deacon John J. Fitzpatrick.
Res.: 370 Middleboro, P.O. Box 619, 02718. Tel: 508-824-5707; Fax: 508-824-5665.
Catechesis/Religious Program—Tel: 508-824-3578; Fax: 508-824-5665. Margaret Ormond, D.R.E. Students 525.

EDGARTOWN, DUKES CO., ST. ELIZABETH (1925), Revs. Michael R. Nagle, D.Min.; John C. Ozug; Deacon Fred Lapiana.
Res.: 86 Main St., P.O. Box 1536, 02539. Tel: 508-627-5017; Fax: 508-627-6021.
Catechesis/Religious Program—School St., Oak Bluffs, 02557. Tel: 508-693-0342; Fax: 508-693-8517 Consolidated with Sacred Heart, Oak Bluffs.

FAIRHAVEN, BRISTOL CO.

1—ST. JOSEPH'S (1905), Rev. Robert Charlton, SS.CC.; Deacons Robert Lorenzo; Douglas Medeiros.
Res.: 41 Walnut St., 02719. Tel: 508-994-9714; Fax: 508-979-4659.
School—Spring St. and Homestead Ave., 02719. Tel: 508-996-1983; Fax: 508-996-1998. Dorothea Coderre, Prin. Lay Teachers 11; Students 194.
Catechesis/Religious Program—Tel: 508-994-8679. Mary Lorenzo, D.R.E. Students 327.

2—ST MARY'S (1933), Rev. Patrick Killilea, SS.CC.
Res.: 41 Harding Rd., 02719. Tel: 508-992-7300; Fax: 508-992-0685.
Catechesis/Religious Program—Tel: 508-992-8721. Sr. Eleanor Cyr, SS.CC., D.R.E. Students 285.

FALMOUTH, BARNSTABLE CO., ST. PATRICK'S (1928), [CEM] Rev. Msgr. John A. Perry, V.G.; Rev. Tadeusz Pacholczyk; Deacons Patrick J. Mahoney; John E. Simonis.
Res.: 511 Main St., P.O. Box 569, 02541. Tel: 508-548-1065; Fax: 508-495-0875.
Catechesis/Religious Program—Tel: 508-548-2306. Cynthia O'Connor, D.R.E. Students 373.
Chapel—Falmouth Heights, St. Thomas

HYANNIS, BARNSTABLE CO., ST. FRANCIS XAVIER'S (1904), [CEM 2] Revs. Thomas A. Frechette; Paul T. Lamb; Roger J. Landry; Deacons Richard M. Dresser; Richard J. Murphy.
Res.: 21 Cross St., 02601. Tel: 508-775-0818; Fax: 508-771-5940.
School—Tel: 508-771-7200; Fax: 508-771-7233. Robert H. Deburro, Headmaster. Lay Teachers 14; Students 220.
Catechesis/Religious Program—Tel: 508-775-6200; Fax: 508-771-7233. Mrs. Mary Offiler, D.R.E. Students 190.
Mission—Sacred Heart Chapel Summer St., Yarmouth Port, Barnstable Co. 02675.

MANSFIELD, BRISTOL CO., ST. MARY'S (1894), [CEM] Very Rev. George C. Bellenoit, V.F.; Revs. Michael Joseph Fitzpatrick; Dariusz Kalinowski; Sr. Ann William Publicover, M.S.B.T., Pastoral Min.; Deacons Thomas P. Palanza; Walter D. Thomas.
Res.: 330 Pratt St., 02048-1581. Tel: 508-339-2981; Fax: 508-339-0612.
School—Tel: 508-339-4800. Lay Teachers 6; Students 119.
Catechesis/Religious Program—Tel: 508-339-4621. Mrs. Ellen Westlund, D.R.E. Students 2,345.

MARION, PLYMOUTH CO., ST. RITA'S (1972), Rev. William G. Campbell.
Res.: 113 Front St., Box 902, 02738. Tel: 508-748-1497; Fax: 508-748-0604.
Catechesis/Religious Program—Tel: 508-748-0576. Students 200.

MASHPEE, BARNSTABLE CO., CHRIST THE KING (1984), Rev. Msgr. Ronald A. Tosti; Rev. Lawrence A. Jerge, C.S.C., P.V.; Deacons Robert D. Lemay, Pastoral Assoc.; Gregory J. Beckel; Frank D. Fantasia.
The Commons: P.O. Box 1800, 02649. Tel: 508-477-7700; Fax: 508-477-8158.
Catechesis/Religious Program—Tel: 508-477-6565. Sisters Annette Roach, O.P., D.R.E.; Claire Sinotte, O.P., D.R.E. Students 790.

MATTAPOISETT, PLYMOUTH CO., ST. ANTHONY'S (1908), [CEM] Rev. Leonard M. Mullaney; Deacon Robert L. Surprenant.
Mailing Address: P.O. Box 501, 02739-0501. Fax: 508-758-3019.
Res.: 22 Barstow St., 02739. Tel: 508-758-3719.
Catechesis/Religious Program—Tel: 508-758-3735. Mrs. Mary Chaplain, D.R.E. Students 353.

NANTUCKET, NANTUCKET CO., ST. MARY'S, OUR LADY OF THE ISLE (1903), [CEM] Rev. Paul A. Caron; Deacon Donald L. Battiston.
Res.: 6 Orange St., P.O. Box 1168, 02554. Tel: 508-228-0100; Fax: 508-325-7991.
Catechesis/Religious Program—Tel: 508-228-4852. Ms. Elaine Boehm, D.R.E. Students 214.
Station— Siasconset.

NEW BEDFORD, BRISTOL CO.

1—ST. ANNE (1908), (French), Rev. Martin L. Buote; Deacon Marcel Morency.
Res.: 890 Brock Ave., 02744. Tel: 508-997-9271.
Catechesis/Religious Program—Students 11.

2—ST. ANTHONY OF PADUA'S (1895), (French), Rev. Msgr. Edmond R. Levesque; Rev. Christopher Gomes, O.F.M.
Res.: 1359 Acushnet Ave., 02746. Tel: 508-993-1691; Fax: 508-999-4775.
School—109 Ashley Blvd., 02746. Tel: 508-994-5121; Fax: 508-979-5923. Mrs. Elizabeth Lavigne, Prin. Lay Teachers 13; Students 300.
Catechesis/Religious Program—Students 82.
Convent—106 Bullard St., 02746.

3—ST. CASIMIR (1927), (Polish), Closed., For inquiries for parish records, please see Our Lady of Perpetual Help, New Bedford.

4—ST. FRANCIS OF ASSISI (1928), (Italian), Rev. Kevin Harrington.
Res.: 247 North St., 02740. Tel: 508-997-7732; Fax: 508-991-6630.
Catechesis/Religious Program—Mrs. Pamela Herbert, D.R.E. Students 30.

5—ST. HEDWIG (1908), (Polish), Rev. Ramon Dominguez, Admin.
Mailing Address: P.O. Box 40605, 02744-0006.
Res.: 42 Chicago St., 02721. Tel: 508-996-8703; Fax: 508-992-2208.
Catechesis/Religious Program— Sr. Margarita Ocana, M.G.Sp.S., D.R.E. Students 7.

6—HOLY NAME, Merged, with Sacred Heart, New

Bedford to form Holy Name of the Sacred Heart of Jesus, New Bedford.

7—HOLY NAME OF THE SACRED HEART OF JESUS (1999), Rev. Msgr. Thomas J. Harrington, J.C.L.; Rev. Andrzej J. Kozanko; Deacon Eugene H. Sasseville.
Res.: 121 Mt. Pleasant St., 02740. Tel: 508-992-3184; Fax: 508-984-3406.
School—Sisters 2; Lay Teachers 11; Students 275.
Catechesis / Religious Program—Tel: 508-996-8654. Mrs. Heidi Kuliga, D.R.E. Students 260.

8—ST. JAMES (1888), Very Rev. Edward E. Correia, V.F.; Deacon Lawrence St. Onge.
02740Web: www.saintjames-nb.org. In Res., Revs. Herbert T. Nichols; Michael S. Racine.
Res.: 233 County St., 02740. Tel: 508-992-9408; Fax: 508-990-0575.
School—St. James-St. John, 180 Orchard St., 02740. Tel: 508-996-0534. Lay Teachers 10; Students 266.
Catechesis / Religious Program—Students 156.

9—ST. JOHN THE BAPTIST (1871), (Portuguese), [CEM] Revs. Maurice O. Gauvin; Rodney E. Thibault; Deacon Paul J. Macedo, P.D.
Res.: 344 County St., 02740. Tel: 508-992-7727; Fax: 508-997-1462.
School—Tel: 508-996-0534; Fax: 508-996-0534. See listing for St. James, New Bedford.
Catechesis / Religious Program—Tel: 508-996-3087. Ms. Marge Ferreira, D.R.E. Students 193.

10—ST. JOSEPH (1910), Merged, with St. Theresa, New Bedford to form St. Joseph-St. Therese, New Bedford.

11—ST. JOSEPH-ST. THERESE (1999), Rev. Roger J. Levesque; Deacons Maurice Lavallee; Leo W. Racine.
Res.: 51 Duncan St., 02745-6108. Tel: 508-995-5235; Fax: 508-995-7266.
School—35 Kearsarge St., 02745-6117. Tel: 508-995-2264; Fax: 508-995-0038. Mary Beth Moriarty, Prin. Lay Teachers 8; Students 142.
Catechesis / Religious Program—Students 104.

12—ST. KILIAN (1896), Revs. Jose G. Giunta, I.V.E., Pastor; Pablo Ruani, I.V.E.
Res.: 306 Ashley Blvd., 02746. Tel: 508-992-7587; Fax: 508-994-0281.
Catechesis / Religious Program—Fax: 508-994-0281. Julie Carbor, D.R.E. Students 72.

13—ST. LAWRENCE MARTYR (1821), Rev. John M. Sullivan.
Res.: 110 Summer St., 02740. Tel: 508-992-4251; Fax: 508-984-4136.
School—Holy Family-Holy Name, 91 Summer St., 02740. Tel: 508-993-3547; Fax: 508-993-8277. Sisters 2; Lay Teachers 17; Students 275.
Catechesis / Religious Program—Tel: 508-993-3547. Mrs. Teresa Ouellette, D.R.E.; Ms. Cecilia Felix, D.R.E. Students 130.

14—ST. MARY'S (1923), Rev. Msgr. John J. Oliveira, P.A.; Deacon David B. Pepin.
Res.: 106 Illinois St., 02745. Tel: 508-995-3593; Fax: 508-995-2453.
School—115 Illinois St., 02745. Tel: 508-995-3696; Fax: 508-995-0840. Web: www.saintjames-nb.org. Lay Teachers 10; Students 235.
Catechesis / Religious Program—Tel: 508-995-3693. Students 250.

15—NUESTRA SENORA DE GUADALUPE (1993), (Hispanic), Rev. Ramon Dominguez, Admin.
Mailing Address: P.O. Box 40605, 02744-0006. Tel: 508-996-5862; Fax: 508-992-2208.
Res.: 42 Chicago St., 02721. Tel: 508-996-5862; Fax: 508-992-2208.
Catechesis / Religious Program—Tel: 508-997-8729. Sr. Margarita Ocana, M.G.Sp.S., D.R.E. Students 84.

16—OUR LADY OF FATIMA (1966), Rev. Stephen A. Fernandes.
Res.: 4256 Acushnet Ave., 02745. Tel: 508-995-7351; Fax: 508-995-4401.
Parish Center—980 Tobey St., 02745.
Catechesis / Religious Program—Tel: 508-995-6685. Mrs. Pearl Enos, D.R.E. Students 143.

17—OUR LADY OF MT. CARMEL (1902), (Portuguese), Revs. John J. Oliveira; Michael M. Camara; Kevin A. Cook; Deacon Abilio Pires. In Res., Rev. Msgr. Antonino C. Tavares (Retired).
Res.: 230 Bonney St., 02744. Tel: 508-993-4704; Fax: 508-991-5536.
School—103 Crapo St., 02744. Tel: 508-997-9612; Fax: 508-997-2485. Mr. Joseph P. Sullivan, Prin. Lay Teachers 9; Students 117.
Catechesis / Religious Program—Tel: 508-984-7097. Students 535.

18—OUR LADY OF PERPETUAL HELP (1905), (Polish), Revs. Roman Chwaliszewski, O.F.M.Conv.; Sebastian Slesinski, O.F.M.Conv.
Res.: 235 N. Front St., 02746. Tel: 508-992-9378; Fax: 508-993-4881.
Catechesis / Religious Program—Students 64.

19—OUR LADY OF THE ASSUMPTION (1905), (Cape Verdean), Rev. Stanley Kolasa, SS.CC.; Deacons Eduardo M. Pacheco; Antonio M. Da Cruz.
Res.: 54 S. 6th St., 02740. Tel: 508-994-0106; Fax: 508-994-9461.
Parish Center—47 S. 6th St., 02740. Tel: 508-994-7602.
Catechesis / Religious Program—Tel: 508-994-7602. Students 178.

20—OUR LADY OF THE IMMACULATE CONCEPTION (1914), (Portuguese), Revs. Daniel O. Reis; Timothy Paul Driscoll; Deacon Albertino F. Pires.
Res.: 136 Earle St., 02746. Tel: 508-992-9892; Fax: 508-992-9907.
Catechesis / Religious Program—156 Davis St., 02746. Tel: 508-990-0249. Students 635.

21—SACRED HEART (1874), (French), Merged, With Holy Name, New Bedford to form Holy Name of the Sacred Heart of Jesus, New Bedford.

22—ST. THERESA (1926), (French), Merged, with St. Joseph's, New Bedford to form St. Joseph-St. Therese, New Bedford.

NORTH ATTLEBORO, BRISTOL CO.

1—ST. MARY'S (1890), [CEM] Rev. James M. Fitzpatrick; Deacon James J. Meloni Jr.
Res.: 14 Park St., 02760. Tel: 508-695-6161.
School—Tel: 508-695-3072; Fax: 508-695-9074. See St. Mary-Sacred Heart.
Catechesis / Religious Program—14 Park St., 02761. Tel: 508-695-3823. Students 387.

2—SACRED HEART (1904), (French), Rev. David A. Costa.
Res.: 58 Church St., 02760. Tel: 508-699-8383; Fax: 508-699-7016.
School—St. Mary's-Sacred Heart Consolidated School, 57 Richards Ave., 02760. Tel: 508-695-3072; Fax: 508-695-9074. Mrs. Denise M. Peixoto, Prin. Lay Teachers 12; Students 250.
Catechesis / Religious Program—Tel: 508-643-9009. Students 288.

NORTH DARTMOUTH, BRISTOL CO., ST. JULIE BILLIART (1969), Revs. Brian J. Harrington, Pastor; David A. Pignato; Deacon Claude A. LeBlanc.
Res.: 494 Slocum Rd., 02747. Tel: 508-993-2351; Fax: 508-993-2437.
Catechesis / Religious Program—Tel: 508-990-0287. Peter Healy, D.R.E. Students 573.

NORTH DIGHTON, BRISTOL CO., ST. JOSEPH'S (1913), Rev. James R. McLellan.
Res.: 499 Spring St., P.O. Box 564, 02764-0564. Tel: 508-822-1425; Fax: 508-822-3886.
Catechesis / Religious Program—Tel: 508-824-6581. Sr. Judith Costa, S.S.D., D.R.E. Students 384.

NORTH EASTON, BRISTOL CO., IMMACULATE CONCEPTION (1871), [CEM] Revs. Thomas C. Lopes; Ethan Garrett McCarthy; Deacon Paul M. Fournier.
Res.: 193 Main St., 02356. Tel: 508-238-3232; Fax: 508-238-7849. Email: rectory@icceaston.org.
Catechesis / Religious Program—Tel: 508-238-3230; Fax: 508-238-7849. Kathleen Hohl, D.R.E. Students 577.

NORTH FALMOUTH, BARNSTABLE CO., ST. ELIZABETH SETON (1977), Rev. Msgr. John F. Moore; Deacons Paul K. Roma; William A. Martin; Vincent J. Coates Jr.; Peter M. Guresh.
Res.: 481 Quaker Rd., Box 861, 02556. Tel: 508-563-7770; Fax: 508-563-7794. Email: seton@capecod.net.
Catechesis / Religious Program—Tel: 508-563-7774. Students 393.

NORTON, BRISTOL CO., ST. MARY'S (1925), Rev. Robert A. Oliveira; Deacon Michael E. Murray.
Res.: 133 S. Worcester St., Box 430, 02766-0430. Tel: 508-285-4462; Fax: 508-285-5589.
Catechesis / Religious Program—Tel: 508-285-3237. Mrs. Midge Melendy, D.R.E.; Deb Demers, D.R.E. Students 1,097.

OAK BLUFFS, DUKES CO., SACRED HEART (1880), [CEM] Revs. Michael R. Nagle, D.Min.; John C. Ozug; Deacon Fred Lapiana.
Res.: 156 Circuit Ave., P.O. Box 1565, 02557. Tel: 508-693-0342; Fax: 508-696-8408.
Catechesis / Religious Program—Fax: 508-693-8517. Students 339.

ORLEANS, BARNSTABLE CO., ST. JOAN OF ARC (1947), Rev. Richard M. Roy; Deacons Norman McEnaney; John Twerago.
Res.: 61 Canal Rd., P.O. Box 336, 02653. Tel: 508-255-0170; Fax: 508-240-6741.
Catechesis / Religious Program—Tel: 508-255-1257. Judith Burt Walker, D.R.E. Students 260.

OSTERVILLE, BARNSTABLE CO., OUR LADY OF THE ASSUMPTION (1928), Revs. Philip A. Davignon; Pawel A. Swiercz. In Res., Rev. Roger Nolette.
Res.: 76 Wianno Ave., P.O. Box E., 02655. Tel: 508-428-2011; Fax: 508-428-2891.
Catechesis / Religious Program—Tel: 508-428-0797. Students 182.

POCASSET, BARNSTABLE CO., ST. JOHN THE EVANGELIST (1969), Rev. Robert C. Donovan, Pastor; Deacons Leonard C. Dexter Jr.; James Marzelli Jr.
Res.: 15 Virginia Rd., P.O. Box 1558, 02559. Tel: 508-563-3121; 508-563-5887; Fax: 508-563-3102.
Catechesis / Religious Program—841 Shore Rd., P.O. Box 1558, 02559. Tel: 508-563-5536; Fax: 508-563-5536. Liz Henry, D.R.E. Students 294.

PROVINCETOWN, BARNSTABLE CO., ST. PETER THE APOSTLE (1874), [CEM] Rev. Henry J. Dahl; Deacon Chester O. Cook.
Res.: 11 Prince St., 02657. Tel: 508-487-0095; Fax: 508-487-2564.
Catechesis / Religious Program—Students 92.
Mission—Our Lady of Perpetual Help, North Truro, Barnstable Co. 02652.

RAYNHAM, BRISTOL CO., ST. ANN (1961), Revs. Michael K. McManus; David A. Pregana; Deacon John Welch.
Res.: 660 N. Main St., P.O. Box 247, 02768. Tel: 508-823-9833; 508-823-9834; Fax: 508-823-8935.
Catechesis / Religious Program—725 N. Main St. Box 247, Raynham Center, 02768. Tel: 508-824-9021; Fax: 508-824-1090. Catherine Goudreau, D.R.E.; Paul Gilchrist, D.R.E. Students 1,036.

SANDWICH, BARNSTABLE CO., CORPUS CHRISTI (1830), [CEM] Very Rev. Marcel H. Bouchard, V.F.; Rev. Rodney E. Thibault; Deacons David Boucher; Robert Alence; Arthur LaChance; Dennis O'Connell.
Res.: 251 Service Rd., P.O. Box 1170, East Sandwich, 02537-2170. Tel: 508-888-0209; Fax: 508-888-8961.
Parish Center—324 Quaker Meetinghouse Rd., East Sandwich, 02537.
Catechesis / Religious Program—Tel: 508-888-8267. Deborah M. Boucher, D.R.E.; Jane Amaral, D.R.E. Students 1,268.
Mission—St. Theresa Sagamore, Barnstable Co.

SEEKONK, BRISTOL CO.

1—ST. MARY'S (1906), Revs. George Scales, Pastor; Robert J. Powell, O.S.B.Cam.
Res.: 385 Central Ave., 02771. Tel: 508-399-8440; Fax: 508-399-7398.
Catechesis / Religious Program—Tel: 508-399-7534. Students 601.

2—OUR LADY OF MT. CARMEL (1922), Revs. George E. Harrison; Michael O'Hearn; Deacon Robert W. Pelland.
Res.: 984 Taunton Ave., 02771. Tel: 508-336-9022; Fax: 508-336-9010.
Catechesis / Religious Program—1040 Taunton Ave., 02771. Tel: 508-336-8608. Christine Gregorek, D.R.E.; Sr. Irene Rivard, F.C.S.C.J., D.R.E. Students 788.

SOMERSET, BRISTOL CO.

1—ST. JOHN OF GOD (1928), (Portuguese), [CEM] Rev. Raul M. Lagoa. In Res., Rev. Luciano J. de M. Pereira (Retired).
Res.: 996 Brayton Ave., Box 113, 02726. Tel: 508-678-5513; Fax: 508-678-6458.
Catechesis / Religious Program—1036 Brayton Ave., 02726. Tel: 508-678-5139. Edward Medeiros, D.R.E.; Agnes Barboza, D.R.E. Students 492.

2—ST. PATRICK'S (1883), [CEM] Rev. Marc P. Tremblay; Deacon Edward Hussey.
Res.: 306 South St., 02726-5617. Tel: 508-672-1523; Fax: 508-675-5787.
Catechesis / Religious Program—Tel: 508-675-1073. Students 292.

3—ST. THOMAS MORE (1949), Rev. Edward J. Byington; Deacon Victor Haddad.
Res.: 386 Luther Ave., 02726. Tel: 508-673-7831; Fax: 508-730-1396.
Catechesis / Religious Program—Tel: 508-679-1236. Mr. Dennis Griffin, D.R.E. Students 260.

SOUTH DARTMOUTH, BRISTOL CO., ST. MARY'S (1930), Revs. Terence Keenan; Philip N. Hamel; Deacon Jeremiah J. Reardon.
Res.: 783 Dartmouth St., 02748. Tel: 508-992-7163; Fax: 508-992-5209.
Catechesis / Religious Program—Tel: 508-992-7505. Dr. Theresa Lewis, D.R.E. (Grades 1-6); Ken Sylvia, D.R.E. (Grades 7-9). Students 550.

SOUTH EASTON, BRISTOL CO., HOLY CROSS (1967), Revs. R. Bradley Beaupre, C.S.C.; Kenneth J. Silvia, C.S.C.; Deacon George Zarella.
Res.: 225 Purchase St., 02375. Tel: 508-238-2235; Fax: 508-238-0500. Email: rbeaupre@holycrosseaston.org.
Catechesis / Religious Program—Tel: 508-238-2131. Anna Tarallo, D.R.E. Students 975.

SOUTH YARMOUTH, BARNSTABLE CO., ST. PIUS TENTH (1954), Rev. Msgr. John J. Smith; Revs. Paul Bernier; Hugh McCullough; Deacons David Akin; Richard J. Hasey; Thomas Bailey. In Res., Rev. Jose Alfonso de Lima.
Res.: 5 Barbara St., 02664. Tel: 508-398-2248; Fax: 508-398-7233.
Catechesis / Religious Program—Station Ave., 02664. Tel: 508-394-0709; 508-394-0708. Mrs. Joan Robinson, D.R.E.; Mrs. Jean Kelly, D.R.E. Students 618.
Chapel—Bass River, Our Lady of the Highway, Tel: 508-760-3332.

SWANSEA, BRISTOL CO.

1—ST. DOMINIC'S (1911), Rev. Joseph F. Viveiros, Pastor; Deacon Anthony A. Cipriano.

Res.: 1277 Grand Army Hwy., 02777. Tel: 508-675-7206; Fax: 508-675-4626.
Catechesis/Religious Program—Tel: 508-675-7002. Students 276.
2—ST. LOUIS DE FRANCE (1928), (French), Rev. Richard R. Gendreau, Pastor; Deacon Robert G.L. Normandin.
Res.: 56 Buffington St., 02777. Tel: 508-674-1103; Fax: 508-672-8889.
Catechesis/Religious Program—66 Buffington St., 02777. Tel: 508-672-0615. Mrs. Paulette J. Normandin, D.R.E. Students 314.
3—ST. MICHAEL'S (1922), Rev. Dermot P. Rodgers; Deacon Thomas F. Prevost.
Res.: 270 Ocean Grove Ave., 02777. Tel: 508-673-2808; Fax: 508-672-1642.
Catechesis/Religious Program—Tel: 508-674-0024. Students 446.
Mission—Our Lady of Fatima, Bristol Co. Tel: 508-674-0024.
4—OUR LADY OF FATIMA (1958), Closed., For inquiries for parish records, please see St. Michael's, Swansea.
TAUNTON, BRISTOL CO.
1—ANNUNCIATION OF THE LORD (2001), Rev. John A. Gomes; Deacon Joseph P. Medeiros.
Res.: 311 Somerset Ave., 02780. Tel: 508-823-2521; Fax: 508-823-2522.
School—52 First St., 02780. Tel: 508-822-3746; Fax: 508-822-1450. Mrs. Arleen Booker, Prin. Sisters 2; Lay Teachers 6; Students 179.
Catechesis/Religious Program—Tel: 508-824-6791; Fax: 508-824-6791. Students 175.
Convent—49 First St., 02780. Tel: 508-822-0357.
2—ST. ANTHONY'S (1904), (Portuguese), Revs. Henry S. Arruda, Pastor; Jeffrey Cabral; Deacon Jose H. Medina.
Res.: 126 School St., 02780. Tel: 508-822-0714; Fax: 508-828-5844.
Catechesis/Religious Program—Tel: 508-824-6241. Students 325.
3—ST. JAMES (1904), (French), Rev. Thomas E. Morrissey.
Res.: 249 Whittenton St., 02780. Tel: 508-824-7794; Fax: 508-822-8014.
Catechesis/Religious Program—Tel: 508-824-7808. Students 90.
Convent—279 Whittenton St., 02780. Tel: 508-824-8946.
4—ST. JOSEPH'S (1896), Rev. Timothy P. Reis
Res.: 19 Kilmer Ave., 02780. Tel: 508-824-5435; Fax: 508-880-1903.
Catechesis/Religious Program—Tel: 508-823-6819. Students 276.
5—ST. MARY'S (1828), Revs. Francis Zlotkowski, C.S.C.; William H. Kelley, C.S.C.
Res.: 14 St. Mary's Square, 02780. Tel: 508-822-7116; Fax: 508-822-7117.
School—Tel: 508-822-9480; Fax: 508-822-7164. Mr. Brian Cote, Prin.; Mrs. Sandra Parker, Asst. Prin. Lay Teachers 19; Students 402.
Catechesis/Religious Program—Tel: 508-880-5062. Students 160.
Dolan Parish Center—Tel: 508-880-5062.
6—OUR LADY OF LOURDES (1905), (Portuguese), Merged, with Sacred Heart, Taunton to form Annunciation of the Lord, Taunton.
7—OUR LADY OF THE HOLY ROSARY (1909), (Polish), [JC] Rev. David M. Stopyra, O.F.M.Conv.
Res.: 80 Bay St., 02780. Tel: 508-823-3046; Fax: 508-823-0585.
Catechesis/Religious Program—Tel: 508-824-3910. Students 92.
8—OUR LADY OF THE IMMACULATE CONCEPTION (1883), Rev. Richard E. Degagne.
In Res—Rev. Edward A. Murphy.
Res.: 387 Bay St., 02780-1718. Tel: 508-824-8794; Fax: 508-821-7616.
Catechesis/Religious Program—Tel: 508-824-4545. Mrs. Kathleen A. Peterson, D.R.E. Students 227.
9—ST. PAUL'S (1904), Very Rev. Bento R. Fraga, V.F.; Deacon Robet J. Hill.
Res.: 261 Tremont St., 02780. Tel: 508-824-7166; Fax: 508-822-9618.
Catechesis/Religious Program—Tel: 508-822-9672. Students 435.
10—SACRED HEART (1873), Merged, with Our Lady of Lourdes, Taunton to form Annunciation of the Lord, Taunton.
VINEYARD HAVEN, DUKES CO., ST. AUGUSTINE (1962), Revs. Michael R. Nagle, D.Min.; John C. Ozug; Deacon Fred Lapiana.
Res.: 56 Franklin St., P.O. Box 1058, 02568. Tel: 508-693-0103; Fax: 508-693-8517.
Catechesis/Religious Program—School St., Oak Bluffs, 02557. Tel: 508-693-0342; Fax: 508-696-8408. Consolidated with Sacred Heart, Oak Bluffs.
WAREHAM, PLYMOUTH CO., ST. PATRICK'S (1911), [CEM] Revs. Arnold R. Medeiros; Paul C. Fedak.
Res.: 82 High St., P.O. Box 271, 02571-0271. Tel: 508-295-2411; Fax: 508-295-2417.
Catechesis/Religious Program—Tel: 508-295-0780; Fax: 508-295-2417. Mrs. Priscilla Silva, D.R.E. Students 540.
Mission—St. Anthony P.O. Box 271, West Wareham, Plymouth Co. 02571-0271.
WELLFLEET, BARNSTABLE CO., OUR LADY OF LOURDES (1910), [CEM 2] Rev. John P. Andrews.
Res.: 137 Fresh Brook Ln., P.O. Box 1414, 02667-1414. Tel: 508-349-2222; Fax: 508-349-9612.
Catechesis/Religious Program—Students 26.
Mission—Visitation Church 930 Massasoit Rd., North Eastham, Barnstable Co. 02651.
WEST HARWICH, BARNSTABLE CO., HOLY TRINITY (1918), Revs. Thomas L. Rita, Pastor; Marek Chmurski; Michael O'Hearn. In Res., Rev. William Rodrigues; Deacons Ralph F. Cox; Dana G. McCarthy; Vincent P. Walsh.
Res.: S. Main St., 02671. Tel: 508-432-4000; Fax: 508-432-3494.
School—Tel: 508-432-8216. Sisters 2; Lay Teachers 9; Students 184.
Catechesis/Religious Program—Tel: 508-432-2898; Fax: 508-432-2898. Marie Mann, D.R.E. Students 260.
Mission—Our Lady of the Annunciation [CEM] P.O. Box 428, Dennis Port, Barnstable Co. 02671.
WESTPORT, BRISTOL CO.
1—ST. GEORGE'S (1914), Rev. Gerard A. Hebert, J.C.L.
Res.: 12 Highland Ave., 02790. Tel: 508-636-4965; Fax: 508-636-4188.
Catechesis/Religious Program—Students 240.
2—ST. JOHN THE BAPTIST (1930), Rev. Msgr. Edmund J. Fitzgerald, V.F.
Res.: 945 Main Rd., Box 3328, 02790. Tel: 508-636-2251; Fax: 508-636-8306.
Catechesis/Religious Program—924 Main Rd., P.O. Box 3328, 02790. Tel: 508-636-5506. Students 283.
3—OUR LADY OF GRACE (1954), Rev. Horace J. Travassos.
Res.: 569 Sanford Rd., 02790. Tel: 508-674-6271; Fax: 508-675-4128.
Catechesis/Religious Program—Tel: 508-675-5857. Students 329.
WOODS HOLE, BARNSTABLE CO., ST. JOSEPH'S (1882), Rev. Joseph H. Mauritzen.
Res.: 33 Millfield St., P.O. Box 3, 02543. Tel: 508-548-0990.
Catechesis/Religious Program—Tel: 508-540-3723. Students 52.

Chaplains of Public Institutions

BARNSTABLE. *Barnstable County House of Correction*. 347 South St., Hyannis, 02601. Deacon Richard J. Murphy, Coord.
NEW BEDFORD. *Bristol Co. House of Correction & Eastern Massachusetts Correctional Alcohol Center*.
824 Tucker Rd., North Dartmouth, 02747. Tel: 508-996-2413. Rev. Marc Fallon, C.S.C.

Special Assignment:
Revs.—
Blyskosz, Joseph, St. Rose of Lima & St. Francis of Assisi, Casa Cural, Guaimaca, Honduras.
Canuel, Paul E., St. Rose of Lima & St. Francis of Assisi, Casa Cural, Guaimaca, Honduras.
Engo, David, F.P.O., Priests Hostel, 2402 Highland Ave., 02720.
Magee, Patrick, 18 Cottage St., 1st Floor, 02721. Tel: 508-675-9980
Robinson, Paul F., O.Carm. Tel: 508-675-7150

Graduate Studies:
Revs.—
Mathias, Gregory A., Little Flower Rectory, 5607 Massachusetts Ave., Bethesda, MD 20816.
O'Connor, Gerard, Villa Stritch, Via Della Nocetta, 63, Rome, Italy.

On Duty Outside the Diocese:
Revs.—
Kocik, Thomas, Omaha, NE
Sharland, David, McLean, VA

Absent on Leave:
Revs.—
Herrera, Hernando
Sousa, Jose

Absent on Sick Leave:
Rev.—
Beaulieu, Richard

Retired:
Rev. Msgrs.—
Munroe, Henry T., P.A., P.O. Box 1310, Sagamore Beach, 02542.
Regan, John J., P.O. Box 1094, North Falmouth, 02556.
Tavares, Antonino C., 230 Bonney St., 02744.
Revs.—
Almeida, George F., 375 Elsbree St., 02720.
Boivin, Louis R., 375 Elsbree St., 02720.
Boule, Roland B., 2446 Highland Ave., 02720.
Bousquet, Roland, 53 California St., 02723.
Buckley, James F., 209 Union St., Yarmouthport, 02675.
Burns, Edward J., 4234 N. Main St., 02720.
Delano, Kenneth J., 22 Ingell St., Taunton, 02780.
Dos Santos, Jose A.F., 375 Elsbree St., 02720.
Driscoll, John P., 800 Pleasant St., 02740.
Dufour, Clement E., 77 Cottonwood St., Fairhaven, 02719-5596.
Ferreira, Manuel P., 375 Elsbree St., 02720.
Freitas, Daniel L., P.O. Box 411154, Melbourne, FL 32941-1154.
Kelly, Bernard R.
Kirby, Robert F., P.O. Box 169, Cotuit, 02635.
Kropiwnicki, Henry, 19 Rutland St., 02745-5830.
LeDuc, Roger D., P.O. Box 2538, Tehachapi, CA 93581-2538.
Lyons, James F., 375 Elsbree St., 02720.
McCarthy, James, 375 Elsbree St., 02720.
Murphy, Clarence, 375 Elsbree St., 02720.
Murphy, John J., 375 Elsbree St., 02720.
Norton, William W., 375 Elsbree St., 02720.
Pereira, Luciano J., 996 Brayton Ave., Somerset, 02726.
Ryan, Albert J., 375 Elsbree St., 02720.
Shovelton, Gerald T., 419 Chula Vista Ave., Lady Lake, FL 32159.
Shovelton, William J., 419 Chula Vista Ave., Lady Lake, FL 32159.
Tetrault, Ralph D., 375 Elsbree St., 02720.
Wallace, Francis X., P.O. Box 3737, Pocasset, 02559.
Wingate, Arthur K., 375 Elsbree St., 02720.

Permanent Deacons:
Akin, David P., St. Pius X, South Yarmouth
Alence, Robert, Corpus Christi, East Sandwich
Bailey, Thomas C., St. Pius Tenth, South Yarmouth
Barrett, James M., Our Lady of Victory, Centerville
Battiston, Donald L., St. Mary/O.L. of the Isle, Nantucket
Beckel, Gregory J., Christ the King, Mashpee
Bedard, Philip E., St. Jacques, Taunton
Biron, Donald R., Our Lady of the Cape, Brewster
Bonneau, Bruce J., St. John Neumann, East Freetown
Boucher, David R., Corpus Christi, Sandwich
Bousquet, Louis A., St. Anne, Fall River
Branco, John F., Good Shepherd, Fall River
Camacho, Francis, Florida
Cipriano, A. Anthony, St. Dominic, Swansea
Coates, Vincent, Jr., St. Elizabeth Seton, North Falmouth
Cook, Chester O., St. Peter the Apostle, Provincetown
Cox, Ralph F., Holy Trinity, West Harwich
daCruz, Antonio, Our Lady of the Assumption, New Bedford
Dexter, Leonard C., Jr., St. John the Evangelist, Pocasset
Dresser, Richard M., St. Francis Xavier, Hyannis
Drinkwater, Oscar T., So. Carolina
Emmert, John J., (Unassigned)
Fantasia, Frank D., Christ the King, Mashpee
Faria, Robert A., Our Lady of Health, Fall River
Fitzpatrick, John J., Holy Family, East Taunton
Fournier, Paul M., Immaculate Conception, North Easton
Gardyna, Henry A., St. Patrick, Wareham; Boston, MA
Gendron, Ernest J., St. Margaret, Buzzards Bay
Gundlach, Richard J., St. Mark, Attleboro Falls
Guresh, Peter M., St. Elizabeth Seton, North Falmouth
Guy, Michael P., St. Francis Xavier, Acushnet
Haddad, Victor, St. Thomas More, Somerset
Hassey, Richard J., St. Pius Tenth, So. Yarmouth
Hill, Robert J., St. Paul, Taunton
Hussey, Edward J., St. Patrick, Somerset
LaChance, Arthur L., Jr., Corpus Christi, Sandwich
Ladroga, William, Florida
LaPiana, Fred G., III, St. Augustine, Vineyard Haven
Lavallee, Maurice, St. Joseph and St. Therese, New Bedford
Leavitt, James P., Our Lady of the Cape, Brewster
LeBlanc, Claude A., St. Julie Billiart, North Dartmouth
Lemay, Robert D., Christ the King, Mashpee
Liegey, Gabriel J., Holy Redeemer, Chatham
Lorenzo, Robert G., Camden, NJ; St. Joseph, Fairhaven
Lukac, Theodore E., Our Lady of Victory, Centerville
Macedo, Paul J., P.D., St. John the Baptist, New Bedford

Mador, Joseph F., Holy Redeemer, Chatham
Mahoney, Patrick J., St. Patrick, Falmouth
Martin, William A., St. Elizabeth Seton, North Falmouth
Marzelli, James, Jr., St. John the Evangelist, Pocasset
Massoud, Donald P., St. Anthony of the Desert, Fall River
Mattar, Jean E., Our Lady of Purgatory, New Bedford
McCarthy, Dana G., Holy Trinity, West Harwich
McEnaney, Norman F., St. Joan of Arc, Orleans
Medeiros, Douglas R., St. Joseph, Fairhaven
Medeiros, Joseph P., Annunciation of the Lord, Taunton
Medina, Jose H., St. Anthony, Taunton
Meloni, James J., Jr., St. Mary's, North Attleboro
Metilly, Paul, Florida
Mis, Franciszek W., St. Stanislaus Church, Fall River
Moniz, John de A., Espirito Santo, Fall River
Morency, Marcel G., St. Anne, New Bedford
Murphy, Richard J., St. Francis Xavier, Hyannis
Murray, Michael E., St. Mary, Norton
Nasser, Andre P., St. Anthony of the Desert, Fall River
Nogueira, Benjamin, Fitchburg, MA
Normandin, Robert G.L., St. Louis de France, Swansea
O'Connell, Dennis G., Corpus Christi, Sandwich
Ouellette, Maurice A., St. Lawrence, New Bedford
Pacheco, Eduardo M., Our Lady of the Assumption, New Bedford
Palanza, Thomas P., St. Mary, Mansfield
Pelland, Robert W., Our Lady of Mount Carmel, Seekonk
Pepin, David B., St. Mary, New Bedford
Pires, Abilio dos A., Our Lady of Mt. Carmel, New Bedford
Pires, Albertino F., Our Lady of the Immaculate Conception, New Bedford
Prevost, Thomas F., St. Michael, Swansea
Racine, Leo W., St. Joseph-St. Therese, New Bedford
Raymond, Robert, (Retired), Arizona
Reardon, Jeremiah J., St. Mary, South Dartmouth
Regali, Joseph E., Sacred Heart, North Attleboro
Roma, Paul K., St. Elizabeth Seton, North Falmouth
Sasseville, Eugene H., Holy Name of the Sacred Heart of Jesus, New Bedford
Simonis, John E., St. Patrick, Falmouth
Souza, Thomas J., Espirito Santo, Fall River
St. Onge, Lawrence A., St. James, New Bedford
Stanley, Joseph P., Our Lady of Victory, Centerville
Stenberg, Richard S., Holy Redeemer, Chatham; Bridgeport CT
Surprenant, Robert L., St. Anthony, Mattapoisett
Thomas, Walter D., St. Mary, Mansfield
Twerago, John P., St. Joan of Arc, Orleans
Wallace, Forrest, Cincinnati, Ohio
Walsh, Vincent, Holy Trinity, West Harwich
Welch, John, St. Ann, Raynham
Zarella, George H., Holy Cross, South Easton
Zeich, Richard C., St. Pius X, South Yarmouth

INSTITUTIONS LOCATED IN THE DIOCESE

[A] COLLEGES AND UNIVERSITIES

EASTON. *Villa Nazareth USA, Inc.*, 320 Washington St., 02537. Tel: 508-230-5738; Fax: 508-565-1420. Email: rrossi@stonehill.edu. Web: www.holycrosscsc.org/csc/villanazarethusa.html. Rick Rossi, Dir. Students 13.

NORTH EASTON. *Holy Cross Fathers Religious*, 480 Washington St., 02356. Tel: 508-238-5942; Fax: 508-230-7455. Email: tbertone@stonehill.edu. Web: www.holycrosscsc.org. Revs. Thomas P. Gariepy, C.S.C., Supr.; Thomas C. Bertone, C.S.C., Asst. Supr.; Richard E. Gribble, C.S.C., Asst. Supr.; Genaro P. Aguilar, C.S.C.; David J. Arthur, C.S.C.; Bro. Lawrence Atkinson, C.S.C.; Revs. Joseph F. Callahan, C.S.C.; Thomas L. Campbell; Rudolph V. Carchidi, C.S.C.; James W. Chichetto, C.S.C.; Bro. Stephan Clarke, C.S.C.; Revs. Mark T. Cregan, C.S.C.; John F. Denning, C.S.C.; Paul J. Duff, C.S.C.; Harry B. Eichorn, C.S.C.; Thomas M. Feeley; James Fenstermaker, C.S.C.; Thomas M. Halkovic, C.S.C.; Francis J. Hurley, C.S.C.; Robert J. Kruse, C.S.C.; Bro. James W. Madigan, C.S.C.; Revs. John E. McCarthy, C.S.C.; John J. Murphy, C.S.C.; George B. Mulligan, C.S.C.; Leo Polselli, C.S.C.; Bro. Paul Rahaim, C.S.C.; Revs. Richard J. Segreve, C.S.C.; Kevin P. Spicer, C.S.C.; Thaddeus T. Swertz, C.S.C.; James E. Tobin, C.S.C.; Francis M. Walsh, C.S.C.; Peter J. Walsh, C.S.C.

Stonehill College 02357. Tel: 508-565-1301; Fax: 508-565-1432. Email: mcregan@stonehill.edu. Web: www.stonehill.edu. Revs. Mark T. Cregan, C.S.C., Pres.; Genaro P. Aguilar, C.S.C.; Rudolph V. Carchidi, C.S.C.; James W. Chichetto, C.S.C.; Harry B. Eichorn, C.S.C.; John F. Denning, C.S.C., College Chap.; Thomas P. Gariepy, C.S.C.; Richard Gribble, C.S.C.; Thomas M. Halkovic, C.S.C.; Francis J. Hurley, C.S.C.; Robert J. Kruse, C.S.C.; Bartley MacPhaidin, C.S.C.; John E. McCarthy, C.S.C.; George B. Mulligan, C.S.C.; Kevin Spicer, C.S.C.; Francis M. Walsh, C.S.C.; Peter Walsh, C.S.C.; Deacon Walter Jenkins, C.S.C; Bros. Paul Rahaim, C.S.C.; Herman Zaccarelli, C.S.C. Priests 16; Brothers 2; Deacons 1; Lay Teachers 178; Students 2,344.

[B] HIGH SCHOOLS, DIOCESAN

FALL RIVER. *Bishop Connolly High School*, 373 Elsbree St., 02720. Tel: 508-676-1071; Fax: 508-676-8594. Email: bchs@bishopconnolly.com. Web: www.bishopconnolly.com. Mr. James McNamee, Prin.; Paul Cartier, Academic Vice Prin.; Rev. Michael A. Ciryak, O.F.M. Priests 1; Brothers 2; (Part-Time) 1; Lay Teachers 40; Students 418.

ATTLEBORO. *Bishop Feehan High School*, 70 Holcott Dr., 02703. Tel: 508-226-6223; Fax: 508-226-7696. Email: webmaster@bishopfeehan.com. Web: www.bishopfeehan.com. Mr. Christopher E. Servant, Prin.; Rev. Michael F. Kuhn, Chap. Priests 1; Sisters 1; Lay Teachers 74; Students 996.

Our Lady of Mercy Convent, 70 Holcott Dr., 02703. Tel: 508-226-4608; Fax: 508-226-7696. Sr. Rose Angela McLellan, R.S.M., Supr. Sisters 13.

NORTH DARTMOUTH. *Bishop Stang High School*, 500 Slocum Rd., 02747-2999. Tel: 508-996-5602; Fax: 508-994-6756. Email: tdougall@bishopstang.com. Web: www.bishopstang.com. Theresa E. Dougall, Pres.; Mary Ann Miskel, Academic Prin.; Michael P. O'Brien, Prin. of Students; Rev. David Pignato, Chap. Priests 1; Lay Teachers 59; Support Staff 19; Students 781.

TAUNTON. *Coyle and Cassidy High School*, 2 Hamilton St., 02780. Tel: 508-823-6164; Fax: 508-823-2530. Web: www.coylecassidy.com. Bro. Harold Hathaway, C.S.C., Pres. Priests 2; Brothers 2; Sisters 2; Lay Teachers 56; Students 732.

[C] ELEMENTARY SCHOOLS, DIOCESAN

TAUNTON. *Taunton Catholic Middle School*, 61 Summer St., 02780. Tel: 508-822-0491; Fax: 508-824-0469. Email: tcms@catholicmiddle.com. Web: www.catholicmiddle.com. Robert A. Jefferey, Prin. Lay Teachers 14; Students 303.

[D] RESIDENTIAL CHILD CARE FACILITIES

FALL RIVER. *St. Vincent's Home Corp.*, Main Campus: 2425 Highland Ave., 02720. Tel: 508-679-8511; Fax: 508-672-2558. Web: www.stvincentshome.org. Mr. John T. Weldon, Exec. Dir. Sisters 8; Total Staff 483; Children Residents 160.

[E] NURSERIES

NEW BEDFORD. *St. Saviour's Day Nursery* Closed

[F] GENERAL HOSPITALS

FALL RIVER. *Saint Anne's Health Care Management Services, Inc.*, 795 Middle St., 02721-1798. Tel: 508-674-5741; Fax: 508-675-5647. Web: www.saintanneshospital.com. Michael W. Metzler, Pres.

Saint Anne's Health Care System, Inc., 795 Middle St., 02721-1798. Tel: 508-674-5741; Fax: 508-675-5647. Email: saintanneshospital.org. Web: www.saintanneshospital.com. Michael W. Metzler, Pres.

Saint Anne's Hospital, 795 Middle St., 02721-1798. Tel: 508-674-5741; Fax: 508-675-5647. Web: www.saintanneshospital.org. Michael W. Metzler, Pres. Dominican Sisters of Charity of the Presentation of the Blessed Virgin Mary Sisters 6; Total Staff 1,176; Bed Capacity 144; Patients Assisted Annually 141,463.

[G] HOMES FOR AGED

FALL RIVER. *Catholic Memorial Home Inc.*, 2446 Highland Ave., 02720-4599. Tel: 508-679-0011; Fax: 508-672-5858. Email: thealy@dhfo.org. Thomas F. Healy, Supr. & Admin.; Rev. William P. Blottman; Sr. Catherine Donovan, R.S.M., Dir. Pastoral Care. Total Assisted 300; Total Staff 425.

FAIRHAVEN. *Our Lady's Haven of Fairhaven Inc.*, 71 Center St., 02719. Tel: 508-999-4561; Fax: 508-997-0254. Email: mbenevides@dhfo.org. Web: www.dhfo.org. Manuel Benevides, Admin.; Rev. Ambrose Forgit, SS.CC., Chap. Residents 117; Total Staff 165.

NEW BEDFORD. *Sacred Heart Home*, 359 Summer St., 02740. Tel: 508-996-6751; Fax: 508-992-3145. Web: www.dhfo.org. Jean M. Golitz, R.N., M.S. Sisters of Charity of Quebec 3; Total Staff 286; Residents 217.

NORTH ATTLEBORO. *Madonna Manor Inc.*, 85 N. Washington St., 02760. Tel: 508-699-2740; Fax: 508-699-0481. Email: jroque@dhfo.org. Web: www.dhfo.org. Joanne M. Roque, R.N., B.S.N., Admin.; Rev. Thaddeus T. Swertz, C.S.C.; Sr. Mary Duffy, S.S.J., Dir. of Pastoral Care. Total Staff 189; Residents 129.

TAUNTON. *Bethany House Adult Day Care*, 72 Church Green, 02780. Tel: 508-822-9200. Mrs. Laura Faria, Admin. Total Staff 7; Total Assisted 47.

Marian Manor Inc., 33 Summer St., 02780. Tel: 508-822-4885; Fax: 508-677-4361. Email: Lfaria@dhfo.org. Mrs. Laura Faria, Admin.; Rev. Bernard Vanasse, Chap.; Sr. Paulina Cardenas, O.P., Dir. Pastoral Care. Dominican Sisters of Charity of the Presentation of the Blessed Virgin Mary 1; Total Staff 175; Patients Assisted Annually 116.

[H] MONASTERIES AND RESIDENCES OF PRIESTS AND BROTHERS

FALL RIVER. *Brothers of Christian Instruction*, 555 Eastern Ave., 02723. Tel: 508-672-5763. Bros. Daniel Caron, Prov.; Walter Zwierchowski, Supr.; Roger Millette, F.I.C.; Norman Simoneau. Brothers 4; Faculty of Bishop Connolly High 3.

Cardinal Medeiros Residence-Retirement Facility for Priests, 375 Elsbree St., 02720-7211. Tel: 508-675-1050; Fax: 508-675-2181.

Dominican House, 818 Middle St., 02721. Tel: 508-678-5322.

St. John Vianney House, 818 Middle St., 02721-1734. Tel: 508-673-0377; Fax: 508-672-0939. Revs. Marc H. Bergeron; Christopher Stanibula. Priests 2; Total Staff 2.

Priests' Hostel, 2402 Highland Ave., 02720. Tel: 508-672-1632; Fax: 508-679-1422. In Res. Revs. David Engo, F.P.O.; Bernard Vanasse.

ATTLEBORO. *La Salette Missionary Association*, 947 Park St., 02703. Tel: 508-222-0027; Fax: 508-222-2504. Email: lsmajp@aol.com. Very Rev. Dennis J. Loomis, M.S., Dir.

Legal Title: *The Province of the Immaculate Heart of Mary, Inc.*

La Salette Shrine, 947 Park St., 02703. Tel: 508-222-5410; Fax: 508-222-6770. Email: lspgmsoffice@juno.com. Web: lasalette.shrine.tripod.com. Revs. Raymond Vaillancourt, M.S., Supr.; George Brennan, M.S., Dir. Priests 11; Brothers 9. In Res. Revs. Daniel Bradley, M.S.; Fernand Cassista, M.S.; Victor Chaupetta, M.S.; Gerald Forest, M.S.; John Gabriel, M.S.; Richard Lavoie, M.S.; Roger Leroux, M.S.; Donald Paradis, M.S.; Thomas Paris, M.S.; Bros. Paul Boucher, M.S.; Lucien Brodeur, M.S.; Jean-Paul Champagne, M.S.; Leonard Melanson, M.S.; Roger Moreau, M.S.; Robert Nichols, M.S.; Roger St. Germain, M.S.; Ronald Taylor, M.S.; Raymond Tetreault, M.S.

FAIRHAVEN. *Sacred Hearts Provincial House*, 77 Adams St., P.O. Box 111, 02719-0111. Tel: 508-993-2442; Fax: 508-996-5499. Web: www.sscc.org. Very Rev. David P. Reid, SS.CC., Prov.; Bro. Paul R. Alves, SS.CC., Treas.; Revs. Gabriel Healy, SS.CC., Mission Procurator; Donald Demers, Dir., Devel.; Andrew Healey, SS.CC., (On Sabbatical); Albert Dagnoli, SS.CC.; Ambrose Forgit, SS.CC.; William F. Petrie, SS.CC., Vocation Dir. Congregation of the Sacred Hearts of Jesus and Mary Fathers 3.

National Center of the Enthronement, P.O. Box 111, 02719-0111. Tel: 508-999-2680; Fax: 508-993-8233. Email: necenter@juno.com. Web: www.sscc.org. Rev. Columban Crotty, SS.CC., Natl. Dir. Congregation of the Sacred Hearts of Jesus and Mary Total Staff 2.

Damien Residence, 73 Adams St., P.O. Box 111, 02719-0111. Tel: 508-999-0500; Fax: 508-990-7173. Revs. William Heffron, SS.CC., Dir.; Gabriel Healy, SS.CC.; William Davis, SS.CC.; William Mitchell, SS.CC.; Owen F. Goodwin, SS.CC.; Henry Creighton, SS.CC.; Brian Marggraf, SS.CC.; Leo King, SS.CC.; Paul Deyo, SS.CC.; Thomas McElroy, SS.CC.; Bros. James Rukavina, SS.CC.; Joseph Fandel, SS.CC. Fathers 12; Brothers 2.

Priests of the Province Serving Abroad - In Japanese Missions: Most Rev. Michiaki Chihara, SS.CC.; Revs. Cornelius Biffar, SS.CC.; Michael Coleman, SS.CC.; Lawrence Craig, SS.CC.; Kenji Honma, SS.CC.; Louis Kawamata, SS.CC.; Edward Keeney, SS.CC.; Augustine Kobayashi, SS.CC.; Peter Kusunoki, SS.CC.; Philip Murphy, SS.CC.; Michael Narita, SS.CC.; Very Rev. John Yamada, SS.CC., Vice Prov.; Bro. Francis Nakazawa, SS.CC.

In the Philippines: Rev. Fintan Sheeran, SS.CC.

In Nassau, Bahamas: Revs. Patrick F. Fanning, SS.CC.; Martin Gomes, SS.CC.; Christopher Santangelo, SS.CC.

In India: Revs. Columban Crotty, SS.CC.; Alexis Nayak, SS.CC.; Subal Nayak, SS.CC.; Sudhir Nayak, SS.CC.; Michael Shanahan, SS.CC.
In Rome, Italy: Revs. William Donegan, SS.CC., Gen. Councilor; Alfredo Garcia, SS.CC.
Chaplain in Military Facilities: Rev. Austin Nagle, SS.CC., Campello Station, P.O. Box 3555, Brockton, 02303.
On Sabbatical: Rev. Michael Kelly, SS.CC., Sangre De Christo Center, 410 Atate Rd., 592, Santa Fe, NM 87501. Tel: 505-983-7291.
Our Lady of Grace Rectory, 1111 N. Roselawn St., Artesia, NM 88210. Tel: 505-748-1536; Fax: 505-748-1049. Revs. Richard Lifrak, SS.CC.; Benedict Folger, SS.CC.
P.O. Box 9054, Hidalgo, TX 78557-9054. Tel: 011-52-89-9922-5371; Fax: 011-52-89-9922-5371. Rev. Gerry Shanley, SS.CC.
Our Lady's Haven, 71 Center St., 02719. Rev. Roy Yurco, SS.CC.

NEW BEDFORD. *Franciscans of Primitive Observance*, Immaculate Conception Friary, 107 Rivet St., 02744. Revs. Peter Giroux, F.P.O.; Francis Joseph Kelly, F.P.O.; Joseph Paul Medio, F.P.O.; John Maria Sweeney, F.P.O.
Marian Friary of Our Lady, Queen of the Seraphic Order, 600 Pleasant St., 02740-6299. Tel: 508-996-8274; Fax: 508-996-8296. Email: ffi@marymediatrix.com. Web: www.marymediatrix.com. P.O. Box 3003, 02741-3003. Revs. George M. Roth, F.F.I., Guardian; Martin M. Fonte, F.F.I., Vicar and Guard.; Alphonsus M. Sutton, F.F.I.; Michael M. Gauxreau; Angelo Michael M. Guarin, F.F.I. Priests 4; Brothers 2.

NORTH DARTMOUTH. *Holy Cross Residence*, 824 Tucker Rd., 02747. Tel: 508-993-2238; Fax: 508-984-4339. Revs. J. Robert Rioux, C.S.C., Supr.; Thomas J. Tobin, C.S.C., Asst. Supr.; Henry Bourgeois, C.S.C.; J. Marc Hebert, C.S.C.; Marc F. Fallon, C.S.C.; Joseph M. Quinn, C.S.C.; Donald W. Whipple, C.S.C.; James J. Doyle, C.S.C.; Bro. Lewis Morrow, C.S.C.
St. Joseph's Hall, 800 Tucker Rd., 02747-3599. Tel: 508-996-2413; Fax: 508-984-4339. Email: cscda@aol.com. Revs. J. Robert Rioux, C.S.C., Dir.; Albert A. Croce, C.S.C.; John F. Dias, C.S.C.; William G. Condon, C.S.C.; Bro. Joseph L. Morris, C.S.C.

ONSET. *St. Joseph Friary-Franciscan Friars*, 46 Robinwood Rd., P.O. Box 63, 02558. Tel: 508-759-7280; Fax: 508-743-9551. Email: gjsilverio@hotmail.com. Revs. Gilbert J. Silverio, O.F.M.; Brennan Egan, O.F.M.; Richard Passeri, O.F.M. Total Staff 3; Total in Residence 3.

[I] CONVENTS AND RESIDENCES FOR SISTERS

FALL RIVER. *Bishop's Residence Convent*, 394 Highland Ave., 02720. Tel: 508-675-1311. Sisters of St. Jeanne d'Arc Sisters 2.
St. Patrick's Convent Closed Sr. M. Romana Murphy, R.S.M., Coord.

ATTLEBORO. *Our Lady of Mercy Convent*, 70 Holcott Dr., 02703. Tel: 508-226-4608; Fax: 508-222-2713. Email: srosea@earthlink.net sisterrose@comcast.net. Sr. Rose Angela McLellan, R.S.M., Local Coord. Sisters 13.

DIGHTON. *Dominican Sisters of Charity of the Presentation of the Blessed Virgin*, 3012 Elm St., 02715. Tel: 508-669-5425; 508-669-5023 (Novitiate); Fax: 508-669-6521. Email: domsis@dominicansistersofthepresentation.org. Web: www.dominicansistersofthepresentation.org. Sr. Joanna Fernandes, O.P., Prov. Supr. Provincial House-Residence, Residence for Aged Sisters, Novitiate. Sisters 23.

FAIRHAVEN. *Franciscan Sisters of the Immaculate Convent Church of the Sacred Hearts of Jesus & Mary*, 382 Main St., 02719. Tel: 508-992-0482; Fax: 508-992-0482. Email: sfi@marymediatrix.com. Web: www.marymediatrix.com.
Sisters of the Sacred Hearts, Community Headquarters, 35 Huttleston Ave., 02719-3154. Tel: 508-994-9341; Fax: 508-990-1967. Email: srdolorespavao@cs.com.
Legal Title: *Sisters of the Sacred Hearts of Jesus and Mary and of Perpetual Adoration, SS.CC.* Sisters in Community 5.

HARWICHPORT. *Contemplative Sisters of the Good Shepherd*, 88 Bank St., 02646. Tel: 508-432-5582; Fax: 508-432-6293. Email: aureenb@aol.com.

NEW BEDFORD. *Misioneras Guadalupanas del Espiritu Santo*, 2 Acushnet Ave., 02744. Tel: 508-997-8729; Fax: 508-997-4537. Email: guadalupananb@aol.com. Sr. Margarita Ocana, Supr. Sisters 5.
Our Lady of Mercy Convent, 144 Summer St., 02740. Tel: 508-992-3694. Email: summerstnb@aol.com. Sr. Mary Nora Smith, R.S.M., Coord. Sisters 4.
Sisters of Mercy, 15 Lemos St., 02740. Tel: 508-992-4947. Sr. M. Nathan Doherty, R.S.M., Contact Person. Sisters 3.

NORTH DARTMOUTH. *Diocesan Family Life Center*, 500 Slocum Rd., 02747. Tel: 508-993-4930; Fax: 508-999-6430. Total Staff 3.
Dominican Sisters of Hope, 856 Tucker Rd., 02747. Tel: 508-993-1305. Web: www.ophope.org. Sisters 5.

TAUNTON. *Villa Fatima*, 90 County St., 02780. Tel: 508-822-6282; Fax: 508-823-0825. Email: sr.dot@att.net. Web: www.ssdmission.org. Sr. Rosalie Patrello, S.S.D., Local Coord. Sisters of St. Dorothy Professed Sisters 6.

WAREHAM. *St. Patrick's Missionary Cenacle*, 86 High St., 02571. Tel: 508-295-0799. Outreach to the homebound handicapped.

[J] RETREAT HOUSES

ATTLEBORO. *La Salette Center for Christian Living*, 947 Park St., 02703-0965. Tel: 508-222-8530; Fax: 508-236-9089. Email: lasalett@rcn.com. Web: www.lasalette.org. Revs. Fernand Cassista, M.S.; Daniel Bradley, M.S.; Sr. Anna Marie Kane, S.S.J., Retreat Ministry Coord.; Bro. Roger A. Moreau, M.S.; Mrs. Karen Laroche. Priests 2; Total Staff 10; Total Assisted 4,200.

EAST FREETOWN. *Cathedral Camp and Retreat Center*, 167 Middleboro Rd., P.O. Box 428, 02717-0428. Tel: 508-763-3394; 508-763-8874; Fax: 508-763-3768. Email: joseph_marie2@juno.com. Web: www.cathedralcamp.com. Sr. Joseph Marie Levesque, O.P., Dir. Total Staff 80; Total in Residence 2.
Cathedral Camp Retreat Center, 167 Middleboro Rd., P.O. Box 428, 02717-0428. Tel: 508-763-3994; Fax: 508-763-3768. Email: joseph_marie2@juno.com. Sr. Joseph Marie Levesque, O.P., Dir. Total Staff 7; Total in Residence 2.

NORTH EASTON. *Holy Cross Retreat House*, 490 Washington St., 02356-1294. Tel: 508-238-2051; Fax: 508-238-0164. Email: jfcal44@hotmail.com. Web: www.retreathouse.org. Rev. Joseph F. Callahan, C.S.C., Spiritual Dir. Priests 1.

WAREHAM. *Sacred Hearts Retreat Center*, 226 Great Neck Rd., 02571. Tel: 508-295-0100; Fax: 508-291-2624. Email: retreats@sscc.org. Web: www.sscc.org/wareham. Revs. James E. McDonough, SS.CC., Dir.; William Penderghest, SS.CC.; Bro. Damien O'Hare, SS.CC.; Deacon Frank Tremblay, Admin. Congregation of the Sacred Hearts of Jesus and Mary and of the Perpetual Adoration of the Most Blessed Sacrement. Priests 2; Brothers 1; Deacons 1.

[K] DEPARTMENT OF CATHOLIC SOCIAL SERVICES AND SPECIAL APOSTOLATES

FALL RIVER. *Campaign For Human Development Apostolate*, 1600 Bay St., P.O. Box M-S, Station, 02724. Tel: 508-674-4681; Fax: 508-675-2224. Email: aam@cssdioc.org. Arlene A. McNamee, L.C.S.W., Exec. Dir.
Office for Persons with Disabilities Tel: 508-679-8373; 508-997-7337 (Voice); 508-679-4277 (TTY); Fax: 508-984-1667. Mathew Dansereau, Coord.; Dennis Caruela.
Spanish Apostolate, P.O. Box 2577, 02722. Tel: 508-675-1311; Fax: 508-679-9220. Sr. Aida Sansor, M.G.Sp.S.; Rev. Richard Wilson, Dir.
P.O. Box 40605, New Bedford, 02744-0006. Tel: 508-675-1311; Fax: 508-679-9220.
Catholic Social Services of Fall River, 1600 Bay St., P.O. Box M-S, Station, 02724. Tel: 508-674-4681; Fax: 508-675-2224. Email: arlmac@aol.com. Arlene A. McNamee, L.C.S.W., Exec. Dir.
Program Directors: Susan E. Desrosiers, M.S.W., L.I.S.C.W., Sexual Abuse Prevention; Mary Lou Mancini, M.Ed., L.I.S.C.W., Pregnancy & Adoption Svcs.; Mary McGrail, M.A., M.A., Women's Residences; Maria A. Pereira, L.I.S.C.W., Counseling Svcs.; Sheila Sullivan, Volunteer Coord.
Catholic Social Services of Attleboro, 10 Maple St., Attleboro, 02703. Tel: 508-226-4780; Fax: 508-226-5813.
Catholic Social Services of New Bedford, 238 Bonney St., New Bedford, 02744. Tel: 508-997-7337; Fax: 508-984-1667.
Catholic Social Services of Cape Cod, 261 South St., Hyannis, 02601. Tel: 508-771-6771; Fax: 508-771-4711.
Catholic Social Services of Taunton, 78 Broadway, Taunton, 02780. Tel: 508-824-3264; Fax: 508-880-1903.
Reaching Out, 311 Hooper St., Tiverton, RI 02878. Tel: 401-624-9270; Fax: 508-675-2224.
St. Clare Chabot, 189 Wellington St., 02720. Tel: 508-675-1868; Fax: 508-675-1868. Email: clarechabo@aol.com.

HYANNIS. *St. Clare's Residence for Women*, 949 Pitcher's Way, 02601. Tel: 508-775-5096; Fax: 508-775-5096.

[L] CAMPS AND COMMUNITY CENTERS

EAST TAUNTON. *Diocesan Catholic Youth Organization*, P.O. Box 619, 02718. Tel: 508-824-5707; Fax: 508-824-5665. Rev. Jay T. Maddock, J.C.L., Diocesan & Area Dir.
Fall River Area Catholic Youth Organization, Sullivan-McCarrick CYO Center, 403 Anawan St., 02720. Tel: 508-672-9644; Fax: 508-824-5665.
New Bedford Area Catholic Youth Organization, Kennedy Youth Center, 377 County St., New Bedford, 02740. Tel: 508-996-0536; Fax: 508-824-5665. Mr. George Viveiros, Acting Area Dir.
Taunton Area Catholic Youth Organization, 61 Summer St., Taunton, 02780. Tel: 508-822-5218; Fax: 508-824-5665. Mr. Donald Morrison, Acting Area Dir.

[M] NEWMAN CENTERS AND CAMPUS MINISTRY

FALL RIVER. *Bristol Community College Newman Center* 777 Elsbree St., 02720-7395. Tel: 508-678-2811, Ext. 2247; Fax: 508-730-3286. Web: www.bristol.mass.edu/students/counseling/min_cath.html. Rev. Scott A. Ciosek. Total Staff 1.
Diocesan Education Center 423 Highland Ave., 02720. Tel: 508-678-2828; Fax: 508-674-4218. Email: director@dfrcec.com. Web: www.dfrcec.com. Mr. George A. Milot, Supt. of Schools; Dr. Donna Boyle, Asst. Supt. Curriculum; Kathleen A. Simpson, Asst. Supt. Personnel; Rev. Henry J. Dahl, Dir. of R.C.I.A.; Deacon Bruce Bonneau, Dir. Religious Education; Lisa M. Gulino, Dir. Adult Education & Evangelization; Bud Miller, Dir. Youth & Young Adult Ministry. Tel: 508-675-3847; Fax: 508-675-3864; Rev. George E. Harrison, Dir. Youth & Young Adult Min.

BUZZARDS BAY. *Massachusetts Maritime Academy Newman Center* 141 Main St., 02532.

NORTH DARTMOUTH. *Catholic Campus Ministry University of Massachusetts Dartmouth* 285 Old Westport Rd., 02747-2300. Tel: 508-999-8872. Email: cpregana@umassd.edu. Web: www.catholiccampusministries.com. Rev. Craig Pregana, Campus Min.; Sr. Madeleine Tacy, O.P., Campus Min. Total Staff 2.

NORTON. *Wheaton College Newman Center* Tel: 508-675-1311; Fax: 508-679-9220. Email: cap@diocfr.org. Web: catholiccampusministry.com.
Catholic Campus Ministry P.O. Box 2577, 02722. Rev. Craig A. Pregana.

TAUNTON. *Paul A. Dever State School (For Retarded) Newman Center* Box 631, 02780. Tel: 508-824-5881.

WEST BARNSTABLE. *Cape Cod Community College Newman Center*

[N] MISCELLANEOUS LISTINGS

FALL RIVER. *Carmelite Convent of Dartmouth, Inc.*, c/o P.O. Box 2577, 02722.
Community Action for Better Housing, Inc., 1600 Bay St., P.O. Box M, S. Station, 02724. Tel: 508-674-4681; Fax: 508-675-2224. Email: AAM@cssdioc.org.
Diocesan Facilities Self-Insurance Group, Inc., P.O. Box 1110, 02722.
Saint Mary's Education Fund, Inc., P.O. Box 2577, 02722. Tel: 508-675-1311.
Rose Hawthorne Lathrop Home (Servants of Relief for Incurable Cancer), P.O. Box 2577, 02724. Tel: 508-675-1311; Fax: 508-730-2447.
Youth Apostles, 42 Chicago St., 02721-2007. Tel: 508-672-2755; Fax: 508-672-2755. Email: yas-fr@excite.com. Web: www.youthapostles.org. Rev. Michael F. Kuhn, Dir. Total in Residence 3.

ATTLEBORO. *Priestly Fraternity of the Missionaries of St. Charles Borromeo*, 208 S. Main St., 02703. Tel: 508-226-1115; Fax: 917-464-9065. Email: m.carvill@fscb.org. Web: www.fscb.org/. Revs. Michael Carvill; Vincent Nagle, F.S.C.B.; Luca Brancolini.

NEW BEDFORD. *The Institute of the Incarnate Word, Inc.*, 306 Ashley Blvd., 02746. Tel: 508-992-7587; Fax: 508-994-0281. Email: jggiunta@aol.com josegiunta@ive.org. Web: www.ive.org. Rev. Jose Giunta, I.V.E. Tel: 508-992-7587.
St. Mary's Home of New Bedford, Inc., c/o P.O. Box 2577, 02722. Tel: 508-675-1311.
Missionaries of Charity, 556 County St., 02740. Tel: 508-997-7847. Shelter for homeless women. Total in Residence 4; Total Assisted 203.

NORTH EASTON. *Holy Cross Family Ministries*, 518 Washington St., 02356-1200. Tel: 508-238-4095; Fax: 508-238-3953. Email: mission@HCFM.org. Web: www.hcfm.org. William Riley, COO; Revs. John P. Phalen, C.S.C., Pres.; Thomas Feeley, C.S.C., Vice Postulator; Wilfred Raymond, C.S.C., Natl. Dir. of Family Theater Producations; Bro. Joseph Esparza, C.S.C., Family Institute; Beth Mahoney, Mission Dir. Corporate Name: The Family Rosary, Inc.; Sponsored by Congregation of

Holy Cross (Eastern Province)

RELIGIOUS INSTITUTES OF MEN REPRESENTED IN THE DIOCESE

For further details refer to the corresponding bracketed number in the Religious Institutes of Men or Women section.

[0320]—*Brothers of Christian Instruction*—F.I.C.
[0330]—*Brothers of the Christian Schools*
[0600]—*Brothers of the Congregation of Holy Cross*
[1330]—*Congregation of the Mission*—C.M.
[1140]—*Congregation of the Sacred Hearts of Jesus and Mary*—SS.CC.
[0480]—*Conventual Franciscans* (Buffalo, NY)—O.F.M.Conv
[0520]—*Franciscan Friars* (Immaculate Conception Prov.)—O.F.M.
[0533]—*Franciscan Friars of the Immaculate*—F.F.I.
[0470]—*Franciscan (Order of Friars Minor Capuchin)* (St. Augustine Prov.)—O.F.M.Cap.
[]—*The Institute of the Incarnate Word*—I.V.E.
[]—*The Institute of the Incarnate Word*
[0690]—*Jesuit Fathers and Brothers*—S.J.
[0720]—*The Missionaries of Our Lady of La Salette*—M.S.
[0430]—*Order of Preachers (Dominicans)*—O.P.
[]—*Priestly Fraternity of the Missionaries of St. Charles Borromeo Order*—F.S.C.B.
[0610]—*Priests of the Congregation of the Holy Cross* (Eastern Prov.)—C.S.C.

RELIGIOUS INSTITUTES OF WOMEN REPRESENTED IN THE DIOCESE

[0330]—*Carmelite Sisters of the Aged and Infirm*—O.Carm.
[3815]—*Congregation of the Sisters of St. Joan of Arc*—S.J.A.
[1830]—*Contemplative Sisters of the Good Shepherd*—C.G.S.
[0750]—*Daughters of the Charity of the Sacred Heart of Jesus* (Sacred Heart Prov.)—F.C.S.C.J.
[1070-23]—*Dominican Sisters*—O.P.
[1100]—*Dominican Sisters of Charity of the Presentation of the Blessed Virgin*—O.P.
[]—*Dominican Sisters of Hope*—O.P.
[2580]—*Institute of the Sisters of Mercy of the Americas* (Hartford, CT; Manchester, NH; Buffalo, NY)—R.S.M.
[3790]—*Institute of the Sisters of St. Dorothy*—S.S.D.
[2790]—*Missionary Servants of the Most Blessed Trinity*—M.S.B.T.
[]—*Missioneras Guadalupanas del Espirito Santo*
[3410]—*Religious of Christian Education*—R.C.E.
[3450]—*Religious of Jesus and Mary*—R.J.M.
[2070]—*Religious of the Holy Union of the Sacred Hearts* (Immaculate Heart and Sacred Heart Provs.)—S.U.S.C.
[3650]—*Servants of Our Lady, Queen of the Clergy*—S.R.C.
[0560]—*Sisters of Charity of Quebec (Grey Nuns)*—S.C.Q.
[0590]—*Sisters of Charity of Saint Elizabeth (Convent Station)*—S.C.
[0640]—*Sisters of Charity of St. Vincent de Paul (Halifax)*—S.C.
[3720]—*Sisters of Saint Anne*—S.S.A.
[1705]—*The Sisters of St. Francis of Assisi*—O.S.F.
[3830-16]—*Sisters of St. Joseph*—S.S.J.
[3860]—*Sisters of St. Joseph of Cluny*—S.J.C.
[2980]—*Sisters of the Congregation of Notre Dame*—C.N.D.
[1830]—*Sisters of the Good Shepherd*—R.G.S.
[]—*Sisters of the Holy Cross*
[]—*Sisters of the Holy Cross and of the Seven Dolors*—C.S.C.
[3690]—*Sisters of the Sacred Hearts of Perpetual Adoration*—SS.CC.
[4048]—*Society of the Sisters, Faithful Companions of Jesus*—F.C.J.

DIOCESAN CEMETERIES

FALL RIVER. *St. John*
St. Mary
Notre Dame
St. Patrick
ATTLEBORO. *St. John*
St. Stephen
EAST FALMOUTH. *St. Anthony*
HYANNIS. *St. Francis*
MANSFIELD. *St. Mary*
MATTAPOISETT. *St. Anthony*
NANTUCKET. *St. Mary*
NEW BEDFORD. *St. John Sacred Heart*
St. Mary
NORTH ATTLEBORO. *St. Mary*
NORTH EASTON. *Immaculate Conception*
OAK BLUFFS. *Sacred Heart*
PROVINCETOWN. *St. Peter*
SANDWICH. *St. Peter*
SOMERSET. *St. Patrick*
TAUNTON. *St. Francis*
St. James
St. Joseph
St. Mary
TRURO. *Sacred Heart*
WAREHAM. *St. Patrick*
WELLFLEET. *Our Lady of Lourdes*
WEST HARWICH. *Holy Trinity*

NECROLOGY

† Denehy, Rev. Msgr. John F.—Died Aug. 21, 2003
† Connors, Francis B. (Retired)—Died Jan. 4, 2003
† Jussaume, Andre P. (Retired)—Died Oct. 14, 2003
† Munro, Hugh J. (Retired)—Died July 31, 2003
† Robida, Raymond A., (Retired)—Died May 5, 2003

Diocese of Fargo

(Dioecesis Fargensis)

Most Reverend

SAMUEL J. AQUILA, D.D.

Bishop of Fargo; ordained June 5, 1976; appointed Coadjutor Bishop of Fargo June 12, 2001; ordained August 24, 2001; appointed Bishop of Fargo March 18, 2002 *5201 Bishops Blvd., Ste. A, Fargo, ND 58104-7298.*

Most Reverend

JAMES S. SULLIVAN, D.D.

Retired Bishop of Fargo; ordained June 4, 1955; consecrated Auxiliary Bishop of Lansing September 21, 1972; appointed Bishop of Fargo April 2, 1985 installed May 30, 1985; retired March 18, 2002 *Res.: Holy Spirit Parish*, 1420 7th St. N., Fargo, ND 58102.

Square Miles 35,786.

Corporate Title: The Diocese of Fargo.

Formerly Diocese of Jamestown.

Established November 12, 1889; Transfered to Fargo, April 6, 1897.

Comprises the Counties of Barnes, Benson, Bottineau, Cass, Cavalier, Dickey, Eddy, Foster, Grand Forks, Griggs, Kidder, LaMoure, Logan, McHenry, McIntosh, Nelson, Pembina, Pierce, Ramsey, Ransom, Richland, Rolette, Sargent, Sheridan, Steele, Stutsman, Towner, Traill, Walsh and Wells in the State of North Dakota.

Legal Title: For legal titles of parishes and diocesan institutions, consult the Chancery Office.

Chancery Office: 5201 Bishops Blvd., Ste. A, Fargo, ND 58104-7298. Tel: 701-235-6429; Fax: 701-356-7999.

Web: www.fargodiocese.org

Email: web@fargodiocese.org

STATISTICAL OVERVIEW

Personnel	
Bishop	1
Retired Bishops	1
Priests: Diocesan Active in Diocese	92
Priests: Diocesan Active Outside Diocese	14
Priests: Diocesan in Foreign Missions	1
Priests: Retired, Sick or Absent	46
Number of Diocesan Priests	153
Religious Priests in Diocese	7
Total Priests in Diocese	160
Extern Priests in Diocese	4
Ordinations:	
Diocesan Priests	3
Permanent Deacons	7
Permanent Deacons in Diocese	40
Total Sisters	201
Parishes	
Parishes	158
With Resident Pastor:	
Resident Diocesan Priests	72
Resident Religious Priests	2
Without Resident Pastor:	
Administered by Priests	84
Professional Ministry Personnel:	
Sisters	10
Lay Ministers	53
Welfare	
Catholic Hospitals	9
Total Assisted	108,732
Homes for the Aged	12
Total Assisted	1,222
Day Care Centers	1
Total Assisted	18
Specialized Homes	1
Special Centers for Social Services	5
Total Assisted	7,941
Educational	
Seminaries, Diocesan	1
Students from This Diocese	2
Students from Other Diocese	7
Diocesan Students in Other Seminaries	10
Total Seminarians	12
High Schools, Diocesan and Parish	1
Total Students	292
Elementary Schools, Diocesan and Parish	13
Total Students	1,895
Catechesis/Religious Education:	
High School Students	3,247
Elementary Students	7,571
Total Students under Catholic Instruction	13,017
Teachers in the Diocese:	
Priests	1
Lay Teachers	137
Vital Statistics	
Receptions into the Church:	
Infant Baptism Totals	1,483
Adult Baptism Totals	70
Received into Full Communion	168
First Communions	1,344
Confirmations	2,571
Marriages:	
Catholic	275
Interfaith	200
Total Marriages	475
Deaths	968
Total Catholic Population	84,190
Total Population	374,256

Former Bishops—Rt. Rev. JOHN SHANLEY, D.D., ord. 1874; consecrated Dec. 27, 1889; died July 16, 1909; Most Rev. JAMES O'REILLY, D.D., ord. June 24, 1880; consecrated May 19, 1910; installed June 1, 1910; died Dec. 19, 1934; His Eminence ALOISIUS CARDINAL MUENCH, ord. June 8, 1913; appt. Bishop of Fargo, Aug. 10, 1935; consecrated Oct. 15, 1935; installed Nov. 6, 1935; appt. Apostolic Visitator for Germany, July 8, 1946;; granted personal title of Archbishop, Nov. 1, 1950;; appt. Papal Nuncio to Germany, March 10, 1951; created Cardinal Priest and elevated to the Roman Curia, Dec. 14, 1959; died Feb. 15, 1962; Most Revs. LEO F. DWORSCHAK, D.D. (Retired), ord. May 29, 1926; appt. Coadjutor Bishop of Rapid City, June 23, 1946; consecrated August 22, 1946; appt. Auxiliary Bishop of Fargo, April 10, 1947; succeeded to See, May 10, 1960; retired Sept. 8, 1970; died Nov. 5, 1976; JUSTIN A. DRISCOLL, D.D., ord. July 28, 1945; appt. Bishop of Fargo, Sept. 8, 1970; consecrated and installed Oct. 28, 1970; died Nov. 19, 1984; JAMES S. SULLIVAN, D.D. (Retired), ord. June 4, 1955; consecrated Auxiliary Bishop of Lansing Sept. 21, 1972; appt. Bishop of Fargo April 2, 1985; installed May 30, 1985; retired March 18, 2002.

Chancery Office—5201 Bishops Blvd., Fargo, 58104. Tel: 701-235-6429; Fax: 701-356-7999.

Moderator of the Curia—Rev. Msgr. BRIAN G. DONAHUE, V.G.

Vicars General—Rev. Msgr. BRIAN G. DONAHUE, V.G.; Very Rev. GREGORY J. SCHLESSELMANN.

Chancellor and Secretary to the Bishop—Very Rev. JOSEPH P. GOERING.

Vicar for Clergy—Rev. Msgr. BRIAN G. DONAHUE, V.G.

Vice-Chancellors—Very Rev. DANIEL PILON, J.C.L.; Rev. JEFFREY WALD; GINNY BAIR, Asst. to Bishop.

Archivist—Very Rev. JOSEPH P. GOERING.

Chief Financial Officer—Mr. SCOTT A. HOSELTON, C.P.A.

Diocesan Tribunal—5201 Bishops Blvd., Fargo, 58104. Tel: 701-235-6429.

Judicial Vicar—Very Rev. DANIEL J. PILON, J.C.L.

Promotor Justitiae—VACANT.

Defensor Vinculi—Revs. JAMES A. LEITH, J.C.D.; JAMES GOODWIN.

Presiding Judge—Very Rev. DANIEL PILON, J.C.L.

Judges—Rev. Msgrs. WENDELYN VETTER; ALLAN F. NILLES (Retired); Revs. CHAD F. WILHELM; THOMAS M. GRANER; JARED KADLEC; AL BETZ.

Advocates—Deacon DONALD TINGUELY; Sr. CELINE FOY, P.B.V.M.; ELLEN O'CONNOR.

Auditor—MARILYN BITTNER.

Notaries—Very Revs. JOSEPH P. GOERING, Chancellor; GREGORY J SCHLESSELMANN; Mr. SCOTT A. HOSELTON, C.P.A.; BERNESIA RADCLIFFE; JOLETTE KRABBENHOFT.

Diocesan College of Consultors—Very Revs. GREGORY J. SCHLESSELMANN; BRIAN BACHMEIER; Rev. JAMES ERMER; Rev. Msgr. BRIAN G. DONAHUE, V.G.; Revs. ROBERT LALIBERTE; JAMES MCKINNEY; DAVID SYVERSON.

Deans—Deanery 1: Very Rev. DALE LAGODINSKI, Wahpeton. Deanery 2: Very Rev. PAUL C. DUCHSCHERE, Fargo. Deanery 3: Very Rev. BERNARD SCHNEIDER, Manvel. Deanery 4: Very Rev. BRIAN M. BACHMEIER, Walhalla. Deanery 5: Very Rev. KEVIN L. WILLIS, Cando. Deanery 6: Very Rev. KEVIN BOUCHER, Rugby. Deanery 7: Very Rev. KEVIN BOUCHER, Interim Dean, Rugby. Deanery 8: Very Rev. GERARD BRAUN, Valley City. Deanery 9: Very Rev. GARY D. LUITEN, Ellendale.

Diocesan Offices and Directors

Corporate Board—Most Rev. SAMUEL J. AQUILA, D.D.; Rev. Msgr. BRIAN G. DONAHUE, V.G.; Very Rev. JOSEPH P. GOERING; Rev. CHAD F. WILHELM; Mr. SCOTT A. HOSELTON, C.P.A.; TERRY W. KNOEPFLE, Esq.

Apostleship of Prayer—Rev. CHAD F. WILHELM, Dir.

Diocesan Finance Council—Most Rev. SAMUEL J. AQUILA, D.D.; Rev. Msgr. BRIAN G. DONAHUE, V.G.; Very Rev. JOSEPH P. GOERING; Revs. MICHAEL PARROTTA; CHAD WILHELM; Mr. GERALD F. HAMERLIK; Mr. GARY DIETZ; Mr. RAY SIMON; Mr. SCOTT A. HOSELTON, C.P.A.; TERRY W. KNOEPFLE, Esq.; FRANCIS KRITZBERGER; KAREN LESTER; WILLIAM HARBEKE.

The Catholic Church Expansion Fund of the Diocese of Fargo— Same as corporate board.

Pension Plan—Mr. SCOTT A. HOSELTON, C.P.A.

Censor Librorum—Rev. ROBERT LALIBERTE, Ph.D.
Office of Worship and Sacraments—Very Rev. JOSEPH P. GOERING.
Continuing Education of Priests—Very Rev. BRIAN BACHMEIER, Chm.
Due Process Board (Conciliators)—VACANT, Chm.
Ecumenical Commission—Rev. PAUL R. SCHUSTER.
Director of Stewardship and Development—WILLIAM HARBEKE.
Holy Childhood Association—Very Rev. JOSEPH P. GOERING.
Communications—TANYA WATTERUD.
The "New Earth" (Diocesan Newspaper)—TANYA WATTERUD, Editor.
North Dakota Catholic Conference—CHRISTOPHER DODSON, 227 W. Broadway, Ste. 2, Bismarck, 58501.
Permanent Diaconate—Very Rev. GREGORY J. SCHLESSELMANN, Rector & Sec. of Diaconate; Revs. ROBERT LALIBERTE, Ph.D.; DENNIS SKONSENG; Deacons DAVID EBLEN, Dir. Formation; MATTHIAS PROM.
Presbyteral Council—Rev. DAVID SYVERSON, Chm.
Propagation of the Faith—Very Rev. JOSEPH P. GOERING.
Rural Life—Rev. THOMAS GRANER, Dir.; Rev. Msgr. WENDELYN VETTER; Very Rev. BERNARD R. SCHNEIDER, P.O. Box 127, Rolette, 58366. Tel: 701-246-3486.
Technology / Computer Office—JOCELYN SLOAN.
Catholic Education and Formation—TOM FREI, Dir.
Evangelization / Catechesis—STELLA JEFFREY.
Healthcare Director—Rev. DALE H. KINZLER.
Youth / Young Adults—KURTIS L. GUNWALL.
Catholic Schools—THOMAS A. FREI.
Education in Parish Service (EPS)—Deacon DAVID EBLEN.
Respect Life Office—RACHELLE L. SAUVAGEAU.
Vocation Director—Rev. ROBERT F. SMITH JR., Cardinal Muench Seminary, 100-35th Ave., N.E., Fargo, 58102. Tel: 701-271-1212.
Catholic Cemeteries—Mr. SCOTT A. HOSELTON, C.P.A.
Hispanic Ministry—Rev. TIMOTHY SCHROEDER, Sacred Heart, P.O. Box 316, Minto, 58261.
Native American Ministries—Rev. EDWARD SHERMAN, Chap. at Large (Retired).
Apostolate for Native Americans—Rev. GERALD A. MCCARTHY (Retired), 304 3rd Ave. W., Box 155, Bisbee, 58317.
Prison Apostolate—Rev. PAUL R. SCHUSTER.
Liaison with Charismatic Movement—Revs. ROBERT L. LALIBERTE, Ph.D.; DONALD A. LEIPHON.

CLERGY, PARISHES, MISSIONS AND PAROCHIAL SCHOOLS

CITY OF FARGO
(CASS COUNTY)

1—ST. MARY CATHEDRAL (1880), [JC], Also serving Argusville. Revs. Peter Hughes, C.S.Sp.; Brian Moen; Deacon George Loegering.
Office—619 7th St. N., 58102. Tel: 701-235-4289; 701-235-4280; Fax: 701-235-2986.
Res.: 679 6th Ave. N., 58102. Tel: 701-235-4280.
Catechesis / Religious Program—Students 175.

2—SS. ANNE & JOACHIM (1995), [JC] Rev. Msgr. Val Gross; Rev. Peter J. Anderl.
5202 25th St. S., 58104. Tel: 701-235-5757; Fax: 701-235-0651.
Res.: 5202 25th St. S., 58104. Tel: 701-235-1514.
Catechesis / Religious Program—Students 300.

3—ST. ANTHONY OF PADUA (1917), [JC] Rev. James R. Ermer; Deacon Stuart Longtin; Rev. Wenceslaus Katanga; Deacon Mathias Prom.
Church: 710 S. 10th St., 58103. Tel: 701-237-6063; Fax: 701-237-6064.
Catechesis / Religious Program—Tel: 701-232-3995. Students 241.

4—HOLY SPIRIT (1951), [JC] Revs. Jeffrey L. Wald; John F. Aerts.
Church: 1420 N. 7th St., 58102. Tel: 701-232-5900; Fax: 701-232-5902.
School—1441 8th St. N., 58102. Tel: 701-232-4087; Fax: 701-232-8240. Jason Kotrba, Prin. Lay Teachers 12; Students 214.
Catechesis / Religious Program—Students 205.

5—NATIVITY (1960), [JC] Revs. Dale Kinzler; Richard Fineo; Tim Mathern, Parish Admin.
Church: 1825 11th St. S., 58103. Tel: 701-232-2414; Fax: 701-232-4491.
School—Tel: 701-232-7461; Fax: 701-298-8981. Cindy Hutchins, Prin. Lay Teachers 24; Students 340.
Catechesis / Religious Program—Students 319.

6—ST. PAUL NEWMAN CENTER, N.D.S.U. (1928), [JC] Rev. Paul Duchschere.
Church: 1141 N. University Dr., 58102. Tel: 701-866-2747.
Church: Tel: 701-235-0142.
Catechesis / Religious Program—Students 27.

OUTSIDE THE CITY OF FARGO

ALICE, CASS CO., ST. HENRY (OF ALICE) (1902), [CEM], Served from Enderlin. Rev. John Fallon.
Mailing Address: c/o St Patrick, 302 Bluff St., Enderlin, 58027.
Church: 58003.
Catechesis / Religious Program—Students 16.

ANAMOOSE, MCHENRY CO., ST. FRANCIS XAVIER (1899), [CEM], Also serving Drake and Orrin. Rev. Leo Kinney.
Church: 605 1st St. W., P.O. Box 49, 58710-0049. Tel: 701-465-3780; Fax: 701-465-0217.

ANETA, NELSON CO., SACRED HEART (1908), [CEM], Served from Cooperstown. Rev. James W. Cheney.
Mailing Address: c/o St. George, P.O. Box 217, Cooperstown, 58425. Tel: 701-797-2624.
Catechesis / Religious Program—Students 4.

ARDOCH, WALSH CO., ST. JOHN THE BAPTIST (1883), [CEM], Served from Minto. Rev. Timothy C. Schroeder.
Mailing Address: c/o Sacred Heart, P.O. Box 316, Minto, 58261. Tel: 701-248-3589; Fax: 701-248-3139.
Catechesis / Religious Program—Students 9.

ARGUSVILLE, CASS CO., ST. WILLIAM (1942), [JC], Served from St. Mary's Cathedral, Fargo. , Mailing Address: P.O. Box 1, Harwood, 58042-0001.
Church: 107 Drake Ave., 58005.
Catechesis / Religious Program—Tel: 701-484-5211. Students 49.

ASHLEY, MCINTOSH CO., ST. DAVID (1960),, Served from Wishek. Rev. Andrew Jasinski.
Mailing Address: c/o St. Patrick, P.O. Box 293, Wishek, 58495. Tel: 701-423-5494.
Catechesis / Religious Program—Students 17.

BALFOUR, MCHENRY CO., ST. JOSEPH (1906), Closed., For inquiries for parish records please contact the Chancellor.

BALTA, PIERCE CO., OUR LADY OF MOUNT CARMEL (1902), [CEM], Served from Rugby. Also serving Fulda and Orrin.
Church: 301 Main St. N, 58313. Tel: 701-542-3326.
Catechesis / Religious Program—Students 22.

BATHGATE, PEMBINA CO., ST. ANTHONY (1883), [CEM], Served from Cavalier. Rev. Jason Lefor.
Mailing Address: c/o St. Brigid, P.O. Box 280, Cavalier, 58220-0280. Tel: 701-265-8877; Fax: 701-265-8848.
Catechesis / Religious Program—Students 11.

BECHYNE, SS. PETER & PAUL (1886), [CEM], Served from Michigan. Rev. Samuel Ezeibekwe.
Mailing Address: c/o St. Lawrence O' Toole, P.O. Box 332, Michigan, 58259. Tel: 701-259-2248; Fax: 701-259-2350.
Catechesis / Religious Program—Students 33.

BELCOURT, ROLETTE CO.

1—ST. ANN (1885), [CEM], Also serving Immaculate Heart of Mary, St. Louis, Dunseith; St. Anthony, St. Benedict, Belcourt, and St. John, St John. Revs. Dale Craig, S.O.L.T.; Robert J. Cronin, S.O.L.T.; Ralph Jones, S.O.L.T., Prin.; John Patterson, S.O.L.T.; Deacon Eddie Johnson.
Church: Box 2000, 58316. Tel: 701-477-5601; Fax: 701-477-0602.
School—St. Ann, P.O. Box 2020, 58316-2020. Priests 1; Sisters 1; Lay Teachers 8; Students 60.
Catechesis / Religious Program—Students 190.

2—ST. ANTHONY (1895), [CEM], Served from Belcourt. Rev. Dale Craig, S.O.L.T.
Mailing Address: c/o St. Ann, P.O. Box 2000, 58316. Tel: 701-477-5601.
Catechesis / Religious Program—Students 20.

BISBEE, TOWNER CO., HOLY ROSARY (1889), [CEM], Served from Rolette. Rev. Thomas Graner.
Mailing Address: c/o Sacred Heart, P.O. Box 127, Rolette, 58366. Tel: 701-246-3449.
Church: 304 3rd Ave. W., 58317. Tel: 701-656-3307; Fax: 701-246-3449.
Catechesis / Religious Program—Students 22.

BOTTINEAU, BOTTINEAU CO., ST. MARK (1905), [CEM], Also serving Westhope. Rev. Paul R. Schuster.
Res.: 322 Sinclair St., 58318. Tel: 701-228-3164.
Catechesis / Religious Program—Students 123.

BREMEN, WELLS CO., ST. JOSEPH (1896), [CEM], Served from Fessenden. Rev. William Callery.
Mailing Address: c/o St. Augustine, 105 7th Ave. S, Fessenden, 58438-7404. Tel: 701-547-3430.
Catechesis / Religious Program—Students 22.

BROCKET, RAMSEY CO., ST. JOSEPH (1910), [CEM], Served from Lakota. Rev. Scott Sautner.
Mailing Address: c/o St. Mary, 109 East Ave. E., P.O. Box 509, Lakota, 58344. Tel: 701-247-2594; Fax: 701-247-2584.
Catechesis / Religious Program—Students 5.

BUCHANAN, STUTSMAN CO., ST. MARGARET ALACOQUE (1924), [CEM], Served from Jamestown Very Rev. Al M. Bitz.
Mailing Address: c/o Basilica of St. James, 622 1st Ave. S., Box 347, Jamestown, 58402. Tel: 701-252-0119; Fax: 701-252-6992.
Catechesis / Religious Program— Twinned with St. Michael in Pingree. Students 18.

BUFFALO, CASS CO., ST. THOMAS (1900), [JC], Served from Casselton Rev. Michael Parrotta.
Mailing Address: c/o St. Leo, P.O. Box 340, Casselton, 58012. Tel: 701-347-4609.
Church: 401 3rd St. N. Buffalo, Casselton, 58012. Tel: 701-633-5150.
Catechesis / Religious Program—Students 11.

BURNSTAD, LOGAN CO., ST. CLARE OF ASSISI (1915),, Served from Napoleon. Rev. Donald A. Leiphon.
Mailing Address: c/o St. Philip Neri, 401 Broadway, Napoleon, 58561-7013. Tel: 701-754-2860.
Catechesis / Religious Program—Students 3.

CANDO, TOWNER CO., SACRED HEART (1893), [CEM] Rev. Kevin Willis; Deacon James Eggl.
Mailing Address: P.O. Box 399, 58324. Tel: 701-968-3462.
Church: 310 3rd Ave., 58324.
Catechesis / Religious Program—Tel: 701-968-3830. Students 75.

CARRINGTON, FOSTER CO., SACRED HEART (1887), [CEM] Rev. Lawrence W. Haas.
Mailing Address: P.O. Box 420, 58421. Tel: 701-652-2519.
Church: 633 1st St. S., 58421.
Catechesis / Religious Program—Tel: 701-652-2072. Students 163.

CASSELTON, CASS CO., ST. LEO (1880), [CEM], Also serving Buffalo. Rev. Michael Parrotta.
Mailing Address: P.O. Box 340, 58012.
Church: 211 Langer Ave., 58012. Tel: 701-347-4609; Fax: 701-347-4611.
Catechesis / Religious Program—Students 212.

CAVALIER, PEMBINA CO., ST. BRIDGET (1881), [CEM], Also serving Neche and Bathgate Rev. Jason Lefor; Deacon Jim Carpenter.
Mailing Address: P.O. Box 280, 58220-0280. Tel: 701-265-8877; Fax: 701-265-8848.
Church: 201 1st Ave. S., 58220.
Catechesis / Religious Program—Students 103.

CAYUGA, SARGENT CO., SS. PETER AND PAUL (1916),, Served from Forman Rev. Franklin Miller.
Mailing Address: 480 4th St., S.W., Forman, 58032-4209. Tel: 701-724-3319; Fax: 701-724-3310.
Church: 229 Franklin Ave. W., 58032.
Catechesis / Religious Program—Students 8.

COGSWELL, SARGENT CO., OUR LADY OF MERCY (1903), [CEM], Served from Forman Rev. Franklin Miller.
Mailing Address: c/o St. Mary, 480 4th St., S.W., Forman, 58032-4209. Tel: 701-724-3319; Fax: 701-724-3310.
Catechesis / Religious Program—Students 3.

CONWAY, WALSH CO., ST. MARK (1884), [CEM], Served from Pisek Rev. John Lewandowski.
Mailing Address: c/o St. John Nepomucene, P.O. Box 27, Pisek, 58273. Tel: 701-284-6060; Fax: 701-284-6331.
Church: 110 Front St. E..
Catechesis / Religious Program—Students 29.

COOPERSTOWN, GRIGGS CO., ST. GEORGE (1939), [CEM], Also serving Aneta, Jessie Rev. James Cheney.
Res.: P.O. Box 217, 808 Foster St., 58425. Tel: 701-797-2624.
Catechesis / Religious Program—Students 25.

COURTENAY, STUTSMAN CO., ST. MARY, [CEM], Served from Wimbledon Rev. Steven Meyer.
Mailing Address: c/o St. Boniface, P.O. Box 9, Wimbledon, 58492. Tel: 701-435-2310.
Church: 1324 95th Ave. S.E..
Catechesis / Religious Program—Students 4.

CRARY, RAMSEY CO., ST. BENEDICT (1910), [CEM], Served from Devils Lake Rev. Chad Wilhelm.
Mailing Address: c/o St. Joseph, Box 898, Devils Lake, 58301. Tel: 701-662-7558; Fax: 701-662-7559.
Church: 5384 91st Ave. N.E..
Catechesis / Religious Program—Students 27.

CROW HILL, BENSON CO., ST. JEROME (1892), [CEM], Served from Fort Totten Rev. Charles Leute, O.P.
Mailing Address: c/o Seven Dolors, Box 299, Fort Totten, 58335. Tel: 701-766-4314.
Catechesis / Religious Program—Students 29.

CRYSTAL, PEMBINA CO., ST. PATRICK (1892), [CEM], Served from Park River Rev. Robert P. Unger.
Mailing Address: c/o St. Mary, P.O. Box 110, Park River, 58270. Tel: 701-284-6165; Fax: 701-284-7789.
Catechesis / Religious Program—Students 19.

DAZEY, BARNES CO., ST. MARY (1899), [CEM], Served from Sanborn Rev. Matthew Attansey.
Church: c/o Sacred Heart, P.O. Box 35, Sanborn, 58480. Tel: 701-646-6306.
Catechesis / Religious Program—Students 3.

DEVILS LAKE, RAMSEY CO., ST. JOSEPH (1884),, Also serving Crary Rev. Chad F. Wilhelm; Most Rev. Joseph Christensen; Deacon Lawrence Lange.

Mailing Address: Box 898, 58301. Tel: 701-662-7558; Fax: 701-662-7559.
Church: 515 4th St..
School—824 10th Ave.. Tel: 701-662-5016; Fax: 701-662-5017. Tom Burckhard, Prin. Lay Teachers 15; Students 184.
Catechesis/Religious Program—Students 334.

DICKEY, LAMOURE CO., ASSUMPTION (1909), [CEM], Served from LaMoure Rev. Jimmy Lim Tiu.
Mailing Address: c/o Holy Rosary, 209 First St., S.E., P.O. Box 217, La Moure, 58458. Tel: 701-883-5987.
Church: 106 Main St..

DRAKE, MCHENRY CO., ST. MARGARET MARY (1910), [CEM], Served by Anamoose Rev. Leo Kinney.
Res.: 605 Main St., P.O. Box 197, 58735-0197. Tel: 701-465-3284.
Catechesis/Religious Program—Students 60.

DRAYTON, PEMBINA CO., ST. EDWARD (1889), [CEM], Also serving Pembina Rev. William T. Ovsak.
Mailing Address: P.O. Box 215, 58225. Tel: 701-454-6171; Fax: 701-454-6171.
Church: 211 N. Main St..
Catechesis/Religious Program—Students 35.

DUNSEITH, ROLETTE CO.
1—IMMACULATE HEART OF MARY (1948), [CEM], Served from Belcourt. Rev. Dale Craig, S.O.L.T.
Mailing Address: *c/o St. Ann*, P.O. Box 2000, Belcourt, 58316-2000. Tel: 701-477-5601; Fax: 701-447-0602.
Catechesis/Religious Program—Tel: 701-244-5784. Twinned with St. Louis, Dunseith.
2—ST. LOUIS KING OF FRANCE (1882), [CEM], Served from Belcourt Rev. Dale Craig, S.O.L.T.
Mailing Address: *c/o St. Ann*, P.O. Box 2000, Belcourt, 58316-2000. Tel: 701-477-5601.
Res.: 112 First St., N.W., Box 160, 58329. Tel: 701-477-5601.
Catechesis/Religious Program—Students 86.

EDGELEY, LAMOURE CO., TRANSFIGURATION (1915), [CEM], Also serving Nortonville and St. Joseph Manor Rev. Duaine M. Cote; Deacon Thurston Ham.
Mailing Address: 205 Second St., P.O. Box 347, 58433. Tel: 701-493-2387; Fax: 701-493-2387.

ELLENDALE, DICKEY CO., ST. HELENA (1888), [CEM], Also serving Fullerton. Very Rev. Gary Luiten.
Mailing Address: P.O. Box 796, 58436. Tel: 701-349-3297; Fax: 701-349-3297.
Church: 421 N. 2nd St..
Catechesis/Religious Program—Tel: 701-349-4128. Students 59.

ENDERLIN, RANSOM CO., ST. PATRICK (1901), [CEM], Also serving Alice, Sheldon Rev. John P. Fallon.
302 Bluff St., 58027. Tel: 701-437-2791; Fax: 701-437-2791.
Catechesis/Religious Program—Students 41.

ESMOND, BENSON CO., ST. BONIFACE (1909), [CEM], Also serving Maddock Rev. Julian Kupisz.
Mailing Address: P.O. Box 37, 58332-0033. Tel: 701-249-8360.
Church: 108 Alta Ave. N..
Catechesis/Religious Program—Students 29.

FAIRMOUNT, RICHLAND CO., ST. ANTHONY (1909), [CEM], Also serving Carmel Convent Rev. Thomas Krupich.
Mailing Address: Box 292, 58030. Tel: 701-474-5518.
Church: 204 2nd St. N..
Catechesis/Religious Program—Students 42.

FESSENDEN, WELLS CO., ST. AUGUSTINE (1896),, Also serving Bremen. Rev. William Callery.
105 7th Ave. S., 58438-7404. Tel: 701-547-3430.
Catechesis/Religious Program—Students 30.

FINGAL, BARNES CO., HOLY TRINITY (1889), [CEM 2], Served by Oriska Rev. K. S. Kopacz.
Mailing Address: c/o St. Bernard, 606 Fifth St., Oriska, 58063. Tel: 701-845-3713; Fax: 701-845-0172.
Catechesis/Religious Program—Students 26.

FINLEY, STEELE CO., ST. OLAF (1949), [JC], Served from Hope. Rev. Armand L. Brooks.
Mailing Address: c/o St. Agatha, P.O. Box 99, Hope, 58046. Tel: 701-945-2652.
Catechesis/Religious Program—Tel: 701-524-1101. Students 28.

FORMAN, SARGENT CO., ST. MARY (1913), [CEM], Also serving Cayuga, Cogswell, Milnor. Rev. Franklin D. Miller; Deacon Richard Biss.
Mailing Address: 480 4th St., S.W., 58032-0175. Tel: 701-724-3319; Fax: 701-724-3310.
Church: 484 4th St. S.W..
Catechesis/Religious Program—Tel: 701-724-3440. Students 40.

FORT TOTTEN, BENSON CO., SEVEN DOLORS (1875), (Native American), [CEM], Also serving Crow Hill, Tokio. Rev. Charles J. Leute, O.P.; Deacon Anthony McDonald.
Mailing Address: P.O. Box 299, 58335. Tel: 701-766-4314.
Catechesis/Religious Program—Tel: 701-766-4314. Students 28.

FRIED, STUTSMAN CO., SACRED HEART (1888), [CEM], Served from Jamestown. Very Rev. Al M. Bitz.
Mailing Address: c/o Basilica of St. James, 622 First Ave. S., Box 347, Jamestown, 58402. Tel: 701-252-0119; Fax: 701-252-6992.
Church: 2548 87th St.E..
Catechesis/Religious Program—Students 7.

FULDA, MCHENRY CO., ST. ANSELM (1901), [CEM] Unassigned., Mailing Address: c/o Our Lady of Mt. Carmel, P.O. Box 428, Balta, 58313. Tel: 701-542-3326. Served from Balta.
Church: 5851 19th Ave. N..
Catechesis/Religious Program—Students 7.

FULLERTON, DICKEY CO., ST. PATRICK (1921), [CEM], Served from Ellendale. Very Rev. Gary Luiten.
Mailing Address: c/o St. Helena, P.O. Box 796, Ellendale, 58436. Tel: 701-349-3297.
Church: 300 W. Cedar.
Catechesis/Religious Program—Students 17.

GACKLE, LOGAN CO., ST. ANNE (1951),, Served from Windsor. Rev. Joseph Okogba.
Mailing Address: c/o St Mathias, 207 Washington Ave., Cleveland, 58424. Tel: 701-763-6192; 701-320-6192 (Cellular).
Catechesis/Religious Program—Students 25.

GENESEO, SARGENT CO., ST. MARTIN OF TOURS (1907), [CEM], Served from Lidgerwood. Rev. J. Vincent Fitzpatrick.
413 Main St., 58053. Tel: 701-538-4821.
Catechesis/Religious Program—Students 17.

GRAFTON, WALSH CO., ST. JOHN THE EVANGELIST (1881), [CEM], Also serving State School. Rev. Bert Miller; Deacon Leonard Buresh.
Mailing Address: P.O. Box 636, 58237.
Church: 344 15th St. W..
St. John's Catechetical Center— 58237. Brent Hermans, D.R.E.; Rose Marie Kerner, D.R.E. Students 272.

GRAND FORKS GRAND FORKS CO.
1—HOLY FAMILY (1960), [JC] Revs. Phil Ackerman; John Kleinschmidt.
1018 18th Ave. S., 58201-6830. Tel: 701-746-1454; Fax: 701-746-1456.
School—Tel: 701-775-9886; Fax: 701-775-0221. Mr. Charles Scherr, Prin. Lay Teachers 6; Students 113.
Catechesis/Religious Program—Tel: 701-746-9386; Fax: 701-746-1456. Students 380.
2—ST. MARY (1914), [JC] Rev. Jerald L.C. Finnestad; Deacon Don Litzinger.
216 Belmont Rd., 58201. Tel: 701-775-9318; Fax: 701-775-7568.
School—Tel: 701-775-4818. Lay Teachers 8; Students 95.
Catechesis/Religious Program—Tel: 701-775-2842. Students 220.
3—ST. MICHAEL (1872), [JC] Revs. Michael Schommer; Augustine Alilonu; Thomas Feltman.
520 N. Sixth St., 58203. Tel: 701-772-2624
School—504 5th Ave. N.. Tel: 701-772-1822; Fax: 701-772-0211. Sharon Litchy, Prin. Lay Teachers 14; Students 109.
Catechesis/Religious Program—Tel: 701-772-2282. Students 383.
4—ST. THOMAS AQUINAS (UNIVERSITY OF NORTH DAKOTA) (1951), [JC] Rev. Raymond P. Courtright; Deacon Samuel Pupino.
Res.: 410 Cambridge St., 58203. Tel: 701-777-6850; Fax: 701-777-0911.
Catechesis/Religious Program—Students 62.

GRANVILLE, MCHENRY CO., OUR LADY OF PERPETUAL HELP (1933), Served from Towner. Rev. Ronald Yee Mon.
Mailing Address: c/o St. Cecilia, 503 First St. S.W., Box 267, Towner, 58788-0267. Tel: 701-537-5133.
Catechesis/Religious Program—Students 17.

GWINNER, SARGENT CO., ST. VINCENT (1908), [CEM], Served from Lisbon. Rev. Andrew Dudzinski.
Mailing Address: c/o St. Aloysius, P.O. Box 226, Lisbon, 58054-0226. Tel: 701-683-4620; Fax: 701-683-5703.
Church: 315 3rd St. S.E., Lisbon, 58054-0226. Tel: 701-683-4620.
Catechesis/Religious Program—Tel: 701-678-2364. Students 41.

HANKINSON, RICHLAND CO., ST. PHILIP (1889), [CEM] Rev. James S. Goodwin.
Res.: 612 S. Main, P.O. Box 419, 58041. Tel: 701-242-7327.
Catechesis/Religious Program—Students 140.

HANSBORO, TOWNER CO., SACRED HEART, Closed., For inquiries for parish records please contact the Chancellor.

HARVEY, WELLS CO., ST. CECILIA (1895), [CEM], Also serving Selz. Rev. Vernon Smith; Deacon Jeffrey M. Faul.
413 E. Brewster St., 58341. Tel: 701-324-2144; Fax: 701-324-4640.
Catechesis/Religious Program—Tel: 701-324-2637. Students 167.

HILLSBORO, TRAILL CO., ST. ROSE OF LIMA (1892), [CEM] Rev. Msgr. Wendelyn Vetter, V.F.; Deacon David Eblen.
Mailing Address: Box 459, 58045-0459. Tel: 701-636-4541; Fax: 701-636-4452.
Church: 503 3rd St. S.E..
Catechesis/Religious Program—Students 116.

HOPE, STEELE CO., ST. AGATHA (1907),, Also serving Finley and Page. Rev. Armand L. Brooks.
Mailing Address: P.O. Box 99, 58046-0099. Tel: 701-945-2652.
Church: 819 Steele Ave..
Catechesis/Religious Program—Students 53.

HUNTER, CASS CO., ST. AGNES (1898),, Served by Mayville. Rev. James A. Meyer.
Mailing Address: c/o Our Lady of Peace, 846 5th St. S.E., Mayville, 58257. Tel: 701-786-3234.
Church: 101 1st St. E.. Tel: 701-874-2226.
Catechesis/Religious Program—Tel: 701-967-8970. Students 49.

HURDSFIELD, WELLS CO., ST. PATRICK (1969),, Served from Sykeston. Rev. Louden Hans Flisk.
Mailing Address: c/o St. Elizabeth, P.O. Box 397, Sykeston, 58486. Tel: 701-984-2266; Fax: 701-981-2261.
Church: 12 3rd St. W., 58451.
Catechesis/Religious Program—Students 17.

JAMESTOWN, STUTSMAN CO., THE BASILICA OF ST. JAMES (1881), [CEM], Also serving Buchanan, Fried, and Pingree. Very Rev. Al M. Bitz; Rev. John Fisher Kizito; Sr. Michaeleen Jantzer, O.S.B., Pastoral Min.
Mailing Address: Box 347, 58402-0347. Tel: 701-252-0119; Fax: 701-252-6992.
Church: 622 1st Ave. S..
School—St. John Grade School, Tel: 701-252-3397; Fax: 701-252-4453. Beverly Jacobson, Prin. Lay Teachers 12; Students (Grades PreK-6) 188.
St. James Religious Education—622 1st Ave. S., P.O. Box 347, 58402-0347. Tel: 701-252-0478; Fax: 701-252-4453. Karen Miller, D.R.E. Lay Teachers 37.
Catechesis/Religious Program—215 5th St., S.E., P.O. Box 347, 58402-0347. Students 292.

JESSIE, GRIGGS CO., ST. LAWRENCE (1888), [CEM], Served from Cooperstown. Rev. James Cheny.
Mailing Address: c/o St. George, P.O. Box 217, Cooperstown, 58425. Tel: 701-797-2624.
Church: 105 Dewey St..
Catechesis/Religious Program—Students 10.

KARLSRUHE, MCHENRY CO., SS. PETER AND PAUL'S (1903), [CEM], Served from Velva. Rev. Daniel Mrnarevic.
Mailing Address: c/o St. Cecilia, 201 Second Ave. W., P.O. Box K, Velva, 58790-0496. Tel: 701-338-2663.
Church: 500 N. Main.
Catechesis/Religious Program—Students 32.

KENSAL, STUTSMAN CO., ST. JOHN (1917), [CEM], Served from Wimbledon. Rev. Steven J. Meyer.
Mailing Address: c/o St. Boniface, P.O. Box 9, Wimbledon, 58492. Tel: 701-435-2310.
Church: 407 Pleasant Ave..
Catechesis/Religious Program—Students 3.

KINDRED, CASS CO., ST. MAURICE (1965),, Served from Wyndmere. Rev. Leonard Loegering.
Mailing Address: P.O. Box 272, 58051. Tel: 701-428-3094; Fax: 701-428-3094.
Church: 5315 165th Ave. S.E..
Catechesis/Religious Program—Tel: 701-428-3094. Students 79.

KINTYRE, LOGAN CO., ST. BONIFACE (1905), [CEM], Served from Napoleon. Rev. Donald A. Leiphon.
7013 26th Ave., S.E., 58549-9614. Tel: 701-332-6636.
Catechesis/Religious Program—Students 8.

KNOX, BENSON CO., ST. MARY (1936), [CEM], Served from Leeds. Very Rev. Mathias Lanz.
Mailing Address: *c/o St. Vincent*, P.O. Box 307, Leeds, 58346-0307. Tel: 701-466-2777.
Church: 129 Morgan.
Catechesis/Religious Program—Tel: 701-583-2382. Students 12.

LA MOURE, LA MOURE CO., HOLY ROSARY (1890), [CEM], Also serving Dickey and Marion. Rev. Jimmy Lim Tiu.
Mailing Address: P.O. Box 217, 58458.
Church: 209 1 St., S.E., 58458. Tel: 701-883-5987; Fax: 701-883-5987.
Catechesis/Religious Program—Students 75.

LAKE WILLIAMS, KIDDER CO., OUR LADY OF THE LAKE (1946),, Served from Steele. Rev. Jerome Hunkler.
Mailing Address: c/o St. Francis de Sales, P.O. Box 87, Steele, 58482-0087. Tel: 701-475-2333.
Church: 222 Monroe St..
Catechesis/Religious Program—Students 0.

LAKOTA, NELSON CO., ST. MARY (1902),, Also serving Brocket and Tolna. Rev. Scott J. Sautner.
Mailing Address: P.O. Box 509, 58344. Tel: 701-247-2594.
Church: 109 East Ave. E..
Catechesis/Religious Program—Tel: 701-247-2584. Students 47.

LANGDON, CAVALIER CO., ST. ALPHONSUS (1888),

[CEM], Also serving Nekoma. Rev. William McDermott.
Mailing Address: 1010 3rd St., P.O. Box 640, 58249. Tel: 701-256-5966; Fax: 701-256-2358.
School—209 10th Ave.. Tel: 701-256-2354. Sr. Anne Frawley, P.B.V.M., Prin. Sisters 1; Lay Teachers 11; Students 80.
Catechesis / Religious Program—Tel: 701-256-5104. Students 126.

LANKIN, WALSH CO., ST. JOSEPH (1906), [CEM], Served by Pisek. Rev. John Lewandowski.
Mailing Address: c/o St. John Nepomucene, P.O. Box 27, Pisek, 58273.
Church: 506 4th St.. Tel: 701-284-6060.
Catechesis / Religious Program—Students 17.

LARIMORE, GRAND FORKS CO., ST. STEPHEN (1885), Rev. Thaines Arulandu.
Mailing Address: P.O. Box 778, 58251. Tel: 701-343-2377; Fax: 701-343-2316.
Church: 311 W. Front St..
Catechesis / Religious Program—Tel: 701-343-2747. Students 153.

LEEDS, BENSON CO., ST. VINCENT DE PAUL (1897), [CEM], Also serving Knox and Minnewaukan. Very Rev. Mathias F. Lanz.
Mailing Address: 315 Central Ave., P.O. Box 307, 58346. Tel: 701-466-2777; Fax: 701-466-2095.
Catechesis / Religious Program—Students 37.

LEROY, PEMBINA CO., ST. JOSEPH (1873), [CEM], Served from Walhalla. Very Rev. Brian Bachmeier.
Mailing Address: c/o St. Boniface, P.O. Box 228, Walhalla, 58282. Tel: 701-549-2729; Fax: 701-549-3256.
Church: 801 Central, 58252.

LIDGERWOOD, RICHLAND CO., ST. BONIFACE (1887), [CEM], Also serving Geneseo. Rev. J. Vincent Fitzpatrick; Deacon Jerome Wisnewski.
Church: P.O. Box 449, 58053. Tel: 701-538-4608.
Church: 230 1st St. N.W..
Catechesis / Religious Program—Tel: 701-538-4604. Students 105.

LISBON, RANSOM CO., ST. ALOYSIUS (1884), [CEM], Also serving Gwinner. Rev. Andrew Dudzinski.
Mailing Address: P.O. Box 226, 58054-0226.
Church: 701 Oak St., 58054-0226. Tel: 701-683-4584; Fax: 701-683-5703.
Catechesis / Religious Program—Tel: 701-683-4620. Students 116.

LOMICE, WALSH CO., ST. CATHERINE (1936), [CEM], Served from Michigan, ND. Rev. Samuel Ezeibekwe.
Mailing Address: c/o St. Lawrence O'Toole, P.O. Box 332, Michigan, 58259. Tel: 701-259-2248; Fax: 701-259-2350.

MADDOCK, BENSON CO., ST. WILLIAM (1954),, Served from Esmond. Rev. Julian Kupisz.
Mailing Address: c/o St. Boniface, P.O. Box 37, Esmond, 58332. Tel: 701-249-8360.
Catechesis / Religious Program—Students 30.

MANTADOR, RICHLAND CO., SS. PETER AND PAUL (1881), [CEM], Served from Mooreton. Rev. Leroy "Jake" Miller.
Mailing Address: c/o St. Anthony, 204 Mooreton Ave. N., Mooreton, 58061. Tel: 701-274-8259.
Church: 609 County Rd. 25.
Catechesis / Religious Program—Students 30.

MANVEL, GRAND FORKS CO., ST. TIMOTHY (1882), [CEM] Very Rev. Bernard Schneider.
Mailing Address: P.O. Box 28, 58256. Tel: 701-696-2219.
Church: 511 8th St. W..
Catechesis / Religious Program—Students 90.

MARION, LA MOURE CO., ST. FRANCIS (1910), [CEM] Rev. Jimmy Lim Tiu.
Mailing Address: Box 217, LaMoure, 58458. Tel: 701-883-5987.
Church: 109 4th St., 58466.

MAYVILLE, TRAILL CO., OUR LADY OF PEACE (1945),, Also serving Hunter. Rev. James Meyer; Very Rev. Bernard R. Schneider.
Church: 846 5th St. S.E., 58257. Tel: 701-788-3234; Fax: 701-788-3234.
Catechesis / Religious Program—Students 95.
Mission—State University Newman Club, Traill Co.

MCCLUSKY, SHERIDAN CO., HOLY FAMILY (1932),, Served from Sykeston. Rev. Louden Hans Flisk.
Mailing Address: c/o St. Elizabeth, P.O. Box 397, Sykeston, 58486. Tel: 701-984-2266; Fax: 701-984-2261.
Church: 409 Ave. B E..
Catechesis / Religious Program—Students 12.

MCHENRY, FOSTER CO., SS. PETER & PAUL (1912), [CEM], Served from New Rockford. Rev. Bernard Pfau.
Mailing Address: c/o St. John, 116 First Ave. N., P.O. Box 389, New Rockford, 58356. Tel: 701-947-5325.
Church: 391 Conn St..
Catechesis / Religious Program—Students 15.

MEDINA, STUTSMAN CO., ST. MARY (1904), [CEM], Served from Windsor. Rev. Joseph Okogba.
Mailing Address: c/o St. Mathias, 207 Washington Ave., Cleveland, 58424. Tel: 701-763-6192.
Church: 105 3rd Ave. S.E..
Catechesis / Religious Program—4142 57th Ave. S.E., 58467. Tel: 701-486-3414. Ellen Rau, D.R.E. Students 20.

MICHIGAN, NELSON CO., ST. LAWRENCE O'TOOLE (1883),, Also serving Bechyne and Lomice. Rev. Samuel Ezeibeke (Nigeria).
Mailing Address: P.O. Box 332, 58259. Tel: 701-259-2248; Fax: 701-259-2350.
Catechesis / Religious Program—Students 38.

MILNOR, SARGENT CO., ST. ARNOLD (1905), [CEM], Served from Forman. Rev. Franklin Miller.
Mailing Address: *c/o St. Mary*, 480 4th St., S.W., Forman, 58032-0175. Tel: 701-724-3319; Fax: 701-724-3310.
Church: 107 3rd St., 58060. Tel: 701-427-9288.
Catechesis / Religious Program—Tel: 701-427-5327. Students 62.

MILTON, CAVALIER CO., ST. CLOTILDE (1893), [CEM], Served from Wales. Rev. Joseph D'Aco.
Mailing Address: c/o St. Michael, P.O. Box 127, Wales, 58281. Tel: 701-283-5352; Fax: 701-283-5133.
Church: 223 Poplar.

MINNEWAUKAN, BENSON CO., ST. JAMES (1899), [CEM], Served from Leeds. Rev. Mathias Lanz.
Mailing Address: c/o St Vincent de Paul, P.O. Box 307, Leeds, 58346. Tel: 701-466-2777.
Catechesis / Religious Program—Students 2.

MINTO, WALSH CO., SACRED HEART (1905), [CEM], Also serving Ardoch. Rev. Timothy Schroeder.
Mailing Address: P.O. Box 316, 58261. Tel: 701-248-3589; 701-248-3139.
Church: 621 3rd St., 58261.
Catechesis / Religious Program—Students 105.

MOORETON, RICHLAND CO., ST. ANTHONY'S (1885), [CEM], Also serving Mantador. Rev. Leroy "Jake" Miller.
204 Mooreton Ave. N., 58061. Tel: 701-274-8259.
Catechesis / Religious Program—Students 63.

MOUNT CARMEL, CAVALIER CO., OUR LADY OF MOUNT CARMEL (1888), [CEM], Served from Wales. Rev. Joseph D'Aco.
Mailing Address: c/o St. Michael, P.O. Box 127, Wales, 58281. Tel: 701-283-5352.

MUNICH, CAVALIER CO., ST. MARY (1916), [CEM 3], Also serving Starkweather. Rev. Anthony Hession.
Mailing Address: P.O. Box 159, 58352-0159. Tel: 701-682-5178; Fax: 701-682-5124.
Church: 607 Main.
Catechesis / Religious Program—Tel: 701-682-5124. Students 74.

NAPOLEON, LOGAN CO., ST. PHILIP NERI (1906), [CEM], Also serving Burnstad and Kintyre. Rev. Donald Leiphon.
Res.: 401 Broadway, 58561-7013. Tel: 701-754-2860.
Catechesis / Religious Program—Students 149.

NECHE, PEMBINA CO., SS. NEREUS AND ACHILLEUS (1884), [CEM], Served from Cavalier. Rev. Jason Lefor.
Mailing Address: c/o St. Brigid, S., P.O. Box 280, Cavalier, 58220-0280. Tel: 701-265-8877; Fax: 701-265-8848.
Catechesis / Religious Program—Students 34.

NEKOMA, CAVALIER CO., ST. EDWARD (1907), [CEM], Served from Langdon. Rev. William McDermott.
Mailing Address: c/o St. Alphonsus, P.O. Box 640, Langdon, 58249. Tel: 701-256-5966; Fax: 701-256-2358.
Church: 323 Main.
Catechesis / Religious Program—Students 9.

NEW ROCKFORD, EDDY CO., ST. JOHN (1896), [CEM], Also serving McHenry. Rev. Bernard Pfau.
Mailing Address: P.O. Box 389, 58356. Tel: 701-947-5325.
Church: 116 1st Ave. N..
Catechesis / Religious Program—Students 126.

NORTONVILLE, LAMOURE CO., HOLY SPIRIT (1912), [JC], Served from Edgeley. Rev. Duaine Cote.
Mailing Address: c/o Transfiguration, P.O. Box 347, Edgeley, 58433. Tel: 701-493-2387; Fax: 701-493-2387.
Church: 705 1st St..
Catechesis / Religious Program—Students 30.

OAKES, DICKEY CO., ST. CHARLES BORROMEO (1905), [CEM], Also serving Verona. Rev. Matthew V. Pamplaniyil (India).
410 N. Seventh St., 58474. Tel: 701-742-2418.
Catechesis / Religious Program—Tel: 701-742-2911. Students 144.

OAKWOOD, WALSH CO., SACRED HEART (1881), [CEM], Also serving St. Thomas. Rev. James P. Lauerman.
7010 County Rd. 4, Grafton, 58237-8860. Tel: 701-352-1392.
Catechesis / Religious Program—Students 21.

OLGA, CAVALIER CO., OUR LADY OF THE SACRED HEART (1882), [CEM 2], Served from Walhalla. Very Rev. Brian Bachmeier.
Mailing Address: *c/o St. Boniface*, P.O. Box 228, Walhalla, 58282. Tel: 701-549-2729; Fax: 701-549-3256.
Church: 11980 95th St. R. N. E., Oakwood.

ORISKA, BARNES CO., ST. BERNARD (1908), [CEM], Also serving Fingal. Rev. Timothy Johnson, Admin.
Res.: 606 Fifth St., 58063-4103. Tel: 701-845-3713; Fax: 701-845-0172.
Catechesis / Religious Program—Students 12.

ORRIN, PIERCE CO., SACRED HEART (1903), [CEM], Served from Anamoose. Rev. Leo Kinney.
Mailing Address: *c/o St. Francis Xavier*, P.O. Box 49, Anamoose, 58710-0049. Tel: 701-542-3326.
Church: 123 Scholl St., 58368.
Catechesis / Religious Program—Students 12.

OSNABROCK, CAVALIER CO., ST. JOSEPH (1909), [CEM], Served from Wales. Rev. Joseph D'Aco.
Mailing Address: c/o St. Michael, P.O. Box 127, Wales, 58281. Tel: 701-282-5352.

PAGE, CASS CO., ST. JAMES (1909), [CEM], Served from Hope. Rev. Armand L. Brooks.
Mailing Address: c/o St. Agatha, P.O. Box 99, Hope, 58046. Tel: 701-945-2652.
Church: Morton Ave., 58064.
Catechesis / Religious Program—Students 7.

PARK RIVER, WALSH CO., ST. MARY (1888), [CEM], Also serving Crystal. Rev. Robert P. Unger; Deacon Gerald F. Sobolik.
Mailing Address: P.O. Box 110, 58270-0110. Tel: 701-284-6165; Fax: 701-284-7789.
Church: 505 Park St. E..
Catechesis / Religious Program—Tel: 701-284-7789. Students 110.

PEMBINA, PEMBINA CO., ASSUMPTION OF THE BLESSED VIRGIN MARY (1818), [CEM], Served from Drayton. Rev. William Ovsak.
Church: 143 Hayden St., 58271. Tel: 701-825-6266; Fax: 701-825-6266.
Catechesis / Religious Program—Students 30.

PENN, RAMSEY CO., IMMACULATE CONCEPTION, Closed., For inquiries for parish records contact St. Vincent de Paul, Leeds.

PINGREE, STUTSMAN CO., ST. MICHAEL (1905), [CEM], Served from Jamestown. Very Rev. Al Bitz.
Mailing Address: c/o Basilica of St. James, P.O. Box 347, Jamestown, 58402. Tel: 701-252-0119; Fax: 701-252-6992.
Church: 518 Bentley Ave., 58476.
Catechesis / Religious Program— Twinned with St. Margaret's, Buchanan.

PISEK, WALSH CO., ST. JOHN NEPOMUCENE (1886), [CEM], Also serving Conway and Lankin. Rev. John Lewandowski.
Mailing Address: P.O. Box 27, 58273. Tel: 701-284-6060; Fax: 701-284-6060.
Catechesis / Religious Program—Students 12.

REYNOLDS, GRAND FORKS CO., OUR LADY OF PERPETUAL HELP (1895), [CEM] Rev. Msgr. Wendelyn Vetter.
Mailing Address: Box 68, 58275. Tel: 701-847-3096.
Church: 424 5th St..
Catechesis / Religious Program—Students 97.

ROCK LAKE, TOWNER CO., IMMACULATE HEART OF MARY (1950),, Served from Rolla. Rev. James McKinney.
Mailing Address: c/o St. Joachim, P.O. Box 788, Rolla, 58367. Tel: 701-477-5277.
Catechesis / Religious Program—Tel: 701-477-3568. Students 13.

ROLETTE, ROLETTE CO., SACRED HEART (1918), [CEM 3], Also serving Willow City and Bisbee. Rev. Thomas M. Graner; Deacon Conrad A. Schuster.
Mailing Address: P.O. Box 127, 58366. Tel: 701-246-3449; Fax: 701-246-3449.
Church: 505 Main.
Catechesis / Religious Program—Students 49.

ROLLA, ROLETTE CO., ST. JOACHIM (1894), [CEM], Also serving Rock Lake. Rev. James McKinney.
Mailing Address: 207 Second Ave. N.E., P.O. Box 788, 58367-0788. Tel: 701-477-5277.
Church: 207 2nd Ave. N. E..
St. Joachim Religious Education Center—Tel: 701-477-3568.
Catechesis / Religious Program—Students 105.

RUGBY, PIERCE CO., ST. THERESE, LITTLE FLOWER (1910), [CEM] Very Rev. Kevin Boucher; Rev. Francis Arthur.
218 Third St., S.E., 58368. Tel: 701-776-5327.
School—306 Third Ave., S.E., 58368. Tel: 701-776-6258; Fax: 701-776-6740. Sisters of St. Francis of the Immaculate Heart of Mary (Hankinson, ND) 3; Lay Teachers 10; Students 95.
Catechesis / Religious Program—Tel: 701-776-5327. Students 221.

ST. JOHN, ROLETTE CO., ST. JOHN THE BAPTIST (1882), [CEM], Served from Belcourt (St. Ann). Revs. Dale Craig, S.O.L.T.; John Patterson, S.O.L.T.
Mailing Address: P.O. Box 170, 58369. Tel: 701-477-3081.
Church: 107 St. Ann St. S.E..
Catechesis / Religious Program—Students 63.

ST. MICHAEL, BENSON CO., ST. MICHAEL (1874), [CEM] Revs. Paul Ruge; Joachim Mudd.

Mailing Address: P.O. Box 84, 58370. Tel: 701-766-4151; Fax: 701-766-1085.
Catechesis / Religious Program—Students 47.

ST. THOMAS, PEMBINA CO., ST. THOMAS (1886) [CEM], Served from Oakwood. Rev. James Lauerman.
Mailing Address: c/o Sacred Heart, 7010 Country Rd. 4, Grafton, 58237. Tel: 701-352-1392.
Church: 640 Main St., 58276. Tel: 701-257-6492.
Catechesis / Religious Program—Students 44.

SANBORN, BARNES CO., SACRED HEART (1904), (German), [CEM], Also serves Dazey. Rev. Matthew Attansey (Nigeria); Deacon Harry Didier.
Mailing Address: P.O. Box 35, 58480. Tel: 701-646-6306; Fax: 701-646-6619.
Church: 711-4th St..
Catechesis / Religious Program—Students 21.

SELZ, PIERCE CO., ST. ANTHONY (1917), [CEM], Served from Harvey. Rev. Vernon Smith.
Mailing Address: c/o St. Cecilia, 413 E. Brewster St., Harvey, 58341-7316. Tel: 701-324-2144; Fax: 701-324-4640.
Catechesis / Religious Program— Twinned with St. Cecilia, Harvey.

SHELDON, RANSOM CO., ST. MARY, OUR LADY OF THE SCAPULAR (1884), [CEM], Served from Enderlin. Rev. John Fallon.
Mailing Address: c/o St. Patrick, 302 Bluff St., Enderlin, 58027. Tel: 701-437-2791.
Church: 14025 55th St. S. E., 58068.
Catechesis / Religious Program—Students 43.

STARKWEATHER, RAMSEY CO., ASSUMPTION OF THE BLESSED VIRGIN MARY (1905), [CEM], Served from Munich. Rev. Anthony Hession.
Mailing Address: c/o St. Mary, P.O. Box 159, Munich, 58352-0159. Tel: 701-682-5178; Fax: 701-682-5124.
Church: 502 Main St., 58377. Tel: 701-292-4301.
Catechesis / Religious Program—Students 25.

STEELE, KIDDER CO., ST. FRANCIS DE SALES (1958), [CEM], Also serves Lake Williams and Tappan. Rev. Jerome Hunkler.
Mailing Address: P.O. Box 87, 58428-0087.
Church: 318 2nd St., Tappen, 58487. Tel: 701-475-2333.
Catechesis / Religious Program—Students 67.

STIRUM, SARGENT CO., ST. VINCENT, Closed, 1986. For inquiries for parish records contact St. Aloysius, Lisbon.

SYKESTON, WELLS CO., ST. ELIZABETH (1905), [CEM], Also serving Hurdsfield and McCluskey Rev. Louden Hans Flisk.
Mailing Address: P.O. Box 397, 58486. Tel: 701-984-2266; Fax: 701-984-2261.
Church: 132 Anson Ave. S. E..
Catechesis / Religious Program—Students 53.

TAPPEN, KIDDER CO., ST. PAUL (1908),, Served from Steele. Rev. Jerome Hunkler.
Mailing Address: *c/o St. Francis*, P.O. Box 87, Steele, 58482-0087.
Church: 218 1st St., N.E., 58487. Tel: 701-475-2333.
Catechesis / Religious Program—Students 19.

THOMPSON, GRAND FORKS CO., ST. JUDE (1895), [CEM], Served from Holy Family, Grand Forks Rev. Phil Ackerman; Deacon Jim West.
Mailing Address: P. O.Box 305, 58278. Tel: 701-599-2574.
Church: 329 Broadway, 58278. Tel: 701-599-2574.
Catechesis / Religious Program—Students 101.

TOKIO, BENSON CO., CHRIST THE KING (1938), (Native American),, Served from Fort Totten. Rev. Charles Leute, O.P.
Mailing Address: c/o Seven Dolors, P.O. Box 299, Fort Totten, 58335. Tel: 701-766-4314.
Church: 134 2nd St..

TOLNA, NELSON CO., ST. JOSEPH (1911), [CEM], Served from Lakota. Rev. Scott Sautner.
Mailing Address: c/o St. Mary, P.O. Box 509, Lakota, 58344.
Church: 220 Main St., 58380.
Catechesis / Religious Program—Students 25.

TOWNER, MCHENRY CO., ST. CECILIA (1903), [CEM], Also serving Granville. Rev. Ronald Yee Mon.
Mailing Address: Box 267, 58788-0263. Tel: 701-537-5133.
Church: 503 1st St. S. W..
Catechesis / Religious Program—Tel: 701-537-5842. Students 57.

VALLEY CITY, BARNES CO., ST. CATHERINE (1882), [CEM] Very Rev. H. Gerard Braun; Deacons Arlie Braunberger; Raphael Grim; Eugene Klein; Edward Didier.
524 Third Ave., N.E., 58072-2628. Tel: 701-845-0354; Fax: 701-845-0556.
School—(Grades K-6) Tel: 701-845-1453; Fax: 701-845-0556. Mr. Ralph Dyrness, Prin. Lay Teachers 6; Students 63.
St. Catherine's Parish Education Center—540 Third Ave., N.E., 58072. Ralph Dyrness, Parish Education Dir. Lay Teachers 20.
Catechesis / Religious Program—Kelley Utt D.R.E. Students 193.

VELVA, MCHENRY CO., ST. CECILIA (1905), [CEM], Also serving Karlsruhe. Rev. Daniel Mrnarevic.
Mailing Address: P.O. Box K, 58790-0196. Tel: 701-338-2663; Fax: 701-338-2455.
Church: 201 2nd Ave. W..
Catechesis / Religious Program—Students 103.

VERONA, LAMOURE CO., ST. RAPHAEL (1898), [CEM], Served from Oakes. Rev. Matthew V. Pamplaniyil (India).
Mailing Address: c/o St. Charles, 410 N. Seventh St., Oakes, 58474. Tel: 701-742-2418.
Church: 205 1st St..
Catechesis / Religious Program—Students 17.

VESELEYVILLE, WALSH CO., ST. LUKE (1880), [CEM], Served from Warsaw. Rev. Damian Hils.
Mailing Address: 14207 63rd St., N.E., Grafton, 58237. Tel: 701-248-3981; Fax: 701-248-3961.
Catechesis / Religious Program—Tel: 701-352-0026. Students 25.

WAHPETON, RICHLAND CO., ST. JOHN'S (1876), [CEM] Rev. Dale Lagodinski.
Mailing Address: *Office*, 115 Second St. N., 58075. Tel: 701-642-6982; Fax: 701-642-2601.
Res.: 222 Dakota Ave., 58075. Tel: 701-642-4985.
School—122 Second St. N., 58075. Tel: 701-642-6116; Fax: 701-642-9134. Renee Goroski, Prin. Lay Teachers 11; Students 151.
School—St. John Day Care Center, Tel: 701-642-4922. Cary Forrester, Dir. Staff 23; Students 120.
Catechesis / Religious Program—Students 340.

WALES, CAVALIER CO., ST. MICHAEL'S (1905), [CEM], Also serving Mount Carmel, Milton, and Osnabrock. Rev. Joseph D'Aco.
Mailing Address: P.O. Box 127, 58281. Tel: 701-283-5352.
Church: 221 2nd Ave..
Catechesis / Religious Program—Students 3.

WALHALLA, PEMBINA CO., ST. BONIFACE (1850), [CEM], Also serving Leroy and Olga. Very Rev. Brian Bachmeier.
Mailing Address: 801 Central Ave., Box 223, 58282. Tel: 701-549-2729; Fax: 701-549-3256.
Church: 805 Central Ave..
Catechesis / Religious Program—Students 110.

WARSAW, WALSH CO., ST. STANISLAUS (1882), [CEM], Also serves Veselyville. Rev. Damian J. Hils.
6098 County Rd. 4, Minto, 58261. Tel: 701-248-3981; Fax: 701-248-3961.
Catechesis / Religious Program—Tel: 701-699-2181. Students 42.

WEST FARGO, CASS CO.
1—BLESSED SACRAMENT, [CEM] Rev. John Cavanaugh; Deacons James Perius; James Uline.
210 Fifth Ave. W., 58078-1799. Tel: 701-282-3321; Fax: 701-282-6503.
Catechesis / Religious Program—Tel: 701-282-4554. Students 354.
2—HOLY CROSS (1981), [CEM] Revs. David Syverson; Ross Laframboise; Deacon John Lane.
1420 16th St. E., 58078-3445. Tel: 701-282-7217; Fax: 701-282-2753.
Catechesis / Religious Program—Students 457.

WESTHOPE, BOTTINEAU CO., ST. ANDREW (1904), [CEM], Served from Bottineau. Rev. Paul R. Schuster.
Mailing Address: Box 365, 58793. Tel: 701-228-3164.
Church: 260 1st Ave. E.. Tel: 701-245-6171.
Catechesis / Religious Program—Students 44.

WILD RICE, CASS CO., ST. BENEDICT (1870), [CEM] Very Rev. Daniel J. Pilon, J.C.L.; Melissa Wornarowicz, Parish Life Coord.
Mailing Address: 11705 38th St. S., Horace, 58047-9512. Tel: 701-588-4288; Fax: 701-588-4154.
Catechesis / Religious Program—Tel: 701-588-9290. Students 165.

WILLOW CITY BOTTINEAU CO., NOTRE DAME DES VICTOIRES (1895), [CEM 2], Served by Rolette. Rev. Thomas Graner; Deacon Conrad Shuster.
Church: P.O. Box 115, 58384. Tel: 701-366-4601.
Catechesis / Religious Program—Students 12.

WIMBLEDON, BARNES CO., ST. BONIFACE (1886), [CEM], Also serving Kensal and Courtenay. Rev. Steven J. Meyer.
Mailing Address: P.O. Box 9, 58492. Tel: 701-435-2310.
Church: 301 1st Ave..
Catechesis / Religious Program—Students 47.

WINDSOR, STUTSMAN CO., ST. MATHIAS (1910), [CEM], Also serving Gackle and Medina. Rev Joseph Okogba.
207 Washington Ave., Cleveland, 58424. Tel: 701-763-6192.
Catechesis / Religious Program—Students 7.

WISHEK, MCINTOSH CO., ST. PATRICK (1952), [CEM], Also serving Zeeland and Ashley. Rev. Andrew Jasinski.
Mailing Address: P.O. Box 293, 58495-0295.
Church: 322 Centennial St. S., 58495. Tel: 701-452-2970.
Catechesis / Religious Program—Students 52.

WYNDMERE, RICHLAND CO., ST. JOHN THE BAPTIST (1912), [CEM], Also serving Kindred. Rev. Leonard Loegering.
630 Sixth St., 58081. Tel: 701-439-2200.
Catechesis / Religious Program—Students 96.

ZEELAND, MCINTOSH CO., ST. ANDREW (1906), [CEM 2], Served from Wishek. Rev. Andrew Jasinski.
Mailing Address: c/o St. Patrick, P.O. Box 293, Wishek, 58495. Tel: 701-452-2970.
Church: 301 1st Ave. S.E..
Catechesis / Religious Program—Students 46.

INDIAN MISSIONS

FORT TOTTEN RESERVATION, (SPIRIT LAKE SIOUX) (1875),
Mission—Christ the King (1938), Fort Totten, Tokio, Benson Co. 58335. Tel: 701-766-4314. Rev. Charles J. Leute, O.P.
Mission—St. Jerome (1892), c/o Box 299, Benson Co. 58334-0299. Tel: 701-766-4314. (Crow Hill District)
Mission—Seven Dolors Indian Mission [CEM] Seven Sorrows Dr., Box 299, Benson Co. 58335-0299. Tel: 701-766-4314. Rev. Charles J. Leute, O.P. Also serving Crow Hill, Tokio.

ST. MICHAEL, ST. MICHAEL'S INDIAN MISSION, Revs. Paul Ruge; Joachim Mudd.

TURTLE MOUNTAIN RESERVATION, (TURTLE MOUNTAIN BAND OF CHIPPEWA),
Mission—St. Ann Belcourt, Rolette Co. Revs. Dale Craig, S.O.L.T.; Robert J. Cronin, S.O.L.T.; Daniel Estes, S.O.L.T.; John Patterson, S.O.L.T.; Bro. John DeMay, S.O.L.T.
Mission—St. Anthony St. Anthony, Rolette Co. Served from Belcourt.

Chaplains of Public Institutions

FARGO. *Prairie St. John's*, 510 4th St. S., 58103-1914. Rev. John Evans II.

GRAND FORKS. *Altru Hospital*. Very Rev. Bernard Schneider, Chap., P.O. Box 6002, 58206-6002.
Grand Forks Air Force Base. Vacant.
Our Lady of the Snows: 345 Tuskegee Airman Blvd., 58205-6335. Tel: 701-747-3092.

Special Assignment:
Rev. Msgr.—
Donahue, Brian G., V.G., 5201 Bishops Blvd., Ste. A, 58104-7298.
Revs.—
Evans, John, II, Dir. Pastoral Care, Prairie St. John's, 510 4th St., S., 58103-1914.
Fischer, Charles M., Jr., S.T.D., Sisters of St. Francis Provincial Motherhouse, P.O. Box 447, Hankinson, 58041.
Very Rev.—
Goering, Joseph P., Chancellor & Priest Sec. to the Bishop, 5201 Bishops Blvd., Ste. A, 58104-7298.
Revs.—
Gross, Richard J., Chap. (Retired), Altru Hospital, 1220 S. Columbia Rd., 58201.
Laliberte, Robert L., Ph.D., Cardinal Muench Seminary, 100 35th Ave. N.E., 58102.
Very Rev.—
Schlesselmann, Gregory J., Vicar Gen. & Rector of Cardinal Muench Seminary
Revs.—
Skonseng, Dennis A., Cardinal Muench Seminary, 100 35th Ave., N.E., 58102.
Smith, Robert F., Jr., 100 35th Ave., N.E., 58102.

On Duty Outside the Diocese:
Revs.—
Campbell, Joseph (SPC), Sacred Heart Church: 605 Ward Ave., Caruthersville, MO 63830.
Davis, John E., Apartado 134, Chimbote, Peru.
Graven, John P. (Retired), St. Polycarp Church, 8100 Chapman Ave., Stanton, CA 90680.
Heck, Quintin, St. Mary Parish: N89W 16297 Cleveland Ave., Menomonee Falls, WI 53051.
Irwin, Robert (SD), P.O. Box 85728, San Diego, CA 92186-5728.
Mikes, Pavel, Dekcnsky urad, 763 25 Ujezd u Volasskych, Klobouk 5, Czech Republic.
Myers, Gerald, St. Francis de Sales: 1375 S. Camino Seco, Tucson, AZ 85710.
Odozi, Anthony, Jr., J.C.L. (SD)
Okonmah, Emmanuel (RCK), 3225 Cavendish Dr., Rockford, IL 61109-1898.
Schill, Damien (STP), 769 Scheffer Ave., St. Paul, MN 55102.

Graduate Studies:
Revs.—
Hickin, Michael, Rome
Kadlec, Jared, Rome
Kopacz, Kazimierz, Rome

Military Chaplains:
Revs.—
Goellen, Richard M., 21 Myer Dr., Augusta, GA 30905.

Herron, Jack B. (MAJ), Chap., USACHCS, CHOAC, 305-B Sudut St., Wahiawa, HI 96786-3836. Tel: 808-655-9417
Kawczynski, Ronald (LT), Chap., LCDR, USN, 10720 El Camono Nuevo, Monterey, CA 93940.

Absent on Leave:
Revs.—
Leith, James A., J.C.D., P.O. Box 1750, 58107.
Reiske, Steven R.W.
Vos, Jude

Retired:
Most Rev.—
Sullivan, James S., D.D., c/o Holy Spirit, 1420 7th St. N., 58102-2697.
Rev. Msgrs.—
Anderson, John D., 5320 12th St. S., #317, 58104.
Nilles, Allan F., 200 8th St. S., #402, 58103. Tel: 701-239-5939
Schneider, George D., 1020 Devine Ave., #5, Harvey, 58341.
Revs.—
Allmaras, Alfred, 115 49th St., N.E., 58259.
Bachmeier, Bernard A., 7027 Camino Degrazia, #203, San Diego, CA 92111.
Cosentino, Jack A., Epiphany Cathedral Parish House, 310 Sarasota St., Venice, FL 34285.
Dickinson, Stephen, P.O. Box 667, Valley City, 58072-0667.
Fish, Eugene J., St. Luke Rectory, 14207 63rd St., N.E., Grafton, 58237.
Grady, Peter W., Riverview Pl., 5220-12th St. S, #201, 58104.
Graven, John P., 320 N. Park Vista St., #154, Anaheim, CA 92806.
Gross, Richard J., 1335 11th Ave., 58201.
Huebsch, Joseph R., 514 First Ave., S.W., P.O. Box 98, Hankinson, 58041-0098.
Jeffrey, James C., 3309 Eastridge Dr., Belleville, IL 62221.
Krile, George F., Brentwood West, 3104 E. Broadway, #211, Mesa, AZ 85204.
Lang, Julius, P.O. Box 126, Naples, FL 34106.
Lommel, George D., 509 Almeron Ave., Drayton, 58225.
McCarthy, Gerald A., 304 3rd Ave. W., P.O. Box 155, Bisbee, 58317.
Moore, John E.
Mullins, Robert J., 1451 Third St., S.E., Apt. 306B, St. Cloud, MN 56301.
Potter, Gerald, 615 39th St. N., #204C, 58203.
Richard, Antonio J., 772 Leisure World, Meza, AZ 85206.
Sandell, John, 2115 32nd Ave. S., 58103.
Schill, Victor J., P.O. Box 12, Walhalla, 58282.
Schue, Dennis L., Mercy Hospital, 1031 Seventh St., Devils Lake, 58301.
Sherman, Edward, 106 N. 3rd St., #609, 58203-3700.
Sherman, William C.
Snell, Roger K., P.O. Box 305, Edgeley, 58433.
Stelten, Leo F., 50981 Good Oak Loop, Frazee, MN 56544.

Permanent Deacons:
Biss, Richard, St. Arnold, Milnor
Blessum, Arlen, St. Therese Little Flower, Rugby
Braumberger, Arlie, St. Catherine, Valley City
Buresh, Leonard, St. John the Evangelist, Grafton
Carpenter, Stanley, St. Boniface, Walhalla
Davis, Francis R., St. Ann, Belcourt
Didier, Edward, St. Catherine, Valley City
Didier, Harry, Jr., Sacred Heart, Sanborn
Eberle, Edward, St. Therese Little Flower, Rugby
Eblen, David, St. Rose of Lima, Hillsboro
Eggl, James, Sacred Heart, Cando
Ethier, George, (Retired), St. John, Wahpeton
Faul, Jeffrey, St. Cecilia, Harvey
Geffre, Thomas, Our Lady of Peace, Mayville
Grim, Raphael, St. Catherine, Valley City
Ham, Thurston, Transfiguration, Edgeley
Hoefs, Gene, St. John, Wahpeton
Johnson, Eddie, St. Ann, Belcourt
Klein, Eugene, St. Catherine, Valley City
Lane, John, Holy Cross, West Fargo
Lange, Lawrence, St. Joseph, Devils Lake
Litzinger, Donald, St. Mary, Grand Forks
Loegering, George, St. Mary Cathedral, Fargo
Longtin, Stuart, St. Anthony, Fargo
Marcy, Timothy
McDonald, Anthony, Seven Dolors, Fort Totten
Mears, Emery, St. Joachim, Rolla
Perius, James, Blessed Sacrament, West Fargo
Prom, Mathias, St. Anthony, Fargo
Pupino, Samuel, St. Thomas Aquinas Newman Center, Grand Forks
Schuster, Conrad, Notre Dame, Willow City
Sobolick, Gerald, St. Mary, Park River
Tinguely, Donald, St. Leo, Casselton
Uline, James, Blessed Sacrament, West Fargo
West, James, St. Jude, Thompson
Wisnewski, Jerome, St. Boniface, Lidgerwood
Zach, Ignatz

INSTITUTIONS LOCATED IN THE DIOCESE

[A] SEMINARIES, DIOCESAN

FARGO. *Cardinal Muench Seminary*, 100 35th Ave., N.E., 58102. Tel: 701-232-8969; Fax: 701-271-1250. Email: cms@cardinalmuench.org. Web: www.cardinalmuench.org. Very Rev. Gregory J. Schlesselmann, Rector; Revs. Dennis A. Skonseng; Robert L. Laliberte, Ph.D. Corporate Title: The Cardinal Muench Seminary. Sisters 1; Priests 3; Lay Teachers 4; 4-year College Students 10.

[B] HIGH SCHOOLS, DIOCESAN

FARGO. *Fargo Catholic Schools Network*, 5600 25th St. SW, 58104. Tel: 701-293-7910; Fax: 701-293-0729. Email: jerry.bartholomay@sendit.nodal.edu. Web: www.fcsn.k12.nd.us. Most Rev. Samuel J. Aquila, D.D., Pres.; Rev. James R. Ermer, Chair; Jerry Bartholomay, Supt. Priests 1; Lay Teachers 80; Total Enrollment 1,045.

Shanley High School and Sullivan Middle School, Formerly Shanley High School, 5600 25th St. SW, 58104. Tel: 701-293-7910; Fax: 701-293-0729. Email: kent.r.packer@sendit.nodak.edu. Web: www.fcsn.k12.nd.us. Mr. Kent Packer, Prin.; Rev. James Gross, Chap. Priests 1; Lay Teachers 25; Students 292.

[C] PROTECTIVE INSTITUTIONS

FARGO. *Villa Nazareth* dba Friendship, Inc. , 801 Page Dr., 58103. Tel: 701-235-8217; Fax: 701-235-7538. Email: jeffpederson@catholichealth.net. Sr. Paula Ringuette, P.B.V.M., Dir. Presentation Sisters (P.B.V.M.). Catholic Health Initiatives , A community-based facility providing an array of residential, vocational, educational, social and clinical services for children and adults with mental retardation and other developmental disabilities. Total Assisted 220; Total Staff 300.

[D] GENERAL HOSPITALS

FARGO. *Prairie St. John's*, Formerly Prairie Psychiatric Center, 510 4th St. S., 58103-1914. Tel: 701-476-7200; Fax: 701-476-7261. Email: jevans@prairie-stjohns.com. Web: www.praire-stjohns.com. Marshall Korman, CEO; Rev. John Evans II, Parish Svcs. Dir. Bed Capacity 53; Patients Assisted Annually 2,508; Staff 325.

BOTTINEAU. *St. Andrew's Health Center*, 316 Ohmer St., 58318. Tel: 701-228-2255; Fax: 701-228-9384. Email: sahc@utma.com. Web: www.standrewshealth.us. Sr. Miriam Braun, S.M.P., Chap.; Jodi Atkinson, C.E.O. Sisters of Mary of the Presentation 1; Bed Capacity 25; Staff 115; Patients Assisted Annually 9,244.

CARRINGTON. *Carrington Health Center* Catholic Health Initiatives. , 800 N. Fourth St., 58421. Tel: 701-652-3141; Fax: 701-652-3034. Web: www.carringtonhealthcenter.com. Johnson L. Smith, CEO. Bed Capacity 25; Staff 155; Patients Assisted Annually 17,985.

DEVILS LAKE. *Mercy Hospital*, 1031 Seventh St., 58301-2798. Tel: 701-662-2131; Fax: 701-662-9651. Email: marlenekrein@catholichealth.net. Web: www.mercyhospitaldl.com. Marlene Krein, CEO & Pres. Sisters of Mercy of the Americas 3; Staff 207; Bed Capacity 50; Bassinets 7; Patients Assisted Annually 22,064. In Res. Rev. Dennis L. Schue (Retired).

HARVEY. *St. Aloisius Medical Center*, 325 E. Brewster St., 58341. Tel: 701-324-4651; Fax: 701-324-4651. Email: rvolk@stacoisius.com. Web: www.stacoisius.com. Ronald J. Volk, Admin. & Pres.; Greg Wilson, CFO. Sisters of Mary of the Presentation. Staff 301; Bed Capacity 25; Long Term Care 106; Patients Assisted Annually 5,735.

LISBON. *Lisbon Area Health Services, Catholic Health Initiatives*, 905 Main St., 58054. Tel: 701-683-5241; Fax: 701-683-4345. Sr. Peggy Ann Martin, O.P., J.C.L., Senior Vice Pres. Sponsorship & Governance. Bed Capacity 25; Total Assisted Annually 9,500; Total Staff 104; Home Health Care Agency 1.

OAKES. *Oakes Community Hospital*, 314 S. Eighth St., 58474-2099. Tel: 701-742-3291; Fax: 701-742-3632. Email: bradburris@catholichealth.net. Sr. M. Dianna Hell, O.S.F., Supr.; Bradley D. Burris, CEO & Pres. Sisters of St. Francis of the Immaculate Heart of Mary (Hankinson, ND) 3; Total Staff 90; Bed Capacity 25; Bassinets 4; Patients Assisted Annually 6,999.

ROLLA. *Presentation Medical Center*, 213 Second Ave., N.E., P.O. Box 759, 58367. Tel: 701-477-3161; Fax: 701-477-5564. Email: pmc@utma.com. Web: www.pmc-rolla.com. Kimber L. Wraalstad, Pres. & CEO. Sisters of Mary of the Presentation 3; Total Staff 130; Acute Beds 25; Patients Assisted Annually 14,882.

VALLEY CITY. *Mercy Hospital* Catholic Health Initiatives. , 570 Chautauqua Blvd., 58072. Tel: 701-845-6400; Fax: 701-845-6413. Email: johnsonsmith@chi-midwest.org. Johnson Smith, Pres. & CEO. Sisters of Mercy 1; Bed Capacity 25; Bassinets 15; Patients Assisted 19,815; Staff 160.

[E] HOMES FOR AGED

FARGO. *Riverview Place*, 5300 12th St. S., 58104. Tel: 701-237-4700; Fax: 701-235-5738. Email: Jeffpederson@chi-midwest.org. Jeff Pederson, CEO. Residents 180; Staff 60; Total Assisted Annually 250.

Rosewood on Broadway, SMP Health System, 1351 Broadway, 58102. Tel: 701-277-2999; Fax: 701-277-7989. Email: shawn.stuhaug@smphs.org. Shawn Stuhaug, CEO. Bed Capacity 102; Total Staff 108; Resident Days 36,402.

Villa Maria, SMP Health System, 3102 University Dr. S., 58103. Tel: 701-293-7750; Fax: 701-293-5845. Email: sue.grove@smphs.org. Susan Grove, CEO. Bed Capacity 138; Total Staff 150; Resident Days 48,800.

EDGELEY. *Manor St. Joseph*, 404 Fourth Ave., 58433. Tel: 701-493-2477; Fax: 701-493-2477. Email: stjoseph@drtel.net. Tammy Jangula, Admin. Sister Servants of Christ the King 2; Total Assisted Annually 40; Bed Capacity 40; Staff 33.

ELLENDALE. *Prince of Peace Care Center*, 201 8th St. N., 58436. Tel: 701-349-3312; Fax: 701-349-3944. Mr. Tony Hanson, Admin. Operated by Benedictine Living Communities, Inc. Bed Capacity 64; Staff 90; Total Assisted Annually 200.

ENDERLIN. *Maryhill Manor, SMP Health System*, 110 Hillcrest Dr., 58027. Tel: 701-437-3544; Fax: 701-437-3816. Email: nancy.farnham@smphs.org. Nancy Farnham, CEO. Bed Capacity 54; Total Staff 56; Resident Days 18,546.

GRAND FORKS. *St. Anne's Guest Home*, 524 N. 17th St., 58203. Tel: 701-746-9401; Fax: 701-795-7825. Email: stannes@midconetwork.com. Sr. Rebecca Metzger, O.S.F., Admin. Sisters of St. Francis of the Immaculate Heart of Mary (Hankinson, ND) 7; Staff 36; Guests 86; Total Assisted Annually 150.

HANKINSON. *St. Gerard Community Nursing Home*, 613 First Ave. S.W., 58041. Tel: 701-242-7891; Fax: 701-242-7896. Sr. Rose Marie Freund, O.S.F., Admin. Sisters of St. Francis of the Immaculate Heart of Mary (Hankinson, ND) 4; Bed Capacity 37; Patients Assisted Annually 54; Independent Living Unit Beds 12; Children in Daycare 18; Staff 70.

JAMESTOWN. *Central Dakota Village, SMP Health System*, 501 19th St., N.E., 58401. Tel: 701-252-5660; Fax: 701-251-2643. Email: tim.walpole@smphs.org. Timothy Wapole, CEO. Bed Capacity 100; Total Staff 118; Resident Days 36,077.

LA MOURE. *St. Rose Care Center*, 315 1st St., S.E., 58458. Tel: 701-883-5363; Fax: 701-883-5711. Email: tony-hanson@bhshealth.org. Mr. Tony Hanson, Admin. Operated by Benedictine Living Communities, Inc. Bed Capacity 50; Staff 70.

ROLETTE. *Presentation Care Center*, 304 John St., P.O. Box 218, 58366. Tel: 701-246-3786; Fax: 701-246-3422. Kimber Wraalstad, Pres. & CEO. Bed Capacity 48; Patients Assisted 65; Staff 60.

VALLEY CITY. *Sheyenne Care Center, SMP Health System*, 979 N. Central Ave., 58072. Tel: 701-845-8222; Fax: 701-845-8270. Email: craig.christianson@smphs.org. Craig Christianson, CEO. Bed Capacity 170; Total Staff 186; Resident Days 60,534.

WAHPETON. *St. Catherine's Living Center*, 1307 N. Seventh St., 58075. Tel: 701-642-6667; Fax: 701-642-2485. Steve Williams, Admin. Operated by Benedictine Living Communities, Inc. Residents 160; Long-term Care Beds 132; Basic Care Beds 16; Staff 185.

[F] CATHOLIC CHARITIES

FARGO. *Catholic Charities North Dakota*, Formerly Catholic Family Service, 5201 Bishops Blvd., 58104. Tel: 701-235-4457; Fax: 701-239-8266. Email: fargo@catholiccharitiesnd.org. Web: www.catholiccharitiesnd.org. Briston Fernandes, Exec. Dir.

St. Vincent de Paul Society, 1425 First Ave. S., 58102. Tel: 701-235-5944; Fax: 701-232-6576. James Pyle, Contact Person.

GRAND FORKS. *Catholic Family Service*, 311 4th St. S.

Suite 105, 58201. Tel: 701-775-4196; Fax: 701-775-0129. Email: grandforks@cfsnd.org. Web: www.cfsnd.org.

St. Vincent de Paul, 620 8th Ave. S., 58201. Tel: 701-795-8614; Fax: 701-746-6648. Email: svdpofgf@yahoo.com. Jo Ann Brundin, Dir. Total Assisted Annually 6,291.

MINTO. *Blessed Gianna's Home Inc.* Residence for pregnant women and their children 15605 Country Rd. 15, 58261. Tel: 701-248-3077; Fax: 701-248-3961. Email: marypatjahner@hotmail.com. Mary Pat Jahner, Contact Person.

[G] CONVENTS AND RESIDENCES FOR SISTERS

FARGO. *Presentation Center-Sacred Heart Convent*, 1101 32nd Ave. S., 58103. Tel: 701-237-4857; Fax: 701-237-9822. Email: foundation@presentationsistersfargo.com. Web: www.presentationsistersfargo.com. Sr. Paula Ringuette, Pres. Sisters 57.

BELCOURT. *Queen of Peace Monastery*, Sisters of St. Benedict, P.O. Box 370, 58316. Tel: 701-477-6167; Fax: 701-477-5575. Email: qop@utma.com. Sr. Judith Emge, O.S.B., Prioress. Sisters 4.

HANKINSON. *Sisters of St. Francis of the Immaculate Heart of Mary*, P.O. Box 447, 58041-0447. Tel: 701-242-7195; Fax: 701-242-7198. Email: osfhank@rrt.net. Web: www.fargodiocese.org/sfc/index.html. Sr. Donna Welder, O.S.F., Prov. Sisters 56.

VALLEY CITY. *Sisters of Mary of the Presentation*, 11550 River R. Rd., 58072. Tel: 701-845-2864; Fax: 701-845-0805. Email: srmarlyss@fargodiocese.org. Sr. Marlyss Dionne, S.M.P., Prov. Supr.; Rev. John Odermann, O.S.B., Chap. Sisters 52.

WAHPETON. *Carmel of Mary*, 17765 78th St. S.E., 58075. Tel: 701-642-2360. Web: www.masstransit.com/nd/carmelmary-nd-wahpeton. Sr. Maria of Divine Mercy, O.Carm., Prioress; Rev. Thomas Krupich, Chap. Carmelite Nuns of the Ancient Observance Solemn Professed Nuns 10; Junior Professed Nuns 1.

[H] RETREAT HOUSES

FARGO. *Presentation Prayer Center*, 3001 11th St. S., 58103. Tel: 701-235-8246; Fax: 701-237-9822. Email: presprayerctr@cableone.net. Web: www.presentationsistersfargo.com. Sr. Andrea Arendt, P.B.V.M., Dir. Sisters 2.

[I] NEWMAN FOUNDATIONS

FARGO. *St. Paul's Catholic Chapel* 1141 N. University Dr., 58102. Tel: 701-235-0142. Email: ndsu.newman.center@ndsu.nodak.edu. Web: www.acm.ndsu.nodak.edu/ndsu_newman/. Very Rev. Paul Duchschere, Dir. Campus Ministry. Staff 3.

GRAND FORKS. *Univ. of North Dakota Newman Center* St. Thomas Aquinas Parish, UND. Tel: 701-777-6850; Fax: 701-775-0911. Email: rcourtri@sage.und.nodak.edu. Web: www.und.nodak.edu/dept/newman. Staff 2; Catholic Students 2,500.

St. Thomas Aquinas Newman Center, UND 410 Cambridge St., 58203. Tel: 701-777-6850; Fax: 701-775-0911. Rev. Raymond P. Courtright.

WAHPETON. *State College of Science Newman Student Parish* 701 N. Seventh St., 58075. Tel: 701-642-3415; Fax: 701-642-2601. Rev. Dale Lagodinski.

[J] MISCELLANEOUS LISTINGS

FARGO. *Catholic Chaplains Association, Diocese of Fargo*, Pastoral Center, 5201 Bishops Blvd., 58104. Tel: 701-235-6429. Email: josephgoering@fargodiocese.org. Very Rev. Joseph P. Goering.

Catholic Charities North Dakota, Formerly Catholic Family Service5201 Bishops Blvd., 58104. Tel: 701-235-4457; Fax: 701-239-8266. Email: fargo@catholiccharitiesnd.org. Web: www.catholiccharitiesnd.org. Briston Fernandes, Exec. Dir Statewide social service agency, providing Adoption Services, Child Welfare, Guardianship Services, Pregnancy Services and Adults Adopting Special Kids (AASK). Staff 32.

Catholic Development Foundation, Diocese of Fargo, Pastoral Center, 5201 Bishops Blvd., 58104. Tel: 701-235-6429; Fax: 701-235-0296. Email: scott.hoselton@fargodiocese.org. Web: www.fargodiocese.org. A non-profit foundation for religious charitable and educational purposes

Catholic School Network Foundation, c/o Laura Huth, 5600 25th St. S., 58104. Tel: 701-293-7910; Fax: 701-293-0729. Email: laura.huth@sendit.nodak.edu. Web: www.fcsn.k12.nd.us. A nonprofit foundation for religious charitable and educational purposes. The Foundation is organized to financially support, assist, promote, expand and strengthen religious educational institutions affiliated with and under the governance of the Fargo Catholic Schools Network.

Cursillo Movement, 113 21st Ave. N., 58102. Tel: 701-237-0251. Web: www.natl-cursillo.org. Rev. Duaine M. Cote.

Engaged Encounter, 3319 Par St., 58102. Tel: 701-234-9602. John Pollard, Contact Person; Sharon Pollard, Contact Person.

Hughes, Inc. 1101 32nd Ave. S., 58103. Tel: 701-237-4857; Fax: 701-237-9822. Email: foundation@presentationsistersfargo.com. Web: www.presentationsistersfargo.com. Sr. Paula Ringuette, Pres. Assisting, providing and expanding low-cost housing (in part for senior citizens along with other groups).

Marriage Encounter, Nativity, 1825 11th St. S., 58103. Tel: 701-232-2414. Rev. Dale H. Kinzler.

Prairieland Home Health Agency, Inc., 1102 Page Dr., S.W., 58103. Tel: 701-232-1245; Fax: 701-232-0813. Email: bbourasso@cableone.net. Web: www.prairielandhomecare.org.

The Presentation Foundation, Sacred Heart Convent, 1101 32nd Ave. S., 58103. Tel: 701-237-4857; Fax: 701-237-9822. Email: foundation@presentationsistersfargo.com. Web: www.presentationsistersfargo.com. Sr. Paula Ringuette, Supr. & Pres.

BATHGATE. *Bethlehem Community*, 10194 Garfield St., S., 58216. Tel: 701-265-3717; Fax: 701-265-3716. Email: inquiry@bethlehembooks.com. Web: www.vmcenter.org. Lydia Reynolds, Contact Person.

BOTTINEAU. *Minot State University-Bottineau*, c/o St. Mark, 322 Sinclair St., 58318. Tel: 701-228-3164. Rev. Paul Schuster. Catholic Students 70

DEVILS LAKE. *UND-Lake Region*, c/o St. Joseph's, 515 Fourth St., P.O. Box 898, 58301. Tel: 701-662-7558; Fax: 701-662-7559. Email: stjosephchurch@stellarnet.com. Rev. Chad F. Wilhelm. Catholic Students 92.

GRAND FORKS. *Air Force Base, Our Lady of the Snows Catholic Community*, 319 ARW/HC, 345 Tuskegee Airman Blvd., 58205-6335. Tel: 701-747-3147; Fax: 701-747-4102.

Grand Forks Catholic Schools Association, 216 Belmont Rd., 58201. Tel: 701-775-4818; Fax: 701-775-7568. Sharon Litchy, Contact Person. A non-profit organization developing, curriculum study, scholarship, transportation, personnel and fund raising.

HANKINSON. *Friends of the International Seminary John Paul II*, c/o Sisters of St. Francis Provincial Motherhouse, P.O. Box 447, 58041-0447. Tel: 701-242-7720. Rev. Charles J. Fischer Jr., S.T.D., Pres. A non-profit foundation for the sole purpose of raising funds in order to financially support, assist, promote, expand and strengthen the International Seminary John Paul II, whose primary purpose is to prepare young men from the third world and eastern Europe for the priesthood. The seminary is located in Rome, Italy.

JAMESTOWN. *Jamestown College*, 6052 College Ln., 58405. Tel: 701-252-0119; Fax: 701-252-6992. Email: michaeleen@buffalocity.net. Very Rev. Al Bitz; Sr. Michaeleen Jantzer, O.S.B., Pastoral Min. & Campus Min. Catholic Students 240.

LANGDON. *St. Alphonsus School Foundation*, 1419 11th Ave., 58249-1919. Tel: 701-256-2141. Gerald Mikkelsen, Pres.

MARYVILLE. *Beginning Experience Apostolate, c/o St. Timothy*, P.O. Box 28, Manvel, 58256-0028. Tel: 701-786-3234. Email: bernard.schneider@fargodiocese.org. Very Rev. Bernard Schneider.

VALLEY CITY. *Valley City State University*, c/o St. Catherine, 540 3rd Ave. N.E., 58072. Tel: 701-845-0354; Fax: 701-845-0556. Email: kelley.utt@sendit.nodak.edu. Kelley Utt, Dir. Catholic Students 150.

RELIGIOUS INSTITUTES OF MEN REPRESENTED IN THE DIOCESE

For further details refer to the corresponding bracketed number in the Religious Institutes of Men or Women section.

[0200]—*Benedictine Monks* (St. Meinrad, Meinrad, IN)—O.S.B.

[0650]—*Holy Ghost Fathers*—C.S.Sp.

[0430]—*Order of Preachers-Dominicans*—O.P.

[0975]—*Society of Our Lady of the Holy Trinity*—S.O.L.T.

RELIGIOUS INSTITUTES OF WOMEN REPRESENTED IN THE DIOCESE

[0230]—*Benedictine Sisters of the Pontifical Jurisdiction* (Belcourt, ND)—O.S.B.

[0300]—*Calced Carmelites*—O.Carm.

[1310]—*Franciscan Sisters of Little Falls, MN*

[2575]—*Institute of the Sisters of Mercy of the Americas* (Omaha, NE)—R.S.M.

[3510]—*Sister Servants of Christ the King*

[2450]—*Sisters of Mary of the Presentation* (Maryvale, R.F.D. 1)—S.M.P.

[1590]—*Sisters of St. Francis of the Immaculate Heart of Mary* (Hankinson, ND)—O.S.F.

[3320]—*Sisters of the Presentation of the B.V.M.* (Fargo, ND)—P.B.V.M.

NECROLOGY

† Neva, Rev. Msgr. Roman G., (Retired)—Died Nov. 25, 2002

† Studzinski, Rev. Msgr. Lambert V., (Retired)—Died Jan. 12, 2003

† Aleksonis, Vladas, (Retired)—Died Dec. 6, 2002

† Mentel, Joseph C., (Retired)—Died July 7, 2003

Diocese of Fort Wayne - South Bend

(Dioecesis Wayne Castrensis-South Bendensis)

Most Reverend

JOHN M. D'ARCY, D.D., M.D., S.T.D.

Bishop of Fort Wayne-South Bend; ordained February 2, 1957; appointed Auxiliary Bishop of Boston and Titular Bishop of Mediana December 31, 1974; consecrated February 11, 1975; appointed Bishop of Fort Wayne-South Bend February 26, 1985; installed May 1, 1985. *P.O. Box 390, Fort Wayne, IN 46801.*

Chancery Office: 1103 S. Calhoun St., P.O. Box 390, Fort Wayne, IN 46801. Tel: 260-422-4611; Fax: 260-423-3382.

Web: www.diocesefwsb.org

Email: jkoch@fw.diocesefwsb.org

ESTABLISHED SEPTEMBER 22, 1857.

Square Miles 5,792.

Redesignated Diocese of Fort Wayne-South Bend on July 22, 1960.

Comprises the Counties of Adams, Allen, Dekalb, Elkhart, Huntington, Kosciusko, La Grange, Marshall, Noble, St. Joseph, Steuben, Wabash, Wells, Whitley in the State of Indiana.

For legal titles of parishes and diocesan institutions, consult the Chancery Office.

STATISTICAL OVERVIEW

Personnel	
Bishop	1
Priests: Diocesan Active in Diocese	62
Priests: Diocesan Active Outside Diocese	1
Priests: Retired, Sick or Absent	30
Number of Diocesan Priests	93
Religious Priests in Diocese	160
Total Priests in Diocese	253
Extern Priests in Diocese	19
Ordinations:	
Religious Priests	2
Transitional Deacons	1
Permanent Deacons in Diocese	20
Total Brothers	134
Total Sisters	581
Parishes	
Parishes	84
With Resident Pastor:	
Resident Diocesan Priests	60
Resident Religious Priests	15
Without Resident Pastor:	
Administered by Priests	9
Pastoral Centers	1
Closed Parishes	3
Professional Ministry Personnel:	
Sisters	24
Lay Ministers	117
Welfare	
Catholic Hospitals	4
Total Assisted	245,237
Health Care Centers	5
Total Assisted	51,343
Homes for the Aged	7
Total Assisted	1,747
Day Care Centers	2
Total Assisted	303
Special Centers for Social Services	9
Total Assisted	138,711
Residential Care of Disabled	1
Total Assisted	38
Other Institutions	4
Total Assisted	3,174
Educational	
Diocesan Students in Other Seminaries	14
Seminaries, Religious	1
Students Religious	15
Total Seminarians	29
Colleges and Universities	5
Total Students	15,639
High Schools, Diocesan and Parish	4
Total Students	3,097
Elementary Schools, Diocesan and Parish	41
Total Students	10,681
Catechesis/Religious Education:	
High School Students	1,448
Elementary Students	9,545
Total Students under Catholic Instruction	40,439
Teachers in the Diocese:	
Priests	2
Sisters	15
Lay Teachers	828
Vital Statistics	
Receptions into the Church:	
Infant Baptism Totals	2,723
Adult Baptism Totals	356
Received into Full Communion	354
First Communions	3,031
Confirmations	2,947
Marriages:	
Catholic	566
Interfaith	373
Total Marriages	939
Deaths	1,536
Total Catholic Population	162,043
Total Population	1,217,932

Former Bishops—Rt. Revs. JOHN HENRY LUERS, D.D., consecrated Jan. 10, 1858; died June 29, 1871; JOSEPH DWENGER, C.PP.S., D.D., consecrated April 14, 1872; died Jan. 27, 1893; JOSEPH RADEMACHER, D.D., consecrated Bishop of Nashville, June 24, 1883; transferred to Fort Wayne, July 14, 1893; died Jan. 12, 1900; HERMAN JOSEPH ALERDING, D.D., consecrated Nov. 30, 1900; died Dec. 6, 1924; Most Revs. JOHN FRANCIS NOLL, D.D., consecrated June 30, 1925; promoted to rank of Archbishop "ad personam," Sept. 2, 1953; died July 31, 1956; LEO A. PURSLEY, D.D. (Retired), consecrated Sept. 19, 1950; retired Oct. 19, 1976; died Nov. 15, 1998; WILLIAM E. MCMANUS, D.D. (Retired), ord. April 15, 1939; appt. Auxiliary Bishop of Chicago, June 21, 1967; appt. Bishop of Fort Wayne, Aug. 31, 1976; installed as 7th Bishop of Fort Wayne, Oct. 19, 1976; retired Feb. 25, 1985; died March 3, 1997.

Diocese of Fort Wayne-South Bend, Inc.—(Incorporated Aug. 29, 1955). Board of Directors: Most Rev. JOHN M. D'ARCY, D.D., M.A., S.T.D., Pres.; Rev. ROBERT C. SCHULTE, Vice Pres.; JOSEPH RYAN, Sec. & Treas., Finance Council:. Finance Council: Most Rev. JOHN M. D'ARCY, D.D., M.A., S.T.D.; Rev. ROBERT C. SCHULTE; Mr. JOSEPH RYAN, Sec. & Treas.; ARTHUR DECIO; Sr. JANE MARIE KLEIN, O.S.F.; Mr. JERRY HAMMES; JOSEPH DAHM; MICHAEL HAMMES; THOMAS BLEE; RICHARD DOERMER; VINCENT TIPPMANN; JEROME KEARNS; ALICE KOPFER; SCOTT MALPASS; RONALD KAUFMAN.

Chancery Office—1103 S. Calhoun St., P.O. Box 390, Fort Wayne, 46801. Tel: 260-422-4611; Fax: 260-423-3382. Office Hours: Mon.-Fri. 8:30-4:30. Other times by appointment

Vicar General-Chancellor—Rev. ROBERT C. SCHULTE.

Vicar for Retired Clergy—Rev. Msgr. J. WILLIAM LESTER, P.A. (Retired).

Episcopal Vicar for Education—Rev. ROBERT C. SCHULTE, 1103 S. Clinton St., Box 390, Fort Wayne, 46801. Tel: 260-422-4611; Fax: 260-423-3382.

South Bend Chancery—114 W. Wayne St., South Bend, 46601. Tel: 574-234-0687; Fax: 574-232-8483.

Diocesan Tribunal—1103 S. Calhoun St., P.O. Box 390, Fort Wayne, 46801. Tel: 260-422-4611; Fax: 260-423-3382. *South Bend Office, 114 W. Wayne St, P.O. Box 1432, South Bend, 46624.* Tel: 574-287-6531; Fax: 574-287-9391.

Judicial Vicar—Rev. BRUCE PIECHOCKI.

Defender of the Bond—SANDRA LA VIOLETTE.

Pro-Synodal Judges—Revs. PHILIP DEVOLDER; LAWRENCE KRAMER; GARY SIGLER; ELDEN MILLER; BRUCE PIECHOCKI.

Court Consultant—Dr. PHIL SUTTON.

Fort Wayne Office—JANICE BRELL, Admin. Sec. Advocates: VICKI FERRIER; MONICA KLUESNER. Auditors: SUE WILSON; KAY NELSON.

Notary—JANICE BRELL.

South Bend Office Manager—DIANA HEIDT. Office Auditors: BARBARA SZYMANSKI; EUGENE LAVIOLETTE.

Advocate—ELIZABETH LIES.

Consultors—Rev. ROBERT C. SCHULTE; Rev. Msgr. JAMES J. WOLF; Revs. MARK GURTNER; TERRY FISHER; WILLIAM SCHOOLER; THOMAS SHOEMAKER; MICHAEL HEINTZ; JAMES SHAFER.

Diocesan Offices and Directors

Business Administration Office—JOSEPH RYAN, Chief Fin. Officer, P.O. Box 390, Fort Wayne, 46801. Tel: 260-422-4611; Fax: 260-423-3382.

Buildings and Improvements—Advisory Board: Rev. ROBERT SCHULTE; Rev. Msgr. JAMES WOLF; Revs. DOMINIQUE CARBONEAU; DERRICK SNEYD; WILLIAM SULLIVAN; JOHN OVERMYER; DALE BAUMAN; JOHN DELANEY; DAVID CARKENORD; ELDEN J. MILLER (Retired); Mr. JOSEPH RYAN; Mr. JAMES SCHENKEL.

Budget Committee—Revs. ROBERT C. SCHULTE; JOHN PFISTER; Rev. Msgr. JOHN SUELZER; Rev. BERNARD GALIC; Mr. JOSEPH RYAN.

Diocesan Services Agency—JOHN KLEIN; MARY LOU O'KEEFFE, Purchasing, P.O. Box 390, Fort Wayne, 46801. Tel: 260-422-4611; 800-856-4611; Fax: 260-420-6306.

Diocesan Office of Development—HARRY W. VERHILEY, Dir., 1328 W. Dragoon Trail, Mishawaka, 46544. Tel: 574-258-6571; Fax: 574-256-2709.

Campus Ministry—LINDA FURGE, Dir., 1330 E. Washington Center Rd., Fort Wayne, 46825. Tel: 260-483-3661; Fax: 260-483-1881.

Catholic Campaign for Human Development—Rev. ROBERT C. SCHULTE, P.O. Box 390, 1103 S. Calhoun St., Fort Wayne, 46801. Tel: 260-422-4611; Fax: 260-423-3382.

Catholic Charities—DEBRA SCHMIDT, Dir., 315 E. Washington, Fort Wayne, 46802. Tel: 260-422-5625; 800-686-7459; Fax: 260-422-5657.

Censor Librorum—Rev. MICHAEL HEINTZ, 1701 Miami St., South Bend, 46613. Tel: 574-289-5539; Fax: 574-289-0227.

Cemeteries—Rev. DAVID CARKENORD, Dir., 1098 County Rd. 39, Waterloo, 46793-9779. Tel: 260-837-7115; 800-570-8080; Fax: 260-837-7727.

Catholic Cemetery Association of Fort Wayne, Inc.—3500 Lake Ave., Fort Wayne, 46805. Tel: 260-426-2044.

Communications—CHRISTINE BONAHOOM-NIX, Dir., 150 Doan Dr., Fort Wayne, 46816. Tel: 260-744-0012; Fax: 260-744-1473.

Continuing Education of the Clergy—Rev. ROBERT C. SCHULTE, P.O. Box 390, Fort Wayne, 46801. Tel: 260-422-4611; Fax: 260-423-3382.

Council of Priests—Revs. ROBERT C. SCHULTE; STEPHEN COLCHIN; ROBERT D'SOUZA; BERNARD GALIC; GLENN KOHRMAN; LAWRENCE KRAMER; WILLIAM KUMMER; Rev. Msgr. J. WILLIAM LESTER, P.A. (Retired); Revs. MICHAEL MATHEWS, C.S.C.; JOHN OVERMYER; JOSEPH RULLI; THOMAS SHOEMAKER; WILLIAM SULLIVAN; TIMOTHY WROZEK; CHRISTOPHER YOUNG.

Cursillo—Rev. PAUL BUETER. Tel: 574-267-5842 (Spanish); Fax: 574-268-1030; MARY FULASKI, Contact. Tel: 574-243-8854 (English).

Hispanic Ministry Services—Rev. PAUL R. BUETER, Vicar for Hispanic Ministry, 125 N. Harrison, Warsaw, 46580. Tel: 574-267-5842; 574-658-9384; Fax: 574-256-2709; ENID ROMAN-DEJESUS, Diocesan Coord., 1328 W. Dragoon Trail, Mishawaka, 46544. Tel: 574-259-9994, Ext. 211.

Angola—St. Anthony of Padua, 700 W. Maumee St., Angola, 46703. Tel: 260-665-2259. Rev. PHILLIP LEY, O.F.M.Conv.

Bluffton—St. Joseph, 1300 N. Main St., Blufton, 46714. Tel: 260-824-1380. Rev. LAWRENCE KRAMER. Ministry to Migrant Catholics.

Bremen—St. Dominic, 803 W. Bike St., Bremen, 46506. Tel: 574-546-3601.

Decatur—St. Mary of the Assumption, 414 W. Madison St., Decatur, 46733. Tel: 260-724-9159. Deacon ISAAC MCDONALD.

Elkhart—St. Vincent de Paul, 1108 S. Main St., Elkhart, 46516. Tel: 574-389-9634. Revs. JOHN OVERMYER; WILSON CORZO.

Fort Wayne—St. Patrick, 2120 Harrison St., Fort Wayne, 46802. Tel: 260-744-1450. Rev. ANGEL VALDEZ, O.F.M.

Geneva—St. Mary of the Presentation, 5790 E. 11105, Geneva, 46740. Tel: 260-724-9159. Deacon ISAAC MCDONALD.

Goshen—St. John the Evangelist, 109 W. Monroe St., Goshen, 46526-3957. Tel: 574-534-7554. Rev. CONSTANTINO ROCHA.

LaGrange—St. Joseph, P.O. Box 69, LaGrange, 46761. Tel: 260-463-3472. Rev. PHILLIP LEY, O.F.M.Conv.

Ligonier—St. Patrick, 300 Ravine Park Dr., Ligonier, 46767-1301. Tel: 260-894-4946. Rev. JOSE VILLANUEVA.

Milford—Our Lady of Guadalupe, 4th & Main St., P.O. Box 605, Milford, 46542. Tel: 574-658-9384. Rev. PAUL R. BUETER; Sr. JOAN HASTREITER, S.S.J.

Plymouth—St. Michael, 612 N. Walnut St., Plymouth, 46563. Tel: 574-936-4935.

South Bend—St. Adalbert, 2420 W. Huron, South Bend, 46619-3395. Tel: 574-288-5708. Revs. CHRISTOPHER COX, C.S.C.; DAVID PORTERFIELD, C.S.C.

Warsaw—Sacred Heart, 125 N. Harrison St., Warsaw, 46580. Tel: 574-267-5842. Rev. PAUL BUETER; Sr. JOAN HASTREITER, S.S.J.

Other Services Rendered to the Hispanic in Spanish—

Elkhart & South Bend Area—Deacon RICARDO MEDINA III. Tel: 574-295-5284; 800-875-5286.

Encuentro Matrimonial - (Marriage Encounters)—CIRILO PONCE; ROSARIO PONCE. Tel: 574-267-4024. Elkhart/South Bend & Warsaw areas:

Diocesan Council of Catholic Women—Rev. EDWARD NARCOWICH (Retired), St. Mary's of the Assumption 228 N. Main St., Avilla, 46710. Tel: 260-897-4254; GEORGETTA GUNTHORP, Pres., 0240 N. 850 E., LaGrange, 46761. Tel: 260-367-2359.

Diocesan Family Life—FRED EVERETT; LISA EVERETT, 114 W. Wayne St., South Bend, 46601. Tel: 574-234-0687; Fax: 574-232-8483. Email: everettfam@aol.com.

Ecumenical Affairs—Rev. ROBERT C. SCHULTE, Dir., East, P.O. Box 390, Fort Wayne, 46801. Tel: 260-422-4611; Fax: 260-423-3382. Email: rschulte@fw.diocesefwsb.org.

Liturgical Commission—Revs. WILLIAM KUMMER; PETER ROCCA, C.S.C.; JAMES SHAFER; WILLIAM SCHOOLER, Chm.; Deacon ART BLEAU; JAMES FITZPATRICK; Rev. MICHAEL DRISCOLL; GERVAISE BASTIAN; Mrs. JUDY MOCKENHAUPT; BEVERLY RIEGER; Mr. STEVE WARNER.

Environment and Art—CHRISTOPHER SCHENKEL; Revs. JAMES FLANIGAN, C.S.C., Chm.; DAVID CARKENORD; Sr. AGNES MARIE REGAN O.S.F.; SAM JONES, A.I.A.; BEVERLY RIEGER.

Diocesan Music Committee—Sr. PHYLLIS GRZECZKA, S.S.N.D.; BEVERLY RIEGER; JEREMY HOW; KEVIN DEMETROFF; TIM ROBISON; JUDY THROM; CAROLYN SHERMAN; MICHAEL BECHTOL; ANN BECHTOL.

Diocesan Initiation Committee—GERVAISE BASTIAN; BEVERLY RIEGER; MARY BARNES; CAROL CONE; Sr. EILEEN DAUDLIN, S.S.N.D.; DONNA MACINO; CHRIS MILLER; Mrs. JUDY MOCKENHAUPT; REGINA WILSON; Rev. TIMOTHY WROZEK.

Office of Worship—BEVERLY RIEGER, Dir., 1103 S. Calhoun St., Box 390, Fort Wayne, 46801. Tel: 260-422-4611.

Official Publication "Today's Catholic"—TIMOTHY JOHNSON, Acting Editor, 150 Doan Dr., Fort Wayne, 46806. Mailing Address, P.O. Box 11169, Fort Wayne, 46856. Tel: 260-456-2824; 260-456-2900; Fax: 260-744-1473.

Permanent Diaconate—Rev. WILLIAM KUMMER, St. Michael Church, 612 N. Walnut St., Plymouth, 46563-1548. Tel: 574-936-4935; Fax: 574-936-9293.

Pro-Life—FRED EVERETT; LISA EVERETT, 114 W. Wayne St., South Bend, 46601. Tel: 574-234-0687. Birthline phones. Tel: 260-422-1818 (Fort Wayne); 260-356-3322 (Huntington); 574-289-1034 (South Bend).

Propagation of the Faith and Holy Childhood Association—Rev. PHILLIP WIDMANN, St. Peter Catholic Church, 518 E. DeWald St., Fort Wayne, 46803. Tel: 260-744-2765; Fax: 260-744-1972.

Office of Catechesis—Sr. M. JANE CAREW, O.V., Diocesan Dir., Religious Education; JANE CORS SMITH, Coord. Hispanic Catechesis, Fort Wayne:; DONNA MACINO, Assoc. Dir., P.O. Box 390, Fort Wayne, 46801. Tel: 260-422-4611; Fax: 260-420-6306.

South Bend-Mishawaka Office of Catechesis—KIM CUNNINGHAM, Assoc. Dir. Catechesis, 1328 W. Dragoon Trail, Mishawaka, 46554. Tel 574-259-9994; Fax: 574-256-2709.

Refugee Resettlement Program—DEBRA SMITH, Dir., 315 E. Washington, Fort Wayne, 46802 Tel: 260-422-5625; 800-686-7459; Fax: 260-422-5557.

Retired Clergy Committee—Rev. Msgrs. J WILLIAM LESTER, P.A. (Retired); JOHN SUELZER; Revs. RAYMOND BALZER; WILLIAM HODDE (Retired); ROBERT HOEVEL; ROBERT SCHULTE; PHILLIP WIDMANN; Rev. Msgr. JAMES WOLF.

Retired Senior Volunteer Program (RSVP)—Auburn: 107 W. 5th St., Auburn, 46706. Tel: 260-925-0917; Fax: 260-925-1732.

Serra International—Fort Wayne: EUGENE DONNELLY, Pres., 2402 Broadway, Fort Wayne, 46807. Tel: 260-456-2083; Rev. GLENN KOHRMAN, Chap., 124 College Ave., Culver, 46511. Tel: 574-842-2522. South Bend Office: Dr. JOHN B. TOEPP, Pres. Serra Club, 63991 Miami Rd., South Bend, 46614. Tel: 574-287-5542; 574-291-3181; Rev. ROBERT YAST, Chap., 225 S. Mill St., Mishawaka, 46544. Tel: 574-255-6134.

Single Catholic Adult Club—VACANT.

Schools—MICHELLE HITTIE, Supt.; JO ANN ROSCOE, Assoc. Supt.; REBECCA ELSWERKY, Assoc. Supt. Personnel; JOHN GAUGHAN, Asst. Dir. High Schools, 1102 S. Clinton St., Box 390, Fort Wayne, 46801. Tel: 260-422-4611; Fax: 260-426-3077.

South Bend Office: BARBARA JEMIELITY, Assoc. Supt., 1328 W. Dragoon Trail, Mishawaka, 46544. Tel: 574-255-1387; Fax: 574-256-2709.

School Board, Diocesan—Rev. TERRY FISHER; GENE ANDERT; MICHELLE HITTIE, Supt.; BARBARA JEMIELITY; JOHN GAUGHAN; JO ANN ROSCOE; MARIJO KELLY; AL DOWNING; DENISE CROWEL; REBECCA ELSWERKY; JERRY HENRY; JOYCE JOHNSTONE.

Ex Officio Member—Most Rev. JOHN M. D'ARCY, D.D., M.A., S.T.D.

Scouting—Fort Wayne: VACANT, Chap.; GARY WEAVER, Vice Chm. Tel: 260-485-5229. South Bend: VACANT, Chap.

St. Vincent de Paul Society—Rev. THOMAS O'CONNOR, 1101 S. Lafayette St., Fort Wayne, 46802-3202. Tel: 260-424-8231; Fax: 260-426-2406. Mailing Address, P.O. Box 11383, Fort Wayne, 46857-1383.

Spiritual Development—Fort Wayne: Sr. JOLENE HEIDEN, S.S.N.D.; GINNY KOHRMAN, 1102 S. Clinton St., P.O. Box 390, Fort Wayne, 46801. Tel: 260-422-4611; Fax: 260-420-6306. South Bend: Sr. MARY BROOKS, 114 W. Wayne St., South Bend, 46601. Tel: 574-234-0687; Fax: 574-232-8483.

Office of Youth Ministry and Spiritual Formation—STEVE WEIGAND, Dir., 1102 S. Clinton St., P.O. Box 390, Fort Wayne, 46801. Tel: 260-422-4611; Fax: 260-420-6306; CHRIS CULVER, Assoc. Dir., 1328 W. Dragoon Trail, Mishawaka, 46544. Tel: 574-257-4294.

Vocations—Rev. BERNARD GALIC, Dir., 114 W. Wayne St., South Bend, 46601. Tel: 574-234-0687; Fax: 574-232-8483.

Youth Organizations—VACANT, Moderator.

CYO Office—AVA MEYER, Business Mgr., P.O. Box 445, Monroeville, 46773. Tel: 260-623-6007; Fax: 260-623-6007; MARY SCHREIBER, Pres., 2021 Reckeweg Rd., Fort Wayne, 46804. Tel: 260-432-1921.

Inter City Catholic League—Rev. MICHAEL HEINTZ, Moderator, St. Matthew Cathedral, 1701 Miami St., South Bend, 46613. Tel: 574-289-5539; TONY VIOLI, Pres., 225 Omer Ave., Mishawaka, 46545. Tel: 574-259-1638; 574-255-9776; Fax: 574-259-0995.

Victim Assistance Coordinator—Rev. ROBERT C. SCHULTE, Vicar Gen. & Chancellor. Tel: 260-422-4611. Email: mraatz@fw.diocesefwsb.org.

CLERGY, PARISHES, MISSIONS AND PAROCHIAL SCHOOLS

CITY OF FORT WAYNE

(ALLEN COUNTY)

1—CATHEDRAL OF THE IMMACULATE CONCEPTION (1836),, (Calhoun, between Lewis and Jefferson Sts.) Revs. Robert C. Schulte, Rector; Benedict Jayatilake; Sr. Sally Soules, S.F.C.C., Pastoral Min.; Deacon Joseph R. Zickgraf. In Res., Rev. Msgr. J. William Lester, P.A. (Retired).
Res.: 1122 Clinton St., P.O. Box 10898, 46854. Tel: 260-424-1485; Fax: 260-424-7625.
Catechesis/Religious Program—Fax: 260-424-7625. Teresa Wedler, D.R.E. Students 163.
Chapel—MacDougall Memorial Chapel

2—ST. ANDREW (1910), Closed., For inquiries for parish records please contact the Diocesan Archives Office, Tel: 260-745-5340. , 518 E. DeWald, 46803. Tel: 260-422-0380.

3—ST. CHARLES BORROMEO (1957), [CEM] Rev. Msgrs. John N. Suelzer; Edward I. Hession, Pastor Emeritus (Retired); Revs. Christopher L. Smith; Gabriel Coelho; Sr. Kathleen Morrissey, O.P., Pastoral Assoc.; Margaret Sorg, Business Admin.
Res.: 4916 Trier Rd., 46815. Tel: 260-482-2186; Fax: 260-471-2144.
School—4910 Trier Rd., 46815. Tel: 260-484-3392; Fax: 260-482-2006. Robert Sordelet, Prin. Franciscan Sisters of the Sacred Heart 1; Lay Teachers 39; Students 784.
Catechesis/Religious Program—Tel: 260-484-7322. Kathy Monagle, D.R.E. Students 205.

4—ST. ELIZABETH ANN SETON (1988), Revs. James A. Shafer; Thomas Kodakassery, O.S.B. (India).
Office—10700 Aboite Center Rd., 46804. Tel: 260-432-0268; Fax: 260-436-5851.
Res.: 10517 Unita Dr., 46804. Tel: 260-436-9819.
Catechesis/Religious Program—Mary Behe, D.R.E. Students 362.

5—ST. HENRY (1956), Rev. Emmanuel Chikezie.
Res.: 2929 E. Paulding Rd., 46816. Tel: 260-447-4100; Fax: 260-447-2519.
Catechesis/Religious Program—Tel: 260-744-1450; Fax: 260-745-3643. Students 62.

6—ST. HYACINTH (1910), Closed. For inquiries for parish records contact the chancery.

7—ST. JOHN THE BAPTIST (1929), Rev. Daryl Rybicki; Mary L. Glowaski, Pastoral Assoc.
Res.: 4525 Arlington Ave., 46807. Tel: 260-744-4393; Fax: 260-456-3072.
School—4500 Fairfield Ave., 46807. Tel: 260-456-3321. Ms. Peggy Richardson, Prin. Lay Teachers 24; Students 349.
Catechesis/Religious Program—4501 Arlington Ave., 46807. Tel: 260-744-3578. Elizabeth Balbo-Ryan, D.R.E. Students 75.

8—ST. JOSEPH (1914), (Italian), Rev. Timothy A. Wrozek. In Res., Rev. Adam Schmitt (Retired).
Office: 2213 Brooklyn Ave., 46802.
Res.: 1910 Hale Ave., 46802. Tel: 260-432-5113; Fax: 260-432-4711.
School—2211 Brooklyn Ave., 46802. Tel: 260-432-4000; Fax: 260-432-8642. Ms. Lois Widner, Prin. Lay Teachers 27; Students 450.
Catechesis/Religious Program—Students 37.

9—ST. JOSEPH (1851), (German), [CEM] Rev. Edward Erpelding.
Res.: 11337 Old U.S. 27 S., 46816. Tel: 260-639-3748; Fax: 260-639-3331.
School—11521 Old U.S. 27 S., 46816. Tel: 260-639-3580; Fax: 260-639-3675. Lay Teachers 13; Students 189.
Catechesis/Religious Program—Students 37.

10—ST. JUDE (1929), Revs. Thomas Shoemaker; Robert D'Souza (India); Mary Pohlman, Pastoral Assoc.; Deacon Fred J. Larson.
Res.: 2130 Pemberton Dr., 46805. Tel: 260-484-6609; Fax: 260-969-1607.
School—2110 Pemberton Dr., 46805. Tel: 260-484-4611. Sr. Kathleen Marie Knueven, Prin. Sisters of Notre Dame 3; Lay Teachers 38; Students 625.
Catechesis/Religious Program—Mary Barnes, D.R.E. Students 179.

11—St. Mary (1848), (German), Rev. Thomas P. O'Connor.
Mailing Address: P.O. Box 11383, 46857-1383. Tel: 260-424-8231; Fax: 260-426-2604.
Res.: 1101 S. Lafayette St., 46802.
Catechesis / Religious Program—Students 30.

12—Most Precious Blood (1897), Rev. John C. Mencsik, C.PP.S.; Deacon Peter Loving.
Res.: 1515 Barthold St., 46808. Tel: 260-424-5535; Fax: 260-426-7765.
School—1529 Barthold St., 46808. Tel: 260-424-4832. Corinne Tessman, Prin. Lay Teachers 12; Students 190.
Catechesis / Religious Program—Students 30.

13—Our Lady of Good Hope (1969), Rev. David Voors.
Res.: 7215 St. Joe Rd., 46835. Tel: 260-485-9615; Fax: 260-485-4463.
Catechesis / Religious Program—Tel: 260-485-9615, Ext. 17. Mary Kay Matasky, D.R.E. Students 250.

14—St. Patrick (1889), (Vietnamese), Rev. Angel Valdez, O.F.M.
Res.: 2120 S. Harrison St., 46802. Tel: 260-744-1450; Fax: 260-745-3643.
Catechesis / Religious Program—Fax: 260-745-3546. Students 60.

15—St. Paul (1865), (Hispanic), Merged, with St. Patrick's, Fort Wayne.

16—St. Peter (1872), (German), Rev. Phillip A. Widmann.
Res.: 518 E. De Wald St., 46803. Tel: 260-744-2765; Fax: 260-744-1972.
Catechesis / Religious Program—Students 25.

17—Queen of Angels (1947), [CEM] Rev. John F. Pfister. In Res., Rev. Bruce Piechocki.
Res.: 1500 W. State St., 46808. Tel: 260-482-9411; Fax: 260-471-0005.
School—1600 W. State Blvd., 46808. Tel: 260-483-8214. Mrs. Marsha Jordan, Prin. Lay Teachers 19; Students 319.
Catechesis / Religious Program—Students 57.

18—Sacred Heart (1947), Rev. Emmanuel Chikezie.
Res.: 2929 E. Paulding Rd., 46816. Tel: 260-447-4100; Fax: 260-744-2519.
Catechesis / Religious Program—Tel: 260-744-1450; Fax: 260-745-3643. Students 37.

19—St. Therese (1947), Rev. Joseph A. Rulli.
Res.: 2304 Lower Huntington Rd., 46819. Tel: 260-747-9139; Fax: 260-747-1494.
School—2222 Lower Huntington Rd., 46819. Tel: 260-747-2343; Fax: 260-747-4767. Michael Briggs, Prin. Lay Teachers 14; Students 187.
Catechesis / Religious Program—Students 86.

20—St. Vincent de Paul (1846), [CEM] Revs. John M. Kuzmich; Joseph Gaughan; Mark Allen Gurtner; Sr. Mary Catherine Jarema, S.S.N.D., Pastoral Assoc.; Sherry Miller, Pastoral Assoc. & Admin.; Mrs. Judy Mockenhaupt, Pastoral Assoc.
Res.: 1502 E. Wallen Rd., 46825. Tel: 260-489-3537; Fax: 260-497-9405.
School—1720 E. Wallen Rd., 46825. Tel: 260-489-3537, Ext. 213; Fax: 260-489-5318. Mrs. Sandra Guffey, Prin. Lay Teachers 40; Students 709.
Catechesis / Religious Program—Tel: 260-489-3537, Ext. 235. Beth Amick, D.R.E. Students 600.

CITY OF SOUTH BEND
(St. Joseph County)

1—St. Adalbert (1910), (Polish), Revs. David J. Porterfield, C.S.C., Admin.; Christopher Cox, C.S.C.; Thomas McDermott, C.S.C. In Res., Revs. Charles J. Lavely, C.S.C.; Thomas Smith, C.S.C.
Res.: 2420 W. Huron St., 46619. Tel: 574-288-5708; Fax: 574-251-2786.
School—519 S. Olive St., 46619. Tel: 574-288-6645; Fax: 574-251-2788. Sr. Dian Majsterek, S.S.J.-T.O.S.F., Prin. Felician Sisters 2; Sisters of St. Joseph 1; Lay Teachers 10; Students 107.
Catechesis / Religious Program—Students 214.

2—St. Anthony de Padua (1949), Rev. Terry Fisher; Deacon Brian Miller.
Res.: 2120 E. Jefferson Blvd., 46617. Tel: 574-282-2308; Fax: 574-288-8877.
School—2310 E. Jefferson Blvd., 46615. Tel: 574-233-7169; Fax: 574-233-7290. Ms. Martha Lewallen, Prin. Lay Teachers 22; Students 455.
Catechesis / Religious Program—Students 88.

3—St. Augustine (1928), (African American), Rev. Charles J. Lavely, C.S.C.; Deacon Paul Baumgartner.
Mailing Address: P.O. Box 3198, 46619-0198. Tel: 574-234-6334; Fax: 574-251-2786.
Res.: 1501 W. Washington St., 46628. Tel: 574-234-7082.
Catechesis / Religious Program—Students 15.

4—St. Casimir (1899), (Polish), Revs. David J. Porterfield, C.S.C.; Christopher Cox, C.S.C.
Res.: 1308 W. Dunham St., 46619. Tel: 574-287-9551; Fax: 574-287-0329.
Catechesis / Religious Program—Students 17.

5—Christ the King (1933), Revs. Thomas J. Jones, C.S.C.; Stephen Kempinger, C.S.C.; Ronald Tripi, C.S.C.
Res.: 52473 Indiana State Rte. 933, 46637. Tel: 574-272-3113; Fax: 574-273-6702.
School—Tel: 574-272-3922; Fax: 574-273-6707. Lay Teachers 25; Students 500.
Catechesis / Religious Program—Students 120.

6—Corpus Christi (1961), Rev. Camillo Tirabassi. In Res., Rev. Walter J. Bly.
Res.: 2822 Corpus Christi Dr., 46628. Tel: 574-272-9982; Fax: 574-272-2545.
School—2817 Corpus Christi Dr., 46628. Tel: 574-272-9868; Fax: 574-272-9894. Mrs. Marilyn Gibbs, Prin. Daughters of Divine Charity 1; Lay Teachers 26; Students 460.
Catechesis / Religious Program—Students 20.

7—Faith & Hope & Charity Chapel (1975), Revs. William C. O'Connor, C.S.C.; David H. Verhalen, C.S.C.
Res.: 114 W. Wayne St., 46624. Tel: 574-289-4263.

8—St. Hedwig (1877), (Polish), Rev. Leonard F. Chrobot.
Res.: 331 S. Scott St., 46601. Tel: 574-287-8932; Fax: 574-232-9787.
Catechesis / Religious Program—Students 5.

9—Holy Cross (1929), Revs. Michael Mathews, C.S.C.; James Rigert, C.S.C. In Res., Revs. Richard Laurick, C.S.C.; Donald F. Guertin, C.S.C.; James J. Ferguson, C.S.C.
Parish Office—920 Wilber St., 46628.
Res.: 1520 Vassar Ave., 46628. Tel: 574-233-2179; Fax: 574-237-6736.
School—(Grades PreK-8), 1020 Wilber St., 46628. Tel: 574-234-3422; Fax: 574-237-6725. Mrs. Angela Budzinski, Prin. Lay Teachers 24; Students 358.
Catechesis / Religious Program—920 Wilber St., 46628. Tel: 219-233-2954. Gloria Kucela, D.R.E. Students 31.

10—Holy Family (1945), [JC] Revs. Bernard J. Galic; Christopher Young; Deacon Eugene Szynski, Pastoral Assoc.
Res.: 56405 Mayflower Rd., 46619. Tel: 574-282-2317; Fax: 574-282-2318.
School—Tel: 574-289-7375; Fax: 574-289-7386. Sr. Joan Marie Shillinger, C.S.S.F., Prin. Felician Sisters of Livonia, MI 2; Lay Teachers 28; Students 470.
Catechesis / Religious Program—Linda Lagodney, D.R.E. Students 210.

11—St. John the Baptist (1956), Rev. Lourdino Fernandes.
Res.: 3526 St. John Way, 46628. Tel: 574-233-5414; Fax: 574-233-5414.
School—3616 St. John Way, 46628. Tel: 574-232-9849; Fax: 574-232-9849. Janet Wroblewski, Prin. Lay Teachers 11; Students 210.
Catechesis / Religious Program—Students 15.

12—St. Joseph (1853), Rev. Michael D. Couhig, C.S.C.; Regina Wilson, M.Div., Pastoral Assoc. In Res., Revs. William Neidhart, C.S.C.; Brent A. Kruger.
Res.: 226 N. Hill St., 46617. Tel: 574-234-3135.
Parish Office—211 N. St. Louis Blvd., 46617. Tel: 574-234-3134; Fax: 574-234-2822.
School—216 N. Hill St., 46617. Tel: 574-234-0451; Fax: 574-234-0524. Mrs. Suzanne Wiwi, Prin. Lay Teachers 25; Students 440.
Catechesis / Religious Program—Students 31.

13—St. Jude (1948), Rev. Derrick Sneyd.
Res.: 19704 Johnson Rd., 46614. Tel: 574-291-0570; Fax: 574-299-3051.
School—19657 Hildebrand St., 46614. Tel: 574-291-3820. Ms. Judi Cole, Prin. Lay Teachers 15; Students 223.
Catechesis / Religious Program—Tel: 574-291-2797. Students 60.

14—St. Mary of the Assumption (1882), (German), Rev. Derrick Sneyd.
Res.: 3501 S. Locust Rd., 46614. Tel: 574-287-0225; Fax: 574-287-8781.
School—3402 S. Locust Rd., 46614. Tel: 574-287-1472; Fax: 574-287-9883. Lay Teachers 10; Students 124.
Catechesis / Religious Program—Students 20.

15—St. Matthew Cathedral (1921), Revs. Michael Heintz, Admin.; Robert Van Kempen; Sr. Agnes Marie Regan, O.S.F., Pastoral Assoc.; Deacon Emilio Gizzi; David Laux, Business Mgr.
Res.: 1701 Miami St., 46613. Tel: 574-289-5539; Fax: 574-289-0227.
School—1015 E. Dayton, 46613. Tel: 574-289-4535; Fax: 574-289-5439. Ms. Mary Ann Retseck, Prin. Lay Teachers 23; Students 399.
Catechesis / Religious Program—1721 Miami St., 46613. Tel: 574-289-0940; Fax: 574-289-0940. Students 65.

16—Our Lady of Hungary (1921), [CEM] Revs. Thaddeus Kwak; Lawrence Teteh, C.S.Sp.; Deacon Ervin Kuspa.
Res.: 829 W. Calvert St., 46613. Tel: 574-287-1700; Fax: 574-289-6704.
School—735 W. Calvert St., 46613. Tel: 574-289-3272; Fax: 574-289-3272. Mr. Clem Wroblewski, Prin. Lay Teachers 10; Students 117.
Catechesis / Religious Program—Tel: 574-288-3169. Students 117.

17—St. Patrick (1858), [JC] Rev. Leonard Chrobot, Ph.D. In Res., Revs. Donald J. Bielby, C.S.C. (Canada); Raymond Likupe (Africa).
Res.: 309 S. Taylor St., 46625. Tel: 574-232-5839; Fax: 574-232-5830.
Catechesis / Religious Program—Tel: 574-277-2006. Students 37.

18—St. Stanislaus (1899), (Polish), Revs. Michael C. Matthews, C.S.C.; James A. Rigert, C.S.C. In Res., Revs. James J. Ferguson, C.S.C.; Donald F. Guertin, C.S.C.; Richard Laurick, C.S.C.
Res.: 1520 Vassar St., 46628. Tel: 574-233-2179; Fax: 574-237-6736.

19—St. Stephen (1909), (Hispanic—Hungarian), Closed., For inquiries for parish records, contact St. Adalbert, South Bend.

20—St. Therese, Little Flower (1937), Revs. Andre E. Leveille, C.S.C.; Cornelius Ryan, C.S.C.
54191 N. Ironwood Dr., 46635. Tel: 574-272-7070; Fax: 574-243-3434.
Catechesis / Religious Program—Tel: 574-243-3439. Students 225.

OUTSIDE THE CITIES OF FORT WAYNE AND SOUTH BEND

Albion, Noble Co., Blessed Sacrament (1875), [JC] Rev. Babasino Fernandes (India).
Res.: 403 Ravine Park Dr., Ligonier, 46767-1301. Tel: 260-894-4946.
Church: State Rd. 9 S., Box 102, 46701-0102. Tel: 260-636-2072; Fax: 260-894-4911.
Catechesis / Religious Program—Students 54.

Angola, Steuben Co., St. Anthony (1926), Revs. Fred Pasche, O.F.M.Conv.; Phillip Ley, O.F.M-.Conv.; Philip Schneider, O.F.M.Conv.
Res.: 700 W. Maumee St., 46703. Tel: 260-665-2259; Fax: 260-665-2268.
Catechesis / Religious Program—Cathy Bryan, D.R.E. Students 200.
Mission—St. Paul Chapel Clear Lake, Steuben Co. 46703. Tel: 260-495-9913. 8780 E. 700 N. Freemont, Fremont, 46737.

Arcola, Allen Co., St. Patrick (1846), [CEM] Rev. Cyril Fernandes.
Res.: 12305 Arcola Rd., 46818. Tel: 260-625-4151; Fax: 260-625-3095.
Catechesis / Religious Program—Tel: 260-625-4104. Students 100.

Auburn, De Kalb Co., Immaculate Conception (1872), [CEM] Rev. Charles A. Herman.
Res.: 500 E. 7th St., 46706. Tel: 260-925-3930; Fax: 260-925-3186.
Catechesis / Religious Program—Tel: 260-925-1621. Phyllis Gurtner, D.R.E.; Karen Wrona, D.R.E. Students 215.

Avilla, Noble Co., St. Mary of the Assumption (1853), [CEM] Rev. Daniel Durkin.
Res.: 228 N. Main St., Box 700, 46710-0700. Tel: 260-897-3261; Fax: 260-897-3261.
School—232 N. Main St., 46710. Tel: 260-897-3481; Fax: 260-897-3706. Mrs. Kathy Garlitz, Prin. Franciscan Sisters of the Sacred Heart 2; Lay Teachers 8; Students 183.
Catechesis / Religious Program—Students 105.

Besancon, Allen Co., St. Louis (1846), (French), [CEM 2] Rev. Stephen E. Colchin.
Res.: 15535 Lincoln Hwy. E., New Haven, 46774. Tel: 260-749-4525.
School—(Grades PreK-8), 15529 Lincoln Hwy. E., New Haven, 46774. Tel: 260-749-5815; Fax: 260-749-5815. Ms. Agnes Hart, Prin. Lay Teachers 6; Students 85.

Big Long Lake, LaGrange Co., St. Mary of the Angels (1937), Rev. Phillip Ley, O.F.M.Conv.
Rectory—St. Anthony Rectory, 700 W. Maumee, Angola, 46703. Tel: 260-665-2259; Fax: 260-665-2268.
Church: Hudson, 46747. Tel: 260-351-2404.
Catechesis / Religious Program—Tel: 260-351-2964. Students 18.

Bluffton, Wells Co., St. Joseph (1875), Rev. Dale Bauman.
Res.: 1300 N. Main St., 46714. Tel: 260-824-3597; Fax: 260-824-2792.
Catechesis / Religious Program—Tel: 260-824-5395. Students 139.

Bremen, Marshall Co., St. Dominic (1947), [JC] Rev. Polycarp Fernando.
Church: 212 N. Maryland St., 46506. Tel: 574-546-3601; Fax: 574-546-3659.
Catechesis / Religious Program—803 W. Bike St., 46506. Students 302.

Bristol, Elkhart Co., St. Mary of the Annunciation (1942), [JC] Rev. James F. Seculoff.
Res.: 411 W. Vistula St., Box 245, 46507. Tel: 574-848-4305; Fax: 574-848-4305.
Catechesis / Religious Program—Students 346.

Churubusco, Whitley Co., St. John Bosco (1971), Rev. Danny Pinto (Sri Lanka), Admin.

Res.: 216 N. Main St., 46723. Tel: 260-693-9578; Fax: 260-693-1608.
Catechesis/Religious Program—Tel: 260-693-3332. Students 132.

CLEAR LAKE, STEUBEN CO., ST. PAUL CHAPEL (1941), Rev. Philip Schneider, O.F.M.Conv., Admin.
Rectory—St. Anthony Rectory, 700 W. Maumee, Angola, 46703. Tel: 260-665-2259; Fax: 260-665-2268.
Church: 8780 E. 700 N., 46703. Tel: 260-495-9913.
Catechesis/Religious Program—Tel: 260-238-2047. Joyce Hook, D.R.E. Students 44.

COLUMBIA CITY, WHITLEY CO., ST. PAUL OF THE CROSS (1860), [CEM] [JC] Rev. Lawrence A. Kramer.
Mailing Address: 315 S. Line St., 46725.
Res.: 308 S. Chaucey St., 46725. Tel: 260-244-5723; Fax: 260-244-2833.
Catechesis/Religious Program—Tel: 260-244-2926. Students 218.

CULVER, MARSHALL CO., ST. MARY OF THE LAKE, [JC] Rev. Glenn Kohrman.
Res.: 124 College Ave., 46511. Tel: 574-842-2522; Fax: 574-842-2549.
Catechesis/Religious Program—Tel: 574-842-3667. Students 137.

DECATUR, ADAMS CO., ST. MARY (1840), (German), [CEM] Rev. Philip DeVolder; Sisters Margaret Rose Donnelly, S.S.N.D., Pastoral Assoc.; M. Rosellyn Theisen, S.N.D., Small Christian Communities; Deacon Isaac McDonald; Kristine Poque, Devel. Dir.
Res.: 414 W. Madison St., P.O. Box 207, 46733. Tel: 260-724-9159; Fax: 260-724-8948.
School—St. Joseph, 127 N. Fourth St., 46733. Tel: 260-724-2765; Fax: 260-724-4953. Karla Hormann, Prin. Lay Teachers 20; Students 362.
Catechesis/Religious Program—Fax: 260-724-9380. Teresa Schurger, D.R.E. Students 175.

EGE, NOBLE CO., IMMACULATE CONCEPTION (1876), [CEM] Attended by, St. John Bosco, Churubusco. Rev. Danny Pinto (Sri Lanka), Admin.
216 N. Main St., Churubusco, 46723. Tel: 260-693-9578; Fax: 260-693-1608.
Catechesis/Religious Program—Students 74.

ELKHART, ELKHART CO.
1—ST. THOMAS THE APOSTLE (1949), [JC] Rev. William Sullivan.
Res.: 1405 N. Main St., 46514. Tel: 574-262-1505; Fax: 574-264-4186.
School—1331 N. Main St., 46514. Tel: 574-264-4855; Fax: 574-262-8477. Lay Teachers 24; Students 370.
Catechesis/Religious Program—Tel: 574-264-0491. Students 133.

2—ST. VINCENT DE PAUL (1868), [CEM] Revs. John Overmyer; Wilson O. Corzo (Colombia); Deacon Ramiro Reyes.
Res.: 1108 S. Main St., 46516. Tel: 574-293-8231; Fax: 574-293-1105.
School—(Grades PreK-6), 1114 S. Main St., 46516. Tel: 574-293-8451; Fax: 574-295-9702. Ms. Donna Quinn, Prin. Lay Teachers 8; Students 175.
Catechesis/Religious Program—Tel: 574-293-8071. Sr. Eileen Daudlin, S.S.N.D., D.R.E.; Mrs. Vickie Bayer, D.R.E. Students 373.

GARRETT, DE KALB CO., ST. JOSEPH (1876), [CEM] Rev. Thomas Lombardi; Deacon Harris Hoeffel.
Office—300 W. Houston, 46738-1424. Tel: 260-357-3122.
Res.: 307 S. Ijams St., 46738.
School—(Grades PreK-6), 301 W. Houston, 46738. Tel: 260-357-5137; Fax: 260-357-5138. Ms. Linda Speer, Prin. Lay Teachers 7; Students 123.
Catechesis/Religious Program—Tel: 260-357-1604. Students 21.

GENEVA, ADAMS CO., ST. MARY OF THE PRESENTATION (1883), [CEM] Rev. J. Bosco Perera (Sri Lanka).
Res.: 5790 E. 1100 S., 46740-9132. Tel: 260-997-6558; Fax: 260-997-6558.
Catechesis/Religious Program—Students 30.

GOSHEN, ELKHART CO., ST. JOHN THE EVANGELIST (1840), [CEM] Revs. John H. Delaney; Constantina Rocha (Mexico); Deacon N. Arthur Bleau.
Res.: 109 W. Monroe St., 46526. Tel: 574-533-3385; Fax: 574-533-1814.
School—117 W. Monroe, 46526. Tel: 574-533-9480. Rose Smith, Prin. Sisters 1; Lay Teachers 8; Students 150.
Catechesis/Religious Program—Jodi Magallanes, D.R.E. Students 239.

GRANGER, ST. JOSEPH CO., ST. PIUS X (1955), Revs. William C. Schooler; Daniel D. Scheidt.
Res.: 52553 Fir Rd., 46530. Tel: 574-272-8462; Fax: 574-272-8493.
Catechesis/Religious Program—Tel: 574-277-5760. Students 1,080.

HUNTINGTON, HUNTINGTON CO.
1—ST. MARY (1896), [JC] Rev. Gary L. Sigler.
Office & Res.: 903 N. Jefferson St., 46750. Tel: 260-356-4398; Fax: 260-356-3529.
School—Huntington Catholic School, Primary Building, 820 Cherry St., 46750. Tel: 260-356-2320. (Consolidated with SS. Peter and Paul) Lay Teachers 15; Students 227.
Middle Building—960 Warren St., 46750. Tel: 260-356-1926; Fax: 260-356-8419. Mr. Jason Schiffli, Prin.
Catechesis/Religious Program—Students 145.

2—SS. PETER AND PAUL (1843), [JC] Revs. Ronald Rieder, O.F.M.Cap.; John C. Guimond, O.F.M.Cap. (Retired).
Res.: 860 Cherry St., 46750. Tel: 260-356-4798; Fax: 260-356-7154.
School—Huntington Catholic School, Tel: 260-356-2320; Fax: 260-359-8419. (See St. Mary for details)
Catechesis/Religious Program—Sr. Miriam Gill, S.S.N.D., D.R.E. Students 225.

KENDALLVILLE, NOBLE CO., IMMACULATE CONCEPTION (1867), Rev. Jacob M. Gall.
Res.: 319 E. Diamond St., 46755. Tel: 260-347-2522; Fax: 260-347-9829.
Catechesis/Religious Program—Tel: 260-347-2635. Students 67.

LAGRANGE, LAGRANGE CO., ST. JOSEPH (1930), [JC] Rev. Paul Faroh, O.F.M.Conv.
Res.: 050 N. 100 E., 46761. Tel: 260-463-3472.
Catechesis/Religious Program—Students 120.

LAGRO, WABASH CO., ST. PATRICK (1838), Closed. For inquiries for parish records contact the chancery.

LAKEVILLE, ST. JOSEPH CO., SACRED HEART (1932), [JC] Rev. Thomas King, C.S.C.
Res.: 63568 U.S. 31 S., 46614-9409. Tel: 574-291-2826; Fax: 574-291-3775.
Catechesis/Religious Program—Tel: 574-784-2579. Students 79.

LIGONIER, NOBLE CO., ST. PATRICK (1860), [JC] Revs. Babasino Fernandes (India); Jose Villanueva (Mexico).
Res.: 403 Ravine Park Dr., 46767-1301. Tel: 260-894-4946; Fax: 260-894-4911.
Catechesis/Religious Program—Students 198.

MILFORD, KOSCIUSKO CO., OUR LADY OF GUADALUPE (1972), (Hispanic), Rev. Paul Bueter.
Res.: 125 N. Harrison, Warsaw, 46580. Tel: 574-267-5842, Ext. 115; Fax: 574-268-1030.
Church: P.O. Box 605, 46542. Tel: 574-658-9384.
Catechesis/Religious Program—Students 59.

MISHAWAKA, ST. JOSEPH CO.
1—ST. BAVO (1903), Rev. Barry C. England; Deacon Kevin M. Ranaghan.
Res.: 511 W. 7th St., 46544. Tel: 574-255-1437; Fax: 574-255-0404.
School—524 W. 8th St., 46544. Tel: 574-259-4214; Fax: 574-258-0403. Linda Hixon, Prin. Lay Teachers 13; Students 270.
Catechesis/Religious Program—Students 119.

2—ST. JOSEPH (1848), [CEM] Rev. Robert A. Yast; Deacon Ronald Moser.
Res.: 225 S. Mill St., 46544. Tel: 574-255-6134; Fax: 574-255-6387.
School—220 W. 4th St., 46544. Tel: 574-255-5554; Fax: 574-255-6381. Mrs. Mary Geist, Prin. Lay Teachers 13; Students 229.
Catechesis/Religious Program—Students 85.

3—ST. MICHAEL UKRAINIAN CATHOLIC CHURCH (1916), (Ukrainian), [CEM] [JC] Rev. Thomas R. Dobrowolski.
Res.: 712 E. Lawrence St., 46545-6835. Tel: 574-259-7173.
Catechesis/Religious Program—Students 13.

4—ST. MONICA (1915), Rev. James Stoyle. In Res., Rev. Paulinus Odozor, C.S.Sp.
Res.: 222 W. Mishawaka Ave., 46545. Tel: 574-255-2247; Fax: 574-255-8375.
Ministries Bldg.—214 W. Mishawaka Ave., 46545. Tel: 574-255-1957.
School—223 W. Grove St., 46545. Tel: 574-255-0709; Fax: 574-258-5969. Sr. Pat Gavin, S.S.N.D., Prin. Sisters 1; Lay Teachers 15; Students 228.
Catechesis/Religious Program—Scott Hibbs, D.R.E. Students 39.

5—QUEEN OF PEACE (1957), Rev. Richard Hire; Carol Cone, Pastoral Assoc.
Res.: 4508 Vistula Rd., 46544. Tel: 574-255-9674; Fax: 574-255-9675.
Catechesis/Religious Program—Tel: 574-255-0392; Fax: 574-255-1029. Students 150.

MONROEVILLE, ALLEN CO., ST. ROSE OF LIMA (1888), [CEM] Rev. Stephen Colchin.
Res.: P.O. Box 406, 46773. Tel: 260-623-3437.
School—St. Joseph, 209 Mulberry St., 46773. Tel: 260-623-3447; Fax: 260-623-3447. Ms. Carolyn Kirkendall, Prin. Lay Teachers 5; Students 76.
Catechesis/Religious Program—Tel: 260-749-2841. Students 27.

NAPANEE, ELKHART CO., ST. ISIDORE, Closed. For inquiries for parish records contact the chancery.

NEW CARLISLE, ST. JOSEPH CO., ST. STANISLAUS KOSTKA (1884), (Polish), Rev. John Klimczyk.
Res.: 55756 Tulip Rd., 46552. Tel: 574-654-3781; Fax: 574-654-3781.
Catechesis/Religious Program—Tel: 574-654-8738. Mrs. Elisa Berger, D.R.E. Students 96.

NEW HAVEN, ALLEN CO., ST. JOHN THE BAPTIST (1859), [CEM] Rev. Paul McCarthy.
Res.: 943 Powers St., 46774. Tel: 260-493-4553; Fax: 260-749-6164.
School—206 Rufus St., 46774. Tel: 260-749-9903; Fax: 260-749-6047. Janice Comito, Prin. Lay Teachers 20; Students 378.
Catechesis/Religious Program—Tel: 260-493-3044. Students 165.

NIX SETTLEMENT, WHITLEY CO., ST. CATHARINE (1850), [CEM] Rev. Kenneth J. Sarrazine.
St. Joseph Rectory: 641 N. Main St., P.O. Box 250, Roanoke, 46783-0250. Tel: 260-672-2838; Fax: 260-672-3069.
Church: Ind. Hwy. 9 & Whitley Co. Rd., 1,000 S., 46783.
Catechesis/Religious Program—Dr. Kathleen Schneider, D.R.E. Students 32.

NORTH MANCHESTER, WABASH CO., ST. ROBERT BELLARMINE (1963), [JC] Rev. Ronald Ramenaden.
Res.: 1203 State Rd., 114 E., 46962. Tel: 260-982-4404; Fax: 260-982-6979.
Catechesis/Religious Program—Students 53.

NOTRE DAME, ST. JOSEPH CO., SACRED HEART (1842), [CEM] [JC] Rev. John Patrick Riley, C.S.C.
Res.: 104 The Presbytery, 46556-5658. Tel: 574-631-7511; 574-631-7512; Fax: 574-631-8080.
Catechesis/Religious Program—Tel: 574-631-9436; Fax: 574-631-9687. Students 30.

PIERCETON, KOSCIUSKO CO., ST. FRANCIS XAVIER (1841), [CEM] Rev. Bruce Piechocki.
Mailing Address: P.O. Box 376, 46562.
Church: 408 W. Catholic St., 46562. Tel: 574-594-5750; Fax: 574-594-2347.
Catechesis/Religious Program—Tel: 574-594-5750, Ext. 12. Students 68.

PLYMOUTH, MARSHALL CO., ST. MICHAEL (1862), [CEM] Revs. William Kummer; Edward Ssebbowa.
Office: 611 N. Center St., 46563.
Res.: 612 N. Walnut St., 46563. Tel: 574-936-4935; Fax: 574-936-9293.
School—(Grades PreK-8), 612 N. Center St., 46563. Tel: 574-936-4329; Fax: 574-936-1151. Miss Gertrude Nawara, Prin. Lay Teachers 12; Students 231.
Catechesis/Religious Program—Sr. Rose Andre Miller, D.R.E. Students 143.

ROANOKE, HUNTINGTON CO., ST. JOSEPH (1867), [CEM] Rev. Kenneth J. Sarrazine.
Res.: 641 N. Main St., P.O. Box 250, 46783-0250. Tel: 260-672-2838; Fax: 260-672-3069.
Catechesis/Religious Program—Dr. Kathleen Schneider, D.R.E. Students 53.

ROME CITY, NOBLE CO., ST. GASPAR DEL BUFALO (1957), [CEM] Rev. Charles F. Mullen, C.PP.S.
Res.: 10871 N. State Rd. 9, 46784. Tel: 260-854-3100.
Catechesis/Religious Program—Tel: 260-854-2106. Students 57.

SYRACUSE, KOSCIUSKO CO., ST. MARTIN DE PORRES (1966), Rev. Terry E. Place.
Res.: 6941 E. Waco Dr., 46567-9496. Tel: 574-457-3528; Fax: 574-457-3542.
Catechesis/Religious Program—Tel: 574-457-8176. Students 100.

WABASH, WABASH CO., ST. BERNARD (1864), Rev. Sextus Don (Sri Lanka); Deacon Ted Krizman.
Res.: 207 N. Cass St., 46992. Tel: 260-563-4750; Fax: 260-563-0313.
School—(Grades PreK-4), 191 N. Cass St., 46992. Tel: 260-563-5746; Fax: 260-563-4898. Sr. Marilyn Ellert, Prin. Lay Teachers 6; Students 86.
Catechesis/Religious Program—Students 49.

WALKERTON, ST. JOSEPH CO., ST. PATRICK (1856), Rev. Michael J. Winkowski, C.PP.S.
Office—807 Tyler St., 46574. Tel: 574-586-7401; Fax: 574-586-7401.
Res.: 801 Tyler St., 46574. Tel: 574-586-7404.
School—811 Tyler St., 46574. Tel: 574-586-7405; Fax: 574-586-7405. Patricia Morris, Prin. Sisters of St. Joseph of the Third Order of St. Francis 1; Lay Teachers 4; Students 48.
Catechesis/Religious Program—Tel: 574-586-3590. Mrs. Evelyn Rudecki, D.R.E. Students 60.

WARSAW, KOSCIUSKO CO., SACRED HEART (1852), [JC] Rev. Msgr. James J. Wolf.
Res.: 125 N. Harrison St., 46580. Tel: 574-267-5842; Fax: 574-268-1030.
School—135 N. Harrison, 46590. Tel: 574-267-5874; Fax: 574-267-5136. Mr. William Landrigan, Prin. Lay Teachers 13; Students 210.
Catechesis/Religious Program—Students 369.

WATERLOO, DEKALB CO., ST. MICHAEL THE ARCHANGEL (1880), Rev. David Carkenord.
Res.: 1098 County Road 39, 46793-9779. Tel: 260-837-7115; Fax: 260-837-7727.
Catechesis/Religious Program—Students 147.

YODER, ALLEN CO., ST. ALOYSIUS (1859), Rev. Dominique A. Carboneau.
Res.: 14623 Bluffton Rd., 46798-9741. Tel: 260-622-4491.

School—14607 Bluffton Rd., 46798-9741. Tel: 260-622-7151; Fax: 260-622-7961. Kimberly Reber, Prin. Lay Teachers 8; Students 112.
Catechesis/Religious Program—Students 60.

Chaplains of Public Institutions

FORT WAYNE. *St. Joseph Medical Center*, 700 Broadway, 46802-1402. Tel: 260-425-3000. Rev. Daniel Chukwuleta, Chap.
Lutheran Hospital, Tel: 260-435-7001. Roseann Bloomfield. Tel: 260-435-7722.
Parkview Memorial Hospital, Tel: 260-484-6636, Ext. 26311. Rev. Robert D'Souza (India), Chap.
Veterans Administration Hospital. Rev. Daniel R. Leeuw, Chap.

On Special Assignment:
Revs.—
McNulty, Patrick J., Madonna House, Combermere ON K0J 1L0 Canada.
Piechocki, Bruce, Officialis of Diocese, Chancery

Retired:
Rev. Msgrs.—
Contant, Robert, St. Charles Seminary, Carthagena, OH 45822. Tel: 419-925-4516, Ext. 304
Faber, William, St. Anne Home, 1900 Randallia Dr., 46805. Tel: 260-471-0795
Hession, Edward I., 4827 Woodmark Ct., 46815. Tel: 260-483-2567
Lester, J. William, P.A., Cathedral of the Immaculate Conception, 1122 S. Clinton St., P.O. Box 10898, 46854-0898. Tel: 260-424-1485
Revs.—
Balzer, Raymond, 2 Northway Dr., Huntington, 46750. Tel: 260-355-0140
Cis, James, Albertine Home, 1501 Hoffman St., Hammond, 46327. Tel: 219-933-4378
Dombrowski, Robert J., 190 Hummingbird Ln., Eureka Springs, AR 72632. Tel: 479-253-5491
Doriot, Thomas E., 2637 Fulton Ave., #232, Sacramento, CA 95821. Tel: 916-484-6145
Hammond, Robert, St. Anne Home, 1900 Randallia Dr., 46805. Tel: 260-482-7954
Hodde, William, Saint Anne Home, 1900 Randallia Dr., 46805. Tel: 260-483-7708
Hoevel, Robert J., St. Anne Home, 1900 Randallia Dr., #1023, 46805. Tel: 260-484-0051
Isenbarger, Donald, 1523 Summit St., Apt. 7, New Haven, 46774. Tel: 260-750-5775
Kazmekcziak, Eugene, 1407 Vans Rd., Fulton, IL 61252. Tel: 309-887-9506
Koers, Eugene, 510 E. Dewald, 46803. Tel: 260-745-7101
Miller, Elden J., 10701 N. Oak Knoll E., Rome City, 46784.
Miller, Paul D., 1023 Daly Dr., New Haven, 46774.
Molnar, Anthony
Narcowich, Edward, St. Mary Assumption, 228 N. Main St., P.O. Box 700, Avilla, 46710-0700. Tel: 260-897-4254
O'Connor, James J., 6006 Chapel Pines Run, 46804. Tel: 260-436-1703
Peil, William, 1841 N. Anthony, 46805. Tel: 260-422-1950
Rose, James, 2781 Huycks, Coldwater, MI 49036. Tel: 518-238-5522
Ruetz, Edward J., 621 Portage, 46616. Tel: 574-234-5652
Schmitt, Adam, St. Joseph Church, 190 Hale Ave., 46802. Tel: 260-432-5113
Sienkiewicz, Matthew, 10980 Three Oaks Rd., Three Oaks, MI 49128. Tel: 616-756-6316
Tippmann, Laurence, 113 W. Wayne, Ste. 209, 46802.
Traub, Robert, Saint Anne Home, 1900 Randallia Dr., 46805. Tel: 260-272-9982

Permanent Deacons:
Baumgartner, Paul E., 417 Howard St., 46617.
Bleau, N. Arthur, 64429 Pleasant Pl., Goshen, 46526.
Dits, Paul, 17433 Battles Rd., Mishawaka, 46544.
Egendoerfer, Eugene, 218 Palm Blvd., Parish, FL 32419-9107.
Folds, Milton, P.O. Box 202, Churubusco, 46723.
Gizzi, Emilio, 238 Eckman, 46614.
Hilger, Edward, 30865 Hunters Dr., Apt. 2, Farmington Hills, MI 48334.
Hoeffel, Harris H., 401 S. Harrison, Garrett, 46738.
Krizman, Ted, Box 134 W. Sinclair, Wabash, 46992.
Kuspa, Ervin, 434 S. Liberty, 46619.
Larson, Fred J., 1001 Bell, New Haven, 46774.
Loving, Peter, 3730 Stillwater Pl., 46808.
Lyczak, Edward, 4645 Mariner Blvd., Brooksville, FL 34609.
McDougall, Louis, 3419 Sanibel Dr., 46815.
Medina, Ricardo, III, Elkhart Community Center, 201 S. Second St., Elkhart, 46516.
Messina, Joseph, 1443 Loman Court, Palm Harbor, FL 34683.
Miller, Brian L., 2120 E. Jefferson, 46617.
Moser, Ronald J., 51812 Whitestable, 46627.
Ranaghan, Kevin, 1003 St. Vincent, 46617.
Salinas, Rogelio, 30492 Co. Rd. 38, Wakarusa, 46573.
Szynski, Eugene, Holy Family, 56405 Mayflower Rd., 46619.
Tucker, Dean, 4808 6th St. W., Lehigh Acres, FL 33971.
Walsh, Francis, 2515 Clifton Hills Dr., 46808.
Walsh, James M., 2212 Broadmoor Dr., Elkhart, 46514.
Zickgraf, Joseph R., P.O. Box 515, Columbia City, 46725.

INSTITUTIONS LOCATED IN THE DIOCESE

[A] SEMINARIES, RELIGIOUS, OR SCHOLASTICATES

NOTRE DAME. *Moreau Seminary*, P.O. Box 668, 46556. Tel: 574-631-7735; Fax: 574-631-9233. This is a college level and Theological Seminary run by the Indiana Province of the Congregation of Holy Cross for Religious Priesthood and Brotherhood candidates. Priests 15; Seminarians 35; Total Staff 12.
Formation Staff: Revs. James Flanigan, C.S.C.; James K. Foster, C.S.C.; Charles B. Gordon, C.S.C.; Wilson D. Miscamble, C.S.C., Supr. & Rector; Patrick M. Neary, C.S.C., Asst. Supr.; Peter D. Rocca, C.S.C.; Sisters Susan Bruno, O.S.F.; Susan Dunn, O.P.; Carrine Etheridge, I.H.M.; Jean Lenz, O.S.F.; Bros. Edward C. Luther, C.S.C; Jerome Meyer, C.S.C. In Res. Revs. Michael Baxter, C.S.C.; David B. Burrell, C.S.C.; Alfred F. D'Alonzo, C.S.C.; Maurice D'Souza, C.S.C.; James Flanigan, C.S.C.; Mark Ghyselinck, C.S.C.; Paul V. Kollman, C.S.C.; Anthony Lee; Thomas McNally, C.S.C.; Wilson D. Miscamble, C.S.C.; Patrick Neary, C.S.C.; Martin Lan Nguyen, C.S.C.; Roberta Rivera; Peter D. Rocca, C.S.C.; David Schlaver, C.S.C.; Thomas Tusingwire; Herbert Yost, C.S.C.; Bros. Thomas Dziekan, C.S.C.; Robert Ewald, C.S.C.; James E. Gormley, C.S.C.; James Lakofka, C.S.C.; John Platte, C.S.C.
Vocations Office: Revs. James B. King, C.S.C., Dir.; Kevin Russeau, C.S.C.
Old College, Box 638, 46556-0638. Tel: 574-631-7881; Fax: 574-631-0111. Email: CharlesB.Gordon.20@nd.edu. Web: www.nd.edu/7Evocation/OldCollege.html. Rev. Charles B. Gordon, C.S.C., Dir. & Contact Person. College candidates study here for up to three years before entering Moreau Seminary. Priests 1; Brothers 2; Candidates for the Priesthood in the First Three Years of Undergraduate Formation 9; Sisters 1; Lay Teachers 2; Total Staff 5.

[B] COLLEGES AND UNIVERSITIES

FORT WAYNE. *University of Saint Francis*, 2701 Spring St., 46808-3994. Tel: 260-434-3100; Fax: 260-434-3246. Email: ekriss@sf.edu. Web: www.sf.edu. Sr. M. Elise Kriss, O.S.F., Pres.; Rev. James Sapp (WH), Resident Chap. Conducted by Sisters of St. Francis of Perpetual Adoration. Priests 1; Sisters 7; Students 1,800; Lay Teachers 112; Total Staff 141.

DONALDSON. *Ancilla Domini College* Tel: 574-936-8898; Fax: 574-935-1773. Email: admissions@ancilla.edu. Web: www.ancilla.edu. P.O. Box 1, 46513. Dr. Robert Abene, Pres.; Rev. Samuel Boys, Coord. Pastoral Min.; Raymond Girres, Business Officer; Dr. Dianne Rasch, Academic Dean; Sharon Blubaugh, Registrar; Steven Olson, Dir. Enrollment Mgmt.; Glenda Bockman, Head Librarian; Donna Pontius, Dir. Institute Advancement. Poor Handmaids of Jesus Christ (Ancilla Domini Sisters) Sisters 4; Lay Teachers 46; Students 546.

NOTRE DAME. *Holy Cross College, Holy Cross College, Inc.*, 54515 State Rd., 933 N., 46556-0308. Tel: 574-239-8400; Fax: 574-233-7427. Email: rgilman@hcc-nd.edu. Web: www.hcc-nd.edu. Bro. Richard Gilman, C.S.C., Pres.; R. Douglas Irvine, Dir. Financial Aid; Mark P. Mullaney, Vice Pres. Admin.; Bro. Charles Gregg, C.S.C., Librarian; Richard J. Sullivan, Registrar; Vincent M. Duke, Dir. Admissions; Robert Kloska, Dir. Campus Ministry; Tina Holland, Vice Pres. Student Affairs; Daniel Cochran, Dir. Residence Life; William Mangan, Vice Pres. Academic Affairs; Bro. Chris Dreyer, C.S.C., Dir. Student Counseling Svcs.
Legal Title: *Holy Cross College, Inc.* Priests 5; Sisters 3; Brothers 10; Lay Professors 28; Lay Teachers 16; Students 491; Total Staff 31.
Saint Mary's College 46556. Tel: 574-284-4556; Fax: 574-284-4707. Email: lhitch@stmarys.edu. Web: www.saintmarys.edu. Marilou Eldred, Pres. Sisters of the Holy Cross, An institution of higher education for women. Sisters 1; Lay Professors 143; Students 1,475.
**University of Notre Dame Du Lac* (1842), Provost Office, 300 Main Bldg., 46556. Tel: 574-631-5000; 574-631-5090 (Provost); Fax: 574-631-6897. Email: rodebush.1@nd.edu. Web: www.nd.edu. The Graduate School (29 departments). The Law School. The Undergraduate School (four colleges, 36 departments). Institutes and Radiation Laboratory, Center for Study of Man, Institute for Urban Studies and Institute for International Studies. Priests 71; Sisters 7; Total Staff 1,606; Total Enrollment 11,311.
Officers Group: Revs. Peter A. Jarret, C.S.C., Counselor to the Pres.; John I. Jenkins, C.S.C., Vice Pres. & Assoc. Provost; Edward A. Malloy, C.S.C., Pres.; Mark L. Poorman, C.S.C., Vice Pres. Student Affairs; William D. Seetch, C.S.C., Rel. Supr.; John Affleck-Graves, Ph.D., Vice Pres. & Assoc. Provost; Matthew S. Cullinan, Exec. Asst. to Pres.; J. Roberto Gutierrez, Vice Pres. for Public Affairs & Communications; Nathan O. Hatch, Ph.D., Provost; Chandra Johnson, Asst. to the Pres.; Carol C. Kaesebier, J.D., Vice Pres. & General Counsel; Jeffrey C. Kantor, Ph.D., Vice Pres. Graduate Studies & Research; James J. Lyphout, Vice Pres. for Business Operations; Scott C. Malpass, M.B.A., Vice Pres. & Chief Investment Officer; Carol A. Mooney, J.D., Vice Pres. & Assoc. Provost; Louis M. Nanni, Vice Pres. Univ. Rels.; Maura A. Ryan, Assoc. Provost; John A. Sejdinaj, Vice Pres. for Finance.
Administrative Group: Sisters Mary L. Gude, C.S.C., Asst. Vice Pres. Student Affairs; Jean Lenz, O.S.F., Asst. Vice Pres. for Student Affairs; Jill Bodensteiner, Assoc. Vice Pres. & Counsel; Gilberto Cardenas, Asst. Provost for Inst. Relations & Diversity; William Hoye, Assoc. Vice Pres. & Deputy Gen. Counsel; Dr. Anthony Hyder, Assoc. Vice Pres. Graduate School; Philip J. Iapalucci Jr., Dir. Audit & Advisory Svcs.; William W. Kirk, Assoc. Vice Pres. for Residence Life; Jennifer Monahan, Asst. to the Vice Pres. Student Affairs; David Moss, Asst. Vice Pres. Student Affairs; Iris Outlaw, Multicultural Student Programs & Svcs.; Dr. James H. Powell, Assoc. Dean & Dir. Summer Session; Daniel J. Saracino, Asst. Provost, Admissions; Joy Vann-Hamilton, Asst. Provost; Kevin M. White, Dir. Athletics; Jennifer Younger, Dir. Univ. Libraries.
Assistant Vice Presidents & Counsels: Terrence J. Akai, Assoc. Dean Graduate School; Rhonda L. Brown, Dir. Institute Equity; Shannon Cullinan, Univ. Relations; Peter Diffley, Assoc. Dean Graduate School; Timothy J. Flanagan; David Harr, Asst. Vice Pres. Auxiliary Svcs.; Lois C. Jackson; Charles F. Lennon Jr., Assoc. Vice Pres. Univ. Rels.; Carl T. Magel, Dir. Univ. Communications Design; Mary Ellen McGillian, Asst. Vice Pres. for Devel.; Dennis K. Moore, Assoc. Vice Pres. Public Relations; Harold L. Pace, Registrar; Andrew M. Paluf, Asst. Vice Pres. Finance & Controller; Janice Poorman, Assoc. Dean Graduate Admissions; Donald B. Pope-Davis, Assoc.Vice Pres. & Assoc. Dean Graduate School; Mary E. Pugel, Exec. Asst. to the Provost; Daniel G. Reagan, Assoc. Vice Pres. for Univ. Relations; Tim Rippinger, Vice. Pres. for Devel.; Joseph A. Russo, Dir. Financial Aid; Matthew V. Storin, Assoc. Vice Pres News & Information; Barbara Turpin, Assoc. Dean Graduate School; Kevin White, Dir. Athletics; Diane Wilson, Asst. Dean Graduate School; Gordon D. Wishon, Assoc. Vice Pres. & Chief Information Officer.
C.S.C. Faculty & Personnel: Revs. Robert J. Austgen, C.S.C.; Nicholas Ayo, C.S.C.; Leonard N. Banas, C.S.C.; Ernest J. Bartell, C.S.C.; Michael J. Baxter, C.S.C.; Thomas E. Blantz, C.S.C.; James Bracke, C.S.C. (CHI); Richard S. Bullene, C.S.C.; David B. Burrell, C.S.C.; Joe Carey, C.S.C.; Austin I. Collins, C.S.C.; John E. Conley, C.S.C.; Michael Connors, C.S.C.; Alfred F. D'Alonzo, C.S.C.; Robert A. Dowd, C.S.C; Paul F. Doyle, C.S.C.; John S. Dunne, C.S.C.; Clarence R. Durbin, C.S.C.; Carl F. Ebey, C.S.C.; Tom Eckert, C.S.C.; James F. Flanigan, C.S.C.; James K. Foster, C.S.C.; Patrick Gaffney, C.S.C.; Thomas E. Gaughan, C.S.C.; Charles Gordon, C.S.C.; Eugene F. Gorski, C.S.C.; Gregory A. Green, C.S.C.; Daniel Groody, C.S.C.; Theodore M. Hesburgh, C.S.C.; Peter A. Jarret, C.S.C.; John I. Jenkins, C.S.C., Vice. Pres. & Assoc. Provost; David Kashangaki, C.S.C.; James King, C.S.C.; Thomas P. King, C.S.C.; Jerome E. Knoll, C.S.C.; William Lies, C.S.C.; Edward A. Malloy, C.S.C., Pres.; Patrick H. Maloney, C.S.C.; James J. McGrath,

C.S.C.; Leon J. Mertensotto, C.S.C.; Matthew M. Miceli, C.S.C.; Wilson D. Miscamble, C.S.C.; Robert H. Moss, C.S.C.; Michael J. Murphy, C.S.C.; Pat Neary, C.S.C.; Martin Lam Nguyen, C.S.C.; Edward D. O'Connor, C.S.C.; William O'Connor, C.S.C.; Dan Parrish, C.S.C.; John H. Pearson, C.S.C.; Robert S. Pelton, C.S.C.; Mark L. Poorman, C.S.C., Vice Pres. Student Affairs; James L. Riehle, C.S.C.; John Riley, C.S.C.; Peter Rocca, C.S.C.; George A. Rozum, C.S.C.; Kevin Russeau, C.S.C.; Jeffrey Schneibel, C.S.C.; Timothy R. Scully, C.S.C.; William D. Seetch, C.S.C., Religious Supr.; William Simmons, C.S.C.; John Steele, C.S.C.; Thomas G. Streit, C.S.C.; Michael Bruce Sullivan, C.S.C.; Thomas Tallarida, C.S.C.; Mark Thesing, C.S.C.; Merwyn J. Thomas, C.S.C.; Joseph L. Walter, C.S.C.; Oliver F. Williams, C.S.C.; Bros. Francis Gorch, C.S.C.; Louis Hurcik, C.S.C.; Edward Luther, C.S.C.; Jerome Meyer, C.S.C.; Dennis Meyers, C.S.C.; Thomas Tucker, C.S.C.

Non-C.S.C. Religious Faculty: Revs. Joseph P. Amar (SAM); Paul F. Bradshaw; John J. Coughlin, O.F.M.; Brian Daley, S.J.; Michael Driscoll; Virgilio P. Elizondo; C. Lincoln Johnson; Maxwell E. Johnson; Richard P. McBrien; Ernan McMullin; John P. Meier; John A. Melloh, S.M.; Jerome H. Neyrey, S.J.; Marvin R. O'Connell; Thomas O'Meara, O.P.; Paulinus I. Odozor, C.S.Sp.; Hugh R. Page; Robert E. Sullivan; Joseph E. Weiss, S.J.; Sisters Eleanor Bernstein, C.S.J.; Kathleen Cannon, O.P.; Regina Coll, C.S.J.; Mary Catherine Hilkert, O.P.; Jean Lenz, O.S.F.; Mary Ann Mueninghoff, O.P.

[C] HIGH SCHOOLS, DIOCESAN

SOUTH BEND. *Saint Joseph's High School*, 1441 N. Michigan St., 46617. Tel: 574-233-6137; Fax: 574-232-3482. Email: sbdstjoehs@stjoe.k12.in.us. Web: www.SaintJoeHigh.com. Mrs. Kathleen Ratliff, Prin.; Mr. Jim Fitzpatrick, Vice Prin. Operations; Revs. Walter J. Bly; Christopher Young. Priests 2; Brothers of Holy Cross 1; Sisters of the Holy Cross 2; Lay Teachers 58; Students 754.

FORT WAYNE. *Bishop Dwenger High School*, 1300 E. Washington Center Rd., 46825. Tel: 260-496-4700; Fax: 260-496-4702. Email: bdhs@bishopdwenger.com. Web: www.bishopdwenger.com. Mr. J. Fred Tone, Prin.; Mr. Dan Swygart, Asst. Prin. Priests 1; Lay Teachers 67; Students 1,027; Total Staff 105.

Bishop Luers High School, 333 E. Paulding Rd., 46816. Tel: 260-456-1261; Fax: 260-456-1262. Email: mkeefer@bishopluers.org. Web: www.bishopluers.org. Mary Keefer, Prin.; Tracy Edgerton, Asst. Prin.; Revs. Lawrence A. Kramer, Chap.; Dominique Carboneau, Chap.; Joseph Rulli, Chap. Priests 1; Lay Teachers 40; Students 546.

MISHAWAKA. *Marian High School*, 1311 S. Logan St., 46544. Tel: 574-259-5257; Fax: 574-258-7668. Email: cmoretti@marianhs.org. Web: www.marianhs.org. Mr. Joseph Brettnacher, Prin.; Carol Miller, Pastoral Min. Priests 1; Sisters 3; Lay Teachers 51; Students 770.

[D] DIOCESAN ELEMENTARY SCHOOLS

FORT WAYNE. *Monsignor Julian Benoit Academy*, 3029 E. Paulding Rd., 46816. Tel: 260-447-5121; Fax: 260-447-4606. Email: baoffice@benoitacademy.com. Ms. Mary Schreiber, Prin. (Consolidation of Sacred Heart, St. Patrick's & St. Henry's Schools.) Lay Teachers 12; Students 134.

[E] GENERAL HOSPITALS

SOUTH BEND. *Saint Joseph Regional Medical Center - South Bend*, 801 E. LaSalle St., 46617. Tel: 574-237-7111; Fax: 574-271-7077. Email: breedenm@sjrmc.com. Web: www.sjmed.com. Nancy R. Hellyer, Pres. & CEO; Gary Perecko, Exec. Vice Pres.; Martin G. Breeden, P.H.J.C., Vice Pres., Mission Integration. Bed Capacity 339; Total Staff 1,479; Patients Assisted Annually 105,079.

Our Lady of Peace Hospital, Inc., 801 E. LaSalle Ave., 46617. Tel: 574-237-7457; Fax: 574-280-5889. Email: voordec@sjrmc.com. Web: www.sjmed.com. Christine T. Voorde, CEO; Sr. Gertrude Dolores, C.S.C., Pres.; Edward I. Friend, Vice Pres. Bed Capacity 32; Patients Assisted Annually 275; Total Staff 78.

MISHAWAKA. **Saint Joseph Regional Medical Center-Mishawaka*, 215 W. 4th St., 46544. Tel: 574-259-2431; Fax: 574-257-2831. Email: breedenm@sjrmc.com. Web: www.sjmed.com. Nancy R. Hellyer, Pres. & CEO; Lori Price, Exec. Vice Pres. & COO; Martin G. Breeden, P.H.J.C., Vice Pres. Mission Integration. Bed Capacity 100; Total Staff 554; Patients Assisted Annually 73,357.

PLYMOUTH. *Saint Joseph Regional Medical Center - Plymouth*, 1915 Lake Ave., P.O. Box 670, 46563. Tel: 574-936-3181; Fax: 574-935-2235. Email: breedenm@sjmc.com. Web: www.sjmed.com. Nancy R. Hellyer, Pres. & CEO; Lori Price, Exec. Vice Pres. & CEO; Martin G. Breeden, P.H.J.C., Vice Pres. Mission Integration. Staff 313; Bed Capacity 58; Patients Assisted Annually 66,526.

[F] SPECIAL HOSPITALS

NOTRE DAME. *University Health Services* 46556. Tel: 574-239-8013; Fax: 574-631-6047. Email: Ann.E.Kleva.4@nd.edu. Web: www.nd.edu/~uhs. Rev. Robert J. Austgen, C.S.C., Health Center Chap. Total Staff 47; Patients Assisted Annually 17,500.

[G] HOMES FOR THE AGED

FORT WAYNE. *Saint Anne Home & Retirement Community*, 1900 Randallia Dr., 46805. Tel: 260-484-5555; Fax: 260-482-8929. Email: sah1900@aol.com. Web: www.saintannehome.com. Mary E. Haverstick, Admin.; Rev. Frank Kronewitter, Chap. A Service of the Fort Wayne-South Bend Diocese, Inc. Staff 246; Residents 254. In Res. Revs. Robert Hammond; William Hodde (Retired); Robert Traub (Retired).

St. Anne Home of the Diocese of Fort Wayne - South Bend, Inc., 1900 Randalia Dr., 46805. Tel: 260-484-5555; Fax: 260-482-8929. Email: sah1900@aol.com. Web: www.saintannehome.com. Rev. Msgr. J. William Lester, P.A., Contact (Retired). Purpose: Nursing Home, Independent Living Units and Assisted Living Total Staff 246; Total in residence 153. In Res. Revs. Robert Fosselman; Robert Hammond; William Hodde (Retired); Robert Traub (Retired).

AVILLA. *Provena LaVerna Terrace*, 517 N. Main St., 46710. Tel: 260-897-2093; Fax: 260-897-2086. Email: sharonmckinley@provenahealth.com. Linda A. Simon, System Vice Pres. Mktg. & Planning; Sharon McKinley, Mgr.

Legal Title: *LaVerna Terrace Housing Corp.*, Conducted by Franciscan Sisters Health Care Corp. whose sole member is Provena Health. Total Staff 2; Apartments 51; Total Assisted 51. In Res. Rev. Daniel Leeuw. Tel: 260-897-3822.

Provena Sacred Heart Home, 515 N. Main St., 46710-9602. Tel: 260-897-2841; Fax: 260-897-3724. Email: CraigJProkupek@provenahealth.com. Web: www.provenahealth.com. Craig Prokupek, Admin.; Sr. Corde Miranda, O.S.F., Religious Leader; Rev. Daniel Leeuw, Chap.

Legal Title: *Provena Senior Services* Staff 160; Residents 128.

[H] PERSONAL PRELATURES

SOUTH BEND. *Prelature of the Holy Cross and Opus Dei*, Windmoor Center, 1121 N. Notre Dame Ave., 46617. Tel: 574-232-0550; Fax: 574-287-4798. Web: www.opusdei.org. Rev. Mark S. Mannion. Staff 4; Total in Residence 11.

[I] MONASTERIES AND RESIDENCES OF PRIESTS AND BROTHERS

SOUTH BEND. *Congregation of Holy Cross, Indiana Province, Provincial House*, 1304 E. Jefferson Blvd., 46617. Tel: 574-289-6850; Fax: 574-287-7307. Web: www.nd.edu/~vocation. *Provincial Administrative Offices*, 54515 State Rd. 933 N., P.O. Box 1064, Notre Dame, 46556-1064. Tel: 574-631-6196; Fax: 574-631-2999. Email: david.t.tyson.4@nd.edu. Revs. David T. Tyson, C.S.C., Prov.; Kenneth M. Molinaro, C.S.C., First Asst. Prov.; Anthony V. Szakaly, C.S.C., Second Asst. Prov.; E. William Beauchamp, C.S.C., Councilor; Thomas P. Doyle, C.S.C., Councilor; Thomas E. Chambers, C.S.C. (NO), Councilor; Peter A. Jarret, C.S.C., Councilor; John I. Jenkins, C.S.C., Councilor; Patrick M. Neary, C.S.C., Councilor; Claude Pomerleau, C.S.C. (A.), Councilor; Bro. Edward C. Lucher, C.S.C, Councilor.

Legal Title: *Priests of Holy Cross, Indiana Province, Inc.*

Holy Cross Priests Serving in Foreign Countries:

Chile:

Congregacion de Santa Cruz, Casilla 1271, Santiago 1, Chile. Tel: 56-2-673-3278; Fax: 56-2-206-9339. Revs. Donald G. Fetters, C.S.C., Dist. Supr.; Jose E. Ahumanda, C.S.C.; Gerald R. Barmasse, C.S.C.; Jorge A. Canepa, C.S.C.; Charles A. Delaney, C.S.C.; Fermin J. Donoso, C.S.C.; Joseph A. Dorsey, C.S.C.; Erwin A. Fonseca, C.S.C.; Roberto M. Gilbo, C.S.C.; Malcolm D. Johnson, C.S.C.; James E. McDonald, C.S.C.; Gerald T. Papen, C.S.C.; Pedro Parra, C.S.C.; Bro. Joaquin R. Parada, C.S.C.; Revs. Jorge Urtubia, C.S.C.; Robert L. Plasker, C.S.C.; Robert G. Simon, C.S.C.; Romulo E. Vera, C.S.C.; Gerald J. Whelan, C.S.C.

Peru:

Instituto de Estudios Aymaras, Apartado 295, Puno, Peru. Fax: 011-51-54-351574. Rev. Diego J. Yrarrazaval, C.S.C.

Apartado 313, Lima 36, Peru. Rev. Philip T. Devlin, C.S.C.

District of East Africa (Uganda):

Holy Cross Bugembe, P.O. Box 1037, Jinja, Uganda. Tel: 011-256-43-120013; Fax: 011-256-43-121322. Revs. Robert T. Hesse, C.S.C.; James E. Kelly, C.S.C.; Russell K. McDougall, C.S.C.; Robert Mugera, C.S.C.

Kyarusozi Parish Community, P.O. Box 46, Fort Portal, Uganda. Tel: 011-256-077-548-307. Revs. Lucius Atwine, C.S.C.; Aristides Massawe, C.S.C.; Richard L. Potthast, C.S.C.

Holy Cross Novitiate, Lake Saaka, P.O. Box 176, Fort Portal, Uganda. Tel: 011-256-77-609469. Revs. Francis J. Murphy, C.S.C.; Richard E. Stout, C.S.C.

Bishop McCauley House, P.O. Box 25827, Kampala, Uganda. Tel: 011-256-41-268325. Revs. James Burasa, C.S.C., District Supr.; Fulgentius Katende, C.S.C.

District of East Africa (Kenya):

P.O. Box 58078-00200, Nairobi, Kenya. Tel: 011-254-2-791157; Fax: 011-254-2-780506. Revs. Richard Kyazze, C.S.C.; Silvester Makwali, C.S.C.

Tanzania:

St. Brendan, P.O. Box 39, Karatu, Arusha, Tanzania. Revs. Andrew Massawe, C.S.C.; George Muganyizi, C.S.C.

McCauley House of Formation, Box 355-00517 Uhuru Gardens, Nairobi, Kenya. Tel: 011-254-2-601014. Rev. Willy Frank Lukati, C.S.C., McCauley House of Formation, Box 355-00517 Uhuru Gardens, Nairobi, Kenya. Tel: 011-254-2-601014.

On Leave for Higher Studies:

St. Anthony Parish, 1029 Monroe St., N.E., Washington, DC 20017. Tel: 202-635-0815. Revs. Gary S. Chamberland, C.S.C.; Stephen S. Wilbricht, C.S.C.

Holy Trinity Parish, 213 W. 82nd St., New York, NY 10024. Tel: 212-787-0634. Rev. William R. Dailey, C.S.C.

Our Lady Help of Christians Parish, 573 Washington St., Newton, MA 02458. Tel: 617-527-7560, Ext. 25. Revs. Thomas P. Doyle, C.S.C.; Sean D. McGraw, C.S.C.

Corby Hall, P.O. Box 514, Notre Dame, 46556. Tel: 574-631-7325; Fax: 574-631-6715. Rev. David Kashangaki, C.S.C.

325 Prior Ave. S., Saint Paul, MN 55105. Tel: 651-696-5426. Rev. James M. Lies, C.S.C.

Corpus Christi, 529 W. 121st St., New York, NY 10027. Tel: 212-662-6739. Rev. Randall C. Renter, C.S.C.

Military Chaplains:

LTCDR, CHC, USNR Commander, 1021 Daniel Ct., Jacksonville, NC 28540-6803. Tel: 910-455-0503. Rev. S. Douglas Smith, C.S.C.

411th BSB Chaplain's Office, CMR 419, Box 1811, APO AE09102. Tel: 011-49-06221-57-1570. Rev. Robert E. Roetzel, C.S.C.

Priests of the Province in Residences Not Listed Elsewhere:

c/o Provincial Administration Center, P.O. Box 1064, Notre Dame, 46556. Rev. J. David Burke, C.S.C.

Mathis House, P.O. Box 5, Dhaka 1000, Bangladesh. Tel: 011-880-2-832-695. Rev. James T. Banas, C.S.C.

3320 Toledo Pl. Apt. G, Hyattsville, MD 20782. Tel: 240-893-7273. Rev. Michael T. Belinsky, C.S.C.

Servants of the Paraclete, Louis Martin Villa, P.O. Box 10, Jemez Springs, NM 87025. Tel: 505-829-9606. Rev. Harold L. Bride, C.S.C.

Sacred Heart of Jesus, 139 S. Lopez, New Orleans, LA 70119-5109. Tel: 504-827-1481. Rev. Thomas E. Chambers, C.S.C. (NO).

Columba Hall, P.O. Box 47, Notre Dame, 46556. Tel: 219-631-8440. Rev. Maurice E. Amen, C.S.C.

Holy Cross Mission House, P.O. Box 929, Notre Dame, 46556-0929. Tel: 574-631-4757. Rev. Donald W. Dilg, C.S.C.

13645 Riverside Dr., Sherman Oaks, CA 91423. Tel: 818-386-1931. Rev. Lawrence E. Calhoun, C.S.C.

Stonehill College, 480 Washington St., North Easton, MA 02356. Tel: 508-238-4515. Revs. Harry B. Eichorn, C.S.C.; Richard E. Gribble, C.S.C.

Archdiocese of Anchorage, 225 Cordova St., Anchorage, AK 99501. Tel: 907-297-7734; Fax: 907-279-3885. Rev. LeRoy E. Clementich, C.S.C.

1406 Buffalo, Michigan City, 46360. Tel: 219-877-1532. Rev. Henry J. Lawrence, C.S.C.

Box 3908, Fremont, CA 94539. Tel: 510-659-9717. Rev. Charles W. Corso, C.S.C.

1800 E. Libra Dr., Tempe, AZ 85283-3216. Tel: 480-838-7474. Rev. Edward J. Kaminski, C.S.C.

Holy Cross Center, 2597 Virginia St., Berkeley, CA 94709. Tel: 510-548-8515; Fax: 510-548-7903. Revs. Harry C. Cronin, C.S.C.; William W. Faiella, C.S.C.

2033 N.E. Fifteen Ave., Portland, OR 97212. Tel: 971-404-6716. Rev. Dennis J. O'Hare, C.S.C.

Sacred Heart of Jesus Parish, 139 S. Lopez, New Orleans, LA 70119-5109. Tel: 504-827-1481. Rev. James J. Denn, C.S.C.

330 W. Colfax St., 46601. Tel: 574-233-7057. Rev.

Stephen P. Nani, C.S.C.
School Sisters of Notre Dame, 345 Belden Hill Rd., Wilton, CT 06896. Tel: 203-762-3318. Rev. Thomas F. Elliott, C.S.C.
P.O. Box 1064, Notre Dame, 46556-1064. Tel: 574-631-6196. Revs. William G. Blum, C.S.C.; J. David Burke, C.S.C.; William D. Dorwart, C.S.C.
Catholic University, Cardinal Station, Box 236, Washington, DC 20064. Tel: 202-319-6501; Fax: 202-319-5875. Rev. John T. Ford, C.S.C.
55 Elk St., San Francisco, CA 91431. Tel: 415-337-5073. Rev. William J. Dohar, C.S.C.
St. Edward, 5303 River Rd., N., Salem, OR 97303. Tel: 503-393-5323. Rev. Philip G. Sopke, C.S.C.
Calle Esmeralda, 1822 Ote., Col. Valle Verde, Ciudad Obregon Sonora 85097 Mexico. Tel: 011-52-6444-1777-21; Fax: 011-52-6444-1777-21. Rev. James W. Irwin, C.S.C.
St. Paul's Retirement Community, 3602 S. Ironwood Dr., 46614. Tel: 219-291-8205; Fax: 219-291-0858. Rev. Michael W. Glockner, C.S.C.
Holy Cross College, P.O. Box 308, Notre Dame, 46556. Fax: 219-631-9233. Revs. Mark R. Ghyselinck, C.S.C. Tel: 219-631-9484; Kenneth E. Grabner, C.S.C. Tel: 219-251-2232.
Gannon University, Erie, PA 16541. Tel: 814-871-7702. Rev. Edward C. Krause, C.S.C.
St. Cletus, 600 W. 55th St., La Grange, IL 60525. Tel: 708-352-6209. Rev. Stephen P. Newton, C.S.C.
1439 Gold Ct., Traverse City, MI 49686. Tel: 231-922-2668; Fax: 231-922-2668. Rev. Leonard D. Paul, C.S.C.
St. Paul Catholic Church: 91 E. Main St., Norwalk, OH 44857. Tel: 419-668-6044; Fax: 419-663-5770. Rev. William A. Pifher, C.S.C.
Holy Cross Mission Center, P.O. Box 543, Notre Dame, 46556. Fax: 219-631-6813. Revs. David E. Schlaver, C.S.C. Tel: 219-631-8884; Thomas W. Smith, C.S.C. Tel: 219-631-6814.
Holy Cross Scholasticate, Road 4, Banashree Prokalpo, Rampura, Dhaka 119, Bangladesh. Bro. J. Rodney Struble, C.S.C.
Valley Missionary Program, 52-565 Oasis Palms St., Coachella, CA 92236. Tel: 760-398-9277; Fax: 760-398-9281. Rev. Jose M. Martelli, C.S.C.
Morris Camp, Box 550, Atikokan ON Canada. Tel: 807-929-2341; Fax: 807-929-7181. Rev. John M. Mulcahy, C.S.C.
Congregazione di Santa Croce, Via Framura, 85, Rome 00168 Italy. Tel: 011-39-06-612-962-10; Fax: 011-39-06-614-7547. Most Rev. Charles A. Schleck, C.S.C.
319 Ave. C, Apt. 2B, New York, NY 10009. Tel: 212-673-1101. Rev. Norbert J. Sinski, C.S.C.
St. Francis of Rome, 501 E. Foothill Blvd., Azusa, CA 91702. Tel: 626-969-1829. Rev. John A. Struzzo, C.S.C., (2).
St. Francis High School, 1885 Miramonte Ave., Mountain View, CA 94040. Tel: 650-961-4276. Rev. John V. VandenBossche, C.S.C.
Holy Cross Mission House, P.O. Box 929, Notre Dame, TX 46556. Tel: 574-631-4757. Rev. David H. Verhalen, C.S.C.
400 E. Randolph St., Apt. 3230, Chicago, IL 60601. Tel: 312-861-0651. Rev. James N. Watzke, C.S.C.
Holy Cross Association, P.O. Box K, Notre Dame, 46556. Tel: 219-631-6022; Fax: 219-631-7291. Rev. Herbert C. Yost, C.S.C.
El Cristo Rey Catholic Chapel 44 Albright Ave., P.O. Box 505, Grand Canyon, AZ 86023-0505. Tel: 928-638-2390. Revs. Francis D. Zagorc, C.S.C.; Richard P. Zang, C.S.C.
Carmelite, qUIDENHAM, Norwich NR16 2PH England. Tel: 011-01953-887-202.
Holy Cross House, P.O. Box 1048, Notre Dame, 46556. Tel: 219-631-6337; Fax: 219-631-5172. Revs. Charles W. Kohlerman, C.S.C., Supr.; William P. Melody, C.S.C., Asst. Supr.; Lawrence T. Bauer, C.S.C.; William J. Beston, C.S.C.; Paul E. Beichner, C.S.C.; James F. Blaes, C.S.C.; Leon J. Boarman, C.S.C.; Claude L. Boehm, C.S.C.; William A. Botzum, C.S.C.; Eugene A. Burke, C.S.C. (PHX); Daniel C. Coughlin, C.S.C.; Joseph H. Fey, C.S.C.; Bernard P. Foley, C.S.C.; James B. Gillis, C.S.C.; Casimir F. Grabarz, C.S.C.; Arthur S. Harvey, C.S.C.; Norbert F. Hess, C.S.C.; William F. Hickens, C.S.C.; Robert M. Hoffman, C.S.C.; Edmund P. Joyce, C.S.C.; George G. Kahle, C.S.C.; William F. Keegan, C.S.C.; John F. Lahey, C.S.C.; Jerome R. Lawyer, C.S.C.; Robert J. Lochner, C.S.C. (Retired); John W. Lubbers, C.S.C.; James B. Mannis, C.S.C.; Walter L. McInerney, C.S.C.; Walter G. Michalik, C.S.C.; Michael G. O'Brien, C.S.C.; Augustine J. Peverada, C.S.C.; Paul B. Rankin, C.S.C.; Joseph W. Rehage, C.S.C.; Herman R. Reith, C.S.C.; Louis W. Rink, C.S.C.; Joseph A. Rogusz, C.S.C.; William M. Schreiner, C.S.C.; G. Michael Scully, C.S.C.; Chester A. Soleta, C.S.C.; Adrien Ste. Marie, C.S.C. (P); Denis B. Sughrue, C.S.C.; Richard H. Sullivan, C.S.C.; James E. Tobin, C.S.C. (FR); Charles F. Weiher, C.S.C.; George C. Wiskirchen, C.S.C.; Bros. Clarence J. Breitenbach, C.S.C.; Thomas J. Combs, C.S.C.; Andrew Corsini Fowler, C.S.C.; Orlando Gozdowski, C.S.C.; Paul H. Loos, C.S.C.; Beatus Schlenker, C.S.C.; Chester J. Ziemba, C.S.C.
LeMans Academy, 5901 N. 500 East, P.O. Box 7, Rolling Prairie, 46371. Tel: 219-778-2521. Rev. James R. Blantz, C.S.C.
Gilmour Academy, 34001 Cedar Rd., Gates Mills, OH 44040-9356. Tel: 440-473-3560. Rev. John J. Blazek, C.S.C.
St. Mary, 9168 Silver Falls S.E. Highway, P.O. Box 338, Aumsville, OR 97325-0338. Tel: 503-362-6159. Rev. G. James Brady, C.S.C.
St. Birgitta Parish: 11820 N.W. St. Helens Rd., Portland, OR 97231-2319. Tel: 503-286-3929. Rev. Joseph P. Browne, C.S.C.
Our Lady Queen of Martyrs Parish: 32340 Pierce, Beverly Hills, MI 48025. Tel: 248-644-8620. Rev. Michael J. Heppen, C.S.C.
St. Mark Parish: 3 N. 19th St., Niles, MI 49120-2117. Tel: 269-683-8650. Rev. Joseph W. Koma, C.S.C.
Our Lady of the Rosary Cathedral: 265 W. 25th St., San Bernardino, CA 92405. Tel: 909-648-1562. Rev. Robert J. Nogosek, C.S.C.
Sacred Heart of Jesus Parish: 201 S. Walnut St., Bangor, MI 49013. Tel: 269-427-7514. Rev. Thomas E. Seidel, C.S.C.

NOTRE DAME. *Congregation of Holy Cross, Midwest Province*, Provincial Admin., 54515 State Rd. 933 North, P.O. Box 460, 46556-0460. Tel: 574-631-4000; Fax: 574-631-2999. Email: rfillmore@hcc-nd.edu. Web: www.hcc-nd.edu/mwp. Bro. Robert Fillmore, C.S.C., Prov.; Rev. Raymond Papenfuss, C.S.C., Asst. Prov. & Vicar; Bros. Lawrence Skitzki, C.S.C., Prov. Steward; Robert Livernois, C.S.C., Prov. Sec.; Philip R. Smith, C.S.C., Prov. Councilor; Joseph Fox, C.S.C., Dir.
Legal Title: *Brothers of Holy Cross, Inc.*
Holy Cross Village, P.O. Box 609, 46556. Tel: 574-631-4000; Fax: 574-631-2999. Rev. Kenneth Grabner, C.S.C., Chap. Total in Residence 30.
Dujarie House, Infirmary, P.O. Box 706, 46556. Tel: 574-287-1838; Fax: 574-289-7277. Stephen Kastner, Admin. Total in Residence 28.
Helen D. Schubert Villa, Assisted Living, P.O. Box 1020, 46556-1020. Tel: 574-287-1986; Fax: 574-289-7277. Stephen Kastner, Admin. Total in Residence 15.
Columba Hall, P.O. Box N, 46556. Tel: 574-631-6284; Fax: 574-631-9882. Bro. Thomas Shaughnessy, C.S.C., Supr.; Rev. Maurice Amen, C.S.C., Chap. Total in Residence 41.
Holy Cross Community, Corby Hall, University of Notre Dame 46556. Tel: 574-631-7325; Fax: 574-631-6715. Revs. Robert J. Austgen, C.S.C.; Nicholas Ayo, C.S.C.; Leonard N. Banas, C.S.C.; Ernest J. Bartell, C.S.C.; James Bracke, C.S.C. (CHI); Thomas E. Blantz, C.S.C.; Richard S. Bullene, C.S.C.; Joseph H. Carey, C.S.C.; Austin I. Collins, C.S.C.; John E. Conley, C.S.C.; Michael E. Connors, C.S.C.; Robert A. Dowd, C.S.C; Paul F. Doyle, C.S.C.; John S. Dunne, C.S.C.; Clarence R. Durbin, C.S.C.; Carl F. Ebey, C.S.C.; James K. Foster, C.S.C.; Patrick Gaffney, C.S.C.; Thomas E. Gaughan, C.S.C.; Bro. Francis J. Gorch, C.S.C.; Revs. Charles B. Gordon, C.S.C.; Eugene F. Gorski, C.S.C.; Gregory A. Green, C.S.C.; Daniel Groody, C.S.C.; Theodore M. Hesburgh, C.S.C.; Bro. Louis F. Hurcik, C.S.C.; Revs. Peter A. Jarret, C.S.C.; John I. Jenkins, C.S.C., Religious Supr.; David Kashangaki, C.S.C.; Thomas P. King, C.S.C.; Jim B. King, C.S.C.; Jerome E. Knoll, C.S.C.; William Lies, C.S.C.; Bro. Edward C. Luther, C.S.C; Revs. James J. McGrath, C.S.C.; Edward A. Malloy, C.S.C.; Patrick H. Maloney, C.S.C.; Leon J. Mertensotto, C.S.C.; Bros. Dennis Meyers, C.S.C.; Jerome Meyer, C.S.C.; Revs. Matthew M. Miceli, C.S.C.; Robert H. Moss, C.S.C.; Michael J. Murphy, C.S.C.; Edward D. O'Connor, C.S.C.; William O'Connor, C.S.C.; Dan Parrish, C.S.C.; John H. Pearson, C.S.C.; Robert S. Pelton, C.S.C.; Mark L. Poorman, C.S.C.; James L. Riehle, C.S.C.; John P. Riley, C.S.C.; George A. Rozum, C.S.C.; Kevin Russeau, C.S.C.; Jeffrey Schneibel, C.S.C.; Timothy R. Scully, C.S.C.; William D. Seetch, C.S.C., Rel. Supr. Corby Hall; William Simmons, C.S.C.; J. Steele, C.S.C.; Thomas G. Streit, C.S.C.; Michael Bruce Sullivan, C.S.C.; Thomas Tallarida, C.S.C.; Mark Thesing, C.S.C.; Merwyn J. Thomas, C.S.C.; Bro. Thomas P. Tucker, C.S.C.; Revs. Joseph L. Walter, C.S.C.; Richard V. Warner, C.S.C.; Oliver F. Williams, C.S.C.

[J] CONVENTS AND RESIDENCES OF SISTERS

SOUTH BEND. *Handmaids of the Most Holy Trinity Monastery-Hermitage*, 23089 Adams Rd., 46628-9674. Tel: 574-272-9425. Sr. Mary Emmanuel Baggoo, H.T., Representative. Contemplative Community; Prayer Ministry; Prayer Witness which includes Retreats and Spiritual Direction.
Sara House, 1213 E. Bronson, 46615. Tel: 574-287-8342; Fax: 574-287-8342. Email: cbach3@juno.com. Sr. Margaret Anne Henss, Treas. Owned by the Poor Handmaids of Jesus Christ.
The Sisters of St. Joseph of the Third Order of St. Francis, S.S.J.-T.O.S.F., 1208 Thomas St., 46601-2645. Tel: 574-289-7341. Email: rfirkus4@cs.com. Web: www.ssj-tosf.org. Sr. Rose Margaret Firkus, Novice Min.

FORT WAYNE. *Marian Convent* (St. Joseph Hospital), 4138 S. Harrison, 46807. Tel: 260-745-4041. Email: MarianConvent@juno.com. Poor Handmaids of Jesus Christ 4.
Sisters of Providence Residences, 813 1-2 Kinnaird Ave., 46807-1829. Tel: 260-744-0780.
Other Location:
2440 Fairfield Ave., Apt. 212, 46807-1250. Tel: 260-744-5586.
Sisters of St. Benedict, 802 E. Tenth St., Ferdinand, 47532-9239. Tel: 812-367-1411; Fax: 812-367-2313. Email: sisters@thedome.org. Web: www.thedome.org.
Sisters of St. Joseph of the Third Order of St. Francis Residences S.S.J.-T.O.S.F., 5123 Truemper Way, 46835. Tel: 260-492-6520. Email: trueway@msn.com. Sisters 3.
Other Location:
2222 Abbey Dr., 46835. Tel: 260-485-4616. Sisters 2.

AVILLA. *St. Mary Convent*, 226 N. Main St., P.O. Box 109, 46710. Tel: 260-897-3484; Fax: 260-897-3706. Email: srtheresa@excite.com. Sr. Theresa Renninger, O.S.F., Supr. Franciscan Sisters of the Sacred Heart Sisters 2.

DONALDSON. *Convent Ancilla Domini* 46513. Tel: 574-936-9936; Fax: 574-935-1785. Email: sjolisem@poorhandmaids.org. Web: www.poorhandmaids.org. Sr. Jolise May, P.H.J.C., Prov. Provincialate, Poor Handmaids of Jesus Christ (The Ancilla Domini Sisters) Professed Sisters 41.
Catherine Kasper Home Tel: 574-935-1742; Fax: 574-935-1755. Retired Sisters 51.
Ancilla Domini Hospitals Insurance Trust Tel: 574-947-8544; Fax: 574-947-5274.
Maria Center 46513. Tel: 574-936-9936; Fax: 574-935-1790. Senior Apartments (Efficiency and Singles) Apartments 27.
Poor Handmaids of Jesus Christ Community Support Trust Tel: 574-936-9936; Fax: 574-935-1785.
Ancilla College Tel: 574-936-8898; Fax: 574-935-1773.
Lindenwood, Retreat & Conference Center Tel: 574-935-1780; Fax: 574-935-1728.
St. Joseph Community Foundation Tel: 260-969-2001; Fax: 260-969-2004.

HUNTINGTON. *Victory Noll--Motherhouse of Our Lady of Victory Missionary Sisters* (1922), 1900 W. Park Dr., P.O. Box 109, 46750-0109. Tel: 260-356-0628; Fax: 260-358-1504. Email: victorynoll@olvm.org. Web: www.olvm.org. Rev. Thomas C. Fahey, O.F.M. (CHY), Chap. (Retired). Legal Holding: Victory Noll Sisters Community Support Trust. Professed Sisters 160.

MISHAWAKA. *St. Francis Provincialate*, 1515 Dragoon Tr., Box 766, 46546-0766. Tel: 574-259-5427; Fax: 574-256-0822. Web: www.ssfpa.org. Sr. M. Blanche Rausch, O.S.F., Prov.; Rev. Francis Affelt, O.F.M., Chap. Sisters of St. Francis of Perpetual Adoration, Inc., St. Francis Convent and Novitiate of Immaculate Heart of Mary Province. Sisters 132; Novices 3; Postulants 1.
Our Lady of the Angels Convent, 1515 Dragoon Tr., P.O. Box 766, 46546-0766. Tel: 574-259-5427; Fax: 574-256-0822. Web: www.ssfpa.org. Sr. M. Jacqueline Kozlowski, O.S.F., Supr.; Rev. Dacian Bluma, O.F.M., Chap. Convent for retired and infirm sisters. Sisters 44.

NOTRE DAME. *Sisters of the Holy Cross, Inc.*, Saint Mary's of the Immaculate Conception, 309 Bertrand Hall, 46556-5000. Tel: 574-284-5550; Fax: 574-284-5779. Sisters Aline Marie, C.S.C., Pres.; Joan Marie Steadman, C.S.C., Vice Pres.; Mary Eliza, C.S.C., Leadership Team, Finance; Marilyn Zugish, C.S.C., Leadership Team, Ministry; Veronique, C.S.C., Leadership Team, Holistic Living; Anna Mae Golden, C.S.C., Leadership Team, Holistic Living.
Legal Title: *Sisters of the Holy Cross, Inc.; Sisters of the Holy Cross, Inc dba CSC Consultation Services; The Corporation of Saint Mary's College, Notre Dame; Holy Cross Services Corporation.*, Generalate, Candidate Program, Associate Program. Professed Sisters in Congregation 565; Temporarily Incorporated 18; Novices 13.
Sisters of the Holy Cross Other Residences and Programs:
Rainbow House, 114 River Ave., Mishawaka, 46544-1572. Tel: 574-255-4516. Sisters 2.

190 Village Dr., Mishawaka, 46545. Tel: 574-258-5974.
Basil Moreau Convent, 18325 Bailey Ave., 46637. Tel: 574-271-1376. Sisters 15.
Our Lady of Hungary Convent, 731 W. Calvert St., 46613. Tel: 574-289-2531. Sisters 3.
3211 Rue Voltaire, 46615. Tel: 574-289-9154.
303 Waterfall Dr., P.O. Box 50, Elkhart, 46516.
St. Joseph's Tower, 316 S. St. Joseph St., #116, 46601-2342. Tel: 574-232-8170.
3921 Irish Hills Dr., 46614. Tel: 574-299-9246.
52700 Shellbark Ave., 46628-4082. Tel: 574-273-9598. Sisters 2.
727 Forest Ave., 46601. Tel: 574-246-0673. Sisters 3.
413 W. Navarre, 46616. Tel: 574-234-3208. Sisters 2.
2924 Rue Renoir, 46615. Tel: 574-287-6071.
Immaculata Convent Tel: 574-284-5707. Sisters 3.
Lourdes Convent Tel: 574-284-5589. Sisters 18.
Marian Convent Tel: 574-284-5710. Sisters 4.
Mary's Solitude Tel: 574-284-5599.
Moreau Convent Tel: 574-284-5663. Sisters 4.
Rosary Convent Tel: 574-284-5845. Sisters 27.
House of Shalem, Formerly Shalem House Tel: 574-284-5358. Sisters 3.
St. Bridget's Convent Tel: 574-232-2683. Sisters 2.
St. John's Convent Tel: 574-284-5695. Sisters 5.
Bethany House Tel: 574-284-5674. Sisters 4.
Saint Mary's Convent Tel: 574-284-5688; 574-284-5689; 574-284-5736. Sisters 76.
Loretto Convent Tel: 574-284-5667. Sisters 6.
Holy Spirit Convent, Saint Mary's. Tel 574-284-5715. Sisters 4.
Kateri Convent, Saint Mary's, 46556. Tel: 574-284-5993. Sisters 3.
Madonna Convent, St. Mary's, 46556. Tel: 574-284-5890. Sisters 4.
Nazareth Convent, Saint Mary's, 46556. Tel: 574-284-5822. Sisters 2.
Saint Ann's Convent, Formerly Saint Ann's Convent - East Saint Mary's, 46556. Tel: 574-284-5713. Sisters 2.
Saint Claire Convent, Saint Mary's, 46556. Tel: 574-284-5892. Sisters 2.
Visitation Convent, Saint Mary's, 46556. Tel: 574-284-5820. Sisters 2.
Guadalupe Convent, St. Mary's, 46556. Tel: 574-284-5717. Sisters 2.
Andre House - East, St. Mary's, 46556. Tel: 574-284-5644. Sisters 4.
Andre House - West, St. Mary's, 46556. Tel: 574-284-5644. Sisters 4.
Faith Convent, St. Mary's, 46556. Tel: 574-284-5870. Sisters 4.
Marian Convent, Saint Mary's, 46556. Tel: 574-284-5710. Sisters 7.
Mary's Song, Saint Mary's, 46556. Tel: 574-284-5998. Sisters 2.
Saint Mary's Convent, 46556. Tel: 574-284-5689. Sisters 82.
Sisters of the Holy Cross, P.O. Box 327, University of Notre Dame, 46556. Tel: 574-631-7072.

[K] MISSION HOUSES

NOTRE DAME. *Holy Cross Mission House* 46556. Tel: 574-631-4757; Fax: 574-631-5239. Revs. John J. Croston, C.S.C.; Stephen C. Gibson, C.S.C., Supr.; Andrew Guljas, C.S.C.; Robert M. Hoffman, C.S.C.; Roman Ladewski, C.S.C.; Robert C. Steigmeyer, C.S.C.; Paul G. Wendel, C.S.C., Asst. Supr.

[L] RETREAT HOUSES & EDUCATIONAL CENTERS

SOUTH BEND. *Forever Learning Institute, Inc.*, 308 S. Scott St., 46601. Tel: 574-282-1901; Fax: 574-282-1901. Email: backles@mvillage.com. Sr. Jeanne Finske, C.S.C., Pres.; Mary Jane Chase, Vice Pres.; Pilar Nacu-Brandewie, Sec.; Beverly Ackles, Exec. Dir. To promote and support the quality and dignity of older adults and to assist older adults in finding enrichment, joy and fellowship through educational and recreational activities.

DONALDSON. *Lindenwood Retreat & Conference Center*, Formerly Lindenwood Retreat, PHJC Ministry Center, 46513. Tel: 574-935-1780; Fax: 574-935-1728. Email: lw@lindenwood.org. Web: www.lindenwood.org. P.O. Box 1, 46513. Tel: 574-935-1780; Fax: 574-935-1728. Loretta Peters, Dir. Overnight facilities for 100, Conference rooms for 250, Handicapped accessibility. Total Staff 8; Total in Residence 2.

NOTRE DAME. *Mary's Solitude*, St. Mary's, 100 Lourdes Hall, 46556-5014. Tel: 574-284-5599; Fax: 574-284-5701. Email: msolitude@cscsisters.org. Sisters Michaeleen Frieders, C.S.C., Dir.; Gladys Marie Martin, C.S.C., Asst. Dir. A retreat and conference center offering: Spiritual direction, days and evenings of reflection, week-end retreats, individually directed retreats, private and group retreats, Scripture, and special interest programs, 30-day directed retreats and the Nineteenth Annotation. Sixteen rooms are available; 14 single and 2 double. Total Staff 2.
Our Lady of Fatima Retreat Center, P.O. Box 929, 46556-0929. Tel: 574-631-8288; Fax: 574-631-5239. Email: nd.fatima.1@nd.edu. Web: www.nd.edu/~Fatima. James F. Kavanagh, Interim Dir.; Revs. Stephen C. Gibson, C.S.C., Dir.; Paul G. Wendel, C.S.C., Spiritual Dir. in Res.; Sr. Rose Edward Goodrow, C.S.C., Dir. Retreats for men, women, husbands and wives, special interest groups, professional groups, youth groups and religious. Total Staff 4; Total in Residence 10.

[M] MISCELLANEOUS

SOUTH BEND. *Chiara Home, Inc.*, 1105 W Jefferson Blvd., 46601-2618. Tel: 574-287-5435; Fax: 574-287-3184. Email: chiarahome@att.net. Web: www.chiarahome.org. Sr. Gretchen Clark, S.S.J.-T.O.S.F., Contact Person. Respite Care for people with special needs. Total Staff 4; Total Families Assisted 180.
Christ Child Society of South Bend, Tel: 574-288-6028. P.O Box 1286, 46624. Total Assisted 4,000.
Saint Joseph Regional Medical Center, Inc., 801 E. LaSalle, 46617. Tel: 574-237-7989; Fax: 574-237-7077. Email: breedenm@sjrmc.com. Web: www.sjmed.com. Nancy R. Hellyer, Pres. & CEO; Martin C. Breeden, P.H.J.C., Vice Pres. Mission Integration. Total Staff 604; Total Assisted 245,237.
Trinity Health Corporation and Trinity Continuing Care Services-Indiana, Inc., 3575 Moreau Ct., 46628-4320. Tel: 248-305-7921. Karen Struve, Pres. & CEO. Total Staff 1,000; Total in Residence 1,200.
St. Vincent de Paul Society of St. Joseph County, Inc., 3408 Ardmore Tr., 46628. Tel: 574-251-4908; Fax: 574-234-6248. Email: jackiebsvdp@aol.com. Web: www.stvinnie.org. Ms. Jacqueline Beverly, Exec. Dir.; Mrs. Joan M. Eash, Asst. Dir. Total Staff 45; Volunteers 350; Total Assisted 27,000.
St. Vincent de Paul Thrift Shop, 3408 Ardmore Tr., 46628-1802. Tel: 574-234-6000; Fax: 574-234-6248. Email: jackiebsudp@aol.com. Web: www.stvinnies.org. Alicia McMurtrie, Dir. Thrift Store Oper.

FORT WAYNE. *Cathedral Museum*, P.O. Box 10898, 46854. Tel: 260-744-2765; Fax: 260-744-1972. Rev. Phillip A. Widmann, Dir.
Catholic Charities, Tel: 260-422-5625; Fax: 260-422-5657. Email: fwoffice@fw.diocesefwsb.org. Web: www.diocesefwsb.org/charity.
Fort Wayne Community Service Center, 315 E. Washington Blvd., 46802. Tel: 260-422-5625; Fax: 260-422-5657. Debbie Schmidt, Dir. Total Staff 46; Total Assisted 12,369.
South Bend Community Service Center, 1817 Miami Rd., 46613. Tel: 574-234-3111; Fax: 574-289-1034. Total Staff 9; Total Assisted 2,377.
Elkhart Community Service Center, 201 S. Second St., Elkhart, 46516. Tel: 574-295-5284; Fax: 574-294-1428.
Villa of the Woods-Catholic Charities Residential Living, 5610 Noll Ave., 48606. Tel: 260-745-7039; Fax: 260-744-4887. Cheryl Smith, Admin. Residential facilities for the elderly including housing, meals, laundry services and planned activities. Total Staff 10; Residents 35.
Children's Cottage, 2820 Reed St., 46803. Tel: 260-745-4929; Fax: 260-456-6100. Day care center serving children 6 weeks- 12 years old, year round. Total Staff 25; Students 138.
Circle of Mercy, 120 S. Taylor St., 46601. Tel: 574-287-0500. Day care center, serving children 2-6 years old, year round. Total Staff 10; Students 33.
RSVP (Retired Senior Volunteer Program), 107 W. 5th St., Auburn, 46706. Tel: 260-925-0917; Fax: 260-925-1732. Total Staff 4; Volunteers Placed 432.
Catholic Charities Children's Services, 2820 Reed St., 46806. Tel: 260-745-4929; Fax: 260-456-6100. Email: tervin@ccfwsb.org. Web: www.diocesefwsb.org/charity/ccottage.html. Toyi Ervin, Admin. Lay Teachers 13; Aides 8; Enrollment 125.
**The Christ Child Society of Fort Wayne, Inc.*, P.O. Box 12708, 46864. Tel: 260-422-4611; Fax: 260-423-3382. Ann Marie Wislon, Contact Person.
Crosier Fathers of Fort Wayne, 1721 Magnavox Way, 46802 Tel: 320-532-5225; Fax: 320-532-5222. Email ABecker@Crosiers.org. William G. Niezer, Registered Agent. Total Staff 1.
Diocese of Fort Wayne-South Bend Investment Trust, Inc., to invest money received from qualified 501(c)(3) organizations that buy shares offered by the organization. All investments of share purchase proceeds shall be directed and conducted consistent with the investment policies and objectives established by the organization that are applicable to the type of share(s) sold to the participating 501 (c)(3) entities. All gains and any losses on investments, after administrative and money management fees, shall be reflected in share values.1102 S. Calhoun St., P.O. Box 390, 46801. Tel: 260-422-4611. Most Rev. John M. D'Arcy, D.D., M.A., S.T.D., Admin.; Joseph Ryan, Contact Person.
The Diocese of Fort Wayne-South Bend, Endowment Trust, Inc., 1103 S. Calhoun Street, P.O. Box 390, 46801. Tel: 260-422-4611; Fax: 260-423-3382. Email: rschulte@fw.diocesefwsb.org. Web: www.diocesefwsb.org. Most Rev. John M. D'Arcy, D.D., M.A., S.T.D., Contact Person.
Foundation For Catholic Secondary Schools of Fort Wayne, Inc., P.O. Box 11632, 46859-1632. Tel: 260-424-8112; Fax: 260-424-7630. Donald J. Mauch, Pres.; Michael E. Millikan, Dir. & Contact Person.
The St. Joseph Community Health Foundation, Inc., 500 W. Main St., 46802. Tel: 260-969-2001; Fax: 260-969-2004. Email: mdistler@st.josephhealthfdn.org ckronstain@stjosephhealthfdn.org. Web: www.poorhandmaids.org. Meg Distler, Exec. Dir.; Connie Kronstain, Office Program Asst. Total Staff 2.
St. Vincent de Paul Society Store, 1600 S. Calhoun St., 46802. Tel: 260-456-3561. Steve R. App, Mgr. Total Staff 10; Total Assisted 1,000.

GRANGER. *Jesuit Community*, 16203 Candlewycke Ct., 46530. Tel: 574-243-0601; Fax: 574-631-8092. Email: neyrey.1@nd.edu daley.3@nd.edu. Web: www.nd.edu/~jneyrey1. Revs. Jerome H. Neyrey, S.J., Contact Person; Brian Daley, S.J.
St. Joseph's Farm, 52682 Current Rd., 46530. Tel: 574-272-0962. Email: albeke5@aol.com. Bro. Donald Dunleavy, C.S.C., Dir. Brothers of the Congregation of Holy Cross, South-West Province, This farm is operated in the interests of the Congregation of Holy Cross, South-West Province. Brothers 2; Total Staff 2.

HUNTINGTON. *Our Sunday Visitor, Inc.*, 200 Noll Plaza, 46750. Tel: 260-356-8400; Fax: 260-359-9117. Email: osvinc@osv.com. Web: www.osv.com. Most Rev. John M. D'Arcy, D.D., M.A., S.T.D., Bd. Chm. Publishers of Catholic Periodicals, Books, Religious Education Materials and Offering Envelopes

MISHAWAKA. *The Foundation of Saint Joseph Regional Medical Center, Inc.*, 4215 Edison Lakes Pkwy. Ste. 300, 46546. Mr. Tim Sexton, Vice Pres. Community Devel.
Legal Title: *The Foundation of Saint Joseph Regional Medical Center, Inc.*
Saint Joseph Care Foundation, Inc., 4215 Edison Lakes Pkwy., Ste. 300, 46545. Tel: 574-247-8790; Fax: 574-247-8798. Email: sextont@sjrmc.com. Web: www.sjmed.com.
Saint Joseph Regional Medical Center-Mishawaka, 215 W. Fourth St., 46544. Tel: 574-935-2263; Fax: 574-257-2831. Email: breedenm@sjrmc.com. Web: www.sjmed.com. Lori Price, Exec. Vice Pres.; Martin Breeden, Vice Pres. Mission Integration. Bed Capacity 25; Total Staff 644.
Saint Joseph's Visiting Nurse Association, Inc., 810 E. Park Pl., P.O. Box 5006, 46546-5006. Tel: 574-472-6500; Fax: 574-472-6501. Email: lambb@sjrmc.com. Web: www.sjvna.org. Ms. Bea Lamb, Exec. Dir. dba Saint Joseph VNA Home Care. Total Staff 155; Total Assisted 2,364.
Sisters of St. Francis Health Services, Inc. dba Alverno Information Services, P.O. Box 1290, 46546-1290. Tel: 574-256-3935; Fax: 574-256-0267. Web: www.ssfhs.org.
Alverno Health Corporation, 1515 Dragoon Tr., P.O. Box 1290, 46546-1290.
St. Anthony Medical Center Foundation, 1515 Dragoon Tr., P.O. Box 1290, 46546-1290.
Sisters of St. Francis of Perpetual Adoration, Inc., Mailing Address: P.O. Box 766, 46546-0766. Tel: 574-259-5427; Fax: 574-256-0822. Web: www.ssfpa,org.
Sisters of St. Francis of Perpetual Adoration, Inc., Medical Benefits Trust Tel: 574-259-5427; Fax: 574-256-0822.
Sisters of St. Francis of Perpetual Adoration, Inc. Capital Improvements Trust, 1515 Dragoon Tr., Box 766, 46546-0766. Tel: 574-259-5427; Fax: 574-256-0822. Web: www.ssfpa.org.
Sisters of St. Francis Charitable Mission Trust Tel: 574-259-5427; Fax: 574-256-0822.
Sisters of St. Francis Retirement Fund Tel: 574-259-5427; Fax: 574-256-0822.
SSFPA Ministry Corporation, 1515 Dragoon Trail, P.O. Box 766, 46546. Tel: 574-259-5427; Fax: 574-256-0822. Web: www.ssfpa.org. Sr. M. Blanche Rausch, O.S.F., Prov. Supr.
Yves R. Simon Institute, 3921 Glenview Dr., 46628. Tel: 574-271-1187; Fax: 574-271-1292. Email: aosimon@michiana.org. Mr. Anthony O. Simon,

Dir. & Contact Person. Catholic academic institute. Total Staff 2.

NOTRE DAME. *Andre Residential Services, Inc.*, Dujarie House-200 W. River Ridge Rd., P.O. Box 706, 46556-0706. Tel: 574-287-1838; Fax: 574-289-7277. Email: skastner@hcc-nd.edu. Stephen Kastner, Admin.; Bro. Richard Daly, C.S.C., Pres. of Board. Sponsored by Brothers of the Holy Cross, Inc., Purpose: to establish and maintain a health facility for members and persons associated with the Congregation.

Ave Maria Press, Inc., P.O. Box 428, 46556. Tel: 574-287-2831; Fax: 574-239-2904. Email: avemariapress.1@nd.edu. Web: www.avemariapress.com. Frank J. Cunningham, Pres. & Publisher. Owned and operated by the Congregation of Holy Cross, Indiana Province, Inc.

Brothers of Holy Cross Life Development Trust, Mailing Address: P.O. Box 460, 46556. Tel: 574-631-4000; Fax: 574-631-2999. Bros. Donald Bailer, Trustees; William Dygert, Trustees; Paul Kelly, Trustees; Robert Lavelle, C.S.C., Trustees; Lawrence Skitzki, C.S.C., Trustees.

Holy Cross Associates, Mailing Address: Moreau Seminary, P.O. Box 668, 46556. Tel: 574-631-5521; Fax: 574-631-9233. Email: hca@nd.edu. Web: www.holycrossassociates.nd.edu. John Pinter, Contact Person & Dir. Total Staff 3; Total in Residence 45.

Holy Cross Ministry Net-Work, Inc., Bertrand Hall - St. Mary's, 46556-5000. Tel: 574-284-5551; Fax: 574-284-5779. Sisters Geneva Rolf, C.S.C., Dir.; Mary Eliza Martin, C.S.C., Admin.

Holy Cross Services Corp., 402 Bertrand Hall, St. Mary's, 46556. Tel: 574-284-5551; Fax: 574-284-5779. Email: maryeliza@cscsisters.org. Web: www.holycrossservicescorp.org. Sisters of the Holy Cross

Holy Cross Village at Notre Dame, Inc., 54515 State Rd. 933 N., P.O. Box 460, 46556-0460. Tel: 574-251-3250; Fax: 574-631-2999. Web: www.hcc-nd.edu/hcvillage. Bro. Robert Fillmore, C.S.C., Prov.

PLYMOUTH. *Catherine Kasper Life Center, Inc.*, 9601 Union Rd., 46563. Tel: 574-936-9936; Fax: 574-936-9366. Email: sjolisem@poorhandmaids.org. Sr. Jolise May, P.H.J.C., Pres. & Prov.; Linda Burt, Vice Pres.; Sr. Rosemary Jurkowski, P.H.J.C., Sec. Sponsored by the Poor Handmaids of Jesus Christ, Purpose: To provide quality care and address the spiritual, emotional, and physical needs of the aged, sick and disabled.

Earthworks, Inc., 9815 Union Rd., 46563. Tel: 574-935-4164. Email: earthworks@skyenet.net. Web: www.earthworksonline.org. Sr. Suzanne Rogers, Dir. An environmental education center; a sponsored entity of the Poor Handmaids of Jesus Christ (P.H.J.C.) affiliated with Convent Ancilla Domini, Donaldson, IN.

RELIGIOUS INSTITUTES OF MEN REPRESENTED IN THE DIOCESE

For further details refer to the corresponding bracketed number in the Religious Institutes of Men or Women section.

[0600]—*Brothers of the Congregation of Holy Cross* (Midwest Province)—C.S.C.

[0470]—*The Capuchin Friars* (Prov. of St. Joseph)—O.F.M.Cap.

[0480]—*Conventual Franciscans* (Prov. of Our Lady of Consolation)—O.F.M.Conv

[0520]—*Franciscan Friars* (Prov. of St. John the Baptist)—O.F.M.

[0690]—*Jesuit Fathers and Brothers*—S.J.

[0610]—*Priests of the Congregation of Holy Cross* (Indiana Province)—C.S.C.

[1060]—*Society of the Precious Blood* (Cincinnati Province)—C.PP.S.

RELIGIOUS INSTITUTES OF WOMEN REPRESENTED IN THE DIOCESE

[0230]—*Benedictine Sisters of Pontifical Jurisdiction* (Ferdinand, IN)—O.S.B.

[3710]—*Congregation of the Sisters of Saint Agnes*—C.S.A.

[1920]—*Congregation of the Sisters of the Holy Cross*—C.S.C.

[1710]—*Congregation of the Third Order of St. Francis of Mary Immaculate* (Joliet, IL)—O.S.F.

[0760]—*Daughters of Charity of St. Vincent de Paul* (East Central Province)—D.C.

[0790]—*Daughters of Divine Charity* (Holy Trinity Province)—F.D.C.

[1070-03]—*Dominican Sisters*—O.P.

[1070-13]—*Dominican Sisters*—O.P.

[1170]—*Felician Sisters* (Presentation of the B.V.M. Province)—C.S.S.F.

[1450]—*Franciscan Sisters of the Sacred Heart*—O.S.F.

[]—*Handmaids of the Most Holy Trinity*—H.T.

[3130]—*Our Lady of Victory Missionary Sisters*—O.L.V.M.

[3230]—*Poor Handmaids of Jesus Christ*—P.H.J.C.

[2970]—*School Sisters of Notre Dame*—S.S.N.D.

[2990]—*Sisters of Notre Dame* (Province of Toledo)—S.N.D.

[3000]—*Sisters of Notre Dame de Namur* (Chesapeake Province)—S.N.D.deN.

[3360]—*Sisters of Providence of Saint Mary-of-the-Woods, Indiana*—S.P.

[1640]—*Sisters of St. Francis of Perpetual Adoration* (Province of the Immaculate Heart of Mary)—O.S.F.

[3830]—*Sisters of St. Joseph*—C.S.J.

[3880]—*Sisters of St. Joseph of Medaille* (New Orleans)—C.S.J.

[3930]—*Sisters of St. Joseph of the Third Order of St. Francis*—S.S.J.-T.O

[2110]—*Sisters of the Humility of Mary*—H.M.

[3260]—*Sisters of the Precious Blood* (Dayton, OH)—C.PP.S.

DIOCESAN CEMETERY

FORT WAYNE. *Catholic*, 3500 Lake Ave., 46805. Tel: 260-426-2044.

NECROLOGY

✠ Crowley, Most Rev. Joseph R., Retired Auxiliary Bishop of Fort Wayne-South Bend—Died Feb. 4, 2003

✠ Sheets, Most Rev. John R., Retired Auxiliary Bishop of Fort Wayne-South Bend—Died April 16, 2003

† Cardinali, Fred, (Retired)—Died May 17, 2003

† Fosselman, Robert, (Retired)—Died May 27, 2003

† Jacobs, Joseph A., (Retired)—Died July 14, 2003

Diocese of Fort Worth

(Dioecesis Arcis-Vorthensis)

Most Reverend

JOSEPH P. DELANEY, D.D.

Bishop of Fort Worth; ordained December 18, 1960; appointed Bishop of Fort Worth July 10, 1981; ordained Bishop September 13, 1981. *800 West Loop 820 S., Fort Worth, TX 76108.* Tel: 817-560-3300.

PRAISED BE JESUS CHRIST

The Catholic Center: 800 West Loop 820 S., Fort Worth, TX 76108. Tel: 817-560-3300; Fax: 817-244-8839.

Web: www.fwdioc.org

Email: rwilson@fwdioc.org

ESTABLISHED AUGUST 22, 1969.

Square Miles 23,950.

Comprises the following twenty-eight Counties in the State of Texas: Archer, Baylor, Bosque, Clay, Comanche, Cooke, Denton, Eastland, Erath, Foard, Hardeman, Hill, Hood, Jack, Johnson, Knox, Montague, Palo Pinto, Parker, Shackleford, Stephens, Somervell, Tarrant, Throckmorton, Wichita, Wilbarger, Wise and Young.

For legal titles of parishes and diocesan institutions, consult the Chancery Office.

STATISTICAL OVERVIEW

Personnel	
Bishop	1
Priests: Diocesan Active in Diocese	43
Priests: Diocesan Active Outside Diocese	2
Priests: Diocesan in Foreign Missions	1
Priests: Retired, Sick or Absent	17
Number of Diocesan Priests	63
Religious Priests in Diocese	51
Total Priests in Diocese	114
Extern Priests in Diocese	10
Ordinations:	
Transitional Deacons	1
Permanent Deacons	20
Permanent Deacons in Diocese	80
Total Brothers	13
Total Sisters	93
Parishes	
Parishes	88
With Resident Pastor:	
Resident Diocesan Priests	37
Resident Religious Priests	22
Without Resident Pastor:	
Administered by Priests	19
Administered by Deacons	7
Administered by Professed Religious Men	1
Administered by Religious Women	1
Missions	3
Closed Parishes	3
Professional Ministry Personnel:	
Brothers	12
Sisters	91
Lay Ministers	300
Welfare	
Catholic Hospitals	1
Total Assisted	140,075
Health Care Centers	1
Total Assisted	3,100
Homes for the Aged	6
Total Assisted	398
Specialized Homes	16
Total Assisted	35,200
Educational	
Diocesan Students in Other Seminaries	15
Total Seminarians	15
High Schools, Diocesan and Parish	4
Total Students	1,463
Elementary Schools, Diocesan and Parish	15
Total Students	5,353
Elementary Schools, Private	1
Total Students	238
Catechesis/Religious Education:	
High School Students	7,452
Elementary Students	19,786
Total Students under Catholic Instruction	34,307
Teachers in the Diocese:	
Priests	2
Brothers	5
Sisters	12
Lay Teachers	541
Vital Statistics	
Receptions into the Church:	
Infant Baptism Totals	6,066
Adult Baptism Totals	430
Received into Full Communion	714
First Communions	5,859
Confirmations	3,174
Marriages:	
Catholic	820
Interfaith	379
Total Marriages	1,199
Deaths	1,197
Total Catholic Population	400,500
Total Population	2,098,443

Former Bishops—Most Rev. JOHN J. CASSATA, D.D. (Retired), ord. Dec. 8, 1932; Titular Bishop of Bida and Auxiliary of Dallas-Fort Worth; appt. March 20, 1968; consecrated June 5, 1968; first Bishop, Fort Worth; appt. Aug. 22, 1969; retired Sept. 16, 1980; died Sept. 8, 1989.

Vicar General—Rev. Msgr. JOSEPH A. SCHUMACHER.

Chancellor and Moderator of the Curia—Rev. ROBERT WILSON.

Deans—Revs. JOSEPH SCANTLIN, Arlington Area Deanery; KEN ROBINSON, Northeast Deanery; JOSEPH PEMBERTON, West Central Deanery; DAVID BRISTOW, East Central Deanery; JOHN SWISTOVICH, Northwest Deanery; WILLIAM HOPKINS, Southwest Deanery; Rev. Msgr. CHARLES KING, North Deanery; Rev. JUAN RIVERO, South Deanery.

Diocesan Pastoral Advisory Council— (Includes Presbyteral Council listed below) Lay Persons: Ms. MARY ALVAREZ; Ms. JO-LEE BUNCIC; Mr. DAN DELGADO; Mr. STEVE GARCIA; Mr. MARK SHADOWENS; Ms. JENNIFER TAYAG; Mr. LONG TRAN; Mr. RUSSELL OVERBY. Career Ministers: Ms. KAREN DEFILIPPIS; Mr. JEFF HEDGLEN; Deacon JIM NOVAK; Ms. ALICE CURRAN; Mr. ERIC GRAY; Ms. BETSY MILLIGAN; Mr. BRYAN WEBB; Bro. PAUL MCMULLEN, T.O.R.; Ms. CHARMAINE WILLIAMS, Facilitator.

Presbyteral Council and Consultors—Revs. MEL BESSELLIEU; RICHARD ELDREDGE, T.O.R.; WILLIAM HOPKINS; HECTOR MEDINA; Rev. Msgr. JOSEPH A. SCHUMACHER; Revs. D. TIMOTHY THOMPSON; ROBERT WILSON; DANIEL KELLEY; HOA NGUYEN; JOHN OHNER, O.S.A.

Diocesan Finance Council—Mr. CHUCK BARTUSH JR.; Mr. JOHN HERNANDEZ; Rev. PHILIP L. JOHNSON; Ms. BARBARA MAY; Mr. DAVID MORITZ; Ms. ELAINE PETRUS; Mr. ROBERT SCHUMACHER; Mr. EARLE SHIELDS JR.; Mr. PETER FLYNN, Staff; Rev. ROBERT WILSON, Ex Officio; Rev. Msgr. JOSEPH A. SCHUMACHER, Chm. Ex Officio.

Catholic Foundation of North Texas—Mr. PETER FLYNN, Exec. Dir.; Mr. CHUCK BARTUSH JR.; Mr. JOHN HERNANDEZ; Rev. PHILIP L. JOHNSON; Ms. BARBARA MAY; Mr. DAVID MORITZ; Ms. ELAINE PETRUS; Mr. ROBERT SCHUMACHER; Mr. EARLE SHIELDS JR.; Rev. ROBERT WILSON; Rev. Msgr. JOSEPH A. SCHUMACHER.

Catholic Schools' Trust—Mr. EARLE SHIELDS JR., Chm.; Mr. KEVIN SHORT; Mr. CHARLES GAPPA; Mr. HOWARD RATTLIFF; Mr. JOHN BAILEY; Mr. TIM CONNOLLY; Mr. CHRISTOPHER PORTER; Sr. MARGUERITE CONNORS, S.H.Sp., Supt. of Schools; Mr. PETER FLYNN, Exec. Officer.

Catholic Cemeteries Trust—Mr. HENRY PENNARTZ; Mr. BILL METZLER; Mr. DAN SHINE; Mr. PAUL HOLUB; Mr. JOHN ECKELKAMP; Ms. JOLEEN RAMPY; Mr. RAY LINDEMANN; Mr. MALCOLM GORRIE, Staff.

St. Joseph's Health Care Trust—Rev. ROBERT W. WILSON.

North Texas San Benito, Inc.—Mr. PETER FLYNN.

Division Directors, Diocesan Offices

Christian Formation—Dr. DAN LUBY.

Clergy and Religious Personnel Services—Rev. Msgr. JOSEPH A. SCHUMACHER.

Executive Services—Rev. ROBERT WILSON.

Financial Services—Mr. PETER FLYNN.

Pastoral and Community Services—Mr. RALPH MCCLOUD.

Pastoral Planning and Human Resources—Ms. CHARMAINE WILLIAMS.

Schools—Sr. MARGUERITE CONNORS, S.H.Sp.

The Catholic Center—800 West Loop 820 S., Fort Worth, 76108. Tel: 817-560-3300; Fax: 817-244-8839. Departments and programs below, which are part of one of the divisions above, are listed alphabetically. Unless specifically noted the address and phone numbers are as above.

Boards and Associations

Board of Arbitration and Conciliation—Mr. PHIL RECORD, Chm.; Ms. SANDRA LEIGHTON; Mr. STEVE WILCOX; Mr. CLE ROYAL; Ms. THERESA TAYLOR.

Building Commission—Rev. Msgrs. HUBERT NEU, Chm. Emeritus; JOSEPH A. SCHUMACHER, Chm.; Mr. JACK DREWETT; Mr. CREIGHTON PICKETT; Mr. BRAD RUPAY; Mr. RONALD NIENAS; Mr. GARY FRAGOSSO, Staff.

Diocesan Pastoral Finance Council (Budgets)—Rev. ROBERT WILSON, Chm.

Diocesan School Advisory Council—Mrs. EILEEN STANKUCAS.

Mission Council—Mr. DARRYL CLEMENTS; Ms. JUANITA CLEMENTS; Mr. JAMES CRITES; Mr. PETER FLYNN; Mr. MICHAEL FAY; Mr. RALPH MCCLOUD; Sr. DOROTHY POWERS; Ms. LETTY ZATARAIN; Ms. AMY ZEDER; Mr. STEVE ZEDER; Revs. THOMAS CRAIG; ROBERT W. WILSON; JOHN GREMMELS; Mr. TOM GHESQUIERE; Ms. HILDA FLORES, Staff.

Priests' Personnel Board—Rev. JOSEPH SCANTLIN, Chm., 2100 N. Davis Dr., Arlington, 76012-1803. Tel: 817-460-2751.

Priests' Retirement Board—Rev. Msgr. JOSEPH A. SCHUMACHER, Chm.; Ms. BARBARA MAY; Mr. FRANKLIN MOORE; Rev. Msgr. HUBERT NEU; Mr.

EARLE SHIELDS; Mr. MARK SIMEROTH.

Diocesan Programs

Christian Formation—Dr. DAN LUBY, Div. Dir.
Adult Formation—Dr. DAN LUBY, Dir.
Campus Ministry—Mr. PAUL COMBEST, Contact Person.
Children's Catechesis—Ms. TERRY CASEY, Dir., Children's Catechesis & Catechetical Ministry; Sr. YOLANDA CRUZ, S.S.M.N., Assoc. Dir.
Cursillo—Rev. FRANCIS X. FERNANDEZ, O.F.M.Cap., Cursillo Center, 2221 N.W. 26th St., Fort Worth, 76106. Tel: 817-624-9411.
Hispanic Pastoral Services—Mr. ANDRES ARANDA, Dir.; Sr. ELVIRA MATA, M.C.V.P., Assoc. Dir.
Light of Christ Institute for Lay Ministry Development—Mr. PEDRO MORENO, Dir.
Media Library—Ms. RITA PHELPS; Ms. SALLY HUBBARD.
Permanent Diaconate Formation Program—Dr. ANN HEALEY, Dir.
Scouting—Rev. ANH TRAN, The Catholic Center, 800 W. Loop 820 S., Fort Worth, 76108. Tel: 817-560-3300.
Worship—Ms. MARY MCLARRY, Dir.; Mr. JOSEPH COLEMAN, Assoc. Dir.
Young Adult Ministry—Mr. PAUL COMBEST, Dir.
Youth Ministry and Adolescent Catechesis—Mr. KEVIN PREVOU, Dir.
Clergy and Religious Personnel Services—Rev. Msgr. JOSEPH A. SCHUMACHER, Div. Dir.
Clergy Relief Association—Rev. Msgr. JOSEPH A. SCHUMACHER.
Continuing Pastoral Formation—Rev. JOSEPH PEMBERTON.
Permanent Diaconate, Office of—Deacon DON WARNER, Dir.
Seminarians—Sr. DONNA FERGUSON, S.S.M.N., Dir.
Vicar for Religious—Sr. THERESA KHIRALLAH, S.S.N.D.
Vocations—Rev. ANH TRAN, Dir.
Executive Services—Rev. ROBERT WILSON, Div. Dir.
Office of Development and Stewardship—Mr. JOHN HONAMAN, Dir.; Ms. LAURA JUDD, Assoc. Dir.
Stewardship and Planning for Spanish Speaking—Ms. MARY PESQUEDA, Coord.
Newspaper—Mr. JEFF HENSLEY, Editor; Ms. MARY MARTIN, M.A., Assoc. Editor. "North Texas Catholic"
Propagation of the Faith—Rev. ROBERT WILSON, Dir.
Tribunal—Rev. TIMOTHY THOMPSON, Judicial Vicar; Ms. SANDRA LEIGHTON, Dir.; Ms. DENISE SNIDER, Case Coord.
Financial Services—Mr. PETER FLYNN, Div. Dir.; Mr. MALCOLM GORRIE, Assoc. Dir.
Accounting/Budgeting—Ms. CAROLYN JONES.
Construction and Property Management—Mr. GARY FRAGOSSO, Dir.
Cemeteries—Mr. MALCOLM GORRIE, Dir.
Planning and Human Resources—Ms. CHARMAINE WILLIAMS, Div. Dir.
Pastoral Planning Office—Ms. CHARMAINE WILLIAMS, Dir.
Benefits Coordinator—Ms. SHARON FIELDER.
Parish Pastoral Planning—Mr. JOE RODRIGUEZ.
Personnel Officer—Ms. KATHLEEN ANDREWS.
Pastoral and Community Services—Mr. RALPH MCCLOUD, Div. Dir.
African American Ministries—Mr. RALPH MCCLOUD, Dir.
Catholic Women, Council of—Rev. IVOR KOCH, Sacred Heart Parish, 1504 10th St., Wichita Falls, 76301. Tel: 817-723-5288.
Campaign for Human Development—Mr. RALPH MCCLOUD.
Ecumenism, Office of—Rev. Msgr. CHARLES KING, Immaculate Conception Church, 1215 N. Elm, Denton, 76201. Tel: 940-565-1770.
Family Life and Pre-Cana—Deacon RICHARD STOJAK.
Hospital Chaplaincy—Rev. VINCENT ELSEN, O.F.M., St. Mary of the Assumption, 509 W. Magnolia Ave., Fort Worth, 76104. Tel: 817-923-1911; Sr. TERESA NASCHE, S.H.Sp., 3416 Brady, Fort Worth, 76109. Tel: 817-926-7180.
Jail Ministry—Mr. RALPH MCCLOUD, Dir.
Peace and Justice Office—Mr. RALPH MCCLOUD, Dir.
Prolife Ministries—Deacon RICHARD STOJAK.
Rural Life—Mr. RALPH MCCLOUD, Contact Person.
St. Vincent de Paul—Mr. RALPH E. HASSEL, 3005 Phoenix Dr., Fort Worth, 76116. Tel: 817-244-4624.
Wichita Falls-United Regional Health Care System-Chaplain—Rev. AIDAN DONLON, S.A.C., 1600 11th St., Wichita Falls, 76301. Tel: 817-723-4111.
Schools—Sr. MARGUERITE CONNORS, S.H.Sp., Div. Dir. & Supt. of Catholic Schools.
Associate Superintendent of Schools—Ms. DIANE STARKOVICH.
Holy Childhood Association—Sr. MARGUERITE CONNORS, S.H.Sp., Dir.
Sexual Misconduct Review Board—Rev. ROBERT W. WILSON, Chancellor & Moderator of the Curia, 800 W. Loop 820 S., Fort Worth, 76108. Tel: 817-560-3300; Fax: 817-244-8839. Email: rwilson@fwdioc.org.
Victim Assistance Coordinator—Ms. JUDY LOCKE. Tel: 817-560-3300, Ext. 201. Email: jlocke@fwdioc.org.

CLERGY, PARISHES, MISSIONS AND PAROCHIAL SCHOOLS

CITY OF FORT WORTH
(TARRANT COUNTY)

1—ST. PATRICK CATHEDRAL (1870), Rev. Msgr. Hubert Neu; Rev. Albert Tyl. In Res., Rev. Anthanasius Kasekende.
Res.: 1206 Throckmorton St., 76102. Tel: 817-332-4915; Fax: 817-338-1988.
Catechesis/Religious Program—Tel: 817-338-4441. Students 425.

2—ALL SAINTS (1902), Revs. Stephen Jasso, T.O.R.; Ernesto De los Santos.
Res.: 214 N.W. 20th St., 76106. Tel: 817-626-3055; Fax: 817-626-3050.
School—2006 N. Houston St., 76106-8195. Tel: 817-624-2670; Fax: 817-624-1221. Lay Teachers 11; Students 165.
Catechesis/Religious Program—2022 Houston St., 76106. Tel: 817-626-1711. Students 943.

3—ST. ANDREW (1953), Revs. Warren Murphy, T.O.R.; Shawn Robertson, T.O.R.; Carl Szura. In Res., Revs. Benjamin Medeiros, T.O.R.; Theodore J. Bradower, T.O.R.
Res.: 46 Chelsea Dr., 76134. Tel: 817-927-5383; Fax: 817-927-8507.
School—St. Andrew Catholic School, 3304 Dryden Rd., 76109. Tel: 817-924-8917; Fax: 817-927-8507. Lay Teachers 38; Students 692.
Catechesis/Religious Program—Students 540.

4—ST. BARTHOLOMEW (1969), Bro. Paul McMullen, T.O.R., Pastoral Admin.; Deacons Gary Brooks; Manuel Pereda. In Res., Rev. Raohael Eagle, TOR.
Res.: 3601 Altamesa Blvd., 76133. Tel: 817-292-7703; Fax: 817-292-2568.
Catechesis/Religious Program—Students 415.

5—CHRIST THE KING, Rev. Polycarp Nguyen, C.M.C.
Res.: 1112 Eagle Dr., 76111. Tel: 817-831-7200; Fax: 817-222-3410.

6—ST. GEORGE (1941), Rev. Daniel Kelley; Deacon Ruben Curiel.
Res.: 825 Karnes, 76111. Tel: 817-831-4404; Fax: 817-834-0121.
School—824 Hudgins St., 76111. Tel: 817-222-1221; Fax: 817-838-0424. Lay Teachers 13; Students 325.
Catechesis/Religious Program—Tel: 817-831-4404. Students 200.

7—HOLY FAMILY (1942), Revs. Joseph Pemberton; Antony Mathew Pottananickal, T.O.R.; Deacons Joseph L. Milligan Jr.; Michael Mocek.
Res.: 6150 Pershing Ave., 76107. Tel: 817-737-6768; Fax: 817-737-6876.
School—Tel: 817-737-4201. Lay Teachers 20; Students 222.
Catechesis/Religious Program—Students 233.

8—HOLY NAME OF JESUS (1952), Revs. Lawrence Breedlove; Rodrigo Serrano.
Res.: 2637 Avenue L., 76105. Tel: 817-536-9604.
Catechesis/Religious Program—Tel: 817-535-8495. Students 783.

9—IMMACULATE HEART OF MARY (1961), Revs. Antonio Bandres, O.F.M.Cap.; Domingo Romero, O.F.M-.Cap.; Greg Goicoechea, O.F.M.
Res.: 100 E. Pafford St., 76110. Tel: 817-923-6323; Fax: 817-923-6523.
Catechesis/Religious Program—Tel: 817-923-8582. Students 1,562.

10—ST. JOHN THE APOSTLE (North Richland Hills) (1964), Revs. D. Timothy Thompson; Sojan George; Rodolfo Ramirez, TOR.
Res.: 7341 Glenview Dr., 76180. Tel: 817-284-4811; Fax: 817-284-1729.
School—7421 Glenview Dr., 76180. Tel: 817-284-2228; Fax: 807-284-1800. Lay Teachers 37; Students 454.
Catechesis/Religious Program—Tel: 817-590-0915. Students 900.

11—ST. MARY OF THE ASSUMPTION (1909), Rev. David Bristow. In Res., Rev. Vincent Elsen, O.F.M.
Res.: 509 W. Magnolia Ave., 76104. Tel: 817-923-1911; Fax: 817-923-0769.
Catechesis/Religious Program—Students 491.

12—OUR LADY OF FATIMA, Rev. Ignatius M. Hai Duong, C.M.C.
Mailing Address: 5109 E. Lancaster Ave., 76112. Tel: 817-446-4196.

13—OUR LADY OF GUADALUPE (1977), (Hispanic), Revs. Claudio Zudaire, O.F.M.Cap.; Francis Garces, O.F.M.Cap. In Res., Revs. Francis Fernandez, O.F.M.Cap.; Jesse Torre, O.F.M.Cap.
Res.: 4100 Blue Mound Rd., 76106. Tel: 817-626-7421; Fax: 817-626-4461.
Catechesis/Religious Program—Tel: 817-624-3240. Students 941.

14—OUR MOTHER OF MERCY (1929), (African American), Rev. Michael J. Farrell, S.S.J.
Res.: 1007 E. Terrell Ave., 76104-3788. Tel: 817-335-1695.
School—1003 E. Terrell Ave., 76104-3799. Tel: 817-336-2880; Fax: 817-338-4227. Lay Teachers 12; Students 120.

15—ST. PAUL (1952), Rev. Ellsworth T. Wigginton; Deacon Ron Aziere.
Res.: 925 Yale St., 76114. Tel: 817-738-9925; Fax: 817-735-8579.
Church: 5508-B Black Oak Ln., 76114.
Catechesis/Religious Program—Students 154.

16—ST. PETER THE APOSTLE (1952), Rev. James Hart; Deacon Pat Bresler. In Res., Rev. Anh Tran.
Office—1201 S. Cherry Ln., 76108. Tel: 817-246-3622.
School—Tel: 817-246-2032; Fax: 817-246-3686. Mrs. Deborah Herrera, Prin. Lay Teachers 18; Students 196.
Catechesis/Religious Program—Students 229.

17—ST. RITA (1910), Rev. Richard Flores.
Res.: 5550 E. Lancaster, 76112. Tel: 817-451-9395; Fax: 817-451-9421.
School—712 Weiler Blvd., 76112. Tel: 817-451-9383. Lay Teachers 15; Students 196.
Catechesis/Religious Program—Students 209.

18—SAN MATEO (1939), Rev. Robert Strittmatter.
Mailing Address: c/o 1206 Throckmorton St., 76102.
Office: 2909 Photo Ave., 76107. Tel: 817-737-5470.
Catechesis/Religious Program—Students 128.

19—ST. THOMAS (1937), Rev. Salvator Stefula, T.O.R.
Mailing Address: P.O. Box 136038, Forth Worth, 76136.
Res.: 2920 Azle Ave., 76106. Tel: 817-624-2184; Fax: 817-624-9688.
Catechesis/Religious Program—Students 635.
Mission—Holy Trinity 800 Highcrest, Azle, Tarrant Co. 76020. Tel: 817-444-3063; Fax: 817-444-2217.

20—ST. THOMAS MORE, Closed. For inquiries for parish records contact the chancery.

OUTSIDE THE CITY OF FORT WORTH

ABBOTT, HILL CO., IMMACULATE HEART OF MARY (1946), [CEM] Unassigned. In Res., Rev. Bruno Mikolajczk.
Res.: 601 W. Houston St., 76621. Tel: 254-582-3092; Fax: 254-582-0613.
Catechesis/Religious Program—Students 85.

ALBANY, SHACKELFORD CO., JESUS OF NAZARETH (1970), Rev. George Foley.
Catechesis/Religious Program—Students 54.

ALEDO, PARKER CO., HOLY REDEEMER PARISH, Rev. Robert W. Wilson; Ms. Judie Woodall, Pastoral Assoc.
Mailing Address: P.O. Box 550, 76008. Tel: 817-441-3500.
Catechesis/Religious Program—Students 144.

ARLINGTON, TARRANT CO.

1—CHURCH OF ST. MARY THE VIRGIN (1994), Rev. Allan R.G. Hawkins.
Res.: 1408 N. Davis Dr., 76012. Tel: 817-460-2278; Fax: 817-277-9927. Email: stmaryark@aol.com.
Catechesis/Religious Program—Students 42.

2—CHURCH OF THE VIETNAMESE MARTYRS (2000), Revs. Bartholomew M. Thai Hoa Do, C.M.C.; Basil M. Toan Doan, C.M.C.
801 E. Mayfield Rd., 76014. Tel: 817-557-6885.

3—ST. JOSEPH'S (1988), Deacon Dean Hermann, Pastoral Admin.; Ms. Biana Levesque, Pastoral Admin.
Office—1927 S.W. Green Oaks Blvd., 76017-2734. Tel: 817-472-5181; Fax: 817-467-9319.
Res.: 5108 Winterberry, 76018. Tel: 817-468-7521.
Catechesis/Religious Program—Students 611.

4—ST. MARIA GORETTI (1941), Revs. James Gigliotti, T.O.R.; Michael Ciski, T.O.R.
Res.: 1200 S. Davis Dr., 76013. Tel: 817-274-0643; Fax: 817-277-4193.
School—Tel: 817-275-5081. Lay Teachers 26; Students 437.
Catechesis/Religious Program—Tel: 817-274-0643, Ext. 226. Students 340.

5—ST. MATTHEW (1964), Rev. Msgr. Joseph A. Schumacher; Rev. Kyle R. Walterscheid; Deacons Eduardo Garcia; Benito Serenil; Rev. Aloysius Muthaya, SAC.
Res.: 2021 New York Ave., 76010-6097. Tel: 817-860-0130; Fax: 817-277-7159.
Catechesis/Religious Program—Students 1,672.

6—MOST BLESSED SACRAMENT (1978), Revs. Joseph S. Scantlin; Gonzalo Morales; Deacon Jim Blackmore.
Res.: 2100 N. Davis Dr., 76012. Tel: 817-460-2751; Fax: 817-460-2761.

Catechesis/Religious Program—Students 733.
7—ST. VINCENT DE PAUL (1976), Revs. Thomas Craig; Thobiyas Perianayagam; Deacon Charles Castleberry.
Res.: 5819 W. Pleasant Ridge Rd., 76016. Tel: 817-478-8206; Fax: 817-478-8513.
Catechesis/Religious Program—Tel: 817-478-8208; Fax: 817-478-8513. Students 1,570.

BEDFORD, TARRANT CO., ST. MICHAEL (1977), Revs. Philip Johnson; Jeff Poirot; Deacon Harry Heinz.
Res.: 3713 Harwood, 76021-4097. Tel: 817-283-8746; Fax: 817-283-9306.
School—Holy Trinity Catholic School Please see section [D] Elementary and Secondary Schools, Parochial, in the Institution Section for more information.
Catechesis/Religious Program—Students 923.

BOWIE, MONTAGUE CO., ST. JEROME (1986), Attended by, St. Mary, Henrietta. Rev. Stephen Berg.
Mailing Address: 105 S. Barrett, Henrietta, 76365. Tel: 940-538-4214.
Catechesis/Religious Program—Students 40.

BRECKENRIDGE, STEPHENS CO., SACRED HEART (1920), Rev. George Foley.
Res.: 208 S. Miller St., 76424. Tel: 254-559-2860; Fax: 254-559-5289.
Catechesis/Religious Program—Students 107.

BRIDGEPORT, WISE CO., ST. JOHN THE BAPTIZER (1889), Rev. Gilbert Pansza.
Res.: 1801 Irvin, 76426. Tel: 940-683-2743; Fax: 940-683-5958.
Catechesis/Religious Program—Students 43.

BURKBURNETT, WICHITA CO., ST. JUDE THADDEUS (1965), Rev. Hoa Nguyen.
Res.: 600 Davey Dr., 76354. Tel: 940-569-1222; Fax: 940-569-2714.
Catechesis/Religious Program—Students 110.

BURLESON, TARRANT CO., ST. ANN (1971), Rev. John Hennessy.
Res.: 100 S.W. Alsbury Blvd., 76028. Tel: 817-295-5621; Fax: 817-295-5482.
Catechesis/Religious Program—Tel: 817-426-1101; Fax: 817-426-1106. Students 388.

CARROLLTON, DENTON CO., ST. CATHERINE OF SIENA (1981), Rev. George Thennattil, T.O.R.; Deacons Philip Webb; Robert Stuart.
Mailing Address: 1705 Peters Colony, 75007-3704. Tel: 972-492-3237; Fax: 972-394-0676.
Catechesis/Religious Program—Students 721.

CISCO, EASTLAND CO., HOLY ROSARY (1920), Attended by, St. Rita, Ranger. , 1109 Blackwell St., Ranger, 76470. Tel: 254-647-3167.
Catechesis/Religious Program—Students 31.

CLEBURNE, JOHNSON CO., ST. JOSEPH (1888), Rev. Sergio Rizo.
Mailing Address: 807 N. Anglin St., 76031. Tel: 817-645-4478; Fax: 817-558-9938.
Catechesis/Religious Program—Tel: 817-558-9938. Students 315.

CLIFTON, BOSQUE CO., HOLY ANGELS (1954), Attended by, Our Lady of Mercy, Hillsboro. Rev. Alberto Bueno, T.O.R.; Bro. John Patrick Coley, TOR, Pastoral Assoc.; Deacon James Poole.
Church: 1915 W. Fifth St., 76634. Tel: 254-675-8877; Fax: 254-675-2298.
Catechesis/Religious Program—Tel: 254-675-3165. Students 96.

COLLEYVILLE, TARRANT CO., GOOD SHEPHERD (1992), Sisters Dorothy Eggering, S.S.N.D., Pastoral Admin.; Theresa Khirallah, S.S.N.D., Pastoral Admin.
1000 Tinker Rd., 76034. Tel: 817-421-1387; Fax: 817-421-4709.
School—Holy Trinity Catholic School Please see section [D] Elementary and Secondary Schools, Parochial, in the Institutions Section for more information.

COMANCHE, COMANCHE CO., SACRED HEART (1964), Attended by, St. Brendan, Stephenville.
Church: 1444 W. Washington Ave., Stephenville, 76401. Tel: 254-965-5693.
Catechesis/Religious Program—Tel: 915-356-2040. Students 77.

CROWELL, FOARD CO., ST. JOSEPH (1910), Attended by, Holy Family, Vernon. Rev. Oren W. Key, S.J.
Church: 2200 Roberts, P.O. Box 1377, Vernon, 76384. Tel: 940-552-2895; 940-552-9370 (Rel. Ed.); Fax: 940-552-6084.

DE LEON, COMANCHE CO., OUR LADY OF GUADALUPE (1975), Attended by, St. Brendan, Stephenville. , Mailing Address: *c/o St. Brendan*, 1444 W. Washington, Stephenville, 76401. Tel: 254-965-5693.
Church: Hwy. 16, 2 miles S. of Hwy. 6, 76444. Tel: 817-893-5511.
Catechesis/Religious Program—Students 50.

DECATUR, WISE CO., ASSUMPTION OF THE BLESSED VIRGIN MARY (1938), Rev. Gilbert Pansza.
1305 Deer Park Rd., 76234-9701. Tel: 940-627-3307; Fax: 940-683-5958.
Church Rectory: 1801 Irvin, Bridgeport, 76426.
Catechesis/Religious Program—Tel: 940-683-2743. Students 369.

DENTON, DENTON CO.
1—IMMACULATE CONCEPTION (1894), Rev. Msgr. Charles King; Rev. Rigoberto Contreras; Deacon Popo Gonzalez.
Res.: 1215 N. Elm St., 76201. Tel: 940-565-1770; Fax: 940-382-7939.
Catechesis/Religious Program—Sr. Helen Stejskal, S.S.N.D., D.R.E. Students 648.
2—ST. MARK (1995), Revs. Eugene Sweeney, S.M.; Daniel Trulzi, S.M.
2800 Pennsylvania, 76205. Tel: 940-387-6223; Fax: 940-382-1641.
Catechesis/Religious Program—Students 406.

DODSON PRAIRIE, PALO PINTO CO., ST. BONIFACE (1913), Closed. For inquiries for parish records contact the chancery.

DUBLIN, ERATH CO., ST. MARY (1916), Attended by, St. Brendan, Stephenville. , 1444 W. Washington Ave., Stephenville, 76401. Tel: 254-965-5693.
Church: 12286 S. U.S. Hwy. 377, 73446. Tel: 254-445-3300.
Catechesis/Religious Program—Tel: 254-445-0237. Students 195.

EASTLAND, EASTLAND CO., ST. FRANCIS XAVIER (1920), Attended by, St. Rita, Ranger. , 1109 Blackwell St., Ranger, 76470. Tel: 254-647-3167; Fax: 254-647-3167.

ELECTRA, WICHITA CO., ST. PAUL (1966), [JC] Deacon Patrick Burke, Admin.
Mailing Address: P.O. Box 991, 76360.
Office—1008 First St., Iowa Park, 76367. Tel: 940-592-2802; Fax: 940-592-2802.
Res.: 709 W. Rebecca St., Iowa Park, 76367. Tel: 940-592-2930.
Church: 500 N. Bailey, 76360. Tel: 940-495-3464; 940-592-2802.

GAINESVILLE, COOKE CO., ST. MARY (1879), Rev. James J. Sheridan, O.S.A. In Res., Rev. Donald Brennan, O.S.A.
Res.: 805 N. Weaver St., 76240. Tel: 940-665-5395, Ext. 2; Fax: 940-665-0957.
School—931 N. Weaver St., 76240. Tel: 940-665-5395; Fax: 940-668-1881. Lay Teachers 15; Students 165.
Catechesis/Religious Program—Tel: 817-665-0957. Students 280.
Convent—825 N. Weaver St., 76240.

GLEN ROSE, SOMERVELL CO., ST. ROSE OF LIMA (1969), [JC] Attended by, St. Frances Cabrini. Rev. Juan Rivero; Deacon Frank Eschbach.
2301 Acton Hwy., Granbury, 76048. Tel: 817-326-2131; Fax: 817-326-3211.
Catechesis/Religious Program—Students 114.

GRAFORD, PALO PINTO CO., ST. FRANCIS OF ASSISI (1949), Attended by, Our Lady of Lourdes, Mineral Wells. Rev. William J. Hopkins.
Res.: P.O. Box 404, 76449. Tel: 254-779-2023.

GRAHAM, YOUNG CO., ST. MARY (1922), [JC] Rev. Raymund A. Mullan.
Res.: 1218 S. Rodgers Dr., Box 547, 76450. Tel: 940-549-4314; Fax: 940-549-5618.
Catechesis/Religious Program—Tel: 940-549-1058. Students 173.

GRANBURY, HOOD CO., ST. FRANCES CABRINI (1976), [JC] Rev. Juan Rivero; Deacons Ed Bevers; Jim Bell; Dick Stojak; Jim Fuller.
Res.: 2301 Acton Hwy., 76049. Tel: 817-326-2131; Fax: 817-326-3211.
Catechesis/Religious Program— 76048. Tel: 817-326-2131. Students 346.

GRAPEVINE, TARRANT CO., ST. FRANCIS OF ASSISI (1949) Rev. Ken Robinson; Deacons Anthony Falbo; M. C. Marquez.
Res.: 861 Wildwood, 76051-3398. Tel: 817-481-2685; Fax: 817-488-3169.
School—Holy Trinity Catholic School Please see section [D] Elementary and Secondary Schools, Parochial, in the Institutions Section for more information.
Catechesis/Religious Program—Students 1,876.

HENRIETTA, CLAY CO., ST. MARY (1879), [CEM] Rev. Stephen Berg.
Res.: 105 S. Barrett St., 76365. Tel: 940-538-4214; Fax: 940-538-6638.

HILLSBORO, HILL CO., OUR LADY OF MERCY (1887), Rev. Alberto Bueno, T.O.R.; Bro. John Patrick Calvey, TOR, Pastoral Assoc.; Deacon James Poole.
Res.: Interstate 35, P.O. Box 567, 76645. Tel: 254-582-5640; Fax: 254-582-0347.
Catechesis/Religious Program—Students 120.

HURST, TARRANT CO., KOREAN MARTYRS CATHOLIC CHURCH, Rev. Felix Hyo-UN Lee.
415 Brown Tr., 76053. Tel: 817-268-0181; Fax: 817-485-2460. Email: leefelix@hanmail.net.

IOWA PARK, WICHITA CO., CHRIST THE KING (1980), Deacon Patrick Burke, Pastoral Admin.
Mailing Address: P.O. Box 239, 76367.
Office—1008 First St., 76367. Tel: 940-592-2802.
Res. 709 W. Rebecca St., 76367. Tel: 940-592-2930; Fax: 940-592-2802.
Catechesis/Religious Program—Students 45.

JACKSBORO, JACK CO., ST. MARY (1911), Rev. Gilbert Pansza.
Mailing Address: *c/o St. John the Baptizer*, 1801 Irvin St., Bridgeport, 76426. Tel: 940-683-2743; 940-683-2743 (Rel. Ed.); Fax: 940-683-5958; 940-683-2743 (Rel. Ed.).
Church: Hwy. 148 N., 76458.

KELLER, TARRANT CO., ST. ELIZABETH ANN SETON (1985), Revs. John Gremmels; Dennis Smith; Gary Geurtz; Deacons Klaus Gutbier; Donald E. Warner; Myles Miller; Robert Montini.
Office—2016 Willis Ln., 76248. Tel: 817-431-3857; Fax: 817-431-9568.
School—(Grades PreK-4) Tel: 817-431-4845. Kay Burrell, Prin. Students 469.
Catechesis/Religious Program—Tel: 817-431-6023; Fax: 817-431-3871. Students 1,840.

KNOX CITY, KNOX CO., SANTA ROSA (1948), [JC] Attended by, St. Joseph, Rhineland Rev. Leo Schloemer, G.H.M.; Deacon Ben Vasquez.
Mailing Address: P.O. Box 428, 79529. Tel: 940-658-5062.
Church: N. 3rd and Ave. G, 79529. Tel: 940-658-5062.
Catechesis/Religious Program—Students 40.

LEWISVILLE, DENTON CO., ST. PHILIP THE APOSTLE (1976), Rev. John Stasiowski; Deacons Raymond G. Lamarre; Bart Supino; John Kerrigan.
Office—1897 W. Main St., 75067. Tel: 972-436-9581; Fax: 972-436-5302.
Catechesis/Religious Program—Tel: 972-219-7448. Students 816.

LINDSAY, COOKE CO., ST. PETER (1902), [CEM] Rev. Ronald Scheible, O.S.A.
Res.: 424 Main St., P.O. Box 148, 76250. Tel: 940-668-7609; Fax: 940-668-7723.
Catechesis/Religious Program—Tel: 940-665-6763. Students 291.

MANSFIELD, TARRANT CO., ST. JUDE (1898), [CEM] Revs. Joseph S. Scantlin; John Robert Skeldon.
Res.: 500 E. Dallas St., 76063. Tel: 817-473-6709; Fax: 817-477-2088.
Catechesis/Religious Program—Tel: 817-473-0768. Students 663.

MEGARGEL, ARCHER CO., ST. MARY (1909), [CEM] Attended by, Sacred Heart, Seymour. Rev. Richard Eldredge, T.O.R.
207 W. Pecan, Seymour, 76380. Tel: 940-889-5252; Fax: 940-889-2136.

MINERAL WELLS, PALO PINTO CO., OUR LADY OF LOURDES (1960), Rev. William J. Hopkins.
Res.: 108 N.W. 4th Ave., P.O. Box 1327, 76068. Tel: 940-325-4789; Fax: 940-327-8170.
Catechesis/Religious Program—Students 202.

MONTAGUE, MONTAGUE CO., ST. WILLIAM (1899), [CEM] Attended by, St. Mary, Henrietta. Rev. Stephen Berg.
Mailing Address: 105 S. Barrett, Henrietta, 76365. Tel: 940-538-4214; Fax: 940-538-6638.
Catechesis/Religious Program—Students 29.

MORGAN, BOSQUE CO., OUR LADY OF GUADALUPE (1987), Attended by, Our Lady of Mercy, Hillsboro. Rev. Alberto Bueno, T.O.R.; Bro. John Patrick Calvey, TOR; Deacon James Poole.
Mailing Address: 304 Charles St., P.O. Box 470, 76671. Tel: 254-635-0145; Fax: 254-675-2298.

MUENSTER, COOKE CO., SACRED HEART (1889), [CEM] Rev. John Ohner, O.S.A.
Res.: 714 N. Main St., 76252. Tel: 940-759-2511; Fax: 940-759-4422.
School—Preschool Lay Teachers 3; Students 24.
School—Benedictine Sisters 2; Lay Teachers 13; Students 191.
High School—Benedictine Sisters 2; Lay Teachers 11; Students 141.
Catechesis/Religious Program—Tel: 940-759-2511, Ext. 37. Students 263.

NOCONA, MONTAGUE CO., ST. JOSEPH (1948), Attended by, St. Mary, Henrietta. Rev. Stephen Berg.
105 S. Barrett, Henrietta, 76365. Tel: 940-538-4214; Fax: 940-538-6638.

OLNEY, YOUNG CO., ST. THERESA OF THE INFANT JESUS (1935), [JC] Attended by, St. Mary, Graham. Rev. Raymund A. Mullan.
Mailing Address: P.O. Box 547, Graham, 76450. Tel: 940-549-4314.
Church: Oak & Ave. E, 76374. Tel: 940-564-5426.

PENELOPE, HILL CO., NATIVITY OF THE BLESSED VIRGIN MARY (1909), [CEM 2] Attended by, Immaculate Heart of Mary, Abbot. , Mailing Address: P.O. Box 98, 76676. Tel: 254-582-3092; Fax: 254-582-3092. In Res., Rev. Bruno Mikolajczk.
Catechesis/Religious Program—Tel: 254-533-2486. Students 50.

PILOT POINT, DENTON CO., ST. THOMAS AQUINAS (1891), [CEM] Rev. Mel Bessellieu.
Res.: 925 N. Charcut, 76258. Tel: 940-686-2088; Fax: 940-686-3044.
Catechesis/Religious Program—400 E. Gibbons, 76258. Tel: 940-686-2360. Students 215.

QUANAH, HARDEMAN CO., ST. MARY (1914), [JC] Attended by, Holy Family, Vernon. Rev. Oren W.

Key, S.J.
2200 Roberts, P.O. Box 1377, Vernon, 76384. Tel: 940-552-2895; Fax: 940-552-6084.

RANGER, EASTLAND CO., ST. RITA (1919), Deacon Ruben Castaneda, Pastoral Admin.
Res.: 1109 Blackwell St., 76470. Tel: 254-647-3167; Fax: 254-647-3167.

RHINELAND, KNOX CO., ST. JOSEPH (1895), [CEM] Rev. Leo Schloemer, G.H.M.; Deacon Julian Estrada.
Res.: 10180 CR 6010, Munday, 76371. Tel: 940-422-4994; Fax: 940-422-4994.
Catechesis / Religious Program—Students 130.

SCOTLAND, ARCHER CO., ST. BONIFACE (1911), [CEM] Attended by, St. Mary, Windthorst. Rev. David Kraeger, T.O.R.
Church: 76379. Tel: 940-423-6687; Fax: 940-423-6657.

SEYMOUR, BAYLOR CO., SACRED HEART (1910), [CEM] Rev. Richard Eldredge, T.O.R.
Res.: 207 W. Pecan St., 76380. Tel: 940-889-5252.
Sacred Heart Pastoral Center—207 W. Pecan, 76380. Fax: 940-889-2136.
Catechesis / Religious Program—Students 92.

STEPHENVILLE, ERATH CO., ST. BRENDAN (1958), Rev. Philip McNamara, S.A.C.; Deacon William Bolf.
Res.: 1444 W. Washington Ave., 76401. Tel: 254-965-5693.
Catechesis / Religious Program—Students 250.

STRAWN, PALO PINTO CO., ST. JOHN (1912), Attended by, St. Rita.
Res.: 1109 Blackwell Rd., Ranger, 76470. Tel: 254-647-3167.

THE COLONY, DENTON CO., HOLY CROSS (1981), Rev. Publius Xuereb.
Church: 7000 Morning Star, P.O. Box 560156, 75056. Tel: 972-625-5252; Fax: 972-370-5524.
Catechesis / Religious Program—Students 420.

THROCKMORTON, THROCKMORTON CO., SAN PATRICIO (1964), Closed. For inquiries for parish records contact the chancery., Sacred Heart, Breckenridge.

VALLEY VIEW, COOKE CO., ST. JOHN (1946), [JC] Unassigned. In Res., Rev. Joseph Meledom.
Res.: 709 Lee St., 76272. Tel: 940-726-3524.

VERNON, WILBARGER CO., HOLY FAMILY (1891), Rev. Oren W. Key, S.J.
Res.: 2200 Roberts, P.O. Box 1377, 76384. Tel: 940-552-2895; Fax: 940-552-6084.
Catechesis / Religious Program—Tel: 940-553-1580. Students 76.

WEATHERFORD, PARKER CO., ST. STEPHEN (1882), Rev. John Casey, S.A.C.; Deacon Carlos Frias.
Mailing Address: P.O. Box 1743, 76086.
Office—1802 Bethel Rd., 76086. Tel: 817-596-9585.
Res.: 1904 Bethel Rd., 76086. Tel: 817-596-9586.
Catechesis / Religious Program—Students 477.

WICHITA FALLS, WICHITA CO.

1—OUR LADY OF GUADALUPE (1927), [JC] Rev. Hector Medina; Deacon Anastasio Perez.
Res.: 421 Marconi, 76301. Tel: 940-766-2735; Fax: 940-766-4052.
Parish Hall—Tel: 940-322-0143.
Catechesis / Religious Program—Students 200.

2—OUR LADY QUEEN OF PEACE (1956), [JC] Rev. John Swistovich; Deacons Richard A. Arndt; Larry W. Bills.
Res.: 4040 York Ave., 76309. Tel: 940-696-1253; Fax: 940-696-1216.
Catechesis / Religious Program—Fax: 940-696-1253. Students 218.

3—SACRED HEART (1891), [JC] Revs. Ivor Koch; Atanasio M. Linh Uy, C.M.C.
Mailing Address: 1504 Tenth St., 76301. Tel: 940-723-5288; Fax: 940-767-0160.
Res.: 1505 Ninth St., 76301. Tel: 940-723-5288; Fax: 940-767-0160.
Catechesis / Religious Program—Students 306.
Mission—The Assumption of Mary [CEM] [JC] 2901 Barnett Rd., Wichita Co. 76310. Tel: 940-692-1825.

WINDTHORST, ARCHER CO., ST. MARY (1892), [CEM] Rev. David Kraeger, T.O.R.
Res.: P.O. Drawer 230, 76389. Tel: 940-423-6687; Fax: 940-423-6657.
Catechesis / Religious Program—Students 305.

Chaplains of Public Institutions

FORT WORTH. *Federal Medical Center, Carswell.* 76199. Revs. Vincent Inametti, M.S.P. (HON), Krsysztof Bauta (HON).

DENTON. *State School*, 1215 E. Elm St., 76201. Tel: 817-387-1755. Deacon Emilio (Popo) Gonzalez.

GAINESVILLE. *Texas Youth Council Youth Facility*, 805 N. Weaver, 76240. Tel: 817-665-2413. Rev. James Sheridan, O.S.A.

WICHITA FALLS. *State Hospital*, Tel: 817-723-4111. Rev. Aidan Donlon, S.A.C.

On Duty Outside the Diocese:
Revs.—
Olson, Michael
Spong, William, Ogdensburg, NY
Thames, Robert, Residencia de Arzobispado, Casilla 25, Santa Cruz, Bolivia.

Graduate Studies:
Rev.—
Olson, Michael

Retired:
Revs.—
Beaumont, Richard
Blank, Severius, 1022 Sheridan St., Burkburnett, 76354.
Cooney, Gerald, c/o 1824 Clark Rd., Crowley, 76036-9714.
Curtsinger, George, 3015 Lubbock, #5, 76109.
Edwards, Dale
Fisher, Harry, 1002 John Reagan St., 76126.
Landwermeyer, Bart, St. Subiaco Abbey, Subiaco, AR 72865.
Magaldi, Philip, 22982 Lone Oak Dr., Estero, FL 33928.
Miller, James
Miranda, Luke, 3240 Daniels, Apt. 101, Dallas, 75205.
O'Toole, James, c/o The Catholic Center, 800 W. Loop 820 S., 76108.
Perez, Salvador, Calle 22 #678, N. con Avenida Guerrero, Torreon, Coah 27000 Mexico.
Stephens, Gerald, 208 Martin St., Wylie, 75098.

Permanent Deacons:
Amos, Clarence
Arndt, Richard
Aziere, Ronald
Barry, Gerald
Bell, James
Benoit, Roland
Bevers, Eddy
Bills, Larry
Blackmore, Jim
Bolf, William
Bowden, Edgar
Bressler, Patrick
Brooks, Gary
Burke, Patrick
Camargo, Moises
Casias, Arturo
Castaneda, Ruben
Castellon, Damaso
Castleberry, Charles
Curiel, Ruben
Detwiler, Russell
Dorsey, Tim
Escamilla, Juan
Eschbach, Frank
Estrada, Julian
Falbo, Tony
Firth, John
Frias, Carlos
Fuller, Jim
Garcia, Eduardo
Garcia, Pedro
Garcia, Raul
Germann, Joe
Giovannitti, Thomas
Gonzalez, Adolfo
Gonzalez, Emilio
Greene, Clifford
Griego, Richard
Gutbier, Klaus
Guzman, John
Hatch, Larry
Heinz, Harry
Hermann, Dean
Hoang, Dominic
Hoang, Michael
Huerta, Lauro
Kerrigan, John
Krempp, Michael
Kunath, Wolfgang
Lamarre, Raymond
Laremore, Robert
Marquez, Mario
Maskow, Kurt
McDermott, John
Miller, Myles
Milligan, Joseph
Mocek, Michael
Montini, Robert
Novak, Jim
Onofre, Jose
Pereda, Manuel
Perez, Anastasio
Poole, James
Poth, Louis J.
Reyes, Juan
Ruiz, Jesus
Salva, Hector
Serenil, Benito
Standridge, Joe
Stojak, Dick
Stuart, Robert
Supino, Bart
Torrez, Simon
Vasquez, Ben
Warner, Don
Weaver, Lonnie, Jr.
Webb, Philip
Wolf, George
Wuenschel, Douglas F.

INSTITUTIONS LOCATED IN THE DIOCESE

[A] COLLEGES & UNIVERSITIES

FORT WORTH. *The College of St. Thomas More*, 3013 Lubbock St., 76109.

[B] HIGH SCHOOLS, DIOCESAN

FORT WORTH. *Cassata High School* (Coed Secondary). , 1400 Hemphill St., 76104-4796. Tel: 817-926-1745; Fax: 817-926-3132. Email: cassata@hotmail.com. Web: www.expage.com/page/cassata. Mr. Bob Stephens, Exec. Dir. Teachers 11; Students 387.

Nolan Catholic High School, (Grades 7-12) , (Coed) , 4501 Bridge St., 76103. Tel: 817-457-2920; Fax: 817-496-9775. Email: rthompson@nolancatholichs.org. Web: www.nolancatholichs.org. Rev. Lawrence Doersching, S.M., Pres.; Bro. Richard Thompson, S.M., Prin.; Rev. James Mueller, S.M. Society of Mary Priests 2; Brothers 6; Sisters 1; Lay Teachers 70; Students 1,035.
Nolan School Trust

WICHITA FALLS. *Notre Dame Middle-High School*, 2821 Lansing Blvd., 76309. Tel: 940-692-6041; Fax: 940-692-2811. Email: nd.ubdie@esc9.net. Web: www.notredamecatholic.org. Mr. Chris Neeb, Prin. Lay Teachers 22; Students 134.

[C] HIGH SCHOOLS, PAROCHIAL

MUENSTER. *Sacred Heart School*, (Grades PreK-12), 141 E. Sixth, Box 588, 76252. Tel: 940-759-2511; Fax: 940-759-4422. Email: jmurdock@nortexinfo.net. Web: www.nortexinfo.net/sacredheart/schools.html. Mr. Jon LeBrasseur, Prin. Priests 1; Olivetan Benedictine Sisters 3; Lay Teachers 24; Students 253.
**Sacred Heart Teachers Trust Fund*

[D] ELEMENTARY AND SECONDARY SCHOOLS, PAROCHIAL

ARLINGTON. *Holy Rosary Catholic School*, 2015 S.W. Green Oaks Blvd., 76017. Tel: 817-419-6800; Fax: 817-419-7080. Email: lday@hrestx.com. Mr. Lynn L. Day, Prin. Total Staff 37; Students 433.

DENTON. *Immaculate Conception Catholic School*, 2301 N. Bonnie Brae, 76201. Tel: 940-381-1155; Fax: 940-381-1837. Email: eschad@escll.net. Web: www.catholicschooldenton.org. Ms. Elaine Schad, Prin. Lay Teachers 13; Students 255.

GRAPEVINE. *Holy Trinity Catholic School*, .. 3750 William D. Tate Ave., 76051. Tel: 817-421-8000; Fax: 817-421-4468. Email: htcs2@airmail.net. Dr. Jack Murdock, Prin. Lay Teachers 36; Students 549.

WICHITA FALLS. *Notre Dame Elementary School*, 4060 York Ave., 76309. Tel: 940-696-1011; Fax: 940-691-6913. Web: www.notredamecatholic.org. Mr. Chris Neeb, Prin. Sisters 1; Lay Teachers 13; Students 195.

[E] ELEMENTARY SCHOOLS, PRIVATE

FORT WORTH. *Our Lady of Victory Elementary*, 3320 S. Hemphill St., 76110. Tel: 817-924-5123; Fax: 817-922-6598. Email: tmiller@olvfw.com. Web: www.olvfw.com. Ms. Trudy Miller, Prin. Sisters 2; Lay Teachers 14; Students 247.

[F] CHILDREN'S GROUP CARE

FORT WORTH. *Catholic Charities, Inc.* An Independent Corporation Founded by the Diocese of Fort Worth. , 2701 Burchill Rd. N., 76105-3012. Tel: 817-534-0814; Fax: 817-535-8779. Email: webmaster@ccdofw.org. Web: www.ccdofw.org. Karen Spicer, L.M.S.W., A.C.P., Exec. Dir. Provides direct financial and material assistance to families in financial crisis.
Emergency Financial Assistance, 1404 Hemphill, 76104. Tel: 817-921-5381; Fax: 817-923-6818.
Office Sites:
401 W. Sanford, Arlington, 76011. Tel: 817-274-2560; Fax: 817-274-1797.

Harvest House, 349 N.W. Renfro, Burleson, 76028. Tel: 817-295-6675; Fax: 817-295-2392.

Westaid, 4701 Bryant Irwin Rd. N., Ste. 100, 76107. Tel: 817-737-9338; Fax: 817-732-4331.

Senior Disabled Housing, 2701 Burchill Rd. N., 76105-3012. Tel: 817-534-0814; Fax: 817-535-8779. Administers residential programs for the elderly, and disabled.

Program Sites:

Nuestro Hogar, Inc., 709 Magnolia St., Arlington, 76012. Tel: 817-216-0608; Fax: 817-861-6178.

CASA, Inc., 3201 Sondra Dr., 76107. Tel: 817-332-7276; Fax: 817-877-0487.

CASA Brendan & CASA II, Inc., 1300 Hyman St., Stephenville, 76401. Tel: 817-965-6964; Fax: 817-968-3072.

Program Sites:

Healthy Start, 2001 Beach St., Ste. 800, 76103. Tel: 817-534-8372; Fax: 817-534-8812.

Assessment Center of Tarrant County, 2000 McKenzie, 76105. Tel: 871-534-0814. (Children's Shelter)

Extended Day Treatment & Family Support Services, 2701 Burchhill Rd., 76105. Tel: 817-534-0814; Fax: 817-535-8779.

Therapeutic Foster and Respite Care, 2701 Burchill Rd. N., 76105. Tel: 817-534-0814; Fax: 817-535-8779.

Family Preservation Unit, 2701 Buchill Rd., 76104. Tel: 817-534-0814; Fax: 817-535-8779.

Anne Simon Reeves Children's Center, 2641 Ave. L, 76105. Tel: 817-534-0814; Fax: 817-535-8779.

Clinical Counseling Department, 2701Burchill Rd., 76104. Tel: 817-534-0814; Fax: 817-535-8779.

Immigration and Refugee Services Department, 1216 W. Magnolia, 76104. Tel: 817-338-0774; Fax: 817-335-9749. Janie Hermosillo, Co-Dir.; Ahmed Aquino, Co-Dir.

Community and Parish Support Services, 1404 Hemphill, 76104. Tel: 807-921-5381; Fax: 817-923-6818. Lylette Pharr, L.M.S.W., Dept. Dir.

[G] GENERAL HOSPITALS

WICHITA FALLS. *United Regional Health Care System*, Eleventh Street Campus, 1600 Eleventh St., 76301. Tel: 940-723-4111. Email: dwitcker@urhcs.org. Web: www.urhcs.org. Mr. David D. Whitaker, Pres. & CEO; Sr. M. Irena, C.S.F.N., Supr.; Rev. Aidan Donlon, S.A.C., Chap. Sisters of the Holy Family of Nazareth Sisters 5; Bed Capacity 542; Patients Assisted Annually 160,000.

[H] RETIREMENT & DISABILITY HOUSING

FORT WORTH. *Casa del Cor, Inc.*, 2701 Burchill Rd. N., 76105. Tel: 817-534-0814; Fax: 817-535-8779. Email: webmaster@ccdofw.org. Web: www.ccdofw.org.

Casa, Inc. Housing for the Elderly and Handicapped, 3201 Sondra Dr., 76107. Tel: 817-332-7276; Fax: 817-877-0487. Email casainc1@plash.net. Web: www.ccdofw.org. Units 200; Total in Residence 189; Total Staff 10.

ARLINGTON. *Nuestro Hogar, Inc. Catholic Charities*, 709 Magnolia St., 76012. Tel: 817-261-0608. Email: nuestrol@flash.net. Web: www.ccdofw.org. 65 unit apartment complex for the elderly and disabled. Total in Residence 65; Total Staff 5.

CROWLEY. *St. Francis Village, Inc.*, 1 Chapel Plaza, 76036. Tel: 817-292-5786; Fax: 817-294-2989. Email: deanamh@mindspring.com. Web: www.saintfrancisvillage.com. Deana Harris, Admin.; Rev. Lambert Leykam, O.F.M., Chap. Active Retirement village, on shores of Lake Benbrook near Fort Worth, for retirees and the elderly sponsored by Franciscan Tertiary Provinces Foundation & SFV, Inc. (Illinois). Residents 420. In Res. Rev. Msgr. W. Robert Johnson (Retired); Revs. Augustine Healey, O.C.D.; James Miller.

Franciscan Tertiary Provinces Foundation, 1 Chapel Plaza, 76036. Tel: 817-292-5786. Sponsor corporation of St. Francis Village (retirement village) in Crowley, TX. Total Staff 12.

STEPHENVILLE. *CASA Brendan & CASA II, Inc. Catholic Charities*, 1300 Hyman, 76401. Tel: 254-965-6964; Fax: 254-968-3072. Email: casab@our-town.net. Web: www.ccdofw.org. 86 unit apartment complex for the elderly and handicapped. Total in Residence 88; Total Staff 9.

[I] MONASTERIES AND RESIDENCES OF PRIESTS AND BROTHERS

CROWLEY. *St. Maximilian Kolbe Friary* (Fort Worth), One Marquard Cir. & Two Marquard Cir., St. Francis Village, 76036. Tel: 817-370-9747; Fax: 817-361-9522. Email: maxkolby@aol.com. Revs. Peter Fritz, O.F.M.; Raymar Bobber O.F.M.; Vincent Eisen, O.F.M; Jovian Lang, O.F.M; Cal Giesen; Kenan Dulzer; Lambert Leykam, O.F.M.; Bros. Camillus Smith, O.F.M., Guardian; Allan Haiar, O.F.M.; Lester Kocklin; Michel LeMier.

[J] CONVENTS AND RESIDENCES FOR SISTERS

FORT WORTH. *Hermanas Catequistas Guadalupanas*, 1001 Altamont Dr., 76106. Tel: 817-740-0038. Sisters 2.

Missionary Catechists of the Sacred Hearts of Jesus and Mary, 2640 Avenue L., 76105. Tel 817-535-8495. Sr. Lucia Flores, Supr. Sisters 3.

Provincialate, Our Lady of Victory Center, 909 W. Shaw St., 76110. Tel: 817-923-8393; Fax: 817-921-5064. Email: dorothypowers@sbcglobal.net. Web: web2.airmail.net/ssmn. Sr. Dorothy Powers, S.S.M.N., Prov. Supr. Provincial House of the Western Province, Sisters of St. Mary of Namur

Sisters of St. Mary Namur, 909 W. Shaw, 76110. Tel: 817-921-0305; 817-923-8393; Fax: 817-921-5064. Email: dorothypowers@sbcglobal.net. Web: web2.airmail.net/ssmn/. Sr. Dorothy Powers. Sisters of St. Mary of Namur

ARLINGTON. *Monastery of the Most Holy Trinity, Discalced Carmelites*, 5801 Mt. Carmel Dr., 76017. Tel: 817-468-1781; Fax: 817-468-1782. Email: arcarmel@ix.netcom.com. Web: www.carmelnuns.com. Sr. Anne Teresa Kulinski, O.C.D., Prioress. Solemn Professed Nuns 9; Temporary Professed Nuns 2.

WICHITA FALLS. *Mercy Convent*, 3000 Lansing Blvd., 76309. Tel: 940-692-9770; Fax: 940-696-1216. Email: mercycom@aol.com. Web: web2.airmail.net/ssmn. Sisters 2.

Notre Dame House of Prayer and Hospitality, 2820 Lansing Blvd., 76309. Tel: 940-692-2043. Email: sjstewar79@aol.com. Sisters 2.

[K] RETREAT HOUSES

LAKE DALLAS. *Montserrat Jesuit Retreat House*, 600 N. Shady Shores Rd., P.O. Box 398, 75065. Tel: 940-321-6020; 940-321-6030; Fax: 940-321-6040. Email: retreat1@airmail.net. Web: web2.airmail.net/retreat1. Revs. Hernando Ramirez, S.J., Dir.; Walter C. McCauley, S.J., Assoc. Dir.; John L. Vessels, S.J.

Montserrat Foundation, Inc. Tel: 940-321-6020; Fax: 940-321-6040.

Board Members & Directors: Rev. George Wiltz, S.J.; Mr. Adam Auten; Mr. Archy Roper.

[L] RENEWAL CENTERS

FORT WORTH. *The Catholic Renewal Center of North Texas, Inc.*, 4503 Bridge St., 76103. Tel: 817-429-2920 (Metro); Fax: 817-492-3668. Email: crcwomen@aol.com. Web: www.catholiccrc.org. Ms. Gail Schatzman, Dir.

Beginning Experience Tel: 817-429-2920; Fax: 817-492-8668.

Retorno Tel: 817-485-9764.

Special Days for Special People Tel: 807-429-2920; Fax: 817-492-8668.

National Marriage Encounter of North Texas Tel: 817-451-6005.

Engaged Encounter of North Texas Tel: 817-429-2920; Fax: 817-492-8668.

CRC Ministries Outreach Tel: 940-382-3594. Sisters Pat Miller, S.S.N.D.; Kay Kolb, S.S.N.D.

Rachel's Vineyard Post Abortion Ministry Tel: 817-457-4757.

[M] SOCIETY OF ST. VINCENT DE PAUL

FORT WORTH. *St. Vincent de Paul Diocesan Council of Fort Worth*, 8504 Redwing Lane, 76123. Tel: 817-361-8704; Fax: 817-361-8704. Email: rehassel@aol.com. Mr. Ralph E. Hassel, Pres.

WICHITA FALLS. *Particular Council of Wichita Falls, St. Vincent de Paul Society*, 4516 Lake Park Dr., 76302. Tel: 817-322-2920. Mr. Walter Brady.

[N] NEWMAN CENTERS

FORT WORTH. *Texas Christian University Catholic Community* TCU Box 297310, 76129-0001. Tel: 817-257-7830; Fax: 817-257-7333. Email: c.calabrese@tcu.edu. Web: www.catholic.tcu.edu. Rev. Charles L. Calabrese (STU).

ARLINGTON. *UTA Catholic Campus Center* 303 Lampe, 76010. Tel: 817-460-1155. Email: egray@fwdioc.org.

Legal Title: *University of Texas at Arlington University Catholic Community*

DENTON. *University of North Texas and Texas Woman's University* 1303 Eagle Dr., 76201. Tel: 940-566-0004; Fax: 817-244-8839. Email: egray@fwdioc.org. Web: orgs.unt.edu/unt_ccm. Rev. Marc Clifford, O.S.F.S.; Mr. Eric Gray, Campus Min.

Legal Title: *University of North Texas and Texas Woman's University*

HEWITT. *Hill College Newman Center* 810 Rolling Hills Dr., 76643. Email: poole646@aol.com. Deacon Jim Poole, Campus Min.

WICHITA FALLS. *Catholic Campus Ministry* Midwestern State University, 3410 Louis Rodriguez Dr., 76308. Tel: 940-692-9778. Email: msuccc@yahoo.com. Web: www.mwsu.edu/htmldocs/departments/organizations/catholic/framehomepage.htm. Ms. Debbie Neely.

[O] MISCELLANEOUS

FORT WORTH. *Community Hospice of North Texas*, 6100 Western Place, Ste. 500, 76107. Tel: 817-870-2795; Fax: 817-878-3713. Email: agreen@chot.org. Ms. Andrea Green.

Ministry to Gay & Lesbians, 3312 Dryden Rd., 76109. Tel: 817-927-5383; Fax: 817-927-8507. Email: frwarren@standrewsch.org. Web: www.standrewcc.org. Rev. Warren L. Murphy, T.O.R.

North Texas San Benito, Inc., The Catholic Center, 800 W. Loop, 820 S., 76108. Tel: 817-560-3300; Fax: 817-244-8839. Email: pflynn@fwdioc.org. Web: www.fwdioc.org.

Sisters of St. Mary of Namur, 909 W. Shaw, 76110. Tel: 817-923-8393; Fax: 817-921-5064. Email: dorothypowers@sbcglobal.net.

GRAPEVINE. *Magnificat, Grapevine Chapter*, 2217 Branchwood Dr., 76051. Tel: 817-329-3218; Fax: 817-724-0252. Email: rjofulton@hotmail.com. Mrs. JoAnn Fulton, Coord.

RELIGIOUS INSTITUTES OF MEN REPRESENTED IN THE DIOCESE

For further details refer to the corresponding bracketed number in the Religious Institutes of Men or Women section.

[0140]—*The Augustinians*—O.S.A.
[0470]—*The Capuchin Friars*—O.F.M.Cap.
[0520]—*Franciscan Friars*—O.F.M.
[0570]—*Glenmary Home Missioners*—G.H.M.
[]—*Heralds of Good News*—H.G.N.
[0690]—*Jesuit Fathers and Brothers*—S.J.
[]—*Oblates of St. Francis de Sales*—O.S.F.S.
[]—*Priests and Brothers of the Congregation of Mother Coredemptrix*—C.M.C.
[0760]—*Society of Mary (Marianists)*—S.M.
[0990]—*Society of the Catholic Apostolate*—S.A.C.
[0700]—*St. Joseph's Society of the Sacred Heart*—S.S.J.
[0560]—*Third Order Regular of Saint Francis*—T.O.R.

RELIGIOUS INSTITUTES OF WOMEN REPRESENTED IN THE DIOCESE

[]—*Hermanas Franciscanas de la Inmaculada Concepcion*—H.F.I.C.
[]—*Missionary Catechist Sisters of the Sacred Heart of Jesus and Mary*—M.C.S.H.
[0100]—*Adorers of the Blood of Christ*—A.S.C.
[0230]—*Benedictine Sisters of Pontifical Jurisdiction*—O.S.B.
[1110]—*Cabra Dominican Sisters*—O.P.
[0460]—*Congregation of Sisters of Charity of the Incarnate Word*—C.C.V.I.
[0420]—*Discalced Carmelite Nuns*—O.C.D.
[1900]—*Hermanas Catequistas Guadalupanas*—H.C.G.
[2690]—*Missionary Catechists of Divine Providence*—M.C.D.P.
[2970]—*School Sisters of Notre Dame*—S.S.N.D.
[3950]—*Sisters of Saint Mary of Namur*—S.S.M.N.
[1970]—*Sisters of the Holy Family of Nazareth*—C.S.F.N.
[2050]—*Sisters of the Holy Spirit and Mary Immaculate*—S.H.Sp.

NECROLOGY

(No Deaths)

Diocese of Fresno

(Dioecesis Fresnensis)

Most Reverend

JOHN T. STEINBOCK, D.D.

Bishop of Fresno; ordained May 1, 1963; appointed Titular Bishop of Midila and Auxiliary Bishop of Orange May 29, 1984; consecrated July 14, 1984; installed as Bishop of Santa Rosa March 31, 1987; installed as Bishop of Fresno November 24, 1991. *Office: 1550 N. Fresno St., Fresno, CA 93703-3788.* Tel: 559-488-7400; Fax: 559-488-7464.

Chancery Office: 1550 N. Fresno St., Fresno, CA 93703-3788. Tel: 559-488-7400; Fax: 559-488-7464.

ESTABLISHED DECEMBER 15, 1967.

Square Miles 35,239.

Formerly Diocese of Monterey-Fresno.

Comprises the Counties of Fresno, Inyo, Kern, Kings, Madera, Mariposa, Merced and Tulare in the State of California.

Diocesan Patroness: St. Therese of the Child Jesus.

Legal Title: Legal titles of parishes and institutions, the Roman Catholic Bishop of Fresno, a Corporation Sole, Diocese of Fresno Education Corporation (for schools).

STATISTICAL OVERVIEW

Personnel	
Bishop	1
Priests: Diocesan Active in Diocese	85
Priests: Diocesan Active Outside Diocese	1
Priests: Retired, Sick or Absent	29
Number of Diocesan Priests	115
Religious Priests in Diocese	31
Total Priests in Diocese	146
Extern Priests in Diocese	18
Ordinations:	
Diocesan Priests	3
Permanent Deacons	22
Permanent Deacons in Diocese	31
Total Sisters	124
Parishes	
Parishes	86
With Resident Pastor:	
Resident Diocesan Priests	59
Resident Religious Priests	8
Without Resident Pastor:	
Administered by Priests	19
Missions	40
Professional Ministry Personnel:	
Sisters	23
Lay Ministers	311
Welfare	
Catholic Hospitals	3
Total Assisted	573,780
Homes for the Aged	2
Total Assisted	216
Special Centers for Social Services	2
Total Assisted	351,718
Educational	
Diocesan Students in Other Seminaries	23
Total Seminarians	23
High Schools, Diocesan and Parish	2
Total Students	1,369
Elementary Schools, Diocesan and Parish	23
Total Students	5,331
Catechesis/Religious Education:	
High School Students	7,329
Elementary Students	23,665
Total Students under Catholic Instruction	37,717
Teachers in the Diocese:	
Priests	3
Sisters	23
Lay Teachers	368
Vital Statistics	
Receptions into the Church:	
Infant Baptism Totals	17,209
Adult Baptism Totals	579
Received into Full Communion	523
First Communions	12,147
Confirmations	4,020
Marriages:	
Catholic	1,823
Interfaith	307
Total Marriages	2,130
Deaths	3,135
Total Catholic Population	581,000
Total Population	2,327,272

Former Prelates of Diocese of Monterey-Fresno—Most Revs. JOHN B. MACGINLEY, D.D., ord. June 8, 1895; consecrated May 10, 1910; First Bishop of Monterey-Fresno, July 31, 1924; resigned Sept. 30, 1932; died Oct. 18, 1969; PHILIP G. SCHER, ord. June 6, 1903; appt. April 28, 1933; consecrated June 29, 1933; died Jan. 3, 1953; ALOYSIUS J. WILLINGER, C.Ss.R., ord. July 2, 1911; consecrated Bishop of Ponce, Puerto Rico, Oct. 28, 1929; Coadjutor Bishop of Monterey/Fresno ""cum jure successionis," Dec. 12, 1946; succeeded to the See, Jan. 3, 1953; resigned Oct. 25, 1967; died July 25, 1973; HARRY ANSELM CLINCH, D.D., ord. June 6, 1936; consecrated Feb. 27, 1957; appt. Auxiliary to the Bishop of Monterey-Fresno, Dec. 5, 1956; transferred to the See of Monterey, Dec. 14, 1967; retired Jan. 19, 1982; died March 8, 2003.

Former Bishops of the Diocese of Fresno—His Eminence TIMOTHY CARDINAL MANNING, D.D., J.C.D., ord. June 16, 1934; appt. Titular Bishop of Lesvi and Auxiliary of Los Angeles, Aug. 3, 1946; consecrated Oct. 15, 1946; installed as First Bishop of Fresno, Dec. 15, 1967; elevated to Coadjutor Archbishop of Los Angeles "cum jure successionis," May 26, 1969; succeeded to the See, Jan. 21, 1970; created Cardinal, March 5, 1973; died June 23, 1989; Most Rev. HUGH A. DONOHOE, D.D., Ph.D., ord. June 14, 1930; appt. Auxiliary in San Francisco, Aug. 2, 1947; consecrated Oct. 7, 1947; appt. Bishop of Stockton, Feb. 21, 1962; appt. Second Bishop of Fresno, Aug. 28, 1969; resigned July 1, 1980; died Oct. 26, 1987; His Eminence ROGER CARDINAL MAHONY, D.D., ord. May 1, 1962; appt. Auxiliary Bishop of Fresno, Jan. 7, 1975; ord. Bishop, March 19, 1975; transferred to Diocese of Stockton, Feb. 26, 1980; installed April 17, 1980; appt. Archbishop of Los Angeles, July 16, 1985; installed Sept. 5, 1985; created Cardinal, June 28, 1991; Most Rev. JOSEPH J. MADERA, M.Sp.S., D.D., ord. June 15, 1957; consecrated March 4, 1980; succeeded to the See on July 1, 1980; transferred to Archdiocese for the Military Services, Washington, DC May 28, 1991.

Vicar General and Moderator of the Curia—Rev. Msgr. MYRON J. COTTA, V.G.

Chancellor—Sr. ROSA MARIA GUEMBE, R.C.M.

Chancery Office—1550 N. Fresno St., Fresno, 93703-3788. Tel: 559-488-7400; Fax: 559-488-7464.

Diocesan Tribunal—1550 N. Fresno St., Fresno, 93703-3788. Tel: 559-488-7490; Fax: 559-488-7498. Email: tribunal@dioceseoffresno.org.

Satellite Tribunal—Christ the King Center, 1800 Bedford Way, Bakersfield, 93308. Tel: 661-391-4640; Fax: 661-391-4649.

Judicial Vicar—Rev. Msgr. STEPHEN A. FROST, J.C.L., Satellite Tribunal Dir.. Email: safrost@juno.com.

Adjutant Judicial Vicar—Rev. MICHAEL A. BURCHFIELD, J.C.L., Asst. Tribunal Dir.. Email: fathermichael@dioceseoffresno.org.

Tribunal Director—NANCY S. STEVENS, J.C.L.. Email: nstevens@dioceseoffresno.org.

Tribunal Office Assistant & Tribunal Bilingual Auditor—Mrs. PATRICIA RUIZ. Tel: 559-488-7425. Email: pruiz@dioceseoffresno.org.

Tribunal Secretaries—Mrs. NANCY CLEMONS. Email: nclemons@dioceseoffresno.org; Mrs. CUAUHTEMOC "TEMO" DIAZ. Email: temo@dioceseoffresno.org.

Satellite Tribunal Secretary—Mrs. DIANE FRAILEY. Email: dianefrailey@christtheking.ws.

Ecclesiastical Notaries—Mrs. NANCY CLEMONS; Mrs. DIANE FRAILEY; Mrs. PATRICIA RUIZ; Revs. THOMAS TIMMINGS; PERRY KAVOOKJIAN; Mrs. MARIA ALANIS FLORES.

Defenders of the Bond—Rev. Msgrs. MICHAEL BRAUN; PATRICK MCCORMICK.

Advocates—Rev. Msgrs. JOHN ESQUIVEL; JOHN GRIESBACH; RICHARD URIZALQUI; WALTER F. MINHOTO (Retired).

Diocesan Consultors—Rev. Msgrs. RONALD SWETT, V.F.; DANIEL LOPEZ, V.F.; Revs. ERIC SWEARINGEN; GERRY CHAVEZ, V.F.; STEVE BULFER, V.F.; Rev. Msgrs. MYRON COTTA, V.G.; JAMES T. LOGAN (Retired).

Vicars Forane—Rev. ERIC SWEARINGEN; Rev. Msgr. RONALD SWETT, V.F.; Revs. GERRY CHAVEZ, V.F.; STEVE BULFER, V.F.; Rev. Msgr. DANIEL LOPEZ, V.F.

Diocesan Offices and Directors

Catholic Charities—PHILIP TRAYNOR, Dir., 149 N. Fulton, Fresno, 93701. Tel: 559-237-0851; Fax: 559-237-7144.

Channel 49 (KNXT)—MARV HARRISON, Gen. Mgr., 1550 N. Fresno St., Fresno, 93703-3788. Tel: 559-488-7440; Fax: 559-488-7444.

Cursillo Movement—Rev. Msgr. ANTHONY JANELLI, 1550 N. Fresno St., Fresno, 93703-3788. Tel: 559-488-7424.

Diocese of Fresno Education Corporation—1550 N. Fresno St., Fresno, 93703-3788.

Diocesan Newspaper—BILL LUCIDO, Editor, 1550 N. Fresno St., Fresno, 93703-3788. "Central California Catholic Life"

Finance Committee—Rev. Msgrs. MYRON J. COTTA, V.G.; J. WAYNE HAYES, P.A.; MICHAEL BRAUN; LEROY GILSDORF; GARY BETHKE; LARRY STEFANI; GARY RENNER; PAUL R. WORSLEY JR., 1550 N. Fresno St., Fresno, 93703-3788. Tel: 559-488-7400.

Deposit and Loan Fund—Rev. Msgrs. MYRON J. COTTA, V.G.; MICHAEL BRAUN; J. WAYNE HAYES, P.A.; Mr. JAMES F. SWEENEY; Mrs. ROSEMARY MCCAVE; Mr. GARY BETHKE.

Detention Ministry—ELAINE LOPES, 1550 N. Fresno St., Fresno, 93703-3788. Tel: 559-493-2851.

Holy Childhood, Pontifical Association—Rev. Msgr. MYRON J. COTTA, V.G., Dir., 1550 N. Fresno St., Fresno, 93703-3788. Tel: 559-488-7400; Fax: 559-488-7464.

Italian Catholic Federation—Rev. Msgr. J. WAYNE HAYES, P.A., Diocesan Chap.

Legion of Mary—Rev. Msgr. LASERIAN BYRNE, Diocesan Dir., 5770 N. Maroa, Fresno, 93704. Tel: 559-439-0124.

Marian Federation of Guadalupe—Rev. Msgr. DANIEL LOPEZ, Diocesan Chap., 2441 Dockery Ave., Selma, 93662.

Newman Apostolate—Rev. PERRY KAVOOKJIAN, 1572 E. Barstow Ave., Fresno, 93710. Tel: 559-436-3434.

Office of Catholic Education—RICHARD SEXTON, Supt.; Miss PATRICIA BAILEY, Asst. Supt.

Diocesan Advisory Board of Education—Mrs. DEBORAH LEARY, Pres., 1510 N. Fresno St.,

Fresno, 93703-3711. Tel: 559-488-7420; Fax: 559-488-7422.

Office of Diocesan Properties—TIM TILLMAN, 1550 N. Fresno St., Fresno, 93703-3788. Tel: 559-488-7470.

Office of Finances—GARY BETHKE, Fiscal Mgr., 1550 N. Fresno St., Fresno, 93703-3788. Tel: 559-488-7426; Fax: 559-488-7461.

Office of Insurance and Human Resources—Mr. PAT GORDON, S.P.H.R., Dir., 1550 N. Fresno St., Fresno, 93703-3788. Tel: 559-488-7488.

Office of Ministries—Sr. CLARA ANN BUDENZ, O.P.; PAUL MENTLEWSKI, Admin. Asst. Tel: 559-488-7474.

Campesino Ministry (Spanish)—Mr. ZEFERINO GONZALEZ. Tel: 559-488-7455.

Family Life Ministry—VACANT. Vacant

Lay Ministry Formation Coord.—Sr. CLARA ANN BUDENZ, O.P.

Youth Ministry—LUCIA RANGEL, Bilingual Youth Ministry Coord.

Office of Liturgy, Worship and Evangelization—Rev. TIMOTHY GALLEMORE, Dir., P.O. Box 119, Laton, 93242. Tel: 559-923-4935; Fax: 559-923-2284. Email: fathertim@ourladyoffatima.com.

Ecumenical Affairs—Rev. GREGORY J. BEAUMONT, 19 Follett St., Lemoore, 93245. Tel: 559-924-2562.

Master of Ceremonies—Rev. Msgr. PATRICK MCCORMICK, Mailing Address:, 4636 W Dakota Ave., Fresno, 93722-4699. Tel: 559-275-2022; Fax: 559-275-2040. Email: fatherpat@stmarysfresno.org.

Pastoral Center / St. Anthony Retreat House—DEAN DAVISON, 1530 N. Fresno St., Fresno, 93703. Tel: 559-488-7470.

Permanent Diaconate Office—Deacon EDWARD HARMON, Dir., 1550 N. Fresno St., Fresno, 93703-3788. Tel: 559-493-2840.

Personnel Committee—Rev. RAUL SANCHEZ; Rev. Msgrs. STEPHEN FROST; J. WAYNE HAYES, P.A.; JOHN HARGUINDEGUY; MYRON J. COTTA, V.G.; Rev. ERIC SWEARINGEN; Rev. Msgr. DANIEL LOPEZ, V.F.; Revs. GERRY CHAVEZ, V.F.; STEPHEN BULFER, V.F.; Rev. Msgr. RONALD SWETT, V.F.

Priests' Council—Rev. Msgr. MYRON J. COTTA, V.G.; Rev. ERIC SWEARINGEN; Rev. Msgr. DANIEL LOPEZ, V.F.; Revs. GERRY CHAVEZ, V.F.; STEVE BULFER, V.F.; Rev. Msgr. RONALD SWETT, V.F.; Rev. HARVEY FONSECA; Rev. Msgrs. STEPHEN FROST; PAT MCCORMICK; JAMES LOGAN; Revs. TIM GALLEMORE; VITO DIMARZIO, R.C.J.; Sr. ROSA MARIA GUEMBE, R.C.M.; Rev. Msgr. JOHN ESQUIVEL.

Propagation of the Faith and St. Peter Society—Rev. Msgr. MYRON J. COTTA, V.G., 1550 N. Fresno St., Fresno, 93703-3788.

Retreats—Retreat Master: Rev. Msgr. JOHN GRIESBACH, Dir., P.O. Box 249, Three Rivers, 93271. Tel: 559-561-4595.

Scouting—Revs. GERALD NORTHRUP, Chap., Sequoia Council, P.O. Box 410, Bass Lake, 93604; JOHN FLUETSCH, Chap., Southern Sierra Council, 1300 9th Pl., Wasco, 93280. Tel: 661-758-6688.

Vicar for Clergy—Rev. Msgr. MYRON J. COTTA, V.G.

Continuing Formation of Priests—Rev. Msgr. MYRON J. COTTA, V.G., 1550 N. Fresno St., Fresno, 93703-3788. Tel: 559-488-7400; Fax: 559-488-7464; Rev. JEAN-MICHAEL LASTIRI, P.O. Box 2087, Merced, 95344. Tel: 209-383-3924.

Vicar for Insurance and Retirement Affairs—Rev. Msgr. J. WAYNE HAYES, P.A., 1621 Center Ave., Los Banos, 93635. Tel: 209-826-4246; Fax: 209-826-5335.

Vicar for Religious—Sr. ROSA MARIA GUEMBE, R.C.M., 1550 N. Fresno St., Fresno, 93703. Tel: 559-488-7400; Fax: 559-488-7464.

Victim Assistance Coordinator—Rev. Msgr. MYRON J. COTTA, V.G. Tel: 559-488-7400. Email: msgrmyron@dioceseoffresno.org; Mr. PAT GORDON, Human Resource Dir.. Email: pat@dioceseoffresno.org.

Vocations—Rev. Msgr. ANTHONY JANELLI, Dir., 1550 N. Fresno St., Fresno, 93703-3788. Tel: 559-488-7424; Fax: 559-488-7475.

CLERGY, PARISHES, MISSIONS AND PAROCHIAL SCHOOLS

CITY OF FRESNO
(FRESNO COUNTY)

1—ST. JOHN CATHEDRAL (1882), Rev. Msgr. John Esquivel, Rector; Rev. Francisco Diaz. In Res., Rev. Msgr. Walter F. Minhoto (Retired); Rev. Jose Luis Rico.
Res.: 2814 Mariposa St., 93721. Tel: 559-485-6210; Fax: 559-485-8409.
Catechesis / Religious Program—Tel: 559-485-0161. Students 1,857.
Mission—St. Francis Ninth & Lowe, Fresno Co. 93702. Tel: 559-485-9467; Fax: 559-453-0165. Rev. Joseph Nguyen, (Vietnamese Ministry).

2—ST. ALPHONSUS (1908), Rev. Raul Sanchez.
351 E. Kearney Blvd., 93706. Tel: 559-233-8275; Fax: 559-233-9379.
Catechesis / Religious Program—Students 95.

3—ST. ANTHONY CLARET (Calwa Area) (1952), Revs. Brian Culley, C.M.F.; Valentino Ramon, C.M.F.
Res.: 2494 S. Chestnut Ave., 93725. Tel: 559-255-4260; Fax: 559-255-6329.
Catechesis / Religious Program—Tel: 559-255-0223. Students 491.
Mission—Christ the King 3565 Calvin St., Malaga, Fresno Co. 93725. Tel: 559-498-3819; Fax: 559-255-6329.

4—ST. ANTHONY OF PADUA (1953), Rev. Msgr. John Coelho-Harguindeguy; Rev. Loren Blessing.
Office—5770 N. Maroa St., 93704. Tel: 559-439-0124; Fax: 559-439-3050.
School—Tel: 559-435-0700; Fax: 559-435-6749. Mr. Shawn Carey, Prin. Lay Teachers 24; Students 631.
Catechesis / Religious Program—5770 N. Maroa St., 93704. Tel: 559-439-0124. Students 800.
Mission—St. Agnes 111 W. Birch, Pinedale, Fresno Co. 93650. Tel: 559-439-2100. Rev. Israel Avila.

5—ST. GENEVIEVE (1941), [CEM] Rev. Vincent Lau (Hong Kong).
Res.: 1127 Tulare St., 93706. Tel: 559-486-2988; Fax: 559-486-2988. Res.: P.O. Box 12324, 93777-2324.

6—ST. HELEN (1955), Rev. David J. Norris, D.Min. In Res., Revs. Joseph Nguyen Hoan (Vietnam); Gerald Amerando.
Office—4875 E. Grant Ave., 93727. Tel: 559-255-3871; Fax: 559-255-7625.
Res.: 4870 E. Belmont, 93727.
School—4888 E. Belmont, 93727. Tel: 559-251-5855; Fax: 559-251-5948. Dr. Toni Amodio, Prin. Lay Teachers 13; Students 362.
School—Junior Kindergarten, Tel: 209-251-2422. Monica Kay, Dir.
Catechesis / Religious Program—Students 181.

7—HOLY SPIRIT (1981), Rev. Eric Swearingen; Sharon Tellifson, Business Mgr.
Mailing Address: 355 E. Champlain Dr., 93720-1273. Tel: 559-434-7701; Fax: 559-434-7734.
Res.: 8781 N. Millbrook, 93720-1718. Tel: 559-439-2159 (Rectory).
Catechesis / Religious Program—Tel: 559-434-3522. Judy Bedrosian, D.R.E. Students 450.
Mission—Infant Jesus of Prague Tollhouse, Tollhouse, Fresno Co. 93667. Tel: 559-855-4659.
Station—Holy Spirit Tollhouse, Shaver Lake. Tel: 559-841-3524.

8—ST. MARY (1967), [CEM] Rev. Msgr. Patrick Joseph McCormick.
Res.: 4636 W. Dakota, 93722. Tel: 559-275-2022; Fax: 559-275-2040.
Catechesis / Religious Program—Tel: 559-271-1459. Students 304.

9—OUR LADY OF MT. CARMEL (1955), Rev. Warren Hengel Jr.
Office—816 Pottle Ave., 93706. Tel: 559-264-2587; Fax: 559-264-2539.
Catechesis / Religious Program—Students 100.
Mission—Mission de Guadalupe Raisin City, Fresno Co.

10—OUR LADY OF VICTORY (1950), Rev. Msgr. John Moreton.
Res.: 1215 W. Michigan Ave., 93705. Tel: 559-226-1163.
Parish Center—2850 N. Crystal, 93705. Fax: 559-226-2093.
School—1626 W. Princeton Ave., 93705. Tel: 559-229-0205; Fax: 559-229-3230. Mr. Terry Lane, Prin. Lay Teachers 11; Students 224; Total Enrollment 317.
Catechesis / Religious Program—Tel: 559-229-2084. Students 317.

11—ST. PAUL (1964), Rev. Perry Kavookjian. In Res., Rev. Michael Burchfield; Deacon John Supino.
California State University: *St. Paul Newman Center*, 1572 E. Barstow Ave., 93710. Tel: 559-436-3434; Fax: 559-436-3430.
Catechesis / Religious Program—Students 297.

12—SACRED HEART (1947), Rev. Leslie F Shenoy.
Res.: 2240 N. Cedar Ave., 93703-2668. Tel: 559-237-4121; Fax: 559-237-0122.
School—4460 E. Yale, 93703. Tel: 559-251-3171; Fax: 559-251-7778. Sr. Kathleen Drilling, S.S.N.D., Prin. Lay Teachers 8; Students 150.
Catechesis / Religious Program—Tel: 559-237-4365. Students 256.

13—ST. THERESE (1925), Rev. Msgr. E. James Petersen; Revs. John Congdon; Flordito Redulla, S.V.D.
Mailing & Res.: 855 E. Floradora Ave., 93728. Tel: 559-268-6388; Fax: 559-268-0852.
Catechesis / Religious Program—Students 313.

OUTSIDE THE CITY OF FRESNO

ARVIN, KERN CO., ST. THOMAS (1941), Rev. Lucas Azpericueta.
Res.: 350 E. Bear Mountain Blvd., 93203. Tel: 661-854-6150; Fax: 661-854-2564.
Catechesis / Religious Program—Students 210.

ATWATER, MERCED CO., ST. ANTHONY (1909), Rev. Thomas Timmings.
Office—1799 Winton Way, 95301. Tel: 209-358-5743; Fax: 209-358-2423.
Res.: 1999 Juniper Ave., 95301.
School—Tel: 209-358-3341. Miss Dianne Silva, Prin. Lay Teachers 8; Students 155.
School—Preschool, Tel: 209-358-3341 Mary Oliveira, Dir.
Catechesis / Religious Program—Tel: 209-357-3259. Students 820.
Mission—Immaculate Conception 1799 Winton Way, Buhach, Merced Co. 95301.

AVENAL, KINGS CO., ST. JOSEPH (1941), Revs. Juan Franco, M.S.C. (Mexico); Juan Pineda, M.S.C. (Mexico).
Res.: 428 E. Kern St., 93204. Tel: 559-386-9523; Fax: 559-386-1068.
Catechesis / Religious Program—Students 58.
Mission—St. Cecilia Milham & 8th St., Kettleman City, Kings Co. 93239.

BAKERSFIELD, KERN CO.

1—ST. FRANCIS (1878), Revs. Craig F. Harrison; Victor Dinh.
Res.: 900 H St., 93304. Tel: 661-327-4734; Fax: 661-327-4930.
School—2516 Palm St., 93304. Tel: 661-326-7955; Fax: 661-327-0395. Mrs. Cynthia Meek, Prin. Lay Teachers 21; Students 530.
School—Day Care / Preschool, Tel: 661-326-7958. Mrs. Mary Johnson, Dir. Students 78.
Catechesis / Religious Program—Tel: 661-323-8800. Mrs. Alice Fry, D.R.E. Students 844.

2—ST. JOSEPH (1907), Revs. Robert D. Wenzinger; Ricardo Magdaleno.
Res.: 1515 Baker St., 93305. Tel: 661-327-2744; Fax: 661-327-0133.
Catechesis / Religious Program—Tel: 661-325-2581. Students 1,699.

3—OUR LADY OF GUADALUPE (1925), Revs. James Catalano, O.S.J.; Chummar Chirayath, O.S.J. (India).
Res.: 601 E. California Ave., 93307. Tel: 661-323-3148; Fax: 661-323-6016.
School—609 E. California Ave., 93307. Tel: 661-323-6059. Sr. Margarita Gallardo, S.J.S., Prin. Sisters 3; Lay Teachers 12; Students 170.
Catechesis / Religious Program—Tel: 661-323-7642. Luis Maldonado, D.R.E. Students 1,253.
Mission—Holy Spirit 720 E. Belle Terrace, Kern Co. 93307. Tel: 661-834-7095.
Mission—St. Jude 825 Chapman, Kern Co. 93307. Tel: 661-323-2347.

4—OUR LADY OF PERPETUAL HELP (1948), Rev. Msgr. Michael R. Braun.
Res.: 124 Columbus St., 93305. Tel: 661-323-3108; Fax: 661-325-7067.
School—Tel: 661-327-7741. Mrs. Eleanor Etcheverry, Prin. Lay Teachers 15; Students 289.
Catechesis / Religious Program—Tel: 661-327-0712. Students 152.
Mission—San Clemente 1305 Water St., Kern Co. 93305. Tel: 661-871-9190. Rev. Angel Sotelo.

5—SACRED HEART (1953), Rev. Dan Coyle.
Res.: 9915 Ramos St., 93307. Tel: 661-831-8905; Fax: 661-837-8075.
Catechesis / Religious Program—Tel: 661-831-6223; Fax: 661-837-8073. Students 290.

6—ST. PHILIP THE APOSTLE, Rev. Msgr. Ronald J. Swett; Rev. Titus Rodrigo, O.S.B.
Mailing Address: 7100 Stockdale Hwy., 93309-1399. Tel: 661-834-7483; Fax: 661-834-2214.
School—Preschool Mrs. Karen Cerri, Dir.
Catechesis / Religious Program—Leila Hinzman, D.R.E. Students 1,200.

BASS LAKE, MADERA CO., OUR LADY OF THE SIERRA (1999), Rev. Gerald Northrup.
40180 Indian Springs Rd., Oakhurst, 93644.
Res. & Mailing Address: P.O. Box 410, 93604. Tel: 559-642-3452; Fax: 559-642-3452.
Mission—St. Joseph the Worker 56522 Rd. 200, North Fork, Madera Co. 93643.
Mission—St. Dominic Savio (1961), 40077 Rd. 222, Madera Co. 93604.

BISHOP, INYO CO., OUR LADY OF PERPETUAL HELP, Rev. Charles B. Casale.
Res.: 849 N. Home St., 93514. Tel: 760-872-7231; Fax: 760-872-9222.
Catechesis / Religious Program—Tel: 760-873-8862; Fax: 760-873-8862. Students 96.
Mission—St. Stephen 461 S. Main St., Big Pine, Inyo Co. 93513. Tel: 760-872-7231.

BUTTONWILLOW, KERN CO., ST. MARY (1941), Rev.

Msgr. Loydell J. Marth, Admin.
Res.: 420 N. Main St., Box 875, 93206. Tel: 661-764-5486.
Catechesis/Religious Program—Students 57.
CALIFORNIA CITY, KERN CO., OUR LADY OF LOURDES (1982), Rev. John Gracey.
Mailing Address: P.O. Box 2060, California City, 93505. Tel: 760-373-2256; Fax: 760-373-2206.
Catechesis/Religious Program—Karen Thomas, D.R.E. Students 54.
Mission—St. Joseph (1969), P.O. Box 1080, Boron, Kern Co. 93596. Tel: 760-762-5453.
CHOWCHILLA, MADERA CO., ST. COLUMBA (1921), [JC] Rev. Kenneth J. Bozzo.
Res.: 213 Orange Ave., 93610. Tel: 559-665-3376; Fax: 559-665-0546.
Catechesis/Religious Program—Tel: 559-665-5104. Students 265.
CLOVIS, FRESNO CO., OUR LADY OF PERPETUAL HELP (1929), Rev. Msgr. Raymond C. Dreiling.
Res.: 929 Harvard, 93612. Tel: 559-299-4270; Fax: 559-299-7126.
Church: Ninth & DeWitt, 93612.
School—836 DeWitt, 93612. Tel: 559-299-7504; Fax: 559-299-4627. Immaculate Conception Sisters 4; Lay Teachers 8; Students 272.
Catechesis/Religious Program—Students 700.
COALINGA, FRESNO CO., ST. PAUL THE APOSTLE (1907), (Mexican-English), [JC] Rev. Nobert Rackensperger, O.F.M.Conv.
Res.: 637 Sunset St., P.O. Box 812, 93210. Tel: 559-935-1872; Fax: 559-935-3763.
Catechesis/Religious Program—Students 200.
CORCORAN, KINGS CO., OUR LADY OF LOURDES (1941), (Hispanic), Rev. Gerald F. Chavez.
Res.: 1404 Hanna, 93212. Tel: 559-992-4414; Fax: 559-992-2512.
Catechesis/Religious Program—Tel: 559-992-4698. Students 376.
CUTLER, TULARE CO., ST. MARY (1953), Rev. Jose Luis Vega.
Res.: 12588 Avenue 407, P.O. Box 6, 93615. Tel: 559-528-3566.
Catechesis/Religious Program—Tel: 559-528-3077; Fax: 559-528-3535. Students 400.
DEL REY, FRESNO CO., ST. KATHERINE, , (Quasi-parish included with St. Mary, Sanger). Rev. Vito DiMarzio, R.C.J.
Res.: 828 "O" St., P.O. Box 335, Sanger, 93657. Tel: 559-888-2889; 559-875-2025; Fax: 559-875-2618.
Catechesis/Religious Program—Students 68.
DELANO, KERN CO.
1—ST. MARY'S OF THE MIRACULOUS MEDAL (1920), Revs. Rick Fierros, M.Div.; James Kyrie, O.F.M. (Retired).
Res.: 916 Lexington St., 93215. Tel: 661-725-8456; Fax: 661-725-8485.
School—Tel: 661-725-9055; Fax: 661-725-3224. Ms. Luci DeAvila, Prin. Lay Teachers 4; Students 50.
Catechesis/Religious Program—Tel: 661-725-9041. Students 625.
Mission—St. Vincent 1716 11th Ave., Richgrove, Tulare Co. 93215.
2—OUR LADY OF GUADALUPE (1954), Revs. Emerito Gomez, O.F.M.; Ervan Beers, O.F.M.
Res.: 1015 Clinton St., 93215. Tel: 661-725-9087; 661-725-9115; Fax: 661-725-5128.
Catechesis/Religious Program—Tel: 661-725-2777; Fax: 661-725-7129. Students 550.
DINUBA, TULARE CO., ST. CATHERINE (1948), Rev. Rod L. Craig.
Res.: 356 N. Villa Ave., 93618. Tel: 559-591-0931; Fax: 559-591-2965.
Catechesis/Religious Program—Tel: 559-591-2988. Tomi Castilleja, D.R.E.; Laura Rico, D.R.E. Students 550.
DOS PALOS, MERCED CO., SACRED HEART (1924), Rev. Robert R. Vanoncini; Deacon David Mumby.
Res.: 1655 Lucerne, 93620-2623. Tel: 209-392-2724; Fax: 209-392-1037.
Catechesis/Religious Program—Students 500.
EARLIMART, TULARE CO., ST. JUDE THADDEUS (1968), Rev. Jorge Luis de la Torre, M.S.C. (Mexico).
Mailing Address: P.O. Box 12187, 93219. Tel: 661-849-3170; Fax: 661-849-0704.
Res.: 964 Dove St., 93219. Tel: 661-849-2858.
Catechesis/Religious Program—Students 166.
EASTON, FRESNO CO., ST. JUDE MISSION (1967), Rev. Jerry Amerando.
208 W. Jefferson, 93706. Tel: 559-485-3870; Fax: 559-485-3880.
Catechesis/Religious Program—Students 160.
EXETER, TULARE CO., SACRED HEART (1950), Rev. Michael Moore.
Res.: 417 North E St., 93221. Tel: 559-592-2465; Fax: 559-592-6075.
Catechesis/Religious Program—Tel: 559-592-1020. Students 565.
Mission—St. Anthony of Egypt 821 W. Visalia Rd., Farmersville, Tulare Co. 93223. Tel: 559-747-0234.
FIREBAUGH, FRESNO CO., ST. JOSEPH (1950), Rev. Timothy A. Gallemore.
Res.: 1558 12th St., 93622. Tel: 559-659-2225; Fax: 559-659-0408.
School—1900 Saipan, 93622. Tel: 559-659-2841; Fax: 559-659-0726. Lay Teachers 6; Students 80.
Catechesis/Religious Program—Tel: 559-659-2943. Students 285.
FOWLER, FRESNO CO., ST. LUCY (1965), Rev. Joaquin S. Arriaga.
Res.: 512 S. 5th, 93625. Tel: 559-834-2624; Fax: 559-834-6814.
Catechesis/Religious Program—Students 123.
FRAZIER PARK, KERN CO., OUR LADY OF THE SNOWS (1946),, (Quasi-parish) Rev. James Kirchner.
7115 Lakewood Dr. Lake of the Woods, P.O. Box 995, 93225. Tel: 661-245-3741; Fax: 661-245-1680.
Catechesis/Religious Program—Students 90.
GOSHEN, TULARE CO., ST. THOMAS THE APOSTLE (1963), Rev. Raphael G. Farrow; Deacons Julian Ponce; Paul Hernandez; James Rooney.
Res.: 1908 N. Court, Visalia, 93291. Tel: 559-732-8089; Fax: 559-732-0969.
Catechesis/Religious Program—Students 84.
GUSTINE, MERCED CO., OUR LADY OF MIRACLES (1924), Rev. Leonard J. Trindade; Mary Aguirre - Bohnen, Lay Parish Admin.
Res.: 370 Linden Ave., 95322. Tel: 209-854-6692; Fax: 209-854-1344.
School—Tel: 209-854-3180; Fax: 209-854-3961. Mr. Michael Gillitzer, Prin. Lay Teachers 10; Students 180.
School—Preschool, Tel: 209-854-3180. Mrs. Connie Rayan, Dir. Students 39.
Catechesis/Religious Program—Tel: 209-854-2834. Karen Souza, D.R.E. Students 220.
HANFORD, KINGS CO.
1—ST. BRIGID (1886), [CEM] Revs. Daniel C. Avila; Onyema Okorie; Deacon Anthony Silveira.
Office & Mailing Address: 200 E. Florinda, 93230. Tel: 559-582-2533; Fax: 559-582-9193.
Res.: 1005 N. Douty St., 93230. Tel: 559-584-9799.
School—St. Rose-McCarthy Catholic School, 1000 N. Harris St., 93230. Tel: 559-584-5218; Fax: 559-584-5273. Mr. Jim Carpenter, Prin. Sisters of Our Lady of Nazareth 1; Lay Teachers 9; Students 200.
Catechesis/Religious Program—Tel: 559-583-6563; Fax: 559-582-9193. Students 351.
2—IMMACULATE HEART OF MARY (1948), Revs. Guillermo Preciado; Stephen M. Devine.
Res.: 10355 Hanford Armona Rd., 93230. Tel: 559-584-8576; Fax: 559-584-0436.
Catechesis/Religious Program—Tel: 559-582-5688. Students 255.
HILMAR, MERCED CO., HOLY ROSARY (1948), Rev. Hilary Silva.
Res.: P.O. Box 429, 95324. Tel: 209-667-8961; Fax: 209-667-5239.
Catechesis/Religious Program—Tel: 209-632-7163. Students 302.
Mission—St. Mary Stevinson, Merced Co. 95374.
HURON, FRESNO CO., ST. FRANCES CABRINI (1961), Rev. Juan Pineda, M.S.C. (Mexico).
Res.: 36986 Los Angeles St., P.O. Box 939, 93234. Tel: 559-945-2507; Fax: 559-945-2630.
Catechesis/Religious Program—Students 123.
KERMAN, FRESNO CO., ST. PATRICK (1953), Rev. Houng Sik Cheon.
Mailing Address: P.O. Box 375, 93630. Tel: 559-846-8190; Fax: 559-846-7705.
Res.: 567 S. Sixth St., 93630.
Catechesis/Religious Program—Tel: 559-846-9106. Students 400.
KINGSBURG, FRESNO CO., HOLY FAMILY (1950), [JC] Rev. Salvador Gonzalez.
Res.: 1301 Smith St., P.O. Box 798, 93631-0798. Tel: 559-897-5953; Fax: 559-897-8599.
Catechesis/Religious Program—Students 215.
Mission—Santa Cruz 5625 Ave. 378, London, Tulare Co. 93631.
Mission—St. John the Baptist Educational Center 4204 Merritt Dr., Traver, Tulare Co. 93673.
LAMONT, KERN CO., ST. AUGUSTINE (1962), (Mexican), Rev. John Schmoll.
Res.: 10601 Myrtle Ave., 93241-2198. Tel: 661-845-0003; Fax: 661-845-0259.
Catechesis/Religious Program—Tel: 661-845-3622. Students 900.
LATON, FRESNO CO., SHRINE OF OUR LADY OF FATIMA (1953), Rev. Richard Smith.
Res.: P.O. Box 119, 93242. Tel: 559-923-4935; Fax: 559-923-2284.
Catechesis/Religious Program—Tel: 559-923-3715. Students 270.
LEMOORE, KINGS CO., ST. PETER (1912), Rev. Gregory J. Beaumont.
Res.: 19 Follett St., 93245. Tel: 559-924-2562; Fax: 559-924-5727.
School—884 N. Lemoore Ave., 93245. Tel: 559-924-3424; Fax: 559-924-7848. Tessy Pius, Prin. Carmelite Sisters of St. Teresa 4; Lay Teachers 6; Students 235.
Catechesis/Religious Program—Tel: 559-924-2826. Edna Rowell, D.R.E. Students 348.
Mission—St. Joseph 19359 Empire St., Stratford, Kings Co. 93266.
Mission—St. Rosa [CEM] 16111 Alkaki, Tache Indian Reservation, Kings Co. 93245.
Chapel—St. Rose of Lima
LINDSAY, TULARE CO., SACRED HEART (1925), Rev. Alex C. Ignacio.
Res.: 217 Lindero Ave., 93247-2623. Tel: 559-562-4008; Fax: 559-562-5511.
Catechesis/Religious Program—Tel: 559-562-2295. Students 531.
Mission—St. Anthony Church 21631 Brooks Ave., Tonyville, Tulare Co. 93247.
Mission—St. James Catholic Church 19752 Guthrie Rd., Strathmore, Tulare Co. 93267. Tel: 559-568-0435.
Station—Plainview, Santa Cruz Plainview.
LIVINGSTON, MERCED CO., ST. JUDE THADDEUS (1937), Rev. Harvey Fonseca.
Res.: 330 Franci St., 95334. Tel: 209-394-7512; Fax: 209-394-3089.
Catechesis/Religious Program—Tel: 209-394-7516. Rosa Maria Mercado, D.R.E. Students 872.
Mission—Blessed Teresa of Calcutta P.O. Box 86, Delhi, Merced Co. 95315. Tel: 209-667-7742.
LONE PINE, INYO CO., SANTA ROSA (1919), Rev. John P. Burns, Admin.
Res.: P.O. Box 246, 93545. Tel: 760-876-4350; Fax: 760-876-4350.
Catechesis/Religious Program—Students 30.
Mission—St. John the Baptist P.O. Box 246, Shoshone-Tecopa, Inyo Co. 93545.
Mission—St. Vivian Independence, Inyo Co.
Station— Death Valley.
LOS BANOS, MERCED CO., ST. JOSEPH (1905), Rev. Msgr. J. Wayne Hayes, P.A.; Rev. Jose Luis Varo.
Res.: 1545 Center Ave., 93635. Tel: 209-826-4246; Fax: 209-827-3457.
School—Tel: 209-826-2709; Fax: 209-826-7320. Miss Connie McGhee, Prin. Lay Teachers 11; Students 203.
Catechesis/Religious Program—1625 Center Ave., 93635. Tel: 209-826-1512. Students 605.
MADERA, MADERA CO., ST. JOACHIM (1881), Revs. Larry Toschi, O.S.J.; Guadalupe Sanchez, O.S.J.; Jim Kledzik.
Res.: 401 W. Fifth St., 93637. Tel: 559-673-3290; Fax: 559-673-6471.
School—Tel: 559-674-7628; Fax: 559-674-8770. Claudia Roack, Prin. Immaculate Conception Sisters 4; Lay Teachers 7; Students 268.
Catechesis/Religious Program—Tel: 559-674-5871. Students 1,300.
Mission—St. Agnes 7308 Hwy. 145, Madera Co. 93637.
Mission—St. Anne Raymond-Knowles, Raymond, Madera Co. 93653.
MARIPOSA, MARIPOSA CO., ST. JOSEPH (1863), [CEM 3] Rev. Stephen C. Bulfer.
Mailing Address: P.O. Box 215, 95338-0215. Tel: 209-966-2522; Fax: 209-966-2522.
Res.: 4985 Bullion St., 95338.
Catechesis/Religious Program—Tel: 209-742-6817. Students 38.
Mission—St. Catherine of Sienna Hornitos, Mariposa Co.
MCFARLAND, KERN CO., ST. ELIZABETH (1966), (Hispanic), Rev. Antero Sanchez, M.S.C.
Res.: 835 E. Perkins, 93250. Tel: 661-792-3225; Fax: 661-792-5645.
Catechesis/Religious Program—Tel: 661-792-3429. Socorro Munoz, D.R.E. Students 407.
MENDOTA, FRESNO CO., OUR LADY OF GUADALUPE (1953), (Hispanic), Rev. Gaspar Bautista.
Res.: P.O. Box 248, 93640. Tel: 559-655-3631; 559-655-4237 (Rectory); Fax: 559-655-3785.
Catechesis/Religious Program—Students 145.
Mission—Our Lady of Lourdes 161015 S. Derrick, Three Rocks, Fresno Co. 93608. Tel: 559-829-3358.
MERCED, MERCED CO.
1—OUR LADY OF MERCY/ST. PATRICK'S (1868), [JC] Revs. Jean-Michael Lastiri; Joseph Baca; Josep Smith.
Mailing Address: P.O. Box 2087, 95344.
(1867), Our Lady of Mercy: 435 W. 21st St., 95340. Tel: 209-383-3924; 209-383-3930 (Mass Recording); Fax: 209-723-6510.
(1968), St. Patrick: 671 E. Yosemite, 95340. Tel: 209-726-3216. Rev. Douglas Walker.
Res.: 334 & 338 Snowhaven Ct., 95348. Tel: 209-383-3924; Fax: 209-723-6510.
School—Our Lady of Mercy Elementary, 1400 E. 27th St., 95340. Tel: 209-722-7496; Fax: 209-722-7532. Mrs. Judy Blackburn, Prin. Lay Teachers 18; Students 403.
School—Preschool, Tel: 209-722-6657. Mrs. Jill Serpa, Dir.
Catechesis/Religious Program—Tel: 209-723-8888.

Sr. Mary Kinsinger, D.R.E. Students 735.
Mission—St. John the Baptist Hopeton, Merced Co.
2—SACRED HEART (1945), Rev. Jose M. Montiel.
Res.: 519 W. 12th St., 95340. Tel: 209-383-6604; Fax: 209-383-6147.
Catechesis/Religious Program—Tel: 209-383-1528. Sr. Judith Galicia, D.R.E. Students 594.
Mission—El Nido, Merced Co.
Mission—St. George, Merced Co.

OILDALE, KERN CO., CHRIST THE KING (1952), Rev. Msgr. Stephen A. Frost, J.C.L.; Rev. David Rodriguez.
Res.: 1800 Bedford Way, 93308. Tel: 661-391-4640; Fax: 661-391-4649.
Catechesis/Religious Program—Tel: 661-399-1956. Students 160.

ORANGE COVE, FRESNO CO., ST. ISIDORE THE FARMER (1978), (Hispanic), Rev. Robert Davis.
Mailing & Res. Address: 480 Adams Ave., 93646. Tel: 559-626-4943; Fax: 559-626-4648.
Catechesis/Religious Program—Tel: 559-626-2420. Students 177.
Mission—St. Rita 30673 George Smith Rd., Squaw Valley, Fresno Co. 93675.

PARLIER, FRESNO CO., OUR LADY OF SORROWS (1965), Rev. Raul Diaz.
Res.: 830 Tulare St., 93648. Tel: 559-646-2161; Fax: 559-646-9511.
Catechesis/Religious Program—Students 230.

PLANADA, MERCED CO., SACRED HEART (1966), [JC] Rev. Jorge Gomez.
Res.: 9317 Amistad, P.O. Box 278, 95365. Tel: 209-382-0459; 209-382-0814; Fax: 209-382-0814.
Catechesis/Religious Program—Students 130.
Mission—Our Lady of Lourdes 13141 Le Grand Rd., LeGrand, Merced Co. 95333.

PORTERVILLE, TULARE CO., ST. ANNE (1896), Revs. Scott Daugherty; Martin A. McGagh (Retired); Jose Luis Rico; Rev. Msgr. Ronald Royer; Rev. Juan Manuel Flores (YAK); Deacon James Dieterle.
Res.: 378 North F St., 93257. Tel: 559-784-2800; Fax: 559-784-4338.
School—369 North F St., 93257. Tel: 559-784-4096. Sr. Rosario Mediavilla, R.A.D., Prin. Sisters of the Love of God 4; Lay Teachers 7; Students 197.
School—Preschool, Tel: 559-781-8614. Mrs. Rhonda Dotters, Dir.
Catechesis/Religious Program—Students 950.
Mission—Our Lady of Guadalupe 217 S. Wallace, Tulare Co. 93257.
Mission—Mater Dolorosa Tule Indian Reservation, Tulare Co. Tel: 559-784-2800.
Mission—Blessed Miguel Agustin Pro 9120 Rd. 236, Terra Bella, Tulare Co. 93270.
Station—Springville, Community Church 35725 Hwy. 190, Springville, 93265.

REEDLEY, FRESNO CO., ST. ANTHONY (1906), Rev. Msgr. Francis G. Tasy, V.S.; Rev. Angel Gonzalez.
Res.: P.O. Box 188, 93654. Tel: 559-638-2012; Fax: 559-638-8211.
School—LaSalle Preschool/Child Care Center, Tel: 559-638-2621; Fax: 559-638-5542. Sr. Lucy Cassarino, F.D.Z., Dir.
School—St. La Salle Grammar School, 404 E. Manning Ave., 93654. Tel: 559-638-2621; Fax: 559-638-5542. Sisters 5; Lay Teachers 8; Students 274.
Catechesis/Religious Program—Tel: 559-638-5608. Sr. Kathleen Garcia, S.H.F., D.R.E. Students 485.

RIDGECREST, KERN CO., ST. ANN (1965), [JC] Rev. Robert E. Gamel.
Res.: 446 W. Church St., P.O. Box 127, 93556. Tel: 760-375-2110; Fax: 760-375-6345.
School—(Grades K-8) Tel: 760-375-4713. Lay Teachers 19; Students 136.
Catechesis/Religious Program—Students 260.
Mission—Santa Barbara 72 Lexington Ave., Randsburg, Kern Co. 93554.

RIVERDALE, FRESNO CO., ST. ANN (1928), [JC] Rev. Victor Piansay.
Res.: P.O. Box 335, 93656. Tel: 559-867-3035; Fax: 559-867-7205.
Catechesis/Religious Program—Tel: 559-867-4996. Students 86.
Mission—Holy Family Chapel Diener Ranch At Five Points, Fresno Co.
Mission—Our Lady of the Assumption West & Herndon, P.O. Box 335, Fresno Co. 93656-0335.

ROSAMOND, KERN CO., ST. MARY (1999), Rev. Jim Kudilil.
Mailing Address: 3100 Fifteenth St., 93560. Tel: 661-256-4505; Fax: 661-256-7127.
Catechesis/Religious Program—Students 120.
Mission—St. Francis of Assisi Church 15382 Myer Rd., Mojave, Kern Co. 93501. Tel: 661-256-4505.

SANGER, FRESNO CO., ST. MARY (1922), [JC] Revs. Vito Di Marzio, R.C.J.; Fillippo Puntrello, R.C.J. In Res., Rev. Salvatore Ciranni, R.C.J. (Retired).
Res.: 828 O St., P.O. Box 335, 93657. Tel: 559-875-2025; Fax: 559-875-1281.
Catechesis/Religious Program—2590 North Ave., 93657. Tel: 559-875-6340; Fax: 559-875-2618. Students 788.
Mission—St. Katherine's 5375 Carmel, Del Rey, Fresno Co. 93616. Tel: 559-888-2889; Fax: 559-888-2889.
Catechesis/Religious Program—Students 68.

SELMA, FRESNO CO., ST. JOSEPH (1913), Rev. Msgr. Daniel Lopez; Deacons Ed Harmon III; Jim Nunez.
Res.: 2441 Dockery Ave., 93662. Tel: 209-896-1052; Fax: 209-896-3975.
Catechesis/Religious Program—Tel: 559-896-2620. Students 564.

SHAFTER, KERN CO., ST. THERESE (1952), Rev. Thomas O'Neill.
Res.: 300 W. Lerdo, P.O. Box 1448, 93263. Tel: 661-746-4471; Fax: 661-746-0945.
Catechesis/Religious Program—Tel: 661-746-9937. Students 419.

TAFT, KERN CO., ST. MARY (1918), Rev. Msgr. Loydell J. Marth.
Res.: 110 E. Woodrow St., 93268. Tel: 661-765-4292.
Catechesis/Religious Program—Students 89.

TEHACHAPI, KERN CO., ST. MALACHY (1887), Rev. Joel Davadilla.
Res.: 407 W. "E" St., 93561-1642. Tel: 661-822-3060; Fax: 661-822-3159.
Catechesis/Religious Program—Tel: 661-822-6327. Students 252.

TIPTON, TULARE CO., ST. JOHN THE EVANGELIST (1945), (Portuguese—Spanish), Rev. Jorge Luis de la Torre, M.S.C. (Mexico).
Res.: 232 S. Adams Rd., Box 159, 93272. Tel: 559-752-4544; Fax: 559-752-1409.
Catechesis/Religious Program—Tel: 559-752-4313. Students 400.
Mission—St. Francis of Assisi 16410 Ave. 168, Woodville, Tulare Co. 93258. Tel: 559-688-8412.
Station— Tipton-Pixley.

TRANQUILLITY, FRESNO CO., ST. PAUL (1924), (English—Spanish), Rev. Edgar Jimenez.
Res.: P.O. Box 575, 93668. Tel: 559-698-7429; Fax: 559-698-1059.
Catechesis/Religious Program—Tel: 559-693-4320. Students 190.
Mission—St. Vincent de Paul San Joaquin, Fresno Co.

TULARE, TULARE CO.
1—ST. ALOYSIUS (1905), Rev. Msgr. Richard Urizalqui; Rev. Raul Marta.
Res.: 125 E. Pleasant Ave., 93274. Tel: 559-688-1796; 559-688-1797; Fax: 559-688-0948.
School—Tel: 559-686-6250; Fax: 559-686-0479. Sr. Kay O'Brien, O.P., Prin. Dominican Sisters of Tacoma, WA 1; Lay Teachers 12; Students 217.
Catechesis/Religious Program—Tel: 559-688-8644. Students 550.
2—ST. RITA (1967), Rev. Timothy N. Cardoza.
Res.: 954 S. O St., 93274. Tel: 559-686-3847; Fax: 559-686-9672.
Catechesis/Religious Program—Tel: 559-686-0802. Students 452.

VISALIA, TULARE CO.
1—HOLY FAMILY (1950), [JC] Rev. Raphael G. Farrow; Deacons Paul Hernandez; Julian Ponce; James Rooney.
Res.: 1908 N. Court St., 93291. Tel: 559-732-8089; Fax: 559-732-0969.
Catechesis/Religious Program—Tel: 559-732-9651. Rebecca Arrona, D.R.E. Students 984.
Mission—San Felipe de Jesus 32809 Rd. 159, Ivanhoe, Tulare Co. 93235. Tel: 559-798-1359.
2—ST. MARY (1861), Rev. Shelton Fernando; Deacon Kevin Ramage.
Res.: 506 N. Garden, P.O. Box 237, 93279. Tel: 559-734-9522; Fax: 559-734-3435.
School—George McCann Memorial School, 200 E. Race St., 93291. Tel: 559-732-5831; Fax: 559-741-1562. Mrs. Sheila Rast, Prin. Lay Teachers 10; Students 222.
Catechesis/Religious Program—Tel: 559-733-3929; Fax: 559-733-1255. Mrs. Joan Bell, D.R.E. Preschool 86; Students 783.

WASCO, KERN CO., ST. JOHN THE EVANGELIST (1913), Rev. John P. Fluetsch.
Res.: 1300 Ninth Pl., 93280. Tel: 661-758-6688; Fax: 661-758-7751.
School—Tel: 661-758-6467. Mrs. Teresa Juarez, Prin. Lay Teachers 4; Students 53.
School—Preschool, Tel: 661-758-6829. Kathy Giesy, Dir.
Catechesis/Religious Program—Tel: 661-758-8174. Students 325.
Mission—Nuestra Senora de la Paz Lost Hills. 14846 Hwy. 33, Blackwell's Corner, Kern Co. 93249.

WOFFORD HEIGHTS, KERN CO., ST. JUDE (1969), Rev. Patrick Persinger.
Res.: 86 Nellie Dent Dr., 93285. Tel: 760-376-2416; Fax: 760-376-2253.
Catechesis/Religious Program—Students 33.

WOODLAKE, TULARE CO., ST. FRANCES CABRINI (1963), (Spanish), Rev. Jesse C. Venzor.
Res.: 599 N. Valencia Blvd., P.O. Box 459, 93286. Tel: 559-564-2647; Fax: 559-564-2647.
Catechesis/Religious Program—Students 260.
Mission—St. Clair Alta Acres Dr., Three Rivers, Tulare Co. 93271.

YOSEMITE NATIONAL PARK, MARIPOSA CO., OUR LADY OF THE SNOWS (1963), Rev. Raymond Duffy.
Res.: P.O. Box 457, 95389. Tel: 209-372-4729; Fax: 209-372-4767.
Station—Yosemite National Park Wawona.

Chaplains of Public Institutions

FRESNO. *Community Hospital, Veterans' Hospital & University Medical Center*. Revs. Flordito Redulla, S.V.D., Supr., Alejandro Magallanes, O.F.M.Cap., Donal Burke, O.F.M.Cap.
Valley Children's Hospital. (Vacant)

AVENAL. *California State Prison, Kings Co.*. Deacon Ned Quigley.

BAKERSFIELD. *Kern Medical Center, Bakersfield Memorial Hospital & San Joaquin Community Hospital*. Rev. Msgr. Ralph Belluomini.

BORON. *Federal Prison Camp*, P.O. Box 500, 93561. (Vacant)

CALIFORNIA CITY. *California City Correctional Center*, P.O. Box 2590, 93550. (Vacant)

CHOWCHILLA. *Department of Corrections, Central California Women's Facility*, P.O. Box 1501, 93610. Sr. Kathleen McCarthy, R.S.M.
Valley State Prison for Women, P.O. Box 99, 93610-9361. Sr. Mary Adele Appleby, B.V.M.

COALINGA. *Pleasant Valley State Prison*. Gary Egeberg.

CORCORAN. *Calif. State Prison*, P.O. Box 8800, 93212. Tel: 559-992-8800. (Vacant)
California Substance Abuse Treatment Facility & State Prison - Corcoran, P.O. Box 7100, 93212-7100. Sisters Carolyn Whited, S.H.F., Christine McNamara, S.S.L.

DELANO. *North Kern State Prison*, 2737 W. Cecil Ave., 93216-0567. Tel: 661-721-2345, Ext. 6862. John Messina, Chap.

MARIPOSA. *Mt. Bullion Conservation Camp*, P.O. Box 5006, 95338. Rev. Jose Montiel.

PORTERVILLE. *Developmental Center*, P.O. Box 2000, 93258. Sr. Patrick Malani, S.O.L.N.

TAFT. *Correctional Institution*, P.O. Box 7000, 93268. Tel: 661-763-2510. (Vacant)

TEHACHAPI. *California Correctional Institution*, Tel: 661-822-4402, Ext. 4387. Deacon Clyde Davis.

WASCO. *Prison Facility*, P.O. Box 8800, 93280-8800. Tel: 661-758-8400. Rev. Daniel Bringas.

On Special Assignment:
Rev. Msgrs.—
Griesbach, John, St. Anthony Retreat House
Janelli, Anthony, Vocations Dir.
Revs.—
Amerando, Jerry, Chap., San Joaquin Memorial H.S.
Burchfield, Michael, J.C.L., Asst. Tribunal Dir. & Adjutant Vicar, Canada.
Congdon, John, Chap., San Joaquin Memorial High School, Fresno
Cotta, Myron, V.G., 1550 N. Fresno St., 93703-3788.
La Casse, James, S.J.
Lopez, Vincent, O.P., Prin., San Joaquin Memorial High School

---

Faculties Only:
Rev.—
Olmos, Pedro

On Duty Outside the Diocese:
Rev.—
Flickinger, Don D., 15333 Woodard Rd., San Jose, 95124.

Absent on Sick Leave:
Rev.—
Bray, Kevin

Retired:
Rev. Msgrs.—
Balker, Joseph W., 2121 N. First St., 93703.
Byrne, Laserian, 5770 N. Marda, 93704.
Cleary, Kevin, P.O. Box 1407, Ridgecrest, 93556.
Doherty, Patrick G., 2121 N. 1st. St., 93703.
Flood, Patrick, 2121 N. 1st. St., 93703.
Herdegen, Anthony, 5660 N. River Forrest Dr., Milwaukee, WI 53209.
Herrero, Nicolas
Lahey, Maurice, 2121 N. 1st St., 93703.
Lee, Howard T.
Logan, James T.
Meyer, Gilbert, 328 del Mar Ln., Ridgecrest, 93555.
Minhoto, Walter F., 2814 Mariposa, 93721.
O'Connor, Michael, 5804 Indian Wells Ave., Bakersfield, 93309.

O'Friel, John, 181 W. Bush St., Lemoore, 93245.
Pointek, Francis J., P.O. Box 1240, Tehachapi, 93581.
Poschen, Ed, 390 N. Winchester Blvd., 5-4A, Santa Clara, 95050.
Riccomini, Dino, Morro Bay.
Revs.—
Alabart, Francis X., 722 Dover Pl., Delano, 93215.
Alvernaz, Dennis
Barron, Cecil, C.M.F., 2494 S. Chestnut, 93721.
Bezunartea, Herman O., Spain
Burkhart, Roy, C.S.S.P., Bakersfield, CA
Ciranni, Salvatore, R.C.J.
Cummins, Timothy, 2121 N. First St., 93703.
Dreici, Patrick, C.SS.R., 2121 N. 1st St., 93703.
Gonzalez, Antonio, Santa Maria, CA
Heffernan, Joseph A.
Kurea, Pius, Fresno, CA
Kyrie, James, O.F.M.
McGagh, Martin A., P.O. Box 52, Porterville, 93258.
Orozco, Rodolfo, Strathmore, CA
Pascual, Manuel, 4701 S. Mooney Blvd., Sp.R7, Visalia, 93277.
Raffel, Godfrey, P.O. Box 387, Bakersfield, 93390.
Simeone, Francis
Vogt, William, Nazareth House

INSTITUTIONS LOCATED IN THE DIOCESE

[A] HIGH SCHOOLS, DIOCESAN

FRESNO. *San Joaquin Memorial High School*, 1406 N. Fresno St., 93703-3789. Tel: 559-268-9251; Fax: 559-268-1351. Email: mqualls@sjmhs.org. Web: www.sjmhs.org. Rev. Vincent Lopez, O.P., Prin. Priest Teachers 2; Lay Teachers 42; Students 623.

BAKERSFIELD. *Garces Memorial High School*, 2800 Loma Linda Dr., 93305. Tel: 661-327-2578; Fax: 661-327-5427. Email: jkvasnicka@garces.org. Web: www.garces.org. John Kvasnicka, Prin.; Susan Rizo, Dir. Campus Ministry. Lay Teachers 40; Students 699.

[B] GENERAL HOSPITALS

FRESNO. *Saint Agnes' Medical Center*, 1303 E. Herndon, 93720. Tel: 559-450-3000; Fax: 559-450-5699. Email: rnickerson@samc.com. Web: www.samc.com. Sr. Ruth Marie Nickerson, C.S.C., Pres. & CEO; Lowell Carruth, Chm., Bd. of Trustees. Sisters of the Holy Cross Sisters 10; Nurses 707; Bed Capacity 330; Patients Assisted Annually 377,584.

Professional Office Corporation, Saint Agnes Medical Center, 1303 E. Herndon Ave., 93720. Tel: 559-449-3000; Fax: 559-449-2143. Sr. Ruth Marie Nickerson, C.S.C., CEO; Thomas Mac Michael, Chm. Bd. of Trustees.

BAKERSFIELD. *Catholic Healthcare West* dba Mercy Hospital , 2215 Truxtun Ave., 93301. Tel: 661-632-5000; Fax: 661-327-2592. Web: www.chwhealth.com. P.O. Box 119, 93302. Paul R. Luehrs, COO. Sponsored by the Burlingame Regional Community of the Sisters of Mercy Patients Assisted Annually 111,450; Bed Capacity 279; Sisters 1; Staff 1,118.

Mercy Southwest Hospital dba Catholic Healthcare West , 400 Old River Rd., 93311. Tel: 661-663-6000; Fax: 661-663-6570. Web: www.chwhealth.com. P.O. Box 119, 93302.

Friends of Mercy Foundation, 2215 Truxtun Ave., 93301. Tel: 661-632-5683; Fax: 661-322-8543. Web: www.chwhealth.com. Stephanie Weber, Exec. Dir.

MERCED. *Mercy Medical Center Merced - Dominican Campus* dba Mater Misericodiae Hospital , 2740 M St., 95340. Tel: 209-384-6444; Fax: 209-722-2902. Web: www.mercymercedCARES.org. John Headding, Pres. Sponsored by the Dominican Sisters of St. Catherine of Siena of Kenosha, Wisconsin Sisters 2; Bed Capacity 129; Staff 670; Patients Assisted Annually 84,746.

[C] HOMES FOR INVALID AND AGED

FRESNO. *Nazareth House*, 2121 N. First St., 93703. Tel: 559-237-2257; Fax: 559-237-1958. Sr. Antionette Farrell, P.S.N., Supr.; Rev. Pius Kurera, Chap. Sisters of Nazareth of Fresno Inc. 3; Residential Care 65; Skilled Nursing 39; Total Staff 90.

LOS BANOS. *New Bethany*, 1441 Berkeley Dr., 93635. Tel: 209-827-8933; Fax: 209-827-8975. Email: jaf2003@grid.com. Sisters Helen Petrovich, F.H.I.C., Dir. Skilled Nursing; Julia Fonseca, F.H.I.C., Dir. Residential Care; Lucinda Fonseca, F.H.I.C., Dir. Community Representative; Rev. Manuel Soares, Dir. & Chap. Franciscan Hospitaller Sisters of the Immaculate Conception 14; Residential Care 76; Skilled Nursing 35; Total Staff 68; Capacity 111.

[D] CATHOLIC CHARITIES

FRESNO. *Catholic Charities of the Diocese of Fresno*, 149 N. Fulton St., 93701. Tel: 559-264-6434; Fax: 559-237-7144. Email: ptraynor@ccdof.org. Philip Traynor, Exec Dir.

Catholic Charities Thrift Store, 149 N. Fulton St., 93701-1607. Tel: 559-237-0851; Fax: 559-264-0655. Email: mdiaz@ccdof.org. Nancy Fournet, Prog. Mgr. Total Staff 2.

Catholic Social Services, 149 N. Fulton St., 93701. Tel: 559-237-0851; Fax: 559-264-0655. Email: socialservices@ccdof.org. Web: www.ccdof.org. Sandra Fournet, Prog. Mgr. Total Staff 1; Total Assisted 5,584.

Francis X. Singleton Emergency Food Assistance Program, 149 N. Fulton St., 93701. Tel: 559-237-0851; Fax: 559-264-0655. Greg Sultz, Prog. Mgr. Total Staff 3; Total Assisted 75,000.

Immigration Services, 149 N. Fulton St., 93701. Tel: 559-264-6400; Fax: 559-264-0655. Email: FRESM@lightspeed.net. Web: www.ccdof.org. Anna Rodriguez, Prog. Manager. Total Staff 3; Total Assisted 102,500.

Senior Companion Program Tel: 559-498-6377. Email: ccaples@ccdof.org. Catherine Caples, Prog. Mgr. Total Staff 6; Total Assisted 324.

BAKERSFIELD. *Catholic Social Services*, 525 18th St., 93301. Tel: 661-281-2130; Fax: 661-281-2139. Email: 1calderon@ccdof.org. Liz Calderon, Prog. Mgr. Total Staff 2; Total Assisted 78,000.

FARMERSVILLE. *St. Vincent de Paul Center*, 468 E. Visalia Rd., P.O. Box 106, 93223. Tel: 559-594-4932; Fax: 559-594-5632. Mary G. Flores, Prog. Mgr. Total Staff 1; Total Assisted 4,144.

MERCED. *Catholic Charities*, 366 W. Main #1, 95340. Tel: 209-383-2494; 209-383-5220; Fax: 209-383-3975. Email: rcoronado@ccdof.org. Ramiro G. Coronado, Prog. Mgr. Total Staff 5; Total Assisted 25,000.

Catholic Charities Social Services, 366 W. Main, #1, 95340. Tel: 209-383-2494; Fax: 209-383-3975.

Immigration Program, 336 W. Main, #1, 95340. Tel: 209-383-2494; 209-383-5220; Fax: 209-383-3975. Email: rcoronado@ccdof.org.

PORTERVILLE. *Catholic Social Services*, 1309 W. Main, Bldg. B, 93257. Tel: 559-781-5555; Fax: 559-781-3415. Sr. Sesilia Taulanga, S.O.L.N., Prog. Mgr. Total Staff 2; Total assisted annually 42,500.

VISALIA. *Catholic Social Services*, 1638 N. Dinuba Blvd., 93291. Tel: 559-734-1572; Fax: 559-734-4921. Deacon Paul Hernandez, Dir. Total Staff 13; Total Assisted 94,000.

Good News Center (Sr. Ursula's Kitchen & Thrift Store), 1638 N. Dinuba Blvd., 93291. Tel: 559-738-8922.

Good News Inn (Shelter), 1718 & 1722 N. Dinuba Blvd., 93291. Tel: 559-734-6470; Fax: 559-734-4921. Total Families Assisted Annually 150.

Immigration Services, 1638 N. Dinuba Blvd., 93291. Tel: 559-713-0658.

[E] CONVENTS AND RESIDENCES FOR SISTERS

FRESNO. *St. Agnes Hospital Convent*, 1261 E. Los Altos Ave., 93710. Tel: 559-431-3376. Sisters of the Holy Cross, Inc. 11.

Congregation of the Sisters of Nazareth of Fresno, Formerly Poor Sisters of Nazareth, 2121 N. First St., 93703. Tel: 559-237-2257; Fax: 559-237-2323. Email: nazfresno@aol.com. Sr. Antionette Farrell, P.S.N., Supr. Sisters 3.

Sister Disciples of the Divine Master, 3700 N. Cornelia Ave., 93722. Tel: 559-275-1656; Fax: 559-275-2725. Sr. M. Lucille VanHoogmoed, P.D.D.M., Supr. Sisters 14.

ATWATER. *Our Lady of the Atonement Convent*, 1694 Grove Ave., 95301. Tel: 209-358-2109. Franciscan Sisters of the Atonement 2.

BAKERSFIELD. *Sister Servants of the Blessed Sacrament (SJS)*, 1100 S. Kern St., 93307. Tel: 661-631-1061 (Convent); 661-323-6059 (School); Fax: 661-323-1860. Email: sjsbakers@aol.com. Sisters 5.

CLOVIS. *Sisters of the Immaculate Conception (RCM)*, 859 Harvard Ave., 93612. Tel: 559-299-8407; Fax: 559-299-4627. Email: rcmclovis@cvip.net. Web: www.rc.net/conception. Sisters 4.

LEMOORE. *Carmelite Sisters of St. Teresa (CSST)*, 884 N. Lemoore Ave., 93245. Tel: 559-924-2347; Fax: 559-924-7848. Email: carmel@lemoorenet.com. Sisters 4.

LOS BANOS. *Franciscan Hospitallers of the Immaculate Conception (FHIC)*, 1441 Berkeley Dr., 93635-9599. Tel: 209-826-0770; Fax: 209-827-8989. Email: confhic@sbglobal.net. Sisters 13.

MERCED. *Dominican Sisters (OP)*, 2635 Piedmont Dr., 95340-9679. Tel: 209-723-6564; Fax: 209-388-9423. Sisters 6.

REEDLEY. *Daughters of Divine Zeal (FDZ)*, 379 E. Manning Ave., 93654. Tel: 559-638-1916; Fax: 559-638-5542. Email: srlucy45@hotmail.com. Web: www.figliedivinozelo.it. Sisters 5.

[F] RETREAT HOUSES

THREE RIVERS. *St. Anthony's Retreat House*, P.O. Box 249, 93271. Tel: 559-561-4595; Fax: 559-561-4493. Email: stanthonyretreatcenter_Francis@yahoo.com. Web: www.stanthonyretreat.org. Priests 1.

[G] NEWMAN CENTERS

FRESNO. *St. Paul Newman Center* 1572 E. Barstow Ave., 93710. Tel: 559-436-3434; Fax: 559-436-3430. Email: pkavookjian@hotmail.com. Web: www.csufnewman.com. Revs. Perry Kavookjian; Michael Burchfield; Deacon John Supino; Sr. Joanne Bauer, C.S.C., Adult Education.

California State University at Fresno Tel: 559-436-3434; Fax: 559-436-3430. Karena Steiner, Campus Min.

Fresno City College

BAKERSFIELD. *California State University at Bakersfield Newman Center* 710 Stockdale Hwy., 93309-1399. Tel: 661-834-7483; Fax: 661-834-2214. Email: csub_newman@hotmail.com.

[H] MISCELLANEOUS & AGENCIES

MERCED. *Catholic Professional & Business Breakfast Club of the Fresno Diocese*, 23 W. Alexander Ave., PMB #450, 95348-3404. Tel: 209-394-7984; Fax: 209-394-4988. Email: tmendez@josephfarms.com. 1550 N. Fresno St., 93703-3788. E.J. Almo Lorenzi, Pres.

SANGER. *Fr. Hannibal House Social Service Center*, 1501 14th St., P.O. Box 37, 93657. Tel: 559-875-0564; Fax: 559-875-1281. Email: hannibalhouse.@aol.com. Jerry Sanchez, Dir. Total Assisted: Food Distribution 11,853.

RELIGIOUS INSTITUTES OF MEN REPRESENTED IN THE DIOCESE

For further details refer to the corresponding bracketed number in the Religious Institutes of Men or Women section.

[0200]—*Benedictine Monks*—O.S.B.
[]—*Carmelite*—O.C.D.
[0360]—*Claretian Missionaries* (Western Prov.)—C.M.F.
[0480]—*Conventual Franciscans* (St. Joseph Cupertino Prov.)—O.F.M.Conv
[0520]—*Franciscan Friars* (St. Barbara Prov.)—O.F.M.
[0650]—*Holy Ghost Fathers* (Western Prov.)—C.S.Sp.
[0690]—*Jesuit Fathers and Brothers*—S.J.
[]—*Missioneros del Sagrado Corazon y Santa Maria de Guadalupe*—M.S.C.
[0930]—*Oblates of St. Joseph* (Asti, Italy)—O.S.J.
[0430]—*Order of Preachers*—O.P.
[1070]—*Redemptorists*—C.SS.R.
[1090]—*Rogationist Fathers*—R.C.J.

RELIGIOUS INSTITUTES OF WOMEN REPRESENTED IN THE DIOCESE

[]—*Adrian Dominican Sisters*—O.P.
[]—*Carmelite Sisters of St. Teresa* (Gidellahalli, Bangalore-India)—C.S.S.T.
[]—*Congregation of the Carmelite Sisters of St. Therese*—C.S.S.T.
[3242]—*Congregation of the Sisters of Nazareth* (Los Angeles, CA)—C.S.N.
[3935]—*Congregation of the Sisters of St. Louis* (Juilly, Monaghan)—S.S.L.
[1920]—*Congregation of the Sisters of the Holy Cross* (Notre Dame, IN)—C.S.C.
[0760]—*Daughters of Charity of St. Vincent de Paul* (Los Altos Hills, CA) (Western Prov.)—D.C.
[0795]—*Daughters of Divine Zeal* (Rome, Italy)—F.D.Z.
[0820]—*Daughters of the Holy Spirit* (France) (Putnam, CT Prov. House)—D.H.S.
[1070-20]—*Dominican Sisters* (Congregation of St. Thomas Aquinas, Marymount, Tacoma, WA)—O.P.
[1070-25]—*Dominican Sisters* (Congregation of the Dominican Sisters of St. Catherine of Siena of Kenosha)—O.P.
[1270]—*Franciscan Hospitaller Sisters of the Immaculate Conception* (San Jose, CA)—F.H.I.C.
[1190]—*Franciscan Sisters of the Atonement* Garrison, NY)—S.A.
[]—*Hijas del Sagrado Corazon de Jesusy Santa Maria* (Mexico)—H.S.C.M.
[2180]—*Immaculate Heart Community* (Los Angeles, CA)—I.H.M.
[2570]—*Institute of the Sisters of Mercy of the Americas* (Burlingame, CA)—R.S.M.
[]—*Instituto Misionero Apostoles de la Palabra*—I.M.A.P.

[]—*Misioneras Carmelitas de Santa Teresa del Nino Jesus*—M.L.S.T.N.

[3130]—*Our Lady of Victory Missionary Sisters*—O.L.V.M.

[0980]—*Pious Disciples of the Divine Master* (Staten Island, NY)—P.D.D.M.

[2970]—*School Sisters of Notre Dame* (St. Louis, MO)—S.S.N.D.

[3499]—*Servants of the Blessed Sacrament* (El Segundo, CA)—S.J.S.

[0430]—*Sisters of Charity of Blessed Virgin Mary* (Dubuque, IA)—B.V.M.

[]—*Sisters of Our Lady of Nazareth* (Fiji, South Pacific)—S.O.L.N.

[3840]—*Sisters of St. Joseph of Carondelet* (Los Angeles, CA)—C.S.J.

[1960]—*Sisters of the Holy Family* (Mission San Jose, CA)—S.H.F.

[2130]—*Sisters of the Immaculate Conception* (San Francisco, CA)—R.C.M.

[]—*Sisters of the Love of God* (La Puente, CA)—R.A.D.

[4120-06]—*Ursuline Nuns of the Congregation of Paris* (Toledo, OH)—O.S.U.

DIOCESAN CEMETERIES

FRESNO. *Fresno Catholic Cemeteries*, 264 N. Blythe, 93706. Tel: 559-488-7449; Fax: 559-488-7485. Richard A. Davis, Dir.

NECROLOGY

† Kleinhans, Rev. Msgr. Thomas G., Visalia, CA St. Mary—Died Jan. 4, 2004

Diocese of Gallup

(Dioecesis Gallupiensis)

Most Reverend

DONALD E. PELOTTE, S.S.S., D.D., PH.D.

Bishop of Gallup; ordained September 2, 1972; appointed Coadjutor Bishop of Gallup February 24, 1986; consecrated May 6, 1986; succeeded to See, March 20, 1990. *Office: P.O. Box 1338, Gallup, NM 87305. Res.: P.O. Box 1317, Gallup, NM 87305.* Tel: 505-722-3047.

Chancery: 711 S. Puerco Dr., P.O. Box 1338, Gallup, NM 87305. Tel: 505-863-4406; Fax: 505-722-9131.

ESTABLISHED DECEMBER 16, 1939.

Square Miles 55,468.

Comprises Apache, Navajo and those parts of the Navajo and Hopi Reservations in Coconino Counties in the State of Arizona; San Juan, McKinley, Catron, Cibola and those parts of Rio Arriba, Sandoval, Bernalillo and Valencia Counties lying west of 106, 52', 41" meridian in the State of New Mexico.

Legal Title: New Mexico: Roman Catholic Church of the Diocese of Gallup. Arizona: Bishop of the Roman Catholic Church of the Diocese of Gallup.

For legal titles of parishes and diocesan institutions, consult the Chancery Office.

STATISTICAL OVERVIEW

Personnel	
Bishop	1
Priests: Diocesan Active in Diocese	28
Priests: Diocesan Active Outside Diocese	3
Priests: Retired, Sick or Absent	10
Number of Diocesan Priests	41
Religious Priests in Diocese	25
Total Priests in Diocese	66
Ordinations:	
Permanent Deacons	4
Permanent Deacons in Diocese	33
Total Brothers	12
Total Sisters	142
Parishes	
Parishes	53
With Resident Pastor:	
Resident Diocesan Priests	22
Resident Religious Priests	18
Without Resident Pastor:	
Administered by Priests	9
Administered by Deacons	2
Administered by Religious Women	2
Missions	25
Professional Ministry Personnel:	
Brothers	5
Sisters	32
Lay Ministers	14
Welfare	
Homes for the Aged	1
Total Assisted	54
Residential Care of Children	1
Total Assisted	62
Day Care Centers	3
Total Assisted	66
Specialized Homes	1
Total Assisted	24
Special Centers for Social Services	24
Total Assisted	64,853
Other Institutions	1
Total Assisted	49,199
Educational	
Diocesan Students in Other Seminaries	4
Total Seminarians	4
High Schools, Private	2
Total Students	242
Elementary Schools, Private	10
Total Students	1,420
Catechesis/Religious Education:	
High School Students	1,006
Elementary Students	3,350
Total Students under Catholic Instruction	6,022
Teachers in the Diocese:	
Priests	1
Brothers	4
Sisters	25
Lay Teachers	109
Vital Statistics	
Receptions into the Church:	
Infant Baptism Totals	917
Adult Baptism Totals	235
Received into Full Communion	124
First Communions	881
Confirmations	708
Marriages:	
Catholic	133
Interfaith	49
Total Marriages	182
Deaths	613
Total Catholic Population	48,488
Total Population	449,485

Former Bishop—Most Revs. BERNARD T. ESPELAGE, O.F.M., D.D., ord. May 16, 1918; appt. Bishop of Gallup, July 20, 1940; consecrated Oct. 9, 1940; resigned Sept. 3, 1969; died Feb. 19, 1971; JEROME J. HASTRICH, D.D. (Retired), ord. Feb. 9, 1941; consecrated Auxiliary Bishop of Madison and Titular Bishop of Gurza, July 31, 1963; transferred to the See of Gallup, Sept. 3, 1969; installed Dec. 3, 1969; retired March 20, 1990; died May 12, 1995.

Vicar General—Rev. Msgr. LEO GOMEZ, V.G.

Judicial Vicar—Rev. LAWRENCE J. O'KEEFE, J.C.D.

Vicar for Indian Affairs—Rev. CARON VOLLMER, O.F.M.

Office of the Bishop—711 S. Puerco Dr., P.O. Box 1338, Gallup, 87305. Tel: 505-863-4406.

Chancery—711 S. Puerco Dr., P.O. Box 1338, Gallup, 87305. Tel: 505-863-4406; Fax: 505-722-9131. Office Hours: Mon.-Thurs. 8:30-12 & 1-4:30; Fri. 8:30-12

Chancellor and Administrative Assistant—Deacon TIMOTEO LUJAN.

Financial Secretary—Mrs. ANNA J. DIGREGORIO.

Diocesan Tribunal (First Instance)—711 S. Puerco Dr., P.O. Box 1338, Gallup, 87305. Tel: 505-863-4406; Fax: 505-722-9324.

Adjutant Judicial Vicar—Rev. MICHAEL VIGIL, J.C.L.

Judges—Revs. ALFRED A. TACHIAS, J.C.L.; LAWRENCE J. O'KEEFE, J.C.D.; MICHAEL VIGIL, J.C.L.; Deacon JIM HOY.

Defenders of the Bond—Revs. THOMAS MAIKOWSKI, Ph.D.; RONALD WALTERS, O.F.M.; JOHN BOLAND; JERRY HERFF, C.M.

Notary—MARY MARES.

Vicars Forane—Revs. MICHAEL VIGIL, J.C.L., McKinley Vicariate; MELDON HICKEY, O.E.M., Apache Vicariate; Very Revs. CLAYTON KILBURN, C.M., Navajo Vicariate; WILLIAM WELCH, Lower Arizona Vicariate; Rev. LAWRENCE SMITH, S.J., San Juan Vicariate; Very Rev. ALBERTO AVELLA, Cibola Vicariate.

Bishop's Delegate for Women Religious—Sr. MARGUERITE MCGRANAHAN, R.S.M.

Presbyteral Council—Most Rev. DONALD E. PELOTTE, S.S.S., D.D., Ph.D.; Rev. Msgr. LEO GOMEZ, V.G.; Revs. LAWRENCE SMITH, S.J., Moderator; DIEGO MAZON, O.F.M.; ALBERTO AVELLA; LOUIS FRANZ, C.M.; LAWRENCE O'KEEFE, J.C.D.; THOMAS MAIKOWSKI, Ph.D.; CLAY KILBURN, C.M.; MELDON HICKEY, O.E.M.; Very Rev. WILLIAM WELCH; Revs. EDWARD FRONSKE, O.F.M.; FRANK CHACON; TIMOTHY FARRELL; Deacon TIMOTEO LUJAN, Sec., P.O. Box 1338, Gallup, 87305.

Diocesan Consultors—Rev. Msgr. LEO GOMEZ, V.G.; Revs. LAWRENCE O'KEEFE, J.C.D.; EDWARD FRONSKE, O.F.M.; THOMAS MAIKOWSKI, Ph.D.; DIEGO MAZON, O.F.M.; LOUIS FRANZ, C.M.; FRANK CHACON.

Diocesan Navajo Mission Board—Most Rev. DONALD E. PELOTTE, S.S.S., D.D., Ph.D.; Rev. CARON VOLLMER, O.F.M.

Diocesan Offices and Directors

Archivist—Dr. EMERINE GLOWIENKA, Ph.D.

Boy Scouts—Rev. THOMAS MAIKOWSKI, Ph.D., Dir. & Chap., P.O. Box 1028, Gallup, 87305. Tel: 505-863-3563.

Budget and Finance—Deacon JAMES P. HOY, Dir.

Cemeteries—VACANT, Box 2840, Farmington, 87401.

Catholic Charities—Sr. BETTY MARIE DUNKEL, D.C., Dir., Main Office, Gallup: P.O. Box 1589, Gallup, 87305. Tel: 505-722-5272. Chinle: P.O. Box 417, Chinle, AZ 86053. Tel: 928-674-3238. Grants-Milan: 2595 W. Hwy. 66, Grants, 87020. Tel: 505-285-5451. Farmington: 119 W. Broadway, Farmington, 87401. Tel: 505-325-3724. Holbrook: P.O. Box 41, Holbrook, AZ 86025. Tel: 928-524-9720. White Mountain: P.O. Box 600, McNary, AZ 85930. Tel: 928-334-2219.

Cursillos—Rev. MELDON HICKEY, O.E.M., P.O. Box 680, St. Michael's, AZ 86511. Tel: 928-871-4171.

Diocesan Pastoral Council—Most Rev. DONALD E. PELOTTE, S.S.S., D.D., Ph.D.; ROMY RODRIQUEZ, Chm.; JAMES SCOTT, Vice Chm.; GERRY LABASH, Sec.; Rev. THOMAS MAIKOWSKI, Ph.D.; Deacons MARCELLINO MORRIS JR.; LAWRENCE VALDO; TIMOTEO LUJAN, Ex Officio; Sisters BETTY DUNKEL, D.C.; VIRGINIA ADLER, C.S.A.; ANDREA BORG; MARY CAMPELL; FRANK CHAVEZ; EMILY FREELAND; GREGORY JARRIN, M.D.; MARY ANN MONTOYA; BARBARA PRESSON; ERNEST TSOSIE JR.

Director of Education, (Catholic Schools and Religious Education)—Rev. THOMAS MAIKOWSKI, Ph.D., Dir. Educ., P.O. Box 1028, Gallup, 87305. Tel: 505-863-3563.

Ecumenical Affairs in Arizona, Arizona Ecumenical Council—Rev. WILLIAM F. DAY, P.O. Box 1449, Showlow, 85901. Tel: 928-537-2543.

Ecumenical Affairs in New Mexico, New Mexico Council of Churches—Rev. DANIEL DALEY, 307 N. Church St., Bloomfield, 87413. Tel: 505-632-2014.

Newspaper—P.O. Box 1338, Gallup, 87305. Tel: 505-863-4406. "Voice of the Southwest"

Priests' Retirement Fund—MICHAEL VIGIL, J.C.L., Chm.; Revs. MATTHEW KELLER; ROBERT MATHIEU.

Propagation of the Faith—Deacon JOSEPH F. KRIKAWA, Dir., P.O. Box 1338, Gallup, 87305.

Radio and Television—Rev. CORMAC ANTRAM, O.F.M., P.O. Box 48, Hauck, AZ 86506-0048.

Search—TED GOMEZ, Dir., 2103 Lynwood Dr., Farmington, 87401.

Social Justice and Outreach—Sr. ROSE MARIE CECCHINI, M.M., M.M., P.O. Box 3146, Gallup, 87305.

Vocations— For Priesthood: Rev. TIMOTHY W. FARRELL, 414 N. Allen Ave., Farmington, 87401. Deacon Vocations:; Deacon MARCELLINO MORRIS JR., P.O. Box 768, Fort Defiance, AZ 86505. Bishop's Delegate for Women Religious; Sr. MARGUERITE MCGRANAHAN, R.S.M.

Youth Ministry—VACANT. Tel: 505-863-4406.

Ministry Formation Program—Rev. BLAINE GREIN, O.F.M., Builders of the New Earth & Native American Formation; Deacons MARCELLINO MORRIS JR., Dir. Deacon Formation; TIMOTEO

Lujan, Dir. Diaconate Life & Ministry; Sr. Rose Marie Cecchini, M.M., M.M., Lay Spirituality; Dr. Emerine Glowienka, Ph.D., Academics.

Diocesan Review Board for Sexual Abuse & Misconduct by Clergy, Religious and Other Church Personnel—Rev. Jerome R. Herff, C.M.; Gregory Thomas Jarrin, M.D., F.A.C.S.; Margie Trujillo, Ph.D.; Floyd J. Kezele, J.D.

Victim Assistance Coordinator—Sr. Mary Thurllough, D.C. Tel: 505-722-4406.

CLERGY, PARISHES, MISSIONS AND PAROCHIAL SCHOOLS

CITY OF GALLUP
(McKinley County)

1—Cathedral of the Sacred Heart (1939), (Dedicated June 19, 1955 Revs. Lawrence O'Keefe, J.C.D., Rector; James E. Walker; Deacons Thomas Richtsmeier, M.D.; James P. Hoy. In Res., Rev. Michael Vigil.
Res. & Mailing Address: 415 E. Green Ave., 87301. Tel: 505-722-6644; Fax: 505-722-6645.
Catechesis/Religious Program—Tel: 505-722-5485. Barbara Kozeliski, D.R.E. Students 456.

2—St. Francis of Assisi (1943), (Hispanic), Revs. Diego Mazon, O.F.M.; Gonzalo Guzman, O.F.M.; Joseph Redinbo, O.F.M.; Bro. Maynard Shurley, O.F.M. In Res., Rev. Conall Lynch, O.F.M.
Res.: 411 N. Second, 87301. Tel: 505-863-3033; Fax: 505-863-6887.
Catechesis/Religious Program—Tel: 505-863-5291. Students 111.
Mission—St. Joseph the Worker Gamerco, McKinley Co.

3—St. Jerome, Closed., For inquiries for parish records contact Sacred Heart Cathedral.

4—St. John Vianney (1973), Rev. Walter Opalewski.
Res.: 3408 Zia Dr., 87301. Tel: 505-722-3361.
Catechesis/Religious Program—Tel: 505-722-5085. Students 81.

OUTSIDE THE CITY OF GALLUP, NEW MEXICO

Acoma, Cibola Co., San Esteban, Acoma Catholic Indian Mission (1629), (Native American), [CEM 3] Revs. Larry Bernard, O.F.M.; Ulric Pax, O.F.M.; Deacon Larry Valdo; Ernest Vallo, Pastoral Team.
Res.: P.O. Box 448, Pueblo of Acoma, 87034-0448. Tel: 505-552-6403; Fax: 505-522-6221.
Catechesis/Religious Program—Students 41.
Mission—St. Anne Pueblo of Acoma, P.O. Box 448, Acomita, Cibola Co. 87034.
Mission—Santa Maria de Acoma McCartys, Cibola Co. 87034.

Aragon, Catron Co., Santo Nino (1910), (Hispanic), Deacon Juan Aragon.
Res.: P.O. Box 489, Reserve, 87830-0489. Tel: 505-533-6240.
Mission—San Isidro Lower San Francisco, Catron Co.
Mission—St. Francis Reserve, Catron Co.
Mission—St. Anne Horse Springs, Catron Co.
Station— Apache Creek.

Aztec, San Juan Co., St. Joseph (1946), (Hispanic), Rev. Joachim Blonski; Deacon Charles Peterson, Pastoral Assoc.
Res.: 500 N. Mesa Verde St., 87410. Tel: 505-334-6535; Fax: 505-334-5902.
Catechesis/Religious Program—Tel: 505-334-3542. Sr. Sara Marie Gomez, O.S.U., D.R.E. Students 255.

Blanco, San Juan Co., St. Rose of Lima (1900), [CEM] Rev. Daniel P. Daley; Deacon Roger Garcia.
Res.: 307 N. Church St., Bloomfield, 87413. Tel: 505-632-2014; Fax: 505-633-1986.
Catechesis/Religious Program—Students 102.
Catechesis/Religious Program—Joann Valdez, D.R.E.; Monique Bryant, D.R.E. Students 75.
Mission—Our Lady of Guadalupe Los Martinez, Torrance Co.

Bloomfield, San Juan Co., St. Mary (1960), [CEM] Rev. Daniel P. Daley; Deacon Roger Garcia.
Res.: 307 N. Church St., 87413. Tel: 505-632-2014.
Catechesis/Religious Program—Roselie Valdez, D.R.E. Students 200.

Chichiltah, McKinley Co., St. Patrick (1965), (Native American), Rev. Jeffrey King.
Res.: P.O. Box 267, Vanderwagen, 87326. Tel: 505-778-5410.
Catechesis/Religious Program—Students 25.
Mission—Good Shepherd Catholic Mission

Church Rock, McKinley Co., St. Philip Benizi, Closed., For inquiries for parish records please see Sacred Heart Cathedral, Gallup.
Station— Pindale.

Crownpoint, McKinley Co., St. Paul (1961), (Native American), [JC] Rev. Lawrence O'Keefe, J.C.D., Canonical Pastor; Sisters Barbara Smith, A.S.C., Pastoral Admin.; Maureen Farrar, A.S.C., Pastoral Admin.; Deacon Sherman Manuelito, Pastoral Admin.
Res.: P.O. Box 268, 87313. Tel: 505-786-5376; Fax: 505-786-5376.
Catechesis/Religious Program—Christine Smith, D.R.E. Students 32.
Mission—Risen Savior Thoreau. HC 62, Box 8146, Bluewater, McKinley Co. 87323-9410.
Station— Lake Valley.
Station—St. Bonaventure Thoreau.

Cuba, Sandoval Co., Immaculate Conception (Nacimiento) (1914), [CEM 4] Rev. John Boland.
Res.: P.O. Box 40, 87013. Tel: 505-289-3803; Fax: 505-289-3236.
Catechesis/Religious Program—Students 60.
Mission—Santo Nino La Jara, Sandoval Co.
Mission—Saint Aloysius Gonzaga San Luis, Sandoval Co.
Mission—San Jose Cabezon, Sandoval Co.

Farmington, San Juan Co.

1—St. Mary's (1976), (Hispanic), Rev. Msgr. Leo Gomez; Deacons Frank Chavez; John Lucero.
Res.: P.O. Box 2840, 87499-2840. Tel: 505-325-0287; Fax: 505-534-8515.
Catechesis/Religious Program—Tel: 505-325-0287, Ext. 147. Sr. Ruth Battagila, D.R.E. Students 464.

2—Sacred Heart (1929), Rev. Timothy Farrell. In Res., Rev. Raymond Mahlmann.
Res.: 414 N. Allen Ave., 87401. Tel: 505-325-9743; Fax: 505-325-8860.
Catechesis/Religious Program—Tel: 505-564-8164. Cindy Blanco, D.R.E. Students 365.

Flora Vista, San Juan Co., Holy Trinity (1986), (Hispanic), Rev. Joachim Blonski; Deacon Charles Peterson, Pastoral Assoc.
Res.: 500 N. Mesa Verde Ave., Aztec, 87410. Tel: 505-334-6535; Fax: 505-334-5902.

Fort Wingate, McKinley Co., St. Eleanor, Closed., For inquiries for parish records contact Sacred Heart Cathedral.
Station— Iyanbito.

Grants, Cibola Co., St. Teresa (1942), Very Rev. Alberto Avella; Revs. Mathew Keller; Timothy Cervantes; Deacons Michael Lente; Timoteo Lujan; Rogelio Fernandez; Paul Sanchez; Larry Chavez.
Res.: 213 Smith St., P.O. Box 668, 87020. Tel: 505-285-6645; Fax: 505-285-6646.
Catechesis/Religious Program—Tel: 505-287-3549. Socorro Jackson, D.R.E. Students 298.

Laguna, Cibola Co., St. Joseph (Laguna Indian Pueblo) (1699), Revs. Ulric Pax, O.F.M.; Larry Barnard, O.F.M.; Sr. Virginia Adler, C.S.A., Pastoral Assoc.
Res.: P.O. Box 1000, 87026. Tel: 505-552-9330.
Catechesis/Religious Program—Tel: 505-552-7464; Fax: 505-552-9429. Florence Chino, D.R.E.; Virginia Siow, D.R.E. Students 84.
Mission—Nativity of the Blessed Virgin Mary Encinal, Valencia Co.
Mission—Sacred Heart Mesita, Valencia Co.
Mission—St. Elizabeth Paguate, Valencia Co.
Mission—St. Mary Margaret Paraje, Valencia Co.
Mission—St. Anne Seama, Valencia Co.

Lumberton, Rio Arriba Co., St. Francis of Assisi (1910), (Hispanic—Native American), Rev. Lawrence Smith, S.J., Admin.
Res.: P.O. Box 490, Dulce, 87528. Tel 505-759-1307; Fax 505-759-1392.
Catechesis/Religious Program—Students 27.
Mission—St. Anthony 3760 Sandhill, Dulce, Rio Arriba Co.

Milan, Cibola Co., St. Vivian (1969), Very Rev. Alberto Avella; Rev. Matthew Keller Deacons Larry Chavez; Paul Sanchez; Timoteo Lujan; Michel Lente; Rogelio Fernandez.
Res.: P.O. Box 2938, 87201-2938. Tel: 505-287-9327.
Catechesis/Religious Program—Students 93.

Navajo, McKinley Co., St. Berard (1963), (Native American), [JC] Rev. Gilbert Schneider, O.F.M.; Deacon Wilson Gorman.
Res.: P.O. Box 1284, 87328. Tel: 505-777-2251.
Catechesis/Religious Program—Tel: 505-777-2490. Sr. Marquerite Bartz, S.B.S., D.R.E. Students 96.
Mission—St. Francis Mission P.O. Box 41, Sawmill, Apache Co., AZ 86549. Tel: 602-729-5224.
Station— Crystal.

Pinehaven, McKinley Co., Good Shepherd Catholic Mission (1972), (Native American), [CEM] Rev. Jeffrey King.
Res.: P.O. Box 2170, 87305. Tel: 505-778-5658.
Catechesis/Religious Program—Students 12.
Convent—Missionaries of Charity, Box 267, Vanderwagen, 87326. Tel: 505-778-5740. Sisters 4.

Quemado, Catron Co., Sacred Heart (1881), (Hispanic), [CEM] Rev. Patrick J. Universal.
Res.: P.O. Box 339, 87829. Tel: 505-773-4631.
Catechesis/Religious Program—Students 5.

San Fidel, Cibola Co., St. Joseph Mission (1920), (Hispanic), [CEM] Attended by, Acoma, NM.
Res.: P.O. Box 448, Acoma, 87034. Tel: 505-552-6403.

San Mateo, Cibola and McKinley Cos., San Mateo, Very Rev. Alberto Avella; Rev. Matthew Keller; Deacons Larry Chavez; Paul Sanchez; Timoteo Lujan; Michael Lente; Rogelio Fernandez.
Mailing Address: P.O. Box 2938, Milan, 87021. Tel: 505-287-9327.
Catechesis/Religious Program—Students 10.

San Rafael, Cibola Co., San Rafael, Very Rev. Alberto Avella; Rev. Matthew Keller; Deacons Larry Chavez; Paul Sanchez; Timoteo Lujan; Michael Lente; Rogelio Fernandez.
Mailing Address: P.O. Box 2938, Milan, 87201.
Catechesis/Religious Program—Students 48.

Seboyeta, Cibola Co., Our Lady of Sorrows (1974), (Hispanic), [CEM] Deacon William P. Beaton, Admin.
Res.: H.C. 77, P.O. Box 13, 87014. Tel: 505-552-6301.
Catechesis/Religious Program—Students 8.
Mission—Our Lady of Loretto Bibo, Cibola Co.
Mission—Santa Rosalia Moquino, Valencia Co.
Station— Marquez.

Shiprock, San Juan Co., Christ the King (1924), (Native American), [JC] Rev. John Sauter; Deacon Earl Rogers.
Res.: P.O. Box 610, 87420. Tel: 505-368-4532.
Catechesis/Religious Program—Tel: 505-368-5845. Students 45.

Thoreau, McKinley Co., St. Bonaventure, Unassigned., Mailing Address: P.O. Box 268, Crownpoint, 87313. Tel: 505-786-7110.
Station—Holy Spirit Smith Lake.

Tinaja, Cibola Co., San Lorenzo (1935), (Hispanic—Native American), Attended by, Chichiltah, NM. Rev. Jeffrey King.
Res.: State Rte. 2, Box 47, Ramah, 87321. Tel: 505-783-4301.
Catechesis/Religious Program—Students 4.
Mission—El Morro Fence Lake, Valencia Co.

Tohatchi, McKinley Co., St. Mary Church (1920), (Native American), [CEM] Rev. John Mittelstadt, O.F.M.; Bro. Michael Haag, O.F.M.; Deacon Marcellino Morris.
Res.: Box 39, 87325. Tel: 505-733-2243; Fax: 505-733-2243.
Catechesis/Religious Program—Tel: 505-733-2468. Sisters Marlene Kochert, O.S.F., D.R.E.; Donna Marie Evans, O.S.F., D.R.E.; Mildred Speed, O.S.F., D.R.E.
Mission—St. Anthony Naschitti, San Juan Co. Tel: 505-732-4344.
Station— Coyote Canyon.
Station— Mexican Springs.
Station— Twin Lakes.
Station— Sheep Springs.
Station— Chuska.

Waterflow, San Juan Co., Sacred Heart (1917), [CEM] Rev. Patrick Wedeking, Admin.; Deacon Joseph Didde.
Res.: 9 Rd. 6820, 87421. Tel: 505-598-5454.
Catechesis/Religious Program—Tel: 505-598-9856. Sr. Ann Reges Barrett, M.S.B.T. Students 70.
Mission—San Juan Catholic Center P.O. Box 857, Kirtland, San Juan Co. 87417. Tel: 505-598-6799.
Mission—Sacred Heart Missionary Cenacle Fruitland. P.O. Box 1037, Ojo Armarillo, San Juan Co. 87416. Tel: 505-598-9856. Sr. Ann Regis Barrett, M.S.B.T., Dir.

Zuni, McKinley Co., St. Anthony, Our Lady of Guadalupe (Zuni Indian Pueblo) (1923), Rev. Sean Murnan, O.F.M.; Sr. Clara Scherr, S.C.L., Pastoral Min. In Res., Rev. Terance Rhoades, O.F.M.
Res.: P.O. Box 486, 87327. Tel: 505-782-2888; Fax: 505-782-2888.
Catechesis/Religious Program—Tel: 505-782-2527. Students 6.

ARIZONA

Alpine, Apache Co., St. Helena (1971), Rev. Msgr. Arthur F. MacDonald.
Res.: P.O. Box 229, AZ 85920. Tel: 928-339-4363.
Catechesis/Religious Program—Students 6.
Mission—Santo Nino Glenwood, Catron Co.

Chinle, Apache Co., Our Lady of Fatima (1905), (Native American), Rev. Blane Grein, O.F.M.
Res.: P.O. Box 2119, AZ 86503. Tel: 928-674-5413; Fax: 928-674-5813.
Mission—St. Anthony P.O. Box 578, Many Farms, Apache Co., AZ 86538. Tel: 928-781-6350.
Mission—St. Mary of the Rosary P.O. Box 432, Pinon, Navajo Co., AZ 86510. Tel: 928-725-3365.
Catechesis/Religious Program—Tel: 928-674-5029. Students 32.

Cibecue, Navajo Co., St. Catherine (1929), (Native American), Rev. Bernard Green, S.D.S., Admin.
Res.: P.O. Box 80156, AZ 85911. Tel: 928-332-2311; Fax: 928-332-2528.
Mission—St. Anthony Cedar Creek, Gila Co., AZ. (TUC)

CONCHO, APACHE CO., SAN RAFAEL (1977), Rev. Frank Chacon.
Church: P.O. Drawer C, AZ 85924. Tel: 928-337-2515.
Catechesis/Religious Program—Students 14.

FORT DEFIANCE, APACHE CO., OUR LADY OF BLESSED SACRAMENT (1915), (Native American), [JC] Revs. Gilbert Schneider, O.F.M.; Meldon Hickey, O.E.M.; Deacon Dan Martin.
Res.: P.O. Box 70, AZ 86504-0070. Tel: 928-729-5068.
Catechesis/Religious Program—Sr. Mary Hotten Roth, S.B.S., D.R.E. Students 62.

GANADO, APACHE CO., ALL SAINTS (1968), (Native American), Rev. Flann O'Neil, O.F.M.
Res.: P.O. Box 119, AZ 86505. Tel: 928-755-3401.
Catechesis/Religious Program—Tel: 928-652-3236; Fax: 928-652-3236. Sr. Monica Dubois, O.P., D.R.E. Students 30.
Mission—St. Anne Klagetoh, AZ. #50, HC 58, P.O. Box 90, Apache Co., AZ 86505. Tel: 928-652-3264. Bro. John Hotstream, S.C. In Res., Rev. Will McCue, S.C.
Mission—Our Lady of the Rosary #161, HC 58, Box 70, Greasewood, Navajo Co., AZ 86505. Tel: 928-654-3236. Bro. Paul O'Brien, O.F.M.
Station— Cornfields, AZ.
Station— Wide Ruins, AZ.

HOLBROOK, NAVAJO CO., OUR LADY OF GUADALUPE (1923), Rev. Robert Mathieu; Deacon Robert Racicot.
Res.: 212 E. Arizona St., P.O. Box 849, AZ 86025. Tel: 928-524-3261; Fax: 928-524-1507.
Catechesis/Religious Program—Tel: 928-524-2920; 928-524-6724. Students 90.

HOUCK, APACHE CO., ST. JOHN THE EVANGELIST (Tekakwitha Mission) (1927), (Native American), Rev. Cormac Antram, O.F.M.
Res.: P.O. Box 48, AZ 86506. Tel: 928-688-2921; Fax: 928-688-2921.
Catechesis/Religious Program—Students 18.
Mission—St. Rose Pine Springs, Apache Co., AZ.

KAYENTA, NAVAJO CO., OUR LADY OF GUADALUPE (1967), Rev. Jerome Herff, C.M.
Res.: P.O. Box 517, AZ 86033. Tel: 928-697-3429.
Catechesis/Religious Program—Students 8.

KEAMS CANYON, NAVAJO CO., ST. JOSEPH'S INDIAN MISSION (1920), (Hopi-Navajo), Rev. Clayton F. Kilburn, C.M.
Res.: P.O. Box 128, AZ 86034. Tel: 928-738-2325; Fax: 928-738-2325.
Catechesis/Religious Program—Students 15.
Station— Toyei, AZ.

LUKACHUKAI, APACHE CO., ST. ISABEL (1910), (Native American), Rev. Caron Vollmer, O.F.M.
Res.: P.O. Box 128, AZ 86507. Tel: 928-787-2322.
Catechesis/Religious Program—Students 15.
Mission—Our Lady of Guadalupe Round Rock, Apache Co., AZ.
Mission—St. Ann Tsaile, Apache Co., AZ.
Mission—Our Lady of the Lake Wheatfields, Apache Co., AZ.

MCNARY, APACHE CO., ST. ANTHONY (1922), Rev. Cyril Levy.
Res.: P.O. Box 628, AZ 85930. Tel: 928-334-2394.
Catechesis/Religious Program—Students 6.
Station— Hawley Lake, AZ.
Station— Vernon, AZ. (Vernon)
Station—Sunrise Ski Lodge Greer, AZ. (Winter)

OVERGAARD, NAVAJO CO., OUR LADY OF ASSUMPTION (1982), Rev. William F. Day; Deacon Charles Hetter.
Res.: P.O. Box 628, AZ 85933. Tel: 928-535-5329; Fax: 928-535-6602.
Catechesis/Religious Program—Students 28.

PAGE, COCONINO CO., IMMACULATE HEART OF MARY (1958), Deacons Roy Stringfellow, Pastoral Admin.; Jerry Lindsay.
Res.: P.O. Box 1387, AZ 86040. Tel: 928-645-2301; Fax: 928-645-1261.
Catechesis/Religious Program—Tel: 928-645-3124. Students 80.

PINETOP, NAVAJO CO., ST. MARY OF THE ANGELS (1974), Rev. Oliver Curran; Deacon Richard Conn.
Res.: Box 819, AZ 85935. Tel: 928-367-2080; Fax: 928-367-2085. Web: www.stmaryoftheanegls.us.
Catechesis/Religious Program—Fax: 928-367-2085. Shannon Barton, D.R.E.; Mary Knaust, D.R.E. Students 215.

PINON, NAVAJO CO., ST. MARY OF THE ROSARY (1937), (Native American), Attended by, Chinle, AZ.
Res.: P.O. Box 432, AZ 86510. Tel: 928-725-3365.
Catechesis/Religious Program—Students 6.
Station— Tachee, AZ.
Station— Blue Gap, AZ.
Station— Forest Lake, AZ.
Station— Whippoorwill Spring, AZ.
Station— Hardrock, AZ.
Station— Kits'iiLi, AZ.

ST. JOHNS, APACHE CO., ST. JOHN THE BAPTIST (1890), Rev. Frank Chacon; Deacon Filomeno Ulibarri.
Res.: P.O. Box 309, AZ 85936. Tel: 928-337-4390.
Catechesis/Religious Program—Tel: 928-337-4461. Students 232.

ST. MICHAELS, APACHE CO., ST. MICHAEL (1898), (Native American), [JC] Revs. Gilbert Schneider, O.F.M.; Meldon Hickey, O.E.M. In Res., Revs. Ronald Walters, O.F.M.; Berard Doerger, O.F.M.; Jack Clark Robinson, O.F.M.; Bros. John Friebel, O.F.M.; Jos[00e9] Rodriguez.
Res.: P.O. Box 680, AZ 86511-0680. Tel: 928-871-4171; Fax: 928-871-4186.
Catechesis/Religious Program—Tel: 928-871-4173. Sr. Frances Rose Dinkel, C.S.A, D.R.E.; Chris Rayner, Youth Minister. Students 73.
Mission—St. Michael's Mission for Navajo Indians, Apache Co., AZ.

SHOW LOW, NAVAJO CO., ST. RITA (1962), Rev. Gil Mangampo; Deacon John Heal.
Res.: P.O. Box 1449, AZ 85901. Tel: 928-537-2543; Fax: 928-532-8441.
Catechesis/Religious Program—Susan Olsen, D.R.E. Students 104.

SNOWFLAKE, NAVAJO CO., OUR LADY OF THE SNOWS (1963), Rev. William J. Welch; Deacons William J. Rogers; Raymond Melcher.
Res.: 1655 S. Main St., AZ 85937. Tel: 928-536-4559; Fax: 928-536-5852.
Catechesis/Religious Program—Tel: 928-337-4067. Denise Castillo, D.R.E. Students 113.

SPRINGERVILLE, APACHE CO., ST. PETER (1880), (Hispanic), Rev. Patrick J. Universal; Deacon George Campos.
Res.: P.O. Box 1566, AZ 85938. Tel: 928-333-4423; Fax: 928-333-0448.
Catechesis/Religious Program—Tel: 928-333-5328. Students 68.

TUBA CITY, COCONINO CO., ST. JUDE (1956), Rev. J. Godden Menard, C.M.
Res.: P.O. Box 248, AZ 86045. Tel: 928-283-5391.
Catechesis/Religious Program—Students 27.

WHITERIVER, NAVAJO CO., ST. FRANCIS (1921), (Native American), Rev. Edward Fronske, O.F.M.
Res.: P.O. Box 679, AZ 85941. Tel: 928-338-4432.
Catechesis/Religious Program—Fax: 928-338-1568. Phyllis Esquibel, D.R.E. Students 42.

WINSLOW, NAVAJO CO.
1—ST. JOSEPH'S (1896), Rev. Daniel C. Hussey.
Res.: 300 W. Hillview St., AZ 86047. Tel: 928-289-2350; Fax: 928-289-9226.
Catechesis/Religious Program—Anita Henling, D.R.E. Students 252.
2—MADRE DE DIOS (1950), (Hispanic), Rev. Daniel C. Hussey.
Res.: 300 W. Hillview St., AZ 86047. Tel: 928-289-2350; Fax: 928-289-9226.
Catechesis/Religious Program— Twinned with St. Joseph's, Winslow.

Chaplains of Public Institutions

GALLUP. *Gallup Area Hospitals & Nursing Homes*, 506 W. 66 Ave., 87301. Tel: 505-722-0999. Rev. Hugh O'Neill.

FARMINGTON. *Farmington Area Hospitals*, 414 N. Allen Ave., 87401. Tel: 505-325-9743. Rev. Raymond Mahlmann.

Special Assignment:
Rev.—
Maikowski, Thomas R., Dir. of Education

On Duty Outside of Diocese:
Revs.—
Bowski, Eugene, 901 Brother Matthias Pl NW, Albuquerque, 87102.
Morello, Peter
Sanchez, Raul N., Ch. Capt., 1267 Hurst Dr., Van Air Force Base, Enid, OK 73703-8557. Tel: 210-670-7373 USAF
Turner, Robert, Blessed Sacrament Parish, 3100 S. 41st St., Milwaukee, WI 53215.

On Leave of Absence:
Revs.—
Buckley, James, P.O. Box 71037, Sanger, TX 76266.
Kassis, Daniel F., P.O. Box 4742, Laguna Beach, CA 92652-4742.
Kugler, Michael, Milwaukee, WI.
McConvey, Michael, 3 Argyll Ave., Bustin Brae Larne, Co. Antrim Ireland.
Mesley, Jerry
Obersteiner, Ernest, 67-918 Arden Dr., Cathedral City, CA 92234.

Retired:
Revs.—
Downie, Arley T., #15 Rd. 6015, 87401.
Hart, William, P.O. Box 413, Castine, ME 04421.
Lindenmeyer, James, 4600 San Medina, 87401.
Pispeky, Steve
Richardson, Donald
Smith, Norman, Mullen Home, 3629 W. 29th Ave., Denver, CO 80211.
Stanfield, Francis E., 309 E. Logan Ave., 87301.

Permanent Deacons:
Aragon, Juan, Gen. Del., Aragon.
Aragon, Vidal, 324 Jane N.E., Albuquerque, 87123.
Beaton, William P., P.O. Box 425, San Fidel, 87049.
Berhost, Paul, 2104 E. 17th St., 87020.
Campos, George, P.O. Box 1254, Eagar, AZ 85925.
Chavez, Frank, 341 Arnold Dr., Aztec, 87410.
Chavez, Larry, P.O. Box 1883, Grants, 87020.
Conn, Richard, 3060 Rainbow Lake Dr., Lakeside, AZ 85929.
Didde, Joseph, 12 CR 6A27, Kirtland, 87417.
Fernandez, Rogelio, 80011 Lobo Canyon Rd., Grants, 87020.
Garcia, Roger, 14 CR 5359, Bloomfield, 87413.
Gorman, Wilson C., P.O. Box 218, Fort Defiance, AZ 86504-0218.
Guoladdle, Bobby
Heal, John, P.O. Box 1429, Snowflake, AZ 85937.
Hoy, James, P.O Box 1084, 87305.
Kelley, Timothy, P.O. Box 360, Bulverde, TX 78163.
Krikawa, Joseph, P.O. Box 1338, 87305.
Lane, John F.
Lente, Michael, 610 E. High St., Grants, 87020.
Lindsay, Jerry, P.O. Box 3607, Page, AZ 86040-3607.
Lucero, John
Lucero, Levy, 414 San Andreas, Alamogordo, 88310.
Lujan, Timoteo, P.O. Box 2612, Milan, 87021-2612.
Majesky, Russel, P.O. Box 139, Greer, AZ 85927.
Manuelito, Sherman, P.O. Box 296, Tohatchi, 87325-0296.
Martin, Daniel Nez, P.O. Box 724, Window Rock, AZ 86515.
Melcher, Raymond, P.O. Box 1266, Snowflake, AZ 85937-1226.
Morris, Marcelino, P.O. Box 768, Fort Defiance, AZ 86505.
Peterson, Charles, 28 Rd. 3009, Aztec, 87410.
Racicot, Robert, P.O. 892, Holbrook, AZ 86025-0892.
Richtsmeier, Thomas, 1134 Boggie Dr., 87301.
Rogers, Earl, P.O. Box 283, La Plata, 87418.
Rogers, William, P.O. Box 217, Taylor, AZ 85939-0217.
Sanchez, Paul, 203 N. Nimitz, Grants, 89020.
Stando, Matthew, 2446 Harlem Rd., Cheektowaga, NY 14225.
Starrs, William, 103 Lampliter Village, Clarkdale, AZ 86324.
Stringfellow, Roy, P.O. Box 2559, Page, AZ 86040.
Ulibarri, Fiomeno, P.O. Box 453, Concho, AZ 85924.
Valdo, Larry
Valencia, Ernest, P.O. Box 461, Blanco, 87412.

INSTITUTIONS LOCATED IN THE DIOCESE

[A] SEMINARIES, DIOCESAN

GALLUP. *Diocesan Diaconate and Lay Ecclesial Ministry Formation Program*, P.O. Box 1338, 87305. Tel: 505-863-4406; Fax: 505-722-9131. Email: officeofbishop@cnetco.com. Most Rev. Donald E. Pelotte, S.S.S., Ph.D. see Ministry Formation Program.

CHINLE. *Native American Lay Ministry and Diaconate Program*, P.O. Box 2119, AZ 86503. Tel: 928-674-5413; Fax: 928-674-5813. Email: clownOFM@cybertrails.com. Rev. Blane Grein, O.F.M., Dir. Students 32.
Faculty: Rev. John Sauter; Bro. John Hotstream, S.C.; Sisters Maureen Farrar, A.S.C.; Barbara Smith, A.S.C.; Mary Sullivan, S.B.S.; Marquerite Bartz, S.B.S.; Mildred Speed, O.S.F.; Annette O'Donnell, S.B.S.; Mary Hottenroth, S.B.S.; Chris Rayner.

[B] HIGH SCHOOLS, PRIVATE

GALLUP. *Gallup Catholic High School*, 515 Park Ave., 87301. Tel: 505-722-6089; Fax: 505-726-8142. Email: gcschool@cnetco.com. Web: www.gcschool.pvt.k12.nm.us. Donald Sparks, Prin. Lay Teachers 8; Students 78.

ST. MICHAELS. *St. Michael High School*, P.O. Box 650, AZ 86511. Tel: 928-871-4443; Fax: 928-871-3191. Email: smis@aol.com. Sr. Kathleen Ries, Prin. Brothers 3; Sisters 6; Lay Teachers 9; Students 164.

[C] ELEMENTARY SCHOOLS, PRIVATE

GALLUP. *St. Francis of Assisi School*, 215 W. Wilson, 87305. Tel: 505-863-3145; Fax: 505-863-8150. Rev. Thomas R. Maikowski, Prin. Priests 1; Sisters 11; Lay Teachers 2; Students 140.
Gallup Catholic School, (Grades PreK-8), 515 Park Ave., 87301. Tel: 505-863-6652; Fax: 505-726-8142.

Email: gcshool@cnetco.com. Web: www.gcschool.pvt.k12.nm.us. Donald Sparks, Prin. Lay Teachers 11; Students 172.

CUBA. *Immaculate Conception School*, (Grades K-5), P.O. Box 218, 87013. Tel: 505-289-3749; Fax: 505-289-0031. Email: PJholliscuba@yahoo.com. Lay Teachers 3; Students 10.

FARMINGTON. *Sacred Heart School*, (Grades PreK-6), 404 N. Allen Ave., 87401. Tel: 505-325-7152; Fax: 505-325-6157. Email: shesk5@hotmail.com. Dr. J. Atanasoff, Prin. Lay Teachers 12; Students 135.

GRANTS. *St. Teresa of Avila School*, (Grades PreK-8), P.O. Box 729, 87020. Tel: 505-287-2261; Fax: 505-285-4350. Email: stteresa@hotmail.com. Jerry Garcia, Prin. Lay Teachers 11; Students 161.

LUMBERTON. *St. Francis School*, (Grades K-8), HC 71, Box 26, 87528. Tel: 505-759-3252; Fax: 505-759-3844. Email: lumbertonschool@yahoo.com. Kristelle Talamante, Prin. Lay Teachers 7; Students 96.

ST. MICHAELS. *St. Michael Elementary School*, P.O. Box 650, AZ 86511. Tel: 928-871-4636; Fax: 928-871-3027. Email: smis1902@aol.com. Web: www.rc.net/gallup/stmichael. Sr. Kathleen Kajer, Prin. Sisters 4; Lay Teachers 9; Students 255.

SAN FIDEL. *St. Joseph School*, (Grades PreK-8), P.O. Box 370, 87049. Tel: 505-552-6362; Fax: 505-552-6362. Email: stjosephmissionschools@hotmail.com. David R. Jiron, Prin. Sisters 1; Lay Teachers 5; Students 69.

THOREAU. *St. Bonaventure School*, (Grades PreK-8), 25 Navarre Blvd., W., P.O. Box 909, 87323. Tel: 505-862-7847; Fax: 505-862-7790. Web: www.sbms.k12.nm.us. Sr. Natalie Bussiere, S.N.D.deN., Prin. Brothers 1; Sisters 3; Lay Teachers 11; Students 212.

ZUNI. *St. Anthony Indian School*, P.O. Box 486, 87327. Tel: 505-782-4596; Fax: 505-782-2013. Gus Keene Jr., Prin. Lay Teachers 12; Students 170.

[D] CONVENTS AND RESIDENCES FOR SISTERS

GALLUP. *Casa Reina*, 217 E. Wilson, 87301. Tel: 505-722-5511; Fax: 505-863-0075. Email: guadalupesjsrs@cnet.com. Sr. Magda, H.N.S.G., Supr. Sisters of Guadalupe and St. Joseph, Perpetual Adoration Chapel. Immigration and Naturalization Services, Hispanic Ministry. Sisters 14.

Catholic Indian Center, 506 W. 66th Ave., 87301. Tel: 505-722-0999; Fax: 505-722-7512. Email: cathcharties@yahoo.com. Web: www.cnetco.com/~cathcharities. Sr. Betty Marie Dunkel, D.C., Exec. Dir.

[E] HOMES FOR THE AGED

GALLUP. *Villa Guadalupe Home for the Aged*, 1900 Mark Ave., 87301. Tel: 505-863-6894; Fax: 505-722-4121. Sr. Gerard M. O'Connor, L.S.P.; Rev. Alfred A. Tachias, J.C.L., Chap. Little Sisters of the Poor 8; Total Assisted 54; Total Staff 50.

[F] MISCELLANEOUS LISTINGS

GALLUP. *Blue Army* (Fatima Apostolate) , 217 E. Wilson Ave., 87301. Tel: 505-722-5511; Fax: 505-863-0075. Email: guadalupesjsrs@cnetco.com. Sisters Magda Leticia Garcia, Spiritual Dir.; Rosa M. Zuniga, H.N.S.G., Contact Person; Lorena Osuna, H.N.S.G., Contact Person.

Casa San Martin, 207 W. Wilson St., 87301. Tel: 505-722-5156. Sr. M. Damascene, M.C., Supr. & Contact Person. Missionaries of Charity, Soup Kitchen & Shelter for Native American Clients. Total Assisted 49,199.

207 E. Wilson Ave., 87301. Tel: 505-722-5261.

Catholic Peoples' Initiative, Inc., P.O. Box 369, 87305. Tel: 505-726-8295; Fax: 505-726-8295. Email: cpf@cpfnm.org. Web: www.cpfnm.org. Mr. Daniel J. Sanchez, Exec. Dir.

Gallup Catholic School Foundation, Inc., 515 Park Ave., 87301. Tel: 505-722-6966; Fax: 505-726-8142. Email: gcschoolfnd@cnetco.com. Web: www.gcschool.pvt.k12.nm.us. Elizabeth Sparks, Dir.

Our Lady of Mt. Carmel (Residential Treatment Center for Native American Girls and Children), 200 Mount Carmel Ave., 87301. Tel: 505-722-9411; Fax: 505-863-5017. Sr. Rose Marie Holden, O.S.F., Dir. Residence for Indian girls. Total Assisted 62; Staff 12.

Sacred Heart Retreat, Zuni Hwy. S., P.O. Box 1338, 87305. Tel: 505-722-6755. Michael Sullivan, Facility Dir.; Sr. Mary Matthias Ward, O.S.U., Program Dir.

Southwest Indian Foundation, 100 W. Coal Ave., P.O. Box 307, 87305. Tel: 505-863-2125; Fax: 505-726-8327. Email: swif@cia-g.com Web: www.southwestindian.com. Mr. William McCarthy, Chief Exec. Officer.

Board of Directors: Most Rev. Donald E. Pelotte, S.S.S., Ph.D., Ex Officio; Mr. James Mason, Pres.; Mr. John Dowling, Vice Pres.; Mrs. Mary Constant, Sec.; Rev. Gilbert Schneider, O.F.M.; Deacon Robert Racicot; Sr. Angela Aldi, O.S.F.; Hon. Judge Marie Nezwood; Mr. Martin Neal; Mr. Leonard Shirley; Mrs. Fred Melton; Ronald Denney, Rear Admin.

CHINLE. *Talbot House-Catholic Charities*, P.O. Box 417, AZ 86503. Tel: 928-674-3238; Fax: 928-674-5813. Email: alinksfp@yahoo.com. Web: www.cnetco.com/catholiccharities. Sr. Adelaide Link, S.F.P., C.I.S.W., Dir. (Affiliated with Catholic Charities) Total Assisted 2,533; Staff 3.

GRANTS-MILAN. *Casa San Jose*, 2595 W. Hwy. 66, 87020-9626. Tel: 505-285-5451; Fax: 505-285-6436. Email: casa@7cities.com. Web: www.cnetco/~Catholiccharities.com. Sr. Francine Schuster, A.S.C., Admin. Residence of pregnant & parenting teenagers Operated by Catholic Charities. Sisters Adorers of the Blood of Christ 1; Sinsinawa Dominican of the Most Holy Rosary 1; Total Staff 8; Total Assisted 24.

PINETOP. *St. Vincent DePaul Society* Thrift Shop & Emergency Aid Office. , St. Mary of the Angels, P.O. Box 319, AZ 85935. Tel: 928-367-2029; 928-367-3057. Kay McNeff, Pres.; Bill Schultz, Shop Mgr.; Lucy Wallace, Emergency Aid Contact Person. Total Assisted 1,080; Total Staff 4.

THOREAU. *St. Bonaventure Indian Mission & School*, 25 Navarre Blvd. W., P.O. Box 610, 87323. Tel: 505-862-7847; Fax: 505-862-7029 Email: boconnell@sbms.k12.nm.us. Web: www.sbms.k12.nm.us. Paul Leche, Chm.; Barbara Morales, Sec.; Suzanne Slankard, Vice Chm.; Frank Thompson, Treas.

TUBA CITY. *Life Sharing Center, Inc., St. Jude Food Bank*, P.O. Box 1277, AZ 86045. Tel: 928-283-6886; Fax: 928-283-6614. Email: stjudefoodbank@cybertrails.com. Sr. Frances Vista, D.C., M.S.W., Contact Person.

WINSLOW. *La Casa de Nuestra Senora* Mission of Madonna House Apostolate Combermere, Ontario, Canada. , 213 Jefferson St., AZ 86047. Tel: 928-289-9284 Web: www.madonnahouse.org. Kathy McVady, Dir., Pro-Tem. Prayer and Community Service Center; Catechesis of the Good Shepherd Program for 3 - 5 yr. olds. Total Residents 6.

RELIGIOUS INSTITUTES OF MEN REPRESENTED IN THE DIOCESE

For further details refer to the corresponding bracketed number in the Religious Institutes of Men or Women section.

[1100]—*Brothers of the Sacred Heart*—S.C.
[1330]—*Congregation of the Mission*—C.M.
[0490]—*Franciscan Brothers of Brooklyn, NY*—O.S.F.
[0520]—*Franciscan Friars* (Provs. of Our Lady of Guadalupe & St. Barbara)—O.F.M.
[0690]—*Jesuit Fathers and Brothers*—S.J.
[1200]—*Society of the Divine Savior*—S.D.S.

RELIGIOUS INSTITUTES OF WOMEN REPRESENTED IN THE DIOCESE

[0100]—*Adorers of the Blood of Christ*—A.S.C.
[3710]—*Congregation of the Sisters of Saint Agnes*—C.S.A.
[1780]—*Congregation of the Sisters of the Third Order of St. Francis of Perpetual Adoration*—F.S.P.A.
[0760]—*Daughters of Charity of St. Vincent de Paul*—D.C.
[[0420]]—*Discalced Carmelite Nuns*—O.C.D.
[1070-13]—*Dominican Sisters (Adrian, MI)*—O.P.
[1070-09]—*Dominican Sisters (Racine, WI)*—O.P.
[1390]—*Franciscan Missionary Sisters of Our Lady of Sorrow*—O.S.F.
[1350]—*Franciscan Missionary Sisters of the Immaculate Conception*—O.S.F.
[1180]—*Franciscan Sisters of Allegany* (New York)—O.S.F.
[1425]—*Franciscan Sisters of Peace*—F.S.P.
[2340]—*Little Sisters of the Poor*—L.S.P.
[2470]—*Maryknoll Sisters of St. Dominic*—M.M.
[2710]—*Missionaries of Charity*—M.C.
[2790]—*Missionary Servants of the Most Blessed Trinity*—M.S.B.T.
[2760]—*Missionary Sisters of the Immaculate Conception of the Mother of God*—S.M.I.C.
[3640]—*Poor Servants of the Mother of God*—S.M.G.
[[]]—*Rosarian Dominicans* Philippines
[2970]—*School Sisters of Notre Dame*—S.S.N.D.
[0480]—*Sisters of Charity of Leavenworth, KS*—S.C.L.
[0600]—*Sisters of Charity of St. Joan Antide*
[2570]—*Sisters of Mercy* (Erie, PA)—R.S.M.
[3000]—*Sisters of Notre Dame de Namur*—S.N.D.deN.
[]—*Sisters of Our Lady of Guadalupe and St. Joseph, Inc.*
[1510]—*Sisters of St. Francis*—O.S.F.
[1705]—*Sisters of St. Francis of Assisi*—O.S.F.
[1730]—*Sisters of St. Francis of Oldenburg*—O.S.F.
[1650]—*The Sisters of St. Francis of Philadelphia*—O.S.F.
[3830-13]—*Sisters of St. Joseph of Boden, PA*—C.S.J.
[0260]—*Sisters of the Blessed Sacrament for Indians and Colored People*—S.B.S.
[1830]—*The Sisters of the Good Shepherd*—R.G.S.
[1990]—*Sisters of the Holy Name of Jesus and Mary*—S.N.J.M.
[]—*Sisters of the Immaculate Heart of Mary* Nigeria
[2940]—*Sisters of the Most Holy Sacrament*—M.H.S.
[1440]—*Sisters of the Poor of St. Francis*—S.F.P.
[3260]—*Sisters of the Precious Blood* (Dayton, OH)—C.PP.S.
[4120-05]—*Ursuline Nuns of the Congregation of Paris*—O.S.U.

NECROLOGY

† Konechne, Louis, (Retired)—Died June 5, 2003

Diocese of Galveston—Houston

(Dioecesis Galvestoniensis Houstoniensis)

Most Reverend

JOSEPH A. FIORENZA, D.D.

Bishop of Galveston-Houston; ordained May 29, 1954; appointed Bishop of San Angelo September 4, 1979; consecrated and installed October 25, 1979; appointed Bishop of Galveston-Houston December 18, 1984; installed February 18, 1985. *Office: 1700 San Jacinto, Houston, TX 77002-8291. P.O. Box 907, Houston, TX 77001-0907.* Tel: 713-659-5461.

Chancery Ofice: P.O. Box 907, Houston, TX 77001-0907. Tel: 713-659-5461; Fax: 713-759-9151.

Most Reverend

DANIEL N. DINARDO

Coadjutor Bishop of Galveston-Houston; ordained July 16, 1977; appointed Coadjutor Bishop of Sioux City August 19, 1997; consecrated October 7, 1997; appointed Bishop of Sioux City November 28, 1998; appointed Coadjutor Bishop of Galveston-Houston January 16, 2004; installed March 26, 2004

.Most Reverend

VINCENT M. RIZZOTTO, J.C.L.

Auxiliary Bishop of Galveston-Houston; ordained May 26, 1956; appointed Auxiliary Bishop of Galveston-Houston June 22, 2001; ordained July 31, 2001.

Most Reverend

JOE S. VASQUEZ

Auxiliary Bishop of Galveston-Houston; ordained June 30, 1984; appointed Auxiliary Bishop of Galveston-Houston November 30, 2001; ordained January 23, 2002.

ESTABLISHED IN 1847.

Square Miles 8,880.

Redesignated Diocese of Galveston-Houston on July 25, 1959.

Comprises the Counties of Walker, San Jacinto, Galveston, Grimes, Montgomery, Waller, Harris, Fort Bend, Brazoria and Austin in the State of Texas.

For legal titles of parishes and diocesan institutions, consult the Chancery Office.

STATISTICAL OVERVIEW

Personnel	
Bishop	1
Auxiliary Bishops	2
Priests: Diocesan Active in Diocese	146
Priests: Diocesan Active Outside Diocese	3
Priests: Diocesan in Foreign Missions	1
Priests: Retired, Sick or Absent	49
Number of Diocesan Priests	199
Religious Priests in Diocese	217
Total Priests in Diocese	416
Extern Priests in Diocese	33
Ordinations:	
Permanent Deacons	89
Permanent Deacons in Diocese	362
Total Brothers	12
Total Sisters	499
Parishes	
Parishes	150
With Resident Pastor:	
Resident Diocesan Priests	100
Resident Religious Priests	48
Missions	8
Pastoral Centers	17
Welfare	
Catholic Hospitals	3
Total Assisted	526,232
Health Care Centers	7
Total Assisted	55,447
Homes for the Aged	3
Total Assisted	493
Residential Care of Children	2
Total Assisted	2,009
Day Care Centers	39
Total Assisted	3,973
Specialized Homes	4
Total Assisted	2,354
Special Centers for Social Services	11
Total Assisted	329,985
Educational	
Seminaries, Diocesan	1
Students from This Diocese	23
Students from Other Diocese	30
Diocesan Students in Other Seminaries	13
Seminaries, Religious	5
Students Religious	21
Total Seminarians	57
Colleges and Universities	1
Total Students	7,694
High Schools, Diocesan and Parish	2
Total Students	320
High Schools, Private	6
Total Students	3,362
Elementary Schools, Diocesan and Parish	43
Total Students	10,019
Elementary Schools, Private	6
Total Students	2,017
Catechesis/Religious Education:	
High School Students	16,127
Elementary Students	67,813
Total Students under Catholic Instruction	107,409
Teachers in the Diocese:	
Priests	13
Scholastics	2
Brothers	2
Sisters	53
Lay Teachers	1,460
Vital Statistics	
Receptions into the Church:	
Infant Baptism Totals	20,744
Adult Baptism Totals	1,834
Received into Full Communion	838
First Communions	18,401
Confirmations	9,283
Marriages:	
Catholic	2,765
Interfaith	859
Total Marriages	3,624
Deaths	3,534
Total Catholic Population	1,041,123
Total Population	4,972,544

Former Bishops—Rt. Revs. J. M. ODIN, C.M., D.D., consecrated Bishop of Claudiopolis and Vicar-Apostolic of Texas, March 6, 1842; transferred to Galveston 1847; promoted to New Orleans in 1861; died in Ambierle, France, May 25, 1870; C. M. DUBUIS, D.D., consecrated Nov. 23, 1862; resigned 1881; remained Titular Bishop of Galveston till 1892, when he was promoted to an Archbishopric i.p.i.;; died May 21, 1895; at Vernaison, France; P. DUFAL, C.S.C., D.D., consecrated Nov. 25, 1860; Bishop of Delcon, and Vicar-Apostolic of Eastern Bengal; transferred to Galveston; as Coadjutor of Rt. Rev. C. M. Dubuis, cum jure successionis, May 14, 1878;; resigned 1880; died in Paris 1898; NICHOLAS A. GALLAGHER, D.D., consecrated Titular Bishop of Canopus, April 30, 1882; succeeded to Galveston, Dec. 16, 1892; died Jan. 21, 1918; Most Revs. CHRISTOPHER E. BYRNE, D.D., appt. July 18, 1918; consecrated Nov. 10, 1918;; made Assistant at the Pontifical Throne, May 8, 1941;; died April 1, 1950; WENDELIN J. NOLD, S.T.D., appt. Nov. 29, 1947; consecrated Feb. 25, 1948; died Oct. 1, 1981; JOHN L. MORKOVSKY, S.T.D. (Retired), ord. Dec. 5, 1933; Titular Bishop of Hieron and Auxiliary Bishop of Amarillo; appt. Dec. 22, 1955; consecrated Feb. 22, 1956; succeeded to See Aug. 18, 1958; transferred to Galveston-Houston as Titular Bishop of Tigava and Coadjutor and Apostolic Administrator "cum jure successionis"April 1963; installed June 11, 1963; succeeded to the See of Galveston-Houston, April 22, 1975; retired Aug. 16, 1984; died March 24, 1990.

Chancery Office—1700 San Jacinto St., Houston, 77002-8291. P.O. Box 907, Houston, 77001-0907. Tel: 713-659-5461; Fax: 713-759-9151. Office Hours: Mon.-Fri. 8:30-4:30

Chancellor and Moderator of the Curia—Rev. Msgr. FRANK H. ROSSI, S.T.L., 1700 San Jacinto St., Houston, 77002-8291. Tel: 713-659-5461.

Vice Chancellor—Rev. R. TROY GATELY, 1700 San Jacinto St., Houston, 77002-8291. Tel: 713-659-5461.

Vicars General—Most Revs. VINCENT M. RIZZOTTO, D.D., J.C.L.; JOE S. VASQUEZ, D.D.

Ethnic Vicars—Most Revs. VINCENT M. RIZZOTTO, D.D., J.C.L., Vicar of African American Catholics; JOSEPH S. VASQUEZ, Vicar of Hispanic Catholics; Rev. JOHN KHA TRAN, Vicar of Vietnamese Catholics; Rev. Msgr. SETH HERMOSO, Vicar of Filipino Catholics.

Vicar for Religious—Sr. M. ADELINE O'DONOGHUE, C.C.V.I., 6510 Lawndale, Houston, 77023. Tel: 713-928-6053.

Deans and Vicariates—

Central Vicariate—Rev. Msgr. PATRICK WELLS, Episcopal Vicar. Tel: 713-659-5461; Revs. TIM GRAY, S.C.J., V.F., Central Dean. Tel: 713-222-0203; LOUIS PIRAN, C.S., Northeast Dean. Tel: 281-449-2344; PAUL CHOVANEC, V.F., Southeast Dean. Tel: 713-645-6614.

Northern Vicariate—Rev. Msgrs. GEORGE A. SHELTZ, E.V., Episcopal Vicar. Tel: 281-419-8700; DAVID W. KENNEDY, V.F., Northern Dean. Tel: 409-756-8186; Revs. JOHN A. ZABELSKAS, V.F., Eastern Dean. Tel: 281-843-2422; PAUL PROCELLA, V.F., San Jacinto Dean. Tel: 281-446-8211.

Southern Vicariate—Rev. Msgr. T. JOSEPH CULVER, E.V., Episcopal Vicar. Tel: 409-744-3561; Rev. BILL BARTNISKI, V.F., Galveston-Mainland Dean. Tel: 281-337-4112; Rev. Msgr. REGINALD R. NESVADBA, V.F., Bay Area Dean. Tel: 281-485-2421; Rev. VINCENT DULOCK, C.S.B., V.F., Southern Dean. Tel: 409-849-2421.

Western Vicariate—Rev. Msgr. ED RANDALL, E.V., Episcopal Vicar. Tel: 713-621-4370; Rev. WENCIL C. PAVLOVSKY, C.S.B., V.F., Western Dean. Tel: 281-342-5092; Rev. Msgrs. BILL YOUNG, V.F., Southwest Dean. Tel: 713-729-0221; DANIEL SCHEEL, Northwest Dean. Tel: 713-468-9555; Rev. ROBERT BARRAS, V.F., Bluebonnet Dean. Tel: 409-826-2275.

Secretariat Directors—

Secretariat For Administration—Rev. Msgr. FRANK ROSSI, Dir., 1700 San Jacinto St., Houston, 77002-8291. Tel: 713-659-5461.

Secretariat For Clergy Formation and Chaplaincy

Services—Most Rev. VINCENT M. RIZZOTTO, D.D., J.C.L., Dir., 1700 San Jacinto St., Houston, 77002-8291. Tel: 713-659-5461.
Secretariat For Communication—Mrs. ANNETTE GONZALES-TAYLOR, 1700 San Jacinto St., Houston, 77002-8291. Tel: 713-659-5461.
Secretariat For Finance—Mr. STUART HENDRIX, 1700 San Jacinto St., Houston, 77002-8291. Tel: 713-659-5461.
Secretariat For Pastoral and Educational Ministries—Bro. JIM BARRETTE, S.M., Dir., 2403 Holcombe, Houston, 77021-2099. Tel: 713-741-8786.
Secretariat for Social Concerns—Mrs. SUSAN STROMATT, Dir., 2403 Holcombe, Houston, 77021-2099. Tel: 713-741-8769.

Tribunal Judicial—Rev. LAWRENCE JOZWIAK, J.C.L., Vicar, P.O. Box 907, Houston, 77001-0907. Tel: 713-807-9286.
Adjutant Judicial Vicar—Rev. RICHARD WAHL, C.S.B., P.O. Box 907, Houston, 77001-0907. Tel: 713-807-9286; Fax: 713-807-9296. Email: tribunal@diogh.org.
Diocesan Judges—Rev. Msgrs. T. JOSEPH CULVER, E.V.; PHILIPPE LE-XUAN THUONG, J.C.D.; Revs. TRUNG V. NGUYEN; ERIC PITRE, M.Div.; JOHN CAHOON, J.C.L.; NGOC NGUYEN, J.C.L.; Sr. ROSEMARY SMITH, S.C., J.C.D.; Ms. MEG ROMANO-HOGAN, J.C.L.
Promoter of Justice—VACANT.
Defenders of the Bond—Rev. Msgrs. DAVID KENNEDY, J.C.L.; WILLIAM PICKARD, J.C.D.; Rev. RICHARD WAHL, J.C.L.
Censor Librorum—Rev. TERENCE BRINKMAN, S.T.D., 2302 Oak Shores Dr., Kingwood, 77339-1801. Tel: 281-358-6637.

Diocesan Councils, Commissions and Committees Diocesan Presbyteral Council—1700 San Jacinto St., Houston, 77002-8291.
Presbyteral Council—Most Rev. JOSEPH A. FIORENZA, Pres. Ex Officio Members: Most Revs. VINCENT M. RIZZOTTO, D.D., J.C.L., Vicar Gen.; JOE S. VASQUEZ, D.D., Vicar Gen.; Rev. Msgr. FRANK H. ROSSI, S.T.L., Chancellor. Appointees: Rev. Msgrs. T. JOSEPH CULVER, E.V.; PATRICK WELLS; ED RANDALL, E.V.; GEORGE A. SHELTZ, E.V.; CHESTER L. BORSKI, S.T.L. Elected Members: Revs. PAGE POLK, O.F.M., Chap.; CARL L. BELISCH, C.S.B., Educational; PHIL "SKIP" NEGLEY, M.S., Spiritual and Admin. Area Representatives: Revs. WENCIL C. PAVLOVSKY, C.S.B., V.F., Northern, Western and Bluebonnet; WILLIAM D. BARTNISKI, Galveston-Mainland and Southern; NORBERT J. MADUZIA JR., Bay Area and Southeast; Rev. Msgr. JAMES B. ANDERSON, Southwest and Northwest; Revs. NICHOLAS J. HARDING, Central and Northeast; JOHN T. KELLER, Eastern and San Jacinto.
College of Consultors—Rev. Msgrs. T. JOSEPH CULVER, E.V.; WILLIAM M. PICKARD, J.C.D.; Most Rev. VINCENT M. RIZZOTTO, D.D., J.C.L.; Rev. Msgrs. DANIEL SCHEEL; FRANK H. ROSSI, S.T.L.; GEORGE A. SHELTZ, E.V.; Rev. JOHN WEYER; Rev. Msgr. ED RANDALL, E.V.
Priests Personnel Committee—Most Revs. VINCENT M. RIZZOTTO, D.D., J.C.L., Chm., 1700 San Jacinto, Houston, 77002. Tel: 713-659-5461, Ext. 257; JOE S. VASQUEZ, D.D.; Rev. Msgr. REGINALD R. NESVADBA, V.F.; Rev. ERIC PITRE, M.Div.; Rev. Msgr. FRANK H. ROSSI, S.T.L.; Revs. ALBERT A. MAULLON JR.; BRENDAN CAHILL; SEAN HORRIGAN; PHIL M. NEGLEY, M.S.
Building Commission—Rev. Msgrs. CHARLES C. DOMEC, Chm., 26777 Glen Loch Rd., The Woodlands, 77381-2921. Tel: 281-367-9885; T. JOSEPH CULVER, E.V.; EDWARD RANDALL; Rev. GEORGE SHELTZ; Mr. JAMES GRIBBLE; Mr. TONY ROURKE; Mr. STANLEY SARMAN; Mr. STEVE FAUGHT.
Board of Education—Mr. PAUL ESPENAN, Pres., 11 Swallow Tail Ct., The Woodland, 77381-3816. Tel: 281-298-5877.
Ecumenism and Interreligious Affairs Commission—Rev. JOHN ROONEY, Chm., 1801 Sage Rd., Houston, 77036-6403. Tel: 713-774-0097.
Liturgical Commission—Rev. BILL OLIVER, Chm., 800 W. Baker Rd., Baytown, 77521-2311. Tel: 281-837-8180.

Secretariat for Administration—Rev. Msgr. FRANK ROSSI, Dir., 1700 San Jacinto St., Houston, 77002-8291. Tel: 713-659-5461.
Archives and Current Records—Ms. LISA MAY, Dir., 1700 San Jacinto St., Houston, 77002-8291. Tel: 713-659-5461.
Catholic Cemeteries—Mr. GUS HOLLIS, Dir., P.O. Box 965 (Gulf Fwy. at Hughes Rd.), Dickinson, 77539. Tel: 281-337-1641; 409-948-1455.
Construction / Preventative Maintenance—Mr. STEVE FAUGHT, Dir.; DON SENGER, Preventive Maintenance, 1700 San Jacinto St., Houston, 77002-8291. Tel: 713-659-5461.
Information Services—Mr. ED HERRERA, 1700 San Jacinto St., Houston, 77002-8921. Tel: 713-659-5461.
Insurance & Risk Manager—MEREDITH L. SMITH, CPCU, ARM Dir., 1700 San Jacinto St., Houston, 77002-8291. Tel: 713-659-5461.
Claims Risk Manager—CHRISTINA SANDOVAL, Dir., 2403 Holcombe, Houston, 77021-2099. Tel: 713-741-8758; 800-856-4040; Fax: 713-748-8205.
Internal Auditor—WILLIAM PRIME, 1700 San Jacinto St., Houston, 77002-8291. Tel: 713-659-5461.
Legal Services—JOHN SIEGER, Dir. Gen. Council, 1700 San Jacinto St., Houston, 77002-8291. Tel: 713-659-5461.
Real Estate—Mr. KEN SYKES, 1700 San Jacinto St., Houston, 77002-8291. Tel: 713-659-5461.
Human Resources—Mr. FRED SHETZ, Dir.; Mrs. DAWN GIBLIN, Dir. Benefits, 1700 San Jacinto St., Houston, 77002. Tel: 713-659-5461.

Secretariat for Clergy Formation and Chaplaincy Services—Most Rev. VINCENT M. RIZZOTTO, D.D., J.C.L., Dir., 1700 San Jacinto St., Houston, 77002-8291. P.O. Box 907, Houston, 77001-0907. Tel: 713-659-5461.
African American Ministry—VACANT, Dir., 1700 San Jacinto, Houston, 77002-8291. Tel: 713-659-5461.
Apostleship of the Sea (Port Ministry)—Rev. RIVERS PATOUT, Houston Dir. Tel: 713-923-5843. Houston International Seaman's Center, P.O. Box 9506, Houston, 77261. Tel: 713-672-0511; Mrs. KAREN LAI Galveston: 2002 Mechanic, Galveston, 77550. Tel: 409-762-0021.
Catholic Chaplain Corps (Hospital Chaplains)—Rev. PAGE POLK, O.F.M., 4206 MacGregor Way S., Houston, 77021-1598. Tel: 713-526-6433.
Catholic Relief Services—Mrs. HILDA HERNANDEZ, Dir., 1700 San Jacinto St., Houston, 77002-8921. Tel: 713-659-5461.
Correctional Ministries (Jail Chaplains)—Rev. RONALD F. CLOUTIER, Dir. (Chaplain Office at Harris County Jail), Office and Mailing Address, 2403 E. Holcombe, Houston, 77021-2098. Tel: 713-741-8745; 713-755-5326 (Jail).
Director of Ministry to Priests—Rev. PHIL NEGLEY, M.S., Dir., 5918 Wigton Dr., Houston, 77096. Tel: 713-729-3906.
Diaconal Formation / Diaconal Ministry—Deacon GERALD DUPONT, Dir., 1530 Norwalk Dr., Katy, 77450-4999. Tel: 281-578-0707.
Permanent Deacons—Deacon GERALD DUPONT, Dir., 1700 San Jacinto St., Houston, 77002-8291. Tel: 713-659-5461.
Mission Office—Mrs. HILDA HERNANDEZ, Dir. *Holy Childhood, Propagation of the Faith* 1700 San Jacinto St., Houston, 77002-8291. Tel: 713-659-5461 Holy Childhood, Propagation of the Faith.
Seminarian Support—Rev. CLINT RESSLER, Dir., 1700 San Jacinto St., Houston, 77002-8291. Tel: 713-659-5461.
Vocations Office—Rev. CLINT RESSLER, Dir., 1700 San Jacinto St., Houston, 77002-8291. Tel: 713-659-5461.

Secretariat for Communication—Mrs. ANNETTE GONZALES TAYLOR, Dir., 1700 San Jacinto St., Houston, 77002-8291. Tel: 713-659-5461.
Radio—Mrs. MADELINE JOHNSON, Dir., 1700 San Jacinto St., Houston, 77002-8291. Tel: 713-659-5461.
Texas Catholic Herald—Mr. ERIK NORIEGA, Editor, 1700 San Jacinto St., Houston, 77002-8291. Tel: 713-659-5461; Tel: 713-659-3702 Sat. & Holidays; Fax: 713-659-3444.

Secretariat for Finance—Mr. STUART HENDRIX, Dir., 1700 San Jacinto St., Houston, 77002-8291. Tel: 713-659-5461.
Accounting Department—MICHAEL ZABKIEWICZ, Dir., 1700 San Jacinto St., Houston, 77002-8291. Tel: 713-659-5461.
Development Office—Rev. CARL PIEBER, C.M., Dir., 1700 San Jacinto St., Houston, 77002-8291. Tel: 713-659-5461.
Parish Accounting Services (PAS)—Mrs. JANIE MORALES, Dir., 1700 San Jacinto St., Houston, 77002-8291. Tel: 713-659-5461.

Secretariat for Pastoral and Educational Ministries—Bro. JIM BARRETTE, S.M., Dir., 2403 Holcombe, Houston, 77021-2099. Tel: 713-741-8786.
Aging Ministry—Mrs. KATHY BINGHAM, Dir., 2403 Holcombe, Houston, 77021-2098. Tel: 713-741-8712.
Boy and Girl Scouts—Rev. Msgr. WILLIAM L. YOUNG, Dir., 8600 Brinkman Rd., Houston, 77018-6329. Tel: 713-692-9123.
Campus Ministry and Young Adults—Mr. WILLIAM CORK, Dir., 2403 Holcombe Houston, 77021-2098. Tel: 713-741-8786.
Continuing Christian Education—Mrs. ANNE COMEAUX, Dir., 2403 Holcombe, Houston, 77021-2099. Tel: 713-741-8730.
Circle Lake Retreat Center—BOB SCHMIDT, Dir., P.O. Box 1408, Pinehurst, 77362-1408. Tel: 281-356-6764, Ext. 11.
Deaf Apostolate—Rev. LEONARD BRONIAK, C.Ss.R., Dir., 2401 Holcombe Blvd., Houston, 77021-2099. Tel: 713-741-8721.
Family Life Ministry—Mrs. WINIFRED HONEYWELL, Dir., 2403 Holcombe, Houston, 77021-2099. Tel: 713-741-8710.
Resource Center—Mrs. DIANE O'CONNOR, 2403 E. Holcombe, Houston, 77021-2099. Tel: 713-741-8781.
Respect Life Office—Mrs. MARCELLA COLBERT, Dir., 2403 Holcombe, Houston, 77021-2098. Tel: 713-741-8730 (Main Tel.).
Catholic School Office—Mr. NORMAN GLISSMAN, Supt., 2403 Holcombe, Houston, 77021-2099. Tel: 713-741-8704.
School of Environmental Education - Camp Kappe—Sr. THOMAS ANN LACOUR, O.P., Dir., 7738 Camp Kappe Rd., Navasota, 77363. Tel: 936-894-2141.
Worship—Mr. DAVID WOOD, Dir., 2403 Holcombe, Houston, 77021-2099. Tel: 713-741-8760.
Youth Ministry—Mr. BRIAN JOHNSON, Dir., 2403 Holcombe, Houston, 77021-2099. Tel: 713-741-8723.
Special Youth Services (Juvenile Detention Ministry)—MARILU BALLOW, Dir., 2403 Holcombe, Houston, 77021-2099. Tel: 713-527-1894; Pager: 713-762-7192.

Secretariat for Social Concerns—Mrs. SUSAN STROMATT, Dir., 2403 Holcombe, Houston, 77021-2099. Tel: 713-741-8769.
Campaign for Human Development—Mr. SAM DUNNING, Dir., 2403 Holcombe, Houston, 77021-2098. Tel: 713-741-8731.
Catholic Charities—ANNA M. BABIN, C.P.A., Pres. & CEO, 2900 Louisiana St., P.O. Box 66508, Houston, 77266. Tel: 713-526-4611; Fax: 713-526-1546.
Program Services—BOB FLEMING. Tel: 713-874-6739.
Finance and Support Services—MICHAEL J. PIERI, C.P.A., Vice Pres.
Fund Development / Marketing—DONNA FORMAN PERILLO, Dir.
Parish Relation and Advocacy—Deacon JOE RUBIO, Vice Pres.
Human Resources—RITA VILLANUEVA.
Children & Family Services—VALERIE PERALES, L.M.S.W.-A.C.P., Admin.
Children Placement Services Adoption and Foster Care—SHARON JORGESON, L.M.S.W., Supvr.
Services to Pregnant Adolescents and Their Families—MICHELLE MITCHELL, L.M.S.W.-A.C.P., A.C.S.W., C.C.A. Supvr.
Post Adoption Services—LILLIAN SALINAS, L.M.S.W. Tel: 800-BABY-DUE.
Community Outreach Services—GREG PATIN, Admin.
Diocesan AIDS Ministry—GEOFFREY BENNETT, Supvr., 2900 Louisiana St., Houston, 77266. Tel: 713-526-4611.
Guadalupe Center—YOLANDA GUTIERREZ, L.M.S.W., Site Coord., 326 S. Jensen, Houston, 77003-1599. Family Assistance Program, La Casita, Villa Guadalupe-Transitional Housing for Women.
Parish Social Ministry—ESMERALDA CERVANTES, Coord. Tel: 713-526-4611.
Services to the Alone and Frail Elderly—AYE KHINE, Supvr. Tel: 713-520-7835.
Family Counseling—VALERIE PERALES, L.M.S.W., A.C.P., Dir. Admin.; ENCARNITA GOMEZ, M.S., L.M.F.T., L.C.D.C., Supvr. Tel: 713-668-5763; 713-526-4611, Ext. 3500 (Appointments); Fax: 713-527-9198 (Family Counseling).
Immigration and Refugee Services—JANET WAITES, Admin.
St. Frances Cabrini Center for Immigrant Legal Assistance—WAFA ABDIN, Supvr. Tel: 713-526-4611, Ext. 3406.
Refugee Resettlement Services—DANIELLE BOLKS, Supvr. Tel: 713-526-4611.
St. Michael Home for Children—LETICIA HARMON, Supvr. Tel: 713-526-4611.
Serenity House—CHIWANDA IRVING. Tel: 713-526-4611, Ext. 3268.
Galveston County Center—ELIZABETH KINARD, Supvr., 4418 Ave. M, Galveston, 77550-3726. Tel: 409-762-2143; Fax: 409-762-2088.
Catholic Campaign for Human Development—Mr. SAM DUNNING, Dir., 2403 E. Holcombe, Houston, 77021-2099. Tel: 713-741-8730.
Justice and Peace—Mr. SAM DUNNING, Dir., 2403 E. Holcombe, Houston, 77021-2099. Tel: 713-741-8730.
St. Vincent de Paul Society—ROZ HILL, Exec. Dir., 2403 Holcombe, Houston, 77021-2099. Tel: 713-741-8783.

Council of Catholic Women—Rev. Msgr. DANIEL SCHEEL, Dir., 3600 Brinkman Rd., Houston, 77018-6329. Tel: 713-692-9123.

Cursillos in Christianity—HECTOR MORALES, Dir., St. Paul Cursillo Center, 4000 Belk St., Houston, 77087. Tel: 713-643-7682.

Disaster Relief—Rev. Msgr. FRANK H. ROSSI, S.T.L., Dir., 1700 San Jacinto, Houston, 77002. Tel: 713-659-5461.

Oremus Pro Invicem—Rev. Msgr. FRANCIS G. WEARDEN, Dir. (Retired), 1100 Parthenon Pl., New Caney, 77357-3039. Tel: 281-399-0270.

Rural Life Bureau—Rev. Msgr. FRANK H. ROSSI, S.T.L., 1700 San Jacinto St., Houston, 77002-8291. Tel: 713-659-5461.

Victim Assistance Coordinator—Sr. MAUREEN O'CONNELL, O.P. Tel: 713-659-5461, Ext. 499. Email: moconnell@diogh.org.

CLERGY, PARISHES, MISSIONS AND PAROCHIAL SCHOOLS

CITY OF GALVESTON
(GALVESTON COUNTY)

1—ST. MARY'S CATHEDRAL BASILICA (1847), Rev. John N. LaBauve, S.V.D. In Res., Revs. Gerald Lewis, S.V.D.; Benignus "Bennie" Wego, S.V.D. (LAF); Deacon John S. Pistone.
Res., Church & Mailing Address: 2011 Church St., 77550-2091. Tel: 409-762-9611; Fax: 409-765-8585.

2—HOLY ROSARY (1888), Revs. Paul H. Banet, S.S.J.; Joseph Onuoha; Deacon Douglas W. Matthews.
Church & Mailing Address: 1420 31st St., 77550-4399. Tel: 409-762-2478; Fax: 409-762-8383.
Catechesis/Religious Program—Tel: 409-935-4372. Thomasine Allen, D.R.E. Students 34.

3—OUR LADY OF GUADALUPE, Closed., August 1992. Contact St Patrick, Galveston for further information.

4—ST. PATRICK (1870), Revs. John Bok, O.F.M.; John Flajole, O.F.M.; Sylvester Heppner, O.F.M.; Bro. Luke Dung Lee, O.F.M.
Mailing Address: 1010 35th St., 77550-4058. Tel: 409-762-9646; Fax: 409-765-7636.
Res.: 3420 Avenue K, 77550.
Church: 34th and Avenue K, 77550-4058.
Catechesis/Religious Program—Jo Anita Jefferies, D.R.E. Students 224.
Mission—Queen of Peace Mission 706 51st St., Galveston Co. 77551-4106. Tel: 409-762-2833; Fax: 409-765-9747. Rev. Serafin Cejudo.

5—ST. PETER THE APOSTLE (1965), Rev. William D. Bartniski; Deacons William J. Bobb; Henry Becker Jr.; Louis Sam Dell'Olio.
Church & Mailing Address: 1804 69th St., 77551-1326.
Rectory—1805 Driftwood Ln., 77551-1326. Tel: 409-744-3561; Fax: 409-744-4286.
Catechesis/Religious Program—Tel: 409-744-7250. Mrs. Miriam Dell'Olio, D.R.E. Students 127.
Mission—Mary, Star of the Sea 16626 San Luis Pass Rd., Jamaica Beach, Galveston Co. 77551-1399.

6—SACRED HEART (1884), Rev. Frank T. Fabj.
Church & Mailing Address: 1302 Broadway, 77550-6198. Tel: 409-762-6374; Fax: 409-762-0919.
Catechesis/Religious Program— Michelle Gonzalez, D.R.E. Students 146.

CITY OF HOUSTON
(HARRIS COUNTY)

1—ST. ALBERT OF TRAPANI (1970), Rev. Philip A. Wilhite, S.T.L.; Deacons Carlito Buhay; Alvaro Casas Jr.; Donald Rapp; Antonio Flores Jr.; Larry T. Longley. In Res., Rev. Joseph Manapuram.
Church & Mailing Address: 11027 S. Gessner Rd., 77071-3599. Tel: 713-771-3596; Fax: 713-270-0441.
Catechesis/Religious Program— Peggy Popkey, D.R.E. Students 372.

2—ALL SAINTS (1908), Rev. Msgr. Adam S. McClosky; Deacons Fancis L. Matula; Gary Hilbig; Juan M. Contla. In Res., Rev. Ronald F. Cloutier.
Res., Church & Mailing Address: 215 E. 10th St., 77008-7025. Tel: 713-864-2653; Fax: 713-864-0761.
Catechesis/Religious Program— Daniel Schwieterman, D.R.E. Students 239.

3—ST. ALPHONSUS (1966), Rev. Rivers A. Patout, Admin.
Res., Church & Mailing Address: 9217 E. Ave. L, 77012-2727. Tel: 713-923-5843; Fax: 713-923-5866.
Catechesis/Religious Program—Tel: 713-644-7008. Ophelia Martinez, D.R.E. Students 324.

4—ST. AMBROSE (1958), Revs. Benjamin Smaistrla; Alfonso Delgado, SS.CC.; Deacons Jose Melendez; Ronald Vance. In Res., Rev. Franklin Simmons.
Res., Church & Mailing Address: 4213 Mangum Rd., 77092-5599. Tel: 713-686-3497; Fax: 713-686-6604.
School—Tel: 713-686-6990; Fax: 713-686-6902. Judy A. Fritsch, Prin. Sisters 1; Lay Teachers 30; Students 382.
Catechesis/Religious Program—Tel: 713-686-3857. Miguel Venes, D.R.E. Students 345.

5—ST. ANDREW KIM (1977), (Korean), Rev. Augustine Hyeok-Ku Yeo.
Church & Mailing Address: 1706 Bingle Rd., 77055-2336. Tel: 713-465-2682; Fax: 713-465-5974.
Rectory—8557 Hiridge St., 77055. Tel: 713-465-2926.
Convent—Handmaids of the Sacred Heart of Jesus (H.S.H.), Tel: 713-465-1196; Fax: 713-465-2682. Email: sea4628@hotmail.com. Sisters 2.
Catechesis/Religious Program—Tel: 281-646-8228. Byung Go, D.R.E. Students 173.

6—ST. ANNE (1925), Revs. John F. Robbins, C.S.B.; Paul F. English, C.S.B.; Thomas B. Mailloux, C.S.B.; Jay Francis Walsh, C.S.B.; Deacons William Garrett; Jean-Paul Budinger; Joan O'Leary, Pastoral Assoc.
Res., Church & Mailing Address: 2140 Westheimer, 77098-1496. Tel: 713-526-3276; Fax: 713-526-3079.
School—Tel: 713-526-3279. Kathy Barnosky, Prin. Sisters 1; Lay Teachers 31; Students 414.
Catechesis/Religious Program—Tel: 713-526-2936. Mrs. Rose Schick, D.R.E. Students 525.

7—ST. ANNE DE BEAUPRE (1948), Rev. Felix Elosi, M.S.P.
Res., Church & Mailing Address: 2810 Link Rd., 77009-1196. Tel: 713-869-1319; Fax: 713-869-4527.
Catechesis/Religious Program—Tel: 281-537-6825. Elizabeth Julivette, D.R.E. Students 44.

8—ANNUNCIATION (1869), Rev. Msgr. James L. Golasinski; Deacon Robert George Alexander.
Mailing Address: P.O. Box 214, 77001-0214. Tel: 713-222-2289; Fax: 713-222-2280. In Res., Rev. Patrick J. Cummings; Deacons Joseph A. Jachimczyk; David Adame.
Church: 1618 Texas Ave., 77001-0214.
Catechesis/Religious Program—Herman Jadloski, S.T.L., D.R.E. Students 55.

9—ASCENSION CHINESE MISSION (1988), (Chinese), Rev. Louis C. Zee; Deacon Paul Kiang.
Office Mailing Address: P.O. Box 749, Alief, 77411-0749.
Church: 4605 Jetty Ln., 77411-0749. Tel: 713-575-8855; Fax: 713-575-6940.
Catechesis/Religious Program—Tel: 281-531-4513. Elizabeth Yang, D.R.E. Students 53.

10—ASSUMPTION (1948), Revs. Narciso Bordignon, C.R.S.; John P. Borsari, C.R.S.; Deacon Albert Bottjer. In Res., Rev. Albert Zanatta, C.R.S.
Res., Church & Mailing Address: 901 Rose Ln., 77037-4699. Tel: 281-447-6381; Fax: 281-447-6382.
Catechesis/Religious Program—Tel: 281-931-1460. Mario Ortega, D.R.E. Students 626.

11—ST. AUGUSTINE (1955), Rev. Msgr. Seth Hermoso, (Vicar for Filipinos); Deacon Benito Meza.
Mailing Address: 5438 Laurel Creek Way, 77017-6746.
Church & Res.: 5560 Laurel Creek Way, 77017-6729. Tel: 713-946-8968; Fax: 713-946-0080.
School—5500 Laurel Creek Way, 77017. Tel: 713-946-9050; Fax: 713-943-3444. Patricia Mulvey, Prin. Lay Teachers 22; Students 189.
Catechesis/Religious Program—Tel: 713-946-7636. Karen Jones, D.R.E. Students 461.

12—ST. BENEDICT THE ABBOT (1963), Revs. Benoit K. Mukamba, C.S.Sp.; Renatus J. Assenga; Deacon Frank Laugermann Jr.
Church & Mailing Address: 4025 Grapevine, 77045-6320. Tel: 713-433-9836; Fax: 713-433-3949.
Rectory—3931 Grapevine, 77045.
Catechesis/Religious Program—Tel: 713-433-2436. Deacon Frank J. Laugermann Jr. Students 387.

13—ST. BERNADETTE SOUBIROUS (1977), Revs. Joseph J. McCarthy, O.Carm.; Adrian M. Wilde, O.Carm.; Christopher J. Kulig, O.Carm.
Church & Mailing Address: 15500 El Camino Real, 77062-5793. Tel: 281-486-0337; Fax: 281-218-9440.
Rectory—959 El Dorado Blvd., 77062.
School— Pam Calandra, Prin. Lay Teachers 15; Students 136.
Catechesis/Religious Program—Tel: 281-486-0337. Sheryl Dalpe, D.R.E. (Junior High); Barbara Aubushon, D.R.E. (Elementary). Students 1,248.

14—BLESSED SACRAMENT (1910), Rev. Jose Isidore Garcia, O.M.I.; Deacon Pedro Lerma Sr.
Res., Church & Mailing Address: 4015 Sherman, 77003-2695. Tel: 713-224-5291; Fax: 713-224-5292.
Catechesis/Religious Program—Tel: 713-928-6484. Carmen T. Hernandez, D.R.E. Students 334.

15—ST. CATHERINE OF SIENA (1975), Rev. Michael J. Carmody; Deacons F. Jay Vocelka Jr.; John F. Coussirat.
Church & Mailing Address: 10688 Shadow Wood Dr., 77043-2826. Tel: 713-467-8170; Fax: 713-467-7149.
Rectory—1902 Stebbins Dr., 77043-2417.
Catechesis/Religious Program— Robert McInturff, D.R.E. Students 87.

16—ST. CECILIA (1956), Revs. John E. Cahoon; Jesus Lizalde; Joseph Thu Le; Deacons Don E. Bradley; D. Cade Nelms; Gregory Evans; Carlos Porras. In Res., Rev. Jacques Weber, S.J.
Church & Mailing Address: 11720 Joan of Arc Dr., 77024-2602. Tel: 713-465-3414; Fax: 713-465-1305.
Rectory—11701 Joan of Arc Dr., 77024.
School—Tel: 713-468-9515; Fax: 713-468-4698. Ms. Bridget Collins, Prin. Lay Teachers 45; Students 479.
Catechesis/Religious Program— Lettie Gillespie, D.R.E. Students 940.

17—ST. CHARLES BORROMEO (1962), Revs. Nicholas J. Harding; Eduardo Lopez, C.M.; Deacon Rodrigo Lozano. In Res., Rev. Ruben Nwankwar; Deacon Charles R. Conant.
Res., Church & Mailing Address: 501 Tidwell, 77022-2121. Tel: 713-692-6303; Fax: 713-692-6314.
School—Tel: 713-692-4898; Fax: 713-692-1376. Ann Henthorn, Prin. Sisters 1; Lay Teachers 13; Students 248.
Catechesis/Religious Program—Tel: 281-522-0632. Sr. Beatrice Cruz, I.W.B.S., D.R.E. Students 928.

18—CHRIST THE KING (1928), Revs. Giulio Veronesi, C.R.S.; Julian Gerosa, C.R.S.; Deacon Gerardo J. Garcia. In Res., Rev. Italo Dell'Oro, C.R.S.
Res., Church & Mailing Address: 4419 N. Main St., 77009-5199. Tel: 713-869-1449; Fax: 713-869-1491.
Catechesis/Religious Program—Tel: 713-869-3140. Students 1,205.

19—CHRIST THE REDEEMER (1980), Revs. Leonard F. Elder, S.C.J.; Ralph Intranuovo, S.C.J.; Deacons James H. Osterhaus; Richard L. Leach.
Church and Mailing Address: 11507 Huffmeister Rd., 77065-1051. Tel: 281-469-5533; Fax: 281-469-8441.
Rectory—12402 Bexhill, 77065.
Catechesis/Religious Program—Tel: 281-469-5533. Fredna Kilcommins, D.R.E. Students 1,432.

20—CHRIST, THE INCARNATE WORD (1997), (Vietnamese), Rev. Msgr. Philippe Le-Xuan Thuong, J.C.D.; Rev. Joseph T.P. Bui; Deacons Dinh Van Nguyen; Joseph SiBach Nguyen.
Res., Church & Mailing Address: 8503 S. Kirkwood Rd., 77099-4056. Tel: 281-495-3741; Fax: 281-495-4220.
Catechesis/Religious Program—Tel: 281-495-4571. Joseph Bui, D.R.E. Students 571.

21—ST. CHRISTOPHER (1924), Revs. Paul R. Chovanec; Joseph Phiet The Nguyen; Deacons Benito Tristan; Merce C. Leal Jr.
Res., Church & Mailing Address: 8150 Park Place Blvd., 77017-3033. Tel: 713-645-6614; Fax: 713-640-1640.
School—8134 Park Place Blvd., 77017. Tel: 713-649-0009; Fax: 713-649-1104. Jo Ann Prater, Prin. Sisters 1; Lay Teachers 14; Students 239.
Catechesis/Religious Program—Tel: 713-645-6142. Gloria Leal, D.R.E. Students 798.

22—ST. CLARE OF ASSISI (1990), Rev. Dominic J. Pistone Jr.; Deacons Donathan Durden; John H. Dean; Jim Wright. In Res., Rev. Robert J. Matzinger, C.S.B.
Res.: 3131 El Dorado Blvd., 77059-5100.
Church & Mailing Address: 3131 El Dorado Blvd., 77059-5100. Tel: 281-286-7729; Fax: 281-286-1256.
School—Tel: 281-286-3395. Brenda Fricks, Prin. Lay Teachers 15; Students 110.
Catechesis/Religious Program—Tel: 281-486-0874. Christy Wright, D.R.E. Students 587.

23—CORPUS CHRISTI (1956), Revs. Scott Haig, S.S.S. (CLV); Dana Pelotte, S.S.S. In Res., Revs. Frederico J.G. Ablog, S.S.S.; William F. Fickel, S.S.S. (CLV); Bro. Joseph M. Patrick, S.S.S.
Res., Church & Mailing Address: 9900 Stella Link Rd., 77025-4798. Tel: 713-667-0497; Fax: 713-668-4742.
School—4005 Cheena St., 77025. Tel: 713-664-3351; Fax: 713-664-6095. Mrs. Mary Ramirez, Prin. Lay Teachers 18; Students 151.
Catechesis/Religious Program—Cary Nunn, D.R.E.; Leonor Castillo, D.R.E. Students 387.

24—ST. CYRIL OF ALEXANDRIA (1963), Revs. Mario J. Arroyo; Ralph O. Roberts; Deacons Edward Thompson; Eduardo M. Dolpher; Alberto Ospina; Ernesto Abedejos.
Res., Church & Mailing Address: 10503 Westheimer Rd., 77042-3502. Tel: 713-789-1250; Fax: 713-780-0967.
Catechesis/Religious Program—Tel: 713-789-1250. Ms. Margaret McDermott, D.R.E. Students 943.

25—ST. DOMINIC (1965), Rev. Chacko Puthomayil; Deacon Philip Arlen Wiles.
Res., Church & Mailing Address: 8215 Reservoir St., 77049-1728. Tel: 281-458-2910; Fax: 281-458-7114.
Catechesis/Religious Program—Tel: 713-453-6719. George T. McDonald, D.R.E. Students 138.

26—ST. ELIZABETH ANN SETON (1977), Revs. Frank Wittouck, S.C.J.; Quang A. Nguyen, S.C.J.; David Szatkowski, S.C.J.; Deacons Francis E. Adams;

Charles G. Pennell; Jose Guadalupe Trevino; Ed Tripp; Joe Zamora; Bernard Lambert; Gilbert R. Johnson; Alfonse Sosa.
Church & Mailing Address: 6646 Addicks-Satsuma Rd., 77084-1599. Tel: 281-463-7878; Fax: 281-463-4822.
Rectory—14843 Willow Hearth, 77084.
School—Tel: 281-463-1444; Fax: 281-463-8707. Jan Krametbauer, Prin. Lay Teachers 23; Students 345.
Catechesis/Religious Program—Tel: 281-463-7356. Carm Cline, D.R.E. Students 2,370.

27—St. Frances Cabrini (1962), Revs. Norbert J. Maduzia Jr.; Jose Maria Fernandez; Deacons Robert Gregory Stevens; Charles F. Roessler Jr.; Jose Fuentez.
Church & Mailing Address: 10727 Hartsook St., 77034-3523. Tel: 713-946-5768; Fax: 713-946-3282.
Res.: 10726 Bessemer St., 77034.
Catechesis/Religious Program—Mrs. Nancy Patyrak, D.R.E. Students 985.

28—St. Francis de Sales (1962), Revs. Joseph A. Limanni; Ferley de Jesus Bedoya; Vincent Vuong-Ouoc Nguyen; Deacon David W. Illingworth.
Church & Mailing Address: 8200 Roos Rd., 77036-6399.
Res.: 8018 Roos Rd., 77036. Tel: 713-774-7475; Fax: 713-774-6591.
School—8100 Roos Rd., 77036. Tel: 713-774-4447; Fax: 713-271-6744. Sandra Mendez, Prin. Lay Teachers 45; Students 510.
Catechesis/Religious Program—Tel: 713-774-9631. Diane Wooten, D.R.E. Students 934.

29—St. Francis of Assisi (1950), Rev. Msgr. Patrick R. Wells; Rev. John C. Ndubuisi; Deacons Ignatius Joseph; Michael St. Julian.
Res., Church & Mailing Address: 5102 Dabney St., 77026-3015. Tel: 713-672-7773; Fax: 713-673-1913.
School—5100 Dabney St., 77026. Tel: 832-325-0480; Fax: 713-674-9901. Clarice Campbell, Prin. Priests 2; Sisters 4; Lay Teachers 8; Students 166.
Catechesis/Religious Program—Tel: 713-672-7773, Ext. 105. Mrs. Delores Melvin, D.R.E. Students 106.

30—St. Francis Xavier (1952), Very Rev. Kenneth J. Howard, S.S.; Rev. Joseph Varghese; Deacons Albert Henry; Michael V. Jenkins.
Res., Church & Mailing Address: 4600 Reed Rd., 77051-2857. Tel: 713-738-2311; Fax: 713-738-3337.
Catechesis/Religious Program—Tel: 713-734-5646. Mrs. Dorothy Reado, D.R.E. Students 172.

31—St. Gregory the Great (1962), Revs. Francis Huan Ton Ngo; Frank Guenter; Deacons Julio M. Ramirez; Abner Brown.
Res., Church & Mailing Address: 10500 Nold Dr., 77016-2921. Tel: 713-631-3681; Fax: 713-631-6114.
Catechesis/Religious Program—Tel: 713-631-0058. Sr. Ann Theresa Nguyen, D.R.E. Students 365.

32—Holy Cross Chapel (Downtown) (1982), Rev. Michael J. Barrett, S.T.D.
Chapel— 905 Main St., 77002-6408. Tel: 713-650-1323; Fax: 713-650-8836.

33—Holy Ghost (1946), Revs. Gregory May, C.Ss.R.; Gan Minh Peter Nguyen, C.Ss.R.; Peter H. Voelker, C.Ss.R.; Edward Glebe, C.Ss.R.; Joseph Chuong Van Cao, C.Ss.R. In Res., Rev. Leonard Broniak, C.Ss.R.; Bro. Michael Rhodes, C.Ss.R.; Deacon Robert T. Brueggerhoff.
Res., Church & Mailing Address: 6921 Chetwood Dr., 77081-5697. Tel: 713-668-0463; Fax: 713-661-4645.
School—6920 Chimney Rock Rd., 77081. Tel: 713-668-5327; Fax: 713-667-4410. Yvonne Clark, Prin. Lay Teachers 14; Students 138.
Catechesis/Religious Program—Tel: 713-668-8001. Ms. Marilynn Wilson, D.R.E. Students 913.

34—Holy Name (1920), Revs. Oscar Cantu; Dat Hoang; Deacon Juan Francisco Pareja.
Church: 1920 Marion St., 77009.
Res.: 1917 Cochran St., 77009-8497. Tel: 713-222-1255; Fax: 713-222-1260.
School—1912 Marion St., 77009-8649 Tel: 713-227-9529; Fax: 713-227-0224. Tina Lewis. Prin. Sisters 3; Lay Teachers 12; Students 145.
Catechesis/Religious Program—Tel: 713-223-4059. Mrs. Alicia Bernal, D.R.E. Students 446.

35—Holy Rosary (1913), Revs. Joseph D. Konkel, O.P.; William H. Brenda, O.P.; Joseph Ngoc Tu Nguyen, O.P.; Victor F.A. Celio. In Res., Rev. Albert S. Moraczewski, O.P.
Res., Church & Mailing Address: 3600 Travis St., 77002-9591. Tel: 713-529-4854; Fax: 713-522-3967.
Catechesis/Religious Program— Rev. Joseph D. Konkel, O.P., D.R.E. Students 110.

36—Immaculate Conception (1911), Revs. Kevin A. Collins, O.M.I.; Andrew Small, O.M.I.; Deacons Joseph G. Morin; Leslie Bart Hock; Luis A. Rodriguez.
Res., Church & Mailing Address: 7250 Harrisburg Blvd., 77011-4791. Tel: 713-921-1261; Fax: 713-921-2304.
Catechesis/Religious Program—Tel: 713-923-7153. Angeles Diaz, C.R.E., D.R.E. Students 800.

37—Immaculate Heart of Mary (1926), Revs. William C. Davis, O.M.I.; Timothy Paulsen, O.M.I.; Deacon Bob Rumford.
Res., Church & Mailing Address: 7539 Ave. K, 77012-1033. Tel: 713-923-2394; Fax: 713-923-6497.
Catechesis/Religious Program—Tel: 713-921-5431. Norma Torok, D.R.E. Students 572.

38—St. Jerome (1960), Rev. Msgr. Daniel Scheel; Revs. Michael S. Van Cleve; Christopher Shackelford; Deacons Alden J. Knobloch; James E. Rutledge.
Church & Mailing Address: 8825 Hempwood, 77080-4199. Tel: 713-468-9555; Fax: 713-464-0325.
Rectory—9011 Friendship, 77080.
School—Tel: 713-468-7946; Fax: 713-464-0324. Sharon Makulski, Prin. Sisters 1; Lay Teachers 23; Students 373.
Catechesis/Religious Program—Tel: 713-464-5029. Sr. Imelda Alcober, D.R.E. Students 923.

39—St. John Neumann (1977), Rev. Msgr. Eugene G. Francis; Rev. Alberto A. Rodriguez.
Church & Mailing Address: 2730 Nelwood Dr., 77038-1025. Tel: 281-931-0684; Fax: 281-931-5363.
Rectory—2715 Nelwood Dr., 77038-1025.
Catechesis/Religious Program—Tel: 281-580-5415. Ms. Ofelia Carrasco, D.R.E. Students 621.

40—St. John Vianney (1966), Revs. John N. Morfin; Niall Nolan; Sean P. Horrigan; Deacons Dale W. Steffes; Albert E. Vacek Jr.; Fred J. Kosegi; Robert J. Hesse; Rolando J. Garcia; German Godoy.
Res., Church & Mailing Address: 625 Nottingham Oaks Tr., 77079-6299. Tel: 281-497-1500; Fax: 281-584-2024.
Catechesis/Religious Program—Tel: 281-497-6665. Mrs. Frances Contello, D.R.E. Students 1,103.

41—St. Joseph (1880), Rev. Philip R. Howard, C.S.Sp.; Deacons Geronimo Flores; Martin G. Sanchez; Reynaldo S. Gil; Francisco M. Rangel.
Res., Church & Mailing Address: 1505 Kane St., 77007-7711. Tel: 713-222-6193; Fax: 713-222-1729.
Catechesis/Religious Program—Tel: 713-222-6579. Marina Ramirez, D.R.E. Students 305.

42—St. Justin Martyr (1982), Revs. Thomas F. Rafferty Dominic Chinh Van Pham, I.C.M.; Deacons Gene Festa; Cornelius C. Llorens; J. M. Baker; Louis Provenzano; Nhat Tran; Michael A. Vasquez.
Church & Mailing Address: 13350 Ashford Point Dr., 77082-5100. Tel: 281-556-5116; Fax: 281-556-6932.
Rectory—3142 W. Hampton, 77082.
Catechesis/Religious Program— Melanie Naeger, D.R.E. Students 945.

43—St. Leo the Great (1973), Revs. Louis Piran, C.S.; Carlo A. Titotto, C.S.; Deacon Ralph R. Gregory. In Res., Rev. Guillermo Garcia, C.S.
Res., Church & Mailing Address: 2131 Lauder Rd., 77039-3199. Tel: 281-449-2344; Fax: 281-449-3664.
Catechesis/Religious Program—Students 780.

44—St. Luke the Evangelist (1975), Revs. Stephen R. Horn; Joseph Loc D. Phan; Deacons John E. Devine Jr.; James Sharpless; Alvin Birsinger; Jessie Tollett; Rainaldo J. Egusquiza.
Church & Mailing Address: 11011 Hall Rd., 77089-2999. Tel: 281-481-6816; Fax: 281-481-8780.
Rectory: 8402 Kirkville, 77089.
Catechesis/Religious Program—Marilyn Kiel, D.R.E. Students 925.

45—St. Mark the Evangelist (1974), Rev. Roosevelt Martin; Deacons John Benoit; Marcelino Villarreal.
Church and Mailing Address: 5430 W. Ridgecreek Dr., 77053-3211.
Rectory—5302 Castlecreek Ln., 77053. Tel: 281-437-9114; 281-437-4828; Fax: 281-835-6303.
Catechesis/Religious Program—Tel: 281-438-9677. Zulema Perez, D.R.E. Students 358.

46—St. Mary of the Purification (1929), Rev. Borgia Aubespin, S.V.D.; Deacons Leonard P. Lockett; Andrew B. Malveaux.
Res., Church & Mailing Address: 3006 Rosedale Ave., 77004-6199. Tel: 713-528-0571; Fax: 713-528-0572.
School—3002 Rosedale, 77004. Tel: 713-522-9276; Fax: 713-522-1879. Mrs. Mazie McCoy, Prin. Sisters 1; Lay Teachers 11; Students 230.
Catechesis/Religious Program—Tel: 281-437-4110. Dr. Evelyn Hunter, D.R.E. Students 194.

47—St. Matthew the Evangelist (1974), Revs. Robert Tucker, S.C.J.; Jack Cavanaugh, S.C.J.; Deacon John W. Adams.
Res., Church & Mailing Address: 9915 Hollister Dr., 77040-1702. Tel: 713-466-4030; Fax: 713-896-7235.
Catechesis/Religious Program—Tel: 713-466-0510. Virginia Diehl, D.R.E. Students 416.

48—St. Maximilian Kolbe (1983), Rev. John F. Ulm; Deacons Ronald J. Frazier; Auburn Higgins; Gary Walsh; Adrian F. Dinges. In Res., Rev. Msgr. Milam Kleas.
Church and Mailing Address: 10135 West Rd., 77064-5361. Tel: 281-955-7324; Fax: 281-955-7328.
Rectory—10218 Great Plains, 77064.
Catechesis/Religious Program—Rosemary Munoz, D.R.E. Students 1,005.

49—St. Michael (1925), Rev. Msgr. Edward Randall; Revs. Stephen V. Cooley, O.Carm.; John Rooney; Deacons Thomas C. Newhouse; Henry Woods Martin; Craig Cashio, Pastoral Assoc. In Res., Rev. Leon Strider.
Res., Church & Mailing Address: 1801 Sage Rd., 77056-3598. Tel: 713-621-4370; Fax: 713-850-8341.
School—1833 Sage Rd., 77056-3599. Tel: 713-621-6847; Fax: 713-877-8812. Stephen P. Parsons, Prin. Sisters 2; Lay Teachers 27; Students 472.
Catechesis/Religious Program—Tel: 713-840-8213. Mrs. Mary Jo Wilt, D.R.E. Students 470.

50—St. Monica (1960), Rev. Neal Stull, S.O.L.T.
Res., Church & Mailing Address: 8421 W. Montgomery Rd., 77088-7116. Tel: 281-447-5837; Fax: 281-447-8410.
Catechesis/Religious Program—Tel: 281-445-0334. Jennifer Sims, D.R.E. Students 171.

51—St. Nicholas (1887), Rev. Brian Okon, M.S.P.
Res., Church & Mailing Address: 2508 Clay Ave., 77003-4498. Tel: 713-223-5210; Fax: 713-222-0424.
Catechesis/Religious Program— Lourdes Gomez, D.R.E. Students 25.

52—Notre Dame (1969), Rev. Nicholas O. Pasadilla; Rev. Msgr. Rolando V. Diokno; Deacons F.L. Ostrowski; Ernesto Abadejos; Jose F. Sandoval.
Rectory—11226 Pompano Ln., 77072-3595.
Church & Mailing Address: 7720 Boone Rd., 77072-3595. Tel: 281-498-4653; Fax: 281-879-1527.
Catechesis/Religious Program—Tel: 281-498-1256. Cyndy O'Connor, D.R.E.; Josephine Lowell, D.R.E. Students 556.

53—Our Lady of Czestochowa (1982), (Polish), Rev. Jan Fiedurek, S.Chr. (MIA); Deacon Anthony Rudnicki.
Mailing Address: 1712 Oak Tree, 77080-7240. Tel: 713-973-1081; Fax: 713-984-9501.
Church: 1731 Blalock Rd., 77080.
Catechesis/Religious Program—Rev. Jerzy Frydrych, S.Ch., D.R.E. Students 10.

54—Our Lady of Guadalupe (1912), [JC] Revs. Timothy J. Gray, S.C.J.; Richard Dileo, S.C.J.; Joseph Thien Dinh, S.C.J.; Peter Mastrobuono, S.C.J.; Deacons Guadalupe L. Gonzalez; Manuel A. Laurel; Gabriel Z. Quiroga.
Res., Church & Mailing Address: 2405 Navigation Blvd., 77003-1599. Tel: 713-222-0203; Fax: 713-225-2235.
School—Tel: 713-224-6904; Fax: 713-225-2122. Chris Skowronek, Prin. Sisters 3; Lay Teachers 16; Students 225.
Catechesis/Religious Program— Sr. Lelia Martinez, M.C.D.P., D.R.E. Students 986.

55—Our Lady of Lavang Church (1985), (Vietnamese), Revs. Dominic Huy The Trinh, O.P.; Joseph Chung Van Do, O.P.; Bro. Peter To Van Mai, O.P.; Deacon Michael Kim Khanh Nguyen.
Mailing Address: 12320 Old Foltin Rd., 77086-3513. Tel: 281-999-1672; Fax: 281-820-7095.
Church: 12311 Old Foltin Rd., 77086-3513.
Catechesis/Religious Program—Tel: 281-955-9395. Students 596.

56—Our Lady of Lourdes (1994), Revs. Joseph Luc Van Do, O.P.; Peter Thien Van Hoang, O.P.; Deacon Joseph Chuong Nguyen Do.
Church & Mailing Address: 6550 Fairbanks N. Houston, 77040-4307. Tel: 713-939-1906; Fax: 713-939-0771.
Catechesis/Religious Program—Rev. Dominic Huy The Trinh, O.P. Students 479.

57—Our Lady of Mt. Carmel (1952), Rev. Ronald Oakham, O.Carm.; Deacons Frederico Guajardo; Arturo Monterruhio; Eric Bell, O.Carm.
Mailing Address: 6723 Whitefriars Dr., 77087-6598. Tel: 713-645-6673; Fax: 713-645-6674.
Church: 6725-A Reed Rd., 77087.
School—6703 Whitefriars Dr., 77087. Tel: 713-643-0676; Fax: 713-649-1835. Mrs. Elizabeth Anthony, Prin. Lay Teachers 18; Students 230.
Catechesis/Religious Program—Esperanza Moterrubio, D.R.E. Students 305.

58—Our Lady of Sorrows (1936), Rev. Norberto Conde.
Church & Mailing Address: 3006 Kashmere St., 77026-5999. Tel: 713-673-5600; Fax: 713-673-5667.
Catechesis/Religious Program—Tel: 713-695-3928. Mrs. Rose Mary Cadena, Prin. Students 201.

59—Our Lady of St. John (1947), Rev. Edwin A. Coreas.
Church & Mailing Address: 7500 Hirsch Rd., 77016-6215. Tel: 713-631-0810; Fax: 713-631-0781.
Catechesis/Religious Program—Mary Lou Gonzales, D.R.E. Students 234.

60—Our Lady of Walsingham (1984), Rev. James T. Moore; Deacon James Barnett.
Church & Mailing Address: 7809 Shady Villa Ln., 77055-5011. Tel: 713-683-9407; Fax: 713-683-1518.
Rectory—21806 Galewood Lane, 77073.

Catechesis/Religious Program—Kaye Roewe, D.R.E. Students 55.

61—OUR LADY STAR OF THE SEA (1950), Revs. Charles Andrus, S.S.J.; Walter A. Cerbin, S.S.J.; Dominic A. Adama; Deacons Charles J. Allen Sr.; Irvin Johnson Jr.; Rick L. Simon.
Church & Mailing Address: 1401 Fidelity St., 77029-4624. Tel: 713-674-9206; Fax: 713-675-7842.
Catechesis/Religious Program—Daisy Fields, D.R.E. Students 55.

62—OUR MOTHER OF MERCY (1930), Revs. Charles Andrus, S.S.J.; Walter A. Cerbin, S.S.J.; Dominic V. Adama; Deacons Charles J. Allen Sr.; Irvin Johnson Jr.; Rick L. Simon.
Res., Church & Mailing Address: 4000 Sumpter St., 77020-2497. Tel: 713-672-0026; Fax: 713-672-2031.
School—2010 Benson St., 77020. Tel: 713-673-1862; Fax: 713-673-1041. Linda Mabrie, Prin. Sisters 3; Lay Teachers 11; Students 125.
Catechesis/Religious Program—Tel: 713-672-2037. Sr. Theresa Healy, D.R.E. Students 328.

63—ST. PATRICK (1880), Rev. Henry B. Walker, O.M.I.
Church & Mailing Address: 4918 Cochran St., 77009-2117. Tel: 713-695-0631; Fax: 713-695-6255.
Catechesis/Religious Program—Beatrice Perez, D.R.E. Students 871.

64—ST. PAUL (1964), Revs. Albert A. Maullon Jr.; Yong Huyk Lee. In Res., Rev. Walter N. Sheffield; Deacons Richard Labrecque; James A. Lockwood.
Church & Mailing Address: 18223 Point Lookout Dr., 77058-3594. Tel: 281-333-3891; Fax: 281-333-3815.
Rectory:—18326 Point Lookout Dr., 77058.
Catechesis/Religious Program—Tel: 281-335-5701. Laura Hicks, D.R.E. Students 652.

65—ST. PETER CLAVER (1964), Rev. Rawlin B. Enette, S.S.J.; Deacon Raymond L. Despania Sr.
Church & Mailing Address: 6005 N. Wayside Dr., 77028-4494. Tel: 713-674-3338; Fax: 713-674-6524.
Catechesis/Religious Program—Helen H. Wilson, D.R.E. Students 175.

66—ST. PETER THE APOSTLE (1941), Revs. Raphael Asika, M.S.P.; Felix I. Osasona, M.S.P.; Deacons Clarence B. Johnson; Dan Gilbert.
Res., Church & Mailing Address: 6220 La Salette Dr., 77021-1323. Tel: 713-747-7800; Fax: 713-747-9671.
School—Tel: 713-747-9484; Fax: 713-747-2621. Mr. Eugene Roussell, Prin. Sisters 2; Lay Teachers 9; Students 78.
Catechesis/Religious Program—Tel: 713-842-1226. Virgie Ricardo, D.R.E. Students 84.

67—ST. PHILIP NERI (1961), Rev. Emmanuel E. Agbor, M.S.P. (BR); Deacons Ronald Simon; James Brooks; Orrin D. Burroughs.
Mailing Address: P.O. Box 330190, 77233-0190. Tel: 713-734-0320; Fax: 713-734-0331.
Church: 10960 Martin Luther King Jr. Blvd., 77048.
School—Tel: 713-733-2343. Mrs. Melina Harris, Prin. Priests 1; Sisters 1; Lay Teachers 8; Students 81.
Catechesis/Religious Program—Tel: 713-734-0320. Mary E. Freeman, D.R.E. Students 130.

68—ST. PHILIP OF JESUS (1958), Rev. Miguel A. Solorzano; Deacon Roy Breaux.
Res.: 3526 La Retama Dr., 77013-3818. Tel: 713-672-6141; Fax: 713-672-8675.
Church & Mailing Address: 9700 Villita St., 77013-3851.
Catechesis/Religious Program— Enrique Herrera, D.R.E. Students 522.

69—PRINCE OF PEACE (1971), Revs. John T. Keller; Aberlado Cabos; Kurian Stephen Chooshukunnel, O.S.H.; Abelardo Cobos; Deacons Allen W. Prescott; Chuck Butler; Jeronimo R. Bazan.
Church & Mailing Address: 19222 Tomball Pkwy., 77070-3510. Tel: 281-469-2686; Fax: 281-469-8418.
Catechesis/Religious Program—Domenica Weir, D.R.E. Students 1,605.

70—QUEEN OF PEACE (1942), Revs. Christian H.F. Riesbeck; Daren Bryk; Randall C. Hendriks; Deacons Jose L. Liendo; Juan Aguilar; Jose M. Galvan. In Res., Revs. Francis A. Frankovich; Ed Wade.
Res., Church & Mailing Address: 3011 Telephone Rd., 77023-5312. Tel: 713-921-6127; Fax: 713-921-6128.
School—2320 Oakcliff St., 77023. Tel: 713-921-1558; Fax: 713-921-0855. Brian Kissell, Prin. Sisters 1; Lay Teachers 11; Students 132.
Catechesis/Religious Program—Tel: 713-921-1917. Mr. Julio Cordova, C.M.S.T., D.R.E. Students 507.

71—ST. RAPHAEL THE ARCHANGEL (1961), Rev. Jaime C. Arrambide, C.Ss.R.; Deacons Antonio Marquez; Juan De Dios Perez.
Mailing Address: P.O. Box 630787, 77263-0787. Tel: 713-781-9511; Fax: 713-278-9705.
Res. & Church Address: 3915 Ocee, 77063-5417.
Catechesis/Religious Program—Tel: 281-584-9133. Mrs. Maria Lucio, D.R.E. Students 420.

72—RESURRECTION (1920), Revs. David J. Cardenas; Blas P. Herrador; Deacon Gregory C. Garcia.
Res., Church & Mailing Address: 915 Zoe St., 77020-6898. Tel: 713-675-5333; Fax: 713-673-3605.
School—916 Majestic St., 77019. Tel: 713-674-5545; Fax: 713-678-4036. Dora Tillman, Prin. Priests 2; Sisters 1; Lay Teachers 12; Students 155.
Catechesis/Religious Program—Tel: 713-673-1443. Gloria Hewitt, D.R.E. Students 512.
Station—La Divina Providencia Port Houston.

73—ST. ROSE OF LIMA (1947), Rev. Msgr. James B. Anderson; Rev. Thuy Quang Nguyen; Deacon John T. Murrell; Connie Swenceski, Pastoral Assoc. In Res., Rev. Luis P. Chia.
Church & Mailing Address: 3600 Brinkman St., 77018-6329. Tel: 713-692-9123; Fax: 713-692-5638.
Rectory—802 Judiway, 77018-6329.
School—Tel: 713-691-0104; Fax: 713-692-8073. Barbara Foltyn, Prin. Lay Teachers 20; Students 198.
Catechesis/Religious Program— Ms. Rosa Guerrero, D.R.E. Students 211.

74—SACRED HEART CO-CATHEDRAL (1896), Revs. R. Troy Gately; Thu Ngoc Nguyen; Edmund P. Eduarte; Deacons Marvin R. Fikac; Julio Suriano; Bob Rumford. In Res., Rev. Charles Talar.
Res.: 1111 Pierce St., 77002-8195. Tel: 713-659-1561; Fax: 713-739-1185.
Catechesis/Religious Program—Tel: 281-447-4848. Jaclyn Jarzanbek, D.R.E. Students 170.

75—ST. STEPHEN (1941), Revs. Gabriel Camilo, M.J.; Salvador Meza, M.J.
Rectory—Rectory & Mailing Address: 2019 Center St., 77007-6106.
Church: 1910 Center St., 77007. Tel: 713-864-4075; Fax: 713-880-8611.
Catechesis/Religious Program—Tel: 713-880-0041. Mr. John Guzman, D.R.E.; Mrs. John Guzman, D.R.E. Students 250.

76—ST. THERESA (1946), Rev. Stephen E. Tiemann; Rev. Msgr. William M. Pickard, J.C.D.; Deacons Larry A. Vaclavik; J. M. Baker; Antonio Moya. In Res., Rev. Dennis L. Peterson.
Church & Mailing Address: 6622 Haskell St., 77007-2097. Tel: 713-869-3783; Fax: 713-869-3784.
School—Tel: 713-864-4536; Fax: 713-869-5184. Ms. Frances Ramsey, Prin. Lay Teachers 19; Students 224.
Catechesis/Religious Program—Tel: 713-869-9725. Ginger Tamborello, D.R.E. Students 243.

77—ST. THOMAS MORE (1962), Rev. Msgr. William L. Young; Revs. Isaac O. Francis; Alberto A. Rodriguez; Rodolfo Sanchez; Deacons Edwin F. Gosline; Edward T. Stoessel; John Pelletier.
Church & Mailing Address: 10330 Hillcroft, 77096-4795. Tel: 713-729-0221; Fax: 713-729-3294.
School—5927 Wigton, 77096. Tel: 713-729-3434. Mrs. Nadine Mouser, Prin. Lay Teachers 39; Students 630.
Catechesis/Religious Program—Tel: 713-729-3435. Barbara Mackie, D.R.E. Students 935.

78—VIETNAMESE MARTYRS (1986), (Vietnamese), Revs. John Minh Toan Hoang; Daokim Nguyen; Deacon Joseph Pham Nguyen.
Mailing Address: 10612 Kingspoint Rd., 77075-4114.
Rectory—10614 Kingspoint Rd., 77075-4114. Tel: 713-941-0521.
Church: 10610 Kingspoint Rd., 77075-4114. Fax: 713-941-2464.

79—ST. VINCENT DE PAUL (1939), Revs. John T. Weyer; Rodrigo R. Maata; Witold Kania. In Res., Rev. Romanus O. Muoneke; Deacon George A. Sheltz Sr.
Church & Mailing Address: 6800 Buffalo Speedway, 77025-1499. Tel: 713-667-9111; Fax: 713-667-3453.
School—6802 Buffalo Speedway, 77025. Tel: 713-666-2345; Fax: 713-663-3562. Mary Getschow, Prin. Sisters 1; Lay Teachers 40; Students 506.
Catechesis/Religious Program—Tel: 713-663-3524. Sr. Jean Marie Goukas, C.V.I., D.R.E. Students 932.

OUTSIDE THE CITIES OF GALVESTON AND HOUSTON

ALVIN, BRAZORIA CO., ST. JOHN THE BAPTIST (1952), Revs. Charles J. Borski, O.M.I.; John Franko, O.M.I.; Deacons Robert Kacz; David Bowman. In Res., Rev. Hendrik Laenen, O.M.I. (SAN).
Res., Church & Mailing Address: 110 E. South St., 77511-3500. Tel: 281-331-3751; Fax: 281-331-5430.
Catechesis/Religious Program—Tel: 281-824-0877. Sr. Charles Marie Flores, S.S.C.J., D.R.E. Students 738.

ANDERSON, GRIMES CO., ST. STANISLAUS (1866), [CEM] Rev. Louis S. Sikorski.
Mailing Address: P.O. Box 210, 77830-0210.
Church: 1511 Hwy. 90 S., 77830. Tel: 936-873-2291; Fax: 936-873-3304.
Catechesis/Religious Program—Students 81.

ANGLETON, BRAZORIA CO., MOST HOLY TRINITY (1960), Revs. Vincent J. Dulock, C.S.B.; Jamie M. Abercrombie, C.S.B.; Deacon Andrew J. Shefts.
Church & Mailing Address: 1713 N. Tinsley St., 77515-3598. Tel: 979-849-2421; Fax: 979-849-2425.
Catechesis/Religious Program—Tel: 979-849-1764. Cheryl Scott, D.R.E. Students 444.

BARRETT STATION, HARRIS CO., ST. MARTIN DE PORRES (1944), [JC] Rev. Anthony Ekanem, M.S.P.
Mailing Address: P.O. Box 3459, 77532-2459.
Res. & Church Address: 12606 Crosby-Lynchburg Rd., 77532-2459. Tel: 281-328-4451; Fax: 281-328-7306.
Catechesis/Religious Program—Tel: 281-328-1972. Mrs. Louisa Salandy, D.R.E. Students 235.

BAYTOWN, HARRIS CO.

1—ST. JOHN THE EVANGELIST (1974), Rev. William A. Oliver; Deacons Justin J. Wewer; Robert Hennessy. In Res., Rev. Msgr. Fred P. O'Connor.
Church & Mailing Address: 800 W. Baker Rd., 77521-2311. Tel: 281-837-8180; Fax: 281-837-8181.
Catechesis/Religious Program—Tel: 281-837-0532. Jan Allison, D.R.E. Students 320.

2—ST. JOSEPH (1924), Rev. Dwight M. Canizares; Deacons John William Singer Jr.; Rudy Venegas. In Res., Rev. Paul Marterior, O.P.
Res., Church & Mailing Address: 1907 Carolina St., 77520-6098. Tel: 281-420-3588; Fax: 281-422-3044.
School—1811 Carolina St., 77520-6099. Tel: 281-422-9749. Ms. Ann Mullins, Prin. Lay Teachers 14; Students 113.
Catechesis/Religious Program—Tel: 281-427-5720. Mrs. Jude Arceneaux, D.R.E. Students 228.

3—OUR LADY OF GUADALUPE (1958), Revs. Luis E. Hernandez, O.S.A.; Jesus Torres, O.S.A.; Deacons Fernando Gonzalez Bangs; Rudy Venegas; George Rincon.
Church & Mailing Address: 1124 Beech St., 77520-4198. Tel: 281-428-1507; Fax: 281-422-4554.
Catechesis/Religious Program—Tel: 281-427-5836. Dahlia & Hector Meza, D.R.E. Students 647.

BEASLEY, FT. BEND CO., ST. WENCESLAUS MISSION (1923), [CEM], (Independent Mission) Rev. Henry C. Rachunek.
Mailing Address: P.O. Box 121, Hungerford, 77448-0121. Tel: 979-532-4747; Fax: 979-532-8713.
Church: 407 S. 3rd St., 77448-0121.
Catechesis/Religious Program—Students 141.

BELLVILLE, AUSTIN CO., SS. PETER & PAUL (1860), Rev. Timothy P. Bucek; Deacon Gerald DuPont.
Mailing Address: P.O. Box 808, 77418-0808. Tel: 979-865-2368; Fax: 979-865-9929.
Church: 936 S. Front St., 77418-0176.
Catechesis/Religious Program—Tel: 979-865-8601. Cristina Pier, D.R.E. Students 184.
Mission—Immaculate Conception (1875), Industry, Austin Co.

BRAZORIA, BRAZORIA CO., ST. JOSEPH ON THE BRAZOS (1840), Rev. Tin Cosmas Kim Pham; Deacons Raul A. Castillo; Jimmy Smith.
Church & Mailing Address: 219 Country Rd. 762, 77422-8699. Tel: 979-798-2288; Fax: 979-798-2271.
Catechesis/Religious Program—Tel: 979-798-4702. Students 193.

CHANNELVIEW, HARRIS CO., ST. ANDREW (1970), Rev. Stephen P. Zigrang; Deacons R. Jack Rook; John Santos; Stephen Miller; Javier Gomez; Carlos Vences.
Res., Church & Mailing Address: 827 Sheldon Rd., 77530-3511. Tel: 281-452-9865; Fax: 281-452-2157.
Catechesis/Religious Program—Tel: 281-452-0618. Sr. Helen Spanos, C.V.I., D.R.E. Students 1,024.

CLUTE, BRAZORIA CO., ST. JEROME (1969), Rev. James F. Lynes; Deacon Julio Garcia; Dina Tonche, Pastoral Assoc.
Mailing Address: 201 N. Lazy Ln., 77531-4001. Tel: 979-265-5179; Fax: 979-265-4601.
Rectory—100 Oak Dr. S., Lake Jackson, 77566-5630.
Church: 107 N. Lazy Ln., 77531-4000.
Catechesis/Religious Program—Tel: 979-266-8634. Dina Tonche, D.R.E. Students 430.

CONROE, MONTGOMERY CO., SACRED HEART (1916), Rev. Msgr. David W. Kennedy, V.F.; Rev. Oscar M. Castro, SS.CC.; Deacons Leo F. St. Aubin; John W. Ehrman Jr.
Church & Mailing Address: 109 N. Frazier St., 77301-2889. Tel: 936-756-8186; Fax: 936-756-8105.
School—615 McDade St., 77301-2890. Tel: 936-756-3848. Gerard Kubelka, Prin. Sisters 4; Lay Teachers 21; Students 308.
Spanish Ministry—Tel: 936-756-8288. Sr. Isidra Hernandez.
Catechesis/Religious Program—Becki Lipari, D.R.E. Students 998.

CROSBY, HARRIS CO., SACRED HEART (1935), Rev. Terence P. Brinkman; Deacon Archie Benham.
Res., Church & Mailing Address: 915 Runneburg Rd., 77532-5826. Tel: 281-328-4871; Fax: 281-328-1075.
School—907 Runneberg Rd., 77532. Tel: 281-328-6561; Fax: 281-462-0072. Deborah Francis, Prin. Sisters 3; Lay Teachers 12; Students 131.
Catechesis/Religious Program—Tel: 281-328-4871, Ext. 16. Mrs. Margaret Benham, D.R.E. Students 201.

DAMON, BRAZORIA CO., STS. CYRIL AND METHODIUS

(1925), [CEM] Rev. James Ramsey.
Mailing Address: P.O. Box 309, 77430-0309.
Rectory—P.O. Box 95, Needville, 77461.
Church: 603 Parrott Ave., 77430-0309. Tel: 979-742-3383; Fax: 979-742-3395.
Catechesis/Religious Program—Tel: 979-742-3288. Linda Pavlicek, D.R.E. Students 61.

DANBURY, BRAZORIA CO., ST. ANTHONY DE PADUA (1911), [CEM] Rev. William T. Kelly; Deacon Gerald Peltier.
Mailing Address: P.O. Box 299, 77534-0299. Tel: 979-922-1240; Fax: 979-922-8643.
Rectory—1603 Main St., 77534. Tel: 979-922-1253.
Church: 1523 Main St., 77534-0299.
Catechesis/Religious Program—Tel: 409-922-1241. Mary LeCompte, D.R.E. Students 165.

DEER PARK, HARRIS CO., ST. HYACINTH (1965), Revs. Kenneth Heberlein; Richard E. Barker Deacons Dennis M. Hickey; Richard F. Camunez; Tom C. Mesa Jr.
Church & Mailing Address: 2921 Center St., 77536-4997. Tel: 281-479-4298; Fax: 281-478-6123.
Catechesis/Religious Program—Joseph F. Marie, D.R.E. Students 868.

DICKINSON, GALVESTON CO., SHRINE OF THE TRUE CROSS (1909), Revs. Paul G. Felix, Admin.; Antonio G. Perez; Deacons Sam Ausmus III; Jose Duplan Jr.; Harold B. Eskew Jr.; Jesus J. Rubio.
Mailing Address: P.O. Box 687, 77539-0687.
Res.: 3720 Spruce, 77539. Tel: 281-337-4112; Fax: 281-337-5779.
Church: 300 FM 517 E., 77539.
School—400 Pine Dr., 77539. Tel: 281-337-5212. Susan Callaway, Prin. Lay Teachers 15; Students 345.
Catechesis/Religious Program—Tel: 281-337-3130. Cynthia Newman, D.R.E. Students 694.

FREEPORT, BRAZORIA CO.

1—ST. HENRY (1932), Rev. Jose M. Sanchez.
Mailing Address: P.O. Box 857, 77542-0857.
Church: 318 E. 5th St., 77541-5913. Tel: 979-233-2887; Fax: 979-233-0293.
Catechesis/Religious Program—Tel: 979-233-4374. Margaret Garcia, D.R.E. Students 89.

2—ST. MARY: STAR OF THE SEA (1926), Rev William P. Sommerville; Deacon Wallace Shaw.
Church & Mailing Address: 1019 West 6th St., 77541-5423. Tel: 979-233-5271; Fax: 979-233-4418.
Rectory—914 W. 7th St., 77541.
Catechesis/Religious Program—Tel: 979-480-9789. Barbara Flores, D.R.E. Students 231.

FRIENDSWOOD, GALVESTON CO., MARY, QUEEN (1964), Rev. Ronald A. Beauchemin, M.S.; Deacon Darrell Moulton; Rev. James Winiarski, M.S.
Mailing Address: P.O. Box 207, 77549-0207. Tel: 281-482-1391; Fax: 281-482-4886. In Res., Rev. Ronald Groschen, M.S.
Church: 606 Cedarwood Dr., 77546.
Catechesis/Religious Program—Tel: 281-482-1391, Ext. 329. Donna Patlach, D.R.E. Students 1,113.

FRYDEK, AUSTIN CO., ST. MARY'S (1908), [CEM] Rev. Bernard C. Snock.
Church & Mailing Address: 10471 Grotto Rd., Sealy, 77474-9801. Tel: 979-885-3131; Fax: 979-885-4555.
Catechesis/Religious Program—Tel: 979-885-3178. Leona Buchala, D.R.E. Students 125.

GALENA PARK, HARRIS CO., OUR LADY OF FATIMA (1946), Revs. Robert D. Carlson, Admin.; Francis M. Macatangay; Deacon Hector Hernando Morales.
Mailing Address: P.O. Box 644, 77547-0644. In Res., Rev. Rivers A. Potout III.
Res. & Church Address: 1705 Eighth St., 77547-0644. Tel: 713-675-0981; Fax: 713-675-0982.
School—1702 Ninth St., 77547. Tel: 713-674-5832; Fax: 713-674-3877. Dorene Whitmer, Prin. Lay Teachers 12; Students 169.
Catechesis/Religious Program—Mrs. Rachel Gonzalez, D.R.E. Students 540.

HEMPSTEAD, WALLER CO.

1—ST. KATHERINE DREXEL (2001), Rev. James Burkart. In Res., Rev. Kenneth E. Mikclik; Deacon William Leonard Sheffield.
Church: 1346 Wilkins St., 77445-4402. Tel: 979-826-2275; Fax: 979-826-8057.
Rectory—604 14th St., 77445.
Catechesis/Religious Program— Lucille Pavlock, D.R.E. Students 419.

2—MARY, MOTHER OF GOD (1879), Merged, with St. Martin de Porres, Prairie View to form St. Katherine Drexel, Hempstead.

HIGHLANDS, HARRIS CO., ST. JUDE THADDEUS (1946), Rev. John A. Zabelskas, V.F.
Church & Mailing Address: 800 S. Main St., 77562-4236. Tel: 281-843-2422; Fax: 281-426-3671.
Catechesis/Religious Program—Tel: 281-426-6800. Mrs. Claudine Lewis, D.R.E. Students 144.

HITCHCOCK, GALVESTON CO., OUR LADY OF LOURDES (1953), Rev. John H. Kappe.
Church & Mailing Address: 10114 Hwy. 6, 77563-4515. Tel: 409-925-3579; Fax: 409-925-5094.
School—Tel: 409-925-3224. Mrs. Patti Dyda, Prin. Sisters 2; Lay Teachers 6; Students 129.
Catechesis/Religious Program—Ms. Celia Guardian, D.R.E. Students 218.

HUFFMAN, HARRIS CO., ST. PHILIP THE APOSTLE (1977), Rev. George J. Olsovsky; Deacon John Schuster.
Mailing Address: P.O. Box 292, 77336-0292.
Church: 2308 Third St., 77336. Tel: 281-324-1478; Fax: 281-324-2775.
Catechesis/Religious Program—Tel: 281-334-4401. Maureen Schuster, D.R.E. Students 126

HUMBLE, HARRIS CO., ST. MARY MAGDALENE (1911), Rev. Msgr. Paul Procella; Rev. Juan Pablo Pena; Deacons James Nicholas Caruso; Thomas K. McKinney; Robert MacFarlane; Miguel A. Gonzalez.
Church & Mailing Address: 527 S. Houston Ave., 77338-4763. Tel: 281-446-8211; Fax: 281-446-8213.
Rectory—525 S. Houston Ave., 77338-4753.
School—530 Ferguson, 77338. Tel: 281-446-8535; Fax: 281-446-8527. Jean Johnson, Prin. Lay Teachers 14; Students 140.
Catechesis/Religious Program—Tel: 281-446-2933. Ms. Deborah Jones, D.R.E. Students 1,294.

HUNTSVILLE, WALKER CO., ST. THOMAS THE APOSTLE (1963), Rev. Stephen J. Payne; Deacons Frank P. Ortego; Ivy C. Floyd; Richard Lopez; Gene Warzecha.
Church & Mailing Address: 1323 16th St., 77340-4431. Tel: 936-295-8159; Fax: 936-295-3543.
Rectory—1608 Ave. M, 77340-4431.
Catechesis/Religious Program— Sharyn Pezant, D.R.E.; Ana Diaz, D.R.E.; Sondra Conner, D.R.E. Students 375.

KATY, HARRIS CO.

1—ST. BARTHOLOMEW THE APOSTLE (1965), Revs. John Kha Tran; Josefino P. Templado; Deacons William C. Wagner; L. William Hamilton; Michael J. McGuire; Arthur Chin-Fatt.
Church & Mailing Address: 5356 11th St., 77493-1748. Tel: 281-391-4758; Fax: 281-391-3978.
Rectory—1419 Watts Ave., 77493.
Catechesis/Religious Program—Tel: 281-391-0839. Students 952.

2—ST. EDITH STEIN (1999), Rev. Robert S. Barras; Deacons Leonard J. Broussard; Timothy Borbas.
Church & Mailing Address: 3311 N. Fry Rd., 77449. Tel: 281-492-7500; Fax: 281-492-0266.
Rectory—2903 Sinton Ct., 77449.
Catechesis/Religious Program—Christine Twardowski, D.R.E. Students 570.

3—EPIPHANY OF THE LORD (1981), Rev. Msgr. Jack M. Dinkins Deacon Don Kish.
Church & Mailing Address: 1530 Norwalk Dr., 77450-4999. Tel: 281-578-0707; Fax: 281-578-9161.
Catechesis/Religious Program—Tel: 281-578-8271. Debbie Ziegler, D.R.E. Students 2,582

KINGWOOD, HARRIS CO., ST. MARTHA (1979), Rev. Msgr. Chester L. Borski, S.T.L.; Revs. Ryszard Kulma; Joseph Phan; Deacons Gerald Ostrand; Tom Vicknair; Ralph A. Rittenhouse; James Meshell.
Mailing Address: 2302 Oak Shores Dr. 77339-1801. Tel: 281-358-6637; Fax: 281-358-7973.
Church 3702 Woodland Hills Dr., 77339-1801.
School—2411 Oakshores Dr., 77339. Tel: 281-358-5523; Fax: 281-358-5526. Leslie Flickenger, Prin. Lay Teachers 24; Students 269.
Catechesis/Religious Program—Tel: 713-358-1959, Ext. 212. Jeff Crandle, D.R.E. Students 2,091.

LA MARQUE, GALVESTON CO., OUR LADY QUEEN OF PEACE (1951), Rev. Msgr. T. Joseph Culver, E.V.; Deacon James L. Bonura Sr.; Armando G. Tapia.
Mailing Address: 1224 Cedar Dr., 77568. In Res., Rev. A. Peter Whitney.
Rectory—626 Laurel, 77568. Tel: 409-938-7000; Fax: 409-935-9791.
Church: 1200 Cedar Dr., 77568.
Catechesis/Religious Program—Tel: 409-935-3535. Armando G. Tapia, D.R.E. Students 159.

LA PORTE, HARRIS CO., ST. MARY OF THE IMMACULATE CONCEPTION (1954), Rev. Eric J. Fitre; Deacons Hector Cantu; Edward Thomas Lewis; Julio C. Matallana. In Res., Rev. Msgr. Boleslaus Zientek.
Church & Mailing Address: 816 Park Dr., 77571-5811. Tel: 281-471-2000; Fax: 281-471-9365.
Catechesis/Religious Program—Tel: 281-471-2316. Diane Koonce, D.R.E. Students 358.

LAKE JACKSON, BRAZORIA CO., ST. MICHAEL (1966), Rev. Msgr. Leo Wleczyk.
Church & Mailing Address: 100 Oak Dr. S., 77566-5630. Tel: 979-297-3041; Fax: 979-297-7895.
Catechesis/Religious Program—Tel: 979-297-3043. Marsha Jacklitsch, D.R.E. Students 678.

LEAGUE CITY, GALVESTON CO., ST. MARY (1910), Rev. Msgr. Eugene Cargill; Deacons Robert Garza; George Blanford Jr.
Church & Mailing Address: 1612 E. Walker St., 77573-4137. Tel: 281-332-3031; 281-332-7211 (Rectory); Fax: 281-332-8328.
School—Tel: 281-332-4014. Lay Teachers 21; Students 170.
Catechesis/Religious Program—Tel 281-332-7459. Sr. Camilla Micheletti, O.P., D.R.E. Students 791.

MAGNOLIA, MONTGOMERY CO., ST. MATTHIAS THE APOSTLE (1978), Rev. Frank W. Jones; Deacons George Troscfair; Richard L. Clough.
Church & Mailing Address: 302 S. Magnolia Blvd., 77355-8535. Tel: 281-356-2000; Fax: 281-356-7818.
Catechesis/Religious Program—Barbara Bezub, D.R.E. Students 474.

MANVEL, BRAZORIA CO., SACRED HEART OF JESUS (1945), Revs. James J. Gaunt, C.S.B.; John S. Broussard, C.S.B.; Deacon Robert Reed Leicht Jr.
Mailing Address: 6502 Co. Rd. 48, 77578-2908. Tel: 281-489-8720; Fax: 281-489-8727.
Catechesis/Religious Program—Tel: 281-489-7603. Connie Bowers, D.R.E. Students 721.

MCNAIR, HARRIS CO., HOLY FAMILY (1945), [JC] Rev. Rodney J. Armstrong, S.S.J.; Deacon Steve Arceneaux Jr.
Church & Mailing Address: 7122 Whiting Rock Dr., Baytown, 77521-1124. Tel: 281-426-8448; Fax: 281-426-8449.
Catechesis/Religious Program—Tel: 281-426-4688. Catherine Lemelle, D.R.E. Students 75.

MISSOURI CITY, FT. BEND CO., HOLY FAMILY (1915), Revs. Thaddeus Valencia, C.S.B.; David J. Zapalac, C.S.B.; Damian Hinojosa, C.S.B.; Deacons William E. Seifert Jr.; Alfred Abram Sr.; Pedro Solas.
Church & Mailing Address: 1510 Fifth St., 77489-1298. Tel: 281-499-9688; Fax: 281-499-9680.
Catechesis/Religious Program—Tel: 281-499-4612. Yolanda Pena, D.R.E. Students 415.

NAVASOTA, GRIMES CO., CHRIST OUR LIGHT (1869), Rev. Antonio Castro, Admin.; Deacons Grant E. Holt; Gregory N. Jelinek, M.D.
Mailing Address: 510 Manley St., 77868-3926.
Res.: 615 Church St., 77868-3905.
Church: 9677 Hwy. 6, 77868. Tel: 936-825-3920; Fax: 936-825-7612.
Catechesis/Religious Program—Mrs. Jodi Alejandro, D.R.E. Students 228.

NEEDVILLE, FORT BEND CO., ST. MICHAEL (1913), [CEM] Rev. James Ramsey.
Mailing Address: P.O. Box 95, 77461-0095.
Church: 9202 Main St., 77461. Tel: 979-793-4477; Fax: 979-793-7456.
Catechesis/Religious Program—Tel: 281-232-4006. Lynn Sury, D.R.E. Students 490.

NEW CANEY, MONTGOMERY CO., ST. JOHN OF THE CROSS (1989), Rev. Gary Rickles; Deacon Winfield S. Matz.
Church & Mailing Address: 20000 Loop 494, 77357-9804. Tel: 281-399-9008; 281-399-3384 (Rectory); Fax: 281-399-1500.
Catechesis/Religious Program—Tel: 281-399-9127. Debbie Davis, D.R.E. Students 266.

NEW WAVERLY, WALKER CO., ST. JOSEPH (1869), [CEM 2] Rev. Joseph K. Kalladan; Deacons Klaus Petereit; Paul A. Wichman.
Church & Mailing Address: 101 Elmore, 77358-4105. Tel: 936-344-6104 (Res.); Fax: 936-344-2818 (Res.).
Catechesis/Religious Program—Tel: 936-856-3713. Students 124.
Mission—St. Stephen the Martyr 101 Stagecoach, Pointblank, San Jacinto Co. 77364.

PASADENA, HARRIS CO.

1—ST. JUAN DIEGO (1954), (Hispanic),, (Formerly Guardian Angel) Revs. Francisco Leon, O.S.A.; Leonel Martinez, O.S.A. (Mexico); Deacons Valeriano Leija; Jose Jimenez; Miguel Hernandez; Adolfo Mejia-Parada; Servando Rojas.
Church & Mailing Address: 3301 Pasadena Blvd., 77503-3201. Tel: 713-477-6693; Fax: 713-477-0523.
Catechesis/Religious Program—Tel: 713-472-0356. Beatrice Canas, D.R.E. Students 514.

2—ST. PIUS THE FIFTH (1941), Revs. Hubert J. Kealy; Jesus E Suarez; Deacons Enrique Herrera; Celestino M. Perez; James L. Bart; Sr. Felice Mojica, M.C.D.P., Pastoral Assoc.
Church & Mailing Address: 824 S. Main St., 77506-3532. Tel: 713-473-9484; Fax: 713-473-2731.
School—812 S. Main St., Pasaena, 77506. Tel: 713-472-5172. Becky Gleasman, Prin. Lay Teachers 18; Students 250.
Catechesis/Religious Program— Sr. Felice Mojica, M.C.D.P., Pastoral Assoc. Students 1,058.

PATTISON/BROOKSHIRE, WALLER CO., SACRED HEART (1914), Rev. David DuBois.
Mailing Address: P.O. Box 300, 77466-0300.
Church: 4445 F.M. 359 N., 77466. Tel: 281-375-6799; Fax: 281-375-5799.
Catechesis/Religious Program—Tel: 281-375-6638. Mrs. Marie Pattison, D.R.E. Students 209.

PEARLAND, BRAZORIA CO., ST. HELEN (1952), Rev. Msgr. Reginald R. Nesvadba, V.F.; Rev. Francisco R. Ordonez; Deacons Darvin A. Bordelon; Pete Calvillo; Hector Ibarra; J. Cruz Trujillo.
Res., Church & Mailing Address: 2209 Old Alvin Rd., 77581. Tel: 281-485-2421; Fax: 281-485-6789.
School—2213 Old Alvin Rd., 77581. Tel: 281-485-2845; Fax: 281-485-7607. Mary Margaret Hitt, Prin. Lay Teachers 21; Students 248.

Catechesis/Religious Program—Tel: 281-485-5457. Julie Martinez, D.R.E. Students 1,512.

PLANTERSVILLE, GRIMES CO., ST. MARY (1894), [CEM] Rev. Edward C Kucera Jr.; Deacon Peter Sechelski.
Mailing Address: P.O. Box 388, 77363-0388.
Church: 8227 County Rd. 205, 77363. Tel: 936-894-2223; Fax: 936-894-3613.
Catechesis/Religious Program—Frances Marek, D.R.E. Students 127.
Mission—St. Joseph Stonehan, Grimes Co. Fax: 936-894-3614. 11323 County Rd. 304, 77363-0388.

PORT BOLIVAR, GALVESTON CO., OUR MOTHER OF MERCY (1968), Rev. Msgr. Fred P. O'Connor.
Mailing Address: P.O. Box 900, 77650-0900.
Church: 18th St. at Madison, Port Boliver, 77650-0900. Tel: 409-684-8962; Fax: 409-684-3274.
Rectory—1313 18th St., 77650.
Catechesis/Religious Program—Tel: 409-684-5713. Maryanne Rogers, D.R.E. Students 20.
Mission—St. Therese of Lisieux (1994), 2400 Hwy. 87, Crystal Beach, Galveston Co. 77650. Tel: 409-684-6824.

PRAIRIE VIEW, WALLER CO., ST. MARTIN DE PORRES (1962), Merged, with Mary, Mother of God, Hempstead to form St. Katherine Drexel, Hempstead.

RICHMOND, FORT BEND CO.

1—ST. JOHN FISHER (1952), Rev. Wencil C. Pavlovsky, C.S.B., V.F.; Deacons Ben Munguia; Billy Guerrero Jr.; Ruben Torres; Hector Rodriguez.
Church & Mailing Address: 410 Clay St., 77469-1708. Tel: 281-342-5092; Fax: 281-633-9465.
Rectory—610 North Fourth St., 77469.
Catechesis/Religious Program—Tel: 281-342-8371. Virginia Ewald, D.R.E. Students 335.

2—SACRED HEART (1935), Rev. Howard E. Drabek. In Res., Rev. J. Donald Schwarting; Deacons Donald G. Ries; Joseph R. Kelly Sr.; Brick Hodge.
Church & Mailing Address: 507 S. Fourth St., 77469-3599. Tel: 281-342-3609; Fax: 281-342-9833.
Rectory—303 Houston, 77469.
Catechesis/Religious Program—Tel: 281-342-8371. Virginia Ewald, D.R.E. Students 1,320.

ROSENBERG, FORT BEND CO.

1—HOLY ROSARY (1911), Rev. Daniel L. Warden, V.F.
Church & Mailing Address: 1416 George St., 77471-3198. Tel: 281-342-3089; Fax: 281-342-7688.
School—1408 James St., 77471. Tel: 281-342-5813; Fax: 281-762-3013. Mrs. Nancy Moore, Prin. Sisters 2; Lay Teachers 21; Students 235.
Catechesis/Religious Program—Barbara Respondek, D.R.E. Students 287.

2—OUR LADY OF GUADALUPE (1936), [CEM] Revs. James Blocher, C.S.B.; Charles Lynch, C.S.B.; Deacon Enrique G. Avila.
Mailing Address: P.O. Box 748, 77471-0748.
Church: 514 Carlisle St., 77471-1822. Tel: 281-232-5113; Fax: 281-342-4008.
Catechesis/Religious Program—Tel: 281-232-4322. Pauline Cano, D.R.E. Students 724.

SEALY, AUSTIN CO., IMMACULATE CONCEPTION (1889), [CEM] Rev. Octavio A. Muguerza; Deacons Frank Laredo; Jerome Losack Sr.
Mailing Address: P.O. Box 337, 77474-0337.
Rectory—517 Fifth St., 77474-0337. Tel: 979-885-3868; Fax: 979-885-2246.
Church: 525 5th St., 77474.
Catechesis/Religious Program—Tel: 979-885-6902. Ms. Carolyn Rapsilver, D.R.E. Students 332.

SOUTH HOUSTON, HARRIS CO., OUR LADY OF GRACE (1971), Rev. Jose Maria Asenjo.
Mailing Address: P.O. Box 164, 77587-0164.
Church: 1211 Michigan St., 77587.
Res.: 1204 Michigan St., 77587. Tel: 979-946-6461; Fax: 979-946-0647.
Catechesis/Religious Program—Tel: 281-461-9417. Amalia Durran Parra, D.R.E. Students 239.

SPRING, HARRIS CO.

1—CHRIST THE GOOD SHEPHERD (1978), Revs. John Upton; Mathew Sunny Joseph Plammoottil, O.S.H.; Deacons Steve L. La Bonte; Pat W. Camerino; Alberto J. Patetta.
Church & Mailing Address: 18511 Klein Church Rd., 77379-4998. Tel: 281-376-6831; Fax: 281-376-8945.
Catechesis/Religious Program—Ms. Kathy Kelley, D.R.E. Students 937.

2—ST. EDWARD (1969), Revs. Joseph A. Gietl; Joseph Thanh Vu; Matthai K. Thomman, O.S.H.; Deacons Nicholas Thompson; Kenneth Martin.
Church & Mailing Address: 2601 Spring Stuebner Rd., 77389-4824. Tel: 281-353-9774; Fax: 281-353-9786.
School—Tel: 281-353-4570; Fax: 281-353-8255. Loretta Orlando, Prin. Lay Teachers 26; Students 399.
Catechesis/Religious Program—Tel: 281-353-4930. Linda Cussen, D.R.E. Students 542.

3—ST. IGNATIUS OF LOYOLA (1985), Revs. Francis X. Pistorius, S.J.; Daniel A. Creagan, S.J.; Deacons Glen H. Cupier; Michael E. Higgins.
Church & Mailing Address: 7810 Cypresswood Dr., 77379-7101. Tel: 281-370-3401 (Office); Fax: 281-370-9306.
Rectory—7802 King Arthur Ct., 77379.
Catechesis/Religious Program—Joe Wappelhorst, D.R.E. Students 1,485.

4—ST. JAMES THE APOSTLE (1976), Revs. Charles J. Samperi; Rafael Eugene Chakkalakal; Deacon Ray Oden.
Church & Mailing Address: 22800 Aldine Westfield Rd., 77373-6565. Tel: 281-353-5053; Fax: 281-355-8847.
Catechesis/Religious Program—Tel: 281-353-3497. Students 722.

SUGAR LAND, FORT BEND CO.

1—ST. LAURENCE (1985), Revs. William Andrew Wood; Philip P. Lloyd; Trung V. Nguyen; Deacons Don Burns; Robert K. Dunham; Paul Robinson Jr.; Albert G. Bothe.
Church & Mailing Address: 3100 Sweetwater Blvd., 77479-2630. Tel: 281-980-9812; Fax: 281-980-0686.
School—2630 Austin Pkwy., 77479. Tel: 281-980-0500; Fax: 281-980-0026. Nancy Taylor, Prin. Lay Teachers 53; Students 684.
Catechesis/Religious Program—Tel: 281-265-5774. Mrs. Eleanor Notz, D.R.E. Students 1,937.

2—ST. THERESA (1924), Revs. Stephen B. Reynolds; Mathew Thottiyil, M.S.F.S.; Deacons Glenn F. Haller; Frank Cromer; Joaquin Garcia.
Mailing Address: P.O. Box 968, 77487-0968. In Res., Rev. Ligori Johnson Philip.
Res. & Church Address: 115 Seventh St., 77487-0968. Tel: 281-494-1156; Fax: 281-242-1393.
Catechesis/Religious Program—Tel: 281-494-2717. Christy Wright, D.R.E. Students 1,393.

3—ST. THOMAS AQUINAS (1978), Rev. Kevin C. Thissen, O.P.; Verna Patout, Pastoral Assoc.; Deacons Sam Dunning; Robert Kirkpatrick; Danilo C. Narnajo.
Church & Mailing Address: 12627 W. Bellfort Ave., 77478-1844. Tel: 281-240-6721; Fax: 281-240-6733.
Rectory—10415 Huntington Wood Dr., 77099-3721.
Catechesis/Religious Program—John Masterson, D.R.E. Students 523.

SWEENY, BRAZORIA CO., OUR LADY OF PERPETUAL HELP (1954), Rev. Lee Flores; Deacon Jerry J. Michalec.
Church & Mailing Address: 310 N. McKinney St., 77480-2899. Tel: 979-548-2020; Fax: 979-548-4253.
Catechesis/Religious Program—Tel: 979-798-8129. Chris Kasper, D.R.E. Students 136.
Mission—St. John the Apostle 807 Loggins, West Columbia, Brazoria Co. 77486-3843. Tel: 979-345-3600.

TEXAS CITY, GALVESTON CO., ST. MARY (1911), Revs. Thomas V. Ponzini; Jan Kubisa; Deacons Joseph A. Hensley; Stephen A. Mistretta.
Mailing Address: 1604 Ninth Ave. N., 77590-5468.
Church: 722 Third Ave. N., 77590. Tel: 409-948-8448; Fax: 409-945-8662.
School—Our Lady of Fatima, 1600 Ninth Ave. N., 77590. Tel: 409-945-3326; Fax: 409-945-3389. Sr. Kathleen Daly, Prin. Sisters 4; Lay Teachers 7; Students 167.
Catechesis/Religious Program—Mr. Joe Hensley, D.R.E. Students 433.

THE WOODLANDS, MONTGOMERY CO.

1—ST. ANTHONY OF PADUA (1997), Rev. Msgr. George A. Sheltz, E.V.; Revs. Albert Walsh; Cyuracus Onyejegbu; Cyuracus Onyejegbu; Deacons Joe Mignogna; Glendon Michael Schmidt; Robert Dalecki; Leon M. Arceneaux Jr.; Charles Duck.
Church & Mailing Address: 7801 Bay Branch Dr., 77382-5312. Tel: 281-296-2800; Fax: 281-296-7238.
Rectory—7979 Bay Branch Dr., 77382-5312.
School—7901 Bay Branch Dr., 77382. Tel: 281-296-0300. Renee Nunez, Prin. Lay Teachers 15; Students 158.
Catechesis/Religious Program—Mrs. Ann Tadvick, D.R.E. Students 2,024.

2—STS. SIMON AND JUDE (1979), Rev. Msgr. Charles C. Domec; Rev. Hai Duc Dang; Deacons Kenneth D. Carlson; Robert E. Flynn Sr.; Fred T. Shetz; Sid Sandiford; Anthony G. Cantania.
Res., Church & Mailing Address: 26777 Glen Loch Dr., 77381-2921. Tel: 281-367-9885; Fax: 281-367-9888.
Catechesis/Religious Program—Tel: 281-292-9801. Robin Walker, D.R.E. Students 1,013.

TOMBALL, HARRIS CO., ST. ANNE (1964), Rev. Fred W. Valone; Deacons Ted F. Heap; Collie J. Mangano Jr.
Church & Mailing Address: 1111 S. Cherry St., 77375-6675. Tel: 281-351-8106; Fax: 281-351-8142.
School—Tel: 281-351-0093. Ken Waguespack, Prin. Lay Teachers 25; Students 282.
Catechesis/Religious Program—Laura Hinton, D.R.E. Students 492.

WALLIS, AUSTIN CO., GUARDIAN ANGEL (1892), [CEM] Rev. Richard A. Johnston, S.C.J.
Mailing Address: P.O. Box 487, 77485-0487. Tel: 979-478-6532; Fax: 979-478-7275.
Church and Res.: 5610 Demel St., 77485.
Catechesis/Religious Program—Tel: 979-478-6717. Steve Williams, D.R.E. (PreK-8); Angie Flores, D.R.E.; Nita Sulak, D.R.E. Students 181.

Chaplains of Public Institutions
Prison Chaplains

GALVESTON. *Galveston County Jail*, 715 19th St., 77550. Tel: 409-766-2315. Deacon Javier Gomez.
John Sealy Hospital. Tel: 409-772-6108. Deacon Javier Gomez. Prison Unit

HOUSTON. *Federal Correctional Center*, 1200 Texas Ave., 77002. Tel: 713-755-5326. Rev. Ronald F. Cloutier.
George Bush Intercontinental Airport. Rev. Msgr. Paul Procella, Chap.
William P. Hobby Airport. Rev. Norbert Manduzia, Chap.

ANGLETON. *Brazoria County Jail*, Tel: 409-849-2441. Evelyn Nachtegaele.
Pam Lychner State Jail.
2350 Atoscocita Rd., Humble, 77396. Tel: 281-454-5036, Ext. 358. Deacon Tom McKiney.
Retrieve Unit. Vacant.
Rte. 4, Box 1500, 77515. Tel: 409-849-9306.

BRAZORIA. *Clemens Unit*.
Rte. 1, Box 1077, 77422. Tel: 409-798-2188. Deacon David Mitchell.

HUNTSVILLE. *Diagnostic Unit*.
P.O. Box 100, 77340. Tel: 409-295-8459. Anthony Velasquez.
Eastham Unit.
P.O. Box 1974, 77342. Tel: 409-636-7321. Rev. Virginio C. Vazquez.
Ellis I Unit, Rt. 6, 77343. Tel: 409-295-5756, Ext. 217. Deacon John Stanley.
Estelle Unit 77343. Tel: 409-291-4200, Ext. 2274. Deacon Gene Warzecha.
Goree Unit.
Box 38, 77340. Tel: 409-295-8159. Mr. Anthony Velasquez.
Huntsville Walls Unit, P.O. Box 32, 77340. Tel: 409-295-8159; 409-291-4200. Vacant.
Texas Department of Criminal Justice, 2503 Lake Rd., Ste. #19, 77340. Tel: 409-294-6548 (Regl. Program Admin.). Deacon Richard Lopez.
Walls Unit.
Box 32, 77340. Tel: 409-295-8159. Mrs. Linda Hill.
Wynne Unit.
Rte. 1, Box 1, 77340. Tel: 409-295-8159. Deacon Jose Trujillo.

MIDWAY. *Ferguson Unit*. Vacant.
Rte. 2, Box 20, Huntsville, 75852. Tel: 409-348-3751, Ext. 333.

NAVASOTA. *Pack I Unit*.
Rte. 3, Box 300, 77686. Tel: 409-825-3728. Deacon Peter Sechelski.
Pack II Unit.
Rte. 1, Box 1000, 77686. Tel: 409-825-7548. Deacon Peter L. Sechelski.

RICHMOND. *Jester I, II, III, IV Unit*.
Rte. 2, 77469. Tel: 281-277-3700.

ROSHARON. *Darrington Unit*.
Rte. 3, Box 59, 77583. Tel: 281-595-2465, Ext. 275. Deacon Gerardo Garcia.
Ramsey I Unit.
Rte. 4, Box 1100, 77583. Tel: 281-595-3491. Deacon Ron Simon.
Ramsey II Unit.
Rte. 4, Box 1200, 77583. Tel: 281-595-3413. Deacon Bob Leicht.
Ramsey III Unit. (Vacant)
Rte. 4, Box 1300, 77583. Tel: 281-595-3481.

SUGAR LAND. *Central Unit*.
One Circle Dr., Richmond, 77478. Tel: 281-491-2146. Bryant Laesen. Vacant.

Jail Chaplains

HOUSTON. *Harris County Jail*. Rev. Ronald F. Cloutier. Tel: 713-755-5326.
Res.: 215 E. 10th St.. Tel: 713-755-5326.
701 Bldg.. Tel: 713-755-8562.
Juvenile Detention Center. Ms. Marilu Ballow. Tel: 713-741-8779. Special Youth Svcs.

CONROE. *Montgomery County Jail*. Deacon Leo St. Alban. Tel: 409-756-8186.

On Special or Other Diocesan Assignment:
Revs.—
Gately, R. Troy, Vice Chancellor
Jozwiak, Lawrence, Tribunal
Nguyen, Trung V., Tribunal
Rossi, Frank H., Chancellor
Russler, Clint, Vocation Dir.

On Duty Outside the Diocese:
Rev. Msgrs.—
Broussard, William L.
Fruge, Donald J., P.O. Box 13327, Capitol Station, Austin, 78711.
Revs.—
Cantu, Oscar, Casa Santa Maria, Via dell'Umilta, 30 00187, Rome, Italy. Tel: 68-69-441 (06)

Corrigan, Michael T., St. Anne, 300 Ashton Ave., Kingstree, SC 29556. Tel: 803-354-7798
McGinnis, Jack P., Chap., P.O. Box 2456, Idyllwild, CA 92549-2456.
Nguyen, Trung, Divine Word College, Catholic University of America, Washington, DC.
Perez, Joseph, The Chancery, P.O. Box 907, 77001.

Retired:
Rev. Msgrs.—
Beck, Albert, Holy Cross Chapel, 77021.
Braden, Leroy H., Pope John XXIII Residence, 2407 Holcombe Blvd., 77021-2023. Tel: 713-440-7540
Crosthwait, Joseph H., P.O. Box 1302, New Ulm, 78950. Tel: 409-992-3821
Donovan, Thomas A., Pope John XXIII Residence, 2407 Holcombe Blvd., 77021-2023. Tel: 713-741-9471
Fuchs, Sylvester, Lost Prairie Villa, 9901 FM 2086, Temple, 76501-3528. Tel: 817-984-2312
Jones, John B., Pope John XXIII Residence, 2407 E. Holcombe Blvd., 77021-2023. Tel: 713-747-1746
Madden, James J., Pope John XXIII Residence, 2407 E. Holcombe Blvd., 77021-2023. Tel: 713-748-1761
Rhein, George V., 2407 Holcombe Blvd., 77021-2023. Tel: 713-747-7308
Wearden, Francis G., 1100 Parthenen Pl., New Caney, 77357-3039. Tel: 713-399-0270
Revs.—
Anton, Ronald J., S.J. (BAL), Pope John XXIII Residence, 2407 Holcombe Blvd., 77021-2023. Tel: 713-748-1553
Burns, Charles E., 343 Bobolink, New Braunfels, 78130-3868.
Chu, Peter Ngoc Thanh, Pope John XXIII Residence, 2407 Holcombe Blvd., 77021-2023. Tel: 713-747-8774
Connelly, Laurence D., 7 Tourney Cove, Austin, 78738-1119.
Daigle, Robert E., 6505 O'Bannon Dr., Las Vegas, NV 89102-0854. Tel: 619-268-3249
Freret, Warren Joseph, P.O. Box 8691, Gulfport, MS 39506. Tel: 228-868-1687
Gillece, Eugene J., Pope John XXIII, 2407 Holcombe Blvd., 77021-2023. Tel: 713-748-7201
Greenwald, Alfred E., 630 N. Via Lucia, Tucson, AZ 85745. Tel: 602-792-0122
Hebert, Marvin A., c/o Mr. Jude C. Hebert, 415 Jeannette Dr., Bridge City, 77611-3742.
Hughes, Royce, 745 E. U.S. Hwy. 90, Schulenberg, 78956-5233. Tel: 409-743-3722
Kellick, John W., 6517 Burdock Dr., Santa Fe, 77510-9340. Tel: 409-925-6817
Lee, Lawrence, Pope John XXIII Residence, 2407 Holcombe Blvd., 77021-2023. Tel: 713-741-7267
Linan, Jesse S., P.O. Box 250, Anderson, 77830-0250. Tel: 409-873-2945
Natho, Clifton J., 8326 Autumn Wind Dr., 77040-1474. Tel: 713-856-8469
O'Malley, Joseph T., St. Thomas More, 10330 Hillcroft Ave., 77096-4795. Tel: 713-729-0021
Schwarting, Donald J., 3972 Jackdaw #115, San Diego, CA 92103. Tel: 619-298-5464
Tran, John Chinh Chan, 8138 Lynn St., 77017-3050. Tel: 713-645-2834
Walker, Anselm, 1815 Parker, 77093. Tel: 713-697-7109

Permanent Deacons:
Abadejos, Ernesto, Notre Dame, Houston
Abram, Alfred, Sr., Unassigned
Acosta, Angel R., St. Mary, Texas City
Adame, David, Annunciation/St. Joseph Hospital, Houston
Adams, Francis E., St. Elizabeth Anne Seton, Houston
Adams, John W., St. Matthew the Evangelist, Houston
Aiuvalasit, Anthony George, St. John Vianney, Houston
Alessi, Anthony V., St. Thomas More, Houston
Alexander, Robert George, Annunciation and St. Paul, Houston
Allen, Charles J., Sr., Our Mother of Mercy, Houston
Aranda, Jose Francisco, St. Christopher, Houston
Arceneaux, Leon M., Jr., St. Pius V, Pasadena
Arceneaux, Steve, Jr., St. Martin de Porres, Barrett Station
Arellano, Jose, Immaculate Heart of Mary, Houston
Ausmus, Sam, III, Shrine of the True Cross, Dickinson
Baker, J. M., St. Theresa and St. Justin Martyr, Houston
Baker, Theodore Otis, St. Matthias the Apostle, Magnolia
Barnett, James, Our Lady of Walsingham, Houston
Bart, James L., St. Augustine, Houston
Bazan, Jeronimo, Prince of Peace, Houston
Becker, Henry, St. Peter the Apostle, Galveston
Betancourt, Manuel, Unassigned
Birsinger, Alvin, St. Luke the Evangelist, Houston
Blanford, George, St.Mary, League City
Bobb, William J., St. Peter the Apostle, Galveston
Bonura, James L., Sr., TDC/Queen of Peace, La Marque
Bordelon, Darvin A., St. Helen, Pearland
Bothe, Albert G., St. Francis de Sales, Houston
Bottjer, Albert, Assumption, Houston; Ben Taub Hospital Jail Chap.
Bowman, David, St. John the Baptist, Alvin
Bradley, Donald E., St. Cecilia, Houston
Breaux, Roy, St. Phillip of Jesus, Houston
Brinkman Fred H., TDC-Ramsey Units I, II, III/Drug Trustee Camp
Broussard, Leonard J., Epiphany of the Lord, Katy; Holy Name Retreat Center, Houston
Brown, Albert, Sr., St. Gregory
Brueggerhoff, Robert T., Holy Ghost, Houston
Budinger, Jean-Paul, St. Anne, Houston
Buhay, Carlito, St. Albert, Houston
Burns, Don, St. Theresa, Sugar Land
Butler, Charles, Prince of Peace, Houston
Cabler, Paul Stephen, Unassigned
Calonge, Elie, Texas Dept. of Corrections, Palestine, TX
Calvo, Clement S., Hispanic Ministry Office, Houston
Camerino, Pat W., Christ the Good Shepherd, Spring
Camunez, Richard F., St. Hyacinth, Deer Park
Cantu, Hector, St. Mary, La Porte
Carlson, Kenneth D., Sts. Simon & Jude, The Woodlands
Caruso, James, St. Mary, Humble
Casas, Alvaro, Jr., St. Albert, Houston
Castaneda, Guillermo F., Jr., Diocese of Brownsville
Castillo, Raul A., St. Joseph, Brazoria
Charnisky, John E., Jr., Diocese of Beaumont
Chin-Fatt, Arthur, St. Bartholomew
Coehen, Jerry, St. Luke the Evangelist, Houston
Cooper, Leslie F., Unassigned
Coussirat, John F., St. Catherine, Houston
Crawford, J. R., St. Anne, Tomball
Cromer, Frank P., St. Theresa, Sugarland
Cuiper, Glen H., St. Ignatius of Loyola, Spring
Dalecki, Robert, Prince of Peace, Houston
Davis, Roger, St. Luke the Evangelist, Houston
Dell-Olio, L. S., St. Peter, Galveston
Despania, Raymond L., Sr., St. Peter Claver, Houston
Devine, John E., Jr., St. Luke the Evangelist, Houston
Do, Joseph Chuong Nguyen, Our Lady of Lourdes, Houston
Duck, Charles, Prince of Peace, Houston
Dunham, Robert K., St. Laurence, Sugarland
Dunning, Sam, St. Thomas
Duplan, Jose, Jr., St. Mary's, Texas City
Dupont, Gerald W., St. Theresa, Sugar Land
Durden, Jonathon, St. Clare
Ehrman, John W., Jr., Sacred Heart, Conroe
Evon, William J., Sr., St. Ignatius of Loyola, Spring
Festa, Gene, St. Justin Martyr, Houston
Fikac, Marvin R., Sacred Heart Co-Cathedral, Houston
Flores, Geronimo, St. Joseph, Houston
Floyd, Ivy C., St. Thomas the Apostle, Huntsville
Flynn, Robert E., Sr., Sts. Simon & Jude, The Woodlands
Fraser, Ronald J., St. Maximilian Kolbe, Houston
Garcia, Gerardo J., Christ the King, Houston
Garcia, Gregory C., Resurrection, Houston
Garcia, Julio, St. Jerome, Clute
Garrett, William, St. Anne, Houston
Garza, Robert, St. Mary, League City
Gilbert, Daniel W., St. Francis Xavier, Houston
Glor, Richard J.L., Unassigned
Gomez, Arturo M., Notre Dame, Houston
Gomez, Javier, St. Andrew, Channelview
Gonzales, Emiliano, TDC Prison Chaplain, Houston
Gonzalez, Enrique, St. Charles Borromeo, Houston
Gonzalez, Guadalupe, Our Lady of Guadalupe, Houston
Gonzalez Bangs, Fernando, Our Lady of Guadalupe, Baytown
Gosline, Edwin F., St. Thomas More, Houston
Graham, Michael G., Unassigned
Gramann, Henry T., St. Christopher, Houston
Granado, Alfred E., Jr., Leave of Absence
Griesmyer, Steven, Sr., St. James the Apostle, Spring
Guajardo, Fredrico, Our Lady of Mt. Carmel, Houston
Guerra, Daniel, Sr., St. Clare of Assisi, Houston
Gutierrez, Diego, Sr., St. John the Baptist, Alvin
Hall, Raymond J., Unassigned
Hamilton, L. William, St. Bartholomew, Katy
Hargraves, Wilfred J., Jr., Transfer to Austin, TX
Harper, Stephen Edwin, St. Laurence, Sugarland
Hennessy, Robert, St. John the Evangelist, Baytown
Henry, Albert, St. Francis Xavier, Houston
Herrera, Rolando, Archdiocese of San Antonio
Hickey, Dennis, St. Hyacinth, Deer Park
Higgins, Auburn, St. Maximilian Kolbe, Houston
Hite, James, St. Ignatius Loyola, Spring
Hock, Leslie Bart, Immaculate Conception, Houston
Hodapp, Cyril J., St. Bernadette, Houston
Hodge, Brick, Sacred Heart, Richmond
Holt, Grant E., Christ Our Light, Navasota
Horbowy, Thaddeus J., Chap. Fed. Bureau of Prisons and Medical Center, Lexington, KY
Horr, Louis Eugene, St. Jerome, Houston
Housholder, John, St. Helen, Pearland
Hubisz, John, St. Laurence
Hunter, Thomas Alexander, Hospital Port St. Patrick, Galveston
Husch, John M., Unassigned
Jachimczyk, Joseph A., Annunciation, Houston
Jackson, Clifford X., Our Lady of Sorrows, Houston
Jelinek, Gregory N., M.D., Christ Our Light-Navasota; O.C. Luther TDC
Jenkins, Michael V., St. Francis Xavier, Houston
Johnson, Clarence B., St. Peter the Apostle, Houston
Johnson, Irvin, Jr., Our Mother of Mercy, Houston
Joseph, Ignatius, St. Francis of Assisi, Houston
Kacz, Robert, St. John the Baptist, Alvin
Kelleher, Peter J., St. Christopher, Houston
Keller, Robert C., St. Justin Martyr, Houston
Kelly, Joseph R., Sr., Sacred Heart, Richmond
Kish, Don, Epiphany of the Lord, Katy
Klein, Hugo L., St. Francis de Sales, Houston
Knobloch, Alden J., St. Jerome, Houston
Koch, William E., Sr., Unassigned
Kulhanek, Jerry Peter, Sr., Our Lady of Fatima, Galena Park
Kutach, Emil W., Leave of Absence
LaBonte, Stephen L., Christ the Good Shepherd, Spring
Labrecque, Richard, St. Paul, Houston
Landry, Burke J., St. Elizabeth Ann Seton, Madisonville
Lansch, John, St. Justin Martyr, Houston
Laredo, Frank, Immaculate Conception, Sealy
Laugermann, Frank J., Jr., St. Benedict the Abbot, Houston
Leach, Richard L., Christ the Redeemer; St. John Neumann, Houston
Leal, Merce C., Jr., St. Christopher, Houston
Leblanc, Irvin, Unassigned
Leicht, Robert Reed, Jr., Sacred Heart, Manvel
Leija, Valeriano, Blessed Juan Diego, Pasadena
Lerma, Pedro, Sr., Blessed Sacrament, Houston
Lewis, Edward Thomas, St. Mary, La Porte
Liendo, Jose L., Queen of Peace, Houston
Llewellyn, Earl, Jr., TDCJ Hospital Chaplain, Galveston; Queen of Peace, LaMarque
Llorens, Cornelius C., St. Justin Martyr, Houston
Lopez, Richard, St. Thomas the Apostle, Huntsville
Lorino, Joseph E., St. Vincent de Paul, Houston
Losack, Jerome, Sr., Immaculate Conception, Sealy
Lozano, Rodrigo, St. Charles Borromeo, Houston
Lugo, Loni G., Unassigned
Lynch, Philip F., Unassigned
MacFarlane, Robert, St. Mary, Humble
Marquez, Antonio, St. Raphael, Houston
Martin, Henry Woods, St. Michael, Houston
Martin, Kenneth, St. Edward, Spring
Matula, Francis L., All Saints, Houston
McAllister, Jerome, St. Mary, League City
McKinney, Thomas K., Ellis Unit TDC; St. Mary Magdalene, Humble
Meshell, James, Holy Ghost, Houston
Mignogna, Joe, St. Anthony of Padua, The Woodlands
Miller, Arthur, Unassigned
Miller, Steve, St. Andrew, Channelview
Mitchell, David D., Holy Rosary, Rosenberg
Morales, Hector Hernando, Our Lady of Fatima, Galena Park
Moreno, Aurelio Frank, Jr., St. Frances Cabrini, Houston
Moreno, Leopold R., Catholic Charismatic Center, Houston
Morin, Joseph G., Immaculate Conception, Houston
Motley, John M., Unassigned
Moulton, Darrell, Mary Queen, Friendswood; Covenant House, Houston
Mulcare, Terrance D., St. Christopher, Houston
Munguia, Ben, St. John, Fischer
Navarro, Raul G., Immaculate Heart of Mary, Houston
Nelms, D. Cade, St. Cecilia, Houston
Newhouse, Thomas C., St. Michael, Houston

Nguyen Kim Khanh, Michael, Our Lady of Lavang, Houston
Nguyen Pham, Joseph, Vietnamese Martyrs, Houston
Nguyen Si Bach, Joseph, Christ the Incarnate Word, Houston
O'Brien, Alfred J., Prison Chaplain Stiles Unit-Beaumont
Ortego, Frank P., St. Thomas the Apostle, Huntsville
Osterhaus, James H., Christ the Redeemer, Houston
Ostrand, Gerard, St. Martha, Kingwood
Ostrowski, F. L., Notre Dame, Houston
Pareja, Juan Francisco, St. Jerome, Houston
Parr, Kenneth, Catholic Charismatic Center, Houston
Payne, George, Leave of Absence
Pelletier, John, St. Thomas More, Houston
Peltier, Gerald, St. Anthony, Danbury
Pennell, Charles G., St. Elizabeth Ann Seton, Houston
Petereit, Klaus, St. John Newmann, Houston
Pistone, John Salvadore, St. Mary's Cathedral Basilica, Galveston
Provenzano, Luis, St. Justin Martyr, Houston
Ramirez, Fernando, St. Frances Cabrini, Houston
Ramirez, Jose J., Resurrection, Houston
Ramirez, Julio M., St. Gregory the Great, Houston
Ramirez, Leonard, Holy Family, Missouri City
Rapp, Donald, St. Thomas More, Houston
Reish, Thomas, Christ the Redeemer, Houston
Ries, Donald G., Sacred Heart, Richmond
Rincon, George, Our Lady of Guadalupe, Baytown
Robison, Paul L., Jr., St. Luke the Evangelist, Houston
Rodriguez, Luis, Immaculate Conception, Houston
Roessler, Charles F., Jr., St. Frances Cabrini, Houston
Romeu, Hector J., St. John Vianney, Houston
Rook, R. Jack, St. Andrew, Channelview
Rooney, John, St. Frances Cabrini, Houston
Rowan, Vincent A., St. Michael, Lake Jackson
Rumford, Robert, St. Bernadette
Rutledge, James E., St. Jerome, Houston
Salazar, Mariano, St. Joseph, Houston
Saltzmann, Peter, Catholic Charismatic Center, Houston
Sanchez, Martin G., St. Joseph, Houston
Sanders, Raymond L., Jr., Diocese of Austin
Sandiford, Sid, Sts. Simon & Jude, The Woodlands
Santos, John, St. Andrew, Channelview
Satterwhite, Michael, St. Mary, Texas City
Schmidt, Glendon Michael, St. James, Spring
Sechelski, Peter, TDC/St. Stanislaus, Anderson
Seifert, William E., Jr., Holy Family, Missouri City
Sharpless, James, St. Luke the Evangelist, Houston
Shaw, Wallace, St. Mary Star of the Sea, Freeport
Sheffield, William Leonard, Christ Our Light, Navasota; St. Matthias, Magnolia
Shefts, Andrew, St. Basil, Angleton
Sheltz, George A., Sr., St. Joseph Hospital/St. Vincent de Paul, Houston
Shetz, Fred T., Dir. Permanent Deacons, Sts. Simon & Jude, The Woodlands
Sicinski, Anton, St. Stanislaus, Anderson
Simon, Ronald, St. Philip Neri, Houston
Singer, John William, Jr., St. Joseph, Baytown
Smaistrla, Denis J., St. Mary's Seminary, Houston
Smith, Jimmy, St. Joseph, Brazoria
St. Aubin, Leo F., Sacred Heart, Conroe
St. Julian, Michael, St. Francis of Assisi
Steffes, Dale W., St. John Vianney, Houston
Stevens, Robert Gregory, St. Francis Cabrini, Houston
Stoessel, Edward T., St. Thomas More, Houston
Sullivan, John, Queen of Peace, Houston
Suriano, Julio S., Our Lady of St. John, Houston
Thompson, Edward, St. Cyril
Thomson, Nicholas, St. Andrew, Channelview
Tollett, Jesse, St. Luke, Houston
Tollett, Lee Joseph, St. Laurence, Sugar Land
Tripp, Edwin, St. Elizabeth, Houston
Trosclair, George, Prince of Peace, Houston; St. Mary, Plantersville
Vacek, Albert E., Jr., St. John Vianney, Houston
Vaclavik, Larry A., St. Theresa, Houston
Vanderslice, Ron, Diocese of Tulsa
Venegas, Rudy, Our Lady of Guadalupe
Vicknair, Tom Jude, Catholic Charismatic Center, Houston
Villarreal, Gilbert R., St. Helen, Pearland
Villarreal, Marcelino, St. Benedict the Abbot, Houston
Vocelka, Frank Jay, Jr., St. Theresa, Houston
Wagner, William C., St. Bartholomew, Katy
Waterman, John H., St. Anthony of Padua, The Woodlands
Watkins, Rollo J., Christ the King, Houston
Weaver, William A., St. Elizabeth Ann Seton, Houston
Wewer, Justin J., St. John the Evangelist, Baytown
Wiles, Philip Arlen, St. Dominic, Houston
Wright, Jim, Unassigned
Zamora, Joe, St. Augustine, Houston
Zuk, Adolph J., St. Matthew the Evangelist, Houston

INSTITUTIONS LOCATED IN THE DIOCESE

[A] SEMINARIES, DIOCESAN

HOUSTON. *St. Mary's Seminary*, 9845 Memorial Dr., 77024-3498. Tel: 713-686-4345; Fax: 713-681-7550. Email: sms@stthom.edu. Rev. Msgrs. Daniel Flores (CC), Vice Rector; Joseph Crosthwait; Charles Elmer (AUS); Very Rev. Brendan J. Cahill, Rector; Revs. Robert McTeigue, S.J.; Raphael Davila, M.M.; Edward Abell; Ivan C. Marsh, O.Carm; Michael Olson (FWT); Sr. Barbara Tovar, M.C.D.P., Dir. Cultural Formation; Deacon Denis J. Smaistrla, Treas. & Plant Mgr.; Sandra Magie, S.T.D., Dean School of Theology. Priests 11; Sisters 2; Lay Teachers 5; Diocesan Seminarians 53; Religious Seminarians 10; Total Enrollment 63.

[B] SEMINARIES, RELIGIOUS OR SCHOLASTICATES

HOUSTON. *Casa San Basilio*, 1910 W. Alabama, 77098. Tel: 713-522-7610; Fax: 713-522-1917. Email: restivm@stthom.edu. Revs. Maurice L. Restivo, C.S.B., Rector; Alvin A. Sinasac, C.S.B. Purpose: House of formation for Hispanic men in Religious life discernment. Apostolate of the Basilian Fathers. Priests 2; Total Enrollment 2.

Holy Ghost Fathers and Brothers, Holy Spirit Seminary, 4410 Yoakum Blvd., 77006-5820. Tel: 713-529-0405; Fax: 713-529-4236. Web: www.spiritans.org. Revs. John J. Walsh, C.S.Sp.; Binh T. Quach, C.S.Sp.; Donald S. Nesti, C.S.Sp. Priests 3; Consecrated Religious 5.

SUGAR LAND. *Basilian Fathers House of Prayer*, 106 Fifth St., 77478. Tel: 281-491-8700; Fax: 281-491-1799. Priests 1.

[C] COLLEGES AND UNIVERSITIES

HOUSTON. **University of St. Thomas*, 3800 Montrose Blvd., 77006-4696. Tel: 713-522-7911; Fax: 713-525-2125. Email: president@stthom.edu. Web: www.stthom.edu. Rev. J. Michael Miller, C.S.B., Pres.; Dr. Kurt F. Geisinger, Vice Pres. Academic Affairs; Ms. Helen Hays-Thomas, Registrar; Mr. James Piccininni, Dir., Doherty Library; Dr. Sandra C. Magie, Dean School of Theology; Dr. Jared Ashraf, Dean Cameron School of Business; Dr. Ruth Strudler, Dean School of Education; Mr. Brian Pomeroy, Dean Scholarships & Financial Aid; Rev. Daniel Callam, C.S.B., Univ. Chap.; Ms. Susan Greensage, Dir. Alumni Rels. and Annual Giving; Dr. Colleen Hester, Vice Pres. Strategic Planning, Institutional Research and Evaluation; Mr. James Booth, Vice Pres. Finance & Acting Vice Pres. Student Affairs; Dr. Jerome A. Kramer, Dean School of Arts & Sciences, Assoc. Vice Pres. Academic Affairs; Dr. Janice Gordon-Kelter, Dean Master in Liberal Arts Program; Dr. Rose Signorello, Dir. Counseling Svcs.; Dr. Mary Catherine Sommers, Dir. Center for Thomistic Studies; Mr. Gary McCormack, Vice Pres. Information Technology; Mr. H. Ken DeDominicis, Vice Pres. Inst. Advancement; Mr. Matthew Prasifka, Dir. Recreation and Sports Svcs.; Mr. Brian Allen, Dir. Security; Ms. Kristie Gerber, Dir. Student Activities; Ms. Elinor Collier, Dir. Volunteer Opportunities; Mr. Howard Rose, Asst. Vice Pres. Facilities Opers.; Ms. Karen Burns, Controller; Ms. Susan Byford, Treas.; Rev. Donald Nesti, C.S.Sp., Dir. Center for Faith and Culture; Dr. Daryl Koehn, Dir. Center for Business Ethics; Ms. Patricia McKinley, Dir. Career Svcs. and Testing; Mr. Thomas Overton, Dir. Public Affairs; Ms. Marionette Mitchell, Dir. Publications; Ms. Laura Dozier, Dir. Advancement Projects; Ms. Susan Bradford, Exec. Dir. Institute Advancement; Mr. Frank Souto, Dir. Network and Campus Computing; Ms. Christine Barry, Dir. Central Computing Svcs.; Ms. Joanna Palasota, Dir. Admin. Computing Svcs.; Dr. Timothy Murphy, Dir. Inst. Technology & Web Svcs.; Ms. Bobbe Ames, Vice Pres. Enrollment Svcs.; Sr. Paula Jean Miller, FSE, Dir. Catholic Studies Prog.; Ms. Laura P. Olejnik, Dir. Cardinal Beran Library; Dr. Terry Hall, Dir. Honors Prog.; Dr. Sophia Esquiff, Dir. Learning and Writing Center; Ms. Deborah Crofoot-Morley, Dir. Major Constituents; Ms. Roya Esfandi, Dir. Information Resources; Ms. Jan Schultz, Dir. Residence Life; Ms. Diane Thornton, Dir. Planned Giving; Mr. Eduardo Prieto, Dean Admissions; Ms. Marie-Peire Stien, Dir. Human Resources; Dr. Sherra Theisen, Dir. Academic Advising; Dir. Living Learning Center. Founded in 1947, Graduate Division (Four Schools). Undergraduate Division (21 Departments). Center for Thomistic Studies. Center for International Studies. Center for Business Ethics. Priests 11; Sisters 3; Lay Professors 103; Total Staff 158; Total Enrollment 7,694.

[D] HIGH SCHOOLS, DIOCESAN

GALVESTON. *O'Connell Catholic High School*, 1320 Tremont St., 77550-4513. Tel: 409-765-5534; Fax: 409-765-5536. Email: chauvette@hotmail.com. Web: www.ochs-dgh.org. Rev. Frank T. Fabj; Mr. David Chauvette, Prin. Priests 1; Lay Teachers 20; Total Staff 34; Students 153.

HOUSTON. *Mt. Carmel High School*, 6700 Mt. Carmel Dr., 77087-6699. Tel: 713-649-2745; Fax: 713-649-6851. Dr. Thomas W. O'Neill. Priests 1; Sisters 1; Lay Teachers 13; Total Staff 20; Students 167.

[E] JUNIOR HIGH SCHOOLS, DIOCESAN

HOUSTON. *Seton Catholic Jr. High School*, 801 Rose Ln., 77037-4696. Tel: 281-447-2132; Fax: 281-447-1825. Email: PWClark@setoncatholicjh.org. Web: www.setoncatholicjh.org. Mr. Patrick W. Clark, Prin. Sisters 2; Principals 1; Counselors 1; Development Directors 1; Lay Teachers 13; Total Staff 15; Students 207.

[F] HIGH SCHOOLS, PRIVATE

HOUSTON. *St. Agnes Academy*, 9000 Bellaire Blvd., 77036-4683. Tel: 713-219-5400; Fax: 713-219-5499. Email: sjmeyer@st-agnes.org. Web: www.st-agnes.org. Sr. Jane Meyer, O.P., Prin. Tel: 713-219-5400; Fax: 713-219-5499. Dominican Sisters 2; Lay Teachers 51; Girls 785.

Duchesne Academy of the Sacred Heart, 10202 Memorial Dr., 77024-3299. Tel: 713-468-8211; Fax: 713-465-9809. Email: Jan_Dunn@duchesne.org. Web: www.duchesne.org. Sr. Jan Dunn, R.S.C.J., Headmistress. Religious of the Sacred Heart Sisters 4; Lay Teachers 83; Girls (Grades 9-12) 246; Total Enrollment (Grades PK-12) 651.

Incarnate Word Academy, 609 Crawford St., 77002-3668. Tel: 713-227-3637; Fax: 713-227-1014. Email: ssanchez@incarnateword.org. Web: www.incarnateword.org. Mrs. Susan Sanchez. Sisters of the Incarnate Word and Blessed Sacrament Sisters 3; Lay Teachers 20; Girls 237.

St. Pius X High School, Inc., 811 W. Donovan, 77091-5699. Tel: 713-692-3581; Fax: 713-692-5725. Email: pollardd@stpiusx.org. Web: www.stpiusx.org. Sr. Donna M. Pollard, O.P., Prin. Dominican Sisters 2; Lay Teachers 52; Students 689; Total Staff 54.

Pope John XXIII High School, Inc. School will re-open Aug. 2004 , 13707 Cottrell Ct., 7077. Tel: 281-558-5824; Fax: 281-558-5461. Email: theresa@swbell.net. Web: www.pj23.org. Ms. Theresa Bramanti, Contact Person. Teachers 1.

Strake, Jesuit College Preparatory Inc., 8900 Bellaire Blvd., 77036-4699. Tel: 713-774-7651; Fax: 713-774-6427. Email: webmaster@strakejesuit.org. Web: www.strakejesuit.org. Mr. Richard Nevle, Prin.; Revs. Christopher A. Billac, S.J.; A. Ferdinand Derrera, S.J.; John N. Folzenlogen, S.J.; Daniel K. Lahart, S.J., Pres.; Joseph B. Leininger, S.J.; Mark E. Thibodeaux; Bros. Castenzio A. Ferlita, S.J., Scholastics; A. Joseph Martin, S.J. Priests 6; Brothers 1; Scholastics 1; Lay Teachers 64; Boys 822.

St. Thomas High School, 4500 Memorial Dr., 77007-7332. Tel: 713-864-6348 (School); 713-868-9209 (Residence); Fax: 713-864-5750. Web: www.sths.org. Revs. Jack H. Hanna, C.S.B., Supr.; Carl L. Belisch, C.S.B.; William Vela, C.S.B.; Ronald G. Schwenzer, C.S.B.; Albert R. Gaelens, C.S.B.; Richard A. Wahl, C.S.B. Basilian Residence, Basilian Fathers Priests 5; Lay Teachers 57; Total Staff 85; Total Enrollment 643.

[G] ELEMENTARY SCHOOLS, PRIVATE

HOUSTON. *St. Catherine's Montessori*, 2510 Westridge, 77054-1508. Tel: 713-665-2195; Fax: 713-665-1478. Email: scms@io.com. Judy McCullough, Prin. Lay Teachers 11; Students 198; Total Staff 28.

Duchesne Academy of the Sacred Heart, 10101 Memorial Dr., 77024-3299. Tel: 713-468-8211; Fax: 713-465-9809. Email: Jan.Dunn@duchesne.org. Web: www.duchesne.org. Sr. Jan Dunn, R.S.C.J., Headmistress. Sisters 4; Lay Teachers 83; Total Teaching Staff 84; Girls 651.

John Paul II Catholic School, 1400 Parkway Plaza Dr., 77077-1503. Tel: 281-496-1500; Fax: 281-496-2943. Email: principal@jp2.org. Web: www.jp2.org. Debra Haney, Prin.; Janie Hengst, Asst. Prin.

Sisters 1; Lay Teachers 35; Students 631; Total Staff 61.

The Regis School, 7330 Westview Dr., 77055-5122. Tel: 713-682-8383; Fax: 713-682-8388. Email: ascarty@theregisschool.org. Web: www.theregisschool.org. Anne Storey Carty, Headmistress. Catholic School for Boys. Lay Teachers 31; Students 186; Total Staff 40.

[H] ELEMENTARY SCHOOLS, CONSOLIDATED

GALVESTON. *Galveston Catholic School*, 2601 Ursuline Ave., 77550-4398. Tel: 409-765-6607; Fax: 409-765-5154. Email: gcschol@flash.net. Mrs. Mary Frances Bernardoni, Prin. Sisters 1; Lay Teachers 25; Students 295; Total Staff 35.

GALVESTON//HOUSTON. *School of Environmental Education - Camp Kappe*, (Grades 5-5) Tel: 936-894-2141; Fax: 936-894-2198. Email: stalsee@aol.com. 7738 Camp Kappe Rd., Plantersville, 77363. Sr. Thomas Ann LaCour, O.P., Prin. Sisters 1; Lay Teachers 3; Total Staff 4; Total Enrollment 1,400.

RICHWOOD. *Our Lady Queen of Peace*, 1600 Hwy. 2004, 77531. Tel: 979-265-3909; Fax: 979-265-9780. Email: olqp@olqpschool.org. Web: www.olqpschool.org. Mrs. Deborah Kyle, Prin. Serving the parishes of Holy Trinity, Angleton; St. Jerome, Clute; St. Anthony, Danbury; St. Henry; St. Mary, Star of the Sea, Freeport; St. Michael, Lake Jackson; Our Lady of Perpetual Help, Sweeney; St. John the Apostle Mission, West Columbia; St. Joseph's, Brazoria, TX. Lay Teachers 25; Students 311.

[I] SOCIAL AGENCIES CATHOLIC CHARITIES

HOUSTON. *Catholic Charities of the Diocese of Galveston-Houston*, 2900 Louisiana St., P.O. Box 66508, 77266. Tel: 713-526-4611; Fax: 713-526-1546. Web: www.catholiccharities.org. Anna M. Babin, C.P.A., Pres. Total Assisted 38,871.

AIDS Ministry Tel: 713-526-4611; Fax: 713-526-1546.

Catholic Charities, Galveston County Center. Tel: 409-762-2143; Fax: 409-762-2088.

Guadalupe Center, Formerly Guadalupe Area Social Services Tel: 713-227-9981; Fax: 713-225-1242. (Family Assistance)

Children's and Family Services Tel: 713-526-4611; Fax: 713-526-1546. (Adoption and Foster Care)

Services to Pregnant and Parenting Adolescents Tel: 713-526-4611; Fax: 713-526-1546.

Post Adoption Services Tel: 713-526-4611; Fax: 713-526-1546.

Family Counseling Tel: 713-526-4611; Fax: 713-526-1546.

St. Frances Cabrini Center for Immigrant Legal Assistance, Formerly Texas Center for Immigrant Legal Assistance Tel: 713-526-4611; Fax: 713-526-1546.

Refugee Resettlement Program Tel: 713-526-4611; Fax: 713-526-1546.

St. Michael's Home for Children, Formerly Unaccompanied Juvenile Foster Care Program Tel: 713-526-4611; Fax: 713-526-1546.

Services to the Alone and Frail Elderly Tel: 713-526-4611; Fax: 713-526-1546.

Serenity House Tel: 713-526-4611; Fax: 713-526-1546.

Parish Social Ministry Tel: 713-526-4611; Fax: 713-526-1546.

Villa Guadalupe Tel: 713-227-4971; Fax: 713-225-1242. (Transitional Housing)

[J] HEALTH AND HOSPITALS

HOUSTON. *CHRISTUS Health Gulf Coast*, 1401 St. Joseph Pkwy., 77002. Tel: 713-756-5008; Fax: 713-657-7123. Email: rae.korczynski@christushealth.org. Web: www.christushealth.org. Rich Williams, Interim Pres. Total Staff 3,213; Total Assisted Annually 446,259; Bed Capacity 985.

CHRISTUS Medical Group, Formerly CHRISTUS Southwest Community Health Center

CHRISTUS Our Daily Bread, Formerly CHRISTUS Galveston Ministries Tel: 409-765-3971; Fax: 409-765-8547.

CHRISTUS New Horizons Tel: 409-765-1479; Fax: 409-763-5924.

CHRISTUS St. Joseph Hospital, 1401 St. Joseph Pkwy., 77002. Tel: 713-757-1000; Fax: 713-657-7123. Web: www.christushealth.org. Jeff Webster, Admin. Staff 2,200; Patients Assisted Annually 311,978; Bed Capacity 792.

KATY. *CHRISTUS St. Catherine Hospital*, 701 S. Fry Rd., 77450. Tel: 281-559-5700. Dan Brown, Admin. Bed Capacity 58; Patients Assisted Annually 50,254; Total Staff 434.

NASSAU BAY. *CHRISTUS St. John Hospital*, 18300 St. John Dr., 77058. Tel: 281-333-8898; Fax: 281-333-8891. Email: tom.permetti@christushealth.org. Web: www.christusstjohn.org. Tom Permetti, Admin. Bed Capacity 135; Patients Assisted Annually 150,000; Total Staff 712.

[K] CATHOLIC CHAPLAIN CORPS

HOUSTON. *The Catholic Chaplain Corps*, 4206 S. MacGregor Way, 77021-1598. Tel: 713-747-8445; Fax: 713-747-3642. Houston Hospitals: St. Luke's Episcopal Texas Heart Institute, Texas Children's Hospital, Methodist, M. D. Anderson Cancer Center - Hospital of University of Texas, Diagnostic, The Institute of Rehabilitation and Research, Ben Taub Hospital, Hermann Memorial Hospital, Diagnostic Center Hospital, Kindred Hospital.

Catholic Chaplain Corps, Texas Medical Center Tel: 713-526-6438; Fax: 713-747-3642. Revs. Rodolfo Cal-Ortiz; Saverio Murano, O.S.S.T; Joseph Bang-Doan; Elias E. Doroin; Bruce H. Noble; David H. Noble; Don A. Neumann; Donald E. Kuder, C.S.B.; Teodoro Tim Y. Prado; Patrick Cummings; Frederico J.G. Ablog, S.S.S.; Joshua R. Alvero, D.S.; Michael Barrosa, D.S.; John Ndubuisi; Page E. Polk, O.F.M.; Franklin E. Simmons; Luis Evardoni, D.S.; Sisters Beatrice Cruz, I.W.B.S.; Martha Christina Mejia, C.V.I.

Chaplain Corps, Memorial Southwest Center Complex, 10330 Hillcroft, 77096-4795. Tel: 713-776-5000; Fax: 713-776-5369. Rev. Michael Barrosa, D.S. Cell: 713-922-0700.

Chaplain Corps, Lyndon B. Johnson Hospital Tel: 713-566-5000 (24-hour paging); Fax: 713-747-3642. Rev. John Ndubuisi; Sr. Martha Christina Mejia, C.V.I.

Chaplain Corps Tel: 713-526-6438 (24 hour paging); Fax: 713-747-3642. Rev. Franklin Simmons. Memorial City/Spring Branch Medical Complexes: Memorial City Medical Center Hospital.

Chaplain Corps: John Sealy Medical Center, U.T.M.B. Hospital, 2011 Ave. F (Church St.), 77550-2091. Tel: 409-762-9612; Fax: 409-762-9612. Revs. Gerald Lewis, S.V.D.; Benignus "Bennie" Wego, S.V.D. (LAF).

[L] CLINICS

HOUSTON. *Holy Family Clinic*, 7539 Ave. K, 77012-1033. Tel: 713-926-8057; Fax: 713-923-6497. Email: hfclinic@msn.wm. Rev. William C. Davis, O.M.I., Contact Person.

San Jose Clinic, 301 Hamilton St., 77002. Tel: 713-228-9411; Fax: 713-228-6371. Email: staciecokinos@sanjoseclinic.org. Web: www.sanjoseclinic.org. Stacie Cokinos, Exec. Dir. Patients Assisted Annually 6,000; Lay Staff 30.

[M] PROTECTIVE INSTITUTIONS

HOUSTON. *Casa de Esperanza, De Los Ninos, Inc.*, Mailing Address: P.O. Box 66581, 77266-6581. Tel: 713-529-0639; Fax: 713-529-9179. Email: casa@casahope.org. Web: www.casahope.org. Kathleen Foster, Dir.; Mr. William Jones, Assoc. Dir. Homes for children in crisis situations, foster care, adoption. Sisters 5; Served 2,000; Total Assisted 200; Total Staff 40.

Casa Juan Diego, 4818 Rose, 77007 Tel: 713-869-7376; Fax: 713-864-7295. Email: info@cjd.org. Web: www.cjd.org. P.O. Box 70113, 77270. Mr. Mark Zwick, Dir. Houses 16; People Served Annually 21,000.

Casa Maria de Guadalupe Medical Clinic and Social Service Center, 6101 Edgemoor, 77081. Tel: 713-995-9414; Fax: 713-272-0510. Email: info@cjd.com. Web: www.cjd.org. (Catholic Worker) Patients Assisted Annually 17,500 Total Staff 10.

Covenant House Texas, 1111 Lovett Blvd., 77006. Tel: 713-523-2231; Fax: 713-523-6904. Email: rrobinson@covenanthouse.org. Web: www.covenanthousetx.org. Sr. Tricia Cruise, Pres.; Ronca G. Robinson, Exec. Dir. & CEO; Julian Solis, Pastoral Min. Total Assisted 5,114; Total Staff 97.

Magnificat Houses Inc., 3300 Caroline St., 77004. Tel: 713-520-0461; Fax: 713-520-0461. Email: magnificat@surfree.com. Web: www.magnificathouse.com. Rose Mary Badami, Contact Person.

Santa Maria Hostel, 807 Paschall St., 77009. Tel: 713-228-0125; Fax: 713-222-0595. Email: cempey@hotmail.com. Web: www.santamariahostel.org. Ms. Cheryl Empey, Exec. Dir. Intensive residential treatment and outpatient services (substance abuse) for women ages 18 and above. Residents 88; Patients Assisted Annually 800; Total Staff 60.

[N] HOMES FOR THE AGED

HOUSTON. *St. Dominic Village*, 2401 Holcombe Blvd., 77021-2099. Tel: 713-741-8701; Fax: 713-741-9811. Email: rstanley@stdominicvillage.org. Ruth Stanley, Dir.

Pope John Paul XXIII Priests' Residence, 2407 Holcombe Blvd., 77021-2023. Tel: 713-748-4608. Revs. Gabre-Tinsaye Adhana (Retired). Tel: 713-748-4425; Ronald J. Anton, S.J. (BAL) (Retired). Tel: 713-748-1553; Rev. Msgr. Leroy H. Braden (Retired). Tel: 713-440-7540; Rev. Peter Chu (Retired). Tel: 713-747-8774; Rev. Msgr. Thomas A. Donovan (Retired). Tel: 713-741-9471; Revs. Lawrence Lee (Retired). Tel: 713-741-7267; James J. Madden (Retired). Tel: 713-748-1761; Joseph T. O'Malley (Retired). Tel: 713-842-2728 (Maloney Hall); George V. Rhein (Retired). Tel: 713-747-7308; Armando J Rodriguez (Retired). Tel: 713-842-2053; Charles K. Schoeppe (Retired). Tel: 713-748-4596; Alcuin E. Greenburg. Tel: 713-748-8852; Felician del Val, (Maloney Hall). Total Residents 15; Total Staff 2.

St. Dominic Nursing Home, 2409 Holcombe Blvd., 7721--023. Tel: 713-741-8701; Fax: 713-741-9811. Ruth Stanley, Admin. Aged Residents 300; Total Staff 140.

St. Dominic Residence Hall, 2401 Holcombe Blvd., 77021-2023. Tel: 713-741-8700; Fax: 713-748-8305. Ruth Stanley, Admin. Total Residents 150; Total Staff 35.

[O] RESIDENTIAL TREATMENT AND RENEWAL CENTERS

SPLENDORA. *Shalom Center, Inc.*, 13516 Morgan Dr., 77372-3121. Tel: 281-399-0520; Fax: 281-399-3366. Email: sca@shalomcenterinc.org. Web: www.shalomcenterinc.org. Sr. Gina Marie Iadanza, M.S.C., Exec. Dir. A residential treatment center for priests, brothers and sisters.

[P] PERSONAL PRELATURES

HOUSTON. *Opus Dei* Prelature of the Holy Cross and Opus Dei , 5505 Chaucer Dr., 77005-2631. Tel: 713-528-4081; Fax: 713-523-6829. Web: www.opusdei.org. Very Rev. Gerald Kolf, Vicar of the delegation of Texas; Revs. Jack Solarski; Michael Barrett.

[Q] MONASTERIES AND RESIDENCES OF PRIESTS AND BROTHERS

HOUSTON. *Carmelite Priory*, Casa Santa Teresita, 6725 Reed Rd., 77087-6830. Tel: 713-644-8400; Fax: 713-649-6955. Email: casa@carmelnet.org. Revs. Gregory Houck, O.Carm., Dir. & Prior; Bernard Lickteig, O.Carm.; Deacon Eric Bell, O.Carm. Prenovitiate house for students in the Most Pure Heart Province of the Carmelite Order (O.Carm.). Students 5; Total in Residence 8; Total Staff 1.

Companions of the Cross (Texas), 1949 Cullen Blvd., P.O. Box 230287, 77023-5395. Tel: 713-236-9977; Fax: 713-236-0073. Email: compcros@cyberus.ca. Web: www.companionscross.ca. Rev. Francis A. Frankovich, Dir.

Congregation of the Passion, Holy Name Retreat Center, 430 Bunker Hill Rd., 77024-6399. Tel: 713-464-4932; Fax: 713-932-7303. Email: steinmillerusa@juno.com. Very Rev. Alexander Steinmiller, C.P., Local Supr.; Revs. Peter Berendt, C.P., Retreat Dir.; Simon Herbers, C.P.; Cedric Pisegna, C.P.; George Stanfield, C.P. (LA); Joseph Moons, C.P.

Dillon House, 1302 Kipling, 77006-4297. Tel: 713-529-3994; Fax: 713-942-7623. Revs. Donald E. Kuder, C.S.B., Supr.; Enrique Bravo, C.S.B.; Wilfred S. Canning, C.S.B. (Retired); Charles A. Christopher, C.S.B.; Joseph B. Courtney, C.S.B. (Retired); Hugh J. Curran; Gerald F. Dillon, C.S.B.; Thomas J. McReavy, C.S.B.; Robert G. Ritz, C.S.B.; Frederick H. Sohn; John C. Wick; John M. Wilson, C.S.B. (Retired). Basilian Fathers

Disciples of Hope (Texas), 15403 Palmway St., 77071. Tel: 713-721-2873; 713-721-2894; 713-721-2879; Fax: 713-721-2894. Email: diciplesofhope2000@yahoo.com. Web: www.geocities.com/disciplesofhope/. Revs. Julian Michael A. Barrosa, D.S., Community Supr.; Luis Paolo Agostino V. Evardoni, D.S., Procurator; Rodolfo Cal-Ortiz, Assoc. Member.

Dominican Friars, St. Mark Priory, Inc., 1702 Bolsover St., 77005-1726. Tel: 713-526-6411; Fax: 713-528-6795. Revs. Robert A. Bordenkircher, O.P.; Thomas A. Clifford, O.P., Subprior; Brian G. Donovan, O.P.; Richard Martin Patrick, O.P., Prior; Joseph Ngoc Tu Nguyen, O.P.; John J. Boll, O.P.; Anthony Hung Ngoc Tran, O.P.; James Fontenot, O.P.; Bro. John Cosgrove, O.P.

Marianist Community, 6409 Brookside Dr., 77023-3323. Tel: 713-926-5925. Email: wnvw88b@worldnet.att.net. Web: www.marianist.org/usa. Bro. James E. Barrette, S.M. Society of Mary

Marianist Community, P.O. Box 1408, Pinehurst, 77362-1408. Tel: 281-356-1740. Rev. Robert E. Hackel, S.M.; Bro. Fred A.R. Stovall, S.M. Tel: 281-356-6764, Ext. 13 (Work).

Maryknoll Fathers and Brothers, 2360 Rice Blvd., 77005-2652. Tel: 713-529-1912; Fax: 713-529-0372.

Email: mklhouston@maryknoll.org. Web: www.maryknoll.org. Revs. Gerald E. Kelly, M.M., Dir.; Edward R. Schoellmann, M.M.; Bro. Leo Shedy, M.M.
Priests Residing Elsewhere:
St. Mary Seminary, 9845 Memorial Dr., 77024-3498. Tel: 713-686-4345; Fax: 713-681-7550. Rev. Rafael R. Davila, M.M.
P.O. Box 9592, 77261. Tel: 713-921-2736. Rev. Richard E. Paulissen, M.M.
Residence of the Basilian Fathers of the University of St. Thomas, 4019 Yoakum Blvd., 77006-4833. Tel: 713-525-3515; Fax: 713-529-0844. Revs. Dennis M. Andrews, C.S.B., Supr.; Edward A. Bader, C.S.B.; Edward J. Baenziger, C.S.B.; Patrick O. Braden, C.S.B.; Victor B. Brezik, C.S.B.; Daniel D. Callam, C.S.B.; Robert W. Crooker, C.S.B.; Anthony E. Giampietro, C.S.B.; Michael T. Grey, C.S.Sp.; George H. Hosko, C.S.B.; Janusz Ihnatowicz (Poland); James J. Keon, C.S.B.; J. Michael Miller, C.S.B.; Harold V. O'Leary, C.S.B.; Joseph E. Pilsner, C.S.B.; Richard J. Schiefen, C.S.B.; T. Patrick Warden, C.S.B.; Walter M. Werbylo, C.S.B.; William J. Young, C.S.B.
Western Province of the Congregation of the Holy Ghost, 1700 West Alabama St., 77098-2808. Tel: 713-522-2882; Fax: 713-522-8063. Email: spiritans@aol.com. Web: www.spiritans.org. Very Rev. Michael T. White, C.S.Sp., Supr. Total in Residence 3.

BARRETT STATION. *Missionary Society of St. Paul, Inc. - U.S. Region*Rev. Paul N. Ofoha, M.S.P., Local Supr.

NEW CANEY. *Congregation of the Mother Coredemptrix*, 23404 Oak Shadows Pl., 77357-8516. Tel: 281-354-4764. Rev. Joseph Doan Huy Chuong. Total in Residence 1.

SPRING. *The Society of the Oblates of Sacred Heart*, 2601 Spring Stuebner Rd., 77389-4824. Tel: 281-353-9774; Fax: 281-353-9786. Email: frkuzhuppillil@yahoo.com. Web: www.askcongregation.org. Revs. Matthai K. Thomman, O.S.H., Supr.; Sunny Joseph Plammoottil, O.S.H.; Kurian Stephen Choozhukunnel, O.S.H.

SUGAR LAND. *Basilian Mission Center*, 414 Main St., P.O. Box 708, 77487-0708. Tel: 218-242-3148; Fax: 281-242-3149. Email: basmissions@earthlink.net. Web: www.basilianfathersmissions.org. Revs. John R. Whitley, C.S.B., Mission Procurator, Treas.; Robert J. Klem, C.S.B.; Joseph P. Shannon, C.S.B.; Roy J. Oggero, C.S.B., Supr. Associates 5; Scholastics 4; Novices 6.
Priests Serving in Foreign Missions: Revs. Francis A. Amico, C.S.B.; Ernesto Arriaga, C.S.B.; Robert J. Barringer, C.S.B.; John L. Boscoe, C.S.B.; Jose D. Delgado, C.S.B.; Thomas P. Dugan, C.S.B.; Rene J. Espejel, C.S.B.; Alberto A. Ferrara, C.S.B.; William J. Frankenberger, C.S.B.; Jose Herrera, O.S.B.; Rafael I. Lopera, C.S.B.; Francisco S. Mauricio, C.S.B.; Pedro M. Mora, C.S.B.; Francois J. Morfin, C.S.B.; Bernard C. Owens, C.S.B.; Roberto P. Rojas, C.S.B.; Alejandro Romero, C.S.B.; Robert J. Seguin, C.S.B.; Thomas W. Sepulveda, C.S.B.; J. Vincent Thompson, C.S.B.; Clarence E. Watrin, C.S.B.

[R] CONVENTS AND RESIDENCES FOR SISTERS

HOUSTON. *Carmelite Sisters of the Sacred Heart (C.S.H.)*, 22 Farrell, 77022. Tel: 713-697-6020; Fax: 713-697-6020. Email: Carmelitas20@hotmail.com. Sr. Antonia Albarran, Supr. Total Staff 3.
Casa Providencia, 3907 Rotman, 77003. Tel: 713-227-2555; Fax: 713-923-5866.
Congregation of Divine Providence (C.D.P.), 2008 Southgate, 77030-2126. Tel: 713-659-5461; Fax: 713-759-9151. Email: Karstedt@diogh.org. Web: www.diogh.org. Sisters 4.
1111 Blalock #61, 77055. Tel: 713-621-4370. Email: fklinger@ev1.net.
Congregation of the Incarnate Word & Blessed Sacrament (C.V.I.) (Houston), Incarnate Word Convent, 3400 Bradford Pl., 77025-1398. Tel: 713-668-0423; Fax: 713-668-1857. Email: lbeck@incarnateword.org. Web: www.incarnateword.org. Sisters 37.
Casa Pacis Convent, 3428 Bradford Pl., 77025. Tel: 713-661-3785. Sisters 2.
Incarnate Word Academy, 609 Crawford St., 77002. Tel: 713-227-3637; Fax: 713-227-1014. Email: ssanchez@incarnateword.org. Web: www.incarnate-word.org.
St. Christopher Convent, 8711 Glen Loch, 77061. Tel: 713-649-4700. Sisters 2.
Visitation Convent, 3418A Bradford Pl., 77025-1398. Tel: 713-664-8370. Sisters 4.
Our Lady of Lourdes Convent, 10114 Hwy 6, Hitchcock, 77563. Tel: 409-925-7237. Sisters 3.
Sacred Heart Convent, 615 McDade, Conroe, 77301. Tel: 936-756-3051. Sisters 2.
St. Joseph Convent, 1811 Carolina, Baytown, 77520. Tel: 281-422-7700. Sisters 3.
St. Michael Convent, 5515 W. 43rd, 77092. Tel: 713-682-2242. Sisters 1.
Congregation of the Sisters of Charity of the Incarnate Word (C.C.V.I.), 6510 Lawndale, P.O. Box 230969, 77223-0969. Tel: 713-928-6053; Fax: 713-928-8148. Email: obordelon@ccvi-vdm.org. Web: www.sistersofcharity.org. Total Sisters in Congregation (professed sisters) 184.
St. Jeanne Convent Tel: 713-928-6053; Fax: 713-928-8148. Sisters 2.
Marian Convent Tel: 713-928-8148; Fax: 713-928-8148. Sisters 23.
St. Anne Convent Tel: 713-928-6053; Fax: 713-921-1070. Sisters 12.
Ruah Community Tel: 713-928-6053; Fax: 713-928-9962. Sisters 2.
Villa de Matel, 6510 Lawndale Ave., 77023. Tel: 713-928-6053; Fax: 713-928-8148. Sisters 9.
St. Placidus Convent, 1500 S. Wayside Dr., P.O. Box 230969, 77223-0969. Tel: 713-928-6053; Fax: 713-928-8148. Sisters 27.
Edith Stein Convent, 6405 Pinehurst, 77023. Tel: 713-926-6024; Fax: 713-926-6024. Sisters 2.
St. John Convent, 1623 Antigua Ln., 77058. Tel: 713-333-9363; Fax: 281-333-2489. Sisters 2.
St. Mary's Convent, 4400 Ave. N., 77550. Tel: 409-763-1971; Fax: 409-762-0599.
Incarnate Word Charitable Trust, 6510 Lawndale, P.O. Box 230969, 77223-0969. Tel: 713-928-6053; Fax: 713-926-3085. Sr. Elizabeth Ann Hayes, C.C.V.I., Chairperson.
Dominican Sisters of Houston, Motherhouse Complex & Administrative Offices: 6501 Almeda Rd., 77021-2095. Tel: 713-747-3310; Fax: 713-747-4707. Email: houstonop@domhou.org. Web: www.houstonop.org. Sr. Heloise Cruzat, O.P., Prioress.
Legal Title: *Dominican Sisters of Houston, Texas Inc. (O.P.)*, The Sacred Heart Convent Retirement Trust.; St. Agnes Academy, Inc.; St. Agnes Academy Foundation, Inc.; St. Pius X High School, Inc.; St. Pius X High School Foundation, Inc.; The Sacred Heart Convent Retirement Trust.
Dominican Sisters-Vietnamese (O.P.), Inc., Provincial House, 5250 Gasmer Dr., 77035. Tel: 713-723-8250; Fax: 713-723-8229. Sisters 53.
Vietnamese Dominican Sisters House of Study, 5250 Gasmer Dr., 77035. Tel: 713-723-8250; 713-723-8208; Fax: 713-723-8229.
Mary Immaculate Convent, 5900 Chippewa Blvd., 77086. Tel: 281-445-9574; Fax: 281-445-6716. Sisters 10.
Our Lady of the Rosary Convent (Novititate), 1602 Adams St., Missouri City, 77489. Tel: 281-403-9300; Fax: 281-403-9300. Sisters 16.
Incarnate Word Convent, 3400 Bradford Pl., 77025-1398. Tel: 713-668-0423; Fax: 713-668-1857. Email: lbeck@incarnateword.org. Web: www.incarnateword.org.
Maryknoll Sisters of St. Dominic (M.M.), 7490 Brompton, No. 265, 77025. Tel: 713-873-2480 (Office); 713-666-5245 (Home); Fax: 713-666-5245.
Missionary Carmelites of St. Teresa (C.M.S.T.), Holy Family Provincial House, 9548 Deer Trail Dr., 77038. Tel: 281-445-5520; Fax: 281-445-5748. Email: martimm22@yahoo.com. Sisters 4.
Divine Providence Convent, 9600 Deer Trail Dr., 77038. Tel: 281-847-3328; Fax: 281-445-5748. Sisters 2.
Mt. Carmel House of Prayer 9600 Deer Trail Dr., 77038. Tel: 281-445-8830; Fax: 281-260-0460. Sisters 11.
St. Therese Novitiate, 9608 Deer Trail Dr., 77038. Tel: 281-820-3732; Fax: 281-445-5748. Sisters 6.
Missionary Catechists of the Sacred Hearts of Jesus and Mary (M.C.S.H.J.M.) Tel: 281-232-5500. Sisters 3.
Our Lady of Guadalupe Convent, 502 Carlisle St., Rosenberg, 77471. Tel: 281-232-5500; Fax: 281-342-4008. Sisters 3.
Missionary Sisters of the Immaculate Conception (S.M.I.C.), 6414 Ludington Dr., 77035-3919. Tel: 713-729-6971. Email: angmenta@hal-pc.org.
Our Lady of the Cenacle (R.C.), Cenacle Retreat House, 420 N. Kirkwood, 77079. Tel: 281-497-3131; Fax: 281-497-7632. Email: cenacle.retreat@pdq.net. Web: www.cenacleretreathouse.org. Sisters 7.
Religious of the Sacred Heart (R.S.C.J.), Duchesne Community, 10204 Memorial Dr., 77024. Tel: 713-467-5312; Fax: 713-465-9809. Email: acaire@rscj.org. Web: www.rscj.org. Sisters 10.
2020 Harvard St., 77008. Tel: 713-868-9607. Sisters 11.
Sisters for Christian Community (S.F.C.C.) Tel: 936-756-8288; Fax: 936-756-8105.
SFCC Community, 109 N. Frazier, Conroe, 77301. Tel: 409-756-3051; Fax: 409-756-8105.
Sacred Heart Convent, 105 N. Frazier St., Conroe, 77301. Tel: 936-756-8288; Fax: 936-756-8105.
3709 Lilia St., 77026. Tel: 713-674-7342; Fax: 281-356-7818.
Sisters of Providence of St. Mary of the Woods (Indiana) (S.P.), 4727 Oakshire, No. 2, 77027. Tel: 713-850-1687; Fax: 713-745-0349. Email: apotts@mda.org. Web: www.spsmw.org.
Sisters of the Holy Family (S.S.F.), Our Mother of Mercy Convent, 2000 Benson St., 77020. Tel: 713-674-6560; Fax: 713-674-3696. Email: Mercy2000@aol.com. Sisters 3.
Sisters of the Holy Spirit and Mary Immaculate (S.H.Sp.), St. Charles Borromeo Convent, 9601 McGallon, 77076-5122. Tel: 713-694-4264 (Convent); 713-692-4898 (School); Fax: 713-692-1376. Sr. Veronica Cahill, S.H.Sp., Gen. Supr. Tel: 210-533-5149; 210-533-5522; Fax: 210-533-3434.
Sisters of the Sacred Heart (S.S.C.J.), Holy Name Convent, 1217 Hogan, 77009-8642. Tel: 713-225-2309; Fax: 713-227-0224. Email: josiebv@juno.com.

MISSOURI CITY. *Schoenstatt Sisters of Mary (I.S.S.M.)*, Holy Family Church, 1510 Fifth St., 77489. Tel: 281-499-6246, Ext. 339; Fax: 281-499-9680. Sr. M. Carmen Rodriguez, Coord., Social Min.

NEW CANEY. *Discalced Carmelite Nuns (O.C.D.) Carmel of the Holy Trinity*, 1100 Parthenon Pl., 77357-3276. Tel: 281-399-0270; Fax: 281-689-3615. Web: www.icansurf.com/ocdnewcaney. Sisters 9.

PEARLAND. *Handmaids of the Holy Child of Jesus*, 3614 Englewood Dr., 77584. Tel: 281-692-0098; Fax: 281-692-0049; 713-995-6706. Email: missiondev@handmaidsisters.org. Web: www.handmaidsisters.org. Sr. Felicia Agibi, H.H.C.J., Dir.

[S] RETREAT HOUSES

HOUSTON. *Cenacle Retreat House*, 420 N. Kirkwood, 77079. Tel: 281-497-3131; Fax: 281-497-7632. Email: ministry@cenacleretreathouse.org. Web: www.cenacleretreathouse.org. Sisters Dorothy Briscoe; Lois Dideon; Mary Dennison; Thressa Heard, Ministry Coord.; Lucille Kunz; Elizabeth Mozina; Margaret Byrne. Congregation of Our Lady of the Retreat in the Cenacle Sisters 7.
Holy Name Retreat Center, 430 Bunker Hill Rd., 77024-6399. Tel: 713-464-0211; Fax: 713-464-0671. Email: holynamerc@yahoo.com. Revs. Peter Berendt, C.P., Assoc.Dir.; Ronald Corl, C.P., Retreat Staff; Joseph Moons, C.P., Dir.; George Stanfield, C.P. (LA), Staff. Total in Residence 1; Total Staff 3.
Shalom House of Prayer, 6510 Lawndale Ave., P.O. Box 230969, 77223. Tel: 713-921-5305. Sr. Genevieve Marheineke, Hermit. Total in Residence 2.

DICKINSON. *Christian Renewal Center*, 1515 Hughes Rd., P.O. Box 699, 77539-0699. Tel: 281-337-1312 (Center); Fax: 281-337-2615. Email: crc1515@wt.net. Web: www.retreatcentercrc.org. Revs. Tom Ovalle, O.M.I. (SAT), Dir.; William Martin, O.M.I., Assoc. Dir. Total in Residence 4; Total Staff 17. In Res. Revs. Richard Beck, O.M.I.; Gerald Fogarty, O.M.I.

[T] NEWMAN CENTERS

GALVESTON. *Galveston Newman Center* 1402 Broadway, 77550-4938. Tel: 409-762-4202; Fax: 409-762-4233. Rev. Dennis Bosse (O.F.M), Dir. Texas A & M University at Galveston; University of Texas Medical Branch; Galveston College; College of the Mainland.

HOUSTON. *Catholic Newman Association at the University of Houston Central Campus* Catholic Center, 4805 Calhoun Rd., 77004. Tel: 713-748-2529; Fax: 713-748-8412. Email: catholic@uh.edu. Web: www.uh.edu/catholic.
Satellite Office, 203 AD Bruce Religion Center, 77204. Tel: 713-748-2529; Fax: 713-748-8412. Revs. John J. Boll, O.P., Campus Min. & Dir.; Lubna Nabi, Campus Min.; Dolores Perez, Sec.
Rice University/Texas Medical Center Schools; Catholic Student Center 1703 Bolsover Rd., 77005. Tel: 713-526-3809; Fax: 713-526-6010. Email: cathcen@rice.edu. Web: www.rice.edu/catholic. Rev. Michael T. Grey, C.S.Sp., Chap.; Sr. Antoinette "Kitty" Carter, O.P., Dir. Total Staff 3.
Texas Southern University Catholic Newman Hall 3535 Wheeler Ave., 77004. Tel: 713-747-9595; Fax: 713-747-3198. Email: tsunewmanhall@aol.com. Rev. Brian Okon, M.S.P. Total Staff 1.
University of St. Thomas Campus Ministry 3800 Montrose Blvd., 77006. Tel: 713-525-3589; Fax: 713-525-3524. Email: thompson@stthom.edu. Web: www.stthom.edu. Sr. Clare Hunter, F.S.E., Coord. of Campus Ministry; Rev. Daniel Callam, C.S.B., Chap.

HEMPSTEAD. *Prairie View A & M University Catholic Center* 1346 Wilkins St., 77445. Tel: 979-826-2275; Fax: 979-826-8057. Total Staff 1.

HUNTSVILLE. *Catholic Student Center, S.H.S.U.* 1310 17th St., 77340-4415. Tel: 936-291-2620; Fax: 936-291-2620. Email: org-cath@shsu.edu. Web: www.shsu-catholic.org. Joseph Magee, Ph.D., Dir. Total Assisted 350; Total Staff 3.

[U] MISCELLANEOUS

GALVESTON. *The Bishop's Palace,* 1402 Broadway, 77550. Tel: 409-762-2475; Fax: 409-762-1801. Rev. H. James Bartlett, S.M. (CIN), Exec. Dir.

HOUSTON. *Catholic Charismatic Center,* 1949 Cullen P.O. Box 230287, 77223-0287. Tel: 713-236-9977; Fax: 713-236-0073. Email: catholiccharismatic@earthlink.net. Web: www.cathoicharismatic.org. Revs. Francis A. Frankovich, Dir.; Ed Wade, Assoc. Dir.

Catholic Clerical Student Fund, 9845 Memorial, 77024. Tel: 713-686-4345, Ext. 273; 281-437-8188; Fax: 713-681-7550. Email: caroleupdyke@att.net. Most Rev. Joseph A. Fiorenza, Chm.; Carole Updyke, Pres. Higher learning for the priesthood.

The Catholic Endowment Foundation of Galveston-Houston, P.O. Box 907, 77001-0907. Tel: 713-963-8008. Harold Hidalgo, Pres.

Charity Guild of Catholic Women, 1203 Lovett Blvd., 77006. Tel: 713-529-0995; Fax: 713-529-9263.

Charity Guild of St. Joseph, P.O. Box 570728-319, 77257-0728. Tel: 713-965-0965.

CHRISTUS Health, 2600 N. Loop W., 77092. Tel: 713-680-4835; Fax: 713-812-6867. Email: margieconyers@christushealth.org. Web: www.christushealth.org. Thomas C. Royer, M.D., Pres. & CEO; Margaret Conyers, Corp. Sec.

CHRISTUS Health Liability Retention Trust
CHRISTUS Health Cash Balance Plan Trust
CHRISTUS Health Matched Savings Plan
CHRISTUS Tax-Deferred Annuity Plans
CHRISTUS Health Rabbi Trust
CHRISTUS Health Employee Benefits Trust

St. Dominic Center, Inc., 2401 E. Holcombe, 77021. Tel: 713-741-8743; Fax: 713-741-8705. Email: wknight@diogh.org. Wayne Knight, Facility Admin.

Equestrian Order of the Holy Sepulchre of Jerusalem, 309 Knipp Rd., 77024. Tel: 713-468-5602; Fax: 713-468-1218. Email: theokendall@earthlink.net. Mr. F. Russell Kendall, Knight of the Collar, Vice Gov. Gen. of Honor; Mr. Michael Earthman, Lt.

Southwestern Lieutenancy, Equestrian Order of the Holy Sepulchre of Jerusalem, 2240 Chilton Rd., 77019-1402. Tel: 713-523-5442; Fax: 713-523-5442.

St. Francis de Sales School Foundation, 8100 Roos, 77036. Tel: 713-774-4447; Fax: 713-271-6744. Email: webmaster@st-francis-de-sales.org. Web: www.st-francis-de-sales.org.

Jesuit Volunteer Corps: South, P.O. Box 3126, 77253-3126. Tel: 713-756-5095; Fax: 713-756-8928. Email: jvcsouth@jesuitvolunteers.org. Web: www.jesuitvolunteers.org. Ms. Pam Krinock, Dir. Volunteer service organizations.

Kolbe Project, Inc., 1030 Heights Blvd. 77008-6914. Tel: 713-861-1800; Fax: 713-861-7212. Email: info@kolbeproject.org. Web: www.kolbeproject.org. P.O. Box 7765, 77270-7765. Tel: 713-861-1800; Fax: 713-861-7212.

Martha's Kitchen Food Services, 322 S. Jensen Dr., 77003. Tel: 713-224-2522; Fax: 713-224-7814. 2302 Oak Shores Dr., Kingwood, 77339. Rev. Msgr. Chester L. Borski, S.T.L. Sisters 2.

St. Mary's Children's Relief Fund, Chancery Bldg., 1700 San Jacinto, P.O. Box 907, 77001-0907. Tel: 713-659-5461; Fax: 713-759-9151 Most Rev. Joseph A. Fiorenza, Pres.

St. Pius X High School Foundation, Inc., 811 W. Donovan, 77091-5699. Tel: 713-692-3581; Fax: 713-692-5725. Email: pollardd@stpiusx.org. Web: www.stpiusx.org. Harold Hidalgo, Pres.

Sacred Military Constantinian Order of Saint George, American Delegation, P.O. Box 56328, 77256-6328. Tel: 713-888-0242; Fax: 713-888-0345. Email: dlgarrison@houston.r.com. Web: www.realcasadiborbone.it. Mr. David Garrison, Delegate.

Sociedad San Martin de Porres, P.O. Box 7788, 77270-7788. Tel: 713-869-0999. Email: ccampbell@abhllp.com.

Southern Dominican Volunteer Program
Corporate Office:
6501 Almeda Rd., 77021-2095. Tel: 713-747-3310; Fax: 713-747-4707.

The Society of the Holy Spirit, 4410 Yoakum Rd., 77006. Tel: 713-529-0405. Email: nesti@ssthom.edu. Rev. Donald S. Nesti, C.S.Sp., Contact Person.

SEALY. *Asociacion Nacional de Sacerdotes Hispanos,* P.O. Box 337, 77474. Tel: 979-885-3868; Fax: 979-885-2246. Email: info@ansh.org Web: www.ansh.org. Revs. Octavio Muguerza; Enrique J. Sera (CRG).

RELIGIOUS INSTITUTES OF MEN REPRESENTED IN THE DIOCESE

For further details refer to the corresponding bracketed number in the Religious Institutes of Men or Women section.

[0140]—*The Augustinians*—O.S.A.
[0170]—*Basilian Fathers* (Toronto, Canada)—C.S.B.
[0470]—*The Capuchin Friars*—O.F.M.Cap.
[0270]—*Carmelite Fathers & Brothers* (Prov. of Most Pure Heart of Mary)—O.Carm.
[0275]—*Carmelites of Mary Immaculate*—C.M.I.
[0360]—*Claretian Missionaries*—C.M.F.
[0220]—*Congregation of the Blessed Sacrament*—S.S.S.
[1330]—*Congregation of the Mission* (Southern Prov.)—C.M.
[]—*Congregation of the Mother Coredemptrix*—C.M.C.
[1000]—*Congregation of the Passion* (Chicago)—C.P.
[1130]—*Congregation of the Priests of the Sacred Heart*—S.C.J.
[0520]—*Franciscan Friars*—O.F.M.
[0650]—*Holy Ghost Fathers* (Western Prov.)—C.S.Sp.
[0690]—*Jesuit Fathers and Brothers* (New Orleans Prov.)—S.J.
[0800]—*Maryknoll*—M.M.
[0720]—*The Missionaries of Our Lady of La Salette* (Prov. of Mary Queen)—M.S.
[]—*Missionaries of St. Joseph* (Mexico)—M.J.
[]—*Missionaries of St. Paul*—M.S.P.
[1110]—*Missionaries of the Sacred Heart*—M.S.C.
[0910]—*Oblates of Mary Immaculate*—O.M.I.
[0920]—*Oblates of St. Francis de Sales*—O.S.F.S.
[0430]—*Order of Preachers-Dominicans* (Prov. of St. Albert the Great)—O.P.
[1070]—*Redemptorist Fathers* (New Orleans Vice Prov.)—C.SS.R.
[]—*Scalabrinians*—C.S.
[1260]—*Society of Christ*—S.Ch.
[0975]—*Society of Our Lady of the Most Holy Trinity*—S.O.L.T.
[0420]—*Society of the Divine Word*—S.V.D.
[]—*Society of the Precious Blood Sanguinist Fathers*—C.PP.S.
[1250]—*Somascan Fathers*—C.R.S.
[0700]—*St. Joseph's Society of the Sacred Heart* (Baltimore, MD)—S.S.J.

RELIGIOUS INSTITUTES OF WOMEN REPRESENTED IN THE DIOCESE

[0230]—*Benedictine Sisters of the Sacred Heart*—O.S.B.
[0390]—*Carmelite Missionaries of St. Teresa*—C.M.S.T.
[]—*Carmelite Sisters of the Sacred Heart*—C.S.C.
[]—*Comunidad Apostolica de Maria Siempre Virgen*—C.A.M.S.V.
[1010]—*Congregation of Divine Providence*—C.D.P.
[3110]—*Congregation of Our Lady of the Retreat in the Cenacle*—R.C.
[3830-08]—*Congregation of St. Joseph* (Cleveland, OH)—C.S.J.
[3830-01]—*Congregation of St. Joseph* (Boston, MA)—C.S.J.
[]—*Congregation of the Lovers of the Cross* (N. Vietnam)—H.C.L.
[]—*Daughters of Divine Love* (Nigeria)—D.D.L.
[0420]—*Discalced Carmelite Nuns*—O.C.D.
[1070-13]—*Dominican Sisters* (Adrian, MI)—O.P.
[1070-21]—*Dominican Sisters* (Edmonds, WA)—O.P.
[1070-19]—*Dominican Sisters, Congregation of the Sacred Heart* (Houston)—O.P.
[]—*Eucharistic Missionaries of St. Theresa* (Mexico)—M.E.S.T.
[]—*Handmaids of the Holy Child Jesus* (Nigeria)—H.H.C.J.
[]—*Handmaids of the Sacred Heart* (N. Korea)—H.S.H.
[2410]—*Marianites of the Holy Cross*—M.S.C.
[2470]—*Maryknoll Sisters of St. Dominic*—M.M.
[2690]—*Missionary Catechists of Divine Providence*—M.C.D.P.
[2700]—*Missionary Catechists of the Sacred Hearts of Jesus and Mary*—M.C.SS.CC.
[2760]—*Missionary Sisters of the Immaculate Conception*—S.M.I.C.
[2860]—*Missionary Sisters of the Sacred Heart*—M.S.C.
[1145]—*The Religious Missionaries of St. Dominic, Inc.*—O.P.
[4070]—*Religious of the Sacred Heart*—R.S.C.J.
[4110]—*Roman Union of the Order of St. Ursula*—O.S.U.
[]—*Schoenstatt Sisters of Mary*—I.S.S.M.
[2970]—*School Sisters of Notre Dame*—S.S.N.D.
[]—*Sisters for Christian Community*—S.F.C.C.
[0440]—*Sisters of Charity* (Cincinnati, OH)—S.C.
[0590]—*Sisters of Charity of St. Elizabeth* (Northern Prov.)—S.C.
[0470]—*Sisters of Charity of the Incarnate Word* (Houston)—C.C.V.I.
[0460]—*Sisters of Charity of the Incarnate Word* (San Antonio)—C.C.V.I.
[3360]—*Sisters of Providence* (St. Mary of the Woods, IN)—S.P.
[]—*Sisters of St. Francis of the Providence of God* (Whitehall, PA)—O.S.F.
[]—*Sisters of St. Joseph* (Boston)—C.S.J.
[3830-08]—*Sisters of St. Joseph* (Cleveland, OH)—C.S.J.
[3950]—*Sisters of St. Mary of Namur*—S.S.M.N.
[1950]—*Sisters of the Holy Family*—S.S.F.
[2050]—*Sisters of the Holy Spirit and Mary Immaculate*—S.H.Sp.
[2150]—*Sisters of the Immaculate Heart of Mary*—I.H.M.
[2190]—*Sisters of the Incarnate Word and Blessed Sacrament* (Houston)—C.V.I.
[2200]—*Sisters of the Incarnate Word and Blessed Sacrament* (Corpus Christi)—I.W.B.S.
[2205]—*Sisters of the Incarnate Word and Blessed Sacrament* (Victoria)—I.W.B.S.
[3310]—*Sisters of the Presentation of Mary*—P.M.
[3670]—*Sisters of the Sacred Heart of Jesus*—S.S.C.J.
[]—*Vietnamese Dominican Sisters*—O.P.

DIOCESAN CEMETERIES

GALVESTON. *Old Catholic, Calvary*
HOUSTON. *Holy Cross*
St. Vincent
DICKINSON. *Mount Olivet*

NECROLOGY

† Alleman, Rev. Msgr. C. J., (Retired)—Died July 10, 2003
† Lagana, Rev. Msgr. Frank A. (Retired), Houston, TX Vice Pres., St. Mary's Children's Relief Fund—Died Oct. 20, 2003
† Quinters, Rev. Msgr. Elmer T., (Retired)—Died Aug. 26, 2003
† Burns, David E., (Retired)—Died May 11, 2003
† del Val, Feliciano, (Retired)—Died Aug. 30, 2003
† Sheltz, Anton R., Houston, TX St. Dominic—Died May 9, 2003

Diocese of Gary

(Dioecesis Gariensis)

Most Reverend

DALE J. MELCZEK, D.D.

Bishop of Gary; ordained June 6, 1964; appointed Auxiliary Bishop of Detroit and Titular Bishop of Trau December 3, 1982; consecrated January 27, 1983; appointed Apostolic Administrator of Gary August 19, 1992; appointed Coadjutor Bishop of Gary October 20, 1995; succeeded to the See of Gary June 1, 1996 *Office: 9292 Broadway, Merrillville, IN 46410.* Tel: 219-769-9292; Fax: 219-769-2066.

Chancery: 9292 Broadway, Merrillville, IN 46410. Tel: 219-769-9292; Fax: 219-738-9034.

Web: www.dcgary.org

ESTABLISHED DECEMBER 17, 1956.

Square Miles 1,807.

Comprises the Counties of Lake, LaPorte, Porter and Starke in the State of Indiana.

Legal Title: For legal titles of parishes and diocesan institutions, consult the Chancery.

STATISTICAL OVERVIEW

Personnel	
Bishop	1
Priests: Diocesan Active in Diocese	73
Priests: Diocesan Active Outside Diocese	8
Priests: Diocesan in Foreign Missions	1
Priests: Retired, Sick or Absent	31
Number of Diocesan Priests	113
Religious Priests in Diocese	43
Total Priests in Diocese	156
Extern Priests in Diocese	8
Ordinations:	
Transitional Deacons	1
Permanent Deacons	9
Permanent Deacons in Diocese	50
Total Brothers	9
Total Sisters	100
Parishes	
Parishes	73
With Resident Pastor:	
Resident Diocesan Priests	60
Resident Religious Priests	4
Without Resident Pastor:	
Administered by Priests	9
Missions	4
Pastoral Centers	6
Closed Parishes	1
Professional Ministry Personnel:	
Brothers	1
Sisters	4
Lay Ministers	69
Welfare	
Catholic Hospitals	6
Total Assisted	1,024,720
Homes for the Aged	3
Total Assisted	462
Residential Care of Children	3
Total Assisted	78
Day Care Centers	2
Total Assisted	500
Specialized Homes	1
Total Assisted	700
Special Centers for Social Services	7
Total Assisted	10,000
Educational	
Diocesan Students in Other Seminaries	11
Seminaries, Religious	1
Students Religious	7
Total Seminarians	18
Colleges and Universities	1
Total Students	1,230
High Schools, Diocesan and Parish	1
Total Students	1,413
Elementary Schools, Diocesan and Parish	24
Total Students	6,562
Catechesis/Religious Education:	
High School Students	500
Elementary Students	9,650
Total Students under Catholic Instruction	19,373
Teachers in the Diocese:	
Priests	2
Sisters	7
Lay Teachers	442
Vital Statistics	
Receptions into the Church:	
Infant Baptism Totals	2,174
Adult Baptism Totals	127
Received into Full Communion	228
First Communions	2,154
Confirmations	1,932
Marriages:	
Catholic	467
Interfaith	202
Total Marriages	669
Deaths	1,742
Total Catholic Population	185,700
Total Population	770,635

Former Bishops—Most Revs. ANDREW GREGORY GRUTKA, D.D. (Retired), ord. Dec. 5, 1933; appt. Bishop of Gary Dec. 29, 1956; consecrated February 25, 1957; retired July 9, 1984; died Nov. 11, 1993; NORBERT F. GAUGHAN, D.D., Ph.D. (Retired), ord. Nov. 4, 1945; appt. Auxiliary Bishop of Greensburg April 2, 1975; consecrated June 26, 1975; appt. Bishop of Gary July 9, 1984; retired June 1, 1996; died Oct. 1, 1999.

Vicar General—Rev. STANLEY J. DOMINIK.

Deans—Revs. DOMINIC V. BERTINO, Gary-Hobart Deanery; STANLEY J. DOMINIK, North Lake County Deanery; DENNIS J. TELES, South Lake County Deanery; GERALD H. SCHWEITZER, Porter-Starke County Deanery; THEODORE A. NORDQUIST, LaPorte County Deanery.

Chancery—9292 Broadway, Merrillville, 46410. Tel: 219-769-9292; Fax: 219-738-9034.

Administrative Assistant to the Bishop—Rev. JON J. PLAVCAN.

Bishop's Delegate for Sexual Misconduct Matters—KENNETH M. FLANAGAN, M.S.W., Ph.D.

Director of Finance and Administration—KARL P. DYTRYCH.

Executive Secretary to the Bishop—VALERIE D. MCMANUS. Tel: 219-769-9181; Fax: 219-769-2066.

Diocesan Tribunal—9292 Broadway, Merrillville, 46410. Tel: 219-769-9292.

Judicial Vicar—Rev. MICHAEL L. MAGINOT, S.T.L., J.C.L.

Judges—Revs. MATTHEW C. IWUJI, J.U.D.; JAMES W. MEADE, J.D., S.T.L., J.C.L.

Second Instance—Rev. Msgrs. EDWARD F. LITOT (Retired); VINCENT L. LENGERICH (Retired); Rev. LOURDU PASALA.

Defender of the Bond—EVELYN OVALLES, S.P., J.C.L.

Auditors—Rev. BRIAN D. CHADWICK; Deacon SHERMAN BROWN; DONNA V. CALLAWAY; LINDA A. PLANER.

Notaries—VALERIE MCMANUS; MARY ANN O'CONNELL; JEAN DAVID.

Bishop's Council of Priests—Revs. ROBERT P. GEHRING; DOMINIC V. BERTINO; DAVID H. GOSNELL; KEVIN P. MCCARTHY; BRIAN D. CHADWICK; STANLEY J. DOMINIK; DERRICK F. DUDASH; EDWARD J. KENNEDY; THEODORE A. NORDQUIST; FRANCIS M. LAZAR; RICHARD A. ORLINSKI; JON J. PLAVCAN; GERALD H. SCHWEITZER; JOHN V. SCOTT; DENNIS J. TELES; GARY SCHERER, C.PP.S.; MICHAEL J. YADRON.

Consultors—Revs. GERALD H. SCHWEITZER; DOMINIC V. BERTINO; STANLEY J. DOMINIK; DENNIS J. TELES; THEODORE A. NORDQUIST; JON J. PLAVCAN.

Priests' Personnel Board—Revs. GERALD H. SCHWEITZER; DENNIS J. TELES; JOSEPH E. VAMOS; STANLEY J. DOMINIK; DOMINIC V. BERTINO; JON J. PLAVCAN; THEODORE J. MENS; ROY T. BEECHING; THEODORE A. NORDQUIST; KEVIN R. HUBER.

Diocesan Offices and Directors

African American Catholic Ministry—PEARLETTE SPRINGER, Dir., 9292 Broadway, Merrillville, 46410. Tel: 219-769-9292; Fax: 219-738-9034.

Blue Army—Rev. WALTER M. CIESLA, Chap., P.O. Box 3036, Munster, 46321. Tel: 219-836-8779.

Boy Scouts Liaison—Rev. ROBERT T. NAGLICH, S.C.J., Chap.; SUSAN BARRIBALL, Chm., 919 Foxpoint Dr., Chesterton, 46304. Tel: 219-926-3028.

Catholic Campaign for Human Development—Rev. THOMAS M. GANNON, S.J., 7128 Arizona Ave., Hammond, 46323. Tel: 219-844-7515; Fax: 219-844-7566.

Campus Ministry— St. Teresa of Avila Catholic Student Center (Valparaiso University) Rev. KEVIN P. MCCARTHY, Chap., 1511 LaPorte St., Valparaiso, 46383. Tel: 219-464-4042.

Catholic Relief Services— Operation Rice Bowl, annual Lenten collection, and disaster relief collections. KENNETH FLANAGAN, M.S.W., Ph.D., 973 W. Sixth Ave., Gary, 46402. Tel: 219-882-2720; Fax: 219-886-2428.

Global Solidarity Partnership Program—Rev. THOMAS M. GANNON, S.J., 7128 Arizona Ave., Hammond, 46323. Tel: 219-844-7515; Fax: 219-844-7566.

Catholic Services Appeal—JOYCE ILLYES, 9292 Broadway, Merrillville, 46410. Tel: 219-769-9292; Fax: 219-738-9034.

Catholic Youth Organization (CYO) Office—PAUL WENGEL, 7725 Broadway, Ste. G, Merrillville, 46410. Tel: 219-736-8931; Fax: 219-736-9457.

Cemeteries—Rev. STANLEY J. DOMINIK, Dir., 1731 LaPorte Ave., Whiting, 46394. Tel: 219-659-0733; HENRY DRUX, 1547 167th St., Hammond, 46324. Tel: 219-844-9475.

Charismatic Apostolate—Rev. JOHN V. SCOTT, Dir., 406 E. Washington St., Knox, 46534. Tel: 219-772-4134; Deacon JOHN D. ROSCOE SR., 2402 Willowwood Ave., Valparaiso, 46383. Tel: 219-477-3616.

Charities—KENNETH M. FLANAGAN, M.S.W., Ph.D., Dir., 973 W. Sixth Ave., Gary, 46402. Tel: 219-882-2720; Fax: 219-886-2428.

Communications Office—BRIAN T. OLSZEWSKI, Dir., 9292 Broadway, Merrillville, 46410. Tel: 219-769-9292; Fax: 219-738-9034.

Council of Catholic Women—Rev. ROY T. BEECHING, Diocesan Moderator, 5304 Hohman Ave., Hammond, 46320. Tel: 219-932-0702.

Cursillos in Christianity—Revs. JUAN GONZALEZ, C.PP.S., Chap. (Spanish); EDWARD J. KENNEDY, (English), 11000 W. 133rd Ave., Cedar Lake, 46303. Tel: 219-374-7160.

Diaconate—Rev. MICHAEL J. YADRON, Deacon Formation Dir., 8501 Calumet Ave., Munster, 46321. Tel: 219-836-8610; Deacon JOSEPH CODESPOTI, Diaconate Dir. - Post Ordination, 5884 Roosevelt St., Merrillville, 46410. Tel: 219-980-3038.

Ecumenical Officer—Mr. MARK PLAISS, 4137 W. Andrea Dr., LaPorte, 46350. Tel: 219-324-6026.

Employee Benefits—KAREN WALSH, Coord., 9292 Broadway, Merrillville, 46410. Tel: 219-769-9292; Fax: 219-738-9034.

Family Life Ministry—973 W. Sixth Ave., Gary, 46402. Tel: 219-882-2720.

Finance Council—DENNIS BIELFELDT; CALVIN E. BELLAMY; T. CLIFFORD FLEMING; JOSEPH F. GLOTZBACH, C.P.A.; KARL DYTRYCH; FELICIA FLOWERS SMITH; Rev. JOSEPH M. PAWLOWSKI; DENISE CARRASQUILLO; JOSEPH ALVARADO.

Girl Scout Liaison—Rev. THEODORE A. NORDQUIST; JACKIE KRILICH, Chm., 10621 State Line Rd., Dyer, 46311. Tel: 219-365-5217.

Heartland Center—Revs. THOMAS M. GANNON, S.J.; JAMES DIXON, S.J., 7128 Arizona Ave., Hammond, 46323. Tel: 219-844-7515; Fax: 219-844-7566.

Holy Childhood Association— cf. Mission Office

Hispanic Diocesan Ministries—ADELINE TORRES, P.O. Box 3027, East Chicago, 46312. Tel: 219-397-2125; Fax: 219-397-2168.

Indiana Catholic Conference—Rev. JAMES DIXON, S.J., Diocesan Coord., 7128 Arizona Ave., Hammond, 46323. Tel: 219-844-7515; Fax: 219-844-7566.

Lay Ministry Formation Office—ANNE VERBEKE, Dir., 9292 Broadway, Merrillville, 46410. Tel: 219-769-9292; Fax: 219-738-9034.

Legal Counsel—ROBERT M. SCHWERD, 2637 45th St., Highland, 46322. Tel: 219-924-2427.

Marriage Dispensations—Rev. GERALD H. SCHWEITZER, P.O. Box 336, Wanatah, 46390. Tel: 219-733-2955.

Marriage Encounter—BRIAN OTTO; DEBBIE OTTO, 0674 E. 600 N., LaPorte, 46350. Tel: 219-778-4712.

Ministry to Hearing Impaired—Rev. JOHN J. ZEMELKO, Coord., 303 Keller Ave., North Judson, 46366. Tel: 219-896-2195.

Mission Office—Rev. JOSEPH E. VAMOS, Dir., 9292 Broadway Merrillville, 46410. Tel: 219-769-9292.

Newspaper—BRIAN T. OLSZEWSKI, Editor; CAROL MACINGA, Circulation Mgr., 9292 Broadway, Merrillville, 46410. Tel: 219-769-9292; Fax: 219-738-9034. "Northwest Indiana Catholic"

Parish Pastoral Councils—ANNE VERBEKE, Dir., 9292 Broadway, Merrillville, 46410. Tel: 219-769-9292; Fax: 219-738-9034.

Peace and Social Justice, Office of—Revs. THOMAS M. GANNON, S.J., Dir.; JAMES M. DIXON, S.J., 7128 Arizona Ave., Hammond, 46323. Tel: 219-844-7515; Fax: 219-844-7566.

Priestly Life—Rev. EDWARD J. KENNEDY, Dir., 11000 W. 133rd Ave., Cedar Lake, 46303. Tel: 219-374-7160.

Pro-Life Activities—Rev. THEODORE J. MENS, Dir., 525 N. Broad St., Griffith, 46319. Tel: 219-924-4163.

Propagation of the Faith and Holy Childhood Association— cf. Mission Office

Religious Education Office—FRANK J. ZOLVINSKI, Dir., 9292 Broadway, Merrillville, 46410. Tel: 219-769-9292; Fax: 219-738-9034.

Religious, Liaison for Women and Men—Sr. KAREN WALTHER, S.S.N.D., 5861 Van Buren St., Merrillville, 46410. Tel: 219-980-3478.

Retirement Plan of the Diocese of Gary, Indiana—JOSEPH F. GLOTZBACH, C.P.A., 9292 Broadway, Merrillville, 46410. Tel: 219-769-9292.

Rural Life Conference—Rev. JAMES M. DIXON, S.J., Dir., 7128 Arizona Ave., Hammond, 46323. Tel: 219-844-7515.

Safe Environment Program—KENNETH FLANAGAN, Ph.D., Bishop's Delegate for Sexual Misconduct Cases, 973 W. Sixth Ave., Gary, 46402. Tel: 219-882-2720.

Victim Assistance Coordinator—MARCELLA WALTERS, 6919 Indianapolis Blvd., Hammond, 46324. Tel: 219-844-4883.

Safe Environment Program—KIM PRYZBYLSKI, Ph.D., Coord., 9292 Broadway, Merrillville, 46410. Tel: 219-769-9292.

St. Vincent de Paul Society—STANLEY WROBEL, Pres., 7132 Arizona Ave., Hammond, 46324. Tel: 219-845-7531.

Schools Office—KIM PRYZBYLSKI, Ph.D., Supt. Schools, 9292 Broadway, Merrillville, 46410. Tel: 219-769-9292; Fax: 219-738-9034.

Spiritual Life/Seimetz Center—1441 Hoffman St., Hammond, 46327. Tel: 219-932-8321.

Stewardship—ANNE VERBEKE, Dir., 9292 Broadway, Merrillville, 46410. Tel: 219-769-9292; Fax: 219-738-9034.

Vocations—Rev. KEVIN R. HUBER, Dir., 9292 Broadway, Merrillville, 46410. Tel: 219-769-9292; Fax: 219-738-9034.

Worship and Spirituality, Office of—Rev. MARTIN J. DOBRZYNSKI, Dir.; KRISTOPHER SEAMAN, Assoc. Dir., 9292 Broadway, Merrillville, 46410. Tel: 219-769-9292; Fax: 219-738-9034.

Youth Ministry—KEVIN DRISCOLL, Dir., 9292 Broadway, Merrillville, 46410. Tel: 219-769-9292; Fax: 219-738-9034.

CLERGY, PARISHES, MISSIONS AND PAROCHIAL SCHOOLS

CITY OF GARY
(LAKE COUNTY)

1—CATHEDRAL OF HOLY ANGELS (1907), Rev. Robert P. Gehring.
Res.: 640 Tyler St., Gary, 46402-2299. Tel: 219-882-6079; Fax: 219-882-0133.
Catechesis/Religious Program—Tel: 219-882-1553. Students 20.

2—ST. ANTHONY (1918), Closed., For inquiries for parish records contact Cathedral of Holy Angels, Gary.

3—BLESSED SACRAMENT (1947), Revs. Dennis J. Teles, Admin.; Lourdu Pasala; Deacon Joseph Kwitko.
Res.: 1775 W. 41st Ave., Gary, 46408. Tel: 219-980-3081; Fax: 219-980-1510.
Catechesis/Religious Program—Tel: 219-887-2940. Students 10.

4—ST. CASIMIR (1916), (Lithuanian), Closed., For inquiries for parish records contact Holy Angels Cathedral.

5—ST. EMERIC (1911), Closed., For inquiries for parish records contact Holy Trinity (Hungarian), East Chicago.

6—ST. HEDWIG (1908), (Polish), [JC], 1746 Pennsylvania St., Gary, 46407. Tel: 219-882-2584. 5755 Pennsylvania St., 46410. Tel: 219-884-0714; Fax: 219-981-9224.

7—HOLY FAMILY (1926), (Polish), Closed., For inquiries for parish records, contact St. Bridget, Hobart.

8—HOLY ROSARY (1931), Rev. Robert P. Gehring, Admin.; Deacon Martin Gomez.
Res.: 719 Clark Rd., Gary, 46406. Tel: 219-944-1084; Fax: 219-949-7465.
Catechesis/Religious Program— Mary Ellen Sendejas, D.R.E. Students 50.

9—HOLY TRINITY (1911), (African American), Closed., For inquiries for parish records contact Cathedral of Holy Angels, Gary.

10—ST. JOSEPH THE WORKER (1912), (Croatian), Revs. Stephen Loncar, O.F.M.Conv.; Benedict Benakovic, O.F.M.Conv.
Res.: 330 E. 45th Ave., Gary, 46409. Tel: 219-980-1846.

11—ST. LUKE (1917),, See St. Monica, Gary.

12—ST. MARK (1921), Rev. John T. Ambre.
Mailing Address: P.O. Box 2100, Gary, 46409-0100. Tel: 219-887-0514; Fax: 219-887-0515.
Res.: 640 Tyler St., Gary, 46402. Tel: 219-882-0573.
Catechesis/Religious Program—Tel: 219-886-0511. Students 20.
Convent—509 W. Ridge Rd., Gary, 46408. Tel: 219-884-2140. Missionaries of Charity 4.

13—ST. MARY OF THE LAKE (1929), Rev. Thomas E. Mischler.
Res.: 6060 Miller Ave., Gary, 46403. Tel: 219-938-1373; Fax: 219-938-1316.
Catechesis/Religious Program—Tel: 219-938-9115. Debra Lightsey, D.R.E. Students 39.

14—SS. MONICA-ST. LUKE (1927; 1917), Rev. J. Patrick Gaza; Deacons Melvin Clark; Michael Richardson.
Res.: 645 Rhode Island, Gary, 46402. Tel: 219-883-1861.
Catechesis/Religious Program—Students 76.

15—SACRED HEART (1918), (Polish), Closed., For inquiries for parish records contact Cathedral of Holy Angels, Gary.

16—ST. ANN (1942), Revs. Theodore J. Mens, Admin.; James E. Wozniak, Assoc.
6025 W. 25th Ave., Gary, 46406.
Res.: 525 N. Broad St., Griffith, 46319. Tel: 219-924-4163; Fax: 219-922-2291.

OUTSIDE THE CITY OF GARY

BEVERLY SHORES, PORTER CO., ST ANN (1950), (Lithuanian), Rev. John B. Barasinski.
Res.: P.O. Box 727, 46301. Tel: 219-879-7565; Fax: 219-879-8893.
Catechesis/Religious Program—Students 16.

CEDAR LAKE, LAKE CO., HOLY NAME (1859), [CEM] Rev. Edward J. Kennedy.
Res.: 11000 W. 133rd Ave., 46303. Tel: 219-374-7160; Fax: 219-374-7165.
Parish Center—13209 Schneider St., 46303. Tel: 219-374-8798.
Catechesis/Religious Program—Tel: 219-374-8798. Students 153.

CHESTERTON, PORTER CO., ST. PATRICK (1858), [CEM] Revs. James W. Meade, J.D., S.T.L., J.C.L.; Ian J. Williams; Deacons Nicholas Juracevich; William Jones.
Res.: 638 N. Calumet Rd., 46304. Tel: 219-926-1282; Fax: 219-395-1560.
School—640 N. Calumet Rd., 46304. Tel: 219-926-1707; Fax: 219-921-1922. Ruth McCullough, Prin. Lay Teachers 14; Students 296.
Catechesis/Religious Program—Tel: 219-926-1265. Norma Dvorscak, D.R.E. Students 545.

CROWN POINT, LAKE CO.

1—ST. MARY (1865), (German), [CEM] Rev. Msgr. Don C. Grass; Rev. Patrick J. Kalich; Deacon Robert Angelich.
Res.: 321 E. Joliet St., 46307. Tel: 219-663-0044; Fax: 219-663-1027.
School—405 E. Joliet St., 46307. Tel: 219-663-0676; Fax: 219-663-1347. Suzan LaPeer, Prin. Lay Teachers 22; Students 561.
Catechesis/Religious Program—Tel: 219-663-7934. Mrs. Jan Mucha, D.R.E. Students 340.

2—ST. MATTHIAS (1967), Rev. Terrence J. Steffens; Deacon Gregory Fabian.
Mailing Address: 101 W. Burrell Dr., 46307. Tel: 219-663-2201; Fax: 219-663-2567.
Res.: 12505 Marshall St., 46307.
Catechesis/Religious Program—Tel: 219-663-4281. Christine Nienhaus, D.R.E. Students 184.

DYER, LAKE CO.

1—ST. JOSEPH (1867), [CEM] Rev. Mark S. Pavlina.
Res.: 440 Joliet St., 46311. Tel: 219-865-2271; Fax: 219-865-2350.
School—Tel: 219-865-2750; Fax: 219-865-2750. James Wiltshire, Prin. Lay Teachers 18; Students 138.
Catechesis/Religious Program—430 Joliet St., 46311. Tel: 219-865-2355. Students 339.

2—ST. MARIA GORETTI (1977), Rev. Charles W. Niblick.
Res.: 500 Northgate Dr., 46311. Tel: 219-865-8956; Fax: 219-322-1670.
Catechesis/Religious Program—Tel: 219-322-6124; Fax: 219-865-5482. Patricia Sidor, D.R.E. Students 368.

EAST CHICAGO, LAKE CO.

1—ASSUMPTION (1915), (Slovak), Closed., For inquiries for parish records contact St. Patrick, East Chicago.

2—ST. FRANCIS (1913), (Lithuanian), Closed., For inquiries for parish records contact St. John Cantius, East Chicago.

3—HOLY TRINITY (1916), (Croatian), Rev. Stanley J. Dominik, Admin.; Deacon John Bacon.
Res.: 4754 Carey St., 46312. Tel: 219-398-3061.

4—HOLY TRINITY (1906), (Hungarian), Rev. Alphonse Skerl.
Res.: 4759 McCook Ave., 46312. Tel: 219-397-1907; Fax: 219-397-1907.

5—IMMACULATE CONCEPTION (1933), (Italian), Closed., For inquiries for parish records contact St. Stanislaus, East Chicago.

6—ST. JOHN CANTIUS (1906), (Polish), Rev. Joseph R. Niezgoda.
Res.: 3903 Main St., 46312. Tel: 219-398-1370; Fax: 219-398-4302.
School—Indiana Harbor Catholic Elementary School, Tel: 219-397-1122; Fax: 219-397-1972.
Catechesis/Religious Program—3916 Pulaski. Tel: 219-397-3293. Students 14.

7—ST. JOSEPH (1916), (Polish), Closed., For inquiries for parish records contact St. John Cantius, East Chicago.

8—ST. JUDE (1933), Closed., For inquiries for parish records contact Our Lady of Guadalupe, East Chicago.

9—ST. MARY (1890), Revs. Stephen G. Gibson; Frank D. Torres.
822 W. 144th St., 46312. Tel: 219-398-2409; Fax: 219-391-8999.
School—Tel: 219-397-4404; Fax: 219-397-0924. Lay Teachers 4; Students 68.
Catechesis/Religious Program—Students 277.

10—OUR LADY OF GUADALUPE (1927), (Hispanic), Rev. Juan Gonzalez, C.PP.S.
Res.: 3510 Deodar St., P.O. Box 3400, 46312. Tel: 219-398-0253; Fax: 219-398-0266.
School—Interparochial Consolidated, Tel: 219-397-1122; Fax: 219-397-1972.
Catechesis/Religious Program—3916 Pulaski St.,

46312. Tel: 219-397-3293; Fax: 219-397-3293. Marilyn A. Baron, D.R.E. Students 153.
11—ST. PATRICK (1902), (Hispanic), Rev. Fernando de Cristobal.
Res.: 3810 Grand Blvd., 46312. Tel: 219-398-1036; Fax: 219-398-1036.
School—Interparochial, Tel: 219-397-1122.
Catechesis/Religious Program—3916 Pulaski St., 46312. Tel: 219-397-3293. Students 54.
12—SACRED HEART (1926), (Slovak), Rev. Msgr. Joseph F. Semancik.
Res.: 4423 Olcott Ave., 46312. Tel: 219-397-5857.
Catechesis/Religious Program—Students 24.
13—ST. STANISLAUS (1900), (Polish), Rev. Msgr. John J. Siekierski.
Res.: 808 W. 150th St., 46312. Tel: 219-398-2341; Fax: 219-398-2388.
School—4930 Indianapolis Blvd., 46312. Tel: 219-398-1316; Fax: 219-398-9080. Kathleen A. Lowry, Prin. Lay Teachers 11; Students 162.
Catechesis/Religious Program—Tel: 219-397-7059. Students 20.
Convent—4940 Indianapolis Blvd., 46312. Tel: 219-397-7059.
EAST GARY, LAKE CO., , NAME CHANGE - REFER TO LAKE STATION, LAKE CO., IN, FOR ALL INFORMATION
FISH LAKE, LA PORTE CO., ST. ANTHONY (1948), Rev. Michael G. Heimer.
Res.: 7732 E. State Rd. 4, Walkerton, 46574. Tel: 219-369-1210; Fax: 219-369-9500. (Fish Lake)
GRIFFITH, LAKE CO., ST. MARY (1928), Revs. Theodore J. Mens; James E. Wozniak. In Res., Rev. Charles A. Mosley.
Res.: 525 N. Broad St., 46319. Tel: 219-924-4163; Fax: 219-922-2291.
School—(Grades PreK-8) Tel: 219-924-8633; Fax: 219-922-2279. Mrs. Rebecca Maskovich, Prin. Sisters of St. Francis of Perpetual Adoration 1; Lay Teachers 11; Students 305.
Catechesis/Religious Program—Tel: 219-922-2277. Students 289.
Convent—508 N. Lafayette St., 46319. Tel: 219-922-2278.
HAMLET, STARKE CO., HOLY CROSS (1888), [CEM] Rev. Anthony L. Spanley.
Res.: P.O. Box 230, 46532. Tel: 574-867-2461; Fax: 574-867-2461.
Catechesis/Religious Program—Students 11.
Mission—St. Dominic (1981), P.O. Box 230, Koontz Lake, Starke Co. 46532.
HAMMOND, LAKE CO.
1—ALL SAINTS (1896), Rev. Stephen D. Kosinski.
Res.: 570 Sibley St., P.O. Box 836, 46325-0836. Tel: 219-932-0204; Fax: 219-932-4507.
Catechesis/Religious Program—Josephine Perez, D.R.E. Students 160.
2—ST. CASIMIR (1890), (Polish), [JC] Rev. Vladimir Janeczek.
Res.: 4340 Johnson St., 46327. Tel: 219-931-2589; Fax: 219-931-2589.
School—4329 Cameron St., 46327. Tel: 219-932-2686; Fax: 219-932-2686. Mrs. Stasia Krempa, Prin. Lay Teachers 11; Students 266.
Catechesis/Religious Program—Tel: 219-931-8466. Students 65.
3—ST. CATHERINE OF SIENA (1956), Rev. Larry J. Kew; Sr. Margaret Urban, P.H.J.C., Pastoral Assoc.
Res.: 6605 Kentucky Ave., 46323. Tel: 219-845-1939; Fax: 219-845-4772.
School—6525 Kentucky Ave., 46323. Tel: 219-845-1217; Fax: 219-845-1591. Christine Nielsen, Prin. Poor Handmaids of Jesus Christ 1; Lay Teachers 6; Students 144.
Catechesis/Religious Program—Tel: 219-845-2207. Mrs. Shirley Brown, D.R.E. Students 100.
Convent—Tel: 219-845-5341.
4—ST. JOHN BOSCO (1934), Rev. Richard Orlinski.
Res.: 7113 Columbia Ave., 46324. Tel: 219-844-9027; Fax: 219-844-6986.
Pastoral Center—1247 171st Pl., 46324. Fax: 219-989-7947.
School—(Grades PreK-8), 1231 171st Pl., 46324. Tel: 219-845-6226; Fax: 219-989-7946. James O'Donnell, Prin. Lay Teachers 14; Students 292.
Catechesis/Religious Program—Tel: 219-844-9027, Ext. 310. Mrs. Vickie Blackwood, D.R.E. Students 100.
5—ST. JOSEPH (1879), Rev. Roy T. Beeching.
Res.: 5304 Hohman Ave., 46320. Tel: 219-932-0702; Fax: 219-932-0059. Email: saintjoe@peoplepc.com.
Catechesis/Religious Program—Tel: 219-932-7294. Bryan Lazorik, D.R.E. Students 74.
6—ST. MARGARET MARY (1947), [CEM] Rev. James W. Schulz, S.J., Admin.
Res.: 1445 Hoffman St., 46327. Tel: 219-931-5229; Fax: 219-937-4357.
Catechesis/Religious Program—Students 120.
7—ST. MARY (1912), Unassigned.
Res.: 931 Merrill St., 46320. Tel: 219-838-3680. Church: Morris & Tapper Aves., 46320. Tel: 219-933-9772.
Catechesis/Religious Program—Tel: 219-844-9027; Fax: 219-989-7947. Students 1.
8—OUR LADY OF PERPETUAL HELP (1937), Rev. John R. Winterlin; Deacon Thomas Kreidler.
Res.: 7132 Arizona St., 46323. Tel: 219-844-3438; Fax: 219-844-3580.
Catechesis/Religious Program—7128 Arizona St., 46323. Ruth Rossi, D.R.E. Students 245.
HEBRON, PORTER CO., ST. HELEN (1946), Rev. Derrick F. Dudash.
Res.: 302 N. Madison St., 46341. Tel: 219-996-4611.
Catechesis/Religious Program—Tel: 219-996-4612. Susan Witt, D.R.E.; Karen Yankauskas, D.R.E. Students 107.
HIGHLAND, LAKE CO.
1—ST. JAMES THE LESS (1967), Rev. Francis M. Lazar; Deacons Martin Denkhoff; Raymond Dec.
Mailing Address: 9640 Kennedy Ave., 46322.
Res.: 2703 45th St., 46322. Tel: 219-924-4220; Fax: 219-924-4295.
Catechesis/Religious Program—Tel: 219-924-4222. Marie Pavnica, D.R.E. Students 465.
2—OUR LADY OF GRACE (1949), Rev. Edward J. Moszur; Deacon Charles Patrick.
Office—3005 Condit St., 46322. Tel: 219-838-0395; Fax: 219-972-6372.
School—3025 Highway Ave., 46322. Tel: 219-838-2901; Fax: 219-972-6389. Marilyn Tomko, Prin. Lay Teachers 14; Students 192.
Catechesis/Religious Program—Tel: 219-838-6790. Patricia Franz, D.R.E. Students 191.
HOBART, LAKE CO., ST. BRIDGET (1873), Rev. Dominic V. Bertino; Deacon Richard W. Huber.
Res.: 568 E. Second St., 46342. Tel: 219-942-6441; Fax: 219-942-4573.
School—(Grades PreK-8), 107 Main St., 46342. Tel: 219-942-1894. Sr. Rita Marie Malachinski, S.S.J., Prin. Lay Teachers 15; Students 285.
Catechesis/Religious Program—Tel: 219-955-0186. Students 162.
KINGSFORD HEIGHTS, LA PORTE CO., IMMACULATE HEART OF MARY (1953), Closed., For inquiries for parish records contact St. Anthony, Fish Lake.
KNOX, STARKE CO., ST. THOMAS AQUINAS (1923), Rev. John V. Scott.
Res.: 406 E. Washington St., 46534. Tel: 574-772-4134.
Catechesis/Religious Program—Tel: 574-772-3237. Students 100.
KOUTS, PORTER CO., ST. MARY (1884), [CEM] Rev. Thomas T. Tibbs.
Res.: P.O. Box 663, 46347. Tel: 219-766-3680.
Catechesis/Religious Program—Susan Keller, D.R.E. Students 110.
LA PORTE, LA PORTE CO.
1—ST. JOSEPH (1858), [CEM] Revs. Theodore A. Nordquist; David W. Kime; Deacon Robert Bucheit.
Res.: 109 C St., 46350. Tel: 219-362-9595; Fax: 219-325-9021.
School—101 C St., 46350. Tel: 219-362-6472; Fax: 219-362-2707. Dr. Patricia Schroeder, Prin. Sisters of St. Francis of Perpetual Adoration 2; Lay Teachers 10; Students 184.
Catechesis/Religious Program—Students 134.
Convent—102 B St., 46350. Tel: 219-362-2587.
2—ST. PETER (1853), Rev. George M. Vrabely.
Res.: 1104 Monroe St., 46350. Tel: 219-362-6186.
Catechesis/Religious Program—1110 Monroe St., 46350. Tel: 219-362-2509; Fax: 219-362-2748. Patricia Poleski, D.R.E. Students 189.
3—SACRED HEART (1912), (Polish), [JC] Rev. Gerald A. Sroka.
Res.: 130 Bach St., 46350. Tel: 219-362-2815; Fax: 219-362-4822.
Catechesis/Religious Program—Tel: 219-362-4822. Irene Konieczny, D.R.E. Students 85.
LAKE STATION, LAKE CO., ST. FRANCIS XAVIER (1930), [CEM] Rev. J. Antonio Valtierra; Deacon Leonard Holland.
Res.: 2447 Putnam St., 46405. Tel: 219-962-8626; Fax: 219-962-8627.
School—2453 Putnam St., 46405. Tel: 219-962-4507. Carol Brendza, Prin. Lay Teachers 5; Students 115.
Catechesis/Religious Program— LaVerne Papich, D.R.E. Students 185.
LOWELL, LAKE CO., ST. EDWARD (1870), [CEM] Rev. Peter J. Muha.
Res.: 216 S. Nichols St., 46356. Tel: 219-696-7307; Fax: 219-696-3525.
School—210 S. Nichols St., 46356. Tel: 219-696-9876; Fax: 219-696-2524. Lay Teachers 7; Students 120.
Catechesis/Religious Program—Tel: 219-696-4282; Fax: 219-696-3525. Sylvia Downing, D.R.E. Students 320.
Mission—St. Theresa 23315 Shelby Rd., Shelby, Lake Co. 46377.
MERRILLVILLE, LAKE CO.
1—ST. ANDREW (1965), Rev. Richard H. Ameling; Deacons George V. Modrak; Thomas Gryzbek. In Res., Rev. Kevin R. Huber.
Res.: 801 W. 73rd Ave., 46410. Tel: 219-769-8534; Fax: 219-769-8543.
School—Tel: 219-769-2049. June Kachur, Prin. Lay Teachers 11; Students 181.
Catechesis/Religious Program—Tel: 219-769-2049. Students 146.
Mission—St. Hedwig 1746 Pennsylvania St., Gary, 46407.
2—ST. JOAN OF ARC (1968), Rev. Andrew J. Corona; MaryAnn Dienes, Pastoral Assoc.
Res.: 200 E. 78th Ave., 46410. Tel: 219-769-1973; Fax: 219-769-9056.
Catechesis/Religious Program—Tel: 219-769-2037. Alan Wartman, D.R.E.; Janet Wartman, D.R.E. Students 90.
St. Joan of Arc Center—
3—OUR LADY OF CONSOLATION (1947), Rev. Joseph E. Vamos; Deacon Robert E. Gill.
Res.: 8303 Taft St., 46410. Tel: 219-769-2785; Fax: 219-769-2177.
Catechesis/Religious Program—Tel: 219-769-2295. Bernadette Burosh, D.R.E. Students 359.
4—SS. PETER AND PAUL (1841), [CEM] Rev. Dennis J. Teles.
Res.: 5885 Harrison St., 46410. Tel: 219-980-2693; Fax: 219-980-2851.
Catechesis/Religious Program—Tel: 219-887-2940. Paula Burrell, D.R.E. Students 115.
5—ST. STEPHEN, MARTYR (1968), Rev. Michael L. Maginot, S.T.L., J.C.L.
Res.: 5920 Waite St., 46410. Tel: 219-980-9348; Fax: 219-980-9354.
Catechesis/Religious Program—5885 Harrison, 46410. Tel: 219-887-2940. Students 24.
MICHIGAN CITY, LA PORTE CO.
1—ST. MARY OF THE IMMACULATE CONCEPTION (1867), Rev. James P. McGrogan.
Res.: 411 W. 11th St., 46360. Tel: 219-874-7231.
Catechesis/Religious Program—Students 20.
Mission—Sacred Heart 1001 W. Eighth St., 46360.
2—NOTRE DAME (1953), Rev. Richard A. Emerson.
Res.: 1010 Moore Rd., 46360. Tel: 219-872-4844; Fax: 219-872-2510.
School—(Grades PreK-8) Tel: 219-872-6216; Fax: 219-872-6216. Mrs. Karen Breen, Prin. Lay Teachers 18; Students 255.
Catechesis/Religious Program—Students 19.
3—QUEEN OF ALL SAINTS (1950), Revs. Terrence R. Chase; Keith McClellan, Assoc.; Deacon Mark Plaiss.
Res.: 606 S. Woodland Ave., 46360. Tel: 219-872-9196; Fax: 219-872-9176.
School—1715 E. Barker Ave., 46360. Tel: 219-872-4420; Fax: 219-872-1943. Chet A. Nordyke, Prin. Sisters of Holy Cross 1; Lay Teachers 22; Students 460.
Catechesis/Religious Program—Tel: 219-878-9348. Kathy Schroeder, D.R.E. Students 200.
Convent—Tel: 219-872-5401.
4—SACRED HEART MISSION (1915), (Lebanese), Rev. James P. McGrogan, Admin.
Res.: 411 W. 11th St., 46360. Tel: 219-874-7231; Fax: 219-873-1322.
Catechesis/Religious Program—Students 4.
5—ST. STANISLAUS KOSTKA (1891), (Polish), Rev. Walter M. Ciesla; Deacon Daniel Bowmar.
Mailing Address: 1506 Washington St., 46360.
Res.: 109 Ann St., 46360. Tel: 219-879-9281; Fax: 219-879-6501.
School—1506 Washington St., 46360. Tel: 219-872-2258; Fax: 219-872-2295. Lay Teachers 16; Students 206.
Catechesis/Religious Program—203 Benton St., 46360. Tel: 219-872-1257. Antoinette Sajewski, D.R.E. Students 76.
MUNSTER, LAKE CO., ST. THOMAS MORE (1945), Revs. David G. Nowak; Michael J. Yadron; Keith M. Virus; Deacon Joseph Sobek.
Res.: 8501 Calumet Ave., 46321. Tel: 219-836-8610; Fax: 219-836-9185.
School—Tel: 219-836-9151; Fax: 219-836-0982. Kevin T. Zajdel, Ed.D., Prin. Lay Teachers 30; Students 641.
Catechesis/Religious Program—Tel: 219-836-9152. Sr. Marilyn Hettinger, D.R.E. Students 634.
NEW CHICAGO, LAKE CO., ASSUMPTION OF THE BLESSED VIRGIN MARY (P.O. Hobart) (1917), (Polish), Rev. Jon J. Plavcan, Admin.
Res.: 3530 Illinois St., Hobart, 46342. Tel: 219-962-1073; Fax: 219-962-1073.
Catechesis/Religious Program—Tel: 219-962-6678. Students 50.
NORTH JUDSON, STARKE CO., SS. CYRIL AND METHODIUS (1881), [CEM] Rev. John J. Zemelko.
Res.: 303 Keller Ave., 46366. Tel: 574-896-2195; Fax: 574-896-5131.
Catechesis/Religious Program—Students 60.
OTIS, LA PORTE CO., ST. MARY (1873), (Polish), [CEM] Rev. Joseph E. Pusateri.
Res.: 101 N. Church St., 46391. Tel: 219-785-2212;

Fax: 219-785-4743.
Catechesis/Religious Program—Tel: 219-785-2160; Fax: 219-785-4743. Students 67.

PORTAGE, PORTER CO., NATIVITY OF OUR SAVIOR (1964), Revs. Walter J. Rakoczy; William F. O'Toole; Deacons Alexander A. Saims; Joseph Wilczynski; Robert J. Bonta.
Res.: 2949 Willowcreek Rd., 46368. Tel: 219-762-4858; Fax: 219-762-3094.
School—2929 Willowcreek Rd., 46368. Tel: 219-763-2400. Jo Ann Abbott, Prin. Lay Teachers 10; Students 202.
Catechesis/Religious Program—Tel: 219-764-3143. Marian Weeks, D.R.E. Students 608.

ROLLING PRAIRIE, LAPORTE CO., ST. JOHN KANTY (1888), (Polish), [CEM] Rev. Michael G Heimer, Admin.
Res.: 7732 E. State Rd. 4, Walkerton, 46574. Tel: 219-369-1210; Fax: 219-369-9500.
Catechesis/Religious Program—Students 78.

SAINT JOHN, LAKE CO., ST. JOHN EVANGELIST (1839), [CEM] Rev. Sammie L. Maletta.
Mailing Address: 11301 W. 93rd. Ave., St. John, 46373.
Res.: Tel: 219-365-5678; Fax: 219-365-2703.
Parish Office—11301 W. 93rd Ave., St. John, 46373.
School—9400 Wicker Ave., St. John, 46373. Tel: 219-365-5451; Fax: 219-365-6173. Mary Jane Bartley, Prin. Lay Teachers 22; Students 327.
Catechesis/Religious Program—Tel: 219-365-3709. Colleen Anderson, D.R.E. Students 377.

SAN PIERRE, STARKE CO., ALL SAINTS (1858), [CEM] Rev. William J. Spranger.
Res.: P.O. Box 56, 46374. Tel: 219-828-4281.
Catechesis/Religious Program—Tel: 219-828-4111. Students 8.

SCHERERVILLE, LAKE CO., ST. MICHAEL (1874), [CEM] Revs. Martin J. Dobrzynski; Selvaraj Selladurai; Deacons Edwin Gatons; Jack Krol.
Res.: One Wilhelm St., 46375. Tel: 219-322-4505; Fax: 219-322-4508.
School—Preschool, Tel: 219-322-3077. (Good Shepherd Program) Students 43.
School—16 W. Wilhelm St., 46375. Tel: 219-322-4531; Fax: 219-322-1710. Franciscan Sisters of the Sacred Heart 1; Lay Teachers 25; Students 326.
Catechesis/Religious Program—Tel: 219-322-3077. Students 634.

SHELBY, LAKE CO., ST. THERESA (1939), Rev. Peter J. Muha.
Res.: 216 S. Nichols St., Lowell, 46356. Tel: 219-696-7307; Fax: 219-696-3525.
Catechesis/Religious Program— Kelly Braun, D.R.E. Students 20.

VALPARAISO, PORTER CO.
1—ST. ELIZABETH SETON (1978), Rev. David H. Gosnell; Deacons James J. Keough; Michael Prendergast; Brian Nosbusch.
Res.: 509 W. Division Rd., 46385. Tel: 219-464-1624; Fax: 219-465-7673.
Catechesis/Religious Program—Tel: 219-462-2202. Students 344.
2—OUR LADY OF SORROWS (South Haven) (1967), Rev. Douglas J. Mayer; Deacon Sherman Brown.
Res.: 356 W. Seven Mile Rd., 46385. Tel: 219-759-2400; Fax: 219-759-0054.
Catechesis/Religious Program—Tel: 219-759-2286. Students 110.
3—ST. PAUL (1858), [CEM] Revs. Joseph M. Pawlowski; Robert T. Naglich, S.C.J.; Deacons John McGuckin; John Roscoe; Michael Foster.
Mailing Address: P.O. Box 1475, 46384-1475. Tel: 219-464-4831; Fax: 219-464-4833.
Res.: 452 W. Chicago St., 46383. Tel: 219-465-3723. Church: P.O. Box 1475, 46384-1475. Tel: 219-464-4831; Fax: 219-464-4833.
School—352 W. Chicago St., 46383. Tel: 219-462-3374; Fax: 219-477-1763. Mary Knarr, Prin. Lay Teachers 13; Students 197.
Catechesis/Religious Program—Tel: 219-464-8502. Students 669.
Child Development Center—Tel: 219-465-0882; Fax: 219-531-2047. Janet McCorkle, Dir.
St. Agnes Day Service Center—1859 Harrison Blvd., 46383. Tel: 219-477-5433. Barbara Kubiszak, Dir.

WANATAH, LA PORTE CO., SACRED HEART (1887), [CEM] Rev. Gerald H. Schweitzer; Deacon Dale Walsh.
Res.: 202 N. Ohio St, P.O. Box 386, 46390. Tel: 219-733-2955; Fax: 219-733-0001.
Catechesis/Religious Program—Tel: 219-733-2315. Students 185.
Mission—St. Martin (1860), Lowell & Dominic Sts., LaCrosse, LaPorte Co. 46348.

WHITING, LAKE CO.
1—ST. ADALBERT (1902), (Polish), Revs. Stanley J. Dominik, Admin.; Eduardo Malagon.
Res.: 1340 121st St., 46394. Tel: 219-659-3848; Fax: 219-473-0133.
Catechesis Religious Program—Sacred Heart Parish, 1731 LaPorte Ave., 46394. Tel: 219-659-0733; Fax: 219-659-0195.
2—IMMACULATE CONCEPTION (1922), (Slovak), Revs. Stanley J. Dominik, Admin.; Eduardo Malagon.
Res.: 1731 La Parre Ave., 46394. Tel: 219-659-0733; Fax: 219-659-0195.
Catechesis/Religious Program—1723 LaPorte Ave.. Tel: 219-659-1088. Students 8.
3—ST. JOHN THE BAPTIST (1897), (Slovak), Revs. John E. Kalicky, C.PP.S.; Gary Scherer, C.PP.S.; Bro. Gabriel Bridges, C.PP.S.; Deacons David Hajduch; Joseph Manchak. In Res., Rev. John J. Zvijak, C.PP.S.; Bro. Terrence Nufer, C.PP.S.
Res.: 1849 Lincoln Ave., P.O. Box 711, 46394. Tel: 219-659-0023; Fax: 219-473-7551.
School—1844 Lincoln Ave., 46394. Tel: 219-659-3042; Fax: 219-473-7553. Thomas J. Puplava, Prin. Lay Teachers 23; Students 485.
Catechesis/Religious Program—Tel: 219-659-1088; Fax: 219-473-7553. Students 183.
4—STS. PETER AND PAUL (1910), Closed., For inquiries of parish records, contact Sacred Heart, Whiting.
5—SACRED HEART (1889), Revs. Stanley Dominik; Eduardo Malagon.
Res.: 1731 Laporte Ave., 46394. Tel: 219-659-0733; Fax: 219-659-0195.
Catechesis/Religious Program—1723 LaPorte Ave.. Tel: 219-659-1088. Students 173.

WINFIELD TOWNSHIP, LAKE CO., HOLY SPIRIT (1998), Rev. Joseph V. Murphy.
Res.: 7667 E. 109th Ave., Crown Point, 46307. Tel: 219-661-0644; Fax: 219-662-2611.
Catechesis/Religious Program—Students 300.

Chaplains of Public Institutions

MICHIGAN CITY. *Indiana State Prison*. Deacon Michael Prendergast.
123 Shorewood Dr., Valparaiso, 46385.

ROLLING PRAIRIE. *Sharing Meadows*. Dennis J. Blaney. P.O. Box 400, 46371. Tel: 219-778-9130

WESTVILLE. *Westville Correctional Center*. Deacon James Etter.
P.O. Box 473, 46391. Tel: 219-785-2511.

On Duty Outside the Diocese:
Revs.—
Chadwick, Brian D., Santa Maria, Rome, Italy.
Coriden, James A., 6896 Laurel St., N.W., Washington, DC 20012.
Hand, Dennis M., Pje. 6, Poligno E-Casa #101, Col. San Luis, San Martin, Depto. de San Salvador, El Salvador.
Hendricks, Clare, 1428 Lyon St., Columbia, TN 38401.
Iwuji, Matthew C., J.U.D., P.O. Box 300192, Austin, TX 78703.
Malarz, Andrew, Diocese of Venice
Mazza, Mark G., Archdiocese of San Francisco

Military Chaplains:
Revs.—
Angotti, Joseph A., HHC 9 ENG, CMR 457, Box 1204, Apo, AE 09033-1204.
Nondorf, Aloysius J., 1962 Bay City Pl., El Paso, TX 79936.

Retired:
Rev. Msgrs.—
Charlebois, John J., P.O. Box 2342, Chesterton, 46304.
Charlebois, Robert L., 161 E. Chicago Ave., Chicago, IL 60611.
Dowdy, Timothy F., 1501 Hoffman St., Hammond, 46327.
Fowerbaugh, F. Raymond, 1501 Hoffman St., Hammond, 46327.
Lengerich, Vincent L., 2860 U.S. Route 127, Carthagena, OH 45822.
Litot, Edward F., 317 Waverly Rd., La Porte, 46350.
Martin, William F., 419 Autumn Tr., Michigan City, 46360.
Malevage, F. J., 3214 Milestone Creek Ct., Valparaiso, 46383.
Morales, John F., 333 N. Palm Dr., #305, Beverly Hills, CA 90210.
Tomaszewski, Michael J., 2605 Hermoine Dr., Michigan City, 46360.
Urbonas, Ignatius L., 14911 127th St., Lemont, IL 60439.
Witte, John C., 3713 S. State Rd. 104, La Porte, 46350.
Zollinger, Richard, 301 South Main St., Knox, 46534.
Revs.—
Blaney, Dennis J., P.O. Box 400, Rolling Prairie, 46371.
Daniels, John W., 425 Birch St., N.W., DeMotte, 46310.
Dettmer, Alfred J., 1134 Bluebird Lane, Munster, 46321.
Doyle, Charles E., 105 Autumn Tr., Michigan City, 46360.
Evers, Robert B.
Heeg, Lawrence, 327 E. Burdick Rd., Chesterton, 46304.
Hogan, John A., 11620 N. Quicksilver, Tucson, AZ 46534.
Kashmer, George B., 6101 Osuna Rd., N.E., #24, Albuquerque, NM 87109.
Kish, Matthew J., 1501 Hoffman St., Hammond, 46327.
Kronkowski, Leonard J., 1 Cambridge Ct., Apt. 8, Michigan City, 46360.
Meneghello, Serafino, Via Oliosi, 13 San Massimo, Verona, Italy.
Minnich, John F., P.O. Box 537, Georgetown, 47122.
Murzyn, John A., P.O. Box 6189, Hilo, HI 96720.
Peil, William L., 1841 N. Anthony Blvd., Fort Wayne, 46805.
Strebig, John J., 135 Kingsbury Ave., LaPorte, 46350.
Till, Joseph E., 417 Autumn Trail S., Michigan City, 46360.
Vogt, William E., 2121 North First St., Fresno, CA 93650.

Permanent Deacons:
Angelich, Robert, St. Mary, Crown Point
Bacon, John
Bonta, Robert J.
Bowmar, Daniel L., Senior Deacon
Brown, Sherman, Senior Deacon
Bucheit, Robert J.
Cichoracki, Eugene
Clark, Melvin
Codespoti, Joseph
Dec, Raymond, Senior Deacon
Delgado, Victor
Denkhoff, Martin J.
Etter, James
Fabian, Gregory G.
Foster, Michael
Gatons, Edwin
Gill, Robert E.
Gomez, Martin, Senior Deacon
Gryzbek, Thomas
Hajduch, David A.
Haugh, James
Hawkins, Dennis, Senior Deacon
Holland, Leonard D.
Huber, Richard
Janowski, Victor
Jones, William E., Jr.
Jurasevich, Nicholas J.
Keough, James J., Senior Deacon
Kozub, Edward
Kreidler, Thomas
Krol, Jack
Kwitko, Joseph
Lunsford, Malcolm
Maldonado, Felipe
Manchak, Joseph C.
McGuckin, John D.
Modrak, George V.
Nosbusch, Brian
Patrick, Charles
Plaiss, Mark
Prendergast, Michael
Richardson, Michael E.
Roscoe, John
Saims, Alexander, Senior Deacon
Sobek, Joseph J., Sr.
Stodola, Joseph, St. Thomas More, Munster
Tabion, Napoleon, St. Thomas More, Munster
Walsh, Dale
Wilczynski, Joseph
Zubel, Steven, St. Joan of Arc, Merrillville

INSTITUTIONS LOCATED IN THE DIOCESE

[A] COLLEGES AND UNIVERSITIES

WHITING. *Calumet College of St. Joseph*, 2400 New York Ave., 46394. Tel: 219-473-7770; Fax: 219-473-4259. Web: www.ccsj.edu. Dr. Dennis Rittenmeyer, Pres.; Revs. Ernest Krantz, C.PP.S., Chap.; Alphonse Spilly, C.PP.S.; Bros James Ballmann, C.PP.S., Religious Supr. & Computer Svcs.; Jerry Schwieterman, C.PP.S., Campus Ministry; Gerard Hall, C.PP.S., Faculty; Basie Benjamin, C.PP.S.

Priests 2; Brothers 3; Sisters 1; Lay Teachers 126; Total Staff 132; Enrollment 1,230.

[B] HIGH SCHOOLS, DIOCESAN

HAMMOND. *Bishop Noll Institute*, 1519 Hoffman St., 46327. Tel: 219-932-9058; Fax: 219-853-1736. Email: fechsl@calumet.purdue.edu. Web: www.bishopnoll.com. Scott D. Fech, Prin. Priests 1; Students 533; Lay Teachers 41; Total Staff 55; Total Enrollment 533.

MERRILLVILLE. *Andrean High School*, 5959 Broadway, 46410. Tel: 219-887-5281; Fax: 219-981-5072. Web: www.andreanhs.com. Rev. Paul E. Quanz, C.S.B., Prin.; Julie Herr, Asst. Prin.; Rev. John J. Fiore, C.S.B. Basilian Fathers 2; Sisters of Sts. Cyril and Methodius 3; Lay Teachers 50; Total Staff 55; Students 679.

MICHIGAN CITY. *Marquette Catholic High School*, 306 W. Tenth St., 46360. Tel: 219-873-1325; Fax: 219-873-1327. Email: info@marquette-hs.org. Web: www.marquette-hs.org. Patrick Cannon, Prin. Lay Teachers 21; Total Staff 31; Students 208.

[C] ELEMENTARY SCHOOLS, PRIVATE

ROLLING PRAIRIE. *Le Mans Academy*, (Grades 5-9) 46371. Tel: 219-778-2521; Fax: 219-778-4801. Email: kelly@lemansacademy.net. Bro. William Dygent, C.S.C., Pres.; Mr. Steve Cash, Headmaster. Private boarding school for boys. Brothers 2; Total Staff 3.

[D] ELEMENTARY SCHOOLS, INTERPAROCHIAL

EAST CHICAGO. *Indiana Harbor Catholic Elementary School*, 3916 Pulaski St., 46312. Tel: 219-397-1122; Fax: 219-397-1972. Email: fpihces3916@aol.com. Mrs. Francisca C. Phelps, Prin. Serving the parishes of Our Lady of Guadalupe, St John Cantius, and St. Patrick in East Chicago. Lay Teachers 5; Students 80.

[E] GENERAL HOSPITALS

CROWN POINT. *St. Anthony Medical Center of Crown Point*, 1201 S. Main St., 46307-8483. Tel: 219-738-2100; Fax: 219-757-6242. Email: susan.nordstrom.lopez@ssfhs.org. Web: www.stanthonymedicalcenter.com. Mrs. Susan Nordstrom Lopez, Pres. & CEO; Sr. Aline Shultz, O.S.F., Chap. Sisters of St. Francis Health Services, Inc. Sister of St. Francis of Perpetual Adoration 2; Franciscan Sisters of Chicago 2; Bed Capacity 266; Total Staff 1,470; Patients Assisted Annually 241,000.

DYER. *St. Margaret Mercy Healthcare Centers, South Campus* (Div. of the Sisters of St. Francis Health Services, Inc.) , 24 Joliet, 46311. Tel: 219-865-2141; Fax: 219-933-2585. Email: gene.diamond@ssfhs.org. Web: www.smmhc.com. Rev. Ignatius Ijere, Chap. Sisters of St. Francis of Perpetual Adoration 2; Bed Capacity 337; Bassinets 20; Total Staff 830; Patients Assisted Annually 225,174.

EAST CHICAGO. *St. Catherine Hospital*, 4321 Fir St., 46312. Tel: 219-392-1700; Fax: 219-392-7002. Web: www.comhs.org. Joann Birdzell, Admin.; Mark Rogers, COO & CFO; Ms. Susan Miller, Dir. Mission Effectiveness. Sisters 2; Bed Capacity 200; Bassinets 9; Total Staff 776; Patients Assisted Annually 100,042.

Transitional Care Unit (TCU) Tel: 219-392-7530; Fax: 219-392-7540.

HAMMOND. *St. Margaret Mercy Healthcare Centers - North Campus*, 5454 Hohman Ave., 46320. Tel: 219-932-2300; Fax: 219-933-2585. Email: gene.diamond@ssfhs.org. Web: www.smmhc.com. Rev. Gregory Holicky. Sisters of St. Francis Health Services, Inc. Sisters of St. Francis of Perpetual Adoration 5; Bed Capacity 465; Bassinets 45; Total Staff 1,350; Patients Assisted Annually 133,118.

HOBART. *St. Mary Medical Center*, 1500 S. Lake Park Ave., 46342. Tel: 219-942-0551; Fax: 219-947-6037. Web: www.stmary-hobart.com. Milton Triana, Admin.; Sr. Mary Ellen Goeller, PHJC, Div. Dir., Mission Integration; Rev. Joseph M. Kelchak, Chap. Sisters 3; Bed Capacity 194; Bassinets 12; Total Staff 913; Patients Assisted Annually 78,430.

MICHIGAN CITY. *St. Anthony Memorial Health Centers*, 301 W. Homer St., 46360. Tel: 219-879-8511; Fax: 219-877-1409. Email: linda.skinner@ssfhs.org. Web: www.samhc.org. Rev. Jose Pottokaran, C.M.I. Sisters of St. Francis Health Services, Inc. Sisters of St. Francis of Perpetual Adoration 4; Bed Capacity 310; Bassinets 20; Total Staff 1,053; Patients Assisted Annually 246,956.

[F] PROTECTIVE INSTITUTIONS

EAST CHICAGO. *Carmelite Home for Girls/Holy Innocents Shelter*, 4840 Grasselli Ave., 46312. Tel: 219-397-1085; Fax: 219-392-3574. Email: carmeliteec@aol.com. Sr. Maria Giuseppe Moxley, Supr. Carmelite Sisters of the Divine Heart of Jesus 6; Total Staff 60; Girls 30; Total Assisted Annually 295.

Nazareth Home, 4301 Elm St., 46312. Tel: 219-392-7692; Fax: 219-397-2021. Email: bkuper349@aol.com. Web: www.nazarethhome.com. Sr. Barbara Kuper, P.H.J.C., Supvr. Total Staff 8.

HAMMOND. *St. Joseph's Home for Boys, Inc.*, 4007 Sheffield Ave., 46327. Tel: 219-931-6451; Fax: 219-931-2241. Email: dfrazier@catholic-Charities.Org. Jerri Palmer-Glass, Admin. Dir. Total Staff 33; Boys 19; Total Assisted Annually 43.

[G] HOMES FOR THE AGED

CROWN POINT. *Franciscan Communities at St. Anthony Campus*, Formerly Franciscan Homes & Community Services, Inc., 203 Franciscan Dr., 46307-4824. Tel: 219-661-5100; Fax: 219-661-5102. Web: www.franciscancommunities.com. Linda O'Neill, Exec. Dir.; Rev. Myron Lowisz, O.F.M., Pastoral Care. Priests 1; Franciscan Sisters of Chicago 14; Total Staff 471.

St. Anthony Home Tel: 219-661-5100; Fax: 219-661-5102. Capacity 212.

St. Anthony Assisted Living Apartments Tel: 219-661-5150. Capacity 60.

St. Anthony Hospice Tel: 219-661-5306; Fax: 219-661-5305.

Franciscan Community Services Adult Day Care, Formerly Caritas Adult Day Health Services Tel: 219-661-5200. Capacity 25.

Holy Family Child Care Center Tel: 219-661-5250. Children 212.

HAMMOND. *Albertine Home*, 1501 Hoffman St., 46327. Tel: 219-937-0575; Fax: 219-937-0575. Email: albertineusa@aol.com. Sr. Loretta Soja, Dir. Albertine Sisters 9; Guests 36.

SAN PIERRE. *Trinity Continuing Care Services-Ind fka Holy Cross Care*, Formerly Holy Cross Care Services dba Little Company of Mary Health Facility, Inc., 7520 S. U.S. Hwy. 421, 46374-4275. Tel: 219-828-4111; Fax: 219-828-4275. Email: pego@trinity-health.org. James May, Admin.; Rev. William J. Spranger, Chap. Comprehensive Nursing Care Home. Priests 1; Bed Capacity 200; Patients Assisted Annually 214.

[H] PERSONAL PRELATURES

VALPARAISO. *Opus Dei*, 359 West 200 North, 46385. Tel: 219-462-6594; 219-462-0931; Fax: 219-465-6241. Email: shellbourne2@aol.com. Web: www.shellbourne.org. Prelature of the Holy Cross and Opus Dei, Shellbourne Conference Center.

[I] MONASTERIES AND RESIDENCES OF PRIESTS AND BROTHERS

CEDAR LAKE. *Our Lady of Lourdes Friary*, 12915 Parrish St., P.O. Box 156, 46303. Tel: 219-374-5931. Revs. Anthony F. Janik, O.F.M.; Francis Appelt; Bronislaus Jaskulski, O.F.M.; Myron Lowisz, O.F.M., Guardian; Andrew Meronek; Bert Pepowski; Dacian Bluma. Franciscan Friars of the Assumption of the B.V.M. Province (Order of Friars Minor) Priests 7; Brothers 2.

San Damiano Friary, 12921 Parrish St., P.O. Box 500, 46303. Tel: 219-374-5741; Fax: 219-374-9650. Email: jimlause@hotmail.com. Web: www.ofmnovitiate.org. Revs. James A. Lause, O.F.M. (STL), Guardian & Asst. Novice Dir.; Edward G. Tlucek, O.F.M., Dir. Novices; Dennet Jung, O.F.M. (CIN), Asst. Novice Dir. & Vicar. Cedar Lake Franciscan Friars (Order of Friars Minor). Interprovinicial Novitiate Priests 3; Novices 7.

EAST CHICAGO. *Roque Gonzalez Residence-Jesuit Fathers*, 3905 Fir St., 46312. Tel: 219-397-1885; 219-397-3906; Fax: 219-844-7566. Email: tmgannonsj@aol.com. Revs. Thomas M. Gannon, S.J.; James M. Dixon, S.J.

MERRILLVILLE. *Basilian Fathers Residence*, 5959 Broadway, 46410. Tel: 219-887-5284; Fax: 219-981-5072. Email: pquanz@andreanhs.com. Revs. John J. Fiore, C.S.B.; Paul E. Quanz, C.S.B., Rector. Priests 2.

Salvatorian Fathers (Society of the Divine Savior), 5755 Pennsylvania St., 46410. Tel: 219-884-0714; Fax: 219-981-9224. Email: wpawlik@attglobal.net. Web: www.sds.org. Revs. Joseph R. Zuziak, S.D.S.; Edward Kawa, S.D.S.; Walter M. Pawlik, S.D.S.; Jozef Musiol, S.D.S. (Poland) (AUS), Supr. Mission House for Polish Priests and Brothers. Priests 4.

MUNSTER. *Discalced Carmelite Fathers Monastery*, 1628 Ridge Rd., 46321. Tel: 219-838-7111; Fax: 219-838-7214. Email: ocdmunster@direcway.com. Revs. Robert Andrzej Strojny, O.C.D., Prior; Jacek Palica, O.C.D.; Thomas I. Balys, O.C.D.; Casimir Adalbert Borcz, O.C.D.; Joseph Ivans, O.C.D.; Edward C. Spyrka, O.C.D.; Waclaw L. Lech, O.C.D.; Bronislaw F. Socha, O.C.D.; Michael G. Veneklase, O.C.D.; John L. Gibson; Franciszek Czaicki, O.C.D.; Andrzej Gbur, O.C.D.; Bros. Tomasz S. Paczek, O.C.D.; Jan Reszka, O.C.D. Priests 12; Brothers 2.

[J] CONVENTS AND RESIDENCES OF SISTERS

GARY. *Missionaries of Charity, St. Mark Convent*, 509 W. Ridge Rd., 46408. Tel: 219-884-2140. Sr. M. Alokesh, M.C., Supr. Sisters 4.

EAST CHICAGO. *St. Catherine Convent*, 4325 Elm St., 46312. Tel: 219-398-0403; Fax: 219-398-9232. Email: stcathec@aol.com. Web: poorhandmaids.org. Poor Handmaids of Jesus Christ 4.

HAMMOND. *Albertine Sisters (Prov. of Krakow, Poland)*, 1501 Hoffman St., 46327. Tel: 219-937-0575; Fax: 219-937-0575. Email: albertineusa@aol.com. Sr. Danuta Karwacka, Supr. Sisters 9.

MERRILLVILLE. *Andrean H.S. Sisters' Residence* Sisters of SS. Cyril and Methodius , 5959 Broadway, 46410. Tel: 219-887-5287. Email: jambresscm@hotmail.com. Web: www.sscm.org. Teaching at Andrean High School.; Working at Catholic Charities, Diocese of Gary; Working at St. Mary Medical Center Sisters 3; Sisters 1; Sisters 1.

[K] RETREAT HOUSES

EAST CHICAGO. *Bethany Retreat House*, 2202 Lituanica Ave., 46312. Tel: 219-398-5047; Fax: 219-398-9329. Email: bethanyrh@sprynet.com. Web: www.bethanyretreathouse.org. Sr. Joyce Diltz, P.H.J.C. Total Staff 2; Guests 236.

MICHIGAN CITY. *Angela House*, 412 W. 10th St., 46360. Tel: 219-873-1324. Email: angela@atsnet.com. Sisters Anna Clare O'Connor, C.S.C., Dir.; Cyril Dubala, C.S.C. Total Staff 2; Total in Residence 2.

[L] DIOCESAN CHARITIES

GARY. *Catholic Charities*, 973 W. Sixth Ave., 46402. Tel: 219-882-2720; Fax: 219-886-2428. Email: kflanagan@catholic-charities.org. Web: www.catholic-charities.org/. Kenneth M. Flanagan, M.S.W., Ph.D., Diocesan Dir.

Catholic Family Service, 973 W. Sixth Ave., 46402. Tel: 219-882-2723; Fax: 219-886-2428.

973 W. 6th Ave., 46402. Tel: 219-882-2723; Fax: 219-886-2428.

3901 Fir St., East Chicago, 46312. Tel: 219-397-5803; Fax: 219-397-5804.

6919 Indianapolis Blvd., Hammond, 46324. Tel: 219-844-4883; Fax: 219-844-4885.

2967 Willowcreek Rd., Portage, 46368. Tel: 219-762-1177; Fax: 219-762-1827.

1501 Franklin St., Michigan City, 46360. Tel: 219-879-9312; Fax: 219-879-9073.

166 S. West St., Crown Point, 46307. Tel: 219-662-7677; Fax: 219-662-7678.

Family Life Ministry Tel: 219-882-2759; Fax: 219-886-2428.

Legal Title: *Family Life Ministry, Refugee Assistance Program, Marriage Preparation, Rainbows, Pastor's Emergency Fund & Elizabeth Ministry.*

973 W. Sixth Ave., 46402. Tel: 219-882-2720; Fax: 219-886-2428.

Services to the Aging, Retired & Senior Volunteer Program Tel: 219-882-2737; Fax: 219-886-2428.

LaPorte & Starke Co., 1501 Franklin St., Michigan City, 46360. Tel: 219-874-8195; Fax: 219-879-9073.

Lake Co., 973 W. Sixth Ave., 46402. Tel: 219-882-2737; Fax: 219-886-2428.

Senior Companion Program, 1128 Broadway, 46402. Tel: 219-882-7331; Fax: 219-886-2428.

Lake Co., 973 W. Sixth Ave., 46402. Tel: 219-882-7331; Fax: 219-886-2428.

Foster Grandparent Program, 1128 Broadway, 46402. Tel: 219-882-2720; Fax: 219-886-2428.

[M] NEWMAN APOSTOLATES

VALPARAISO. *Newman Apostolate-Valparaiso University* 1511 La Porte Ave., 46383-5818. Tel: 219-464-4042; Fax: 219-462-2711. Email: kevin.mccarthy@valpo.edu. Web: www.valpo.edu/student/stt/. Rev. Kevin P. McCarthy, Chap. St. Teresa, Catholic Student Center of Avila; Chapel and Center for Students attending Valparaiso University Students 836.

[N] MISCELLANEOUS

GARY. *Sojourner Truth House*, 410 W. 13th Ave., 46407. Tel: 219-885-2282; 219-880-2915 (H); Fax: 219-885-1984. Email: sthjopeg@aol.com. Web: www.sojournertruthhouse.com. A ministry for women and children (Professional Clothes Closet, Computer, Parenting, Lifeskill Classes, Hospitality Center, Laundry Facilities, connection to agencies....)

CROWN POINT. *Franciscan Home Care Services, Inc.*,

203 Franciscan Dr., 46307. Tel: 219-661-5321; Fax: 219-661-5305. Email: cgrantner@franciscancommunities.com. Sr. M. Madonna Rougeau, O.S.F., Corp. Sec.

EAST CHICAGO. *HealthVisions Midwest*, 4522 Indianapolis Blvd., 46312. Tel: 219-397-4335; Fax: 219-397-4651. Email: akampwerth@hvusa.org. Web: www.hvusa.org. Mr. Donald G. Barnes, Pres. & CEO.

Office of Hispanic Ministry, 1709 E. 138th St., P.O. Box 3027, 46312. Tel: 219-397-2125; Fax 219-397-2168. Email: atorres@dcgary.org. Web: www.dcgary.org. Adeline Torres, Co-Dir.

HAMMOND. *Alverno Clinical Laboratories, Inc.*, 2434 Interstate Plaza, 46324-3361. Tel: 219-989-3700; Fax: 219-989-3900. Email: jim.sparks@ssfhs.org. Web: ssfhs.org.

Heartland Center, 7128 Arizona Ave., 46323. Tel: 219-844-7515; Fax: 219-844-7566. Email: mail@heartlandctr.org. Web: www.thetimesonline.com/org/Heartland. Revs. Thomas M. Gannon, S.J.; James W. Schulz, S.J.; James M. Dixon, S.J. Office of Peace and Social Justice of the Diocese of Gary. Total Staff 5.

Spiritual Life/Seimetz Center, 1441 Hoffman St., 46327. Tel: 219-932-8321; Fax: 219-932-8321. Email: xctb29c@prodigy.com. Total Staff 3.

HOBART. *Ancilla Systems Incorporated*, 1000 S. Lake Park Ave., 46342. Tel: 219-947-8552; Fax: 219-947-3708. Email: bkaminski@ancilla.org. Web: www.ancilla.org. Sr. Jolise May, P.H.J.C., Chairperson; Beth Kaminski, Pres. & CEO.

Ancilla Systems Foundation, Inc., 46342. Tel: 219-947-8559; Fax: 219-947-3708.

MICHIGAN CITY. *Alverno-Michigan City Corp.*, 1515 Dragoon Tr., P.O. Box 1290, Mishawaka, 46546-1290.

VALPARAISO. *Camp Lawrence* Diocesan Spiritual Center and Youth Camp. , 68 E. 700 N., 46383. Tel: 219-462-8243; 219-462-5261; Fax: 219-477-4452. Email: thorstad@gte.net.

Catholic Youth Organization, 5284 Broadway, 46410. Tel: 219-887-9581.

RELIGIOUS INSTITUTES OF MEN REPRESENTED IN THE DIOCESE

For further details refer to the corresponding bracketed number in the Religious Institutes of Men or Women section.

[0170]—*Basilian Fathers* (Toronto)—C.S.B.
[0200]—*Benedictine Monks*—O.S.B.
[0600]—*Brothers of the Congregation of Holy Cross*—C.S.C.
[0275]—*Carmelites of Mary Immaculate*—C.M.I.
[1130]—*Congregation of the Priests of the Sacred Heart*—S.C.J.
[0480]—*Conventual Franciscans* (Croatia)—O.F.M.Conv
[0260]—*Discalced Carmelite Friars* (Holy Ghost Prov., Poland)—O.C.D.
[0520]—*Franciscan Friars* (Prov. of Assumption of B.V.M.; Prov. of St. John the Baptist; Prov. of the Sacred Heart)—O.F.M.
[0690]—*Jesuit Fathers*—S.J.
[0610]—*Priests of the Congregation of Holy Cross*—C.S.C.
[1200]—*Society of the Divine Savior*—S.D.S.
[1060]—*Society of the Precious Blood*—C.PP.S.

RELIGIOUS INSTITUTES OF WOMEN REPRESENTED IN THE DIOCESE

[]—*Albertine Sisters* (Prov. of Krakow, Poland)—C.S.A.
[0230]—*Benedictine Sisters of the Pontifical Jurisdiction*—O.S.B.
[0360]—*Carmelite Sisters of the Divine Heart of Jesus*—Carmel D.C
[3710]—*Congregation of the Sisters of Saint Agnes*—C.S.A.
[1920]—*Congregation of the Sisters of the Holy Cross*—C.S.C.
[1070-03]—*Dominican Sisters*—O.P.
[1070-13]—*Dominican Sisters*—O.P.
[1210]—*Franciscan Sisters of Chicago*—O.S.F.
[1450]—*Franciscan Sisters of the Sacred Heart*—O.S.F.
[2710]—*Missionaries of Charity*—M.C.
[3130]—*Our Lady of Victory Missionary Sisters*—O.L.V.M.
[3230]—*Poor Handmaids of Jesus Christ*—P.H.J.C.
[2970]—*School Sisters of Notre Dame*—S.S.N.D.
[3340]—*Sisters of Providence*—S.P.
[3780]—*Sisters of Saints Cyril and Methodius*—SS.C.M.
[]—*Sisters of St. Anne of Bangalore*—S.A.B.
[1640]—*Sisters of St. Francis of Perpetual Adoration*—O.S.F.
[3930]—*Sisters of St. Joseph of the Third Order of St. Francis* (Immaculate Conception Prov.)—S.S.J.-T.O

DIOCESAN CEMETERIES

HAMMOND. *Saint John-Saint Joseph*, 1547 167th St., 46324. Tel: 219-844-9475.

MICHIGAN CITY. *Saint Stanislaus*, 1015 Greenwood, 46360. Tel: 219-874-4310.

NECROLOGY

† Bargielski, John, (Retired)—Died Dec. 24, 2002
† Connolly, Patrick, (Retired)—Died Dec. 28, 2002
† Danforth, Clarence, (Retired)—Died June 25, 2003
† Lukaszewski, Leonard, (Retired)—Died July 8, 2003

Diocese of Gaylord

(Dioecesis Gaylordensis)

Most Reverend

PATRICK R. COONEY, S.T.D., S.T.D.

Bishop of Gaylord; ordained December 20, 1959; appointed Titular Bishop of Hodelm and Auxiliary Bishop of Detroit December 3, 1982; consecrated January 27, 1983; appointed Bishop of Gaylord November 21, 1989; installed January 28, 1990 *Res.: 611 W. North St., Gaylord, MI 49735-8349.*

Diocesan Pastoral Center: 611 W. North St., Gaylord, MI 49735-8349. Tel: 989-732-5147; Fax: 989-705-3589.

Web: www.dioceseofgaylord.org

Email: msteffel@dioceseofgaylord.org

ESTABLISHED JULY 20, 1971.

Square Miles 11,171.

Comprises the following 21 Counties in the State of Michigan: Alcona, Alpena, Antrim, Benzie, Charlevoix, Cheboygan, Crawford, Emmet, Grand Traverse, Iosco, Kalkaska, Leelanau, Manistee, Missaukee, Montmorency, Ogemaw, Oscoda, Otsego, Presque Isle, Roscommon and Wexford.

Legal Title: For legal titles of parishes and diocesan institutions, consult the Chancery Office.

STATISTICAL OVERVIEW

Personnel	
Bishop	1
Priests: Diocesan Active in Diocese	44
Priests: Diocesan Active Outside Diocese	2
Priests: Retired, Sick or Absent	20
Number of Diocesan Priests	66
Religious Priests in Diocese	11
Total Priests in Diocese	77
Extern Priests in Diocese	5
Ordinations:	
Diocesan Priests	1
Transitional Deacons	1
Permanent Deacons in Diocese	14
Total Brothers	1
Total Sisters	41
Parishes	
Parishes	81
With Resident Pastor:	
Resident Diocesan Priests	42
Resident Religious Priests	7
Without Resident Pastor:	
Administered by Priests	16
Administered by Deacons	6
Administered by Religious Women	3
Administered by Lay People	7
Professional Ministry Personnel:	
Brothers	1
Sisters	10
Lay Ministers	51
Welfare	
Catholic Hospitals	3
Total Assisted	369,500
Residential Care of Children	2
Total Assisted	45
Day Care Centers	6
Total Assisted	267
Specialized Homes	1
Total Assisted	250
Special Centers for Social Services	23
Total Assisted	5,818
Educational	
Diocesan Students in Other Seminaries	13
Total Seminarians	13
High Schools, Diocesan and Parish	4
Total Students	662
Elementary Schools, Diocesan and Parish	16
Total Students	2,406
Catechesis/Religious Education:	
High School Students	1,720
Elementary Students	4,310
Total Students under Catholic Instruction	9,111
Teachers in the Diocese:	
Sisters	2
Lay Teachers	198
Vital Statistics	
Receptions into the Church:	
Infant Baptism Totals	901
Adult Baptism Totals	110
Received into Full Communion	175
First Communions	1,170
Confirmations	2,232
Marriages:	
Catholic	275
Interfaith	129
Total Marriages	404
Deaths	933
Total Catholic Population	76,060
Total Population	497,264

Former Bishops—Most Revs. EDMUND C. SZOKA, J.C.L., D.D., First Bishop of Gaylord; ord. June 5, 1954; consecrated July 20, 1971; installed July 20, 1971; appt. Archbishop of Detroit March 28, 1981; installed May 17, 1981; named Cardinal Priest May 29, 1988; elevated June 28, 1988; Assigned to the Vatican, 1990; ROBERT J. ROSE, S.T.L., D.D., ord. Dec. 21, 1955; appt. Bishop of Gaylord Oct. 13, 1981; installed Dec. 6, 1981; transferred to Diocese of Grand Rapids July 11, 1989; installed Aug. 30, 1989.

Vicar General—Rev. FRANCIS J. MURPHY, St. Ann Parish, 800 W. 13th, Cadillac, 49601. Tel: 231-775-2471.

Diocesan Offices and Departments

Diocesan Pastoral Center—611 W. North St., Gaylord, 49735-8349. Tel: 989-732-5147; Fax: 989-705-3589. Office Hours: Mon.-Fri. 8-4:30; All business should be directed to this office.

Consultors, Diocesan Board of—Revs. JAMES L. BRUCKSCH; JAMES P. HAYDEN; FRANCIS J. MURPHY; THOMAS A. NEIS; JOHN E. MCCRACKEN; GERALD F. MICKETTI.

Members of the Presbyteral Council—

Elected Members—Revs. JAMES P. HAYDEN; VIANNEY SIPULSKI, O.F.M.; CLARENCE D. SMOLINSKI (Retired); FRANCIS J. MURPHY; THOMAS A. NEIS; GREGORY P. MCCALLUM; PAUL MEGGE.

Appointed Members—Revs. JAMES L. BRUCKSCH; GERALD F. MICKETTI; JOHN E. MCCRACKEN.

Vicars (by region)—Revs. CHARLES G. DONAJKOWSKI, Alpena; ANTHONY M. CITRO, Gaylord; MICHAEL P. CONNER, Manistee; DENNIS R. STILWELL, Petoskey; JAMES K. GARDINER, Traverse City; J. AUGUST FRANCZEK, West Branch.

Administrative Services, Secretariat for—MICHAEL E. STEFFEL, Dir., 611 W. North St., Gaylord, 49735. Tel: 989-732-5147.

Audio-Visual Resource Center—Sr. BARBARA MATIEVICH, O.P., 611 W. North St., Gaylord, 49735. Tel: 989-732-5147.

Archivist—Rev. GERALD F. MICKETTI, 611 W. North St., Gaylord, 49735. Tel: 989-732-5147.

Catechesis— (See Faith Formation of Children and Youth.)

Communications, Secretariat for—CANDACE NEFF, Dir., 611 W. North St., Gaylord, 49735. Tel: 989-732-5147.

Council of Catholic Women, Diocesan—TONI LARSON, Pres., 11411 Lakeshore Dr., Fife Lake, 49633. Tel: 231-879-4490.

Cursillo—Rev. PAUL MEGGE, P.O. Box 40, Cheboygan, 49721. Tel: 231-627-2105.

Ecumenical and Interreligious Affairs, Delegate for—VACANT.

Faith Formation of Adults, Secretariat for—Sr. BARBARA MATIEVICH, O.P., Dir., 611 W. North St., Gaylord, 49735. Tel: 989-732-5147.

Faith Formation of Children and Youth, Secretariat for—Rev. DANIEL B. GALLAGHER, Dir., 611 W. North St., Gaylord, 49735-8349. Tel: 989-732-5147.

Finance Council, Diocesan—Most Rev. PATRICK R. COONEY, S.T.D., S.T.L.; Rev. FRANCIS J. MURPHY; BARBARA BENSON; ALFRED J. GODFREY; EDWARD CARLSON; ROSEMARY SMITH; KIM SMITH; JAMES MERENDA; GERALD G. CASSIDY.

Holy Childhood Pontifical Association—Rev. Msgr. GERARD F. GUZIKOWSKI, 371 Fifth St., Manistee, 49660. Tel: 231-723-2165.

Native American Apostolate—Rev. ANDREW G. BUVALA, O.F.M., Coord., Blessed Kateri Tekakwitha Parish, P.O. Box 369, Suttons Bay, 49682. Tel: 231-271-6651.

Knights of Columbus—MICHAEL J. STANCHINA, Eastern Diocesan Prog. Dir., 937 Joyce Court, Mio, 48647. Tel: 989-848-5322; ROGER HANSEN, Western Diocesan Prog. Dir., 2853 Victoria Dr., Traverse City, 49684. Tel: 231-947-6884.

Worship and Liturgical Formation, Secretariat for—Rev. DUANE A. WACHOWIAK, Dir., 611 W. North St., Gaylord, 49735. Tel: 989-732-5147.

Marriage Enrichment, Secretariat for—Sr. ARLENE BENNETT, R.S.M., Dir., 611 W. North St., Gaylord, 49735. Tel: 517-732-5147.

Migrant Apostolate—Revs. REYNALDO GARCIA, S.J., St. Wenceslaus Parish, 8500 E. Kolarik, Suttons Bay, 49682. Tel: 231-271-3574; WAYNE H. DZIEKAN, St. Michael Church, P.O. Box 9, Suttons Bay, 49682. Tel: 231-271-3744; SYLVIA CORTEZ, Immaculate Conception Parish, 720 W. Second St., Traverse City, 49684. Tel: 231-946-1205.

Justice and Peace—BETH A. BAUER, Dir., 611 W. North St., Gaylord, 49735. Tel: 989-732-5147.

Continuing Spiritual Formation of Clergy, Pastoral Administrators and Women Religious—Rev. JOHN E. MCCRACKEN, Delegate, 611 W. North St., Gaylord, 49735. Tel: 989-732-5147.

Priests' Retirement Fund—Most Rev. PATRICK R. COONEY, S.T.D., S.T.L. Elected Members: Revs. ROBERT W. NALLEY, Chm.; JAMES L. BRUCKSCH; JAMES P. HAYDEN. Appointed Members: DON BARTOSH; Rev. JOHN E. MCCRACKEN.

Vocations and Pastoral Care of Seminarians, Delegate for—Rev. JOSEPH A. BLASKO, Diocese of Gaylord, 611 W. North St., Gaylord, 49735. Tel: 989-732-5147.

Propagation of the Faith—Rev. Msgr. GERARD F. GUZIKOWSKI, Dir., Guardian Angels Parish, 317 Fifth St., Manistee, 49660. Tel: 231-723-2165.

St. Vincent De Paul, Society of—Particular Council of Tawas, 115 First St., Tawas City, 49763. Roscommon County, Box 644, Prudenville, 48651. Tel: 989-366-7613. *P.O. Box 37, Roscommon,*

48653. Tel: 989-275-3036. *Grand Traverse County: Traverse Bay Conference, 715 Beitner St., Traverse City, 49686*. Also particular councils in Cheboygan, Hillman, Hale, Prescott, Mikado and Alpena.

Spiritual Formation—MICHAEL FONSECA, Dir., 611 W. North St., Gaylord, 49735. Tel: 989-732-5147.

Tribunal Diocesan—Rev. ROBERT W. NALLEY Judicial Vicar. Judges: Revs. DENNIS R. STILWELL; R. DALE MAGOON; WILLIAM L. ZWIEFKA. Procurators-Advocates: Revs. JAMES P. HAYDEN; CHARLES G. DONAJKOWSKI; PATRICIA WARD, Auditor; MARY DICKERSON, Notary Inquiries may be made through the local pastors or directed to this office: 611 W. North St., Gaylord, 49735. Tel: 989-732-5147.

Victim Assistance Coordinator—CANDACE NEFF. Tel: 989-732-5147. Email: cneff@dioceseofgaylord.org.

CLERGY, PARISHES, MISSIONS AND PAROCHIAL SCHOOLS

CITY OF GAYLORD
(OTSEGO COUNTY)

ST. MARY CATHEDRAL, [CEM] Rev. John E. McCracken, Rector; Sr. Cecilia Faber, O.P., Pastoral Min.
Res.: 606 N. Ohio Ave., 49735. Tel: 989-732-5448; Fax: 989-705-3585.
Catechesis/Religious Program—Students 379.

OUTSIDE THE CITY OF GAYLORD

ACME, GRAND TRAVERSE CO., CHRIST THE KING, Rev. Garth L. Hilmer.
Res.: P.O. Box 95, 49610. Tel: 231-938-9214; Fax: 231-938-3266.
Church: 3801 Shore Rd., 49610.
School—Grand Traverse Area Schools See separate listing under Institutions Located in the Diocese.
Catechesis/Religious Program—Patricia Cesere, D.R.E. Students 252.

AFTON, CHEBOYGAN CO., ST. MONICA, [CEM] Rev. Thomas M. Dominiak.
Res.: P.O. Box 130, Onaway, 49765. Tel: 989-733-4043; Fax: 989-733-6053.
Church: M-68, 49705.

ALPENA, ALPENA CO.
1—ST. ANNE, [JC] Rev. Daniel G. Madigan.
Res.: 817 Sable, 49707. Tel: 989-356-0622; Fax: 989-354-3918.
Church: 201 S. Ninth Ave., 49707.
Catechesis/Religious Program—T.J. Achatz, D.R.E. Students 91.
2—ST. BERNARD, [JC] Rev. David E. Grzeka.
Res.: 322 Chisholm St., 49707. Tel: 989-354-2676; Fax: 989-354-5142.
Catechesis/Religious Program—Tel: 989-354-8018. Anne Kelley, D.R.E. Students 50.
3—ST. JOHN THE BAPTIST, Rev. Kenneth R. Stachnik.
Res.: 2550 S. First Ave., 49707. Tel: 989-354-3019; Fax: 989-358-9079.
4—ST. MARY, [JC] Rev. Gregory P. McCallum.
Res.: 516 N. Second Ave., 49707. Tel: 989-354-2322; Fax: 989-354-2030.
Catechesis/Religious Program—Tel: 989-354-8655. Anne Kelley, D.R.E. Students 120.

ALVERNO, CHEBOYGAN CO., ST. FRANCIS OF ASSISI, Closed., For sacramental records contact St. Mary-St. Charles Parish, Cheboygan.

ATLANTA, MONTMORENCY CO., JESUS THE GOOD SHEPHERD, Rev. Vianney C. Sipulski, O.F.M.
Res.: P.O. Box 216, Hillman, 49746. Tel: 989-742-4542; Fax: 989-742-8090.
Church: 4521 County Rd. 491, 49746.

BAY SHORE, EMMET CO., ST. FRANCIS SOLANUS, Rev. Dennis R. Stilwell.
Res.: 513 Howard St., Petoskey, 49770. Tel: 231-347-4133; Fax: 231-347-4134.
Church: Townline Rd., 49770.

BEAVER ISLAND, CHARLEVOIX CO., HOLY CROSS, [CEM] Rev. Patrick T. Cawley.
Res.: P.O. Box 145, St. James, 49782.
St. James: Kings Hwy., 49782. Tel: 231-448-2230; Fax: 231-448-2230.

BELLAIRE, ANTRIM CO., ST. LUKE, Sisters Celine Goessl, S.C.S.C., Admin.; Joelle Mauer, S.C.S.C., Pastoral Liturgist.
Res.: 3078 M-88, P.O. Box 799, 49615-0799. Tel: 231-533-8121; Fax: 231-533-8759.

BLACK RIVER, ALCONA CO., ST. GABRIEL, [CEM] Rev. Lawrence A. Kelleher.
Res.: 2188 W. Nicholson Hill Rd., Ossineke, 49766-9736. Tel: 989-471-2555; Fax: 989-471-3221.
Church: 5570 N. Lake Shore Dr., 48721.

BOYNE CITY, CHARLEVOIX CO., ST. MATTHEW, [JC] Rev. Francis C. Partridge.
Res.: 1303 Boyne Ave., 49712. Tel: 231-582-7718; Fax: 231-582-7490.
Catechesis/Religious Program—Tel: 231-582-6589. Suzanne Dzwik, D.R.E. Students 135.

BOYNE FALLS, CHARLEVOIX CO., ST. AUGUSTINE, [CEM] Rev. Francis C. Partridge.
Res.: 1303 Boyne Ave., Boyne City, 49712. Tel: 231-582-7718; Fax: 231-582-7490.
Church: Grove St., 49713. Tel: 231-549-2350.
Catechesis/Religious Program—Frank Wasylewski, D.R.E. Students 62.

BURT LAKE, CHEBOYGAN CO., ASSUMPTION OF ST. MARY, Raymond Griffith, Lay Admin.
Res.: P.O. Box 122, Pellston, 49769. Tel: 231-539-8805; Fax: 231-539-8572.

CADILLAC, WEXFORD CO., ST. ANN, [CEM] Revs. Francis J. Murphy; Artur F. Duchnowicz; Deacon James Barton, Pastoral Min.
Res.: 800 W. 13th St., 49601-9281. Tel: 231-775-2471; Fax: 231-775-0161.

CEDAR, LEELANAU CO., HOLY ROSARY, [CEM] Deacon John Moeggenberg, Admin.
Res.: 3919 E. Gatzke Rd., 49621. Tel: 231-228-5429; Fax: 231-228-5529.

CHARLEVOIX, CHARLEVOIX CO., ST. MARY, Rev. Thomas A. Neis.
Res.: 102 W. Garfield, 49720. Tel: 231-547-6652.
Catechesis/Religious Program—Students 97.

CHEBOYGAN, CHEBOYGAN CO., ST. MARY-ST. CHARLES, [JC] Rev. Paul Megge; Deacon Stan Szczepanski, Pastoral Assoc.; Mrs. Patricia Watson, Pastoral Assoc.
Mailing Address: P.O. Box 40, 49721. Tel: 231-627-2105; Fax: 231-627-5362.
Catechesis/Religious Program—Students 132.

COPEMISH, MANISTEE CO., ST. RAPHAEL, [CEM] Rev. Richard A. Kosterman.
Res.: P.O. Box 56, 49625. Tel: 231-864-4141; Fax: 231-378-4953.
Church: M-115, 49765.

CROSS VILLAGE, EMMET CO., HOLY CROSS, [CEM] Deacon Joseph Nelson, Pastoral Admin.
Mailing Address: P.O. Box 120, 49723.
Res.: 6624 N. Lake Shore, 49740-9745. Tel: 231-526-2030.

EAST JORDAN, CHARLEVOIX CO., ST. JOSEPH, [CEM] Deacon Timothy J. Pilon, Pastoral Admin.
Res.: P.O. Box 379, 49727. Tel: 231-536-2934; Fax: 231-536-2988.

EAST TAWAS, IOSCO CO.
1—HOLY FAMILY, Rev. Donald R. Geyman.
Res.: P.O. Box 472, 48730.
Church: 516 W. Lincoln, 48730. Tel: 989-362-3162; Fax: 989-362-9077.
2—ST. JOSEPH, Merged, with Immaculate Heart of Mary, Tawas City to form Holy Family, East Tawas.

ELK RAPIDS, ANTRIM CO., SACRED HEART, [CEM] Rev. Robert J. Zuchowski.
Res.: 143 Charles St., 49629. Tel: 231-264-8087; Fax: 231-264-6350.
Catechesis/Religious Program—John Drury, D.R.E. Students 78.

ELMIRA, ANTRIM CO., ST. THOMAS AQUINAS, [CEM] Rev. Richard T. Hannon.
Res.: P.O. Box 128, 49730. Tel: 231-546-3326.
Church: M-32, 49730.

EMPIRE, LEELANAU CO., ST. PHILIP NERI, [CEM] Rev. William W. Lipscomb.
Res.: P.O. Box 257, 49630. Tel: 231-326-5255; Fax: 231-326-5839.
Church: 11411 La Core Ave., 49630.

FIFE LAKE, GRAND TRAVERSE CO., ST. ALOYSIUS, [CEM] Rev. James K. Gardiner.
Res.: 0438 County Rd. 612, Kalkaska, 49646. Tel: 231-258-5021; Fax: 231-258-2842.
Church: Merritt St., 49633. Tel: 231-258-2752.

FRANKFORT, BENZIE CO., ST. ANN, Rev. Raymond C. Cotter.
Res.: P.O. Box 1168, 508 Crystal Ave., 49635. Tel: 231-352-4421; Fax: 231-352-9940
Catechesis/Religious Program—Tel: 231-352-4541. Students 35.

GILLS PIER, LEELANAU CO., ST. WENCESLAUS, [CEM] Rev. Reynaldo Garcia, S.J.; Gary Zemaitis, Lay Admin.
Church & Res.: 8500 E. Kolarik Rd., Suttons Bay, 49682. Tel: 231-271-3574.

GLENNIE, ALCONA CO., ST. FRANCIS OF ASSISI, Closed. For inquiries for parish records contact the chancery.

GOOD HART, EMMET CO., ST. IGNATIUS, [CEM] Deacon Joseph Nelson, Pastoral Admin.
Mailing Address: P.O. Box 120, Cross Village, 49723.
Res.: 6624 N. Lake Shore Dr., Cross Village, 49740. Tel: 231-526-2030.

GRAYLING, CRAWFORD CO., ST. MARY, Rev. Robert W. Nalley.
Res.: 708 Peninsular St., 49738. Tel: 989-348-7291; 989-348-7657 (Office); Fax: 989-348-7658.
Catechesis/Religious Program—Students 61.

HALE, IOSCO CO., ST. PIUS X, Rev. J. August Franczek.
Res.: P.O. Box 428, 48739. Tel: 989-728-2278; Fax: 989-728-7487.
Church: 3900 M-65, 48739.
Catechesis/Religious Program—Tel: 989-728-2278; Fax: 989-728-7487. Karol Shellenbarger, D.R.E. Students 40.

HANNAH, GRAND TRAVERSE CO., ST. MARY, [CEM] Revs. James P. Hayden; Michael S. Janowski.
Res.: 2962 M-113 West Rd., Kingsley, 49649. Tel: 231-263-2430.
Catechesis/Religious Program—Nancy Horton, D.R.E. Students 36.
Convent—2912 M-113 West Rd., Kingsley, 49649. Tel: 616-263-5287.

HARBOR SPRINGS, EMMET CO., HOLY CHILDHOOD OF JESUS, [CEM] Rev. Joseph P. Graff.
Res.: 150 W. Main St., 49740. Tel: 231-526-2017; Fax: 231-526-9299.
Catechesis/Religious Program—Tel: 616-526-7181. Robert Chapdelaine, D.R.E. Students 243.

HARRIETTA, WEXFORD CO., ST. EDWARD, Rev. Francis J. Murphy.
Res.: 800 W. 13th St., Cadillac, 49601-9281. Tel: 231-775-2471; Fax: 231-775-2452.
Church: 207 W. Gaston, 49638.

HARRISVILLE, ALCONA CO., ST. ANNE, [CEM] Rev. Lawrence E. Boks.
Res.: P.O. Box 345, 48740. Tel: 989-724-6713.
Church: 110 State St., 48740.

HERRON, ALPENA CO., ST. ROSE OF LIMA, Agnes Dubie, Lay Admin.
Church: 3439 Herron Rd., 49744. Tel: 989-379-4316.

HIGGINS LAKE, ROSCOMMON CO., ST. HUBERT, Rev. Lawrence J. Sergott.
Res.: P.O. Box 75, 48627. Tel: 989-821-5591; Fax: 989-821-5895.
Church: 7612 W. Higgins Lake Dr., 48627.

HILLMAN, MONTMORENCY CO., ST. AUGUSTINE, [CEM] Rev. Vianney C. Sipulski, O.F.M.
Res.: P.O. Box 216, 49746. Tel: 989-742-4542; Fax: 989-742-8090.
Church: 24140 Veterans Memorial Hwy., 49746.
Catechesis/Religious Program—Patty Gressick, D.R.E. Students 65.

HOUGHTON LAKE, ROSCOMMON CO., ST. JAMES, Rev. Lawrence J. Sergott.
Res.: P.O. Box 75, Higgins Lake, 48627. Tel: 989-821-5591; Fax: 989-821-5895.
Church: 7878 E. Houghton Lake Dr., 48629. Tel: 989-422-3925.

INDIAN RIVER, CHEBOYGAN CO., CROSS IN THE WOODS CATHOLIC SHRINE, [CEM] Revs. Harry Speckman, O.F.M.; Donard Paulus, O.F.M.; Albert Langheim, O.F.M.; Sylvester Micek, O.F.M.; Bro. Thom Smith, O.F.M.
Res.: 7078 M-68, 49749. Tel: 231-238-8973; Fax: 231-238-7012.
Catechesis/Religious Program— 49749. Tel: 231-238-8542. Elizabeth Gengle, D.R.E. Students 85.

KALKASKA, KALKASKA CO., ST. MARY OF THE WOODS, [CEM] Rev. James K. Gardiner.
Res.: 0438 County Rd. 612, 49646. Tel: 231-258-5021; Fax: 231-258-2842.
Catechesis/Religious Program—Robert Bowersox, D.R.E. Students 47.

KLACKING CREEK, OGEMAW CO., HOLY FAMILY, [CEM] Rev. Miro Wiese, O.F.M.
Res.: 402 W. Peters Rd., West Branch, 48661. Tel: 989-345-3422.
Catechesis/Religious Program—Glen Painter, D.R.E. Students 50.

LAKE CITY, MISSAUKEE CO., ST. STEPHEN, Revs. Francis J. Murphy; Artur F. Duchnowicz.
Res.: P.O. Box 379, 49651. Tel: 231-839-2121; Fax: 231-839-3755.
Church: 506 Union St., 49651.
Catechesis/Religious Program—Students 35.

LAKE LEELANAU, LEELANAU CO., ST. MARY, [CEM] Rev. Gerard A. Hunko.
Mailing Address: P.O. Box 340, 49653. Tel: 231-256-9676; Fax: 231-256-7812.
Res.: 307 S. St. Mary St., 49653.
Church: 403 S. St. Mary St., 49653.

LARKS LAKE, EMMET CO., ST. NICHOLAS, [CEM] Deacon Joseph Nelson, Pastoral Admin.
Mailing Address: P.O. Box 120, Cross Village, 49723.
Res.: 6624 N. Lake Shore Dr., Cross Village, 49740. Tel: 231-526-2030.

LEWISTON, MONTMORENCY CO., ST. FRANCIS OF ASSISI, [CEM] Rev. Gregory Kurutz, O.F.M.
Res.: P.O. Box 182, 49756. Tel: 989-786-2235; Fax: 989-786-7685.
Church: 4086 Salling Ave., 49756. Tel: 989-786-3081.
Catechesis/Religious Program—Laura Bartle, D.R.E. Students 35.

MACKINAW CITY, EMMET CO., ST. ANTHONY OF PADUA, [CEM] Sr. Chris Herald, O.P., Pastoral Admin.

Res.: P.O. Box 460, 49701. Tel: 231-436-5561; 231-436-5601; Fax: 231-436-5699.
Church: 600 W. Central Ave., 49701.

MANCELONA, ANTRIM CO., ST. ANTHONY, [CEM] Rev. R. Dale Magoon.
Mailing Address: P.O. Box 677, 49659-0677.
Church: 209 Jefferson St., 49659. Tel: 231-587-8401; Fax: 231-587-5643.

MANISTEE, MANISTEE CO.

1—GUARDIAN ANGELS, [JC] Rev. Msgr. Gerard Guzikowski.
Res.: 371 Fifth St., 49660. Tel: 231-723-2165.
Convent—501 Michael St., 49660. Tel: 231-723-6332.

2—ST. JOSEPH, [JC] Rev. William L. Zwiefka.
Res.: 254 Sixth St., 49660. Tel: 231-723-2619; Fax: 231-723-6827.
Catechesis/Religious Program—Tel: 231-723-3732. Liz Hainstock, D.R.E. Students 200.

3—ST. MARY OF MT. CARMEL SHRINE, [JC] Rev. James M. Bearss.
Res.: 260 St. Mary Pkwy., 49660. Tel: 231-723-3345; Fax: 231-723-2157.
Catechesis/Religious Program—Students 95.

MANTON, WEXFORD CO., ST. THERESA, Revs. Francis J. Murphy; Artur F. Duchnowicz.
Res.: P.O. Box 379, Lake City, 49651. Tel: 231-839-2121.
Church: 9475 14th & 1/4 Rd., 49663.

MAPLE CITY, LEELANAU CO., ST. RITA-ST. JOSEPH, Rev. William W. Lipscomb.
Mailing Address: P.O. Box 75, 49664-0075. Tel: 231-228-5823; Fax: 231-228-5823.
Church: 8707 Hill St., 49664. Tel: 231-228-5823.

MAPLETON, GRAND TRAVERSE CO., ST. JOSEPH, [CEM] Rev. Edwin A. Thome, Admin. (Retired).
Mailing Address: 13400 Center Rd., Traverse City, 49686. Tel: 231-223-4303.
Catechesis/Religious Program—Denise Elsenheimer, D.R.E. Students 65.

MCBAIN, MISSAUKEE CO., ST. RITA, Closed. For inquiries for parish records contact the chancery.

METZ, PRESQUE ISLE CO., ST. DOMINIC, [CEM] Sr. Rita Epple, R.S.M., Pastoral Admin.
Res.: 9269 County Rd. 441, Posen, 49776. Tel: 989-766-2694; Fax: 989-766-2694.
Catechesis/Religious Program—Carolyn Haske, D.R.E. Students 37.

MIKADO, ALOCONA CO., ST. RAPHAEL, [CEM] Rev. Lawrence E. Boks.
Res.: P.O. Box 345, Harrisville, 48740. Tel: 989-724-6713.
Church: 2531 E. Mikado Rd., 48745. Tel: 989-736-6071.

MIO, OSCODA CO., ST. MARY, Rev. Joseph A. Blasko.
Res.: P.O. Box 189, 48647. Tel: 989-826-5509; Fax: 989-826-1333.
Ministry Office—Tel: 989-826-6057.

NORTHPORT, LEELANAU CO., ST. GERTRUDE, Rev. Wayne H. Dziekan.
Res.: P.O. Box 9, Suttons Bay, 49682. Tel: 231-271-3744.
Church: 701 Warren, 49670.

ONAWAY, PRESQUE ISLE CO., ST. PAUL, [CEM] Rev. Thomas M. Dominiak.
Res.: 3856 Oak St., P.O. Box 130, 49765. Tel: 989-733-4043; Fax: 989-733-6053.

ONEKAMA, MANISTEE CO., ST. JOSEPH, [CEM] Rev. Michael P. Conner.
Res.: P.O. Box 150, 49675. Tel: 231-889-4254; Fax: 231-889-3706.
Church: 8380 Fifth St., 49675.

OSCODA, IOSCO CO., SACRED HEART, [CEM] Rev. James L. Brucksch.
Res.: 5300 N. U.S.-23, 48750. Tel: 989-739-9511; Fax: 989-739-3010.
Catechesis/Religious Program—Tel: 989-739-5523. Mrs. Jackie Welles, D.R.E. Students 62.

OSSINEKE, ALPENA CO., ST. CATHERINE, [CEM] Rev. Lawrence A. Kelleher.
Res.: 2188 W. Nicholson Hill Rd., 49766-9736. Tel: 989-471-2556; Fax: 989-471-3221.
Catechesis/Religious Program—Tel: 989-471-5121. Ann Skuse, D.R.E.; Valerie LaBell, D.R.E. Students 75.

PELLSTON, EMMET CO., ST. CLEMENT, [CEM] Raymond Griffith, Lay Admin.
Res.: P.O. Box 122, 49769. Tel: 231-539-8805; Fax: 231-539-8572.
Church: 202 Maple, 49769.

PESHABESTOWN, LEELANAU CO., BLESSED KATERI TEKAKWITHA, Rev. Andrew Buvala, O.F.M.
Res.: P.O. Box 369, Suttons Bay, 49682. Tel: 231-271-6651; Fax: 231-271-4954.

PETOSKEY, EMMET CO., ST. FRANCIS XAVIER, [CEM] Rev. Dennis R. Stilwell.
Res.: 513 Howard St., 49770. Tel: 231-347-4133; Fax: 231-347-4134.
School—414 Michigan St., 49770. Tel: 231-347-3651; Fax: 231-347-3610. Jon Moore, Prin. Students 169.
Catechesis/Religious Program—Tel: 231-347-2681. Students 90.

POSEN, PRESQUE ISLE CO., ST. CASIMIR, [CEM] Rev. Stanislaw J. Bereda.
Res.: P.O. Box 217, 49776. Tel: 989-766-2660.
Church: 10075 M-65 N.,, 49776-0217.
Catechesis/Religious Program—Joan Chappa, D.R.E. Students 108.

PRAGA, ANTRIM CO., ST. JOHN NEPOMUCENE, [CEM] Deacon Timothy J. Pilon, Pastoral Admin.
Res.: P.O. Box 379, East Jordan, 49727. Tel: 231-536-2934; Fax: 231-536-2988.

PRUDENVILLE, ROSCOMMON CO., OUR LADY OF THE LAKE, Rev. John O. Ladd.
Res.: 1037 W. Houghton Lake Dr., P.O. Box 800, 48651. Tel: 989-366-5533; Fax: 989-366-5988.
Catechesis/Religious Program—Barbara Falls, D.R.E. Students 55.

RIGGSVILLE, CHEBOYGAN CO., SACRED HEART, Richard Jankoviak, Lay Admin.
Church: 4989 Polish Line Rd., Cheboygan, 49721. Tel: 231-627-9663 (Parish); Fax: 231-627-7836.

ROGERS CITY, PRESQUE ISLE CO., ST. IGNATIUS, [CEM] Rev. Charles G. Donajkowski.
Business Office & Mailing Address: 585 S. Third St., 49779. Tel: 989-734-2753; Fax: 989-734-7671.
Catechesis/Religious Program—Tel: 989-734-7768. Students 26.

ROSCOMMON, ROSCOMMON CO., ST. MICHAEL, Rev. Anthony M. Citro.
Res.: 104 N. 6th St., P.O. Box 248, 48653. Tel: 989-275-5212; Fax: 989-275-9020.
Catechesis/Religious Program—Tel: 989-275-5212. Kathleen Butler, D.R.E. Students 110.

ST. HELEN, ROSCOMMON CO., ST. HELEN, Rev. Albert Couturier.
Res.: 737 N. St. Helen Rd., 48646. Tel: 989-389-3495; 989-389-4959 (Office); 989-389-3441 (Church); Fax: 989-389-3495.

SKIDWAY LAKE, OGEMAW CO., ST. STEPHEN OF HUNGARY, Rev. Alexander Boruta, O.F.M.
Mailing Address: P.O. Box 4430, Prescott, 48756.
Res.: 2811 E. Greenwood Rd., Prescott, 48756. Tel: 989-873-3340; Fax: 989-873-5209.

SUTTONS BAY, LEELANAU CO., ST. MICHAEL THE ARCHANGEL, [CEM] Rev. Wayne H. Dziekan.
Res.: P.O. Box 9, 49682. Tel: 231-271-3744.
Church: 315 Broadway, 49682.

TAWAS CITY, IOSCO CO., IMMACULATE HEART OF MARY, Merged, with St. Joseph, East Tawas to form Holy Family, East Tawas.

TRAVERSE CITY, GRAND TRAVERSE CO.

1—ST. FRANCIS OF ASSISI, Revs. James K. Gardiner; Thomas Patrick Maher; Sr. Katherine Murphy, R.S.M., Pastoral Assoc.
Res.: 1025 S. Union St., 49684. Tel: 231-947-4620; Fax: 231-947-4693.

2—IMMACULATE CONCEPTION, Revs. James P. Hayden; Michael S. Janowski.
Res.: 720 W. Second, 49684. Tel: 231-946-4211; Fax: 231-946-0567.
Catechesis/Religious Program—Tel: 231-946-2782. Dannie Brzezinski, D.R.E. Students 240.

3—ST. PATRICK, Rev. Gerald F. Micketti.
Res.: 630 W. Silver Lake Rd. S., 49684-8526. Tel: 231-943-4633; Fax: 231-943-8886.
Catechesis/Religious Program—Students 106.

VANDERBILT, OTSEGO CO., HOLY REDEEMER, Rev. John E. McCracken.
Res.: 606 N. Ohio St., 49735. Tel: 989-732-5448.

WEST BRANCH, OGEMAW CO., ST. JOSEPH, [CEM] Rev. Robert H. Bissot.
Mailing Address: 961 W. Houghton, 48661. Tel: 989-345-0064; Fax: 989-345-8757.
Res.: 907 Houghton Ave., 48661.
School—Tel: 989-345-0220; Fax: 989-345-3030.
Catechesis/Religious Program—Tel: 989-345-0670. Students 80.

WHITTEMORE, IOSCO CO., ST. JAMES, [CEM] Rev. James Krasman, O.F.M.
Res.: P.O. Box 206, 48770. Tel: 989-756-2591; Fax: 989-756-3255.
Church: 202 E. Sherman, 48770.

Special Assignment:
Revs.—
Derylo, Walter W., Ministry with Food for the Poor
Zielinski, Chad W., Military Service

Absent on Leave:
Revs.—
Greene, John C.
Suchocki, James A.

Retired:
Revs.—
Fox, Gabriel, 305 Care Center Dr., #225, Manistee, 49660.
Gietzen, Albin J., P.O. Box 311, Buckley, 49620.
Jocys, Leonard, 71 Chelsea Ln., Cheboygan, 49721.
Machcinski, Anthony J., 7826 Homer Ave., Hudson, FL 34667.
Marek, Walter, P.O. Box 203, Whitehall, 49461.
Mausolf, James H., 1421 Veterans Dr., Traverse City, 49684.
Mikulski, Isadore J., 7718 Westwood Dr., Oscoda, 48750.
Mulka, Arthur C., 2388 Emmett, Alpena, 49707.
Mulka, Raymond C., 300 Washington, Alpena, 49707.
Reitz, Joseph A., 52 Marble Rd., Lowell, 49331.
Rushman, John, Iosco Medical Care Facility, 1201 Harris, Tawas City, 48763.
Sarosiek, John H., 4468 Lincoln, Dearborn Heights, 48125.
Seifferly, Richard R., P.O. Box 422, West Branch, 48661-0422.
Sitar, Richard T., 12039 Leer Rd., Posen, 49776.
Smolinski, Clarence D., 14692 Lakeside Dr., Presque Isle, 49777.
Tamulis, John J., 1189 S. 35 Mile Rd., Cadillac, 49601.
Thome, Edwin A., 6844 Deepwater Point Rd., Acme, 49610.
Wiekierak, Joseph F., 1470 West Norton, Apt. H-5, Muskegon, 49441-4362.

Permanent Deacons:
Barton, James, St. Ann, Cadillac
Bousamra, Thomas, St. Patrick, Traverse City
Friend, Harry, St. Philip, Empire
Goetz, Robert, (Unassigned)
Krupka, James, St. Joseph of Mapleton, Traverse City
LoVetere, Arthur, Jesus the Good Shepherd, Atlanta
Moeggenberg, John, Holy Rosary, Cedar
Nelson, Joseph B., Holy Cross, Cross Village
Pilon, Timothy J., St. Joseph, East Jordon
Szczepanski, Stanley T., St. Mary-St. Charles, Cheboygan
Trapp, Richard, (Retired)
Vondra, Edward, (Unassigned)
Wallace, John, (Retired)
Wendell, Max, (Unassigned)

INSTITUTIONS LOCATED IN THE DIOCESE

[A] INTERPAROCHIAL SCHOOLS

MANISTEE. *Manistee Catholic Central Schools*, (Grades PreK-12), 1200 U.S. 31 South (at 12th St.), 49660. Tel: 231-723-2529; Fax: 231-723-0669. Chris Smith, Prin. Sisters 1; Lay Teachers 19; Students 230; Preschool 48.

TRAVERSE CITY. *St. Elizabeth Ann Seton Middle School*, (Grades 6-8), 1601 Three Mile Rd. N., 49686. Tel: 231-932-4810; Fax: 231-932-4814. Michael P. Wilson, Prin.; Deborah Haase, Sec. Lay Teachers 17; Students 270.

St. Francis High School, 123 E. 11th St., 49684. Tel: 231-946-8038; Fax: 231-946-1878. Email: rbridg@gtacs.org. Web: www.gtacs.org. Robert Bridges, Prin. Lay Teachers 16; Students 327.

Grand Traverse Area Catholic Schools, 123 E. 11th St., 49684. Tel: 231-946-8100. Michael R. Buell, Supt. Lay Teachers 56; Students 1,038.

Holy Angels Elementary, (Grades K-2), 130 E. 10th, 49684. Tel: 231-946-5961; Fax: 231-946-1878. Maureen DeYoung, Prin. Lay Teachers 13; Students 206.

Immaculate Conception Elementary School, (Grades 3-5), 218 Vine, 49684. Tel: 231-947-1252. Charles Taylor, Prin. Lay Teachers 10; Students 235.

[B] PAROCHIAL SCHOOLS

GAYLORD. *St. Mary Cathedral Elementary School*, (Grades K-6), 321 N. Otsego Ave., 49735. Tel: 989-732-5801; Fax: 989-732-7812. Deanna Couture, Prin. Lay Teachers 14; Students 194.

St. Mary Cathedral High School, (Grades 7-12), 310 W. Mitchell, 49735. Tel: 989-732-5303; Fax: 989-732-2085. Email: stmarys@northland.lib.mi.us. Mr. James Kerfoot, Prin. Lay Teachers 13; Students 184.

ALPENA. *All Saints Catholic School* (Consolidation of St. Anne Elementary, Alpena and St. Mary Elementary, Alpena) , 205 S. Ninth St., 49707.

Tel: 989-354-4911; Fax: 989-354-3752. Email: allsaints@speednet.com. Mary Lightner, Prin. Lay Teachers 7; Students 124.

CADILLAC. *St. Ann Elementary*, (Grades K-7), 800 W. 13th, 49601. Tel: 231-775-1301; Fax: 231-775-0161. Mary Ann Palacios, Prin. Lay Teachers 11; Students 188.

CHARLEVOIX. *St. Mary Elementary*, (Grades K-6), 1005 Bridge St., 49720. Tel: 231-547-9441; Fax: 231-547-6658. Email: stmary@freeway.net. Janet M. Troppman, Prin. Lay Teachers 6; Students 80.

CHEBOYGAN. *Bishop Baraga Elementary*, (Grades K-6), 421 State St., 49721. Email: principal@nmo.net. Web: www.bishopbaraga.com. James Leinbach, Prin. Lay Teachers 13; Students 168.

EAST TAWAS. *Holy Family Elementary School*, (Grades K-6), 411 N. Wilkinson, 48730. Tel: 989-362-5651; Fax: 989-362-9077. Email: hfschool@voyager.net. Linda Howe, Prin. Lay Teachers 7; Students 96.

HANNAH. *St. Mary's Hannah School*, (Grades K-8), 2912 M-113, 49649. Tel: 231-263-5288; Fax: 231-263-5288. Lisa Medina, Prin. Lay Teachers 5; Students 42.

LAKE LEELANAU. *St. Mary's Schools*, (Grades K-12), 303 S. St. Mary St., 49653. Tel: 231-256-9636; Fax: 231-256-7239. Email: stmarys@microageetc.com. P.O. Box 340, 49653. Patrick Gaudard, Prin. Lay Teachers 13; Students 221.

PETOSKEY. *St. Francis Xavier Elementary*, (Grades K-8), 414 Michigan, 49770. Tel: 231-347-3651; Fax: 231-347-3610. Jon Moore, Prin. Lay Teachers 15; Students 187.

PRUDENVILLE. *Our Lady of the Lake Elementary*, (Grades K-8), 1039 W. Houghton Lake, 48651. Tel: 989-366-5592; Fax: 989-366-1348. Email: olls@freeway.net. Lea Ann Anderson, Prin. Lay Teachers 8; Students 78.

ROGERS CITY. *St. Ignatius Elementary*, (Grades 1-8), 545 S. Third, 49779. Tel: 989-734-3443. Amy Rabeau, Prin. Sisters 1; Lay Teachers 7; Students 100.

WEST BRANCH. *St. Joseph Elementary*, (Grades K-8), 935 W. Houghton Ave., 48661. Tel: 989-345-0220; Fax: 989-345-3030. Lorrene Spaulding, Prin. Lay Teachers 10; Students 180.

[C] GENERAL HOSPITALS

CADILLAC. *Mercy Hospital* Mercy Health Services North, Division of Sisters of Mercy Health Corp., Trinity Health, Novi, MI , 400 Hobart St., 49601. Tel: 231-876-7200; Fax: 231-876-7439. Email: mercycadillac@munsonhealthcare.org. Web: www.mercycadillac.com. Mr. John L. MacLeod, CEO. Bed Capacity 97; Patients Assisted Annually 72,653.

GRAYLING. *Mercy Hospital*, 1100 E. Michigan Ave., 49738. Tel: 989-348-5461; Fax: 989-348-0479. Email: BenderM@trinity-health.org. Stephanie J. Riemer-Matuzak, CEO. Member Organization of Trinity Health. Bed Capacity 128; Patients Assisted Annually 96,847.

TAWAS CITY. *St. Joseph Health System*, 200 Hemlock, P.O. Box 659, 48764-0659. Tel: 989-362-3411; 989-362-4611; Fax: 989-362-7277. Email: v.balser@sjhsys.org. Web: www.sjhsys.org. Mr. Patrick J. Murtha, Pres. & CEO; Sisters Margot Eder, S.S.J., Chap.; Patricia Mullen, S.S.J., Vice Pres. Mission Integration. Associated with Ascension Health, St. Louis, MO. Sisters of St. Joseph (Nazareth, MI) 2; Bed Capacity 49; Patients Assisted Annually 200,000.

[D] CONVENTS AND RESIDENCES FOR SISTERS

CONWAY. *Sacramentine Monastery of Perpetual Adoration*, P.O. Box 86, 49722. Tel: 231-347-0447. Sr. Mary Rosalie, O.S.S., Prioress. Sacramentine Sisters 2.

TRAVERSE CITY. *Infant Jesus of Prague Monastery*, 3501 Silver Lake Rd., 49684-8949. Tel: 231-946-4960; Fax: 231-947-7729. Rev. George B. Billman, Chap. Tel: 231-947-6935; Sr. Celine Sook, O.C.D. Carmelite Nuns 6; Solemn Vows 2.

[E] CHILD CARE FACILITIES

ALPENA. *Huron House/Holy Cross Children's Services*, 4761 U.S. 23 N., 49707. Tel: 989-356-3573; Fax: 989-356-4910. *Holy Cross Childrens Services*, 8759 Clinton-Macon Rd., Clinton, 49236. Bro. Francis Boylan, C.S.C., Pres. Residential and community-based treatment programs for troubled youth and families, with facilities located throughout the state of Michigan. Boys 30; Staff 17.

ONAWAY. *Russell House/Holy Cross Children's Services*, P.O. Box 599, 49765. Tel: 989-733-5201; Fax: 989-733-8678. Boys 15; Staff 17.

TRAVERSE CITY. *Holy Cross Children's Services*, 207 W. Grandview Pkwy., Ste. 200, 49684. Tel: 231-922-9664; 800-235-9664; Fax: 231-922-9675. Web: www.hcsnet.org. Bro. Francis Boylan, C.S.C., Pres.; Rick Boone, Regl. Dir. Youth 250.

[F] RETREAT CENTERS AND CAMPS

GAYLORD. *Camp Sancta Maria*, P.O. Box 338, 49734. Tel: 231-546-3878; Fax: 231-546-3171. Email: office@campsanctamaria.org. Web: www.campsanctamaria.org. Michael Hickey, Exec. Dir.; James Berigan, Contact Person. Staff 50; Campers 555.

CONWAY. *Augustine Center*, P.O. Box 84, 49722-0084. Tel: 231-347-3657; Fax: 231-347-9502. Email: huberyop@freeway.net. Sr. Barbara Hubeny, O.P., Dir.

[G] CATHOLIC SOCIAL SERVICE AGENCIES

GAYLORD. *Catholic Human Services*, 611 W. North St., 49735. Tel: 989-732-5147; Fax: 989-705-3589. Email: chshast@freeway.net. Mr. David Martin, Pres. & CEO.

Area Offices:

154 S. Ripley Blvd., Alpena, 49707. Tel: 989-356-6385; Fax: 989-356-4909. Joseph Carant, Admin.

421 S. Mitchell, Cadillac, 49601. Tel: 231-775-6581; Fax: 231-775-5421. Nancy Morgridge, Admin.

1169 Elkview #3, 49735. Tel: 989-732-6761; Fax: 989-732-6763. Nancy Morgridge, Admin.

1000 Hastings St., Traverse City, 49686. Tel: 231-947-8110; Fax: 231-947-3522. Mr. David Martin, Admin.

[H] MISCELLANEOUS

GAYLORD. *Northern Michigan Catholic Foundation, Inc.*, 611 W. North St., 49735. Tel: 989-732-5147; Fax: 989-705-3589. Email: msteffel@dioceseofgaylord.org. H. Charles Nelson, Pres.; Ken Kleinrichert, Vice Pres.; Joel Myler, Sec.; James Kelly, Treas.; Most Rev. Patrick R. Cooney, S.T.D., S.T.L.; Ann Mawby; David M. Penrod; Michael Mulcahy; Gene Skiba.

ALPENA. *Madonna House Apostolate*, 309 Lockwood, 49707-2543. Tel: 989-354-4073. Rosemary Horan, Dir.

HARBOR SPRINGS. *Christ Child Society of Northern Michigan, Inc.*, P.O. Box 132, 49740-0132. Tel: 231-526-7271. Ann Kroha, Pres.

JOHANNESBURG. *Stella Maris Hermitage*, 19920 Black River Rd., 49751-9645. Tel: 989-732-9580. Email: rwkropf@stellamar.net. Web: www.stellamar.net. Rev. Richard Kropf.

PRESCOTT. *House of the Holy Shroud*, 1629 Beach Rd., 48756. Tel: 989-873-4000. Bro. Michael W. Whitman, Dir.

RELIGIOUS INSTITUTES OF MEN REPRESENTED IN THE DIOCESE

For further details refer to the corresponding bracketed number in the Religious Institutes of Men or Women section.

[0520]—*Franciscan Friars* (Assumption, Sacred Heart Provs.)—O.F.M.

[0690]—*Jesuit Fathers and Brothers*—S.J.

RELIGIOUS INSTITUTES OF WOMEN REPRESENTED IN THE DIOCESE

[0420]—*Discalced Carmelite Nuns*—O.C.D.

[1070]—*Dominican Sisters*—O.P.

[2580]—*Institute of the Sisters of Mercy of the Americas*—R.S.M.

[3490]—*Sacramentine Nuns*—O.S.S.

[3560]—*Servants of Jesus*—S.J.

[3590]—*Servants of Mary*—O.S.M.

[2630]—*Sisters of Mercy of the Holy Cross* (Merill, WI)—S.C.S.C.

[3830]—*Sisters of St. Joseph*—S.S.J.

NECROLOGY

(No Deaths)

Diocese of Grand Island

(Dioecesis Insulae Grandis)

Most Reverend

LAWRENCE J. MCNAMARA, D.D., S.T.L.

Bishop of Grand Island; ordained May 30, 1953; appointed January 10, 1978; consecrated and installed March 28, 1978. *Mailing Address: Box 1531, Grand Island, NE 68802.*

Chancery Office: 311 W. 17th St., P.O. Box 996, Grand Island, NE 68802. Tel: 308-382-6565; Fax: 308-382-6569.

Square Miles 40,000.

Erected at Kearney, March 8, 1912; See Transferred to Grand Island, April 11, 1917.

Comprises the Counties of Arthur, Banner, Blaine, Box Butte, Brown, Buffalo, Cherry, Cheyenne, Custer, Dawes, Deuel, Garden, Garfield, Grant, Greeley, Hooker, Howard Keyapaha, Kimball, Logan, Loup, McPherson, Morrill, Rock, Scotts Bluff, Sheridan, Sherman, Wheeler, Sioux, Thomas, Valley, and those portions of Dawson, Hall, Lincoln and Keith lying north of the South Platte River in the State of Nebraska.

Legal Title: For legal titles of parishes and diocesan institutions, consult the Chancery Office.

STATISTICAL OVERVIEW

Personnel	
Bishop	1
Priests: Diocesan Active in Diocese	41
Priests: Diocesan Active Outside Diocese	3
Priests: Diocesan in Foreign Missions	1
Priests: Retired, Sick or Absent	30
Number of Diocesan Priests	75
Total Priests in Diocese	75
Ordinations:	
Transitional Deacons	1
Total Sisters	73
Parishes	
Parishes	36
With Resident Pastor:	
Resident Diocesan Priests	36
Missions	37
Closed Parishes	9
Welfare	
Health Care Centers	2
Total Assisted	168,811
Homes for the Aged	1
Total Assisted	75
Educational	
Diocesan Students in Other Seminaries	4
Total Seminarians	4
High Schools, Diocesan and Parish	4
Total Students	539
Elementary Schools, Diocesan and Parish	7
Total Students	981
Catechesis/Religious Education:	
High School Students	2,849
Elementary Students	4,208
Total Students under Catholic Instruction	8,581
Teachers in the Diocese:	
Lay Teachers	123
Vital Statistics	
Receptions into the Church:	
Infant Baptism Totals	1,288
Adult Baptism Totals	103
Received into Full Communion	140
First Communions	1,088
Confirmations	895
Marriages:	
Catholic	133
Interfaith	170
Total Marriages	303
Deaths	521
Total Catholic Population	57,460
Total Population	295,176

Former Bishops—Most Revs. JAMES ALBERT DUFFY, D.D., consecrated April 16, 1913; resigned See, May 7, 1931; appt. Titular Bishop of Silando; died Feb. 12, 1968; STANISLAUS V. BONA, D.D., appt. Bishop of Grand Island, Dec. 18, 1931; consecrated Feb. 25, 1932; appt. Coadjutor Bishop of Green Bay and Titular Bishop of Mela, Dec. 2, 1944; succeeded to See, March 3, 1945; died Dec. 1, 1967; EDWARD J. HUNKELER, D.D., ord. June 14, 1919; appt. March 10, 1945; consecrated May 1, 1945; transferred to Kansas City in Kansas, March 31, 1951; died Oct. 1, 1970; JOHN L. PASCHANG, D.D., Ph.D., J.C.D., ord. June 12, 1921; appt. July 28, 1951; consecrated October 9, 1951; resigned July 25, 1972; died March 21, 1999; JOHN J. SULLIVAN, D.D., ord. Sept. 23, 1944; appt. July 25, 1972; consecrated Sept. 19, 1972; transferred to Kansas City-St. Joseph in Missouri, Aug. 17, 1977; died Feb. 11, 2001.

Vicar General—Rev. CHARLES L. TORPEY, S.T.L., J.C.L., St. James, P.O. Box 128, Kearney, 68848. Tel: 308-234-5536.

Chancery Office—311 W. 17th St., P.O. Box 996, Grand Island, 68802. Tel: 308-382-6565; Fax: 308-382-6569. Office Hours: 9-5

Chancellor—Rev. MICHAEL F. MCDERMOTT, J.C.L.

Vice Chancellor—LINDA L. WEMHOFF.

Moderator of the Curia—Rev. RICHARD L. PIONTKOWSKI JR., S.T.L., J.C.L.

Diocesan Tribunal—P.O. Box 5405, Grand Island, 68802. Tel: 308-382-6364.

Vicar-Judicial—Rev. MICHAEL F. MCDERMOTT, J.C.L.

Adjutant Vicars-Judicial—Revs. RICHARD L. PIONTKOWSKI JR., S.T.L., J.C.L.; CHARLES L. TORPEY, S.T.L., J.C.L.

Defenders of the Bond—Revs. THOMAS RYAN; DONALD E. LARMORE, J.C.D.

Promoter Justitiae—Rev. CHARLES L. TORPEY, S.T.L., J.C.L.

Judges—Revs. CHARLES L. TORPEY, S.T.L., J.C.L.; RICHARD PIONTKOWSKI JR., S.T.L., J.C.L.; MICHAEL F. MCDERMOTT, J.C.L.

Procurator—Rev. JAMES M. HUNT.

Advocates—Rev. JAMES M. HUNT; CONNIE RUHLMAN; KATHLEEN HAHN.

Associate Director-Notary—RUTH NOZISKA.

Diocesan Consultors—Revs. NEAL P. NOLLETTE; MICHAEL D. MCDONALD; VINCENT L. PARSONS; MICHAEL F. MCDERMOTT, J.C.L.; CHARLES L. TORPEY, S.T.L., J.C.L.; MARTIN L. EGGING.

Vicar for Religious Communities of Women—VACANT. Vacant.

Diocesan Offices and Directors

Building Committee—Revs. ANDREW GONDA (Retired); STANLEY GORAK; JOHN SCHLAF; JAMES D. O'KANE (Retired).

Charismatic Renewal—Rev. HAROLD KURTENBACH, Dir., 2136 W. 11th St., Grand Island, 68802.

Charities—Revs. JOSEPH M. WALSH, Dir., Catholic Soc. Svc.; CHRISTOPHER KUBAT, Asst. Dir., Catholic Soc. Svcs., 515 W. 3rd St., Hastings, 68901. Tel: 402-463-2112.

Communications—Most Rev. LAWRENCE J. MCNAMARA, D.D., S.T.L., Dir.

Continuing Education for the Clergy—Revs. JAMES R. GOLKA, P.O. Box 2485, Scottsbluff, 69361. Tel: 308-632-7507; HAROLD R. KURTENBACH (Retired), 2136 W. 11th St., Grand Island, 68803.

Council of Catholic Women, Diocesan—Rev. STEPHEN F. DEAVER, Diocesan Moderator.

Hispanic Ministry—

Justice and Peace Office—P.O. Box 651, Lexington, 68850. Tel: 308-532-2707. Rev. PAUL J. COLLING, Asst. Dir., P.O. Box 578, Lexington, 68850. Tel: 308-324-4647.

Liturgical Commission—Revs. CHARLES L. TORPEY, S.T.L., J.C.L., Chm.; JAMES D. O'KANE, Vice Chm. (Retired).

Newspaper—MARY PARLIN, Editor, P.O. Box 608, Grand Island, 68802. Tel: 308-382-4660; Fax: 308-382-4746 Address all correspondence to:. "The West Nebraska Register"

Personnel Board—Revs. BRYAN D. ERNEST; BERNARD M. BERGER; CHARLES L. TORPEY, S.T.L., J.C.L.; JOHN E. SCHLAF; JAMES R. GOLKA; DONALD A. BUHRMAN; ROBERT A. KARNISH; JAMES H. HEITHOFF.

Priests' Advisory Board (Presbyteral Council)—Revs. MICHAEL F. MCDERMOTT, J.C.L.; ROBERT A. KARNISH; PAUL J. COLLING; JOSEPH A. HANNAPPEL; CHARLES L. TORPEY, S.T.L., J.C.L.; NEAL NOLLETTE; MICHAEL D. MCDONALD; JAMES O'KANE; RICHARD L. PIONTKOWSKI JR., S.T.L., J.C.L.; MARTIN L. EGGING.

Catholic Relief Services—Most Rev. LAWRENCE J. MCNAMARA, D.D., S.T.L., Dir.

Priests' Pension and Welfare Board— Address all mail to: Rev. LAWRENCE W. COULTER, P.O. Box 99, Greeley, 68842.

Propagation of the Faith—Rev. MICHAEL D. MCDONALD, Dir., 1210 E. 11th, Kearney, 68847. Tel: 308-236-9171.

Remex-Media Center—CYNTHIA MUENCHRATH, Dir., 214 W. 5th St., P.O. Box 1617, North Platte, 69103. Tel: 308-532-2707.

Religious Education—DONALD KURRE, Dir.; CYNTHIA MUENCHRATH, Assoc. Dir., 214 W. 5th St., P.O. Box 1617, North Platte, 69103. Tel: 308-532-2707.

Rural Life Conference—Rev. NEAL P. NOLLETTE, Dir., P.O. Box 309, Stapleton, 69163.

Schools—Rev. THOMAS A. RYAN, Diocesan Supt. of Schools, 311 W. 17th, P.O. Box 996, Grand Island, 68802. Tel: 308-682-6565; Fax: 308-382-6569.

Vocations—Rev. BRYAN D. ERNEST, Dir., 1104 Cheyenne Ave., Alliance, 69301. Tel: 308-762-1418.

Youth & Young Adult— Vacant. *P.O. Box 1721, Grand Island, 68802.* Tel: 308-382-4660; Fax: 308-382-4746.

Cursillo—Rev. PAUL J. COLLING, Spiritual Dir., P.O. Box 578, Lexington, 68850.

Community Mental Health—MICHAEL F. MCDERMOTT, L.M.H.P., P.O. Box 996, Grand Island, 68802.

Victim Assistance Coordinator—AILEEN D. GRUENDEL, Ph.D. Tel: 308-382-2233. Email: gruendel@hamilton.net.

CLERGY, PARISHES, MISSIONS AND PAROCHIAL SCHOOLS

CITY OF GRAND ISLAND
(HALL COUNTY)

1—CATHEDRAL OF THE NATIVITY OF THE BLESSED VIRGIN MARY (1864), Revs. Thomas A. Ryan; Philip M. Flott.
Res.: 207 S. Elm St., 68801. Tel: 308-384-2523; Fax: 308-384-2527.
Catechesis/Religious Program—502 West Division, 68801. Tel: 308-382-1198. Sr. Barbara Bader, C.S.J., D.R.E. Students 345.

2—BLESSED SACRAMENT (1949), Revs. Francis T. Curran; Vincent L. Parsons.
Res.: 1724 N. Walnut, 68801. Tel: 308-381-1361.
Church: 518 W. State St., 68801. Tel: 308-384-0532; Fax: 308-384-0424.
Catechesis/Religious Program—518 W. State St., 68801. Tel: 308-395-8521. Ms. Debra Wetzel, D.R.E. Students 440.
Chapel—Geer-Sterne 801 Stoeger Dr., 68803.

3—ST. LEO (1972), Rev. John R. Rademacher; Sr. Leona Augustyn, Pastoral Min.
Res.: 2410 S. Blaine, 68801. Tel: 308-382-4753.
Catechesis/Religious Program—Jodi Stauffer, D.R.E. Students 301.

4—RESURRECTION (1973), Rev. Michael F. McDermott, J.C.L.
Res.: 4110 Cannon Rd., 68803. Tel: 308-382-8644; Fax: 308-382-8644.
Catechesis/Religious Program—Tel: 308-382-0976. Therese Stump, D.R.E. Students 268.

OUTSIDE THE CITY OF GRAND ISLAND

AINSWORTH, BROWN CO., ST. PIUS X (1955), Rev. James M. Hunt.
Res.: P.O. Box 7, 69210. Tel: 402-387-1275.
Catechesis/Religious Program—Tel: 402-387-2260. Lorraine Pozehl, D.R.E. Students 111
Mission—Holy Cross P.O. Box 7, Bassett, Rock Co. 69210. Tel: 402-684-3640.

ALLIANCE, BOX BUTTE CO., HOLY ROSARY (1894), [CEM] Rev. Bryan D. Ernest.
Parish Offices—1104 Cheyenne Ave , 69301. Tel: 308-762-2009; Fax: 308-762-7474.
Res.: 916 Cheyenne Ave., 69301. Tel: 308-762-1418.
School—St. Agnes Academy, Tel: 308-762-2315. Sisters 3; Lay Teachers 14; Students 180.
Catechesis/Religious Program—Tel: 308-762-2830. Noreen Placek, D.R.E.; Kyle Lierk. Students 250.
Mission—St. Bridget (1888), 801 Niobrara Ave., P.O. Box 67, Hemingford, Box Butte Co. 69348. Tel: 308-487-3617. Sr. Sarah Manchester, O.S.F., Pastoral Min.
Catechesis/Religious Program—Students 114.

ANSELMO, CUSTER CO., ST. ANSELM'S (1905),, See St. Joseph, Broken Bow.

BRIDGEPORT, MORRILL CO., ALL SOULS (1919), [CEM] Rev. David L. Rykwalder.
Res.: P.O. Box 250, 69336-0250. Tel: 308-262-0709.
Catechesis/Religious Program— Colleen Cruise, D.R.E.; Peg Backer, D.R.E.; Paula Contraras, D.R.E.; Deb Wise, D.R.E.; Veronica Miller, D.R.E. Students 145.
Mission—St. Mary P.O. Box 346, Dalton, Cheyenne Co. 69131-0346. Tel: 308-377-2440.
Mission—Sacred Heart P.O. Box 190, Bayard, Morrill Co. 69334-0190. Tel: 308-586-1160.

BROADWATER, CHEYENNE CO., ST. DOMINIC, Closed. For inquiries for parish records contact the chancery.

BROKEN BOW, CUSTER CO., ST. JOSEPH'S (1888), [CEM] Rev. Todd K. Philipsen.
Mailing Address: P.O. Box 405, 68822. Tel: 308-872-5809 (Office); Fax: 308-872-5809.
Res.: 1407 S. E St., 68822. Tel: 308-872-5716; Fax: 308-872-5809.
Catechesis/Religious Program— Rashelle Ryan, D.R.E. Students 143.
Mission—Sacred Heart Ansley, Custer Co.
Mission—St. Thomas Mason City, Custer Co. 68822.
Mission—St. Anselm's [CEM 2] Anselmo, Custer Co. 68822.
Catechesis/Religious Program— Makayla Hunt, (Preschool-6); Bobbi Kirkpatrick, (Grades 7-12); Carol Porter, (Grades 7-12). Students 105.
Mission—St. Paul Merna, Custer Co. 68822.

BURWELL, GARFIELD CO., SACRED HEART (1910), Rev. Bernard M. Berger.
Res.: 747 I St., P.O. Box 667, 68823. Tel: 308-346-4190; Fax: 308-346-5480.
Catechesis/Religious Program—Tel: 308-346-4360. Betty Kovarik, D.R.E. Students 88.
Mission—St. Theresa of the Child Jesus Box 667, Ericson, Wheeler Co. 68823. Tel: 308-346-4190.
Catechesis/Religious Program—Tel: 308-654-3331. Students 48.
Mission—Assumption of the Blessed Virgin Mary [CEM] P.O. Box 397, Sargent, Custer Co. 68874.
Catechesis/Religious Program—Tel: 308-527-3523. Students 51.

CHADRON, DAWES CO., ST. PATRICK'S (1886), [CEM] Rev. Edward P. Cortney.
Office—340 Cedar St., P.O. Box 231, 69337. Tel: 308-432-2326; Fax: 308-432-4969.
Catechesis/Religious Program—Tel: 308-432-2161. Linda Yeradi, D.R.E. Students 150.

CHAPPELL, DEUEL CO., ST. JOSEPH'S (1909), [CEM] Rev. Martin L. Egging.
Office—Tel: 308-874-3407.
Res.: 1069 2nd St., P.O. Box 586, 69129. Tel: 308-874-3221.
Catechesis/Religious Program—Students 61.
Mission—St. Elizabeth 300 W. 4th, P.O. Box 586, Oshkosh Garden Co. 69154. Tel: 308-772-3221.
Catechesis/Religious Program—Tel: 308-722-3445. Students 34.
Mission—St. Gall 307 1st St., Lisco, Garden Co. 69148.

COZAD, DAWSON CO., CHRIST THE KING (1951), (Irish), Rev. Donald J. O'Brien; Sr. Pat Eichner, C.S.J., Pastoral Assoc. Tel: 308-537-3364.
Res.: 1220 Ave. M, 69130. Tel: 308-784-3959.
Catechesis/Religious Program—512 E. 19th. Tel: 308-784-2696. Donna Kolbo, D.R.E. Students 205.
Mission—Our Lady of Good Counsel 1915 Ave. J, Gothenburg, Dawson Co. 69138.

CRAWFORD, DAWES CO., ST. JOHN THE BAPTIST (1896), (German—Irish), [CEM 2] Rev. Loren Pohlmeier.
Res.: 808 4th St., 69339. Tel: 308-665-1584.
Catechesis/Religious Program—Tel: 308-665-2240. Linda Moloney, D.R.E. Students 37.
Mission—Church of the Nativity of the Blessed Virgin Mary 426 Kate St., Harrison, Sioux Co. 69339. Tel: 308-668-2181.
Catechesis/Religious Program—Students 14.

ELM CREEK, BUFFALO CO., IMMACULATE CONCEPTION (1879) [CEM] Rev. Mark Maresh.
Res.: P.O. Box 530, 68836. Tel: 308-856-4375; Fax: 308-856-4375.
Catechesis/Religious Program—Students 139.
Mission—Holy Rosary 6th and D, Overton, Dawson Co. 68863. Tel: 308-987-2379.
Mission—St. John Capistran Jefferson & Ash, Amherst, Buffalo Co. 68812.

ELYRIA, VALLEY CO., ST. MARY'S, Closed. For inquiries for parish records contact the chancery.

FARWELL, HOWARD CO., ST. ANTHONY OF PADUA (1877),, Now a mission of SS. Peter and Paul, St. Paul

GERING, SCOTTS BLUFF CO., CHRIST THE KING (1958), Rev. Gerald J. Harr.
Res.: 1730 North St., P.O. Box 33, 69341. Tel: 308-436-4000; Fax: 308-436-2923.
Catechesis/Religious Program—18th & North St., P.O. Box 33, 69341. Tel: 308-436-2290. Micki Walker, D.R.E. & Dir. Youth Ministry. Students 279.

GORDON, SHERIDAN CO., ST. LEO'S (1887), [JC] Rev. Timothy L. Stoner.
Res.: 228 N. Maverick, 69343. Tel: 308-282-0427.
Catechesis/Religious Program—Students 143.
Mission—Immaculate Conception 606 Church St., Rushville, Sheridan Co. 69360. Tel: 308-327-2430.
Mission—St. Columbkille 545 N. Main, Hay Springs, Sheridan Co. 69347.

GREELEY, GREELEY CO., SACRED HEART (1893), (Irish), [CEM 2] [JC] Rev. Larry Coulter.
Res.: 302 W. Wicklow, P.O. Box 99, 68842. Tel: 308-428-2855.
School—Sacred Heart School 68842. Tel: 308-428-3015; Fax: 308-428-2405. Students 15.
Catechesis/Religious Program—Students 113.
Mission—St. Patrick Scotia, Greeley Co.

HEMINGFORD, BOX BUTTE CO., ST BRIDGET (1888),, See Holy Rosary, Alliance

KEARNEY, BUFFALO CO.

1—ST. JAMES (1881), Revs. Charles L. Torpey, S.T.L., J.C.L.; Jose Chavez; Sr. Pat Finn, O.P., Admin. Asst.
Church Office: 3801 Ave. A, P.O. Box 128, 68847. Tel: 308-234-5536.
Res.: 7 Sioux Ln., 68847. Tel: 308-233-5051.
High School—Kearney Catholic (Grades 6-12) Tel: 308-234-2610; Fax: 308-234-4986. Mr. Terrence Torson, Admin. Sisters 1; Lay Teachers 24; Students 309.
Catechesis/Religious Program—Tel: 308-234-9695. Deb Kratochvil, D.R.E. Students 580.

2—PRINCE OF PEACE (1986), Rev. Michael D. McDonald; Sr. Mary Chamberlain, O.S.M., Pastoral Min.
Res.: 1210 E. 11th St., 68847. Tel: 308-236-9171.
Catechesis/Religious Program— Ms. Jane Bettles, D.R.E. Students 153.

KIMBALL, KIMBALL CO., ST. JOSEPH'S (1921), Rev. Robert Karnish.
Res.: 507 S. Howard, 69145. Tel: 308-235-2162.
Catechesis/Religious Program—Students 85.

LEXINGTON, DAWSON CO., ST. ANN'S (1883), [CEM] Rev. Paul J. Colling. Tel: 308-324-4648; Sisters Dottie Moss, C.S.J., Pastoral Min. Tel: 308-324-2450; Regina McCarthy, O.P., Pastoral Min.
Res.: 303 E. 6th St., P.O. Box 578, 68850. Tel: 308-324-4648.
Catechesis/Religious Program—St. Ann's Parish Center, 10th & Taft St., 68850. Tel: 308-324-4647; Fax: 308-324-5320. Joan Karre, D.R.E. (Grades K-5); Andrew Finch, D.R.E. (Grades 6-12). Students 715.

LOUP CITY, SHERMAN CO., ST. JOSAPHAT'S (1882), (Polish), Rev. Louis A. Nollette.
Res.: P.O. Box 626, 68853. Tel: 308-745-0315.
Catechesis/Religious Program—Tel: 308-745-1235. Students 165.
Mission—St. Francis [CEM] Ashton, Sherman Co. 68817. P.O. Box 626, 68853.
Catechesis/Religious Program—Mrs. Eddy Krzycki, D.R.E. Students 55.
Mission—St. Gabriel Hazard, 68844. P.O. Box 626, 68853. Tel: 308-745-0315.
Catechesis/Religious Program—Annette Siegel, D.R.E. Students 10.

MERNA, CUSTER CO., ST. PAUL'S, , See St. Joseph, Broken Bow

MERRIMAN, CHERRY CO., ST. ELIZABETH, Closed. For inquiries for parish records contact the chancery.

MINATARE, SCOTTS BLUFF CO., ST. MARY, Closed. For inquiries for parish records contact the chancery.

MITCHELL, SCOTTS BLUFF CO., ST. THERESA'S (1930), Rev. Stephen F. Deaver.
Res.: 1715 17th St., 69357. Tel: 308-623-1745.
Catechesis/Religious Program—Tel: 308-623-2245. Students 50.
Mission—St. Ann Hwy. 26 & Walsh, Morrill, Scotts Bluff Co. 69358. Tel: 308-247-3238.
Mission—Sacred Heart 203 East "O" St., Lyman, Scotts Bluff Co. 69352.

MULLEN, HOOKER CO., ST. MARY'S (1910), Rev. James L. Warner.
Res.: 302 S. Blaine, P.O. Box 191, 69152. Tel: 308-546-2250; Fax: 308-546-2250.
Catechesis/Religious Program—Students 49.
Mission—All Saint's Hyannis, Grant Co. 69152.
Mission—St. Thomas of Canterbury Thedford, Thomas Co. 69152.

NORTH PLATTE, LINCOLN CO.

1—HOLY SPIRIT (1973), Rev. Arthur A. Faesser.
Res.: P.O. Box 427, 69103. Tel: 308-534-4334.
Church: Tel: 308-534-6623.
Catechesis/Religious Program—Tel: 308-534-7906; Fax: 308-534-6525. Traci McKeon, D.R.E. Students 102.
Mission—Sacred Heart Sutherland, Lincoln Co. 69165.
Mission—Our Lady of Guadalupe Hershey, Lincoln Co. 69143.

2—ST. PATRICK (1875), [CEM] Rev. Richard L. Piontkowski Jr., S.T.L., J.C.L.
Res.: 415 N. Chestnut, P.O. Box 399, 69103. Tel: 308-532-0942; Fax: 308-532-0944.
School—(Grades K-6) Tel: 308-532-0622; Fax: 308-532-8015. Mr. Rick Carpenter, Prin. Lay Teachers 17; Students 231.
High School—(Grades 7-12) Tel: 308-532-1874. Mr. William McGahan Jr., Supt. Lay Teachers 17; Students 199.
Catechesis/Religious Program—Tel: 308-532-6388. Mary Wyatt, D.R.E. Students 91.

OGALLALA, KEITH CO., ST. LUKE'S (1887), [JC] Rev. John E. Schlaf.
Res.: 417 E. Third, 69153. Tel: 308-284-3196.
School—Tel: 308-284-4841; Fax: 308-284-9839. Lay Teachers 4; Students 50.
Catechesis/Religious Program—Lay Teachers 23; Students 160.
Mission—St. Patrick's Church Paxton, Keith Co. 69155.

ORD, VALLEY CO., OUR LADY OF PERPETUAL HELP (1908), [CEM] Revs. James H. Heithoff; Hubert J. Spanel, Parochial Admin. (Retired).
Res.: P.O. Box 123, 68862. Tel: 308-728-3351.
School—Tel: 308-728-5389. Sisters 1; Lay Teachers 5; Students 76.
Catechesis/Religious Program—Students 125.
Mission—Sacred Heart Burwell, Garfield Co. 68823.
Mission—Assumption of the Blessed Virgin Mary Sargent, Custer Co. 68874.

PLEASANTON, BUFFALO CO., ST. MARY'S (1909), (German), [CEM] [JC], Now a mission of Our Lady of Lourdes, Ravenna
Res.: 504 N. Sycamore St., Box 134, 68866. Tel: 308-388-2181.

RAVENNA, BUFFALO CO., OUR LADY OF LOURDES (1887), (German), Rev. Rodney Lee A. Pruss.
Res.: 515 Sicily Ave., Box 90, 68869. Tel: 308-452-3314.
Catechesis/Religious Program—Tel: 308-452-3109; Fax: 308-452-9102. Students 123.
Mission—St. Mary's [CEM] 406 Fair St., Rockville,

Sherman Co. 68871.
Mission—St. Mary's (1909), [CEM] [JC] 504 N. Syracuse St., Box 134, Pleasanton, Buffalo Co. 68866. Tel: 308-388-2181.
Catechesis / Religious Program—Tel: 308-388-3062. Sr. Paulette Kuta, D.R.E. Students 52.

ST. LIBORY, HOWARD CO., ST. LIBORY'S (1884), [CEM] Rev. Michael F. McDermott, J.C.L.
Res.: P.O. Box 7, 68872. Tel: 308-687-6276; Fax: 308-687-6093.
Catechesis / Religious Program—Tel: 308-687-6421. Teri Supencheck, D.R.E. Students 100.

ST. PAUL, HOWARD CO., SS. PETER AND PAUL (1878), [JC] Revs. Michael F. McDermott, J.C.L.; Raymond Kosmicki.
Res.: 405 7th St., 68873. Tel: 308-754-4649; Fax: 308-754-4002.
Catechesis / Religious Program—713 Elm St., 68873. Tel: 308-754-4002. Students 200.
Mission—St. Joseph 1803 Hwy. 11, Elba, Howard Co. 68838. Tel: 308-336-3323.
Mission—St. Anthony of Padua (1877), [CEM 3] 103 Kearns Ave., Box 156,, Farwell, Howard Co. 68838. Tel: 308-336-3323. Rev. Lawrence W. Coulter.
Catechesis / Religious Program—Tel: 308-754-5544. Kathy Gorecki, D.R.E. Tel: 308-336-3351; Victor Dush, D.R.E. Tel: 308-968-3421; Shelly Wolinski, D.R.E. Tel: 308-863-2232. Students 337.

SCOTTSBLUFF, SCOTTS BLUFF CO.
1—ST. AGNES (1912), Rev. Donald A. Buhrman.
Res.: 2314 3rd Ave., P.O. Box 349, 69363. Tel: 308-632-2541; Fax: 308-632-2146.
School—Tel: 308-632-6918; Fax: 308-632-6918. Lay Teachers 9; Students 75.
Catechesis / Religious Program— Terri Calvert, D.R.E. Students 171.
2—OUR LADY OF GUADALUPE (1955), (Hispanic), Rev. James R. Golka.
Res.: 1103 12th Ave., P.O. Box 2485, 69361. Tel: 308-632-2845; Fax: 308-632-7356.
Catechesis / Religious Program— Elizabeth Salazar, D.R.E. Students 133.

SIDNEY, CHEYENNE CO., ST. PATRICK'S (1878), [JC] Rev. James E. Novakowski; Sisters Marietta Spenner, O.S.F., Pastoral Assoc.; Clarice Gentrup, O.S.F., Pastoral Assoc.
Res.: 1039 14th Ave., P.O. Box 99, 69162. Tel: 308-254-2828; Fax: 308-254-2830.
Catechesis / Religious Program— Sr. Marietta Spenner, O.S.F., D.R.E.; Pat Mertz, D.R.E. Students 266.

SPALDING, GREELEY CO., ST. MICHAEL'S (1887), [CEM 2] Rev. Joseph A. Hannappel.
Res.: 150 E. Marguerite, P.O. Box 310, 68665. Tel: 308-497-2662.
School—Spalding Academy, Tel: 308-497-2103; Fax: 308-497-2105. Sisters of St. Dominic 1; Lay Teachers 14; Students 99.
School—(Grades K-6) Lay Teachers 4; Students 56.
High School—Lay Teachers 10; Students 43.
Catechesis / Religious Program—Students 97.
Mission—St. Theresa of the Child Jesus Ericson, 68637.
Catechesis / Religious Program—Students 37.

STAPLETON, LOGAN CO., ST. JOHN THE EVANGELIST (1913), (German), [CEM] Rev. Neal P. Nollette.
Res.: P.O. Box 309, 69163. Tel: 308-636-2421.
Catechesis / Religious Program—Students 36.
Mission—St. Agnes Box 309, Arnold, Custer Co. 69163. Tel: 308-848-2442.
Catechesis / Religious Program—Students 22.
Mission—St. Boniface Callaway, Logan Co. Tel: 308-836-2606.
Catechesis / Religious Program—Students 30.

SUTHERLAND, LINCOLN CO., SACRED HEART, Rev. James J. Janovec.
Res.: 69165. Tel: 308-386-4300.
Catechesis / Religious Program—Tel: 308-386-2401. Students 228.
Mission—St. Patrick P.O. Box 398, Paxton, Keith Co. 69165. Fax: 308-386-4300.
Mission—Our Lady of Guadalupe [JC] Hershey, Lincoln Co. 69165.

VALENTINE, CHERRY CO., ST. NICHOLAS (1893), [JC] Rev. Bernard M. Berger.
Res.: 69201. Tel: 402-376-1672; Fax: 402-376-1672.
Catechesis / Religious Program—Tel: 402-376-1938. Mary Lou Stauffer, D.R.E. Students 180.
Mission—St. Mary [CEM] P.O. Box 510, Nenzel, Cherry Co. 69201.

WOOD RIVER, HALL CO., ST. MARY'S (1884), [CEM] Rev. James J. Janovec.
Res.: P.O. Box 37, 68883. Tel: 308-583-2464.
Catechesis / Religious Program—Students 132.
Mission—Sacred Heart P.O. Box 190, Shelton, Buffalo Co. 68876.
Catechesis / Religious Program—Tel: 308-647-6970. Students 91.

Chaplains of Public Institutions

GRAND ISLAND. *Nebraska Veterans Home*. Rev. James C. Schmitt (Retired).
U.S. Veterans' Hospital. Rev. Walter M. Phelan (Retired).

KEARNEY. *Youth Development Center*, W. Hwy. 30, 68847. Tel: 308-237-3181. Rev. Michael D. McDonald, Chap.

On Duty Outside the Diocese:
Revs.—
Larmore, Donald E., J.C.D., Box 867, Dares Salaam, Tanzania.
Urban, Reginald A., P.O. Box 673, La Crosse, KS 67548.
Whalen, Joseph E., 308 Albany Rd., Lexington, KY 40503.

Military Chaplains:
Rev.—
Borzych, Alexander J.

Retired:
Rev. Msgr.—
Hayden, Carl T., 111 Emerson #1225, Denver, CO 80201.
Revs.—
Abele, Joseph P., Box 168, Oshkosh, 69154.
Augustyn, Andrew M., 2517 W. Phoenix, 68803.
Bauer, Jacob F., 2106 W. Cottage, 68803.
Carlson, Gerald J., 3720 State St., Apt C-12, 68803.
Chamberlain, Robert F., 1520 East 43 St., 68847.
Cook, John N., Box 242, Greeley, 68842.
Dillon, Thomas J., 1200 S. Oak, Apt. 2C, North Platte, 69101.
Dowd, Thomas M., 2516 Commerce Ave., 68801.
Fenton, Lawrence E., 10351 Sprague St., Omaha, 68134.
Ferris, Carl A., Valentine, 69201.
Gonda, Andrew, 1111 E. Nebraska Ave., 68801.
Gorak, Stanley C., 318 E. 22nd St., 68847.
Guevara, Miguel H., 1010 W. 8th St., North Platte, 69103.
Koprowski, Mitchell J., Mullen, 69152.
Kremeier, James, 60 2nd St., Apt. 13, Las Animas, CO 81054.
Krystosek, Robert H., Box 425, Clara City, MN 56222.
Kurtenbach, Harold R., 2136 W. 11th St., 68803.
Mullowney, Thomas E., 3915 Ave. H, 68847.
Murphy, James E., Rte. 1, Box 131, Spalding, 68665.
Nekoliczak, Ted A., 1516 E. 43rd St., 68848.
O'Kane, James D., 708 Monument Cir., Scottsbluff, 69361.
Phelan, Walter M., 515 N. Cluster, 68803.
Phillips, Walter W., 701 Student Dr., Ogallala, 69153.
Rooney, Robert B., 6910 Eastshore Dr., Lincoln, 68516.
Schmitt, James C., 23 Chantilly, 68803.
Smutny, Jan, Box 194, Pleasanton, 68866.
Snyder, Frederick, St. Mary's Convent, 2649-US20, Swanton, OH 43558.
Spanel, Hubert J., 745 N. 5th Ave., Broken Bow, 68822.
Whalen, James R., c/o 701 Student Dr., Ogallala, 69153.

INSTITUTIONS LOCATED IN THE DIOCESE

[A] HIGH SCHOOLS, DIOCESAN

GRAND ISLAND. *Central Catholic Schools*, (Grades 6-12), 1200 Ruby Ave., 68803. Tel: 308-384-2440; Fax: 308-389-3274. Email: jseitz@gicentralcatholic.org. Web: www.gicentralcatholic.org. Gerald P. Seitz, Supt.; John Golka, Prin.; Howard Schumann, Asst. Prin. Sisters 1; Lay Teachers 30; Students 313.

[B] GENERAL HOSPITALS

GRAND ISLAND. *Saint Francis Medical Center, Affiliate of Catholic Health Initiatives*, 2620 W. Faidley Ave., P.O. Box 9804, 68802. Tel: 308-398-4600; Fax: 308-389-5589. Email: dsanders@sfmc-gi.org. Web: www.saintfrancisgi.org. Mr. Michael Gloor, Pres. Catholic Health Initiatives. Bed Capacity 189; Bassinets 17; Patients Assisted Annually 113,406; Total Staff 1,190.

KEARNEY. *Good Samaritan Hospital, Affiliate of Catholic Health Initiatives*, 10 E. 31st St., P.O. Box 1990, 68848-1990. Tel: 308-865-7100. Email: rbeason@chi-midwest.org. Web: www.gshs.org. Ken Tomlon, Pres. & CEO. Sisters 2; Total Staff 1,698; Bed Capacity 220; Patients Assisted Annually 54,530.
Richard H. Young Hospital, 4600 17th Ave., 68847. Tel: 308-865-2000. Bed Capacity 80; Patients Assisted Annually 875.

[C] HOMES FOR THE AGED

KEARNEY. *Mount Carmel Home-Keens' Memorial*, 412 W. 18th St., 68847. Tel: 308-237-2287; Fax: 308-236-9380. Email: brownun@yahoo.com. Web: www.corpuschristicarmelites.org. Sr. Delphine Napoleoni, O.Carm., Supr. Carmelites 10; Residents 75; Total Staff 95.

[D] NEWMAN CENTERS

CHADRON. *Chadron State College-Newman House* 907 Main St., 69337. Tel: 308-432-4286. Email: newmanhousecsc@yahoo.com. Total in Residence 1; Total Staff 2.

KEARNEY. *University of Nebraska at Kearney Newman Apostolate* 821 W. 27th St., 68845. Tel: 308-234-1539; Fax: 308-233-5718. Email: cathnewman@unk.edu. Web: www.unk.edu/related/newman. Shirley Wallace, Dir.; Rev. Michael D. McDonald. Total in Residence 4; Total Staff 5.

RELIGIOUS INSTITUTES OF WOMEN REPRESENTED IN THE DIOCESE

For further details refer to the corresponding bracketed number in the Religious Institutes of Men or Women section.

[0350]—*Carmelite Sisters (Corpus Christi)*—O.Carm.
[1070-01]—*Dominican Sisters*—O.P.
[1070-13]—*Dominican Sisters*—O.P.
[2960]—*Notre Dame Sisters*—N.D.
[3580]—*Servants of Mary* (Omaha, NE)—O.S.M.
[1630]—*Sisters of St. Francis of Penance and Christian Charity*—O.S.F.
[1640]—*Sisters of St. Francis of Perpetual Adoration*—O.S.F.
[3830]—*Sisters of St. Joseph*—C.S.J.
[3930]—*Sisters of St. Joseph of the Third Order of St. Francis P*—S.S.J.-T.O
[2110]—*Sisters of the Humility of Mary*—H.M.
[4120-03]—*Ursuline Nuns of the Congregation of Paris* (Louisville, KY)—O.S.U.

NECROLOGY

† Portrey, Rev. Msgr. Lawrence A., (Retired)—Died April 7, 2003
† Dennett, John A., (Retired)—Died Oct. 6, 2003
† Hoelck, Frank L., Grand Island, NE Central Catholic Schools—Died April 16, 2003
† Szczesny, Michael S., (Retired)—Died Nov. 23, 2003

Diocese of Grand Rapids

(Dioecesis Grandormensis)

Most Reverend

KEVIN M. BRITT, D.D.

Bishop of Grand Rapids; ordained June 28, 1970; appointed Auxiliary Bishop of Detroit, Titular Bishop of Esco November 23, 1993; consecrated January 6, 1994; appointed Coadjutor Bishop of Grand Rapids December 10, 2002; Succeeded to See October 13, 2003 *Office: 660 Burton St., S.E., Grand Rapids, MI 49507*. Tel: 616-243-0491.

Most Reverend

ROBERT J. ROSE, S.T.L., D.D.

Retired Bishop of Grand Rapids; ordained December 21, 1955; appointed Bishop of Gaylord October 13, 1981; consecrated December 6, 1981; appointed Bishop of Grand Rapids July 11, 1989; installed August 30, 1989; retired October 13, 2003 *Res.: 1200 104th, Apt. A, Byron Center, MI 49315*. Tel: 616-583-1260.

Most Reverend

JOSEPH M. BREITENBECK, D.D.

Retired Bishop of Grand Rapids; ordained May 30, 1942; appointed Titular Bishop of Tepelta and Auxiliary of Detroit October 18, 1965; consecrated December 20, 1965; appointed Bishop of Grand Rapids October 15, 1969; installed December 2, 1969; retired August 3, 1989 *Mailing Address: 660 Burton St., S.E., Grand Rapids, MI 49507*.

Administrative Office of Diocese of Grand Rapids: 660 Burton St., S.E., Grand Rapids, MI 49507. Tel: 616-243-0491; Fax: 616-243-4910.

Web: www.dioceseofgrandrapids.org

Most Reverend

JOSEPH C. MCKINNEY, D.D.

Retired Auxiliary Bishop of Grand Rapids; ordained December 20, 1953; appointed Titular Bishop of Lentini and Auxiliary of Grand Rapids July 24, 1968; consecrated September 26, 1968; retired October 3, 2001 *Res.: Villa Maria #5110*, 1315 Walker, N.W., Grand Rapids, MI 49504. Tel: 616-776-8506; Fax: 616-776-8413.

ESTABLISHED MAY 19, 1882.

Square Miles 6,795.

Comprises the following Counties of the Lower Peninsula of the State of Michigan: Ionia, Kent, Lake, Mason, Mecosta, Montcalm, Muskegon, Newaygo, Oceana, Osceola, Ottawa.

Legal Title: For legal titles of parishes and diocesan institutions, consult the Chancery Office.

STATISTICAL OVERVIEW

Personnel	
Bishop	1
Auxiliary Bishops	1
Retired Bishops	2
Priests: Diocesan Active in Diocese	76
Priests: Diocesan Active Outside Diocese	3
Priests: Retired, Sick or Absent	28
Number of Diocesan Priests	107
Religious Priests in Diocese	15
Total Priests in Diocese	122
Extern Priests in Diocese	12
Ordinations:	
Diocesan Priests	3
Religious Priests	1
Transitional Deacons	1
Permanent Deacons	1
Permanent Deacons in Diocese	29
Total Brothers	1
Total Sisters	273
Parishes	
Parishes	90
With Resident Pastor:	
Resident Diocesan Priests	81
Resident Religious Priests	1
Without Resident Pastor:	
Administered by Priests	8
Missions	12
Pastoral Centers	2
Welfare	
Catholic Hospitals	2
Total Assisted	593,000
Homes for the Aged	1
Total Assisted	145
Specialized Homes	2
Total Assisted	5,894
Special Centers for Social Services	8
Total Assisted	18,655
Other Institutions	9
Total Assisted	11,532
Educational	
Diocesan Students in Other Seminaries	9
Total Seminarians	9
Colleges and Universities	1
Total Students	2,338
High Schools, Diocesan and Parish	4
Total Students	1,895
Elementary Schools, Diocesan and Parish	39
Total Students	6,847
Catechesis/Religious Education:	
High School Students	1,992
Elementary Students	14,288
Total Students under Catholic Instruction	27,369
Teachers in the Diocese:	
Sisters	9
Lay Teachers	506
Vital Statistics	
Receptions into the Church:	
Infant Baptism Totals	2,604
Adult Baptism Totals	309
First Communions	2,858
Confirmations	2,856
Marriages:	
Catholic	574
Interfaith	366
Total Marriages	940
Deaths	1,384
Total Catholic Population	162,670
Total Population	1,283,717

Former Bishops—Most Revs. HENRY JOSEPH RICHTER, D.D., consecrated April 22, 1883; died Dec. 26, 1916; MICHAEL JAMES GALLAGHER, D.D., ord. March 19, 1893; appt. titular Bishop of Tipasa and Coadjutor Bishop of Grand Rapids July 5, 1915; consecrated Sept. 8, 1915; succeeded to the Diocese of Grand Rapids, Dec. 26, 1916; transferred to the See of Detroit, July 18, 1918; died Jan. 20, 1937; EDWARD D. KELLY, ord. June 16, 1886; consecrated auxiliary Bishop of Detroit, Jan. 26, 1911; transferred to the See of Grand Rapids, Jan. 16, 1919; died March 26, 1926; JOSEPH G. PINTEN, D.D., ord. Nov. 1, 1890; consecrated Bishop of Superior May 3, 1922; transferred to See of Grand Rapids June 25, 1926; resigned and appt. Titular Bishop of Sela Nov. 1, 1940; died Nov. 6, 1945; JOSEPH CASIMIR PLAGENS, ord. July 5, 1903; consecrated Sept. 30, 1924, Auxiliary Bishop of Detroit and Titular Bishop of Rhodiopolis; transferred to See of Marquette Nov. 16, 1935; transferred to See of Grand Rapids Dec. 16, 1940; installed as Bishop of Grand Rapids Feb. 18, 1941; died March 31, 1943; FRANCIS J. HAAS, D.D., ord. June 11, 1913; appt. Sept. 26, 1943; consecrated and installed as Bishop of Grand Rapids, Nov. 18, 1943; died Aug. 29, 1953; ALLEN J. BABCOCK, D.D., ord. March 7, 1925; appt. Titular Bishop of Irenopolis and Auxiliary of Detroit Feb. 15, 1947; consecrated March 25, 1947; appt. to Grand Rapids March 23, 1954; died June 27, 1969; JOSEPH M. BREITENBECK, D.D. (Retired), ord. May 30, 1942; appt. Titular Bishop of Tepelta and Auxiliary of Detroit Oct. 18, 1965; consecrated Dec. 20, 1965; appt. Bishop of Grand Rapids Oct. 15, 1969; installed Dec. 2, 1969; retired Aug. 3, 1989; ROBERT J ROSE, D.D., S.T.L. (Retired), ord. Dec. 21, 1955; appt. Bishop of Gaylord Oct. 13, 1981; consecrated Dec. 6, 1981; appt. Bishop of Grand Rapids July 11, 1989; installed Aug. 30, 1989; retired Oct. 13, 2003.

Administrative Office of Diocese of Grand Rapids—660 Burton St., S.E., Grand Rapids, 49507. Tel: 616-243-0491; Fax: 616-243-4910. Office Hours: Mon.-Fri. 8-4:30; All official communications to be directed to this office.

Moderator of the Curia—Rev. WILLIAM H. DUNCAN.

Chancellor—Sr. PATRICE KONWINSKI, O.P.

Director of Finance—JOHN S. CZACHORSKI.

Vicar General—Rev. WILLIAM H. DUNCAN, 660 Burton St., S.E., Grand Rapids, 49507. Tel: 616-243-0491; Fax: 616-243-4910.

Clergy Fund—Rev. R. LOUIS STASKER. Tel: 616-949-4170.

Deans—Revs. WAYNE WHEELER, Big Rapids, 1 Damascus Rd., Big Rapids, 49307-2396. Tel: 231-796-7393; JOSEPH W. KENSHOL, Grand Rapids North, 1 Maple St., P.O. Box 140, Sand Lake, 49343. Tel: 616-636-5671; THEODORE KOZLOWSKI, Grand Rapids South, 101 Hall, S.E., Grand Rapids, 49507. Tel: 616-243-0222; JAMES KOWALSKI, Grand Rapids East, 6477 Ada Dr., P.O. Box 369, Ada, 49301. Tel: 616-676-9111; THOMAS J. DE YOUNG, Grand Rapids West, 701 4th St., N.W., Grand Rapids, 49504. Tel: 616-459-2984; THOMAS F. BOUFFORD, Ionia, 531 Jordan Lake St., Lake Odessa, 48849. Tel: 616-374-7253; RONALD E. SCHNEIDER, Northwest Lake Shore Deanery, 316 Peach St., Hart, 49420. Tel: 231-893-2660; ANTHONY VAINAVICZ, Grand Haven Deanery, 406 E. Savidge St., Spring Lake, 49456. Tel: 616-842-1702; JAMES WYSE, Muskegon, 1292 Jefferson St., Muskegon, 49441-2027. Tel: 231-722-2793.

Presbyteral Council—Rev. JOSEPH KENSHOL, P.O. Box 140, Sand Lake, 49343. Tel: 616-636-5671.

College of Consultors—Rev. Msgr. TERRENCE L. STEWART; Revs. DONALD E. WEBER, Vicar for Priests; THOMAS F. BOUFFORD, Dean, Ionia Deanery; THEODORE J. KOZLOWSKI, Dean, GR South Deanery; RICHARD VAN LENTE; WILLIAM H. DUNCAN, Vicar Gen.

Finance Council—Most Rev. KEVIN M. BRITT, D.D., 660 Burton St., S.E., Grand Rapids, 49507. Tel: 616-243-0491.

Vicar for Religious—VACANT.

Catholic Services Appeal—660 Burton St., S.E., Grand Rapids, 49507. Tel: 616-243-0491.

Tribunal Office—Rev. JOHN PORTER, Officialis, 265

Sheldon Ave., S.E., Grand Rapids, 49503. Tel: 616-459-4509.

Vicar For Priests—Rev. DONALD E. WEBER, 7523 Pinegrove Dr., Jenison, 49428.

Moderator of the Curia—Rev. WILLIAM H. DUNCAN, 660 Burton St., S.E., Grand Rapids, 49507. Tel: 616-243-0491.

Secretariat for Christian Life and Ministry Formation

Secretary—Dr. WILLIAM JOHNSTON. Tel: 616-243-0491, Ext. 540.

Bishop Baraga Bookstore and Religious Education Resource Center—MARGARET A. DEVITO, Coord. Tel: 616-245-2251.

Youth, Young Adult and Family—Mr. MARK MANN. Tel: 616-243-0491, Ext. 539.

Worship and Spirituality—MICHELLE OGREN, Dir. Tel: 616-243-0491, Ext. 550.

Permanent Diaconate—Deacon MICHAEL DORDAN. Tel: 616-243-0491, Ext. 551.

Director of Spiritual Formation for Permanent Diaconate Program—Rev. PHILLIP SHANGRAW.

Director of Seminarians—Rev. MICHAEL DANNER, 600 Burton, S.E., Grand Rapids, 49507. Tel: 616-243-0491; Fax: 616-243-1442.

Volunteer Formation—VACANT.

Continuing Formation of Priests—Rev. MARK C. PRZYBYSZ, 1776 Acacia Dr., N.W., Grand Rapids, 49504. Tel: 616-453-8229; Fax: 616-453-8053.

Vocation Director—Rev. PAUL MILANOWSKI, 600 Burton, S.E., Grand Rapids, 49507. Tel: 616-243-0491, Ext. 530.

Pastoral Council Formation—VACANT.

Secretariat for Diocesan Schools

Secretary—JAMES O'DONNELL.

Supt. of Schools—JAMES O'DONNELL, 600 Burton St., S.E., Grand Rapids, 49507. Tel: 616-243-0491.

Associate Superintendent—BERNARD STANKO, 600 Burton, S.E., Grand Rapids, 49507.

Secretariat for Social Justice

Secretary—JAMES RADEMAKER, Dir., 650 Burton St., S.E., Grand Rapids, 49507. Tel: 616-243-0491.

Catholic Social Services, Grand Rapids—RICHARD V. LIBERATORE, Exec. Dir., 40 Jefferson Ave., S.E., Grand Rapids, 49503. Tel: 616-456-1443.

Catholic Social Services, Muskegon—ROBERT H. MILLS, Exec. Dir., 1095 Third St., Ste. 125, Muskegon, 49441. Tel: 616-726-4735.

Catholic Human Development Outreach—SUSAN COOK, Pres., 650 Burton St., S.E., Grand Rapids, 49507. Tel: 616-248-3030; Fax: 616-248-3437.

Christian Community Center—540 E. Hackley, Muskegon, 49444. Tel: 231-725-7579.

Rose Haven Ministry—2303 Kalamazoo, S.E., Grand Rapids, 49507. Tel: 616-247-8826; Fax: 616-247-8871.

Office of Social Justice—650 Burton St., S.E., Grand Rapids, 49507. Tel: 616-243-0491.

Bishops Overseas Appeal—

Catholic Relief Services—

Project Rachel—PATRICIA RYAN, Dir., 650 Burton St., S.E., Grand Rapids, 49507. Tel: 616-243-0491, Ext. 520.

Office of Black Catholic Ministry—ROBERT ELLIS, 650 Burton St., S.E., Grand Rapids, 49507. Tel: 616-243-0491, Ext. 564.

Native American Ministry—SHARRON DETZ, Dir., 650 Burton St., S.E., Grand Rapids, 49507. Tel: 616-243-0491, Ext. 517.

Hispanic Ministry—LUIS BETETA, Dir., 650 Burton S.W., Grand Rapids, 49507. Tel: 616-243-0491, Ext. 557.

Vietnamese Ministry—Rev. PETER NGHIEM, Our Lady of Lavang, 2420 Avon, S.W., Wyoming, 49509. Tel: 616-531-5213; Fax: 616-261-0232.

Prison/Jail Ministry—JUDITH GRANSTROM, Dir., 650 Burton St., S.E., Grand Rapids, 49507. Tel: 616-243-0491, Ext. 523.

Secretariat for Administration

Secretary—Sr. PATRICE KONWINSKI, O.P., 660 Burton St., S.E., Grand Rapids, 49507. Tel: 616-243-0491; Fax: 616-243-4910.

Archivist—Rev. DENNIS W. MORROW, 660 Burton St., S.E., Grand Rapids, 49507. Tel: 616-243-0491; Fax: 616-243-4910.

Building and Planning Committee—Sr. PATRICE KONWINSKI, O.P., 660 Burton St., S.E., Grand Rapids, 49507. Tel: 616-243-0491.

Cemeteries—ROBERT MENZEL, 4100 Clyde Park, S.W., Wyoming, 49509-0063. Tel: 616-531-9320; Fax: 616-531-9780. Resurrection Cemetery; Mt. Calvary Cemetery; St. Andrew Cemetery; Holy Cross Cemetery: ROBERT R. MENZEL, Mgr., Res.: 4100 Clyde Park, S.W., Grand Rapids, 49509. Tel: 616-531-9320.

Director of Finance—JOHN S. CZACHORSKI, 660 Burton St., S.E., Grand Rapids, 49507. Tel: 616-243-0491.

Self-Insurance Program—Sr. PATRICE KONWINSKI, O.P., 660 Burton St., S.E., Grand Rapids, 49507. Tel: 616-243-0491.

Tribunal—Rev. JOHN PORTER, Officialis, 265 Sheldon, S.E., Grand Rapids, 49503. Tel: 616-459-4509; Fax: 616-459-7488.

Diocesan Council of Catholic Women—MARY BURK, 650 Burton St., S.E., Grand Rapids, 49507. Tel: 616-243-0491, Ext. 536.

Ecumenical Commission—Rev. CHARLES R. DAUTREMONT, 50 Bellevue St., S.W., Wyoming, 49548-3144. Tel: 616-531-1480.

Hospital Apostolate—Rev. MARK E. MITCHELL, Chap., Res.: 628 Diamond N.E., Grand Rapids, 49503. Tel: 616-454-7899.

Director of Communications—MARY HAARMAN.

Director of Stewardship—STANLEY ROTH.

Director of Research & Planning—KEVIN WOODS.

Director of Development—MARK MORROW.

Victim Assistance Coordinator—EDGAR R. DONATELLI. Tel: 616-942-8396.

CLERGY, PARISHES, MISSIONS AND PAROCHIAL SCHOOLS

CITY OF GRAND RAPIDS
(KENT COUNTY)

1—CATHERDRAL OF ST. ANDREW, [CEM] Rev. Steven D. Cron, Rector.
Res.: 267 Sheldon Ave., S.E., 49503. Tel: 616-456-1454; Fax: 616-456-5110.
School—302 Sheldon Ave., S.E., 49503. Tel: 616-451-8463; Fax: 616-451-2354. Sisters 2; Lay Teachers 12; Students 139.
Catechesis/Religious Program—Students 139.

2—ST. ALPHONSUS, [JC] Revs. Thomas Donaldson, C.SS.R.; Bernard Rooney, C.SS.R.; Rudy Papes, C.SS.R.; Robert Balser, C.SS.R.; Durkin Fitzgerald, C.SS.R.; Eugene R. Harrison, C.SS.R.
Res.: 224 Carrier St., N.E., 49505. Tel: 616-451-3043; Fax: 616-458-5667.
School—228 Carrier St., N.E., 49505. Tel: 616-454-4904. Brothers 1; Lay Teachers 14; Students 228.
Catechesis/Religious Program—Tel: 616-459-5472; Fax: 616-454-5213. Maureen Geglio, D.R.E. Students 183.

3—ST. ANTHONY OF PADUA, Rev. Mark C. Przybysz; Deacon Leo Ferguson. In Res., Rev. Peter Nickels, O.F.M.Conv. (LAN).
Res.: 2510 Richmond St., N.W., 49504. Tel: 616-453-8229; Fax: 616-453-8053.
School— Ellen Schwartzfisher, Prin. Lay Teachers 20; Students 381.
Catechesis/Religious Program— Sandra Ten Hagen, D.R.E. Students 264.

4—BASILICA OF ST. ADALBERT, (Polish), [JC] Rev. Thomas J. De Young.
Parish Office:—701 4th St., N.W., 49504-5199. Tel: 616-458-3065; Fax: 616-458-0563.
Church: 4th and Davis, N.W., 49504.

5—BLESSED SACRAMENT, [JC] Rev. John J. Wisneski; Deacon George LeMire.
Res.: 2275 Diamond Ave., N.E., 49505-4313. Tel: 616-361-7339; Fax: 616-361-1327.
School—2233 Diamond Ave., N.E., 49505-4313. Tel: 616-364-9453; Fax: 616-361-6991. Lay Teachers 11; Students 258.
Catechesis/Religious Program—Tel: 616-361-7738; Fax: 616-361-1327. Jody DeGraw, D.R.E. Students 126.

6—ST. DOMINIC, Rev. Charles R. Dautremont.
Office—50 Bellevue, S.W., 49548-3144. Tel: 616-531-1480; Fax: 616-531-0759.
Catechesis/Religious Program—Students 48.

7—HOLY NAME OF JESUS, [JC] Rev. Stephen S. Dudek.
Res.: 1630 Godfrey Ave., S.W., 49509. Tel: 616-241-6489; Fax: 616-241-6480.
School—1650 Godfrey Ave., S.W., 49509. Tel: 616-243-1126; Fax: 616-243-0862. Sr. Adele Labiotka, Prin. Lay Teachers 9; Students 124.
Catechesis/Religious Program—Tel: 616-245-3359. Students 56.

8—HOLY SPIRIT, Rev. Leonard Sudlik; Daryl E. Nowicki, Business Mgr.
Res.: 2230 Lake Michigan Dr., N.W., 49504. Tel: 616-453-6369; Fax: 616-453-0244.
School—Tel: 616-453-2772; Fax: 616-453-0018. Lay Teachers 20; Students 503.
Catechesis/Religious Program—Tel: 616-453-1591. Students 212.

9—IMMACULATE HEART OF MARY, Rev. Donn Tufts.
Res.: 1935 Plymouth Rd., S.E., 49506. Tel: 616-241-4477; Fax: 616-241-2832.
School—Tel: 616-241-4633; Fax: 616-241-4418. Lay Teachers 20; Students 457.
Catechesis/Religious Program—Tel: 616-241-0863. Teri D'Orazio, D.R.E. Students 133.

10—ST. ISIDORE, (Polish), [JC] Rev. Donald E. Lomasiewicz.
Res.: 628 Diamond Ave., N.E., 49503. Tel: 616-459-4731; Fax: 616-454-5832.
School—625 Spring Ave., N.E., 49503. Tel: 616-454-1236; Fax: 616-454-6746. Lay Teachers 12; Students 131.
Catechesis/Religious Program—Students 63.

11—ST. JAMES, Rev. M. Thomas Bolster.
Res.: 733 Bridge St., N.W., 49504. Tel: 616-458-3213; Fax: 616-458-9002.
School—750 First St., N.W., 49504. Tel: 616-454-2567; Fax: 616-988-2852. Lay Teachers 7; Students 110.
Catechesis/Religious Program—671 Davis N.W., 49504. Tel: 616-451-4215; Fax: 616-451-4215. Students 130.

12—ST. JOHN VIANNEY, [JC] Revs. Larry King; Edward J. Bielskas (Retired); Deacon Dale Hollern.
Res.: 4101 Clyde Park, S.W., 49509. Tel: 616-534-5449; Fax: 616-530-8224.
School—Tel: 616-532-7001; Fax: 616-532-1884. Catherine Prietz, Prin. Lay Teachers 23; Students 415.
Catechesis/Religious Program—Tel: 616-532-2397. Jan Cook, Dir. Students 236.

13—ST. JOSEPH THE WORKER, Rev. Stephen S. Dudek.
Res.: 333 Rumsey St., S.W., 49503-4935. Tel: 616-456-7982; Fax: 616-456-1445.

14—ST. JUDE, Revs. Godfrey Onyekwere; Michael Danner, Dir. Diocese Seminarians.
Office—1120 Four Mile, N.E., 49505. Tel: 616-363-6885; Fax: 616-363-1470.
School—Tel: 616-363-7725; Fax: 616-363-3086. Lay Teachers 15; Students 200.
Catechesis/Religious Program—1120 Four Mile, N.E., 49505. Tel: 616-363-6897; Fax: 616-363-1470. Patricia Cebelak, D.R.E. Students 255.

15—ST. MARY MAGDALEN, Rev. Phong Pham; Barbara Kerkhoff, Pastoral Assoc.; Deacon Michael L. Wood.
Res.: 1213 52nd St., S.E., 49508. Tel: 616-455-9310; Fax: 616-455-4139.
Catechesis/Religious Program—Students 504.

16—ST. MARY'S, Rev. Dick Host.
Res.: 423 First St., N.W., 49504. Tel: 616-459-7390; Fax: 616-459-9630.
Catechesis/Religious Program—Tel: 616-451-4215; Fax: 616-451-4215. Dick Bulkowski, D.R.E. Students 98.

17—OUR LADY OF SORROWS, (Italian), Rev. Theodore Kozlowski.
Res.: 101 Hall St., S.E., 49507. Tel: 616-243-0222.
Catechesis/Religious Program—Sr. Adriana Gazzera, M.C., D.R.E. Students 60.

18—ST. PAUL THE APOSTLE, Rev. Msgr. Ernest Schneider; Deacon Richard Radecki; Fran Gilhoran, Pastoral Assoc.
Res.: 2750 Burton St., S.E., 49546. Tel: 616-949-4170; Fax: 616-949-5295.
School—Fax: 616-949-1690. Lay Teachers 16; Students 169.
Catechesis/Religious Program— Beth Kolenda, D.R.E. Students 248.

19—SS. PETER AND PAUL, (Lithuanian), [CEM] Rev. Dennis W. Morrow; Deacon Manuel E. Herrera.
Res.: 520 Myrtle St., N.W., 49504-3277. Tel: 616-454-6000; Fax: 616-454-4532.
School—1433 Hamilton Ave., N.W., 49504. Tel: 616-454-5611. Lori Salva, Prin. Lay Teachers 9; Students 105.
Catechesis/Religious Program—Students 33.

20—SACRED HEART OF JESUS, Formerly Sacred Heart [JC] Rev. Edward A. Hankiewicz; Sr. Marie Bernarde Salazar, O.P., Pastoral Assoc. In Res., Rev. Msgr. James P. Moran, P.A. (Retired); Rev. Joseph Pettit (Retired).
Res.: 156 Valley Ave., S.W., 49504. Tel: 616-459-8362; Fax: 616-458-0602.
School—Tel: 616-459-0948; Fax: 616-459-0899. Richard E. Kosla, Prin. Lay Teachers 9; Students 120.
Catechesis/Religious Program—Jacquiline Kozal, D.R.E. Students 60.

21—SHRINE OF ST. FRANCIS XAVIER AND OUR LADY OF GUADALUPE, [JC] Rev. Jose Quintana.
Res.: 250 Brown St., S.E., 49507. Tel: 616-241-2485; Fax: 616-241-2079.
School—240 Brown St., S.E., 49507. Tel: 616-241-5474; Fax: 616-241-5493. Mr. Tom Priest, Prin. Lay Teachers 11; Students 180.
Catechesis/Religious Program—Angie Ciccone, D.R.E. Students 120.

22—ST. STEPHEN'S, [JC] Unassigned.

Res.: 750 Gladstone Ave., S.E., 49506. Tel: 616-243-8998; Fax: 616-245-7360.
School—740 Rosewood Ave., S.E., 49506. Fax: 616-243-0451. Peter Chan, Ph.D., Prin. Lay Teachers 12; Students 290.
Catechesis/Religious Program—Mrs. Rhonda Lomonaco, D.R.E. Students 420.

23—ST. THOMAS THE APOSTLE, [JC] Rev. James A. Chelich.
Res.: 1449 Wilcox Park Dr., S.E., 49506. Tel: 616-459-4662; Fax: 616-458-4047.
School—Tel: 616-458-4228; Fax: 616-458-4583. David A. Faber, Prin. Lay Teachers 14; Students 309.
Catechesis/Religious Program—Students 143.

OUTSIDE THE CITY OF GRAND RAPIDS

ADA, KENT CO., ST. ROBERT, Revs. R. Louis Stasker; James C. Kowalski; Sisters Joan Brown, O.P., Pastoral Assoc.; Ann Michael Farnsworth, O.P., Pastoral Assoc.
Res.: P.O. Box 369, 49301. Tel: 616-676-9111; Fax: 616-676-0950.
Catechesis/Religious Program—Tel: 616-676-1488. Mary Ann Snyder, D.R.E. Students 1,213.

ALPINE, KENT CO., HOLY TRINITY, Rev. Daniel R. DePew.
Res.: 1200 Alpine Church Rd., N.W., 49321. Tel: 616-784-0677; Fax: 616-784-0678.
School—Comstock Park, 49321. Tel: 616-784-0696. Nancy Kryger, Prin. Lay Teachers 9; Students 220.
Catechesis/Religious Program—Tel: 616-784-3242. Jackie Lyals, D.R.E. Students 235.

BALDWIN, LAKE CO., ST. ANN'S, Rev. Thomas J. Brown.
Res.: 740 E. Ninth St., P.O. Box 729, 49304. Tel: 231-745-7997; Fax: 231-745-9844.
Mission—St. Ignatius Luther, Lake Co.

BELDING, IONIA CO., ST. JOSEPH'S, [CEM] Rev. Troy Nevins.
Office—409 S. Bridge St., 48809. Tel: 616-794-2145; Fax: 616-794-2145.
School—St. Joseph-St. Mary, Tel: 616-794-1910. Ted Cusack, Prin. Lay Teachers 5; Students 75.
Catechesis/Religious Program—Students 71.

BELMONT, KENT CO., ASSUMPTION OF THE BLESSED VIRGIN MARY, [CEM] Rev. Peter G. Vu.
Res.: 6369 Belmont Ave., 49306. Tel: 616-361-5126; Fax: 616-361-5503.
School—6393 Belmont Ave., 49306. Tel: 616-361-5483; Fax: 616-361-2553. Sr. Rosemary Smith, R.S.M., Prin. Lay Teachers 9; Students 201.
Catechesis/Religious Program—Students 327.

BIG RAPIDS, MECOSTA CO.

1—ST. MARY'S, [CEM] Rev. Wayne B. Wheeler Jr. 1009 Marion Ave., 49307. Tel: 231-796-5202; Fax: 231-796-9231.
School—Tel: 231-796-6731; Fax: 231-976-9293. Pamela Dickerson, Prin. Lay Teachers 6; Students 87.
Catechesis/Religious Program—Students 87.

2—ST. PAUL'S CAMPUS PARISH, Rev. Wayne B. Wheeler Jr.
Res.: One Damascus Rd., 49307. Tel: 231-796-7393; Fax: 231-796-3990.
Catechesis/Religious Program—Students 180.

BRUNSWICK, NEWAYGO CO., ST. MICHAEL'S, [CEM] Rev. Michael Alber.
Res.: 6382 S. Maple Island Rd., Fremont, 49412. Tel: 231-924-3389; 231-924-9803; Fax: 231-924-0402.
School—Tel: 231-924-0268; Fax: 231-924-0268. Anne Featherstone. Lay Teachers 5; Students 60.
Catechesis/Religious Program—Students 65.
Mission—Christ the King Hesperia, Oceana Co.

BYRON CENTER, KENT CO., ST. SEBASTIAN'S, [CEM] Rev. Msgr. Gaspar F. Ancona.
Res.: 9408 Wilson, 49315. Tel: 616-878-1893; Fax: 616-878-4019.
Catechesis/Religious Program—Tel: 616-878-1619; Fax: 616-878-0715. Theresa Dekker, D.R.E. Students 206.

CALEDONIA, KENT CO., HOLY FAMILY, [CEM 3] Rev. David E. LeBlanc.
Res.: 9669 Kraft Ave., S.E., 49316. Tel: 616-891-1160; 616-891-9259 (Office); Fax: 616-891-1346.
Catechesis/Religious Program—Tel: 616-891-8867. Christine Shafer, D.R.E. Students 593.

CARSON CITY, MONTCALM CO., ST. MARY'S, [CEM] Rev. William J. Reitz.
Res.: 404 N. Division St., 48811. Tel: 989-584-3553; Fax: 989-584-6044.
Catechesis/Religious Program—Tel: 517-981-6668. Nancy Woodcock, D.R.E. Students 81.

CONKLIN, OTTAWA CO., ST. FRANCIS XAVIER, Rev. John F. Porter.
Res.: 2044 Gooding Rd., 49403. Tel: 616-899-2471; Fax: 231-853-2191.
Catechesis/Religious Program—Students 35.

COOPERSVILLE, OTTAWA CO., ST. MICHAEL'S, [CEM] [JC] Rev. John F. Vallier.
Res.: 17151 88th Ave., 49404. Tel: 616-837-8792; 616-837-8158 (Parish Office); Fax: 616-837-7893.
School—Tel: 616-837-6346. Kevin Varner, Prin. Lay Teachers 5; Students 82.
Catechesis/Religious Program—Tel: 616-837-8580. Students 209.
Mission—Grand Valley State University - Catholic Campus Ministry

CUSTER, MASON CO., ST. MARY'S, [CEM] [JC] Rev. Isidro Gangatiel (Philippines).
Res.: 85 S. Madison, P.O. Box 68, 49405. Tel: 231-757-4709.
Catechesis/Religious Program—Tel: 231-757-9562. Ann Glencoe, D.R.E. Students 32.

EDMORE, MONTCALM CO., ST. MARGARET MARY, Rev. Eugene Okoli (Nigeria).
Res.: 1051 E. Howard City Rd., 48829. Tel: 989-427-5645; Fax: 989-427-3268.
Catechesis/Religious Program—Students 50.

EVART, OSCEOLA CO., SACRED HEART, Rev. Joseph J. Fix.
Res.: 9878 E. US 10, P.O. Box 778, 49631. Tel: 231-734-3171; Fax: 231-734-6880.
Catechesis/Religious Program—Tel: 231-834-3175. Students 75.

FREE SOIL, MASON CO., ST. JOHN CANTIUS, [CEM] Rev. David L. Harpe.
Res.: 2845 E. Michigan, 49411-9602. Tel: 231-464-5672.
Catechesis/Religious Program—Tel: 231-464-5567. Mary Kovalcik, D.R.E. Students 38.

FREMONT, NEWAYGO CO., ALL SAINTS, [CEM] Rev. Anthony Russo.
Res.: 510 Iroquois Dr., 49412. Tel: 231-924-7705; Fax: 231-924-7708.
Catechesis/Religious Program—Tel: 231-924-7571. Students 161.

GRAND HAVEN, OTTAWA CO., ST. PATRICK'S, Rev. William A. Langlois; Deacon Richard Fett.
Res.: 920 Fulton St., 49417. Tel: 616-842-0001; Fax: 616-842-1174.
Catechesis/Religious Program—Tel: 616-842-8230. Jeff Andrini, D.R.E. Students 400.
Mission—St. Anthony 13421 Green St., Robinson Township, Ottawa Co. 49417. Tel: 616-846-3548; Fax: 616-846-1085.

GRANDVILLE, KENT CO., ST. PIUS X, Rev. George E. Darling; Deacon Norman Riksen, Pastoral Assoc.
Res.: 3937 Wilson Ave., S.W., 49418 Tel: 616-532-9344; Fax: 616-538-6340.
Catechesis/Religious Program—Tel: 616-538-2600. Students 487.

GREENVILLE, MONTCALM CO., ST. CHARLES, [CEM] Rev. Philip Salmonowicz, Admin.
Res.: 505 S. Lafayette, 48838. Tel: 616-754-4194; Fax: 616-754-2357.
School—502 S. Franklin St., 48838. Tel: 616-754-3416 Fax: 616-754-9262. Sr. David Therese Korson, O.P., Prin. Sisters of St. Dominic (Grand Rapids, MI) 1; Lay Teachers 8; Students 127.
Catechesis/Religious Program—Tel: 616-754-3196. Joseph Velie, D.R.E. Students 121.
Mission—St. Margaret [CEM] Cedar Springs. 10195 16 Mile Rd., Harvard, Kent Co. 49319. Tel: 616-696-3904.

HART, OCEANA CO., ST. GREGORY'S, Rev. Ronald F. Schneider.
Res.: 316 Peach St., 49420. Tel: 231-873-2660; Fax: 231-873-7601.
Catechesis/Religious Program—Tel: 231-873-2578; Fax: 231-873-2578. Andrea Bosse, D.R.E. Students 72.
Mission—Kateri Tekawitha Native American Center & St. Joseph Center Elbridge, Oceana Co.

HOLLAND, OTTAWA CO.

1—ST. FRANCIS DE SALES, Revs. Charles D. Brown; Fred Hoesli, O.P. (Retired); Sr. Ann Thielen, O.P., Pastoral Assoc.; Deacon Juan Garcia.
Office—195 W. 13th St., 49423. Tel: 616-396-7641; Fax: 616-392-2474.
School—12100 Quincy St., 49424. Tel: 616-994-9864; Fax: 616-994-9870. Judi Koepnick, Prin. Holland Area Catholic Schools Lay Teachers 15; Students 286.
Catechesis/Religious Program—195 W. 13th St., 49423. Tel: 616-392-6700. Marilyn Torborg, D.R.E. Students 389.

2—OUR LADY OF THE LAKE, Rev. Phillip Nguyen.
Res.: 480 152nd Ave., 49424. Tel: 616-399-1062; Fax: 616-399-5766.
Catechesis/Religious Program— David Johnson, D.R.E. Students 641.

HOWARD CITY, MONTCALM CO., CHRIST THE KING, Rev. Raymond E. Bruck, Admin. (Retired).
Res.: 9596 Reed Rd., 49329. Tel: 231-937-5757; Fax: 231-937-8211.
Catechesis/Religious Program— Sandy Weiks, D.R.E. Students 44.
Mission—St. Frances de Sales 829 E. Richardson, Lakeview, Montcalm Co. 48850. Tel: 989-352-7293.

HUBBARDSTON, IONIA CO., ST. JOHN THE BAPTIST, [CEM] Rev. William J. Reitz.
Res.: 404 N. Division, Carson City, 48811. Tel: 989-584-3553; Fax: 989-584-6044.
Catechesis/Religious Program—Tel: 517-981-6668. Nancy Woodcock, D.R.E. Students 38.

IONIA, IONIA CO., SS. PETER AND PAUL, [CEM] Rev. Melvin E. Fox; Deacon Zenon Cardenas Sr.
Parish Office—434 High St., 48846. Tel: 616-527-3610; Fax: 616-527-3697.
School—317 Baldie St., 48846. Tel: 616-527-3561; Fax: 616-527-3562. Lay Teachers 12; Students 189.
Catechesis/Religious Program—Tel: 616-527-3575. Students 122.

IRONS, LAKE CO., ST. BERNARD'S, Rev. David L. Harpe.
Res.: One Oak St., P.O. Box 155, 49644. Tel: 231-266-5155; Fax: 231-266-8948.
Catechesis/Religious Program—Students 13.

JENISON, OTTAWA CO., HOLY REDEEMER, Rev. Ronald D. Hutchinson.
Res.: 2700 Baldwin Dr., 49428. Tel: 616-669-9220; Fax: 616-669-9360.
Catechesis/Religious Program—Tel: 616-669-0820. Donna Francisco, D.R.E. Students 510.

LAKE ODESSA, IONIA CO., ST. EDWARD'S, Rev. Thomas F. Boufford.
Res.: 531 Jordan Lake St., 48849-6200. Tel: 616-374-7253; Fax: 616-374-1559.
Catechesis/Religious Program—Dee Manshum, D.R.E. Students 108.

LAKEVIEW, MONTCALM CO., ST. FRANCIS DE SALES, Rev. Raymond E. Bruck, Admin. (Retired).
Res.: 9596 N. Reed Rd., Howard City, 49329. Tel: 231-937-5757; Fax: 231-937-8211.
Church: 829 E. Richardson, 48850.
Catechesis/Religious Program— Patricia Berry, D.R.E. Students 42.

LAKEWOOD CLUB, MUSKEGON CO., ST. MARY OF THE WOODS, Rev. Paul T. Johnson.
Res.: 150 Church St., Twin Lake, 49457. Tel: 231-894-5887.

LOWELL, KENT CO., ST. MARY'S, [CEM] Rev. George J. Fekete.
Res.: 402 Amity St., 49331-1308. Tel: 616-897-9820; Fax: 616-897-9683.
Catechesis/Religious Program—Tel: 616-897-7915; Fax: 616-897-7915. Brenda Berding, D.R.E. Students 163.

LUDINGTON, MASON CO.

1—ST. SIMON'S, [CEM] Rev. Kenneth H. Schichtel.
Res.: 702 E. Bryant Rd., 49431. Tel: 231-843-8606; Fax: 231-843-2052.
School—Tel: 231-843-3188. Collin Thompson, Prin. Lay Teachers 10; Students 220.
Catechesis/Religious Program—Tel: 231-843-3497. Students 276.

2—ST. STANISLAUS, [JC] Rev. Kenneth H. Schichtel.
Res.: 702 E. Bryant Rd., 49431. Tel: 231-843-8606; Fax: 231-843-2052.

MARION, OSCEOLA CO., ST. AGNES, Rev. Joseph J. Fix.
Res.: P.O. Box 778, Evart, 49631. Tel: 231-734-3171.
Church: Tel: 231-743-6401; Fax: 231-734-6880.
Catechesis/Religious Program—Students 71.

MARNE, OTTAWA CO., ST. MARY'S, [CEM] Rev. William F. Zink.
Res.: 15164 Juniper Dr., 49435. Tel: 616-677-3934; Fax: 616-677-5866.
Catechesis/Religious Program—Tel: 616-677-3753. Students 190.

MIRIAM, IONIA CO., ST. MARY'S, [CEM] Rev. Troy Nevins.
Office—409 S. Bridge St., Belding, 48809. Tel: 616-794-2145; Fax: 616-794-2145.
School—St. Joseph-St. Mary, Tel: 616-794-1910. See St. Joseph, Belding.
Catechesis/Religious Program— Twinned with St. Joseph, Belding. Students 31.

MONTAGUE, MUSKEGON CO., ST. JAMES, [CEM] Rev. Chris Rouech.
Res.: 5179 Dowling St., 49437. Tel: 231-893-3085; Fax: 231-894-9929.
School—Tel: 231-893-2972. Stephen Habetler, Prin. Lay Teachers 5; Students 59.
Catechesis/Religious Program—Tel: 231-894-8771. Brenda Runyan, D.R.E. Students 186.
Mission—St. John 5179 Dowling St., Claybanks, Oceana Co. 49437.

MUSKEGON HEIGHTS, MUSKEGON CO., SACRED HEART, [JC] Revs. James Wyse; Mark Bauer.
Res.: 150 E. Summit Ave., 49444. Tel: 231-733-2440; Fax: 231-733-5128.
Catechesis/Religious Program—Tel: 231-733-2455. Students 64.

MUSKEGON, MUSKEGON CO.

1—ST. FRANCIS DE SALES, Revs. Thomas G. Simons; Julian Reginato; Deacon William McCabe.
Res.: 2929 McCracken St., 49441. Tel: 231-755-1953; Fax: 231-759-7074.
Catechesis/Religious Program—Tel: 231-755-1307. Rick Grinstead, D.R.E. Students 175.

2—ST. JEAN BAPTISTE, [JC] Revs. Mark Bauer; James B. Wyse; Michael Pekar, Pastoral Assoc.
Res.: 1292 Jefferson St., 49441. Tel: 231-722-2793; Fax: 231-726-5976.
Catechesis/Religious Program—Barbara Miles, D.R.E. Students 94.

3—ST. JOSEPH'S, Closed. For inquiries for parish records contact the chancery.
4—ST. MARY'S, [JC] Revs. James B. Wyse; Mark Bauer. In Res., Rev. Ernest J. Bernott, Admin.
Res.: 239 W. Clay Ave., 49440-1213. Tel: 231-722-2844; Fax: 231-722-0733.
Catechesis/Religious Program—Students 60.
5—ST. MICHAEL'S, [JC] Revs. James Wyse; Mark Bauer.
Res.: 1716 Sixth St., 49441. Tel: 231-722-3071; Fax: 231-722-3243.
Catechesis/Religious Program— Sr. Agnes Mary Wojtkowiak, O.P., D.R.E. Students 57.
6—OUR LADY OF GRACE, [JC] Rev. Michael P. Olson; Michael A. Pekar Jr., Pastoral Assoc.
Res.: 451 S. Getty St., 49442. Tel: 231-722-2803; Fax: 231-722-3622.
Catechesis/Religious Program—Students 60.
7—ST. THOMAS THE APOSTLE, Deacon David Kasprzyk.
Office:—3252 Apple Ave., 49442. Tel: 231-773-3160; Fax: 231-777-7866.
Catechesis/Religious Program—Students 175.
NEWAYGO, NEWAYGO CO., ST. BARTHOLOMEW'S, [CEM] Rev. Loc Trinh.
Res.: 599 Brooks St., 49337. Tel: 231-652-1286; Fax: 231-652-6669.
Catechesis/Religious Program—Billie Haskin, D.R.E. Students 268.
Mission—Our Lady of Guadalupe Church Grant, Newaygo Co.
NORTH MUSKEGON, MUSKEGON CO., PRINCE OF PEACE, Rev. Robert A. Hart; Deacon Wesley Hewitt; Barbara Perri, Pastoral Assoc.
Res.: 1110 Dykstra, 49445. Tel: 231-744-3321; Fax: 231-744-4859.
Catechesis/Religious Program—Tel: 231-744-5445. Joann McQuone, D.R.E. Students 184.
PARNELL, KENT CO., ST. PATRICK'S, [CEM] Rev. Rock Badgerow.
Res.: 4351 Parnell Ada, 49301. Tel: 616-691-8541; Fax: 616-691-6309.
School—Tel: 616-691-8833. Suzanne Deugaw, Prin. Students 180.
Catechesis/Religious Program—Students 312.
PEWAMO, IONIA CO., ST. JOSEPH'S, [CEM] Rev. Charlon O. Mason, Admin.
Res.: 106 East St., 48873. Tel: 989-593-3440; Fax: 989-593-3184.
School—Tel: 989-593-3400. Lorie Salisbury, Prin. Lay Teachers 5; Students 111.
Catechesis/Religious Program—840 N. Norway Dr., P.O. Box 372, Fowler, 48835. Tel: 989-593-3488. Aaron Epkey. Students 99.
PORTLAND, IONIA CO., ST. PATRICK'S, Revs. Charles D. Hall; Shamaun Beas (Pakistan), Assoc. Pastor.
Res.: 140 Church St., 48875. Tel: 517-647-6505; Fax: 517-647-7807.
School—122 West St., 48875. Tel: 517-647-7551; Fax: 517-647-4545. Lay Teachers 15; Students 282.
High School—Lay Teachers 13; Students 127.
Catechesis/Religious Program—Tel: 517-647-0040. Thomas Jandernoa, D.R.E. Students 310.
RAVENNA, MUSKEGON CO., ST. CATHERINE, [CEM] Rev. John F. Porter.
Res.: P.O. Box 216, 49451. Tel: 231-853-6222; Fax: 231-853-2191.
School—Tel: 231-853-6743; Fax: 231-853-8673. Sr. Peter Mary Korson, O.P., Prin. Lay Teachers 4; Students 46.
Catechesis/Religious Program—Tel: 231-853-6222. Students 63.
REED CITY, OSCEOLA CO., ST. PHILIP NERI, [CEM] Rev. Philip Shangraw, Admin.
Res.: 831 S. Chestnut, 49677. Tel: 231-832-5544; Fax: 231-832-5545.
Catechesis/Religious Program—Elizabeth Marek, D.R.E. Students 97.
Mission—St. Anne 23949 22 Mile Rd., Paris, Mecosta Co. 49338.
REMUS, MECOSTA CO., ST. MICHAEL'S, [CEM] Rev. Thomas Hack (Retired); Deacon Robert Cathcart.
Res.: 5045 Nine Mile Rd., 49340. Tel: 989-967-3520; Fax: 989-967-8246.
School—(Grades PreK-6) Mrs. Mary Schoner, Prin. Sisters 2; Lay Teachers 9; Students 135.
Catechesis/Religious Program—Students 85.
ROCKFORD, KENT CO., OUR LADY OF CONSOLATION, Revs. Thomas P. Page; Anthony Pelak; Mary Ellen Koziol, Pastoral Assoc.
Office—4865 Eleven Mile Rd., 49341. Tel: 616-866-0931; Fax: 616-866-3668.
School—(Grades K-6) Tel: 616-866-2427; Fax: 616-866-5475. Carolyn Hardy, Prin. Lay Teachers 7; Students 187.
Catechesis/Religious Program—Tel: 616-866-2577. Students 674.
ROTHBURY, OCEANA CO., OUR LADY OF THE ASSUMPTION, [CEM] Rev. Phillip J. Witkowski.
Res.: 1372 S. Oceana Dr., Shelby, 49455. Tel: 231-861-2620; Fax: 231-861-6878.
Church: 3000 Winston Rd., P.O. Box 8, 49452. Tel: 231-893-0905.
SAND LAKE, KENT CO., MARY QUEEN OF APOSTLES, [CEM 2] Rev. Joseph W. Kenshol.
Res.: 1 Maple St., 49343. Tel: 616-636-5671; Fax: 616-636-4570.
Catechesis/Religious Program—Tel: 616-636-5923. Pat Patin, D.R.E. Students 160.
Mission—St. Clara 4584 N. Bailey Rd., Coral, Montcalm Co. 49322.
SARANAC, IONIA CO., ST. ANTHONY (1981), Rev. Thomas Boufford.
Res.: 3927 Jackson Rd., 48881. Tel: 616-642-6119; Fax: 616-642-0390.
Catechesis/Religious Program—Tel: 616-642-6402. Janice Diaz, D.R.E.; Sharon Bassett, D.R.E. Students 85.
SCOTTVILLE, MASON CO., ST. JEROME, Rev. Isidro T. Gargantiel.
Res.: 203 W. State St., 49454. Tel: 231-757-2855.
Catechesis/Religious Program—Kathy Papes, D.R.E. Students 66.
SHELBY, OCEANA CO., OUR LADY OF FATIMA, Rev. Phillip J. Witkowski.
Res.: 1372 S. Oceana Dr., 49455. Tel: 231-861-2620; Fax: 231-861-6878.
Catechesis/Religious Program—Students 70.
SPARTA, KENT CO., HOLY FAMILY, Rev. Msgr. Terrence L. Stewart.
Res.: 425 S. State St., 49345. Tel: 616-887-8222; Fax: 616-887-0681.
Catechesis/Religious Program—Tel: 616-887-8857. Students 258.
SPRING LAKE, OTTAWA CO., ST. MARY'S, Rev. Anthony C. Vainavicz. In Res., Rev. James M. Bozung (Retired). Tel: 616-862-6635.
Res.: 406 E. Savidge, 49456. Tel: 616-842-1702; Fax: 616-842-3392.
School—Tel: 616-842-1282; Fax: 616-842-8048. Wendy Sipka, Prin. Dominican Sisters 3; Lay Teachers 11; Students 218.
Catechesis/Religious Program—Tel: 616-842-2840. Jim Penrice, D.R.E. Students 258.
Convent—421 E. Exchange St., 49456. Tel: 616-842-1615.
STANTON, MONTCALM CO., ST. BERNADETTE OF LOURDES, Rev. Eugene Okoli (Nigeria).
Res.: 1051 E. Howard City, Edmore, 48829. Tel: 989-427-5645; Fax: 989-427-3268.
Catechesis/Religious Program—Students 75.
WEARE TWP., OCEANA CO., ST. JOSEPH'S, [CEM] Rev. Dung Anton Tran.
Res.: 2380 W. Jackson Rd., Hart, 49420. Tel: 231-873-2683; Fax: 231-873-5327.
Catechesis/Religious Program—Tel: 231-869-5231. Clara Jean Monton, D.R.E. Students 120.
Mission—St. Vincent 637 E. Sixth, Pentwater, Oceana Co. 49449. Tel: 231-869-2601.
WHITE CLOUD, NEWAYGO CO., ST. JOSEPH'S, [CEM] Rev. Anthony S. Russo.
965 Newell St., P.O. Box 175, 49349. Tel: 231-689-6061; Fax: 231-689-6225.
WRIGHT TOWNSHIP, OTTAWA CO., ST. JOSEPH'S, Rev. Leo S. Rosloniec.
Res.: 18876 Eighth Ave., Conklin, 49403. Tel: 616-899-2286; Fax: 616-899-2212.
School—Tel: 616-899-5300; Fax: 616-899-5491. Mrs. Ann Rutowski, Prin. Dominican Sisters 1; Lay Teachers 5; Students 75.
Catechesis/Religious Program—Tel: 616-899-2384. Students 143.
WYOMING, OUR LADY OF LAVANG (1999), Rev. Peter Nghiem.
2420 Avon S.W., 49509. Tel: 616-531-5213; Fax: 616-261-9906.

CHAPELS

GRAND RAPIDS. *Chapel of Our Lady of Aglona, Latvian Apostolate*, 507 Broadway Ave., N.W., 49504. Tel: 616-363-2337.
Chapel of St. Paul-Catholic Information Center, 246 Ionia, N.W., 49503. Tel: 616-459-7267. Revs. Robert M. Cary, C.S.P. (KNX), Joseph W. Gallagher, C.S.P., Charles Cunniff, C.S.P., John Kenny, C.S.P., Deacon Michael Mauer.
Michigan Veterans' Facility Catholic Chapel, 3000 Monroe Ave., N.E., 49505. Tel: 616-364-5323.

On Special Assignment:
Revs.—
Brucker, G. Fredrick, Tribunal Office. Tel: 616-459-4509
Danner, Michael A., Dir. Christopher House, Christopher House, 723 Rosewood, S.E., 45906. Tel: 616-243-6538
Dudek, Stephen S., Dir. Diocesan Hispanic Ministry
Duncan, William H., Vicar Gen. & Moderator of the Curia, 660 Burton, S.E., 49507. Tel: 616-243-0491
Fekete, George J., 402 Amity, Lowell, 49331. Tel: 616-897-9820 Dir. Missions
Hankiewicz, Edward, Tribunal Office. Tel: 616-459-4509
Milanowski, Paul A., Dir. of Priestly Vocations. Tel: 616-243-0491
Mitchell, Mark E., Chap., Blodgett & Butterworth Hospitals, 628 Diamond, N.E., 49503. Tel: 616-242-4832
Morrow, Dennis, Adjutant Judicial Vicar for the Tribunal; Diocesan Archivist; Chap. Grand Rapids Fire Dept. & Grand Rapids Police Dept.
Nghiem, Peter Hoan-Xuan, Dir. Vietnamese Apostolate, 2420 Avon S.W., 49509. Tel: 616-531-5213 National service to community of Vietnamese Clergy and Religious; Serving Vietnamese Catholic Federation of USA.
Page, Thomas P., Assoc. Vicar for Priests. Tel: 616-866-0931
Porter, John, Judicial Vicar, 265 Sheldon, S.E., 49503. Tel: 616-459-4509
Przybysz, Mark C., Dir. of Continuing Formation of Priests. Tel: 616-243-8998, Ext. 201
Van Lente, Richard, Diocesan Tribunal. Tel: 616-459-4509
Weber, Donald E., Vicar Priests. Tel: 616-241-6489
Wyse, James, special attention to Diocesan Hispanic Ministry Office

---

On Duty Outside the Diocese:
Revs.—
Cook, Daniel
Kurylowicz, Martin
Turner, Robert

Retired:
Rev. Msgrs.—
Brophy, Charles D., St. Ann's Home, 2161 Leonard, N.W., #128, 49504.
Giammona, John J., 3803 Old Elm Dr., S.E., Kentwood, 49512.
Jude, Walter F., 105 W.11 Mile Rd., Irons, 49644.
Moran, James P., P.A., 156 Valley, S.W., 49504.
Zerfas, Herman H., 1200 104th, S.W., Byron Center, 49315.
Revs.—
Anderson, Louis, St. Mary's, Big Rapids, 49307.
Antekeier, Charles R.
Bielskas, Edward J., 4101 Clyde Park, S.W., Wyoming, 49509.
Bozung, James M., 406 E. Savidge St., Spring Lake, 49456.
Bruck, Raymond E., 1200 104th, S.W., Byron Center, 49315.
Cawley, Patrick, c/o General Delivery, Vanderbilt, 49795.
Dondzila, Henry J., 628 Diamond N.E., 49503.
Droski, Norman, Sacred Heart, Muskegon.
Garcia, Pedro, St. Joseph the Worker, Parnell.
Gillespie, Robert B., St. Ann's Home, 2161 Leonard, N.W., 49504.
Golas, Eugene S., 2110 Leonard N.E., Apt. #416, 49505.
Hack, Thomas, 1630 Godfrey, S.W., Wyoming, 49509.
La Goe, John P., 3119 Scenic Dr., North Muskegon, 49445.
Leyrita, Norbert, 6253 E. Woodrow Rd., Hesperia, 49421.
McKinney, Thomas A., St. Ann's Home, 2161 Leonard, N.W., Rm. 109, 49504.
Nash, Denis P., 4487 Glenhollow, Hudsonville, 49426.
Pettit, Joseph
Schiller, Thomas A., 3816 Fountain R., Ludington, 49431.
Toolis, Martin, 3028 Piney Ridge Rd., Ludington, 49431.
Vesbit, Thomas, St. Jude.
Weber, Donald
Wing, Kenneth A., 2093 Barclay, #209, Muskegon, 49441.

Permanent Deacons:
Ashmore, John, Holy Family, Caledonia
Baldwin, Kenneth, Shrine of St. Francis Xavier, Grand Rapids
Cardenas, Zenon, SS. Peter and Paul, Ionia & St. Patrick, Grand Haven
Cathcart, Robert, St. Michael, Ramus
Conigliaro, Pietro, St. Patrick, Parnell & Jail Ministry
Dordan, Michael, Director Diocean Program for Permanent Diaconate
Ferguson, Leo, St. Anthony of Padua
Fett, Richard, Jail Ministry, Ottawa Co.
Garcia, Juan, St. Francis de Sales, Holland
Gutierrez, Carlos, Cathedral of St. Andrew, Grand Rapids
Herrera, Manuel E., SS. Peter and Paul, Grand Rapids
Hewitt, Wesley, Prince of Peace, North Muskegon
Hollern, Dale, St. John Vianney, Wyoming, MI

Jankowski, Leon, (Retired)
Jurek, Thomas, Holy Name of Jesus, Wyoming, MI
Kasprzyk, David, St. Thomas the Apostle, Muskegon
LeMire, George, Blessed Sacrament, Grand Rapids
Mauer, Michael J., Catholic Information Center, Grand Rapids
McCabe, William, St. Francis de Sales, Muskegon
McGinnity, Michael, All Saints, Fremont
Pitt, Richard, Holy Redeemer, Jenison
Radecki, Richard, St. Paul the Apostle, Grand Rapids
Riksen, Norman, St. Pius X, Grandville
Scheid, Howard, St. Joseph, Belding
Schneider, Daniel
Simon, Edward, St. Joseph, Weare
VandeVoren, Lawrence, Saint Mary's Mercy Medical Center Hospital Ministry
Wood, Michael, St. Mary Magdalen, Grand Rapids

INSTITUTIONS LOCATED IN THE DIOCESE

[A] COLLEGES AND UNIVERSITIES

GRAND RAPIDS. *Aquinas College*, 1607 Robinson Rd., S.E., 49506. Tel: 616-459-8281, Ext. 2491; Fax: 616-732-4589. Web: www.aquinas.edu. Harry J. Knopke, Ph.D., Pres.; C. Edward Balog, Ph.D., Provost & Dean of Faculty; Michael C. Keller, M.S.A., Vice Pres. Planning & Analysis; Mr. William Shefferly, Vice Pres. Finance & Operations; Julie Ridenour, B.A., Vice Pres. Devel.; Sr. M. Aquinas Weber, O.P., M.A., Chancellor; Cynthia Vangeideren, Ph.D., Dean of School Mgmt.; Dr. V. James Garofalo, Ph.D., Dean School Education; Dr. Shirley Lewis, Dean School Arts & Sciences; Ms. Paula Meehan, Dean Admissions; Mr. Bradford Winkler, Dean Student Affairs; Marty Fahey, A.P.R., Dir. College Relations; Cecilia Mesler, Registrar; Mr. David J. Steffee, Dir. Financial Aid; Mrs. Mary Clark-Kaiser, Dir. of Campus Min.; Mrs. Terry Marshall, Liturgist; Rev. Charles Santoro, O.P., Chaplain; Mr. Eric Bridge, Outreach; Mr. Dennis Rybicki, Music Dir. Sisters 10; Lay Teachers 87; Students 2,571.

[B] HIGH SCHOOLS, DIOCESAN

GRAND RAPIDS. *Catholic Central High School*, 319 Sheldon Ave., S.E., 49503. Tel: 616-459-4559; Fax: 616-459-0257. Web: www.remc8.k12.mi.us/cathsec/cchome. Mr. Steve Passinault, Prin.; Tom Maj, Asst. Prin. Sisters of St. Dominic 3; Lay Teachers 49; Students 975.

West Catholic High School, 1801 Bristol, N.W., 49504. Tel: 616-233-5800; Fax: 616-453-4320. Web: www.westcath.put.k12.mi. Mr. Stan Spetoskey, Prin. Lay Teachers 36; Students 614.

MUSKEGON. *Muskegon Catholic Middle and High School*, 1145 W. Laketon, 49441. Tel: 231-755-2201; Fax: 231-755-2415. Thomas Powers, Chief School Officer & Exec. Dir.; Patricia O'Toole, Prin., High School; Julie Whelan, Prin., Middle School. Greater Muskegon Catholic Schools. Brothers 1; Lay Teachers 37; High School Students 262; Middle School Students 208.

[C] GRADE SCHOOL INTERPAROCHIAL

MUSKEGON. *St. Francis de Sales Elementary School*, (Grades PreK-5) , Greater Muskegon Consolidated Catholic School. , 2947 McCracken Ave., 49441. Tel: 231-755-1045; Fax: 231-759-7009 Email: cthomas@muskegon-cath.pvt.K12.mi.us. Web: www.gmcs.org. Miss Cindy Thomas, Prin. Lay Teachers 11; Students 203.

St. Michael Elementary School, (Grades PreK-5) , Greater Muskegon Consolidated School. , 215 W. Dale Ave., 49441. Tel: 231-722-4666; Fax: 231-725-7282. Web: www.gmcs.org. Miss Cindy Thomas, Prin. Lay Teachers 5; Students 93.

[D] GENERAL HOSPITALS

GRAND RAPIDS. *Saint Mary's Mercy Medical Center*, 200 Jefferson, S.E., 49503. Tel: 616-752-6090; Fax: 616-752-6151. Web: www.smmmc.org. Philip McCorkle, Pres. & CEO; Rev. Ayub Nasar, Chap.; Sr. Myra Bergman, R.S.M., Vice Pres. Mission Svcs. Sponsored by Catholic Health Ministries. Bed Capacity 324; Patients assisted annually 358,435.

MUSKEGON. *Mercy General Health Partners* Web: www.mghp.com. Sponsored by Trinity Health.

Sherman Campus, 1500 E. Sherman Blvd., P.O. Box 358, 49443. Tel: 231-739-9341; Fax: 231-733-0957.

Oak Campus, 1700 Oak Ave., 49242Web: www.mghp.com. Roger Spoelman, Pres. & CEO; Larry Ehren, Vice Pres. Mission Svcs. Sisters 1; Bed Capacity 322; Patients assisted annually 234,175.

[E] HOMES FOR THE AGED

GRAND RAPIDS. *St. Ann's Home*, 2161 Leonard St., N.W., 49504. Tel: 616-453-7715; Fax: 616-453-7359. Email: stanns@iserv.net. Carmelite Sisters of the Divine Heart of Jesus Sisters 3; Residents 140; Adult Day Care 5; Total Assisted 145.

[F] CONVENTS AND RESIDENCES FOR SISTERS

GRAND RAPIDS. *Aquinata Hall*, 2025 E. Fulton, 49503-3894. Tel: 616-456-5038; Fax: 616-454-6105. Sisters 42 Bed Capacity 54.

Dominican Center, 2025 E. Fulton St., 49503-3895. Tel: 616-454-1241; Fax: 616-454-2861. Web: www.dominicancenter.org. Mark Clarke, Dir.

Motherhouse of the Dominican Sisters, Marywood, 2025 E. Fulton St., 49503-3895. Tel: 616-459-2910; Fax: 616-454-6105. Web: www.grdominicans.org. Sr. Maribeth Holst, O.P., Prioress; Rev. Robert M. Kelly, O.P.; Sisters Carmelita Switzer, O.P., Coord. Pastoral Life; Darlene Sikorski, O.P., Treas.

Legal Title: *Sisters of St. Dominic of the Congregation of Our Lady of the Sacred Heart (The Religious Institute)*

Legal Title: *Sisters of the Order of St. Dominic of Grand Rapids, Michigan (The Corporation).*, Motherhouse and Novitiate for the Sisters of the Order of St. Dominic of the Congregation of Our Lady of the Sacred Heart. Sisters 305.

ADA. *Discalced Carmelite Nuns, Monastery of Our Lady of Guadalupe* (Parnell) , 4300 Mount Carmel Dr., N.E., 49301-9784. Tel: 616-691-7625; Fax: 616-691-8538. Sr. Agnes Therese, O.C.D., Prioress. Professed Carmelite Nuns 14; Extern Sisters 2; Novices 1.

BELMONT. *Motherhouse of the Consolata Missionary Sisters*, 6801 Belmont Rd., P.O. Box 371, 49306. Tel: 616-361-2072; Fax: 616-361-2049. Email: reusa.mc@iserv.net. Web: www.consolatasisters.org. Sr. Zelia Cordeiro, M.C., Supr. Consolata Sisters 15.

[G] RETREAT HOUSES

SPRING LAKE. *St. Lazare Retreat House*, 18600 W. Spring Lake Rd., P.O. Box 462, 49456-0462. Tel: 616-842-3370; Fax: 616-842-6815. Email: mjs_stlazare@triton.net. Revs. Michael J. Shea, C.M.; Robert J. Prior, C.M.

[H] NEWMAN CENTERS

COOPERSVILLE. *Grand Valley State University Catholic Campus Ministry* Allendale Campus, 10150-88th Ave., 49404-9413. Tel: 616-837-8158; Fax: 616-837-7893. Email: catholic@student.gvsu.edu. Web: www2.gvsu.edu/micatholic. Rev. John F. Vallier, Campus Priest.

[I] MISCELLANEOUS LISTINGS

GRAND RAPIDS. *Basilica of St. Adalbert Education Foundation*, 701 4th St. N.W., 49504. Tel: 616-458-3065; Fax: 616-458-0563. Web: basilcagr.org.

Bishops' Housing Corporation, 660 Burton St., S.E., 49507. Tel: 616-243-0491; Fax: 616-243-4910.

The Catholic Foundation of West Michigan, 660 Burton, S.E., 49507. Tel: 616-243-0491; Fax: 616-243-4910. Sr. Patrice Konwinski, O.P.

Educational Foundation of St. Francis Xavier School, Inc., 240 Brown St., S.E., 49507. Tel: 616-241-5474; Fax: 616-241-5493. Web: saintfrancisxavier.org.

The Foundation for Catholic Education of Greater Grand Rapids, Inc., 359 S. Division Ave., P.O. Box 327, 49501-0327. Tel: 616-233-5986; Fax: 616-233-5986. Email: mayfce@yahoo.com. Web: foundation@grcss.org. Duane E. Feldpausch, Exec. Dir.

Fund for Faith, 660 Burton St., S.E., 49507. Tel: 616-243-0491; Fax: 616-243-4910. Foundation established in 1976 for various apostolic works.

Marywood Academy, 2025 E. Fulton St., 49503-3895. Tel: 616-454-2910; Fax: 616-454-6105.

Ministry Ventures, 2025 E. Fulton St., 49503-3895. Tel: 616-454-4548; Fax: 616-454-6105. Email: dsikorski@grdominicans.org. Sr. Darlene Sikorski, Treas.; Carole Nugent, Operations Admin.

SS. Peter and Paul Parish Education Endowment Fund, 520 Myrtle St., N.W., 49504. Tel: 616-454-6000; Fax: 616-454-4532.

Sisters of St. Dominic Charitable Trust, 2025 E. Fulton Rd., 49503-3895. Tel: 616-459-2910; Fax: 616-454-6105. Sr. Maribeth Holst, O.P.

Legal Title: *Sisters of St. Dominic of the Congregation of Our Lady of the Sacred Heart Charitable Trust (The Trust).*

The Society of the Redemptorists of the City of Grand Rapids Represented in the Diocese. , 224 Carrier St., N.E., 49505. Tel: 616-451-3043; Fax: 616-458-5667. Revs. Thomas Donaldson, C.SS.R., Supr.; Bernard Rooney, C.SS.R.; Rudy Papes, C.SS.R.; Thomas O'Connor, C.SS.R.; Robert Balser, C.SS.R.; Durkin Fitzgerald, C.SS.R.; Eugene R. Harrison, C.SS.R.; Bro. Andrew Patin.

Steepletown Neighborhood Services, Inc., 671 Davis, N.W., Steepletown Center, 49504. Tel: 616-451-4215; Fax: 616-451-0557. Email: steeplet@iserv.net. Special Center for Social Service and Assistance.

LOWELL. *Franciscan Life Process Center*, 11650 Downes St., 49331-9489. Tel: 616-897-7842; Fax: 616-897-7054. Email: scanagle@lifeprocesscenter.org. Sr. Colleen Ann Nagle, F.S.E., Dir.

MUSKEGON HEIGHTS. *Christian Community Center*, 540 E. Hackley, 49444. Tel: 231-728-6402; Fax: 231-725-7579.

PORTLAND. *The Father Flohe Foundation*, 140 Church St., 48875. Tel: 517-647-6505; Fax: 517-647-7807.

VESTABURG. *Emmaus Monastery*, 10154 N. Pine Grove Rd., 48891. Tel: 989-268-5494; Fax: 989-268-5373. Email: emmaus@compuserv.com. Web: www.nethawk.com/emmaus. Sr. Diane Steir, E.C., Prioress.

WYOMING. *Catholic Cemeteries Extended Care Fund*, 4100 Clyde Park, S.W., 49509-0063. Tel: 616-531-9320; Fax: 616-531-9780. Robert Menzel, Dir. & Mgr.

RELIGIOUS INSTITUTES OF MEN REPRESENTED IN THE DIOCESE

For further details refer to the corresponding bracketed number in the Religious Institutes of Men or Women section.

[1330]—*Congregation of the Mission* (Eastern Prov.)—C.M.
[0430]—*Order of Preachers-Dominicans* (Central Prov.)—O.P.
[1030]—*Paulist Fathers*—C.S.P.
[1070]—*Redemptorist Fathers* (Denver Prov.)—C.SS.R.

RELIGIOUS INSTITUTES OF WOMEN REPRESENTED IN THE DIOCESE

[0360]—*Carmelite Sisters of the Divine Heart of Jesus*—Carmel.D.C
[0720]—*Consolata Missionary Sisters*—M.C.
[0420]—*Discalced Carmelite Nuns*—O.C.D.
[1070-14]—*Dominican Sisters*—O.P.
[2575]—*Institute of the Sisters of Mercy of the Americas*—R.S.M.
[2970]—*School Sisters of Notre Dame*—S.S.N.D.
[3560]—*Servants of Jesus*—S.J.
[]—*Sisters for Christian Community*—S.F.C.C.
[0460]—*Sisters of Charity of the Incarnate Word*—C.C.V.I.
[2990]—*Sisters of Notre Dame*—S.N.D.
[3830-11]—*Sisters of St. Joseph of Nazareth*—S.S.J.
[1830]—*Sisters of the Good Shepherd*—R.G.S.-C.G
[2150]—*Sisters of the Immaculate Heart of Mary*—I.H.M.
[3260]—*Sisters of the Precious Blood*—C.PP.S.

NECROLOGY

† Powers, Rev. Msgr. William E., (Retired)—Died Feb. 18, 2003
† Bernott, Albert R., (Retired)—Died June 27, 2003
† Feltman, Harold R., (Retired)—Died Aug. 17, 2003
† Kubiak, Edward J., (Retired)—Died Feb. 4, 2003
† McKnight, William—Died June 25, 2003
† Yager, James P., (Retired)—Died Aug. 20, 2003

Diocese of Great Falls - Billings

(Dioecesis Magnocataractensis-Billingensis)

Most Reverend

ANTHONY M. MILONE, D.D.

Bishop of Great Falls-Billings; ordained December 15, 1957; appointed Titular Bishop Plestia and Auxiliary of Omaha November 10, 1981; Episcopal ordination January 6, 1982; appointed Bishop of Great Falls-Billings December 14, 1987; installed February 23, 1988 *Office: 121-23rd St. S., Great Falls, MT 59401-3939*. Tel: 406-727-6683.

Pastoral Office: 121 23rd St. S., Great Falls, MT 59401-3939P.O. Box 1399, Great Falls, MT 59403-1399. Tel: 406-727-6683; 800-332-9998 (Toll Free Montana only); Fax: 406-454-3480.

Web: www.dioceseofgfb.org

Email: chancery@dioceseofgfb.org

ERECTED MAY 18, 1904.

Square Miles 94,158.

Corporation Title: "Roman Catholic Bishop of Great Falls, Montana, a corporation sole."

Comprises the eastern part of the State of Montana and is made up of the following Counties: Big Horn, Blaine, Carbon, Carter, Cascade, Chouteau, Custer, Daniels, Dawson, Fallon, Fergus, Garfield, Golden Valley, Hill, Judith Basin, Liberty, McCone, Musselshell, Park, Petroleum, Phillips, Powder River, Prairie, Richland, Roosevelt, Rosebud, Sheridan, Stillwater, Sweet Grass, Treasure, Valley, Wibaux, Yellowstone and parts of Toole.

Legal Title: For legal titles of parishes and diocesan institutions, consult the Pastoral Office.

STATISTICAL OVERVIEW

Personnel	
Bishop	1
Priests: Diocesan Active in Diocese	35
Priests: Diocesan Active Outside Diocese	5
Priests: Diocesan in Foreign Missions	1
Priests: Retired, Sick or Absent	27
Number of Diocesan Priests	68
Religious Priests in Diocese	14
Total Priests in Diocese	82
Extern Priests in Diocese	8
Permanent Deacons in Diocese	4
Total Brothers	1
Total Sisters	71
Parishes	
Parishes	65
With Resident Pastor:	
Resident Diocesan Priests	30
Resident Religious Priests	10
Without Resident Pastor:	
Administered by Priests	19
Administered by Deacons	3
Administered by Religious Women	2
Administered by Lay People	1
Missions	45
Professional Ministry Personnel:	
Brothers	1
Sisters	13
Lay Ministers	49
Welfare	
Catholic Hospitals	3
Total Assisted	513,955
Health Care Centers	1
Total Assisted	313
Homes for the Aged	2
Total Assisted	321
Day Care Centers	8
Total Assisted	208
Special Centers for Social Services	3
Total Assisted	59,803
Educational	
Diocesan Students in Other Seminaries	6
Total Seminarians	6
Colleges and Universities	1
Total Students	801
High Schools, Diocesan and Parish	2
Total Students	368
High Schools, Private	1
Total Students	187
Elementary Schools, Diocesan and Parish	8
Total Students	1,507
Elementary Schools, Private	4
Total Students	657
Catechesis/Religious Education:	
High School Students	1,297
Elementary Students	3,601
Total Students under Catholic Instruction	8,424
Teachers in the Diocese:	
Priests	2
Sisters	5
Lay Teachers	289
Vital Statistics	
Receptions into the Church:	
Infant Baptism Totals	849
Adult Baptism Totals	116
Received into Full Communion	103
First Communions	817
Confirmations	1,127
Marriages:	
Catholic	124
Interfaith	132
Total Marriages	256
Deaths	749
Total Catholic Population	53,824
Total Population	391,360

Former Bishops—Most Revs. MATHIAS C. LENIHAN, D.D., ord. Dec. 20, 1879; consecrated First Bishop of Great Falls, Sept. 21, 1904; resigned Jan. 18, 1930; created Titular Archbishop of Preslavo, Feb. 14, 1930; died Aug. 19, 1943; EDWIN V. O'HARA, D.D., ord. June 10, 1905; appt. Aug. 1, 1930; consecrated Oct. 28, 1930; appt. Bishop of Kansas City April 15, 1939; made asst. at the Pontifical Throne Jan. 5, 1949; appt. Archbishop "Ad Personam" June 29, 1954; died Sept. 11, 1956, Milan, Italy; WILLIAM J. CONDON, D.D., ord. Oct. 14, 1917; appt. Aug. 5, 1939; consecrated Oct. 18, 1939; asst. at the Pontifical Throne Dec. 9, 1964; died Aug. 17, 1967; ELDON BERNARD SCHUSTER, D.D., ord. May 27, 1937; appt. Titular Bishop of Amblada; consecrated Dec. 21, 1961; appt. Bishop of Great Falls Dec. 2, 1967; resigned Dec. 27, 1977; died Sept. 4, 1998; THOMAS JOSEPH MURPHY, D.D., S.T.D., ord. April 12, 1958; appt. Bishop of Great Falls July 5, 1978; Episcopal ordination and installation Aug. 21, 1978; appt. coadjutor Archbishop of Seattle May 26, 1987; died June 26, 1997.

Vicar General—Very Rev. JAY PETERSON, V.G.. Email: vicargeneral@dioceseofgfb.org.

Pastoral Office—121 23rd St. S., P.O. Box 1399, Great Falls, 59403. Tel: 406-727-6683; 800-332-9998 (Montana Toll Free Number Only); Fax: 406-454-3480. All applications for dispensations and official communications should be addressed to this office.

Chancellor—Sr. MARY MURRAY, O.P.. Email: chancellor@dioceseofgfb.org. Direct all Matrimonial Correspondence to the Tribunal.

Moderator of the Curia—Very Rev. JAY PETERSON, V.G.

Business Manager/Fiscal Officer—JOSEPH LONCKI. Email: business@dioceseofgfb.org.

Diocesan Tribunal—121 23rd St. S., P.O. Box 1399, Great Falls, 59403. Tel: 406-727-6683; 800-332-9998 (Montana Toll Free Number Only). Email: tribunal@dioceseofgfb.org.

Judicial Vicar—Rev. ROBERT D. GROSCH, J.C.L.

Promoter of Justice—Rev. JOHN W. ROBERTSON, J.C.L.

Defenders of the Bond—Rev. ROBERT J. FOX (Retired); Sr. DIANE MASSON, C.S.S.F., J.C.L.

Director of the Tribunal—TERRYAL ANN REAVLEY.

Notary—TERRYAL ANN REAVLEY.

Diocesan Consultors—Revs. JOSEPH DIEKHANS; ROBERT GROSCH; JAY PETERSON; JOSEPH PONESSA; LEO MCDOWELL; STEPHEN TOKARSKI; ROB OSWALD; TERRY REGAN; ANTHONY SCHUSTER.

Personnel Board—Most Rev. ANTHONY M. MILONE, D.D.; Revs. JERRY CONNOLLY; JAMES O'NEIL; THOMAS HARNEY; THAD KOZIKOWSKI; WAYNE PITTARD; Very Rev. JAY PETERSON, V.G., Ex Officio; Rev. ROGER VEIK, O.F.M.Cap., Ex Officio.

Vicars Forane—Revs. WILLIAM HOGAN, Billings; RICHARD SCHLOSSER, Great Falls; MARCEL VOGEL, Havre; GILBERT HEMAUER, O.F.M.Cap., Miles City; STEPHEN ZABROCKI, Wolf Point.

Cemetery Board—Very Rev. JAY PETERSON, V.G., Great Falls; JOSEPH LONCKI.

Vicar for Clergy—VACANT.

Cum Christo/Cursillo—Rev. FRANCIS MCINNIS, Spiritual Dir., 1701-26th St. S., Apt. #3, Great Falls, 59405-5173. Tel: 406-453-0258.

Vicar for Ministry to Native Americans—Rev. PETER E. GUTHNECK, P.O. Box 3009, Box Elder, 59521-3009. Tel: 406-395-4380. Email: peterg@attc-cmc.net.

Diocesan Offices and Directors

Boy Scouts—Rev. LEO MCDOWELL, Chap., P.O. Box 160, Circle, 59215-0160. Tel: 406-485-3520. Email: frleo@justcatholic.net.

Catholic Campaign for Human Development—Very Rev. JAY PETERSON, V.G., Diocesan Dir., 121 23rd St. S., Great Falls, 59401. P.O. Box 1399, Great Falls, 59403. Tel: 406-727-6683; Fax: 406-454-3480.

Stewardship Committee—STELLA ZIEGLER, Chm.. Email: stewardship@dioceseofgfb.org.

Catechesis—ANTHONY ALLEN, Dir. Youth Ministry & Catechesis, Pastoral Center, P.O. Box 1399, Great Falls, 59403. Tel: 406-727-3386. Email: catechesis@dioceseofgfb.org.

Catholic Relief Services—Very Rev. JAY H. PETERSON, V.G., Dir.

Clerical Benefit Association—Most Rev. ANTHONY M. MILONE, D.D., Ex Officio; Revs. JAMES BIRKMAIER, Pres.; PATRICK ZABROCKI, Vice Pres.; JAMES SIKORA, Sec.; JOSEPH DIEKHANS; STEPHEN ZABROCKI; THOMAS HARNEY; JOSEPH LONCKI, Consultant; Rev. ROBERT J. FOX, Retired Priests' Rep. (Retired).

Continuing Formation of Clergy—Revs. JOHN J. HOULIHAN. Tel: 406-259-3389; Fax: 406-248-1185. St. Patrick's Co-Cathedral, 215 N. 31st St., Billings, 59101-9920; ROGER VEIK, O.F.M.Cap., 1122 N. 30th St., Billing, 59101-0124. Tel: 406-259-9920; JERRY CONNOLLY, Immaculate Conception Church, P.O. Box 166, Forsyth, 59327-0166. Tel: 406-356-2101.

Diocesan Pastoral Council—Sr. MARY MURRAY, O.P.,

Exec. Coord.; SANDRA BILLS, Chm., 121 23rd St. S., P.O. Box 1399, Great Falls, 59403-1399. Tel: 406-727-6683; Fax: 406-454-3480.

Diocesan School Board—Sr. JEAN M. DAWSON, S.C.L., Supt.. Email: jdawson@billingscatholicschools.org; VACANT, Chm., P.O. Box 31158, Billings, 59107-1158. Tel: 406-252-9595; Fax: 406-252-9875.

D.C.C.W.—COREEN GLEN, Pres.; Most Rev. ANTHONY M. MILONE, D.D., Episcopal Moderator.

Ecumenical Officer—PAUL F. KAISER.

Education—Sr. JEAN DAWSON, S.C.L., Diocesan School Supt., P.O. Box 31158, Billings, 59107-1158. Tel: 406-252-9595; 800-682-2218 (Montana Toll Free Number Only); Fax: 406-252-9875. Email: jdawson@billingscatholicschools.org.

Engaged Encounter—PAIGE NICHOLSON; DOUG NICHOLSON. Tel: 406-771-8013.

Big Sky Marriage Encounter—Rev. FRANCIS MCINNIS; DALE BOESPFLUG; PAM BOESPFLUG. Tel: 406-761-0987.

Finance Council—Most Rev. ANTHONY M. MILONE, D.D.; CHRIS BOLAND; Sr. JEAN DAWSON, S.C.L.; JOSEPH LONCKI, Consultant; Very Rev. JAY PETERSON, V.G., Ex Officio; MARILYN HARMON; JOHN NELSON; ALBERT MARTENS; THOMAS PELATT; MARILYN ROSE; ELLEN SOLEM; Rev. LEO MCDOWELL.

Holy Childhood Association—Very Rev. JAY H. PETERSON, V.G.

Lay Ministry Programs—Sr. EILEEN HURLEY, S.C.L.. Email: layministry@dioceseofgfb.org.

Liturgical Commission—CAROL FALBO; CARRIE GRACE; Deacon WILLIAM MEDVED; Revs. THEODORE SZUDERA; STEPHEN ZABROCKI; BARBARA OLSON; ANN O'BRIEN; TONY VARAS; Most Rev ANTHONY MILONE.

Office of Worship—TONY VARAS. Email: worship@dioceseofgfb.org.

Newspaper—Very Rev. JAY PETERSON, V.G., Editor. "The Harvest"

Social Justice and Peace Office—VACANT, Dir., P.O. Box 1399 Great Falls, 59403-1399. Tel: 406-727-6683; Fax 406-454-3480.

RCIA—Sr. EILEEN HURLEY, S.C.L.

Pastoral Outreach—Very Rev. JAY PETERSON, V.G., Coord.; ANTHONY ALLEN; Sisters EILEEN HURLEY, S.C.L.; JEAN DAWSON, S.C.L.; Bro. BEDE BALDRY, F.S.C.; LINDA KOVAR; PAUL F. KAISER; TONY VARAS; Sr. MARY MURRAY, O.P.

Priests' Council—Most Rev. ANTHONY M MILONE, D.D.; Very Rev. JAY PETERSON, V.G.; Revs. ROB OSWALD; STEPHEN ZABROCKI, Chm. JOSEPH PONESSA; LEO MCDOWELL; STEPHEN TOKARSKI; ANTHONY SCHUSTER; JOSEPH DIEKHANS; ROBERT GROSCH; TERRY REGAN.

Sister's Council—Liaisons: Sisters EILEEN HURLEY, S.C.L.; MARY MURRAY, O.P.

Director of Vocations—Rev. DALE E. YURKOVIC, St. Mary's Church, P.O. Box 646, Livingston, 59047. Tel: 406-222-1393; Fax: 406-222-1405. Email: ddaled@mcn.net.

Inter-Diocesan Organizations

Montana Catholic Conference—FRANCIS CLINCH, Dir., P.O. Box 1708, Helena, 59624. Tel: 406-442-5761; Fax: 406-442-9047. Email: mcc@mt.net.

Catholic Social Services of Montana—ROSEMARY MILLER, Dir., P.O. Box 907, Helena, 59624-0907. Tel: 406-442-4130; Fax: 406-442-4192. Web: www.catholicsocialservicesofmontana.org. Email: ann@catholicsocialservicesofmontana.org.
Provides adoption and counseling services for families, children and infants.

Billings Office—BECKY HUBBERT, 1048 N. 30th St., Billings, 59101. Tel: 406-252-3399; Fax: 406-252-9174. Email: beckyh@180com.net.

Great Falls Office—KYLA WRIGHT, P.O. Box 7410, Great Falls, 59403. Tel: 406-771-7805. Email: cssmgtf@imt.net.

Helena Office—SHIRLEY COLE, P.O. Box 907, Helena, 59601. Tel: 406-442-4130; Fax: 406-442-4192. Email: shirley@treasurebook.org.

Missoula Office—BETSY ROBEL, 420 W. Pine St., Missoula, 59802. Tel: 406-728-5429; Fax: 406-327-8537. Email: betsymsl@montana.com.

Montana Association of Churches—Rev. JAY PETERSON, Pres.; MARGARET E. MACDONALD, Exec. Dir., 180-24th St. W., Ste. G, Billings, 59102. Tel: 406-656-9779.

Victim Assistance Coordinator—Sr. KATHLEEN KANE, O.P. Tel: 406-378-2369. Email: kkop@ttc-cmc.net.

CLERGY, PARISHES, MISSIONS AND PAROCHIAL SCHOOLS

CITY OF GREAT FALLS
(CASCADE COUNTY)

1—ST. ANN'S CATHEDRAL, Most Rev. Anthony M. Milone, D.D.; Rev. Oliver Doyle, Admin.
Res.: 715 Third Ave. N., P.O. Box 1708, 59403. Tel: 406-761-5456; Fax: 406-761-5457.
Catechesis/Religious Program—Students 70.

2—ST. GERARD MAJELLA, Closed. For inquiries for parish records contact the chancery.

3—HOLY FAMILY, Closed., See Holy Spirit.

4—HOLY SPIRIT, Rev. Richard Schlosser; Sr. Catherine Kinsella, O.P., Pastoral Assoc.
Parish Office—2816 Central Ave., 59401-3498. Tel: 406-452-6491; 406-761-4805 (Worship Center); Fax: 406-452-6495.
School—(Grades PreK-8), 2820 Central Ave , 59401. Tel: 406-761-5775; Fax: 406-761-5887. Linda Traxinger, Prin. Lay Teachers 23; Students 313.
Catechesis/Religious Program—Rodi Pitstick, Youth Minister. Students 170.
Chapel—*Holy Family* 2800 Central Ave., 59401.
Sts. Peter & Paul Worship Center—200-44th St. S., 59405.

5—ST. JOSEPH'S, Revs. Patrick R. Zabrocki; John Neneman (ORG); Jean Sobolik, Pastoral Assoc.
Church and Res.: 500-2nd. Ave., S.W., 59404. Tel: 406-453-9331; Fax: 406-453-5558.
Catechesis/Religious Program—Tel: 406-453-9331. Carmen Thorsen, D.R.E. Students 80.

6—ST. LUKE THE EVANGELIST, Revs. Patrick R. Zabrocki; John Neneman (ORG); Donna Wilson, Pastoral Assoc.; Mary Lynn Wojtowick, Pastoral Assoc.
Res.: 410 22nd Ave. N.E., 59404. Tel: 406-453-6546; Fax: 406-453-0323.
Catechesis/Religious Program—Jeanne Tonkovich, D.R.E.; Aubrey Rearden, D.R.E. Students 185.

7—OUR LADY OF LOURDES, Rev. Lothar Krauth; Sr. Marian Lorang, O.S.U., Pastoral Assoc.
Res.: 409 13th St. S., 59405. Tel: 406-452-6464; Fax: 406-452-6464.
School—(Grades PreK-8), 1305 Fifth Ave. S., 59405. Tel: 406-452-0551. Mrs. Sherri Schmitz, Prin. Ursuline Nuns 1; Lay Teachers 17; Students 229.
Catechesis/Religious Program—Barbara Brown, D.R.E.; Roslyn Gallagher, D.R.E.; Mary Jo Bailly. Students 68.

8—STS. PETER & PAUL, Closed., See Holy Spirit.

CITY OF BILLINGS
(YELLOWSTONE COUNTY)

1—LITTLE FLOWER, Rev. Paul Reichling, O.F.M.Cap.
Res.: 209 S. 35th St., 59101. Tel: 406-245-4717.
Catechesis/Religious Program—Amy Aguirre, D.R.E. Tel: 406-855-0273. Students 45.

2—ST. BERNARD'S, Rev. David Reichling, O.F.M.Cap.
Office—226 Wicks Ln., 59105. Tel: 406-259-4350; Fax: 406-259-0443.
Catechesis/Religious Program—Becky Krkosa, D.R.E.; Brain Shea, D.R.E.; Bob Murphy, D.R.E. Students 340.
Mission—*Sts. Cyril & Methodius* c/o St. Bernard's Church, 226 Wicks Ln., Ballantine, Yellowstone Co. 59105.

3—HOLY ROSARY, Deacon Melvin A. Melius, Pastoral Admin.; Lynne Gillig, Pastoral Assoc.
Office—521 Custer Ave., 59101. Tel: 406-259-7611; Fax: 406-248-8921.
Catechesis/Religious Program—Students 32.

4—OUR LADY OF GUADALUPE, Rev. Paul Reichling, O.F.M.Cap
Res.: 209 S. 35th St., 59101. Tel: 406-245-4717.
Catechesis/Religious Program—Tel: 406-855-0273. Students 100.

5—ST. PATRICK'S CO-CATHEDRAL, Revs. John J. Houlihan; Richard J. Hopkins (Retired); Jose Valliparambil, Sacramental Min.; Deacon Timothy J. Birkle.
Res.: 215 N. 31st St., 59101. Tel: 406-259-3389; Fax: 406-248-1185.
Catechesis/Religious Program— Brenda Estill, D.R.E. Students 140.

6—ST. PIUS X, Rev. Stephen L. Tokarski Deacon Robert W. Daem; Bob Bender, Pastoral Assoc.
Parish Center—717 18th St. W., 59102. Tel: 406-656-2522; Fax: 406-656-2584.
Catechesis/Religious Program— Cheryl Daem, D.R.E. Students 291.

7—ST. THOMAS THE APOSTLE, Rev. William A. Hogan; Sr. Genevieve Garvin, R.S.M., Pastoral Assoc.; Jim Downs, Pastoral Assoc.
Res.: 2101-24th St. W., 59102. Tel: 406-656-5578.
Church: 2055 Woody Dr., 59102. Tel: 406-656-5800; Fax: 406-656-8260.
Catechesis/Religious Program—Joyce Hollowell, D.R.E. Students 190.

OUTSIDE THE CITIES OF GREAT FALLS AND BILLINGS

ASHLAND, ROSEBUD CO., ST. LABRE'S, Revs. Paschal Siler, O.F.M.Cap.; William D'Souza.
Res.: Tongue River Rd., P.O. Box 228, 59003. Tel: 406-784-4536.
Station— Ashland-Birney Post.

BAKER, FALLON CO., ST. JOHN THE EVANGELIST, Rev. Thomas Tobin.
Res.: P.O. Box 1519, 59313. Tel: 406-778-2297.
Catechesis/Religious Program—Nancy Schillinger, D.R.E. Students 104.
Mission—*St Joan of Arc* Ekalaka, Carter Co.
Mission—*St Anthony* [CEM] Plevna, Fallon Co.

BELT, CASCADE CO., ST. MARK THE EVANGELIST, Rev. Ted F. Szudera.
Res.: P.O. Box 213, 59412. Tel: 406-277-3527.
Catechesis/Religious Program—Tel: 406-277-3366. Kim Pierson, D.R.E. Students 62.
Mission—*St. Clement* Monarch, Cascade Co.
Mission—*St. Mary* Raynesford, Judith Basin Co.
Mission—*Holy Trinity* Centerville, Cascade Co.

BIG SANDY, CHOUTEAU CO., ST. MARGARET MARY, Rev. Peter E. Guthneck; Sisters Margaret Mary O'Doherty, O.P., Pastoral Assoc. & D.R.E.; Kathleen Kane, O.P., Pastoral Assoc.
St. Mary's Rocky Boy Indian Reservation: P.O. Box 3009, Box Elder, 59521. Tel: 406-395-4380.
Catechesis/Religious Program—Students 87.
Mission—*St. Anthony* Box Elder, Hill Co.
Mission—*St. Mary* Rocky Boys Indian Reservation, Hill Co.

BIG TIMBER, SWEET GRASS CO., ST. JOSEPH, Tom Schleder, Pastoral Admin.
Res.: P.O. Box 871, 59011. Tel: 406-932-4723.

BLACK EAGLE, CASCADE CO., MOST BLESSED SACRAMENT, Rev. Raymond J. Nyquist.
Res.: 1325 Smelter Ave., 59414. Tel: 406-453-8425; Fax: 406-453-8425.
Catechesis/Religious Program—Students 20.

BRIDGER, CARBON CO., SACRED HEART, Sr. Mary Lou Mendel, S.C.L., Pastoral Admin.
Mailing Address: P.O. Box 309, 59014-0309.
Res.: 209 S. 4th St., 59014-0309. Tel: 406-662-3550.
Catechesis/Religious Program—Students 102.
Mission—*St. Joseph* Fromberg, Carbon Co.
Mission—*St. John* Joliet, Carbon Co.

BROADUS, POWDER RIVER CO., ST. DAVID'S, Rev. Chester Poppa, O.F.M.Cap.
Mailing Address: P.O. Box 52, 59317. Tel: 406-436-2348.
Catechesis/Religious Program—Students 30.

CHESTER, LIBERTY CO., ST. MARY'S, Rev. Joseph Diekhans; Natalie Ghekiere, Parish Coord.
Res.: P.O. Box 647, 504 Main, 59522. Tel: 406-759-5377; Fax: 406-759-5568.
Catechesis/Religious Program—Tel: 406-759-5389. Natalie Ghekiere, D.R.E.; Dianne Folk, D.R.E. Students 110.
Mission—*Holy Family Center* Rudyard, Hill Co.

CHINOOK, BLAINE CO., ST. GABRIEL'S, Rev. Marcel J. Vogel.
Res.: 152 Eighth St., P.O. Box 1089, 59523. Tel: 406-357-2073; Fax: 406-357-2173.
Catechesis/Religious Program—Mrs. Ellen Pyette, D.R.E., (Elementary); Mrs. Carol Elliot, D.R.E., (High School). Students 62.
Mission—*St. Thomas the Apostle* P.O. Box 819, Harlem, Blaine Co. 59526. Tel: 406-353-4643.
Mission—*St. Thomas Aquinas* c/o Mary Ann Olszewski, HC 80-Box 1, Hogeland, Blaine Co. 59529. Tel: 406-379-2582; Fax: 406-379-2582.

CIRCLE, MCCONE CO., ST. FRANCIS XAVIER, Rev. Leo G. McDowell.
Res.: 1102 C Ave., P.O. Box 160, 59215-0160. Tel: 406-485-3520; Fax: 406-485-3520.
Catechesis/Religious Program—Estelle Nagel, D.R.E. Students 45.
Mission—*St. John the Baptist* Jordan, Garfield Co. Tel: 406-557-6135.
Catechesis/Religious Program—Students 38.
Mission—*St. Francis de Sales* Richey, Dawson Co.

COLSTRIP, ROSEBUD CO., ST. MARGARET MARY, Deacon William Medved, Pastoral Admin.; Terri McDonald, Pastoral Assoc.
Res.: P.O. Box 305, 59323. Tel: 406-748-2234; Fax: 406-748-2234.
Catechesis/Religious Program—Sue McKamey, D.R.E. Students 106.

COLUMBUS, STILLWATER CO., ST. MARY'S, Rev. Charles Gorman, Admin.
Mailing Address: P.O. Box 956, 59019. Tel: 406-322-5541.
Catechesis/Religious Program—Margie Brooks, D.R.E.; Anne Smith, D.R.E.; Pam Kightlinger, D.R.E.; Andrea Stampfel, D.R.E. Students 99.
Mission—*St. Michael* Absarokee, Stillwater Co.

CROW AGENCY, BIG HORN CO., ST. DENNIS, Rev. Charles Robinson, O.F.M.Cap.; Sr. Loretta Sedlmayer, R.S.M., Pastoral Assoc.
Res.: P.O. Box 57, 59022. Tel: 406-638-2641.
Catechesis/Religious Program—Students 85.
Mission—*St. Francis Xavier* P.O. Box 138, St.

Xavier, Big Horn Co. 59075. Tel: 406-666-2380. Coleen Couture, Pastoral Assoc.

CULBERTSON, ROOSEVELT CO., ST. ANTHONY'S, , Now a mission of St. Matthew, Sidney.

FORSYTH, ROSEBUD CO., IMMACULATE CONCEPTION, Rev. Jerry Connolly.
Res.: 591 N. 12th Ave. N., P.O. Box 166, 59327. Tel: 406-356-2101 (Church); 406-356-9239 (Parish Center).
Catechesis/Religious Program—Students 44.
Mission—St. Joseph Hysham, Treasure Co.

FORT BENTON, CHOUTEAU CO., IMMACULATE CONCEPTION, Rev. Jim Birkmaier; Trish Eklund, Pastoral Assoc.
Res.: P.O. Box 868, 59442. Tel: 406-622-3726.
Catechesis/Religious Program—Tel: 406-622-5288. Students 35.
Mission—St. Margaret P.O. Box 50, Geraldine, Chouteau Co. 59446-0050. Tel: 406-737-4573.

FORT SHAW, CASCADE CO., ST. ANN, Rev. Eugene P. Hruska.
Res.: 13327 MT. Hwy 200, 59443. Tel: 406-264-5554.
Catechesis/Religious Program—JoAnn Holmes, D.R.E., (St. Ann). Tel: 406-264-5495; David Konecny, D.R.E., (Sacred Heart). Tel: 406-468-2368. Students 97.
Mission—Sacred Heart Cascade, Cascade Co.

GLASGOW, VALLEY CO., ST. RAPHAEL'S, Rev. Thad Kozikowski.
Office—412 Third Ave. N., P.O. Box 1047, 59230. Tel: 406-228-4651; Fax: 406-228-9800.
Catechesis/Religious Program—Tel: 406-228-4651. Sr. Margaret Chambers, D.R.E. Students 131.
Mission—Our Lady of the Lake Fort Peck, Valley Co.
Mission—St. Albert Hinsdale, Valley Co.
Mission—Queen of the Angels Nashua, Valley Co.

GLENDIVE, DAWSON CO., SACRED HEART, Rev. Joseph Ponessa.
Res.: 316 W. Benham St., P.O. Box 36, 59330. Tel: 406-377-2585; Fax: 406-377-4033.
Catechesis/Religious Program—Tel: 406-377-4569. Monica Christianson, D.R.E. (Sacred Heart); Kim Miske, D.R.E. (St. Peter); LaNee Sokoloski, D.R.E. Students 170.
Mission—St. Peter P.O. Box 217, Wibaux, Wibaux Co. 59353. Tel: 406-796-2215.
Mission—St. Philip Wibaux. P.O. Box 217, Wibaux, Wibaux Co. 59353. Tel: 406-796-8188.

HARDIN, BIG HORN CO., ST. JOSEPH'S, Rev. Fabian Fehring, O.F.M.Cap.
Res.: 710 N. Custer, P.O. Box 510, 59034. Tel: 406-665-1432; Fax: 406-665-1432.
Catechesis/Religious Program—Students 85.
Mission—St. Mary Custer, Yellowstone Co.

HAVRE, HILL CO., ST. JUDE THADDEUS, Rev. Robert D. Grosch, J.C.L.; Timothy Maroney, Pastoral Assoc.
Res.: 624 Fourth St., P.O. Box 407, 59501. Tel: 406-265-4261; Fax: 406-265-4408.
School—(Grades PreK-8) Tel: 406-265-4613. Mrs. Therese Cowdery, Prin. Lay Teachers 12; Students 185.
Catechesis/Religious Program—Students 145.
Mission—St. John the Baptist Cottonwood, Hill Co.

HAYS, BLAINE CO., ST. PAUL'S INDIAN MISSION, Revs. Joseph R. Retzel, S.J.; Robert L. Erickson, S.J.; Sisters Barbara Bogenschutz, O.P., Pastoral Assoc.; Laura Fucito, O.P., Pastoral Assoc.
Res.: P.O. Box 40, 59527. Tel: 406-673-3300.
School—Tel: 406-673-3123. Sr. Helen Durso, O.P., Prin. Sisters 3; Lay Teachers 6; Students 80.
Catechesis/Religious Program—Students 90.
Mission—St. Joseph Zortman, Phillips Co.
Mission—St. Thomas Dodson. HC63-Box 5240, Lodgepole, Blaine Co. 59524. Tel: 406-673-3454; Fax: 406-673-3454. Sr. Laura Fucito, O.P., Pastoral Assoc.
Mission—Sacred Heart P.O. Box 42, Fort Belknap Agency, Blaine Co. 59526. Tel: 406-353-2927; Fax: 406-353-2927. Sr. Nancy Maclean, S.P., Pastoral Assoc.

HINGHAM, HILL CO., OUR LADY OF RANSOM (1910), Rev. Joseph Diekhans.
Mailing Address: P.O. Box 647, Chester, 59522-0647.
Res.: 201-2nd. St., 59528. Tel: 406-759-5377; Fax: 406-759-5568.
Catechesis/Religious Program—Dianne Folk, D.R.E. Students 42.
Mission—Sacred Heart Inverness, Hill Co.

LAME DEER, ROSEBUD CO., BLESSED SACRAMENT, Deacon Joseph Kristufek, Pastoral Admin.
Res.: P.O. Box 100, 59043. Tel: 406-477-6384; Fax: 406-477-6224.
Catechesis/Religious Program—Students 20.
Mission—Christ the King Busby, Big Horn Co.

LAUREL, YELLOWSTONE CO., ST. ANTHONY'S, [CEM] Rev. Thomas C. Harney.
Res.: P.O. Box 955, 59044. Tel: 406-628-7182.
Catechesis/Religious Program—Tel: 406-628-7484. Barb Hoppel, D.R.E. Students 139.

LEWISTOWN, FERGUS CO., ST. LEO'S, [CEM] Rev. Daniel O'Rourke.
Res.: P.O. Box 421, 59457. Tel: 406-538-9306; Fax: 406-538-7624.
Catechesis/Religious Program— Pam Zerr, D.R.E., (Grades K-6); Ron Hrubes, D.R.E. Students 140.
Mission—Holy Family Winifred, Fergus CoP.O. Box 421, 59457.
Chapel—Danvers, St. Wenceslaus
Chapel—Roy, Sacred Heart

LIVINGSTON, PARK CO., ST. MARY'S, [CEM] Rev. Dale E. Yurkovic; Joannie Lee, Pastoral Assoc.
Res.: S. F St., P.O. Box 646, 59047-0646. Tel: 406-222-1393; Fax: 406-222-1405.
School—(Grades PreK-8) Tel: 406-222-3303. Michelle Moore, Prin. Lay Teachers 13; Students 130.
Catechesis/Religious Program—Students 39.
Mission—St. Margaret 206 1st. Ave. N., Clyde Park, Park Co. 59018.
Mission—St. William 704 Scott St., W., Gardiner, Park Co. 59030.

LODGE GRASS, BIG HORN CO., OUR LADY OF LORETTO, Rev. James Antoine, O.F.M.Cap.
Res.: P.O. Box 509, 59050. Tel: 406-639-2254; Fax: 406-639-2254.
Catechesis/Religious Program—Rosaline Old Bear, D.R.E. Students 30.
Mission—Blessed Kateri Tekakwitha Wyola, Big Horn Co.

MALTA, PHILLIPS CO., ST. MARY'S, Rev. Jim O'Neil.
Res.: 27 S. Seventh St. W., P.O. Box 70, 59538. Tel: 406-654-1446; Fax: 406-654-1467.
Catechesis/Religious Program—Tel: 406-654-1311. Dianne Salsbery, D.R.E. Students 85.
Mission—Sacred Heart Dodson, Phillips Co.
Mission—St. Francis of Assisi Saco, Phillips Co.
Mission—St. John Whitewater, Phillips Co.

MILES CITY, CUSTER CO., SACRED HEART, Revs. Gil Hemauer, O.F.M.Cap.; Thomas Pittappilly; Wilfred Splonskowski, O.S.B.
Mailing Address: P.O. Box 1016, 59301. Tel: 406-234-1691; Fax: 406-234-5687.
Church: 110 N. Montana. Tel: 406-234-7585.
School—(Grades K-8) Tel: 406-234-3850. Bart Freese, Prin. Lay Teachers 6; Students 85.
Catechesis/Religious Program—Students 130.
Mission—Sacred Heart P.O. Box 526, Terry, Prairie Co. 59349. Tel: 406-635-5569.
Station—Pine Hills School Helena. Tel: 406-232-1377; Fax: 406-232-7432.
Station—Holy Rosary Extended Care, Tel: 406-233-2600; Fax: 406-233-2621.
Station—Holy Rosary Healthcare, Tel: 406-233-2601.
Station—Veterans' Administration Hospital Fort Harrison. Tel: 406-232-3060.
Station—Friendship Villa Rest Home, Tel: 406-232-2687.

PLENTYWOOD, SHERIDAN CO., ST. JOSEPH'S, Rev. Robert J. Sewvello; Kordelia French.
Res.: P.O. Box 6, 59254. Tel: 406-765-2250; Fax: 406-765-2345.
Catechesis/Religious Program—Tel: 406-765-2251. Nancy Bennett, D.R.E. Students 60.
Mission—St. Patrick Medicine Lane, Sheridan Co.
Chapel—Outlook, St. Boniface

POPLAR, ROOSEVELT CO., OUR LADY OF LOURDES, Rev. Michael Schneider.
Res.: P.O. Box 187, 59255. Tel: 406-768-3244 (Rectory); 406-768-3305 (Office); Fax: 406-768-5703.
Catechesis/Religious Program—Deacon Joseph T. McPherson, D.R.E. Students 82.
Mission—St. Thomas Brockton, Roosevelt Co.
Chapel—Fort Kipp, St. Anthony

PRYOR, BIG HORN CO., ST. CHARLES BORROMEO MISSION, Rev. Randolph Graczyk, O.F.M.Cap. (DET).
Res.: P.O. Box 29, 59066. Tel: 406-259-9747; Fax: 406-259-7092.
School—(Grades K-8) Tel: 406-259-9976; Fax: 406-259-7092. Nicole Trahan, Prin. Lay Teachers 15; Students 88.

RED LODGE, CARBON CO., ST. AGNES, Rev. Denis J. Keane.
Res.: P.O. Box 1067, 59068. Tel: 406-446-1237; Fax: 406-446-1237.
Catechesis/Religious Program—Students 59.

ROUNDUP, MUSSELSHELL CO., ST. BENEDICT'S, Rev. Anthony Schuster.
Res.: 503 Main St., 59072. Tel: 406-323-1019; Fax: 406-323-1054.
Catechesis/Religious Program—Debbie Mosdal, D.R.E.; Laurie Shanks, D.R.E. Students 75.
Mission—Our Lady of Mercy Melstone, Musselshell Co.
Mission—St. Aloysius Winnett, Petroleum Co.
Mission—Little Flower Broadview, Yellowstone Co.
Mission—St Mathias Ryegate, Golden Valley Co.
Chapel—St. Honorata Musselshell, .

SCOBEY, DANIELS CO., ST. PHILIP BONITUS, Rev. Robert Michael Oswald.
Res.: P.O. Box 827, 59263. Tel: 406-487-5525; Fax: 406-487-5566.
Catechesis/Religious Program—Julie French, D.R.E.; Karen Schaefer, D.R.E. Students 54.
Mission—St. Louis Flaxville, Daniels Co.
Mission—Holy Family Glentana, Valley Co.
Mission—St. Ann [CEM] Peerless, Daniels Co.

SIDNEY, RICHLAND CO., ST. MATTHEW'S, Formerly St. Anthony's, Culbertson [CEM] Revs. Greg Staudinger; Francis Anton Schreiber; Linda Latka, Parish Admin.
Res.: 219 Seventh St. S.E., 59270. Tel: 406-433-1068; Fax: 406-433-4373.
Catechesis/Religious Program—Tel: 406-433-2510. Barbara Olson, D.R.E. Students 184.
Mission—St. Catherine P.O. Box 494, Fairview, Richland Co. 59221. Tel: 406-742-5293.
Mission—St. Theresa P.O. Box 153, Lambert, Richland Co. 59243. Tel: 406-774-3360.
Mission—St. Bernard's Charley Creek, Richland Co.
Mission—St. Michael P.O. Box 95, Savage, Richland Co. 59262.
Mission—St. Anthony's P.O. Box 30, Culbertson, Roosevelt Co. 59218. Tel: 406-787-6666.
Mission—Sacred Heart Bainville, Roosevelt Co.
Chapel—Immaculate Conception Froid.

STANFORD, JUDITH BASIN CO., ST. ROSE OF LIMA, Rev. Terrence P. Regan.
Mailing Address: P.O. Box 250, 59479. Tel: 406-566-2531.
Catechesis/Religious Program—Students 80.
Mission—St. Anthony P.O. Box 384, Denton, Fergus Co. 59430. Tel: 406-567-2438.
Mission—St. Cyril RR 1-Box 50A, Geyser, Judith Basin Co. 59447. Tel: 406-735-4388.
Mission—St. Mathias P.O. Box 104, Moore, Fergus Co. 59464. Tel: 406-374-2477.
Mission—Sacred Heart P.O. Box 225, Hobson, Judith Basin Co. 59452. Tel: 406-423-5613.

WOLF POINT, ROOSEVELT CO., IMMACULATE CONCEPTION, [CEM] Rev. Stephen J. Zabrocki.
Res.: 500 Fifth Ave. S., P.O. Box 789, 59201. Tel: 406-653-2610.
Catechesis/Religious Program—Linda Johnson, D.R.E. Students 120.
Mission—St. Joseph Frazer, Valley Co.
Mission—St. Ann Vida, McCone Co.
Mission—Sacred Heart Riverside, McCone Co.

Special Assignment:
Revs.—
Bochnak, Zenon A., 315 72nd St. N., Malmstrom AFB, 59402-7514.
D'Souza, William, St. Labre, P.O. Box 228, Ashland, 59003-0228.
Doyle, Oliver, St. Ann's Cathedral, P.O. Box 1708, 59403-1708.
Pittapilly, Thomas, Sacred Heart, P.O. Box 1016, Miles City, 59301-1016.
Sewvello, Robert, St. Joseph's Church, P.O. Box 6, Plentywood, 59254-0006.
Taylor, Jon, University of Great Falls, 1301 20th St. S., 59405-4996.
Valliparambil, Jose, 2003 Woody Dr., #3, 59102-2891.
Veik, Roger A., O.F.M.Cap., 1122 N. 30th St., 59101-0124. Tel: 406-259-9920

On Duty Outside of the Diocese:
Revs.—
Cawley, William M., St. Patrick Rectory, 231 S. Beaver St., York, PA 17403-5499.
Dobbin, Jay D., Historical Preservation Office for Yap State, P.O. Box 714, Yap, FM 96943.
Kirkness, Michael D., 104 Palm Court Dr., Santa Maria, CA 93454-6644.
Krier, John P., Immaculate Conception Church, P.O. Box 910, Davenport, WA 99122-0910.

Military Chaplains:
Rev.—
Munsell, Richard F., 1028 Wellbrook, Schertz, TX 78154-2822.

Retired:
Revs.—
Arbanas, Harold P., 3475 16th St., #6, San Francisco, CA 94114-1751.
Beggin, Thomas M., 1242 Custer Ave., 59102-5218.
Bofto, Robert C., 3001 S. 288th St., #230, Federal Way, WA 98003-8017.
Bourke, Nathaniel J., 2003 Woody Dr., #2, 59102-2891.
Clausen, Kenneth J., 3729 Second Ave. S., 59101-3603.
Coady, John, 5734 E. 19th St., Tucson, AZ 85711-5163.
Dimke, John, 1701-26th St. S., #2, 59405-5173.
Fisher, Martin, 507 Parkhill Dr., 59102-3619.
Fox, Robert J., 1000-6th St. N., Apt. 16, 59201-1867.
Gedvila, Izidorius, 1718 Haverhill Cir., Chipley, FL 32428-3179.

Gregori, Anthony F., 1711 Smelter Ave., 59414-1222.
Guinan, Michael, 1701 26th St. S., #4, 59405-5173.
Hoffman, Emmett G., 745 Indian Trail, 59105-2750.
Hopkins, Richard J., St. Patrick's Co-Cathedral, 215 N. 31st St., 59101-1908.
Janson, Leo F., 2351 Solomon Ave., #106, 59102-2884.
Kaminski, Joseph M., 2300-30th Ave. N.E., Black Eagle, 59414-2040.
Kelly, Frank F., 2621-15th Ave. S., 59405-5201.
McInnis, Francis L., 1701-26th St. S. #3, 59404-5173.
McTague, Thomas, 2003 Woody Dr., #4, 59102-2891.
Moore, John J., 18140 Medford Ave., Stratford, CA 93266-9748.
O'Hanlon, Michael A., Danesfort, Dromahane Mallow, County Cork 022-50140 Ireland.
O'Reilly, Patrick J., c/o John Rice, Chapel Land, Athboy, County Meath Ireland.
Osterman, Richard, P.O. Box 1093, Red Lodge, 59068-1093.
Papes, Joseph T., 5201 Raubinger Rd., Swartz Creek, MI 48473-1620.
Rutan, Albert E., P.O. Box 50, Liberty Center, IA 50145-0050.
Shinnick, Edward P., RR 2 - Box 156A, Savage, 59262-9706.
Tarrant, Patrick J., P.O. Box 275, Yarmouth Port, MA 02675-0275.

Permanent Deacons:

Birkle, Timothy J., 3820 Towhee Lane, 59102-7723.
Bunce, Donald A., 444 Judith Ln., 59105-1760.
Daem, Robert W., 220 34th St. W., 59102-4473.
Kristufek, Joseph M., P.O. Box 100, Lame Deer, 59043-0100.
McPherson, Joe, P.O. Box 256, Poplar, 59255-0256.
Medved, William, P.O. Box 305, Colstrip, 59323-0305.
Melius, Melvin A., 1437 Avenue D, 59102-3124.

INSTITUTIONS LOCATED IN THE DIOCESE

[A] COLLEGES AND UNIVERSITIES

GREAT FALLS. *University of Great Falls* (1932), 1301 20th St. S., 59405. Tel: 406-761-8210; Fax: 406-791-5393. Email: adminrec@ugf.edu. Web: www.ugf.edu. Sr. Mary Kaye Nealen, S.P., Provost; Eugene J. McAllister, Pres.; James B. Washburn Jr., Vice Pres. for Admin. & Finance; Cherri Brown, Campus Min.; Rev. James R. Sikora, Chap. Sponsored by the Sisters of Providence Priests 2; Lay Teachers 35; Students 801.

Associate Professors of Religious Studies: Revs. James R. Sikora; Jon Taylor; Sr. Mary Kaye Nealen, S.P.

[B] HIGH SCHOOLS, DIOCESAN

GREAT FALLS. *Great Falls Central Catholic High School*, P.O. Box 1399, 59403. Tel: 406-791-5940; Fax: 406-454-3480. Email: hughsmith@mcn.net. Web: greatfallscentral.org. Hugh Smith, Prin.; Rev. Francis McInnis, Chap. Lay Teachers 14; Students 64.

BILLINGS. *Central Catholic High School*, 3 Broadwater Ave., 59101. Tel: 406-245-6651; Fax: 406-259-3124. Email: she1hanser@billingscatholicschools.org. Sheldon Hanser, Prin.; Jim Stanton, Assoc. Prin. Sisters 1; Lay Teachers 25; Students 315.

[C] HIGH SCHOOLS, PRIVATE

ASHLAND. *St. Labre Indian Catholic High School*, Mission Rd., 59003. Tel: 406-784-4500; Fax: 406-784-4565. Email: ralexander@stlabre.org. Web: www.stlabre.org. Dr. Russell Alexander, Dir. Schools; John Salois, Assoc. Prin. Lay Teachers 19; Students 187.

[D] ELEMENTARY SCHOOLS, DIOCESAN

BILLINGS. *St. Francis Intermediate School*, (Grades 3-5), 1734 Yellowstone Ave., 59102. Tel: 406-656-2300; Fax: 406-656-2301. Email: cread@billingscatholicschools.org. Chris Read, Prin. Lay Teachers 12; Students 175.

St. Francis Primary School, (Grades PreK-2), 511 Custer Ave., 59101. Tel: 406-259-6421. Email: kpetermann@billingscatholicschools.org. Web: www.bcs.pvt.k12.mt.us. Karen Petermann, Prin. Lay Teachers 11; Students 234.

St. Francis Upper School, (Grades 6-8), 205 N. 32nd St., 59101. Tel: 406-259-5037; Fax: 406-259-7981. Email: mzauher@billingscatholicschools.org. Martha Zauher, Prin. Lay Teachers 16; Students 180.

[E] ELEMENTARY SCHOOLS, PRIVATE

ASHLAND. *St. Labre Indian Catholic Elementary School*, Mission Rd., 59003. Tel: 406-784-4500; Fax: 406-784-4565. Dr. Russell Alexander, Dir. of Schools; Scott Gion, Prin., Middle School; Chris Schmid, Prin., PreK-5. Lay Teachers 25; Students 377.

PRYOR. *St. Charles Mission School*, P.O. Box 29, 59066. Tel: 406-259-9976; Fax: 406-259-7092. Email: ntrahan@stlabre.org. Nicole Trahan, Prin. Priests 1; Lay Teachers 16; Students 88.

ST. XAVIER. *Pretty Eagle Catholic School*, P.O. Box 257, 59075. Tel: 406-666-2215; Fax: 406-666-2245. Email: smccandless@stlabre.org. Suzanne McCandless, Prin. Sisters 1; Lay Teachers 16; Students 112.

[F] CHILD CARE & YOUTH SERVICES

GREAT FALLS. *St. Thomas Child and Family Center*, 1710 Benefis Ct., 59405. Tel: 406-761-6538; Fax: 406-727-0670. Email: stcfc@mcn.net. Web: stthomaskids.org. Marg Greer, Acting Dir. Sisters of Providence, Child Care Center; Family Life Education; Prevention and Treatment of Child Abuse; Education, Information, and Referral Service; Summer Food Program for Low-Income Children; Before- and After-School Care Programs. Lay Staff 50; Child Care & Nursery Children 188.

BILLINGS. *Little Flower Day Care*, 120 S. 34th St., P.O. Box 31158, 59107. Tel: 406-252-0997; Fax: 406-252-5697. Email: lpurcell@billingscatholicschools.org. Web: www.billingscatholicschools.org. Katie Seibel, Dir.

St. Francis Day Care, 511 Custer Ave., 59101. Tel: 406-259-6421; Fax: 406-252-5697. Katie Seibel, Dir.

Saint Francis Day Care West, 2821 Augusta Ln., 59102. Tel: 406-256-3562; Fax: 406-252-5697. Katie Seibel, Dir.

[G] GENERAL HOSPITALS

GREAT FALLS. *Benefis Healthcare*, 1101-26th St. S., P.O. Box 5013, 59403. Tel: 406-455-5000; Fax: 406-455-4587. Email: benefis@benefis.org. Web: www.benefis.org. Rev. Wayne Pittard, Chap. & Coord.; John Goodnow, Pres. & CEO. Sisters of Providence Sisters 2; Patients Assisted Annually 102,066.

BILLINGS. *St. Vincent Healthcare*, 1233 N. 30th St., P.O. Box 35200, 59107-5200. Tel: 406-657-7000; Fax: 406-237-3078. Email: michelle.hood@svh_mt.org. Web: www.svh-mt.org. M. Michelle Hood, Pres. & CEO; Sr. Judy Tralnes, C.S.J.P., Dir. & Spiritual Care; Rev. Anthony J. Ozimek, O.S.B., Spiritual Care. Sisters of Charity of Leavenworth, Kansas Sisters 6; Bed Capacity 314; Patients Assisted Annually 64,286.

MILES CITY. *Holy Rosary Healthcare*, 2600 Wilson St., 59301. Tel: 406-233-2600; 800-843-3820; Fax: 406-233-2611. Web: www.hrh-mt.org. Gregory Nielson, Chief Adm. Officer. Sponsored by Sisters of Charity of Leavenworth. Sisters 1; Beds: Acute Care 44; Extended Care 107; Patients Assisted Annually 13,500.

[H] CONVENTS AND RESIDENCES FOR SISTERS

GREAT FALLS. *Poor Clares of Montana, Inc.* 416-2nd Ave., S.W., 59404-2904. Tel: 406-453-7891; Fax: 406-453-8639. Email: sisters@poorclaresmt.org. Web: www.poorclaresmt.org. Sisters 4.

Ursuline Convent, 2300 Central Ave., 59401. Tel: 406-452-8585; Fax: 406-452-8586. Email: bresnan.net. Sr. Dolores Helbling, O.S.U., Supr. Ursuline Sisters 12.

BILLINGS. *Mercy Convent*, 2420 Elm St., 59101. Tel: 406-259-2550; Fax: 406-259-2550. Email: mccormilla@yahoo.com. Web: www.sistersofmercy.ie. Sisters of Mercy 2.

Sisters of Charity of Leavenworth, 1134 N. 31st St., 59101. Tel: 406-252-0395. Sisters 4.

[I] RENEWAL CENTERS

BILLINGS. *Sacred Heart Renewal Center*, 26 Wyoming Ave., P.O. Box 153, 59103-0153. Tel: 406-252-0322. Email: shrcspd@mcn.net. Kathleen O'Neal, Exec. Dir.; Sandra McKee, Dir. of Program & Spiritual Dev.

[J] RETREAT HOUSES

GREAT FALLS. *Ursuline Retreat Centre*, 2300 Central Ave., 59401. Tel: 406-452-8585; Fax: 406-452-8586. Email: ursuline@in-tch.com. Web: www.ursulinecentre.com. Harry J. Tholen, Dir.

[K] MISCELLANEOUS LISTINGS

BILLINGS. *Beginning Experience of Central MT*, P.O. Box 2223, 59103. Tel: 406-294-8000. Virginia Jeanotte, Spiritual Coord.

Billings Area Catholic Education Trust (BACET), P.O. Box 31158, 59107-1158. Tel: 406-252-0252; Fax: 406-252-5731. Email: bacet@billingscatholicschools.org. Kristie Asay, Exec. Dir.; Dan Merry, Chair; Patrick W. Hanley, Vice Chair; Dave Rigg, Treas.

Billings Catholic Engaged Encounter, 3203 Morledge St., 59102. Tel: 406-656-1308. Email: jandapatterson@msn.com.

Kateri Indian Ministry, 215 N. 31st St., 59101-1908. Tel: 406-256-5142; Fax: 406-248-1185. Email: kateri2000@juno.com Bbaldryfsc@aol.com. Bro. Bede Baldry, F.S.C., Dir.

Mayfair Auction, Billings Catholic Schools, P.O. Box 31158, 59107. Tel: 406-245-5463; Fax: 406-252-9875. Vicki Davison, Exec. Dir.

Newman Center, MSU-Billings, 1500 University Dr., #55, 59101. Tel: 406-657-2276; Fax: 406-657-2388. Email: blgsnewmancntr@hotmail.com.

Regina Cleri (Retired Priests Living)

Pastoral Center, P.O. Box 1399, 59403. Tel: 406-727-6683; Fax: 406-454-3480. Email: business@dioceseofgfb.org. Web: www.dioceseofgfb.org.

2003 Woody Dr., 59102. Joseph Loncki, Contact Person.

St. Vincent de Paul Society of Yellowstone County, 2610 Montana Ave., 59101-2340. Tel: 406-252-1855; Fax: 406-259-3979. Email: stvincentdpmt@aol.com. Harold W. Merchant, Exec. Dir.; Bro. Bede Baldry, Spiritual Advisor.

St. Vincent Healthcare Foundation, 1106 N. 30th St., 59101. Tel: 406-237-3600; Fax: 406-237-3619. Email: david.irion@svh-mt.org. Web: www.svfoundation.org. David Irion, Exec. Dir.; Dr. Kathleen Ryan M.D., Chm.

GREAT FALLS. *American Indian Outreach*, 121 23rd St. S., P.O. Box 1399, 59403. Tel: 406-727-6683; Fax: 406-454-3480. Email: nativeoutreach@dioceseofgfb.org. Web: www.dioceseofgfb.org. Linda Kovar, Dir.

Big Sky Cum Christo/Cursillo, P.O. Box 1399, 59403-1399. Bob Meyers, Contact Person. Tel: 406-453-5304; Vern Boyer, Contact Person. Tel: 406-628-4753.

Cascade County Council of the St. Vincent de Paul Society, P.O. Box 1562, 500 Central Ave. W., 59403. Tel: 406-761-0870. Email: svdp@in-tch.com. Dione Leidholt, Operations Dir.

Catholic Foundation of Eastern Montana, Inc., P.O. Box 1399, 59403-1399. Tel: 406-727-6683; Fax: 406-454-3480. Email: stewardship@dioceseofgfb.org. Web: www.dioceseofgfb.org. Joseph Pipinich, Contact Person.

Committee for a Great Falls Catholic High School, P.O. Box 1399, 59403-1399. Tel: 406-727-6683; Fax: 406-454-3480. Email: business@dioceseofgfb.org. Web: www.dioceseofgfb.org. Joseph Loncki, Diocesan Finance Officer.

Frank & Isabell Stites Memorial Center (Retired Priests & Lay People Living), *Pastoral Center*, P.O. Box 1399, 59403. Tel: 406-727-6683; Fax: 406-454-3480. Email: business@dioceseofgfb.org. Web: www.dioceseofgfb.org.

1701 26th St. S., 59403. Joseph Loncki, Contact Person.

Heisey Memorial Trust Fund, 313 Seventh St. N., 59401. Tel: 406-453-1211; Fax: 406-453-1211. Mr. Kirby Crosley, Dir.

Heisey Memorial Youth Center, 313 Seventh St. N., 59401. Tel: 406-453-1211; Fax: 406-453-1211. Mr. Kirby Crosley, Dir. Recreation center serving the adults and youth of the community.

Holy Spirit Catholic School Endowment Trust, 2820 Central Ave., 59401-3412. Tel: 406-761-5775; Fax: 406-761-5887. Email: parshscs@hotmail.com. Peggy Tremper, Pres.

St. Joseph's Education Trust, 500 2nd Ave. S.W., 59404. Tel: 406-453-9331. Rev. Patrick R. Zabrocki, Chm.

Retrouvaille of Montana, P.O. Box 4, 59403-0004. Tel: 800-470-2330; 406-761-4830. Email: MT1Retrouvaille@aol.com. Gary Quinn, Co-Coord.; Mary Quinn, Co-Coord.

Tekakwitha Conference, P.O. Box 6768, 59406-6768. Tel: 406-727-0147; 800-842-9635; Fax: 406-452-9845. Email: tekakwitha.conference@worldnet.att.net. Web: www.tekconf.org. Sr. Kateri Mitchell, S.S.A., Exec. Dir.

ASHLAND. *St. Labre Indian School Educational Association*, P.O. Box 216, 59003. Tel: 406-784-4500; Fax: 406-784-6161. Email: executivedirector@atlabre.org. Web: www.stlabre.org. Mr. Curtis Yarlott, Pres. & Exec. Dir.; Rev. Emmett G. Hoffmann, Retired. A nonprofit Corporation.; Four Catholic schools for Native Americans: St. Labre Indian School at

Ashland (PreK-8 Students 364); (High School Students 179); Pretty Eagle Catholic School, St. Xavier (Students 109); St. Charles Mission School, Pryor (Students 88).

St. Labre Youth & Family Services/Youth Group Homes, P.O. Box 458, 59003. Tel: 406-784-4521; 877-785-4457; Fax: 406-784-4527. Web: www.stlabre.org. Clay A. Ramey, Dir. Eagle's Nest for Girls; Tallwhiteman for Boys; Licensed for 8 children each.

HAVRE. *St. Jude's Education Trust*, P.O. Box 407, 59501. Tel: 406-265-4261; Fax: 406-265-4408. Email: stjude@ttc.cmc.net. Web: www.stjudethaddeusschool.org. Rev. Robert D. Grosch, J.C.L.

LEWISTOWN. *St. Leo's Catholic Education Trust*, P.O. Box 421, 59457. Tel: 406-538-9306; Fax: 406-538-7624. Email: stleos@tein.net. Rev. Daniel O'Rourke, Chm.

MALTA. *St. Mary's Catholic Education Trust*, P.O. Box 70, 59538. Tel: 406-654-1446; Fax: 406-654-1467. Web: www.saintmarysmalta.com. Rev. James O'Neil.

MILES CITY. *Custer County Conference of the Society of Saint Vincent de Paul and Thrift Store*, 407 Main St., 59301. Tel: 406-234-3011. Dorothy Buck, Pres.; Linda Life, Exec. Dir.; Jane O'Donnell, Store Mgr.; Lori Loomis, Store Mgr.; Joann Kanenwischer, Store Mgr.

MONARCH. *Thieltges-St. Thomas Camp*, P.O. Box 46, 59463. Tel: 406-236-5385. Email: jhox@3rivers.net.

RELIGIOUS INSTITUTES OF MEN REPRESENTED IN THE DIOCESE

For further details refer to the corresponding bracketed number in the Religious Institutes of Men or Women section.

[0200]—*Benedictine Monks* (Assumption Abbey, Richardton, ND; Cleveland, OH)—O.S.B.

[0330]—*Brothers of the Christian Schools* (Midwest Province)—F.S.C.

[0470]—*The Capuchin Friars* (Prov. of St. Joseph, Detroit)—O.F.M.Cap.

[0690]—*Jesuit Fathers and Brothers* (Oregon Prov.)—S.J.

RELIGIOUS INSTITUTES OF WOMEN REPRESENTED IN THE DIOCESE

[0230]—*Benedictine Sisters of Pontifical Jurisdiction* (Rapid City, SD and St. Paul, MN)—O.S.B.

[2100]—*Congregation of the Humility of Mary* (Davenport, IA)—C.H.M.

[1730]—*Congregation of the Sisters of the Third Order of St. Francis* (Oldenburg, IN)—O.S.F.

[1070-10]—*Dominican Sisters of Springfield in Illinois*—O.P.

[1070-11]—*Dominican Sisters, Congregation of Our Lady of the Rosary* (Sparkill, NY)—O.P.

[1070-03]—*Dominican Sisters, Sinsinawa Dominican Congregation of the Most Holy Rosary* (Sinsinawa, WI)—O.P.

[3760]—*Order of St. Clares, Holy Name Federation* (Great Falls, MT)—O.S.C.

[0480]—*Sisters of Charity of Leavenworth, Kansas*—S.C.L.

[2560]—*Sisters of Mercy - US Prov.* (Redlands, CA)—R.S.M.

[2575]—*Sisters of Mercy of the Americas* (Omaha, NE)—R.S.M.

[3350]—*Sisters of Providence* (Spokane, WA)—S.P.

[3720]—*Sisters of Saint Anne* (Marlboro, MA)—S.S.A.

[]—*Sisters of Sainte Anne* (Victoria, BC, Canada)—S.S.A.

[3890]—*Sisters of St. Joseph of Peace* (Bellvue, WA)—C.S.J.P.

[3320]—*Sisters of the Presentation of the B.V.M.* (Aberdeen, SD)—P.B.V.M.

[1720]—*Sisters of the Third Order Regular of St. Francis of the Congregation of Our Lady of Lourdes* (Rochester, MN)—O.S.F.

[4110]—*Ursuline Nuns* (Santa Rosa, CA)—O.S.U.

[4120-07]—*Ursuline Nuns of Youngstown* (Canfield, OH)—O.S.U.

DIOCESAN CEMETERIES

BILLINGS. *Holy Cross*

GREAT FALLS. *Calvary*

Mount Olivet

NECROLOGY

† Sampson, Patrick, (Retired)—Died July 4, 2003

Diocese of Green Bay

(Dioecesis Sinus Viridis)

Most Reverend

DAVID A. ZUBIK

Bishop of Green Bay; ordained May 3, 1975; appointed Auxiliary Bishop of Pittsburgh and Titular Bishop of Jamestown February 18, 1997; consecrated April 6, 1997; appointed Bishop of Green Bay October 10, 2003; installed December 12, 2003. *Office: 1910 S. Webster Ave,. P.O. Box 23825, Green Bay, WI 54305-3825.* Tel: 920-437-7531.

Most Reverend

ROBERT J. BANKS, D.D.

Retired Bishop of Green Bay; ordained December 20, 1952; consecrated September 19, 1985; appointed Auxiliary Bishop to the Archbishop of Boston and Titular Bishop of Taraqua on June 26, 1985; appointed to Green Bay October 16, 1990; installed December 5, 1990; retired December 12, 2003. *Office. 1910 S. Webster Ave., P.O. Box 23825, Green Bay, WI 54305-3825.*

Most Reverend

ALOYSIUS J. WYCISLO, D.D.

Retired Bishop of Green Bay; ordained April 7, 1934; appointed Titular Bishop of Stadia and Auxiliary of Chicago October 17, 1960; consecrated December 21, 1960; appointed to Green Bay March 8, 1968; retired May 10, 1983; appointed Apostolic Administrator of Green Bay Diocese June 16, 1983. *Res.: 1825 Riverside Dr., Green Bay, WI 54301.* Tel: 920-435-3685.

Chancery: 1910 S. Webster Ave., P.O. Box 23825, Green Bay, WI 54305-3825. Tel: 920-437-7531; Fax: 920-435-1330.

Web: www.gbdioc.org

Email: jdewane@gbdioc.org

Most Reverend

ROBERT F. MORNEAU, D.D.

Auxiliary Bishop of Green Bay; ordained May 28, 1966; appointed Auxiliary Bishop of Green Bay and Titular Bishop of Massa Lubrense December 19, 1978; consecrated February 22, 1979. *Res.: 1825 Riverside Dr., P.O. Box 23825, Green Bay, WI 54305-3825. Office: 1910 S. Webster, P.O. Box 23825, Green Bay, WI 54305-3825.* Tel: 920-437-7531.

ESTABLISHED MARCH 3, 1868.

Square Miles 10,728.

Incorporated January 16, 1907.

Comprises these 16 Counties: Brown, Calumet, Door, Florence, Forest, Kewaunee, Langlade, Manitowoc, Marinette, Menominee, Oconto, Outagamie, Shawano, Waupaca, Waushara and Winnebago in the State of Wisconsin.

Legal Title: Catholic Diocese of Green Bay.

For legal titles of parishes and diocesan institutions, consult the Chancery Office.

STATISTICAL OVERVIEW

Personnel	
Bishop	1
Auxiliary Bishops	1
Retired Bishops	1
Abbots	1
Retired Abbots	3
Priests: Diocesan Active in Diocese	111
Priests: Diocesan Active Outside Diocese	7
Priests: Diocesan in Foreign Missions	3
Priests: Retired, Sick or Absent	81
Number of Diocesan Priests	202
Religious Priests in Diocese	115
Total Priests in Diocese	317
Extern Priests in Diocese	8
Ordinations:	
Transitional Deacons	2
Permanent Deacons	4
Permanent Deacons in Diocese	108
Total Brothers	34
Total Sisters	653
Parishes	
Parishes	185
With Resident Pastor:	
Resident Diocesan Priests	95
Resident Religious Priests	23
Without Resident Pastor:	
Administered by Priests	55
Administered by Deacons	1
Administered by Religious Women	8
Administered by Lay People	3
Missions	3
Pastoral Centers	14
Professional Ministry Personnel:	
Sisters	65
Lay Ministers	174
Welfare	
Catholic Hospitals	7
Total Assisted	977,606
Homes for the Aged	15
Total Assisted	1,413
Day Care Centers	2
Total Assisted	111
Specialized Homes	4
Total Assisted	8,081
Special Centers for Social Services	8
Total Assisted	182,276
Residential Care of Disabled	1
Total Assisted	6
Educational	
Diocesan Students in Other Seminaries	14
Seminaries, Religious	1
Students Religious	9
Total Seminarians	23
Colleges and Universities	2
Total Students	4,908
High Schools, Diocesan and Parish	5
Total Students	1,405
High Schools, Private	1
Total Students	741
Elementary Schools, Diocesan and Parish	70
Total Students	10,519
Catechesis/Religious Education:	
High School Students	12,118
Elementary Students	22,700
Total Students under Catholic Instruction	52,414
Teachers in the Diocese:	
Priests	1
Brothers	4
Sisters	27
Lay Teachers	916
Vital Statistics	
Receptions into the Church:	
Infant Baptism Totals	4,284
Adult Baptism Totals	544
Received into Full Communion	318
First Communions	4,373
Confirmations	3,814
Marriages:	
Catholic	1,135
Interfaith	448
Total Marriages	1,583
Deaths	3,176
Total Catholic Population	358,211
Total Population	930,419

Former Bishops—Rt. Revs. JOSEPH MELCHER, D.D., consecrated July 12, 1868; died Dec. 20, 1873; FRANCIS XAVIER KRAUTBAUER, D.D., consecrated June 29, 1875; died Dec. 17, 1885; FREDERICK XAVIER KATZER, D.D., appt. July 13, 1886; consecrated Sept. 21, 1886; appt. Archbishop of Milwaukee, Jan. 30, 1891; died July 20, 1903; SEBASTIAN GEBHARD MESSMER, D.D., consecrated Bishop of Green Bay, March 27, 1892; appt. Archbishop of Milwaukee, Nov. 28, 1903; died Aug. 4, 1930; JOSEPH J. FOX, D.D., consecrated Bishop of Green Bay, July 25, 1904; resigned Dec. 4, 1914; appt. Titular Bishop of Ionopolis; died March 14, 1915; Most Revs. PAUL P. RHODE, D.D., ord. June 17, 1894; consecrated Titular Bishop of Barca and Auxiliary to the Archbishop of Chicago, July 29, 1908; transferred to the See of Green Bay, July 5, 1915; died March 3, 1945; STANISLAUS V. BONA, D.D., ord. Nov. 1, 1912; appt. Bishop of Grand Island, NE Dec. 18, 1931; consecrated Feb. 25, 1932; appt. Coadjutor Bishop of Green Bay, Dec. 2, 1944; succeeded to See, March 3, 1945; died Dec. 1, 1967; ALOYSIUS J. WYCISLO, D.D., ord. April 7, 1934; appt. Titular Bishop of Stadia and Auxiliary Bishop of Chicago Oct. 17, 1960; consecrated Dec. 21, 1960; appt. to Green Bay, March 8, 1968; retired May 10, 1983; ADAM J. MAIDA, J.C.L., J.D., S.T.L., ord. May 26, 1956; appt. to Green Bay, Nov. 8, 1983; consecrated Jan. 25, 1984; installed as Archbishop of Detroit, June 12, 1990; created Cardinal on Nov. 26, 1994; ROBERT J. BANKS, D.D. (Retired), ordained Dec. 20, 1952; consecrated September 19, 1985; appointed Auxiliary Bishop to the Archbishop of Boston and Titular Bishop of Taraqua on June 26, 1985; appointed to Green Bay October 16, 1990; installed December 5, 1990; retired December 12, 2003.

Vicars General—Most Rev. ROBERT F. MORNEAU, D.D.; Rev. Msgr. JOHN B. DEWANE, M.A., S.T.L., D.Min.

Chancery—1910 S. Webster Ave., P.O. Box 23825, Green Bay, 54305-3825. Tel: 920-437-7531; Fax: 920-435-1330. Office Hours: Mon.-Fri. 9-5; other times by appointment only

Vicar for Administration—Rev. Msgr. JOHN B. DEWANE, M.A., S.T.L., D.Min.

Chancellor—Sr. MARY BRIDE GRUBBS, A.N.G.

Vice-Chancellor—Rev. Msgr. JOHN H. SCHUH.

Assistant Chancellor—Rev. JOHN DOERFLER, J.C.L., S.T.L.

Archivist—Mr. JOHN LEDOUX.

Secretary to Bishop—TERRI WICKMAN. Tel: 216-696-6525, Ext. 8194.

Chancery Secretary—MARY JO KRUEGER. Tel: 216-696-6525, Ext. 8188.

Diocesan Tribunal—Mailing Address, 1910 S. Webster Ave., P.O. Box 23825, Green Bay, 54305-3825. Tel: 920-437-7531.

Judicial Vicar—Rev. ROBERT J. KABAT, J.C.L.

Adjutant Judicial Vicars—Rev. RICHARD GETCHEL, J.C.L.; Rev. Msgr. BRIAN P. COLEMAN, J.C.L.

Judges in First Instance—Revs. ROBERT J. KABAT, J.C.L.; JOHN F. DOERFLER, J.C.L., S.T.L.; Rev. Msgr. DENNIS M. LALLY, B.A.

Judges in Second Instance—Rev. ROBERT J. KABAT, J.C.L.; Rev. Msgrs. DENNIS M. LALLY, B.A.;

BRIAN P. COLEMAN, J.C.L.; Revs. RICHARD GETCHEL, J.C.L.; ARTHUR DANKS, M.A.; Rt. Rev. GARY NEVILLE, O.Praem, J.C.D.; Rev. WILLIAM VAN DE KREEKE, J.C.L.

Defenders of the Bond—Rev. LEE J. KAHRS, B.A.; Sr. ANN BEHRAUER, J.C.L., M.A.

Notaries—CATHLEEN NICK; KATHLEEN SCHUMACHER; MARGE PAVLAT.

Diocesan Consultors—Most Rev. ROBERT F. MORNEAU, D.D.; Rev. Msgrs. JOHN B. DEWANE, M.A., S.T.L., D.Min.; JAMES DILLENBURG; JAMES FEELY (Retired); PETER KLAUCK (Retired); PAUL KOSZAREK; ROY KLISTER, S.T.D., J.C.L., S.T.L.; Revs. JOHN BERGSTADT; MICHAEL O'ROURKE.

Secretary to Consultors—Sr. MARY BRIDE GRUBBS, A.N.G.

Pastor Consultors—Rev. Msgr. PETER N. KLAUCK; Revs. JOHN P. BERGSTADT; JAMES A. HABLEWITZ; JOSEPH A. MATTERN; PAUL A. SCHUMACHER; WILLARD J. VAN DE LOO (Retired).

Regional Vicars—Revs. MICHAEL BETLEY, Vicariate I; DAVID S. BARRETT, Vicariate II; JOHN M. GALLAGHER, Vicariate III; PHILIP DINH-VAN-THIEP, Vicariate IV; DENNIS M. RYAN, Vicariate V; DAVID J. PLIER, Vicariate VI; ANTHONY J. BIRDSALL, Vicariate VII; ROY J. GEENEN, Vicariate VIII; DENNIS L. BERGSBAKEN, Vicariate IX; JOSEPH A. MATTERN, Vicariate X; GARY NEW, S.D.S., Vicariate XI; DAVID HOFFMAN, Vicariate XII.

Diocesan Pastoral Council—Rev. Msgr. JOHN B. DEWANE, M.A., S.T.L., D.Min., Contact Person.

Presbyteral Council—Rev. JOHN DOERFLER, Chm.

Appointed Representatives—Rev. Msgrs. PETER KLAUCK (Retired); PAUL KOSZAREK; Revs. JOHN DOERFLER; PATRICK GAWRYLEWSKI, O.F.M.; JOHN GIROTTI; DANE RADECKI, O.Praem.; JAMES JUGENHEIMER; MICHAEL O'ROURKE.

Elected Representatives—Revs. JEROME PASTORS, Vicariate I; JEREMIAH WORMAN, Vicariate II; LAWRENCE MARTO, Vicariate III; JOHN BECKER, Vicariate IV; GERALD PRUSAKOWSKI, O.F.M., Vicariate V; LARRY J. SEIDL, Vicariate VI; DENNIS G. DRURY, Vicariate VII; MARK VANDER STEEG, Vicariate VIII; DAVID SCHMIDT, Vicariate IX; THOMAS REYNEBEAU, Vicariate X; W. THOMAS LONG, Vicariate XI; CAMILLUS JANAS, O.F.M., Vicariate XII. Ex Officios: Most Rev. ROBERT F. MORNEAU, D.D.; Rev. Msgr. JOHN B. DEWANE, M.A., S.T.L., D.Min.

Bishop's Finance Council—Rev. ROBERT K. FINNEGAN, O.Praem.; Ms. MARY STAUDENMAIER; Mr. MICHAEL ARIENS; Mr. JOHN F. BERGSTROM; Mr. ROBERT C. GALLAGHER; Mr. PAUL GEHL; Mr. THOMAS VORPAHL; Rev. Msgr. JOHN B. DEWANE, M.A., S.T.L., D.Min.

Resource—Most Rev. ROBERT F. MORNEAU, D.D.; THOMAS KURKOWSKI.

Ministry Personnel

Vicar for Religious—Rev. Msgr. JOHN H. SCHUH, P.O. Box 23825, Green Bay, 54305-3825. Tel: 920-437-7531, Ext. 8179.

Representative for Religious—Sr. MARY JO KIRT, P.O. Box 23825, Green Bay, 54305-3825. Tel: 920-437-7531, Ext. 8292.

Vicar for Priests—Most Rev. ROBERT F. MORNEAU, D.D., P.O. Box 23825, Green Bay, 54305-3825. Tel: 920-437-7531, Ext. 8322.

Bishop's Representative to Senior Priests—Rev. WILLARD VAN DE LOO, 825 E. River Dr., #4, De Pere, 54115. Tel: 920-338-1113.

Ministry to Priests Program—Most Rev. ROBERT F. MORNEAU, D.D., Dir., P.O. Box 23825, Green Bay, 54305-3825. Tel: 920-437-7531, Ext. 8322.

Department of the Permanent Diaconate—Deacon PAUL GRIMM, Dir., Prog. Coord. & Vicar for Deacons, P.O. Box 23825, Green Bay, 54305-3825. Tel: 920-437-7531, Ext. 8290.

Vocations—Rev. DOUGLAS LECAPTAIN, Dir., P.O. Box 23825, Green Bay, 54305-3825. Tel: 920-437-7531, Ext. 8293.

Department for Parish Ministers—TONY PICHLER, Dir., P.O. Box 23825, Green Bay, 54305-3825. Tel: 920-437-7531, Ext. 8268.

Education

Total Catholic Education Department—Mr. LELAND NAGEL, Dir., 1825 Riverside Dr., P.O. Box 23825, Green Bay, 54305-3825. Tel: 920-437-7531, Ext. 8309; Fax: 920-437-0694.

Consultants—

Youth Ministry—VACANT. Tel: 920-437-7531, Ext. 8281.

Scouts—Rev. ROGER STREBEL, W. 10530 Cole St., P.O. Box 128, Elcho, 54428-0128.

Administrative Development—Sr. PAT MCCORMICK. Tel: 920-437-7531, Ext. 8271.

Administrative Services—ANN FOX. Tel: 920-437-7531, Ext. 8273.

Educational Leadership/School Program Development—Rev. ROBERT KROLL, O.F.M. Tel: 920-437-7531, Ext. 8284.

Staff Development/Educational Programs—CHRIS BROSLAVICK. Tel: 920-437-7531, Ext. 8283.

Young Adult/Adult Catechesis—Sr. PEG GABIK. Tel: 920-437-7531, Ext. 8274.

Religious Education (K-6)—ANDREA SABOR. Tel: 920-437-7531, Ext. 8270.

Liaisons-Office of Education—

Priests Eucharistic League—Rev. DONALD FELLER, 2496 Mary Jo Dr., Green Bay, 54311-5208. Tel: 920-465-3460.

The Diocesan Charismatic Renewal Center—Rev. Msgr. JAMES VANDEN HOGEN, St. John Nepomucene Parish, 323 S. Pine St., Little Chute, 54140-1854. Tel: 920-788-9061.

Serra Clubs—Rev. DOUGLAS LECAPTAIN, P.O. Box 23825, Green Bay, 54305-3825. Tel: 920-437-7531.

Blue Army - World Apostolate of Fatima—Deacon ROBERT ELLIS, 1372 Nienhaus Dr., De Pere, 54115-8600. Tel: 920-337-6263.

Cursillo—Rev. DAVID PLEIER, 2040 Hillside Ln., Green Bay, 54302-4098. Tel: 920-468-4811.

Xavier Guild—Rev. DENNIS M. RYAN, Chap., St. Nicholas Parish (Freedom), N4088 Cty. Rd. E., Kaukauna, 54130-7592. Tel: 920-788-1492.

Diocesan Council of Catholic Women—MARGIE WESTERN, Pres., 9208 Hwy. G, Suring, 54174. Tel: 920-897-3632.

Pastoral Services

Pastoral Services—1825 Riverside Dr., P.O. Box 23825, Green Bay, 54305-3825. Tel: 920-437-7531; Fax: 920-437-0694. Email: pastserv@gbdioc.org. MARK MOGILKA, Dir. Tel: 920-437-7531, Ext. 8297. Email: mmogilka@gbdioc.org.

Marriage Preparation, Parenting—MARY STUBLER. Tel: 920-437-7531, Ext. 8315.

Consultants—

Campaign for Human Development—Deacon PAUL GRIMM. Tel: 920-437-7531, Ext. 8299.

Deaf & Hard of Hearing—SUE PERRAULT. Tel: 920-437-7531, Ext. 8306.

Ecumenism—Rev. GREGORY J. SMITH, Ecumenical Officer.

Evangelization—ANISSA MELOTTE. Tel: 920-437-7531, Ext. 8301.

Family Life—MARY STUBLER, Dir. Tel: 920-437-7531, Ext. 8315.

Hispanic Ministry—RUDY PINEDA. Tel: 920-437-7531, Ext. 8308.

Hmong/Lao Pastoral Care—DON CHANG. Tel: 920-437-7531, Ext. 8307.

Ministry with Persons with Disabilities—SUE PERRAULT. Tel: 920-437-7531, Ext. 8306.

Parish Planning & Collaboration—TOM DONOVAN. Tel: 920-437-7531, Ext. 8286.

Pastoral Care—MARY SHERMAN. Tel: 920-437-7531, Ext. 8300.

Pastoral Councils—TOM DONOVAN. Tel: 920-437-7531, Ext. 8286.

Prison Ministry—MARY SHERMAN. Tel: 920-437-7531, Ext. 8300.

Respect Life—TOM DONOVAN. Tel: 920-437-7531, Ext. 8286.

Rural Life—MARY STUBLER. Tel: 920-437-7531, Ext. 8315.

Social Concerns—Deacon PAUL GRIMM. Tel: 920-437-7531, Ext. 8299.

Stewardship—TOM DONOVAN. Tel: 920-437-7531, Ext. 8286.

Worship Department—DIANN WIMMER, Dir. Tel: 920-437-7531, Ext. 8311.

RCIA & Sacred Music—ANISSA MELOTTE. Tel: 920-437-7531, Ext. 8301.

Campus Ministry—LAURIE SVATEK, UWGB Ecumenical Center, 2420 Nicolet Dr., Green Bay, 54311-7011. Tel: 920-465-5133.

Holy Name Retreat House—BOB PENZENSTADLER; MONICA PENZENSTADLER. Tel: 920-437-7531, Ext. 8296.

Liturgical Commission—DIANN WIMMER.

Ecumenical Commission—Rev. GREGORY J. SMITH.

Justice & Peace Commission—Deacon PAUL GRIMM.

Dominican Republic Mission—Rev. MICHAEL SEIS.

Community Services

Catholic Charities—KAREN JOHNSTON, Dir., 1825 Riverside Dr., P.O. Box 23825, Green Bay, 54305-3825. Tel: 920-437-7531, Ext. 8234; Fax: 920-437-0694.

Resettlement & Immigration Services—BARBARA B. BIEBEL, Program Mgr. Tel: 920-437-7531, Ext. 8252.

Apostleship of the Sea—Deacon GLENN TESKE, Port Chap., 2839 S. Broadway, Green Bay, 54304-5309. Tel: 920-499-0035.

Diocesan Health Services—Rev. RICHARD KLINGEISEN, Coord., 1110 S. 10th St., Manitowoc, 54220-5288. Tel: 920-684-3718.

McCormick Memorial Home for the Aged—212 Iroquois St., Green Bay, 54301-1995. Tel: 920-437-0883. JAMES GENRICH, Admin.; Rev. THADDEUS J. KOSZAREK, Chap. (Retired).

Liaisons - Community Services—

Sign of God Deaf Ministry—MARY E. ZUPANSIC, Pastoral Assoc., 1016 N. Broadway, De Pere, 54115-2697. Tel: 920-337-9454 (V/TDD).

Society of St. Vincent de Paul—JAMES MATOUSEK, Pres. & Trustee, 3135 St. Gregory Dr., Green Bay, 54311; Rev. JOSEPH DORNER, Chap. (Council of the Green Bay Diocesan, Society of St. Vincent de Paul, Inc.); EVERETT JOHNSON, Exec. Sec.

Knights of Columbus—MEL STEINER, 8145 Donna St., Chilton, 53014-1585.

Our Lady of Charity Center, Inc.—Sr. DEANA KOHLMAN, O.L.C., Dir., 2560 Shawano Ave., P.O. Box 10357, Green Bay, 54307-0357. Tel: 920-434-8208.

Catholic Veterans of War—RAYMOND WOZNICK, Commander, 418 Forrest Ave., Fond du Lac, 54935.

Menominee Pastoral Program—Rev. DAVID S. BARRETT, St. Michael Church, P.O. Box 610, Keshena, 54135-0160. Tel: 715-799-3811.

Support Services

Support Services—P.O. Box 23825, Green Bay, 54305-3825. Tel: 920-437-7531; Fax: 920-435-1330. Rev. Msgr. JOHN B. DEWANE, M.A., S.T.L., D.Min., Vicar for Admin. Tel: 920-437-7531, Ext. 8171.

Department of World Mission Services—CINDI BRAWNER, Dir., P.O. Box 23825, Green Bay, 54305-3825. Tel: 920-437-7531, Ext. 8173; Fax: 920-435-1330.

Agencies— Propagation of the Faith, St. Peter the Apostle, Holy Childhood Association, Catholic Relief Services

Annual Bishop's Appeal—RON SHAHA. Tel: 920-437-7531, Ext. 8196.

Medical Insurance and Benefits—MARY VANKAUWENBERG, Box 23825, Green Bay, 54305-3825. Tel: 920-437-7531, Ext. 8260.

Bishop's Charities Game—JAMES HOGAN, P.O. Box 23825, Green Bay, 54305-3825. Tel: 920-437-7531, Ext. 8219.

Camp Tekawitha Retreat and Conference Center—ROBERTA LARSON, P.O. Box 23825, Green Bay, 54305-3825. Tel: 920-437-7531, Ext. 8511.

Cemeteries—JON RUATTI, 1825 Riverside Dr., P.O. Box 23825, Green Bay, 54305-3825. Tel: 920-437-7531, Ext. 8229.

Communications—P.O. Box 23825, Green Bay, 54305-3825. Tel: 920-437-7531, Ext. 8213. TONY KUICK, Dir. Tel: 920-437-7531, Ext. 8214; RENAE BAUER, Communications Specialist. Tel: 920-437-7531, Ext. 8213.

Diocesan Newspaper—P.O. Box 23825, Green Bay, 54305-3825. Tel: 920-437-7531. *Appleton Area.* Tel: 920-233-5555. TONY KUICK, Gen. Mgr. Tel: 920-437-7531, Ext. 8214; ANTON STALEY, Editor. Tel: 920-437-7531, Ext. 8210. "The Compass"

Computer Services—TONY KUICK, Dir. Tel: 920-437-7531, Ext. 8214; BEA SEIDL, Database Admin. Tel: 920-437-7531, Ext. 8255; DAN LEE, P.C. Specialist, Box 23825, Green Bay, 54305-3825. Tel: 920-437-7531, Ext. 8253.

Financial Services—THOMAS KURKOWSKI, Dir. Tel: 920-437-7531, Ext. 8267; MIKE SPEEL, Sr. Acct., P.O. Box 23825, Green Bay, 54305-3825. Tel: 920-437-7531, Ext. 8259.

Human Resources—CATHY LARSON, Dir., P.O. Box 23825, Green Bay, 54305-3825. Tel: 920-437-7531, Ext. 8219.

Property Management and Real Estate—KEVIN M. BRUNNER, Dir. Diocesan Properties, P.O. Box 23825, Green Bay, 54305-3825. Tel: 920-437-7531, Ext. 8277.

Sacred Heart Seminary, Inc.—P.O. Box 23825, Green Bay, 54305-3825. Tel: 920-437-7531.

Sacrificial Giving Program—CINDI BRAWNER, Dir., P.O. Box 23825, Green Bay, 54305-3825. Tel: 920-437-7531, Ext. 8173.

St. Joseph Corporation and Central Services—KEVIN BRUNNER, P.O. Box 23825, Green Bay, 54305-3825. Tel: 920-437-7531, Ext. 8260.

Development—CINDI BRAWNER, P.O. Box 23825, Green Bay, 54305-3825. Tel: 920-437-7531, Ext. 8173.

Priests' Personnel Board—Revs. PAUL DEMUTH; RONALD BELITZ; DEAN DOMBROSKI; TOM FARRELL; DAVID KIEFER; WILLARD VAN DE LOO; Rev. Msgr. JOHN H. SCHUH; Most Rev. ROBERT F. MORNEAU, D.D., Resource Person.

Conciliation and Arbitration Board—Revs. JOHN T. MULLARKEY, Pres.; ROBERT J. KABAT, J.C.L., Clerk, P.O. Box 23825, Green Bay, 54305-3825. Tel: 920-437-7531.

Liaisons--Personnel—

Association of Pastoral Associates—KATHLEEN DENOBLE, 2020 Cottonwood Ct., De Pere, 54115. Tel: 920-339-8839.

Leo Benevolent Association—Rev. ROBERT H.

VANDENBERG, Treas., 410 Wallace St., Combined Locks, 54113. Tel: 920-788-4553.

Clergy Credit Union—Rev. CHARLES W. MOCCO, Treas., P.O. Box 70, De Pere, 54115. Tel: 920-983-2926.

Community of Our Lady—Very Rev. REGIS N. BARWIG, Prior, 2804 Oakwood Ln., Oshkosh, 54904-8406. Tel: 920-233-5633.

A New Genesis—Sr. CAROL HAANEN, Moderator, 1017 E. Florida Ave., Appleton, 54911 Tel: 920-749-9838; Most Rev. ALOYSIUS J. WYCISLO, D.D., Chap.

Victim Assistance Coordinator—Sr. MARY BRIDE GRUBBS, A.N.G. Tel: 920-437-7531, Ext. 8174. Email: mgrubbs@gbdioc.org.

CLERGY, PARISHES, MISSIONS AND PAROCHIAL SCHOOLS

CITY OF GREEN BAY
(BROWN COUNTY)

1—ST. FRANCIS XAVIER CATHEDRAL, , Also serves St. John, Green Bay Rev. Douglas LeCaptain, Admin.
Res.: 139 S. Madison St., 54301-4501. Tel: 920-432-4348; Fax: 920-435-5068.
School—St. Thomas More, 650 S. Irwin Ave., 54301. Tel: 920-432-8242. Barbara Schneider, Prin. Consolidated with SS. Peter & Paul and St. Mary of the Angels.
Catechesis/Religious Program—1420 Harvey St., 54302-1999. Tel: 920-437-0651. Michael Vincent, D.R.E. Associated with St. John, Green Bay. Students 77.

2—ST. AGNES, Rev. Richard Getchel; Deacon Robert Nooker.
Res.: 1484 9th St., 54304-3061. Tel: 920-494-2534.
School—Holy Family, 1204 S. Fisk St., 54304. Tel: 920-494-1931. Daniel Malmberg, Prin. Franciscan Sisters of Christian Charity 4; Lay Teachers 26; Students 477.
Catechesis/Religious Program—Tel: 920-494-6450. Ellen Mommaerts, D.R.E. Students 377.

3—ANNUNCIATION OF THE BLESSED VIRGIN MARY, , Served from St. Jude, Green Bay. Rev. Ronald C. Belitz.
Mailing Address: 1423 Kellogg St., 54303-3113. Tel: 920-496-2160; Fax: 920-496-2167.
Res.: 401 Gray St., 54303-3013. Tel: 920-499-2333.
School—Trinity Catholic Schools, (Grades 5-8), 1087 Kellogg St., 54303. Tel: 920-499-1919; Fax: 920-499-9166. Daniel O'Rourke, Prin. Lay Teachers 12; Students 221.
Catechesis/Religious Program—Tel: 920-496-2164. Carolyn Whitcomb, D.R.E. Students 111.

4—ST. BERNARD, Rev. David Pleier; Deacons Keith P. Holschbach; John Laurant; Larry Mastalish.
Res.: 2040 Hillside Ln., 54302-4098. Tel: 920-468-4811; Fax: 920-468-1396.
School—2020 Hillside Ln., 54302. Tel: 920-468-5026; Fax: 920-468-3478. Sr. Patricia Clement, Prin. Sisters 1; Lay Teachers 20; Students 488.
Catechesis/Religious Program—Tel: 920-468-4390. Andrew J. Russell, D.R.E. Students 752.

5—ST. ELIZABETH ANN SETON, Rev. Msgr. James E. Dillenburg; Deacon James Gauthier.
Res.: 2771 Oakwood Dr., 54304-1618. Tel: 920-499-1546; Fax: 920-499-2207.
School—Holy Family, 1204 Fisk St., 54304. Tel: 920-494-1931. Daniel Malmberg, Prin. Consolidated with St. Agnes. Religious 5; Lay Teachers 26; Students 259.
Catechesis/Religious Program—Carol A. VandenBush, D.R.E. Students 675.

6—HOLY MARTYRS OF GORCUM, [CEM] Revs. Ronald C. Belitz; Robert E. Rhyner; Deacon William Burkel.
Res.: 3562 Finger Rd., 54311-7733. Tel: 920-468-5718; Fax: 920-468-5713.
School—Holy Martyrs School, 3542 Finger Rd., 54311-7733. Tel: 920-468-7262. Theresa M. Williams, Prin. Lay Teachers 9; Students 141.
Catechesis/Religious Program—Mary Holzberger, D.R.E. Students 138.

7—ST. JOHN, , Served from St. Francis Xavier Cathedral, Green Bay Rev. Douglas LeCaptain, Admin.
Res.: 413 St. John St., 54301-4116. Tel: 920-436-6380; Fax: 920-436-6382.
Catechesis/Religious Program—Tel: 920-432-4348. Doris Vincent, D.R.E.

8—ST. JOSEPH, Rev. Michael Ingold.
Res.: 936 9th St., 54304-3439. Tel: 920-497-7042; Fax: 920-497-7240.
School—1224 12th Ave., 54304. Tel: 920-497-7085. Patrice Wadzinski, Prin. Lay Teachers 13 Students 174.
Catechesis/Religious Program—1434 12th Ave., 54304. Mr. Eugene Mailhiot, D.R.E. Students 128.

9—ST. JUDE, , Also serves Annunciation of the Blessed Virgin Mary, Green Bay Rev. Michael Lngold.
Res.: 1423 Kellogg St., 54303-3113. Tel: 920-496-2160; Fax: 920-496-2167.
School—Trinity Catholic Schools, (Grades PreK-4), 1420 Division St., 54303-3113. Tel: 920-496-2162. Jane Schueller, Prin. Religious 1; Lay Teachers 14; Students 259.
Catechesis/Religious Program—Tel: 920-496-2164. Carolyn Whitcomb, D.R.E. Students 246

10—ST. MARY OF THE ANGELS, Rev. Albert Lis, O.F.M.; Deacon Paul P. Umentum. In Res., Rev. Nathan Jaskulski, O.F.M.
Res.: 645 S. Irwin Ave., 54301-33. Tel 920-437-1979; Fax 920-437-8990.
School—St. Thomas More, (Grades PreK-8), 650 S. Irwin, 54301. Tel: 920-432-8242. Barbara Schneider, Prin. Consolidated with St. Francis Xavier Cathedral and SS. Peter & Paul. Religious 1; Lay Teachers 22; Students 255.
Catechesis/Religious Program—Tel: 920-432-2747. Mary (Nelson) Sedlacek, D.R.E. High school associated with St. John. Students 105.

11—ST. MATTHEW, Rev. Larry J. Seidl.
Res.: 130 St. Matthews St., 54301-2910 Tel: 920-435-6811; Fax: 920-435-0065.
School—2575 S. Webster Ave., 54301. Tel: 920-432-5223. Donald J. Graff, Prin. Religious 1; Lay Teachers 15; Students 198.
Catechesis/Religious Program—Michael Westenberg, D.R.E. Students 275.

12—NATIVITY OF OUR LORD, Revs. James A. Hablewitz; John W. Girotti; Deacons Manuel Torres; Michael E. Schmidt.
Res.: 2270 S. Oneida St., 54304-4712. Tel: 920-499-5156; Fax 920-490-9285.
Catechesis/Religious Program—Tel: 920-499-6012. James Whalen, D.R.E. Students 1,433.

13—ST. PATRICK, Rev. Msgr. Brian P. Coleman, J.C.L., Admin.
Res.: 211 N. Maple Ave., 54303-2749. Tel: 920-437-3911; Fax 920-437-3274.
Catechesis/Religious Program—Marjory E. Vander Steeg, D.R.E. Students 165.

14—SS. PETER AND PAUL, Rev. Thomas Farrell; Deacon Michael Vincent.
Res.: 710 N. Baird St., 54302-1902. Tel: 920-435-7548; Fax 920-432-1321.
School—St. Thomas More Elementary Consolidated with St. Mary of the Angels & St. Francis Xavier Cathedral. Sisters 1; Lay Teachers 24; SSPP Students 81.
School—St. Thomas More School System, (Grades PreK-8), 650 S. Irwin Ave., 54301. Tel: 920-432-8242. Mrs. Barbara Schneider, Prin. Lay Teachers 7; SSPP Students 42.
Catechesis/Religious Program—1420 Harvey St., 54302. Tel: 920-437-0651. Associated with Holy Martyrs (for Confirmation). Students 234.

15—ST. PHILIP THE APOSTLE, Rev. Lawrence J. Canavera; Deacon Kenneth Clark.
Res.: 312 Victoria St., 54302-2818. Tel: 920-468-7848; Fax 920-468-1025.
School—Tel: 920-468-7755. M. Suzanne Amtmann, Prin. Sisters 2; Lay Teachers 14; Students 279.
Catechesis/Religious Program—Tel: 920-468-4368. Mary VanDenHeuvel, D.R.E.; Lenore LeRoy, D.R.E. Students 354.

16—RESURRECTION, Rev. Paul E. Demuth; Deacons Michael Grzeca; Timothy Reilly.
Res.: 333 Hilltop Dr., 54301-2713. Tel: 920-336-7768; Fax 920-336-1949.
School—Tel: 920-336-3230. Rose Adler, Prin. Lay Teachers 18; Students 229.
Catechesis/Religious Program—Jane Lyon, D.R.E. Students 374.

17—ST. WILLEBRORD, Revs. Kenneth J. De Groot, O.Praem.; Gery G. Meehan, O.Praem.; Deacon Luis Sanchez.
Res.: 209 S. Adams St., 54301-4584. Tel: 920-435-2016; Fax 920-435-2039.

OUTSIDE THE CITY OF GREEN BAY

ABRAMS, OCONTO CO., ST. LOUIS, [JC], Served from St. John Cantius, Sobieski Rev. Gerald Prusakowski, O.F.M.
Mailing Address: 6051 Noble St., Sobieski, 54171-9724. Tel: 920-826-7425; Fax: 920-822-1859.
Catechesis/Religious Program—P.O. Box 87, 54101-0087. Tel: 920-822-8795. Donna Rae VanKauwenbergh, D.R.E. Associated with St. John Cantius, Sobieski. Students 65.

ALGOMA, KEWAUNEE CO., ST. MARY, [CEM], Also serves Holy Rosary, Kewaunee. Rev. William M. Kuhr, Admin.
Res.: 118 Church St., 54201-1033. Tel: 920-487-5005; Fax: 920-487-5002. Email: smp@itol.com.
School—214 Church St., 54201-1035. Tel: 920-487-5004. Mrs. Monica Nelson, Prin. Lay Teachers 9; Students 115.
Catechesis/Religious Program— Rosearn Kubicek, D.R.E. Students 130.

ALVERNO, MANITOWOC CO., ST. JOSEPH, Merged, with St. Casimir, Northeim; St. Isidore, Osman; and St. Wendel, Cleveland to form St. Thomas the Apostle, Northeim.

AMBERG, MARINETTE CO., ST. AGNES, Unassigned., Served from St. Augustine, Wausaukee. , Mailing Address: 507 Church St., Wausaukee, 54177-9749. Tel: 715-856-5276; Fax: 715-856-5276. In Res., Rev. Vincent Ssewagudde, Temp. Admin.
Catechesis/Religious Program—Tel: 920-856-5066. Sherri L. Schlies, D.R.E.

ANIWA, SHAWANO CO., ST. BONIFACE, [CEM], Served from St. Philomena, Birnamwood. Rev. Everard Scesney, O.F.M.
Res.: P.O. Box K, Birnamwood, 54414-0911. Tel: 715-449-2104.
Catechesis/Religious Program—Students 84.

ANTIGO, LANGLADE CO.

1—ST. HYACINTH, Merged, with St. Mary, Antigo to form SS. Mary & Hyacinth, Antigo.

2—ST. JOHN, [JC] Rev. Charles G. Hoffmann.
Res.: 426 Hudson St., 54409-2109. Tel: 715-623-2024; Fax: 715-627-0234.
School—All Saints Catholic School, 420 Fulton St., 54409. Tel: 715-623-4835. Marie A. Millsaps, Prin. Lay Teachers 12; Students 261.
Catechesis/Religious Program—Joyce Wagner, D.R.E. Students 249.

3—ST. MARY, Merged, with St. Hyacinth, Antigo to form SS. Mary & Hyacinth, Antigo.

4—SS. MARY & HYACINTH, [JC], Also serves St. Wenceslaus, Neva. (Has records for St. Mary and St. Hyacinth, Antigo) Rev. Jeremiah F. Worman; Deacon Thomas Hanley.
Res.: 734 Deleglise St., 54409-1424. Tel: 715-623-4938; Fax: 715-623-3202.
School—All Saints Catholic School, 723 Deleglise St. / 419 Fulton St., 54409. Tel: 715-623-4835; Fax: 715-627-2969. Marie A. Millsaps, Prin.
Catechesis/Religious Program—819 3rd Ave., 54409-1930. Tel: 715-623-5255. Thomas Hanley, D.R.E.; Susan Brettingen, D.R.E.

APPLETON, OUTAGAMIE CO.

1—ST. BERNADETTE, Rev. Harold L. Berryman; Deacon Michael A. Madden.
Church: 2331 E. Lourdes Dr., 54915-3615. Tel: 920-739-4157; Fax: 920-739-2795.
School—(ACES), Tel: 920-739-5391; Fax: 920-739-0061. Margaret Carey, Prin. Lay Teachers 26; Students 218.
Catechesis/Religious Program—Tel: 920-734-7502. Shirley Riley, D.R.E.; Peter Gagnon, D.R.E. Students 510.

2—ST. BERNARD, Rev. John P. Bergstadt; Deacons Maurice Reed; Robert Vincent. In Res., Rev. Michael Simonini.
Parish Center:—1617 W. Pine St., 54914-5118. Tel: 920-739-0331; Fax: 920-749-9771.
School—ACES/Xavier Educational System Inc., 101 E. Northland Ave., 54911. Tel: 920-735-9380; Fax: 920-735-1787. Sr. Patrice Hughes, S.C., Pres.
Catechesis/Religious Program—Tel: 920-739-8912. Jane Angha, D.R.E.; Lisa Hecht, D.R.E.; Pat Stefancic, D.R.E. Students 697.

3—ST. JOSEPH, Rev. Lawrence E. Abler, O.F.M.Cap.; Deacons Mark Farrell; Roy Baumruk. In Res., Rev. Kenneth Reinhart, O.F.M.Cap.
Res.: 404 W. Lawrence St., 54911-5817. Tel: 920-734-7195; Fax: 920-734-0227.
School—(ACES), 2626 N. Oneida St., 54914. Tel: 920-730-8849. Anthony Abts, Prin.
Catechesis/Religious Program—Tel: 920-738-7413. Mary Ann Bayer, D.R.E. Associated with St. Mary's, Appleton. Students 167.

4—ST. MARY, [CEM] Rev. Michael K. O'Rourke; Deacon William J. Burke.
Church: 312 S. State St., 54911-5930. Tel: 920-739-5119; Fax: 920-739-5111.
School—Catholic Central (ACES), 313 S. State St., 54911. Tel: 920-733-3709; Fax: 920-733-8142. Rosemary F. Perrino, Prin. Religious 1; Lay Teachers 23; Students 226.
Catechesis/Religious Program—404 W. Lawrence St., 54911. Tel: 920-738-7413. Mary Ann Bayer, D.R.E. Associated with St. Joseph-St. Mary Interparish. Students 307.

5—ST. PIUS X, Revs. Donald M. Zuleger; Mark Vander Steeg.
Office:—500 W. Marquette St., 54911-1917. Tel: 920-733-0575; Fax: 920-749-8056.
School—(ACES), Tel: 920-733-4918; Fax: 920-733-7269. Sr. Carol Jean Peterson, C.S.J., Prin. Lay Teachers 16; Students 332.
Catechesis/Religious Program—Tel: 920-733-4919. Carol Burns, D.R.E. Students 726.

6—SACRED HEART, Rev. Robert J. Karuhn; Deacons Gilbert Schmidt; Donald Gigure.

Res.: 222 E. Fremont St., 54915-1827. Tel: 920-739-3196; Fax: 920-739-4062.
School—Preschool (ACES), 101 E. Northland Ave., 54911. Tel: 920-735-9380.
Catechesis/Religious Program—Tel: 920-739-0889. Georgia M. Bretl, D.R.E.; Kelly Koszalinski, D.R.E. Students 304.

7—ST. THERESE, Rev. William A. Hoffman; Deacon Patrick J. Whitcomb.
Office:—213 E. Wisconsin Ave., 54911-4875. Tel: 920-733-8568; Fax: 920-954-5727.
School—(ACES), 101 E. Northland Ave., 54911. Tel: 920-735-9380; Fax: 920-735-1787. Sr. Patrice Hughes, S.C., Pres.

8—ST. THOMAS MORE, Rev. Gerald R. Falk; Deacons Donald J, Wetzel; Craig W. Merrick; Reinhart J. Wessing; Paul J. Klein.
Res.: 1810B N. McDonald St., 54911-3450. Tel: 920-739-7758; Fax: 920-739-2376.
School—1810 N. McDonald St., 54911. Tel: 920-739-7826; Fax: 920-739-1787. Mr. David L. Callan, Prin. Sisters 2; Lay Teachers 19; Students 229.
Catechesis/Religious Program—Tel: 920-739-8172. Irene Skarban, D.R.E. Students 415.
Convent—1226 E. Pauline St., 54911.

ARGONNE, FOREST CO., ST. MARY, Merged, with St. Joseph, Crandon.

ARMSTRONG CREEK, FOREST CO., ST. STANISLAUS KOSTKA, , Also serves St. Joan of Arc, Goodman. Rev. Edward S. Nowakowski.
Mailing Address: P.O. Box 39, 54103-0039. Tel: 715-336-2334.
Catechesis/Religious Program—Deborah Thompson, D.R.E. Associated with St. Joan of Arc, Goodman. Students 67.

ASKEATON, BROWN CO., ST. PATRICK, [CEM] Rev. Allen Geiser.
Res.: 7815 St. Patrick's Church Rd., Greenleaf, 54126-9611. Tel: 920-532-6665; Fax: 920-532-6665.
Catechesis/Religious Program—Tel: 920-735-4721. Terry Lark, D.R.E.

AURORA, FLORENCE CO., SACRED HEART, , Served from St. Anthony, Niagara Rev. Michael E. Betley.
Mailing Address: c/o 1432 River Rd., Niagara, 54151-1544. Tel: 715-251-3879; Fax: 715-251-3875.
Catechesis/Religious Program—P.O. Box 166, Florence, 54121. Tel: 715-528-4992. Students 63.

BAILEYS HARBOR, DOOR CO., ST. MARY OF THE LAKE, [CEM], Served from St. John the Baptist, Egg Harbor. Rev. Mathew J. Simonar.
Mailing Address: P.O. Box 49, Egg Harbor, 54209-0049. Tel: 920-868-3241; Fax: 920-868-1481.
Catechesis/Religious Program—Tel: 920-839-2041.

BAY SETTLEMENT, BROWN CO., HOLY CROSS, [CEM] Rev. Thomas A. Hagendorf, O.Praem.; Deacon Richard Nowak.
Res.: 3009 Bay Settlement Rd., 54311-7301. Tel: 920-468-0595; Fax: 920-468-4764.
School—3002 Bay Settlement Rd., 54311. Tel: 920-468-0625; Fax: 920-468-0625. Ms. Kathleen VanVonderen, Prin. Lay Teachers 10; Students 193.
Catechesis/Religious Program—Tel: 920-468-6554. Patricia Davister, D.R.E. Students 195.

BEAR CREEK, OUTAGAMIE CO., ST. MARY, [CEM], Served from St. Rose, Clintonville Rev. Donald E. Everts, Admin.; Deacons Thomas Jozwiak; Joseph Lehman.
Mailing Address: P.O. Box 27, 54922-0027. Tel: 715-752-4177; Fax: 715-752-3249.
Catechesis/Religious Program—Sr. Sandra Peterson, S.S.N.D., D.R.E.; Toni V. Tomlyanovich, D.R.E. Associated with St. Rose, Clintonville. Students 68.

BIRNAMWOOD, SHAWANO CO., ST. PHILOMENA, [CEM], Also serves St. Boniface, Aniwa Rev. Everard Scesney, O.F.M.
Res.: P.O. Box K, 54414-0911. Tel: 715-449-2104.
Catechesis/Religious Program—George Brunecker, D.R.E. Students 170.

BLACK CREEK, OUTAGAMIE CO., ST. MARY, [CEM] Rev. Theodore J. Hendricks.
Res.: P.O. Box 217, 54106-0217. Tel: 920-984-3319.
Catechesis/Religious Program—Rita Theobald, D.R.E.

BRILLION, CALUMET CO.

1—HOLY FAMILY, [JC], Merger of St. Mary, Brillion and St. Mary-St. Patrick, Reedsville. Rev. W. Thomas Long. Merger of St. Mary, Brillion and St. Mary-St. Patrick, Reedsville.
Res.: 1100 W. Ryan St., 54110-1074. Tel: 920-756-2535; Fax: 920-756-9802.
School—209 N. Custer St., 54110. Tel: 920-756-2502. Richard Krainz, Prin.
Catechesis/Religious Program—Roberta Whittaker, D.R.E.

2—ST. MARY, Merged, with St. Mary-St. Patrick, Reedsville to form Holy Family, Brillion.

BRUSSELS, DOOR CO.

1—ST. FRANCIS XAVIER, Merged, with St. Mary, Namur to form St. Francis-St. Mary, Brussels.

2—ST. FRANCIS-ST. MARY PARISH, [CEM 3], Merger of St. Francis Xavier, Brussels and St. Mary, Namur. (Has records for St. Francis Xavier, Brussels and St. Mary, Namur) Rev. Pius Cotter, O.F.M.Cap., Admin.
Res.: 9716 Cemetery Rd., 54204-9749. Tel: 920-825-7555; Fax: 920-825-1492.
Catechesis/Religious Program—Tel: 920-825-7713. Sue Johnson, D.R.E. Students 247.

CASCO/SLOVAN, KEWAUNEE CO., HOLY TRINITY, [CEM] Merged Rev. John F. Doerfler, J.C.L., S.T.L., Admin. Merger of Holy Trinity, Casco and Mission of St. Adalbert, Slovan. (Has records for Holy Trinity, Casco and St. Adalbert, Slovan)
Res.: 506 Church Ave., 54205-9712. Tel: 920-837-7531; Fax: 920-837-2361.
School—510 Church Ave., 54205-9700. Mrs. Kaye Jacobs, Prin. Lay Teachers 7; Students 111.
Catechesis/Religious Program—Timothy Younk, D.R.E. Students 152.

CECIL, SHAWANO CO., ST. MARTIN, [CEM], Served from Sacred Heart, Shawano Deacon Thomas Craig, Parish Dir.; Rev. Leonard M. Evers, Moderator.
Mailing Address: *Mailing Address:*, P.O. Box 144, 54111-0144. Tel: 715-745-6681; Fax: 715-745-4289. Church: 107 S. Warrington, P.O. Box 157, 54111.
Catechesis/Religious Program—Tel: 715-526-2023. Associated with Sacred Heart, Shawano.

CHAMPION, BROWN CO., ST. JOSEPH, [CEM] Unassigned. Rev. Milton M. Suess.
Mailing Address: 5996 County Rd. K, New Franken, 54229-9456. Tel: 920-866-9961. Served from Immaculate Conception, Luxemburg. (Has records for St. Amand, Walhain; St. Martin, Tonet and St. Odile, Thiry Daems)
Catechesis/Religious Program—Lisa Laurent, D.R.E. Students 125.

CHARLESBURG, CALUMET CO., ST. CHARLES BORROMEO, [CEM], Served from St. Mary, Chilton Revs. Gary New, S.D.S.; Thomas Akpen, C.S.SP., Part-time; Deacon Dennis Bennin.
Mailing Address: 62 E. Main St., Chilton, 53014-1428. Tel: 920-849-9363; Fax: 920-849-7270.
Catechesis/Religious Program—Tel: 920-849-4613. Associated with Chilton area parishes. See St. Mary, Chilton.

CHARLESTOWN, CALUMET CO., ST. MARTIN, [CEM], Served from St. Mary, Chilton Revs. Gary New, S.D.S.; Thomas Akpen, C.S.SP., Part-time; Deacon Dennis Bennin.
Mailing Address: 62 E. Main St., Chilton, 53014-1428. Tel: 920-849-9363; Fax: 920-849-7270.
School—Chilton Catholic, Tel: 920-849-4141. Mrs. Patricia Leuknecht, Prin. (Consolidated)
Catechesis/Religious Program—Tel: 920-849-4613. Associated with Chilton area parishes. See St. Mary, Chilton.

CHASE, OCONTO CO., ST. JOSEPH, [CEM], Served from St. John Cantius, Sobieski. Rev. Gerald Prusakowski, O.F.M.
Res.: 6051 Noble St., Sobieski, 54171-9724. Tel: 920-822-5255; Fax: 920-822-1859.
Catechesis/Religious Program—Tel: 920-822-8795. Donna Rae VanKauwenbergh, D.R.E. Associated with St. John Cantius, Sobieski.

CHILTON, CALUMET CO.

1—ST. AUGUSTINE, [CEM], Served from St. Mary, Chilton. Revs. Gary New, S.D.S.; Thomas Akpen, C.S.SP., Part-time; Deacon Dennis Bennin.
Mailing Address: 62 E. Main St., 53014-1428. Tel: 920-849-9363; Fax: 920-849-7270.
School—Chilton Catholic, 60 E. Washington St., 53014. Tel: 920-849-4141. Mrs. Patricia Leuknecht, Prin. (Consolidated)
Catechesis/Religious Program—Tel: 920-849-4613. Associated with Chilton area parishes. See St. Mary, Chilton.

2—ST. MARY, [CEM], Also serves St. Augustine, Chilton; St. Charles Borromeo, Charlesburg; St. Elizabeth, Kloten; St. Martin, Charlestown; and Holy Trinity, Jericho Revs. Gary New, S.D.S.; Thomas Akpen, C.S.SP., Part-time; Deacon Dennis Bennin.
Res.: 62 E. Main St., 53014-1428. Tel: 920-849-9363; Fax: 920-849-7270.
School—Chilton Catholic, 60 E. Washington St., 53014. Tel: 920-849-4141. Mrs. Patricia Leuknecht, Prin. (Consolidated) Sisters 1; Lay Teachers 10; Students 155.
Catechesis/Religious Program—Tel: 920-849-4613. Consolidated with all area parishes. Students 574.

CLARKS MILLS, MANITOWOC CO., IMMACULATE CONCEPTION, [CEM] Rev. James R. Jugenheimer (PH); Deacon Thomas J. Koch.
Res.: 15 S. County Rd. J, Cato, 54230-8329. Tel: 920-775-4365; Fax: 920-775-4365.
School—, Formerly St. Mary, 19 S. County Rd. J, Cato, 54230. Tel: 920-775-4366. Patricia Dougherty, Prin. Franciscan Sisters of Christian Charity 4; Lay Teachers 5; Students 88.
Catechesis/Religious Program—Tel: 920-775-4876. Teresa Pederson, D.R.E. (Elementary). Students 116.

CLEVELAND, MANITOWOC CO., ST. WENDEL, Merged, with St. Isidore, Osman; St. Joseph, Alverno; and St. Casimir, Northeim to form St. Thomas the Apostle, Northeim.

CLINTONVILLE, WAUPACA CO., ST. ROSE, [CEM], Also serves St. Mary, Bear Creek Rev. Donald E. Everts, Admin.; Deacons Joseph Lehman; Thomas Jozwiak.
Res.: 24 7th St., 54929-1733. Tel: 715-823-3416; Fax: 715-823-3249.
School—140 Auto St., 54929. Tel: 715-823-4360; Fax: 715-823-7160. Robert Bootz, Prin. Lay Teachers 9; Students 77.
Catechesis/Religious Program—P.O. Box, Bear Creek, 54922. Tel: 715-823-5266. Dawn Kratzke, D.R.E. Students 149.

COLEMAN, MARINETTE CO.

1—ST. FRANCIS OF ASSISI, Merged, with St. Wenceslaus, Klondike to form SS. Francis-Wenceslaus, Coleman.

2—SS. FRANCIS-WENCESLAUS, [CEM 2], (Has records for St. Leo, Pound; St. John, Coleman; St. Francis of Assisi, Coleman and St. Wenceslaus, Klondike) Rev. Lawrence Marto.
Res.: 228 E. Main St., 54112-9407. Tel: 920-897-3226; Fax: 920-897-4677.
Catechesis/Religious Program—Joyce M. Woulf, D.R.E. Students 221.

COMBINED LOCKS, OUTAGAMIE CO., ST. PAUL, [CEM] Rev. Robert H. Vandenberg; Deacon George Schraufnagel.
Res.: 410 Wallace St., 54113-1128. Tel: 920-788-4553; Fax: 920-788-6822. Email: stpaulcl@aol.com.
Catechesis/Religious Program—Tel: 920-788-5711. Deborah Peters, D.R.E. Students 254.

COOPERSTOWN, MANITOWOC CO., ST. JAMES, [CEM] Rev. Ronald A. Colombo; Deacon Clarence Naidl. Served from All Saints, Denmark.
Res.: 18228 County Rd. R, Denmark, 54208-9554. Tel: 920-863-2585; Fax: 920-863-5445.
Catechesis/Religious Program—Susan Angoli, D.R.E. Students 224.

CRANDON, FOREST CO., ST. JOSEPH, , Also serves St. Ambrose, Wabeno. (Has records for St. Mary, Argonne and St. Michael Station, Hiles) Rev. Ralph J. Gillis.
Res.: 208 N. Park Ave., 54520-1351. Tel: 715-478-3396.
Catechesis/Religious Program—Lynn Edwards-Barker, D.R.E. Students 155.

CRIVITZ, MARINETTE CO., ST. MARY, [CEM], Also serves Station at Caldron Falls Rev. Donald R. Burkart.
Mailing Address: P.O. Box 159, 54114-0159. Tel: 715-854-2501.
Catechesis/Religious Program—Students 265.

DARBOY, OUTAGAMIE CO. (APPLETON P.O.), HOLY ANGELS, [CEM] Rev. Thomas Pomeroy.
Res.: W2796 County Hwy. KK, Appleton, 54915-9407. Tel: 920-733-6214; Fax: 920-733-5440.
School—Tel: 920-733-2651. Sue Simonsen, Prin. Religious 1; Lay Teachers 16; Students 280.
Catechesis/Religious Program—W2806 County Rd., KK, Appleton, 54915. Tel: 920-734-6470. Sr. Elise Cholewinski, D.R.E. Students 311.

DE PERE, BROWN CO.

1—ST. BONIFACE, Merged, with St. Joseph, De Pere to form Our Lady of Lourdes, De Pere.

2—ST. FRANCIS XAVIER, [JC] Rev. V. Anthony Dolski.
Res.: 220 S. Michigan St., 54115-2730. Tel: 920-336-1813; Fax: 920-336-1814.

3—ST. JOSEPH, Merged, with St. Boniface, De Pere to form Our Lady of Lourdes, De Pere.

4—ST. MARY, [JC] Rev. John H. Harper.
Mailing Address: P.O. Box 70, 54115-0070. Tel: 920-337-2330; Fax: 920-337-2332.
School—Notre Dame, 100 S. Huron St., 54115. Tel: 920-337-1103. Mary Vanden Busch, Prin. Consolidated with St. Francis Xavier, De Pere. Sisters of St. Francis of the Holy Cross 1; Lay Teachers 26; Students 484.
Catechesis/Religious Program—Jennifer Nooker, D.R.E.; Jean Stein, D.R.E. Students 266.

5—ST. NORBERT COLLEGE, Revs. Brian J. Prunty, O.Praem.; Salvatore H. Cuccia, O.Praem.
Mailing Address: 100 Grant St., 54115-2099. Tel: 920-403-3010; Fax: 920-403-4432.
Res.: 402 3rd St., 54115-2142. Tel: 920-403-3010; Fax: 920-403-4432.
Catechesis/Religious Program—Tel: 920-403-3559. Daniel Robinson, D.R.E. Students 78.

6—OUR LADY OF LOURDES (1996), [CEM], Has records for St. Joseph, De Pere and St. Boniface, De Pere Rev. Conrad J. Kratz, O.Praem.; Deacons Michael D. Vander Bloomen; Harvey Quinette.
Res.: 1307 Lourdes Ave., 54115-1018. Tel: 920-336-4033; Fax: 920-336-3910.
School—1305 Lourdes Ave., 54115-1018. Tel: 920-336-3091; Fax: 920-337-6806. Mrs. Susan Sands, Prin. Lay Teachers 25; Students 311.

Catechesis/Religious Program—Tel: 920-337-0443. Mrs. Karen Nienhaus, D.R.E. Students 407.

DENMARK, BROWN CO., ALL SAINTS, [CEM] Rev. Ronald A. Colombo. Also serves St. James, Cooperstown and Holy Trinity Mission, New Denmark.
Res.: P.O. Box 787, 54208-0787. Tel: 920-863-2357; Fax: 920-863-5425.
School—Tel: 920-863-2449. Deanna Johnson, Prin. Lay Teachers 8; Students 112.
Catechesis/Religious Program—Tel: 920-863-5256. Lori Wagner, D.R.E.; Mary Burns-Carriveau, D.R.E. Associated with Holy Trinity, New Denmark. Students 191.

DYCKESVILLE, KEWAUNEE CO., ST. LOUIS, [CEM 2] Sr. Marlene M. Dimmerling, O.P., Dir.; Rev. Joseph L. Bestler, Moderator & Sacramental Min.
Res.: N8726 County Line Rd., Luxemburg, 54217-8629. Tel: 920-866-2410; Fax: 920-866-3591.
School—N8710 County Line Rd., Luxemburg, 54217. Tel: 920-866-2611. Mrs. Mary Rechek, Prin. Lay Teachers 6; Students 60.
Catechesis/Religious Program—Tel: 920-866-2842. Mrs. Kathleen Cornette, D.R.E. Students 125.

EATON, BROWN CO., SS. CYRIL AND METHODIUS, Merged, with Our Lady Queen of Peace, Humboldt to form St. Thomas the Apostle, Humboldt

EGG HARBOR, DOOR CO., ST. JOHN THE BAPTIST, [CEM], Also serves St. Mary of the Lake, Baileys Harbor; St. Paul, Fish Creek; St. Michael, Jacksonport; St. Rosalia, Sister Bay; and the Station at Washington Island Rev. Mathew J. Simonar.
Mailing Address: P.O. Box 49, 54209-0049. Tel: 920-868-3241; Fax: 920-868-1481.

ELAND, SHAWANO CO., ST. WILLIAM, Merged, with Holy Family, Wittenberg to form Holy Family-St. William, Wittenberg.

ELCHO, LANGLADE CO., HOLY FAMILY, [CEM], Also serves St. Mary Mission, Pickerel and SS James/Stanislaus, White Lake/Langlade Rev. Roger W. Strebel, Admin.
Mailing Address: P.O. Box 128, 54428-0128. Tel: 715-275-3750.

FISH CREEK, DOOR CO., ST. PAUL, [CEM], Served from St. John the Baptist, Egg Harbor Rev. Mathew J. Simonar.
Mailing Address: P.O. Box 49, Egg Harbor, 54209-0049. Tel: 920-868-3241; Fax: 920-868-1481.

FLINTVILLE, BROWN CO., SS. EDWARD AND ISIDORE, [CEM] Rev. David D. Kasperek; Deacon Earl Kunzer.
Office:—3752 Elm Tree Rd., 54313.
Res.: 3667 Flintville Rd., 54313-8330. Tel: 920-865-7844; Fax: 920-865-4375.
Catechesis/Religious Program—Tel: 920-865-7677. June Ingold, D.R.E. Students 656.

FLORENCE, FLORENCE CO., IMMACULATE CONCEPTION, [CEM], Served from St. Anthony, Niagara Sr. Marla J. Clercx, A.N.G., Dir.; Rev. Michael E. Betley, Moderator, Sacramental Min.
Res.: P.O. Box 166, 54121-0166. Tel: 715-528-3310; Fax: 715-528-3052.
Catechesis/Religious Program—Tel: 715-582-4992. Sr. Marla J. Clercx, A.N.G., D.R.E. Students 139.

FRANCIS CREEK, MANITOWOC CO., ST. ANNE, [CEM], Also serves St. Augustine, Kossuth Rev. Paul Paider.
Res.: P.O. Box 217, 54214-0217. Tel: 920-682-6640.
School—202 Packer Dr., P.O. Box 218, 54214. Tel: 920-682-1454. Mr. Charles Vaughan, Prin. Franciscan Sisters of Christian Charity 4; Lay Teachers 4; Students 95.
Catechesis/Religious Program—803 Forest Home Dr., 54214. Tel: 920-682-4393. Linda Klessig, D.R.E. Students 109.

FREEDOM, OUTAGAMIE CO., ST. NICHOLAS, [CEM] Rev. Dennis M. Ryan; Deacon Donald Newhouse.
Res.: N4088 County Rd. E., Kaukauna, 54130-7592. Tel: 920-788-1492; Fax: 920-788-1492.
School—W2035 County Rd. S., Kaukauna, 54130. Tel: 920-788-9371. Phyllis G. Techlin, Prin. Lay Teachers 12; Students 189.
Catechesis/Religious Program—Tel: 920-788-1451. Sr. Charlene Hockers, D.R.E. Students 355.

GILLETT, OCONTO CO., ST. JOHN, [CEM] Rev. John M. Gallagher; Deacon William Doran.
Res.: P.O. Box 377, 54124-0377. Tel: 920-855-2542.
Catechesis/Religious Program—Wendy Wozniak, D.R.E. Students 122.
Station—Chute Lake, Chute Lake Station P.O. Box 248, Suring, 54174-248.

GLENMORE, BROWN CO., IMMACULATE CONCEPTION, Merged, with St. Mary, Stark to form St. Mary, Glenmore/Stark.

GLENMORE/STARK, BROWN CO., ST. MARY, [CEM 2], Merger of Immaculate Conception, Glenmore and St. Mary, Stark. (Has records for St. Mary, Stark) Rev. Lee J. Kahrs, B.A.
Mailing Address: 5840 Big Apple Rd., De Pere, 54115-9766. Tel: 920-864-7641.
Catechesis/Religious Program—Denis Lotto, D.R.E.

GOODMAN, MARINETTE CO., ST. JOAN OF ARC, , Served from St. Stanislaus Kostka, Armstrong Creek Rev. Edward S. Nowakowski.
Mailing Address: P.O. Box 39, Armstrong Creek, 54103-0039. Tel: 715-336-2334.
Catechesis/Religious Program—Deborah Thompson, D.R.E. Associated with St. Stanislaus Kosta, Armstrong Creek. Students 50.

GREENLEAF, BROWN CO., ST. MARY, [CEM 2] Rev. Robert J. Eabat, J.C.L.
Res.: 2212 Day St., 54126-9200. Tel: 920-864-2550; Fax: 920-864-2979.
School—2218 Day St., 54126-9200. Tel: 920-864-2586. Gloria Kennedy, Prin. Religious 1; Lay Teachers 6; Students 64.
Catechesis/Religious Program—Michael Lotto, D.R.E. Students 159.

GREENVILLE, OUTAGAMIE CO., ST. MARY, [CEM] Deacons David DeYoung; Richard Miech.
Mailing Address: N2385 Municipal Dr., 54942-9713. Tel: 920-757-6555; Fax: 920-757-6560.
Res.: N2343 Municipal Dr., 54942. Tel: 920-757-6333.
School—(Grades PreK-8), N2387 Municipal Dr., 54942. Tel 920-757-5516. Steve T. Zangl, Prin. Lay Teachers 10; Students 158.
Catechesis/Religious Program—Lee Ann Lella, D.R.E. Students 305.

GRESHAM, SHAWANO CO., ST. FRANCIS SOLANUS, [CEM], Served from St. Michael, Keshena Rev. David S. Barrett, Admin.
Mailing Address: P.O. Box 177, 54128-0177. Tel: 715-787-3250.
Catechesis/Religious Program—Sr. Mary S. Brunner, D.R.E. Students 63.

HILBERT, CALUMET CO., ST. MARY, [CEM], Served from St. John-Sacred Heart, Sherwood Rev. Kenneth R. Frozena.
Res.: P.O. Box 386, 54129-0386. Tel: 920-853-3252.
School—P.O. Box 249, 54129-0249. Tel: 920-853-3216. Laura M. Hill, Prin. Religious 1; Lay Teachers 4; Students 51.
Catechesis/Religious Program—Eugene Sinner, D.R.E. Students 155.

HOFA PARK, SHAWANO CO., ST. STANISLAUS, [CEM], Served from Assumption BVM, Pulaski Rev. Patrick Gawrylewski, O.F.M., Admin.
Res.: W1888 Hofa Park Rd., Seymour, 54165-9510. Tel: 920-822-5512; Fax: 920-822-8030.
Catechesis/Religious Program—N1302 Maple Rd., Seymour, 54165-9506. Tel: 920-822-5650. Deanne Wilinski, D.R.E. Students 69.

HOLLANDTOWN, BROWN CO., ST. FRANCIS, [CEM], Served from Holy Cross, Kaukauna Rev. John T. Mullarkey; Deacon Gerald Kuborn.
Res.: 433 County Rd. CE, Kaukauna, 54130-8964. Tel: 920-766-1222.
School—431 County Rd. CE, Kaukauna, 54130. Tel: 920-766-3469. Ms. Laurie Fale, Prin. Franciscan Sisters of Christian Charity 2; Lay Teachers 5; Students 54.
Catechesis/Religious Program—Sharon Bouressa, D.R.E.; Jacqueline Wallace, D.R.E.

HORTONVILLE, OUTAGAMIE CO., SS. PETER AND PAUL, [CEM] Deacon Kenneth D. Bilgrien.
Res.: P.O. Box 238, 54944-0238. Tel: 920-779-6133; Fax: 920-779-6164.
Catechesis/Religious Program—105 N. Olk St., 54944-0238. Tel: 920-779-0551. Sr. Clarice Sevegney, O.P., D.R.E. Students 214.

HOWARD, BROWN CO., ST. JOHN THE BAPTIST, [CEM] Revs. William D. Swichtenberg, Co-Pastor; Gregory J. Smith, Co-Pastor; Deacons James M. Patton; Nicholas Williams.
Res.: 2597 Glendale Ave., 54313-6821. Tel: 920-434-2145; Fax: 920-434-5015.
School—2561 Glendale Ave., 54313. Tel: 920-434-3822; Fax: 920-434-5016. Kay L. Franz, Prin. Lay Teachers 21; Students 342.
Catechesis/Religious Program—880 Cardinal Ln., 54313. Tel: 920-434-2417. Patricia Vanden Boogaard, D.R.E.; Margaret Mary Schiffer, D.R.E. Students 652.

HUMBOLDT, BROWN CO.

1—OUR LADY QUEEN OF PEACE, Merged, with SS. Cyril & Methodius, Eaton to form St. Thomas the Apostle, Humbolt.

2—ST. THOMAS THE APOSTLE, [JC 4], Also serves St. Kilian, New Franken. (Has records for SS Cyril & Methodius, Eaton and Our Lady Queen of Peace, Humboldt Rev. Dean W. Dombroski.
Res.: 5930 Humboldt Rd., Luxemburg, 54217-9325. Tel: 920-863-6113; Fax: 920-845-5180
Catechesis/Religious Program—3041 S. County Rd. T, 54311. Tel: 920-863-5297. Betty Schwandt, D.R.E. Students 229.

INSTITUTE, DOOR CO., SS. PETER AND PAUL, [CEM], Served from St. Joseph, Sturgeon Bay Deacon Roger Madsen.
Res.: 4767 E. Dunn Rd., Sturgeon Bay, 54235-8822. Tel: 920-743-4842; Fax: 920-743-3885.
School—4761 Dunn Rd., Sturgeon Bay, 54235. Tel: 920-743-6335. Michael W. Taylor, Prin. Sisters of St. Francis of the Holy Cross 1; Lay Teachers 6; Students 119.

ISAAR, OUTAGAMIE CO., ST. SEBASTIAN, [CEM] Rev. David K. Ashbeck, Admin.
Res.: N9269 Isaar Rd., Seymour, 54165-9428. Tel: 920-833-2558.
Catechesis/Religious Program—Ms. Chris Stedl, D.R.E. Students 161.

JACKSONPORT, DOOR CO., ST. MICHAEL, [CEM], Served from St. John the Baptist, Egg Harbor Rev. Mathew J. Simonar.
Mailing Address: P.O. Box 49, Egg Harbor, 54209-0049. Tel: 920-868-3241; Fax: 920-868-1481. Served from St. John the Baptist, Egg Harbor.

JERICHO, CALUMET CO., HOLY TRINITY, [CEM] Revs. Gary New, S.D.S.; Thomas Akpen, C.S.SP., Part-time; Deacon Dennis Bennin.
Mailing Address: 62 E. Main St., Chilton, 53014-1428. Tel: 920-849-9363; Fax: 920-849-7270. Served from St. Mary, Chilton.
Catechesis/Religious Program—Tel: 920-849-4613.

KAUKAUNA, OUTAGAMIE CO.

1—ST. ALOYSIUS, Rev. David R. Schmidt, Admin.; Deacon Peter Reinl.
Res.: 2401 Main Ave., 54130-3599. Tel: 920-766-5111; Fax: 920-766-5229.
School—Kaukauna Catholic Schools System, Tel: 920-766-5199. Gayle Reider, Prin. Franciscan Sisters of Christian Charity 3; Lay Teachers 12; Students 125.
Catechesis/Religious Program—Tel: 920-766-5379. Maxine Geiger, D.R.E. Students 309.

2—HOLY CROSS, [CEM], Also serves St. Francis, Hollandtown Revs. John T. Mullarkey; James Lucas; Deacon Gerald Kuborn.
Res.: 309 Desnoyer St., 54130-2103. Tel: 920-766-3773; Fax: 920-766-3774.
School—Kaukauna Catholic Schools System, 220 Doty St., 54130-2188. Tel: 920-766-0186. Sr. Camilla Wolfgram, O.S.F., Prin. Sisters 5; Lay Teachers 14; Students 237.
Catechesis/Religious Program—212 Doty St., 54130-2108. Tel: 920-766-3510. Sharon Bouressa, D.R.E.; Jacqueline Wallace, D.R.E. Students 502.

3—ST. MARY OF THE ANNUNCIATION, [JC] Rev. Robert Udulutsch, O.F.M.Cap.; Deacons Randall Haak; Steven VandeHey. In Res., Revs. Leopold Gleissner, O.F.M.Cap.; Kieran Hickey, O.F.M.Cap.
Res.: 119 W. 7th St., 54130-2356. Tel: 920-766-1445; Fax: 920-766-1476.
School—Kaukauna Catholic Schools System, 112 W. 8th St., 54130. Tel: 920-766-1545. Mrs. Rita A. Schmidt, Prin. Sisters 1; Lay Teachers 13; Students 153.
Catechesis/Religious Program—Tel: 920-766-1545. Jean Olson, D.R.E. Students 369.
Convent—Franciscan Sisters of Christian Charity, Tel: 414-766-2952.

KELLNERSVILLE, MANITOWOC CO., ST. JOSEPH, [CEM 2] Sr. Marlene Greatens, A.N.G., Parish Dir.; Rev. Ronald A. Colombo, Moderator; Rev. Msgr. Robert F. Gulig, Sacramental Min.
Res.: P.O. Box 27, 54215-0027. Tel: 920-732-3770; Fax: 920-732-3770.
Catechesis/Religious Program—Tel: 920-732-3462. Jane Kalies, D.R.E. Students 68.

KESHENA, MENOMINEE CO., ST. MICHAEL, (Native American), [CEM], Also serves St. Francis Solanus, Gresham Rev. David S. Barrett.
Mailing Address: P.O. Box 610, 54135-0610. Tel: 715-799-3811; Fax: 715-799-5092.
Catechesis/Religious Program—Tel: 715-799-3234. Students 113.

KEWAUNEE, KEWAUNEE CO., HOLY ROSARY, [CEM] Rev. William M. Kuhr.
Res.: 521 Juneau St., 54216-1397. Tel: 920-388-2285; Fax: 920-388-3822.
School—519 Kilbourn St., 54216. Tel: 920-388-2431. Jeff Williams, Prin. Lay Teachers 11; Students 175.
Catechesis/Religious Program—Theresa Vandervest, D.R.E. Students 178.

KIEL, MANITOWOC CO., SS. PETER AND PAUL, [CEM] Rev. Loren Nys, S.D.S.; Deacon Bernard P. Knier. In Res., Bro. Paul Bauer, S.D.S.; Rev. Cletus LaMere, S.D.S.
Res.: 413 Fremont St., 53042-1398. Tel: 920-894-3553; Fax: 920-894-4462.
School—423 Fremont St., 53042. Tel: 920-894-3533; Fax: 920-894-4959. Dr. Wayne T. Haasl, Prin. Sisters 2; Lay Teachers 9; Students 135.
Catechesis/Religious Program—409 Fremont St., 53042. Tel: 920-894-2280. Mary Jo Meyer, D.R.E. Students 254.

KIMBERLY, OUTAGAMIE CO., HOLY NAME OF JESUS, [CEM] Deacon Cyril J. Klister.
Res.: 602 E. Kimberly Ave., 54136-1599. Tel: 920-788-7640; Fax: 920-788-7658.
School—614 E. Kimberly Ave., 54136. Tel: 920-788-7650. Jeanine Leege-Jankowski, Prin. Lay Teachers 24; Students 276.

Catechesis/Religious Program—Tel: 920-788-7655. Mary A. Jasiak, D.R.E. Students 436.

KING, WAUPACA CO., ST. GEORGE, Closed., For inquiries for parish records, please see St. Mary Magdalene, Waupaca.

KLONDIKE, OCONTO CO., ST. WENCESLAUS, Merged, with St. Francis of Assisi, Coleman, to form SS. Francis-Wenceslaus, Coleman.

KLOTEN, CALUMET CO., ST. ELIZABETH, [CEM] Revs. Gary New, S.D.S.; Thomas Akpen, C.S.SP., Part-time; Deacon Dennis Bennin.
Mailing Address: 62 E. Main St., Chilton, 53014-1428. Tel: 920-849-9363; Fax: 920-849-7270. Served from St. Mary, Chilton.
Catechesis/Religious Program— Associated with Chilton area parishes. See St. Mary, Chilton.

KOSSUTH, MANITOWOC CO., ST. AUGUSTINE, [CEM], Served from St. Anne, Francis Creek Rev. Paul Paider.
Mailing Address: P.O. Box 217, Francis Creek, 54214-0217. Tel: 920-682-6640.
Catechesis/Religious Program—Linda Klessig, D.R.E. Associated with St. Anne, Francis Creek.

KRAKOW, SHAWANO CO., ST. CASIMIR, [CEM] Rev. James Esser, O.F.M.
Mailing Address: P.O. Box 66, 54137-0066. Tel: 920-899-3621.
Catechesis/Religious Program—William Mihalski, D.R.E. Students 106.

KROK, KEWAUNEE CO., ST. JOHN, Merged, with St. Joseph, Montpelier to form St. Joseph-St. John, Montpelier.

LAKEWOOD, OCONTO CO., ST. MARY OF THE LAKE, [CEM] Unassigned.
Res.: P.O. Box 219, 54138-0219. Tel: 715-276-7364.
Catechesis/Religious Program—Students 75.
Station—Crooked Lake, Crooked Lake Station
Station—Silver Cliff, Silver Cliff Station

LANGLADE, LANGLADE CO., ST. STANISLAUS KOSTKA, Merged, with St. James, White Lake to form SS. James-Stanislaus, White Lake.

LAONA, FOREST CO., ST. LEONARD, [JC], Also serves St. Norbert, Long Lake and St. Hubert Mission, Newald Rev. John W. Cerkas.
Res.: 5330 Beech St., 54541-9340. Tel: 715-674-3241; Fax: 715-674-3401.
Catechesis/Religious Program—Tel: 715-674-3306. Cynthia Beairl, D.R.E. Students 137.

LEBANON TOWNSHIP, WAUPACA CO., ST. PATRICK, [CEM] Rev. Msgr. Dennis M. Lally, B.A., Admin.
Res.: N5705 County Rd. T, New London, 54961-8464. Tel: 920-982-5475.
Catechesis/Religious Program—Diane Urban, D.R.E. Students 99.

LENA, OCONTO CO., ST. CHARLES BORROMEO, Merged, with Sacred Heart, Spruce to form Holy Cross, Lena.

LENA/SPRUCE, OCONTO CO., HOLY CROSS, [JC 2], Merger of (and holder of records for) St. Charles Borromeo, Lena and Sacred Heart, Spruce. Deacon Byron Otradovec.
Res.: P.O. Box 30, 54139-0030. Tel: 920-829-5222.
Catechesis/Religious Program—Theresa M. Alberts, D.R.E. Students 211.

LEOPOLIS, SHAWANO CO., ST. MARY, [CEM] Rev. Harry G. Hafeman.
Res.: P.O. Box 39, 54948-0039. Tel: 715-787-3377.
Catechesis/Religious Program—P.O. Box 38, 54948-0038. Students 64.

LINCOLN, KEWAUNEE CO., ST. PETER, Merged, with St. Hubert, Rosiere to form St. Peter-St. Hubert, Rosiere.

LITTLE CHUTE, OUTAGAMIE CO., ST. JOHN NEPOMUCENE, [CEM] Rev. Msgr. James Vanden Hogen; Deacon Vincent DeGroot.
Res.: 323 Pine St., 54140-1854. Tel: 920-788-9061; Fax: 920-687-0851.
School—328 Grand Ave., 54140. Tel: 920-788-9082. Holly Rottier, Co-Prin.; Mary Terrien, Co-Prin. Sisters 4; Lay Teachers 25; Students 584.
Catechesis/Religious Program—325 Pine St., 54140-1854. Tel: 920-788-9033. Nancy Schmoll, D.R.E. Students 533.

LITTLE SUAMICO, OCONTO CO., ST. PIUS, , Served from St. Benedict, Suamico Rev. Gary J. Dantinne.
Mailing Address: P.O. Box 66, Suamico, 54173-0066. Tel: 920-434-2024; Fax: 920-622-2301.
Catechesis/Religious Program—Joan Koehne, D.R.E. Students 80.

LONG LAKE, FLORENCE CO., ST. NORBERT, , Served from St. Leonard, Laona Rev. John W. Cerkas.
Res.: 5330 Beech St., Laona, 54541-9340. Tel: 715-674-3241.
Catechesis/Religious Program—Cynthia Beairl, D.R.E. Associated with St. Leonard, Laona.

LUXEMBURG, KEWAUNEE CO., IMMACULATE CONCEPTION, [CEM], Also serves St. Joseph, Champion Rev. Milton M. Suess.
Res.: 1412 Main St., 54217-1308. Tel: 920-845-2056; Fax: 920-845-5581.
School—St. Mary, 1406 Main St., 54217-1308. Tel: 920-845-2224. William Matchefts, Prin. Lay Teachers 8; Students 161.
Catechesis/Religious Program—Lee Treml, D.R.E. Students 232.

MACKVILLE, OUTAGAMIE CO., ST. EDWARD, [CEM] Rev. Charles R. Brooks.
Res.: N2921 State Rd. 47, Appleton, 54913-9564. Tel: 920-733-9266; Fax: 920-733-7964.
School—N2944 State Rd. 47, Appleton, 54913-9564. Tel: 920-733-6276. Candee L. Schmalzer, Prin. Lay Teachers 6; Students 45.
Catechesis/Religious Program—Tel: 920-733-6070. Sabrina G. Schmidt, D.R.E. Students 232.

MANAWA, WAUPACA CO., SACRED HEART, [JC], Served from SS. Peter & Paul, Weyauwega Rev. Bertin L. Samsa, O.F.M.Cap., Admin.
Res.: P.O. Box 10, 54949-0010. Tel: 920-596-3323; Fax: 920-596-3323.
Catechesis/Religious Program—Sr. Marie Rose VanDeurzen, S.S.N.D., D.R.E. Students 118.

MANITOWOC, MANITOWOC CO.

1—ST. ANDREW, Rev. Camillus W. Janas, O.F.M.
Res.: 1416 Grand Ave., 54220-6130. Tel: 920-682-0023; Fax: 920-682-1452.
School—Manitowoc Area Catholic System, Formerly St. Francis Xavier, 1418 Grand Ave., 54220. Tel: 920-682-0802. Joseph L. Steepleton, Prin. See Consolidated Schools under Institutions Located in the Diocese. Religious 2; Lay Teachers 11; Students 216.
Catechesis/Religious Program—1001 Marshall St., 54220. Tel: 920-683-3897. Christine Kouba, D.R.E. Associated with St. Boniface, St. Paul, St. Mary, and St. Andrew. Students 60.

2—ST. BONIFACE, , Served from St. Andrew, Manitowoc Rev. Camillus W. Janas, O.F.M. In Res., Rev. Richard H. Klingeisen.
Res.: 1110 S. 10th St., 54220-5212. Tel: 920-684-3718; Fax: 920-652-0659.
School—Member of MACS For further information please see Manitowoc Area Catholic System, Manitowoc
Catechesis/Religious Program—1001 Marshall St., 54220. Tel: 920-683-3897. Christine Kouba, D.R.E. Associated with St. Paul, St. Mary & St. Andrew. Students 60.

3—HOLY INNOCENTS, Rev. Gerald J. Foley; Deacons Robert L. Beehner; Paul Kieffer; Kenneth R. Nelesen.
Res.: 1121 N. 14th St., 54220-3236. Tel: 920-682-0031; Fax: 920-682-1096.
School—St. Francis de Sales, 1408 Waldo Blvd., 54220. Tel: 920-682-0802. Joseph L. Steepleton, Prin. See Consolidated Schools under Institutions Located in the Diocese. Religious 1; Lay Teachers 22; Students 381.
Catechesis/Religious Program—1122 N. 14th St., 54220. Tel: 920-684-4313. Claudia A. Malley, D.R.E. Students 354.

4—ST. MARY, Rev. Thomas Wojciechowski, O.F.M.; Deacons Phillip Andrastek; Robert Drobka. In Res., Rev. Joachim Swarick, O.F.M.
Res.: 1114 S. 21st St., 54220-4917. Tel: 920-684-3558; Fax: 920-684-3255.
School—St. Frances Cabrini Middle School (MACS) For further information please see Manitowoc Area Catholic System, Manitowoc
Catechesis/Religious Program—1110 S. 10th St., 54220. Tel: 920-683-3867. Christine Kouba, D.R.E. Associated with St. Boniface, Manitowoc. Students 210.

5—ST. PAUL, Rev. Ronald P. Reimer; Deacons Alan Boeldt; William D. Klein.
Res.: 712 S. 24th St., 54220-4498. Tel: 920-684-6714.
School—Member of MACS For further information please see Manitowoc Area Catholic System, Manitowoc
Catechesis/Religious Program—1110 S. 10th St., 54220. Tel: 920-684-3718. Christine Kouba, D.R.E. Associated with St. Boniface, St. Mary, St. Andrew. Students 72.

6—SACRED HEART, [JC] Rev. David Hoffman, Admin.; Deacon Richard Bahnaman.
Res.: 702 State St., 54220-4034. Tel: 920-684-8692; Fax: 920-684-8667.
School—-Member of MACS For further information please see St. Andrew, Manitowoc
Catechesis/Religious Program—702 State St., 54220-4034. Tel: 920-683-2165. Barbara K. Kratz, D.R.E. Students 220.

MAPLE GROVE, MANITOWOC CO., ST. PATRICK, Merged, with St. Mary, Reedsville to form St. Mary-St. Patrick, Reedsville.

MAPLEWOOD, DOOR CO., ST. MARY, [CEM 2] Rev. Wilbert L. Buhl.
Mailing Address: P.O. Box 308, 54226-0308. Tel: 920-856-6440.
Catechesis/Religious Program—Students 209.

MARCHAND, DOOR CO., ST. FRANCIS DE PAUL (Duvall), Closed., For inquiries for parish records contact St. Louis, Dyckesville.

MARINETTE, MARINETTE CO.

1—ST. ANTHONY, Merged, with St. Joseph, Sacred Heart, and Our Lady of Lourdes, Marinette to form Holy Family, Marinette.

2—HOLY FAMILY, [CEM 2], Has records for St. Anthony, St. Joseph, Our Lady of Lourdes and Sacred Heart, Marinette) Rev. Joseph E. Dorner; Deacons Mark Gribowski; Jerome Thetreau.
Office:—1223 Carney Blvd., 54143-2512. Tel: 715-735-9100; Fax: 715-735-9650.
School—1232 Garfield Ave., 54143. Tel: 715-735-7174; Fax: 715-735-7146. Mrs. Patricia E. Lane, Prin. Students 210.
Catechesis/Religious Program—Martha A. Karban, D.R.E. Students 470.

3—ST. JOSEPH, Merged, with Our Lady of Lourdes, St. Anthony, and Sacred Heart, Marinette to form Holy Family, Marinette.

4—OUR LADY OF LOURDES, Merged, with St. Joseph, St. Anthony, and Sacred Heart, Marinette to form Holy Family, Marinette.

5—SACRED HEART CONGREGATION, Merged, with St. Anthony, St. Joseph, and Our Lady of Lourdes, Marinette to form Holy Family, Marinette.

MARION, WAUPACA CO., ST. MARY, [CEM], Served from St. Anthony, Tigerton Rev. Charles G. Hoffmann, Moderator; Deacon Kenneth Sambs.
Mailing Address: P.O. Box 206, 54950-0206. Tel: 715-754-2116; Fax: 715-754-2116.
Catechesis/Religious Program—P.O. Box 106, Tigerton, 54486-0106. Jon Ann Kasson, D.R.E. Associated with St. Anthony, Tigerton. Students 87.

MATTOON, SHAWANO CO., HOLY FAMILY, [CEM], Served from St. Anthony, Neopit Rev. R. David Kiefer; Deacon Thomas Hartman.
Mailing Address: P.O. Box 21, 54450-0021. Tel: 715-489-3330.
Catechesis/Religious Program—P.O. Box 73, Phlox, 54464-0073. Tel: 715-489-3418. Joyce Fuller, D.R.E.

MENASHA, WINNEBAGO CO.

1—ST. JOHN, [CEM] Rev. Paul J. Radetski, Admin.; Deacon Gerald Cross.
Res.: 516 De Pere St., 54952-2899. Tel: 920-722-8922; Fax: 920-729-9248.
School—Twin City Catholic Education System For further information please see St. Gabriel the Archangel, Neenah
Catechesis/Religious Program—628 Fifth St., 54952. Tel: 920-722-4830. Deborah A. Spielbauer, D.R.E. Students 163.

2—ST. MARY, [CEM] Rev. Paul J. Radetski; Deacon Gerald Cross.
Res.: 528 2nd St., 54952-3112. Tel: 920-725-7714; Fax: 920-725-7612.
School—Twin City Catholic Education System For further information please see St. Gabriel the Archangel, Neenah
Catechesis/Religious Program—Tel: 920-722-6491. Cathy Hein, D.R.E. Students 175.

3—ST. PATRICK, [JC] Rev. Roy J. Geenen; Deacon Howard R. Bricco.
Res.: 324 Nicolet Blvd., 54952-3334. Tel: 920-725-8381; Fax: 920-725-5544.
School—Seton Catholic Middle School For further information please see St. Gabriel the Archangel, Neenah
Catechesis/Religious Program—Barbara Mauthe, D.R.E. Students 205.

MISHICOT, MANITOWOC CO., HOLY CROSS, [JC] Rev. John C. Neuser.
Res.: 423 S. Main St., 54228-9777. Tel: 920-755-2550.
School—423 Church St., 54228. Tel: 920-755-2487. Joseph Stodola, Prin. Lay Teachers 6; Students 102.
Catechesis/Religious Program—3210 Tannery Rd., Two Rivers, 54241. Tel: 920-793-1755. Corrine Duffek, D.R.E. Students 180.

MONTPELIER, KEWAUNEE CO.

1—ST. JOSEPH, Merged, with St. John, Krok to form St. Joseph-St. John, Montpelier.

2—ST. JOSEPH-ST. JOHN, Merged, with St. Lawrence, Stangelville and St. Hedwig, West Kewaunee to form St. Therese de Lisieux, Stangelville.

NAMUR, DOOR CO., ST. MARY, Merged, with St. Francis Xavier, Brussels to form St. Francis-St. Mary, Brussels.

NAVARINO, SHAWANO CO., ST. LAWRENCE, [CEM] Sr. Charlotte Rebbe, O.P., Parish Dir.; Revs. David K. Ashbeck, Moderator; Theodore J. Hendricks.
Res.: W5125 State Hwy. 156, Bonduel, 54107-8614. Tel: 715-758-8161; Fax: 715-758-7562.
Catechesis/Religious Program—Sr. Charlotte Rebbe, D.R.E. Students 90.

NEENAH, WINNEBAGO CO.

1—ST. GABRIEL, [JC] Rev. Richard L. Allen.
Res.: 900 Geiger St., 54956-2302. Tel: 920-722-4914; Fax: 920-722-2566.
School—Twin City Catholic Education System, 1050 Zephyr Dr., 54956-1389. Tel: 920-722-7796. Julie Klein, Prin. Lay Teachers 18; Students 224.

Catechesis/Religious Program—Tel: 920-725-0660. Kurt Grube, D.R.E. Students 688.

2—ST. MARGARET MARY, [JC] Rev. David J. Koch; Deacon Norman Spielbauer.
Res.: 439 Washington Ave., 54956-3340. Tel: 920-729-4560; Fax: 920-729-4572.
Church: 666 Division St., 54956-3398.
School— For further information please see St. Gabriel the Archangel, Neenah
Catechesis/Religious Program—Tel: 920-729-4562. Jeannine Goggin, D.R.E.; Sr. Diane Baumann, D.R.E. Students 230.

NEOPIT, MENOMINEE CO., ST. ANTHONY, [CEM], Also serves St. Joseph, Phlox and Holy Family, Mattoon Rev. R. David Kiefer; Deacon Thomas W. Hartman.
Mailing Address: P.O. Box 241, 54150-0241. Tel: 715-756-2361; Fax: 715-756-2756.
Catechesis/Religious Program—Tel: 715-756-2218. Charlotte Ann Wagner, D.R.E. Students 104.

NEVA, LANGLADE CO., ST. WENCESLAUS, [CEM], Served from SS. Mary & Hyacinth, Antigo Rev. Jeremiah F. Worman; Deacon Thomas Hanley.
Mailing Address: P.O. Box 50, Deerbrook, 54424-0050. Tel: 715-627-2126.
Res.: N5340 Church Rd., Deerbrook, 54424-9413. Tel: 715-623-7019.
School—All Saints Catholic School For further information please see Ss Mary & Hyacinth Parish, Antigo Marie A. Millsaps, Admin.
Catechesis/Religious Program—Students 160.

NEW DENMARK, BROWN CO., HOLY TRINITY, [CEM], Served from All Saints, Denmark Rev. Ronald A. Colombo.
Res.: P.O. Box 787, Denmark, 54208-0787. Tel: 920-863-2357; Fax: 920-863-5425.
Catechesis/Religious Program—Tel: 920-863-5256. Mary L. Burns-Carriveau, D.R.E.

NEW FRANKEN, BROWN CO., ST. KILIAN, [CEM], Served from St. Thomas the Apostle, Humboldt Rev. Dean W. Dombroski.
Res.: P.O. Box 83, 54229-0083. Tel: 920-866-3541.
Catechesis/Religious Program—Nancy Meltzer, D.R.E. Students 122.

NEW HOLSTEIN, CALUMET CO., HOLY ROSARY, [CEM], Also serves St. Ann, St. Anna. Rev. Donald Weber (GR) (Retired).
Res.: 1724 Madison St., 53061-1326. Tel: 920-898-4884; Fax: 920-898-4884.
School—1814 Madison St., 53061-1347. Tel: 920-898-4210; Fax: 920-898-4220. Lawrence Konetzke, Prin. Sisters 4; Lay Teachers 10; Students 150.
Catechesis/Religious Program—Tel: 920-898-9248. Andrew Glaza, D.R.E. Students 158.

NEW LONDON, WAUPACA CO., MOST PRECIOUS BLOOD, [CEM] Rev. David J. Lewis.
Res.: 808 S. Pearl St., 54961-1863. Tel: 920-982-2346.
School—102 E. Washington St., 54961. Tel: 414-982-2134. Mr. Donald Stuebs, Prin. Lay Teachers 12; Students 156.
Catechesis/Religious Program—Kim A. Schroeder, D.R.E.; Ellen Clarke, D.R.E. Students 332.

NEWALD, ARGONNE CO., ST. HUBERT, , Served from St. Leonard, Laona Rev. John W. Cerkas.
Res.: 5330 Beech St., Laona, 54541-9340. Tel: 715-674-3241; Fax: 715-674-3401.
Catechesis/Religious Program—Cynthia Beairl, D.R.E.

NEWTON, MANITOWOC CO., ST. THOMAS THE APOSTLE (2000), [CEM] Rev. David B. Beaudry.
Res.: 8100 Brunner Rd., 53063-9607. Tel: 920-726-4228; Fax: 920-726-4229.
Catechesis/Religious Program—Tel: 920-726-4287. Pamela Fischer, D.R.E.

NIAGARA, MARINETTE CO., ST. ANTHONY, , Also serves St. Margaret, Pembine; Immaculate Conception, Florence; and Sacred Heart, Aurora Rev. Michael E. Betley.
Res.: 1432 River St., 54151-1544. Tel: 715-251-3879; Fax: 715-251-3875.
Catechesis/Religious Program—Dawn L. Johnson, D.R.E. Students 251.

NORMAN, KEWAUNEE CO., ST. JOSEPH, Merged, with Nativity of the Blessed Virgin Mary, Tisch Mills to form St. Isidore the Farmer, Tisch Mills.

NORTHEIM, MANITOWOC CO., ST. CASIMIR, Merged, with St. Joseph, Alverno; St. Wendel, Cleveland; and St. Isidore, Osman to form St. Thomas the Apostle, Northeim.

OCONTO FALLS, OCONTO CO., ST. ANTHONY, [CEM], Also serves from St. Patrick, Stiles Mrs. Patricia DeGroot, Parish Dir.; Rev. Msgr. James E. Dillenburg, Moderator; Rev. Harold A. Beerntsen, Sacramental Min.
Church: 239 N. Franklin St., 54154-1042. Tel: 920-846-2276; Fax: 920-846-8254.
School—253 N. Franklin St., 54154. Tel: 414-846-2276; Fax: 920-846-8254. Ms. Rosemary Marifke, Prin. Lay Teachers 5; Students 48.
Catechesis/Religious Program—Tina Meyer, D.R.E. Associated with St. Patrick, Stiles. Students 191.

OCONTO, OCONTO CO.

1—HOLY TRINITY (1996),, (Has records for St. Joseph, Oconto and St. Peter, Oconto Rev. David Ruby; Deacon Walter P. Kaszynski.
Res.: 716 Madison St., 54153-1668. Tel 920-835-5900; Fax: 920-835-5907.
Catechesis/Religious Program—Jan Vande Hei, D.R.E.

2—ST. JOSEPH, Merged, with St. Peter, Oconto to form Holy Trinity, Oconto.

3—ST. PETER, Merged, with St. Joseph, Oconto to form Holy Trinity, Oconto.

OMRO, WINNEBAGO CO., ST. MARY, Rev. Joseph A. Mattern.
Res.: 233 E. Scott St., 54963-1705. Tel: 920-685-2258; Fax: 920-685-7343.
Catechesis/Religious Program—Jane Abalan, D.R.E. Students 218.

ONEIDA TOWNSHIP, OUTAGAMIE CO., IMMACULATE CONCEPTION, [CEM], Served from St. John the Baptist, Howard Revs. Gregory J. Smith; William D. Swichtenberg.
Res.: N5889 County Rd. E., De Pere, 54115-8529. Tel: 920-869-2626.
Catechesis/Religious Program—Tel: 920-869-2950. Rochelle Bastien, D.R.E. Students 83.

ONEIDA, BROWN CO., ST. JOSEPH, [CEM], Served from St. John the Baptist, Howard Revs. William D. Swichtenberg; Gregory J. Smith.
Res.: 145 St. Joseph Dr., 54155-8914. Tel: 920-869-2244.
Catechesis/Religious Program—Tel: 920-869-2219. Darlene Wertel, D.R.E.; Mary Van Schyndel, D.R.E. Students 258.

OSHKOSH, WINNEBAGO CO.

1—ST. JOHN, [JC], Also serves St. Vincent de Paul, Oshkosh Rev. William L. Van De Kreeke.
Res.: 434 W. South Park Ave., 54902-6597. Tel: 920-231-3596; Fax: 920-237-0432.
Unified Catholic Schools of Oshkosh—Business Office: 110 N. Sawyer St., 54902-5657. Tel: 920-426-3626.
Catechesis/Religious Program—450 W 12th Ave., 54902. Tel: 920-231-7526. Robin Flanigan, D.R.E. Students 232.

2—ST. JOSAPHAT, Rev. Robert Stegmann.
Res.: 1333 Walnut St., 54901-3655. Tel: 920-235-3363; Fax: 920-235-3863.
Unified Catholic Schools of Oshkosh—Business Office: 110 N. Sawyer St., 54902-5657. Tel: 920-426-3626.
Catechesis/Religious Program—Tel: 920-235-3371. Mary Wichmann, D.R.E. Students 173

3—ST. MARY, Sr. Judith Ann Miller, C.S.J., Parish Dir.; Revs. Thomas Reynebeau, Moderator; Robert Stegmann, Sacramental Min.; Deacon Robert Penzenstadler.
Res.: 432 Monroe St., 54901-5146. Tel: 920-231-5317; Fax: 920-231-1344.
Unified Catholic Schools of Oshkosh—
Catechesis/Religious Program—Tel: 920-235-4266. Mrs. Jenny Thorn, D.R.E. Students 150.
Convent—441 Boyd St., 54901-5135. Tel: 414-231-3388.

4—ST. PETER, [JC] Rev. Robert Kollath; Deacon Joseph F. Gates.
Res.: 449 High Ave., 54901-4708. Tel: 920-231-9782; Fax: 920-231-9808.
School—(Unified Catholic Schools of Oshkosh), 110 N. Sawyer St., 54901. Tel: 920-426-3626. Mr. Stan Spanbauer, Prin.
Catechesis/Religious Program—Tel: 920-235-6156. Patricia Birling, D.R.E. Students 274

5—ST. RAPHAEL THE ARCHANGEL, [JC] Rev. Daniel J. Felton.
2355 W. Ninth Ave., 54904. Tel: 920-235-7158.
Church & Mailing Address: 830 S. Westhaven Dr., 54904-7977. Tel: 920-233-8044; Fax: 920-233-2360.
School—(Unified Catholic Schools of Oshkosh), 110 N. Sawyer St., 54902-5657. Tel: 920-235-5670. Mr. Stan Spanbauer, Pres.
Catechesis/Religious Program—Amy Matz, D.R.E.; Sr. Pamela A. Biehl, O.S.F., D.R.E. Students 785.

6—SACRED HEART, [CEM] Rev. Thomas Reynebeau; Deacon Frederick C. Fischer.
Res.: 1020 W. 6th Ave., 54902-5732. Tel: 920-235-2073; Fax: 920-235-7412.
(Unified Catholic Schools of Oshkosh)—Business Office: 110 N. Sawyer St., 54902-5657. Tel: 920-426-3626.
Catechesis/Religious Program—Tel: 920-235-5236. Cynthia Hable, D.R.E. Students 112

7—ST. VINCENT DE PAUL, [JC], Served from St. John, Oshkosh Rev. William L. Van De Kreeke; Deacon Raymond Brandenstein.
Res.: 1216 W. South Park Ave., 54902-6538. Tel: 920-231-8855; Fax: 920-237-0432.
School—St. Elizabeth Seton Elementary, 110 N. Sawyer St., 54902-3626. Tel: 920-426-3626. Mr. Stan Spanbauer, Prin. (Part of the Unified Catholic Schools of Oshkosh.) Religious 1; Lay Teachers 10; Students 233.

Catechesis/Religious Program—James Rasmussen, D.R.E. Students 109.

OSMAN, MANITOWOC CO., ST. ISIDORE, Merged, with St. Wendel, Cleveland; St. Joseph, Alverno; and St. Casimir, Northeim to form St. Thomas the Apostle, Northeim.

PEMBINE, MARINETTE CO., ST. MARGARET, , Served from St. Anthony, Niagara Rev. Michael E. Betley.
Mailing Address: P.O. Box 235, 54156-0235. Tel: 715-251-3879; Fax: 715-251-3875.
Res.: 1432 River St., Niagara, 54151-1544.
Catechesis/Religious Program—N18844 Hwy. 141 & 8, 54156. Tel: 715-324-5595. Tamie England, D.R.E.

PESHTIGO, MARINETTE CO., ST. MARY, , Also serves St. Edward, Wagner and St. Joseph, Walsh Rev. James P. Massart.
Res.: 171 S. Wood Ave., 54157-1426. Tel: 715-582-3876; Fax: 715-582-0970.
School—141 S. Wood, 54157. Tel: 715-582-4041. Frank C. Kotecki, Prin. Sisters 1; Lay Teachers 7; Students 89.
Catechesis/Religious Program—717 S. Wood Ave., 54157. Tel: 715-582-4897. Alice A. Boyce, D.R.E. Students 251.

PHLOX, LANGLADE CO., ST. JOSEPH, [CEM], Served from St. Anthony, Neopit Rev. R. David Kiefer; Deacon Thomas Hartman.
Mailing Address: P.O. Box 73, 54464-0073. Tel: 715-489-3330.
Catechesis/Religious Program—Eileen Hartl, D.R.E. Students 83.

PICKEREL, LANGLADE CO., ST. MARY MISSION, [CEM], Served from Holy Family, Elcho Rev. Roger W. Strebel, Admin.
Mailing Address: P.O. Box 77, 54465-0077. Tel: 715-275-3750.
Catechesis/Religious Program—P.O. Box 128, Elcho, 54428-0128. Tel: 715-484-2732. Sherri Thiede, D.R.E.

PINE GROVE, BROWN CO., HOLY TRINITY, [CEM] Rev. Ronald C. Belitz. In Res., Rev. Finian Zaucha, O.F.M.
Res.: 4767 Stagecoach Rd., Denmark, 54208-9181. Tel: 920-863-2545.
Catechesis/Religious Program—JoAnne Adrians, D.R.E. Students 340.

PLAINFIELD, WAUSHARA CO., ST. PAUL, [CEM] Unassigned.
Res.: 622 S. Beach St., 54966-9637. Tel: 715-335-4314; Fax: 715-335-6016.
Catechesis/Religious Program—Kate Drmolka, D.R.E. Students 200.

POY SIPPI, WAUSHARA CO., SACRED HEART OF JESUS, , Served from St. Mark, Redgranite Rev. Jerome J. Taddy.
Mailing Address: P.O. Box 273, Redgranite, 54970-0273. Tel: 920-566-4442; Fax: 920-566-4559.
Catechesis/Religious Program—Karen Neuman, D.R.E.; Barb Niklinski, D.R.E.

PULASKI, BROWN CO., ASSUMPTION OF THE BLESSED VIRGIN MARY, [CEM], Also serves St. Stanislaus, Hofa Park Revs. Patrick Gawrylewski, O.F.M., Admin.; Brendan Wroblewski, O.F.M.; Deacon Dennis G. Majewski.
Res.: P.O. Box 379, 54162-0379. Tel: 920-822-3279; Fax: 920-822-8030.
School—109 E. Pulaski St., 54162. Tel: 920-822-5650; Fax: 920-822-8003. Mrs. Deanne Wilinski, Prin. Sisters 2; Lay Teachers 10; Students 125.
Catechesis/Religious Program—Deanne Wilinski, D.R.E. Students 290.

REDGRANITE, WAUSHARA CO., ST. MARK, [CEM], Also serves Sacred Heart of Jesus, Poy Sippi Rev. Jerome J. Taddy.
Mailing Address: P.O. Box 273, 54970-0273. Tel: 920-566-4442; Fax: 920-566-4559.
Catechesis/Religious Program—Karen Neuman, D.R.E. Students 72.

REEDSVILLE, MANITOWOC CO.

1—ST. MARY, Merged, with St. Patrick's, Maple Grove to form St. Mary-St. Patrick, Reedsville.

2—ST. MARY-ST. PATRICK, Merged, with St. Mary, Brillion to form Holy Family, Brillion.

ROSIERE, KEWAUNEE CO., ST. HUBERT, Merged, with St. Peter, Lincoln to form St. Peter-St. Hubert, Rosiere.

ROSIERE/LINCOLN, KEWAUNEE CO., ST. PETER-ST. HUBERT, [JC 4], Merger of St. Peter, Lincoln and St. Hubert, Rosiere. (Has records for St. Peter, Lincoln) Rev. Dennis G. Drury.
Res.: E3085 County Rd. X, Casco, 54205-9787. Tel: 920-837-2852.
Catechesis/Religious Program—Donna L. Bredael, D.R.E. Students 279.

ST. ANNA, CALUMET CO., ST. ANN, [CEM], Served from Holy Rosary, New Holstein Rev. Donald Weber (GR) (Retired).
Res.: N188 School St., New Holstein, 53061-9776. Tel: 920-894-3147; Fax: 920-894-3147.
Catechesis/Religious Program—1724 Madison St., New Holstein, 53061-1326. Tel: 920-894-3166. June

Winkel, D.R.E. Students 54.

ST. JOHN, CALUMET CO., ST. JOHN THE BAPTIST, Merged, with Sacred Heart, Sherwood, to form St. John-Sacred Heart, Sherwood.

ST. NAZIANZ, MANITOWOC CO., ST. GREGORY, [CEM], Also serves Holy Trinity, School Hill. Rev. Gregory Coulthard, S.D.S.; Deacon James Steffen.
Mailing Address: P.O. Box 199, 54232-0199. Tel: 920-773-2511; Fax: 920-773-3086.
School—212 School St., 54232. Tel: 920-773-2530. Rosie Bartel, Prin. Lay Teachers 10; Students 90.
Catechesis/Religious Program—11928 Marken Rd., Kiel, 53042. Tel: 920-849-9045. Rosie Bartel, D.R.E. Students 154.

SCHOOL HILL, MANITOWOC CO., HOLY TRINITY, [CEM], Served from St. Gregory, St. Nazianz Rev. Gregory Coulthard, S.D.S.; Deacon James Steffen.
Res.: 11928 Marken Rd., Kiel, 53042-9731. Tel: 920-773-2380.
Catechesis/Religious Program—11928 Marken Rd., Kiel, 53042. Tel: 920-773-2380. Rosemary G. Bartel, D.R.E. Students 168.

SEYMOUR, OUTAGAMIE CO., ST. JOHN, [CEM] Rev. Martin F. Fox, Admin.; Deacons Paul Grimm; Orvell A. DeBruin.
Mailing Address: 915 Ivory St., 54165-1629.
Res.: 915 Ivory St., 54165-1629. Tel: 920-833-6140; Fax: 920-833-7098.
School—928 S. Main St., 54165. Tel: 920-833-2122; Fax: 920-833-6568. Jaclyn J. Behnke, Prin. Lay Teachers 8; Students 109.
Catechesis/Religious Program—1002 S. Main St., 54165. Tel: 920-833-2504. Mary Carter, D.R.E. Students 222.

SHAWANO, SHAWANO CO., SACRED HEART, [CEM 2] Rev. Leonard M. Evers.
Office & Mailing Address: 321 S. Sawyer St., 54166-2437. Tel: 715-526-2023; Fax: 715-526-4105.
Res.: 321 S. Sawyer St., 54166-2437. Tel: 715-526-4106.
School—124 E. Center St., 54166-2499. Tel: 715-526-5328. Lois R. Maczuzak, Prin. Lay Teachers 13; Students 220.
Catechesis/Religious Program—Mary Ellen Waldvogel, D.R.E. Students 350.

SHERWOOD, CALUMET CO.
1—ST. JOHN-SACRED HEART, Rev. Kenneth R. Frozena.
Res.: N369 Military Rd., 54169-9661. Tel: 920-989-1515; Fax: 920-989-8585.
School—N361 Military Rd., 54169. Tel: 920-989-1373. Kerry Sievert, Prin. Lay Teachers 9; Students 125.
Catechesis/Religious Program—Tel: 920-989-2400. Eugene Sinner, D.R.E. Students 113.
2—SACRED HEART, Merged, with St. John the Baptist, St. John to form St. John-Sacred Heart, Sherwood.

SHIOCTON, OUTAGAMIE CO., ST. DENIS, [CEM], Also serves St. Patrick, Stephensville Sr. Pauline Feiner, S.D.S., Parish Dir.; Rev. Dennis M. Ryan, Moderator.
Mailing Address: N5591 2nd St., 54170-8652. Tel: 920-986-3369; Fax: 920-986-3634.
Catechesis/Religious Program—Tel: 920-757-5090. Mrs. Donna Cherry, D.R.E. Students 166.

SISTER BAY, DOOR CO., ST. ROSALIA, [CEM], Served from St. John the Baptist, Egg Harbor Rev. Mathew J. Simonar.
Mailing Address: P.O. Box 49, Egg Harbor, 54209-0049. Tel: 920-854-5264; Fax: 920-868-1481.

SLOVAN, KEWAUNEE CO., ST. ADALBERT, Merged, with Holy Trinity, Casco.

SOBIESKI, OCONTO CO., ST. JOHN CANTIUS, [CEM], Also serves St. Joseph, Chase, and St. Louis, Abrams. Rev. Gerald Prusakowski, O.F.M.
Res.: 6051 Noble St., 54171-9724. Tel: 920-822-5255; Fax: 920-822-1859.
Catechesis/Religious Program—Tel: 920-822-8795. Donna Rae VanKauwenbergh, D.R.E. Students 101.

SOUTH BRANCH, MENOMINEE RESERVATION, ST. JOSEPH OF THE LAKE, Closed. For inquiries for parish records contact the chancery.

SPRUCE, OCONTO CO., SACRED HEART OF JESUS, Merged, with St. Charles Borromeo, Lena to form Holy Cross, Lena.

STANGELVILLE, KEWAUNEE CO.
1—ST. LAWRENCE, Merged, with St. Joseph-St. John, Montpelier and St. Hedwig, West Kewaunee to form St. Therese de Lisieux, Stangelville.
2—ST. THERESE DE LISIEUX (2000), [JC], Has records for St. Joseph-St. John, Montpelier/Krok; St. Lawrence, Strangelville and St. Hedwig, West Kewaunee) Rev. C. Terrence LaCombe, Admin.
Mailing Address: N2085 County Rd. AB, Denmark, 54208-7705. Tel: 920-863-8747; Fax: 920-863-5768.
Catechesis/Religious Program—Anna Mae Schlies, D.R.E.

STEPHENSVILLE, OUTAGAMIE CO., ST. PATRICK, [CEM], Served from St. Denis, Shiocton Sr. Pauline Feiner, S.D.S., Parish Dir.; Rev. Dennis M. Ryan, Moderator.
Res.: N3686 State Rd. 76, Hortonville, 54944-8320. Tel: 920-757-5090; Fax: 920-986-3634.
Catechesis/Religious Program—Mrs. Donna Cherry, D.R.E. Students 120.

STILES, OCONTO CO., ST. PATRICK, [JC], Served from St. Anthony, Oconto Falls Mrs. Patricia DeGroot, Parish Dir.; Rev. Msgr. James E. Dillenburg, Moderator; Rev. Harold A. Beerntsen, Sacramental Min.
Res.: 5246 St. Patrick's Rd., Lena, 54139-9105. Tel: 920-834-2575; Fax: 920-834-2575.
Catechesis/Religious Program—253 N. Franklin, Oconto Falls, 54154. Tel: 920-846-2276. Tina Meyer, D.R.E. Associated with St. Anthony, Oconto Falls. Students 51.

STOCKBRIDGE, CALUMET CO., ST. MARY, [CEM], Served from St. John-Sacred Heart, Sherwood/ Saint John Rev. Kenneth R. Frozena.
Res.: P.O. Box 8, 53088-0008. Tel: 920-439-1515.
Catechesis/Religious Program—Tel: 920-989-2400. Eugene Sinner, D.R.E. Students 125.

STURGEON BAY, DOOR CO.
1—CORPUS CHRISTI, [JC] Rev. Anthony J. Birdsall; Deacon Paul Zenefski.
Oratory— [JC] Mailing Address & Oratory: 25 N. Elgin Ave., 54235-2963. Tel: 920-743-4716; Fax: 920-743-3711.
Res.: 722 W. Maple St., 54235.
School—15 N. Elgin Ave., 54235. Tel: 920-743-4144; Fax: 920-743-3157. Jan Scoville, Prin. Lay Teachers 9; Students 171.
Catechesis/Religious Program—Amy Alberts, D.R.E. Students 169.
2—ST. JOSEPH, , Also serves SS. Peter & Paul, Institute Rev. Dominic Peluse, S.C.J.; Deacons Roger Madsen; Kenneth L. Hunsader.
Church & Office Address: 526 Louisiana St., 54235-1738. Tel: 920-743-2062; Fax: 920-743-6786.
School—130 N. 5th Ave., 54235. Tel: 920-743-9219; Fax: 920-743-9297. Richard C. Aebly, Prin. Lay Teachers 11; Students 112.
Catechesis/Religious Program—Pamela Marsh, D.R.E. Students 263.

SUAMICO, BROWN CO., ST. BENEDICT, [CEM], Also serves St. Pius, Little Suamico. Rev. Gary J. Dantinne; Deacon John Maloney.
Mailing Address: P.O. Box 66, 54173-0066. Tel: 920-434-2024; Fax: 920-662-2301.
Catechesis/Religious Program—Tel: 920-434-1219. Betty Nier, D.R.E. Students 143.

SURING, OCONTO CO., ST. MICHAEL, [CEM], Served from St. John, Gillett Rev. John M. Gallagher, Admin.; Deacon William Doran.
Mailing Address: P.O. Box 248, 54174-0248. Tel: 920-842-2580.
Catechesis/Religious Program—Tel: 920-842-9825. Dee Kramer, D.R.E. Students 128.

THIRY DAEMS, KEWAUNEE CO., ST. ODILE, Closed., For inquiries for parish records, please see St. Joseph, Champion.

TIGERTON, SHAWANO CO., ST. ANTHONY, , Also serves St. Mary, Marion and Holy Family-St. William, Wittenberg/Eland Rev. Charles G. Hoffmann, Moderator; Deacons Kenneth Sambs; Hilary Hayek.
Mailing Address: P.O. Box 206, 54486-0206. Tel: 715-535-2571; Fax: 715-535-2953.
Catechesis/Religious Program—Tel: 715-535-2067. Rosalie Dudzik, D.R.E. Students 70.

TISCH MILLS, MANITOWOC CO.
1—ST. ISIDORE THE FARMER (2002),, (Has records for St. Joseph, Norman and Nativity of the BVM, Tisch Mills Rev. Joseph R. Coopmans, O.Praem., Admin.
Mailing Address: 18424 Tisch Mills Rd., Denmark, 54208-9508. Tel: 920-776-1555; Fax: 920-776-1555.
Catechesis/Religious Program—Christal Wavrunek, D.R.E.
2—NATIVITY OF THE BLESSED VIRGIN MARY, Merged, with St. Joseph, Norman to form St. Isidore the Farmer, Tisch Mills.

TONET, KEWAUNEE CO., ST. MARTIN, Closed., For inquiries for parish records, please see St. Joseph, Champion.

TWO RIVERS, MANITOWOC CO.
1—HOLY REDEEMER - SACRED HEART (2000), Merged, with St. Luke and St. Mark, Two Rivers to form St. Peter the Fisherman, Two Rivers.
2—ST. LUKE, Merged, with St. Mark and Holy Redeemer-Sacred Heart, Two Rivers to form St. Peter the Fisherman, Two Rivers.
3—ST. MARK, Merged, with St. Luke and Holy Redeemer-Sacred Heart, Two Rivers to form St. Peter the Fisherman, Two Rivers.
4—MOST HOLY REDEEMER, Merged, with Sacred Heart, Two Rivers to form Holy Redeemer-Sacred Heart, Two Rivers.
5—SACRED HEART, Merged, with Most Holy Redeemer, Two Rivers to form Holy Redeemer-Sacred Heart, Two Rivers.

TWO RIVERS, MANITOWOK CO., ST. PETER THE FISHERMAN (2002), [CEM], Merger of St. Luke, St. Mark and Holy Redeemer-Sacred Heart, Two Rivers Rev. William O'Brien; Deacon Kenneth T. Coenen.
Mailing Address: 3218 Tannery Rd., 54241-1699. Tel: 920-793-4531; Fax: 920-793-8067.
School—Two Rivers Catholic Schools (TRCCS), 2203 12th St., 54241.
Catechesis/Religious Program—Sr. Jacqueline Spaniola, O.S.F., D.R.E.

WABENO, FOREST CO., ST. AMBROSE, [CEM], Served from St. Joseph, Crandon Rev. Ralph J. Gillis; Deacon Harold Orlowski.
Mailing Address: P.O. Box 280, 54566-0280. Tel: 715-473-2511.
Catechesis/Religious Program—Linda McEwen, D.R.E. Students 67.

WAGNER, MARINETTE CO., ST. EDWARD, [CEM], Served from St. Mary, Peshtigo. Rev. James P. Massart.
Res.: W3308 County Rd. G, Porterfield, 54159-9736. Tel: 715-789-2254; Fax: 715-789-2293.
Catechesis/Religious Program—Tel: 715-735-9228. Alice A. Boyce, D.R.E.

WALHAIN, KEWAUNEE CO., ST. AMAND, Closed., For inquiries for parish records, please see St. Joseph, Champion.

WALSH, MARINETTE CO., ST. JOSEPH, [CEM], Served from St. Mary, Peshtigo. Rev. James P. Massart.
Res.: W3308 County Rd. G, Porterfield, 54159-9736. Tel: 715-789-2254; Fax: 715-789-2293.
Catechesis/Religious Program—W5303 County Rd. G, Porterfield, 54159. Tel: 715-735-9228. Alice A. Boyce, D.R.E.

WAUPACA, WAUPACA CO., ST. MARY MAGDALENE, [CEM] Rev. John J. Becker.
Office & Mailing Address: 223 S. Division St., 54981-1508. Tel: 715-258-3000; Fax: 715-258-5708.
Res.: 1277 E. Cleghorn Rd., 54981. Tel: 715-258-4928.
Catechesis/Religious Program—Tel: 715-258-3000. Catherine Miller, D.R.E.; Betty Manion, D.R.E. Students 440.

WAUSAUKEE, MARINETTE CO., ST. AUGUSTINE, Unassigned., Mailing Address: 507 Church St., 54177-9749. Tel: 715-856-5276; Fax: 715-856-5276. Also serves St. Agnes, Amberg.
Catechesis/Religious Program—Tel: 715-856-5066. Sherri L. Schlies, D.R.E. Students 170.

WAUTOMA, WAUSHARA CO., ST. JOSEPH, [CEM] Rev. Philip Dinh-Van-Thiep.
Res.: 364 S. Cambridge St., 54982-8101. Tel: 920-787-3848; Fax: 920-787-4781.
Catechesis/Religious Program—Ellen Scheibe, D.R.E. Students 236.

WEST KEWAUNEE, KEWAUNEE CO., ST. HEDWIG, Merged, with St. Joseph-St. John, Montpelier and St. Lawrence, Stangelville to form St. Therese de Lisieux, Stangelville.

WEYAUWEGA, WAUPACA CO., SS. PETER AND PAUL, [CEM], Also serves Sacred Heart, Manawa Rev. Bertin L. Samsa, O.F.M.Cap.
Res.: P.O. Box 548, 54983-0548. Tel: 920-867-2179; Fax: 920-867-2074.
Catechesis/Religious Program—Tel: 920-867-2170. Sr. Marie Rose Van Deurzen, S.S.N.D., D.R.E. Students 175.

WHITE LAKE, LANGLADE CO.
1—ST. JAMES, Merged, with St. Stanislaus, Langdale to form SS. James-Stanislaus, White Lake.
2—SS. JAMES-STANISLAUS, [CEM 2] Unassigned., Mailing Address: P.O. Box 36, 54491-0036. Tel: 715-882-2551. Served from Holy Family, Elcho.
Res.: 252 Bissell St., 54491.
Catechesis/Religious Program—Sr. Marie A. Miszewski, S.S.N.D., D.R.E.

WHITELAW, MANITOWOC CO., ST. MICHAEL, [CEM] Rev. James R. Jugenheimer (PH).
Mailing Address: P.O. Box 206, 54247-0206. Tel: 920-732-3901.
School—132 W. Menasha Ave., P.O. Box 27, 54247. Tel: 920-732-4442. Mrs. Arlene Rhein, Prin. Lay Teachers 5; Students 53.
Catechesis/Religious Program—110 W. Menasha Ave., P.O. Box 27, 54247. Students 124.

WINNECONNE, WINNEBAGO CO., ST. MARY, [JC] Rev. Leroy R. Smet.
Res.: 205 Pleasant Dr., P.O. Box 640, 54986-0640. Tel: 920-582-4246.
Church: P.O. Box 640, 54986-0640. Tel: 920-582-7712; Fax: 920-582-0181.
Catechesis/Religious Program—Tel: 920-582-4601. Erica Liddle, D.R.E. Students 291.

WITTENBERG, SHAWANO CO., HOLY FAMILY, Merged, with St. William, Eland to form Holy Family-St. William, Wittenberg/Eland.

WITTENBERG/ELAND, SHAWANO CO., HOLY FAMILY-ST. WILLIAM (2000), [CEM], Served from St. Anthony, Tigerton. (Has records for St. William, Eland Rev. Charles G. Hoffmann, Moderator; Deacon Kenneth Sambs.
Res.: 106 N. Ellms St., 54499-9099. Tel: 715-253-2050; Fax: 715-253-3020.
Catechesis/Religious Program—Karen Hendrikson, D.R.E.

WRIGHTSTOWN, BROWN CO., ST. PAUL, [JC] Ms. Joan Bartman, Parish Dir.; Revs. Dennis L. Bergsbaken, Moderator; Robert J. Kabat, J.C.L., Sacramental Min.; Deacon Kenneth Kabat.

Res.: 437 Main St., 54180-1057. Tel: 920-532-4374; Fax: 920-532-0149.

School—425 Main St., 54180. Tel: 920-532-4833. Mrs. Carol Hoard, Prin. Lay Teachers 8; Students 105.

Catechesis/Religious Program—429 Main St., 54180-1057. Tel: 920-532-0319. Marjorie M. Frase, D.R.E. Students 131.

Special Assignment:

Rev. Msgrs.—

Dewane, John B., M.A., S.T.L., D.Min., P.O. Box 23825, 54305-3825.
Gulig, Robert, 224 Iroquois Ave., #7, 54301-1998.
Maufort, Richard A., Charlestown Pointe I, 1975 Ridgeway Dr., Apt. 30, De Pere, 54115-4109.
Schuh, John H., P.O. Box 23825, 54305-3825.

Revs.—

Baeten, David, 224 Nicolet Pl., De Pere, 54115.
Bauschka, Joseph, 250 S. 9th St., #112, De Pere, 54115.
Carr, Martin P., 1965 Oshkosh Ave., Oshkosh, 54901-2659.
Gilsdorf, Gordon J., Notre Dame de la Baie Academy, 610 Maryhill Dr., 54303-2092.
Golden, Thomas, 1162 McCormick St., 54301.
Groher, Robert C., 6202 Dogwood Ln., Oconto, 54153-9590.
Thomas, Richard, P.O. Box 23825, 54305-3825.

On Duty Outside the Diocese:

Rev. Msgrs.—

Dewane, Frank J., Pontifical Council for Justice and Peace, 00120 Vatican City, Rome, Italy. Tel: 011-39-06-698-79912
Klister, Roy, S.T.D., J.C.D., S.T.L., The Liturgical Institute, 1000 E. Maple Ave., Mundelein, IL 60060.
Polc, Jaroslav, Thakurova 3, 16000 Prague 6, Czech Republic.

Revs.—

Mayefske, Thomas J., 833 Arizona, S.E., Albuquerqe, NM 87108.
Rank, Robert F., Our Lady of Corpus Christi, P.O. Box 9785, 1200 Luntana, Corpus Christi, TX 78469.
Reuter, John F., Apartado 46, Tlaxiaco, Oaxaca Mexico.
Schiavone, Robert W., sacred Heart School of Theology, P.O. Box 429, Hales Corners, 53130-0429. Tel: 414-425-0630
Seis, Michael, BM # 7047, 6911 N.W. 87th St., Miami, FL 33178-1625.
Vander Heyden, William F., Chap., V.A. Medical Center, 3001 Green Bay Rd., North Chicago, IL 60064-3049.

Military Chaplains:

Rev.—

Dory, Michael, Lt. Cmdr., 1214 Capella S., Newport, RI 02840-1584.

Absent on Leave:

Revs.—

Browne, Stanley
Carroll, Michael
Conrad, John
Gilsdorf, Daniel
Hoffmann, Philip
Mastalir, Peter
Pawelski, John
Schneider, Ronald
Schuetze, John
Shebuski, Charles
Somers, Michael
Zimmerman, David

Retired:

Most Rev.—

Wycislo, Aloysius, P.O. Box 23825, 54305-3825.

Rev. Msgrs.—

Feely, James, 2785 Taurus Rd., 54311.
Klauck, Peter, 825 East River Dr., Apt. 1, De Pere, 54115.
Rose, Donald, 865 Mill Rd., Sturgeon Bay, 54235-9267.
Schneider, Alfred, 1903 Division St. #214, Manitowoc, 54220.
Schommer, Mark, N2614 Bughs Lake Rd., Wautoma, 54982.

Revs.—

Barcome, Earl, 7026 Co. Y, Oconto, 54153.
Bedessem, Henry W., 1851 Eldorado Dr., Apt. 6, 54302-5554.
Beerntsen, Harold, 10544 W. Rost Lake Rd., Coleman, 54112.
Bernardy, Patrick, 2626 W. Shore Ln., Crandon, 54520.
Bestler, Joseph, 5319B Sturgeon Bay Rd., 54311.
Clifford, Michael J., 4775 Pine Ridge Tr., Abrams, 54101.
Conard, Ray J. 48005 Almaty Apostolic Administration, Tlendieva St. 9, 480005, almaty, Kazakhstan.
Danks, Arthur J., 2616 He Nis Ra Ln., 54304-1308.
Dewane, Daniel, 1613 Waldo Blvd., Manitowoc, 54220.
Dowling, Raymond, 3404 American Dr., #3201, Lago Vista, TX 78645.
DuCharme Paul, 224 Iroquois Ave., #8, 54301-1998.
Feeney, John P., P.O. Box 23825, 54305-3825.
Feller, Donald J., 2496 Mary Jo Dr., 54311-5208.
Geigel, Francis, 2937 Trump Lake Rd., Wabeno, 54566-9273.
Gerend, Lawrence, 216 Catherine St., Kaukauna, 54130-2136.
Gilsdorf, Richard, N9599 Bay Shore Ln., Luxemburg, 54217-9630.
Hephner, John, N15211 Beazley Rd., Amberg, 54102-9[illegible]77.
Heymen, Richard, South Brook Manor, [illegible]400 Yorkshire Ln., Apt. 318, Manitowoc, 54220.
Hogan, LeRoy, 220 W. 4th St., Kaukauna, 54130.
Jacobs, James T., 2792 W. Shore Ln., Crandon, 54520.
Johanek, John, 224 Iroquois Ave., #9, 54301.
Kelley, Omer C., P.O. Box 33, White Lake, 54491-0033.
Kerscher, Francis, 2408 W. River St., Two Rivers, 54241-1943.
Koch, Michael R., 2156 W. 9th Ave., Apt. 2, Oshkosh, 54904.
Koehne, David, 224 Iroquois Ave., #12, 54301-1970.
Koszarek Paul P., 2788 W. Shore Ln., Crandon, 54520.
Koszarek Thaddeus J., 224 Iroquois Ave., #1, 54301-1994.
Krutzik, Norman, 622 Pershing St., Appleton, 54911-2870.
Kutiuk, Casimir, 1246 W. 20th Ave., Oshkosh, 54902-5620.
Lenzner, George, 1157 Packerland Dr., 54304-1376.
Lessard, Leo, 17725 Munger Lake Ln., Lakewood, 54138-9615.
Lexa, Robert, 232 S. Pleasant Dr., Appleton, 54914-4205.
Marquardt, Donald, 224 Iroquois Ave., #3, 54301-1994.
Mauthe, Richard, 315 Breezy Acres Rd., Luxemburg, 54127
Melchior, Frank, E2783 Rockledge Rd., Casco, 54205
Merkatoris, Ralph, 2808 Taurus Rd., 54311-4600.
Mocco, Charles, P.O. Box 70, De Pere, 54115-0070.
Neuser, John, 627 S. 31st St., Manitowoc, 54220.
Nickel, Leander, 224 Iroquois Ave., # 6, 54301-1998.
O'Brien John, 502 N. Front St., Apt. 4, De Pere, 54115-2546.
Reinke, Francis P., 1820 Ridgeway Dr., Apt. 12B, De Pere, 54115.
Resheske, Florian, 224 Iroquois Ave., #15, 54301-1969.
Rickert, William, 224 Iroquois Ave., #5, 54301-1998.
Rodgers, Kenneth, 441 St. Mary Blvd., 54301-2607.
Sammut, Tito, P.O. Box 193, Davisburg, MI 48350.
Samter, James W., 1600 Rustic Oaks Ct., #11, 54301-2465.
Schmidt, Eugene, 2650 Vinland Rd., Oshkosh, 54901-1524.
Schmitt, John P., 2819 35th St., Two Rivers, 54241-1521.
Schreiner, Daniel A., 4616 Basswood St., Land O'Lakes, FL 34639-5603.
Schuh Earl, 2470 Mary Jo Dr., 54311-5208.
Schumacher, Paul, 2427 County Rd. J, Abrams, 54101.
Staudenmaier, Wilbert, 626 Fifth St., Menasha, 54952.
Stencil, Rallen, 224 Iroquois Ave., #16, 54301.
Stengel, William, W8445 Germantown Rd., Crivitz, 54114.
Stingle, Lawrence A., 2777 He Nis Ra Ln., 54304-1357.
Van De Loo, Willard J., 825 E. River Dr., # 4, De Pere, 54115.
Van Der Horst, John, 224 Iroquois Ave., # 10, 54301-1994.
Van Deuren, John H., 1490 Capitol Dr., # 12, 54303.
Vanden Hogen, Paul, 689 Evans St., Apt. 8, Waupaca, 54981.
Vennix, James J., E1277 Cleghorn Rd., Waupaca, 54981-9552.
Werner, Justin, N1682 Ridgeway Dr., Greenville, 54942.
Worzalla, Dennis A., St. Peter Parish, 800 4th Ave., Stevens Point, 54481-1627.

Permanent Deacons:

Andrastek, Phillip, St. Mary Church, Manitowoc
Asmuth, James, (Retired), Neenah
Bahnaman, Richard, Sacred Heart Church, Manitowoc
Baumruk, Roy, St. Joseph Church, Appleton
Beehner, Robert, Holy Innocents Church, Manitowoc
Bennin, Dennis, St. Mary Church, Chilton
Bilgrien, Kenneth, Ss. Peter & Paul Church, Hortonville
Boeldt, Alan, St. Paul Church, Manitowoc
Boucher, Paul, (Retired), Gresham
Brandenstein, Raymond, St. Vincent de Paul Church, Oshkosh
Bricco, Howard, St. Patrick Church, Menasha
Burke, William, St. Mary Church, Appleton
Burkel, William, Holy Martyrs of Gorcum Church, Green Bay
Charlier, Earl, (Retired), Green Bay
Cheskie, Peter, Oshkosh
Clark, Kenneth, St. Philip the Apostle Church, Green Bay
Coenen, Kenneth, St. Peter the Fisherman Church, Two Rivers
Craig, Thomas, Parish Dir., St. Martin, Cecil
Cross, Gerald, St. Mary Church, Menasha
Dahlen, Joseph, Appleton
De Bruin, Orvell, St. John Church, Seymour
De Groot, Vincent M., St. John Nepomucene Church, Little Chute
DeYoung, David, St. Mary Church, Greenville
Doran, William, St. John Church, Gillet; St. Michael Church, Suring
Drobka, Robert, St. Mary Church, Manitowoc
Ellis, Robert, De Pere
Farrell, Mark, St. Joseph Church, Appleton
Fischer, Frederick, Sacred Heart Church, Oshkosh
Garcia, Benjamin, (Retired), Shawano
Gates, Joseph, St. Peter Church, Oshkosh
Gauthier, James, St. Elizabeth Ann Seton Church, Green Bay
Gigure, Donald, Sacred Heart Church, Appleton
Gribowski, Mark, Holy Family Church, Marinette
Grimm, Paul, Dir. Office of Permanent Diaconate, St. John Church, Seymour
Grzeca, Michael, Resurrection Church, Green Bay
Haak, Randall, St. Mary of the Annunciation Church, Kaukauna
Hanley, Thomas, SS. Mary & Hyacinth Church, Antigo and St. Wenceslaus Church, Neva
Hartman, Thomas
Hayek, Hilary, St. Anthony Church, Tigerton
Holschbach, Keith, St. Bernard Church, Green Bay
Hunsader, Kenneth, St. Joseph Church, Sturgeon Bay and SS. Peter & Paul Church, Institute
Jacqmin, Robert, (Retired), De Pere
Jozwiak, Thomas, St. Rose Church, Clintonville; St. Mary Church, Bear Creek
Kabat, Ken, St. Paul Church, Wrightstown
Kaszynski, Walter, Holy Trinity Church, Oconto
Kieffer, Paul, Holy Innocents Church, Manitowoc
Klein, Paul, St. Thomas More Church, Appleton
Klein, William
Klister, Cyril, Holy Name of Jesus Church, Kimberly
Knier, Bernard P., SS. Peter & Paul Chuch, Kiel
Koch, Thomas J., Immaculate Conception Church, Clarks Mills
Kopydlowski, Kenneth, Green Bay
Kuborn, Gerald, St. Francis Church, Hollandtown and Holy Cross Church, Kaukauna
Kunzer, Earl, Ss. Edward/Isidore Church, Flintville
Laurant, John
Le Mere, David, Cresham
Lehman, Joseph, St. Mary Church, Bear Creek; St. Rose Church, Clintonville
Lobdell, Donald, Waupaca
Lowe, Russ, (Retired), Waupaca
Madden, Michael, St. Bernadette Church, Appleton
Madsen, Roger, Ss. Peter/Paul Church, Institute; St. Joseph Church, Sturgeon Bay
Majewski, Dennis, Assumption of the BVM Church, Pulaski
Maloney, John, St. Benedict Church, Suamico
Mastalish, Larry, St. Bernard Church, Green Bay
Meidl, Richard, Peoria, AZ
Merrick, Craig, St. Thomas More Church, Appleton
Miech, Richard, St. Mary, Greenville
Naidl, Clarence, St. James Church, Cooperstown
Nass, Donald, (Retired), Redgranite
Nelesen, Ken, Holy Innocents Church, Manitowoc
Newhouse, Don, St. Nicholas Church, Freedom
Nooker, Robert, St. Agnes Church, Green Bay
Nowak, Richard, Holy Cross Church, Coreen Bay
Orlowski, Harold, St. Ambrose Church, Wabeno
Otradovec, Byron, Holy Cross Church, Lena
Patton, James, St. John the Baptist Church, Howard

Penzenstadler, Robert, St. Mary Church, Oshkosh; Holy Name Retreat House, Chambers Island
Plantico, Paul, (Retired), DePere
Proulx, Rahlf, Manitowoc
Quinette, Harvey, Our Lady of Lourdes Church, De Pere
Reed, Maurice, St. Bernard Church, Appleton
Reilly, Timothy, Ressurection Church, Green Bay
Reinl, Peter, Appleton
Rocchi, Steven, (Retired), Wild Rose
Sambs, Kenneth, St. Anthony Church, Tigerton; St. Mary Church, Marion and Holy Family-St. William, Wittenberg
Sanchez, Luis, St. Willebrord Church, Green Bay
Schmidt, Gilbert, Sacred Heart Church, Appleton
Schmidt, Michael, Nativity of Our Lord Church, Green Bay
Schraufnagel, George, St. Paul Church, Combined Locks
Spielbauer, Norman, St. Margaret Mary Church, Neenah
Steffen, James, Holy Trinity Church, School Hill and St. Gregory Church, St. Nazianz
Sustman, James, Mishicot
Swinford, Norval, (Retired), Hortonville
Teske, Glenn, Port Chap., Apostleship of the Sea, Green Bay
Thetreau, Jerome, Holy Family Church, Marinette
Torres, Manuel, Nativity of Our Lord Church, Green Bay
Umentum, Paul, St. Mary of the Angels Church, Green Bay
Vande Hey, Steven, St. Mary of the Annunciation Church, Kaukauna
Vanden Heuvel, Lee P., St. Raphael the Archangel Church, Oshkosh
Vander Bloomen, Michael D., Our Lady of Lourdes Church, DePere
Vincent, Michael, SS. Peter & Paul Church, Green Bay
Vincent, Robert, St. Bernard Church, Appleton
Wessing, Reinhart, St. Thomas More Church, Appleton
Wetzel, Donald J,, St. Thomas More Church, Appleton
Whitcomb, Patrick, St. Therese Church, Appleton
Wildenberg, Clay, Gresham
Williams, Nicholas, St. John the Baptist Church, Howard
Zenefski, Paul, Corpus Christi Church, Sturgeon Bay

INSTITUTIONS LOCATED IN THE DIOCESE

[A] SEMINARIES, RELIGIOUS OR SCHOLASTICATES

GREEN BAY. *St. Mary of the Angels Friary*, 645 S. Irwin Ave., 54301-3397. Tel: 920-437-7411; Fax: 920-437-7411. Bro. James Buda, O.F.M., Guardian. Priests 4; Brothers 1.

DE PERE. *St. Norbert Abbey*, 1016 N. Broadway, 54115-2697. Tel: 920-337-4300; Fax: 920-337-4328. Email: gjn@netnet.net. Web: www.norbertines.org. Rt. Revs. Gary J. Neville, O.Praem., Abbot; John P. Kastenholz, O.Praem., Treas.; E. Thomas De Wane, O.Praem., Abbot; Benjamin T. Mackin, O.Praem., Abbot Emeritus; Jerome G. Tremel, O.Praem., Abbot Emeritus; Very Rev. David M. Komatz, O.Praem., Prior; Revs. James T. Baraniak, O.Praem., Vocation Coord.; Gilbert H. Jacobs, O.Praem., Subprior & House Supr.; Andrew G. Cribben, O.Praem., Dir. Formation & Novice Master; Thomas O. Muelemans, O.Praem., Mission Procurator; Xavier G. Colavechio, O.Praem., Dir. Norbertine Center for Spirituality. Priests 77; Brothers 4; Seminarians 9; Total Staff 90.

[B] COLLEGES AND UNIVERSITIES

DE PERE. *St. Norbert College* 54115-2099. Tel: 920-403-3165; Fax: 920-403-4063. Email: amy.sorenson@snc.edu. Web: www.snc.edu. Dr. William J. Hynes, Pres.; Dr. Michael Marsdes, Vice Pres. Academic Affairs & Dean of College; Mr. Greg Garber, Interim Vice Pres. Business & Finance; Dr. Richard Rankin, Vice Pres. Student Life; Mr. Donald L. Salmon, Vice Pres. Institutional Advancement; Revs. Dane J. Radecki, O.Praem., Vice Pres. Mission & Heritage; Brian Prunty, O.Praem., Dir. Campus Min. & Pastor, St. Norbert College Parish.
Legal Title: *St. Norbert College, Inc.* Priests 5; Sisters 2; ROTC 1; Lay Teachers 120; Students 2,030.
Faculty: Revs. Robert J. Cornell, O.Praem.; John P. Kastenholz, O.Praem.; David R. McElroy, O.Praem.; James Nielsen, O.Praem.; Very Rev. David M. Komatz, O.Praem.; Revs. Jay M. Fostner, O.Praem.; John Bostwick, O.Praem.
St. Norbert College Summer School Tel: 920-403-3051; Fax: 920-403-4096. Dr. John Sutton, Assoc. Dean Instructional Svcs.

MANITOWOC. *Silver Lake College of the Holy Family*, 2406 S. Alverno Rd., 54220-9319. Tel: 920-684-6691; Fax: 920-684-7082. Email: mshepard@silver.sl.edu. Web: www.sl.edu. Sr. Maureen Anne Shepard, O.S.F., Pres. Sponsored by the Franciscan Sisters of Christian Charity. Priests 4; Sisters 47; Lay Teachers 113; Students 2,878.

[C] HIGH SCHOOLS, DIOCESAN

APPLETON. *Xavier High School* Coed , 1600 W. Prospect Ave., 54914. Tel: 920-733-6632; Fax: 920-733-5513. Email: mreynebeau@xavier.k12.wi.us. Web: www.xavier.k12.wi.us. Mr. Matt Reynebeau, Prin.; Mrs. Donna Fahrenkrug, Assoc. Prin.; Andrew Mahoney, Dir. Guidance Dept.; Ms. Sarah Simon, Campus Min. (Part of ACES/Xavier Educational System, Inc.) Lay Teachers 30; Students 532.

MANITOWOC. *Roncalli High School*, 2000 Mirro Dr., 54220-6799. Tel: 920-682-8801; Fax: 920-686-8110. Bro. Roger Betzold, F.S.C., Prin.; Mr. Tim Olson, Assoc. Prin.; Ms. Sara Morrison, Campus Min. Christian Brothers and Franciscan Sisters of Christian Charity Brothers 4; Sisters 2; Lay Teachers 27; Students 336.

MARINETTE. *Marinette Catholic Central High School*, 1200 Main St., 54143-2594. Tel: 715-735-7481; Fax: 715-735-3375. Email: mcchs@hotmail.com. Rev. Robert Kroll, O.F.M., Admin. Council Chairperson. Lay Teachers 14; Students 70.

NEENAH/MENASHA. *St. Mary Central High School* 54956. Tel: 920-722-7796; Fax: 920-722-5940. Email: pbeach@smc.k12.wi.us. Web: www.smc.k12.wi.us. 1050 Zephyr Dr., 54956-1389. Tel: 920-722-7796; Fax: 920-722-5940. Lewis Malczewski, Prin. Lay Teachers 23; Students 273.

OSHKOSH. *Lourdes High School* (Coed.) , 110 N. Sawyer St., 54902. Tel: 920-235-5670; Fax: 920-235-7453. Web: www.lourdeshs.org. (Part of Unified Catholic Schools of Oshkosh) Lay Teachers 22; Students 194.

[D] HIGH SCHOOLS, PRIVATE

GREEN BAY. *Notre Dame de la Baie Academy*, 610 Maryhill Dr., 54303-2092. Tel: 920-429-6100; Fax: 920-429-6168. Email: bherlache@notredameacademy.com. Web: www.notredameacademy.com. Dick Hietpas, Assoc. Prin. Priests 1; Lay Teachers 46; Students 741.

[E] CONSOLIDATED SCHOOLS

ANTIGO. *All Saints Catholic Schools, Inc.* Tel: 715-623-5629; Fax: 715-623-3202. Email: ascs@antigopro.net. Marie A. Millsaps, Prin.
St. John Site:, 419 6th Ave., 54409. Tel: 715-623-4835; Fax: 715-627-2969.
St. Mary Site:, 723 Deleglise St., 54409. Tel: 715-623-5629; Fax: 715-623-3202. Lay Teachers 17; Total Enrollment 253.

APPLETON. *ACES/Xavier Catholic Educational System, Inc.*, 101 E. Northland Ave., 54911. Tel: 920-735-9380; Fax: 920-735-1787. Email: aces@acesys.org. Web: www.acesys.org. Sr. Patrice Hughes, S.C., Pres. Lay Teachers 85; Total Enrollment 2,201.

MANITOWOC. *Manitowoc Area Catholic System (MACS)*, 1418 Grand Ave., 54220-6130. Tel: 920-683-6880; Fax: 920-683-6881. Email: jstecple@mps.k12.wi.us. Joseph L. Steepleton, MACS System Admin. Sisters 5; Lay Teachers 47; Total Enrollment 639.
St. Francis de Sales School (Grades K-5), 1408 Waldo Blvd., 54220-2610. Tel: 920-683-6892; Fax: 920-683-6889. Sr. Paulyn Vanden Hogen, Prin.
St. Francis Xavier School (Grades PreK-5), 1418 Grand Ave., 54220-6197. Tel: 920-683-6888; Fax: 920-683-6881. Mrs. Linda Bender, Prin.
St. Frances Cabrini Middle School (Grades 6-8), 2109 Marshall St., 54220-4959. Tel: 920-683-6884; Fax: 920-683-6882. Mr. James Clark, Prin. Consolidation of Holy Innocents, Sacred Heart, St. Andrew, St. Paul, St. Mary and St. Boniface grade schools in Manitowoc.

NEENAH/MENASHA. *Twin Cities Catholic Educational System (TCCES)* Tel: 920-967-0021; Fax: 920-722-5940. Email: jklein@.tcces.k12.wi.us. 1050 Zephyr Dr., 54956. Tel: 920-967-0021; Fax: 920-722-5940. Julie Klein, Contact Person. Consolidation of St. Gabriel, St. Margaret Mary, St. Mary Elementary, Seton Catholic Middle School and St. Mary Central High School. Lay Teachers 89; Total Enrollment 942.

OSHKOSH. *Unified Catholic Schools of Oshkosh*, 110 N. Sawyer St., 54902. Tel: 920-426-3626; Fax: 920-303-6682. Mr. Stan Spanbauer, Prin. Sisters 3; Lay Teachers 51; Total Enrollment 731.

TWO RIVERS. *Two Rivers Catholic Schools (TRCCS)*, (Grades K-8), 2203 12th St., 54241. Tel: 920-794-7622; Fax: 920-794-7266. Sr. Valerie Lemansky, Prin. Consolidation of St. Luke and St. Mark Schools. Sisters 2; Lay Teachers 20; Students 123.

[F] GENERAL HOSPITALS

GREEN BAY. *Libertas Treatment Center for Chemically Dependent*, 1701 Dousman St., 54303-3282. Tel: 920-498-8600; Fax: 920-496-2027. David B. Fish, Exec. Vice Pres.; Patrick W. Ryan, Prog. Dir. Hospital Sisters of the Third Order of St. Francis, Hospital Sisters Health System. Bed Capacity 24; Patients Assisted Annually 8,000; Total Staff 31.
St. Mary's Hospital-Medical Center, 1726 Shawano Ave., 54303-3282. Tel: 920-498-4200; Fax: 920-498-1861. Email: cstaubin@stmgb.org. Web: www.stmgb.org. Mr. James G. Coller, Admin.; David J. Schmidt, Dir. Pastoral Care & Case Mgmt. Depts.; Deacon Nick Williams, Pastoral Care Assoc. Hospital Sisters of Third Order of St. Francis Bed Capacity 158; Staff 950; Patients Assisted Annually 92,997.
St. Vincent Hospital, P.O. Box 13508, 54307-3508. Tel: 920-433-0111; 920-433-8163; Fax: 920-431-3275. Email: msalm@stvgb.org. Web: www.stvgb.org; www.stvincenthospital .org. Mr. Joseph J. Neidenbach, Exec. Vice Pres. & CEO; Mary J. Salm, Dir. Pastoral Care; Sisters Paulette Hupfauf, O.S.F., Chap.; Monica Bongert, O.S.F., Chap.; Marilyn Herr, O.S.F., Chap. Hospital Sisters of the Third Order of St. Francis 3; Bassinets 25; Bed Capacity 517; Patients Assisted Annually 174,591; Total Staff 1,941.

ANTIGO. *Langlade Memorial Hospital*, 112 E. 5th Ave., 55409. Tel: 715-623-2331; Fax: 715-623-9359. Email: jbricco@langmemhosp.org rhsj@antigopro.net. Web: www.langladememorial.com. Sr. Dolores Demulling, Mission & Philosophy Advocate & Trustee, Dir. of LeRoyer Hospice; Mr. David Schneider, Exec. Dir.; Sisters Jean Bricco, Dir. Pastoral Care, Trustee & Contact Person; Adele Demulling, R.H.S.J., Supr., Coord. LeRoyer Hospice; Rev. Omer C. Kelley, Part-time Chap. (Retired). Religious Hospitallers of St. Joseph
Sisters Res.: 644 Longlade Rd., 55409. Tel: 715-623-4615; Fax: 715-623-4615. Sisters 3; Priests 1; Bed Capacity 49; Patients Assisted Annually 54,126.

APPLETON. *St. Elizabeth Hospital*, 1506 S. Oneida St., 54915-1305. Tel: 920-831-8913; Fax: 920-738-8916. Email: Bturner@affinityhealth.org. Kevin Nolan, Pres.; Bob Turner, COO; Revs. Thomas Oie, Chap.; Darrel Diers, Assoc. Chap.; Sisters Germaine Hietpas, Chap.; Gerri Krautkramer, Chap.; Anne Arthur Klinker, Chap.
Legal Title: *St. Elizabeth Hospital, Inc.*, Corporate Sponsors: Wheaton Franciscan Services, Inc. (Wheaton, IL) and Affinity Health System (Menasha, WI) Franciscan Sisters, Daughters of the Sacred Hearts of Jesus and Mary (Wheaton, IL) 2; Bed Capacity 203; Total Staff 1,070; Patients Assisted Annually 136,966.

MANITOWOC. *Holy Family Memorial, Inc.*, 2300 Western Ave., P.O. Box 1450, 54221-1450. Tel: 920-684-2011; Fax: 920-684-2522. Email: services@hfmhealth.org. Web: www.hfmhealth.org. Mr. Mark Herzog, Pres.; Revs. Richard Klingeisen, Dir. Pastoral Care; Richard H. Klingeisen, Chap.; Bob Bleeke, Chap.; Sr. Jean Herman Dykstra, Chap.; Deacon Rahlf Proulx, Chap.; Molly La Fond, Chap. Franciscan Sisters of Christian Charity Sisters 4; Licensed Beds 216; Bassinets 26; Patients Assisted Annually 202,367; Total Staff 1,278.

OSHKOSH. *Mercy Medical Center*, 500 S. Oakwood Rd., P.O. Box 3370, 54902-3370. Tel: 920-223-0504; Fax: 920-223-0508. Email: clehman@affinityhealth.org. Mr. Kevin Nolan, CEO; Clifford Lehman, COO; Sr. Johnette Marek, S.S.M., Chap.; Revs. Calvin Rayburn, Chap.; Phil Dewit, Chap.; Donna Greischar, Chap.; Gordon MacDonald, Chap.
Legal Title: *Mercy Medical Center of Oshkosh, Inc.*, Corporate Sponsors: Ministry Health Care, Inc. (Milwaukee, WI) and Affinity Health System (Menasha, WI) Sisters of the Sorrowful Mother 1; Bed Capacity 172; Staff 1,131; Bassinets 25; Patients Assisted Annually 153,725.

STURGEON BAY. **Door County Memorial Hospital*, 323 S. 18th Ave., 54235. Tel: 920-743-5566; Fax: 920-743-8165. Email: gworrick@dcmh.org. Web: www.ministryhealth.org. Gerald M. Worrick, Pres. Corporate Sponsor: Ministry Health Care, Inc.(Milwaukee, WI); Sponsored by Sisters of the Sorrowful Mother. Bed Capacity 75; Patients Assisted Annually 162,834; Total Staff 410.

[G] PROTECTIVE INSTITUTIONS

GREEN BAY. *McClosky Program, Inc.*, 2560 Shawano Ave., P.O. Box 10357, 54313. Tel: 920-434-8208; Fax: 920-662-0047. Sr. Barbara Jean Arnsmeyer, O.L.C., Dir. A Community based residential facility for women 18 years old and over who are pregnant or in a crisis situation and in need of transitional supervision and guidance. Needs addressed are personal and family problems. Also, shelter offered during crisis or unemployment. Total Staff 3; Total Assisted 10.

Our Lady of Charity Center, Inc., 2560 Shawano Ave., P.O. Box 10357, 54313. Tel: 920-434-8208; Fax: 920-662-0047. Sr. Patrick Dolan, O.L.C., Admin. Total Staff 4; Total Assisted 20.

OSHKOSH. *The Convent Project, Inc.*, 449 High Ave., 54901. Tel: 920-233-1894. Email: bbakerl@new.rr.com. Barbara Baker, Treas. For victims of domestic abuse Total Assisted 51.

TWO RIVERS. *Sisters Treatment Group Home*, 3904 Martin Ln., 54241. Tel: 920-553-1524; Fax: 920-553-2442. Sisters Irmina Bula, S.S.J.-T.O.S.F., Co-Dir.; Edmund Antoniewicz, S.S.J.-T.O.S.F., Co-Dir. For physically and mentally handicapped children. Children 4; Adults 2; Staff 8; Total Assisted 6.

[H] HOMES FOR AGED

GREEN BAY. *The McCormick Memorial Home for the Aged*, 212 Iroquois Ave., 54301-1918. Tel: 920-437-0883; Fax: 920-437-2696. Email: jgenrich@netnet.net. James Genrich, Admin.; Rev. Thaddeus J. Koszarek, Chap. (Retired). Staff 27; Nursing Staff 6; Residents 55.

APPLETON. **Franciscan Care and Rehabilitation Center, Inc.*, 2915 N. Meade St., 54911-1598. Tel: 920-831-8700; Fax: 920-731-3206. Email: nbassett@affinityhealth.org. Todd Greeneway, Admin. Corporate Sponsors: Wheaton Franciscan Services, Inc. (Wheaton, IL) and Affinity Health System (Menasha, WI) Residents 400; Total Staff 282.

KAUKAUNA. *St. Paul Elder Services, Inc.*, 316 E. Fourteenth St., 54130. Tel: 920-766-6020; Fax: 920-766-7945. Email: jimf@stpaulelders.org. Web: stpaulelders.org. James J. Fett, Pres.; Sandra Randall, Admin.

St. Paul Home, 1211 Oakridge Ave., 54130. Tel: 920-766-6020; Fax: 920-766-9161. Residents 129.

St. Paul Villa, 312 E. Fourteenth St., 54130. Tel: 920-766-6020; Fax: 920-766-7945. Residents 89.

St. Paul Manor, 509 W. Wisconsin Ave., 54130. Tel: 920-766-6027; Fax: 920-766-6035. Residents 27.

MANITOWOC. *Felician Senior Living Community* Tel: 920-684-7171. Web: www.feliciancommunity.org.

Felician Village Inc., 1700 S. 18th St., 54220. Tel: 920-684-7171, Ext. 231; Fax: 920-684-0240. Email: jgospodarek@lakefield.net. Jack A. Gospodarek, CEO. Apartments 134.

St. Mary's Home, 2005 Division St., 54220. Tel: 920-684-7171, Ext. 231; Fax: 920-684-0240. Email: jgospodarek@lakefield.net. Jack A. Gospodarek, CEO. Sisters 10; Aged Residents 191.

Sacred Heart Assisted Living Apartments, 1903 Division St., 54220. Tel: 920-684-7171, Ext. 231; Fax: 920-684-0240. Email: jgospodarek@lakefield.net. Jack A. Gospodarek, CEO. Apartments 32.

NEENAH. *Assisi Homes of Neenah, Inc.*, 210 Byrd Ave., 54956. Tel: 920-722-5100; Fax: 920-722-5171. Web: www.wfs-inc.org. (An independent living community for Seniors.) Total Staff 4; Total in residence 38.

Villa St. Clare, Inc., 130 Byrd Ave., 54946. Tel: 920-722-5100; Fax: 920-722-5171. Web: www.wfs-inc.org. Mariann Baumann, Mgr. Special care facility, affordable housing with supportive accommodations in an independent setting for seniors 55+. Total in Residence 45; Total Assisted 50; Staff 20.

NEW LONDON. *St. Joseph Residence, Inc., New London*, 107 E. Beckert Rd., 54961. Tel: 920-982-5354; Fax: 920-982-5420. Email: sjradm@athenet.net. Mr. Daniel W. Orr, CEO. Residents 107.

St. Joseph Residence, Inc. Residents 107.

Trinity Terrace, 107 E. Beckert Rd., 54961. Tel: 920-982-5354. Email: sjradm@athenet.net. Total in Residence 32; Staff 23; Nursing Care Staff 170.

Marion Heights Apartments Residents 26.

St. Joseph Residence - The Washington Center, Inc., 500 Washington St., 54961. Tel: 920-982-9200. Email: sjradm@athenet.net. Mr. Daniel W. Orr, CEO. Apartments 33.

NIAGARA. *Maryhill Manor (SNF)*, 501 Madison Ave., 54151. Tel: 715-251-3172; Fax: 715-251-1200. Email: maryhill@netnet.net. Jana Clement, Admin. Sponsored by School Sisters of St. Francis, Milwaukee. Nursing Care: Residents 75; Total Staff 100.

[I] MONASTERIES AND RESIDENCES OF PRIESTS AND BROTHERS

GREEN BAY. *St. Mary of the Angels Friary*, 645 S. Irwin Ave., 54301-3303. Tel: 920-437-7411; 920-437-1979 (Res.); Fax: 920-437-7411. Rev. Albert Lis O.F.M. Franciscan Friars, Assumption of the Blessed Virgin Mary Province (Order of Friars Minor) Priests 4; Brothers 1. In Res. Revs. Bede Hepnar; Nathan Jaskulski, O.F.M.; Robert Kroll; Bro. James Buda, O.F.M., Guardian.

APPLETON. *St. Fidelis Friary*, 1100 N. Ballard Rd., 54911-5100. Tel: 920-954-8954; Fax: 920-954-1095. Revs. William Alcuin, O.F.M.Cap.; Silas Baumann, O.F.M.Cap.; David Belongea, O.F.M.Cap.; Donald Brody, O.F.M.Cap.; Reynold Rynda, O.F.M.Cap.; Ambrose Simon, O.F.M.Cap.; Bros. John Gau, O.F.M.Cap.; Conrad Heinen, O.F.M.Cap.; Cyrus Toschik, O.F.M.Cap.; Dan Vena, O.F.M.Cap. Order of Friars Minor Capuchin Priests 6; Brothers 4; Staff 3.

St. Joseph Friary, 404 W. Lawrence St., 54911-5855. Tel: 920-734-7195; Fax: 920-734-0227. Web: www.stjosephparish.org. Revs. Larry Abler, O.F.M.; Kenneth Reinhart, O.F.M.Cap. Order of Friars Minor Capuchin

DE PERE. *St. Joseph Priory*, 103 Grant St., 54115-2001. Tel: 920-403-3572 (Office); Fax: 920-403-4430. Revs. James T. Baraniak, O.Praem.; John Bostwick, O.Praem.; Robert J. Cornell, O.Praem.; Rowland C. De Peaux, O.Praem.; Jay M. Fostner, O.Praem.; Conrad J. Kratz, O.Praem.; Brendan J. McKeough, O.Praem.; Gery G. Meehan, O.Praem.; Thomas O. Meulemans, O.Praem.; Brian J. Prunty, O.Praem., House Supr.; Dane Radecki, O.Praem.; Joseph S. Rekasi, O.Praem.; Timothy D. Shillcox, O.Praem.; Harvey H. Tonnen, O.Praem.; Robert Vande Hey, O.Praem. Residence for Norbertine Community. Priests 15.

St. Norbert Abbey, 1016 N. Broadway 54115-2697. Tel: 920-337-4300; Fax: 920-337-4328. Email: gjn@netnet.net. Web: www.norbertines.org. Rt. Revs. Gary J. Neville, O.Praem., Abbot; E. Thomas De Wane, O.Praem., Abbot; Benjamin T. Mackin, O.Praem., Abbot Emeritus; Jerome G. Tremel, O.Praem., Abbot Emeritus; Very Rev. David M. Komatz, O.Praem., Prior; Revs. John P. Kastenholz, O.Praem., Treas.; Gilbert H. Jacobs, O.Praem., Subprior & House Supr.; Thomas O. Meulemans, O.Praem., Mission Procurator; Bartholomew A. Agar, O.Praem.; Jordan R. Blecha, O.Praem.; Bernard M. Brunette, O.Praem.; Robert E. Carson, O.Praem.; Andrew G. Cribben, O.Praem.; Salvatore H. Cuccia, O.Praem.; Mark D. Falcone, O.Praem.; Angelo J. Feldkamp, O.Praem.; Roderick R. Fenzl, O.Praem.; Robert K. Finnegan, O.Praem.; Michael F. Frisch, O.Praem., Graduate Studies, Univ. of MI Ann Arbor, MI; Guy E. Guyon, O.Praem.; Thomas A. Hagendorf, O.Praem.; James B. Herring, O.Praem., Graduate Studies, St. Paul Univ., Ottowa, ON Canada; Robert L. Hyde, O.Praem.; Gerald B. Kempen, O.Praem.; David R. McElroy, O.Praem.; Gilbert Mihayli, O.Praem., Headmaster, Archmere Academy, Claymont, DE; Timothy F. Mullen, O.Praem.; Conan P. Mulrooney, O.Praem.; James P. Nielson, O.Praem.; Donald C. Noel, O.Praem.; Ambrose J. Peeters, O.Praem.; Robert B. Reppen, O.Praem.; Julian C. Resch, O.Praem.; William H. Ribbens, O.Praem.; Stephen J. Rossey, O.Praem.; James W. Stein, O.Praem.; Roman R. Vanasse, O.Praem., Admin., St. Joseph Priory, Queen Park, Australia; Steven J. Vanden Boogard, O.Praem., (Chap.,United States Navy, Jacksonville, FL); Achilles E. Van Hoof, O.Praem., (Tongerlo, Belgium); Albin V. Veszelovszky, O.Praem., (Godollo, Hungary); Michael J. Weber, O.Praem., Chap., United States Air Force, Grand Forks AFB, ND); Bros. Robert J. Craanen, O.Praem.; Steven J. Herro, O.Praem.; Terrence R. Lauerman, O.Praem.; Clement G. Tourangeau, O.Praem.

Legal Title: *The Premonstratensian Fathers*

Legal Title: *NORBERT & CO., a nominee of The Premonstratensian Fathers, Norbertine Fathers*

Legal Title: *St. Norbert Abbey, Inc.*

Legal Title: *Augustine Stewardship Fund Trust*

Legal Title: *Norbertine Retirement Fund Trust*

Legal Title: *St. Norbert Abbey Seminary and Education Fund Trust*

Legal Title: *The Walnut Market, Inc.*

Legal Title: *Los Amigos del Peru, Inc.* Canons Regular of Premontre Brothers 4; Priests 77; Priests at St. Norbert Abbey 35; Seminarians 4; Novices 5.

Priests serving in foreign countries:

Archdiocese of Iquitos, Peru, Santa Clotilde, Rio Napo, Apartado 216, Iquitos, Peru. Tel: 011-51-94-25-1932; Fax: 011-51-94-25-1922. Revs. Lambert C. Baeten, O.Praem.; John P. MacCarthy, O.Praem.

Archdiocese of Cape Town, South Africa, St. Norbert's Priory, Rubbi Rd., P.O. Box 48106, 7976 Kommetjie, Cape Province, South Africa. Tel: 011-27-21-783-17-68. Rev. Milton C. Strebel, O.Praem.

Diocese of Cuernavaca, Mexico, c/o 413 Interamerica Blvd., WH1, PMB 21-63, Laredo, TX 78045. Tel: 011-52-777-312-42-62; Fax: 011-52-777-312-93-92. Rev. Brendan J. McKeough, O.Praem.

NEW HOLSTEIN. *Salvatorian Center Residence* 53061-0001. Tel: 920-898-5635. Email: mission@salvatoriancenter.com. Web: www.weinschenk.com/mission. Brothers 4.

Salvatorian Public Relations, Salvatorian Center, 53062. Tel: 920-898-4201; Fax: 920-898-4736. Rev. Gregory Coulthardt, S.D.S.

Salvatorian Mission Warehouse, 53061. Tel: 920-898-5898; Fax: 920-898-4736. Bro. Regis Fust, S.D.S., Dir. Mission Supply Prog.

OSHKOSH. *Community of Our Lady* (Diocesan Pious Union) , 2804 Oakwood Ln., 54904-8406. Tel: 920-233-5633; Fax: 920-233-5604. Very Rev. Regis N. Barwig, Prior; Revs. Eugene E. Kalinski; Augustine Serafini; Bro. Joseph G. Le Sanche.

PULASKI. *Assumption of B.V.M. Friary*, 143 E. Pulaski St., P.O. Box 100, 54162-0100. Tel: 920-822-5422; Fax: 920-822-5423. Email: abvm@execpc.com. Web: www.ofm.abvm.org. (Order of Franciscan Fathers, Order of Friars Minor).

Friary, 54162. Tel: 920-822-8125; Fax: 920-822-5423. Revs. Melvin Wierzbicki, O.F.M.; Finian Zaucha, O.F.M.; Richard Tulko, O.F.M., Guardian; Maynard Kolodziej, O.F.M.; Lawrence Karcz, O.F.M.; James Heinsch, O.F.M.; Bros. Anthony Gancarz, O.F.M.; Theodore Tokarz, O.F.M.; Peter Rydza, O.F.M.; Gregory Stasinski, O.F.M.; David Typek, O.F.M.; Sebastian Nocinski, O.F.M.; Henry Kolbok, O.F.M.; Austin Mysliwiec, O.F.M.; Michael Janiak, O.F.M.; Andrew Giba, O.F.M.

Retired-Infirm - Elsewhere: St. Mary's Home, Manitowoc: Revs. Josaphat Ledwon, O.F.M.; Raynold Jarecki, O.F.M.; Michael Lacienski, O.F.M.; James Verdick, O.F.M.; Humphrey Tobias, O.F.M.; Pater Machesky, O.F.M.; Bro. Miles Brainer, O.F.M.

Villa Alverna, N. 11450 Rademaker Rd., Wausaukee, 54177. Tel: 715-732-6612. Bro. David Typek, O.F.M., Dir.

Outside of Diocese: Revs. Ladislaus Szepe, S.F.O., Sarasota, FL; Lazarus Macior, O.F.M.

Univ. of Akron, Biology Dept., Akron, OH 44325-3908. Tel: 330-972-7155. Rev. Adam Szufel, O.F.M.

Warner Robins, GA 31088. Tel: 478-328-6481; Fax: 478-328-3876. Rev. Robert Kroll.

St. Mary of the Angels Friary, 645 S. Irwin Ave., 54301. Tel: 920-437-7411. Bros. John Brice, O.F.M., South Africa; Mario Nagy, O.F.M., Novo Sibirsk, Russia; Andre Lemay, O.F.M., Las Vegas, NV; Augustine Fraszczak, O.F.M., Philippines.

Priests of the Province Serving Abroad: Revs. Sergius Wroblewski, O.F.M., South Africa; Lyle Chrobak, O.F.M., Guaymas, Mexico; Arcadius Smolinski, O.F.M., Europe; Henry Howaniec, O.F.M., Apostolic Admin. in Almaty, Kazakstan; Barnabas Gorski, O.F.M., Morocco.

St. Francis of Assisi Friary, Hwy. 82 E., Greenwood, MS 38930-5966. Tel: 662-453-0623. Revs. Conrad Targonski, O.F.M., Military Chap.; Randall Roberts, O.F.M., Military Chap.

[J] CONVENTS AND RESIDENCES FOR SISTERS

GREEN BAY. *St. Francis Convent of Sisters of St. Francis of the Holy Cross*, 3025 Bay Settlement Rd., 54311-7301. Tel: 920-468-1828; Fax: 920-468-1207. Email: CommSecretary@gbfranciscanscans.org. Web: www.gbfranciscanscans.org. Sr. Ann Rehrauer, Pres. Sisters 82; Novices 1; In Diocese 80.

Hospital Sisters of the Third Order of St. Francis Web: www.springfieldfranciscans.org. 1015 S. Webster St., 54301. Tel: 920-432-0337. Sr. Maureen O'Connor, O.S.F., Prov. Sec. & Treas. Sisters 3.

Sisters of Our Lady of Charity of the North American Union, Inc., 2560 Shawano Ave., P.O. Box 10357, 54307-0357. Tel: 920-434-8208; Fax: 920-662-0047. Sr. Patrick Dolan, Supr. Sisters 19.

DENMARK. *Monastery of the Holy Name of Jesus, Ltd.* Discalced Carmelite Nuns , 6100 Pepper Rd., 54208. Tel: 920-863-5055. Email: carmel@catholicfamilies.net. Sr. Mary Elizabeth, O.C.D., Prioress. Total 11.

MANITOWOC. *St. Clare Convent*, 3 Riverview Dr., 54220. Tel: 920-682-5145. Email: smnbrown@juno.com. Sr. Michael Majeskie, Dir. Franciscan Sisters of Christian Charity Sisters 6.

St. Francis Convent, 6835 Hwy. 151, 54220. Tel: 920-684-7884; Fax: 920-682-4195. Web: www.sl.edu/FSCC. Sr. Debra Shepeck, Sec. Franciscan Sisters of Christian Charity Sisters 42.

Holy Family Convent of Franciscan Sisters of Christian Charity Motherhouse and Novitiate dedicated to the Holy Family , 2409 S. Alverno Rd., 54220-9320. Tel: 920-682-7728; Fax: 920-682-4195. Email: slouiseh@fscc.sl.edu. Web: www.sl.edu/FSCC/. Revs. DePaul Sobotka, O.F.M., Chap.; Samuel D. Jadin, O.Praem.; Sr. Louise Hembrecht, Community Dir. Sisters 422; In Diocese 340; Novices 1; Total in Residence 192.

OSHKOSH. *SSM Franciscan Courts*, 815 S. Westhaven Dr., 54904-7978. Tel: 920-426-2440; Fax: 920-426-3196. Email: skomp@northnet.net. Steve Komp, Admin.; Sr. Helen Marie Brand, Local Community Leader; Leslie Raddatz, Admin. Coord.; Rev. Michael R. Koch, Chap. (Retired). Sisters of the Sorrowful Mother Sisters 39.

[K] SHRINES

CHILTON. *St. Peregrine Shrine* 54 E. Main St., 53014. Tel: 920-849-9363; Fax: 920-849-7270. Rev. Gary New, S.D.S., Pastor St. Mary Church, Chilton.

NEW FRANKEN. *The Chapel of Our Lady of Good Help (Diocesan Shrine)-Robinsonville* 4047 Chapel Dr., 54229-9768. Tel: 920-866-2571.

[L] RETREAT HOUSES

APPLETON. *Monte Alverno Retreat Center*, 1000 N. Ballard Rd., 54911-5148. Tel: 920-733-8526; Fax: 920-733-7562. Email: montealverno@juno.com. Web: www.montealverno.org. Revs. Werner Wolf, O.F.M.Cap., Dir.; Lester Bach, O.F.M.Cap.; Adrian Staehler, O.F.M.Cap.; Ellis Zimmer, O.F.M.Cap.; Bro. John Kocian, O.F.M.Cap. The Province of St. Joseph of the Capuchin Order, Inc. Priests 4; Brothers 1; Retreatants Annually 3,000; Total in residence 5; Total Staff 16.

BAILEYS HARBOR. *St. Joseph Retreat Center*, 3035 O'Brien Rd., 54202-9132. Tel: 920-839-2391; Fax: 920-839-2391. Email: malbert@itol.com. Sr. Mary Anne Albert, S.S.S.F., Dir.; Rev. Byron Haaland, S.C.J., Admin. Retreat; Sr. Lorraine Aspenleiter, S.S.S.F.; Bros. John Monek, S.C.J.; Andrew Lewandowski, S.C.J. Priests 3; Brothers 2; Sisters 3; Total in residence 8; Total Staff 12. In Res. Revs. Joseph Dean, S.C.J., Community Coord.; Mark Fortner, S.C.J.; Sr. Irene Zimmerman, S.S.S.F.

CHAMBERS ISLAND. *Holy Name Retreat House* Tel: 920-493-2792. 1825 Riverside Dr., P.O. Box 23825, 54305-3825. Tel: 920-437-7531; Fax: 920-437-0694. Conducted by Diocese of Green Bay.

DE PERE. *Norbertine Center for Spirituality* (An Apostolate of the Norbertine Fathers) , St. Norbert Abbey, 1016 N. Broadway, 54115-2697. Tel: 920-337-4315; Fax: 920-337-4328. Email: norbertinecenter@yahoo.com. Web: www.norbertines.org. Rev. Xavier G. Colavechio, O.Praem., Dir. Total in residence 2; Total Staff 6.

MENASHA. *Mount Tabor Center*, 522 2nd St., 54952-3112. Tel: 920-722-8918; Fax: 920-722-8918. Email: mttabor@athenet.net. Web: mttabor.net. Eden Foord, Retreat Dir. & Admin.; Theresa Collier, Admin. Asst.; Katherine Foord, Youth Retreat Dir. Total Staff 4.

OSHKOSH. *Jesuit Retreat House*, 4800 Fahrnwald Rd., 54902-7598. Tel: 920-231-9060; Fax: 920-231-9094. Email: office@jesuitretreathouse.org. Web: www.jesuitretreathouse.org. Revs. John Schwantes, S.J., Dir.; Robert Dufford, S.J.; Sr. Mary Jacqueline Pratt, O.S.U.; Rev. Eugene F. Zimmerman, S.J. Society of Jesus

SHAWANO. *Camp Tekawitha Retreat and Conference Center*, Tel: 920-437-7531, Ext. 8234. P.O. Box 23825, 54305-3825. Tel: 920-437-7531, Ext. 8234. Mrs. Roberta Larson, Dir. (Located on Loon Lake, Shawano); (Boys & Girls ages 7 to 14) Capacity 160.

[M] NEWMAN CENTERS

GREEN BAY. *Ecumenical Center-UWGB* 2420 Nicolet Dr., 54311-7001. Tel: 920-465-5133; Fax: 920-465-0128. Email: info@ecumenical-center.org. Web: www.ecumenical-center.org. Lauric Sratek, Campus Min.; Rev. W. Thomas Long, Chap.

Lawrence University Newman Center (Appleton)

University of Wisconsin Manitowoc Campus Newman Center Tel: 920-684-6691. (Manitowoc)

University of Wisconsin Marinette Campus Newman Center (Marinette)

University of Wisconsin Fox Valley Campus Newman Center (Menasha)

University of Wisconsin Newman Center, 750 Elmwood Ave., Oshkosh, 54901. Tel: 920-233-5555. Tina Koch, Office Mgr.; Rev. Robert Kollath, Dir. & Chap.

[N] MISCELLANEOUS LISTINGS

GREEN BAY. *The Catholic Foundation of the Diocese of Green Bay, Inc.*, 1910 S. Webster Ave., P.O. Box 23825, 54305-3825. Tel: 920-437-7531, Ext. 8173; Fax: 920-435-1330. Email: cbrawner@gbdioc.org. Web: www.gbdioc.org. Cindi Brawner, Exec. Dir.

The Diocesan Charismatic Renewal Center, 1227 13th Ave., 54304. Tel: 920-405-1960. Rev. Msgr. James Vanden Hogen, Liaison; Mrs. Karen Wautlet, Asst. Liaison; Judy Goolsbey, Office Mgr.

St. Francis Xavier Investment Corp., 1910 S. Webster Ave., P.O. Box 23825, 54305-3825. Tel: 920-437-7531, Ext. 8267; Fax: 920-437-0694. Email: tkurkowski@gbdioc.org. Web: gbdioc.org. Tom Kurkowski, Diocesan Finance Officer.

Green Bay Area Catholic High School Foundation, L.T.D., P.O. Box 23825, 54305-3825. Tel: 920-437-7531. Mr. Thomas Olejniczak, Pres.

Green Bay Diocese Cemetery Corporation, 1910 S. Webster Ave., P.O. Box 23825, 54305-3825. Tel: 920-437-7531, Ext. 8229; Fax: 920-437-9296. Email: jruatti@gbdioc.org. Mr. Jon C. Ruatti, Dir. of Cemeteries.

St. Joseph Corporation, Diocesan Central Offices, P.O. Box 23825, 54305-3825. Tel: 920-437-7531; Fax: 920-437-0694. Email: kbrunner@gbdioc.org. Web: www.gbdioc.org. Mr. Kevin Brunner, Admin.

Latin Mass Apostolate Institute of Christ the King , 413 St. John St., 54301. Tel: 920-437-9660; Fax: 920-437-5154. Email: institutegreenbay@pngusq.net. Web: institute-christ-king.org/greebay.htm. Rev. Andreas Hellmann, Chap.

Notre Dame de la Baie Foundation, Inc., 610 Maryhill Dr., 54303. Tel: 920-429-6100; Fax: 920-429-6168. Email: eblumreich@notredameacademy.com. Web: www.NDAFdn.org. Deacon Tim Reilly, Pres.

Sacred Heart Seminary, Inc., P.O. Box 23825, 54305-3825. Tel: 920-437-7531; Fax: 920-435-1330. Rev. Msgr. John B. Dewane, M.A., S.T.L., D.Min., Admin.; Sr. Mary Bride Grubbs, A.N.G., Chancellor.

Teens Encounter Christ (TEC), Green Bay Chapter, P.O. Box 23825, 54305-3825. Tel: 920-437-7531; Fax: 920-437-0694. Email: tpichler@gbdioc.org. Mr. Tony Pichler, Diocesan Liaison.

APPLETON. *St. Elizabeth Hospital Community Foundation, Inc.*, 1506 S. Oneida St., 54915-1397. Tel: 920-738-2859; Fax: 920-738-2061. Email: btincher@affinityhealth.org. Mr. Kevin Nolan, CEO Affinity Health System; Barbara J. Tincher, Exec. Dir. Franciscan Sisters, Daughters of the Sacred Heart of Jesus and Mary (Wheaton, IL)

**ISECP, Inc.*, 418 E. Grant St., 54911. Tel: 920-733-3210. Email: jroemer1@msn.com. Web: www.isecp.org. Sr. Judith A. Roemer, Pres.

A New Genesis (ANG) An Association of the Faithful , 1017 E. Florida Ave., 54911. Tel: 920-437-7531; Fax: 920-437-0694. Email: schaanen@hotmail.com. Web: www.anewgenesis.org. Sr. Carol Haanen, Moderator, St. Joseph Chapel; Most Rev. Aloysius J. Wycislo, D.D. Total Members 28.

DE PERE. *Augustine Stewardship Fund Trust*, 1016 N. Broadway, 54115-2697. Tel: 920-337-4300; Fax: 920-337-4328. Email: gjn@netnet.net. Web: www.norbertines.org.

Canons Regular of Magnovarad, Ltd., 1016 N. Broadway, 54115-2697. Tel: 920-337-4300; Fax: 920-337-4328. Email: rkfinn@netnet.net. Web: www.norbertines.org. Rev. Albin V. Veszelovszky, O.Praem., Pres.; Rt. Rev. Jerome G. Tremel, O.Praem., Vice Pres.; Revs. Joseph S. Rekasi, O.Praem.; Robert K. Finnegan, O.Praem., Sec. & Treas.

Los Amigos del Peru, Inc., 1016 N. Broadway St., 54115-2697. Tel: 920-337-4300; Fax: 920-337-4328. Email: gjn@netnet.net. Web: www.norbertines.org.

NORBERT & CO. A nominee of The Premonstratensian Fathers , 1016 N. Broadway, 54115-2697. Tel: 920-337-4300; Fax: 920-337-4328. Email: gjn@netnet.net. Web: www.norbertines.org. Rt. Rev. Gary Neville, O.Praem, J.C.D.; Very Rev. David M. Komatz, O.Praem.; Rev. John P. Kastenholz, O.Praem.

St. Norbert Abbey Seminary and Education Fund Trust, 1016 N. Broadway, 54115-2697. Tel: 920-337-4300; Fax: 920-337-4328. Email: gjn@netnet.net. Web: www.norbertines.org.

Norbertine Generalate, Inc., 1016 N. Broadway, 54115-2697. Tel: 920-337-4300; Fax: 920-337-4328. Email: rkfinn@netnet.net. Web: www.premontre.org. Most Rev. Thomas A. Handgratinger, O.Praem., Pres., Rome, Italy; Rt. Rev. Gary Neville, O.Praem, J.C.D., Vice Pres.; Rev. Robert K. Finnegan, O.Praem., Sec. & Treas.

Norbertine Retirement Fund Trust, 1016 N. Broadway, 54115-2697. Tel: 920-337-4300; Fax: 920-337-4328. Email: gjn@netnet.net. Web: www.norbertines.org.

Thea Bowman Spirituality Center, Inc., 1016 N. Broadway, 54115. Tel: 920-337-4398. Email: GJN@netnet.net. Rt. Rev. Gary Neville, O.Praem.

DEERBROOK. **Living Waters International, Inc.*, N7544 County Rd. S., 54424. Tel: 715-627-4782; Fax: 715-627-4782. Email: livingh20@livingwatersinternational.org. Web: www.livingwatersinternatioanl.org. Dr. Stephen L. Zimmerman, Ph.D., Pres.

MANITOWOC. *Franciscan Sisters of Christian Charity HealthCare Ministry, Inc.*, 1415 S. Rapids Rd., 54220-9302. Tel: 920-684-7071; Fax: 920-684-6417. Email: lwolf@fhcm.org. Web: www.fhcm.org. Sr. Laura J. Wolf, O.S.F., Pres.

MENASHA. *Affinity Health System*, 1570 Midway Pl., 54952. Tel: 920-720-1713; Fax: 920-720-1720. Email: Knolan@affinityhealth.org. Web: www.affinityhealth.org. Kevin Nolan, Pres. & CEO. Sponsored by Wheaton Franciscan Services, Inc. (Wheaton, IL) and Ministry Health Care, Inc. (Milwaukee, WI).

**Network Health System, Inc.*, 1165 Appleton Rd., P.O. Box 8005, 54952-8005. Tel: 920-720-1712. Kevin Nolan, Pres.

NEENAH. *Global Outreach, Inc.*, 433 Hawthorne St., 54956. Tel: 920-727-1207. Email: globalmom35@sbcglobal.net. Web: www.globaloutreachprogram.com. Gary Elmer, Pres. & Treas.; Tom Kropidlowski, Vice Pres.; Carol Catlin, Sec.; Mary Piette, Dir.

St. Mary High School Foundation, Inc., 1050 Zephyr Dr., 54956-1389. Tel: 920-722-7796; Fax: 920-722-5940. Web: www.smc.k12.wi.us.

STURGEON BAY. *Christ Child Society of Door County*, 5594 Daubner Ln., 54235-9557. Tel: 920-743-8076. Patricia L. Mock, Contact Person.

[O] CLOSED AND MERGED PARISHES

GREEN BAY. *Green Bay Diocesan Archives*, 1910 S. Webster Ave., P.O. Box 23825, 54305-3825. Tel: 920-437-7531, Ext. 8186; Fax: 920-435-1330. Email: jledoux@gbdioc.org. Web: www.gbdioc.org. Parish sacramental records for parishes that have closed or merged can be found at the locations listed below. As the location of sacramental records can change periodically, inquiries for records of parishes on this list should be directed to the above address.

St. Joseph, Alverno Tel: 920-726-4228; Fax: 920-726-4229. Please see St. Thomas the Apostle, Newton.

St. Mary, Argonne Tel: 715-478-3396. Please see St. Joseph, Crandon

St. Mary, Brillion Tel: 920-753-2535; Fax: 920-753-9802. Please see Holy Family, Brillion

St Wendel, Cleveland Tel: 920-726-4228; Fax: 920-726-4229. Please see St. Thomas the Apostle, Newton.

St. John the Baptist, Coleman Tel: 920-897-3226; Fax: 920-897-4677. Please see SS. Francis and Wenceslaus, Coleman.

St. Francis of Assisi, Coleman Tel: 920-897-3226; Fax: 920-897-4677. Please see SS. Francis and Wenceslaus, Coleman.

St. Boniface, De Pere Tel: 920-336-4033; Fax: 920-336-3910. Please see Our Lady of Lourdes, De Pere.

St. Joseph, De Pere Tel: 920-336-4033; Fax: 920-336-3910. Please see Our Lady of Lourdes, De Pere.

SS. Cyril and Methodius, Eaton Tel: 920-863-2593; Fax: 920-845-5180. Please see St. Thomas the Apostle, Humboldt.

St. William, Eland Tel: 715-253-2050; Fax: 715-253-3020. Please see Holy Family-St. William, Wittenberg

St. Michael, Hiles Tel: 715-478-3396. Please see St Joseph, Crandon

Our Lady Queen of Peace, Humboldt Tel: 920-863-2593; Fax: 920-845-5180. Please see St. Thomas the Apostle, Humboldt.

St. George, King Tel: 715-258-3000; Fax: 715-258-5708. Please see St. Mary Magdalene, Waupaca.

St. Wenceslaus, Klondike Tel: 920-897-3226; Fax: 920-897-4677. Please see SS. Francis and Wenceslaus, Coleman.

St. John, Krok Tel: 920-863-8747; Fax: 920-863-5768. Please see St. Therese de Lisieux, Stangelville.

St. Stanislaus Kostka, Langlade Tel: 715-882-2551. Please see SS. James and Stanislaus, White Lake.

St. Charles Borromeo, Lena Tel: 920-829-5222. Please see Holy Cross, Lena.

St. Peter, Lincoln Tel: 920-837-2852. Please see St. Peter and St. Hubert, Rosiere.

St. Patrick, Maple Grove Tel: 920-756-2535; Fax: 920-756-9802. Please see Holy Family, Brillion/Reedsville.

St. Francis De Paul, Marchand (Duvall) Tel: 920-866-2410; Fax: 920-866-3591. Please see St. Louis, Dyckesville.

Our Lady of Lourdes, Marinette Tel: 715-735-9100; Fax: 715-735-9650. Please see Holy Family, Marinette.

Sacred Heart of Jesus, Marinette Tel: 715-735-9100; Fax: 715-735-9650. Please see Holy Family, Marinette.

St. Anthony, Marinette Tel: 715-735-9100; Fax:

715-735-9650. Please see Holy Family, Marinette.

St. Joseph, Marinette Tel: 715-735-9100; Fax: 715-735-9650. Please see Holy Family, Marinette.

St. Joseph, Montpelier Tel: 920-863-8747; Fax: 920-863-5768. Please see St. Therese de Lisieux, Stangelville.

St. Joseph-St. John, Montpelier Tel: 920-863-8747; Fax: 920-863-5768. Please see St. Therese de Lisieux, Stangelville.

St. Mary, Namur Tel: 920-825-7555; Fax: 920-825-1492. Please see St. Francis and St. Mary, Brussels.

St. Joseph, Norman Tel: 920-776-1555; Fax: 920-776-1555. Please see St. Isidore the Farmer, Tisch Mills

St. Casimir, Northeim Tel: 920-726-4228; Fax: 920-726-4229. Please see St. Thomas the Apostle, Newton.

St. Joseph, Oconto Tel: 920-835-5900; Fax: 920-835-5907. Please see Holy Trinity, Oconto.

St. Peter, Oconto Tel: 920-835-5900; Fax: 920-835-5907. Please see Holy Trinity, Oconto.

St. Isidore, Osman Tel: 920-726-4228; Fax 920-726-4229. Please see St. Thomas the Apostle, Newton.

St. Leo, Pound Tel: 920-897-3226; Fax: 920-897-4677. Please see SS. Francis and Wenceslaus, Coleman.

St. Mary, Reedsville Tel: 920-756-2535; Fax: 920-756-9802. Please see Holy Family, Brillion

St. Mary-St. Patrick, Reedsville/ Maple Grove Tel: 920-756-2535; Fax: 920-756-9802. Please see Holy Family, Brillion

St. Adalbert, Slovan Tel: 920-837-7234; Fax: 920-837-2361. Please see Holy Trinity, Casco.

St. Joseph of the Lake, South Branch Tel: 715-799-3811; Fax: 715-799-5092. Please see St. Michael, Keshena

Sacred Heart, Spruce Tel: 920-829-5222. Please see Holy Cross, Lena.

St. John the Baptist, St. John Tel: 920-989-1515; Fax: 920-989-8585. Please see St. John-Sacred Heart, Sherwood.

St. Lawrence, Stangelville Tel: 920-863-8747; Fax: 920-863-5768. Please see St. Therese de Lisieux, Stangelville.

St. Mary, Stark Tel: 920-864-7641. Please see St. Mary, Glenmore.

St. Odile, Thiry Daems Tel: 920-866-9961. Please see St. Joseph, Champion.

Nativity of the BVM, Tisch Mills Tel: 920-776-1555; Fax: 920-776-1555. Please see St. Isidore the Farmer, Tisch Mills

St. Martin, Tonet Tel: 920-866-9961. Please see St. Joseph, Champion.

Holy Redeemer-Sacred Heart, Two Rivers Tel: 920-793-4531; Fax: 920-793-8067. Please see St. Peter the Fisherman, Two Rivers

Sacred Heart, Two Rivers Tel: 920-793-4531; Fax: 920-793-8067. Please see St. Peter the Fisherman, Two Rivers

St. Luke, Two Rivers Tel: 920-793-4531; Fax: 920-793-8067. Please see St. Peter the Fisherman, Two Rivers

St. Mark, Two Rivers Tel: 920-793-4531; Fax: 920-793-8067. Please see St. Peter the Fisherman, Two Rivers

St. Amand, Walhain Tel: 920-866-9961. Please see St. Joseph Champion.

St. Hedwig, West Kewaunee Tel: 920-863-8747; Fax: 920-863-5768. Please see St. Therese de Lisieux, Stangelville.

RELIGIOUS INSTITUTES OF MEN REPRESENTED IN THE DIOCESE

For further details refer to the corresponding bracketed number in the Religious Institutes of Men or Women section.

[0330]—*Brothers of the Christian Schools* (Midwest Province), Burr Ridge, IL—F.S.C.

[0900]—*Canons Regular of Premontre*—O.Praem.

[0470]—*The Capuchin Friars* (Province of St. Joseph)—O.F.M.Cap.

[1130]—*Congregation of the Priests of the Sacred Heart*—S.C.J.

[0690]—*Franciscan Friars*—O.F.M.

[]—*Holy Ghost Fathers*—C.S.SP.

[0305]—*Institute of Christ the King*

[0690]—*Jesuit Fathers and Brothers* (Wisconsin Province)—S.J.

[0910]—*Oblates of Mary Immaculate*—O.M.I.

[1200]—*Society of the Divine Savior*—S.D.S.

RELIGIOUS INSTITUTES OF WOMEN REPRESENTED IN THE DIOCESE

[3710]—*Congregation of the Sisters of St. Agnes*—C.S.A.

[0420]—*Discalced Carmelite Nuns*—O.C.D.

[1070-03]—*Dominican Sisters*—O.P.

[1070-09]—*Dominican Sisters*—O.P.

[1070-14]—*Dominican Sisters*—O.P.

[1070-13]—*Dominican Sisters*—O.P.

[1170]—*Felician Sisters*—C.S.S.F.

[1230]—*Franciscan Sisters of Christian Charity*—O.S.F.

[]—*Franciscan Sisters of Perpetual Adoration*—F.S.P.A.

[1240]—*Franciscan Sisters, Daughters of the Sacred Hearts of Jesus and Mary*—O.S.F.

[1820]—*Hospital Sisters of the Third Order of St. Francis*—O.S.F.

[3070]—*North American Union Sisters of Our Lady of Charity*—N.A.U.-O.L

[3440]—*Religious Hospitallers of Saint Joseph*—R.H.S.J.

[2970]—*School Sisters of Notre Dame*—S.S.N.D.

[1680]—*School Sisters of St. Francis*—S.S.S.F.

[2630]—*Sisters of Mercy of the Holy Cross*—S.C.S.C.

[3800]—*Sisters of St. Elizabeth*—S.S.E.

[1705]—*The Sisters of St. Francis of Assisi*—O.S.F.

[1550]—*Sisters of St. Francis of the Holy Cross*—O.S.F.

[3840]—*Sisters of St. Joseph of Carondelet* (Prov. of St. Louis)—C.S.J.

[3930]—*Sisters of St. Joseph of the Third Order of St. Francis*—S.S.J.-T.O

[1030]—*Sisters of the Divine Savior*—S.D.S.

[4100]—*Sisters of the Sorrowful Mother (Third Order of St. Francis)*—S.S.M.

DIOCESAN CEMETERIES

GREEN BAY. *Diocesan Cemeteries*, P.O. Box 23825, 54305-3825. Tel: 920-437-7531, Ext. 8229. Mr. Jon C. Ruatti, Diocesan Dir.

Allouez Catholic Cemetery and Mausoleum, 2121 Riverside Dr., 54301.

Queen of Peace Cemetery & Mausoleum, 101 6th St., P.O. Box 535, Antigo, 54409.

St. Joseph Cemetery, P.O. Box 2676, Appleton, 54913-2676.

Mount Olivet Cemetery, S. Erie St., De Pere, 54115.

Calvary Cemetery & Calvary Chapel Mausoleum, 2601 S. 14th St., Manitowoc, 54220-6467.

Oconto Catholic Cemetery, c/o 716 Madison St., Oconto, 54153. Tel: 920-835-5900.

Oshkosh Catholic Cemetery, 1905 Roosevelt Ave., Oshkosh, 54901.

St. Joseph Cemetery & Mausoleum, 25 N. Elgin, Sturgeon Bay, 54235.

NECROLOGY

† Gilsoul, James M., Institute, WI SS. Peter and Paul; Sturgeon Bay, WI St. Joseph.—Died Feb. 12, 2003

† Kilsdonk, Edward, (Retired)—Died July 14, 2003

† Knier, Aloysius M., (Retired)—Died Feb. 20, 2003

† Kolbusz, Stanley, (Retired)—Died June 23, 2003

† Laux, Donald, (Retired)—Died June 28, 2003

† McLaughlin, John, (Retired)—Died Sept. 22, 2003

† Schrage, Frank P., Little Chute, WI St. John Nepomucene.—Died May 5, 2003

† Ver Bust, Richard, (Retired)—Died July 11, 2003

Diocese of Greensburg

(Dioecesis Greensburgensis)

Most Reverend

LAWRENCE E. BRANDT

Bishop of Greensburg; ordained December 19, 1969; appointed Bishop of Greensburg January 2, 2004; installed March 4, 2004. *Office: 723 E. Pittsburgh St., Greensburg, PA 15601.*

Pastoral Center: 723 E. Pittsburgh St., Greensburg, PA 15601. Tel: 724-837-0901; Fax: 724-837-0857.

Web: www.catholicgbg.org

Most Reverend

ANTHONY G. BOSCO, D.D., J.C.L.

Retired Bishop of Greensburg; ordained June 7, 1952; appointed Auxiliary Bishop of Pittsburgh and Titular Bishop of Labico May 14, 1970; consecrated June 30, 1970; appointed Bishop of Greensburg April 14, 1987; installed June 30, 1987; retired January 2, 2004.

ESTABLISHED MARCH 10, 1951.

Square Miles 3,334.

Comprises the Counties of Armstrong, Fayette, Indiana and Westmoreland in the State of Pennsylvania.

For legal titles of parishes and diocesan institutions, consult the Chancery Office.

STATISTICAL OVERVIEW

Personnel	
Bishop	1
Abbots	1
Priests: Diocesan Active in Diocese	93
Priests: Diocesan Active Outside Diocese	8
Priests: Retired, Sick or Absent	37
Number of Diocesan Priests	138
Religious Priests in Diocese	79
Total Priests in Diocese	217
Ordinations:	
Religious Priests	3
Transitional Deacons	3
Total Brothers	23
Total Sisters	325
Parishes	
Parishes	102
With Resident Pastor:	
Resident Diocesan Priests	74
Resident Religious Priests	8
Without Resident Pastor:	
Administered by Priests	20
Closed Parishes	1
Professional Ministry Personnel:	
Sisters	20
Lay Ministers	65
Welfare	
Catholic Hospitals	1
Total Assisted	20,347
Homes for the Aged	2
Total Assisted	129
Special Centers for Social Services	6
Total Assisted	11,231
Residential Care of Disabled	1
Total Assisted	40
Other Institutions	2
Total Assisted	3
Educational	
Diocesan Students in Other Seminaries	4
Seminaries, Religious	1
Students Religious	26
Total Seminarians	30
Colleges and Universities	2
Total Students	5,141
High Schools, Diocesan and Parish	2
Total Students	780
Elementary Schools, Diocesan and Parish	20
Total Students	4,224
Elementary Schools, Private	3
Total Students	235
Catechesis/Religious Education:	
High School Students	2,895
Elementary Students	8,923
Total Students under Catholic Instruction	22,228
Teachers in the Diocese:	
Priests	25
Brothers	24
Sisters	44
Lay Teachers	482
Vital Statistics	
Receptions into the Church:	
Infant Baptism Totals	1,729
Adult Baptism Totals	140
Received into Full Communion	219
First Communions	2,247
Confirmations	2,369
Marriages:	
Catholic	466
Interfaith	344
Total Marriages	810
Deaths	2,739
Total Catholic Population	181,167
Total Population	679,990

Former Bishops—Most Revs. HUGH L. LAMB, S.T.D., First Bishop of Greensburg; ord. May 29, 1915; appt. Titular Bishop of Helos and Auxiliary of Philadelphia Dec. 19, 1935; consecrated March 19, 1936; promoted to Greensburg May 28, 1951; installed Jan. 16, 1952; died Dec. 8, 1959; WILLIAM G. CONNARE, D.D. (Retired), ord. June 14, 1936; appt. Feb. 23, 1960; consecrated May 4, 1960; retired Jan. 20, 1987; died June 12, 1995.

Pastoral Center—723 E. Pittsburgh St., Greensburg, 15601-2697. Tel: 724-837-0901; Fax: 724-837-0857. Office Hours: Mon.-Fri. 8:45-5

Vicar General/General Executive Director, Moderator of the Curia—Rev. ROGER A. STATNICK, V.G., S.T.L., Ph.D. Tel: 724-837-0901.

Chancellor/Associate General Executive Director—Rev. LAWRENCE T. PERSICO, J.C.L. Tel: 724-837-0901.

Executive Director of Finance—Mr. MICHAEL J. MCGEE.

Deaneries—Rev. JAMES T. GASTON, V.F., Deanery 1; Rev. Msgrs. WILLIAM G. CHARNOKI, V.F., J.C.L., Deanery 2; JOHN L. CONWAY, V.F., Deanery 3; Rev. JOSEPH P. MADDALENA, S.T.L., V.F., Deanery 4; VACANT, Deanery 5; Rev. KENNETH G. ZACCAGNINI, V.F., Deanery 6.

Director for Religious—VACANT, Office, 723 E. Pittsburgh St., Greensburg, 15601-2697. Tel: 724-837-0901.

Tribunal— Address all correspondence to *723 E. Pittsburgh St., Greensburg, 15601-2697.* Tel: 724-837-0901.

Judicial Vicar—Rev. WILLIAM R. RATHGEB, J.C.L.

Defender of Bond—Rev. LAWRENCE T. PERSICO, J.C.L.

Judges—Rev. RICHARD J. KOSISKO, J.C.L.; Rev. Msgr. WILLIAM G. CHARNOKI, V.F., J.C.L.; Rev. ANTHONY J. CARBONE, J.C.L.

Advocate—Rev. DANIEL C. MAHONEY.

Notaries—Mrs. CINDY J. OZZELLO; Ms. KATHLEEN POLOSKY.

Tribunal Coordinator—Ms. KATHLEEN POLOSKY.

Advisory Bodies

College of Consultors—Most Rev. ANTHONY G. BOSCO, D.D., J.C.L., Presider (Retired); Revs. ROGER A. STATNICK, V.G., S.T.L., Ph.D.; KENNETH G. ZACCAGNINI, V.F.; Rev. Msgr. JOHN L. CONWAY, V.F.; Revs. LAWRENCE R. KINIRY; MICHAEL W. MATUSAK; JOHN A. MOINEAU; LEONARD W. STOVIAK; LARRY J. KULICK.

Diocesan Pastoral Council—Ms. SHIRLEY A. MAKUTA, Region 1; VACANT, Region 2; Miss JUDY LATIMER, Region 3; Mrs. ARLENE R. SMITH, Region 4; Rev. ANDREW M. KAWECKI, Region 5; Mr. CARL BELTRAM, Region 6; Mr. WILLIAM G. MERCHANT, Region 7; Mr. LUCIUS P. MANNS, Region 8; Rev. MARTIN R. BARTEL, O.S.B., Region 9; Ms. COLLEEN M. YOTHERS, Region 10; Mr. CLAUDE G. MYERS, Region 11; Rev. JONATHAN WISNESKI, Region 12; Mrs. DARLA A. LABUDA, Region 13; Mr. CHRISTOPHER R. SPARKS, Region 14; Rev. PAUL A. LISIK, Region 15; Mr. RICHARD J. MLINARCIK JR., Region 16; Mrs. ELAINE M. SWANEY, Region 17; Mr. DAVID KENNEY, Region 18; Very Rev. EARL HENRY, O.S.B.; Sr. LOIS SCULCO, S.C.

Special Appointment—Rev. LARRY J. KULICK; Very Rev. EARL HENRY, O.S.B.; Sr. LOIS SCULCO, S.C.

Bishop's Priests Council—Rev. ROGER A. STATNICK, V.G., S.T.L., Ph.D.; Rev. Msgr. JOHN L. CONWAY, V.F.; Revs. JOSEPH P. MADDALENA, S.T.L., V.F.; JAMES T. GASTON, V.F.; Rev. Msgr. WILLIAM G. CHARNOKI, V.F., J.C.L.; Rev. KENNETH G. ZACCAGNINI, V.F.; Rev. Msgr. ROBERT J. SHUDA; Revs. J. EDWARD MCCULLOUGH; LEONARD W. STOVIAK; JOHN A. MOINEAU; JOHN A. REGOLI; LAWRENCE R. KINIRY; MICHAEL W. MATUSAK; RICHARD J. KOSISKO, J.C.L.; LARRY J. KULICK.

Finance Council—Most Rev. ANTHONY G. BOSCO, D.D., J.C.L. (Retired); Rev. ROGER A. STATNICK, V.G., S.T.L., Ph.D.; Mr. JOSEPH G. KLOCEK; Mr. JOHN A. ROBERTSHAW JR.; Mrs. NORMA F. SCHERER; Rev. THADDEUS J. KACZMAREK; Mr. CHARLES A. FAGAN III; Mr. B. PATRICK COSTELLO.

Diocesan Offices, Commissions and Special Programs

The Catholic Foundation for the Diocese of Greensburg— Under Declaration of Trust dated 1st day of November, 1988, as amended 2nd day of November 1992 having as its purpose the support of any Roman Catholic benevolent, charitable, educational or missionary undertaking. Most Rev. ANTHONY G. BOSCO, D.D., J.C.L., Chm. Board of Trustees (Retired); Revs. ROGER A. STATNICK, V.G., S.T.L., Ph.D., Vice Chm.; LAWRENCE T. PERSICO, J.C.L., Assoc. Vice Chm.; Mr. JOHN A. ROBERTSHAW JR., Pres.; Mr. CHARLES A. FAGAN III, Sec.; Mr. MICHAEL J. MCGEE, Treas., 723 E. Pittsburgh St., Greensburg, 15601-2697.

The Catholic Institute of Greensburg— A Corporation, not-for-profit, incorporated under the law of the Commonwealth of Pennsylvania on the 4th day of June, 1954 having as its purpose the support of any Roman Catholic benevolent, charitable, educational or missionary undertaking.

Board of Members of the Corporation—Most Rev. ANTHONY G. BOSCO, D.D., J.C.L., Pres. (Retired); Revs. ROGER A. STATNICK, V.G., S.T.L., Ph.D., Vice Pres.; LAWRENCE T. PERSICO, J.C.L., Sec.

Board of Trustees—Mr. MARK E. LOPUSHANSKY, Pres.; Mr. MICHAEL J. MCGEE, Sec.; Mr. LAWRENCE S. BUSCH; Mrs. SHEILA R. MURRAY, Staff Member, 723 E. Pittsburgh St., Greensburg, 15601-2697.

Greensburg Catholic Accent and Communications, Inc.— A corporation, not-for-profit, under the laws of the Commonwealth of Pennsylvania having as its purpose the support of any Roman Catholic benevolent, charitable, educational or missionary undertaking. Most Rev. ANTHONY G. BOSCO, D.D., J.C.L., CEO (Retired); Rev. ROGER A. STATNICK, V.G., S.T.L., Ph.D., Vice Pres.; Mr. MICHAEL J. MCGEE, Treas., 723 E. Pittsburgh St., Greensburg, 15601-2697. Tel: 724-837-0901; Fax: 724-837-0857.

Catholic Charities of the Diocese of Greensburg, PA, Inc.— A corporation not-for-profit incorporated under the law of the Commonwealth of Pennsylvania on the 27th day of August, 1954, having as its purpose, the support of any Roman Catholic benevolent, charitable, educational or missionary undertaking. Most Rev. ANTHONY G. BOSCO, D.D., J.C.L., Chm. Bd. Members of the Corp. (Retired); Judge DEBRA PEZZE, Pres. Bd. of Trustees; Rev. RAYMOND E. RIFFLE, M.P.A., Exec. Dir., 711 E. Pittsburgh St., Greensburg, 15601-2636. Tel: 724-837-1840; Fax: 724-837-4077.

Archives—723 E. Pittsburgh St., Greensburg, 15601. Tel: 724-837-0901.

Catholic Charities—Rev. RAYMOND E. RIFFLE, M.P.A., Exec. Dir.; Mr. ROBERT MCHENRY, Dir. Oper. & Finance; Mrs. JUDY MODECKI, Dir., Coordinated Svcs. & Devel., 711 E. Pittsburgh St., Greensburg, 15601-2636. Tel: 724-837-1840; Fax: 724-837-4077.

Catholic Relief Services Representative—Rev. J. EDWARD MCCULLOUGH, 723 E. Pittsburgh St., Greensburg, 15601-2697. Tel: 724-837-0901.

Communications—Ms. ANGELA J. BURROWS, Exec. Dir., 725 E. Pittsburgh St., P.O. Box 850, Greensburg, 15601-2697. Tel: 724-834-4010; Fax: 724-836-5650.

Office of IT & Telecommunications—Ms. KAREN CORNELL, Dir.; Mr. BRIAN LOOSZ, Network Analyst; Mr. TONY KRANCE, Internet/Lotus Notes System Admin.; Mr. GREGG WHITFIELD, Client Technology Analyst & Telecommunication Specialist; Mr. DARREN DORN, Client Technology Specialist; JORDAN GOVI, Database & System Admin.; Mrs. NINA MANNO, Instructional Technology Analyst; Mrs. CINDY STICKLE, IT Asset Management & Contract Admin.

Purchasing and Services Office—Mr. RICHARD LITTLE, Coord., 723 E. Pittsburgh St., Greensburg, 15601-2697. Tel: 724-837-0901; Fax: 724-837-0857.

Office of Pastoral Life and Planning—Dr. MARY ANN GUBISH, Dir.; Rev. WILLIAM J. LECHNAR, Assoc. Dir., 723 E. Pittsburgh St., Greensburg, 15601-2697. Tel: 724-837-0901; Fax: 724-837-0857.

Department of Education and Spiritual Formation—Sr. GERTRUDE FOLEY, S.C., Exec. Dir., 723 E. Pittsburgh St., Greensburg, 15601-2697. Tel: 724-837-0901; Fax: 724-837-0857. Email: gfoley@dioceseofgreensburg.org.

Office of Catholic Schools—Mr. JOHN BECK, Assoc. Supt.; Ms. DEBORAH WOJCIECHOWSKI, Coord. Govt. Programs & Technology. Email: dwojciech@catholicgbg.org; Miss THERESE TELEPAK, Dir. Youth & Youth Adult Ministry, 723 E. Pittsburgh St., Greensburg, 15601-2697. Tel: 724-837-0901; Fax: 724-837-0857.

Office for Worship—Dr. FRED MOLECK, Dir.

Office for Catechesis—Sr. JOAN SUPEL, O.P., Dir.

Youth Formation—Miss THERESE TELEPAK, Dir. Youth & Youth Adult Ministry.

Marriage Formation—Coordinators: RICHARD RYBA; LEEANNA RYBA.

Athletics—Mr. ANGELO DIPPOLITO, Coord.

Diocesan Catholic Scoutmaster—Rev. LAWRENCE L. MANCHAS, Coord., 723 E. Pittsburgh St., Greensburg, 15601-2697. Tel: 724-837-0901; Fax: 724-837-0857.

Office for Ministry Development—Ms. MARSHA KABLE, Dir.; Revs. LARRY J. KULICK, Consultant, Priestly Vocations; JOSEPH P. MADDALENA, S.T.L., V.F., Consultant Continuing Clergy Formation, 723 E. Pittsburgh St., Greensburg, 15601-2697. Tel: 724-837-0901; Fax: 724-837-0857.

Missions— Society for the Propagation of the Faith and Holy Childhood, Rev. J. EDWARD MCCULLOUGH, 723 E. Pittsburgh St., Greensburg, 15601-2697. Tel: 724-837-0901; Fax: 724-837-0857.

Newspaper—725 E. Pittsburgh St., P.O. Box 850, Greensburg, 15601-2697. Tel: 724-834-4010; Fax: 724-836-5650. Mr. VINCENT A. CAPOZZI, Editor; Mr. JEROME ZUFELT, Mng. Editor. "The Catholic Accent"

Engineering and Facility Management Office—Mr. EDGAR R. TURNER, Dir.; Mr. RUSSELL FORAN, Assoc. Dir., 723 E. Pittsburgh St., Greensburg, 15601-2697. Tel: 724-837-0901; 724-552-2570; Fax: 724-836-5592.

Stewardship—Mr. MICHAEL LUCOTCH, Dir. Stewardship & Devel.; Mr. JAMES A. SCHUCOLSKY, Assoc. Dir. Stewardship & Devel., 723 E. Pittsburgh St., Greensburg, 15601-2697. Tel: 724-837-0901; Fax: 724-837-0857.

SPECIAL PROGRAMS—

Apostleship of Prayer—Rev. J. EDWARD MCCULLOUGH, Dir., 459 Ranch Rd., Dunbar, 15431. Tel: 724-277-4236; Fax: 724-277-0192.

Apostolate for the Deaf—VACANT, Diocese of Greensburg, 723 E. Pittsburgh St., Greensburg, 15601. Tel: 724-837-0901.

Catholic Business and Professional Women's Association—VACANT, 723 E. Pittsburgh St., Greensburg, 15601-2697. Tel: 724-837-0901; Fax: 724-837-0857.

Catholic Daughters of America—Rev. J. EDWARD MCCULLOUGH, Dir., 459 Ranch Rd., Dunbar, 15431. Tel: 724-277-4236; Fax: 724-277-0192.

Cemeteries—723 E. Pittsburgh St., Greensburg, 15601-2697. Tel: 724-837-0901.

Charismatic—Sr. ANN INFANGER, S.C., Moderator, Seton Hill College, Greensburg, 15601. Tel: 724-834-2200, Ext. 374.

Cursillo—VACANT.

Diocesan Council of Catholic Women—Rev. DONALD J. MONDELLO, Dir., 1204 Ligonier St., Latrobe, 15650. Tel: 724-539-9751.

Holy Childhood Association—Rev. J. EDWARD MCCULLOUGH, Dir., 723 E. Pittsburgh St., Greensburg, 15601-2697. Tel: 724-837-0901; Fax: 724-837-0857.

Holy Name Society—Rev. PATRICK J. O'CONNOR, Dir., 61 Mill St., Uniontown, 15401. Tel: 724-438-2341.

Legion of Mary—Rev. HENRY P. DINICCO, Dir., 135 Carriage Dr., North Huntington, 15642. Tel: 724-861-5424.

Pilgrimages—Rev. J. EDWARD MCCULLOUGH, Dir., 459 Ranch Rd., Dunbar, 15431. Tel: 724-277-4236.

Priests' Eucharistic League—Rev. J. EDWARD MCCULLOUGH, 459 Ranch Rd., Dunbar, 15431. Tel: 724-277-4236.

St. Thomas More Guild for Lawyers—723 E. Pittsburgh St., Greensburg, 15601-2697. Tel: 724-837-0901.

St. Vincent de Paul Society—Rev. JOHN A. SEDLAK, Spiritual Dir., St. Hedwig Church, Church St., Box 251, Smock, 15480. Tel: 724-677-2110.

Victim Assistance Coordinator—Rev. ROGER A. STATNICK, V.G., S.T.L., Ph.D. Tel: 724-837-0901. Email: rstatnick@dioceseofgreensburg.org.

CLERGY, PARISHES, MISSIONS AND PAROCHIAL SCHOOLS

CITY OF GREENSBURG
(WESTMORELAND COUNTY)

1—BLESSED SACRAMENT CATHEDRAL, [CEM] Revs. Michael J. Begolly, D.Min., M.A.; Jonathan J. Wisneski, M.Div., M.A.; Helene Paharik, Pastoral Assoc.; Jack W. Simon, Business Mgr.
Res.: 300 N. Main St., 15601. Tel: 724-834-3710; Fax: 724-834-1518.
School—Aquinas Academy See separate listing under Elementary Schools in the Institution section.
Catechesis/Religious Program—Sr. Susan Jenny, S.C., D.R.E. Students 239.

2—ST. BRUNO, Rev. Blane L. Resko, O.S.B.
Res.: 1707 Poplar St., 15601. Tel: 724-836-0690; Fax: 724-834-9980.
School—Aquinas Academy See separate listing under Elementary Schools in the Institution section.
Catechesis/Religious Program—Tel: 724-836-0690, Ext. 11. Donna DeLoretta, D.R.E. Students 88.

3—OUR LADY OF GRACE, Revs. Raymond E. Riffle, M.P.A.; Daniel L. Blout.
Res.: 1001 Mount Pleasant Rd., 15601. Tel: 724-838-9480; Fax: 724-838-1842.
School—Aquinas Academy See separate listing under Elementary Schools in the Institution section.
Catechesis/Religious Program—Tel: 724-832-6738. Patricia Santia, D.R.E. Tel: 724-836-5356. Students 343.

4—ST. PAUL, Rev. Daniel C. Mahoney.
Res.: 820 Carbon Rd., 15601. Tel: 724-834-6880; Fax: 724-834-1492.
School—Aquinas Academy See separate listing under Elementary Schools in the Institution section.
Catechesis/Religious Program—Sharon Balchus, D.R.E. Students 170.

OUTSIDE THE CITY OF GREENSBURG

APOLLO, ARMSTRONG CO., ST. JAMES THE GREATER, Rev. John T. Sweeney.
Res.: 109 Owens View, 15613. Tel: 724-478-4958; Fax: 724-478-3551.

ARNOLD, WESTMORELAND CO., ALL SAINTS, (Slovak), Rev. Richard G. Curci, Admin.
Res.: 1700 Leishman Ave., 15068. Tel: 724-335-8232.

AVONMORE, WESTMORELAND CO., ST. AMBROSE, Rev. Peter L. Peretti.
Res.: P.O. Box 617, 505 Cambria Ave., 15618. Tel: 724-697-4129; Fax: 724-697-5116.

BELLE VERNON, WESTMORELAND CO., ST. SEBASTIAN, Revs. Lawrence L. Manchas, Admin.; Ronald L. Cyktor Jr.
Res.: 801 Broad Ave., 15012. Tel: 724-929-9300; Fax: 724-930-7611.
School—815 Broad Ave., 15012. Tel: 724-929-5143; Fax: 724-929-3038. Dr. Mathew F. Harris, Prin. Lay Teachers 17; Students 267.

BLAIRSVILLE, INDIANA CO., SS. SIMON AND JUDE, Rev. Chester J. Raimer.
Res.: 155 N. Brady St., 15717. Tel: 724-459-7103; Fax: 724-459-5314.
Catechesis/Religious Program—Becky Feldbusch, D.R.E. Students 59.

BOVARD, WESTMORELAND CO., ST. BEDE, Rev. Claude Pollak, O.S.B.
c/o St. Vincent Archabbey: 300 Fraser Purchase Rd.,, Latrobe, 15650. Tel: 724-532-6752; Fax: 724-537-3690.

BRADY'S BEND, ARMSTRONG CO., ST. PATRICK, [CEM 2] Rev. Anthony W. Ditto.
Res.: R.D. 1, Box 78, 16028. Tel: 724-526-5079; Fax: 724-526-3028.
Chapel—Sugar Creek, Chapel of St. Patrick, Brady's Bend [CEM]Tel: 724-445-2459.

BROWNSVILLE, FAYETTE CO.

1—ST. MARY, (Slovak), [CEM] Rev. Vincent J. Gigliotti.
Res.: 118 Church St., 15417 Tel: 724-785-7781; Fax: 724-785-0844.
Catechesis/Religious Program—Tel: 724-632-6316. Anita LaMendola, D.R.E. Students 12.

2—ST. PETER, [CEM 2] Rev. Vincent J. Gigliotti.
Res.: 304 Shaffner Ave., 15417. Tel: 724-785-7781; Fax: 724-785-0844.

CADOGAN, ARMSTRONG CO., ST. LAWRENCE, [CEM] Rev. Edward Volz, O.S.P.P.E.
Res.: P.O. Box 114, 16212. Tel: 724-763-1089; Fax: 724-763-8100.
Catechesis/Religious Program—Tel: 724-763-7973. Patricia Shevchuk, D.R.E. Students 125.
Chapel—Nicholson Run, Guardian Angel Cemetery and Chapel

CALUMET, WESTMORELAND CO., ST. STANISLAUS, (Polish), [CEM] Rev. William C. McGuirk, Admin.
Res.: P.O. Box 56, 15621. Tel: 724-423-4052; Fax: 724-423-4438.

CARDALE, FAYETTE CO., MADONNA OF CZESTOCHOWA, (Polish), [CEM] Rev. Stephen R. Bugay, Admin.
Res.: 212 Filbert-Orient Rd., New Salem, 15468. Tel: 724-246-9639. In Res., Rev. James W. Clark.

CLYMER, INDIANA CO., CHURCH OF THE RESURRECTION, [CEM] Revs. Andrew M. Kawecki; Dennis E. Sheehy; Rudolph J. Koser.
Administration Center—349 Morris St., 15728-1266. Tel: 724-254-3041; Fax: 724-254-3045.
Catechesis/Religious Program—Gregory Petrucci, D.R.E. Students 95.
Chapel—Camerons Bottom, Chapel of Church of the Resurrection, Clymer

CONNELLSVILLE, FAYETTE CO.

1—HOLY TRINITY, (Polish), [CEM] Rev. John M. Butler, Admin. In Res., Rev. Dennis A. Bogusz. Tel: 724-626-0736.
Res.: 109 N. Seventh St., 15425. Tel: 724-628-7061; Fax: 724-628-8601.
School—Conn-Area Catholic School See separate listing under Elementary Schools in the Institution section.

2—IMMACULATE CONCEPTION, [CEM 5] Rev. Terry A. Hercik.
Res.: 148 E. Crawford Ave., 15425. Tel: 724-628-8550; Fax: 724-628-3410.
School—Conn-Area Catholic School See separate listing under Elementary Schools in the Institution section.
Chapel—Dawson, Sacred Heart Chapel
3—ST. JOHN THE EVANGELIST, (Slovak), [CEM] Rev. John M. Butler.
Res.: 908 W. Crawford Ave., 15425. Tel: 724-628-2112.
School—Conn-Area Catholic School See separate listing under Elementary Schools in the Institution section.
4—ST. RITA, (Italian), [CEM] Rev. Francis A. Lesniowski.
Res.: 116 S. Second St., 15425. Tel: 724-628-4015.
School—Conn-Area Catholic School See separate listing under Elementary Schools in the Institution section.
Catechesis/Religious Program—Tel: 724-628-0979. Raymond Gallo, D.R.E. Students 104.
CORAL, INDIANA CO., ST. FRANCIS, [CEM] Rev. Lawrence R. Kiniry.
Res.: P.O. Box G, 15731. Tel: 724-479-9542; Fax: 724-479-1130.
Catechesis/Religious Program—Tel: 724-479-8885; Fax: 724-479-1130. Sr. Donna Mulligan, D.R.E.; Jackie Zoldak, D.R.E. Students 60.
CRABTREE, WESTMORELAND CO., ST. BARTHOLOMEW, [CEM] Rev. Richard Ulam, O.S.B. (PIT).
Res.: P.O. Box A, 15624. Tel: 724-834-0709; Fax: 724-832-3768.
DELMONT, WESTMORELAND CO., ST. JOHN BAPTIST DE LA SALLE, Rev. James M. Goldberg.
Res.: 497 Athena Dr., 15626. Tel: 724-468-4221; Fax: 724-468-6206.
DERRY, WESTMORELAND CO., ST. JOSEPH, [CEM] Rev. Stephen C. West.
Rectory—117 S. Ligonier St., 15627. Tel: 724-694-5359; Fax: 724-694-6215.
DONEGAL, WESTMORELAND CO., ST. RAYMOND OF THE MOUNTAINS, [CEM] Rev. John J. Harrold.
Res.: P.O. Box 330, 15628. Tel: 724-593-7479; Fax: 724-593-5934.
DUNBAR, FAYETTE CO., ST. ALOYSIUS, [CEM] Rev. J. Edward McCullough.
Res.: 459 Ranch Rd., 15431. Tel: 724-277-4236; Fax: 724-277-0192.
Catechesis/Religious Program—Tel: 724-277-8102. Elizabeth Jaynes, D.R.E. Students 68.
EAST VANDERGRIFT, WESTMORELAND CO., OUR LADY, QUEEN OF PEACE, Rev. Michael J. Sciberras.
Res.: 400 Kennedy Ave., P.O. Box 429, 15629. Tel: 724-567-7603; Fax: 724-568-3365.
Catechesis/Religious Program—Fax: 724-568-3365. Carol Hollenbaugh, D.R.E. Students 55.
ERNEST, INDIANA CO., CHURCH OF THE ASSUMPTION, Closed., For inquiries for parish records contact Church of the Resurrection, Clymer.
EVERSON, FAYETTE CO., ST. JOSEPH, (Polish), [CEM] Rev. Robert M. Washko.
Res.: 201 Painter St., 15631. Tel: 724-887-6714.
EXPORT, WESTMORELAND CO., ST. MARY, Rev. James M. Goldberg, Admin.; Sr. Georgia Litzenberg, S.C., Pastoral Assoc.
Res.: 5900 Kennedy Ave., 15632. Tel: 724-327-0647; Fax: 724-325-3784.
Catechesis/Religious Program—Tel: 724-733-4976; 327-253-; Fax: 724-327-2532. Linda Kuchar, D.R.E. Students 236.
FAIRCHANCE, FAYETTE CO., SS. CYRIL AND METHODIUS, [CEM] Rev. David Nazimek.
Res.: 50 Morgantown St., 15436. Tel: 724-564-7436; Fax: 724-564-7435.
Catechesis/Religious Program—Tel: 724-438-5271. Joyce Burkhart, D.R.E. Students 39.
Chapel—Shoaf, Chapel of SS. Cyril & Methodius, Fairchance
FARMINGTON, FAYETTE CO., ST. JOAN OF ARC, [CEM] Rev. Paul A. Whalen.
Res.: 3523 National Pike, P.O. Box 92, 15437. Tel: 724-329-4522; Fax: 724-329-4955.
FAYETTE CITY, FAYETTE CO., HOLY SPIRIT, Rev. Leonard McAlpin.
Res.: 143 S. High St., P.O. Box 639, 15438. Tel: 724-326-4352; Fax: 724-326-4221.
Catechesis/Religious Program—Tel: 724-930-8504; Fax: 724-930-7611. Scott Martin, D.R.E. Students 20.
FOOTEDALE, FAYETTE CO., ST. THOMAS, (Polish), [CEM] Rev. James L. Popochock, Admin.
Res.: 528 Footedale Rd., P.O. Box 547, New Salem, 15468. Tel: 724-245-9244; Fax: 724-245-9289.
FORBES ROAD, WESTMORELAND CO., ST. MARY, Rev. Claude Pollak, O.S.B.
c/o St. Vincent Archabbey: 300 Fraser Purchase Rd., Latrobe, 15650. Tel: 724-532-6752; Fax: 724-837-3690.
FORD CITY, ARMSTRONG CO.
1—CHRIST, PRINCE OF PEACE PARISH, Rev. Edward J. Lewis.
Res.: 1008 Sixth Ave., 16226. Tel: 724-763-9141; Fax: 724-763-9142.
Catechesis/Religious Program—Tel: 724-763-7380. Jacqueline Smith, D.R.E. Students 120.
2—ST. FRANCIS OF PAOLA, (Polish), Merged, with St. Mary and Holy Trinity, Ford City to form Christ, Prince of Peace Parish, Ford City.
3—HOLY TRINITY, (Slovak), Merged, St. Mary and St. Francis of Paola, Ford City to form Christ, Prince of Peace Parish, Ford City.
4—ST. MARY, Merged, with St. Francis of Paola and Holy Trinity, Ford City to form Christ, Prince of Peace Parish, Ford City.
FREEPORT, ARMSTRONG CO., ST. MARY, [CEM] Rev. Thomas A. Federline.
Res.: 608 High St., 16229. Tel: 724-295-2281; Fax: 724-295-3090.
School—610 High St., 16229. Tel: 724-295-3003; Fax: 724-295-2790. Mrs. Adrienne Ofcharsky, Prin. Lay Teachers 9; Students 105.
GLEN CAMPBELL, INDIANA CO., ST. MICHAEL, Closed., For inquiries for parish records contact Church of the Resurrection, Clymer.
GRINDSTONE, FAYETTE CO., ST. CECILIA, (Slovak), Rev. John A. Sedlak, Admin.
Mailing Address: c/o P.O. Box 251, Smock, 15480. Tel: 724-677-2110; Fax: 724-677-0146.
HARRISON CITY, WESTMORELAND CO., ST. BARBARA, [CEM] Revs. V. Paul Fitzmaurice; Robert T. Lubic.
Res.: 34 Raymaley Rd., 15636. Tel: 724-744-7474; Fax: 724-744-3056.
Catechesis/Religious Program—Tel: 724-744-4885. Kenneth M. Meyer, D.R.E. Students 900.
HEILWOOD, INDIANA CO., ST. JOHN THE BAPTIST, Closed., For inquiries for parish records contact Church of the Resurrection, Clymer.
HERMINIE, WESTMORELAND CO., ST. EDWARD, Rev. Thomas S. Trupkovich.
Res.: 87 Sixth St. Ext., 15637. Tel: 724-446-5197; Fax: 724-446-1433.
School—89 Sixth St. Ext., 15637. Tel: 724-446-5381. Sr. MaryLou Witkowski, S.H.S., Prin. Sisters of the Holy Spirit 2; Lay Teachers 9; Students 137.
Convent—Sisters of the Holy Spirit, 89 Sixth St. Ext., 15637. Tel: 724-446-5359.
INDIANA, INDIANA CO.
1—ST. BERNARD, [CEM] Rev. Msgr. William G. Charnoki, V.F., J.C.L.; Rev. Douglas E. Dorula.
Res.: 200 Clairvaux Dr., 15701. Tel: 724-465-2210; Fax: 724-465-0422.
School—300 Clairvaux Dr., 15701. Tel: 724-465-7139; Fax: 724-465-0803. Bridget Everett, Prin. Lay Teachers 14; Students 177.
Catechesis/Religious Program—Tel: 724-349-9145. Greg Petrucci, D.R.E. Students 206.
2—ST. THOMAS MORE UNIVERSITY PARISH, , (Newman Center) Rev. Michael J. Crookston.
Indiana University of PA: 1200 Oakland Ave., 15701. Tel: 724-463-2277; Fax: 724-463-7116.
IRWIN, WESTMORELAND CO., IMMACULATE CONCEPTION, [CEM] Rev. Msgr. John L. Conway, V.F.
Res.: 305 Second St., 15642. Tel: 724-863-9550; Fax: 724-863-9552.
School—Queen of Angels Regional Catholic School See separate listing under Elementary Schools in the Institution section.
ISELIN, INDIANA CO., HOLY CROSS, Closed., For inquiries for parish records contact Church of the Good Shepherd, Kent.
JEANNETTE, WESTMORELAND CO.
1—ASCENSION, (Italian), Rev. John M. Foriska.
Res.: 615 Division St., 15644. Tel: 724-523-6567; 724-523-6568.
2—SACRED HEART, [CEM] Rev. Leon Hont, O.S.B. In Res., Rev. Dominic J. Petroy, O.S.B.
Res.: 504 Cowan Ave., 15644. Tel: 724-523-2560; Fax: 724-523-9400.
Catechesis/Religious Program—Students 36.
KENT, INDIANA CO., CHURCH OF THE GOOD SHEPHERD, Rev. E. George Saletrik.
Res.: 100 Good Sheperd Dr., P.O. Box 99, 15752. Tel: 724-479-3881; Fax: 724-479-3882.
Catechesis/Religious Program—Denise Pencola, D.R.E. Students 66.
KITTANNING, ARMSTRONG CO., ST. MARY, OUR LADY OF GUADALUPE, [CEM] Rev. Emil S. Payer.
Res.: 101 W. High St., 16201. Tel: 724-548-7649; Fax: 724-543-2938.
Catechesis/Religious Program—Tel: 724-543-2107. Sr. Honora McCawley, D.R.E. Students 174.
Convent—Sisters of St. Joseph, 348 N. Water St., 16201. Tel: 724-543-4518.
LATROBE, WESTMORELAND CO.
1—ST. BONIFACE, , (Chestnut Ridge) Rev. Simon J. Toth, O.S.B. Tel: 724-532-6735.
Res.: *c/o St. Vincent Archabbey*, 300 Fraser Purchase Rd., 15650. Tel: 724-532-6600.
School—Christ the Divine Teacher School See separate listing under Elementary Schools in the Institution section.
Catechesis/Religious Program—Tel: 724-537-9750. Mrs. Ruth Apone, D.R.E. Students 102.
2—HOLY FAMILY, [CEM] Revs. Donald J. Mondello; Alan W. Grote.
Res.: 1204 Ligonier St., 15650. Tel: 724-539-9751; Fax: 724-539-8044.
School—Christ the Divine Teacher School See separate listing under Elementary Schools in the Institution section.
Catechesis/Religious Program—Tel: 724-539-3638. Elizabeth Wechtenhiser, D.R.E. Students 190.
3—ST. JOHN THE EVANGELIST, Rev. Thomas M. Lukac.
Res.: 306 St. John Dr., 15650. Tel: 724-537-8909; Fax: 724-537-2788.
School—Christ the Divine Teacher School See separate listing under Elementary Schools in the Institution section.
Catechesis/Religious Program—Cindy Shifflett, D.R.E. Students 195.
4—ST. ROSE, [CEM] Rev. William P. Donahue.
Res.: 1112 Hillview Ave., 15650. Tel: 724-537-3709.
School—Christ the Divine Teacher School See separate listing under Elementary Schools in the Institution section.
5—ST. VINCENT BASILICA, [CEM] Revs. Gilbert J. Burke, O.S.B.; Thomas P. Curry, O.S.B.
Res.: 300 Fraser Purchase Rd., 15650. Tel: 724-539-8629; Fax: 724-539-3810.
School—Christ the Divine Teacher School See separate listing under Elementary Schools in the Institution section.
Catechesis/Religious Program—Tel: 724-539-8629, Ext. 16. Darlene Argall, D.R.E. Students 179.
LECKRONE, FAYETTE CO., OUR LADY OF PERPETUAL HELP (ST. MARY), [CEM] Rev. Donald Trexler.
Res.: P.O. Box 248, 15454. Tel: 724-737-5736; Fax: 724-737-1042.
LEECHBURG, ARMSTRONG CO.
1—ST. CATHERINE OF ALEXANDRIA, Closed., For inquiries for parish records contact Christ the King, Leechburg.
2—CHRIST THE KING, [CEM] Rev. Joseph V. Trupkovich.
Administrative Center—630 Second St., 15656. Tel: 724-845-8191; 724-842-1791; Fax: 724-845-5480.
3—CHURCH OF THE ASSUMPTION, Closed., For inquiries for parish records contact Christ the King, Leechburg.
4—ST. MARTHA, (Slovak), Closed., For inquiries for parish records contact Christ the King, Leechburg
LEISENRING, FAYETTE CO., ST. VINCENT DE PAUL, [CEM] Rev. J. Edward McCullough, Admin.
Res.: Box 24, 15455. Tel: 724-628-7361; Fax: 724-628-7361.
LIGONIER, WESTMORELAND CO., HOLY TRINITY, [CEM] Rev. Joseph P. Maddalena, S.T.L., V.F.
Res.: 342 W. Main St., 15658. Tel: 724-238-6434; Fax: 724-238-6688.
School—327 W. Vincent St., 15658. Tel: 724-238-6430; Fax: 724-238-6341. Mrs. Barbara Sabo, Prin. Lay Teachers 9; Students 109.
Catechesis/Religious Program—Tel: 724-238-6341. Mrs. Carol A. Serafin, D.R.E. Students 85.
Chapel—Wilpen, Chapel of Holy Trinity, Ligonier
LOWER BURRELL, WESTMORELAND CO., ST. MARGARET MARY, Revs. James T. Gaston, V.F.; William G. Berkey; Sr. Joan Marie Keller, M.S.B.T., Coord. Pastoral Ministries.
Res.: 201 Park Dr., 15068. Tel: 724-335-2336; Fax: 724-337-6676.
Catechesis/Religious Program—Tel: 724-335-8946; Fax: 724-335-0353. Joan Duncan, D.R.E. Students 278.
LUCERNEMINES, INDIANA CO., ST. LOUIS, [CEM] Rev. Lawrence R. Kiniry.
Res.: 403 Lucerne Rd., P.O. Box 197, 15754. Tel: 724-479-9542; Fax: 724-479-1130.
MARGUERITE, WESTMORELAND CO., ST. BENEDICT, Rev. John Murtha, O.S.B.
Res.: R.D. 8, P.O. Box 560, Bruno Rd.,, 15601. Tel: 724-834-9045; Fax: 724-834-1880.
Catechesis/Religious Program—Tel: 724-537-9750; 837-847-; Fax: 724-537-9750. Ruth Apone, D.R.E.; L. DiDonato, D.R.E. Students 95.
MASONTOWN, FAYETTE CO., ALL SAINTS, [CEM] Rev. James F. Bump.
Res.: 101 W. Church Ave., 15461. Tel: 724-583-7866; Fax: 724-583-0373.
School—100 S. Washington St., 15461. Tel: 724-583-2141; Fax: 724-583-2141. Mrs. Lori Sagosky, Acting Prin. Lay Teachers 7; Students 112.
Catechesis/Religious Program—Tel: 724-583-1149. Ms. Wanda Wokulich, D.R.E. Students 34.
Chapel—McClellandtown, Chapel of All Saints, Masontown
MAXWELL, FAYETTE CO., ST. JAMES, Rev. James F. Petrovsky.
Res.: P.O. Box 247, LaBelle, 15450. Tel: 724-785-3617.
Chapel—Isabella, Chapel of St. James, Maxwell
MONESSEN, WESTMORELAND CO., THE EPIPHANY OF

OUR LORD, [CEM 2] Revs. Paul A. Lisik; Ronald. L. Cyktor Jr.
Res.: 618 Knox Ave., 15062. Tel: 724-684-7661; Fax: 724-684-8981.
Catechesis/Religious Program—Scott Martin, D.R.E. Students 56.

MOUNT PLEASANT, WESTMORELAND CO.
1—ST. PIUS X, [CEM] Rev. Michael W. Matusak.
Res.: 216 Spruce St., 15666. Tel: 724-547-1911; Fax: 724-547-2930.
Catechesis/Religious Program—Erin Colcombe, D.R.E. Students 150.
2—TRANSFIGURATION, (Polish), [CEM] Closed. Rev. Michael W. Matusak, Admin.
Res.: 35 N. Hitchman St., 15666. Tel: 724-547-2556; Fax: 724-547-2930.
3—VISITATION OF THE BLESSED VIRGIN MARY, (Slovak), [CEM] Rev. Michael W. Matusak, Admin. In Res., Rev. William J. Lechnar.
Res.: 740 Walnut St., 15666. Tel: 724-547-5735; Fax: 724-547-2930.

MURRYSVILLE, WESTMORELAND CO., MOTHER OF SORROWS, Revs. John A. Moineau; Charles Esposito.
Res.: 4200 Old William Penn Hwy., 15668. Tel: 724-733-8870; Fax: 724-733-8108.
School—3264 Evergreen Dr., 15668. Tel: 724-733-8840; Fax: 724-325-1144. Patricia A. Sheahan, Ed.D., Prin. Lay Teachers 30; Students 362.

NEW ALEXANDRIA, WESTMORELAND CO., ST. JAMES, Rev. Lawrence T. Persico, J.C.L.
Res.: R.D. 3, Box 400, 15670. Tel: 724-668-2829; Fax: 724-668-7327.
Catechesis/Religious Program—William J. D'Angelo, D.R.E. Students 63.

NEW DERRY, WESTMORELAND CO., ST. MARTIN, [CEM] Rev. Martin Bartel, O.S.B.
Res.: R.D. 1, Box 100, 15671-9717. Tel: 724-694-5716; Fax: 724-694-5716.

NEW KENSINGTON, WESTMORELAND CO.
1—ST. JOSEPH, Rev. Larry J. Kulick.
Res.: 1125 Leishman Ave., 15068. Tel: 724-337-6412; Fax: 724-337-4022.
2—ST. MARY OF CZESTOCHOWA, (Polish), [CEM] Rev. Richard P. Karenbauer; Sr. Mary Carol Kardell, C.S.S.F., Pastoral Min.
Res.: 857 Kenneth Ave., 15068. Tel: 724-335-8212; Fax: 724-335-1314.
Convent—Felician Sisters, 837 Kenneth Ave., 15068. Tel: 724-339-9868. Sr. Mary Carol Kardell, C.S.S.F., Pastoral Min.
3—MT. ST. PETER, (Italian), Revs. Richard G. Curci; William G. Berkey.
Res.: 100 Freeport Rd., 15068. Tel: 724-335-9877; Fax: 724-335-9138.

NEW SALEM, FAYETTE CO., ST. PROCOPIUS, [CEM] Rev. James L. Popochock.
Res.: 20 Church St., P.O. Box 547, 15468. Tel: 724-245-9244; Fax: 724-245-9289.
Catechesis/Religious Program—Students 83.

NORTH HUNTINGDON, WESTMORELAND CO.
1—ST. AGNES, Rev. Thaddeus J. Kaczmarek.
Res.: 11400 St. Agnes Ln., 15642. Tel: 724-863-2626; 724-863-2630; Fax: 724-863-1057.
School—Queen of Angels Catholic School See separate listing under Elementary Schools in the Institution section.
Catechesis/Religious Program—Tel: 724-864-5393. Mary Blythe, D.R.E. Students 498.
2—ST. ELIZABETH ANN SETON, Rev. Richard J. Kosisko, J.C.L.
Res.: 200 Leger Rd., 15642. Tel: 724-864-6364; Fax: 724-864-4580.

PALMER, FAYETTE CO., ST. ALBERT, Rev. Donald Trexler.
Res.: Box 295, Adah, 15410. Tel: 724-737-6720.

PARKER, ARMSTRONG CO., ST. MARY, OUR LADY OF THE SNOWS, Rev. Anthony W. Ditto, Admin.
Res.: c/o R.D. 1, Box 78, Brady's Bend, 16028. Tel: 724-526-5079; Fax: 724-526-3028.

PENN, WESTMORELAND CO., ST. BONIFACE, [CEM] Rev. John Foriska, Admin.
Res.: 201 Church St., Box 398, 15675. Tel: 724-523-3450; Fax: 724-523-6468. In Res., Rev. Bernard Survil.

PERRYOPOLIS, FAYETTE CO., ST. JOHN THE BAPTIST, [CEM] Rev. John T. Euker.
Res.: P.O. Box 606, 15473. Tel: 724-736-4442; Fax: 724-736-8403.
Catechesis/Religious Program—Tel: 724-736-0158. Sr. Loretta Topper, D.R.E. Students 114.

POINT MARION, FAYETTE CO., ST. HUBERT, Rev. Joseph L. Sredzinski, M.Div.
Res.: 9 Sadler St., 15474. Tel: 724-725-3655.
Catechesis/Religious Program—Students 58.

REPUBLIC, FAYETTE CO., HOLY ROSARY, [CEM] Rev. Stephen R. Bugay.
Res.: Main St., P.O. Box 400, 15475. Tel: 724-246-9639; Fax: 724-246-8081.
School—Abigail St., P.O. Box 797, 15475. Tel: 724-246-9083; Fax: 724-246-2500. Sr. Corrine Giel, V.S.C., Prin. Sisters 2; Lay Teachers 10; Students 167.
Catechesis/Religious Program—Sr. Phyllis Gembarosky, D.R.E. Students 20.
Convent—Vincentian Sisters of Charity, P.O. Box 797, 15475. Tel: 724-246-2500.

ROSSITER, INDIANA CO., ST. FRANCIS OF ASSISI, Closed., For inquiries for parish records contact the Church of the Resurrection, Clymer.

ROSTRAVER, WESTMORELAND CO., ST. ANNE, Rev. Ronald L. Simboli.
Res.: 1870 Rostraver Rd., Belle Vernon, 15012. Tel: 724-872-3555; Fax: 724-872-3373.

SAGAMORE, ARMSTRONG CO., SACRED HEART, [CEM] Rev. Michael P. Sikon, Admin.
Res.: c/o Box 327, Yatesboro, 16263. Tel: 724-783-7191; Fax: 724-783-7783.

SALTSBURG, INDIANA CO., ST. MATTHEW, (Italian), [CEM] Rev. Richard E. Mackiewicz.
Res.: 703 Indiana Ave., 15681. Tel: 724-639-3690; Fax: 724-639-3966.
Catechesis/Religious Program—Ray Brannon, D.R.E. Tel: 724-639-9796; Jan Brannon, D.R.E.; Jim Bowers, D.R.E. Tel: 724-639-9854; Marie Bowers, D.R.E. Students 43.

SCOTTDALE, WESTMORELAND CO., ST. JOHN THE BAPTIST, [CEM] Rev. Leonard W. Stoviak.
Res.: 416 S. Broadway, 15683. Tel: 724-887-6321; Fax: 724-887-6324.
School—504 S. Broadway, 15683. Tel: 724-887-9550; Fax: 724-887-9553. Lay Teachers 15; Students 191.
Catechesis/Religious Program—Dr. Joseph Dreliszak, Prin. & D.R.E. Students 75.
Convent—Benedictine Sisters, 408 S. Broadway, 15683. Tel: 724-887-6612.

SEWARD, WESTMORELAND CO., HOLY FAMILY, [CEM 3] Rev. John E. Wilt.
Res.: Box 481, 15954. Tel: 814-446-5759; Fax: 814-446-4481.
Chapel—New Florence, Chapel of Holy Family, Seward Tel: 724-235-2290.
Chapel—Bolivar, Chapel of Holy Family, Seward, Tel: 724-676-4781.

SLICKVILLE, WESTMORELAND CO., ST. SYLVESTER, Rev. Anthony J. Carbone, J.C.L.
Res.: Box 307, 15684. Tel: 724-468-5794; Fax: 724-468-5765.

SMITHTON, WESTMORELAND CO., ST. TIMOTHY, [CEM] Rev. Paul R. Stivason, Admin.
Res.: Center & Hill Streets, P.O. Box 308, Yukon, 15698. Tel: 724-722-3141; Fax: 724-722-3140.
Parish Administration Center—Tel: 724-722-3141; Fax: 724-722-3140.
Catechesis/Religious Program—Rogers Hall, 106 Center St., Yukon, 15698. Tel: 724-722-3143. Martha Hazlinsky, D.R.E. Students 15.

SMOCK, FAYETTE CO., ST. HEDWIG, (Slovak), [CEM 2] Rev. John A. Sedlak.
Res.: Box 251, 15480. Tel: 724-677-2110; Fax: 724-677-0146.

STARFORD, INDIANA CO., ST. ELIZABETH, Closed., For inquiries for parish records contact Church of the Resurrection, Clymer.

SUTERSVILLE, WESTMORELAND CO., ST CHARLES BORROMEO, Rev. John A. Regoli, Admin.
Res.: 419 Fifth Ave., P.O. Box 413, 15083. Tel: 724-872-5286; Fax: 724-872-3650.
Catechesis/Religious Program—Tel: 724-872-6986. Rita M. Keegan, D.R.E. Students 65.

TRAFFORD, WESTMORELAND CO., ST. REGIS, Rev. James D. Tinghese.
Res. 517 Homewood Ave., 15085. Tel: 412-372-4577; Fax: 412-373-5979.
Catechesis/Religious Program—Tel: 412-372-7609. Kathy Wawrzeniak, D.R.E. Students 150.

TRAUGER, WESTMORELAND CO., FORTY MARTYRS, (Hungarian), [CEM] Rev. Joachim R. Fatora, O.S.B. c/o St. Vincent Archabbey: 300 Fraser Purchase Rd. Latrobe, 15650. Tel: 724-423-3282; 724-532-6623; Fax: 724-537-4554.

UNIONTOWN, FAYETTE CO.
1—ST. JOHN THE EVANGELIST, Rev. William J. Kiel.
Res.: 50 Jefferson St., 15401. Tel: 724-437-7569; Fax: 724-437-6277.
School—52 Jefferson St., 15401. Tel: 724-438-8598; Fax: 724-438-8585. Christine Roskovensky, Prin. Sisters 1; Lay Teachers 15; Students 245.
Catechesis/Religious Program—Sr. M. Joyce Burkhart, O.S.F., D.R.E. (1-6). Students 162.
Convent—School Sisters of St. Francis, 88 Pennsylvania Ave., 15401. Tel: 724-438-8271.
2—ST. JOSEPH, (Polish), [CEM] Rev. Alexander L. Pleban, S.T.L.
Res.: 180 Old Walnut Hill Rd., 15401. Tel: 724-437-3927; Fax: 724-437-5354.
Catechesis/Religious Program—Tel: 724-438-2236. Patricia Neel, D.R.E. Students 216.
3—NATIVITY OF THE BLESSED VIRGIN MARY, (Slovak), [CEM] Rev. Micah E. Kozoil.
Res.: 61 N. Mount Vernon Ave., 15401. Tel: 724-437-1513; Fax: 724-437-7482.
School—17 Gilmore St., 15401. Tel: 724-438-8471; Fax: 724-438-8338. Melvyn Sepic, Prin. Lay Teachers 12; Students 176.
Catechesis/Religious Program—Sr. LaVerne Sihelnik, D.R.E. Students 80.
Convent—Vincentian Sisters of Charity, 7 Gilmore St., 15401. Tel: 724-437-5478.
Chapel—Lemont Furnace, Chapel of St. Mary, Uniontown
4—ST. THERESE, THE LITTLE FLOWER OF JESUS, (Italian), Rev. Kenneth G. Zaccagnini, V.F. In Res., Rev. Patrick J. O'Connor, Senior Priest.
Res.: 61 Mill St., 15401. Tel: 724-438-2341; Fax: 724-438-2361.

UNITED, WESTMORELAND CO., ST. FLORIAN, [CEM] Rev. William C. McGuirk.
Res.: P.O. Box 187, 15689. Tel: 724-423-4431; Fax: 724-423-4438.
School—(Grades PreSchool), P.O. Box 188, 15689. Tel: 724-423-4437. Lay Teachers 1; Students 30.

VANDERGRIFT, WESTMORELAND CO., ST. GERTRUDE, [CEM] Revs. Thaddeus E. Rettger, O.S.B.; Leo Rothrauff, O.S.B.
Res.: 303 Franklin Ave., 15690. Tel: 724-568-2331.
School—315 Franklin Ave., 15690. Tel: 724-568-3304; Fax: 724-567-1900. Mr. John Courey, Prin. Lay Teachers 10; Students 85.

WEST NEWTON, WESTMORELAND CO., HOLY FAMILY, Rev. John A. Regoli.
Res.: 225 N. Second St., 15089. Tel: 724-872-6123; Fax: 724-872-6133.
Catechesis/Religious Program—Tel: 724-872-2106. Michalene Lovato, D.R.E. Students 67.

WHITNEY, WESTMORELAND CO., ST. CECILIA, Revs. Aaron N. Buzzelli, O.S.B.; William A. Beaver, O.S.B.
Res.: P.O. Box 80, 15693. Tel: 724-423-3777; 724-423-2289; Fax: 724-423-3778.
Catechesis/Religious Program—Tel: 724-423-3777, Ext. 15. Maria Nave, D.R.E. Students 55.

YATESBORO, ARMSTRONG CO., ST. MARY, [CEM] Rev. Michael Sikon.
Res.: P.O. Box 327, 16263. Tel: 724-783-7191; Fax: 724-783-7783.

YOUNGSTOWN, WESTMORELAND CO., SACRED HEART, Revs. Aaron N. Buzzelli, O.S.B.; William A. Beaver, O.S.B.
Res.: P.O. Box 328, 15696. Tel: 724-537-7358; Fax: 724-537-6988.
School—P.O. Box 328, 15696. Tel: 724-539-5561; Fax: 724-539-6338. Sr. Grace Marie Spera, C.S.S.F., Prin. Felician Sisters 2; Lay Teachers 5; Students 101.
Convent—Felician Sisters, Main St., P.O. Box 328, 15696. Tel: 724-537-8958.

YOUNGWOOD, WESTMORELAND CO., HOLY CROSS, Rev. John S. Szczesny.
Res.: 711 Depot St., 15697. Tel: 724-925-7811; Fax: 724-925-6170.
School—S. Eighth St., 15697. Tel: 724-925-7253; Fax: 724-925-7707. Lay Teachers 7; Students 110.
Catechesis/Religious Program—Tel: 724-925-6966. Cheryle Helble, D.R.E. Students 34.

YUKON, WESTMORELAND CO., SEVEN DOLORS, [CEM] Rev. Paul R. Stivason.
Res.: Center St. & Hill St., P.O. Box 308, 15698. Tel: 724-722-3141; 724-722-3140 (Hall); Fax: 724-722-3140.
Catechesis/Religious Program—Tel: 724-722-3143. Martha Hazlinsky, D.R.E. Partner Parishes of Seven Dolors & St. Timothy Students 24.

Chaplains of Public Institutions

GREENSBURG. *Westmoreland Hospital*, Tel: 724-832-4000. Rev. Jacques de Paul Daley, O.S.B., Chap., Rev. Msgr. Robert J. Shuda, Assoc. Chap., Revs. Robert R. Byrnes, Assoc. Chap., Justin Withrow, O.S.B., Assoc. Chap.

BROWNSVILLE. *Brownsville General Hospital*. Attended by St. Peter, Brownsville, Tel: 724-785-7200; 785-7781 (Res.).

CONNELLSVILLE. *Highlands Hospital & Health Center*, Tel: 724-628-0736. Revs. William C. McGuirk, Chap. Tel: 724-423-4431 (Res.), Dennis A. Bogusz, Asst. Chap.

INDIANA. *Indiana Hospital*, Tel: 724-465-7000. Attended by St. Bernard, Indiana, Tel: 724-465-3900 (Hospital); 724-465-2210 (Res.).

JEANNETTE. *Mercy Jeannette Hospital*, Tel: 724-527-3551. Revs. Dominic J. Petroy, O.S.B., Chap. Tel: 724-523-2560 (Res.), Justin Withrow, O.S.B., Assoc. Chap. Tel: 724-539-9761 (Res.).
Monsour Medical Center, Tel: 724-527-1511 (Hospital). Revs. Dominic J. Petroy, O.S.B., Chap. Tel: 724-523-2560 (Res.), Justin Withrow, O.S.B., Assoc. Chap. Tel: 724-539-9761 (Res.).

KITTANNING. *Armstrong County Hospital*, Tel: 724-543-8500. Rev. Raphael K. Glinkowski, O.S.P.P.E., Chap. Tel: 724-763-1375 (Res.).

LATROBE. *Latrobe Area Hospital*, Tel: 724-537-1000.

Revs. Michael A. McIlwain, O.S.B., Chap., Damian Warnock, O.S.B., Chap., Justin Withrow, O.S.B., Assoc. Chap., Daniel O'Keefe, O.S.B., Assoc. Chap. Tel: 724-539-9761 (Res.).

MOUNT PLEASANT. *Frick Community Health Center*, Tel: 724-547-1500 (Hospital). Revs. William C. McGuirk, Chap., Dennis A. Bogusz, Asst. Chap.

NEW KENSINGTON. *Citizens General Hospital*, Tel: 724-337-3541. Attended by St. Mary, New Kensington, Tel: 724-335-8212 (Res.); St. Joseph, New Kensington, Tel: 724-337-6412 (Res.); Mount St. Peter, New Kensington, Tel: 724-335-9877 (Res.).

TORRANCE. *Torrance State Hospital*, Tel: 724-459-8000. Rev. Chester J. Raimer, Chap. Tel: 724-459-7103 (Res.).

UNIONTOWN. *Uniontown Hospital*, Tel: 724-430-5000 (Res.); 724-246-9657. Rev. James W. Clark, Chap.

On Duty Outside the Diocese:

Rev. Msgr.—

Dylag, Michael R., One Kenberton Dr., Pleasant Ridge, MI 48069. Tel: 248-547-2006

Revs.—

Bonafed, Joseph E., Holy Redeemer Church, 9705 Summit Ave., Kensington, MD 20895. Tel: 301-942-6515

Conroy, Donald B., S.T.L., Ph.D., 3019 4th St., N.E., Washington, DC 20017. Tel: 202-462-2591 Dir., Nat'l. Institute for Family

Lamendola, Salvatore R., M.Div., Mt. St. Mary Seminary, Emmitsburg, MD 21727-7797. Tel: 301-447-5295, Ext. 4129

Preneta, Henry S. (Retired), St. Paul Church, 128 N. McKean St., Butler, 16001.

Military Chaplains:

Rev.—

Mandock, Patrick H., CH. (LTC), P.O. Box 497, Elephant Butte, NM 87935.

Retired:

Rev. Msgrs.—

McCarren, Stephen A., 307 Avenue of Dukes, Nokomis, FL 34275.

Ramellini, P. Lino, 19 Rex Blvd., Monessen, 15062.

Revs.—

Bahleda, Aloysius J., Neumann House, 2900 Seminary Dr., 15601.

Bienia, Michael A., Neumann House, 2900 Seminary Dr., 15601.

Borkowski, Aloysius J., R.D. 3, Box 138D, Derry, 15627.

Bratus, Walter N., 723 East Pittsburgh St., 15601.

Bucci, Michael J., 1319 Walnut St., South Connellsville, 15425.

Casaliggi, John R., Casa Del Clero Cerati, Via Torta 28, 29100 Piacenza, Italy.

Cheatham, Louis W., Neumann House, 2900 Seminary Dr., 15601.

Dinnico, Henry P., 135 Carriage Dr., North Huntington, 15642.

Gearing, Edward P., 37 Pocono Dr., Pittsburgh, 15220.

Higgins, Edward F., St. James, 200 Walnut St., Sewickley, 15143.

Marzilli, Raphael, c/o Waterview Villa, 1275 S. Broadway, East Providence, RI 02914. Tel: 401-467-9875

Murphy, Harry J., 203 Nazareth House-St. Michael's, 6333 Rancho Mission Rd., San Diego, CA 92108-2099.

Oris, Fabian G., 79 N. Morgantown St., Fairchance, 15436.

Rivi, Geno G., Sailwind Condo #416, 1200 Shoreline Dr., Gulf Breeze, FL 32561.

Sweeney, Denis, 900 Washington Rd., Apt. 105, Pittsburgh, 15228.

Waczula, Michael F., 1415 Main St., #252, Dunedin, FL 34698.

Weiksner, Jerome M., P.O. Box 875, 15601.

INSTITUTIONS LOCATED IN THE DIOCESE

[A] SEMINARIES, RELIGIOUS OR SCHOLASTICATES

LATROBE. *St. Vincent Seminary*, 300 Fraser Purchase Rd., 15650. Tel: 724-537-4592; Fax: 724-532-5052. Email: kbelsole@stvincent.edu. Web: www.benedictine.stvincent.edu/seminary. Very Rev. Kurt Belsole, O.S.B., Rector; Revs. Charles A. Byrd Jr. (ATL), Dir. Spiritual Formation; Justin M. Matro, O.S.B., Vice Rector; Kevin Dominik, Dean of Students; Sr. Cecilia Murphy, R.S.M., Academic Dean; Mrs. Ellen Cavanaugh, Interim Dir. of Pastoral Formation. Professors 25; Lay Students 12; Seminarians 70; Benedictines 17; Other Religious 5.

[B] COLLEGES AND UNIVERSITIES

GREENSBURG. *Seton Hill University* 15601. Tel: 724-834-2200; Fax: 724-830-4611. Email: admit@setonhill.edu. Web: www.setonhill.edu. Dr. JoAnne W. Boyle, Pres.; Mary Ann Gawelek, Ed.D., Vice Pres. Academic Affairs & Dean of Faculty. Sisters of Charity of Seton Hill Sisters 5; Lay Teachers 67; Students 1,679.

LATROBE. *Saint Vincent College*, 300 Fraser Purchase Rd., 15650-2690. Tel: 724-539-9761; Fax: 724-537-4587. Rt. Rev. Douglas R. Nowicki, O.S.B., Chancellor; James F. Will, Pres.; Bro. Norman W. Hipps, O.S.B., Sr. Vice Pres., Student Affairs.

Legal Title: *Saint Vincent College Corporation* Priests 20; Brothers 8; Lay Teachers 63; Students 1,371.

[C] HIGH SCHOOLS, DIOCESAN

GREENSBURG. *Greensburg Central Catholic High School*, 901 Armory Dr., 15601. Tel: 724-834-0310; Fax: 724-834-2472. Email: info@gcchs.org. Web: www.gcchs.org. Mr. Terence P. Meehan, Prin.; Rev. Daniel L. Blout, Pres. Priests 1; Sisters 3; Lay Teachers 39; Students 524.

CONNELLSVILLE. *Geibel Catholic High School*, 611 E. Crawford Ave., 15425. Tel: 724-628-5600; Fax: 724-626-5700. Web: www.geibelcatholic.org. Rev. Daniel L. Blout, Pres.; Mr. Vincent Mascia, Prin. Priests 1; Lay Teachers 22; Students 255.

[D] ELEMENTARY SCHOOLS, INTER-PAROCHIAL

GREENSBURG. *Aquinas Academy*, 330 N. Main St., 15601. Tel: 724-834-7940; Fax: 724-836-0497. Email: beyler@aquinasacademy.org. Sr. Brycelyn Eyler, S.C., Prin.; Mr. Daniel Mahoney, Vice Prin. Lay Teachers 29; Students 454.

CONNELLSVILLE. *Conn-Area Catholic School*, 110 N. Prospect St., 15425. Tel: 724-628-5090; Fax: 724-628-5023. Email: connarea@cvzoom.net. Web: www.connareacatholic.org. Sr. Catherine Meinert, S.C., Prin. Lay Teachers 11; Students 170.

FORD CITY. *Divine Redeemer School*, 726 Fourth Ave., 16226. Tel: 724-763-3761; Fax: 724-763-4112. Joseph A. Mauro, Prin. Lay Teachers 9; Students 188.

JEANNETTE. *Queen of Angels Regional Catholic School*, 320 N. 7th St., 15644. Tel: 724-523-3780; 863-958-; Fax: 724-523-3783. Email: qofaschool@aol.com. Web: www.queenofangelssch.org. Sharyn Zalno, Acting Prin. Lay Teachers 24; Students 373.

LATROBE. *Christ the Divine Teacher School*, (Grades PreK-8), 323 Chestnut St., 15650. Tel: 724-539-1561; Fax: 724-532-3873. Email: cdt@cdtschool.org. Web: www.cdtschool.org. Sr. Donna Marie Palya, V.S.C., Prin. Sisters 1; Lay Teachers 23; Students 329.

[E] SPECIAL EDUCATION

GREENSBURG. *Clelian Heights School for Exceptional Children*, R.D. 9, Box 607, 15601. Tel: 724-837-8120; Fax: 724-837-6480. Email: clelian@aol.com. Web: www.clelianheights.org. Sisters Rosemary Zaffuto, A.C.S.J., Dir.; Linda Pettinella, A.S.C.J., Prin.; Rev. William R. Rathgeb, J.C.L., Chap. Apostles of the Sacred Heart of Jesus Sisters 13; Lay Teachers 10; Students 73.

Elizabeth Seton Montessori School of Westmoreland County, Inc., R.D. 7, P.O. Box 268, 15601. Tel: 724-837-8500; Fax: 724-836-0772. Email: esmontsch@aol.com. Sr. Anita Schulte, S.C., Dir. Sisters of Charity Sisters 1; Lay Teachers 2; Students 50.

MOUNT PLEASANT. *Verna Montessori School*, 268 Prittstown Rd., 15666. Tel: 724-887-8810; Fax: 724-887-2977. Email: vmsami@a1usa.net. Sisters M. Letizia Tribuzio, S.C.I.C., Prin.; Maria Letizia Garruba, Admin. Ivrea Sisters of Charity of the Immaculate Conception Sisters 5; Lay Teachers 4; Students 115.

[F] GENERAL HOSPITALS

JEANNETTE. *Mercy Jeannette Hospital*, 600 Jefferson Ave., 15644. Tel: 724-527-3551; Fax: 724-527-9430. Email: nmagee@mercy.pmhs.org. Web: jdmh.org. Nancy J. Magee, Admin.; Revs. Dominic J. Petroy, O.S.B., Chap.; Justin Withrow, O.S.B., Assoc. Chap. Sisters of Charity of Seton Hill 4; Bed Capacity 159.

[G] HOMES FOR AGED

GREENSBURG. *St. Anne Home*, 685 Angela Dr., 15601. Tel: 724-837-6070; Fax: 724-837-6099. Email: bfiedor@stannehome.org. Web: www.stannehome.org. Rev. Anthony Wozniak, Chap.; Sr. Bernice M. Fiedor, C.S.S.F., Admin. Felician Sisters 6; Capacity 125.

Neumann House, 2900 Seminary Dr., 15601. Tel: 724-834-7350; Fax: 724-834-7351. Email: jbertig@dioceseofgreensburg.org. Residence for retired Priests. In Res. Revs. Aloysius J. Bahleda (Retired). Tel: 724-834-5953; Michael A. Bienia (Retired). Tel: 724-836-1017; Robert F. Brannon. Tel: 724-853-4307; Louis W. Cheatham (Retired). Tel: 724-850-7619; John R. Cindric, V.F.; Robert E. Feeney. Tel: 724-850-1643; William J. Homolak; Edward J. Kretz. Tel: 724-832-1516.

[H] MONASTERIES AND RESIDENCES OF PRIESTS AND BROTHERS

BOLIVER. *Mount Carmel Hermitage*, 244 Baileys Rd., 15923. Tel: 724-238-0423; Fax: 724-238-0423. Revs. Bede J.K. Mulligan, O.Carm.; Simeon D. Marro, O.Carm. Priests 2; Brothers 1.

KITTANNING. *Pauline Fathers Monastery*, Bunker Hill Rd., P.O. Box 66, 16201. Tel: 724-763-1375; Fax: 724-763-8100. Revs. Edward Volz, O.S.P.P.E.; Raphael K. Glinkowski, O.S.P.P.E., Admin. Priests 2.

LATROBE. *Saint Vincent Archabbey*, 300 Fraser Purchase Rd., 15650-2690. Tel: 724-532-6600; Fax: 724-539-2110. Email: nowicki@acadl.stvincent.edu. Web: benedict.stvincent.edu/archabbey. Rt. Revs. Douglas R. Nowicki, O.S.B., Archabbot; Paul R. Maher, O.S.B., Archabbot (Retired); Very Rev. Earl J. Henry, O.S.B., Prior; Bro. Anthony Kirsch, O.S.B., Subprior; Revs. Sebastian A. Samay, Master of Novices; Reginald G. Bender, O.S.B., Procurator; Kurt J. Belsole, O.S.B., Rector of the Seminary; Brian D. Boosel, O.S.B., Dir. of College Campus Ministry; Joseph P. Bronder, O.S.B.; Gilbert J. Burke, O.S.B.; Godfrey F. Burkhardt, O.S.B.; Frederick Byrne, O.S.B.; Andrew S. Campbell, O.S.B.; Athanasius C. Cherry, O.S.B.; Wulfstan F. Clough, O.S.B.; Cyprian G. Constantine, O.S.B.; Patrick T. Cronauer, O.S.B.; Thomas P. Curry, O.S.B.; Jacques de Paul Daley, O.S.B.; Thomas W. Devereux, O.S.B.; Alvin T. Downey, O.S.B.; Demetrius R. Dumm, O.S.B.; John R. Erickson, O.S.B.; Joachim R. Fatora, O.S.B.; Conan E. Feigh, O.S.B.; Augustine A. Flood; Campion P. Gavaler, O.S.B.; Joseph U. Gerg, O.S.B.; Anthony J. Grossi, O.S.B.; Mark F.X. Gruber, O.S.B.; Thomas M. Hart, O.S.B.; Bede J. Hasso, O.S.B.; Clement J. Heid, O.S.B.; Vernon A. Holtz, O.S.B.; Cuthbert A. Jack, O.S.B.; Philip M. Kanfush, O.S.B.; Myron M. Kirsch, O.S.B.; Omer U. Kline, O.S.B.; Rene M. Kollar, O.S.B.; Meinrad J. Lawson, O.S.B., Admin. Asst. to the Archabbot; Christian LeFrois, O.S.B (SAV); Germain L. Lieb, O.S.B.; Stanley T. Markiewicz, O.S.B.; Justin M. Matro, O.S.B., Vice Rector of Seminary; Michael A. McIlwain, O.S.B.; Alphonse H. Meier, O.S.B.; Richard B. Michel, O.S.B.; Nathan J. Munsch, O.S.B.; Jonathan J. Murrman, O.S.B.; Warren D. Murrman, O.S.B.; Justin Nolan, O.S.B.; Daniel Paul O'Keefe, O.S.B.; Dominic J. Petroy, O.S.B.; Claude W. Pollak, O.S.B. (E); Jerome J. Purta, O.S.B.; Donald Raila, O.S.B.; Roland R. Ripoli, O.S.B.; Noel H. Rothrauff, O.S.B., Dir. of Foreign Missions; Paul E. Rubadue, O.S.B.; Chrysostom V. Schlimm, O.S.B.; Louis S. Sedlacko, O.S.B.; Paulinus J. Selle, O.S.B.; Thomas More Sikora, O.S.B.; Paul-Alexander Shutt, O.S.B.; Ermin R. Smith, O.S.B.; Brinstan G. Takach, O.S.B.; Paul R. Taylor, O.S.B.; Simon J. Toth, O.S.B.; Damian J. Warnock, O.S.B.; Mark Edward Wenzinger, O.S.B.; Justin Withrow, O.S.B.; Flavian G. Yelinko, O.S.B.; Lee R. Yoakam, O.S.B.

Legal Title: *The Benedictine Society of Westmoreland County*

Legal Title: *Saint Vincent College Corporation*

Legal Title: *The Wimmer Corporation*

Legal Title: *The Saint Vincent Cemetery Corporation* Priests in Archabbey 72; Community: Priests 126; Brothers 6; Deacons 3; Solemn Professed Choir-Monks 26; Junior Professed Monks 10; Choir Novices 4.

Priests of the Archabbey Serving Abroad: Very Rev. Lucas Torrell deAlmeida Costa, O.S.B., Prior; Revs. Paulo Sergio Panza, O.S.B.; Mauro de Souza Fernandes, O.S.B.; Claudio Moraes, O.S.B.

Priests on Leave: Revs. Vincent R. Crosby, O.S.B.; Becket G. Senchur, O.S.B.; Millard Cook, O.S.B.; William Wurm, O.S.B.

Priests on Loan: Rev. Cornelius P. Chang, O.S.B., Archdiocese of New York.

Priests on Leave for Study and Teaching: Revs. Edward M. Mazich, O.S.B., Gregorian University, Rome; Cajetan P. Homick, O.S.B., Lateran University, Rome.

UNIONTOWN. *St. Anthony Friary*, 115 Oakland Ave., 15401-2818. Tel: 724-438-0500; Fax: 724-438-4251. Bros. Richard A. Portasik, O.F.M., Local Min.;

Damian Cesanek, O.F.M.; Matthew Brozovic, O.F.M., Spiritual Asst.; Damien Murkley, O.F.M., Asst.

[I] CONVENTS AND RESIDENCES FOR SISTERS

GREENSBURG. *Apostles of the Sacred Heart of Jesus*, Clelian Heights Convent, R.D. 9, P.O. Box 607, 15601-9231. Tel: 724-837-8120; Fax: 724-837-6480. Email: clelian@aol.com. Web: www.clelianheights.org. Sr. Rosemary Zaffuto, A.C.S.J., Local Supr.; Rev. William R. Rathgeb, J.C.L., Chap. Sisters 13.

Benedictine Nuns (Eichstatt, Bavaria), St. Emma Monastery, 1001 Harvey Ave., 15601-1494. Tel: 724-834-3060; Fax: 724-834-5772. Email: benedictinenuns@stemma.org. Web: www.stemma.org. Sr. Mary Anne Noll, O.S.B., Prioress; Rev. Msgr. Robert J. Shuda, Chap. Sisters 15; Novices 4; Postulants 1.

Doran Hall, 443 Mount Thor Rd., 15601. Tel: 724-837-8645. Web: www.scsh.org. Sisters of Charity 26.

Ennis Hall, 447 Mount Thor Rd., 15601. Tel: 724-836-7940. Sisters of Charity 8.

Regina House (Sisters of Charity) , 465 Mt. Thor Rd., 15601. Tel: 724-836-0406; Fax: 724-836-8280. Web: www.scsh.org. Sr. Vivien Linkhauer, S.C., Prov. Supr.

Sisters of Charity, Caritas Christi, Motherhouse, 459 Mount Thor Rd., 15601. Tel: 724-853-7948; Fax: 724-838-1512. Web: www.scsh.org. Sr. Mary Janice Grindle, Senior Servant. Sisters 92.

Sisters of Charity, Marian Hall, 451 Mount Thor Rd., 15601. Tel: 724-837-5863. Web: www.scsh.org. Sisters of Charity 2.

Sisters of Charity of Seton Hill, Greensburg, Pennsylvania, 463 Mount Thor Rd., 15601. Tel: 724-836-0406; Fax: 724-836-8280. Web: www.scsh.org.

Regina House: 465 Mt. Thor Rd..

DePaul Center, 463 Mt. Thor Rd.. Tel: 724-836-0406; Fax: 724-836-8280. Administrative offices.

Caritias Christi Tel: 724-853-7948; Fax: 724-838-1512.

Doran Hall Tel: 724-837-8645.

Ennis Hall Tel: 724-836-7940.

Marian Hall Tel: 724-837-5863.

Bayley House Tel: 724-836-6398. A Pennsylvania nonprofit corporation. Sisters 479; Novices 10; Postulants 9.

Sisters of Mary Immaculate (Krishnagar, India), St. Joseph Center Convent, 2900 Seminary Dr., 15601. Tel: 724-836-0449. Email: smigbg@westol.com. Sr. Dora Fernandes, S.M.I., Local Supr. Sisters 2.

LATROBE. *Discalced Carmelite Nuns*, Carmel of the Assumption, R.D. 6, P.O. Box 28, Center Dr., 15650. Tel: 724-539-1056. Email: carmelite.monastary@verizon.net. Sr. Barbara Sitter, O.C.D., Prioress; Rev. Meirad Lawson, O.S.B., Chap. Professed Nuns of Solemn Vows 12; Extern 1.

LEECHBURG. *Sisters of Mary Immaculate (Krishnagar, India)*, R.D. 5, Box 1231, 15656. Tel: 724-845-2828; Fax: 724-845-1658. Email: smi@kiski.net. Sr. Dora Fernandes, S.M.I., Local Supr. Sisters 4.

MOUNT PLEASANT. *Ivrea Sisters of Charity of the Immaculate Conception*, Immaculate Virgin of Miracles Convent, 268 Prittstown Rd., #348, 15666. Tel: 724-887-6753; Fax: 724-887-0220. Email: scicpa@charterpa.net. Sr. Letizia Garruba, S.C.I.C., Local Supr. Sisters 10.

[J] RETREAT HOUSES

GREENSBURG. *St. Emma Retreat House*, 1001 Harvey Ave., 15601. Tel: 724-834-3060; Fax: 724-834-5772. Email: benedictinenuns@stemma.org. Web: www.stemma.org. Sr. Mary Anne Noll, O.S.B., Prioress. Benedictine Nuns (Eichstatt, Bavaria)

[K] MISCELLANEOUS LISTINGS

GREENSBURG. *Gilbert Straub Plaza*, 620 Reamer Ave., 15601. Tel: 724-832-2280; Fax: 724-832-9511. Email: samgsp@aol.com. Sr. Andrew Mary, S.C., Mgr. Sisters of Charity Sisters 1.

St. Joseph Center, 2900 Seminary Dr., 15601. Tel: 724-834-7350; Fax: 724-834-7351. Email: jbertig@diocesegreensburg.org. Web: www.dioceseofgreensburg.org. Mr. Gerald R. Bertig, Dir. Facilities Mgmt.

INDIANA. *Clairvaux Commons*, 100 Clairvaux Dr., 15701. Tel: 724-349-2920; Fax: 724-349-2921. Sisters of St. Joseph 2.

LEECHBURG. *Bishop Morrow Personal Care Home*, R.D. #5, Box 1231, 15656. Tel: 724-845-2828; Fax: 724-845-1658. Email: smi@kiski.net. Sr. Dora Fernandes, S.M.I., Dir. Sisters of Mary Immaculate

NEW SALEM. *Rendu Services, Inc.*, 528 Footedale Rd., 15468. Tel: 724-628-6334; Fax: 724-628-6335. Email: mgtuley@yahoo.com. Web: www.renduservices.org. Sr. Margaret Tuley, D.C., Exec. Dir.

SMOCK. *Ladies of Charity*, P.O. Box 251, 15480. Tel: 724-677-2110; Fax: 724-677-0146. Email: sthedwig@charterpa.net. Rev. John A. Sedlak, Spiritual Dir.

RELIGIOUS INSTITUTES OF MEN REPRESENTED IN THE DIOCESE

For further details refer to the corresponding bracketed number in the Religious Institutes of Men or Women section.

[0200]—*Benedictine Monks* (St. Vincent Archabbey)—O.S.B.

[0270]—*Carmelite Fathers and Brothers*—O.Carm.

[0520]—*Franciscan Friars*—O.F.M.

[1010]—*Pauline Fathers*—O.S.P.P.E.

RELIGIOUS INSTITUTES OF WOMEN REPRESENTED IN THE DIOCESE

[0130]—*Apostles of the Sacred Heart of Jesus*—A.S.C.J.

[0190]—*Benedictine Sisters*—O.S.B.

[0230]—*Benedictine Sisters of Pontifical Jurisdiction*—O.S.B.

[0420]—*Discalced Carmelite Nuns*—O.C.D.

[1070]—*Dominican Sisters, St. Mary of the Springs* (Columbus, OH)—O.P.

[1170]—*Felician Sisters*—C.S.S.F.

[2575]—*Institute of the Sisters of Mercy of the Americas* (Pittsburgh, PA)—R.S.M.

[1690]—*School Sisters of the Third Order of St. Francis*—O.S.F.

[0570]—*Sisters of Charity of Seton Hill, Greensburg, Pennsylvania*—S.C.

[0450]—*Sisters of Charity of the Immaculate Conception of Ivrea*—S.C.I.C.

[0990]—*Sisters of Divine Providence* (St. Peter Prov.)—C.D.P.

[2440]—*Sisters of Mary Immaculate*—S.M.I.

[1660]—*Sisters of Saint Francis of the Providence of God*—O.S.F.

[1620]—*Sisters of Saint Francis, Millvale, Pennsylvania*—O.S.F.

[3830-13]—*Sisters of St. Joseph*—C.S.J.

[2040]—*Sisters of the Holy Spirit*—S.H.S.

[3730]—*Sisters of the Order of St. Basil the Great*—O.S.B.M.

[4160]—*Vincentian Sisters of Charity*—V.S.C.

NECROLOGY

† Chupela, Rev. Msgr. Andrew A., (Retired)—Died Oct. 8, 2003

† Charnoki, Andrew J., (Retired)—Died Aug. 5, 2003

† Drab, Stephen J., (Retired)—Died May 16, 2003

Diocese of Harrisburg

(Dioecesis Harrisburgensis)

ESTABLISHED MARCH 3, 1868.

Square Miles 7,660.

Comprises the Counties of Dauphin, Lebanon, Lancaster, York, Adams, Franklin, Cumberland, Perry, Juniata, Mifflin, Snyder, Northumberland, Union, Montour and Columbia in the State of Pennsylvania.

Patron of Diocese: St. Patrick, Bishop and Confessor.

For legal titles of parishes and diocesan institutions, consult the General Secretariat.

(VACANT SEE)

Diocesan Center: P.O. Box 2153, Harrisburg, PA 17105-2153. Tel: 717-657-4804; Fax: 717-657-2453.

Web: www.hbgdiocese.org

Email: general@hbgdiocese.org

STATISTICAL OVERVIEW

Personnel	
Bishop	1
Priests: Diocesan Active in Diocese	106
Priests: Diocesan Active Outside Diocese	7
Priests: Retired, Sick or Absent	36
Number of Diocesan Priests	149
Religious Priests in Diocese	30
Total Priests in Diocese	179
Extern Priests in Diocese	16
Ordinations:	
Diocesan Priests	2
Transitional Deacons	3
Permanent Deacons in Diocese	47
Total Sisters	447
Parishes	
Parishes	89
With Resident Pastor:	
Resident Diocesan Priests	76
Resident Religious Priests	12
Without Resident Pastor:	
Administered by Priests	4
Missions	7
Welfare	
Catholic Hospitals	1
Total Assisted	203,562
Homes for the Aged	4
Total Assisted	1,093
Residential Care of Children	1
Total Assisted	107
Specialized Homes	5
Total Assisted	88
Special Centers for Social Services	14
Total Assisted	3,005
Educational	
Diocesan Students in Other Seminaries	17
Total Seminarians	17
High Schools, Diocesan and Parish	7
Total Students	3,932
Elementary Schools, Diocesan and Parish	39
Total Students	10,160
Elementary Schools, Private	3
Total Students	125
Catechesis/Religious Education:	
High School Students	1,894
Elementary Students	19,795
Total Students under Catholic Instruction	35,923
Teachers in the Diocese:	
Priests	1
Sisters	55
Lay Teachers	800
Vital Statistics	
Receptions into the Church:	
Infant Baptism Totals	2,977
Adult Baptism Totals	411
Received into Full Communion	428
First Communions	3,484
Confirmations	3,380
Marriages:	
Catholic	505
Interfaith	554
Total Marriages	1,059
Deaths	2,271
Total Catholic Population	247,194
Total Population	2,027,835

Former Bishops—Rt. Revs. JEREMIAH F. SHANAHAN, D.D., consecrated July 12, 1868; died Sept. 24, 1886; THOMAS MCGOVERN, D.D., consecrated March 11, 1888; died July 25, 1898; JOHN W. SHANAHAN, D.D., consecrated May 1, 1899; died Feb. 19, 1916; Most Revs. PHILIP R. MCDEVITT, D.D., consecrated Sept. 21, 1916; died Nov. 11, 1935; GEORGE L. LEECH, D.D., J.C.D. (Retired), appt. Auxiliary of Harrisburg July 6, 1935; consecrated Oct. 17, 1935; succeeded to See Dec. 19, 1935; retired Oct. 19, 1971; died March 12, 1985; JOSEPH T. DALEY, D.D., consecrated Jan. 7, 1964; appt. Coadjutor Bishop July 31, 1967; succeeded to See Oct. 19, 1971; died Sept. 2, 1983; WILLIAM H. KEELER, ord. July 17, 1955; consecrated Sept. 21, 1979; appt. Bishop of Harrisburg, Nov. 10, 1983; succeeded to See Jan. 4, 1984; transferred to Baltimore May 23, 1989; NICHOLAS C. DATTILO, D.D., ord. May 31, 1958; appt. Eighth Bishop of Harrisburg Nov. 21, 1989; cons. Jan. 26, 1990; died March 5, 2004.

Diocese of Harrisburg Officials

Vicar General—Very Rev. JAMES M. LYONS, V.G., 4800 Union Deposit Rd., Box 2153, Harrisburg, 17105-2153. Tel: 717-657-4804.

General Secretary—Very Rev. JAMES M. LYONS, V.G., P.O. Box 2153, Harrisburg, 17105-2153.

Secretary for Canonical Services—Very Rev. WILLIAM J. KING, J.C.D., M.Div., M.A., P.O. Box 2557, Harrisburg, 17105-2557. Tel: 717-657-4804.

Secretary for Catholic Charities—P.O. Box 3551, Harrisburg, 17105-3551. Tel: 717-657-4804.

Secretary for Clergy and Religious Life—Very Rev. J. MICHAEL MCFADDEN, M.Div., P.O. Box 2161, Harrisburg, 17105-2161.

Secretary for Communications—Very Rev. T. RONALD HANEY, M.A., 4800 Union Deposit Rd., P.O. Box 2555, Harrisburg, 17105-2555. Tel: 717-657-4804.

Secretary for Education—Very Rev. EDWARD J. QUINLAN III, M.Div., M.A., M.S., P.O. Box 3553, Harrisburg, 17105-3553. Tel: 717-657-4804; 717-921-2363 (Res.).

Secretary for Parish and Special Ministries—Very Rev. WILLIAM C. FORREY JR., M.A., M.Div., P.O. Box 3557, Harrisburg, 17105-3557. Tel: 717-657-4804.

Judicial Vicar—Very Rev. WILLIAM J. KING, J.C.D., M.Div., M.A., P.O. Box 2557, Harrisburg, 17105-2557. Tel: 717-657-4804.

Chancellor—CAROL HOUGHTON, S.T.D., J.C.D., P.O. Box 2557, Harrisburg, 17105-2557. Tel: 717-657-4804.

Diocesan Offices, Commissions, Boards and Programs

Adult Religious Formation, Department for—MARY ANN BOYARSKI, Ed.D., Dir., P.O. Box 2161, Harrisburg, 17105-2161.

Catholic History and Archives, Office of—Rev. Msgr. THOMAS J. KUJOVSKY, Dir. (Retired); VACANT, Archivist & Asst. Chancellor Archives, 4800 Union Deposit Rd., P.O. Box 2153, Harrisburg, 17105. Tel: 717-657-4804.

Black Catholic Ministry—GWEN SUMMERS, Coord., 4800 Union Deposit Rd., P.O. Box 3557, Harrisburg, 17105. Tel: 717-657-4804.

Buildings and Properties—LES ZIMMERMAN, Dir., 4800 Union Deposit Rd., P.O. Box 2153, Harrisburg, 17105. Tel: 717-657-4804.

Campus Ministry—Very Rev. WILLIAM C. FORREY JR., M.A., M.Div., Coord., P.O. Box 3557, Harrisburg, 17105. Tel: 717-657-4804.

Catholic Charities Administration, Department for—VACANT, Dir., P.O. Box 3551, Harrisburg, 17105.

Catholic Charities Counseling/Field Services, Department for—Associate Executive Directors: PHILIP J. VERRECCHIA, Ph.D.; FRANK KOEBER, M.S.W., M.F., R.P.R.P.; THOMAS THORPE, M.P.A., C.A.C., P.O. Box 3551, Harrisburg, 17105.

Catholic Schools, Department for—Sr. SUE ANN STEVES, I.H.M., Supt., P.O. Box 3553, Harrisburg, 17105.

The "Catholic Witness"—Very Rev. T. RONALD HANEY, M.A., Exec. Editor, 4800 Union Deposit Rd., Box 2555, Harrisburg, 17105. Tel: 717-657-4804.

Catholic Women, Diocesan Council of—BETTY KRESS, 160 Chester St., Carlisle, 17103. Tel: 717-249-5612.

Cemeteries—EDWARD G. FARADAY, Dir., 4800 Union Deposit Rd., Box 3651, Harrisburg, 17105. Tel: 717-652-0539.

Charismatic Movement—Rev. FRANCIS KARWACKI, Liaison, 863 W. Chestnut St., Coal Township, 17866.

Consultors, College—Revs. JOHN BATEMAN; ROBERT GILLELAN, V.F.; Rev. Msgr. LAWRENCE OVERBAUGH; Rev. PATRICK A. DEVINE; Very Revs. PAUL C. HELWIG, V.F.; KENNETH F. LAWRENCE, V.F.; JAMES M. LYONS, V.G.; J. MICHAEL MCFADDEN, M.Div.; Revs. SAMUEL HOUSER; THOMAS LANGAN; Very Rev. ROBERT YOHE, V.F.; Rev. CHESTER A. SNYDER.

Cursillo Movement—Rev. Msgr. THOMAS H. SMITH, V.F., Moderator.

Deans—Rev. JOSEPH F. GOTWALT, Adams Deanery; Very Revs. PAUL C. HELWIG, V.F., Cumberland/ Perry Deanery; DANIEL C. MITZEL, V.F., Dauphin Deanery; Rev. ROBERT A. YOHE JR., V.F., Franklin Deanery; Very Rev. KENNETH F. LAWRENCE, V.F.,

North Lancaster Deanery; Rev. Msgr. THOMAS H. SMITH, V.F., South Lancaster Deanery; Very Revs. DAVID T. MCANDREW, V.F., Lebanon Deanery; DENNIS G. DALESSANDRO, Northern Deanery; Rev. Msgr. LAWRENCE R. OVERBAUGH, Northumberland Deanery; Rev. ROBERT M. GILLELAN JR., V.F., York Deanery.

Diocesan Center—DONNA GREGORITS, Coord., 4800 Union Deposit Rd., P.O. Box 3651, Harrisburg, 17105. Tel: 717-657-4804.

Ecumenical and Interreligious Affairs—Deacon CHARLES CLARK, Dir., P.O. Box 3557, Harrisburg, 17105.

Family Ministries, Department for—VICTORIA LASKOWSKI, J.D., Dir., P.O. Box 3557, Harrisburg, 17105. Tel: 717-657-4804.

Finance Council

Financial Administration, Department for—EDWARD G. FARADAY, Dir., 4800 Union Deposit Rd., P.O. Box 3651, Harrisburg, 17105. Tel: 717-657-4804.

Health Care Ministry—MARY ANN O'DONNELL, P.O. Box 3557, Harrisburg, 17105.

Holy Name Societies—THOMAS AUMEN, Liaison, 5055 Grandview Rd., Hanover, 17331. Tel: 717-637-5236.

Knights of Columbus—ALPHONSUS A. CHERRY, Coord., 408 Shield St., Harrisburg, 17109. Tel: 717-564-1404.

Ministry Development, Department for—MARY ANN O'DONNELL, Dir., 4800 Union Deposit Rd., P.O. Box 3557, Harrisburg, 17105. Tel: 717-657-4804.

Lay Personnel, Department for—Very Rev. JAMES M. LYONS, V.G., Box 2153, Harrisburg, 17105. Tel: 717-657-4804.

Legion of Mary—Rev. PAUL R. SHUDA, Moderator, 2121 N. Third St., Harrisburg, 17110. Tel: 717-233-1014.

Mediation Services, Office of—Mrs. BARBARA A. ROTH, Clerk, P.O. Box 2557, Harrisburg, 17105. Tel: 717-657-4804.

Missions, Office of (Home and Foreign)—Rev. ROBERT F. SHARMAN, S.T.L., Dir., P.O. Box 3657, Harrisburg, 17105. Tel: 717-657-4804.

Pastoral Council, Diocesan—INES CARROLL; PETER A. CICCOCIOPPO; JAMES R. CORBIN; STEPHEN P. DESJARDINS; MARIA T. DISANTO; SANDRA L. ESHENOWER; Rev. PAUL FISHER; GEORGE GARBER; WALTER J. LEGENSTEIN; DONALD MARKLE; C. CLAIR MCCORMICK; ALLEN F. NEIDERER; Deacon JOHN L. PARUSO; CARMEN I. RIVERA; Rev. MICHAEL REID; PATRICIA A. SHIRATO; JOSEPH SWATSKI; JULIO E. TORO; JACQUELINE WATERS; EDMUND A. WICKENHEISER; MARY C. ZALES; CHARLES L. ZITNICK JR.; JOHN J. ZOGBY; Sr. FRANCINE GAGNE, I.H.M.

Permanent Diaconate, Office for—Very Rev. J. MICHAEL MCFADDEN, M.Div., Dir., P.O. Box 2161, Harrisburg, 17105. Tel: 717-657-4804.

Presbyteral Council—Revs. THOMAS F. LANGAN, Adams; CHESTER P. SNYDER, Cumberland/Perry; Very Rev. DANIEL C. MITZEL, V.F., Dauphin; Revs. ROBERT A. YOHE JR., V.F., Franklin; RAYMOND COLLINS, C.SS.R., North Lancaster; Rev. Msgr. THOMAS H. SMITH, V.F., South Lancaster; Rev. THOMAS A. SCALA, Northern; Rev. Msgr. LAWRENCE R. OVERBAUGH, Northumberland; Rev. ROBERT M. GILLELAN JR., V.F., York.

Appointed—Revs. JOHN B. BATEMAN; SYLVAN P. CAPITANI, D.Min.; PATRICK A. DEVINE; Very Rev. PAUL C. HELWIG, V.F.; Rev. SAMUEL E. HOUSER; Very Revs. KENNETH F. LAWRENCE, V.F.; DANIEL F.X. POWELL; Rev. JOHN D. SCHMALHOFER.

Prison Ministry—Very Rev. WILLIAM C. FORREY JR., M.A., M.Div., P.O. Box 3557, Harrisburg, 17105.

Senior Adult Ministry—VICTORIA LASKOWSKI, Coord., P.O. Box 3557, Harrisburg, 17105.

Respect Life, Office for—MARY SHRIVER, M.A., Dir., P.O. Box 3557, Harrisburg, 17105.

Public Relations, Department for—Very Rev. T. RONALD HANEY, M.A., Dir., P.O. Box 2555, Harrisburg, 17105.

Religious Education (CCD), Department for—JAMES GONTIS, P.O. Box 3553, Harrisburg, 17105.

Religious Life, Department for—P.O. Box 2161, Harrisburg, 17105.

Resource Center—PATRICIA BOTTIGLIA, Mgr., P.O. Box 3553, Harrisburg, 17105. Tel: 717-657-4804, Ext. 381.

Saint Thomas More Society—LOREN PRESCOTT, Esq., P.O. Box 2557, Harrisburg, 17105. Tel: 717-657-4804, Ext. 305.

Saint Vincent de Paul Society—RICHARD HORN, Pres., 28 S. 11th St., Columbia, 17512. Tel: 717-684-5167.

Spanish Speaking Ministry—Very Rev. BERNARD PISTONE, Vicar, St. Francis Xavier Parish, 22 W. High St., Gettysburg, 17325. Tel: 717-334-3919.

Special Ministries, Department for—Very Rev. WILLIAM C. FORREY JR., M.A., M.Div., Dir., P.O. Box 3557, Harrisburg, 17105.

Telecommunications—JOSEPH APONICK, Dir., 4800 Union Deposit Rd., Box 2555, Harrisburg, 17105. Tel: 717-657-4804.

Tribunal—4800 Union Deposit Rd., P.O. Box 2557, Harrisburg, 17105. Tel: 717-657-4804; Fax: 717-657-1573.

Judicial Vicar—Very Rev. WILLIAM J. KING, J.C.D., M.Div., M.A.

Adjutant Judicial Vicar—Rev. EDWARD C. MALESIC.

Case Services Administrator—Mrs. BARBARA A. ROTH.

Diocesan Judges—Rev. Msgr. RICHARD A. YOUTZ, J.C.L.; Dr. CAROL L. HOUGHTON, S.T.D., J.C.D.

Defender of the Bond—Rev. EDWARD R. LAVELLE.

Promoter of Justice—Rev. WILLIAM J. NESSEL, O.S.F.S., J.C.D.

Advocates—Rev. Msgr. THOMAS J. KUJOVSKY (Retired); Mr. ROBERT F. O'DONNELL; Mrs. BARBARA A. ROTH; LOREN D. PRESCOTT JR., Esq.

Auditor—Rev. MICHAEL E. MESSNER.

Notaries—KATHRYN GOULDY; RITA PATACKIS.

Mediation Services, Office of—Dr. CAROL L. HOUGHTON, S.T.D., J.C.D., Dir.; Mrs. BARBARA A. ROTH, Clerk.

Victim Assistance Coordinator—TOM THORPE. Tel: 717-657-4804. Email: tthorpe@hbgdiocese.org.

Vietnamese Ministry—Rev. JOSEPH HOA VAN NGUYEN, Coord., Our Lady of the Blessed Sacrament, 2121 N. Third St., Harrisburg, 17110. Tel: 717-233-1014.

Vocations, Office for—Rev. MICHAEL E. MESSNER, Dir.; Sr. DEBORAH MARIE BORNEMAN, S.S.C.M., Coord., P.O. Box 2161, Harrisburg, 17105. Tel: 717-657-4804.

World Apostolate of Fatima—Rev. JOHN A. SZADA JR., Spiritual Moderator, St. Vincent de Paul, 224 Third St., Hanover, 17331. Tel: 717-637-5190.

Worship, Office of—Rev. NEIL SULLIVAN, Dir., P.O. Box 2161, Harrisburg, 17105. Tel: 717-657-4804.

Youth and Young Adult Ministry, Department for—ROBERT WILLIAMS, Dir., 4800 Union Deposit Rd., Box 3551, Harrisburg, 17105. Tel: 717-657-4804.

Youth Protection Program—Very Rev. WILLIAM J. KING, M.Div., M.A., J.C.D., Dir., P.O. Box 2557, Harrisburg, 17105. Tel: 717-657-4804.

CLERGY, PARISHES, MISSIONS AND PAROCHIAL SCHOOLS

CITY OF HARRISBURG
(DAUPHIN COUNTY)

1—CATHEDRAL PARISH OF ST. PATRICK (1995), Rev. Thomas J. Rozman; Deacons J. Leo Dunn; Charles W. Clark. In Res., Very Rev. J. Michael McFadden, M.Div.
Res.: 212 State St., 17101. Tel: 717-232-2169; Fax: 717-232-2799.
Catechesis/Religious Program—Students 90.

2—ST. CATHERINE LABOURE (1948),, (Shrine of the Miraculous Medal) Rev. Msgr. Hugh A. Overbaugh; Rev. Neil S. Sullivan; Deacons Thomas H. Flannery; Thomas A. Fedor. In Res., Very Rev. James M. Lyons, V.G.; Rev. Curtis R. Delarm; Rev. Msgr. Vincent J. Topper (Retired).
Res.: 4000 Derry St., 17111. Tel: 717-564-1321; Fax: 717-564-8822.
School—4020 Derry St., 17111. Tel: 717-564-1760; Fax: 717-564-3010. Sr. Suzanne Duzen, SS.C.M., Prin. Sisters of SS. Cyril and Methodius 3; Lay Teachers 31; Students 512.
Catechesis/Religious Program— Sr. Carol Marie, SS.C.M., D.R.E. Students 399.
Convent—4010 Derry St., 17111. Tel: 717-564-0721.

3—ST. FRANCIS OF ASSISI (1901), Very Rev. Daniel C. Mitzel, V.F.; Deacons Miguel Marroquin; Francis Enderle. In Res., Rev. Michael Messner.
Res.: 1439 Market St., 17103. Tel: 717-232-1003; Fax: 717-232-4536.
Catechesis/Religious Program—Tel: 717-233-7912. Students 101.

4—HOLY FAMILY (1958), Rev. Bernard P. McGinley, M.A.
Church: 555 S. 25th St., 17104. Tel: 717-232-4237; Fax: 717-232-9661.
Rectory—2501 Barkley Ln., 17104. Tel: 717-561-8250.
School—Tel: 717-232-2551. Sr. Joseph Marie Carter, I.H.M., Prin. Sisters Servants of the Immaculate Heart of Mary 2; Lay Teachers 10; Students 184.
Catechesis/Religious Program—Tel: 717-232-2551. Students 232.
Convent—2473 Adrian St., 17104. Tel: 717-564-7236.

5—HOLY NAME OF JESUS (Lower Paxton Twp.) (1960), Rev. Msgr. Robert E. Lawrence; Rev. Walter F. Guzman; Deacons Jerome Foerster; Joseph J. Wrabel.
Res.: 6150 Allentown Blvd., 17112. Tel: 717-652-4211; Fax: 717-652-2033.
School—(Grades K-8), 6190 Allentown Blvd., 17112. Tel: 717-657-1704; Fax: 717-657-9135. Tom Nissley, Prin. (Lower Paxton Twp.) Sisters of St. Joseph 1; Lay Teachers 51; Students 633.
Catechesis/Religious Program—Tel: 717-545-1154; Fax: 717-545-4642. Evelyn Alviani, D.R.E. Students 603.
Convent—Tel: 717-545-4357. Pastoral Associates 2; Teachers 1; Diocesan Administrators 1.

6—ST. LAWRENCE (1859), (German), Closed., See St. Patrick Cathedral, Harrisburg.

7—ST. MARGARET MARY ALACOQUE (Penbrook) (1948), Very Rev. Daniel F.X. Powell; Mrs. Karen Hurley, Pastoral Assoc. In Res., Very Rev. William C. Forrey Jr., M.A., M.Div.
Res.: 2848 Herr St., 17103-1817. Tel: 717-233-3062; Fax: 717-238-5633.
School—Tel: 717-232-3771; Fax: 717-232-0776. Mrs. Joyce Haug, Prin. Sisters of Mercy 2; Lay Teachers 19; Students 331.
Catechesis/Religious Program—Tel: 717-232-3800. Mrs. Margaret Puerzer, D.R.E. Students 135.

8—OUR LADY OF THE BLESSED SACRAMENT (1906), Rev. Paul R. Shuda; Cecelia Jackson, Pastoral Assoc. In Res., Rev. Joseph Hoa Nguyen.
Res.: 2121 N. Third St., 17110-1812. Tel: 717-233-1014; Fax: 717-234-5652.
Catechesis/Religious Program—Tel: 717-234-8656. Students 41.

9—SACRED HEART OF JESUS (1901), Closed., See St. Patrick Cathedral, Harrisburg.

OUTSIDE THE CITY OF HARRISBURG

ABBOTTSTOWN, YORK CO., IMMACULATE HEART OF MARY (1809), [CEM] Rev. Thomas F. Langan; Deacon Raymond J. Smith. In Res., Rev. Msgr. Robert C. Gribbin.
Res.: 6084 W. Canal Rd., 17301. Tel: 717-259-0611; Fax: 717-259-6371.
Catechesis/Religious Program—Tel: 717-259-9426. Students 208.

ANNVILLE, LEBANON CO., ST. PAUL THE APOSTLE (1928), Rev. John D. Peck, O.S.B.
Res.: 125 S. Spruce St., 17003. Tel: 717-867-1525; Fax: 717-867-5318.
Catechesis/Religious Program—Tel: 717-867-7471. Students 262.
Station—Lebanon Valley College, Miller Chapel, Tel: 717-867-6135.

BERWICK, COLUMBIA CO.

1—IMMACULATE CONCEPTION OF THE BLESSED VIRGIN MARY (1906), [CEM] Rev. Francis J. Tamburro.
Res.: 1730 Fowler Ave., 18603-1462. Tel: 570-759-8113; Fax: 570-759-6637.
School—Holy Family Consolidated School, Tel: 570-752-2021; Fax: 570-752-2914. Please refer to Consolidated Elementary Schools located in the Institutions Located in the Diocese for details.
Catechesis/Religious Program—Tel: 570-759-9225. Students 180.

2—ST. JOSEPH'S (1928), Very Rev. Dennis G. Dalessandro; Sisters M. Carmelina, D.M., Pastoral Assoc.; M. Amelia, D.M., Pastoral Assoc.
Res.: 721 Monroe St., 18603. Tel: 570-752-5684; Fax: 570-752-7765.
School—Holy Family Consolidated School, Tel: 570-752-2021; Fax: 570-752-5623. Sr. M. Judith Tarozzi, D.M., Prin. Please refer to Consolidated Elementary Schools located in the Institutions Located in the Diocese for details.
Catechesis/Religious Program—Students 206.
Convent—Daughters of Mercy, 728 Washington St., 18603. Tel: 570-752-2112. Sisters 4.

BLOOMSBURG, COLUMBIA CO., ST. COLUMBA (1882), (Irish), [CEM] Rev. Patrick A. Devine.
Mailing Address: P.O. Box 829, 17815. Tel: 570-784-0801; Fax: 570-387-2604.
Res.: 42 E. Third St., 17815.
School—(Grades PreK-6), 40 E. Third St., 17815. Tel: 570-784-5932. Mrs. Margaret Jessick, Prin. Sisters 1; Lay Teachers 6; Students 163.
Catechesis/Religious Program—Tel: 570-387-4068. Students 350.
Convent—342 Iron St., 17815. Tel: 570-784-1385.
Mission—Christ the King Mendenhall Ln., Benton, Columbia Co. 17814. Tel: 570-925-6969.

BLUE RIDGE SUMMIT, FRANKLIN CO., ST. RITA (1919), [JC] Revs. Michael A. Messaro, M.SS.CC.; Sigfrido Troche, M.SS.CC.
Mailing Address: *Immaculate Conception*, P.O. Box 704, Fairfield, 17320. Tel: 717-642-8815; Fax: 717-642-9616.
Catechesis/Religious Program—Tel: 717-794-2067. Students 90.

BONNEAUVILLE, ADAM CO., ST. JOSEPH (1859), [CEM]

Rev. Philip DeChico; Deacon Richard J. Weaver.
Res.: 12 E. Hanover St., Gettysburg, 17325-7750. Tel: 717-334-2510; Fax: 717-337-1968.
Catechesis / Religious Program—Students 50.

BUCHANAN VALLEY, ADAMS CO., ST. IGNATIUS LOYOLA (Orrtanna) (1817), [CEM] Rev. Carl J. Steffen.
Res.: 1095 Church Rd., Orrtanna, 17353. Tel: 717-677-8012.
Catechesis / Religious Program—Tel: 717-677-8012. Students 80.

CAMP HILL, CUMBERLAND CO., GOOD SHEPHERD (1951), Very Rev. Paul C. Helwig, V.F.; Rev. Donald W. Cramer II; Deacon Francis Gorman. In Res., Very Rev. William J. King, M.Div., M.A., J.C.D.
Res.: 3435 Trindle Rd., 17011. Tel: 717-761-1167; Fax: 717-761-5313.
School—Tel: 717-737-7261; Fax: 717-761-4673. Mrs. Maretta K. Schmidt, Prin. Lay Teachers 20; Students 266.
Catechesis / Religious Program—3400 Market St., 17011. Tel: 717-737-8216. Mrs. Lucille Smith, D.R.E. Students 272.

CARLISLE, CUMBERLAND CO., ST. PATRICK (1779), [CEM 2] Revs. William J. Waltersheid; Andre J. Meluskey; David M. Hereshko.
Res.: 140 E. Pomfret St., 17013. Tel: 717-243-4411; Fax: 717-258-9281.
School—87 Marsh Dr., 17013. Tel: 717-249-4826; Fax: 717-245-0522. Sr. Karen Washabaugh, S.S.J., Prin. Lay Teachers 37; Students 448.
Catechesis / Religious Program—Tel: 717-243-4891; Fax: 717-245-0552. Mrs. Helen Richards, D.R.E. Students 353.
Chapel—Pine Grove Furnace, St. Eleanor Regina
Chapel—St. Katherine Drexel Chapel - Perpetual Adoration

CENTRALIA, COLUMBIA CO., ST. IGNATIUS (1869), Closed., See Our Lady of Mount Carmel, Mount Carmel.

CHAMBERSBURG, FRANKLIN CO., CORPUS CHRISTI (1792), [CEM] Revs. James R. O'Brien; Rodrigo A. Arrazola.
Res.: 320 Philadelphia Ave., 17201. Tel: 717-264-6317; Fax: 717-264-1787.
School—305 N. Second St., 17201. Tel: 717-263-5036; Fax: 717-263-6079. Mr. Robert G. Dortenzo, Prin. Lay Teachers 22; Students 288.
Catechesis / Religious Program—Tel: 717-263-9541. Mr. David C. Cheslock, D.R.E. Students 215.
Mission—Our Lady of Refuge 21169 Cross Rd., Doylesburg, Franklin Co. 17219. Tel: 717-349-7953. Rev. John R. Campion, Admin. (Retired).
Station—Scotland School for Veterans' Children Scotland. Tel: 717-264-7187; Fax: 717-264-0322.

COAL TOWNSHIP, NORTHUMBERLAND CO.

1—OUR LADY OF HOPE (1995), Revs. Francis J. Karwacki; Michael Letteer.
Res.: 863 W. Chestnut St., 17866-1995. Tel: 570-648-4432; Fax: 570-648-8944.
Catechesis / Religious Program—Students 153.

2—ST. STEPHEN PROTOMARTYR (1898), (Polish), Closed., See Our Lady of Hope, Coal Township.

COLUMBIA, LANCASTER CO.

1—HOLY TRINITY (1860), [CEM] Very Rev. Kenneth F. Lawrence, V.F.; Sr. Anna Cosgrave, O.S.F., Pastoral Assoc.
Res.: 409 Cherry St., 17512. Tel: 717-684-2711; Fax: 717-684-9612.
School—404 Cherry St., 17512. Tel: 717-684-2664; Fax: 717-684-5039. Theresa Burg, Prin. (Consolidated) Lay Teachers 13; Students 112.
Catechesis / Religious Program—Tel: 717-684-2232. Students 141.
Convent—Sisters of St. Francis of Philadelphia, 548 Cherry St., 17512. Tel: 717-684-2232.

2—ST. PETER (1828), [CEM 2] Rev. Peter I. Hahn.
Res.: 121 S. Second St., 17512. Tel: 717-684-7070.
School—Our Lady of the Angels Please refer to Consolidated Elementary Schools located in the Institutions Located in the Diocese for details.
Catechesis / Religious Program—Tel: 717-684-7070. Richard Groff, D.R.E. Students 70.
Convent—Tel: 717-684-2707.

CONEWAGO TOWNSHIP, ADAMS CO., BASILICA OF THE SACRED HEART OF JESUS (1730), [CEM] Rev. Lawrence J. McNeil, D.Min.
Res.: 30 Basilica Dr., Hanover, 17331-8924. Tel: 717-637-2721.
School—Tel: 717-632-8715. Sr. Eileen Kean, Prin. Sisters of St. Joseph 4; Lay Teachers 8; Students 245.
Catechesis / Religious Program—Students 50.
Convent—Sisters of St. Joseph, 55 Basilica Dr., Hanover, 17331. Tel: 717-637-3370. Sisters 6.

CORNWALL, LEBANON CO., SACRED HEART OF JESUS (1886), [CEM] Revs. Andrew P. Marinak; Paul R. Fisher, O.Pream.
Res.: 2596 Cornwall Rd., P.O. Box 136, 17016-0136. Tel: 717-273-1574.
Parish Center—Tel: 717-274-3239; Fax: 717-273-9588.
Catechesis / Religious Program—Tel: 717-273-2160. Becky Broderic, D.R.E. Students 102.

DALLASTOWN, YORK CO., ST. JOSEPH (1850), [CEM] [JC] Rev. Charles L. Persing; Deacon John Weaver.
Res.: 251 E. Main St., 17313. Tel: 717-246-3007; Fax: 717-244-5278.
School—271 E. Main St., 17313. Tel: 717-244-9386; Fax: 717-244-9478. Bernadette L. Snook, Prin. Lay Teachers 10; Students 162.
Catechesis / Religious Program—Tel: 717-244-6279. Students 465.

DANVILLE, MONTOUR CO., ST. JOSEPH (1848), [CEM 3] Rev. William M. Weary.
Res.: 18 E. Center St., 17821. Tel: 570-275-2512; Fax: 570-275-6840.
School—511 Ferry St., 17821. Tel: 717-275-2435; Fax: 570-275-3947. Lay Teachers 11; Students 134.
Catechesis / Religious Program—Tel: 570-275-0345. Students 228.

DAUPHIN, DAUPHIN CO., ST. MATTHEW, APOSTLE AND EVANGELIST (1976), Very Rev. Edward J. Quinlan III, M.Div., M.A., M.S.; Deacon Richard Aull.
Res.: 420 Stony Creek Rd., P.O. Box 459, 17018. Tel: 717-921-2363; Fax: 717-921-2364.
Catechesis / Religious Program—Students 61.

DOYLESBURG, FRANKLIN CO., OUR LADY OF REFUGE MISSION (1802), [CEM] Rev. John R. Campion, Admin. (Retired).
Res.: 21169 Cross Rd., 17219. Tel: 717-349-7953; Fax: 717-349-7942.
Catechesis / Religious Program—Students 11.

ELIZABETHTOWN, LANCASTER CO., ST. PETER (1752), [CEM] Rev. David L. Danneker, Ph.D. In Res., Rev. Msgr. Thomas J. Kujovsky (Retired); Deacon Richard A. Ryan.
Parish Office—1840 Marshall Dr., 17022. Tel: 717-367-1255; Fax: 717-367-1270.
Res.: 1 Saint Peter's Pl., 17022-1956.
School—61 E. Washington St., 17022. Tel: 717-367-1678; Fax: 717-367-1270. Mrs. Susan Miklos, Prin. Lay Teachers 5; Students 86.
Catechesis / Religious Program—Students 263.

ELYSBURG, NORTHUMBERLAND CO., QUEEN OF THE MOST HOLY ROSARY (1950), [JC] Rev. Charles R. Slough.
Res.: 103 W. Center St., 17824. Tel: 750-672-2302; Fax: 570-672-3310.
Catechesis / Religious Program—Tel: 570-672-9930. Students 199.

ENHAUT, DAUPHIN CO., ST. JOHN THE EVANGELIST (1902), Closed., See Prince of Peace, Steelton.

ENOLA, CUMBERLAND CO., OUR LADY OF LOURDES (1926), Rev. John A. Acri; Ms. Celeste Hamilton, Pastoral Assoc.; Deacon Edwin L. Fitzpatrick.
Res.: 225 Salt Rd., 17025. Tel: 717-732-9642; Fax: 717-732-8184.
Catechesis / Religious Program—Students 555.

EPHRATA, LANCASTER CO., MOTHER OF PERPETUAL HELP (1914), [JC] Very Rev. Raymond F. Collins, C.SS.R.; Revs. Brendan P. Greany, C.SS.R.; William G. Geiger, C.SS.R.
Church Office: 320 Church Ave., 17522. Tel: 717-733-9641; Fax: 717-733-2119.
Res.: 300 W. Pine St., P.O. Box 209, 17522. Tel: 717-733-6596; Fax: 717-733-0502.
School—330 Church Ave., 17522. Tel: 717-738-2414; Fax: 717-738-3280. Sr. Marie Gayda, O.S.F., Prin. Bernardine Sisters of the Third Order of St. Francis 3; Lay Teachers 10; Students 335.
Catechesis / Religious Program—Tel: 717-738-4517; Fax: 717-733-2119. Students 380.
Convent—310 Church Ave., 17522. Tel: 717-733-1291.

FAIRFIELD, ADAMS CO., IMMACULATE CONCEPTION OF THE BLESSED VIRGIN MARY (1823), [CEM] [JC] Revs. Michael A. Messaro, M.SS.CC.; Sigfrido Troche, M.SS.CC.
256 Tract Rd., P.O. Box 704, 17320.
Res.: Tel: 717-642-8815; Fax: 717-642-9616.
Catechesis / Religious Program—Students 150.

GETTYSBURG, ADAMS CO., ST. FRANCIS XAVIER'S (1831), [CEM] Revs. Benardo Pistone; Michael P. Reid II; Deacon James Sneeringer.
Res.: 22 W. High St., 17325. Tel: 717-334-3919; 717-334-7711; Fax: 717-334-3919.
School—45 W. High St., 17325. Tel: 717-334-4221; Fax: 717-334-8883. Sr. Phyllis, R.S.M., Prin. Sisters of Mercy 2; Sisters of St. Joseph 1; Lay Teachers 13; Students 281.
Catechesis / Religious Program—Tel: 717-334-1221. Students 523.
Convent—Sisters of Mercy Convent, Tel: 717-334-4310. Sisters 4.

GREENCASTLE, FRANKLIN CO., ST. MARK THE EVANGELIST (1965), [JC] Rev. Joseph L. Stahura.
Res.: 395 S. Ridge Ave., P.O. Box 218, 17225. Tel: 717-597-2705.
Catechesis / Religious Program—Tel: 717-597-2705. Students 162.
Mission—St. Luke the Evangelist Overhill Dr. & Black Rd., Mercersburg, Franklin Co. 17236.

HANOVER, YORK CO.

1—ST. JOSEPH (1864), [CEM] Revs. Joseph F. Gotwalt; Steven W. Fauser.
Res.: 5055 Grandview Rd., 17331. Tel: 717-637-5236; Fax: 717-637-6615.
School—236 Baltimore St., 17331. Tel: 717-632-1335; Fax: 717-632-5147. Mrs. Susan M. Mummert, Prin. Lay Teachers 16; Students 216.
School—Middle School, 5125 Grandview Rd., 17331. Tel: 717-632-0118; Fax: 717-632-0030.
Catechesis / Religious Program—Students 400.

2—ST. VINCENT (1904), [CEM] Rev. John A. Szada Jr.
Res.: 220 Third St., 17331. Tel: 717-637-4625; Fax: 717-637-6650.
School—224 Third St., 17331. Tel: 717-637-5190. Lay Teachers 10; Students 201.
Catechesis / Religious Program—Students 60.

HERSHEY, DAUPHIN CO., ST. JOAN OF ARC (1920), Revs. Philip G. Burger; Paul M. Clark; Martin Aitsebaomo, O.P.; Paul M. Clark.
Res.: 359 W. Areba Ave., 17033. Tel: 717-533-7168; Fax: 717-520-0526.
School—329 W. Areba Ave., 17033. Tel: 717-533-2854; Fax: 717-534-0755. Sr. Eileen M. McGowan, Prin. Daughters of Our Lady of Mercy 1; Lay Teachers 24; Students 293.
Catechesis / Religious Program—Tel: 717-533-8578. Students 723.
Convent—Tel: 717-533-2864. Sisters 6.

KULPMONT, NORTHUMBERLAND CO.

1—ASSUMPTION OF THE BLESSED VIRGIN MARY (1909), Closed., See Holy Angels, Kulpmont.

2—ST. CASIMIR (1915), Closed., See Holy Angels, Kulpmont.

3—HOLY ANGELS (1955), [CEM 3] Rev. Raymond J. Orloski.
Res.: 855 Scott St., 17834. Tel: 570-373-1221; Fax: 570-373-1226.
Catechesis / Religious Program—863 Scott St., 17834. Tel: 570-373-1512. Students 346.

LANCASTER, LANCASTER CO.

1—ST. ANNE (1923), Rev. Msgr. Richard A. Youtz, J.C.L.; Deacons Frank Eckman; Joseph L. Anders.
Res.: 929 N. Duke St., 17602. Tel: 717-392-2225.
School— Please refer to Consolidated Elementary Schools located in the Institutions in the Diocese for details.
Catechesis / Religious Program—Tel: 717-509-8554. Mrs. Catherine Trusz, D.R.E. Students 114.

2—ST. ANTHONY OF PADUA (1870), [CEM] Revs. Patrick McGarrity, C.SS.R.; James Small, C.SS.R.; Patrick Flynn, C.SS.R.
Res.: 501 E. Orange St., 17602. Tel: 717-394-0669; Fax: 717-394-4507.
School—Resurrection Please refer to Consolidated Elementary Schools located in the Institutions in the Diocese for details.
Catechesis / Religious Program—Tel: 717-392-2930. Patricia Meyer, D.R.E. Students 129.
Convent—Sisters of the Holy Cross, 533 E. Orange St., 17602. Tel: 717-397-1043.
Station—Lancaster County Prison, Tel: 717-299-7800.
Station—Conestoga View Nursing Home, Tel: 717-299-7850.

3—ASSUMPTION OF THE BLESSED VIRGIN MARY (1741), Revs. Leo M. Goodman; Thomas J. Gralinski; Mrs. Frances Sescilla, Pastoral Assoc.; Deacon Manuel Velazquez.
Res.: 119 S. Prince St., 17603. Tel: 717-392-2578; Fax: 717-394-6549.
School—Resurrection Please refer to Consolidated Elementary Schools located in the Institutions in the Diocese for details.
Catechesis / Religious Program—Ann Bleistine, D.R.E. Students 250.
Iglesia Catolica San Juan Bautista—425 S. Duke St., 17602. Tel: 717-392-4118; Fax: 717-392-4789. Email: p127sanjuan@hbgdiocese.org. Revs. Allan F. Wolfe; Ignacio Palomino; Sr. Therese Marie Smith, A.S.C., Pastoral Asst.; Deacons Expedito Santos; Manuel Velazquez; Felix Ramos.

4—ST. JOHN NEUMANN (1978), Rev. Msgr. Richard A. Youtz, J.C.L.; Rev. David A. Hillier (TR); Sr. Helen E. McCormac, Pastoral Assoc.
Res.: 601 E. Delp Rd., 17601. Tel: 717-569-8531; Fax: 717-569-2135.
Catechesis / Religious Program—Tel: 717-569-8533. Mr. Alan H. Schwartz, D.R.E. Students 1,335.

5—ST. JOSEPH (1849), [CEM] Rev. Msgr. Thomas H. Smith, V.F.; Mrs. Patricia Weaver, Pastoral Assoc. In Res., Rev. Joseph C. Hilbert.
Res.: 440 St. Joseph St., 17603-5298. Tel: 717-397-6921; Fax: 717-397-2120.
School—Resurrection Please refer to Consolidated Elementary Schools located in the Institutions in the Diocese for details.
Catechesis / Religious Program—Students 132.

6—SACRED HEART OF JESUS (1900), Rev. Michael J. Grab. In Res., Rev. Bernard Quinn (Retired).
Res.: 558 W. Walnut St., 17603. Tel: 717-394-0757; Fax: 717-394-3589.

School—235 Nevin St., 17603. Tel: 717-393-8433. Sr. Patricia McKee, I.H.M., Prin. Servants of the Immaculate Heart of Mary 3; Lay Teachers 14; Students 199.
Catechesis/Religious Program—Sr. Mary Elizabeth Schmidt, I.H.M., D.R.E. Students 90.
Convent—565 W. Walnut St., 17603. Tel: 717-392-4522.

LEBANON, LEBANON CO.
1—ASSUMPTION OF THE BLESSED VIRGIN MARY (1812), [CEM] [JC] Very Rev. David T. McAndrew, V.F.; Rev. Jeffrey Thoms; Deacon Richard Wentzel.
Office & Res.: 2 N. Eighth St., 17046. Tel: 717-272-5674; Fax: 717-270-2734.
Catechesis/Religious Program—Debra Herr, D.R.E. Students 384.
Mission—Our Lady of Fatima 2 N. 8th St., Lebanon Co. 17046.
2—ST. BENEDICT THE ABBOT (1995), Rev Luis R. Rodriguez.
Res.: 1300 Lehman St., 17046-3331. Tel 717-272-0623; Fax: 717-270-6926.
Catechesis/Religious Program—Tel: 717-272-1242. Students 173.
3—ST. CECILIA (1995), [CEM] Revs. Joseph T. Scanlin; Walter A. Sempko (Retired).
Res.: 202 E. Lehman St., 17046. Tel: 717-272-4412; Fax: 717-272-3966.
Catechesis/Religious Program—Tel: 717-272-4352. Sisters 2; Students 157.
4—SS. CYRIL AND METHODIUS (1905), (Slovak), Closed., See St. Benedict the Abbot, Lebanon.
5—ST. GERTRUDE (1906), Closed., See St. Cecilia, Lebanon.
6—ST. GREGORY THE GREAT (1965), Closed., See St. Cecilia, Lebanon.

LEWISBURG, UNION CO., SACRED HEART OF JESUS (1935), Revs. William J. Nessel, O.S.F.S., J.C.D.; Patrick J. Shannon, O.S.F.S.
Res.: 814 St. Louis St., 17837. Tel: 570-523-3104; Fax: 570-524-5156.
Catechesis/Religious Program— Sisters Karen Wilson, SS.C.M., D.R.E., Pastoral Sister; Thomas More Dzurnak, SS.C.M., D.R.E., Pastoral Sister. Students 371.
Mission—Saint George Church 775 Forest Hill Rd., P.O. Box 47, Mifflinburg, Union Co 17844. Tel: 570-966-3088.

LEWISTOWN, MIFFLIN CO., SACRED HEART OF JESUS (1830), [CEM] Rev. John B. Bateman
Res.: 106 N. Dorcas St., 17044. Tel: 717-242-2781; Fax: 717-242-2781.
School—110 N. Dorcas St., 17044. Tel: 717-248-5351; 717-248-0260; Fax: 717-248-5351. Lay Teachers 6; Students 97.
Catechesis/Religious Program—Students 128.

LITITZ, LANCASTER CO., ST. JAMES (1977), Rev. James O'Blaney, C.SS.R.
Res.: 505 Woodcrest Ave., 17543. Tel: 717-626-5580; Fax: 717-626-2146.
Catechesis/Religious Program—Tel: 717-626-0244. Joseph Trainor, D.R.E. Students 509.

LITTLESTOWN, ADAMS CO., ST. ALOYSIUS (1884), [CEM] Rev. James M. Sterner.
Res.: 29 S. Queen St., 17340. Tel 717-359-4513; Fax: 717-359-0683.
Catechesis/Religious Program—Faith Redding, D.R.E. Students 112.

LOCUST GAP, NORTHUMBERLAND CO., ST. JOSEPH (1870), Closed., See Our Lady of Mount Carmel, Mount Carmel.

LOCUSTDALE, COLUMBIA CO., ST. JOSEPH (1913), Closed., See Our Lady of Mount Carmel, Mount Carmel.

LYKENS, DAUPHIN CO., OUR LADY HELP OF CHRISTIANS (1853), [CEM 2] [JC 3] Rev. Tri Luong.
Res.: 732 E. Main St., 17048. Tel: 717-453-7895; Fax: 717-453-9426.
Catechesis/Religious Program—Tel: 717-453-9931. Students 220.
Mission—Sacred Heart of Jesus 140 E. Market St., Williamstown, Dauphin Co. 17098. Tel: 717-647-2645; 717-647-2447.

MANHEIM, LANCASTER CO., ST. RICHARD (1978), [JC] Rev. Francis Menei; Deacon James J. Rush.
Res.: 201 Adele Ave., 17545. Tel: 717-665-2465; Fax: 717-665-7119.
Catechesis/Religious Program—Jeannette Mastromatteo, D.R.E. Students 75.

MARIETTA, LANCASTER CO., PRESENTATION OF THE BLESSED VIRGIN MARY (1869), Closed., See Mary, Mother of the Church, Mount Joy.

MARION HEIGHTS, NORTHUMBERLAND CO., OUR LADY OF PERPETUAL HELP (1905), Closed., See Holy Angels, Kulpmont.

MARYSVILLE, PERRY CO.
1—OUR LADY OF GOOD COUNSEL (1965), Rev. John P. Trigilio Jr.
Res.: 121 William St., 17053. Tel: 717-957-2662; Fax: 717-957-4247.
Catechesis/Religious Program—Tel: 717-957-9218. Mary Olley, D.R.E.; Jack Zogby, D.R.E. Students 33.
Mission—St. Bernadette (1954), 901 High St., Duncannon Perry Co. 17020. Tel: 717-834-4519.

MCSHERRYSTOWN, ADAMS CO., ANNUNCIATION OF THE BLESSED VIRGIN MARY (1899), [CEM] Rev. Lawrence W. Sherdel; Deacon Joseph F. Lawrence.
Res.: 26 N. Third St., 17344. Tel: 717-637-1191; Fax: 717-637-1715.
School—316 North St., 17344. Tel: 717-337-3135. Sr. Ann Marie Wierman, S.S.J., Prin. Lay Teachers 22; Students 387.
Catechesis/Religious Program—Students 90.

MECHANICSBURG, CUMBERLAND CO.
1—ST. ELIZABETH ANN SETON (1977), Rev. Richard P. Waldron. In Res., Rev. Edward C. Malesic.
Res.: 310 Hertzler Rd., 17055. Tel: 717-697-2614; Fax: 717-795-0800.
Catechesis/Religious Program—Tel: 717-697-3545. Candice Straka, D.R.E.; Judy Olinger, D.R.E. Students 399.
2—ST. JOSEPH (1950), Rev. Chester P. Snyder; Rose Baker, Pastoral Assoc.; Deacon Jack Paruso; William Reilly, Parish Mgr.
Res.: 200 S. Filbert St., P.O. Box 2012, 17055. Tel: 717-766-9433; Fax: 717-795-9123.
Church: 400 E. Simpson St., 17055.
School—410 E. Simpson St., 17055. Tel: 717-766-2564; Fax: 717-766-1226. Sisters of SS. Cyril and Methodius 3; Lay Teachers 21; Students 464.
Catechesis/Religious Program—Tel: 717-766-2472; Fax: 717-766-2856. Sr. Joseph Therese, D.R.E. Students 420.
Convent—302 S. Chestnut St., 17055.
3—SAINT KATHARINE DREXEL (1988), Rev. Stephen D. Weitzel; Deacon Joseph Gorini.
Mailing Address: One Peter Dr., 17050. In Res., Rev. Msgr. Vincent J. Smith (Retired).
Res.: 87 Skyline Dr., 17050. Tel: 717-697-8716; Fax: 717-697-3702.
Catechesis/Religious Program—Tel: 717-795-8572. Christopher Adams, D.R.E. Students 430.

MIDDLETOWN, DAUPHIN CO., SEVEN SORROWS OF THE BLESSED VIRGIN MARY (1855), [CEM] Revs. Louis P. Ogden David S. Keller.
Res.: 280 N. Race St., 17057. Tel: 717-944-3133; Fax: 717-944-1170.
School—(Grades PreK-8), Race & Conewago St., 17057 Tel: 717-944-5371; Fax: 717-944-5419. Mrs. Suzanne Gausman, Prin. Lay Teachers 16; Students 209.
Catechesis/Religious Program—Students 258.

MIFFLINTOWN, JUNIATA CO., ST. JUDE (1959), Revs. John Bateman Jr.; Bernerad Mary Ohiwee, O.P.
Res.: Box 187, 17059. Tel: 717-436-6722.
Catechesis/Religious Program—Students 61.

MILLERSBURG, DAUPHIN CO., QUEEN OF PEACE (1952), Rev. Darius G. C. Moss.
Res.: 202 Zimmerman, 17061. Tel: 717-692-3504.
Catechesis/Religious Program—Tel: 717-692-3504. Mrs. Dolores Wertz, D.R.E. Students 106.

MILLERSVILLE, LANCASTER CO., ST. PHILIP THE APOSTLE (1965), Rev. Brian P. Conrad; Deacons Martin C. Light Sr.; Ross Beighley. In Res., Rev. Lawrence C. Gross.
Res.: 2111 Millersville Pike, Lancaster, 17603. Tel: 717-872-2166; Fax: 717-872-2587.
Catechesis/Religious Program—Tel: 717-872-5653. Miss Christine M. Miller, D.R.E. Students 364.

MILTON, NORTHUMBERLAND CO., ST. JOSEPH (1805), [CEM] Rev. Thomas A. Scala.
Res.: 109 Broadway, 17847. Tel: 570-742-4356; Fax: 570-742-3475.
Catechesis/Religious Program—Tel: 570-724-4302. Belinda Stefl, D.R.E. Students 177.

MOUNT CARMEL, NORTHUMBERLAND CO.
1—DIVINE REDEEMER (1995), [CEM 4] Rev. Norman C. Hohenwarter Jr.
Res.: 438 West Ave., 17851. Tel: 570-339-3450; Fax: 570-339-5759.
Catechesis/Religious Program—250 West Ave., 17851. Tel: 570-339-4420. Students 90.
2—HOLY CROSS (1892), (Lithuanian), Closed., See Divine Redeemer, Mount Carmel.
3—ST. JOHN THE BAPTIST (1892) (Slovak), Closed., See Divine Redeemer, Mount Carmel.
4—ST. JOSEPH (1875), (Polish), Closed., See Our Lady of Mount Carmel, Mount Carmel.
5—OUR LADY OF MOUNT CARMEL (1886), [JC 4] Rev. Msgrs. Lawrence R. Overbaugh; Francis J. Hudak.
Res.: 47 S. Market St., 17851 Tel: 717-339-1031; Fax: 717-339-4814.
Catechesis/Religious Program—Tel: 717-339-4420. Ms. Victoria Calabretta, D.R.E. Students 151.
6—OUR MOTHER OF CONSOLATION (1895), (Polish), Closed., See Divine Redeemer, Mount Carmel.
7—ST. PETER (1905), (Italian), Closed., See Divine Redeemer, Mount Carmel.

MOUNT JOY, LANCASTER CO.
1—ASSUMPTION OF B.V.M. (1979), Closed., See Mary, Mother of the Church, Mount Joy.
2—MARY, MOTHER OF THE CHURCH (1995), Rev. Paul T. Rindos.
Res.: 625 Union School Rd., 17552-9712. Tel: 717-653-4903; Fax: 717-653-4058.
Catechesis/Religious Program—Students 221.

MYERSTOWN, LEBANON COUNTY, MARY, GATE OF HEAVEN (1926), Rev. Robert F. Berger.
Res.: 188 W. McKinley Ave., P.O. Box 227, 17067. Tel: 717-866-5640.
Catechesis/Religious Program—Students 153.

NEW BLOOMFIELD, PERRY CO., ST. BERNARD (1942), Rev. Robert F. Sharman, S.T.L.
Res.: 120 W. McClure St., P.O. Box 25, 17068. Tel: 717-582-4113; Fax: 717-582-3797.
Catechesis/Religious Program— Alice Vilk, D.R.E. Students 250.

NEW CUMBERLAND, CUMBERLAND CO., ST. THERESA OF THE INFANT JESUS (1928), Rev. Msgr. Willilam M. Richardson; Deacon Joseph J. Kramer. In Res., Very Rev. Thomas R. Haney.
Res.: 1300 Bridge St., 17070. Tel: 717-774-5918; Fax: 717-774-5915.
School—1200 Bridge St., 17070. Tel: 717-774-7464; Fax: 717-774-3154. Sisters Margaret Mary Barrett, Prin. (Elementary); Francine Gagne, I.H.M., Prin. (High School). Lay Teachers 32; Students 498.
Catechesis/Religious Program—Tel: 717-774-7296. Students 464.

NEW FREEDOM, YORK CO., ST. JOHN THE BAPTIST (1841), [CEM] Revs. Sylvan P. Capitani, D.Min.; Michael P. Reid II; Stan U. Ukwe, O.P.; Deacon Michael Bahn.
Res.: 315 N. Constitution Ave., 17349. Tel: 717-235-2156; Fax: 717-235-2223.
Catechesis/Religious Program—Tel: 717-235-2439. Students 615.

NEW HOLLAND, LANCASTER CO., OUR LADY OF LOURDES (1972), Rev. John D. Schmalhofer.
Res.: 737 Walnut St., 17557. Tel: 717-354-2540; Fax: 717-354-4170.
Catechesis/Religious Program—Tel: 717-354-3338. Students 297.

NEW OXFORD, ADAMS CO., IMMACULATE CONCEPTION OF THE BLESSED VIRGIN MARY (1852), [CEM] Rev. Daniel P. O'Brien.
Res.: 106 Carlisle St., 17350. Tel: 717-624-4121; Fax: 717-624-4221.
School—101 N. Peter St., 17350. Tel: 717-624-2061; Fax: 717-624-9711. Dianne Giampietro, Prin. Lay Teachers 14; Students 193.
Catechesis/Religious Program—Tel: 717-624-7531; Fax: 717-624-4221. Sr. Paula Mary Aumen, D.R.E. Students 121.
Convent—5 Carlisle St., 17350. Tel: 717-624-7531.

NORTHUMBERLAND, NORTHUMBERLAND CO., ST. THOMAS MORE (1955), Closed., See St. Monica, Sunbury.

PALMYRA, LEBANON CO., HOLY SPIRIT (1955), Rev. James F. Podlesny, O.S.B.
Res.: 245 W. Pine St., 17078. Tel: 717-838-3369; Fax: 717-838-3065.
Catechesis/Religious Program— Mrs. Helen Remington, D.R.E. Students 242.

QUARRYVILLE, LANCASTER CO., ST. CATHERINE OF SIENA (1843), [CEM] Rev. Ronald J. Moratelli.
Res.: 955 Robert Fulton Hwy., 17566-9543. Tel: 717-786-2695; Fax: 717-786-0374.
Catechesis/Religious Program—Mrs. Diane Dalgaard, D.R.E. Students 186.

RANSHAW, NORTHUMBERLAND CO., ST. ANTHONY OF PADUA (1919), Closed., See Mother Cabrini, Shamokin.

ROARING CREEK, COLUMBIA CO., OUR LADY OF MERCY (1923), [CEM] Rev. Thomas Ignatius Mannion.
Res.: 304 Slabtown Rd., Catawissa, 17820. Tel: 570-799-5642.
Catechesis/Religious Program—Mrs. Margaret Jessick, D.R.E. Students 94.

ROHRERSTOWN, LANCASTER CO., ST. LEO THE GREAT (1964), Revs. William J. Sullivan; Jose Celia, O.Carm. (JOL); Deacon Eugene Vannucci.
Res.: 2427 Marietta Ave., Lancaster, 17601. Tel: 717-394-1742; Fax: 717-394-1779.
School—Tel: 717-392-2441; Fax: 717-392-4080. Mrs. Joyce Redington, Prin. Lay Teachers 15; Students 256.
Catechesis/Religious Program—Tel: 717-394-7354. Students 546.

SELINSGROVE, SNYDER CO., ST. PIUS X (1964), Rev. Edward J. Keating Jr.
Res.: 610 University Ave., 17870. Tel: 570-374-4113; Fax: 570-374-4113.
Catechesis/Religious Program—Students 264.
Mission—Susquehanna University 610 University Ave., Snyder Co. 17870. Tel: 570-372-4113.
Mission—Selinsgrove Center, Snyder Co. 17870. Tel: 570-374-4113.
Mission—Snyder County Prison, Snyder Co.

SHAMOKIN, NORTHUMBERLAND CO.
1—ASSUMPTION OF THE BLESSED VIRGIN MARY (1892), (Slovak), Closed., See Mother Cabrini, Shamokin.

2—ST. EDWARD (1866), Closed., See Mother Cabrini, Shamokin.
3—ST. JOSEPH (1913), Closed., See Our Lady of Hope, Coal Township.
4—ST. MICHAEL ARCHANGEL (1894), (Lithuanian), Closed., See Mother Cabrini, Shamokin.
5—MOTHER CABRINI (1995), [JC 4] Revs. Dennis Grumsey, O.F.M.Conv.; Adam Ziolkowski, O.F.M-.Conv.; Robert Plociennik, O.F.M.Conv.; Robert Grybowski, O.F.M.Conv.
Res.: 214 N. Shamokin St., 17872. Tel: 570-648-4512; Fax: 570-648-1209.
Catechesis / Religious Program—Students 135.
6—ST. STANISLAUS KOSTKA (1874), (Polish), Closed., See Mother Cabrini, Shamokin.
SHIPPENSBURG, CUMBERLAND CO., OUR LADY OF THE VISITATION (1950), Rev. Robert A. Yohe Jr., V.F.
Res.: 305 N. Prince St., 17257. Tel: 717-532-2912; Fax: 717-532-3905.
Catechesis / Religious Program—Students 128.
SOUTH MOUNTAIN, FRANKLIN CO., MOST HOLY ROSARY, Closed., See St. Ignatius, Buchannon Valley.
SPRING GROVE, YORK CO., SACRED HEART (1976), Rev. Hugh J. McLaughlin.
Res.: 152 N. Main St., Box 42, 17362. Tel: 717-225-1704; Fax: 717-225-9570.
Catechesis / Religious Program—Tel: 717-225-1997. Peggy Rizzuto, D.R.E. Students 71.
STEELTON, DAUPHIN CO.
1—ST. ANN (1901), (Italian), Closed., See Prince of Peace, Steelton.
2—ASSUMPTION OF THE BLESSED VIRGIN MARY (1898), (Croatian), Closed., See Prince of Peace, Steelton.
3—ST. JAMES (1878), Closed., See Prince of Peace, Steelton.
4—ST. PETER (1909), (Slovenian), Closed., See Prince of Peace, Steelton.
5—PRINCE OF PEACE (1995), Rev. Samuel E. Houser; Deacon Michael Grella.
Res.: 815 S. Second St., 17113. Tel: 717-985-1330; Fax: 717-985-1333.
School—245 Reynders Ave., 17113. Tel: 717-939-6357; Fax: 717-939-3660. Mr. James Collins, Prin. Daughters of Our Lady of Mercy 1; Religious Sisters of Mercy 2; Lay Teachers 8; Students 144.
Catechesis / Religious Program—Fax: 717-985-1331. Students 61.
SUNBURY, NORTHUMBERLAND CO.
1—ST. MICHAEL ARCHANGEL (1863), Closed., See St. Monica, Sunbury.
2—ST. MONICA (1995), Rev. William T. Haviland.
Res.: 20 N. Front St., 17801. Tel: 570-286-0761; Fax: 570-286-8588.
School—109 Market St., 17801. Tel: 570-286-5983; Fax: 570-286-7351. Martin McCarthy, Prin. Lay Teachers 14; Students 175.
Catechesis / Religious Program— Mrs. Peggy Walker, D.R.E. Students 110.
TREVORTON, NORTHUMBERLAND CO., ST. PATRICK (1850), [CEM] Revs. Francis J. Karwacki; Michael C. Letteer.
Res.: 331 W. Shamokin St., 17881-1523. Tel: 570-797-8251; Fax: 570-797-3990.
Catechesis / Religious Program—Tel: 570-648-8437. Mrs. Margaret Conrad, D.R.E. Students 70.
WAYNESBORO, FRANKLIN CO., ST. ANDREW (1893), [CEM] Rev. Thomas J. Hemler.
Res.: 12 N. Broad St., P.O. Box 167, 17268. Tel: 717-762-1914; Fax: 717-762-3319.
School—213 E. Main St., 17268. Tel: 717-762-3221. Mrs. Connie Richwine, Prin. Lay Teachers 12; Students 146.
Catechesis / Religious Program—Fax: 717-762-3319. Margaret E. Wagaman, D.R.E. Students 109.
WILLIAMSTOWN, DAUPHIN CO., SACRED HEART OF JESUS (1875), [CEM] [JC] Rev. Tri Luong.
Church: 140 E. Market St., 17098. Tel: 717-453-7895; Fax: 717-453-9426.
Res.: 732 Main St., Lykens, 17048.
Catechesis / Religious Program—Tel: 717-647-2645; Fax: 717-647-0641. Earl Roberts, D.R.E. Students 61.
YORK HAVEN, YORK CO., HOLY INFANT (1972), Rev. Clarence A. Olszewski; Rebecca Papa, Pastoral Asst.
Res.: 34 Third St., 17370. Tel: 717-266-5286; Fax: 717-266-2177.
Catechesis / Religious Program—Students 178.
YORK, YORK CO.
1—IMMACULATE CONCEPTION OF THE BLESSED VIRGIN MARY (1852), [CEM] [JC] Rev. Robert M. Gillelan Jr., V.F.; Deacon Catalino Gonzalez, Pastoral Assoc. In Res., Rev. John Mary Mooka, A.J. (Uganda).
Res.: 309 S. George St., 17403. Tel: 717-845-7629; Fax: 717-845-2433.
Catechesis / Religious Program—Tel: 717-846-6001. Ms. Karen Kreller, D.R.E. Students 153.
2—ST. JOSEPH (1913), [JC] Revs. Louis Petruha, O.F.M.Cap.; Robert E. McCreary, O.F.M.Cap. (CLV); Most Rev. Mark Carter, O.F.M.Cap; Rev. John McCloskey, O.F.M.Cap. In Res., Rev. James Froehlich, O.F.M.Cap.; Bro. Michael Rubus, O.F.M.Cap.
Res.: 2935 Kingston Rd., 17402-4003. Tel: 717-755-7503; Fax: 717-757-1900.
School—2945 Kingston Rd., 17402. Tel: 717-755-1797; Fax: 717-751-0136. Mrs. Patricia A. Byrnes, Prin. Sisters 2; Lay Teachers 22; Students 380.
Catechesis / Religious Program— Sr. Jean Holtz, S.S.J., D.R.E.; Mrs. Patricia Trevino, D.R.E. Students 660.
Convent—Sisters of St. Francis, 405 Quaker Dr., 17402. Tel: 717-757-3667. Sisters 5.
3—ST. PATRICK (1776), [CEM] Rev. C. Anthony Miller; Deacon Sam Moschella; Sr. Monica Imgrund, R.S.M., Pastoral Assoc. In Res., Rev. William M. Cawley (GF).
Res.: 231 S. Beaver St., 17403. Tel: 717-848-2007.
School—235 S. Beaver St., 17403. Tel: 717-854-8263; Fax: 717-846-6049. Sr. Noreen Joseph, I.H.M., Prin. Sisters, Servants of the Immaculate Heart of Mary 2; Lay Teachers 12; Students 164.
Catechesis / Religious Program—Tel: 717-854-6653. Mrs. Connie Egan, D.R.E. Students 150.
Convent—Sisters, Servants of the Immaculate Heart of Mary, Tel: 717-848-1911. Sisters 7.
4—ST. ROSE OF LIMA (1907), [JC] Rev. John R. Hoke; Deacon Joseph Sferrella. In Res., Rev. Carl T. Tancredi.
Res.: 950 W. Market St., 17404. Tel: 717-846-4935; Fax: 717-699-0715.
School—115 N. Biesecker Rd., Thomasville, 17364. Tel: 717-792-0889; Fax: 717-792-3959. Marlene Blake, Prin. Sisters of St. Joseph 1; Lay Teachers 13; Students 186.
Catechesis / Religious Program—Tel: 717-843-3043. Sr. Jane Keller, S.S.J., D.R.E. Students 417.
Convent—Sisters of St. Joseph, 944 W. Market St., 17404. Tel: 717-854-0378. Sisters 5.

Chaplains of Public Institutions

HARRISBURG. *Community General Osteopathic Hospital*. Rev. Kenneth G. Smith. Vacant
Harrisburg Hospital, Tel: 717-782-3333. Rev. Kenneth G. Smith.
Polyclinic Medical Clinic, Tel: 717-782-4141. Rev. Kenneth G. Smith.
State Hospital, Pouch A, 17105. Tel: 717-787-9232. Deacon Frank Parr.
CAMP HILL. *State Correctional Institution*, P.O. Box 200, 17011. Tel: 717-737-4531, Ext. 307. Deacon Manuel Velazquez.
DANVILLE. *Geisinger Medical Center*, Tel: 717-275-2512. Rev. Thomas C. Marickovic.
State Hospital, P.O. Box 219, 17821. Tel: 717-275-7011. Rev. Thomas Ignatius Mannion. Tel: 717-799-5642.
HERSHEY. *Milton J. Hershey Medical Center*, 500 University Blvd., 17033. Tel: 717-534-8177.
LANCASTER. *Lancaster County Prison*, 625 E. King St., 17602. Tel: 717-534-8177. Vacant
Lancaster General Hospital and Lancaster Community Hospital. Rev. Michael Culkin.
LEBANON. *Veterans Administration Hospital*, R.D. No. 1, 17042. Tel: 717-272-6621. Rev. James N. Drucker (PSC).
LEWISBURG. *U.S. Penitentiary*, Tel: 717-523-1251. Sr. Patricia Weidman, Chap.
SELINSGROVE. *Selinsgrove Center*, Box 500, 17870. Tel: 717-374-2911, Ext. 425. Rev. Edward J. Keating Jr.
SOUTH MOUNTAIN. *Restoration Center*, Tel: 717-749-5773. Rev. Joeseph C. Carolin.
YORK. *York Hospital*, 1001 S. George St., 17405. Tel: 717-771-2345. Rev. Carl T. Tancredi.

On Duty Outside the Diocese:
Very Rev.—
Rhoades, Kevin C., S.T.L., J.C.L., Mount St. Mary's Seminary, Emmitsburg, MD 21727. Mount St. Mary's Seminary Emmitsburg, MD
Revs.—
Bennett, Michael X., St. Mary Church, Ottawa ON Canada.
Blackwell, Edward A., 520 N.E. 20th St., #408, Fort Lauderdale, FL 33305-2195.
Hoke, John R., U.S. Navy
Kemper, John C., S.S., Sts. Cyril & Methodius Seminary, 3535 Indian Tr., Orchard Lake, MI 48324.
McLernon, Thomas M., Sacred Heart School of Theology, P.O. Box 429, Hales Corners, WI 53130-0429.
Topper, Charles J., 467 Bloomfield Ave., Bloomfield, CT 06002.

Retired:
Rev. Msgrs.—
Kujovsky, Thomas J.
Smith, Vincent J.
Topper, Vincent J. Tel: 717-273-1295
Revs.—
Farace, Frederick A., P.O. Box 276, Mount Carmel, 17851.
Fennessy, Joseph H.
Mammarella, Dominick
Miller, Paul
Quinn, Bernard
Sawdy, Wallace E., 115 North St., 17101.

Permanent Deacons:
Anders, Joseph L., St. Anne, Lancaster
Aull, Richard H., St. Matthew's, Dauphin
Bahn, Michael P., St. Joseph, York
Beighley, Ross W., St. Catherine of Siena, Quarryville
Bertollo, Edward L., Jr., Immaculate Conception BVM, Berwick
Clark, Charles W., St. Patrick, Harrisburg
Dunn, J. Leo, St. Patrick, Harrisburg
Eckman, Frank M., St. Anne, Lancaster
Enderle, Francis X.
Fedor, Thomas A., Holy Family, Harrisburg
Fitzpatrick, Edwin L., Our Lady of Lourdes, Enola
Flannery, Thomas H., St. Catherine, Harrisburg
Foerster, Jerome T., Holy Name of Jesus, Harrisburg
Gonzales, Catalino, Spanish-Speaking Apostolate, Harrisburg; Cristo Salvador, York
Gorini, Joseph B., St. Katharine Drexel, Mechanicsburg
Gorman, Francis, Good Shepherd, Camp Hill
Grella, Michael A., Prince of Peace, Steelton
Jordan, William J., St. Peter, Columbia
Kenski, Francis G.
Kramer, Joseph J., St. Theresa, New Cumberland
Lawrence, Joseph F., Annunciation BVM, McSherrystown
Light, Martin C., Sr., St. Philip, Millersville
Mack, Robert P., St. Edward, Shamokin
Marroquin, Miguel, Spanish-Speaking Apostolate, Harrisburg
Miller, Gene R., Immaculate Conception BVM, New Oxford
Mordecai, Philip B.
Moschella, Sabino E., St. Patrick, York
Mowery, John A.
Parr, Frank J., Harrisburg State Hospital, Harrisburg
Paruso, John L., St. Joseph, Mechanicsburg
Ramos, Felix, San Juan Bautista, Lancaster
Runkle, Ralph H., St. Patrick, York
Ryan, Richard A., St. Paul the Apostle, Annville
Santiago, Expidito, San Juan Bautista, Lancaster
Sferrella, Joseph, St. Rose of Lima, York
Smith, Raymond, Immaculate Heart, Abbottstown
Sneeringer, James, St. Francis Xavier, Gettysburg
Vannucci, Eugene D., St. Leo the Great, Rohrerstown
Velazquez, Manuel, Camp Hill State Correctional Institution, Camp Hill
Weaver, John A., St. Joseph, Dallastown
Weaver, Richard J., St. Joseph, Bonneauville
Weaver, Robert E., St. Joseph Hospital, Lancaster
Wentzel, Richard W., Assumption BVM & Lebanon Catholic High School, Lebanon
Wrabel, Joseph J., Holy Name, Harrisburg

INSTITUTIONS LOCATED IN THE DIOCESE

[A] HIGH SCHOOLS

HARRISBURG. *Bishop McDevitt High School*, 2200 Market St., 17103-2499. Tel: 717-236-7973; Fax: 717-234-1270. Email: mcdevitthbg@juno.com. Web: www.bishopmcdevitt.org. Sr. Mary Anne Bedner, I.H.M., Prin. Sisters 8; Lay Teachers 52; Students 811.

CAMP HILL. *Trinity High School*, 3601 Simpson Ferry Rd., 17011. Tel: 717-761-1116; Fax: 717-761-7309. Email: fgagne@trinityhs.k12.pa.us. Web: www.trinityhs.k12.pa.us. Sr. Francine Gagne, I.H.M., Prin. Sisters 2; Lay Teachers 44; Students 624.

COAL TOWNSHIP. *Our Lady of Lourdes Regional High School*, 2001 Clinton Ave., 17866-1699. Tel: 570-644-0375; Fax: 570-644-7655. Email: lourdes@ptd.net. Web: www.lourdes.k12.pa.us. Mr. John A. McKay, Prin. Lay Teachers 26; Students 206.

LANCASTER. *Lancaster Catholic High School*, 650 Juliette Ave., 17601. Tel: 717-509-0315; Fax: 717-509-0312. Email: dgarrett@lancatholichs.pvt.k12.pa.us. Mr. Dermot Garrett, Prin. Sisters 4; Lay Teachers 46; Students 740.

LEBANON. *Lebanon Catholic School*, (Grades K-12),

1400 Chestnut St., 17042. Tel: 717-273-3731; Fax: 717-274-5167. Deacon Richard Wentzel. Deacons 1; Lay Teachers 43; Students 519.

MCSHERRYSTOWN. *Delone Catholic High School*, 140 S. Oxford Ave., 17042. Tel: 717-637-5969; Fax: 717-637-0442. Dr. Maureen Thiec, Prin.

YORK. *York Catholic High School*, 601 E. Springettsbury Ave., 17403. Tel: 717-846-8871; Fax: 717-843-4588. Email: yorkcatholic@blazenet.net. Web: www.yorkcatholic.org. George E. Andrews, Prin.; Rev. William M. Cawley (GF), Teacher. Priests 1; Sisters 3; Lay Teachers 49; Total Staff 85; Students 708.

[B] CONSOLIDATED ELEMENTARY SCHOOLS

HARRISBURG. *Cathedral School*, 212 State St., 17101. Tel: 717-234-3797; Fax: 717-213-2000. Email: cathedralcs@paonline.com. Web: www.paonline.com/cathedrl. Sr. Mary Agnes Shurer, S.C.C., Prin.

Upper School (Grades PreK-4) Tel: 717-234-3797; Fax: 717-213-2000. Lay Teachers 6.

Lower School Tel: 717-234-3797. Lay Teachers 4; Total Students 167.

BERWICK. *Holy Family Consolidated School*, 728 Washington St., 18603. Tel: 570-752-2021; Fax: 570-752-5623. Email: prince@evenlink.com. Sr. Judith Tarozzi, D.M., Prin.

COLUMBIA. *Our Lady of the Angels School, Primary Bldg.*, 215 Union St., 17512. *Elementary Bldg.*, 404 Cherry St., 17512. Tel: 717-684-2433; 717-684-2664; Fax: 717-684-5039. Email: tburg@ourladyoftheangels.org. Mrs. Theresa M. Burg, Prin.

LANCASTER. *Resurrection School, Primary Bldg.*, 32 W. Vine St., 17603. *Elementary Bldg.*, 521 E. Orange St., 17603. Tel: 717-397-3136; 717-392-3083; Fax: 717-295-8475; 717-735-7793. Email dphilipps@resurrectioncatholicschool.net. Ms. Donna Philipps, Prin.

MOUNT CARMEL. *Holy Spirit Consolidated School*, 250 West Ave., 17851. Tel: 570-339-3823; Fax: 570-339-0606. Email: dove@sunlink.net hss@sunlink.net. Web: www.sunlink.net/~dove. Joseph Litchko, Prin. Sisters 1; Lay Teachers 8; Students 161.

SHAMOKIN. *Queen of Peace Consolidated School*, (Grades K-8), 201 N. Shamokin St., 17872. Tel: 570-648-6672; 570-648-0182 (Convent); Fax: 570-644-4737. Email: squeenofpeace@hbgdiocese.org. Sr. Margaret McCullough, I.H.M., Prin. Serves the parishes of Our Lady of Hope, Coal Township; Queen of the Most Holy Rosary, Elysburg; Mother Cabrini, Shamokin; and St. Patrick, Treverton. Sisters 3; Lay Teachers 12; Students 191.

[C] PRESCHOOLS AND DAY NURSERIES

MCSHERRYSTOWN. *St. Joseph Academy Preschool*, 90 Main St., 17344. Tel: 717-630-9990. Email: sjaprek@netrax.net. Sr. Anne Leonard Freed, S.S.J., Dir. Sisters of St. Joseph Sisters 1; Students 38; Aide 1.

YORK. *Holy Child Nursery*, 1141 E. Market St., 17403. Tel: 717-848-1691; Fax: 717-848-5181. Email: hcn1141@juno.com. Sr. Mary Grace, D.M., Admin. Daughters of Our Lady of Mercy Sisters 5; Lay Aides 5; Students 50.

[D] RELIGIOUS RESOURCE CENTERS

CAMP HILL. *Trinity High School* 17011. Tel: 717-761-1116; Fax: 717-761-7309. Email: trinity@trinityhs.k12.pa.us. Web: www.trinityhs.k12.pa.us.

DANVILLE. *Villa Sacred Heart* 17821-1698. Tel: 570-275-3581 (Motherhouse); 570-275-4929 (Generalate); Fax: 570-275-5997. Email: smtmsscm@hotmail.com. Web: www.sscm.org.

[E] CATHOLIC CHARITIES COUNSELING & FIELD SERVICES

HARRISBURG. *Department for Catholic Charities Administrative Office*, P.O. Box 3551, 17105. Tel: 717-657-4804; Fax: 717-657-8683. Web: www.hbgdiocese.org.

Adoption Services, 214 State St., 17101. Tel: 717-238-5944; Fax: 717-238-6050. Peter Biasucci, L.S.W., L.S.W., Dir.

Capital Region Office, 223 North St., 17101. Tel: 717-233-7978; Fax: 717-233-4194. Larry Belmont, L.S.W., Dir.; Donna Dillon, M.S. M.S., A.A.M.F.T., Dir.

Evergreen House Program, 100 Evergreen St., 17104. Tel: 717-238-6343; Fax: 717-238-4161. Lydia Porter, M.S., Dir.

Specialized Foster Care, 806-C S. 29th St., 17111. Tel: 717-654-7115; Fax: 717-564-7180. Nancy Jamison, M.S.W., Prog. Dir.

Immigration and Refugee Services, 900 N. 17th St., 17103. Tel: 717-232-0568; Fax: 717-234-1742. Norman Lederer, M.A., M.S., Prog. Dir.

Interfaith Shelter for Homeless Families, Harrisburg St. Hospital, Hemlock Bldg. #26, 17105. Tel: 717-236-6783; Fax: 717-236-3271. Linda Grudi, Prog. Dir.

Lourdeshouse Maternity Services, 100 B. Livingston St., Enhaut, 17113. Tel: 717-986-9510; Fax: 717-986-1030. Annette Martin, M.H.S., Prog. Dir.

Paradise School, 6156 West Canal Rd., Abbottstown, 17301. Tel: 717-259-9537; Fax: 717-259-9262. Michael Langley, M.S., Prog. Dir.

Chambersburg Office, 336 Philadelphia Ave., Chambersburg, 17201. Tel: 717-263-3765; Fax: 717-263-3226. Carolyn George, M.Div., Dir.

Chambersburg Family Outreach, 336 Philadelphia Ave., Chambersburg, 17201. Tel: 717-264-2332; Fax: 717-264-0654. Sheila Gross, M.A., Prog. Dir.

Lancaster Office, 925 N. Duke St., Lancaster, 17602. Tel: 717-299-3659; Fax: 717-299-1328. Kirk Reider, A.C.S.W, L.I.S.W., Dir.

Lancaster Latino Office, 925 N. Duke St., Lancaster, 17602. Tel: 717-395-2113; Fax: 717-299-1328.

Intensive Day Treatment, 47 S. Mulberry St., Lancaster, 17603. Tel: 717-295-9630; Fax: 717-295-9525. Laurence Reid, M.S.W., Prog. Dir.

Lancaster In-Home Intensive Services, 417 Poplar St., Lancaster, 17603. Tel: 717-392-3619; Fax: 717-392-4198. Chris Vandenberg, M.H.S., Prog. Dir.

Lebanon Office, 779 Cumberland St., Lebanon, 17042. Tel: 717-273-8514; Fax: 717-273-7518. Heather Teter, M.S.W., L.S.W., Prog. Dir.; Kirk Reider, A.C.S.W, L.I.S.W., L.C.S.W., A.C.S.W.

Lebanon Family FOCUS, 1431 Walnut St., Lebanon, 17042. Tel: 717-273-3011; Fax: 717-273-8518. Aimee Myers, M.A., N.C.C., L.P.C., Prog. Dir.

Northern Office, 815 W. Chestnut St., Coal Township, 17872. Tel: 570-648-6431; Fax: 570-648-9610. Loretta Stefanovage, M.S.W., L.S.W., Dir.

York Office, 253 E. Market St., York, 17403. Tel: 717-845-2696; Fax: 717-843-3941. Donna Dillon, M.S., Dir.

York/Adams Family Based Services, 253 E. Market St., York, 17403. Tel: 717-512-3228; Fax: 717-843-3941. Heather Teter, M.S.W., L.S.W. Prog. Dir.

York Intensive Family Services, 253 E. Market St., York, 17403. Tel: 717-843-7986; Fax: 717-699-0020. Connie Dodson, M.H.S., Prog. Dir.

HOPE House, 1509 Cresent Ave., Lancaster, 17601. Tel: 717-293-9089; Fax: 717-293-1425. Sr. Marie Aimee Finnegan, R.S.M., Prog. Dir. Total Staff 300; Total Assisted 9,700.

[F] GENERAL HOSPITALS

CAMP HILL. *Holy Spirit Hospital and Behavioral Health Center*, Formerly Holy Spirit Hospital and Community Mental Health Center, 503 N. 21st St., 17011-2288. Tel: 717-763-2100 Fax: 717-763-2183 Email: jfegan@hsh.org. Web: www.hsh.org. Sr. Romaine Niemeyer, S.C.C., Pres.

Legal Title: *Sisters of Christian Charity Health Care Corporation.*

Legal Title: *Comfort Care of Holy Spirit Hospital, Inc.*

Legal Title: *Holy Spirit Ventures, Inc.*

Legal Title: *Holy Spirit Corporation.*

Legal Title: *West Shore ALS, Inc.*

Legal Title: *Holy Spirit Hospital.*

Legal Title: *Spirit Physician Services, Inc.* Sisters of Christian Charity Inpatient admissions 15,241; Outpatient Visits 192,932; Bed Capacity 296; Bassinets 14; Sisters 27; Total Staff 2,140.

[G] CONVALESCENT & RETIREMENT HOMES

HARRISBURG. *Priests' Retirement Residence*, 675 Rutherford Rd., 17109. Tel: 717-657-3147; Fax: 717-657-3167. Email: mwood@hbgdiocese.org. Maria Wood, Contact Person.

Villa Teresa Nursing Home, 1051 Avila Rd., 17109. Tel: 717-652-5900; Fax: 717-652-5941. Email: villateresa@panetwork.com. Sr. Diane M. Mack, Admin.; Rev. Edward R. Lavelle Chap. Carmelite Sisters Sisters 6; Bed Capacity 184; Total Staff 275.

COLUMBIA. *St. Anne's Home*, 3952 Columbia Ave., 17512-9715. Tel: 717-285-5443; Fax: 717-285-5950. Email: johnc@saintanneshome.org. Sr. M. Carmela Guito, A.S.C., CEO; John A Clancy, Admin. Adorers of the Blood of Christ Sisters 19; Total Staff 214; Personal Care Staff 18; Residents 121; Cottages 36; Apartments 36; Residents in Retirement Village 45; Residents in Apartments 41; Personal Care 50.

DANVILLE. *Holy Family Convent and Infirmary*, One Montour St., 17821. Tel: 570-275-3141; Fax: 570-275-9511. Sr. Mary Mark Smith, S.C.C., Local Coord.; Rev. Thaddeus Strzelec, Chap. Tel: 717-275-0103. Home for the Aged Sisters of Christian Charity. Sisters of Christian Charity 75; Patients Assisted Annually 38; Total Staff 48.

Maria Hall, Maria Hall Dr., 17821. Tel: 570-275-1120; Fax: 570-275-1134. Email: sscmarhl@aol.com. Sr. Margaret Mary, SS.C.M., Admin.; Rev. Cyril J. Rable. Home for retired Sisters of SS. Cyril and Methodius. Sisters 32; Total Assisted 30; Total Staff 22.

Maria Joseph Manor, 875 Montour Blvd., 17821. Tel: 570-275-4221; Fax: 570-275-4711. Email: meadows@mail.ptdprolog.net. Sr. M. Marguerite, SS.C.M., Admin.; Rev. Thomas C. Marickovic. Nursing Home Beds 90; Personal Card Beds 95; Sisters 9.

The Meadows at Maria Joseph Manor, 875 Montour Blvd., 17821. Tel: 570-271-1000; Fax: 570-271-0848. Sr. Elizabeth Ann Matonak, SS.C.M., Dir. Independent Living Units 100; Total Staff 5; Residents 135.

YORK. *Misericordia Convalescent Home*, 998 S. Russell St., 17402. Tel: 717-755-1964; Fax: 717-840-0010. Email: misericordia@blazenet.net. Sr. Carmel Marie, D.M., Admin. Daughters of Our Lady of Mercy Sisters 7; Bed Capacity 53; Total Assisted 76; Total Staff 76.

[H] MONASTERIES AND RESIDENCES OF PRIESTS AND BROTHERS

EPHRATA. *St. Clement's Mission House*, 300 W. Pine St., 17522-0209. Tel: 717-733-6596; Fax: 717-733-0502. Email: omph@ptd.net. Very Rev. Raymond Collins, C.SS.R.; Revs. John J. Creaven, C.SS.R.; James O'Blaney, C.SS.R.; William Geiger, C.SS.R.; James Small, C.SS.R.; Brendan Greany, C.SS.R. Redemptorist Fathers and Brothers Total in Residence 8.

Mission Preaching Band: Revs. Paul Bryan, C.SS.R.; John W. Kelly, C.SS.R.

[I] CONVENTS AND RESIDENCES FOR SISTERS

HARRISBURG. *Bishops' Residence*, 4800-A Union Deposit Rd., 17105. Tel: 717-671-9323. Sisters of Christian Charity 2.

Immaculate Heart of Mary Convent, 603 N. Second St., 17101. Tel: 717-236-4821. Email: ihm603@aol.com. Sr. Catherine McElroy, I.H.M., Supr. Sisters, Servants of the Immaculate Heart of Mary 11.

St. Joseph Convent, 605 N. Second St., 17101. Tel: 717-232-0204. Email: mashurer@paonline.com. Sr. Jude Biank, S.C.C., Supr. Sisters of Christian Charity Sisters of St. Francis (Aston, PA) 1; Total in Residence 7; Total Staff 7.

Saint Margaret Mary Convent, 2836 Herr St., 17103. Tel: 717-230-9411. Email: Juno.com. Adorers of the Blood of Christ Total in Residence 3.

COLUMBIA. *Adorers of the Blood of Christ, Columbia Center*, 3950 Columbia Ave., 17512-9714. Tel: 717-285-4536; Fax: 717-285-9789. Web: www.adorers.org. Sr. Joan Hornick, Dir. Comm. Life & Mission. Columbia Center of the Adorers of the Blood of Christ

The Precious Blood Spiritual Center, 3950 Columbia Ave., 17512-9714. Tel: 717-285-2215; Fax: 717-285-4415. Email: pbsc@redrose.net. S. Constance Sophy, R.S.M., Dir. US Province 466; Columbia Sisters 75.

DANVILLE. *Villa Sacred Heart* 17821-1698. Tel: 570-275-3581; 570-275-4929; Fax: 570-275-5997. Email: smtmsscm@hotmail.com. Web: www.sscm.org. Sr. Pamela Smith, SS.C.M., Gen. Supr. Motherhouse of the Sisters of SS. Cyril and Methodius. Sisters 136.

Villa Sacred Heart Formation Center Tel: 570-275-3702; Fax: 570-275-5997.

Vocation Office/SCA Spiritual Center Tel: 570-275-1093; Fax: 570-275-5997. Sr. Deborah Marie, SS.C.M., Vocation Dir.

Villa Sacred Heart Music Conservatory, 17821-1698. Tel: 570-275-5185; Fax: 570-275-5997.

St. Cyril Academy Preschool and Kindergarten, 17821-1698. Tel: 570-275-1667; Fax: 570-275-8303. Sr. Donna Marie, SS.C.M., Prin.

ELYSBURG. *Carmelite Monastery*, 70 Monastery Rd., 17824-9697. Tel: 570-672-2935; Fax: 570-672-0278. Email: elysburgcarmel@juno.com. Sisters Patricia Boyd, O.C.D., Vocation Dir.; Angela Pikus, O.C.D., Prioress. Discalced Carmelite Nuns Nuns in Solemn Vows 14.

LANCASTER. *Dominican Nuns of the Perpetual Rosary, Incorporated*, 1834 Lititz Pike, 17601-6585. Tel: 717-569-2104; Fax: 717-569-1598. Email: monlanc@aol.com. Sr. Marie Clare, O.P., Prioress; Rev. Edward M. Gaffney, O.P., Chap. Solemnly Professed Nuns 11.

[J] NEWMAN CENTERS

HARRISBURG. *Catholic Campus Ministry* P.O. Box 3557, 17105-3557. Tel: 717-657-4804; Fax: 717-657-4041. Email: frforrey@hbgdiocese.org. Web: www.hbgdiocese.org. Very Rev. William C. Forrey Jr., M.A., M.Div.

Lebanon Valley College, 125 S. Spruce St., Annville, 17003. Tel: 717-867-1525. Rev. John D. Peck, O.S.B.

Bloomsburg University of Pennsylvania, 353 College Hill, Bloomsburg, 17815. Tel: 570-784-3123; Fax: 570-784-3123. Rev. Alfred P. Sceski; Christina Mento.

Dickinson School of Law, 140 E. Pomfret St., Carlisle, 17013. Tel: 717-243-4411; Fax: 717-258-9281. Rev. David M. Hereshko.

Wilson College Chambersburg, Corpus Christi, 320 Philadelphia Ave., Chambersburg, 17201. Tel: 717-264-6317. Rev. James O'Brien.

Elizabethtown College, 1840 Marshall Dr., Elizabethtown, 17022. Tel: 717-367-1255. Rev. David L. Danneker, Ph.D.

Gettysburg College, 12 E. Hanover St., Gettysburg, 17325-0136. Tel: 717-334-2510. Rev. Philip DeChico; Susan Collinge.

Hershey Medical Center, St. Joan of Arc, 359 W. Areba Ave., 17033. Tel: 717-533-7168. Rev. Philip Burger.

Messiah College, One College Ave., Grantham, 17027. Tel: 717-766-2511. Cathy Poiesz; Anita Voelker; Christopher Couch.

Franklin and Marshall College, Lancaster, 227 N. George St., Millersville, 17551. Tel: 717-872-3350. Rev. Raymond J. LaVoie; Very Rev. Daniel F.X. Powell; Melanie Mascarenas.

Bucknell University, Newman Center, 610 St. George St., Lewisburg, 17837. Tel: 570-577-3766; Fax: 570-577-2760. Rev. Martin O. Moran III.

Penn State University, Harrisburg Campus, Seven Sorrows BVM, 401 Conewago St., Middletown, 17057. Tel: 717-944-3133. Rev. Louis P. Ogden.

Millersville University, Newman Center, 227 N. George St., Millersville, 17551. Tel: 717-872-3350. Very Rev. Daniel F.X. Powell; Rev. Raymond J. LaVoie.

Susquehanna University Catholic Campus Ministry, 610 University Ave., Selinsgrove, 17870. Tel: 570-374-4113. Rev. Edward J. Keating Jr.

Shippensburg University, 305 N. Prince St., Shippensburg, 17257. Tel: 717-477-1244. Rev. Robert A. Yohe Jr., V.F.; Roxanne Dennis.

Penn State University, Mont Alto Campus, South Mountain, 1 Campus Dr., Mont Alto, 17237. Tel: 717-749-6021. Roxanne Dennis.

Penn State University, York Campus, 931 S. Pershing Ave., York, 17403. Tel: 717-873-5163. Rev. Carl T. Tancredi.

York College, 931 S. Pershing Ave., York, 17403. Tel: 717-846-7591. Rev. Carl T. Tancredi.

[K] MISCELLANEOUS LISTINGS

HARRISBURG. *The Neumann Scholarship Foundation*, 4800 Union Deposit Rd., P.O. Box 3553, 17105. Tel: 717-657-4804; Fax: 717-657-3790. Very Rev. Edward J. Quinlan III, M.Div., M.A., M.S., Sec. for Educ.

Pennsylvania Catholic Conference, 223 North St., P.O. Box 2835, 17105. Tel: 717-238-9613; Fax: 717-238-1473. Email: staff@pacatholic.org. Web: www.pacatholic.org.

Pennsylvania Catholic Conference Scholarship Foundation, 223 North St., P.O. Box 2835, 17105. Tel: 717-238-9613; Fax: 717-238-1473. Email: rjoh@pacatholic.org. Web: www@pacatholic.org. Dr. Robert J. O'Hara Jr., Exec. Dir.

Pennsylvania Catholic Health Association, 223 North St., P.O. Box 2835, 17105. Tel: 717-238-9613; Fax: 717-238-1473. Email: PCHA@pacatholic.org. Web: www.pacatholic.org/pcha. Sr. Clare Christi Schiefer, O.S.F., Pres.

ELYSBURG. *Carmelite Monastery of Wheeling Corp.*, c/o Carmelite Monastery, 70 Monastery Rd., 17824-9697. Tel: 570-672-2935; Fax: 570-672-0278. Email: elysburgcarmel@juno.com. Sr. Angela Pikus, O.C.D., Pres.

LANCASTER. *Bachmann Realty Corporation*, 830 Marietta Ave., 17603. Tel: 610-378-2729; Fax: 610-208-8875.

Saint Joseph Health Ministries & Saint Joseph Health Ministries Foundation, 832 Marietta Ave., 17603. Tel: 717-397-7625; Fax: 717-397-6057. Email: sjhm@catholichealth.net. Web: www.sjhm.org. Jennifer L. Thompson, Exec. Dir.

PHILADELPHIA. *St. Joseph Village Corporation*, Mount Saint Joseph Convent, 9701 Germantown Ave., 19118-2694. Tel: 215-248-7200; Fax: 215-248-7277. Email: msjc@ssjphila.org. Web: www.ssjphila.org. Sisters of St. Joseph., Residence for Senior Citizens

Village location, 90 Main St., McSherrystown, 17344. Tel: 717-637-2227; Fax: 717-637-2441. Sr. Joanne Fehrenbach, S.S.J., Gen. Sec. Total Staff 3; Total in Residence 40.

RELIGIOUS INSTITUTES OF MEN REPRESENTED IN THE DIOCESE

For further details refer to the corresponding bracketed number in the Religious Institutes of Men or Women section.

[0200]—*Benedictine Monks*—O.S.B.
[0470]—*The Capuchin Friars*—O.F.M.Cap.
[0480]—*Conventual Franciscans* (Buffalo, NY)—O.F.M.Conv
[0650]—*Holy Ghost Fathers* (Eastern Prov.)—C.S.Sp.
[0690]—*Jesuit Fathers and Brothers*—S.J.
[1120]—*Missionaries of the Sacred Hearts of Jesus and Mary*—M.SS.CC.
[0920]—*Oblates of St. Francis De Sales* (American Prov.)—O.S.F.S.
[0430]—*Order of Preachers (Dominicans)*—O.P.
[1070]—*Redemptorist Fathers* (Baltimore Prov.)—C.SS.R.
[1060]—*Society of the Precious Blood* (Cincinnati Prov.)—C.PP.S.
[0700]—*St. Joseph's Society of the Sacred Heart*—S.S.J.
[0560]—*Third Order Regular of Saint Francis* (Prov. of the Most Sacred Heart)—T.O.R.

RELIGIOUS INSTITUTES OF WOMEN REPRESENTED IN THE DIOCESE

[0100]—*Adorers of the Blood of Christ*—A.S.C.
[1810]—*Bernardine Sisters of the Third Order of St. Francis*—O.S.F.
[1920]—*Congregation of the Sisters of Holy Cross*—C.S.C.
[0890]—*Daughters of Our Lady of Mercy*—D.M.
[0420]—*Discalced Carmelite Nuns*—O.C.D.
[1050]—*Dominican Contemplative Nuns*—O.P.
[1170]—*Felician Sisters*—C.S.S.F.
[1470]—*Franciscan Sisters of St. Joseph*—F.S.S.J.
[2575]—*Institute of the Sisters of Mercy of the Americas*—R.S.M.
[0660]—*Sisters of Christian Charity*—S.C.C.
[3780]—*Sisters of Saints Cyril and Methodius*—SS.C.M.
[1650]—*The Sisters of St. Francis of Philadelphia*—O.S.F.
[3830-13]—*Sisters of St. Joseph*—C.S.J.
[2170]—*Sisters, Servants of the Immaculate Heart of Mary*—I.H.M.

NECROLOGY

✠ Dattilo, Most Rev. Nicholas C., Bishop of Harrisburg—Died March 5, 2004
† McGuire, Rev. Msgr. Hubert (Retired)—Died May 16, 2003
† Homola, Michael E. (Retired)—Died Jan. 18, 2003
† Lahout, Francis (Retired)—Died Aug. 11, 2003

Archdiocese of Hartford

(Archidioecesis Hartfortiensis)

Most Reverend

HENRY J. MANSELL

Archbishop of Hartford; ordained December 19, 1962; appointed Titular Bishop of Marazane and Auxiliary of New York November 24, 1992; installed January 6, 1993; appointed Bishop of Buffalo April 18, 1995; installed June 12, 1995; appointed Archbishop of Hartford October 20, 2003; installed December 18, 2003. *Res.: 1109 Prospect Ave., West Hartford, CT 06105.*

Chancery Office: 134 Farmington Ave., Hartford, CT 06105-3784 Tel: 860-541-6491; Fax: 860-541-6309.

Web: www.archdiocese-hartford.org

Email: chancllr@mindspring.com

Most Reverend

DANIEL A. CRONIN, D.D., S.T.D.

Archbishop Emeritus of Hartford; ordained December 20, 1952; appointed Titular Bishop of Egnatia and Auxiliary of Boston June 10, 1968; ordained Bishop September 12, 1968; Transferred to Fall River October 30, 1970; installed December 16, 1970; Transfered to Hartford December 10, 1991; installed January 28, 1992; retired October 20, 2003. *Office: 469 Bloomfield Ave., Bloomfield, CT 06002.*

Most Reverend

PETER A. ROSAZZA, D.D., V.G.

Auxiliary Bishop of Hartford; ordained June 29, 1961; appointed Auxiliary Bishop of Hartford and Titular Bishop of Oppido Nuovo February 28, 1978; ordained Bishop June 24, 1978. *Office & Res.: 1450 Chapel St., New Haven, CT 06511.* Tel: 203-789-5970.

Most Reverend

CHRISTIE A. MACALUSO, D.D., V.G.

Auxiliary Bishop of Hartford; ordained May 22, 1971; appointed Auxiliary Bishop of Hartford and Titular Bishop of Grassy Valley March 18, 1997; ordained Bishop June 10, 1997. *Office: 134 Farmington Ave., Hartford, CT 06105-3784.* Tel: 860-541-6491; Fax: 860-541-6293.

Square Miles 2,288.

Established November 28, 1843; created Archdiocese August 6, 1953.

Corporate Title: "The Hartford Roman Catholic Diocesan Corporation."

Comprises the Counties of Hartford, Litchfield and New Haven in the State of Connecticut.

For legal titles of parishes and archdiocesan institutions, consult the Chancery Office.

STATISTICAL OVERVIEW

Personnel	
Archbishops	1
Retired Archbishops	1
Auxiliary Bishops	2
Priests: Diocesan Active in Diocese	239
Priests: Diocesan Active Outside Diocese	15
Priests: Retired, Sick or Absent	100
Number of Diocesan Priests	354
Religious Priests in Diocese	121
Total Priests in Diocese	475
Extern Priests in Diocese	30
Ordinations:	
Diocesan Priests	3
Transitional Deacons	1
Permanent Deacons in Diocese	300
Total Brothers	52
Total Sisters	833
Parishes	
Parishes	216
With Resident Pastor:	
Resident Diocesan Priests	176
Resident Religious Priests	20
Without Resident Pastor:	
Administered by Priests	20
Missions	1
Closed Parishes	1
Professional Ministry Personnel:	
Brothers	4
Sisters	31
Lay Ministers	122
Welfare	
Catholic Hospitals	3
Total Assisted	843,693
Health Care Centers	1
Total Assisted	60
Homes for the Aged	2
Total Assisted	350
Residential Care of Children	1
Total Assisted	95
Day Care Centers	9
Total Assisted	393
Specialized Homes	1
Total Assisted	50
Special Centers for Social Services	28
Total Assisted	19,138
Residential Care of Disabled	9
Total Assisted	33
Educational	
Seminaries, Diocesan	1
Diocesan Students in Other Seminaries	9
Seminaries, Religious	1
Students Religious	112
Total Seminarians	121
Colleges and Universities	2
Total Students	3,922
High Schools, Diocesan and Parish	4
Total Students	2,063
High Schools, Private	5
Total Students	2,840
Elementary Schools, Diocesan and Parish	66
Total Students	1,584
Elementary Schools, Private	3
Total Students	342
Catechesis/Religious Education:	
High School Students	14,363
Elementary Students	55,436
Total Students under Catholic Instruction	94,928
Teachers in the Diocese:	
Priests	15
Brothers	19
Sisters	67
Lay Teachers	1,371
Vital Statistics	
Receptions into the Church:	
Infant Baptism Totals	8,975
Adult Baptism Totals	210
Received into Full Communion	739
First Communions	9,793
Confirmations	8,072
Marriages:	
Catholic	1,824
Interfaith	390
Total Marriages	2,214
Deaths	10,724
Total Catholic Population	694,220
Total Population	1,873,986

Former Bishops—Rt. Revs. WILLIAM TYLER, D.D., first Bishop; consecrated March 17, 1844; died June 18, 1849; BERNARD O'REILLY, D.D., second Bishop; consecrated Nov. 10, 1850;; perished at sea, Jan., 1856.; FRANCIS P. MCFARLAND, D.D., third Bishop; consecrated March 14, 1858; died Oct. 12, 1874; THOMAS GALBERRY, D.D., fourth Bishop; consecrated March 19, 1876; died Oct. 10, 1878; LAWRENCE S. MCMAHON, D.D., fifth Bishop; consecrated Aug. 10, 1879; died Aug. 21, 1893; MICHAEL TIERNEY, D.D., sixth Bishop; consecrated Feb. 22, 1894; died Oct. 5, 1908; Most Revs. JOHN J. NILAN, D.D., seventh Bishop; consecrated April 28, 1910; died April 13, 1934; MAURICE F. MCAULIFFE, D.D., eighth Bishop; ord. July 29, 1900; appt. Auxiliary to the Bishop of Hartford, Dec. 17, 1925; consecrated April 28, 1926; appt. Bishop of Hartford, April 25, 1934; installed May 29, 1934; died Dec. 15, 1944; HENRY J. O'BRIEN, D.D., ninth Bishop, first Archbishop; ord. July 8, 1923; appt. Titular Bishop of Sita and Auxiliary to Bishop of Hartford, March 19, 1940; consecrated May 14, 1940; appt. Bishop of Hartford, April 7, 1945; appt. Archbishop of Hartford, Aug. 6, 1953; appt. at Pontifical Throne, April 29, 1955; resigned and appt. Titular Archbishop of Utina, Nov. 20, 1968;; Given title "Former Archbishop of Hartford", Nov. 14, 1970;; died July 23, 1976; JOHN F. WHEALON, D.D., S.T.L., S.S.L., tenth Bishop second Archbishop; ord. May 26, 1945; appt. Titular Bishop of Andrapa and Auxiliary of Cleveland, June 2, 1961; consecrated July 6, 1961; appt. Bishop of Erie, Nov. 30, 1966; installed March 7, 1967; appt. Archbishop of Hartford, Dec. 28, 1968; installed March 19, 1969; died Aug. 2, 1991.

Vicars General—Most Revs. PETER A. ROSAZZA, D.D., V.G.; CHRISTIE A. MACALUSO, D.D., V.G.

Episcopal Vicars—Most Rev. PETER A. ROSAZZA, D.D., V.G., Vicar for Hispanics; Rev. Msgrs. JOHN P. CONTE New Haven Vicariate; JAMES G. COLEMAN, Waterbury Vicariate.

Chancery Office—134 Farmington Ave., Hartford, 06105-3784. Tel: 860-541-6491; Fax: 860-541-6293 (Bishop's Office); 860-541-6309 (Chancery). All applications for dispensations and correspondence on diocesan business should be sent to this address. Office Hours: Mon.-Fri. 8:30-4:30.

Moderator of the Curia—Most Rev. CHRISTIE A. MACALUSO, D.D., V.G.

Chancellor—Rev. Msgr. THOMAS M. GINTY.

Ministry for Healing and Assistance—Sr. MARY KELLY, C.S.J., Dir., 134 Farmington Ave., Hartford, 06105-3784. Tel: 860-541-6491; Fax: 860-541-6293.

Archdiocesan Liturgical Consultant—Sr. MARY KATHLEEN RONAN, R.S.M. Fax: 860-541-6521.

Archivist—F. MARIA MEDINA, M.L.S.

Fiscal Office—Most Rev. CHRISTIE A. MACALUSO, D.D., V.G., Finance Officer; MICHAEL R. ST. DENIS, C.P.A., Fiscal Coord., Internal Affairs; THERESA MROCZKOWSKI, Accounts Mgr.; CATHERINE COOK, Accounts Payable; MARY-ALICE SULLIVAN, Accounts Receivable; LESLI-ANN ANDERSON, Group Benefits; MATTHEW A. BYRNE, C.P.A., Fiscal Coord., External Affairs; BRENDA ROCK, Asst. to Fiscal Coord., External Affairs.

Secretary to the Archbishop—Rev. Msgr. THOMAS M. GINTY.

Metropolitan Tribunal—134 Farmington Ave., *Hartford, 06105-3784*. Tel: 860-541-6491.
Judicial Vicar (Officialis)—Rev. ROBERT B. VARGO, J.C.L.
Adjutant Judicial Vicar—Rev. JAMES F. KINNANE.
Defender of the Bond—Rev. M. JUAN-DIEGO BRUNETTA, O.P., J.C.D.
Promoter of Justice—Rev. Msgr. JOHN J. MCCARTHY.
Judges—Rev. Msgrs. JOHN J. MCCARTHY; WILLIAM J. MULLEN (Retired); Revs. LAWRENCE G. WRENN (Retired); JAMES F. KINNANE; M. JUAN-DIEGO BRUNETTA, O.P., J.C.D.; PAUL LUNIW, J.C.L.; RICHARD L. WELCH, C.S.S.R., J.C.D.
Accessor—Sr. PATRICK MARIE DOHERTY, I.H.M.
Auditors (Part-time Case Instructors)—Revs. LAWRENCE R. BOCK; HENRY P. CODY; GENE E. GIANELLI; BERNARD KILLEEN; LEONARD KVEDAS; DANIEL J. MCLEAREN; TIMOTHY A. O'BRIEN; ADAM C. SUBOCZ; ROBERT F. TUCKER; Deacon PAUL B. LAUER.
Secretary and Notary—CAROL M. HATTEN.

College of Consultors—Most Revs. PETER A. ROSAZZA, D.D., V.G.; CHRISTIE A. MACALUSO, D.D., V.G.; Rev. Msgrs. JAMES G. COLEMAN; THOMAS M. GINTY; JOHN D. REGAN (Retired); Revs. JAMES B. GUNNOUD; JAMES H. SMITH.

Deans— Hartford Vicariate: Revs. JOHN S. GOLAS, Farmington Valley; THOMAS F. GAFFNEY, New Britain; JOSEPH T. DEVINE, Hartford; JOHN F. EDWARDS, Suburban Hartford; KEVIN P. CAVANAUGH, Manchester; ROBERT T. O'GRADY, Enfield, New Haven Vicariate:; ROBERT J. ST. MARTIN, Hamden-North Haven; LAWRENCE S. SYMOLON, East Shore Line; SHAWN T. DALY, Meriden; PETER S. DARGAN, West Shore Line; PHILIP J. SHARKEY, New Haven, Waterbury Vicariate:; ROBERT M. KWIATKOWSKI, Suburban Waterbury; LEONARD J. KVEDAS, Ansonia-Derby; JOSEPH F. GORMAN, Waterbury; ROBERT F. TUCKER, Litchfield; JOHN J. GEORGIA, Bristol; WILLIAM J. BRENZA, Naugatuck-Cheshire.

Ecumenical Affairs, Commission for—Rev. AIDAN N. DONAHUE, Ecumenical Officer, Sacred Heart Rectory, 26 Wintonbury Ave., Bloomfield, 06002-2488. Tel: 860-242-4142.

Evangelization Office—Rev. Msgr. MICHAEL J. MOTTA, Dir., 650 Willard Ave., Newington, 06111-2614. Tel: 860-667-0891; Fax: 860-667-2595.

Office of Stewardship—COLLEEN BOCCACCIO-CORRIVEAU, Dir., 467 Bloomfield Ave., Bloomfield, 06002-2999. Email: stewardshiphtfd@aol.com.

Holy Childhood Association—Rev. BRIAN W. MONNERAT, Dir., 467 Bloomfield Ave., Bloomfield, 06002-2999. Tel: 860-243-9184; Fax: 860-243-9460.

Office for Divine Worship—Rev. Msgr. THOMAS M. GINTY, Dir.; LUCY ZOCCO, Asst. to the Dir., 467 Bloomfield Ave., Bloomfield, 06002-2999. Tel: 860-242-4020; Fax: 860-286-0513.

Newspaper—Rev. Msgr. DAVID Q. LIPTAK, Exec. Editor, 467 Bloomfield Ave., Bloomfield, 06002-2999. Tel: 860-286-2828; 800-726-2391; Fax: 860-726-0000; Most Rev. HENRY J. MANSELL, D.D., Pres. & Publisher; ROBERTA TUTTLE, Assoc. Editor; CAROLE CRONSELL, Business Mgr. & Advertising; SUSAN MELLOON, Graphic Design & Layout Mgr.; JOYCE H. BOUDREAU, Circulation Supvr. "The Catholic Transcript"

Office for AIDS Ministries—Sr. DOROTHY STRELCHUN, S.N.D.deN., Catholic Charities, 467 Bloomfield Ave., Bloomfield, 06002-2999. Tel: 860-242-9577.

Office for Black Catholics—Mr. MYLES N. HUBBARD, Dir. St. Thomas Seminary, 467 Bloomfield Ave., Bloomfield, 06002-2999. Tel: 860-243-0648; Fax: 860-243-0648.

Office of Continuing Formation of Priests—Rev. AIDAN N. DONAHUE, Dir., 134 Farmington Ave., Hartford, 06105-3784. Tel: 860-541-6491.

Office of Radio and Television—Rev. JOHN P. GATZAK, Exec. Dir., 15 Peach Orchard Rd., Prospect, 06712-1052. Tel: 203-758-7367; Fax: 203-758-7371.

Office of Family Life, Marriage and Family Apostolate—Co-Directors: DONALD PAGLIA; CHRISTINE PAGLIA, 412 Ridge Rd., Hamden, 06517-2941. Tel: 203-230-2460; Fax: 203-230-2472.

Archbishop's Annual Appeal—Rev. Msgr. DOUGLAS P. CLANCY, Exec. Dir., 134 Farmington Ave., Hartford, 06105-3784. Tel: 800-781-2550; Fax: 203-294-1596.

Office of Religious Education (CCD)—Rev. Msgr. MICHAEL J. MOTTA, Dir., 650 Willard Ave., Newington, 06111-2614. Tel: 860-667-0891; Fax: 860-667-2595.

Commission for Priests' Retreats—Revs. FREDERICK M. ANIELLO, Chm.; ALEXIS PAUL, C.P.; Rev. Msgr. GERARD G. SCHMITZ; Rev. DANIEL JEREMIAH SULLIVAN.

Office of Ministry for Priests—Rev. ROBERT F. TUCKER, Min. for Priests, St. Thomas Seminary, 467 Bloomfield Ave., Bloomfield, 06002-2999. Tel: 860-286-8644; Fax: 860-286-7651.

Mission Cooperative Planning Office—Rev. BRIAN W. MONNERAT, Dir., 467 Bloomfield Ave., Bloomfield, 06002-2999. Tel: 860-243-9184; Fax: 860-243-9460.
Priests Retirement Plan for Secular Priests of the Archdiocese of Hartford— The Secular Priests of the Archdiocese of Hartford Retirement Trust. Rev. Msgr. JOSEPH A. DEVINE, Chm., 134 Farmington Ave., Hartford, 06105-3784. Tel: 860-541-6491.

Pro-Life Activities—Rev. JAMES J. CRONIN, Dir., 70 Gulf St., P.O. Box 230, Milford, 06460-0230. Tel: 203-878-3571; Sr. SUZANNE GROSS, F.S.E., Program Coord., P.O. Box 417, Meriden, 06450. Tel: 203-238-1441.

Propagation of the Faith, Society for— (The Catholic Mission Aid Society of Hartford)-- Rev. BRIAN W. MONNERAT, Dir., 467 Bloomfield Ave., Bloomfield, 06002-2999. Tel: 860-243-9184; Fax: 860-243-9460.

Radio Apostolate— Radio Station WJMJ-- JOHN L. ELLINGER, Station Mgr., 467 Bloomfield Ave., Bloomfield, 06002-2999. Tel: 860-242-8800 Licensed by St. Thomas Seminary, Bloomfield. (Hartford).

Office of Catholic Schools—Rev. ZIGFORD J. KRISS, Supt.; Dr. JOSEPH A. BOUND, Asst. Supt. Spec. Svcs. & Secondary Schools; Sr. LORETTA FRANCIS MANN, O.S.F., Asst. Supt. Elementary Educ.; JEANNINE V. DASH, Dir. Devel., 467 Bloomfield Ave., Bloomfield, 06002-2999. Tel: 860-242-4362; Fax: 860-242-8683.

Diocesan Labor Institute—Rev. DANIEL E. JOHNSON, Dir. (Retired), 115 Pond Hill Rd., Wallingford, 06492-4836. Tel: 203-265-1694.

Social Service—ROSE ALMA SENATORE, Dir., 467 Bloomfield Ave., Bloomfield, 06002-2999. Tel: 860-242-9577; Fax: 860-286-2800.

Office for Catholic Relief Services—ROSE ALMA SENATORE, Coord., 467 Bloomfield Ave., Bloomfield, 06002-2999. Tel: 860-242-9577; Fax: 860-286-2800.

Vocations—Rev. ALPHONSO R. FONTANA, Dir., St. Thomas Seminary, 467 Bloomfield Ave., Bloomfield, 06002-2999. Tel: 860-286-7670; Fax: 860-242-9701.

Office of the Permanent Diaconate—Deacon RICHARD L. SANTELLO, Dir., 467 Bloomfield Ave., Bloomfield, 06002-2999. Tel: 860-243-8005; Fax: 860-243-5287.

Office for Religious—Rev. JAMES F. KINNANE, Vicar; Sr. MARY KELLY, C.S.J., Dir., 134 Farmington Ave., Hartford, 06105-3784. Tel: 860-541-6491; Fax: 860-541-6309.

Office of Vicar For Priests—Rev. Msgr. GERARD G. SCHMITZ, 467 Bloomfield Ave., Bloomfield, 06002-2999. Tel: 860-242-2510; Fax: 860-242-3785.

Censor Librorum—Rev. Msgr. DAVID Q. LIPTAK.

Archdiocesan Offices and Directors

Archdiocesan Dispute Resolution Office—Most Rev. CHRISTIE A. MACALUSO, D.D., V.G., Moderator of the Curia, 134 Farmington Ave., Hartford, 06105-3784. Tel: 860-541-6491.

Archdiocesan Office of Urban Affairs—P. JOSEPH SMYTH, Exec. Dir., 81 Saltonstall Ave., New Haven, 06513-4356. Tel: 203-777-7279; Fax: 203-776-3233.

Office for Hispanic Evangelization—Most Rev. PETER A. ROSAZZA, D.D., V.G., Vicar; LUZ YANEZ, Office Mgr., 467 Bloomfield Ave., Bloomfield, 06002-2999. Tel: 860-243-0940; Fax: 860-286-2797.

Cana Conferences—DONALD PAGLIA; CHRISTINE PAGLIA, 412 Ridge Rd., Hamden, 06517-2941. Tel: 203-230-2460; Fax: 203-230-2472.

Catholic Cemeteries Association—Rev. Msgr. DAVID M. WALKER, Dir.; ROBERT S. MAREK, Exec. Dir., 700 Middletown Ave., P.O. Box 517, North Haven, 06473-0517. Tel: 203-239-2557; Fax: 203-239-5035.

Catholic Deaf Apostolate—Rev. Msgr. ROBERT D. BERGIN, Dir.; Sr. MAURA JOSEPH, R.S.M., Coord., 243 Steele Rd., West Hartford, 06117-2797. Tel: 860-523-7530 (TDD or Voice); 860-236-3503.

Catholic Library and Information Center—Rev. EDWARD J. MCLEAN, Dir., 125 Market St., Hartford, 06103-1397. Tel: 860-522-0602; 860-246-5628; 800-308-3300; Fax: 860-247-3490.

Connecticut Catholic Conference—Dr. MARIE HILLIARD, Exec. Dir., 134 Farmington Ave., Hartford, 06105-3784. Tel: 860-524-7882; Fax: 860-525-0750.

Office for People with Disabilities—Co-Directors: GEORGE DUCHARME, Ph.D.; MARY N. MCGRATH, 467 Bloomfield Ave., Bloomfield, 06002-2999. Tel: 860-242-3304.

Small Christian Communities—Bro. ROBERT K. MORIARTY, S.M., Coord., 467 Bloomfield Ave., Bloomfield, 06002-2999. Tel: 860-243-9642; Fax: 860-286-0289.

Cursillo Movement, Archdiocesan Director of—Rev. JOHN M. COONEY, Dir., St. John the Evangelist, 21 Academy Hill, Watertown, 06795-2101. Tel: 860-274-8836.

CLERGY, PARISHES, MISSIONS AND PAROCHIAL SCHOOLS

CITY OF HARTFORD
(HARTFORD COUNTY)

1—CATHEDRAL OF ST. JOSEPH (1872), Rev. Msgr. Robert D. Bergin; Rev. John P. Melnick. In Res., Revs. John P. Gatzak; Lawrence G. Wrenn (Retired); David Q. Liptak.
Res.: 140 Farmington Ave., 06105-3708. Tel: 860-249-8431; Fax: 860-249-5910.
Catechesis / Religious Program—Students 35.

2—ST. ANNE (1889), (French), Closed., For inquiries for sacramental records contact St. Anne-Immaculate Conception, Hartford.

3—ST. ANNE-IMMACULATE CONCEPTION (2000), (French—Spanish), Rev. James T. Lowery, M.S.; Deacon Pedro L. Rivera.
Res.: 820 Park St., 06106-2388. Tel: 860-728-7445; Fax: 860-728-1973.
Catechesis / Religious Program—Tel: 860-525-1522. Students 105.

4—ST. AUGUSTINE (1902), Rev. Nicholas J. Cesaro; Deacons Valentin Perez; John F. Dempsey. In Res., Revs. Gustavo B. Sepulveda (Colombia); James O. Ibekwe (Nigeria); Deacon Adolfo G. Carrero.
Res.: 10 Campfield Ave., 06114-1832. Tel: 860-522-7128; Fax: 860-246-1753.
School—20 Clifford St., 06114-1798. Tel: 860-249-5661; Fax: 860-293-2981. Sr. Patricia Dora, C.S.J., Prin. Priests 3; Brothers 1; Sisters 2; Lay Teachers 11; Students 240.
Catechesis / Religious Program—Tel: 860-249-3430; Fax: 860-246-1753. Students 130.

5—SS. CYRIL AND METHODIUS (1902), (Polish), Revs. William P. Przybylo; Kazimierz Heisig (Poland).
Res.: 55 Charter Oak Ave., 06106-1902. Tel: 860-522-9157; Fax: 860-524-9433.
School—35 Groton St., 06106-2799. Tel: 860-522-8490; Fax: 860-493-7409. Sisters 5; Lay Teachers 11; Students 218.
Catechesis / Religious Program—Tel: 860-527-3775. Students 306.
Convent—Felician Sisters, 45 Groton St., 06106-2798. Tel: 860-527-3775.

6—HOLY TRINITY (1900), (Lithuanian), Rev. Charles E. Jacobs.
Res.: 53 Capitol Ave., 06106-1798. Tel: 860-246-4162; Fax: 860-246-4162.

7—IMMACULATE CONCEPTION (1899), Closed. For inquiries for parish records contact the chancery., For inquiries for sacramental records contact St. Anne-Immaculate Conception, Hartford.

8—ST. JUSTIN (1924), (African American—West Indian), Revs. David M. McDonald, Team Ministry; James Manship, Team Ministry; Guillermo Velez (Colombia), Team Ministry; Arlin Jean-Louis, O.M.I., Team Ministry; Deacons Isidro DeJesus; Thomas F. Breen III, (2).
Res.: 230 Blue Hills Ave., 06112-1836. Tel: 860-246-6897; Fax: 860-246-6898.
Catechesis / Religious Program—Tel: 860-524-5239. Students 95.

9—ST. LAWRENCE O'TOOLE (1885), Revs. Joseph T. Devine; Paul F. Kenefick; Deacon Domingo Delgado. In Res., Rev. Pedro Liss (Brazil).
Res.: 494 New Britain Ave., 06106-3797. Tel: 860-522-1129; Fax: 860-549-4261.
Catechesis / Religious Program—Students 72.

10—ST. LUKE (1930), Rev. Thomas G. Anglim (VEN); Deacon James E. Hickey Jr. In Res., Rev. Msgr. Charles W. Daly (Retired).
Res.: 66 Bolton St., 06114. Tel: 860-296-8681; Fax: 860-296-1983.
Catechesis / Religious Program—Tel: 860-296-2233. Students 55.

11—ST. MICHAEL (1900), (African American—Hispanic), Revs. David M. McDonald, Team Ministry; James Manship, Team Ministry; Guillermo Velez (Colombia), Team Ministry; Deacons Thomas F. Breen III, Team Ministry; Isidro DeJesus; Sr. Elizabeth Secord, R.S.M., Pastoral Assoc.
Res.: 98 Capen St., 06120-2010. Tel: 860-522-6184; Fax: 860-278-8410.
Catechesis / Religious Program—Tel: 860-522-6184; Fax: 860-278-8410. Students 70.

12—OUR LADY OF FATIMA (1958), (Portuguese), Revs. Jose D. Silva; Antonio Jorge Tchinqui (Angola).
Res.: Fatima Sq., 06106-2042. Tel: 860-236-1443; Fax: 860-232-4455.

Catechesis/Religious Program—Students 240.
13—Our Lady of Sorrows (1895), Revs. Joseph M. O'Neil, M.S., Co-Pastor & Admin.; Francis C. Cooney, M.S., Co-Pastor; Deacons Peter J. Klimanowski; Carmelo Hernandez.
Res.: 16 Greenwood St., 06106-2109. Tel: 860-233-4424; Fax: 860-236-0149.
Church: 79 New Park Ave., 06106-2109.
Catechesis/Religious Program—Students 55.
14—St. Patrick-St. Anthony (1829), Revs. James F. Hynes, O.F.M.; John Murphy, O.F.M.; Andrew Giardino, O.F.M.; Michael P. Jones, O.F.M.; Patricia Curtis, Pastoral Assoc.
Franciscan Center for Urban Ministry—285 Church St., 06103. Tel: 860-756-4034; Fax: 860-249-6487.
Catechesis/Religious Program—Students 221.
15—St. Peter (1859), (Irish), Rev. Michael S. Galasso. Mercedarian Missionary Sisters (Spanish)
Res.: 160 Main St., 06106-1894. Tel: 860-547-1187.
Catechesis/Religious Program—Tel: 860-525-2684. Students 350.
Convent—Sisters of Mercy, 11 Charter Oak Pl., 06106. Tel: 860-522-8428.
16—Sacred Heart (1872), (Spanish), Revs. David M. McDonald, Team Ministry; James C. Manship, Team Ministry; Guillermo Velez (Colombia), Team Ministry; Deacons Isidro DeJesus, Team Ministry; Edwin Ortiz, Team Ministry.
Res.: 49 Winthrop St., 06103-1030. Tel: 860-527-6459; Fax: 860-527-6450.
Catechesis/Religious Program—Students 115.

OUTSIDE THE CITY OF HARTFORD

Ansonia, New Haven Co.
1—St. Anthony's (1915), (Lithuanian), Rev. Patrick J. Berkery.
Res.: 199 N. Main St., 06401-1696. Tel: 203-734-4759; Fax: 203-734-2259.
Catechesis/Religious Program—Tel: 203-734-6723. Students 30.
2—Assumption (1870), Revs. George P. Burnett, Team Ministry; Robert F. Condron, Team Ministry; Deacons John F. Brady Jr., Team Ministry; Robert C. Johnson, Team Ministry; Joseph Dipiro, Team Ministry (Retired). In Res., Rev. Albert J. Zanavich (Retired).
Res.: 61 N. Cliff St., 06401-1698. Tel: 203-735-7857; Fax: 203-734-5521.
School—Tel: 203-734-0855; Fax: 203-734-5521. Mrs. Kathleen Molner, Prin. Lay Teachers 11; Students 201.
Catechesis/Religious Program—51 N. Cliff St., 06401-1698. Tel: 203-735-2701; Fax: 203-734-5521. Students 259.
3—Holy Rosary (1908), (Italian), Revs. Ronald L. Genua; Dominic Thomas, M.C.B.S. (India); Deacon Mario DiRienzo.
Res.: Fr. Salemi Dr., 06401-2396. Tel: 203-735-7875; Fax: 203-732-2212.
Catechesis/Religious Program—Tel: 203-736-0242; Fax: 203-732-2212. Verna Ingrassia, D.R.E. Students 288.
4—St. Joseph's (1925), (Polish), Revs. Marek W. Sobczak, C.M.; Joseph Szpilski, C.M. In Res., Rev. Henry Czekala, C.M.
Res.: 32 Jewett St., 06401-2499. Tel: 203-734-0402.
School—36 Jewett St., 06401. Tel: 203-734-3821; Fax: 203-734-4884. Mrs. Carmel Brown, Prin. Lay Teachers 10; Students 139.
Catechesis/Religious Program—Students 105.
Avon, Hartford Co., St. Ann's (1917), [CEM] Rev. Thomas J. Sas; Deacons Alan D. Campbell; John J. Mylott. In Res., Rev. Thomas E. McCarthy (Retired).
Res.: 289 Arch Rd., 06001-4209. Tel: 860-673-9858; Fax: 860-675-4350.
Catechesis/Religious Program—Tel: 860-673-2137; Fax: 860-675-4350. Janine Cote, D.R.E. Students 975.
Bantam, Litchfield Co., Our Lady of Grace (1970), [CEM] Rev. John H. McCann, S.M.M., Admin.
Res.: P.O. Box 427, Rte. 202, 06750. Tel: 860-567-9522; Fax: 860-567-9522.
Catechesis/Religious Program—Students 37.
Beacon Falls, New Haven Co., St. Michael's (1899), Rev. Leonard J. Kvedas; Deacon Victor M. Lembo. In Res., Rev. Richard C. Bollea.
Res.: 25 Maple Ave., 06403-1145. Tel: 203-729-2504.
Catechesis/Religious Program—Tel: 203-729-2504. Students 255.
Bethlehem, Litchfield Co., Church of the Nativity (1921), Rev. Richard L. Shellman; Deacon Daniel W. Polansky.
Res.: 48 East St., Box 192, 06751-0192. Tel: 203-266-5211.
Catechesis/Religious Program—Tel: 203-266-5212. Students 297.
Bloomfield, Hartford Co.
1—Christ the King (1936), Closed., For inquiries for sacramental records contact Sacred Heart, Bloomfield.
2—Sacred Heart (1878), Rev. Aidan N. Donahue; Deacon Barry T. Skipp.
Rectory—25 Foothills Way, 06002-2488. Tel: 860-242-1942; Fax: 860-286-0044.
Church: 26 Wintonbury Ave., 06002. Tel: 860-242-4142; Fax: 860-286-0044.
Catechesis/Religious Program—Students 90.
Branford, New Haven Co.
1—St. Elizabeth (1966), Rev. Robert G. Heffernan; Deacons Joseph F. Coyne; Wayne E. Sandford.
Res.: 65 Burban Dr., 06405. Tel: 203-488-1361; Fax: 203-483-9248.
Catechesis/Religious Program—Tel: 203-483-1997; Fax: 203-483-9248. Students 165.
2—St. Mary (1868), [CEM 2] Revs. Christopher M. Ford; Faron Calumba (Philippines); William O. Seery; Deacons Robert P. Tartaris; Norman H. Singer.
Res.: 731 Main St., 06405-3693. Tel: 203-488-1607; Fax: 203-483-9208.
School—(Grades PreK-8) Tel: 203-488-8386; Fax: 203-488-2347. Lay Teachers 16; Students 234.
Catechesis/Religious Program—Tel: 203-488-7412. Students 715.
3—St. Therese (1947), Rev. Raymond J. Barry; Deacon Gerald S. Walton.
Office—105 Leetes Island Rd., 06405. Tel: 203-488-2998; Fax: 203-488-8542.
Res.: 39 Acorn Rd., 06405. Tel: 203-483-9304.
Catechesis/Religious Program—Students 272.
Bristol, Hartford Co.
1—St. Ann (1908), (French), Rev. Robert J. Rousseau; Deacons Joseph E. Levesque; Albert Lozier.
Mailing Address: *Parish Center*, 180 Laurel St., 06010.
Res.: 215 West St., 06010-5754. Tel: 860-589-9080; Fax: 860-585-7139.
Catechesis/Religious Program—Tel: 860-582-3524. Carol Gignac, D.R.E. Students 234.
2—St. Anthony's (1920), (Italian), Rev. Nicholas P. Melo; Deacon Laurent J. Cote.
Res.: 111 School St., 06010-6078. Tel: 860-583-1349; Fax: 860-582-3861.
School—30 Pleasant St., 06010. Tel: 860-582-7874; Fax: 860-582-3861. Lay Teachers 16; Students 296.
Catechesis/Religious Program—20 Pleasant St., 06010. Tel: 860-583-4495; Fax: 860-582-3861. Students 234.
3—St. Gregory's (1957), Rev. John J. Georgia; Deacon Roger Albert. In Res., Rev. Carmine B. Raneri (Retired).
Res. & Mailing Address: St. Gregory Rectory, 235 Maltby St., 06010-3892. Tel: 860-589-2295; Fax: 860-589-6692.
Catechesis/Religious Program—1043 Stafford Ave., 06010. Tel: 860-589-4232; Fax: 860-584-4786. Barbara Sergio, D.R.E. Students 1,067.
4—St. Joseph (1864), [CEM] Revs. James F. Leary; Robert Villa; Deacon Robert M. Pallotti.
Res.: 149 Goodwin St., 06010-5115. Tel: 860-583-1369; Fax: 860-589-5374.
School—335 Center St., 06010. Tel: 860-582-8696; Fax: 860-584-9907. Mark J. Monnerat, Prin. Lay Teachers 18; Students 273.
Catechesis/Religious Program—Tel: 860-582-2888. Students 558.
5—St. Stanislaus (1919), (Polish), Revs. Raymond S. Smialowski; Ronald P. Zepecki; Deacons Roy C. Dungan; Leonard R. Lewandoski.
Res.: 510 West St., P.O. Box 1860, 06011-1860. Tel: 860-583-4242; Fax: 860-583-9464.
Catechesis/Religious Program—Tel: 860-584-5378. Students 250.
Broad Brook, Hartford Co., St. Catherine (1886), [CEM] Rev. Emilio P. Padelli; Deacons Vincent Motto; John Abdalla, (Retired).
Res.: 6 Windsorville Rd., P.O. Box 359, 06016-0359. Tel: 860-623-4636; Fax: 860-623-4636.
Catechesis/Religious Program—7 Rye St., 06016. Tel: 860-623-1974. Students 220.
Canaan, Litchfield Co., St. Joseph's (1920), [CEM] [JC] Rev. James Merlino, O.F.M.
Res.: 4 Main St., P.O. Box 845, 06018-2459. Tel: 860-824-7078; Fax: 860-824-4925.
Catechesis/Religious Program—Students 88.
Cheshire, New Haven Co.
1—St. Bridget's (1871), [CEM] Revs. James B. Gunnoud; Robert P. Ricciardi; Deacon Richard Wilber.
Res.: 175 Main St., 06410-2446. Tel: 203-272-3531; Fax: 203-271-3356.
Parish Center—Tel: 203-271-9994.
School—171 Main St., 06410. Tel: 203-272-5860; Fax: 203-271-7031. Mrs. Sharon Tarrant, Prin. Lay Teachers 31; Students 425.
Catechesis/Religious Program—Tel: 203-272-6504. Students 900.
2—Church of the Epiphany (1967), Rev. Norman L. Brockett.
Res.: 1777 Old Waterbury Rd., 06410-1399. Tel: 203-272-5211.
Church & Parish Center: 1750 Huckins Rd., 06410. Tel: 203-272-4355; Fax: 203-272-4878.
Catechesis/Religious Program—Tel: 203-272-4355, Ext. 2. Students 325.
3—St. Thomas Becket (1971), Rev. Eugene J. Charman.
Res.: 511 Sharon Dr., 06410-4244. Tel: 203-272-3324; Fax: 203-271-9210.
Catechesis/Religious Program—Tel: 203-272-5777. Students 409.
Collinsville, Hartford Co., St. Patrick's (1856), [CEM] [JC 2] Rev. Ronald P. May; Deacon Timothy E. Healey.
Res.: 7 Burlington Ave., P.O. Box 287, 06022-0287. Tel: 860-693-8727; Fax: 860-693-4538.
Catechesis/Religious Program—Tel: 860-693-1068; Fax: 860-693-4538. Marguerite Janille, D.R.E. Students 528.
Cornwall Bridge, Litchfield Co., St. Bridget (1883), [CEM] Rev. Francis R. Fador; Deacon Stephen M. Beecher.
Res.: 7 River Rd., P.O. Box 52, 06754-1903. Tel: 860-672-6515; Fax: 860-364-9893.
Catechesis/Religious Program—Students 48.
Derby, New Haven Co.
1—St. Jude (1961), Rev. William J. Killeen.
Res.: 71 Pleasant View Rd., 06418-2455. Tel: 203-735-8725; Fax: 203-735-4402.
Catechesis/Religious Program—Tel: 203-735-8725; Fax: 203-735-4402. Students 73.
2—St. Mary's (1851), Rev. Edward G. Pfnausch; Deacon Robert C. Johnson.
Res.: 212 Elizabeth St., 06418-1834. Tel: 203-735-3341; Fax: 203-736-6492.
School—St. Mary-St. Michael, (Grades K-8), St. Mary Campus, 14 Seymour Ave., 06418. Tel: 203-735-6471; Fax: 203-732-9009. Lay Teachers 12; Students 237.
St. Michael Campus—73 Derby Ave., 06418. Tel: 203-734-2017; Fax: 203-734-8166.
Catechesis/Religious Program—Students 220.
3—St. Michael (1905), (Polish), [CEM] Rev. Michael Wanat, C.M. In Res., Rev. John Kuczynski, C.M.
Res.: 75 Derby Ave., 06418-2098. Tel: 203-734-0005.
School—St. Mary-St. Michael, (Grades 4-8), St. Michael Campus, 73 Derby Ave., P.O. Box 397, 06418. Tel: 203-734-2017. Lay Teachers 5; Students 121.
Catechesis/Religious Program—Fax: 203-736-2044. Students 236.
East Berlin, Hartford Co., Sacred Heart (1896), Rev. Thomas C. Culotta.
Res.: 48 Cottage St., 06023. Tel: 860-828-0159; Fax: 860-828-5305.
Church: 66 Cottage St., 06023. Tel: 860-828-0154; Fax: 860-828-5305.
Catechesis/Religious Program—Students 149.
East Hartford, Hartford Co.
1—Blessed Sacrament (1948), Rev. James J. Nock.
Mailing Address: 36 Cambridge Dr., 06118. Tel: 860-568-2747; Fax: 860-568-4133.
Catechesis/Religious Program—Tel: 860-568-2001. Students 60.
2—St. Christopher (1965), Revs. James G. Fanelli; William E. McGrath, Pastor Emeritus (Retired); Deacon William J. Gilles.
Res.: 538 Brewer St., 06118-2399. Tel: 860-568-5240; Fax: 860-568-0673.
School—570 Brewer St., 06118. Tel: 860-568-4100; Fax: 860-568-1070. Sr. Valerie Noone, O.P., Prin. Lay Teachers 14; Students 283.
Catechesis/Religious Program—Tel: 860-568-0546 (Rel. Educ.); 860-895-8692 (Youth Min.); Fax: 860-568-0242. Students 314.
3—St. Isaac Jogues (1964), Rev. James H. Smith.
Res.: 1 Community St., 06108-2808. Tel: 860-528-6749; Fax: 860-282-2730.
Catechesis/Religious Program—Tel: 860-528-7976. Students 155.
4—St. Mary's (1873), Revs. Martin J. Scholsky; Frank E. Papa, S.O.L.T.; Augustine Owusu-Sekyere, (Min. to Ghanainan Catholic Community); Deacon William H. Bartlett.
Res.: 15 Maplewood Ave., 06108-4021. Tel: 860-289-7916; Fax: 860-289-3224.
Parish Center—30 Maplewood Ave., 06108. Tel: 860-289-7510.
Catechesis/Religious Program—Students 155.
5—Our Lady of Peace (1971), Rev. James J. Nock; Deacon Raymond A. Parenteau.
Res.: 370 May Rd., 06118-3496. Tel: 860-568-4414.
Catechesis/Religious Program—Students 225.
6—St. Rose's (1920), Rev. Thomas R. Mitchell. In Res., Rev. John P. Rohan.
Res.: 33 Church St., 06108-3794. Tel: 860-289-8616; Fax: 860-289-3966.
School—Tel: 860-528-4169; Fax: 860-528-4160. Lay Teachers 9; Students 167.
Catechesis/Religious Program—Students 210.
East Haven, New Haven Co.
1—St. Clare (1947), Rev. Robert G. Heffernan; Deacons Wayne E. Sandford; Joseph F. Coyne.
Res.: 234 Coe Ave., 06512-4112. Tel: 203-467-5136;

Fax: 203-469-0241.
Catechesis/Religious Program—Tel: 203-467-0600. Students 287.

2—OUR LADY OF POMPEII (1947), Revs. David J. Borino; James A. Shanley; Deacon Joseph W. LaPierre.
Res.: 355 Foxon Rd., 06513. Tel: 203-469-0764; Fax: 203-469-3645.
Catechesis/Religious Program—Fax: 203-469-0764. Students 526.

3—ST. VINCENT DE PAUL'S (1915), Revs. Gary F. Simeone; Robert J. Burbank, Pastor Emeritus; Dariusz Gosciniak; Deacon William Eyles.
Res.: 80 Taylor Ave., 06512. Tel: 203-467-6394; Fax: 203-467-6716.
School—35 Bishop St., 06512. Tel: 203-467-1606; 203-467-1607; Fax: 203-467-8851. Lay Teachers 10; Students 239.
Catechesis/Religious Program—Students 581.

EAST WINDSOR, HARTFORD CO., ST. PHILIP'S (1959), Rev. Adam C. Subocz.
Res.: 150 S. Main St., 06088-9760. Tel: 860-623-0408; Fax: 860-623-8937.
Catechesis/Religious Program—Students 79.

ENFIELD, HARTFORD CO.

1—ST. ADALBERT'S (1915), (Polish), [CEM] Rev. Edmund M. O'Brien; Deacon Robert E. Lambert. In Res., Rev. Anthony J. Bruno. Tel: 860-745-9966.
Res.: 90 Alden Ave., 06082-2865. Tel: 860-745-4837; Fax: 860-745-1787.
School—Tel: 860-745-6135; Fax: 860-741-7358. Sisters 2; Lay Teachers 8; Students 161.
Catechesis/Religious Program—Students 70.

2—ST. BERNARD'S (1870), [CEM] Revs. Joseph E. Vujs; William F. O'Keefe; Deacons Hobart Stadtlander, (Retired); Donald H. Pond.
Res.: 426 Hazard Ave., 06082-4719. Tel: 860-749-8353; Fax: 860-749-6456.
School—Tel: 860-749-8182 (East Campus); 860-745-5275 (West Campus); Fax: 860-749-8182. Sisters 3; Lay Teachers 21; Students 300.
Catechesis/Religious Program—Tel: 860-749-2993. Students 320.
Convent—Felician Sisters, 376 Hazard Ave., 06082. Tel: 860-749-4214.

3—HOLY FAMILY (1965), Rev. Francis T. Kerwan; Deacon Arthur J. Dickman. In Res., Rev. William J. Hilliard.
Res.: 23 Simon Rd., 06082-5903. Tel: 860-741-2101; Fax: 860-741-7411.
Catechesis/Religious Program—Tel: 860-745-7770. Elizabeth McGivney, D.R.E.; Carole Frappier, D.R.E. Students 770.

4—ST. MARTHA'S (1961), Revs. John P. Gwozdz; W. Edward Jissera (Sri Lanka) (DAV); Deacons Robert Bernd; Joseph S. Sloan.
Res.: 214 Brainard Rd., 06082-2609. Tel: 860-745-5616; Fax: 860-741-6731.
School—Tel: 860-745-3833; Fax: 860-745-3329. Felician Sisters 1; Lay Teachers 11; Students 250.
Catechesis/Religious Program—Tel: 860-745-5616. Students 335.

5—ST. PATRICK'S (1866), [CEM] Revs. Richard L. Welch, C.S.S.R., J.C.D.; Thomas G. Sullivan, C.S.S.R.
Res.: 64 Pearl St., 06082-3594. Tel: 860-745-2411; Fax: 860-253-9483.
Catechesis/Religious Program—Tel: 860-741-0572. Students 290.

FARMINGTON, HARTFORD CO., ST. PATRICK'S (1871), Revs. Mark F. Flynn; Mark S. Suslenko; Deacon William A.. Farrell.
Res.: 110 Main St., P.O. Box 523, 06034-0523. Tel: 860-677-2639; Fax: 860-677-2672.
Catechesis/Religious Program—Tel: 860-676-0253; Fax: 860-677-2672. Eileen Dignazio, D.R.E. Students 835.

FORESTVILLE, HARTFORD CO., ST. MATTHEW (1891), Revs. Brian W. Monnerat; Peter Dwomik; Francis W. Wright, C.S.S.R.; Deacons John E. Pahl; Michael P. Szumigala.
Res.: 120 Church Ave., Box 9216, 06011-9216. Tel: 860-583-1833; Fax: 860-582-6152.
School—Welch Dr., 06010. Tel: 860-583-5214; Fax: 860-314-1541. Sisters 5; Lay Teachers 14; Students 311.
Parish Resource Center—101 Church Ave., 06010. Tel: 860-583-1241.
Catechesis/Religious Program—Tel: 860-583-7806. Students 533.
Convent—Sisters, Servants of the Immaculate Heart of Mary, 119 Church Ave., 06010. Tel: 860-583-2004.

GLASTONBURY, HARTFORD CO.

1—ST. DUNSTAN (1971), Revs. William L. Traxl; Arthur J. Audet; Sr. Mary O'Neill, R.S.M., Pastoral Assoc.
Res.: 1345 Manchester Rd., 06033-2604. Tel: 860-633-3317; Fax: 860-659-8611.
Catechesis/Religious Program—Tel: 860-633-6876. Students 760.

2—ST. PAUL'S (1954), Revs. Kevin P. Cavanaugh; Jeffery V. Romans; Deacons Peter J. Klein; Stephen L. Weaver.
Res.: 2577 Main St., 06033-2023. Tel: 860-633-9419; Fax: 860-633-0040.
Catechesis/Religious Program—Tel: 860-659-3029. Students 1,190.

GOSHEN, LITCHFIELD CO., ST. THOMAS OF VILLANOVA (1877), [CEM] Rev. Raymond G. Proulx; Deacons Nick Diorio; Kenneth Dos Santos.
Res.: 71 North St., P.O. Box 177, 06756-0177. Tel: 860-491-2756; Fax: 860-491-3780.
Catechesis/Religious Program—Tel: 860-491-9276. Students 180.

GRANBY, HARTFORD CO., ST. THERESE'S (1958), Rev. Ronald R. Yelle; Deacons Robert D. Newbery; Robert D. Navickas.
Res.: 120 W. Granby Rd., 06035-2907. Tel: 860-653-3371.
Catechesis/Religious Program—Tel: 860-653-5780. Students 380.

GUILFORD, NEW HAVEN CO., ST. GEORGE (1870), [CEM] Rev. Lawrence S. Symolon; Deacons Adam J. Michaele; William A. Elder.
Res.: 33 Whitfield St., 06437-2698. Tel: 203-453-2788; Fax: 203-453-1707.
Catechesis/Religious Program—Tel: 203-453-3496. Students 1,217.

HAMDEN, NEW HAVEN CO.

1—ST. ANN'S (1919), (Italian), Rev. Kenneth P. Bonadies.
Res.: 930 Dixwell Ave., 06514-4990. Tel: 203-865-0886.
Catechesis/Religious Program—Students 26.

2—ASCENSION (1964), Rev. Thomas J. O'Rourke; Deacon Kenneth McCusker.
Res.: 1040 Dunbar Hill Rd., 06514-1410. Tel: 203-288-7516; Fax: 203-288-7516.
Catechesis/Religious Program—Tel: 203-288-7516. Students 105.

3—BLESSED SACRAMENT (1939), Rev. Donald J. French; Deacon Joseph R. Ryzewski.
Res.: 321 Circular Ave., 06514-3428. Tel: 203-288-1652; Fax: 203-248-0873.
Catechesis/Religious Program—306 Circular Ave., 06514. Tel: 203-288-5228. Students 214.

4—ST. JOAN OF ARC (1971), Rev. Daniel G. Keefe; Deacons Paul T. Koch; James Trippi Sr.
Res.: 450 W. Todd St., 06518. Tel: 203-288-4543; Fax: 203-288-1130.
Catechesis/Religious Program—Tel: 203-230-1926. Students 228.

5—OUR LADY OF MT. CARMEL (1869), [CEM] Revs. Daniel James Sullivan; Ralph M. Colicchio; Deacons John O'Donovan; James H. Stanley.
Res.: 2819 Whitney Ave., 06518-2598. Tel: 203-248-0141; Fax: 203-248-8658.
Parish Center—2809 Whitney Ave., 06518. Tel: 203-287-9017.
Catechesis/Religious Program—Tel: 203-287-9017. Sr. Ann O'Neill, R.S.M., D.R.E. Students 940.

6—ST. RITA'S (1928), Rev. Msgr. David M. Walker; Rev. Vincent J. Curran. In Res., Rev. Geoffrey C. Smith.
Res.: 1620 Whitney Ave., 06517. Tel: 203-248-5513; Fax: 203-248-2684.
School—1601 Whitney Ave., 06517. Tel: 203-248-3114; Fax: 203-248-1016. Priests 1; Apostles of the Sacred Heart 2; Lay Teachers 24; Students 489.
Catechesis/Religious Program—Tel: 203-281-7522; Fax: 203-248-2684. Dianne Breen, D.R.E. Students 428.

7—ST. STEPHEN'S (1953), Rev. David J. Baranowski; Deacon Richard Santello.
Res.: 400 Ridge Rd., 06517-2941. Tel: 203-288-6439; Fax: 203-288-4152.
School—Tel: 203-288-6792; Fax: 203-287-9158. Lay Teachers 12; Students 218.
Catechesis/Religious Program—Tel: 203-288-1305. Students 81.

HARWINTON, LITCHFIELD CO., IMMACULATE HEART OF MARY (1956), Rev. Allan J. Hill; Deacons Gerald Wootton; Lee Conrad.
Res.: 78 Litchfield Rd., 06791-2230. Tel: 860-485-1588; Fax: 860-485-1004.
Catechesis/Religious Program—Tel: 860-485-9264. Christine Rousseau, D.R.E. Students 299.

KENSINGTON, HARTFORD CO., ST. PAUL'S (1878), Revs. Herman Czaster, O.F.M.Conv., Team Ministry; Herbert Obijiski, O.F.M.Conv., Team Ministry; Michael Englert, O.F.M.Conv., Team Ministry; Marion Tolczyk, O.F.M.Conv., Team Ministry; Deacon Carmen Guzzardi, Team Ministry.
Res.: 479 Alling St., 06037-2170. Tel: 860-828-0331; Fax: 860-828-7620.
Parish Center—467 Alling St., Kesington, 06037-2170.
School—(Grades PreK-8) Tel: 860-828-4343; Fax: 860-828-1226. Mrs. Patricia O'Neil Tiezzi, Prin. Lay Teachers 20; Students 295.
Catechesis/Religious Program—Tel: 860-828-1934. Louann Warren, D.R.E. Students 1,193.

KENT, LITCHFIELD CO., SACRED HEART (1970), [CEM] Rev. Thomas E. Berberich.
Res.: 90 Cobble Rd., P.O. Box 186, 06757-0186. Tel: 860-927-3003; Fax: 860-927-3985.
Church: 17 Bridge St., 06757.
Catechesis/Religious Program—Students 70.

LAKEVILLE, LITCHFIELD CO., ST. MARY'S (1874), [CEM] Rev. Thomas Kelly.
Res.: 76 Sharon Rd., 06039-0466. Tel: 860-435-2659; Fax: 860-435-1042.
Catechesis/Religious Program—Students 79.

LITCHFIELD, LITCHFIELD CO., ST. ANTHONY'S (1882), [CEM] Revs. Robert F. Tucker; Nathaniel C. Labarda; Deacon John R. Maffeo.
Res.: 49 South St., P.O. Box 97, 06759-0097. Tel: 860-567-5209; Fax: 860-567-2052.
Catechesis/Religious Program—Tel: 860-567-4188. Students 455.

MADISON, NEW HAVEN CO., ST. MARGARET (1937), Rev. Msgr. John P. Conte; Rev. Joseph F. Keough; Sr. Patricia Cigrand, A.S.C.J.; Deacons Joseph M. Regan; P. Terrence Moran; Paul Prete.
Res.: 24 Academy St., P.O. Box 814, 06443-2647. Tel: 203-245-7301; Fax: 203-245-8568.
Catechesis/Religious Program—Tel: 203-245-7971; Fax: 203-245-3387. Students 1,163.

MANCHESTER, HARTFORD CO.

1—ASSUMPTION (1955), Rev. John F. Brinsmade; Deacon J. Fernand Chamberland.
Res.: 285 W. Center St., 06040-4898. Tel: 860-643-2195; Fax: 860-646-4360.
School—Tel: 860-649-0889; Fax: 860-643-0559. Sr. Mary Mark, Prin. Sisters 3; Lay Teachers 8; Students 170.
Catechesis/Religious Program—Tel: 860-643-7596. Students 224.
Convent—Sisters of Charity of Our Lady, Mother of the Church, 21 S. Adams St., 06040. Tel: 860-643-0452.

2—ST. BARTHOLOMEW'S (1958), Rev. Thomas A. Sievel; Deacon Edward J. Giard.
Res.: 45 Ludlow Rd., 06040-4542. Tel: 860-646-1613; Fax: 860-646-7121.
Catechesis/Religious Program—Tel: 860-643-9178. Students 360.

3—ST. BRIDGET'S (1870), Rev. Stephen M. Sledesky.
Res.: 80 Main St., 06040-3180. Tel: 860-643-2403; Fax: 860-646-6936.
School—74 Main St., 06040. Tel: 860-649-7731. Lay Teachers 18; Students 220.
Catechesis/Religious Program—Tel: 860-643-5454. Students 400.

4—ST. JAMES (1874), Rev. Msgrs. Douglas P. Clancy; Charles B. Johnson, Pastor Emeritus; Rev. Louis D. Cremonie; Deacon William J. Brown.
Res.: 896 Main St., 06040-6079. Tel: 860-643-4129; Fax: 860-643-4130.
School—Tel: 860-643-5088; Fax: 860-649-6462. Mrs. Patricia Kanute, Prin. Sisters 1; Lay Teachers 27; Students 401.
Catechesis/Religious Program—73 Park St., 06040. Tel: 860-643-9605. Students 260.

MARLBOROUGH, HARTFORD CO., ST. JOHN FISHER (1972), Revs. William L. Traxl; Arthur J. Audet; Deacon John W. McKaig.
Res.: 24 Cheney Rd., 06447-1327. Tel: 860-295-0067; 860-295-0001 (Office); Fax: 860-295-0001.
Catechesis/Religious Program—Tel: 860-295-0007. Students 325.

MERIDEN, NEW HAVEN CO.

1—ST. JOSEPH (1900), Revs. Shawn T. Daly; Robert P. Roy.
Res.: 22 Goodwill Ave., 06451. Tel: 203-237-5593.
School—Tel: 203-237-6800; Fax: 203-238-2963. Kathy Spencer, Prin. Sisters of Mercy 1; Lay Teachers 8; Students 219.
Catechesis/Religious Program—Tel: 203-237-5593. Students 377.

2—ST. LAURENT (1880), (French), Rev. Joseph V. DiSciacca; Deacon Robert P. Gale.
Res.: 121 Camp St., 06450-3279. Tel: 203-634-1583; Fax: 203-238-3629.
Catechesis/Religious Program—Students 85.

3—ST. MARY (1890), (German), [CEM] Revs. Shawn T. Daly; Robert P. Roy.
Res.: 5 Sherman Pl., 06451. Tel: 203-235-0519.
School—Tel: 203-237-2931; Fax: 203-237-9013. Lay Teachers 9; Students 106.
Catechesis/Religious Program—Students 5.

4—OUR LADY OF MOUNT CARMEL (1894), (Italian), Rev. Joseph V. DiSciacca; Deacon Robert Gale.
Res.: 109 Goodwill Ave., 06451-3000. Tel: 203-235-6381; Fax: 203-238-3629.
School—Tel: 203-235-2959. Lay Teachers 10; Students 166.
Catechesis/Religious Program—Students 250.
Convent—Apostles of the Sacred Heart of Jesus, 17 North St., 06451. Tel: 203-235-3622. Sisters 3.

5—ST. ROSE OF LIMA (1848), Revs. Paul Rotondi, O.F.M.; Isaac J. Calicchio, O.F.M.; Deacon Jacinto Ortiz.

Res.: 35 Center St., 06450-5685. Tel: 203-235-1644; Fax: 203-235-1360.
Catechesis/Religious Program—Tel: 203-235-6887. Students 237.
6—ST. STANISLAUS (1891), (Polish), [CEM] Rev. Edmund S. Nadolny.
Res.: 82 Akron St., 06450-5796. Tel: 203-235-6341; Fax: 203-235-6342.
School—Tel: 203-235-1005; Fax: 203-630-3424. Sisters of St. Joseph of the Third of St. Francis (Garfield Heights, OH) 3; Lay Teachers 25; Students 394.
Catechesis/Religious Program—Tel: 203-235-6341. Students 240.
MIDDLEBURY, NEW HAVEN CO., ST. JOHN OF THE CROSS (1904), Rev. Thomas J. Barry; Deacon Neil Culhane.
Res.: 1089 Whittemore Rd., P.O. Box 361, 06762-0361. Tel: 203-758-2659; Fax: 203-758-1121.
Catechesis/Religious Program—Tel: 203-758-1326; Fax: 203-758-1852. Students 501.
MILFORD, NEW HAVEN CO.
1—ST. ANN'S (1924), Rev. Thomas E. Ptaszynski; Deacon Edmund J. Ramos.
Res.: 501 Naugatuck Ave., 06460-5095. Tel: 203-874-0634; Fax: 203-874-1919.
School—Tel: 203-878-2738; Fax: 203-878-5473. Lay Teachers 11; Students 170.
Catechesis/Religious Program—Tel: 203-878-8130. Students 380.
2—CHRIST THE REDEEMER (1966), Rev. Daniel H. Connaghan. In Res., Rev. Stephen A. Krugel; Deacon George A. Puskas.
Res.: 325 Oronoque Rd., 06460-1798. Tel: 203-878-7431; Fax: 203-878-0677.
Catechesis/Religious Program—Students 154.
3—ST. GABRIEL (Wildemere Beach) (1946), Rev. Maurice J. Maroney; Deacons Calvin Croll; Henry Doyle.
Res.: 26 Shorefront, 06460-5968. Tel: 203-877-6096; Fax: 203-878-9700.
School—(Grades PreK-8), 1 Tudor Rd., 06460. Tel: 203-874-3811; Fax: 203-874-0416. Lay Teachers 18; Students 218.
Catechesis/Religious Program—Tel: 203-876-9355; Fax: 203-876-9355. Students 126.
4—ST. MARY (1874), [CEM] Revs. James J. Cronin; Kevin G. Donovan; Deacons Richard M. Sennett; Paul Lauer.
Res.: 70 Gulf St., Box 230, 06460-0230. Tel: 203-878-3571; Fax: 203-877-8741.
School—Tel: 203-878-6539; Fax: 203-878-1866. Sisters of Mercy 2; Lay Teachers 30; Students 480.
Catechesis/Religious Program—Tel: 203-877-5874. Sue Marra, D.R.E. Students 921.
NAUGATUCK, NEW HAVEN CO.
1—ST. FRANCIS OF ASSISI (1866), Revs. William J. Brenza; Michael J. Slusz; Deacon Nicholas Iassogna.
Res.: 318 Church St., 06770. Tel: 203-729-4543; Fax: 203-729-6216.
School—Tel: 203-729-2247; Fax: 203-729-0512. Mrs. Margaret Carabelli, Prin. Lay Teachers 9; Students 213.
Catechesis/Religious Program—Mrs. Joyce Luzio; Mr. John Paret. Students 613.
2—ST. VINCENT FERRER (1975), Rev. Kevin J. Forsyth; Sr. Cecilia Baranowski, R.S.M., Pastoral Min.
Res.: 1006 New Haven Rd., 06770-4731. Tel: 203-723-7497; Fax: 203-729-2978.
Catechesis/Religious Program—Carol Beebe, D.R.E. Students 300.
NEW BRITAIN, HARTFORD CO.
1—ALL SAINTS (1918), (Slovak), Closed., For inquiries for sacramental records, contact St. Ann, New Britain.
2—ST. ANDREW'S (1895), (Lithuanian), Rev. Ronald T. Smith.
Res.: 396 Church St., Box 515, 06050-0515. Tel: 860-224-0341; Fax: 860-826-6201.
Catechesis/Religious Program—Tel: 860-223-3667. Students 19.
3—ST. ANN (1938), (Italian), Rev. Thomas J. Walsh; Deacon Carl Lickwar. In Res., Rev. Augustine H. Giusani (Retired).
Res.: 47 Clark St., 06051-1903. Tel: 860-225-7625; Fax: 860-224-4283; 860-229-1929.
Catechesis/Religious Program—Tel: 860-229-1929; Fax: 860-229-1929. Students 111.
4—ST. FRANCIS OF ASSISI (1941), Rev. Paul R. Guido, O.F.M. In Res., Rev. Patrick J. Donovan, O.S.M. (ORG).
Res.: 1755 Stanley St., 06053-2099. Tel: 860-225-6449; Fax: 860-225-2315.
School—Middle School, Tel: 860-225-8729. School Sisters of Notre Dame 2; Lay Teachers 7; Students 97.
Catechesis/Religious Program—Students 97.
5—HOLY CROSS (1927), (Polish), Revs. Brian A. Shaw, D.Min.; Lech Kuna (Poland); Edward Ziemnicki; Deacon Michael J. Rubitz.
Res.: 31 Biruta St., 06053-2899. Tel: 860-229-2011; Fax: 860-826-5887.
School—221 Farmington Ave., 06053. Tel: 860-225-4275; Fax: 860-225-5073. Sisters of St. Joseph of the Third Order of St. Francis 4; Lay Teachers 27; Students 271.
Catechesis/Religious Program—Students 220.
6—ST. JEROME'S (1958), Rev. Thomas J. Cieslikowski; Deacon Reginald Roy.
Res.: 1010 Slater Rd., 06053-1698. Tel: 860-224-2411; Fax: 860-224-6838.
Catechesis/Religious Program—Students 159.
7—ST. JOHN THE EVANGELIST (1916), Rev. Ronald T. Smith.
Res.: 655 East St., 06051-2108. Tel: 860-223-3667; 860-223-3658; Fax: 860-348-1488.
Catechesis/Religious Program—Students 115.
8—ST. JOSEPH'S (1896), Rev. Thomas F. Gaffney; Deacon Gerald S. Geraci.
Res.: 195 S. Main St., 06051-3199. Tel: 860-229-4851; Fax: 860-225-1403.
School—Tel: 860-223-5959. Lay Teachers 11; Students 174.
Catechesis/Religious Program—Students 128.
9—ST. MARY'S (1848), Rev. Thomas J. Walsh; Deacons John E. Thayer; Raul Cardona.
Res.: 544 Main St., 06051-1814. Tel: 860-229-4894; Fax: 860-223-2756.
Catechesis/Religious Program—Students 130.
10—ST. MAURICE (1946), Rev. Joseph V. Napolitano.
Res.: 100 Wightman Rd., 06052-1597. Tel: 860-225-8419; Fax: 860-224-1947.
Catechesis/Religious Program—Tel: 860-225-4477. Linda E. Tower, D.R.E. Students 176.
11—ST. PETER'S (1873), (German—French) Rev. Thomas F. Gaffney; Deacon Gerald S. Geraci, (2).
Catechesis/Religious Program—Students 28.
Res.: 98 Franklin Sq., 06051-2607. Tel: 860-224-1446; Fax: 860-223-8717.
12—SACRED HEART OF JESUS (1894), (Polish), [CEM] Rev. Msgr. Daniel J. Plocharczyk; Rev. Peter S. Sobiecki. In Res., Rev. Henry P. Fiedorczyk (Retired).
Res.: 158 Broad St., 06053-4195. Tel: 860-229-0081; Fax: 860-826-4721.
School—Tel: 860-229-7663; Fax: 860-832-6098. Sr. M. Alma Sakowicz, Prin. Daughters of Mary of the Immaculate Conception 2; Lay Teachers 20; Students 465.
Catechesis/Religious Program—Students 230.
NEW HARTFORD, LITCHFIELD CO., IMMACULATE CONCEPTION (1869), [CEM] Rev. Timothy A. O'Brien; Deacon Robert N. Blair.
Res.: 60 Town Hill Rd., P.O. Box 285, 06057. Tel: 860-379-5215; Fax: 860-379-9587.
Catechesis/Religious Program—Students 362.
NEW HAVEN, NEW HAVEN CO.
1—ST. AEDAN'S (1900), Revs. Joseph H. McCann; Cyriac Maliekal; Deacons William H. Parkinson; Robert J. Brunell; Edward Taddei, (Retired).
Res.: 112 Fountain St., 06515-0156. Tel: 203-389-2619; Fax: 203-389-1235.
School—Tel: 203-387-5693; Fax: 203-387-1609. Miss Nancy Bourgoin, Prin. Lay Teachers 17; Students 247.
Catechesis/Religious Program—Students 76.
2—ST. ANTHONY'S (1904), (Italian), Revs. Joseph G. Moffo, C.S.; Antonio Licastro.
Res.: 25 Gold St., 06519. Tel: 203-624-1418; Fax: 203-624-3420.
3—ST. BERNADETTE, Formerly St. Bernadette's (1938), (Italian), Rev. Philip J. Sharkey; Deacon Martin J. O'Connor.
Res.: 385 Townsend Ave., 06512-3998. Tel: 203-467-1007; Fax: 203-467-3719.
School—Tel: 203-469-2271; Fax: 203-469-4615. Lay Teachers 15; Students 198.
Catechesis/Religious Program—Tel: 203-467-8763. Students 81.
4—ST. BONIFACE'S (1868), (German), Rev. John D. Casey.
Res.: 630 State St., 06511-6599. Tel: 203-865-3365.
Catechesis/Religious Program—Students 4.
5—ST. BRENDAN'S (1913), Revs. Joseph H. McCann; Cyriac Maliekal; Deacons Robert Brunell; Willaim H. Parkinson.
Res.: 455 Whalley Ave., 06511-3080. Tel: 203-865-0561; Fax: 203-865-0562.
School—342 Ellsworth Ave., 06511. Tel: 203-562-6128; Fax: 203-562-6129. Sisters 4; Lay Teachers 9; Students 225.
Convent—Sisters of Our Lady of the Garden, 455 1/2 Whalley Ave., 06511. Tel: 203-787-4631.
6—ST. CASIMIR'S (1912), (Lithuanian), Closed., For inquiries for sacramental records, contact St. Boniface, New Haven.
7—ST. DONATO'S (1915), (Italian), Rev. Louis Anthony Evangelisto.
Res.: 505 Lombard St., 06513-2910. Tel: 203-789-1576; Fax: 203-789-1576.
Catechesis/Religious Program—Students 45.
8—ST. FRANCIS (1868), Rev. Daniel J. McLearen.
Res.: 397 Ferry St., 06513-3698. Tel: 203-777-5356; Fax: 203-777-0874.
School—Tel: 203-777-5352; Fax: 203-865-1271. Mr. Frank P. Smith, Prin. Religious 1; Lay Teachers 11; Students 234.
Catechesis/Religious Program—Tel: 203-865-5179. Students 55.
9—ST. JOHN THE BAPTIST (1893), Rev. John J. Keane; Deacon Ronald Gurr. In Res., Rev. Daniel J. Scott, M.S.
Res.: 782 Dixwell Ave., 06511-1098. Tel: 203-624-3097; Fax: 203-562-0433.
Parish Center—20 Elizabeth St., 06511. Tel: 203-562-3908. Sr. Rosalie Shields, O.P., Pastoral Min.
Catechesis/Religious Program—Tel: 203-562-5587. Students 53.
10—ST. JOHN THE EVANGELIST, Closed., For inquiries for sacramental records contact Sacred Heart, New Haven.
11—ST. JOSEPH'S (1900), Rev. John P. Sullivan, Temp. Admin.
Res.: 129 Edwards St., 06511-2299. Tel: 203-777-2548.
Catechesis/Religious Program—Students 30.
12—SAINT MARTIN DE PORRES (1942), (African American), Rev. Joseph M. Elko.
Res.: 136 Dixwell Ave., 06511-3400. Tel: 203-624-9944.
Catechesis/Religious Program—Students 50.
13—ST. MARY'S PRIORY (1832), Very Rev. William A. Holt, O.P., Prior.
Mailing Address: P.O. Box 1202, 06505-1202. In Res., Revs. Bernard T. Confer, O.P.; Gabriel O'Donnell, O.P.; Albert A. Caprio, O.P.; M. Juan-Diego Brunetta, O.P., J.C.D.; Bros. Gerard Thayer, O.P.; William Ng, O.F.M.
Res.: 5 Hillhouse Ave., 06511. Tel: 203-562-6193; Fax: 203-562-1273.
Catechesis/Religious Program—Students 42.
Shrine—The Shrine of the Infant Prague (Inc.), Tel: 203-562-9326; Fax: 203-562-1273.
14—ST. MICHAEL'S (1889), (Italian), Rev. Andrew Brizzolara, C.S.
Res.: 29 Wooster Pl., 06511-6998. Tel: 203-562-7178; Fax: 203-752-0157.
Catechesis/Religious Program—Students 4.
Parish Center—Tel: 203-789-9453.
15—ST. PETER (1902), Closed., For inquiries for sacramental records contact Sacred Heart, New Haven.
16—ST. ROSE OF LIMA (1907), Revs. William Burbank; Agustin Rojas (Mexico); Deacon Julius Marcarelli.
Res.: 115 Blatchley Ave., 06513-4298. Tel: 203-865-6149; Fax: 203-865-6140.
School—12 Richard St., 06513. Tel: 203-624-5075; Fax: 203-624-1586. Salvatore Ferro, Prin. Lay Teachers 10; Students 177.
Catechesis/Religious Program—Students 138.
17—SACRED HEART (1876), Revs. James Richardson, S.C.; Lorenzo Lortie, S.C. (Canada).
Res.: 74 Liberty St., 06519-2299. Tel: 203-562-7592; Fax: 203-562-1737.
School—208 Columbus Ave., 06519. Tel: 203-777-8137; Fax: 203-776-5018. Lay Teachers 12; Students 209.
Catechesis/Religious Program—Students 111.
18—ST. STANISLAUS (1901), (Polish), Revs. Waclaw Hlond, C.M.; Boleslaw Potomski, C.M.; Stanley Miekina, C.M.
Res.: 9 Eld St., 06511-3815. Tel: 203-562-2828; Fax: 203-752-0217.
Catechesis/Religious Program—Students 92.
Convent—Sisters Minor of Mary Immaculate, 15 Eld St., 06511. Tel: 203-562-2751.
NEW MILFORD, LITCHFIELD CO.
1—ST. FRANCIS XAVIER, Formerly St. Francis Xavier's (1871), Revs. Mario F. Julian, O.F.M.; Jack W. Hoak, O.F.M.; Deacon George H. Streib.
Mailing Address: 1 Elm St., 06776-4009. Tel: 860-354-2202; Fax: 860-355-9485.
Res.: 48 Old Park Ln., 06776-2508. Tel: 860-350-1611; Fax: 860-335-3214.
Catechesis/Religious Program—Tel: 860-354-5372. Students 869.
2—OUR LADY OF THE LAKES (1990), Rev. Frederick M. Langlois; Deacon Robert E. Muro Sr. Tel: 860-354-9062.
Res.: 3 Old Town Park Rd., 06776-4212. Tel: 860-354-5239; Fax: 860-354-2968.
Catechesis/Religious Program—Tel: 860-355-5365. Students 388.
NEWINGTON, HARTFORD CO.
1—HOLY SPIRIT (1964), Rev. Lawrence R. Bock; Deacons James H. Shiels; James Fortier.
Res.: 183 Church St., 06111-4898. Tel: 860-666-5671; Fax: 860-666-9784.
Catechesis/Religious Program—Tel: 860-666-3562. Susan Skipp, D.R.E. Students 728.
2—ST. MARY (1924), Revs. George M. Couturier; Michael J. Dolan; Deacons Bruce R. Thompson; Michael J. O'Toole, (Retired).
Res.: 626 Willard Ave., 06111. Tel: 860-666-1591;

Fax: 860-666-5720.
School—Tel: 860-666-3844; Fax: 860-666-5570. Religious 1; Lay Teachers 10; Students 245.
Catechesis/Religious Program—Tel: 860-666-6347. Students 780.
Convent—Sisters of Charity, 168 Cedar St., 06111. Tel: 860-667-1790; Fax: 860-667-9881.

NORFOLK, LITCHFIELD CO., IMMACULATE CONCEPTION (1889), [CEM] Rev. John S. Ahern.
Res.: 4 North St., P.O. Box 583, 06058-0583. Tel: 860-542-5442.
Catechesis/Religious Program—Students 98.

NORTH BRANFORD, NEW HAVEN CO., ST. AUGUSTINE (1941), Rev. Joseph T. Kaminsky; Deacons John Hart; William J. Lovelace.
Res.: 30 Caputo Rd., 06471-1027. Tel: 203-484-0403; Fax: 203-484-0132.
Catechesis/Religious Program—Students 670.

NORTH HAVEN, NEW HAVEN CO.
1—ST. BARNABAS (1922), Revs. Hugh J. MacDonald; John J. Daly, Pastor Emeritus; Deacon Joseph Cretella.
Res.: 44 Washington Ave., 06473-1799. Tel: 203-239-5378; Fax: 203-239-3510.
Catechesis/Religious Program—Tel: 203-239-3804. Karin Tierney, D.R.E. Students 345.
2—ST. FRANCES CABRINI (1967), Rev. Robert J. St. Martin; Deacon George R. Stephens.
Res.: 6 Welch Rd., 06473-2896. Tel: 203-239-5700; Fax: 203-239-6463.
Church & Parish Center: Pond Hill Rd., 06473. Tel: 203-239-5644.
Catechesis/Religious Program—94 Chapel Hill Rd., 06473. Tel: 203-239-8012. Students 423.
School—Nursery School, 90 Chapel Hill Rd., 06473. Tel: 203-239-8012.
Convent—Sisters of the Sacred Heart of Jesus, Fax: 203-239-8012.
3—ST. THERESE (1925), Revs. Timothy A. Meehan; Alexander J. Cherukarakunnel (India); Deacon Louis J. Florio.
Res.: 555 Middletown Ave., 06473-4000. Tel: 203-239-1671; Fax: 203-234-2220.
Catechesis/Religious Program—Tel: 203-234-9287. Students 642.

NORTHFORD, NEW HAVEN CO., ST. MONICA'S (1964), Rev. Joseph Parel; Deacons Louis P. Fusco; William B. Bergers.
Res.: 1331 Middletown Ave., Box 160, 06472-0160. Tel: 203-484-9226; Fax: 203-484-1189.
Catechesis/Religious Program—Tel: 203-484-2434. Students 437.

OAKVILLE, LITCHFIELD CO., ST. MARY MAGDALEN (1900), Rev. Stuart H. Pinette; Deacon George M. Pettinico.
Res.: 145 Buckingham St., 06779-1797. Tel: 860-274-9273; Fax: 860-274-2013.
School—Tel: 860-945-0621; Fax: 860-945-6162. Lay Teachers 12; Students 294.
Catechesis/Religious Program—Students 402.

ORANGE, NEW HAVEN CO., HOLY INFANT (1952), Rev. Peter S. Dargan; Deacons Bernard J. Hayden; Harold J. Hoffman; Joseph D. Sullivan. In Res., Rev. Bernard D. Killeen (Retired).
Res.: 450 Race Brook Rd., 06477. Tel: 203-799-2379; Fax: 203-799-9720.
Catechesis/Religious Program—Tel: 203-777-2417. Students 957.

OXFORD, NEW HAVEN CO., ST. THOMAS THE APOSTLE (1966), Rev. Dominic J. Valla.
Res.: 733 Oxford Rd., 06478. Tel: 203-888-2382; Fax: 203-881-5518.
Catechesis/Religious Program—Tel: 203-888-4951. Students 798.

PLAINVILLE, HARTFORD CO., OUR LADY OF MERCY (1881), [CEM] Revs. Richard P. McGann; Edmund K. Karwowski; Sebastian Kochupurkal (India).
Res.: 15 S. Canal St., 06062-2799. Tel: 860-793-1399; Fax: 860-747-5407.
Parish Center—19 S. Canal St., 06062. Tel: 860-747-6825.
Catechesis/Religious Program—Tel: 860-747-6010. Jeanne Gionfriddo, D.R.E. Students 230.

PLANTSVILLE, HARTFORD CO.
1—ST. ALOYSIUS (1961), [JC] Rev. John P. Blanchfield. In Res., Rev. Donald J. O'Leary (Retired); Deacon Angelo J. Coppola.
Res.: 254 Burritt St., 06479-1426. Tel: 860-276-9208; Fax: 860-628-7650.
Catechesis/Religious Program—Tel: 860-621-2454. Students 818.
2—MARY OUR QUEEN (1961), Rev. Arthur J. DuPont; Deacons James P. Quinn; Paul J. Kulas.
Res.: 248 Savage St., P.O. Box 46, 06479-0046. Tel: 860-628-4901; Fax: 860-621-0610.
Catechesis/Religious Program—Tel: 860-628-0437. Students 476.

POQUONOCK, HARTFORD CO., ST. JOSEPH'S (1874), [CEM] Rev. Robert B. Vargo, J.C.L.; Deacons Leo R. LaRocque; Ronald Biamonte, (2).
Res.: 1747 Poquonock Ave., P.O. Box 253, 06064-0253. Tel: 860-688-9566; Fax: 860-683-2225.
Catechesis/Religious Program—Tel: 860-683-0366. Gayle Brick, D.R.E. Students 382.

PROSPECT, NEW HAVEN CO., ST. ANTHONY'S (1939), Revs. Philip J. Cascia; Joseph R. DeCarolis; Deacons Domenic Stolfi; George Dinkle.
Res.: 4 Union City Rd., P.O. Box 7117, 06712-0117. Tel: 203-758-4056; Fax: 203-758-4594. Email: revpcascia@aol.com.
Catechesis/Religious Program—Tel: 203-758-4848. Students 611.

ROCKY HILL, HARTFORD CO.
1—ST. ELIZABETH SETON (1985), Rev. Alvin J. Be-Blanc; Deacon Michael A. Shelto.
Res.: 280 Brook St., 06067-0485. Tel: 860-529-3222; Fax: 860-529-6421.
Catechesis/Religious Program—Students 676.
2—ST. JAMES (1880), Rev. Thomas B. Shepard.
Res.: 767 Elm St., 06067-1902. Tel: 860-529-8655; Fax: 860-257-1754. Web: stjamesrh.org.
Catechesis/Religious Program—(Grades K-10) Tel: 860-529-1274. Patricia Boorman, D.R.E. Students 741.

SEYMOUR, NEW HAVEN CO.
1—ST. AUGUSTINE'S (1866), [CEM] Rev. Brian E. Jeffries; Deacon Richard Renker.
Res.: 35 Washington Ave., 06483-3198. Tel: 203-888-2081; Fax: 203-888-9681.
Catechesis/Religious Program—Tel: 203-888-7003. Students 227.
2—GOOD SHEPHERD (1967), Rev. Edward S. Jaksina; Deacon Frank J. Krasnicki.
Res.: 135 Mountain Rd., 06483-2038. Tel: 203-888-9243; Fax: 203-888-6016.
Catechesis/Religious Program—Tel: 203-735-3190. Glenn Durette, D.R.E.; Debra Durette, D.R.E. Students 374.

SHARON, LITCHFIELD CO., ST. BERNARD'S (1885), [CEM] Rev. Francis R. Fador; Deacon Stephen Beecher.
Res.: 52 New St., Box 218, 06069-0218. Tel: 860-364-5244; Fax: 860-364-9893.
Catechesis/Religious Program—Students 28.

SIMSBURY, HARTFORD CO., ST. MARY'S (1921), Revs. William R. Metzler; John W. McHugh; Deacons John Sweeney; Joseph Gabriele.
Res.: 940 Hopmeadow St., P.O. Box 575, 06070-0575.
Parish Office—3 Massaco St., P.O. Box 575, 06070. Tel: 860-658-7627; Fax: 860-658-7626.
School—St. Mary School, 946 Hopmeadow St., 06070. Tel: 860-658-9412; Fax: 860-658-1737. Mrs. Maria Maynard, Prin. Lay Teachers 12; Students 299.
Catechesis/Religious Program—Tel: 860-658-5919. Students 974.

SOUTH GLASTONBURY, HARTFORD CO., ST. AUGUSTINE (1877), [CEM] Revs. Kevin P. Cavanaugh; Jettery V. Romans; Deacons Stephen L. Weaver; Peter J. Klein.
Res.: 55 Hopewell Rd., P.O. Box 175, 06073-0175. Tel: 860-633-9505; Fax: 860-633-1341.
Catechesis/Religious Program—Hopewell School, (Grades K-8) Tel: 860-633-9505. Students 311.

SOUTH MERIDEN, NEW HAVEN CO., HOLY ANGELS (1887), Rev. Roland M. LaPlante; Deacon Donald H. Smith.
Res.: 915 Main St., 06451-4999. Tel: 203-235-5311 (Rectory); 203-235-3822 (Office); Fax: 203-630-3041.
Catechesis/Religious Program—585 Main St.. Tel: 203-237-8697. Laura DelVecchio, D.R.E. Students 163.

SOUTH WINDSOR, HARTFORD CO.
1—ST. FRANCIS OF ASSISI (1941), Rev. Jeremiah N. Murasso; Deacon Ronald Daigle.
Res.: 673 Ellington Rd., 06074-4166. Tel: 860-528-8288; Fax: 860-528-1685.
Catechesis/Religious Program—Tel: 860-289-3671. Mark F. Cerrato, D.R.E. Students 594.
2—ST. MARGARET MARY (1961), Rev. Daniel Jeremiah Sullivan; Deacons Thomas J. Conklin; Rene J. Kieda.
Res.: 80 Hayes Rd., 06074-1499. Tel: 860-644-2411; Fax: 860-644-5765.
Catechesis/Religious Program—Tel: 860-644-2549. Students 1,325.

SOUTHBURY, NEW HAVEN CO., SACRED HEART (1884), [CEM] Rev. Joseph T. Donnelly; Deacons Charles Dietsch; Michael Kulas.
Res.: 68 Georges Hill Rd., 06488-0686. Tel: 203-264-5071; Fax: 203-264-9562.
Catechesis/Religious Program—Tel: 203-264-5065; Fax: 203-264-4271. Ann Sharkey, D.R.E.; Margaret Griffin, D.R.E. Students 983.
Station—Southbury, Southbury Training School, Tel: 203-264-8231.

SOUTHINGTON, HARTFORD CO.
1—ST. DOMINIC (1971), Rev. Henry C. Frascadore; Deacons John L. Crowley; Eugene P. Nebiolo.
Res.: 1050 Flanders Rd., 06489-1344. Tel: 860-628-0349; Fax: 860-276-8390.
Catechesis/Religious Program—Tel: 860-628-5159; Fax: 860-628-5159. Jacqueline Marenholz, D.R.E. Students 865.
2—IMMACULATE CONCEPTION (1915), (Polish), [CEM] Rev. David J. Lewandowski; Deacon Neil B. Richter.
Res.: 130 Summer St., 06489. Tel: 860-628-2181.
Catechesis/Religious Program—Judy Telesmanic, D.R.E. Students 201.
Father Kolbe Catechetical Center—50 Knowles Ave., Plantsville, 06479. Tel: 860-628-6973; Fax: 860-628-6973.
3—ST. THOMAS (1860), [CEM] Revs. George F. Lauretti; Christopher Meade; Deacon Wesley F. Baxter.
Res.: 99 Bristol St., 06489-4599. Tel: 860-628-4713; Fax: 860-628-7341.
School—Tel: 860-628-2485. Mrs. Joan Murphy, Prin. Lay Teachers 8; Students 137.
Catechesis/Religious Program—Tel: 860-628-9679. Students 281.

SUFFIELD, HARTFORD CO.
1—ST. JOSEPH'S (1916), (Polish), [CEM] Rev. William L. Baldyga; Deacon Edward Szewczyk.
Res.: 140 S. Main St., 06078-2218. Tel: 860-668-2880.
Catechesis/Religious Program—Students 40.
Convent—Felician Sisters, 156 S. Main St., 06078. Tel: 860-668-2503.
2—SACRED HEART (1884), [JC] Revs. Theodore T. Raczynski; Dennis J. Vincenzo.
Res.: 446 Mountain Rd., P.O. Box 626, 06078-0626. Tel: 860-668-4246; Fax: 860-668-1337.
Catechesis/Religious Program—Tel: 860-668-7766. Students 805.

TARIFFVILLE, HARTFORD CO., ST. BERNARD'S (1878), [CEM] Rev. Thomas A. Flower; Deacon Thomas P. Scanlon.
Res.: 7 Maple St., P.O. Box 85, 06081-0085. Tel: 860-658-5142; Fax: 860-658-2804.
Catechesis/Religious Program—Students 157.

TERRYVILLE, LITCHFIELD CO.
1—ST. CASIMIR (1906), (Polish), Rev. Gerald H. Dziedzic; Deacon John W. Makara.
Mailing Address: 21 Maple St..
Res.: 19 Allen St., 06786-1503. Tel: 860-583-4697.
Catechesis/Religious Program—Students 98.
2—IMMACULATE CONCEPTION (1882), [CEM 2] Rev. Gerald H. Dziedzic; Deacon John W. Makara.
Res.: 21 Maple St., 06786-1197. Tel: 860-583-4697.
Catechesis/Religious Program—Fax: 860-584-8656. Students 176.

THOMASTON, LITCHFIELD CO., ST. THOMAS (1869), Revs. Harold M. Kearns; John E. Cockayne; Deacons Jose L. Dlugokinski; Robert Gordon.
Parish Center—19 Electric Ave., 06787-1651. Tel: 860-283-5817; Fax: 860-283-1009. (CEM)
Catechesis/Religious Program—Tel: 860-283-4296. Students 474.

TORRINGTON, LITCHFIELD CO.
1—ST. FRANCIS OF ASSISI (1877), Revs. John G. Weaver; Gerard G. Masters; James T. Gregory; Deacon Edward Dickson; Sr. Helen Marie Clark, R.S.M., Pastoral Assoc.
Res.: 160 Main St., 06790-5299. Tel: 860-482-5571; Fax: 860-482-1972.
School—Tel: 860-489-4177; Fax: 860-489-1590. Mrs. Jo-Anne Gauger, Prin. Lay Teachers 10; Students 130.
Catechesis/Religious Program—360 Prospect St., 06790. Tel: 860-482-3121. Students 450.
2—ST. MARY'S (1919), (Polish), Revs. John G. Weaver; Gerard G. Masters; James T. Gregory; Deacon Edward J. Dickson.
Mailing Address: 160 Main St., 06790-5201. Tel: 860-482-5571; Fax: 860-482-1972.
Res.: 61 Forest Ct., 06790-4698. Tel: 860-482-3583; Fax: 860-482-1972.
Catechesis/Religious Program—Tel: 860-482-3121. Students 55.
3—ST. PETER'S (1910), (Italian), Revs. John G. Weaver; Gerard G. Masters; James T. Gregory, (2); Deacon John L. Dembishack.
Res.: 107 E. Main St., 06790-5493. Tel: 860-482-4433; Fax: 860-482-1891.
School—Tel: 860-489-8735; Fax: 860-482-9406. Maestre Pie Filippini 2; Lay Teachers 8; Students 150.
Catechesis/Religious Program—Tel: 860-482-3121. Students 190.
4—SACRED HEART (1910), (Slovak), Revs. John G. Weaver; Gerard G. Masters; James T. Gregory; Deacon John L. Dembishack.
Res.: 116 Grove St., 06790-5047. Tel: 860-482-8246; Fax: 860-482-1863.
Parish Center—119 Grove St., 06790. Tel: 860-489-4070.
Catechesis/Religious Program—Tel: 860-482-3121. Students 58.

UNION CITY, NEW HAVEN CO.
1—ST. HEDWIG (Naugatuck) (1906), (Polish), Rev. Stephen H. Bzdyra; Deacon Thomas J. Clifford.
Res.: 32 Golden Hill St., 06770-3099. Tel: 203-729-2490; Fax: 203-720-2161.
School—Tel: 203-729-2403; Fax: 203-723-7954. Ms. Patricia Dayner, Prin. Lay Teachers 9; Students

173.
Catechesis/Religious Program—Students 43.
2—St. Mary's (Naugatuck) (1907), Rev. Richard M. Taberski; Deacon Earle A. Kimball.
Res.: 338 N. Main St., 06770-3235. Tel: 203-729-2279; Fax: 203-729-2270.
Catechesis/Religious Program—Tel: 203-729-1392; Fax: 203-729-1392. Students 164.

Unionville, Hartford Co., St. Mary's (1874), [CEM] Rev. John S. Golas; Deacon Thomas S. Sutak.
Res.: 16 Bidwell Sq., 06085-1116. Tel: 860-673-2422; Fax: 860-673-2001.
Catechesis/Religious Program—Tel: 860-675-8522. Students 723.

Wallingford, New Haven Co.
1—Holy Trinity (1869), Revs. Charles J. MacDonald; Dairo Quinchia-Diaz; Deacon Eugene Riotte.
Res.: 68 N. Colony St., 06492-3696. Tel: 203-269-8791; Fax: 203-269-0880.
School—11 N. Whittlesey Ave., 06492. Tel: 203-269-4476; Fax: 203-294-4983. Sr. Kathleen Kelly, R.S.M., Prin. Sisters of Mercy 1; Lay Teachers 9; Students 263.
Catechesis/Religious Program—Tel: 203-265-6300. Frances Selmecki, D.R.E. Students 953.
2—SS. Peter and Paul (1924), [CEM] Revs. Joseph K. Parzymies; Daniel J. Karpiey; Deacon Louis P. Sill Jr.
Res.: 139 N. Orchard St., 06492-3617. Tel: 203-269-4617; Fax: 203-265-6751.
Catechesis/Religious Program—Tel: 203-269-0271. Students 55.
3—Resurrection (1963), Rev. Msgr. John J. McCarthy. In Res., Rev. Daniel E. Johnson, Pastor Emeritus (Retired); Deacon Wayne F. Griffin.
Res.: 115 Pond Hill Rd., 06492-4836. Tel: 203-265-1694; Fax: 203-284-9766.
Catechesis/Religious Program—Tel: 203-269-4683; Fax: 203-269-4683. Mary Ann Marchitto, D.R.E. Students 614.

Washington Depot, Litchfield Co., Our Lady of Perpetual Help (1893), [CEM] Rev. Thomas F. Bennett; Deacon Roland G. Miller.
Res.: 34 Green Hill Rd., P.O. Box 303, 06794. Tel: 860-868-2600.
Catechesis/Religious Program—Students 125.
Mission—St. Patrick's Church St., Roxbury, Litchfield Co. 06783.

Waterbury, New Haven Co.
1—St. Anne (1886), (French), Revs. Kevin J. Gray, Admin.; Dennis C. Gingras; Deacons Francis X. Bandeira; Gaspard D. LeBlanc.
Res.: 515 S. Main St., 06706-1089. Tel 203-756-4439; Fax: 203-754-3244.
Catechesis/Religious Program—Tel: 203-756-8981; Fax: 203-756-2074. Students 14.
2—Blessed Sacrament (1911), Rev. Michael F.X. Hinkley; Deacon William M. McGrath.
Res.: 182 Robbins St., 06708. Tel: 203-753-3149; Fax: 203-596-0740.
School—Tel: 203-756-5313; Fax: 203-756-5313. Lay Teachers 9; Students 266.
Catechesis/Religious Program—Students 78.
3—St. Cecilia's (1893), (German), Closed., For inquiries for sacramental records, contact Sacred Heart-Segrado Corazon, Waterbury
4—St. Francis Xavier's (1896), Rev. Paul J. Pace.
Res.: 625 Baldwin St., 06706-1597. Tel: 203-756-7804.
School—605 Baldwin St., 06706. Tel: 203-753-3197; Fax: 203-574-0128. Mr. J. Brian Lally, Prin. Lay Teachers 10; Students 215.
Catechesis/Religious Program—Tel: 203-754-6996. Students 200.
5—Immaculate Conception (1848), Revs. John J. Bevins; George M. White, O.M.I.; John Curry Gay; Maximo Asencios-Pablo, M.Ss.A.; Thomas Simon, M.Ss.A; Deacon Carl Vecca. In Res., Rev. Michael Burke.
Res.: 74 W. Main St., 06721-1670. Tel: 203-574-0017; Fax: 203-756-8748.
School—St. Mary's, Tel: 203-753-2574; Fax: 203-596-2498. Lay Teachers 18; Students 500.
Catechesis/Religious Program—Students 500.
6—St. Joseph (1894), (Lithuanian), Rev. John L. Williams.
Mailing Address: 46 Congress Ave., P.O. Box 271, 06720-0271.
Res.: 50 Churles St., 06708. Tel: 203-754-1557; Fax: 203-756-4690.
Catechesis/Religious Program—Students 5.
7—St. Leo the Great (1974), Rev. Joseph F. Gorman; Deacons Robert F. Wallin; Modesto A. Rosello, (Retired).
Res.: 14 Bentwood Dr., 06705-3612. Tel: 203-573-0511.
Catechesis/Religious Program—Students 180.
8—St. Lucy's (1926), (Italian), Rev. Ronald A. Ferraro.
Res.: 24 Branch St., 06704-3626. Tel: 203-574-5903.
School—58 Griggs St., 06704. Tel: 203-753-3708; Fax: 203-755-6134. Mr. Joseph W. Meaney, Prin. Lay Teachers 10; Students 160.
Parish Center—64 Division St., 06704. Tel: 203-755-8420.
Catechesis/Religious Program—Students 17.
9—St. Margaret's (1910), (Hispanic), Revs. Joseph E. Looney; Zacarias Pushpanathan; Deacon Paul P. Iadarola.
Res.: 289 Willow St., 06710. Tel: 203-754-6101; Fax: 203-754-2006.
School—Tel: 203-755-6134; Fax: 203-753-1360. Donna Binkoski, Prin. Lay Teachers 8; Students 221.
Catechesis/Religious Program—Students 221.
10—St. Michael (1897), Rev. Ronald Gliatta, O.F.M.; Deacon George D. Hajjar.
Res.: 62 St. Michael Dr., 06704-1295. Tel: 203-753-0689; Fax: 203-573-9101.
Catechesis/Religious Program—Students 164.
11—Our Lady of Fatima (1971), (Portuguese), Rev. Nelson Ribeiro, C.M.
Res.: 2071 Baldwin St., P.O. Box 1787, 06721. Tel: 203-753-1424; Fax: 203-753-1424.
Catechesis/Religious Program—Students 380.
12—Our Lady of Loreto (1971), Rev. Msgr. Joseph A. Devine.
Res.: 12 Ardsley Rd., 06708-1825. Tel: 203-757-6112; Fax: 203-756-9656.
Catechesis/Religious Program—Students 275.
13—Our Lady of Lourdes (1899), (Italian), Rev. Ronald A. Ferraro.
Res.: 309 S. Main St., 06706-1014. Tel: 203-754-4134; Fax: 203-755-0456.
Catechesis/Religious Program—Students 66.
14—Our Lady of Mt. Carmel (1923), (Italian), Rev. David J. Eorino.
Res.: 785 Highland Ave., 06708-4199. Tel: 203-756-8981; Fax: 203-756-2074.
School—645 Congress Ave., 06708. Tel 203-755-6809; Fax: 203-755-5850. Mrs. Robin A. Booth, Prin. Lay Teachers 9; Students 237.
Catechesis/Religious Program—Tel: 203-753-1713. Students 240.
Convent—656 Congress Ave., 06708. Tel: 203-753-1408.
15—St. Patrick (1880), (Irish), Rev. John L. Williams; Deacon Thomas F. Johnson.
Mailing Address: P.O. Box 271, 06720-0271. Tel: 203-756-8837; Fax: 203-756-4690.
Res.: 50 Charles St., 06708. Tel: 203-756 8837; Fax: 203-756-4620.
Catechesis/Religious Program—645 Highland Ave., 06708. Tel: 203-753-1713. Students 31.
16—SS. Peter and Paul (1920), Rev. Msgr. James G. Coleman; Rev. Dennis C. Gingras; Deacons Charles Colella; Albert J. DeHippolytis.
Res.: 67 Southmayd Rd., 06705. Tel: 203-756-7919; Fax: 203-755-3535.
School—Tel: 203-755-0881. Janet Curry, Prin. Lay Teachers 12; Students 278.
Catechesis/Religious Program—116 Beecher Ave., 06705. Tel: 203-753-4242. Students 104.
17—Sacred Heart-Sagrado Corazon, Formerly Sacred Heart-Segrado Corazon (1885), Rev. Kevin J. Gray. In Res., Rev. Alfred J. Jaenicke (Retired).
Res.: 13 Wolcott St., 06702-1790. Tel: 203-757-8737; Fax: 203-754-5862.
Catechesis/Religious Program—Students 217.
18—St. Stanislaus Kostka (1913), (Polish), Rev. Stephen H. Bzdyra.
Mailing Address: 32 Golden Hill St., Union City, 06770. Tel: 203-729-2490; Fax: 203-720-2161.
Office—86 E. Farm St., 06704. Tel: 203-574-0871; Fax: 203-575-0107.
19—St. Thomas (1898), Closed., For inquiries for sacramental records contact St. Michael, Waterbury.

Watertown, Litchfield Co., St. John the Evangelist (1878), [CEM] Revs. John M. Cooney; J. Daniel McElheron; Deacons John Charles; Daniel Cameroca.
Res.: 21 Academy Hill, 06795-2101. Tel: 860-274-8836; Fax: 860-274-0667.
School—Tel: 860-274-9208; Fax: 860-945-1082. John Petto, Prin. School Sisters of Notre Dame 2; Lay Teachers 12; Students 195.
Catechesis/Religious Program—Tel: 860-274-4123. Therese N. Morgado, D.R.E. Students 507.

West Hartford, Hartford Co.
1—St. Brigid's (1919), Revs. Francis T. Carter; Alphonso R. Fontana. In Res., Rev. Edward J. McLean; Deacon Andrew Moemeka.
Res.: 1088 New Britain Ave., 06110-2489. Tel: 860-236-5965; Fax: 860-233-8016.
School—100 Mayflower St., 06110. Tel: 860-561-2130; Fax: 860-561-0011. Sisters 1; Lay Teachers 18; Students 245.
Catechesis/Religious Program—Tel: 860-521-8523. Students 300.
2—St. Helena (1966), Revs. Francis P. Johnson; Eugene M. Kilbride; Deacon Robert J. Hilliard. In Res., Rev. Zigford J. Kriss.
Res.: 30 Echo Ln., 06107-3698. Tel: 860-521-1921.
Catechesis/Religious Program—Tel: 860-521-3661. Students 244.
3—St. John the Evangelist (1942), (Spanish), Closed., For inquiries for sacramental records contact St. Lawrence O'Toole, Hartford.
4—St. Mark the Evangelist (1942), Rev. Thomas J. Sas; Rev. Msgr. Michael J. Motta; Rev. Michael G. Whyte; Deacon Raymond J. Fugere.
Res.: 467 S. Quaker Ln., 06110-1042. Tel: 860-233-1269; Fax: 860-233-5791.
Catechesis/Religious Program—491 S. Quaker Ln., 06110. Tel: 860-236-3545. Catherine Umanetz, D.R.E.; Peter Chabot, D.R.E. Students 207.
5—St. Peter Claver (1966), Revs. Joseph P. McGarry; Kevin M. Dillon.
Res.: 47 Pleasant St., 06107-1600. Tel: 860-561-4235; Fax: 860-561-4235.
Catechesis/Religious Program—Tel: 860-521-2904. Students 526.
6—St. Thomas the Apostle Church (1921), Revs. Arthur J. Murphy; Patrick J. Curran (SLC); Edward M. Moran. In Res., Rev. John J. Stack (Retired).
Res.: 872 Farmington Ave., 06119-1499. Tel: 860-233-8269; Fax: 860-523-8794.
School—25 Dover Rd., 06119. Tel: 860-236-6257; Fax: 860-236-8865. Lay Teachers 29; Students 295.
Catechesis/Religious Program—Tel: 860-523-4209; Fax: 860-570-0273. Students 259.
7—St. Timothy's (1958), Rev. Henry P. Cody; Deacon Anthony Nwankwo; Patricia A. Piano, Pastoral Assoc. Tel: 860-232-8594.
Res.: 1116 N. Main St., 06117-1209. Tel: 860-233-5131; Fax: 860-232-2189.
School—St. Timothy Middle School, 225 King Philip Dr., 06117. Tel: 860-236-0614; Fax: 860-920-0293. Lay Teachers 16; Students 148.
Catechesis/Religious Program—Tel: 860-232-3952. Students 334.

West Haven, New Haven Co.
1—St. John Vianney (1965), Revs. Christopher M. Tiano; Joseph R. Cronin; Deacons Frank J. Bevvino; Charles W. Parlee Jr.; Paul E. Sabo.
Res.: 300 Capt. Thomas Blvd., 06516-5974. Tel: 203-934-6000; Fax: 203-931-8747.
Catechesis/Religious Program—Tel: 203-933-8471. Students 128.
2—St. Lawrence's (1886), Rev. Mark R. Jette; Deacons Anthony P. Solli; John E. Wheeler. In Res., Rev. Chacko K. Kumplam (India).
Res.: 207 Main St., 06516-4599. Tel: 203-934-8351; Fax: 203-937-7858.
School—233 Main St., 06516. Tel: 203-933-2518; Fax: 203-932-2058. Mary Pat Wirkus, Prin. Lay Teachers 11; Students 243.
Catechesis/Religious Program—231 Main St., 06516. Tel: 203-933-2519. Students 187.
3—St. Louis (1886), (French Territorial), Rev. Peter J. Pinto; Deacons Salvatore DeFilippo; Edward J. Mancini.
Res.: 89 Bull Hill Ln., 06516-3998. Tel: 203-934-5249; Fax: 203-934-1055.
Catechesis/Religious Program—Students 117.
4—Our Lady of Victory (1935), Revs. Christopher M. Tiano; Joseph R. Cronin. In Res., Rev. Gregory M. Altermatt; Deacons Paul E. Sabo; Frank J. Bevvino; Charles W. Parlee Jr.
Res.: 600 Jones Hill Rd., 06516-6399. Tel: 203-934-6357; Fax: 203-932-3315.
School—Tel: 203-932-6457; Fax: 203-932-6456. Lay Teachers 17; Students 174.
Catechesis/Religious Program—Tel: 203-933-0044. Students 503.
5—St. Paul's (1916), (Italian), Revs. Salvatore J. Rosa; Augustine Mangalath (India); Deacon Richard Fournier.
Res.: 41 Alling St., 06516-2799. Tel: 203-933-1024; Fax: 203-931-9416.
Catechesis/Religious Program—Tel: 203-934-1357. Sisters Carolyn Severino, A.S.C.J., D.R.E.; Lany Jo Smith, A.S.C.J., D.R.E. Students 160.
Parish Center:—45 Alling St., 06516. Tel: 203-934-1357.

West Simsbury, Hartford Co., St. Catherine of Siena (1971), Rev. Richard R. Russell; Deacon Thomas F. Delehanty.
Res.: Box 184, 06092. Tel: 860-658-1642; Fax: 860-658-0668.
Catechesis/Religious Program—Tel: 860-658-4737. Students 550.

Wethersfield, Hartford Co.
1—Corpus Christi (1941), Revs. Thomas B. Campion, Co-Pastor & Team Ministry; David W. Lonergan, Co-Pastor & Team Ministry; Deacon Seth M. English, Team Ministry. In Res., Rev. Bradford Colton, Pastor Emeritus.
Res.: 84 Somerset St., 06109-3068. Tel: 860-529-2545; Fax: 860-529-5861.
School—Tel: 860-529-5487; Fax: 860-257-9106. Mrs. Eileen Sampiere, Prin. Religious 1; Lay Teachers

29; Students 463.
Catechesis/Religious Program—581 Silas Deane Hwy., 06109. Tel: 860-721-9419; Fax: 860-721-9418. Students 604.

2—INCARNATION (1963), Revs. John F. Edwards; James M. Moran; Deacon Robert J. D'Efemia.
Res.: 544 Prospect St., 06109-3696. Tel: 860-529-2533; Fax: 860-721-6595.
Catechesis/Religious Program—Tel: 860-529-6765. Noranne Wamester, D.R.E. Students 551.

3—SACRED HEART (1876), Revs. Thomas B. Campion, Co-Pastor & Team Ministry; David W. Lonergan, Co-Pastor & Team Ministry; Deacon Cornelius D. O'Connell, Team Ministry.
Res.: 56 Hartford Ave., 06109-1800. Tel: 860-529-1991.
Catechesis/Religious Program—Tel: 860-529-2545. Students 145.

WINDSOR LOCKS, HARTFORD CO.

1—ST. MARY (1852), [CEM] Revs. Robert A. O'Grady; Francis P. McDonnell; Deacons Donald Norton; Benedict L. Winiarski.
Res.: 42 Spring St., 06096-2311. Tel: 860-623-2524; Fax: 860-623-5684.
Parish Center—45 Church St., 06096. Tel: 860-627-9469.
Catechesis/Religious Program—Students 591.

2—ST. ROBERT BELLARMINE (1962), Rev. Thomas F. Farrell.
Res.: 52 S. Elm St., P.O. Box 315, 06096-0315. Tel: 860-623-0240; Fax: 860-623-0240.
Catechesis/Religious Program—Students 26.

WINDSOR, HARTFORD CO.

1—ST. GABRIEL'S (1894), Revs. Richard J. Neumann; Robert J. Grant.
Res.: 379 Broad St., 06095-3004. Tel: 860-688-4905; Fax: 860-688-2638.
School—77 Bloomfield Ave., 06095. Tel: 860-688-6401; Fax: 860-298-8668. Lay Teachers 12; Students 255.
Catechesis/Religious Program—Students 235.

2—ST. GERTRUDE'S (1947), Rev. Maurice J. Barry; Deacon Vincent Thorney.
Res.: 550 Matianuck Ave., 06095-3599. Tel: 860-522-6163; Fax: 860-525-2320.
Catechesis/Religious Program—Students 139.

WINSTED, LITCHFIELD CO., ST. JOSEPH'S (1853), [CEM] Rev. Bruce C. Czapla, O.F.M.; Deacon William H. Wilcox.
Res.: 31 Oak St., P.O. Box 808, 06098-0808. Tel: 860-379-3369; Fax: 860-379-4194.
School—St. Anthony's, 55 Oak St., 06098. Tel: 860-379-7521; Fax: 860-379-7522. Patricia Devanney, Prin. Lay Teachers 10; Students 201.
Catechesis/Religious Program—Tel: 860-379-5968. Students 273.

WOLCOTT, NEW HAVEN CO.

1—ST. MARIA GORETTI (1973), Rev. William R. Sokolowski.
Res.: 1300 Woodtick Rd., P.O. Box 6291, 06716-0291. Tel: 203-879-4608; Fax: 203-879-4609.
Catechesis/Religious Program—Tel: 203-879-5242. Students 467.

2—ST. PIUS X (1955), Rev. Henry A. Balchunas; Deacon Stephen J. Kelly.
Res.: 525 Woodtick Rd., 06716-2898. Tel: 203-879-2544; Fax: 203-879-2545.
Catechesis/Religious Program—Tel: 203-879-9030. Students 580.

WOODBRIDGE, NEW HAVEN CO., CHURCH OF THE ASSUMPTION (1924), Rev. Gene E. Gianelli; Deacons Joseph P. Borland; John J. Conte Jr.
Res.: 81 Center Rd., 06525-1699. Tel: 203-387-7119; Fax: 203-387-4281. Web: www.assumptionchurch.com.
Catechesis/Religious Program—Tel: 203-389-9863. Sr. Dorellen Sullivan, R.S.M., D.R.E.; Deacons John J. Conte Jr., D.R.E.; Joseph P. Borland, D.R.E. Students 805.

WOODBURY, LITCHFIELD CO., ST. TERESA'S (1902), Rev. Robert M. Kwiatkowski; Deacons Ralph Rescildo; Terence M. Nolan.
Res.: P.O. Box A, 11 Washington Ave., 06798-0417. Tel: 203-263-2008; Fax: 203-263-7259.
Catechesis/Religious Program—Tel: 203-263-0608. Students 412.

WOODMONT, NEW HAVEN CO., ST. AGNES (1906), Rev. Francis X. Callahan. In Res., Rev. George J. Raffaeta (Retired); Deacon Nicholas A. Genovese.
Res.: 400 Merwin Ave., 06460-7198. Tel: 203-878-1617; Fax: 203-878-5545.
Catechesis/Religious Program—Students 530.

YALESVILLE, NEW HAVEN CO., OUR LADY OF FATIMA (1956), Rev. Salvatore F. Cavagnuolo. In Res., Rev. Leo J. Daily (Retired).
Res.: 382 Hope Hill Rd., 06492-2270. Tel: 203-265-0961; Fax: 203-269-9386.
Catechesis/Religious Program—Tel: 203-265-6426; 203-265-6818 (Youth Minister). Tracy Blum, D.R.E. Students 574.

Chaplains of Public Institutions

HARTFORD. *Hartford Correctional Institution*, 177 Weston St., 06120. Tel: 860-240-1857. Rev. Robert O'Grady, Chap., Deacon Carl Vecca, Chap.
Hartford Hospital, 80 Seymour St., 06102-5037. Tel: 860-545-2251; Fax: 860-545-3594. Rev. Gerard Pelletier, S.M., Chap., Deacon Paul Koch, Chap.

BRISTOL. *Bristol Hospital*, Brewster Rd., 06011-0977. Tel: 860-585-3431. Rev. J. Richard Fowler, Interfaith Chap.

CHESHIRE. *Cheshire Correctional Institution*, 900 Highland Ave., 06410-1698. Tel: 203-250-2787. Rev. Stephen A. Krugel, Chap., Deacon Robert P. Gale, Chap.
Manson Youth Institution, 42 Jarvis St., 06510. Tel: 203-272-5391. Deacon Carl Vecca.

ENFIELD. *Carl Robinson Correctional Institution*, P.O. Box 1400, 06083-1400. Tel: 860-763-6200. Rev. Robert J. Grant, Chap., Deacon Robert Blair, Chap.
Enfield Correctional Institute, 289 Shaker Rd., 06083. Tel: 860-763-7318. Rev. William Hilliard, Chap., Deacon George Hajjar, Chap.
Willard-Cybulski Correction Institute, 391 Shaker Rd., P.O. Box 2400, 06082. Tel: 860-763-6140. Revs. Robert J. Grant, Chap., William J. Hilliard, Chap., Deacon Robert Lambert, Chap.

NEW BRITAIN. *New Britain General Hospital*, 100 Grand St., 06050. Tel: 860-224-5011. Rev. Ronald T. Smith, Chap.
Res.: 396 Church St., 06051.

NEW HAVEN. *Yale-New Haven Hospital*, 20 York St., 06504-1001. Tel: 203-688-2152. Rev. Geoffrey C. Smith, Chap.

NEWINGTON. *Department of Veteran Affairs Medical Center*, 555 Willard Ave., 06111. Tel: 860-666-6951. Rev. Francis M. Vella, Chap.

ROCKY HILL. *Veterans' Home and Hospital*, West St., 06067. Rev. Francis J. Kula, M.S.

SUFFIELD. *Macdougall Correctional Institute*, 1153 E. St. S., 06080-0002. Tel: 860-627-2148; Fax: 860-627-2152. Rev. Louis S. Paturzo, Chap., Deacon Rene Kieda, Chap.
Walker RSMU, 1151 East St. S., 06080-0002. Tel: 860-292-3429. Revs. Robert Grant, Chap., William Hilliard, Chap., Deacon Robert Blair, Chap.

WATERBURY. *Waterbury Hospital*, 64 Robbins St., 06708. Tel: 203-573-7213; Fax: 203-573-7326. Rev. Richard C. Bollea, Chap.

WEST HAVEN. *V.A. CT Health Care System*, 950 Campbell Ave., 06516. Tel: 203-932-5711. Rev. Daniel V. Scott, M.S.

WETHERSFIELD. *Connecticut Department of Correction*, 24 Wolcott Hill Rd., 06109-1152. Tel: 860-692-7577. Rev. Anthony J. Bruno, Dir. Religious Svcs.

Special and other Archdiocesan Assignment:
Rev. Msgrs.—
Bergin, Robert D., Deaf Apostolate, Mercyknoll, 243 Steele Rd., West Hartford, 06117. Dir.
Ginty, Thomas M., 467 Bloomfield Ave., Bloomfield, 06002. Sec. to the Archbishop, Chancellor, Dir. Office for Divine Worship
Liptak, David Q., "The Catholic Transcript", 785 Asylum Ave., 06105. Editor
Motta, Michael J., Dir., Office of Religious Education, 650 Willard Ave., Newington, 06111.
Schmitz, Gerard G., St. Thomas Seminary, 467 Bloomfield Ave., Bloomfield, 06002. Vicar for Priests & Dir., Vocations
Walker, David M., Dir., Catholic Cemeteries Assoc., P.O. Box 517,, North Haven, 06473-0517.
Revs.—
Couturier, George M., St. Thomas Seminary, 467 Bloomfield Ave., Bloomfield, 06002. Office of Ministry for Priests; Coord., Office to Study Restructuring Parishes and Asst. to Vicar for Priests
Gatzak, John P., 15 Peach Orchard Rd., Prospect, 06712-1052. Exec. Dir., Office of Communications (Radio/Television)
Kinnane, James F., 134 Farmington Ave., 06105-3784. Vicar for Religious and Adjutant Judicial Vicar
Kriss, Zigford J., 467 Bloomfield Ave., Bloomfield, 06002. Supt. of Schools
McLean, Edward J., Catholic Library and Information Center, 125 Market St., 06103. Dir.
Monnerat, Brian W., Propagation of the Faith, 467 Bloomfield Ave., Bloomfield, 06002-2999.
Tucker, Robert F., Office of Minister for Priests, 467 Bloomfield Ave., Bloomfield, 06002-2999.
Vargo, Robert B., J.C.L., Judical Vicar(Officalis), Chancery, 134 Farmington Ave., 06105-3784.

On Duty Outside the Archdiocese:
Rev. Msgr.—
Sokolowski, Robert S., Catholic University of America, School of Philosophy, Washington, DC 20064.
Revs.—
Birmingham, Robert F. (Retired), P.O. Box 177, Shenorock, NY 10587.
Charbonneau, William R., HGB/HC, 1411 Jefferson Davis Hwy., Ste. 9502, Arlington, VA 22202-3231.
Cwiekowski, Frederick J., S.S., S.T.D. (SFR), St. Patrick Seminary, 320 Middlefield Rd., Menlo Park, CA 94025.
Dietrich, John J., Mt. St. Mary Seminary, Emmitsburg, MD 21727-7797.
Leavitt, Robert F., S.S., St. Mary Seminary, 5400 Roland Ave., Baltimore, MD 21210.
Malave, Will-Roger, St. Joseph Rectory, 333 N. Main St. P.O. Box 35, Amsterdam, OH 43903.
Matera, Frank J., Catholic University of America, Dept. of Theology, Washington, DC 20064.
McBrien, Richard P., University of Notre Dame, Notre Dame, IN 46556.
McKearney, James L., Casa Santa Maria, Via dell Umilta 30, Rome 00187 Italy.
Morrison, Douglas A., 24 Courthouse Sq., Apt. 805, Rockville, MD 20850-2340.
Smolenski, Stanley, 119 Broad St., Charleston, SC 29402.
Thayer, David D., S.S., Theological College of Catholic University of America, 401 Michigan Ave., N.E., Washington, DC 20064.
ViHorio, Guerrera, 25 E. 39th St., New York, NY 10016.

Military Chaplains:
Revs.—
Hanley, Dennis P., 6 ABW/HC, 2204 Administration Ave., MacDill AFB, FL 33621-5403. U.S. Air Force
Hellwig, Lee W., 91-1141 Kaileolea Dr., #3D1, Ewa Beach, HI 96706. U.S. Navy

---

Medical Leave:
Revs.—
Chow, Louis Y.
Halovatch, Paul J.
Kurnath, Joseph G.M.
Mangiafico, Paul J.
Rohan, John P.
Shanley, Matthew R.

Unassigned:
Revs.—
Burns, William L.
Hagearty, Charles B.
Kappalumakkel, Mathew

Retired:
Rev. Msgrs.—
Daly, Charles W., St. Luke Rectory, 66 Bolton St., 06114-2698.
Mullen, William J., St. Thomas Seminary, 467 Bloomfield Ave., Bloomfield, 06002.
Regan, John D., 409 A Heritage Village, Southbury, 06488.
Revs.—
Archambault, James H., 2003 49th St. W., Bradenton, FL 34209.
Bieluch, Chester A., St. Mary Home, 2021 Albany Ave., West Hartford, 06117-2701.
Birmingham, Robert F., P.O. Box 177, Shenorock, NY 10587.
Blackall, John C., 1027 Farmington Ave., West Hartford, 06107.
Blackall, Randall L., 1027 Farmington Ave., West Hartford, 06107.
Boyle, James M., St. Mary Home, 2021 Albany Ave., West Hartford, 06117-2701.
Castellani, John J., 81 Reservoir Ridge Dr., Southington, 06489-1356.
Clarkin, Herbert J., St. Mary Home, 2021 Albany Ave., West Hartford, 06117.
Colton, Bradford, Corpus Christi Rectory, 84 Somerset St., 06109.
Cook, John P., Mercyknoll, 243 Steele Rd., West Hartford, 06117.
Cronin, W. Vincent, St. Mary Home, 2021 Albany Ave., West Hartford, 06117.
Croteau, Francois A., St. Mary Home, 2021 Albany Ave., West Hartford, 06117.
Crowley, Stephen L., 156 Circular Ave., Hamden, 06514.
Daily, Leo J., Our Lady of Fatima Rectory, 382 Hope Hill Rd., Yalesville, 06492.
DeCarolis, Vito C., Box 1325, Union City, 06770.
DeMuro, S. Patrick, 31 Northside Dr., Torrington, 06790.
Dery, Henry R., St. Thomas Seminary, 467 Bloomfield Ave., Bloomfield, 06002.
Dilion, Joseph A., 13 Leeway Dr., Westbrook, 06498.
Donahue, Joseph P., 2513 Lakeville Dr., Vienna, VA 22181.
Emerling, James R., 376 Goshen Rd., Torrington, 06790.

Fiedorczyk, Henry P., Sacred Heart Rectory, 158 Broad St., New Britain, 06053.
Flynn, Joseph A., 7 Horsepond Rd., Madison, 06443.
Frisbie, Kenneth J., St. Thomas Seminary, 467 Bloomfield Ave., Bloomfield, 06002.
Gengras, Joseph C., St. Thomas Seminary, 467 Bloomfield Ave., Bloomfield, 06002.
Giusani, Augustine H., St. Ann, 47 Clark St., New Britain, 06051.
Graziani, Joseph A., 380 Lake Plymouth Blvd., Plymouth, 06728.
Hannon, John P., 64 Pearl St., Enfield, 06082.
Hayes, William J., The Lodge, 50 Cold Spring Rd., #328, Rocky Hill, 06067. Tel: 860-721-1940
Heinrich, Harold D., 216 Bristol St., Southington, 06489.
Hussey, Dennis R., 7 Brookwood Dr., Branford, 06405.
Hyland, Edward F., 272 Todd Rd., Wolcott, 06716.
Jaenicke, Alfred J., Sacred Heart Sagrado Corazon Rectory, 13 Wolcott St., Waterbury, 06702-1790.
Johnson, Daniel E., Resurrection, 115 Fond Hill Rd., Wallingford, 06492.
Kaminski, Ladislaus J., St. Lucian's Residence, 532 Burritt St., New Britain, 06503.
Karvelis, Francis V., 14 Deepwood Dr., Southington, 06489-3442.
Keating, Joseph H., 574 Easton St., New Haven, 06513.
Killeen, Bernard D., Holy Infant Rectory, 450 Race Brook Rd., Orange, 06477-2599.
Krupnik, Marion I., 548 Eddy GloverBlvd., New Brirain, 06053.
Ladamus, Robert G., 38 Marshall St., Milford, 06460.
Ladish, Robert W., 255 W. Shore Rd., New Preston, 06777.
Laliberte, George G., 948 Villeroy Greens Dr., Sun City Center, FL 33573.
LeClair, Lawrence J., Spring Lake Village, 661 Ledgeview Ct., Southington, 06489.
Lynch, John K., 211 Wintonburg Ave., Bloomfield, 06002.
Malley, Michael A., 9 Sunset Ave., Terryville, 06786.
Maynard, Leo E., 123 Maple St., Somers, 06071.
McCarthy, Thomas E., St. Ann Rectory, 289 Arch Rd., Avon, 06001.
McDonald, John F., St. Thomas Seminary, 467 Bloomfield Ave., Bloomfield, 06002.
McGrath, Robert D., 873 Durham Rd. Madison, 06443.
McGrath, William E., St. Christopher Rectory, 538 Brewer St., East Hartford, 06118-2399.
Mitchell, Peter G., 30 Woodland St. #11-P, 06105.
Montgomery, Joseph T., 30 Royal Oak Rd., 06053.
Moskus, John T., 42 Maplewood Ave., Storrs Mansfield, 06268.
Murphy, Joseph G., The McAuley, 275 Steele Rd., B312, West Hartford, 06117.
O'Connell, John B., St. Joseph Residence, 1365 Enfield St., Enfield, 06082.
O'Leary, Donald J., St. Aloysius Rectory, 254 Burritt St., Plantsville, 06479.
Paul, Raymond F., 314 Osgood Ave., Ansonia, 06053.
Pepe, Mario P., St. Mary Home, 2021 Albany Ave., West Hartford, 06117-2701.
Pettit, Joseph H., 433 Lakeview Dr., Southington, 06489.
Ptaszynski, Stephen F., 90 Wolcott St., Box 1271, Bristol, 06011-1271.
Quinn, Thomas P., 218 Mountain Rd., Windsor, 06095.
Raffaeta, George J., St. Agnes Rectory, 400 Merwin Ave., Milford, 06460.
Raneri, Carmine B., St. Gregory the Great, 235 Maltby St., Bristol, 06010-3892.
Rikteraitis, John E., 1039 Maple Ave, P.O. Box 341361, 06134-1361.
Rush, James C., 161 Brunswick Ave., West Hartford, 06107-1715.
Russo, Robert T., 55 Park Hill, Broad Brook, 06016-9740.
Shaw, Charles E., P.O. Box 10158, Phoenix, AZ 85064.
Sherer, Richard B., 40 Niantic Rive Rd., Waterford, 06385.
Sheridan, Philip A., St. Joseph Manor, 20 Carmel Ridge Estates, Trumbull, 06611-2072.
Sikora, Stanley J., St. Thomas Seminary, 467 Bloomfield Ave., Bloomfied, 06002-2999.
Smith, William C., 82 W. Rocks Rd., Norwalk, 06851.
Speer, Patrick J., St. Joseph Manor, 6448 Main St., Trumbull, 06611.
Spodnik, A. Leo, P.O. Box 456, Higganum, 06441.
Stack, John J., St. Thomas the Apostle, 872 Farmington Ave., West Hartford, 06107.
Testa, Genaro J., 5233 S.W. 11th Ct., Cape Coral, FL 33914
Thuer, William J., Visitation Plaza, 100 Jefferson Sq., Apt. 6-A, Waterbury, 06706. (Mailing Address: P.O. Box 1027, Woodbury, CT 06798)
Toscano, Pasquale A., St. Joseph Residence, 1365 Enfield St., Enfield, 06082-4900.
Tracy, John P., St. Thomas Seminary, 467 Bloomfield Ave. Bloomfield, 06002.
Ventura, Anthony C., St. Thomas Seminary, 467 Bloomfield Ave., Bloomfield, 06002.
Vichas, Walter A., P.O. Box 92, Watertown, 06795.
Wrenn, Lawrence G., Cathedral of St. Joseph Rectory, 140 Farmington Ave., 06105.
Zanavich, Albert J., Assumption Rectory, 61 N. Cliff St., Ansonia, 06401.
Ziezulewicz, George F., 5 Whitewood Rd., Killingworth, 06419.

Permanent Deacons:
Abdalla, John, (Retired)
Aconfora, Ralph A., (Retired)
Albert, Roger R., St. Gregory the Great, Bristol
Angeloni, Carmine, (Retired)
Anthony, Andrew, (Retired)
Arena, Paul, Leave of Absence
Azzaro, Gabriel S., (Retired)
Bailey, Thomas
Bandeira, Francis, St. Anne, Waterbury
Bartlett, William H., St. Mary, East Hartford, 06108.
Bartlett, William, Jr., (Retired)
Battiston, Donald, (Retired)
Baxter, Wesley F., St. Thomas, Southington
Beecher, Stephen M., St. Bridget, Corwall Bridge and St. Bernard, Sharon
Bergers, William, (Retired)
Bernd, Robert E., St. Martha, Enfield
Bevvino, Frank J., St. John Vianney, West Haven and Our Lady of Victory, West Haven
Biamonte, Ronald, St. Joseph, Poquonock
Bichi, Americo, (Retired)
Blair, Robert N., Immaculate Conception, New Hartford
Borland, Joseph P., Assumption, Woodbridge
Brady, John F., Jr., Assumption, Ansonia
Breen, Thomas F., III, Sacred Heart, St. Justin and Michael, Hartford
Brown, George S., (Retired)
Brown, William J., St. James, Manchester
Brunell, Robert J., St. Brendan, New Haven and St. Aedan, New Haven
Camerota, Daniel A., St. John the Evangelist, Watertown
Campbell, Alan D., St. Ann, Avon
Cardona Raul, St. Mary, New Britain
Carrero, Adolfo G., St. Augustine, Hartford
Cassidy, Vincent, (Retired)
Charles, John H., St. John the Evangelist, Watertown
Chope, Robert C.
Clifford, Thomas J., St. Hedwig, Union City and St. Stanislaus, Waterbury
Colella, Charles, SS. Peter and Paul, Waterbury
Conard, Leo B., Immaculate Heart of Mary, Harwinton
Conklin Thomas J., St. Margaret Mary, South Windsor
Conte, John J.M., Jr., Assumption, Woodbridge
Cooke, Joseph J., (Retired)
Coppola, Angelo J., St. Aloysius, Plantsville
Cornell Thomas
Cote, Laurent L., St. Anthony, Bristol
Coyne, Joseph F., St. Elizabeth, Branford and St. Clare East Haven
Cretella, Joseph J., Jr., St. Barnabas, North Haven
Croll, Calvin S., St. Gabriel, Milford
Crowley, John, St. Dominic, Southington
Cruess Donald E., (Retired)
Culhane, Neil, St. John of the Cross, Middlebury
Cunniff, Charles E., Jr., (Retired)
D'Eferria, Robert J., Incarnation, Wethersfield
Daigle, Ronald R., St. Francis of Assisi, South Windsor
DeFilippo, Salvatore A., St. Louis, West Haven
DeHippolytis, Albert J., SS. Peter and Paul, Waterbury
DeJesus, Isidiro, Sacred Heart, St. Justin and St. Michael, Hartford
DelCorte, Nicholas, (Retired)
Delehanty, Thomas F., St. Catherine of Siena, West Simsbury
Delgado, Domingo, St. Lawrence O'Toole, Hartford
Delmonte, Richard F., (Retired)
Dembishack, John L., Sacred Heart and St. Peter, Torrington
Dempsey, John F., St. Augustine, Hartford
Dickman, Arthur J., Holy Family, Enfield
Dickson, Edward, St. Francis of Assisi, Torrington and St. Mary, Torrington
Dietsch, Charles C., Sacred Heart, Southbury
DiMauro, Joseph, (Retired)
Dinkle, George J., St. Anthony, Prospect
Diorio, Nicholas J., St. Thomas, Goshen
DiPiro, Joseph L., (Retired)
DiRienzo, Mario, Holy Rosary, Ansonia
DiSalvo, Aldo
Dlugokinski, Jose L., St. Thomas, Thomaston
DosSantos, Kenneth, St. Thomas Villanova, Goshen
Doyle, Henry, St. Gabriel, Milford
Driscoll, Frank M., Unassigned
Dudzic, Anthony
Dungan, Roy C., St. Stanislaus, Bristol
Elder, William A., St. George, Guilford
English, Seth M., Corpus Christi, Wethersfield
Eschrich, Paul C., (Retired)
Eyles, William H., St. Vincent de Paul, East Haven
Falbo, Anthony
Farrell, William A., St. Patrick, Farmington
Fiederlein, Frank H., (Retired)
Firth, John
Fitzgerald, Robert W., (Retired)
Florio, Louis J., St. Therese, North Haven
Fournier, Richard G., St. Paul, West Haven
Fracasso, Robert G., (Retired)
Fugere, Raymond J., St. Mark the Evangelist, West Hartford
Fusco, Louis P., St. Monica, Northford
Gabriele, Joseph G., (Retired)
Gale, Robert P., Our Lady of Mt. Carmel, Meriden and Laurent, Meriden
Gallucci, Donald
Genovese, Nicholas A., St. Agnes, Woodmont
Geraci, Gerald S., St. Joseph and St. Peter, New Britain
Giaimo, Thomas, Clelian Adult Day Care, Hamden
Giard, Edward J., St. Bartholomew, Manchester
Gilles, William J., St. Christopher, East Hartford
Giusto, Oreste M., (Retired)
Gluhosky, Frank
Godlewsky, Robert H., (Retired)
Gonzalez, Ricardo
Gordon, Robert D., Unassigned
Gosselin, Raymond
Grant, Frederick M., (Retired)
Griffin, Wayne F., Resurrection, Wallingford
Gurr, Ronald, St. John the Baptist, New Haven
Guzzardi, Carmelo A., St. Paul, Kensington
Hajjar, George D., St. Michael, Waterbury
Hart, John L., St. Augustine, North Branford
Hayden, Bernard J., Holy Infant, Orange
Healy, Timothy E., St. Patrick, Collinsville
Hernandez, Carmelo, Our Lady of Sorrows, Hartford
Hickey, James E., Jr., St. Luke, Hartford
Higgs, Kenneth
Hilliard, Robert J., St. Helena, West Hartford
Hoffman, Harold, Holy Infant, Orange
Iadarola, Paul P., St. Margaret, Waterbury
Iassogna, Nicholas J., Jr., St. Francis of Assisi, Naugatuck
Impellitteri, Michael, Sr., (Retired)
Jacobs, James
Jacques, J. Martin, (Retired)
Johnson, Robert C., St. Mary, Derby
Johnson, Thomas F., St. Patrick, Waterbury
Kane, Joseph E., (Retired)
Kelly, Stephen J., St. Pius X, Wolcott
Kieda, Rene J., St. Margaret Mary, South Windsor
Kimball, Earle A., St. Mary, Union City
Klein, Peter J., Jr., St. Paul, Glastonbury; St. Augustine, South Glastonbury
Klimanowski, Peter J., Our Lady of Sorrows, Hartford
Koch, Paul T., St. Joan of Arc, Hamden
Krasnicki, Frank J., Good Shepherd, Seymour
Kraussman, George A., (Retired)
Krikawa, Joseph
Kulas, Michael J., Sacred Heart, Southbury
Kulas, Paul J., Mary Our Queen, Plantsville
Kwon, Peter
Lafleur, Carl
Lambert, Robert E., St. Adalbert, Enfield
LaPierre, Joseph W., Our Lady of Pompeii, East Haven
LaRocque, Leo R., St. Joseph, Poquonock
Lauer, Paul B., St. Mary, Milford
Lavoie, Joseph V., (Retired)
LeBlanc, Gaspard D., St. Anne, Waterbury
Lembo, Victor M., St. Michael, Beacon Falls
Lepkowski, Henry M., (Retired)
Levesque, Joseph J., (Retired)
Lewandoski, Leonard R., St. Stanislaus, Bristol
Lickwar, R. Carl, St. Ann, New Britain
Linehan, F. Robert, (Retired)
Lopatosky, Thomas J., (Retired)
Lotto, Henry, St. Francis, New Haven
Lovelace, William, St. Augustine, North Branford
Lovetre, Arthur
Lowe, Burdon G., (Retired)
Lozier, Albert J., St. Ann, Bristol

Maffeo, John R., St. Anthony of Padua, Litchfield
Mahoney, Patrick
Makara, John W., Immaculate Conception & St. Casimir, Terryville
Mancini, Edward J., St. Louis, West Haven
Marcarelli, Julius R., St. Rose of Lima, New Haven
McGivney, Raymond J., Jr., (Unassigned)
McGrath, William M., Blessed Sacrament, Waterbury
McInnis, John P., (Retired)
McKaig, John W., St. John Fisher, Marlborough
Michaele, Adam J., St. George, Guilford
Midwood, Barry
Miller, Roland G., Our Lady of Perpetual Help, Washington Depot
Mingrone, William F., (Retired)
Mitchell, Richard
Moemeka, Andrew A., St. Brigid, Elmwood
Monahan, William
Morales, Jose A., (Retired)
Moran, Patrick T., St. Margaret, Madison
Motto, Vincent J., St. Catherine, Broad Brook
Muro, Robert E., Sr., Our Lady of the Lakes, New Milford
Murray, Thomas
Mylott, John J., St. Ann, Avon
Navickas, Robert D., St. Therese, Granby
Nebiolo, Eugene, (Retired)
Neris, Susano
Newbery, Robert D., St. Therese, Granby
Nolan, Terence M., St. Teresa, Woodbury
Norton, Donald E., St. Mary, Windsor Locks
Nwanko, Anthony, St. Timothy, West Hartford
O'Connell, Cornelius D., Sacred Heart, Wethersfield
O'Connor, Martin J., St. Bernadette, New Haven
O'Donovan, John, Our Lady of Mt. Carmel, Hamden
O'Neill, James F., (Retired)
O'Toole, Michael J., (Retired)
Ortiz, Edwin, Leave of Absence
Ortiz, Jacinto, St. Rose of Lima, Meriden
Pahl, John E., St. Matthew, Forestville
Pallotti, Robert M., St. Joseph, Bristol
Pantalena, Edward J., (Retired)
Parenteau, Raymond A., Our Lady of Peace, East Hartford
Parkinson, William H., St. Aedan and St. Brendan, New Haven
Parlee, Charles, St. John Vianney & Our Lady of Victory, West Haven
Perez, Valentin, St. Augustine, Hartford
Pettinico, George, St. Mary Magdalen, Oakville
Phaneuf, Eugene E., (Retired)
Poland, James K., (Retired)
Polansky, Daniel W., Nativity, Bethlehem
Pond, Donald H., Jr., St. Bernard, Enfield
Poulin, Gerald
Prete, Paul V., St. Margaret, Madison
Puskas, George A., Christ the Redeemer, Milford
Quinn, James P., Mary Our Queen, Plantville
Ramos, Edmund J., St. Ann, Milford
Regan, Joseph M., Jr., St. Margaret, Madison
Renker, Richard E., St. Augustine, Seymour
Rescildo, Ralph, St. Teresa, Woodbury
Richter, Neil B., Immaculate Conception, Southington
Riotte, Eugene C., St. Augustine, Seymour
Rivera, Jose A., Leave of Absence
Rivera, Pedro L., St. Anne-Immaculate Conception, Hartford
Rogers, Joseph K., (Retired)
Rogers, Thomas D., (Retired)
Rolando, Joseph E., (Retired)
Rosello, Modesto A., (Retired)
Roy, Reginald, St. Jerome, New Britain
Rubitz, Michael, Holy Cross, New Britain
Ruiz, Candelario, (Retired)
Ryan, Richard
Ryzewski, Joseph R., Blessed Sacrament, Hamden
Sabo, Paul E., Our Lady of Victory & St. John Vianney, West Haven
Sandford, Wayne E., St. Clare, East Haven & St. Elizabeth, Branford
Santello, Richard L., Dir. Office Permanent Diaconate, St. Stephen, Hamden
Scanlon, Thomas P., St. Bernard, Tariffville
Sennett, Richard M., St. Mary, Milford
Serafini, Ferdinand T., (Retired)
Shelto, Michael A., St. Elizabeth Seton, Rocky Hill
Shiels, James H., Holy Spirit, Newington
Sill, Louis P., Jr., SS. Peter and Paul, Wallingford
Singer, Norman H., St. Mary, Branford
Skipp, Barry T., Sacred Heart, Bloomfield
Sloan, Daniel A., (Retired)
Sloan, Joseph S., St. Martha, Enfield
Smith, Donald H., Holy Angels, South Meriden
Solli, Anthony P., St. Lawrence, West Haven
Sponzo, Michael T., (Retired)
Stadtlander, Hobart, (Retired)
Stanley, James H., Our Lady of Mt. Carmel, Hamden
Stephens, George R., St. Francis Cabrini, North Haven
Stolfi, Domenic N., St. Anthony, Prospect
Streib, George H., St. Francis Xavier, New Milford
Sullivan, Joseph, Holy Infant, Orange
Sutak, Thomas S., St. Mary, Unionville
Suzio, John J., (Retired)
Sweeney, John M., St. Mary, Simsbury
Szewczyk, Edward J., St. Joseph, Suffield
Szumigala, Michael P., St. Matthew, Forestville
Taddei, Edward D., (Retired)
Talbot, Oral A., (Retired)
Tanski, William J., St. Dunstan, Glastonbury
Tartaris, Robert P., St. Mary, Branford
Taylor, James P., Our Lady of Fatima, Yalesville
Thayer, John E., St. Mary, New Britain
Thompson, Bruce R., St. Mary, Newington
Thorney, Vincent M., (Retired)
Tolassi, Bernard
Tomasiello, Frank R., (Retired)
Tripp, James A., Sr., St. Joan of Arc, Hamden
Twerago, John P., (Retired)
Vazquez, Julio, (Retired)
Vecca, Carl M., Immaculate Conception, Waterbury
Violette, Carroll, Unassigned
Wallin, Robert F., SS. Leo the Great, Waterbury
Walsh, Maurice
Walton, Gerald S., St. Therese, Branford
Weaver, Stephen L., St. Augustine, South Glastonbury; St. Paul Glastonbury
Wheeler, John E., St. Lawrence, West Haven
Wilber, Richard, St. Bridget, Cheshire
Wilcox, William H., St. Joseph, Winsted
Winiarski, Benedict L., St. Mary, Windsor Locks
Wootton, Gerald R., Immaculate Heart of Mary, Harwinton
Zammett, Anthony

INSTITUTIONS LOCATED IN THE ARCHDIOCESE

[A] SEMINARIES, ARCHDIOCESAN

BLOOMFIELD. *St. Thomas Seminary*, 467 Bloomfield Ave., 06002-2999. Tel: 860-242-5573; Fax: 860-242-4886. Email: stsggs@aol.com. Rev. Msgr. Gerard G. Schmitz, Rector & Contact. Fathers 10; Candidates for Diaconate Studies 27. In Res. Most Rev. Christie A. Macaluso, D.D.; Rev. Msgr. William J. Mullen (Retired); Revs. Henry R. Dery (Retired); Kenneth J. Frisbie (Retired); Joseph C. Gengras (Retired); John F. McDonald (Retired); Stanley J. Sikora (Retired); John P. Tracy (Retired); Anthony C. Ventura (Retired).

[B] SEMINARIES, RELIGIOUS OR SCHOLASTICATES

CHESHIRE. *Novitiate of the Legion of Christ*, 475 Oak Ave., 06410. Tel: 203-271-0805; Fax: 203-271-3845. Email: chehire@legionaries.org. Web: www.legionofchrist.org. Revs. Christopher Brackett, L.C., Rector; Kevin Lixey, L.C., Vice Rector; Anthony Bailleres, L.C., Asst. to the Natl. Dir. & Vice Rector; Julio Marti, L.C., Novice Instructor. Priests 9; Religious 8; Juniors 56; Novices 56.
Studies: Revs. Owen Kearns, L.C.; Andreas Kramarz, L.C.; Edward McImail, L.C.; Anthony Rodriguez, L.C.; Walter Schu, L.C.

[C] COLLEGES AND UNIVERSITIES

HAMDEN. *Mt. Sacred Heart College*, 265 Benham St., 06514-2801. Tel: 203-248-4225; Fax: 203-230-8341. Email: smgascj@aol.com. Sisters Clare Millea, A.S.C.J., Pres.; Mary Grace Giaimo, A.S.C.J., Dean. Chartered by the State of Connecticut for Sisters of Community of Apostles of the Sacred Heart of Jesus.

NEW HAVEN. *Albertus Magnus College*, 700 Prospect St., 06511-1189. Tel: 203-773-8550; Fax: 203-785-8652. Email: admissions@albertus.edu. Web: www.albertus.edu. Dr. Julia M. McNamara, Pres.; Dr. William C. Schulz, Vice Pres. Academic Affairs; Jeanne Mann, Treas.; Eileen Perillo, Registrar; Maureen Morrison, Dean Student Svcs. Dominican Sisters (St. Mary of the Springs, Columbus, OH) Sisters 6; Lay Teachers 31; Total Enrollment 2,222.

WEST HARTFORD. *Saint Joseph College*, 1678 Asylum Ave., 06117. Tel: 860-232-4571; Fax: 860-233-5695. Email: admissions@sjc.edu. Web: www.sjc.edu. Winifred E. Coleman, M.A., Pres.; Dr. Clark Hendley, Ph.D., Vice Pres. Academic; Dr. Maureen Reardon, Exec. Vice Pres., COO & Contact; Mary C. Demo, Dean of Students; Brenda Sebastianell, Registrar; Revs. David Cinquegrani, C.P.; Charles J. Topper, Ed.D.; Aidan Donahue, S.T.M., S.T.L. Sisters of Mercy, Women.; Chartered by the State of Connecticut.; Undergraduates: Priests 2; Sisters 13; Lay Teachers 85; Students 1,966; Women 1,175; Men 18; Graduates Coed 643; School for Young Children 160; Gengras Center for Exceptional Children 124.

[D] HIGH SCHOOLS, ARCHDIOCESAN

BRISTOL. *St. Paul Catholic High School*, 1001 Stafford Ave., 06010-3894. Tel: 860-584-0911; Fax: 860-585-8815. Web: www.stpaulchs.com. Craig Hill, Pres. & Prin.; Sharon Mielcarz, Asst. Prin. Faculty: Lay Teachers 27; Students 314.

MANCHESTER. *East Catholic High School*, 115 New State Rd., 06040. Tel: 860-649-5336; Fax: 860-649-7191. Email: pegsieg@aol.com. Web: ECHS.com. Peggy Siegmund, Prin. Sisters of Notre Dame de Namur 6; Lay Teachers 53; Students 675.

WATERBURY. *Sacred Heart High School*, 142 S. Elm St., 06722. Tel: 203-753-1605; Fax: 203-597-1686. Email: jc.jennings@snet.net sandy.murphy@snet.net. Web: sacredhearthighschool.org. Mr. Francis(Sandy) Murphy, Prin.; Mrs. Eileen Regan, Dir. Devel.; Mrs. Jacqueline Jennings, Vice Prin. Priests 1; Lay Teachers 36; Students 508.

WEST HARTFORD. *Northwest Catholic High School*, 29 Wampanoag Dr., 06117. Tel: 860-236-4221; Fax: 860-586-0911. Email: callahan@nwcath.org. Web: www.nwcath.org. Dr. Michael S. Griffin, Pres.; Mrs. Margaret R. Williamson, Prin.; Mr. Richard Callahan, Vice Prin.; Mr. John Cusson, Academic Dean. Priests 1; Lay Teachers 49; Students 625.

[E] HIGH SCHOOLS, PRIVATE

HAMDEN. *Sacred Heart Academy*, 265 Benham St., 06514-2833. Tel: 203-288-2309; Fax: 203-230-9680. Email: Principal@SHA-Excelsior.org. Web: www.sha-excelsior.org. Sr. Ritamary Schulz, A.S.C.J., Prin. & Contact. Apostles of the Sacred Heart of Jesus Sisters 4; Lay Teachers 46; Students 504.

MILFORD. *Academy of Our Lady of Mercy*, Lauralton Hall, 200 High St., 06460. Tel: 203-877-2786; Fax: 203-876-9760. Email: dkosiewicz@lauraltonhall.org. Web: www.lauraltonhall.org. Mrs. Barbara C. Griffin, Pres. & Contact. Sisters of Mercy Sisters 1; Lay Teachers 51; Students 459.

NEW MILFORD. *Canterbury School*, Aspetuck Ave., 06776-1739. Tel: 860-210-3800; Fax: 860-350-4425. Email: tsheeny@cbury.org. Web: www.cbury.org. Thomas J. Sheehy III, Headmaster; Patricia L. Hiro, Headmaster's Asst. & Contact; Rev. Sebastian Leonard, O.S.B., Chap. Coed. Boarding and day students Priests 1; Lay Teachers 69; Students 345.

WATERBURY. *Holy Cross High School*, 587 Oronoke Rd., 06708. Tel: 203-757-9248; Fax: 203-757-3423. Email: jdjbcsc@hol.com. Web: HolyCrosshs-ct.com. Bro. Jerome Donnelly, C.S.C., Chief Admin., Head of School & Contact; Mr. Timothy McDonald, Prin. Brothers of the Congregation of Holy Cross Brothers 1; Sisters 3; Lay Teachers 55; Students 810.

WEST HAVEN. *Notre Dame High School*, 24 Ricardo St., 06516. Tel: 203-933-1673; Fax: 203-933-2474. Email: ralph@notredamehs.com. Web: www.notredamehs.com. Bro. James Branigan, C.S.C., Headmaster; Mr. Ralph Proto, Prin.; Mr. Patrick Clifford, Asst. Prin. for Academics; Mr. Thomas Marcucci, Asst. Prin. for Student Life; Mr. Joseph Ramirez, Asst. Prin., Pupil Personnel Svcs.; Mrs. Gail Bellucci, Campus Min. Holy Cross Brothers Brothers 6; Sisters 2; Lay Teachers 47; Students 712.

Notre Dame Loyalty & Endowment Fund, Inc., 24 Ricardo St., 06516. Tel: 203-933-1673; Fax: 203-933-2474.

[F] ELEMENTARY SCHOOLS, PRIVATE

MADISON. *Our Lady of Mercy School, Incorporated*, 149 Neck Rd., 06443-2728. Tel: 203-245-4393; Fax: 203-245-3498. Email: office@olmschool.com. Web: olmschool.homestead.com. Francine Coss, Prin. & Contact. Sisters of Mercy 2; Lay Teachers 18; Students 178.

WEST HARTFORD. *Cedar Court School, Inc.*, 27 Park Rd., 06119. Tel: 860-523-0060; Fax: 860-523-1310. Email: thecedarcourt@juno.com. Dr. Fleming Allaire, Prin. & Contact. Sisters of St. Joseph of Chambery 10; Lay Teachers 10; Children 50.

[G] SPECIALIZED CHILD CARING HOME

NEW BRITAIN. *Marian Educational Clinic*, 314 Osgood Ave., 06053. Tel: 860-223-0501. Sr. Mary Edmunda, D.M., Dir. & Contact. Daughters of Mary of the Immaculate Conception Sisters 2.

NEW HAVEN. *St. Francis Home for Children, Inc.*, 651 Prospect St., 06511. Tel: 203-777-5513; Fax: 203-777-0644. Email: psalerno1@aol.com. Mr. Peter T.

Salerno, Exec. Dir. & Contact. Residential extended day treatment, group home, special education, and theraputic preschool. Lay Staff 135; Children 52; Extended Day Treatment 25; Preschool 25; Special Education School 70.

[H] DAY CARE CENTER

HAMDEN. *Clelian Adult Day Center*, 261 Benham St., 06514. Tel: 203-288-4151; Fax: 203-288-0551. Sr. Shawn Lyons, A.S.C.J., Dir. & Contact. Apostles of the Sacred Heart of Jesus, A day health care facility for elderly and disabled adults. Total Assisted 86; Total Staff 20.

Sacred Heart Manor Nursery and Kindergarten, 261 Benham St., 06514. Tel: 203-230-4889. Email: sealat@yahoo.com. Sr. Elaine Ann Lattanzi, Contact. Apostles of the Sacred Heart of Jesus 1; Lay Teachers 4; Students 80; Total Assisted 98.

[I] GENERAL HOSPITALS

HARTFORD. *Saint Francis Hospital and Medical Center*, 114 Woodland St., 06105-1299. Tel: 860-714-4000; Fax: 860-714-7809. Email: pastoralcare@stfranciscare.org. Web: www.stfranciscare.org. Dr. David D'Eramo, Pres. & CEO; Revs. Liam C. Casey, Dir. Pastoral Care & Chap.; Mark Bonsignore, Chap.; Thomas Puthiyadom, Chap. Licensed Beds 617; Bassinets 65; Out-Patient Visits 299,456; In-Patient Visits 28,880; Staff 3,850.

The Women's Auxiliary of Saint Francis Hospital and Medical Center Tel: 860-714-4558; Fax: 860-714-7809. Mrs. Carol Proom, Pres.

Asylum Hill Family Medicine Center, Inc. Tel: 860-714-4212; Fax: 860-714-8079.

Woodland Physician Associates, Inc.

Camillus Corporation

The One Thousand Corporation Tel: 860-714-4793.

One Thousand One Corporation

Saint Francis Hospital and Medical Center Foundation, Inc., 114 Woodland St., 06105-1299. Tel: 860-714-4901; Fax: 860-714-8069. Peter G. Kelly Esq., Pres.; Richard Popilowski, Senior Vice Pres. Philanthropy.

The Rehabilitation Hospital of Connecticut, Inc., 480 Blue Hills Ave., 06112. Tel: 860-714-4000; Fax: 860-714-8550.

NEW HAVEN. *Hospital of St. Raphael*, 1450 Chapel St., 06511. Tel: 203-789-3000; Fax: 203-789-3107. Email: jgranville@srhs.org. Web: www.srhs.org. David W. Benfer, Pres.; Sisters Joan Granville, S.C., Admin. & Contact; Colette Hanlon, S.C., Dir. Pastoral Care & Chap.; Marjorie Crean, S.C., Chap.; Revs. Chacko K. Kumplam (India), Chap.; Gregory M. Altermatt, Chap.; Augustine Mangalath (India), Chap.; Steven Voytovich, Orthodox Church in America & Chap.; William West, UCC & Chap.; Rev. Sandy Alves Belcher, Episcopal Priest & Chap.; Rabbi Steve Steinberg, Chap. Sisters of Charity (Convent Station), Legal Holdings: Saint Raphael Healthcare System; Saint Raphael Foundation, Inc.; DePaul Health Services Corporation; Saint Regis Health Center, Inc. (Nonprofit charitable corporations affiliated with the Hospital of Saint Raphael). Chaplains 9; Sisters 6; Bed Capacity 511; Bassinets 22; Patients Assisted Annually 300,000; Staff 3,500; CPE Residents 5.

Saint Regis Health Center, Inc. dba Sister Anne Virginia Grimes Health Center , 1354 Chapel St., 06511. Tel: 203-867-8300; Fax: 203-867-8370. Email: acasagrande@srhs.org. Web: www.srhs.org. Sr. Ann Casagrande, Exec. Dir. 125-bed skilled nursing facility. Annually assisted 45,000; Staff 135.

WATERBURY. *St. Mary Hospital*, 56 Franklin St., 06706. Tel: 203-574-6000; Fax: 203-597-3238. Email: community@stmh.org. Web: stmh.org. Robert P. Ritz, Pres. & CEO; Revs. Edmund Aku; Stanley R. Staron. Sisters of St. Joseph of Chambery, The Slocum Corporation-St. Mary's Hospital Foundation, Inc., Non-profit corporations for the exclusive benefit of St. Mary Hospital. Sisters 10; Bed Capacity 347; Licensed 347; Bassinets 24; Neonatal ICU 9; Patients Assisted Annually 227,562; Staff 1,825.

St. Mary's Hospital Foundation, Inc., 56 Franklin St., 06706. Tel: 203-574-6390; Fax: 203-597-3272. Margaret J. Lawlor, Vice Pres., Corporate Svcs. & Community Affairs.

Slocum Corporation, 56 Franklin St., 06706. Tel: 203-574-6000. Margaret J. Lawlor, Vice Pres., Corporate Svcs. & Community Affairs.

St. Mary's Hospital Auxiliary, 56 Franklin St., 06706. Tel: 203-597-3271. Tess Beauchomp, Pres.

[J] SPECIAL HOSPITALS

WEST HARTFORD. *Saint Agnes Home, Inc.*, 104 Mayflower St., 06110. Tel: 860-521-7516; Fax: 860-521-6160. Email: safc@aol.com. Web: www.stagnes.org. M. Keegan, Exec. Dir. For adolescent single mothers and their infants Bed Capacity 16; Patients Assisted Annually 53; Total Staff 46.

[K] HOMES FOR AGED

ENFIELD. *The Home for the Aged of the Little Sisters of the Poor* Incorporated Operating as St. Joseph's Residence 1365 Enfield St., 06082-4900 Tel: 860-741-0791; Fax: 860-741-3982. Email: enmslsp@attglobal.net. Rev. Julian Szumilo, C.M.; Sr. Margaret Hogarty, L.S.P. Little Sisters of the Poor 13; Residents 85; Senior Day Center 10; Total Assisted 85.

NEW BRITAIN. *St. Lucian's Residence, Inc.*, 532 Burritt St., 06053-3699. Tel: 860-223-2123; Fax: 860-612-0321. Email: stlucian.res.inc@snet.net. Rev. Augustine Pilatowski, O.F.M.Conv., Chap.; Halina A. Marut, Contact. Daughters of Mary of the Immaculate Conception Sisters 2; Residents 42.

Monsignor Bojnowski Manor, Inc., 50 Pulaski St., 06053. Tel: 860-229-0336; Fax: 860-229-3252. Email: dhlados@snet.net. Sr. Mary Deborah, D.M., Exec. Dir. Owned and operated by the Daughters of Mary of the Immaculate Conception. Skilled Nursing Beds 60; Total Staff 110.

WEST HARTFORD. *Saint Mary Home*, 2021 Albany Ave., 06117. Tel: 860-570-8200; Fax: 860-570-8205. Web: www.saintmaryhome.org. Mrs. Patricia Morse, Admin.; Mrs. Anne Pratson, Asst. Admin.; Mrs. Patricia Duclos-Miller, R.N., Dir. Nursing Svcs. Sisters of Mercy 5; Sisters in Res. 3; Residents 97; Patients Assisted Annually 322. In Res. Revs. Herbert Clarkin, Resident Chap.; Mario P. Pepe (Retired).

[L] HEALTH CARE CENTERS FOR AGED

WEST HARTFORD. *McAuley Center, Inc.*, 275 Steele Rd., 06117. Tel: 860-920-6300; Fax: 860-232-4077. Stephen Surprenant, Exec. Dir. & Contact. Continuing care retirement community; Sisters of Mercy. 229 residential apartment units for individuals age 62 and over. Nursing care at St. Mary's Home included.

[M] MONASTERIES AND RESIDENCES OF PRIESTS AND BROTHERS

HARTFORD. *Missionaries of LaSalette*, 915 Maple Ave., 06114-2330. Tel: 860-956-8870; Fax: 860-956-8849. Email: mlsadmin@aol.com. Web: www.lasalette.org. Revs. Dennis J. Loomis, M.S., Prov. Supr.; James H. Kuczynski, M.S., Vicar & Prov. Sec.; Rev. Peter D. Kohler, M.S., Asst.; Rev. John J. O'Neill, M.S., Asst.; Bro. Claude F. Rheaume, M.S., Pro. Treas.

Legal Title: *Missionaries of La Salette Corp.*

Legal Title: *MLS Trust* Province of Mary, Mother of the Americas, Religious Trust of the Missionaries of Our Lady of LaSalette. Priests 4.

Missionaries of LaSalette, 85 New Park Ave., 06106-2184. Tel: 860-523-8275; Fax: 860-586-0754. Revs. Richard R. Boucher, M.S., Supr. & Treas.; Salvatore D. Altavista, M.S.; William H. Crane, M.S.; Joseph A. Decoteau, M.S.; Stephen G. Dressell, M.S.; Frederick R. Flaherty, M.S.; Charles A. Gendron, M.S.; Stanley T. Kennedy, M.S.; William J. Kinney, M.S.; Maurice F. Linehan, M.S.; Alan B. McGuirk, M.S.; William W. Mulcair, M.S.; James P. Hurley, M.S.; James P. O'Reilly, M.S.; Daniel J. Scott, M.S.; John G. Toner, M.S.; Louis M. Ouellette, M.S.; Donald D. Simonds, M.S.; William D. LaFosse, M.S.; John J. McCarthy, M.S.; John P. Sullivan, M.S. Donald K. Thomas, M.S.; Roland G. Vandal, M.S. Bros. Ronald R. Beaudoin, M.S.; G. Peter Collins, M.S.; David J. Cook, M.S.; Alexander J. Delaney, M.S.; Andre J. Hamel, M.S.; Paul Maceyka, Oblate; Edmund A. Normantowicz, M.S.; Jean-Denis Roy, M.S.; Bonaventure Russell, M.S.; Francis K. Smith, M.S.; Peter P. Staskiewicz, M.S.; Alfred D. Tetrault, M.S.; Donald J Wininski, M.S. Priests 23; Brothers 12; Oblates 1.

Military Chaplains:

302 K Signer Blvd., Honolulu, HI 96818-4975. Tel: 808-449-1754. Rev. Robert F. Ippolito, M.S.

Priests-Brothers of Province Serving Abroad:

Missionaries in Argentina: Revs. Eugene P. Brennan, M.S.; Robert R. Butler, M.S.; John M. Garvey, M.S.; John F. Higgins, M.S.

Bolivia: Revs. Norman H. Butler, M.S.; James M. Weeks, M.S.

St. Anne-Immaculate Conception 820 Park St., 06106-2388. Tel: 860-728-7445; Fax: 860-728-1973. Rev. James T. Lowery, M.S.

Our Lady of Sorrows Rectory, 16 Greenwood St., 06106-2109. Tel: 860-233-4424; Fax: 860-236-0149. Revs. Joseph M. O'Neil, M.S., Co-Pastor; Francis C. Cooney, M.S., Co-Pastor.

Rome, Italy: Revs. Rene J. Butler, M.S.; Roland S. Nadeau, M.S.; Paul A. Roy, M.S.; James R. Stajkowski, M.S.

North American La Salette Mission Center, 85 New Park Ave., 06106-2184. Tel: 860-523-4017; Fax: 860-523-4074. Rev. John R. Nuelle, M.S., Dir.; Bro. Roger F. Clement, M.S., Asst.

St. Patrick-St. Anthony Friary (Holy Name Prov.) , 285 Church St., 06103-1105. Tel: 860-756-4034; Fax: 860-249-6487. Web: stpatrick-stanthony.org. Franciscan Friars

BLOOMFIELD. *Brothers of the Sacred Heart*, 1153 Blue Hills Ave., 06002-1971. Tel: 860-242-3342. Email: plgauvinsc@hotmail.com. Total in Residence 4.

CHESHIRE. *Legionaries of Christ*, 475 Oak Ave., 06410. Tel: 203-271-0805; Fax: 203-271-3845. Email: cheshire@legionaries.org. Web: www.legionofchrist.org.

393 Derby Ave., Orange, 06477. Tel: 203-795-2800; Fax: 203-795-2808.

EAST HARTFORD. *Society of Our Lady of the Most Holy Trinity*, 15 Maplewood Ave., 06108. Tel: 860-289-7916.

ENFIELD. *St. Patrick Rectory*, 64 Pearl St., 06082. Tel: 860-745-2411; Fax: 860-253-9483. Web: www.stpatrickparish.net. Rev. Richard L. Welch, C.S.S.R., J.C.D. Redemptorist Fathers and Brothers Priests 2; Brothers 1.

LITCHFIELD. *Montfort Missionaries*, 83 Montfort Rd., P.O. Box 667, 06759. Tel: 860-567-8434; Fax: 860-567-9670. Web: www.lourdes-in-litchfield.org. Revs. Thomas Poth, S.M.M., Supr. & Novice Dir.; Eugene Lynch, S.M.M., Contact; Donald Lasalle, S.M.M. Priests 3.

Lourdes in Litchfield Tel: 860-567-1041.

Legal Title: *Lourdes Shrine Guild, Inc.*

Montfort House (Center for Spiritual Renewal) Tel: 860-567-8434; Fax: 860-567-9670.

Monfort Novitiate Revs. Thomas Poth, S.M.M., Supr. & Novice Dir.; Eugene Lynch, S.M.M., Contact Person; Donald Lasalle, S.M.M. Priests 3.

MANCHESTER. *DePaul Provincial Residence* (Vincentian Fathers and Brothers) , 234 Keeney St., 06040-7048. Tel: 860-643-2828; Fax: 860-533-9462. Email: nepcm@snet.net. Very Rev. John S. Sledziona, C.M., Prov. & Contact; Revs. Roman Gorowski, C.M. (BRK), Supr.; Chester R. Mrowka, C.M., Procurator.

Legal Title: *The New England Province of the Congregation of the Mission Incorporated*

Congregation of the Mission, New England Province

Charitable Trust of the New England Province of the Congregation of the Mission

Special Assignments: Revs. Henry Czekala, C.M.; George J. Dabrowski, C.M.; Edward Gicewicz, C.M.; Casimir Kiczuk, C.M.; Anthony F. Kuzia, C.M.; Joseph C. Paciorek, C.M.; Walenty Pieczka, C.M.; Stanley Staniszewski, C.M.; Julian Szumilo, C.M.; Ronald Wiktor, C.M.; Bros. Henry Wojtkiewicz, C.M.; Joseph S. Zurowski, C.M.

St. Joseph Rectory, 32 Jewett St., Ansonia, 06401-2499. Tel: 203-734-0402; Fax: 203-734-4884.

St. Michael the Archangel Rectory: 75 Derby Ave., Derby, 06418-2098. Tel: 203-734-0005; Fax: 203-736-2044.

St. Stanislaus Rectory, 9 Eld St., New Haven, 06511-3899. Tel: 203-562-2828; Fax: 203-752-0217.

MILFORD. *Brothers of the Congregation of Holy Cross*, 400 Merwin Ave., 06460. Tel: 203-876-9355; Fax: 203-876-9355. Email: lar587@aol.com. Brothers of Holy Cross

24 Ricardo St., West Haven, 06516-2499. Tel: 203-932-2101. Bros. Thomas Gorman, C.S.C.; Benjamin Sunday, C.S.C.; Francis Ensign, C.S.C.; Theodore Oliveira, C.S.C.; William Farrell, C.S.C.

236A Cherry St., Naugatuck, 06770. Tel: 203-723-5137. Bros. Jerome Donnelly, C.S.C.; James Branigan, C.S.C.

NEW BRITAIN. *Conventual Franciscans*, 548 Burritt St., 06053-2869. Tel: 860-225-5786. Revs. Augustine Pilatowski, O.F.M.Conv., Supr., Delegate & Contact; Walter Leon Mruk, O.F.M.Conv., Chap. Daughters of Mary Motherhouse

St. Paul Friary, 479 Alling St., Kensington, 06037-2100. Tel: 860-828-0331; Fax: 860-828-7620.

NEW HAVEN. *St. Anthony Rectory*, 25 Gold St., 06519. Tel: 203-624-1418; Fax: 203-624-3420. Email: revmoffocs@aol.com. Web: www.stanthony-church.org. Missionaries of St. Charles-Scalabrinians

St. Michael Rectory, 29 Wooster Pl., 06511. Tel: 203-562-7178; Fax: 203-752-0157.

St. Mary Priory, 5 Hillhouse Ave., 06505-1202. Tel: 203-562-6193; Fax: 203-562-1273. Email: church@stmarys-priory.com. Web: www.stmarys-priory.com. Very Rev. William A. Holt, O.P., Contact. Order of Preachers (Dominicans) Total in Residence 6.

Priests of the Congregation of Holy Cross, 203 Maple St., 06511. Tel: 203-776-2405. Email: jlmyoung@pol.net. Rev. John L. Young, C.S.C.

Sacred Heart Rectory, 74 Liberty St., 06519-2299. Tel: 203-562-7592; Fax: 203-562-1737. Email: sacredheartnh@snet.net. Sons of Charity

NEW MILFORD. *Canterbury School*, Aspetuck Ave., 06776. Tel: 860-210-3832; Fax: 860-350-1120. Email: admissions@cbury.org. Web: www.cbury.org. Keith R. Holton, Contact. Benedictine Monks

NORTH GUILFORD. *Our Lady of Grace Monastery*, 11 Race Hill Rd., 06437-1099. Tel: 203-457-0599; Fax: 203-457-1948. Web: www.op-stjoseph.org/nuns/olgrace//olgrace.htm. Sr. Lee, O.P., Contact. Order of Preachers (Dominicans) Total in Residence 37.

WATERBURY. *Immaculate Conception Rectory*, 74 W. Main St., 06702. Tel: 203-574-0017; Fax: 203-756-8748. Web: www.TheImmaculate.com. Missionaries of the Holy Apostles; Oblates of Mary Immaculate;

St. Michael Rectory (Immaculate Conception Prov.) , 62 St. Michael Dr., 06704-1295. Tel: 203-753-0689; Fax: 203-573-9101. Web: www.stmichaelwtby.com.

WEST HARTFORD. *Holy Family Monastery/Retreat*, 303 Tunxis Rd., 06107. Tel: 860-521-0440; Fax: 860-521-0883 (Community); 860-521-1929. Email: holyfamilyretreat@ccprov.org. Web: www.holyfamilyretreat.org. Revs. Alexis Paul, C.P., Prov. Vicar; Ronan Callahan, C.P., Asst. Supr. Congregation of the Passion of Jesus Christ Monastery Staff: Revs. Quentin Amrhein, C.P.; Cajetan Bendernagel, C.P.; Victor Donovan, C.P.; Kiernan Earley, C.P.; Daniel Free, C.P.; Nicholas Gill, C.P.; Peter Hallisy, C.P.; Julian Morgan, C.P.; Columkille O'Grady, C.P.; Florian Pekar, C.P.; John Baptist Pesce, C.P.; Owen Sharkey, C.P.; Basil Trahon, C.P.; Simon Paul Wood, C.P.; Bros. Frederick Barton, C.P.; Louis Bouchard, C.P.; Charles Dell, C.P.; William Drotar, C.P.; Conrad Federspiel, C.P.; Louis Mitchell, C.P.; Joseph Rogers, C.P. Retreat Center: Revs. David Cinquegrani, C.P.; Alexis Paul, C.P.

WOLCOTT. *Maryknoll*, 8 S. View St., 06716. Tel: 203-879-3936.

[N] CONVENTS AND RESIDENCES FOR SISTERS

HARTFORD. *SS. Cyril & Methodius Convent*, 45 Groton St., 06106. Tel: 860-527-3775. Rev. William P. Przybylo. Felician Sisters of the Order of St. Francis of Connecticut

Dominican Oblates of Jesus, 510 New Britain Ave., 06106. Tel: 860-249-2912; 860-249-3735. Sisters 4.

Medical Mission Sisters, 92 Sherman St., 06105. Tel: 860-233-0875; Fax: 860-509-9509. Email: mms@hartsem.edu. Web: www.medicalmissionsisters.org.

Mercyhouse, 102 Putnam St., 06106-1324. Tel: 860-560-9590. Email: maryhouse6@juno.com. Sisters of Mercy of the Americas

St. Peter Convent, 11 Charter Oak Pl., 06106. Tel: 860-522-8428. Email: rsmstpeter@aol.com. Sisters of Mercy of the Americas of Connecticut, Sisters of the Blessed Korean Martyrs

Sisters of Notre Dame de Namur, 18 Dover St., 06114. Tel: 860-296-5498.
217 Laurel St., 06105. Tel: 860-246-0678.

Sisters of St. Joseph of Chambery Email: csjusa@juno.com.
27 Park Rd., West Hartford, 06119. Tel: 860-233-5126; Fax: 860-232-4649.
145 Elizabeth St., 06105. Tel: 860-523-5704.
40 Clifford St., 06114. Tel: 860-246-4086; Fax: 860-548-9635.

Formation House, 40 Clifford St., 06114. Tel: 860-246-4083.

Shalom Community, 33 Freeman St., 06114. Tel: 860-956-9247.
35B Freeman St., 06114. Tel: 860-956-9248.
35A Freeman St., 06114. Tel: 860-956-8157; Fax: 860-525-2439.
14 Ringgold St., 06114. Tel: 860-231-8272.
66 Freeman St., 06114. Tel: 860-956-1939.

Spirit of Mercy Community, 410 Campfield Ave., 06114-2807. Tel: 860-956-3030. Sisters of Mercy

BETHLEHEM. *Abbey of Regina Laudis*, 237 Flanders Rd., 06751. Tel: 203-266-7727; Fax: 203-266-5915. Web: www.abbeyofreginalaudis.com. Sisters Benedict Duss, O.S.B., Abbess Emerita; David Serna, O.S.B., Abbess & Mailing Contact. Bendictine Nuns of the Primitive Observance Professed Nuns 29; In First Vows 4; Novices 6; Postulants 1. In Res. Rev. Don Stefano Concordia, O.S.B.

St. Catherine's Convent of Mercy, 63 Crane Hollow Rd., 06751. Tel: 203-266-5411; Fax: 203-266-5421. Religious Sisters of Mercy (Alma, MI) Sisters 6.

BLOOMFIELD. *Sisters of Mercy of the Americas of Connecticut*, 5 Garrison Ter., 06002. Tel: 860-243-8524.

Sisters of Notre Dame de Namur (Connecticut Province) , 5 Garrison Ter., 06002. Tel: 860-243-8524; Fax: 860-683-1351. Email: sndbloom@aol.com. Total in Residence 3.

BRISTOL. *Queen of Apostles Provincial House*, 474 East Rd., 06010. Tel: 860-584-2138; Fax: 860-582-1119. Email: Ltflower@Erols.com. Web: queenofapostles.com. Sisters Frances Stavalo, M.P.F., Prov. Supr.; Josephine Riccio, M.P.F., Community Archivist & Contact. Religious Teachers Filippini Sisters in Diocese 15.

CHESHIRE. *Sisters of St. Joseph of Chambery*, 441 E. Mitchell Ave., 06410. Tel: 203-699-9421. Email: luscata@aol.com.

EAST HARTFORD. *Sisters of Notre Dame de Namur*, 21 Highview St., 06108. Tel: 860-289-5295.
50 Larrabee St. #F, 06108. Tel: 860-528-1024.
50 Larrabee St. #G, 06108. Tel: 860-289-2421.
52 Elms Village Rd., 06118. Tel: 860-569-0022.
908 Forbes St., 06118. Tel: 860-568-6958.

Sisters of Notre Dame de Namur, 908 Forbes St., 06118-1924. Tel: 860-568-6958. Email: ellisnd@aol.com. Total in Residence 4.

EAST HAVEN. *Provincial House*, 32 Tuttle Pl., 06512. Tel: 203-469-7872; Fax: 203-469-8819. Email: scmm_eh@snet.net.
87 Gerrish Ave., 06512. Fax: 203-468-9112.

ENFIELD. *Felician Sisters - Our Lady of the Angels*, Provincial House, 1315 Enfield St., 06082-4929. Tel: 860-745-7791; 860-745-4946; Fax: 860-741-0819. Email: cssfct@aol.com. Sr. Mary Laureann Alexandrowicz, C.S.S.F., Contact. Felician Sisters of the Order of St. Francis of Connecticut

Provincial House and Novitiate Tel: 860-745-7791; Fax: 860-741-0819. Sr. Mary Laureann Alexandrowicz, C.S.S.F., Prov. Min.; Rev. Adolphe T. Renkiewicz, Chap. Felician Sisters In Province: Professed Sisters 104.

Felician Adult Day Care, 1333A Enfield St., 06082-4929. Tel: 860-745-2542; Fax: 860-745-2542. Email: fadcmail@juno.com. Sr. Patricia Marie Iagrosso, C.S.S.F., Dir. Felician Sisters, A day respite health care facility for Caregivers of the Frail, elderly and Alzheimer Clients Total Assisted 25; Total Staff 11.

Felician Sisters Infirmary, 1315 Enfield St., 06082-4929. Tel: 860-745-0217; Fax: 860-741-6474. Email: snmfs@.att.net.

Mother Angela Residence, 1333-B Enfield St., 06082-4929. Tel: 860-745-5705. Email: angela.res@snet.net.

Child Jesus Convent, 1370 Enfield St., 06082-5526. Tel: 860-745-5847; Fax: 860-745-2010.

Enfield Montessori School, 1370 Enfield St., 06082-5526. Tel: 860-745-5847; Fax: 860-745-2010. Email: Montessori@snet.net. Sr. Mary Anastasia, C.S.S.F., Contact. Students 117.

St. Bernard Convent, 376 Hazard Ave., 06082-4709. Tel: 860-749-4214; Fax: 860-745-0167 (at school). Email: st.bernards.west@snet.net.

Little Sisters of the Poor, 1365 Enfield St., 06082-4900. Tel: 860-741-0791; Fax: 860-741-3982. Email: enmslsp@attglobal.net.

FARMINGTON. *St. Gabriel House*, 31 Colton St., 06032. Tel: 860-678-7274.

Sisters of the Cross and Passion, St. Gabriel's House, 31 Colton St., 06032. Tel: 860-678-7274; Fax: 860-677-2873. Web: www.cptryon.org/scp; passionistsisters.org. Sisters 4.

FORESTVILLE. *St. Matthew Convent*, 119 Church Ave., 06010. Tel: 860-583-2004; Fax: 860-314-1541 (School). Email: matthewct1@home.com. Sisters, Servants of the Immaculate Heart of Mary

Sisters of St. Joseph of the Third Order of St. Francis, 105 Kenney St., 06010. Tel: 860-582-1635. Email: ctmlw@aol.com. Web: ssj-tosf.org. Total in Residence 7; Total Staff 14.
82 Kenney St., 06010. Tel: 860-584-2985; Fax: 860-585-6192.

HAMDEN. *Dominican Sisters of Hope*, 1204 Whitney Ave., #217, 06517-2873. Tel: 203-248-2601.

Mary, Mother of the Church Convent, 115 Denslow Hill Rd., 06514. Tel: 203-407-1042; Fax: 203-230-9903. Sisters 4.

Mount Sacred Heart Provincial House and Novitiate, 265 Benham St., 06514. Tel: 203-248-4225; Fax: 203-230-8341. Email: smgascj@aol.com. Web: www.ascjus.org. Sisters M. Clare Millea, Prov. Supr.; Barbara Matazzaro, Vicaress. Sisters in Province 162; Resident Sisters 15.

St. Rita Convent, 30 Gillies Rd., 06517. Tel: 203-288-4707. Email: melboyle1@juno.com. Dominican Sisters (Columbus, OH)

Sisters of Mercy of the Americas of Connecticut, 2809 Whitney Ave., 06518-2544. Tel: 203-287-9017.

HARTFORD. *Sisters of Mercy of the Americas, Mercyhouse*, 102 Putnam St., 06106-1324. Tel: 860-560-9590.

LITCHFIELD. *Daughters of Wisdom*, 229 E. Litchfield Rd., 06759. Tel: 860-567-3163; Fax: 860-567-3166. Email: info@wisdomhouse.org. Web: www.wisdomhouse.org. Sisters Rosemarie Greco, D.W., Contact; Jo-Ann Iannotti, O.P.

MADISON. *Sisters of Mercy of the Americas of Connecticut*, 149 Neck Rd., 06443. Tel: 203-245-4261. Email: emmanuel115@juno.com.

Sisters of St. Joseph of Brentwood, 62 Kelsey Pl., 06443. Tel: 203-245-1329.

MANCHESTER. *Assumption Convent*, 21 S. Adams St., 06040. Tel: 860-643-0452; Fax: 860-643-0559. Email: mothermarymark@assumption-parish.com. Web: www.assumption-parish.com. Sr. Mary Mark, S.C.M.C., Contact. Sisters of Charity of Our Lady, Mother of the Church

Sisters of Notre Dame de Namur, 9 Plano Pl., 06040-4907. Tel: 860-647-8544. Email: frandall01@aol.com. Web: www.snadden.org. Total in Residence 1.

Sisters of St. Joseph of Chambery, 572F Hilliard St., 06040. Tel: 860-645-9750. Email: stjoan@juno.com.
572 F Hilliard St., 06040. Tel: 860-645-9750.

MERIDEN. *Generalate and Motherhouse of the Franciscan Sisters of the Eucharist*, 405 Allen Ave., 06451. Tel: 203-238-2243; Fax: 203-237-3734. Email: fseinfo@fsecommunity.org. Web: fsecommunity.org. Sisters Suzanne Gross, F.S.E., Contact; Rosemae Pender, F.S.E., Mother Gen. Legal Title: *Franciscan Sisters of the Eucharist, Inc.* The Institute of the Franciscan Sisters of the Eucharist Professed 24; Novices 2.
275 Finch Ave., 06451. Tel: 203-238-2400; Fax: 203-237-3739.
269 Finch Ave., 06451. Tel: 203-630-1771; Fax: 203-630-1776.

St. Joseph Convent, 19 Goodwill Ave., 06451. Tel: 203-235-8551. Email: stjosephconvent4@cox.net.

Mt. Carmel Convent, 109 Goodwill Ave., 06451. Tel: 203-235-3622. Sr. Matthew Maria Rancilio, A.S.C.J. Apostles of the Sacred Heart of Jesus

St. Stanislaus Convent, 70 Akron St., 06450. Tel: 203-237-1559. Sr. Laura Nowakowski, S.S.J.-T.O.S.F., Contact. Sisters of St. Joseph of the Third Order of St. Francis, Sisters of Mercy

Ursuline Sisters of the Congregation of Tildonk, Belgium, 64 Springdale Ave., 06451. Tel: 203-686-1702.

MILFORD. *Sisters of Mercy of the Americas of Connecticut*, 23 Jones Ct., 06460. Tel: 203-877-1171. Email: Patsio@aol.com.

St. Mary Convent, 74 Gulf St., 06460. Tel: 203-874-8427.

NEW BRITAIN. *Cana*, 1190 Slater Rd., 06053-1614. Tel: 860-826-1655. Sisters of St. Joseph of Chambery Total in Residence 2.

St. Francis of Assisi Convent, School Sisters of Notre Dame, 1757 Stanley St., 06053. Tel: 860-225-7143. Email: stfrancis@snet.net. Sisters 2.

Holy Cross Convent, 225 Farmington Ave., 06053-2929. Tel: 860-229-0677; Fax: 860-225-5073. Email: marlenepearl123@aol.com. Sisters of St. Joseph of the Third Order of St. Francis

Motherhouse of Daughters of Mary of the Immaculate Conception, 314 Osgood Ave., 06053. Tel: 860-225-9406; Fax: 860-225-4321. Web: www.crossfire.org/daughtersofmary. Sisters Mary Mark Pizzotti, D.M., Supr. Gen.; Mary Clare, D.M., Sec. & Contact; Rev. Walter Leon Mruk, O.F.M.Conv., Chap. Tel: 860-225-5786. Daughters of Mary of the Immaculate Conception Sisters in Community 52; Residence at the Motherhouse 19.

Sacred Heart Convent, 23 Orange St., 06053. Tel: 860-225-3989.

Msgr. Bojnowski Manor, 50 Pulaski St., 06053. Tel: 860-229-0336; Fax: 860-229-3252.

St. Lucian Home, 532 Burritt St., 06053. Tel: 860-223-2123; Fax: 860-612-0321.

Marian Educational Clinic, 314 Osgood Ave., 06053. Tel: 860-223-0501.

Sisters of Mercy of the Americas, 37 Carlton St., 06053. Tel: 860-229-7575.

The Sisters of St. Francis of Philadelphia, 15 Wilcox St., 06051. Tel: 860-229-0463; Fax: 860-242-8683. Email: lmann@adh-ocs.org.

Sisters of the Cross and Passion, 25 Streamside Ln., 06052. Tel: 860-224-1193.

NEW HARTFORD. *Missionary Servants of the Most Blessed Trinity*, 595 Town Hill Rd., 06057. Tel: 860-379-4329; Fax: 860-379-4329. Email: amgmsbt@juno.com. Total in Residence 2.

NEW HAVEN. *St. Brendan Convent*, 455 1/2 Whalley Ave., 06511. Tel: 203-787-4631; Fax: 203-785-1781. Email: marineap@hotmail.com. Sisters of Our Lady of the Garden

Dominican Sisters, St. Mary's Convent, 15 Lincoln St., 06511. Tel: 203-865-7305.

St. Joseph Convent, 135 Edwards St., 06511. Tel: 203-562-9202; Fax: 203-562-4042. Email: peggy.sause@juno.com. Web: www.columbusdominicans.org.
15 Lincoln St., 06511. Tel: 203-865-7305. Email: melboyle1@juno.com.
1914 Chapel St., 06515. Tel: 203-389-9428.

Albertus Magnus College, 790 Prospect St., 06511. Tel: 203-777-7484; Fax: 203-773-3117.

Sisters of Charity of St. Elizabeth, Convent Station,

1450 Chapel St., 06511. Tel: 203-789-4172; 203-789-3402; 203-789-3283; 203-789-4194; 203-789-4198.
480 Central Ave., 06515. Tel: 203-397-5243.
80 Whittier Ave., 06515. Tel: 203-389-4400.
Sisters of Notre Dame de Namur
311 Eastern St. #917E, 06513. Tel: 203-469-8385.
83 Porter St., 06519-5528. Tel: 203-498-9569.
Sisters of St. Joseph of Chambery, 83 Porter St., 06519. Tel: 203-498-9569.
St. Mary's Convent, 15 Lincolan St., 06511. Tel: 203-865-7305. Email: melboylel@juno.com. Dominican Sisters (Columbus, OH)

NEWINGTON. *Sisters of Notre Dame de Namur*, 42 E. Robbins Ave., 06111.

NORTH GUILFORD. *Monastery of Our Lady of Grace*, 11 Race Hill Rd., 06437-1099. Tel: 203-457-0599; Fax: 203-457-1248. Web: op-stjoseph.org/nuns/olgrace/olgrace.htm. Dominican Contemplative Nuns (Cloistered). Professed Sisters 39.
A contemplative community with solemn vows and papal enclosure. Perpetual Adoration. Sr. Lee, O.P., J.C.L., Prioress & Contact; Rev. Thomas B. Confer, O.P., Chap.
Dominican Contemplative Nuns (Cloistered). Sr. Lee, O.P., Prioress & Contact; Rev. Thomas B. Confer, O.P., Chap. Tel: 203-562-6193.

NORTH HAVEN. *St. Francis Cabrini Convent*, 94 Chapel Hill Rd., 06473. Tel: 203-239-8012; Fax: 203-239-8012. Sisters of the Sacred Heart of Jesus of Ragura Total in Residence 4.

SUFFIELD. *St. Joseph Convent*, 156 S. Main St., 06078. Tel: 860-668-2503.

TERRYVILLE. *Daughters of Wisdom*
Our Lady of Province, 41 Allen St., 06786-6301. Tel: 860-582-7676.

TORRINGTON. *St. Francis of Assisi Convent* 93 Marcia Dr., 06790. Tel: 860-489-7405; Fax: 860-482-1972. Email: shmclark@mwisp.net elrrsm@mwisp.net. Sisters of Mercy of the Americas of Connecticut Sisters 2.
St. Peter Convent, 25 St. John Pl., 06790. Tel: 860-489-4035. Email: spsweb@snet.net. Religious Teachers Filippini

WALLINGFORD. *Holy Trinity Convent*, 247 S. Main St., 06492. Tel: 203-265-6999; Fax: 203-294-4983. Sisters of Mercy of the Americas of Connecticut, Sisters of Notre Dame de Namur

WATERBURY. *Anawim Community*, 129 Grandview Ave., 06708. Tel: 203-753-0867. Email: chuot2@juno.com. Daughters of the Holy Spirit
92 Bucks Hill Rd., 06704. Tel: 203-754-0844.
Holy Land Convent, 60 Slocum St., 06706. Tel: 203-755-2456. Religious Teachers Filippini
St. Mary Hospital, 56 Franklin St., 06706-1200. Tel: 203-574-6455. Sr. Patricia Corcoran, C.S.J., Contact. Sisters of St. Joseph of Chambery
284 Windy Dr., 06705-2543. Tel: 203-574-6374.
31 Marita Dr., 06705-2527. Tel: 203-574-6482.
Maryknoll Sisters of St. Dominic, 55 Cole St., 06706. Tel: 203-754-2913. Total in Residence 8.
Notre Dame Convent, 119 Southmayd Rd., 06705. Tel: 203-753-1095; Fax: 203-753-4431. Sr. Edith Laflamme, C.N.D., Contact. Sisters of the Congregation of Notre Dame Sisters 3.
587 Oronoke Rd., 06708. Tel: 203-755-8828. Sisters 8.
28 Devon Wood Dr., 06708. Tel: 203-753-3073. Sisters 2.
Sisters of Charity of St. Elizabeth, Convent Station
100 Jefferson Sq. #6H, 06706. Tel: 203-596-1331.
Sisters of Mercy of the Americas, 1054 Meriden Rd., 06705-3137. Tel: 203-753-3507.
Visitation Plaza, 100 Jefferson Sq. #7J, 06706. Tel: 203-755-7236.
36 Irving St. #2, 06710. Tel: 203-753-4503.
Sisters of Notre Dame de Namur, 131 Herschel Ave., 06708. Tel: 203-757-1444; Fax: 860-945-0892.
38 Summer St., 06704. Tel: 203-755-0012.
28 Devin Wood Dr., 06708. Tel: 203-753-3073.

WATERTOWN. *St. John the Evangelist Convent*, 9 Academy Hill, 06795-2101. Tel: 860-274-1820; Fax: 860-945-6418. Email: bvaluckas@cs.com. School Sisters of Notre Dame Sisters 3.

WEST HARTFORD. *Convent of Mary Immaculate, Provincial House of the Sisters of St. Joseph of Chambery* (North American Province) , 27 Park Rd., 06119. Tel: 860-233-5126; Fax: 860-232-4649. Email: csjusa@juno.com. Sisters Sally Hodgdon, C.S.J., Prov.; Presentation Hoye, C.S.J., Contact.
Legal Title: *The Sisters of St. Joseph Corporation* Sisters of St. Joseph of Chambery, In Community: Professed Sisters 153.
Religious Trust of the Sisters of St. Joseph of Chambery (the "Trust")
Saint Mary Home, 2021 Albany Ave., 06117. Tel: 860-570-8200; Fax: 860-570-8205. Web: www.saintmaryhome.org.
Mercyknoll, Incorporated, 243 Steele Rd., 06117. Tel: 860-236-3503; Fax: 860-233-1737. Email: amanning-mk@mchct.org. Anne Manning Admin. & Contact; Rev. Msgr. Robert D. Bergin, Chap. Sisters of Mercy of the Americas, Connecticut Regional Community, A retirement and health care facility for the Sisters of Mercy; skilled nursing open to all. Bed Capacity 88; Skilled Nursing 59; RHNS 1; HFA 29.
Sisters of Mercy of the Americas, 249 Steele Rd., 06117-2796. Tel: 860-232-8602; Fax: 860-233-0065. Email: sistersofmercy@rsmct.org. Patricia Pelletier, Contact. Connecticut Regional Community.
Mercy Administrative Office, 249 Steele Rd., 06117-2796. Tel: 860-232-8602; Fax: 860-233-0065. Email: sistersofmercy@rsmct.org. Sr. Eileen Dooling, R.S.M., Regl. Pres. Sisters in Community 168.
Sisters of Mercy of the Americas of Connecticut, 132 Milton St., 06119-1218. Tel: 860-523-0707.
St. Joseph College, Lourdes Hall, 1678 Asylum Ave., 06117-2791. Tel: 860-232-6730.
St. Paul Convent, 243 Steele Rd., 06117-2741. Tel: 860-232-7745.
Trocaire, 243 Steele Rd., 06117-2796. Tel: 860-233-2195.
Sacred Heart Convent, 243 Steele Rd., 06117-2797. Tel: 860-236-3503.
Maranatha, 243 Steele Rd., 06117-2797. Tel: 860-236-9448.
54 Boulanger Ave. #1, 06110-1103. Tel: 860-231-8472.
54 Boulanger Ave. #2, 06110-1103. Tel: 860-233-6679.
Sisters of Mercy of the Americas of Vermont, 54 Clifford Dr., 06107-1208. Tel: 860-586-8402.
Sisters of Notre Dame de Namur, 21 Prescott St., 06110. Tel: 860-231-7979.
Sisters of St. Joseph (Springfield, MA) , 50 Crescent St., 06119. Tel: 860-233-8708.
Vietnamese Dominican Sisters, 78 Westpoint Ter., 06107. Tel: 860-521-8296; Fax: 860-521-8296. Email: magdalenekimhue@hotmail.com. Sr. Magdalene Nguyen, O.P., Supr. & Contact. Total in Residence 3.

WEST HAVEN. *Our Lady of Victory Convent*, 634 Jones Hill Rd., 06516-6398. Tel: 203-934-8601. Sr. Denise Farrands, O.S.U. Ursuline Sisters of the Congregation of Tildonk, Belgium
St. Paul Parish Center, 45 Alling St., 06516. Tel: 203-934-1357; Fax: 203-931-9416.
Sisters of the Assumption, 491 Washington Ave. #3W, 06516. Tel: 203-932-6449; Fax: 203-777-0144. Email: jo-ann.veillette@yale.edu. Web: www.sasv.org.

WETHERSFIELD. *Daughters of Wisdom*, 78 Fairlane Dr., 06109. Tel: 860-529-8419; Fax: 860-563-5152. Web: daughtersofwisdom.org.
Maryknoll Sisters of St. Dominic, 547 Goff Rd., 06109. Tel: 860-529-1483.
96 Victoria Rd., 06114. Tel: 860-296-1826. Sr. Joan Metzner, M.M., Contact.
Sisters of Notre Dame de Namur, 98-1 Folly Brook Blvd., 06109. Tel: 860-529-3525. Email: tkreibick@aol.com.

WINCHESTER CENTER. *Villa Ferretti, Religious Teachers Filippini*, 438 Winchester Rd., Box 55, 06094. Tel: 860-379-3279; Fax: 860-379-3279. Email: ltflower@erols.com.

WINDSOR. *Sisters of Notre Dame de Namur*, Province Center, 468 Poquonock Ave., 06095-2473. Tel: 860-688-1832; Fax: 860-683-1741. Email: sndct@aol.com. Web: www.sndden.org. Sisters Mary Beth Johnston, S.N.D., Administrative Team. Tel: 860-285-0554; Patricia J. Chappell, S.N.D., Administrative Team. Tel: 860-285-8901; Ann-Louise Nadeau, S.N.D., Administrative Team & Contact. Tel: 860-285-8441.
Community, 468 Poquonock Ave., 06095-2473. Tel: 860-285-0038; Fax: 860-683-1741
Julie House, 425 Poquonock Ave., 06095-2465. Tel: 860-298-8320; Fax: 860-683-1351. Assisted living home for S.N.D.'s only Residents 18; Staff 4.
Sisters of St. Joseph of Chambery, 67 Bloomfield Ave., 06095. Tel: 860-285-0890; Fax: 860-285-0883. Email: windwomen@aol.com.

WINSTED. *St. Anthony Convent*, 66 Oak St., 06098. Tel: 860-379-8375; Fax: 860-379-7522. Email: sas-principal@snet.net. Franciscan Missionaries of the Divine Motherhood Sisters 3.

WOLCOTT. *Daughters of Wisdom*, 18 Munson Rd. #2, 06716. Tel: 203-879-3432. Email: gueretted2@aol.com.

[O] COUNSELING CENTERS

MERIDEN. *Franciscan Life Center* 271 Finch Ave., 06451. Tel: 203-237-8084; Fax: 203-639-1333. Web: www.flcenter.org. Sr. Shaun Vergauwen, F.S.E., Dir. & Contact.
Legal Title: *Franciscan Life Center Network, Inc.* Franciscan Sisters of the Eucharist 7; Total Assisted 1,200; Total Staff 20.

[P] ADOPTION SERVICES-HOME CARE

MERIDEN. *Franciscan Family Care Center*, 267 Finch Ave., 06451. Tel: 203-237-8084; Fax: 203-639-1333. Email: ssuzanne@franciscanhc.org. Sisters Shaun Vergauwen, F.S.E., Dir.; Suzanne Gross, F.S.E., Dir. Franciscan Home Care & Contact. Tel: 203-237-8084; Fax: 203-639-1333.
Legal Title: *Franciscan Family Care Center, Inc.* Franciscan Sisters of the Eucharist 8; Total Assisted 600; Total Staff 90.

[Q] RETREAT HOUSES-RENEWAL CENTERS

FARMINGTON. *Our Lady of Calvary Retreat House* Conducted by the Sisters of the Cross and Passion for Religious and Lay Persons , 31 Colton St., 06032. Tel: 860-677-8519; Fax: 860-677-2873. Email: olcret@mindspring.com. Web: www.ourladyofcalvary.com.
Staff: Sisters Mary O'Brien, C.P.; Ann Rodgers, C.P., Prog. Dir.; Pauline Semkow, R.S.M.; Jeanne Snyder, R.S.M., Asst. Admin.; Andrea T. Urbano, Admin. & Contact; Joanne Ceccarelli-Egan; Marie DiBenedetto; Hanna Grymek; Beverly Montana.

LITCHFIELD. *Wisdom House Retreat Center*, 229 E. Litchfield Rd., 06759-3002. Tel: 860-567-3163; Fax: 860-567-3166. Email: info@wisdomhouse.com. Web: www.wisdomhouse.org. Sisters Rosemarie Greco, D.W., Admin.; Jo-Ann Iannotti, O.P., Art & Spirituality Coord. A retreat center which presents programs in spirituality, education & the arts. Use of space is available for non-profit organizations when their purpose corresponds to the Mission of Wisdom House. The Center is a sponsored ministry of the Daughters of Wisdom

MADISON. *Mercy Center, Incorporated*, 167 Neck Rd., P.O. Box 191, 06443. Tel: 203-245-0401; Fax: 203-245-8718. Email: mercymad@aol.com. Web: www.mercyctrmadison.com. Sr. Eugenie Guterch, R.S.M., Exec. Dir. & Contact. Sisters of Mercy Sisters 10; Total in Residence 6; Total Staff 25.

WEST HARTFORD. *Holy Family Passionist Retreat Center*, 303 Tunxis Rd., 06107. Tel: 860-521-0440; Fax: 860-521-1929. Email: holyfamilyretreat@cpprov.org. Web: www.holyfamilyretreat.org. Rev. David Cinquegrani, C.P., Retreat Dir.; Christian Cashman, Assoc. Dir.; Cirstin Connors, Assoc. Dir.; Sr. Mary Ann Strain, C.P., Assoc. Dir.; Brandon Nappi, Assoc. Dir. For laymen and laywomen. Conducted by the Passionist Community Priests 1; Sisters 1; Lay Staff 3.

[R] NEWMAN CENTERS

HARTFORD. *University of Hartford Newman Center* 200 Bloomfield Ave., 06117-1599. Tel: 860-768-4899. Web: www.trincoll.edu/orgs/newman-club/. Rev. Michael J. Dolan, Chap.
St. Mary Rectory, 626 Willard Ave., Newington, 06111. Tel: 860-666-1591; Fax: 860-666-5720.
Trinity College Chapel 300 Summit St., 06106-3186. Tel: 860-297-2015.

HAMDEN. *Catholic Community at Quinnipiac University* P.O. Box 340, 06518-1908. Tel: 203-582-8257. Email: gracchus@hotmail.com. Rev. Louis Anthony Evangelisto, Chap. & Contact.

NEW BRITAIN. *Central Connecticut State University Newman House* 145 Paul J. Manafort Dr., 06053-2552. Tel: 860-832-3795; Fax: 860-225-2315. Email: donovanr@ccsu.ctstateu.edu. Rev. Patrick J. Donovan, O.S.M. (ORG). Total Staff 1.
St. Francis of Assisi Friary, 1755 Stanley St., 06053-2099. Tel: 860-225-6449; Fax: 860-225-2315.

NEW HAVEN. *Southern Connecticut State University Catholic Center* 129 Edwards St., 06511. Tel: 203-392-5331; 203-624-5297. Email: sullivanJ9@southernct.edu. Rev. John P. Sullivan.
Yale University-St. Thomas More Catholic Center and Chapel 268 Park St., 06511-4714. Tel: 203-777-5537; Fax: 203-777-0144. Email: morehouse@yale.edu. Web: www.yale.edu/stm. Rev. Robert L. Beloin, Ph.D., Chap. & Contact; Sr. Jo-Ann Veillette, S.A.S.V., Assoc. Chap.

[S] ORGANIZED CHARITIES

HARTFORD. *Catholic Charities-Catholic Family Services (Archdiocese of Hartford)* Central Office Email: blmfld.cc.cfs@snet.net. Web: www.cccfs.org.
Archdiocesan Center, 467 Bloomfield Ave., Bloomfield, 06002-2999. Tel: 860-242-9577; Fax: 860-286-2800. Rose Alma Senatore, Dir. Charities & Exec. Dir.; Sr. Dorothy Strelchun, Assoc. Dir.; Linda S. Smith, C.I.S.W., Asst. Exec. Dir. Programs; Edgar Bernier, C.P.A., Controller; Francis Laffin, Dir. Group Home Svcs.; Ana Malave-Ortiz, Human Resources Dir.; J. Peter O'Donnell, Devel. Dir; John R. Morrison, Dir. of Operations.
Network Connecticut, Inc., c/o Catholic Charities, 467 Bloomfield Ave., Bloomfield, 06002-2999. Tel: 860-242-9577; Fax: 860-286-2800. Rose Alma Senatore, Dir. Charities.

Capitol Region:
Hartford, 896 Asylum Ave., 06105. Tel: 860-522-8241; Fax: 860-527-1919. Dr. Galo Rodriguez, Regl. Dir.
Child Development Center, 449 Silas Dean Hwy., Wethersfield, 06109. Tel: 860-563-3747; Fax: 860-573-5640.
Hartford Street Youth Project, 15 Ely St., 06103. Tel: 860-728-0117; Fax: 860-249-5398.
Adoption Office, 2433 Main St., Ste. # 6, Rocky Hill, 06067. Tel: 860-257-4335; Fax: 860-257-4339. Mary Beth Dobmeier, Contact Person.
Institute for the Hispanic Family, 80 Jefferson St., 06105. Tel: 860-527-1124; Fax: 806-724-2539.
The Hispanic Child Guidance Clinic, 80 Jefferson St., 06105. Tel: 860-524-8974.
Empowering People for Success, 999 Asylum Ave., 06105. Tel: 860-548-0030. Judi Gough, Contact Person.
Jobs First Employment Services Program, 3580 Main St., 06120.
Jobs First Employment Services Program, 620 Enfield St., Enfield, 06082. Tel: 860-745-8097; Fax: 860-741-4290.
Jobs First Employment Services Program, Goodwin College, 06105. Tel: 860-622-0766.
Hispanic Senior Center, 95 Park St., 06106. Tel: 860-246-9322; Fax: 860-293-2662.
New Haven, 478 Orange St., New Haven, 06502. Tel: 203-787-2207; Fax: 203-773-3626. Brent Porges, M.S.W., Regl. Dir.
South Region:
Workforce Development, 3580 Main St., 06106. Tel: 860-522-0025.
Project Apoyo, 790 Grand Ave., New Haven, 06511. Tel: 203-772-1131; Fax: 203-772-1058.
Centro San Jose, Inc., 290 Grand Ave., New Haven, 06513. Tel: 203-562-3135; Fax: 203-777-5290.
Step Ahead Pre-School, 357 Pine Rock Ave., Hamden, 06514. Tel: 203-389-5609; Fax: 203-389-6230.
Ansonia, 205 Wakelee Ave., P.O. Box 364, Ansonia, 06401. Tel: 203-735-7481; Fax: 203-735-5021.
Meriden, 61 Colony St., Meriden, 06450. Tel: 203-235-2707; Fax: 203-639-6509.
Catholic Family Services, 357 Pine Rock Ave., Ste. 2, Hamden, 06514. Tel: 203-389-6230; Fax: 203-389-6246.
Milford, 203 High St., P.O. Box 147, Milford, 06460. Tel: 203-874-6270; Fax: 203-874-3301.
Long Hill Center-School Readiness, 514 Long Hill Rd., Waterbury, 06708. Tel: 203-596-9359.
School Readiness, 88 Cook St., Waterbury, 06708. Tel: 203-755-0691.
Guilford Office, 652 Boston Post Rd., Guilford, 06437. Tel: 203-453-5746; Fax: 203-773-3626.
School Readiness, Our Lady of Mt. Carmel, 785 Highland Ave., Waterbury, 06708. Tel: 203-757-4308.
West Region:
Torrington, 132 Grove St., Torrington, 06790. Tel: 860-482-5558; Fax: 860-489-2984.
New Britain, 90 Franklin Sq., New Britain, 06051. Tel: 860-225-3561; Fax: 860-225-2558. Rev. Wanda Brown-Claitty, A.C.S.W, Regl. Dir.
School Readiness, 29 John St., Waterbury, 06708. Tel: 203-575-0182.
Waterbury, 56 Church St., Waterbury, 06702. Tel: 203-755-1196; Fax: 203-575-9675.
Bristol Office, 440C North Main St., Bristol, 06010. Tel: 860-589-8662.
Migration and Refugee Service, 125 Market St., 06103. Tel: 860-548-0059; Fax: 860-549-8697. Sr. Dorothy Strelchun, Acting Dir.

[T] SOCIAL SERVICE CENTERS FOR SPANISH-SPEAKING AND BLACK PEOPLE

BLOOMFIELD. *Office for Hispanic Evangelization*, 467 Bloomfield Ave., 06002-2999. Tel: 860-243-0940; Fax: 860-286-2797. Email: hispanic.evnglztn@snet.net. Most Rev. Peter A. Rosazza, Vicar for Hispanics; Luz Yunes, Office Mgr. & Asst. to Vicar.

WATERBURY. *Spanish-Speaking Center*, 13 Wolcott St., 06702-1790. Tel: 203-757-8737. Rev. Kevin J. Gray, Contact. Total Assisted 350; Total Staff 1.

[U] SOCIETY OF ST. VINCENT DE PAUL

HARTFORD. *Particular Council of the St. Vincent de Paul Society* Greater Hartford , 134 Farmington Ave., 06105-3784. Tel: 860-541-6491.
Legal Title: *Particular Council of the St. Vincent de Paul Society of the Archdiocese of Hartford*

[V] MISCELLANEOUS

HARTFORD. *Mercy Housing & Shelter Corporation*, 211 Wethersfield Ave., 06114. Tel: 860-724-7988; Fax: 860-548-0692. Email: pmckeon@mercyhousingct.org. Web: www.mercyhousingct.org. Patricia McKeon, R.S.M., Pres. & Exec. Dir.; Christopher Montemayor, Finance Dir.; Sr. P. McKeon, R.S.M., Contact. Special Centers for Social Service and Assistance. Total Assisted 4,500; Total Staff 84.
North American La Salette Mission Center, Inc., 85 New Park Ave., 06106-2184. Tel: 860-523-4017; Fax: 860-523-4074. Email: lsmc1997@comcast.net. Web: www.lasalette.org ission. Rev. John R. Nuelle, M.S., Pres. & Exec. Dir.; Bro. Roger Clement, M.S., Asst. Dir.
Religious Trust of the Missionaries of Our Lady of LaSalette MLS Trust , 915 Maple Ave., 06114-2330. Tel: 860-956-8870; Fax: 860-956-8849. Email: mlstrust@aol.com. Rev. James H. Kuczynski, M.S., Contact.

BLOOMFIELD. *Foundation for the Advancement of Catholic Schools*, 467 Bloomfield Ave., 06002-2999. Tel: 860-242-4362; Fax: 860-242-8683. Email: jdash@adh-ocs.org. Peter G. Carey, Pres.; Jeannine V. Dash, Exec. Dir. & Contact.

LITCHFIELD. *Lourdes Shrine Guild, Inc.*, 83 Montfort Rd., 06759. Tel: 860-567-1041; Fax: 860-567-9670. Rev. Gerald Fitzsimmons, S.S.M., Prov. & Contact Person.

MERIDEN. *Franciscan Life Center Network, Incorporated*, 405 Allen Ave., 06451. Tel: 203-237-8084; Fax: 203-639-1333. Web: www.flcenter.org.
Franciscan Life Center, 271 Finch Ave., 06451. Tel: 203-237-8084; Fax: 203-639-1333.
Franciscan Life Process Center, 11650 Downes St., Lowell, MI 49331. Tel: 616-897-7842; Fax: 616-897-7054.
Franciscan Montessori Earth School, 14750 S.E. Clinton St., Portland, OR 97236. Tel: 503-760-8220; Fax: 503-760-8333.
Franciscan Northwoods Computer Center, 5601 Lilac Hill Rd., Duluth, MN 55810. Tel: 218-624-5478; Fax: 218-624-4649.
John S. Duss Memorial Music Center, 2211 Greysolon Rd., Duluth, MN 55812. Tel: 203-724-6912; Fax: 218-724-3318.
Franciscan Cre-Act School, 526 Grant St., P.O. Box 723, Pocatello, ID 83204. Tel: 208-233-4747; Fax: 208-233-4114.
Franciscan Family Life Center, 1745 Pocatello Creek Rd., Pocatello, ID 83201. Tel: 208-233-9383; Fax: 208-233-2707.
Creative Acting, 526 S. Grant St., Pocatello, ID 83204. Tel: 208-233-4747.

NEW HAVEN. *The Children's Foundation at St. Francis Home, Inc.*, 651 Prospect St., 06511. Tel: 203-777-5513; Fax: 203-777-0644. Email: psalerno1@aol.com. Mr. Peter T. Salerno, Exec. Dir.

NEW MILFORD. *Our Lady of the Lakes Corporation*, 3 Old Town Park Rd., 06776-4212. Tel: 860-354-5239; Fax: 860-354-2968. Email: byrdolol@aol.com. Rev. Frederick M. Langlois, Contact.

ORANGE. *Helping Hand Investments, Inc*, 393 Derby Ave., 06477. Tel: 203-795-2800; Fax: 203-795-2808. Rev. Juan Sabadell, L.C. (LA).
Horizons Institute, Inc., 393 Derby Ave., 06477. Tel: 203-795-2800; Fax: 203-795-2808. Rev. Juan Sabadell, L.C., Contact.
Legion of Christ, Inc., 393 Derby Ave., 06477. Tel: 203-795-2800; Fax: 203-795-2808. Email: vhiggins@legionaries.org. Revs. Anthony Bannon, L.C., Territorial Dir.; Vincent Higgins, L.C., Sec.; Emilio Diaz Torre, L.C.; Edward McIlmail, L.C. Priests 4; Religious 4.
Logos, Inc., 393 Derby Ave., 06477. Tel: 203-795-2800; Fax: 203-795-2808. Email: cheshire@legionaries.org. Rev. Jose Felix Ortega, L.C.
LUX ET VITA, INC., 393 Derby Ave., 06477. Tel: 203-795-2800. Rev. Jose Felix Ortega, L.C., Contact.
Racebrook, Inc., 393 Derby Ave., 06477. Tel: 203-795-2800; Fax: 203-795-2808. Rev. Emilio Diaz-Torre, L.C.
Rossotto, Inc., 393 Derby Ave., 06477. Tel: 203-795-2800; Fax: 203-795-2808. Rev. Jose Felix Ortega, L.C., Sec.

WEST HARTFORD. *Mercy Community Health, Inc.*, 2021 Albany Ave., 06117-2796. Tel: 860-570-8300; Fax: 860-233-8849. Email: Mchwh@aol.com. Web: www.merrycommunityhealth.org. Jane Marie Murphy, Bd. Chm.
Mercy Community Home Care Services, Inc., 275 Steele Rd., 06117. Tel: 860-236-0695; 860-586-8318. Email: debg@themoauleyct.com. Web: www.mercycommunityhomecare.org. Debra Gates, Admin.
Mercy Services, Inc., 2021 Albany Ave., 06117-2796. Tel: 860-570-8300; Fax: 860-233-8849. Email: mchwh@aol.com. Mr. Richard J. Kisner, Pres. & CEO.
Sisters of St. Joseph of Chambery, Business Office & Mailing, 27 Park Rd.. Tel: 860-233-1526.

WINDSOR. *The Connecticut Province of the Sisters of Notre Dame de Namur, Inc.*, 468 Poquonock Ave., 06095-2473. Tel: 860-688-1832; Fax: 860-683-1741. Email: sndct@aol.com. Web: www.sndden.org. Sr. Anne-Louise Nadeau, S.N.D., Contact.

RELIGIOUS INSTITUTES OF MEN REPRESENTED IN THE ARCHDIOCESE

For further details refer to the corresponding bracketed number in the Religious Institutes of Men or Women section.

[0200]—*Benedictine Monks*—O.S.B.
[0600]—*Brothers of the Congregation of Holy Cross* (Notre Dame, IN)—C.S.C.
[1100]—*Brothers of the Sacred Heart*—S.C.
[0650]—*Congregation of the Holy Spirit, Spiritans*—C.S.Sp.
[1330]—*Congregation of the Mission (Vincentian Fathers)*—C.M.
[1000]—*Congregation of the Passion* (Prov. of St. Paul of the Cross)—C.P.
[0480]—*Conventual Franciscans* (St. Anthony of Padua Prov.)—O.F.M.Conv
[0520]—*Franciscan Friars* (Immaculate Conception, Holy Name Provs.)—O.F.M.
[0690]—*Jesuit Fathers and Brothers*—S.J.
[0730]—*Legionaries of Christ*—L.C.
[0780]—*Marist Fathers*—S.M.
[0800]—*Maryknoll*—M.M.
[0720]—*The Missionaries of Our Lady of La Salette* (Prov. O.L. of Seven Dolors)—M.S.
[1210]—*Missionaries of St. Charles-Scalabrinians*—C.S.
[0590]—*Missionaries of the Holy Apostles*—M.S.A.
[]—*Missionary Congregation of the Blessed Sacrament*—M.C.B.S.
[0860]—*Missionhurst Congregation of the Immaculate Heart of Mary*—C.I.C.M.
[0870]—*Montfort Missionaries*—S.M.M.
[0430]—*Order of Preachers-Dominicans* (Eastern Prov.)—O.P.
[1030]—*Paulist Fathers*
[0610]—*Priests of the Congregation of Holy Cross*—C.S.C.
[1070]—*Redemptorist Fathers* (Baltimore Prov.)—C.SS.R.
[0760]—*Society of Mary (Marianists)*—S.M.
[0975]—*Society of Our Lady of the Most Holy Trinity*—S.O.L.T.
[]—*Sons of Charity*—S.C.

RELIGIOUS INSTITUTES OF WOMEN REPRESENTED IN THE ARCHDIOCESE

[0130]—*Apostles of the Sacred Heart of Jesus*—A.S.C.J.
[0180]—*Benedictine Nuns of the Primitive Observance*—O.S.B.
[2250]—*Congregation of Benedictines of Jesus Crucified*—O.S.B.
[0860]—*Daughters of Mary of the Immaculate Conception*—D.M.
[0820]—*Daughters of the Holy Spirit*—D.H.S.
[0960]—*Daughters of Wisdom*—D.W.
[1050]—*Dominican Contemplative Nuns*—O.P.
[]—*Dominican Oblates of Jesus* (Madrid, Spain)—D.O.O.P.
[1070-02]—*Dominican Sisters (Congregation of St. Mary of the Springs)*—O.P.
[]—*Dominican Sisters of Fatima*—O.P.
[1070-15]—*Dominican Sisters of Hope*—O.P.
[]—*Dominican Sisters (Vietnamese Congregation of St. Catherine of Siena)*—O.P.
[1170]—*Felician Sisters* (Our Lady of the Angels Province)—C.S.S.F.
[]—*Franciscan Missionaries of the Divine Motherhood*—F.M.D.M.
[1250]—*Institutes of the Franciscan Sisters of the Eucharist*—F.S.E.
[2340]—*Little Sisters of the Poor*—l.s.p.
[2470]—*Maryknoll Sisters of St. Dominic*—M.M.
[2490]—*Medical Mission Sisters*—M.M.S.
[2790]—*Missionary Servants of the Most Blessed Trinity*—M.S.B.T.
[2519]—*Religious Sisters of Mercy of Alma* (MI)—R.S.M.
[3430]—*Religious Teachers Filippini*—M.P.F.
[2970]—*School Sisters of Notre Dame*—S.S.N.D.
[]—*Sisters Minor of Mary Immaculate*—S.M.M.I.
[0520]—*Sisters of Charity of Our Lady, Mother of Mercy*—S.C.M.M.
[0530]—*Sisters of Charity of Our Lady, Mother of the Church*—S.C.M.C.
[0590]—*Sisters of Charity of Saint Elizabeth, Convent Station*—S.C.
[2575]—*Sisters of Mercy of the Americas* (Albany, Vermont, Detroit & Connecticut)—R.S.M.
[3000]—*Sisters of Notre Dame de Namur* (Connecticut, Boston, California & Base Community)—S.N.D.deN.
[]—*Sisters of Our Lady of the Garden*—O.L.G.

[1650]—*Sisters of St. Francis of Philadelphia*—O.S.F.
[3830-16]—*Sisters of St. Joseph* (Springfield)—S.S.J.
[3830-05]—*Sisters of St. Joseph of Brentwood*—C.S.J.
[3850]—*Sisters of St. Joseph of Chambery*—C.S.J.
[3930]—*Sisters of St. Joseph of the Third Order of St. Francis*—S.S.J.-T.O
[0150]—*Sisters of the Assumption B.V.*—S.A.S.V.
[2980]—*Sisters of the Congregation de Notre Dame*—C.N.D.
[3180]—*Sisters of the Cross and Passion*—C.P.
[1830]—*The Sisters of the Good Shepherd*
[]—*Sisters of the Sacred Heart of Jesus of Ragura*—S.S.H.J.
[2170]—*Sisters, Servants of the Immaculate Heart of Mary*—I.H.M.
[4060]—*Society of the Holy Child Jesus*—S.H.C.J.
[4130]—*Ursuline Sisters of The Congregation of Tildonk, Belgium*—O.S.U.

ARCHDIOCESAN CEMETERIES

HARTFORD. *Catholic Cemeteries Association of the Archdiocese of Hartford, Inc.*, 700 Middletown Ave., P.O. Box 517, North Haven, 06473-0517. Tel: 203-239-2557; Fax: 203-239-5035. Rev. Msgr. David M. Walker, Dir.; Robert Marek, Exec. Dir.
Holy Cross
Holy Trinity
St. Patrick

ANSONIA. *St. Mary*
Old St. Mary
BLOOMFIELD. *Mount Saint Benedict*
DERBY. *Mount St. Peter*
EAST HARTFORD. *St. Mary*
GLASTONBURY. *Holy Cross*
MANCHESTER. *St. Bridget*
St. James
MERIDEN. *St. Patrick*
Sacred Heart
NAUGATUCK. *St. Francis* (New Haven Region)
St. James
NEW BRITAIN. *St. Mary*
Old St. Mary
NEW HAVEN. *St. Bernard*
NORTH HAVEN. *All Saints*
TORRINGTON. *St. Francis*
Old St. Francis
St. Peter
WALLINGFORD. *Holy Trinity*
St. John
WATERBURY. *Calvary*
St. Joseph
Old St. Joseph
WATERTOWN. *Mount Olivet*
WEST HAVEN. *St. Lawrence*

NECROLOGY

† Brown, Vincent A., Branford, CT St. Mary Rectory.—Died July 10, 2003
† Fitzgerald, Neil F., (Retired)—Died Oct. 2, 2003
† Hewitt, Charles L., (Retired)—Died March 18, 2003
† Lynch, William F.—Died Jan. 1, 2003
† O'Connor, John T., (Retired)—Died Dec. 1, 2003
† Quinn, John J., (Retired)—Died Oct. 27, 2003
† Wysocki, Paul P., New Britain, CT Sacred Heart Rectory—Died March 14, 2003

Diocese of Helena

(Dioecesis Helenensis)

Most Reverend

GEORGE L. THOMAS, D.D., Ph.D.

Bishop of Helena; ordained May 22, 1976; appointed Auxiliary Bishop of Seattle November 19, 1999; appointed Bishop of Helena March 23, 2004; installed June 4, 2004.

Chancery and Diocesan Pastoral Center Office: 515 N. Ewing, P.O. Box 1729, Helena, MT 59624-1729. Tel: 406-442-5820; Fax: 406-442-5191.

Web: www.diocesehelena.org

Email: chancery@diocesehelena.org

ERECTED MARCH 7, 1884.

Square Miles 51,922.

Comprises the western part of the State of Montana, and is made up of the following Counties: Lewis and Clark, Glacier, Pondera, Flathead, Lake, Lincoln, Missoula, Mineral, Sanders, Powell, Granite, Ravalli, Deer Lodge, Silver Bow, Jefferson, Broadwater, Gallatin, Madison, Beaverhead, Meagher, Wheatland and parts of Teton and Toole.

Diocesan Legal Title--Roman Catholic Bishop of Helena, Montana, a Corporation Sole.

For legal titles of parishes and diocesan institutions, consult the Chancery Office.

STATISTICAL OVERVIEW

Personnel	
Retired Archbishops	1
Priests: Diocesan Active in Diocese	52
Priests: Diocesan Active Outside Diocese	12
Priests: Diocesan in Foreign Missions	1
Priests: Retired, Sick or Absent	24
Number of Diocesan Priests	89
Religious Priests in Diocese	6
Total Priests in Diocese	95
Extern Priests in Diocese	5
Ordinations:	
Diocesan Priests	2
Permanent Deacons in Diocese	33
Total Brothers	2
Total Sisters	35
Parishes	
Parishes	58
With Resident Pastor:	
Resident Diocesan Priests	41
Resident Religious Priests	3
Without Resident Pastor:	
Administered by Priests	10
Administered by Deacons	2
Administered by Religious Women	3
Missions	39
Pastoral Centers	14
Professional Ministry Personnel:	
Brothers	2
Sisters	34
Welfare	
Catholic Hospitals	3
Total Assisted	160,856
Day Care Centers	3
Total Assisted	135
Educational	
Diocesan Students in Other Seminaries	8
Total Seminarians	8
Colleges and Universities	1
Total Students	1,469
High Schools, Diocesan and Parish	2
Total Students	323
Elementary Schools, Diocesan and Parish	3
Total Students	895
Catechesis/Religious Education:	
High School Students	1,227
Elementary Students	4,065
Total Students under Catholic Instruction	7,987
Teachers in the Diocese:	
Priests	7
Brothers	2
Sisters	3
Lay Teachers	237
Vital Statistics	
Receptions into the Church:	
Infant Baptism Totals	623
Adult Baptism Totals	465
Received into Full Communion	155
First Communions	820
Confirmations	1,182
Marriages:	
Catholic	142
Interfaith	136
Total Marriages	278
Deaths	815
Total Catholic Population	49,527
Total Population	506,002

Former Bishops—Rt. Revs. JOHN B. BRONDEL, consecrated Bishop of Victoria, V.I., Dec. 14, 1879; appt. Vicar Apostolic of Montana, April 17, 1883; Bishop of Helena, March 7, 1884; died Nov. 3, 1903; JOHN P. CARROLL, D.D., consecrated Bishop of Helena, Dec. 21, 1904; died Nov. 4, 1925; Most Revs. GEORGE J. FINNIGAN, C.S.C., D.D., consecrated Bishop of Helena, Aug. 1, 1927; died Aug. 14, 1932; RALPH L. HAYES, D.D., consecrated Bishop of Helena, Sept. 21, 1933; transferred to Rectorship North American College, Rome, Italy, September 11, 1935; transferred to Titular See of Hierapolis, Oct. 26, 1935; transferred to Davenport, Nov. 16, 1944; appt. Assistant at the Pontifical Throne, April 30, 1958; transferred to Titular See of Naraggara and retired, Oct. 20, 1966; died July 4, 1970; JOSEPH M. GILMORE, S.T.D., consecrated Bishop of Helena, Feb. 19, 1936; died April 2, 1962; RAYMOND G. HUNTHAUSEN (Retired), ord. June 1, 1946; appt. July 8, 1962; consecrated Bishop of Helena, Aug. 30, 1962; transferred to Archdiocese of Seattle, Feb. 25, 1975; installed Archbishop of Seattle, May 22, 1975; retired Aug. 21, 1991; ELDEN F. CURTISS, D.D., ord. May 24, 1958; appt. March 4, 1976; consecrated Bishop of Helena, April 28, 1976; transferred to Archdiocese of Omaha, May 4, 1993; installed Archbishop of Omaha, June 25, 1993; ALEXANDER J. BRUNETT, Ph.D., ord. July 13, 1958; appt. April 19, 1994; consecrated Bishop of Helena, July 6, 1994; transferred to Archdiocese of Seattle Oct. 28, 1997; installed Archbishop of Seattle Dec. 18, 1997; ROBERT C. MORLINO, ord. June 1, 1974; consecrated Bishop of Helena Sept. 21, 1999; transferred to Diocese of Madison Aug. 1, 2003.

Apostolic Administrator—Rev. Msgr. KEVIN S. O'NEILL.

Liaison to Senior Status Priests—Rev. Msgr. JOSEPH D. HARRINGTON (Retired), Carroll College, Helena, 59625. Tel: 406-447-4459.

Episcopal Vicar for Canonical Services—Rev. JOHN ROBERTSON, P.O. Box 3269, Butte, 59701. Tel: 406-723-1255; Fax: 406-723-0182. Email: jrobertson@diocesehelena.org.

Chancery and Diocesan Pastoral Office—515 N. Ewing St., P.O. Box 1729, Helena, 59624. Tel: 406-442-5820; Fax: 406-442-5191. Email: chancery@diocesehelena.org. Web: www.diocesehelena.org.

Moderator of the Curia—Rev. Msgr. KEVIN S. O'NEILL.

Chancellor—Mr. KEVIN R. PHELAN.

Director of Pastoral Office—Deacon J. ANTHONY DUVERNAY.

Archivist—Sr. DOLORES BRINKEL, S.C.L.

Business Administration Office—PETER MCNAMEE, Diocesan Finance Officer, 515 N. Ewing St., P.O. Box 1729, Helena, 59624. Tel: 406-442-5820.

Development Office—GLENNA OBIE, Dir. Stewardship, P.O. Box 1729, Helena, 59624. Tel: 406-442-5820.

Western Montana Catholic Foundation—PHILIP GRAINEY, Pres.; Deacon GERALD KUHL, Exec. Dir., P.O. Box 1729, Helena, 59624. Tel: 406-442-5820.

Diocesan Tribunal—Rev. JOHN W. ROBERTSON, P.O. Box 3269, Butte, 59701. Tel: 406-723-1255; Fax: 406-723-0182.

Judicial Vicar—Rev. JOHN W. ROBERTSON.

Associate Judges—Revs. JEFFREY M. FLEMING; RAYMOND V. GILMORE; THOMAS P. HAFFEY; MATTHEW P. HUBER; PATRICK C. MCGURK.

Promoter of Justice—Rev. ROBERT GROSCH, J.C.L.

Defenders of the Bond—Revs. ROBERT BEAULIEU; ROBERT NOONAN; KEVIN O'NEILL; GARY RELLER.

Notary—SUE ZEZEUS.

Diocesan Consultors—Very Rev. KEVIN S. O'NEILL, V.G.; Revs. THOMAS F. HEALY, S.J.; THOMAS HAFFEY; MATTHEW HUBER; CHARLES ROMAN; Rev. Msgr. DONALD SHEA; Rev. JEREMIAH SULLIVAN.

Presbyteral Council—Rev. Msgr. KEVIN S. O'NEILL, Apostolic Admin.; Revs. THOMAS F. HEALY, S.J.; JOHN J. DARRAGH; THOMAS HAFFEY; EDWARD HISLOP; MATTHEW HUBER; ROBERT NOONAN; JOHN ROBERTSON; CHARLES ROMAN; Rev. Msgr. DONALD SHEA; Rev. JEREMIAH SULLIVAN; Mr. KEVIN R. PHELAN, Chancellor, Sec.

Diocesan Finance Council—PETER MCNAMEE; JEANNE AHMANN; TONI BROADBENT; ROBERT BUGNI; EDWARD CASNE; THOMAS DOWNEY; KEVIN PHELAN; PETER JOHNSON; Rev. Msgr. KEVIN S. O'NEILL, Apostolic Admin.; HUGH MCWHORTER; Rev. DANIEL SHEA; DENNIS LOVELESS.

Vicariates—Revs. ROBERT NOONAN, Conrad; LEO PROXELL, Helena; MATTHEW HUBER, Missoula; GARY W. RELLER, Kalispell; THOMAS HAFFEY, Butte.

Personnel Board—Rev. Msgr. KEVIN S. O'NEILL, Apostolic Admin.; Revs. THOMAS P. HAFFEY; MATTHEW HUBER; JOHN MURRAY; ROBERT NOONAN; DANIEL SHEA.

Inter-Diocesan Organizations

Montana Catholic Conference—P.O. Box 1708, Helena, 59624. Tel: 406-442-5761; Fax: 406-442-9047. Email: mcc@mt.net. Web: www.mt.net/mcc.

Board of Directors—Rev. Msgr. KEVIN S. O'NEILL, (Helena); Most Rev. ANTHONY MILONE, (Great Falls); KIM LARSEN, (Great Falls); Rev. JAY PETERSON, (Great Falls); Sr. MARY JOE MCDONALD, S.C.L., (Butte).

Catholic Social Services for Montana, Inc.—ROSEMARY MILLER, Dir., 22 S. Ewing St., P.O. Box 907, Helena, 59601. Tel: 406-442-4130; Fax:

406-442-4192 Coordinates and supervises all Catholic Social welfare in the State of Montana.

Board of Directors—Rev. Msgr. KEVIN S. O'NEILL, (Helena); Most Rev. ANTHONY MILONE, (Great Falls); Rev. JAY PETERSON, (Great Falls); Sisters EILEEN JOHNSON, S.C.L., (Helena); LILLIAN MCGUIRE, (Great Falls); Rev. MATTHEW HUBER, (Helena); WAYNE BEANER, (Great Falls); KEVIN MEEK, (Great Falls); THERESE COWDERY, (Great Falls); JOE SHEVLIN, (Helena); KEVIN PHELAN, (Helena).

Helena Office—ROSEMARY MILLER, Dir., Adoptions; HELEN BEAUSOLEIL, Social Worker; PAULA CORY, Project Rachel; SHIRLEY COLE, Treasure Book, 22 S. Ewing , P.O. Box 907, Helena, 59624. Tel: 406-442-4130.

Billings Office—Social Workers: BECKY HUBBERT, (Billings); SAM HUBBERT, (Columbus), St. Vincent's Hospital, 2703 11th Ave. N. Billings, 59101. Tel: 406-252-3399.

Great Falls Office—KYLA KALANICK, Social Worker, 1601 Second Ave. N., Ste. 640, Great Falls, 59401. Tel: 406-771-7805.

Missoula Office—BETSY ROBEL-GOMEZ, Social Worker, 420 W. Pine St., Missoula, 59802. Tel: 406-728-5429.

Montana Association of Churches—MARGARET MACDONALD, Exec. Dir., 180 24th St. W., Ste. G, Billings, 59102. Tel: 406-656-9779; Rev. GARY W. RELLER, Diocesan Ecumenical Officer, P.O. Box 1477, Polson, 59860. Tel: 406-883-4607.

Diocesan Offices and Organizations

Borromeo Pre-Seminary Program—Rev. Msgr. KEVIN S. O'NEILL, Carroll College, P.O. Box 1729, Helena, 59624. Tel: 406-442-5820.

Catholic Campaign for Human Development—Deacon J. ANTHONY DUVERNAY, P.O. Box 1729, Helena, 59624. Tel: 406-442-5820.

Catholic Committee on Scouting—JAMES TUCKER, Contact, P.O. Box 1729, Helena, 59624. Tel: 406-442-5820.

Catholic Youth Coalition—ERIC SOVA, P.O. Box 1729, Helena, 59624. Tel: 406-442-5820.

Charismatic Renewal—J. ANTHONY DUVERNAY, Diocesan Pastoral Office, P.O. Box 1729, Helena, 59624.

Christian Family Movement—Diocesan Pastoral Office, P.O. Box 1729, Helena, 59624.

Clergy Senior Status and Security Trust Board—Rev. ROBERT C. BEAULIEU; Rev. Msgr. JOSEPH HARRINGTON; Revs. JOHN DARRAGH; JOHN HUNTHAUSEN; KEVIN O'NEILL; DANIEL SHEA.

Continuing Formation of the Clergy—Rev. THOMAS P. HAFFEY, Dir., 2100 Farragut, Butte, 59701. Tel: 406-723-4303.

Assembly of Women Religious—Sr. MARY JO MCDONALD, S.C.L., 438 W. Porphyry, Butte, 59701. Tel: 406-723-4303.

Cursillo Movement, Journey and Search—Deacon J. ANTHONY DUVERNAY, Diocesan Dir., Diocesan Pastoral Office, P.O. Box 1729, Helena, 59624. Tel: 406-442-5820.

Daughters of Isabella—SUSAN COSTLE, State Regent, 1019 E. 5th St., Anaconda, 59711.

Diocesan Attorney—WARD SHANAHAN, Gough, Shanahan, Johnson & Waterman, P.O. Box 1715, Helena, 59624. Tel: 406-442-8560.

Diocesan Buildings—SCOTT FITZPATRICK, Mgr., P.O. Box 1729, Helena, 59624.

Diocesan Council of Catholic Women—KATHY CAMPBELL, Pres., 21 8th Ave., S.E., Cutbank, 59429.

Diocesan Ecumenical Officer—Rev. GARY W. RELLER, P.O. Box 1477, Polson, 59860. Tel: 406-883-4607.

Friends of The Catholic University—Rev. Msgr. JOSEPH HARRINGTON, Chm., Carroll College, Helena, 59625. Tel: 406-447-4459.

Guatemala Missions—Deacon J. ANTHONY DUVERNAY, Dir., P.O. Box 1729, Helena, 59624. Tel: 406-442-5820.

Holy Childhood Association—Rev. JOSEPH L. BYRNE, Dir., P.O. Box 610, Townsend, 59644. Tel: 406-266-3973.

Legendary Lodge (Diocesan Summer Camp)—JAMES TUCKER, P.O. Box 1729, Helena, 59624. Tel: 406-442-5820.

Marriage Encounter—DAN PHILLIPS; MARY BETH PHILLIPS, 4614 A Ironwood, Great Falls, 59405.

Office of Due Process—Rev. JOHN ROBERTSON, P.O. Box 3269, Butte, 59701. Tel: 406-723-1255.

Permanent Deacons—Deacon J. ANTHONY DUVERNAY, Dir., P.O. Box 1729, Helena, 59624. Tel: 406-442-5820.

Program of Formation for Lay Ministry—JAMES TUCKER, P.O. Box 1729, Helena, 59624. Tel: 406-442-5820.

Program of Formation for the Permanent Diaconate—Deacon J. ANTHONY DUVERNAY, Coord., P.O. Box 1729, Helena, 59624. Tel: 406-442-5820.

Office of Worship—Rev. Msgr. KEVIN S. O'NEILL, Liturgy Consultant, P.O. Box 1729, Helena, 59624. Tel: 406-442-5820.

Propagation of the Faith—Rev. JOSEPH L. BYRNE, Diocesan Dir., P.O. Box 610, Townsend, 59644. Tel: 406-266-3973.

Christian Formation Department—JAMES TUCKER, Dir., 515 N. Ewing St., P.O. Box 1729, Helena, 59624. Tel: 406-442-5820.

Resource Center—KATHY WARD, Mgr., 515 N. Ewing St., P.O. Box 1729, Helena, 59624. Tel: 406-442-5820.

Vicar for Catholic Schools—PATRICK HAGGARTY, Supt., 515 N. Ewing St., P.O. Box 1729, Helena, 59624. Tel: 406-442-5820; Fax: 406-442-5191.

Third Order of St. Francis—KATHY POLEMAN, S.F.O., 1702 Peosta, Helena, 59601.

Victim Assistance Coordinator—KEVIN PHELAN. Tel: 406-442-5820. Email: kphelan@diocesehelena.org.

Vocations Office—P.O. Box 1729, Helena, 59624. Tel: 406-442-5820. Rev. THOMAS O'DONNELL, Dir., P.O. Box 1110, East Helena, 59635. Tel: 406-227-5334.

"Montana Catholic" (Diocesan Newspaper)—ERIC SCHIEDERMAYER, Editor. Assistant Editors: RENEE ST. MARTIN-WISEMAN; M. CATHERINE TILZEY, 515 N. Ewing St., P.O. Box 1729, Helena, 59624. Tel: 406-442-5820; Fax: 406-442-5191.

CLERGY, PARISHES, MISSIONS AND PAROCHIAL SCHOOLS

CITY OF HELENA
(LEWIS AND CLARK COUNTY)

1—CATHEDRAL OF ST. HELENA (1866), Very Rev. Kevin S. O'Neill, V.G., Rector; Rev. Timothy Moriarty; Michael Vreeberg, Pastoral Assoc.; Tracey Johnson, Pastoral Assoc.; Bob Fishman, Pastoral Assoc.
Office—530 N. Ewing St., 59601. Tel: 406-442-5825; 406-442-7094 (after hours); Fax: 406-449-5113.
Catechesis/Religious Program—Deb Kralicek, D.R.E. Students 484.
Good Samaritan Thrift Store— (Assistance to those in need.) , 3065 N. Montana Ave., 59601. Tel: 406-442-0780.

2—ST. MARY (1910), Rev. James Connor; Deacon Richard Miller, Pastoral Assoc.; Joanie Volesky, Pastoral Assoc.; Janice Nankivel, Pastoral Assoc.; Jay Stimac, Pastoral Assoc.
Office—1700 Missoula Ave., 59601. Tel: 406-442-5268; Fax: 406-449-0860.

3—OUR LADY OF THE VALLEY, Rev. Daniel B. Shea; Deacon Randy Fraser.
Office—1502 Shirley Rd., 59601. Tel: 406-458-6114; Fax: 406-458-8179.
Mission—Sacred Heart Wolf Creek, Lewis and Clark Co.
Mission—Our Lady of Lourdes Marysville, Lewis and Clark Co.

OUTSIDE THE CITY OF HELENA

ANACONDA, DEER LODGE CO.

1—ANACONDA CATHOLIC COMMUNITY (1980),, Serves the entire community of Anaconda Revs. John E. Murray; Jeffrey Benusa; Sr. Eileen Johnson, S.C.L., Pastoral Assoc.; Patricia A. Ricci Pastoral Assoc.; Mr. John McKenna, Admin.
Office:—217 W. Pennsylvania, 59711. Tel: 406-563-8406; Fax: 406-563-5912.
Res.: 405 Alder St., 59711. Tel: 406-563-6633.
Holy Family: 217 W. Pennsylvania, 58711.
St. Peter: 401 Alder St., 59711.
Catechesis/Religious Program—Patricia A. Ricci, D.R.E.
Station—Georgetown Lake

2—ST. JOSEPH'S (1957),, Closed 1977. For inquiries for parish records contact Anaconda Catholic Community, Anaconda

3—ST. PAUL'S (1888),, Closed 1980. For inquiries for parish records contact Anaconda Catholic Community, Anaconda

4—ST. PETER'S (1898),, Closed 1980. For inquiries for parish records contact Anaconda Catholic Community, Anaconda

BIGFORK, FLATHEAD CO., ST. CATHERINE (1958), Rev. Msgr. Donald Shea; Deacons James Butts; Anthony Martin.
Res.: P.O. Box 277, 59911. Tel: 406-837-4846; Fax: 406-837-4909.
Church: 105 Oliver Ln., 59911.
Mission—St. Ann Somers.

BONNER, MISSOULA CO., ST. ANN (1940), Rev. Raymond V. Gilmore.
Res.: P.O. Box 1008, 59823. Tel: 406-258-6815; Fax: 406-258-2943.
Catechesis/Religious Program—Josephine Labbe, D.R.E.

BOULDER, JEFFERSON CO., ST. CATHERINE (1894), Rev. William Greytak.
Res.: 214 S. Elder St., P.O. Box 205, 59632. Tel: 406-225-3222; Fax: 406-225-9152.
Catechesis/Religious Program—Tel: 406-225-3541. Michelle St. George, D.R.E. Students 52.
Mission—St. John the Evangelist Boulder Valley, Jefferson Co.

BOZEMAN, GALLATIN CO.

1—HOLY ROSARY (1885), Rev. Leo Proxell; Laurie Croghan, Pastoral Assoc.; Timothy Bell, Pastoral Assoc.
Office—220 W. Main St., P.O. Box 96, 59771-0096. Tel: 406-587-4581; Fax: 406-582-0248.

2—RESURRECTION (1965),, (Newman Parish) Rev. Robert Hall; Marge O'Leary, Pastoral Assoc.; Diane Dwyer, Pastoral Assoc.
Office—1725 S. 11th, 59715. Tel: 406-586-9243; 406-587-8667 (Res.); Fax: 406-586-2886.
Catechesis/Religious Program—Diane Dwyer, D.R.E.

BROWNING, GLACIER CO., CHURCH OF THE LITTLE FLOWER (1904), Rev. Edward Kohler; Sr. Edna Hunthausen, S.C.L., Pastoral Assoc.; Deacons Robert Bremner; John Gobert.
Office—P.O. Box 519, 59417. Tel: 406-338-5775; Fax: 406-338-5506.
Church: 204 First St. N.W., 59417.
Catechesis/Religious Program—Valarie Goss, D.R.E.
School—De La Salle Blackfeet Middle School, Tel: 406-338-5290. Bro. Paul Ackerman, Prin.
Mission—St. Mary, Queen of the World Babb, Glacier Co.
Mission—Sacred Heart Starr School.
Mission—Church of the Ascension East Glacier, Glacier Co.

BUTTE, SILVER BOW CO.

1—ST. ANN (1917), Rev. Thomas P. Haffey; Sr. Mary Jo McDonald, S.C.L., Pastoral Assoc.; Deacon H. J. Johnson.
Res.: 2100 Farragut, 59701. Tel: 406-723-4303; Fax: 406-723-5172.
Catechesis/Religious Program—Rosie Richards, D.R.E.

2—BUTTE CATHOLIC COMMUNITY NORTH, , Includes Immaculate Conception, St. Joseph, and St. Patrick Parishes. See individual listings. Rev. William F. Vernon; Sr. Patricia Field, S.C.L., Pastoral Assoc. In Res., Rev. Harry Butori; Deacons Ronald Fournier; Stan Gould.
Office & Res.: 102 S. Washington St., 59701. Tel: 406-723-5407; Fax: 406-782-8082.
Catechesis/Religious Program—Fax: 406-723-5408. Seaneen Prendergast, D.R.E.

3—ST. HELENA (1921), Closed., 1966. For inquiries for parish records contact Butte Catholic Community North, Butte.

4—HOLY SAVIOR (1904),, Closed 1974. For inquiries for parish records contact Butte Catholic Community North, Butte.

5—HOLY SPIRIT (1978), Rev. John W. Robertson; Deacon Dan McGrath.
Office:—3930 East Lake, 59701. Tel: 406-494-5078; Fax: 406-494-5726.
Catechesis/Religious Program—Theresa O'Leary, D.R.E.

6—IMMACULATE CONCEPTION (1907),, (Butte Catholic Community North) Rev. William F. Vernon.
Office & Res.: 102 S. Washington, 59701. Tel: 406-723-5407; Fax: 406-782-8082.
Church: Western & Caledonia St., 59701.

7—ST. JOHN THE EVANGELIST (1917), Rev. Edward Courtney; Kathy Walter, Pastoral Assoc.
Office—1500 Cobban Ave., 59701.
Res.: 2040 Whitman, 59701. Tel: 406-782-8349; Fax: 406-782-1660.
Church: 1500 Majors Ave., 59701.

8—ST. JOSEPH (1905),, (Butte Catholic Community North) Rev. William F. Vernon.
Office & Res.: 102 S. Washington, 59701. Tel: 406-723-5407 (Office); Fax: 406-782-8082.
Church: Utah & Second St., 59701.

9—ST. MARY (1903), Closed., 1986. For inquiries for parish records contact Butte Catholic Community North, Butte.

10—ST. PATRICK (1881),, (Butte Catholic Community North) Rev. William F. Vernon.
Office & Res.: 102 S. Washington St., 59701. Tel: 406-723-5407; Fax: 406-782-8082.
Church: Mercury & Washington St., 59701.

11—SACRED HEART PARISH (1903), Closed., 1970. For inquiries for parish records contact Butte Catholic Community North, Butte.

CHOTEAU, TETON CO., ST. JOSEPH (1898), Rev. Robert C. Noonan, Pastor.
Res.: P.O. Box 640, 59422. Tel: 406-466-2961; Fax: 406-466-5157.
Church: 320 Main St., 59422.

Catechesis/Religious Program—Tel: 406-469-2312. Frankie Hanson, D.R.E.

COLUMBIA FALLS, FLATHEAD CO., ST. RICHARD (1941), Rev. Joseph P. Moran; Deacon Robert Pearce.
Res.: P.O. Box 2073, 59912. Tel: 406-892-5142; Fax: 406-892-2147.
Church: 1210 Ninth St. W., 59912.
Mission— West Glacier, Flathead Co.
Station—Apgar

CONRAD, PONDERA CO., ST. MICHAEL (1909), Rev. Michael Poole.
Res.: 106 S. Maryland St., 59425. Tel: 406-278-7517; Fax: 406-278-9106.
Catechesis/Religious Program—Kathy Hauer, D.R.E.
Station—Stations Brady Ledger

CUT BANK, GLACIER CO., ST. MARGARET (1914), Rev. Stanley Popowski; Kathy Campbell, Pastoral Assoc.; Deacon James E. Hayes.
Res.: 207 Second St., S.E., 59427. Tel: 406-873-4413; Fax: 406-873-9256.

DEER LODGE, POWELL CO., IMMACULATE CONCEPTION (1911), Rev. Robert G. Porter.
Res.: 605 Clark St., P.O. Box 786, 59722. Tel: 406-846-1444; Fax: 406-846-1444.
Catechesis/Religious Program—Tel: 406-563-2949; Fax: 406-846-1999. Mary Fox, D.R.E.
Mission—St. Theodore Avon, Powell Co.

DILLON, BEAVERHEAD CO., ST. ROSE OF LIMA (1901), Rev. Jeffrey M. Fleming; Cecilia Tarleton, Pastoral Assoc.
Office—226 S. Atlantic St., 59725. Tel: 406-683-4391; 406-683-6753 (Rectory); Fax: 406-683-4391.
Catechesis/Religious Program—Nancy Johnson, D.R.E.
Mission—St. John The Apostle Melrose, Silver Bow Co.
Mission—Our Lady of Wisdom Wisdom, Beaverhead Co.

DRUMMOND, GRANITE CO., ST. MICHAEL (1919), Rev. Herbert J. Pins (SEA).
Res.: P.O. Box 329, 59832. Tel: 406-288-3847; Fax: 406-288-3847.
Mission—St. Mary Goldcreek, Powell Co.

DUTTON, TETON CO., ST. WILLIAM (1962), Rev. Michael Poole, Sacramental Min.
Res.: 107-1st Ave. N.E., 59433. Tel: 406-476-3429; Fax: 406-476-3392.
Mission—Guardian Angel Power, Teton Co.

EAST HELENA, LEWIS AND CLARK CO., SS. CYRIL AND METHODIUS (1907), Rev. Thomas M. O'Donnell; Deacons Gerald Kuhl; Bob Miller.
Res.: 214 W. Riggs St., P.O. Box 1110, 59635. Tel: 406-227-5334; Fax: 406-227-5891.
Catechesis/Religious Program—Tel: 406-227-6260. Marie Moran, D.R.E.
Mission—Our Lady of the Lake Canyon Ferry, Lewis and Clark Co.
Mission—St. John's Clancy, Jefferson Co.
Station—Alhambra

EUREKA, LINCOLN CO., OUR LADY OF MERCY (1916), Rev. Henry Steinhoff (B) (Retired); Deacon Dan Casazza, Pastoral Admin.
Res.: 500 Dewey Ave., P.O. Box 626, 59917. Tel: 406-296-2118; Fax: 406-296-5247.
Catechesis/Religious Program—Betty Peltier, D.R.E.

FAIRFIELD, TETON CO., ST. JOHN (1941), Rev. Robert C. Noonan.
Res.: 514 First Ave. S., P.O. Box 397, 59436. Tel: 406-467-2481.
Mission—St. Matthias Augusta, Lewis and Clark Co.

FRENCHTOWN, MISSOULA CO., ST. JOHN THE BAPTIST (1884), [CEM] Rev. Kevin Christofferson; Deacon Van Wolverton.
Res.: P.O. Box 329, 59834. Tel: 406-626-4492; Fax: 406-626-1970.
Catechesis/Religious Program—Donna Haacke, D.R.E.
Mission—St. Mary Queen of Heaven Superior, Mineral Co.
Mission—St. Albert the Great Alberton, Mineral Co.

HAMILTON, RAVALLI CO., ST. FRANCIS (1896), Rev. John J. Darragh; Sr. Margaret Hogan, S.C.L., Pastoral Assoc.
Res.: 411 S. Fifth St., 59840. Tel: 406-363-1385; Fax: 406-375-0967.
Mission—St. Philip Benizi Darby, Ravalli Co.

HARLOWTON, WHEATLAND CO., ST. JOSEPH (1909), Unassigned.
Res.: 26 Third St., N.W., Box 286, 59036. Tel: 406-632-5538; Fax: 406-632-4897.
Mission—Immaculate Conception Judith Gap, Wheatland Co.
Mission—Blessed Sacrament Shawmut, Wheatland Co.

HEART BUTTE, GLACIER CO., ST. ANNE (1911), Rev. Daniel Powers, S.J.; Bev Bullshoe, Pastoral Assoc.; Deacon Melvin Rutherford, Pastoral Assoc.
Blackfeet Reservation: P.O. Box 160, 59448. Tel: 406-338-2312; Fax: 406-338-2362.
Mission—Holy Family Mission [CEM], Glacier Co.

HELMVILLE, POWELL CO., ST. THOMAS (1889), [CEM] Rev. Jozef Perehubka.
Res.: P.O. Box 90, 59843. Tel: 406-793-5697; Fax: 406-793-5697.
Mission—St. Jude's Lincoln, Lewis and Clark Co.
Mission—Living Water 465 Highland Dr., P.O. Box 995, Seeley Lake, Missoula Co. 59868.

KALISPELL, FLATHEAD CO.

1—ST. MATTHEW (1895), Rev. Victor E. Langhans; Deacon Fred Topp, Pastoral Assoc.
Office—602 S. Main St., 59901. Tel: 406-752-6788; Fax: 406-756-8248.
Res.: 644 First Ave. W., 59901. Tel: 406-755-1357.

2—RISEN CHRIST (1978), Rev. Rudy Bullman.
Res.: 65 W. Evergreen Dr., 59901. Tel: 406-752-4219; Fax: 406-752-4226.
Catechesis/Religious Program—Marj DeZort, D.R.E.; Laurie Kollmann, D.R.E.

LIBBY, LINCOLN CO., ST. JOSEPH (1911), Rev. Daniel Driscoll; Deacon David Weisbeck.
Res.: 719 Utah Ave., P.O. Box 1467, 59923. Tel: 406-293-4322; Fax: 406-293-7231.
Mission—Immaculate Conception Troy, Lincoln Co.

MADISON, MADISON CO., MADISON COUNTY CATHOLIC COMMUNITY, , Comprised of St. Mary of the Assumption, Laurin; St. Joseph, Sheridan; and St. Patrick, Ennis. Rev. Edward L. Stupca.
Res.: 105 Poppleton, P.O. Box 17, Sheridan, 59749. Tel: 406-842-5588; Fax: 406-842-7433.
Catechesis/Religious Program—Laurie Bartoletti, D.R.E.

MISSOULA, MISSOULA CO.

1—ST. ANTHONY (1921), Rev. John P. Miller; Terry Jimmerson, Pastoral Assoc.
Office—217 Tremont St., 59801. Tel: 406-543-3129; Fax: 406-549-6009.

2—CHRIST THE KING (1966),, (Newman Parish) Rev. James J. Hogan; Sr. Doris Faber, Pastoral Assoc.; Richard A. Bishop, Pastoral Assoc.
Office—1400 Gerald Ave., 59801. Tel: 406-728-3845; Fax: 406-829-8797.
Catechesis/Religious Program—Devon Honzel, D.R.E.

3—ST. FRANCIS XAVIER (1881), Revs. Richard Perry, S.J.; James Meehan, S.J.; Deacons Michael Bloomdahl; Carlton Quamme. In Res., Revs. Thomas F. Healy, S.J.; George J. Dumais, S.J.; William Burke, S.J.; Jerry S. Graham, S.J. (P).
Office:—420 W. Pine St., 59802. Tel: 406-542-0321; Fax: 406-327-8537.
Catechesis/Religious Program—Erin Eisenman-Turner, D.R.E.

4—HOLY FAMILY (1972), Rev. Matthew Huber; Sr. Kathleen O'Sullivan, B.V.M., Pastoral Assoc.; Deacon Thomas McCarthy.
Res.: 4616 Gharrett St., 59803. Tel: 406-251-2692; Fax: 406-251-0324.
Catechesis/Religious Program—Tel: 406-251-2027. Patti Cassidy, D.R.E.
Mission—Spirit of Christ 4200 Farm Ln., P.O. Box 743, Lolo, Missoula Co. 59847. Tel: 406-273-2748.

5—POPE JOHN XXIII (1971), Rev. Edward Hislop.
Office—1475 Eaton St., 59801. Tel: 406-721-2405; Fax: 406-721-0025.
Catechesis/Religious Program—Scott Kappes, D.R.E.

PHILIPSBURG, GRANITE CO., ST. PHILIP (1892), Rev. Herbert J. Pins.
Res.: 307 W. Kearney, P.O. Box 397, 59858. Tel: 406-859-3908; Fax: 406-859-3960.

PLAINS, SANDERS CO., ST. JAMES (1889), Rev. Kenneth E. Fortney; Deacon Lynn F. McAtee.
Res.: 107 Meany St., P.O. Box 745, 59859. Tel: 406-826-3668; Fax: 406-826-0029.
Catechesis/Religious Program—Tel: 406-826-5602 (St. James); 741-300- (Sacred Heart Mission). Bonnie Ziegler, D.R.E. (Sacred Heart Mission).
Mission—Sacred Heart Hot Springs, Sanders Co.

POLSON, LAKE CO., IMMACULATE CONCEPTION (1909), [CEM 3] Rev. Gary W. Reller; Deacons Wesley Vert; Daniel Gullotta.
Res.: 908 Fifth Ave. E., P.O. Box 1477, 59860. Tel: 406-883-4607; 406-883-2506 (Office); Fax: 406-883-4607.
Church: 1002 Fourth Ave. E., 59860.
Catechesis/Religious Program—Ellen Hoyt, D.R.E.

RONAN, LAKE CO., SACRED HEART (1911), Rev. Gary W. Reller; Sr. Barbara Bell, O.P., Pastoral Admin.
Res.: 325 Round Butte W., 59864. Tel: 406-676-4511; Fax: 406-676-4515.
Mission—St. Joseph's Charlo, Mount Lake Co.

ST. IGNATIUS, LAKE CO., ST. IGNATIUS MISSION (1854), Rev. Andrew Maddock, S.J.; Sisters Dolores Shortal, O.P., Pastoral Assoc.; Joan Bartin, O.P., Pastoral Assoc.
Res.: #1 Church St., P.O. Box 667, 59865. Tel: 406-745-2768; Fax: 406-745-0010.
Mission—Sacred Heart 434 HI Francis, Arlee, Lake Co. 59821. Tel: 406-726-3450; Fax: 406-726-0012.
Mission—St. John Berchman's Jocko, Lake Co.

SHELBY, TOOLE CO., ST. WILLIAM (1924), Rev. Gregory Lively.
Res.: 531 Main St., 59474. Tel: 406-434-2988; Fax: 406-434-9133.
Catechesis/Religious Program—Tammy Hauschultz, D.R.E.
Mission—St. Thomas Aquinas (1917), Sunburst.

STEVENSVILLE, RAVALLI CO., ST. MARY (1842), [CEM] Rev. Michael M. Smith.
Res.: 333 Charlos St., 59870. Tel: 406-777-5574; Fax: 406-777-1032.
Catechesis/Religious Program—Betsy Mercer, D.R.E.
Mission—St. Joseph Florence, Ravalli Co.

SWAN VALLEY, LAKE CO., SWAN VALLEY CATHOLIC COMMUNITY, Rev. Dusan A. Okorn, Admin. (Retired); Michelle Jenkins, Pastoral Assoc.
Res.: The Sycamore Tree, Swan Lake, 59911. Tel: 406-754-2429; Fax: 406-754-2429.

THOMPSON FALLS, SANDERS CO., ST. WILLIAM (1955), Rev. Kenneth E. Fortney; Deacon Ronald Kazmierezak.
Res.: 416 Preston Ave., P.O. Box 186, 59873. Tel: 406-827-4433; Fax: 406-827-4422.
Catechesis/Religious Program—Tel: 406-827-4119. Tina Fausett, D.R.E.
Mission— Noxon.

THREE FORKS, GALLATIN CO., HOLY FAMILY (1886), Rev. Stephen Cocca; Deacon Robert Lane.
Res.: 104 Birch St., P.O. Box 99, 59752. Tel: 406-285-3592; Fax: 406-285-0838.
Catechesis/Religious Program—Mary Olson, D.R.E.
Mission—Valley of Flowers 609 Quaw Blvd., Belgrade, Gallatin Co. 59714.

TOWNSEND, BROADWATER CO., HOLY CROSS (1903), Rev. Joseph L. Byrne; Deacon Donald Marks.
Res.: 101 S. Walnut, P.O. Box 610, 59644. Tel: 406-266-4811; Fax: 406-266-4811.
Catechesis/Religious Program—Tel: 406-266-4845. Elizabeth Ferris, D.R.E.
Mission—Immaculate Conception Toston, Broadwater Co.
St. Joseph's Historical Church—Canton.

VALIER, PONDERA CO., ST. FRANCIS (1909), Rev. Stanley Popowski; Mary Jean Brophy, Pastoral Assoc.
Res.: 701-4th St., P.O. Box 338, 59486. Tel: 406-279-3327.
Mission—Holy Cross Dupuyer, Pondera Co.

WALKERVILLE, SILVER BOW CO., ST. LAWRENCE O'TOOLE (1896), Closed., 1986. For inquiries for parish records contact Butte Catholic Community North, Butte.

WEST YELLOWSTONE, GALLATIN CO., OUR LADY OF THE PINES, Rev. Joseph B. Oblinger (Retired); Sr. Patricia Toeckes, S.C.L., Pastoral Admin.
Res.: Madison Ave. & Geyser St., P.O. Box 577, 59758. Tel: 406-646-7755; Fax: 406-646-4590.
Mission—Big Sky

WHITE SULPHUR SPRINGS, MEAGHER CO., ST. BARTHOLOMEW (1916), Unassigned.
Res.: 407 Second Ave. S.E., P.O. Box 422, 59645. Tel: 406-547-3737; Fax: 406-547-2581.

WHITEFISH, FLATHEAD CO., ST. CHARLES (1890), Rev. Charles Roman.
Res.: 230 Baker, P.O. Box 128, 59937. Tel: 406-862-2051; Fax: 406-862-9897.
Catechesis/Religious Program—Wendy Lengstorf, D.R.E.

WHITEHALL, JEFFERSON CO., ST. TERESA (1911), Rev. Richard H. Sodja.
Res.: 109 Second Ave. E., P.O. Box 430, 59759. Tel: 406-287-3893; Fax: 406-287-9213.
Mission—Notre Dame Twin Bridges, Jefferson Co.

DIOCESAN MISSIONS

GUATEMALA, SANTO TOMAS LA UNION, Rev. James Hazelton; Sisters Mary Waddell, B.V.M., Clinic Dir.; Anna Priester, B.V.M., D.R.E.
10017 Departmento Suchitepequez, Mexico.

HELENA, LEWIS AND CLARK CO., GUATEMALA MISSION MEDICAL FUND,

Chaplains of Public Institutions

HELENA. *U.S. Veteran's Hospital*, Fort Harrison. Served by Helena Area Parishes.

BOULDER. *Boulder River School and Hospital*. Rev. William Greytak. Attended from St. Catherine, Boulder.

DEER LODGE. *Montana State Prison*. Rev. Herbert J. Pins (SEA).

WARM SPRINGS. *Warm Springs State Hospital*. Rev. Herbert J. Pins (SEA).

Special Assignments:
Revs.—
Dornbos, William, Diocesan Chancery, 100 E. Broadway, Butte, 59701.
Dumais, George J., S.J., Dir., Rochmont, Inc., 1700 Madeline, Missoula, 59801.

Malnar, Stan, 4220 W. Fremont Rd., Spokane, WA 99204. P.O. Box 1729, 59624.
McCallum, Dougald, North American College, Rome
Robertson, John W., Judicial Vicar & Vicar for Canonical Concerns

On Duty Outside the Diocese:
Rev. Msgr.—
McCarthy, John F., P.A., Oblates of Wisdom, P.O. Box 109, Eastman, WI 54626.
Revs.—
Driscoll, Michael, Notre Dame University, Department of Theology, Notre Dame, IN 46556.
Flynn, Thomas, Emory University, 1278 Oakdale Rd., N.E., Atlanta, GA 30307.
Hazelton, James, Santo Tomas La Union, Departmento Suchitepuez 10017 Guatemala.
Sullivan, James M., Creighton University, 2500 California St., Omaha, NE 68178.

On Leave of Absence:
Rev.—
McCarthy, James C., 1123 Maryland, Butte, 59701.

Military Chaplains:
Revs.—
Diphe, Juan M., U.S. Air Force
Patton, Patrick G., U.S. Army

Retired:
Rev. Msgrs.—
Brown, Anthony M., 30 Penny Ln., Butte, 59701.
Harrington, Joseph D., Carroll College, 59625.
Revs.—
Beaulieu, Robert, 4307 Gharrett St., Missoula, 59803.
Burke, Gregory, 105 Rampart Dr., #215, Butte, 59701.
Burns, Ernest, 100 E. Broadway #601, Butte, 59701.
Butori, Harry, 102 S. Washington St., Butte, 59701.
Fenlon, Thomas J., 100 E. Broadway, Butte, 59701.
Finnegan, Joseph, P.O. Box 503, Whitehall, 59759.
Hunthausen, John F., Carroll College, 59625.
Koenig, Bernard, P.O. Box 765, Ronan, 59864.
Lynam, Gerald J., 915 Saddle Dr., #115 59625.
McGurk, Patrick, 534 Gold Creek Rd., Gold Creek, 59733.
O'Sullivan, Sarsfield, 410 N. Western Ave., Butte, 59701.
Oblinger, Joseph B., 2400 Durston Rd., #37, Bozeman, 59715.
Okorn, Dusan A., Sycamore Tree, Swan Lake, 59701.
Plummer, J. Bruce, 261 Half Circle Way, Polson, 59860
Simons, Lawrence D., P.O. Box 696, Honaunau, HI 96726.
Strom, Charles W., 341 Lupfer Ave., Whitefish, 59937.
Sullivan, J. Bernard, 915 Saddle Dr., #309, 59601.
Tallman, Stephen, 5630 Lower Woodchuck Rd., Florence, 59833.
Waggener, William L., 300 Mt. Highland Dr., #221, Butte, 59701.
Wang, John, 425 Ford St., Missoula, 59801.
Ward, John, 776 Asteroid, Billings, 59105.
Wiegenstein, Francis, 4309 Gharett Ave., Missoula, 59803.

Permanent Deacons:
Blake, Stephen, Little Flower, Browning
Bloomdahl, Michael, St. Francis Xavier, Missoula
Bremner, Robert, Sr., Little Flower, Browning
Britton, Michael, (Retired)
Butts, James, St. Catherine, Bigfork
Curry, James, (Retired)
Duvernay, J. Anthony, Dir. Diocesan Pastoral Office, St. Helena Cathedral
Fournier, Ronald, Butte Catholic Community North, Butte
Fraser, Randall, Our Lady of the Valley, Helena
Gobert, John, Little Flower, Browning
Gould, Stanley F., St. Patrick, Butte
Gullotta, Daniel, Immaculate Conception, Polson
Hayes, James E., St. Margaret, Cut Bank
Johnson, H. J., St. Ann's, Butte
Kazmierczak, Ronald, St. William, Thompson Falls
Kelley, Robert, St. William, Thompson Falls
Kuhl, Gerald, Sts. Cyril and Methodius, East Helena
Lane, Robert, Holy Family, Three Forks
Marks, Donald, Holy Cross, Townsend
Martin, Anthony, St. Catherine, Bigfork
McAtee, Lynn F., St. James, Plains
McCarthy, Thomas, Holy Family, Missoula
McGrath, Daniel, Holy Spirit, Butte
Miller, Richard, St. Mary, Helena
Miller, Robert, Sts. Cyril and Methodius, East Helena
Pearce, Robert, St. Richard, Columbia Falls
Peterson, Roland, St. Francis Parish, Hamilton
Quamme, Carlton, St. Francis, Missoula
Roos, Fritz, Cathedral of St. Helena, Helena
Rutherford, Melvin, (On Duty Outside the Diocese)
Topp, Frederick, St. Matthew, Kalispell
Vert, Wesley, Immaculate Conception, Polson
Weisbeck, David, St. Joseph, Libby
Wolverton, Van, St. John the Baptist, Frenchtown

INSTITUTIONS LOCATED IN THE DIOCESE

[A] SEMINARIES, DIOCESAN

HELENA. *Carroll College*, 1601 N. Benton Ave., 59625. Tel: 406-447-4300; Fax: 406-447-4533. Email: rturner@carroll.edu. Rev. Robert Turner, Dir. Diocesan Pre-Seminary Prog. Students 1.

[B] COLLEGES AND UNIVERSITIES

HELENA. *Carroll College* (1909), 1601 N. Benton Ave., 59625. Tel: 406-447-4300; Fax: 406-447-4533. Web: www.carroll.edu. Rev. Robert Turner, Chap. & Campus Min.; Dr. Thomas Trebon, Pres.; Ms. Lynn Etchart, Vice Pres. Finance & Admin.; Mr. Thomas J. McCarvel, Vice Pres. Institutional Advancement; Dr. James Hardwick, Vice Pres. Student Affairs; Revs. Jeremiah Lowney; J. Eugene Peoples; Daniel B. Shea; Jeremiah T. Sullivan. Four year Diocesan College of Liberal Arts and Sciences. Priests 5; Lay Professors 69; Students 1,469; Total Staff 135. In Res. Rev. Msgr. Joseph D. Harrington (Retired); Rev. John F. Hunthausen (Retired).

[C] HIGH SCHOOLS, DIOCESAN

BUTTE. *Central High School*, 9 S. Idaho St., 59701. Tel: 406-782-6761; Fax: 406-723-3873. Tim Norbeck, Prin. Lay Teachers 17; Students 140.

MISSOULA. *Loyola Sacred Heart High School* (Missoula Catholic Schools) , 320 Edith St., 59801. Tel: 406-549-6101; Fax: 406-542-1432. Email: lsh@blackfoot.net. Web: www.montana.com/loyola/index2.html. Patrick Haggarty, Supt., Schools; Jeremy Beck, Prin.; Kathy Schneider, Vice Prin. Priests 1; Lay Teachers 23; Students 182.

[D] SCHOOLS, ELEMENTARY

BROWNING. *De La Salle Blackfeet Middle School*, P.O. Box 1489, 59417. Tel: 406-338-5290. Email: principal@delasalleblackfeet.org Bro. Paul Ackerman, Prin. Students 50.

BUTTE. *Central Elementary School*, (Grades PreK-5), 1100 Delaware, 59701. Tel: 406-782-4500; Fax: 406-723-4845. Email: bcelem@in-tch.com. Carolyn Trudnowski, Prin. Sisters 2; Lay Teachers 14; Students 298.

After School Care Tel: 406-782-4500; Fax: 406-723-4845. Mary Carol Hogart, Dir. Students (Ages 5-12) 30.

Central Junior High School, (Grades 6-8), 1100 Delaware, 59701. Tel: 406-782-4500; Fax: 406-723-4845. Carolyn Trudnowski, Prin. Lay Teachers 5; Students 97.

KALISPELL. *St. Matthew School*, 602 S. Main St., 59901. Tel: 406-752-6303; Fax: 406-756-8248. Email: office@stmattsaints.org. Web: www.digisys.net. Eugene Boyle, Prin. Sisters 1; Lay Teachers 19; Preschool (Age 4) 40; Students 203.

Day Care Center Tel: 406-756-6807; Fax: 406-756-8248. Merlene Stephens, Dir (Ages 2-6) Students 60.

MISSOULA. *St. Joseph Elementary School* (Missoula Catholic Schools) , 503 Edith St., 59801. Tel: 406-549-1290; Fax: 406-543-4034. Email: mdougherty@sjs.k12.mt.us. Web: www.montana.com/stjoe. Scott Anderson, Prin. Lay Teachers 21; Students 260.

Child Care Center Tel: 406-549-1290; Fax: 406-543-4034. Evalie Hankinson, Dir. (Ages 2-12) Students 45.

[E] GENERAL HOSPITALS

BUTTE. *St. James Health System, Sisters of Charity of Leavenworth Health System*, 400 S. Clark St., 59701. Tel: 406-723-2500; Fax: 406-723-2443. Email: jkaiser@sjch.org. Web: www.sj-mt.org. P.O. Box 3300, 59702. James Kaiser, Admin.; Sisters Mary Agnes Hogan, S.C.L., Dir. & Pastoral Care; Joy Duff, S.C.L., Pastoral Care; Rev. Gregory Burke, Chap. & Pastoral Care. Bed Capacity 100; Sisters of Charity of Leavenworth 4; Lay Staff 491; Patients Assisted Annually 21,416.

MISSOULA. *St. Patrick Hospital and Health Sciences Center, Sisters of Providence of Montana Corporation*, 500 W. Broadway, 59802. Tel: 406-543-7271; Fax: 406-329-5693. Email: witz@saintpatrick.org. Web: www.saintpatrick.org. P.O. Box 4587, 59806. Steven Witz, Pres.; Revs. William Burke, S.J.; George Dumias, S.J.; Frank McCormick; Sr. Elizabeth Olsen, B.V.M., Pastoral Care. Sisters 1; Lay Staff 1,350; Bed Capacity 213; Patients Assisted Annually 115,000.

POLSON. *St. Joseph Hospital Corporation*, #6 Thirteenth Ave. E., P.O. Box 1010, 59860. Tel: 406-883-5377; Fax: 406-883-8488. Email: whealon@saintjoes.org. Web: saintjoes.org. John W. Glueckert, Admin.; Rev. Gary Reller, Chap.; Deacon Wes Vert; Joan Christensen, Pastoral Care. Bed Capacity 22; Lay Staff 155; Patients Assisted Annually 24,440.

[F] CONVENTS AND RESIDENCES OF SISTERS

COLUMBIA FALLS. *Epiphany Monastery*, P.O. Box 8177, 59912. Tel: 406-892-4670. Monastery dependent upon St. Martin Monastery, Rapid City, SD. Sisters 2.

[G] HOUSES OF PRAYER

SWAN LAKE. *The Sycamore Tree Contemplative Prayer Center* 59911. Tel: 406-754-2429. Email: sycamoretree@blackfoot.net. Rev. Dusan A. Okorn, Dir. (Retired); Michelle Jenkins, Asst.

[H] NEWMAN CHAPLAINS

BOZEMAN. *Montana State University* , (Resurrection Parish) , Office: 1725 S. Eleventh, 59715-4218. Tel: 406-586-9243; Fax: 406-586-2886. Rev. Robert Hall.

BUTTE. *Montana College of Mineral Science and Technology* Office: 102 S. Washington St., 59701. Tel: 406-723-5407; Fax: 406-723-8082. Email: bccn@in-tch.com. Rev. William F. Vernon, Chap.; Seaneen Prendergast, Campus Min.

DILLON. *University of Montana - Western* 226 S. Atlantic St., 59725. Tel: 406-683-4391; Fax: 406-683-6244. Email: jfleming@diocesehelena.org. Web: www.strosedillon.org. Rev. Jeffrey M. Fleming.

MISSOULA. *University of Montana* , (Christ the King Parish) , 1400 Gerald Ave., 59801-4230. Tel: 406-728-3845; Fax: 406-829-8797. Email: ctkccm@christthekingccm.org. Web: www.christthekingccm.org. Rev. James J. Hogan; Sr. Doris Faber, Pastoral Assoc.; Suzanne A. Monroe, Admin. Asst.

[I] FOUNDATIONS

BUTTE. *St. James Healthcare Foundation*, 400 S. Clark St., 59701. Tel: 406-723-2500; Fax: 406-723-2443. Email: jameskaiser@sjch.org. James Kaiser, Admin.

MISSOULA. *St. Patrick Health and Hospital Foundation*, 500 W. Broadway, 59806. Tel: 406-329-5630; Fax: 406-329-5693. Email: witz@stpatrick.org. Tom Wozniak, Pres.

[J] MISCELLANEOUS

HELENA. *The St. Helena Cathedral Foundation, Inc.*, 530 N. Ewing St., 59601-4001. Tel: 406-442-5825; Fax: 406-449-5113. Terry B. Cosgrove, Chmn.

BROWNING. *St. Vincent de Paul Thrift Store*, 112 First Ave., N.W., P.O. Box 974, 59417. Tel: 406-338-5403. Mona Kipling, Mgr.

BUTTE. *Central Education Foundation*, P.O. Box 634, 59703-0634. Tel: 406-723-6706; Fax: 406-723-3873. Don Peoples Jr., Exec. Dir.

**Maternal Life International*, 434 N. Main St, 59701-8804. Tel: 406-782-1719. Email: usacares@in-tch.com. Web: Maternallifeintl.com. Dr. George Mulcaire-Jones, Medical Dir. & Bd. Pres.

St. Vincent de Paul Thrift Store, 123 E. Park St., 59701. Tel: 406-782-0233. Frank Cotton, Dir.

MISSOULA. *Loyola-Sacred Heart High School Foundation*, 300 Edith St., 59801-3916. Tel: 406-728-2367; 406-728-2353; Fax: 406-542-9900. Email: lshftjf@montana.com. Steve Hall, Pres.; Tim Furey, Exec. Dir.

STEVENSVILLE. *Historic St. Mary's Mission*, P.O. Box 211, 59870-0211. Tel: 406-777-5734; Fax: 406-777-5734. Email: stmary@cybernet1.com. Web: saintmarysmission.org.

RELIGIOUS INSTITUTES OF MEN REPRESENTED IN THE DIOCESE

For further details refer to the corresponding bracketed number in the Religious Institutes of Men or Women section.

[0330]—*Brothers of the Christian Schools* (Midwest Prov.)—F.S.C.

[0690]—*Jesuit Fathers and Brothers* (Oregon Prov.)—S.J.

RELIGIOUS INSTITUTES OF WOMEN REPRESENTED IN THE DIOCESE

[0230]—*Benedictine Sisters of Pontifical Jurisdiction* (Rapid City)—O.S.B.

[1070-03]—*Dominican Sisters*—O.P.

[1070-13]—*Dominican Sisters*—O.P.

[1070-11]—*Dominican Sisters*—O.P.

[2575]—*Institute of the Sisters of Mercy of the Americas* (Cedar Rapids, IA)—R.S.M.

[0440]—*Sisters of Charity of Cincinnati, Ohio*—S.C.

[0480]—*Sisters of Charity of Leavenworth, Kansas*—S.C.L.

[0430]—*Sisters of Charity of the Blessed Virgin Mary*—B.V.M.

[3840]—*Sisters of St. Joseph of Carondelet*—C.S.J.

[1720]—*Sisters of the Third Order Regular of St. Francis of the Congregation of Our Lady of Lourdes*—O.S.F.

DIOCESAN CEMETERIES

HELENA. *Resurrection*, 3700 N. Montana Ave., P.O. Box 5029, 59604. Tel: 406-442-1782; Fax: 406-443-7036. Mr. Scott Fitzpatrick, Dir. Cemeteries; Kathy Redd, Office Mgr.

Resurrection Cemetery Association, 3700 N. Montana Ave., P.O. Box 5029, 59604. Tel: 406-442-1782; Fax: 406-443-7036. Mr. Scott Fitzpatrick, Exec. Dir.; Kathy Redd, Office Mgr. (Corporate Name for Diocesan Cemeteries)

BUTTE. *Holy Cross*, Office: 4700 Harrison Ave., 59701. Tel: 406-494-3812.

St. Patrick, Office: 4700 Harrison Ave., 59701. Tel: 406-494-3812.

MISSOULA. *St. Mary*, Office: 641 Turner St., 59802. Tel: 406-543-7951.

NECROLOGY

† Hillen, Rev. Daniel (Retired), (Retired)

† McCarthy, Bernard, (Retired)—Died Sept. 16, 2003

Diocese of Honolulu

(Dioecesis Honoluluensis)

(VACANT SEE)

Chancery Office: 1184 Bishop St., Honolulu, HI 96813. Tel: 808-533-1791; Fax: 808-521-8428.

Web: www.catholichawaii.com

Email: bishop@pono.net

Square Miles 6,435.

Corporate Title: The Roman Catholic Church In The State Of Hawaii.

Comprises all of the Hawaiian Islands.

The Hawaiian Islands were annexed as a Territory of the United States in 1898. Hawaii became the 50th State of the Union on August 21, 1959.

In 1826, a Prefecture-Apostolic was erected for the Hawaiian Islands, then called Sandwich Islands, and entrusted to the Fathers of the Sacred Hearts of Jesus and Mary (Picpus). The Very Rev. Alexis Bachelot, SS.CC., was the first Prefect-Apostolic. He arrived with his companions at Honolulu on the 7th of July, 1827. In 1844, the Islands were erected a Vicariate. Diocese erected Sept. 10, 1941.

Legal Title: For legal titles of parishes and diocesan institutions, consult the Chancery Office.

STATISTICAL OVERVIEW

Personnel	
Bishop	1
Retired Bishops	1
Priests: Diocesan Active in Diocese	28
Priests: Diocesan Active Outside Diocese	13
Priests: Retired, Sick or Absent	25
Number of Diocesan Priests	66
Religious Priests in Diocese	78
Total Priests in Diocese	144
Extern Priests in Diocese	26
Ordinations:	
Transitional Deacons	1
Permanent Deacons in Diocese	51
Total Brothers	47
Total Sisters	153
Parishes	
Parishes	66
With Resident Pastor:	
Resident Diocesan Priests	24
Resident Religious Priests	14
Without Resident Pastor:	
Administered by Priests	22
Administered by Deacons	1
Missions	24
Professional Ministry Personnel:	
Brothers	1
Sisters	7
Lay Ministers	41
Welfare	
Catholic Hospitals	2
Total Assisted	421,745
Health Care Centers	4
Total Assisted	32,006
Specialized Homes	1
Total Assisted	66
Special Centers for Social Services	17
Total Assisted	14,730
Other Institutions	1
Total Assisted	101
Educational	
Students from This Diocese	1
Total Seminarians	1
Colleges and Universities	1
Total Students	4,270
High Schools, Diocesan and Parish	3
Total Students	1,892
High Schools, Private	4
Total Students	2,709
Elementary Schools, Diocesan and Parish	33
Total Students	6,967
Catechesis/Religious Education:	
High School Students	2,300
Elementary Students	6,640
Total Students under Catholic Instruction	24,779
Teachers in the Diocese:	
Priests	4
Brothers	13
Sisters	71
Lay Teachers	868
Vital Statistics	
Receptions into the Church:	
Infant Baptism Totals	2,862
Adult Baptism Totals	409
Received into Full Communion	252
First Communions	2,442
Confirmations	1,248
Marriages:	
Catholic	579
Interfaith	285
Total Marriages	864
Deaths	1,870
Total Catholic Population	234,588
Total Population	1,244,898

Former Prelates—Very Revs. ALEXIS BACHELOT, SS.CC., Pref. Apost.; died Dec. 5, 1837; LOUIS MAIGRET, SS.CC. Pref. Apost. till 1844; Rt. Revs. VINCENT FERRIER DUBOIZE, SS.CC., resigned before he was consecrated; LOUIS MAIGRET, SS.CC., Titular Bishop of Arathia; consecrated at Santiago, Oct. 31, 1847; died June 11, 1882; HERMAN KOECKEMANN, SS.CC., Titular Bishop of Olba; consecrated at San Francisco Aug. 21, 1881; died Feb. 18, 1892; GULSTAN ROPERT, SS.CC., Titular Bishop of Panopolis; consecrated at San Francisco, Sept. 25, 1892; died Jan. 3, 1903; LIBERT H. BOEYNAEMS, SS.CC., Titular Bishop of Zeugma; consecrated at San Francisco, July 25, 1903; died May 13, 1926; Most Revs. STEPHEN P. ALENCASTRE, SS.CC., Titular Bishop of Arabissus; consecrated at Los Angeles, Aug. 24, 1924; died Nov. 9, 1940; JAMES J. SWEENEY, D.D., ord. June 20, 1925; appt. May 20, 1941, consecrated at San Francisco, July 25, 1941; died June 19, 1968; JOHN J. SCANLAN, D.D. (Retired), Retired Bishop of Honolulu; ord. June 22, 1930; succeeded to see March 6, 1968; retired June 30, 1981; died Jan. 31, 1997; JOSEPH A. FERRARIO, D.D., Retired Bishop of Honolulu; ord. May 19, 1951; succeeded to see June 25, 1982; retired Oct. 12, 1993; FRANCIS X. DILORENZO, ordained May 18, 1968; appointed Titular Bishop of Tigia and Auxiliary Bishop of Scranton January 26, 1988; cons. March 8, 1988; appt. Apostolic Admin. October 12, 1993; succeeded to See November 29, 1994; appt. Bishop of Richmond March 31, 2004; installed May 24, 2004.

Vicars General—Very Revs. JOSEPH A. GRIMALDI, J.C.L., V.G., M.A.; THOMAS L. GROSS, V.G.

Chancery Office—1184 Bishop St., Honolulu, 96813-2858. Tel: 808-533-1791; Fax: 808-521-8428; 808-585-3382 (Chancellor's Office). Office Hours: Mon.-Fri. 8-4

Chancellor—JOHN N. RINGROSE, J.C.L.

Vice-Chancellor—Very Rev. JOSEPH A. GRIMALDI, J.C.L., V.G., M.A.

Tribunal—1184 Bishop St., Honolulu, 96813-2858. Tel: 808-533-1791; Fax: 808-585-3382. Office Hours: Mon.-Fri 8-4

Judicial Vicar—Very Rev. JOSEPH A. GRIMALDI, J.C.L., V.G., M.A.

Promoter of Justice—Rev. MATTHEW LOCHS, SS.CC., S.T.L.

Defender of the Bond—Rev. WILLIAM O'CONNELL, S.M.

Judges—Very Rev. JOSEPH A. GRIMALDI, J.C.L., V.G., M.A.; Revs. ROBERT MAHER, O.F.M.Cap.; JOHN N. RINGROSE, J.C.L.

Notaries and Secretaries—NETTIE LOU PEILER; KATHY SNIFFEN; TERESITA FONTANILLA.

Diocesan Theologian—Rev. MARC ALEXANDER, S.T.D.

Diocesan Theological Commission—Rev. MARC R. ALEXANDER, S.T.D., Chm. Commission Members: DAVID COLEMAN, M.A., Ph.D.; Very Rev. JOSEPH A. GRIMALDI, J.C.L., V.G. M.A.; Rev. HALBERT WEIDNER, C.O., M.A., Ph.D.; Sr. GRETCHEN GILROY, O.S.F., M.S.; CELESTE O'BRIEN, M.A.

Master of Ceremonies for Episcopal Functions—Rev. Msgr. TERRENCE WATANABE.

Coordinator of Diocesan Major Events—Rev. Msgr. TERRENCE WATANABE.

Administrative Council—Most Rev. FRANCIS X. DILORENZO, D.D., S.T.D.; Very Revs. JOSEPH A. GRIMALDI, J.C.L., V.G., M.A.; THOMAS L. GROSS, V.G.

Bishop's Administrative Advisory Council—Very Revs. JOSEPH A. GRIMALDI, J.C.L., V.G., M.A.; THOMAS L. GROSS, V.G.; Rev. MICHEL DALTON, O.F.M.Cap.; Deacon WALTER YOSHIMITSU; WILLIAM BURTON; PATRICIA S. TOSSEY.

Administrative Assistant to the Bishop—PATRICIA S. TOSSEY.

Vicar for Clergy—Rev. GARY SECOR.

Vocations Director—Rev. GARY SECOR.

Clergy Personnel Board—Revs. GARY SECOR, Chm.; JAMES BERRY; Very Revs. JOSEPH A. GRIMALDI, J.C.L., V.G., M.A.; THOMAS L. GROSS, V.G.; Revs. KONELIO FALETOI; CLARENCE FISHER; STEVE NGUYEN.

Permanent Deacon Council—Deacon WALLACE MITSUI, Chm.

Permanent Deacon Formation—Coordinators: Deacon WILLIAM MCPEEK; FLORENCE MCPEEK.

Priestly Life and Ministry—Rev. GARY SECOR.

Consulting Pastors—Rev. MICHEL DALTON, O.F.M.Cap.

College of Consultors—Very Revs. JOSEPH A. GRIMALDI, J.C.L., V.G., M.A.; THOMAS L. GROSS, V.G.; Rev. MICHEL DALTON, O.F.M.Cap.; Rev. Msgr. WILLIAM F. MATTIMORE; Revs. JAMES BERRY; ALPHONSE LAROCHELLE, M.S.; ANASTACIO POSTRANO; HALBERT WEIDNER, C.O., M.A., Ph.D.; SCOTT BUSH; Rev. Msgr. TERRENCE WATANABE.

Finance Committee—Most Rev. FRANCIS X. DILORENZO, D.D., S.T.D.; Very Rev. JOSEPH A. GRIMALDI, J.C.L., V.G., M.A.; Rev. JOHN F. BOLIN, S.M.; ALFRED FERNANDES; JOSEPH GOLDCAMP; ROBERT BRUCE GRAHAM JR.; REGINALD

MALDONADO; JUDITH ROSTRON; JAMES SEVERSON; PHYLLIS SHEA; EUGENE N. TIWANAK; JOHN TOLMIE JR.; MELVIN VENTURA; LAN TRAN.

Diocesan Planning and Building Commission—Deacon WALTER YOSHIMITSU, Chm.; Rev. JOHN BOLIN, S.M.; Rev. Msgr. TERRENCE WATANABE; Sr. HELENE WOOD, SS.CC.; GARY BATCHELLER; WILLIAM BURTON; Rev. GARY COLTON; MICHAEL DARCEY; FRANK FELIX JR.; LUKE YASAKA; Rev. JAMES BERRY; ANNE KUSAO; MARK LIVELY; Rev. ROBERT WYNNE, M.M.; MANOLO QUIASON; LUKE YASAKA.

Ethnic Ministry Advisory Board—Rev. GARY SECOR, Chm.

Ethnic Ministries—

Chinese Ministry—Rev. ANDREW NG, S.D.B., Coord.

Japanese Ministry—Rev. FRANCIS NAKAGAWA, S.M., Coord.

Filipino Ministry—Rev. Msgr. EDGAR BRILLANTES; Revs. EDGARDO BONGHANOY; SALVADOR BRINGAS JR.; JOSEPH DIAZ; GREGORIO DEDAL JR.; PETER DUMAG; RAYMUND ELLORIN; MANUEL HEWE; JOVEN JUNIO, M.S.; ANTONIO MANLIGUES; JOSEPHINO ORILLA; ANASTACIO POSTRANO.

Hispanic Ministry-Oahu—Rev. DONALD P. MERRIFIELD, S.J., Coord.

Hispanic Ministry-Maui—Rev. GERARDO DE TOMASI, M.C.C.J., Coord.

Hispanic Ministry-Kailua Kona—Rev. JACK RYAN, Coord.

Korean Ministry—Rev. JOHN SOLTIS, M.M., Coord.

Samoan Ministry—Rev. SEBASTIAN CHACKO, Coord.

Tongan Ministry—Rev. LANE AKIONA, SS.CC., Coord.

Vietnamese Ministry—Rev. VINCENT KIEN NGUYEN, Coord. (Hsin-Chu).

Business Office—1184 Bishop St., Honolulu, 96813-2858. Tel: 808-533-1791; Fax: 808-521-8428. Office Hours: Mon.-Fri. 8-4

Business Manager—WILLIAM L. BURTON JR.

Diocesan Offices and Directors

Archivist—JOHN N. RINGROSE, J.C.L.

Censor Liborum—Rev. MARC R. ALEXANDER, S.T.D.

Vicars Forane—Rev. HALBERT WEIDNER, C.O., M.A., Ph.D., East Honolulu; Rev. Msgr. TERRENCE WATANABE, West Honolulu; Rev. MICHEL DALTON, O.F.M.Cap., Leeward; Rev. Msgr. WILLIAM MATTIMORE, Windward; Revs. ANASTACIO POSTRANO, West Hawaii; ALPHONSE LAROCHELLE, M.S., Kauai; JAMES BERRY, Maui, Molokai, Lanai; SCOTT BUSH, East Hawaii.

Presbyteral Council—Very Revs. JOSEPH A. GRIMALDI, J.C.L., V.G., M.A.; THOMAS GROSS, V.G.; Revs. MARC ALEXANDER, S.T.D.; SCOTT BUSH; ANASTACIO POSTRANO; GORDIAN CARVALHO; GARY COLTON; MICHEL DALTON, O.F.M.Cap.; KONELIO FALETOI; JOHN BOLIN, S.M.; ALAPAKI KIM; Rev. Msgr. WILLIAM F. MATTIMORE; Rev. GARY SECOR; Rev. Msgrs. TERRENCE WATANABE; EDGAR BRILLANTES; Revs. HALBERT WEIDNER, C.O., M.A., Ph.D.; CHRISTOPHER M. CARTWRIGHT, S.J.

Diocesan Pastoral Council—PAULETTE GOMES, Contact, 1184 Bishop St., Honolulu, 96813. Tel: 808-533-1791, Ext. 342.

Delegate of the Bishop for Religious—Sr. BEATRICE TOM, O.S.F., Delegate; Bro. THOMAS SPRING, S.M., Assoc. Delegate.

Senior Priests' Committee—Revs. GARY SECOR, Chm.; JOHN BERGER; Rev. Msgr. DANIEL DEVER; Very Rev. JOSEPH A. GRIMALDI, J.C.L., V.G., M.A.; Rev. Msgr. TERRENCE WATANABE.

Hawaii Catholic Herald—1184 Bishop St., Honolulu, 96813-2858. Tel: 808-533-1791; Fax: 808-521-8428. Most Rev. FRANCIS X. DILORENZO, D.D., S.T.D., Publisher; PATRICK DOWNES, Editor.

Saint Stephen Diocesan Center—6301 Pali Hwy., Kaneohe, 96744-5298. Tel: 808-263-8844, Ext. 324; Fax: 808-261-7022. Deacon WALTER YOSHIMITSU, Admin. Office Hours: Mon.-Fri, 8-4

Religious Education—LORI CREPEAU, Dir. Tel: 808-263-8844, Ext. 341.

Servant Leadership Education Program—LORI CREPEAU, Dir.

Hawaii Catholic Conference—Most Rev. FRANCIS X. DILORENZO, D.D., S.T.D.; PATRICK DOWNES; JEROME E. RAUCKHORST; Rev. TIMOTHY EDEN, S.M.; CARMEN HIMENES; BETTY LOU LARSON; Sr. GRETCHEN GILROY, O.S.F., M.S.; EVA MARIE SIMMONS; Deacon WALTER YOSHIMITSU, Dir.

Hawaii Catholic Schools—CARMEN HIMENES, Supt.; LOUISE WONG, Assoc. Supt. Tel: 808-263-8844, Ext. 364.

Office of Development—ROBERT J. STILLWELL, Ed.D. Tel: 808-263-8844, Ext. 323.

Diocesan Development Committee—JOAN BICKSON; R. CHARLES BOCKEN; JOHN BROGAN, Chm.; WILLIAM BURTON; ROBERT BRUCE GRAHAM JR.; STANLEY HONG; JON THOMAS HUNTER; ROBERT STILLWELL; LILA MARANTZ.

Office for the Welcoming Parish—SHARON CHIARUCCI, Coord. Tel: 808-263-8844, Ext. 333.

Office of Worship—Sr. HELENE WOOD, SS.CC., Dir. Tel: 808-263-8844, Ext. 328.

Diocesan Liturgical Commission—Sr. HELENE WOOD, SS.CC., Dir.; Rev. JOHN BERGER, Chm.; ROSE BRITO; BARBARA ISODA; ROBERT MONDOY; REGINA PFEIFFER; CORA ROLLINS; WENDELL APOSTOL; CECIL FARIN; JONILA KIM.

Respect Life Office—Deacon GEORGE THORP, Dir. Tel: 808-263-8844, Ext. 322.

Natural Family Planning—ED CODA; BETTY CODA; Deacon WALTER YOSHIMITSU; FRANCES YOSHIMITSU.

Other Diocesan Offices—

Apostleship of the Sea—579-D Keolu Dr., Kailua, 96734. Tel: 808-262-5422. Rev. JOHN G. NEWTON, Chap.

**Catholic Charities Hawaii—250 Vineyard St., Honolulu, 96813-2495*. Tel: 808-537-6321; Fax: 808-523-8773. JEROME E. RAUCKHORST, Diocesan Dir. Tel: 808-537-6321, Ext. 301.

Board of Advisors—MICHAEL E. O'NEILL, Chm.; STEVEN AI; EDWIN C. CADMAN, M.D.; WALTER A. DODS JR.; H. MITCHELL D'OLIER; NONIE TOLEDO; KEITH VIEIRA; JENAI WALL; CHATT G. WRIGHT; Adm. R.J. "ZAP" ZLATOPER, USN (Ret.).

Board of Trustees—Most Rev. FRANCIS X. DILORENZO, D.D., S.T.D., Pres.; Very Rev. JOSEPH A. GRIMALDI, J.C.L., V.G., M.A.; JEROME RAUCKHORST, Diocesan Dir.; WILLIAM BURTON; MARIANITA LOPEZ; CLIFF K. CISCO; BRANDT FARIAS, Bd. Chm.

Board of Directors—Most Rev. FRANCIS X. DILORENZO, D.D., S.T.D., Pres.; BRANDT FARIAS, Bd. Chm.; MARIANITA LOPEZ, Bd. Vice Chm.; ROGER WALL, Bd. Sec.; I. PATRICK GRIGGS, Bd. Treas.; Very Rev. JOSEPH A. GRIMALDI, J.C.L., V.G., M.A.; Revs. JOHN BOLIN, S.M.; GARY SECOR; ROBBIE ALM; Mr. DAVID BELLO; STAN BROWN; JEFFREY CASE; VIRGIE CHATTERGY; CLIFF K. CISCO; Dr. LESLIE CORREA; CHRISTOPHER R. DANG; BETH FRANCISCA; WILLIAM BURTON; JAN OHTANI; PAULA HARRIS; Dr. KENT KEITH; RUSSELL J. LAU; JEFFREY LOO; MICHAEL MAGAOAY; RIX MAURER; LINDA MCKENZIE; CYNTHIA D. QUINN; JAMES SERNA; RICHARD STACK JR.; DOUGLAS C. SMITH; KEVIN SYPNIEWSKI; MARY PAT WATERHOUSE; JAMES WALSH; Dr. THOMAS WESSELKAMPER; DANIEL WHITFORD.

Catholic Charities Community and Immigrant Services—JONI CHUN, Interim Exec. Dir., 712 N. School St., Honolulu, 96817. Tel: 808-528-5233, Ext. 18; Fax: 808-531-1970.

Catholic Charities Elderly Services—2745 Pali Hwy., Honolulu, 96817. Tel: 808-595-0077; Fax: 808-595-0811. STELLA WONG, Exec. Dir.

Catholic Charities Housing Development Corporation—250 Vineyard St., Honolulu, 96813-2495. Tel: 808-537-6321; Fax: 808-585-7408. JEROME RAUCKHORST, Diocesan Dir.

Catholic Charities Family Services—200 N. Vineyard Blvd., Ste. 200, Honolulu, 96817. Tel: 808-536-1794; Fax: 808-599-8761. ANA ROSAL, Exec. Dir.

Hospital Ministry—1717 Ala Wai Blvd. #1806, Honolulu, 96815. Tel: 808-949-7939; Fax: 808-949-7939. Revs. PAUL SMITH, Dir.; TEODULO GAQUIT.

Prison Ministry—1184 Bishop St., Honolulu, 96813. Tel: 808-533-1791, Ext. 341. Deacon WALTER YOSHIMITSU, Diocesan Rep.

Association of Religious Congregations in Hawaii—91-1048 Aawa Dr., Ewa Beach, 96706. Tel: 808-547-6855. Sisters NORISE KAISER, O.S.F., Coord.; ROCHELLE LIU, O.S.F.; JUDY RESTA, S.F.C.C.; MARIAN TUNG, O.S.J.; Bro. THOMAS SPRINGER, S.M.

Office for Social Ministry—140 B Holomua St., Hilo, 96720. Tel: 808-935-3050; 877-935-3050 (Toll Free); Fax: 808-935-3794. CAROL IGNACIO, Diocesan Dir.

Oahu Branch—6301 Pali Hwy., Kaneohe, 96744-5298. Tel: 808-263-8844, Ext. 302. IWIE TAMASHIRO, Program Dir.

Maui County Branch—95 Mahalani St., Wailuku, 96793. Tel: 808-244-8106; Fax: 808-244-9270. Sr. ROSELANI ENOMOTO, C.S.J., Program Dir.

Hawaii Island Branch—CAROL IGNACIO, Exec. Dir.

Care-a-Van—BRANDEE CACHOLA, Program Admin.

Campaign for Human Development—Sr. ROSELANI ENOMOTO, C.S.J., Dir.

Catholic Relief Services—CAROL IGNACIO, Diocesan Dir.

Hawaii Island Food Bank—DIANE SANCHEZ HEIMAN, Mng. Dir.

Mobile Health Project—KAYE LUNDBURG, Program Dir.

Ministry to Persons with Disabilities—IWIE TAMASHIRO, Program Dir.

Boards and Commissions—

Bishop's Advisory Board for Persons with Disabilities—Members: SHARON CHIARUCCI; MARVIN CHOY, Vice Chm.; Sr. ROSELANI ENOMOTO, C.S.J., Staff Rep.; NANI FIFE; VALERY O'BRIEN; CAROLE SUAPAIA, Chm.; IWIE TAMASHIRO, Program Dir.; CAROL IGNACIO, Staff Rep.; PATRICIA TOSSEY, Bishop's Rep.

Diocesan Board of Education—Most Rev. FRANCIS X. DILORENZO, D.D., S.T.D., Pres. Members: VIVIAN AIONA; ROEANA ALEXANDER; ANTHONY BOQUER; Rev. GORDIAN CARVALHO; DAVID GARCIA; Rev. TIMOTHY EDEN, S.M.; DAPHNE KAUHANE; Dr. HAROLD KOZUMA; Dr. MARY SHERIDAN; CAROLA SOUZA, Chm.; Sisters BERNARDA SINDOL, O.P.; JOAN OF ARC SOUZA, O.S.F.; CAROL WEST; Rev. Msgr. TERRENCE WATANABE; KURT WRIGHT; Very Rev. THOMAS L. GROSS, V.G., Ex Officio; CARMEN HIMENES, Supt., Ex Officio; LOUISE WONG, Assoc. Supt., Ex Officio.

Ecumenical Commission—Rev. Msgr. DANIEL DEVER; Revs. CLARENCE L. FISHER; HALBERT WEIDNER, C.O., M.A., Ph.D., Chm.; REGINA PFEIFFER; Dr. DAVID COLEMAN; Rev. WILLIAM KUNISCH.

Diocesan Synod Implementation Committee—Deacon WALTER YOSHIMITSU, Coord.

Women's Concerns Committee—Co-Coordinators: JUDI BRAMLETT; Sr. BRENDA LAU, C.S.J.

Lay Associations—

Apostleship of Prayer—

Basic Christian Community of Hawaii—Spiritual Directors: Rev. MICHAEL SAWYER, O.S.B.; Sr. MARY JO MCENANY, O.S.B.

Beginning Experience-Hawaii—Rev. BERNARD CASSIDY, S.J., Spiritual Dir.

Catholic Committee on Scouting—42 Puiwa Rd., Honolulu, 96808. Tel: 808-595-6366. Rev. CHARLES J. SCHMIDT, M.M., Scout Chaplain.

Catholic Women's Guild—Rev. FRANCIS PETERSON, Chap. (Retired), P.O. Box 10284, Honolulu, 96816-0284. Tel: 808-234-0500.

Chinese Catholic Club—Rev. Msgr. ROY PETERS, Spiritual Dir.

Confraternity of Our Lady of Mt. Carmel—Rev. PAUL ZEGERS, SS.CC.

Confraternity of the Most Holy Rosary—Deacon ANDREW GERAKAS, Pres.

Cursillos of Hawaii—VACANT.

Engaged Encounter—Coordinators: Deacon RONALD PAGLINAWAN; EUNICE PAGLINAWAN.

Filipino Catholic Clubs, Diocesan Congress of—Rev. JOVEN JUNIO, M.S., Diocesan Dir.; Sr. ROSALINDA BARROZA, M.M., Assoc. Spiritual Diocesan Dir.

Oahu—Rev. CLARENCE L. FISHER, Spiritual Dir.

Kauai—Rev. ALPHONSE LAROCHELLE, M.S., Spiritual Dir.

Maui—Deacon CORNELIO PULIDO, Spiritual Dir.

Hawaii—VACANT, Spiritual Dir.

Hawaii Catholic Charismatic Renewal—Deacon DANIEL GUINAUGH.

Holy Childhood Association—

Holy Name Society, Diocesan Union of the—Rev. THOMAS CHOO, SS.CC., Spiritual Dir.

Knights of Columbus—Most Rev. FRANCIS X. DILORENZO, D.D., S.T.D., Honorary State Chap.; Rev. LANE AKIONA, SS.CC., State Chap.; BILLY E. INGELS, State Deputy.

Legion of Mary—

Oahu—Rev. AUGUSTINE CHEERAKATHIL, M.S., Spiritual Dir.; Bro. PATRICK D. MCCORMACK, C.F.C., Asst. Spiritual Dir.

Missionary Basic Christian Community of Hawaii—Sr. GRACE DOROTHY LIM, M.M., Spiritual Dir.

Nocturnal Adoration Society—Rev. Msgr. ROY PETERS, Spiritual Dir.

The Oratory in Hawaii, Inc.—Rev. HALBERT WEIDNER, C.O., M.A., Ph.D., Pres.

Reparation of the Immaculate Heart of Mary Association—Very Rev. JOSEPH A. GRIMALDI, J.C.L., V.G., M.A., Spiritual Dir.

St. Francis Xavier Clubs—

Oahu—Rev. FRANCIS NAKAGAWA, S.M., Spiritual Dir.

Maui—Rev. RAYMOND E. MALLEY, S.M., Spiritual Dir.

St. Vincent de Paul Society—Honolulu District Council, 1708 Hoohulu St., Pearl City, 96782. Tel: 808-456-1029. HENRY SUMIDA, Dir.

Secular Franciscan Order—Rev. GORDON COMBS, O.F.M.Cap., Reg. Spiritual Asst.

Secular Order of Discalced Carmelites—GWENDOLYN B. LAW, O.C.D.S., Group Leader.

Serra Club of Honolulu—Rev. GARY L. SECOR, Chap.

Worldwide Marriage Encounter—Rev. FRANCIS PETERSON, Spiritual Dir. (Retired).

Young Ladies' Institute—

Honolulu Institute No. 84—Rev. MARK CONSALVI, SS.CC., Spiritual Dir.

Ana Malia Institute No. 208—Rev. PATRICK FREITAS, Spiritual Dir.

Kailua Institute No. 213—Rev. GARY SECOR, Spiritual Dir.

Young Men's Institute—Rev. ROBERT SCHWARZHAUPT,

Chap.

CLERGY, PARISHES, MISSIONS AND PAROCHIAL SCHOOLS

ISLAND OF OAHU
CITY OF HONOLULU

1—CATHEDRAL OF OUR LADY OF PEACE (1843), (Portuguese—Filipino), Most Rev. Francis X. DiLorenzo, D.D., S.T.D.; Rev. John Berger, Admin.; Mrs. Ann Hannan, M.R.E., Pastoral Assoc. & D.R.E. In Res., Revs. Robert Hannon; Gary Secor; Marvin Samiano.
Res.: 1184 Bishop St., 96813-2838. Tel: 808-536-7036; Fax: 808-536-7039.
School—Cathedral School, 1728 Nuuanu Ave., 96817. Tel: 808-533-2069; Fax: 808-533-2069. Mrs. Mary Ann Lopes, Prin. Lay Teachers 13; Students 150.
Catechesis/Religious Program—Tel: 808-952-7220; Fax: 808-952-7201. Students 45.

2—ST. ANTHONY (1916), (Filipino), Revs. Augustine Cheerakathil, M.S.; Geronimo Castro, M.S.; Deacon George W. Thorp Jr. In Res., Rev. Teodulo Gaquit.
Res.: 640 Puuhale Rd., 96819. Tel: 808-845-3255; Fax: 808-845-3664.
School—Tel: 808-845-2769; Fax: 808-853-2234. Sr. Ruth Linaac, R.V.M., Prin. Sisters 5; Lay Teachers 8; Students 160.
Catechesis/Religious Program—Students 139.
Convent—702 Puuhale Rd., 96819. Tel: 808-845-4888. Religious of the Blessed Virgin Mary (R.V.M.) Sisters 6.

3—ST. AUGUSTINE (1854), Rev. Thomas Choo, SS.CC., Admin.; Deacon Robert Cobb.
Res.: 130 Ohua Ave., 96815. Tel: 808-923-7024; Fax: 808-922-4086.
Catechesis/Religious Program—Students 28.

4—BLESSED SACRAMENT (1938), Rev. Mark Consalvi, SS.CC.; Deacon Ronald Choo.
Res.: 2124 Pauoa Rd., 96813. Tel: 808-531-6980.
Catechesis/Religious Program—Students 50.

5—CO-CATHEDRAL OF ST. THERESA OF THE CHILD JESUS (1931), (Filipino), Revs. Gary Colton; Anthony Rosario. In Res., Rev. Vincent Kien Nguyen.
Res.: 712 N. School St., 96817. Tel: 808-521-1700; Fax: 808-599-3629.
School—Tel: 808-536-4703; Fax: 808-524-6861. Sr. John Joseph Gilligan, C.S.J., Prin. Sisters 7; Lay Teachers 20; Students 560.
Catechesis/Religious Program—Students 140.
Convent—Sisters of St. Joseph of Carondelet, Tel: 808-533-3101.

6—HOLY FAMILY (1950), Rev. Owen Mullen.
Res.: 830 Main St., 96818. Tel: 808-422-1135; Fax: 808-421-1702.
School—Tel: 808-423-9612; Fax: 808-422-5030. Antonio J. Boquer, Prin. Lay Teachers 51; Students 630.
Catechesis/Religious Program—Fax: 808-423-9611. Bonnie Boquer, D.R.E. Students 120.

7—HOLY TRINITY (1939), Revs. Halbert Weidner, C.O.; James Moran, C.O.; Deacons Samuel Taylor; Daniel R. Guinaugh.
Res.: 5919 Kalanianaole Hwy., 96821. Tel: 808-396-0551; Fax: 808-396-1380.
School—Tel: 808-396-8466; Fax: 808-396-3310. Monica Des Jarlais, Prin. Sisters 2; Lay Teachers 14; Students 149.
Catechesis/Religious Program—Tel: 808-396-0551, Ext. 11; Fax: 808-396-1380. Students 56.

8—ST. JOHN THE BAPTIST (1844), (Filipino-Samoan), [CEM] Rev. Msgr. Edgar B. Brillantes, Admin.; Rev. Donald P. Merrifield, S.J. In Res., Rev. Mario Raquepo.
Res.: 2324 Omilo Ln., 96819. Tel: 808-845-0984; Fax: 808-841-6643.
School—Tel: 808-841-5551; Fax: 808-842-6104. Mary Lou Superio, Prin. Dominican Sisters 6; Lay Teachers 11; Students 180.
Catechesis/Religious Program—Tel: 808-845-3304. Students 179.
Convent—2330 Omilo Ln., 96819. Tel: 808-845-2622. Dominican Sisters of the Most Holy Rosary 6.

9—NEWMAN CENTER-HOLY SPIRIT PARISH (1981), Revs. Christopher M. Cartwright, S J.; James A. Rude, S.J.
Mailing Address: 1941 East West Rd., 96822-2321. Tel: 808-988-6222; Fax: 808-988-1752.
Jesuit House: 2727 Pamoa Rd., 96822-1838. Tel: 808-988-3464; Fax: 808-988-7627.
Catechesis/Religious Program—Students 18.

10—OUR LADY OF THE MOUNT (1870), [CEM] Rev. Jose R. Nacu, M.S. In Res., Rev. Spatz Silva.
Res.: 1614 Monte St., 96819. Tel: 808-845-0828; Fax: 808-845-0828.
Catechesis/Religious Program—Tel: 808-845-0223. Students 109.

11—ST. PATRICK (1929), Rev. Lane K. Akiona, SS.CC. Please refer to the listing for St. Patrick Monastery under Monasteries and Residences for Priests and Brothers for additional residents.
Res.: 1124 Seventh Ave., 96816. Tel: 808-732-5565; Fax: 808-737-2477.
School—Tel: 808-734-8979; Fax: 808-732-2851. Sr. Rose Miriam Schillinger, C.S.J., Prin Sisters 5; Lay Teachers 30; Students 545.
Catechesis/Religious Program—Tel: 808-732-5505. Students 180.

12—SS PETER AND PAUL (1969), Rev. David O. Travers, S.J., Admin.; Rev. Msgr. Roy V. Peters; Deacon Richard Port.
Mailing Address: 800 Kaheka St., 96814. Tel: 808-941 0675; Fax: 808-945-0689.
Res.: 1561 Kanunu St., #1006, 96814. Tel: 808-955-8830.
Catechesis/Religious Program—Students 53.

13—ST. PHILOMENA (1942), Rev. Msgr. Terrence A.M. Watanabe. In Res., Rev. Conrado Lomibao, Hospital Ministry.
Res.: 3300 Ala Laulani St., 96818-2837. Tel: 808-839-1876; Fax: 808-834-6888.
School—Tel: 808-833-8080; Fax: 808-834-3438. Angeline A.V. Thomas, Prin. Lay Teachers 19; Teacher Aids 10; Students 224.
Catechesis/Religious Program—Students 88.

14—ST. PIUS X (1958), Rev. Marc R. Alexander, S.T.D. In Res., Rev. John F. Soltis, M.M., Korean Catholic Community Admin.; Deacons Sidney Townsley, Ph.D., (Retired); Vincent Wozniak; Dominic Kang, (Retired).
Res. & Mailing Address: 2821 Lowrey Ave., 96822-1644. Tel: 808-988-3308; Fax: 808-988-9313.
Catechesis/Religious Program—Students 131.

15—SACRED HEART (1914), Rev. Marc R. Alexander, S.T.D.; Deacons Sidney Townsley, Ph.D., (Retired); Vincent Wozniak.
Res.: 1701 Wilder Ave., 96822. Tel 808-973-2211; Fax: 808-973-2209.
School—Maryknoll Grade School, 1526 Alexander St., 96822. Tel: 808-952-8400; 808-952-7100; Fax: 808-972-7101. Paul O'Brien, Prin.; Carole Ota, Vice Prin Teacher Aides 7; Lay Teachers 46; Students 829.
High School—1526 Alexander St., 96822. Tel: 808-952-7200; Fax: 808-952-7201. Ms. Betsy Gunderson, Prin.; Mr. Evanson Chang, Vice Prin. Sisters 2; Lay Teachers 53; Students 564.
Catechesis/Religious Program—Tel: 808-952-7120; Fax: 808-952-7121. Joanne Dougherty, D.R.E. Students 121.

16—STAR OF THE SEA (1946), Revs. John Sullivan, S.M.; John F. McGregor, S.M.; Andrew Ng, S.D.B.; Bro. Roy Madigan, S.M.; Deacons Thomas Rienzi, (Retired); Andrew Gerakas; Leslie Victor.
Res.: 4470 Aliikoa St., 96821. Tel: 808-734-0396; Fax: 808-735-6017.
School—Tel: 808-734-0208; Fax: 808-735-9790. Carola Souza, Prin. Lay Teachers 22; Students 238.
School—Early Learning Center, Tel: 808-734-3840; Fax: 808-732-1738. Lisa Foster, Prin. Lay Teachers 10; Assistants 9; Students 142.
Catechesis/Religious Program—Tel: 808-735-0259. Darlene Ah Yo, D.R.E. Students 156.

17—ST. STEPHEN (1932), (Japanese), Rev. Alan Nagai.
Res.: 2747 Pali Hwy., 96817. Tel. 808-595-3105.
Catechesis/Religious Program—Students 21.

OUTSIDE THE CITY OF HONOLULU

County of Honolulu

AIEA, ST. ELIZABETH (1926), Revs. Michel Dalton, O.F.M.Cap.; Robert Maher, O.F.M.Cap.; Deacon Fernando V. Ona. In Res., Rev. Gordon Combs, O.F.M.Cap.
Res.: 99-312 Moanalua Rd., 96701. Tel: 808-487-2414; Fax: 808-487-2168.
School—Tel: 808-488-5322; Fax: 808-486-0856. Sr. Bernarda Sindol, O.P., Prin. Sisters 4; Lay Teachers 11; Students 249.
Catechesis/Religious Program—Tel: 808-487-7994. Will Layden, D.R.E.; Missy Layden, D.R.E. Students 225.
Convent—99-310 Moanalua Rd., 96701. Tel: 808-487-3131. Dominican Sisters of the Most Holy Rosary 4.

EWA, IMMACULATE CONCEPTION (1929), (Filipino), Rev. Frank Bourgeois, M.S.; Deacon Ernest Libarios.
Res.: 91-1298 Renton Rd., 96706. Tel: 808-681-3701; Fax: 808-681-3117.
Catechesis/Religious Program—Students 150.

EWA BEACH, OUR LADY OF PERPETUAL HELP (1969), Revs. Konelio Faletoi; Patrick Freitas; Deacon Ron Paglinawan.
Res.: 91-1004 North Rd., 96706-2796. Tel: 808-689-8681.
School—91-1010 North Rd. 96706. Tel: 808-689-0474; Fax: 808-689-4847. Sr. Davilyn AhChick, O.S.F., Prin. Lay Teachers 9; Students 204.
Catechesis/Religious Program—Remi Cabrera, D.R.E.; Julia Torres, D.R.E. Students 210.

KAHUKU, ST. ROCH (1928), (Filipino-Hawaiian), [CEM] Rev. Sydney Fernandes, Admin.
Res.: P.O. Box 295, 96731. Tel: 808-293-5026; Fax: 808-293-1737.
Catechesis/Religious Program—Tel: 808-293-5026. Students 76.
Mission—St. Joachim (1917), P.O. Box 295, Honolulu Co. 96731. Tel: 808-293-8590.

KAILUA

1—ST. ANTHONY (1933), Revs. Dennis Koshko; Trung D. Hoang; Deacon Robert Cyr.
Res.: 148-A Makawao St., 96734-2334. Tel: 808-266-2222; Fax: 808-266-2229.
School—148 Makawao St., 96734-2334. Tel: 808-261-3331; Fax: 808-263-3518. Mrs. Lovey DeRego, Prin. Sisters 1; Lay Teachers 24; Students 342.
Catechesis/Religious Program—Tel: 808-266-2222, Ext. 14. Lisa Gomes, D.R.E. Students 250.

2—ST. JOHN VIANNEY (1962), Very Rev. Thomas L. Gross, V.G.; Deacons Lauren S.F. Wong; Walter H. Yoshimitsu; Sr. Clarence DeCaires.
Res.: 920 Keolu Dr., 96734-3842. Tel: 808-262-8317; Fax: 808-261-4039.
School—940 Keolu Dr., 96734-3842. Tel: 808-261-4651; Fax: 808-263-0505. Mrs. Jane Ann Quinn, Prin. Lay Teachers 22; Staff 12; Students 281.
Catechesis/Religious Program—Students 151.

KANEOHE, ST. ANN (1841), [CEM] Very Rev. Clarence L. Guerreiro, SS.CC.; Revs. Bertram Lock, SS.CC.; Herman Gomes, SS.CC.
Res.: 46-129 Haiku Rd., 96744. Tel: 808-247-3092; Fax: 808-235-0717.
School and Early Learning Center, 46-125 Haiku Rd., 96744. Sr. Anne Clare DeCosta, SS.CC., Dir. Education; Daphne Kauhane, Prin. (School); Mrs. Frances Vasquez, Prin. (Early Learning Center). Sisters 2; Lay Teachers 33; Students 493.
Catechesis/Religious Program—Tel: 808-235-5682. Students 328.

MAKAKILO, ST. JUDE (1988), Rev. Khanh Hoang (SD), Admin.; Deacon Edward Vargas.
Res.: 92-104 Leipapa Hwy., Kapolei, 96707. Tel: 808-672-9041.
Church: 92-455 Makakilo Dr., Kapolei, 96707. Tel: 808-672-8669.
Catechesis/Religious Program—Tel: 808-672-8669, Ext. 12; Fax: 808-672-3779. Caren Argenzia, D.R.E. Students 212.

MILILANI TOWN, ST. JOHN APOSTLE AND EVANGELIST (1969), Revs. Gordian J. Carvalho Jr.; Salvador Bringas; Deacons Wally Mitsui; Ronald Nelson. In Res., Rev. Thomas B. Killackey, M.M.
Res.: 95-370 Kuahelani Ave., 96789. Tel: 808-623-3332, Ext. 100; Fax: 808-623-3286.
School—St. John Catholic Preschool, Tel: 808-623-3332, Ext. 200; Fax: 808-623-6496. Monica Caldeira, Interm. Prin.
Catechesis/Religious Program—Tel: 808-623-3332, Ext. 204,. Gwen Mitsui, D.R.E. Students 459.

NANAKULI, ST. RITA (1963), (Hawaiian), Rev. Alapaki Kim; Deacon Harold S. Levy Jr.
Res.: 89-318 Farrington Hwy., 96792. Tel: 808-668-7833; Fax: 808-668-7716.
Catechesis/Religious Program—Tel: 808-672-5359. Cathy Agor, D.R.E. Students 83.

PEARL CITY, OUR LADY OF GOOD COUNSEL (1958), [CEM] Revs. John Niland, O.F.M.Cap; Paulo R. Kosaka, O.F.M.Cap; Deacons Thomas Miyashiro; Efrain Andrews. In Res., Rev. Eymard McKinnon, O.F.M.Cap.
Office—1525 Waimano Home Rd., 96782. Tel: 808-455-3012; Fax: 808-456-9443.
School—1530 Hoolana St., 96782. Tel: 808-455-4533; Fax: 808-455-5587. Mrs. Cindy Olaso, Prin. Lay Teachers 14; Students 286.
Catechesis/Religious Program—Mr. Reggie Comilang, D.R.E. Students 377.
Friary—1525 Waimano Home Rd., 96782. Tel: 808-455-9039.

WAHIAWA, OUR LADY OF SORROWS (1939), Rev. Clarence L. Fisher; Deacons Benjamin A. Awana; George Kagehiro.
Res.: 1403-A California Ave., 96786-2595. Tel: 808-621-5109; Fax: 808-622-5073. Email: ourladyofsorrows@rcchawaii.org.
Catechesis/Religious Program—Fax: 808-622-5703. Mr. Jack Kampfer, D.R.E. Students 215.

WAIALUA, ST. MICHAEL (1853), (Filipino—Portuguese), Revs. Christopher Keahi, SS.CC.; Felix J. Vandebroek, SS.CC.
Res.: 67-390 Goodale Ave., 96791. Tel: 808-637-4040; Fax: 808-637-4287.
School—67-340 Haona St., 96791. Tel: 808-637-7772; Fax: 808-637-7722. Sr. William Marie Eleniki, O.S.F., Prin. Sisters 3; Lay Teachers 11; Students

207.
Catechesis/Religious Program—Tel: 808-637-4040, Ext. 5. Priscilla Tampon, D.R.E. Students 117.
Convent—Tel: 808-637-7772; Fax: 808-637-7722. Sisters 3.
Mission—SS. Peter and Paul 67-390 Goodale, Waimea Bay, Honolulu Co. 96791.

WAIANAE, SACRED HEART (1838), [CEM] Rev. Sebastian Chacko, Admin.; Deacon Jerome Vito.
Res.: 85-786 Old Government Rd., 96792. Tel: 808-696-3773; Fax: 808-696-2242.
Parish Outreach—Tel: 808-696-3746; Fax: 808-696-3746.
Catechesis/Religious Program—Tel: 808-696-2242. Students 200.

WAIKANE, OUR LADY OF MT. CARMEL (1850), [CEM] Rev. Sydney Fernandes, Admin.
Res.: 48-422 Kamehaineha Hwy., Kaneohe, 96744. Tel: 808-239-9269; Fax: 808-239-8561.
Catechesis/Religious Program—Students 60.

WAIMANALO, ST. GEORGE (1954), Rev. Msgr. William F. Mattimore, Admin.; Deacon Edward Cho.
Res.: 41-1323 Kalanianaole Hwy., 96795. Tel: 808-259-7188; Fax: 808-259-0169.
Catechesis/Religious Program—Tel: 808-259-8979. Students 161.

WAIPAHU, ST. JOSEPH (1940), (Filipino), [CEM] Revs. Joven Junio, M.S.; Geronimo Castro, M.S.; Wilfredo Iminga, M.S. (SB).
Res.: 94-675 Farrington Hwy., 96797. Tel: 808-677-4276; Fax: 808-671-3215.
School—Tel: 808-677-4475; Fax: 808-677-8937. Miss Beverly Sandobal, Prin. Sisters 1; Lay Teachers 24; Students 435.
Catechesis/Religious Program—Tel: 808-676-3493; Fax: 808-676-3493. Geraldine Simbahon, D.R.E. Students 602.
Convent—Sisters of St. Joseph of Carondelet, 91-807 Poowai Pl., Ewa Beach, 96706. Tel: 808-681-4610.

WAIPIO, RESURRECTION OF THE LORD (1986), Rev. Paul L. Minchak, O.F.M.Cap., Admin.
Mailing Address: 94-1260 Lumikula St., Waipahu, 96797. Tel: 808-676-4700; Fax: 808-676-4534.
Catechesis/Religious Program—Yuko D. Ornellas, D.R.E. Students 160.

ISLAND OF HAWAII

County of Hawaii

HAWI, SACRED HEART (1926), [CEM 2] Rev. Maurice Cardinal, M.S., Admin.; Deacon Thomas J. Adams.
Res.: 1048 Kapaau, Kapaau, 96755. Tel: 808-889-6436; Fax: 808-889-5698.
Catechesis/Religious Program—Tel: 808-889-0674; Fax: 808-880-5698. Students 144.
Mission—Our Lady of Grace Halaula, Hawaii Co.

HILO, ST. JOSEPH (1860), [CEM] Revs. Scott Bush; Josephino Orilla (Philippines); Deacons Harvey Kawaihae; Don Aanavi.
Res.: 43 Kapiolani St., 96720. Tel: 808-935-1465; Fax: 808-969-1665.
School—1000 Ululani St., 96720. Tel: 808-935-4935; Fax: 808-969-9019. Mr. Anson Chong, Interm. Prin. Franciscan Sisters of Third Order 3; Lay Teachers 39; Students 388.
Catechesis/Religious Program—Tel: 808-935-1202. Marianne Panoff, D.R.E. Students 222.
Convent—49 Iiwipolena Rd., 96720. Tel: 808-935-1388.

HONAUNAU, ST. BENEDICT (1899), [CEM 5] [JC 5] Rev. Jack Ryan.
Res.: 84-5140 Painted Church Rd., Captain Cook, 96704. Tel: 808-328-2227; Fax: 808-328-8482.
Catechesis/Religious Program—Marjorie Fujimoto, D.R.E. Students 60.
Mission— P.O. Box 209, Honaunau Co. 96726. Tel: 808-323-3711; Fax: 808-328-8482.
Mission— Milolii, Honaunau Co.

HONOKAA, OUR LADY OF LOURDES (1870), [CEM 6] Rev. Joseph Diaz, Admin.
Mailing Address: P.O. Box 129, 96727. Tel: 808-775-9591; Fax: 808-775-0591.
Res.: 45-5028 Plumeria St., 96727.
Catechesis/Religious Program—Students 137.
Mission—St. Joseph Paauilo, Hawaii Co.

KAILUA-KONA, ST. MICHAEL THE ARCHANGEL (1840), [CEM 4] Rev. Anastacio Postrano, Admin.; Deacon John K. Shuster. In Res., Rev. John B. Stawasz (Retired).
Res.: 75-5769 Alii Dr., 96740. Tel: 808-326-7771; Fax: 808-326-7096.
Catechesis/Religious Program—Students 196.
Mission—Holy Rosary Kalaoa, Hawaii Co.
Mission—Immaculate Conception P.O. Box 275, Holualoa, Hawaii Co. 96725.
Mission—St. Paul Honalo, Hawaii Co.
Mission—St. Peter Kahaluu, Hawaii Co.

KAMUELA, CHURCH OF THE ANNUNCIATION (1965), [CEM] Rev. Robert F. Wynne, M.M.; Deacon William McPeek. In Res., Rev. Thomas Donnelly, M.M.
Res.: P.O. Box 301, 96743. Tel: 808-885-4196; Fax: 808-887-1220.
Catechesis/Religious Program—Tel: 808-887-1203. Students 150.
Mission—Church of the Ascension, Puako Puako, Hawaii Co. 96743.

KEAUKAHA, HILO, MALIA PUKA'O KALANI (MARY GATE OF HEAVEN) (1929), (Hawaiian), Rev. Scott Bush, Admin.
Res.: 326 Desha Ave., 96720. Tel: 808-935-9338; Fax: 808-935-3865.
School—Montessori Preschool Marie Roberts, Prin., D.R.E. & Pastorial Assoc.; Joseph Camacho, Coord.
Catechesis/Religious Program—Students 44.

MOUNTAIN VIEW, ST. THERESA (1930), (Portuguese—Filipino), Rev. Edgardo C. Bonghanoy, Admin.
Res.: P.O. Box 37, 96771. Tel: 808-968-6233.
Catechesis/Religious Program—Students 66.
Mission—Holy Rosary Keaau, Hawaii Co.

NAALEHU, SACRED HEART (1846), [CEM] Rev. Manuel A. Hewe (Philippines), Admin.
Office:—P.O. Box 760, Pahala, 96772. Tel: 808-929-7474; 808-928-8208; Fax: 808-928-8208.
Catechesis/Religious Program— 96772. Tel: 808-929-7686. Margorie Pedra, D.R.E. Students 33.

PAHALA, HOLY ROSARY (1885), [CEM] Rev. Manuel A. Hewe (Philippines), Admin.
Res.: P.O. Box 760, 96777. Tel: 808-929-8208; Fax: 808-929-8208.
Catechesis/Religious Program—Tel: 808-928-9054. Jeanette Castillo, D.R.E. Students 46.

PAHOA, SACRED HEART (1882), [CEM 2] Rev. Gregorio Dedal Jr., Admin.
Res.: P.O. Box 17, 96778. Tel: 808-965-8202; Fax: 808-965-8202.
Catechesis/Religious Program—Tel: 808-965-8202; Fax: 808-965-5144. Sr. Eva Joseph Mesina, D.R.E. Students 114.

PAPAALOA, ST. ANTHONY (1926), [CEM 2] Rev. Robert Schwarzhaupt.
Oratory— [CEM 2] P.O. Box 339, Laupahoehoe, 96764. Tel: 808-962-6538; Fax: 808-962-6971.
Catechesis/Religious Program—Dorothy DeConte, D.R.E. Students 25.

PAPAIKOU, IMMACULATE HEART OF MARY (1950), Rev. Robert Schwarzhaupt.
Church: P.O. Box 79, 96781. Tel: 808-964-1240; 808-963-5434; Fax: 808-964-1240.
Catechesis/Religious Program—Laura Kanoa, D.R.E. Students 90.
Mission—Good Shepherd [CEM] Honomu, Hawaii Co. 96728.

ISLAND OF KAUAI

County of Kauai

KALAHEO, HOLY CROSS (1909), (Portuguese—Filipino), [CEM] Revs. Napoleon Andres, M.S., M.S., Admin.; Rene Bisaillon, M.S.
Mailing Address: P.O. Box 487, 96741. Tel: 808-332-8011; Fax: 808-332-7749.
Res.: 2-2370 Kaumualii Hwy., 96741. Tel: 808-332-8011; Fax: 808-332-7749.
Catechesis/Religious Program—Students 139.
Mission—Sacred Heart P.O. Box 487, Eleele, Kauai Co. 96741.

KAPAA, ST. CATHERINE (1887), [CEM 2] Rev. James Orsini.
Res.: 5021-A Kawaihau Rd., 96746. Tel: 808-822-4804; 808-882-7900 (Office); Fax: 808-822-3014.
School—Tel: 808-822-4212; Fax: 808-822-0991. Carol West, Prin. Lay Teachers 12; Students 140.
Catechesis/Religious Program—Students 105.
Mission—St. Sylvester 2390 Kolo Rd., Kilauea, Kauai Co. 96754. Tel: 808-828-2818.
Mission—St. William 5292 Kuhio Hwy., Hanalei, Kauai Co. 96714. Tel: 808-826-4163.

KEKAHA, ST. THERESA (1944), (Filipino), [JC] Rev. Alphonse Larochelle, M.S.; Deacon James Bostick.
Res.: P.O. Box 159, 96752. Tel: 808-337-1784 (Rectory); 808-337-1548 (Office); Fax: 808-337-1548.
School—8311 Kaumualii Hwy, 96752. Tel: 808-337-1351; Fax: 808-337-1351. Sisters 6; Lay Teachers 7; Students 164.
Catechesis/Religious Program—Tel: 808-338-1725. Beverly Johnston, D.R.E. Students 77.
Convent—P.O. Box 277, 96752. Tel: 808-337-9661. Sr. Jerianne Stelmach, Supr. Franciscan Sisters of Christian Charity 6.
Mission—Sacred Hearts of Jesus & Mary 9500 Kaumualii Hwy., Waimea, Kauai Co. 96796.
Mission—St. Joseph Village Main St., Kaumakani, Kauai Co. 96747.

KOLOA, ST. RAPHAEL (1841), [CEM 2] Revs. Napoleon Andres, M.S., M.S., Admin.; Rene Bisaillon, M.S.
Res.: 3011 Hapa Rd., 96756. Tel: 808-742-1955; Fax: 808-742-1845.
Catechesis/Religious Program—Students 81.

LIHUE, IMMACULATE CONCEPTION (1884), (Filipino—Portuguese), [CEM 2] Rev. Joseph Carroll (Retired).
Mailing Address: 4453 Kapaia Rd., 96766. Tel: 808-245-2432; Fax: 808-246-2571.
Catechesis/Religious Program—Tel: 808-632-0638; Fax: 808-245-5628. Sr. Florence Remata, O.S.F., D.R.E. Students 173.

ISLAND OF LANAI

LANAI CITY, SACRED HEARTS (1930), (Filipino), [JC] Rev. Raymund Ellorin, Admin.
Res.: P.O. Box 784, 96763. Tel: 808-565-6837; Fax: 808-565-6897.
Catechesis/Religious Program—Tel: 808-565-6051. Rosita Camero, D.R.E.; Priscilla Felipe, D.R.E. Students 93.

ISLAND OF MAUI

County of Maui

HAIKU, ST. RITA (1950), (Hawaiian—Portuguese), [CEM] Rev. Teodoro Magpayo, Admin.; Deacon Patrick Constantino.
Res.: 655 Haiku Rd., 96708. Tel: 808-575-2601; Fax: 808-575-2063.
Catechesis/Religious Program—Sandra Silva, D.R.E. Students 75.
Mission—St. Gabriel 655 Haiku Rd., Keanae, Maui Co. 96708. Tel: 808-248-8658; Fax: 808-248-7097.

HANA, ST. MARY (1859), (Hawaiian), [CEM] [JC 2] Rev. Paul A. Zegers, SS.CC.
Res.: P.O. Box 219, 96713. Tel: 808-248-8030; Fax: 808-248-7654.
Catechesis/Religious Program—Tel: 808-248-7417. Esse Sinenci, D.R.E. Students 36.
Mission—St. Peter Puuiki, Maui Co.
Mission—St. Paul Kipahulu, Maui Co.
Mission—St. Joseph Kaupo, Maui Co.

KAHULUI, CHRIST THE KING (1932), (Filipino), Revs. William Shannon; Steve Nguyen; Deacons Frank R. Singson Sr.; Cornelio Pulido.
Res.: 20 W. Wakea Ave., 96732. Tel: 808-877-6098; Fax: 808-871-6296.
School—(Grades PreK-6) Tel: 808-877-6618; Fax: 808-871-8101. Sisters 3; Lay Teachers 10; Students 159.
Catechesis/Religious Program—Tel: 808-877-3674. Sr. Angela Laurenzo, C.S.J, D.R.E. Students 232.
Convent—Sisters of St. Joseph of Carondelet, 211 S. Kaulawahine St., 96732. Tel: 808-877-0790.

KIHEI, MAUI CO., ST. THERESA (1908), Revs. James A. Berry; Peter Dumag (Philippines); Deacon Lawrence S. Franco.
Res.: 25 W. Lipoa St., 96753. Tel: 808-879-2649; Fax: 808-879-0045.
Catechesis/Religious Program—Students 189.

KULA, HAWAII CO., OUR LADY QUEEN OF THE ANGELS (1944), (Portuguese), [CEM 2] Rev. Thomas R. Heinzel.
Res.: 9177 Kula Hwy., 96790-9464. Tel: 808-878-1261; Fax: 808-878-3105.
Catechesis/Religious Program—Tel: 808-878-3838. Mrs. Mary Jean Bega, D.R.E. Students 45.
Mission—Holy Ghost 9 Lower Kula Rd., Waiakoa, Maui Co. 96790-9464. Tel: 808-878-1091.
Mission—St. James the Less Ulupalakua, Maui Co.

LAHAINA, MAUI CO., MARIA LANAKILA (1846), [CEM] Revs. William Kunisch II, Admin.; Gerardo De Tomasi, M.C.C.J., Dir. Hispanic Min.
Res.: 712 Wainee St., 96761-1511. Tel: 808-661-0552; Fax: 808-661-1670.
School—Tel: 808-661-4720; Fax: 808-661-1670. Susan Hendricks, Interm. Prin. Lay Teachers 13; Students 208.
Catechesis/Religious Program—Tel: 808-661-6607. Students 141.
Mission—Sacred Hearts of Jesus and Mary Office Rd., Honokahua (Kapalua), Maui Co. 96761. Tel: 808-669-7022.

MAKAWAO, HONOLULU, ST. JOSEPH (1851), [CEM] Revs. Eugene Keusal (CHI), Admin. (Retired); Alfred Rebuldela; Deacon Albert Phillips Jr.
Res.: 1294 Makawao Ave., 96768. Tel: 808-572-7652; Fax: 808-573-2278.
School—(Grades PreK-6) Tel: 808-572-8675; Fax: 808-572-0748. Edward Alexander, Prin. Sisters 3; Lay Teachers 7; Students 114.
Catechesis/Religious Program—Laura Paresa, D.R.E. Students 163.
Convent—57 Dominican Ln., 96768. Tel: 808-572-8454. Dominican Sisters of the Most Holy Rosary 3.

PAIA, MAUI CO., HOLY ROSARY (1915), (Portuguese—Filipino), [CEM] Rev. Teodoro Magpayo; Deacon Patrick Constantino.
Church: 954 Baldwin Ave., 96779-9605. Tel: 808-579-9551; Fax: 808-579-8714.
Catechesis/Religious Program—Tel: 808-579-9551; Fax: 808-575-2063. Students 34.

WAIHEE, HONOLULU, ST. ANN (1935), [CEM] [JC] Deacon James R. Gonsalves, Admin.
Res.: 40 Kuhinia St., 96793-9216. Tel: 808-244-3284; Fax: 808-244-3284.
Catechesis/Religious Program—Students 70.
Mission—St. Joseph [CEM] [JC] Waikapu, Maui

Co. 96793.
Mission—St. Francis Xavier [CEM] [JC] Kahakuloa, Maui Co. 96793.

WAILUKU, MAUI CO., ST. ANTHONY (1846), [CEM] Rev. Raymond E. Malley, S.M.; Deacons Joseph Borges; Hiram Haupu; Stephen Maglente.
Res.: 1627 B Mill St., 96793-1999. Tel: 808-244-4148; Fax: 808-242-9375.
School—(Grades PreK-6) Tel: 808-244-4976; 808-242-9024 (PreK); Fax: 808-244-7950. Mrs. Winona Martinez, Prin.; Mrs. Carlene Santos, Dir. (PreK). Lay Teachers 18; Students 246.
Catechesis/Religious Program—Tel: 808-242-6040. Kathy DeLima, D.R.E. Students 258.

ISLAND OF MOLOKAI

KALAUPAPA, KALAWAOLAHAINA CO., ST. FRANCIS (1873), (Hawaiian), [CEM] Rev. Joseph Hendriks, SS.CC.
Res.: P.O. Box 9, 96742. Tel: 808-567-6238.
Mission—St. Philomena P.O. Box 9, Kalawao, Molokai Co. 96742.

KAUNAKAKAI, MAUI CO., MOLOKAI CATHOLIC COMMUNITY (1874), [CEM 2] Attended by, Our Lady of Sorrows, Kalua'aha; St. Joseph, Kamalo (Shrine); St. Sophia, Kaunakakai; and St. Vincent Ferrer, Maunaloa. Rev. Antonio Manligues (Philippines), Admin.
Mailing Address: P.O. Box 1948, 96748-1948. Tel: 808-553-5220; Fax: 808-553-5556.
Office—115 Ala Malama St., 96748.
Catechesis/Religious Program—Students 132.

Chaplains of Public Institutions

HONOLULU. *Prison Ministry*, 1184 Bishop St., 96813. Tel: 808-533-1791, Ext. 341. Deacon Walter Yoshimitsu, Diocesan Representative.

On Duty Outside the Diocese:
Revs.—
Blazek, Eugene
Butler, John
Coughlin, Thomas
Drew, James F.
Etuale, Etuale
Evers, Paul H.
Gervacio, Adrian R. (LA)
Lanuevo, Victor
Lee, William, Chicago, IL
O'Mahony, James
Owens, Michael J.
Santry, Robert

Military Chaplains:
Rev. Msgrs.—
Gomulka, Eugene T., U.S. Navy
McCormick, Patrick U.S. Navy
Revs.—
Estabrook, Joseph W., U.S. Navy
Hellwig, Lee, U.S. Navy
Herron, Jack, U.S. Army
Ippolito, Robert, U.S. Air Force
Kopec, Rajmind, U.S. Army

Leave of Absence:
Revs.—
Bolger, Anthony (Retired)
Hannon, Robert E. (Retired)

Kaleikoa, Charles
O'Brien, Arthur (Retired)
Turner, Edward (Retired)
deOtero, Roberto

Retired:
Rev. Msgrs—
Dever, Daniel J., 6301 Pali Hwy., Kaneohe, 96744.
Eikmeier, Bernard J., 801 S. King St. # 1006, 96813.
Marzen, Francis A., P.O. Box 4935, Kaneohe, 96744.
Nishigaya, Raymond, 801 S. King St. #1011, 96813.
Revs.—
Bolger, Anthony
Burke, Ronald
Carroll, Joseph, 801 S. King St. # 1007, 96813.
Ching, Herbert, 86-660 Lualualei Homestead, Maili, 96792.
DeCosta, George
Duffy, Edwin J., Alexander Towers, 1226 Alexander St., Apt. 601, 96826.
Halloran, John, Our Lady of Peace, 2800 Mission College Blvd., Santa Clara, CA 95054.
McNeely, Maurice
McNichol, Daniel, 1738 Elua St., 96817.
Peterson, Francis, 1511 Nuuanu Ave., PT 122, 96817.
Sabog, Henry, 2909 Kalihi St., 96819.
Siu, Robert K.C., P.O. Box 1047, Lander, WY 82520.
Stawasz, James, 75-5769 Alii Dr., Kailua-Kona, 96740.
Thomas, Donald, P.O. Box 0358, Haleiwa, 96812.
Yim, Louis H., 801 S. King St. #1002, 96813.
daPorte, Robert, 4730 N. Mesa St. #59, El Paso, TX 79912.

Permanent Deacons:
Aanavi, Don, St. Joseph Church, P.O. Box 165, Ninole, 96773.
Adams, Thomas J., Sacred Heart-Hawi, P.O. Box 1048, Kapaau, 96755.
Andrews, Efrain, Our Lady of Good Counsel, 98-1366 Oni Kiniki Pl., Aiea, 96701.
Andrews, LeRoy, St. Joseph, 136 Ululani St., Hilo, 96720.
Awana, Benjamin A., 89-104 A Haleakala Ave., Nannakuli, 96792. Our Lady of Sorrows, Wahiawa
Benet, Alfonso, On Leave
Bostick, James E., St. Theresa-Kauai, P.O. Box 874, Kekaha, 96752.
Carlbom, Ernest F., St. George, 41-865 Mahailua St., Waimanalo, 96795.
Carroll, James, (Retired)
Cho, Edward, Sacre Heart; St. Pius X, 41-1403 Humuula St., Waimanalo, 96795.
Choo, Ronald T.Y., Blessed Sacrament, 46-144 Hilinama St., Kaneoha, 96744.
Cobb, Robert C., St. Augustine 2500 Kalakaua Ave., #2305, Honalulu, 96815.
Constantino, Patrick R., 3188 Kilani Pl., Pukalani, 96734. Holy Rosary, Paia; St. Rita, Haiku
Cyr, Robert, St. Antony, 701 Keolu Dr., Kailua, 96734.
DeCaires, Clarence, Jr., St. Anthony, 1131 Kupau St., Kailua, 96734.

Franco, Lawrence Stanley, St. Theresa - Maui, 452 Kaiola Pl., Kihei, Maui 96753.
Gerakas, Andrew J., Star of the Sea, 4524 Waikui St., 96821.
Gonsalves, James R., 2534 Main St., Wailuku, 96793. St. Ann, Waihee, Maui
Guinaugh, Daniel R., Holy Trinity, 1005 Mokuhano St., 96825.
Hart, Christopher L., On Leave
Haupu, Hiram B., St. Anthony, 398-A Puunene Ave., Kahului, 96732.
Hope, Jack M., On Leave
Ignacio, Lawrence, St. Anthony, Papaaloa, P.O. Box 317, Paauilo, 96776.
Kagehiro, George K., Our Lady of Sorrows, 916 Lemi St., Wahiawa, 96786.
Kang, Dominic S., St. Pius X, 2750 Kalawao St., 96822.
Kawaihae, Harvey, St. Joseph, 24 Poni Mai Pl., Hilo, 96720.
Levy, Harold S., Jr., St. Rita, 87-2214 Farrington Hwy., Waianae, 96792.
Libarios, Ernest, Sr., Immaculate Conception, 98-1470 Kaonohi St., Aiea, 96701.
Maglente, Stephen, St. Anthony, 50 E. Waiko Rd., Wailuku, 96793-9319.
Matsuo, Roy T., On Leave
McPeek, William, Anunciation Parish, Kamuela, P.O. Box 278, Kapaau, 96755.
Mitsui, Wallace M., St. John Apostle & Evangelist, 95-690 Lewanuu St., Mililani, 97689.
Miyashiro, Thomas H., Our Lady of Good Counsel, 2054 Hoohai St, Pearl City, 96782.
Paglinawan, Ronald, Our Lady of Perpetual Help, 94-348 Kioele Pl., Miliani, 96789.
Phillips, Albert C., St. Joseph, Makaweo, Maui, 3297 Haleakala Hwy., Pukalani, 96788.
Port, Richard J., Sts. Peter and Paul, 1600 Ala Moana Blvd., #3100, 96815.
Pulido, Cornelio, Christ the King, 624 Mlolkai Hema St., Kahului, 96732.
Rienzi, Thomas M., Star of the Sea, 676 Elepaio St., 96816.
Seagraves, Veral M. N., (On Duty Outside the Diocese)
Shuster, John K., St. Michael, P.O. Box 2495, Kealakekua, 96750.
Singson, Frank R., Sr., Christ the King, 468 Kipuka Pl., Kahului, 96732.
Taylor, Samuel, Holy Trinity, 7218 Pikoni Pl., 96825.
Thorp, George, St. Anthony-Kalihi, 1459 Akamai St., Kailua, 96734.
Townsley, Sidney J., (Retired)
Vargas, Edward, St. Jude, 92-1051 Makakilo Dr. #96, Kapolei, 96707.
Victor, Leslie, Star of the Sea, 7255 Kuhono St., 96825.
Vito, Jerome, Sacred Heart-Waianae, 87-150 Helelua St.#6, Waianae, 96792.
Waldemar, Donald, St. Catherine, P.O. Box 401, Kilauea, 96754. (On Duty Outside the Diocese)
Wong, Lauren H., St. John Vianney, 1309 Kupau St., Kailua, 96734.
Wozniak, Vincent, Star of the Sea, 1524 Halekula Way #D, 96822-4918.
Yoshimitsu, Walter H., St. John Vianney, 681 Akoakoa St., Kailua, 96734.

INSTITUTIONS LOCATED IN THE DIOCESE

[A] COLLEGES AND UNIVERSITIES

HONOLULU. **Chaminade University of Honolulu*, 3140 Waialae Ave., 96816. Tel: 808-735-4711; Fax: 808-735-7748. Email: cuhadm@lava.net. Web: www.chaminade.edu. Dr. Sue Wesselkamper, Pres.; Bro. Jerome Bommer, S.M.; Revs. Timothy E. Eden, S.M., Chap.; Kenneth A. Templin, S.M., Dir. Campus Ministry; Mrs. Catherine Agor, Campus Ministry; Kay Stone, Campus Ministry. Priests 3; Brothers 12; Lay Teachers 57; Students 4,270; Total Staff 208; Total Enrollment 4,270.

[B] HIGH SCHOOLS, DIOCESAN AND PAROCHIAL

HONOLULU. *Maryknoll School*, 1526 Alexander St., 96822. Tel: 808-952-7330; Fax: 808-952-7331. Email: admission@maryknollschool.org. Web: www.maryknollschool.org. Michael E. Baker, Pres.; Paul O'Brien, Grade School Prin.; Betsey Gunderson, High School Prin.; Scott Siegfried, Contact Person/Dir. Admission. Sisters 2; Lay Teachers 106; Students 1,398.

HILO. *St. Joseph Junior-Senior High School*, 1000 Ululani St., 96720. Tel: 808-935-4936; Fax: 808-969-9019. Email: ansonchong@pobox.com. Web: www.sjhshilo.org. Mr. Anson Chong, Interm Prin. Sisters 2; Lay Teachers 20; Students 207; Total Staff 15.

WAILUKU. *St. Anthony Junior-Senior High School*, 1618 Lower Main St., 96793. Tel: 808-244-4190; Fax: 808-242-8081. Email: sas@ccmaui.com. Web: www.sasmaui.org/. Daina Collins, Prin. Sisters 2; Lay Teachers 22; Students 287.

[C] HIGH SCHOOLS, PRIVATE

HONOLULU. *Damien Memorial School*, 1401 Houghtailing St., 96817. Tel: 808-841-0195; Fax: 808-847-1401. Email: odonnell@damien.edu. Web: www.damien.edu. Bro. W. Greg O'Donnell, C.F.C., Pres.; Michael Weaver, Prin. (High School); Burton Tomita, Prin. (Middle School).
Legal Title: *The Congregation of Christian Brothers of Hawaii, Inc.* The Congregation of Christian Brothers of Hawaii, Inc. Brothers 5; Lay Teachers 24; Boys 400.

St. Francis School, (Grades 6-12), 2707 Pamoa Rd., 96822. Tel: 808-988-4111; Fax: 808-988-5497. Email: admin@stfrancis-oahu.org. Web: www.stfrancis-oahu.org. Sr. Joan of Arc Souza, O.S.F., Prin.; Louise Gerboc, Contact Person. Sisters 10; Lay Teachers 29; Girls 405.

**Saint Louis School*, 3142 Waialae Ave., 96816-1578. Tel: 808-739-7777; Fax: 808-739-4853. Email: jdelong123@aol.com. Web: www.saintlouishawaii.org. Rev. James Allen DeLong, S.M., Pres. & Chap. Priests 1; Brothers 2; Lay Teachers 57; Boys 754.

Sacred Hearts Academy, (Grades PreK-12), 3253 Waialae Ave., 96816. Tel: 808-734-5058; Fax: 808-737-7867. Email: bwhite@sacredhearts.org. Web: www.sacredhearts.org. Mrs. Betty White, Prin. Sisters 4; Lay Teachers 87; Girls 1,150; Support Staff, Counselors, Administrators 30.

[D] PRESCHOOL CENTERS

HONOLULU. *St. Philomena Early Learning Center*, 3300 Ala Laulani St., 96818. Tel: 808-833-8080; Fax: 808-834-3438; 888-889-8418 (Toll Free). Email: stphilomenaelc@aol.com. Angie A. Thomas, Prin. Lay Teachers 10; Teachers Aids 9; Students 224; Total Staff 15.

HILO. *Hale O Kamalii Montessori Preschool*, 326 Desha Ave., 96720. Tel: 808-935-9338; Fax: 808-935-3865. Email: maliap@aloha.net. Marie Roberts, Co-Dir.; Joe Camacho, Co-Dir. Students 6; Total Staff 3.

MILILANI TOWN. *St. John Catholic Preschool*, 95-370 Kuahelani Ave., 96789. Tel: 808-623-3332, Ext. 200; Fax: 808-623-6496. Web: stjohnmililani.org. Email: preschool@stjohnmililani.org. Monica Caldeira, Dir. Total Staff 12; Lay Teachers 3; Students 67.

[E] GENERAL HOSPITALS

HONOLULU. *St. Francis Health Care System of Hawaii, St. Francis Residential Care Community*, 2226 Liliha St., Ste. 225, 96817. Tel: 808-547-6877; Fax: 808-547-6872. Email: EugeneT@sfhs-hi.org. Web: stfrancishawaii.org. Eugene N. Tiwanak, Pres.; Sisters Francis Regis Hadano, O.S.F., Vice Pres.;

Norise Kaiser, O.S.F., Sec. & Treas.
St. Francis Healthcare System of Hawaii, P.O. Box 29380, 96820. Tel: 808-547-6883; Fax: 808-547-6616. Web: www.sfhs.hi.org. Sr. Beatrice Tom, O.S.F., CEO & Pres. Total Staff 147.
St. Francis Home Care Services, 2230 Liliha St., 96817. Tel: 808-547-6511; Fax: 808-534-0798.
St. Francis Home Care Services-Kauai, 3224-B Elua St., Lihue, 96766. Tel: 808-245-6430; Fax: 808-246-8620.
Mobile Care Health Project, 140-B Holomua St., Hilo, 96720. Tel: 808-935-3050; Fax: 808-935-3794.
St. Francis Residential Care Community, P.O. Box 29380. Tel: 808-547-6874.
St. Francis Medical Center, 2230 Liliha St., 96817. Tel: 808-547-6011; Fax: 808-547-6616. Raleigh Awaya, COO & Exec. Vice Pres.; Revs. Mario Raquepo, Chap.; Joseph E. Specht, S.J., Chap.; Sr. Candida Oroc, O.S.F., Chap. Bed Capacity 240; Patients Assisted Annually 287,017; Total Staff 805.
St. Francis Medical Center - West, 91-2141 Fort Weaver Rd., Ewa Beach, 96706. Tel: 808-678-7000; Fax: 808-678-7054. Roger Eitelman, Admin. & Senior V.P.; Revs. Silva Spatz; Marvin Samiano. Bed Capacity 102; Patients Assisted Annually 134,728; Total Staff 152.
St. Francis Healthcare Foundation of Hawaii, P.O. Box 30100, 96820. Tel: 808-547-6877; Fax: 808-547-6872. Mr. Eugene Tiwanak, Pres. Total Staff 5.
St. Francis Community Health Service, P.O. Box 29380, 96820. Tel: 808-595-7566; Fax: 808-595-6996. Michael Warren, Senior Vice Pres. Total Staff 125.
The Sister Maureen Keleher Center (Hospice), 24 Puiwa Rd.. Tel: 808-595-7566; Fax: 808-595-6996. Sr. Francine Gries, O.S.F., Exec. Dir. Bed Capacity 12; Patients Assisted Annually 486.
Sister Maureen Intergenerational Learning Environment, 2715 Pamoa Rd., 96822. Tel: 808-988-5678; Fax: 808-988-1179. Alexandra Au, Dir. Total Staff 9; Capacity 35; Patients Assisted Annually 69.
The Maurice J. Sullivan Family Hospice Center, 91-2127 Fort Weaver Rd., Ewa Beach, 96706. Tel: 808-678-7580; Fax: 808-678-7597. Sr. Francine Gries, O.S.F., Exec. Dir. Bed Capacity 24; Patients Assisted Annually 585.
Health Services for Senior Citizens, 2230 Liliha Street, 96817. Tel: 808-547-6120; Fax: 808-547-6130. Patients Assisted Annually 30,866.

Renal Satellites

Hilo Renal Facility, 140 Rainbow Dr., Hilo, 96720. Tel: 808-935-3422; Fax: 808-934-7901.
Kona Renal Facility, 79-1020 Haukapila St., Ste. 213, Kealakekua, 96750. Tel: 808-322-2131; Fax: 808-322-0605.
Maui Renal Facility, 255 Mahalani St., Wailuku, 96793. Tel: 808-244-9600; Fax: 808-244-5712.
Kahana Renal Facility, 10 Hoohui Rd., Ste. 100, Lahaina, 96761. Tel: 808-669-6628; Fax: 808-669-1272.
Kauai Renal Facility, 3224 Elua St., Lihue, 96766. Tel: 808-245-3700; Fax: 808-245-2390.
West Kauai Renal Facility, 4643-A Waimea Canyon, Waimea, 96796. Tel: 808-338-1100; Fax: 808-338-1185.
Leeward Renal Facility, 91-2137 Ft. Weaver Rd., Ewa Beach, 96706. Tel: 808-671-3042; Fax: 808-677-7903.
Waianae Renal Facility, 86-080 Farrington Hwy., Waianae, 96792. Tel: 808-696-0216; Fax: 808-696-0345.
Molokai Renal Facility, 28 Kamoi St., Ste. 400, Kaunakakai, 96748. Tel: 808-553-8088; Fax: 808-553-3210.

[F] SPECIAL HOSPITALS AND SANATORIA FOR INVALIDS

KALAUPAPA. *Kalaupapa Care Home*, Formerly Kalaupapa Settlement (Molokai), P.O. Box 3333, 96742. Tel: 808-567-6911; Fax: 808-567-6916. Email: kch@lava.net. Sachi Taketa, Nursing Supvr.; Dr. W. Philip Jones, Settlement Medical Dir.; Rev. Joseph Hendriks, SS.CC., Pastor. Operated by the State Dept. of Health for Hansen's Disease Branch. Franciscan Sisters of the Third Order 1; Bed Capacity 14; Patients Assisted Annually 40.

[G] MONASTERIES AND RESIDENCES OF PRIESTS AND BROTHERS

HONOLULU. *The Christian Brothers of Ireland, Inc.*, 1401 Houghtailing St., 96817. Tel: 808-845-2330; Fax: 808-847-1401. Email: frick@damien.edu cullerton@damien.edu. Bros. F. Louis Frick, C.F.C., Supr.. Email: frick@damien.edu; B. John Cullerton, C.F.C., Community Leader. Email: cullerton@damien.edu; Karl C. Berndlmaier, C.F.C.; Liam V. Nolan, C.F.C.; W. Greg O'Donnell, C.F.C.; Patrick L. O'Hare, C.F.C.; F. M. Popish, C.F.C.; K. J. Reilly, C.F.C.; T. Patrick Rowland, C.F.C.; Patrick D. McCormack, C.F.C. Brothers 10.
Jesuit Fathers House, 2727 Pamoa Rd., 96822-1838. Tel: 808-988-3464; Fax: 808-988-7627. Email: bcassidy@calprov.org. Web: www.newmanhawaii.org. Revs. Christopher M. Cartwright, S.J., Regl. Supr.; Bernard F. Cassidy, S.J.; James A. Rude, S.J.; Donald P. Merrifield, S.J.; Joseph E. Specht, S.J.
Legal Title: *California Province of the Society of Jesus*
Marianist Communities
3140 Waialae Ave., 96816-1578. Rev. Francis Nakagawa, S.M.; Bro. Robert G. Hoppe, S.M.
Center Marianist Community, 3140 Waialae Ave., 96816. Tel: 808-735-2711; Fax: 808-734-3117. Revs. Allen DeLong, S.M.; Timothy Eden, S.M.; Kenneth A. Templin, S.M. Priests 4; Brothers 12; Total in Residence 15.
Marianist Hall Community, 3140 Waialae Ave., 96816. Tel: 808-739-8300; Fax: 808-739-8320. Revs. William O'Connell, S.M., Dir.; Joseph Priestly, S.M.; John Bolin, S.M.; Robert W. Hertweck, S.M. Priests 4; Brothers 7.
Chaminade Pohaku Marianist Community, 3140 Waialae Ave., 96816. Tel: 808-735-4857; Fax: 808-739-8333. Bro. Thomas Spring, S.M., Dir.; Rev. Robert Bouffier, S.M. Priests 1; Brothers 3.
Wailuku Marianist Community, 1627 B Mill St., Wailuku, 96793. Tel: 808-244-4148; Fax: 808-242-9375. Revs. Raymond E. Malley, S.M.; Stephen R. Tutas, S.M. Priests 2.
Maryknoll Fathers House (M.M.), Honolulu Society House, 1721 Dole St, 96822. Tel: 808-949-7737; Fax: 808-943-6392. Email: mklhnl@aol.com. Revs. Charles W. Schmidt, M.M.; Elias Tederous, M.M.; Robert Donnelly, M.M.; Ralph Christman, M.M. Priests 4; Total in Residence 4.
Annunciation Church: P.O. Box 301, Kamuela, 96743. Tel: 808-885-4196; Fax: 808-887-1220. Revs. Robert F. Wynne, M.M.; Thomas Donnelly, M.M.
1721 Dole St., 96822-4906. Tel: 808-973-2211, Ext. 29. Bro. Venard F. Ruane, M.M.
St. John Apostle and Evangelist: 95-370 Kuahelani Ave., Mililani, 96789. Tel: 808-623-3332. Rev. Thomas B. Killackey, M.M.
The Oratory Community, P.O. Box 26113, 96825. Tel: 808-396-0551; Fax: 808-396-1380. Email: htoratory@aol.com. Web: http://oratoryhawaii.org. Rev. Halbert G. Weidner, C.O., Moderator. Priests 2; Brothers 4.
KANEOHE. *Congregation of the Sacred Hearts of Jesus and Mary (Hawaii Province SS.CC.)*, P.O. Box 1365, 96744-1365. Tel: 808-247-5035; Fax: 808-235-8849. Email: sacredhearts@hawaii.rr.com. Very Rev. Clarence L. Guerreiro, SS.CC., Prov. Priests 27; Brothers 10.
Sacred Hearts Center, P.O. Box 1365, 96744-1365. Tel: 808-247-3647; Fax: 808-235-8849. Email: sacredhearts@hawaii.rr.com. Revs. Clyde Guerreiro, SS.CC.; Nobincio Fernandez, SS.CC.; Francis Schellemans, SS.CC.; Joseph Bukoski III, SS.CC.; Marisi Palepale, SS.CC.; Paul Zaccone, SS.CC.; James Anguay, SS.CC.; Albert Garcia, SS.CC.; Paul McLeod, SS.CC.; Edward Popish, SS.CC.; Bros. Charles Kaahanui, SS.CC.; Richard Kupo, SS.CC., Supr.; Jonathan Hurrell, SS.CC., (Deacon in Transit); Gaston Gosselin, SS.CC.; Anthony Rapozo, SS.CC. Total in Residence 11; Total Staff 2.
St. Patrick's Monastery, 1124-A Seventh Ave., 96816. Tel: 808-732-0281. Revs. Lane K. Akiona, SS.CC., Supr.; Gaston Diels, SS.CC.; Clement Geysen, SS.CC.; Timothy Jacobs, SS.CC.; Matthew Lochs, SS.CC.; Albert Miechielsen, SS.CC.; Raphael Smulders, SS.CC.; Gabriel Vanden Brouke, SS.CC.; Stephen Van den Eynde, SS.CC.; Ildephonse Kuntz, SS.CC.; Bros. James Dunn, SS.CC.; Leo Vendiola, SS.CC.; Patrick Hughes, SS.CC; Dominic Stone, SS.CC.; George Apo, SS.CC.; Anthony Rapozo, SS.CC. Total in Residence 13; Total Staff 11.
WAIALUA, OAHU. *Benedictine Monastery of Hawaii/Retreat Center*, 67-290 Farrington Hwy., P.O. Box 490, 96791. Tel: 808-637-7887; Fax: 808-637-8601. Email: benedicthi@aol.com. Web: www.catholichawaii.com/religious/benedictine. Revs. Michael Sawyer, O.S.B.; Timothy Ottman, O.S.B.; David Barfknecht, O.S.B., Supr.; Sisters Mary Jo McEnany, O.S.B.; Geraldine Keirnan, O.S.B.; Celeste Cabral, O.S.B.; Geralyn Spaulding, O.S.B.; Bro. Gregory Foret, O.S.B. Benedictine Congregation of Our Lady of Mounte Oliveto, O.S.B.

[H] CONVENTS AND RESIDENCES FOR SISTERS

HONOLULU. *St. Anthony Retreat Center*, 3351 Kalihi St,, 96819. Tel: 808-845-4353; Fax: 808-848-2696. Sr. Rose Kathleen Lenchanko, SS.CC., Contact. Sisters 4.
Congregation of the Sacred Hearts and of Perpetual Adoration, 1120 Fifth Ave., 96816. Tel: 808-737-5822; Fax: 808-735-0878. Web: www.glauco.it/sscc. (Sisters of the Congregation of the Sacred Hearts of Jesus and Mary of Perpetual Adoration, SS.CC.)
Regina Pacis Community, 1120 Fifth Ave., 96816. Tel: 808-737-5822; Fax: 808-735-0878. Sisters Helene Wood, SS.CC., Pres. & Prov. Supr.; Regina Mary Jenkins, SS.CC., Vice Pres.; Anne Clare DeCosta, SS.CC., Sec.; Irene Barboza, SS.CC., Auditor; Mary Josephine Araki, Treas.; Jessie Kai, SS.CC., Contact Person. Sisters 6.
Puawakea Community, 3351 Kalihi St., 96819. Tel: 808-845-4353; Fax: 808-848-2696. Sr. Anne Clare DeCosta, SS.CC., Contact Person. Sisters 4.
Paewalani Community, 45-901 Wailele Rd., 96744. Tel: 808-247-3688; Fax: 808-235-0717. Sr. Anne Clare DeCosta, SS.CC., Contact Person. Sisters 5.
Malia o ka Malu Community, 1117 Fourth Ave., 96816. Tel: 808-734-2048. Sr. Anne-Marie Tamanaha, SS.CC., Contact Person. Sisters 13.
Na Leo Ho'onani Community, 2151 Kauhana St., 96816. Tel: 808-739-5566. Sr. Irene Barboza, SS.CC., Contact Person. Sisters 3.
Our Lady of Grace Community, 1110 N. Roselawn Ave., Artesia, NM 88210-1441. Tel: 505-746-6747; Fax: 505-748-1049. Sr. Marie Lemert, SS.CC., Contact Person. Sisters 3.
Sacred Hearts Community, 35 Huttleston Ave., Fairhaven, MA 02719-3154. Tel: 508-994-9341; Fax: 508-990-1967. Sr. Dolores Marie Pavao, SS.CC., Contact Person. Sisters 5.
Maryknoll Sisters of St. Dominic M.M. Tel: 808-261-0276; Fax: 808-261-1283. Email: mksrscpr@lava.net.
125 Ainoni St., Kailua, 96734-2138. Tel: 808-261-0267; 808-261-6356 Residence; Fax: 808-261-1283. Sr. Rosalinda Barrozo, M.M., Contact Person. Sisters 3.
2880 Oahu Ave., 96822-1726. Tel: 808-988-6540; Fax: 808-988-7938. Email: mkmanoa@lava.net. Sisters 5.
1617B Nakula St., Wahiawa, 96786-2630. Tel: 808-621-1677. Sisters 2.
1720 Huna St. #313, 96817-2463. Tel: 808-528-3328. Sisters 3.
1634 Makiki St., 96822-4439. Tel: 808-949-8448. Sisters 2.
271 Silva St., Hilo, 96720-4729. Tel: 808-961-2415.
P.O. Box 305, Pahala, 96777. Tel: 808-928-0410.
P.O. Box 1287, Kaunakakai, 96748. Tel: 808-558-8120.
1570 Mokulua Dr., Kailua, 96734-3254. Tel: 808-261-1674. Sisters 3.
87-204 Holomalia Pl., Nanakuli, 96792-3706. Tel: 808-668-1603. Sisters 3.
St. Anthony Convent, 702 Puuhale Rd., 96819-3305. Tel: 808-841-5652.
Sisters of St. Joseph of Carondelet CSJ, Hawaii Vice-Province Administration Center , 5311 Apo Dr., 96821-1829. Tel: 808-373-2096; Fax: 808-373-5341. Email: sandersar@aol.com. Sr. Brenda Lau, C.S.J., Dir.
The following are listings of residences and the number of sisters residing at each:
Carondelet Community, 5311 Apo Dr., 96821-1829. Tel: 808-373-3850; Fax: 808-373-5341. Email: sanderssar@aol.com csjh@hgea.org meleana@hgea.org. Sisters 3.
Hale Medaille Community, 2220 E. Kalaiwa Way #19, 96819-2711. Tel: 808-847-7807; Fax: 808-847-7807. Email: pjcsjsl@aol.com palenacsj@aol.com. Sisters 2.
Hale San Jose Comminity, 730 Captain Cook Ave., 96813. Tel: 808-545-8385; Fax: 808-545-8385. Email: hsjcsj@juno.com.
Holy Trinity Community, 6590 Hawaii Kai Dr., 96825-1112. Tel: 808-396-9182. Email: htcsj@juno.com. Sisters 2.
Ho'omaluhia Community, 1735 Ala Aolani St., 96819-1413. Tel: 808-836-8575. Email: maluhia9@hawaii.rr.com. Sisters 3.
Mana'Olana Community, 1046 6th Ave., 96816-1644. Tel: 808-737-2130; Fax: 808-732-2851. Email: srm@kahala.net. Sisters 3.
St. Joseph by the Sea Community, 206 Kailua Rd., Kailua, 96734-2398. Tel: 808-262-0575. Email: sjbts@hawaii.rr.com. Sisters 3.
St. Joseph the Worker Community, 15-2773 Niuhi St., Pahoa, 96778-8951. Tel: 808-965-8426; Fax: 808-965-8916. Email: opalrose@interpac.net. Sisters 2.
St. Theresa Community, 712 N. School St., 96817-3098. Tel: 808-533-3101. Email: stccsj@pixi.com. Sisters 7.
Christ the King Community, 211 A. South Kaulawahine St., Kahului, 96732-2200. Tel: 808-877-0790. Email: LePuycsj@aol.com. Sisters 5.
Hale Iokepa Community, 828 Analio St., Waiehu, 96793-9610. Tel: 808-244-8123; Fax: 808-244-5474. Email: roselani@gte.net. Sisters 2.
La'ialoha Community, P.O. Box 23858, 96823-3514. Tel: 808-848-4970; Fax: 808-833-5264. Email:

sisterew@yahoo.com. Web: www.compassionate.us.

Sisters of the Third Franciscan Order; Hawaii Region, St. Francis Convent, 2715 Pamoa Rd., 96822-1885. Tel: 808-988-4432; Fax: 808-988-1486. Email: elenikiswm@aol.com. Sr. William Marie Eleniki, O.S.F., Contact Person. Franciscan Sisters of Syracuse (O.S.F.) Sisters 23.

The following are listings of residences and the number of sisters residing at each:

Immaculate Conception Convent, 4453 Kapaia Rd., Lihue, Kauai, 96766. Tel: 808-246-4600.

Marianne Cope Convent, 2102 Liliha St., 96817-1642. Tel: 808-538-1526. Sisters 7.

St. Elizabeth Convent, Bishop Home and Hospital, Kalaupapa, 96742-0129. Tel: 808-567-6079. Sisters 2.

St. Theresa Convent, 712 N. School St., 96817-3030. Tel: 808-533-3101.

St. Joseph Convent, 49 Iwipolina Rd., Hilo, 96720-1777. Tel: 808-935-1388. Sisters 3.

St. Francis Medical Center - West, St. Clare Convent, 91-1048 A'awa Dr., Ewa Beach, 96706-3900. Tel: 808-687-3420. Sisters 6.

St. Michael Convent, 67-340 Haona St., Waialua, 96791-9689. Tel: 808-637-7772; Fax: 808-637-7722. Sisters 3.

KANEOHE. *Carmel of the Holy Trinity (Carmelite Monastery)*, 6301 Pali Hwy., 96744-5224. Tel: 808-261-6542. Sr. Agnes Marie Wong, Prioress. Order of Discalced Carmelite Nuns of Our Lady of Mount Carmel (O.C.D.) Sisters 7.

WAIPAHU. *Dominican Center Hawaii*, 94-1249 Lumikula St., 96797. Tel: 808-676-1452; 808-677-1202; Fax: 808-677-1202. Email: srmauraliaop@juno.com. Web: www.ophawiiregion.com. Sr. M. Aurelia Sanchez, O.P., Regl. Sec. Please refer to the following parish convents for additional residences: St. Elizabeth, Aiea; St. John, Honolulu; St. Joseph, Makawao. Sisters 8.

[I] MISCELLANEOUS

HONOLULU. *Catholic Charities Housing Development Corporation*, 250 Vineyard St., 96813. Tel: 808-537-6321; Fax: 808-585-7408. Email: jerry@catholiccharitieshawaii.org. Web: www.catholiccharitieshawaii.org. Jerome E. Rauckhorst, Diocesan Dir.

**Marianist Center of Hawaii*, 3140 Waialae Ave., 96816. Tel: 808-738-5887; Fax: 808 732-3374. Email: brohoppe@aol.com. Bro. Robert G. Hoppe, S.M., Contact Person. Total Staff 15.

Our Lady the Mystical Rose Chapel (Oratory) , c/o Marianist Center of Hawaii, 3140 Waialae Ave., 96816. Tel: 808-739-4738; 808-738-5887 (direct line); Fax: 808-732-3374. Email: brohoppe@aol.com. Rev. Timothy E. Eden, S.M., Chap.; Bro. Robert G Hoppe, S.M., Contact Person. Tel: 808-738-5887

KANEOHE. *Augustine Educational Foundation*, St. Stephen Diocesan Center, 6301 Pali Hwy., 96744. Tel: 808-230-2440; Fax: 808-230-2441. Email: aef@aloha.net. Web: www.planet-hawaii.com/~aef/. Most Rev. Francis X. DiLorenzo, D.D., S.T.D., Pres.; Rev. Msgr. Daniel J. Dever, Second Vice Pres. (Retired); Very Rev. Joseph A. Grimaldi, J.C.L., V.G., M.A., Sec.; Wendall K. Pang, Treas.; Susan Ferandin, Dir.

PEARL CITY. *St. Vincent de Paul Society Honolulu District Council*, 949 Luehu St., 96782. Tel: 808-454-1290; Fax: 808-247-4784. Email: svdphawaii@aol.com. Harold W. Westphalan Jr., Pres., Treas. & Contact Person; Henry Sumida, Pres.

WAILUKU. *Maui Helio Endowment Fund*, c/o St. Anthony Church, 1627-B Mill St., 96793. Tel: 808-572-4593. Lloyd Sodentani, Pres. & Contact Person; John Kim, Vice Pres.; Joseph W. Andrews, Treas.; Stephanie Hall, Sec.

RELIGIOUS INSTITUTES OF MEN REPRESENTED IN THE DIOCESE

For further details refer to the corresponding bracketed number in the Religious Institutes of Men or Women section.

[0200]—*Benedictine Monks* (Olivetan)—O.S.B.
[0470]—*The Capuchin Friars*—O.F.M.Cap.
[0310]—*Congregation of Christian Brothers*—C.F.C.
[1140]—*Fathers of the Sacred Hearts* (Hawaii Prov.)—SS.CC.
[0520]—*Franciscan Friars*—O.F.M.
[0690]—*Jesuit Fathers and Brothers*—S.J.
[0780]—*Marist Fathers*—S.M.
[0800]—*Maryknoll*—M.M.
[0720]—*The Missionaries of Our Lady of La Salette* (Pacific Region)—M.S.
[0950]—*Oratorians*—C.O.
[1030]—*Paulist Fathers*—C.S.P.
[0760]—*Society of Mary* (Prov. of the Pacific)—S.M.

RELIGIOUS INSTITUTES OF WOMEN REPRESENTED IN THE DIOCESE

[]—*Benedictine Congregation of Our Lady of Mounte Oliveto*—O.S.B.
[0870]—*Congregation of the Daughters of Mary Immaculate (Marianist Sisters)*—F.M.I.
[0950]—*Daughters of Saint Paul*—F.S.P.
[0420]—*Discalced Carmelite Nuns*—O.C.D.
[1070-03]—*Dominican Sisters of the Most Holy Rosary*—O.P.
[1230]—*Franciscan Sisters of Christian Charity*—O.S.F.
[1780]—*Franciscan Sisters of Perpetual Adoration*—F.S.P.A.
[2420]—*Marist Missionary Sisters*—S.M.S.M.
[2470]—*Maryknoll Sisters of St. Dominic*—M.M.
[]—*Religious of the Blessed Virgin Mary*—R.V.M.
[]—*Sacred Hearts Community*
[0430]—*Sisters of Charity of the Blessed Virgin Mary*—B.V.M.
[3000]—*Sisters of Notre Dame de Namur*—S.N.D.deN.
[3840]—*Sisters of St. Joseph of Carondelet*—C.S.J.
[1960]—*Sisters of the Holy Family*—S.H.F.
[3690]—*Sisters of the Sacred Hearts and of Perpetual Adoration*—SS.CC.
[1490]—*Sisters of the Third Franciscan Order* (Syracuse, NY)—O.S.F

NECROLOGY

✠ Ferrario, Most Rev. Joseph A., Retired Bishop of Honolulu—Died Dec. 12, 2003
† MacGregor, Donald, Makawao, Maui, HI St. Joseph—Died April 12, 2003
† O'Leary, Bartholomew, (Retired)—Died June 22, 2003
† Pascale, Anthony, (Retired)—Died Jan. 9, 2003

Diocese of Houma-Thibodaux

(Dioecesis Humensis-Thibodensis)

Most Reverend

SAM G. JACOBS, D.D.

Bishop of Houma-Thibodaux; ordained June 6, 1964; appointed Bishop of Alexandria July 1, 1989; ordained and installed August 24, 1989; appointed third Bishop of Houma-Thibodaux August 1, 2003; installed October 10, 2003 *Office: 2779 Hwy. 311, Schriever, LA 70395.*

Chancery: P.O. Box 505, Schriever, LA 70395. Tel: 985-868-7720; Fax: 985-868-7727.

Email: mmitchell@htdiocese.org

ERECTED JUNE 5, 1977.

Square Miles 3,440.

Comprises the parishes of Lafourche, Terrebonne, parts of St. Mary and Jefferson.

Legal Title: For legal titles of parishes and diocesan institutions, consult the Chancery Office.

STATISTICAL OVERVIEW

Personnel	
Bishop	1
Priests: Diocesan Active in Diocese	44
Priests: Diocesan Active Outside Diocese	2
Priests: Retired, Sick or Absent	17
Number of Diocesan Priests	63
Religious Priests in Diocese	8
Total Priests in Diocese	71
Extern Priests in Diocese	3
Ordinations:	
Diocesan Priests	1
Transitional Deacons	1
Permanent Deacons in Diocese	27
Total Brothers	2
Total Sisters	26
Parishes	
Parishes	39
With Resident Pastor:	
Resident Diocesan Priests	33
Resident Religious Priests	2
Without Resident Pastor:	
Administered by Priests	4
Missions	2
Professional Ministry Personnel:	
Sisters	10
Lay Ministers	36
Welfare	
Day Care Centers	1
Total Assisted	136
Specialized Homes	2
Total Assisted	65
Special Centers for Social Services	4
Total Assisted	25,000
Educational	
Diocesan Students in Other Seminaries	4
Total Seminarians	4
High Schools, Diocesan and Parish	3
Total Students	1,930
Elementary Schools, Diocesan and Parish	10
Total Students	4,060
Catechesis/Religious Education:	
High School Students	3,115
Elementary Students	6,283
Total Students under Catholic Instruction	15,392
Teachers in the Diocese:	
Brothers	2
Sisters	5
Lay Teachers	373
Vital Statistics	
Receptions into the Church:	
Infant Baptism Totals	1,546
Adult Baptism Totals	54
Received into Full Communion	64
First Communions	1,475
Confirmations	1,259
Marriages:	
Catholic	363
Interfaith	58
Total Marriages	421
Deaths	1,194
Total Catholic Population	126,000
Total Population	202,000

Former Bishops—Most Revs. WARREN L. BOUDREAUX, J.C.D., D.D. (Retired), First Bishop of Houma-Thibodaux; ord. May 30, 1942; retired Dec. 29, 1992; died Oct. 6, 1997; MICHAEL JARRELL, D.D., Second Bishop of Houma-Thibodaux; ord. June 3, 1967; appt. Dec. 29, 1992; consecrated and installed March 4, 1993; appt. 6th Bishop of Lafayette, Louisiana Nov. 8, 2002.

Chancery

Chancery—Address all correspondence to: P.O. Box 505, Schriever, 70395. Office, 2779 Hwy. 311, Schriever, 70395. Tel: 985-868-7720; Fax: 985-868-7727. Office Hours: Mon.-Fri. 8-5.

Vicar General—Rev. Msgr. JAMES B. SONGY (Retired).

Chancellor—Sr. MIRIAM MITCHELL, S.H.Sp.

Finance Officer—Rev. Msgr. FREDERICK BRUNET.

Judicial Vicar—Very Rev. VICENTE DELA CRUZ.

Director of Tribunal—Sr. BONNIE KOEHNE, S.E.

Diocesan Tribunal— Address all correspondence to: *P.O. Box 505, Schriever, 70395. Office, 2779 Hwy. 311, Schriever, 70395*. Tel: 985-850-3126.

Departments of the Diocesan Curia

Department of Administration Ministries

Judges—Rev. Msgr. WILLIAM KONINKX; Very Rev. VICENTE DELA CRUZ, J.V.; Revs. BRENDAN FOLEY; JAY BAKER.

Defenders of the Bond—Revs. DANIEL M. POCHE; ROLAND TIMBRE; Deacon CHARLES GIROIR.

Counselor—Mrs. NANCY DIEDRICH.

Priests Council—Revs. FRANCIS QUYET BUI; SABINO REBOSURA; CHARLES PERKINS; OSCAR SOLIS; DEAN DANOS, V.F.; PATRICK O'BRIEN; CLYDE MAHLER; ROBERT CRUZ; ROGER "JERRY" E. VILLARRUBIA JR., At Large 2000-2005; Rev. Msgr. JAMES B. SONGY, Ex Officio (Retired); JAY BAKER, Ex Officio, Mailing Address, P.O. Box 505, Schriever, 70395. 2779 Hwy. 311, Schriever, 70395.

College of Consultors—Revs. FRANCIS Q. BUI; ROBERT CRUZ; DEAN DANOS; CLYDE MAHLER; CHARLES PERKINS; JERRY VILLARRUBIA.

Deans—

Upper Lafourche Deanery—Very Rev. OSCAR A. SOLIS, 721 Canal Blvd., Thibodaux, 70301.

South Lafourche Deanery—Rev. DEAN DANOS, P.O. Box 10, Larose, 70373.

Terrebonne Deanery—Rev. PATRICK O'BRIEN, 409 Funderburk Ave., Houma, 70364-1895.

Diocesan Finance Council—WILLIAM J. BARBERA; Rev. Msgr. FREDERIC J. BRUNET; Rev. PATRICK O'BRIEN; A. J. CHAMPAGNE JR.; ROBERT NAQUIN; Sr. MIRIAM MITCHELL, S.H.Sp.

Coordinator—Sr. MIRIAM MITCHELL, S.H.Sp., 2779 Hwy. 311, Schriever, 70395. Mailing Address, P.O. Box 505, Schriever, 70395. Tel: 985-850-3122.

Accounting, Business Office, Finance—WILLIAM J. BARBERA, Business Mgr., 2779 Hwy. 311, Schriever, 70395. Mailing Address, P.O. Box 505, Schriever, 70395. Tel: 985-868-7720.

Archives and Historical Research Center—Sr. MIRIAM MITCHELL, S.H.Sp., 205 Audubon St., Thibodaux, 70301. Tel: 985-446-2383.

Building Commission—JAMES J. DANOS, Dir., 2779 Hwy. 311, Schriever, 70395. Mailing Address, P.O. Box 505, Schriever, 70395. Tel: 985-868-7720.

Cemeteries—GEORGE COOKE, Dir., 949 Menard St., Thibodaux, 70301. Tel: 985-446-0280.

Legal Services—Rev. Msgr. JAMES B. SONGY, Dir. (Retired), 2779 Hwy. 311, Schriever, 70395. Mailing Address, P.O. Box 505, Schriever, 70395. Tel: 985-868-7720. Attorneys: KENNETH WATKINS; DANIEL WALKER, 501 Roussell St., P.O. Box 5095, Houma, 70361. Tel: 985-868-2333.

Stewardship and Development—JEREMY BECKER, Dir., 2779 Hwy. 311, Schriever, 70395. Mailing Address, P.O. Box 505, Schriever, 70395. Tel: 985-868-7720.

Human Resources & Employment Benefits—KATHLEEN THERIOT, Dir., 2779 Hwy. 311, Schriever, 70395. Mailing Address, P.O. Box 505, Schriever, 70395. Tel: 985-868-7720.

Insurance - Property, Casualty & Liability—PENNY BREAUX, Dir., 2779 Hwy. 311, Schriever, 70395. Mailing Address, P.O. Box 505, Schriever, 70395. Tel: 985-868-7720.

Operations - Computers & Technology—HOLLY BECNEL, Dir., 2779 Hwy. 311, Schriever, 70395. Mailing Address, P.O. Box 505, Schriever, 70395. Tel: 985-868-7720.

Department for Clergy and Religious

Coordinator—Rev. JAY L. BAKER, 2779 Hwy. 311, Schriever, 70395. Mailing Address, P.O. Box 505, Schriever, 70395. Tel: 985-868-7720.

Clergy Personnel—Rev. JAY L. BAKER, Mailing Address, P.O. Box 505, Schriever, 70395. Tel: 985-868-7720.

Continuing Education of the Clergy-Ministry to Priests Program—Rev. ETIENNE LEBLANC, P.O. Box 505, Schriever, 70395. Tel: 985-868-7720.

Vicar for Priests—Rev. Msgr. FRANCIS LEGENDRE, 15300 W. Main St., Cutoff, 70345. Tel: 985-632-3858.

Permanent Diaconate—Deacon ROBERT DUSSE, 514 Gaynell Dr., Houma, 70364. Tel: 985-876-5122. 2779 Hwy. 311, Schriever, 70395. Mailing Address, P.O. Box 505, Schriever, 70395. Tel: 985-868-7720.

Vocations—Rev. MARK TOUPS, Dir., P.O. Box 10, Larose, 70373.

Seminarians—Rev. JAMES MORRISON, Dir., 204 NSU Madewood Dr., Thibodaux, 70310. Mailing Address, NSU Box 2051, Thibodaux, 70310. Tel: 985-446-2606.

Women Religious—Sr. MIRIAM MITCHELL, S.H.Sp., P.O. Box 505, Schriever, 70395. Tel: 985-850-3122.

Department of Formation Ministries

Coordinator—LOUIS G. AGUIRRE, 2779 Hwy. 311, Schriever, 70395. Mailing Address, P.O. Box 505, Schriever, 70395. Tel: 985-868-7720.

Campus Ministry—Rev. JAMES MORRISON, Dir., N.S.U., Box 2051, Thibodaux, 70310. Tel: 985-446-6201.

Catholic Schools—Sr. IMMACULATA PAISANT, M.S.C., Supt., 2779 Hwy. 311, Schriever, 70395. Mailing Address, P.O. Box 505, Schriever, 70395. Tel: 985-868-7720.

Communications, Public Relations, Publications, Radio & Television—LOUIS G. AGUIRRE, Dir., 2779 Hwy. 311, Schriever, 70395. Mailing Address, P.O. Box 505, Schriever, 70395. Tel: 985-868-7720.

Religious Education—Sr. FIONNUALA QUINN, O.P., Dir., 2779 Hwy. 311, Schriever, 70395. Mailing Address, P.O. Box 505, Schriever, 70395. Tel: 985-368-7720.

Pastoral Staffing—Dr. MARIAN SCHWAB, Dir., 2779 Hwy. 311, Schriever, 70395. Mailing Address, P.O. Box 505, Schriever, 70395. Tel: 985-868-7720.

"The Bayou Catholic"—LOUIS G. AGUIRRE, Editor, 2779 Hwy. 311, Schriever, 70395. Mailing Address, P.O. Box 505, Schriever, 70395. Tel: 985-868-7720. (Diocesan Newspaper)-

Youth Ministries—MICHAEL DISALVO, 2779 Hwy. 311, Schriever, 70395. Mailing Address, P.O. Box 505, Schriever, 70395. Tel: 985-868-7720.

Family Ministries—CATHERINE KLINGMAN, 2779 Hwy. 311, Schriever, 70395. P.O. Box 505, Schriever, 70395. Tel: 985-868-7720.

Worship—Rev. ETIENNE LEBLANC, Dir., 2779 Hwy. 311, Schriever, 70395. Mailing Address, P.O. Box 505, Schriever, 70395. Tel: 985-868-7720.

Rite of Chiristian Initiation of Adults—Sr. KATHLEEN STAKELUM, M.S.C., Dir., Mailing Address, 409 Funderburk Ave., Houma, 70364. Tel: 985-879-1506.

Young Adult Ministries—Rev. CHARLES J. PERKINS, Dir., Mailing Address, P.O. Box 310, Amelia, 70340. Tel: 985-631-2333.

Department of Social Ministries

Coordinator—Sr. MIRIAM MITCHELL, S.H.Sp., 2779 Hwy. 311 P.O. Box 505, Schriever, 70395. Tel: 985-850-3122.

Assisi Bridge House—BERNADETTE THIBODAUX, Admin., 600 Bull Run Rd., Schriever, 70395. Tel: 985-872-5529.

Catholic Campaign for Human Development—ROBERT GORMAN, Diocesan Dir., 1220 Aycock St., P.O. Box 3894, Houma, 70361. Tel: 985-876-0490

Catholic Relief Service Director—Sr. CELESTE COTTER, C.S.J.

Catholic Social Services; Justice & Peace—ROBERT D. GORMAN, A.C.S.W., B.C.S.W., Dir. Assoc. Directors: Sr. CELESTE COTTER, C.S.J.; GERMAINE JACKSON, 1220 Aycock St., P.O. Box 3894, Houma, 70361. Tel: 985-876-0490.

Disaster Relief—ROBERT D. GORMAN, A.C.S.W., B.C.S.W, Dir., 1220 Aycock St., P.O Box 3894, Houma, 70361. Tel: 985-876-0490.

St. Lucy's Day Care Center—CAROLYN WOODS, Admin., 1220 Aycock St., P.O. Box 3894, Houma, 70361. Tel: 985-876-1246.

Other Offices and Commissions

Charismatic Renewal—Deacon MELVIN MARTS, Charismatic Renewal Liaison, 2779 Hwy. 311, Schriever, 70394. Tel: 985-868-7720.

Cursillo—Rev. ROCH R. NAQUIN, Dir., 5101 Grand Caillou Rd., Dulac, 70353. Tel: 985-563-2325.

Ecumenism—P.O. Box 505, Schriever, 70395. Tel: 985-868-7720; Fax: 985-868-7727.

*Pontifical Societies for the Propagation of the Faith—*Holy Childhood Association; Society of St. Peter the Apostle Rev. NGUYEN VAN TY, Dir., 1027 Hwy. 308, Thibodaux, 70301. Tel: 985-446-6663.

Scouting—MICHAEL J. DISALVO, Dir., 2779 Hwy. 311, Schriever, 70395. Mailing Address, P.O. Box 505, Schriever, 70395. Tel: 985-868-7720.

Organizations

Catholic Daughters of the Americas—Rev. GREGORY FRATT, Diocesan Advisor to State Court Officers, 15300 W. Main, Cut Off, 70345. Tel: 985-632-3858.

Diocesan Council of St. Vincent de Paul Societies—NORMAN SIMON, Pres., 901 Liberty St., Houma, 70360. Tel: 985-851-2432.

Knights of Columbus—VACANT, Diocesan Chap., P.O. Box 4014, Houma, 70361. Tel: 985-876-6904.

Legion of Mary—KATE WOOD, Pres.; VACANT, Spiritual Dir.

St. Vincent de Paul Store—Mr. PETE CAVALIER, Pres.; Mr. ROY BURNS, Vice Pres.; Mr. CULLEN BOUDREAUX, Treas. Store Managers: JIM LAGARDE; PHYLLIS LAGARDE, 107 Point St., Houma, 70360. Tel: 985-872-9373.

Serra Club of South Lafourche—Mr. BOBBY CHERAMIE, Pres.

Serra Club of Thibodaux—Rev. JAMES MORRISON, Spiritual Advisor; Mr. DON HARRIS, Pres.

Anawim—EVELYN RUCKSTUHL, Pres., 501 Grinage St., Houma, 70360. Tel: 985-872-4761.

Victim Assistance Coordinator—Sr. MIRIAM MITCHELL, S.H.Sp Tel: 985-850-3122. Email: mmitchell@htdiocese.org.

CLERGY, PARISHES, MISSIONS AND PAROCHIAL SCHOOLS

CITY OF HOUMA
(PARISH TERREBONNE)

1—CATHEDRAL OF ST. FRANCIS DE SALES (1847), [CEM 2] Revs. Roger E. (Jerry) Villarrubia Jr., Admin.; Scott Dugas. In Res., Rev. Van Constant.
Res.: P.O. Box 4014, Houma, 70361. Tel: 985-876-6904; Fax: 985-851-4204.
School—300 Verret St., Houma, 70361. Tel: 985-868-6646; Fax: 985-851-5896. Lay Teachers 35; Students 827.
Catechesis/Religious Program—Students 184.
Convent—501 Grinage St., Houma, 70361. Tel: 985-876-7260.

2—ANNUNZIATA (1963), Rev. Wilfredo Decal; Sr. Paula Richard, O.P., Pastoral Assoc. In Res., Rev. Rodolfo Fernandez.
Res.: 2011 Acadian Dr., Houma, 70363. Tel: 985-876-2971; Fax: 985-868-6414.
Catechesis/Religious Program—Tel: 985-876-2865. Students 345.

3—ST. BERNADETTE (1958), Very Rev. Patrick O'Brien; Rev. Clyde Mahler; Sr. Kathleen Stakelum, M.S.C., Pastoral Assoc.
Res.: 409 Funderburk Ave., Houma, 70364. Tel: 985-879-1506; Fax: 985-876-9654.
School—309 Funderburk Ave., Houma, 70364. Tel: 985-872-3854. Sisters 1; Lay Teachers 18; Students 484.
Catechesis/Religious Program—Miss Amy Lirette, D.R.E. Students 737.

4—ST. GREGORY BARBARIGO (1963), Rev. Francis Bui. Mailing Address: P.O. Box 1066, Houma, 70361.
Res.: 439 Sixth St., Houma, 70364. Tel: 504-876-2003.
Administration Bldg.—1005 Williams Ave., Houma, 70364. Tel: 985-876-2047; Fax: 985-876-0628.
School—441 Sixth St., Houma, 70364. Tel: 985-876-2038; Fax: 985-879-2789. Lay Teachers 11; Students 203.
Catechesis/Religious Program—Students 205.

5—ST. LOUIS (1965), [CEM] Rev. Guy Zeringue.
Res.: 2226 Bayou Blue Rd.. Tel: 985-876-3449; Fax: 504-876-6810.
Catechesis/Religious Program—Tel: 985-876-6686; Fax: 985-876-6810. Nancy P. Champton, D.R.E. Students 286.

6—ST. LUCY, Revs. Bert Heise, O.F.M. (CIN); William Ollendick, O.F.M.; Reynolds Garland, O.F.M.
Mailing Address: P.O. Box 3508, Houma, 70361. Tel: 985-879-2632; Fax: 985-876-4054.
Res.: 8594 Main Street, Houma, 70360. Tel: 985-879-2632.
Church: 1220 Aycock St., Houma, 70360.
Catechesis/Religious Program—Bernadette Travis, D.R.E. Students 36.

7—MARIA IMMACOLATA (1963), Rev. Caesar Silva; Deacon Douglas Authement.
Administration Office—246 Corporate Dr., Houma, 70360. Tel: 985-876-3313; Fax: 985-879-2137.
Res.: 326 Estate Dr., Houma, 70360. Tel: 985-868-4915.
School—324 Estate Dr., Houma, 70360. Tel: 985-876-1631; Fax: 985-876-1608 Lay Teachers 12; Students 187.
Catechesis/Religious Program—Students 265.

8—OUR LADY OF THE MOST HOLY ROSARY (1948), [CEM], (Holy Rosary Church) Revs. Bert Heise, O.F.M.; Reynolds Garland, O.F.M.; William Ollendick, O.F.M.; Deacons Linwood Liner; Harold Kurtz.
Res.: 8594 Main St., Houma, 70363. Tel: 985-876-7652; Fax: 985-876-7647.
Catechesis/Religious Program—Tel: 985-879-2815. Debbie Hotard, D.R.E. Students 22[illegible].

CITY OF THIBODAUX
(LAFOURCHE PARISH)

1—ST. CHARLES BORROMEO (1912), [CEM] Rev. Nguyen Van Ty.
Res.: 1027 Hwy. 308, Thibodaux, 70301. Tel: 985-446-6663; Fax: 985-447-3348.
Catechesis/Religious Program—Students 185.

2—CHRIST THE REDEEMER (1983), [CEM] Rev. John Gallen; Deacon Charles Giroir.
Res.: 720 Talbot Ave., Thibodaux, 70301. Tel: 985-447-2013; Fax: 985-447-4422.
Catechesis/Religious Program—Students 262.

3—ST. GENEVIEVE (1959), Very Rev. Wilmer L. Todd; Rev. Mike Viet Manh Tran.
Res.: 815 Barbier Ave., Thibodaux, 70301. Tel: 985-446-5571; Fax: 985-449-1939.
School—807 Barbier Ave., Thibodaux, 70301. Tel: 985-447-9291; Fax: 985-447-9883. Lay Teachers 27; Students 454.
Catechesis/Religious Program—Tel: 985-446-5127. Students 196.

4—ST. JOHN THE EVANGELIST (1919), [CEM] Rev. Florentino Santiago, Pastor.
Res.: 2085 St. Mary St., Thibodaux, 70301. Tel: 985-447-3995; Fax: 985-447-2092.
Catechesis/Religious Program—Fax: 985-447-2092. Elaine Benoit, D.R.E. Students 254.

5—ST. JOSEPH CO-CATHEDRAL (1817), Revs. Oscar Solis (Philippines); Jeremias T. Jadulco (Philippines); Lonnie James Cheramie; Deacons Willie R. Orgeron; Ambrose J. Ayzinne; Pedro Pujals.
Res.: 721 Canal Blvd., P.O. Box 966, Thibodaux, 70302. Tel: 985-446-1387; Fax: 985-446-6571.
School—501 Cardinal Dr., Thibodaux, 70301. Tel: 504-446-1346; Fax: 504-449-0730. Lay Teachers 37; Students 681.
Catechesis/Religious Program—Students 151.

6—ST. LUKE (1923), Very Rev. Wilmer Todd; Sr. Terry Falco, R.S.M., Pastoral Assoc.
Office:—P.O. Box 1819, Thibodaux, 70302. Tel: 985-446-0487; Fax: 985-446-0430.
Catechesis/Religious Program—Students 63.

7—ST. THOMAS AQUINAS (1970), Rev. James Morrison. Nicholls Sta.: NSU Box 2051 Thibodaux, 70310. Tel: 985-446-6201; Fax: 985-449-0710.
Catechesis/Religious Program—Tel: 985-446-6201; Fax: 985-449-0710. Students 12.

OUTSIDE THE CITIES OF HOUMA AND THIBODAUX

AMELIA, ST. MARY PARISH

1—ST. ANDREW (1965), [CEM] Rev. Gregory Perkins Fratt, Pastor.
Res.: P.O. Box 310, 70340. Tel: 985-631-2333; Fax: 985-631-2334.
Catechesis/Religious Program—Students 129.

2—THANH GIA (1981), Personal Parish for Vietnamese Community. Revs. Anthony Lap Nguyen; Dominic Dieu Tran. Personal Parish for Vietnamese Community.
Res.: 711 Magnolia St., Morgan City, 70380. Tel: 985-631-3194; Fax: 985-631-2634.
Catechesis/Religious Program—Students 170.
Domus Dei Institute, Inc.—1002 Aycock St., Houma, 70360. Tel: 985-851-1351.

BAYOU BLACK, TERREBONNE PARISH, ST. ANTHONY (1876), Rev. Gerard C. Hayes.
Res.: 3897 Bayou Black Dr., Houma, 70360. Tel: 985-872-0922; Fax: 985-872-2001.
Catechesis/Religious Program—Students 207.

BOURG, TERREBONNE PARISH, ST. ANN (1908), [CEM] Very Rev. Vicente DeLa Cruz; Deacon Gerald Belanger.
Res.: 4355 Hwy. 24, P.O. Box 700, 70343. Tel: 985-594-3548; Fax: 985-594-3570.
Catechesis/Religious Program—Tel: 985-594-5088. Students 403.

CHACAHOULA, TERREBONNE PARISH, ST. LAWRENCE (1858), [CEM 2] Rev. Michael Bergeron; Deacon Raymond Le Boeuf.
Res.: P.O. Box 426, 70395. Tel: 985-449-1732; Fax: 985-448-2764.
Catechesis/Religious Program—Tel: 985-449-1732; Fax: 985-448-2764. Students 38.

CHACKBAY, LAFOURCHE PARISH, OUR LADY OF PROMPT SUCCOR (1892), [CEM 2] Rev. Roland Timbre.
Res.: 529 Hwy. 20, Thibodaux, 70301. Tel: 985-633-2903; Fax: 985-633-9225.
Catechesis/Religious Program—Students 368.

CHAUVIN, TERREBONNE PARISH, ST. JOSEPH (1948), [CEM] Rev. Msgr. Frederic J. Brunet; Rev. Peter Tai Le.
Res.: 5232 Hwy. 56, 70344. Tel: 985-594-5859; Fax: 985-594-2116.
Catechesis/Religious Program—Veralyn Price, D.R.E. Students 526.

CUT-OFF, LAFOURCHE PARISH, SACRED HEART (1923), [CEM] Rev. Msgr. Francis J. Legendre; Deacons Sam J. Burregi; Eldon Frazier.
Res.: 15300 W. Main, 70345. Tel: 985-632-3858; Fax: 985-632-4452.
Catechesis/Religious Program—Tel: 985-632-6322; Fax: 985-632-4452. Students 525.

GALLIANO, LAFOURCHE PARISH, ST. JOSEPH (1958), [CEM] Rev. Shenan J. Boquet.
Res.: P.O. Box 519, 70354. Tel: 985-632-7321; Fax: 985-632-7345.
Catechesis/Religious Program—Students 230.

GHEENS, LAFOURCHE PARISH, COMMUNITY OF ST. ANTHONY (1987), [CEM], (Quasi Parish) Revs. Daniel M. Poche, Admin.; Carlos Talavera.
Res.: 333 Twin Oaks Dr., Raceland, 70394. Tel: 985-537-6002; Fax: 985-537-4408.
Catechesis/Religious Program—Tel: 985-537-6002; Fax: 985-337-4408. Students 109.

GIBSON, TERREBONNE PARISH, ST. PATRICK (1920), Merged, with St. Lawrence, Chacahoula.

GOLDEN MEADOW, LAFOURCHE PARISH, OUR LADY OF PROMPT SUCCOR (1916) [CEM] Rev. Carl Collins; Sr. Gayle Williams, M.S.C., Pastoral Assoc.
Res.: 723 N. Bayou Dr., 70357. Tel: 985-475-5428; Fax: 985-475-7699.
Catechesis/Religious Program—Tel: 985-475-5886; Fax: 985-475-7699. Students 400.

GRAND CAILLOU, TERREBONNE PARISH, HOLY FAMILY (1952), [CEM 2] Revs. Etienne LeBlanc; Joseph Pilola; Deacon Bernard A. Harold Fanguy; Sr. Diane McOsker, Pastoral Assoc.
Res.: P.O. Box 87, Dulac, 70353. Tel: 985-563-2325; Fax: 985-563-4980.
Catechesis/Religious Program—Students 167.

GRAND ISLE, WEST JEFFERSON PARISH, OUR LADY OF THE ISLE (1933), [CEM] Rev. Warren F. Chassaniol.
Res.: P.O. Box 885, 70358. Tel: 504-787-2385; Fax: 504-787-4530.
Catechesis/Religious Program—Tel: 985-787-2385; Fax: 985-787-4530. Students 100.

KRAEMER, LAFOURCHE PARISH, ST. LAWRENCE THE MARTYR (1962), [JC 2] Rev. Domingo Cruz.
Res.: 3723 Hwy. 307, Thibodaux, 70301. Tel: 985-633-9431; Fax: 985-633-5706.
Mission—St. James [CEM] Thibodaux. 1278 Choctaw Rd., Choctaw, Lafourche Parish 70301. Tel: 985-633-9855.
Catechesis/Religious Program—Tel: 504-633-5714. Students 206.

LAROSE, LAFOURCHE PARISH, OUR LADY OF THE ROSARY (1873), [CEM] Revs. Dean F. Danos; Mark Anthony Toups; Deacon Michael Cantrelle.
Res.: P.O. Box 10, 70373. Tel: 985-693-3433; Fax: 985-693-7551.
School—P.O. Box 40, 70373. Tel: 985-693-3342; Fax: 985-693-3348. Sisters 1; Lay Teachers 12; Students 252.
Catechesis/Religious Program—Tel: 985-693-3125. Jennifer Sanamo, D.R.E. Students 325.

LOCKPORT, LAFOURCHE PARISH, HOLY SAVIOR (1850), [CEM] Rev. Robert Joel Cruz.
Res.: 612 Main St., 70374. Tel: 985-532-3533; Fax: 985-532-2010.
School—201 Church St., 70374. Tel: 985-532-2536; Fax: 985-532-2269. Lay Teachers 23; Students 310.
Catechesis/Religious Program—Tel: 985-532-6111; Fax: 985-532-2010. Students 366.

MONTEGUT, TERREBONNE PARISH, SACRED HEART (1864), [CEM 2] Revs. Robert C. Rogers; Joseph Tu Tran.
Res.: P.O. Box 2, 70377. Tel: 985-594-5856; Fax: 985-594-8087.
Catechesis/Religious Program—Tel: 985-594-5856; Fax: 985-594-8087. Students 87.

MORGAN CITY, ST. MARY PARISH
1—HOLY CROSS (1964), Revs. Jay L. Baker; Joshua John Rodrigue; Deacon Andrew Dragna.
Res.: 2100 Cedar St., Unit 3, 70380. Tel: 985-384-3551; Fax: 985-384-5790.
School—2100 Cedar St., Unit 2, 70381. Tel: 985-384-1933; Fax: 985-384-3270. Lay Teachers 18; Students 360.
Catechesis/Religious Program—Tel: 985-384-3551; Fax: 985-384-5970. Students 196.
Mission—St. Rosalie 1315 Stephensville Rd., St. Mary Parish 70380. Tel: 504-385-5713.
2—SACRED HEART OF JESUS (1859), Revs. Sabino B. Rebosura II; Roque Anquilero Jr. (Philippines).
Res.: 415 Union St., P.O. Box 632, 70381. Tel: 985-385-0770; Fax: 985-384-7176.
Catechesis/Religious Program—Tel: 985-384-8108. Students 301.

POINTE-AUX-CHENES, LAFOURCHE PARISH, ST. CHARLES BORROMEO (1971), [CEM] Revs. Robert C. Rogers; Joseph Tu Tran.
Mailing Address: P.O. Box 54, Montegut, 70377.
Res.: 1237 Hwy. 665, Montegut, 70377. Tel: 985-594-6801; Fax: 985-594-6802.
Catechesis/Religious Program—Fax: 985-594-6802. Students 106.

RACELAND, LAFOURCHE PARISH
1—ST. HILARY OF POITIERS (1965), Revs. Daniel M. Poche; Carlos Talavera.
Res.: 333 Twin Oaks, 70394. Tel: 985-537-6002; Fax: 985-537-4408.
Catechesis/Religious Program—Fax: 985-537-4408. Students 441.
2—ST. MARY'S NATIVITY (1850), [CEM] Revs. Charles J. Perkins, Admin.; Dat Huu Pham.
Res.: 3500 Hwy. 1, 70394. Tel: 985-537-3204; Fax: 985-537-3235.
School—(Grades PreK-8), 3492 Nies St., 70394. Tel: 985-537-7544; Fax: 985-537-4020. Lay Teachers 13; Students 292.
Catechesis/Religious Program—Students 148.

SCHRIEVER, TERREBONNE PARISH, ST. BRIDGET (1911), [CEM] Rev. Michael Bergeron; Deacon Raymond LeBouef.
Res.: 100 Hwy. 311, 70395. Tel: 985-446-6801; Fax: 985-448-2764.
Catechesis/Religious Program—Tel: 985-446-1985. Students 286.

THERIOT, TERREBONNE PARISH, ST. ELOI (1875), [CEM] Revs. Etienne LeBlanc; Joseph Pilola; Deacon Daniel Bascle; Sr. Mary Teresa O'Donnell, R.S.M., Pastoral Assoc.
Res.: 1335 Bayou Dularge Rd., 70397. Tel: 985-872-2946; Fax: 985-872-9961.
Catechesis/Religious Program—Tel: 504-851-6893. Students 143.

Chaplains of Public Institutions

HOUMA. *Terrebonne Parish General Hospital*. Rev. Van Constant.
THIBODAUX. *Nicholls State University*. Rev. James Morrison.
Thibodaux General Hospital. Rev. John Ruiz, (Philippines).

On Duty Outside the Diocese:
Rev.—
LeCompte, Glenn David, M.Div., S.T.L., Prof. Scripture, Notre Dame Seminary, New Orleans.

On Sabbatical:
Rev.—
Bouterie, Thomas

Administrative Leave:
Rev.—
Cavell, Lawrence Arthur

Retired:
Rev. Msgrs.—
Amedee, Francis, 725 St. Philip St., 70301.
Bergeron, Albert G., Hollywood Park Apartments, 546 Ave. B, Marrero, 70072.
Fossier, Emile, Cheateau Creole, 273 Monarch Dr., A-13, Houma, 70364.
Koninkx, William, P.O. Box 1066, Houma, 70361.
Ledet, Donald, P.O. Box 617, Gibson, 70356.
Newfield, John L., 2832 Burdette St., Apt. 428, New Orleans, 70125-2514.
Songy, James B., 410 Ninth St., Lockport, 70374.
Revs.—
Brewerton, Peter H., 1201 Cardinal Dr., Apt. L113, 70301.
Broussard, Hubert C., Chateau Creole, 273 Monarch Dr., Apt. J13, Houma, 70360.
Daigle, H.C. Paul, Hollywood Park Apts., 4000 West Bank Expwy., Apt. 12, Marrero, 70072.
Foley, Brendan P., 182 E. 110th St., Galliano, 70354.
Loresco, Alfredo, 155 Church St., Lockport, 70374.
Luu, Joseph
Naquin, Roch, 539 Island Rd., Montegut, 70377.
Sevigny, Robert J., St. Joseph Manor, 70301.

Permanent Deacons:
Authement, Douglas, Maria Immacolata, Houma
Ayzinne, Ambrose Joseph, St. Joseph, Thibodaux
Bascle, Daniel, St. Eloi, Theriot
Belanger, Gerald, St. Ann, Bourg
Blanchard, Gerald, St. Ann, Bourg
Burregi, Sammy, Sacred Heart, Cut-Off
Cantrelle, Michael, Holy Rosary, Larose
Dragna, Andrew J., Holy Cross, Morgan City
Dufrene, Roland, St. Hilary of Poitiers, Raceland
Dusse, Robert, St. Bernadette, Houma
Duthu, James, Annunziata, Houma
Fanguy, Bernard A. Harold, Holy Family, Grand Caillou
Frazier, Eldon, Cut-Off
Giroir, Charles, Christ the Redeemer, Thibodaux
Haddad, Gregory, Lafourche Parish Detention Center
Kurtz, Harold, Our Lady of the Most Holy Rosary, Houma
Landry, Alduce, St. Charles, Thibodaux
LeBouef, Raymond, Holy Rosary, Houma
Legendre, Paul Joseph, Jr., St. Genevieve, Thibodaux
Liner, Linwood Paul, Sr., St. Lucy, Houma
Marts, Melvin, St. Joseph, Galliano
Messina, Nick, St. Anthony, Bayou Black
Orgeron, Willie R., St. Joseph Co-Cathedral, Thibodaux
Porche, Glenn, St. Eloi, Theriot
Pujals, Pedro P., St. Thomas Aquinas, Thibodaux
Rabalais, Bertrand A., Annunziata, Houma
Uzee, Dickey, St. Mary's Nativity, Raceland

INSTITUTIONS LOCATED IN THE DIOCESE

[A] HIGH SCHOOLS, DIOCESAN

HOUMA. *Vandebilt Catholic High*, 209 S. Hollywood Rd., 70360. Tel: 985-876-2551; Fax: 985-868-9774. Email: vchs@archdiocese-no.org. Web: www.vandebiltcatholic.org. Mr. James Reiss, Prin.; Bro. Carl Evans, S.C., Chap. Brothers of the Sacred Heart Priest/Brother 1; Brothers 1; Lay Teachers 67; Students 940.

THIBODAUX. *Edward Douglas White Catholic High* (Coed) , 555 Cardinal Dr., 70301. Tel: 985-446-8486; Fax: 985-448-1275. Email: edwhitehi@htdiocese.org. 70301. Mr. David Boudreaux, Prin. Brothers of the Sacred Heart Brothers 1; Sisters 1; Lay Teachers 50; Students 774.
E.D. White Catholic High School Foundation, Inc. Tel: 985-449-1859; Fax: 985-448-1275.
E.D. White Catholic High School Alumni Assn. Tel: 985-446-8486; Fax: 985-448-1275.

MORGAN CITY. *Central Catholic High*, 2100 Cedar St., 70380. Tel: 985-385-5372; Fax: 985-385-3444. Email: centcathi@archdiocese-no.org. Web: www.cchseagles.com. Mr. John P. Weimer, Prin.; Patricia Roland, Guidance Counselor. Lay Teachers 21; Students 216.

[B] DAY CARE CENTERS

HOUMA. *St. Lucy Day Care and Child Development Center*, P.O. Box 3894, 70361. Tel: 985-876-1246; Fax: 985-876-7751. Email: enfants@mobiltel.com. Staff 11; Children 65.

[C] RETREAT CENTERS

SCHRIEVER. *Lumen Christi Retreat Center*, 100 Lumen Christi Ln., Hwy. 311, 70395. Tel: 985-868-1523; Fax: 985-868-1525. Rev. Rock Travnikar, O.F.M., Dir.

[D] CONVENTS

LOCKPORT. *Monastery of the Heart of Jesus*, 155 Church St., 70374. Tel: 985-532-2411. Sr. Marie Therese, O.P., Vicaress. Dominican Contemplative Sisters of the Heart of Jesus of the Diocese of Houma-Thibodaux

[E] PRIVATE ASSOCIATIONS OF THE FAITHFUL

THIBODAUX. *Marian Servants of the Word*, 506 Cardinal Dr., 70361. Tel: 504-447-6564; Fax: 504-447-5734. Email: marianserviants@mobiletel.com. Rev. Michael Bergeron, Chap.; Dr. Bonnie J. Bourg, Dir.; Dr. Margaret Jolley, Asst. Dir.; Ms. Yvonne Scignet, Sec.; Mrs. Rose Adams, Treas.

[F] MISCELLANEOUS

THIBODAUX. *The Diocese of Houma-Thibodaux Historical Research Center*, 205 Audubon Ave., 70301. Tel: 985-446-2383; Fax: 985-449-0574. Email: htchancllor@htdiocese.org. Sr. Miriam Mitchell, S.H.Sp., Chancellor & Archivist.
St. Joseph Manor (Retirement Community) , 1201 Cardinal Dr., 70301. Tel: 985-446-9050; Fax: 985-449-0047. Email: annt@stjosephmanor.org. Web: www.stjosephmanor.org. Ann Thibodaux, Admin.
Magnificat of the Houma-Thibodaux Diocese, 830 Laurel Valley Rd., 70301. Tel: 985-446-5001; Fax: 985-447-4261. Mrs. Mina McKee, Coord., Bayou River Chapter.

SCHRIEVER. *Cemeteries Trust*, P.O. Box 505, 70395. Tel: 985-850-3149; Fax: 985-850-3164. Email: pbreaux@htdiocese.org.

RELIGIOUS INSTITUTES OF MEN REPRESENTED IN THE DIOCESE

For further details refer to the corresponding bracketed number in the Religious Institutes of Men or Women section.

[1100]—*Brothers of the Sacred Heart*—S.C.

[0520]—*Franciscan Friars*—O.F.M.

[0770]—*Marist Brothers*—F.M.S.

RELIGIOUS INSTITUTES OF WOMEN REPRESENTED IN THE DIOCESE

[0400]—*Congregation of Our Lady of Mount Carmel*—O.Carm.

[2410]—*Congregation of the Marianites of Holy Cross*—M.S.C.

[]—*Dominican Contemplative Sisters*—O.P.

[]—*Dominican Sisters* (Cabra, Ireland)—O.P.

[1140]—*Eucharistic Missionaries of St. Dominic*—O.P.

[2970]—*School Sisters of Notre Dame*—S.S.N.D.

[2550]—*Sisters of Mercy*—R.S.M.

[3830]—*Sisters of St. Joseph*—C.S.J.

[2050]—*Sisters of the Holy Spirit and Mary Immaculate*—S.H.Sp.

[2120]—*Sisters of the Immaculate Conception*—C.I.C.

NECROLOGY

† Pol, Dom Te (Retired)—Died April 10, 2003
† Skorogod, Leopold (Retired)—Died Sept. 14, 2003
† Toth, Victor (Retired)—Died Aug. 8, 2003

Archdiocese of Indianapolis

(Archidioecesis Indianapolitana)

Most Reverend

DANIEL MARK BUECHLEIN, O.S.B., D.D.

Archbishop of Indianapolis; ordained May 3, 1964; appointed to Memphis January 16, 1987; consecrated Bishop March 2, 1987; installed March 2, 1987; appointed Archbishop of Indianapolis July 14, 1992; installed September 9, 1992.

The Archbishop Edward T. O'Meara Catholic Center: 1400 N. Meridian St., P.O. Box 1410, Indianapolis, IN 46206. Tel: 317-236-1400; Fax: 317-236-1401.

Web: www.archindy.org

Email: chancery@archindy.org

Square Miles 13,758.

Established a Diocese in 1834; established an Archdiocese December 19, 1944 by decree of Pope Pius XII.

Comprises the Counties of Bartholomew, Brown, Clark, Clay, Crawford, Dearborn, Decatur, Fayette, Floyd, Franklin, Hancock, Harrison, Hendricks, Henry, Jackson, Jefferson, Jennings, Johnson, Lawrence, Marion, Monroe, Morgan, Ohio, Orange, Owen, Parke, Perry, Putnam, Ripley, Rush, Scott, Shelby, Switzerland, Union, Vermillion, Vigo, Washington and Wayne, and the township of Harrison in Spencer County, in the southern part of Indiana.

For legal titles of parishes and archdiocesan institutions, consult the Chancery Office.

STATISTICAL OVERVIEW

Personnel	
Archbishops	1
Abbots	1
Retired Abbots	2
Priests: Diocesan Active in Diocese	116
Priests: Diocesan Active Outside Diocese	2
Priests: Retired, Sick or Absent	41
Number of Diocesan Priests	159
Religious Priests in Diocese	111
Total Priests in Diocese	270
Extern Priests in Diocese	9
Ordinations:	
Diocesan Priests	2
Total Brothers	42
Total Sisters	457
Parishes	
Parishes	139
With Resident Pastor:	
Resident Diocesan Priests	100
Resident Religious Priests	18
Without Resident Pastor:	
Administered by Priests	9
Administered by Religious Women	11
Administered by Lay People	1
Missions	11
Professional Ministry Personnel:	
Sisters	23
Lay Ministers	135
Welfare	
Catholic Hospitals	2
Total Assisted	1,007,475
Homes for the Aged	4
Total Assisted	580
Day Care Centers	2
Total Assisted	205
Specialized Homes	3
Total Assisted	608
Special Centers for Social Services	5
Total Assisted	144,987
Educational	
Diocesan Students in Other Seminaries	18
Seminaries, Religious	1
Students Religious	11
Total Seminarians	29
Colleges and Universities	2
Total Students	3,039
High Schools, Diocesan and Parish	7
Total Students	3,392
High Schools, Private	3
Total Students	2,108
Elementary Schools, Diocesan and Parish	63
Total Students	18,701
Catechesis/Religious Education:	
High School Students	3,498
Elementary Students	13,920
Total Students under Catholic Instruction	44,687
Teachers in the Diocese:	
Priests	8
Brothers	4
Sisters	25
Lay Teachers	1,490
Vital Statistics	
Receptions into the Church:	
Infant Baptism Totals	4,183
Adult Baptism Totals	624
Received into Full Communion	700
First Communions	4,041
Confirmations	2,824
Marriages:	
Catholic	697
Interfaith	548
Total Marriages	1,245
Deaths	2,060
Total Catholic Population	230,938
Total Population	2,430,606

The Diocese of Vincennes (now Indianapolis) was established by decree of Pope Gregory XVI, May 6, 1834, and the See was fixed at Vincennes. The territory then comprised the entire State of Indiana and the eastern third of Illinois. By decree of Pope Pius IX, January 8, 1857, the northern half of the State became the Diocese of Fort Wayne. The southern half of the State remained the Diocese of Vincennes.

The second Bishop of Vincennes, by Apostolic Brief, was permitted to establish his residence either at Vincennes, Madison, Lafayette or Indianapolis; the See city, however, was to remain at Vincennes. This permission was renewed to the fourth Bishop, with the exception of Lafayette. On the appointment of the fifth Bishop, he was directed to fix his residence at Indianapolis, but the Cathedral and title of the See were continued at Vincennes. By an Apostolic Brief dated March 28, 1898, the title of the Diocese was changed to that of "Diocese of Indianapolis" with the city of Indianapolis as the Episcopal See. By the same Brief the Patron Saint of the Diocese was to remain St. Francis Xavier, the title of the old Cathedral in Vincennes.

On December 19, 1944, Most Reverend Amleto Giovanni Cicognani, Apostolic Delegate to the United States, solemnly proclaimed the Papal Decree of Pope Pius XII in SS. Peter and Paul Cathedral, Indianapolis, elevating Indianapolis to the status of an Archdiocese, the State of Indiana being the Metropolitan Area. The Dioceses of Evansville and Lafayette-in-Indiana were created by the same decree and were made Suffragan Sees of Indianapolis. Upon the establishment of the Diocese of Gary on December 17, 1956, it too became a Suffragan See.

Former Bishops—Rt. Revs. SIMON GUILLAUME GABRIEL BRUTE DE REMUR, S.S., D.D., consecrated 1834; died 1839; CELESTIN DE LA HAILANDIERE, D.D., consecrated 1839; resigned 1847; died in France, 1882; JOHN S. BAZIN, D.D., consecrated 1847; died 1848; MAURICE DE SAINT PALAIS D.D., consecrated Jan. 14, 1849; died June 28, 1877; FRANCIS SILAS CHATARD, D.D., consecrated May 12, 1878; died Sept. 7, 1918; Most Revs. JOSEPH CHARTRAND, D.D., consecrated Titular Bishop of Flavias and Coadjutor Bishop, Sept. 15, 1910; succeeded to the See of Indianapolis, Sept. 7, 1918; died Dec. 8, 1933; JOSEPH ELMER RITTER, S.T.D., consecrated Titular Bishop of Hippo and Auxiliary Bishop, March 28, 1933; succeeded to the See March 24, 1934; installed as Archbishop Dec. 19, 1944; transferred to Metropolitan See of St. Louis, July 20, 1946; named Cardinal, Jan. 16, 1961; died June 10, 1967; PAUL C. SCHULTE, D.D., consecrated Bishop of Leavenworth, Sept. 21, 1937; appt. Archbishop of Indianapolis, July 20, 1946; installed Oct. 10, 1946; resigned Jan. 14, 1970; died Feb. 17, 1984; GEORGE J. BISKUP, consecrated Titular Bishop of Hemeria and Auxiliary of Dubuque, April 24, 1957;; transferred to Des Moines Feb. 3, 1965; transferred to Indianapolis "cum jure successionis," July 26, 1967;; succeeded to See Jan. 14, 1970; resigned March 26, 1979; died Oct. 17, 1979; EDWARD T. O'MEARA, S.T.D., appt. Titular Bishop of Thisiduo and Auxiliary of St. Louis Jan. 28, 1972; consecrated in the Basilica of St. Peter, Rome, Feb. 13, 1972; appt. Archbishop of Indianapolis Nov. 27, 1979; installed Jan. 10, 1980; died Jan. 10, 1992.

Archdiocesan Administration— Secretariats/ Vicariates/Agencies and Offices can be contacted through The Archbishop Edward T. O'Meara Catholic Center. *1400 N. Meridian St., Indianapolis, 46202. Address all mail unless otherwise indicated to, P.O. Box 1410, Indianapolis, 46206-1410.* Tel: 317-236-1400; Fax: 317-236-1401.

Vicar General and Moderator of the Curia—Rev. Msgr. JOSEPH F. SCHAEDEL, M.S., M.Div., V.G.

Chancellor—SUZANNE L. YAKIMCHICK.

Assistant Chancellor—Rev. WILLIAM STUMPF.

Chief Financial Officer—JEFFREY D. STUMPF.

Board of Consultors—Most Rev. DANIEL M. BUECHLEIN, O.S.B., D.D., Chm.; Rev. Msgrs. JOSEPH F. SCHAEDEL, M.S., M.Div., V.G.; FRANCIS R. TUOHY; Revs. WILLIAM STUMPF; CLIFFORD VOGELSANG, V.F.; PAUL ETIENNE; PAUL KOETTER; DANIEL MAHAN, V.F.; DANIEL STAUBLIN.

Deaneries and Deans—Revs. PATRICK DOYLE, V.F., Indianapolis North; JOSEPH RIEDMAN, V.F., Indianapolis East; JAMES WILMOTH, V.F., Indianapolis South; Rev. Msgr. JOHN RYAN, V.F., Indianapolis West; Revs. DANIEL MAHAN, V.F., Batesville; CHARLES S. CHESEBROUGH, V.F., Bloomington; STANLEY J. HERBER, M.A., V.F., Connersville; CLIFFORD VOGELSANG, V.F., New Albany; JOHN A. MEYER, V.F., Seymour; CARL DEITCHMAN, O.S.B., V.F., Tell City; JOSEPH KERN, V.F., Terre Haute.

Council of Priests—Most Rev. DANIEL M. BUECHLEIN, O.S.B., D.D., Pres.; SUZANNE YAKIMCHICK; Rev.

Msgr. JOSEPH F. SCHAEDEL, M.S., M.Div., V.G.; Revs. STEPHEN JARRELL; RICHARD GINTHER; ROBERT GILDAY; LOUIS MANNA; BRENDAN MOSS, O.S.B.; RUSSELL ZINT; DANIEL STAUBLIN; ROGER RUDOLF; THOMAS SCHLIESSMANN; WILLIAM STUMPF; Rev. Msgr. FRANCIS R. TUOHY; Revs. WILLIAM EHALT; VINCENT LAMPERT; DONALD SCHMIDLIN; BEDE CISCO, O.S.B.; DANIEL DONOHOO; PAUL KOETTER; WILLIAM MARKS; DAN ATKINS.

Finance Council—Most Rev. DANIEL M. BUECHLEIN, O.S.B., D.D., Chm.; Rev. Msgr. JOSEPH F. SCHAEDEL, M.S., M.Div., V.G.; JEFFREY D. STUMPF, C.F.O.; JAY BREHM; JACKIE BYERS; CLARK BYRUM; PATRICK CARR; MICHAEL DILTS; DALE GETTELFINGER; MARY HORN; PHILIP B. MCKEIRNAN; DAVID MILROY; DENNIS J. SCHLICHTE; JAMES SHANAHAN. Tel: 317-236-1410.

Priests' Personnel Board—Most Rev. DANIEL M. BUECHLEIN, O.S.B., D.D.; Revs. PATRICK BEIDELMAN; THOMAS CLEGG; PATRICK DOYLE; JAMES FARRELL; JOHN GEIS; STEPHEN GIANNINI, M.Div., M.A., M.S.; WILLIAM STUMPF; HENRY TULLY.

Archdiocesan Review Board—ANN M. DELANEY; Rev. JAMES BONKE; CATHLEEN GRAHAM; RICHARD K. GRANA; SUZANNE YAKIMCHICK; JOHN "JAY" S. MERCER; Rev. PAUL D. ETIENNE; Rev. Msgr. JOSEPH F. SCHAEDEL, M.S., M.Div., V.G.; Rev. WILLIAM F. STUMPF; JOHN "JACK" M. WHELAN; WILLIAM J. WOOD; MICHAEL H. ZUNK.

Archdiocesan Pastoral Council—Most Rev. DANIEL M. BUECHLEIN, O.S.B., D.D.; Rev. Msgr. JOSEPH SCHAEDEL, Vicar Gen.; SUZANNE YAKIMCHICK, Chancellor; L. H. BAYLEY; MILLY BREHOB; WILLIAM R. BRUNS; RON DOXSEE; Rev. Msgr. FREDERICK EASTON, J.C.L.; CHARLES GARDNER; ROBERT W. GOLOBISH; Rev. PAUL KOETTER; ANNETTE "MICKEY" LENTZ; KAREN ODDI; DAVID J. SILER; MICHAEL SLAUGHTER; AMANDA STRONG; JEFFREY STUMPF; Rev. WILLIAM STUMPF; JOSEPH THERBER. Tel: 317-236-7325.

Secretariat for Catholic Charities and Family Ministries—DAVID J. SILER, Exec. Dir. Tel: 317-236-7325.

Family Ministries—DAVID BETHURAM, Assoc. Exec. Dir. Tel: 317-236-1595.

Archdiocesan Deaf Ministry—DAVID BETHURAM, Contact Person. Tel: 317-236-1595.

Bloomington Catholic Social Services—KAREN BROSIUIS, M.S.W., Dir., 635 N. College Ave., Bloomington, 47404. Tel: 812-332-1262.

Catholic Campaign for Human Development—DAVID J. SILER, Dir. Tel: 317-236-7325.

Catholic Social Services of Central Indiana—DAVID BETHURAM, Assoc. Exec. Dir. Tel: 317-236-1500.

Commission for Multicultural Ministry—Rev. KENNETH TAYLOR, Dir. Tel: 317-236-1562.

Pro-Life Activities—Sr. DIANE CAROLLO, S.G.L., Dir. Tel: 317-236-1569.

St. Elizabeth's Pregnancy and Adoption Services—MICHELLE MEER, Dir., 2500 Churchman Ave., Indianapolis, 46203. Tel: 317-787-3412.

St. Elizabeth - Catholic Charities—KEITH E. STORMES, Dir., 601 E. Market St., New Albany, 47150. Tel: 812-949-7305.

Tell City Catholic Charities—802 Ninth St., Tell City, 47586. Tel: 812-547-6414.

Terre Haute Catholic Charities—JOHN ETLING, M.S., Dir., Corporate Square Annex, 2931 Ohio Blvd., Terre Haute, 47803. Tel: 812-232-1447.

Family Ministries—DAVID BETHURAM, Assoc. Exec. Dir. Tel: 317-236-1596.

Secretariat for Catholic Education and Faith Formation—ANNETTE "MICKEY" LENTZ, Exec. Dir. Tel: 317-236-1438.

Catholic Education—G. JOSEPH PETERS, Assoc. Exec. Dir. Tel: 317-236-1437.

Faith Formation—Dr. HARRY DUDLEY, Assoc. Exec. Dir. Tel: 317-236-1446.

Catholic Education, School Improvement, Project Exceed—RONALD COSTELLO, Assoc. Exec. Dir. Tel: 317-236-1486.

Catholic Youth Organization—EDWARD TINDER, Dir., 580 E. Stevens St., Indianapolis, 46203. Tel: 317-632-9311.

Ministry to Youth and Young Adults—Rev. ROBERT J. ROBESON, Dir. Tel: 317-236-1477.

St. Mary's Child Center—CONSTANCE SHERMAN, Dir., 901 Dr. Martin Luther King, Jr. St., Indianapolis, 46202. Tel: 317-635-1491.

Secretariat for Communications—WILLIAM R. BRUNS, Exec. Dir. Tel: 317-236-1585.

Archdiocesan Newspaper, "The Criterion"—Most Rev. DANIEL M. BUECHLEIN, O.S.B., D.D., Publisher; WILLIAM R. BRUNS, Assoc. Publisher; GREG A. OTOLSKI, Editor. Tel: 317-236-1570.

Catholic Communications Center—SUSAN BORCHERTS, Dir. Tel: 317-236-1585.

Secretariat for Finance and Administrative Services—JEFFREY D. STUMPF, CFO & Exec. Dir. Tel: 317-236-1410.

Accounting Services—JULIE SHEWMAKER, Controller. Tel: 317-236-1410.

Information Services—TOM O'DROBINAK, Dir. Tel: 317-236-1420.

Management Services—DAVID L. HODDE, Dir. Tel: 317-236-1452.

Purchasing Office—STEPHEN M. JAMES, Dir. Tel: 317-236-1451.

Catholic Cemeteries Assoc.—TONY LLOYD, Buchanan Group, 9001 N. Haverstick Rd., Indianapolis, 46240. Tel: 317-574-8898.

Roman Catholic Archdiocese of Indianapolis Properties—Most Rev. DANIEL M. BUECHLEIN, O.S.B., D.D., Pres.; Rev. Msgr. JOSEPH F. SCHAEDEL, M.S., M.Div., V.G., Vice Pres. Secretaries: SUZANNE L. YAKIMCHICK; JEFFREY D. STUMPF. Tel: 317-236-1410.

Secretariat for Lay Ministry and Pastoral Services—SUZANNE L. YAKIMCHICK, Chancellor & Exec. Dir. Tel: 317-236-7325.

Archives—JANET NEWLAND, Assoc. Archivist. Tel: 317-236-1429.

Archdiocesan Historian—Rev. JACK W. PORTER, Ph.D.

Human Resources—ED ISAKSON, Dir. Tel: 317-236-1594.

Lay Ministry—SUZANNE YAKIMCHICK, Dir. Tel: 317-236-7325.

Parish Planning and Organizational Development—SUZANNE YAKIMCHICK, Dir. Tel: 317-236-7325.

Secretariat for Spiritual Life and Worship—CHARLES GARDNER, Exec. Dir. Tel: 317-236-1483.

Archdiocesan Cathedral—Rev. RICHARD GINTHER, Pastor & Rector, 1347 N. Meridian St., Indianapolis, 46202-2396. Tel: 317-634-4519.

Evangelization Commission—KAREN ODDI, Coord. Tel: 317-236-1489.

Office of Worship—CHARLES GARDNER, Dir. Tel: 317-236-1483.

Retreat & Renewal Ministries and Fatima Retreat House—STEPHEN JAMES, Interim Dir., 5353 E. 56th St., Indianapolis, 46226. Tel: 317-545-7681; Fax: 317-545-0095.

Secretariat for Stewardship and Development—JOSEPH THERBER, Exec. Dir. Tel: 317-236-1415.

Office of Stewardship and Development—VACANT, Dir., School & Agency Svcs. Tel: 317-236-1447; DANA TOWNSEND, Dir., Donor Svcs. Tel: 317-236-1498; DENA PERRY, Dir., Stewardship. Tel: 317-236-1578; MICHAEL KIRK, Assoc. Dir. Stewardship. Tel: 317-236-1546; RON GREULICH, Dir. Major Gifts. Tel: 317-236-1426.

Catholic Community Foundation, Inc.—Most Rev. DANIEL M. BUECHLEIN, O.S.B., D.D., Chm.; JAMES WATHEN, Assoc. Dir. Gift Planning. Tel: 317-236-1427.

Mission Office—Rev. Msgr. JOSEPH F. SCHAEDEL, M.S., M.Div., V.G., Dir. Tel: 317-236-1485.

Vicariate of Clergy and Parish Life Coordinators: Formation and Personnel—Rev. WILLIAM STUMPF, Vicar. Tel: 317-236-1495.

Deacon Formation—Rev. BEDE CISCO, Dir. Tel: 317-236-1491.

Ministry to Priests—Associates: Revs. JOHN GEIS. Tel: 812-923-3011; GERALD KIRKHOFF. Tel: 317-255-4534; J. LAWRENCE RICHARDT. Tel: 765-647-1994; JOSEPH RAUTENBERG, Ethics & Bioethics Consultant. Tel: 317-647-1994.

Personnel: Priests and Parish Life Coordinators—Rev. WILLIAM STUMPF, Dir. Tel: 317-236-1495.

Priestly and Religious Vocations—Rev. JOSEPH B. MORIARTY, Dir. Tel: 317-236-1490.

Vicariate Judicial Metropolitan Tribunal—Rev. Msgr. FREDERICK EASTON, J.C.L., Judicial Vicar. Tel: 317-236-1460.

Adjunct Vice Vicars Judicial—Revs. ROBERT J. GILDAY, S.T.B.; PAUL M. SHIKANY, J.C.L.

Judge Instructor—KATHARINE LOZANO, B.A., J.D.; ANN TULLY, B.S., M.T.S.

Defenders of the Bond—Revs. JAMES R. BONKE, J.C.L.; MYLES H. SMITH, J.C.L.

Deputy Defender of the Bond—PATRICIA JEFFERS.

Archdiocesan Judges—Revs. JOHN DEDE, J.C.D., M.A., Emeritus; BERNARD HEAD, Emeritus; HERMAN LUTZ, S.T.L., J.C.L.; RICHARD MUELLER, S.T.L.; Rev. Msgr. FRANCIS TUOHY, J.C.L., P.A.; Revs. JOHN SCIARRA; DANIEL DONOHOO, M.A., M.Div.; STEPHEN GIANNINI, M.Div., M.A., M.S.; STANLEY PONDO, J.D., M.A., A.B., M.Div.

Auditor—Rev. ROBERT MAZZOLA.

Notaries—KAREN CLEMENT; KAY SUMMERS; MARY ELLEN HAUCK.

Victim Assistance Coordinator—SUZANNE L. YAKIMCHICK. Tel: 317-236-7325; 800-382-9836,.

CLERGY, PARISHES, MISSIONS AND PAROCHIAL SCHOOLS

CITY OF INDIANAPOLIS
(MARION COUNTY)

1—SS. PETER AND PAUL CATHEDRAL (1892), [JC] Rev. Richard M. Ginther. In Res., Revs. James R. Bonke, J.C.L.; Joseph F. Schaedel; Dennis M. Duvelius, F.S.S.P.
Res.: 1347 N. Meridian St., 46202. Tel: 317-634-4519; Fax: 317-630-9621.
Catechesis/Religious Program—Students 50.

2—ST. ANDREW THE APOSTLE (1946), Sr. Marilyn Herber, S.P., Parish Life Coord.; Rev. Patrick Doyle, Priest Moderator.
Parish Office—4052 E. 38th St., 46218-1444. Tel: 317-546-1571; Fax: 317-549-6311.
School—St. Andrew & St. Rita Catholic Academy, 4050 E. 38th St., 46218. Tel: 317-549-6305; Fax: 317-549-6306. (school & daycare) Lay Teachers 25; Students 200.
Catechesis/Religious Program—Tel: 317-549-6301. Students 28.

3—ST. ANN (1917), [JC] Rev. Glenn L. O'Connor.
Office & Mailing Address: 2862 S. Holt Rd., 46241. Tel: 317-244-3750; Fax: 317-244-9841.
Res.: 2850 S. Holt Rd., 46241.
Catechesis/Religious Program—Steven Nicholas, D.R.E. Students 43.

4—ST. ANTHONY (1891), (Irish—German), [JC] Rev. Msgr. John T. Ryan, V.F.
379 N. Warman Ave., 46222. Tel: 317-636-4828; Fax: 317-636-3140.
School—All Saints Consolidated, 75 N. Belleview Pl., 46222-4145. Tel: 317-636-3739; Fax: 317-636-1928. Lay Teachers 9; Students 123.
Catechesis/Religious Program—Students 160.

5—ST. BARNABAS (1965), Revs. James Farrell; John Patrick McCaslin.
Res.: 8300 Rahke Rd., 46217. Tel: 317-882-0724; Fax: 317-887-8932.
School—Tel: 317-881-7422; Fax: 317-887-8933. Debra Perkins, Prin. Lay Teachers 31; Students 627.
Catechesis/Religious Program—Students 320.

6—ST. BERNADETTE (1952), [CEM] Rev. J. Nicholas Dant.
Church & Parish Office: 4838 Fletcher Ave., 46203. Tel: 317-356-5867; Fax: 317-356-2460.
Res.: 4826 Fletcher Ave., 46203. Tel: 317-356-5867.
Catechesis/Religious Program—Students 20.

7—CHRIST THE KING (1939), Rev. Msgr. Francis R. Tuohy; Rev. James Bonke. In Res., Rev. Thomas J. Murphy (Retired).
Parish Office—5884 Crittenden Ave., 46220. Tel: 317-255-3666; Fax: 317-475-6579.
Res.: 1827 E. Kessler Blvd., 46220. Tel: 317-475-6582.
School—5858 Crittenden Ave., 46220. Tel: 317-257-9366; Fax: 317-475-6581. Lay Teachers 25; Students 362.
Catechesis/Religious Program—Tel: 317-255-3666; Fax: 317-475-6579. Students 110.

8—ST. CHRISTOPHER (Speedway City) (1937), Revs. D. Michael Welch; David Lawler, Assoc. Pastor; Sr. Sue Bradshaw, O.S.F., Pastoral Assoc.; Mr. Bill Szolek Van Valkenburgh, Pastoral Assoc.; Nancy L. Meyer, Pastoral Assoc.
Res.: 5301 W. 16th St., 46224. Tel: 317-241-6314; Fax: 317-241-6587.
School—5335 W. 16th St., 46224. Fax: 317-244-6678. Mrs. Barbara Leek, Prin. Lay Teachers 16; Students 272.
Catechesis/Religious Program—Mr. David J. Burkhard, D.R.E. Students 295.

9—ST. GABRIEL THE ARCHANGEL (1963), Rev. Larry P. Crawford; Sr. Mary Timothy Kavanaugh, O.S.F., Pastoral Assoc. In Res., Rev. Msgr. Frederick C. Easton.
Parish Center:—6000 W. 34th St., 46224. Tel: 317-291-7014; Fax: 317-297-6455.
School—(Grades PreK-8) Tel: 317-297-1414; Fax: 317-297-6453. Teachers 21; Students 226.
Catechesis/Religious Program—Tel: 317-299-9924. Students 98.

10—GOOD SHEPHERD (1993), [JC], (St. Catherine, 1909, and St. James the Greater, 1951, were closed, merged, and renamed in 1993) Thomas Meier, Parish Life Coord.; Rev. Joseph Moriarty.
Church & Parish Office: 1109 E. Cameron St., 46203. Tel: 317-783-3158; Fax: 317-781-5961.
School—Central Catholic School, 1155 E. Cameron St., 46203. Tel: 317-783-7759; Fax: 317-781-5964. Students 170.
Catechesis/Religious Program—Students 21.

11—HOLY ANGELS (1903), (African American), [JC] Rev. Clarence R. Waldon.
Res.: 740 W. 28th St., 46208-5099. Tel: 317-926-3324; Fax: 317-926-3325.
School—2822 Dr. Martin Luther King, Jr. St.,

46208. Tel: 317-926-5211; Fax: 317-926-5219. Sisters Theresa Ann Boland, S.P., Prin.; Gerry O'Laughlin, C.S.J., Prin. Sisters of St. Joseph 2; Sisters of I.H.M. Reparatrix 1; Lay Teachers 7; Students 130.
Catechesis/Religious Program—Students 75.

12—HOLY CROSS (1895), Rev. Lawrence Voelker.
Church: 125 N. Oriental St., 46202. Tel: 317-637-2620; Fax: 317-637-0112.
School—Tel: 317-638-9068; Fax: 317-638-0116. Lay Teachers 14; Students 168.
Catechesis/Religious Program—Students 36.

13—HOLY ROSARY (1909), (Italian), [JC] Rev. Msgr. Joseph Schaedel; Rev. Dennis M. Duvelius, F.S.S.P.
Office—520 Stevens St., 46203. Tel: 317-636-4478; Fax: 317-636-2522.

14—HOLY SPIRIT (1946), Revs. Joseph G. Riedman; Harold Warren Rightor III.
Res.: 7243 E. 10th St., 46219. Tel: 317-353-9404; Fax: 317-351-1707.
School—7241 E. 10th St., 46219. Tel: 317-352-1243; Fax: 317-351-1822. Lay Teachers 23; Students 411.
Catechesis/Religious Program—Tel: 317-357-6915. Students 588.

15—HOLY TRINITY (1906), [JC] Rev. Kenneth E. Taylor.
Res.: 2618 W. St. Clair St., 46222. Tel: 317-631-2939; Fax: 317-631-2921.
School—All Saints, Tel: 317-636-3739; Fax: 317-636-3740. Consolidated. See St. Anthony listing.
Catechesis/Religious Program—Students 12.

16—IMMACULATE HEART OF MARY (1946), [JC] Rev. Jeffery H. Godecker.
Parish Center—5692 N. Central Ave., 46220. Tel: 317-257-2266; Fax: 317-475-7380.
School—317 E. 57th St., 46220. Tel: 317-255-5468; Fax: 317-475-7379. Lay Teachers 24; Students 403.
Catechesis/Religious Program—Students 26.

17—ST. JOAN OF ARC (1921), [JC] Rev. Patrick A. Doyle.
Res.: 4217 Central Ave., 46205. Tel: 317-283-5508; Fax: 317-283-5511.
School—500 E. 42nd St., 46205. Tel: 317-283-1518; Fax: 317-931-3380. Lay Teachers 9; Students 146.
Catechesis/Religious Program—Fax: 317-283-5511. Students 87.

18—ST. JOHN THE EVANGELIST (1837), (Irish), [JC] Revs. Thomas J. Murphy (Retired); Noah J. Casey, O.S.B.; Ephrem Carr, O.S.B.
Res.: 126 W. Georgia St., 46225. Tel: 317-635-2021; Fax: 317-635-2014.
Catechesis/Religious Program—Students 6.

19—ST. JOSEPH (1949), [JC] Rev. Glenn L. O'Connor.
Res.: 1375 S. Mickley Ave., 46241. Tel: 317-244-9002; Fax: 317-244-0278.
School—All Saints Consolidated, Tel: 317-636-3739; Fax: 317-636-3740. See St. Anthony Listing.
Catechesis/Religious Program—Students 37.

20—ST. JUDE (1959), Rev. Stephen Banet; Peggy Clegg, Pastoral Assoc.
Res.: 5353 McFarland Rd., 46227. Tel: 317-786-4371; 317-780-7588; Fax: 317-780-7592.
School—5375 McFarland Rd, 46227. Tel: 317-784-6828; Fax: 317-780-7594. Sisters of Providence 2; Lay Teachers 20; Students 500.
Catechesis/Religious Program—Tel: 317-780-7591. Students 246.

21—ST. LAWRENCE (1949), Revs. John Beitans; Stephano Pang.
Office—6944 E. 46th St., 46226-3704. Tel: 317-546-4065; Fax: 317-543-4926.
Res.: 4650 N. Shadeland Ave., 46226. Tel: 317-543-4921.
School—6950 E. 46th St., 46226. Tel: 317-543-4923; Fax: 317-543-4924. Lay Teachers 23; Students 424.
Catechesis/Religious Program—Tel: 317-543-2935. Students 175.

22—ST. LUKE (1961), [JC] Revs. Stephen W. Giannini; Justin David Martin.
Res.: 7575 Holliday Dr. E., 46260. Tel: 317-259-4373; Fax: 317-254-3210.
School—7650 N. Illinois St., 46260. Tel: 317-255-3912. Lay Teachers 34; Students 535.
Catechesis/Religious Program—Tel: 317-479-7373. Students 280.

23—ST. MARK THE EVANGELIST (1946), Rev. Henry F. Tully.
Res.: 535 E. Edgewood, 46227. Tel: 317-787-8246; Fax: 317-781-6466.
School—541 E. Edgewood Ave., 46227. Tel: 317-786-4013; Fax: 317-783-9574. Web: www.stmarkindy-.org. Lay Teachers 22; Students 336.
Catechesis/Religious Program—Tel: 317-784-7155. Students 149.

24—ST. MARY/IMMACULATE CONCEPTION (1858), (Hispanic), [JC] Rev. Michael E. O'Mara; Sr. Therese Wente, O.S.F.; Teresa Trujillo de Aguayo, Pastoral Assoc.
Res.: 317 N. New Jersey St., 46204-2174. Tel: 317-637-3983; Fax: 317-637-0111.
Catechesis/Religious Program—The Marian Center, 311 N. New Jersey St., 46204. Students 105.

25—ST. MATTHEW (1958), Rev. Daniel B. Donohoo. In Res., Rev. Robert E. Mazzola.
Res.: 4100 E. 56th St., 46220. Tel: 317-257-4297; Fax: 317-479-2381.
School—(Grades PreK-8) Tel: 317-251-3997. Lay Teachers 24; Students 480.
Catechesis/Religious Program—Tel: 317-257-9733. Students 50.

26—ST. MICHAEL THE ARCHANGEL (1948), Rev. Anthony Volz. In Res., Rev. Bede Cisco, O.S.B.
Res.: 3354 W. 30th St., 46222. Tel: 317-926-7359; Fax: 317-921-3282.
School—3352 W. 30th St., 46222. Tel: 317-926-0516; Fax: 317-921-3280. Lay Teachers 23 Students 350.
Catechesis/Religious Program—Tel: 317-925-7597. Students 59.

27—ST. MONICA (1956), Revs. Paul D. Koetter; Robert Hausladen; Robert J. Robeson.
Res.: 6131 N. Michigan Rd., 46228. Tel: 317-253-2193; Fax: 317-253-3342.
School—Tel: 317-255-7153; Fax: 317-259-5570. Lay Teachers 31; Students 333.
Catechesis/Religious Program—Students 344.

28—NATIVITY OF OUR LORD JESUS CHRIST (1947), [JC] Rev. Steven Schwab.
7225 Southeastern Ave., 46239. Tel: 317-357-1200.
School—3310 S. Meadow Dr., 46239. Tel: 317-357-1459; Fax: 317-357-9175. Sisters of Providence 1; Lay Teachers 16; Students 317.
Catechesis/Religious Program—Tel: 317-359-6075. Students 145.

29—OUR LADY OF LOURDES (1909), Rev. J. Nicholas Dant; Mr. Charles Eble, Pastoral Assoc.
Parish Office: 5333 E. Washington St., 46219. Tel: 317-356-7291; Fax: 317-356-2358.
School—30 S. Downey St., 46219. Tel: 317-357-3316; Fax: 317-357-0980. Lay Teachers 22 Students 310.
Catechesis/Religious Program—Beverly Hansberry, D.R.E. Students 28.

30—ST. PATRICK (1865), (Irish—Hispanic), Revs. Lawrence Voelker; Al Jost, O.F.M; Thomas Fox, O.F.M., (Hispanic Ministry).
Church: 950 Prospect St., 46203. Tel: 317-631-5824; Fax: 317-631-5828.
School—Consolidated See Central Catholic Good Shepherd Parish.
Catechesis/Religious Program—Students 120.

31—ST. PHILIP NERI (1909), (Irish—Hispanic), [JC] Rev. Carlton J. Beever.
Res.: 550 N. Rural St., 46201. Tel: 317-631-8746; Fax: 317-632-8161.
School—545 Eastern Ave., 46201. Tel: 317-636-0134; Fax: 317-636-3231. Lay Teachers 14 Students 160.
Catechesis/Religious Program—Students 160.

32—ST. PIUS X (1955), Revs. Gerald J. Kirkhoff; Eric Matthew Johnson.
Res.: 7200 Sarto Dr., 46240. Tel: 317-255-4534; Fax: 317-466-3354; 317-466-3369.
School—Tel: 317-466-3361. Lay Teachers 28; Students 449.
Catechesis/Religious Program—Tel: 317-257-1085; Fax: 317-466-3377. Students 263.

33—ST. RITA (1919), (African American—Vietnamese), [JC] Revs. Stephan Brown, S.V.D.; Hien Pham, S.V.D., Dir. Vietnamese Apostolate. In Res., Revs. Chester Smith, S.V.D.; Charles Smith, S.V.D.
Res.: 1733 Dr. Andrew J. Brown Ave., 46202. Tel: 317-632-9349; Fax: 317-687-0973.
Catechesis/Religious Program—Students 71.

34—ST. ROCH (1922), [JC] Rev. James R. Wilmoth.
Res.: 3600 S. Pennsylvania St., 46227. Tel: 317-784-1763; Fax: 317-783-9617.
School—3603 S. Meridian St., 46217. Tel 317-784-9144. Lay Teachers 19; Students 281.
Catechesis/Religious Program—Students 84.

35—SACRED HEART OF JESUS (1875), (German), [CEM 2] [JC] Revs. Michael G. Barrett, O.F.M.; Justin Belitz, O.F.M.; Frank Jasper, O.F.M.; Al Jost, O.F.M; Tom Fox, O.F.M.
Res.: 1530 S. Union St., 46225. Tel: 317-638-5551 (TTY); Fax: 317-637-9741.
School—Central Catholic Consolidated., Tel: 317-783-7759; Fax: 317-781-5964. See Good Shepherd Listing.
Catechesis/Religious Program—Students 24.

36—ST. SIMON THE APOSTLE (1961), Rev. Robert W. Sims. In Res., Rev. Peter Gallagher.
Res.: 8155 Oaklandon Rd., 46236-8578. Tel: 317-826-6000; Fax: 317-826-6010.
School—Tel: 317-826-6000, Ext. 107; Fax: 317-826-6020. Lay Teachers 37; Students 760.
Catechesis/Religious Program—Tel: 317-826-6000, Ext. 113. Students 262.

37—ST. THERESE OF THE INFANT JESUS (LITTLE FLOWER) (1925), [JC] Revs. Vincent P. Lampert; Robert J. Gilday, S.T.B.
Res.: 4720 E. 13th St., 46201. Tel: 317 357-8352; Fax: 317-357-5316.
School—(Grades PreSchool-8), 1401 N. Bosart Ave, 46202. Tel: 317-353-2282. Lay Teachers 22; Students 430.
Catechesis/Religious Program—Students 40.

38—ST. THOMAS AQUINAS (1939), Rev. William G. Munshower.
Office—4625 N. Kenwood Ave., 46208. Tel: 317-253-1461; Fax: 317-253-1410.
Res.: 4650 N. Illinois St., 46208.
School—4600 N. Illinois St., 46208. Tel: 317-255-6244; Fax: 317-255-6106. Lay Teachers 16; Students 221.
Catechesis/Religious Program—Students 55.

OUTSIDE THE CITY OF INDIANAPOLIS

AURORA, DEARBORN CO., ST. MARY OF THE IMMACULATE CONCEPTION (1857), Rev. Christopher A. Craig.
Parish Office—203 Fourth St., 47001. Tel: 812-926-0644; 812-926-0060; Fax: 812-926-4439.
School—211 Fourth St., 47001. Tel: 812-926-1558; Fax: 812-926-2590. Lay Teachers 9; Students 149.
Catechesis/Religious Program—Students 60.

BATESVILLE, RIPLEY CO., ST. LOUIS (1868), (German), [CEM] Revs. Daniel J. Mahan; Christiaan Wesley Kappes.
Res.: 13 St. Louis Pl., 47006. Tel: 812-934-3204; Fax: 812-933-0667.
School—17 St. Louis Pl., 47006. Tel: 812-934-3310; Fax: 812-934-6202. Lay Teachers 27; Students 425.
Catechesis/Religious Program—Tel: 812-934-3204, Ext. 38. Terri Meyer, D.R.E. Students 247.

BEDFORD, LAWRENCE CO., ST. VINCENT DE PAUL (1864), Rev. Bernard Cox, Parish/Mailing Office: 1723 I St., 47421.
Res.: 1711 I St., 47421. Tel: 812-275-6539; Fax: 812-275-3493.
School—923 18th St., 47421. Tel: 812-279-2540; Fax: 812-276-4880. Lay Teachers 10; Students 223.
Catechesis/Religious Program—Students 83.

BEECH GROVE, MARION CO., HOLY NAME (1908), [JC] Rev. Gerald F. Burkert. In Res., Rev. Joseph F. Rautenberg.
Res.: 89 N. 17th Ave., 46107. Tel: 317-784-5454; Fax: 317-784-1834.
School—21 N. 17th Ave., 46107. Tel: 317-784-9078; Fax: 317-784-9103. Kent Schwartz, Prin. Lay Teachers 19; Students 251.
Catechesis/Religious Program—Students 100.

BLOOMINGTON, MONROE CO.

1—ST. CHARLES BORROMEO (1864), [JC] Revs. Charles S. Chesebrough, V.F.; Don Davison, C.P.P.S.
Res.: 2222 E. Third St., 47401. Tel: 812-336-6846; Fax: 812-331-6732.
School—(Grades PreK-8), 2224 E. Third St., 47401. Tel: 812-336-5853; Fax: 812-349-0300. Lay Teachers 35; Students 509.
Catechesis/Religious Program—Tel: 812-334-1664. Students 155.

2—ST. JOHN THE APOSTLE (1970), Rev. Michael C. Fritsch.
Res.: 4607 W. State Rd. 46, 47404-9255. Tel: 812-876-1974; Fax: 812-876-9494.
Catechesis/Religious Program—Tel: 812-876-0718, Ext. 203. Joseph Brake, D.R.E. Students 165.

3—ST. PAUL CATHOLIC CENTER (1969), Rev. Daniel Atkins.
Res.: 1413 E. 17th St., 47408. Tel: 812-339-5561; Fax: 812-333-4846.
Catechesis/Religious Program—Students 215.

BRADFORD, HARRISON CO., ST. MICHAEL (1835), [CEM] Rev. John L. Fink.
Mailing Address: P.O. Box 22, 47107. Tel: 812-364-6646; Fax: 812-364-6614.
Catechesis/Religious Program—Tel: 812-364-6173. Students 232.

BRAZIL, CLAY CO., ANNUNCIATION OF THE BLESSED VIRGIN MARY (1865), Rev. Robert Hausladen.
Office—19 N. Alabama St., 47834. Tel: 812-448-1901; Fax: 812-448-1901.
School—(Grades PreK-5), 415 E. Church St., 47834. Tel: 812-448-1394; Fax: 812-443-3089. Lay Teachers 6; Students 50.
Catechesis/Religious Program—Students 44.

BRIGHT, DEARBORN CO., ST. TERESA BENEDICTA OF THE CROSS (2000), Rev. William Marks.
Parish Office: 24486 State Line Rd. "B", Lawrenceburg, 47025-8372.
Church: 23670 Salt Ford Rd., Lawrenceburg, 47025.
Rectory—Rectory: 23455 Gavin Ln., Lawrenceburg, 47025-8372.
Catechesis/Religious Program—Students 187.

BROOKVILLE, FRANKLIN CO., ST. MICHAEL (1845), (German), [CEM] Rev. Patrick J. Beidelman.
Mailing Address: *St. Francis Center*, 145 St. Michael Blvd., P.O. Box J, 47012.
Church: 250 High St., 47012. Tel: 765-647-5462; Fax: 765-647-1634.
School—275 High St., 47012. Tel: 765-647-4961; Fax: 317-647-4961. Sisters of the Third Order Regular of St. Francis 2; Lay Teachers 14; Students 227.

Catechesis/Religious Program—Tel: 765-647-0513. Students 59.

BROWNSBURG, HENDRICKS CO., ST. MALACHY (1869), (Irish), [CEM 2] Revs. Daniel J. Staublin; Robert Jason Hankee.
Parish Center—326 N. Green St., 46112. Tel: 317-852-3195; Fax: 317-852-8939.
School—330 N. Green St., 46112. Tel: 317-852-2242; Fax: 317-852-3604. Lay Teachers 30; Students 440.
Catechesis/Religious Program—Tel: 317-852-8476. Students 587.

BROWNSTOWN, JACKSON CO., OUR LADY OF PROVIDENCE (1934), Attended by, St. Ambrose, Seymour. Rev. John M. Hall, Admin.
Mailing Address: c/o St. Ambrose Church, 325 S. Chestnut St., Seymour, 47274. Tel: 812-522-5304; Fax: 812-522-8959.
Church: Hwy. 50, 47220.
Catechesis/Religious Program—Students 22.

CAMBRIDGE CITY, WAYNE CO., ST. ELIZABETH OF HUNGARY (1852), Rev. William L. Ehalt.
Res.: 333 W. Maple St., 47327. Tel: 765-478-3242; Fax: 765-478-3585.
Catechesis/Religious Program—Students 87.

CANNELTON, PERRY CO., ST. MICHAEL (1859), [CEM] Rev. Barnabas Gillespie, O.S.B.
Parish Office—c/o Catholic Ministry Center, 802 Ninth St., Tell City, 47586-2114. Tel: 812-547-7994; Fax: 812-547-6985.
Res.: 814 Jefferson St., Tell City, 47586. Tel: 812-547-9901.
Church: Eighth St., 47520.

CEDAR GROVE, FRANKLIN CO., HOLY GUARDIAN ANGELS (1874), (German), [CEM] Rev. Patrick Beidelman.
Mailing Address: P.O. Box 38, 47016. Tel: 765-647-6981; Fax: 765-647-1634. Mailing Address: *Shipping address*, St. Francis Center,145 St. Michael Blvd., Brookville, 47012.
Church: 405 U.S. Hwy. 52, 47016.
Catechesis/Religious Program—Tel: 765-647-3122. Students 79.

CHARLESTOWN, CLARK CO., ST. MICHAEL (1860), [CEM] Rev. Stephen Schaftlein.
Res.: 101 St. Michael Dr., 47111. Tel: 812-256-3200; Fax: 317-256-9066.
School—Child Care Center, 102 St. Michael Dr., 47111. Tel: 812-256-3503. (PreK-K) Students 74.
Catechesis/Religious Program—Students 52.
Mission—St. Francis Xavier (1869), Hwy. 31 & 160, P.O. Box 368, Henryville, Clark Co. 47126.

CLARKSVILLE, CLARK CO., ST. ANTHONY OF PADUA (1851), [CEM] Rev. Dismas J. Veeneman, O.F.M.Conv. In Res., Bro. Bruno Nemcosky, O.F.M-.Conv.; Rev. David Lenz, O.F.M.Conv.; Bro. Ray Ramos, O.F.M.Conv.; Rev. Troy Overton, O.F.M.Conv.
Res.: 316 N. Sherwood Ave., 47129. Tel: 812-282-2290; Fax: 812-283-3924.
School—320 N. Sherwood Ave., 47129. Tel: 812-282-2144; Fax: 812-282-2169. Sisters of St. Benedict 1; Lay Teachers 22; Students 388.
Catechesis/Religious Program—Students 31.

CLINTON, VERMILLION CO., SACRED HEART (1891), Rev. Joseph L. Villa.
Office—619 S. Fifth St., 47842-2016. Tel: 765-832-8468; Fax: 765-832-5092.
Rectory—558 Nebeker St., 47842.
School—(Grades PreK-5), 610 S. Sixth St., 47842. Tel: 317-832-3228; Fax: 765-832-2549. Lay Teachers 7; Students 53.
Mission—St. Joseph (1920), 270 E. Wood Ave., Universal, Vermillion Co. 47884.
Catechesis/Religious Program—Elizabeth Davis, D.R.E. Students 71.

COLUMBUS, BARTHOLOMEW CO., ST. BARTHOLOMEW (1994),, St. Bartholomew (1841) and St. Columba (1963) were closed, merged, and renamed St. Bartholomew. Revs. Clement T. Davis; Todd Michael Goodson.
Mailing Address: 1306 27th St., 47201. Tel: 812-379-9353; Fax: 812-375-0720.
School—Preschool Center, 845 8th St., 47201. Tel: 812-376-0468.
School—(Grades K-8), 1306 27th St., 47201. Tel: 812-372-6830; Fax: 812-376-0377. Lay Teachers 24; Students 387.
Catechesis/Religious Program—Tel: 812-372-2207. Students 367.

CONNERSVILLE, FAYETTE CO., ST. GABRIEL (1851), [JC] Rev. Stanley J. Herber, M.A., V.F.; Pamela S. Rader, Business Mgr.
Res.: 232 W. Ninth St., 47331-2099. Tel: 765-825-8578; Fax: 765-825-7060.
School—(Grades PreK-6), 224 W. Ninth St., 47331. Tel: 765-825-7951; Fax: 765-827-4347. Sue Barth, Prin. Lay Teachers 8; Students 179.
Catechesis/Religious Program—Students 70.

CORYDON, HARRISON CO., ST. JOSEPH (1896), [CEM] Rev. Louis Manna.
Res.: 312 E. High St., 47112. Tel: 812-738-2742; Fax: 812-738-2718.
School—512 N. Mulberry St., 47112. Tel: 812-738-4549; Fax: 812-738-2722. Lay Teachers 6; Students 75.
Catechesis/Religious Program—Tel: 812-738-2759. Students 146.
Mission—Most Precious Blood (1880), [CEM] Corydon-New Middletown Rd., New Middletown, Harrison Co. 47160.
Mission—St. Peter (1849), [CEM] Buena Vista Rd., Elizabeth, Harrison Co. 47117.

DANVILLE, HENDRICKS CO., MARY QUEEN OF PEACE (1939), Rev. Thomas K. Stepanski.
Res.: 1005 W. Main St., 46122. Tel: 317-745-4284; Fax: 317-745-7090.
Catechesis/Religious Program—Tel: 317-745-4284, Ext. 13. Peg Klein, D.R.E. Students 226.

DOVER, DEARBORN CO., ST. JOHN THE BAPTIST (1824), [CEM] Unassigned.
Church & Mailing Address: 25743 State Rte.1, Guilford, 47022. Tel: 812-576-4302; Fax: 812-576-2324.
Catechesis/Religious Program—Students 116.

EDINBURGH, JOHNSON CO., HOLY TRINITY (1851), Rev. Paul M. Shikany, J.C.L.
Res.: Keely Dr. & Main Cross, P.O. Box 216, 46124. Tel: 812-526-9460; Fax: 812-526-2477.
Catechesis/Religious Program—Tel: 812-526-9470. Students 44.

ENOCHSBURG, DECATUR CO., ST. JOHN THE EVANGELIST (1844), (German), [CEM] Rev. Gregory Bramlage.
Mailing Address: 5267 N. Hamburg Rd., Oldenburg, 47036. Tel: 812-934-5854; Fax: 812-934-5854.
Church: 9995 E. Base Rd., Greensburg, 47240.
Catechesis/Religious Program—Tel: 812-933-0923; Fax: 812-934-2880. Students 98.

FORTVILLE, HANCOCK CO., ST. THOMAS (1869), Rev. Joseph G. Pesola.
Res.: 523 S. Merrill St., 46040. Tel: 317-485-5101; Fax: 317-485-0022.
Catechesis/Religious Program—Tel: 317-485-5103; Fax: 317-485-0022. Students 146.

FRANKLIN, JOHNSON CO., ST. ROSE OF LIMA (1868), Rev. Paul M. Shikany, J.C.L.; Jean Martin, Pastoral Assoc. Tel: 317-738-2965.
Res.: 114 Lancelot Dr., 46131. Tel: 317-738-3929; Fax: 317-738-3583.
School—(Grades PreK-8) Tel: 317-738-3451. Laura Riley, Prin.
Catechesis/Religious Program—Tel: 317-736-6754. Students 232.

FRENCH LICK, ORANGE CO., OUR LADY OF THE SPRINGS (1887), Revs. Joseph F. Routenberg; Charles S. Chesebrough, V.F.; Ms. Deberah L. Fleck, Parish Life Coordinator.
Res.: 8796 W. State Rd. 56, 47432. Tel: 812-936-4568; Fax: 812-936-4568.
Catechesis/Religious Program—Tel: 812-936-2185. Students 21.
Mission—Our Lord Jesus Christ the King (1948), Hwy 150, E., Paoli, Orange Co. 47454. Tel: 812-723-3900.
Catechesis/Religious Program—Students 22.

FRENCHTOWN, HARRISON CO., ST. BERNARD (1849), [CEM] Rev. Frederick J. Denison.
Church: State Road 337.
Res.: 7600 Hwy. 337 N.W., Depauw, 47115. Tel: 812-347-2326.
Catechesis/Religious Program—Students 88.
Mission—St. Joseph (1855), State Road 66, Marengo, Crawford Co. 47140.

FULDA, SPENCER CO., ST. BONIFACE (1847), [CEM] Rev. Brendan Moss, O.S.B.
Mailing Address: P.O. Box 8, St. Meinrad, 47577. Tel: 812-357-5533; Fax: 812-357-2862.
Church: 15529 N. State Rd. 545, 47536.
Catechesis/Religious Program—Students 99.

GREENCASTLE, PUTNAM CO., ST. PAUL THE APOSTLE (1853), Rev. Stephen Jarrell.
Res.: 202 E. Washington St., 46135. Tel: 765-653-5678; Fax: 765-653-4377.
Catechesis/Religious Program—Students 118.

GREENFIELD, HANCOCK CO., ST. MICHAEL (1860), Rev. Severin Messick, O.S.B.
Res.: 519 Jefferson Blvd., 46140. Tel: 317-462-4240; Fax: 317-462-2571.
School—Tel: 317-462-6380; Fax: 317-467-2864. Lay Teachers 19; Students 269.
Catechesis/Religious Program—Students 305.

GREENSBURG, DECATUR CO., ST. MARY (1858), [CEM] Rev. Msgr. Harold L. Knueven (Retired).
Res.: 302 E. McKee St., 47240. Tel: 812-663-8427; Fax: 812-663-6088.
School—(Grades PreK-6), 210 S. East St., 47240. Tel: 812-663-2804. Lay Teachers 16; Students 265.
Catechesis/Religious Program—Students 273.

GREENWOOD, JOHNSON CO.

1—SS. FRANCIS AND CLARE OF ASSISI (1993), Rev. Vincent P. Lampert.
Church & Parish Office: 5901 Olive Branch Rd., 46143. Tel: 317-859-4673; Fax: 317-859-4678.
Catechesis/Religious Program—Students 350.

2—OUR LADY OF THE GREENWOOD (1948), [JC] Rev. Msgr. Mark Svarczkopf; Rev. Jonathan Meyer. In Res., Rev. Alvin Fong Ben.
Res.: 335 S. Meridian St., 46143. Tel: 317-888-2861; Fax: 317-885-5006.
School—399 S. Meridian St., 46143. Tel: 317-881-1300. Lay Teachers 25; Students 521.
Catechesis/Religious Program—Tel: 317-885-5007. Students 308.

HAMBURG, FRANKLIN CO., ST. ANNE (1869), [CEM] Rev. Gregory Bramlage.
Res.: 5267 N. Hamburg Rd., Oldenburg, 47036. Tel: 812-934-5854; Fax: 812-934-2077.
Catechesis/Religious Program—Tel: 812-934-2077. Students 53.

HENRYVILLE, CLARK CO., ST. FRANCIS XAVIER (1869),, Attended from St. Michael's, 101 St. Michael Dr., Charlestown, IN 47111. Tel: 812-256-3200. Rev. Stephen Schaftlein.
Church: Hwy. 31& Hwy.160, P.O. Box 368, 47126.

JEFFERSONVILLE, CLARK CO.

1—ST. AUGUSTINE (1851), [CEM] Rev. Clifford R. Vogelsang.
Res.: 315 E. Chestnut St., P.O. Box 447, 47130. Tel: 812-282-2677; Fax: 812-282-8821.
Catechesis/Religious Program—316 E. Maple St.. Tel: 812-282-1231; Fax: 812-282-1605. Students 118.

2—SACRED HEART (1953), Revs. Thomas Clegg; Michael Hilderbrand.
Church & Parish Office: 1840 E. 8th St., 47103. Tel: 812-282-0423; Fax: 812-284-6673.
School—1842 E. 8th St., 47130. Tel: 812-283-3123. Lay Teachers 13; Students 202.
Catechesis/Religious Program—Tel: 812-283-6914. Students 52.

KNIGHTSTOWN, HENRY CO., ST. ROSE (1872), Sr. Shirley Gerth, O.S.F., Parish Life Coord.; Revs. William L. Ehalt; Stanley J. Herber, M.A., V.F.
Mailing Address: P.O. Box 209, 46148. Tel: 765-345-5595.
Church: 8144 W. U.S. Hwy. 40, 46148.
Catechesis/Religious Program—Students 31.

LANESVILLE, HARRISON CO., ST. MARY (1843), (German), [CEM] Rev. Harold A. Ripperger.
Res.: 2500 St. Mary's Dr., 47136. Tel: 812-952-2853; Fax: 812-952-2852.
Catechesis/Religious Program—Tel: 812-952-2854. Students 162.

LAWRENCEBURG, DEARBORN CO., ST. LAWRENCE (1842), (German), Rev. John Hartzer.
Parish Office—542 Walnut St., 47025. Tel: 812-537-3992.
Rectory—526 Walnut St., 47025. Tel: 812-537-1297.
School—524 Walnut St., 47025. Tel: 812-537-3690; Fax: 812-537-9685. Lay Teachers 18; Students 250.
Catechesis/Religious Program—Tel: 812-537-1112. Students 130.

LEOPOLD, PERRY CO., ST. AUGUSTINE (1837), [CEM] Rev. Sean Hoppe, O.S.B.
Res.: 18020 Lafayette St., 47551. Tel: 812-843-5143; Fax: 812-843-5143.
Catechesis/Religious Program—Students 180.

LIBERTY, UNION CO., ST. BRIDGET (1854), [CEM] Rev. John O'Brien.
Res.: 404 E. Vine St., 47353. Tel: 765-458-7170.
Catechesis/Religious Program—Tel: 765-458-5412. Students 30.

MADISON, JEFFERSON CO., PRINCE OF PEACE (1993), [CEM 2], St. Michael (1837), St. Mary (1851), St. Patrick (1853), Madison, and St. Anthony, China (1861) were closed; merged and renamed Prince of Peace Rev. John A. Meyer.
Mailing Address: *Catholic Community Center*, 305 W. State St., 47250. Tel: 812-265-4166; Fax: 812-273-3427.
Res.: 415 E. Second St., 47250. Tel: 812-265-4166.
School—Pope John XXIII, (Grades K-6), 221 State St., 47250. Tel: 812-273-3957; Fax: 812-265-4566.
High School—Shawe Memorial Junior-Senior High School, Tel: 812-273-2150; Fax: 812-273-6694. See High Schools, Inter-Parochial, under Institutions Located in the Archdiocese.
Catechesis/Religious Program—Students 75.

MARTINSVILLE, MORGAN CO., ST. MARTIN OF TOURS (1848), [CEM] Rev. Mark Gottemoeller.
Res.: 1709 E. Harrison St., 46151. Tel: 765-342-6379.
Catechesis/Religious Program—Tel: 765-352-0602; Fax: 765-342-1263. Students 150.

MILAN, RIPLEY CO., ST. CHARLES BORROMEO (1908), Rev. Msgr. Bernard R. Schmitz.
Mailing Address: c/o St. Anthony, P.O. Box 3, Morris, 47033. Fax: 812-934-5936.
Church: 213 Ripley St., 47031.
Catechesis/Religious Program—Tel: 812-744-3882. Students 82.

MILLHOUSEN, DECATUR CO., IMMACULATE CONCEPTION (1834), Sr. Christine Ernstes, O.S.F., Parish Life Coord.; Revs. Larry D. Borders, Sacramental Min.; Paul E. Landwerlen.
Mailing Address: 2081 E. County Rd., 820 S.,

Greensburg, 47240-9636. Tel: 812-591-2362; Fax: 812-591-2362.
Mission—St. Denis (1894), [CEM] Westport. 12155 N. County Rd., 600 E., St. Denis, Jennings Co. 47283.
Catechesis/Religious Program—Students 126.
MITCHELL, LAWRENCE CO., ST. MARY/ASSUMPTION (1869), Rev. Bernard Cox.
Res.: 777 S. 11th St., 47446. Tel: 812-849-3570; Fax: 812-275-3493.
Catechesis/Religious Program—Fax: 812-849-6024. Students 50.
MONTEZUMA, PARKE CO., IMMACULATE CONCEPTION (1867), Closed. For inquiries for parish records contact the chancery.
MOORESVILLE, MORGAN CO., ST. THOMAS MORE (1967), Rev. Richard Eldred, Admin.
Res.: 1200 N. Indiana St., 46158. Tel: 317-831-4142; Fax: 317-834-2947.
Catechesis/Religious Program—Tel: 317-831-1431. Students 315.
MORRIS, RIPLEY CO., ST. ANTHONY OF PADUA (1856), [CEM] Rev. Msgr. Bernard R. Schmitz.
Mailing Address: P.O. Box 3, 47033. Tel: 812-934-6218; Fax: 812-934-5936.
Parish Office:—4781 E. Morris Church St., 47033.
Church: 4773 E. Morris Church St., 47033.
Catechesis/Religious Program—Students 106.
Mission—St. Pius (1859), St. Pius, Ripley Co.
NAPOLEON, RIPLEY CO., ST. MAURICE (1848), [CEM] Rev. Larry D. Borders, Admin.
Mailing Address: 8874 Harrison St., P.O. Box 17, 47034. Tel: 812-852-4237.
Catechesis/Religious Program—Students 163.
NASHVILLE, BROWN CO., ST. AGNES (1940), [JC] Sr. Mildred Wannemuehler, O.S.B., Parish Life Coord.; Rev. William F. Stumpf.
Mailing Address: 1008 McLary Rd., 47448. Tel: 812-988-2778; Fax: 812-988-2778.
Catechesis/Religious Program—Tel: 812-988-1432. Students 115.
NAVILLETON, FLOYD CO., ST. MARY (1845), (German), [CEM] Daniel B. Sarell, Parish Life Coord.; Rev. Michael Hilderbrand.
Res.: 7500 Navilleton Rd., Floyds Knobs, 47119. Tel: 812-923-5419; Fax: 812-923-3430.
Catechesis/Religious Program—Tel: 812-923-9957. Students 250.
NEW ALBANY, FLOYD CO.
1—HOLY FAMILY (1954), [JC] Rev. Wilfred E. Day.
Res.: 129 W. Daisy Ln., 47150. Tel: 812-944-8283; Fax: 812-945-0180.
School—217 W. Daisy Ln., 47150. Tel: 812-944-6090; Fax: 812-944-7299. Lay Teachers 23; Students 446.
Catechesis/Religious Program—Students 92.
2—ST. MARY (1858), (German), [CEM] [JC] Rev. William W. Ernst, V.F.
Res.: 415 E. Eighth St., 47150. Tel: 812-944-0417; Fax: 812-944-9557.
School—420 E. 8th St., 47150. Tel: 812-944-0888; Fax: 812-945-4770. Lay Teachers 14; Students 167.
Catechesis/Religious Program—Tel: 812-945-7337. Students 70.
3—OUR LADY OF PERPETUAL HELP (1950), Rev. Paul D. Etienne; Tom Yost, Pastoral Assoc.
Res.: 1752 Scheller Ln., 47150. Tel: 812-944-1184; Fax: 812-944-3326.
School—Tel: 812-944-7676; Fax: 812-948-2944. Lay Teachers 23; Students 371.
Catechesis/Religious Program—Tel: 812-948-0185. Students 84.
NEW ALSACE, DEARBORN CO., ST. PAUL (1833), [CEM] Rev. William J. Turner.
Mailing Address: 8044 Yorkridge Rd., Guilford, 47022. Tel: 812-623-3408; Fax: 812-623-4879.
Res.: 8044 Yorkridge Rd., Guilford, 47022. Tel: 812-623-3408.
School—(Grades K-6), 9788 N. Dearborn Rd., Guilford, 47022. Tel: 812-623-2631. Lay Teachers 5; Students 70.
Catechesis/Religious Program—Tel: 812-623-2662. Students 110.
NEW CASTLE, HENRY CO., ST. ANNE (1873), [CEM] Sr. Shirley Gerth, O.S.F., Parish Life Coord.; Revs. William L. Ehalt, Sacramental Min.; Stanley J. Herber, M.A., V.F.
Parish Office—102 N. 19th St., 47362. Tel: 765-529-0933; Fax: 765-529-8976.
Church: 1904 Broad St., 47362. Tel: 765-529-7413; Fax: 765-529-2879.
Catechesis/Religious Program—Tel: 765-529-8976. Students 102.
NEW MARION, RIPLEY CO., ST. MAGDALEN (1847),, Attended from St. John, Osgood. Rev. Darvin E. Winters.
Res.: Tel: 812-689-4244.
NEW MIDDLETOWN, HARRISON CO., MOST PRECIOUS BLOOD (1880), [CEM], Attended from St. Joseph, 312 E. High St., Corydon, IN 47112. Tel: 812-738-2742. Rev. Louis Manna.
Mailing Address: 312 E. High St., Corydon, 47112.
Church: Corydon-New Middletown Rd., 47160. Fax: 812-738-2718.
Catechesis/Religious Program—Tel: 812-738-2759. Students 16.
NORTH VERNON, JENNINGS CO., ST. MARY/NATIVITY OF THE BLESSED VIRGIN MARY (1861), [CEM] Rev. Stephen D. Donahue.
212 Washington St., 47265. Tel: 812-346-3604; Fax: 812-346-3506.
School—209 Washington St., 47265. Tel: 812-346-3445; Fax: 812-346-5930. Lay Teachers 8; Students 219.
Catechesis/Religious Program—Students 97.
OAK FOREST, FRANKLIN CO., ST. CECILIA OF ROME/ FORMERLY ST. PHILOMENA (1844), (German), Closed., Parish is now an oratory of St. Mary-of-the-Rock Church, St Mary-of-the-Rock.
OLDENBURG, FRANKLIN CO., HOLY FAMILY (1837), [CEM] Rev John Turnbull, O.F.M. In Res., Revs. Raymar Middendorf, O.F.M.; Benno Heidlage, O.F.M.
Res.: 3027 Pearl St., P.O. Box 98, 47036. Tel: 812-934-3013; Fax: 812-933-0728.
Catechesis/Religious Program—Students 195.
OSGOOD, RIPLEY CO., ST. JOHN (1867), (German), [CEM] Rev Darvin E. Winters.
Res.: 331 S Buckeye St., 47037. Tel: 812-689-4244; Fax: 812-689-4244.
Mission—St. Mary Magdalen (1847), [CEM] New Marion, Ripley Co. 47037.
Catechesis/Religious Program—349 S. Buckeye St., 47037. Tel: 812-689-6670; Fax: 812-689-5954. Students 153.
PAOLI, ORANGE CO., OUR LORD JESUS CHRIST THE KING (1943),, Attended from Our Lady of the Springs, French Lick. Revs. Joseph Rautenburg; Charles S. Chesebrough, V.F.; Ms. Deborah L. Fleck, Parish Life Coord.
Church: Hwy. 150 E., 47454. Tel: 812-936-4568.
Catechesis/Religious Program—Tel: 812-723-5506. Jim O'Connell, D.R.E. Students 18.
PLAINFIELD, HENDRICKS CO., ST. SUSANNA (1953), Rev. Kevin Morris.
Res.: 1210 E. Main St., 46168. Tel: 317-839-3333; Fax: 317-839-0732.
School—(Grades PreK-6), 1212 E. Main St., 46168. Tel: 317-839-3713; Fax: 317-838-7718. Lay Teachers 13; Students 256.
Catechesis/Religious Program—Tel: 317-838-7722; Fax: 317-838-7720. Students 438.
RICHMOND, WAYNE CO.
1—ST. ANDREW (1846), [JC] Revs. Todd M. Riebe; Joseph Michael Feltz.
Res.: 720 A North St., 47374. Tel: 765-962-3569.
Church: 235 S. 5th St., 47374.
Parish Center & Mailing Address: 240 S. 6th St., 47374. Tel: 765-966-0916.
Catechesis/Religious Program—Tel: 765-966-0916. Marcy Valentini, D.R.E. Students 147.
2—HOLY FAMILY (1953), Revs. Todd M. Riebe; Joseph Michael Feltz.
Mailing Address: 240 S. 6th St., 47374. Tel: 765-962-3902; Fax: 765-966-0820.
Res.: 720 N. A St., 47374. Tel: 765-962-3569.
Church: 815 W. Main St., 47374.
School—St Elizabeth Ann Seton, (Grades 3-6), 801 W. Main St., 47374. Tel: 765-962-4877; Fax: 765-962-5381. Lay Teachers 9; Students 165.
Catechesis/Religious Program—Marcy Valentini, D.R.E. Students 147.
3—ST. MARY (1859), [JC] Revs. Todd M. Riebe; Joseph Michael Feltz.
Mailing Address: 240 S. 6th St., 47374. Tel: 765-962-3902; Fax: 765-966-0820.
Church & Res.: 720 N. A St., 47374. Tel: 765-962-3569.
School—St Elizabeth Ann Seton, (Grades K-2), 700 N. A St., 47374. Tel: 765-962-5010; Fax: 765-962-3692. Lay Teachers 5; Students 145.
Catechesis/Religious Program—233 S. 5th St., 47374. Tel 765-966-0916. Marcy Valentini, D.R.E. Students 147.
ROCKVILLE, PARKE CO., ST. JOSEPH (1867), Rev. Joseph L. Villa.
Res.: 217 E. Ohio St., 47872. Tel: 765-569-5406.
Catechesis/Religious Program—Tel: 765-548-2101. Students 27.
RUSHVILLE, RUSH CO., IMMACULATE CONCEPTION/ST. MARY (1857), [CEM] Rev. Roger G. Rudolf.
Res.: 512 N. Perkins St., 46173. Tel: 765-932-2588.
School—(Grades PreK-6), 226 E. 5th St., 46173. Tel: 765-932-3639; Fax: 765-938-1322. Lay Teachers 11; Students 179.
Catechesis/Religious Program—Fax: 765-932-2458. Students 216.
ST. ANNE, JENNINGS CO., ST. ANNE (1841), [CEM], Attended from St. Joseph, North Vernon. Rev. C. Ryan McCarthy, Admin.
Mailing Address: 1875 S. County Rd. 700 W., North Vernon, 47265. Tel: 812-346-4783.
Church: 150E 450N, North Vernon, 47265.
ST. CROIX, PERRY CO.
1—HOLY CROSS (1860), [CEM] Rev. Guy Mansini, O.S.B.
Res.: State Rd. 62, Gen. Delivery, 47576. Tel: 812-843-5701.
Catechesis/Religious Program—Students 31.
2—ST. ISIDORE THE FARMER (1968), [CEM], St. John, (1875), and St. Joseph, (1891), Perry Co., were closed; merged and renamed St. Isidore in 1968. Rev. Guy Mansini, O.S.B.
Res.: 6501 St. Isidore Rd., Bristow, 47515. Tel: 812-843-5713; Fax: 812-843-3103.
Catechesis/Religious Program—Students 97.
ST. DENIS, JENNINGS CO., ST. DENIS (1894), [CEM] Attended by, Immaculate Conception, Millhousen. Revs. Larry D. Borders, Sacramental Min.; Paul E. Landwerlen; Sr. Christine Ernstes, O.S.F., Parish Life Coord.
Mailing Address: 2081 E. County Rd. 820S, Greensburg, 47240. Tel: 812-591-2362.
Church: 12155 N. County Rd. 600E, Westport, 47283.
Catechesis/Religious Program— Clustered with Immaculate Conception, Milhousen.
ST. JOSEPH, CRAWFORD CO., ST. JOSEPH (1855), [CEM] Attended by, St. Bernard, Frenchtown. Rev. Frederick J. Denison, Admin.
Mailing Address: 7600 Hwy. 337 N.W., Depauw, 47115. Tel: 812-347-2326.
Church: State Rd. 66, Marengo, 47140.
Catechesis/Religious Program—Students 26.
ST. JOSEPH, JENNINGS CO., ST. JOSEPH (1850), [CEM 2] Rev. C. Ryan McCarthy, Admin.
Mailing Address: 1875 S. County Rd. 700 W., North Vernon, 47265. Tel: 812-346-4783; Fax: 812-352-9033.
Mission—St. Anne (1841), 150 E. 450 N., North Vernon, Jennings Co. 47265.
Catechesis/Religious Program—Students 55.
ST. JOSEPH HILL, CLARK CO., ST. JOSEPH (1853), [CEM] Rev. John Raphael Hadnagy, O.F.M.Conv.
Res.: 2605 St. Joe Rd. W., Sellersburg, 47172. Tel: 812-246-2512; Fax: 812-246-2671.
Catechesis/Religious Program—Tel: 812-246-3969. Students 125.
ST. LEON, DEARBORN CO., ST. JOSEPH (1841), [CEM] Unassigned.
Res.: 7536 Church Ln., West Harrison, 47060. Tel: 812-576-3593; Fax: 812-576-2304.
Catechesis/Religious Program—29060 State Rte. 1, West Harrison, 47060. Tel: 812-576-3234. Students 141.
ST. MARK, PERRY CO., ST. MARK (1863), (German), [CEM] [JC] Rev. Sean Hoppe, O.S.B.
Res.: 5377 Acorn Rd., Tell City, 47586. Tel: 812-836-2481.
Catechesis/Religious Program—Students 104.
ST. MARY-OF-THE-KNOBS, FLOYD CO., ST. MARY-OF-THE-KNOBS (1823), [CEM] Rev. John F. Geis.
Res.: 3033 Martin Rd., Floyds Knobs, 47119. Tel: 812-923-3011; Fax: 812-923-1431.
School—(Grades PreSchool-2) Tel: 812-923-1630; Fax: 812-923-0310. Students 137.
Catechesis/Religious Program—Students 420.
ST. MARY-OF-THE-ROCK, FRANKLIN CO., ST. MARY-OF-THE-ROCK (1844), (German), [CEM] Unassigned. Sr. Patricia Campbell, Parish Life Coord.
Office—17440 St. Mary's Rd., Batesville, 47006. Tel: 812-934-4165; Fax: 812-934-0111.
Catechesis/Religious Program—Tel: 812-934-3219. Students 50.
Oratory—St. Cecilia of Rome (1844), Oak Forest, Franklin Co. 47006.
ST. MARY-OF-THE-WOODS, VIGO CO., ST. MARY (1837), [CEM] Sr. Peggy Lynch, S.P., Parish Life Coord.; Revs. Bernard Head, Sacramental Min.; Anthony Volz.
Mailing Address: P.O. Box 155, 47876. Tel: 812-535-1261; Fax: 812-535-1561.
Catechesis/Religious Program—Diana Bird, D.R.E. Students 80.
ST. MAURICE, DECATUR CO., ST. MAURICE (1859), [CEM] Rev. Gregory Bramlage.
Church: 1963 N. St. John St., Greensburg, 47240. Tel: 812-663-4754; Fax: 812-663-4754.
Catechesis/Religious Program—Students 126.
ST. MEINRAD, SPENCER CO., ST. MEINRAD (1854), [CEM] Rev. Brendan Moss, O.S.B.
Mailing Address: P.O. Box 8, 47577. Tel: 812-357-5533; Fax: 812-357-2862.
Church: 19630 N. 4th St., 47577.
Catechesis/Religious Program—Students 143.
ST. NICHOLAS, RIPLEY CO., ST. NICHOLAS (1836), [CEM] Rev. Gregory D. Bramlage.
Res.: 6461 E. St. Nicholas Dr., Sunman, 47041. Tel: 812-623-2964 (Office); 812-623-4231 (Rectory); Fax: 812-623-2964.
School—(Grades K-8), 6459 E. St. Nicholas Dr., Sunman, 47041. Tel: 812-623-2348. Lay Teachers 11; Students 187.

Catechesis/Religious Program—Students 98.

ST. PETER, FRANKLIN CO., ST. PETER (1838), (German), [CEM] Sr. Margie Niemer, O.S.F., Parish Life Coord.; Rev. William Stumpf, Mod.
Res.: 1207 East Rd., Brookville, 47012. Tel: 812-623-3670; Fax: 812-623-5261.
Catechesis/Religious Program—Tel: 812-623-3670. Students 68.

ST. PETER, HARRISON CO., ST. PETER (1849), [CEM], Attended from St. Joseph, Corydon, St. Peter, 312 E. High St., Corydon, Harrison Co., IN 47112. Rev. Louis Manna.
Mailing Address: 312 E. High St., Corydon, 47112. Tel: 812-738-2742; Fax: 812-738-2718.
Church: Buena Vista Rd., Elizabeth, 47117.
Catechesis/Religious Program—Tel: 812-738-2759. Students 9.

ST. PIUS, RIPLEY CO., ST. PIUS (1859), [CEM], Attended from St. Anthony, Morris Rev. Msgr. Bernard R. Schmitz, Admin.
Mailing Address: P.O. Box 3, Morris, 47033. Tel: 812-934-6218; Fax: 812-934-5936.

ST. VINCENT DE PAUL, SHELBY CO., ST. VINCENT DE PAUL (1837), [CEM] Rev. Paul E. Landwerlen.
Res.: 4218 E. Michigan Rd., Shelbyville, 46176. Tel: 317-398-4028.
Catechesis/Religious Program—Tel: 317-392-3879; Fax: 317-392-3879. Students 93.
Mission— [CEM]

SALEM, WASHINGTON CO., ST. PATRICK (1942), [CEM] Rev. Thomas L. Schliessmann.
208 S. Shelby St., P.O. Box 273, 47167. Tel: 812-752-3693.
Catechesis/Religious Program—Tel: 812-883-3589. Students 75.

SCOTTSBURG, SCOTT CO., AMERICAN MARTYRS (1938), Rev. Thomas L. Schliessmann.
270 S. Bond St., 47170-2009. Tel: 812-752-3693; Fax: 812-752-0969.
Parish Office Address: 262 W. Cherry St., 47170.
Catechesis/Religious Program—Students 54.
Mission—St. Patrick (1942), 208 S. Shelby St., Salem, Washington Co. 47167. Tel: 812-883-3589.

SEELYVILLE, VIGO CO., HOLY ROSARY (1908), Rev. Ken Ciano.
Church & Mailing Address: 2585 N. Main, P.O. Box 151, 47878. Tel: 812-877-1279.
Catechesis/Religious Program—Students 35.

SELLERSBURG, CLARK CO., ST. PAUL (1948), Rev. Paul F. Richart.
Church: 218 Scheller Ave., 47172. Tel: 812-246-3522; Fax: 812-246-7635.
School—(Grades K-6), 105 St. Paul St., 47172. Tel: 812-246-3266; Fax: 812-246-7632. Web: http://stpauls.school.home.insightbb.com. Lay Teachers 18; Students 298.
Catechesis/Religious Program—216 Scheller Ave., 47172. Tel: 812-246-5088. Students 60.

SEYMOUR, JACKSON CO., ST. AMBROSE (1860), [CEM] Rev. John M. Hall.
Res.: 325 S. Chestnut St., 47274. Tel: 812-522-5304; Fax: 812-522-8959.
School—(Grades PreK-7), 301 S. Chestnut St., 47274. Tel: 812-522-3522. Lay Teachers 13; Students 140.
Catechesis/Religious Program—Tel: 812-522-2686. Students 80.
Mission—Our Lady of Providence (1934), 325 S. Chestnut St., Brownstown, Jackson Co. 47274.

SHELBYVILLE, SHELBY CO., ST. JOSEPH (1868), [CEM] [JC] Rev. Don Quinn.
Res.: 125 E. Broadway, 46176. Tel: 317-398-8227; Fax: 317-392-7820.
School—(Grades PreK-5), 127 E. Broadway, 46176. Tel: 317-398-4202; Fax: 317-398-0270. Lay Teachers 11; Students 188.
Catechesis/Religious Program—Tel: 317-398-0530. Students 200.

SIBERIA, PERRY CO., ST. MARTIN OF TOURS (1869), [CEM] Rev. Brendan Moss, O.S.B.
Mailing Address: P.O. Box 8, St. Meinrad, 47577. Tel: 812-357-5533; Fax: 812-357-2862.
Church: 27246 Perry St., 47515.
Catechesis/Religious Program—Students 45.

SPENCER, OWEN CO., ST. JUDE THE APOSTLE (1951), Rev. Paul M. Dede.
300 W. Hillside Ave., P.O. Box 317, 47460. Tel: 812-829-3082; Fax: 812-829-0888.
Catechesis/Religious Program—Students 50.

STARLIGHT, CLARK CO., ST. JOHN THE BAPTIST (1861), (German), [CEM] [JC] Rev. Richard Hindel, O.S.B.
Res.: 8310 St. John's Rd., Floyds Knobs, 47119. Tel: 812-923-5785; Fax: 812-923-5785.
Catechesis/Religious Program—Tel: 812-923-0445; Fax: 812-923-5785. Students 84.

TELL CITY, PERRY CO., ST. PAUL (1859), [CEM] Rev. Carl Deitchman, O.S.B.
Parish Office—Catholic Ministry Center, 802 9th St., 47586. Tel: 812-547-7994; Fax: 812-547-6985.
In Res., Rev. Barnabas Gillespie, O.S.B.
Church: 814 Jefferson St., 47586. Tel: 812-547-9901.
Catechesis/Religious Program—Tel: 812-547-7102. Students 378.

TERRE HAUTE, VIGO CO.

1—ST. ANN (1876), [JC] Sr. Constance Kramer, S.P., Parish Life Coord.; Rev. Russell Zint, Sacramental Min.
Res.: 1440 Locust St., 47807. Tel: 812-232-6832; Fax: 812-232-2444.
Catechesis/Religious Program—Students 30.

2—ST. BENEDICT (1865), (German), [JC] Rev. Joel Burget, O.F.M.Conv.
Parish Office—111 S. Ninth St., 47807. Tel: 812-235-3041; Fax: 812-238-9203.
Church: 118 S. Ninth St., 47807. Church: Tel: 812-238-9109.
Catechesis/Religious Program—Tel: 812-232-8421. Students 118.

3—ST. JOSEPH UNIVERSITY PARISH (1838), [JC] Rev. Richard Kaley, O.F.M.Conv.
Res.: 113 S. Fifth St., 47807. Tel: 812-232-7011; Fax: 812-232-7012.
Catechesis/Religious Program—Students 223.

4—ST. MARGARET MARY (1920), [JC] Revs. Ronald M. Ashmore; Joseph Kern, V.F., Admin.
Res.: 2405 S. Seventh St., 47802. Tel: 812-232-3512; Fax: 812-232-6921.
Catechesis/Religious Program—Students 119.

5—ST. PATRICK (1881), Rev. Lawrence J. Moran; John Fuller, Pastoral Assoc.
Church: 1807 Poplar St., 47803. Tel: 812-232-8518; Fax: 812-234-3312.
School—(Grades PreK-8), 449 S. 19th St., 47803. Tel: 812-232-2157; Fax: 812-478-9384. Julie Bowers, Prin. Lay Teachers 17; Students 272.
Catechesis/Religious Program—Tel: 812-232-2827. Students 212.

6—SACRED HEART OF JESUS (1924), Rev. Russell Zint.
Res.: 2322 N. 13 1/2 St., 47804. Tel: 812-466-1231; Fax: 812-466-9683.
School—1330 Lafayette Ave., 47804. Tel: 812-232-8901. Sisters 1; Lay Teachers 9; Students 120.
Catechesis/Religious Program—Students 111.

TROY, PERRY CO., ST. PIUS (1849), [CEM] Rev. Barnabas Gillespie, O.S.B.
Parish Office & Mailing Address: Catholic Ministry Center, 802 9th St., Tell City, 47586. Tel: 812-547-7994; Fax: 812-547-6985.
Church: State Rd. 66, 47588.

UNIVERSAL, VERMILLION CO., ST. JOSEPH (1920),, Attended from Sacred Heart, 619 S. Fifth St., Clinton, IN 47842-2016. Tel: 765-832-8468. Rev. Joseph L. Villa, Admin.
Church: 270 E. Wood Ave., 47884.
Catechesis/Religious Program—Students 4.

VEVAY, SWITZERLAND CO., MOST SORROWFUL MOTHER OF GOD (1876), Rev. John A. Meyer, V.F.
Mailing Address: *Catholic Community Center*, 305 W. State St., Madison, 47250. Tel: 812-265-4166; Fax: 812-273-3427.
Church: Ferry St., 47043.
Catechesis/Religious Program—Students 5.

WEST TERRE HAUTE, VIGO CO., ST. LEONARD OF PORT MAURICE (1912), Sr. Margaret M. Lynch, S.P., Parish Life Coord.; Revs. Bernard Head, Sacramental Min.; Anthony Volz.
126 N. Eighth St., 47885. Tel: 812-533-1240.

YORKVILLE, DEARBORN CO., ST. MARTIN (1850), [CEM] Rev. William J. Turner.
Res.: 8044 Yorkridge Rd., Guilford, 47022. Tel: 812-487-2096; 812-623-3408; Fax: 812-623-4879.
Catechesis/Religious Program—Tel: 812-623-2662. Students 110.

Chaplains of Public Institutions

INDIANAPOLIS. *Community Hospital North*. Rev. Jack Emrich.
Indiana University Hospital/Riley Hospital for Children. Rev. George Henninger.
Indiana Women's Prison. Rev. Lawrence Voelker.
Indianapolis Fire Department.
Indianapolis International Airport. Rev. Glenn L. O'Connor.
Marion County Sheriff Department. Rev. James R. Wilmoth.
Methodist Hospital. Rev. David Lawler.
Veterans' Administration Hospital. Revs. Joachim Keine, O.F.M.Conv., Gordon P. Wagoner.
Winona Medical Center. Rev. Jack Emrich.
Wishard Memorial Hospital. Vacant.

PUTNAMVILLE. *Indiana State Farm*. Rev. Stephen Jarrell.

RICHMOND. *Richmond State Hospital*. Rev. Todd M. Riebe.

TERRE HAUTE. *Regional Hospital/Union Hospital*. Rev. Joel Burget, O.F.M.Conv.
U.S. Penitentiary. Rev. Francis Roof.

Unassigned:
Revs.—
Ashmore, Ronald M.
Brown, W. Joseph
Emrich, Jack
Kelley, Michael
Schafer, Raymond E.
Stewart, Jonathan

Graduate Studies:
Rev.—
Pondo, Stanley, J.D., M.A., A.B., M.Div.

On Special or Other Archdiocesan Assignment:
Revs.—
Mazzola, Robert E., Auditor, Metropolitan Tribunal
Porter, Jack W., Archdiocesan Historian
Smith, Myles H., J.C.L., Defender of the Bond, Metropolitan Tribunal

---

On Disability Leave:
Rev.—
Mader, Joseph

Retired:
Rev. Msgrs.—
Dooley, Joseph W., St. Augustine Home, 2345 W. 86th St., 46260.
Kavanagh, Richard T., St. Paul Hermitage, 501 N. 17th Ave., Beech Grove, 46107-1196.
Knueven, Harold L.
Marchino, Louis H., 127 Rossmore Dr., New Albany, 47150.
Wright, John M., CHC, USN, 9253 Regents Rd., La Jolla, CA 92037.
Revs.—
Ajamie, Albert, Fatima Retreat House, 5353 E. 56th St., 46226.
Armstrong, Daniel F., St. Paul Hermitage, 50 N. 17th Ave., Beech Grove, 46107-1196.
Arneson, James E., 1868 Shore Dr. S., #114, South Pasadena, FL 33707.
Brown, Henry P., St. Paul Hermitage, 501 N. 17th Ave., Beech Grove, 46107.
Buchanan, LCDR Donald E., P.O. Box 367, Austin, 47102-0367.
Burwinkel, Elmer J., M.Ed., M.Div., 3991 W.C.R. 925 S., Madison, 47250.
Cleary, William D., P.O. Box 430, Rushville, 46137-0430.
Commons, Patrick M., 210 Hunter Ct., Apt. 5, Milan, 47031.
Dede, John F., 2421 S. Seventh St., 47802.
Eckstein, Francis J., P.O. Box 336, Milan, 47031.
Evard, Paul A., 718 Bitterbark Ln., 46227.
Evrard, Donald J., P.O. Box 723, Tell City, 47306-0723.
Gayso, Edward V., 5235 E. Greenbriar Dr., Apt. 5A, 47802.
Head, Bernard, 3461 St. Mary's Rd., #331, West Terre Haute, 47885.
Kern, Joseph R., 936 Springdale Ln., 47802.
Kraeszig, Charles J., 7901 Castle Dr., Lakewood Estates, New Port Richey, FL 34653.
Luerman, John H., 823 S.W. 15th St., Richmond, 47374.
Lutz, Herman, 59 Allendale, 47802.
McNally, Joseph J., 219 E. Eagle Dr., Ninevah, 46164.
Meny, Hilary G., P.O. Box 245, Haubstadt, 47639.
Mueller, Richard J., 2722 B Marquette Manor W. Dr., 46268.
Murphy, Thomas J., 1827 Kessler Blvd. E. Dr., 46220.
O'Riley, James K., 3388 Rothshire Cir., North Vernon, 47265.
Peter, Martin A., 12935 W. Sawmill Rd., Columbus, 47201.
Porter, Jack W., 7432-D Lions Head Dr., 46260-3445.
Ripperger, William, 38220 Boxwood Dr., Zephyrhills, FL 33542.
Rodas, Mauro, 736 Royal St. George Dr., Greenwood, 46143.
Schmidlin, Donald L., St. Paul Catholic Center, 1413 E. 17th St., Bloomington, 47408.
Sciarra, John N., 8300 Rahke Rd., 46217.
Sheets, Joseph B., 436 Mutton Creek Dr., Seymour, 47274.
Stineman, William F., 7432-D Lions Head Dr., 46260.
Terrill, Richard F., 1391 Gardner Ave., Newago, MI 49337.
Zore, Richard I., 5254 McFarland Rd., 46227.

INSTITUTIONS LOCATED IN THE ARCHDIOCESE

[A] SEMINARIES, RELIGIOUS OR SCHOLASTICATES

ST. MEINRAD. *St. Meinrad School of Theology*, 200 Hill Dr., 47577. Tel: 812-357-6611; Fax: 812-357-6964. Email: rector@saintmeinrad.edu. Web: www.saintmeinrad.edu. Revs. Mark O'Keefe, O.S.B., Pres. & Rector; Justin Duvall, O.S.B., Vice Rector & Provost; Adrian Burke, O.S.B.; Bede Cisco, O.S.B.; Patrick Cooney, O.S.B.; Cyprian Davis, O.S.B.; Kenneth Davis, O.F.M.Conv.; Guerric DeBona, O.S.B.; Damian Dietlein, O.S.B.; Jonathan Fassero, O.S.B.; Harry Hagan, O.S.B.; Eugene Hensell, O.S.B.; Columba Kelly, O.S.B.; Alaric Lewis, O.S.B.; Bernard Lutz (EVN) (Retired); Guy Mansini, O.S.B.; Noel Mueller, O.S.B.; Godfrey Mullen, O.S.B.; Thomas Richstatter, O.F.M.; Denis Robinson, O.S.B.; Kurt Stasiak, O.S.B.; Charles C. Thompson, J.C.L. (L); Joseph A. Weigman (TOL). School of Theology. Other Faculty and Staff 27; Students 88.

[B] COLLEGES AND UNIVERSITIES

INDIANAPOLIS. *Marian College* (Coed) , 3200 Cold Spring Rd., 46222. Tel: 317-955-6000; Fax: 317-955-6448. Email: admit@marian.edu. Web: www.marian.edu. Sr. Norma Rocklage, O.S.F., Ph.D., Senior Vice Pres. Mission Effectiveness & Student Life; Michael Maxwell Jr., Ph.D., J.D., Vice Pres. for Academic Affairs; Daniel J. Elsener, Pres.; Revs. Francis E. Bryan; Leopold Keffler, O.F.M.Conv. Sisters of the Third Order Regular of St. Francis Priests 2; Sisters 3; Lay Teachers 62; Students 1,425.

SAINT MARY-OF-THE-WOODS. *Saint Mary-of-the-Woods College*, St. Mary-of-the-Woods, 47876. Tel: 812-535-5151; Fax: 812-535-4613. Email: smeier@woods.smwc.edu. Web: www.smwc.edu. Dr. Joan Lescinski, C.S.J., Pres. Sponsored by the Sisters of Providence, St. Mary-of-the-Woods. Priests 1; Sisters of Providence 4; Sisters of St. Francis 1; Lay Teachers 53; Students 1,510.

[C] HIGH SCHOOLS, INTER-PAROCHIAL

INDIANAPOLIS. *Bishop Chatard High School*, 5885 N. Crittenden Ave., 46220. Tel: 317-251-1451; Fax: 317-254-5427. Email: jkedra@bishopchatard.org. Web: www.chatard.org. Bro. Joseph Umile, C.S.C., Pres.; James Kedra, Vice Pres. Academics; Rev. Eric Matthew Johnson, Chap. Priests 1; Sisters of St. Benedict 4; Brothers of Holy Cross 1; Lay Teachers 56; Students 828.

Cardinal Ritter High School, 3360 W. 30th St., 46222. Tel: 317-924-4333; Fax: 317-927-7822. Paul Lockard, Pres.; E. Jo Hoy, Prin. Brothers 1; Lay Teachers 23; Students 388.

Father Thomas Scecina Memorial High School, 5000 Nowland Ave., 46201-1836. Tel: 317-356-6377; Fax: 317-322-4287. Email: rruhl@scecina.org. Web: www.scecina.org. Mr. Ricky J. Ruhl, Prin.; Rev. J. Peter Gallagher. Priests 1; Lay Teachers 30; Students 360.

Roncalli High School, 3300 Prague Rd., 46227. Tel: 317-787-8277; Fax: 317-788-4095. Email: cweisenbach@roncallihs.org. Web: www.roncalli.org. Mr. Joseph D. Hollowell, Pres.; Charles Weisenbach. Priests 1; Lay Teachers 64; Students 951.

CLARKSVILLE. *Our Lady of Providence Junior & Senior High School*, 707 W. Hwy. 131, 47129. Tel: 812-945-2538; Fax: 812-945-3460. Email: jwilkinson@providencehigh.net. Web: www.providencehigh.net. Mrs. Melinda Ernstberger, Prin.; Mr. Gerald Wilkinson, Pres.; Rev. Michael Hilderbrand, Chap. Priests 1; Lay Teachers 42; Students (Grades 9-12) 539; Students (Grades 7-12) 583.

MADISON. *Shawe Memorial Junior-Senior High School*, 201 W. State St., 47250. Tel: 812-273-2150; Fax: 812-273-6694. Email: shaweprincipal@popeace.org. Priests 1; Lay Teachers 18; Students 142.

RICHMOND. *Seton Catholic High School*, 233 S. 5th St., 47374. Tel: 765-965-6956; Fax: 765-935-9930. Email: dmusial@setoncatholichighschool.org. Web:. Dennis Musial, Prin.; Rev. Joseph Michael Feltz, Chap. Priests 1; Lay Teachers 10; Students 88.

[D] HIGH SCHOOLS, PRIVATE

INDIANAPOLIS. *Brebeuf Jesuit Preparatory School, Inc.*, 2801 W. 86th St., 46268-1925. Tel: 317-872-7050; Fax: 317-876-4712. Email: principalsoffice@brebeuf.org. Web: www.brebeuf.org. Rev. Benjamin Hawley, S.J., Pres.; Mr. Andrew F. Noga, Prin. Society of Jesus Community
2823 W. 86 St., 46268-1926. Tel: 317-876-4700; Fax: 317-870-2753. Revs. J. Peter Carey, S.J., Rector; J. Paul O'Brien, S.J.; Richard L. Millbourn, S.J.; Frederick J. Deters, S.J.; George R. Menke, S.J.; Benjamin Hawley, S.J.; Bro. John F. Buchman, S.J.; Rev. Michael S. Christiana, S.J. Priests 7; Sisters 1; Brothers 1; Lay Teachers 61; Students 806.

Cathedral High School (Cathedral Trustees, Inc.), 5225 E. 56th St., 46226. Tel: 317-542-1418; Fax: 317-542-1434. Email: chsjtp@indy.net. Web: www.cathedral-irish.org. Stephen J. Helmich, M.S., Pres.; David Worland, Prin. Sisters 4; Priests 2; Lay Teachers 95; Students 1,210.

OLDENBURG. *Oldenburg Academy of the Immaculate Conception* One Twister Cir., P.O. Box 200, 47036-0200. Tel: 812-934-4440; Fax: 812-934-4838. Email: connie_deardorff@oa.batesville.k12.in.us. Web: www.batesville.k12.in.us/oa/. Connie Deardorff, Prin. Lay Teachers 20; Students 192.

[E] DAY CARE

SAINT MARY-OF-THE-WOODS. *Woods Day Care/ Preschool, Inc.*, St. Mary-of-the-Woods, 47876-1099. Tel: 812-535-4610. Total Staff 16; Children 45.

[F] RELIGIOUS EDUCATION CENTERS

CLARKSVILLE. *Aquinas Center for Continuing Religious Education*, 707 W. Hwy. 131, 47129. Tel: 812-945-0354; Fax: 812-945-2929. Email: bobnadac@aol.com. Web: aquinascenter.org. Mr. Robert K. Leonard, Dir. Catechetical Ministry & Religious Education.

TERRE HAUTE. *Terre Haute Deanery Pastoral Center*, 2931 Ohio Blvd., 47803. Tel: 812-232-8400; Fax: 812-234-2655. Email: sueethdeanery.org. Web: www.thdeanery.org. Sue Butwin, Dir.; Janet Cianteo, Admin. Asst. Total Staff 2.

[G] GENERAL HOSPITALS

INDIANAPOLIS. *Central Indiana Health System Cardiac Services, Inc.*, 8425 N. Harcourt Rd., 46260. Tel: 317-415-6042; Fax: 317-415-6051. M. Lynne O'Day, Chm.; Vincent C. Caponi, Chm.

**St. Vincent Children's Special Hospital, Inc.* dba St. Vincent Pediatric Rehabilitation Center , (A member of St. Vincent Health & Ascension Health.) , 1707 W. 86th St., 46260. Tel: 317-415-5500; Fax: 317-415-5595. Email: akmott@stvincent.org. James C. Van Dyke, CEO; Andrea Mott, CFO

St. Vincent Hospital and Health Care Center, Inc., 2001 W. 86th St., 46260. Tel: 317-338-7000; Fax: 317-338-7005. Email: jbford@stvincent.org. Web: www.stvincent.org. Sr. Mary Francis Loftin, D.C., Chairperson; Vincent C. Caponi, CEO, St. Vincent Health, Inc.; Dr. Patricia A. Maryland, PH., Pres., St. Vincent Hospital and Health Care Center, Inc.; Vincent C. Caponi, Interim Pres., St Vincent Hospital and Health Care Center, Inc.; Sr. Sharon Richardt, D.C., Vice Pres. Mission Svcs.; Revs. Joseph Rautenberg; Ben Okonkwo; Ms. Joan M. Bumpus, Dir. Pastoral Care. Daughters of Charity of St. Vincent de Paul. Sisters 8; Bed Capacity 851; Total Staff 5,623; Inpatient Admissions 39,933; Outpatient Visits 900,262; Emergency Visits 66,424; Chaplains 27.

**St. Vincent New Hope, Inc.*, 8450 N. Payne Rd., 46268. Tel: 317-872-4210; Fax: 317-338-4585. Daughters of Charity of St. Vincent de Paul. Bed Capacity 69; Total Annually Assisted 263; Total Staff 424.

BEECH GROVE. *St. Francis Hospital and Health Centers*, 1600 Albany St., 46107. Tel: 317-787-3311; Fax: 317-782-6731. Web: www.stfrancishospitals.org. Mr. Robert J. Brody, Pres. & CEO; Sr. Corita Last, Vice Pres. Mission Integration Svcs., Supr.; Revs. Frederick J. Deters, S.J., Chap.; Ruta A. Cabazi (Tanzania), Chap.; John H. Mannion (LFT), Chap. Sisters of St. Francis Health Services, Inc. Sisters 7; Staff 4,146; Bed Capacity 600; Patients Assisted Annually 209,000.
8111 S. Emerson Ave., 46237. Tel: 317-865-5000; Fax: 317-865-5061.
1201 Hadley Rd., Mooresville, 46158. Tel: 317-834-1160; Fax: 317-831-9315.

BRAZIL. *St. Vincent Clay Hospitals, Inc.* (A member of St. Vincent Health & Ascension Health) , 1206 E. National Ave., 47834. Tel: 812-442-2500; Fax: 812-442-2605. Email: rjohans@stvincent.org. Richard L. Johansen, CEO.

NORTH VERNON. **St. Vincent Jennings Hospital, Inc.* (A member of St. Vincent Health & Ascension Health) , 301 Henry St., 47265. Tel: 812-352-4200; Fax: 812-352-4201. Email: kheffel@stvincent.org. Joseph E. Roche, CEO; Kent Heffelbower, Contact Person.

[H] PROTECTIVE INSTITUTIONS

TERRE HAUTE. *Gibault*, 6301 S. U.S. Hwy. 41, P.O. Box 2316, 47802-0316. Tel: 812-299-1156; Fax: 812-299-0019. Email: gibault@gibault.org. Web: www.gibault.org. Mr. James M. Sinclair, M.S.S.W., J.D., Exec. Dir. Residential treatment facility for males and females between the ages of 8 and 18, sponsored by the Knights of Columbus of Indiana Licensed Youth 147; Total Staff 200.

[I] HOMES FOR AGED

INDIANAPOLIS. *St. Augustine Home, Little Sisters of the Poor*, 2345 W. 86th St., 46260. Tel: 317-872-6420; Fax: 317-875-9883. Sisters Geraldine Harvie, Supr.; Celestine Meade, Admin.; Rev. Adrian Figuerola, Chap. Sisters 12; Total Staff 97; Residents 92.

BEECH GROVE. *St. Paul Hermitage*, 501 N. 17th Ave., 46107. Tel: 317-786-2261; Fax: 317-782-1411. Email: srbierman@aol.com. Rev. Msgr. Richard Kavanaugh; Revs. Henry Brown; John Sciarra; Herman Lutz (Retired); Sr. Sharon Bierman, O.S.B., Admin.
Legal Title: *Sisters of St. Benedict of Beech Grove, Ind., Inc.* Sisters 10; Total Staff 110; Residents 108.

NEW ALBANY. *Mercy Long Term Care Initiatives* dba Providence Retirement Home , 4915 Charlestown Rd., 47150. Tel: 812-945-5221; Fax: 812-945-2614. Email: www.prhonline.org. Mary Jo Cavanaugh, Admin. Sisters of Mercy Priests 1; Sisters 1; Total Staff 180; Residents 176; Adult Day Care clients 32.

[J] RETREAT HOUSES

INDIANAPOLIS. *Our Lady of Fatima Retreat House, Inc.*, 5353 E. 56th St., 46226. Tel: 317-545-7681; Fax: 317-545-0095. Email: fatima@archindy.org. Web: www.archindy.org/fatima. Mr. Brian Doyle, Dir. Used by both clergy and laity. Priests 1; Total in Residence 1; Total Staff 9; Served 7,472.

BEECH GROVE. *Benedict Inn Retreat & Conference Center*, 1402 Southern Ave., 46107-1197. Tel: 317-788-7581; Fax: 317-782-3142. Email: benedict@indy.net. Web: www.benedictinn.org. Sr. Mark Luke Jones, O.S.B., Admin. Retreats and workshops for clergy, religious, and laity. Sisters 5.

MOUNT SAINT FRANCIS. *Mount Saint Francis Friary and Retreat Center*, 101 St. Anthony Dr., Mount St. Francis, 47146-9999. Tel: 812-923-8817; Fax: 812-923-0177. Revs. John Raphael Hadnagy, O.F.M.Conv., St. Joe Hill Church; Jim Van Dorn, O.F.M.Conv., Parish Missions; Eliot Comstock, O.F.M.Conv., Devel. Office de familia; Simeon Yates, O.F.M.Conv., Retreat Staff; Florian Tiell, O.F.M.Conv., Nursing Home Chap.; Kenneth Davis, O.F.M.Conv., Prof., St. Meinrad's; Germain Belen, O.F.M.Conv. (LAN) (Retired) In Res. Revs. Maximilian Korecki, O.F.M.Conv., Chap., Archives, de familia; John Columban Sattler, O.F.M.Conv. (Retired); Bros. Robert Baxter, O.F.M.Conv., Sec. of the Province; Angelo Catania, O.F.M.Conv., Retreat Staff; Ambrose Eischens, O.F.M.Conv., Guardian & Retreat Dir.; Jose Reyes, O.F.M.Conv., de familia; Aloysius Wagener, O.F.M.Conv., (Retired); James Worchuck, O.F.M.Conv., Studies; Deacon Donald R. Hart, O.F.M.Conv.

Province of Our Lady of Consolation, Inc., Mount St. Francis. Tel: 812-923-8444; Fax: 812-923-8145. Very Rev. Peter Damian Massengill, O.F.M.Conv., Min. Prov.; Rev. David Lenz, O.F.M.Conv., Vicar; Bro. Robert Baxter, O.F.M.Conv., Sec. of Prov. (Provincial Office) Total Staff 5; Total in Residence 14.

ST. MEINRAD. *Archabbey Guest House*, 200 Hill Dr., 47577. Tel: 812-357-6585; 800-581-6905; Fax: 812-357-6325. Email: mzoeller@saintmeinrad.edu. Web: www.saintmeinrad.edu/abbey/ghouse.htm. Retreat House for Men, Women, Couples Double Rooms 25.

[K] MONASTERIES AND RESIDENCES OF PRIESTS AND BROTHERS

MOUNT SAINT FRANCIS. *Provincial Headquarters for the Conventual Franciscan Province*, 101 Anthony Dr., Mount St. Francis, 47146. Tel: 812-923-8444; Fax: 812-923-8145. Email: ProvOffOLC@aol.com. Web: www.olcprovince.com. Very Rev. Peter Damian Massengill, O.F.M.Conv., Min. Prov.; Rev. David Lenz, O.F.M.Conv., Vicar Prov.; Bro. Robert B. Baxter, O.F.M.Conv., Sec. of Prov.
Legal Title: *Province of Our Lady of Consolation* Priests 2.

Development Office, 103 St. Francis Blvd., Mount St. Francis, 47146. Tel: 812-923-5250; Fax: 812-923-3200.

Vocation Office of the Province Tel: 502-933-4439; Fax: 502-933-7747.

St. Paul Friary, 6901 Dixie Hwy., Pleasure Ridge

Park, KY 40258. Tel: 502-933-4439; Fax: 502-933-7747. Rev. James Kent, O.F.M.Conv., Vocation Dir.
Curia Generalizia, Piazza Ss. Apostoli, 51, Rome 00187 Italy. Tel: 0113906699571; Fax: 011390669957321. Rev. Basil Heiser, O.F.M.Conv.

ST. MEINRAD. *St. Meinrad Archabbey*, 200 Hill Dr., 47577-1010. Tel: 812-357-6611; Fax: 812-357-6551. Email: abbot@saintmeinrad.edu. Web: www.saintmeinrad.edu. Rt. Revs. Lambert Reilly, O.S.B., Archabbot; Bonaventure Knaebel, O.S.B., Resigned Archabbot; Revs. Tobias Colgan, O.S.B., Prior; Harry Hagan, O.S.B., Master of Novices & Junior Master; Benet Amato, O.S.B.; Gavin Barnes, O.S.B.; Alban Berling, O.S.B.; Aurelius Boberek, O.S.B.; Meinrad Brune, O.S.B.; Aelred Cody, O.S.B.; Patrick Cooney, O.S.B.; Joseph Cox, O.S.B.; Simeon Daly, O.S.B.; Augustine Davis, O.S.B.; Cyprian Davis, O.S.B.; Guerrie DeBona, O.S.B.; Justin DuVall, O.S.B.; Jonathan Fassero, O.S.B.; Malachy Fulton, O.S.B.; Rembert Gehant, O.S.B.; Colman Grabert, O.S.B.; Theodore Heck, O.S.B.; Warren Heitz, O.S.B.; Eugene Hensell, O.S.B.; Columba Kelly, O.S.B.; Jeramy King, O.S.B.; Alcuin Leibold, O.S.B.; Eric Lies, O.S.B.; Prosper Lindauer, O.S.B.; Simon McTighe, O.S.B.; Guy Mansini, O.S.B.; Noel Mueller, O.S.B.; Louis Mulcahy, O.S.B.; Godfrey Mullen, O.S.B.; Mark O'Keefe, O.S.B., Pres. & Rector, School of Theology; Rupert Ostdick, O.S.B.; Julian Peters, O.S.B.; Kevin Ryan, O.S.B.; Stephen Snoich, O.S.B.; Kurt Stasiak, O.S.B.; Germain Swisshelm, O.S.B.; Donald Walpole, O.S.B.; Peter Yock, O.S.B.; Marion C. Walsh, O.S.B. (Retired). Archabbey of the Order of St. Benedict, including School of Theology (St. Meinrad Seminary). Priests 81; Brothers 30.
Priests of the Archabbey Teaching, Studying at Universities, or on Special Assignment:
Collegio Sant'Anselmo, Piazza Cavalieri di Malta, 5, Roma 1-00153 Italy. Rev. Adrian Burke, O.S.B.
Collegio Sant'Anselmo, Piazza Cavalieri di Malta 5, Rome I-00153 Italy. Rev. Ephrem Carr, O.S.B.
St. John the Evangelist: 126 W. Georgia St., 46225-1004. Rev. Noah Casey, O.S.B.
St. Benedict Church: 1328 Lincoln Ave., Evansville, 47714-1598. Rev. Gregory D. Chamberlin, O.S.B. (EVN).
St. Michael Parish: 3354 W. 30th St., 46222. Rev. Bede Cisco, O.S.B.
Monastero San Benedetto, Via Reguardati, 22, Norcia (pg) 06046 Italy. Rev. Cassian Folsom, O.S.B.
St. Paul Parish: 814 Jefferson St., Tell City, 47586. Rev. Carl Deitchman, O.S.B.
St. Anthony Church: 604 S. Center, Casper, WY 82601. Rev. Camillus Ellspermann, O.S.B.
St. Paul Church: 802 Ninth St., Tell City, 47586. Rev. Barnabas Gillespie, O.S.B.
701 S. Boeke, Evansville, 47714. Rev. Harold Hammerstein, O.S.B.
2171 Avondale Pl., P.O. Box 18567, 46218. Rev. Boniface Hardin, O.S.B.
St. John the Baptist Parish: 8310 St. John Rd., Floyds Knobs, 47119. Rev. Richard Hindel, O.S.B.
St. Augustine Church: General Delivery, Leopold, 47551. Rev. Sean Hoppe, O.S.B.
208 Carmalt Rd., Hamden, CT 06157. Rev. Aidan Kavanagh, O.S.B.
St. Mary Rectory, 313 Washington St., Huntingburg, 47532. Rev. Pius Klein, O.S.B.
The Hollows, 1300 Longcreek Dr., Apt. 713, Columbia, SC 29210. Rev. Micheas Langston, O.S.B.
Canterbury School, Aspetuck Ave., New Milford, CT 06776. Rev. Sebastian Leonard, O.S.B.
St. James Parish: 2942 S. Wabash, Chicago, IL 60616. Rev. Edward Linton, O.S.B.
Collegio Sant'Anselmo, Piazza Cavalieri di Malta, 5, Roma I-00153 Italy. Rev. Alaric Lewis, O.S.B.
St. Martin de Porres Dominicans: 3050 Knob Gap Rd., New Hope, KY 40052. Rev. Ralph Lynch, O.S.B.
Queen of All Saints Parish: 606 South Woodland Ave., Michigan City, 46360. Rev. Keith J. McClellan, O.S.B.
St. Mary of the Assumption: 8120 Lincoln Ave., Apt. D, Evansville, 47715. Rev. Alan R. McIntosh, O.S.B.
St. Michael Church: 519 Jefferson Blvd., Greenfield, 46140. Rev. Severin Messick, O.S.B.
St. John the Baptist Parish: 203 W. Ash, Brinkley, AR 72021. Rev. Benedict Meyer, O.S.B.
Saint Meinrad Parish: 47577. Rev. Brendan Moss, O.S.B.
1414 Southern Ave., Beech Grove, 46107. Rev. Matthias Neuman, O.S.B.
Sacred Heart Monastery, 1005 W. Eighth St., Yankton, SD 57078. Rev. Mel Patton, O.S.B.
P.O. Box 326, Manchester, KY 40962. Rev. David Rabenecker, O.S.B.
The Ameican College, Naamsestraadt, 100, Leuven, B-3000, Belgium. Rev. Denis Robinson, O.S.B.
St. James Parish: 2942 S.Wabash, Chicago, IL 60616. Rev. Anselm Russell, O.S.B.
St. Henry Parish: 1311 W. 1100 S., Ferdinand, 47532. Rev. Damian Schmelz, O.S.B.
Curley Hall, Catholic University of America, Washington, DC 20064. Rev. Raymond Studzinski, O.S.B.
Parish of the Immaculate Rev. Timothy Sweeney, O.S.B.2516 Christie Place, Owensboro, KY 42301.
The American College, 00120, Vatican City State. Rev. Vincent Tobin, O.S.B.
Our Lady Queen Monastery, 50352 Antioch Rd., Tickfaw, LA 70466. Rev. Marion C. Walsh, O.S.B. (Retired).
Wake Forest Divinity School, P.O. Box 7719, Winston-Salem, NC 27109-7719. Rev. Samuel Weber, O.S.B.

[L] CONVENTS AND RESIDENCES FOR SISTERS

INDIANAPOLIS. *F.I.H. Convent*, 3356 W. 30th St., 46222. Tel: 317-924-0573; Fax: 317-924-0573. Email: franciscansisters@yahoo.com. Sr. Delphine Mary. Franciscan Sisters of the Immaculate Heart of Mary Sisters 13.
Servants of the Gospel of Life, Inc, 1400 N. Meridian St., 46202. Tel: 317-236-1521. Email: dcarollo@archindy.org. Sr. Diane Carollo, Senior Servant.
Sisters of Our Lady of Mount Carmel Carmelite Monastery, 2500 Cold Spring Rd., 46222-2323. Tel: 317-926-5654; Fax: 317-926-1492. Email: indycarm@praythenews.com. Web: www.praythenews.com. Sr. Jean Alice McGoff, O.C.D., Prioress. Professed Religious 11.

BEECH GROVE. *Our Lady of Grace Monastery*, 1402 Southern Ave., 46107-1197. Tel: 317-787-3287; Fax: 317-780-2368. Email: olgprioress@aol.com. Web: www.benedictine.com.
Legal Title: *Sisters of St. Benedict of Beech Grove, IN, Inc.*
1414 Southern Ave., 46107-1197. Tel: 317-786-0338; Fax: 317-780-2368. Email: mnewman@dellnet.com. Rev. Matthias Newman, O.S.B., Chap. Sisters 81.

OLDENBURG. *Motherhouse of the Congregation of the Sisters of the Third Order of St. Francis* 47036. Tel: 812-934-2475; Fax: 812-933-6403. Email: oldenburgosf.com. Sr. Jean Marie Cleveland, O.S.F., Congregational Min.; Revs. Raymar Middendorf, O.F.M.; John Turnbull, O.F.M., Assoc. Chap., Holy Family Friary. Professed Sisters in Congregation 312; Professed Sisters in Archdiocese 228; Total in Residence 139.
Sisters of St. Francis Community Support Trust Tel: 812-934-2475. Email: osf@seidata.com.

SAINT MARY-OF-THE-WOODS. *Sisters of Providence General Administration*, St. Mary-of-the-Woods, 47876-1089. Tel: 812-535-4193; Fax: 812-535-4727. Web: www.sistersofprovidence.org. Sr. Ann Margaret O'Hara, S.P., Gen. Supr.; Rev. Daniel R. Hopcus, Chap. Professed in Congregation 513; Professed Residing in Archdiocese 317; Novices 2; Postulants 3.

TERRE HAUTE. *Sisters of Our Lady of Mount Carmel of Terre Haute, Carmelite Monastery*, Carmelite Monastery, 59 Allendale, 47802-4751. Tel: 812-299-1410; Fax: 812-299-5820. Email: carmelth@heartsawake.org. Web: www.heartsawake.org. Sr. Anne Brackmann, O.C.D., Prioress. Solemnly Professed 11; Novices 2.

[M] ARCHDIOCESAN CHARITIES

INDIANAPOLIS. *Adult Day Services*, 1400 N. Meridian, P.O. Box 1410, 46202-2367. Tel: 317-236-1527; Fax: 317-261-3375. Email: lbaxter@archindy.org. Lula E. Baxter, Prog. Dir.
A Caring Place - Adult Day Services, c/o Fairview Presbyterian Church, 4609 N. Capitol Ave., 46208. Tel: 317-466-0015; Fax: 317-475-3093. Sr. Susan Dinnin, Site Mgr.
Holy Trinity Place - Adult Day Services, 907 Holmes Ave., 46222. Tel: 317-638-8322; Fax: 317-638-9215. Joan Gootee, Site Mgr.
Catholic Social Services of Central Indiana, The Catholic Center, 1400 N. Meridian St., P.O. Box 1410, 46206. Tel: 317-236-1500; Fax: 317-261-3375. Email: css@archindy.org. Web: www.archindy.org; indycss.org. David Bethuram, Exec. Dir. Total Staff 69; Total Assisted 15,784.
Holy Family Services, 30 E. Palmer St., 46225. Tel: 317-635-7830; Fax: 317-684-9702. Email: hf-shelter@iquest.net. Bill Bickel, M.T.S., Dir. Total Staff 16; Total Assisted 1,206.

NEW ALBANY. *Catholic Charities of South Central Indiana*, 601 E. Market St., 47150. Tel: 812-948-0438; Fax: 812-948-0400. Email: stelizabeths@juno.com. Web: www.catholiccharities-sci.org. Keith E. Storms, Dir. Total Staff 3; Total Assisted 660.
St. Elizabeth's Regional Maternity Center, 601 E. Market St., 47150. Tel: 812-949-7305; Fax: 812-941-7008. Email: stelizabeths@juno.com. Web: www.stelizabeths1.org. Keith E. Stormes, Dir. Full-range maternity home and adoption agency offering residential and outreach services. Total Staff 15; Total in Residence 36.

TELL CITY. *Catholic Charities*, 802 9th St., 47586. Tel: 812-547-7994; Fax: 812-547-6985.
Rainbow Cottage Latch Key Program Tel: 812-547-6414. Susan Hughes, Supvr. Total Staff 5; Total Assisted 60.
Martins Cloak, Siberia. Tel: 812-357-5533. Food Pantry. Total Staff 1.
Matrix Lifeline Tel: 812-836-2587. Assistance to mothers and their children. Total Staff 1.

TERRE HAUTE. *Catholic Charities of Terre Haute*, Corporate Square Annex, 2931 Ohio Blvd., 47803. Tel: 812-232-1447; Fax: 812-232-1447. Email: cath.char@verizon.net. Web: www.abcs.com/ryveshall/thcc.html. John Etling, M.A., Dir. Total Staff 3.
Bethany House, 1402 Locust Ave., 47807. Tel: 812-232-4978. Marty Green, Mgr. Total Staff 3; Total Assisted 10,000.
Christmas House, 829 N. 14th St., 47808. Tel: 812-234-7242. Pat Armstrong, Dir. Total Staff 1; Total Assisted 3,855.
Household Exchange, 829 N. 14th St., 47807. Tel: 812-234-1132. Pat Armstrong, Dir. Total Staff 1; Total Assisted 1,644.
Ryves Hall Youth Center, 1356 Locust St., 47807. Tel: 812-235-1261. Jim Edwards, Youth Center Dir. Total Staff 6; Total Assisted 1,600.
Simeon House I (St. Patrick Parish), 1801 Poplar St., 47803. Tel: 812-232-6144. Harriett Johnson, Dir. Total Staff 4; Total Assisted 175.
Terre Haute Catholic Charities Foodbank, 1356 Locust St., 47807. Tel: 812-232-1447. Pat Etling, Dir. Total Staff 4; Total Assisted 80,000.

[N] CATHOLIC YOUTH ORGANIZATIONS

INDIANAPOLIS. *Catholic Youth Organization*, Related Ministries, 580 E. Stevens St., 46203. Tel: 317-632-9311. Web: www.cyoarchindy.org. Mr. Edward J. Tinder, Dir.; Mr. Gerald R. Ross, Asst. Dir.
Monsignor Downey Athletic Field
Perkins & Raymond St., 46203.

NASHVILLE. *C.Y.O. Camp Rancho Framasa*, 2230 N. Clay Lick Rd., 47448-4641. Tel: 888-998-2839; Fax: 812-988-4842. Email: cyocamp@aol.com. Web: www.members.aol.com/cyocamp. Mr. Kevin Sullivan, Camp Dir.

[O] CAMPUS MINISTRIES

INDIANAPOLIS. *Butler University c/o St. Thomas Aquinas Parish*, 4625 N. Kenwood, 46208. Tel: 317-253-1461. Rev. William G. Munshower.
Indiana University-Purdue University at Indianapolis c/o SS. Peter & Paul Cathedral, 1347 N. Meridian, 46202. Tel: 317-634-4519. *c/o Holy Trinity Parish*, 2618 W. St. Clair St., 46222. Tel: 317-631-2939. Rev. Kenneth Taylor.

BLOOMINGTON. *Indiana University, Bloomington c/o St. Paul Catholic Center*, 1413 E. 17th St., 47408. Tel: 812-339-5561. Rev. J. Daniel Atkins.

FRANKLIN. *Franklin College c/o St. Rose of Lima Parish*, 114 Lancelot Dr., 46131. Tel: 317-738-3929. Rev. Paul M. Shikany, J.C.L.

GREENCASTLE. *DePauw University c/o St. Paul the Apostle Parish*, 202 E. Washington St., 46135. Tel: 765-653-5678. Rev. Stephen Jarrell.

MADISON. *Hanover College c/o Prince of Peace Parish*, 415 E. Second St., 47250. Tel: 812-265-4166. Rev. John Meyer.

RICHMOND. *Earlham College c/o St. Andrew Parish*, 240 S. 6th St., 47374. Tel: 765-962-3902. Rev. Todd M. Riebe.

SHELBYVILLE. *University of Indianapolis c/o St. Joseph Parish*, 125 E. Broadway, 46176. Tel: 317-398-8227. Rev. Donald Quinn.

TERRE HAUTE. *Indiana State University/Rose-Hulman Institute c/o St. Joseph University Parish*, 113 Fifth St., 47807. Tel: 812-232-8088. Sr. Carmen Gillick, S.F.C.C., Pastoral Assoc. for Students.

[P] MISCELLANEOUS

INDIANAPOLIS. *Association of Contemplative Sisters*, c/o Carmelite Monastery, 2500 Cold Spring Rd., 46222. Tel: 317-926-5654; Fax: 317-926-1492. Email: jean@praythenews.com. Web: www.laycontemplative.org/ACS.htm. Deborah Gebhardt, Pres. Membership 425.
Christ Child Society of Indianapolis, 5825 Crittenden Ave., 46220. Tel: 317-257-8211. Email: jodybruce1@hotmail.com. Jody Bruce, Pres.
Hispanic Education Center Sponsored by the Sisters of Providence, Saint Mary-of-the-Woods. Tel: 317-634-5022; Fax: 317-535-0442. *Sisters of Providence General Administration*, St. Mary-of-the-Woods, 47876-1089.
580 E. Stevens St., 46203-1740. Tel: 317-634-5022; Fax: 317-634-0442. Email: hecindy@iquest.net. Total Staff 10; Total Assisted 5,000.

Society of St. Vincent de Paul, Archdiocesan Council of Indianapolis, Inc., P.O. Box 19133, 46219. Tel: 317-805-4766; Fax: 317-805-4723. Web: www.web.net/stvdepaul/index.html. Mr. Jake Asher, Pres. Total Assisted 67,000.

SVSM, Inc., 2001 W. 86th St., 46260. Tel: 317-415-6042; Fax: 517-415-6051. Email: jbford@stvincent.org. Web: www.stvincent.org. Vincent Caponi, CEO, St. Vincent Health, Inc.

**St. Vincent Health, Inc.*, 2001 W. 86th St., 46260. Tel: 317-338-7000; Fax: 317-338-7005. Email: mocannon@stvincent.org. Web: www.stvincent.org. Vincent Caponi, CEO; Joseph B. Ford, Mgr. Finance & Contact Person.

BEECH GROVE. *Alverno Information Services*, 1300 Albany St., 46107. Tel: 317-532-7800; Fax: 317-532-7801. Email: don.keller@ssfhs.org. Web: www.alverno.org. Mr. William G. Laker, Vice Pres. & CIO. Sponsored by Sisters of St. Francis Health Services, Inc.

Alverno-Beech Grove Corp., 1600 Albany St., 46107. Tel: 317-783-8133; Fax: 317-782-6731. Mr. Robert J. Brody, Pres. & CEO.

Charitable Trust of the Monastery of Our Lady of Grace, 1402 Southern Ave., 46107-1197. Tel: 317-787-3287; Fax: 317-780-2368. Email: olgprioress@aol.com. Web: www.benedictine.com.
Legal Title: *Charitable Trust of the Monastery of Our Lady of Grace, Sisters of the Order of St. Benedict*

CLARKSVILLE. *New Albany Deanery-Catholic Youth Ministries*, 707 W. Hwy. 131, 47129. Tel: 812-945-2000; Fax: 812-945-2995. Email: nadcym@aye.net. Web: www.nadyouth.org.

GEORGETOWN. *Providence Self-Sufficiency Ministries, Inc.*, 8037 Unruh Dr., 47122-8759. Tel: 812-951-1878; Fax: 812-951-1659. Email: sbarannz@pssm.win.net. Web: www.pssm.org. Sr. Barbara Ann Zeller, Pres. Sponsored by The Sisters of Providence, Saint Mary-of-the-Woods Total Staff 229; Total Assisted 7,943.

MOUNT SAINT FRANCIS. *Mount Saint Francis Sanctuary, Inc., Marian College*, 3200 Cold Spring Rd., 46222. Tel: 812-923-8817; Fax: 812-923-0177. Samuel L. Smith, Pres.; Leo Messmer, Vice Pres.; Thomas A. Smith, O.F.M.Conv., Treas.; Rev. Leopold Keffler, O.F.M.Conv., Sec.

ST. MARY-OF-THE-WOODS. *Providence Health Care, Inc.*, 1 Sisters of Providence, Owen's Hall, 47876-1089. Tel: 812-535-3131; Fax: 812-535-4727. Email: rborntra@spsmw.org. Sponsored by the Sisters of Providence of Saint Mary-of-the-Woods.

SAINT MARY-OF-THE-WOODS. *Sisters of Providence Community Support Trust*, St. Mary-of-the-Woods. Tel: 812-535-4193; Fax: 812-535-4727. Sr. Rosemary Borntrager, S.P., Corp. Sec.

TERRE HAUTE. *St. Ann Community Outreach Services of Terre Haute*, 1436 Locust St., 47807. Tel: 812-232-6832. Email: StAnnChurch@aol.com. Sr. Constance Kramer, S.P., Dir.

[Q] CLOSED PARISHES, SCHOOLS AND OTHER INSTITUTIONS

INDIANAPOLIS. *Archives of the Archdiocese of Indianapolis*, 1400 N. Meridian St., 46202. Tel: 317-236-1429; Fax: 317-236-1406. Email: archives@archindy.org. Sacramental and other records may be found where indicated.
Closed Parishes and Missions:
Indianapolis:
Assumption (1894-1994), Merged with St. Anthony, where sacramental records are kept.
St. Bridget (1880-1994), Merged with SS. Peter & Paul, where sacramental records are kept.
St. Catherine of Siena (1909-1993), Merged with St. James and renamed Good Shepherd, where sacramental records are kept.
St. Francis de Sales (1881-1983), Merged with four neighboring parishes. Sacramental records are located in the archives.
St. James the Greater (1951-1993), Merged with St. Catherine and renamed Good Shepherd, where sacramental records are kept.
St. Joseph (1873-1949), Sacramental records kept at the new St. Joseph parish.
Acton:
St. John the Evangelist (1855-1936), Sacramental records are located in the archives.
Adyeville:
St. Jude Thaddeus (1889-1898),
Bainbridge:
St. Patrick (1865-1973),
Blanford:
Queen of the Most Holy Rosary (1917-1942),
Cannelton:
St. Patrick (1847-1902), Merged with St. Michael, Cannelton, where sacramental records are kept.
Carbon:
St. Joseph (1870-1970), Sacramental records are located in the archives.
Centenary:
St. Anthony (1917-1942),
China:
St. Anthony (1861-1993), Merged with Prince of Peace, Madison, where sacramental records are kept.
Columbus:
St. Columba (1963-1994), Merged with St. Bartholomew, Columbus, where sacramental records are kept.
Cypress Dale:
Sacred Heart (1868-1918),
Derby:
St. Mary (1824-1973), Sacramental records kept at St. Augustine, Leopold.
Diamond:
St. John Baptist (Greek Uniate Catholic) (1897-1926), Sacaramental records are located in the archives.
St. Mary (1897-1991), Sacramental records are located in the archives.
Dogwood:
St. Michael (1820-1928),
Dugger:
Our Lady of Perpetual Help (1911-1982), Sacramental records kept at St. Mary, Sullivan Co., Diocese of Evansville.
Ellsworth:
St. John (1910-1912),
Eureka:
Mattingly Chapel (1874-1886),
Fontanet:
St. Augustine (1891-1980), Sacramental records are located in the archives.
Hovey:
All Souls Chapel (1900-1915),
Indian Creek:
St. Columban (1848-1868),
Knightsville:
St. Patrick (1868-1890),
Laconia:
Sacred Heart of Mary (1854-1922),
Laurel:
St. Raphael (1869-1958), Sacramental records kept at St. Gabriel, Connersville.
Lexington:
Mother of God (1854-1941),
Locust Point:
St. Joachim (1888-1930),
Madison:
St. Mary (1851-1993), Merged with St. Patrick (1853-1993) and St. Michael (1837-1993) and renamed Prince of Peace, where sacramental records are kept.
Magnet:
Sacred Heart Sacramental recrods kept at St. Augustine, Leopold.
McCutcheonville:
St. Patrick (1842-1881),
Mecca:
St. Mary (1905-1936),
Milltown:
St. Joseph (1855-1974), Sacramental records kept at St. Joseph, Crawford Co..
Montezuma:
Parke Co., Immaculate Conception (1867-2001) Sacramental records kept at St. Joseph, Rockville.
Mount Erin:
St. John Baptist (1852-1885),
Mount Pleasant:
St. Rose (1821-1883),
Nebraska:
St. Bridget (1845-1936),
New Albany:
Holy Trinity (1836-1975), Merged with St. Mary, New Albany, where sacramental records are kept.
Oak Forest:
Franklin Co., St. Cecilia of Rome (Formerly St. Philomena) (1844-2000) Sacramental records are kept at St. Mary of the Rock.
Rome:
St. Peter (1868-1885), Sacramental records are located in the archives.
St. Catherine
St. Catherine (1841-1871), Sacramental records are located in the archives.
St. James
St. James (1844-1850), Merged with St. Joseph, Perry Co. (1891-1968) and renamed St. Isidore, Perry Co., where sacramental records are kept.
St. Magdalen
St. Magdalen (1847-1941), Sacramental records kept at St. John, Osgood.
St. Paul
St. Paul (1859-1996), Sacramental records kept at St. Vincent, Shelby Co..
Perry Co.:
St. Peter
St. Rose
St. Rose 1840-1903), Merged with St. Thomas, Knox Co., Diocese of Evansville, where sacramental records are kept.
Salem
St. Mary (1871-1902),
Scipio:
St. Patrick (1841-1958), Sacramental records are located in the archives.
Shelburn:
St. Ann (1909-1978), Sacramental records kept at St. Mary, Sullivan, Diocese of Evansville.
Shirley:
Mother of God (1900-1920), Sacramental records are located in the archives.
Taylorsville (Selvin):
St. Thomas (1845-1875),
Valley Mills:
St. John the Baptist (1855-1903), Sacramental records are located in the archives.
West Baden Springs:
Our Lady of Lourdes (1900-1929),
Willow Valley:
St. Stephen (1906-1944),
Closed Parish Grade Schools:
Indianapolis:
Assumption, All Saints Catholic School, 75 N. Belleview Pl., 46222. Tel: 317-636-3739.
Cathedral, Holy Cross Central School, 125 N. Oriental St., 46201. Tel: 317-638-9068.
Holy Rosary, Holy Rosary Rectory, 520 Stevens St., 46203. Tel: 317-636-4478.
Holy Trinity, All Saints Catholic School, 75 N. Belleview Pl., 46222. Tel: 317-636-3739.
Sacred Heart, Sacred Heart Rectory, 1530 Union St., 46225. Tel: 317-638-5551.
St. Ann, St. Ann Rectory, 2862 S. Holt Rd., 46241. Tel: 317-244-3750.
St. Anthony, All Saints Catholic School, 75 N. Belleview Pl., 46222. Tel: 317-636-3739.
St. Bernadette
St. Bridget Sacramental records are located in the archives.
St. Catherine, Central Catholic School, 1155 Cameron St., 46203. Tel: 317-783-7759.
St. Francis de Sales Sacramental records are located in the archives.
St. James the Greater, Central Catholic School, 1155 Cameron St., 46203. Tel: 317-783-7759.
St. Joseph, All Saints Catholic School, 75 N. Belleview Pl., 46222. Tel: 317-636-3739.
St. Mary, Holy Cross Central School, 125 N. Oriental St., 46201. Tel: 317-638-9068.
St. Patrick, Central Catholic School, 1155 Cameron St., 46203. Tel: 317-783-7759.
Madison:
St. Mary; St. Michael, Pope John XXIII Grade School, 221 State St., Madison, 47250. Tel: 812-273-3957.
Morris:
St. Anthony, St. Anthony Rectory, P.O. Box 3, Morris, 47033. Tel: 812-934-6218.
New Castle:
St. Anne, St. Anne Rectory, 102 N. 19th St., New Castle, 47362. Tel: 765-529-0933.
Richmond:
Holy Family; St. Andrew; St. Mary, Elizabeth Ann Seton School, 801 W. Main St., Richmond, 47374. Tel: 765-962-4877.
Terre Haute:
St. Ann; St. Joseph, Student Services, Vigo County School Corp., P.O. Box 3703, Terre Haute, 47803. Tel: 812-462-4224.
St. Benedict, Terre Haute. Sacramental records are located in the archives.
St. Margaret Mary, St. Margaret Mary Rectory, 2405 S. Seventh St., Terre Haute, 47802. Tel: 812-232-3512.
Closed High Schools and Academies.
Brute Latin School School records are located in the archives.
Chartrand; Kennedy; Sacred Heart, Roncalli High School, 3300 Prague Rd., 46227. Tel: 317-787-8277.
St. John; St. Agnes; Ladywood; Ladywood / St. Agnes Academies, Sisters of Providence, Records Office - Owens Hall, St. Mary-of-the-Woods, 47876. Tel: 812-535-3131.
St. Mary Academy, Registrar, Franciscan Motherhouse, Oldenburg, 47036. Tel: 812-934-2475.
Our Lady of Grace Academy, Our Lady of Grace Monastery, 1402 Southern Ave., Beech Grove, 46107. Tel: 317-787-3287.
Terre Haute:
Central Catholic High School for Girls
St. Patrick High School for Girls
St. Vincent Academy Renamed St. Joseph Academy.
Schulte High School, Student Services, Vigo County School Corp., P.O. Box 3703, Terre Haute, 47803. Tel: 812-462-4224.
Other Closed Institutions:
Indianapolis:
Sisters of the Good Shepherd Convent Sacramental records are located in the archives.
Angel Guardian School for Orphans Entrance records, 1924-1937, are located in the archives.
Marydale School For Girls Sacramental records,

1875-1953, are located in the archives. School records are locate in the archives of the Archdiocese of Indianapolis.

New Albany:

St. Edward Hospital, New Albany, Sisters of St. Francis of Perpetual Adoration (O.S.F.), Box 766, Mishawaka, 46546. Tel: 219-259-5427.

Terre Haute:

St. Anthony Hospital Baptismal records are located in the archives.

RELIGIOUS INSTITUTES OF MEN REPRESENTED IN THE ARCHDIOCESE

For further details refer to the corresponding bracketed number in the Religious Institutes of Men or Women section.

[0200]—*Benedictine Monks of St. Maur & St. Meinrad*—O.S.B.

[0600]—*Brothers of the Congregation of Holy Cross (Midwest & Eastern Provinces)*—C.S.C.

[0480]—*Conventual Franciscans* (Our Lady of Consolation Prov.)—O.F.M.Conv

[0520]—*Franciscan Friars (St. John the Baptist & Sacred Heart Province)*—O.F.M.

[0690]—*Jesuit Fathers and Brothers* (Chicago Prov.)—S.J.

[1065]—*Priestly Fraternity of Saint Peter*—F.S.S.P.

[0420]—*Society of the Divine Word* (Chicago Province)—S.V.D.

[1060]—*Society of the Precious Blood* Cincinnati, Province—C.PP.S.

RELIGIOUS INSTITUTES OF WOMEN REPRESENTED IN THE ARCHDIOCESE

[0230]—*Benedictine Sisters of Pontifical Jurisdiction* (Ferdinand, IN)—O.S.B.

[]—*Congreation of Divine Providence (CDP)* Melbourne, Ky—CDP

[1920]—*Congregation of the Sisters of the Holy Cross*—C.S.C.

[1730]—*Congregation of the Sisters of the Third Order of St. Francis, Oldenburg, IN*—O.S.F.

[0760]—*Daughters of Charity of St. Vincent De Paul* (Evansville, IN)—D.C.

[0420]—*Discalced Carmelite Nuns*—O.C.D.

[1070-03]—*Dominican Sisters*—O.P.

[]—*Franciscan Sisters of the Immaculate Heart of Mary* (Kerala, India)—F.I.H.

[2340]—*Little Sisters of the Poor* (Baltimore, MD)—L.S.P.

[2710]—*Missionaries of Charity*—M.C.

[2820]—*Missionary Sisters of Our Lady of Africa* (American Headquarters, Winooski, VT)—M.S.O.L.A.

[]—*Poor Handmaids of Jesus Christ* (Donaldson, IN)—(PHJC)

[]—*Servants of the Gospel of Life*—S.G.L.

[0440]—*Sisters of Charity of Cincinnati, Ohio* (Central Region)—S.C.

[0500]—*Sisters of Charity of Nazareth* (Nazareth, KY)—S.C.N.

[]—*Sisters of Loretto at the Foot of the Cross* Nerinx, KY—S.L.

[3360]—*Sisters of Providence of Saint Mary-of-the-Woods, IN*—S.P.

[]—*Sisters of St. Benedict of Our Lady of Grace Monastery* (Beech Grove, IN)—O.S.B.

[1620]—*Sisters of St. Francis of Millvale*—O.S.F.

[1640]—*Sisters of St. Francis of Perpetual Adoration*—O.S.F.

[3840]—*Sisters of St. Joseph Carondelet* (St. Louis, MO)—C.S.J.

[]—*Sisters of St. Joseph of Tipton* (Tipton, IN)—C.S.J.

[]—*Sisters Of The Immaculate Heart Of Mary Reparatrix* Kisubi, Uganda—(IHMR)

[1720]—*Sisters of the Third Order Regular of St. Francis of the Congregation of Our Lady of Lourdes*—O.S.F.

[4120-03]—*Ursuline Nuns of the Congregation of Paris*—O.S.U.

ARCHDIOCESAN CEMETERIES

INDIANAPOLIS. *Catholic Cemeteries*, 9001 Haverstick Rd., 46240.

Indianapolis Deanery

Holy Cross

St. Joseph

Calvary

Our Lady of Peace, 46240.

St. Malachy, Brownsburg.

St. Malachy, Pittsboro.

BATESVILLE. *Batesville Deanery*

St. Mary, Greensburg.

St. John, Osgood.

St. Charles, Milan.

St. Maurice, Napoleon.

BLOOMINGTON. *Bloomington Deanery*

Catholic, Martinsville.

CONNERSVILLE. *Connersville Deanery*

St. Raphael, Laurel.

St. Michael, Brookville.

Holy Family, Oldenburg.

Holy Family Shrine Oldenburg.

Cemetery North, Brookville.

Calvary, Rushville.

St. Bridget, Liberty.

St. Mary, Richmond.

NEW ALBANY. *New Albany Deanery*

St. Joseph, Corydon.

St. Michael, Dogwood.

St. Peter, Taylor Twp.

Cemetery South West, Bradford.

St. Bernard, Frenchtown.

St. Joachim, Locust Point.

St. Anthony, Jeffersonville.

Queen of Heaven

St. Michael

SEYMOUR. *Seymour Deanery*

St. Ambrose

St. Mary, North Vernon.

St. Catherine

Old St. James

St. Joseph

St. Patrick

St. Magdalen

TELL CITY. *Tell City Deanery*

St. Joseph, St. Croix.

St. Croix, St. Croix. (Cemetery on original parish site.)

St. Meinrad, St. Meinrad.

St. Paul

St. Peter, Cannelton.

TERRE HAUTE. *Terre Haute Deanery*

Catholic, Brazil.

Calvary

St. Joseph

St. Mary of the Woods

NECROLOGY

† Minta, Rev. Msgr. John J. (Retired)—Died Aug. 31, 2003

† Happel, Stephen P., Washington, DC The Catholic University of America—Died Oct. 4, 2003

† Hubler, Tony, Navilleton, IN St. Mary—Died Oct. 14, 2003

† Kelly, Patrick J., Indianapolis, IN St. Andrew the Apostle—Died Dec. 30, 2003

† Shappard, Christopher, St. Meinrad Archabbey St. Meinrad, IN—Died 2003

Diocese of Jackson

(Dioecesis Jacksoniensis)

Most Reverend

JOSEPH LATINO

Bishop of Jackson; ordained May 25, 1963; appointed Bishop of Jackson January 3, 2003; consecrated March 7, 2003. *P.O. Box 2248, Jackson, MS 39225-2248.*

Most Reverend

WILLIAM R. HOUCK, D.D.

Bishop Emeritus of Jackson; ordained May 19, 1951; appointed Auxiliary Bishop of Jackson and Titular Bishop of Allessano on March 28, 1979; consecrated May 27, 1979; appointed Bishop of Jackson April 24, 1984; installed June 5, 1984; retired January 3, 2003. *Catholic Extension Society*, 150 S. Wacker Dr., 20th Fl., Chicago, IL 60606-4200.

Chancery Office: 237 E. Amite St., P.O. Box 2248, Jackson, MS 39225-2248. Tel: 601-969-1880; Fax: 601-960-8455.

Web: www.jacksondiocese.org

Email: chancery@jacksondiocese.org

Square Miles 37,643.

Established July 28, 1837 as Diocese of Natchez. Name changed to Dioceseof Natchez-Jackson, March 7, 1957. Name changed to Diocese of Jackson, June 6, 1977.

Comprises 65 Counties in the State of Mississippi, namely: Adams, Alcorn,Amite, Attala, Benton, Bolivar, Calhoun, Carroll, Chickasaw, Choctaw, Claiborne, Clarke, Clay, Coahoma, Copiah, De Soto, Franklin, Grenada, Hinds, Holmes, Humphreys, Issaquena, Itawamba, Jasper, Jefferson, Kemper, Lafayette, Lauderdale, Leake, Lee, Leflore, Lincoln, Lowndes, Madison, Marshall, Monroe, Montgomery, Neshoba, Newton, Noxubee, Oktibbeha, Panola, Pike, Pontotoc, Prentiss, Quitman, Rankin, Scott, Sharkey, Simpson, Smith, Sunflower, Tallahatchie, Tate, Tippah, Tishomingo, Tunica, Union, Warren, Washington, Webster, Wilkinson, Winston, Yalobusha and Yazoo.

Legal Title: "Catholic Diocese of Jackson".

STATISTICAL OVERVIEW

Personnel	
Bishop	1
Retired Bishops	1
Priests: Diocesan Active in Diocese	44
Priests: Diocesan Active Outside Diocese	3
Priests: Retired, Sick or Absent	15
Number of Diocesan Priests	62
Religious Priests in Diocese	29
Total Priests in Diocese	91
Ordinations:	
Diocesan Priests	2
Transitional Deacons	1
Permanent Deacons in Diocese	6
Total Brothers	13
Total Sisters	212
Parishes	
Parishes	74
With Resident Pastor:	
Resident Diocesan Priests	122
Resident Religious Priests	3
Without Resident Pastor:	
Administered by Priests	11
Administered by Deacons	1
Administered by Professed Religious Men	1
Administered by Religious Women	4
Administered by Lay People	4
Missions	29
Professional Ministry Personnel:	
Brothers	4
Sisters	27
Lay Ministers	27
Welfare	
Catholic Hospitals	1
Total Assisted	96,616
Health Care Centers	2
Total Assisted	9,458
Homes for the Aged	1
Total Assisted	225
Residential Care of Children	2
Total Assisted	315
Day Care Centers	2
Total Assisted	435
Specialized Homes	7
Total Assisted	2,001
Special Centers for Social Services	5
Total Assisted	16,890
Residential Care of Disabled	3
Total Assisted	60
Other Institutions	3
Total Assisted	75
Educational	
Diocesan Students in Other Seminaries	4
Total Seminarians	4
Colleges and Universities	1
Total Students	42
High Schools, Diocesan and Parish	4
Total Students	772
Elementary Schools, Diocesan and Parish	15
Total Students	3,872
Catechesis/Religious Education:	
High School Students	8,166
Elementary Students	24,208
Total Students under Catholic Instruction	37,064
Teachers in the Diocese:	
Brothers	2
Sisters	15
Lay Teachers	312
Vital Statistics	
Receptions into the Church:	
Infant Baptism Totals	927
Adult Baptism Totals	132
Received into Full Communion	276
First Communions	653
Confirmations	374
Marriages:	
Catholic	88
Interfaith	183
Total Marriages	271
Deaths	440
Total Catholic Population	51,992
Total Population	1,980,025

Former Bishops—Rt. Revs. JOHN J. CHANCHE, S.S., D.D., consecrated March 14, 1841; died July 22, 1852; J. O. VAN DE VELDE, S.J., D.D., transferred to from Chicago, July 29, 1853; died Nov. 13, 1855; Most Revs. WILLIAM HENRY ELDER, D.D., consecrated May 3, 1857; transferred to Cincinnati, 1880; died Oct. 31, 1904; FRANCIS JANSSENS, D.D., consecrated May 1, 1881; transferred to New Orleans, Aug. 7, 1888; died June 9, 1897; Rt. Revs. THOMAS HESLIN, D.D., consecrated June 18, 1889; died Feb. 22, 1911; JOHN EDWARD GUNN, S.M., D.D., consecrated Aug. 29, 1911; died Feb. 19, 1924; Most Revs. RICHARD OLIVER GEROW, LL.D., S.T.D. (Retired), ord. June 5, 1909; appt. June 25, 1924; consecrated Oct. 15, 1924; retired Dec. 2, 1967; died Dec. 20, 1976; JOSEPH B. BRUNINI, D.D., LL.D., J.C.D. (Retired), ord. Dec. 5, 1933; consecrated Jan. 29, 1957; appt. Bishop, Dec. 2, 1967; installed Jan. 29, 1968; retired Jan. 24, 1984; died Jan. 7, 1996; WILLIAM R. HOUCK, D.D. (Retired), 237 E. Amite St., P.O. Box 2248, Jackson, 39225-2248. Tel: 601-969-1880; Fax: 601-960-8455 ord. May 19, 1951; appt. Auxiliary Bishop of Jackson and Titular Bishop of Allessano on March 28, 1979; consecrated May 27, 1979; appt. Bishop of Jackson April 24, 1984; installed June 5, 1984; retired Jan. 3, 2003; The telephone number for all Diocesan Offices is 601-969-1880, unless otherwise listed. Office Hours: 8:30-4:30.; JOSEPH LATINO, 237 E. Amite St., P.O. Box 2248, Jackson, 39225-2248.

Office of Vicar General—Rev. Msgr. MICHAEL FLANNERY, J.C.L.; Rev. FRANCIS J. COSGROVE.

Department of Ecclesiastical Affairs—

Chancellor—Rev. Msgr. MICHAEL FLANNERY, J.C.L., 237 E. Amite St., P.O. Box 2248, Jackson, 39225-2248.

Vice Chancellor—Rev. KEVIN SLATTERY, J.C.L.

Office of Child Protection—Mrs. VICKIE CAROLLO.

Director of Vocations—Rev. KENT BOWLDS.

Director of Permanent Diaconate—Deacon KEVIN J. MCCARTHY.

Propagation of the Faith—Rev. BRIAN KASKIE, Dir., St. Peter Cathedral, P.O. Box 57, Jackson, 39205-0057. Tel: 601-969-3125.

Archivist—JO ANN BOMAR.

Judicial Vicar—Rev. KEVIN SLATTERY, J.C.L.

Engaged Encounter—Rev. KEVIN SLATTERY, J.C.L., Dir.

Ecumenism—Rev. RICHARD SMITH, St. Michael, P.O. Box 388, Forest, 39074-0388. Tel: 601-469-1916.

Promoters of Justice—Rev. THOMAS MCGING, J.C.L.

Continuing Formation Committee—Revs. KEVIN SLATTERY, J.C.L., Coord.; DAVID O'CONNOR; ERIC GRONER, S.V.D.; THOMAS LALOR; JEFFREY WALDREP; MATTHEW P. SIMMONS; Rev. Msgr. MICHAEL FLANNERY, J.C.L., Ex Officio.

Defenders of the Bond—Rev. Msgr. MICHAEL FLANNERY, J.C.L.; Revs. JOHN BOHN; JEFFREY WALDREP; DANIEL GALLAGHER; THOMAS MCGING, J.C.L. at the 2nd Instance; XAVIER COLAVECHIO, O.Praem., S.T.L.; RICARDO M. PHIPPS; Sr. JOYCE HOBEN, S.N.D.N., J.C.L.

Notaries—Rev. ROBERT OLIVIER; MARYBETH RABERT; JUDY CANNON.

Diocesan Judges—Revs. PATRICK FARRELL; KEVIN SLATTERY, J.C.L.

Approved Advocate and Auditors—Revs. CHARLES BUCCIANTINI; THOMAS DELANEY; DON DERIVAUX, S.T.L.; ROBERT GOODYEAR, S.T.; BRIAN KASKIE; TIMOTHY MURPHY, M.A.; MICHAEL O'BRIEN.

Priests' Council—Most Rev. JOSEPH LATINO, Pres.; Revs. BRIAN KASKIE, Chm.; ERIC GRONER, S.V.D., Vice Chm.; KENT BOWLDS, Sec.; KEVIN SLATTERY, J.C.L., Treas.; WALTER BROWN; BRIAN CARROLL; Rev. Msgr. MICHAEL FLANNERY, J.C.L.; Revs. THOMAS DELANEY; PATRICK FARRELL; JOHN

McSpiritt, S.T.; Patrick Noonan; Henry Shelton; Elvin Sunds.

Diocesan Consultors—Most Rev. Joseph Latino, Pres.; Rev. Msgr. Michael Flannery, J.C.L.; Revs. Brian Carroll; Francis Cosgrove; Kevin Slattery, J.C.L.; Elvin Sunds; Patrick Farrell.

Association of Priests—Most Revs. Joseph Latino, Co-Chm.; Thomas J. Rodi, Co-Chm.; Revs. Thomas Conway, Pres.; Charles Bucciantini, Sec., Treas. & Pres.-Elect. Trustees: Revs. Patrick Farrell; George Murphy; Ken Ramon-Landry; Elvin Sunds.

Diocesan Pastoral Council—Most Rev. Joseph Latino, Pres.

Personnel Board—Rev. Msgr. Michael Flannery, J.C.L., Personnel Dir.; Revs. Patrick Curley; Michael O'Brien; Patrick Noonan; John Bohn.

Department of Administration & Finance—William P. Dunning, Dir., Admin. Affairs, 237 E. Amite St., P.O. Box 2248, Jackson, 39225-2248.

Department of Stewardship - Development—Mr. George Roman, Dir.

Catholic Foundation—Mr. George Roman, Dir., 237 E. Amite St., P.O. Box 2248, Jackson, 39225-2248.

Department of Catholic Charities and Community Services—

Catholic Charities, Inc.—Linda Raff, Dir., 530 George St., P.O. Box 2248, Jackson, 39225-2248. Tel: 601-355-8634; Fax: 601-960-8493.

Parish-Based Ministries—Sr. Donna Gunn, C.S.J., Dir. Parish Social Ministry. Tel: 601-355-8634; Mrs. Louise Dillon, Dir. Family Ministry.

Peace and Justice—Linda Raff, Dir., P.O. Box 2248, Jackson, 39225-2248.

Victim Assistance Coordinator—Linda Raff. Tel: 601-355-8634. Email: linda.raff@catholiccharitiesjackson.org.

Department of Educational Services—Sr. Deborah Hughes, S.S.J., Dir., 237 E. Amite St., P.O. Box 2248, Jackson, 39225-2248.

Superintendent of Schools—Sr. Deborah Hughes, S.S.J.

Assistant Superintendent—Ms. Catherine D. Cook.

Director of Religious Education—Mr. John Valenti.

Director of Spring Hill Theology Program—Mr. John Valenti.

Holy Childhood Pontifical Association—Ms. Catherine D. Cook, Dir.

Early Child Development, Health and Education Projects—Sr. Deborah Hughes, S.S.J.

Department of Evangelization—Miss Mary Woodward, Dir.

Charismatic Renewal—Rev. William Henry.

Cursillo Movement—Rev. Daniel Gallagher, Spiritual Dir.

Youth Ministry—Mrs. Molly McCarthy, Diocesan Dir.

Campus Ministry—Sr. Sharon Glumb, S.L.W., Dir.

Parish Pastoral Councils—Miss Mary Woodward, Dir.

"Mississippi Catholic"—Janna Avalon, Editor.

Black Catholic Ministry—Joyce Hart, Dir.

Hispanic Ministry—Bro. Theodore Dausch, C.F.C., Dir.

CLERGY, PARISHES, MISSIONS AND PAROCHIAL SCHOOLS

CITY OF JACKSON
(Hinds County)

1—St. Peter Cathedral (1846), Rev. Brian Kaskie, Rector. In Res., Rev. Msgr. Michael Flannery; Rev. Daniel Gallagher.
Res.: 123 N. West St., P.O. Box 57, 39205-0057. Tel: 601-969-3125; Fax: 601-969-3130.

2—Christ the King (1945), Rev. Richard P. Chiles, O.Praem.
Res.: 2303 J.R. Lynch St., 39209. Tel: 601-948-8867.
School—Preschool and Montessori, Tel: 601-352-5441; Fax: 601-352-5136. Mrs. Janie Paige, Dir. Students 132.

3—Holy Family (1957), Revs. Edward Balser (Retired); Michael O'Brien; Kent Bowlds.
Church: 820 Forest Ave., 39206-3299. Tel: 601-362-1888.

4—Holy Ghost (1908), Rev. Ryszard Kalinowski, S.V.D.; Deacon Sam Baker.
Res.: 1151 Cloister St., 39202. Tel: 601-353-1339; Fax: 601-353-9607.

5—St. Mary (1948), Rev. Richard P. Chiles, O.Praem.
Res.: 653 Claiborne Ave., 39209. Tel: 601-353-2292; Fax: 601-944-1606.
School—Tel: 601-353-7357; Fax: 601-352-5164. Ms. Pamela Osborne, Prin. Lay Teachers 7; Students 152.

6—St. Richard (1953), Revs. Michael O'Brien; Kent Bowlds. In Res., Rev. Msgr. Michael Glynn (Retired).
Res.: 1242 Lynnwood Dr., P.O. Box 16547, 39236. Tel: 601-366-2335; Fax: 601-366-0438.
School—Tel: 601-366-1157; Fax: 601-366-4344. Lay Teachers 35; Students 497.

7—St. Therese (1955), Rev. Anthony Quyet.
Church: 309 McDowell Rd., P.O. Box 8642, 39284-8642. Tel: 601-372-4481; Fax: 601-376-0094.
Res.: 3111 Tynes Dr., 39272. Tel: 601-372-3441.
School—Tel: 601-372-3323; Fax: 601-372-3365. Lay Teachers 10; Students 101.

OUTSIDE THE CITY OF JACKSON

Aberdeen, Monroe Co., St. Francis of Assisi (1977), Rev. Timothy Murphy, G.H.M.; Bro. Terry O'Rourke, G.H.M., Outreach Worker; Susan Sweet, Pastoral Assoc.
Res.: 104 S. James St., P.O. Box 134, 39730-0134. Tel: 662-369-2897.
Mission—Immaculate Heart of Mary (1942), P.O. Box 309, Houston, Chickasaw Co. 38851. Tel: 662-456-5450. Sisters Rosemary Empen, O.P., Mission Coord.; Pat Sullivan, O.P., Mission Coord.
Mission—St. Theresa 116 N. Fleming St., Okolona, Chickasaw Co. 38860. Tel: 662-447-3008. Sr. Elizabeth Brown, C.S.J., Mission Coord.

Ackerman, Choctaw Co., St. Mark (2001), Sr. Alies Therese.
Mailing Address: P.O. Box 1293, 38935. Tel: 662-285-3347.

Amory, Monroe Co., St. Helen (1977), Sisters Florita Rodman, C.D.P., Resident Pastoral Min.; Mary Agatha Ruhe, C.D.P., Pastoral Assoc.
Res.: 401 Eighth Ave. S., P.O. Box 97, 38821-0097. Tel: 662-256-8392; Fax: 662-256-8392.
Mission—Christ the King 100 E. Main St., Fulton, Itawamba Co. 38843-1207. Tel: 662-862-2239; Fax: 662-862-2239. Mr. Jerry Woods, Mission Coord.

Batesville, Panola Co., St. Mary (1960), Rev. Samuel Messina.
Res.: P.O. Box 569, 38606-0569. Tel: 662-563-2273; Fax: 662-563-9788. Sharon Hodge, D.R.E.
Catechesis/Religious Program—Tel: 662-563-1197. Students 27.
Mission—St. John the Baptist 110 N. Main St., Sardis, Panola Co. 38666.

Belzoni, Humphreys Co., All Saints (1953), Rev. James O'Riordan.
Res.: 200 Bowles St., 39038-3602. Tel: 662-247-1408; Fax: 662-247-1504.
Mission—Our Mother of Mercy 119 Jefferson St., Anguilla, Sharkey Co. 38721. Tel: 662-873-2712.

Booneville, Prentiss Co., St. Francis of Assisi (1962), Rev. Thomas L. Burns, S.C.J., Admin.; Sr. Dorothy Pashuta, C.S.J., Pastoral Min.
Res.: P.O. Box 654, 38829. Tel: 662-728-7509; Fax: 662-728-7503.
Mission—St. Mary P.O. Box 651, Iuka, Tishomingo Co. 38852. Tel: 662-423-9358; Fax: 662-423-9358.

Brandon, Rankin Co., St. Paul (1978), Revs. Brian Carroll; Patrick Smith; Deacon Frank Agosta.
Church: 5971 Hwy. 25, 39047. Tel: 601-992-9547; Fax: 601-992-9972.
Res.: 108 Twin Oaks Dr., 39047. Tel: 601-992-3222; Fax: 601-992-9972.
School—Learning Center, Tel: 601-992-2876; Fax: 601-992-8741. Ellen Treadaway, Dir. Students 102.

Brookhaven, Lincoln Co., St. Francis (1887), Rev. Patrick Noonan.
Res.: 227 E. Cherokee St., P.O. Box 196, 39602. Tel: 601-833-1799; Fax: 601-833-7756.
Catechesis/Religious Program—Tel: 601-833-2709. Christy Sims, D.R.E. Students 84.
Mission—St. Ann Meadville, Franklin Co.

Bruce, Calhoun Co., St. Luke the Evangelist (1997), Sr. Mary Jean Morris, O.S.F., Mission Coord.
Church: 209 W. Calhoun St., P.O. Box 230, 38915-0230. Tel: 662-983-4600; Fax: 662-983-4600.

Camden, Madison Co., Immaculate Conception (1850), Unassigned. In Res., Bros. Finbarr Ray, S.T.; Michael Lobo, S.T.
Res.: 1363 Hwy. 17, 39045. Tel: 662-468-2354; Fax: 662-468-2488.

Canton, Madison Co.

1—Holy Child Jesus (1946), Rev. Joseph Dyer; Sr. Mary Ann Poeschl, R.S.M., Pastoral Assoc.
Res.: 315 Garrett St., P.O. Box 366, 39046. Tel: 601-859-2957; Fax: 601-859-5257.
School—Tel: 601-859-4168; Fax: 601-859-4140. Sr. Anita Henning, C.S.A., Prin. Sisters 2; Lay Teachers 6; Students 132.

2—Sacred Heart (1859), Rev. Joseph Dyer; Sr. Mary Ann Poeschl, R.S.M., Pastoral Assoc. In Res., Rev. Kevin Slattery, J.C.L.
Res.: 238 E. Center St., P.O. Box 361, 39046-0361. Tel: 601-859-3749; Fax: 601-859-5257.

Carthage, Leake Co., St. Anne (1954), Sr. Patricia Godri, S.C., Pastoral Min.; Rev. Kevin Slattery, J.C.L.
Res.: 207 Red Dog Rd., 39051. Tel: 601-267-7190; Fax: 601-267-8972.
Catechesis/Religious Program—Students 50.

Charleston, Tallahatchie Co., St. John (1973), Unassigned.
Church: 304 W. Cypress St., P.O. Box 30, 38921-0030. Tel: 662-647-3170.
Catechesis/Religious Program—Students 2.

Chatawa, Pike Co., St. Teresa (1868), Rev. Robert Dore.
Res.: P.O. Box 11, 39632-0011. Tel: 601-783-5931; Fax: 601-783-3984.
Mission—St. James Bay St., Magnolia, Pike Co. 39652.

Clarksdale, Coahoma Co.

1—St. Elizabeth (1891), Rev. Alfred L. Camp.
Res.: 130 Florence Ave., 38614-2720. Tel: 662-624-4301; Fax: 662-627-7856.
School—150 Florence Ave., 38614-2720. Tel: 662-624-4239; Fax: 662-624-2072. Sr. Carolyn Zionce, R.S.M., Prin. Lay Teachers 9; Students 128.

2—Immaculate Conception (1950), Rev. Alfred L. Camp.
Res.: 510 Ritchie Ave., 38614. Tel: 662-624-4029; Fax: 662-627-4867.

Cleveland, Bolivar Co., Our Lady of Victories (1924), Rev. Thomas Lalor.
Res.: 215 Bishop Rd., P.O. Box 1450, 38732-1450. Tel: 662-846-6273.
Station—Delta State University

Clinton, Hinds Co., Holy Savior (1966), Rev. Thomas McGing, J.C.L.
Church: 714 Lyndale St., P.O. Box 85, 39060-0085. Tel: 601-924-6344; Fax: 601-924-6344.
Res.: 129 Villa Way, 39056. Tel: 601-924-7228.
Catechesis/Religious Program—Tel: 601-853-7650; Fax: 601-750-8144. Maureen Griffin, D.R.E. Students 158.
Mission—Immaculate Conception Raymond, Hinds Co.

Columbus, Lowndes Co., Annunciation (1863), Rev. Gerard Hurley.
Res.: 808 College St., 39701. Tel: 662-328-2927; Fax: 662-329-8270.
School—223 N. Browder St., 39701. Tel: 662-328-4479; Fax: 662-328-0430. Lay Teachers 14; Students 156.

Corinth, Alcorn Co., St. James (1956), Rev. Thomas L. Burns, S.C.J.
Res.: 3187 Harper Rd., P.O. Box 660, 38835-0660. Tel: 662-287-1385.
Church: 3189 Harper Rd., 38835. Tel: 662-287-1051.
Catechesis/Religious Program—Linda Gunther, D.R.E. Students 32.

Crystal Springs, Copiah Co., St. John (1953), Rev. Jerry Mattingly.
Church: 219 E. Georgetown St., P.O. Box 167, 39059-0167. Tel: 601-892-1717; Fax: 601-892-0746.
Rectory—Rectory: 221 E. Georgetown St., 39059.
Catechesis/Religious Program—Celeste Caro, D.R.E. Students 35.
Mission—St. Martin Hazlehurst, Copiah Co.

Europa, Webster Co., St. John Neumann, Formerly St. John
Church: 201 W. Roane St., 39744. Tel: 662-258-7539. Sr. Alies Therese, Mission Coord.

Fayette, Jefferson Co., St. Anne (1969), Rev. Joseph McKinley, S.S.J. (NO), Admin.
Res.: 195 New Harriston Rd., P.O. Box 159, 39069. Tel: 601-445-5700; Fax: 601-442-6030.

Forest, Scott Co., St. Michael (1957), Rev. Richard Smith.
Res.: P.O. Box 388, 39074. Tel: 601-469-1916.
Catechesis/Religious Program—Students 43.
Mission—St. Anne 608 Decatur St., Newton, Newton Co. 39045.

Greenville, Washington Co.

1—St. Joseph (1868), Rev. Richard Somers.
Res.: 410 Main St., P.O. Box 1220, 38702-1220. Tel: 662-335-5251; Fax: 662-332-1178.
School—Our Lady of Lourdes, (Grades PreK-6) Tel: 662-334-3287; Fax: 662-332-9877. Sr. Marie Elizabeth Alspaugh, S.S.J., Prin. Sisters 2; Lay Teachers 23; Students 285.
School—Junior & Senior High School, Tel: 662-378-9711; Fax: 662-378-3496. Agnes Campbell, Prin. (7-12) Students 245.

2—Sacred Heart (1909), Rev. Eric Groner, S.V.D.
Res.: 560 E. Gloster St., 38701-3836. Tel: 662-332-0891; Fax: 662-332-0891.

Greenwood, LeFlore Co.

1—St. Francis of Assisi (1951), Rev. Gregory Plata, O.F.M.; Bros. Andrew Brophy, O.F.M.; Jose Gandarilla, O.F.M.
Res.: 2613 Hwy. 82 E., 38930-5966. Tel: 662-453-0623; Fax: 662-453-9060.
School—2607 Hwy. 82 E., 38930-5966. Tel: 662-453-9511; Fax: 662-453-9060. Sisters 7; Lay Teachers 9; Students 125.
Catechesis/Religious Program—Maxine Ford,

D.R.E.; Sr. Thelma, D.R.E. Students 34.
Convent—Franciscan Sisters of Christian Charity, 2603 Hwy. 82 E., 38930-5966. Tel: 662-453-1221; Fax: 662-453-9060.
2—IMMACULATE HEART OF MARY (1909), Rev. Thomas Delaney; Sr. Christiana Hofmann, S.C.N., Pastoral Min.
Res.: 511 W. Washington St., P.O. Box 313, 38935-0313. Tel: 662-453-3980; Fax: 662-453-3970.
Parish Center—310 Henderson St., 38935-0313. Tel: 662-453-9535.
GRENADA, GRENADA CO., ST. PETER (1943), Rev. John Brock.
Res.: 320 College Blvd., 38901-3808. Tel: 662-226-2490.
HERNANDO, DESOTO CO., HOLY SPIRIT (1961), Rev. James A. Cunniffe, S.C.J.
Res.: P.O. Box 424, 38632-0424. Tel: 662-429-7851; Fax: 662-429-7882.
Catechesis/Religious Program—Tel: 662-429-3467. Amanda Ready, D.R.E. Students 63.
HOLLY SPRINGS, MARSHALL CO., ST. JOSEPH (1857), Revs. John E. Young, S.C.J., Admin.; James R. Schifano, S.C.J., Assoc. Pastor.
Church: 305 Van Dorn Ave., P.O. Box 430, 38635-0430. Tel: 662-252-3138; Fax: 662-252-3138. Email: stjoseph@dixie-net.com.
School—Holy Family School, (Grades K-8), 395 N. West St., 38635-1922. Tel: 662-252-1612; Fax: 662-252-3694. Ketia Francis, Prin. Students 193.
School—Holy Family Early Childhood Center, Formerly Holy Family Child CareTel: 662-252-1366; Fax: 662-252-1576. Toy E. Harris, Dir. Students 70.
Catechesis/Religious Program—Kata Gysendorfer, D.R.E. Students 25.
INDIANOLA, SUNFLOWER CO.
1—ST. BENEDICT THE MOOR (1953), Rev. Sean Atkinson.
Res.: 403 Church Ave., P.O. Box 407, 38751. Tel: 662-887-4659.
2—IMMACULATE CONCEPTION (1955), Rev. Sean Atkinson.
Res.: Hwy. 448, P.O. Box 944, 38751-9665. Tel: 662-887-4659.
KOSCIUSKO, ATTALA CO., ST. THERESE (1956), Barbara A. Sturbaum, Ph.D., Resident Pastoral Min.
Res.: 108 Bell St., P.O. Box 628, 39090. Tel: 662-289-1193.
Catechesis/Religious Program—Students 17.
LELAND, WASHINGTON CO., ST. JAMES (1944), Rev. Charles Bucciantini.
Res.: 312 E. Third St., P.O. Box 352, 38756-0352. Tel: 662-686-7352; Fax: 662-686-7352.
Mission—Immaculate Conception Hwy. 12 E., Hollandale, Washington Co. 38748.
LEXINGTON, HOLMES CO., ST. THOMAS (1936), Rev. Gregory Plata, O.F.M., Admin.
Church: 200 Boulevard St., 39095. Tel: 662-453-0623; Fax: 662-453-9060.
Catechesis/Religious Program—Students 3.
Mission—Sacred Heart 304 Jones St., Winona, Montgomery Co. 38967. Tel: 662-453-0623. Rev. Gregory Plata, O.F.M.
LOUISVILLE, WINSTON CO., SACRED HEART (1966), Barbara A. Sturbaum, Ph.D., Resident Pastoral Min.
Res.: 410 Spring Ave., 39339. Tel: 662-773-6062.
Catechesis/Religious Program—Students 8.
MADISON, MADISON CO., ST. FRANCIS OF ASSISI (1983), Revs. Francis J. Cosgrove; Ricardo M. Phipps.
Office—4000 W. Tidewater Ln., 39110-8942. Tel: 601-856-5556; Fax: 601-856-2849.
School—Learning Center, Tel: 601-856-9494. Sr. Paula Blouin, S.S.N.D., Dir. Students 168.
Mission—St. Joseph 127 Church Rd., Gluckstadt, Madison Co. 39110. Tel: 601-856-2054; Fax: 601-859-6868. Sr. Jane Desaulniers, S.S.N.D., Pastoral Assoc.; Deacon Kevin J. McCarthy.
MAGEE, SIMPSON CO., ST. STEPHEN (1958), Rev. Robert Goodyear, S.T.
Res.: 594 Simpson Hwy. 149, P.O. Box 427, 39111-0427. Tel: 601-849-3237; Fax: 601-849-3398.
Catechesis/Religious Program—Alicia Keith, D.R.E. Tel: 601-849-3539; Eula Purvis, D.R.E. Tel: 601-847-2799. Students 41.
Mission—St. Paul Hwy. 35 S., Raleigh, Smith Co. 39153.
MCCOMB, PIKE CO., ST. ALPHONSUS (1876), Rev. William F. Henry.
Church: 509 Delaware Ave., P.O. Box 1105, 39648-1105. Tel: 601-684-5648; Fax: 601-684-1924.
School—Elementary and Preschool, 104 S. 5th St., 39648. Tel: 601-684-1843; Fax: 601-684-1831. Ms. Catherine Barrilleaux, Prin. Students 225.
MERIDIAN, LAUDERDALE CO.
1—ST. JOSEPH (1910), Rev. Elvin Sunds; Sr. Andre Burkhart, O.S.F., Pastoral Assoc.
Res.: 1914 18th Ave., P.O. Box 532, 39302-0532. Tel: 601-485-5349; Fax: 601-484-8953.
2—ST. PATRICK (1865), Revs. Elvin Sunds; Matthew P. Simmons; Matthew P. Simmons.
Church & Mailing Address: 2601 Davis St., P.O. Box 529, 39302. Tel: 601-693-1321; Fax: 601-484-8953.
Res.: 204-39th Ct., 39301. Tel: 601-693-2574.
School—Tel: 601-482-6044; Fax: 601-485-2762. Lay Teachers 9; Students 146.
Catechesis/Religious Program—Randy Munoz, D.R.E. Students 270.
Mission—Good Shepherd 1004 N. ArchUSA, Quitman, Clarke Co. 39355.
MOUND BAYOU, BOLIVAR CO., ST. GABRIEL (1949), Rev. Don Derivaux, Sacramental Min.; Bro. Pius Kamphefner, F.S.C., Resident Pastoral Min.
Res.: P.O. Box 53, 38762-0053. Tel: 662-741-2439.
NATCHEZ, ADAMS CO.
1—ASSUMPTION OF THE B.V.M. (1957), Rev. David O'Connor.
Res.: 10 Morgantown Rd., 39120-2788. Tel: 601-442-7250; Fax: 601-442-7250.
2—HOLY FAMILY (1891), Rev. Joseph McKinley, S.S.J. (NO), Admin.
Res.: 16 Orange Ave., 39120. Tel: 601-445-5700; Fax: 601-442-6030.
School—Tel: 601-442-3947; Fax: 601-442-3973. Sisters 2; Lay Teachers 9; Students 126.
Convent—Sisters of the Holy Spirit, 26 Orange Ave., 39120. Tel: 601-445-4257; Fax: 601-442-6030.
Mission—St. John the Baptist Cranfield, Adams Co.
3—ST. MARY BASILICA (1842), Rev. David O'Connor.
Res.: 107 S. Union St., P.O. Box 1044, 39121-1044. Tel: 601-445-5616; Fax: 601-445-9631.
School—Cathedral Unit School, Tel: 601-442-2531; Fax: 601-442-0960. See High Schools, Inter-Parochial under Institutions Located in the Diocese.
Catechesis/Religious Program—Mr. Mike Roboski, D.R.E. Students 10.
NEW ALBANY, UNION CO., ST. FRANCIS OF ASSISI (1949), Rev. Don Tranel.
Res.: 1507 S. Central Ave., P.O. Box 887, 38652-0887. Tel: 662-534-9205.
Church: 650 Hwy. 15 S., P.O. Box 887, 38652-0887. Tel: 662-534-4654; Fax: 662-534-4654.
Mission—St. Christopher S. Main St., P.O. Box 67, Pontotoc, Pontotoc Co. 38863-0067. Tel: 662-489-7749. In Res., Rev. Gerald Peterson (Retired), 107 N. Montgomery St., Pontotoc, 38864. Tel: 662-509-9591.
OLIVE BRANCH, DESOTO CO., QUEEN OF PEACE (1983), Rev. John Young, S.C.J.; Deacon Henry Rabin.
Res.: 8455 Germantown Rd., P.O. Box 65, 38654-0065. Tel: 662-895-5007; Fax: 662-895-5036.
Catechesis/Religious Program—Sr. Eileen Sheehy, D.R.E. Students 179.
OXFORD, LAFAYETTE CO., ST. JOHN (1943), Rev. Joseph Tonos; Deacon Theodore Klingen.
Church: 403 University Ave., 38655-4329. Tel: 662-234-6073; 662-234-1940 (Res.); Fax: 662-234-6079.
Catechesis/Religious Program—Fax: 662-234-6079. Mary Schoberg, I.H.M., D.R.E. Students 150.
PAULDING, JASPER CO., ST. MICHAEL (1843), Rev. Richard Smith.
Mailing Address: P.O. Box 388, Forest, 39074-0388. Tel: 601-469-1916.
Church: Star Rte., P.O. Box 15, 39348. Fax: 601-469-1916.
PEARL, RANKIN CO., ST. JUDE (1962), Rev. Martin Ruane.
(Rectory): 399 Barrow St., P.O. Box 5526, 39288-5525. Tel: 601-939-3181 (Office); 601-939-1863; Fax: 601-939-3160.
Station—Mississippi State Mental Hospital Whitfield.
PHILADELPHIA, NESHOBA CO.
1—HOLY CROSS (1860), Rev. Kenan Ryan, S.T.
Res.: 406 Wilson St., 39350-2906. Tel 601-656-1841; Fax 601-650-9098.
2—HOLY ROSARY (Tucker Community) (1884), Rev. David A. Hamm, S.T.
Res.: 10181 Holy Rosary Rd., P.O. Box 37, 39350. Tel: 601-656-2880; Fax: 601-656-2829.
Mission—St. Catherine 9857 Hwy. 489, Conehatta, Newton Co. 39057.
Mission—St. Theresa, Neshoba Co.
PORT GIBSON, CLAIBORNE CO., ST. JOSEPH (1849), Rev. Msgr. Thaddeus Harkins.
Res.: 411 Coffee St., P.O. Box 1012, 39150. Tel: 601-437-5790.
RIPLEY, TIPPAH CO., ST. MATTHEW (1997), Sr. Kate Regan, C.S.J., Mission Coord.
Res.: P.O. Box 452, 38663. Tel: 662-837-3529; Fax: 662-837-3529.
ROSEDALE, BOLIVAR CO., SACRED HEART (1938), Sisters Celia Evers, O.P., Pastoral Ministry Team; Catherine Leamy, S.N.J.M., Pastoral Ministry Team; Rev. Thomas Lalor, Pastoral Ministry Team.
Res.: P.O. Box 307, 38769. Tel: 662-759-6341.
SENATOBIA, TATE CO., ST. GREGORY THE GREAT (1978), Rev. Dermot Twomey, S.C.J.
Church: P.O. Box 129, 705 Strayhorn St., 38668-0129. Tel: 662-562-5318; Fax: 662-562-6649.
SHAW, BOLIVAR CO., ST. FRANCIS OF ASSISI (1949), Rev. Donald F. Derivaux, Sacramental Min. (Retired); Barbara Reginelli, Pastoral Assoc.
Res.: 303 Dean Blvd., P.O. Box 239, 38773. Tel: 662-754-5561; Fax: 662-754-5561.
SHELBY, BOLIVAR CO., ST. MARY (1905), Mrs. Bernadette Johnson, Pastoral Min.; Rev. Don Derivaux, Sacramental Min.
Res.: 700 Second St., P.O. Box 208, 38774-0208. Tel: 662-398-7964; Fax: 662-398-7892.
Station—Parchman State Penitentiary, Tel: 662-745-6611.
SOUTHAVEN, DESOTO CO., CHRIST THE KING (1974), Revs. Patrick J. LLoyd, S.C.J.; Edward J. Zemlik, S.C.J.; Deacon Lawrence M. Campbell.
Office: 785 Church Rd., West Southaven, 38671. Tel: 662-342-1073; Fax: 662-342-7733.
School—Sacred Heart Elementary School, 5150 Tchulahoma Rd., 38671. Tel: 662-349-0900; Fax: 662-349-0690.
STARKVILLE, OKTIBBEHA CO., ST. JOSEPH (1930), Rev. Jeffrey Waldrep.
Res.: 607 University Dr., 39759. Tel: 662-323-2257; Fax: 662-323-2258.
Catechesis/Religious Program—Geraldine Orgler, D.R.E. Students 168.
Mission—Corpus Christi P.O. Box 533, Macon, Noxubee Co. 39341.
Chaplaincy—Mississippi State University.
TUPELO, LEE CO., ST. JAMES (1908), Rev. Henry Shelton. In Res., Rev. August Langenkamp, S.V.D.
Res.: 820 Lakeshire Dr., P.O. Box 734, 38802-0734. Tel: 662-842-4881; Fax: 662-844-0327.
Catechesis/Religious Program—Dawn Steinman, D.R.E.; Mary Ann Plasensia, D.R.E. Students 400.
Mission—St. Thomas Aquinas Saltillo, Lee Co.
VICKSBURG, WARREN CO.
1—ST. MARY (1906), Rev. Charles Boykins, S.V.D.
Res.: 1512 Main St., 39183. Tel: 601-636-0115; Fax: 601-661-0677.
Catechesis/Religious Program—Tel: 601-638-3890; Fax: 601-638-3822. Leona Barnes Stringer, D.R.E. Students 43.
2—ST. MICHAEL (1966), Rev. Patrick Curley.
Res.: 100 St. Michael Pl., 39180-8246. Tel: 601-636-3445; Fax: 601-636-3534.
3—ST. PAUL (1848), Rev. Patrick Farrell.
Res.: 713 Crawford St., P.O. Box 646, 39180-0646. Tel: 601-636-0140; Fax: 601-638-5021.
High School—Vicksburg Catholic School, (Grades PreK-12) Tel: 601-636-2256; Fax: 601-631-0430. See High Schools, Inter-Parochial under Institutions Located in the Diocese.
WALLS, DESOTO CO., SACRED HEART (1944), Revs. Dermot J. Twomey, S.C.J.; Francis J. Burshnick, S.C.J.
Res.: 6473 Hwy. 161 N., P.O. Box 60, 38680-0060. Tel: 662-781-0450; Fax: 662-781-7766.
Convent—School Sisters of St. Francis, P.O. Box 237, 38680. Tel: 662-781-0807.
Mission—St. Anthony of Padua P.O. Box 2026, Tunica, Tunica Co. 38676. Tel: 662-363-0140; Fax: 662-363-3596.
WEST POINT, CLAY CO., IMMACULATE CONCEPTION (1965), Rev. John Vollor.
Res.: 617 E. Main, 39773-3007. Tel: 662-494-3486; Fax: 662-494-1829.
WOODVILLE, WILKINSON CO., ST. JOSEPH (1873), Rev. Walter W. Brown, Admin.
Res.: 338 Church St., P.O. Box 668, 39669. Tel: 601-888-3261; Fax: 601-888-3289.
Mission—St. Patrick Fort Adams, Wilkinson Co.
Mission—Holy Family P.O. Box 548, Gloster, Amite Co. 39638. Tel: 601-225-4171.
YAZOO CITY, YAZOO CO.
1—ST. FRANCIS (1940), Rev. Noel Prendergast.
Res.: 735 E. Powell St., 39194-4398. Tel: 662-746-1680.
2—ST. MARY (1851), Rev. Noel Prendergast.
Res.: 129 N. Washington St., P.O. Box 27, 39194-0027. Tel: 662-746-1680; Fax: 662-746-8407.

Chaplains of Public Institutions

JACKSON. *Institute for the Blind, Institute for the Deaf and Speech Impaired*. Rev. Michael O'Brien.
University of Mississippi Medical Center. Rev. Daniel Gallagher, Mrs. Molly McCarthy, Campus Min.
Veterans Administration Hospital. Rev. Daniel Gallagher.
MERIDIAN. *East Mississippi State Hospital*. Rev. Elvin Sunds.
PARCHMAN. *Mississippi State Penitentiary*. Sr. Catherine Leamy, S.N.J.M.
PEARL. *Rankin County Prison*. Rev. Martin Ruane.
SANATORIUM. *Boswell Retardation Center*. Rev. Robert Goodyear, S.T.
WHITFIELD. *Mississippi State Hospital*. Rev. Martin Ruane.

On Leave::

Revs.—
Bohn, John Joseph
Daniels, Jerrell Michael

On Duty Outside the Diocese:
Revs.—
Lopez, Jose
Niemira, Thomas
Schmit, Meyrl

Retired:
Most Rev.—
Houck, William R.
Rev. Msgrs.—
Glynn, Michael, St. Richard Church, P.O. Box 16547, 39236-6547.
Koury, Joseph A., 105 Abby Oak Dr., Clinton, 39056.
Revs.—
Balser, Edward
Carroll, James, 2544 Vintage Dr., Apt. 102, Cordova, TN 38016.
Corcoran, Frank, 948 Bellevue Pl., Apt. 102, 39202.
Derivaux, Donald F., 2440 Ballground Rd., Vicksburg, 39183.
Johnson, Howard, St. Joseph Seminary, 1200 Varnum St., N.E., Washington, DC 20017.
Loyacono, Charles, Williamsburg Retirement Community, 5445 Government St., Apt. 138, Baton Rouge, LA 70806.
Pentony, Liam, St. Peter's Church, Dromiskin, Co. Louth, Ireland.
Quinn, Peter, 674 Beach Blvd., Biloxi, 39530.
Rietti, John, 5180 Forest Ave., Bay St. Louis, 39520.
Spadini, Marian, Ave Maria Nursing Home, 2805 Charles Bryan Road, Memphis, TN 38134.

Permanent Deacons:
Agosta, Frank, St. Paul, Brandon
Babin, Henry, Queen of Peace, Olive Branch
Baker, Sam, Holy Ghost, Jackson
Campbell, Lawrence M., Christ the King, Southhaven
Klingen, Dr. Theodore, St. John, Oxford
McCarthy, Kevin J., St. Joseph Mission, Gluckstadt

INSTITUTIONS LOCATED IN THE DIOCESE

[A] HIGH SCHOOLS, INTER-PAROCHIAL

GREENVILLE. *St. Joseph Junior-Senior High School*, (Grades 7-12) , (Coed) , 700 Golf St., 38701. Tel: 601-378-9711; Fax: 601-378-3496. Ms. Agnes Campbell, Prin. Lay Teachers 24; Students 262.

MADISON. *St. Joseph Catholic School*, (Grades 7-12) , (Coed) , 308 New Mannsdale Rd., P.O. Box 2027, 39130-2027. Tel: 601-898-4800; Fax: 601-898-4689. Email: info@stjoebruins.com. Web: www.stjoebruins.com. Mr. William M. Heller, Prin. Brothers 2; Sisters 1; Lay Teachers 39; Students 384.

NATCHEZ. *Cathedral School*, (Grades PreK-12) , (Coed) , 701 Martin Luther King, Jr. St., 39120. Tel: 601-442-2531; Fax: 601-442-0960. Mr. Pat Sanguinetti, Prin. Lay Teachers 57; Students 666.

VICKSBURG. *Vicksburg Catholic School*, (Grades PreK-12) , (Coed) , 1900 Grove St., 39183. Tel: 601-636-2256; Fax: 601-631-0430. Email: pikul@vicksburgcatholic.org. Web: www.vicksburgcatholic.org. Mr. Peter Pikul, Prin. Lay Teachers 52; Students 652.

[B] ELEMENTARY SCHOOLS INTER-PAROCHIAL

SOUTHHAVEN. *Sacred Heart School*, (Grades PreK-8), 5150 Tchulahoma Rd., 38671. Tel: 662-349-0900; Fax: 662-349-0690. Email: lclark@shsm.org. Mrs. Laura Blackwell Clark, Prin. Sisters 3; Lay Teachers 16; Students 309.

[C] SPECIAL SCHOOLS

JACKSON. *St. Richard's Special Kids Program*, 10 Glen Eagles Dr., 39211. Tel: 601-956-4124; Fax: 601-956-8051. John Tracy, Coord. Lay Teachers 2; Aides 2; Students 17.

[D] GENERAL HOSPITALS

JACKSON. *St. Dominic-Jackson Memorial Hospital*, 969 Lakeland Dr., 39216. Tel: 601-200-2000; Fax: 601-200-6800. Email: charbarger@stdom.com. Web: www.stdom.com. Sr. Mary Trinita Eddington, Prioress; Mr. Claude W. Harbarger, Pres.; Rev. Robert Olivier, Resident Chap. Sisters of St. Dominic of Springfield, IL 9; Bed Capacity 571; Patients Assisted Annually 96,616.

GLENDORA. *Glendora Clinic (Satellite of Tutwiler Clinic)*, Gipson & Westbrook Sts., P.O. Box 189, 38928. Tel: 662-375-8878. Patients Assisted Annually 1,193.

JONESTOWN. *Jonestown Health Center (Satellite of Tutwiler Clinic)*, Formerly Jonestown Health Center (Satellite of DePorres Health Center), 280 2nd St., P.O. Box 79, 38639. Tel: 662-358-4377. Sr. Manette Durand, C.S.J., Dir.

TUTWILER. *Tutwiler Clinic, Inc.*, 205 Alma St., P.O. Box 462, 38963-0462. Tel: 662-345-8334; Fax: 662-345-8336. Sr. Anne Brooks, S.N.J.M., D.O., Dir. Patients Assisted Annually 8,265.

[E] ORPHANAGES AND INFANT HOMES

JACKSON. *D'Evereaux Hall Home, Inc.*, P.O. Box 2248, 39225. Tel: 601-355-8634; Fax: 601-960-8493. Email: linda.raff@catholiccharitiesjackson.org. Mrs. Linda Raff, Exec. Dir.

St. Mary Orphan Home, Inc., P.O. Box 2248, 39225. Tel: 601-355-8634; Fax: 601-960-8493. Email: linda.raff@catholiccharitiesjackson.org. Mrs. Linda Raff, Exec. Dir.

[F] MONASTERIES AND RESIDENCES OF PRIESTS AND BROTHERS

JACKSON. *Christian Brothers Residence*, 820 Forest Ave., 39206-3299. Tel: 601-362-3861; Fax: 601-362-1382. Bros. John Brennan, C.F.C.; Theodore Dausch, C.F.C., Local Supr.; Daniel Lauber, C.F.C.; Daniel McDonough, C.F.C. Congregation of Christian Brothers

Priory of St. Moses the Black, 653 Claiborne Ave., 39209. Tel: 601-354-3287. Revs. Richard P. Chiles, O.Praem., Prior; Norbert N'Zilamba, O.Praem.; Jeremy Tobin, O.Praem.; Sebastian Schalk. Canons Regular of Premontre (The Premonstratensian Fathers) Priests 4.

NESBIT. *St. Michael Community House*, 1360 Nesbit Rd., P.O. Box 38, 38651. Tel: 662-429-8424; Fax: 662-429-8423. Email: jcunniffe@juno.com. Revs. Francis J. Burshnick, S.C.J.; James A. Cunniffe, S.C.J., Coord.; Thomas Lind, S.C.J.; Patrick J. Lloyd, S.C.J.; Dermot J. Twomey, S.C.J.; Charles Yost, S.C.J.; Edward Zemlik, S.C.J.

[G] CONVENTS AND RESIDENCES FOR SISTERS

JACKSON. *St. Dominic Convent*, Formerly St. Dominick Convent, 969 Lakeland Dr., 39216. Tel: 601-200-6729; Fax: 601-944-0096. Email: strinita@stdom.com. Web: www.stdom.com. Dominican Sisters of Springfield, IL 9.

St. Elizabeth Ann Seton, 4642 Trawick St., 39211-5834. Tel: 601-982-5183; Fax: 601-982-1097. Email: sambdc@bellsouth.net. Web: www.doc-ecp.org. Daughters of Charity 5.

Our Lady of Mount Carmel and Little Flower Monastery, 2155 Terry Rd., 39204. Tel: 601-373-1460; Fax: 601-372-1369. Email: jm2155jt@aol.com. Sr. Margaret Mary Flynn, O.C.D., Prioress. Discalced Carmelites Nuns with Solemn Vows 5.

BROOKSVILLE. *The Dwelling Place*, 2824 Dwelling Place Rd., 39739-9537. Tel: 662-738-5348; Fax: 662-738-5345. Email: dwellpl@crawdat.com. Web: dwellingplace.com. Morag Burgess, Dir.

CHATAWA. *St. Mary of the Pines*, 3167 Old Hwy. 51 S., P.O. Box 38, 39632. Tel: 601-783-3494; Fax: 601-783-5758. Email: smpines@telapex.com. Sr. Suzanne Pescay, S.S.N.D., Admin. Home for the Retired Sisters of the Dallas Province of the School Sisters of Notre Dame. Retreat Center for Lay and Religious Groups. Sisters in Residence 64.

GREENVILLE. *Our Lady of Lourdes Convent*, 1600 E. Reed Rd., 38703-7229. Tel: 662-334-4337; Fax: 662-332-9877. Email: alspaughn@tecinfo.com. Web: http://lourdes.greenville.msus. Sisters of St. Joseph

GREENWOOD. *St. Francis Convent*, 2603 Hwy. 82 E., 38930-5966. Tel: 662-453-1221. Franciscan Sisters of Christian Charity 7.

PHILADELPHIA. *Holy Rosary Convent*, P.O. Box 496, 39350. Tel: 601-656-2949; Fax: 601-656-2829. Email: glorias@netdoor.com. Sister Servants of the I.H.M.

WALLS. *Sacred Heart Convent*, P.O. Box 237, 38680. Tel: 662-781-0807. School Sisters of St. Francis 3.

[H] RETREAT CENTERS

BROOKSVILLE. *The Dwelling Place*, 2824 Dwelling Place Rd., 39739-9796. Tel: 662-738-5348; Fax: 662-738-5345. Email: dwellpl@crawdat.com. Web: www.dwellingplace.com. Clare Van Lent, Dir.

CHATAWA. *St. Mary of the Pines*, 3167 Old Hwy. 51 S., P.O. Box 38, 39632. Tel: 601-783-3494; Fax: 601-783-5758. Email: smpines@telalpex.com. Sr. Suzanne Pescay, S.S.N.D., Admin. Home for the Retired Sisters of the Dallas Province of the School Sisters of Notre Dame. Retreat Center for Lay and Religious Groups. Sisters in Residence 64.

[I] NEWMAN CENTERS

JACKSON. *Belhaven College Newman Center* P.O. Box 57, 39205-0057. Tel: 601-974-1239; Fax: 601-974-1229. Email: mccarmm@millsaps.edu. Rev. Brian Kaskie.

Jackson State University Newman Center 2303 Lynch St., 32909. Rev. Richard P. Chiles, O.Praem.

Millsaps College Newman Center P.O. Box 57, 39205-0057. Tel: 601-974-1239; Fax: 601-974-1229. Email: mccarmm@millsaps.edu. Rev. Brian Kaskie.

Tougaloo College Newman Center Holy Ghost Church, 1151 Cloister St., 39202. Tel: 601-353-1339. Rev. Ryszard Kalinowski, S.V.D.

University of Mississippi Medical Center - Newman Center P.O. Box 57, 39205-0057. Tel: 601-974-1239; Fax: 601-974-1229. Email: mccarmm@millsaps.edu. Rev. Brian Kaskie.

BOONEVILLE. *Northeast Mississippi Community College Catholic Student Center* St. Francis of Assisi, P.O. Box 654, 38829. Tel: 662-728-7509; Fax: 662-728-7503. Email: stfrancischurch@shsm.org. Web: www.avsia.com/rhh/stfrancis/index.html. Sr. Dorothy Pashuta, C.S.J.

BROOKHAVEN. *Lincoln Junior College Newman Center* P.O. Box 196, 39602-0196. Tel: 601-833-1799. Rev. Patrick Noonan.

CLEVELAND. *Delta State University Newman Center* Our Lady of Victories, 215 Bishop Rd., P.O. Box 1450, 38732-1450. Tel: 662-846-6273. Rev. Thomas Lalor.

CLINTON. *Mississippi College Newman Center* Holy Savior Church, P.O. Box 85, 39060. Tel: 601-924-6344. Rev. Thomas McGing, J.C.L.

COLUMBUS. *Mississippi University for Women Student Center* Annunciation Church, 808 College St., 39701. Tel: 662-328-2927; Fax: 662-329-8270. Email: annunchr@bellsouth.net. Web: www.annunciationcatholicchurch.com. Rev. Gerard Hurley.

FOREST. *East Central Community College Newman Center* St. Michael's Church, P.O. Box 388, 39074. Tel: 601-469-1916. Email: res@localink4.com. Rev. Richard Smith.

GOODMAN. *Holmes Community College Newman Center St. Thomas*, 200 Boulevard St., Lexington, 39095. Tel: 662-453-0623; Fax: 662-453-9060. Rev. Gregory Plata, O.F.M.

HOLLY SPRINGS. *Rust College Newman Center* St. Joseph's, P.O. Box 430, 38635. Tel: 662-252-3138; Fax: 662-252-3138 *51. Email: stjoseph@dixie-net.com. Mr. James Rayford Sr.

OXFORD. *University of Mississippi Newman Center* St. John Church, 403 University Ave., 38655. Tel: 662-915-3169; Fax: 662-234-6079. Email: stjohns@watervalley.net. Rev. Joseph Tonos; Deacon Theodore Klingen.

RAYMOND. *Hinds Community College Catholic Student Organization* Denise Scifres, P.O. Box 11269 - Hinds Community College, 39154. Tel: 601-857-3302; Fax: 601-857-3406. Email: dlscifres@hinds.cc.ms.us.

SENATOBIA. *Northwest Mississippi Community College Newman Center* St. Gregory Church, P.O. Box 129, 38668-0129. Tel: 662-562-5318. Rev. Dermot J. Twomey, S.C.J.

STARKVILLE. *Mississippi State University Catholic Student Association* St. Joseph Church, 607 University Dr., 39759. Tel: 662-323-2257; Fax: 662-323-2258. Email: falavelle@hotmail.com. Web: www.msstate.edu/org/csa. Rev. Jeffrey Waldrep; Fran Lavelle, Campus Min.

[J] MISCELLANEOUS

JACKSON. *Jackson Diocese Educational Services, Inc.*, P.O. Box 2248, 39225-2248. Tel: 601-969-2742; Fax: 601-960-8469. Email: education.office@jacksondiocese.org. Sr. Deborah Hughes, S.S.J., Dir. & Contact Person.

Parroquia De San Miguel Del Arcangel, P.O. Box 2248, 39225-2248. Rev. Msgr. Michael Thornton; Rev. William Cullen. Saltillo Mission Sponsored by Dioceses of Jackson and Biloxi.
Suc. "A" Apdo. 52, Saltillo, Coahuilla C.P. 25000 Mexico. Tel: 011-52-84-44-82-2207.

Pax Christi Franciscans, LaVerna House, 2108 Alta Woods Blvd., 39204. Tel: 601-373-4463. Genevieve Feyen, Pres.; Rhoda Kalscheur, House Dir. A Private Association of the Christian faithful, living a consecrated life, engaged in social and educational works. Consecrated Members 7.

ABERDEEN. *Catholic Committee of the South, Inc.*, St.

Francis of Assisi, Box 134, 39730. Tel: 662-369-2897. Email: stfa@juno.com. Sr. Mary Priniski, O.P., Coord.

CANTON. *Notre Dame Education Center, Inc.*, 153 E. Center St., P.O. Box 505, 39046. Tel: 601-859-6826; Fax: 601-859-6898. Email: ndec@netdoor.com.

GREENWOOD. *Pax Christi Franciscans*, St. Francis Information Center, 709 Ave. I, 38930. Tel: 662-453-1465. Genevieve Feyen, Pres.; Bessie Willburn, Center Dir. A Private Association of the Christian faithful, living a consecrated life, engaged in social and educational works. Consecrated Members 8.

MADISON. **St. Catherine's Village, Inc.*, 200 Dominican Dr., 39110. Tel: 601-856-0100; Fax: 601-200-0823.

MOUND BAYOU. *St. Gabriel Mercy Center*, P.O. Box 0824, 38762-0824. Tel: 662-741-3255; Fax: 662-741-3494. Email: moundbayou@tecinfo.com. Sisters Donald Mary Lynch, R.S.M., Dir.; Cyrena Harkins, R.S.M., Coord. Outreach Program of the Sisters of Mercy Health System (Mercycare) and Educational Services, Inc; Mercy Computer Learning Lab, Indianola, MS, 662-887-1033 (phone & fax), Sr. Rita May Killian, R.S.M., Coord.; Mercy Learning and Recreation Center, Rolling Fork, MS 39159-2626, 662-873-4880 (phone), 662-873-4881 (fax), James Balder, Coord.

ROSEDALE. *Delta Catholic Ministries*, 113 Railroad St., P.O. Box 307, 38769-0307. Tel: 662-759-6341. Email: dcmsh@juno.com. Sisters Catherine Leamy, S.N.J.M., Pres. & Dir.; Kay Burton, S.N.J.M., Vice Pres. & Dir.; Celia Evers, O.P., Sec., Treas. & Dir.; Dorothy Oursler, C.S.J., Board Member; Joanne Blomme, O.P., Board Member.

WALLS. *Sacred Heart League*, 6050 Hwy. 161 N., P.O. Box 300, 38680-0300. Tel: 662-781-1360; Fax: 662-781-3340. Email: esavage@shl.org. Web: www.sacredheartleague.org. Rev. Charles Yost, S.C.J., Spiritual Dir.; Mr. Ed Savage, Exec. Dir.

Sacred Heart Southern Missions Housing Corporation, P.O. Box 365, 38680-0365. Tel: 662-781-1472; Fax: 662-781-3534. Email: badams@shsm.org. Sr. Elizabeth A. Adams, C.S.J., Dir. of Social Svcs. & Housing; Rev. Jack Kurps, S.C.J., Pres.

Sacred Heart Southern Missions, Inc., 6473 Hwy. 161 N., P.O. Box 190, 38680-0190. Tel: 662-781-1472; Fax: 662-781-0842. Email: jkurps@shsm.org. Rev. Jack Kurps, S.C.J., Exec. Dir.

RELIGIOUS INSTITUTES OF MEN REPRESENTED IN THE DIOCESE

For further details refer to the corresponding bracketed number in the Religious Institutes of Men or Women section.

[0330]—*Brothers of the Christian Schools* (Prov. of St. Louis, MO)—F.S.C.

[0900]—*Canons Regular of Premontre*—O.Praem.

[0310]—*Congregation of Christian Brothers*—C.F.C.

[1130]—*Congregation of the Priests of the Sacred Heart*—S.C.J.

[0520]—*Franciscan Friars* (Pulaski, WI)—O.F.M.

[0570]—*Glenmary Home Missioners*—G.H.M.

[0840]—*Missionary Servants of the Most Holy Trinity*—S.T.

[0420]—*Society of the Divine Word*—S.V.D.

[0700]—*St. Joseph's Society of the Sacred Heart*—S.S.J.

RELIGIOUS INSTITUTES OF WOMEN REPRESENTED IN THE DIOCESE

[]—*Congregation of Sisters of Charity of St. Charles Borromeo*—C.B.

[2410]—*Congregation of the Marianites of the Holy Cross*—M.S.C.

[3710]—*Congregation of the Sisters of Saint Agnes*—C.S.A.

[1780]—*Congregation of the Sisters of the Third Order of St. Francis of Perpetual Adoration*—F.S.P.A.

[0760]—*Daughters of Charity of St. Vincent de Paul*—D.C.

[0420]—*Discalced Carmelite Nuns*—O.C.D.

[1070-03]—*Dominican Sisters* (Sinsinawa, WI)—O.P.

[1070-06]—*Dominican Sisters* (Newburgh, NY)—O.P.

[1070-09]—*Dominican Sisters* (Racine, WI)—O.P.

[1070-13]—*Dominican Sisters* (Adrian, MI)—O.P.

[1070-10]—*Dominican Sisters* (Springfield, IL)—O.P.

[1230]—*Franciscan Sisters of Christian Charity*—O.S.F.

[1310]—*Franciscan Sisters of Little Falls, Minnesota*—O.S.F.

[2575]—*Institute of the Sisters of Mercy of the Americas* (St. Louis, MO)—R.S.M.

[]—*Literary Society of St. Catherine of Sienna Kentucky Dominican*—O.P.

[2800]—*Missionary Sisters of the Most Sacred Heart of Jesus*—M.S.C.

[2970]—*School Sisters of Notre Dame* (Baltimore & Dallas Provs., Mankato)—S.S.N.D.

[1680]—*School Sisters of St. Francis*—O.S.F.

[0500]—*Sisters of Charity of Nazareth* (Kentucky)—S.C.N.

[0430]—*Sisters of Charity of the Blessed Virgin Mary* (Dubuque, IA)—B.V.M.

[]—*Sisters of Christian Community*—S.F.C.C.

[0990]—*Sisters of Divine Providence*—C.D.P.

[2100]—*Sisters of Humility of Mary*—C.H.M.

[]—*Sisters of Mercy of Mississippi, Inc.*—R.S.M.

[3360]—*Sisters of Providence of Saint Mary-of-the-Woods, Indiana*—S.P.

[3893]—*Sisters of Saint Joseph of Chestnut Hill, Philadelphia*—S.S.J.

[]—*Sisters of St. Francis of Dubuque*

[]—*Sisters of St. Francis of Sylvania, Ohio*—O.S.F.

[1570]—*Sisters of St. Francis of the Holy Family* (Dubuque)—O.S.F.

[3830-02]—*Sisters of St. Joseph* (La Grange Park, IL)—C.S.J.

[3830-15]—*Sisters of St. Joseph* (Concordia, KS)—C.S.J.

[3840]—*Sisters of St. Joseph of Carondelet* (St. Louis & St. Paul Provs.)—C.S.J.

[3930]—*Sisters of St. Joseph of the Third Order of St. Francis* (Marymount Prov.)—S.S.J.-T.O

[1030]—*Sisters of the Divine Savior*—S.D.S.

[1990]—*Sisters of the Holy Names of Jesus and Mary* (Albany, NY; Spokane, WA; Los Gatos, CA; Marylhurst, OR)—S.N.J.M.

[2050]—*Sisters of the Holy Spirit and Mary Immaculate*—S.H.Sp.

[2350]—*Sisters of the Living Word*—S.L.W.

[2160]—*Sisters, Servants of the Immaculate Heart of Mary*—I.H.M.

[4120-03]—*Ursuline Nuns, of the Congregation of Paris*—O.S.U.

NECROLOGY

† Foley, Rev. Msgr. Noel, Jackson, MS St. Richard
† Boyce, Thomas, (Retired)—Died Dec. 13, 2002
† Englehart, William, (Retired)—Died April 29, 2003
† Leonard, John, (Retired)—Died April 28, 2003
† Maloney, Walter, (Retired)—Died Feb. 25, 2003

Diocese of Jefferson City

(Dioecesis Civitatis Jeffersoniensis)

Most Reverend

JOHN RAYMOND GAYDOS, D.D.

Bishop of Jefferson City; ordained December 20, 1968; appointed June 25, 1997; consecrated August 27, 1997 *Res.: Bishop's House*, P.O. Box 417, Jefferson City, MO 65102.

Chancery: 605 Clark Ave., P.O. Box 417, Jefferson City, MO 65102. Tel: 573-635-9127; Fax: 573-635-0386.

Web: www.diojeffcity.org

Email: chancellor@diojeffcity.org

ESTABLISHED JULY 2, 1956.

Square Miles 22,127.

Comprises the Counties of Adair, Audrain, Benton, Boone, Callaway, Camden, Chariton, Clark, Cole, Cooper, Crawford, Gasconade, Hickory, Howard, Knox, Lewis, Linn, Macon, Maries, Marion, Miller, Moniteau, Monroe, Montgomery, Morgan, Osage, Pettis, Phelps, Pike, Pulaski, Putnam, Ralls, Randolph, Saline, Schuyler, Scotland, Shelby and Sullivan in the State of Missouri.

Legal Title: For legal titles of parishes and diocesan institutions, consult the Chancery Office.

STATISTICAL OVERVIEW

Personnel	
Bishop	1
Retired Bishops	1
Priests: Diocesan Active in Diocese	75
Priests: Diocesan Active Outside Diocese	2
Priests: Diocesan in Foreign Missions	1
Priests: Retired, Sick or Absent	24
Number of Diocesan Priests	102
Religious Priests in Diocese	6
Total Priests in Diocese	108
Extern Priests in Diocese	9
Ordinations:	
Diocesan Priests	1
Transitional Deacons	1
Permanent Deacons	3
Permanent Deacons in Diocese	57
Total Brothers	2
Total Sisters	86
Parishes	
Parishes	95
With Resident Pastor:	
Resident Diocesan Priests	65
Resident Religious Priests	6
Without Resident Pastor:	
Administered by Priests	18
Administered by Deacons	2
Administered by Religious Women	3
Administered by Lay People	1
Missions	15
Professional Ministry Personnel:	
Brothers	2
Sisters	86
Lay Ministers	26
Welfare	
Catholic Hospitals	1
Total Assisted	265,000
Health Care Centers	13
Total Assisted	150,000
Homes for the Aged	2
Total Assisted	215
Special Centers for Social Services	2
Total Assisted	36,000
Educational	
Diocesan Students in Other Seminaries	15
Total Seminarians	15
High Schools, Diocesan and Parish	2
Total Students	1,032
Elementary Schools, Diocesan and Parish	38
Total Students	6,582
Non-residential Schools for the Disabled	1
Total Students	20
Catechesis/Religious Education:	
High School Students	2,688
Elementary Students	4,607
Total Students under Catholic Instruction	14,944
Teachers in the Diocese:	
Brothers	2
Sisters	19
Lay Teachers	511
Vital Statistics	
Receptions into the Church:	
Infant Baptism Totals	1,396
Adult Baptism Totals	292
Received into Full Communion	310
First Communions	1,507
Confirmations	1,437
Marriages:	
Catholic	299
Interfaith	272
Total Marriages	571
Deaths	808
Total Catholic Population	86,457
Total Population	851,131

Former Bishops—Most Revs. JOSEPH M. MARLING, C.PP.S., D.D. (Retired), ord. Feb. 21, 1929; appt. Auxiliary of Kansas City, June 9, 1947; consecrated Aug. 6, 1947; appt. Bishop of Jefferson City, Aug. 24, 1956; retired July 2, 1969; died Oct. 2, 1979; MICHAEL F. MCAULIFFE, S.T.D. (Retired), ord. May 31, 1945; appt. July 2, 1969; consecrated Aug. 18, 1969; retired August 27, 1997.

Vicar General—Rev. GREGORY L. HIGLEY, V.G., P.O. Box 417, Jefferson City, 65102-0417.

Episcopal Vicars—Rev. Msgrs. MICHAEL T. FLANAGAN, E.V.; MICHAEL J. WILBERS, E.V.

Chancery Office—605 Clark Ave., P.O. Box 417, Jefferson City, 65102-0417. Tel: 573-635-9127; Fax: 573-635-0386. All offices are at this address unless noted otherwise.

Chancellor—Sr. ETHEL-MARIE BIRI, S.S.N.D., M.R.Ed., M.A.

Secretary to the Bishop—Rev. ROBERT A. KURWICKI.

Vice-Chancellors—Revs. BRENDAN DOYLE; ROBERT A. KURWICKI.

Moderator of the Curia—Rev. GREGORY L. HIGLEY, V.G.

Diocesan Tribunal—

Judicial Vicar—Rev. BRENDAN DOYLE.

Adjutant Judicial Vicar—Rev. GREGORY L. HIGLEY, V.G.

Defenders of the Bond—Rev. ROBERT W. DUESDIEKER; Deacon JAMES R. BUTLER; Mrs. CONSTANCE SCHEPERS.

Promoter of Justice—Rev. MARK A. PORTERFIELD, J.C.L.

Judges—Rev. Msgr. FRANCIS G. GILLGANNON (Retired); Revs. J. JAMES OFFUTT; MARK A. PORTERFIELD, J.C.L.; MICHAEL F. QUINN.

Notaries—Mrs. JULIE LAUNE; Sr. ETHEL-MARIE BIRI, S.S.N.D.

Diocesan Consultors—Rev. Msgr. MICHAEL T. FLANAGAN, E.V.; Revs. PHILIP M. KANE; GREGORY L. HIGLEY, V.G.; DANIEL I.J. LUECKENOTTE; THOMAS E. MCGRATH; GREGORY C. MEYSTRIK; Rev. Msgr. MICHAEL J. WILBERS, E.V.

Deans—I. Brookfield: Rev. LEONARD S. MISEY Dean: Brookfield, Brunswick, Clarence, Indian Grove, Macon (Bevier), Marceline (Hurricane Branch/ Mendon), Salisbury, Shelbina, Wien. II. Columbia: Rev. MICHAEL A. COLEMAN Dean: Boonville, Columbia, Fayette, Moberly, Pilot Grove. III. Hannibal: Rev. MICHAEL F. QUINN Dean: Canton (La Grange), Ewing, Hannibal, Indian Creek, Kahoka (Wayland), Louisiana (Clarksville), Monroe City, Palmyra, Perry (Paris), St. Clement, St. Patrick. IV. Jefferson City: Rev. LOUIS E. DORN Dean: California, Holts Summit, Jefferson City, Osage Bend, Russellville, St. Martins, St. Thomas, Taos, Wardsville. V. Kirksville: Rev. R. WILLIAM PECKMAN Dean: Baring, Edina, Kirksville (Novinger), Memphis, Milan (Unionville). VI. Lake Ozark: Rev. CLARENCE E. WIEDERHOLT Dean: Camdenton, Eldon, Laurie (Versailles), Hermitage (Climax Springs), Lake Ozark, Mary's Home, St. Anthony, St. Elizabeth. VII. Marshall: Rev. THOMAS L. ALBERS, C.PP.S. Dean: Glasgow, Marshall (Sweet Springs), Sedalia, Slater, Tipton, Warsaw (Cole Camp). VIII. Mexico: Rev. WAYNE M. BOYER Dean: Centralia, Fulton, Hermann, Jonesburg, Martinsburg, Mexico, Mokane, Montgomery City, Morrison, Rhineland, Vandalia (Laddonia), Wellsville. IX. Osage: Rev. JOHN J. SCHUTTY Dean: Argyle (Koeltztown), Bonnots Mill, Chamois, Folk, Frankenstein, Freeburg, Linn, Loose Creek, Meta, Rich Fountain, Westphalia. X. Rolla: Rev. DAVID D. COX Dean: Belle, Bourbon, Brinktown, Crocker, Cuba, Dixon, Owensville, Richland, Rolla, Rosati, St. James, Steelville, Vienna, St. Robert.

Masters of Ceremonies—

To The Bishop—Revs. ROBERT A. KURWICKI; DAVID J. VEIT.

Personnel Board—Most Rev. JOHN RAYMOND GAYDOS, D.D.; Revs. FRED J. ELSKAMP; L. JAMES FINDER; Rev. Msgr. MICHAEL T. FLANAGAN, E.V.; Revs. ROBERT A. KURWICKI; GREGORY L. HIGLEY, V.G.; DONALD W. LAMMERS; Rev. Msgr. MICHAEL J. WILBERS, E.V.

Presbyteral Council—Most Rev. JOHN RAYMOND GAYDOS, D.D., Pres. Senators: Revs. WILLIAM L. KORTE; THOMAS J. SEIFNER; PHILIP M. KANE; DAVID D. COX, Treas.; R. WILLIAM PECKMAN; J. DAVID MAHER; CLARENCE E. WIEDERHOLT, Vice-Chm.; JOHN W. GRONER; LOUIS E. DORN; JOHN J. SCHUTTY; RICHARD A. COLBERT, C.PP.S., Rel. Rep.; Rev. Msgr. GERARD L. POELKER, Retired Rep. (Retired); Revs. W. PAUL JONES; EDWARD A. DOYLE. Appointed Members: Revs. EDWIN J. COLE; CHRISTOPHER L. CORDES, Chm.; RAPHAEL P. KEYES; MARION J. MAKAREWICZ; IGNAZIO C. MEDINA; DAVID J. VEIT. Ex Officio Members: Rev. Msgrs. MICHAEL J. WILBERS, E.V.; MICHAEL T. FLANAGAN, E.V.; Rev. GREGORY L. HIGLEY, V.G.

Diocesan Offices and Directors

Buildings and Properties—Mr. BARRY VOLLMER, Coord.

Campus Ministry—Rev. CHARLES D. PARDEE.

Catholic Relief Overseas Fund—Mrs. ALICE J. WOLTERS, Dir.

Cemeteries—Rev. ROBERT A. KURWICKI, Dir.

Charismatic Renewal Program—Deacon KENNETH

BERRY, Diocesan Representative, 201 N. Cottey, Edina, 63537. Tel: 660-397-2636.

Communication—Mr. MARK D. SAUCIER, Dir.

Cursillo Movement—Mr. JIM SOWASH, Lay Dir.; Rev. R. WILLIAM PECKMAN, Spiritual Dir., 1211 Torrey Pines, Columbia, 65203. Tel: 573-442-9084.

Diocesan Excellence in Education Fund, Inc.—Most Revs. JOHN RAYMOND GAYDOS, D.D., Chm.; MICHAEL F. MCAULIFFE, S.T.D. (Retired); Mr. LOUIS J. LEONATTI, Pres.; Sr. ETHEL-MARIE BIRI, S.S.N.D.; Rev. GREGORY L. HIGLEY, V.G.; Mr. JOHN KOLB; Mrs. MILLIE SCHELL; Deacon DONALD W. ORSCHELN, Vice Pres.; Mr. GARY SCHELL; Mr. DONALD NOVOTNEY; Mr. NORMAN P. STUCKENSCHNEIDER; Rev. Msgr. MICHAEL J. WILBERS, E.V.

Diaconate Office—Rev. FRED J. ELSKAMP Vicar; Deacon ROBERT RACKERS.

Engaged Encounter—Coords.: RICHARD SPORLEDER; BERNICE SPORLEDER, Rte. 3, Box 22, Marshall, 65340; Rev. MICHAEL F. QUINN, Spiritual Dir.; JIM VEIT; ARLENE VEIT, 5908 County Rd. 324, Palmyra, 63461.

Family Life—Mr. MICHAEL A. VAN GUNDY, Dir.; Dr. STEPHANA LANDWHER, Pro-Life.

Finance—Rev. JOSEPH BRADDOCK, CFO.

Stewardship—Mrs. JANE RUTTER, Dir.

Finance Committee—Most Revs. JOHN RAYMOND GAYDOS, D.D.; MICHAEL F. MCAULIFFE, S.T.D. (Retired); Sr. ETHEL-MARIE BIRI, S.S.N.D.; Miss OLIVIA BUERSMEYER; Mr. CHARLES CASSMEYER; Rev. Msgr. MICHAEL T. FLANAGAN, E.V.; Mr. CHRIS HERMANN; Rev. GREGORY L. HIGLEY, V.G.; Mr. RICHARD KAMPETER; Mr. MICHAEL KELLY; Mr. RODNEY LOESCH; Deacon DONALD ORSCHELN; Rev. CHARLES D. PARDEE; Mr. JAMES E. WESTERBROOK; Mrs. HELEN VOSSEN; Rev. Msgr. MICHAEL J. WILBERS, E.V.; Mrs. BETTY ZIMMER.

Hispanic Ministry—Sr. JOYCE SCHRAMM, C.PP.S., Coord., P.O. Box 417, Jefferson City, 65102. Tel: 573-635-9127, Ext. 250.

El Puente—Sisters PEGGY BONNOT, C.C.V.I.; MARGARET SNYDER, C.C.V.I., 1106 Swifts Hwy., Jefferson City, 65109. Tel: 573-635-2540; EILEEN SCHIEBER, C.PP.S., 415 E. Fourth St., Sedalia, 65301-4598. Tel: 660-829-0981.

Historical Archivist—Rev. ROBERT A. KURWICKI.

Holy Childhood— (See Mission Office)

Human Development Campaign—Ms. BARBARA ROSS.

Leadership Services—Sr. ETHEL-MARIE BIRI, S.S.N.D.

Legion of Mary—Rev. WILLIAM L. KORTE, 301 W. Williams, Salisbury, 65281. Tel: 660-388-5590.

Liturgical Commission—Rev. LOUIS E. DORN, Chm., 508 N. Third St., Louisiana, 63353. Tel: 573-754-4757.

Mediation and Arbitration Board—VACANT 508 N. Third St., Louisiana, 63353. Tel: 573-754-4757.

Marriage Encounter—Chair Couple: BOB JARMAN; KATHY JARMAN, 7713 Clarose Dr., Jefferson City, 65109. Tel: 573-893-3318; Rev. GREGORY C. MEYSTRIK, Spiritual Dir., 6410 Rt. W, Jefferson City, 65101. Tel: 573-636-4925.

Ministry Formation—Rev. GEORGE KRAMER, Dir., P.O. Box 68, Bonnots Mill, 65016. Tel: 573-897-2061.

Ministry to Priests—Rev. J. DAVID MAHER; Most Rev. JOHN RAYMOND GAYDOS, D.D.; Revs. CHRISTOPHER L. CORDES; JOSEPH S. COREL, Chm.; DAVID D. COX; PATRICK G. DOLAN; KEVIN GORMLEY; GERALD J. KAIMANN; ROBERT A. KURWICKI, Sec.; GREGORY C. MEYSTRIK.

Mission Office (Peru Missions, Propagation of the Faith, Holy Childhood, Catholic Relief Services)—Mrs. ALICE J. WOLTERS, Dir.; Mr. MARK D. SAUCIER, P.O. Box 417, Jefferson City, 65102.

Newspaper-"Catholic Missourian"—Mr. JAY NIES, Editor, P.O. Box 1107, Jefferson City, 65102.

Priestly and Religious Vocations Committee—Rev. ROBERT A. KURWICKI, Chair.

Priests' Eucharistic League—Rev. FRED J. ELSKAMP, Dir.

Priests' Mutual Benefit Society—Board of Trustees: Most Revs. JOHN R. GAYDOS; MICHAEL F. MCAULIFFE, S.T.D., Advisor (Retired); Revs. WAYNE M. BOYER; EDWIN J. COLE, Board of Truste; Rev. Msgr. MICHAEL T. FLANAGAN, E.V.; Revs. KEVIN GORMLEY; GREGORY L. HIGLEY, V.G., Sec. & Treas.; Rev. Msgrs. GERARD L. POELKER, Chm. (Retired); MICHAEL J. WILBERS, E.V., Ex Officio.

Propagation of Faith & Holy Childhood—Mrs. ALICE J. WOLTERS, Dir., P.O. Box 417, Jefferson City, 65102.

Religious Education Office—Mr. JAMES M. KEMNA, Dir.; Mrs. CAROLYN A. SAUCIER.

Refugee and Immigration Services—Mrs. ALICE J. WOLTERS, Dir.

Columbia Office—201 W. Broadway, Bldg. 3, Columbia, 65203. Tel: 573-442-7568.

Residents Encounter Christ—Ms. BARBARA ROSS, Diocesan Liaison; Rev. LOUIS E. DORN, Spiritual Dir.

School Office—Mr. DONALD F. NOVOTNEY, Supt.

Diocesan Schools Technology Foundation—Mr. DONALD F. NOVOTNEY, Supt., 605 Clark Ave., P.O. Box 417, Jefferson City, 65102. Tel: 573-635-9127; Fax: 573-635-0153.

Scouting—Rev. GREGORY C. MEYSTRIK, Chap., 6410 Rt. W, Jefferson City, 65101. Tel: 573-636-4925.

Diocesan Sisters' Organization—Sr. VIRGINIA GRUMICH, S.S.N.D., 120 Hayden, Hannibal, 63401. Tel: 573-221-3241.

Social Concerns Office—Ms. BARBARA ROSS, Dir.

Prison Ministry—Sr. FRAN BUSCHELL, S.S.N.D.

Spiritual Renewal for the Laity—VACANT.

Stewardship—Mrs. JANE RUTTER, Dir.

Teens Encounter Christ (TEC)—Mrs. PAM WHITNEY, Lay Dir., 1801 Miami Ave., Marshall, 65340; Rev. MICHAEL A. COLEMAN, Spiritual Dir., P.O. Box 310, Moberly, 65270.

Victim Assistance Coordinator—Sr. ETHEL-MARIE BIRI, S.S.N.D. Tel: 573-635-9127, Ext. 201. Email: chancellor@diojeffcity.org.

Youth Ministry—VACANT.

CLERGY, PARISHES, MISSIONS AND PAROCHIAL SCHOOLS

JEFFERSON CITY
(COLE COUNTY)

1—ST. JOSEPH CATHEDRAL (1959), [JC] Revs Frederick J. Elskamp, Rector; Joseph S. Corel; Daniel I.J. Lueckenotte; Deacons Robert J. Rackers; Joseph Braddock; Dana K. Joyce. In Res., Revs. David G. Buescher; Thomas E. McGrath.
Office:—Tel: 573-635-7991; Fax: 573-635-0842.
School—2305 W. Main St., 65109. Tel: 573-635-5024; Fax: 573-635-5238. Lay Teachers 27; Students 500.
Catechesis/Religious Program—Students 75.

2—IMMACULATE CONCEPTION (1913), [JC] Revs. Patrick G. Dolan; Marion J. Makarewicz. In Res., Revs. Thomas L. Alber; Brendan Doyle; Deacons Larry Hildebrand; Mark Albur; Raymond L. Purvis.
Res.: 1206 E. McCarty St., 65101. Tel: 573-635-6143; 573-635-6144; Fax: 573-635-6036.
School—Tel: 573-636-7680; Fax: 573-635-6036. Sisters 1; Lay Teachers 38; Students 578.
Catechesis/Religious Program—Students 112.

3—ST. PETER (1846), [JC] Revs. Donald W. Lammers; James M. Smith; Deacons Robert L. Dulle; Anthony J. Valdes; Thomas M. Whalen. In Res., Rev. Robert H. Fields.
Res.: 216 Broadway, 65101. Tel: 573-636-8159; Fax: 573-634-6079.
School—Tel: 573-636-8922; Fax: 573-636-8410. Sisters 2; School Sisters of Notre Dame 1; Sisters of Charity of the Incarnate Word 1; Lay Teachers 28; Students 514.
Catechesis/Religious Program—Students 185.

OUTSIDE JEFFERSON CITY

ARGYLE, OSAGE CO., ST. ALOYSIUS (1910), [CEM 2] Rev. John J. Schmitz.
Mailing Address: P.O. Box 6, 65001. Tel: 573-728-6212; Fax: 573-728-6217.
Catechesis/Religious Program—Students 73.
Mission—St. Boniface (1866), P.O. Box 53, Koeltztown, Osage Co. 65001. Tel: 314-728-6919.

BARING, KNOX CO., ST. ALOYSIUS (1894), [CEM] Attended by, Edina Rev. R. William Peckman.
Res.: 509 N. Main St., Edina, 63537-1239. Tel: 660-397-2183; Fax: 660-397-3680.
Catechesis/Religious Program— Twinned with St. Joseph, Edina.

BELLE, MARIES CO., ST. ALEXANDER (1908), [CEM] Attended by, Immaculate Conception, Owensville Rev. Joseph Hoi.
Mailing Address: 400 W. Third St., P.O. Box 606, 65013. Tel: 573-859-6231.
Catechesis/Religious Program—Students 17.

BONNOTS MILL, OSAGE CO., ST. LOUIS (1905), [CEM] Rev. Joseph S. Corel.
Mailing Address: P.O. Box 8, 65016. Tel: 573-897-2922; Fax: 573-897-4528.
Church: 211 Church Hill, 65016.
Catechesis/Religious Program—Students 27.

BOONVILLE, COOPER CO., SS. PETER AND PAUL (1856), [CEM] Rev. Robert W. Duesdieker; Deacon David Miller.
Res.: 322 7th St., 65233. Tel: 660-882-6468; Fax: 660-882-6757.
School—Tel: 660-882-2589; Fax: 660-882-3020. Sisters 1; Lay Teachers 11; Students 248.
Catechesis/Religious Program—Tel: 660-882-7920. Students 135.

BOURBON, CRAWFORD CO., ST. FRANCIS (1915), [CEM 2] Rev. James Finder; Sr. Mary Ferrar, S.S.J., Pastoral Admin.
Res.: 1098 Old Hwy. 66 W., Box 419, 65441. Tel: 573-732-4494; Fax: 573-732-4494.
Catechesis/Religious Program—Students 11.

BRINKTOWN, MARIES CO., HOLY GUARDIAN ANGELS (1891), [CEM] Attended by, Visitation, Vienna Rev. John J. Schmitz.
Res. & Mailing Address: P.O. Box 226, Vienna, 65582. Tel: 573-422-3950; Fax: 573-422-3950.
Church: 37515 Hwy.. Tel: 573-422-3105.
Catechesis/Religious Program—Students 10.
Convent—Franciscan Sisters of Mary, Tel 573-422-3921.

BROOKFIELD, LINN CO., IMMACULATE CONCEPTION (1859), [CEM] Rev. Thomas Duggan.
Res.: 313 N. Livingston St., 64628. Tel: 660-258-2507; Fax: 660-258-5637.
Catechesis/Religious Program—Tel: 660-258-3956. Students 90.

BRUNSWICK, CHARITON CO., ST. BONIFACE (1860), [CEM] Rev. Leonard S. Misey.
Res.: 203 E. Vine St., P.O. Box 5, 65236. Tel: 660-548-3267.
Catechesis/Religious Program—Students 50.

CALIFORNIA, MONITEAU CO., ANNUNCIATION (1872), [CEM] Rev. Gregory L. Higley, V.G.
Res.: 414 W. Patrick St., 65018. Tel: 573-796-4842.
Catechesis/Religious Program—Tel: 573-796-4842. Students 130.

CAMDENTON, CAMDEN CO., ST. ANTHONY (1946), Rev. Raphael P. Keyes; Deacons Martin J. Towey; Richard A. Von Gunten; Theodore E. Staal.
Church & Mailing: 1874 N. State Hwy. 5, 65020. Tel: 573-346-2716; Fax: 573-346-0625.
Catechesis/Religious Program—Students 275.

CANTON, LEWIS CO., ST. JOSEPH (1865), Rev. Donald E. Siciliano; Deacon Robert DePyper, Pastoral Admin.
Res.: 812 Lewis St., 63435. Tel: 573-288-3198; Fax: 573-288-3198.
Catechesis/Religious Program—Students 72.
Mission—Notre Dame (1868), Rte. C, La Grange, Lewis Co. 63448. Tel: 573-655-4296.

CENTRALIA, BOONE CO., HOLY SPIRIT (1897), Rev. J. James Offutt.
Res.: 404 S. Rollins St., 65240. Tel: 573-682-2815.
Catechesis/Religious Program—Students 77.

CHAMOIS, OSAGE CO., MOST PURE HEART OF MARY (1865), [CEM 2] Rev. Patrick Dowling.
Res.: P.O. Box 156, 65024. Tel: 573-763-5345.
Catechesis/Religious Program—Students 54.

CLARENCE, SHELBY CO., ST. PATRICK (1884), [CEM] Rev. Paul M. Hartley.
Mailing and Res. Address: 307 E. Chestnut, P.O. Box 306, Shelbina, 63468. Tel: 573-588-4458; Fax: 573-588-4728.
Church: 201 Grand St., 63437. Tel: 573-699-3805.

COLUMBIA, BOONE CO.

1—OUR LADY OF LOURDES (1958), Rev. Msgr. Michael T. Flanagan, E.V.; Rev. Michael W. Penn; Deacon Fred Fritsch.
Res.: 903 Bernadette Dr., 65203. Tel: 573-445-7915; Fax: 573-446-7402.
School—817 Bernadette Dr., 65203. Tel: 573-445-6516; Fax: 573-445-9887. Sisters 1; Lay Teachers 34; Students 515.
Catechesis/Religious Program—Tel: 573-445-9602. Students 475.

2—SACRED HEART (1876), Rev. Edwin J. Cole; Deacon John D. Weber.
Res.: 1115 Locust St., 65201. Tel: 573-443-3470; Fax: 573-875-3947.
Catechesis/Religious Program—Students 100.

3—ST. THOMAS MORE NEWMAN CENTER, UNIVERSITY OF MISSOURI (1963), Revs. Charles D. Pardee; Mark S. Smith; Deacon Eugene S. Kazmierczak.
Res.: 701 Maryland, 65201. Tel: 573-445-8068.
Church: Tel: 573-449-5514; 573-449-5424; Fax: 573-874-2777.
Catechesis/Religious Program—Students 340.

CROCKER, PULASKI CO., ST. CORNELIUS (1966), [CEM] Attended by, Dixon. Rev. Walter J. Reisinger, C.M.
Res.: P.O. Box 310, Dixon, 65459. Tel: 573-759-7521.

CUBA, CRAWFORD CO., HOLY CROSS (1880), [CEM] Rev. James Finder; Deacon Earl Horsefield.
Res.: 415 W. School Ave., 65453. Tel: 573-885-3520; 573-885-3291 (Rectory); Fax: 573-885-3501.
School—407 W. School Ave., 65453. Tel: 573-885-4727. Sisters 2; Lay Teachers 5; Students 53.
Catechesis/Religious Program—Teresa Leicht, D.R.E. Students 61.

DIXON, PULASKI CO., ST. THERESA (1928), [CEM] Rev. Walter J. Reisinger, C.M.
Res.: 506 Oak St., P.O. Box 310, 65459. Tel: 573-759-7521.
Catechesis/Religious Program—Students 22.

EDINA, KNOX CO., ST. JOSEPH (1844), [CEM 2] Rev. R.

William Peckman; Deacon Kenneth Berry.
Res.: 509 N. Main St., 63537-1239. Tel: 660-397-2183; Fax: 660-397-3680.
Catechesis/Religious Program—Tel: 660-397-3128; Fax: 660-397-3680. Students 95.

ELDON, MILLER CO., SACRED HEART (1910), Rev. James J. O'Sullivan.
Res.: 540 N. Mill St., 65026. Tel: 573-392-5334; Fax: 573-392-3493.
Catechesis/Religious Program—Students 125.

EWING, LEWIS CO., QUEEN OF PEACE (1887), [CEM 2] Rev. Donald E. Siciliano.
Res.: 307 N. Main, P.O. Box 347, 63440. Tel: 573-209-3343.
Catechesis/Religious Program—Students 56.

FAYETTE, HOWARD CO., ST. JOSEPH (1956), Rev. Robert W. Duesdieker.
Res.: 300 S. Cleveland, 65248. Tel: 660-248-2439; Fax: 660-248-2439.
Catechesis/Religious Program—Students 15.

FOLK, OSAGE CO., ST. ANTHONY OF PADUA (1905), [CEM] Rev. Robert A. Kurwicki.
Mailing Address: P.O. Box 157, Westphalia, 65085. Tel: 573-455-2888; Fax: 573-455-2482.
Catechesis/Religious Program—Tel: 573-455-2482. Students 54.

FRANKENSTEIN, OSAGE CO., OUR LADY OF HELP (1863), [CEM 3] Rev. Ignazio C. Medina.
Mailing Address: Rte. 1, Box 201, Bonnots Mill, 65016. Tel: 573-897-2587.
Church: County Road C.
School—Tel: 573-897-2567; Fax: 573-897-4143. Lay Teachers 4; Students 43.
Catechesis/Religious Program—Students 24.

FREEBURG, OSAGE CO., HOLY FAMILY (1904), [CEM] Rev. Michael P. Murphy.
Res.: 104 Oliver St., P.O. Box 97, 65035. Tel: 573-744-5254; Fax: 573-744-5254.
School—Tel: 573-744-5200; Fax: 573-744-5200. Sisters 1; Lay Teachers 3; Students 68.
Catechesis/Religious Program—Students 36.

FULTON, CALLAWAY CO., ST. PETER (1875), Rev. Greg Oligschlaeger; Deacon John L. Nuedecker.
Parish Center—700 Hwy. Z, 65251. Tel: 573-642-5562; Fax: 573-642-2839.
School—Tel: 573-642-2839; Fax: 573-642-2839. Sisters of Christian Charity 2; Lay Teachers 9; Students 130.
Catechesis/Religious Program—Students 65.

GLASGOW, HOWARD CO., ST. MARY (1866), [CEM] Rev. Philip M. Kane; Deacon Jerome C. Brucks.
Res.: 421 Third St., P.O. Box 44, 65254. Tel: 660-338-2053; Fax: 660-338-2598.
School—Tel: 660-338-2258; Fax: 660-338-9930. Lay Teachers 11; Students 119.
Catechesis/Religious Program—Students 8.

HANNIBAL, MARION CO., HOLY FAMILY (1845), [JC] Rev. Michael F. Quinn; Deacon Eugene Pierceall.
Office—2103 Broadway, 63401. Tel: 573-221-1078; Fax: 573-248-1662.
School—Tel: 573-221-0456; Fax: 573-221-6357. Lay Teachers 18; Students 226.
Catechesis/Religious Program—Students 80.

HERMANN, GASCONADE CO., ST. GEORGE (1845), [CEM] Rev. William D. Debo.
Res.: 128 W. 4th St., 65041-1099. Tel: 573-486-2723.
School—Tel: 573-486-5914; Fax: 573-486-2434. Lay Teachers 13; Students 173.
Catechesis/Religious Program—Tel: 573-486-2157. Students 87.

HERMITAGE, HICKORY CO., ST. BERNADETTE (1973), Rev. W. Paul Jones.
Church: Hwy. 254, P.O. Box 167, 65668. Tel: 417-745-6361.
Catechesis/Religious Program—Students 22.

HOLTS SUMMIT, CALLAWAY CO., ST. ANDREW (1975), [CEM] Rev. Brendan P. Doyle; Deacons Daniel J. Ramsay; Lawrence A. Weber.
Church: 400 St. Andrew Dr., 65043. Tel: 573-896-5810.
Catechesis/Religious Program—Students 72.
Mission—Our Lady of the Snows P.O. Box 21, Climax Springs, Camden Co. 65324. Tel: 573-345-4223.

ILASCO, RALLS CO., HOLY CROSS, Closed., For inquires for parish records please see Holy Family, Hannibal.

INDIAN CREEK, MONROE CO., ST. STEPHEN (1833), [CEM] Rev. Donald J. Antweiler.
Res.: 27519 Monroe Rd. 533, Monroe City, 63456. Tel: 573-735-4033.

INDIAN GROVE, CHARITON CO., ST. RAPHAEL (1886), [CEM] Attended by, St. Boniface, Brunswick. Rev. Leonard S. Misey.
Mailing Address: 203 E. Vine St., P.O. Box 5, Brunswick, 65236-0005. Tel: 660-548-3267.

JONESBURG, MONTGOMERY CO., ST. PATRICK (1862), [CEM] Rev. Christopher L. Cordes; Ms. Kristin Roth, Pastoral Admin.
Res.: 505 First St., 63351. Tel: 636-488-5623; Fax: 636-488-5623.
Catechesis/Religious Program—Students 56.

KAHOKA, CLARK CO., ST. MICHAEL THE ARCHANGEL (1891), Rev. Roland J. Carbone, O.S.B.
Church: 622 W. Exchange St., P.O. Box 216, 63445. Tel: 660-727-3472.
Catechesis/Religious Program—Students 34.
Mission—St. Martha (1887), 202 S. Main St., Wayland, Clark Co. 63472. Tel: 660-754-6011.
Catechesis/Religious Program—Students 7.

KIRKSVILLE, ADAIR CO., MARY IMMACULATE (1888), [CEM] Revs. Patrick J. Shortt; William P. Kottenstette; Deacons Thomas Capuano; David D. Ream.
716 E. Washington St., 63501. Tel: 660-665-2466; Fax: 660-665-8955.
School—Tel: 660-665-1006; Fax: 660-665-1006. Lay Teachers 8; Students 135.
Catechesis/Religious Program—Tel: 660-665-2466. Students 153.
Mission—St. Rose of Lima (1903), Hwy. 149, Novinger, Adair Co. 63559. Tel: 660-488-6680.

LAKE OZARK, MILLER CO., OUR LADY OF THE LAKE (1940), Rev. Msgr. Michael J. Wilbers, E.V.; Deacon Francis P. Zimmerman.
Church: 2411 Bagnell Dam Blvd., P.O. Box 2390, 65049. Tel: 573-365-2241; Fax: 573-365-4458.
Catechesis/Religious Program—Students 91.

LAURIE, MORGAN CO., SHRINE OF ST. PATRICK (1870), [CEM] Rev. Fred J. Barnett.
Office—P.O. Box 1098, 65038-1098. Tel: 573-374-7855; Fax: 573-374-0627.
Catechesis/Religious Program—Students 42.
Mission—St. Philip Benizi (1963), 17034 Hwy. D, Versailles, Morgan Co. 65084. Tel: 573-378-5958; Fax: 573-374-4825. Rev. C. Duane Ryan.
Catechesis/Religious Program—Students 43.
Shrine—Mary Mother of the Church P.O. Box 1250, 65038. Tel: 573-374-6279; Fax: 573-374-0627.

LINN, OSAGE CO., ST. GEORGE (1866), [CEM] Rev. Ignazio C. Medina.
Res.: 613 E. Main St., P.O. Box 49, 65051. Tel: 573-897-2293.
School—Tel: 573-897-3645; Fax: 573-897-2148. Lay Teachers 12; Students 168.
Catechesis/Religious Program—Tel: 573-897-2009. Students 88.

LOOSE CREEK, OSAGE CO., IMMACULATE CONCEPTION (1845), [CEM 2] Rev. Joseph S. Corel.
Res.: P.O. Box 8, 65054. Tel: 573-897-2922; Fax: 573-897-4528.
School—Tel: 573-897-3516; Fax: 573-897-4271. School Sisters of Notre Dame 1; Lay Teachers 8; Students 92.
Catechesis/Religious Program—Students 79.

LOUISIANA, PIKE CO., ST. JOSEPH (1865), [CEM] Rev. Louis E. Dorn; Deacon Mark J. Dobelmann.
Res.: 508 N. 3rd St., 63353. Tel: 573-754-4757.
Catechesis/Religious Program—Tel: 573-754-6609. Students 47.
Mission—Mary Queen of Peace (1951), South Second St., Clarksville, Pike Co. 63336. Tel: 573-242-3730.

MACON, MACON CO., IMMACULATE CONCEPTION (1857), [CEM] Rev. Paul M. Hartley; Deacons Leo Prenger; Bernhard Toll.
Res.: 402 N. Rollins St., 63552. Tel: 660-385-3792; Fax: 660-385-6523.
School—Tel: 660-385-2711. Lay Teachers 5; Students 72.
Catechesis/Religious Program—Students 40.
Mission—Sacred Heart (1880), Bevier, Macon Co. 63532.

MARCELINE, LINN CO., ST. BONAVENTURE (1888), [CEM 2] Rev. Gerald J. Kaimann.
Res.: 409 S. Kansas Ave., 64658-1301. Tel: 660-376-3239.
School—Tel: 660-376-3580; Fax: 660-376-2836. Lay Teachers 6; Students 57.
Catechesis/Religious Program—Students 85.
Mission—St. Joseph (1870), Hurricane Branch, Chariton Co.

MARSHALL, SALINE CO., ST. PETER (1870), [CEM] Rev. Kevin Gormley; Deacons Richard H. Luebbering; Joseph R. Mitchell.
Res.: 1801 S. Miami Ave., P.O. Box 220, 65340. Tel: 660-886-7960; Fax: 660-831-1723.
School—Tel: 660-886-6390; Fax: 660-866-6606. Lay Teachers 11; Students 100.
Catechesis/Religious Program—Students 79.
Mission—Holy Family (1945), 200 Ruby St., Sweet Springs, Saline Co. 65351.

MARTINSBURG, AUDRAIN CO., ST. JOSEPH (1876), [CEM] Rev. Wayne M. Boyer; Deacon Vincent E. Garufi.
Res.: 408 E. Kellett, 65264. Tel: 573-492-6595; Fax: 573-492-6105.
School—Tel: 573-492-6283. Lay Teachers 6; Students 66.
Catechesis/Religious Program—Students 45.

MARY'S HOME, MILLER CO., OUR LADY OF THE SNOWS (1883), [CEM] Rev. Clarence E. Wiederholt.
Res.: 274 Hwy. H, Eugene, 65032-4231. Tel: 573-498-3820; Fax: 573-498-3779.
School—Tel: 573-498-3574; Fax: 573-498-3776. Lay Teachers 7; Students 94.
Catechesis/Religious Program—Students 125.

MEMPHIS, SCOTLAND CO., ST. JOHN (1952), [CEM] Rev. William P. Kottenstette.
Rectory—Rectory: Rte. 3, Box 34 H, 63555. Tel: 660-465-7130.
c/o Mary Immaculate Parish: 716 E. Washington, Kirksville, 63501. Tel: 660-665-5269; 660-665-2466.
Catechesis/Religious Program—Students 30.

META, OSAGE CO., ST. CECILIA (1904), [CEM] Rev. John J. Schutty.
Res.: P.O. Box 96, 65058-0096. Tel: 573-229-4811; Fax: 573-229-4699.
Catechesis/Religious Program—Students 72.

MEXICO, AUDRAIN CO., ST. BRENDAN (1857), [CEM] Rev. Henry J. Reichert. In Res., Rev. Lyndon Jong.
Res.: 615 S. Washington St., 65265. Tel: 573-581-4720.
School—Tel: 573-581-2443; Fax: 573-581-2571. Lay Teachers 11; Students 138.
Catechesis/Religious Program—Students 73.

MILAN, SULLIVAN CO., ST. MARY (1868), [CEM 2] Rev. Brendan Griffey; Deacon Terence L. Reibenspies.
Res.: 101 W. Baker St., P.O. Box 147, 63556. Tel: 660-265-4110; Fax: 660-265-4110.
Catechesis/Religious Program—Tel: 660-265-4110. Students 51.
Mission—St. Mary (1868), Unionville, Putnam Co. Tel: 660-947-2599.
Catechesis/Religious Program—Students 17.

MOBERLY, RANDOLPH CO., ST. PIUS X (1888), [CEM] Rev. Michael A. Coleman; Deacons Donald W. Orscheln; David F. Ritter.
Res.: 217 S. Williams St., P.O. Box 310, 65270. Tel: 660-263-5243; Fax: 660-263-0101.
School—Tel: 660-263-5500; Fax: 660-263-5744. Lay Teachers 15; Students 208.
Catechesis/Religious Program—Students 105.

MOKANE, CALLAWAY CO., ST. JUDE THADDEUS (1900), Rev. Greg Oligschlaeger; Deacon Lawrence A. Weber.
Mailing Address: 700 Hwy 2, Fulton, 65251.
Church: P.O. Box 128, 65059. Tel: 573-676-3238.
Catechesis/Religious Program—401 Adams, 65059. Students 40.

MONROE CITY, MONROE CO., HOLY ROSARY (1884), [CEM] Rev. Donald J. Antweiler.
Res.: 405 S. Main St., 63456. Tel: 573-735-4718; Fax: 573-735-4718.
School—Tel: 573-735-2422; Fax: 573-735-3091. Sisters of St. Dominic 1; Lay Teachers 10; Students 153.
Catechesis/Religious Program—Students 115.

MONTGOMERY CITY, MONTGOMERY CO., IMMACULATE CONCEPTION (1861), [CEM 2] Rev. Christopher L. Cordes.
Res.: 307 N. Walker, 63361. Tel: 573-564-2375; Fax: 573-564-2375.
School—407 W. Third St., 63361. Tel: 573-564-2679; Fax: 573-564-2679. School Sisters of Notre Dame 1; Lay Teachers 6; Students 53.
Catechesis/Religious Program—Students 75.

MORRISON, GASCONADE CO., ASSUMPTION (1875), [CEM 2] Attended by, Chamois. Rev. Patrick Dowling.
Mailing Address: P.O. Box 156, Chamois, 65024. Tel: 573-763-5345.
Catechesis/Religious Program—Students 12.

OSAGE BEND, COLE CO., ST. MARGARET OF ANTIOCH (1907), [CEM] Rev. Mark A. Porterfield, J.C.L.; Deacon Robert Smerek, Pastoral Admin.
Mailing Address: *Mailing Address*, 12025 Rte. W., 65101. Tel: 573-496-3404.

OWENSVILLE, GASCONADE CO., IMMACULATE CONCEPTION (1893), [CEM 2] Rev. Joseph Hoi.
Res.: 404 S. First St., 65066. Tel: 573-437-2494; Fax: 573-437-7494.
Catechesis/Religious Program—Tel: 573-437-3086. Students 140.

PALMYRA, MARION CO., ST. JOSEPH (1866), Rev. Patrick L. Pierceall; Sr. Marlene Buese, S.S.N.D., Pastoral Min.
Res.: 411 S. Lane St., P.O. Box 606, 63461. Tel: 573-769-3270; Fax: 573-769-3176.
Catechesis/Religious Program—Tel: 573-769-2837. Students 130.

PERRY, RALLS CO., ST. WILLIAM (1901), [CEM] Rev. John A. Henderson.
Res.: P.O. Box 339, 63462. Tel: 573-565-2852; Fax: 573-565-8012.
Catechesis/Religious Program—Students 55.
Mission—St. Frances Cabrini (1953), Hwy. 24, Paris, Monroe Co. Tel: 660-327-4448; Fax: 573-565-8012.
Mission—St. Paul (Historic Church) Hwy. EE, Center, Ralls Co. 63436.

PILOT GROVE, COOPER CO., ST. JOSEPH (1894), [CEM 3] Rev. Thomas J. Seifner.
Res.: 407 Harris St., 65276. Tel: 660-834-4251; Fax: 660-834-5601.
School—Tel: 660-834-5600; Fax: 660-834-5601.

Lay Teachers 7; Students 62.
Catechesis/Religious Program—Students 95.
Station—St. John the Baptist (1840), Clear Creek. (Mass)

RHINELAND, MONTGOMERY CO., CHURCH OF THE RISEN SAVIOR (1979), [CEM 2] Rev. William D. Debo; Deacons Joseph E. Horton; Gerald W. Korman.
Res.: 605 Bluff St., 65069. Tel: 573-236-4390; Fax: 573-236-4747.
Pilgrimage Site— (1888), Shrine of Our Lady of Sorrows, 65069. Tel: 573-236-4390.

RICH FOUNTAIN, OSAGE CO., SACRED HEART (1838), [CEM] Rev. Michael P. Murphy.
Church: Rte. 1, Box 118, 65035. Tel: 573-744-5987.
School—Tel: 573-744-5898; Fax: 573-744-5761. Sisters of Notre Dame 2; Lay Teachers 5; Students 88.
Catechesis/Religious Program—Students 42.

RICHLAND, PULASKI CO., ST. JUDE (1972), Rev. John W. Groner.
Res. & Mailing Address: 367 Old Hwy. 66, St. Robert, 65584. Tel: 573-336-3662.
Church: P.O. Box 8, 65556.

ROLLA, PHELPS CO., ST. PATRICK (1862), [CEM] Rev. David D. Cox; Deacons Michael S. Brooks; Thomas C. Manion.
Res.: 17 St. Patrick Ln., 65401. Tel: 573-364-1435; 573-341-9004; Fax: 573-364-2073.
School—Tel: 573-364-1162; Fax: 573-364-2073. Sisters of St. Francis of Our Lady of Perpetual Help 1; Lay Teachers 13; Students 230.
Catechesis/Religious Program—Students 170.

ROSATI, PHELPS CO., ST. ANTHONY (1908), [CEM] Rev. Brendan Lawless; Sr. Virginia Meyer, S.S.N.D., Pastoral Admin.
Res.: 21670 County Rd. 3640, St. James, 65559. Tel: 573-265-7247.

RUSSELLVILLE, COLE CO., ST. MICHAEL (1906), [CEM 2] Rev. Robert H. Fields; Sr. Donna Eggering, O.S.F., Pastoral Admin.; Deacon Gary Christhoff.
Res.: 13321 Railroad Ave., 65074-9447. Tel: 573-782-4503.
Catechesis/Religious Program—Tel: 573-782-3171. Students 47.

ST. ANTHONY, MILLER CO., ST. ANTHONY (1906), [CEM] Rev. M. Christopher Smith.
Church: 132 Main St., Iberia, 65486. Tel: 573-793-6550; Fax: 573-793-6550.
Catechesis/Religious Program—Students 57.

ST. CLEMENT, PIKE CO., ST. CLEMENT (1871), [CEM 2] Rev. Richard W. Frank.
Res.: 21509 Hwy. 161, Bowling Green, 63334. Tel: 573-324-5545; Fax: 573-324-5155.
School—Tel: 573-324-2166; Fax: 573-324-6159. Lay Teachers 7; Students 86.
Catechesis/Religious Program—Students 115.

ST. ELIZABETH, MILLER CO., ST. LAWRENCE (1871), [CEM] Rev. M. Christopher Smith.
Res.: 246 Main, P.O. Box 128, 65075. Tel: 573-493-2301.
Catechesis/Religious Program—Tel: 573-793-6550. Students 140.

ST. JAMES, PHELPS CO., IMMACULATE CONCEPTION (1870), Rev. P. Brendan Lawless.
Oratory— [CEM] 316 E. Scioto, 65559. Tel: 573-265-7276; Fax: 573-265-7269.
Catechesis/Religious Program—Tel: 573-265-7247. Students 50.

ST. MARTINS, COLE CO., ST. MARTIN (1885), [CEM] Rev. Edwin A. Schmidt; Deacons Francis J. Butel; Stephan J. Kliethermes.
Res.: 7148 St. Martins Ave., 65109. Tel: 573-893-2923; Fax: 573-893-3865.
School—Tel: 573-893-3519; Fax: 573-893-7404. Lay Teachers 13; Students 221.
Catechesis/Religious Program—Tel: 573-893-2352; Fax: 573-893-9587. Students 96.

ST. PATRICK, CLARK CO., THE SHRINE OF ST. PATRICK (1839), [CEM] Attended by, Canton. Rev. Ronald J. Carbone, O.S.B.; Deacon Robert DePyper, Pastoral Admin.
Parish Office:—812 Lewis St., Canton, 63435. Tel: 573-288-3198; Fax: 573-228-3198.
Catechesis/Religious Program—Students 12.

ST. ROBERT, PULASKI CO., ST. ROBERT BELLARMINE (1941), [CEM] Rev. John W. Groner.
Res.: 367 Old Hwy. 66, 65584. Tel: 573-336-3662.

ST. THOMAS, COLE CO., ST. THOMAS THE APOSTLE (1869), [CEM] Rev. Mark A. Porterfield, J.C.L.
Res.: 14814 Rt. B, P.O. Box 146, 65076. Tel: 573-477-3315; Fax: 573-477-0177.
School—P.O. Box 211, 65076. Tel: 573-477-3322; Fax: 573-477-3700. Lay Teachers 6; Students 72.
Catechesis/Religious Program—Students 50.

SALISBURY, CHARITON CO., ST. JOSEPH (1870), [CEM] Rev. William L. Korte.
Res.: 301 W. Williams, 65281. Tel: 660-388-5590; Fax: 660-388-6088.
School—Tel: 660-388-5518; Fax: 660-388-5518. Lay Teachers 10; Students 108.
Catechesis/Religious Program—Tel: 660-388-6180. Students 108.

SEDALIA, PETTIS CO.

1—ST. PATRICK (1866), Revs. Thomas Albers, C.PP.S.; Timothy J. Guthridge, C.PP.S.; Deacon Jerome Connery.
Res.: 415 E. Fourth St., 65301. Tel: 660-826-2062; Fax: 660-829-1085.
Catechesis/Religious Program—Students 68.
Station—St. Joseph Clifton City. (Mass)

2—SACRED HEART (1882), [CEM] Revs. Thomas L. Albers, C.PP.S.; Timothy J. Guthridge, C.PP.S.; Deacon Jerome Connery.
Res.: 421 W. Third St., 65301. Tel: 660-827-2311; Fax: 660-827-3941.
School—Tel: 660-827-3800; Fax: 660-827-3806. Sisters of Divine Providence 1; Lay Teachers 11; Students 202.
High School—Lay Teachers 21; Students 211.
Catechesis/Religious Program—Students 49.
Mission—St. John (1845), Bahner, Pettis Co.
Station—St. Patrick (1876), Spring Fork. (Mass)

SHELBINA, SHELBY CO., ST. MARY (1879), [CEM] Rev. Paul M. Hartley.
Res.: 307 E. Chestnut St., P.O. Box 306, 63468. Tel: 573-588-4498; Fax: 573-588-4728.
Catechesis/Religious Program—Tel: 573-588-4045. Students 90.

SLATER, SALINE CO., ST. JOSEPH (1882), Attended by, Glasgow. Rev. Philip M. Kane.
Res.: 325 W. Emma St., 65349. Tel: 660-529-2588.
Catechesis/Religious Program—Students 23.

STEELVILLE, CRAWFORD CO., ST. MICHAEL (1949), Rev. James Finder; Sr. Mary Ferraer, S.S.J., Pastoral Admin.
Mailing Address: 1098 Old Hwy. 66 W. Box 419, Bourbon, 65441. Tel: 573-732-4494; Fax: 573-732-4494.
Church: Hwy. 8 E., 65565.
Catechesis/Religious Program—Tel: 573-775-2029. Students 13.

TAOS, COLE CO., ST. FRANCIS XAVIER (1838), [CEM] Rev. J. David Maher; Deacon James E. Skahan. In Res., Rev. Roberto Ike.
Res.: 7319 Rte. M, 65101. Tel: 573-395-4401; Fax: 573-395-4302.
School—Tel: 573-395-4612. Lay Teachers 14; Students 220.
Catechesis/Religious Program—Students 46.

TIPTON, MONITEAU CO., ST. ANDREW (1857), [CEM] Rev. David J. Veit.
Res.: 106 W. Cooper St., P.O. Box 598, 65081. Tel: 660-433-2162.
School—Tel: 660-433-2232; Fax: 660-433-5432. Lay Teachers 11; Students 139.
Catechesis/Religious Program—Students 73.

VANDALIA, AUDRAIN CO., SACRED HEART (1891), Rev. Russell R. Judge.
Res.: 203 W. Home, 63382. Tel: 573-594-2717; Fax: 573-594-2556.
Catechesis/Religious Program—Students 37.
Mission—St. John (1889), 7th and Elm, Laddonia, Audrain Co. 63352. Tel: 573-373-5351; Fax: 573-373-2221.

VIENNA, MARIES CO., VISITATION (1867), [CEM] Rev. John J. Schmitz.
Res.: 105 N. Main St., P.O. Box 171, 65582. Tel: 573-422-3950; Fax: 573-422-3950.
School—105 N. Coffey St., P.O. Box 269, 65582. Tel: 573-422-3375; Fax: 573-422-3537. Sisters of Sacred Heart of Jesus 1; Lay Teachers 6; Students 76.
Catechesis/Religious Program—Students 31.

WARDSVILLE, COLE CO., ST. STANISLAUS (1880), [CEM] Rev. Gregory C. Meystrik.
Res.: 6410 Rte. W., 65101. Tel: 573-636-4925; Fax: 573-636-2534.
School—Tel: 573-636-7802; Fax: 573-635-4782. Lay Teachers 21; Students 338.
Catechesis/Religious Program—Students 22.

WARSAW, BENTON CO., ST. ANN (1945), [CEM] Rev. Richard Colbert, C.PP.S.
Res.: Rte. 2, Box 29-20, 65355. Tel: 660-438-3844 (Church); 660-438-5870 (Rectory); Fax: 660-438-5870.
Catechesis/Religious Program—Tel: 660-438-3843. Students 40.
Mission—SS. Peter & Paul (1878), Rte. 2, P.O. Box 248, Cole Camp, Benton Co. 65325. Tel: 660-668-3952.

WELLSVILLE, MONTGOMERY CO., RESURRECTION (1873), [CEM] Rev. Wayne M. Boyer; Deacon Vincent Garufi.
Church: 109 E. Bates.
Res. & Mailing Address: 408 E. Kellett, Martinsburg, 65264. Tel: 573-492-6595; Fax: 573-492-6105.
Catechesis/Religious Program—Students 54.

WESTPHALIA, OSAGE CO., ST. JOSEPH (1835), [CEM 2] Rev. Robert A. Kurwicki.
Res.: P.O. Box 116, 65085-0116. Tel: 573-455-2320; Fax: 573-455-2984.
School—Tel: 573-455-2339; Fax: 573-455-2287. Lay Teachers 10; Students 132.
Catechesis/Religious Program—Students 55.

WIEN, CHARITON CO., ST. MARY OF THE ANGELS (1876), [CEM 2] Rev. Philip M. Moriarty.
Res.: 12520 St. Mary's Blvd., New Cambria, 63558. Tel: 660-226-5243; Fax: 660-226-5207.
Catechesis/Religious Program—Students 61.
Station—Immaculate Conception Hamden. (Mass)

Chaplains of Public Institutions
Prisons

JEFFERSON CITY. *Algoa Correctional Center*, Algoa Rd., P.O. Box 538, 65102. Tel: 573-751-3911. Rev. Sylvester W. Bauer, Chap. Tel: 573-744-5913, Sr. Fran Buschell, S.S.N.D., Chap. Tel: 573-635-9127, Ext. 226.
Central Missouri Correctional Center, Hwy. 179, 65109. Tel: 573-751-2053. Rev. Patrick Dowling, Catholic Chap.
Jefferson City Correctional Center, 631 State St., P.O. Box 900, 65102. Tel: 573-751-3224. Rev. Joseph S. Corel, Chap. Tel: 573-635-7991, Sr. Ruth Heaney, O.S.B., Chap. Tel: 573-635-8123.

BOONVILLE. *Boonville Correctional Center*.
E. Morgan St., 65233. Tel: 660-882-6521. Rev. John A. Henderson, Chap. Tel: 573-565-2852.

BOWLING GREEN. *Northeast Correctional Center*, 13698 Pike 46, Airport Rd., 63334. Tel: 573-324-5545. Rev. Richard W. Frank, Chap.

FULTON. *Diagnostic and Reception Center*, P.O. Box 581, 65251. Tel: 573-592-4040. Rev. Patrick Dowling, Chap., Deacon Robert L. Dulle, Chap.

MOBERLY. *Moberly Correctional Center*, P.O. Box 7, 65270. Tel: 660-263-3778. Rev. Michael A. Coleman, Chap. Tel: 660-263-5243.

TIPTON. *Tipton Treatment Center* 65081. Tel: 660-433-2031. Rev. David J. Veit, Chap. Tel: 660-433-2162.

VANDALIA. *Women's Eastern Missouri Reception, Diagnostic and Correctional Center*, P.O. Box 300, 63382. Tel: 573-594-6686. Rev. Russell R. Judge, Chap., Sr. Fran Buschell, S.S.N.D., Chap. Tel: 573-635-9127, Ext. 226.

Hospitals and Schools

JEFFERSON CITY. *Capital Region Medical Center*, 1125 Madison St., 65101. Tel: 573-635-7100. Rev. Daniel I.J. Lueckenotte.

COLUMBIA. *Boone Hospital Center*, 1600 E. Broadway, 65201. Tel: 573-815-8000.
Columbia Catholic Hospital Ministry, 1115 Locust, 65201. Ms. Mary Salois, Dir. Tel: 573-443-3470, Ext. 1006; Fax: 573-875-3947. Email: hospitalmin@diojeffcity.org, Rev. Edwin J. Cole. Tel: 578-443-2892, Eleanor S. Braddock, M.D., P.R.N. Tel: 573-445-6701, Deacon Gene Kazmierczak, Volunteer. Tel: 573-446-0387.
Columbia Regional Hospital, 404 Keene St., 65201. Tel: 573-875-9000.
Ellis Fischel State Cancer Hospital, 115 Business Loop 70 W., 65201. Tel: 573-882-2100.
Mid-Missouri Mental Health Center, Three Hospital Dr., 65201. Tel: 573-449-2511.
Rusk Rehabilitation Center, 315 Business Loop 70 W., 65203. Tel: 573-817-2703.
University Hospital & Clinics, One Hospital Dr., 65201. Tel: 573-882-4141.
Veterans' Administration Medical Center, 800 Stadium Rd., 65201. Tel: 573-443-2511. Rev. Edwin J. Cole, Chap. Tel: 573-443-2892. (Harry S. Truman Memorial)

FULTON. *Fulton State Hospital*, 600 Fifth St., 65251. Tel: 573-592-4100. Deacon Robert L. Dulle, Chap.
Missouri School for the Deaf, 505 E. Fifth St., 65251. Tel: 573-592-4000. Rev. William L. Korte, Chap. Tel: 573-642-5562.

MARCELINE. *Pershing Regional Health Care Center*, 225 W. Hayden, 64658. Tel: 660-376-3521. Attended by St. Boniventure Rectory, 409 S. Kansas, Marceline, 64658. Tel.:660-376-3239.

MARSHALL. *Marshall State School-Hospital*, E. Slater St., 65340. Tel: 660-886-2202. Rev. Kevin Gormley, Chap. Tel: 660-886-7960.

ST. JAMES. *Missouri Veterans' Home*, 620 N. Jefferson St., 65559. Tel: 573-265-3271. Rev. Brendan Lawless, Chap. Tel: 573-265-7250. Vacant.

On Duty Outside the Diocese:
Revs.—
Hereford, Thomas D.
Keogh, William

Missionary Assignment in Peru:
Rev.—
Lawlor, Joseph

Absent on Leave:
Revs.—
Behan, Hugh F.
Daly, Manus P.
Driscoll, Brian J.
Schlachter, Eric A.

Tatro, Timothy M.
Wallace, Donald L. (Retired)

Retired:
Rev. Msgrs.—
Gillgannon, Francis G., Little Sisters of the Poor, 8475 James A. Reed Rd., Rm. 1003, Kansas City, 64138. Tel: 816-965-0994
McCorkle, Louis W., 107 Shepherd Dr., Hannibal, 63401. Tel: 573-221-0947
Poelker, Gerard L., P.O. Box 39, Holts Summit, 65043. Tel: 573-896-4748
Sommer, Jerome, Regina Cleri, 10 Archbishop May Dr., St. Louis, 63119. Tel: 314-961-0271
Wenting, J. Jacques, St. Joseph Home, 1306 W. Main St., 65109. Tel: 573-634-4936
Revs.—
Bonn, Ferdinand C., Wyandott Apartments, 2717 Wyandotte A5, Las Vegas, NV 89102. Tel: 702-364-0554
Buhman, Leo T., 1513 43rd St., St. Joseph, 64506. Tel: 816-233-7775
Cronin, Richard, c/o Mr. & Mrs. Tim O'Leary, 8 Ashleigh Dr., Skehard Rd., Cork City, Ireland. Tel: 011-353-21-292006
Flanagan, William F., 27519 Monroe Rd. 533, Monroe City, 63456.
Forst, William, St. Patrick's Apts., 555 Bluff Park Dr., #7203, St. Louis, 63031. Tel: 314-921-5430
Fuemmeler, James R., 1567 Resorts Rd., Camdenton, 65020.
Konrad, Erwin, 901 Missouri Blvd., PMB 107, 65109-1759. Tel: 573-659-8694
Long, John, The Cathedral Presbytery, Roman Street, Cork, Ireland. Tel: 011-353-21-4831103
Stangl, Frank J., 4229 Shelly Dr., Rocky Mount, NC 27804. Tel: 252-451-1844
Starmann, Joseph W., 25 Ackermann Rd., Winfield, 63389-3106. Tel: 636-566-8420
Stockman, Gerald W., 718 Randolph St., Glasgow, 65254. Tel: 660-338-2188
Waickman, Thomas L., 265 St. Joseph Hill Rd., Pacific, 63069.
Walsh, Peter, 97 New St., Ballinrobe, Co. Mayo Ireland. Tel: 011-353-92-42371
Wheeler, Clarence, M.S., 612 Norris Dr., 65109. Tel: 573-635-0648

Permanent Deacons:
Agniel, Harry M., (Retired)
Anderberg, Peter K., (Retired)
Aulbur, Mark
Berry, Kenneth
Bilgrien, Kenneth D., (On Duty Outside the Diocese)
Braddock, Joseph
Breazile, James E., On Duty Outside the Diocese)
Brooks, Michael
Brown, William J., (Retired)
Brucks, Jerome C., (Retired)
Butel, Francis J.
Capuano, Tom
Chaplin, Mark, (On Duty Outside the Diocese)
Christoff, Gary
Connery, Jerome
Daly, Michael M., (Leave of Absence)
Davis, Howard E., (On Duty Outside the Diocese)
DePyper, Robert
Dobelman, Mark J.
Dulle, Robert L.
Fritsch, Frederick
Garufi, Vincent E.
Gerling, Thomas J., (On Duty Outside the Diocese)
Heidlage, Walter F., (Retired)
Hildebrand, Larry
Horsefield, Earl R.
Horton, Joseph E.
Houston, John D., (On Duty Outside the Diocese)
Joyce, Dana K.
Kazmierczak, Eugene S.
Kinney, William J., (Retired)
Kliethermes, Stephan J.
Korman, Gerald W.
Luebbering, Richard H.
Manion, Thomas C.
McEvoy, Tim, (On Duty Outside the Diocese)
Miller, David
Mitchell, Joseph R.
Neudecker, John L.
Orscheln, Donald W., (Retired)
Parn, Harold L., (On Duty Outside the Diocese)
Pierceall, Eugene E., (Retired)
Prenger, Leo F., (Retired)
Purvis, Raymond L.
Rackers, Robert J.
Ramsay, Daniel J.
Ream, David D.
Reibenspies, Terence L.
Reuter, Ralph V., (Retired)
Ritter, David F.
Rockhold, Jess L., (Retired)
Shumake, Lindell P., (Retired)
Skahan, James E.
Smerek, Robert
Snooks, Richard W., (Retired)
Stahl, Theodore E.
Tebbe, John J., (Retired)
Toll, Bernhard F.
Towey, Martin G., Ph.D.
Valdes, Anthony J.
Visot, Luis R., (On Duty Outside the Diocese)
Von Gunten, Richard A.
Warden, Donald E., (Retired)
Watson, G. Robert, (Leave of Absence)
Weaver, John D.
Weber, Lawrence A.
Weisel, Fred M., (Leave of Absence)
Whalen, Tom
Zimmerman, Francis P.

INSTITUTIONS LOCATED IN THE DIOCESE

[A] HIGH SCHOOLS, DIOCESAN

JEFFERSON CITY. *Helias High School*, 1305 Swift's Hwy., 65109. Tel: 573-635-6139; Fax: 573-635-5615. Mr. Stan Ochsner, Dean of Students; Sr. Jean Dietrich, Prin.; Mr. Dennis Hughes, Admin.; Mr. Ron Vossen, Campus Ministry; Rev. Brendan Doyle, Spiritual Dir. Brothers of the Christian Schools 2; School Sisters of Notre Dame 1; Lay Teachers 47; Students 907.

[B] GENERAL HOSPITALS

JEFFERSON CITY. *St. Mary's Health Center*, 100 St. Mary's Medical Plaza, 65101. Tel: 573-761-7000; Fax: 573-636-5733. Web: www.stmarys-jeffcity.com. Elizabeth Anderholt, Pres.; Rev. James Carter, American Baptist Min., APC Certified Chap.; Mrs. Marge Doyle, NACC Certified & Chap.; Rev. Robert Fields, Chap.; Mrs. Peggy Van Gundy, Chap.; Sr. Evelyn Marie Peterman, F.S.M., Chap.; Rev. Harvel Sanders, Episcopal Priest & Chap. Member of SSM Health Care Bed Capacity 167; Patients Assisted Annually 245,684; Clinics 12; Clinic visits 128,684.

[C] NURSING HOMES

JEFFERSON CITY. *St. Joseph's Home*, 1306 W. Main St., 65109. Tel: 573-635-0166; Fax: 573-635-1405. Grace Hoffmann, Admin.; Sr. Lydia Ann Braun, Supr.; Denise Sommerer, Dir. Nurses; Rev. Msgr. Charles Patterson, Chap. Conducted by the Carmelite Sisters of the Divine Heart of Jesus. Sisters 3; Residents 90.

Villa Marie Skilled Nursing Facility, 1030 Edmonds St., 65109. Tel: 573-761-6700; Fax: 573-635-6685. William Popp, Admin.; Sr. Angelina Terrio, F.S.M., Pastoral Care. Member of SSM Health Care Franciscan Sisters of Mary, St Louis 4; Bed Capacity 120.

[D] CONVENTS AND RESIDENCES FOR SISTERS

JEFFERSON CITY. *Discalced Carmelite Monastery*, 2201 W. Main St., 65109. Tel: 573-636-3364. Sr. Marie Therese Dubois, O.C.D., Prioress. Professed of Solemn Vows 8.

Franciscan Sisters of Mary, Jericho Community, 202 Binder Dr., 65109-0815. Tel: 573-635-8123. Sisters 3.

COLUMBIA. *Our Lady of Peace Monastery*, 3710 W. Broadway Blvd., 65203-0116. Tel: 573-446-2300; Fax: 573-446-2312. Email: administration@benedictinesister.org. Web: www.benedictinesister.org. Benedictine Sisters of Pontifical Jurisdiction 12.

[E] NEWMAN CENTERS

COLUMBIA. *University of Missouri-Columbia, Campus Ministry* 701 Maryland, 65201. Tel: 573-449-5424; Fax: 573-874-2777. Email: pardeech@socket.net. Web: www.students.missouri.edu/~newman/. Revs. Charles D. Pardee, Dir. & Pastor; Mark S. Smith.

FAYETTE. *Central Methodist College* c/o St. Joseph Church, 300 S. Cleveland, 65248. Tel: 660-248-2439; Fax: 660-248-2439. Rev. Robert W. Duesdieker, Dir.

KIRKSVILLE. *Catholic Newman Center, Truman State University* 709 S. Davis, 63501. Tel: 660-665-4357; Fax: 660-665-3592. Email: tsnewman@socket.net. Web: www.kirksvillenewman.org. Mrs. Bettie Lesczynski, Dir.; Rev. William P. Kottenstette, Chap.

ROLLA. *University of Missouri-Rolla* 2 Vichy Rd., P.O. Box 838, 65402. Tel: 573-364-2133; Fax: 573-368-3560. Email: newman@umr.edu. Web: www.umr.edu/~newman. Sr. Renita Brummer, O.S.F., Dir.

[F] SOCIAL SERVICES

JEFFERSON CITY. *Samaritan Center*, 1310 E. McCarty St., P.O. Box 1687, 65102. Tel: 573-634-7776; Fax: 573-761-5948. Email: samlady@socket.net. Marylyn DeFeo, Exec. Dir.

[G] MISCELLANEOUS

JEFFERSON CITY. *Diocesan Excellence in Education Fund, Inc.*, P.O. Box 417, 65102. Tel: 573-635-9127.

St. Mary's Health Center, Jefferson City, Missouri, Foundation, 100 St. Mary's Medical Plaza, 65101. Tel: 573-761-7198. Ms. Beverly Stafford, Dir. Member of SSM Health Care

Missouri Catholic Conference, 600 Clark Ave., P.O. Box 1022, 65102. Tel: 573-635-7239; Fax: 573-635-7431. Email: mocatholic@mocatholic.org. Web: www.mocatholic.org. Lawrence A. Weber, Exec. Dir. & Gen. Council.

LINN. *Good Shepherd Center*, 1208 B E. Lee St., 65051. Tel: 573-897-0525. P.O. Box 763, 65051. Bernice Voss, Volunteer Dir.; Bill Voss, Volunteer Dir.

ST. JAMES. *Boys and Girls Town of Missouri*, 13160 County Rd. 3610, 65559. Tel: 800-737-3251. Web: www.bgtm.org.

ST. LOUIS. *Residents Encounter Christ*, Missouri State Board, 7522 Big Bend Blvd., 63119. Tel: 314-647-7060; Fax: 314-647-8380. Mr. Joseph Hedley, Exec. Dir.

RELIGIOUS INSTITUTES OF MEN REPRESENTED IN THE DIOCESE

For further details refer to the corresponding bracketed number in the Religious Institutes of Men or Women section.

[0330]—*Brothers of the Christian Schools* (Midwest Prov.)—F.S.C.

[1330]—*Congregation of the Mission* (Midwest Prov.)—C.M.

[0720]—*The Missionaries of Our Lady of La Salette* (Prov. of Mary Queen)—M.S.

[]—*Order of St. Benedict* (Conception Abbey)

[1060]—*Society of the Precious Blood* (Kansas City Prov.)—C.PP.S.

RELIGIOUS INSTITUTES OF WOMEN REPRESENTED IN THE DIOCESE

[0230]—*Benedictine Sisters of Pontifical Jurisdiction* (Columbia, MO)—O.S.B.

[0360]—*Carmelite Sisters of the Divine Heart of Jesus*—Carmel.D.C

[3670]—*Congregation of the Sacred Heart of Jesus of Saint Jacut* (San Antonio, TX)—S.S.C.J.

[0460]—*Congregation of the Sisters of Charity of the Incarnate Word*—C.C.V.I.

[1730]—*Congregation of the Sisters of the Third Order of St. Francis* (Oldenburg, IN)—O.S.F.

[0420]—*Discalced Carmelite Nuns (Second Order of the Carmel)* Jefferson City, MO—O.C.D.

[1070-11]—*Dominican Sisters* (Sparkill, NY)—O.P.

[1415]—*Franciscan Sisters of Mary*—F.S.M.

[1430]—*Franciscan Sisters of Our Lady of Perpetual Help*—O.S.F.

[2970]—*School Sisters of Notre Dame* (Milwaukee Prov.)—S.S.N.D.

[2970]—*School Sisters of Notre Dame* (Dallas, TX Prov.)—S.S.N.D.

[2970]—*School Sisters of Notre Dame* (St. Louis Prov.)—S.S.N.D.

[1680]—*School Sisters of St. Francis* (Milwaukee, WI)—O.S.F.

[0480]—*Sisters of Charity of Leavenworth, Kansas* (Leavenworth, KS)—S.C.L.

[0660]—*Sisters of Christian Charity* (Wilmette, IL)—S.C.C.

[0990]—*Sisters of Divine Providence* (Allison Park, PA)—C.D.P.

[3830-15]—*Sisters of St. Joseph* (Concordia, KS)—C.S.J.

[3840]—*Sisters of St. Joseph of Carondelet* (St. Paul, MN)—C.S.J.

[3893]—*Sisters of St. Joseph of Chestnut Hill* (Philadelphia, PA)—S.S.J.

[3270]—*Sisters of the Most Precious Blood* (O'Fallon, MO)—C.PP.S.

DIOCESAN CEMETERIES

JEFFERSON CITY. *St. Peter's Catholic Cemetery Association*, c/o Resurrection Cemetery, 3015 W. Truman Blvd., 65109. Tel: 573-893-2751. Mr. Harry Otto, Pres.

NECROLOGY

† Chenoweth, Robert J., (Retired)—Died April 7, 2003

† Mersinger, Arthur, (Retired)—Died July 24, 2003

Diocese of Joliet in Illinois

(Dioecesis Joliettensis in Illinois)

Most Reverend

JOSEPH J. IMESCH, D.D.

Bishop of Joliet; ordained December 16, 1956; ordained Auxiliary Bishop of Detroit April 3, 1973; appointed Bishop of Joliet June 30, 1979; installed August 28, 1979. *Res.: 425 Summit St., Joliet, IL 60435.*

Most Reverend

ROGER L. KAFFER, D.D.

Retired Auxiliary Bishop of Joliet; ordained May 1, 1954; appointed Auxiliary Bishop of Joliet and Titular Bishop of Dusa April 25, 1985; consecrated June 26, 1985; retired August 15, 2002. *Res.: 425 Summit St., Joliet, IL 60435.*

ESTABLISHED BY BULL DATED DECEMBER 11, 1948.

Square Miles 4,218.

Canonically Erected March 24, 1949.

Comprises the Counties of Du Page, Kankakee, Will, Grundy, Ford, Iroquois and Kendall in the State of Illinois.

Patron of Diocese: St. Francis Xavier.

Legal Title: For legal titles of parishes and diocesan institutions, consult the Chancery.

Chancery: 425 Summit St., Joliet, IL 60435. Tel: 815-722-6606; Fax: 815-722-6602.

Web: www.dioceseofjoliet.org

Email: jdavies@dioceseofjoliet.org

STATISTICAL OVERVIEW

Personnel	
Bishop	1
Retired Bishops	2
Retired Abbots	1
Priests: Diocesan Active in Diocese	134
Priests: Diocesan Active Outside Diocese	5
Priests: Diocesan in Foreign Missions	2
Priests: Retired, Sick or Absent	52
Number of Diocesan Priests	193
Religious Priests in Diocese	113
Total Priests in Diocese	306
Extern Priests in Diocese	13
Ordinations:	
Diocesan Priests	1
Religious Priests	2
Transitional Deacons	5
Permanent Deacons	24
Permanent Deacons in Diocese	171
Total Brothers	76
Total Sisters	631
Parishes	
Parishes	122
With Resident Pastor:	
Resident Diocesan Priests	98
Resident Religious Priests	16
Without Resident Pastor:	
Administered by Priests	8
Missions	11
Professional Ministry Personnel:	
Sisters	65
Lay Ministers	225
Welfare	
Catholic Hospitals	3
Total Assisted	629,415
Homes for the Aged	13
Total Assisted	2,363
Day Care Centers	4
Total Assisted	1,056
Specialized Homes	1
Total Assisted	2,000
Special Centers for Social Services	5
Total Assisted	53,882
Residential Care of Disabled	1
Total Assisted	120
Educational	
Diocesan Students in Other Seminaries	24
Total Seminarians	24
Colleges and Universities	3
Total Students	10,736
High Schools, Diocesan and Parish	4
Total Students	2,498
High Schools, Private	4
Total Students	3,366
Elementary Schools, Diocesan and Parish	56
Total Students	18,892
Catechesis/Religious Education:	
High School Students	4,575
Elementary Students	54,155
Total Students under Catholic Instruction	94,246
Teachers in the Diocese:	
Priests	24
Brothers	20
Sisters	75
Lay Teachers	1,722
Vital Statistics	
Receptions into the Church:	
Infant Baptism Totals	9,932
Adult Baptism Totals	330
Received into Full Communion	423
First Communions	10,340
Confirmations	7,546
Marriages:	
Catholic	1,503
Interfaith	500
Total Marriages	2,003
Deaths	3,708
Total Catholic Population	625,189
Total Population	1,734,304

Former Bishops—Most Revs. MARTIN D. MCNAMARA, D.D., appt. first Bishop of Joliet; ord. Dec. 3, 1922; appt. Dec. 17, 1948; consecrated March 7, 1949; died May 23, 1966; ROMEO BLANCHETTE, D.D., appt. Auxiliary Bishop of Joliet and Titular Bishop of Maxita Feb. 8, 1965; consecrated April 3, 1965; appt. Bishop of Joliet July 19, 1966; installed Aug. 31, 1966; resigned Jan. 30, 1979; died Jan. 10, 1982.

Chancery—425 Summit St., Joliet, 60435. Tel: 815-722-6606; Fax: 815-722-6602. Office Hours: Mon.-Fri. 8:30-4:30

Vicar General—Very Rev. JOSEPH TAPELLA, J.C.L.

Chancellor—Sr. JUDITH A. DAVIES, O.S.F.

Moderator of the Curia—Very Rev. JOSEPH TAPELLA, J.C.L.

Director of Administration—Mr. JAMES P. LYNCH.

Director of Finance—Mr. GUY A. SELL.

Matrimonial Tribunal—310 Bridge St., Joliet, 60435. Tel: 815-722-2256.

Judicial Vicar—Very Rev. JOSEPH TAPELLA, J.C.L.

Adjutant Judicial Vicar—Rev. MICHAEL GINTER, J.C.L.

Notaries—Mrs. SYLVIA CARBONI; Mrs. MARIE SMEETS; Mrs. BETTY JOUTRAS; Mrs. HELEN MILCHERSKA; Mrs. DELORES AICHELE.

Defender of the Bond—Sr. MARILYN PHILLIPS, O.S.F., Ph.D., J.C.D.

Judges—Very Rev. JOSEPH TAPELLA, J.C.L.; Rev. MICHAEL W. GINTER, J.C.L.; Mr. THOMAS E. KERBER, J.C.L.

Advocates—Mrs. VIRGINIA L. LAUTZ; Sr. CLARE VAN VOOREN, O.S.F.

Diocesan Offices and Directors

Board of Conciliation and Arbitration—425 Summit St., Joliet, 60435.

Campaign for Human Development—Mrs. ELIZABETH FRANKLIN, St. Charles Borromeo Pastoral Center, 402 S. Independence Blvd., Romeoville, 60441. Tel: 815-834-4027.

Catholic Cemeteries—Mr. RICHARD TAPELLA, Dir., St. Charles Borromeo Pastoral Center, 402 S. Independence Blvd., Romeoville, 60441. Tel: 815-838-0395.

Catholic Charities— Legal Title: Catholic Charities of the Diocese of Joliet Ms. KATHLEEN MCGOWAN, Exec. Dir., 203 N. Ottawa St., Joliet, 60432. Tel: 815-723-3405.

The Catholic Education Foundation of the Diocese of Joliet—Mrs. PEGGY KOBE, Dir., St. Charles Borromeo Pastoral Center, 402 S. Independence Blvd., Romeoville, 60441. Tel: 815-834-4033.

Catholic Relief Services—Mr. THOMAS GARLITZ, Dir., St. Charles Center, 402 S. Independence Blvd., Romeoville, 60441. Tel: 815-834-4026.

Council of Catholic Women—Mrs. ROSE MARTINET, Office: St. Charles Borromeo Pastoral Center, 402 S. Independence Blvd., Romeoville, 60441. Tel: 815-834-4070.

Communications Office—Mr. JOHN CULLEN, Chancery, 425 Summit St., Joliet, 60435. Tel: 815-722-6606.

Cursillo Movement—Rev. MARK JENDRYSIK, Moderator, St. Charles Borromeo Pastoral Center, 405 S. Independence Blvd., Romeoville, 60441. Tel: 815-838-8100.

Deans—Revs. THOMAS SULARZ, East Dupage; JOEL FORTIER, West Dupage Kendall; JOSEPH SIEGEL, East Will; RICHARD BENNETT, West Will; CHARLES WHEELER, Kankakee-Grundy; F. LEE RYAN, Ford-Iroquois.

Development—Mr. KEVIN DELABRE, Dir., St. Charles Borromeo Pastoral Center, 402 S. Independence Blvd., Romeoville, 60441. Tel: 815-838-8515.

Coordinator for Health Affairs—Sr. JUDITH A. DAVIES, O.S.F., Chancery, 425 Summit St., Joliet, 60435. Tel: 815-722-6606.

Vicar for Religious—VACANT, St. Charles Borromeo Pastoral Center, 402 S. Independence Blvd., Romeoville, 60441. Tel: 815-834-4009.

Diaconate—Deacon WILL WORDEN, Dir., St. Charles Borromeo Pastoral Center, 402 S. Independence Blvd., Romeoville, 60441. Tel: 815-834-4091.

Divine Worship—Sr. SHARON MARIE STOLA, O.S.B., Dir., St. Charles Borromeo Pastoral Center, 402 S. Independence Blvd., Romeoville, 60441. Tel: 815-834-4010.

Ecumenism—Rev. STANLEY ORLIKIEWICZ, Dir., St. John Vianney Villa, 1464 Green Trails Dr., Naperville, 60540. Tel: 630-305-8819.

Family Ministry—Dr. JAMES HEALY, Dir., St. Charles Borromeo Pastoral Center, 402 S. Independence Blvd., Romeoville, 60441. Tel: 815-838-5334.

Hispanic Ministry—Sr. JUDY CALLAHAN, B.V.M., Dir., St. Charles Borromeo Center, 402 S. Independence Blvd., Romeoville, 60441. Tel: 815-834-4037.

Catholic Explorer—Mrs. MARY BRESLIN, Editor, Office, 402 S. Independence Blvd., Romeoville, 60441. Tel: 815-838-6475; Fax: 815-834-4068.

Diocesan Life Office—Mrs. FRAN FORTIER, Dir., St. Charles Borromeo Pastoral Center, 402 S. Independence Blvd., Romeoville, 60441. Tel: 815-838-1002.

Marriage Encounter—Leadership Couple: ANDY JOBST; BRIDGET JOBST, 6 Camden Ct., Cary, 60013. Tel: 847-516-0005.

Marriage Preparation—Dr. JAMES HEALY, Dir., St. Charles Borromeo Pastoral Center, 402 S. Independence Blvd., Romeoville, 60441. Tel: 815-838-5334.

Ministry Formation—Mrs. YVONNE DE BRUIN, Dir., St. Charles Borromeo Pastoral Center, 402 S. Independence Blvd., Romeoville, 60441. Tel: 815-834-4001.

College Campus Ministry—Mr. KEVIN O'DONNELL, 402 S. Independence Blvd., Romeoville, 60446-2264. Tel: 815-834-4022.

Peace and Social Justice Ministry—Mr. THOMAS GARLITZ, Dir. Tel: 815-834-4026. St. Charles Borromeo Pastoral Center, 402 S. Independence Blvd., Romeoville, 60441.

Personnel—Mr. MICHAEL SVACH, Dir. Tel: 815-834-4077.

Presbyteral Council—Rev. CHRIS GROH, Pres., 425 Summit, Joliet, 60435. Tel: 815-722-6606.

Propagation of the Faith—Rev. DAMIEN GRAZIANO, Dir., 1531 Summit St., Oakbrook Terrace, 60181. Tel: 630-629-5810.

Religious Education—Mr. THOMAS QUINLAN, Dir., 430 N. Center St., Joliet, 60435. Tel: 815-727-6411.

Rural Life—Rev. LEE BACCHI, St. Peter, 450 E. 3rd, P.O. Box 25, Clifton, 60927. Tel: 815-694-2027.

St. Vincent de Paul Society—213 Main St., West Chicago, 60185. Tel: 630-293-9420.

Catholic Schools—Sr. HELEN JEAN KORMELINK, O.S.B., Supt., St. Charles Borromeo Pastoral Center, 402 S. Independence Blvd., Romeoville, 60441. Tel: 815-838-2181.

Scouts—Rev. JOHN OUPER, Office: St. James the Apostle, 480 S. Park Blvd., Glen Ellyn, 60137. Tel: 630-469-7540.

Stewardship—Mrs. MARIANNE MURPHY, Dir., St. Charles Borromeo Pastoral Center, 402 S. Independence Blvd., Romeoville, 60441. Tel: 815-834-4030.

Victim Assistance Coordinator—Sr. MARY FRANCES SEELEY, O.S.F. Tel: 815-263-6467.

Vocations—Rev. JOHN REGAN, Dir., St. Charles Borromeo, 402 S. Independence Blvd., Romeoville, 60441. Tel: 815-834-4002.

CLERGY, PARISHES, MISSIONS AND PAROCHIAL SCHOOLS

CITY OF JOLIET
(WILL COUNTY)

1—THE CATHEDRAL OF ST. RAYMOND (1917), Revs. Joseph Siegel; James Burnett, Rector. In Res., Rev. Joseph J. Tapella.
Res.: 604 N. Raynor Ave., 60435. Tel: 815-722-6653; Fax: 815-722-6175.
School—713 Douglas St., 60435. Tel: 815-722-6626; Fax: 815-727-4668. Lay Teachers 22; Students 532.
Catechesis / Religious Program—Fax: 815-722-3137. Students 303.

2—ST. AMBROSE (1965), Rev. John J. Doyle.
Res.: 1711 Burry Cir., Crest Hill, 60435. Tel: 815-722-3748; Fax: 815-722-4950.
Catechesis / Religious Program—Tel: 815-722-9193. Students 150.

3—ST. ANNE (1953), Rev. John J. Doyle.
Res.: 1702 N. Dearborn St., Crest Hill, 60435. Tel: 815-722-3222; Fax: 815-722-1955.
Catechesis / Religious Program—Students 125.

4—ST. ANTHONY (1902), (Italian), Rev. Arthur LaPore.
Res.: 100 N. Scott St., 60431-1210. Tel: 815-722-1057; Fax: 815-722-9805.

5—ST. BERNARD (1921), Rev. Richard Ross.
Res.: 1313 Ridgewood Ave., 60432. Tel: 815-726-4474; Fax: 815-726-4520.
Catechesis / Religious Program—Tel: 815-722-7653; Fax: 815-724-1720. Clustered with St. Mary Magdalene, Joliet. Students 20.

6—SS. CYRIL AND METHODIUS (1900), (Slovak), Revs. Branislav Caniga, Admin.; James Pajkos, O.F.M.
Res.: 704 Landau Ave., 60432. Tel: 815-722-3586; Fax: 815-722-7276.
Catechesis / Religious Program—Tel: 815-723-0061; Fax: 815-722-6276. Students 35.

7—HOLY CROSS (1893), (Polish), [CEM] Rev. Chris Groh.
Res.: 901 Elizabeth St., 60435. Tel: 815-722-0785; Fax: 815-723-0679.

8—ST. JOHN THE BAPTIST (1852), [CEM] Revs. John Dombrowski, O.F.M.; Medard Buvala, O.F.M.; Tom Shaughnessy, O.F.M.; Deacon Jose Lopez In Res., Revs. Lawrence Jagdfeld, O.F.M.; Louis B. Antl, O.F.M.; Bros. Ducanh Pham, O.F.M.; Theophane Ballman, O.F.M.
Res.: 404 N. Hickory St., 60435. Tel: 815-727-4788; Fax: 815-740-1521.
Catechesis / Religious Program—403 N. Hickory St., 60435. Tel: 815-727-9077; Fax: 815-727-1729. Students 250.

9—ST. JOSEPH (1891), (Slovenian), [CEM] Rev. James Radek.
Res.: 416 N. Chicago St., 60432. Tel: 815-727-9378; Fax: 815-727-9580.
School—409 N. Scott St., 60432. Tel: 815-722-1005; Fax: 815-722-1213. Sisters 2; Lay Teachers 11; Students 181.
Catechesis / Religious Program—Students 65.

10—ST. JUDE (1954), Rev. James A. Schwab Deacons Raymond Clark; William Hetzel.
Res.: 2212 McDonough St., 60436. Tel: 815-725-2209; Fax: 815-741-8844.
School—2204 McDonough St., 60436. Tel: 815-729-0288; Fax: 815-729-0344. Sisters of St. Francis of Mary Immaculate 1; Lay Teachers 14; Students 239.
Catechesis / Religious Program—Tel: 815-729-0288; Fax: 815-729-0344. Students 239.

11—ST. MARY, Closed. For inquiries for parish records contact the chancery.

12—ST. MARY MAGDALENE (1953), Rev. Ron P. Neitzke.
Res.: 127 S. Briggs St., 60433. Tel: 815-722-7653; Fax: 815-724-1720.
School—Tel: 815-727-9079; Fax: 815-727-2059. Lay Teachers 9; Students 100.
Catechesis / Religious Program—Students 110.

13—ST. MARY NATIVITY (1906), (Croatian), Revs. Christopher Groh; John T. McGeean Stanley Drewniak (Poland); Deacon Daniel Mahoney Sr.
Res.: 706 N. Broadway, 60435. Tel: 815-726-4031; Fax: 815-727-4393.
School—702 N. Broadway, 60435. Tel: 815-722-8518. Sisters of St. Francis of Christ the King 2; Lay Teachers 16; Students 251.
Catechesis / Religious Program—Tel: 815-726-4073. Students 180.

14—MOUNT CARMEL (1939), (Mexican-American), Revs. Raymond Corkery, O.Carm.; Charles Countie, O.Carm.; Jose Cilia, O.Carm.
Res.: 409 Irving St., 60432. Tel: 815-726-5208; Fax: 815-727-7225.
Catechesis / Religious Program—Tel: 815-727-7187. Students 465.

15—ST. PATRICK (1838), Rev. James M Lennon; Deacons Paul Kolodziej; Charles Peterson. In Res., Rev. Eugene Bucciferro.
Res.: 710 W. Marion St., 60436. Tel: 815-727-4746; Fax: 815-727-4798.
School—110 Willow Ave., 60436. Tel: 815-726-2924; Fax: 815-726-9289. Lay Teachers 15; Students 300.
Catechesis / Religious Program—Tel: 815-727-4746; Fax: 815-727-4746. Students 125.

16—ST. PAUL THE APOSTLE (1950), Revs. George Klepec; Gregory Rothfuchs; Deacons James Bouldin, (Retired); William Bevan.
Res.: 18 Woodlawn Ave., 60435. Tel: 815-725-1527; Fax: 815-730-9907.
School—130 N. Woodlawn Ave., 60435. Tel: 815-725-3390; Fax: 815-725-3180. Lay Teachers 20; Students 400.
Catechesis / Religious Program—120 Woodlawn Ave., 60435. Tel: 815-725-6927. Students 200.

17—SACRED HEART (1886), (African American), Rev. Raymond C. Lescher; Deacon Ralph Bias.
Res.: 337 S. Ottawa St., 60436. Tel: 815-722-0295; Fax: 815-722-6088.
Catechesis / Religious Program—Students 40.

18—ST. THADDEUS (1927), (Polish), Rev. Edward P. Rowland.
Res.: 501 Liberty St., 60432. Tel: 815-727-7212.
Hall—510 Columbia St., 60432. Tel: 815-727-7806.

OUTSIDE THE CITY OF JOLIET

ADDISON, DU PAGE CO.
1—ST. JOSEPH (1956), (Hispanic), Rev. Thomas Cargo; Deacon Gabriel Gamboa.
Res.: 330 E. Fullerton, 60101. Tel: 630-279-6553; Fax: 630-279-4925.
School—Tel: 630-279-4211; Fax: 630-279-4032. Mrs. Mary Rehfield, Prin. Lay Teachers 13; Students 208.
Catechesis / Religious Program—Tel: 630-832-5514. Dolly Matthews, D.R.E. Students 615.

2—ST. PHILIP THE APOSTLE (1963), Revs. Tom Sularz; Scott Huggins; Deacon Philip Heitz; Deacon James Dixon.
Res.: 1223 W. Holtz Ave., 60101. Tel: 630-628-0900; Fax: 630-543-9858.
School—Tel: 630-543-4130; Fax: 630-458-8750. Denise Sedlak, Prin. Lay Teachers 19; Students 329.
Catechesis / Religious Program—Tel: 630-543-1754; Fax: 630-543-4672. Students 422.

ASHKUM, IROQUOIS CO., ASSUMPTION OF THE BLESSED VIRGIN MARY (1903), [CEM] [JC 2] Rev. James Holup.
Res.: N. Second St., Box 218, 60911. Tel: 815-698-2262; Fax: 815-698-2262.
Mission—St. John the Baptist (1856), Box 218, L'Erable, Iroquois Co. 60911. Tel: 815-698-2262.
Catechesis / Religious Program—Tel: 815-698-2224. Students 130.

AURORA, DU PAGE CO., OUR LADY OF MERCY (1988), Rev. Hugh Fullmer; Most Rev. Peter G. Jankowski, Vicar.
Res.: 801 S. Eola Rd., 60504. Tel: 630-851-3444; Fax: 630-851-3468.
Catechesis / Religious Program—Tel: 630-851-3444, Ext. 6222. Students 1,500.

BEAVERVILLE, IROQUOIS CO., ST. MARY (1857), (French), [CEM] [JC] Rev. Robert J. Coleman.
Res.: 308 St. Charles St., P.O. Box 152, 60912. Tel: 815-435-2432.
Catechesis / Religious Program—Students 45.

BENSENVILLE, DU PAGE CO.
1—ST. ALEXIS (1926), Rev. Agustin Ortega, Admin.; Sr. Laurina Kahne, C.S.J., Pastoral Assoc.
Res.: 400 W. Wood St., 60106. Tel: 630-766-3530; Fax: 630-766-3536.
Catechesis / Religious Program—410 W. Wood St., 60106. Tel: 630-766-4417. Elizabeth Marquez, D.R.E.; Tere Hescott, D.R.E. Students 284.

2—ST. CHARLES BORROMEO (1959), Rev. Martin M. Gabel; Deacon Michael Principe.
Res.: 1135 Daniel, 60106-3467. Tel: 630-860-1120; Fax: 630-860-5029.
School—Tel: 630-766-0116; Fax: 630-766-0181. Lay Teachers 9; Students 239.
Catechesis / Religious Program—Tel: 630-766-8822; Fax: 630-766-0181. Students 172.

BLOOMINGDALE, DUPAGE CO., ST. ISIDORE (1920), [CEM] Revs. Felipe Legarreta; Anthony Taschetta; Frank Infanger; Sr. Helen Mantovani, O.P., Pastoral Assoc.; Deacons Ken Jackson; John Freund; Terry Cummiskey, Pastoral Assoc.; Don Randolph.
Res.: 427 W. Army Trail Rd., 60108. Tel: 630-529-3045; Fax: 630-529-2940.
School—Tel: 630-529-9323; Fax: 630-529-8882. Lay Teachers 23; Students 352.
Catechesis / Religious Program—Tel: 630-529-9191. Students 1,350.

BOLINGBROOK, WILL CO.
1—ST. DOMINIC (1964), Revs. Mark Jendrysik; Luis Gutierrez; Deacons Robert Wallace; Paul Walen.
Res.: 440 E. Briarcliff Rd., 60440. Tel: 630-739-5703; Fax: 630-739-2036.
School—420 E. Briarcliff Rd., 60440. Tel: 630-739-1633; Fax: 630-739-5989. Franciscans of the Sacred Heart 1; Lay Teachers 25; Students 380.
Catechesis / Religious Program—Tel: 630-739-2102. Students 733.

2—ST. FRANCIS OF ASSISI (1980), Revs. David J. Hankus; Mario S. Quejadas; Deacons Raymond Hamilton; Rudulfo Molano; Marco Lovero.
Res.: 325 Whitewater Dr., 60440. Tel: 630-759-7588; Fax: 630-759-5257.
Catechesis / Religious Program—Tel: 630-759-7611. Theresa Palicka, D.R.E. Students 635.

BOURBONNAIS, KANKAKEE CO., MATERNITY OF THE BLESSED VIRGIN MARY (1847), [CEM] Revs. John Linnan, C.S.V.; James E. Michaletz, C.S.V.; Deacons Euchrist J. Marcotte; Francis Chamness; Dale Barth.
Res.: 308 E. Marsile St., 60914. Tel: 815-933-8285; Fax: 815-933-8289.
School—Tel: 815-933-7758; Fax: 815-933-1884. Lay Teachers 16; Students 231.
Catechesis / Religious Program—Tel: 815-933-8226; Fax: 815-933-1884. Students 242.

BRADLEY, KANKAKEE CO., ST. JOSEPH (1904), Rev. William G. Dewan; Deacons Bob LaMotte; Leon Fritz; Andrew Berg. In Res., Rev. John Antczak.
Res.: 211 N. Center Ave., 60915. Tel: 815-939-3573;

Fax: 815-939-3138.
School—Tel: 815-933-8013; Fax: 815-933-2775. Sisters 2; Lay Teachers 17; Students 269.
Catechesis/Religious Program—247 N. Center Ave., 60915. Tel: 815-937-9340. Students 297.
Convent—247 N. Center Ave., 60915. Tel: 815-932-0112.

BRAIDWOOD, WILL CO., IMMACULATE CONCEPTION (1869), (Irish—Italian), [CEM] Rev. Steven Bondi.
Res.: 110 S. School St., 60408. Tel: 815-458-2125; Fax: 815-458-2836.
Catechesis/Religious Program—Students 250.
Mission—St. Lawrence O'Toole Essex, Kankakee Co.

CABERY, FORD CO., ST. JOSEPH (1867), (German), [CEM] Rev. Richard F. Kostelz.
Res.: 112 W. Main St., P.O. Box 77, 60919. Tel: 815-949-1568.
Catechesis/Religious Program—Students 26.
Mission—St. Mary (1899), 216 E. Lincoln, Reddick, Kankakee Co. 60961.

CAROL STREAM, DU PAGE CO.

1—CORPUS CHRISTI (1989), Rev. Charles A. Gemskie; Deacon Tom Thiltgen, Pastoral Assoc.; Kathie Brewer, Pastoral Assoc. In Res., Rev. Henry Wilkening (Retired).
Res.: 1415 W. Lies Rd., 60188-0453. Tel: 630-483-4673; Fax: 630-483-4679.
Catechesis/Religious Program—Tel: 630-483-4222. Students 977.

2—ST. LUKE (1963), Rev. Thomas Schutter; Sr. Barbara Rowan, S.S.S.F., Pastoral Assoc.
Res.: 421 Cochise Ct., 60188. Tel: 630-668-1325; Fax: 630-668-1356.
Catechesis/Religious Program—Tel: 630-665-2322. Students 436.

CHANNAHON, WILL CO., ST. ANN PARISH (1990), Rev. Jeff Stoneberg.
Res.: 24500 S. Navajo Dr., 60410. Tel: 815-467-6962; Fax: 815-467-2320.
Catechesis/Religious Program—Tel: 815-467-6992. Students 521.

CHEBANSE, IROQUOIS CO., SS. MARY AND JOSEPH'S (1869), [CEM] Rev. Lee F. Bacchi.
Res.: 525 S. Chestnut, P.O. Box 5, 60922. Tel: 815-697-2654; Fax: 815-694-3507.
Catechesis/Religious Program—Students 65.

CLARENDON HILLS, DU PAGE CO., NOTRE DAME (1954), Revs. Robert J. Schuler; Venard Kommer, O.F.M.; Sundar Raj Kocherla (India); David Lifka; Deacons Neill Carson; Frank Foys; David Lifka; Alan Symonanis.
Res.: 64 Norfolk Ave., 60514. Tel: 630-654-3365; Fax: 630-654-8701.
School—Tel: 630-323-1642; Fax: 630-654-3255. Lay Teachers 19; Students 277.
Catechesis/Religious Program—Tel: 630-654-3365, Ext. 237. Students 525.

CLIFTON, IROQUOIS CO., ST. PETER'S (1869), [CEM] [JC] Rev. Lee F. Bacchi.
Res.: 450 E. Third Ave., Box 25, 60927. Tel: 815-694-2027; Fax: 815-694-3507.
Catechesis/Religious Program—Tel: 815-694-2970. Students 100.

COAL CITY, GRUNDY CO., ASSUMPTION (1889), Rev. Michael Pennock; Deacon John Schimandle.
Res.: 245 S. Kankakee St., 60416. Tel: 815-634-4171; Fax: 815-634-4186.
Catechesis/Religious Program—Tel: 815-634-8020. Judith Kaluzny, D.R.E. Students 345.

DARIEN, DU PAGE CO.

1—OUR LADY OF KOREAN MARTYRS MISSION (1999), (Korean), Rev. Simeon Je Chan-Kyu.
7121 Clarendon Hills Rd., 60561. Tel: 630-794-0203; Fax: 630-794-9364.

2—OUR LADY OF MOUNT CARMEL (1970), Revs. Gavin Quinn, O.Carm.; Edward Ward, O.Carm. (CHI); Robert Boley, O.Carm.; Deacon John Farrell.
Res.: 8404 Cass Ave., 60561. Tel: 630-852-3303; Fax: 630-852-5227.
Catechesis/Religious Program—Tel: 630-963-3053. Students 1,564.

3—OUR LADY OF PEACE (1970), Revs. Alphonse Micka, M.I.C.; Anthony Kelpsas, M.I.C.; Dan Cambra, M.I.C.; Deacons Frank Bina; Paul Brachle; Dennis Stolarz.
Res.: 701 Plainfield Rd., 60561. Tel: 630-323-4333; Fax: 630-323-4354.
School—709 Plainfield Rd., 60561. Tel: 630-325-9220; Fax: 630-325-1995. Lay Teachers 30; Students 509.
Catechesis/Religious Program—Tel: 630-986-8430; 630-986-8446; Fax: 630-986-1214. Students 708.

DOWNERS GROVE, DU PAGE CO.

1—DIVINE SAVIOR (1968), Rev. Robert E. Pietras; Deacon Paul S. Newey. In Res., Rev. Leonard J. Guz.
Res.: 6700 Main St., 60516. Tel: 630-969-1532; Fax: 630-969-1724.
Catechesis/Religious Program—Tel: 630-969-1673. Students 644.

2—ST. JOSEPH (1907), Revs. Paul Hottinger; John Joseph Hornicak.
Res.: 4824 Highland, 60515. Tel: 630-964-0216; Fax: 630-964-0867.
School—Franklin & Highland, 60515. Tel: 630-969-4306; Fax: 630-969-3946. Lay Teachers 24; Students 460.
Catechesis/Religious Program—Tel: 630-971-1740; Fax: 630-964-0867. Students 495.

3—ST. MARY OF GOSTYN (1891), Revs. Thomas Paul; Tri Van Tran.
Res.: 444 Wilson St., 60515. Tel: 630-969-1063; Fax: 630-969-1259.
School—440 Prairie Ave., 60515. Tel: 630-968-6155; Fax: 630-968-6208. Felician Sisters 2; Lay Teachers 25; Students 628.
Catechesis/Religious Program—Tel: 630-960-3565; Fax: 630-969-1289. Students 625.

ELMHURST, DU PAGE CO.

1—IMMACULATE CONCEPTION (1876), Revs. James Murphy; Raymond Garbin; Brad Baker; Deacon Thomas Goebel.
Res.: 134 Arthur St., 60126. Tel: 630-530-8515; Fax: 630-530-9346.
School—Tel: 630-530-3490; Fax: 630-530-9787. Grace Benner, Prin. Lay Teachers 22; Students 592.
High School—217 Cottage Hill Ave., 60126. Tel: 630-530-3460; Fax: 630-530-2290. Ms. Pamela M. Levar, Prin. Lay Teachers 21; Students 225.
Catechesis/Religious Program—Tel: 630-530-3480. Students 715.

2—MARY, QUEEN OF HEAVEN (1957), (Irish—German), Rev. John Barrett. In Res., Rev. Thomas Wolter; Deacons John Maloney; Thomas Nolan.
Res.: 426 N. West Ave., 60126. Tel: 630-279-5700; Fax: 630-279-4667.
Catechesis/Religious Program—442 N. West Ave., 60126. Tel: 630-832-8962. Students 483.

3—VISITATION (1953), Revs. Michael Lane; John Oliver Klein; Robert Noesen; Deacons Jay Janousek; Anthony Spatafore; Charles Nunez.
Res.: 779 S. York St., 60126. Tel: 630-834-6700; Fax: 630-834-6711.
School—Tel: 630-834-4931; Fax: 630-834-4936. Sisters of St. Adrian Dominican 4; Lay Teachers 23; Students 540.
Catechesis/Religious Program—851 S. York, 60126. Tel: 630-279-7058; Fax: 630-279-9340. Students 530.

FRANKFORT, WILL CO., ST. ANTHONY (1929), Rev. Thomas A. Corbino; Deacon Donald Berkey, Pastoral Assoc.; Katie Augustynowicz, Pastoral Assoc.; Deacons Daniel Danahey; Richard Rosko.
Res.: 7659 W. Sauk Trail, 60423. Tel: 815-469-3750; Fax: 815-469-6514.
Catechesis/Religious Program—Tel: 815-469-6072; Fax: 815-806-9421. Barbara Bekker, D.R.E. Students 1,539.

GIBSON CITY, FORD CO., OUR LADY OF LOURDES (1875), [JC] Revs. Joseph A. Mundakal, C.M.I., Gibson City, IL Our Lady of Lourdes; William Smith, O.Carm.
Res.: 534 N. Wood St., 60936. Tel: 217-784-4671; Fax: 217-784-4671.
Catechesis/Religious Program—Students 80.
Mission—St. George Melvin, Ford Co.

GILMAN, IROQUOIS CO., IMMACULATE CONCEPTION (1872), [CEM] Rev. John Balluff.
Res.: 224 N. Secor St., 60938. Tel: 815-265-7236; Fax: 815-265-7236.
Catechesis/Religious Program—Students 98.
Mission—Our Lady of Guadalupe 504 W. Seminary Ave.,, Onarga, Iroquois Co. 60955.

GLEN ELLYN, DU PAGE CO.

1—ST. JAMES THE APOSTLE (1965), Revs. John J. Ouper; Mathew Maniampra, C.M.I. (India); Deacons John W. Moeller; Matthew Pidgeon.
Res.: 480 S. Park Blvd., 60137. Tel: 630-469-7540; Fax: 630-469-7590.
School—Tel: 630-469-8060; Fax: 630-469-1107. Lay Teachers 19; Students 258.
Catechesis/Religious Program—490 S. Park Blvd., 60137. Tel: 630-858-5646; Fax: 630-858-5687. Students 920.

2—ST. PETRONILLE (1925), Revs. James Dougherty; Michael A. O'Keefe, Pastor Emeritus; John Sullivan; David Lawrence; Deacons Ronald Yurcus; John Spiezio; Bob Cassey. In Res., Rev. Nguyen Huy Quyen.
Res.: 420 Glenwood Ave., 60137. Tel: 630-469-0404; Fax: 630-469-0412.
School—Tel: 630-469-5041; Fax: 630-469-5071. Lay Teachers 33; Students 540.
Catechesis/Religious Program—Tel: 630-858-3796; Fax: 630-858-6232. Students 1,200.

3—QUEENSHIP OF MARY (1993), (Vietnamese), Rev. Nguyen Huy Quyen.
Res.: 23W371 Armitage, 60137. Tel: 630-469-7494; Fax: 630-752-0332.
Catechesis/Religious Program—Tel: 630-752-0332. Students 191.

GLENDALE HEIGHTS, DU PAGE CO., ST. MATTHEW (1960), Revs. David Dillon, O.Carm.; Michael O'Keefe, O.Carm.; Deacon Robert Malek; Mr. Alex Gervacio, Pastoral Assoc.
Res.: 1555 Glen Ellyn Rd., 60139. Tel: 630-469-6300; Fax: 630-469-6302.
School—Tel: 630-858-3112; Fax: 630-858-0623. Lay Teachers 25; Students 377.
Catechesis/Religious Program—Tel: 630-469-5178; Fax: 630-469-6302. Students 467.

GOODRICH, KANKAKEE CO., SACRED HEART (1895), [CEM] Rev. Ronald Hart.
Res.: 588 S. 10000 W. Road, Bonfield, 60913-7019. Tel: 815-426-2221.
Catechesis/Religious Program—Tel: 815-426-2770. Students 31.

HERSCHER, KANKAKEE CO., ST. MARGARET MARY, [CEM] Rev. Ronald Hart.
Res.: 207 E. Fifth St., 60941. Tel: 815-426-2153; Fax: 815-426-2136.
Catechesis/Religious Program—Tel: 815-426-2720. Students 92.

HINSDALE, DU PAGE CO., ST. ISAAC JOGUES (1930), (Irish—Italian), Revs. William Donnelly; Richard Lundgren.
Res.: 306 W. Fourth St., 60521. Tel: 630-323-1248; Fax: 630-323-6373.
School—Tel: 630-323-3244; Fax: 630-655-6676. Religious 1; Lay Teachers 49; Students 717.
Catechesis/Religious Program—421 S. Clay St., 60521. Tel: 630-323-0265. Students 1,102.

HOMER GLEN, WILL CO., OUR MOTHER OF GOOD COUNSEL (1996), Revs. Thomas Osborne, O.S.A.; Donald Lewandowski, O.S.A.
Church: 16043 S. Bell Rd., 60441. Tel: 708-301-6246; Fax: 708-301-6356.
Catechesis/Religious Program—Tel: 708-301-0214. Students 623.

HOPKINS PARK, KANKAKEE CO., SACRED HEART (1939), (African American), Rev. Vernon Arseneau; Deacon Norman Neher.
Res. & Mailing Address: P.O. Box 557, 60944. Tel: 815-944-5562; Fax: 815-472-3043.
Catechesis/Religious Program—16485 E. Birch, P.O. Box 557, 60944. Students 11.

IRWIN, KANKAKEE CO., ST. JAMES THE APOSTLE, [CEM] Rev. Ronald Hart.
Res.: 4372 Main St., Kankakee, 60901. Tel: 815-933-8807; Fax: 815-426-2136.
Catechesis/Religious Program—Tel: 815-933-5443. Students 69.

ITASCA, DU PAGE CO.

1—ST. ANDREW KIM (1981), (Korean), [JC] Rev. Josephus Y. Kim (Korea, South).
Res.: 1275 Arlington Hts. Rd., 60143. Tel: 630-250-0576; Fax: 630-250-2502.

2—ST. PETER THE APOSTLE (1956), Revs. Douglas L. Hauber; Scaria T. Thoppil, C.M.I. (India); Deacon Steven A. Fox.
Res.: 524 N. Rush St., 60143-1698. Tel: 630-773-1272; Fax: 630-773-1720.
School—500 N. Cherry St., 60143-1699. Tel: 630-773-1979; Fax: 630-773-2826. Lay Teachers 14; Students 200.
Catechesis/Religious Program—Tel: 630-773-1959; Fax: 630-773-2624. Students 320.

KANKAKEE, KANKAKEE CO.

1—ST. MARTIN OF TOURS (1950), [JC] Rev. Dennis F. Settles.
Res.: 953 S. Ninth Ave., 60901. Tel: 815-933-7177; Fax: 815-933-2171.
School—907 S. Ninth Ave., 60901. Tel: 815-932-7911; Fax: 815-932-7296. Lay Teachers 9; Students 138.
Catechesis/Religious Program—Students 230.

2—ST. PATRICK (1893), (Irish), Rev. Richard Pighini, C.S.V.; Sr. Theresa Galvan, C.N.D., Pastoral Min.; Deacon Joseph Cotugno, Pastoral Assoc.; Marilyn Mulcahy, Pastoral Assoc. In Res., Revs. Joseph Tremonti, C.S.V.; Francis Czerwionka, C.S.V.; Donald R. Wehnert.
Res.: 428 S. Indiana Ave., 60901. Tel: 815-932-6716; Fax: 815-932-2585.
School—Tel: 815-932-8124; Fax: 815-932-0485. Lay Teachers 14; Students 231.
Catechesis/Religious Program—Students 248.

3—ST. ROSE OF LIMA (1855), Rev. Charles Wheeler.
Res.: 486 W. Merchant St., 60901. Tel: 815-933-9391; Fax: 815-933-9393.
Catechesis/Religious Program—Students 92.

4—ST. STANISLAUS, (Polish), Closed. For inquiries for parish records contact the chancery.

5—ST. TERESA (1949), Rev. Gregor Gorsic; Sr. Mary McElmeel, B.V.M., Pastoral Assoc.; Deacon Ronald Whitman; Barbara Staniszeski, Pastoral Assoc.
Res.: 361 N. St. Joseph Ave., 60901. Tel: 815-933-7683; Fax: 815-933-7692.
Lisieux Pastoral Center—371 St. Joseph Ave., 60901. Tel: 815-939-2913.
School—Tel: 815-932-8124. School and Religious Program combined with St. Patrick, Kankakee.

KINSMAN, GRUNDY CO., SACRED HEART (1880), Rev.

Robert Maternoski, Admin.
Res.: 219 Emmett St., P.O. Box 824, 60437. Tel: 815-392-4245; Fax: 815-392-4307.
Catechesis/Religious Program—Students 68.

LISLE, DU PAGE CO., ST. JOAN OF ARC (1924), Revs. Gerald Tivy; Kenneth Zigmond, O.S.B.; Thomas Botheroyd; Deacons Denis Stucko; Joseph Dalpiaz.
Office—820 Division St., 60532. Tel: 630-963-4500; Fax: 630-963-4568.
School—Tel: 630-969-1732; Fax: 630-963-9070. Religious 3; Lay Teachers 25; Students 714.
Catechesis/Religious Program—Students 508.

LOCKPORT, WILL CO.

1—ST. BERNARD (1978), Rev. Richard B. Prodehl; Sr. Mary Carr, O.P., Pastoral Assoc.
Res.: 14135 Parker Rd., Homer Glen, 60441. Tel: 708-301-3020; Fax: 708-301-0738.
Catechesis/Religious Program—14724 S Arboretum Dr., Homer Glen, 60441. Tel: 708-301-6952; Fax: 708-301-8870. Students 621.

2—ST. DENNIS (1846), Revs. Jim Curtin; Thomson Panakal; Sr. Joanne Vallaro, C.S.J., Pastoral Assoc.; Deacons Rob Weierman, Pastoral Assoc.; William Uffman.
Res.: 1214 Hamilton St., 60441. Tel: 815-838-2592; Fax: 815-838-2401.
School—1201 S. Washington St., 60441. Tel: 815-838-4494; Fax: 815-838-5435. Lay Teachers 11; Students 260.
Catechesis/Religious Program—Students 450.

3—ST. JOHN VIANNEY (1958), Rev. Andrew L. Buczyna.
Res.: 401 Brassel, 60441. Tel: 815-723-3291; Fax: 815-724-0566.
Catechesis/Religious Program—Students 20.

4—ST. JOSEPH (1868), Rev. Thomas McGivney Jr.; Dr. Jeanne M. Cosgrove, Pastoral Assoc. In Res., Rev. Lawrence Mudduse.
Res.: 410 S. Jefferson St., 60441. Tel: 815-838-0187; Fax: 815-838-5379.
School—529 Madison, 60441. Tel: 815-838-8173; Fax: 815-838-0504. Franciscan Sisters of the Sacred Heart 1; Lay Teachers 14; Students 257.
Catechesis/Religious Program—529 Madison St., 60441. Tel: 815-838-2112. Students 330.
Convent—531 E. Fourth St., 60441. Tel: 815-838-0186.

LOMBARD, DU PAGE CO.

1—CHRIST THE KING (1960), Rev. Peter Jarosz; Deacons Fred Francl; Frank Lillig; John Freund; Wayne Storrs.
Res.: 1501 S. Main St., 60148. Tel: 630-629-1717; Fax: 630-629-1717.
School—Tel: 630-627-0640; Fax: 630-627-0640. Lay Teachers 16; Students 175.
Catechesis/Religious Program—Tel: 630-629-1717, Ext. 16; Fax: 630-629-1717. Students 375.

2—DIVINE MERCY POLISH MISSION, Rev. Adam Bobola, S.Ch. (CHI).
21 W. 411 Sunset Ave., 60148. Tel: 630-268-8766; Fax: 630-268-8712.

3—ST. PIUS X (1954), Revs. Herbert Essig; Scaria T. Thoppil, C.M.I. (India); Sr. Pauline Schultz, O.S.F., Pastoral Assoc.; Deacons Thomas Rachubinski; Ron Knecht; William Crane; Larry Lissak.
Res.: 1025 E. Madison, 60148. Tel: 630-627-4526; Fax: 630-495-5926.
School—Tel: 630-627-2353; Fax: 630-627-1810. Patricia Walther, Prin. Lay Teachers 28; Students 440.
Catechesis/Religious Program—Tel: 630-627-1551. Sr. Helen Susan, D.R.E. Students 505.

4—SACRED HEART (1912), Revs. Arno A. Dennerlein; Jess Testa; Deacon Thomas Bailey.
Res.: 114 S. Elizabeth St., 60148. Tel: 630-627-0687; Fax: 630-627-0688.
School—Tel: 630-629-0536; Fax: 630-629-4752. Lay Teachers 12; Students 270.
Catechesis/Religious Program—328 W. Maple St., 60148. Tel: 630-495-0843. Students 450.

MANHATTAN, WILL CO., ST. JOSEPH (1891), [CEM 2] Rev. Edward J. O'Malley; Deacon John Putman.
Res.: 235 W. North, P.O. Box 25, 60442. Tel: 815-478-3341; Fax: 815-478-7046.
School—Tel: 815-478-3951; Fax: 815-478-7412. Lay Teachers 12; Students 150.
Catechesis/Religious Program—Tel: 815-478-4419. Students 468.

MANTENO, KANKAKEE CO., ST. JOSEPH (1855), [CEM] [JC] Rev. Ed Grotovsky; Deacons Francis Henrisey; John Hindes; Richard Balgeman; John Leonas.
Res.: 207 S. Main St., 60950. Tel: 815-468-3403; Fax: 815-468-7089.
Catechesis/Religious Program—Tel: 815-468-8116. Students 413.

MARTINTON, IROQUOIS CO., ST. MARTIN (1899), [CEM] Rev. Robert J. Coleman.
Res.: P.O. Box 152, Beaverville, 60912. Tel: 815-435-2432.

MINOOKA, GRUNDY CO., ST. MARY (1862), (Irish), [CEM] Rev. Mark Fracaro.
Res.: 303 St. Mary St., P.O. Box 456, 60447. Tel: 815-467-2233; Fax: 815-467-1760.
Catechesis/Religious Program—Tel: 815-467-2769. Students 615.

MOKENA, WILL CO., ST. MARY CHURCH (1864), [CEM] Revs. James Dvorscak; Scott McCawley; Sr. Dolores Zemont, O.S.F., Pastoral Assoc.; Deacons Donald Bernardin; Robert Kaminski; Duane Hahn; Gary Bednar.
Res.: 19515 S. 115th Ave., P.O. Box 2, 60448. Tel: 708-326-9300; Fax: 708-326-9301.
School—Tel: 708-326-9330; Fax: 708-326-9331. Franciscan Sisters of the Sacred Heart 1; Lay Teachers 13; Students 308.
Catechesis/Religious Program—11409 W. 195th St., 60448 Tel: 708-326-9350; Fax: 708-326-9351. Students 1,630.

MOMENCE, KANKAKEE CO., ST. PATRICK (1859), [CEM] Rev. Vernon Arseneau; Deacon Norman Weher.
Res.: 119 Market St., 60954. Tel: 815-472-2864; Fax: 815-472-3043.
School—404 W. Second St., 60954. Tel 815-472-2469. Lay Teachers 5; Students 135.
Catechesis/Religious Program—Students 120.
Mission—*Sacred Heart* P.O. Box 557, Hopkins Park, Kankakee Co. 60944. Tel: 815-944-5562.

MONEE, WILL CO., ST. BONIFACE (1868), (Irish—Polish), Rev. Mark Menezes; Deacon Robert Jossey.
Church: 5304 W. Main St., P.O. Box 217, 60449. Tel: 708-534-9682; Fax: 708-534-9683.
Rectory—Rectory: 25942 S. Middlepoint Ln., 60449.
Catechesis/Religious Program—Students 140.

MORRIS, GRUNDY CO., IMMACULATE CONCEPTION OF THE BLESSED VIRGIN MARY (1852), [CEM] Rev. Robert A. Hoffenkamp; Deacons Robert Stansberry Jr.; Dennis Kobs.
Res.: 516 E. Jackson St., 60450. Tel: 815-942-0620; Fax: 815-942-3171.
School—Tel: 815-942-4111; Fax: 815-942-5094. Lay Teachers 19; Students 272.
Catechesis/Religious Program—505 E. North St., 60450. Tel: 815-942-4177; Fax: 815-942-4177. Students 307.

NAPERVILLE, DUPAGE CO.

1—ST. ELIZABETH SETON (1986), Rev. Ernest Norbeck; Sr. Frances McCarron, I.B.V.M., Pastoral Assoc.; Deacons Bart Federici; Thomas Ross; Gary Swauger.
Res.: 2220 Lisson Rd., 60565. Tel: 630-416-3325; Fax: 630-416-3642.
Catechesis/Religious Program—Tel: 630-416-1992; Fax: 630-416-4086. Students 1,845.

2—HOLY SPIRIT CATHOLIC COMMUNITY (1998), Rev. Richard Bennett; Deacon Tom Schroeder.
Res.: 2225 Snow Creek Rd., 60564. Tel: 630-922-0081; Fax: 630-922-0085.
Catechesis/Religious Program—Students 1,802.

3—ST. MARGARET MARY (1980), Revs. William J. O'Shea; Danilo Soriano, C.P.; Sr. Madelyn Gould, S.S.S.F., Pastoral Assoc.; Deacons Kenneth J. Miles; James Perry; Terry Taylor.
1450 Green Trails Dr., 60540. Tel: 630-369-0777; Fax: 630-369-1493.
Catechesis/Religious Program—Tel: 630 369-0833. Students 1,486.

4—STS. PETER AND PAUL (1856), [CEM] Revs. James A. Nowak; Jerome Kish; Gordon Mahoney; Most Rev. Slawomir Ignasik; Sr. Aniceta Stube, O.P., Pastoral Assoc.; Deacons William Girard; Ronald Brown.
Res.: 36 N. Ellsworth St., 60540. Tel: 630-355-1081; Fax: 630-355-1179.
School—201 E. Franklin, 60540. Tel: 630-355-0113; Fax: 630-355-9803. Mr. Frank Glowaty Prin. Lay Teachers 25; Students 622.
Catechesis/Religious Program—36 N. Ellsworth St., Ste. 104, 60540. Tel: 630-357-2436 Fax: 630-357-2458 Students 1,250.

5—ST. RAPHAEL (1963), Revs. Theodore Weitzel; Dennis Paul; Deacons William Blessing; John McHugh; Andrew Repak; Charles Woods.
Mailing Address: 1215 Modaff Rd., 60540-7818. Tel: 630-355-4545; Fax: 630-355-7470.
Res.: 416 Gartner, 60540. Tel: 630-355 4545; Fax: 630-355-7470.
School—Tel: 630-355-4545, Ext. 135; Fax: 630-428-4974. Lay Teachers 19; Students 310.
Catechesis/Religious Program—Tel: 630-355-4545, Ext. 121. Students 2,547.

6—ST. THOMAS THE APOSTLE (1984), Revs. Joel Fortier; Matthew Pozen; Deacons William Worden; Charles Lane; James Breen.
Res.: 1500 Brookdale Rd., 60563. Tel: 630-355-8980; Fax: 630-355-0521.
Catechesis/Religious Program—Tel: 630-305-6318. Students 1,741.

NEW LENOX, WILL CO., ST. JUDE (1934), Revs. Michael Slattery, O.S.A.; R. William Sullivan, O.S.A.; Michael Schweifler, O.S.A. In Res., Rev. John Merkelis, O.S.A.; Bro. Mark Emken, O.S.A.; Deacons Robert Fitt; William Ciston; Dennis Theriault.
Res.: 241 W. Second Ave., 60451. Tel: 815-485-8049; Fax: 815-485-7754.
School—Tel: 815-485-2549; Fax: 815-485-0234. Lay Teachers 12; Students 221.
Catechesis/Religious Program—Tel: 815-485-4852; Fax: 815-485-2623. Students 1,913.

OAKBROOK TERRACE, DUPAGE CO., ASCENSION OF OUR LORD (1967), Rev. J. Damien Graziano; Deacon William J. Tansey, M.D.
Res.: 1 S. 314 Summit Ave., 60181. Tel: 630-629-5810; Fax: 630-953-8251.
Catechesis/Religious Program—Tel: 630-629-5810, Ext. 215;. Students 197.

OSWEGO, KENDALL CO., ST. ANNE (1963), Revs. Daniel F. Stempora; Robert Collogan; Deacons William Dunn; Duane Wozek.
Res.: 551 Boulder Hill Pass, P.O. Box 670, 60543. Tel: 630-554-3331; Fax: 630-554-0530.
Catechesis/Religious Program—(Grades K-8) Tel: 630-554-1425; Fax: 630-554-9797. Students 1,220.

PARK FOREST, WILL CO., ST. MARY (1953), Rev. John Ryan; Deacon John Drechny.
Res.: 212 Monee Rd., 60466. Tel: 708-747-1600; Fax: 708-748-6907.
School—227 Monee Rd., 60466-2403. Tel: 708-748-6686. Franciscan Sisters of the Sacred Heart 1; Lay Teachers 8; Students 190.
Catechesis/Religious Program—Students 15.

PAXTON, FORD CO., ST. MARY (1910), Rev. Denis White.
Res.: 407 W. Pells, 60957-1920. Tel: 217-379-4033; Fax: 217-379-6303.
Mission—*St. Joseph* c/o St. Mary, 407 W. Pells, Loda, Iroquois Co. 60957-1920.
Catechesis/Religious Program—Tel: 217-379-2983. Students 145.

PEOTONE, WILL CO., ST. PAUL THE APOSTLE (1961), Rev. Michael Ginter; Deacon Thomas McCarthy.
Res.: 501 N. Conrad St., P.O. Box 700, 60468-0700. Tel: 708-258-6917; Fax: 708-258-3031.
Catechesis/Religious Program—Tel: 708-258-9580; Fax: 708-258-3031. Students 260.

PIPER CITY, FORD CO., ST. PETER (1887), Rev. John Balluff.
Res. & Mailing Address: 212 Pine St., 60959. Tel: 815-686-2595.
Catechesis/Religious Program—1245 E. 2800 N., 60959. Tel: 815-686-9270. Students 74.
Mission—*Immaculate Conception* [CEM 2] Roberts, Ford Co.

PLAINFIELD, WILL CO.

1—ST. FRANCIS XAVIER, Formerly Catholic Center of Plainfield (2002), [CEM] Rev. Dennis Lewandowski.
Mailing Address: 7140 Caton Farm Rd., Unit A, 60544. Tel: 815-609-8077; Fax: 815-609-8078.
Catechesis/Religious Program—Students 200.

2—ST. MARY IMMACULATE (1909), [CEM] Revs. Anthony A. Nugent; David Medow; Sr. Margaret Ann Spagnola, O.S.M., Pastoral Assoc.; Deacons James Sossong, Pastoral Assoc.; Terry Sakfo, Pastoral Assoc.; James Walters, Pastoral Assoc.; Jerry Krupowicz, Pastoral Assoc.; Patrick Lombardo, Pastoral Assoc.; Thomas Sheridan, Pastoral Assoc.; Peni Heffernan, Pastoral Assoc.
Mailing Address: 129 S. Division St. (Rte. 59), 60544.
Res.: 116 Frederick, 60544. Tel: 815-436-2651; Fax: 815-436-5017.
School—129 S. Division St., 60544-8806. Tel: 815-436-3953; Fax: 815-439-8045. Lay Teachers 29; Students 544.
Catechesis/Religious Program—Tel: 815-436-4501. Students 2,361.

PLANO, KENDALL CO., ST. MARY (1885), [CEM] Revs. Jerome A. Zalonis, M.I.C.; Victor S. Incardona, M.I.C.; Boniface Vaisnoras, M.I.C.; Anthony Nockumas, M.I.C.; Deacon Santos Martinez.
Res.: 901 N. Center St., 60545. Tel: 630-552-3448; Fax: 630-552-3450.
School—817 N. Center Ave., 60545. Tel: 630-552-3345; Fax: 630-552-4385. Lay Teachers 15; Students 273.
Catechesis/Religious Program—810 N. Center Ave., 60545. Tel: 630-552-1505. Sr. Kathryn Frankovich, O.S.F., D.R.E. Students 245.

ROCKDALE, WILL CO., ST. JOSEPH (1914), Rev. John J. Zanoni.
Res.: 1329 Belleview Ave., 60436. Tel: 815-725-4469; Fax: 815-725-1820.
Catechesis/Religious Program—Tel: 815-729-9149. Students 65.

ROMEOVILLE, WILL CO., ST. ANDREW THE APOSTLE (1959), Rev. Gerald Simonelli; Deacons Jose Mendoza; Herb Waldron; Rich Ford; Jerry Clark; Leo Borkowicz.
530 Glen Ave., 60446. In Res., Rev. John Driscoll.
Res.: 219 Arlington Dr., 60446. Tel: 815-886-4165; Fax: 815-886-6119.
School—Tel: 815-886-5953; Fax: 815-293-2016. Sisters 2; Lay Teachers 16; Students 315.
Catechesis/Religious Program—505 Kingston Dr.,

60446. Tel: 815-886-5962; Fax: 815-886-6624. Students 850.

ROSELLE, DU PAGE CO., ST. WALTER (1946), Revs. Francis B. McDonald; Dennis Spies; Deacons Ron Searls; Charles Pistorio; Richard Foy.
Res.: 130 W. Pine Ave., 60172. Tel: 630-894-2461; Fax: 630-582-4206.
School—201 W. Maple Ave., 60172. Tel: 630-529-1721; Fax: 630-529-9290. Lay Teachers 29; Students 742.
Catechesis/Religious Program—140 W. Pine, 60172. Tel: 630-894-5880; Fax: 630-582-4206. Kenneth Ortega, D.R.E. Students 1,004.

ST. ANNE, KANKAKEE CO., ST. ANNE (1872), (French-Canadian), [CEM] Rev. James Fanale, C.S.V.
Res.: 230 N. Sixth Ave., 60964. Tel: 815-427-8265; Fax: 815-427-6403.
Catechesis/Religious Program—Students 35.

ST. GEORGE, KANKAKEE CO., ST. GEORGE (1853), (French-Canadian), [CEM] Rev. Kenneth Yarno, C.S.V.
Res.: 5272 E. 5000 North Rd., Bourbonnais, 60914-9725. Tel: 815-939-1851; Fax: 815-939-2777.

SHOREWOOD, WILL CO., HOLY FAMILY (1959), Rev. John L. Dennerlein; Deacon Fred Straub.
Church: 600 N. Brookforest Ave., 60431. Tel: 815-725-6880; Fax: 815-725-8649.
Res.: 604 Edgebrook Dr., 60431. Tel: 815-725-6880.
School—Tel: 815-725-8149. Lay Teachers 12; Students 316.
Catechesis/Religious Program—Tel: 815-729-2243. Students 316.

SOUTH WILMINGTON, GRUNDY CO., ST. LAWRENCE (1904), Rev. Robert Maternoski; Deacons Joseph Riggi; Steven Frazier.
Res.: 165 Rice St., Box 190, 60474. Tel: 815-237-2230; Fax: 815-237-2201.
Catechesis/Religious Program—Students 104.

STEGER, WILL CO., ST. LIBORIUS (1902), Revs. Joseph Burns; Roger Kutzner; Deacons Len Olszak; Loren Bowns.
Res.: 71 W. 35th St., 60475. Tel: 708-754-1363; Fax: 708-754-7577.
School—3436 Halsted Blvd., 60475. Tel: 708-754-0192; Fax: 708-755-3982. (Steger Campus) Lay Teachers 15; Students 246.
Catechesis/Religious Program—Tel: 708-754-3460. Students 262.

VILLA PARK, DU PAGE CO.

1—ST. ALEXANDER (1924), Rev. Tuan Van Nguyen; Deacons John Boyle; Christopher Cochran; James Krueger; John Gibbons.
Res.: 300 S. Cornell Ave., 60181. Tel: 630-833-7730; Fax: 630-833-3127.
School—136 S. Cornell Ave., 60181. Tel: 630-834-3787; Fax: 630-834-1961. Lay Teachers 19; Students 271.
Catechesis/Religious Program—130 S. Cornell Ave., 60181. Tel: 630-832-0506. Students 236.

2—ST. JOHN THE APOSTLE (1959), (Italian—Polish), Rev. Robert Duda.
Res.: 330 N. Westmore, 60181. Tel: 630-279-7404; Fax: 630-530-9910.
Catechesis/Religious Program—Tel: 630-832-7588; Fax: 630-832-7588. Students 118.

WARRENVILLE, DU PAGE CO., ST. IRENE (1927), Rev. James Antiporek; Sr. Roseann Eck, C.S.J., Pastoral Assoc.; Deacons William Murphy, Pastoral Assoc.; Robert True, Pastoral Assoc.; Joseph Urso, Pastoral Assoc.; Annette Kubalanza, Pastoral Assoc.
Res.: 28 W. 441 Warrenville Rd., 60555. Tel: 630-393-2400; Fax: 630-393-9680.
School—3S601 Warren Ave., 60555. Tel: 630-393-9303; Fax: 630-393-7009. Maureen White, Prin. Lay Teachers 15; Students 221.
Catechesis/Religious Program—Tel: 630-393-2400, Ext. 22. Students 323.

WATSEKA, IROQUOIS CO., ST. EDMUND (1872), Rev. F. Lee Ryan.
Res.: 219 E. Locust St., 60970. Tel: 815-432-3274; Fax: 815-432-3275.
Catechesis/Religious Program—Tel: 815-432-5569. Students 170.
Mission—*St. Joseph* P.O. Box 173, Crescent City, Iroquois Co. 60928.

WAYNE, DU PAGE CO., RESURRECTION (1964), Rev. Laurian Janicki, O.F.M.
Res.: 30 W. 350 Army Tr., 60184. Tel: 630-289-5400, Ext. 203; Fax: 630-289-5407.
Catechesis/Religious Program—Tel: 630-289-5400, Ext. 215;. Students 580.

WEST CHICAGO, DU PAGE CO., ST. MARY (1894), [CEM] Revs. William Conway; Burke Masters; Deacons Bruce Carlson; Harry Sheaffer; George Valdez; Luis Saltigerald.
Res.: 140 N. Oakwood Ave., 60185. Tel: 630-231-0013; Fax: 630-293-2671.
School—147 Garden St., 60185. Tel: 630-231-1776. Lay Teachers 13; Students 176.
Catechesis/Religious Program—Tel: 630-231-5704. Students 360.

WESTMONT, DU PAGE CO., HOLY TRINITY (1938), Revs. William DeSalvo; Albert Heidecke.
Res.: 111 S. Cass Ave., 60559. Tel: 630-968-1366; Fax: 630-968-7846.
School—108 S. Linden, 60559. Tel: 630-971-0184; Fax: 630-971-1175. Lay Teachers 18; Students 406.
Catechesis/Religious Program—Tel: 630-968-5978. Students 475.

WHEATON, DU PAGE CO.

1—ST. DANIEL THE PROPHET CHURCH (1989), Rev. Thomas J. White; Sisters Josephine Sincak, Pastoral Assoc.; Mary Potthast, Pastoral Assoc.; Margaret M. Ivers, I.B.V.M., Pastoral Assoc.
Res.: 101 W. Loop Rd., 60187. Tel: 630-682-5003; Fax: 630-682-5004.
Catechesis/Religious Program—Tel: 630-682-5003, Ext. 121. Students 800.

2—ST. MARK (1962), Rev. John Ducaji.
Res.: 303 E. Parkway Dr., 60187. Tel: 630-665-0030; Fax: 630-665-0303.
Catechesis/Religious Program—300 E. Cole St., 60187. Tel: 630-668-4614. Students 165.

3—ST. MICHAEL (1882), [CEM] Rev. Don E. McLaughlin; Deacons John Cozzens; William Stroner; David Meador.
Res.: 315 W. Illinois St., 60187. Tel: 630-665-2250; Fax: 630-510-8891.
School—314 W. Willow Ave., 60187. Tel: 630-653-1454; Fax: 630-665-1491. Notre Dame Sisters of Toledo 2; Lay Teachers 26; Students 580.
Catechesis/Religious Program—Tel: 630-682-3650; Fax: 630-690-3324. Students 755.

WILMINGTON, WILL CO., ST. ROSE (1855), [CEM] Rev. Frank Vitus; Sr. Ann Ellen Quirk, B.V.M., Pastoral Assoc.; Deacon Don Dyer.
Res.: 603 S. Main St., 60481. Tel: 815-476-7491; Fax: 815-476-1085.
School—Tel: 815-476-6220; Fax: 815-476-2154. Lay Teachers 12; Students 129.
Catechesis/Religious Program—Students 154.

WILTON CENTER, WILL CO., ST. PATRICK (1905), (Irish), [CEM] Rev. S. C. Giunta.
Res.: 14936 Wilmington Peotone Rd., Manhattan, 60442. Tel: 815-478-3440; Fax: 815-478-4186.
Catechesis/Religious Program—Students 28.

WINFIELD, DU PAGE CO., ST. JOHN THE BAPTIST (1867), [CEM] [JC 2] Revs. Guy Vaccaro; John Bosco Panakal; John Sponder; Deacons Andrew Nielo; Rod Accardi.
Res.: O.S. 233 Church St., 60190. Tel: 630-668-0918; Fax: 630-668-1074.
School—O.S. 259 Church St., 60190. Tel: 630-668-2625; Fax: 630-668-7176. Julie Tobin, Prin. Lay Teachers 20; Students 340.
Catechesis/Religious Program—Tel: 630-682-4400; Fax: 630-668-1074. Maureen Brennan, D.R.E. Students 700.

WOOD DALE, DU PAGE CO., HOLY GHOST (1946), Rev. Kevin R. Farrell; Deacon Dino Franch.
Res.: 254 N. Wood Dale Rd., 60191. Tel: 630-860-2975; Fax: 630-860-9482.
School—Tel: 630-766-4508; Fax: 630-860-7697. Lay Teachers 18; Students 230.
Catechesis/Religious Program—Tel: 630-766-1045. Students 540.

WOODRIDGE, DU PAGE CO.

1—CHRIST THE SERVANT PARISH (1990), Rev. Philip Danaher; Deacon Thomas Fricke.
Mailing Address: 8700 Havens Dr., 60517. Tel: 630-910-0770; Fax: 630-910-6060.
Catechesis/Religious Program—Students 149.

2—ST. SCHOLASTICA (1962), Revs. Gerald Riva; Reynaldo Treyes, C.I.C.M.; Sr. Regina Ann Weissmann, O.S.B., Pastoral Assoc.; Deacons Roger Schmith; Terry Zarembka.
Res.: 7800 S. Janes Ave., 60517. Tel: 630-985-2351; Fax: 630-985-8770.
School—Tel: 630-985-2515; Fax: 630-985-2395. Gail Kueper, Prin. Lay Teachers 11; Students 280.
Catechesis/Religious Program—7720 Janes Ave., 60517. Tel: 630-985-9255. Sr. Suzanne Lesniewski, O.S.F., D.R.E. Students 602.

YORKVILLE, KENDALL CO., ST. PATRICK (1885), (Irish), [CEM] [JC] Rev. Jerome Zalonis, M.I.C.; Deacons Dale Metcalfe; Donald Cyr; David English.
406 Walnut St., 60560. Tel: 630-553-6671; Fax: 630-553-2695.
Catechesis/Religious Program—Students 450.

Chaplains of Public Institutions

JOLIET. *Dept. of Corrections*, McDonough St., 60436. Rev. Richard Ross.
Illinois State Penitentiary, P.O. Box 1122, 60435. Deacon Charles Peterson.
Illinois Youth Commission, Reception and Diagnostic Center, McDonough St., 60435. Deacon Joseph O'Connor.
Silver Cross Hospital, 1200 Maple Rd., 60432. Rev. Andrew L. Buczyna.

DOWNERS GROVE. *Good Samaritan Hospital*, 3821 Highland Ave., 60515. Rev. Philip Danaher.

ELMHURST. *Elmhurst Memorial Hospital*, 200 Berteau Ave., 60126. Rev. Michael McMillen, S.C.J.

HINSDALE. *Hinsdale Hospital*, 120 N. Oak, 60521. Rev. James Walton, O.F.M.

KANKAKEE. *Riverside Medical Center*, 350 N. Wells, 60901. Rev. John Antczak.
Shapiro Development Center, 100 E. Jeffrey, 60901. Rev. Richard Jacklin.

NAPERVILLE. *Edward Hospital*, S. Washington St., 60540. Rev. Thomas Wolter.

WINFIELD. *Central DuPage Hospital*, 0N025 Winfield, 60190. Deacon Rod Accardi. (Vacant)

On Duty Outside the Diocese:
Revs.—
Butters, Joseph, St. Patrick, P.O. Box 860, Arroyo Grande, CA 93421.
Caruso, Carmen A.
Dieter, Thomas M.
Hemrick, Eugene F.
Martis, Douglas, Mundelein Seminary Seminary, Mundelein, 60060.
Milota, Thomas, North American College, Rome, Italy.
Moriarty, John J. ((JOL)), Society of St. James the Apostle, 24 Clark St., Boston, MA 02109.
Mumper, Edward, N. 4515 Sawdust Rd., Bruce, WI 54819.
Schoenstene, Robert L., S.S.L., St. Mary of the Lake Seminary, Mundelein, 60060.

Absent on Sick Leave:
Revs.—
Best, Richard
Dugal, William
Joyce, Edwin
Stalzer, Joseph

Absent on Leave:
Revs.—
Kempfer, James
Smith, Richard
Walsh, Richard
Werling, Keith

Retired:
Most Rev.—
Kaffer, Roger L., 425 Summit St., 60435.
Revs.—
Bowden, Lloyd, 115 N. May St., 60435.
Corley, Thomas, St. John Vianney Villa, 1464 Green Trails Dr., Naperville, 60540.
Cullen, William, 6267 Trinity Dr., #2D, Lisle, 60532.
Driscoll, John, St. Andrew the Apostle, 530 Glen Ave., Romeoville, 60446.
Duffy, James, 6340 Americana Dr., #110, Willowbrook, 60514.
Emerson, Robert F., St. John Vianney Villa, 1464 Green Trails Dr., Naperville, 60540.
Fleming, Thomas, St. John Vianney Villa, 1464 Green Trails Dr., Naperville, 60540.
Formusa, Salvatore, P.O. Box 46010, Chicago, 60646.
Guiney, John, S.M.A., 256 Forest, Glen Ellyn, 60137.
Hurley, George, 5 Oak Brook Dr., Oakbrook, 60521-1314.
Kenny, Donald, Bolivia
Kloepfer, John S., Box 1742, Clarksville, VA 23927.
Maher, Arthur, 1115 Lorraine Rd., #32, Wheaton, 60187.
Maher, Francis, 740 Donald Rd., Colorado Springs, CO 80930.
Mahoney, Gordon, Sts. Peter & Paul, 36 N. Ellsworth, Naperville, 60540.
Memenas, Vytas, 29 S. Delaplaine Rd., Riverside, 60546.
Morrissette, Dominic, P.O. Box 851, Indian Springs, NV 89018.
Mulloy, Sylvester, St. Patrick Residence, 1400 Brookdale, Naperville, 60563-2126.
O'Keefe, Michael, St. John Vianney Villa, 1464 Green Trails Dr., Naperville, 60540.
Orlikiewicz, Stanley, St. John Vianney Villa, 1464 Green Trails Dr., Naperville, 60540.
Ryan, William, St. John Vianney Villa, 1464 Green Trails Dr., Naperville, 60540.
Sebahar, John, St. John Vianney Villa, Naperville.
Shimanek, Joseph, 438 N. LaGrange Rd., LaGrange Park, 60526.
Stonich, Raymond, St. John Vianney Villa, 1464 Green Trails Dr., Naperville, 60540.
Valente, Michael, St. Priscilla, 6949 W. Addison St., Chicago, 60634.
Wilkening, Henry, Corpus Christi, 1415 Lies Rd., Carol Stream, 60188-4841.

Permanent Deacons:

Accardi, Rodger F., Central DuPage Hospital and St. John the Baptist, Winfield
Agurkis, Albert, St. Mary of Gostyn, Downers Grove
Anchor, Robert, (On Duty Outside the Diocese)
Anderson, Roy D., (Residing Outside the Diocese)
Bailey, Thomas, Sacred Heart, Lombard
Balgeman, Richard, St. Joseph, Manteno
Beabout, Norman, (On Duty Outside the Diocese)
Bednar, Gary, St. Mary, Mokena
Berg, Andrew, St. Joseph, Bradley
Berkey, Donald, St. Anthony, Frankfort
Bernardin, Donald, St. Mary, Mokena
Bevan, William F., III, St. Paul the Apostle, Joliet
Bias, Ralph, Sacred Heart, Joliet
Bina, Frank, Our Lady of Peace, Darien
Blessing, William, St. Raphael, Naperville
Bonacci, Nicholas, Cathedral of St. Raymond, Joliet
Borkowicz, Leo M., St. Andrew the Apostle, Romeoville
Bouldin, James, St. Paul the Apostle, Joliet
Bowns, Loren, St. Liborius, Steger
Boyle, John R., St. Alexander, Villa Park
Brachle, Paul L., Jr., Our Lady of Peace, Darien
Brechtel, Scott, Corpus Christi, Carol Stream
Breen, James, St.Thomas the Apostle, Naperville
Brockman, David, (Unassigned)
Brown, Ronald, Sts. Peter & Paul, Naperville
Carlson, Bruce, St. Mary, West Chicago
Carson, Neill, Notre Dame, Claredon Hills
Casey, William, Holy Trinity, Westmont
Cassey, Robert, St. Petronille, Glen Ellyn
Chambers, Frank A., (On Duty Outside the Diocese)
Chamness, Francis J., Maternity BVM, Bourbonnais
Christensen, Gerald G., (Leave of Absence)
Ciston, William, St. Jude, New Lenox
Clark, Gordon, St. Andrew, Romeoville
Clark, Raymond, St. Jude, Joliet
Clodi, Gregory, St. Martin of Tours, Kankakee
Cochran, Christopher, St. Alexander, Villa Park
Cole, John, (Unassigned)
Cook, Michael, Cathedral of St. Raymond, Joliet
Cooley, Stephen, (On Duty Outside the Diocese)
Cotugno, Joseph, St. Patrick, Kankakee
Cozzens, John, St. Michael, Wheaton
Crane, William H., St. Pius X, Lombard
Cummiskey, Terry, St. Isidore, Bloomingdale
Cyr, Donald, St. Patrick, Yorkville
Dalpiaz, Joseph C., St. Joan of Arc, Lisle
Danahey, Daniel, St. Anthony, Frankfort
Darschewski, Ronald, (On Duty Outside the Diocese)
Dennison, James, St. James, Irwin
Dixon, James A., St. Philip, Addison
Donahue, James, (Retired)
Dougherty, Michael, (On Duty Outside the Diocese)
Drechny, John, St.Mary, Park Forest
Drinan, Russell, St. Isaac Jogues, Hinsdale
Dunn, William, St. Anne, Oswego
Dyer, Donald L., St. Rose, Wilmington
Eastburn, Lloyd D., St. Edmund, Watseka
Ellman, Edward, (On Duty Outside the Diocese)
English, David, St. Patrick, Yorkville
Farrell, John, Our Lady of Mt. Carmel, Darien
Federici, Bart, St. Elizabeth Seton, Naperville
Fitt, Robert, St. Jude, New Lenox
Ford, Richard, St. Andrew, Romeoville
Fox, Steven A., St. Peter the Apostle, Itasca
Foy, Richard, St. Walter, Roselle
Foys, Frank F., Notre Dame, Clarendon Hills
Franch, Dino J., Holy Ghost, Wooddale
Francl, Frederick, Christ the King, Lombard
Frazier, Steven, St. Lawrence, South Wilmington
Freund, John, St. Isidore, Bloomington
Fricke, Thomas E., Christ the Servant, Woodridge
Fritz, Leon P., St. Joseph, Bradley
Gagnon, Ronnie, St. Patrick, Kankakee
Gamboa, Gabriel, St. Joseph, Addison
Gavin, Philip, (Retired)
Gibbons, John, St. Alexander, Villa Park
Girard, William, Sts. Peter and Paul, Naperville
Goebel, Thomas, Immaculate Conception, Elmhurst
Hahn, Duane, St. Mary, Mokena
Hamilton, Raymond, St. Francis of Assisi, Bolingbrook
Hamrlick, James, (On Duty Outside the Diocese)
Hanley, Terrance R., St. Francis of Assisi, Bolingbrook
Heitz, Philip, St. Philip, Addison
Henrissey, Francis R., St. Joseph, Manteno
Hessling, Danny E., Sacred Heart Seminary, Hales Corner, WI
Hetzel, William, St. Jude, Joliet
Hindes, John T., St. Joseph, Manteno
Jackson, Kenneth, St. Isidore, Bloomingdale
Jacob, Jeffrey, (Unassigned)
Jagielo, Thomas, Holy Trinity, Westmont
Janousek, Jay, Visitation, Elmhurst
Jazdzewski, Melvin J., (Unassigned)
Jossey, Robert, St. Boniface, Monee
Kaminski, Robert, St. Mary, Mokena
Kenes, Michael, Annunciation Byzantine Catholic, Lockport
Kinsella, James, Cathedral of St. Raymond, Joliet
Knecht, Ronald, St. Pius X, Lombard
Kobs, Dennis, Immaculate Conception, Morris
Kolodziej, Paul, St. Patrick, Joliet
Kowalski, Henry, (Retired)
Krostenko, Alexander, (On Duty Outside the Diocese)
Krueger, James, St. Alexander, Villa Park
Lamon, John D., (On Duty Outside the Diocese)
LaMotte, Robert, St. Joseph, Bradley
Lane, Charles, St. Thomas, Naperville
Leonas, John, St. Joseph, Manteno
Lifka, David, Notre Dame, Clarendon Hills
Lillig, Francis, Christ the King, Lombard
Lissak, Lawrence, St. Pius X, Lombard
Lombardo, Patrick, St. Mary Immaculate, Plainfield
Lopez, Jose L., St. John the Baptist, Joliet
Lovero, Marco, St. Francis of Assisi, Bolingbrook
Lysaght, Evan, (On Duty Outside the Diocese)
Mahoney, Daniel, Sr., St. Mary Nativity, Joliet
Malek, Robert, St. Matthew, Glendale Heights
Maloney, John, Mary Queen of Heaven, Elmhurst
Marcotte, Euchrist, Maternity B.V.M., Bourbonnais
Marrow, Philip J., (Unassigned)
Martinez, Santos H., St. Mary, Plano
McCarthy, Thomas, St. Paul the Apostle, Peotone
McHugh, John, St. Raphael, Naperville
Meador, David, St. Michael, Wheaton
Mendoza, Jose, St. Andrew, Romeoville
Metcalfe, Dale R., St. Patrick, Plano
Miles, Kenneth J., St. Margaret Mary, Naperville
Moeller, John, St. James, Glen Ellyn
Molano, Rodulfo N., St. Francis of Assisi, Bolingbrook
Molinaro, Serafin, Resurrection, Wayne
Murphy, William E., St. Irene, Warrenville
Murray, John, St. Mary Magdalene, Joliet
Naso, James, St. Francis Xavier, Plainfield
Neher, Norman, Sacred Heart, Hopkins Park
Newey, Paul, Divine Savior, Downers Grove
Nguyen, Anthony, Queenship of Mary, Glen Ellyn
Nielo, Andrew, St. John the Baptist, Winfield
Nolan, Thomas J., Mary, Queen of Heaven, Elmhurst
Nowak, Richard, (On Duty Outside the Diocese)
Nunez, Charles, Visitation, Elmhurst
O'Connor, Joseph, St. Joseph, Downers Grove
Olszak, Leonard, St. Liborius, Steger
Ouska, Gregory, St. Joseph Downers Grove
Pecka, Lawrence, St. Mary, Downers Grove
Pellack, Robert J., (On Duty Outside the Diocese)
Perry, James, St. Margaret Mary, Naperville
Petak, Edwin, Cathedral of St. Raymond, Joliet
Peterson, Charles M., St. Patrick, Joliet
Pidgeon, Matthew, St. James, Glen Ellyn
Pineiro, Ismael, (On Duty Outside the Diocese)
Pistorio, Charles, St. Walter, Roselle
Principe, Michael, St. Charles Borromeo, Bensenville
Putman, John, St. Joseph, Manhattan
Rachubinski, Thomas, St. Pius X, Lombard
Randolph, Donald, St. Isidore, Bloomingdale
Raskowski, David, St. Joseph, Joliet
Rehmer, Philip, Our Lady of Mercy, Aurora
Repak, Andrew, St. Raphael, Naperville
Riggi, Joseph, St. Lawrence, South Wilimington
Rosko, Richard, St. Anthony, Frankfort
Ross, Thomas, St. Elizabeth Seton, Naperville
Ryan, Kevin, St. Bernard, Homer Glen
Safko, Terry L., St. Mary, Plainfield
Saltigerald, Luis, St. Mary, West Chicago
Scavone, Emmanuel J., (Retired)
Schimandle, John, Assumption, Coal City
Schlund, James, (On Duty Outside the Diocese)
Schmidt, Walter F., (On Leave of Absence)
Schmith, Roger, St. Scholastica, Woodridge
Schneider, Paul A., (On Duty Outside the Diocese)
Schubert, Anthony, (On Duty Outside the Diocese)
Schumacher, Carl N.J., St. Joseph, Downers Grove
Searls, Ronald, St. Walter, Roselle
Sebastian, John, St. Isaac Jogues, Hinsdale
Sheaffer, Harry, St. Mary, West Chicago
Sheridan, Thomas, St. Mary Immaculate, Plainfield
Sipek, Sr., Robert, (Retired)
Siwek, Raymond, (Retired)
Sossong, James R., St. Mary Immaculate, Plainfield
Spatafore, Anthony, Visitation, Elmhurst
Spiezio, John, St. Petronille, Glen Ellyn
Stansberry, Robert T., Jr., Immaculate Conception, Morris
Stevens, Richard R., (On Duty Outside the Diocese)
Stolarz, Dennis, Our Lady of Peace, Darien
Storrs, Wayne, Christ the King, Lombard
Straub, Fred, Holy Family, Shorewood
Stroner, William, St. Michael, Wheaton
Stucko, Denis, St. Joan of Arc, Lisle
Sullivan, Robert, St. Joseph, Downers Grove
Swauger, Gary, St. Elizabeth Seton, Naperville
Symonanis, Alan, Notre Dame, Clarendon Hills
Tansey, William, Ascension, Oakbrook Terrace
Taylor, Terrance, St. Margaret Mary, Naperville
Tetrault, Robert L., (On Duty Outside the Diocese)
Theriault, Dennis, St. Jude, New Lenox
Thiltgen, Thomas, Corpus Christi, Carol Stream
Tkach, J. Timothy, Annunciation Byzantine, Lockport
Troy, Daniel, St. Joseph, Downers Grove
True, Robert, St. Irene, Warrenville
Uffmann, William, St. Dennis, Lockport
Urso, Joseph, St. Irene, Warrenville
Valdez, George, St. Mary, West Chicago
Van Dril, William, (On Duty Outside the Diocese)
Vavra, Robert, Our Lady of Mercy, Aurora
Waldron, Herbert, St. Andrew, Romeoville
Walen, Paul J., Sr., St. Dominic, Bolingbrook
Wallace, Robert, St. Dominic, Bolingbrook
Walsh, Thomas, (On Duty Outside the Diocese)
Walters, James C., St. Mary, Plainfield
Weierman, Robert, St. Dennis, Lockport
Wharry, James, (On Duty Outside the Diocese)
Whitman, Ronald, St. Teresa, Kankakee
Winblad, Joseph, Marian Village, Lockport
Woods, Charles, St. Raphael, Naperville
Worden, William, St. Thomas the Apostle, Naperville
Wozek, Duane, St. Anne, Oswego
Yarshen, Richard, (Unassigned)
Yurcus, Ronald J., St. Petronille, Glen Ellyn
Zarembka, Terrance, St. Scholastica, Woodridge

INSTITUTIONS LOCATED IN THE DIOCESE

[A] COLLEGES AND UNIVERSITIES

JOLIET. *University of St. Francis*, 500 N. Wilcox, 60435. Tel: 815-740-3360; Fax: 815-740-6366. Email: jhicks@stfrancis.edu. Web: www.stfrancis.edu. Dr. Michael J. Vinceguerra, Pres.; Sr. Rosemary Small, O.S.F., Pres. Mission Integration. A coed resident and commuter school. Priests 1; Sisters of St. Francis of Mary Immaculate 4; Lay Teachers 79; Students 4,233; Total Staff 332.

LISLE. *Benedictine University*, 5700 College Rd., 60532-0900. Tel: 630-829-6000; Fax: 630-960-1126. Web: www.ben.edu. Rt. Rev. Dismas B. Kalcic, O.S.B., Chancellor; Dr. William J. Carroll, Pres.; Dr. John Mickus, College of Arts and Sciences; Charles Gregory, Exec. Vice Pres.; Dr. John Cicero, Dean, College of Business, Technology and Professional Programs; Dr. Charlotte Ross, Dean, School of Education; Dr. Daniel J. Julius, Provost & Vice Pres. Academic Affairs; Revs. David Turner, O.S.B., Dir. Institute Mission; Kevin J. Sheeran, O.S.B., Sec. & Treas. & Dir. Univ. Ministry; Philip S. Timko, O.S.B.; Michael E. Komechak, O.S.B.; Odilo Crkva, O.S.B; Theodore D. Suchy O.S.B.; John Palmer, C.S.V.; Julian von Duerbeck, O.S.B.; James Flint, O.S.B.; Bro. Richard Poro, O.S.B., Asst. Campus Min. Fathers 9; Brothers 1; Sisters 1; Lay Teachers 89; Administrators 139; Students 2,044.

ROMEOVILLE. *Lewis University* (Coed University) , One University Pkwy., 60446-2200. Tel: 815-838-0500; Fax: 815-838-5979. Email: wassbeca@lewisu.edu. Web: www.lewisu.edu/. Bros. James Gaffney, F.S.C., Pres.; Philip Johnson, F.S.C., Dir. University Ministry. Priests 4; Brothers of the Christian Schools 13; Lay Teachers 161; Students 4,459.

[B] HIGH SCHOOLS, DIOCESAN

KANKAKEE. *Bishop McNamara High School*, 550 W. Brookmont Blvd., 60901. Tel: 815-932-7413; Fax: 815-932-0926. Email: mcnamararas@hotmail.com. Web: www.bishopmac.com. Sr. Madeleine LaMarre, C.N.D., Alumni Coord. Sisters 1; Lay Teachers 30; Students 428; Total Staff 55.

[C] HIGH SCHOOLS, PRIVATE

JOLIET. *Joliet Catholic Academy* (Coed) , 1200 N. Larkin Ave., 60435. Tel: 815-741-0500; Fax: 815-741-8825. Email: faith@jca-online.org. Web: www.jca-online.org. Sr. Faith Szambelanczyk, O.S.F., Pres. & CEO; Michael Nadeau, Prin. & COO; Dr. Robert Jenkins, Asst. Prin. Carmelites

& Joliet Franciscans Priests 2; Brothers 1; Sisters 3; Lay Teachers 49; Students 970.

ADDISON. *Driscoll Catholic High School*, 555 N. Lombard Rd., 60101. Tel: 630-543-6310; Fax: 630-543-2913. Email: smarth@driscollcatholic.com. Web: www.driscollcatholic.com. Mr. Stephen A. Marth, Pres.; Mr. Fred Muehleman, Prin.; Mr. Michael Neis, Asst. Prin.; Mr. Peter Lewek, Admin. Asst.; Mr. Tim Racki, Dean Students; Mrs. Laraine Parker, Campus Min. Brothers of Christian Schools 1; Lay Teachers 30; Students 466.

LISLE. *Benet Academy*, 2200 Maple Ave., 60532. Tel: 630-969-6550; Fax: 630-719-0929. Email: webmaster@benet.org. Web: www.benet.org. Rt. Rev. Dismas B. Kalcic, O.S.B., Chancellor; Rev. Jude D. Randall, O.S.B., Pres.; Mr. Ernest Stark, Prin.; Mr. James Brown, Asst. Prin.; Mr. Tim Turner, Dir. Devel.; Rev. Anthony J. Jacob, O.S.B., Business Mgr. Priests 6; Sisters 1; Brothers 2; Lay Teachers 67; Students 1,294.

LOMBARD. *Montini Catholic High School*, 19 W. 070 16th St., 60148-4797. Tel: 630-627-6930; Fax: 630-627-6965. Web: www.montini.org. Bro. Thomas A. Harding, F.S.C., Pres. Brothers of the Christian Schools 3; Lay Teachers 52; Students 636.

NEW LENOX. *Providence Catholic High School* (Coed) , 1800 W. Lincoln Hwy., 60451. Tel: 815-485-2136; Fax: 815-485-2709. Email: fmcg123@aol.com. Web: www.providencecatholic.org. Rev. Richard J. McGrath, O.S.A., Pres.; Mr. Donald E. Sebestyen, Prin.; Ms. Judith Legan, Asst. Prin.; Revs. Roland F. Follmann, O.S.A.; Edward A. Andrews, O.S.A. (CHI); Gerald A. Nicholas, O.S.A.; Michael J. O'Connor, O.S.A. Priests 5; Lay Teachers 75; Students 1,119.

WHEATON. *St. Francis High School*, 2130 W. Roosevelt Rd., 60187. Tel: 630-668-5800; Fax: 630-668-5893. Email: csorentino@sfhsnet.org. Web: www.sfhsnet.org. Charles Sorentino Jr., Prin. Lay Teachers 57; Students 715.

[D] ELEMENTARY SCHOOLS, DIOCESAN

Naperville Regional Catholic School, 2220 Lisson Rd., Naperville, 60565-5234. Tel: 630-416-3325; Fax: 630-416-3642. Rev. Ernest Norbeck.

[E] AGENCIES AND INSTITUTIONS OF THE CHARITIES OF THE DIOCESE

JOLIET. *Catholic Charities*, 203 N. Ottawa St., 60432. Tel: 815-723-3405; Fax: 815-723-3452. Email: kmcgowan@cc-doj.org. Web: www.cc-doj.org. Ms. Kathleen McGowan, Exec. Dir. Diocesan Administrative Office and Regional Office for Will, Grundy and Kendall Counties.

KANKAKEE. *Catholic Charities*, 270 N. Schuyler Ave., 60901. Tel: 815-933-7791; Fax: 815-932-3030. Web: www.cc-doj.org. Regional Office for Kankakee, Ford, and Iroquois Counties.

LOMBARD. *Catholic Charities*, 26 W. St. Charles Rd., 60148. Tel: 630-495-8008; Fax: 630-495-9854. Email: pterrell@cc-doj.org. Web: www.cc-doj.org. Regional Office for DuPage County.

[F] PROTECTIVE INSTITUTIONS

JOLIET. *Guardian Angel Home*, 1550 Plainfield Rd., 60435. Tel: 815-729-0930; Fax: 815-744-6087. Email: sas726@aol.com. Web: www.guardianangelhome.org. Sponsored by the Sisters of St. Francis of Mary Immaculate.; Child and family welfare agency: therapeutic school, foster care, domestic violence shelter, child abuse prevention center, and counselling.

MOMENCE. *Good Shepherd Manor*, P.O. Box 260, 60954. Tel: 815-472-6492; Fax: 815-472-2160. Email: gsmanor@prairieinet.net. Web: www.goodshepherdmanor.org. Dr. James Czerwionka, Pres.; Bruce Fitzpatrick, Admin.; Bro. Alphonsus Brown, B.G.S., Asst. Admin. Adult Male DD-MR. Brothers of the Good Shepherd 2; Bed Capacity 120; Permanent Residents 120.

[G] DAY CARE

JOLIET. *Vilaseca Josephine Center*, 351 N. Chicago St., 60432. Tel: 815-727-1467; Fax: 815-727-1480. Email: josemvilaseca@hotmail.com. Josephine Sisters Students 88.

[H] LEARNING CENTERS

JOLIET. *Franciscan Learning Center*, 1734 Theodore St., 60435. Tel: 815-744-7634; Fax: 815-744-2152. Email: lillppl@corecom.net. Sr. Margaret McGuckin, Dir. Students 84.

BOURBONNAIS. *Provena Fortin Villa*, 615 S. Main St., 60914. Tel: 815-932-8411; Fax: 815-932-9002. Email: rhondakgreen@provenahealth.com. Rhonda K. Green, Dir. Childcare with Preschool for children 15 months to 12 years. Staff 23; Students 121.

[I] GENERAL HOSPITALS

JOLIET. *Provena Saint Joseph Medical Center*, 333 N. Madison St., 60435-6595. Tel: 815-741-7236; Fax: 815-741-7579. Email: name@provena.org. Web: www.provenasaintjoe.org. Thomas A. Reitinger, Pres. & CEO; Deacon Ed Petak, Dir. Pastoral Care.

Legal Title: *Provena Hospitals dba Provena St. Joseph Medical Center* Sisters 8; Chaplains 10; Bed Capacity 401; Patients Assisted Annually 414,751; Total Staff 2,310.

Provena Industrial Rehabilitation Center, Joliet Tel: 815-436-4545; Fax: 815-741-0774.

Provena Physical Rehab & Sports Injury Center, Joliet Tel: 815-741-7114; Fax: 815-725-6997.

KANKAKEE. *Provena St. Mary's Hospital*, 500 West Court St., 60901. Tel: 815-937-2490; Fax: 815-937-8772. Web: www.provenastmarys.com. Sr. Virginia Marie Derk, Dir. Pastoral Care. Tel: 815-937-2384; George Miller, B.A., M.M., Pres.; Rev. Michael Powell, Chap.

Legal Title: *Provena Hospitals dba Provena St. Mary Hospital* Bed Capacity 210; Patients Assisted Annually 211,164; Staff 917; Chaplains 1; Sisters (SSCM) 3; Sisters (Holy Family) 3.

MOKENA. *Provena Health (Jol)*, 19065 Hickory Creek Dr., Ste. 300, 60448. Tel: 708-478-6300; Fax: 708-478-5960. Web: www.provena.org.

Provena Hospitals (Jol), 19065 Hickory Creek Dr., Ste. 300, 60448. Tel: 708-478-6300; Fax: 708-478-5960. Web: www.provena.org.

[J] REHABILITATION CENTERS

WHEATON. *Marianjoy Rehabilitation Hospital & Clinics, Inc.*, 26 W. 171 Roosevelt Rd., P.O. Box 795, 60189. Tel: 630-462-4000; Fax: 630-462-0112. Web: www.marianjoy.org. Sr. Mariette Kalbac, Chap. Franciscan Sisters, Daughters of the Sacred Hearts of Jesus and Mary (Wheaton, IL) Bed Capacity 120; Patients Assisted Annually 3,500.

[K] HOMES FOR AGED

JOLIET. *Our Lady of Angels Retirement Home*, 1201 Wyoming, 60435. Tel: 815-725-6631; Fax: 815-725-1451. Rev. Louis Antl, O.F.M., Chap.; Stephen E. McMillin, Admin. Sisters of St. Francis of Mary Immaculate Sister Staff 12; Lay Employees 184; Retired Sisters 75; Residents 102. In Res. Sr. Lourdes Boyer, O.S.F., Local Coord.

Provena Villa Franciscan, 210 N. Springfield Ave., 60435. Tel: 815-725-3400; Fax: 815-725-2160. Ann Dodge, Admin.

Legal Title: *Provena Senior Services*, Extended, Intermediate, and Skilled Care, Respite Care. Bed Capacity 176.

BOURBONNAIS. *Provena Our Lady of Victory*, 20 Briarcliff Ln., 60914. Tel: 815-937-2022; Fax: 815-936-3231. Email: julieacadle@provenahealth.com. Julie A. Cadle, Admin.; Rev. Joseph Tremonti, C.S.V., Chap.

Legal Title: *Provena Senior Services* Bed Capacity 107.

CLIFTON. *Merkle-Knipprath Countryside Home*, 1190 E. 2900 N Rd., 60927-7103. Tel: 815-694-2306. Bro. Damien DeBraekeleer, O.S.F., Admin. Apartment Community and Nursing Center. Religious 4; Total in Nursing Care 100; Apartment Living 30.

CRETE. *St. James Manor & Villas (Sub. of Franciscan Communities, Inc.)* Sponsored by Franciscan Sisters of Chicago , 1251 Richton Rd., 60417. Tel: 708-672-6700; Fax: 708-672-4939. Email: dstrutynski@franciscancommunities.com. Dianne Strutynski, Exec. Dir. Care of the Elderly. Bed Capacity 181; Total Assisted Annually 34,589; Total Staff 180.

DARIEN. *Carmelite Carefree Retirement Village*, 8419 Bailey Rd., 60561-5361. Tel: 630-960-4060; Fax: 630-960-4071. Email: carmelitecarefree@earthlink.net. Web: carmelitecarefree.org. Rev. Roger Bonneau, O.Carm., Dir. Residents 97.

KANKAKEE. *Provena Heritage Village*, 901 North Entrance Ave., 60901. Tel: 815-939-4506; Fax: 815-939-4761. Email: caroldmcintyre@provenahealth.com. Carol McIntyre, Admin.

Legal Title: *Provena Senior Services dba Provena Heritage Village* Bed Capacity 87.

Provena Meadowview Lodge, 995 North Entrance Ave., 60901. Tel: 815-939-4506; Fax: 815-939-4761. Email: caroldmcintyre@provenahealth.com. Carol McIntyre, Admin.

Legal Title: *Provena Senior Services dba Provena Meadowview Lodge* Bed Capacity 26.

Provena Senior Services (Jol), Kankakee Tel: 815-939-4506; Fax: 815-939-4761.

LISLE. *Villa St. Benedict*, 1920 Maple Ave., 60532. Tel: 630-852-5360; Fax: 630-852-3196. Email: gtrembley@villastben.org. Web: www.villastben.org. Mr. Glenn Trembley, Admin. Retirement home. Lay Staff 20; Residents 32.

NAPERVILLE. *St. John Vianney Villa*, 1464 Green Trails Dr., 60540-8372. Tel: 630-983-0533; Fax: 630-983-6375. Revs. Thomas Corley; Thomas Fleming (Retired); Robert F. Emerson (Retired); John Sebahar (Retired); Michael O'Keefe; Stanley Orlikiewicz; Raymond Stonich (Retired). Retirement home for priests. Residents 7.

St. Patrick's Residence, 1400 Brookdale Rd., 60563-2125. Tel: 630-416-6565; Fax: 630-416-8755. Email: stpatres@earthlink.net. Web: Stpatricksresidence.org. Sr. Jeanne Francis Haley, Admin. Carmelite Sisters 8; Bed Capacity 210; Residents 210; Total Staff 242.

OAK BROOK. *Cedarlake Village, Plainfield Campus, Inc.*, Formerly Mayslake Village, Plainfield Campus, Inc., 1801 35th St., 60523. Tel: 630-850-8232; Fax: 630-850-8233. Email: mayslakvlg@aol.com. Web: www.mayslake.com. Rev. Larry Dreffein, O.F.M., Pres.; Mr. Michael A. Frigo, Admin. Senior Citizen Retirement Community. Total Staff 45.

WHEATON. *Marian Park, Inc.*, 2126 W. Roosevelt Rd., 60187. Tel: 630-665-9100; Fax: 630-665-9357. Web: www.wfs-inc.org. *Franciscan Ministries, Inc.*, 26 W. 171 Roosevelt Rd., P.O. Box 667, 60189-0667.

[L] MONASTERIES AND RESIDENCES OF PRIESTS AND BROTHERS

JOLIET. *Congregation of Christian Brothers, Brother Rice Province Center*, 958 Western Ave., 60435-6954. Tel: 815-723-5464; Fax: 815-723-5278. Email: cjgattone@brprovince.org. Web: www.brprovince.org. Bros. Charles J. Gattone, C.F.C., Prov. Leader; James Keane, C.F.C., Deputy Prov. Leader; Daniel J. Casey, C.F.C., Councilor; George G. Gremley, C.F.C., Councilor; Michael S. Segvich, C.F.C., Councilor.

Legal Title: *The Christian Brothers of Ireland, Inc.* In Res. Bro. M. David Lucas.

St. Elias Carmelites, 3504 Lake Shore Dr., 60431-8819. Tel: 815-439-8246; Fax: 815-439-8633. Email: steliascarmelites@comcast.net. Revs. William Wert, O.Carm., Prior; Raymond Foster, O.Carm.; Rocco DiLeonardi, O.Carm. (Retired); Louis Rogge, O.Carm. (Retired); Leopold Glueckert, O.Carm.; John J. Comerford, O.Carm.; Bros. Lawrence Fidelus, O.Carm.; Andrew White, O.Carm. Priests 6; Brothers 2.

St. John the Baptist Friary, 404 N. Hickory St., 60435. Tel: 815-727-9783; Fax: 815-740-1521. Revs. John Dombrowski, O.F.M.; Thomas Shaughnessy, O.F.M.; Lawrence Jagdfeld, O.F.M.; Louis B. Antl, O.F.M.; Medard Buvala, O.F.M.; Gerold Schubert, O.F.M.; Venard Kommer, O.F.M.; Bros. Theophane Ballman, O.F.M.; Ducanh Pham, O.F.M. Priests 7; Brothers 2.

Westcourt Corporation, 958 Western Ave., 60435. Tel: 815-723-5464. Email: cjgattone@hotmail.com. Bro. George G. Gremley, C.F.C.

BURR RIDGE. *Christian Brothers Provincial Office (Midwest Province)*, 7650 S. County Line Rd., 60527-4718. Tel: 630-323-3725; Fax: 630-323-3779. Email: info@cbmidwest.org. Web: www.cbmidwest.org. Bros. Francis Carr, F.S.C., Prov.; Michael Flaherty, F.S.C., Auxiliary Prov.; Mr. Leo Hirsch, Dir. Devel.; Karin McClelland-Anderer, Dir. Shared Mission & Formation; Bros. Joseph Saurbier, F.S.C., Dir. Finance; Robert Veselsky, F.S.C., Dir. Vocations & Formation; Nicholas Schumer, F.S.C., Dir. St. La Salle Auxiliary; Martin Spellman, F.S.C., Dir. Senior Brothers.

DARIEN. *Carmelite Community*, St. Simon Stock Priory, 8501 Bailey Rd., 60561. Tel: 630-241-1802; Fax: 630-969-3376. Revs. John-Benedict Weber, O.Carm., Prior; John Russell, O.Carm.; Bro. Charles Kwiatkowski, O.Carm.; Revs. Robert E. Lee, O.Carm.; Bernhard Bauerle, O.Carm.; Robert E. Colaresi, O.Carm.; Roger Bonneau, O.Carm. Priests 6; Brothers 1.

Carmelite Provincial Office, 1317 Frontage Rd., 60561. Tel: 630-971-0050; Fax: 630-971-0195. Email: provincial@carmelnet.org. Web: www.carmelnet.org. Very Rev. John F. Russell, O.Carm., Prior Prov.; Revs. Bernhard Bauerle, O.Carm., Prov. Procurator; Joseph R. Wallroth, O.Carm., Military Chap.; Bro. Charles Kwiatkowski, O.Carm.

Legal Title: *Society of Mt. Carmel of Illinois*

Carmelites Serving in Italy: Revs. William Harry, O.Carm.; Raul Maravi, O.Carm.; Patrick McMahon, O.Carm., Ph.D. (WDC); Craig Morrison, O.Carm.; Joachim Smet, O.Carm.

Carmelites Serving in Canada: Revs. Bruce Baker, O.Carm.; Thomas Hakala, O.Carm.; Leo Huard, O.Carm.; Anthony McNamara, O.Carm.; Gerard Power, O.Carm.; Jordon Rooney, O.Carm.; David Simpson, O.Carm.; Bro. Gabriel Murray, O.Carm.

Carmelites Serving in Peru:

Prelate Nullius, Sicuani, Peru. Tel: 011-51-8-435-11611; Fax: 011-51-8-435-1089. Most Rev. Michael LaFay, O.Carm.; Revs. Salvador Bartolo, O.Carm.;

Michael Brown, O.Carm.; Kevin Lafey, O.Carm.; Alban Quinn, O.Carm.; Enrique Laguna-Vargas, O.Carm.; James Geaney, O.Carm.; Edward Adelmann, O.Carm.; Eduardo Rivero, O.Carm.; Jorge Remuzgo, O.Carm.; Raul Maravi, O.Carm.; Bros. Miguel Bacigalupo-Del Corrall, O.Carm.; Jorge Villegas, O.Carm.; Adolfo Medrano, O.Carm.; Carlos Valdez, O.Carm.

Carmelites Serving in Australia: Bro. Sean Keefe, O.Carm.

Carmelites Serving in Mexico: Revs. Thomas Alkire, O.Carm.; John Hertel, O.Carm.; Peter Hinde, O.Carm.; Thomas Jordan, O.Carm.; Joel Moelter, O.Carm.; William Smith, O.Carm.; Bros. Rodolfo Aznaran, O.Carm.; Emilio Rodriguez, O.Carm.; Jose Luis Torres P., O.Carm.

Carmelites Serving in Puerto Rico Rev. Felix Rivera, O.Carm.

Carmelites Serving in El Salvador Rev. David Blanchard, O.Carm. (WDC).

Carmelites Serving Elsewhere: Revs. Tim Andres, O.Carm.; Jerome Callahan, O.Carm; Warren Carlin, O.Carm.; John F. Donohue, O.Carm.; Jeffry Fairfield, O.Carm.; Michael Greenwell, O.Carm.; Myron Judy, O.Carm.; Paul Kirchner, O.Carm.; Gregory Klein, O.Carm.; Anton Kollar, O.Carm.; Albert P. Koppes, O.Carm.; Barry Kremer O.Carm. (VEN); Charles Kurgan, O.Carm. (LA); James Lewis, O.Carm.; Francis E. McCarthy, O.Carm. (VEN); Blaise McInerney, O.Carm.; Zack Monet, O.Carm.; Phillip Nessinger, O.Carm.; Kieran O'Hara, O.Carm.; Henry Ormond, O.Carm.; Venard Poslusney, O.Carm.; Thomas Schaefer, O.Carm.; Bertin Smith, O.Carm.; Frank Weil, O.Carm.; Bros. Stephen Cooley, O.Carm.; Ivan Cormac Marsh, O.Carm.; William O'Brien O.Carm.; Paul Robinson, O.Carm.

LISLE. *St. Procopius Abbey*, 5601 College Rd., 60532. Tel: 630-969-6410; Fax: 630-969-6426. Email: stprocopius@hotmail.com. Web: www.procopius.org. Rt. Rev. Dismas B. Kalcic, O.S.B., Abbot; Bro. Very Ven. Columban Trojan, O.S.B., Prior; Revs. Thomas Chisholm, O.S.B., Subprior; Roman Galiardi, O.S.B., Master of Novices; Kevin J. Sheeran, O.S.B., Procurator & Business Mgr.; Benedict Alva, O.S.B.; Gabriel Baltes, O.S.B.; Frederic J. Beller, O.S.B.; Joseph Chang, O.S.B.; Odilo Crkva, O.S.B.; Ivan Dobnikar, O.S.B.; Jerome Dobry, O.S.B.; Julian von Duerbeck, O.S.B.; Terence Fitzmaurice, O.S.B.; James Flint, O.S.B.; T. Becket Franks, O.S.B.; Rt. Rev. Thomas J. Havlik, O.S.B., Abbot, (Retired); Revs. Paschal D. Honner, O.S.B.; Alban Hrebic, O.S.B.; Zachary Hrisko, O.S.B.; Anthony J. Jacob, O.S.B.; Michael E. Komechak, O.S.B.; Edward J. Kucera, O.S.B.; Timothy R. Marceau, O.S.B.; Jude D. Randall, O.S.B., Pres., Benet Academy; James Saul, O.S.B.; Theodore D. Suchy, O.S.B.; Philip S. Timko, O.S.B.; David Turner, O.S.B.; Mel R. Uzdrowski, O.S.B.; Kenneth Zigmond, O.S.B.; Francis Laurence; Most Rev. Daniel W. Kucera, O.S.B., Archbishop of Dubuque, IA (Retired). Benedictine Monks Monks 49; Priests 32; Brothers 14; Bishops 1; Oblates 2.

Benedictine Chinese Mission 24 W. 350 Maple Ave., Naperville, 60540. Tel: 630-968-4264. Rev. James Saul, O.S.B., Dir.

Slav Missions 5601 College Dr., 60532. Tel: 630-969-6410; Fax: 630-969-6426.

Benedictine University, 5700 College Rd., 60532. Tel: 630-829-6000; Fax: 630-829-6242.

Benet Academy, 2200 Maple Ave., 60532. Tel: 630-969-6550; Fax: 630-719-0929.

St. Scholastica Mission House 24 W. 350 Maple Ave., Naperville, 60540. Tel: 630-968-4264. Missionary Oblates of St. Benedict

St. Procopius Abbey Endowment, 5601 College Rd., 60532. Tel: 630-969-6410; Fax: 630-969-6426.

MOMENCE. *Brother Mathias Barrett Inc. of Illinois*, P.O. Box 260, 60954. Tel: 815-472-3700; Fax: 815-472-2160. Bro. Michael P. Brown, Pres. Brothers 2.

NEW LENOX. *Augustinian Friary*, 1800 W. Lincoln Hwy., 60451. Tel: 815-485-6880; Fax: 815-485-2709. (See separate listing for Providence High School) In Res. Revs. Edward A. Andrews, O.S.A. (CHI); Roland F. Follmann, O.S.A.; Richard J. McGrath, O.S.A., Pres.; Gerald A Nicholas, O.S.A., Prior; Michael J. O'Connor, O.S.A.; Bro. John Patrick Currier, O.S.A.

ROMEOVILLE. *La Salle House Community*, 100 Faculty Lane, 60446-1178. Tel: 815-836-5530 Fax: 815-836-5858. Email: johnsoph@lewisu.edu. Bro. Philip Johnson, F.S.C., Dir. Brothers 17.

WESTMONT. *Westmont North Community*, Formerly Christian Brothers Center, 222 S. Cass Ave., 60559. Tel: 630-724-1976; Fax: 630-724-1978. Bro. Thomas Vance, F.S.C., Dir. Brothers 4.

[M] CONVENTS AND RESIDENCES FOR SISTERS

JOLIET. *St. Francis Convent*, Formerly St. Francis Convent (Motherhouse), 801 N. Larkin Ave. Ste. 101, 60435-3442. Tel: 815-725-8735; Fax 815-725-8648. Web: www.jolietfranciscans.org. Sr. Maria Pesavento, O.S.F., Pres.

Legal Title: *Retirement Plan Trust of the Congregation of the Third Order of St. Francis of Mary Immaculate* Congregation of the Third Order of St. Francis of Mary Immaculate, Joliet, IL

Josephine Sisters, 351 N. Chicago St., 60432. Tel: 815-727-1467; Fax: 815-727-1480. Email: josephiness@hotmail.com. Josephine Sisters of Mexico (Hermanas Josefinas) Sisters 7.

FRANKFORT. *Franciscan Sisters of the Sacred Heart*, St. Francis Woods, 9201 W. St. Francis Rd., 60423-8335. Tel: 815-469-4895; Fax: 815 464-3809. Email: smeimler@aol.com. Web: www.fssh.com. Sr. Mary Elizabeth Imler, O.S.F., Gen. Supr

Legal Title: *An Association of Franciscan Sisters of the Sacred Heart and the Franciscan Sisters of the Sacred Heart in California; Franciscan Foundation.* Sisters 120.

KANKAKEE. *St. Clare House of Prayer*, 2041 W. Rte. 113, 60901-7411. Tel: 815-933-3945; Fax: 815-933-3945. Email: stclare@mailstation.com. Sisters of St. Francis of Mary Immaculate 6.

Servants of the Holy Heart of Mary, Holy Family Prov., U.S.A., Provincial Administration, 15 Elmwood Dr., 60901. Tel: 815-937-2380; Fax: 815-937-5520. Email: maryahettel@provenahealth.com. Web: inil.com/users/hatton. Sr. Mary Ann Hettel, Prov. Supr.

Legal Title: *Servants of the Holy Heart of Mary Charitable Trust*, Provena Health including 7 hospitals and 13 long term care institutions. Professed Sisters 49.

LISLE. *Benedictine Sisters of the Sacred Heart, Sacred Heart Monastery*, 1910 Maple Ave., 60532-2164. Tel: 630-969-7040; Fax: 630-969-5814. Email: jheble@aol.com. Web: www.shmlisle.org. Sr. Judith Ann Heble, O.S.B., Prioress; Rev. Becket Franks, Chap.

Legal Title: *Benedictine Sisters of the Sacred Heart Charitable Trust* Professed Sisters 43.

MINOOKA. *The Poor Clares of Joliet, Annunciation Monastery*, 6200 E. Minooka Rd., 60447. Tel: 815-467-0032 Fax: 815-467-0032. Email: paxbonum@aol.com. Sr. M. Dorothy Urschalitz, P.C., Contact Person. Cloistered Sisters 8; Extern Sisters 2.

NEW LENOX *Mother of Good Counsel Monastery* Augustinian Nuns. , 440 N. Marley Rd., 60451. Tel: 815-463-9662. Sr. Mary Grace Kuppe, O.S.A., Prioress.

PLAINFIELD. *Mantellate Sisters Servants of Mary of Plainfield*, 16949 S. Drauden Rd., 60544-9219. Tel: 815-436-5796; Fax: 815-436-7486. Sr. Francis Gresser, O.S.M., Regl. Supr. Ministry in the field of Academic Education, Parish Ministry, Social Work, Nursing, Homes for the Aged, and Foreign Missions; Homes for the Aged and Foreign Missions Sisters 9.

WHEATON. *St. Clara Province Charitable Trust*, 26 W. 171 Roosevelt Rd., P.O. Box 667, 60189-0667. Tel: 630-462-7422; Fax: 630-462-9065.

Convent of Our Lady of the Angels Motherhouse and Novitiate Franciscan Sisters, Daughters of the Sacred Hearts of Jesus and Mary (Wheaton, IL) , P.O. Box 667, 60189-0667. Tel: 630-462-7422; Fax: 630-462-7148. Email: danderson@wheatonfranciscan.org. Web: www.wheatonfranciscan.org. Sr. Margaret Grempka, O.S.F., Prov. Dir.

Legal Title: *Wheaton Franciscan Sisters Corp.* Sisters 95.

Loretto Convent, Religious of the Institute of the Blessed Virgin Mary, P.O. Box 508, 60189. Tel: 630-653-4740; Fax: 630-653-4885. Email: spatzibvm@aol.com. Web: www.ibvm.org. Sisters 22.

Loretto Center, Formerly Loretto Conference Center Tel: 630-653-7918; Fax: 630-653-0845.

Office of Development Tel: 630-682-9097; Fax: 630-868-8258.

Loretto Extension Service Tel: 630-462-8860.

Loretto Early Childhood Center Tel: 630-690-8410; Fax: 630-868-2764.

Children of God Retreats Tel: 630-588-8501.

United States Province Administration, Formerly American Regional Administration Tel: 630-665-3814 (Superior); 630-653-6113 (Treas.); Fax: 630-653-4881.

[N] HOUSES OF RETREAT/PRAYER

DARIEN. *Carmelite Spiritual Center*, 8433 Bailey Rd., 60561. Tel: 630-969-4141; Fax: 630-969-3376. Email: cscretreat@aol.com. Revs. Kevin Shanley, O.Carm.; Robert E. Colaresi, O.Carm., Dir. Total Staff 16.

FRANKFORT. *Portiuncula Center for Prayer*, 9263 W. St. Francis Rd., 60423-8330. Tel: 815-464-3880; Fax: 815-469-4880. Email: portc4p@aol.com. Web: www.portc4p.com.

PLANO. *La Salle Manor Christian Brothers Retreat House*, 12480 Galena Rd., 60545. Tel: 630-552-3224; Fax: 630-552-9160. Email: info@lasallemanor.org. Web: www.lasallemanor.org. Robert Dressel, Pres.

WARRENVILLE. *Congregation of Our Lady of the Retreat in the Cenacle*, 29W012 Batavia Rd., P.O. Box 797, 60555-0797. Tel: 630-393-1231; Fax: 630-393-2646. Email: ministry@cenacle.org. Web: www.cenacle.org. Sisters Mary Sharon Riley, R.C., Supr.; Marguerite Gautreau, R.C., Novice Dir. Novices 3; Sisters 11.

WESTMONT. *Mayslake Ministries, Inc.*, 760 Pasquinelli Dr., Ste. 304, 60559. Tel: 630-323-1620; Fax: 630-323-1621. Email: info@mayslakeministries.org. Web: mayslakeministries.org. Rev. Jonathan D. Foster, O.F.M.; David E. Nowak, Exec. Dir. Priests 1; Lay Staff 3.

[O] MISCELLANEOUS

JOLIET. *Fiat House of Discernment*, 113 N. Ottawa, 60432. Tel: 815-723-2089; Fax: 815-724-0632. Email: frjohnr@dioceseofjoliet.org. Web: www.vocations.com. Rev. John Regan, Dir. Vocations.

St. Vincent Thrift Shop, 307 N. Chicago St., 60432. Tel: 815-722-1140.

211 Main St., West Chicago, 60185. Tel: 630-293-9755; Fax: 630-293-9881.

AURORA. *Assisi Homes - Constitution House, Inc.*, 401 Constitution Dr., 60506. Tel: 630-396-2100; Fax: 630-896-0313. Web: www.wfs-inc.org. *Franciscan Ministries, Inc.*, 26 W. 171 Roosevelt Rd., P.O. Box 667, Wheaton, 60189-0667.

BURR RIDGE. *Christian Brothers Fund, Inc.*, 7650 S. County Line Rd., 60527-4718. Tel: 630-323-3725; Fax: 630-323-3779. Email: info@cbmidwest.org. Web: cbmidwest.org. Bros. Thomas Hetland, Pres.; Fred Dillenburg, Treas.

CAROL STREAM. *Assisi Homes - Colony Park, Inc.*, 550 E. Thornhill Dr., 60188. Tel: 630-682-9000; Fax: 630-682-9008. Web: www.wfs-inc.org. *Franciscan Ministries, Inc.*, 26 W. 171 Roosevelt Rd., P.O. Box 667, Wheaton, 60189-0667.

DARIEN. *Carmelite Mission Office*, 8501 Bailey Rd., 60561. Tel: 630-969-5220; Fax: 630-969-5266. Email: jemalley@juno.com. Web: www.carmelnet.org/missions/missions/htm. Rev. John Malley, O.Carm., Dir.

National Shrine of St. Therese, 8501 Bailey Rd., 60561. Tel: 630-969-3311; Fax: 630-969-5536. Email: webmaster@saint-therese.org. Web: www.saint-therese.org. Rev. Roger Bonneau, O.Carm., Dir.

Provincial Office of Lay Carmelites and Scapular Confraternity, 8501 Bailey Rd., 60561. Tel: 630-969-5050; Fax: 630-969-7519. Email: laycarmelites@carmelnet.org. Web: carmelnet.org. Sr. Libby Dahlstrom, O.Carm., Assoc. Dir.; Rev. John-Benedict Weber, O.Carm., Delegate & Dir.

Society of the Little Flower, 1313 Frontage Rd., 60561-5341. Tel: 630-968-9400; Fax: 630-968-9542. Email: webmaster@littleflower.org. Web: www.littleflower.org. Rev. Robert E. Colaresi, O.Carm., Dir.

FRANKFORT. *Provena Care @ Home Inc.*, 9223 West St. Francis Rd., 60423-8334. Tel: 815-806-2300; Fax: 815-806-0409. Email: edwardmolare@provenahealth.com. Web: www.provenahealth.com. Edward Molare, Pres. & Contact Person.

Provena Home Health, Inc., 9223 West St. Francis Rd., 60423-8334. Tel: 815-806-2300; Fax: 815-806-0409. Email: edwardmolare@provenahealth.com. Web: www.provenahealth.com. Edward Molare, Pres. & Contact Person.

GURNEE. *Assisi Homes of Gurnee, Inc.*, 3495 W. Grand Ave., 60031. Tel: 847-336-4428; Fax: 847-336-3778. Web: www.wfs-inc.org. *Franciscan Ministries, Inc.*, 26 W. 171 Roosevelt Rd., P.O. Box 667, Wheaton, 60189-0667.

KANKAKEE. *Lisieux Pastoral Outreach Center*, 371 N. St. Joseph Ave., 60901-2741. Tel: 815-939-2913; Fax: 815-933-7692; 815-939-2452. Email: lisieuxpc@aol.com.

LISLE. *Catholic CEO Healthcare Connection (CCHC)*, 3333 Warrenville Rd, Ste. 200, 60532. Tel: 630-799-8315; Fax: 630-799-8316. Email: rbutler@cchcnet.com. Roger N. Butler, Exec. Dir.

National Association of Catholic Nurses-U.S.A., P.O. Box 3016, 60532-3016. Tel: 520-624-4654; Fax: 520-872-4909. Email: sookie-escandon@msn.com. Web: www.nacn-usa.org. P.O. Box 3016, 60532. Socorro Escandon-Dominguez, R.N., Ph.D., Pres.

MOKENA. *Provena Senior Services*, 19065 Hickory Creek Dr., Ste. 310, 60448-8507. Tel: 708-478-7900; Fax: 708-478-5143. Web:

www.provenahealth.com. Ms. Connie March, Pres.

MOMENCE. *B.G.S. Charitable Trust*, P.O. Box 736, 60954-0736. Tel: 815-472-3131; Fax: 815-472-6914. Michael Brown, Contact Person.

Little Brothers of the Good Shepherd, Inc. of Illinois, 4129 N. Dixie Hwy., P.O. Box 736, 60954. Tel: 815-472-3131; Fax: 815-472-6914. Email: jabrinkman@aol.com. Web: www.lbgs.org. Bro. Richard MacPhee, Treas. Gen.; Judy Brinkmann, Dir. of Finance.

OAK BROOK. *Catholic Community Investment Retirement Trust* Christian Brothers of the Midwest, Inc. , 1200 Jorie Blvd. Ste. 210, 60523. Tel: 630-571-2182; Fax: 630-571-2723. Email: skeldingd@cbisonline.com. Bro. Joseph Saurbier, F.S.C.

Mayslake East Wing, Inc., 1801 35th St., 60523. Tel: 630-850-8232. Email: mayslakvlg@aol.com. Web: www.mayslake.com. Rev. Larry Dreffein, O.F.M., Pres. Units 150.

MV Benevolent Fund, Inc., 1801 35th St., 60523. Tel: 630-214-1858; Fax: 630-850-8233.

PLAINFIELD. *Housing Options for Religious, Clergy and Laity, NFP*, 16949 S. Drauden Rd., 60544-9291. Tel: 314-241-9090. Email: bch@greensfelder.com. Mr. Bernard C. Huger, Contact Person.

ROMEOVILLE. *Charitable Trust of the Brothers of the Christian Schools*, 1205 Windham Pkwy., 60446-1679. Tel: 630-378-2900; Fax: 630-378-2501. Email: info@cbservices.org. Web: www.cbservices.org.

Christian Brothers Employee Benefit Trust, 1205 Windham Pkwy., 60446-1679. Tel: 630-378-2900; Fax: 630-378-2501. Email: info@cbservices.org. Web: www.cbservices.org.

Christian Brothers Employee Retirement Plan Trust, 1205 Windham Pkwy., 60446-1679. Tel: 630-378-2900; Fax: 630-378-2501. Email: info@cbservices.org. Web: www.cbservices.org.

Christian Brothers Religious Community Deductible Trust, 1205 Windham Pkwy., 60446-1679. Tel: 630-378-2900; Fax: 630-378-2501. Email: info@cbservices.org. Web: www.cbservices.org.

Christian Brothers Religious Comprehensive Trust, 1205 Windham Pkwy., 60446-1679. Tel: 630-378-2900; Fax: 630-378-2501. Email: info@cbservices.org. Web: www.cbservices.org.

Christian Brothers Retirement Savings Plan Trust, 1205 Windham Pkwy., 60446-1679. Tel: 630-378-2900; Fax: 630-378-2501. Email: info@cbservices.org. Web: www.cbservices.org.

**Christian Brothers Services*, 1205 Windham Pkwy., 60446-1679. Tel: 630-378-2900; Fax: 630-378-2501. Email: info@cbservices.org. Web: www.cbservices.org. Bro. William Walz, F.S.C.

Religious & Charitable Risk Pooling Trust of the Brothers of the Christian Schools, 1205 Windham Pkwy., 60446-1679. Tel: 630-378-2900; Fax: 630-378-2501. Email: info@cbservices.org. Web: www.cbservices.org.

WEST CHICAGO. *Society of St. Vincent de Paul*, Diocesan Council of Joliet, 211 Main St., 60185. Tel: 630-293-9755; Fax: 630-293-9881. Email: svdpjoliet@aol.com.

WHEATON. *Assisi Homes of Illinois, Inc.*, Tel: 630-665-9100; Fax: 630-665-9357. Web: www.wfs-inc.org. *Franciscan Ministries, Inc.*, 26 W. 171 Roosevelt Rd., P.O. Box 667, 60189-0667.

Canticle Ministries, Inc., 26 W. 171 Roosevelt Rd., P.O. Box 667, 60189. Tel: 630-588-9165; Fax: 630-588-9167. Email: info@canticleministries.org. Web: www.canticleministries.org. Brad Ogilvie, Contact Person. Tel: 630-784-2722.

Canticle Place, Inc., 26 W. 105 Roosevelt Rd., #13, 60187. Tel: 630-588-9165; Fax: 630-588-9167. Web: www.canticleplace.org. *Franciscan Ministries, Inc.*, 26 W. Roosevelt Rd., P.O. Box 667, 60189-0667.

Clara Pfaender Fund, Inc., 26 W. 171 Roosevelt Rd., P.O. Box 667, 60189. Tel: 630-462-9271; Fax: 630-462-4977. Sr. Patricia Norton, Chairperson & Pres. Franciscan Sisters, Daughters of the Sacred Hearts of Jesus and Mary (Wheaton, IL)

Franciscan Health & Education Corp., Inc., 26 W. 171 Roosevelt Rd., P.O. Box 667, 60189. Tel: 630-462-7422; Fax: 630-462-9065.

**Franciscan Ministries Community Foundation, Inc.*, 26 W. 171 Roosevelt Rd., 60189. Tel: 630-462-9271; Fax: 630-462-4977. Web: www.wfs-inc.org.

Franciscan Ministries, Inc. Property & Mailing Address: , P.O. Box 667, 26 W. 171 Roosevelt Rd., 60189-0667. Tel: 630-462-9271; Fax: 630-784-2485. Web: www.wfs-inc.org.

Institute of the Blessed Virgin Mary Charitable Trust, P.O. Box 508, 60189. Tel: 630-653-6113; Fax: 630-653-4886. Email: ibvmjfryel@aol.com. Web: ibvm.org.

Marianjoy Rehabilitation Hospital Auxiliary, Formerly Marianjoy Rehabilitation Center AuxiliaryP.O. Box 795, 60189. Tel: 630-462-4081; Fax: 630-462-4262. Email: lsheridan@marianjoy.org. Web: www.marianjoy.org. Lois Sheridan, Dir.

**Marianjoy, Inc.*, 26 W. 171 Roosevelt Rd., P.O. Box 667, 60189. Tel: 630-462-9271; Fax: 630-462-0112. Web: www.marianjoy.org. Kathleen Yosko, Pres. & CEO.

**Rehabilitation Medicine Clinic, Inc.*, 26 W. 171 Roosevelt Rd., 60189. Tel: 630-462-9271; Fax: 630-462-0112. Web: www.marianjoy.org.

Wheaton Franciscan Services, Inc., 26 W. 171 Roosevelt Rd., P.O. Box 667, 60189. Tel: 630-462-9271; Fax: 630-462-4977. Web: www.wfs-inc.org. Joseph Lewis, Chm.; John D. Oliverio, Pres. & CEO.

RELIGIOUS INSTITUTES OF MEN REPRESENTED IN THE DIOCESE

For further details refer to the corresponding bracketed number in the Religious Institutes of Men or Women section.

[0140]—*The Augustinians* (Mother of Good Counsel Prov.)—O.S.A.

[0200]—*Benedictine Monks*—O.S.B.

[0330]—*Brothers of the Christian Schools* (Midwest Prov.)—F.S.C.

[0580]—*Brothers of the Good Shepherd*—B.G.S.

[0270]—*Carmelite Fathers & Brothers* (Prov. of Pure Heart of Mary)—O.Carm.

[0275]—*Carmelites of Mary Immaculate*—C.M.I.

[1320]—*Clerics of St. Viator*—C.S.V.

[0310]—*Congregation of Christian Brothers*—C.F.C.

[1130]—*Congregation of the Priests of the Sacred Heart*—S.C.J.

[0430]—*Dominicans* (Prov. of Albert the Great)—O.P.

[0520]—*Franciscan Friars* (Sacred Heart, Assumption Provs.)—O.F.M.

[0540]—*Franciscan Missionary Brothers of the Sacred Heart of Jesus*—O.S.F.

[0520]—*Franciscans* (Order of Friars Minor, Sacred Heart Prov.)—O.F.M.

[0740]—*Marian Fathers* (Prov. of St. Casimer)—M.I.C.

[0610]—*Priests of the Congregation of Holy Cross*—C.S.C.

[0110]—*Society of African Missions*—S.M.A.

[1260]—*Society of Christ*—S.Ch.

[0690]—*Society of Jesus* (Chicago and St. Louis Prov.)—S.J.

RELIGIOUS INSTITUTES OF WOMEN REPRESENTED IN THE DIOCESE

[0230]—*Benedictine Sisters of Pontifical Jurisdiction* (Lisle, IL; Ferdinand, IN)—O.S.B.

[0330]—*Carmelite Sisters for the Aged and Infirm* (Germantown, NY)—O.Carm.

[0400]—*Congregation of Our Lady of Mount Carmel* (Lacombe, LA)—O.Carm.

[3110]—*Congregation of Our Lady of the Retreat in the Cenacle*—R.C.

[3710]—*Congregation of the Sisters of Saint Agnes*—C.S.A.

[1920]—*Congregation of the Sisters of the Holy Cross*—C.S.C.

[2052]—*Congregation of the Sisters of the Third Order of St. Francis* Oldenburg, IN—O.S.F.

[1710]—*Congregation of the Third Order of St. Francis of Mary Immaculate, Joliet, IL*—O.S.F.

[1070-01]—*Dominican Sisters* (St. Catharine, KY)—O.P.

[1070-13]—*Dominican Sisters* (Adrian)—O.P.

[1070-10]—*Dominican Sisters* (Springfield)—O.P.

[1070-03]—*Dominican Sisters* (Sinsinawa)—O.P.

[1170]—*Felician Sisters*—C.S.S.F.

[1450]—*Franciscan Sisters of the Sacred Heart*—O.S.F.

[1240]—*Franciscan Sisters, Daughters of the Sacred Hearts of Jesus and Mary*—O.S.F.

[1910]—*Hermanas Josefinas*—H.J.

[2370]—*Institute of the Blessed Virgin Mary (Loretto Sisters)*—I.B.V.M.

[2575]—*Institute of the Sisters of Mercy of the Americas* (Chicago, IL)—R.S.M.

[3570]—*Mantellate Sisters, Servants of Mary* (Plainfield, IL)—O.S.M.

[]—*Missionary Sisters of the Holy Family* (Komorrow-Warsaw, Poland)—M.S.H.F.

[3760]—*Order of St. Clare*—P.C.C.

[3230]—*Poor Handmaids of Jesus Christ*—P.H.J.C.

[2970]—*School Sisters of Notre Dame* (Chicago Prov.)—S.S.N.D.

[1680]—*School Sisters of St. Francis* (U.S. Prov.)—O.S.F.

[3590]—*Servants of Mary* (Ladysmith, WI)—O.S.M.

[3520]—*Servants of the Holy Heart of Mary*—S.S.C.M.

[0460]—*Sisters of Charity of Incarnate Word*—C.C.V.I.

[0430]—*Sisters of Charity of the Blessed Virgin Mary*—B.V.M.

[1010]—*Sisters of Divine Providence of San Antonio* Texas—C.D.P.

[]—*Sisters of Korean Martyrs*—S.K.M.

[2990]—*Sisters of Notre Dame* (Toledo, OH)—S.N.D.

[3000]—*Sisters of Notre Dame de Namur* (Cincinnati Prov.)—S.N.D.deN.

[3360]—*Sisters of Providence of Saint Mary-of-the-Woods, IN*—S.P.

[3740]—*Sisters of St. Casimir*—S.S.C.

[1540]—*Sisters of St. Francis* (Clinton, IA)—O.S.F.

[1705]—*The Sisters of St. Francis of Assisi* (St. Francis)—O.S.F.

[1520]—*Sisters of St. Francis of Christ the King*—O.S.F.

[1570]—*Sisters of St. Francis of Dubuque* (Iowa)—O.S.F.

[3830-02]—*Sisters of St. Joseph*—C.S.J.

[3930]—*Sisters of St. Joseph of the Third Order of St. Francis* (Prov. of Immaculate Conception)—S.S.J.-T.O

[2980]—*Sisters of the Congregation de Notre Dame*—C.N.D.

[1720]—*Sisters of the Third Order Regular of St. Francis of the Congregation of Our Lady of Lourdes* (Rochester, MN)—O.S.F.

[2150]—*Sisters Servants of the Immaculate Heart of Mary*—I.H.M.

DIOCESAN CEMETERIES

JOLIET. *SS. Cyril and Methodius*, Rte. 6 & Maple Rd.. Tel: 815-838-0395.

Holy Cross, Theodore St.. Tel: 815-838-0395.

St. John the Baptist, Ruby St. & Clemet St.. Tel: 815-838-0395.

St. Mary Nativity, Caton Farm Rd. & Oakland Ave.. Tel: 815-838-0395.

Mount Olivet, 1320 E. Cass St.. Tel: 815-838-0395.

St. Patrick, Hunter St. & Jefferson St.. Tel: 815-838-0395.

BOURBONNAIS. *All Saints*, 1839 W. Rte. 102. Tel: 815-936-9378.

Maternity/BVM, Canberry Ln.. Tel: 815-933-2342.

CAROL STREAM. *St. Stephen*, St. Charles Rd.. Tel: 630-668-3313.

DOWNERS GROVE. *St. Bernard*, Hobson & Belmont Roads. Tel: 630-668-3313.

ELMHURST. *St. Mary*, Alexander Blvd.. Tel: 630-668-3313.

KANKAKEE. *Mt. Calvary*, 2000 E. Court St.. Tel: 815-933-2342.

St. Rose, Rte. 50. Tel: 815-933-2342.

LOCKPORT. *Calvary*, Rte. 171 & High Rd.. Tel: 815-838-0395.

LOCKPORT SOUTH. *Lockport South Cemetery*, Formerly St. Dennis16th St. & Washington St.. Tel: 815-838-0395.

LOMBARD. *St. Mary*, Finley Rd.. Tel: 630-668-3313.

NAPERVILLE. *SS. Peter & Paul*, Columbia St. & North Ave.. Tel: 630-668-3313.

ROMEOVILLE. *Catholic Cemeteries Monument Sales*, Formerly St. Charles Borromeo402 S. Independence Blvd., 60446-2264. Tel: 815-838-0395.

Resurrection, 135th St. & Rte. 53. Tel: 815-838-0395.

WHEATON. *Assumption*, One S. 510 Winfield Rd.. Tel: 630-668-3313.

WINFIELD. *St. John the Baptist*, Summit Rd. & Gary Mill Rd.. Tel: 630-668-3313.

NECROLOGY

✠ Fitzgerald, Most Rev. James E., Retired Auxiliary Bishop of Joliet—Died Sept. 11, 2003

† Podesta, Rev. Msgr. John F., (Retired)—Died May 6, 2003

† Davis, Raymond, (Retired)—Died March 17, 2003

† Dochstader, Richard, Plainfield, IL St. Mary—Died Sept. 5, 2003

Diocese of Juneau

(Dioecesis Junellensis)

Most Reverend

MICHAEL W. WARFEL

Bishop of Juneau; ordained April 26, 1980; appointed November 19, 1996; installed December 17, 1996.

Chancery: 415 Sixth St., #300, Juneau, AK 99801. Tel: 907-586-2227; Fax: 907-463-3237.

Web: www.dioceseofjuneau.org

Email: junodio@gci.net

ESTABLISHED JUNE 23, 1951.

Square Miles 37,566.

Corporate Title: "Corporation of the Catholic Bishop of Juneau."

Comprises the entire southeastern part of the State of Alaska known legally as The First Judicial District.

For legal titles of parishes and diocesan institutions, consult the Chancery Office.

STATISTICAL OVERVIEW

Personnel	
Bishop	1
Priests: Diocesan Active in Diocese	5
Priests: Diocesan Active Outside Diocese	2
Priests: Retired, Sick or Absent	4
Number of Diocesan Priests	11
Religious Priests in Diocese	2
Total Priests in Diocese	13
Extern Priests in Diocese	2
Permanent Deacons in Diocese	3
Total Sisters	4
Parishes	
Parishes	11
With Resident Pastor:	
Resident Diocesan Priests	4
Resident Religious Priests	4
Without Resident Pastor:	
Administered by Priests	3
Professional Ministry Personnel:	
Sisters	3
Lay Ministers	9
Welfare	
Catholic Hospitals	1
Total Assisted	38,979
Day Care Centers	1
Total Assisted	100
Special Centers for Social Services	1
Total Assisted	9,590
Other Institutions	1
Total Assisted	14,163
Educational	
Elementary Schools, Diocesan and Parish	1
Total Students	135
Catechesis/Religious Education:	
High School Students	139
Elementary Students	554
Total Students under Catholic Instruction	828
Teachers in the Diocese:	
Lay Teachers	14
Vital Statistics	
Receptions into the Church:	
Infant Baptism Totals	89
Adult Baptism Totals	15
Received into Full Communion	19
First Communions	56
Confirmations	87
Marriages:	
Catholic	8
Interfaith	12
Total Marriages	20
Deaths	20
Total Catholic Population	5,366
Total Population	71,972

Former Bishops—Most Revs. DERMOT O'FLANAGAN, D.D., ord. Aug. 27, 1929; appt. Bishop July 9, 1951; consecrated Oct. 3, 1951; resigned June 19, 1968; appt. Titular Bishop of Trecalae; died Dec. 31, 1972; FRANCIS T. HURLEY, D.D., ord. June 16, 1951; appt. Titular Bishop of Daimlaig and Auxiliary of Juneau, Feb. 4, 1970; consecrated March 19, 1970; Ordinary of See, July 20, 1971; appt. Archbishop of Anchorage, May 4, 1976; MICHAEL H. KENNY, D.D., ord. March 30, 1963; appt. March 20, 1979; consecrated May 27, 1979; installed June 15, 1979; died Feb. 19, 1995.

Diocesan Pastoral Center

Chancery—415 Sixth St., #300, Juneau, 99801. Tel: 907-586-2227; Fax: 907-463-3237.

Chancellor—Rev. PATRICK J. TRAVERS, J.C.L., J.D.

Diocesan Consultors—Revs. PETER GORGES (Retired); JEAN-PAULIN LOCKULU; PERRY KENASTON; PATRICK J. TRAVERS, J.C.L., J.D.; MICHAEL SCHWARTE; ANTHONY B. DUMMER, O.M.I.; EDMUND J. PENISTEN; THOMAS J. WEISE.

Tribunal—433 Jackson St., Ketchikan, 99901. Tel: 907-247-2755; Fax: 907-225-2571.

Judicial Vicar—Rev. PATRICK J. TRAVERS, J.C.L., J.D.

Defender of the Bond—Sr. CAROLYN ROEBER, O.P., J.C.L., J.D.

Auditor—ALETHEA JOHNSON.

Notaries—Mrs. LINDA KELLEY; ALETHEA JOHNSON; Mrs. KATHLEEN SVENSON.

Administration—415 Sixth St., #300, Juneau, 99801. Tel: 907-586-2227; Fax: 907-463-3237.

Business Manager and Finance Officer—JAMES DONAGHEY.

Director of Administrative Services—ROBERTA IZZARD.

Assistant to the Finance Officer—DENISE GRANT.

Finance Council—WILLIAM PETERS; THOMAS KOHAN; HUGH GRANT; Rev. PERRY KENASTON; Ms. JEAN ANTIOQUIA; Mr. RICH CONNEEN; Most Rev. MICHAEL WARFEL; JAMES DONAGHEY

Diocesan Offices and Directors

Apostleship of the Sea—Port Chaplains: Revs. ANASTASIUS IWUOHA, 416 Fifth St., Juneau, 99801; PATRICK TRAVERS, 433 Jackson St., Ketchikan, 99801; JEAN-PAULIN LOCKULU, P.O. Box 495, Sitka, 99835; MICHAEL SCHWARTE, P.O. Box 469, Wrangell, 99929. P.O. Box 508, Petersburg, 99833.

Catholic Community Service, Inc.—ROSEMARY HAGEVIG, Exec. Dir., 419 Sixth St., Juneau, 99801. Tel: 907-463-6151.

Board of Directors—Most Rev. MICHAEL W. WARFEL, Pres.; PATRICIA CLASBY; JOHN GREELY; SHARON KELLY; FRAN KINNEY; ETHEL LUND; MARY LOU MEINERS; MARJORIE MENZI; THOMAS SLAGLE; KEVIN SULLIVAN; TONY YORBA.

Southeast Senior Services—JILL SANDLEBEN, Prog. Dir., 419 Sixth St., Juneau, 99801 Tel: 907-463-6153.

Diocesan Publication "Inside Passage"—KARLA DONAGHEY, Editor, 415 Sixth St., #300, Juneau, 99801. Tel: 907-586-2237, Ext. 32.

Ministry Support Center—Sr. JILL JAEB, O.S.U., Dir., 415 Sixth St., #300, Juneau, 99801. Tel: 907-586-2227.

Commission for Liturgy—Rev. EDMUND PENISTEN, 433 Jackson St., Ketchikan, 99901. Tel: 907-225-2570.

Commission for Social Justice—Rev. PERRY KENASTON, 415 Sixth St., Juneau, 99801. Tel: 907-586-2227, Ext. 29.

Commission for Christian Formation—CHARLES ROHRBACHER, 416 Fifth St., Juneau, 99801. Tel: 907-586-8046.

Permanent Deacon Program—Deacon GARY HORTON, 415 6th St., #300, Juneau, 99801. Tel: 907-586-2227, Ext. 36.

School—STEVEN CLOSSICK, Prin., Holy Name School, 433 Jackson St., Ketchikan, 99901. Tel: 907-225-2400.

Shrine of St. Therese—THOMAS FITTERER, 5933 Lund St., Juneau, 99801. Tel: 907-780-6112. Caretakers: JODIE LILIEDAHL; MARCIA LILIEDAHL, 8695 Short Ct., Juneau, 99801. Tel: 907-789-9815.

St. Vincent de Paul Society—DAN AUSTIN, 8617 Teal St., Juneau, 99801. Tel: 907-789-5535.

Special Collections and Archivist—Deacon GARY HORTON, 415 6th St., #300, Juneau, 99801. Tel: 907-586-2227, Ext. 36.

Victim Assistance Coordinator—ROBERTA IZZARD. Tel: 907-586-2227, Ext. 25. Email: robbiei@gci.net.

Vocations—Most Rev. MICHAEL WARFEL, 415 6th St., #300, Juneau, 99801. Tel: 907-586-2227, Ext. 25.

CLERGY, PARISHES, MISSIONS AND PAROCHIAL SCHOOLS

CITY AND BOROUGH OF JUNEAU

1—CATHEDRAL OF THE NATIVITY OF THE BLESSED VIRGIN MARY, Rev. Anastasius Iwuoha, Admin.

Res.: 416 Fifth St., 99801. Tel: 907-586-1513; Fax: 907-586-8091.

Catechesis/Religious Program—Charles Rohrbacher, D.R.E. Students 97.

2—ST. PAUL THE APOSTLE, Revs. Anthony B. Dummer, O.M.I.; Thomas J. Weise.

Res.: 9055 Atlin Ave., 99801. Tel 907-789-2648 (Rectory); 907-789-7307 (Office); Fax: 907-790-3430.

Catechesis/Religious Program—Tel 907-789-7303. Marilyn Monagle, D.R.E. Students 321.

OUTSIDE THE CITY AND BOROUGH OF JUNEAU

CRAIG, MATANUSKA-SUSITNA CO., ST. JOHN BY THE SEA, Sr. Zita Simon, O.P., Admin.

Res.: P.O. Box 245, Klawock, 99925. Tel: 907-755-2345; Fax: 907-755-2350.

Mission— Thorne Bay, 99919. Tel: 907-828-3324.
Mission— Coffman Cove.
Mission— Hydaburg.
Mission— Klawock.
Mission— Kasaan.
Mission— Whale Pass.
Mission— Naukati.
Mission— Hollis.

HAINES, FAIRBANKS NORTH STAR CO., SACRED HEART, Rev. Jim Blaney, O.M.I.
Res.: Box 326, 99827. Tel: 907-766-2241.

HOONAH, SKAGWAY-HOONAH-ANGOONA(CA) CO., SACRED HEART, Rev. Perry Kenaston.
Res.: P.O. Box 368, 99829. Tel: 907-945-3323.

KETCHIKAN, KETCHIKAN GATEWAY CO., HOLY NAME, Revs. Patrick J. Travers, J.C.L., J.D.; Edmund Penisten.
Res.: 433 Jackson St., 99901. Tel: 907-225-2570; 907-225-5352 (Rectory); Fax: 907-225-2571.
School—Tel: 907-225-2400. Lay Teachers 10; Students 135.
Catechesis/Religious Program—Tel: 907-225-2120; Fax: 907-225-2570. Alethea Johnson, D.R.E. Students 115.
Mission—Holy Family P.O. Box 228, Metlakatla, 99926.

PETERSBURG, WRANGELL-PETERSBURG(CA) CO., ST. CATHERINE OF SIENA, Rev. Michael Schwarte.
Res.: P.O. Box 508, 99833. Tel: 907-772-3257; Fax: 907-772-3020.
Mission— Kake.

SITKA, SITKA CO., ST. GREGORY OF NAZIANZEN, Rev. Jean-Paulin Lockulu.
Res.: P.O. Box 495, 99835. Tel: 907-747-8371; 907-747-6997; Fax: 907-747-8051.
Mission— Angoon.

SKAGWAY, SKAGWAY-HOONAH-ANGOON (CA) CO., ST. THERESE OF THE CHILD JESUS, Rev. Jim Blaney, O.M.I.
Res.: Box 496, 99840. Tel: 907-983-2271.

WRANGELL, WRANGELL-PETERSBURG (CA) CO., ST. ROSE OF LIMA, Rev. Michael Schwarte.
Res.: Box 469, 99929. Tel: 907-874-3771; Fax: 907-874-3744.

YAKUTAT, YAKUTAT CO., ST. ANN, Rev. Perry Kenaston; Sr. Josephine Aloralrea, O.S.U., Parish Admin.
Res.: P.O. Box 323, 99689. Tel: 907-784-3406.
Mission— Hobart Bay.
Mission— Cube Cove.
Mission— Elfin Cove.
Mission— Gustavus.
Mission— Pelican.
Mission— Tenakee Springs.

On Duty Outside the Diocese:
Rev.—
Saba, Joseph, 5660 W. Placita Del Risco, Tuscon, AZ 85745.

Retired:
Revs.—
Cronin, James D., 1870-A Vista del Sur, Sante Fe, NM 87505.
Frister, Jerome, 3621 Vista Campana S. #70, Oceanside, CA 92057.
Gorges, Peter, St. Gregory, P.O. Box 495, Sitka, 99835-0495.
Ryan, James, 2828 Sloat Rd., Pebble Beach, CA 93953.

Permanent Deacons:
Horton, Gary, Cathedral of the Nativity of the Blessed Virgin Mary, Juneau
Johnson, Charles, St. Gregory's, Sitka
Mackin, Francis, St. Gregory's, Sitka
Paradis, Paul, (Retired)
Seslar, Charles, Cathedral of the Nativity of the Blessed Virgin Mary, Juneau

INSTITUTIONS LOCATED IN THE DIOCESE

[A] HOSPITALS

KETCHIKAN. *Ketchikan General Hospital*, 3100 Tongass, 99901. Tel: 907-225-5171; Fax: 907-228-8322. Licensed Bed Capacity 85; Patients Assisted Annually 38,843.
Island View Nursing Home

[B] CONVENTS AND RESIDENCES FOR SISTERS

JUNEAU. *St. Joseph Convent*, 2971 Douglas Hwy., 99801. Tel: 907-586-2085. Intercommunity residence of various religious orders of women.

KETCHIKAN. *Sisters of St. Joseph of Peace*, 234 Carlanna Lake Rd., 99901. Tel: 907-225-5171; Fax: 907-228-8322.

RELIGIOUS INSTITUTES OF WOMEN REPRESENTED IN THE DIOCESE

For further details refer to the corresponding bracketed number in the Religious Institutes of Men or Women section.

[1070]—*Dominican Sisters*—O.P.

[3890]—*Sisters of St. Joseph of Peace*—C.S.J.P.

[]—*Ursuline Sisters of the Roman Union*—O.S.U.

NECROLOGY

(No Deaths)

Diocese of Kalamazoo

(Dioecesis Kalamazuensis)

Most Reverend

JAMES A. MURRAY

Bishop of Kalamazoo; ordained June 7, 1958; appointed Bishop of Kalamazoo November 18, 1997; ordained and installed January 27, 1998.

Most Reverend

PAUL V. DONOVAN, D.D.

Former Bishop of Kalamazoo; ordained May 20, 1950; appointed Bishop of Kalamazoo June 15, 1971; ordained and installed July 21, 1971; resigned November 22, 1994. *Mailing Address: 238 Falkirk Ct., Kalamazoo, MI 49006.*

ESTABLISHED JULY 21, 1971.

Square Miles 5,337.

Comprises the following nine Counties in the State of Michigan: Allegan, Barry, Berrien, Branch, Calhoun, Cass, Kalamazoo, St. Joseph and Van Buren.

For legal titles of parishes and diocesan institutions, consult the Chancery.

Chancery: 215 N. Westnedge Ave., Kalamazoo, MI 49007-3760. Tel: 269-349-8714; Fax: 269-349-6440.

STATISTICAL OVERVIEW

Personnel	
Bishop	1
Retired Bishops	1
Priests: Diocesan Active in Diocese	41
Priests: Diocesan Active Outside Diocese	1
Priests: Retired, Sick or Absent	14
Number of Diocesan Priests	56
Religious Priests in Diocese	12
Total Priests in Diocese	68
Extern Priests in Diocese	7
Ordinations:	
Diocesan Priests	2
Transitional Deacons	1
Permanent Deacons in Diocese	27
Total Brothers	2
Total Sisters	170
Parishes	
Parishes	46
With Resident Pastor:	
Resident Diocesan Priests	38
Resident Religious Priests	8
Without Resident Pastor:	
Administered by Priests	1
Administered by Deacons	3
Administered by Religious Women	2
Missions	13
Pastoral Centers	1
Professional Ministry Personnel:	
Brothers	1
Sisters	8
Lay Ministers	39
Welfare	
Catholic Hospitals	3
Total Assisted	757,008
Homes for the Aged	5
Total Assisted	440
Day Care Centers	15
Total Assisted	453
Specialized Homes	1
Total Assisted	236
Special Centers for Social Services	5
Total Assisted	38,414
Educational	
Diocesan Students in Other Seminaries	12
Total Seminarians	12
High Schools, Diocesan and Parish	3
Total Students	775
Elementary Schools, Diocesan and Parish	22
Total Students	3,152
Catechesis/Religious Education:	
High School Students	1,213
Elementary Students	6,150
Total Students under Catholic Instruction	11,302
Teachers in the Diocese:	
Priests	1
Sisters	5
Lay Teachers	269
Vital Statistics	
Receptions into the Church:	
Infant Baptism Totals	1,430
Adult Baptism Totals	209
Received into Full Communion	264
First Communions	1,444
Confirmations	1,325
Marriages:	
Catholic	257
Interfaith	158
Total Marriages	415
Deaths	862
Total Catholic Population	117,088
Total Population	840,352

Former Bishops—Most Revs. PAUL V. DONOVAN, D.D., ord. May 20, 1950; appt. Bishop of Kalamazoo June 15, 1971; installed July 21, 1971; resigned Nov. 22, 1994; ALFRED J. MARKIEWICZ, D.D., ord. June 6, 1953; appt. Titular Bishop of Afufenia and Auxiliary to the Bishop of Rockville Centre, July 7, 1986; ord. Bishop, Sept. 17, 1986; appt. Bishop of Kalamazoo, Nov. 22, 1994; installed Jan. 31, 1995; died Jan. 9, 1997.

Vicar General—Rev. Msgr. EUGENE A. SEARS, 211 Church St., St. Joseph, 49085. Tel: 269-983-1575; Fax: 269-983-1576.

Chancery—215 N. Westnedge Ave., Kalamazoo, 49007-3760. Tel: 269-349-8714; Fax: 269-349-6440. Web: dioceseofkalamazoo.org. Office Hours: 8:30-4; Address all communications to this office.

Chancellor—Mr. T. EDWARD CAREY JR., 215 N. Westnedge Ave., Kalamazoo, 49007. Tel: 269-349-8714, Ext. 116; Fax: 269-349-6440.

Diocesan Tribunal—215 N. Westnedge Ave., Kalamazoo, 49007-3760. Tel: 269-349-8714, Ext. 115; Fax: 269-349-6440.

Judicial Vicar—Rev. THOMAS A. MARTIN, J.C.D.

Defenders of the Bond—Revs. MICHAEL A. HACK, J.C.D.; KENNETH W. SCHMIDT, J.C.D.

Promoter of Justice—Rev. KENNETH W. SCHMIDT, J.C.D.

Judges—Revs. JEFFREY A. KASSIAN, J.C.O.L.; EDWARD A. HANKIEWICZ, J.C.L.; Sr. JOYCE HOBEN, S.N.D.N., J.C.L.

Advocates—Revs. ROBERT E. FLICKINGER; MICHAEL D. HAZARD; CHARLES H. FISCHER.

Chief Notary and Administrative Assistant—Mrs. MARLENE J. PRANSKATIS.

Ecclesiastical Notaries—Mrs. NANCY L. BOOTHBY; Mrs. DENISE ABRAHAM; Revs. THOMAS MARTIN; KENNETH SCHMIDT.

Archivist—Rev. ROBERT F. CREAGAN, 209 S. Brown St., Paw Paw, 49079. Tel: 269-657-4459; Fax: 269-657-4260.

Diocesan Consultors—Revs. DAVID C. ADAMS; ROBERT E. FLICKINGER; THOMAS A. MARTIN, J.C.D.; JAMES BARRETT; DONALD TURCICH, O.S.A.; Rev. Msgr. EUGENE A. SEARS; Rev. MARK J. VYVERMAN.

Vicar for Religious—Sr. MARY JOAN WALSH, O.L.L., 4111 Nazareth Rd., Kalamazoo, 49004. Tel: 269-226-4839.

Diocesan Offices and Directors

Campaign for Human Development—Sr. SUSAN RIDLEY, O.P., Dir., 215 N. Westnedge Ave., Kalamazoo, 49007-3760. Tel: 269-349-8714, Ext. 238; Fax: 269-349-6440.

Catholic Family Services—Mrs. FRANCES H. DENNY, A.C.S.W, M.B.A., Exec. Dir., 1819 Gull Rd., Kalamazoo, 49001. Tel: 269-381-9800; Fax: 269-381-2932.

Catholic Relief Services—Sr. SUSAN RIDLEY, O.P., Dir., 215 N. Westnedge Ave., Kalamazoo, 49007-3760. Tel: 269-349-8714, Ext. 238; Fax: 269-349-6440.

Cemeteries—Mr. T. EDWARD CAREY JR., 215 N. Westnedge Ave., Kalamazoo, 49007. Tel: 269-349-8714, Ext. 116; Fax: 269-349-6440.

Diocesan Cemetery - Kalamazoo—Mt. Olivet.

Evangelization, Catechesis & Initiation—Mr. D. J. FLORIAN, Dir. Tel: 269-349-8714, Ext. 227. Assoc. Directors: LISA IRWIN. Tel: 269-349-8714, Ext. 228; KURT LUCAS. Tel: 269-349-8714, Ext. 234. 215 N. Westnedge Ave., Kalamazoo, 49007-3760. Tel: 269-349-8714, Ext. 227; Fax: 269-349-6440.

Christian Service—Sr. SUSAN RIDLEY, O.P., Dir., 215 N. Westnedge Ave., Kalamazoo, 49007-3760. Tel: 269-349-8714, Ext. 238; Fax: 269-349-6440.

Communications—Mr. BRENT KING, Dir., 215 N. Westnedge Ave., Kalamazoo, 49007-3760. Tel: 269-349-8714, Ext. 350.

Audio-Visual Resources—Mr. D. J. FLORIAN, Coord., 215 N. Westnedge Ave., Kalamazoo, 49007-3760. Tel: 269-349-8714, Ext. 227.

Diocesan Council of Catholic Women (D.C.C.W.)—Rev. DONALD P. KLINGER, Spiritual Dir., St. Margaret's Church, 245 Court St., Otsego, 49078. Tel: 269-694-6311.

Diocesan Development and Stewardship Office—Mr. DAVID BAERWALDE, Dir., 215 N. Westnedge Ave., Kalamazoo, 49007-3760. Tel: 269-349-8714, Ext. 349; MARY JANE DOERR, Assoc. Dir. Tel: 269-349-8714, Ext. 246.

Delegate for Ecumenical and Interreligious Concerns—Rev. THOMAS A. MARTIN, J.C.D., Dir., 215 N. Westnedge Ave., Kalamazoo, 49007-3760. Tel: 269-349-8714, Ext. 118.

Diocesan Pastoral Council—Mr. JOSEPH PAWLANTA, 215 N. Westnedge Ave., Kalamazoo, 49007-3760. Tel: 269-349-8714, Ext. 354.

Diocesan-Parish Council Ministry—VACANT, 215 N. Westnedge Ave., Kalamazoo, 49007-3760. Tel: 269-349-8714.

Diocesan Pilgrimages—Rev. ROBERT F. CREAGAN, Diocesan Coord., 209 S. Brown St., Paw Paw, 49079. Tel: 269-657-4459; Fax: 269-657-4260.

Education—FRANK C. WIPPEL, Ed.D., Supt. of Schools. Associate Superintendents: Mrs. MARGARET ERICH. Tel: 269-349-8714, Ext. 239; Sr. MARY ANN DALTON, S.S.J. Tel: 269-349-8714, Ext. 248. 215 N. Westnedge Ave., Kalamazoo, 49007-3760. Tel: 269-349-8714, Ext. 235; Fax: 269-349-6440.

Finance Council—Revs. DAVID C. ADAMS; LAWRENCE FARRELL; Mr. T. EDWARD CAREY JR.; Mr. LEN AMAT; Mr. ED KOWIESKI; Mr. DANIEL KUNITZER; Mr. JERRY B. LOVE; Mr. JOHN A. PANFIL; Mr. BRUCE RAGAN; Mr. LEO A. SWIAT.

Diocesan Finance Office—Mr. BRUCE D. RAGAN, Dir., 215 N. Westnedge Ave., Kalamazoo, 49007-3760. Tel: 269-349-8714, Ext. 353; Fax: 269-349-6440.

Holy Childhood Association—Rev. LAWRENCE FARRELL, Dir., 215 N. Westnedge Ave., Kalamazoo, 49007-3760. Tel: 269-349-8714, Ext. 119.

Inner City Ministry—Sisters RITA SCHAFER, S.S.J.; MARY PUNG, S.S.J., Catholic Community Center, 589 Pearl St., Benton Harbor, 49022. Tel: 269-926-6424; Fax: 269-926-2870.

Jail Ministry—Sr. SUSAN RIDLEY, O.P., Coord., 215 N. Westnedge Ave., Kalamazoo, 49007-3760. Tel: 269-349-8714, Ext. 238.

Knights of Columbus—Rev. ROBERT F. CREAGAN, Diocesan Chap., 209 S. Brown St., Paw Paw, 49079. Tel: 269-657-4459; Fax: 269-657-4260.

Marriage and Family Ministry, Office of—Mr. JOE SCHMITT, Dir. Tel: 269-349-8714, Ext. 112; Mrs. JANE BODWAY, Asst. Dir. Tel: 269-349-8714, Ext. 113. 215 N. Westnedge Ave., Kalamazoo, 49007-3760. Fax: 269-349-6440.

Ministry with Persons with Disabilities—Miss ANN SHERZER, Dir., 215 N. Westnedge Ave., Kalamazoo, 49007-3760. Tel: 269-349-7276, Ext. 229.

Missions—Rev. LAWRENCE FARRELL, Dir., 215 N. Westnedge Ave., Kalamazoo, 49007-3760. Tel: 269-349-8714, Ext. 119; Fax: 269-349-6440.

Natural Family Planning Center of Southwestern Michigan—Mrs. MARY CULP, Dir., 165 N. Washington St., Battle Creek, 49017. Tel: 269-964-9474; Fax: 269-964-0431.

Permanent Diaconate—Mr. D. J. FLORIAN, Dir.; Deacon JOHN BODWAY, Pastoral Coord., 215 N. Westnedge Ave., Kalamazoo, 49007-3760. Tel: 269-349-8714, Ext. 227; Fax: 269-349-6440.

Presbyteral Council—Revs. DAVID C. ADAMS; ROBERT E. FLICKINGER; THOMAS A. MARTIN, J.C.D.; JAMES L. BARRETT (Retired); DONALD TURCICH, O.S.A.; Rev. Msgr. EUGENE A. SEARS; Rev. MARK J. VYVERMAN.

Priestly Life and Ministry Office—Rev. KENNETH SCHMIDT, Dir., 421 Monroe St., Kalamazoo, 49006. Tel: 269-381-8917; Fax: 269-381-0195.

Respect Life—Sr. SUSAN RIDLEY, O.P., Dir., 215 N. Westnedge Ave., Kalamazoo, 49007-3760. Tel: 269-349-8714, Ext. 238; Fax: 269-349-6440.

St. Vincent DePaul Society—Rev. LAWRENCE W. KROLL, Spiritual Advisor, 128 Cedar St., Wayland, 49348. Tel: 616-792-2138; Fax: 616-792-2908.

Office of Immigration Services—Ms. KISH ENSTICE, Dir., 1128 Race St., Kalamazoo, 49001. Tel: 269-385-1019; Fax: 269-344-6602.

Office of Strategic Planning—Mr. JOSEPH PAWLANTA, Dir., 215 N. Westnedge Ave., Kalamazoo, 49007-3760. Tel: 269-349-8714, Ext. 354.

Scouting Apostolate—Rev. RICHARD L. ALTINE, Chap., 939 Charlotte Ave., Kalamazoo, 49001.

Spanish-Speaking Apostolate—Ms. FANNY TABARES, Dir., 215 N. Westnedge Ave., Kalamazoo, 49007-3760. Tel: 269-349-8714, Ext. 236; Fax: 269-349-6440.

Victim Assistance Coordinator—Mr. T. EDWARD CAREY JR. Tel: 269-349-8714, Ext. 116. Email: edcarey@dioceseofkalamazoo.org.

Vocations—Rev. ROBERT F. CREAGAN, Dir., 215 N. Westnedge Ave., Kalamazoo, 49007-3760. Tel: 269-349-8714, Ext. 242; Fax: 269-349-6440.

Office of Christian Worship—Mr. DAVID J. REILLY, Dir., 215 N. Westnedge Ave., Kalamazoo, 49007-3760. Tel: 269-349-8714, Ext. 245; Fax: 269-349-6440.

Address communications for all other offices to: *Chancery, Diocese of Kalamazoo, 215 N. Westnedge Ave., Kalamazoo, 49007-3760*. Tel: 269-349-8714; Fax: 269-349-6440.

CLERGY, PARISHES, MISSIONS AND PAROCHIAL SCHOOLS

CITY OF KALAMAZOO
(KALAMAZOO COUNTY)

1—ST. AUGUSTINE CATHEDRAL (1856), Revs. Mark J. Vyverman; A. Thomas Fernando (India); Jeffery Kassian.
Res.: 542 W. Michigan Ave., 49007. Tel: 269-345-5147; Fax: 269-349-0166.
School—600 W. Michigan Ave., 49007. Tel: 269-349-1945; Fax: 269-349-1085. Sisters 1; Lay Teachers 17; Students 265.
Catechesis/Religious Program—Students 75.

2—ST. JOSEPH (1904), Revs. Michael D. Hazard; Mark J. Nojeck.
Res.: 936 Lake St., 26949-01. Tel: 269-343-6256; Fax: 269-343-1214.
School—930 Lake St., 49001. Tel: 269-342-9441; Fax: 269-349-1934. Lay Teachers 12; Students 110.
Catechesis/Religious Program—Students 165.

3—ST. MARY (1935), Revs. Richard L. Altine; Michael Rejent, O.S.F.S.; Jacob Vadakkekudy (India).
Res.: 939 Charlotte Ave., 49048. Tel: 269-342-0621; Fax: 269-342-4132.
School—929 Charlotte Ave., 49048. Tel: 269-342-2884; Fax: 269-342-2033. Lay Teachers 10; Students 82.
Catechesis/Religious Program—

4—ST. MONICA (1955), Rev. Lawrence M. Farrell. In Res., Revs. Robert E. Consani (Retired); Massimiliano Camporese (Italy); Wieslaw Lipka (Poland); Deacon Robert Stevens.
Res.: 534 W. Kilgore Rd., 49008. Tel: 269-345-4389; Fax: 269-345-5211.
Church Office: 4408 S. Westnedge, 49008.
School—530 W. Kilgore Rd., 49008. Tel: 269-345-2444; Fax: 269-345-8534. Lay Teachers 23; Students 475.
Catechesis/Religious Program—Students 632.

5—ST. THOMAS MORE STUDENT PARISH (1956), Rev. Kenneth W. Schmidt, J.C.D.; Sr. Susan McCrery, S.S.J., Pastoral Assoc.; Mrs. Marian Nelson, Pastoral Assoc.; Patrick Hall, Pastoral Assoc.
Office—421 Monroe St., 49006. Tel: 616-381-8917; Fax: 616-381-0195.
Catechesis/Religious Program—936 Lake St., 49001. Tel: 616-343-6258; Fax: 616-343-1214. Students 93.

OUTSIDE THE CITY OF KALAMAZOO

ALBION, CALHOUN CO., ST. JOHN THE EVANGELIST (1873), [CEM] Rev. Gordon L. Greene.
Office:—879 Finley Dr., 49224-9712. Tel: 517-629-4532; Fax: 517-629-5462.
Catechesis/Religious Program—Students 52.

ALLEGAN, ALLEGAN CO., BLESSED SACRAMENT (1934), [CEM] Rev. Jerome M. Heyman, O.S.A.
Res.: 422 Hubbard St., 49010-1246. Tel: 616-673-4455; Fax: 616-673-5869.
Church: 110 Cedar St., 49010-1244. Tel: 269-673-4455; Fax: 269-673-5869.
Catechesis/Religious Program—Students 155.

BANGOR, VAN BUREN CO., SACRED HEART OF JESUS (1932), [CEM] Rev. Thomas Seidel, C.S.C., Admin.
Res.: 201 S. Walnut St., 49013. Tel: 616-427-7514; Fax: 616-427-5558.
Catechesis/Religious Program—Tel: 616-427-8202. Students 52.
Chapel—Grand Junction, St. Cyril, (Summer)

BATTLE CREEK, CALHOUN CO.

1—ST. JEROME (1955), [JC] Deacon Albert W. Patrick, Admin.
Res.: 229 Collier Ave., 49017. Tel: 269-968-2218; Fax: 269-968-2233.
Catechesis/Religious Program—Students 40.

2—ST. JOSEPH (1942), [JC] Revs. James S. O'Leary; Mario Aquirre (Colombia). In Res., Revs. Donn J. Taylor (Retired); Joseph Thachet (India) (Retired).
Res.: 61 N. 23rd St., 49015. Tel: 269-962-0165; Fax: 269-962-5937.
School—63 N. 24th St., 49015. Tel: 269-965-7749; Fax: 269-965-0790. Lay Teachers 23; Students 352.
Catechesis/Religious Program—Tel: 269-465-4079. Students 218.

3—ST. PHILIP (1869), [CEM] Revs. Charles H. Fischer; John Fleckenstein; Deacons Al Bell; Hal Bohan; Bernie Mileski.
Office—126 Capital Ave., N.E., 49017. Tel: 269-968-6645; Fax: 269-968-0632.
Res.: 92 Capital Ave., N.E., 49017.
School—(Grades 6-12), 20 Cherry St., 49017. Tel: 269-963-4935; Fax: 269-963-5590. Lay Teachers 25; Students 280.
Catechesis/Religious Program—Tel: 269-962-9506. Students 173.

BENTON HARBOR, BERRIEN CO.

1—ST. BERNARD, Merged, with St. John, Benton Harbor.

2—SS. JOHN & BERNARD (1996), [CEM] Rev. William J. Jacobs Jr.; Deacon Al Lazaga.
Res.: 600 Columbus Ave., 49022. Tel: 616-925-2425; Fax: 616-925-4678.
Catechesis/Religious Program—220 Church St., St. Joseph, 49085. Tel: 616-983-7797. Students 141.

3—ST. JOHN THE EVANGELIST, Merged, with St. Bernard, Benton Harbor.

BRIDGMAN, BERRIEN CO., OUR LADY QUEEN OF PEACE (1939), Rev. Raymond J. Barth.
Res.: 3903 Lake St., P.O. Box 747, 49106-0747. Tel: 269-465-6252; Fax: 269-465-4930.
Catechesis/Religious Program—Students 119.

BRONSON, BRANCH CO., ST. MARY'S (1867), (Polish), [CEM] Rev. Richard A. Fritz; Deacon Gerald Smoker.
Res.: 602 W. Chicago, 49028. Tel: 517-369-2120; Fax: 517-369-8707.
School—204 Albers Rd., 49028. Tel: 517-369-4625; Fax: 517-369-1652. Lay Teachers 6; Students 103.
Mission—St. Barbara Colon, St. Joseph Co. Tel: 616-432-2109.
Catechesis/Religious Program—Tel: 269-432-3122. Students 63.

BUCHANAN, BERRIEN CO., ST. ANTHONY (1963), Rev. Charles T. Page.
Res.: 509 W. 4th St., 49107. Tel: 269-695-3863; Fax: 269-695-3864.
Catechesis/Religious Program—Students 70.

BYRON CENTER, KENT CO., ST. MARY'S VISITATION (1866), (German), [CEM 2] [JC 2] Rev. Stephen Rodrigo, S.J. (India).
Res.: 2459 146th Ave., 49315. Tel: 616-681-9701; Fax: 616-681-9919.
School—2455 146th Ave., 49315. Lay Teachers 7; Students 104.
Catechesis/Religious Program—Students 200.

CASSOPOLIS, CASS CO., ST. ANN (1915), Rev. Donald G. Potts.
Church & Mailing Address: 421 N. Broadway, P.O. Box 247, 49031. Tel: 269-445-3000; Fax: 269-445-5787.
Res.: 312 N. Disbrow, P.O. Box 247, 49031. Tel: 616-445-3140.
Catechesis/Religious Program—Students 47.

COLDWATER, BRANCH CO., ST. CHARLES BORROMEO (1849), Revs. Brian L. Stanley; Leon H. Pohl, Pastor Emeritus; Deacon Alvin Provot.
Res.: 150 Taylor St., 49036. Tel: 517-278-2650; Fax: 517-278-5800.
School—79 Harrison St., 49036. Tel: 517-279-0404; Fax: 517-278-0505. Lay Teachers 8; Students 98.
Catechesis/Religious Program—Students 160.
Mission—Our Lady of Fatima Union City, Branch Co. Tel: 517-741-7275.

DECATUR, VAN BUREN CO., HOLY FAMILY (1938), Rev. Richard Valls.
Res.: 500 W. St. Mary St., 49045. Tel: 269-423-3151; Fax: 269-423-7755.
Catechesis/Religious Program—Students 31.

DELTON, BARRY CO., ST. AMBROSE (1950), Rev. Carl F. Peltz; Sr. Constance Fifelski, Parish Coord.
Res.: 11252 Floria Rd., 49046. Tel: 269-623-2490; Fax: 269-623-2498.
Catechesis/Religious Program—Students 51.
Mission—Our Lady of Great Oak Lacey, Barry Co.

DORR, ALLEGAN CO., ST. STANISLAUS (1892), (Polish), [CEM] Rev. James Vinh Le.
Res.: 1871 136th Ave., 49323. Tel: 269-793-7268; Fax: 269-793-3325.
School—1861 136th Ave., 49323. Tel: 269-793-7204; Fax: 269-793-3264. Lay Teachers 5; Students 88.
Catechesis/Religious Program—Students 123.
Mission—Sacred Heart [CEM] 2036 20th St., Watson, Allegan Co. 49010.

DOUGLAS, ALLEGAN CO., ST. PETER (1894), [CEM] Rev. Ronald R. Turcich, O.S.A.
Res.: St. Peter's Dr., 49406. Tel: 269-857-7951; 269-857-8175; Fax: 269-857-8164.

DOWAGIAC, CASS CO., HOLY MATERNITY OF MARY (1892), [CEM] Rev. Leo A. Taubitz.
Res.: 210 N. Front St., 49047. Tel: 616-782-2808; Fax: 616-782-3558.
Catechesis/Religious Program—Tel: 616-782-3558. Students 109.
Mission—Sacred Heart of Mary Silver Creek, MI, Cass Co51841 Leach Rd., 49047. Tel: 616-782-5740.

EDWARDSBURG, CASS CO., OUR LADY OF THE LAKE (1923), Rev. David C. Otto.
Res.: 24832 U.S. 12 E., 49112. Tel: 616-699-5870; Fax: 616-699-5474.
Catechesis/Religious Program—Students 151.

GOBLES, VAN BUREN CO., ST. JUDE (1985), Rev. Robert F. Creagan; Deacon John R. Bodway, Pastoral Admin.
Church and Mailing: 13809 M-40 N., P.O. Box 102, 49055. Tel: 269-628-2219; Fax: 269-628-7479.
Res.: 2802 Nichols Rd., 49004. Tel: 269-382-2379.
Catechesis/Religious Program—Students 39.

GULL LAKE, KALAMAZOO CO., ST. ANN (1958), Rev. David C. Adams.
Res.: 12648 E. D Ave., Augusta, 49012. Tel: 616-731-4721; Fax: 616-731-4147.
Catechesis/Religious Program—Tel: 616-731-0295; Fax: 616-731-4147. Students 327.

HARTFORD, VAN BUREN CO., IMMACULATE CONCEPTION (1946), (Hispanic), Rev. German Perez Diaz.
Res.: 63559 60th Ave., 49057. Tel: 269-621-4106; Fax: 269-621-2138.
Catechesis/Religious Program—Students 172.

HASTINGS, BARRY CO., ST. ROSE OF LIMA (1873), [CEM] Rev. Alfred J. Russell.
Res.: 805 S. Jefferson Ave., 49058. Tel: 269-945-4246; Fax: 269-945-0005.

School—707 S. Jefferson St., 49058. Tel: 269-945-3164. Sisters of St. Joseph 1; Lay Teachers 6; Students 111.
Catechesis/Religious Program—Students 135.
Mission—*St. Cyril* 203 N. State St., Nashville, Barry Co. 49073.

MARSHALL, CALHOUN CO., ST. MARY (1852), [CEM] Rev. Stephen Naas.
Res.: 212 Hanover St., 49068. Tel: 269-781-3949; 269-781-7341.
Catechesis/Religious Program—Tel: 269-781-5656. Students 251.

MATTAWAN, VAN BUREN CO., ST. JOHN BOSCO (1953), Rev. Bogdan Werra.
Res.: 23830 Front Ave., 49071. Tel: 269-668-3312; Fax: 269-668-3313.
Catechesis/Religious Program—Tel: 269-668-3266. Students 205.
Mission—*St. Margaret Mary* 296 E. Dibble St., Marcellus, Cass Co. 49067.

MENDON, ST. JOSEPH CO., ST. EDWARD (1872), [CEM] Rev. Thomas A. Martin, J.C.D. In Res., Rev. Robert E. Flickinger.
Res.: 332 W. State, P.O. Box 368, 49072. Tel: 269-496-3525; Fax: 269-496-8640.
Catechesis/Religious Program—Students 77.

NEW BUFFALO, BERRIEN CO., ST. MARY OF THE LAKE (1857), Rev. James A. Morris.
Res.: 718 W. Buffalo St., 49117. Tel: 269-469-2637; Fax: 269-469-7393.
School—704 W. Merchant St., 49117. Tel: 616-469-1515; Fax: 616-469-3772. Lay Teachers 10; Students 203.
Catechesis/Religious Program—Students 22.

NILES, BERRIEN CO.

1—ST. MARK (1955), Rev. Joseph W. Koma, C.S.C.
Res.: 3 N. 19th St., 49120-2117. Tel: 616-683-8650; Fax: 616-683-9314.
Catechesis/Religious Program—Tel: 269-683-8650; Fax: 269-683-9314. Students 61.

2—ST. MARY (1870), [CEM 2] Rev. Canon Marian M. Kencik (Poland).
Res.: 211 S. Lincoln Ave., 49120. Tel: 269-683-5087; Fax: 269-683-5089.
School—217 S. Lincoln Ave., 49120. Tel: 269-683-9191; Fax: 269-683-6612. Sisters 1; Lay Teachers 8; Students 124.
Catechesis/Religious Program—Students 130.
Convent—219 S. State St., 49120. Tel: 269-683-8630.
Mission—*St. Gabriel Mission Church* 429 Rose Hill, Berrien Springs, Berrien Co. 49103. Tel: 269-471-2424.

OTSEGO, ALLEGAN CO., ST. MARGARET (1887), [CEM] Rev. Donald P. Klingler.
Res.: 245 Court St., 49078. Tel: 616-694-6311; Fax: 616-694-5415.
School—736 S. Farmer, 49078. Tel: 616-694-2951; Fax: 616-694-4520. Lay Teachers 12; Students 102.
Catechesis/Religious Program—Tel: 616-692-2234. Students 150.

PARCHMENT, KALAMAZOO CO., ST. AMBROSE (1955), Rev. Carl F. Peltz.
Res.: 1628 E. G Ave., 49004. Tel: 269-385-4152; Fax: 269-385-2527.
Catechesis/Religious Program—Tel: 269-343-0099. Students 129.

PAW PAW, VAN BUREN CO., ST. MARY (1887), [CEM] Rev. Robert F. Creagan; Friar Robert Dentzman, O.F.M.
Res.: 500 Paw Paw St., 49079. Tel: 269-657-4459; Fax: 269-657-4260.
School—508 Paw Paw St., 49079. Tel: 616-657-3750. Lay Teachers 9; Students 114.
Catechesis/Religious Program—Tel: 269-657-3497. Students 266.
Mission—*St. Jude's Church* 13809 N. M-40, Gobles, Van Buren Co. 49055. Tel: 269-628-2219; Fax: 269-628-7479.

PEARL, ALLEGAN CO., SAN FELIPE DE JESUS (1986), (Hispanic), Revs. German Perez-Diaz; Juan Chaverria; Deacons Juan Barbosa; Maximino Rodriguez. Mailing Address: P.O. Box 588, Fennville, 49408. Tel: 269-561-5029; Fax: 269-561-5029.
Res.: 63559 60th Ave., Hartford, 49057. Tel: 269-621-4106; Fax: 269-621-2138.
Catechesis/Religious Program—Students 95.

PORTAGE, KALAMAZOO CO., ST. CATHERINE OF SIENA (1966), Rev. Kevin A. Covert. In Res., Rev. John M. Grathwohl (Retired).
Res.: 1150 W. Centre St., 49024-5385. Tel: 269-327-5962; Fax: 269-327-7266.
Catechesis/Religious Program—Tel: 269-327-0861. Students 1,235.

ST. JOSEPH, BERRIEN CO., ST. JOSEPH (1720), Rev. Msgr. Eugene A. Sears; Revs. Robert Johansen; Chinnappareddy (Paul) Yeruva (India); Deacon Michael Gallagher.
Res.: 211 Church St., 49085. Tel: 269-983-1575; Fax: 269-983-6305.
Annex—Stevensville, 5353 S. Roosevelt Rd., 49085. Tel: 269-429-1074.
Catechesis/Religious Program—220 Church St., 49085. Students 1,022.

SILVER CREEK, CASS CO., SACRED HEART OF MARY (1838), (Native American), [CEM] Deacon Frank Wesolowski, Admin.
Res.: 51841 Leach Rd., Dowagiac, 49047. Tel: 269-782-5740; Fax: 269-782-5692.
Catechesis/Religious Program—Tel: 269-782-8048. Students 98.

SOUTH HAVEN, VAN BUREN CO., ST. BASIL (1900), [CEM] Rev. John E. Young.
Res.: 513 Monroe Blvd., 49090. Tel: 616-637-2404; Fax: 616-637-8374.
School—94 Superior St., 49090. Tel: 269-637-3529; Fax: 269-639-1242. Lay Teachers 9; Students 148.
Catechesis/Religious Program—Tel: 269-637-4732. Students 55.

STURGIS, ST. JOSEPH CO., HOLY ANGELS (1921), Rev. Stanley Witek, Admin.
Res.: 402 S. Nottawa St., 49091. Tel: 269-651-5200; Fax: 269-659-8366.
School—Tel: 269-651-2088; Fax: 269-651-9503. Lay Teachers 9; Students 140.
Mission—*St. Joseph* P.O. Box 344, White Pigeon, St. Joseph Co. 49099. Tel: 269-483-7621.
Catechesis/Religious Program—Tel: 269-483-7621; Fax: 269-483-7891. Students 100.

THREE OAKS, BERRIEN CO., ST. MARY OF THE ASSUMPTION (1880), Rev. Donald Suberlak, C.R.
Res.: 28 W. Ash St., 49128. Tel: 269-756-2041; Fax: 269-756-2212.
Catechesis/Religious Program—Students 60.
Mission—*St. Agnes* Sawyer, Berrien Co.

THREE RIVERS, ST. JOSEPH CO., IMMACULATE CONCEPTION (1885), Rev. Mathew K. Illikattil.
Res.: 645 S. Douglas Ave., 49093. Tel: 269-273-8953; Fax: 269-273-2114.
School—601 S. Douglas Ave., 49093-2044. Tel: 269-273-2085; Fax: 269-273-2114. Lay Teachers 7; Students 87.
Catechesis/Religious Program—Tel: 269-273-8953; Fax: 269-273-2114. Rick Demars, D.R.E. Students 87.
Mission—*St. Clare* 229 N. Dean, Centreville, St. Joseph Co. 49032. Tel: 269-273-8953.

VICKSBURG, KALAMAZOO CO., ST. MARTIN (1951), Rev. Thomas A. Martin, J.C.D.
Res.: 5855 E. W Ave., 49097. Tel: 269-649-1629; Fax: 269-649-2877.
Catechesis/Religious Program—5835 East W. Ave., 49097. Tel: 269-649-3626. Students 209.

WATERVLIET, BERRIEN CO., ST. JOSEPH (1886), [CEM] Rev. Donald A. Wieber.
Res.: 179 Lucinda Ln., Box 157, 49098. Tel: 269-463-5470; Fax: 269-463-4642.
School—Tel: 269-463-3941; Fax: 269-463-4525. Lay Teachers 9; Students 159.
Catechesis/Religious Program—Tel: 269-463-5540. Students 95.

WAYLAND, ALLEGAN CO.

1—SS. CYRIL AND METHODIUS (1917), [CEM] Revs. Larry Krol; Gaylord Shimnoski.
Church: 150-131st Ave., 49348. Tel: 269-792-3543; Fax: 269-792-9062.
Catechesis/Religious Program—Students 70.

2—ST. THERESE (1942), Rev. Lawrence W. Kroll.
Res.: 128 Cedar St., 49348. Tel: 269-792-2138; 269-792-9315; Fax: 269-792-2908.
School—Tel: 269-792-2016; Fax: 269-792-6778. Lay Teachers 5; Students 62.
Catechesis/Religious Program—Tel: 616-681-2430. Students 132.

WHITE PIGEON, ST. JOSEPH CO., ST. JOSEPH (1832), [CEM] Sr. Maxine McGee, S.S.J., Admin.
Res.: 16603 E. U.S. 12, P.O. Box 344, 49099-0344. Tel: 269-483-7621; Fax: 269-483-7891.
Catechesis/Religious Program—Tel: 269-483-7622. Students 47.

Chaplains of Public Institutions

COLDWATER. *Camp Branch*. Rev. Brian L. Stanley, Volunteer Chap.
St. Charles Church, 150 Taylor St., 49036. Tel: 517-278-2650; Fax: 517-278-5800.
Florence Crane Correctional Facility for Women. Rev. Brian L. Stanley, Volunteer Chap.
Lakeland Correctional Facility for Men. Rev. Brian L. Stanley, Volunteer Chap.

Retired:
Rev. Msgr.—
Fitzgerald, William (LAN), 8700 Spicer Rd., Brighton, 48116.
Revs.—
Barrett, James L., "F" Dr., Marshall, 49068.
Bogdan, Leonard A., P.O. Box 5753, Sun City Center, AZ 85376-5753.
Burger, Frank J., P.O. Box 143, Grand Junction, 49506.
Consani, Robert E., 1604 Laughton Pl., Sun City Center, FL 33573.
Grathwohl, John M., St. Catherine Church, 1150 W. Centre St., Portage, 49024.
Limbert, William G., 11859 Marquette Dr., New Buffalo, 49117.
Sonefeld, Raymond G., 814 Engleman St., Manistee, 49660.
Spillane, Walter J., 63 Centennial Dr., #17, Norwood, MA 02062.
Taylor, Donn J., 29 LaVista, Battle Creek, 49015.
Thachet, Joseph (India), St. Joseph Church, 61 N. 23rd St., Battle Creek, 49015.
Weller, Joseph W., P.O. Box 231, New Buffalo, 49117.

Permanent Deacons:
Bartholomew, David, St. Augustine, Kalamazoo
Bell, Alfred
Bodway, John, St. Jude, Gobles
Bohan, Hal
Connolly, Bart, Holy Angels, Sturgis
Gallagher, Michael, St. Joseph, St. Joseph
Gregorski, Roger
Haas, Gene
Kasuboski, Larry
Lazaga, Alfred C., St. Joseph, St. Joseph
Mileski, Bernard, Battle Creek, MI
Moreno, Michael, St. Joseph, Battle Creek
Morsaw, Art, Immaculate Conception, Hartford
Nethercott, Anthony
Patrick, Albert W., St. Jerome, Battle Creek
Prendergast, John, St. Catherine of Siena, Portage
Provot, Alvin, St. Charles, Coldwater
Radford, Alfred
Rauner, James D., St. Joseph, Watervliet
Rodriguez, Maximino, San Felipe de Jesus, Pearl
Smoker, Gerald J., St. Mary, Bronson
Stevens, Robert, St. Monica, Kalamazoo
Thamann, Tom
Van Dril, William, Blessed Sacrament, Allegan
Wesolowski, Frank, Sacred Heart, Dowagiac
Whitehouse, Howard, St. Mary, Niles
Wright, Gary, St. Jerome, Battle Creek

INSTITUTIONS LOCATED IN THE DIOCESE

[A] HIGH SCHOOLS, DIOCESAN

KALAMAZOO. *Msgr. Hackett Catholic Central High School*, 1000 W. Kilgore Rd., 49008. Tel: 269-381-2646; Fax: 269-381-3919. Email: hackett@hackettcc.org. Web: www.hackettcc.org. Mr. Tim Eastman, Prin. Lay Teachers 27; Students 468.

BATTLE CREEK. *St. Philip Catholic Central High School*, 20 Cherry St., 49017. Tel: 616-963-4503; Fax: 616-963-5590. Mr. Cliff Curtis, Prin. Total Staff 20.

ST. JOSEPH. *Lake Michigan Catholic Middle and High School*, (Grades 6-12), 915 Pleasant St., 49085. Tel: 616-983-2511; Fax: 616-983-0883. Email: dbooth@remcII.k12.MI.US. Web: www./mc/akers.com. Mrs. Paula Mattis, Prin., (Middle School); Mr. Phil Brooks, Prin. (High School). Adrian Dominican Sisters of Immaculate Conception Province 1; Lay Teachers 16; Students 271.

[B] GRADE SCHOOLS, INTERPAROCHIAL

ST. JOSEPH. *Lake Michigan Catholic Schools*, (Grades PreK-5), 2165 Washington Ave., 49085 Tel: 269-429-0227; Fax: 269-429-1461. Email: catholicprincipal@yahoo.com. Web: lmclakers.com. Mrs. Jody G. Maher, Prin. Lay Teachers 13; Students 293.

[C] CATHOLIC SOCIAL AGENCIES

KALAMAZOO. *Catholic Family Services*, 1819 Gull Rd., 49048. Tel: 269-381-9800; Fax: 269-381-2932. Email: frandenny@catholicfamilyservices.org. Web: www.catholicfamilyservices.org. Mrs. Frances H. Denny, A.C.S.W, M.B.A., Exec. Dir.

[D] GENERAL HOSPITALS

KALAMAZOO. *Borgess Medical Center*, 1521 Gull Rd., 49048-1640. Tel: 269-226-7000; Fax: 269-226-7396. Email: rstasik@borgess.com. Mr. Randall Stasik, Pres. & CEO. Bed Capacity 424; (Inpatient descharges plus Outpatient visits) 492,324.

BATTLE CREEK. *Battle Creek Health System*, 300 North Ave., 49016. Tel: 269-966-8000; Fax: 269-966-8008. Mr. Patrick R. Garrett, Pres. & CEO. Div. of Mercy Health Services Bed Capacity 172; Patients Assisted Annually 218,491.

DOWAGIAC. *Lee Memorial Hospital*, 420 W. High St., 49047. Tel: 269-782-8681; Fax: 269-782-7611. Mr. William Daam, CEO. Bed Capacity 74; Patients Assisted Annually 45,215.

[E] RESIDENCES OF PRIESTS AND BROTHERS

KALAMAZOO. *St. Philip Neri House*, 219 Woodward Ave., 49007. Tel: 269-385-9933; Fax: 269-553-9497. Email: frrobert@stphilipnerihouse.org. Web: www.stphilipnerihouse.org. Rev. Robert Sirico; Bros. David Grondz; James Richardson.

DOUGLAS. *Order of St. Augustine* (Chicago Prov.) , 100 St. Peter Dr., Box 248, 49406. Tel: 269-857-8175; 269-857-7951 (Parish); Fax: 269-857-8164. Rev. Ronald R. Turcich, O.S.A.; Bro. Lawrence Sparacino, O.S.A., Parish Sec. Brothers 1.

[F] HOMES FOR SENIOR CITIZENS

KALAMAZOO. *Borgess Nursing Home*, 537 Chicago Ave., 49048. Tel: 269-382-2392; Fax: 269-382-0843. Email: tmunson@borgess.com. Web: www.borgess.com. Bart Carrel, Admin. Total Staff 140; Total Assisted 121.

BATTLE CREEK. *Mercy Pavilion Skilled Nursing Home and Senior Care Residence*, 80 N. 20 St., 49015. Tel: 269-964-5400; Fax: 269-964-5559. Mr. Robert M. Irwin, Admin. Sub. of Battle Creek Health System. Bed Capacity 77; Senior Care Residence Beds 64.

DOWAGIAC. *Dowagiac Nursing Home*, 610 Uneta St., 49047. Tel: 616-782-3471; Fax: 616-782-1681. Bart Carrel, Admin. Total Staff 112; Bed Capacity 108.

NAZARETH. *Dillon Complex for Independent Living, Inc., Dillion Hall*, 3307 Gulf Rd., P.O. Box 21, 49074. Tel: 269-342-0263; Fax: 269-342-1814. Email: rheynssj@msn.com. Sr. Ruth A. Heyn, S.S.J., Mgr. Sponsored by the Sisters of St. Joseph Total In Residence 80; Total Staff 4; Residents 76.

OTSEGO. *Otsego Senior Apts., Inc.*, Baraga Manor, 301 Washington St., 49078. Tel: 269-694-9711; Fax: 269-694-5857. Patrick Topping, Mgr. Managed by Catholic Family Services, Diocese of Kalamazoo. 1819 Gull Rd., 49048. Apartments 48.

[G] CONVENTS AND RESIDENCES FOR SISTERS

NAZARETH. *Sisters of St. Joseph* 49074. Tel: 269-381-6290; Fax: 269-381-4909. Email: ssjnaz@aol.com. Web: www.ssjnazareth.org. Sr. Janet Fleischhacker, S.S.J., Pres. Congregation; Rev. Michael J. Howell, Chap. Ministry in the field of Education; Social Services; Parish and Church-related Ministries; Healthcare & Foreign Missions Sisters in the Community 280.

[H] NEWMAN CENTERS

KALAMAZOO. *Western Michigan University, Kalamazoo College-Kalamazoo Valley Community College* , Davenport University, Kalamazoo Center for Medical Studies , St. Thomas More Catholic Student Parish, 421 Monroe St., 49006. Tel: 616-381-8917; Fax: 616-381-0195. Email: st_toms@wmich.edu. Web: www.sttomskazoo.org. Rev. Kenneth W. Schmidt, J.C.D.; Sr. Sue McCrery, S.S.J., Pastoral Assoc.; Marian Nelson, Pastoral Assoc.; Patrick Hall, Pastoral Assoc.

[I] MISCELLANEOUS LISTINGS

KALAMAZOO. *Borgess Health Alliance, Inc.*, 1521 Gull Rd., 49048. Tel: 269-226-7000; Fax: 269-226-7396. Web: www.borgess.com. Randall J. Stasik, Pres. & CEO; Michael Alfred, Exec. Dir., Business Devel. & Public Rels.; Lawrence Cain, Chmn.; Sidney B. Williams, Vice Chmn.; D. Craig Martin, Sec.; Shirley Larkins, Treas. Borgess Health Care Alliance is a Health Care System sponsored by Ascension Health which operates Borgess Ambulatory Care, Inc., Borgess Foundation, Borgess Medical Center, Borgess Nursing Home, Borgess-Pipp Health Center, Care Link of Jackson, Borgess-Lee Memorial Hospital, ProMed Healthcare, Borgess Visiting Nurse & Hospice Services; Borgess VNA Home Care, Textile Systems, Inc. and other related companies. Incorporated in the State of Michigan.

Kalamazoo Regional Catholic Schools Foundation, 1000 W. Kilgore Rd., 49008. Tel: 616-381-2646; Fax: 616-381-3919. Email: teastman@hackettcc.org. Web: hackettcc.org.

Secular Franciscan Order, 2903 E. Main St., 49001. Tel: 616-467-8114. Mr. James Goethals, Spiritual Dir.

BATTLE CREEK. *BCACS Foundation, Inc.* (Battle Creek Area Catholic Schools Foundation, Inc.) , 63 N. 24th St., 49015. Tel: 269-963-4771; Fax: 269-963-3917. Email: gallagherk_bcacs@yahoo.com.

Diocesan Council of St. Vincent dePaul, 136 E. Hill, 49017. Tel: 269-660-9579; Fax: 269-372-0908. Email: MFC7@home.com. Mr. Fred Clark, Pres.

HASTINGS. *St. Rose Lima Trust Fund*, 805 S. Jefferson St., 49058. Tel: 269-945-4246; Fax: 269-945-0005.

ST. JOSEPH. *Twin-City Area Catholic School Fund, Inc.*, 915 Pleasant St., 49085. Tel: 616-983-5529; Fax: 616-983-5520. Email: bethstanley51@hotmail.com.

SOUTH HAVEN. *St. Basil Educational Endowment Fund*, 94 Superior St., 49090. Tel: 616-637-3529.

STURGIS. **Holy Angels School Foundation, Inc.*, P.O. Box 24, 49091-0024. Tel: 616-467-8114.

RELIGIOUS INSTITUTES OF MEN REPRESENTED IN THE DIOCESE

For further details refer to the corresponding bracketed number in the Religious Institutes of Men or Women section.

[0140]—*The Augustinians*—O.S.A.
[0200]—*Benedictine Monks*—O.S.B.
[0470]—*The Capuchin Friars* (Province of St. Joseph, Detroit)—O.F.M.Cap.
[1330]—*Congregation of the Mission*—C.M.
[1080]—*Congregation of the Resurrection*—C.R.
[0260]—*Discalced Carmelite Fathers*—O.C.D.
[0520]—*Franciscan Friars* (Prov. of the Sacred Heart)—O.F.M.
[0920]—*Oblates of St. Francis deSales* (Toledo-Detroit Prov.)—O.S.F.S.
[0610]—*Priests of the Congregation of the Holy Cross* (Indiana Prov.)—C.S.C.

RELIGIOUS INSTITUTES OF WOMEN REPRESENTED IN THE DIOCESE

[1920]—*Congregation of the Sisters of the Holy Cross*—C.S.C.
[1070-05]—*Dominican Sisters*—O.P.
[1070-13]—*Dominican Sisters*—O.P.
[1070-14]—*Dominican Sisters*—O.P.
[2575]—*Sisters of Mercy of the Americas*—R.S.M.
[3830-11]—*Sisters of St. Joseph* (Nazareth, MI)—S.S.J.
[3930]—*Sisters of St. Joseph of the Third Order of St. Francis*—S.S.J.-T.O
[3260]—*Sisters of the Precious Blood* (Dayton, OH)—C.PP.S.
[2150]—*Sisters, Servants of the Immaculate Heart of Mary* (Monroe, MI)—I.H.M.

NECROLOGY

† Atchison, Donald W., (Retired)—Died Jan. 24, 2003
† Crenner, William A., (Retired)—Died Nov. 9, 2003
† Steffey, John M., (Retired)—Died Aug. 9, 2003
† Wieber, Elmer F., (Retired)—Died Oct. 2, 2003

Archdiocese of Kansas City in Kansas

(Archidiœcesis Kansanopolitana in Kansas)

Most Reverend

JAMES P. KELEHER, S.T.D.

Archbishop of Kansas City in Kansas; ordained April 12, 1958; appointed Bishop of Belleville October 23, 1984; consecrated December 11, 1984; transferred to Kansas City in Kansas September 8, 1993 *Office: 12615 Parallel Pkwy., Kansas City, KS 66109.* Tel: 913-721-1570.

Most Reverend

JOSEPH F. NAUMANN

Coadjutor Archbishop of Kansas City in Kansas; ordained May 24, 1975; appointed Titular Bishop of Caput Cilla and Auxiliary Bishop of St. Louis July 9, 1997; consecrated September 3, 1997; appointed Coadjutor Archbishop of Kansas City in Kansas January 7, 2004; installed March 19, 2004

Most Reverend

MARION F. FORST, D.D.

Retired Auxiliary Bishop of Kansas City in Kansas; ordained June 10, 1934; consecrated Bishop of Dodge City, March 24, 1960; installed April 5, 1960; resigned from Dodge City; appointed Auxiliary Bishop of Kansas City in Kansas October 16, 1976; retired December 23, 1986 *Res.: 16600 W. 126th, Olathe, KS 66062.*

Square Miles 12,524.

Established Vicariate Apostolic July 19, 1850. Diocese of Leavenworth established May 22, 1877. See changed to Kansas City in Kansas May 10, 1947; created Archdiocese August 9, 1952.

Comprises the following 21 Counties of Kansas: Anderson, Atchison, Brown, Coffey, Doniphan, Douglas, Franklin, Jackson, Jefferson, Johnson, Leavenworth, Linn, Lyon, Marshall, Miami, Nemaha, Osage, Pottawatomie, Shawnee, Wabaunsee and Wyandotte.

Patrons of the Diocese: I. Blessed Virgin Mary (Immaculate Conception); II. St. John Baptist Vianney.

Catholic Chancery Offices: 12615 Parallel Pkwy., Kansas City, KS 66109. Tel: 913-721-1570; Fax: 913-721-1577.

Web: www.archkck.org

Email: archkck@archkck.org

STATISTICAL OVERVIEW

Personnel	
Archbishops	1
Retired Bishops	1
Abbots	1
Retired Abbots	2
Priests: Diocesan Active in Diocese	72
Priests: Diocesan Active Outside Diocese	4
Priests: Diocesan in Foreign Missions	2
Priests: Retired, Sick or Absent	20
Number of Diocesan Priests	98
Religious Priests in Diocese	59
Total Priests in Diocese	157
Extern Priests in Diocese	11
Ordinations:	
Diocesan Priests	5
Transitional Deacons	4
Total Brothers	15
Total Sisters	644
Parishes	
Parishes	118
With Resident Pastor:	
Resident Diocesan Priests	57
Resident Religious Priests	15
Without Resident Pastor:	
Administered by Priests	41
Administered by Religious Women	3
Administered by Lay People	1
Completely Vacant	1
Closed Parishes	1
Professional Ministry Personnel:	
Brothers	1
Sisters	18
Lay Ministers	93
Welfare	
Catholic Hospitals	4
Total Assisted	363,691
Health Care Centers	4
Total Assisted	25,712
Homes for the Aged	3
Total Assisted	486
Special Centers for Social Services	18
Total Assisted	75,339
Residential Care of Disabled	1
Total Assisted	503
Educational	
Diocesan Students in Other Seminaries	21
Students Religious	2
Total Seminarians	23
Colleges and Universities	3
Total Students	3,923
High Schools, Diocesan and Parish	5
Total Students	3,263
High Schools, Private	1
Total Students	248
Elementary Schools, Diocesan and Parish	43
Total Students	12,708
Elementary Schools, Private	1
Total Students	37
Catechesis/Religious Education:	
High School Students	2,900
Elementary Students	14,991
Total Students under Catholic Instruction	38,093
Teachers in the Diocese:	
Sisters	19
Lay Teachers	1,107
Vital Statistics	
Receptions into the Church:	
Infant Baptism Totals	3,981
Adult Baptism Totals	336
Received into Full Communion	545
First Communions	3,910
Confirmations	3,394
Marriages:	
Catholic	647
Interfaith	450
Total Marriages	1,097
Deaths	1,483
Total Catholic Population	191,203
Total Population	1,193,425

Predecessors—Rt. Revs. J. B. MIEGE, S.J., consecrated Bishop of Messenia, Vicar-Apostolic, March 25, 1851; resignation accepted by Pope Pius IX Nov. 8, 1874;; died July 21, 1884; LOUIS M. FINK, O.S.B., D.D., consecrated Bishop of Eucarpia June 11, 1871; appt. first Bishop of Leavenworth May 22, 1877; died March 17, 1904; THOMAS F. LILLIS, O.D., consecrated Bishop of Leavenworth, Dec. 27, 1904; appt. Coadjutor Bishop of Kansas City, with right of succession March 14, 1910; succeeded to the See of Kansas City, Feb. 21, 1913; JOHN WARD, D.D., ord. July 17, 1884; appt. Bishop of Leavenworth Nov. 25, 1910; consecrated Feb. 22, 1911; died April 20, 1929; Most Revs. FRANCIS JOHANNES, D.D., LL.D., consecrated May 1, 1928; succeeded to the See, April 20, 1929; died March 13, 1937; PAUL C. SCHULTE, D.D., ord. June 11, 1915; appt. Bishop of Leavenworth May 29, 1937; consecrated Sept. 21, 1937; appt. Archbishop of Indianapolis July 20, 1946; installed Oct. 10, 1946; GEORGE J. DONNELLY, S.T.D., ord. June 12, 1921; appt. Titular Bishop of Coela and Auxiliary of St. Louis March 19, 1940; consecrated April 23, 1940; appt. Bishop of Leavenworth Nov. 9, 1946; died Dec. 13, 1950; EDWARD J. HUNKELER, D.D. (Retired), ord. June 14, 1919; appt Bishop of Grand Island March 10, 1945; consecrated May 1, 1945; transferred to Kansas City March 28, 1951; elevated to Archiepiscopal dignity Aug. 9, 1952; retired Sept. 10, 1969; died Oct. 1, 1970; IGNATIUS J. STRECKER, D.D., S.T.D., ord. Dec. 19, 1942; appt. Bishop of Springfield-Cape Girardeau April 7, 1962; consecrated June 20, 1962; transferred to Kansas City Sept. 10, 1969; retired Sept. 8, 1993; died Oct. 16, 2003.

Catholic Chancery Offices—12615 Parallel Pkwy., Kansas City, 66109. Tel: 913-721-1570; Fax: 913-721-1577. Office Hours: 8:30-5

Vicars General—Revs. CHARLES MCGLINN; THOMAS TANK.

Chancellor—Rev. THOMAS TANK.

Vice-Chancellor—Rev. RAYMOND BURGER.

Metropolitan Tribunal—12615 Parallel Pkwy., Kansas City, 66109. Tel: 913-721-1570; Fax: 913-721-1577.

Judicial Vicar—Rev. PHILIP KENDALL, C.S.V.

Pro-Synodal Judges—Revs. PHILIP E. KENDALL, C.S.V., J.C.D.; GEORGE BERTELS, J.C.L.

Defenders of the Bond—Revs. GARY APPLEGATE, J.C.L.; THOMAS TANK; RAYMOND BURGER; MICHAEL MULLEN.

Advocates— Selected priests, Sr. MARY ANN BARTOLAC, S.C.L., selected Lay Advocates.

Director Notary—JOAN DEBAUGE.

Archdiocesan Consultors—Revs. RAYMOND DAVERN; THOMAS TANK; Rt. Rev. BARNABAS SENECAL, O.S.B.; Revs. FRANCIS KRISCHE; CHARLES MCGLINN; NORBERT LICKTEIG; GARY APPLEGATE.

Archdiocesan Council on Finances—Rev. THOMAS TANK, Chancellor; Mr. RICH DICKASON; Mr. JERRY MAYNE; Mr. MICHAEL MORRISSEY; Mr. JOHN MENGHINI; Mr. MAL ROBINSON.

Archdiocesan Finance Officer—Mr. JERRY MAYNE.

Regional Pastoral Leaders—Revs. GERARD SENECAL, O.S.B., Atchison; GERALD VOLZ, Emporia; FRANK BURGER, Johnson Co.; CHARLES POLIFKA, O.F.M.Cap., Lawrence; MICHAEL STUBBS, Leavenworth; JON HULLINGER, Nortonville; GEORGE BERTELS, Topeka; GEORGE MATZ, Garnett; BILL BRUNING, Nemah-Marshall; JOHN TORREZ, St. Mary's; MICHAEL HERMES, Wyandotte Co.

Archdiocesan Administrative Team—Mrs. JENNIFER DAMIANO; Rev. CHARLES MCGLINN; Dr. KATHLEEN O'HARA; Mr. JERRY MAYNE; Rev. THOMAS TANK; Mr. MARK HENKE.

Catholic Foundation of Northeast Kansas—12615 Parallel Pkwy., Kansas City, 66109.

Catholic Education Foundation—11413 Pflumm, Overland Park, 66215.
Minister to Priests—Rev. JAMES WHITE, S.J., 12600 Hollingsworth Rd., Kansas City, 66109. Tel: 913-721-3966.
Archdiocesan Archivist—Rev. LEO COOPER.

Archdiocesan Offices and Directors

Savior Pastoral Center—12601 Parallel, Kansas City, 66109. Tel: 913-721-1097.
Black Catholics—REGINA BARGER, Dir., 2203 Parallel, Kansas City, 66104. Tel: 913-321-1958.
Department of Parish Ministries—Rev. THOMAS TANK, Dir., 12615 Parallel Pkwy., Kansas City, 66109. Tel: 913-721-1570.
Adult Faith Formation—Mr. LAWRENCE LIVINGSTON.
Deaf Ministry—Mrs. PAT RICHEY.
Family Life—Mrs. JACKI CORRIGAN.
Liturgy—Mr. MICHAEL PODREBARAC.
Pro-life / Respect Life—Mr. DAVID GITTRICH.
Religious Education—Mrs. JEANNE BRADY.
Youth—Mr. DANA NEARMYER; Ms. TERRI BARNETT, Assoc. Consultant.
Hispanic Ministry—Rev. PATRICK MURPHY, C.S.
Administrative Services / Human Resources—Mrs. SUSAN CARROLL.
Stewardship and Development Office—Mrs. JENNIFER DAMIANO, Dir., 12615 Parallel Pkwy., Kansas City, 66109. Tel: 913-721-1570.
Catholic Youth Organization—DAVE NICK, Athletic Dir., 5041 Reinhardt Dr., P.O. Box 721, Shawnee Mission, 66201. Tel: 913-384-7377.
Catholic Charities—Mr. MARK HENKE, Dir., 2220 Central Ave., Kansas City, 66102. Tel: 913-621-1504.
Council for Catholic Charismatic Renewal—Rev. MARK MERTES.
Catholic Community Service—2220 Central Ave., Kansas City, 66102. Tel: 913-621-1504.
Communications—12615 Parallel Pkwy., Kansas City, 66109. Tel: 913-721-1570.
Catholic Scouts—Rev. MARK BROSKI, O.S.B., Chap.
Holy Childhood Association—Rev. NORBERT LICKTEIG, 12615 Parallel Pkwy., Kansas City, 66109. Tel: 913-721-1570.
Hospitals—Rev. JEREMIAH L. SPENCER, Dir., 16 S. Iowa, Kansas City, 66103.
Kansas Catholic Conference—Mr. MIKE FARMER, Exec. Dir., 6301 Antioch, Shawnee Mission, 66202. Tel: 913-722-6633.
Legion of Mary—Rev. ROBERT BURGER, Spiritual Moderator, Vianney Center, Ste. 205, 12601 Parallel Pkwy., Kansas City, 66109.
Missions—Rev. NORBERT LICKTEIG, 12615 Parallel Pkwy., Kansas City, 66109.
Newspaper "The Leaven"—Rev. MARK GOLDASICH, Editor, 12615 Parallel Pkwy., Kansas City, 66109. Tel: 913-721-1570; Fax: 913-721-5276.
Nurses Association—Rev. JEREMIAH L. SPENCER, Dir., 16 S. Iowa, Kansas City, 66103.
Priests' Council—Revs. GARY APPLEGATE, Chm.; BILL BRUNING, Vice Chm.
Pontifical Mission Societies in the United States—Rev. NORBERT LICKTEIG, 12615 Parallel Pkwy., Kansas City, 66109.
Schools—Dr. KATHLEEN O'HARA, Supt.; Mrs. KARLA LEIBHAM, Assoc. Supt.; Sr. CHARLOTTE WHITE, S.C.L., Asst. Supt. & Dir. Mission, 12615 Parallel Pkwy., Kansas City, 66109. Tel: 913-721-1570.
Victim Assistance Coordinator—Mr. DAN W. POPE, Ed.D. Tel: 913-681-1863. Email: dm@sprintmail.com.
Vocations Office—Directors: Revs. BRIAN SCHIEBER; MICHAEL MULLEN, 12615 Parallel Pkwy., Kansas City, 66109. Tel: 913-721-1570.

CLERGY, PARISHES, MISSIONS AND PAROCHIAL SCHOOLS

CITY OF KANSAS CITY
(WYANDOTTE COUNTY)

1—CATHEDRAL OF ST. PETER THE APOSTLE, Revs. Gary Applegate; Philip Kendall, C.S.V.; Brian Klingele.
Res.: 409 N. 15th St., 66102. Tel: 913-371-2345; Fax: 913-371-2151.
Business Office:—431 N. 15th St., 66102. Tel: 913-371-0840; Fax: 913-371-2151.
School—422 N. 14th, 66102. Tel: 913-371-8101; Fax: 913-371-1014. Lay Teachers 17; Students 220.
Catechesis / Religious Program—Jeanette Michalski, D.R.E. Students 33.

2—BLESSED SACRAMENT, Rev. William McEvoy.
Res.: 2203 Parallel Ave., 66104. Tel: 913-321-1958; Fax: 913-321-1997.

3—CHRIST THE KING, Rev. Raymond J. Davern.
Res.: 3024 N. 53rd St., 66104. Tel: 913-287-8823; Fax: 913-287-8711.
School—3027 N. 54th St., 66104. Tel: 913-287-8883; Fax: 913-287-7409. Lay Teachers 14; Students 243.
Catechesis / Religious Program—Tel: 913-287-9046. Nancy Rottinghaus, D.R.E. Students 45.

4—SS. CYRIL AND METHODIUS, (Slovak), Attended by, St. Joseph-St. Benedict, Kansas City. Rev. Michael Hermes.
Res.: 801 Vermont, 66101. Tel: 913-371-3549; Fax: 913-621-2709.
Catechesis / Religious Program—Students 23.

5—HOLY FAMILY, (Slovenian), Rev. Msgr. Heliodore Mejak.
Res.: 274 Orchard Ave., 66101. Tel: 913-371-1561.
School—St. John and Holy Family, Tel: 913-371-3923; Fax: 913-321-5001. (Consolidated). See separate listing under St. John the Baptist.

6—HOLY NAME, Rev. Jeremiah L. Spencer.
Res.: 16 S. Iowa St., 66103. Tel: 913-236-9219; Fax: 913-403-8834.
School—1007 S.W. Blvd., 66103. Tel: 913-722-1032; Fax: 913-722-4175. Lay Teachers 10; Students 172.
Catechesis / Religious Program—Tel: 913-236-9219; Fax: 913-404-8834. Bette Maslak, D.R.E. Students 36.

7—ST. JOHN THE BAPTIST, (Croatian), Rev. Francis Horvat.
Res.: 708 N. Fourth St., 66101. Tel: 913-371-0627; Fax: 913-342-3324.
School—St. John the Baptist and Holy Family, 515 Ohio, 66101. Tel: 913-371-3923; Fax: 913-321-5001. (Consolidated) Lay Teachers 11; Students 98.

8—ST. JOHN THE EVANGELIST, Rev. Charles Andalikiewicz.
Res.: 2910 Strong Ave., 66106. Tel: 913-677-4621.
School—Our Lady of Unity Consolidated with Sacred Heart. See separate listing for further details.
Catechesis / Religious Program—Tel: 913-262-7022. Ruth Campos, D.R.E. Students 120.

9—ST. JOSEPH AND ST. BENEDICT, Rev. Michael Hermes.
Res.: 229 S. 8th St., 66101. Tel: 913-371-1837; Fax: 913-621-2709.
School—All Saints (Consolidated). See separate listing.
Catechesis / Religious Program—Gabriela Torres, D.R.E. Students 425.

10—ST. MARY-ST. ANTHONY, Rev. Matt J. Horvat.
Res.: 615 N. Seventh St., 66101. Tel: 913-371-1408; Fax: 913-371-4177.

11—OUR LADY AND ST. ROSE, Attended by, Blessed Sacrament, Kansas City. Rev. William McEvoy.
Church: 2300 N. Eighth St., 66101. Tel: 913-321-1958; Fax: 913-321-1997.
Catechesis / Religious Program—Tel: 913-321-1958; Fax: 913-321-1997. Students 15.

12—ST. PATRICK'S, Revs. Michael Mullen; Roger Schmit, O.S.B., Assoc. Pastor.
Res.: 1086 N. 94th St., 66112. Tel: 913-299-3370; Fax: 913-299-3422.
School—1066 N. 94th, 66112. Tel: 913-299-8131; Fax: 913-299-2845. Sisters 1; Lay Teachers 20; Students 331.
Catechesis / Religious Program—Tel: 913-299-3728. Susan Buck, D.R.E. Students 197.

13—SACRED HEART, Attended by, St. John the Evangelist, Kansas City. Rev. Charles Andalikiewicz.
Res.: 2910 Strong Ave., 66106. Tel: 913-677-4621.
Church: 2646 S. 34th, 66106. Tel: 913-677-1277.
School—Our Lady of Unity, Tel: 913-262-7022; Fax: 913-262-7836. See separate listing.
Catechesis / Religious Program—Tel: 913-859-9912. Ruth Campos, D.R.E. Students 100.

14—ST. THOMAS THE APOSTLE, Closed. For inquiries for parish records contact the chancery.

OUTSIDE THE CITY OF KANSAS CITY

ALMA, WABAUNSEE CO., HOLY FAMILY, [CEM] Attended by, Wamego Rev. John Pilcher.
Church: 66401.
Catechesis / Religious Program—Tel: 785-765-2316. Dan Deiter, D.R.E. Students 41.

ATCHISON, ATCHISON CO.
1—ST. BENEDICT'S, [JC] Rev. Gerard Senecal, O.S.B.
Res.: 1001 N. Second St., 66002. Tel: 913-367-0671; Fax: 913-367-0797.
School—Atchison Catholic Elementary (Consolidated). See separate listing.
Catechesis / Religious Program—Tel: 913-367-3503. Students 15.
Mission—St. John the Baptist Doniphan, Doniphan Co. (Stational Church)

2—ST. JOSEPH'S, [JC] Rev. Bertrand LaNoue, O.S.B.
Res.: 705 Spring Garden St., 66002. Tel: 913-367-4271.
School—Atchison Catholic Elementary (Consolidated). See separate listing.
Catechesis / Religious Program—Tel: 913-367-3503; Fax: 913-367-0797. Nicki DeMint, D.R.E. Students 28.

3—SACRED HEART, [JC] Rev. Gerard Senecal, O.S.B.
Office:—1427 Main St., 66002. Tel: 913-367-0387; Fax: 913-367-0797.
Church: 1439 Kansas Ave., Atchinson, 66002.
School—Atchison Catholic Elementary (Consolidated). See separate listing.
Catechesis / Religious Program—Rick Weber, D.R.E. Students 55.

AXTELL, MARSHALL CO., ST. MICHAEL'S, Rev. Albert Hauser, O.S.B.
Mailing Address: P.O. Box K, 66403. Tel: 785-736-2220; Fax: 785-736-2230.
School—605 Elm St., 66403. Tel: 785-736-2257. Lay Teachers 4; Students 32.
Catechesis / Religious Program—Tel: 785-736-2260. Janice Koch, D.R.E. Students 94.

BAILEYVILLE, NEMAHA CO., SACRED HEART, [CEM] Rev. Albert J. Fey, C.PP.S.
Church: Box 36, 66404. Tel: 785-336-6464.
Catechesis / Religious Program—Tel: 785-336-6415. Debbie Waller, D.R.E. Students 143.

BALDWIN, DOUGLAS CO., ANNUNCIATION, [CEM] Attended by, Assumption, Edgerton Rev. William Fisher.
Church: P.O. Box 293, 66006. Tel: 785-594-3700.

BASEHOR, LEAVENWORTH CO., HOLY ANGELS, [CEM] Rev. Anthony C. Williams.
Res.: 15440 Leavenworth Rd., Box 295, 66007. Tel: 913-724-3122; 913-724-1665 (Offices). Web: www.HolyAngelsBasehor.org.
Catechesis / Religious Program—Fax: 913-724-3114. Marilyn Hauschild, D.R.E. Students 255.

BEATTIE, MARSHALL CO., ST. MALACHY'S, Attended by, St. Michael, Axtell. Rev. Albert Hauser, O.S.B.
Church: 1012 Main St., 66406. Tel: 785-353-2280.
Catechesis / Religious Program—Tel: 785-292-4576. Judy Studer, D.R.E. Students 51.

BENDENA, DONIPHAN CO., ST. BENEDICT'S, [CEM] Attended by, St. Joseph, Wathena. Rev. Dayananda Prabhu (India), Admin.
Church: P.O. Box 128, 66008. Tel: 785-359-6725; Fax: 785-989-2313.
Catechesis / Religious Program—Tel: 785-359-6725. Greg Bevis, D.R.E. Students 50.

BLAINE, POTTAWATOMIE CO., ST. COLUMBKILLE, Attended by, St. Vincent de Paul, Onaga. Rev. Edwin Nwabugwu.
Church: 66480.
Catechesis / Religious Program—Tel: 785-457-2164. Susan Snapp, D.R.E. Students 19.

BLUE RAPIDS, MARSHALL CO., ST. MONICA - ST. ELIZABETH, Attended by, Annunciation, Frankfort. Revs. William Bruning; John Cordes.
Catechesis / Religious Program—Tel: 785-363-7587. Mike Minihan, D.R.E. Students 13.

BURLINGTON, COFFEY CO., ST. FRANCIS XAVIER'S, [CEM] Rev. Michael Hawken.
Res.: 214 Juniatta, 66839. Tel: 620-364-2416; Fax: 620-364-2416.
Catechesis / Religious Program—Tel: 316-364-5220. Kimberly Robrahn, D.R.E. Students 127.

CORNING, NEMAHA CO., ST. PATRICK'S, [CEM] Attended by, St. Mary's, St. Benedict. Rev. Earl Deket; Sr. Mary Beth Niehaus, O.S.B., Parish Min. Tel: 785-868-2790.

DELIA, JACKSON CO., SACRED HEART OF JESUS, , (Stational Church)

DONIPHAN, DONIPHAN CO., ST. JOHN'S, , (Stational Church)

EASTON, LEAVENWORTH CO., ST. LAWRENCE, [CEM] Rev. John Ayang, S.O.L.T.
Res.: P.O. Box 129, 66020. Tel: 913-773-5712; Fax: 913-773-8401.
Catechesis / Religious Program—Tel: 913-774-2511. Mary Naumann, D.R.E. Students 75.

EDGERTON, JOHNSON CO., ASSUMPTION OF THE BLESSED VIRGIN MARY, [CEM] Rev. William Fisher.
Church: P.O. Box 74, 66021. Tel: 913-893-6272; Fax: 785-594-3700.
Catechesis / Religious Program—Tel: 913-592-2875; Fax: 913-893-6061. Melissa McCarthy, D.R.E. Students 48.

EFFINGHAM, ATCHISON CO., ST. ANN'S, [CEM] Rev. Benjamin Tremmel, O.S.B.
Res.: 301 William, Box 54, 66023. Tel: 913-833-5660.
Catechesis / Religious Program—Jacki Reichart, D.R.E. Students 48.

EMERALD, ANDERSON CO., ST. PATRICK'S, , Served by St. Francis Xavier, Burlington. Rev. Michael Hawken.
Church: 66095. Tel: 620-364-2416; Fax: 620-364-2416.
Catechesis / Religious Program—Cindy Rubick, D.R.E. Students 27.

EMMETT, POTTAWATOMIE CO., HOLY CROSS, Attended by, Immaculate Conception, St. Marys. Rev. John Torrez.

EMPORIA, LYON CO.

1—ST. CATHERINE, [CEM] Attended by, Sacred Heart, Emporia. Rev. Daniel L. Gardner.
Church: 205 S. Lawrence St., 66801. Tel: 620-342-1061; Fax: 620-342-0450.
Catechesis/Religious Program—Tel: 620-342-1368. Sr. Aurora Villamar, D.R.E. Students 250.

2—SACRED HEART, [CEM] Rev. Daniel L. Gardner.
Office—101 Cottonwood St., 66801. Tel: 620-342-1061; Fax: 620-342-0450.
School—102 Cottonwood St., 66801. Tel: 620-343-7394; Fax: 620-343-7395. Lay Teachers 11; Students 133.
Rectory—123 Cottonwood St., 66801. Tel: 620-342-3328.
Catechesis/Religious Program—Tel: 620-342-4878. Linda DeDonder, D.R.E. Students 230.

ESKRIDGE, WABAUNSEE CO., ST. JOHN VIANNEY, Attended by, Immaculate Conception, St. Marys. Revs. John Torrez; Balaswamy Guvvala (India).
Catechesis/Religious Program—Students 8.

EUDORA, DOUGLAS CO., HOLY FAMILY, [CEM] Rev. Raymond Burger.
Res.: 311 E. 9th St., 66025. Tel: 785-542-2788; Fax: 785-542-1908.
Catechesis/Religious Program—Steve Eggers, D.R.E. Students 166.

FIDELITY, BROWN CO., ST. AUGUSTINE'S, Attended by, Sacred Heart, Sabetha. Rev. Richard J. McDonald.
Catechesis/Religious Program—Tel: 785-284-3329. Teresa Baumgartner, D.R.E. Students 24.

FLUSH, POTTAWATOMIE CO., ST. JOSEPH'S, Attended by, St. Bernard, Wamego. Rev. John Pilcher. Tel: 785-494-8234.
Catechesis/Religious Program—Tel: 785-456-2431. Rich Cheek, D.R.E. Students 89.

FORT LEAVENWORTH, LEAVENWORTH CO., ST. IGNATIUS CHAPEL, Rev. Jose Herrera, Military Services Army Chap.
Church: 66027. Tel: 913-684-8983; Fax: 913-684-8994. [Natl. CEM]

FRANKFORT, MARSHALL CO., ANNUNCIATION, [CEM] Revs. William Bruning; John Cordes.
Res.: 213 E. Fifth St., 66427. Tel: 785-292-4462; Fax: 785-292-5095.
Catechesis/Religious Program—Tel: 785-382-6376. Connie Broxterman, D.R.E. Students 109.

GARDNER, JOHNSON CO., SACRED HEART, [CEM] Rev. Gerald E. Sheeds.
Res.: 122 E. Warren, 66030. Tel: 913-856-7781; Fax: 913-856-7781.
Catechesis/Religious Program—Tel: 913-884-7788. Judy Orth, D.R.E. Students 240.

GARNETT, ANDERSON CO., HOLY ANGELS, [CEM] Rev. George A. Matz.
Res.: 514 E. Fourth, 66032. Tel: 785-448-3846.
School—530 E. Fourth, 66032. Tel: 785-448-3423; Fax: 785-448-3164. Sisters 2; Lay Teachers 4; Students 60.
Catechesis/Religious Program—Linda Huettenmueller, D.R.E. Students 21.

GREELEY, ANDERSON CO., ST. JOHN THE BAPTIST'S, [CEM] Attended by, Holy Angels, Garnett. Rev. George A. Matz.
Mailing Address: P.O. Box 94, 66033.
Res.: 66033. Tel: 785-867-3474.
School—Tel: 785-867-2680; Fax: 785-867-3160. Sisters 2; Lay Teachers 4; Students 28.
Catechesis/Religious Program—Tel: 785-867-2821. Betty Gellhaus, D.R.E. Students 25.

HARTFORD, LYON CO., ST. MARY'S, Attended by, St. Joseph's, Olpe. Rev. Timothy A. Haberkorn.
Catechesis/Religious Program—Linda Griffiths, D.R.E. Students 35.

HIAWATHA, BROWN CO., ST. ANN'S, Rev. Ralph Koehler, O.S.B.
Res.: 800 Hiawatha Ave., 66434. Tel: 785-742-3010.
Catechesis/Religious Program— Debbie Wilson, D.R.E. Students 125.

HOLTON, JACKSON CO., ST. DOMINIC'S, [CEM] Attended by, St. Joseph, Nortonville. Revs. Jon Hullinger, Admin.; Thomas Hesse, Sacramental Min. (Retired).
Res.: 416 Ohio Ave., 66436. Tel: 785-364-3262.
Catechesis/Religious Program—Tel: 785-364-3621. Tina Haefke, D.R.E. Students 150.

HORTON, BROWN CO., ST. LEO'S, [CEM 3] Rev. Kunduru Joji, S.J.
Res.: 1340 First Ave. E., 66439. Tel: 785-486-3971; Fax: 785-486-3971.
Catechesis/Religious Program—Tel: 785-486-2886; Fax: 785-486-2402. Sherry Wellman, D.R.E. Students 93.

KELLY, NEMAHA CO., ST. BEDE'S (1901), [CEM] Rev. Earl Dekat. Tel: 785-336-3189; Sr. Mary Beth Niehaus, O.S.B.
Catechesis/Religious Program—Connie Winkler, D.R.E. Students 100.

LACYGNE, LINN CO., OUR LADY OF LOURDES, Attended by, St. Philip Neri, Osawatomie Rev. Joseph Cramer.
Mailing Address: c/o St. Philip Neri, P.O. Box 4, Osawatomie, 66064. Tel: 913-755-2652.
Church: 66040.

LANSING, LEAVENWORTH CO., ST. FRANCIS DE SALES, [JC] Rev. Michael C. Stubbs.
Res.: 119 Woodland Rd., 66043. Tel: 913-727-3768.
Church: 900 Ida St., 66043. Tel: 913-727-3742; Fax: 913-727-1281.
Catechesis/Religious Program—Tel: 913-727-3742; Fax: 913-727-2536. Sr. Roberta O'Leary, D.R.E. Students 134.

LAPEER, DOUGLAS CO., ST. FRANCIS, [CEM] Attended by, St. Patrick, Osage City. Rev. Michael Mulvany.
Catechesis/Religious Program—Tel: 785-256-2752. Mary Bond-Lueske, D.R.E. Students 30.

LAWRENCE, DOUGLAS CO.

1—CORPUS CHRISTI, [JC] Rev. James E. Shaughnessy.
Church & Office: 6001 W. 15th St., 66049-5200. Tel: 785-843-6286; Fax: 785-865-3933.
School—The Lawrence Catholic School, Tel: 785-331-3374; Fax: 785-331-3904. (Consolidated). See separate listing.
Catechesis/Religious Program—Tel: 785-843-6604. Nancy Nelson, D.R.E. Students 391.

2—ST. JOHN THE EVANGELIST, [CEM] Rev. Charles Polifka, O.F.M.Cap.
Office—1229 Vermont St., 66044. Tel: 785-843-0109; Fax: 785-749-5064.
School—The Lawrence Catholic School (Consolidated). See separate listing.
Catechesis/Religious Program—Heather Coates, D.R.E. Students 325.

LEAVENWORTH, LEAVENWORTH CO.

1—ST. CASIMIR'S, (Polish), Rev. Phillip J. Winkelbauer.
Res.: 1401 Second Ave., 66048. Tel: 913 772-1787; Fax: 913-651-2150.
School—Xavier Elementary, Tel: 913-682-3135. (Consolidated). See separate listing.
Catechesis/Religious Program—Tel: 913-772-1672; Fax: 913-758-7678. Rick Toretto, D.R.E Students 25.

2—IMMACULATE CONCEPTION, , (Old Cathedral) Rev. David McEvoy, O.Carm. In Res., Rev. Fergus Lickteig, O.Carm.; Bro. David McGinnis O.Carm., Pastoral Assoc.
Office & Mailing: 747 Osage, 66048. Tel: 913-682-3953; Fax 913-682-5599.
Church: 711 N. 5th St., 66048.
School—Xavier Elementary (Consolidated). See separate listing.
Rectory—[illegible]00 N. Broadway, 66048. Tel: 913-682-0809.
Catechesis/Religious Program—Tel: 913-772-1672; Fax: 913-758-7678. Rick Toretto, D.R.E. Students 84.

3—ST. JOSEPH OF THE VALLEY, [CEM] Attended by, St. Lawrence, Easton. Rev. John Ayang S.O.L.T.
Mailing Address: P.O. Box 129, Easton, 66020. Tel: 913-773-5712; Fax: 913-773-8401.
Church: [illegible]1151 207th St., 66048.
Catechesis/Religious Program—Tel: 913-682-8127. Karen Ernzen, D.R.E. Students 31.

4—ST. JOSEPH'S, Rev. David McEvoy, O.Carm.; Bro. David Mc Ginnis, O.Carm., Pastoral Assoc. In Res., Rev. Fergus Lickteig, O.Carm.
Office—747 Osage, 66048. Tel: 913-682-3953; 913-682-0809 (Res.); Fax: 913-682-5599.
School—Xavier Elementary (Consolidated). See separate listing.

5—SACRED HEART OF JESUS, [CEM] Rev. Phillip J. Winkelbauer.
Res.: 1401 Second Ave., 66048. Tel: 913-772-1787; Fax: 913-651-2150.
School—Xavier Elementary, Tel: 913-682-3135. (Consolidated). See separate listing.
Catechesis/Religious Program—Tel: 913-772-1672; Fax: 913-758-7678. Rick Toretto, D.R.E. Students 35.

LEAWOOD, JOHNSON CO.

1—CHURCH OF THE NATIVITY, Revs. Alfred Rockers; Gerardo Arano-Ponce.
Church: 3800 W. 119th St., 66209. Tel: 913-491-5017; Fax: 913-491-5065.
School—3700 W. 119th St., 66209. Tel: 913-338-4330; Fax: 913-338-2050. Lay Teachers 32; Students 569.
Catechesis/Religious Program—Peggy Schrick, D.R.E. Students 436.
Christian Formation Office—Tel: 913-338-4367; Fax: 913-338-0285.

2—CURE OF ARS, Revs. Charles McGlinn; Kenneth O'Connor.
Res.: 9401 Mission Rd., 66206. Tel: 913-649-1337; Fax: 913-649-1339.
School—9403 Mission Rd., 66206. Tel: 913-648-2620; Fax: 913-648-3810. Lay Teachers 42; Students 681.
Vianney Center for Ministries—Tel: 913-649-8625; Fax: 913-649-1339.

Catechesis/Religious Program—Sr. Julie Galan, D.R.E. Students 810.

3—ST. MICHAEL THE ARCHANGEL, Rev. William Porter.
Church: 14201 Nall Ave., 66224. Tel: 913-402-3900; Fax: 913-851-8220.
School—Tel: 913-402-3950. Lay Teachers 19; Students 293.
Catechesis/Religious Program—Denise Ogilvee, D.R.E. Students 1,000.

LENEXA, JOHNSON CO., HOLY TRINITY, Rev. Thomas Dolezal. In Res., Rev. Richard Osei Bempah (Ghana).
Office—9150 Pflumm Rd., 66215. Tel: 913-888-2770; Fax: 913-888-4403.
School—13600 W. 92nd St., 66215. Tel: 913-888-3250; Fax: 913-438-2572. Lay Teachers 35; Students 705.
Catechesis/Religious Program—Tel: 913-492-6068. Stuart Holland, D.R.E. Students 296.

LILLIS, MARSHALL CO., ST. JOSEPH'S, [CEM] Attended by, St. Vincent de Paul, Onaga. Rev. Edwin Nwabugwu. Tel: 785-889-4896.
Catechesis/Religious Program—Tel: 785-292-4848. Jean Boeckman, D.R.E. Students 16.

LOUISBURG, MIAMI CO., IMMACULATE CONCEPTION, [CEM] Rev. Anthony Lickteig, Sacramental Min. (Retired).
Res.: Box 118, 66053. Tel: 913-837-2295; Fax: 913-837-3309.
Catechesis/Religious Program—Jackie Dunn, D.R.E. Students 112.

MARYSVILLE, MARSHALL CO., ST. GREGORY'S, [CEM] Revs. William Bruning; John Cordes.
Res.: 206 N. 14th, 66508. Tel: 785-562-3302; Fax: 785-562-4039.
School—207 N. 14th, 66508. Tel: 785-562-2831; Fax: 785-562-4039. Lay Teachers 8; Students 119.
Catechesis/Religious Program—Tel: 785-562-2635. Rick McCormack, D.R.E. Students 64.

MAYETTA, JACKSON CO., ST. FRANCIS XAVIER, [CEM] Attended by, St. Joseph, Nortonville. Revs. Jon Hullinger, Admin.; Thomas Hesse, Sacramental Min. (Retired).
Mailing Address: *c/o St. Dominic*, 416 Ohio, Holton, 66436. Tel: 785-364-3262.
Catechesis/Religious Program—Tel: 785-986-2690. Eileen Lake, D.R.E. Students 90.

MERIDEN, JEFFERSON CO., ST. ALOYSIUS, [CEM] Attended by, St. Theresa, Perry Rev. Robert Hasenkamp.
Res.: P.O. Box 364, 66512. Tel: 785-484-3312; Fax: 785-484-3338.
Catechesis/Religious Program—Nita Jensen, D.R.E. Students 184.

MISSION, JOHNSON CO., ST. PIUS X, Rev. Kenneth W. Kelly.
Res.: 5601 Woodson Ave., 66202. Tel: 913-432-4808; Fax: 913-432-4855.
School—5500 Woodson, 66202. Tel: 913-432-9355; Fax: 913-432-2086. Lay Teachers 17; Students 133.
Catechesis/Religious Program—Tel: 913-491-3538; Fax: 913-362-3504. Deborah Alexander, D.R.E. Students 70.

MOONEY CREEK, JEFFERSON CO., CORPUS CHRISTI, [CEM] Unassigned., Mailing Address: 18760 Rogers Rd., Atchison, 66002. Tel: 913-774-2385.
Catechesis/Religious Program—Tel: 913-886-8611. Charles Noll, D.R.E.; Sara Noll, D.R.E. Students 36.

MOUND CITY, LINN CO., SACRED HEART SHRINE TO ST. PHILIPPINE DUCHESNE, [CEM] Attended by, St. Philip Neri, Osawatomie Rev. Joseph Cramer.
Mailing Address: *c/o St. Philip Neri*, P.O. Box 4, Osawatomie, 66064. Tel: 913-755-2652.
Res.: 66056. Tel: 913-795-2724.

NORTONVILLE, JEFFERSON CO., ST. JOSEPH'S, [CEM] Rev. Jon Hullinger.
Mailing Address: P.O. Box 236, 66060. Tel: 913-886-2030.
Church: 221 N. Sycamore St., 66060. Tel: 913-886-2030.
School—222 N. Sycamore St., 66060-4014. Tel: 913-886-3510. Religious 1; Lay Teachers 2; Students 28.
Catechesis/Religious Program—Shawn Gigstad, D.R.E. Students 54.

OLATHE, JOHNSON CO.

1—ST. PAUL'S, Rev. Peter Jaramillo.
Office:—900 S. Honeysuckle, 66061. Tel: 913-764-0323; Fax: 913-782-2998.
Res.: 840 Larkspur, 66061. Tel: 913-782-6062.
School—920 W. Honeysuckle, 66061. Tel: 913-764-0619; Fax: 913-768-6040. Lay Teachers 14; Students 190.
Catechesis/Religious Program—Tel: 913-782-2991; Fax: 913-782-2998. Sally Sanem, D.R.E. Students 541.

2—PRINCE OF PEACE, Revs. Frank Burger; Ron Cornish.
Office:—Tel: 913-782-8864; Fax: 913-780-9658.
School—16000 W. 143rd St., 66062. Tel: 913-764-0650; Fax: 913-393-0819. Lay Teachers 28; Students

555.
Catechesis/Religious Program—Tel: 913-829-1147. Mark Schuetz, D.R.E. Students 1,052.

OLPE, LYON CO., ST. JOSEPH'S, [CEM] Rev. Timothy A. Haberkorn.
Res.: P.O. Box 165, 66865. Tel: 620-475-3326.
School—Tel: 620-475-3416. Lay Teachers 5; Students 60.

ONAGA, POTTAWATOMIE CO., ST. VINCENT DE PAUL, Rev. Edwin Nwabugwu.
Res.: Box 396, 66521. Tel: 785-889-4896.
Catechesis/Religious Program—Lisa Meyer, D.R.E. Students 95.

OSAGE CITY, OSAGE CO., ST. PATRICK'S, [CEM 3] Rev. Michael Mulvany.
Mailing Address: 309 S. 6th St., 66523. Tel: 785-528-3424; Fax: 785-528-3381.
Catechesis/Religious Program—Tel: 785-528-3424. Nancy Schroeder, D.R.E.; Kare Schwieger, D.R.E.; Martha Badger, D.R.E. Students 256.

OSAWATOMIE, MIAMI CO., ST. PHILIP NERI, Rev. Joseph Cramer.
Church: 500 Parker Ave., 66064. Tel: 913-755-2652.
Chaplaincy—State Hospital for Mentally Ill, 66064.

OTTAWA, FRANKLIN CO., SACRED HEART, [CEM] Rev. Tod Ziegler.
Res.: 408 S. Cedar St., 66067. Tel: 785-242-2174.
School—426 S. Cedar, 66067. Tel: 785-242-4297; Fax: 785-242-0820. Lay Teachers 6; Students 93.
Catechesis/Religious Program—Tel: 785-242-7258. Emily Davis, D.R.E. Students 92.

OVERLAND PARK, JOHNSON CO.

1—CHURCH OF THE ASCENSION, Revs. Thomas Tank; Alvin Herber, C.PP.S.; Gary Pennings.
Res.: 9510 W. 127th St., 66213. Tel: 913-681-3348; Fax: 913-681-3517.
School—Tel: 913-851-2531; Fax: 913-851-2518. Lay Teachers 37; Students 644.
Catechesis/Religious Program—Tel: 913-681-7683; Fax: 913-681-7634. Sharon Andres, D.R.E. Students 1,569.

2—HOLY CROSS, Rev. Mark Mertes.
Office—8311 W. 93rd St., 66212. Tel: 913-381-2755; Fax: 913-381-2766.
Res.: 8315 W. 93rd St., 66212. Tel: 913-341-5618; Fax: 913-381-2766.
School—8101 W. 95th, 66212. Tel: 913-381-7408; Fax: 913-381-1312. Lay Teachers 30; Students 433.
Catechesis/Religious Program—Tel: 913-381-2757. Julie Dresser, D.R.E. Students 292.

3—HOLY SPIRIT, Revs. Harold F. Schneider; Tom Aduri.
Res.: 11300 W. 103rd St., 66214. Tel: 913-492-7318; Fax: 913-492-7370.
School—Tel: 913-492-2582; Fax: 913-492-9613. Lay Teachers 26; Students 452.
Catechesis/Religious Program—Tel: 913-492-7382; Fax: 913-888-4403. Clare Thorne, D.R.E. Students 135.

4—QUEEN OF THE HOLY ROSARY, Rev. Ronald Livojevich.
Res.: 7023 W. 71st St., 66204. Tel: 913-432-4616; Fax: 913-432-0620.
School—6915 W. 71st, 66204. Tel: 913-432-6350; Fax: 913-432-5081. Lay Teachers 17; Students 185.
Catechesis/Religious Program—Tel: 913-722-2206; Fax: 913-432-0620. Kathy O'Bryan, D.R.E. Students 200.

PAOLA, MIAMI CO., HOLY TRINITY, [CEM] Rev. Thomas Kearns.
Res.: 409 E. Chippewa, 66071. Tel: 913-557-2067; Fax: 913-294-9607.
School—Tel: 913-294-3286; Fax: 913-294-9286. Lay Teachers 8; Students 135.
Catechesis/Religious Program—Tel: 913-557-4741. Sr. Carleen Richards, D.R.E. Students 101.

PAXICO, WABAUNSEE CO., SACRED HEART, [CEM] Attended by, Immaculate Conception, St. Marys. Rev. John M. Torrez.
Res.: 22871 Newbury Rd., 66526. Tel: 785-636-5547.
Catechesis/Religious Program—Tel: 785-437-2408; Fax: 785-437-2938. Michelle Cebulski, D.R.E. Students 59.

PERRY, JEFFERSON CO., ST. THERESA'S, [CEM 2] Rev. Robert Hasenkamp.
Res.: P.O.Box 42, 66073. Tel: 785-597-5656.
Catechesis/Religious Program—Tel: 785-597-5138. Lisa Whitechair-Carver, D.R.E. Students 104.
Mission—Our Lady of Snows Potawatomi Reservation, Jackson Co.

PRAIRIE VILLAGE, JOHNSON CO., ST. ANN'S, Rev. Steven Beseau, S.T.L.
Res.: 7231 Mission Rd., 66208. Tel: 913-660-1182; Fax: 913-660-1194.
School—7241 Mission Rd., 66208. Tel: 913-660-1101; Fax: 913-660-1132. Lay Teachers 30; Students 436.
Catechesis/Religious Program—Betsy Rushton, D.R.E. Students 244.

PURCELL, DONIPHAN CO., ST. MARY'S, [CEM] Attended by, St. Leo's, Horton. Rev. Kunduru Joji, S.J.
446 Hwy 137, 66041. Tel: 785-486-3971; Fax: 785-486-3971.
Catechesis/Religious Program—Tel: 785-847-6749. Jim Handke, D.R.E. Students 32.

READING, LYON CO., ASSUMPTION, Closed. For inquiries for parish records contact the chancery.

RICHMOND, FRANKLIN CO., ST. THERESE, Attended by, St. Boniface, Scipio. Rev. Emil Agostino, O.Carm.
Res.: 32320 N.E. Nevada Rd., Garnett, 66032. Tel: 785-835-6273; Fax: 785-835-6112.

ROELAND PARK, JOHNSON CO., ST. AGNES, Revs. Donald Cullen; John H. Wisner.
Res.: 5250 Mission Rd., 66205. Tel: 913-262-2400; Fax: 913-262-1050.
School—5130 Mission Rd., 66205. Tel: 913-262-1686; Fax: 913-384-1567. Lay Teachers 34; Students 418.
Catechesis/Religious Program—John English, D.R.E. Students 120.

ROSSVILLE, SHAWNEE CO., ST. STANISLAUS, Attended by, Immaculate Conception, St. Marys Revs. John Torrez, Admin.; Balaswamy Guvvala (India).
Catechesis/Religious Program—Tel: 785-296-5253. Connie Fischer, D.R.E. Students 134.

ST. BENEDICT, NEMAHA CO., ST. MARY'S, [CEM] Rt. Rev. Owen Purcell, O.S.B., Sacramental Min.; Sr. Mary Beth Niehaus, O.S.B., Parish Min.
Res.: R.R. 1, Box 59, Seneca, 66538. Tel: 785-336-3174.
Catechesis/Religious Program—Tel: 785-336-2792. Betty Olberding, D.R.E. Students 173.

ST. LOUIS, ATCHISON CO., ST. LOUIS, [CEM] Attended by, St. Ann's, Effingham. Rt. Rev. Benjamin Tremmel, O.S.B.
Mailing Address: c/o St. Ann's, 301 William, Box 54, Effingham, 66023. Tel: 913-833-5660.
Church: 11321 Morton Rd., Atchison, 66002. Tel: 913-847-6849.
Catechesis/Religious Program—Tel: 913-874-5191. Jane Halling, D.R.E. Students 53.

ST. MARYS, POTTAWATOMIE CO., IMMACULATE CONCEPTION, [CEM] Rev. John Torrez.
Res.: 208 W. Bertrand, 66536. Tel: 785-437-2408; Fax: 785-437-2938.
Catechesis/Religious Program—Tel: 785-437-6223. Peggy Wehner, D.R.E. Students 220.

ST. PATRICK, ATCHISON CO., ST. PATRICK'S, [CEM] Attended by, St. Joseph. Rev. Bertrand LaNoue, O.S.B.

SABETHA, NEMAHA CO., SACRED HEART, Rev. Richard J. McDonald.
Office:—1031 S. 12th, 66534. Tel: 785-284-0888.
Res.: 1042 S. 14th, 66534. Tel: 785-284-3068.
Catechesis/Religious Program—Pam Wysong, D.R.E. Students 100.

SCIPIO, ANDERSON CO., ST. BONIFACE, [CEM] Rev. Emil Agostino, O.Carm.
Res.: 32320 N.E. Nevada Rd., Garnett, 66032. Tel: 785-835-6273; Fax: 785-835-6112.
Catechesis/Religious Program—Tel: 785-448-6122. Peg Pearson, D.R.E. Students 70.

SCRANTON, OSAGE CO., ST. PATRICK'S, [CEM] Attended by, St. Patrick's, Osage City. Rev. Michael Mulvany. Tel: 785-528-3424.
Catechesis/Religious Program—Tel: 785-256-2001. Carol Runnebaum, D.R.E. Students 210.

SENECA, NEMAHA CO., SS. PETER AND PAUL'S, [CEM] Revs. Roderic Giller, O.S.B.; Earl Dekat, Assoc. Pastor.
Res.: 411 Pioneer, 66538. Tel: 785-336-2208; Fax: 785-336-3666.
School—401 Pioneer, 66538. Tel: 785-336-2727; Fax: 785-336-3817. Benedictine Sisters 1; Lay Teachers 13; Students 148.
Catechesis/Religious Program—Tel: 785-336-2685. Susan Stallbaumer, D.R.E. Students 148.

SHAWNEE, JOHNSON CO.

1—GOOD SHEPHERD, Rev. Francis Hund.
Office—12800 W. 75th St., 66216. Tel: 913-631-7116; Fax: 913-631-3539.
Res.: 12509 W. 73rd Terr, 66216. Tel: 913-631-5661.
Parish Center:—12800 W. 75th St., 66216.
School—12800 W. 75th St., 66216. Tel: 913-631-0400. Lay Teachers 25; Students 338.
Catechesis/Religious Program—Tel: 913-631-7356. Deb Carmody, D.R.E. Students 970.

2—ST. JOSEPH'S, Rev. Msgr. Robert Bergman; Rev. Thomas Cawley, C.M.
Res.: 5832 King St., 66203. Tel: 913-631-5983; Fax: 913-631-5973.
School—(Grades K-8), 11505 Johnson Dr., 66203. Tel: 913-631-7730; Fax: 913-631-3608. Lay Teachers 39; Students 657.
School—Early Education Center, 5900 Bond St., 66203. Tel: 913-631-0004; Fax: 913-631-4364. (Day Care & Preschool) Auxiliary Teachers 56; Students 362.
Catechesis/Religious Program—Tel: 913-631-8923; Fax: 913-631-5973. Kathleen Clevinger, D.R.E. Students 264.

3—SACRED HEART, Rev. Craig Maxim.
Office—21801 Johnson Dr., 66226. Tel: 913-422-5700; Fax: 913-422-5723.
School—Tel: 913-422-5700; Fax: 913-422-5723. Lay Teachers 20; Students 230.
Catechesis/Religious Program—Fax: 913-422-5700. Trish Miller, D.R.E. Students 279.

SUMMERFIELD, MARSHALL CO., HOLY FAMILY, Attended by, St. Michael's, Axtell. Rev. Albert Hauser, O.S.B.
Church: P.O. Box 136, 66541. Tel: 785-736-2220.
Catechesis/Religious Program—Tel: 785-244-6450. Janet Helmerichs, D.R.E. Students 37.

TONGANOXIE, LEAVENWORTH CO., SACRED HEART, [JC] Rev. Mark Goldasich.
Res.: 703 E. River, P.O. Box 539, 66086-0539. Tel: 913-369-2851.
Catechesis/Religious Program—Tel: 913-845-2881. Students 170.

TOPEKA, SHAWNEE CO.

1—ASSUMPTION, [JC] Rev. John F. Rossiter.
Res.: 204 S.W. Eighth Ave., 66603. Tel: 785-232-2907; Fax: 785-232-8147.
School—735 S.W. Jackson, 66603. Tel: 785-235-0953. Sisters 3; Lay Teachers 10; Students 183.
Catechesis/Religious Program—Tel: 785-246-0436. Marci Lechner, D.R.E. Students 135.

2—CHRIST THE KING, Rev. Peter O' Sullivan.
Res.: 5972 W. 25th St., 66614. Tel: 785-273-0710; 785-273-0715; Fax: 785-273-4766.
School—5973 S.W. 25th St., 66614. Tel: 785-272-2220; Fax: 785-273-4766. Lay Teachers 28; Students 390.
Catechesis/Religious Program—Tel: 785-273-2917. Debbie White, D.R.E. Students 185.

3—HOLY NAME, Revs. John C. Reynolds; Stephen Owusu-Achaw (Ghana).
Res.: 1114 W. 10th Ave., 66604. Tel: 785-232-7744; Fax: 785-232-2341.
School—934 Clay St., 66606. Tel: 785-233-1727; Fax: 785-233-1728. Sisters of Charity of Leavenworth 1; Lay Teachers 17; Students 180.
Catechesis/Religious Program—Tel: 785-233-3727. Linda Mlynek, D.R.E. Students 203.

4—ST. JOSEPH'S, Rev. Carl Dekat.
Res.: 227 S.W. Van Buren St., 66603. Tel: 785-232-2863; Fax: 785-357-7844.
Catechesis/Religious Program—Tel: 785-234-5231. Mary Schneider, D.R.E. Students 53.

5—ST. MATTHEW, Rev. Patric Riley.
Res.: 2700 S.E. Virginia Ave., 66605. Tel: 785-232-5012; Fax: 785-232-0028.
School—1000 S.E. 28th, 66605. Tel: 785-235-2188. Lay Teachers 14; Students 186.
Catechesis/Religious Program—Jaclyn Laffleur, D.R.E. Students 274.

6—MOST PURE HEART OF MARY, Revs. Francis Krische; John Riley; Michael Kantanka (Ghana).
Church Office: 1800 S.W. Stone, 66604. Tel: 785-272-5590; Fax: 785-272-2801.
School—1750 S.W. Stone, 66604. Tel: 785-272-4313; Fax: 785-272-1138. Lay Teachers 37; Students 532.
Catechesis/Religious Program—Tel: 785-272-4727; Fax: 785-272-2801. Marie Apel, D.R.E. Students 262.

7—OUR LADY OF GUADALUPE, (Mexican), [CEM] Rev. Raymond May.
Office—134 N.E. Lake St., 66616. Tel: 785-232-5088; Fax: 785-232-8834.
School—210 N.E. Branner St., 66616. Tel: 785-233-9171; Fax: 785-232-8800. Lay Teachers 9; Students 120.
Catechesis/Religious Program—Tel: 785-233-4593. Monica Agosto, D.R.E. Students 120.

8—SACRED HEART, Rev. George Bertels.
Res.: 333 N.E. Freeman Ave., 66616. Tel: 785-234-3338; Fax: 785-234-6778.
School—1733 Seward Ave., 66616. Tel: 785-234-8980; Fax: 785-234-8980. Lay Teachers 12; Students 145.
Catechesis/Religious Program—Tel: 785-266-7300. Mary Jane Morrissey, D.R.E. Students 80.

TROY, DONIPHAN CO., ST. CHARLES, [CEM] Attended by, St. Joseph's, Wathena. Rev. Dayananda Prabhu (India).
Mailing Address: P.O. Box 456, 66087.
Church: 133 S. Park, P.O. Box 456, 66087. Tel: 785-985-2271.
Catechesis/Religious Program—Barb Greaser, D.R.E. Students 25.

VALLEY FALLS, JEFFERSON CO., ST. MARY'S IMMACULATE CONCEPTION, [CEM] Attended by, St. Joseph's, Nortonville. Rev. Jon Hullinger.
Mailing Address: *c/o St Joseph Church*, P.O. Box 236, Nortonville, 66060. Tel: 913-886-2030.
Church: Broadway at Linn, 66088. Tel: 913-945-3544.
Catechesis/Religious Program—Tel: 785-945-3787; Fax: 785-945-4021. JoLina Wildeman, D.R.E. Students 81.

WAMEGO, POTTAWATOMIE CO., ST. BERNARD'S, [CEM]

Rev. John Pilcher.
Res.: 1006 8th St., 66547. Tel: 785-456-7869; Fax: 785-456-7862.
Catechesis/Religious Program—Rick Cheek, D.R.E. Students 183.

WATERVILLE, MARSHALL CO., ST. MONICA'S, Closed., For inquiries see St. Monica - St. Elizabeth, Blue Rapids
Catechesis/Religious Program—Students 11.

WATHENA, DONIPHAN CO., ST. JOSEPH'S, [CEM] Rev. Dayananda Prabhu (India).
Res.: P.O. Box 159, 66090. Tel: 785-989-4818; Fax: 785-989-2313.
Catechesis/Religious Program—Tel: 785-989-3567. Students 49.

WAVERLY, COFFEY CO., ST. JOSEPH'S, Attended by, St. Francis Xavier, Burlington. Rev. Michael Hawken. Tel: 316-364-2416; Fax: 316-364-2416.
Catechesis/Religious Program—Tel: 785-733-2278. Amy Johnson, D.R.E. Students 58.

WEA, MIAMI CO., QUEEN OF THE HOLY ROSARY (Bucyrus P.O.), [CEM] Rev. Lawrence Albertson.
Res.: 22779 Metcalf Rd., Bucyrus, 66013. Tel: 913-533-2462; Fax: 913-533-2460.
School—22705 Metcalf Rd., Bucyrus, 66013. Tel: 913-533-2462; Fax: 913-533-2460. Lay Teachers 18; Students 230.
Catechesis/Religious Program—Sr. Marie William, D.R.E.; Mrs. Kriste Pickert. Students 253.

WESTPHALIA, ANDERSON CO., ST. TERESA'S, Attended by, St. Francis Xavier, Burlington. Rev. Michael Hawken.
Tel: 316-364-2416; Fax: 316-364-2416.
Catechesis/Religious Program—Tel: 785-489-2324. Marilyn Brooks, D.R.E. Students 72.

WETMORE, NEMAHA CO., ST. JAMES, Attended by, Sacred Heart, Sabetha. Tel.: 785-284-3068 (Rectory); 785-284-0888 (Office) Rev. Richard J. McDonald.

WHEATON, POTTAWATOMIE CO., ST. MICHAEL'S, Closed. For inquiries for parish records contact the chancery.

Chaplains of Public Institutions

KANSAS CITY. *K.U. Medical Center and Chapel*, Holy Name Church. Rev. Jeremiah L. Spencer, Chap.

LAWRENCE. *Haskell Institute*. Rev. Duane E. Reinert, O.F.M.Cap. (KC). (Government Indian School)

TOPEKA. *Kansas Neurological Institute and Kansas Reception and Diagnostic Center*. (Vacant)
Topeka State Hospital. State Reform School attended from Holy Name Church. Menninger Clinic attended from Holy Name Church. Veterans Administration Hospital.

Special Assignment:
Revs.—
Chontos, Joseph, 901 N. 52nd St., 66102.
Cooper, Leo, Archdiocesan Archivist, 12615 Parallel, 66109.
Lee, Matthew Seung Young, 8331 Hall St., Lenexa, 66219.
Wait, Dennis, Sanctuary of Hope, 2601 Ridge Ave., 66102-4317.

On Duty Outside the Archdiocese:
Revs.—
Okoye, Joseph, Africa
Tillia, Marc, Bahia, Brazil

Military Chaplains:
Rev.—
Ludwikoski, James E., U.S.A.F.

Administrative Leave:
Rev.—
Haeglin, William

Retired:
Rev. Msgrs.—
Culhane, Thomas, Overland Park, KS
Loncaric, Stanley, Olathe, KS
Revs.—
Blaufuss, Tony, Garnett, KS
Burger, Robert, Kansas City, KS
Dunnivan, John, Overland Park, KS
Finnerty, William, Kansas City, KS
Gardner, Maurice, Kansas City, KS
Hayes, Edward, Leavenworth, KS
Hesse, Thomas, Lecompton, KS
Klasinski, George, Topeka, KS
Lickteig, Anthony, Louisburg, KS
Melchior, Thomas, Topeka, KS
Pflumm, Robert, Overland Park, KS
Pool, Robert, Mound City, KS
Schwalm, Donald, Minnesota
Seuferling, George, Meriden, KS
Stitz, John, Leavenworth, KS
Wempe, Richard C., Seneca, KS
Wickey, Harold, Bonner Springs, KS

INSTITUTIONS LOCATED IN THE ARCHDIOCESE

[A] COLLEGES AND UNIVERSITIES

KANSAS CITY. *Donnelly College*, 608 N. 18th St., 66102. Tel: 913-621-6070; Fax: 913-621-0354. Email: kgibson@donnelly.cc.ks.us. Web: www.donnelly.edu. Dr. Ken Gibson, Pres.; Sr. Mary Agnes Patterson, Vice Pres.; Frances Sanders, Dean; Sr. Fran Cross, Registrar. Benedictine Sisters 5; Lay Teachers 59; Students 1,650.

ATCHISON. *Benedictine College*, 1020 N. 2nd St., 66002. Tel: 913-367-5340; Fax: 913-367-6566. Web: www.benedictine.edu. Daniel J. Carey, Ph.D., Pres.; John McClaflin, CFO; Kimberly C. Shankman, Ph.D., Dean of College; James Moore, Ph.D., Dean of Students; Kelly J. Vowels, Dean of Enrollment Mgmt.; Bev McConaughey, Registrar; Rev. Blaine Schultz, O.S.B.; Very Rev. James R. Albers, O.S.B.; Revs. Bruce Swift, O.S.B.; Meinrad Miller, O.S.B., Chap.; Brendan Rolling, O.S.B.; Sisters Mary Blaise Cillessen, O.S.B., Assoc. Dean of College; Thomasita Homan, O.S.B., English Dept.; JoAnn Fellin, O.S.B., Math & Computer Science Dept.; Linda Herndon, O.S.B., Chair Math & Computer Science Dept.; Theresa Torres, O.S.B., Religious Studies Dept.; Deborah Peters, O.S.B., English Dept.; Eleanor Suther, O.S.B., Dir. Institute of Religious Studies; Bros. Lawrence Bradford, O.S.B.; Joseph Ryan, O.S.B. Columba McNeill, O.S.B. Coed College of St. Benedict's & Mount St. Scholastica. Priests 5; Brothers 3; Benedictine Sisters 7; Laypeople 57; Students 1,330.

LEAVENWORTH. *University of Saint Mary*, Formerly Saint Mary College 66048. Tel: 913-682-5151; Fax: 913-758-6140. Email: admis@stmary.edu. Web: www.stmary.edu. Sr. Diane Steele, S.C.L., Ph.D., Pres.; Dr. Sandra Van Hoose, Academic Vice Pres. Sisters of Charity of Leavenworth 9; Lay Teachers 30; Students 943.

[B] HIGH SCHOOLS, INTERPAROCHIAL

KANSAS CITY. *Bishop Miege High School*, 5041 Reinhardt Dr., Shawnee Mission, 66205. Tel: 913-262-2700; Fax: 913-262-3754. Email: lgerard@bishopmiege.com. Web: www.bishopmiege.com. Joseph Passantino, Ed.D., Pres.; Stanley Herbic, Prin. Sisters 2; Lay Teachers 55; Students 887.
Bishop Miege High School Foundation Tel: 913-262-2700; Fax: 913-262-3754.
Bishop Ward High School, 708 N. 18th St., 66102. Tel: 913-371-1201; Fax: 913-371-2145. Email: wardhigh@wardhigh.org. Web: www.wardhigh.org. Mr. Dennis Dorr, Prin.; Rev. Brian Klingele, Chap. Sisters of Charity of Leavenworth 2; Benedictines 1; Ursulines 1; Lay Teachers 32; Students 451.
Bishop Ward High School Foundation Tel: 913-371-1201; Fax: 913-371-2145.

LEAVENWORTH. *Immaculata High School* 66048. Tel: 913-682-3900; Fax: 913-682-9036. Email: immaculata@archkckcs.org. Mr. Michael Connelly, Dir.; Peter McDonald, Prin. Lay Teachers 21; Students 169.

OVERLAND PARK. *Saint Thomas Aquinas High School, Inc.*, 11411 Pflumm Rd., 66215. Tel: 913-345-1411; Fax: 913-345-2319. Email: wpford@stasaints.net. Web: www.stasaints.net. Dr. William P. Ford, Pres.; Rev. Gary Pennings, Chap. Lay Teachers 87; Students 1,271.
St. Thomas Aquinas High School Foundation Tel: 913-345-1411; Fax: 913-345-2319.

TOPEKA. *Hayden High School*, 401 Gage Blvd., 66606. Tel: 785-272-5210; Fax: 785-272-2975. Email: streckerr@haydenhigh.org. Web: www.haydenhigh.org. Mr. Rick Strecker, Pres.; Mr. Mark Madsen, Prin. Religious 1; Lay Teachers 37; Students 492.
Hayden High School Foundation Tel: 785-272-5210; Fax: 785-272-2975.

[C] HIGH SCHOOLS, PRIVATE

ATCHISON. *Maur Hill - Mount Academy* 66002. Tel: 913-367-5482; Fax: 913-367-5096 Email: pcairney@mh-ma.com. Web: www.maurhill-mountacademy.com. Mr. Patrick Cairney, Pres.; Sr. Bridget Dickason, O.S.B., Prin.; Rev. Camillus Wurtz, O.S.B. Religious 3; Lay Teachers 16; Students 250.

[D] ELEMENTARY SCHOOLS, INTERPAROCHIAL

KANSAS CITY. *All Saints School* Consolidated , 809 Vermont, 66101. Tel: 913-342-3669; Fax: 913-342-3705. Email: mdelac@archkckcswy.org. Mary Delac, Prin. Lay Teachers 20; Students 389.
St. John/Holy Family School (Consolidated) , 515 Ohio & 420 Barnett, 66101. Tel: 913-321-0649; Fax: 913-321-5001. Email: jsears72@cs.com. Jennifer Sears, Prin. Lay Teachers 10; Students 97.
Our Lady of Unity School, 2646 S. 34th, 66106. Tel: 913-262-7022; Fax: 913-262-7836. Email: sdrlong@hotmail.com. Sr. Delores Long, Prin. Sisters 3; Lay Teachers 9; Students 90.

ATCHISON. *Atchison Catholic Elementary*, 201 Division, 66002. Tel: 913-367-3503; Fax: 913-367-0797. Email: rweber@aces.pvt.k12.ks.us. Mr. Rick Weber, Prin. Lay Teachers 19; Students 297.

LAWRENCE. *The Lawrence Catholic School* Tel: 785-843-9511; Fax: 785-843-7143. Email pnewton@saint-johns.net. Web: www.lcschool.net. Pat Newton, Prin. Sisters 1; Lay Teachers 24; Students 394.
Corpus Christi Campus, 6001 W. 15th St., 66049. Tel: 785-331-3374; Fax: 785-331-9904.
St. John Campus, 1208 Kentucky St., 66044. Tel: 785-843-9511; Fax: 785-843-7143.

LEAVENWORTH. *Xavier Elementary School*, Admin. Office, 320 N. Broadway, 66048. Tel: 913-682-3135; Fax: 913-682-5262. Email: xavier@archkckcs.org. Mr. Michael Connelly, Dir.; Mrs. Susie English, Admin. Consolidation of the following parishes: St. Casimir (Graces PreK-K); Sacred Heart (Grades 1-3); St. Joseph (Grades 7-8); and Immaculate Conception (Grades 4-6), St. Ignatius, St. Francis de Sales, St. Lawrence, and St. Joseph of the Valley. Sisters 1; Lay Teachers 23; Students 364.

[E] ELEMENTARY AND SECONDARY SCHOOLS, PRIVATE

MAPLE HILL. *St. John Vianney Preparatory School*, 14623 Waterman Crossing Rd., 66507. Tel: 785-256-4500; Fax: 785-256-4611. Email: sjvps@juno.com. Rev. Eric Flood, F.S.S.P. (OM). Priests 2; Subdeacons 1; Sisters 1; Lay Teachers 5; Students 37.

[F] GENERAL HOSPITALS

KANSAS CITY. *Providence Medical Center*, 8929 Parallel Pkwy., 66112. Tel: 913-596-4000; Fax: 913-596-4098. Email: catrina.bonesscl@providence-health.org. Web: www.povidence.health.org. Mr. James T. Paquette, Pres. & CEO. An affiliate of the Sisters of Charity of Leavenworth Health System, Inc. Sisters 1; Bed Capacity 400; Bassinets 22; Employees 1,320; Physicians 312; Patients Assisted Annually 117,856.

LEAVENWORTH. *Saint John Hospital*, 3500 S. 4th St., 66048. Tel: 913-680-6000; Fax: 913-680-6013. Mr. Greg Madsen, Admin. Sisters of Charity of Leavenworth 5; Physicians 151; Employees 306; Bassinets 11; Bed Capacity 76; Patients Assisted Annually 33,242.

TOPEKA. *St. Francis Health Center, Inc.*, 1700 W. 7th St., 66606. Tel: 785-295-8000. Sr. Loretto Marie Colwell, S.C.L., Pres. Sisters of Charity of Leavenworth 1; Bed Capacity 378; Total Staff 1,395; Patients Assisted Annually 212,593.

[G] NURSING AND REST HOMES

KANSAS CITY. *Marian Hall*, 1920 Tauromee, 66102. Tel: 913-621-4302; Fax: 913-621-1824. Lynne Serrano, Admin. Total in Residence 46; Total Staff 12.

OLATHE. *Villa St. Francis, Inc.*, 16600 W. 126th St., 66062. Tel: 913-829-5201; Fax: 913-829-5399. Email: villa_st_francis@msn.com. Mr. Jim Bondurant, Admin. Owned and operated by Villa St. Francis, Inc.; Skilled nursing care and independent boarding. Total Staff 170; Total Residents 200; Sisters of Charity of Leavenworth 3. In Res. Most Rev. Marion F. Forst, D.D. (DOD) (Retired); Rev. Msgrs. Thomas Culhane, Chap.; Stanley Loncaric (Retired).

OVERLAND PARK. *Villa St. Joseph Nursing Home*, 11901 Rosewood, 66209. Tel: 913-345-1745; Fax: 913-345-1346. Email: kensign@corondelet.com. Ms. Katharine Ensign, Admin. Total Staff 140; Total Assisted 240.

[H] MONASTERIES AND RESIDENCES FOR PRIESTS AND BROTHERS

ATCHISON. *St. Benedict's Abbey*, 1020 N. 2nd St., 66002. Tel: 913-367-7853; Fax: 913-367-6230. Email: bsenecal@kansasmonks.org. Web: www.kansasmonks.org. Rt. Revs. Barnabas Senecal, O.S.B., Abbot; Owen Purcell, O.S.B.,

(Retired Abbot) (Retired); Ralph Koehler, O.S.B., (Retired Abbot) (Retired); Most Rev. Herbert Hermes, O.S.B.; Very Rev. James R. Albers, O.S.B., Prior; Revs. Meinrad Miller, O.S.B., Subprior; Maurice Haefling, O.S.B., Business Mgr.; Jude Burbach, O.S.B.; Joaquim Carvalho, O.S.B.; Eugene Dehner, O.S.B.; Josias Dias da Costa, O.S.B.; James Downey, O.S.B.; Basil Finken, O.S.B.; Timothy Fry, O.S.B.; Roderic Giller, O.S.B.; Matthew Habiger, O.S.B.; Albert Hauser, O.S.B.; Regis Hickey, O.S.B.; Hugh Keefer, O.S.B.; Bertrand LaNoue, O.S.B.; Benedict J. LaRocque, O.S.B.; Daniel McCarthy, O.S.B.; Kieran McInerny, O.S.B.; Denis Meade, O.S.B.; Aaron Peters, O.S.B.; Donald Redmond, O.S.B; Brendan Rolling, O.S.B.; Duane Roy, O.S.B.; Michael Santa, O.S.B.; Blaine Schultz, O.S.B.; Gerard Senecal, O.S.B.; Paul Steingreaber, O.S.B.; Terence Sullivan, O.S.B.; Bruce Swift, O.S.B.; Benjamin Tremmal, O.S.B.; Gilbert Wolters, O.S.B.; Camillus Wurtz, O.S.B.; Michael Zoellner, O.S.B.; Bros. Lawrence Bradford, O.S.B.; Martin Burkhard, O.S.B.; Dominic Cason, O.S.B.; Marion Charboneau, O.S.B.; Robert Heiman, O.S.B.; Gabriel Landis, O.S.B.; Columba McNeill, O.S.B.; Rodrigo Perissinotto, O.S.B.; John Peto, O.S.B.; Lenilson Rezende, O.S.B.; Joseph Ryan, O.S.B.; Gregory Viscek, O.S.B.; Anthony Vorwerk, O.S.B. Bishops 1; Priests 37; Brothers 13.

LAWRENCE. *St. Conrad's Friary* (Capuchins) , 745 Tennessee, 66044. Tel: 785-843-0188; Fax: 785-843-2214. Web: www.capuchins.org. Total in Residence 5. In Res. Revs. James Moster, O.F.M.Cap.; Charles Polifka, O.F.M.Cap.; Duane F. Reinert, O.F.M.Cap. (KC); John Schmeidler, O.F.M.Cap.; Bro. Joseph McGlynn, O.F.M.Cap.

[I] CONVENTS AND RESIDENCES FOR SISTERS

KANSAS CITY. *Convent of the Sisters, Servants of Mary*, 800 N. 18th St., 66102. Tel: 913-371-3423; 913-621-1147; Fax: 913-621-4962. Ministers to the Sick, Motherhouse of the Congregation for the United States.; Nurses, private duty, and visiting nursing in the homes.

St. Peters Cathedral: Sisters Alfonsa Bellido, S.M., Prov. Supr.; Carmela Sanz, S.M., Local Supr.; Rev. Philip Kendall, C.S.V., Chap. Professed 42.

ATCHISON. *Dooley Center, Inc.*, 801 S. Eighth St., 66002. Tel: 913-360-6200; Fax: 913-360-6275. Benedictine Sisters of Mount St. Scholastica, Inc., Atchison, KS, Nursing care facility for the aged/ infirm members of this religious community.

Mount St. Scholastica, 801 S. 8th St., 66002. Tel: 913-360-6200; Fax: 913-360-6190. Email: collinsm@mountosb.org. Web: www.mountosb.org. Sr. Mary Collins, O.S.B., Prioress. Motherhouse of the Sisters of St. Benedict. Professed Sisters 189; Novices 2.

LEAVENWORTH. *Motherhouse of the Sisters of Charity of Leavenworth* 66048-5054. Tel: 913-758-6501; Fax: 913-682-2128. Email: smiller@scls.org. Web: www.scls.org. Sisters Joan Sue Miller, S.C.L., Community Dir.; Lucy Walter, S.C.L., Local Coord.; Rita Smith, S.C.L., Local Admin.; Rev. Michael Zoellner, O.S.B., Chap. Sisters 372; Total in Residence 114.

PAOLA. *Our Lady of Lourdes Convent*, 901 E. Miami St., 66071. Tel: 913-557-2349; Fax: 913-557-2340. Email: ursuline@paolaursuline.org. Web: www.paolaursuline.org. Sr. Kathleen Condry, O.S.U., Supr.; Rev. Aaron Peters, O.S.B., Chap. Motherhouse of the Ursuline Sisters. Sisters 30.

[J] PRIVATE ASSOCIATIONS OF THE FAITHFUL

KANSAS CITY. *Society of St. Augustine - Public Association of the Faithful*, 3008 S. 34th St., 66106. Tel: 913-384-3583; Fax: 913-782-2998. Email: pmjaramillo@msn.com. Web: www.angelfire.com/pa5/augustinian. Rev. Peter Jaramillo, Dir.; Bro. Thomas Akers, Procurator.

SHAWNEE MISSION. *Franciscan Servants of the Holy Family - Public Association of the Faithful*, P.O. Box 7251, 66207. Tel: 816-729-7065; Fax: 913-299-3422. Email: srd@catholic.org. Sr. Doris Engeman, Contact Person.

[K] CAMPUS MINISTRY

EMPORIA. *Didde Catholic Campus Center, Emporia State University* Office: 1415 Merchant St., 66801. Tel: 620-343-6765; Fax: 620-343-6792. Email: dccc@osprey.net. Web: www.emporia.edu/dccc. 1102 Neosho St., 66801. Tel: 620-342-8727. Rev. Jerry Volz, Chap. Total Staff 6.

LAWRENCE. *Haskell Catholic Campus Center* 2301 Barker Ave., 66046-4813. Tel: 785-842-2401; Fax: 785-843-2214. Email: DEN1588@aol.com. Bro. Joseph McGlynn, O.F.M.Cap., Dir.; Rev. Duane F. Reinert, O.F.M.Cap. (KC), Chap. Total Staff 2.

St. Lawrence Center Foundation

St. Lawrence Catholic Campus Center at the University of Kansas and Residence 1631 Crescent Rd., 66044. Tel: 785-843-0357; Fax: 785-842-2203. Email: slccc@st-lawrence.org. Web: www.st-lawrence.org. Revs. Vincent E. Krische; John Schmeidler, O.F.M.Cap. Total Staff 20.

TOPEKA. *Catholic Campus Center at Washburn University* 1633 Jewell, 66604. Tel: 785-233-2204; Fax: 785-233-2205. Email: wucatholic@hotmail.com. Web: www.wucatholic.homestead.com.

[L] MISCELLANEOUS LISTINGS

KANSAS CITY. *Bethany Community Plaza, Inc.*, 51 N. 12th St., 66102. Tel: 913-596-4000. Email: scbones@providence-health.org. Web: www.providence-health.org. An affiliate of the Sisters of Charity of Leavenworth.

Catholic Community Services, 2220 Central Ave., 66102. Tel: 913-621-1504; Fax: 913-621-4507.

The Catholic Foundation of Northeast Kansas (Formerly known as Archdiocesan Foundation) , 12615 Parallel, 66109. Tel: 913-721-1570; Fax: 913-721-1577. Email: stewdev@archkck.org. Web: www.catholiclegacy.org.

Catholic Housing of Wyandotte County, 400 N. 6th St., 66101. Tel: 913-342-7580; Fax: 913-342-7581. Email: chwc@earthlink.net. Web: www.catholichousing.com.

Duchesne Clinic, 636 Tauromee, 66101. Tel: 913-321-2626; Fax: 913-321-2651. Email: duchesne@kc.rr.com. Web: www.sclhs.org. Sr. Ann McGuire, Exec. Dir.; Gloria Guerra, Mgr. A division of Caritas Clinics, Inc., Leavenworth, KS. Total Staff 12; Total Patients 9,531.

El Centro, Inc., 650 Minnesota Ave., 66101. Tel: 913-677-0100; Fax: 913-362-8513. Web: www.elcentroinc.com. Mr. Richard Ruiz, Pres. & CEO.

ECI Development, Inc., 2100 Metropolitan Ave., 66106. Tel: 913-677-1120; Fax: 913-677-0051.

El Centro, Inc. Argentine, 1333 S. 27th St., 66106. Tel: 913-677-0177; Fax: 913-362-8250.

El Centro, Inc. Family Center, Johnson County, 9525 Metcalf Ave., Overland Park, 66212. Tel: 913-381-2861; Fax: 913-381-2914.

The Gardner Institute, 3021 N. 54th, 66104. Tel: 913-371-8254; Fax: 913-371-8510. Email: svickie@gardnerplan.org. Web: www.gardnerplan.org.

St. Joseph Adoption Referral Services, Inc. (2001), 8160 Parallel Pkwy., Ste.202, 66112. Tel: 913-299-5222; 800-752-1737; Fax: 913-299-5111. Email: hlentz@csjwichita.org. Web: www.csjwichita.org. Sr. Helene Lentz, Pres. & Contact Person.

Lay Employee's Retirement Plan of the Archdiocese of Kansas City in Kansas, 12615 Parallel Pkwy., 66109. Tel: 913-721-1570; Fax: 913-721-2680. Email: insure@archkck.org. Web: www.archkck.org.

Priest's Retirement Plan of the Archdiocese of Kansas City in Kansas, 12615 Parallel Pkwy., 66109. Tel: 912-721-1570; Fax: 912-721-2680. Email: insure@archkck.org. Web: www.archkck.org.

Providence/Saint John Foundation, 8929 Parallel Pkwy., 66112. Tel: 913-596-4151; Fax: 913-596-3418. Email: maryellen.clark@providence-health.org. Web: www.providence-health.org.

Shalom Catholic Worker House, 2100 N. 13th, 66104. Tel: 913-321-2206. Total Staff 5; Total Assisted 2,400.

ATCHISON. *The Maur Hill Prep School Endowment Association, Inc.*, 1000 Green St., 66002. Tel: 913-367-5482.

EASTON. *Shantivanam Archdiocesan House of Prayer*, 22019 Meagher Rd., 66020. Tel: 913-773-8255; Fax: 913-773-5708. Jennifer Sullivan, Dir. Total in Residence 4; Total Staff 8.

EMPORIA. *Community Service Center*, 116 W. 12th, 66801. Tel: 620-343-2296; Fax: 620-343-9517. Total Assisted 578; Staff 9.

FAIRWAY. *Cursillo in Christianity of the Archdiocese of Kansas City in Kansas*, 6115 El Monte, 66205. Tel: 913-722-1789. Email: tanafield@msn.com. Tana Field, Lay Dir.

LAWRENCE. *Catholic Community Services*, 320 Maine St., P.O. Box 342, 66044. Tel: 785-841-0307; Fax: 785-832-1710. Email: ccs@lawrence.ixks.com. Web: www.catholiccharitiesks.org.

LEAVENWORTH. *Caritas Clinics, Inc.*, 511 S. Fifth St., 66048. Tel: 913-651-8860; Fax: 913-682-4409. Email: caritas@kc.rr.com. Web: www.sclhs.org. Joanne Runyon, Pres.; Sr. Ann McGuire, Exec. Dir. Sisters of Charity of Leavenworth, Administrative structure for St. Vincent Clinic, Leavenworth, Duchesne Clinic, Kansas City Total Staff 4.

Catholic Community Services, 716 N. 5th St., 66048. Tel: 913-651-8060; Fax: 913-651-9350. Email: gowens@catholiccharitiesks.org. Staff 11; Patients Assisted Annually 6,716.

Catholic School Foundation of the Leavenworth Region, Inc., 320 N. Broadway, 66048. Tel: 913-682-7801; Fax: 913-682-6019. Email: lcsdev@archkckcs.org. Michael Connelly, Dir.

Saint Vincent Clinic (A division of Caritas Clinics, Inc., Leavenworth, KS.) , 422 Walnut, 66048. Tel: 913-651-8860; Fax: 913-682-4409. Email: saintvincentclinic@kc.rr.com. Web: www.sclhs.org. Sr. Ann McGuire, Exec. Dir.; Tara Ruff, Mgr. Total Staff 5; Total Patients 3,418.

LENEXA. *Sisters of Charity of Leavenworth Health System, Inc.*, 9801 Renner Blvd., Suite 100, 66219. Tel: 913-895-2800; Fax: 913-895-2900. Web: www.sclhs.info. Mr. William M. Murray, Pres.

MAYETTA. *Our Lady of the Snows Catholic Shrine*, Potawatomi Reservation, 66509.

PAOLA. *Lakemary Center, Inc.*, 100 Lakemary Dr., 66071-0449. Tel: 913-557-4000; Fax: 913-557-4910. Email: bcraig@lakemaryctr.org. Web: www.lakemaryctr.org. Dr. William R. Craig, Pres. Ursuline Sisters, Serves children and adults with mental retardation. Total Staff 275; Total Assisted 503.

Ursuline Sisters Charitable Trust, 901 E. Miami, 66071. Tel: 913-557-2349; Fax: 913-557-2340. Email: ursuline@paolaursuline.org. Web: www.paolaursuline.org.

TOPEKA. *Catholic Community Services Inc.*, 306 SW VanBuren, 66603. Tel: 785-233-6300; Fax: 785-233-7234. Email: ccs@cjnetworks.com.

El Centro de Servicios Para Hispanos, 134 N.E. Lake, 66616. Tel: 785-232-8207; Fax: 785-232-8834. Email: mperez6116@aol.com.

St. Francis Hospital Foundation, 1700 W. 7th St., 66606. Tel: 785-295-5356; Fax: 785-295-5479. Email: bjuozitis@stfrancistopeka.org. Web: stfrancitopeka.org.

Marian Clinic, Inc., Medical Plaza Bldg., 1001 S.W. Garfield, 66604. Tel: 785-233-8081; Fax: 785-233-8952. Email: mpage@marianclinic.org. Web: www.marianclinic.org. Mr. William M. Murray, Pres.; Marilyn Page, Exec. Dir. Affiliate of Sisters of Charity of Leavenworth Health Services Total Patients 12,763.

RELIGIOUS INSTITUTES OF MEN REPRESENTED IN THE ARCHDIOCESE

For further details refer to the corresponding bracketed number in the Religious Institutes of Men or Women section.

[0200]—*Benedictine Monks* (St. Benedict's Abbey)—O.S.B.

[0200]—*Benedictine Monks* (Conception Abbey)—O.S.B.

[0470]—*The Capuchin Friars* (Holy Family)—O.F.M.Cap.

[0270]—*Carmelite Fathers & Brothers* (American Prov.)—O.Carm.

[1320]—*Clerics of St. Viator*—C.S.V.

[0520]—*Franciscan Friars* (Cincinnati, OH.)—O.F.M.

[1210]—*Missionaries of St. Charles-Scalabrinians*—C.S.

[]—*Missionaries of St. Francis de Sales*—M.S.F.S.

[1065]—*Priestly Fraternity of St. Peter*—F.S.S.P.

[]—*Society of Jesus*—S.J.

[0975]—*Society of Our Lady of the Trinity*—S.O.L.T.

[1060]—*Society of the Precious Blood*—C.PP.S.

[]—*Vincentian Fathers*—C.M.

RELIGIOUS INSTITUTES OF WOMEN REPRESENTED IN THE ARCHDIOCESE

[0100]—*Adorers of the Blood of Christ*—A.S.C.

[0230]—*Benedictine Sisters of Pontifical Jurisdiction*—O.S.B.

[0725]—*Cordi-Marian Sisters*—M.C-M.

[0760]—*Daughters of Charity of St. Vincent de Paul*—D.C.

[1170]—*Felician Sisters*—C.S.S.F.

[1430]—*Franciscan Sisters of Our Lady of Perpetual Help*—O.S.F.

[2500]—*Medical Sisters of St. Joseph*—M.S.J.

[]—*Missioneras Guadalupanos de Cristo Rey*

[3130]—*Our Lady of Victory Missionary Sisters*—O.L.V.M.

[0480]—*Sisters of Charity of Leavenworth, Kansas*—S.C.L.

[0990]—*Sisters of Divine Providence*—C.D.P.

[2575]—*Sisters of Mercy of the Americas*—R.S.M.

[1520]—*Sisters of St. Francis of Christ the King*—O.S.F.

[1570]—*Sisters of St. Francis of the Holy Family*—O.S.F.

[3840]—*Sisters of St. Joseph of Carondelet* (St. Louis, MO)—C.S.J.

[3830-18]—*Sisters of St. Joseph of Wichita*—C.S.J.

[3600]—*Sisters, Servants of Mary*—S.M.

[4120]—*Ursuline Nuns, of the Congregation of Paris*—O.S.U.

ARCHDIOCESAN CEMETERIES

KANSAS CITY. *Gate of Heaven*
St. John's, Mount Calvary, Resurrection, St. Joseph's, Shawnee, and St. John, Lenexa
ATCHISON. *Mount Calvary*
LEAVENWORTH. *Mount Calvary*
LENEXA. *Holy Trinity*
TOPEKA. *Mount Calvary*

NECROLOGY

✠ Strecker, Most Rev. Ignatius J., Former Archbishop of Kansas City in Kansas—Died Oct. 16, 2003
† Trompeter, Rev. Msgr. Arthur J., (Retired)—Died Oct. 28, 2003
† Pecinovsky, Albert, (Retired)—Died Jan. 24, 2003

Diocese of Kansas City-St. Joseph

(Dioecesis Kansanopolitanae Sancti Josephi)

Most Reverend

RAYMOND J. BOLAND, D.D.

Bishop of Kansas City-St. Joseph; born February 8, 1932; ordained June 16, 1957; appointed Bishop of Birmingham February 2, 1988; consecrated March 25, 1988; appointed Bishop of Kansas City-St. Joseph June 22, 1993; installed September 9, 1993. *P.O. Box 419037, Kansas City, MO 64141-6037.*

Most Reverend

ROBERT W. FINN

Coadjutor Bishop of Kansas City-St. Joseph; ordained July 7, 1979; appointed Coadjutor Bishop of Kansas City-St. Joseph March 9, 2004; installed May 3, 2004 *P.O. Box 419037, Kansas City, MO 64141-6037.*

Square Miles 15,429.

Diocese of Kansas City Established September 10, 1880; Diocese of St. Joseph Established March 3, 1868.

Redesignated Diocese of Kansas City-St. Joseph August 29, 1956.

Comprises the Counties of Andrew, Atchison, Bates, Buchanan, Caldwell, Carroll, Cass, Clay, Clinton, Daviess, DeKalb, Gentry, Grundy, Harrison, Henry, Holt, Jackson, Johnson, Lafayette, Livingston, Mercer, Nodaway, Platte, Ray, Saint Clair, Vernon and Worth in the State of Missouri.

Legal Title: For legal titles of parishes and diocesan institutions, consult the Chancery Office.

Chancery: P.O. Box 419037, Kansas City, MO 64141-6037. Tel: 816-756-1850; Fax: 816-756-0878.

Web: www.diocese-kcsj.org

STATISTICAL OVERVIEW

Personnel	
Bishop	1
Abbots	1
Retired Abbots	2
Priests: Diocesan Active in Diocese	68
Priests: Diocesan Active Outside Diocese	5
Priests: Diocesan in Foreign Missions	2
Priests: Retired, Sick or Absent	39
Number of Diocesan Priests	114
Religious Priests in Diocese	95
Total Priests in Diocese	209
Extern Priests in Diocese	3
Ordinations:	
Transitional Deacons	2
Permanent Deacons in Diocese	59
Total Brothers	27
Total Sisters	300
Parishes	
Parishes	86
With Resident Pastor:	
Resident Diocesan Priests	58
Resident Religious Priests	16
Without Resident Pastor:	
Administered by Priests	3
Administered by Deacons	1
Administered by Religious Women	3
Administered by Lay People	3
Missions	12
New Parishes Created	1
Professional Ministry Personnel:	
Brothers	5
Sisters	35
Lay Ministers	490

Welfare	
Catholic Hospitals	3
Total Assisted	291,291
Homes for the Aged	14
Total Assisted	953
Day Care Centers	12
Total Assisted	763
Special Centers for Social Services	2
Total Assisted	31,000
Residential Care of Disabled	1
Total Assisted	29
Educational	
Diocesan Students in Other Seminaries	10
Seminaries, Religious	1
Total Seminarians	10
Colleges and Universities	2
Total Students	5,146
High Schools, Diocesan and Parish	4
Total Students	1,592
High Schools, Private	3
Total Students	1,532
Elementary Schools, Diocesan and Parish	32
Total Students	8,513
Elementary Schools, Private	1
Total Students	372
Catechesis/Religious Education:	
High School Students	1,002
Elementary Students	9,498
Total Students under Catholic Instruction	27,665
Teachers in the Diocese:	
Priests	3
Sisters	6
Lay Teachers	691

Vital Statistics	
Receptions into the Church:	
Infant Baptism Totals	2,441
Adult Baptism Totals	495
Received into Full Communion	307
First Communions	2,629
Confirmations	2,029
Marriages:	
Catholic	476
Interfaith	351
Total Marriages	827
Deaths	1,324
Total Catholic Population	144,483
Total Population	1,394,040

Former Bishops—Rt. Rev. JOHN JOSEPH HOGAN, D.D., ord. April 10, 1852; consecrated Bishop of St. Joseph, MO, Sept. 13, 1868; transferred to Kansas City, Sept. 10, 1880; died Feb. 21, 1913; Most Revs. THOMAS F. LILLIS, D.D., ord. Aug. 15, 1885; consecrated Bishop of Leavenworth, Dec. 27, 1904; appt. Coadjutor to the Bishop of Kansas City, "cum jure successionis," March 14, 1910; Bishop of Kansas City, Feb. 21, 1913; appt. assistant at the Pontifical Throne, Aug. 19, 1935; died Dec. 29, 1938; EDWIN V. O'HARA, D.D., ord. June 10, 1905; appt. Bishop of Great Falls, MT, August 1, 1930; consecrated Oct. 28, 1930; transferred to the See of Kansas City, April 15, 1939; made assistant at the Pontifical Throne, Jan. 5, 1949; appt. Archbishop "ad personam," June 29, 1954; died Sept. 11, 1956; His Eminence JOHN CARDINAL CODY, S.T.D., ord. Dec. 8, 1931; appt. Titular Bishop of Appollonia and Auxiliary Bishop of St. Louis, May 14, 1947; consecrated July 2, 1947; promoted to coadjutor of St. Joseph "cum jure successionis," Jan. 27, 1954; appt. to Diocese of Kansas City-St. Joseph, Aug. 24, 1956; succeeded to Sept. 11, 1956; transferred to Archdiocese of New Orleans as Coadjutor Archbishop "cum jure successionis," Aug. 10, 1961; acceded to the the See of New Orleans, Nov. 8, 1964; transferred to the Archdiocese of Chicago, June 16, 1965; created Cardinal Priest, June 26, 1967; died April 25, 1982; Most Revs. CHARLES H. HELMSING, D.D. (Retired), ord. June 10, 1933; appt. Titular Bishop of Axomis and Auxiliary Bishop of St. Louis, March 17, 1949; consecrated April 19, 1949; appt. Bishop of Springfield-Cape Girardeau, Aug. 24, 1956; transferred to Diocese of Kansas City-St. Joseph, Jan. 27, 1962; retired Aug. 17, 1977; died Dec. 20, 1993; JOHN J. SULLIVAN, D.D. (Retired), ord. Sept. 23, 1944; appt. Bishop of Grand Island, July 25, 1972; consecrated Sept. 19, 1972; installed Grand Island, Sept. 21, 1972; appt. Bishop of Kansas City-St. Joseph, June 27, 1977; installed Aug. 17, 1977; retired Sept. 9, 1993; died Feb. 8, 2001.

Former Bishops of Diocese of St. Joseph, MO—Rt. Revs. JOHN J. HOGAN, D.D., ord. April 10, 1852; appt. first Bishop of St. Joseph, March 3, 1868; consecrated Sept. 13, 1868; transferred to See of Kansas City, Sept. 10, 1880;; administrator of St. Joseph until 1893;; died Feb. 21, 1913; MAURICE F. BURKE, D.D., born May 5, 1844;; ord. May 22, 1875; appt. first Bishop of Cheyenne, WY, Aug. 9, 1887; consecrated Oct. 28, 1887; transferred to St. Joseph, June 19, 1893; died March 17, 1923; Most Revs. FRANCIS GILFILLAN, D.D., born Feb. 16, 1872;; ord. June 24, 1895; appt. titular Bishop of Spigas and Coadjutor with the right of succession to the See of St. Joseph, July 8, 1922; consecrated Nov. 8, 1922; succeeded to the See of St. Joseph, March 17, 1923; died Jan. 13, 1933; CHARLES H. LEBLOND, D.D., ord. Oct. 27, 1909; appt. Bishop of St. Joseph, July 21, 1933; consecrated Sept. 21, 1933; resigned as Bishop of St. Joseph and appointed Titular Bishop of Orcistus, Aug. 24, 1956; died Dec. 30, 1958.

Vicar General—Rev. PATRICK R. RUSH.

Chancery—P.O. Box 419037, Kansas City, 64141-6037. Tel: 816-756-1850; Fax: 816-756-0878. All official matters should be sent to this address.

Chancellor—GEORGE M. NOONAN.

Vice Chancellor—Sr. JEAN BESTE, B.V.M.

Diocesan Finance Officer—DAVID A. MALANOWSKI.

Diocesan Tribunal—P.O. Box 419037, Kansas City, 64141-6037. Tel: 816-756-1850.

Tribunal Director—Sr. VIRGINIA BARTOLAC, S.C.L., J.C.D.

Judicial Vicar—Rev. C. MICHAEL COLEMAN, J.C.L.

Adjutant Judicial Vicar—Rev. JOSEPH H. MATT, J.C.L.

Defender of the Bond—Sr. RITA KILLACKEY, O.S.B., J.C.L.

Procurators—DONNA EISENBARTH; ALLISON TOWNLEY.

Secretary of the Tribunal—CAROLYN RAMM.

Diocesan Consultors—Revs. J. KENNETH CRIQUI; THOMAS LUDWIG; JOSEPH B. POWERS; ROBERT A. ROST, D.Min.; PATRICK J. RUSH, V.G.; MICHAEL E. TIERNEY; JOHN WEISS; DONALD HELFREY; MICHAEL ROACH; JAMES E. SHEA, C.SS.R.

Presbyteral Council—Revs. ANTHONY PILEGGI, Chm.; TERRELL FINNELL, Sec. & Treas.; MICHAEL CLARY.

Deans—Revs. PHILIP EGAN, Deanery I; JAMES E. SHEA, C.SS.R., Deanery II; THOMAS HOLDER, Deanery III; JOSEPH SHARBEL, Deanery IV; JOSEPH POWERS, Deanery V; BRADLEY S. OFFUTT, Deanery VI; ANTHONY PILEGGI, Deanery VII; TERRELL FINNELL, Deanery VIII; ROBERT KERR, Deanery IX; DANIEL PETSCHE, O.S.B., Deanery X; ROBERT ROST, Deanery XI; THOMAS LUDWIG, Deanery XII; MICHAEL ROACH, Deanery XIII; JOSEPH MANCUSO, Deanery XIV.

Diocesan Offices and Directors

Archivist—Rev. C. MICHAEL COLEMAN, J.C.L.

Building Commission—Revs. MICHAEL RICE; PATRICK J. RUSH, V.G.; DANIEL KENNALEY; BERNARD J. GRAM, Chm.; WILLIAM TURNER; BERNARD JACQUINOT; STEPHEN F. OBARSKI; DAVID A. MALANOWSKI; Sr. JEAN BESTE, B.V.M.; WILLIAM FAGAN; WAYNE ROY; ALLEN MILLER, (See Property Mgmt. Office).

The "Catholic Key" Diocesan Newspaper—ALBERT DE ZUTTER, Editor.

Cemetery (Catholic Cemeteries Associated, Diocese of Kansas City-St. Joseph, Inc.)—Rev. ROBERT M. CAMERON, Diocesan Dir., 7601 Blue Ridge, Kansas City, 64138. Diocesan Cemeteries: Kansas City, Mt. Olivet; Mt. St. Mary; Resurrection; St. Joseph, Mt. Olivet.

Censor Librorum—Rev. Msgr. WILLIAM J. BLACET, J.C.L.

Catholic Charities Foundation—PAULA MOSS, Exec. Dir, 301 E. Armour Blvd., Ste. 620, Kansas City, 64111. Tel: 816-756-1850, Ext. 563; Fax: 816-756-5022.

Catholic Charities of Kansas City-St. Joseph, Inc.—1112 Broadway, Kansas City, 64105-1574. Tel: 816-221-4377; Fax: 816-221-9116. MICHAEL W. HALTERMAN, CEO; GEORGE HANS, CFO; SUSAN JONES, Agency Assoc. Dir.; LAURA WHITE, Exec. Asst. to CEO; ANN PAVLICH, Human Resources/CQI Dir.; ROB SNEAD, MIS Manager; LYNN FLAHERTY, Dir. of Community Rels. Northwest Missouri Branch Office: Deacon MARTIN J. GOEDKEN, Dir., 1302 Faraon, St. Joseph, 64501. Tel: 816-232-2885. Heart of Missouri Office: JACQUELYNN P. MARKUSIC, Dir., 118 Hout St., Ste. F, Warrensburg, 64093. Tel: 660-747-2241.

Center for Pastoral Life and Ministry—DENISE SIMEONE, Dir. Aquinas Masters Program: ROSE THERESE HUELSMAN, I.H.M., Aquinas Masters Program. Catechist Formation: DENISE SIMEONE. Christian Initiation: CELE BREEN, S.C.L.

Continuing Education—VACANT. Evangelization: DALE MOONEY, F.S.C. Hispanic Ministry: DALE MOONEY, F.S.C. Ministry Formation: DAVID BUTEL. New Wine: CLARA DINA HINOJOSA; DALE MOONEY, F.S.C. Parish Life Summer Institute: ROSE THERESE HUELSMAN, I.H.M. Pastoral Leadership (Councils): ROSE THERESE HUELSMAN, I.H.M. Pastoral Leadership (Staffs): CELE BREEN. Religious Education: DENISE SIMEONE.

Small Christian Communities—VACANT.

Central City School Fund Office—BARBARA SCHRADER, S.C.L., Exec. Dir.; JODI BUSCH, Assoc. Dir.

Diocesan Stewardship and Development—Mr. THOMAS MINGES, Dir.; GREG VRANICAR, Assoc. Dir.

Diocesan Ecumenical Officer—GEORGE M. NOONAN.

Diocesan Finance Council—Revs. ROBERT STEWART; JOHN WANDLESS; Sr. HELEN FLEMINGTON, C.S.J.; JOHN CROWE; MICHAEL BROSNAHAN; JAMES STACY; MARGO SHEPARD; MARYELLEN CONNOR; DAVID A. MALANOWSKI, Staff Representative; JOHN DESTEFANO; JOHN HOULEHAN; THOMAS MCCULLOUGH; ED MCSHANE; Mr. THOMAS MINGES; THERESA HUPP; MONICA ADAMS, Staff Representative.

Diocesan Finance Office—DAVID A. MALANOWSKI, Finance Officer; MONICA ADAMS, Internal Auditor; JENNIFER VAN BEBBER, Mgr. Accounting Svcs.

Diocesan Insurance Office—MONICA ADAMS, Risk Mgr.; ROSALEE WIETHARN, Benefits Coord.

Diocesan Ministry for Persons With Disabilities—LYNN FLAHERTY, Program Dir.; JUDY SHUTE, Coord., 4101 E. 105th Ter., Kansas City, 64137. Tel: 816-765-9805.

Education Office—JUDY WARREN, Supt., Schools; Sr. PATRICIA CLUNE, C.S.J., Assoc. Supt.; THOMAS BLAKE, Assoc. Supt. Tel: 816-756-1850.

Family Life Office—Deacon KENNETH GREENE, Dir.

Holy Childhood Association—Rev. ROBERT M. CAMERON, Dir.; Deacon ROSS BEAUDOIN, Coord.

Legion of Mary—Rev. DONALD STURM, Dir.

Office of the Diaconate—Deacon ROSS BEAUDOIN, Dir. Diaconate; BARBARA O'NEILL, Coord. Diaconate Formation; Deacon DONALD L. MCCANDLESS, Coord. Deacons.

Office of Social Concerns—Mr. NEAL COLBY JR., Dir.

Office of Personnel and Planning—Sr. JEAN BESTE, B.V.M., Dir.

Office of Worship—STEPHEN F. OBARSKI, Dir.; CLAUDETTE SCHIRATTI, Assoc. Dir.

Peace and Justice Office—JEAN CHRISTENSEN, R.S.M., Dir.; Rev. FRANCIS SCHUELE, Assoc. Dir.; LINDA ZOERLIN, Assoc. Dir.; PHYLLIS BOWEN, Sec. Tel: 816-756-1850; Fax: 816-756-5221.

Priests' Purgatorial Society—Rev. ROBERT M. CAMERON, Sec.

Priests' Pension Plan—Administrative Committee: Revs. MICHAEL TIERNEY, Chm.; RICHARD F. CARNEY (Retired); JOHN WEIS; ROBERT ROST; Sr. JEAN BESTE, B.V.M.; PATRICIA ISEMAN; JACK SELZER; DAVID A. MALANOWSKI.

Propagation of the Faith— (Pontifical Society for the Propagation of the Faith, Missionary Union of the Clergy and Religious, The Pontifical Society of St. Peter the Apostle for Native Clergy, and Daily World missionaries) Rev. ROBERT M. CAMERON, Dir.

Property Management—WAYNE ROY, Diocesan Property Mgr.; GERI SIRNA, Property Management Coord.; ROBERT JONES, Construction Mgr. Fax: 816-756-5572.

Respect Life Activities—Deacon KENNETH GREENE, Coord.

St. Vincent De Paul Particular Council—FRANK SCHLOEGEL, Moderator.

Victim Assistance Coordinator—Sr. JEANNE CHRISTENSEN, R.S.M. Tel: 816-756-1850, Ext. 534. Email: christensen@diocesekcsj.org.

Vocations—Revs. ROBERT STEWART, Dir. Seminarians; STEPHEN COOK, Assoc. Vocation Dir. & Recruiter; JOSEPH CISETTI, Assoc. Adjunct Recruiter; KEITH JIRON, Vocation Programs Coord.

Youth Office—MARY KELLY MUELLER, Dir.

Young Adult and Campus Ministry—TONY BUTEL, Dir.

CLERGY, PARISHES, MISSIONS AND PAROCHIAL SCHOOLS

KANSAS CITY
(JACKSON COUNTY)

1—CATHEDRAL OF IMMACULATE CONCEPTION (1882),, See listing for Old St. Patrick's. Rev. Msgr. Ernest J. Fiedler, Rector; Rev. Martin DeMeulenaere, O.S.B., Assoc. Pastor.
Res.: 416 W. 12th St., 64105. Tel: 816-842-0416; 816-842-0416, Ext. 112 Cathedral Social Services; 816-842-0416, Ext. 120 Cathedral Center for Faith and Work; Fax: 816-842-3849.

2—ST. ALOYSIUS (1886), (Hispanic), Mr. Anthony Caudillo, Pastoral Admin.
Res.: 2611 E. 11th St., 64127. Tel: 816-231-1886; Fax: 816-241-7010.
Catechesis/Religious Program—Students 81.

3—ST. ANTHONY (1991), Rev. John Schuele.
Res.: 318 Benton Blvd., 64124. Tel: 816-231-5445; Fax: 816-231-5446.
Catechesis/Religious Program—Students 62; Students 62.

4—ST. BERNADETTE'S (1958), Rev. Kenneth A. Riley; Deacons Emory Corrigan; David Townley.
Res.: 9020 E. 51st Ter., 64133. Tel: 816-356-3700; Fax: 816-737-3447.
Catechesis/Religious Program—Students 70.

5—BLESSED SACRAMENT, Closed., For inquiries for parish records contact St. Monica, Kansas City.

6—ST. CATHERINE OF SIENA (1926), Rev. Robert Stone; Deacon William Markey, (Retired); Veronica Ward, Pastoral Assoc. Tel: 816-761-5483, Ext. 110; Diana Rose, Pastoral Assoc. Tel: 816-761-5483, Ext. 109.
Res.: 4101 E. 105th Ter., 64137-1649. Tel: 816-761-5483; Fax: 816-761-8795.
School—Our Lady of Peace Consolidated School, 10526 Grandview Rd., 64137-1699. Tel: 816-761-5605; Fax: 816-761-2797.
Catechesis/Religious Program—Tel: 816-761-5483, Ext. 109. Students 318.

7—ST. CHARLES BORROMEO (1947), Rev. Jack H. McClure, C.PP.S. (DM); Bro. Robert Herman, C.PP.S.; Deacons Jerry Williams; Frank Peak. In Res., Rev. Garry Richmeier, C.PP.S.
Res.: 900 N.E. Shady Lane Dr., Oakview, 64118-4742. Tel: 816-436-0880; Fax: 816-436-0103.
School—804 N.E. Shady Lane Dr., Oakview, 64118. Tel: 816-436-1009; Fax: 816-436-6293. Lay Teachers 50; Students 553.
Catechesis/Religious Program—Students 414.

8—CHRIST THE KING (1938), Rev. John C. Weiss.
Res.: 8510 Wornall Rd., 64114. Tel: 816-363-4888; Fax: 816-363-2315.
School—(Grades K-8), 425 W. 85th St., 64114. Tel: 816-363-1113; Fax: 816-363-2889. Lay Teachers 17; Students 205.
School—Preschool, Tel: 816-363-5313. (Infant/Toddler & Preschool) Lay Teachers 16; Students 62.
Catechesis/Religious Program—Students 20.

9—CHURCH OF THE HOLY MARTYRS (1991), (Vietnamese), Revs. Joseph Phan Trong Hanh; Raymond Tu.
Res.: 7801 Paseo, 64131. Tel: 816-333-3214; Fax: 816-523-8168.
Catechesis/Religious Program—Tel: 816-333-5349. Students 320.

10—ST. ELIZABETH'S (1917), Revs. Robert S. Gregory; Richard Rocha; Deacons Donald Schmit; Mike McClean.
Res.: 7444 Main St., 64114. Tel: 816-523-2405; Fax: 816-444-9858.
School—Tel: 816-523-7100; Fax: 816-523-2566. Lay Teachers 30; Students 539.
Catechesis/Religious Program—Students 15.

11—ST. FRANCIS SERAPH, Closed., For inquiries for parish records contact St. Anthony, Kansas City.

12—ST. FRANCIS XAVIER (1910), Revs. Matthew Ruhl, S.J.; Daniel White, S.J.; James Blumeyer, S.J.
Res.: 1001 E. 52nd St., 64110. Tel: 816-523-5115; Fax: 816-333-0082.
Catechesis/Religious Program—Students 47.

13—ST. GABRIEL ARCHANGEL (1956), Rev. Karl Barmann, O.S.B.
Res.: 4737 N. Cleveland Ave., 64117. Tel: 816-453-1183; Fax: 816-453-6254.
School—Tel: 816-453-4443. Lay Teachers 16; Students 190.
School—Early Childhood Learning Center, Tel: 816-453-4555. Lay Teachers 24; Students 115.
Catechesis/Religious Program—Students 103.

14—GUARDIAN ANGELS (1909), Margaret Lima, Pastoral Admin.; Rev. Glenn R. Mueller, S.J.
Parish Office—1310 Westport Rd., 64111. Tel: 816-931-4351; Fax: 816-531-6396.
School—Our Lady of the Angels School, 211 W. Linwood, 64111. Tel: 816-931-1693; Fax: 816-753-3606.
School—Our Lady of Guadalupe School, 2310 Madison, 64111. Tel: 816-221-2539; Fax: 816-283-3315.
Catechesis/Religious Program—Students 32.

15—HOLY CROSS (1902), Revs. Thomas Holder; Raymond Tu.
Res.: 5106 St. John Ave., 64123. Tel: 816-231-4845; Fax: 816-483-0900.
Catechesis/Religious Program—Students 150.

16—HOLY FAMILY (1981), Rev. Robert H. Stewart.
Res.: 919 N.E. 96th St., 64155. Tel: 816-436-9200; Fax: 816-436-8049.
Catechesis/Religious Program—Students 325.

17—HOLY ROSARY (1891), (Italian), Rev. Joseph Vicentini, C.S. In Res., Revs. Firmo Mantovani, C.S., Northeast Hispanic Ministry; Patrick Murphy, C.S. (KS), Hispanic Ministry.
Res.: 911 Missouri Ave., 64106. Tel: 816-842-0200; Fax: 816-474-3806.
Catechesis/Religious Program—Tel: 816-842-5440. Students 16.

18—HOLY TRINITY, Closed., For inquiries for parish records contact Our Lady of Peace, Kansas City.

19—ST. JAMES (1906), Rev. Garry Richmeier, C.PP.S.; Deacon Philip Ross Beaudoin, Pastoral Admin.
Res.: 3909 Harrison St., 64110. Tel: 816-561-8512; Fax: 816-561-7950.
Catechesis/Religious Program—Students 29.

20—ST. JOHN FRANCIS REGIS (1964), Rev. John Bolderson.
Res.: 8941 James A. Reed Rd., 64138. Tel: 816-761-1608; Fax: 816-966-1350.
School—Tel: 816-763-5837. Lay Teachers 18; Students 278.
Catechesis/Religious Program—Tel: 816-763-1366. Students 80.

21—ST. JOHN THE BAPTIST, Closed., For inquiries for parish records contact St. Anthony, Kansas City, Tel: 816-231-5445.

22—ST. LOUIS (1919), (African American), Rev. John H. Wandless.
Res.: 5930 Swope Pkwy., 64130. Tel: 816-444-6535; Fax: 818-444-6027.
Catechesis/Religious Program—Fax: 816-444-6027. Students 21.

23—ST. MATTHEW THE APOSTLE (1964), Rev. James Taranto.
Res.: 8001 Longview Rd., 64134. Tel: 816-763-0208; Fax: 816-765-2617.
School—Our Lady of Peace Consolidated School, 10526 Grandview Rd., 64134. Tel: 816-761-5605; Fax: 816-761-2797.

Catechesis/Religious Program—Tel: 816-765-7381. Students 80.

24—ST. MICHAEL ARCHANGEL, Closed., For inquiries for parish records contact Our Lady of Peace, Kansas City, Tel: 816-231-1653.

25—ST. MONICA (1995), (African American), Rev. Philip Egan; Deacons Kenneth Greene; Darwin Dupree.
Res.: 1616 The Paseo, 64108. Tel: 816-471-3696; Fax: 816-471-1111.
Catechesis/Religious Program—5809 Michigan, 64130. Tel: 816-444-6736; Fax: 816-444-3591. School, Grades K-8.

26—OLD ST. PATRICK'S (1869),, Public Oratory associated with Cathedral of the Immaculate Conception. Rev. Msgr. Ernest J. Fiedler.
The Cathedral House: 416 W. 12th St., 64105. Tel: 816-842-0416; Fax: 816-842-3849.

27—OUR LADY OF GOOD COUNSEL (1866), Rev. Msgr. William J. Blacet, J.C.L.
Res.: 3934 Washington, 64111-2904. Tel: 816-561-0400; Fax: 816-561-1551.
Catechesis/Religious Program—Students 7.

28—OUR LADY OF GUADALUPE, Closed., For inquiries for parish records contact Sacred Heart - Guadalupe, Kansas City, Tel: 816-842-6146.

29—OUR LADY OF PEACE (1991), (Hispanic), Rev. Stephen Muth (PRM), Admin.; Deacon Al Ohmes, (Retired).
Res.: 1029 Bennington Ave., 64126-2299. Tel: 816-231-0953; Fax: 816-231-8911.
School—Consolidated School St. Stephen's Academy, Tel: 816-231-5227; Fax: 816-231-2824. See separate listing.
Catechesis/Religious Program—Students 85.

30—OUR LADY OF PERPETUAL HELP (1878), Revs. James Shea, C.SS.R.; Frank Kriski, C.Ss.R.; Terry McCloskey, C.Ss.R.; Bros. James Burke, C.Ss.R.; Charles Long, C.SS.R.; Michael Schnittker. In Res., Revs. Joseph Curalli, C.Ss.R.; Edward J. Kane, C.Ss.R.; Eugene Oates, C.Ss.R.; Patrick Power, C.SS.R.
Res.: 3333 Broadway, 64111. Tel: 816-561-3771; Fax: 816-561-3704.
School—Our Lady of the Angels, 211 W. Linwood Blvd., 64111. Tel: 816-931-1693; Fax: 816-931-6713. Mona Price, Prin. Sisters 2; Lay Teachers 17; Students 197.
Catechesis/Religious Program—Students 86.

31—OUR LADY OF SORROWS (1891), Revs. Thomas W. Wiederholt; Francis Kriski, Chap. of Latin Mass Community. Tel: 816-561-3771.
Res.: 2552 Gillham Rd., 64108. Tel: 816-421-2112; Fax: 816-421-6037.

32—ST. PATRICK (1924), Rev. Gerald Waris; Deacon Michael Lewis, Pastoral Assoc.
Res.: 1357 N.E. 42nd Ter., 64116. Tel: 816-453-5510; Fax: 816-453-4458.
School—1401 N.E. 42nd Ter., 64116. Tel: 816-453-0971; Fax: 816-453-5451. Lay Teachers 16; Students 225.
Catechesis/Religious Program—Students 160.

33—ST. PETER'S (1927), Rev. Joseph M. Sharbel. In Res., Rev. Patrick J. Rush, V.G.
Res.: 6415 Holmes St., 64131. Tel: 816-363-2320; Fax: 816-363-2492; 816-363-8157.
School—6400 Charlotte St., 64131. Tel: 816-523-4899; Fax: 816-523-1248. Sisters 1; Lay Teachers 40; Students 625.
Catechesis/Religious Program—Students 40.

34—ST. RAPHAEL THE ARCHANGEL (1963), Rev. Alexander B. Sinclair.
Res.: 7952 N.E. 54th St., 64119. Tel: 816-454-2338.
Catechesis/Religious Program—Students 33.

35—SACRED HEART-GUADALUPE (1887), (Hispanic), Rev. James G. Betzen, C.PP.S.
Res.: 907 Cesar Chavez Ave., 64108. Tel: 816-842-6146; Fax: 816-471-7540.
Catechesis/Religious Program—Students 90.

36—ST. STANISLAUS, Closed., For inquiries for parish records contact Our Lady of Peace, Kansas City, Tel: 816-231-0953.

37—ST. THERESE LITTLE FLOWER (1925), (African American), Rev. John Wandess, Sacramental Min.; Sr. Helen Flemington, C.S.J., Pastoral Admin.
Res.: 5814 Euclid Ave., 64130. Tel: 816-444-5406; Fax: 816-444-9345.
Catechesis/Religious Program—Students 26.

38—ST. THERESE PARISH (Kansas City North) (1949), Revs. Michael Roach; Patrick Tobin.
Res.: 7207 Hwy. 9, N.W., 64152. Tel: 816-741-2800; Fax: 816-741-4959.
School—7277 Hwy. 9 N.W., 64152. Tel: 816-741-5400. Lay Teachers 34; Students 737.
Catechesis/Religious Program—Tel: 816-741-3957. Students 739.

39—ST. THOMAS MORE (1964), Revs. William A. Bauman; Thomas Borkowski; Henry Piacitelli.
Res.: 11822 Holmes St., 64131. Tel: 816-942-2492; Fax: 816-942-8803.
School—Tel: 816-942-5581; Fax: 816-941-2450. Lay Teachers 43; Students 658.
Catechesis/Religious Program—Students 15.

40—VISITATION OF THE BLESSED VIRGIN MARY (1915), (Irish), Rev. Norman Rotert.
Mailing Address: 5141 Main St., 64112. Tel: 816-753-7422; Fax: 816-753-5505.
Res.: 2 E. 51st, 64112. Tel: 816-753-6968.
School—Tel: 816-531-6220; Fax: 816-531-8045. Lay Teachers 33; Students 505.
Catechesis/Religious Program—Preschool 40; Students 80.

CITY OF ST. JOSEPH
(BUCHANAN COUNTY)

ST. JOSEPH

1—ST. FRANCIS XAVIER (1890), Revs. Michael Volkmer, C.PP.S.; Timothy Armbruster, C.PP.S.
Res.: 2618 Seneca St., 64507. Tel: 816-232-8449; Fax: 816-364-5174.
School—2614 Seneca St., 64507. Tel: 816-232-9411; Fax: 816-364-0263. Lay Teachers 22; Students 368.
Catechesis/Religious Program—Students 126.

2—ST. JAMES (1900), Rev. Vincent Rogers.
Res.: 5814 King Hill Ave., 64504. Tel: 816-238-0853; Fax: 816-238-1758.
School—120 Michigan Ave., 64504. Tel: 816-238-0281. Lay Teachers 9; Students 184.
Catechesis/Religious Program—Students 60.

3—ST. JOSEPH'S CO-CATHEDRAL (1845), Rev. Richard Dierkes; Deacons William Dattilo; Richard W. Snooks; Steven Welsh.
Res.: 519 N. 10th St., 64501. Tel: 816-232-7763; Fax: 816-232-2460.
School—518 N. 11th St., 65401. Tel: 816-232-8486; Fax: 816-232-8793. Lay Teachers 17; Students 283.
Catechesis/Religious Program—Students 25.

4—ST. MARY'S (1891), Rev. Thomas K. Ludwig.
Res.: 1606 N. 2nd St., 64505. Tel: 816-279-1154; Fax: 816-279-4078.
Catechesis/Religious Program—Students 50.

5—OUR LADY OF GUADALUPE (1981), Rev. Gregory Haskamp; Jeanne Sample, Business Mgr.; Kathryn Powers, Pastoral Assoc.
Church: 4503 Frederick, 64506. Tel: 816-232-2847; Fax: 816-232-0269.
Catechesis/Religious Program—Tel: 816-232-0112. Toni Hamera, D.R.E. Students 208.

6—ST. PATRICK'S (1869), Rev. Matthew Brumleve; Deacon Elmer Hoppins.
Office:—1813 S. 12th St., 64503. Tel: 816-279-2594; Fax: 816-232-0744.
School—1813 S. 12th St., 64503. Tel: 816-232-9001; Fax: 816-232-7904. Lay Teachers 7; Students 100.
Catechesis/Religious Program—Students 25.

7—QUEEN OF THE APOSTLES, Closed., For inquiries for parish records contact the Co-Cathedral of St. Joseph, Kansas City, Tel: 816-232-7763.

OUTSIDE THE CITIES OF KANSAS CITY AND ST. JOSEPH

BELTON, CASS CO., ST. SABINA'S (1944), Rev. Joseph H. Matt, J.C.L.
Res.: 700 Trevis Ave., 64012. Tel: 816-331-4713; Fax: 816-322-6196.
Catechesis/Religious Program—Students 417.

BETHANY, HARRISON CO., BLESSED SACRAMENT (1945), Sr. Mary Ann T. Schmieding, O.S.F., Pastoral Admin.
Res.: 1208 S. 25th St., 64424. Tel: 660-425-8160; Fax: 660-425-0114.
Catechesis/Religious Program—Students 18.

BLUE SPRINGS, JACKSON CO.

1—ST. JOHN LA LANDE (1938), Revs. Donald P. Farnan; Jeffrey Stephan.
Res.: 805 NW R.D. Mize Rd., 64015. Tel: 816-229-3378; Fax: 816-229-1362.
School—801 NW R.D. Mize Rd., 64015. Tel: 816-228-5895; Fax: 816-228-8979. Lay Teachers 26; Students 451.
Catechesis/Religious Program—Tel: 816-228-4511. Students 389.

2—ST. ROBERT BELLARMINE (1983), Rev. Lloyd E. Opoka.
Res.: 4313 S.W. State Rte. 7, 64014-5701. Tel: 816-229-5168; Fax: 816-229-3981.
Catechesis/Religious Program—Students 258.

BUCKNER, JACKSON CO., CHURCH OF THE SANTA FE (1965), Rev. Ralph L. Kaiser.
Res.: P.O. Box 317, 64016. Tel: 816-650-9341.
Catechesis/Religious Program—Students 43.

BUTLER, BATES CO., ST. PATRICK'S (1882), Rev. Philip Watanabe.
Res.: 400 W. Nursery St., 64730. Tel: 660-679-4482; Fax: 660-679-5646.
Catechesis/Religious Program—Tel: 660-679-5476. Students 54.

CAMERON, CLINTON CO., ST. MUNCHIN (1867), (German—Irish), [CEM 2] Rev. Paul Turner.
Res.: 316 W. Third St., 64429. Tel: 816-632-2768; Fax: 816-632-7997.
Catechesis/Religious Program—Tel: 816-632-6276. Students 133.
Mission—St. Aloysius 301 S. Water, Maysville, DeKalb Co. 64469.

CARROLLTON, CARROLL CO., ST. MARY'S (1867), [CEM] Rev. Kenneth Criqui.
Res.: 211 E. Shanklin St., 64633. Tel: 660-542-1259; Fax: 660-542-1259.
Catechesis/Religious Program—Students 85.
Mission—Sacred Heart 201 E. 5th, Norborne, Carroll Co. 64668. Tel: 660-594-3536.

CHILLICOTHE, LIVINGSTON CO., ST. COLUMBAN (1857), [CEM 2] Rev. J. Matthew Rotert; Deacons Lawrence Schneider, (Retired); Joseph Crookshanks, (Retired); Jerry Davis.
Res.: 1111 Trenton St., 64601-1499. Tel: 660-646-0190.
School—Bishop Hogan Memorial School, 1112 Trenton St., 64601. Tel: 660-646-0705. Jeanne Hinkebein, Prin. Lay Teachers 8; Students 95.
Catechesis/Religious Program—Students 40.

CLINTON, HENRY CO., HOLY ROSARY (1875), Rev. Thomas W. Hermes.
Res.: 610 S. 4th St., 64735. Tel: 660-885-4523; Fax: 660-885-3959.
School—400 E. Wilson, 64735. Tel: 660-885-4412. Lay Teachers 7; Students 73.
Catechesis/Religious Program—Students 53.
Mission—St. Catherine's Hwy. WW, Osceola, St. Clair Co. 64776. Tel: 417-646-2217.
Mission—St. Bartholomew 504 E. Benton, Windsor, Henry Co. 65360. Tel: 660-647-2613.

CONCEPTION JUNCTION, NODAWAY CO., ST. COLUMBA (1860), [CEM] Rev. Augustine Dreiling, O.S.B.; Deacon Martin Goedken.
Res.: 311 Roosevelt, P.O. Box 27, 64434. Tel: 660-944-2301.
Catechesis/Religious Program—Students 134.

EASTON, BUCHANAN CO., ST. JOSEPH'S (1830), (Irish—German), [CEM] Rev. Matthew Brumleve; Sr. Barbara Jennings, C.S.J., Pastoral Admin.
Res.: P.O. Box 197, 64443. Tel: 816-473-2011; Fax: 816-473-2351.
Catechesis/Religious Program—Students 47.

EXCELSIOR SPRINGS, CLAY CO., ST. ANN (1889), Rev. William Caldwell, S.T.B., Pastor; Deacon John Lauhoff.
Res.: 1503 Tracy, 64024. Tel: 816-630-6659.
Catechesis/Religious Program—Tel: 816-630-5874. Connie Davis, D.R.E. Students 189.

GLADSTONE, CLAY CO., ST. ANDREW THE APOSTLE (1964), Rev. Joseph A. Mancuso.
Res.: 6415 N.E. Antioch Rd., 64119. Tel: 816-453-2089; Fax: 816-453-2442.
School—(Grades PreK-4) Tel: 816-454-7377; Fax: 816-453-6393. Students 148.
Catechesis/Religious Program—Tel: 816-453-5179. Students 129.

GRANDVIEW, JACKSON CO., CORONATION OF OUR LADY (1958), Rev. Robert Murphy; Deacon Kenneth Fuenfhausen.
Res.: 13000 Bennington, 64030. Tel: 816-761-8811; Fax: 816-761-8812.
Catechesis/Religious Program—Students 135.

HAMILTON, CALDWELL CO., SACRED HEART (1921), Rev. Robert Kerr.
Res.: 205 E. Middle St., P.O. Box 188, 64644-0188. Tel: 816-583-4413.
Catechesis/Religious Program—Students 29.
Mission—Mary Immaculate 409 S. Main, Gallatin, Daviess Co. 64640. Tel: 816-583-4413. Rev. Robert Kerr.

HARRISONVILLE, CASS CO., OUR LADY OF LOURDES (1941), Rev. Bradley S. Offutt; Deacon Ronald F. Strong.
Res.: 2700 N. Hwy. 7, 64701. Tel: 816-380-5744; Fax: 816-380-5132.
Catechesis/Religious Program—Students 174.

HIGGINSVILLE, LAFAYETTE CO., ST. MARY'S (1879), (German—Irish), [CEM] Rev. Ronald J. Elliott.
Res.: 400 W. 29th, 64037. Tel: 660-584-3038; Fax: 660-584-5081.
Catechesis/Religious Program—Students 62.

HIRLINGEN, BUCHANAN CO., SEVEN DOLORS (1872), (German), [CEM] Rev. Donald E. Sturm.
Res.: 2830 Angelique, 64501. Tel: 816-671-1510.
Catechesis/Religious Program—Students 14.

HOLDEN, JOHNSON CO., ST. PATRICK'S (1896), [CEM 2] Rev. Stephen M. Cook.
Res.: 703 S. Olive St., 64040. Tel: 816-732-4516; Fax: 816-732-5595.
Catechesis/Religious Program—Tel: 816-850-4510. Kathleen Bryant, D.R.E. Students 75.
Mission—Holy Trinity 1372 N.W. Graham Rd., Urich, Henry Co. 64788. Tel: 660-638-4715; Fax: 816-773-2674.

INDEPENDENCE, JACKSON CO.

1—ST. ANN'S (1917), Rev. Terry Bruce.
Res.: 10113 Lexington Ave., 64053. Tel: 816-252-1160; Fax: 816-252-1161.
School—Tel: 816-252-1024; Fax: 816-504-6234. Sisters of St. Francis of the Holy Eucharist 1; Sisters of Charity 1; Benedictine Sisters 1; Lay

Teachers 9; Students 126.
Catechesis/Religious Program—Students 8.
2—St. Joseph the Worker (1976), Rev. John E. Leitner.
Res.: 2200 N. Blue Mills Rd., 64058. Tel: 816-796-6877; Fax: 816-796-6876.
Catechesis/Religious Program—Barbara Ganz, D.R.E. Students 74.
3—St. Mark (1965), Rev. James E. Healy.
Res.: 3736 Lee's Summit Rd., 64055. Tel: 816-373-2600; Fax: 816-373-3816.
Catechesis/Religious Program—Joyce Arthur, D.R.E. Students 495.
4—St. Mary's (1845), [CEM] Rev. Ronald Verhaeghe; Deacon Thomas D. Powell.
Res.: 611 N. Liberty St., 64050. Tel: 816-252-0121; Fax: 816-461-8153.
Catechesis/Religious Program—Students 69.
5—Nativity of the Blessed Virgin Mary (1938), Rev. Robert A. Rost, D.Min.; Deacon Justin M. McMenamy.
Res.: 10017 E. 36th Ter., 64052. Tel: 816-353-2184; Fax: 816-358-4155.
School—10021 E. 36th Ter., 64052. Tel: 816-353-0284; Fax: 816-969-5251. Lay Teachers 14; Students 226.
Catechesis/Religious Program—Tel: 816-353-1638; Fax: 816-353-4155. Students 150.
Kearney, Clay Co., Church of the Annunciation (1980), Rev. John Wolf, C.PP.S.
Mailing Address: P.O. Box 599, 64060-0599. Tel: 816-628-5030; Fax: 816-628-4279.
Catechesis/Religious Program—Students 240.
Lee's Summit, Jackson Co.
1—Holy Spirit (1979), Rev. Michael E. Tierney; Ann Hayles, Pastoral Assoc.
Res.: 800 S.W. Hwy. 150, 64082. Tel: 816-537-6990; Fax: 816-537-8104.
Catechesis/Religious Program—Tel: 816-537-6990. Students 308.
2—St. Margaret's Catholic Community (1999), Rev. Michael D. Rice; Sue Nichols, Business Mgr.
Res.: 777 N.E. Blackwell Rd., 64086. Tel: 816-246-6800; Fax: 816-246-9858.
Catechesis/Religious Program—Tel: 816-246-3912. Cathie Liccar, D.R.E. Students 220.
3—Our Lady of the Presentation (1896), Revs. Michael Clary; Paw Tun Lwin; Deacons Joseph Stueve; Del Wilkinson; Mark Fountain.
Parish Office—130 N.W. Murray Rd., 64081. Tel: 816-251-1100; Fax: 816-251-1199.
School—150 N.W. Murray Rd., 64081. Tel: 816-251-1150; Fax: 816-251-1155. Lay Teachers 30; Students 431.
Catechesis/Religious Program—Tel: 816-251-1135. Jo Engert, D.R.E. Students 406.
Lexington, Lafayette Co., Immaculate Conception (1842), [CEM] Rev. Terrell M. Finnell.
Res.: 107 N. 18th St., 64067. Tel: 660-259-3043; Fax: 660-259-3043.
Catechesis/Religious Program—Kelly Geringer, D.R.E. Students 79.
Chapel—Chapel of Ease, Lexington
Chapel—St. John the Baptist, Lexington
Liberty, Clay Co., St. James (1840), Revs. Ronald Will, C.PP.S.; Keith Branson, C.PP.S.
Res.: 309 S. Stewart Rd., 64068. Tel: 816-781-4343; Fax: 816-792-8691.
School—Tel: 816-781-4428; Fax: 816-781-0747. Lay Teachers 22; Students 316.
Catechesis/Religious Program—Tel: 816-781-4343, Ext. 205. Students 510.
Maryville, Nodaway Co., St. Gregory Barbarigo (1858), [CEM 2] [JC] Rev. Chuck Tobin; Deacon Roy Seipel.
Res.: 333 S. Davis St., 64468. Tel: 660-582-3833; Fax: 660-582-5914.
School—315 S. Davis St., 64468. Tel: 660-582-2462; Fax: 660-582-2496. Sonja Henggeler, Prin. Lay Teachers 18; Students 210.
Newman Center—606 College Ave., 64468. Tel: 660-582-7373.
Catechesis/Religious Program—Tel: 660-582-5914. Students 198.
Montrose, Henry Co., Immaculate Conception (1876), (German), [CEM] [JC 2] Rev. Edward Oen, C.PP.S.
Res.: 606 Kansas Ave.,, 64770-9601. Tel: 660-693-4651; Fax: 660-693-4713.
School—St. Mary School, Tel: 660-693-4502. Lay Teachers 3; Students 33.
Catechesis/Religious Program—Students 37.
Nevada, Vernon Co., St. Mary's (1887), [CEM] Rev. Anthony J. Pileggi.
Res.: 330 N. Main St., 64772. Tel: 417-667-5604; Fax: 417-667-5604.
School—Tel: 417-667-7517; Fax: 417-667-7517. Lay Teachers 3; Students 30.
Catechesis/Religious Program—Students 54.
Mission—St. Bridget's Rich Hill, Bates Co.
Odessa, Lafayette Co., St. George (1882), Rev. Peter M. Savidge; Deacon Harry Rodman.
Res.: 716 S. Third, 64076. Tel: 816-230-4127.
Mission—St. Jude the Apostle 2001 S. Broadway, P.O. Box 590, Oak Grove, Jackson Co. 64075. Tel: 816-690-3155.
Catechesis/Religious Program—Tel: 816-230-7475. Students 67.
Parnell, Nodaway Co., St. Joseph's (1891), [CEM] [JC] Rev. Aidan McSorley, O.S.B.
Res.: 411 S. Main, P.O. Box 78, 64475. Tel: 660-986-3305.
Catechesis/Religious Program—Students 96.
Plattsburg, Clinton Co., St. Ann's (1866), (Irish), [CEM] Rev. Robert E. Crider.
Res.: 700 Maple St., 64477. Tel: 816-539-2634; Fax: 816-539-2964.
Catechesis/Religious Program—Students 55.
Pleasant Hill, Cass Co., St. Bridget (1884), Rev. Joseph I. Cisetti.
Mailing Address: 2103 N. Lexington, P.O. Box 43, 64080. Tel: 816-540-4563; Pager: 816-540-2162.
Raytown, Jackson Co., Our Lady of Lourdes (1948), Rev. Joseph Powers; Deacons Jerry Williams; Samuel Adams.
Res.: 7009 Blue Ridge Blvd., 64133. Tel: 816-353-2380; Fax: 816-353-5737.
School—8312 E. Gregory Blvd., 64133. Tel: 816-353-7062; Fax: 816-353-7650. Lay Teachers 15; Students 152.
Catechesis/Religious Program—Students 56.
Richmond, Ray Co., Immaculate Conception (1869), [CEM] Rev. Ronald J. Elliott.
Res.: 602 S. Camden, 64085. Tel: 816-470-2268; Fax: 816-470-9967.
Catechesis/Religious Program—Students 25.
Savannah, Andrew Co., St. Rose of Lima (1898), Gigi Oram, Pastoral Admin.
Mailing Address: 707 Hall Ave., 64485. Tel: 816-324-5700; Fax: 816-324-5726.
Res.: 705 S. Hall Ave., 64485. Tel: 816-324-3231.
Catechesis/Religious Program—Students 113.
Mission—St. Patrick 303 Grand Ave., Forest City, Holt Co. 64451. Tel: 660-446-2045.
Smithville Clay Co., Church of the Good Shepherd (1974), Rev. Bernard E. Branson.
Res.: 1103 S. Commercial, P.O. Box 653, 64089. Tel: 816-532-4344 (Church); 816-532-0522 Res.); Fax: 816-532-0019.
Catechesis/Religious Program—Tel: 816-734-8925. Students 212.
Stanberry Gentry Co., St. Peter's (1880), [CEM] Rev. Daniel Petsche, O.S.B.
Res.: 614 N. Alanthus Ave., 64489. Tel: 660-783-2159.
Catechesis/Religious Program—Students 116.
Mission—St. Patrick's Ford City, MO. 4201 State Hwy. AA. King City, Gentry Co. 64463.
Sugar Creek, Jackson Co., St. Cyril (1912), (Croatian—Slovak), Rev. Terry Bruce.
Res.: 11231 Chicago Ave., 64054. Tel: 816-252-1160.
Tarkio, Atchison Co., St. Paul the Apostle (1890), [JC] Rev. Reginald Sander, O.S.B.
Res.: 905 Elm St., 64491. Tel: 660-736-4342.
Catechesis/Religious Program—Students 28.
Mission—St. Benedict Catholic Church Burlington Junction, Nodaway Co. 64428. Tel: 660-725-4407.
Trenton, Grundy Co., St. Joseph's (1872), [CEM] Rev. Edgar Probstfield, O.S.B.
Res.: 1728 St. Joseph Ave., 64683. Tel: 660-359-2841.
Mission—Immaculate Heart of Mary Church 1728 St. Joseph Ave., Princeton, Mercer Co. 64683.
Catechesis/Religious Program—Students 31.
Warrensburg, Johnson Co., Sacred Heart (1865), Rev. Dennis Schaab, C.PP.S.
Res.: 300 S. Ridgeview Dr., 64093. Tel: 660-747-6154; Fax: 660-747-5965.
Catechesis/Religious Program—Tel: 660-747-5965; Fax: 660-747-7623. Students 236.
Weston, Platte Co., Holy Trinity (1842), [JC] Rev. Thomas Hawkins.
Res.: 407 Cherry St., 64098. Tel: 816-640-2206.
Catechesis/Religious Program—Students 128.

Special Assignment:
Revs.—
Cameron, Robert M., Cemeteries & Mission Office Dir., 7601 Blue Ridge, 64138.
Coleman, C. Michael, J.C.L., Judicial Vicar & Diocesan Archivist, P.O. Box 419037, 64141-6037.
Davis, Ernest P., Hospital Chap., 6517 Holmes, 64131.
Jankowski, Marcellus A., Hospital Chap. (Retired), 2909 Vista Court, Independence, 64057.
Mahoney, Robert J., 4550 Warwick, 64111.
Rush, Patrick J., V.G., P.O. Box 419037, 64141-6037.
Schuele, Francis J., Staff Assoc. Peace & Justice Office, 640 E. Armour #102, 64109.

On Duty Outside the Diocese:
Revs.—
Cronin, Thomas, Reno, NV
Holloway, David L., Military Chap.
Honhart, Mark (SFE), Albuquerque, NM
Reardon, Daniel, Military Chap.

Mission Duty:
Revs.—
Gillgannon, Michael, Casilla 12162, La Paz, Bolivia.
Walker, Michael, Parroquia San Pedro, Yepocapa Chimaltenango, Guatemala, CA.

Retired:
Rev. Msgrs.—
Bauer, Henry, 6425 Woodson, 64133.
Froeschl, Martin H., 800 E. 21st St., Apt. 57, Falls City, NE 68355.
Huhmann, John F., 10515 Bridlespur Dr., 64114-4712.
Moser, Victor G., 2102 Blue Mills Rd., Independence, 64058.
Summers, R. Emmett, Jeanne Jugan Center, 8745 James A. Reed Rd. #1217, 64138.
Revs.—
Blaes, Paul, M.A., Ph.D., 1589 Carrollwood Dr., Sarasota, FL 34232-3309.
Boyle, Leo A., 4291 Richmond Rd., Cleveland, OH 44122.
Carney, Richard F., 11114 Oak, 64114.
Cleary, Donald R., 411 E. 79th St., 64131.
Coleman, John P., 8745 James A. Reed Rd., 64138.
Ducate, Richard G., 315 E. Elm, Raymore, 64083.
Eldringhoff, John P., 2607 Quail Creek Dr., Independence, 64055.
Faller, Henry E., Jeanne Jugan Center, 8745 James A. Reed Rd., 64138.
Gauthier, Ernest, L.C.S.W., 2920 S.E. Bingham Ct., Lee's Summit, 64063.
Hart, James, 616 E. 120th St., 64145.
Helfrey, Donald C., 414 W. 12th St., 64105.
Jakubowski, Joseph J., 8745 James A. Reed Rd., 64138.
Jankowski, Marcellus A., 2909 Vista Ct., Independence, 64057.
Jones, Charles F., 2120 Norton, Independence, 64052.
Karels, Ambrose G., P.O. Box 410834, 64141.
Lyons, James P., 9001 James A. Reed Rd., 64138.
McCormack, John, 8300 E. 88th Ter., #2010, 64138-4490.
Miller, Donald S., St. Stephen Infirmary, 37174 State Hwy. V.V., Conception, 64433.
Miller, Roger F., 2440 N.W. Shady Bend, Lee's Summit, 64081.
Moscaritolo, Mario, 4019 Warwick, 64111.
Mullin, Hugh J., 10901 Johnson Blvd. J 712, Seminole, FL 33772.
O'Connor, Patrick, 421 Sunset St., Butler, 64730.
Paa, Donald R., 1500 W. 23rd Ter., Apt. C, Independence, 64050.
Pecoraro, James A., 12720 State Line Rd., Leawood, KS 66209.
Pilecki, Walter J., 806 NE Sunnyside School Rd. #711-B, Blue Springs, 64014.
Powell, Harold W., 720 E. 17th St. Apt D., Cheyenne, WY 82001.
Russ, Francis J., 6140 Raytown Rd. #603, Raytown, 64133-5174.
Ryan, C. Duane, Rte. 2, Box 335, Sunrise Beach, 65079.
Saale, Richard T., 8800 Buckingham Ln., Apt. 14, 64138.
Speichinger, Lawrence, 10914 Old Hwy. 190, Chillicothe, 64601.
Ward, Thomas, 1400 E. Mechanic, Independence, 64050.

Permanent Deacons:
Adams, Samuel
Beaudoin, Philip Ross
Bode, William, (Retired)
Bonnarens, Edwin
Browning, Melvin, (Retired)
Clark, Joseph P., (Retired)
Corrigan, Emory S., (Retired)
Crookshanks, Joseph V., (Retired)
Dattilo, William, (Retired)
Davis, F. Jerry
Dupree, Darwin
Falcon, Francis L., (Retired)
Fountain, Mark J., (Retired)
Fuenfhausen, Kenneth
Goedken, Martin J.
Greene, Kenneth
Guerra, Manuel P., (Retired)
Henggeler, Francis J., (Retired)
Hoppins, Elmer E.
Katzer, Dwayne
Koch, John J., (Retired)
Kopp, George C., Jr., (Retired)
Kopp, Harold G., Sr., (Retired)

Kratofil, Lawrence, (Retired)
Langdon, Harry, (Retired)
Lauhoff, John D., (Retired)
Lewis, Michael
Madden, Donald
Markey, William R., (Retired)
Mason, Marvin M., (Retired)
McCandless, Donald L.
McEvoy, Timothy
McKay, Clarence W.
McLean, Michael
McMenamy, Justin M., (Retired)
Muraski, Richard J., (Retired)
Ohmes, Albert J., (Retired)
Peak, Francis L.
Pham, Tuyen
Powell, D. Thomas
Reynolds, James, III
Riead, John T.
Rodman, Harold M., (Retired)
Santellan, Alfred M.
Schieber, Martin L., (Retired)
Schmit, Donald A., (Retired)
Schneider, Lawrence, (Retired)
Seipel, Leroy, (Retired)
Snooks, Richard W., (Retired)
Strong, Ronald F.
Stueve, Joseph E., (Retired)
Thompson, John R., (Retired)
Townley, David
Tran, Doan
Welsh, Steven
West, Larry
Wilkinson, Del
Williams, Jerry

INSTITUTIONS LOCATED IN THE DIOCESE

[A] SEMINARIES, RELIGIOUS OR SCHOLASTICATES

KANSAS CITY. *Gaspar Mission House*, 5221 Rockhill Rd., 64110. Tel: 816-333-7980. Rev. David Matz, C.PP.S.; Bro. Daryl Charron, C.PP.S. Priests 1; Brothers 1; Students 2.

CONCEPTION. *Conception Seminary College*, 37174 State Hwy., P.O. Box 502, 64433. Tel: 660-944-3105; Fax: 660-944-2829. Email: seminary@conception.edu. Web: conceptionabbey.org. Rt. Rev. Gregory Polan, O.S.B., Chancellor; Revs. Benedict Neenan, O.S.B., Pres. & Rector; Sebastian Allgaier, O.S.B.; Albert Bruecken, O.S.B.; Patrick Caveglia, O.S.B.; Donald Grabner, O.S.B.; Quentin Kathol, O.S.B.; Aidan McSorley, O.S.B.; Daniel J. Merz (JC); Xavier Nacke, O.S.B.; Daniel Petsche, O.S.B.; Kenneth Reichert, O.S.B.; Duane F. Reinert, O.F.M.Cap.; Marcel Rooney, O.S.B.; Samuel Russell, O.S.B.; Timothy Schoen, O.S.B.; Isaac True, O.S.B.; Peter Ullrich, O.S.B.; William Whelan (OM). Priests 19; Brothers 8; Sisters 1; Lay Professors 6; Total Staff 43; Students 98.

LIBERTY. *Precious Blood Center* (Kansas City Province) , 2110-2140 Hughes Rd., 64068. Tel: 816-781-4344; Fax: 816-781-3639. Email: KCPROV@sbcglobal.net. Rev. Paul Sattler, C.PP.S., Local Dir. Priests 9; Brothers 2.

Society of the Precious Blood Provincial Offices, P.O. Box 339, 64069-0339. Tel: 816-781-4344; Fax: 816-781-3639. Email: KCProv@sbcglobal.net. Revs. Aloys Ebach, C.PP.S., Prov. Vice; James A. Urbanic, C.PP.S., Prov. Dir.; Garry Richmeier, C.PP.S., Prov. Sec.; Joseph Bathke, C.PP.S. (CHI), 2nd Council.

[B] COLLEGES AND UNIVERSITIES

KANSAS CITY. *Avila University*, 11901 Wornall Rd., 64145-1698. Tel: 816-942-8400; Fax: 816-942-3362. Email: denslowca@mail.avila.edu. Web: www.avila.edu. Thomas F. Gordon, J.D., L.L.M., Pres.; Joseph W. Deighton, J.D., Vice Pres. & Dean for Student Affairs; Sr. Marie Joan Harris, C.S.J., Ph.D., Provost & Vice Pres. for Academic Affairs; Paul G. Bookmeyer, C.P.A., Vice Pres. for Finance & Admin. Svcs.; Philip A. Watson, Vice Pres. Advancement; David Armstrong, Dir. Campus Ministry. Sisters 1; Lay Teachers 61; Students 1,746.

Rockhurst University, 1100 Rockhurst Rd., 64110-2561. Tel: 816-501-4000; Fax: 816-501-4293. Email: cathy.dubois@rockhurst.edu. Web: www.rockhurst.edu. Thomas A. McDonnell, Chm. Bd. of Trustees; Rev. Edward Kinerk, S.J., Pres.; Nan Evanson, Vice Pres. Institutional Advancement; William Haefele, Vice Pres., Academic Affairs; Guy Swanson, Vice Pres. Finance; Elizabeth Brent, Vice Pres. Student Devel.; Jeanne Langdon, Dir. of the Library; Rachael Lierz, Controller. Sisters 2; Priests 7; Brothers 1; Lay Professors 238; Students 3,400.

College of Arts and Sciences Tel: 816-501-4081; Fax: 816-501-4169. Anita Salem, Interim Dean.

School of Graduate and Professional Studies Tel: 816-501-4686; Fax: 816-501-4615. Robin Bowen, Interim Dean.

Helzberg School of Management Tel: 816-501-4087; Fax: 816-501-4650. James Daley, Dean.

Research College of Nursing, 2316 E. Meyer Blvd., 64123. Tel: 816-276-4700; Fax: 816-276-3526. Nancy DeBasio, Pres. & Dean.

Rockhurst University Continuing Education Center/ National Seminars Group, 6901 West 63rd St., KS 66205. Tel: 913-432-7755; Fax: 913-432-2031. Web: www.rockhurst.edu. Mark Truitt, Exec. Dir.; Gary Truitt, Mng. Dir.; Revs. Martin J. Bredeck, S.J.; Edward K. Burger, S.J.; Luke J. Byrne, S.J.; John J. Callahan, S.J.; Thomas J. Casey, S.J.; D. Scott Hendrickson, S.J.; Revs. Edward Kinerk, S.J.; Wilfred L. LaCroix, S.J.; Robert J. Mahoney; Louis J. Oldani, S.J.; John J. Vowells, S.J.; James D. Wheeler, S.J.; Bros. E. Glenn Kerfoot, S.J.; John R. Olson, S.J. Priests 6; Brothers 1; Sisters 1; Lay Teachers 150; Total Enrollment 1,800; Total Staff 233.

[C] HIGH SCHOOLS, DIOCESAN

KANSAS CITY. *Archbishop O'Hara High School* (Coed) , 9001 James A. Reed Rd., 64138. Tel: 816-763-4800; Fax: 816-763-0156. Email: postmaster@oharahs.org. Web: www.oharahs.org. Mr. Walter Bowman, Prin. Christian Brothers 2; Lay Teachers 36; Students 552.

St. Pius X High School, 1500 N.E. 42nd Ter., 64116. Tel: 816-453-3450; Fax: 816-452-7099. Email: jmonachino@stpiusxhs-kc.com. Web: www.stpiusxhs-kc.com. Joseph Monachino Jr., Prin. Sisters 2; Lay Teachers 32; Students 423.

ST. JOSEPH. *Bishop LeBlond High School*, 3529 Frederick Ave., 64506. Tel: 816-279-1629; Fax: 816-279-5488. Email: cconnelly@bishopleblondhs.com. Web: bishopleblond.com. Sr. Corrine Connelly, R.S.M., Prin.; Rev. Thomas K. Ludwig, Chap. Priests 1; Sisters 1; Lay Teachers 22; Students 236.

INDEPENDENCE. *St. Mary's Diocesan High School-Bundschu Memorial*, 622 N. Main St., 64050. Tel: 816-252-8733; Fax: 816-252-2780. Email: gjonas@stmhs.org. Web: www.stmhs.org. Trudy Jonas, Prin. Sisters 1; Lay Teachers 14; Students 235.

[D] HIGH SCHOOLS, PRIVATE

KANSAS CITY. *De La Salle Academy*, 3732 Paseo, 64109. Tel: 816-531-6561; Fax: 816-756-3916. Email: mooney@diocesekcsj.org. Christian Brothers, F.S.C. and LaSallian Volunteers, Special Educational Programs & LaSallian Tutorial Programs. Christian Brothers 3; LaSallian Volunteers 2; Students 65.

Notre Dame de Sion High School, 10631 Wornall Rd., 64114-5096. Tel: 816-942-3282; Fax: 816-942-4052. Email: wor@ndsion.com. Web: www.ndsion.edu. Alice Munninghoff, Head of School; Michelle Olson, Prin. Affiliated with Sisters of Notre Dame de Sion Sisters 1; Lay Teachers 39; Students 440.

Rockhurst High School, 9301 State Line Rd., 64114-3229. Tel: 816-363-2036; Fax: 816-363-3764. Email: tpesci@rockhursths.edu. Web: www.rockhursths.edu. Revs. Thomas A. Pesci, S.J., Pres.; Mark J. Daues, S.J.; Gerard E. Menard, S.J.; John L. Tran, Scholastic. Jesuit Priests 3; Scholastics 1; Lay Teachers 70; Students 1,030.

St. Teresa's Academy, 5600 Main St., 64113. Tel: 816-501-0011; Fax: 816-523-0232. Email: nhand2@stteresasacademy.org. Dr. Faith Wilson, Ph.D., Pres.; Mary Anne Hoecker, M.A., Assoc. Prin.; Nancy Hand, M.A., Assoc. Prin. Affiliated with Sisters of St. Joseph of Carondelet Sisters 2; Lay Teachers 46; Students 528.

[E] CONSOLIDATED SCHOOLS

KANSAS CITY. *Bishop John J. Sullivan Preschool*, 3208 Lexington, 64124. Tel: 816-231-6769. Leslie Bales, Dir. Lay Teachers 14; Students 91.

Holy Cross School, 121 N. Quincy, 64123-1399. Tel: 816-231-8874; Fax: 816-231-7258. Christine Higgins, Prin. Lay Teachers 15; Students 240.

St. Monica School, (Grades PreK-8), Elementary: 5809 Michigan, 64130. Tel: 816-444-6736; Fax: 816-444-6736. Email: stmonicakc@yahoo.com. Charles E. Monckton, Prin. Consolidated with St. Monica of Africa, St. Therese Little Flower, St. Louis, and St. James to form St. Monica's School. Sisters 1; Lay Teachers 14; Students 150.

Our Lady of Guadalupe School, 2310 Madison, 64108. Tel: 816-221-2539; Fax: 816-283-3315. Connie Bowman, Prin. Lay Teachers 5; Total Staff 12; Students 108.

Our Lady of Peace School, (Grades PreK-8), 10526 Grandview Rd., 64137. Tel: 816-761-5605; Fax: 816-761-2797. Email: mmoore@olop-kc.org. Web: www.kansascity.com/.schools. Ms. Barbara J. McCormick, Prin. Consolidated with Coronation, St. Catherine's, St. Matthew's, and St. Sabina's to form Our Lady of Peace School. Lay Teachers 23; Students 318; Preschool Students 48.

Our Lady of the Angels School, (Grades PreK-8), 211 W. Linwood Blvd., 64111. Tel: 816-931-1693; Fax: 816-931-6713. Email: olaprincipal@hotmail.com. Mona R. Price, Prin. Lay Teachers 15; Students 197.

St. Stephen's Academy, 1001 Bennington Ave., 64126. Tel: 816-231-5227; Fax: 816-231-2824. Email: connie.a@micro.com. Web: www.ststephensacademy.org. Connie Armstrong, Prin. Consolidation of Our Lady of Peace, St. Anthony's, Holy Cross, Holy Rosary & St. Aloysius. Sisters 1; Brothers 1; Lay Teachers 13; Students 148.

[F] ELEMENTARY SCHOOLS, PRIVATE

KANSAS CITY. *Notre Dame de Sion Elementary School*, 3823 Locust St., 64109-2697. Tel: 816-753-3810; Fax: 816-753-0806. Email: loc@ndsion.net. Web: www.ndsion.edu. Alice Munninghoff, Head of School; Catherine Butel, Prin.; Barbara Altergott, Asst. Prin. & Admissions Dir. Affiliated with Sisters of Notre Dame de Sion Lay Teachers 32; Students 372.

[G] GENERAL HOSPITALS

KANSAS CITY. *Saint Joseph Health Center*, 1000 Carondelet Dr., 64114. Tel: 816-942-4400; Fax: 816-943-2840. Web: www.carondelethealth.org. Bruce L Van Cleave, M.D., Pres. & CEO; Teresa Rudloff, Chap. Sponsored by the Sisters of St. Joseph of Carondelet. Sisters 5; Bed Capacity 300; Nurses 266; Total Staff 1,644; Patients Assisted Annually 155,258.

Parent Corporation:

Carondelet Health, P.O. Box 8510, 64114. Tel: 816-943-5678; Fax: 816-943-2840. Bruce L Van Cleave, M.D., Pres. & CEO. Parent Co. Sponsored by the Sisters of St. Joseph of Carondelet.

Divisions:

Saint Joseph Health Center Foundation, 1000 Carondelet Dr., 64114. Tel: 816-942-4400; Fax: 816-943-2786. Sr. Patricia Lorenz, Chm.; Bruce L Van Cleave, M.D., Pres. & CEO. Sponsored by the Sisters of St. Joseph of Carondelet.

Carondelet Home Care Services Inc., 11050 Roe Ave., Ste. 120, Overland Park, KS 66211. Tel: 816-943-4700; Fax: 913-345-9129. Karen Steffen, Admin. Home health agency affiliated with Carondelet Health.

BLUE SPRINGS. *St. Mary's Hospital of Blue Springs*, 201 W. R.D. Mize Rd., 64014. Tel: 816-228-5900; Fax: 816-655-5408. Web: www.carondelethealth.com. Gordon Docking, CEO. Sponsored by the Sisters of St. Joseph of Carondelet. Acute care facility, having medical, surgical, obstetrical and pediatric services. Sisters 3; Bed Capacity 134; Patients assisted annually 103,533; Staff 750.

MARYVILLE. *St. Francis Hospital & Health Services*, 2016 S. Main, 64468. Tel: 660-562-2600; Fax: 660-562-7911. Web: www.stfrancismaryville.com. Michael Baumgartner, Pres. Member of SSM Health Care. Sponsored by Franciscan Sisters of Mary, St. Louis, MO. Acute care facility.; Priests of the deanery serve as chaplains. Sisters 1; Bed Capacity 81; Total Staff 410; Patients assisted annually 32,500.

[H] SPECIAL CARE UNITS

KANSAS CITY. *Carondelet Manor*, 621 Carondelet Dr., 64114. Tel: 816-943-4777. Dianne Doctor, Admin. Legal Title: *Carondelet Long Term Care Facilities, Inc.*, Owned and operated by Carondelet Long Term Care Facilities, Inc. Sponsored by Sisters of St. Joseph of Carondelet. Bed Capacity 180.

BLUE SPRINGS. *St. Mary's Manor*, 111 Mock Ave., 64014. Tel: 816-228-5655; Fax: 816-228-8480. Email: pkelley@carondelet.com. Pat Kelley, Admin. Long term care facility with skilled nursing care and residential care. Skilled care 132; Residential care 57; Total Assisted 189; Total Staff 191.

LIBERTY. *Immacolata Manor*, 2101 Hughes Rd., 64068-9397. Tel: 816-781-4332; Fax: 816-781-8820. Email: imanor@sbcglobe.net. Nancy Miller, Exec. Dir.; Peter Brake, Pres. Residential and day habilitation services for women with developmental disabilities.; Operated by the Immacolata Board of Directors. Residents 27; Total Staff 57; Total Assisted 33.

[I] HOMES FOR THE ELDERLY

KANSAS CITY. *Brighton Place*, 2429 Brighton, 64127.

Tel: 816-561-4240; Fax: 816-561-3155. A 31-unit residence for the elderly and disabled. Total Assisted 28; Total Staff 46.

Cathedral Square Towers, 444 W. 12th St., 64105. Tel: 816-471-6555; Fax: 816-421-1279. Email: cath@swbell.net. Jan Carson, Mgr.; Mr. Neal D. Colby Jr., Diocesan Liaison. Apartment residence for the elderly and handicapped. Units 156; Total in Residence 164; Total Staff 8.

Columbus Park Plaza, 801 Pacific, 64106. Tel: 816-472-0887; Fax: 816-472-6105. Email: columbuspark1@swbell.net. Sandy Schaefer, Mgr.; Mr. Neal D. Colby Jr., Diocesan Liaison. Apartment residence for elderly and handicapped. Units 56; Total in Residence 55; Total Staff 4.

Jeanne Jugan Center, 8745 James A. Reed Rd., 64138. Tel: 816-761-4744; Fax: 816-761-4724. Email: mslspkc@hotmail.com. Sr. Marguerite McCarthy, Supr.; Rev. John McCormack, Chap. (Retired).

Legal Title: *Little Sisters of the Poor* Little Sisters of the Poor Apartments 33; Bed Capacity 76; Total in Residence 100; Total Staff 94; Total Assisted 208; Sisters 10.

Marlborough Manor, 1818 E. 79th St., 64132. Tel: 816-333-7761; Fax: 816-523-2388. Email: marlborough01@sbcglobal.net. Louise Shepherd, Mgr. Rental housing for low income (a 31-unit apartment residence for the elderly and disabled). Total in Residence 31; Total Staff 2.

Red Bridge Place, 11300 Colorado, 64137 Tel: 816-761-4667; Fax: 816-761-4769. Email: redbrdgl@swbell.net. Linda Barber, Mgr. Total Staff 3; Total Assisted 45.

Tremont Place, 6161 N. Chatham, 64151. Tel: 816-587-7707; Fax: 816-587-7637. Email: tremont1@swbell.net. Donna Quick, Mgr. A 50-unit apartment residence for the elderly and disabled. Must be sixty two or over.

ST. JOSEPH. *The Living Community of St. Joseph*, 1202 Heartland Rd., 64506. Tel: 816-671-0015. Email: christinekerns@bhshealth.org. Larry Marshall, Corporate Dir.

CAMERON. *St. Patrick's Manor*, 514 Northland Dr., 64429. Tel: 816-632-1684; Fax: 816-632-7624. Email: cpp61587@centurytel.net. Nancy Williams, Mgr.; Mr. Neal D. Colby Jr., Diocesan Dir. A 31-unit apartment residence for the elderly and disabled. Total Staff 3.

LIBERTY. *Our Lady of Mercy Country Home*, 2205 Hughes Rd., 64068. Tel: 816-781-5711; Fax: 816-781-7276. Email: olmadm@ourladyofmercy.net. Web: ourladyofmercy.net. Sr. Sandra Thibodeaux, M.M.B., Regl. Moderator. Mercedarian Missionaries of Berriz Guest Capacity 105; Sisters 16; Total Assisted 44; Total Staff 50.

SAVANNAH. *La Verna Heights Retirement Center, Inc.*, 104 E. Park Ave., P.O. Box 488, 64485-0488. Tel: 816-324-3179; Fax: 816-324-7264. Email: osf@ccp.com. Michael Burak, Admin. Sisters of St. Francis of Savannah Guest Capacity 39; Total Assisted 53; Total Staff 36.

La Verna Village Apartments, 1000-1005 Hall Ave., 64485. Tel: 816-324-3179; Fax: 816-324-7264. Email: osf@ccp.com. Web: www.sistersofstfrancis.org. Rev. Marcel Rooney, O.S.B.; Connie Davison, Mgr. Sisters of St. Francis of Savannah, Apartments for the elderly and handicapped. Units 20; Total in Residence 19; Total Staff 2; Total Assisted 25.

La Verna Village Nursing Home, 904 Hall Ave., P.O. Box 279, 64485. Tel: 816-324-3185; Fax: 816-324-4097. Email: lvv@ponyexpress.net. Michael Burak, Admin. Sisters of St. Francis of Savannah Guest Capacity 120; Total Assisted 148; Total Staff 130.

[J] MONASTERIES AND RESIDENCES OF PRIESTS

KANSAS CITY. *Redemptorists Fathers of Kansas City, Missouri*, 3333 Broadway Blvd., 64111. Tel: 816-561-3771; Fax: 816-561-3704. Email: jshea@olph-kc.org. Revs. James Shea, C.SS.R., Rector; Frank Kriski, C.SS.R.; Joseph Curalli, C.SS.R.; J. Terrence McCloskey, C.SS.R.; Eugene Oates, C.Ss.R.; Patrick Power, C.SS.R.; Bros. James Burke, C.SS.R.; Charles Long, C.SS.R.; Michael Schnittker, C.SS.R. Priests 7; Brothers 3.

Rockhurst Jesuit Community, 5133 Forest Ave., 64110-2513. Tel: 816-501-3300; Fax: 816-501-3250. Web: www.rockhurst.edu/jesuitcommunity. Revs. John J. Callahan, S.J., Rector; Dirk J. Dunfee, S.J., Min.; James A. Blumeyer, S.J.; Martin J. Bredeck, S.J.; Edward K. Burger, S.J.; Luke J. Byrne, S.J.; Thomas J. Casey, S.J.; Mark J. Daues, S.J.; D. Scott Hendrickson, S.J., Scholastic; Revs. Edward Kinerk, S.J.; Wilfred L. LaCroix, S.J.; Gerard E. Menard, S.J.; Glenn R. Mueller, S.J.; Louis J. Oldani, S.J.; Thomas A. Pesci, S.J.; Matthew D. Ruhl, S.J.; John Lan Tran, S.J., Scholastic; Revs. John J. Vowells, S.J.; James D. Wheeler, S.J.; Daniel P. White, S.J.; James J. White, S.J.; Bros. E. Glenn Kerfoot, S.J.; John R. Olson, S.J. Total in Residence 23.

Society of Our Lady of the Most Holy Trinity, 3738 Tracy St., 64109. Tel: 816-561-8849. Web: www.solt3.org.

Vincentian Parish Mission Center, 2100 N. Noland Rd., 64050. Tel: 816-254-3000; Fax: 816-254-2204. Email: mn@vpmc.net. Web: www.vpmc.net. Revs. Richard Gielow, C.M., Supr. Tel: 816-254-3700; Francis Crowley, C.M.; Richard O'Brien, C.M.; Michael Mulhearn, C.M.; Carl G. Schulte, C.M. Total in Residence 5.

CONCEPTION. *Conception Abbey* 64433. Tel 660-944-3100; Fax: 660-944-2800. Email: communications@conception.edu. Web: www.ConceptionAbbey.org. Rt. Rev. Gregory Polan, O.S.B., Abbot; Rev. Kenneth Reichert, O.S.B., Prior; Bro. Bernard Montgomery, O.S.B., Subprior; Rt. Rev. James Jones, O.S.B., Retired Abbot (Retired); Revs. Sebastian Allgaier, O.S.B.; Jerome Werth, O.S.B.; Albert Bruecken, O.S.B.; Patrick Caveglia, O.S.B.; Malachy Riley, O.S.B.; Karl Barmann, O.S.B.; Anthony Shider, O.S.B. Benedictine Monks Priests 41; Brothers 19.

St. Gabriel Parish: 4737 N. Cleveland Ave., 64117. Tel: 816-453-1183. Rev. Martin DeMeulenaere, O.S.B., Assoc. Pastor.

Immaculate Conception Cathedral: 416 W. 12th St., 64105. Tel: 816-842-0416, Ext. 131. Revs. Donald Grabner, O.S.B.; Quentin Kathol, O.S.B.

St. Joseph Parish, P.O. Box 78, Parnell, 64475. Tel: 660-986-3305. Revs. Aidan McSorley, O.S.B., Pastor; Xavier Nacke, O.S.B.; Alexander Luetkemeyer, O.S.B.; Benedict Neenan, O.S.B., Seminary Pres. & Rector; Daniel Petsche, O.S.B.

St. Peter Parish: 614 N. Alanthus Ave. Stanberry, 64489. Tel: 660-783-2159. Revs. Regis Probstfield, O.S.B.; Aelred Rosser, O.S.B.; Samuel Russell, O.S.B.; Adam Ryan, O.S.B.; Norbert Schappler, O.S.B.; Joachim Schieber, O.S.B.; Timothy Schoen, O.S.B.; Gilbert Stack, O.S.B.

8332 Belleview, 64114. Tel: 816-444-3031. Revs. Hugh Tasch, O.S.B.; Paschal Thomas, O.S.B.; Isaac True, O.S.B.; Peter Ullrich, O.S.B.

LIBERTY. *Precious Blood Center*, 2130 Hughes Rd., 64068. Tel: 816-781-4344; Fax: 816-781-3639. Email: kcprov@sbcglobal.net. Revs. Paul Sattler, C.PP.S., Supr.; Bernard Mullen, C.PP.S.; Ralph Bushell, C.PP.S.; Thomas A. Conway, C.PP.S.; Aloys Ebach, C.PP.S.; Edmund Weigel, C.PP.S.; William Dineen, C.PP.S.; George Heinzen, C.PP.S.; Leonard Goettemoeller, C.PP.S.; Bros. Joseph Mary Herzo, C.PP.S.; Stephen Ohnmacht, C.PP.S.

Precious Blood Society Provincial Office, P.O. Box 339, 64069-0339. Tel: 816-781-4344; Fax: 816-781-3639. Email: KCProv@sbcglobal.net. Revs. James A. Urbanic, C.PP.S., Prov. Dir.; Aloys Ebach, C.PP.S. Prov. Sec.; William Dineen, C.PP.S., Prov. Treas. Priests 9; Brothers 2.

Savannah

LaVerna Heights Convent, LaVerna Heights Convent: 101 E. Park Ave., Savannah, 64485. Tel: 816-324-3540. Rev. Marcel Rooney, O.S.B., Retired Abbot, Chap.

[K] CONVENTS AND RESIDENCES FOR SISTERS

KANSAS CITY. *Sisters of the Society of Our Lady of the Most Holy Trinity*, 3738 Tracy, 64109. Tel: 816-561-8849. Society of Apostolic Life. Sisters 2.

CLYDE. *Benedictine Convent of Perpetual Adoration*, 31970 State Hwy. P, 64432. Tel: 660-944-2221; Fax: 660-944-2152. Email: sister@benedictinesisters.org. Web: www.benedictinesisters.org. Sr. Ramona Varela, Prioress Gen. Attended by Conception Abbey.; Three other interdependent monasteries: Tucson, AZ; Sand Springs, OK; and Dayton, WY. Membership in Clyde Community 76; Total in Congregation 110; Novices 1; Sisters 109.

INDEPENDENCE. *St. Francis Convent Novitiate and Prayer Center*, 2100 N. Noland Rd., 64050. Tel: 816-252-1673; Fax: 816-252-5574. Email: STFRAN2100@aol.com. Sr. M. Connie Boulch, O.S.F., Supr. Motherhouse of the Sisters of St. Francis of the Holy Eucharist. Sisters 18.

LIBERTY. *Mercedarian Missionaries of Berriz*, U.S. Regional Headquarters, 2205 Hughes Rd., #101B, 64068-7985. Tel: 816-781-8202; Fax: 816-781-8205. Email: mmbus@earthlink.net. Sr. Betty Preston, M.M.B., Regl. Representative. Mercedarian Missionaries of Berriz 10.

Mercedarian Missionaries of Berriz (M.M.B.), 2209 Hughes Rd., 64068. Tel: 816-415-3024. Sr. Jacinta Fernandez, M.M.B., Local Coord. Sisters 4.

Mercedarian Missionaries of Berriz (M.M.B.), 2213 Hughes Rd., 64068. Tel: 816-415-3133. Email: JSFta@aol.com. Sr. Sandra Thibeau, M.M.B., Local Coord. Sisters 3.

Queen of Angels Monastery - Benedictine Sisters, 23615 N.E. 100th St., 64068-8713. Tel: 816-750-4618; Fax: 816-750-4629. Email: benedictinesisters@earthlink.com. Sr. Mary Imelda Koch, O.S.B., Prioress. Sisters 10; Total in Residence 10.

SAVANNAH. *La Verna Heights Provincial House*, 104 E. Park, Box 488, 64485-0488. Tel: 816-324-3179; Fax: 816-324-7264. Email: osf@ccp.com. Web: sistersofstfrancis.org. Rev. Marcel Rooney, O.S.B. Sisters of St. Francis of Savannah, MO. Motherhouse and Novitiate. Sisters 20.

Maintenance and Custodial Care Trust of the Franciscan Sisters of Savannah, MO Tel: 816-324-3179; Fax: 816-324-7264.

[L] SERVICES

KANSAS CITY. *Bishop Sullivan Center*, 6435 Truman Rd., 64126. Tel: 816-231-0984; Fax: 816-231-3096. Email: tturner@bishopsullivan.org. Web: www.bishopsullivan.org. Rev. Thomas W. Turner, Dir. Total Assisted 17,000; Total Staff 10.

Redemptorist Social Services Center, Inc., 207 Linwood Blvd., 64111-1327. Tel: 816-931-9942; Fax: 816-531-0583. Email: redemptcen@yahoo.com. Loring Henderson, Dir.

**Seton Center Family & Health Services*, 2816 E. 23 St., 64127. Tel: 816-231-3955. Email: rasaro@pei.edu. Rachel A. Asaro, Dir. Total Assisted 14,000; Total Staff 24.

[M] NEWMAN CENTERS

KANSAS CITY. *Avila University Campus Ministry*, Formerly Avila College Campus Ministry 11901 Wornall Rd., 64145. Tel: 816-501-2423; Fax: 816-501-2454. Email: armstrongom@mail.avila.edu. Web: www.avila.edu. David Armstrong, Dir. Campus Ministry.

MARYVILLE. *Newman Catholic Center, Northwest Missouri State University* 606 College Ave., 64468. Tel: 660-582-7373. Email: newman@msc.net.

WARRENSBURG. *Newman Center Catholic Campus Ministry for Central Missouri State University*, Formerly Newman Center Central Missouri State University 106 Broad St., 64093. Tel: 660-747-6997; Fax: 660-747-6997. Email: newman@earthlink. Web: www.cmsuz.cmsu.edu/~newmancenter. Shari Reilly, Dir.

[N] MISCELLANEOUS

KANSAS CITY. *St. Anthony's Home*, 300 E. 36th St., P.O. Box 419037, 64141-6037. Tel: 816-756-1850.

Bishop Boland Institute for Housing and Community Development, P.O. Box 419037, 64141-6037. Tel: 816-756-1850; Fax: 816-756-5221. Mr. Neal Colby Jr., Dir.

Camp Little Flower, 300 E. 36th St., P.O. Box 419037, 64141. Tel: 816-756-1850. Rose-Mary Montemore, Pres.

Catholic Charities Foundation, 301 E. Armour Blvd.- Suite 620, 64111. Tel: 816-756-1858, Ext. 562; Fax: 816-756-5022. Paula Moss, Dir.

Diocesan Council of Catholic Women, 300 E. 36th St., P.O. Box 419037, 64141. Tel: 816-756-1850. Email: kcdietch@aol.com. Rev. Joseph A. Mancuso, Diocesan Moderator; Elizabeth Dietrich, Contact Person.

Diocesan Education Endowment Trust Fund, 300 E. 36th St., P.O. Box 419037, 64111. Tel: 816-756-1850; Fax: 816-756-5089. Email: minges@diocesekcsj.org. Web: www.diocese-kcsj.org. Mr. Thomas Minges, Contact Person.

Friends, Inc., 300 E. 36th St., P.O. Box 419037, 64141-6037. Tel: 816-756-1850.

Immacolata Retreat Center, 300 E. 36th St., P.O. Box 419037, 64141-6037. Tel: 816-756-1850.

St. John's Seminary, Inc., P.O. Box 419037, 64141-6037.

Knights of St. Peter Claver (K.P.C.) Ladies Auxiliary of St. Peter Claver. , 1616 Paseo, St. Monica Parish, 64108. Tel: 816-471-3696.

Ladies of Charity of Metropolitan Kansas City, P.O. Box 480753, 64148-0753. Tel: 816-968-9046. Mrs. Mary Brenneman, Pres. A group of volunteers who work and raise money to help the poor and those in need through Seton Center and other agencies.

Marillac Home for Children, P.O. Box 419037, 64141-6037.

Our Lady of Perpetual Help Charitable Trust, 3333 Broadway, 64111. Tel: 816-561-3771; Fax: 816-561-3704. Email: jshea@olph-kc.org. Web: www.redemptorist.net. Rev. James Shea, C.SS.R., Contact Person.

Siena Club, 300 E. 36th St., P.O. Box 419037, 64141. Tel: 816-756-1850.

CONCEPTION. **The Pontifical Institute of Liturgy Foundation*, Conception Abbey Office, P.O. Box 16, 64433. Tel: 660-944-2820; Fax: 660-944-2800. Email: patrick@conception.edu. Web: www.santanselmo.us. Rev. Patrick Caveglia, O.S.B.

INDEPENDENCE. *Cursillo*, 3623 Harvard, 64052. Tel: 816-254-1528; Fax: 816-358-4155. Email: jmcme1528@aol.com. Deacon Justin McMenamy, Spiritual Dir.

LEE'S SUMMIT. *Mercy Midwest Properties*, Tel: 402-398-6614; Fax: 402-393-2144. Email: cwehrewein@mercyhousing.org. *Mercy Housing Midwest*, 7262 Mercy Rd., Omaha, NE 68124-2348. Tel: 402-398-6614; Fax: 402-393-2144. Email: cwehrwein@mercyhousing.org. Affordable service enriched housing for individuals and families who are economically poor. Total Assisted 141; Total Staff 3.

Mercy Midwest Properties, 920 Northeast Ridgeview Dr., #A, 64086. Tel: 816-525-0990; Fax: 816-525-0078.

LIBERTY. **St. Gaspar Society*, P.O. Box 339, 64069. Tel: 816-781-4344; Fax: 816-781-3639. Email: kcprov@sbcglobal.net. Revs. Ralph Bushell, C.PP.S., Sec.; William Dineen, Treas.

Our Lady of Mercy Home, 2205 Hughes Rd., 64068-9469. Tel: 816-781-5711; Fax: 816-781-7276.

**Queen of Angels Foundation, Inc.*, 23615 N.E. 100th St., 64068. Tel: 816-750-4618; Fax: 816-750-4629. Email: benedictinesisters@earthlink.com.

MARYVILLE. *St. Francis Hospital Foundation*, 2016 S. Main, 64468. Tel: 660-562-7933; Fax: 660-562-7911. Member of SSM Health Care.

RELIGIOUS INSTITUTES OF MEN REPRESENTED IN THE DIOCESE

For further details refer to the corresponding bracketed number in the Religious Institutes of Men or Women section.

[0200]—*Benedictine Monks* (Conception Abbey)—O.S.B.

[]—*Christian Brothers of the Midwest, Burr Ridge, FSC.*

[1330]—*Congregation of the Mission* (Western Prov.)—C.M.

[1210]—*Congregation of the Missionaries of St. Charles*—C.S.

[0690]—*Jesuit Fathers and Brothers* (Missouri Prov.)—S.J.

[1070]—*Redemptorist Fathers of Kansas City, Missouri* (Denver Prov.)—C.SS.R.

[]—*Society of Our Lady of Most Holy Trinity*—S.O.L.T.

[1060]—*Society of the Precious Blood* (Kansas City Prov.)—C.PP.S.

RELIGIOUS INSTITUTES OF WOMEN REPRESENTED IN THE DIOCESE

[0230]—*Benedictine Sisters of Pontifical Jurisdiction* (Atchinson, KS; Columbia, MO; Liberty, MO)—O.S.B.

[]—*Congregation of Mary Queen* (Springfield, MO)—C.M.R.

[0220]—*Congregation of the Benedictine Sisters of Perpetual Adoration of Pontifical Jurisdiction*—O.S.B.

[0760]—*Daughters of Charity of St. Vincent de Paul*—D.C.

[]—*Dominican Sisters* (Sinsinawa, WI)—O.P.

[1415]—*Franciscan Sisters of Mary*—F.S.M.

[2575]—*Institute of the Sisters of Mercy of the Americas* (Omaha, NE)—R.S.M.

[2340]—*Little Sisters of the Poor*—L.S.P.

[2510]—*Mercedarian Missionaries of Berriz*—M.M.B.

[]—*Notre Dame Sisters* (Omaha, NE)—N.D.

[]—*School Sisters of St. Francis* (Milwaukee, WI)—O.S.F.

[]—*Sister Servants of Immaculate Heart of Mary* (Monroe, MI)—I.H.M.

[0480]—*Sisters of Charity of Leavenworth, Kansas*—S.C.L.

[0430]—*Sisters of Charity of the Blessed Virgin Mary*—B.V.M.

[2360]—*Sisters of Loretto at the Foot of the Cross*—S.L.

[1540]—*Sisters of St. Francis* (Clinton, IA)—O.S.F.

[1670]—*Sisters of St. Francis of Savannah, MO*—O.S.F.

[1560]—*Sisters of St. Francis of the Holy Eucharist* (Independence, MO)—O.S.F.

[]—*Sisters of St. Francis of the Holy Eucharist Foundation*

[3830-15]—*Sisters of St. Joseph* (Concordia, KS)—C.S.J.

[3830-18]—*Sisters of St. Joseph* (Wichita, KS)—C.S.J.

[3840]—*Sisters of St. Joseph of Carondelet*—C.S.J.

[]—*Society of Our Lady of the Most Holy Trinity*—S.O.L.T.

[4120-04]—*Ursuline Nuns* (Cleveland, OH)—O.S.U.

[4120-05]—*Ursuline Nuns* (Maple Mount, KY)—O.S.U.

DIOCESAN CEMETERIES

KANSAS CITY. *Mount Olivet & Mount St. Mary*

ST. JOSEPH. *Mount Olivet*

KANSAS CITY NORTH. *Resurrection*

NECROLOGY

† Kearney, Rev. Msgr. Vincent L., (Retired)—Died April 15, 2003

† McCarthy, Thomas H., (Retired)—Died July 2, 2003

† Meisburger, Joseph C., (Retired)—Died Dec. 12, 2002

Diocese of Knoxville

Most Reverend

JOSEPH E. KURTZ, D.D.

Bishop of Knoxville; ordained 1972; appointed Bishop of Knoxville October 26, 1999; ordained and installed December 8, 1999.

Chancery Office: 805 Northshore Dr., S.W., P.O. Box 11127, Knoxville, TN 37939-1127. Tel: 865-584-3307.

ESTABLISHED SEPTEMBER 8, 1988.

Square Miles 14,242.

Comprises the Counties of Anderson, Bledsoe, Blount, Bradley, Campbell, Carter, Claiborne, Cocke, Cumberland, Fentress, Grainger, Greene, Hamblen, Hamilton, Hancock, Hawkins, Jefferson, Johnson, Knox, Loudon, McMinn, Marion, Meigs, Monroe, Morgan, Pickett, Polk, Rhea, Roane, Scott, Sequatchie, Sevier, Sullivan, Unicoi, Union and Washington in the State of Tennessee.

Legal Title: For legal titles of parishes and diocesan institutions, consult the Chancery Office.

STATISTICAL OVERVIEW

Personnel	
Bishop	1
Priests: Diocesan Active in Diocese	45
Priests: Diocesan Active Outside Diocese	2
Priests: Retired, Sick or Absent	7
Number of Diocesan Priests	54
Religious Priests in Diocese	17
Total Priests in Diocese	71
Extern Priests in Diocese	7
Permanent Deacons in Diocese	23
Total Brothers	12
Total Sisters	35
Parishes	
Parishes	44
With Resident Pastor:	
Resident Diocesan Priests	33
Resident Religious Priests	4
Without Resident Pastor:	
Administered by Priests	7
Missions	2
Pastoral Centers	2
Professional Ministry Personnel:	
Brothers	1
Sisters	2
Lay Ministers	34
Welfare	
Catholic Hospitals	2
Total Assisted	426,741
Health Care Centers	1
Total Assisted	429
Homes for the Aged	1
Total Assisted	513
Specialized Homes	1
Total Assisted	85
Special Centers for Social Services	6
Total Assisted	66,138
Educational	
Diocesan Students in Other Seminaries	7
Total Seminarians	7
High Schools, Diocesan and Parish	2
Total Students	1,050
Elementary Schools, Diocesan and Parish	8
Total Students	2,513
Catechesis/Religious Education:	
High School Students	1,339
Elementary Students	3,749
Total Students under Catholic Instruction	8,658
Teachers in the Diocese:	
Priests	2
Brothers	1
Sisters	4
Lay Teachers	265
Vital Statistics	
Receptions into the Church:	
Infant Baptism Totals	857
Adult Baptism Totals	161
Received into Full Communion	173
First Communions	1,137
Confirmations	783
Marriages:	
Catholic	102
Interfaith	106
Total Marriages	208
Deaths	332
Total Catholic Population	50,478
Total Population	2,175,795

Former Bishops—Most Rev. ANTHONY J. O'CONNELL, ord. 1963; appt. Bishop of Knoxville May 27, 1988; installed Sept. 8, 1988; appt. Bishop of Palm Beach Nov. 11, 1998.

Vicar General—Rev. FRANCIS XAVIER MANKEL, V.G., S.T.L.

Deans of the Diocese—Revs. WILLIAM H. GAHAGAN, Five Rivers Deanery; MICHAEL CRESON, Chattanooga Deanery; MICHAEL SWEENEY, Cumberland Mtn. Deanery; T. ALLEN HUMBRECHT, Smoky Mtn. Deanery.

Chancery Office—805 Northshore Dr. S.W., P.O. Box 11127, Knoxville, 37939-1127. Tel: 865-584-3307; Fax: 865-584-7538. Office Hours: Mon-Fri 9-5.; All official business should be directed to this office.

Moderator of the Curia—Rev. J. VANN JOHNSTON JR., J.C.L.

Chancellor—Rev. J. VANN JOHNSTON JR., J.C.L.

Auditors— All priests on assignment in the diocese.

Presbyteral Council—Revs. DAVID BOETTNER; JOSEPH J. BRANDO; PATRICK BROWNELL; WILLIAM C. CASEY; MICHAEL CRESON, Dean; WILLIAM H. GAHAGAN, Dean; G. PATRICK GARRITY; JAMES A. HALEY, C.S.P., Chm.; T. ALLEN HUMBRECHT, Dean; J. VANN JOHNSTON JR., J.C.L.; FRANCIS XAVIER MANKEL, V.G., S.T.L.; CHRISTIAN MATHIS, Recording Sec.; MICHAEL F. NOLAN, Vice Chm.; MICHAEL SWEENEY, Dean.

Diocesan Consultors—Revs. DAVID BOETTNER; JOSEPH J. BRANDO; WILLIAM C. CASEY; WILLIAM H. GAHAGAN, Dean; ROBERT J. HOFSTETTER; T. ALLEN HUMBRECHT, Dean; FRANCIS XAVIER MANKEL, V.G., S.T.L.; CHRIS MICHELSON; TOM VOS, O.F.M.

Diocesan Finance Council—DORMAN BLAINE; J. MICHAEL CONNOR, Chm.; LARRY COOL, Ex Officio, Diocesan Finance Officer; SHARON FOLK; RUDY HOGAN; SUZANNE P. ERPENBACH, Ex Officio, Diocesan Dir., Stewardship & Devel.; Revs. FRANCIS XAVIER MANKEL, V.G., S.T.L., Ex Officio; CHRIS MICHELSON; JOHN T. O'CONNOR, Ex Officio, Diocesan Attorney; PAUL PREMO; SOCRATES SABATER; DAVE SANTI; Rev. GEORGE E. SCHMIDT JR.; SUZANNE SCHRIVER; BILL SWAIN; FRAN THIE, Vice Chm.; FRANK VARALLO; GEORGE WARNE.

Diocesan Offices and Directors

Office of Family Life and Adult Christian Living—DALE D. POWERS, Dir., 805 Northshore Dr., S.W., Knoxville, 37919. Tel: 865-524-9896.

Appalachian Community Development—MARIE CIRILLO, Dir., 281 Roses Creek Rd., Clairfield, 37715. Tel: 423-784-6832 Participants in CORE-Appalachian Ministries, a joint project of Dioceses of Covington, Knoxville, Lexington, Nashville, Richmond and Wheeling-Charleston.

Archives—Rev. J. VANN JOHNSTON JR., J.C.L., 805 Northshore Dr., S.W., Knoxville, 37919. Tel: 865-584-3307.

Campus Ministries—

East Tennessee State University—Rev. WILLIAM H. GAHAGAN, Dean & Chap., Catholic Center, 734 W. Locust St., Johnson City, 37604. Tel: 423-926-7061.

University of Tennessee-Chattanooga—Rev. MICHAEL CRESON, Dean & Dir., 514 Palmetto St., Chattanooga, 37403. Tel: 423-267-3064.

University of Tennessee-Knoxville—Rev. ERIC P. ANDREWS, C.S.P., Dir., 1710 Melrose Pl., Knoxville, 37916. Tel: 865-523-7931.

Catholic Schools Office—Dr. SHERRY G. MORGAN, Supt., 805 Northshore Dr., S.W., Knoxville, 37919. Tel: 865-584-3307.

Catholic Charities of East Tennessee, Inc.—Rev. RAGAN SCHRIVER, Exec. Dir., 119 Dameron Ave., Knoxville, 37917. Tel: 865-524-9896; Fax: 865-971-3575. Email: info@etcatholiccharities.com. The umbrella agency for all Catholic charities of the diocese.

Catholic Campaign for Human Development—Rev. RAGAN SCHRIVER, Dir., 119 Dameron Ave., Knoxville, 37917. Tel: 865-524-9896.

Catholic Charities (Chattanooga Area)—LYNDA DIPRIMA, Admin., 859 McCallie Ave., Chattanooga, 37403. Tel: 423-267-1297.

Catholic Charities (Knoxville Area)—LISA INGLE, Admin., 119 Dameron Ave., Knoxville, 37917. Tel: 865-524-9896.

Catholic Charities (Upper East Tennessee Area)—DEBBIE WOLARY, Admin., 703 East Jackson Blvd., P.O. Box 323, Jonesborough, 37659. Tel: 423-753-3001.

Cemeteries—Revs. J. VANN JOHNSTON JR., J.C.L., Dir., 805 Northshore Dr., S.W., Knoxville, 37919. Tel: 865-584-3307; GEORGE E. SCHMIDT JR., Contact, Mt. Olivet Cemetery in Chattanooga. Tel: 423-266-1618; JAMES A. HALEY, C.S.P., Contact, Calvary Cemetery in Knoxville. Tel: 865-522-1508.

Chancellor—Rev. J. VANN JOHNSTON JR., J.C.L., 805 Northshore Dr., S.W., Knoxville, 37919. Tel: 865-584-3307.

Censor Librorum—Rev. ROBERT J. HOFSTETTER, St. Jude Church, 930 Ashland Ter., Chattanooga, 37415. Tel: 423-870-2386.

Deaf Ministry—Rev. MICHAEL CUMMINS, Dir., St. Mary Church, 2007 Congress Pkwy., Athens, 37303-2813. Tel: 423-745-4277.

Diaconate—Rev. CHARLES BURTON, Dir., 2517 John B. Dennis Hwy., Kingsport, 37660. Tel: 423-288-8101.

Ongoing Formation of Deacons—Rev. GREGORY BOISVERT, A.A., Coord., 2517 John B. Dennis Hwy., Kingsport, 37660. Tel: 423-288-8101.

Diocesan Council of Catholic Women—Rev. FRANCIS XAVIER MANKEL, V.G., S.T.L., Diocesan Spiritual Moderator, P.O. Box 3936, Knoxville, 37927. Tel: 865-522-2205.

Ecumenism—Rev. T. ALLEN HUMBRECHT, Dean & Dir., 805 Northshore Dr., S.W., Knoxville, 37919. Tel: 865-584-3307.

Evangelization—Sr. MARY ALBERTINE PAULUS, R.S.M., Dir., 805 Northshore Dr., S.W., Knoxville, 37919. Tel: 865-584-3307. Email: smaevang@yahoo.com.

Finance Office—LARRY COOL, Diocesan Finance Officer, 805 Northshore Dr., S.W., Knoxville, 37919. Tel: 865-584-3307.

Hispanic Ministry—JACK KRAMER, Dir., 119 Dameron Ave., Knoxville, 37917. Tel: 865-637-4769.

Justice - Peace - Integrity of Creation—GLENDA STRUSS-KEYES, Dir., 119 Dameron Ave., Knoxville, 37917. Tel: 865-540-8348.

Marriage Tribunal—Rev. DEXTER BREWER, J.C.L., J.V., 2400 21st Ave. S., Nashville, 37212-5387. Tel: 615-383-6393 Diocesan marriage tribunal is shared with the Diocese of Nashville.

Ministries of the Chattanooga Deanery—Rev. MICHAEL CRESON, Dean; JANE HUBBARD, Deanery Coord., 859 McCallie Ave., Ste. 302, Chattanooga, 37403. Tel: 423-267-9878.

Ministries of the Five Rivers Deanery—Rev. WILLIAM H. GAHAGAN, Dean, 2211 E. Lakeview Dr., Johnson City, 37601. Tel: 423-282-6367.

Ministries of the Cumberland Mtn. Deanery—Rev. MICHAEL SWEENEY, Dean, 535 Margrave Dr., Harriman, 37748. Tel: 865-882-9838.

Ministries of the Smoky Mtn. Deanery—Rev. T. ALLEN HUMBRECHT, Dean, 711 Northshore Dr., S.W., Knoxville, 37919. Tel: 865-588-0249.

Moderator of the Curia—Rev. J. VANN JOHNSTON JR., J.C.L., 805 Northshore Dr., S.W., Knoxville, 37919. Tel: 865-584-3307.

Priestly Life and Ministry—Rev. PETER IORIO, Dir., 711 Northshore Dr., S.W., Knoxville, 37919. Tel: 865-558-4102.

Propagation of the Faith—Rev. J. VANN JOHNSTON JR., J.C.L., Dir., 805 Northshore Dr., S.W., Knoxville, 37919. Tel: 865-584-3307.

Religious Education—ANNE FREDERICK, Dir., 805 Northshore Dr., S.W., Knoxville, 37919. Tel: 865-584-3307. Email: afrederick@etcatholic.com.

Religious Education Resource Center—ANNE FREDERICK, Dir., 212 Mt. Bethel Rd., Greeneville, 37745. Tel: 800-553-0284 (in state); 423-638-4662 (out of state). Email: caresctr@xtn.net.

Scouting—Deacon OTTO PRESKE, Scout Chap., 535 Buckhorn Rd., Gatlinburg, 37738. Tel: 865-436-5339.

Diocesan Catholic Committee on Scouting—GEORGE C. LECRONE, Chm., 10700 Leeward Lane, Knoxville, 37922. Tel: 865-974-0050.

Stewardship and Development—SUZANNE P. ERPENBACH, Dir., 805 Northshore Dr., S.W., Knoxville, 37919. Tel: 865-584-3307. Email: serpenbach@dioceseofknoxville.org.

"The East Tennessee Catholic"— (Diocesan Newspaper). MARY C. WEAVER, Editor, 805 Northshore Dr., S.W., Knoxville, 37919. Tel: 865-584-3307. Email: mary@etcatholic.com.

Victim Assistance Coordinator—MARLA LENIHAN. Tel: 865-482-1388.

Vocations—Rev. PETER IORIO, Vocation Dir., 805 Northshore Dr., S.W., Knoxville, 37919. Tel: 865-584-3307; Sr. MARY YVETTE GILLEN, R.S.M., Coord. Vocation Promotion for Religious. Tel: 865-457-4073.

Worship and Liturgy—Rev. ALEX WARAKSA, Dir., 805 Northshore Dr., S.W., Knoxville, 37919. Tel: 865-584-3307; 865-982-3672.

Youth Ministry—Rev. MICHAEL CUMMINS, Diocesan Coord., 2007 Congress Pkwy., Athens, 37303-2813. Tel: 423-745-4277; PAT RIECKE, Coord. Chattanooga Deanery, 859 McCallie Ave., Ste. 302, Chattanooga, 37403. Tel: 423-267-9878; LINDA D. MURASKI, Coord., Five Rivers Deanery, 159 Carden Dr., Elizabethton, 37643. Tel: 423-543-7449; ANNE MCGAUGH, Coord., Cumberland Mtn. Deanery, 327 Vermont Ave., Oak Ridge, 37830. Tel: 865-766-8388; THOMAS MIKLUSICAK, Coord., Smoky Mtn. Deanery, 711 Northshore Dr., S.W., Knoxville, 37919. Tel: 865-558-8348.

CLERGY, PARISHES, MISSIONS AND PAROCHIAL SCHOOLS

CITY OF KNOXVILLE
(KNOX COUNTY)

1—CATHEDRAL OF THE SACRED HEART OF JESUS (1956), [JC] Revs. T. Allen Humbrecht; Peter Iorio; William Oruko (Kenya); Deacon James Lawson, Pastoral Assoc. In Res., Rev. J. Vann Johnston Jr., J.C.L.
Res.: 711 Northshore Dr., S.W., 37919. Tel: 865-588-5189; Fax: 865-558-9671.
School—Tel: 865-588-0415; Fax: 865-558-4139. Pamela Bernards, Prin. Brothers 1; Sisters 1; Lay Teachers 67; Students 655.
Catechesis/Religious Program—Tel: 865-584-4528. Brigid Johnson, D.R.E. Students 130.

2—ALL SAINTS CATHOLIC CHURCH (1994), [JC] Revs. Chris Michelson; James Brent Allen Shelton.
Mailing Address: 620 N. Cedar Bluff Rd., 37923. Tel: 865-531-0770; Fax: 865-531-1009. In Res., Rev. Ragan Schriver.
Catechesis/Religious Program—Students 725.

3—HOLY GHOST (1908), [JC] Revs. F. Xavier Mankel, V.G., S.T.L.; John B. Charles O'Neill.
Res.: 111 Hinton Ave., 37917. Tel: 865-522-2205; Fax: 865-525-6051.
School—St. Joseph, 1810 Howard Rd., 37918. Tel: 865-689-3424; Fax: 865-687-7885. Joan Turbyville, Prin. Lay Teachers 22; Students 237.
Catechesis/Religious Program—Betty Krusenklaus, D.R.E. Students 145.

4—IMMACULATE CONCEPTION (1852), (Irish), [CEM] Revs. James A. Haley, C.S.P.; James M. Brucz, C.S.P.
Res.: 414 W. Vine Ave., 37902. Tel: 865-522-1508; Fax: 865-524-8514.
Catechesis/Religious Program—Betty Krusenklaus, D.R.E. Students 133.

5—ST. JOHN NEUMANN (1977), Rev. John R. Dowling; Deacons Donald Amelse; Marquis Syler. In Res., Rev. John Arthur Orr.
Church: 225 Jamestowne Blvd., 37922. Tel: 865-966-4540; Fax: 865-966-4541.
Res.: 300 Dominion Cir., 37922. Tel: 865-966-8924.
School—625 St. John Ct., 37922. Tel: 865-777-0077; Fax: 865-777-0087. Dotti Morris, Prin. Lay Teachers 25; Students 306.
Catechesis/Religious Program—Anita Gouge, D.R.E.; Deacon Donald Amelse, D.R.E. Students 377.

6—JOHN XXIII UNIVERSITY PARISH/CATHOLIC CENTER (1968), [CEM], (Non-territorial parish for the University of Tennessee at Knoxville). Revs. Eric P. Andrews, C.S.P.; Robert M. Cary, C.S.P., Assoc. Pastor; Ruth Queen Smith, Pastoral Assoc.
Res.: 1710 Melrose Pl., 37916. Tel: 865-523-7931; Fax: 865-523-7979.
Catechesis/Religious Program—Students 42.

OUTSIDE THE CITY OF KNOXVILLE

ALCOA, BLOUNT CO., OUR LADY OF FATIMA (1950), Revs. Alex J. Waraksa; William L. McKenzie.
Res.: 860 Louisville Rd., 37701. Tel: 865-982-3672; Fax: 865-977-4183.
Catechesis/Religious Program—Tel: 865-981-2676; Fax: 865-983-3563. LuAnne Zelasko, D.R.E. Students 290.
Mission—St. Francis of Assisi 7717 River Rd., Townsend, Blount Co. 37882. Tel: 865-448-6070. Rev. Joseph W. Julius; Deacon Michael G. Nestor.
Catechesis/Religious Program—Students 21.

ATHENS, MCMINN CO., ST. MARY (1968), Rev. Michael E. Cummins.
Res.: 2007 Congress Pkwy., 37303. Tel: 423-745-4277; Fax: 423-745-4277.
Catechesis/Religious Program—Tel: 423-476-7869. Joyce Spurlin, D.R.E. Students 130.

CHATTANOOGA, HAMILTON CO.

1—ST. JUDE (1958), [JC] Revs. Robert J. Hofstetter; Mark Scholz.
Res.: 930 Ashland Ter., 37415. Tel: 423-870-2386; Fax: 423-876-8960.
School—Tel: 423-877-6022; Fax: 423-875-8920. Jamie Goodhard, Prin. Lay Teachers 30; Students 397.
Catechesis/Religious Program—Students 165.

2—OUR LADY OF PERPETUAL HELP (1937), Revs. Michael F. Nolan; James L. Vick; Deacons Mark Gang Jr.; William Oleck.
Res.: 501 S. Moore Rd., 37412. Tel: 423-622-7232; Fax: 423-624-2686. Web: myolph.com.
School—505 S. Moore Rd., 37412. Tel: 423-622-1418; Fax: 423-622-2016. Mrs. Ray Ann Kurtz, Prin. Lay Teachers 34; Students 413.
Catechesis/Religious Program—Tel: 423-622-7232; Fax: 423-624-2686. Lois Colosia, D.R.E. Students 146.

3—SS. PETER AND PAUL (1852), [JC] Rev. George E. Schmidt Jr.; Deacon James Wilson. In Res., Rev. Bertin Glennon, S.T.
Res.: 214 E. 8th St., 37402. Tel: 423-266-1618.
Catechesis/Religious Program—Tel: 423-935-4518. Students 70.

4—ST. STEPHEN (1961), [JC] Rev. P. J. McGinnity. In Res., Rev. John Appiah.
Res.: 7111 Lee Hwy., 37421. Tel: 423-892-1261; Fax: 423-892-3242.
Catechesis/Religious Program—Tel: 423-892-2957. Students 161.

CLEVELAND, BRADLEY CO., ST. THERESE OF LISIEUX (1914), Revs. Joseph J. Brando; Jesus Antonio Giraldo (Colombia).
Res.: 900 Clingan Ridge Dr., N.W., 37312. Tel: 423-476-8123; Fax: 423-479-3339.
Catechesis/Religious Program—Tel: 423-479-4205. David Wilson, D.R.E. Students 326.

CLINTON, ANDERSON CO., ST. THERESE (1971), Rev. Gerard J. Finucane; Sr. Yvette Gillen, R.S.M., Pastoral Assoc.
Church & Res.: 701 S. Charles G. Seivers Blvd., 37716. Tel: 865-457-4073 (Church); 865-457-1317 (Res.); Fax: 865-463-9734.
Catechesis/Religious Program—Students 60.

COPPERHILL, POLK CO., ST. CATHERINE LABOURE (1977), Attended by, St. Mary, Athens. , Mailing Address: Box 566, 37317. Tel: 423-496-3498. In Res., Rev. Paul A. Hostettler (Retired).
Catechesis/Religious Program—Tel: 706-374-6362. Students 7.

CROSSVILLE, CUMBERLAND CO., ST. ALPHONSUS (1948), Rev. Patrick P. Brownell; Deacon Joseph Solis.
Res.: 151 St. Alphonsus Way, 38555. Tel: 931-484-2358 (Office); 931-456-5005 (Res.); Fax: 931-484-7407.
Catechesis/Religious Program—Tel: 931-456-5227. Sara Carey, D.R.E. Students 180.

DAYTON, RHEA CO., ST. BRIDGET (1969), Rev. Gilbert M. Diaz; Deacons Tom Kiefer; Michael Kucharzak.
Res.: 320 Walnut Grove Church Rd., 37321. Tel: 423-775-2664 (Church); 423-775-5542 (Rectory); Fax: 423-775-2607.
Catechesis/Religious Program—Students 51.

DUNLAP, SEQUATCHIE CO., SHEPHERD OF THE VALLEY (1997), Rev. Thomas W. Moser.
Res.: 110 Old York Hwy., P.O. Box 1747, 37327. Tel: 423-949-6903; Fax: 423-837-7793.
Catechesis/Religious Program—Students 7.

ELIZABETHTON, CARTER CO., ST. ELIZABETH (1916), Rev. Dennis Kress.
Res.: 510 W. C St., 37643. Tel: 423-543-3412; Fax: 423-542-2961.
Catechesis/Religious Program—Donna Townsend, D.R.E. Students 22.

FAIRFIELD GLADE, CUMBERLAND CO., ST. FRANCIS OF ASSISI (1983), [CEM] Rev. Gregory Neuzil; Deacons Mark A. Fredrick; Mark F. White; Keith S. Farber.
Res.: 7503 Peavine Rd., 38571. Tel: 931-484-3628; Fax: 931-707-0186.
Catechesis/Religious Program—Students 6.

GATLINBURG, SEVIER CO., ST. MARY (1935), Rev. Philip F. Thoni (Retired); Deacon Otto Preske.
Res.: 304 Historic Nature Tr., 37738. Tel: 865-436-4907; Fax: 865-430-3623.
Catechesis/Religious Program—Students 26.

GREENEVILLE, GREENE CO., NOTRE DAME (1955), Rev. James P. Harvey. In Res., Rev. Joseph Mary Hammond, C.H.S. (Venezuela).
Res.: 212 Mt. Bethel Rd., 37745. Tel: 423-639-9381; Fax: 423-638-5219.
Catechesis/Religious Program—Tel: 423-638-9510. Susan Collins, D.R.E. Students 87.

HARRIMAN, ROANE CO., BLESSED SACRAMENT (1908), Rev. Michael Sweeney.
Res.: 535 Margrave Dr., 37748. Tel: 865-882-9838; Fax: 865-882-3786 (Rectory); 865-882-5491 (Sec.).
Catechesis/Religious Program—Students 71.
Mission—Mission Catholic Community of Fentress County c/o Jim Romer, 204 Tinch Ave., Jamestown, Fentress Co. 38556-5221. Tel: 931-879-8144; Fax: 931-879-8145.
Catechesis/Religious Program—Students 10.
Station—Brushy Mountain Prison Wartburg. Tel: 865-346-6641.
Station—Morgan County Regional Correctional Facility Wartburg.

HELENWOOD, SCOTT CO., ST. JUDE PARISH (1982), Rev. Joseph Campbell; Sr. Patricia Soete, R.S.M., Pastoral Assoc.
Mailing Address: 13067 Scott Hwy; P.O. Box 555, 37755. Tel: 423-569-9584 (Church).
Catechesis/Religious Program—Students 12.

JEFFERSON CITY, JEFFERSON CO., HOLY TRINITY CATHOLIC CHURCH (1997), Rev. Dan G. Whitman.
475 N. Hwy. 92, P.O. Box 304, 37760. Tel: 865-471-0347; Fax: 865-471-0349.
Catechesis/Religious Program—Students 53.

JOHNSON CITY, WASHINGTON CO., ST. MARY (1906), Revs. William H. Gahagan; Christian Mathis.
Res.: 2211 E. Lakeview Dr., 37601. Tel: 423-282-8696; Fax: 423-282-6145.
School—Tel: 423-282-3397; Fax: 423-282-0224. Michele O'Hare, Prin. Lay Teachers 33; Students 192.
Catechesis/Religious Program—Tel: 423-282-6367. Anne DeVeaux, D.R.E. Students 252.

KINGSPORT, SULLIVAN CO., ST. DOMINIC (1941), Revs. Charles Burton; Gregory Boisvert, A.A. (BO); Deacon Robert Lange.
Res.: 2517 John B. Dennis Hwy., 37660. Tel: 423-288-8101; Fax: 423-288-7183.
School—Tel: 423-245-0362; Fax: 423-245-2907. Debbie DePollo, Prin. Lay Teachers 15; Students 84.
Catechesis/Religious Program—Tel: 423-288-8101. Shirley Parsons, D.R.E. Students 247.

LAFOLLETTE, CAMPBELL CO., OUR LADY OF PERPETUAL HELP (1905), Rev. Joe Campbell.

Mailing Address: 1142 E. Elm St., 37766. Tel: 423-562-0312; Fax: 423-562-0352.
Catechesis/Religious Program—Tel: 423-562-9165. Students 22.

LANCING, MORGAN CO., ST. ANN (1982), Attended by, Blessed Sacrament, Harriman. Rev. Michael Sweeney.
Mailing Address: P.O. Box 77, 37770-0077. Tel: 865-346-6260; Fax: 865-882-5491.
Catechesis/Religious Program—Tel: 865-882-3786. Students 13.

LENOIR CITY, LOUDON CO., ST. THOMAS THE APOSTLE (1973), Rev. David Boettner; Deacon Jose Rivera.
Res.: 1580 St. Thomas Way, 37772. Tel: 865-986-9885; Fax: 865-988-8230.
Catechesis/Religious Program—Students 91.

MADISONVILLE, MONROE CO., ST. JOSEPH THE WORKER (1992),, (Quasi Parish) Rev. Thomas Vos, O.F.M.; Mr. Paul Witte, Pastoral Coord. Tel: 423-442-5530; Rev. Edward Boren, O.F.M. (JOL).
Mailing Address: 649 Old Tellico Hwy. N., P.O. Box 880, 37354. Tel: 423-442-7273; Fax: 423-442-7272.
Catechesis/Religious Program—Students 8.

MORRISTOWN, HAMBLEN CO., ST. PATRICK (1959), Revs. G. Patrick Garrity; Joseph Hammond (Venezuela); Deacon Gerald James Fage.
Res.: 2518 W. Andrew Johnson Hwy., 37814. Tel: 423-586-9174; Fax: 423-318-7044.
Catechesis/Religious Program—Tel: 423-586-4091. Diane McGuire, D.R.E. (High School). Students 177.

MOUNTAIN CITY, JOHNSON CO., ST. ANTHONY OF PADUA CATHOLIC CHURCH (1995),, (Quasi Parish) Rev. John Milewski.
Res.: 513 Hickory St., 37683. Tel: 423-727-7870; Fax: 423-727-5017.
Church: 833 W. Main St., 37683. Tel: 423-727-5156; Fax: 423-727-5017.
Catechesis/Religious Program—Students 11.

NEWPORT, COCKE CO., GOOD SHEPHERD (1967), Attended by, Holy Trinity, Jefferson City Rev. Dan G. Whitman; Mr. Dennis H. Bible, Parish Coord.
Mailing Address: 659 E. Broadway, 37821. Tel: 423-623-5051.
Catechesis/Religious Program—Students 13.

NORRIS, ANDERSON CO., ST. JOSEPH (1949), Rev. Gerard J. Finucane.
Res.: 3452 Andersonville Hwy. 61, P.O. Box 387, 37828. Tel: 865-494-7746.
Catechesis/Religious Program—Laura Seymour, D.R.E. Students 59.

OAK RIDGE, ANDERSON CO., ST. MARY (1943), Revs. Michael A. Woods; Samuel Sturm.
Res.: 327 Vermont Ave., 37830. Tel: 865-482-2875; Fax: 865-482-0443.
School—323 Vermont Ave., 37830. Tel: 865-483-9700; Fax: 865-482-8305. Sr. Mary Charles Sterne, O.P., Prin. Sisters 4; Lay Teachers 18; Students 216.
Catechesis/Religious Program—Tel: 865-483-0958; Fax: 865-482-0443. Students 302.

PIGEON FORGE, SEVIER CO., HOLY CROSS (1992), Rev. Jay M. Flaherty.
Church: 144 Wears Valley Rd., 37863. Tel: 865-429-5587; Fax: 865-453-8951.
Catechesis/Religious Program—Students 101.

ROGERSVILLE, HAWKINS CO., ST. HENRY (1981), Rev. Michael T. Jennings.
Res.: 112-114 Hwy. 70 N., 37857. Tel: 423-272-6897.
Catechesis/Religious Program—Students 27.

SEYMOUR, SEVIER CO., HOLY FAMILY (1984), Rev. Thomas P. O'Connell.
Mailing Address: 407 Overlook Dr., 37865. Tel: 865-609-1081; Fax: 865-579-3645.
Catechesis/Religious Program—Tel: 865-577-3881. Valerie Priddy, D.R.E.; Carol Idol, D.R.E. Students 70.

SIGNAL MOUNTAIN, HAMILTON CO., ST. AUGUSTINE (1938), [JC] Rev. Paul Valleroy; Deacon Gordon Kilburn.
Res.: 1716 Anderson Pike, P.O. Box 10, 37377. Tel: 423-886-3424; Fax: 423-886-3451.
Catechesis/Religious Program—Students 180.

SNEEDVILLE, HANCOCK CO., ST. JAMES THE APOSTLE (1982), Attended by, St. Henry, Rogersville. Rev. Mike Jennings.
Mailing and Res.: P.O. Box 93, 37869. Tel: 423-272-6897.

SODDY DAISY, HAMILTON CO., HOLY SPIRIT CATHOLIC CHURCH (1999), Rev. Michael Creson.
Res. & Mailing Address: 10812 Dayton Pike, P.O. Box 1015, 37384. Tel: 423-332-5300; Fax: 423-332-5391.
Catechesis/Religious Program—Students 37.

SOUTH PITTSBURG, MARION CO., OUR LADY OF LOURDES (1899), Rev. Thomas W. Moser.
Res.: 700 Holly Ave., P.O. Box 288, 37380. Tel: 423-837-7068; Fax: 423-837-7793.
Mission—Virgin of the Poor Shrine Marian, Marian Co.
Catechesis/Religious Program—Students 22.

TAZEWELL, CLAIBORNE CO., CHRIST THE KING (1990), Rev. Joseph Campbell.
Mailing Address: P.O. Box 404, 37879.
Res.: 1142 E. Elm St., LaFollette, 37766. Tel: 423-562-0312.
Catechesis/Religious Program—Students 14.

TOWNSEND, BLOUNT CO., ST. FRANCIS OF ASSISI (1961), Attended by, Our Lady of Fatima, Alcoa. , Mailing Address: 7717 River Rd., 37882. Tel: 423-448-6070.
In Res., Rev. Joseph W. Julius (NSH) (Retired).
Catechesis/Religious Program—Students 21.

Retired:
Rev. Msgr.—
Siener, Leo C., Alexian Village Health Care Center, 100 James Blvd., Rm. 736, Signal Mtn., 37377-1816.
Revs.—
Bowes, David, 1402 Suwanee St., Milton, FL 32583-6527.
Brett, Frank X., 175 Casseekee Trail, Lighthouse Cove, Melbourne Beach, FL 32951-3360.
Casey, William, 670 Shake Rag Rd., Greeneville, 37743.
Hostettler, Paul A., P.O. Box 586, Copperhill, 37317.
Prescott, Herbert W., P.O. Box 15341, Chattanooga, 37415.
Thoni, Philip F., (Retired LTC), 304 Historic Nature Tr., Gatlinburg, 37738.

Permanent Deacons:
Amelse, Donald, St. John Neumann, Knoxville
Bresler, Thomas, St. Augustine Chapel, Signal Mountain; Alexian Village
Diesing, William
Fage, G. James, II, St. Patrick, Morristown
Farber, Keith S., St. Francis of Assisi, Fairfield Glade
Fischer, Robert W.
Fredrick, Mark A., St. Francis of Assisi, Fairfield Glade
Gang, Mark, Jr., Our Lady of Perpetual Help, Chattanooga
Hathaway, Donald F., St. Anthony, Mountain City
Kiefer, Thomas, St. Bridget, Dayton
Kilburn, Gordon, St. Augustine, Signal Mountain
Kucharzak, Michael, St. Bridget, Dayton
Lange, Robert, St. Dominic, Kingsport
Lawson, James, Cathedral of the Sacred Heart of Jesus
Nestor, Michael, St. Francis of Assisi, Townsend
Oleck, William A., Our Lady of Perpetual Help, Chattanooga
Preske, Otto F., St. Mary, Gatlinburg
Rivera, Jose, St. Thomas the Apostle, Lenoir City
Solis, Joseph, St. Alphonsus, Crossville
Syler, Marquis E., St. John Neumann, Knoxville
Volek, Ronald J., Holy Family, Seymour
White, Mark F., St. Francis of Assisi, Fairfield Glade
Wilson, James E., SS. Peter and Paul, Chattanooga

INSTITUTIONS LOCATED IN THE DIOCESE

[A] HIGH SCHOOLS, DIOCESAN

KNOXVILLE. *Knoxville Catholic High School* (1932), (Grades 9-12), 9245 Fox Lonas Rd., 37923. Tel: 865-560-0313; Fax: 865-560-0314. Email: kchs@esper.com. Web: knoxvillecatholic.com. Dr. Aurelia M. Montgomery, Prin. Priests 1; Lay Teachers 35; Students 505.
Knoxville Catholic High School Development Board of Trust Tel: 865-560-0509; Fax: 865-560-0314.

CHATTANOOGA. *Notre Dame High School* (1876), (Grades 9-12), 2701 Vermont Ave., 37404. Tel: 423-624-4618; Fax: 423-624-4621. Email: plstoreyndhs@juno.com. Web: www.myndhs.com. Mr. Perry Storey, Prin. Priests 1; Lay Teachers 41; Students 542; Total Staff 20.
Notre Dame High School Financial Board of Trustees

[B] GENERAL HOSPITALS

KNOXVILLE. *St. Mary's Health System, Inc.* (1930), 900 E. Oak Hill Ave., 37917. Tel: 865-545-8000; Fax: 865-545-6732. Email: dlondon@stmaryshealth.com. Web: www.stmaryshealth.com. Debra London, CEO; Rev. Bertrand Demers, Chap. Conducted by Sisters of Mercy of the Americas Sisters 7; Bed Capacity 473; Patients Assisted Annually 224,775; Total Staff 2,212.
St. Mary's Health System, Inc. Tel: 865-545-8000; Fax: 865-545-6732.

CHATTANOOGA. *Memorial Health Care System, Inc.*, Formerly Memorial Hospital2525 DeSales Ave., 37404. Tel: 423-495-2525; Fax: 423-495-7726. Web: memorial.org. Ruth Williams Brinkley, Pres. & CEO. (Member of Catholic Health Initiatives) Sisters 5; Bed Capacity 420; Patients Assisted Annually 201,966; Total Staff 3,400.
Memorial Health Care System Foundation, Inc., 2525 deSales Ave., 37404.

[C] SPECIAL HOSPITALS

SIGNAL MOUNTAIN. *Alexian Village Health Care Center* (1938), 100 James Blvd., 37377. Tel: 423-886-0338; Fax: 423-886-0470. Email: sfoote@abhses.com. Web: www.alexianvillage.com. Bro. Edward Yochim, C.F.A., Dir. of Community; Rev. Maro Cannon, C.F.A., Chap.; Seneca S. Foote, Admin. Licensed Skilled & Intermediate Care Nursing Home. Brothers 10; Bed Capacity 114; Patients Assisted Annually 429; Assisted Living 207; Total Staff 104.

[D] HOMES FOR THE AGED

CHATTANOOGA. *Alexian Grove, Inc.*, 4025 Carl Swafford, 37419. Tel: 847-640-3296. Email: vitellas@alexian.net. Sandra Vitellaro, Contact Person.

SIGNAL MOUNTAIN. *Alexian Village of Tennessee*, 100 James Blvd., 37377. Tel: 423-886-0100; Fax: 423-886-0470. Email: sfoote@abhses.com. Web: www.alexianvillage.com; www.alexianbrotherssoutheast.org. Seneca S. Foote, CEO; Revs. Bede Aboh, Chap.; Maro Cannon, C.F.A., Assoc. Chap.; Camilius Blazek, Assoc. Chap. Life Care Residences and Nursing Home. Life Care Units 277; Total in Residence 513; Total Staff 160.

[E] PROTECTIVE INSTITUTIONS

KNOXVILLE. *Columbus Home, Inc.*, 3227 Division St., 37919. Tel: 865-971-3560; Fax: 865-546-0433. Kevin Leavy, Admin. Total Assisted Annually 85; Total Staff 12.

[F] MONASTERIES AND RESIDENCES OF PRIESTS AND BROTHERS

KNOXVILLE. *Brothers of Holy Cross*, 816 Creswell Ct., 37919-7444. Tel: 865-588-5566. Bro. Roland Driscoll, C.S.C., (Retired). Total in Residence 1; Total Staff 1.
Franciscan Friars, Alverna Friary, 468 Manor View Dr., 37923. Tel: 865-539-1164. Revs. Evan Eckhoff, O.F.M.; Thomas Vos, O.F.M.
Presentation Brothers of Mary, 1409 Buxton Dr., 37922. Tel: 865-694-3135; Fax: 865-694-5080. Email: brofromknox@yahoo.com. Web: www.presentationbrothers.org. Bros. Gerard Despathy, F.P.M.; Bernard Murphy, F.P.M. Total in Residence 2.

LANCING. *Brothers of Holy Cross*, 297 Davidson Rd., 37770. Tel: 423-965-3392. Bro. Paul Bray, C.S.C., Dir.

SIGNAL MOUNTAIN. *Alexian Brothers*, 198 James Blvd., 37377. Tel: 423-886-0380; Fax: 423-886-0381. Email: eyochim@aol.com. Web: www.alexianbrothers.org/. Bros. Edward Walsh, C.F.A., Supr. Gen.; Anthony J. Ragucci, C.F.A., Asst. Dir. Community; Edward Yochim, C.F.A., Dir. Community; James Johnston, C.F.A.; Brian Murphy, C.F.A.; Simeon Pytel, C.F.A., Sec. (Generalate); Andrew Thome, C.F.A., Admin. Asst.; Neelmino Emmanuel, C.F.A.; Rev. Maro Cannon, C.F.A., Chap. Brothers 9.

[G] CONVENTS AND RESIDENCES FOR SISTERS

KNOXVILLE. *Sisters of Mercy* (Cincinnati Region) Tel: 865-545-8128; Fax: 865-545-6732. Email: snaber@stmaryshealth.com. Web: www.stmaryshealth.com.
St. Mary's Medical Center, 900 E. Oak Hill Ave., 37917. Tel: 865-545-8000; Fax: 865-545-6732. Sisters 9.

CHATTANOOGA. *Missionary Sisters of the Sacred Heart of Jesus "Ad Gentes"*, 430 Glenwood Dr., 37404. Sisters 2.
Sisters of Charity of Nazareth, 425 Glenwood Dr., 37404. Tel: 423-624-2293. Sisters 2.

CLINTON. *St. Therese Convent*, 701 S. Charles G. Seivers Blvd., 37716. Tel: 865-463-8935; Fax: 865-463-9734. Email: smyg42@aol.com.

COPPERHILL. *Monastery of Our Lady of Little Citeaux*, 255 Golf Course Rd., 37317. Tel: 423-496-7373. Sisters 2.

HELENWOOD. *Sisters of Mercy*, P.O. Box 555, 13071 Scott Hwy., 37755. Tel: 423-569-3492.

LANCING. *Sisters of Holy Cross*, 641 Island Ford Rd., 37770. Tel: 423-965-3923. Sisters 2.

MOUNTAIN CITY. *Sisters of St. Joseph, Third Order of St. Francis*, 101 Adams Ln., 37683. Tel: 423-727-8909.

OAK RIDGE. *Dominican Sisters (St. Cecilia Congregation)*, St. Mary's Convent, 323 Vermont Ave., 37830. Tel: 865-483-9700; Fax: 865-483-8305. Web: nashvilledominican.org. Sisters 4.

WASHBURN. *Sisters of the Presentation of the Blessed Virgin Mary*, 1936 Liberty Hill Rd., 37888. Tel: 865-497-3238. Email: dennispbvm@aol.com.

[H] NEWMAN CENTERS

KNOXVILLE. *UT-Knoxville, Newman Foundation, Inc. John XXIII University Parish/Catholic Center*, 1710 Melrose Pl., 37916. Tel: 865-523-7931; Fax: 865-523-7979. Email: john23@utk.edu. Web: www.john23rd.org. Revs. Eric P. Andrews, C.S.P.; Robert M. Cary, C.S.P.

CHATTANOOGA. *Newman Foundation of Chattanooga, Inc.* Catholic Student Center, 514 Palmetto St., 37403. Tel: 423-267-3064. Email: cathstudentctr@chattanooga.net. Web: www.catholicdeaneryofchattanooga.org/utcx.html. Rev. Michael Creson, Dean; Marla H. Thurman, Assoc. Campus Min. Total Staff 2.

JOHNSON CITY. *ETSU-Catholic Center* 734 W. Locust St., 37604. Tel: 423-926-7061. Email: ccenter@chartertn.net. Web: www.etsu.edu/newman. Revs. William H. Gahagan, Chap.; Christian Mathis, Dir. of Campus Ministry. Total Staff 1.

[I] MISCELLANEOUS

KNOXVILLE. *The Catholic Diocese of Knoxville Foundation, Inc.*, 805 Northshore Dr., S.W., 37919. Tel: 865-584-3307; Fax: 865-584-7538.

Catholic Foundation of East Tennessee, 805 Northshore Dr., S.W., 37919. Tel: 865-584-3307; Fax: 865-584-7538.

Diocesan Council of Catholic Women, 805 Northshore Dr., S.W., 37919. Tel: 423-581-1815. Revs. F. Xavier Mankel, V.G., S.T.L., Diocesan Spiritual Moderator; William H. Gahagan, Deanery Spiritual Moderator, Five Rivers; Robert J. Hofstetter, Deanery Spiritual Moderator, Chattanooga; F. Xavier Mankel, V.G., S.T.L., Deanery Spiritual Moderator, Smoky Mountain; Michael Woods, Deanery Spiritual Moderator, Cumberland Mountain.

Ladies of Charity, 1031 Central Ave., 37917. Tel: 865-522-6341; 865-524-0538; Fax: 865-524-0538. Rev. F. Xavier Mankel, V.G., S.T.L., Spiritual Moderator. Total Assisted Annually 27,165; Total Staff 6.

CHATTANOOGA. *Ladies of Charity*, 1800 E. Main St., 37404. Tel: 423-624-3222; Fax: 423-698-2606. Gives emergency assistance in the form of food, medicine, clothing, Lifeline, meals on wheels, layettes to new-born, payment on utilities, rent, glasses, dental work, etc. Total Assisted Annually 18,200.

RELIGIOUS INSTITUTES OF MEN REPRESENTED IN THE DIOCESE

For further details refer to the corresponding bracketed number in the Religious Institutes of Men or Women section.

[0120]—*Alexian Brothers*—C.F.A.
[]—*Apostles of Jesus*—A.J.
[0130]—*Assumptionists*—A.A.
[0600]—*Brothers of the Congregation of Holy Cross*—C.S.C.
[]—*Crusaders of the Holy Spirit*—C.H.S.
[0520]—*Franciscan Friars*—O.F.M.
[0570]—*The Glenmary Home Missioners*—Glmy.
[0840]—*Missionary Servants of the Most Holy Trinity*—S.T.
[1030]—*Paulist Fathers*—C.S.P.
[]—*Presentation Brothers of Mary*—F.P.M.

RELIGIOUS INSTITUTES OF WOMEN REPRESENTED IN THE DIOCESE

[1920]—*Congregation of the Sisters of Holy Cross*—C.S.C.
[1070-07]—*Dominican Sisters (St. Cecilia Congregation)*—O.P.
[2575]—*Institute of the Sisters of Mercy of the Americas* (Cincinnati Prov.)—R.S.M.
[]—*Missionary Sisters of the Sacred Heart of Jesus "Ad Gentes"*—M.A.G.
[0500]—*Sisters of Charity of Nazareth*—S.C.N.
[3930]—*Sisters of St. Joseph, Third Order of St. Francis*—S.S.J.-T.O
[0970]—*Sisters of the Divine Compassion*—R.D.C.
[3320]—*Sisters of the Presentation of the B.V.M.*—P.B.V.M.

INTERPAROCHIAL CEMETERIES

KNOXVILLE. *Calvary*, Martin Luther King Blvd., 37915. Tel: 865-522-1508. Rev. James A. Haley, C.S.P.

CHATTANOOGA. *Mount Olivet*, Ringgold Rd., 37412. Tel: 423-266-1618. Rev. George E. Schmidt Jr.

NECROLOGY

† Junod, Louis J., (Retired)—Died June 6, 2003

Diocese of La Crosse

(Dioecesis Crossensis)

Most Reverend

JOHN J. PAUL, D.D.

Retired Bishop of La Crosse; ordained January 24, 1943; appointed Titular Bishop of Lambese and Auxiliary Bishop of La Crosse May 17, 1977; consecrated August 4, 1977; appointed to the Residential See of La Crosse October 18, 1983; installed as Seventh Bishop of La Crosse December 5, 1983; retired December 10, 1994. *Res.: Holy Cross Diocesan Center,* P.O. Box 4004, La Crosse, WI 54602-4004. Tel: 608-788-8395; 608-788-7700.

(VACANT SEE)

Chancery Office: 3710 East Ave. S., P.O. Box 4004, La Crosse, WI 54602-4004. Tel: 608-788-7700; Fax: 608-788-8413.

Web: www.dioceseoflacrosse.com

Email: mailbox@dioceseoflacrosse.com

Square Miles 15,078.

Erected March 3, 1868. Subdivided May 3, 1905. Subdivided January 15, 1946.

Comprises the following 19 Counties in the State of Wisconsin: Adams, Buffalo, Chippewa, Clark, Crawford, Dunn, Eau Claire, Jackson, Juneau, La Crosse, Marathon, Monroe, Pepin, Pierce, Portage, Richland, Trempealeau, Vernon and Wood.

Legal Title: For legal titles of parishes and diocesan institutions, consult the Chancery Office.

STATISTICAL OVERVIEW

Statistical report was not submitted for 2004.

Personnel	
Bishop	1
Retired Bishops	1
Retired Abbots	1
Priests: Diocesan Active in Diocese	113
Priests: Diocesan Active Outside Diocese	6
Priests: Diocesan in Foreign Missions	2
Priests: Retired, Sick or Absent	70
Number of Diocesan Priests	191
Religious Priests in Diocese	21
Total Priests in Diocese	212
Extern Priests in Diocese	18
Ordinations:	
Diocesan Priests	3
Permanent Deacons in Diocese	31
Total Brothers	4
Total Sisters	483
Parishes	
Parishes	166
With Resident Pastor:	
Resident Diocesan Priests	105
Resident Religious Priests	4
Without Resident Pastor:	
Administered by Priests	50
Administered by Religious Women	5
Administered by Lay People	1
Completely Vacant	1
Closed Parishes	2
Professional Ministry Personnel:	
Sisters	13
Lay Ministers	40
Welfare	
Catholic Hospitals	9
Total Assisted	588,146
Homes for the Aged	12
Total Assisted	1,151
Day Care Centers	2
Total Assisted	204
Specialized Homes	6
Total Assisted	11,326
Special Centers for Social Services	2
Total Assisted	3,125
Educational	
Seminaries, Diocesan	1
Students from This Diocese	2
Students from Other Diocese	4
Diocesan Students in Other Seminaries	25
Total Seminarians	27
Colleges and Universities	1
Total Students	2,167
High Schools, Diocesan and Parish	7
Total Students	1,537
Elementary Schools, Diocesan and Parish	77
Total Students	8,791
Catechesis/Religious Education:	
High School Students	7,711
Elementary Students	14,948
Total Students under Catholic Instruction	35,181
Teachers in the Diocese:	
Priests	7
Sisters	14
Lay Teachers	704
Vital Statistics	
Receptions into the Church:	
Infant Baptism Totals	2,858
Adult Baptism Totals	125
Received into Full Communion	287
First Communions	3,059
Confirmations	3,181
Marriages:	
Catholic	833
Interfaith	474
Total Marriages	1,307
Deaths	2,224
Total Catholic Population	215,573
Total Population	848,455

Former Bishops—Most Rev. MICHAEL HEISS, D.D., consecrated Sept. 6, 1868; appt. Titular Archbishop of Hadrianople, and coadjutor to the Metropolitan of Milwaukee March 14, 1880; promoted to Milwaukee, Sept. 1881; died March 26, 1890; Rt. Revs. KILIAN CASPAR FLASCH, D.D., consecrated Aug. 24, 1881; died Aug. 3, 1891; JAMES SCHWEBACH, D.D., consecrated Feb. 25, 1892; died June 6, 1921; Most Revs. ALEXANDER J. MCGAVICK, D.D., LL.D., consecrated Titular Bishop of Marcopolis and Auxiliary Bishop of Chicago, May 1, 1899; transferred to See of La Crosse, Nov. 21, 1921; died Aug. 25, 1948; JOHN P. TREACY, S.T.D., consecrated Titular Bishop of Metelis and Coadjutor of La Crosse "cum jure successionis," Oct. 2, 1945; succeeded to the See, July 23, 1946; died Oct. 11, 1964 FREDERICK W. FREKING, D.D., J.C.D. (Retired), consecrated Bishop of Salina, KS, November 30, 1957; transferred to the See of La Crosse, Dec. 30, 1964; installed La Crosse, Feb. 24, 1965; retired May 10, 1983; died Nov. 28, 1998; JOHN J. PAUL, D.D. (Retired), appt. Titular Bishop of Lambese and Auxiliary Bishop of La Crosse, May 17, 1977; consecrated Aug. 4, 1977; appt. to the Residential See of La Crosse, Oct. 18, 1983; installed as Bishop of La Crosse, Dec. 5, 1983; retired Dec. 10, 1994; RAYMOND L. BURKE, D.D., J.C.D., appointed to the Residential See of La Crosse Dec. 10, 1994; consecrated Jan. 6, 1995; installed as Eighth Bishop of La Crosse Feb. 22, 1995; appointed Archbishop of the Archdiocese of St. Louis Dec. 2, 2003 installed Jan. 26, 2004.

Chancery Office—3710 East Ave. S., P.O. Box 4004, La Crosse, 54602-4004. Tel: 608-788-7700; Fax: 608-788-8413. Office Hours: Mon.-Fri. 8-4:30

Chancellor—Mr. BENEDICT T. NGUYEN, M.T.S., J.C.L.

Vice-Chancellor—Rev. LEON A. POWELL.

Moderator of the Curia—Rev. RICHARD W. GILLES, J.C.L.

Secretary to the Bishop—VACANT.

Archivist—Rev. ROBERT T. ALTMANN (Retired).

Finance Officer—SONDRA RIEDER.

Ecclesiastical Notaries—Revs. RICHARD W. GILLES, J.C.L.; LEON A. POWELL; Mr. BENEDICT T. NGUYEN, M.T.S., J.C.L.; KELLY MCCARTHY; SHERYL STAPLETON; SUSAN VLASAK, P.O. Box 4004, La Crosse, 54602-4004.

Diocesan Tribunal—3710 East Ave. S., P.O. Box 4004, La Crosse, 54602-4004. Tel: 608-788-7700. (Address all rogatory commissions to the Chancellor).

Judicial Vicar—Very Rev. ROBERT P. HUNDT, J.C.L.

Promoter of Justice—Rev. RICHARD W. GILLES, J.C.L.

Defensor Vinculi—Mr. BENEDICT T. NGUYEN, M.T.S., J.C.L.; Rev. FRANCIS ABUAH QUANSAH, J.C.D.

Auditor—SHERYL STAPLETON.

Diocesan Judges—Very Revs. ROBERT P. HUNDT, J.C.L.; MICHAEL J. GORMAN, J.C.L.; Rev. RICHARD W. GILLES, J.C.L.

Deans—Very Revs. DOUGLAS C. ROBERTSON, Arcadia; WILLIAM P. FELIX, Chippewa Falls; JEFFREY D. BURRILL, Durand; PAUL R. GITTER, Eau Claire; ROGER J. SCHECKEL, La Crosse; CHARLES D. STOETZEL, Marshfield; RONALD T. ZINKLE, S.J., Mauston; Very Rev. Msgr. JOHN F. MCCARTHY, P.A., Prairie du Chien; Very Revs. EMMANUEL FAMIYEH, Richland Center; STEVEN J. KACHEL, Sparta; ROBERT A. SCHALLER, Stevens Point; WOODROW H. PACE, Thorp; JOSEPH DIERMEIER, Wausau; WILLIAM G. MENZEL, Wisconsin Rapids.

Diocesan Offices and Directors

Apostolate for Native Americans—ELEANOR ST. JOHN, Coord.

Boy Scouts—Rev. JOSEPH W. HIRSCH; Mr. ROBERT J. COOPER, Chm., P.O. Box 4004, La Crosse, 54602-4004. Tel: 608-791-2667.

Building Commission—CHRISTOPHER CARSTENS; Revs. RICHARD W. GILLES, J.C.L.; J. FLOYD DWYER (Retired); DIANA L. ROBERTS; Mr. BENEDICT T. NGUYEN, M.T.S., J.C.L.; SONDRA RIEDER; TRAVIS J. SIMPSON.

Catholic Women, Council of—Rev. LAWRENCE G. DUNKLEE, Moderator, P.O. Box 4004, La Crosse, 54602. Tel: 608-791-2689.

Department of Catholic Education—ANN C. LANKFORD, Dir. Catechesis & Evangelization; PETER A. SAVVA, Asst. Dir. Catechesis & Evangelization for Catechumenal Ministry; DIANA L. ROBERTS, Dir. Schools; GARY J. CATALANO, Asst. Dir.; BOUA NENG YANG, La Crosse Area Hmong

Catechist, 3710 East Ave. S., P.O. Box 4004, La Crosse, 54602-4004. Tel: 608-788-7707.

Office of Family Life—SHAWN D. MCMAHON, Dir., P.O. Box 4004, La Crosse, 54602-4004. Tel: 608-791-2665.

Natural Family Planning Program—JEFF HEINZEN, Educator; ALICE HEINZEN, Coord., 711 24th St. N.E., Menomonie, 54751. Tel: 715-235-6226.

Holy Childhood Association—Very Rev. ROGER J. SCHECKEL, Dir., P.O. Box 4004, La Crosse, 54602-4004. Tel: 608-788-7700.

Hospitals and Health Affairs—Revs. EDMUND J. KLIMEK, Coord., Sacred Heart Hospital, 900 W. Clairemont Ave., Eau Claire, 54701. Tel: 715-839-4121; LAWRENCE G. DUNKLEE, Coord., P.O. Box 4004, La Crosse, 54602-4004. Tel: 608-791-2689.

Newman Campus Ministry—Rev. MARK R. PIERCE, Coord., 1732 State St., La Crosse, 54601. Tel: 608-784-4994.

Office of Communications and Public Relations—ROSE A. HAMMES, Dir., P.O. Box 4004, La Crosse, 54602-4004. Tel: 608-791-2663.

Office of Diocesan Buildings and Grounds—TRAVIS J. SIMPSON, Dir., P.O. Box 4004, La Crosse, 54602-4004. Tel: 608-791-2692.

Office of the Consecrated Life—Sr. M. REGINA VANDENBERG, F.S.G.M., Dir., P.O. Box 4004, La Crosse, 54602-4004. Tel: 608-791-2655.

Office of Ecumenism—Very Rev. JEFFREY D. BURRILL, Diocesan Officer, Ecumenical Questions, 911 W. Prospect St., P.O. Box 188, Durand, 54736-1049. Tel: 715-672-5640.

Office of Justice and Peace—Dr. ARTHUR HIPPLER, Dir., P.O. Box 4004, La Crosse, 54602-4004. Tel: 608-791-2675 Justice and Peace Commission Office.

Office of Ministries—CHRISTOPHER J. RUFF, Dir., P.O. Box 4004, La Crosse, 54602-4004. Tel: 608-791-2667 Office of Ministries consists of Permanent Diaconate, Lay Ministries.

Office of Sacred Worship—Mr. CHRISTOPHER J. CARSTENS, Dir., P.O. Box 4004, La Crosse, 54602-4004. Tel: 608-791-2675 Sacred Worship Commission-confer Office.

Office of Youth Ministry—CHRISTOPHER J. STEFANICK, Dir., P.O. Box 4004, La Crosse, 54602-4004.

Pastoral Council—Rev. RICHARD W. GILLES, J.C.L., Exec. Sec., P.O. Box 4004, La Crosse, 54602-4004.

Personnel Council—Revs. DAVID C. KUNZ, Chm.; JOHN T. MCHUGH, Sec.; Very Rev. THOMAS J. DONALDSON; Revs. ALLEN F. JAKUBOWSKI; TERRENCE M. SCHELBLE; Very Rev. WOODROW H. PACE, P.O. Box 4004, La Crosse, 54602-4004. Tel: 608-788-7700. Ex Officio: Revs. LAWRENCE G. DUNKLEE; RICHARD W. GILLES, J.C.L.; JOSEPH W. HIRSCH.

Presbyteral Council—VACANT, Pres. Appointed Members: Revs. KEITH B. APFELBECK; JOHN A. POTACZEK; JOHN A. SCHULTZ. Elected Members: Revs. HENRY R. HOERBURGER; PAUL L. SANKOORIKAL; AMBROSE J. BLENKER; DENNIS J. LYNCH; JOHN W. STEINER; THOMAS M. O'NEILL; JOSEPH W. HIRSCH; JOHN T. MCHUGH; Very Rev. JEFFREY D. BURRILL; Revs. WILLIAM A. DHEIN; BERNARD O. MCGARTY (Retired); OLIVIER MENEY.

Ex Officio Members—Revs. LAWRENCE G. DUNKLEE; RICHARD W. GILLES, J.C.L., Moderator of the Curia; WILLIAM N. GREVATCH; EUGENE A. KLINK; Very Rev. ROGER J. SCHECKEL. Consultors: Rev. RICHARD W. GILLES, J.C.L., Sec.; Very Rev. ROGER J. SCHECKEL; Revs. EUGENE A. KLINK; WILLIAM N. GREVATCH; JOHN W. STEINER; JOHN A. POTACZEK.

Propagation of the Faith—Very Rev. ROGER J. SCHECKEL, Dir., P.O. Box 4004, La Crosse, 54602-4004. Tel: 608-788-7700.

St. Joseph's Priest Fund, Inc., (Benevolent Society)—Very Revs. STEVEN J. KACHEL, Pres.; MICHAEL J. GORMAN, Exec. Sec., P.O. Box 4004, La Crosse, 54602-4004. Tel: 608-788-7700.

"Catholic Times": Diocesan Newspaper—DANIEL J. ROSSINI, Editor, P.O. Box 4004, La Crosse, 54602-4004. Tel: 608-788-1524.

Victim Assistance Coordinator—DANIEL LYNCH. Tel: 715-832-6644.

CLERGY, PARISHES, MISSIONS AND PAROCHIAL SCHOOLS

CITY OF LA CROSSE
(LA CROSSE COUNTY)

1—ST. JOSEPH THE WORKMAN CATHEDRAL (1860), [CEM 2] Very Rev. Michael J. Gorman, Rector. In Res., Rev. Todd A. Mlsna.
Res.: 530 Main St., 54601. Tel: 608-782-0322; Fax: 608-782-8228.
School—Coulee Catholic Schools See Unified Catholic School Systems under Institutions Located in the Diocese.
Catechesis/Religious Program—Tel: 608-782-2953; Fax: 608-785-1064. Pauline Connell, D.R.E. Students 48.

2—BLESSED SACRAMENT (1937), [CEM 2] Very Rev. Robert P. Hundt, J.C.L.; Rev. Francis Thadathil.
Res.: 130 Losey Blvd. S., 54601. Tel: 608-782-2953; Fax: 608-785-1064.
School—Coulee Catholic Schools See Unified Catholic School Systems under Institutions Located in the Diocese.

3—HOLY CROSS, Closed., For inquiries for parish records contact the Diocesan Archive, P.O. Box 4004, La Crosse, WI 54602-4004 Tel: 608-788-7700

4—HOLY TRINITY (1887), [JC] Rev. Lawrence B. Berger.
Res.: 1333 S. 13th St., 54601. Tel: 608-782-2028; Fax: 608-784-2029.
School—Coulee Catholic Schools See Unified Catholic School Systems under Institutions Located in the Diocese.
Catechesis/Religious Program—Fax: 608-784-2029. Jeannie M. Weber, D.R.E. Students 233.

5—ST. JAMES THE LESS (1886), Very Rev. Roger J. Scheckel; Rev. Paul G. Czerwonka, 1032 Caledonia St., 54603.
Res.: 1032 Caledonia St., 54603. Tel: 608-782-7557; Fax: 608-796-0086.
School—Coulee Catholic Schools See Unified Catholic School Systems under Institutions Located in the Diocese.

6—ST. JOHN THE BAPTIST, Closed., For inquiries for parish records contact Diocesan Archives, P.O. Box 4004, La Crosse, WI 54602-4004 Tel: 608-788-7700

7—ST. MARY, Closed., For inquiries for parish records contact The Diocesan Archives, P.O. Box 4004, La Crosse, WI 54602-4004 Tel: 608-788-7700

8—MARY, MOTHER OF THE CHURCH (2000), Rev. David C. Kunz.
Res.: 2006 Weston St., 54601. Tel: 608-788-5483; Fax: 608-788-4070.
School—Coulee Catholic Schools See Unified Catholic School Systems under Institutions Located in the Diocese.

9—ST. PIUS X, Closed., For inquiries for parish records contact Mary, Mother of the Church, La Crosse.Tel: 608-788-7700

10—RONCALLI NEWMAN PARISH, Rev. Mark R. Pierce.
Res.: 1732 State St., 54601. Tel: 608-784-4994; Fax: 608-784-0230.
Catechesis/Religious Program—Kathleen M. Nickiaus, D.R.E. Students 178.

11—ST. THOMAS MORE, Closed., For inquiries for parish records contact Mary, Mother of the Church, La Crosse. Tel: 608-788-7700

12—ST. WENCESLAUS, Closed., For inquiries for parish records contact The Diocesan Archives, P.O. Box 4004, La Crosse, WI 54602-4004 Tel: 608-788-7700

OUTSIDE THE CITY OF LA CROSSE

ABBOTSFORD, CLARK CO., ST. BERNARD, [JC] Attended by, Holy Rosary, Owen. Rev. Eric G. Linzmaier; Sr. Gertrude Rolfes, O.S.B., Pastoral Assoc.
Res.: 101 W. Cedar St., 54405-9558. Tel: 715-223-3331.

ADAMS, ADAMS CO., ST. JOSEPH (1884), [CEM], Also serves St. Ann, Brooks. Very Rev. James P. McNamee; Deacon David Kennedy.
Res.: Box 310, 53910. Tel: 608-339-3485; Fax: 608-339-0225.
Catechesis/Religious Program—Students 112.

ALMA CENTER, JACKSON CO., IMMACULATE CONCEPTION, [CEM] Attended by, St. Joseph, Fairview. Rev. David A. Ziegelmaier.
Mailing Address: Box 188, 54611. Tel: 715-964-5201.
Res.: N13740 Fairview Rd., Fairchild, 54741-8514. Tel: 715-334-2202.

ALMA, BUFFALO CO., ST. LAWRENCE (1867),, Also serves St. Boniface, Waumandee. Rev. John W. Steiner.
Res.: P.O. Box 246, 54610. Tel: 608-685-3253.

ALMOND, PORTAGE CO., HOLY GUARDIAN ANGELS, Closed., For inquiries for parish records contact St. Maximilian Maria Kolbe, Southeastern Portage County.

ALTDORF, WOOD CO., ST. JOSEPH, Closed., For inquiries for parish records contact St. Joachim, Pittsville.

ALTOONA, EAU CLAIRE CO., ST. MARY (1902), [JC] Rev. Donald F. Wilger (Retired).
Res.: 1827 Lynn Ave., 54720. Tel: 715-835-8813; Fax: 715-855-8664.
School—Catholic Area Schools of the Eau Claire Deanery See Unified Catholic School Systems under Institutions Located in the Diocese.
Catechesis/Religious Program—Tel: 715-855-1294. Mary Kneer, D.R.E. Students 233.

AMHERST, PORTAGE CO., ST. JAMES (1905), [CEM], Also serves St. Mary of Mount Carmel, Fancher. Rev. Robert F. Pedretti.
Res.: 453 S. Main, Box 280, 54406-0280. Tel: 715-824-3455; Fax: 715-824-3455. Barbara Lepak, D.R.E.; Dorene Stolpa, D.R.E.

ARCADIA, TREMPEALEAU CO.

1—HOLY FAMILY (2000), [CEM] Sr. Rosemary Rombalski, Pastoral Min.
Res.: 223 E. Maple St., 54612. Tel: 608-323-7116; Fax: 608-323-8346.
Catechesis/Religious Program—Tel: 608-323-8500. Jody Ferguson, D.R.E.; Ruth Manley, D.R.E. Students 161.

2—OUR LADY OF PERPETUAL HELP, Closed., For inquiries for parish records contact Holy Family, Arcadia.

3—ST. STANISLAUS, Closed., For inquiries for parish records contact Holy Family, Arcadia.

ARKANSAW, PEPIN CO., ST. JOSEPH, [CEM 2] Rev. Matthew J. Molinaro.
Res.: W. 7805 County Rd. Z, 54721. Tel: 715-285-5313.
Catechesis/Religious Program—Tel: 715-285-5849. Darlene Huppert, D.R.E. Students 100.

ARPIN, WOOD CO., ST. FRANCIS, Closed., For inquiries for parish records contact St. James, Vesper.

ATHENS, MARATHON CO., ST. ANTHONY DE PADUA (1881), [JC], Also serves Holy Family, Poniatowski and St. Thomas, Milan. Rev. Charles J. Hiebl.
Res.: 417 Caroline St., P.O. Box 206, 54411-0206. Tel: 715-257-7684; Fax: 715-257-7541.
School—Tel: 715-257-7541; Fax: 715-257-7541. Sisters 1; Lay Teachers 7; Students 91.

AUBURNDALE, WOOD CO., NATIVITY OF THE BLESSED VIRGIN MARY (1886), [CEM 2], Also serves St. Michael, Hewitt. Rev. Terrence M. Schelble.
Res.: 5866 Main St., P.O. Box 177, 54412-0177. Tel: 715-652-2806; Fax: 715-652-8020.
School—Tel: 715-652-2196; Fax: 715-652-8020. Sisters of Notre Dame 1; Lay Teachers 6; Students 47.

AUGUSTA, EAU CLAIRE CO., ST. ANTHONY DE PADUA, Closed., For inquiries for Parish Records contact St. Raymond of Penafort, Southern Eau Claire County.

BABCOCK, WOOD CO., ALL SAINTS, Closed., For inquiries for Parish Records contact Sacred Heart of Jesus, Nekoosa.

BAKERVILLE, WOOD CO., CORPUS CHRISTI, Attended by, Sacred Heart, Marshfield Rev. Anthony J. Wolf.
Mailing and Res. address: 112 E. 11th St., Marshfield, 54449. Tel: 715-676-3658 (Mail); 715-384-3213 (Res.).
Church: 10075 Hwy. BB, Marshfield, 54449.
School—Marshfield Area Catholic Schools Please see Unified Catholic School Systems located in the Institutions Section for more information.

BANGOR, LA CROSSE CO., ST. MARY (1899), [CEM] Attended by, St. Leo the Great, West Salem. Rev. Robert S. Hegenbarth.
Mailing Address: 210 W. Hamlin St., West Salem, 54669. Tel: 608-786-0610. In Res., Rev. Paul L. Sankoorikal.
Res.: P.O. Box 290, 54614-0290. Tel: 608-486-2033.

BEAR VALLEY, RICHLAND CO., ST. KILIAN, Closed., For inquiries for parish records contact Nativity, B.V.M., Keyesville.

BEVENT, MARATHON CO., ST. LADISLAUS (1886), [CEM] Attended by, St. Joseph, Galloway. Rev. Rex A. Zimmerman; Sr. Mary Ellen Diermeier, S.S.J.-T.O.S.F., Pastoral Assoc.
Mailing Address: 6455 State Hwy. 153, Hatley, 54440. Tel: 715-446-3060; Fax: 715-446-2668.

BIG RIVER, PIERCE CO., NATIVITY OF THE BLESSED VIRGIN MARY (1872), [CEM 2] Rev. John W. Beckfelt.
Res.: W10137 570th Ave., River Falls, 54022. Tel: 715-425-5806; Fax: 715-425-5806.

BLACK RIVER FALLS, JACKSON CO., ST. JOSEPH (1857), [CEM] Rev. Robert A. Streveler.
Res.: 507 Main St., 54615-1699. Tel: 715-284-5613; Fax: 715-284-8159.
Catechesis/Religious Program— Lauri J. Becker, D.R.E. Tel: 715-284-2660. Students 119.

BLAIR, TREMPEALEAU CO., ST. ANSGAR (1961), Attended by, St. John the Apostle, Whitehall. Rev. Patrick A. Umberger, Parochial Admin.
Mailing Address: 35900 Lee St., Whitehall, 54773. Tel: 715-538-4607; Fax: 715-538-2224.

BLENKER, WOOD CO., ST. KILIAN (1882), [CEM] Attended by, St. Wenceslaus, Milladore. Rev. John A. Wisneski.
Mailing Address: Box 100, Milladore, 54454. Tel: 715-457-2314. In Res., Rev. Edgar Haasl.

BLOOMER, CHIPPEWA CO., ST. PAUL (1902), [CEM 3] Rev. James K. Arthur.
Res.: 1222 Main St., 54724. Tel: 715-568-3255.
School—1210 Main St., 54724. Tel: 715-568-3233; Fax: 715-568-3244. Sisters 2; Lay Teachers 11; Students 187.

Catechesis/Religious Program—Tel: 715-568-3256. Barbara Kostner, D.R.E. Students 192.
Convent—1205 13th Ave., 54724. Tel: 715-568-3266.

BOYCEVILLE, DUNN CO., ST. LUKE (1964), [JC] Attended by, St. Joseph, Menomonie. Rev. Lyle L. Schulte (Retired); Sr. Judith Kramer, O.S.B., Pastoral Min.
Mailing Address: 605 Center St., P.O. Box 316, 54725. Tel: 715-643-3081.
St. Bede Monastery: N 460 City Hwy. D, Eau Galle, 54737. Tel: 715-283-4448.

BOYD, CHIPPEWA CO., SACRED HEART OF JESUS-ST. JOSEPH, [CEM 2] Attended by, Holy Family, Stanley. Rev. Robert W. Nelson. In Res., Rev. Eugene P. Smith (Retired). Tel: 714-667-3038.
Res.: 719 Patten St., P.O. Box 10, 54726-0010. Tel: 715-667-3341.
School—Tel: 715-667-3346. Lay Teachers 6; Students 60.

BRACKETT, EAU CLAIRE CO., HOLY GUARDIAN ANGELS, Closed., For inquiries for Parish Records contact St. Raymond of Penafort, Southern Eau Claire County.

BROOKS, ADAMS CO., ST. ANN, [CEM] Attended by, St. Joseph, Adams. Very Rev. James P. McNamee.
Mailing Address: P.O. Box 132, Oxford, 53952. Tel: 608-584-4900.

BUENA VISTA, PORTAGE CO., ST. MARTIN, Closed., For inquiries for parish records contact St. Maximilian Maria Kolbe, Southeastern Portage County.

CADOTT, CHIPPEWA CO., ST. ROSE OF LIMA, [CEM], Also serves Sacred Heart, Jim Falls. Rev. Kurt J. Apfelbeck.
Res.: Box 160, 54727. Tel: 715-289-4551.
School—Tel: 715-289-4985. Lay Teachers 6; Students 48.

CAMP DOUGLAS, JUNEAU CO., ST. JAMES (1857), [CEM], Also serves Sacred Heart, Jim Falls. Revs. Zbigniew Kucharski; Cheriyan Thomas.
Res.: Box 289, 54618. Tel: 608-427-6762.

CASHTON, MONROE CO., SACRED HEART OF JESUS (1918), [CEM 3] Attended by, Nativity of the Blessed Virgin Mary, St, Mary's Ridge. Revs. Eric R. Berns. Tel: 608-654-7619; Donald J. Bauer.
Res.: 26400 CTH U, 54619-9757. Tel: 608-823-7906; Fax: 608-823-7272.
School—Sacred Heart of Jesus School, 710 Kenyon St., 54619. Tel: 608-654-7733; Fax: 608-654-7733. Lay Teachers 6; Students 37.

CASSEL, MARATHON CO., SACRED HEART, [CEM], Served from St. Patrick, Halder Rev. Barnabas Kyeah.
Res.: 3372 County Rd. S., Marathon City, 54448. Tel: 715-443-3675.

CASTLE ROCK LAKE, JUNEAU CO., OUR LADY OF THE LAKE, [CEM] Attended by, St. Paul, New Lisbon. Rev. Steven H. Baures.
Res.: 408 W. River St., New Lisbon, 53950. Tel: 608-562-3125.

CAZENOVIA, RICHLAND CO., ST. ANTHONY DE PADUA, [CEM] [JC], Also serves Sacred Heart, Lone Rock; and St. Mary, Keyesville. Rev. Andrezej K. Panek.
Res.: 32505 CTH V, 53924. Tel: 608-983-2367.
School—Tel: 608-983-2786. Lay Teachers 5; Students 34.

CHILI, CLARK CO., ST. STEPHEN, Closed., For inquiries for Parish Records contact St. Mary's Parish, Neillsville, WI

CHIPPEWA FALLS, CHIPPEWA CO.

1—ST. CHARLES BORROMEO (1884), [JC], Also serves St. Peter, Tilden. Very Rev. William P. Felix. In Res., Rev. Daniel B. Duchez, O.S.
Res.: 810 Pearl St., 54729. Tel: 715-723-4088; Fax: 715-723-2195.
School—Chippewa Falls Area Catholic Schools See Unified Catholic School Systems under Institutions Located in the Diocese.

2—HOLY GHOST (1886), [JC], Also serves St. Bridget, Springfield. Rev. Edmund J. Doerre.
Res.: 412 S. Main St., 54729. Tel: 715-723-4890; Fax: 715-723-8990.
School—Chippewa Falls Area Catholic Schools See Unified Catholic School Systems under Institutions Located in the Diocese.
Catechesis/Religious Program—Tel: 715-723-4890; Fax: 715-723-8990. Sr. Donna Snyder, D.R.E. Students 230.

3—NOTRE DAME (1856), [JC] Rev. James T. Benzmiller. In Res., Rev. Brian J. Jazdzewski.
Res.: 117 Allen St., 54729-2899. Tel: 715-723-7108; Fax: 715-723-7523.
School—Chippewa Falls Area Catholic Schools See Unified Catholic School Systems under Institutions Located in the Diocese.

COLBY, CLARK CO., ST. MARY HELP OF CHRISTIANS (1877), [CEM] Rev. John E. Malik.
Res.: P.O. Box 436, 54421. Tel: 715-223-3048; Fax: 715-223-0223.
School—Tel: 715-223-3033. Lay Teachers 12; Students 117.
Catechesis/Religious Program—Tel: 715-223-4926. Diane Feiten, D.R.E. Students 140.

COOKS VALLEY, CHIPPEWA CO., ST. JOHN THE BAPTIST (1884), [CEM] Attended by, St. Charles Borromeo, Chippewa Falls. Very Rev. William P. Felix; Rev. James Arthur.
Mailing Address: 4540 State Hwy. 40, Bloomer, 54724. Tel: 715-568-3778; Fax: 715-723-2195.
Res.: 1222 Main St., Bloomer, 54724. Tel 715-568-3255.

COON VALLEY, VERNON CO., ST. MARY, [CEM] Rev. Michael E. Klos.
Res.: 904 Central Ave., 54623. Tel: 608-452-3841.

CORNELL, CHIPPEWA CO., HOLY CROSS (1915), [CEM 2] Rev. Jeremiah Cashman; Deacon Dennis Rivers.
Res.: 107 S. 8th St., P.O. Box 68, 54732. Tel: 715-239-6826.
Catechesis/Religious Program—Tel: 715-239-6759. Pamela Ferrell, D.R.E.; Betty Rivers, D.R.E. Students 84.

CUSTER, PORTAGE CO., IMMACULATE CONCEPTION (1875), [CEM] Rev. Sotico H. Florida Jr.
Res.: 7176 Co. Q, 54423. Tel: 715-592-4300.

CZESTOCHOWA, CLARK CO., ST. MARY OF CZESTOCHOWA, Closed., For inquiries for parish records contact Holy Family, Stanley.

DE SOTO, CRAWFORD CO., SACRED HEART, Closed., For inquiries for parish records contact St. Charles Borromeo, Genoa.

DILLY, VERNON CO., ST. JOHN NEPOMUCENE, Closed., For inquiries for parish records contact Diocesan Archives, P.O. Box 4004, La Crosse,WI 54602-4004 Tel: 608-788-7700

DORCHESTER, CLARK CO., ST. LOUIS (1878), [JC] Rev. James F. Schaefer.
Res.: 133 N. 3rd St., 54425-9577. Tel: 715-654-5089.
School—134 N. 4th St., 54425. Tel: 715-654-5467. Lay Teachers 4; Students 24.
Catechesis/Religious Program—Tel: 715-654-5904. Terri Pinter, D.R.E. Students 121.

DRYWOOD, CHIPPEWA CO., ST. ANTHONY (1886), [CEM] Attended by, St. Rose of Lima, Cadott. Rev. Kurt J. Apfelbeck; Deacon Mark C. Arnold.
Res.: P.O. Box 68, Jim Falls, 54748. Tel: 715-382-4422.

DURAND, PEPIN CO., ST. MARY'S ASSUMPTION (1860), [CEM] Very Rev. Jeffrey D. Burrill; Rev. James R. Kurzynski; Deacon James Weingart.
Mailing Address: 911 W. Prospect St., P.O. Box 188, 54736-1049. Tel: 715-672-5640; Fax: 715 672-4193.
Res.: N6225 CTH V, 54736.
School—901 W. Prospect St., 54736. Tel: 715-672-5617; Fax: 715-672-3931. Lay Teachers 10; Students 108.

EASTMAN, CRAWFORD CO., ST. WENCESLAUS (1883), [CEM] Very Rev. Msgr. John F. McCarthy, P.A.
Res.: P.O. Box 109, 54626-0109. Tel: 608 874-4151.
Catechesis/Religious Program—Tel: 608-874-4221. Barbara Martin, D.R.E. Students 82.

EAU CLAIRE, EAU CLAIRE CO.

1—IMMACULATE CONCEPTION (1945), Rev. Eugene A. Klink.
Res.: 1712 Highland Ave., 54701. Tel 715-835-9935; Fax 715-835-9459.
School—Catholic Area Schools of the Eau Claire Deanery See Unified Catholic School Systems under Institutions Located in the Diocese.
Catechesis/Religious Program—Tel: 715-835-7721; Fax: 715-830-9846. Linda Corey, D.R.E.; Barb Brandner D.R.E. Students 423.

2—ST. JAMES THE GREATER (1948), [JC] Rev. John A. Schultz; Sr. Judie Wagener, S.S.N.D., Pastoral Assoc.
Res.: 2502 Eleventh St., 54703-2700. Tel: 715-835-5887; Fax: 715-835-3110.
School—Catholic Area Schools of the Eau Claire Deanery See Unified Catholic School Systems under Institutions Located in the Diocese.

3—NEWMAN COMMUNITY (1969), [JC] Revs George R. Szews; Edmund J. Klimek.
Res.: 110 Garfield Ave., 54701-4042. Tel: 715-834-3399.
Catechesis/Religious Program—Tel: 715-834-3399. Flo Sheridan, D.R.E. Students 146.

4—ST. OLAF, [JC] Rev. Frank Corradi; Deacon Robert Chittendon.
3220 Monroe St., 54703. Tel: 715-832-2504; Fax: 715-832-0742. Mailing Address: P.O. Box 1203, 54702-1203.
School—Catholic Area Schools of the Eau Claire Deanery See Unified Catholic School Systems under Institutions Located in the Diocese.

5—ST. PATRICK, Merged, with Sacred Heart of Jesus, Eau Claire to form Sacred Heart of Jesus-St. Patrick, Eau Claire. For inquiries for parish records contact Sacred Heart of Jesus-St. Patrick, Eau Claire.

6—SACRED HEART OF JESUS, Merged, with St. Patrick, Eau Claire to form Sacred Heart of Jesus-St. Patrick, Eau Claire. For inquiries for parish records contact Sacred Heart of Jesus-St. Patrick, Eau Claire.

7—SACRED HEART OF JESUS-ST. PATRICK (1999), [CEM 2] Very Rev. Paul R. Gitter; Rev. William A. Dhein; Deacon Larry Agema.
Res.: 318 Fulton St., 54703-5399. Tel: 715-832-0925; Fax: 715-832-0366.

EAU GALLE, DUNN CO., ST. HENRY (1856), [CEM], Also serves St. Luke, Boyceville. Rev. Jerome G. Hoeser.
Res.: N460 CTH D, 54737. Tel: 715-283-4448.
Catechesis/Religious Program—Tel: 715-283-4255. Orpha Baier, D.R.E. Students 59.

EDGAR, MARATHON CO., ST. JOHN THE BAPTIST (1990), [CEM] Rev. Norman D. Boneck. In Res., Rev. Donald M. Berg, Senior Priest (Retired).
Res.: 103 N. Fourth Ave., P.O. Box 35, 54426. Tel: 715-352-3011; Fax: 715-352-3011.
School—Tel: 715-352-3000; Fax: 715-352-7517. Lay Teachers 10; Students 102.
Catechesis/Religious Program—Tel: 715-352-2181. Jean Heidmann, D.R.E. Students 158.

EDSON, CHIPPEWA CO., SACRED HEART OF JESUS, Merged, with St. Joseph, Boyd to form Sacred Heart of Jesus-St. Joseph, Boyd.

ELK MOUND, DUNN CO., ST. JOSEPH, [CEM] Rev. Henry R. Hoerburger.
Res.: P.O. Box 275, 54739. Tel: 715-879-5332.

ELLSWORTH, PIERCE CO., ST. FRANCIS OF ASSISI (1897), [CEM] [JC 4] Very Rev. Thomas J. Donaldson.
Res.: 264 S. Grant St., P.O. Box 839, 54011. Tel: 715-273-4774; Fax: 715-723-4066.
School—Box 250, 54011. Tel: 715-273-4391; Fax: 715-273-4066. Lay Teachers 7; Students 145.

ELMWOOD, PIERCE CO., SACRED HEART, [CEM], Also serves Sacred Heart of Jesus, Spring Valley. Rev. Varkey V. Joseph, S.A.C.
114 W. Wilson Ave., 54740. Tel: 715-639-2741; Fax: 715-639-6031.

ELROY, JUNEAU CO., ST. PATRICK (1877), [CEM] Attended by, St. Joseph, Kendall. Rev. Brian D. Konopa.
Res.: 307 Spring St., Box 155, Kendall, 54638. Tel: 608-462-5875; Fax: 608-462-5876.
Catechesis/Religious Program—Tel: 608-462-5067. Jayne Beaver, D.R.E. Students 36.

ETTRICK, TREMPEALEAU CO., ST. BRIDGET, [CEM], Also serves St. Kevin, Melrose. Rev. Godwin Amah.
Res.: 22650 Washington St., 54627. Tel: 608-525-3811; Fax: 608-525-2909.

FAIRCHILD, EAU CLAIRE CO., ST. JOHN CANTIUS, Attended by, St. Joseph, Fairview. Rev. David A. Ziegelmaier.
Res.: N13740 Fairview Rd., 54741-8514. Tel: 715-334-2202.

FAIRVIEW, EAU CLAIRE CO., ST. JOSEPH, , Also serves Immaculate Conception, Alma Center; and St. John Cantius, Fairchild. Rev. David A. Ziegelmaier.
Res.: N13740 Fairview Rd., Fairchild, 54741-8514. Tel: 715-334-2202.

FALL CREEK, EAU CLAIRE CO.

1—ST. JOHN THE APOSTLE, Closed., For inquiries for Parish Records contact St. Raymond of Penafort, Southern Eau Claire Country.

2—ST. RAYMOND OF PENAFORT (1998), [CEM] Very Rev. Paul R. Gitter; Deacon Larry Agema.
S10444 Hwy. 53, 54742. Tel: 715-878-4183.

FANCHER, PORTAGE CO., ST. MARY OF MOUNT CARMEL (1884), [CEM] Attended by, St. James, Amherst. Rev. Robert F. Pedretti.
Res.: P.O. Box 280, 453 S. Main St., Amherst, 54406. Tel: 715-824-3455; Fax: 715-824-3455.

FOUNTAIN CITY, BUFFALO CO., IMMACULATE CONCEPTION, [CEM] Rev. G. Richard Roberts.
Res.: 1 Wall St., P.O. Box 218, 54629-0218. Tel: 608-687-3496.

GALESVILLE, TREMPEALEAU CO., ST. MARY, Attended by, St. Bartholomew, Trempealeau. Rev. Raymond J. Wagner (Retired).
Res. & Mailling Address: 11646 South St., Trempealeau, 54461-8238. Tel: 608-534-6652.

GALLOWAY, MARATHON CO., ST. JOSEPH (1921), [CEM], Also serves St. Ladislaus, Bevent. Rev. Rex A. Zimmerman; Sr. Mary Ellen Diermeier, S.S.J.-T.O.S.F., Pastoral Assoc.; Deacon David Ashenbrenner.
Res.: 8846 CTH C, Wittenberg, 54499-8936. Tel: 715-454-6431. Dorothy Ashenbrenner, D.R.E.
Catechesis/Religious Program—Tel: 715-454-6432. Students 90.

GAYS MILLS, CRAWFORD CO., ST. MARY (1908), [JC], Also serves St. Philip, Rolling Ground. Rev. Alan P. Wierzba.
Res.: 115 E. School St., 54631. Tel: 608-735-4420; Fax: 608-735-4520.
Catechesis/Religious Program—Tel: 608-734-3054. Barbara Schroeder, D.R.E. Students 23.

GENOA, VERNON CO., ST. CHARLES BORROMEO, [CEM] Rev. Charles Nabwana.
Res.: P.O. Box 130, 54632. Tel: 608-689-2646; Fax: 608-689-2811.

School—Tel: 608-689-2642; Fax: 608-689-2811. Lay Teachers 6; Students 75.

GREENWOOD, CLARK CO., ST. MARY HELP OF CHRISTIANS (1903), [CEM], Also serves Holy Family, Willard. Rev. A. Joseph Follmar.
Res.: 123 N. Main St., P.O. Box 129, 54437. Tel: 715-267-6282.
School—Tel: 715-267-6477. Lay Teachers 3; Students 36.

HALDER, MARATHON CO., ST. PATRICK, [CEM], Also serves Sacred Heart, Cassel. Rev. Barnabas Kyeah.
Mailing Address: 3158 Halder Dr., Mosinee, 54455. Tel: 715-693-2765.
Sacred Heart Rectory: 3372 County Rd. S., Marathon City, 54448-0068. Tel: 715-443-3675.

HATLEY, MARATHON CO., ST. FLORIAN (1885), [CEM] Rev. Thomas J. Abraham.
Res.: 500 Church Ln., P.O. Box 100, 54440. Tel: 715-446-2252; 715-446-3085 (Office); Fax: 715-446-2756.
School—Tel: 715-446-3950; Fax: 715-446-3950. Lay Teachers 6; Students 68.

HEFFRON, PORTAGE CO., ST. JOHN THE BAPTIST, Closed., For inquiries for parish records contact St. Maximilian Maria Kolbe, Southeastern Portage County.

HEWITT, WOOD CO., ST. MICHAEL (1888), [JC] Attended by, St. Mary, Auburndale. Rev. Terrence M. Schelble.
Office:—11100 Main St., 54441. Tel: 715-384-7676; Fax: 715-384-7675.
Res.: 5866 Main St., Box 177, Auburndale, 54412. Tel: 715-652-2806; Fax: 715-652-8020.

HILLSBORO, VERNON CO., ST. ALOYSIUS (1905), [JC] Rev. Wayne R. Kidd.
Res.: 545 Prairie Ave., P.O. Box 466, 54634. Tel: 608-489-2580; Fax: 608-489-2580.
Catechesis/Religious Program—Tel: 608-489-3718; Fax: 608-489-2580. Danna Hera, D.R.E. Students 129.

HOLMEN, LA CROSSE CO., ST. ELIZABETH ANN SETON (1983), Rev. John T. McHugh; Sr. Bridget Donaldson, O.S.B., Pastoral Assoc.
Office—515 N. Main St., 54636. Tel: 608-526-4424; Fax: 608-526-3177.
Res.: 704 Hillcrest Dr., 54636. Tel: 608-526-4624.
Catechesis/Religious Program—Sr. Bridget Donaldson, D.R.E. Students 488.

INDEPENDENCE, TREMPEALEAU CO., SS. PETER AND PAUL (1875), [CEM] Very Rev. Douglas C. Robertson.
Res.: 36028 Osseo Rd., P.O. Box 430, 54747-0430. Tel: 715-985-2227; Fax: 715-985-2649.
School—Tel: 715-985-3719. Lay Teachers 10; Students 150.

INDIAN CREEK, MONROE CO., ST. MICHAEL (1869), [CEM] Attended by, St. James, Camp Douglas. Rev. Cheriyan Thomas.
Mailing Address: P.O. Box 289, Camp Douglas, 54618. Tel: 608-427-6762.

JIM FALLS, CHIPPEWA CO., SACRED HEART, Rev. Brian J. Jazdzewski; Deacon Mark C. Arnold.
Res.: Box 68, 54748. Tel: 715-382-4422.

JUNCTION CITY, PORTAGE CO., ST. MICHAEL (1884), [CEM] Attended by, St. Wenceslaus, Milladore. Rev. John A. Wisneski.
Res.: P.O. Box 100, Milladore, 54454. Tel: 715-457-2314.

KENDALL, MONROE CO., ST. JOSEPH (1883), [CEM], Also serves St. Patrick, Elroy, and St. John the Baptist, Wilton. Rev. Brian D. Konopa.
Res.: 307 Spring St., P.O. Box 155, 54638. Tel: 608-463-7120.
Catechesis/Religious Program—Tel: 608-463-7649. Mary Skolos, D.R.E. Students 43.

KEYESVILLE, RICHLAND CO., NATIVITY OF THE BLESSED VIRGIN MARY, [CEM] Attended by, St. Anthony, Cazenovia. Rev. Andrzej K. Panek.
Mailing Address: 32605 Durst Ln., Richland Center, 53581. Tel: 608-585-4846.
Res.: 32505 Hwy. V, Cazenovia, 53924. Tel: 608-983-2367.

KNOWLTON, MARATHON CO., ST. FRANCIS XAVIER (1853), [CEM], Also serves St. John the Baptist, Peplin. Rev. Joseph A. Grassl.
Res.: 651 Mead Ln., Mosinee, 54455. Tel: 715-693-3120.

LANARK, PORTAGE CO., ST. PATRICK, Closed., For inquiries for parish records contact St. Maximilian Maria Kolbe, Southeastern Portage County.

LIMA, PEPIN CO., HOLY ROSARY, [CEM], Served from: St. Mary's Assumption, Durand. Very Rev. Jeffrey D. Burrill; Rev. James R. Kurzynski; Deacon James Weingart.
Mailing Address: 911 W. Prospect St., Box 188, Durand, 54736-1048. Tel: 715-672-5640; Fax: 715-672-4193.
School—Tel: 715-672-4276. Lay Teachers 4; Students 56.

LONE ROCK, RICHLAND CO., SACRED HEART, Attended by, St. Anthony, Cazenovia. Rev. Andrzej K. Panek.
Mailing Address: 32505 Hwy. V, Cazenovia, 53924. Tel: 608-983-2367.

LOYAL, CLARK CO., ST. ANTHONY OF PADUA (1893), [CEM] Rev. Roman F. Kaiser.
Res.: 407 N. Division St., P.O. Box 69, 54446-0069. Tel: 715-255-8017; Fax: 715-255-8017.
School—212 W. Spring St.. Tel: 715-255-8636; Fax: 715-255-8636. Lay Teachers 7; Students 71.
Catechesis/Religious Program—Tel: 715-255-9938. Marlene Ashbeck, D.R.E.; Michelle Lindner, D.R.E. Students 163.

LYNDON STATION, JUNEAU CO., ST. MARY, [CEM] Very Rev. Ronald T. Zinkle, S.J.
Res.: 117 Juneau St. N., P.O. Box 303, 53944. Tel: 608-666-2421.
Catechesis/Religious Program—Tel: 609-666-4201. Raymonda Blank, D.R.E. Students 54.

MARATHON CITY, MARATHON CO., NATIVITY OF THE BLESSED VIRGIN MARY (1856), [CEM] Very Rev. Joseph Diermeier.
Res.: 712 Market St., Box 7, 54448-0007. Tel: 715-443-2045; Fax: 715-443-3045.
School—Tel: 715-443-3430; Fax: 715-443-2989. Franciscan Sisters of Perpetual Adoration 1; Lay Teachers 14; Students 226.
Catechesis/Religious Program—Tel: 715-443-2433; Fax: 715-443-2575. Barbara Ceranski, D.R.E. Students 276.

MARSHFIELD, WOOD CO.

1—ST. JOHN THE BAPTIST (1877), [JC], Also serves Christ the King, Spencer. Very Rev. Charles D. Stoetzel. In Res., Rev. Daniel H. Hackel.
Res.: 201 W. Blodgett St., P.O. Box 644, 54449-0644. Tel: 715-384-3252; Fax: 715-384-3252.
School—Marshfield Area Catholic Schools See Unified Catholic School systems under Institutions located in The Diocese.
Catechesis/Religious Program—Tel: 715-384-3919. Mari Bohman, D.R.E. Students 252.

2—OUR LADY OF PEACE (1947), [JC] Rev. Donald L. Meuret.
Res.: 1414 W. 5th St., 54449. Tel: 715-384-9414; Fax: 715-384-6606.
School—Marshfield Area Catholic Schools See Unified Catholic School systems under Institutions located in The Diocese.
Catechesis/Religious Program—Tel: 715-676-2549; Fax: 715-384-6606. Corinne Johnson, D.R.E. Students 239.

3—SACRED HEART OF JESUS (1916), [JC], Also serves Corpus Christi, Bakerville. Rev. Anthony J. Wolf.
Res.: 112 E. 11th St., 54449-4216. Tel: 715-384-3213.
School—Marshfield Area Catholic Schools See Unified Catholic School systems under Institutions located in The Diocese.

MAUSTON, JUNEAU CO., ST. PATRICK (1901), [CEM 2] Rev. Daniel J. Kiedinger.
Res.: 401 Mansion St., 53948-1393. Tel: 608-847-6054; Fax: 608-847-3288.
School—325 Mansion St., 53948. Tel: 608-847-5844; Fax: 608-847-4103. Lay Teachers 11; Students 172.

MELROSE, JACKSON CO., ST. KEVIN, [JC] Attended by, St. Bridget, Ettrick. Rev. Godwin Amahi.
Mailing Address: *St. Bridget*, 22650 Washington, Ettrick, 54627. Tel: 608-525-3811; Fax: 608-525-2909.

MENOMONIE, DUNN CO., ST. JOSEPH (1861), [CEM] Rev. Thomas J. Krieg.
Res.: 910 Wilson Ave., 54751. Tel: 715-232-4922; Fax: 715-232-4923.
School—Tel: 715-232-4920. Lay Teachers 13; Students 178.
Catechesis/Religious Program—Mary Lu Bird, D.R.E.; Laure O'Keeffe, D.R.E. Students 127.

MIDDLE RIDGE, LA CROSSE CO., ST. PETER (1869), [CEM], Also serves St. Joseph, St. Joseph Ridge. Rev. Francis Abuah Quansah, J.C.D., Parochial Admin.
Res.: W697 State Rd. 33, #101M, Rockland, 54653. Tel: 608-486-2180.

MILAN, MARATHON CO., ST. THOMAS (1904), [CEM] Attended by, St. Anthony, Athens. Rev. Charles J. Hiebl.
Mailing Address: 417 Caroline St., P.O. Box 206, Athens, 54411. Tel: 715-257-7684; Fax: 715-257-7541.

MILL CREEK, PORTAGE CO., ST. BARTHOLOMEW, [CEM] Attended by, St. Stephen, Stevens Point. Rev. John A. Potaczek.
Res.: 1401 Clark, Stevens Point, 54481. Tel: 715-344-3003.

MILLADORE, WOOD CO., ST. WENCESLAUS (1883), [CEM], Also serves St. Kilian, Blenker & St. Michael, Junction City. Rev. John A. Wisneski.
Res.: 146 Main St., Box 100, 54454. Tel: 715-457-2314.

MONDOVI, BUFFALO CO., SACRED HEART OF JESUS (1896), [JC] Attended by, St. Mary's Assumption, Durand Very Rev. Jeffrey D. Burrill; Rev. James R. Kurzynski; Deacon James Weingart.
Mailing Address: P.O. Box 188, Durand, 54736. Tel: 715-672-5640; Fax: 715-672-4193.

MOSINEE, MARATHON CO., ST. PAUL (1878), [CEM] Rev. Donald L. Przybylski.
Res.: 603 Fourth St., 54455. Tel: 715-693-2650; Fax: 715-692-2650.
School—404 High St., 54455. Tel: 715-693-2675; Fax: 715-693-1332. Lay Teachers 12; Students 148.
Catechesis/Religious Program—Tel: 715-693-4030; Fax: 715-693-1332. Kathryn Lesniak, D.R.E. Students 256.

NECEDAH, JUNEAU CO., ST. FRANCIS OF ASSISI (1876), [CEM] Rev. James J. Lesczynski.
Res.: 2001 S. Main St., 54646-8273. Tel: 608-565-2488.

NEILLSVILLE, CLARK CO., ST. MARY, [CEM] Very Rev. Woodrow H. Pace.
Res.: 1813 Black River Rd., 54456. Tel: 715-743-3840; Fax: 715-743-7963.

NEKOOSA, WOOD CO., SACRED HEART OF JESUS (1900), [JC], Also serves St. Alexander, Port Edwards. Rev. R. John Swing.
Res.: 711 Prospect Ave., 54457. Tel: 715-886-3422; Fax: 715-886-4722.
School—Wisconsin Rapids Area Catholic Schools, Tel: 715-422-0900; Fax: 715-422-0903. See Unified Catholic School Systems under Institutoins Located in the Diocese.

NEW AUBURN, CHIPPEWA CO., ST. JUDE, Closed. For inquiries for parish records contact the chancery.

NEW LISBON, JUNEAU CO., ST. PAUL, [CEM], Also serves Our Lady of the Lake, Castle Rock Lake. Rev. Steven H. Baures.
Res.: 408 W. River St., 53950. Tel: 608-562-3125.
Catechesis/Religious Program—Tel: 608-562-3859. Mary Rubash, D.R.E. Students 81.

NORTH CREEK, TREMPEALEAU CO., ST. MICHAEL (1875), Closed. For inquiries for parish records contact the chancery.

NORWALK, MONROE CO., ST. AUGUSTINE OF HIPPO (1903), [CEM] Attended by, Nativity of the Blessed Virgin Mary, St. Mary's Ridge. Revs. Eric R. Berns; Donald J. Bauer. In Res., Rev. James H. Miller (Retired).
Res.: 26400 CTH U, Cashton, 54619-9757. Tel: 608-823-7906; Fax: 608-823-7272.

ONALASKA, LA CROSSE CO., ST. PATRICK (1949), [JC] Rev. William J. Matzek; Deacon Frank Abnet. In Res., Rev. Edwin J. Thome (Retired).
Res.: 1031 Main St., 54650. Tel: 608-783-5535.
School—Coulee Catholic Schools See Unified Catholic School Systems under Institutions Located in the Diocese.
Catechesis/Religious Program—Tel: 608-783-1099. Cathryn Olson, D.R.E.; Sue Elsen, D.R.E. Students 592.

OWEN, CLARK CO., HOLY ROSARY, , Also serves St. Bernard, Abbotsford Rev. Eric G. Linzmaier.
Res.: 415 W. 3rd St., P.O. Box 309, 54460-0309. Tel: 715-229-2747; Fax: 715-229-4548.
School—Tel: 715-229-2348. Lay Teachers 3; Students 21.

PEPLIN, MARATHON CO., ST. JOHN THE BAPTIST (1916), [CEM] Attended by, St. Francis Xavier, Knowlton. Rev. Joseph A. Grassl.
Mailing Address: 651 Mead Ln., Mosinee, 54455. Tel: 715-693-3120. In Res., Rev. Wladyslaw J. Kowalski (SUP) (Retired).

PINE CREEK, TREMPEALEAU CO., MOST SACRED HEART (1864), [CEM] Rev. Robert F. Polcyn, O.F.M.Cap., Parochial Admin.
Res.: N20555 CTH G, Dodge, 54625-9721. Tel: 608-539-3704; Fax: 608-539-3704.

PITTSVILLE, WOOD CO., ST. JOACHIM, [CEM], Also serves St. James, Vesper and Holy Rosary, Sigel. Rev. Jude Ndugbu.
Res.: 5312 Third Ave., P.O. Box 69, 54466-0069. Tel: 715-884-6815; Fax: 715-884-6160.
Catechesis/Religious Program—Tel: 715-884-2115. Janet Stellmach, D.R.E. Students 129.

PLOVER, PORTAGE CO., ST. BRONISLAVA (1896), [JC] Rev. James F. Trempe.
Res.: 3200 Plover Rd., P.O. Box 158, 54467-0158. Tel: 715-344-4326; Fax: 715-344-6121.
School—3301 Willow Dr., 54467. Tel: 715-342-2015; Fax: 715-342-2016.
Catechesis/Religious Program—Tel: 715-341-6700 (Grades 1-6). Christopher Parker, D.R.E. (Grades 1-6); Michelle Bowe, D.R.E. (Grades 7-10). Students 231.

PLUM CITY, PIERCE CO., ST. JOHN THE BAPTIST (1872), [JC] Rev. Ambrose J. Blenker.
Res.: 212 Church Rd., P.O. Box 206, 54761-0206. Tel: 715-647-2301; Fax: 715-647-2901.
School—Tel: 715-647-2901; Fax: 715-647-2901. Lay Teachers 6; Students 56.

POLONIA, PORTAGE CO., SACRED HEART, [CEM] Attended by, St. Adalbert, Rosholt In Res., Rev. Marcin Mankowski, O.P.
Res.: 7375 Church St., Custer, 54423. Tel: 715-592-4221; Fax: 715-592-4189.

School—7379 Church St., Custer, 54423. Tel: 715-592-4902. Lay Teachers 4; Students 48.
Convent—7381 Church St., Custer, 54423. Tel: 715-592-4213.

PONIATOWSKI, MARATHON CO., HOLY FAMILY (1877), [CEM 2] Attended by, St. Anthony de Padua, Athens. Rev. Charles J. Hiebl; Deacon LeRoy Knauf.
Mailing Address: R444 Hwy. U, Edgar, 54426. Tel: 715-352-3033.

PORT EDWARDS, WOOD CO., ST. ALEXANDER (1941), [JC], Served from: Sacred Heart, Nekoosa Rev. R. John Swing. In Res., Sr. Catherine Kaiser, F.S.P.A., Pastoral Assoc.
Church: 880 First St., 54469. Tel: 715-887-3012; Fax: 715-887-3748.
Res.: 711 Prospect Ave., Nekoosa, 54457.

PRAIRIE DU CHIEN, CRAWFORD CO.

1—ST. GABRIEL (1817), [CEM 2], Served from: St. Nepomucene, Prairie du Chien Revs. Hubert J. Boschert, S.J.; James B. Warosh, S.J.; John W. Wambach, S.J.
Office—506 N. Beaumont Rd., P.O. Box 176, 53821-0176. Tel: 608-326-2404.
School—Prairie Catholic Schools, 515 N. Beaumont Rd., 53821. Tel: 608-326-8624. Lay Teachers 22; Students 323.

2—ST. JOHN NEPOMUCENE (1891),, Also Serves: St. Gabriel, Prairie du Chien Revs. William F. Gerut, S.J.; James B. Warosh, S.J.; John W. Wambach, S.J.
Res.: 710 S. Wacouta St., P.O. Box 28, 53821-0028. Tel: 608-326-6511; Fax: 608-326-4876.
School—Prairie Catholic Schools, 720 S. Wacouta St., 53821. Tel: 608-326-4400.

PRESCOTT, PIERCE CO., ST. JOSEPH, [CEM] Rev. Edward J. Shuttleworth.
Res.: 269 Dakota St. S., P.O. Box 245, 54021-0245. Tel: 715-262-5310; Fax: 715-262-5901.
School—281 Dakota St. S., 54021. Tel: 715-262-5912; Fax: 715-262-5912. Franciscan Sisters of Perpetual Adoration 2; Lay Teachers 8; Students 189.
Convent—268 Dakota St. S., 54021. Tel: 715-262-5105.

RICHLAND CENTER, RICHLAND CO., ST. MARY (ASSUMPTION OF B.V.M.), [CEM] Very Rev. Emmanuel Famiyeh.
160 W. 4th St., P.O. Box 456, 53581. Tel: 608-647-2621; Fax: 608-647-6029.
School—155 W. 5th St., 53581. Tel: 608-647-2422. Lay Teachers 12; Students 124.
Catechesis/Religious Program—Tel: 608-647-4210. Denise Gainor, D.R.E. Students 180.
Convent—789 N. Central Ave., 53581. Tel: 608-647-4210.

RISING SUN, CRAWFORD CO., ST. JAMES, Closed., For inquiries for parish records contact The Diocesan Archive, P.O. Box 4004, La Crosse, WI, 54602-4004

ROCK FALLS, DUNN CO., ST. JOSEPH (1903), [CEM]
Res.: E. 9265 STH 85, Mondovi, 54755-8357. Tel: 715-875-4539.
Catechesis/Religious Program—Sara Lynch, D.R.E. Tel: 715-875-4706; Sue Abing, D.R.E. Tel: 715-875-4527. Students 41.

ROLLING GROUND, CRAWFORD CO., ST. PHILIP (1851), [CEM] Attended by, St. Mary, Gays Mills. Rev. Alan P. Wierzba.
Mailing Address: 115 E. School St., Gays Mills, 54631-0036. Tel: 608-735-4420; Fax: 608-735-4520.
Catechesis/Religious Program—Tel: 608-734-3054. Barbara Schroeder, D.R.E. Students 30.

ROSHOLT, PORTAGE CO., ST. ADALBERT, [CEM], Also serves Sacred Heart, Polonia. In Res., Rev. Marcin Mankowski, O.P.
Res.: 3315 St. Adalbert Rd., 54473. Tel: 715-677-4519; Fax: 715-677-6943.
School—3314 St. Adalbert Rd., 54473. Tel: 715-677-4517. Religious 1; Lay Teachers 5; Students 47.
Catechesis/Religious Program—Christine Check, D.R.E.; Patty Amman, D.R.E. Students 76.

ROTHSCHILD, MARATHON CO.

1—ST. MARK (1937), Rev. Allan L. Slowiak; Deacon Patrick McKeough.
Res.: 602 Military Rd., 54474-1523. Tel: 715-359-5206; Fax: 715-355-8904.
School—Wausau Area Catholic Schools See Unified Catholic School Systems under Institutions Located in the Diocese.
Catechesis/Religious Program—Tel: 715-845-5735; Fax: 715-355-8904. Mary Hart, D.R.E. Students 392.

2—ST. THERESE OF THE CHILD JESUS, [CEM] Rev. Janusz Kowalski.
Res.: 113 Kort St., 54474-1094. Tel: 715-359-2421; Fax: 715-355-3088.
School—Wausau Area Catholic Schools See Consolidated Elementary Schools under Institutions Located in the Diocese.

ROZELLVILLE, MARATHON CO., ST. ANDREW, [CEM] Attended by, St. Joseph, Stratford. Rev. Thomas J. Rudolph. In Res., Rev. Arthur S. Redmond (Retired). Tel: 715-384-7932.
Res.: Box 106, Stratford, 54484. Tel: 715-687-2404.

RUDOLPH, WOOD CO., ST. PHILIP, [CEM] Attended by, St. Lawrence, Wisconsin Rapids. Rev. George Nelson Graham, Parochial Admin.
Office:—6957 Grotto Ave., Box 165, 54475. Tel: 715-435-3286.
Res.: 530 Tenth Ave. N., Wisconsin Rapids, 54495. Tel: 715-421-5777.
School—Wisconsin Rapids Area Catholic Schools See Unified Catholic School Systems under Institutions Located in the Diocese.

SAINT JOSEPH RIDGE, LA CROSSE CO., ST. JOSEPH (1866), [CEM] Attended by, St. Peter, Middle Ridge. Rev. Francis Abuah Quansah, J.C.D., Parochial Admin.
Res.: W2601 Hwy. 33, 54601. Tel: 608-788-1646.

SAINT MARY'S RIDGE, MONROE CO., NATIVITY OF THE BLESSED VIRGIN MARY (1856), [CEM], Also serves St. Augustine, Norwalk; St. John the Baptist, Summit; Sacred Heart of Jesus, Cashton. Revs. Eric R. Berns; Donald J. Bauer.
Res.: 26400 CTH U, Cashton, 54619-9157. Tel: 608-823-7906; Fax: 608-823-7272.
School—Tel: 608-823-7577. Lay Teachers 5; Students 57.

SENECA, CRAWFORD CO., ST. PATRICK (1872), [CEM], Also serves Sacred Heart, Wauzeka. Rev. Eugene J. Wolf.
Res.: Box 18, 54654. Tel: 608-734-3931.

SIGEL, WOOD CO., HOLY ROSARY (1881), [CEM] Attended by, Joachim, Pittsville. Rev. Jude Ndugbu.
Mailing Address: P.O. Box 69, Pittsville, 54466-0069.

SOUTHEASTERN PORTAGE COUNTY, PORTAGE CO., ST. MAXIMILIAN MARIA KOLBE (1996), [CEM 4] Rev. Daniel H. Farley.
Mailing Address: 8909 State Hwy. 54, Amherst, 54406-9157. Tel: 715-824-3380.

SPARTA, MONROE CO., ST. PATRICK (1876), [CEM] Rev. James Leary, O.F.M.Cap.
Res.: 319 W. Main St., 54656-2143. Tel: 608-269-2655; Fax: 608-269-3084.
School—318 W. Oak St., 54654. Tel: 608-269-4748; Fax: 608-269-4748. Lay Teachers 11; Students 153.
Catechesis/Religious Program—Tel: 608-269-7500.

SPAULDING-CITY POINT, JACKSON CO., NORTH AMERICAN MARTYRS, Closed., For inquiries for parish records contact St. Joachim, Pittsville.

SPENCER, MARATHON CO., CHRIST THE KING (1938), [JC] Attended by, St. John , Marshfield. Very Rev. Charles D. Stoetzel.
Res.: 201 W. Blodgett, Marshfield, 54449-2004. Tel: 715-659-4480; Fax: 715-384-3252.

SPRING VALLEY, PIERCE CO., SACRED HEART OF JESUS (1884), [CEM 2] Attended by, Sacred Heart, Elmwood. Rev. Varkey V. Joseph, S.A.C. Terry E. Klages, Pastoral Assoc.
Res.: S. 105 Sabin Ave., P.O. Box 456, 54767-0456. Tel: 715-778-5519; Fax: 715-778-4591.

SPRINGFIELD, EAU CLAIRE CO., ST. BRIDGET (1859), [CEM] Attended by, Holy Ghost, Chippewa Falls. Rev. Edmund J. Doerre.
Office—412 S. Main, Chippewa Falls, 54729. Tel: 715-723-4890.

STANLEY, CHIPPEWA CO., HOLY FAMILY (1896), [CEM], Also serves Sacred Heart of Jesus-St. Joseph, Boyd. Rev. Robert W. Nelson.
Office—P.O. Box 125, 54768. Tel: 715-644-5435.
Res.: 226 E. 3rd Ave., P.O. Box 125, 54768. Tel: 715-644-5435.
School—136 3rd Ave., 54768. Tel: 715-644-3602. Lay Teachers 6; Students 60.

STEVENS POINT, PORTAGE CO.

1—ST. CASIMIR (1871), [CEM], Also serves St. Mary, Torun. Rev. Wesley Janowski (Poland).
Res.: 203 W. Casimir Rd., 54481. Tel: 715-344-9582.

2—ST. JOSEPH (1884), [JC] Rev. Alan T. Burkhardt.
Res.: 1709 Wyatt Ave., 54481-3699. Tel: 715-341-1617; Fax: 715-341-2623.
School—Stevens Point Area Catholic Schools See Unified Catholic School Systems under Institutions Located in the Diocese.
Catechesis/Religious Program—Tel: 715-341-8778; Fax: 715-341-2623. Lynn Meyer, D.R.E. Students 183.

3—NEWMAN UNIVERSITY PARISH (1970), [JC] Rev. Thomas F. Lindner.
Office—2108 Fourth Ave., 54481. Tel: 715-345-6500; Fax: 715-345-5303.
Res.: 1301 6th Ave., #5, 54481. Tel: 715-342-5930.
Catechesis/Religious Program—Bonnie Seidl Bauman, D.R.E. Students 101.

4—ST. PETER (1876), [JC] Very Rev. Robert A. Schaller. In Res., Revs. Derek J. Sakowski; Dennis A. Worzalla (GB) (Retired).
Res.: 800 4th Ave., 54481-1627. Tel: 715-344-6115; Fax: 715-344-6277.
School—Stevens Point Area Catholic Schools See Unified Catholic School Systems under Insitutions Located in Diocese.

5—ST. STANISLAUS (1917), [JC] Rev. Allen F. Jakubowski; Deacons Hugh Walker; Donald Borski; Sr. Carlene Blavat, S.S.J., Pastoral Min.
Res.: 838 N. Fremont St., 54481. Tel: 715-344-9117; Fax: 715-344-1771.
School—Stevens Point Area Catholic Schools See Unified Catholic School Systems under Institutins Located in the Diocese.

6—ST. STEPHEN (1852), [CEM], Also serves St. Bartholomew, Mill Creek. Rev. John A. Potaczek; Deacon Robert Hensen.
Res.: 1401 Clark St., 54481. Tel: 715-344-3319; Fax: 715-344-6101.
School—Stevens Point Area Catholic Schools See Unified Catholic School Systems under Institutions Located in the Diocese.

STRATFORD, MARATHON CO., ST. JOSEPH (1900), [CEM 3], Also serves St. Andrew, Rozellville. Rev. Thomas J. Rudolph.
Res.: 420 Larch St., P.O. Box 6, 54484. Tel: 715-687-2404; Fax: 715-687-2404.
School—P.O. Box 6, 54484. Tel: 715-687-4145; Fax: 715-687-4343. Lay Teachers 11; Students 141.
Catechesis/Religious Program—Tel: 715-687-3392. Ruth Gawlikoski, D.R.E. Students 254.

SUMMIT, MONROE CO., ST. JOHN THE BAPTIST (1877), [CEM] Attended by, Nativity of the Blessed Virgin Mary, St. Mary's Ridge. Revs. Eric R. Berns; Donald J. Bauer.
Mailing Address: 26400 CTH U, Cashton, 54619-9757. Tel: 608-823-7906; Fax: 608-823-7272.

THORP, CLARK CO., ST. BERNARD-ST. HEDWIG PARISH (1884), [CEM] Rev. John W. Puerner.
Res.: Box 329, 54771. Tel: 715-669-5526; Fax: 715-669-5754.
School—Box 369, 54771. Tel: 715-669-5530. Lay Teachers 12; Students 93.
Catechesis/Religious Program—Tel: 715-669-7302. Rosie Alger, D.R.E. Students 229.

TILDEN, CHIPPEWA CO., ST. PETER (1869), [CEM], Attended by St. Charles Borromeo, Chippewa Falls Very Rev. William P. Felix.
Mailing Address: 11358 CTH Q, Chippewa Falls, 54729-6115. Tel: 715-288-6484; Fax: 715-723-2195.
Res.: 11358 CTU Q, Chippewa Falls, 54729-6115. Tel: 715-723-4088; Fax: 715-723-2195.
School—(Grades 1-8), 11370 CTH Q, 54729. Tel: 715-288-6250; Fax: 715-288-6250. Lay Teachers 5; Students 63.

TOMAH, MONROE CO., ST. MARY (IMMACULATE CONCEPTION) (1867), [CEM], Also serves St. Andrew, Warrens. Very Rev. Steven J. Kachel.
Res.: 203 W. Monroe St., 54660. Tel: 608-372-4516; Fax: 608-372-4506.
School—315 W. Monroe St., 54660. Tel: 608-372-5765; Fax: 608-372-4440. Lay Teachers 14; Students 188.
Catechesis/Religious Program—Tel: 608-372-0825. Wanda Thorson, D.R.E. Students 285.

TORUN, PORTAGE CO., ST. MARY, [CEM] Attended by, St. Casimir, Stevens Point. Rev. Wesley Janoski, C.R., Parochial Admin.
Res.: 5589 Dewey Dr., Stevens Point, 54481. Tel: 715-344-2599; Fax: 715-345-1377.

TREMPEALEAU, TREMPEALEAU CO., ST. BARTHOLOMEW, [CEM 2], Also serves St. Mary, Galesville Rev. Raymond J. Wagner (Retired).
Res.: 11646 South St., 54661-8238. Tel: 608-534-6652.

UNION CENTER, JUNEAU CO., ST. THERESA OF AVILA, Closed., For inquiries for parish records contact St. Jerome, Wonewoc.

VESPER, WOOD CO., ST. JAMES, [CEM] Attended by, St. Joachim, Pittsville. Rev. Jude Ndugbu.
6623 N. Church St., Box 68, 54489. Tel: 715-569-4412.
Res.: P.O. Box 69, Pittsville, 54489.
Catechesis/Religious Program—Annette Molepske, D.R.E. Students 58.

VIROQUA, VERNON CO., ANNUNCIATION OF THE BLESSED VIRGIN MARY, Rev. Robert J. Cook.
Res.: 400 Congress Ave., 54665-1309. Tel: 608-637-7711.
Catechesis/Religious Program—Tel: 608-634-3033. Dennis Olson, D.R.E. Students 193.

WARRENS, MONROE CO., ST. ANDREW, Attended by, St. Mary (Immaculate Conception), Tomah. Very Rev. Steven J. Kachel.
Mailing Address: 24798 Atlas Ave., 54666. Tel: 608-378-4397.
Res.: 203 W. Monroe St., Tomah, 54660. Tel: 608-372-4516.

WAUMANDEE, BUFFALO CO., ST. BONIFACE (1867), [CEM 2], Also serves St. Lawrence, Alma. Rev. John W. Steiner.
Res.: 52026 Cty. Rd. U, 54622-0962. Tel: 608-626-2621.
School—Tel: 608-626-2611. Students 22.

WAUSAU, MARATHON CO.

1—ST. ANNE (1949), [JC] Rev. Steven J. Brice; Deacon Robert G. Anderson.

Res.: 700 W. Bridge St., 54401. Tel: 715-849-3930; Fax: 715-849-4679.
School—Wausau Area Catholic Schools See Unified Catholic School Systems under Institutions Located in the Diocese.
Catechesis/Religious Program—Tel: 715-849-3520; Fax: 715-675-4552. M. Kathleen Mero, D.R.E. Students 445.

2—CHURCH OF THE RESURRECTION (1998), [JC] Rev. Stephen F. Gross.
Mailing Address: 621 2nd St., 54403. Tel: 715-845-6715; 715-845-5379; Fax: 715-845-4120.

3—HOLY NAME OF JESUS (1946), Rev. Joseph K. Gyim-Austin; Mrs. Patricia Gaska, Pastoral Assoc.
Res.: 1104 S. 9th Ave., 54401. Tel: 715-842-4543; Fax: 715-845-5059.
School—Wausau Area Catholic Schools See Unified Catholic School Systems under Institutions Located in the Diocese.

4—ST. JAMES THE GREATER, Closed., For inquiries for Parish Records contact Resurrection of Our Lord Jesus Christ, Wausau.

5—ST. MARY (IMMACULATE CONCEPTION), Closed., For inquiries for Parish Records contact Resurrection of Our Lord Jesus Christ, Wausau.

6—ST. MATTHEW, Rev. Robert C. Thorn.
Res.: 2700 Westwood Dr., 54401. Tel: 715-842-3148.
School—Wausau Area Catholic Schools See Consolidated Elementary Schools under Institutions Located in the Diocese.
Catechesis/Religious Program—Sandy Grabko, D.R.E. Students 139.
St. Matthew Parish Education Center—221 S. 28th Ave., 54401. Tel: 715-845-2938.

7—ST. MICHAEL (1887), [CEM] Rev. William N. Grevatch.
Res.: 1315 6th St., 54403-3599. Tel: 715-842-4283; 715-842-2344; Fax: 715-849-2509.
School—Wausau Area Catholic Schools See Unified Catholic School Systems under Institutions Located in the Diocese.
Convent—611 Stark, 54403. Tel: 715-845-6885; Fax: 715-849-2509.

WAUZEKA, CRAWFORD CO., SACRED HEART (1881), [CEM] Attended by, St. Patrick, Seneca. Rev. Eugene J. Wolf; Sr. Donna Weber, F.S.P.A., Pastoral Assoc.
Res.: 711 E. Main St., P.O. Box 237, 53826. Tel: 608-875-5401.

WEST SALEM, LA CROSSE CO., ST. LEO THE GREAT (1957),, Also serves St. Mary, Bangor. Rev. Robert S. Hegenbarth.
Res.: 210 W. Hamlin St., 54669. Tel: 608-786-0610.

WESTON, MARATHON CO., ST. AGNES, [CEM] Rev. Joseph J. Rafacz, D.R.E.
6101 Zinser St., 54476. Tel: 715-359-5675; Fax: 715-359-4392.
Res.: 113 Kort St., Rothschild, 54474. Tel: 715-359-2421; Fax: 715-355-3088.
Catechesis/Religious Program—Students 210.

WHITEHALL, TREMPEALEAU CO., ST. JOHN THE APOSTLE (1948),, Also serves St. Ansgar, Blair. Rev. Patrick A. Umberger, Parochial Admin.
Res.: 35900 Lee St., 54773-0127. Tel: 715-538-4607; Fax: 715-538-2224.

WILLARD, CLARK CO., HOLY FAMILY, [CEM] Attended by, St. Mary Help of Christians, Greenwood. Rev. A. Joseph Follmar.
Res.: 123 N. Main St., Greenwood, 54437. Tel: 715-267-6282; 715-267-6760.

WILSON, EAU CLAIRE CO., ST. PETER, Closed., For inquiries for parish records contact Sacred Heart-St. Joseph, Boyd.

WILTON, MONROE CO., ST. JOHN THE BAPTIST (1875), [CEM] Attended by, St. Joseph, Kendall. Rev. Brian D. Konopa.
Res.: Box 155, Kendall, 54638. Tel: 608-463-7120.
Catechesis/Religious Program—Tel: 608-463-7649. Mary Skolos, D.R.E. Students 49.

WISCONSIN RAPIDS, WOOD CO.

1—ST. LAWRENCE, [JC], Also serves St. Philip, Rudolph Rev. George Nelson Graham, Parochial Admin.; Deacon James L. Landry.
Res.: 530 10th Ave. N., 54495. Tel: 715-421-5777; 715-424-2651; Fax: 715-421-2478.
School—Wisconsin Rapids Area Catholic Schools See Unified Catholic School Systems under Institutions Located in the Diocese.

2—OUR LADY, QUEEN OF HEAVEN (1947), [JC] Rev. Dennis J. Lynch.
Res.: 750 10th Ave. S., 54495. Tel: 715-423-1251; Fax: 715-423-9407.
School—Wisconsin Rapids Area Catholic Schools See Unified Catholic School Systems under Institutions Located in the Diocese.

3—SS. PETER AND PAUL (1837), [CEM] Rev. Andrew K. Karoblis.
Res.: 1150 2nd St. N., 54494. Tel: 715-423-1351.
Catechesis/Religious Program—Tel: 715-423-6045. Charles Peeters, D.R.E. Students 258.

4—ST. VINCENT DE PAUL (1956), Very Rev. William G. Menzel.
Res.: 820 13 St. S., 54494-5336. Tel: 715-423-2111; Fax: 715-423-4227.
School—Wisconsin Rapids Area Catholic Schools See Unified Catholic School Systems under Institutions Located in the Diocese.
Catechesis/Religious Program—Tel: 715-423-2540; Fax: 715-423-4227. Todd Peterson, D.R.E.; Mary Jo Sigourney, D.R.E. Students 265.

WONEWOC, JUNEAU CO., ST. JEROME, [CEM] Attended by, St. Aloysius, Hillsboro. Rev. Wayne R. Kidd.
Office:—528 N. Center St., R.R. 2, Box 87A, 53968. Tel: 608-464-7713; 608-462-5875.

WUERZBURG, MARATHON CO., ST. JOHN THE BAPTIST (1904), Closed., For inquiries for parish records contact the Diocesan Archives.

YUBA, RICHLAND CO., ST. WENCESLAUS, Closed., For inquiries for parish records contact The Diocesan Archives.

Chaplains of Public Institutions

OXFORD. *Federal Correctional Institute*, Tel: 608-584-5511. Vacant

TOMAH. *Veterans Administration Medical Center* 54660. Tel: 608-372-3971. Rev. George Thekkedam.

WAUSAU. *Wausau Hospital Center*, 333 Pine Ridge Blvd., 54401. Tel: 715-847-2121; 715-847-2840. Rev. Michael J. Lynch.
Res.: 4303 Lake Shore Dr., 54401. Tel: 715-355-4499.

Special Assignment:
Revs.—
Apfelbeck, Keith B., Chap. of Hmong Catholics of the Diocese of LaCrosse, St. Adalbert Rectory, 3315 St. Adalbert Rd., Rosholt, 54473. Tel: 715-677-4519
Dunklee, Lawrence G., P.O. Box 4004, 54602-4004. Tel: 608-788-7700
Gilles, Richard W., J.C.L., Sec. to the Diocesan Bishop, Moderator of the Curia, P.O. Box 4004, 54602-4004. Tel: 608-788-7700
Hirsch, Joseph W., Vocations Dir., P.O. Box 4004, 54602-4004. Tel: 608-788-7700
Martin, Samuel A., Dir. of Holy Cross, Seminary House of Formation, P.O. Box 4004, 54602-4004. Tel: 608-788-9095
Powell, Leon A., Vice Chancellor, P.O. Box 4004, 54602-4004. Tel: 608-788-7700
Thorn, Robert C., Diocesan Chap. of Spanish Speaking Catholics, St. Matthew Rectory, 2700 Westwood Dr., 54403. Tel: 715-842-3148; 608-788-6594

On Duty Outside the Diocese:
Revs.—
Fliss, Richard L., 8531 S.W. 185th Terrace, Miami, FL 33157. Tel: 305-969-9964
Heagle, John L., Tara Center, 1037 S. 102nd St., Seattle, WA 98168. Tel: 206-763-8721
Louis, Kevin C., S.T.L., Pontifical College Josephinum, 7625 N. High St., Columbus, OH 43235-1498. Tel: 614-885-5585
Mason, James E., 233 S. Kane St., Burlington, 53105.
Monti, Robert M., 3003 Terramar St., Apt. 201, Fort Lauderdale, FL 33304-4037. Tel: 954-561-5908
Neis, William P., C.H.C., U.S.N.R., 833 Price St., Meridian, MS 39305.
O'Lenny, Patrick J., Pastor of Holy Family Chapel, N. Yorkshire, U.K., PSC 45, Box 1503, APO Europe, AE 09468.

Foreign Missions:
Revs.—
Flock, Robert H., Parroquia de la Santa Cruz, Casilla 713, Santa Cruz, Bolivia. Tel: 011-591-332-6302
Kolodziejczyk, Sebastian J., Casa Hogar Juan Pablo II, Lurin 16, Peru. Tel: 011-5114-30-5646

On Leave of Absence:
Revs.—
Bauer, Scott A.
Dickman, Richard C.
Konopacky, Joseph R.
Olson, Randy G.
Waldbilling, Brian T.

Retired:
Most Rev.—
Paul, John J., P.O. Box 4004, 54602-4004.
Rev. Msgrs.—
Dall, Norbert P., W5735 Timber Trail, New Lisbon, 53950. Tel: 608-565-7714
Finucan, James P., Holy Cross Diocesan Center, 3710 E. Ave. S., P.O. Box 4004, 54602-4004. Tel: 608-788-7151
Very Rev.—
Logan, James J., 706 S. Palmetto Ave., Marshfield, 54449.
Revs.—
Altmann, Robert T., 10080 County Rd. F, P.O. Box 103, Blenker, 54415.
Berg, Donald M., P.O. Box 386, Edgar, 54426. Tel: 715-352-3444
Blazewicz, William J., Holy Cross Diocesan Center, 3710 Fast Ave., S., P.O. Box 4004, 54602-4004.
Blecha, Charles A., 420 Heller Rd., Apt. 322, Menomonie, 54751. Tel: 715-235-1860
Bornbach, Raymond H., 215 W. Upham St., Marshfield, 54449. Tel: 715-384-7571; 608-643-8361
Braun, Michael C., Holy Name Rectory, 1104 South Ninth Ave., 54407-5910. Tel: 715-842-0515
Cassidy, John V., 3325 Solaris Ln., 54601. Tel: 608-788-1196
Doyle, Mark A., 1421 Grove Ave., Wisconsin Rapids, 54494. Tel: 715-424-2298
Dwyer, J. Floyd, Holy Cross Diocesan Center, 3710 East Ave. S., P.O. Box 4004, 54602-4004. Tel: 608-788-6935
Faber, Emmet N., 162 Cynthia Dr., Bastrop, TX 78602.
Finucan, J. Thomas, 315 S. 14th St., LaCrosse, 54601. Tel: 608-785-3167
Geissler, Lloyd F., 309 Hwy. 107 N., Marathon, 54448. Tel: 715-443-3287
Gerum, Jerome G., 1601 N. Palmetto Ave., P.O. Box 673, Marshfield, 54449-0673. Tel: 715-387-4783
Greatorex, Robert W., 1300 Maria Dr., Stevens Point, 54481.
Hemmersbach, Alfred F., Holy Cross Diocesan Center, 3710 East Ave. S., P.O. Box 4004, 54602-4004. Tel: 608-788-8326
Herrmann, Richard J., 309 W. Blodgett St., Marshfield, 54449. Tel: 715-384-5039
Kamla, Jerome J., 6210 E. Arbor Ave., Apt. #155, Mesa, AZ 85206-1696.
Keating, Joseph R., 1001 Klamenski Rd., Wilmington, DE 19804.
Kelly, Bernard T., W. 7407 CTH Z, R.R. 2, Box 284, Onalaska, 54650. Tel: 608-781-0281
Kelly, Daniel J., 417 Thomas St., P.O. Box 162, Westfield, 53964-0162. Tel: 608-206-3170
Knauf, Edwin L., 836 Leroy Ln., River Falls, 54022-1291. Tel: 715-425-9377
Kulovits, Fred A., 221 Scott St., Apt. 412, 54403. Tel: 715-842-4823
Langer, Thomas E., St. Joseph Rectory (Rock Falls), E. 9265 STH 85, Mondovi, 54755. Tel: 715-875-4539
Lee, Henry H., 817 Macomber St., Chippewa Falls, 54729. Tel: 715-723-1151
Leketas, Peter J., 109 N.Oak Ave., Apt. M, Marshfield, 54449. Tel: 715-384-8331
Malin, Delbert J., 909 Western Ave., Holmen, 54636.
Mannion, Thomas J., 10 Ardsallaghmore, Roscommon, Ireland.
McGarty, Bernard O., 109 S. 9th St.,, 54601. Tel: 608-784-4473
McInnis, Thomas J., 19660 Bluffview Pl., P.O. Box 368, Galesville, 54630-6085.
Mertens, Michael G., Holy Cross Diocesan Center, 3710 East Ave. S., P.O. Box 4004, 54602-4004. Tel: 608-788-0311
Miller, James H., 109 CTH U W., Norwalk, 54648. Tel: 608-823-7643
Mish, Roy L., 107 4th Ave., Apt. 2, Strum, 54770.
Nowak, Bernard J., 601 Seneca Manor Dr., Apt. 14L, Rochester, NY 14621.
Osowski, Chester J., St. Philip Rectory, 6597 Grotto Ave., P.O. Box 165, Rudolph, 54475. Tel: 715-569-4412
Papiernik, Roman J., 3460 Woodbridge Ct., 54601. Tel: 608-787-6027
Pedretti, Raymond J., St. Mary of Mt. Carmel Rectory, 3995 Cty. Rd. K, Amherst, 54406. Tel: 715-824-3455
Penchi, Edward J., Casilla 713, Santa Cruz, Bolivia. Tel: 011-591-343-0302
Raschke, Bernard L., Corpus Christi Rectory, 10075 City Hwy. BB, Marshfield, 54449.
Reardon, Thomas J., 405 Grote St., Mauston, 53948. Tel: 608-847-2633
Redmond, Arthur S., St. Andrew Rectory, D1868 CTHC, P.O. Box 106, Stratford, 54484-0106.
Reuter, Arnold F., Holy Cross Diocesan Center, 3710 East Ave. S., P.O. Box 4004, 54602-4004. Tel: 608-788-0717
Schulte, Lyle L., 234 Main St., P.O. Box 287, Junction City, 54443.
Schulte, Oswald W., Bethany-St. Joseph Care Center, 2501 Shelby Rd., 54601. Tel: 608-788-5700
Simmons, Hilary F., (Summer) 2972 Wausau Rd., Rhinelander, 54501. Tel: 751-282-5751
Simmons, Hilary F., (Winter) 404 N.W. 68th Ave.,

Apt. 518, Plantation, FL 33317. Tel: 305-583-8725
Smith, Eugene P., St. Joseph Rectory, P.O. Box 10, Boyd, 54726-0010. Tel: 715-667-3038
Smith, Thomas J., Holy Cross Diocesan Center, 3710 East Ave., P.O. Box 4004, 54602-4004. Tel: 608-788-4555
Sonnberger, Albert W., St. John the Baptist Rectory, 4540 5th 40, Bloomer, 54724. Tel: 715-568-3778
Stanchik, Dennis P., St. Bartholomew Rectory, 2493 CTHM, Stevens Point, 54481. Tel: 715-344-3003
Stashek, Leonard C., 1506 Wuerzburg Rd., Athens, 54411. Tel: 715-257-7092
Theisen, Donald J., 1025 Pine Beach Rd., Apt. 207, Marinette, 54143. Tel: 715-735-3199
Thome, Edwin J., St. Patrick Rectory, 1031 Main St., Onalaska, 54650. Tel: 608-783-5535
Wagner, Raymond J., Holy Cross Diocesan Center, 3710 E. Ave South, P.O. Box 4004, LaCrosse, 54602-4004. Tel: 608-788-1172
Walijewski, Joseph A., Casa Hogar Juan Pablo II, Lurin 16, Peru. Tel: 011-5114-30-5646
Walljasper, Mark A., 505 W. Division, Sparta, 54656. Tel: 608-269-7801
Wilger, Donald F., W8832 Will Loop, Willard, 54493-9420. Tel: 715-267-4573
Wozniak, Aloysius A., St. Joseph's Rehabitation Center, 2902 East Ave. S., 54602-4004.
Zoromski, Herbert P., 8490 Padre Dr., Wittenberg, 54499. Tel: 715-454-6994

Permanent Deacons:
Abnet, Frank, St. Patrick, Onalaska
Agema, Larry, Sacred Heart, Eau Claire
Anderson, Robert, St. Anne, Wausau
Arnold, Mark C., Sacred Heart, Jim Falls; St. Rose of Lima, Cadott; St. Anthony, Drywood
Ashenbrenner, David, St. Joseph, Galloway, St. Ladislaus, Bevent
Beck, Guy, Buckman, MN
Borski, Donald, St. Stanislaus, Stevens Point
Brunner, Norbert, St. Vincent de Paul, Wisconsin Rapids
Burek, Peter, Church of the Resurrection, Wausau, WI
Chittendon, Robert, St. Olaf, Eau Claire
Delgado, Juan, Mauston
Ebben, Ronald, (Retired), Wausau
Hannig, Daniel, Columbus High School, Marshfield; Sacred Heart of Jesus, Marshfield; Corpus Christi, Bakerville
Hensen, Robert, St. Stephen, Stevens Point
Hurrish, Florian, (Retired), Mesa, AZ
Jirous, Thomas, St. James, Amherst, St. Mary of Mt. Carmel, Fancher
Jolliffe, Garry, Chandler, AZ
Kennedy, David, St. Joseph, Adams
Knauf, LeRoy, Holy Family, Poniatowski
Kostner, Richard, St. Paul, Bloomer, St. Jude, New Auburn
Koza, J. Michael, La Crescent, MN
Landry, James, St. Lawrence, Wisconsin Rapids
McKeough, Patrick, St. Mark, Rothschild
Proulx, Rahlf, Holy Family Medical Center, Manitowoc
Richard, Gordon, Winona, MN
Rivers, Dennis, Holy Cross, Cornell
Sage, Richard, Onalaska
Schaller, Arthur, St. Maximillom Kolbe, Southeastern Portage County.
Schaper, Edward, Black River Falls, WI
Slason, Stillman, Office of Ministries, Asst. to the Dir.
Walker, Hugh, St. Stanislaus, Stevens Point
Weingart, James, St. Mary's Assumption, Durand; Holy Rosary, Lima; Sacred Heart, Mondovi

INSTITUTIONS LOCATED IN THE DIOCESE

[A] SEMINARIES, DIOCESAN

LA CROSSE. *Holy Cross Seminary House of Formation*, 3710 East Ave. S., P.O. Box 4004, 54602-4004. Tel: 608-788-9095; Fax: 608-788-8413. Revs. Samuel A. Martin, Dir.; Richard W. Gilles, J.C.L., Spiritual Dir.; Paul G. Czerwonka, Dir.; Mr. Omar F.A. Gutierrez, Prefect. Tel: 608-787-8978. Students 7.

[B] COLLEGES AND UNIVERSITIES

LA CROSSE. *Viterbo University*, 815 Ninth St. South, 54601-8802. Tel: 608-796-3000; Fax: 608-796-3050. Email: admission@viterbo.edu. Web: www.viterbo.edu. William J. Medland, Ph.D., Pres.; John F. Havertape, Academic Vice Pres.; S. Jean Moore, F.S.P.A., Ph.D., Vice Pres. Student Devel.; Todd M. Ericson, C.P.A., Vice Pres. Finance; Patrick G. Kerrigan, Dir. Mktg. & Communications; Amy Gleason, Registrar; Roland Nelson, Ph.D., Vice Pres. of Enrollment; Rev. Thomas M. O'Neill, Chap. & Dir. Campus Ministry. Tel: 608-796-3804. Founded in 1890 by the Franciscan Sisters of Perpetual Adoration, Viterb Univ. is a Catholic, Franciscan Univ. Comprised of Five Undergrauate Schools, A Graduate School, and a School of Extended Learning. Priests 1; Sisters 4; Lay Teachers 113; Students 2,400.

[C] UNIFIED CATHOLIC SCHOOL SYSTEMS

LA CROSSE. *Coulee Catholic Schools* Central Office: , 521 S. 13th St., 54601. Tel: 608-784-8585; Fax: 608-784-9988. Very Rev. Roger J. Scheckel, Dean CCS; Dr. John Lepetit, Pres.

Aquinas Middle School, 315 S. 11th St., 54601. Tel: 608-784-0156; Fax: 608-784-0229. Mrs. Patricia A. Gallagher-Kosmatka, Prin. Lay Teachers 24; Students 222.

Aquinas High School, 315 S. 11th St., 54601. Tel: 608-784-0287; Fax: 608-782-8851. Email: jleonard@aquinas.lacrosse.wi.us. Web: www.centuryinter.net/aquinas. Joan Leonard, Prin. Priests 1; Religious 2; Lay Teachers 46; Students 389.

Blessed Sacrament School, 2404 King St., 54601. Tel: 608-782-5564; Fax: 608-782-7765. Email: kayberra@centurytel.net. Kay Berra, Prin. Lay Teachers 20; Students 267.

Mary, Mother of the Church School, 3710 East Ave. S., 54601. Tel: 608-788-6919; Fax: 608-788-1139. Email: cburnet@centurytel.net. Charles Burnett, Prin. Lay Teachers 15; Students 153.

Mary, Mother of the Church Early Childhood Center, 2000 Weston St., 54601. Tel: 608-788-5225; Fax: 608-788-5230. Anna Fleming, Admin. Students 81.

St. James School, 716 Windsor St., 54603. Tel: 608-784-6167; Fax: 608-793-1599. Email: stjames/@pressenter.com. Patricia Tschumper, Prin. Lay Teachers 10; Students 71.

St. Joseph Cathedral School, 1319 Ferry St., 54601. Tel: 608-782-5998; Fax: 608-784-9933. Email: jstellflue@ccs.k12.wi.us. John Stellflue, Prin. Lay Teachers 16; Students 165.

St. Patrick School, 127 11th Ave. N., Onalaska, 54650. Tel: 608-783-5483; Fax: 608-783-5483. Email: wesely@charter.net. Greg Wesely, Prin. Lay Teachers 16; Students 171.

CHIPPEWA FALLS. *Chippewa Falls Area Catholic Schools* Central Office: 1316 Bel Air Blvd., 54729. Tel: 715-723-0538; Fax: 715-723-1501. Email: msully99@hotmail.com. Web: www.cacs.k12.wi.us. Michael Sullivan, Pres.

Holy Ghost Elementary School (Grades 3-5), 436 S. Main St., 54729. Tel: 715-726-8788; Fax: 715-723-8990. Mary T. Selz, Prin. Lay Teachers 11; Students 148.

McDonell Central Catholic High School, 1316 Bel Air Blvd., 54729. Tel: 715-723-9126; Fax: 715-723-1501. John Flanagan, Prin.; Rev. Brian J. Jazdzewski, Chap. Priests 1; Lay Teachers 22; Students 250.

Notre Dame Middle School (Grades 6-8), 22 S. Prairie, 54729. Tel: 715-723-4777; Fax 715-723-3353. Sue Goslyn, Prin. Lay Teachers 12; Students 171.

St. Charles Primary School (Grades PreK-2), 429 W. Spruce St., 54729. Tel: 715-723-5827; Fax: 715-723-2109. Susan Mohr, Prin. Lay Teachers 12; Students 184.

EAU CLAIRE. *Catholic Area Schools of the Eau Claire Deanery (C.A.S.E.)* Central Office: , 448 N. Dewey St., 54703. Tel: 715-830-2273; Fax: 715-835-4658. Email: chofacker@case.kiz.wi.us. Web: www.case.kiz.wi.us. Cynthia Hofacker, Pres.

Genesis Child Development Center, 418 N. Dewey St., 54701. Tel: 715-830-2275. Gayle Flaig, Dir.

Immaculate Conception School (Grades K-6), 1703 Sherwin Ave., 54701. Tel: 715-830-5816; Fax: 715-835-9459. Sr. Dorothy Brenner, F.S.P.A., Prin. Lay Teachers 18; Students 270.

Regis Child Devel. Center, 2100 Fenwick Ave., 54701. Tel: 715-830-2274; Fax: 715-830-2270. Gayle Flaig, Dir

Regis Middle School (Grades 7-8), 2100 Fenwick Ave., 54701. Tel: 715-830-1327; Fax: 715-835-4658. Renee Cassidy, Prin.; Rev. William A. Dhein, Chap. Lay Teachers 10; Students 125.

Regis High School, 2100 Fenwick Ave., 54701. Tel: 715-830-2271; Fax: 715-830-5461. Thomas Saporito, Prin.; Rev. William A. Dhein, Chap. Priests 1; Lay Teachers 17; Students 209.

St. James School (Grades K-6), 2502 Eleventh St., 54703. Tel: 715-830-2277; Fax: 715-830-9861. Lay Teachers 9; Students 116.

St. Mary School (Grades K-5), 1828 Lynn Ave., Altoona, 54720. Tel: 715-830-2278; Fax: 715-830-9573. Lay Teachers 9; Students 73.

St. Olaf School (Grades K-6), 2407 North Ln., 54703. Tel: 715-830-2279; Fax: 715-832-0742. Faculty 10; Students 123.

MARSHFIELD. *Marshfield Area Catholic Schools (MACS)*, 710 S. Columbus Ave., 54449. Tel: 715-387-1177; Fax: 715-384-4535. Email: hannigd@wctc.net. Deacon Daniel Hannig, Pres.

Columbus High School, 710 S. Columbus Ave., 54449-3413. Tel: 715-387-1177; Fax: 715-384-4535. Email: hannigd@wctc.net. Web: www.columbus-.marshfield.wi.us. Deacon Daniel Hannig, Prin.; Rev. Brian D. Konopa, Chap. Priests 1; Lay Teachers 21; Students 127.

Holy Family Middle School, 710 S. Columbus Ave., 54449. Tel: 715-384-7184; Fax: 715-384-4535. Email: hfms@wctc.net. Web: www.columbus.marshfield.wi.us/hfms. James Weister, Prin.; Rev. Brian D. Konopa, Chap. Priests 1; Lay Teachers 8; Students 78.

Our Lady of Peace School, 1300 W. Fifth St., 54449. Tel: 715-384-5474; Fax: 715-387-8697. Sr. Mary Ann Wutkowski, S.S.N.D., Prin. Students 235.

St. John School, 307 Walnut Ave., 54449. Tel: 715-384-4989; Fax: 715-384-5131. James Weister, Prin. Students 188.

STEVENS POINT. *Stevens Point Area Catholic Schools* Central Office: , 1408 Ellis St., 54481. Tel: 715-341-2445; Fax: 715-342-2001. Email: ghansel@spacs.k12.wi.us. Web: www.spacs.k12.wi.us. Mr. Gregg Hansel, Pres.

St. Bronislava School (Grades PreK-5), 3301 Willow Dr., Plover, 54467. Tel: 715-342-2015; Fax: 715-342-2016. Laura Barnett, Prin. Lay Teachers 7; Students 146.

Pacelli High School, 1301 Maria Dr., 54481. Tel: 715-341-2442; Fax: 715-341-6799. Dr. Robert Lecheler, Prin.; Rev. Derek J. Sakowski, Chap., 800 Fourth St., 54481-1627. Priests 1; Sisters 2; Lay Teachers 25; Students 217.

St. Joseph School Early Childhood Center, 1901 Lincoln Ave., 54481. Tel: 715-341-2878; Fax: 715-342-2013. Laura Barnett, Prin. Lay Teachers 3; Students 104.

St. Peter Middle School (Grades 6-8), 708 First St., 54481. Tel: 715-344-1890; Fax: 715-342-2005. Anne Rogalski, Prin.; Rev. Derek J. Sakowski, Chap. Lay Teachers 15; Students 209.

St. Stanislaus School (Grades K-2), 2150 High St., 54481. Tel: 715-344-3086; Fax: 715-342-2014. Joyce Trebatoski, Prin. Lay Teachers 8; Students 132.

St. Stephen School (Grades 3-5), 1335 Clark St., 54481. Tel: 715-344-3751; Fax: 715-342-2013. Joyce Trebatoski, Prin. Lay Teachers 13; Students 143.

WAUSAU. *Wausau Area Catholic Schools*, 610 Steuben St., 54403. Tel: 715-845-5735; Fax: 715-848-3582. Web: www.wausau.wi.us. Mark Watson, Pres. Central Office:

Holy Name School (Grades PreK-5), 1122 S. 9th Ave., 54401-5910. Tel: 715-848-3281. Jeanne Lang, Prin. Lay Teachers 15; Students 95.

Newman High School, 1130 W. Bridge St., 54401. Tel: 715-845-8274; Fax: 715-842-1302. Janet Klosinski, Prin.; Rev. David Olson, Chap. Priests 1; Lay Teachers 29; Students 229.

St. Anne School (Grades PreK-5), 604 N. 6th Ave., 54401. Tel: 715-845-5754; Fax: 715-842-4021. Sandra Gilge, Prin. Lay Teachers 20; Students 313.

St. Mark School, 602 Military Rd., Rothschild, 54474. Tel: 715-359-9662; Fax: 715-355-8905. Vicki Koeppel, Prin. Lay Teachers 15; Students 149.

St. Matthew Middle School (Grades 6-8), 225 S. 28th Ave., 54401. Tel: 715-842-4857; Fax: 715-845-2937. Tina Meyer, Prin.; Rev. Robert C. Thorn, Chap. Lay Teachers 19; Students 236.

St. Michael School (Grades PreK-5), 614 Steuben St., 54403. Tel: 715-848-0206; Fax: 715-845-6852. Lucille McCarthy, Prin. Felician Sisters 1; Lay Teachers 9; Students 83.

St. Therese School (Grades 4-6), 112 W. Kort St., Schofield, 54476. Tel: 715-359-2131. Vicki Koeppel, Prin. Sisters of St. Joseph Lay Teachers 5; Students 54.

WISCONSIN RAPIDS. *Wisconsin Rapids Area Catholic Schools* Central Office: , 1120 Lincoln, Ste. B, 54494. Tel: 715-422-0900; Fax: 715-422-0903. Email: colson_wracs@hotmail.com. Web: wracs.org. Carol Olson, Administrative Chair.

Assumption Middle School, 440 Mead, 54494. Tel: 715-422-0950; Fax: 715-422-0955. Joan Bond, Prin.; Rev. Brian E. Stashek, Chap. Students 99.

Assumption High School, 445 Chesnut St., 54494. Tel: 715-422-0910; Fax: 715-422-0912. Email: cjmahs@wctc.net. Thomas Reichenbacher, Prin.; Rev. Brian E. Stashek, Chap. Priests 1; Lay Teachers 21; Students 166.

Our Lady Queen of Heaven School, 750 Tenth Ave. S., 54495. Tel: 715-422-0980; Fax: 715-424-2972. Jean Stelzer, Prin. Lay Teachers 9; Students 101.

Sacred Heart of School, 710 Vilas Ave., Nekoosa, 54457. Tel: 715-886-3761; Fax: 715-886-3745. Jean Stelzer, Prin. Lay Teachers 6; Students 55.

St. Lawrence Early Childhood Center, 551 Tenth Ave. N., 54495. Tel: 715-422-0990; Fax: 715-422-0993. Carol Olson, Prin. Lay Teachers 5; Students 101.

St. Philip School, 6975 Grotto Ave., Rudolph, 54475. Tel: 715-435-3386; Fax: 715-435-3346. Carol Olson, Prin. Lay Teachers 7; Students 91.

St. Vincent de Paul School, 831 12th St. S., 54494. Tel: 715-422-0960; Fax: 715-422-0963. Lay Teachers 16; Students 146.

[D] GENERAL HOSPITALS

LA CROSSE. *Franciscan Skemp Healthcare, Mayo Health System, La Crosse Campus Medical Center*, 700 West Ave. S., 54601-4796. Tel: 608-785-0940; Fax: 608-791-9429. Web: www.fransicanskemp.org. David Nesse, Pres. & CEO; Rev. Paul L. Sankoorikal, Chap. Franciscan Sisters of Perpetual Adoration and Mayo Foundation Sisters 7; Total Staff 1,434; Bed Capacity 345; Patients Assisted Annually 118,000.

ARCADIA. *Franciscan Skemp Healthcare, Mayo Health System, Arcadia Campus Hospital*, 464 S. St. Joseph Ave., 54612. Tel: 608-323-3341; Fax: 608-323-3694. Email: tracey.robert@mayo.edu. Web: www.franciscanskemp.org. Robert Tracey, Admin.; Rev. Robert F. Polcyn, O.F.M.Cap., Chap.; Sr. Rose Grabowski, S.S.J., T.O.S.F., Pastoral Care. Franciscan Sisters of Perpetual Adoration and Mayo Foundation Total Staff 94; Bed Capacity 25; Patients Assisted Annually 16,500.

CHIPPEWA FALLS. *St. Joseph's Hospital*, 2661 County Hwy. I, 54729. Tel: 715-723-1811; Fax: 715-726-3204. Web: www.stjoeschipfalls.com. David B. Fish, Exec. Vice Pres.; Rev. Daniel B. Duchez, O.S., Chap. Hospital Sisters of the Third Order of St. Francis, Hospital Sisters Health System. Sisters 4; Total Staff 465; Bed Capacity 84; Patients Assisted Annually 96,486.

EAU CLAIRE. *Sacred Heart Hospital*, 900 W. Clairemont Ave., 54701-6122. Tel: 715-839-4121; Fax: 715-839-8417. Web: www.sacredhearthospital-ec.org. Stephen F. Ronstrom, Exec. Vice Pres.; Rev. Edmund J. Klimek, Chap.; Sr. Augusta Sperl, O.S.F., Dir. Pastoral Care. Hospital Sisters of the Third Order of St. Francis 3; Bed Capacity 344; Patients Assisted Annually 128,751.

HILLSBORO. *St. Joseph's Memorial Hospital, Inc.*, 400 Water Ave., P.O. Box 527, 54634. Tel: 608-489-8000; Fax: 608-489-8181. Email: k.coblentz.stjoseph@mint.net. Web: stjhealthcare.org. Franciscan Sisters of Perpetual Adoration, Connected with the hospital is a home for the aged. Under care 65 infirm and aged men and women. Bed Capacity 25; Patients Assisted Annually 3,440.

MARSHFIELD. *Saint Joseph's Hospital of Marshfield, Inc.*, 611 St. Joseph Ave., 54449. Tel: 715-387-1713; Fax: 715-387-8601. Web: www.ministryhealth.org. Michael Schmidt, Pres.; Michael Krycla, CEO. Corporate Sponsor: Ministry HealthCare, Inc. (Milwaukee, WI); Sponsored by the Sisters of the Sorrowful Mother.; Training School for Nurses (Affiliated with U.W.-Eau Claire).

Spiritual Services Dept. Tel: 715-387-7753. Revs. Edwin Osita Emeli; Nicolas Husain, Chap.; Rebecca Belt, Catholic Lay Chap.; Rita Austin, Pastoral Care Staff; Robert Cassidy, Pastoral Care Staff; Rev. Steven E. Sutterer, Protestant Chap.; Rev. Linden Nelson, Protestant Chap. Sisters of the Sorrowful Mother 1; Bed Capacity 504; Patients Assisted Annually 104,100.

SPARTA. *Franciscan Skemp Healthcare, Mayo Health System, Sparta Campus Hospital*, 310 W. Main St., 54656-2142. Tel: 608-269-2132; Fax: 608-269-1017. Web: www.franciscanskemp.org. Robert M. Tracey, Admin.; Amanda Merlin, Pastoral Care. Franciscan Sisters of Perpetual Adoration and Mayo Foundation Total Staff 160; Bed Capacity 25; Patients Assisted Annually 35,574.

STANLEY. **Victory Medical Center, Inc.*, 1120 Pine St., 54768. Tel: 715-644-5571; Fax: 715-644-5665. Email: eichmanc@olvh.org. Web: www.ministryhealth.org. Mrs. Cynthia Eichman, CEO; Sr. Pat Belongia, Dir. Spiritual Svcs. Corporate Sponsor: Ministry Healthcare, Inc. (Milwaukee, WI); Sponsored by Sisters of the Sorrowful Mother. Hospital 24; Total Staff 150; Patients Assisted Annually 26,000.

STEVENS POINT. *St. Michael's Hospital of Stevens Point, Inc.*, 900 Illinois Ave., 54481. Tel: 715-346-5000; Fax: 715-346-5077. Email: martinj@smhosp.org. Web: www.ministryhealth.org. Jeffrey L. Martin, Regional CEO; Mr. David C. Baker, Dir. Spiritual Svcs.; Mrs. Janet Jacoby, Spiritual Svcs.; Martin Lieber, Spiritual Svcs. Corporate Sponsor: Ministry Health Care, Inc. (Milwaukee, WI); Sponsored by Sisters of the Sorrowful Mother. Bed Capacity 181; Patients Assisted Annually 150,000.

Ministry Medical Group, Inc., 824 Illinois Ave., 54481. Tel: 715-342-7500; Fax: 715-342-7929. Email: spribyl@ricemedical.org. Web: www.ministrymedicalgroup.org. Michael J. Kryda, M.D., Pres.; Stephen J. Pribyl, Admin. Total Staff 650; Patients Assisted Annually 150,000.

WAUSAU. *Saint Clare's Hospital of Weston, Inc.*, 7611 Birch St., Weston, 54476. Tel: 715-346-5079; Fax: 715-346-5088. Web: www.ministryhealth.org. Jeffrey L. Martin, Pres. & CEO; Lori Heiman, Contact Person (Ministry Health Care). Sponsored by Sisters of the Sorrowful Mother, Corporate Sponsor: Ministry Health Care, Inc. (Milwaukee, WI)

[E] REHABILITATION FACILITIES

LA CROSSE. *St. Francis Community Programs, Inc.*, 700 West Ave. S., 54601-4796. Tel: 608-791-9582; Fax: 608-784-7084. Adult Day Care Center 80; Special Centers for Social Services & Assistance 450; Total Staff 77.

Gerard Hall Tel: 608-791-3985; Fax: 608-791-7802. 8 bed home for women with AODA, MH, or Pregnancy and Parenting Issues.

St. Francis Community Housing, Inc. Tel: 608-792-9488; Fax: 608-782-2779. Apartment units for chronically mentally ill; 12 bed apartment unit in Dodgeville, WI; and 12 bed apartment unit in Prairie du Chien, WI.

St. Francis Housing Alternatives, Inc. Tel: 608-791-9488; Fax: 608-782-2779. Apartment units for the chronically mentally ill; 8 bed apartment unit in Arcadia, WI; 8 bed apartment unit in Black River Falls, WI; and 8 bed apartment unit in Mauston, WI.

Siena Hall Tel: 608-784-6010; Fax: 608-784-7084. 20 bed home for mentally ill adults.

LAAR House Tel: 608-782-7700; Fax: 608-791-9431. 24 bed home for chemically dependent adults.

Scarseth House Tel: 608-785-1270; Fax: 608-784-7084. 8 bed home for chemically dependent male adolescents.

Villa Succes, Prairie du Chien, 53821. Tel: 608-326-8424; Fax: 608-326-8638.

CHIPPEWA FALLS. *L.E. Phillips Libertas Treatment Center for the Chemically Dependent*, 2661 County Hwy. I, 54729. Tel: 715-723-5585; 800-680-4578; Fax: 715-726-3504. Email: ddachel@sjcf.hshs.org. Web: www.stjoeschipfalls.com. David B. Fish, Exec. Vice Pres.; Dr. Shawna T. Kovach, Prog. Coord. Hospital Sisters Health System, Hospital Sisters of the Third Order of St. Francis Bed Capacity 44; Patients Assisted Annually 12,628.

Transitus House, 1830 Wheaton St., 54729. Tel: 715-723-1155; Fax: 715-723-1669. Email: transitu@discover-net.net. Web: www.stjoeschipfalls.com. David B. Fish, Chm.; Susan J. Anderson, Ph.D., Prog. Coord.

Legal Title: *Hospital Sisters HealthCare-West, Inc.* Hospital Sisters of the Third Order of St. Francis, Transitional living facility for women recovering from chemical dependency. Bed Capacity 20; Assisted annually 53.

[F] HOMES FOR AGED

LA CROSSE. *Bethany-St. Joseph Care Center*, 2501 Shelby Rd., 54601. Tel: 608-788-5700. Thomas Rand, Admin. Bed Capacity 226; Patients Assisted Annually 247.

Elder Care of North La Crosse, Inc. (Village on St. James), 800 St. James St., 54603. Tel: 608-791-9784; Fax: 608-782-2779. Web: www.franciscanskemp.org. Richard Berendes, Admin. Extended Care. Total Assisted Annually 30; Units 23; Total Staff 3.

Franciscan Elder Care, Inc., 800 West Avenue S., 54601-4796. Tel: 608-791-9505; Fax: 608-782-2779. Richard Berendes, Admin. & Extended Care. Total Staff 17; Subsidized Units 132.

Village on Cass, 225 S. 24th St.. Tel: 608-791-9487; Fax: 608-782-2779. 30 bed assisted living unit for elderly.

Village on 9th, 621 S. 9th St.. Tel: 608-791-9505; Fax: 608-782-2779. 24 bed independent living unit for elderly

Village on St. James, 800 St. James St.. Tel: 608-791-9505; Fax: 608-782-2779.

Village Apartments, Decorah, IA. Tel: 608-791-9505; Fax: 608-782-2779.

Village Apartments, Cresco, IA. Tel: 608-791-9505; Fax: 608-782-2779.

Village Apartments, Sparta. Tel: 608-791-9505; Fax: 608-782-2779.

Franciscan Skemp Healthcare, Mayo Health System, La Crosse Campus Nursing Home, 620 S. 11th St., 54601. Tel: 608-791-9787; Fax: 608-791-9716. Roberta Messer, Admin. Bed Capacity 95; Patients Assisted Annually 315.

St. Joseph's Nursing Home, 2902 East Ave. S., 54601. Tel: 608-788-9870; Fax: 608-788-7373. Mary Clausen, Admin. Operated by Catholic Residential Services, Inc., Diocese of La Crosse. Units 80; Patients Assisted Annually 205.

ARCADIA. *Franciscan Skemp Healthcare, Mayo Health System, Arcadia Campus Nursing Home*, 464 S. St. Joseph Ave., 54612. Tel: 608-323-3341; Fax: 608-323-3694. Darlene Goehner, Admin.; Rev. Robert F. Polcyn, O.F.M.Cap., Chap.; Sr. Arlene Melder, F.S.P.A., Chap. Franciscan Sisters of Perpetual Adoration and Mayo Foundation. Bed Capacity 75; Patients Assisted Annually 125; Total Staff 75.

EAU CLAIRE. *St. Francis Apartment*, 851 University Dr., 54701. Tel: 715-834-1388; Fax: 715-839-8417. Email: stfrancis@cvol.net. David B. Fish, Chm. Legal Title: *Hospital Sisters Health Care-West, Inc.* Units 60; Total in Residence 70.

HILLSBORO. *St. Joseph's Nursing Home*, 400 Water St., P.O. Box 527, 54634. Tel: 608-489-8000; Fax: 608-489-8187. Email: k.coblentz.stjoseph@mwt.net. Web: stjhealthcare.org. (See Hospital Listing.)

ONALASKA. *Franciscan Skemp Healthcare, Mayo Health System, Onalaska Nursing Home*, 1600 Main St., 54650. Tel: 608-783-4681. Larry Alens, Admin. Bed Capacity 112; Patients Assisted Annually 260; Total Staff 160.

SPARTA. *Elder Care of Sparta, Inc.*, 622 S. Court, 54656. Tel: 608-791-9505; Fax: 608-782-2779. Web: www.franciscanskemp.org. Richard Berendes, Admin. Extended Care. Units 24.

Franciscan Skemp Healthcare, Mayo Health System, Sparta Campus Nursing Home, 310 W. Main St., 54656-2142. Tel: 608-269-2132; Fax: 608-269-1017. Susan Steivang, Admin. Bed Capacity 50; Patients Assisted Annually 60; Total Staff 27.

WAUSAU. *Marywood Convalescent Center*, 1821 N. 4th Ave., 54401. Tel: 715-675-9451; Fax: 715-675-9051. Scott W. Rusch, Admin. Operated by Catholic Residential Services, Inc. Units 90; Patients Assisted Annually 131.

[G] RETREAT HOUSES

LA CROSSE. *Franciscan Spirituality Center*, 920 Market St., 54601-8809. Tel: 608-791-5295; Fax: 608-782-6301. Email: fscenter@fspa.org. Web: www.franciscanspiritualitycenter.org. Vince Hatt, Dir. Sisters of the Third Order of St. Francis of Perpetual Adoration

CUSTER. *St. Clare Center for Spirituality*, 7381 Church St., 54423. Tel: 715-592-4099. Email: stclare@coredcs.com. Sr. Mary Therese Lukas, C.S.S.F., Dir. Felician Sisters

EAU CLAIRE. *Saint Bede Retreat and Conference Center*, 1190 Priory Rd., P.O. Box 66, 54702-0066. Tel: 715-834-8642; Fax: 715-834-4292. Email: sisters@saintbede.org. Web: www.saintbede.org. Sr. Hildegarde Geraets, O.S.B., Dir.; Mary Traynor, Asst. Dir. Benedictine Sisters

MARATHON CITY. *St. Anthony Retreat Center*, 300 E. 4th St., 54448-9602. Tel: 715-443-2236; Fax: 715-443-2235. Email: info@sarcenter.com. Web: www.sarcenter.com. Rev. Dan Crosby, O.F.M.Cap., Leadership Team. The Province of St. Joseph of the Capuchin Order, Inc. Priests 3.

[H] MONASTERIES AND RESIDENCES OF PRIESTS AND BROTHERS

LA CROSSE. *Holy Cross (Seminary) Diocesan Center*, 3710 East Ave. S., P.O. Box 4004, 54602-4004. Tel: 608-788-7700; Fax: 608-788-8413. Mr. John J. Newman, Dir. In Res. Most Rev. John J. Paul. Tel: 608-788-8395; Rev. Msgr. James P. Finucan (Retired). Tel: 608-788-7151; Revs. Peter Cops. Tel: 608-787-8739; Lawrence G. Dunklee. Tel: 608-788-4249; J. Floyd Dwyer (Retired). Tel: 608-788-6935; Alfred F. Hemmersbach (Retired). Tel: 608-788-8326; Joseph W. Hirsch. Tel: 608-343-0627; Maryon Jordan, O.S.B. Tel: 608-787-6838; Samuel A. Martin. Tel: 608-788-9095; Michael G. Mertens (Retired). Tel: 608-788-0311; Leon A. Powell. Tel: 608-788-4625; Arnold F. Reuter (Retired). Tel: 608-788-0717; Thomas J. Smith (Retired). Tel: 608-788-4555; Raymond J. Wagner (Retired). Tel: 608-788-1172.

DE SOTO. *Brothers of St. Pius X*, P.O. Box 217, 54624-0217. Tel: 608-648-2087. Bro. Charles Bisenius, Dir.

MARATHON CITY. *St. Anthony Retreat Center*, 300 E. Fourth St., 54448-9602. Tel: 715-443-2236; Fax: 715-443-2235. Email: info@sarcenter.com. Web: www.sarcenter.com. Revs. Dan Crosby, O.F.M.Cap., Leadership Team; Peter Hesse, O.F.M.Cap.; Marty Pable, O.F.M.Cap. The Province of St. Joseph of the Capuchin Order, Inc. Priests 3.

ST. MARY'S RIDGE. *Immaculate Conception Priory*, 429 Grand Ave., Wausau, 54403. Institute of Christ

the King-Sovereign Priest
26384 CTH U, Cashton, 54619-9757. Tel: 608-823-7992. Very Rev. Msgr. Michael R. Schmitz.

SPARTA. *Our Lady of Spring Bank, Cistercian Abbey*, 17304 Havenwood Rd., 54656-9536. Tel: 608-269-8138; Fax: 608-269-2800. Email: Porter@MonksOnline.org. Web: www.MonksOnline.org. Revs. Robert Keffer, O.Cist., Prior Admin.; Bernard McCoy, O.Cist., Subprior & Cellerar; Rt. Rev. Blaise Fuez, O.Cist., Abbott Emeritus. Legal Office for Cistercian Monasteries Auxiliary. Solemnly Professed 4; Simple Professed 2.

WAUSAU. *Institute of Christ the King - Sovereign Priest*, American Headquarters: 429 Grand Ave., 54403. Tel: 715-843-5336; Fax: 715-845-5326. Email: info@institute-christ-king.org. Web: www.institute-christ-king.org. Very Rev. Msgr. Michael R. Schmitz.

[I] CONVENTS AND RESIDENCES FOR SISTERS

LA CROSSE. *St. Rose Convent*, 912 Market St., 54601-8800. Tel: 608-782-5610; Fax: 608-782-6301. Email: fspa@fspa.org. Web: www.fspa.org. Sr. Marlene Weisenbeck, F.S.P.A., Pres. Motherhouse and Novitiate of the Congregation of the Franciscan Sisters of Perpetual Adoration. In Community: Professed 409; Transfers 4; In Motherhouse: Sisters 84.

Villa St. Joseph, W2658 State Rd. 33, 54601-2625. Tel: 608-788-5100; Fax: 608-788-7360. Email: marisk@charter.net. Web: www.fspa.org. Sr. Maris Kerwin, F.S.P.A., Admin. Franciscan Sisters of Perpetual Adoration, A Retirement home for aged and convalescent Franciscan Sisters of Perpetual Adoration. Sisters 9; Lay Staff 105; Under Care 105.

CHIPPEWA FALLS. *St. Francis Convent*, 2509 County Hwy. I, 54729. Tel: 715-723-7476. Sr. Frances Elizabeth Schmitz, Coord. Hospital Sisters of the Third Order of St. Francis Professed Sisters 4.

St. Joseph Convent, 5085 176th St., 54729. Tel: 715-723-7479. Hospital Sisters of the Third Order of St. Francis

EAU CLAIRE. *St. Bede Monastery*, 1190 Priory Rd., P.O. Box 66, 54702-0066. Tel: 715-834-3176; Fax: 715-834-4292. Email: sisters@saintbede.org. Web: www.saintbede.org. Sr. Margaret Michaud, O.S.B., Prioress; Rev. Thomas E. Langer, Chap. (Retired). Motherhouse of Sisters of the Order of St. Benedict. Retreat and Conference Center. Professed 39.

Sacred Heart Hospital Franciscan Sisters Convent, 901 University Ave., 54701. Tel: 715-839-8725; Fax: 715-831-9670. Email: sisteras@juno.com. Sr. Augusta Sperl, O.S.F., Coord. Hospital Sisters of the Third Order of St. Francis Professed Sisters 3.

Sisters of St. Benedict, The Clairemont, 2120 Heights Dr., 54701. Tel: 715-832-9143. Sr. Margaret Michaud, O.S.B., Health Care & House Coord. Residence for Sisters of the Order of St. Benedict. Sisters 7.

POLONIA. *St. Clare Convent*, 7381 Church St., 54423. Tel: 715-592-4213. Sr. M. Ursula Myszka, Local Min. Felician Sisters 5.

STEVENS POINT. *St. Joseph Congregational Home*, 1300 Maria Dr., 54481. Tel: 715-344-2830; Fax: 715-344-2380. Email: lizk@ssj-tosf.org. Rev. Robert W. Greatorex, Chap. (Retired). Tel: 715-344-8346; Sisters Elizabeth Koszarek, S.S.J.-T.O.S.F., Coord.; Janet Smolinski, S.S.J.-T.O.S.F., Coord. Residence of the Sisters of St. Joseph of the Third Order of St. Francis. Sisters 58.

[J] SOCIAL SERVICE AGENCIES

LA CROSSE. *Catholic Charities of the Diocese of La Crosse, Inc.*, 128 S. 6th St., P.O. Box 266, 54601. Tel: 608-782-0710; Fax: 608-782-0702. Email: info@catholiccharitieslax.org. Web: catholiccharitieslax.org. Rev. Richard W. Gilles, J.C.L., Vice Pres. & Treas.; Mr. Benedict T. Nguyen, M.T.S., J.C.L., Sec.; Daniel Idzikowski Jr., Exec. Dir. Counseling and Mental Health Svcs. Counseling and Mental Health Svcs., Fin. Counseling, Pregnancy & Parenting Svcs., Adoption Placement, Emergency Svcs., Immigration & Refugee Svcs. Total Staff 45.

Catholic Residential Services, Inc., 505 King St., Ste. 223, P.O. Box 2394, 54602-2394. Tel: 608-784-5323; Fax: 608-784-7522. Mr. Robert A. Laubach, Exec. Dir.; Sr. Joan Moran, Bd. Pres.; Josephine Smieja, Bd. Vice Pres.; John Newman, Bd. Sec. Total Staff 240; Patients Assisted Annually 420.

WAUSAU. *Northland House*, 102 McClellan St., 54402-0231. Tel: 715-845-4898; Fax: 715-848-0498. Email: nhgh@dwave.net. Web: www.crsinc.org/northland. Janet R. Nissen, Admin. Operated by Catholic Residential Services, Inc., Diocese of La Crosse.; Residential Care of Children.

[K] NEWMAN CAMPUS MINISTRY

LA CROSSE. *Roncalli Newman Parish*, Serving Univ. of Wisconsin-La Crosse and Western Wisconsin Technical College. , 1732 State St., 54601. Tel: 608-784-4994; Fax: 608-784-0280. Email: newmanuw-l@juno.com. Web: www.uwlax.edu/newman. Rev. Mark R. Pierce, Pastor; Jon Stuttgen, Campus Min.

EAU CLAIRE. *Newman Parish*, Serving Univ. of Wisconsin-Eau Claire and Chippewa Valley Technical College. , 110 Garfield Ave., 54701-4042. Tel: 715-834-3399. Email: georges128@aol.com. Web: www.newmanec.com. Revs. George R. Szews, Pastor; Edmund J. Klimek, Assoc.

MENOMONIE. *The Ministry to the University of Wisconsin-Stout* 108 3rd Ave. W., 54751. Tel: 715-235-4258; Fax: 715-235-4258. Rev. Thomas J. Krieg, Chap.

STEVENS POINT. *Newman University Parish*, Serving Univ. of Wisconsin-Stevens Point. , 2108 Fourth Ave., 54481. Tel: 715-345-6500. Email: TomLNewman@aol.com. Web: www.uwsp.edu/stuorg/newman. Rev. Thomas F. Lindner Pastor.

[L] FOUNDATIONS, FUNDS & TRUSTS

LA CROSSE. *Aquinas High School and Aquinas Schools Foundation*, 315 S. 11th St., 54601. Tel: 608-784-0287; Fax: 608-782-8851.

Bishop's Education Endowment Trust, P.O. Box 4004, 54602-4004. Tel: 608-788-7700.

Blessed Sacrament Parish Endowment Trust, 130 S. Losey Blvd., 54601. Tel: 608-782-2953; Fax: 608-785-1064. Email: blessedsacrament@centurytel.net. Web: www.blessedsacrament.catholicweb.com.

Caritas Endowment Trust, 128 S. 6th St., P.O. Box 266, 54602-0266. Tel: 608-782-0710. Daniel Idzikowski Jr., Exec. Dir., Catholic Charities of the Diocese of La Crosse.

Cathedral of St. Joseph the Workman Endowment Trust, 530 Main St., 54601. Tel: 608-782-0322; Fax: 608-782-8228.

Father Joseph Walijewski Orphanage Endowment Trust, 3710 E. Ave S., 54601. Tel: 608-788-7700; Fax: 608-788-8413. Very Rev. Roger J. Scheckel, Exec. Sec.

Franciscan Skemp Foundation, Inc., 700 W. Ave. South, 54601-4796. Tel: 608-784-6449; Fax: 608-791-9799. Email: grabow.peter@mayo.edu. Web: www.franciscanskemp.org. Peter Grabow, Dir.

Holy Cross Seminary Education Fund Endowment Trust, P.O. Box 4004, 54602-4004. Tel: 608-788-7700; Fax: 608-788-8413.

Holy Trinity Catholic Church Endowment Trust, 1333 S. 13th St., 54601. Tel: 608-782-2028.

St. James Parish Endowment Trust, 1032 Caledonia St., 54603. Tel: 608-782-7557; Fax: 608-796-0086. Email: scheckel@execpc.com.

La Crosse Deanery Catholic Education Endowment Trust, P.O. Box 4004, 54602-4004.

Mary, Mother of the Church Parish Endowment Trust, 2006 Weston St., 54601.

Roncalli Newman Parish Student Endowment Trust, 1732 State St., 54601. Tel: 608-784-4994; Fax: 608-784-0230. Email: newmanuw-l@juno.com. Web: www.uwlax.edu/newman.

Shrine of Our Lady of Guadalupe of the Diocese of La Crosse Endowment Trust, 5250 Justin Rd., P.O. Box 1237, 54602-1237. Tel: 608-782-5440; Fax: 608-782-3104. Email: smchrista@shrineofourlady.com. Web: www.shrineofourladyofguadalupe.org.

ALTOONA. *St. Mary Parish Endowment Trust*, 1812 Lynn Ave., 54720. Tel: 715-855-1294; Fax: 715-855-8664. Email: stmary1827@myexcel.com.

ARCADIA. *Arcadia Catholic School Endowment Trust Fund*, 341 S. Washington St., 54612. Tel: 608-323-3676; Fax: 608-323-3786. Email: acs@triwest.net. Web: www.holyfam.com.

Franciscan Skemp Foundation of Arcadia, Inc., 464 S. St. Joseph Ave., 54612. Tel: 608-323-3341; Fax: 608-323-3694. Email: tracey.robert@mayo.edu. Web: www.franciscanskemp.org. Robert Tracey, Ex-Officio.

AUBURNDALE. *St. Mary Education Endowment Trust*, Box 177, 54412-0177. Tel: 715-652-2805; Fax: 715-652-8020.

BIG RIVER. *The St. Mary's-Big River Endowment Trust*, W10137 570th Ave., River Falls 54022. Tel: 715-425-5806.

BLAIR. *The St. Ansgar Catholic Church Endowment Trust*, 35900 Lee St., Whitehall, 54773. Tel: 715-538-4607; Fax: 715-538-2224.

BLOOMER. *St. Paul Catholic Parish of Bloomer Wisconsin Endowment Trust*, 1222 Main St., 54724. Tel: 715-568-3255.

CADOTT. *St. Rose of Lima Catholic Church Endowment Trust*, Box 160, 54727. Tel: 715-289-4551.

CASHTON. *Sacred Heart of Jesus Education Endowment Trust*, 26400 CTH U, 54619-9757. Tel: 608-823-7906; Fax: 608-823-7272.

CHIPPEWA FALLS. *St. Charles Future Fund Trust*, 810 Pearl St., 54729. Tel: 715-723-4088; Fax: 715-723-2195.

The Chippewa Area Catholic Schools Endowment Trust, 1316 Bel Air Blvd., 54729. Tel: 715-723-0538; Fax: 715-723-1501.

The Education/Sustaining Endowment Trust, 412 Main St., 54729. Tel: 715-723-4890; Fax: 715-723-7358.

Friends of St. Joseph's Foundation, St. Joseph's Hospital, 2661 County Hwy. I, 54729. Tel: 715-723-3392; Fax: 715-726-3302. Email: bswanson@sjcf.hshs.org. Web: www.stjoeschipfalls.com.

Notre Dame Children's Endowment Trust, 117 Allen St., 54729-2899. Tel: 715-723-7108; Fax: 715-723-7523. Email: cfnotredame@yahoo.com.

Notre Dame Parish Endowment Trust, 117 Allen St., 54729-2899. Tel: 715-723-7108; Fax: 715-723-7523. Email: cfnotredame@yahoo.com.

COLBY. *St. Mary's Catholic School, Colby Endowment Trust*, P.O. Box 436, 54421. Tel: 715-223-3048.

DURAND. *St. Mary Catholic School Endowment Trust*, 901 W. Prospect St., 54736-1049. Tel: 715-672-5617.

EAU CLAIRE. *Educational Endowment Trust of Eau Claire Coordinated Catholic Schools*, 448 N. Dewey St., 54703. Tel: 715-830-2273; Fax: 715-835-4658.

Friends of St. James the Greater Catholic School at Eau Claire Tuition Endowment Trust, 2502 11th St., 54703-2700. Tel: 715-835-5887; Fax: 715-835-3110. Email: stjameseac@aol.com.

The St. James the Greater Catholic Church Endowment Trust, 2502 11th St., 54703-2700. Tel: 715-835-5887; Fax: 715-835-3110. Email: stjameseac@aol.com. Web: www.stjameseauclaire.catholicweb.com.

The Newman Parish - Eau Claire Endowment Trust, 110 Garfield Ave., 54701-4042. Tel: 715-834-3399. Email: georges128@aol.com. Web: www.newmanec.com.

St. Olaf Parish Endowment Trust, 3220 Monroe St., P.O. Box 1203, 54703-1203. Tel: 715-832-2504; Fax: 715-832-0742. Email: solaf@execpc.com. Web: www.saintolafparish.com.

St. Patrick Parish of Eau Claire Endowment Trust, 318 Fulton St., 54703-5399. Tel: 715-832-0925; Fax: 715-832-0366. Email: sacrdhrt@pressenter.com.

Regis High School Foundation, 2100 Fenwick Ave., 54701-4498. Tel: 715-830-2271; Fax: 715-830-5461.

The Sacred Heart Parish Endowment Trust, 318 Fulton St., 54703. Tel: 715-832-0925; Fax: 715-832-0366. Email: sacrdhrt@pressenter.com.

ELLSWORTH. *The St. Francis Parish Endowment Trust*, 264 S. Grant, Box 839, 54011. Tel: 715-273-4774; Fax: 715-273-4066. Email: francis@pressenter.com.

HATLEY. *St. Ladislaus Parish Bevent Endowment Trust*, 6455 State Rd. 153, 54440. Tel: 715-446-3060.

HOLMEN. *St. Elizabeth Ann Seton Endowment Trust*, 515 N. Main St., 54636. Tel: 608-526-4424; Fax: 608-526-3177. Email: seas@aol.com.

INDEPENDENCE. *The SS. Peter & Paul Parish-Independence Education Endowment Trust*, 36028 Osseo Rd., P.O. Box 430, 54747-0430. Tel: 715-985-2227; Fax: 715-985-2649.

LYNDON STATION. *Troy Quasi-Endowment Trust*, P.O. Box 303, 53944. Tel: 608-666-2421.

MARATHON CITY. *Nativity of the Blessed Virgin Mary, Marathon Endowment Trust*, 712 Market, Box 7, 54448-0007. Tel: 715-443-2045.

MARSHFIELD. *Columbus High School Foundation*, 710 S. Columbus Ave., 54449. Tel: 715-387-2444; Fax: 715-384-4535. Email: chs@wctc.net. Web: www.columbus.marshfield.wi.us. Victoria Tracy, Dir. Devel.

Foundation of Saint Joseph's Hospital of Marshfield, Inc., 611 St. Joseph Ave., 54729. Tel: 715-389-4072; Fax: 715-389-3993. Email: bosona@stjosephs-marshfield.org. Web: www.stjosephs-marshfield.org.

St. John the Baptist Educational Endowment Trust, 201 W. Blodgett, Box 644, 54449-0644. Tel: 715-384-3252; Fax: 715-384-3252. Email: fr-stoetzel@tznet.com.

St. John the Baptist Maintenance Endowment Trust, 201 W. Blodgett, Box 644, 54449-0644. Tel: 715-384-3252; Fax: 715-384-3252. Email: fr-stoetzel@tznet.com.

The Our Lady of Peace Endowment Trust, 1414 W. 5th St., 54449. Tel: 715-384-9414; Fax: 715-384-6606. Email: peacerectory@charter.net. Web: www.olpmarshfield.org.

MAUSTON. *St. Patrick's Congregation Trust*, 401 Mansion St., 53948-1393. Tel: 608-847-6054; Fax:

608-847-3288. Email: patrick@mwt.net. Web: www.stpatrickmauston.com.

MENOMONIE. *The St. Joseph School at Menomonie Endowment Trust*, 910 Wilson Ave., 54751. Tel: 715-232-4922; Fax: 715-232-4923.

MOSINEE. *St. Paul Parish Endowment Trust*, 603 4th St., 54455. Tel: 715-693-2650; Fax: 715-692-2650.

NEILLSVILLE. *The St. Mary's Catholic Church Endowment Trust*, 1813 Black River Rd., 54456. Tel: 715-743-3840; Fax: 715-743-7963. Email: stmaryneillsville@tds.net.

ONALASKA. *Charles Simpson of St. Patrick Parish, Onalaska Endowment Trust*, 1031 Main St., 54650.

Father John Rossiter and Friends Endowment Trust of St. Patrick Parish, 1031 Main St., 54650. Tel: 608-783-5535.

PITTSVILLE. *St. Joachim's Parish Endowment Trust*, P.O. Box 69, 54466-0069. Tel: 715-884-6815.

PLOVER. *St. Bronislava Parish, Plover Endowment Trust*, 3200 Plover Rd., P.O. Box 158, 54467-0158. Tel: 715-344-4326; Fax: 715-344-6121. Web: stbrons.com.

PORT EDWARDS. *St. Alexander's Church, Port Edwards Endowment Trust*, 880 First St., 54469. Tel: 715-887-3012; Fax: 715-887-3748. Rev. R. John Swing.

PRAIRIE DU CHIEN. *The St. Gabriel's Endowment Trust*, 506 N. Beaumont Rd., P.O. Box 176, 53821-0176. Tel: 608-326-2404.

The St. John's Endowment Trust, 710 S. Wacouta St., P.O. Box 28, 53821-0028. Tel: 608-326-6511; Fax: 608-326-4876.

RICHLAND CENTER. *The Assumption of the Blessed Virgin Mary Parish Endowment Trust*, 160 W. 4th St., Box 456, 53581. Tel: 608-647-2621; Fax: 608-647-6029. Email: parishsec@mwt.net. Web: www.mwt.net/~stmarys.

ROTHSCHILD. *The St. Mark Catholic Parish Endowment Trust*, 602 Military Rd., 54474-1523.

St. Therese Catholic Church Endowment Fund, 113 Kort St., 54474. Tel: 715-359-2421; Fax: 715-355-3088.

ST. JOSEPH RIDGE. *St. Joseph Endowment Trust*, W2602 Hwy. 33, 54601. Tel: 608-788-1646.

ST. MARY'S RIDGE. *Holy Family Endowment Trust Fund*

Rectory, 26400 CTH U, Cashton, 54619-9757. Tel: 608-823-7906; Fax: 608-823-7272. Email: SMR1856@centurytel.com.

SPARTA. *Endowment Trust of the Friends and Parishioners of St. Patrick Parish*, 319 W. Main St., 54656-2143. Tel: 608-269-2655.

Franciscan Skemp Foundation of Sparta, Inc., 310 W. Main St., 54656-2142. Tel: 608-269-2132; Fax: 608-269-4562. Web: www.franciscanskemp.org. Robert M. Tracey, Admin.

STEVENS POINT. *Catholic Schools Endowment Trust in Portage County, Wisconsin*, 1408 Ellis St., 54481. Tel: 715-341-2445; Fax: 715-342-2001. Email: ghansel@spacs.k12.wi.us. Web: www.spacs.k12.wi.us.

Community Foundation of Saint Michael's Hospital of Stevens Point, Inc., 900 Illinois Ave., 54481. Tel: 715-346-5337; Fax: 715-346-5298. Email: foundation@smhosp.org. Pam Owens, Dir.

St. Joseph's Congregation, Stevens Point Endowment Trust, 1709 Wyatt Ave., 54481-3699. Tel: 715-341-1617; Fax: 715-341-2623. Web: www.togetherinfaith.org. Rev. Alan T. Burkhardt, Exec. Sec.

Pacelli High School Foundation, 1301 Maria Dr., 54481. Tel: 715-341-2442; Fax: 715-341-6779.

St. Stanislaus Kostka Congregation, Stevens Point Endowment Trust, 838 Fremont St., 54481. Tel: 715-344-9117; Fax: 715-344-1771. Email: ststan@core.com.

St. Stephen Parish Endowment Trust, 1401 Clark St., 54481. Tel: 715-344-3319; Fax: 715-344-6101. Email: stephen@wctc.net. Web: www.geocities.com/dol_saintstephens.

STRATFORD. *St. Joseph Parish Endowment Trust*, Box 6, 54484. Tel: 715-687-2404.

TILDEN. *St. Peter Parish Endowment Trust*, 11358 CTH Q. Tel: 715-288-6484; Fax: 715-723-2195. Chippewa Falls, 54729-6115.

TOMAH. *The St. Mary's Catholic Church Educational Endowment Trust*, 203 W. Monroe St., 54660. Tel: 608-372-4516; Fax: 608-372-4506.

WAUMANDEE. *St. Boniface Parish Catholic School Endowment Trust Fund*, 52026 County Road 4, 54622-0962. Tel: 608-626-2621. Email: stbon@mwt.net. Web: www.mwt.net/~stbon.

WAUSAU. *St. Michael Parish Endowment Trust*, 1315 6th St., 54403-3599. Tel: 715-842-4283; Fax: 715-849-2509. Email: stmichael@dwave.net.

**Wausau Area Catholic Schools Endowment Trust*, 602 Second St., 54403. Tel: 715-845-5735; Fax: 715-845-5735. Mark Watson, Admin.

WHITEHALL. *St. John Parish Endowment Trust*, 35900 Lee St., 54773. Tel: 715-538-4607; Fax: 715-538-2224. Email: johnsgar@triwest.net.

WILLARD. *Holy Family Parish, Willard Endowment Trust* 54493.

WISCONSIN RAPIDS. *St. Lawrence Parish, Wisconsin Rapids Endowment Trust*, 530 10th Ave. N., 54495-2566. Tel: 715-421-5777.

Our Lady Queen of Heaven Parish Endowment Trust, 750 10th Ave. S.,, 54495. Tel: 715-423-1251; Fax: 715-423-9407. Email: heaven@wctc.net.

St. Vincent de Paul Parish, Wisconsin Rapids Endowment Trust, 820 13th St., S., 54494-5336. Tel: 715-423-2111; Fax: 715-423-4227. Email: stvin@wctc.net.

Wisconsin Rapids Area Catholic Schools Endowment Trust, 711 Hill St., 54494.

[M] ASSOCIATIONS OF THE FAITHFUL

LA CROSSE. *Canons Regular of the New Jerusalem*, P.O. Box 4004, 54602-4004. Tel: 608-787-8566. Very Rev. Dom Daniel W. Augustine, C.R.N.J., Oppenheimer.

EASTMAN. *Marian Academy of the Oblates of Holy Tradition*, P.O. Box 109, 54626. Very Rev. Msgr. John F. McCarthy, P.A., Contact Person.

Society of the Oblates of Wisdom, P.O. Box 109, 54626-0109. Tel: 608-874-4733. Email: jfmccarthy@centurytel.net. Very Rev. Msgr. John F. McCarthy, P.A., Dir.

TILDEN. *Institute of St. Joseph*, 11386 CTH Q, Chippewa Falls, 54729-6115. Tel: 715-288-6272; Fax: 715-288-6008. Email: isjbrs@bloomer.net. Very Rev. William P. Felix, Moderator; Rev. John Mary Gilbert, Chap., 11358 Cty. Hwy. Q, Chippewa Falls, 54729.

[N] SOCIETY FOR APOSTOLIC LIFE

WAUSAU. *Institute of Christ the King-Sovereign Priest*, American Headquarters: 429 Grand Ave., 54403. Tel: 715-843-5336; Fax: 715-845-5326. Very Rev. Msgr. Michael R. Schmitz, Vicar Gen. & Supr.

[O] MISCELLANEOUS LISTINGS

LA CROSSE. *Franciscan Skemp Healthcare, Inc., Mayo Health System, Corporate Office*, 700 West Ave. S., 54603. Tel: 608-785-9710; Fax: 608-791-9429. Web: www.franciscanskemp.org. David Nesse, Pres. & CEO, Integrated Healthcare Delivery System. Sponsored by the Congregation of the Sisters of the Third Order of St. Francis of Perpetual Adoration (Franciscan Sisters of Perpetual Adoration) and Mayo Foundation.

Franciscan Skemp Healthcare, Mayo Health System, La Crosse Campus Clinic, 800 West Ave. S., 54601. Tel: 608-782-9760; Fax: 608-791-9429. Web: www.franciscanskemp.org. David Nesse, Pres. & CEO. Total Staff 525; Patient Visits 396,000.

**Franciscan Skemp Medical Center, Inc.*, 700 West Ave. S., 54601-4796. Tel: 608-785-0940; Fax: 608-791-9429. David Nesse, Pres. & CEO.

The Marian Catechist Apostolate, 1032 Caledonia St., 54603. Tel: 608-782-0011; Fax: 608-796-0086. Theresa Ann Krothe, Dir.

Mater Redemptoris House of Formation, 3730 East Ave. S., 54602. Tel: 608-788-2128. Sr. M. Stephania Newell, F.S.G.M., Dir.

Shrine of Our Lady of Guadalupe of the Diocese of La Crosse, Inc., 308 Main St., P.O. Box 1237, 54602-1237. Tel: 608-782-5440; Fax: 608-782-3104. Email: smchrista@shrineofourlady.com. Web: www.shrineofourladyofguadalupe.org. Sr. Christa Marie Halligan, F.S.G.M., Exec. Dir.

ARCADIA. *Franciscan Skemp Healthcare, Mayo Health System, Arcadia Campus Clinic*, 464 St. Joseph Ave., 54612. Tel: 608-323-3341; Fax: 608-323-3694. Email: tracey.robert@mayo.edu. Robert Tracey, Admin.

CHIPPEWA FALLS. *Northern Wisconsin Center for the Developmentally Disabled* State Institution for the Developmentally Disabled , East Park Ave., 54729. Tel: 715-723-5542.

EAU CLAIRE. *Hospital Sisters Health Care-West, Inc.*, St. Francis Apartments, 851 University Dr., 54701. Tel: 715-834-1338; Fax: 715-839-8417. Email: stfrancis@cvol.net.

GENOA. *The Hermitage of St. Mary, Inc.*, W1498 Spring Coulee Rd., 54632. Tel: 608-689-2753. Email: godshermit@hotmail.com. Sr. Mary Dawiczyk, Pres. & Treas.

HILLSBORO. *St. Joseph's Community Health Services* Franciscan Sisters of Perpetual Adoration , 400 Water Ave., P.O. Box 527, 54634. Tel: 608-489-8000; Fax: 608-489-8181. Email: k.coblentz.stjoseph@mwt.net. Web: stjhealthcare.org. Deb Warthan, Pastoral Care Dir.

St. Joseph's Family Clinic, 504 Water Ave., P.O. Box 527, 54634. Tel: 608-489-8280; Fax: 608-489-8189.

St. Joseph's Nursing Home, 400 Water St., P.O. Box 527, 54634. Tel: 608-489-8000; Fax: 608-489-8187. 1705 Omaha St., Elroy, 53929. Tel: 608-489-8720; Fax: 608-489-8188.

St. Joseph's Memorial Hospital Tel: 608-489-8000; Fax: 608-489-8186.

MARSHFIELD. **Ministry Home Care*, 611 St. Joseph Ave., 54449. Tel: 715-389-3802; Fax: 715-387-9950. Web: www.ministryhomecare.org.

SPARTA. *Franciscan Skemp Healthcare, Mayo Health System, Sparta Campus Clinic*, 310 W. Main St., 54656-2142. Tel: 608-269-1770; Fax: 608-269-1017. Email: thompson.kaye@mayo.edu. Robert M. Tracey, Admin.

STEVENS POINT. *Ministry Behavioral Health of St. Michael's Hospital, Inc.*, 209 Prentice St. N., 54481. Tel: 715-344-4611; Fax: 715-344-8127. Email: giffinj@smhosp.org. Web: www.ministrybehavioralhealth.org. JoAnne Griffin, Exec. Dir. Corporate Sponsor: Ministry Health Care, Inc. (Milwaukee, WI); Sponsored by Sisters of the Sorrowful Mother.

TOMAH. *Assisi Homes - Eldr Manor, Inc.*, 1500 Lincoln Ave., 54660. Tel: 608-372-5890. Sr. Susan Dillberg, O.S.F., Pres. Franciscan Sisters, Daughters of the Sacred Hearts of Jesus and Mary of Wheaton, IL., Purpose: to acquire or develop and operate housing projects for low income families and elderly persons.

WILLARD. *The Christine Center*, W8303 Mann Rd., 54493. Tel: 715-267-7507; Fax: 715-267-7512. Email: christinecenter@tds.net. Web: www.christinecenter.org. Sr. Johanna Seubert, F.S.P.A., Pres.

RELIGIOUS INSTITUTES OF MEN REPRESENTED IN THE DIOCESE

For further details refer to the corresponding bracketed number in the Religious Institutes of Men or Women section.

[0200]—*Benedictine Monks, Corpus Christi Abbey* (Sandia, TX; St. David, AZ)—O.S.B.

[1180]—*Brothers of Saint Pius X* (La Crosse)—C.S.P.X.

[0470]—*The Capuchin Friars* (St. Joseph's Prov., Detroit)—O.F.M.Cap.

[0340]—*Cistercian Fathers* (Sparta, WI)—O.Cist.

[]—*Congregation of the Blessed Sacrament*

[0180]—*Congregation of the Resurrection* (Poland)—C.R.

[0690]—*Jesuit Fathers and Brothers* (Missouri Prov. & Wisconsin Prov.)—S.J.

[]—*Missionaries of St. Francis de Sales*

[0430]—*Order of Preachers* Cracow, Poland Province)—O.P.

[990]—*Society of Catholic Apostolate*—S.A.C.

RELIGIOUS INSTITUTES OF WOMEN REPRESENTED IN THE DIOCESE

[]—*Banyatereza Sisters* (Uganda)

[]—*Benedictine Sisters of Mother of God Monastery*

[0230]—*Benedictine Sisters of Pontifical Jurisdiction* (Eau Claire, WI)—O.S.B.

[1010]—*Congregation of Divine Providence* (San Antonio, TX)—C.D.P.

[0470]—*Congregation of Sisters of Charity of the Incarnate Word* (San Antonio, TX)—C.C.V.I.

[1170]—*Congregation of the Sisters of St. Felix of Cantalice, of the III Order of St. Francis* (Chicago, IL)—C.S.S.F.

[1780]—*Congregation of the Sisters of the Third Order of St. Francis of Perpetual Adoration* (La Crosse, WI)—F.S.P.A.

[]—*Daughters of the Redeemer* (Zambia)

[1310]—*Franciscan Sisters of Little Falls, Minnesota*—O.S.F.

[1820]—*Hospital Sisters of the Third Order of St. Francis* (Springfield, IL)—O.S.F.

[]—*Presentation Sisters of the Blessed Virgin Mary* (Philippines)

[2970]—*School Sisters of Notre Dame* (Milwaukee Prov.)—S.S.N.D.

[1680]—*School Sisters of St. Francis* (Milwaukee, WI)—O.S.F.

[3590]—*Servants of Mary* (Ladysmith, WI)—O.S.M.

[1070-03]—*Sinsinawa Dominican Congregation of the Most Holy Rosary*—O.P.

[2630]—*Sisters of Mercy of the Holy Cross* (Merrill, WI)

[]—*Sisters of Our Lady of Good Counsel* (Uganda)

[1620]—*Sisters of St. Francis of Millvale* (Pittsburgh, PA)—O.S.F.

[]—*Sisters of St. Francis of the Martyr St. George* (Alton, IL, Prov. of St. Elizabeth)—O.S.F.

[1720]—*Sisters of St. Francis of the Third Order Regular of St. Francis of the Congregation of Our Lady of* (Rochester, MN)—O.S.F.

[3930]—*Sisters of St. Joseph - Third Order Regular* (Stevens Point, WI)—S.S.J.-T.O

[1030]—*Sisters of the Divine Savior* (Milwaukee, WI)—S.D.S.

[4100]—*Sisters of the Sorrowful Mother* (U.S./ Carribean Prov.)—S.S.M.

[1705]—*Sisters of the Third Order of St. Francis of Assisi of Penance and Charity* (Milwaukee, WI)—O.S.F.

[]—*Tertiary Sisters of St. Francis* (Cameroon Province)

DIOCESAN CEMETERIES

La Crosse. *Catholic Cemetery*, 519 Losey Blvd. S., 54601. Tel: 608-782-0238. Jeffrey Reinhart, Supt. Gate of Heaven Cemetery; French Island Cemetery.

Woodlawn, 3636 Mormon Coulee Rd., 54601. Tel: 608-788-0930. John Reinhart, Supt.

Chippewa Falls. *Hope Cemetery and Mausoleum*, 418 N. State St., 54729. Tel: 715-723-0792. Walter Hurt, Supt.

Eau Claire. *Calvary Cemetery and Mausoleum*, P.O. Box 755, 54702-0755. Tel: 715-832-1411. Rodney Sorenson, Manager.

Marshfield. *Gate of Heaven*, 1803 S. Maple Ave., 54449. Tel: 715-384-3869. Marvin Fait, Pres.; Monica Herman, Sec.; Michael Boltus, Maintenance.

Stevens Point. *Stevens Point Area Catholic Cemetery Association, Inc.*, P.O. Box 497, 54481. Tel: 715-341-3236. Jack Okonek, Supt.; Shirley Suplicki, Exec. Sec. & Treas.

NECROLOGY

† Dockendorff, Carl J., (Retired)—Died Oct. 19, 2003
† Fisher, Gerald E., (Retired)—Died Oct. 2, 2003
† Hansen, Robert H., (Retired)—Died May 5, 2003
† Henseler, Joseph N., (Retired)—Died Aug. 17, 2003
† Kozlowski, Daniel E.—Died Sept. 7, 2003
† Leisle, Charles E., (Retired)—Died Sept. 26, 2003
† Szczerbicki, Thaddeus P., (Retired)—Died 2003

Diocese of Lafayette

(Dioecesis Lafayettensis)

Most Reverend

MICHAEL JARRELL, D.D.

Bishop of Lafayette; ordained June 3, 1967; ordained to the episcopacy and installed as second Bishop of Houma-Thibodaux March 4, 1993; appointed sixth Bishop of Lafayette November 8, 2002; installed December 18, 2002. *Office: 1408 Carmel Ave., Lafayette, LA 70501.*

Most Reverend

GERARD LOUIS FREY, D.D.

Bishop Emeritus of Lafayette; ordained April 2, 1938; appointed Bishop of Savannah May 31, 1967; consecrated August 8, 1967; installed August 10, 1967; appointed third Bishop of Lafayette November 7, 1972; installed January 7, 1973; retired May 13, 1989. *Office: 1408 Carmel Ave., Lafayette, LA 70501.* Tel: 337-261-5613.

Most Reverend

EDWARD JOSEPH O'DONNELL, D.D.

Bishop Emeritus of Lafayette; ordained April 6, 1957; appointed Titular Bishop of Britonia and Auxiliary Bishop of St. Louis December 6, 1983; consecrated February 10, 1984; appointed fifth Bishop of Lafayette November 8, 1994; installed December 16, 1994; retired November 8, 2002. *P.O. Box 3387, Lafayette, LA 70502.*

ESTABLISHED JANUARY 11, 1918.

Square Miles 5,777.

Comprises the civil parishes (Counties) of Acadia, Evangeline, Iberia, Lafayette, St. Landry, St. Martin and St. Mary (west of Atchafalaya River) and Vermilion in the south central part of the State of Louisiana.

For legal titles of Diocese, parishes and diocesan institutions, consult the Chancery Office.

Administrative Offices: Diocesan Office Building, 1408 Carmel Ave., Lafayette, LA 70501. Tel: 337-261-5500; Fax: 337-261-5635.

Web: www.dol-louisiana.org

Email: robins@dol-louisiana.org

STATISTICAL OVERVIEW

Personnel	
Bishop	1
Retired Bishops	2
Priests: Diocesan Active in Diocese	109
Priests: Diocesan Active Outside Diocese	5
Priests: Diocesan in Foreign Missions	1
Priests: Retired, Sick or Absent	43
Number of Diocesan Priests	158
Religious Priests in Diocese	43
Total Priests in Diocese	201
Extern Priests in Diocese	9
Ordinations:	
Diocesan Priests	1
Permanent Deacons in Diocese	70
Total Brothers	28
Total Sisters	159
Parishes	
Parishes	121
With Resident Pastor:	
Resident Diocesan Priests	89
Resident Religious Priests	21
Without Resident Pastor:	
Administered by Priests	7
Administered by Deacons	4
Missions	30
Professional Ministry Personnel:	
Sisters	9
Lay Ministers	62
Welfare	
Catholic Hospitals	1
Total Assisted	139,522
Health Care Centers	1
Total Assisted	19,408
Homes for the Aged	5
Total Assisted	1,200
Specialized Homes	7
Total Assisted	2,300
Special Centers for Social Services	6
Total Assisted	249,554
Educational	
Seminaries, Diocesan	1
Diocesan Students in Other Seminaries	32
Seminaries, Religious	1
Students Religious	20
Total Seminarians	52
High Schools, Diocesan and Parish	9
Total Students	3,737
High Schools, Private	1
Total Students	140
Elementary Schools, Diocesan and Parish	29
Total Students	10,468
Elementary Schools, Private	2
Total Students	576
Catechesis/Religious Education:	
High School Students	9,005
Elementary Students	19,461
Total Students under Catholic Instruction	43,439
Teachers in the Diocese:	
Brothers	1
Sisters	10
Lay Teachers	971
Vital Statistics	
Receptions into the Church:	
Infant Baptism Totals	4,886
Adult Baptism Totals	129
Received into Full Communion	268
First Communions	4,604
Confirmations	3,677
Marriages:	
Catholic	1,152
Interfaith	196
Total Marriages	1,348
Deaths	3,600
Total Catholic Population	322,349
Total Population	568,154

Former Bishops—Most Revs. JULES B. JEANMARD, D.D., LL.D., ord. June 11, 1903; appt. first Bishop of Lafayette, July 18, 1918; consecrated Dec. 8, 1918; installed as first Bishop of Lafayette, Dec. 12, 1918; appt. Assistant at the Pontifical Throne, Dec. 8, 1943; resigned and named Titular Bishop of Bareta, March 13, 1956; died Feb. 23, 1957; ROBERT E. TRACY, D.D., Auxiliary Bishop of Lafayette, March 18, 1959; appt. first Bishop of Baton Rouge, Aug. 10, 1961; WARREN L. BOUDREAUX, D.D., J.C.D., Auxiliary Bishop of Lafayette, May 19, 1962; appt. second Bishop of Beaumont, Texas, June 4, 1971; MAURICE SCHEXNAYDER, D.D., ord. April 11, 1925; appt. Titular Bishop of Tuscamia and Auxiliary of Lafayette, Dec. 11, 1950; consecrated Feb. 22, 1951; appt. second Bishop of Lafayette, March 13, 1956; installed May 24, 1956; resigned Nov. 7, 1972; died Jan. 23, 1981; GERARD L. FREY, D.D., appt. third Bishop of Lafayette, Nov. 7, 1972; installed Jan. 7, 1973; resigned May 13, 1989; HARRY J. FLYNN, D.D., ord. May 28, 1960; appt. Coadjutor Bishop of Lafayette, April 19, 1986, fourth Bishop of Lafayette, May 13, 1989; appt. Coadjutor Archbishop of St. Paul, Minneapolis, Feb. 22, 1994; EDWARD JOSEPH O'DONNELL, D.D. (Retired), ord. April 6, 1957; appt. Titular Bishop of Britonia and Auxiliary Bishop of St. Louis Dec. 6, 1983; consecrated Feb. 10, 1984; appt. fifth Bishop of Lafayette Nov. 8, 1994; installed Dec. 16, 1994; retired Nov. 8, 2002.

Bishop's Office—Diocesan Office Building, P.O. Box 3387, Lafayette, 70502-3387. Tel: 337-261-5614; Fax: 337-261-5603.

Administrative Offices—Diocesan Office Building, 1408 Carmel Ave., Lafayette, 70501-5298. Tel: 337-261-5500; Fax: 337-261-5635.

Vicars General—Rev. Msgrs. H. ALEXANDRE LARROQUE, J.C.D., P.O. Box 3387, Lafayette, 70502-3387. Tel: 337-261-5613; Fax: 337-261-5603; RONALD BROUSSARD, P.O. Box 3387, Lafayette, 70502-3387. Tel: 337-261-5536.

Chancellor—Rev. Msgr. RUSSELL J. HARRINGTON, V.E., P.O. Box 3387, Lafayette, 70502-3387. Tel: 337-261-5611.

Episcopal Vicars and Executives Assistants—Central Region: Rev. THOMAS JAMES, S.V.D.; MARY BERGERON. South Region: Very Rev. Msgr. RICHARD GREENE, V.E.; Deacon GERALD BOURG. North Region: Very Rev. Msgr. J. ROBERT ROMERO, V.E.; JACKIE GRIFFIN. West Region: Very Rev. FREDERICK O. SWENSON; JANETH HARRINGTON.

Director for Religious Brothers and Sisters—Bro. LOUIS WELKER, F.S.C., 1522 Carmel Dr., Lafayette, 70501. Tel: 337-235-3576.

Vicar for Priests—Very Rev. Msgr. RUSSELL HARRINGTON, P.O. Box 3387, Lafayette, 70502-3387. Tel: 337-261-5610; Fax: 337-261-5603.

Tribunal—P.O. Box 3387, Lafayette, 70502-3387. Tel: 337-261-5623; Fax: 337-261-5646.

Judicial Vicar—Very Rev. Msgr. J. DOUGLAS COURVILLE, J.C.L.

Adjutant Judicial Vicars—Revs. ROBIE ROBICHAUX, J.C.L.; ARTHUR M. WARREN.

Advocates—Revs. A. REX BROUSSARD; BILL JOHN MELANCON; ROBERT COURVILLE; JULES ARCENEAUX; PAUL BROUSSARD; JEFFERSON DEBLANC; MITCHELL GUIDRY; KEITH LABOVE; MARK LEDOUX; W. CURTIS MALLET; MALCOLM O'LEARY, S.V.D.; JOSEPH SIMON, S.V.D.

Promoter of Justice—VACANT.

Judges—Rev. Msgrs. GLEN JOHN PROVOST; H. ALEXANDRE LARROQUE, J.C.D.; Rev. HERBERT J. MAY, J.C.L.

Defenders of the Bond—Revs. OVERTON JOSEPH BREAUX; KENNETH R. MORVANT, J.C.L.

Notaries—Mrs. LINDA W. SAVOY; Rev. AUSTIN LEGER.

Diocesan Consultors—Rev. Msgrs. ROBERT ANGELLE; RONALD BROUSSARD; Very Rev. Msgr. RUSSELL HARRINGTON; Rev. Msgrs. H. A. LARROQUE; RICHARD MOUTON; Revs. ROBIE ROBICHAUX, J.C.L.; JULES ARCENEAUX; MITCHELL GUIDRY; CHARLES LANGLOIS; CURTIS MALLET; Rev. Msgr. GLEN PROVOST.

Council of Priests—Rev. HAROLD TRAHAN, St. Elizabeth Seton Church, 610 Raintree Trail, Lafayette, 70507-3722.

Diocesan Offices and Directors

Adult Catechesis—ANN BROUSSARD, Dir., 1408 Carmel Ave., Lafayette, 70501-5298. Tel: 337-261-5550.

Alcohol & Drug Abuse—BEVERLY MIRE, 1408 Carmel Ave., Lafayette, 70501-5298. Tel: 337-261-5578.

Archives, Research and Information—BARBARA C. DEJEAN, 1408 Carmel Ave., Lafayette, 70501-5298. Tel: 337-261-5639; 337-261-5667.

Auxiliary Services—PATSY ARWOOD, 1408 Carmel Ave., Lafayette, 70501-5298. Tel: 337-261-5600.

Bishop's Services Appeal—CONNIE KLEINPETER, 1408 Carmel Ave., Lafayette, 70501-5298. Tel: 337-261-5641.

Black Catholics—Rev. CHESTER ARCENEAUX, Admin.; STEPHANIE BERNARD, Dir., 1408 Carmel Ave., Lafayette, 70501-5298. Tel: 337-261-5694.

Catholic Social Services—PAULA MILNER, 1408 Carmel Ave., Lafayette, 70501-5298. Tel: 337-261-5654.

Catholic Foundation of the Diocese of Lafayette—CONNIE KLEINPETER, 1408 Carmel Ave., Lafayette, 70501-5298. Tel: 337-261-5641.

Catholic Charismatic Renewal—Rev. ALBERT G. NUNEZ, 1408 Carmel Ave., Lafayette, 70501. Tel: 337-265-3773.

Christian Formation—ANN BROUSSARD, Dir., 1408 Carmel Ave., Lafayette, 70501-5298. Tel: 337-261-5550.

Clergy Health Care & Retirement—BEVERLY BROUSSARD, 1408 Carmel Ave., Lafayette, 70501-5298. Tel: 337-261-5629.

Communications— Newspaper-- THOMAS SOMMERS, Editor, 1408 Carmel Ave., Lafayette, 70501-5298. Tel: 337-261-5513; 337-261-5511; 337-261-5518. "Acadiana Catholic"

Data Processing—ROBIN STEVENSON, 1408 Carmel Ave., Lafayette, 70501-5298. Tel: 337-261-5516.

Community Development—Mr. J. BERNEL FONTENOT, 1408 Carmel Ave., Lafayette, 70501-5298. Tel: 337-261-5650.

Deaf Apostolate—MYRA MOUTON, 1408 Carmel Ave., Lafayette, 70501-5298. Tel: 337-232-3463.

Development—CONNIE KLEINPETER, 1408 Carmel Ave., Lafayette, 70501-5298. Tel: 337-261-5641.

Family Life—BARBARA MCCARROLL-WALLEY, Mailing Address, 1408 Carmel Ave., Lafayette, 70501-5298. Tel: 337-261-5653.

Fiscal Administration—MARY PARKER, P.O. Box 3387, Lafayette, 70502-5298. Tel: 337-261-5629.

Hispanic Ministry—Rev. ARTURO LOZANO, S.J., 1408 Carmel Ave., Lafayette, 70501-5298. Tel: 337-261-5543.

Human Resources—GERALD DILL, 1408 Carmel Ave., Lafayette, 70501-5298. Tel: 337-261-5526.

Justice and Peace—UNA HARGRAVE, 1408 Carmel Ave., Lafayette, 70501-5298. Tel: 337-261-5545.

Migration Refugee Services—TINA QUESADA, 1408 Carmel Ave., Lafayette, 70501-5298. Tel: 337-261-5535.

Office for Persons with Disabilities—MYRA MOUTON, 1408 Carmel Ave., Lafayette, 70501-5298. Tel: 337-232-3463.

Parish Finances—JEANNINE REYNOLDS, Dir., P.O. Box 3387, Lafayette, 70502-3387. Tel: 337-261-5632.

Permanent Diaconate—Deacon RONALD A BOREL, 1408 Carmel Ave., Lafayette, 70501-5298. Tel: 337-261-5609.

Pro-Life Issues—KAROL MEYNARD, 1408 Carmel Ave., Lafayette, 70501-5298. Tel: 337-261-5607

Prison Ministry—UNA HARGRAVE, 1408 Carmel Ave., Lafayette, 70501-5298. Tel: 337-261-5545

Radio-TV—DAVID MERGIST, Producer & Dir., 1408 Carmel Ave., Lafayette, 70501-5298. Tel: 337-261-5626.

Religious Brothers and Sisters—Bro. LOUIS WELKER, F.S.C., 1522 Carmel Dr., Lafayette, 70501. Tel: 337-235-3276.

Schools—ANNA LARRIVIERE, Supt., 1408 Carmel Ave., Lafayette, 70501-5298. Tel: 337-261-5529.

Seminarians—Rev. MICHAEL GUIDRY, 1408 Carmel Ave., Lafayette, 70501-5298. Tel: 337-261-5690.

Victim Assistance Coordinator—Ms. CARMEN FALGOUT, R.N., M.S.W., L.C.S.W., B.C.D., 100 Coulee Shore Dr., Lafayette, 70503. Tel: 337-235-5749.

Vocations—Rev. AARON MELANCON, P.O. Box 365, Loreauville, 70552-0365. Tel: 337-229-4254.

Youth Ministry—KATHY STELLY, 1408 Carmel Ave., Lafayette, 70501-5298. Tel: 337-261-5551.

Worship—Rev KEITH DEROUEN, Dir.; FAYE DROBNIC, Asst. Dir., 1408 Carmel Ave., Lafayette, 70501-5298. Tel: 337-261-5554.

Diocesan Commissions and Boards

Abuse Review Board—P.O. Box 3387, Lafayette, 70502-3387. Tel: 337-261-5613.

Building Review Board—GERALD GOSSEN, 1408 Carmel Ave., Lafayette, 70501-5298. Tel: 337-261-5606.

Campus Ministry—Rev. CHESTER ARCENEAUX, Our Lady of Wisdom Catholic Student Center, P.O. Box 42371, Lafayette, 70504-2371. Tel: 337-232-8742; DEBORAH SITTIG, LSU-E Catholic Student Center, P.O. Box 1129, Eunice, 70535-1129.

Catholic Daughters of America—Rev. CEDRIC SONNIER, St. John Church, 18534 LA Hwy. 689 (Henry), Erath, 70533. Tel: 337-937-5108.

Catholic Relief Services—UNA HARGRAVE, 1408 Carmel Ave., Lafayette, 70501-5298. Tel: 337-261-5545.

Clergy Personnel Advisory Board—Rev. MICHAEL ARNAUD, Chm., 130 N. Richelieu Cir., New Iberia, 70560-1598. Tel: 337-364-8360.

Continuing Formation of the Clergy—Rev. JODY SIMONEAUX, 417 E. Simcoe St., Lafayette, 70501. Tel: 337-234-5147.

Credit Union—1600 N. Bertrand Dr., Lafayette, 70506. Tel: 337-261-1151.

Cursillo—3651 Hwy. 104 (Prairie Ronde), Opelousas, 70570. Tel: 337-543-7425.

Diocesan Council of Catholic Women—Rev. MICHAEL RUSSO, Diocesan Moderator, Assumption of the B.V.M. Church, 211 Iberia St., Franklin, 70538. Tel: 337-828-3869.

Diocesan Pastoral Council—1408 Carmel Ave., Lafayette, 70501-5298. Tel: 337-261-5565.

Ecumenism—Rev. CHARLES LANGLOIS, St. Peter Church, P.O. Box 12507, New Iberia, 70562-2507. Tel: 337-369-3816.

Finance Advisory Board—LEON K. POCHE, K.S.G., Chm., 633 W. 17th St., Crowley, 70526. Tel: 337-783-0650.

Holy Childhood—Rev. Msgr. RICHARD MOUTON, 1408 Carmel Ave., Lafayette, 70501-5298. Tel: 337-261-5536.

Hospitals—Rev. KEITH LABOVE, Coord. Health Affairs, St. Joseph Church, P.O. Box 299, Milton, 70558-0299. Tel: 337-856-5997.

Knights of Columbus—Rev. MICHAEL GUIDRY, Diocesan Chap., Our Lady of Perpetual Help, P.O. Box 10110, New Iberia, 70562. Tel: 337-365-5481.

Retreats—Revs. KENNETH BUDDENDORFF, S.J., Our Lady of the Oaks Retreat House, P.O. Box D, Grand Coteau, 70541-1004. Tel: 337-662-5410; WARREN J. BROUSSARD, S.J., Dir., Jesuit Spirituality Center, P.O. Box C, Grand Coteau, 70541-1003. Tel: 337-662-5251.

Scouting—Rev. GARY SCHEXNAYDER, Chap., St. Michael Church, P.O. Box 406, Crowley, 70527-0406. Tel: 337-783-7394; ROBERT T. CLEMENTS, Lay Chm., 204 Crawford, Lafayette, 70506-6028. Tel: 337-981-2519.

Pontifical Mission Societies—Rev. Msgr. RICHARD MOUTON, 1408 Carmel Ave., Lafayette, 70501-5298. Tel: 337-261-5536.

CLERGY, PARISHES, MISSIONS AND PAROCHIAL SCHOOLS

CITY OF LAFAYETTE
(LAFAYETTE PARISH)

1—CATHEDRAL OF ST. JOHN THE EVANGELIST (1821), [CEM] Revs. Keith J. DeRouen; Randal Dale Barras. In Res., Rev. Joseph Kurian Karat (India).
Res.: 515 Cathedral St., P.O. Drawer V, 70502. Tel: 337-232-1322; Fax: 337-232-1379 Email: sjclaf@bellsouth.net.
Church: 914 St. John St., 70501. Email: sjc@bellsouth.net.
School—Cathedral-Carmel Elementary, 848 St. John St., 70502. Tel: 337-235-5577; Fax: 337-261-9493. Mrs. Adele H. Nunez, Prin. Sisters of Mt. Carmel 3; Brothers of the Christian Schools 1; Lay Teachers 50; Students 815.
Catechesis/Religious Program—Tel: 337-232-1325. Email: sjcreligiouseducation@yahoo.com. Students 241.

2—ST. ANTHONY (1955), (African American), [JC] Rev. Michael M. Sucharski, S.V.D.; Deacon Albert Marcel.
Res.: 615 Edison St., 70501. Tel: 337-234-5855; Fax: 337-264-1507.
Catechesis/Religious Program—Students 200.

3—ST. EDMOND (1974), Revs. Timothy Richard; Chris Duhon; Deacon Paul D. Matte.
Res.: 4131 W. Congress St., 70506. Tel: 337-981-0874; Fax: 337-989-1417.
Catechesis/Religious Program—Carol Broglio, (K-8); Phyllis Desormeaux, (9-12). Students 651.

4—ST. ELIZABETH SETON (1975), Rev. Harold Trahan.
Office—610 Raintree Tr., 70507. Tel: 337-235-1483; Fax: 337-235-9645.
Catechesis/Religious Program—Students 238.

5—ST. GENEVIEVE (1929), [CEM] Revs. Jody Simoneaux; Mikel Anthony Polson.
Res.: 417 E. Simcoe St., P.O. Box 90307, 70509. Tel: 337-234-5147; Fax: 337-234-8654.
School—Elementary School, 201 Elizabeth St., 70501. Tel: 337-234-5257; Fax: 337-237-6065. Becky Trouille, Prin. Lay Teachers 20; Students 326.
School—Middle School, 1500 E. Willow St., 70501. Tel: 337-266-5553; Fax: 337-266-5775. Mrs. Susan Stephen, Prin. Lay Teachers 10; Students 154.
Catechesis/Religious Program—Students 192.
Mission—Gift of Mary Chapel Raine St., Lafayette Parish 70501. Tel: 337-234-5147; Fax: 337-234-8654.

6—HOLY CROSS (1965), Rev. Martin Borcherding; Deacons Michael Clark; Richard Picard.
Res.: 505 Broadmoor Blvd., 70503. Tel: 337-984-9636; Fax: 337-988-3790.
Catechesis/Religious Program—Tel: 337-984-9643. Students 904.

7—IMMACULATE HEART OF MARY (1934), (African American), [CEM] Revs. Thomas James, S.V.D.; Maximus Manu, S.V.D.; Bro. Benjamin Tchiyivo; Deacon Anthony Ozene.
Res.: 818-12th St., P.O. Box 2398, 70502. Tel: 337-235-4618; Fax: 337-235-4775.
School—800-12th St., 70502. Tel: 337-235-7843; Fax: 337-233-0070. Herbert Wiltz, Prin. Sisters of Holy Family 3; Lay Teachers 12; Students 154.
Catechesis/Religious Program—Tel: 337-235-6323. Students 405.

8—ST. JULES (1962), Very Rev. Msgr. J. Douglas Courville, J.C.L.
Res.: 116 St. Jules St., 70506. Tel: 337-234-2727; Fax: 337-232-1544.
Catechesis/Religious Program—Students 85.

9—ST. LEO THE GREAT (1960), [CEM] Rev. Paul G. Bienvenu.
Res.: 300 W. Alexander St., 70501. Tel: 337-232-2404; Fax: 337-261-0801.
School—Sts. Leo-Seton, 502 St. Leo St., 70501. Tel: 337-234-5510; Fax: 337-234-3676. William Butcher, Prin. Sisters 1; Lay Teachers 25; Students 544.
Catechesis/Religious Program—Tel: 337-667-7050; Fax: 337-667-6434. Students 117.

10—ST. MARY, MOTHER OF THE CHURCH (1976), Rev. Robie Robichaux, J.C.L.
Res.: 419 Doucet Rd., 70503. Tel: 337-981-3379; Fax: 337-981-5445.
School—St. Mary Early Learning Center, (Grades PreK-PreK) Tel: 337-984-3750. Amy Robideaux, Prin. Students 148.
Catechesis/Religious Program—Tel: 337-984-5396. Students 349.

11—OUR LADY OF FATIMA (1949), Rev. Msgr. Glen John Provost; Rev. Cyprian Eze.
Res.: 2319 Johnston St., 70503. Tel: 337-232-8945; Fax: 337-232-0323.
School—2315 Johnston St., 70503. Tel: 337-235-2464; Fax: 337-235-1320. Mr. Lloyd Guiberteau, Prin. Lay Teachers 62; Students 906.
Catechesis/Religious Program—Students 113.

12—OUR LADY OF WISDOM, UNIVERSITY OF LOUISIANA (1942), Rev. Chester Arceneaux.
Mailing Address: P.O. Box 42371, 70504-2371. Tel: 337-232-8741; Fax: 337-236-6737. In Res., Rev. Thomas Finley.

13—OUR LADY QUEEN OF PEACE (1969), (African American), [CEM] Rev. Thomas Jason Mouton.
Res.: 145 Martin Luther King Jr. Dr., 70501. Tel: 337-233-1591; Fax: 337-232-5961.
Catechesis/Religious Program—Tel: 337-237-6225; Fax: 337-232-5961. Students 205.

14—ST. PATRICK (1952), Rev. Howard Blessing.
Res.: 406 E. Pinhook Rd., 70501. Tel: 337-237-0988; Fax: 337-233-8868.
Catechesis/Religious Program—Students 90.

15—ST. PAUL THE APOSTLE (1911), (African American), Rev. Robert Seay.
Res.: 326 S. Washington St., 70501. Tel: 337-235-0272; Fax: 337-235-3100.
Catechesis/Religious Program—Students 175.
Mission—Our Lady of Good Hope E. Convent, Lafayette Parish 70501. Tel: 337-235-0272; Fax: 337-235-3100.

16—ST. PIUS X (1968), [JC] Rev. Msgr. Richard von Phul Mouton.
Res.: 200 E. Bayou Pkwy., P.O. Box 80489, 70598. Tel: 337-232-4656; Fax: 337-233-9468.
School—201 E. Bayou Pkwy., 70508. Tel: 337-237-3139; Fax: 337-232-3455. Miss Donna Lemaire, Prin. Lay Teachers 48; Students 572.
Catechesis/Religious Program—Tel: 337-237-5059.

Students 290.

OUTSIDE THE CITY OF LAFAYETTE

ABBEVILLE, VERMILION PARISH

1—ST. MARY MAGDALEN (1844), [CEM 2] Revs. William C. Blanda; Thomas E. Habetz; Deacon Chris Mouton.
Mailing Address: P.O. Box 1507, 70511. Tel: 337-893-0244; 337-893-0245; Fax: 337-893-0427.
School—Mt. Carmel Elementary Sr. Janet LeBlanc, O.Carm., Prin. Sisters 1; Lay Teachers 22; Students 413.
High School—Vermilion Catholic, 425 Park Ave., 70511. Tel: 337-893-6636; Fax: 337-893-8718. Gerald Richard, Prin. Lay Teachers 18; Students 161.
Catechesis/Religious Program—Tel: 337-893-0244; Fax: 337-893-0427. Students 342.

2—ST. THERESA OF THE CHILD JESUS (1959), Revs. W. Curtis Mallet; Stephen Chibunda Ugwu; Deacon Benny Morello.
Mailing Address: P.O. Box 609, 70511. Tel: 337-893-5631; Fax: 337-893-9168.

ARNAUDVILLE, ST. LANDRY PARISH

1—ST. CATHERINE (1949), (African American), Rev. Jules M. Aceneaux II; Deacon James B. Davis, Pastoral Assoc.
Mailing Address: P.O. Box 53, 70512. Tel: 337-754-7754; Fax: 337-754-7754.
Catechesis/Religious Program—Tel: 337-754-5912; Fax: 337-754-7754.

2—ST. JOHN FRANCIS REGIS, Formerly St. Francis Regis (1853), [CEM] Rev. Jules M. Aceneaux II.
Mailing Address: P.O. Box 649, 70512. Tel: 337-754-5912; Fax: 337-754-7203.
Catechesis/Religious Program—Tel: 337-754-5912; Fax: 337-754-7203. Students 350.

BALDWIN, ST. MARY PARISH, SACRED HEART (1906), [CEM] Rev. Gregory P. Cormier; Deacon Harry Darce.
Mailing Address: P.O. Box 308, 70514. Tel: 337-923-7781; Fax: 337-923-4966.
Catechesis/Religious Program—Tel: 337-923-4966. Students 124.

BASILE, EVANGELINE PARISH, ST. AUGUSTINE (1921), [CEM] Rev. Kenneth Domingue.
Res.: 2717 Third St., 70515. Tel: 337-432-6817; Fax: 337-432-5203.
Catechesis/Religious Program—Tel: 337-432-5608. Students 324.
Mission—Assumption Glasper St., Evangeline Parish 70515. Tel: 337-432-6817; Fax: 337-432-5203.

BAYOU VISTA, ST. MARY PARISH, ST. BERNADETTE (1963), [CEM] Rev. Barry F. Crochet.
Res.: 1112 Saturn Rd., Morgan City, 70380. Tel: 985-395-2470; Fax: 985-395-6514.
Catechesis/Religious Program—Tel: 985-395-6517. Students 243.

BERWICK, ST. MARY PARISH, ST. STEPHEN (1950), Rev. Emmanuel Fernandez.
Res.: 3217 Second St., 70342. Tel: 985-385-1280; Fax: 985-385-1279.
Catechesis/Religious Program—Tel: 985-385-1283. Students 193.

BREAUX BRIDGE, ST. MARTIN PARISH

1—ST. BERNARD (1847), [CEM 2] [JC 2] Revs. Donald Leger; Allen Breaux; Deacons Harold Richard; Marcel P. Hebert Jr.; Bob McDonner.
Res.: 204 N. Main St., 70517-5096. Tel: 337-332-2159; Fax: 337-332-2276.
School—251 E. Bridge St., 70517. Tel: 337-332-5350; Fax: 337-332-5894. Jeannine Menard, Prin. Lay Teachers 24; Students 519.
Catechesis/Religious Program—219 E. Bridge St., 70517. Tel: 337-332-4488; Fax: 337-332-4488. Students 320.

2—ST. FRANCIS OF ASSISI (1923), (African American), [CEM] Rev. James P. Fallon, S.S.J.; Deacon Lawrence V. Jacobs Jr.
Res.: 610 N. Main St., 70517. Tel: 337-332-2250; Fax: 337-332-0020.
Catechesis/Religious Program—Fax: 337-332-2250. Students 335.

BROUSSARD, LAFAYETTE PARISH

1—ST. JOSEPH (1952), (African American), [CEM 2] Rev. Lambert Lein, S.V.D.
Mailing Address: P.O. Box 278, 70518. Tel: 337-837-6218; Fax: 337-837-2072.
Res.: 232 St. DePorres St., 70518. Tel: 337-837-6218; Fax: 337-837-2072.
Catechesis/Religious Program—Students 98.
Mission—St. Anthony Cade.

2—SACRED HEART OF JESUS (1883), [CEM] Rev. Louis J. Richard; Deacon Joseph I. Trahan.
Mailing Address: P.O. Box 737, 70518. Tel: 337-837-1864; Fax: 337-837-1703.
School—St. Cecilia, P.O. Box 309, 70518. Tel: 337-837-6363; Fax: 337-837-3688. Mr. George Fontenot, Prin. Lay Teachers 26; Students 481.
Catechesis/Religious Program—Students 424.

CANKTON, ST. LANDRY PARISH, ST. JOHN BERCHMANS (1925), [CEM] Rev. Mario Romero.
Res.: 552 Main St., 70584-9722. Tel: 337-668-4413; Fax: 337-668-4505.
Catechesis/Religious Program—Fax: 337-668-4505. Students 200.

CARENCRO, LAFAYETTE PARISH

1—OUR LADY OF THE ASSUMPTION (1925), (African American), [CEM] Rev. William Gearheard; Deacon John Thibodeaux.
Res.: 410 N. Michaud St., P.O. Box 130, 70520-0130. Tel: 337-896-8304; Fax: 337-896-5874.
Catechesis/Religious Program—Tel: 337-896-5874. Students 125.

2—ST. PETER (1874), [CEM] Revs. Bill Melancon; Mathew Mullamangalam (India); Deacon Eugene Waguespack.
Mailing Address: P.O. Box 40, 70520. Tel: 337-896-9408; Fax: 337-896-9414.
School—Carencro Catholic, 200 W. St. Peter St., 70520. Tel: 337-896-8973; Fax: 337-896-1931. Mr. Don Courville, Prin. Lay Teachers 28; Students 462.
Catechesis/Religious Program—Tel: 337-896-8488. Students 500.

CATAHOULA, ST. MARTIN PARISH, ST. RITA (1952), [CEM] Rev. Donald Pelous.
Res.: 1006 St. Rita Hwy., St. Martinville, 70582. Tel: 337-394-4679; Fax: 337-394-7020.
Catechesis/Religious Program—Students 232.

CECILIA, ST. MARTIN PARISH

1—ST. JOSEPH (1893), [CEM] [JC] Rev. Paul Broussard.
Mailing Address: P.O. Box 279, 70521. Tel: 337-667-6344; Fax: 337-667-7073.
Catechesis/Religious Program—Tel: 337-667-8081; Fax: 337-667-7073. Students 342.

2—ST. ROSE OF LIMA (1944), (African American), [CEM] Rev. Gregory M. Simien.
Mailing Address: P.O. Box 126, 70521. Tel: 337-667-6555; Fax: 337-667-6686.
Catechesis/Religious Program—Students 130.

CENTERVILLE, ST. MARY PARISH, ST. JOSEPH (1953), [CEM] Rev. Kenneth Mayne.
Mailing Address: P.O. Box 280, 70522. Tel: 337-836-5659; Fax: 337-836-4600.
Catechesis/Religious Program—P.O. Box 280, 70522. Students 100.

CHARENTON, ST. MARY PARISH, IMMACULATE CONCEPTION (1844), [CEM] Rev. William Crumley, C.S.C.; Deacon Ed Bodin.
Mailing Address: P.O. Box 278, 70523. Tel: 337-923-4281.
Catechesis/Religious Program—Students 27.

CHATAIGNIER, EVANGELINE PARISH, OUR LADY OF MOUNT CARMEL (1869), (French), [CEM] Rev. Lawrence N. Abara; Deacon Thomas J. Richard.
Mailing Address: P.O. Box 100, 70524. Tel: 337-885-3223; Fax: 337-885-3224.
Catechesis/Religious Program—Students 111.

CHURCH POINT, ACADIA PARISH

1—OUR LADY OF THE SACRED HEART (1873), [CEM 3] [JC] Very Rev. Frederick O. Swenson; Deacon James G. Cormier.
Res.: 118 N. Rogers St., P.O. Box 403, 70525. Tel: 337-684-5494; Fax: 337-684-2133.
School—Our Mother of Peace, 218 N. Rogers St., 70525. Tel: 337-684-5780; Fax: 337-684-5780. Mrs. Joni Duos, Prin. Lay Teachers 17; Students 288.
Catechesis/Religious Program—Students 372.
Chapel—Lewisburg, St. John, Tel: 337-684-5494; Fax: 337-687-2133.

2—OUR MOTHER OF MERCY (1941), (African American), [JC] Rev. Francis Butler, S.S.J.
Res.: 693 N. Main St., P.O. Box 237, 70525. Tel: 337-684-2319; Fax: 337-684-3086.
Catechesis/Religious Program—Students 101.

COTEAU HOLMES, ST. MARTIN PARISH, ST. ELIZABETH (1956), [CEM] Rev. Thomas Edapaddy, C.M.I. (India).
Office—1006 St. Elizabeth St., St. Martinville, 70582. Tel: 337-394-6684; Fax: 337-394-6684.
Catechesis/Religious Program—Students 74.

COTEAU, IBERIA PARISH, OUR LADY OF PROMPT SUCCOR (1934), [CEM] Rev. Matthew P. Higginbotham.
Res.: 2409 Coteau Rd., New Iberia, 70560. Tel: 337-369-6993; Fax: 337-560-4475.
Catechesis/Religious Program—Students 380.

COW ISLAND, VERMILION PARISH, ST. ANNE (1933), (Cajun), [CEM] [JC 3] Rev. William G. Rogalla; Deacon Chris Mouton.
Res.: 17315 Lionel Rd., Abbeville, 70510. Tel: 337-643-7714; Fax: 337-643-1021.
Catechesis/Religious Program—Students 130.
Mission—Immaculate Conception Abbeville. 22102 Church Rd., Forked Island, Vermilon Parish 70510.
Mission—Sacred Heart Kaplan. 28220 W. Hwy. 82, Pecan Island, Vermilion Parish 70548.

CROWLEY, ACADIA PARISH

1—IMMACULATE HEART OF MARY (1959), Rev. Rusty P. Richard.
Res.: 901 E. Elm St., 70526. Tel: 337-783-3498; Fax: 337-783-7444.
School—Redemptorist Grade School, 606 South Ave. N., 70526. Tel: 337-783-4466; Fax: 337-788-0961. Gretchen Chaumont, Prin. Lay Teachers 14; Students 262.
Catechesis/Religious Program—Tel: 337-783-3498. Students 150.

2—ST. MICHAEL ARCHANGEL (1895), Revs. Gary Schexnayder; James Bam Nguyen.
Mailing Address: P.O. Box 406, 70527. Tel: 337-783-7394; Fax: 337-788-0237.
School—805 E. Northern Ave., 70527. Tel: 337-783-1410; Fax: 337-783-8547. Mrs. Myra Broussard, Prin. Lay Teachers 35; Students 451.
Catechesis/Religious Program—Tel: 337-783-7393. Students 137.

3—ST. THERESA (1920), (African American), Rev. Richard Sadlier, S.S.J.
Res.: 417 W. 3rd St., 70526. Tel: 337-783-1880; Fax: 337-783-9676.
Catechesis/Religious Program—Tel: 337-783-1311; Fax: 337-783-9676. Students 235.

DELCAMBRE, VERMILION PARISH

1—SAINT MARTIN DE PORRES (1948), (African American), [JC] Rev. Herbert Bennerfield.
Res.: 206 W. Church St., 70528. Tel: 337-685-4426; Fax: 337-685-4426.
Catechesis/Religious Program—Castel School of Religion, 208 S. Peter St., 70528. Tel: 337-685-2549. Students 21.

2—OUR LADY OF THE LAKE (1897), [CEM] Rev. Herbert Bennerfield.
Res.: 206 W. Church St., 70528. Tel: 337-685-4426; Fax: 337-685-4426.
Catechesis/Religious Program—Castel School of Religion, 208 South St. Peter St., 70528. Tel: 337-685-2549. Students 281.

DURALDE, EVANGELINE PARISH, ANNUNCIATION OF THE B.V.M. (1964), (Acadian), Deacon Theo Landry, Admin.
Res.: 4476 Duralde Hwy., Eunice, 70535. Tel: 337-457-4849; Fax: 337-457-4502.
Catechesis/Religious Program—Students 100.

DUSON, LAFAYETTE PARISH

1—ST. BENEDICT THE MOOR, (African American), [CEM] Very Rev. Ronald Broussard, V.G.
Mailing Address: 9135 Cameron St., P.O. Box 127, 70529. Tel: 337-873-6772; Fax: 337-873-3325.
Catechesis/Religious Program—Tel: 337-873-6772; Fax: 337-873-3325. Students 163.

2—ST. THERESA OF THE CHILD JESUS (1928), [CEM] Rev. Martin C. Leonards; Deacon Steve Simon.
Mailing Address: P.O. Box 8, 70529. Tel: 337-873-4962; Fax: 337-873-3023.
Catechesis/Religious Program—Tel: 337-873-4488. Students 187.

ERATH, VERMILION PARISH, OUR LADY OF LOURDES (1928), [CEM 2] Rev. Wayne J. Duet.
Res.: 700 S. Broadway, 70533. Tel: 337-937-6888; Fax: 337-937-8650.
Catechesis/Religious Program—Students 920.

EUNICE, ST. LANDRY PARISH

1—ST. ANTHONY OF PADUA (1902), [CEM] Revs. Thomas P. Voorhies; Keenan Wynn Brown; Deacon Chuck Ortego.
Mailing Address: P.O. Box 31, 70535. Tel: 337-457-5285; Fax: 337-457-7904.
School—St. Edmund Elementary, 331 N. 3rd St., 70535. Tel: 337-457-5988; Fax: 337-457-5989. Mrs. Elizabeth Christ, Asst. Prin.; Mr. Harry Summerlin. Tel: 337-457-3777.
High School—St. Edmund High, 351 W. Magnolia St., 70535. Tel: 337-457-2592; Fax: 337-457-2648. Leon Estes, Asst. Prin. Lay Teachers 40; Students: Elementary 342; High School 279.
Catechesis/Religious Program—Tel: 337-457-7505. Students 324.

2—ST. MATHILDA (1939), (African American), [CEM] Rev. Joseph V. Tyson, S.S.J.
Mailing Address: P.O. Box 346, 70535. Tel: 337-457-3286.
Res.: 800 E. Laurel Ave., 70535.
Catechesis/Religious Program—Tel: 337-457-0108. Students 140.

3—ST. THOMAS MORE (1967), Rev. Matthew G. Roussel; Deacon David Guillory.
Mailing Address: P.O. Box 1022, 70535. Tel: 337-457-8107; Fax: 337-457-1735.
Catechesis/Religious Program—Tel: 337-457-8101; Fax: 337-457-8224. Students 355.

EVANGELINE, ACADIA PARISH, ST. JOSEPH (1938), [CEM 2] Rev. Mark Derise.
Mailing Address: P.O. Box 183, 70537. Tel: 337-824-4995; Fax: 337-824-4995.
Catechesis/Religious Program—Tel: 337-824-8352. Students 131.
Mission—St. Jules Petit Mamou, Acadia Parish. Tel: 337-824-7088. Riverside Rd., Jennings.

FOUR CORNERS, ST. MARY PARISH, ST. PETER THE APOSTLE (1960), Rev. Gregory P. Cormier.
Mailing Address: 1325 Big Four Corners Rd., Franklin, 70538. Tel: 337-923-7781; Fax:

337-923-4966.
Catechesis/Religious Program—Tel: 337-276-2348.
Mission—St. Joan of Arc, (Closed) , Glencoe, St. Mary Parish.

FRANKLIN, ST. MARY PARISH
1—ASSUMPTION B.V.M. (1852), Rev. Michael Russo; Deacon Douglas Hebert.
Mailing Address: 211 Iberia St., 70538. Tel: 337-828-3869; Fax: 337-828-3872.
School—St. John Elementary, 924 Main St., 70538. Tel: 337-828-2648; Fax: 337-828-2112. Mrs. Gayle Clements, Prin. Lay Teachers 13; Students 194.
High School—Hanson High School, 903 Anderson St., 70538. Tel: 337-828-3487; Fax: 337-828-7431. Mr. Scott St. Pierre, Prin. Lay Teachers 22; Students 291.
Catechesis/Religious Program—Tel: 337-828-9499. Students 125.
2—ST. JULES (1950), [CEM] Rev. Thomas Vu; Deacon Joseph Thomas.
Res.: 601 Magnolia St., 70538. Tel: 337-828-1714; Fax: 337-828-1734.
Catechesis/Religious Program—Students 80.
Mission—Immaculate Conception 601 Magnolia, Verdunville, St. Mary Parish 70538.

GRAND COTEAU, ST. LANDRY PARISH, ST. CHARLES BORROMEO (1819), [CEM] [JC] Revs. Thomas J. Madden, S.J.; John Welsh, S.J.; Deacon Samuel Henry.
Mailing Address: P.O. Drawer A, 70541. Tel: 337-662-5279; Fax: 337-662-5270. In Res., Bro. John Puza, S.J.
Res.: 174 Church St., 70541.
School—St. Ignatius, P.O. Drawer J, 70541. Tel: 337-662-3325; Fax: 337-662-3349. Mr. Russell Erickson, Prin. Brothers 1; Lay Teachers 27; Students 360.
Catechesis/Religious Program—Tel: 337-662-5271. Students 383.
Mission—Christ the King Opelousas. 369 Christ the King Rd., Bellevue, St. Landry Parish 70570. Tel: 337-942-6888.

GRAND PRAIRIE, ST. LANDRY PARISH, ST. PETER (1951), [CEM 2] [JC] Rev. Paul J. LaFleur.
Res. & Mailing Address: 1074 Hwy. 748 (Grand Prairie), Washington, 70589-4541. Tel: 337-826-3870; Fax: 337-826-5635.
Catechesis/Religious Program—Students 170.
Mission—St. Andrew Plaisance, St. Landry Parish.

GUEYDAN, VERMILION PARISH, ST. PETER (1907), [JC] Unassigned.
Res.: 603 Main St., P.O. Box 28, 70542. Tel: 337-536-9258; Fax: 337-536-0071.
School—513 6th St., 70542. Tel: 337-536-7930; Fax: 337-536-9460. Mr. Logan "Skip" Gardner, Prin. Sisters 2; Lay Teachers 9; Students 105.
Catechesis/Religious Program—Tel: 337-532-9258. Students 150.
Mission—St. David P.O. Box 28, Mulvey, Vermilion Parish 70542.

HENDERSON, ST. MARTIN PARISH, OUR LADY OF MERCY (1962), [CEM] [JC] Rev. Theodore Broussard.
Res.: Henderson Sta., P.O. Box 587, Breaux Bridge, 70517. Tel: 337-228-2352; Fax: 337-228-2372.
Catechesis/Religious Program—Tel: 337-228-2234. Students 207.
Mission—Sacred Heart Butte La Rose, St. Martin Parish.

HENRY, VERMILION PARISH, ST. JOHN (1939), (French-Acadian), [CEM] Rev. Cedric Sonnier.
Res.: 18534 La. Hwy. 689, Erath, 70533. Tel: 337-937-5108; Fax: 337-937-0002.
Catechesis/Religious Program—Students 218.
Mission—St. James Esther, Vermilion Parish.

IOTA, ACADIA PARISH, ST. JOSEPH (1892), [CEM] Rev. F. David Broussard.
Mailing Address: P.O. Box 710, 70543. Tel: 337-779-2627; Fax: 337-779-2627.
School—St. Francis, P.O. Box 870, 70543. Tel: 337-779-2527. Louis Cramer, Prin. Lay Teachers 10; Students 140.
Catechesis/Religious Program—Students 289.
Mission—St. Michael P.O. Box 298, Egan, Acadia Parish 70531. Tel: 337-788-0529.

JEANERETTE, IBERIA PARISH
1—ST. JOHN THE EVANGELIST (1879), [CEM] Rev. Edward Degeyter.
Res.: 1510 Church St., 70544. Tel: 337-276-4576; Fax: 337-276-5804.
School—St. Joseph, 10917 Old Jeanerette Rd., 70544. Tel: 337-276-3615; Fax: 337-276-3616. Dr. Corinne Hebert, Prin. Lay Teachers 12; Students 166.
Catechesis/Religious Program—Tel: 337-276-6944; Fax: 337-276-5805. Students 300.
2—OUR LADY OF THE ROSARY (1945), (African American), [CEM] [JC] Rev. Agustinus Seran, S.V.D.
Res.: 11200 Old Jeanerette Rd., 70544. Tel: 337-276-6900; Fax: 337-276-6931.
Catechesis/Religious Program—Students 106.

JUDICE, LAFAYETTE PARISH, ST. BASIL (1970) [CEM 2] Rev. Henry J. Broussard.
Res.: 1803 Duhon Rd. (Judice), Duson, 70529. Tel: 337-984-2179; Fax: 337-988-3793.
Catechesis Religious Program—Tel: 337-988-2655. Students 253.

KAPLAN, VERMILION PARISH, OUR LADY OF THE HOLY ROSARY (1896), [JC] Rev. Lloyd F. Benoit; Deacons Paul R. Eleazar; Kendal James Faulk.
Mailing Address: P.O. Box 429, 70548. Tel: 337-643-6472; Fax: 337-643-2516.
School—Maltrait Memorial, One Crusader Square, 70548. Tel: 337-643-7765; Fax: 337-643-7765. Mrs. Renee C. Meaux, Prin. Lay Teachers 11 Students 116.
Catechesis/Religious Program—701 N. Boudreaux Ave., P.O. Box 429, 70548. Students 697.
Mission—St. Frances Xavier Cabrini 705 N. Frederick, P.O. Box 429, Vermilion Parish 70548.

KROTZ SPRINGS, ST. LANDRY PARISH, ST. ANTHONY (1958), [CEM] Rev. Mark Ledoux.
Mailing Address: P.O. Box 425, 70750. Tel: 337-566-3527; Fax: 337-566-2803.
Catechesis/Religious Program—Students 110.

LAWTELL, ST. LANDRY PARISH
1—ST. BRIDGET (1920), [CEM 2] Rev. Daniel Picard.
Mailing Address: P.O. Box 156, 70550. Tel: 337-543-7591; Fax: 337-543-7593.
Catechesis/Religious Program—Students 125.
Mission—Sacred Heart Prairie Ronde, St. Landry Parish.
2—HOLY FAMILY (1953), (African American), Rev. Denis A. Osuagwu (Nigeria).
Mailing Address: P.O. Box 310, 70550. Tel: 337-543-2366; Fax: 337-543-8281.
Catechesis/Religious Program—Students 78.

LEBEAU, ST. LANDRY PARISH, IMMACULATE CONCEPTION (1897), (African American), [CEM] Rev. Ambrose N. Udeze, M.S.P.
Mailing Address: P.O. Box 6, 71345. Tel: 337-623-4783; Fax: 337-623-4783.
Catechesis/Religious Program—Students 65.
Mission—Sacred Heart Rideau Settlement, St. Landry Parish.

LEONVILLE, ST. LANDRY PARISH
1—ST. CATHERINE (1952), (African American), [JC] Rev. Msgr. Paul Metrejean; Deacon Julian Judice.
Mailing Address: P.O. Box 547, 70551. Tel: 337-879-2940; Fax: 337-879-9717.
Catechesis/Religious Program—Tel: 337-879-2347; Fax: 337-879-9717. Students 110.
Mission—St. Jules Prairie Laurent, St. Landry Parish.
2—ST. LEO THE GREAT (1896), [CEM] [JC] Rev. Msgr. Paul Metrejean.
Mailing Address: P.O. Box 8, 70551. Tel: 337-879-2365; Fax: 337-879-3050.
Catechesis/Religious Program—Tel: 337-879-2224. Students 201.

LEROY, VERMILION PARISH, OUR LADY OF PERPETUAL HELP (1922), [CEM] Rev. A. Rex Broussard.
Res.: 12995 Louisiana Hwy. 699, Maurice, 70555. Tel: 337-893-0610; Fax: 337-893-0694
Catechesis/Religious Program—Students 63.

LOREAUVILLE, IBERIA PARISH
1—ST. JOSEPH (1873), [CEM] [JC 2] Rev. Aaron Melancon.
Mailing Address: P.O. Box 365, 70552. Tel: 337-229-4254; Fax: 337-229-4255.
Catechesis/Religious Program—Tel: 337-229-6728. Students 410.
2—OUR LADY OF VICTORY (1953), (African American), [CEM 2] [JC] Rev. Aaron Melancon.
Mailing Address: P.O. Box 387, 70552. Tel: 337-229-8284; Fax: 337-229-4255.
Catechesis/Religious Program—Tel: 337-229-6329. Students 103.

LOUISA, ST. MARY PARISH, ST. HELENA (1890), [CEM] Rev. Thomas Thanh Nguyen.
Res.: 108 St. Helen's Church Ln., Franklin, 70538. Tel: 337-867-4378; Fax: 337-867-5223.
Chapel—St. Francis Cypremort Point.

LYDIA, IBERIA PARISH, ST. NICHOLAS (1867), [CEM 2] Rev. Richard Fabre; Deacon L. J. Frayou.
Mailing Address: P.O. Box 369, 70569. Tel: 337-364-5228; Fax: 337-364-5251.
Catechesis/Religious Program—Tel: 337-367-0562; Fax: 337-364-5251. Students 425.

LYONS POINT, ACADIA PARISH, ST. JOHN THE BAPTIST (1952), [CEM] Rev. Donald Pousson.
Mailing Address: 8021 Lyons Point Hwy., Crowley, 70526. Tel: 337-783-2457; Fax: 337-783-9015.
Catechesis/Religious Program—Tel: 337-783-9875. Students 86.

MALLET, ST. LANDRY PARISH, ST. ANN (1856), (African American), [CEM] Rev. Denis A. Osuagwu (Nigeria).
Mailing Address: P.O. Box 310, Lawtell, 70550. Tel: 337-543-2385; Fax: 337-543-8281.
Catechesis/Religious Program—Tel: 337-543-2366; Fax: 337-543-8182. Students 71.

MAMOU, EVANGELINE PARISH, ST. ANN (1914), [CEM] Revs. Robert Courville; Pius Vallooran, C.M.I. (India).
Parish Center—716 Sixth St., 70554. Tel: 337-468-3159; Fax: 337-468-3427.
Catechesis/Religious Program—Students 466.
Mission—Holy Spirit 5023 Vidrine Rd., Vidrine, Evangeline Parish. Tel: 337-363-7450.

MAURICE, VERMILION PARISH
1—ST. ALPHONSUS (1893), [CEM] Rev. O. Joseph Breaux.
Res.: 8700 Maurice Ave., P.O. Box 190, 70555. Tel: 337-893-4099; Fax: 337-893-2474.
Catechesis/Religious Program—Tel: 337-893-0923; Fax: 337-893-2474. Students 298.
2—ST. JOSEPH (1946), (African American), [JC] Rev. Richard Zawadzki, S.V.D.
Mailing Address: P.O. Box 250, 70555. Tel: 337-893-5428; Fax: 337-893-5441.
Catechesis/Religious Program—Students 122.

MELVILLE, ST. LANDRY PARISH, ST. JOHN THE EVANGELIST (1931), [CEM] Rev. Jose L.F. Padinjarepeedika, C.M.I. (India).
Mailing Address: 318 First St., P.O. Box 256, 71353-0256. Tel: 337-623-4957; Fax: 337-623-4970.
Catechesis/Religious Program—Students 21.
Mission—St. Thomas, the Apostle 340 E. Railroad Ave., Palmetto, St. Landry Parish 71358.

MERMENTAU, ACADIA PARISH, ST. JOHN THE EVANGELIST (1882), [CEM] Rev. Thomas E. Habetz.
Mailing Address: P.O. Box 176, 70556. Tel: 337-824-2278; Fax: 337-824-9624.
Catechesis/Religious Program—Tel: 337-824-2278; Fax: 337-824-9624. Students 117.
Mission—St. Margaret 311 Miller St., Estherwood, Acadia Parish 70534.

MILTON, LAFAYETTE PARISH, ST. JOSEPH (1977), [CEM] Rev. M. Keith LaBove; Deacon Cody Miller.
Mailing Address: P.O. Box 299, 70558. Tel: 337-856-5997; Fax: 337-856-5955.
Catechesis/Religious Program—Tel: 337-856-5997; Fax: 337-856-5955. Students 414.

MIRE, ACADIA PARISH, ASSUMPTION OF THE BLESSED VIRGIN MARY (1954), [CEM] Rev. Msgr. Russell J. Harrington, V.E.; Deacon J. Douglas Melancon.
Res.: 6080 Mire Hwy., Church Point, 70525. Tel: 337-873-6574; Fax: 337-873-3777.
Catechesis/Religious Program—Tel: 337-873-3777. Students 256.

MORROW, ST. LANDRY PARISH, ST. PETER (1947), (French), [CEM] Rev. George Thychery.
Mailing Address: P.O. Box 319, 71356. Tel: 318-346-7010.
Mission—Resurrection Whiteville.

MORSE, ACADIA PARISH, IMMACULATE CONCEPTION (1956), Rev. Donald Pousson.
Mailing Address: P.O. Box 297, 70559-0297. Tel: 337-783-2968.
Catechesis/Religious Program—Tel: 337-783-2968. Students 102.
Mission—St. Aloysius Midland. Tel: 337-783-2968.

MOWATA, ACADIA PARISH, ST. LAWRENCE (1905), [CEM 2] Rev. George Heffner, S.V.D.
Res.: 29031 Crowley-Eunice Hwy., Eunice, 70535. Tel: 337-457-2739; Fax: 337-457-2739.
Catechesis/Religious Program—Students 69.

NEW IBERIA, IBERIA PARISH
1—ST. EDWARD (1917), [CEM] [JC] Rev. Alfred Ayem, S.V.D.
Mailing Address: 175 Ambassador W. Lemelle Dr., 70560. Tel: 337-369-3101; Fax: 337-369-3118.
School—175 Porter St., 70560. Tel: 337-369-6764; Fax: 337-369-9534. Sr. Michelle Callanan, S.B.S., Prin. Sisters of the Blessed Sacrament 2; Lay Teachers 15; Students 375.
Catechesis/Religious Program—Tel: 337-365-3762. Students 248.
Mission—St. Jude 4408 Old Jeanerette Rd., Iberia Parish 70560. Tel: 337-364-2907.
2—NATIVITY OF OUR LADY (1964), [CEM] Rev. Michael Arnaud; Deacon John George Sarkies. In Res., Rev. Albert J. Boumans (Retired).
Res.: Richelieu Circle, 70560. Tel: 337-364-8360; Fax: 337-364-1509.
Catechesis/Religious Program—Tel: 337-365-3759; Fax: 337-364-1509. Students 521.
3—OUR LADY OF PERPETUAL HELP (1949), [JC] Revs. Michael Guidry; Ken Broussard; Deacons Ulysse J. Boudreaux; Ronald Borel; George Sikes.
Res.: 1303 St. Jude Ave., 70560. Tel: 337-365-5481; Fax: 337-365-5483.
Catechesis/Religious Program—Students 352.
4—ST. PETER (1838), (Hispanic—Acadian), [CEM] [JC] Revs. Charles Langlois; Jude Halphen; Deacons Ronald H. Broussard; James Wilson; Wade Joseph Broussard.
Mailing Address: P.O. Box 12507, 70562. Tel: 337-369-3816; Fax: 337-369-3192. In Res., Rev. Msgr. John H. Disch (Retired).
Catechesis/Religious Program—Students 598.
5—SACRED HEART OF JESUS (1960), Rev. Steven C.

LeBlanc.
Res.: 2514 Old Jeanerette Rd., 70563. Tel: 337-364-4439; Fax: 337-364-4474.
Catechesis/Religious Program—Students 460.

OPELOUSAS, ST. LANDRY PARISH

1—HOLY GHOST (1920), (African American), [JC] Rev. Malcolm O'Leary, S.V.D. In Res., Revs. Raymond Jones, S.V.D.; Benignus "Bennie" Wego, S.V.D.
Res.: 732 N. Union St., 70570. Tel: 337-942-2732; Fax: 337-948-4108.
Catechesis/Religious Program—Students 588.

2—ST. LANDRY (1776), [CEM] [JC] Rev. Eugene R. Tremie; Deacons Carlo Cannatella; John W. Miller.
Res.: 1020 N. Main St., 70570. Tel: 337-942-6552; Fax: 337-948-1295.
Catechesis/Religious Program—Students 42.

3—OUR LADY OF MERCY (1942), Rev. Jefferson J. DeBlanc Jr.; Deacons Ulysse Joubert; Thomas Lindsey.
Res.: 124 N. Camille St., 70570. Tel: 337-942-4174; Fax: 337-942-1476.
Catechesis/Religious Program—Tel: 337-942-9404. Students 246.

4—OUR LADY QUEEN OF ANGELS (1967), [JC] Rev. Angelo Cremaldi; Deacon Jerome Collins.
Mailing Address: P.O. Box 508, 70571-0508.
Res.: 2125 S. Union St., 70570. Tel: 337-942-5628; Fax: 337-942-9708.
Catechesis/Religious Program—Tel: 337-942-7831; Fax: 337-942-9708. Students 448.

PARKS, ST. MARTIN PARISH, ST. JOSEPH (1938), Rev. Bryce Sibley.
Mailing Address: P.O. Box 2810, 70582. Tel: 337-845-4168; Fax: 337-845-5079.
Catechesis/Religious Program—Students 320.
Mission—St. Louis, Tel: 337-845-4168.

PATTERSON, ST. MARY PARISH, ST. JOSEPH (1848), [CEM] Very Rev. Msgr. Richard Greene, V.E.
Res.: P.O. Box 219, 70392-0219. Tel: 985-395-3616; Fax: 985-395-9129.
Catechesis/Religious Program—Students 205.

PINE PRAIRIE, EVANGELINE PARISH, ST. PETER (1924), [CEM 2] Rev. Richard Dale Broussard.
Mailing Address: P.O. Box 709, 70576. Tel: 337-599-2224; Fax: 337-599-3003.
Mission—St. Theresa St. Landry, Evangeline Parish.
Catechesis/Religious Program—Tel: 337-599-2229; Fax: 337-599-3003. Students 107.

PLAISANCE, ST. LANDRY PARISH, ST. JOSEPH (1949), (African American), [CEM] Rev. Lawrence N. Abara.
Res.: 3283 Hwy. 167, Opelousas, 70570. Tel: 337-826-3395; Fax: 337-826-3550.
Catechesis/Religious Program—Students 90.
Mission—St. Ann 521 Frilot Cove Rd., Frilot Cove, Evangeline Co. 70570.

PORT BARRE, ST. LANDRY PARISH

1—ST. MARY (1952), (African American), [CEM] [JC] Rev. Raymond Jones, S.V.D.; Deacon Alvin DeJean, Parish Life Coord.
Mailing Address: P.O. Box 338, 70577. Tel: 337-585-2315; Fax: 337-585-2315.
Catechesis/Religious Program—Tel: 337-585-2863; Fax: 337-585-5860. Students 66.

2—SACRED HEART OF JESUS (1871), [CEM] [JC] Rev. Charles N. Trahan.
Mailing Address: P.O. Box 129, 70577. Tel: 337-585-2279; Fax: 337-585-2276.
Catechesis/Religious Program—Tel: 337-585-2279; Fax: 337-585-2215. Students 500.

RAYNE, ACADIA PARISH

1—ST. JOSEPH (1872), [CEM 2] [JC 2] Revs. William Paul Ruskoski; Thomas Hein Vu.
Mailing Address: P.O. Box 199, 70578. Tel: 337-334-2193; Fax: 337-334-2199.
School—Rayne Catholic Elementary, 407 S. Polk St., 70578. Tel: 337-334-5657; 337-334-5658; Fax: 337-334-3301. Blaine Castille, Prin. Lay Teachers 22; Students 434.
Catechesis/Religious Program—Tel: 337-334-9849. Students 248.

2—SHRINE OF OUR MOTHER OF MERCY (1924), (African American), [CEM] Rev. Richard F. Wagner, S.S.J.; Deacon Nolton Senegal Sr.
Mailing Address: 707 Lyman Ave., 70578. Tel: 337-334-3516; Fax: 337-334-4416.
Res.: 707 Lyman Ave., 70578. Tel: 337-334-3516; Fax: 337-334-4416.
Catechesis/Religious Program—Tel: 337-334-4909; Fax: 337-334-4416. Students 166.

RICHARD, ACADIA PARISH, ST. EDWARD (1939), [CEM] [JC] Rev. J. Daniel Edwards.
Res.: 1463 Charlene Hwy., Church Point, 70525. Tel: 337-684-5991; Fax: 337-684-0189.
Catechesis/Religious Program—Students 250.
Mission—St. Thomas Tasso Loop, Savoy, St. Landry Parish 70525.

ROBERT'S COVE, ACADIA PARISH, ST. LEO IV (1883), (German), [CEM] Rev. Francis L. Bourgeois.
Res.: 7166 Roberts Cove Rd., Rayne, 70578-8912. Tel: 337-334-5056; Fax: 337-334-0832.
Catechesis/Religious Program—Tel: 337-334-7458. Students 94.
Mission—St. Edmund Branch, French Parish.

RYNELLA, IBERIA PARISH, ST. MARCELLUS (1960), [CEM] Rev. Donavan J. Labbe.
Res.: 6100 Avery Island Rd., New Iberia, 70560. Tel: 337-364-0818; Fax: 337-364-0824.
Catechesis/Religious Program—Tel: 337-364-9419. Students 187.

ST. MARTINVILLE, ST. MARTIN PARISH

1—ST. MARTIN OF TOURS (1765), [CEM] Revs. P. Austin Leger; Kenneth A. Bienvenu (Retired). In Res., Rev. Jean Marie Jammes (Retired).
Res.: 133 S. Main St., P.O. Drawer 10, 70582. Tel: 337-394-6021; Fax: 337-394-6020.
Catechesis/Religious Program—Tel: 337-394-4203. Students 75.

2—NOTRE DAME DE PERPETUEL SECOURS (1938), (African American), [CEM] [JC] Revs. Thomas A. Mullally, S.V.D.; Arockiam Arockiam, S.V.D.; Deacon Carlton Lee.
Res.: 240 Gary St., 70582. Tel: 337-394-3084; Fax: 337-394-5380.
Catechesis/Religious Program—Tel: 337-394-4749. Students 450.

SCOTT, LAFAYETTE PARISH

1—SAINT MARTIN DE PORRES (1961), (African American), [CEM] Deacon Louis J. Lloyd.
Mailing Address: P.O. Box 1347, 70583-1347. Tel: 337-232-1968; Fax: 337-266-8922.
Catechesis/Religious Program—Students 74.

2—STS. PETER AND PAUL (1904), [CEM] Rev. Gilbert J. Dutel.
Mailing Address: P.O. Box 610, 70583. Tel: 337-235-2433; Fax: 337-233-4868.
Catechesis/Religious Program—Tel: 337-232-6167. Students 757.

VILLE PLATTE, EVANGELINE PARISH

1—ST. JOSEPH (1947), (African American), [CEM] Very Rev. Msgr. J. Robert Romero, V.E.; Rev. Chanh Van Nguyen; Sr. Christina Marie Griggs, O.Carm., Pastoral Assoc.
Res.: 1107 Martin L. King Dr., 70586. Tel: 337-363-1051.
Catechesis/Religious Program—Students 59.

2—OUR LADY QUEEN OF ALL SAINTS (1969), Rev. Randall Moreau; Deacon Eugene Le Boeuf.
Res.: 1135 Parkview St., P.O. Drawer E, 70586. Tel: 337-363-5167; Fax: 337-363-5179.
Catechesis/Religious Program—Students 154.

3—SACRED HEART OF JESUS (1854), [CEM] Very Rev. Msgr. J. Robert Romero, V.E.; Rev. Chanh Nguyen; Deacon Harris Soileau.
Res.: 708 E. Main St., 70586. Tel: 337-363-2989; Fax: 337-363-3500.
School—Sacred Heart Elementary, 532 E. Main St., 70586. Tel: 337-363-3322; Fax: 337-363-2318. Mr. Andrew Ducote, Prin.
High School—Sacred Heart High, 114 Trojan Ln., 70586. Tel: 337-363-1475; Fax: 337-363-0348. Mr. Andrew Ducote, Prin. Lay Teachers 54; Students: Elementary 546; High School 283.
Catechesis/Religious Program—Tel: 337-363-7788; Fax: 337-363-3500. Students 171.
Mission—Sacred Heart Belaire Cove. Tel: 337-363-2989; Fax: 337-363-3500.

WASHINGTON, ST. LANDRY PARISH

1—HOLY TRINITY (1950), (African American), Rev. Albert Gayle Nunez; Deacon Alvin R. DeJean, Parish Life Coord.
Mailing Address: P.O. Box 186, 70589. Tel: 337-826-3376; Fax: 337-826-3376.
Catechesis/Religious Program—Students 36.

2—IMMACULATE CONCEPTION (1756), (French—German), Rev. Albert G. Nunez.
Mailing Address: P.O. Box 116, 70589. Tel: 337-826-7396; Fax: 337-826-0099.
Catechesis/Religious Program—Tel: 337-826-7396; Fax: 337-826-0099. Students 66.

YOUNGSVILLE, LAFAYETTE PARISH, ST. ANNE (1859), [CEM] Rev. Louis Lam Vu.
Mailing Address: P.O. Box 410, 70592. Tel: 337-856-8212; Fax: 337-856-8277.
Catechesis/Religious Program—Tel: 337-856-8242. Students 559.

On Special Assignment:
Revs.—
Boyer, Millard G., Chap., Lafayette General Medical Center, 210 X Long Plantation Blvd., 70508. Tel: 337-289-7483
Champagne, Michael, Chap., Community of Jesus Crucified, 421 1/2 Carmel Ave., 70501. Hospitals/ Health Care Facilities
Finley, John Thomas, Chap., Bethany Health Care, 231 General Gardiner Ave., 70501.
Frey, Jerome V., Community of Jesus Crucified, 421 1/2 Carmel Ave., 70501.
Jones, Raymond, S.V.D., 732 N. Union St., Opelousas, 70570. St. Mary, Port Barre
Kamenski, Thomas, O.F.M., Chap., Our Lady of Lourdes Hospital, 415 Guilbeau Rd., #23, 70506.
Kanat, Joseph Kurian (India), Chap. (Extern-Diocesan), Res.: Cathedral of St. John the Evangelist, P.O. Drawer V, 70502. Diocesan Prison Ministry
Lozano, Arturo, S.J., Dir. Hispanic Ministry, 1408 Carmel Ave., 70501-5298.
Luberti, Richard A., C.SS.R., 1408 Carmel Ave., 70501-5298. Disabilities Office
Morvant, Kenneth R., J.C.L., Office of the Tribunal, P.O. Box 3387, 70502-3387.
O'Neill, Jeremy, O.S.B., 168 Monastery Ln., Opelousas, 70570.
Okwaraocha, Emmanuel, Chap., P.O. Box 429, Kaplan, 70548. Vermilion Parish Nursing Homes & Hospitals
Onuegbe, Paul, Chap., P.O. Box 365, Loreauville, 70552-0365. Iberia Parish Hospitals and Nursing Homes

---

On Duty Outside the Diocese:
Revs.—
Boudreaux, John S., Corpus Christi Church, 6300 McKenna Dr., Mobile, AL 36608-3898.
Davis, Hampton, Notre Dame Seminary, 2901 S. Carrollton Ave., New Orleans, 70118-4391.
Downs, Gregory Todd, P.O. Box 432, Natchitoches, 71458-0432.
Guilbeau, Jeremy, Pontifical North American College, Casa Santa Maria, Dell U Limata, Via Limata 30, Rome 00187 Italy.
Meaux, Glenn, Haiti Mission, P.O. Box 18249, Kansas City, MO 64133.
Voorhies, Bennett J., Diocese of Santa Fe, 4000 Saint Joseph Pl., NW, Albuquerque, NM 87120.

Military Chaplains:
Rev.—
Vidrine, Richard, 68 A. Ridgewood Rd., Middletown, RI 02842.

Absent on Sick Leave:
Rev.—
Delauney, Herbert C.

Retired:
Rev. Msgrs.—
Angelle, Robert G., 205 N. Anita St., 70501.
Barsen, Herman J., 130 N. Richelieu Circle, New Iberia, 70560-1558. Tel: 337-365-0616
Benefiel, Harry E., 301 Eraste Landry Rd., 70506-2321. Tel: 337-235-4373
Disch, John H., P.O. Box 12507, New Iberia, 70562-2507.
Mallet, Charles J., 40 Audobon Oaks Blvd., 70506.
Mouton, Charles Burton, Basilica St. Mary Major 00120 Vatican City State.
Richard, Wayne R., 311 Wayne St., New Iberia, 70563.
Revs.—
Bergeron, C. Paul, 402 Wayside Dr., Houma, 70360.
Betrand, Conley, 1804 W. University Ave., 70506.
Bienvenu, Kenneth A., 1017 Alan Dr., St. Martinville, 70582.
Boumans, Albert, Nativity of Our Lady, 130 B. Richelieu, New Iberia, 70560.
Brennan, Joseph F., 203 Bocage Circle, 70503.
Calais, Floyd J., 313 Rue Louis XIV, Apt. H, 70508. Tel: 318-988-6278
DeLeeuw, John, 526 Raintree Tr., 70507.
Desilets, Viateur, 2319 E. Main St., New Iberia, 70560-4096.
Dugas, Willard, 520 Dugas Rd., 70507-3010.
Dutra, Luis C., 1522 Carmel Ave., 70501. (Extern-Diocesan)
Edwards, Roy D., 308 Sidney Martin Rd., 70507.
Estilette, Grady J., P.O. Box 82315, 70598-2315.
Hebert, Lloyd P., 39100 Orchard Ave., Cherry Valley, CA 92223-3797.
Hebert, T. J., 411 Hanover Sq., 70508.
Jammes, Jean Marie, P.O. Drawer 10, St. Martinville, 70582-0010. Tel: 318-394-6021
Landry, Oneil Anthony, P.O. Box 202, Centerville, 70522.
Landry, Ralph James, 2603 Bodin Rd., New Iberia, 70560.
Ledoux, Louis Vernon, (Retired Armed Forces), 205-21 115th Rd., Jamaica, NY 11412-2907.
Maraist, Martin, 5690 A Resweber Hwy., St. Martinsville, 70582.
Matt, J. Wilson, Res.: St. Landry Church, 1020 N. Main St., Opelousas, 70570.
Montelaro, Thomas, P.O. Box 911, Eunice, 70535-0911.
Robitaille, Raymond, 2319 Main St., New Iberia, 70560-4096.
Senneville, Eugene Joseph, P.O. Box 9, Port Barre, 70577-0009.
Simon, George Howard, 503 Mount Vernon Dr., 70503.

Sonnier, T. Alcide, P.O. Box 100, Chataignier, 70524-0100.
Spekschate, John, De Gauden, 49, 5801 BX Venray, The Netherlands.
Speyrer, Jules, 1530 White St., Basile, 70515. Tel: 337-432-5054
Stemmann, Joseph, 3651 Hwy. 104, Opelousas, 70570.
Theriot, Donald C., 2006 West Summer Dr., Abbeville, 70510.
Thibodeaux, Paul, Res.: 222 Bombardier Ln., Eunice, 70535.
Warren, Arthur, Tribunal Office, 1408 Carmel Ave., 70501.

Permanent Deacons:
Benedetto, Joseph, Northglenn, CO
Bergeron, Harris, Our Lady of Mercy, Henderson
Bodin, Edward J., Immaculate Conception, Charenton
Bodin, Ronnie J., (On Leave)
Borbas, Timothy, Houston, TX
Borel, Ronald, Our Lady of Perpetual Help, New Iberia; Chancery, Lafayette
Boudreaux, Ulysse, Our Lady of Perpetual Help, New Iberia
Bourg, Gerald J., Sacred Heart, Baldwin
Broussard, Ronald H., St. Peter, New Iberia
Broussard, Wade, St. Peter, New Iberia
Cannatella, Carlo, St. Landry, Opelousas
Collins, Jerome, Our Lady Queen of Angels, Opelousas
Comeaux, Joseph, St. Stephen, Berwick
Cormier, James, Our Lady of the Sacred Heart, Church Point
Darce, Harry, Sacred Heart, Broussard
Davis, James, St. John Francis Regis, Arnaudville
DeJean, Alvin Ray, St. Mary, Port Barre; Holy Trinity, Washington
Doumit, Christopher, St. Joseph, Loreauville
Eleazar, Paul R., Holy Rosary, Kaplan
Faulk, Kendal, Our Lady of the Holy Rosary, Kaplan
Freyou, Leonard J., St. Nicholas Church Lydia
Green, Justin, Winona, MN
Guillory, David, St. Thomas More, Eunice
Hanemann, Louis, Fayetteville, NC
Hebert, Douglas J., Assumption, Franklin
Hebert, Marcel, St. Bernard, Breaux Bridge
Henry, Samuel, St. Charles, Grand Coteau
Jacobs, Lawrence, St. Francis of Assisi, Breaux Bridge
Joubert, Ulysse, Our Lady of Mercy, Opelousas
Judice, Julian, St. Catherine, Arnaudville
Kincel, James, Sts. Peter and Paul, Scott
Landry, Theodule, Annunciation of the BVM, Duralde
Lebouef, Eugene J., Queen of All Saints, Ville Platte
Lee, Carlton J., Sr., Notre Dame, St. Martinville
Lejeune, Joseph L., St. John the Evangelist, Mermentau
Leleux, Rodless, St. John the Baptist, Lyons Point; St. Michael, Crowley
Lindsey, Thomas, Our Lady of Mercy, Opelousas
Lloyd, Louis, St. Martin de Porres, Scott
Marcel, Albert, St. Anthony, Lafayette
Mason, Jonas E., (Retired)
Matte, Paul, St. Edmond, Lafayette
McDonner, Robert, St. Bernard, Breux Bridge
Melancon, J. Douglas, Assumption, Mire
Melancon, Roy, Our Lady of Mercy, Henderson
Miller, Cody, St. Joseph, Milton
Miller, John W., St. Landry, Opelousas
Morello, Benedict, St. Theresa, Abbeville
Mouton, Chris, St. Mary Magdalen, Abbeville
Mouton, Melvin, Pasadena, TX
Ortego, Charles, St. Anthony of Padua, Eunice
Perron, Roderick P., (Retired)
Picard, Richard, Holy Cross, Lafayette
Richard, Harold, St. Bernard, Breaux Bridge
Richard, Thomas, Our Lady of Mount Carmel, Chataignier; St. Joseph, Plaisance
Royston, John, (Unassigned)
Sarkies, John, Nativity of Our Lady, New Iberia
Senegal, Nolton, Our Mother of Mercy, Rayne
Sikes, George, Our Lady of Perpetual Help, New Iberia
Simon, Steve, St. Theresa, Duson
Soileau, Harris, Sacred Heart of Jesus, Ville Platte
Sonnier, Adam, (Retired)
Theriot, Samuel, (On Leave)
Thibodeaux, John, Assumption, Carencro
Thomas, Joseph, St. Jules, Franklin
Trahan, Joseph, Sacred Heart, Broussard
Tran, Tam, St. Helena, Louisa
Waguespack, Eugene, St. Peter, Carencro
Waguespack, Kenneth, (Retired)
Wilson, James, St. Peter, New Iberia

INSTITUTIONS LOCATED IN THE DIOCESE

[A] SEMINARIES, RELIGIOUS OR SCHOLASTICATES

GRAND COTEAU. *St. Charles College*, P.O. Box C, 70541-1003. Tel: 337-662-5251; Fax: 337-662-3187. Revs. Francis W. Huete, S.J., Novice Dir. & Supr. of Community; Michael D. Dooley, S.J., Asst. Novice Dir. Novitiate of New Orleans Province of the Society of Jesus. Priests 2; Novices 20.

[B] HIGH SCHOOLS, INTERPAROCHIAL

LAFAYETTE. *Teurlings Catholic High*, 139 Teurlings Dr., 70501. Tel: 337-235-5711; Fax: 337-234-8057. Email: mboyer@tchs.net. Web: www.tchs.net. Mr. Michael H. Boyer, Prin. Lay Teachers 47; Students 591.

St. Thomas More, 450 E. Farrel Rd., 70508. Tel: 337-988-3700; Fax: 337-988-2911. Web: www.stm.k12.la.us/index.html. Mr. Ray Simon, Prin. Brothers 1; Lay Teachers 78; Students 1,080.

CROWLEY. *Notre Dame High School of Acadia Parish*, 910 N. Eastern Ave., 70526. Tel: 337-783-3519; Fax: 337-788-2115. Email: Pios5224@aol.com. Web: www.ndpios.com. Mr. John E. Dailey, Prin. Lay Teachers 42; Students 530.

NEW IBERIA. *Catholic High School*, (Grades 4-12), 1301 DeLaSalle Dr., 70560. Tel: 337-364-5116; Fax: 337-364-5041. Email: ilandry@chspanthers.com. Web: chspanthers.com. Ivy J. Landry, Prin. Lay Teachers 62; Total Staff 81; Students 938.

OPELOUSAS. *Opelousas Catholic School*, (Grades PreK-12) , Elementary: (PreK-5) ; High School: (6-12) , 428 E. Prudhomme St., 70570. Tel: 337-942-5404; Fax: 337-942-5922. Email: ocsvikings@yahoo.com. Mr. Perry Fontenot, Prin. Lay Teachers 13; Students 278; Lay Teachers 30; Students 422; Sisters 1.

[C] ELEMENTARY SCHOOLS, INTERPAROCHIAL

LAFAYETTE. *Holy Family School*, 200 St. John St., 70501. Tel: 337-235-0267; Fax: 337-235-0558. Email: hfs98@aol.com. Sisters of the Holy Family Sisters 1; Lay Teachers 13; Students 203.

ST. MARTINVILLE. *Trinity Catholic School*, (Grades PreK-8), 242 Gary St., 70582. Tel: 337-394-6693; Fax: 337-394-3394. Email: trinity_catholic@stmartin.k12.la.us. Miss Rosemary Pierre, Prin. Lay Teachers 22; Total Staff 39; Students 442.

[D] ELEMENTARY SCHOOLS, PRIVATE

ABBEVILLE. *Mt. Carmel Elementary School*, 405 Park, 70510. Tel: 337-898-0859; Fax: 337-893-5968. Email: sisjanet@vrml.k12.la.us. Web: www.cont.vrml.k12.la.us/mc. Sr. Janet LeBlanc, O.Carm., Prin. Sisters of Mt. Carmel 3; Lay Teachers 23; Students 414.

[E] HIGH AND ELEMENTARY SCHOOLS, PRIVATE

GRAND COTEAU. *Academy of the Sacred Heart*, (Grades PreK-12), P.O. Box 310, 70541. Tel: 337-662-5275; Fax: 337-662-3011. Email: mburns@ashcoteau.org. Web: www.ashcoteau.org. Mary Burns, Head Mistress. Day School for girls. Boarding facilities for girls 8th-12th grade. Religious of the Sacred Heart 2; Lay Teachers 52; Students 353.

[F] GENERAL HOSPITALS

LAFAYETTE. *Our Lady of Lourdes Regional Medical Center, Inc.*, 611 St. Landry St., P.O. Box 4027, 70502. Tel: 337-289-2100; Fax: 337-289-2574. Email: padgettd@lourdesrmc.com bienvenus@lourdesrmc.com. Web: www.lourdes.net. Mr. Frank X. Neuner Jr., Chm. of the Governing Bd.; Mr. Robert Peebles, Pres. & CEO; Rev. Thomas Kamenski, O.F.M. Franciscan Missionaries of Our Lady 2; Bed Capacity 287; Total Staff 1,800; Patients Assisted Annually 139,522.

St. Mary's Imaging Center, Inc., 411 St. Landry St., 70506. Tel: 337-233-6288; Fax: 337-289-2782. A wholly owned, nonprofit subsidiary of Our Lady of Lourdes Regional Medical Center, Inc. Operating as an outpatient diagnostic facility. Patients Assisted Annually 19,408.

Corporate Health Services Incorporated, 611 St. Landry St., 70506. Tel: 337-289-2100; Fax: 337-289-2574.

Acadiana Heart Institute at Our Lady of Lourdes, 611 St. Landry St., 70506. Tel: 337-289-2588; Fax: 337-289-2574.

[G] HOMES FOR THE AGED INFIRM

LAFAYETTE. *Bethany M.H.S. Health Care Center*, P.O. Box 2308, 70502. Tel: 337-234-2459; Fax: 337-234-9483. Sisters of the Most Holy Sacrament 9; Staff 50; Bed Capacity 42; Total Assisted 48.

Village du Lac, Inc., 1404 Carmel Ave., 70501. Tel: 337-234-5106; Fax: 337-234-2630. Mr. J. Bernel Fontenot, Dir. Community housing for the handicapped and elderly with low income. Sponsored by the Diocese. Residents 200.

NEW IBERIA. *Consolata Home*, 2319 E. Main St., 70560. Tel: 337-365-8226; Fax: 337-365-8626. Email: hdlandry@iatel.net. Mr. David Landry, Admin.; Rev. Raymond Robitaille Chap. Tel: 318-365-7477. Residents 114; Bed Capacity 114; Total Staff 112.

OPELOUSAS. *C'est La Vie Center of the Sisters Marianites of Holy Cross*, 960 E. Prudhomme St., 70570. Tel: 337-942-8154; Fax: 337-942-8279. Email promptsuccor@bellsouth.net. Sr. Kay Kinberger, M.S.C., Pres.; Harriet Fisher, Coord.; Michael Purser, Admin. Independent living for the elderly and handicapped. Sisters 2; Total Staff 2; Patients Assisted Annually 34.

Our Lady of Prompt Succor Home, 954 E. Prudhomme St., 70570. Tel: 337-948-3634; Fax: 337-942-8279. Email: promptsuccor@bellsouth.net. Michael Purser, Admin. Sisters 16; Patients Assisted Annually 87; Bed Capacity 120; Total Staff 100.

[H] MONASTERIES AND RESIDENCES PRIESTS AND BROTHERS

LAFAYETTE. *De La Salle Christian Brothers*, 1522 Carmel Dr., 70501. Tel: 337-235-3576; Fax: 337-261-0765. Email: welkerlvw@aol.com. Web: www.magnolia1921.org. Bros. Louis Welker, F.S.C., Dir.; Jerry Vincent, F.S.C., Sub Dir.; C. Daniel Duplantis, F.S.C., Coord.; Rev. Luis C. Dutra, Chap. (Retired). Retired Brothers Home. Brothers 24.

De La Salle Christian Brothers Provincialate Headquarters for the New Orleans-Santa Fe District. , 1522 Carmel Dr., 70501. Tel: 337-234-1973; Fax: 337-261-1014. Email: nosf@BellSouth.net. Bros. Clarence Fioke, F.S.C., Prov.; Richard Kovatch, F.S.C., Auxiliary Prov. & Ed. Dir.; Brendan Hayden, F.S.C., Prov. Bookkeeper & Fin. Dir.
Legal Title: *Brothers of the Christian Schools of Lafayette LA, Inc.*

OPELOUSAS. *Mother of the Redeemer Monastery*, 168 Monastery Ln., 70570. Tel: 337-543-2237; Fax: 337-543-7752. Email: olivetan@banksouth.net. Priests 2; Brothers 2.

[I] CONVENTS AND RESIDENCES FOR SISTERS

LAFAYETTE
Other Addresses:
P.O. Box 298, Egan, 70531-0298. Tel: 337-788-0529.
220 Wilkle St., 70506. Tel: 337-234-4546.
Other Addresses:
317 St. Patrick St., No. 1, 70506-4565. Tel: 337-234-6724.
317 St. Patrick St., No. 3, 70506-4565. Tel: 337-264-1948.
317 St. Patrick St., No. 4, 70506-4565. Tel: 337-232-3443.
317 St. Patrick St., No. 5, 70506-4565. Tel: 337-264-1921.
317 St. Patrick St., No. 6, 70506-4565. Tel: 337-235-1755.
107 Wisteria Dr., 70506-6858. Tel: 337-989-9817. Sisters 2.

Maison Faller Residence, 406 St. Julien St., 70506-4622. Tel: 337-235-4711. Sisters 4.

St. Anne's Annex, 406 St. Julien St., 70506-4622. Tel: 337-233-8901. Sisters 2.

Bethany MHS Health Care Center, 406 St. Julien St., 70506-4622. Sisters 8.
Other Addresses:
506 Surrey St., 70501. Tel: 337-235-1837. Sisters 2.
317 Guilbeau Rd., 70506. Tel: 337-981-4378.

Discalced Carmelites Monastery of Mary, Mother of Grace. , 1250 Carmel Dr., 70501-5299. Tel: 337-232-4651; Fax: 337-232-3540. Sr. Regina Mullins, O.C.D., Prioress; Rev. Msgr. H. Alexandre Larroque, J.C.D., Chap. Cloistered Nuns 14; Extern Sisters 2.

Franciscan Missionaries of Our Lady
Our Lady of Lourdes Hospital, P.O. Box 4027, 70502. Tel: 337-289-2100 (Convent); 337-289-2110 (Hospital); Fax: 337-289-2574; 337-289-2641. Email: lyonsb@lourdesrmc.com. Web: www.lourdes.net.
611 St. Landry St., 70506. Tel: 337-289-2100; Fax: 337-289-2574.

Marianites of Holy Cross, 1417 St. John St., 70506. Tel: 337-234-5454. Email: mwelshmsc@cs.com. Sisters 3.

Missionaries of Charity, 911 St. John St., 70501.

Tel: 337-233-3929. Sisters 4.
School Sisters of Notre Dame, 105 Dogwood, 70501. Tel: 337-232-6975. Email: landrylor@aol.com.
Sisters of Divine Providence, 317 Guilbeau Rd., Apt. 101-E, 70506. Tel: 337-984-8520. Email: mildredleonards@juno.com.
Sisters of Mt. Carmel, 309 Evangeline Dr., 70501. Tel: 337-235-8687. Sisters 4.
Sisters of the Most Holy Sacrament, Convent Generalate, 313 Corona Dr., 70503-4757. Tel: 337-981-8475; Fax: 337-981-9128. Sr. Judine Theriot, M.H.S., Major Supr. Sisters 2.
Administrative Offices, P.O. Box 90037, 70509-0037. Tel: 337-981-8475; Fax: 337-981-9128.
Sisters of the Most Holy Sacrament, P.O. Box 90037, 70509-0037. Tel: 337-981-8475; Fax: 337-981-9128.

ABBEVILLE
Other Addresses:
2326 Camella, 70510. Tel: 337-898-1807. Sisters 3.
108 W. St. Victor St., 70510. Tel: 337-893-0138.
Sisters of Mt. Carmel, 108 Petain St., 70510. Tel: 337-898-0140.

BREAUX BRIDGE. *Sisters of the Most Holy Sacrament*, 221 Berard St., 70517-5023. Tel: 337-332-1951.

CROWLEY. *Marianites of the Holy Cross*, 516 N. Ave. E, 70526. Tel: 337-783-1550.

DUSON. *Eucharistic Missionaries of St. Dominic*, P.O. Box 725, 70529. Tel: 337-873-4159; Fax: 337-873-4159.

GRAND COTEAU
Other Addresses:
P.O. Box 446, 70541. Tel: 337-662-5526. Sisters 6.
P.O. Box 308, 70541. Tel: 337-662-5453. Sisters 5.
Religious of the Sacred Heart, P.O. Box 438, 70541. Tel: 337-662-5454. Sisters 5.

LEBEAU. *Sisters of the Holy Spirit*, P.O. Box 115, 71345. Tel: 337-623-5540.

NEW IBERIA. *Sisters of Providence*, 213 Oak Hill Rd., 70563. Tel: 337-364-3142.
Sisters of the Blessed Sacrament, 720 Providence St., 70560. Tel: 337-369-9534; Fax: 337-369-9534. Email: stedwards@cox-internet.com. Sisters 2.

OPELOUSAS. *Sisters of the Holy Family*, 317 Congress, 70570. Tel: 337-942-2052. Sisters 3.

RAYNE. *Sisters of the Blessed Sacrament*, 710 Malvern Ave., 70578-4632. Tel: 337-334-3606. Email: Roselle6@Juno.com. Sisters 3.

SUNSET. *Sisters of Mt. Carmel*, P.O. Box 1734, 70584-1734. Tel: 337-662-7178.

[J] RETREAT HOUSES

GRAND COTEAU. *Jesuit Spirituality Center (St. Charles College)*, P.O. Box C, 70541-1003. Tel: 337-662-5251; Fax: 337-662-3187. Email: jespirtcen@centurytel.net. Web: http://home.centurytel.net/spiritualitycenter/. Revs. Warren J. Broussard, S.J., Dir.; Louis A. Arceneaux, C.M.; Francis R. Brou, S.J.; John J. Cazenavette, S.J.; Thomas J. Jenniskens, S.J.; Arturo Lozano, S.J.; Thomas J. Madden, S.J.; Fred G. Reynolds, S.J.; Bro. George A. Murphy, S.J.; Sisters Consuelo Champagne, M.S.C.; Marlene Labbe, M.S.C. Year-round directed retreats of 3, 5, 8, or 30 days plus a variety of weekend retreats and/or programs open to men and women. Priests 8; Brothers 1; Sisters 2.
Our Lady of the Oaks Retreat House, P.O. Box D, 70541. Tel: 337-662-5410; Fax: 337-662-5331. Email: olorhgcla@centurytel.net. Web: www.ourladyoftheoaks.com. Revs. Kenneth Buddendorff, S.J., Dir.; Francis J. Coco, S.J., Assoc. Dir.; John T. Condry, S.J., Assoc. Dir.; Joseph P. McGill, S.J., Assoc. Dir. Jesuit Fathers, Preached retreats for men, women and married couples.

[K] CURSILLO CENTERS

OPELOUSAS. *Cursillo Center*, P.O. Box 577, Hayes, 70646-0577. 3651 Hwy. 104, 70570. Tel: 337-622-3562. Email: halhebert@centurytel.net. Rev. Kenneth Morrant, Dir.

[L] NEWMAN CENTERS

LAFAYETTE. *Our Lady of Wisdom Catholic Student Center* Univ. of Louisiana, P.O. Box 43271, 70505. Tel: 337-232-8741; 337-232-8742. Email: wisdom@ourladyofwisdom.org. Rev. Chester Arceneaux.

EUNICE. *Catholic Student Center-Louisiana State Univ.* P.O. Box 1129, 70535. Tel: 337-457-8668. Total Staff 1; Total in Residence 1.

[M] MISCELLANEOUS

LAFAYETTE. *St. Augustine Trust Fund*, P.O. Box 90037, 70509-0037. Tel: 337-981-8475; Fax: 337-981-9128. Sisters of the Most Holy Sacrament
Brothers of the Christian Schools of Lafayette - Retirement Trust, 1522 Carmel Ave., 70501. Tel: 337-234-1973; Fax: 337-261-1014. Email: nosf@BellSouth.net. Total Staff 9; Total in Residence 22.
Come Lord Jesus! Inc., 1804 W. University Ave., 70506. Tel: 337-233-6277; Fax: 337-233-6144. Email: comelord@BellSouth.net. Web: www.comelordjesus.com. Rev. Conley Bertrand, Dir.
Community of Jesus Crucified, 421 1/2 Carmel Dr., 70501. Tel: 337-232-7491; Fax: 337-261-5294. Email: cjc_ols@att.net. Revs. Jerome V. Frey, Spiritual Dir.; Michael Champagne.
St. La Salle Auxiliary, 1522 Carmel Dr., 70501. Tel: 337-234-1973; Fax: 337-261-1014. Email: nosf@bellsouth.net. The St. LaSalle Auxiliary is a development project of "de la Salle Christian Brothers," a nonprofit organization.
Lourdes Foundation, Inc., 611 St. Landry St., 70506. Tel: 337-289-2100; Fax: 337-289-4023. Email: dominguer@lourdesrmc.com. Web: www.lourdes.net. Mr. Robert Peebles, Pres. & CEO.
Sisters of the Eucharistic Covenant, 105 Upperline Ave., 70501. Tel: 337-233-2226; Fax: 337-233-2308. Email: clarroqu@bellsouth.net. Sr. Celeste D. Larroque, S.E.C., Pres.

NEW IBERIA. *Progressive Education Program, Inc.*, P.O. Box 10237, 70562-0237. Tel: 337-365-0933; Fax: 337-364-2555. Email: pepi@cox-internet.com. Sr. Lorraine Landry, S.S.N.D., Dir.

[N] SOCIAL SERVICE CENTERS

LAFAYETTE. *Lafayette Catholic Service Centers, Inc.*, 405 St. John St., P.O. Box 3177, 70502-3177. Tel: 337-235-4972; Fax: 337-234-0953. Web: www.dol-louisiana.org.
Service Centers: Jay Branch, Exec. Dir.
Promised Land Apartments Tel: 337-235-4972; Fax: 337-234-0953.
Msgr. A. O. Sigur Service Center Tel: 337-233-7788; Fax: 337-234-0953.
St. Joseph Shelter for Men Tel: 337-237-6816; Fax: 337-234-0953.
St. Joseph Diner Tel: 337-232-8434; Fax: 337-232-8475.
St. Bernadette Clinic Tel: 337-264-6292.
Msgr. Sigur Thrift Store Tel: 337-232-1166.
New Life Center, Opelousas. Tel: 337-948-3161; Fax: 337-948-0011. Total Assisted Annually 249,554.
New Life Center Thrift Store, Opelousas. Tel: 337-942-4079.

ABBEVILLE. *Christian Service Center*, 701 Chevis St., 70510. Tel: 337-893-9756; Fax: 337-893-0427.

CROWLEY. *Crowley Christian Care Center*, 825 N. Ave. F, P.O. Box 686, 70527-0686. Tel: 337-783-5811; Fax: 337-783-5811. Total Staff 50; Total Assisted 4,800.

NEW IBERIA. *Social Service Center*, 432 Bank Ave., 70560. Tel: 337-369-6384; Fax: 337-369-6384. Paul H. DeClouet, Dir. Total Staff 30; Total Families Assisted 7,500.

OPELOUSAS. *New Life Center*, 411 E. Landry St., P.O. Box 1761, 70571. Tel: 337-948-3161; Fax: 337-948-0011. Sr. Anne Byrne, Dir. Emergency Shelter Transitional Housing and Child Care Center for women & children operated under the direction of the Lafayette Catholic Services Centers, Inc.

VILLE PLATTE. *Christian Care and Share Center*, 129 W. Main St., P.O. Box 901, 70586. Tel: 337-363-8041. Mr. Eugene S. Fontenot, Chm. Total Staff 12.

RELIGIOUS INSTITUTES OF MEN REPRESENTED IN THE DIOCESE

For further details refer to the corresponding bracketed number in the Religious Institutes of Men or Women section.

[0200]—*Benedictines (Olivetan, Subiaco Congregation)*—O.S.B.
[0330]—*Brothers of the Christian Schools* (New Orleans Prov.)—F.S.C.
[]—*Carmelites of Mary Immaculate*—C.M.I.
[]—*Congregation of St. Theresa of the Child Jesus*—C.S.T.
[0520]—*Franciscan Friars*—O.F.M.
[0690]—*Jesuit Fathers and Brothers* (New Orleans Prov.)—S.J.
[]—*Missionaries of St. Paul* (Nigeria)—M.S.P.
[0610]—*Priests of the Congregation of Holy Cross*—C.S.C.
[0420]—*Society of the Divine Word*—S.V.D.
[0700]—*St. Joseph's Society of the Sacred Heart* (Baltimore Prov.)—S.S.J.

RELIGIOUS INSTITUTES OF WOMEN REPRESENTED IN THE DIOCESE

[0400]—*Congregation of Our Lady of Mount Carmel*—O.Carm.
[2410]—*Congregation of the Marianites of Holy Cross*—M.S.C.
[1950]—*Congregation of the Sisters of the Holy Family*—S.S.F.
[0750]—*Daughters of Charity of the Sacred Heart of Jesus*—F.C.S.C.J.
[0420]—*Discalced Carmelite Nuns*—O.C.D.
[1140]—*Eucharistic Missionaries of St. Dominic*—O.P.
[1380]—*Franciscan Missionaries of Our Lady*—O.S.F.
[2710]—*Missionaries of Charity* (Bronx, NY)—M.C.
[4070]—*Religious of the Sacred Heart*—R.S.C.J.
[2970]—*School Sisters of Notre Dame* (South Central)—S.S.N.D.
[0990]—*Sisters of Divine Providence* (San Antonio, TX)—C.D.P.
[3360]—*Sisters of Providence of Saint Mary-of-the-Woods, Indiana* (Prov. of St. Joseph)—S.P.
[3880]—*Sisters of St. Joseph of Medaille*—C.S.J.
[0260]—*Sisters of the Blessed Sacrament for Indians and Colored People*—S.B.S.
[2050]—*Sisters of the Holy Spirit and Mary Immaculate*—S.H.Sp.
[2120]—*Sisters of the Immaculate Conception*—C.R.
[2940]—*Sisters of the Most Holy Sacrament*—M.H.S.

NECROLOGY

† Bourg, Edwin, (Retired)—Died June 9, 2003
† Mau, Joseph, (Retired)—Died July 21, 2003

Diocese of Lafayette in Indiana

(Dioecesis Lafayettensis in Indiana)

Most Reverend

WILLIAM L. HIGI, D.D.

Bishop of Lafayette in Indiana; ordained May 30, 1959; appointed Bishop of Lafayette in Indiana April 7, 1984; consecrated and installed June 6, 1984 *Res.. 610 Lingle Ave., P.O. Box 260, Lafayette, IN 47902-0260.*

Office of Bishop and Chancery: P.O. Box 260, Lafayette, IN 47902-0260. Tel: 765-742-0275; Fax: 765-742-7513.

Web: www.dioceseoflafayette.org

CANONICALLY ERECTED OCTOBER 21, 1944.

Square Miles 9,832.

Comprises the Counties of Benton, Blackford, Boone, Carroll, Cass, Clinton, Delaware, Fountain, Fulton, Grant, Hamilton, Howard, Jasper, Jay, Madison, Miami, Montgomery, Newton, Pulaski, Randolph, Tippecanoe, Tipton, Warren and White in the State of Indiana.

Legal Title: For legal titles of parishes and diocesan institutions, consult the Bishop's Office (Chancery).

STATISTICAL OVERVIEW

Personnel	
Bishop	1
Priests: Diocesan Active in Diocese	74
Priests: Diocesan Active Outside Diocese	22
Priests: Retired, Sick or Absent	16
Number of Diocesan Priests	112
Religious Priests in Diocese	20
Total Priests in Diocese	132
Extern Priests in Diocese	1
Permanent Deacons in Diocese	5
Total Brothers	1
Total Sisters	79
Parishes	
Parishes	62
With Resident Pastor:	
Resident Diocesan Priests	51
Resident Religious Priests	4
Without Resident Pastor:	
Administered by Priests	7
Professional Ministry Personnel:	
Brothers	1
Sisters	7
Lay Ministers	296
Welfare	
Catholic Hospitals	6
Total Assisted	892,569
Homes for the Aged	2
Total Assisted	295
Educational	
Diocesan Students in Other Seminaries	11
Total Seminarians	11
Colleges and Universities	3
Total Students	5,969
High Schools, Diocesan and Parish	1
Total Students	360
Elementary Schools, Diocesan and Parish	23
Total Students	4,579
Catechesis/Religious Education:	
High School Students	3,306
Elementary Students	9,684
Total Students under Catholic Instruction	23,909
Teachers in the Diocese:	
Sisters	6
Lay Teachers	291
Vital Statistics	
Receptions into the Church:	
Infant Baptism Totals	2,155
Adult Baptism Totals	283
Received into Full Communion	350
First Communions	2,075
Confirmations	1,501
Marriages:	
Catholic	274
Interfaith	264
Total Marriages	538
Deaths	841
Total Catholic Population	98,003
Total Population	1,176,736

Former Bishops—Most Rev. JOHN GEORGE BENNETT, D.D., LL.D., ord. June 27, 1914; appt. First Bishop of Lafayette Nov. 11, 1944; consecrated Jan. 10, 1945; died Nov. 20, 1957; His Eminence JOHN CARDINAL CARBERRY, D.D. (Retired), ord. July 28, 1929; appt. Coadjutor with Right of Succession Aug. 22, 1956; appt. Bishop of Lafayette in Indiana Nov. 20, 1957; transferred to Diocese of Columbus, Jan. 20, 1965; transferred to the Archdiocese of St. Louis March 24, 1968; created Cardinal April 28, 1969; retired July 31, 1979; died June 17, 1998; Most Revs. RAYMOND J. GALLAGHER, D.D. (Retired), ord. March 25, 1939; appt. Bishop of Lafayette in Indiana June 23, 1965; consecrated Aug. 11, 1965; installed Aug. 23, 1965; resigned Oct. 26, 1982; retired April 13, 1983; died March 7, 1991; GEORGE A. FULCHER, S.T.D., D.D., ord. Feb. 28, 1948; appt. Auxiliary Bishop of Columbus, OH and Titular Bishop of Morosbido May 24, 1976; consecrated July 18, 1976; appt. Bishop of Lafayette in Indiana Feb. 8, 1983; installed April 14, 1983; died Jan. 25, 1984.

Vicar General—Rev. Msgr. ROBERT L. SELL III, J.C.L., V.G.

Chancellor and Moderator of the Curia—Rev. Msgr. ROBERT L. SELL III, J.C.L., V.G.

Office of Bishop and Chancery—P.O. Box 260, Lafayette, 47902-0260. Tel: 765-742-0275; Fax: 765-742-7513.

Deans—Revs. DANIEL B. GARTLAND, V.F., Lafayette Deanery; ROBERT L. WILLIAMS, V.F., Anderson Deanery; THOMAS E. FOX, V.F., Fowler Deanery; ANTHONY I. LEVI, Carmel Deanery; FRANCIS I. KILCLINE III, V.F., Logansport Deanery; ROBERT E. MORAN, Muncie Deanery.

Diocesan Consultors—Rev. Msgr. ROBERT L. SELL III, J.C.L., V.G.; Revs. DANIEL B. GARTLAND, V.F.; THOMAS H. METZGER, V.F.; THEODORE D. ROTHROCK; PAUL W. COCHRAN; ROBERT L. WILLIAMS, V.F.

Diocesan Pastoral Office for Administration—Mr. ROBERT H. QUINN, Finance Officer; EILEEN HATKE, Financial Svcs. Mgr.; MARILYN DENNE, Accounts Coord.; KATHY ASKINS, Admin. Asst.; WAYNE STEPHENS, Maintenance; ERIC ATKINS, A.I.A., Facilities Mgmt. Dir., P.O. Box 260, Lafayette, 47902-0260. Tel: 765-742-4852 Conducts the financial affairs of the diocese; oversees employee benefit program.

Diocesan Pastoral Office for Planning and Communication—THOMAS A. RUSSELL, Dir., 610 Lingle Ave., P.O. Box 1603, Lafayette, 47902-1603. Tel: 765-742-2050.

Publisher- "The Catholic Moment"—LAURIE CULLEN, Asst. Editor; SEAN SALAI, Contributing Editor; KIM KIRSCHENHEITER, Reporter; CAROLYN MCKINNEY, Advertising/Circulation, Coordinates pastoral planning; serves the communications needs of the diocese primarily through "The Catholic Moment"; maintains the diocesan web page on the world wide web.

Diocesan Pastoral Office for Social Ministry—DAVID R. WILSON, Dir.; CAROLYN BLANKENBERGER, Sec., 836 S. Purdum, Kokomo, 46901-5546. Tel: 765-457-1172 Assists parishes in developing parish social ministry; coordinates the work of the Campaign for Human Development and the Indiana Catholic Conference; liaison with St. Elizabeth Home (Indianapolis) relative to adoption services, Pro-Life Service Centers, St. Vincent dePaul and Ladies of Charity, and coordinates the Premarital Evaluation program.

Diocesan Pastoral Office for Formation—Rev. Msgr. ROBERT L. SELL III, J.C.L., V.G., Catholic Pastoral Center, 2300 S. Ninth St., Lafayette, 47909-2400. Tel: 765-474-6644; Fax: 765-474-3403.

Family Life and Evangelization—JOSEPH DANO.

Youth & Parish Religious Education Programs—LINDA PIZZA.

Worship & Liturgy—JULIE MALES.

Resource Center—LISA ROBINSON.

Administrative Assistants—CHARLENE KUHN; HEATHER KELLY, Coordinates marriage preparation conferences and programs, Natural Family Planning, Separated-Divorced Catholic programs, Sacramental preparation with families, implementation of Family Perspective and Family Catechesis. Additional responsibilities include all programs (Religious Education, Youth Ministry, Pre-schools, Sacramental Preparation, Scouts, Athletics, etc.) for young people in the local church. That responsibility extends to the formation of those who minister to young people as catechists, coaches, youth leaders and administrators.

Pastoral Office for Stewardship and Development—PAMELA STORMS-BARRETT, Dir.; JOSEPH BONNER, Planned Giving; KATHY WALDREP, Admin. Asst., Promotes and encourages Christian stewardship as a way of life by cultivating parish and individual stewardship as a first priority. The office oversees the planning, preparation of materials, training of volunteers, promotion and direction of the biennial Fruitful Harvest fund drive. The office also helps organize and present wills seminars and estate planning programs. Other responsibilities include the marketing and direction of the Catholic Foundation of Northcentral Indiana, Inc., and helping to fund the future needs of the diocese, its parishes and institutions. Provides assistance to parishes or other pastoral offices in writing proposals for grants and consultation with parishes wishing to conduct capital campaigns.

Pastoral Office for Catholic Schools—Sr. LOIS ANN MEYER, S.N.D.deNur, Supt.; PAM PEROUTKY, Asst. Supt.; LOUISE SMITH, Admin. Asst.

Diocesan Tribunal—Catholic Pastoral Center, 2300 S. Ninth St., Lafayette, 47909-2400. Tel: 765-474-0506.

Officialis—Rev. DAVID L. RASNER, J.C.L.

Vice Officialis—Rev. DAVID J. BUCKLES, J.C.L.

First Instance—

Presiding Judge—Rev. DAVID L. RASNER, J.C.L.

Associate Judge—Rev. PETER VANDERKOLK.

Defenders of the Bond—Revs. RICHARD E. MILLER, J.C.L.; DONALD L. GROSS; WILLIAM R. VATH, Appelate Court.

Ecclesiastical Notary—VERNA S. MEEK.

Full-Time Advocates—BRIDGET O'BRIEN; LOU CUFFING.
Periti—Dr. MICHAEL MILLARD, Ph.D.
Second Instance—
Presiding Judge—Rev. DAVID J. BUCKLES, J.C.L.
Associate Judges—Rev. Msgrs. JOHN C. DUNCAN; FRED E. POTTHOFF (Retired); Rev. MELVIN BENNETT; Very Rev. GERALD J. BORAWSKI; Revs. JAMES R. GOODRUM; FRED H. GSCHWIND; DONALD B. VERNON; EDWARD F. DHONDT; THOMAS J. ZIMMER (Retired); JOHN J. CUMMINGS.
Defender of the Bond—Rev. WILLIAM R. VATH.
Ecclesiastical Notary—VERNA S. MEEK.
Advocates— Refer to Court of First Instance.
Lay Advocates— Refer to Court of First Instance.
Periti— Refer to Court of First Instance.
Administrative Causes—Rev. Msgr. ROBERT L. SELL III, J.C.L., V.G.

Diocesan Offices and Directors

Archivist—VACANT.

Building Commission—KEN MCGINITY, Chm.; Rev. THEODORE ROTHROCK; Rev. Msgr. ROBERT SELL, V.G.; ROBERT GLOYESKE; Dr. DOUGLAS SUTTON; WILL WRIGHT; NORBERT STRANSKY; DANIEL MADER; DENNIS G. PAGE.

Finance Officer—Mr. ROBERT H. QUINN, P.O. Box 260, Lafayette, 47902-0260. Tel: 765-742-4852.

Administration— Refer to Diocesan Pastoral Office.

Corporation— Roman Catholic Diocese of Lafayette in Indiana, Inc.(Incorporated, March 21, 1958) Most Rev. WILLIAM L. HIGI, D.D., Pres. & Treas.; Rev. Msgr. ROBERT L. SELL III, J.C.L., V.G., Vice Pres. & Sec.; Mr. ROBERT H. QUINN, Asst. Sec. & Treas.

Director of Development—PAMELIA STORMS-BARRETT, Bishop's Office, P.O. Box 1687, Lafayette, 47902-1687. Tel: 765-742-7000; Fax: 765-742-7513.

Director of Planned Giving—JOSEPH A. BONNER, Bishop's Office, P.O. Box 1687, Lafayette, 47902-1687. Tel: 765-742-7000; Fax: 765-742-7513.

Fruitful Harvest Office—P.O. Box 1687, Lafayette, 47902. Tel: 765-742-4852.

Finance Council—Most Rev. WILLIAM L. HIGI, D.D.; Rev. Msgr. ROBERT L. SELL III, J.C.L., V.G.; Mr. ROBERT H. QUINN, Dir. Pastoral Office for Admin.; LEON CYR; LEO DIERCKMAN; LYNN LADEN; MARIANNE MCLEAN; LEE SNIDER; DON GOETZ; EDWARD LOPKE; JOHN F. BODLE, Legal Advisor.

Human Resources Department—HELEN BENDER, Dir., P.O. Box 260, Lafayette, 47902-0260. Tel: 765-742-4852.

Legal Council—JOHN C. DUFFEY, Life Building, P.O. Box 1010, Lafayette, 47902. Tel: 765-423-1561; Fax: 765-742-8175.

Presbyteral Council—Revs. DANIEL B. GARTLAND, V.F., Chm.; ROBERT L. WILLIAMS, V.F., Vice Chm.
Members—Rev. Msgr. ROBERT L. SELL III, J.C.L., V.G.; Revs. MARTIN J. SANDHAGE; FRANCIS I. KILCLINE III, V.F.; DANIEL B. GARTLAND, V.F.; JOSEPH E. JACOB; ANTHONY I. LEVI; ROBERT L. WILLIAMS, V.F.; THOMAS E. FOX, V.F.; MELVIN J. BENNETT; PAUL WICKLUM; PAUL W. COCHRAN; THEODORE ROTHROCK.

Catholic Relief Services—VACANT.

Censor Librorum—Rev. DAVID L. RASNER, J.C.L., Catholic Pastoral Center, 2300 S. Ninth St., Lafayette, 47909-2400. Tel: 765-474-0506.

Aquinas Educational Foundation, Inc.—Rev. DANIEL C. DAVIS, O.P., Res. Agent, 535 State St., West Lafayette, 47906. Tel: 765-743-4653.

Clergy Relief Association— Board of Directors: Revs. PHILIP T. BOWERS, Pres.; PAUL WICKLUM, Vice Pres.; EDWARD T. KACENA, Sec.; THOMAS FOX, Treas.; ROBERT J. BERNOTAS, Asst. Treas.
Members—Revs. CHARLES KLINE; MICHAEL MCKINLEY; RICHARD MILLER, J.C.L.

Catholic Charities Central Office— Refer to Diocesan Pastoral Office.
Social Ministry—DAVID R. WILSON, Diocesan Dir., Diocesan Catholic Offices, 836 S. Purdum, Kokomo, 46901. Tel: 765-457-1172.

Superintendent for Catholic Schools—Sr. LOIS ANN MEYER, S.N.D.deNur, The Catholic Pastoral Center, 2300 S. Ninth St., Lafayette, 47909-2400. Tel: 765-474-6644.

Society of St. Vincent de Paul—DAVID R. WILSON, Diocesan Dir., Diocesan Catholic Offices, 836 S. Purdum St., Kokomo, 46901. Tel: 765-457-1172.
Association of Ladies of Charity—DAVID R. WILSON, Dir., Diocesan Catholic Offices, 836 Purdum St., Kokomo, 46901. Tel: 765-457-1172.

Liturgical Commission— Refer to Diocesan Pastoral Office.

Eucharistic League—The Chancery, P.O. Box 260, Lafayette, 47902.

Greater Lafayette Catholic School Board—Rev. DANIEL GARTLAND. Tel: 765-742-2107.

Greater Lafayette Catholic School Foundation, Inc.—JOSEPH BONNER, 2410 S. Ninth St., Lafayette, 47905.

Holy Childhood Association—VACANT.

Diocesan Board of Education— In process of reorganization & formation.

D.C.C.W.—VACANT.

Ministry to Priests' Program—Rev. DONALD L. GROSS, Dir., Sacred Heart Church, 107 E. Main St., Fowler, 47944-1148. Tel: 765-884-1818.

Newman Apostolate, Purdue University—Rev. DANIEL C. DAVIS, O.P., Dir., 535 State St., West Lafayette, 47906. Tel: 765-743-4652.

Newman Foundation, Ball State, Inc.—Rev. JOHN J. KEIFER, Dir., 800 Riverside Ave., Muncie, 47303. Tel: 765-288-6180.

Newspaper "The Catholic Moment"—THOMAS RUSSELL, Editor; LAURIE CULLEN, Asst. Editor; SEAN SALAI, Contributing Editor; KIM KIRSCHENHEITER, Reporter; CAROLYN MCKINNEY, Advertising, Editorial Office, P.O. Box 1603, Lafayette, 47902. Tel: 765-742-2050.

Office of the Apostolate to the Spanish Speaking—Deacon DOMINGO CASTILLO, Assoc. Dir., 917 Branson St., Marion, 46952. Tel: 317-662-3288.
Guadalupe Center: . Tel: 765-664-3710.

Propagation of the Faith—DAVID WILSON, Refer to Pastoral Office for Social Ministry.

Religious Education Dept.— Refer to Pastoral Office for Formation.

Rural Life Program—Rev. FRED H. GSCHWIND, Dir., 340 N. Mill St., Tipton, 46072. Tel: 765-675-2422.

Schools— See Superintendent listing.

St. Joseph Memorial Hospital Foundation, Inc.—PEGGY CALDWELL, Exec. Dir., 1907 W. Sycamore St., Kokomo, 46901. Tel: 765-456-5425.

Vicar for Clergy—VACANT.

Vicar for Hispanic Ministry in White County—Rev. CHRISTOPHER T. MILLER, 516 S. Bluff St., Monticello, 47960.

Vicar for Religious—VACANT.

Victim Assistance Coordinator—DAVID WILSON, M.S.W. Tel: 800-533-7018. Email: drwilson@iquest.net.

Vocation Director—Rev. BRIAN DOERR, Dir., St. Joan of Arc, 900 S. Puroum St., Kokomo, 46901-5598. Tel: 765-457-9371.

CLERGY, PARISHES, MISSIONS AND PAROCHIAL SCHOOLS

CITY OF LAFAYETTE
(TIPPECANOE COUNTY)

1—ST. MARY CATHEDRAL (1843), [JC] Rev. Robert Klemme.
Res.: 1207 Columbia St., 47901-1522. Tel: 765-742-4440; Fax: 765-742-8933.
School—(Grades PreK-3) Tel: 765-742-6302. Lay Teachers 8; Students 169.
Catechesis/Religious Program—Tel: 765-742-8336. Students 130.

2—ST. ANN (1884), [JC] Rev. Michael J. McKinley. In Res., Rev. Maurice R. Miller.
Res.: 612 Wabash Ave., 47905-1096. Tel: 765-742-7031; Fax: 765-429-5690.
Catechesis/Religious Program—Tel: 765-423-4635. Students 122.

3—ST. BONIFACE (1853), (German), [CEM] Rev. Timothy M. Alkire; Deacon Ron Nevinger. In Res., Revs. William R. Vath; Richard E. Miller, J.C.L.
Res.: 318 N. Ninth St., 47904-2597. Tel: 765-742-5063; Fax: 765-742-5018.
School—Lafayette Catholic School, (Grades 4-6) Tel: 765-742-7913; Fax: 765-423-4988. Sr. M. Lenore Schwartz, O.S.F., Prin. Sisters 3; Lay Teachers 4; Students 137.
Catechesis/Religious Program—Tel: 765-742-1351. Students 452.

4—ST. LAWRENCE (1895), Revs. Daniel B. Gartland, V.F.; Jack Trippel.
Res.: 1916 Meharry St., 47904-1442. Tel: 765-742-2107; Fax: 765-742-1347.
School—1902 Meharry St., 47904-1497. Tel: 765-742-4450. Jody Williams, Prin. Lay Teachers 12; Students 265.
Catechesis/Religious Program—Tel: 765-423-2396. Carl Wagner, D.R.E. Students 289.

OUTSIDE THE CITY OF LAFAYETTE

ALEXANDRIA, MADISON CO., ST. MARY (1896), Rev. Paul W. Cochran.
Res.: 820 W. Madison St., 46001-1520. Tel: 765-724-2483; 765-724-4459; Fax: 765-724-9711.
School—Tel: 765-724-4459. Sisters 2; Lay Teachers 7; Students 94.
Catechesis/Religious Program—Students 80.

ANDERSON, MADISON CO.
1—ST. AMBROSE (1947), Rev. Edward F. Dhondt.
Res.: 2801 Lincoln St., 46016-5067. Tel: 765-644-5956; Fax: 765-642-9439.
School—Tel: 765-642-8428; Fax: 765-642-7348. Lay Teachers 15; Students 171.
Catechesis/Religious Program—Students 155.
2—ST. MARY (1858), [CEM] Rev. Robert L. Williams, V.F.; Elaine Bowers, Pastoral Assoc.
Res.: 1115 Pearl St., 46016-1789. Tel: 765-644-8467; Fax: 765-648-4000.
School—Tel: 765-642-1848; Fax: 765-642-1828. Sr. Barbara Hudock, A.S.C., Prin. Lay Teachers 20; Students 202.
Station—St. John Medical Center Chapel , KY. Tel: 765-649-2511.
Catechesis/Religious Program—Tel: 765-642-5339. Students 61.

ATTICA, FOUNTAIN CO., ST. FRANCIS XAVIER (1890), [CEM] Rev. Charles Kline.
Res.: 407 S. Perry St., P.O. Box 55, 47918-0001. Tel: 765-762-3330; Fax: 765-762-1810.
Catechesis/Religious Program—Students 90.

BRYANT, JAY CO., HOLY TRINITY (1860), (German), [CEM] Rev. Robert C. Reinhart, C.PP.S.
Res.: 7321 E. SR 67, 47326-9637. Tel: 219-997-6450.
Catechesis/Religious Program—Tel: 219-997-6450. Students 179.

CARMEL, HAMILTON CO.
1—ST. ELIZABETH ANN SETON (1981), Revs. Theodore D. Rothrock; Fred A. Schroeder; Brian A. Dudzinski.
Res.: 10655 Haverstick Rd., 46033-3800. Tel: 317-846-3850; Fax: 317-846-3710.
Catechesis/Religious Program—Tel: 317-846-3850. Students 799.
2—OUR LADY OF MOUNT CARMEL (1955), Rev. Msgr. John C. Duncan; Revs. Dominic Young; Richard J. Doerr; Deacon William Rahill.
Office—14598 Oak Ridge Rd., 46032-1198. Tel: 317-846-3475; Fax: 317-846-3477.
School—Tel: 317-846-1118; Fax: 317-582-2375. Sisters of Notre Dame 2; Lay Teachers 41; Students 677.
Catechesis/Religious Program—Tel: 317-846-3878. Students 1,281.

CICERO, HAMILTON CO., SACRED HEART (1898), (German—Irish), Rev. W. Michael Kettron.
Res.: 429 S. Main St., 46034-9680. Tel: 317-984-5117; Fax: 317-984-5117.
Catechesis/Religious Program—Tel: 317-984-2115. Students 76.

COVINGTON, FOUNTAIN CO., ST. JOSEPH (1861), [CEM] Rev. Charles Kline.
Res.: 308 Pearl St., 47932-1062. Tel: 765-793-3289.
Catechesis/Religious Program—Tel: 765-793-4628. Students 17.

CRAWFORDSVILLE, MONTGOMERY CO., ST. BERNARD (1859), [CEM] Rev. Melvin J. Bennett; Tim Grino, Pastoral Assoc.
Res.: 1306 E. Main St., 47933-0719. Tel: 765-362-6121; Fax: 765-361-0796.
Catechesis/Religious Program—Tel: 765-362-5472; Fax: 765-361-0967. Students 206.

DE MOTTE, JASPER CO., ST. CECILIA (1952), [CEM] Rev. Paul R. Wicklum.
Res.: 334 Fifteenth St., S.W., 46310-9269. Tel: 219-987-3511; Fax: 219-987-7755.
Catechesis/Religious Program—Tel: 219-987-3514. Students 138.

DELPHI, CARROLL CO., ST. JOSEPH (1859), [CEM] Rev. Peter J. Vanderkolk.
Res.: 207 N. Washington St., 46923-1297. Tel: 765-564-2407.
Catechesis/Religious Program—Tel: 765-564-3439. Students 192.

DUNKIRK, JAY CO., ST. MARY (1896), David R. Wilson, Parish Coord.
Res.: 346 S. Broad St., 47336-1310. Tel: 765-768-6157.
Catechesis/Religious Program—Students 31.

DUNNINGTON, BENTON CO., ST. MARY (1876), [CEM] Rev. Donald Gross.
Mailing Address: 2961 South SR71, Ambia, 47917. Tel: 765-884-1818.
Catechesis/Religious Program—Students 34.

EARL PARK, BENTON CO., ST. JOHN THE BAPTIST (1888), [CEM] Merged, Mailing Address: c/o Rev. Robert J. Bernotas, P.O. Box 131, Kentland, 47951-1322. with St. Joseph, Kentland.
Church: 205 S. Chestnut St., 47942-8692.
Catechesis/Religious Program—Students 32.

ELWOOD, MADISON CO., ST. JOSEPH (1889), (Irish—German), [CEM] [JC] Rev. Kenneth T. Raczek.
Res.: 1306 S. A St., 46036-1941. Tel: 765-552-6753.
Catechesis/Religious Program—Tel: 765-552-6753.

Mary Pat Miller, D.R.E. Students 168.
FISHERS, HAMILTON CO.
1—HOLY SPIRIT CHURCH (1991), Revs. Phillip T. Bowers; Patrick R. Click.
Mailing Address: 10350 Glaser Way, 46038. Tel: 317-849-9245; Fax: 317-849-9388.
Res.: 10868 Geist Woods Ln., Indianapolis, 46256. Tel: 317-845-0992.
Catechesis/Religious Program—Tel: 317-849-8016. Students 1,637.
2—ST. LOUIS DE MONTFORT (1978), Revs. Timothy D. Kroeger; David E. Hellman.
Res.: 11441 Hague Rd., 46038-1876. Tel: 317-842-6778; Fax: 317-576-1932.
School—11421 Hague Rd., 46038. Tel: 317-842-1125; Fax: 317-842-1126. Mary Banta, Prin. Lay Teachers 25; Students 328.
Catechesis/Religious Program—Students 921.
FOWLER, BENTON CO., SACRED HEART OF JESUS (1872), [CEM] Rev. Donald L. Gross.
Res.: 107 E. Main St., 47944-1148. Tel: 765-884-1818; Fax: 765-884-1583.
School—Tel: 765-884-0710; Fax: 765-884-0710. Mrs. Terri Goodman, Prin. Lay Teachers 8; Students 114.
Catechesis/Religious Program—Students 98.
FRANCESVILLE, PULASKI CO., ST. FRANCIS SOLANO (1867), Rev. Paul R. White, C.PP.S., Admin. (Retired).
St. Joseph's College: P.O. Box 852, Rensselaer, 47978. Tel: 219-866-6271.
Catechesis/Religious Program—Students 16.
FRANKFORT, CLINTON CO., ST. MARY (1875), [CEM] Very Rev. Gerald J. Borawski.
Res.: 600 St. Mary's Ave., 46041-0181. Tel: 765-654-5796; Fax: 765-654-6589.
School—Preschool, Tel: 765-659-3914.
Catechesis/Religious Program—Tel: 765-654-2913. Students 241.
GAS CITY, GRANT CO., HOLY FAMILY (1906), Rev. David J. Newton.
Res.: 325 E. North A St., 46933-1431. Tel: 765-674-2605; Fax: 765-674-3875.
Catechesis/Religious Program—Students 120.
GOODLAND, NEWTON, SS. PETER AND PAUL (1880), [CEM] Merged, with St. Joseph, Kentland.
Mailing Address: c/o Rev. Robert J. Bernotas, P.O. Box 131, Kentland, 47951-1322.
Church: 421 S. Newton St., 47948-8156.
HARTFORD CITY, BLACKFORD CO., ST. JOHN THE EVANGELIST (1865), Rev. Robert E. Moran.
Res.: 209 S. Spring St., 47348-2551. Tel: 765-348-3123.
School—Tel: 765-348-3889; Fax: 765-348-4399. Lay Teachers 5; Students 62.
Catechesis/Religious Program—Students 39.
KENTLAND, NEWTON, ST. JOSEPH (1864), [CEM] Rev. Robert J. Bernotas.
Res.: 409 E. Allen St., P.O. Box 131, 47951-1322. Tel: 219-474-5514.
St. Joseph School Foundation, Inc.—Tel: 219-474-5514.
Catechesis/Religious Program—Students 135.
KEWANNA, FULTON CO., ST. ANN (1857), [CEM] Rev. Joseph E. Jacob, Admin.
Mailing Address: 1310 Main St., Rochester, 46975.
Res.: 46939-0181. Tel: 574-653-2520.
Catechesis/Religious Program—Tel: 574-223-2808; Fax: 574-224-2808. Students 14.
KOKOMO, HOWARD CO.
1—ST. JOAN OF ARC (1927), Rev. Dennis J. O'Keeffe.
Res.: 900 S. Purdum, 46901-5598. Tel: 765-457-9371; Fax: 765-454-7241.
School—Sts. Joan of Arc & Patrick, 3155 S. - 200 W., 46902. Tel: 765-865-9960 (St. Joan); 765-459-4769 (St. Patrick); Fax: 765-865-9962. (Consolidated School) Lay Teachers 23; Students 352.
Catechesis/Religious Program—923 S. Jay St., 46901. Tel: 765-457-1375; Fax: 765-454-7241. Students 308.
2—ST. PATRICK (1859), [JC] Rev. Theodore Dudzinski; Deacon Truman Stevens, Opers. Mgr.
1230 N. Armstrong St., 46901.
Office & Mailing Address: 320 W. Broadway, 46901-2898. Tel: 765-452-6021; Fax: 765-868-8384.
Res.: 1229 N. Washington, 46901-2898.
School—(Grades PreK-8) Tel: 765-459-4769; Fax: 765-457-3096. Lay Teachers 22; Students 347.
School—SS. Joan of Arc & Patrick, 3155 S. 200 W., 46902. Tel: 765-865-9960; Fax: 765-865-9962. (South Campus)
Catechesis/Religious Program—Students 183.
LAKE VILLAGE, NEWTON, ST. AUGUSTA (1947), [JC] Rev. John J. Cummings.
Res.: 3228 W. St. Rd. 10, 46349-9706. Tel: 219-992-3220; Fax: 219-992-9332.
Catechesis/Religious Program—Students 73.
LEBANON, BOONE CO., ST. JOSEPH (1862), [CEM] Rev. Anthony W. Levi.
Mailing Address: P.O. Box 309, 46052-0309. Tel: 765-482-5558; Fax: 765-482-1436.
Res.: 319 E. South St., 46052-2684. Tel: 765-482-5558.
Catechesis/Religious Program—Marietta "Mimi" Duray, D.R.E. Students 175.
LOGANSPORT, CASS CO., ALL SAINTS (1985), [JC], Consolidation of the following three parishes (Legal Titles): St. Bridget (1875); St. Joseph (1868); and St. Vincent de Paul (1838). Revs. Philip Haslinger; Michael McKinney; Deacon Juan Rodriguez.
Parish Office—112 E. Market St., 46947-3428. Tel: 574-722-4080; Fax: 574-722-5426.
Res.: 114 E. Market St., 46947. Tel: 574-753-3020.
School—All Saints Elementary, 107 Eel River Ave., 46947-3188. Tel: 574-753-3410.
Catechesis/Religious Program—Tel: 574-722-4080; Fax: 574-722-5426. Lori Eubank, D.R.E. Students 225.
LUCERNE, CASS CO., ST. ELIZABETH (1953) Closed., For inquiries for parish records, please see All Saints Church, Logansport
MARION, GRANT CO.
1—OUR LADY OF GUADALUPE, (Hispanic), Closed., For inquiries for parish records contact St. Paul, Marion.
2—ST. PAUL (1868), Rev. Richard J. Weisenberger.
Res.: 1009 W. Kem Rd., 46952-2048. Tel: 765-664-6345; Fax: 765-664-5953.
School—1009 Kem Rd., 46952. Tel: 765-662-2883. Mrs. Jackie Certain, Prin. Lay Teachers 10; Students 118.
Catechesis/Religious Program—Students 106.
MEDARYVILLE, PULASKI CO., ST. HENRY (1868), [CEM] Rev. Paul R. White, C.PP.S., Admin. (Retired).
St. Joseph's College: P.O. Box 852, Rensselaer, 47978. Tel: 219-866-6271.
Catechesis/Religious Program—Students 9.
MONTEREY, PULASKI CO., ST. ANNE (1851), (German), [CEM 2] Rev. Herbert Woolson.
Res.: Church St., P.O. Box 96, 46960-0096. Tel: 574-946-3453; Fax: 574-946-3453.
Catechesis/Religious Program—Tel: 219-542-4711; Fax: 219-542-4711. Students 36.
MONTICELLO, WHITE CO., OUR LADY OF THE LAKES (1948), Rev. James R. Goodrum.
Res.: 543 S. Main St., 47960-2948. Tel: 574-583-5724; Fax: 219-583-4112.
Catechesis/Religious Program—Tel: 574-583-6790. Students 165.
MONTPELIER, BLACKFORD CO., ST. MARGARET OF SCOTLAND (1864), [CEM] Rev. Robert E. Moran, Admin.
Res.: 207 W. Huntington St., P.O. Box 247 47359. Tel: 765-728-5757.
Catechesis/Religious Program—Students 2.
MUNCIE, DELAWARE CO.
1—ST. FRANCIS OF ASSISI (1972),, (Ball State University Parish) Rev. John D. Kiefer.
Res.: 1200 W. Riverside Ave., 47303-3650. Tel: 765-288-6180; Fax: 765-288-7777.
Catechesis/Religious Program—Students 210.
2—ST. LAWRENCE (1869), Rev. Dennis J. Goth.
Res.: 820 E. Charles St., 47305-2699. Tel: 765-288-9223; Fax: 765-289-9262.
School—2801 E. 16th St., 47302. Tel: 765-282-9353; Fax: 765-282-0457. Lay Teachers 12; Students 140.
Catechesis/Religious Program—Tel: 765-28[illegible]-2673. Students 65.
3—ST. MARY (1930), Rev. T. Edward Kacena, Admin. In Res., Revs. James T. Keane; Anthony J. Prosen.
Res.: 2300 W. Jackson St., 47303-4797. Tel: 765-288-5308.
School—2301 W. Gilbert St., 47303-4797. Tel: 765-288-5878; Fax: 765-284-3685. Lay Teachers 20; Students 223.
Catechesis/Religious Program—Students 160.
NOBLESVILLE, HAMILTON CO., OUR LADY OF GRACE (1944), Revs. Thomas H. Metzer; James R. Bates (Retired); John Zahn; Gordon P. Wagoner (IND).
Res.: 9900 E. 191st St., 46060-1998. Tel: 317-773-4275; Fax: 317-773-9344.
School—Tel: 317-770-5660; Fax: 317-770-5663. John Kohan, Prin. Lay Teachers 19; Students 250.
Catechesis/Religious Program—Tel: 317-773-0297; Fax: 317-770-5059. Students 426.
OTTERBEIN, BENTON CO., ST. CHARLES (1902), [JC] Rev. David L. Rasner, J.C.L.
Res.: 108 N. Meadow St., Box 661, 47970-0661. Tel: 765-583-4641.
Catechesis/Religious Program—Students 100.
OXFORD, BENTON CO., ST. PATRICK (1867), Irish), [CEM] [JC] Rev. Donald Eder.
Res.: 502 S. Michigan St., 47971-8562. Tel: 765-385-2587; Fax: 765-385-0225.
Catechesis/Religious Program—Students 74.
PERU, MIAMI CO., ST. CHARLES BORROMEO (1860), [CEM] Rev. Francis I. Kilcline III, V.F.
Res.: 58 W. Fifth St., 46970-2100. Tel: 765-473-5543; Fax: 765-472-2632.
School—(Grades PreK-6) Tel: 765-473-5662; Fax: 765-473-6046. Lay Teachers 10; Students 109.
Catechesis/Religious Program—80 W. Fifth St., 46970. Tel: 765-473-5544; Fax: 765-472-2692. Students 92.
PORTLAND, JAY CO., IMMACULATE CONCEPTION (1876), (German), [JC] Rev. Martin J. Sandhage.
Res.: 506 E. Walnut St., 47371-1599. Tel: 260-726-7341.
Catechesis/Religious Program—Tel: 260-726-7055. Students 236.
REMINGTON, JASPER CO., SACRED HEART (1875), [CEM] Rev. Thomas E. Fox, V.F.
Res.: 124 New York St., P.O. Box 159, 47977-0159. Tel: 219-261-2302.
Catechesis/Religious Program—Tel: 317-279-2656. Students 74.
RENSSELAER, JASPER CO., ST. AUGUSTINE (1883), [CEM] Revs. Mark R. Peres, C.PP.S.; Leonard J. Kostka, C.PP.S. (Retired).
Res.: 318 N. McKinley St., 47978-2599. Tel: 219-866-5351; Fax: 219-866-4310.
School—Tel: 219-866-5480; Fax: 219-866-5663. Religious 1; Lay Teachers 6; Students 135.
Catechesis/Religious Program—Tel: 219-866-5351. Students 170.
REYNOLDS, WHITE CO., ST. JOSEPH (1866), [CEM] Rev. Msgr. Robert L. Sell III, J.C.L., V.G., Admin.
Res.: 601 South Kenton St., 47980-8098. Tel: 219-984-5401; Fax: 219-984-5401.
Catechesis/Religious Program—Students 81.
ROCHESTER, FULTON CO., ST. JOSEPH (1900), [CEM] Rev. Joseph E. Jacob, Pastor & Admin.
Res.: 1310 Main St., 46975-2108. Tel: 574-223-2808; Fax: 574-224-2808.
Catechesis/Religious Program—Tel: 574-223-3246. Students 91.
Mission—St. Ann Kewanna, Fulton Co. 46939. Tel: 574-653-2520.
STAR CITY, PULASKI CO., ST. JOSEPH (1851), [CEM 2] Rev. Ronald J. Schiml, C.PP.S.
Res.: 5895 S. SR 119, 46985-8826. Tel: 219-595-7198.
Catechesis/Religious Program—Students 63.
TIPTON, TIPTON CO., ST. JOHN THE BAPTIST (1866), [CEM] Rev. Leroy G. Kinnaman.
Res.: 340 N. Mill St., 46072-1403. Tel: 765-675-2422.
School—(Grades PreK-5) Tel: 765-675-4741; Fax: 765-675-2163. Lay Teachers 8; Students 86.
Catechesis/Religious Program—Students 121.
UNION CITY, RANDOLPH CO., ST. MARY (1865), (Irish—German), [CEM] Rev. C. Alan Funk.
Res.: 425 W. Hickory St., 47390-1301. Tel: 765-964-4202.
Catechesis/Religious Program—Tel: 765-964-4767. Students 85.
WEST LAFAYETTE, TIPPECANOE CO.
1—BLESSED SACRAMENT (1957), Rev. David M. Douglas.
Res.: 2224 Sacramento Ave., 47906-1998. Tel: 765-463-5733; Fax: 765-497-7866.
Catechesis/Religious Program—Students 310.
Station—Indiana Veterans' Home, Tel: 765-463-1502.
Station—Mary Queen of the Universe Chapel
2—ST. THOMAS AQUINAS (1951),, (Purdue University Parish) Revs. Daniel C. Davis, O.P.; Steven F. Kuhlmann, O.P.; James Q. Barnett, O.P.
Office—535 State St., 47906-3592. Tel: 765-743-4652; Fax: 765-743-0426.
Catechesis/Religious Program—Debbie Nahlik, D.R.E. Students 360.
WESTFIELD, HAMILTON CO., ST. MARIA GORETTI (1995), Rev. Kevin J. Haines; Steve Miller, Pastoral Assoc.; Steve Hood, Financial Controller.
Res.: 17102 Springmill Rd., 46074. Tel: 317-867-3213; Fax: 317-867-3263.
School—Tel: 317-896-5582; Fax: 317-867-0783. Lay Teachers 25; Students 445.
Catechesis/Religious Program—Connie Anderson, D.R.E. Students 455.
WHEATFIELD, JASPER CO., SORROWFUL MOTHER (1887), [CEM] Rev. Philip A. Mahalic.
Res.: P.O. Box 248, 46392-0248. Tel: 219-956-3343; Fax: 219-956-3343.
Church Hall: Tel: 219-956-4648.
Catechesis/Religious Program—Tel: 219-956-3347. Students 154.
WINAMAC, PULASKI CO., ST. PETER (1859), [CEM] Rev. John J. Hoying, C.PP.S.
Res.: 401 N. Monticello St., 46996-1327. Tel: 574-946-4906; Fax: 574-946-4962.
Catechesis/Religious Program—424 N. Market St., 46996. Tel: 574-946-6804. Students 156.
WINCHESTER, RANDOLPH CO., ST. JOSEPH (1952), Rev. Louis S. Heitz.
Res.: 425 W. North St., 47394-1502. Tel: 765-584-2861.
Catechesis/Religious Program—Tel: 765-886-5614. Janis Wiwi, D.R.E. Students 35.
ZIONSVILLE, BOONE CO., ST. ALPHONSUS (1945), [JC] Rev. Douglas McCormack.
Res.: 1870 W. Oak, 46077-1894. Tel: 317-873-2885; 317-873-2700; Fax: 317-873-8746.
Catechesis/Religious Program—Tel: 317-873-9418. Students 527.

Chaplains of Public Institutions

LAFAYETTE. *Indiana Veterans' Home, Queen of the Universe Chapel..* Attended from Blessed Sacrament Church, West Lafayette.

GRISSOM. *Grissom Air Force Base, St. Michael's Chapel* 46971. Tel: 765-688-2191. Rev. Philip S. Hascinger, Auxiliary Civilian Chap.

LOGANSPORT. *Logansport State Hospital*. Vacant.

MARION. *U.S. Veteran's Hospital*. Revs. James Rose (FTW), Chap. (Retired), Joseph W. Grace, Auxiliary Chap.

PENDLETON. *Correctional Industrial Complex Ecumenical Chapel*, P.O. Box 601, 46064. Tel: 765-778-8011. Rev. Anthony J. Prosen.

Indiana State Reformatory, St. Christopher Chapel, P.O. Box 28, 46064. Tel: 765-778-2107. Rev. Anthony J. Prosen.

Special Assignment:

Rev. Msgr.—

Sell, Robert L., III, J.C.L., V.G., Vicar Gen., Chancellor & Moderator of the Curia, 1128 E. State St., 47905. Tel: 765-742-1665

Revs.—

Buckles, David, J.C.L., Diocesan Tribunal, 2300 S. 9th St., 47905. Tel: 765-474-0506

Doerr, Brian, Vocation Dir., 900 S. Purdum St., Kokomo, 46901-5598. Tel: 765-457-9371

Miller, Christopher T., Vicar for Hispanics, 516 S. Bluff St., Monticello, 47960-2435. Tel: 574-583-5500. Email: frchris93@yahoo.com

Miller, Richard E., J.C.L., Diocesan Tribunal, 2300 S. 9th St., 47905. Tel: 765-474-0506

Prosen, Anthony J., 1315 W. University St., Muncie, 47303. Tel: 765-288-6180

Vath, William R., Diocesan Tribunal, 2300 S. 9th St., 47905. Tel: 765-474-0506; 317-742-4440

On Duty Outside the Diocese:

Revs.—

Clegg, Timothy, 3635 Westchester Dr., Holiday, FL 34691.

Comeau, Ronald R., 6 Johnson Rd., Aurora ON L4C 2A2 Canada. Tel: 416-772-1965

Cover, Phillip B., 1600 S. Eads St., #923-S, Arlington, VA 22202.

Cox, Alan B. (B), P.O. Box 10, Post Falls, ID 83877-0010. Tel: 208-773-4715

Gross, Barry, 1601 Georgia Ave., Wheaton, MD 20902.

Holbrook, William M., 6210 W. Bell Plaine, Chicago, IL 60634.

Mannion, John H., 1600 Albany St., Beechgrove, 46107. Tel: 317-787-3311 St. Francis Hospital, Pastoral Care Department

Paternoster, Alejandro, RR2 P.O. Box 2411, Arlington, VT 05250.

Plaster, George F., 1751 - 8436 Viburnum Ct., Indianapolis, 46260. Tel: 317-251-9249

Schultz, John C., P.O. Box 415, Danville, IL 61834. Tel: 217-443-3936

Westfall, Joseph B., P.O. Box 45715, Kansas City, MO 64171.

Military Chaplains:

Rev.—

Kinney, John M., 2520 Crested Hills, Schertz, TX 78154. Tel: 210-658-6825

Unassigned:

Revs.—

Courtney, Patrick E.

Hagan, Paul

Lutkenhoff, Bernard

Retired:

Rev. Msgr.—

Potthoff, Fred E., 37 Wea Oaks St., 47905-3406. Tel: 765-474-7152

Revs.—

Bruetsch, Joseph J., St. Mary Cathedral, 1212 South St., 47901-1576. Tel: 765-742-4440

Eckert, Carl E., Carmel Care Center, 118 Medical Dr., Carmel, 46032.

Hardebeck, Donald E., 5243 N. Crab Apple Loop, Monticello, 47960-7056. Tel: 219-583-6417

Matuszak, Edward S., 619 1/2 E. 10th St., Erie, PA 16503-1315. Tel: 814-455-1166

Puetz, Richard W., St. Elizabeth Healthcare Center, 701 Armory Rd., Rm. 409, Delphi, 46923-1915. Tel: 765-564-2182

Remaklus, Charles W., 708 N. Mohee Dr., Hartford City, 47348-8603. Tel: 765-348-1998

Ruffing, Joseph R., 204 Cedar Creek Rd., Princeton, KY 42445-2341. Tel: 502-365-2932

Schiavone, Jeldo J., P.O. Box 13484, Tampa, FL 33681-3484. Tel: 813-835-0377

Schott, Victor P., 3706 E. Wilson Rd., Muncie, 47303-6203. Tel: 765-284-7355

Weller, Harold E., P.O. Box 235, Kewanna, 46939. Tel: 219-223-2305

Zimmer, Thomas J., 3814 Sunray Dr., Holiday, FL 34691-3239. Tel: 813-943-5112

Permanent Deacons:

Nevinger, Ronald, St. Boniface, Lafayette

Cain, Jerry, Blessed Sacrament, West Lafayette

Castillo, Domingo, St. Paul, Marion

Cloud, H. William, St. Alphonsus, Zionsville

Miller, Mark, Our Lady of Grace, Noblesville

Rahill, William, Our Lady of Mount Carmel, Carmel

Stevens, Truman, St. Patrick, Kokomo

INSTITUTIONS LOCATED IN THE DIOCESE

[A] COLLEGES AND UNIVERSITIES

RENSSELAER. *Saint Joseph's College*, P.O. Box 909, 47978. Tel: 219-866-6000; Fax: 219-866-6100. Web: www.saintjoe.edu. Ernest R. Mills III, J.D., Pres.; Revs. Dominic B. Gerlach, C.PP.S.; Philip F. Gilbert, C.PP.S.; Lawrence F. Heiman, C.PP.S.; Leonard J. Kostka, C.PP.S. (Retired); Edward P. McCarthy, C.PP.S. (Retired); Timothy D. McFarland, C.PP.S.; Charles J. Robbins, C.PP.S. (Retired); William J. Stang, C.PP.S.; Ralph C. Verdi, C.PP.S.; Paul R. White, C.PP.S. (Retired); Bros. Timothy P. Hemm, C.PP.S., Religious Supr.; Robert Reuter, C.PP.S.; Sr. Patricia Robinson, B.V.M. The Society of the Precious Blood Priests 10; Sisters 1; Lay Teachers 80; Brothers 2; Total Staff 220; Students 1,092.

[B] HIGH SCHOOLS, INTER-PAROCHIAL

LAFAYETTE. *Central Catholic Junior-Senior High School*, 2410 S. Ninth St., 47909-2499. Tel: 765-474-2496; Fax: 765-474-8752. Email: delarosa@lcss.org. Web: www.lcss.org/cc/cc_centralcatholic/html. Roberto A. DeLaRosa, Prin.; Joseph M. Wrin, Campus Min. Lay Teachers 35; Students 360.

[C] GENERAL HOSPITALS

LAFAYETTE. *St. Elizabeth Medical Center*, 1501 Hartford St., P.O. Box 7501, 47903. Tel: 765-423-6011; Fax: 765-423-6040. Email: pr@glhsi.org. Web: www.glhsi.org. Mr. Douglas W. Eberle, CEO; Sr. Marilyn Oliver, O.S.F., Vice Pres. Corporate Mission; Revs. Donald Vernon; Paul Graf. Sisters of St. Francis of Perpetual Adoration 3; Operational Beds 188; Patients Assisted Annually 111,200; Staff 1,006.

School of Nursing Tel: 765-423-6408; Fax: 765-423-6385. Students 172.

ANDERSON. *Saint John's Health System*, 2015 Jackson St., 46016. Tel: 765-646-8373; Fax: 765-646-8504. Email: dkdefur@sjhsnet.org. Web: www.stjohnhealthssystem.org. Mr. Kyle DeFur, Pres.; Sr. Kathleen Reilly, C.S.C., Vice Pres. Mission. Sisters of the Holy Cross 4; Bed Capacity 332; Total Assisted 381,208; Total Staff 1,550.

CARMEL. *St. Elizabeth Ann Seton Hospital of Central Indiana, Inc* Tel: 317-582-8560; Fax: 317-582-8565. Email: phalexan@stvincent.org.

St. Elizabeth Ann Seton Hospital of Carmel, 13500 N. Meridian St., 46032. Tel: 317-582-8560; Fax: 317-582-8565. Email: phalexan@stvincent.org. Peter H. Alexander, Exec. Dir. Bed Capacity 38; Patients Assisted Annually 411; Total Staff 150; Bed Capacity 29; Patients Assisted Annually 32; Total Staff 50.

St. Vincent Carmel Hospital, Inc., 13500 N. Meridian St., 46032. Tel: 317-582-7380; Fax: 317-582-7492. Web: www.stvincent.org. (A member of St. Vincent Health, Inc. and Ascension Health.)

CRAWFORDSVILLE. *St. Clare Medical Center*, 1710 Lafayette Rd., 47933. Tel: 765-362-2800; Fax: 765-364-3189. Email: greg.starnes@ssfhs.org. Web: www.stclaremedical.org. Bed Capacity 86; Patients Assisted Annually 42,000; Staff 500; Sisters of St. Francis of Perpetual Adoration 1.

ELWOOD. *St. Vincent Mercy Hospital, Inc.*, 1331 South A St., 46036-1942. Tel: 765-552-4600; Fax: 765-552-4700. Email: rjcoughl@stvincent.org. Web: www.stvmercy.org. Sr. Rosemary J. Coughlin, C.S.J., Chap.

Ascension Health, Formerly Daughters of Charity National Health System Tel: 765-552-4622; Fax: 765-552-4700. Bed Capacity 25; Patients Assisted Annually 43,587; Staff 320.

KOKOMO. *St. Joseph Hospital & Health Center of Kokomo, Indiana, Inc.*, 1907 W. Sycamore St., 46901. Tel: 765-452-5611. Email: kellyc@stjosephhospital.net. Web: www.stjosephhospital.net. P.O. Box 9010, 46904-9010. James M. Full, Pres.; Sr. Catherine Kelly, D.C., Vice Pres./Mission Integration; Luann Young, Dir./Pastoral Care. Total Staff 876; Sisters 2; Bed Capacity 167; Patients Assisted Annually 149,274.

Saint Joseph Foundation of Kokomo, Indiana, Inc. Tel: 765-456-5898; Fax: 765-456-5072.

WILLIAMSPORT. *St. Vincent Williamsport Hospital*, 412 N. Monroe St., 47993-1097. Tel: 765-762-4000; Fax: 765-762-4126. Web: www.stvincent.org. Jane Craigin, CEO. Bed Capacity 16; Patients Assisted Annually 76,800; Total Staff 167.

[D] NURSING HOMES

LAFAYETTE. *St. Anthony Health Care*, 1205 N. 14th St., 47904. Tel: 765-423-4861; Fax: 765-742-8790. Email: kthompson@sahc.net. Web: www.saintanthonyhealthcare.com. Rev. John A. Bach, Chap. Total Staff 135; Bed Capacity 120; Residents 115; Total Assisted Annually 114.

DELPHI. *St. Elizabeth Healthcare Center*, 701 Armory Rd., 46923. Tel: 765-564-6380; 765-464-5689 (Nancy Rich); Fax: 765-564-6384. Email: jgibson@franciscancommunities.com. Web: www.franciscanservices.org. Rev. Richard W. Puetz, Chap. (Retired). Owned by Franciscan Sisters of Chicago. Total Assisted 181; Total Staff 122.

WEST LAFAYETTE. *George Davis Manor*, 1051 Cumberland Ave.. Tel: 765-463-2571; Fax: 765-463-9401. Email: gbaldwin@franciscancommunities.com. Web: www.franciscanservices.org. Owned by Franciscan Sisters of Chicago. Total Assisted 187; Total Staff 213.

[E] MONASTERIES AND RESIDENCES OF PRIESTS AND BROTHERS

LAFAYETTE. *Emmaus House*, 2500 S. Ninth St., 47909. Tel: 317-477-6441.

[F] CONVENTS AND RESIDENCES FOR SISTERS

LAFAYETTE. *Monastery of the Precious Blood*, 1106 State St., E., 47905-1219. Tel: 765-742-8227; Fax: 765-420-7361. Email: saotproc@aol.com. Web: members.aol.com/saotproc/index.htm. Sr. Jacqueline Hayden, A.P.B., Supr.; Rev. John A. Bach, Chap. Sisters Adorers of the Precious Blood Professed 7.

Res.: 155 Durkee's Run Dr., 47905.

ANDERSON. *Sisters of the Holy Cross*, 1007 Raible Ave., 46011. Tel: 765-642-6117. Sisters 2.

2115 Meridian St., 46016. Tel: 765-642-8733. *Sisters of the Holy Cross, Inc.*

KOKOMO. *Maria Regina Mater Monastery*, 1175 N. 300 W., 46901-1799. Tel: 765-457-5743. Web: www.thepoorclares.org. Sr. Miriam, Abbess; Rev. Thomas Dynetius, Chap. Monastery of Poor Clares of the Reform of St. Colette Solemnly Professed Nuns in Cloister 9; Perpetually Professed Extern Sister 1; Temporarily Professed 1.

TIPTON. *St. Joseph Center: Sisters of St. Joseph*, 1440 W. Division Rd., 46072-8584. Tel: 765-675-4146; 765-675-6203; Fax: 765-675-7471; 765-675-7471. Email: sjcenter@csjtipton.org. Web: www.csjtipton.org. Sr. Martin McEntee, C.S.J., Pres.; Rev. Fred H. Gschwind, Chap. Sisters Resident at Motherhouse 23; Total in Residence 20; Total Staff 3.

[G] RETREAT HOUSES

HARTFORD CITY. *John XXIII Center*, 407 W. McDonald St., 47348. Tel: 765-348-4008; Fax: 765-348-5819. Email: john23rd@netusa1.net. Web: www.netusa1.net/~john23rd. Rev. Keith P. Hosey, Dir.; Sr. Maureen Mangen, C.PP.S., Asst. Dir.

[H] NEWMAN CENTERS

MUNCIE. *St. Francis of Assisi University Church* Newman Center, 1200 W. Riverside Ave., 47303. Tel: 765-288-6180; Fax: 765-288-7777. Email: frjohnkiefer@Juno.com. Web: www.stfrancisnewman.org. Rev. John D. Kiefer. Total in Residence 8; Total Staff 8.

WEST LAFAYETTE. *St. Thomas Aquinas Parish and Foundation for Catholic Students Attending Purdue University* 535 State St., 47906. Tel: 765-743-4652; Fax: 765-743-0426. Email: sttomaq@sttoms-purdue.org. Web: www.sttoms-purdue.org. Revs. Daniel C. Davis, O.P., Pastor & Dir., Newman Apostolate; Steven Kuhlmann, O.P., Assoc. Pastor; James Q. Barnett, O.P., Assoc. Pastor.

[I] MISCELLANEOUS

LAFAYETTE. *Catholic Foundation of Northcentral Indiana, Inc.*, P.O. Box 1687, 47902-1687. Tel: 765-742-7000; Fax: 765-742-7513. Email:

pbarrett@dioceseoflafayette.org. Web: www.dioceseoflafayette.org/staff-development.html.

Hamilton County Catholic High School Corporation, P.O. Box 260, 47902-0260. Tel: 317-582-0120; Fax: 317-582-0140. Email: btheodoreguer@indy.rr.com. Web: www.guerinhigh.org. Most Rev. William Higi, Bishop, Diocese of Lafayette in Indiana Board Members: Rev. Msgr. Robert Sell, V.G.; Sr. Lois Ann Meyer, S.N.D.deNur; G. Gary Malone; Robert Quinn.

ANDERSON. *Saint John's Foundation, Inc.*, 2015 Jackson St., 46016. Tel: 765-646-8373; Fax: 765-646-8504. Email: dlapple@sjhsnet.org. Mr. Kyle DeFur, Pres.

CARMEL. *Our Lady of Mount Carmel Parochial School*, 14596 Oak Ridge Rd., 46032. Tel: 317-846-1118; Fax: 317-582-2375. Email: youngc@olmc1.org. Web: olmc1.org. Rev. Msgr. John C. Duncan, Contact Person.

NOBLESVILLE. *Hamilton County Catholic High School Corporation, Blessed Theodore Guerin High School*, P.O. Box 85, 46061-0085. Sr. Lois Ann Meyer, S.N.D.deNur, Contact Person & Supt. Catholic Schools for the Diocese.

RELIGIOUS INSTITUTES OF MEN REPRESENTED IN THE DIOCESE

For further details refer to the corresponding bracketed number in the Religious Institutes of Men or Women section.

[0520]—*Order of St. Francis Minors*—O.F.M.

[1060]—*Society of the Precious Blood*—C.PP.S.

RELIGIOUS INSTITUTES OF WOMEN REPRESENTED IN THE DIOCESE

[1920]—*Congregation of the Sisters of the Holy Cross*—C.S.C.

[1070-09]—*Dominican Sisters*—O.P.

[1780]—*Franciscan Sisters of Peace*—F.S.P.A.

[4150]—*Irish Ursuline Union*—O.S.U.

[0240]—*Olivetan Benedictine Sisters*—O.S.B.

[3230]—*Poor Handmaids of Jesus Christ*—P.H.J.C.

[2970]—*School Sisters of Notre Dame*—S.S.N.D.

[0110]—*Sisters Adorers of the Precious Blood*—A.P.B.

[0430]—*Sisters of Charity of the Blessed Virgin Mary*—B.V.M.

[2990]—*Sisters of Notre Dame* (Toledo Prov.)—S.N.D.

[3000]—*Sisters of Notre Dame de Namur*—S.N.D.deN.

[3360]—*Sisters of Providence of Saint Mary-of-the-Woods, IN*—S.P.

[]—*Sisters of St. Francis* (Sylvania, OH)—O.S.F.

[1640]—*Sisters of St. Francis of Perpetual Adoration*—O.S.F.

[3830-10]—*Sisters of St. Joseph*—C.S.J.

[3260]—*Sisters of the Precious Blood* (Dayton, Ohio)—C.PP.S.

NECROLOGY

† Fosselman, Robert J., (Retired)—Died May 27, 2003

† Grady, William R., Munice, IN, St. Mary—Died Oct. 6, 2003

Diocese of Lake Charles

Most Reverend

EDWARD K. BRAXTON

Bishop of Lake Charles; ordained May 13, 1970; appointed Auxiliary Bishop of St. Louis March 28, 1995; ordained Auxiliary Bishop of St. Louis May 17, 1995; appointed Bishop of Lake Charles December 12, 2000; installed February 22, 2001

ESTABLISHED APRIL 25, 1980.

Square Miles 5,313.

Comprises the civil parishes (or counties) of Allen, Beauregard, Calcasieu, Cameron and Jefferson Davis in the State of Louisiana.

Legal Title: For legal titles of parishes and diocesan institutions, consult the Chancery Office.

Chancery Office: 414 Iris St., P.O. Box 3223, Lake Charles, LA 70602. Tel: 337-439-7400; Fax: 337-439-7413.

Web: lcdiocese.laol.net

Email: lcdiocese@laol.net

STATISTICAL OVERVIEW

Personnel	
Bishop	1
Retired Bishops	1
Priests: Diocesan Active in Diocese	49
Priests: Diocesan Active Outside Diocese	1
Priests: Retired, Sick or Absent	11
Number of Diocesan Priests	61
Religious Priests in Diocese	15
Total Priests in Diocese	76
Ordinations:	
Diocesan Priests	61
Permanent Deacons in Diocese	33
Total Brothers	1
Total Sisters	25
Parishes	
Parishes	38
With Resident Pastor:	
Resident Diocesan Priests	28
Resident Religious Priests	10
Missions	20
Professional Ministry Personnel:	
Brothers	1
Sisters	8
Lay Ministers	58
Welfare	
Catholic Hospitals	1
Total Assisted	135,292
Homes for the Aged	1
Total Assisted	65
Day Care Centers	1
Total Assisted	65
Special Centers for Social Services	1
Total Assisted	135,292
Educational	
High Schools, Diocesan and Parish	1
Total Students	531
Elementary Schools, Diocesan and Parish	7
Total Students	2,061
Catechesis/Religious Education:	
High School Students	3,626
Elementary Students	5,504
Total Students under Catholic Instruction	11,722
Teachers in the Diocese:	
Lay Teachers	263
Vital Statistics	
Receptions into the Church:	
Infant Baptism Totals	1,262
Adult Baptism Totals	85
Received into Full Communion	521
First Communions	1,177
Confirmations	984
Marriages:	
Catholic	304
Interfaith	105
Total Marriages	409
Deaths	936
Total Catholic Population	77,934
Total Population	277,849

Former Bishop—Most Rev. JUDE SPEYRER, D.D., ord. July 25, 1953; appt. First Bishop of Lake Charles Jan. 29, 1980; ord. and installed April 25, 1980; resigned Dec. 12, 2000.

Diocesan Board of Administration— (Legal Title - Society of the Roman Catholic Church of the Diocese of Lake Charles, LA) Most Rev. EDWARD K. BRAXTON; Rev. CHARLES MCMILLIN; Rev. Msgrs. VINCENT A. SEDITA; JAMES GADDY; Deacon GEORGE A. STEARNS; Rev. AUBREY V. GUILBEAU; Rev. Msgr. JACE ESKIND, J.C.L.; Rev. WILLIAM MILLER.

Bishop's Office—414 Iris St., P.O. Box 3223, Lake Charles, 70602. Tel: 337-439-7400, Ext. 14.

Chancery Office—414 Iris St., P.O. Box 3223, Lake Charles, 70602. Tel: 337-439-7400; Fax: 337-439-7413. Office Hours: Mon.-Fri. 8:30-4:30

Perry Building—411 Iris St., Lake Charles, 70601. Tel: 337-439-7426; Fax: 337-439-7428. Office Hours: Mon.-Fri. 8:30-4:30

Vicar General—Rev. AUBREY V. GUILBEAU, P.O. Box 3223, Lake Charles, 70602. Tel: 337-439-7400, Ext. 22.

Chancellor—Deacon GEORGE STEARNS, P.O. Box 3223, Lake Charles, 70602. Tel: 337-439-7400, Ext. 22.

Vicar Judicial—Rev. Msgr. JACE ESKIND, J.C.L., P.O Box 3223, Lake Charles, 70602. Tel: 337-439-7400, Ext. 20.

Tribunal—414 Iris St., P.O. Box 3223, Lake Charles, 70602. Tel: 337-439-7400, Ext. 20.

Judges—Rev. Msgrs. JACE ESKIND, J.C.L.; VINCENT SEDITA; Revs. HERBERT MAY, J.C.L.; ALBERT BOREL, J.C.L.

Advocates—Revs. JOHN POERIO; T. L. HERLONG; Deacons GEORGE CARR; MORRIS CHAPMAN; MAURICE SERICE.

Defenders of the Bond—Rev. Msgr. HARRY D. GREIG II; Rev. JAMES DOYLE.

Notary—PATRICIA SIGUR.

Episcopal Vicars—Rev. HENRY MANCUSO, West Deanery; Rev. Msgr. JAMES GADDY, East Deanery; Rev. WILLIAM MILLER, Central Deanery; Rev. Msgr. JACE ESKIND, J.C.L., Tribunal; Rev. AUBREY V. GUILBEAU, Vicar Gen.

Secretariats—Rev. CHARLES MCMILLIN, Clergy; Deacon EDWARD LAVINE, Black Catholics; Sr. MIRIAM ULM, O.P., Religious; Mrs. SANDRA GAY, Christian Formation.

Priest's Senate—Revs. HERBERT MAY, J.C.L., Chm.; ANTHONY FONTENOT; WAYNE LEBLEU; JOSEPH MCGRATH; DANIEL TORRES; KEITH PELLERIN; JOHN IJEOMA; SUSIL FERNANDO.

Diocesan Consultors—Rev. Msgrs. RONALD GROTH; IRVING DEBLANC; VINCENT SEDITA; Revs. AUBREY V. GUILBEAU, Vicar Gen.; HENRY MANCUSO; HERBERT J. MAY JR., J.C.L.; JOHN GILES; KARL FUSELIER; Rev. Msgr. JACE ESKIND, J.C.L.; Revs. AUBREY GUILBEAU; AUGUSTINE MULANJANANY; Rev. Msgr. JAMES GADDY.

Offices, Boards, Commissions, Committees

Black Catholics—Deacon EDWARD LAVINE, P.O. Box 3223, Lake Charles, 70601. Tel: 337-439-7436, Ext. 11.

Charismatic Renewal—Rev. ORIS BROUSSARD, 2409 2nd St., Lake Charles, 70601. Tel: 337-439-1898.

Christian Formation—Mrs. SANDRA GAY, 411 Iris St., Lake Charles, 70601. Tel: 337-439-7426, Ext. 10.

Clergy Formation—Rev. DON PIRARO, 5121 Sam Houston Jones Pkwy., Lake Charles, 70611. Tel: 337-855-1232.

Communications—MORRIS LEBLEU, P.O. Box 3223, Lake Charles, 70601. Tel: 337-439-7400, Ext. 24.

Counseling—Rev. WHITNEY MILLER, 1620 Bank St., Lake Charles, 70601. Tel: 337-436-7275, Ext. 238.

Deaf Apostolate—Rev. AUBREY GUILBEAU, 418 Iris St., Lake Charles, 70601. Tel: 337-439-4373.

Development Office—MORRIS LEBLEU, P.O. Box 3223, Lake Charles, 70602. Tel: 337-439-7400, Ext. 23.

Diocesan Building Commission—Deacon GEORGE STEARNS, Chm., P.O. Box 3223, Lake Charles, 70602. Tel: 337-439-7400, Ext. 22.

Diocesan Pastoral Council—Most Rev. EDWARD K. BRAXTON, Chm., P.O. Box 3223, Lake Charles, 70602. Tel: 337-439-7400, Ext. 14.

Diocesan Religious Council—Sr. MIRIAM ULM, O.P., 1806 Westwood St., Lake Charles, 70601. Tel: 337-491-7739.

Director of Seminarians—Rev. TIMOTHY GOODLY, 411 Iris St., Lake Charles, 70601. Tel: 337-439-7426.

Education—Deacon MICHAEL MATHEWS, Supt., P.O. Box 3223, Lake Charles, 70602. Tel: 337-439-7426, Ext. 18.

Evangelization—Mrs. SANDRA GAY, 411 Iris St., Lake Charles, 70601. Tel: 337-439-7426, Ext. 10.

Fiscal Administration—Ms. PATRICIA MYERS, P.O. Box 3223, Lake Charles, 70602. Tel: 337-439-7400, Ext. 15.

Hispanic Ministry—Rev. CARLOS GARCIA-CARDOVA, St. Philip Neri Church, P.O. Box 146, Kinder, 70648. Tel: 337-738-5612.

Office For Worship—Rev. Msgr. JACE ESKIND, J.C.L., 414 Iris St., Lake Charles, 70601. Tel: 337-439-7400, Ext. 20.

Parish Boundaries Commission—Deacon GEORGE STEARNS, Chm., P.O. Box 3223, Lake Charles, 70602. Tel: 337-439-7400, Ext. 22.

Permanent Diaconate—Deacon GEORGE CARR, 617 W. Claude St., Lake Charles, 70605. Tel: 337-477-1236.

Personnel Board—Rev. WILLIAM MILLER, Chm., 2500 Enterprise Blvd., Lake Charles, 70601. Tel: 337-439-4585.

Propagation of the Faith & Holy Childhood Association—Deacon GEORGE STEARNS, Dir., P.O. Box 3223, Lake Charles, 70602. Tel: 337-439-7400, Ext. 22.

Religious Education—Mrs. DENISE DONAHOE, 411 Iris

St., Lake Charles, 70601. Tel: 337-439-7426, Ext. 19.

Relief Services Catholic—Rev. V. WAYNE LEBLEU, Dir., P.O. Box 3223, Lake Charles, 70602. Tel: 337-439-7400.

St. Charles Retreat Center—Rev. DON PIRARO, Dir., 2151 Sam Houston Jones Pkwy., Lake Charles, 70611. Tel: 337-855-1232.

Sea, Apostleship of the—Deacon PATRICK LAPOINTE, 160 Marine St., Lake Charles, 70601. Tel: 337-436-1315.

Social Services, Catholic—Deacon EDWARD LAVINE, Dir., 2333 E. Broad St., Lake Charles, 70601. Tel: 337-439-7436, Ext. 11.

Community Services, Catholic—Deacon EDWARD LAVINE, Vicar, 2333 E. Broad St., Lake Charles, 70601. Tel: 337-439-7436, Ext. 11.

Scouting—Rev. ANTHONY FONTENOT, 2500 Enterprise Blvd., Lake Charles, 70601. Tel: 337-439-4585.

Seminary Advisory Board—Rev. TIMOTHY GOODLY, 411 Iris St., Lake Charles, 70601. Tel: 337-439-7426.

Vocation Director—Rev. TIMOTHY GOODLY, 411 Iris St., Lake Charles, 70601. Tel: 337-439-7426.

CLERGY, PARISHES, MISSIONS AND PAROCHIAL SCHOOLS

LAKE CHARLES
(CALCASIEU PARISH)

1—IMMACULATE CONCEPTION CATHEDRAL (1869), [CEM] Revs. Aubrey V. Guilbeau; Richard Adiukwu, Chap.; Deacons Milton P. White; Michael Mathews.
Mailing Address: P.O. Box 1029, 70602. Tel: 337-436-7251; Fax: 337-436-7240. In Res., Rev. Msgr. Jace Eskind.
Church: 935 Bilbo, 70601.
School—Tel: 337-433-3497; Fax: 337-433-5056. Mrs. Dinah Bradford, Prin. Lay Teachers 30; Students 345.

2—CHRIST THE KING, Rev. V. Wayne LeBleu.
Res.: 7680 Gulf Hwy., 70607. Tel: 337-478-0213.

3—ST. HENRY (1942), [JC] Revs. Joseph Angadiath, C.M.I.; Timothy Goodly; Deacon Ray Granger.
Res.: 1021 Eighth Ave., 70601. Tel: 337-436-7223; Fax: 337-436-4614.
Catechesis/Religious Program—Tel: 337-433-6119. Mrs. Anne R. Jacobs, D.R.E. Students 222.

4—IMMACULATE HEART OF MARY (1953), (African American), Rev. Karl Fuselier.
Res.: 2031 Opelousas St., 70601. Tel: 337-436-8093; Fax: 337-436-8033.
Catechesis/Religious Program—Tel: 337-436-8513. Students 310.
Mission—Our Lady of Fatima Chapel 1700 Graham St., Calcasieu Parish 70601.

5—ST. MARGARET (1940), Revs. William Miller; Marcus Johnson; Roger Appuhamy; Deacons Dan Landry; Raymond Menard.
Res.: 2500 Enterprise Blvd., 70601. Tel: 337-439-4585; Fax: 337-433-3186.
School—Tel: 337-436-7959; Fax: 337-436-9932. Mrs. Brenda Dufrene, Prin. Sisters 1; Lay Teachers 40; Students 370.
Catechesis/Religious Program—Tel: 337-436-6358. Betty Timpa, D.R.E.; Joanne Schwem, D.R.E. Students 282.

6—ST. MARTIN DEPORRES, Rev. Keith Pellerin.
Res.: 5326 Elliott Rd., 70605. Tel: 337-478-3845.

7—OUR LADY OF GOOD COUNSEL (1957), Rev. Alan P. Trouille; Deacon Glenn Viau.
Res.: 221 Aqua Dr., 70605. Tel: 337-477-1434; Fax: 337-479-2129.
Catechesis/Religious Program—Students 91.

8—OUR LADY QUEEN OF HEAVEN (1957), [CEM] Rev. Msgrs. Ronald Groth; Irving A. DeBlanc (Retired); Revs. John H. Giles Jr.; Charles McMillin.
Mailing Address: P.O. Box 5940, 70606.
Res.: 617 W. Claude St., 70605. Tel: 337-477-1236; Fax: 337-478-3451.
School—(Grades K-8) Tel: 337-477-7349; Fax: 337-477-7384. Mrs. Mary Ann Hipp, Prin. Tel: 337-477-8438. Lay Teachers 47; Students 781; Students 54.
Catechesis/Religious Program—3909 Creole St., 70605. Tel: 337-477-3937. Mrs. Nancy Chebotsky, D.R.E. (Grades 7-12); Mrs. Robin Suire, D.R.E. (Grades 1-6). Students 1,000.

9—SACRED HEART OF JESUS (1919), (African American), [CEM] Rev. Henry Mancuso; Deacon Ed Lavine.
Res.: 1102 Mill St., 70601. Tel: 337-439-2646; Fax: 337-439-2650.
School—Tel: 337-436-3588; Fax: 337-433-1761. Mr. Herman Metoyer, Prin. Lay Teachers 14; Students 180.
Catechesis/Religious Program—Tel: 337-439-9923. Willa Golden, D.R.E. Students 131.

10—ST. THEODORE'S (1974), Rev. Msgr. Charles J. Dubois; Deacons Jack Reynolds; Glenn Harmon. In Res., Rev. James Doyle.
Res.: 713 Longleaf Dr., 70611. Tel: 337-855-6662; Fax: 337-855-6663.
School—(Grades PreK-8) Tel: 337-855-9465. Mrs. Nancy Authement, Prin. Lay Teachers 28; Students 153.
Catechesis/Religious Program—Tel: 337-855-6664. Victoria Hogan, D.R.E. Students 572.

OUTSIDE THE CITY OF LAKE CHARLES

BELL CITY, CALCASIEU PARISH, ST. JOHN VIANNEY (1939), [CEM] Rev. Albert W. Borel.
Res.: Box 10, 70630. Tel: 337-622-3255; Fax: 337-622-3337.
Catechesis/Religious Program—Lisa Reber, D.R.E. Students 261.
Mission—St. Daniel Chapel Hayes, Calcasieu Parish 70630.

BIG LAKE, CAMERON PARISH, ST. MARY OF THE LAKE (1938), Rev. Msgr. Harry D. Greig II.
Res.: 11054 Hwy. 384, 70607. Tel: 337-598-3101; Fax: 337-598-4298.
Catechesis/Religious Program—Students 145.
Mission—St. Patrick's Sweet Lake, Cameron Parish.

CAMERON, CAMERON PARISH, OUR LADY STAR OF THE SEA (1961), Rev. Msgr. Louis Melancon.
Res.: 135 Our Lady's Road, 70631. Tel: 337-775-5342; Fax: 337-775-7042.
Catechesis/Religious Program—Students 73.

CREOLE, CAMERON PARISH, SACRED HEART OF JESUS (1890), [CEM 3] Rev. E. Joseph McGrath.
Res.: P.O. Drawer 9, 70632. Tel: 337-542-4795; Fax: 337-542-4641.
Catechesis/Religious Program—Tel: 337-542-4078. Stephanie Rodrigue, D.R.E. Students 291.
Mission—St. Rose of Lima 2267 Trosclair Rd., Cameron, Cameron Parish 70631. Tel: 337-542-4795.

DE QUINCY, CALCASIEU PARISH, OUR LADY OF LA SALETTE (1922), (African American), Rev. Scott DesOrmeaux.
Res.: 203 S. Grand, P.O. Box 236, 70633. Tel: 337-786-3500; Fax: 337-786-3500.
Catechesis/Religious Program—Tel: 337-786-3205. Students 133.

DE RIDDER, BEAUREGARD PARISH, ST. JOSEPH'S (1938), Rev. Daniel Torres; Deacon Sumner Kohlhund.
Res.: 1125 Blankenship Dr., 70634. Tel: 337-463-6878; Fax: 337-463-6875.
Catechesis/Religious Program—Sr. Rita Deschenes, S.S.J., D.R.E. Students 273.
Mission—St. Bridget Walker St., Merryville, Beauregard Parish 70634.
Mission—St. Jude 5072 Hwy. 113, Beauregard Parish. Tel: 337-328-8476.

ELTON, JEFFERSON DAVIS PARISH

1—ST. JOSEPH'S (1950), (African American), [CEM] Rev. Jose Vattakunnel; Deacon John Eaves.
Res.: P.O. Box 789, 70532. Tel: 337-584-2038; Fax: 337-584-2038.
Catechesis/Religious Program—Tel: 337-584-2642. Mary Jane Thomas, D.R.E.; Carroll Sue Gobert, D.R.E. Students 62.

2—ST. PAUL (1913), [CEM] Rev. Marshall Boulet; Deacon John Eaves.
Res.: P.O. Box 129, 70532. Tel: 337-584-2818; Fax: 337-584-2818.
Catechesis/Religious Program—Cathy Hollingsworth, D.R.E. Students 152.

FENTON, JEFFERSON DAVIS PARISH, ST. CHARLES BORROMEO (1980), Rev. Augustine Mulanjanany.
Res.: P.O. Box 309, 70640. Tel: 337-756-2529; Fax: 337-756-2706.
Catechesis/Religious Program—Beverly Cormier, D.R.E. Students 49.
Mission—St. John the Evangelist Lacassine Jefferson Davis Parish 70647.

GRAND CHENIER, CAMERON PARISH, ST. EUGENE (1962), [CEM] Rev. Vincent Vadakkedath.
Res.: 5035 Grand Chenier Hwy., 70643. Tel: 337-538-2245; Fax: 337-538-2438.
Catechesis/Religious Program—Students 58.
Mission—Immaculate Conception, Cameron Parish 70643.

HACKBERRY, CAMERON PARISH, ST. PETER APOSTLE (1955), Rev. Roland G. Vaughn.
Res.: 1210 Main St., P.O. Box 236, 70645. Tel: 337-762-3365
Catechesis/Religious Program—Tel: 337-762-4255. Tamra Welch D.R.E. Students 89.
Mission—Holy Trinity Holly Beach, Cameron Parish. Rev. Roland G. Vaughn.
Res.: 6470 Gulf Beach Hwy., Cameron, 70631. Tel: 337-569-2132
Mission—Our Lady of the Assumption Cameron. Johnson Bayou, Cameron Parish.

IOWA, CALCASIEU PARISH, ST. RAPHAEL (1931), [CEM] Rev. Anthony Fontenot.
Res.: P.O. Drawer 849, 70647. Tel: 337-582-3503; Fax: 337-582-3326.
Catechesis/Religious Program—Students 383.
Mission—St. Joseph P.O. Box 849, Le Bleu Settlement, Calcasieu Parish 70647-0849. Tel: 337-582-3483.

JENNINGS, JEFFERSON DAVIS PARISH

1—IMMACULATE CONCEPTION (1956), Rev. Jude Brunnert, M.S.
Res.: 515 Bryan St., P.O. Box 358, 70546. Tel: 337-824-1164; Fax: 337-824-1717.
Catechesis/Religious Program—Bennett McNeal, D.R.E. Students 142.

2—OUR LADY HELP OF CHRISTIANS (1891), [CEM] Rev. Msgr. James Gaddy; Deacon Ed McNally.
Res.: 710 State St., P.O. Drawer 1170, 70546. Tel: 337-824-0168; Fax: 337-824-7597.
School—600 Roberts Ave., 70546. Tel: 337-824-1743; Fax: 337-824-1752. Lay Teachers 26; Students 404.
Catechesis/Religious Program—Tel: 337-824-0168. Janet Guidry, D.R.E. Students 215.

3—OUR LADY OF PERPETUAL HELP (1941), [CEM] Rev. John Vianney Ijeoma.
Res.: 920 S. Broadway, P.O. Box 1331, 70546. Tel: 337-824-3182; 337-824-3186; Fax: 337-824-3186.
Catechesis/Religious Program—Tel: 337-824-3703. Harriet Lawdins, D.R.E.; Maynell Guilbeaux, D.R.E. Students 71.

KINDER, ALLEN PARISH, ST. PHILIP NERI (1937), (Acadian—French), [CEM] Rev. Carlos Garcia Cardona.
Res.: P.O. Box 146, 70648. Tel: 337-738-5612; Fax: 337-738-2728.
Catechesis/Religious Program—Wanda Fontenot, D.R.E. Students 305.
Mission—Sacred Heart 5067 Hwy. 383, Indian Village, Sacred Heart Parish 70648. Tel: 337-666-2788; 337-666-2728.
Mission—St. Maurice 219 4th St., Reeves, Sacred Heart Parish 70634.

LAKE ARTHUR, JEFFERSON DAVIS PARISH, OUR LADY OF THE LAKE (1922), [CEM] [JC 3] Revs. Clyde Thomas; Laus Appuhamy.
Res.: P.O. Drawer P, 70549. Tel: 337-774-2614; Fax: 337-774-3793.
Catechesis/Religious Program—203 Commercial St., 70549. Tel: 337-774-2675. Students 296.

OAKDALE, ALLEN PARISH, SACRED HEART (1948), [CEM] Rev. Fred F. Russi.
Mailing Address: P.O. Box 926, 71463-0926.
Res.: 1208 E. Seventh Ave., 71463. Tel: 318-335-3780.
Catechesis/Religious Program—Students 117.
Mission—St. Frances 204 Poplar St., P.O. Box 926, Elizabeth, Allen Parish 70638.

OBERLIN, ALLEN PARISH, ST. JOAN OF ARC (1920), [CEM] Rev. Michael J. Barras; Deacon Norris Chapman.
Res.: 110 W. Fifth Ave., P.O. Box 479, 70655. Tel: 337-639-4399; 337-639-4798; Fax: 337-639-4799.
Catechesis/Religious Program—Sheryl Reed, D.R.E. Students 242.
Mission—St. Joseph P.O. Box 479, Soileau, Allen Parish 70655.

RAYMOND, JEFFERSON DAVIS PARISH, ST. LAWRENCE (1957), Rev. Eappen Joseph.
Res.: 5505 Pine Island Hwy., Jennings, 70546. Tel: 337-584-2700.
Catechesis/Religious Program—Tel: 337-584-2002; Fax: 337-584-3990. Students 203.

SULPHUR, CALCASIEU PARISH

1—IMMACULATE CONCEPTION OF THE B.V.M. (1959), Rev. Msgr. Vincent Sedita.
Res.: 2700 Maplewood Dr., 70663. Tel: 337-625-3364; Fax: 337-625-9547.
Catechesis/Religious Program—Tel: 337-625-9719. Paula Hunter, D.R.E. Students 289.

2—OUR LADY OF LASALETTE (1961), Rev. Lawrence A. Kohler, M.S.; Deacons Johnny Mounce; Maurice Serice.
Res.: 602 N. Claiborne St., 70663. Tel: 337-527-6722; Fax: 337-527-0909.
Catechesis/Religious Program—Tel: 337-527-8307. Stella Barkate, D.R.E. Students 325.

3—OUR LADY OF PROMPT SUCCOR (1919), Revs. Edward J. Brunnert, M.S.; Raymond Cadran, M.S.; Henry Lenz, M.S.; Bro. Donald V. Smith, M.S.
Res.: 1109 Cypress St., 70663. Tel: 337-527-5261; Fax: 337-528-2991.
School—Tel: 337-527-7828; Fax: 337-528-3778. Mrs. Ranita Peterson, Prin. Lay Teachers 19; Students 226.
Catechesis/Religious Program—1029 Lasalette Dr., 70663. Tel: 337-527-9964. Penny Suarez, D.R.E.; Terry Sittig, D.R.E. Students 311.
Mission—St. Peter Claver 465 Maple St., Calcasieu Parish 70663. Tel: 337-527-5987.

4—ST. THERESA (1971), Rev. Francis Fitzsimmons, M.S.; Mary Little, Admin.
Res.: 4822 Carlyss Dr., 70665. Tel: 337-583-4800; Fax: 337-583-4818.

Catechesis/Religious Program—Tel: 337-583-4010. Cheryl Mouton, D.R.E. Students 400.

VINTON, CALCASIEU PARISH, ST. JOSEPH (1920), Rev. Susil Fernando.
Res.: 1502 Industrial, 70668. Tel: 337-589-7358; Fax: 337-589-7843.
Catechesis/Religious Program—Tel: 337-589-2982. Students 287.
Mission—St. Michael 4679 Evangeline Hwy., Starks, Calcasieu Parish 70661.

WELSH, JEFFERSON DAVIS PARISH
1—ST. JOSEPH (1941), (African American), [JC] Rev. William D. Hogan, S.S.J.
Res.: P.O. Box 607, 70591. Tel: 337-734-3673.
Mission—St. Peter Claver 400 W. 2nd St., Iowa, Calcasieu Parish 70547. Fax: 337-734-4435.
Catechesis/Religious Program—Students 72.
2—OUR LADY OF THE SEVEN DOLORS (1904), [CEM] [JC] Rev. Herbert May; Deacon Richard Hinchee.
Res.: P.O. Box 515, 70591. Tel: 337-734-3446; Fax: 337-734-3697.
Catechesis/Religious Program—Tel: 337-734-3848. Betty LaBouve, D.R.E. Students 303.

WESTLAKE, CALCASIEU PARISH, ST. JOHN BOSCO (1955), Rev. Peter Revel; Deacons Fred Reed Jr.; Garrett Caraway Jr. In Res., Rev. Whitney Miller.
Res.: P.O. Box 66, 70669. Tel: 337-433-2467.
Catechesis/Religious Program—Tel: 337-439-6585; Fax: 337-436-9766. Fred Reed, D.R.E.; Judy Reed, D.R.E. Students 349.

Chaplains of Public Institutions

LAKE CHARLES. *Lake Charles Memorial Hospital*. Rev. Scott DesOrmeaux.

DEQUINCY. *Phelps Correctional Center*. Rev. John Vianney Ijeoma, Chap.

SULPHUR. *West Clacasieu Cameron Hospital*. (Vacant)

On Duty Outside the Diocese:
Revs.—
Harris, Whitney G., 233 Dogwood Ct., Canton, MI 48187-3971.
Miles, James, 115 Gladys Ave., Lansdowne, MD 21227.

Retired:
Rev. Msgrs.—
Bourque, Joseph A., 2960 Lake St., Apt. 142, 70601.
DeBlanc, Irving A., 1505 Jeff Ln., 70605.
Vincent, Amos J., 2319 E. Main St., New Iberia, 70560.
Revs.—
Alers, Juan, P.O. Box 722, Oakdale, 71463.
Broussard, Oris, 1302 California St., 70607.
Herlong, Theophilus L., 5635 B Welcome Rd., 70611.
Smit, Gerard C., 105 Justice Way, Elkton, MD 21921.
Soileau, Charles, 1017 Rose Ann St., Opelousas, 70570.

Permanent Deacons:
Benoit, Mark, Immaculate Conception, Jennings
Broussard, Gordon, St. Raphael, IA
Bushnell, Joseph, Immaculate Heart of Mary, LC
Caraway, Julius G., Jr., St. John Bosco Church, Westlake
Carr, George, Our Lady Queen of Heaven, LC
Chapman, Norris, St. Joan of Arc, Oberlin
Chapman, Wayne, Our Lady of Seven Dolors, Welsh
Deshotel, Dale, St. Joan of Arc, Oberlin
Dronet, Manny, Immaculate Conception, Maplewood
Eaves, John, St. Paul, Elton
Granger, James R., St. Henry, Lake Charles
Harmon, Glenn, St. Theodore, LC
Hebert, Malone, St. Theresa, Carlyss
Hinchee, Richard, Our Lady of Seven Dolors, Welsh
Kohlhund, Sumner, St. Joseph's, De Ridder
Landry, Dan, St. Margaret, Lake Charles
LaPoint, Frederick, St. Philip Neri, Kinder
LaPoint, Patrick Our Lady of Prompt Succor, Sulpher
Lavine, Edward, Sacred Heart, Lake Charles
Mathews, Michael, Supt. of Schools, Diocese of Lake Charles
McNally, Ed, Immaculate Conception, Jennings
McNeal, Bennett, Immaculate Conception, Jennings
Menard, Raymond, St. Margaret, LC
Mounce, Johnny, Our Lady of LaSalette, Sulphur
Nash, Roy, Our Lady Star of the Sea, Cameron & Sacred Heart, Creole
Reed, Frederick, St. John Bosco, Westlake
Reynolds, Jack J., St. Theodore's, Lake Charles
Serice, Maurice, Our Lady of LaSalette, Sulphur
Stearns, George, Our Lady of Good Counsel, Lake Charles
Thompson, Paul, Holy City Community, Lake Charles
Tramel, Michael, St. Lawrence, Jennings
Viau, Glenn, Our Lady of Good Counsel, Lake Charles
Wagner, Harry E., Jr., Lake Charles
White, Milton, Immaculate Conception Cathedral, Lake Charles

INSTITUTIONS LOCATED IN THE DIOCESE

[A] HIGH SCHOOLS, INTERPAROCHIAL

LAKE CHARLES. *St. Louis High School*, 1620 Bank St., 70601. Tel: 337-436-7275. Web: www.stlouishighschool.org. William Simon, Prin. Lay Teachers 44; Students 531.
For Catholic Studies:
920 Seventh St.. Tel: 337-439-7432; Fax: 337-436-6792.

[B] GENERAL HOSPITALS

LAKE CHARLES. *CHRISTUS Health Southwestern Louisiana*, 524 S. Ryan St., 70601. Tel: 337-436-2511; Fax: 337-430-4300. Email: loretta.findley@sph.christushealth.org. Web: www.sph.christushealth.org. Ellen Jones, CEO; Rev. Brian Madison King, Dir. Pastoral Care & Vice Pres. Mission Integration. Sponsored by Christus Health System, Dallas, TX. Sisters 4; Bed Capacity 392; Patients Assisted Annually 135,292; Total Staff 1,213.

[C] RETREAT HOUSES

LAKE CHARLES. *Holy City Community*, 5611 Welcome Rd., 70611. Tel: 337-855-2871; Fax: 337-855-1973. Deacon Ed McNally, Moderator & Admin.; Rev. Oris Broussard, Chap.

MOSS BLUFF. *St. Charles Center*, 2151 Sam Houston Jones Pkwy., 70611. Tel: 337-855-1232; Fax: 337-855-9062. Rev. Don Piraro, Dir.

[D] MONASTERIES AND RESIDENCES OF PRIESTS AND BROTHERS

ELTON. **Herald of Good News, Inc.*, P.O. Box 789, 70532. Tel: 337-584-2038; Fax: 337-584-2038. Rev. Jose Vattakunnel.

[E] SPECIAL RESIDENCES

LAKE CHARLES. *Our Lady Queen of Heaven Manor*, Villa Maria, 3905 Kingston St., 70605. Tel: 337-478-4780; Fax: 337-474-8822. Email: villamaria@xspedius.net. Rev. Msgr. Irving A. DeBlanc, Pres. (Retired). Units 62.

[F] NEWMAN CENTERS

LAKE CHARLES. *Catholic Student Center* McNeese State University, 221 Aqua Dr., 70605. Tel: 337-477-1434; Fax: 337-479-2129. Rev. Alan P. Trouille; Sr. Shirley Gobert, S.E.C., Campus Min.

[G] SOCIAL SERVICE CENTERS

LAKE CHARLES. *Catholic Service Center*, 2333 E. Broad St., 70601. Tel: 337-439-7436, Ext. 11; Fax: 337-439-7435. Deacon Edward Lavine, Dir.

[H] MISCELLANEOUS

LAKE CHARLES. *CHRISTUS St. Patrick Home Care*, 4444 Lake St., 70605. Tel: 337-491-7730. Mr. William A. Hecht, Interim CFO; Deloris Parnell, Admin.
School Food Services of Lake Charles, Inc., 411 Iris St., 70601. Tel: 337-439-7426, Ext. 24; Fax: 337-439-7428. Email: edurio@dolc.org.

RELIGIOUS INSTITUTES OF MEN REPRESENTED IN THE DIOCESE

For further details refer to the corresponding bracketed number in the Religious Institutes of Men or Women section.

[0275]—*Carmelites of Mary Immaculate*—C.M.I.

[]—*Heralds of Good News*

[0690]—*Jesuit Fathers and Brothers*—S.J.

[0720]—*The Missionaries of Our Lady of La Salette* (Prov. of Mary Queen)—M.S.

[0700]—*St. Joseph's Society of the Sacred Heart*—S.S.J.

RELIGIOUS INSTITUTES OF WOMEN REPRESENTED IN THE DIOCESE

[1010]—*Congregation of Divine Providence of San Antonio, Texas*—C.D.P.

[0470]—*Congregation of the Sisters of Charity of the Incarnate Word, Houston, Texas*—C.C.V.I.

[]—*Daughters of Mary, Mother of Mercy*

[1140]—*Eucharistic Missionaries of St. Dominic*—O.P.

[]—*Sisters of Emanuel*—S.E.

[3830-16]—*Sisters of St. Joseph*—S.S.J.

[]—*Sisters of the Eucharistic Covenant*—S.E.C.

[1960]—*Sisters of the Holy Family*—S.H.F.

NECROLOGY

† Volpe, Alfonse, Lake Charles, LA Immaculate Heart of Mary—Died March 26, 2003

Diocese of Lansing

(Dioecesis Lansingensis)

Most Reverend

CARL F. MENGELING, D.D., S.T.D.

Bishop of Lansing; ordained May 25, 1957; appointed Bishop of Lansing November 7, 1995; consecrated and installed January 25, 1996. *Chancery*, 300 W. Ottawa St., Lansing, MI 48933. Tel: 517-342-2452; Fax: 517-342-2505.

Chancery: 300 W. Ottawa, Lansing, MI 48933. Tel: 517-342-2440; Fax: 517-342-2515.

Web: www.dioceseoflansing.org

Email: chancery@dioceseoflansing.org

ESTABLISHED MAY 22, 1937.

Square Miles 6,218.

Canonically Erected August 4, 1937.

Comprises the Counties of Clinton, Eaton, Genesee, Hillsdale, Ingham, Jackson, Lenawee, Livingston, Shiawassee and Washtenaw, in the State of Michigan.

For legal titles of parishes and diocesan institutions, consult the Chancery Office.

STATISTICAL OVERVIEW

Personnel	
Bishop	1
Priests: Diocesan Active in Diocese	98
Priests: Diocesan Active Outside Diocese	9
Priests: Diocesan in Foreign Missions	1
Priests: Retired, Sick or Absent	37
Number of Diocesan Priests	145
Religious Priests in Diocese	35
Total Priests in Diocese	180
Extern Priests in Diocese	22
Ordinations:	
Diocesan Priests	3
Transitional Deacons	3
Permanent Deacons	7
Permanent Deacons in Diocese	84
Total Brothers	7
Total Sisters	456
Parishes	
Parishes	95
With Resident Pastor:	
Resident Diocesan Priests	73
Resident Religious Priests	9
Without Resident Pastor:	
Administered by Priests	5
Administered by Religious Women	6
Administered by Lay People	2
Pastoral Centers	2
Professional Ministry Personnel:	
Brothers	7
Sisters	30
Lay Ministers	165
Welfare	
Catholic Hospitals	4
Total Assisted	1,905,361
Health Care Centers	4
Total Assisted	819
Homes for the Aged	3
Total Assisted	286
Day Care Centers	1
Total Assisted	100
Specialized Homes	3
Total Assisted	217
Special Centers for Social Services	10
Total Assisted	132,493
Residential Care of Disabled	1
Total Assisted	70
Other Institutions	1
Total Assisted	51
Educational	
Diocesan Students in Other Seminaries	15
Seminaries, Religious	4
Total Seminarians	15
Colleges and Universities	3
Total Students	2,680
High Schools, Diocesan and Parish	4
Total Students	2,270
High Schools, Private	2
Total Students	155
Elementary Schools, Diocesan and Parish	38
Total Students	8,897
Elementary Schools, Private	6
Total Students	774
Catechesis/Religious Education:	
High School Students	2,895
Elementary Students	21,650
Total Students under Catholic Instruction	39,336
Teachers in the Diocese:	
Priests	11
Sisters	13
Lay Teachers	757
Vital Statistics	
Receptions into the Church:	
Infant Baptism Totals	3,589
Adult Baptism Totals	492
Received into Full Communion	786
First Communions	4,464
Confirmations	3,463
Marriages:	
Catholic	695
Interfaith	494
Total Marriages	1,189
Deaths	2,074
Total Catholic Population	227,305
Total Population	1,778,475

Former Bishops—Most Revs. JOSEPH H. ALBERS, D.D., J.C.D., appt. Titular Bishop of Lunda and Auxiliary to the Archbishop of Cincinnati, Dec. 16, 1929; consecrated Dec. 27, 1929; appt. first Bishop of Lansing, Aug. 4, 1937; died Dec. 1, 1965; ALEXANDER M. ZALESKI, D.D., S.S.L., appt. Titular Bishop of Lyrbe and Auxiliary of Detroit, March 28, 1950; consecrated May 23, 1950; transferred to Lansing Oct. 7, 1964; acceded to the See Dec. 1, 1965; died May 16, 1975; KENNETH J. POVISH, D.D., appt. Bishop of Crookston, July 28, 1970; consecrated Sept. 29, 1970; appt. Bishop of Lansing, Oct. 8, 1975; installed Dec. 11, 1975; retired Nov. 7, 1995; died Sept. 5, 2003.

Chancery—300 W. Ottawa St., Lansing, 48933. Tel: 517-342-2440; Fax: 517-342-2519. (see Diocesan Departments for additional Fax numbers); Office Hours: Mon.-Fri. 8-12; 1-4:30; Address all communications to this office

Bishop's Office—300 W. Ottawa St., Lansing, 48933. Tel: 517-342-2452; Fax: 517-342-2505. Rev. Msgrs. ROBERT D. LUNSFORD, Chancellor and Administrative Asst. to the Bishop. Tel: 517-342-2454; MICHAEL D. MURPHY, Moderator of the Curia. Tel: 517-342-2450; Rev. GEORGE C. MICHALEK, Vice Chancellor. Tel: 517-485-9902.

Vicar General—Rev. Msgr. RICHARD GROSHEK, St. Pius X Church, G-3139 Hogarth Ave., Flint, 48532. Tel: 810-235-8574; Fax: 810-235-8580.

Regional Vicars—Rev. JOHN KLEIN, Lansing; Rev. Msgr. RICHARD GROSHEK, Genesee/Owosso; Revs. JAMES SHAVER, Jackson; DANIEL WHEELER, Lenawee; DAVID HOWELL, Livingston; THOMAS FIRESTONE, Washtenaw.

College of Consultors—Revs. DWIGHT EZOP; THOMAS NENNEAU; PAUL F. GREHL, O.S.F.S.; DOUGLAS OSBORN; ROGER PROKOP; DAVID J. SPEICHER.

Vicar for Charismatic Communities—Rev. WILLIAM ASHBAUGH, St. Joseph Church, 440 E. Washington, Howell, 48843. Tel: 517-546-0090.

Vicar for Religious—Rev. Msgr. MICHAEL D. MURPHY, Chancery Office, 300 W. Ottawa St., Lansing, 48933. Tel: 517-342-2450; Fax: 517-342-2505.

Ecumenical Officer—Rev. WILLIAM WEGHER, Holy Redeemer Church, 1227 E. Bristol Rd., Burton, 48529. Tel: 810-743-3050; Fax: 810-743-4381.

Commissions and Councils—

Presbyteral Council—Rev. WILLIAM THOMAS Chm., Holy Spirit Church, P.O. Box 610, Hamburg, 48139. Tel: 810-231-9199; Fax: 810-231-6129.

Board of Education and Catechesis—JOHN MANSER, Pres. Tel: 517-768-6487.

Building Commission—Rev. GILBERT O. RAHEIG.

Cursillo—Rev. Msgr. SYLVESTER L. FEDEWA, Spiritual Dir. (Retired), 120 N. Willow St., Box 412, Westphalia, 48894. Tel: 989-587-4378.

Conciliation/Arbitration—WILLIAM D. PARSLEY, 232 S. Capitol, Ste. 1000, Lansing, 48933. Tel: 517-482-2400.

Finance Council—Rev. DANIEL WHEELER, St. Elizabeth, 506 N. Union St., Tecumseh, 49286. Tel: 517-423-2447; Fax: 517-424-7706.

Priest Pension Board—Rev. JONATHAN WEHRLE.

Priest's Assignment Commission—Revs. ANDREW A. CZAJKOWSKI; DOUGLAS OSBORN; THOMAS NENNEAU; JOHN BYERS; GEORGE MICHALEK, J.C.L.; VINCENT VAN DOAN; DAN MCKEAN; ROGER PROKOP; ROY HORNING.

Diocesan Offices And Departments

Moderator of the Curia—Rev. Msgr. MICHAEL D. MURPHY. Tel: 517-342-2450; Fax: 517-342-2505.

Virtus/Protecting God's Children Program—SALLY ELLIS, Coord., 300 W. Ottawa St., Lansing, 48933. Tel: 517-342-2551; Fax: 517-342-2505.

Properties & Cemeteries—PAUL GARRIEPY, Dir. Tel: 517-342-2534.

Diocesan Archivist—Rev. GEORGE C. MICHALEK, 300 W. Ottawa St., Lansing, 48933. Tel: 517-485-9902; Fax: 517-484-8880.

Diocesan Mission Office— (Includes Propagation of the Faith, Holy Childhood Assoc., Inter-Parish Sharing) Rev. MICHAEL J. WILLIAMS, Dir., 300 W. Ottawa St., Lansing, 48933. Tel: 517-342-2541; Fax: 517-342-2519.

Legal Advisor—Mr. MICHAEL MURRAY. Tel: 517-342-2456; Fax: 517-342-2505.

Diocesan Tribunal—

Judicial Vicar—Rev. Msgr. RAYMOND J. GOEHRING, J.C.L., 300 W. Ottawa St., Lansing, 48933. Tel: 517-484-8870; Fax: 517-484-9080 (Address all rogatory commissions to the Diocesan Tribunal.).

Tribunal Judges—Revs. JEFFREY KASSIAN, J.C.O.L.; GEORGE MICHALEK, J.C.L.; PHILLIP SCHWEDA; EILEEN JARAMILLO, J.C.L.

Defenders of the Bond—Rev. BENNETT P. CONSTANTINE, J.C.D.; JOHN CAMERON.

Promoter of Justice—Rev. CHARLES IRVIN (Retired).

Auditor/Assessor—JOHN CAMERON; Rev. WILLIAM THOMAS.
Court Expert—RICHARD G. STRIFE, Ph.D.
Notaries—VIRGINIA A. DELUCA; WANDA D. MILLER.
Victim Assistance Coordinator—Rev. Msgrs. MICHAEL D. MURPHY. Tel: 517-342-2450. Email: mmurph@dioceseoflansing.org; ROBERT D. LUNSFORD. Tel: 517-342-2454. Email: rlunsf&dioceseoflansing.org.
Office of Pastoral Planning—Sr. RITA WENZLICK, O.P., Dir. Tel: 517-342-2502; Fax: 517-342-2468.
Christian Initiation Steering Committee—Sr. RITA WENZLICK, O.P., Chm. Tel: 517-342-2502.
Faith Magazine—Rev. DWIGHT EZOP, Editor in Chief. Tel: 517-669-8335; PATRICK O'BRIEN, Mng. Editor & Creative Dir. Tel: 517-342-2595.
Department of Catholic Charities—CHRISTOPHER ROOT, Chm. Tel: 517-342-2562; Fax: 517-342-2446.
Aging Ministry—ELLEN MCKAY, A.C.S.W., Dir. Tel: 517-342-2467.
Bishop's Council on Alcoholism-Chemical Dependency—ROBERT LAPRAD, Dir. Tel: 517-342-2513.
Befriender Ministry—JUDY SCHARF. Tel: 248-889-0274.
Campaign for Human Development—BARBARA POTT, Coord. Tel: 517-342-2470.
Catholic Relief Services—BARBARA POTT, Coord. Tel: 517-342-2470.
Family Ministry—SANDRA MILLAR. Tel: 517-342-2471.
Natural Family Planning—RITA MICHAELS, R.N., R.N. Tel: 517-342-2587.
Peace and Justice Ministry—VACANT.
Respect Life Ministry—SANDRA MILLAR, Dir. Tel: 517-342-2471.
Separated & Divorced Ministry—BARBARA WHITE. Tel: 517-589-8487.
Project Rachel (Post-Abortion Counseling)—WILSON PERKOWSKI. Tel: 800-968-0968.
Department of Communication—MICHAEL DIEBOLD, Chm. Tel: 517-342-2475; Fax: 517-342-2519.
Department of Diocesan Ministries—Sr. RITA WENZLICK, O.P., Interim Chm. Tel: 517-342-2502; Fax: 517-342-2468.
Black Catholic Ministry/Multicultural Initiative—RONALD LANDFAIR, Dir. Tel: 517-342-2496.
Campus Ministries—Rev. THOMAS FIRESTONE, St. Mary Church, 331 Thompson St., Ann Arbor, 48104. Tel: 734-663-0557; Fax: 734-663-2756.
Ministry with Persons with Disabilities/Deaf Ministry/Catholic Inquiry for the Blind—JOANN DAVIS, Ph.D., Dir. Tel: 517-342-2500; ROSE SMITH, Dir., Catholic Deaf Ministry. Tel: 517-342-2500; Sr. MARLENE TAYLOR, A.D., Outreach Worker. Tel: 517-342-2500; Rev. MICHAEL DEPCIK, O.S.F.S. Tel: 810-233-6992 (TTY); 800-649-3777 (Voice). Email: depcik5@aol.com.
Hispanic/Migrant Ministry—SERAPIO C. HERNANDEZ, Dir. Tel: 517-342-2498.
Worship Office—Rev. DAVID HARVEY, Dir.; RITA THIRON, Assoc. Dir. Tel: 517-342-2480.
Worship Commission—Rev. WILLIAM WEGHER. Tel: 810-238-2679.
Music Consultant—VACANT.
Young Adult Ministry/Restorative Justice—GARY ASHBY, Dir. Tel: 517-342-2495.
Department of Education and Catechesis—Sr. DORITA WOTISKA, O.P., Ph.D., Chm. Tel: 517-342-2481; Fax: 517-342-2515.
Superintendent of Schools—Sr. DORITA WOTISKA, O.P. Tel: 517-342-2481.
Instructional Programs PreK-12—SALLY AMMAN, Dir. Tel: 517-342-2483.
Catechesis—PETER RIES, Dir. Tel: 517-342-2486.
Youth Ministry—PATRICK RINKER. Tel: 517-342-2485.
Department of Finance—THOMAS PASTULA, Chm. & Finance Officer. Tel: 517-342-2442; Fax: 517-342-2519.
Development—JAY JOHNSON, Dir. Tel: 517-342-2503.
Property & Building Services—VACANT. Tel: 517-342-2443.
Technology Administrator—SHARON BYERS. Tel: 517-342-2538; Fax: 517-342-2515.
Department of Formation and Lay Ministry—Rev. MATTHEW FEDEWA, Chm. Tel: 517-342-2509; Fax: 517-342-2515.
Director of Seminarians—Rev. GERALD VINCKE. Tel: 517-342-2507.
Joseph H. Albers Trust Fund for Diocesan Vocations—Rev. MATTHEW FEDEWA. Tel: 517-342-2509.
Lay Ministry—MARY TARDIF, Dir. Tel: 517-342-2512.
Permanent Diaconate—Rev. WILLIAM SIRL, Dir. Tel: 517-342-2451.
Priestly Life and Ministry—Rev. LARRY DELANEY, Dir. Tel: 517-669-8321; 517-669-8279; Fax: 517-669-2708.
Vocation Services—Sr. CARLA MOEGGENBORG, O.P., Dir. Tel: 517-342-2506.
Discernment Houses—
Emmaus House—Rev. GERALD VINCKE, Dir., 320 M.A.C. Ave., East Lansing, 48823. Tel: 517-351-1543.
CHI RHO—Rev. ROGER PROKOP, Dir., St. Thomas the Apostle Church, 520 E. Elizabeth St., Ann Arbor, 48104. Tel: 734-761-8606.

CLERGY, PARISHES, MISSIONS AND PAROCHIAL SCHOOLS

CITY OF LANSING
(INGHAM COUNTY)

1—ST. MARY CATHEDRAL (1866), Rev. Msgr. Michael D. Murphy; Rev. Arockiyasomy Santhiyagu, M.S.F.S. (India). In Res., Rev. Msgr. Robert D. Lunsford; Rev. George C. Michalek.
Res.: 219 Seymour, 48933. Tel: 517-484-5331; Fax: 517-484-0475.

2—ST. ANDREW DUNG-LAC (1998), (Vietnamese), Rev. Joseph Tran.
5430 S. Washington Ave., 48911. Tel: 517-882-8205; Fax: 517-882-8209.
Catechesis/Religious Program—3220 Boston Blvd., 48910. Tel: 517-887-9308. Trang Van Le, D.R.E. Students 44.

3—ST. CASIMIR (1921), Rev. William R. Lugger. In Res., Rev. Phillip Schweda.
Res.: 815 Sparrow Ave., 48910-8003. Tel: 517-482-1346; Fax: 517-482-1313.
Catechesis/Religious Program—Tel: 517-482-1346. Students 163.

4—CRISTO REY (1961), (Hispanic), Rev. Frederick L. Thelen; Deacon Rogelio Alfaro.
Office—201 W. Miller Rd., 48911. Tel: 517-394-4639; Fax: 517-394-8090.
Res.: 6121 Rosedale Rd., 48911. Tel: 517-394-0676.
Catechesis/Religious Program—Students 128.

5—ST. GERARD (Delta Township, Eaton Co.) (1958), [JC] Revs. John P. Klein; John Fain; Deacons Edwin Schneider; Robert McPhilamy; Richard Savage.
Res.: 4437 W. Willow, 48917. Tel: 517-323-2379; Fax: 517-886-1394.
School—4433 W. Willow, 48917. Tel: 517-321-6126; Fax: 517-323-8046. Lynn Fuller, Prin. Lay Teachers 28; Students 523.
Catechesis/Religious Program—Tel: 517-321-4179; Fax: 517-886-1384. Students 453.

6—HOLY CROSS (1924), Rev. Pius Poff, O.F.M.Conv. In Res., Revs. Peter Nickels, O.F.M.Conv.; Timothy Byrnes.
Res.: 1611 Oakland Ave., 48915. Tel: 517-484-7768; Fax: 517-484-5741.
School—1514 W. Saginaw St., 48915. Tel: 517-487-6079; Fax: 517-487-6695. Dr. John Fitzpatrick, Prin. Lay Teachers 5; Students 94.
Catechesis/Religious Program—Tel: 517-371-3705. Students 60.

7—IMMACULATE HEART OF MARY (1949), Rev. John Byers; Deacons William Fudge III; John Cameron.
Office:—3815 S. Cedar, 48910. Tel: 517-393-3030; Fax: 517-393-0855.
School—Tel: 517-882-6631; Fax: 517-882-5536. Mary K. Dalla, Prin. Lay Teachers 13; Students 250.
Catechesis/Religious Program—Tel: 517-393-3033. Students 333.

8—RESURRECTION (1922), Revs. William J. Koenigsknecht; Jeffrey Robideau, Pastoral Assoc. In Res., Rev. Msgr. Raymond Goehring.
Res.: 1531 E. Michigan Ave., 48912. Tel: 517-482-4749; Fax: 517-484-4740.
School—Tel: 517-487-0439; Fax: 517-487-3198. Diane Repichowski, Prin. Lay Teachers 9; Students 170.
Catechesis/Religious Program—1527 E. Michigan Ave., 48912. Tel: 517-482-2605. Students 78.

9—ST. THERESE (1949), [CEM] Rev. Michael J. Williams; Sr. Margaret Ann Roggenbuck, O.P., Pastoral Min.; Deacon David Borzenski.
Res.: 102 W. Randolph St., 48906. Tel: 517-487-3749; Fax: 517-487-3755.
School—2620 N. Turner St., 48906. Tel: 517-482-1634. Mr. Douglas J. Mumby Sr., Prin. Lay Teachers 13; Students 125.
Catechesis/Religious Program—Tel: 517-487-3730. Ms. Patricia Droste, D.R.E. Students 60.

OUTSIDE THE CITY OF LANSING

ADRIAN, LENAWEE CO.

1—ST. JOSEPH (1864), [CEM] Rev. Craig G. Carolan.
Res.: 415 Ormsby St., 49221. Tel: 517-265-8938; Fax: 517-265-1987.
Catechesis/Religious Program—Students 202.

2—ST. MARY OF GOOD COUNSEL (1853), [CEM] Rev. Thomas J. Helfrich, O.S.F.S.; Deacons Richard Bayes Jr.; Calistro Torres. In Res., Rev. Louis A. Komorowski, O.S.F.S.
Office—305 Division St., 49221. Tel: 517-263-4681; Fax: 517-263-4682.
Res.: 320 Division St., 49221. Tel: 517-265-6543.
Catechesis/Religious Program—Tel: 517-265-4160; Fax: 517-263-4682. Students 293.

ANN ARBOR, WASHTENAW CO.

1—CHRIST THE KING (1981), Rev. Edward O. Fride; Deacons Daniel R. Foley; Gerald P. Holowicki; Louis J. Russello, Pastoral Assoc.; Stephen A. Thomashefski.
4000 Ave Maria Dr., 48105. Tel: 734-665-5040; Fax: 734-663-3735.
Catechesis/Religious Program—Tel: 734-663-3873; Fax: 734-663-3735. Students 231.

2—ST. FRANCIS OF ASSISI (1950), [CEM] Revs. James G. McDougall; James Conlon.
Res.: 2150 Frieze Ave., 48104. Tel: 734-769-2550; Fax: 734-821-2102.
School—(Grades K-8) Tel: 734-821-2203; Fax: 734-821-2202. Linda K. Miller, Prin. Lay Teachers 28; Students 500.
Catechesis/Religious Program—Tel: 734-821-2130. Students 850.

3—ST. MARY STUDENT PARISH (1915),, Serving students, faculty, and staff at the University of Michigan Revs. Thomas M. Firestone; Dennis T. Glasgow, S.J.; Grace M. Girvan, Business Mgr.; Susan L. Waters, Devel. Dir.; Gretchen Baumgardt, Pastoral Assoc.; Anita M. Bohn, Pastoral Assoc.; Patrick J. Waters, Pastoral Assoc.; Nicole J. Smith, Pastoral Assoc.; Deacon Romolo J. Leone, Pastoral Assoc.
Office—331 Thompson St., 48104-2295. Tel: 734-663-0557; 734-663-0558; Fax: 734-663-2756.
Catechesis/Religious Program—Students 100.

4—ST. PATRICK (1831), [CEM] Rev. Terrence J. Dumas.
Res.: 5671 Whitmore Lake Rd., 48105. Tel: 734-662-8141; 734-663-1851; Fax: 734-994-9136.
Catechesis/Religious Program—Students 248.

5—ST. THOMAS THE APOSTLE (1835), [CEM] Revs. Roger Prokop; Eric Christopher Weber; Sr. Diane Mueller, Business Mgr.; Deacons James Miles; Warren Hecht; Frank Papp.
517 Elizabeth St., 48104. Tel: 734-761-8606; Fax: 734-997-8432.
School—Tel: 734-769-0911; Fax: 734-769-9078. Patricia Downey, Prin. Sisters 1; Lay Teachers 15; Students 252.
Catechesis/Religious Program—Tel: 734-761-8606; Fax: 734-997-8432. Elizabeth Martin, D.R.E. Students 371.

BELLEVUE, EATON CO., ST. ANN (1923),, (Quasi Parish) Rev. Msgr. Raymond Goehring, Admin.
Res.: 312 S. Main St., 49021. Tel: 616-763-9372; Fax: 616-763-0067.
Catechesis/Religious Program—Students 21.

BLISSFIELD, LENAWEE CO., ST. PETER THE APOSTLE (1910), Rev. Vincent H. Van Doan.
Res.: 309 S. Lane St., 49228. Tel: 517-486-2156; Fax: 517-486-2157.
Catechesis/Religious Program—Students 100.

BRIGHTON, LIVINGSTON CO.

1—ST. MARY MAGDALEN CHURCH (1993),
Res.: 2201 Old U.S. 23, 48114. Tel: 810-229-8624; Fax: 810-229-6471. Rev. David Howell; Deacons H. David Scharf; James Chevalier.
Catechesis/Religious Program—Students 703.

2—ST. PATRICK (1832), (Irish), [CEM] Revs. Dan J. McKean; Jeffrey Njus; Deacon Patrick A. McDonald; Sr. Theresa M. Fifer, O.S.F., Pastoral Min.; Margaret Mullally-Henne, Pastoral Min.; Mary Ann Helie, Pastoral Min.; Robert Wolf, Pastoral Min.; Martha Goode, Pastoral Min.; H. William Smeal, Pastoral Min.
Res.: 711 Rickett Rd., 48116. Tel: 810-229-9863; Fax: 810-220-0730.
School—710 Rickett Rd., 48116. Tel: 810-229-7946; Fax: 810-229-6206. Judy McCusker, Prin. Lay Teachers 16; Students 272.
Catechesis/Religious Program—Tel: 810-229-4221; Fax: 810-229-6206. Sr. Theresa M. Fifer, O.S.F., D.R.E. Students 1,150.

BROOKLYN, LENAWEE CO., ST. JOSEPH'S SHRINE (Irish Hills) (1845), [CEM] Rev. Carl A. Simon; Deacon Eugene Hausmann.
Res.: 8743 U.S. 12, 49230. Tel: 517-467-2183; Fax: 517-467-4285.
Catechesis/Religious Program—Tel: 517-467-2106. Students 121.

BURTON, GENESEE CO.

1—BLESSED SACRAMENT (1957), (Hungarian), Rev. Joseph Sy Kim.
Res.: 6340 Roberta, 48509. Tel: 810-742-3151; Fax: 810-742-1409.
Catechesis/Religious Program—Rev. Joseph S. Kim, D.R.E. Students 60.

2—HOLY REDEEMER (1940), Revs. William Wegher; Gerald Gawronski; Deacon Jim Corder; Sue Meissner, Pastoral Min.

Res.: 1227 E. Bristol Rd., 48529. Tel: 810-743-3050; Fax: 810-743-4381.
School—3468 S. Grand Traverse, 48529. Tel: 810-743-2520; Fax: 810-743-9102. Maureen Carroll, Prin. Lay Teachers 10; Students 152.
Catechesis/Religious Program—Tel: 810-742-9460. Susan Kachel, D.R.E. Students 152.

CHARLOTTE, EATON CO., ST. MARY (1868), Rev. Denis R. Spitzley.
Res.: 807 St. Mary Blvd., 48813. Tel: 517-543-4319; Fax: 517-543-9078.
School—905 St. Mary Blvd., 48813. Tel: 517-543-3460; Fax: 517-541-9798. Susan Davis, Prin. Lay Teachers 7; Students 120.
Catechesis/Religious Program—Tel: 517-541-8223. Students 168.

CHELSEA, WASHTENAW CO., ST. MARY (1845), [CEM] [JC] Rev. William Turner; Deacons Richard Shaneyfelt; Thomas Franklin.
Res.: 14200 E. Old U.S. 12, 48118. Tel: 734-475-7561; Fax: 734-475-3207.
Catechesis/Religious Program—Tel: 734-475-8164; Fax: 734-475-3250. Students 575.

CLARKLAKE, JACKSON CO., ST. RITA (1916), [JC] Rev. Lehr Barkenquest, O.S.F.S.; Deacon Louis Weitzel.
Res.: 10720 Hayes Rd., 49234. Tel: 517-592-5470; Fax: 517-592-5470.
Catechesis/Religious Program—Tel: 517-592-5718. Students 239.

CLINTON, LENAWEE CO., ST. DOMINIC'S (1853), [CEM] Rev. Daniel Wheeler; Sr. Helen Walling, I.H.M., Pastoral Assoc.
Res.: 220 Brown St., 49236. Tel: 517-456-4559; Fax: 517-456-4559.
Catechesis/Religious Program—Tel: 517-456-6036. Students 44.

CLIO, GENESEE CO., SS. CHARLES AND HELENA (1953), Rev. Gerald J. Ploof.
Res.: 230 E. Vienna St., 48420-1423. Tel: 810-686-9861; Fax: 810-686-8070.
Catechesis/Religious Program—Tel: 810-686-6720. Students 301.

CONCORD, JACKSON CO., ST. CATHERINE LABOURE (1953), Rev. John Canavan, Sacramental Min. (Retired); Joyce Rochow, Pastoral Coord.
Res.: 211 Harmon Ave., P.O. Box 188, 49237. Tel: 517-524-7578; Fax: 517-524-7518.
Catechesis/Religious Program—Students 97.

DAVISON, GENESEE CO., ST. JOHN THE EVANGELIST (1871), [CEM] Rev. Andrew A. Czajkowski; Deacons Dan Fairweather; Neil Huiskens.
Res.: 404 N. Dayton St., 48423-1397. Tel: 810-653-2377; 810-653-8015; 810-658-4776 (Voice Mail); Fax: 810-658-1123.
Catechesis/Religious Program—425 N. Genesee, 48423. Tel: 810-653-4056. Elaine Davis, D.R.E.; Elaine Ouellette, D.R.E.; Paul Schlegelmilch, D.R.E. Students 632.

DE WITT, CLINTON CO., ST. JUDE (1971), Rev. Dwight M. Ezop.
Res.: 409 Wilson, P.O. Box 280, 48820. Tel: 517-669-8335; Fax: 517-669-8343.
Catechesis/Religious Program—Tel: 517-669-8341. Students 605.

DEERFIELD, LENAWEE CO., ST. ALPHONSUS (1864), [CEM] Rev. John Loughran, O.S.F.S.
Church Office: 222 Carey St., 49238. Tel: 517-447-3500; Fax: 517-447-3210; 517-447-3766 (Rectory).
Catechesis/Religious Program—Tel: 517-447-3500; Fax: 517-447-3210. Students 124.

DEXTER, WASHTENAW CO., ST. JOSEPH (1840), [CEM] Rev. Brendan J. Walsh; Deacon Romolo Leone.
Res.: 3430 Dover St., 48130. Tel: 734-426-8483; Fax: 734-426-6451.
Catechesis/Religious Program—Tel: 734-426-2674; Fax: 734-426-6451. Students 659.

DURAND, SHIAWASSEE CO., ST. MARY (1900), Rev. J. Thomas Munley.
Res.: 700 Columbia Dr., 48429. Tel: 989-288-6704; Fax: 989-288-0295.
Catechesis/Religious Program—Tel: 989-288-6704. Students 159.

EAST LANSING, INGHAM CO.

1—ST. JOHN THE EVANGELIST, STUDENT PARISH (1958), Rev. Mark Inglot; Angela Liberato, Campus Min.; Michael Liberato, Campus Min.; Liz Schweitzer, Campus Min.; Normand Gouin, Campus Min.; Al Weilbaecher, Campus Min.; Chris Jacobson, Dir. Devel.
Res.: 327 MAC, 48823. Tel: 517-337-9778; Fax: 517-337-8358.
Catechesis/Religious Program—Students 350.

2—ST. THOMAS AQUINAS (1940), Revs. David J. Speicher; David William Hudgins; Chinnappan Kulandai (India); Deacon Stephen Hilker. In Res., Rev. Joseph J. Krupp.
Res.: 955 Alton Rd., 48823. Tel: 517-351-7215; Fax: 517-351-7271.
School—915 Alton Rd., 48823. Tel: 517-332-0813; Fax: 517-332-9490. Jane Bilas, Prin. Lay Teachers 25; Students 395.
Catechesis/Religious Program—Tel: 517-351-5460. Students 228.

EATON RAPIDS, EATON CO., ST. PETER (1891), Rev. Bennett Constantine.
Res.: 515 E. Knight St., 48827. Tel: 517-663-4735; Fax: 517-663-7110.
School—515 E. Knight St., 48827. Tel: 517-663-1799; Fax: 517-663-3799. Matthew Vokun, Prin.
Catechesis/Religious Program—Tel: 517-665-2088. Albert Turkovich, D.R.E. Students 95.

FENTON, GENESEE CO., ST. JOHN (1843), [CEM 2] Revs. David W. Harvey; Peter Clark.
Res.: 600 N. Adelaide St., 48430. Tel: 810-629-2251; Fax: 810-629-2302.
School—514 Lincoln St., 48430. Tel: 810-629-6551; Fax: 810-629-2213. Sr. Patricia Fischer, O.P., Prin. Lay Teachers 25; Students 430.
Catechesis/Religious Program—512 N. Adelaide St., 48430. Tel: 810-629-1850. Elaine Schilling, D.R.E.Web: DREelaine@aol.com; Ronald Kenney, D.R.E.Web: YMKenney@aol.com. Students 709.

FLINT, GENESEE CO.

1—ST. AGNES (1928), Rev. James F. Eisele.
Res.: 500 W. Pierson Rd., 48505. Tel: 810-785-3483; Fax: 810-785-4983.
Catechesis/Religious Program—Students 8.

2—ALL SAINTS (1910), (Polish), [CEM] Rev. Anthony P. Majchrowski.
Res.: G-4063 W. Pierson Rd., 48504. Tel: 810-787-0491.
Catechesis/Religious Program—Students 30.

3—CHRIST THE KING (1929), (African American), Rev. George Puthenpeedika (India), Sacramental Min.; Sr. Joanne Fedewa, S.L.W., Pastoral Coord.
Res.: 1811 Seymour St., 48503. Tel: 810-233-0402; Fax: 810-233-5548.
Catechesis/Religious Program—3202 Forest Hill, 48503. Tel: 810-239-5851; Fax: 810-239-9864.

4—ST. FRANCIS OF ASSISI, Closed. For inquiries for parish records contact the chancery.

5—HOLY ROSARY (1951), Rev. Paul Schwermer.
Res.: 5199 Richfield Rd., 48506. Tel: 810-736-4040; Fax: 810-736-9129.
School—5191 Richfield Rd., 48506. Tel: 810-736-4220; Fax: 810-736-0164. Sharon A. Cuttitta, Prin. Lay Teachers 11; Students 144.
Catechesis/Religious Program—Tel: 810-736-4040, Ext. 22. Students 175.

6—ST. JOHN VIANNEY (1941), Rev. Douglas Osborn.
Res.: 2415 Bagley St., 48504. Tel: 810-235-1812; Fax: 810-235-4911.
School—2319 Bagley St., 48504. Tel: 810-235-5687; Fax: 810-235-2811. Mrs. Kathleen Slattery, Prin. Sisters 2; Lay Teachers 15; Total Staff 17; Students 320.
Catechesis/Religious Program—Students 45.

7—ST. LEO THE GREAT (1957), Rev. James B. Bettendorf.
Res.: 3632 Wyoming Ave., 48506. Tel: 810-736-2150; Fax: 810-736-0122.
Catechesis/Religious Program—Tel: 810-736-7200. Students 28.

8—ST. LUKE (1950), Rev. Gary McInnis, Sacramental Min.; Sr. Judith A. Blake, S.S.J., Pastoral Coord.
Res.: 3202 Forest Hill, 48504. Tel: 810-239-5851; Fax: 810-239-9864.
Catechesis/Religious Program—Tel: 810-232-1015. Students 37.

9—ST. MARY (1919), Rev. Robert F. Copeland.
Res.: 2500 N. Franklin Ave., 48506. Tel: 810-232-4012; Fax: 810-232-3889.
Catechesis/Religious Program—

10—ST. MATTHEW (1911), Rev. Frederick H. Taggart, O.S.A.
Res.: 706 Beach St., 48502. Tel: 810-232-0880; Fax: 810-232-4148.
Catechesis/Religious Program—Students 22.

11—ST. MICHAEL (1843), Rev. Philip P. Gallagher; Deacon Ronald Rowe, Pastoral Assoc.
Res.: 609 E. Fifth Ave., 48503. Tel: 810-238-2679; Fax: 810-232-6820.
Catechesis/Religious Program—Tel: 810-238-7931; Fax: 810-232-6820. Students 139.

12—OUR LADY OF GUADALUPE (1957), (Spanish), Rev. Timothy Nelson.
Res.: G-2316 W. Coldwater Rd., 48505. Tel: 810-787-5701; Fax: 810-787-3198.
Catechesis/Religious Program—Students 160.

13—ST. PIUS X (1955), Rev. Msgr. Richard J. Groshek; Deacon Gary A. Gallagher.
Res.: G-3139 Hogarth Ave., 48532. Tel: 810-235-8574; Fax: 810-235-8580.
School—Tel: 810-235-8572; Fax: 810-235-2675. Sr. Kathleen Avery, O.S.M., Prin. Sisters 3; Lay Teachers 11; Students 185.
Catechesis/Religious Program—Tel: 810-235-8573. Students 141.

14—SACRED HEART (1928), Revs. Philip P. Gallagher; Philip Schmitter, Sacramental Min.; Ethel Hooker, Pastoral Mgr.; Deacon Anthony Verdun.
Res.: 719 E. Moore St., 48505. Tel: 810-789-8579.
Catechesis/Religious Program—Students 7.

FLUSHING, GENESEE CO., ST. ROBERT (1875), [CEM] Revs. Steven F. Makranyi; Robert F. Copeland.
Res.: 310 N. Cherry St., 48433. Tel: 810-659-2501; Fax: 810-659-2564.
School—Tel: 810-659-2503; Fax: 810-659-4002. Susan C. Sharp, Prin. Lay Teachers 18; Students 321.
Catechesis/Religious Program—Tel: 810-659-8556. Students 466.

FOWLER, CLINTON CO., MOST HOLY TRINITY (1881), (German), [CEM] Rev. Timothy E. MacDonald; Deacons Mark Simmon; Michael F. Barrett.
Res.: 545 N. Maple St., Box 349, 48835. Tel: 989-593-2162; Fax: 989-593-2171.
School—11144 Kent St., 48835. Tel: 517-593-2616; Fax: 989-593-2801. Martha Maier, Prin. Lay Teachers 8; Students 94.
Catechesis/Religious Program—Tel: 517-593-3174; Fax: 517-593-2801. Students 387.

FOWLERVILLE, LIVINGSTON CO., ST. AGNES (1891), (Irish—German), [CEM] Rev. James W. Lothamer, S.S.; Deacon Peter Guditas.
Res.: 855 E. Grand River Ave., 48836. Tel: 517-223-8684; Fax: 517-223-0813.
Catechesis/Religious Program—Tel: 517-223-8684. Students 385.

GAINES, GENESSEE CO., ST. JOSEPH (1871), [CEM] Rev. Robert McKeon, Sacramental Min.; Sr. Ann Marie Petri, O.P., Pastoral Coord.; Deacon Currie Cormier.
Res.: 118 E. Lord St., 48436. Tel: 989-271-8434; Fax: 989-271-3017.
Catechesis/Religious Program—Tel: 989-288-0548. Sandy Corrion, D.R.E. Students 182.

GOODRICH, GENESEE CO., ST. MARK THE EVANGELIST (1978), Rev. Joseph Mundadan (India), Sacramental Min.; Sr. Joan M. May, S.S.J., Pastoral Coord.
Church: 7296 Gale Rd., P.O. Box 131, 48438. Tel: 810-636-2216; Fax: 810-636-7319.
Catechesis/Religious Program—Students 226.

GRAND BLANC, GENESEE CO., HOLY FAMILY (1946), Revs. James R. Swiat; Steven D. Anderson.
Res.: 11824 S. Saginaw, 48439. Tel: 810-694-4891; Fax: 810-694-1583.
School—(Grades PreK-8), 215 Orchard St., 48439. Tel: 810-694-9072; Fax: 810-694-9405. Michael McGonigle, Prin. Lay Teachers 30; Students 610.
Catechesis/Religious Program—Tel: 810-694-9072, Ext. 28. Students 477.

GRAND LEDGE, EATON CO., ST. MICHAEL (1901), Rev. Robert H. McGraw.
Res.: 345 Edwards, 48837. Tel: 517-627-8493; 517-627-8494; Fax: 517-627-1289.
School—Tel: 517-627-2167. Mitzi Luttrull, Prin. Lay Teachers 9; Students 147.
Catechesis/Religious Program—Tel: 517-627-8493. Students 185.

HAMBURG, LIVINGSTON CO., HOLY SPIRIT (1979), Rev. William Thomas; Deacon Joseph Lennon; Patrick Flynn, Business Mgr.
Res.: P.O. Box 610, 48139. Tel: 810-231-9199; Fax: 810-231-6129.
School—9565 Musch Rd., Brighton, 48116. Tel: 810-231-9199. Dr. Mary McDonald, Prin.
Catechesis/Religious Program—Tel: 810-231-9199, Ext. 205. Sean Lavell, D.R.E. Students 180.

HARTLAND, LIVINGSTON CO., ST. JOHN THE BAPTIST (1843), [CEM] Rev. Francis M. George; Deacons Francis Wines; David Piggot.
Res.: 2099 Hacker Rd., Howell, 48855. Tel: 517-546-7200; Fax: 517-546-0403.
Catechesis/Religious Program—Tel: 517-548-2540; Fax: 517-546-0403. Students 557.

HILLSDALE, HILLSDALE CO., ST. ANTHONY (1853), [CEM] Rev. Thomas W. Butler.
Res.: 11 N. Broad St., 49242. Tel: 517-437-3305; Fax: 517-437-0034.
Catechesis/Religious Program—Tel: 517-437-2777. Students 275.

HOWELL, LIVINGSTON CO.

1—ST. AUGUSTINE (1843), [CEM], (Quasi Parish) Rev. Gregg A. Pleiness; Deacon William Sirl.
Church: 6481 Faussett Rd., 48855. Tel: 517-546-9807.
Res.: 8011 Faussett Rd., Fenton, 48430.
Parish House—Tel: 810-750-0354.
Catechesis/Religious Program—Students 194.

2—ST. JOSEPH (1888), [CEM] Revs. William A. Ashbaugh; John George Rocus; Deacon Endre Doran.
Res.: 440 E. Washington, 48843. Tel: 517-546-0090; Fax: 517-546-3126.
School—425 E. Washington, 48843. Tel: 517-546-0090, Ext. 200; Fax: 517-546-8939. Sr. Mary Czarnecki, Prin. Lay Teachers 29; Students 460.
Catechesis/Religious Program—Tel: 517-546-0090, Ext. 400. Students 690.

HUDSON, LENAWEE CO., SACRED HEART (1846), [CEM] Rev. Richard Eberle, O.S.F.S.
Res.: 207 S. Market St., 49247. Tel: 517-448-3811; Fax: 517-448-2401.
School—Tel: 517-448-6405. Angela Johnston, Prin.

Lay Teachers 7; Students 99.
Catechesis/Religious Program—Students 133.

JACKSON, JACKSON CO.

1—ST. JOHN THE EVANGELIST (1856), [CEM] [JC] Revs. James R. Shaver; Randall J. Miller; Deacon Joseph A. Kratofil; Sr. Eileen Souva, O.P., Pastoral Assoc.; Patricia Willson, Pastoral Assoc.
Res.: 711 Cooper St., 49201. Tel: 517-784-0553; Fax: 517-788-5381.
School—405 E. North St., 49202. Tel: 517-784-1714; Fax: 517-788-5382. William Devine, Prin. Lay Teachers 17; Students 312.
Catechesis/Religious Program—Tel: 517-784-5746. Students 312.

2—ST. JOSEPH (1902), (Polish—Lithuanian), [JC] Rev. Louis Madey; Deacon Albert Krieger.
Res.: 705 N. Waterloo Ave., 49202. Tel: 517-784-9716; Fax: 517-784-5411.
School—717 N. Waterloo Ave., 49202. Tel: 517-784-4660; Fax: 517-784-3536. Sr. Marie Josephine Lechowicz, C.S.S.F., Prin. Felician Sisters 2; Lay Teachers 4; Students 62.
Catechesis/Religious Program—Students 17.

3—ST. MARY, STAR OF THE SEA (1881), Rev. Bernard Reilly; Deacons Vincent C. Genco; Matthew Shannon.
Res.: 120 E. Wesley St., 49201. Tel: 517-784-7184; Fax: 517-783-2571.
School—116 E. Wesley St., 49201. Tel: 517-784-8811; Fax: 517-788-3425. Julia Hurlburt, Prin. Lay Teachers 18; Students 159.
Catechesis/Religious Program—Tel: 517-788-6153. Students 122.

4—QUEEN OF THE MIRACULOUS MEDAL (1934), Revs. Thomas D. Nenneau; John I. Aduba; Louis T. Ekka; Deacons David Barrett; Ken Spaulding; Jack Kowalski.
Res.: 606 S. Wisner, 49203. Tel: 517-783-2748; Fax: 517-788-4528.
School—811 S. Wisner, 49203. Tel: 517-782-2664; Fax: 517-782-3570. Mary Jo Swartout, Prin. Lay Teachers 20; Students 420.
Catechesis/Religious Program—Tel: 517-782-3609. Students 167.

5—ST. STANISLAUS KOSTKA (1920), (Polish), [CEM] Rev. Canon Darius W. Wyszynski.
Res.: 608 S. Elm Ave., 49203. Tel: 517-784-0551; Fax: 517-784-2639.
School—614 S. Elm Ave., 49203. Tel: 517-784-0551; Fax: 517-784-2639. Julia Hurlburt, Prin. St. Stanislaus Kostka School Cooperative Interparish Venture with St. Mary's Students 12.
Catechesis/Religious Program—116 E. Wesley, 49203. Tel: 517-788-6153; Fax: 517-783-2571. Students 4.

LAINGSBURG, SHIAWASSEE CO., ST. ISIDORE (1902), [CEM] Rev. Duaine H. Pamment.
Res.: 310 Crum St., 48848. Tel: 517-651-6617; 517-651-6722 (Office); Fax: 517-651-6617.
Catechesis/Religious Program—Tel: 517-651-6722. Students 173.

LESLIE, INGHAM CO., SS. CORNELIUS AND CYPRIAN (Bunker Hill) (1863), [CEM] Rev. Michael A. Petroski.
Res.: 1320 Catholic Church Rd., 49251. Tel: 517-589-8492; Fax: 517-589-8470.
Catechesis/Religious Program—Students 110.

MANCHESTER, WASHTENAW CO., ST. MARY (1871), [CEM] Rev. Timothy D. Krzyzaniak.
Res.: 210 W. Main St., P.O. Box 249, 48158. Tel: 734-428-8811; Fax: 734-428-1393.
Catechesis/Religious Program—Students 197.

MANITOU BEACH, LENAWEE CO., ST. MARY ON THE LAKE (1958), Rev. Paul F. Grehl, O.S.F.S., Sacramental Min.; Sr. Jean Schaub, Pastoral Coord.
Res.: 450 Manitou Rd., 49253. Tel: 517-547-7496.
Catechesis/Religious Program—Students 25.

MASON, INGHAM CO., ST. JAMES (1942), Rev. Alan J. Wakefield; Deacon Thomas Feiten.
Office—1010 S. Lansing St., 48854. Tel: 517-676-9111; Fax: 517-676-1343.
Catechesis/Religious Program—Rose Robertson, D.R.E. Students 381.

MICHIGAN CENTER, JACKSON CO., OUR LADY OF FATIMA (1954), Revs. Andrew J. Dunne, O.S.F.S.; Thomas J. Smith, O.S.F.S.
Res.: 913 Napoleon Rd., 49254. Tel: 517-764-2088; 517-764-2112; Fax: 517-764-0461.
School—911 Napoleon Rd., 49254. Tel: 517-764-2563; Fax: 517-764-5411. Joann Kozlowicz, Prin. Lay Teachers 15; Students 116.
Catechesis/Religious Program—Tel: 517-764-1321. Students 172.

MILAN, WASHTENAW CO., IMMACULATE CONCEPTION (1854), Rev. Robert J. Pienta.
Church: 420 North St., 48160. Tel: 734-439-2030; Fax: 734-439-5659.
Catechesis/Religious Program—Tel: 734-439-2030. Students 200.

MONTROSE, GENESEE CO., GOOD SHEPHERD (1979), Rev. Gary L. McInnis; Sr. Josephine McNamara, Pastoral Coord.
Res.: 400 N. Saginaw, P.O. Box 3274, 48457-0974. Tel: 810-639-7600; Fax: 810-639-7600.
Catechesis/Religious Program—Tel: 810-639-3245. Students 118.

MORRICE, SHIAWASSEE CO., ST. MARY (1892), [CEM] Rev. John M. Bosco (India); Deacon Gary Edington.
Res.: 509 N. Main St., P.O. Box 310, 48857. Tel: 517-625-4260; Fax: 517-625-3050.
Catechesis/Religious Program—Tel: 517-625-6140. Students 157.

MOUNT MORRIS, GENESEE CO., ST. MARY (1867), [CEM] Rev. Raymond J. Urbanek.
Res.: 11110 Saginaw St., 48458. Tel: 810-686-3920; Fax: 810-686-0759.
School—11208 N. Saginaw, 48458. Tel: 810-686-4790; Fax: 810-686-4749. Dennis Winchester, Prin. Lay Teachers 12; Students 194.
Catechesis/Religious Program—Tel: 810-686-3920; Fax: 810-686-0759. Students 123.

OKEMOS, INGHAM CO., ST. MARTHA (1988), Rev. Jonathan Wehrle; Deacon Vince Guarnaccia.
Church: 1100 W. Grand River, 48864. Tel: 517-349-1763; Fax: 517-349-7602.
School—Tel: 517-349-3322; Fax: 517-349-3322. Helen Hillman, Prin. Sisters of Charity 3; Lay Teachers 8; Students 145.
Catechesis/Religious Program—Students 647.

OTISVILLE, GENESEE CO., ST. FRANCIS XAVIER (1947), [JC] Rev. Francis Faraci (Retired); Sr. Elaine LaBell, O.P., Pastoral Coord.
212 Center St., 48463. Tel: 810-631-6305; Fax: 810-631-4412.
Catechesis/Religious Program—Tel: 810-631-4237. Students 95.

OVID, SHIAWASSEE CO., HOLY FAMILY (1966),, (Mission) Rev. Paul J. Cummings; Deacon Michael F. Barrett.
Res.: 620 N. Mabbitt Rd., P.O. Box 612, 48866. Tel: 989-834-5855; Fax: 989-834-1208.
Catechesis/Religious Program—Tel: 989-834-2138. Students 113.

OWOSSO, SHIAWASSEE CO.

1—ST. JOSEPH (1923), (Slovak), Rev. David E. Fisher; Mary Ann Dunn, Pastoral Min.
Res.: 915 E. Oliver St., 48867. Tel: 989-725-5215; Fax: 989-725-1519.
St. Joseph Child Care Services—Tel: 989-723-2030. Child Care 133.
Catechesis/Religious Program—811 E. Oliver St., 48867. Tel: 989-723-4765. Students 110.

2—ST. PAUL (1871), [CEM 2] Rev. Robert D. Kolenski; Deacon Tom Moore.
Res.: 111 N. Howell St., 48867. Tel: 989-723-4277; Fax: 989-723-9503.
School—738 W. Main St., 48867. Tel: 517-725-7766. Rita Gregoricka, Prin. Lay Teachers 13; Students 189.
Catechesis/Religious Program—718 W. Main St., 48867. Tel: 517-723-1400. Students 158.

PINCKNEY, LIVINGSTON CO., ST. MARY (1857), [CEM] Rev. Kenneth F. Coughlin.
Res.: 10601 Dexter-Pinckney Rd., 48169. Tel: 734-878-3161; Fax: 734-878-2383.
School—Tel: 734-878-5616. Suzzane Cowdry, Prin. Lay Teachers 14; Students 249.
Catechesis/Religious Program—Tel: 734-878-2217. Students 422.

ST. JOHNS, CLINTON CO., ST. JOSEPH (1874), Revs. Eoin Murphy (Ireland); Innocent Kujur (India); Deacon Marvin Robertson.
Res.: 109 Linden St., 48879. Tel: 989-224-8994; Fax: 989-224-3475.
School—Tel: 989-224-2421; Fax: 989-224-1900. Tomi Ann Scholtheiss, Prin. Lay Teachers 12; Students 309.
Catechesis/Religious Program—Tel: 989-224-8537. Students 329.

SALINE, WASHTENAW CO., ST. ANDREW (1968), Rev. William J. Stevenson; Deacon Paul Ellis.
Res.: 910 Austin Dr., 48176. Tel: 734-429-5210; Fax: 734-429-0680.
Catechesis/Religious Program—Tel: 734-429-7776. Margaret Greca, D.R.E. Students 1,277.

SWARTZ CREEK, GENESEE CO., ST. MARY (1912), (Czech), [CEM] Rev. Amos H. Wischmeyer; Deacon Rodney Amon.
Res.: 7563 Mary St., 48473. Tel: 810-635-3240; Fax: 810-635-0688.
School—4413 Morrish Rd., 48473. Tel: 810-635-4985; Fax: 810-630-1630. Connie Nash, Prin. Lay Teachers 6; Students 65; Kindergarten 12; Preschool 19.
Catechesis/Religious Program—Tel: 810-635-3989. Students 140.

TECUMSEH, LENAWEE CO., ST. ELIZABETH (1947), Rev. Daniel Wheeler; Deacons James Nicholson; Ray Pizana.
Res.: 506 N. Union St., 49286. Tel: 517-423-2447; Fax: 517-424-7706.
Catechesis/Religious Program—512 N. Union St., 49286. Tel: 517-423-4501; Fax: 517-423-1394. Students 312.

WESTPHALIA, CLINTON CO., ST. MARY (1836), (German), [CEM] Rev. Cecilio C. Reyna; Deacon Bernard Pohl.
Res.: 201 N. Westphalia St., P.O. Box 267, 48894. Tel: 989-587-4201; Fax: 989-587-3838.
School—Tel: 989-587-3702; Fax: 989-587-3706. Raymond Rzepecki, Prin. Lay Teachers 13; Students 249.
Catechesis/Religious Program—Tel: 989-587-4201. Students 192.

WILLIAMSTON, INGHAM CO., ST. MARY (1869), [CEM] Rev. Thomas W. Thompson.
Res.: 157 High St., 48895. Tel: 517-655-2620; Fax: 517-655-3933.
School—220 Cedar St., 48895. Tel: 517-655-4038; Fax: 517-655-3855. Katherine White, Prin. Lay Teachers 6; Students 110.
Catechesis/Religious Program—Tel: 517-655-2520. Catherine Draheim, D.R.E. Students 303.

YPSILANTI, WASHTENAW CO.

1—ST. ALEXIS, Closed., For inquiries for parish records contact Transfiguraton Catholic Church.

2—HOLY TRINITY STUDENT PARISH (1965), Revs. Francis D. Mossholder, P.I.M.E.; Sergio Fossati, P.I.M.E. (Italy).
Res.: 511 W. Forest, 48197. Tel: 734-482-1400; 734-487-9756 (Rectory); Fax: 734-482-0542.
Catechesis/Religious Program—Students 114.

3—ST. JOHN (1858), [CEM] Rev. Edmond L. Ertzbischoff; Deacons Wayne Charlton; Robert Chadwick.
Res.: 411 Florence St., 48197. Tel: 734-483-3360; Fax: 734-483-0712.
Catechesis/Religious Program—Tel: 734-483-6378. Students 95.
Convent—411 Florence St., 48197. Tel: 734-483-0742.

4—ST. JOSEPH (1889), [CEM] Rev. Nicholas J. Ritter.
Res.: 9425 Whittaker Rd., 48197. Tel: 734-461-6555; Fax: 734-461-1444.
Catechesis/Religious Program—Tel: 734-461-1800. Students 118.

5—TRANSFIGURATION CATHOLIC CHURCH (1994), Rev. David Franco, O.S.F.S.
Res.: 1705 E. Forest Ave., 48198-4160. Tel: 734-482-6240; Fax: 734-482-1547.
Catechesis/Religious Program—Students 19.

6—ST. URSULA, Closed., For inquiries for parish records contact Transfiguration Catholic Church.

Chaplains of Public Institutions
Hospitals

LANSING. *Michigan Capital Medical Center, Sparrow Hospital*. Alice Hill, Chap. Tel: 517-646-6850.

ANN ARBOR. *University of Michigan Hospitals/Pastoral Care Dept.*. Revs. Darin T. Robert. Tel: 734-936-4041, Ben Werner (Retired). Tel: 734-769-0422, Deacon Wayne Charlton. Tel: 734-434-2546.
Veterans' Hospital.

FLINT. *Hurley Regional Medical Center*. Rev. George Puthenpeedika (India), Chap. Tel: 810-238-2679.
McLaren Regional Medical Center. Rev. George Puthenpeedika (India), Chap. Tel: 810-238-2679.

GRAND BLANC. *Genesys Regional Medical Center*. Rev. Gary McInnis, Chap. Tel: 810-730-4665.

JACKSON. *Foote Hospital*. Rev. John Aduba, Chap. Tel: 517-783-2748.

Prisons

ADRIAN. *Gus Harrison Regional Facility*. Revs. Carl Simon. Tel: 517-263-4681, Vincent Howard. Tel: 517-475-3836, Deacon Don Calistro Torres. Tel: 517-265-8927.
Parr Hwy. Correctional Facility. Rev. Thomas Brennan. Tel: 734-429-3928, Deacons Ray Pizana. Tel: 517-467-7621, Jim Nicholson. Tel: 517-467-2072.

JACKSON. *Cooper Street Correctional Facility*. Revs. Paul F. Grehl, O.S.F.S. Tel: 517-592-4558, Paul Ruddy, O.S.F.S. Tel: 517-592-4558, Deacon Jack Kowalski. Tel: 517-789-8854.
Cotton Facility. Rev. James Shaver. Tel: 517-784-0553.
Egeler Correctional Facility. Rev. Gary McInnis. Tel: 810-232-3639.
Parnell Facility. Rev. Jeffrey Njus. Tel: 810-220-0730, Deacon Vincent Genco. Tel: 517-750-3759.
Southern Michigan Prison. Rev. Paul F. Grehl, O.S.F.S. Tel: 517-592-4558.

MILAN. *Federal Correctional Institution*. Rev. Howard Stunek, O.F.M., Chap. Tel: 734-439-2298.

Special Alternative Incarceration

CHELSEA. *Camp Cassidy Lake*. Revs. Fortunato Turati, S.C. Tel: 734-475-8430, William Turner. Tel: 734-475-1697, Deacon Richard Shaneyfelt. Tel: 517-475-8193.

PICKNEY. *Camp Brighton*. Deacon Endre J. Doran. Tel: 517-546-1137.

WHITMORE LAKE. *W. J. Maxey Boys Training School*. Revs. Bill Thomas. Tel: 810-231-9199, Richard C. Lobert. Tel: 734-662-0496.

Special Assignment:
Rev.—
Schmitter, Philip, 2381 E. Carpenter, Flint, 48505.

On Duty Outside the Diocese:
Rev. Msgr.—
Raica, Steven J., Rome
Revs.—
Bui, Vincent, St. Patrick Seminary, 320 Middlefield Rd., Menlo Park, CA 94025.
Gerl, Robert, P.O. Box 19225, Kalamazoo, 49019.
Irish, Robert, 1501 Boeger Ave., Westchester, IL 60154.
Kersten, Jay J., Navy Chap.
Kropf, Richard, Star Rte. 1, P.O. Box 629, Johannesburg, 49751.
Kuchar, Michael W., Maryknoll Fathers & Brothers, P.O. Box 305, Maryknoll, NY 10545-0305.
Pung, Karl L., Rome
Sessions, Phillip D., St. Catherine Laboure, 4124 Mt. Abraham Ave., San Diego, CA 92111.
Taylor, Jon, The College of Great Falls, 1301-20th St. S., Great Falls, MT 59405.

Retired:
Rev. Msgrs.—
Fedewa, Sylvester L., 120 N. Willow St, Box 412, Westphalia, 48894.
Fitzgerald, William, (Kalamazoo)
Revs.—
Howard, Vincent, 1849 Pierce Rd., Chelsea, 48118.
Aubin, Joseph, 402 E. Madison, #B, DeWitt, 48820.
Bednarski, Mitchell J., Marywood Nursing Care Center, 36975 W. 5 Mile Rd., Livonia, 48154.
Beiter, Eugene J., 402 E. Madison #D, Dewitt, 48820.
Bottazzo, Alex, The Mendelson Home, 2350 Watkins Lake Rd., Apt. 203, Waterford, 48328-9942.
Brennan, Thomas, 468 Lancaster Ct., Saline, 48176.
Canavan, John, (Detroit)
Carlos, Miguel, (On Leave)
Cornelli, Neil, 2501 Via Del Ray, Fernandina, FL 32034-3834.
Dougherty, C. Peter, P.O. Box 14062, 48901.
Dupuis, Philip, 13280 Friendly Dr., Wolverine, 49799.
Eder, Donald, 6090 Oak Creek Dr., Swartz Creek, 48473.
Faraci, Francis, 2214 Blackthorn, Burton, 48509.
Foglio, John, P.O. Box 4098, East Lansing, 48826.
Irvin, Charles, 402 E. Madison, Apt. A, Dewitt, 48820.
Ledwidge, Brendan, 402 E. Madison, Apt. C, DeWitt, 48820.
Lesniak, Marian, 2497 Redwood Dr., Flushing, 48433.
Lorenzo, Eduardo, 6073 Ballard, Flint, 48505.
Martin, Francis, 4437 W. Willow St., 48917.
McDevitt, Thomas, St. Francis Retreat Center, 703 E. Main St., DeWitt, 48820.
McDonald, Kenneth, 401-D E. Madison, DeWitt, 48820.
McKeon, Robert, 10018 Lehring Rd., Box 132, Byron, 48418-0132.
Murray, Francis J., 2146-3 Robinson Rd., Jackson, 49203-8620.
Novak, James, 16269 W. Starry Sky Dr., Surprise, AZ 85374
O'Grady, Edward F., Countryside Manor, 3637 McCain Rd., Apt. 17, Jackson, 49203.
Rahrig, Gilbert, 1873 Eager Rd., Howell, 48843.
Ramer, Leo, 235 Quebec St., Goderich ON N7A 2H2 Canada.
Rusch, Donald, P.O. Box 399, East Pointe, 48021.
Rykowski, Valerian, (Milwaukee)
Schmitt, James, Jr., 215 Banberry North, 48906.
Srebernak, Francis, Houghton County Medical Care Facility, 1100 Quincy St., Hancock, 49930.
Tyler, Bernard
Werner, Ben, 620 Oakdale Dr., Chelsea, 48118.
White, Leroy, (Kalamazoo)
Williams, Francis, 401-B E. Madison, DeWitt, 48820.

Permanent Deacons:
Alfaro, Rogelio R., Cristo Rey, Lansing
Amon, Rodney, St. Mary Queen of Angels Swartz Creek
Barrett, David, Queen of the Miraculous Medal, Jackson
Barrett, Michael, Holy Family, Ovid
Bayes, Richard, St. Mary of Good Counsel, Adrian
Borzenski, David, St. Therese, Lansing
Brown, James, St. Mary, Mt. Morris
Cameron, John, Diocese of Lansing Tribunal; Immaculate Heart of Mary, Lansing
Ceballos, Santos, Hispanic Ministry, Diocese of Lansing
Chadwick, Robert, St. John the Baptist, Ypsilanti
Charlton, Wayne, St. John the Baptist, Ypsilanti
Charlton, Wayne, St. John the Baptist, Ypsilanti
Chevalier, James, St. Mary Maghdalen, Brighton
Corder, James, Holy Redeemer, Burton
Cormier, Currie, St. Joseph, Gaines
Daunt, Jack, Holy Family, Grand Blanc
Doran, Endre, St. Joseph, Howell
Edington, Gary, St. Mary, Morrice
Ellis, Paul, St. Andrew, Saline
Fairweather, Daniel, St. John the Evangelist, Davison
Feiten, Thomas, St. James, Mason
Fleming, Terrence, St. Jude, DeWitt
Foley, Daniel R., Christ the King, Ann Arbor
Franklin, Thomas, St. Mary, Chelsea
Franssen, Carol, St. John the Evangelist, Jackson
Fudge, William, Immaculate Heart of Mary, Lansing
Gallagher, Gary, St. Pius X, Flint
Genco, Vincent, St. Mary Star of the Sea, Jackson
Giesige, Richard, St. Joseph, Ypsilanti
Guarnaccia, Vincent, St. Martha, Okemos
Gudaitis, Peter, St. Agnes, Fowlerville
Hashman, Jim, St. Peter, Blissfield
Hausmann, Eugene, St. Joseph Shrine, Brooklyn
Hecht, Ronald, St. Thomas the Apostle, Ann Arbor
Heutsche, Ted, St. Jude, Dewitt
Hilker, Stephen, St. Thomas Aquinas, East Lansing
Holowicki, Gerry, Christ the King, Ann Arbor
Huiskens, Neil, St. John the Evangelist, Davison
Igoe, James Gerard, Criminal Justice Ministry, Diocese of Lansing
Kowalski, John, Queen of the Miraculous Medal, Jackson
Kratofil, Joseph, St. John the Evangelist, Jackson
Krieger, Albert, St. Joseph, Jackson
Lennon, Joseph, Holy Spirit, Hamburg
Leone, Romolo, St. Joseph, Dexter
McCarthy, John, St. Michael, Grand Ledge
McDonald, Patrick, St. Patrick, Brighton
McPhilamy, Robert, St. Gerard Majella, Lansing
Miles, James, St. Thomas, Ann Arbor
Moore, Thomas, St. Paul, Owosso
Nicholson, James, St. Elizabeth, Tecumseh
Papp, Frank, St. Thomas the Apostle, Ann Arbor
Piggot, David, St. John the Baptist, Hartland
Pigott, David, SS. Charles & Helena, Clio
Pizana, Eulalio, St. Elizabeth, Tecumseh
Pohl, Bernard, St. Mary, Westphalia
Robertson, Marvin, St. Joseph, St. Johns
Rowe, Ronald, St. Michael, Flint
Russello, Lou, Christ the King, Ann Arbor
Savage, Richard, St. Gerard Majella, Lansing
Scharf, David, St. Mary Magdalen, Brighton
Shaneyfelt, Richard, St. Mary, Chelsea
Shannon, Matthew, St. Mary Star of the Sea, Jackson
Simmon, Mark, Most Holy Trinity, Fowler
Sirl, William, St. Augustine, Deerfield Twp.
Spaulding, Kenneth, Queen of the Miraculous Medal, Jackson
Stanford, Richard, St. Mary Cathedral, Lansing
Sundwick, John, St. John Vianney, Flint
Tardif, Andy, St. Michael, Grand Ledge
Thomashefski, Stephen A., Christ the King, Ann Arbor
Torres, Calistro, St. Mary of Good Counsel, Adrian
Verdun, Anthony, Sacred Heart, Flint
Weitzel, Louis, St. Rita, Clarklake
Wines, Frank, St. John the Baptist, Hartland

INSTITUTIONS LOCATED IN THE DIOCESE

[A] COLLEGES AND UNIVERSITIES

ADRIAN. *Siena Heights University*, 1247 E. Siena Heights Dr., 49221-1796. Tel: 517-263-0731; Fax: 517-264-7702. Web: www.sienahts.edu. Richard B. Artman, Ph.D., Pres.; Sr. Sharon R. Weber, O.P., Ph.D., Academic Dean. Sponsored by the Adrian Dominican Sisters. Sisters 11; Faculty 63; Staff 133; Students 2,150.

ANN ARBOR. *Ave Maria School of Law*, 3475 Plymouth Rd., 48105-2550. Tel: 734-827-8040; Fax: 734-622-0123. Email: info@avemarialaw.edu. Web: avemarialaw.edu. Bernard Dobranski, Dean. Students 222; Lay Teachers 27.

YPSILANTI. *Ave Maria College*, 300 W. Forest Ave., 48197. Tel: 734-377-4545; 866-866-3030 (Toll Free); Fax: 734-337-4140. Email: admissions@avemaria.edu. Web: www.avemaria.edu. Ronald Muller, Ph.D., Pres. Priests 1; Lay Teachers 19; Students 308.

[B] HIGH SCHOOLS, DIOCESAN

LANSING. *Lansing Catholic Central High School*, 501 N. Marshall St., 48912. Tel: 517-267-2100; Fax: 517-267-2135. Email: draminsk@lchs.org. Web: lcchs.org. Thomas P. Maloney, Prin. Lansing Catholic Central Board of Education Priests 1; Lay Teachers 30; Students 520.

ANN ARBOR. *Father Gabriel Richard High School*, 4333 Whitehall Dr., 48105. Tel: 734-662-0496; Fax: 734-662-4133. Email: jmaierle@fgrhsaa.org. Web: www.fgrhsaa.org. Gabriel Richard Board of Education Priests 1; Sisters 1; Lay Teachers 29; Students 374.

FLINT. *Luke M. Powers Catholic High School*, G-2040 W. Carpenter Rd., 48505. Tel: 810-591-4741; Fax: 810-591-0383. Email: admin@powerscatholic.org. Web: www.powerscatholic.org. Mr. Thomas Furnas, Prin. Powers Catholic Board of Education Sisters 1; Lay Teachers 40; Students 724; Total Staff 41.

JACKSON. *Lumen Christi Catholic High School*, Formerly Lumen Christi High School 3483 Spring Arbor Rd., 49203. Tel: 517-787-0630; Fax: 517-787-1066. Web: www.lumen-christi.org. Revs. Thomas W. Rieden, O.S.F.S., Prin.; Richard L. McLernan, O.S.F.S.; James Bradley, O.S.F.S.; Paul F. Grehl, O.S.F.S.; Geoff Rose, O.S.F.S.; Bro. John W. Bailey, O.S.F.S. Oblates of St. Francis de Sales Priests 5; Sisters 1; Lay Teachers 36; Students 652.

[C] ELEMENTARY & MIDDLE SCHOOLS, DIOCESAN

FLINT. *Dukette Catholic School*, 530 W. Pierson Rd., 48505. Tel: 810-785-4743; Fax: 810-785-7184. Email: dukettecs@aol.com. Gail Schneider-Negrinelli, Prin. Lay Teachers 11; Aides 4; Total Staff 16; Students 119.

JACKSON. *Jackson Catholic Middle School*, 915 Cooper, 49202. Tel: 517-784-3385; Fax: 517-782-7883. Email: jcms@jacksonareacatholicschools.com. Web: www.jacksonareacatholicschools.com. Mr. Ronald E. Niedzwiecki, Prin. Lay Teachers 19; Students 303.

[D] SCHOOLS, PRIVATE

ADRIAN. *St. Joseph Academy Montessori Children's House*, (Grades PreK-8), 1267 E. Siena Heights, 49221. Tel: 517-263-4898; Fax: 517-265-6470. Email: sjamch@tc3net.com. Web: sjamch.com. Mrs. Deborah Keller, Prin. Sisters of St. Dominic, Congregation of the Most Holy Rosary (Adrian, MI) Lay Teachers 20; Assistants 9; Administrators 7; Students 301; Total Staff 36.

ANN ARBOR. *Spiritus Sanctus Academy*, (Grades K-8), 4101 E. Joy Rd., 48105. Tel: 734-996-3855; Fax: 734-996-4270 Web: www.spiritussanctus.org. Sr. John Dominic, Prin. Priests 1; Sisters 2; Lay Teachers 8; Students 122; Staff 15.

Spiritus Sanctus Academy, (Grades K-8), 2600 Via Sacra, 48105. Tel: 734-995-4770; Fax: 734-930-9885. Email: srmarysamuel@rc.net. Web: www.spiritussanctus.org. Sr. Mary Samuel, Prin. Priests 1; Sisters 2; Lay Teachers 7; Students 87; Staff 12.

BURTON. *St. Thomas More Academy*, (Grades K-12), 6456 E. Bristol Rd., 48519. Tel: 810-742-2411; Fax: 810-742-4803. Email: stma2003@aol.com. Web: stma-mi.org. Dan Le Blanc, Prin. Priests 1; Lay Teachers 11; Administrators 2; Students 125; Total Staff 17.

CLINTON. *St. Thomas More High-Boysville*, 8744 Clinton-Macon Rd., 49236. Tel: 517-423-7451; Fax: 517-423-5214. Email: fboylan@hccsnet.org. Web: www.boysville.org. Mr. Carl LaGore, Prin. Lay Teachers 22; Total Staff 31; Students 120.

PLYMOUTH. *Spiritus Sanctus Academy*, 10450 Joy Rd., 48170. Tel: 734-414-8430; Fax: 734-414-8495. Email: iwottreng@spiritussanctus.org. Irene Wottreng, Prin. Lay Teachers 7; Total Staff 10; Students 89.

YPSILANTI. *Spiritus Sanctus Academy*, (Grades K-8), 3875 Golfside Dr., 48197. Tel: 734-528-3980; Fax: 734-528-3983. Email: apiccirillo@spiritussantus.org. Anna M. Piccirillo, Prin. Lay Teachers 10; Staff 10; Students 85.

[E] SPECIALIZED CHILD CARE FACILITIES & SCHOOLS

LANSING. *Boysville of Michigan/Holy Cross Children's Services, Grants Management Office*, 4601 W. Saginaw Hwy., Ste. A, 48917. Tel: 517-327-0892; Fax: 517-327-0895. Email: fboylan@hccsnet.org. Web: www.hccsnet.org. Bro. Francis Boylan, C.S.C., Exec. Dir.; Adolf Armbruster, Grants Mgr.

CHELSEA. *St. Louis Center for Exceptional Children & Adults*, 16195 Old U.S. 12, 48118. Tel: 734-475-8430; Fax: 734-475-0310. Email: mail@stlouiscenter.org. Web: www.stlouiscenter.org. Revs. Joseph Rinaldo, S.C., Prov. Admin.; Fortunato Turati, S.C.; Matthew Weber, S.C. Operated by the Servants of Charity. Priests 3;

Staff 45; Students 70.

CLINTON. *Boysville of Michigan, Inc./Holy Cross Children's Services*, 8744 Clinton-Macon Rd., 49236. Tel: 517-423-7451; Fax: 517-423-5442. Email: fboylan@hccsnet.org. Web: www.hccsnet.org. Bro. Francis Boylan, C.S.C., Exec. Dir.; Mr. Eugene Hausmann, Pastoral Min.; Bro. Chester Freel, C.S.C., Regl. Dir. Residential and community based treatment programs for troubled youth and families with facilities located throughout the state of Michigan and one in the state of Ohio under the auspices of the Brothers of Holy Cross & Notre Dame. Brothers 5; Boys 148; Total Staff 186.

JACKSON. *St. Joseph Home for Children, Inc.*, 1000 E. Porter, 49202. Tel: 517-787-3320; Fax: 517-787-3704. Sr. Mary Catherine Ryzewicz, C.S.S.F. Felician Sisters (C.S.S.F.), Day Care Center, Retreat-Conference Center (ages 2 months-6 years). Children 100.

MOUNT MORRIS. *Boysville of Michigan/Holy Cross Children's Services: Corcoran House*, 8212 N. Jennings Rd., 48458. Tel: 810-687-5100; Fax: 810-687-5020. Email: fboylan@hccsnet.org. Web: www.hccsnet.org. Bro. Francis Boylan, C.S.C., Pres.; Mr. Rick Boone, Regl. Dir. A day treatment program for 12 boys and girls. Total Assisted 33; Total Staff 27; Total in Residence 6.

YPSILANTI. *Supervised Independent Living Office*, 2310 Packard Ste. 3, 48197. Tel: 734-528-3960; Fax: 734-528-4237. Email: fboylan@hccsnet.org. Web: www.hccsnet.org. Member of Boysville of Michigan/Holy Cross Children's Services. Total Staff 7; Total Assisted Annually 51.

[F] CATHOLIC CHARITIES & SERVICE AGENCIES

LANSING. *Catholic Charities of Michigan*, 4925 Packard St., Ann Arbor, 48108. Tel: 734-971-9781. Robert Javier, Exec. Dir.

Catholic Social Services/St. Vincent Home, Inc., Formerly Catholic Social Services - St. Vincent Home, 913 W. Holmes Rd., Ste. 290, 48910. Tel: 517-272-1524, Ext. 102; Fax: 517-272-1562. Email: phylliskitchell@css-svh.org. Web: www.css-svh.org. Sharon Solomon-Jozwiak, Pres. & CEO. Total Assisted 7,200; Total Staff 245.

Family Counseling Center, 913 W. Holmes Rd., Ste. 179, 48910. Tel: 517-887-8580; Fax: 517-887-9140. Email: dikkehansen@css-svh.org.

Foster Grandparent Program, 6545 Mercantile Way, Ste. 2B-1, 48911. Tel: 517-272-9119; Fax: 517-272-9264. Email: georgegodby@css-svh.org.

International and Refugee Services, 2722 E. Michigan Ave., Ste. 100-B, 48912. Tel: 517-484-1010; Fax: 517-484-2560. Email: peggyroberts@css-svb.org. (Includes Reception, Placement, Health, Employment and Immigration)

St. Vincent Home for Children, 2800 W. Willow St., 48917. Tel: 517-323-4734; Fax: 517-323-0257. Email: millieericson@ccs-svh.org. Web: www.css-svh.org. In Residence 36.

Senior Companion Program, 5815 Wise Rd., 48911. Tel: 517-882-8777; Fax: 517-325-6344. Email: barbarawhite@css-svh.org.

Child Welfare Programs, 2800 W. Willow St., 48917. Tel: 517-323-4734; Fax: 517-323-0257. Email: douglasmiller@css-svh.org. (Includes SHIELD, Foster Care, Intensive Foster Care and Adoption)

Ballentine Stepping Stones, 825 N. Pennsylvania Ave., 48906. Tel: 517-485-4644; Fax: 517-485-6671. Email: pattyjongkind@css-svh.org.

Capital Area Interfaith Respite, 6545 Mercantile Way, Ste. 1-A, 48911. Tel: 517-393-8520; Fax: 517-272-9264. Email: sdubenionsmith@css-svh.org.

Parent Aide, 825 N. Pennsylvania Ave., 48906. Tel: 517-485-4644; Fax: 517-485-6671. Email: pattyjongkind@css-svh.org.

Project CLAY, 201 W. Miller Rd., 48911. Tel: 517-394-3995; Fax: 517-394-1887. Email: markdehetre@ccs-svh.org.

Cristo Rey Community Center, 1717 N. High St., 48906. Tel: 517-372-4700; Fax: 517-372-8499. Email: cristorey@earthlink.net. John Ray Castillo, Exec. Dir. Total Assisted 20,000; Total Staff 60.

Migrant Clinic-Cristo Rey Community Center, 1717 N. High St., 48906. Tel: 517-372-4700; Fax: 517-372-8499. Email: cristorey@earthlink.net. Web: cristo-rey.com. Dr. Carmen Soto, D.O., Migrant Medical Dir.; Dr. Peter Cooke, Medical Dir. Total Assisted 180; Total Staff 10.

ADRIAN. *Catholic Social Services of Lenawee County*, 199 N. Broad St., 49221. Tel: 517-263-2191; Fax: 517-264-6080. Email: cssdir@tc3net.com. Web: www.catholicserviceslenawee.org. Dave Maxwell, Exec. Dir. Total Assisted Annually 750; Total Staff 15.

ANN ARBOR. *C.S.S. of Washtenaw County*, 4925 Packard Rd., 48108. Tel: 734-971-9781; Fax: 734-971-2730. Email: jwisniew@csswashtenaw.org. Web: www.csswashtenaw.org. Lawrence J. Voight, A.C.S.W. Total Assisted Annually 7,000; Total Staff 80.

DAVISON. *Outreach East*, 425 N. Genesee St., P.O. Box 61, 48423. Tel: 810-653-7711. Sr. Rita Berby, S.S.J., Dir. Total Assisted 1,900; Total Staff 1.

FLINT. *Catholic Charities of Shiawassee & Genessee Counties - North End Soup Kitchen*, 901 Chippewa St., 48503. Tel: 810-232-9950; Fax: 810-232-7599. Email: dmccormack@catholiccharities-s-g.org. Web: www.catholiccharities-s-g.org. Deborah J. McCormack, A.C.S.W, Pres. Total Assisted Daily 475; Total Staff 9.

Catholic Charities of Shiawassee and Genesee Counties, 901 Chippewa St., 48503. Tel: 810-232-9950; Fax: 810-232-7599. Email: dmccormack@catholiccharities-s-g.org. Web: contact@catholiccharities-s-g.org. Deborah J. McCormack, A.C.S.W, Pres. Total Assisted Annually 75,388; Total Staff 52.

Catholic Outreach, 509 N. Grand Traverse, P.O. Box 815, 48501. Tel: 810-234-4693; Fax: 810-234-9428. Sr. Claudia Burke, S.F.P., Dir. Total Assisted Annually 9,000; Total Staff 20.

HOWELL. *Livingston County Catholic Social Services*, 2020 E. Grand River Ave., Ste. 103, 48843. Tel: 517-545-5944; Fax: 517-545-7390. Email: lccss@voyager.net. Mark T. Robinson, Exec. Dir. Total Assisted Annually 2,300; Total Staff 17.

JACKSON. *Catholic Charities of Jackson*, 407 S. Mechanic St., 49201. Tel: 517-782-2551; Fax: 517-783-1986. Email: ccjax@modernpool.com. Web: www.ccjax.org. Vicky L. Schultz, Exec. Dir. Total Assisted Annually 8,000; Total Staff 36.

OWOSSO. *Catholic Charities of Shiawassee & Genesee County*, 120 W. Exchange, Ste. 204, 48867. Tel: 989-723-8239; Fax: 989-723-8230. Email: dmccormack@catholiccharities-s-g.org. Web: www.catholiccharities-s-g.org. Total Assisted Annually 480; Total Staff 6.

[G] SOCIETY OF ST. VINCENT DE PAUL

LANSING. *St. Vincent de Paul Society*, St. Vincent de Paul Store & Referral Office, 1020 S. Washington Ave., 48910. Tel: 517-484-5395; 517-484-4228; Fax: 517-484-2426. Email: kvkatko@svdvlansing.org. Web: svdplansing.org. Phillip J. Wippel, Pres.; Karen Katko, Exec. Dir. Total Staff 15.

ANN ARBOR. *Society of St. Vincent de Paul - St. Thomas Conference*, 517 Elizabeth St., 48104. Tel: 734-761-1400; Fax: 734-997-8432. Email: BarbLNorman@aol.com. Barbara Norman, Pres.

FLINT. *Society of St. Vincent de Paul - Particular Council of Flint*, St. Vincent DePaul Store, 1912 N. Franklin, 48506. Tel: 810-234-5381; Fax: 810-234-1697. Margaret Sylvester, Pres.; Richard Twomley, Store Dir.; Kim Kilbride, Asst. Dir.

JACKSON. *Society of St. Vincent de Paul - Jackson District Council Central Office*, 1812 Spring Arbor Rd., 49203. Tel: 517-784-0721; Fax: 517-796-9089. Richard Neuenfelot, Dist. Council Pres.

St. Vincent de Paul Store, 1509 E. Michigan, 49202. Tel: 517-784-0609.

St. Vincent de Paul Store II, 1812 Spring Arbor Rd., 49203. Tel: 517-784-0721.

[H] GENERAL HOSPITALS

ANN ARBOR. *Catherine McAuley Health Services Corporation* (Subsidiary of Mercy Health Services), 5305 E. Huron River Dr., P.O. Box 992, 48106. Tel: 734-712-3791; Fax: 734-712-5459. Health Care Center, Ancillary Care Systems: (Primary Care Physician Practices) Total Staff 187; Total Assisted Annually 140,010.

Saint Joseph Mercy Health System (A Member of Trinity Health), 5305 E. Huron River Dr., Box 992, 48106. Tel: 734-734-4986; Fax: 734-712-5459. Garry C. Faja, Pres. & CEO. Gen. Hospitals 3; Bed Capacity 747; Total Staff 4,369; Total Assisted Annually 1,548,386.

St. Joseph Mercy Hospital, 5301 E. Huron River Dr., P.O. Box 995, 48106. Tel: 734-712-3791; Fax: 734-712-5459. Email: soler@trinityhealth.org. Garry C. Faja, CEO; Revs. Timothy Dombrowski, Chap.; William Lanphear, O.S.F.S., Chap. Gen. Hospitals 1; Bed Capacity 529; Total Staff 3,589; Patients Assisted Annually 986,734.

FLINT. *Center for Gerontology* An affiliate of Genesys Health System., 3919 Beecher Rd., 48532. Tel: 810-762-4550; Fax: 810-762-4576. Email: ssstevens@genesys.org. Web: genesys.org. Greg Murray, Dir.; Sandra Stevens, Admin. Provides adult day care, care management programs, and educational training. Patients Assisted Annually 540; Total Staff 23.

Genesys Ambulatory Health Services, Inc. An affiliate of Genesys Health System., 3935 Beecher Rd., 48532. Tel: 810-762-4340; Fax: 810-762-4283. Email: dcaudle@genesys.org. Web: genesys.org. Dave Caulde, Vice Pres. Provides private duty home care services and manages shared services. Total Staff 424; Total Assisted Annually 7,331.

Genesys Home Health & Hospice An affiliate of Genesys Health System., 3933 Beecher Rd., 48532. Tel: 810-762-4600; Fax: 810-762-0027. Email: dbaker@genesys.org. Web: genesys.org. Dave Baker, Pres. Provides professional home care and rehabilitation services. Bed Capacity 30; Total Staff 250; Total Assisted 4,412.

GOODRICH. *Genesys Hospice* (Affiliate of Genesys Health System), 7280 S. State Rd., 48438. Tel: 810-636-5000; Fax: 810-636-5019. Email: lmccombs@genesys.org. LaVerne McCombs, Admin. & Contact Person. Provides in-home and residential hospice care. Inpatient hospice care for symptom management and respite care. Bed Capacity 28; Care Center 322; Home Program 497; Total Staff 98.

GRAND BLANC. *Genesys Health System*, One Genesys Pkwy., 48439. Tel: 810-606-6600; Fax: 810-606-6605. Email: atucker@genesys.org. Web: genesys.org. Norma Hagenow, Pres. & CEO.

Genesys Regional Medical Center An affiliate of Genesys Health System. Acute care hospital., One Genesys Pkwy., 48439. Tel: 810-606-6600; Fax: 810-606-6605. Email: atucker@genesys.org. Web: www.genesys.org. Allen Tucker, COO. Bed Capacity 410; Total Staff 3,500; Total Assisted Annually 400,000.

HOWELL. *Saint Joseph Mercy Livingston Hospital* (A unit of St. Joseph Mercy Health System), 620 Bryon Rd., 48843-1093. Tel: 517-545-6000; Fax: 517-545-6192. Email: claffeyp@trinity-health.org. Web: trinity-health.org. Patricia Claffey, R.N., Exec. Dir. Bed Capacity 80; General Hospitals 1; Patients Assisted Annually 301,942; Total Staff 740.

SALINE. *Saint Joseph Mercy Saline Hospital* (A unit of Saint Joseph Mercy Health System), 400 W. Russell, 48176. Tel: 734-429-1600; Fax: 734-429-4662. Garry Faja, CEO. General Hospitals 1; Bed Capacity 82; Patients Assisted Annually 216,685; Total Staff 212.

[I] HOMES FOR THE AGED & CONVALESCENT

ANN ARBOR. *Servants of God's Love Ministries: Emmanuel House*, 475 Evergreen, 48103. Tel: 734-669-8825; Fax: 734-669-8261. Email: emmanuelhse@juno.com. Sr. Mary Zalenski, Admin. Total Assisted 7.

GRAND BLANC. *Genesys Convalescent Center, Grand Blanc, Inc.* An affiliate of Genesys Health System., 8481 Holly Rd., 48439-1899. Tel: 810-694-1711; Fax: 810-694-9717. Email: r.stevens@genesys.org. Web: genesys.org. Robert Stevens, Admin. Nursing Home Bed Capacity 140; Patients Assisted Annually 274; Total Staff 202.

YPSILANTI. *Emmanuel House II*, 3341 Hillside Dr., 48197. Tel: 734-528-9031; Fax: 734-528-9086. Email: ehypsi@juno.com. Sr. Mary Zalenski, Admin. Total Assisted 5; Total Staff 38.

[J] CONVENTS AND RESIDENCES FOR SISTERS

LANSING. *Mexican Passionist Sisters*, St. Therese Convent, 109 E. Randolph, 48906-4042. Tel: 517-372-5849; Fax: 517-372-1099. Email: mavialfaro@hotmail.com. Sr. Virginia Alfaro, C.F.P., Prioress. Sisters 4.

ADRIAN. *Adrian Dominican Office of Development*, 1257 E. Siena Heights. Dr., 49221-1793. Tel: 517-266-3417; Fax: 517-266-3545. Email: devoffad@aol.com. Web: www.adriansisters.org. Adrian Dominican Sisters

Dominican Sisters of Adrian, MI, Inc., 1257 E. Siena Heights Dr., 49221. Tel: 517-266-3570. Sr. Janet Capone, O.P., Pres.

Motherhouse of the Sisters of St. Dominic Web: www.adriansisters.org.

Congregation of the Most Holy Rosary, 1257 Siena Heights Dr., 49221-1793. Tel: 517-266-3400; Fax: 517-266-3545. Sr. Janet Capone, O.P., Prioress; Revs. Roland Calvert, O.S.F.S., Chap.; George Ssebadduka, Chap. Total Congregation 1,030.

Dominican Life Center, 1277 Siena Heights Dr., 49221-1755. Tel: 517-266-3650; Fax: 517-266-3656. Sr. Rosemary Abramovich, O.P., Admin.

ANN ARBOR. *Benedictine Sisters of Corpus Christi Monastery*, 4485 Earhart Rd., 48105-9710. Tel: 734-995-3876; Fax: 734-930-9471. Email: benedictines@rc.net. Sr. Regina Mary Kust, O.S.B., Supr.

Dominican Sisters of Mary, Mother of the Eucharist, 4597 Warren Rd., 48105. Tel: 734-994-7437; Fax: 734-994-7438. Email: sjab@rc.net. Web: www.sistersofmary.org. Sr. Mary Assumpta Long, O.P., Prioress Gen.

Dominican SMME Corporation (2002), 4597 Warren

Rd., 48105. Tel: 734-994-7437. Sr. Mary Assumpta Long, O.P., Pres.

Servants of God's Love, 4399 Ford Rd., 48105. Tel: 734-663-6128; Fax: 734-663-6128. Email: servantsofgodslove@catholicweb.com. Sr. Ann Shields, Supr.

DE WITT. *St. Albert the Great House of Studies*, 217 Schavey Rd., 48820. Tel: 517-669-2277; Fax: 517-669-8123. Religious Sisters of Mercy, Alma Michigan 2.

[K] PASTORAL CENTERS

FLUSHING. *Mt. Zion Pastoral Center*, 8228 McKinley Rd., 48433. Tel: 810-639-7175; Fax: 810-639-5262. Email: mtzion@centurytel.net. Web: youthtoyouthcatholic.com. Rev. Dennis Howard, Chap. Tel: 810-639-3563.

JACKSON. *Sacred Heart Chapel*, 1501 E. Michigan, 49202. Tel: 517-783-2772. Email: sacredchapel@aol.com. Sr. Ma. Virginia Alfaro, C.F.P., Pastoral Assoc.; Rudy Flores, Pres. Parish Pastoral Council; Angela Medina, Treas.

[L] RETREAT CENTERS

ADRIAN. *Weber Retreat Center*, 1257 Siena Heights Dr., 49221-1793. Tel: 517-266-4000; Fax: 517-266-4004. Email: webercenter@adriansisters.org. Web: www.adriansisters.org/weber. Sr. Ann Romayne Fallon, O.P., Interim Dir.

BROOKLYN. *Lake Vineyard Camps, Inc., (De Sales Center)*, 1124 Ventura, 49230-9078. Tel: 517-592-8218; Fax: 517-592-8218. Email: mckenna@desales.org. Web: www.desales.org. Rev. Kenneth N. McKenna, O.S.F.S., Contact Person. De Sales Center is a Catholic Retreat Center operated by Lake Vineyard Camps, Inc. for the Oblates of St. Francis de Sales, Inc. Also on the property is the Novitiate House for the Toledo-Detroit Province of the Oblates of St. Francis de Sales. Total in Residence 5; Total Staff 2.

DE WITT. *St. Francis Retreat Center*, 703 E. Main St., 48820. Tel: 517-669-8321; 866-669-8321 (Toll Free); Fax: 517-669-2708. Email: information@stfrancis.ws. Web: www.stfrancis.ws. Revs. Lawrence Delaney, Dir.; Thomas McDevitt, Retreat Team (Retired); Sr. Suzanne Eichhorn, O.P., Assoc. Dir. Total in Residence 4; Total Staff 54.

Bethany House (Spiritual Life Center for Youth), St. Francis Retreat Center, 703 E. Main St., DeWitt, 48820. Tel: 517-669-8321; Fax: 517-669-2708. Rev. Gerald Vincke, Dir.

[M] CAMPUS MINISTRY

ADRIAN. *Siena Heights University* , Campus Ministry. , 1247 E. Siena Heights Dr., 49221. Tel: 517-264-7192; Fax: 517-264-7656. Email: tpuszcze@sienahts.edu. Web: www.sienahts.edu. Tom Puszczewicz, Dir. Campus Ministry.

ANN ARBOR. *St. Mary Student Parish* 331 Thompson St., 48104-2295. Tel: 734-663-0557; Fax: 734-663-2756. Email: stmarys@umich.edu. Web: www.umich.edu/~stmarys. Rev. Thomas M. Firestone. Serving the University of Michigan.; (Refer to the parish section for complete campus ministry staff.) Total Staff 11.

BELLEVUE. *St. Ann* , Serving Olivet College. (Refer to parish section for complete ministry staff.) , 312 S. Main St., 49021. Tel: 616-763-9372; Fax: 616-763-0067. Web: stannbellevue.catholicweb.com.

EAST LANSING. *St. John the Evangelist Student Parish*, Formerly St. John Student Parish , Serving Michigan State University , 327 M.A.C. Ave., 48823-4388. Tel: 517-337-9778; Fax: 517-337-8358. Email: stjohnsp@msu.edu. Web: www.msu.edu/~stjohnsp/. (Refer to the parish section for complete campus ministry staff.)

FLINT. *St. Leo the Great Church* 3632 Wyoming Ave., 48506. Tel: 810-736-2150; Fax: 517-736-0122. Rev. James B. Bettendorf.

HILLSDALE. *St. Anthony Family Center* , (Serving Hillsdale College) , 11 Broad St., 49242. Tel: 517-439-1316; Fax: 517-437-0034. Email: stanthony@dmci.net. Total Assisted 1,300; Total Staff 1.

YPSILANTI. *Holy Trinity Student Parish* 511 W. Forest, 48197. Tel: 734-482-1400; Fax: 734-482-0542. Email: campusminister@htspemu.org. Web: www.htspemu.org. Rev. Francis D. Mossholder, P.I.M.E.; Gregg Costanzo, Campus Min. Serving Eastern Michigan University and Washtenaw Community College.

[N] ENDOWMENTS AND TRUSTS

LANSING. *Chancery Office*, 300 W. Ottawa, 48933. Tel: 517-342-2440.

Blessed Sacrament Educational Trust Fund Tel: 810-742-3151; Fax: 810-742-1409. Rev. Joseph Sy Kim. (Blessed Sacrament Parish, Burton)

Camilla Madden Charitable Trust (Adrian)

Church of the Resurrection Educational Trust Fund (Church of the Resurrection, Lansing) Tel: 517-482-4749; Fax: 517-484-4740.

Father Al Miller Educational Trust Fund (St. Mary Parish, Westphalia) Tel: 517-587-4201; Fax: 517-587-3838.

Father Gabriel Richard High School Trust Fund (Fr. Gabriel Richard H.S., Ann Arbor) Tel: 734-662-0496; Fax: 734-662-4133.

Greater Lansing Catholic Education Foundation (Lansing) Tel: 517-485-8333; Fax: 517-484-8880.

Immaculate Heart of Mary St. Casimir School Mary Goeddeke Educational Trust Fund Tel: 517-882-6631. (IHM-St. Casimir School, Lansing)

Luke M. Powers Educational Trust Fund (Flint) Tel: 810-591-4741; Fax: 810-591-0383.

Lumen Christi High School Endowment Fund (Lumen Christi H.S., Jackson) Tel: 517-787-0630; Fax: 517-787-1066.

Most Holy Trinity Educational Trust Fund (Most Holy Trinity Church, Fowler) Tel: 517-593-2616; Fax: 517-593-2801.

Msgr. Lawrence H. Soest Educational Trust Fund (St. Mary Parish, Flint), , IA 52151. Tel: 810-232-4012; Fax: 810-232-4013.

Rev. Joseph R. Robb Educational Trust Fund (Holy Rosary Parish, Flint) Tel: 810-736-4040; Fax: 810-736-9129.

Sacred Heart Educational Fund (Sacred Heart Parish, Hudson) Tel: 517-448-3811.

St. Francis of Assisi Educational Trust Fund (St. Francis of Assisi Parish, Ann Harbor) Tel: 734-821-2200; Fax: 734-821-2202.

St. John the Evangelist Parish Educational Trust Fund (St. John the Evangelist Parish, Jackson) Tel: 517-784-0553; Fax: 517-788-5381.

St John School Educational Foundation, Inc. (St. John Parish, Fenton) Tel: 810-629-2251; Fax: 810-629-2302.

St. John Vianney Educational Trust Fund (St. John Vianney Parish, Flint) Tel: 810-235-1812; Fax: 810-235-4911.

St. Joseph Church of Howell Trust Fund (St. Joseph Church, Howell) Tel: 517-546-0090.

St. Joseph Educational Trust Fund (St. Joseph Church, Owosso) Tel: 517-725-5215; Fax: 517-725-1519.

St. Joseph Educational Trust Fund (St. Joseph Church, St. Johns) Tel: 517-224-8994; Fax: 517-224-3475.

St. Louis Center for Exceptional Children & Adults Endowment Trust Agreement (St. Louis Center, Chel Tel: 734-475-8430; Fax: 734-475-0310

St. Mary Educational Trust Fund (St. Mary Parish, Mt. Morris) Tel: 810-686-3920; Fax: 810-686-0759.

St. Mary Parish Educational Trust Fund (St. Mary Parish, Charlotte) Tel: 517-543-4319; Fax: 517-543-9078.

St. Mary Star of the Sea Educational Trust Fund (St. Mary Star of the Sea Parish, Jackson) Tel: 517-784-7184; Fax: 517-783-2571.

St. Michael's School Endowment Fund Policy (St. Michael School, Grand Ledge) Tel: 517-627-2167.

St. Paul's School Education Trust Fund (St. Paul Parish, Owosso) Tel: 517-723-4277; Fax: 517-723-9503.

St. Pius X Church Educational Trust Fund (St. Pius X Church, Flint) Tel: 810-235-8574; Fax: 810-235-8580.

St. Robert Bellarmine/Fr. Charles Jacobs Educational Trust Fund (St.Robert Bellarmine Parish, Flushi Tel: 810-659-2501; Fax: 810-659-2564. (St. Robert Bellarmine Parish, Flushing)

St. Therese Educational Trust Fund (St. Therese Parish, Lansing) Tel: 517-487-3749; Fax: 517-487-3755.

St. Thomas Aquinas Educational Foundation Trust (St. Thomas Aquinas Parish, East Lansing) Tel: 517-351-7215; Fax: 517-351-7271.

St. Thomas Grade School Trust Agreement (St. Thomas the Apostle Parish, Ann Arbor) Tel: 734-761-8606; Fax: 734-997-8432.

St. Thomas Scholarship Trust for Father Gabriel Richard H.S. 517 Elizabeth St., Ann Arbor, 48104. Tel: 734-769-0911; Fax: 734-997-8432. Rev. Roger Prokop, Ex-oficio Trustee. (St. Thomas the Apostle Parish, Ann Arbor)

St. Patrick Parish Educational Trust Fund (St. Patrick Parish, Brighton) Tel: 810-229-9863; Fax: 810-220-0730.

St. Gerard Educational Trust Fund (St. Gerard Parish, Lansing) Tel: 517-323-2379; Fax: 517-886-1394.

Holy Redeemer Educational Trust Fund (Holy Redeemer Parish, Burton) Tel: 810-743-3050; Fax: 810-743-4381.

[O] MISCELLANEOUS LISTINGS

LANSING. *Catholic Lawyers Guild*, 219 Seymour St., 48933. Tel: 517-484-5331; Fax: 517-484-0475.

Diocesan Service Committee (Catholic Charismatic Renewal) , 835 Maycroft Rd., 48917. Tel: 517-321-8661. Email: rstamford@hotmail.com. Rev. William Ashbaugh, Bishop's Liaison, St. Joseph, Howell; Ralph Stamford, Assoc. Liaison & Treas.; Patricia Stamford, Sec. Communications & Assoc. Liaison; Jack Karr, Representative to Michigan Svc. Committee.

Liturgical Commission Publishings, 1500 E. Saginaw, Ste. #1, 48906. Tel: 517-484-4449; Fax: 517-484-8880. Email: litcom@worldnet.att.net. Web: www.liturgicalcommission.org. Mary Jo Gillilland, Editor.

Michigan Catholic Conference, 510 S. Capitol Ave., 48933. Tel: 517-372-9310; Fax: 517-372-3940. Email: srmonica@micatholicconference.org. Web: www.micatholicconference.org. Sr. Monica Kostielney, R.S.M., Pres. & CEO.

ADRIAN. *Adrian Dominican Montessori Teacher Education Institute*, 1257 E. Siena Heights Dr., 49221. Tel: 517-266-3415; Fax: 517-266-3545. Email: admtei@tc3net.com. Web: www.tc3net.com/admtei. Sr. Anthonita Porta, O.P., Dir.

ANN ARBOR. *Alma Redemptoris Mater*, 331 Thompson St., 48104-2295. Tel: 734-663-0557; Fax: 734-663-2756. Email: tmf@umich.edu. Rev. Thomas M. Firestone, Contact Person.

Catholic Men's Movement, P.O. Box 466, 48106. Tel: 734-930-4524; Fax: 734-930-3101. Email: cmmdesk@catholic-men.org. Web: www.catholic-men.org. Rev. Patrick Egan, Chap. Tel: 734-930-3246; Bob Roleke, Admin. Tel: 734-930-4524.

The Marnee and John DeVine Foundation Philanthropic arm for CSS of Washtenaw County. , 4925 Packard, 48108. Tel: 734-971-9781; Fax: 734-971-2730. Email: jwisniew@csswashtenaw.org. Web: www.csswashtenaw.org. Jan Wisniewski, Contact Person.

Renewal Ministries Inc., 230 Collingwood Blvd., Ste. 250, 48103. Tel: 734-662-1730; Fax: 734-662-4697. Email: gseromik@renewalministries.net. Web: www.renewalministries.net. Ralph Martin, Pres. Total Staff 13.

BROOKLYN. *Oblate Fathers of St. Francis De Sales, Inc.*, 1124 Ventura Dr., 49230. Tel: 517-592-8218; Fax: 517-592-8218. Email: mckenna@desales.org. Web: www.desales.org. Total in Residence 5.

GRASS LAKE. *The Pious Union of St. Joseph*, 971 E. Michigan Ave., 49240-9210. Tel: 517-522-8017 (Voice/TDD); Fax: 517-522-8387. Email: PiousUnion@stjosephpiousunion.org. Web: www.stjosephpiousunion.org.

"Now and at the Hour" Magazine: Tel: 517-522-8017; Fax: 517-522-8387. Revs. Germano Pegoraro, S.C., Dir. Emeritus; Matthew Weber, S.C., Dir. & Admin.

RELIGIOUS INSTITUTES OF MEN REPRESENTED IN THE DIOCESE

For further details refer to the corresponding bracketed number in the Religious Institutes of Men or Women section.

[0140]—*The Augustinians*—O.S.A.
[0480]—*Conventual Franciscans*—O.F.M.Conv
[0920]—*Oblates of St. Francis de Sales*—O.S.F.S.
[1050]—*Pontifical Institute for Foreign Missions, Inc.*—P.I.M.E.
[1220]—*Servants of Charity*—S.C.

RELIGIOUS INSTITUTES OF WOMEN REPRESENTED IN THE DIOCESE

[1070-13]—*Dominican Sisters*—O.P.
[1070-14]—*Dominican Sisters* (Grand Rapids)—O.P.
[1170]—*Felician Sisters*—C.S.S.F.
[2575]—*Institute of the Sisters of Mercy of the Americas*—R.S.M.
[]—*Mexican Passionist Sisters*—C.F.P.
[3580]—*Servants of Mary*—O.S.M.
[0440]—*Sisters of Charity of Cincinnati, Ohio*—S.C.
[1560]—*Sisters of St. Francis of the Holy Eucharist*—O.S.F.
[3830-11]—*Sisters of St. Joseph*—S.S.J.
[3830]—*Sisters of St. Joseph*—C.S.J.
[2110]—*Sisters of the Humility of Mary*—H.M.
[2260]—*Sisters of the Lamb of God*—A.D.
[2350]—*Sisters of the Living Word*—S.L.W.
[3260]—*Sisters of the Precious Blood (Dayton, OH)*—C.PP.S.
[3320]—*Sisters of the Presentation of the Blessed Virgin Mary*
[2150]—*Sisters Servants of the Immaculate Heart of Mary*—I.H.M.

DIOCESAN CEMETERIES

LANSING. *St. Joseph*
FLINT. *New Calvary*

NECROLOGY

✠ Povish, Most Rev. Kenneth J., Retired Bishop of Lansing—Died Sept. 5, 2003
† Immel, Joseph, (Retired)—Died Oct. 22, 2003

Diocese of Laredo

Most Reverend

JAMES A. TAMAYO, D.D.

Bishop of Laredo; ordained June 11, 1976; appointed Titluar Bishop of Ita and Auxiliary Bishop of Galveston-Houston January 26, 1993; consecrated March 10, 1993; appointed first Bishop of Diocese of Laredo July 3, 2000; installed August 9, 2000 *Office: 1901 Corpus Christi St., Laredo, TX 78043*. Tel: 956-727-2140; Fax: 956-727-2777.

Chancery Office: 1901 Corpus Christi St., Laredo, TX 78043. Tel: 956-727-2140; Fax: 956-727-2777*P.O. Box 2247, Laredo, TX 78044*

ESTABLISHED JULY 3, 2000.

Square Miles 10,905.

Comprises the Counties of Webb, Zapata, Jim Hogg, La Salle, Maverick, Zavala and Dimmitt.

STATISTICAL OVERVIEW

Personnel	
Bishop	1
Priests: Diocesan Active in Diocese	24
Priests: Diocesan Active Outside Diocese	1
Priests: Retired, Sick or Absent	1
Number of Diocesan Priests	26
Religious Priests in Diocese	25
Total Priests in Diocese	51
Extern Priests in Diocese	9
Permanent Deacons in Diocese	27
Total Brothers	8
Total Sisters	76
Parishes	
Parishes	32
With Resident Pastor:	
Resident Diocesan Priests	20
Resident Religious Priests	12
Missions	20
Professional Ministry Personnel:	
Brothers	7
Sisters	66
Lay Ministers	7
Welfare	
Catholic Hospitals	1
Total Assisted	140,000
Residential Care of Children	1
Total Assisted	65
Specialized Homes	1
Total Assisted	663
Special Centers for Social Services	3
Total Assisted	362,284
Educational	
Diocesan Students in Other Seminaries	7
Total Seminarians	7
High Schools, Diocesan and Parish	1
Total Students	650
Elementary Schools, Diocesan and Parish	5
Total Students	956
Elementary Schools, Private	1
Total Students	560
Catechesis/Religious Education:	
High School Students	1,575
Elementary Students	6,410
Total Students under Catholic Instruction	10,158
Teachers in the Diocese:	
Brothers	1
Sisters	8
Lay Teachers	143
Vital Statistics	
Receptions into the Church:	
Infant Baptism Totals	3,388
Adult Baptism Totals	126
Received into Full Communion	52
First Communions	3,357
Confirmations	502
Marriages:	
Catholic	415
Interfaith	19
Total Marriages	434
Deaths	1,097
Total Catholic Population	222,250
Total Population	302,196

Chancery—1901 Corpus Christi St., Laredo, 78043. Tel: 956-727-2140; Fax: 956-727-2777. *Mailing Address, P.O. Box 2247, Laredo, 78044*.

Vicar General—Rev. Msgr. STANLEY A. SLIWIAK, V.G., Ph.D., Blessed Sacrament, 2219 Galveston St., Laredo, 78043. Tel: 956-722-1231; Fax: 956-722-2823.

Chancellor—Bro. JOHN A. ALLEN, F.M.S., 1901 Corpus Christi St., Laredo, 78043. Tel: 956-727-2140; Fax: 956-753-7762.

Tribunal—Sr. MARY WALDEN, O.S.U., Dir., 1901 Corpus Christi St., Laredo, 78043. Tel: 956-727-2140; Fax: 956-712-1343.

Fiscal Officer—PATRICIA GUAJARDO, 1901 Corpus Christi St., Laredo, 78043. Tel: 956-727-2140; Fax: 956-523-0828.

Presbyteral Council—Rev. Msgrs. STANLEY A. SLIWIAK, V.G., Ph.D.; THOMAS A. DAVIS; Revs. P. NOLASCO HINOJOSA JR., Chm.; NOEL DAVIS, Vice Chm.; DANIEL RAMIREZ-PORTUGAL; JOSE M. GUEVARA; Rev. Msgr. ALEJANDRO SALAZAR; Revs. SALVADOR PEDROZA; R. ANTHONY MENDOZA; TORIBIO C. GUERRERO; JOSE L. BALDERAS; WOJCIECH KOSOWICZ; LEONARDO HEREDIA, O.F.M.

College of Consultors—Most Rev. JAMES A. TAMAYO, D.D., Chm.; Rev. Msgrs. STANLEY A. SLIWIAK, V.G., Ph.D.; THOMAS A. DAVIS; Revs. JOSE M. GUEVARA; RICHARD GUERRA, O.M.I.; Rev. Msgr. ALEJANDRO SALAZAR; Rev. P. NOLASCO HINOJOSA JR.

Diocesan Offices and Directors

Campus Ministry— Brothers of St. John, Texas A&M International University

Laredo Catholic Communications, Inc.—BENNETT MCBRIDE, Exec. Vice Pres. & Gen. Mgr.; JOSE A. JIMENEZ, Chief Radio Operator/KHOY; MARIO SEPULVEDA, Part-time Radio Operator; GREGORIO M. LOPEZ, Editor, La Fe Magazine, 1901 Corpus Christi St., Laredo, 78043. Tel: 956-722-4167; Fax: 956-722-4464. Email: KHOY@khoy.org. Web: www.khoy.org.

Catholic Sharing Appeal—CORDELIA ALVARADO, 1901 Corpus Christi St., Laredo, 78043. Tel: 956-727-2140; Fax: 956-523-0828.

Catholic Social Services of Laredo, Inc.—ROXANNA GUERRA, Exec. Dir.; VALERIE SOTO, Office Mgr., 1103 Corpus Christi St., Laredo, 78043. Tel: 956-722-2443; Fax: 956-725-2238.

Adoption Services—SARA THOMPSON. Tel: 956-722-2443.

Emergency Assistance Program—ELIDA GARCIA. Tel: 956-722-2443.

Immigration Services—DANIEL MARTINEZ, Servicios Para Inmigrantes, 1103 Corpus Christi St., Laredo, 78043. Tel: 956-722-2443.

Catholic Cemetery—ROSA ALDAPE, Mgr., 3600 McPherson, P.O. Box 2366, Laredo, 78040. Tel: 956-723-6811; Fax: 956-723-8726.

Charismatic Renewal—Rev. MICHAEL DELEON, Liaison; Deacon ANASTACIO BERNAL. Tel: 956-726-0210; Fax: 956-726-1286.

Cursillo Movement—Rev. PATRICIO DOMINGUEZ, O.M.I., Spiritual Dir.; Bro. JOSEPH E. HERRERA, F.M.S., Young Adults; MARGARITA G. ELIZONDO, Pres. Diocesan Secretariat. Tel: 956-723-3850; Fax: 956-725-6544.

La Frontera Shelter for Battered and Homeless Women—HILARIA DELEON, Night Attendant; CARMEN RENDON, Legal Advocate & Public Rels.; SAN JUANA ARREDONDO, Case Worker; LAURA SALINAS, Program Coord.; SILVIA SANTANA-MEIJA, Outreach Worker; VALERIA SOTO, Office Mgr. Tel: 956-717-7888; Fax: 956-712-0629.

Finance Council—J. PAT HEARN, Chm.; SABAS ZAPATA III; PATRICIA G. GUAJARDO, Fiscal Officer; Bro. JOHN A. ALLEN, F.M.S.; Rev. Msgr. STANLEY SLIWIAK, Ph.D., V.G.; ARMENGOL GUERRA; Rev. P. NOLASCO HINOJOSA JR.; MAR MARTINEZ; HECTOR J. CERNA; LARRY B. MARTIN.

Human Resources—NANETTE DION, 1901 Corpus Christi St., Laredo, 78043. Tel: 956-727-2140; Fax: 956-523-0828.

Natural Family Planning and Understanding Sexuality Instructors—MARICELA HERNANDEZ, Eagle Pass; HELEN MASSEY, Laredo.

Natural Family Planning and Understanding Sexuality—MARIA LOURDES "LULU" SANCHEZ, Instructor & Diocesan Nurse. Tel: 956-727-2140; Fax: 956-753-7762.

Religious Education for Children—Sr. MARIA GUADALUPE HERRERA, R.S.M., Dir.; YOLANDA MOLINA, Program Coord., 1901 Corpus Christi St., Laredo, 78043. Tel: 956-722-0959; Fax: 956-722-0980.

Religious Education for Adults—Mr. REYNALDO MONTEMAYOR, Dir., 1901 Corpus Christi St., Laredo, 78043. Tel: 956-727-2140; Fax: 956-753-7762.

Office of Respect Life—Rev. R. ANTHONY MENDOZA, Dir., St. Joseph Church, P.O. Box 436, La Pryor, 78872-0436. Tel: 830-365-4107; Fax: 830-365-9367.

Persons with Disabilities—MARY MACIAS, Program Coord., 102 W. Hillside Rd., Laredo, 78041. Tel: 956-724-9924; Fax: 956-753-7762.

Priests Personnel Board—Revs. NOEL DAVIS; DANIEL RAMIREZ-PORTUGAL, Sec.; SALVADOR PEDROZA; JOSE LUIS BALDERAS; Rev. Msgr. STANLEY SLIWIAK, Ph.D., V.G.

Victim Assistance Coordinator—Bro. JOHN A. ALLEN, F.M.S. Tel: 956-727-2140. Email: chancellor@dioceseoflaredo.org.

Vocation Office—Rev. TORIBIO C. GUERRERO, Dir., Immaculate Conception Church, P.O. Box 8, Asherton, 78827-0008. Tel: 830-468-3343; Fax: 830-468-3342.

Other Offices and Organizations

Birthright Counseling—ROXANNA GUERRA, Admin, 1103 Corpus Christi St., Laredo, 78043.

Catholic Daughters of the Americas—DOLLY PENA, District 15: Laredo. Tel: 956-723-6792.

Legion of Mary—Mr. MANUEL GARCIA, Laredo Area Contact. Tel: 956-723-4333.

CLERGY, PARISHES, MISSIONS AND PAROCHIAL SCHOOLS

CITY OF LAREDO

(WEBB COUNTY)

1—SAN AGUSTIN CATHEDRAL (1762), (Hispanic), Rev. Jacinto Olguin (VIC); Deacon Miguel Vallarta.
200 San Agustin Ave., 78040. Tel: 956-722-1382; Fax: 956-722-0441.
Parish Office: 214 San Bernardo Ave., 78040.
Catechesis/Religious Program—Students 210.

2—BLESSED SACRAMENT (1950), (Hispanic), Rev. Msgr. Stanley A. Sliwak, Ph.D.; Revs. Wojcielh Przystasz (Poland); Alessandro DiTaddeo (Retired); Deacons David Vargas; Larry Sandlin.
2219 Galveston St., 78043. Tel: 956-722-1231; Fax: 956-722-2823.
Catechesis/Religious Program—Students 147.

3—SAN CARLOS MISSION, Rev. Jorge Krzywda, Admin.
109 N. Meadow Ave., 78040. Tel: 956-723-4172; Fax: 956-728-8824.

4—CHRIST THE KING (1954), Rev. Jose Luis Balderas.
1105 Tilden Ave., 78040. Tel: 956-723-4267; Fax: 956-791-8034.
Catechesis/Religious Program—Tel: 956-722-7821. Students 180.

5—DIVINE MERCY (1998), Rev. Michael De Leon.
Parish Office: 9350 Amber Ave., 78045. Tel: 956-726-9972; Fax: 956-726-1286.
Catechesis/Religious Program—Students 177.

6—ST. FRANCES CABRINI (1958), (Hispanic), Rev. Jose Alfredo Gaytan, S.O.L.T.
3018 Davis Ave., 78040. Tel: 956-722-2919; Fax: 956-724-5232.
Catechesis/Religious Program—Tel: 956-722-8315; Fax: 956-724-5232. Students 165.

7—HOLY FAMILY (1984), (Hispanic), Rev. P. Nolasco Hinojosa Jr.
2705 McPherson, 78040. Tel: 956-724-6881; Fax: 956-724-5581.
Catechesis/Religious Program—Tel: 956-724-5581. Students 110.

8—HOLY REDEEMER (1940), (Hispanic), [JC] Revs. Paulo Aguilar-Ramirez, O.S.A.; Alberto Palmeno, O.S.A.; Deacon Edmundo Lopez.
Mailing Address: P.O. Box 1087, 78040. 1602 Garcia St., 78040. Tel: 956-723-7171; Fax: 956-723-7194.
Mission—Santa Cruz 2002 Lee Ave., Webb Co. 78042.
Catechesis/Religious Program—Students 170.

9—ST. JOHN NEUMANN (1979), Revs. Daniel Ramirez-Portugal (Portugal); Agustin Escalante; Deacon Gerardo Morales.
102 W. Hillside Rd., 78041. Tel: 956-726-9488; Fax: 956-726-0540.
Catechesis/Religious Program—Students 158.

10—ST. JOSEPH (1953), Revs. Jozef Glabinski; Janusz Glabinski; Deacon Crispin O. Soto.
109 N. Meadow, 78040. Tel: 956-723-4172; Fax: 956-728-8824.
Catechesis/Religious Program—Tel: 956-791-6664; Fax: 956-728-8824. Students 159.

11—ST. JUDE (1984), Rev. Santiago Domingo.
Mailing Address: P.O. Box 440502, 78044-0502. Tel: 956-726-6318. 2031 Lowry Rd., 78044-0502. Tel: 956-722-2280; Fax: 956-726-8017.
Catechesis/Religious Program—Tel: 956-722-3717. Students 321.

12—NUESTRA SENORA DEL ROSARIO INDEPENDENT MISSION (2000), Rev. Jan Ziemniak, Admin.
420 Sierra Vista Blvd., 78046. Tel: 956-753-8764; Fax: 956-753-9972.

13—OUR LADY OF GUADALUPE (1926), Revs. Edward Ward, O.M.I.; Edward Vrazel, O.M.I.
Mailing Address: P.O. Box 671, 78042. 1718 San Jorge Ave., 78042. Tel: 956-723-6954; Fax: 956-723-6047.
Catechesis/Religious Program—Students 182.

14—ST. PATRICK (1970), Rev. Msgr. Thomas A. Davis.
555 E. Del Mar Blvd., 78041. Tel: 956-722-6215; Fax: 956-722-6266.
Catechesis/Religious Program—Tel: 956-722-8451. Students 769.
Mission—Apostolate Missions in Northern Mexico

15—ST. PETER THE APOSTLE (1897), Rev. Wojciech Kosowicz, Ph.D.
Mailing Address: P.O. Box 26, 78040. 1502 Matamoros St., 78040. Tel: 956-723-6301; Fax: 956-729-1229.
Catechesis/Religious Program—Students 24.

16—SAGRADO CORAZON DE JESUS MISSION, Rev. Stanley Bieniek.
Mailing Address: P.O. Box 26, 78040-0026. Tel: 956-723-6301; Fax: 956-729-1229.

17—SAN FRANCISCO JAVIER INDEPENDENT MISSION (1966), (Hispanic), Rev. Patricio G. Dominguez, O.M.I.; Deacon Jorge Garza.
Mailing Address: P.O. Box 1175, 78042-1175. 2502 Zaragoza St., 78042-1175. Tel: 956-723-3850; Fax: 956-725-6544.

18—SAN LUIS REY (1958), (Hispanic), Revs. Juan Francisco Munoz, S.D.B.; Thomas Juarez, S.D.B., Vicar.
Mailing Address: P.O. Box 2294, 78044-2294. 3502 Sanders Ave., 78044-2294. Tel: 956-723-6587; Fax: 956-723-6825.
Catechesis/Religious Program—Tel: 956-722-3323. Students 210.

19—SAN MARTIN DE PORRES (1979), (Hispanic), Rev. Msgr. Alejandro Salazar; Deacon Leonel San Miguel.
Mailing Address: P.O. Box 2666, 78044-2666. 1704 Sandman, 78044-2666. Tel: 956-723-5215; Fax: 956-723-9443.
Catechesis/Religious Program—Tel: 956-725-2440. Students 389.

20—SANTA MARGARITA DE ESCOCIA (1991), (Mexican), Rev. Alirio Corrales.
320 Segovia Dr., 78043. Tel: 956-724-9669; Fax: 956-791-2167.
Catechesis/Religious Program—Students 154.

21—SANTO NINO (1985), (Hispanic), Rev. Noel Davis.
2717 Cross St., 78046. Tel: 956-724-6638; Fax: 956-712-8096.
Catechesis/Religious Program—Students 224.

22—SANTA TERISITA MISSION, Rev. Jorge Krzywda, Admin.
109 N. Meadow Ave., 78040. Tel: 956-723-4172; Fax: 956-728-8824.

23—ST. VINCENT DE PAUL (1969), (Hispanic), Rev. Pastor Martinez, O.S.A.
2710 Boulanger St., 78043. Tel: 956-722-3034; Fax: 956-722-4829.
Catechesis/Religious Program—Tel: 956-726-4134. Students 350.

OUTSIDE THE CITY OF LAREDO

ASHERTON, DIMMIT CO., IMMACULATE CONCEPTION (1918), (Hispanic), Rev. Toribio C. Guerrero; Deacons Genaro Ramon; Juan Sauceda.
Mailing Address: P.O. Box 8, 78827. Tel: 830-468-3343; Fax: 830-468-3342.
Mission—St. Michael P.O. Box 266, Big Wells, Dimmit Co. 78830-0266. Tel: 830-457-2698; Fax: 830-468-3342.
Mission—St. Henry P.O. Box 15, Catarina, Dimmit Co. 78836. Tel: 830-468-3343; Fax: 830-468-3342.
Catechesis/Religious Program—Students 200.

CARRIZO SPRINGS, DIMMIT CO., OUR LADY OF GUADALUPE (1881), Rev. Salvador Pedroza; Deacon Jose F. Perez.
1003 N. 6th St., 78834. Tel: 830-876-2239; Fax: 830-876-5023.
Catechesis/Religious Program—Fax: 830-876-5023. Estela Martinez, D.R.E. Students 421.

COTULLA, LA SALLE CO., SACRED HEART (1917), (Hispanic), [JC] Rev. John Van Lare, C.M.; Deacon Jose Patterson.
Mailing Address: P.O. Box 560, 78014. Tel: 830-879-2658.
Catechesis/Religious Program—Tel: 930-879-3196. Students 150
Mission—Our Lady of Guadalupe Millett, La Salle Co.

CRYSTAL CITY, ZAVALA CO., SACRED HEART (1917), (Hispanic), Rev. Jose Maria Guevara; Deacon Jose L. Lopez.
115 E. Kinney St., 78839. Tel: 830-374-3143; Fax: 830-374-2211.
Catechesis/Religious Program—Tel: 830-374-5547. Students 216.

EAGLE PASS, MAVERICK CO.

1—ST. JOSEPH (1967), (Hispanic), Rev. Alfonso Gioppato, O.M.I.
Mailing Address: 800 Comal St., 78852-4029. Tel: 830-773-6114; Fax: 830-773-6608.
Catechesis/Religious Program—Tel: 830-773-6515; Fax: 830-773-6608. Students 336.

2—OUR LADY OF REFUGE (1859), Revs. James A. Loiacono, O.M.I.; Phillip Wagner, O.M.I.; Deacons Efren Maldonado; Miguel Velez.
Mailing Address: P.O. Box 909, 78853-0909. 810 Ceylon St., 78853-0909. Tel: 830-773-8451 (Office); 830-773-8421 (Res.).
Mission—Our Lady of Lourdes Seco Mines, Maverick Co. Tel: 830-773-8288.
Mission—Our Lady of Guadalupe Quemado, Maverick Co. Tel: 830-758-1888.
Catechesis/Religious Program—Tel: 830-773-8915. Students 544.

3—SACRED HEART (1966), (Hispanic), Revs. Richard Guerra, O.M.I.; Alberto Arreola, O.M.I; Roberto Pena, O.M.I.; Deacons Manuel Rene Cardona; Leandro Contreras Jr.; Hector Ricardo Martinez.
Mailing Address: P.O. Box 806, 78853-0806. Tel: 830-773-2451; Fax: 830-773-0643.
Catechesis/Religious Program—Tel: 830-773-5013. Students 903.

ENCINAL, LA SALLE CO., IMMACULATE HEART OF MARY (1898), (Hispanic), Rev. P. Nolasco Hinojosa Jr.
Mailing Address: P.O. Box 5, 78019-0005. 400 Santa Fe St., 78019-0005. Tel: 956-948-5328; Fax: 956-948-5328.
Catechesis/Religious Program—Students 50.

HEBBRONVILLE, JIM HOGG CO., OUR LADY OF GUADALUPE (1926), Revs. Oscar Villalobos; Silvestre Rodriguez, O.F.M.; Christian Sell, O.F.M.; Rodrigo Barba.
504 E. Santa Clara St., 78361. Tel: 361-527-3865; Fax: 361-527-5548.
Mission—St. Agnes Mirando City, Jim Hogg Co.
Mission—St. Bridget Oilton, Jim Hogg Co.
Mission—Sacred Heart Realitos, Duval Co.
Mission—Sacred Heart Bruni, Jim Hogg Co.
Catechesis/Religious Program—Tel: 361-527-3309; Fax: 361-527-5548. Students 310.

LA PRYOR, ZAVALA CO., ST. JOSEPH (1917), Rev. R. Anthony Mendoza; Deacons Gene Corrigan; Juan Gallegos.
Mailing Address: P.O. Box 436, 78872. Tel: 830-365-4107; Fax: 830-365-9367.
Mission—St. Patrick P.O. Box 83, Batesville, Zavala Co. 78829.
Catechesis/Religious Program—Students 175.

RIO BRAVO, WEBB CO., SANTA RITA DE CASIA INDEPENDENT MISSION (1986), Rev. Mariano Martinez.
1001 Espejo Molina, 78043. Tel: 956-725-7215; Fax: 956-728-8539.
Catechesis/Religious Program—Students 204.
Mission—Santa Monica Mission 507 Morales (El Cenizo), Webb Co. 78043.

ZAPATA, ZAPATA CO., OUR LADY OF LOURDES (1940), Revs. Arturo Rodriguez; Francisco J. Hernandez.
Mailing Address: P.O. Box 3213, 78076.
Res.: 1609 Glenn St., 78076. Tel: 956-765-4216; Fax: 956-765-6188.
Catechesis/Religious Program—Students 200.
Mission—Ntra. Sra. Del Refugio P.O. Box 3213, Zapata Co. 78076.
Mission—St. Ignatius San Ignacio, Zapata Co.
Mission—San Pedro Lopeno, Zapata Co.
Mission—Santa Ana Falcon, Zapata Co.

Chaplains of Public Institutions

LAREDO. *Webb County Jail*, 4402 Tilden Ave., 78041. Tel: 956-723-5029. Deacon Jose Rodriguez.
Chaplaincy Apostolate to Refugees & Jail Ministry.

INSTITUTIONS LOCATED IN THE DIOCESE

[A] HIGH SCHOOLS

LAREDO. *St. Augustine High School* (Diocesan) , 1300 Galveston St., 78040. Tel: 956-724-8131; Fax: 956-725-9241. Email: principal@st-augustine.org. Web: st-augustine.org. Sr. Carol Mucha, R.S.M., Prin. Brothers 1; Lay Teachers 35; Students 650.

[B] JUNIOR HIGH AND ELEMENTARY SCHOOLS

LAREDO. *St. Augustine (Elementary School)* (Diocesan) , 1300 Galveston St., 78040. Tel: 956-724-1176; Fax: 956-725-9891. Email: ogentry@st-augustine.org. Web: www.st-augustine.org. Mrs. Olga Gentry, Prin. Lay Teachers 14; Students 240.

Blessed Sacrament, 1501 N. Bartlett St., 78043. Tel: 956-722-1222 Fax: 956-722-5635. Email: school@lmtonline.com cngarcia@blessedsacramentlaredo.org. Mrs. Claudia N. Garcia-Garcia, Prin. Lay Teachers 8; Students 102.

Mary Help of Christians (Private) , 10 E. Del Mar Blvd., 78045. Tel: 956-722-3966; Fax: 956-722-1413. Web: mhsoul.org. Sr. Suzanne Miller, F.M.A., Prin. Sisters 8; Lay Teachers 52; Students 560.

Our Lady of Guadalupe (Parochial) , 400 Callaghan St., 78040-3834. Tel: 956-722-3915; Fax: 956-727-2840. Email: eduardoperales@hotmail.com. Mr. Eduardo Perales, Prin. Sisters 1; Lay Teachers 8; Students 106.

St. Peter Memorial (Diocesan) , 1519 Houston St., P.O. Box 520, 78040. Tel: 956-723-6302; Fax: 956-725-2671. Mrs. Olga R. Ayala, Prin. Sisters 1; Lay Teachers 7; Students 130.

EAGLE PASS. *Our Lady of Refuge*, 577 Washington, 78852. Tel: 830-773-3531; Fax: 830-773-7310. Email: olorschool@msn.com. Sr. Christina M. Conroy, C.S.S.F., Prin. Sisters 2; Lay Teachers 22; Students 378.

[C] ORPHANAGES AND INFANT HOMES

LAREDO. *Sacred Heart Children's Home*, 3310 S.

Zapata Hwy., 78046. Tel: 956-723-3343; Fax: 956-723-3409. Sisters Maria Isidra Valdez, S.S.H.J.P., Supr.; Maria Teresa Grajeda, Admin. Sisters 19; Children 61.

[D] MONASTERIES AND RESIDENCES OF PRIESTS AND BROTHERS

LAREDO. *St. John Priory, F.J.* Congregation of St. John , 505 Century Dr., South, 78046. Tel: 956-722-3399; Fax: 956-722-3299. Email: stjohn@laredo.globalpc.net. Web: www.stjean.com/laredo/hsrc/holy.htm. Revs. Thomas Joachim, F.J., Prior; Marie Joseph Weyne; John Jesus Moloney (LA); Bros. Isaiah Viotte, F.J., Vicar; Louis-Mary Ketterhagen, F.J.; Alexandfe Marie de la Taille; Dominic-Savio Dumalet; Lawrence Therese Ettinger; Joseph Francis Hoffman, F.J. Priests 3; Brothers 5; Deacons 2; Total in Residence 10.

Marist Brothers, 1511 E. Cherry Hill Dr., 78041-3807. Tel: 956-724-2651; Fax: 956-724-1963. Email: fmslaredo@prodigy.net. Bros. Philip R. Degagne, F.M.S.; Joseph E. Herrera, F.M.S.; Thomas W. Coyne, F.M.S., Dir.; John A. Allen, F.M.S. Marist Brothers 4.

[E] CONVENTS AND RESIDENCES FOR SISTERS

LAREDO. *Eucharistic Missionary Society*, 1101 Cortez St., 78040. Tel: 956-726-4085; Fax: 956-726-4085. Email: mesoc@laredo.globalpc.net. Sr. Maria Manuela Susana Pedroza, E.M.S.

Mary Help of Christians Convent, 10 E. Del Mar Blvd., 78045. Tel: 956-791-8617; Fax: 956-712-2191. Email: smartina@fmasuol.org. Web: www.mhsoul.org. Sr. Suzanne Miller, F.M.A., Supr. Daughters of Mary Help of Christians (Salesian Sisters) Sisters 8.

Sacred Heart Children's Home Convent, 3310 S. Zapata Hwy., 78046. Tel: 956-723-3343; Fax: 956-723-3409. Sr. Maria Isidra Valdez, S.S.H.J.P., Supr. Servants of the Sacred Heart of Jesus and of the Poor. Sisters 19.

Sisters of Mercy Convent, 1002 Chihuahua St., 78040-5204. Tel: 956-523-0840. Email: oobregon@laredo.mercy.net sobregon@stx.rr.com liro01@awesomenet.net. Sr. Olivia M. Obregon, Contact Person. Sisters 2.

Sisters of Our Lady of the Most Holy Trinity, 2454 Colonia Loop, 78046. Tel: 956-727-3965. Sisters Leticia Venegas, S.O.L.T., Supr.; Lourdes Venegas, S.O.L.T.

Sisters of St. John, 504 Century Dr., S., 78046. Tel: 956-727-1028; Fax: 956-727-1028. Sisters Laetitia Kremer, Local Supr.; Belinda Mary Cabellero. Total in Residence 5.

Sisters of St. Joseph of Lyons, 1415 N. Jarvis Ave., 78043. Tel: 956-723-8968; Fax: 956-723-4322. Email: mailstation.com. Sr. Aline Roy, C.S.J.

Ursuline Sisters, 2302 Corpus Christi St., 78043. Tel: 956-723-9185; Fax: 956-723-4322. Email: laredoosu@juno.com. Sr. Marianne Mullen, O.S.U., Prioress. Sisters 8.

Roman Union Central Province of the U.S., 1415 N. Jarvis Ave., 78043. Tel: 956-723-8968; Fax: 956-723-4322.

EAGLE PASS. *Benedictine Sisters*, 779 Encinal Dr., 78852. Tel: 830-758-0812.

Felician Sisters, 2250 Maria Del Refugio, 78852. Email: cssfeptx@xramp.net.

Missionary Sisters of Our Lady of Perpetual Help, 895 Webster, 78852. Tel: 830-773-8915; Fax: 830-773-8915. Sisters Teresita Vasquez, M.P.S., Supr.; Caritina Olmos, M.P.S.; Rosa Maria Benarides, M.P.S.

ZAPATA. *Misioneras del Rosario de Fatima*, P.O. Box 3213, 78076. Tel: 956-765-4216; Fax: 956-765-6188. Sisters 2.

[F] RETREAT HOUSES

LAREDO. *Holy Spirit Retreat and Conference Center*, 501 Century Dr., S., 78046. Tel: 956-726-4352; Fax: 956-726-4363. Email: stjohn@laredo.globalpc.net. Web: www.stjean.com/laredo/hsrc/holy.htm. Rev. Thomas Joachim, F.J., Prior; Bros. Alexander Mane de la Tuille, Vicar; Dominic Savio Dumalet, Accountant; Isaie Viotte, Guest Master; Linda Righter, Mgr.; Elizabeth J. Hale, Bookkeeper.

[G] MISCELLANEOUS

LAREDO. *St. Augustine School Endowment Fund, Inc.*, 1300 Galveston, 78040. Tel: 956-724-8131; Fax: 956-725-9241. Email: principal@st_augustine.org. Web: www.st_augustine.org. Sr. Carol Mucha, R.S.M., Prin.

Bethany House, 819 Hidalgo St., 78040. Tel: 956-722-4152; Fax: 956-791-1102. Email: gbkazen@sbcglobal.net. Web: bethanyhouseoflaredo.org. Barbara Kazen, Pres.

Casa de Misericordia Domestic Violence Shelter for Women and Children , P.O. Box 430175, 78044. Tel: 956-712-9590; 877-782-2722; Fax: 956-791-1364. Email: pcramos2000@yahoo.com. Sr. Rosemary Welsh, R.S.M., Exec. Dir.

Casa Frontera, 1103 Corpus Christi St., 78040. Tel: 956-727-7888 (hotline); Fax: 956-712-0629. Email: csslaredo@hotmail.com. Roxanna Guerra, Admin.

Diocese of Laredo Deposit and Loan Fund, Inc., 1901 Corpus Christi St., 78043. Tel: 956-727-2140; Fax: 956-523-0828.

Diocese of Perpetual Benefit Endowment Fund, Inc., 1901 Corpus Christi St., 78043. Tel: 956-727-2140; Fax: 956-523-0828.

International Order of the Alhambras-Zahara Caravan No. 64, P.O. Box 451, 78042-0451. Tel: 956-722-2505. 2601 E. Plum, 78043. His Eminence Rafael Garcia, Grand Commander.

Mercy Ministries of Laredo, 2500 Zacatecas, 78046. Tel: 956-718-6810. Daniel Fiuevora, CEO.

San Agustin Historical Preservation & Restoration Society, Inc., 201 San Agustin Ave., 78040. Tel: 956-722-1382; Fax: 956-722-0441. Email: sanagustin@surfus.net. Deacon Miguel Vallarta, Contact Person.

NECROLOGY

(No Deaths)

Diocese of Las Cruces

(Dioecesis Las Cruces)

Most Reverend

RICARDO RAMIREZ, C.S.B., D.D.

Bishop of Las Cruces; ordained December 10, 1966; appointed Titular Bishop of Vatarba and Auxiliary of San Antonio October 27, 1981; consecrated December 6, 1981; appointed First Bishop of Las Cruces August 31, 1982; installed October 18, 1982 *Res.: 455 W. Palmer Rd., Las Cruces, NM 88005.*

The Pastoral Center: 1280 Med Park Dr., Las Cruces, NM 88005. Tel: 505-523-7577; Fax: 505-524-3874.

Web: www.zianet.com/diocese/

Email: diocese@zianet.com

ESTABLISHED OCTOBER 18, 1982.

Square Miles 44,483.

Comprises the Counties of Dona Ana, Hidalgo, Grant, Luna, Sierra, Otero, Lincoln, Chaves, Eddy and Lea in the State of New Mexico.

Legal Title: For legal titles of parishes and diocesan institutions, consult The Pastoral Center.

STATISTICAL OVERVIEW

Personnel	
Bishop	1
Priests: Diocesan Active in Diocese	16
Priests: Diocesan Active Outside Diocese	1
Priests: Retired, Sick or Absent	11
Number of Diocesan Priests	28
Religious Priests in Diocese	49
Total Priests in Diocese	77
Extern Priests in Diocese	7
Ordinations:	
Permanent Deacons	10
Permanent Deacons in Diocese	38
Total Brothers	6
Total Sisters	38
Parishes	
Parishes	44
With Resident Pastor:	
Resident Diocesan Priests	14
Resident Religious Priests	20
Without Resident Pastor:	
Administered by Priests	8
Administered by Deacons	2
Missions	47
Pastoral Centers	2
Professional Ministry Personnel:	
Brothers	2
Sisters	8
Lay Ministers	24
Welfare	
Health Care Centers	3
Total Assisted	35,000
Day Care Centers	3
Total Assisted	240
Special Centers for Social Services	1
Total Assisted	8,000
Educational	
Seminaries, Diocesan	1
Students from This Diocese	3
Diocesan Students in Other Seminaries	3
Total Seminarians	6
Elementary Schools, Diocesan and Parish	2
Total Students	142
Elementary Schools, Private	3
Total Students	383
Catechesis/Religious Education:	
High School Students	2,275
Elementary Students	7,741
Total Students under Catholic Instruction	10,547
Teachers in the Diocese:	
Sisters	3
Lay Teachers	36
Vital Statistics	
Receptions into the Church:	
Infant Baptism Totals	2,376
Adult Baptism Totals	206
Received into Full Communion	129
First Communions	2,401
Confirmations	1,588
Marriages:	
Catholic	324
Interfaith	57
Total Marriages	381
Deaths	1,123
Total Catholic Population	132,646
Total Population	498,308

The Pastoral Center—1280 Med Park Dr., Las Cruces, 88005. Tel: 505-523-7577; Fax: 505-524-3874. Office Hours: Mon.-Fri. 8:00-5:00

Bishops Administrative Council—Most Rev. RICARDO RAMIREZ, C.S.B., D.D.; Very Rev. Msgr. JOHN E. ANDERSON, V.G.; Rev. ROBERT POWER, C.S.B.; ELIZABETH ENNIS; DAVID MCNAMARA; RICHARD PETRILLO.

Vicar General—Very Rev. Msgr. JOHN E. ANDERSON, V.G.

Episcopal Vicar for Clergy and Personnel—Very Rev. Msgr. ROBERT L. GETZ.

Chancellor—ELIZABETH ENNIS.

Director of Clergy Personnel—Very Rev. Msgr. JOHN E. ANDERSON, V.G.

Diocesan Tribunal—Rev. JOHN S. WEBER, O.F.M.Conv., J.C.L., Judicial Vicar, 1280 Med Park Dr., Las Cruces, 88005.

Promoter of Justice—Rev. ENRIQUE LOPEZ.

Judges—Very Rev. GILES CARIE, O.F.M.Conv.; Revs. JOHN M. WILSON, C.S.B., J.C.L.; ENRIQUE LOPEZ-ESCALERA, J.C.L.; Deacon ALPHONSO F. BOWERS; Sr. CATHERINE C. DARCY, R.S.M., J.C.D.

Defenders of the Bond—Very Rev. Msgr. JOHN E. ANDERSON, V.G.; Revs. DAVID BERGS; RICHARD CATANACH; MICHAEL P. LINDSAY; NOEL KRAMER, O.F.M.Conv.

Administrative Director for Tribunal—IRENE PORTILLO.

Assesor—CHARLOTTE KINCH, Ph.D.

Advocates—IRENE PORTILLO; CHARLOTTE KINCH, Ph.D.

Notaries—IRENE V. PORTILLO; VELIA SALINAS; DOROTHY MEDINA.

Vicars—Revs. ROBERT POWER, C.S.B.; MARCOS REYNA; VALENTINE JANKOWSKI, O.F.M.Conv.; THOMAS DEVINE, O.A.R.; Rev. Msgr. ROBERT GETZ; Rev. DAVID BERGS.

Diocesan Consultors—Very Rev. Msgrs. JOHN E. ANDERSON, V.G.; ROBERT L. GETZ; Revs. ANDRES ALAVA, O.A.R.; DENNIS FOUNTAIN, O.F.M.Conv.; VALENTINE JANKOWSKI, O.F.M.Conv.; MICHAEL LINDSAY; RICHARD CATANACH; ART ROBERTS, C.S.B.

Presbyteral Council—Rev. DAVID BERGS, Pres.; Rev. Msgr. ROBERT GETZ, Vice Pres.; Revs. JOHN WEBER, O.F.M.Conv., J.C.L., Sec.; ENRIQUE LOPEZ; Very Rev. Msgr. JOHN E. ANDERSON, V.G.; Revs. WILLIAM MCCANN; MANUEL IBARRA; MARCOS REYNA; VALENTINE JANKOWSKI, O.F.M.Conv.; ANDY RILEY, P.I.M.E.; ED HERRERA; SEAN GARRITY, C.S.B.; DONALD ADAMSKI, O.F.M.Conv.; ROBERT POWER, C.S.B.; RUBEN ROMERO RUIZ; PAUL MURTAGH, SS.CC.; LARRY GOSSELIN, O.F.M.; BRYANT HAUSFELD, O.F.M.; THOMAS DEVINE, O.A.R.; LARRY SCHREIBER, O.F.M.

Clergy Personnel Board—Most Rev. RICARDO RAMIREZ, C.S.B.; Very Rev. Msgrs. JOHN E. ANDERSON, V.G.; ROBERT L. GETZ; Revs. ED HERRERA; RICHARD CATANACH; ENRIQUE LOPEZ; WILLIAM MCCANN; MARCOS REYNA; MANUEL IBARRA; DAVID BERGS; Deacon PETE VELOTT.

Priestly Life and Ministry Committee—Most Rev. RICARDO RAMIREZ, C.S.B.; Very Rev. Msgr. ROBERT L. GETZ; Revs. DAVID BERGS; RICHARD CATANACH; FRANKLIN EICHHORST, O.F.M.Cap; RICARDO HINOJAL, O.A.R.; VALENTINE JANKOWSKI, O.F.M.Conv.; MICHAEL LINDSAY; ROBERT POWER, C.S.B.

Pastoral Center Personnel Committee—ELIZABETH ENNIS; MAGGIE CANDIA; MARGARET FLORES; IRENE PORTILLO; DEBBIE ISHAM MOORE; SUSAN ROBERTS; PHILIP ALVAREZ.

Priests Retirement Fund Committee—Very Rev. Msgr. ROBERT L. GETZ; Revs. DAVID BERGS; MICHAEL LINDSAY; WILLIAM MCCANN; Mr. DANIEL DOLAN; FELIPE SALCIDO JR.

Permanent Deacon Council—Deacons JOHNNIE PEREZ; PABLO MERAIL; DANIEL CHECK, Chm.; JESUS FARELA; PETE VELOTT; BENJAMIN VIGIL; HECTOR SAMANIEGO.

Director of Deacons—Deacon PETE VELOTT.

Comptroller—FELIPE SALCIDO JR.

Finance Council—Most Rev. RICARDO RAMIREZ, C.S.B.; Very Rev. Msgr. JOHN E. ANDERSON, V.G.; Rev. DAVID BERGS; ELIZABETH ENNIS; CARLOS VIRAMONTES; Rev. BILL MCCANN; DAN DOLAN, Diocesan Attorney; RICHARD FORCE; GILBERT GOMEZ; HAROLD GRANDI; DAVID MCNAMARA; EDWARD PILLAR; FRED VERA; ALFRED PACHECO; Rev. JOHN WEBER, O.F.M.Conv., J.C.L.; SUSAN ROBERTS; FELIPE SALCIDO, Comptroller.

Office of Development, Stewardship and Foundation—SUSAN ROBERTS, Exec. Dir.; PATRICIA PADILLA-TORRES, Devel. Assoc.

Office of Insurance—MARTA ROMERO, Insurance Dir.

Office of Construction and Renovation—MANUEL LEYVA, Dir.

Diocesan Ministries Offices and Directors

Office of Education and Formation—DAVID MCNAMARA, Dir.

Office of Adult Catechesis—DAVID MCNAMARA, Dir.

Office of Vocations—Rev. ENRIQUE LOPEZ, Dir.

Casa San Juan Diego, House of Formation—Rev. ENRIQUE LOPEZ, Dir. Tel: 505-523-0783; 505-523-7577; Fax: 505-524-3874.

Art and Environment Committee—Sr. LUCY MEISSEN, C.PP.S.

Attorneys—DANIEL DOLAN; MIKE LILLEY; DAVID MCNEILL.

Campus Ministry—Revs. MITCHELL DOWALGO, C.S.B.; MARCOS REYNA.

Judicial Vicar—Rev. JOHN WEBER, O.F.M.Conv., J.C.L.

Office of Catholic Social Ministry—CARLOS CORRAL, Dir.; CLAUDIA MITCHELL, Assoc. Dir.

Colonias Development Council—DIANA BUSTAMANTE, Dir.

Office of Parish 2000—DAVID MCNAMARA, Dir.
Cursillo Secretariat—VICTOR RODRIGUEZ, Pres.; BLANCA LUNA, Treas.; VICENTE LUNA, Sec.
Office of Elementary Catechesis—MARY HELEN LLANEZ, Dir.
Lay Ministry Formation—DAVID MCNAMARA, Dir.
Ecumenical Liaison—RICHARD PETRILLO.
Hispanic Ministry—Rev. ROBERT POWER, C.S.B.
Holy Childhood Association—Very Rev. Msgr. JOHN E. ANDERSON, V.G.
Hospital Ministry—MINERVA ROMERO.
Office of Liturgical Education—Sr. LUCY MEISSEN, C.PP.S.
Propogation of the Faith—Very Rev. Msgr. JOHN E. ANDERSON, V.G.
Order of Christian Initiation—Sr. LUCY MEISSEN, C.PP.S., Adult; DAVID MCNAMARA, Children; ROMELIA ENRIQUEZ; ESTEBAN ROAL; SALLY HARPER.
Office of Adolescent Catechesis and Youth Ministry—Sr. LUCY MEISSEN, C.PP.S.
Diocesan Pastoral Council—Members: NONI CONTRERAS; VIRGINIA BELL, Vice Chm.; JESSE SANCHEZ; ROSE GALLEGOS; REY CHAVEZ; GEORGE CRUZ, Chm.; Rev. MARCOS REYNA; Deacon DON DICKMAN; Sr. ROBERT ANN HECKER, O.S.F.; ARTURO NAVARRETE; LESLIE WINGENROTH; Rev. DONALD ADAMSKI, O.F.M.Conv.; ALEX ESTRADA; PATSY GRANTER; CARLOS VIRAMONTES; JAN SETTLES; SUE KOEPP; MARY SALAZAR-HIGHTOWER; JOHN SCHAFFER; LOU ROMAN.
Office of Pastoral Planning and Outreach—RICHARD PETRILLO, Dir.
Diocesan Resource Center—DAVID MCNAMARA, Coord.; DOLORES DIAZ, Librarian.
Diocesan Archives—JOANNA HARMON, Archivist.
Charismatic Renewal Liaisons—LEO MARRUFO, (East); Mr. SAM TOME, (West); Mrs. ENEDINA TOME, (West).
Agua Viva—CHRISTY ANCHONDO, Editor; DAVID MCNAMARA, Special Projects.
Agua Viva Editorial Advisory Board—Rev. ROBERT POWER, C.S.B.; ELIZABETH ENNIS; PHILIP ALVAREZ; RICHARD PETRILLO; CHRISTY ANCHONDO; LALA GONZALEZ; MANUEL LEYVA; DAVID MCNAMARA.
Office of Prison and Jail Ministry—RICHARD PETRILLO, Coord.
Office of Marriage and Family Life—MARY HELEN LLANEZ, Coord.
Office of Catholic Schools—DAVID GARCIA, Supt.
Pro-Life Coordinators—JOSEPH BEHNKE; ELIZABETH BEHNKE.
Victim Assistance Coordinator—ELIZABETH A. ENNIS. Tel: 505-523-7577. Email: eennis@dioceseoflascruces.org.

CLERGY, PARISHES, MISSIONS AND PAROCHIAL SCHOOLS

CITY OF LAS CRUCES
(DONA ANA COUNTY)

1—CATHEDRAL OF IMMACULATE HEART OF MARY, Revs. Robert E. Power, C.S.B., Rector; William Coughlin, C.S.B.
Office—1240 S. Espina St., 88001. Tel: 505-524-8563; Fax: 505-523-2252.
School— See separate listing under Elementary Schools, Private in the Institution section.

2—ST. ALBERT THE GREAT NEWMAN PARISH (1986),, Serving New Mexico State University. Rev. Mitchell G. Dowalgo, C.S.B.; Deacon David McNeill Jr.
Res.: 2615 S. Solano, 88001. Tel: 505-522-6202; Fax: 505-521-3453.

3—ST. GENEVIEVE (1859), [CEM] Revs. Enriqez Lopez Escalera; Juan Moreno; Gerardo Rivera.
Res.: 100 S. Espina, 88001. Tel: 505-524-9649; Fax: 505-524-3263.

4—HOLY CROSS (1970), Very Rev. Msgr. John E. Anderson, V.G.; Rev. Martin Cordero.
Office—1327 N. Miranda St., 88005. Tel: 505-523-0167; Fax: 505-523-8023.
School— See separate listing under Elementary Schools, Private in the Institution section.

5—OUR LADY OF HEALTH (1956), Revs. Ricardo Hinojal, O.A.R.; Francisco Oviedo, O.A.R.
Res.: 1178 N. Mesquite, 88001. Tel: 505-526-9545; Fax: 505-526-9545.

6—SANTA ROSA DE LIMA (1990), Rev. Andres Alava, O.A.R.
Church: 5035 Holsome Rd., 88011. Tel: 505-382-8123.

OUTSIDE THE CITY OF LAS CRUCES

ALAMOGORDO, OTERO CO.

1—IMMACULATE CONCEPTION, [CEM] Revs. Bryant Hausfeld, O.F.M.; Gregg D. Petri, O.F.M.; Bruce Hausfeld, O.F.M.; Deacons Levy Lucero; Donald Dichman.
Res.: 705 Delaware Ave., 88310. Tel: 505-437-3291; Fax: 505-437-3239.
School— See separate listing under Elementary Schools, Private in the Institution section.
Mission—Our Lady of the Desert Boles Acres, Otero Co.
Mission—Our Lady of the Light La Luz, Otero Co.
Mission—Sacred Heart Cloudcroft, Otero Co.

2—ST. JUDE (1965), Very Rev. Wayne D. Herpin, S.J. (NO).
Office—1404 College Ave., 88310. Tel: 505-437-0238; Fax: 505-437-0267.

ANTHONY, DONA ANA CO., ST. ANTHONY'S (1899), [CEM] Rev. Thomas J. Devine, O.A.R.
Res.: P.O. Box 2624, 88021. Tel: 505-882-2239; Fax: 505-882-7343.
Church: 224 Lincoln St., 88021. Tel: 505-882-2239.
Convent—Hermanas Dominicas de la Doctrina Cristiana, Chaparral, MN 88021. Tel: 505-824-0508.
Mission—St. Thomas More 568 Lisa Dr., Chaparral, Dona Ana Co. 88021. Tel: 505-824-4433. Rev. Miguel Echeverria, O.A.R.
Mission—Our Lady of Refuge 1320 Mercantil, La Union, Dona Ana Co. 88021. Tel: 505-589-0542. Evangelina Sainz, Pastoral Team Coord.
Mission—Immaculate Conception San Benito Rd., P.O. Box 155, Berino, Dona Ana Co. 88024.

ARTESIA, EDDY CO.

1—ST. ANTHONY, Rev. Paul Murtagh, SS.CC.
Res.: 502 S. Ninth St., 88210. Tel: 505-746-4471.

2—OUR LADY OF GRACE (1942), Revs. Paul Murtagh, SS.CC.; Richard Lifrak, SS.CC.; Benedict Folger, SS.CC.
Res.: 1111 N. Roselawn Ave., 88210. Tel: 505-748-1356; Fax: 505-748-1049.
Catechesis/Religious Program—Students 452.

BAYARD, GRANT CO., OUR LADY OF FATIMA (1950), Rev. Paulus Kao.
Res.: P.O. Box 1425, 88023. Tel: 505-537-2421.
Mission—St. Anthony c/o Our Lady of Fatima, P.O. Box 1425, 88023. Fierro, NM, Grant Co.
Mission—Holy Family P.O. Box 67, Hanover, Grant Co. 88043.
Mission—San Lorenzo San Lorenzo, Grant Co. Deacon Alfonso Alvarado, Parish Life Coord.
Mission—Black Range Station San Lorenzo, 88057.

CARLSBAD, EDDY CO.

1—ST. EDWARD (1893), Rev. Noel R. Kramer, O.F.M.Conv. In Res., Revs. Maurus Hauer, O.F.M-.Conv.; Alcuin M. Hunter, O.F.M.Conv.; Conrad Sutter, O.F.M.Conv.
Office:—209 N. Guadalupe St., 88220. Tel: 505-885-6600; Fax: 505-885-9992.
Res.: 610 W. Stevens, 88220. Tel: 505-887-6486.
School—(Grades PreK-8), 805 Walter St., 88220. Tel: 505-885-4620; Fax: 505-885-7706. Sandra Cosano, Admin. Religious 1; Lay Teachers 5; Students 70.

2—SAN JOSE (1902), Rev. Valentine M. Jankowski, O.F.M.Conv.
Res.: 1002 DeBaca, 88220. Tel: 505-885-5792; Fax: 505-887-3553.
Religious Education Center—Tel: 505-887-1346. Patsy Grantner, D.R.E.

CARRIZOZO, LINCOLN CO., ST. RITA (1850), [CEM] Rev. David J. Bergs.
Res.: Box 727, 88301. Tel: 505-648-2853; Fax: 505-648-2853.
Mission—Sacred Heart Capitan, Lincoln Co.
Mission—St. Therese of the Little Flower Corona, Lincoln Co.

CHAMBERINO, DONA ANA CO., SAN LUIS REY (1959), Rev. Robert Villegas, C.S.C.
Res.: P.O. Box 230, 88027. Tel: 505-882-2045.
Convent—Our Lady of Guadalupe, 920 Convent Rd., P.O. Box 149, 88027. Tel: 505-882-5811. Franciscan Missionaries of Mary 4.

DEMING, LUNA CO.

1—ST. ANN'S (1918), Rev. Richard Catanach; Deacon Daniel S. Pena.
Res.: 400 S. Ruby St., 88030. Tel: 505-546-3343; Fax: 505-546-3444.
Catechesis/Religious Program—615 S. Copper St., 88030. Tel: 505-546-3905. Alexandra Vigil, D.R.E. Students 368.
Mission—Holy Family 400 S. Ruby St., Columbus, Luna Co. 88030.

2—HOLY FAMILY (1905), Rev. Mike Lindsay.
Res.: 612 S. Copper St., 88030-4115. Tel: 505-546-9783; Fax: 505-546-0123.
Catechesis/Religious Program—615 Copper St., 88030.

DEXTER, CHAVEZ CO., IMMACULATE CONCEPTION (1953), Deacon Jesus Herrera, Admin.
Res.: 400 W. Fifth, P.O. Box 189, 88230. Tel: 505-734-5478.
Mission—Our Lady of Guadalupe 204 Broadway, Lake Arthur, Chavez Co. 88253.
Mission—St. Catherine 200 S. Texas, Hagerman, Chavez Co. 88232.

DONA ANA, DONA ANA CO., OUR LADY OF THE PURIFICATION (1860), [JC] Rev. Miguel Macaya; Deacons Daniel Check; Rigoberto Chavez.
Mailing Address: P.O. Box 706, 88032. Tel: 505-526-2114.
Mission—San Isidro San Isidro, Dona Ana Co.

GARFIELD, DONA ANA CO., SAN ISIDRO (1945), Rev. Robert Power, C.S.B., Canonical Pastor.
Res.: H.C. 31, Box 43, 87936-9701. Tel: 505-267-5111; Fax: 505-267-1887.
Mission—Arrey San Jose, Sierra Co.
Mission—Our Lady of Guadalupe Hillsboro, Sierra Co.

HATCH, DONA ANA CO., OUR LORD OF MERCY (1889), Rev. Narciso Rivera.
Res.: Box 321, 87937. Tel: 505-267-4983; Fax: 505-267-4299.
Mission—Our Lady of All Nations Rincon, Dona Ana Co.

HOBBS, LEA CO.

1—ST. HELENA (1951), Revs. Dennis Fountain; Manuel Ibarra; Sisters Margaret McTaggert, S.S.C.; M. Deborah Romanuski, S.S.C.
Office—100 E. Bender Blvd., 88240. Tel: 505-392-7551; 505-392-7552; Fax: 505-392-3333.
School—Tel: 505-392-5405; Fax: 505-392-0128. Mrs. Sandra Newell, Admin. Lay Teachers 6; Students 82.
Convent—110 E. Bender, 88240. Tel: 505-392-8115.

2—OUR LADY OF GUADALUPE (1981), Rev. Jose Pedro Valdez; Deacon Samuel Navarrette.
Office—914 S. Selman, 88240. Tel: 505-393-4991; Fax: 505-397-1480.

HURLEY, GRANT CO., INFANT JESUS (1916), Rev. Daniel Porter.
Res.: Box 97, 88043. Tel: 505-537-3691; Fax: 505-537-3514.
Mission—San Juan San Juan, Grant Co.
Mission—San Jose Faywood, Luna Co.

JAL, LEA CO., ST. CECILIA (1941), Rev. Roderick J. Garvey, C.SS.R.
Res.: P.O. Box 430, 300 W. Nevada St., 88252. Tel: 505-395-2431; 505-395-2238 (Hall); Fax: 505-395-2431.

LA MESA, DONA ANA CO., SAN JOSE, [JC] Revs. Bonfilio Torres Loeto; Luis Macias Vera.
Res.: P.O. Box 278, 88044. Tel: 505-233-3191; Fax: 505-233-3866.
Mission—San Pedro Del Cerro P.O. Box 281, Vado, Dona Ana Co. 88048. Tel: 505-233-3977.

LORDSBURG, HIDALGO CO., ST. JOSEPH (1900), Rev. Anthony Clark.
Res.: 416 E. Second St., 88045. Tel: 505-542-3268.
Mission—St. Jude Cotton City, Hidalgo Co.
Mission—San Felipe Rodeo, Hidalgo Co.

LOVING, EDDY CO., OUR LADY OF GRACE (1937), Rev. Valentine Jankowski, O.F.M.Conv.
Office—301 4th St., P.O. Box 428, 88256. Tel: 505-745-3341.
Res.: 610 Stevens, Carlsbad, 88220. Tel: 505-885-5792.
Mission—Cristo Rey Malaga, Eddy Co.

LOVINGTON, LEA CO., ST. THOMAS AQUINAS (1919), Rev. Bill McCann.
Res.: 1301 N. Ninth St., 88260. Tel: 505-396-4206; Fax: 505-396-4206.
Mission—Our Lady of the Holy Rosary Tatum, Lea Co.

MESCALERO, OTERO CO., ST. JOSEPH (1895), (Native American), Rev. John Gibbons, O.F.M.; Bro. Peter Boegel, O.F.M.; Sr. Robert Ann Hecker, O.S.F.
Res.: Box 187, 88340. Tel: 505-464-4473; Fax: 505-464-1511.
Mission—Our Lady of Guadalupe 123 Mission Trail, Bent, Otero Co. 88340.
Mission—St. Patrick Three Rivers, Otero Co.

MESILLA PARK, DONA ANA CO., SHRINE AND PARISH OF OUR LADY OF GUADALUPE, Rev. Donald Adamski; Deacon Al Bowers.
Res.: Box 298, 88047. Tel: 505-526-8171; Fax: 505-523-1175.

MESILLA, DONA ANA CO., ST. ALBINO (1852), Rev. Virgilio Flores.
Res.: P.O. Box 26, 88046. Tel: 505-526-9349; Fax: 505-647-1619.
Mission—San Jose Mission P.O. Box 502, Fairacres, Dona Ana Co. 88033. Tel: 505-647-1979. Rev. John Weber.

ROSWELL, CHAVES CO.

1—ASSUMPTION OF THE BLESSED VIRGIN MARY (1963), Rev. Msgr. Robert Getz.
Res.: 2808 N. Kentucky, 88201. Tel: 505-622-9895; Fax: 505-622-6845.

2—ST. JOHN THE BAPTIST (1903), (Hispanic), Rev. Juan Montoya, O.F.M.; Deacons Leopold R. Moreno; Louis Romero; Enrique Salas.

Res.: 506 S. Lincoln, 88201. Tel: 505-622-3531; Fax: 505-623-8933.
3—St. Peter (1903), Rev. Larry Schreiber, O.F.M. Mailing Address: *Franciscan Friary*, 105 E. Mathews, 88203. Tel: 505-622-5742; Fax: 505-623-9228. In Res., Rev. Ramon Smith, O.F.M.
Church: 111 E. Deming, 88302. Tel: 505-622-5742; Fax: 505-623-9228.
Ruidoso, Lincoln Co., St. Eleanor (1939), Rev. Alfred Galvan; Deacon Benjamin Vigil.
Res.: P.O. Box 8300, 120 Junction Rd., 88355. Tel: 505-257-2330; Fax: 505-257-7062.
Mission—St. Jude Thaddeus [CEM] San Patricio, Lincoln Co.
Mission—San Juan Lincoln, Lincoln Co.
Mission—Sacred Heart Fort Stanton, Lincoln Co.
Mission—St. Joseph Picacho, Dona Ana Co.
Mission—San Ysidro Glencoe, Lincoln Co.
San Miguel, Dona Ana Co., San Miguel, Rev. Luis Macias Vera.
Res.: Drawer E, 88058. Tel: 505-233-2453; Fax: 505-233-2453.
Augustinian Recollects: P.O. Box 310, Mesilla, 88046. Tel: 505-523-7030; Fax: 505-233-7030.
Mission—Our Lady of Perpetual Help P.O. Box 48, Mesquite, Dona Ana Co. 88048. Tel: 505-233-4695.
Santa Clara, Grant Co., Santa Clara (1888), Rev. Robert L. Becerra.
Res.: P.O. Box 215, 88026. Tel: 505-537-3713; Fax: 505-537-3715.
Silver City, Grant Co.
1—St. Francis Newman Center Parish (1964),, Serving Western New Mexico University. Rev. Marcos Reyna, Admin.
Res.: 914 W. 13th St., 88061. Tel: 505-538-3662; Fax: 505-534-1059.
2—St. Vincent de Paul (1874), Rev. Rodrick Nichols; Deacons William Holguin; Johnnie Perez; Jeremiah Bustillos.
Res.: 414 Bayard St., P.O. Box 1189, 88062. Tel: 505-538-9373; Fax: 505-388-0870.
Mission—St. Isidore Gila, Grant Co.
Mission—Holy Cross Pinos Altos, Grant Co.
Parish Retreat Center: *St. Mary Theotokos Retreat Center*, 5202 Hwy. 152, 88062. Tel: 505-537-4839.
Sunland Park, Dona Ana Co., St. Martin de Porres (1964), Rev. Edward Herrera; Deacon Jesus Favela.
Res.: 1885 McNutt Rd., 88063. Tel: 505-589-2106; Fax: 505-589-2106.
Mission—Santa Teresa de Avila, Dona Ana Co 88063.
Truth or Consequences, Sierra Co., Our Lady of Perpetual Help (1916), Revs. Art Roberts, C.S.B.; Donald Hyatt, C.S.B.; Sean Garrity, C.S.B.; Deacon Adam L. Sanchez.
Res.: 103 E. Sixth Ave., 87901. Tel: 505-894-7804; Fax: 505-894-0451.
Mission—St. Joseph Cuchillo, Sierra Co.
Mission—San Ysidro Las Palomas, Sierra Co.
Mission—St. Ignatius Montecello, Sierra Co.
Mission—San Lorenzo Placitas, Sierra Co.
Chapel—St. Gregory, Chapels Chise
Chapel—San Miguel, Rancho de San Miguel
Chapel—Winston, St. Jude
Tularosa, Otero Co., St. Francis de Paula (1868), [CEM] [JC] Revs. Gary Swirczynski; Peter A. Verheggen, O.F.M.
Res.: 303 Encino, 88352. Tel: 505-585-2793; Fax: 505-585-3005.

Special Assignment:
Rev.—
Anderson, Joe, O.S.B.

Absent On Leave:
Revs.—
Amezaga, Louis
Beggane, Thomas
Garcia, Samuel

Retired:
Rev. Msgrs.—
Lynch, Richard
VonderHaar, Roland
Revs.—
Griffith, Edwin
Lafrenz, James
Morgan, Arthur
Pytlick, Conrad
Tickle, John

Permanent Deacons:
Alvarado, Alfonso, Blackrange Stations, San Lorenzo
Bowers, Al, Our Lady of Guadalupe, Mesilla Park
Bustillos, Jeramiah Gomes, St. Vincent de Paul, Silver City
Castanon, David M., Santa Clara, Santa Clara
Chavez, Rigoberto, Our Lady of Purification, Dona Ana
Check, Daniel
Crowder, Richard, (Retired)
Daniel, Gregory T., (Leave of Absence)
Dickman, Donald, Our Lady of the Light, La Luz
Dougil, Edward, (Retired)
Favela, Jesus, San Martin de Porres, Sunland Park
Gale, Howard, (Retired)
Herrera, Jesus, Immaculate Conception, Dexter
Holguin, William, St. Vincent de Paul, Silver City
Lucero, John S., (On Duty Outside the Diocese)
Lucero, Levy, Immaculate Conception, Alamogordo
Luevano, Manuel, (On Duty Outside the Diocese)
McNeill, David, Jr., Albert the Great Newman Center, Las Cruces
Medina, Jesus, San Martin de Porres, Sunland Park
Melandrez, Mariano C., St. Francis de Paula, Tularosa
Merjil, Pablo, Our Lady of Grace, Artesia
Miller, Lawrence Fredrick, Holy Cross, Las Cruces
Moreno, Leopoldo, St. Peter, Roswell
Narvaez, Arthur, (Retired)
Navarrette, Sam, Our Lady of Guadalupe, Hobbs
Perez, Johnnie, St. Vincent de Paul, Silver City
Polson, Charles, (On Sabbatical)
Roane, Tom, St. Helena, Hobbs
Rodriguez, Richard Alires, Santa Clara, Santa Clara
Romero, Louis, St. John the Baptist, Roswell
Salas, Enrique, St. John the Baptist, Roswell
Samaniego, Hector S., Immaculate Heart of Mary Cathedral, LasCruces
Sanchez, Adam L., St. Jude, Alamogordo
Schretlen, Frank, (Retired)
Velott, Pete, Director of Deacons
Vigil, Benjamin, St. Eleanors, Ruidoso

INSTITUTIONS LOCATED IN THE DIOCESE

[A] ELEMENTARY SCHOOLS, PRIVATE

Las Cruces. *Las Cruces Catholic School*, (Grades PreK-8), 865 E. Idaho, 88001. Tel: 505-524-2141; Fax: 505-523-2252. Web: www.zianet.com/lcc. Mr. Dino Cervantes, Pres. Bd. of Directors; Mr. John Daniel, Asst. Admin. Lay Teachers 16; Students 263.

Alamogordo. *Fr. James B. Hay, Inc.*, Formerly Rev. James B. Hay School, (Grades 1-6), 1000 E. Eight St., 88310. Tel: 505-437-7821; Fax: 505-443-6129. Email: frhay@wazoo.com. Mrs. Clare Riker, Admin. Lay Teachers 6; Students 80.

Roswell. *Assumption of the Blessed Virgin Mary Catholic School*, 2808 N. Kentucky, 88201. Tel: 505-627-5744; Fax: 505-622-6845. Email: tbear@dfn.com. Vivi Kreitz, Lead Teacher.

[B] HEALTH CARE FACILITIES

Carlsbad. *St. Mary's Health Care Center* (Sub. of St. Mary of the Plains Hospital) , 2330 West Pierce, 88220. Tel: 505-887-0516; Fax: 505-885-8239. Steve Racchito, Mgr.

Hobbs. *Covenant Healthcare Center*, 2410 North Fowler, 88240. Tel: 505-492-2000; Fax: 505-492-2006. Melonie Ankerholz, Practice Mgr.

St. Mary's Family Health Care Center (Sub. of St. Mary of the Plains Hospital) , 515 East Main, 88240. Tel: 505-393-1096; Fax: 505-393-3758. Steve Racchito, Dir.

[C] MONASTERIES & RESIDENCES OF PRIESTS AND BROTHERS

Las Cruces. *Basilian Fathers*, 1682 Alta Vista Pl., 88011. Tel: 505-523-1138; Fax: 505-505-2042. Email: basilian@ziagold.net. Web: www.basilian.org. Revs. Mitchell G. Dowalgo, C.S.B., Rector; Robert E. Power, C.S.B.; William E. Loughlin.

Mesilla. *Augustinian Recollect Fathers* Province of St. Nicholas of Tolentine, Provincial Delegation in the South of U.S.A. , San Alypius House, P.O. Box 310, 88046. Tel: 505-523-7030. Revs. Andres Alava, O.A.R.; Antonio Martinez, O.A.R; Ricardo Hinojal, O.A.R.; Francisco Rivera, O.A.R.

[D] CONVENTS AND RESIDENCES FOR SISTERS

Anthony. *Sisters of Mercy of the Americas (Omaha Region)*, 301 Lincoln St., P.O. Box 2411, 88021. Tel: 505-882-5553; Fax: 505-882-7312. Email: katerickson@zianet.com. Sisters 2.

Chamberino. *Franciscan Missionaries of Mary*, P.O. Box 694, 88027. Tel: 505-882-5811; Fax: 505-882-5374. Email: fmmchamberino@aol.com.

Chaparral. *Dominicas De La Doctrina Cristiana*, 124 Tornillo, 88021. Tel: 505-824-0508. Professed 5; Novices 6.

Religious of the Assumption, 300-2 McCombs Rd., PMB #43, 88021. Tel: 505-824-2850; Fax: 505-824-2850. Email: rachaparral@juno.com. Sr. Maria Isabel Galbe Sada, R.A., Contact Person.

Deming. *Daughters of the Heart of Mary*, P.O. Box 1531, 88030. Tel: 505-546-7599. Email: nazhouse@swnm.com.

Garfield. *Franciscan Missionaries of Mary*, HC 31, Box 43, 87936-9701. Tel: 505-267-5111; Fax: 505-267-1887.

LaUnion. *Sisters of Mercy*, 2675 Salome Hernandez St., 88021. Tel: 505-589-0852. Email: darcyrsm@flash.net.

Roswell. *Poor Clare Monastery of Our Lady of Guadalupe*, 809 E. 19th St., 88201. Tel: 505-622-0868; Fax: 505-627-2184. Web: listserv.american.edu/catholic/franciscan/clares/clares.html. Sisters M. Francis, P.C.C., Abbess; Mary Jeannine, P.C.C., Vicaress. Professed Nuns 27.

Silver City. *Sisters of St. Joseph*, St. Mary's Center, 1801 N. Alabama, 88061. Tel: 505-538-3350; Fax: 505-538-0495. Email: rplante@zianet.com.

[E] RETREAT CENTERS

Mesilla Park. *Holy Cross Retreat and Friary*, P.O. Box 158, 88047. Tel: 505-524-3688; Fax: 505-524-3811. Email: Franciscan@zianet.com. Web: www.zianet.com/franciscan. Rev. Cyprian Uline, O.F.M.Conv.

[F] MISCELLANEOUS

Las Cruces. *Catholic Diocese of Las Cruces Foundation, Inc.*, 1280 Med Park Dr., 80005. Tel: 505-523-7577; Fax: 505-524-3874. Email: ptorres@dioceseoflascruces.org. Web: dioceseoflascruces.org. Susan Roberts, Exec. Dir.

Family Unity and Citizenship Program, 1050 Monte Vista, 88001. Tel: 505-525-6779. Veronica Campos, Dir.

**Order of Secular Discalced Carmelites*, 6100 Robledo Rd., 88012-9566. Tel: 505-382-3795. Email: frogman12@zianet.com. Rita Trujillo, Pres.; Therese Mastrantuono, Contact Person.

Our Lady of Guadalupe Prayer Center, Inc., P.O. Box 6772, 83006. Tel: 505-522-5250. Email: OLOGPC@Catholic.org.

The Priests' Retirement Plan of the Catholic Diocese of Las Cruces, Inc., 1280 Med Park Dr., 88005. Tel: 505-523-7577; Fax: 505-524-3874.

Cloudcroft. **Mount Subasio Hermitage*, 603-16 Springs Canyon, 88317. Tel: 505-687-2507. Email: mtsubasio@yahoo.com. Ms. Helen Riegger, Dir. & Trustee.

San Patricio. *Benedictine Center*, P.O. Box 158, 88348. Tel: 505-653-4709; 505-653-4215. Rev. Colman Heffern, O.S.B.

RELIGIOUS INSTITUTES OF MEN REPRESENTED IN THE DIOCESE

For further details refer to the corresponding bracketed number in the Religious Institutes of Men or Women section.

[0170]—*Basilian Fathers*—C.S.B.
[0200]—*Benedictine Monks*—O.S.B.
[]—*Capuchin Friars* (St. Bonaventure)—O.F.M.Cap.
[0480]—*Conventual Franciscans* (Our Lady of Guadalupe Custody)—O.F.M.Conv
[0520]—*Franciscan Friars* (St. John the Baptist, Our Lady of Guadalupe, St. Barbara Provs.)—O.F.M.
[0690]—*Jesuit Fathers and Brothers* (New Orleans, Wisconsin Provs.)—S.J.
[0150]—*Order of the Augustinian Recollects*—O.A.R.
[0610]—*Priests of the Congregation of Holy Cross* (Southwest Prov.)—C.S.C.

RELIGIOUS INSTITUTES OF WOMEN REPRESENTED IN THE DIOCESE

[0460]—*Congregation of the Sisters of Charity of the Incarnate Word*—C.C.V.I.
[0810]—*Daughters of the Heart of Mary*—D.H.M.
[1110]—*Dominican Sisters of Our Lady of the Rosary and of Saint Catherine of Siena, Cabra*—O.P.
[1070]—*Dominicas de la Doctrina Cristiana*—O.P.
[1370]—*The Franciscan Missionaries of Mary*—F.M.M.
[1430]—*Franciscan Sisters of Our Lady of Perpetual Help*—O.S.F.
[2470]—*Maryknoll Sisters of St. Dominic*—M.M.
[2490]—*Medical Mission Sisters*—M.M.S.
[2710]—*Missionaries of Charity*—M.C.
[3130]—*Our Lady of Victory Missionary Sisters*—O.L.V.M.
[3760]—*Poor Clares Monastery of Our Lady of Guadalupe*—P.C.C.
[]—*Religious of the Assumption*—R.A.
[]—*Sisters for Christian Community*
[0440]—*Sisters of Charity of Cincinnati, Ohio*—S.C.

[2575]—*Sisters of Mercy of the Americas* (Omaha, Vermont, Cincinnati, New Jersey)—R.S.M.
[3740]—*Sisters of St. Casimir*—S.S.C.
[1570]—*Sisters of St. Francis of the Holy Family*—O.S.F.
[3830-15]—*Sisters of St. Joseph*—C.S.J.
[3830-03]—*Sisters of St. Joseph of Orange*—C.S.J.
[3270]—*Sisters of the Most Precious Blood (O'Fallon, MO)*—C.PP.S.
[4060]—*Society of the Holy Child Jesus*—S.H.C.J.

NECROLOGY

(No Deaths)

Diocese of Las Vegas

(Dioecesis Campensis)

Most Reverend

JOSEPH A. PEPE

Bishop of Las Vegas; ordained May 16, 1970; appointed Bishop of Las Vegas April 6, 2001; ordained and installed May 31, 2001 *Mailing Address: P.O. Box 18316, Las Vegas, NV 89114-8316*. Tel: 702-735-3500; Fax: 702-735-8941.

Catholic Center: 336 Cathedral Way, Las Vegas, NV 89109. P.O. Box 18316, Las Vegas, NV 89114-8316. Tel: 702-735-3500; Fax: 702-735-8941.

Square Miles 39,688.

Erected by His Holiness Pope Pius XI March 27, 1931.

Redesignated Diocese of Reno-Las Vegas by Pope Paul VI, October 13, 1976.

Redesignated Diocese of Las Vegas by His Holiness Pope John Paul II March 21, 1995.

For legal titles of parishes and diocesan institutions, consult the Chancery Office.

STATISTICAL OVERVIEW

Personnel	
Bishop	1
Priests: Diocesan Active in Diocese	25
Priests: Diocesan Active Outside Diocese	2
Priests: Retired, Sick or Absent	8
Number of Diocesan Priests	35
Religious Priests in Diocese	20
Total Priests in Diocese	55
Extern Priests in Diocese	30
Permanent Deacons in Diocese	7
Total Brothers	3
Total Sisters	4
Parishes	
Parishes	25
With Resident Pastor:	
Resident Diocesan Priests	15
Resident Religious Priests	4
Without Resident Pastor:	
Administered by Priests	5
Administered by Lay People	1
Missions	7
New Parishes Created	1
Professional Ministry Personnel:	
Brothers	3
Sisters	5
Lay Ministers	50
Welfare	
Catholic Hospitals	1
Total Assisted	150,503
Day Care Centers	1
Total Assisted	6,344
Special Centers for Social Services	19
Total Assisted	1,000,000
Other Institutions	1
Total Assisted	1,700
Educational	
Diocesan Students in Other Seminaries	7
Total Seminarians	7
High Schools, Diocesan and Parish	1
Total Students	853
Elementary Schools, Diocesan and Parish	7
Total Students	2,823
Catechesis/Religious Education:	
High School Students	2,299
Elementary Students	9,503
Total Students under Catholic Instruction	15,485
Teachers in the Diocese:	
Priests	1
Lay Teachers	64
Vital Statistics	
Receptions into the Church:	
Infant Baptism Totals	4,167
Adult Baptism Totals	360
Received into Full Communion	1,752
First Communions	3,809
Confirmations	1,320
Marriages:	
Catholic	462
Interfaith	146
Total Marriages	608
Deaths	772
Total Catholic Population	515,953
Total Population	1,648,422

Former Bishop—Most Rev. DANIEL F. WALSH D.D., ord. March 30, 1963; appt. Titular Bishop of Tigia and Auxiliary of San Francisco Sept. 24, 1981; appt. Bishop of Reno-Las Vegas June 9, 1987; installed Aug. 6, 1987; appt. Bishop of Las Vegas March 21, 1995; installed July 28, 1995; appt. Bishop of Santa Rosa in California, April 11, 2000; installed May 22, 2000.

Catholic Center—336 Cathedral Way, Las Vegas, 89109. Tel: 702-735-3500; Fax: 702-735-8941. *Mailing Address, P.O. Box 18316, Las Vegas, 89114-8316*. Office Hours: Mon.-Fri. 8:30-12 & 1-4:30

Vicar General, Chancellor and Moderator of the Curia—Very Rev. ROBERT E. STOECKIG, V.G. Tel: 702-735-9605.

Diocesan Tribunal Office-Judicial Vicar—Rev. PETER ROMEO, J.C.L. Tel: 702-735-1210; Fax: 702-735-5146.

Notary-Secretary—Mrs. SIDNEY MARSH; Mrs. RUTH SORSAK.

Promoter of Justice—Rev. TOM FRANSISCUS, C.SS.R., J.C.L.

Defender of the Bond—ROBERT J. FLUMMERFELT, J.C.L.

Diocesan Judges—Revs. LAURENCE SPITERI, Ph.D.; KEVIN MCAULIFFE, M.A., J.C.L.; JOHN SULLIVAN, M.A., J.C.L.; DAVID I. FULTON, S.T.D., J.C.L.

Diocesan Advocate—Rev. TOM FRANSISCUS, C.SS.R., J.C.L.

Presbyteral Council for the Diocese of Las Vegas—Most Rev. JOSEPH A. PEPE, D.D., J.C.D., Ex Officio; Very Rev. ROBERT E. STOECKIG, V.G., Ex Officio; Rev. PETER ROMEO, J.C.L., Ex Officio Very Rev. JOSEPH ANNESE; Revs. JAMES BEVAN JR.; FRANCIS TIMONEY; TIMOTHY WEHN; Rev. Msgr. PATRICK LEARY; Revs. KEVIN MCAULIFFE, M.A., J.C.L.; CAESAR CAVIGLIA; GUSTAVO CRUZ; WILLIAM KENNY; WILLIAM HAESAERT, C.S.V.; MANUEL QUINTERO; GREG GORDON.

Diocesan Offices and Directors

Building Committee—Bro. JOHN DODD, C.S.V.; Rev. KEVIN MCAULIFFE, M.A., J.C.L.; Very Rev. ROBERT STOECKIG, V.G.; GIA NGUYEN; HARRY SHULL.

Catholic Charities of Southern Nevada—

Executive Director—Rev. Msgr. PATRICK LEAFY, 1501 Las Vegas Blvd. N., Las Vegas, 89101. Tel: 702-385-2662.

Chief Financial Officer—Bro. JOHN DODD, C.S.V. Tel: 702-735-7865.

Development/Stewardship Office—

Director—Very Rev. ROBERT E. STOECKIG, V.G. Tel: 702-735-9605.

Education Department—

Director of Clergy Education—Very Rev. ROBERT E. STOECKIG, V.G.

Vicar for Education & Superintendent of Schools—Dr. RICHARD FACCIOLO, Ed.D. Tel: 702-697-5918.

Human Resources Department—Dr. RICHARD A. FACCIOLO, Ed.D. Tel: 702-735-3500.

St. Thomas Aquinas Catholic Newman Community - Campus Ministry—

Director—Rev. DOMINIC BRIESE, O.P. Tel: 702-736-0887.

Director of Liturgy—Sr. MARGANNE DRAGO S.S.J. Tel: 702-891-8600.

Office of Catechetical Ministries—

Director—Sr. PATRICIA MCGINLEY, S.S.J. Tel: 702-735-6044.

Associate Director—ANDREA OWEN. Tel: 702-735-6044.

Office of Youth Ministries—

Director—GRACE CASSETTA. Tel: 702-735-2744

Spanish Catechesis and Liaison to Hispanic Ministries—TERESA RUIZ-VELASCO, M.S. Tel: 702-735-3500, Ext. 238.

Office of Peace and Social Justice—Rev. CAESAR J. CAVIGLIA.

Home and Foreign Missions—Very Rev. ROBERT E. STOECKIG, V.G. Tel: 702-735-9605.

Hospital Apostolate—Revs. JESSE CORTES. Tel: 702-870-2767; NOE LAGANSON. Tel: 702-870-2767; INNOCENT ANYANWA. Tel: 702-735-0510.

Information, Communications and Media—Rev. BEDE WEVITA. Tel: 702-657-0200; Fax: 702-648-2327.

Italian Catholic Federation—Rev. Msgr. ELWOOD LAVOY.

Native American and Colored People Commission—Very Rev. ROBERT E. STOECKIG, V.G.

Newspaper—DESERT CLARION.

Pontifical Association of the Holy Childhood—Very Rev. ROBERT E. STOECKIG, V.G.

Priests' Pension Board—Rev. KEVIN MCAULIFFE, M.A., J.C.L.; Very Rev. ROBERT STOECKIG, V.G., Ex Officio; Rev. Msgr. PATRICK LEARY; Rev. JOHN SULLIVAN, J.C.L.

Priests' Personnel Board—Very Rev. ROBERT E. STOECKIG, V.G., Ex Officio; Revs. JOSEPH ANNESE; JAMES BEVAN JR.; Very Rev. FRANCIS TIMONEY; Revs. TIMOTHY WEHN; KEVIN MCAULIFFE, M.A., J.C.L.; GREG GORDON.

Property Management—Bro. JOHN DODD, C.S.V.

Vocations—Rev. ANTHONY VERCELLONE, Dir.

Respect Life Liaison—Mrs. KATHLEEN MILLER, 3510 Leor Court, Las Vegas, 89121.

Natural Family Planning/Fertility Care—MICKEY BACHMAN, R.N., C.N.F.P.P. Tel: 702-616-7550.

Diocesan Finance Committee Members—PHILLIP PECKMAN; PATRICIA MULROY; J. A. TIBERTI; FRANK FERTITTA; LEO FALKENSAMMER; CHUCK KERZETSKI; TED ATENCIO.

Diocesan Loan Board—PAT MULROY; RANDY GARCIA; ARTHUR DEJOYA; ED SKONICKI.

Catholic Charities of Southern Nevada—Board of Trustees: Most Rev. JOSEPH A. PEPE, D.D., J.C.D.; Rev. Msgr. PATRICK LEARY, Exec. Dir. Catholic Charities; Very Rev. ROBERT STOECKIG, V.G.; JEANNE KILDUFF, Pres.; LYNETTE BOGGS MCDONALD; JAMES KROPID; EVA GARCIA MENDOZA; MARY ALICE NIELSEN; LOIS TARKANIAN; CAMILLE RUVO; Dr. CORA MURILLO.

Victim Assistance Coordinator—JOANNE GARRAMONE-HALT. Tel: 702-360-1027. Email: garramonehalt@aol.com

CLERGY, PARISHES, MISSIONS AND PAROCHIAL SCHOOLS

CITY OF LAS VEGAS
(CLARK COUNTY)

1—ST. ANNE (1948), Very Rev. Francis Timoney; Revs. Sabino Lattanzio, O.F.M.Cap., Ph.D.; Innocent Anyanwy, Ph.D. (Nigeria).
Office & Res.: 1901 S. Maryland Pkwy., 89104. Tel: 702-735-0510; Fax: 702-735-5582.
School—1813 S. Maryland Pkwy., 89104. Tel: 702-735-2586; Fax: 702-735-8357. Phyllis Joyce, Prin. Lay Teachers 13; Students 345.
Catechesis/Religious Program—Tel: 702-735-2985; Fax: 702-735-9237. Students 413.

2—ST. BRIDGET (1945), Rev. James L. Swenson.
Office—220 N. 14th St., 89101-4312. Tel: 702-384-3382; Fax: 702-382-9467.
Res.: 215 N. 14th St., 89101. Tel: 702-384-7201.
Catechesis/Religious Program—Students 92.

3—CHRIST THE KING (1978), Revs. William J.M. Kenny; Jerry Nadine.
Mailing Address: 4925 S. Torrey Pines, 89118. Tel: 702-871-1904; Fax: 702-251-4935.
Catechesis/Religious Program—Tel: 702-871-1904, Ext. 230. Beth Summers, D.R.E. Students 557.
Mission—St. Catherine of Siena Jean. P.O. Box 19789, Sandy Valley, Clark Co. 89019. Tel: 702-723-5454.

4—ST. ELIZABETH ANN SETON (1992), Revs. Kevin W. McAuliffe, J.C.L.; Mark J. Gantley, J.C.L. (SY); Deacons Joseph Deegan; Francis Pemper. In Res., Rev. Francis M. Vivona, J.C.L.
Office & Mailing Address: 1811 Pueblo Vista Dr., 89128. Tel: 702-228-8311; Fax: 702-228-8310.
Res.: 2109 Golden Lotus Dr., 89134.
School—1807 Pueblo Vista Dr., 89128. Tel: 702-804-8328; Fax: 702-228-8906. Timothy P. Curtin, Prin. Lay Teachers 18; Students 388.
Catechesis/Religious Program—Tel: 702-228-8311; Fax: 702-228-2154. Students 946.

5—ST. FRANCIS DE SALES (1964), (Hispanic), Revs. Manuel Quintero; Alberto Alzate.
Mailing Address: 1111 Michael Way, 89108. Tel: 702-647-3440; Fax: 702-646-3587.
Res.: 1628 Desert Fort, 89128. Tel: 702-341-7009.
School—Tel: 702-647-2828; Fax: 702-647-0284. Mrs. Catherine Thompson, Prin. Lay Teachers 14; Students 307.
Catechesis/Religious Program—Tel: 702-646-2266; Fax: 702-647-6701. Students 517.

6—GUARDIAN ANGEL CATHEDRAL (1963), Revs. Lawrence Lentz, C.S.V., Rector; Francis P. White, C.S.V.; Joseph Trong; Sr. Timothy Malone, C.H.S., Pastoral Assoc.
Office: 336 Cathedral Way, 89109. Tel: 702-735-5241; Fax: 702-734-7086.
Rectory: 4433 Zev Ct., 89121.

7—HOLY FAMILY (1975), Revs. John Andrew Sullivan; Reginald U. Nwauzor (Nigeria).
Mailing Address: 4490 Mountain Vista, 89121.
Office & Res.: 4528 E. Harmon Ave., 89121-6548. Tel: 702-458-2211 (Office); 702-733-0414 (Res.); Fax: 702-458-0966 (Office).
Catechesis/Religious Program—Tel: 702-458-3575. Students 482.

8—ST. JAMES THE APOSTLE (1942), (African American), Rev. Michael Blackburn, O.F.M.; Sr. Deborah Lockwood, O.S.F., Pastoral Assoc. & D.R.E.; Deacon Peter Gutierrez.
Office & Church: 1920 N. Martin Luther King Blvd., 89106. Tel: 702-648-6606; Fax: 702-648-0352.
Res.: 1420 W. Bartlett, 89106. Tel: 702-648-2798.
Catechesis/Religious Program—Tel: 702-648-6606; Fax: 702-648-0352. Students 158.

9—ST. JOAN OF ARC (1908), Very Rev. Timothy Clark Wehn.
Office & Res.: 315 S. Casino Center Blvd., 89101. Tel: 702-382-9909; Fax: 702-382-6655.
School—1300 Bridger Ave., 89101. Tel: 702-384-6909; Fax: 702-386-0249. Mrs. Lynda Ballard, Prin. Lay Teachers 10; Students 200.
Catechesis/Religious Program— Clustered with St. Bridget's, Las Vegas.

10—ST. JOSEPH, HUSBAND OF MARY (1989), Very Rev. James J. Bevan Jr., V.F.; Revs. Bernard F. Waters (New Zealand); Thomas E. Gallenbach; Oneil A. Monzillo; Kingsley Nonis (Sri Lanka) (TYL).
Office & Mailing Address: 7260 W. Sahara Ave., 89117. Tel: 702-363-1902; Fax: 702-363-7976.
Res.: 10261 Rarity Ave., 89135. Tel: 702-838-6115.
Catechesis/Religious Program—Fax: 702-363-0142. Cynthia O'Connell, D.R.E. Students 980.

11—ST. MARY THE VIRGIN (1983), Closed. For inquiries for parish records contact the chancery.

12—OUR LADY OF LAS VEGAS (1957), Revs. Robert P. Petekiewicz; Robert W. Puhlman; Jesse Cortes; Noe Laganson.
Office—3050 Alta Dr., 89107. Tel: 702-870-2767; Fax: 702-870-1267.
Res.: 3104 Alta Dr., 89107.
School—3046 Alta Dr., 89107. Tel: 702-878-6841; Fax: 702-880-5758. Richard Martinez, Prin. Lay Teachers 25; Students 620.
Catechesis/Religious Program—Tel: 702-870-1882. Robert Flummerfelt, D.R.E. Students 522.

13—ST. PAUL JUNG-HA-SANG (1987), (Korean), Very Rev. Robert E. Stoeckig, V.G. Tel: 702-735-3500; Rev. Ui Song Peter Bang.
5225 Meikle Ln., 89115. Tel: 702-453-0033; Fax: 702-876-2989.
Mission— 3695 Lindell Rd., 89103. Tel: 702-735-3500.

14—PRINCE OF PEACE (1981), Revs. Gustavo Cruz; Sergio Garcia (FRS); Deacon James B. Whittle.
Office—5485 E. Charleston Blvd., 89142. Tel: 702-431-2233; Fax: 702-431-2234.
Res.: 653 Los Feliz, 89110.
Catechesis/Religious Program—Students 1,371.

15—SHRINE OF OUR LADY OF LA VANG, Rev. Joseph Trong Nguyen.
4835 Pearl Ave., 89121. Tel: 702-821-1459.

16—SHRINE OF THE MOST HOLY REDEEMER (1991), Very Rev. Robert E. Stoeckig, V.G. Tel: 702-735-3500.
Office—55 E. Reno Ave., 89119. Tel: 702-891-8600; Fax: 702-891-0339.

17—ST. VIATOR (1954), Revs. Richard A. Rinn, C.S.V.; Wayne G. Dupuis, C.S.V.; William F. Haesaert, C.S.V.; Bro. Michael Rice, C.S.V.; Anita Taylor, Business Mgr.
Office—2461 E. Flamingo Rd., 89121. Tel: 702-733-8323; Fax: 702-733-8154.
School—Tel: 702-732-4477; Fax: 702-732-4418. Mrs. Kathleen Daulton, Prin. Lay Teachers 22; Students 654.
Catechesis/Religious Program—Tel: 702-732-0459. Judie Dawson, D.R.E. Students 308.

OUTSIDE THE CITY OF LAS VEGAS

AMARGOSA VALLEY, NYE CO., CHRIST OF THE DESERT CATHOLIC CHURCH (1987), (Hispanic),, Now a mission of Our Lady of the Valley, Pahrump

BOULDER CITY, CLARK CO., ST. ANDREW'S (1931), [JC] Very Rev. Joseph P. Annese.
1399 San Felipe Dr., 89005. Tel: 702-293-7500; Fax: 702-293-4419.
Catechesis/Religious Program—Barbara Misuraca, D.R.E. Students 165.

BUNKERVILLE, CLARK CO., LA VIRGEN DE GUADALUPE (1992), Rev. Clarence J. Savial.
Mailing Address: P.O. Box 7309, 89007. Corner of 1st W. and 1st S., 89007.
Res.: 121 Falcon St., Mesquite, 89027. Tel: 702-346-7065; Fax: 702-346-0648.
Catechesis/Religious Program—Fax: 702-345-2280. Students 288.

CALIENTE, LINCOLN CO., HOLY CHILD (1870), [CEM] Unassigned., Mailing Address: P.O. Box 748, 89008-0748. Tel: 775-726-3669; Fax: 775-726-3669.
Catechesis/Religious Program—Students 12.

ELY, WHITE PINE CO., SACRED HEART (1869), Rev. Phil Audet.
Mailing Address & Office: P.O. Box 151026, 89301. Tel: 775-289-2201; Fax: 775-289-2207.
Res.: 515 Murry St., 89301.
Catechetical Ministry Center—1100 Park Ave., P.O. Box 26, 89301. Tel: 775-289-8111.
Catechesis/Religious Program—Veronica Williams, D.R.E. Students 92.
Mission—St. Michael's P.O. Box 26, McGill, White Pine Co. 89301. Tel: 775-289-2201.

HENDERSON, CLARK CO.

1—ST. FRANCIS OF ASSISI, Rev. Gregory W. Gordon.
Stonehill Market Pl., Ste 114, 10075 S. Eastern Ave., 89052. Tel: 702-914-2175.

2—ST. PETER THE APOSTLE (1943), Rev. Tony Hughes.
Office:—204 S. Boulder Hwy., 89015. Tel: 702-565-8406; Fax: 702-565-8731.
Rectory—179 Mount St. Helen's Dr., 89012.
Catechesis/Religious Program—Tel: 702-565-0284. Students 496.

3—ST. THOMAS MORE (1986), Revs. Patrick W. Render, C.S.V.; Michael P. Keliher, C.S.V.; Deacon Anthony J. Bravo.
130 N. Pecos Rd., 89074. Tel: 702-361-3022; Fax: 702-361-7784.
Catechesis/Religious Program—Tel: 702-361-8840; Fax: 702-361-5992. Juliann Dwyer, D.R.E.; Dorothy Distel, D.R.E. Students 1,683.

LAUGHLIN, CLARK CO., ST. JOHN THE BAPTIST CATHOLIC MISSION (1992), Rev. Frank Yncierto, Admin.
Mailing Address: P.O. Box 31230, 89028. Tel: 702-298-0440; Fax: 702-298-0279.
Res.: 3115 Terrace View, 89029. Tel: 702-298-5488.
Office: 3055 El Mirage Way, 89029.
Catechesis/Religious Program—Students 27.

NORTH LAS VEGAS, CLARK CO.

1—ST. CHRISTOPHER (1953), [JC] Revs. H. Brian Highfill; Roland Rivera (Mexico).
Mailing Address: 1840 N. Bruce St., 89030. Tel: 702-642-1154; Fax: 702-642-0719.
Res.: 1401 Flower Ave., 89030.
School—Tel: 702-657-8008; Fax: 702-642-2461. Mrs. Mary Gorts-Gugino, Prin. Lay Teachers 11; Students 309.
Catechesis/Religious Program—Tel: 702-657-6779; Fax: 702-657-8406. Mrs. Sharon Pauli, D.R.E. Students 2,350.

2—ST. JOHN NEUMANN (1999), Revs. Bede Wevita; Sean Poland.
Mailing Address: 2575 W. El Campo Grande Ave., 89031. Tel: 702-657-0200; Fax: 702-648-2327.
Res.: 912 Whitehollow Ave., 89031. Tel: 702-642-6750.
Catechesis/Religious Program—Students 391.

OVERTON, CLARK CO., ST. JOHN THE EVANGELIST (1959), Rev. Leo Coughlin, Admin.
Mailing Address: P.O. Box 457, 89040. Fax: 702-397-8098.
Office—150 N. Moapa Valley Blvd., 89040. Tel: 702-397-8096; Fax: 702-397-8264.
Res.: 3228 Taylor St., Logandale, 89021. Tel: 702-398-7275.
Catechesis/Religious Program—Tel: 702-397-2009. Students 66.

PAHRUMP, NYE CO., OUR LADY OF THE VALLEY (1985), Rev. Bruno Mauricci.
Mailing Address: 781 E. Gamebird, 89048.
Rectory: 3031 S. Blagg Rd., 89048. Tel: 775-727-4044; Fax: 775-727-3784.
Catechesis/Religious Program—Students 48.
Mission—Christ the Desert P.O. Box 218, Amargosa Valley, Nye Co. 89020. Tel: 775-372-5337.

TONOPAH, NYE CO., ST. PATRICK (1902), (Native American), [JC] Rev. James P. McCauley, S.J.
Mailing Address: P.O. Box 325, 89049. Tel: 775-482-6746.
Res.: 144 South St., 89049. Fax: 775-482-8446.
Catechesis/Religious Program—Tel: 775-482-6690. Students 30.
Mission—St. Barbara Hadley. P.O. Box 1563, Round Mountain, Nye Co. 89045.
Mission—Our Lady of Guadalupe Fish Lake, Esmeralda Co.

Military Chaplains:
Revs.—
Guico, Manuel R., Wing Chap., Our Lady of the Skies, 4302 N. Washington Blvd., Nellis AFB, 89191.
McNulty, Jerry, Wing Chap., Dept. of Veterans Affairs, VAMC - 125, 1700 Vegas Dr., 89107. Tel: 702-385-3700

Retired:
Revs.—
Caviglia, Caesar
Duff, William
Franzinell, Benjamin
Lavoy, Elwood
McVeigh, John J.
O'Donnell, Philip
Slatterie, Leo

Permanent Deacons:
Bravo, Tony
Deegan, Joseph
Gutierrez, Peter
Halt, Tom
Oettinger, Frank F.
Pemper, Frank
Whittle, James

INSTITUTIONS LOCATED IN THE DIOCESE

[A] HIGH SCHOOLS, DIOCESAN

LAS VEGAS. *Bishop Gorman High School*, 1801 Maryland Pkwy., 89104. Tel: 702-732-1945; Fax: 702-732-2856. Email: principal@bishopgorman.org. Web: www.bishopgorman.org. Connie Gerber, Prin.; Rev. Norbert P. Bibeault, C.S.V. Priests 1; Lay Teachers 64; Students 853.

[B] GENERAL HOSPITALS

HENDERSON. *St. Rose Dominican Hospital Rose de Lima Campus*, 102 E. Lake Mead Dr., 89015. Tel: 702-616-5000; Fax: 702-616-4699. Web: www.strosecares.org. *Catholic Healthcare West*, 185 Berry St., Suite 300, San Francisco, CA 94107. Rod Davis, Pres. Sponsored by Sisters of St. Dominic, Congregation of the Most Holy Rosary (Adrian, MI), a dba of Catholic Healthcare West Sisters 5; Bed Capacity 150; Total Staff 935; Patients Assisted Annually 52,366.

St. Rose Dominican Hospital Siena Campus, 3001 St. Rose Pkwy., 89052-6178. Tel: 702-616-5000; Fax: 702-616-5511. Web: www.strosecares.org. *Catholic Healthcare West*, 185 Berry St., Suite 300, San Francisco, CA 94107. Rod Davis, Pres. Sponsored by Sisters of St. Dominic, Congregation of the Most Holy Rosary (Adrian, MI), a dba of Catholic Healthcare West Sisters 1; Bed Capacity 180; Total Staff 1,066; Patients Assisted Annually 69,181.

[C] DAY NURSERIES

LAS VEGAS. *Catholic Charities Child Care Center*, 451 E. Twain, 89109. Tel: 702-735-4358; Fax: 702-735-6659. Email: childcare@catholiccharities.com. Web: www.catholiccharities.com. Barbara Gray, Admin. Sponsor: Catholic Charities. Enrollment Capacity 150.

[D] MONASTERIES AND RESIDENCES OF PRIESTS AND BROTHERS

LAS VEGAS. *Clerics of St. Viator Retirement Home*, 4219 Pinecrest Cir. E., 89121. Tel: 702-456-8512. Revs. Robert F. Cooney, C.S.V., Dir.; Norbert P. Bibeault, C.S.V.; James Crilly, C.S.V. Priests 3.

Dominican Rectory, Fra Angelico House (Western Dominican Province) , 1701 Chapman Dr., 89104. Tel: 702-369-1215; Fax: 702-369-3742.

[E] CONVENTS AND RESIDENCES FOR SISTERS

LAS VEGAS. *The Franciscan Sisters of Perpetual Adoration*, 1304 E. St. Louis Ave., 89104-3466. Tel: 702-735-5285; Fax: 702-732-8830. Email: lorforster@aol.com.

Holy Family Convent, 5276 S. Lookout St., 89120. Tel: 702-435-1526. Email: srmjulie@333aol.com. Sisters of the Holy Family 2.

HENDERSON. *Convent of the Sisters of St. Joseph Chestnut Hill, Philadelphia*, 507 Chestnut View Pl., 89052-2821. Tel: 702-260-4928; Fax: 702-697-5917. Email: mcginley@dioceseoflasvegas.org. Sr. Patricia McGinley, S.S.J., Dir., Catechetical Min.

[F] MISCELLANEOUS

LAS VEGAS. *Catholic Charities of Southern Nevada*, 1501 Las Vegas Blvd., N., 89101. Tel: 702-385-2662; Fax: 702-384-0677. Email: ccsnweb@catholiccharities.com. Web: www.catholiccharities.com.

Adoption Services Tel: 702-385-3351; Fax: 702-388-8723.

Crossroads Transitional Housing for Senior Men Tel: 702-383-0700; Fax: 702-383-8243.

Deferred Giving Program Tel: 702-385-2662; Fax: 702-384-0677.

Department of Pastoral Ministry, 1501 Las Vegas Blvd. N., 89101. Tel: 702-383-0700; Fax: 702-383-8243. Rev. John McShane, Chap.

Catholic Charities Child Care Center Tel: 702-735-4358; Fax: 702-735-6659.

Immigration Services Tel: 702-388-6908; Fax: 702-436-1579.

Marian Transitional Housing for Senior Women Tel: 702-565-5328; Fax: 702-565-7711.

Migration and Refugee Services Tel: 702-383-8387; Fax: 702-436-1579.

Respite Care Referral Service Tel: 702-385-5284; Fax: 702-385-3206.

RSVP (Retired & Senior Volunteer Program) Tel: 702-385-5284; 702-382-0721; Fax: 702-385-3206.

Senior Community Employment Service Tel: 702-385-5284; Fax: 702-385-3206.

Senior Companion Tel: 702-385-5284; Fax: 702-385-3206.

Senior Nutrition & Meals-on-Wheels Tel: 702-385-5284; Fax: 702-385-3206.

Social Ministry Tel: 702-385-2662; Fax: 702-384-0677.

Social Services Tel: 702-383-0766; Fax: 702-383-9031.

Lied Dining Facility Tel: 702-385-7801; Fax: 702-383-8243.

St. Vincent Shelter Tel: 702-383-0700; Fax: 702-383-8243.

Employment Services Center Tel: 702-384-3837; Fax: 702-385-6085.

Catholic Charities Thrift Stores Tel: 702-385-2662; Fax: 702-384-0677.

NCWB Housing, Inc. Tel: 702-255-0282; Fax: 702-255-0283.

CCSN Mojave Project, Inc. Tel: 702-225-0282; Fax: 702-225-0283.

CCSN-CTS Annex, Inc. Tel: 702-225-0282; Fax: 702-225-0283.

CCSN McFarland Housing Development Corporation, Inc. Tel: 702-255-0282; Fax: 702-255-0283.

CCSN McFarland Housing, Inc., 2021 Loro Ct., 89117. Tel: 702-255-0282; Fax: 702-255-0283. David Elnes, Project Coord.

Diocesan Residence, 5155 W. Tropicana, Unit 2186, 89103. Tel: 702-735-3500; Fax: 702-735-8941.

Serra House (Formation Residence), 1212 E. Oakey Blvd., 89104. Tel: 702-696-1668; Fax: 702-735-8941. Email: lvpriest@aol.com. Rev. Anthony Vercellone, Vocations Dir.

HENDERSON. *Diocesan Residence*, 2378 Rainswept Ave., 89052.

Saint Therese Center HIV/AIDS Outreach Program , 67 E. Lake Mead Blvd., 89009. Tel: 702-564-4224; Fax: 702-564-0604. Email: aidsproject@dioceseoflasvegas.org. Web: sainttheresecenter.org. Rev. Joseph O'Brien, O.P., Exec. Dir.

RELIGIOUS INSTITUTES OF MEN REPRESENTED IN THE DIOCESE

For further details refer to the corresponding bracketed number in the Religious Institutes of Men or Women section.

[1320]—*Clerics of St. Viator*—C.S.V.
[0520]—*Franciscan Friars*—O.F.M.
[0690]—*Jesuit Fathers & Brothers*—S.J.
[]—*Western Dominican Province*—O.P.

RELIGIOUS INSTITUTES OF WOMEN REPRESENTED IN THE DIOCESE

[1780]—*Congregation of the Sisters of the Third Order of St. Francis of Perpetual Adoration*—F.S.P.A.
[1070-04]—*Dominican Sisters*—O.P.
[1630]—*Sisters of St. Francis of the Penance and Christian Charity* (St. Francis Prov.)—O.S.F.
[3893]—*Sisters of St. Joseph of Chestnut Hill*—SSJ
[1960]—*Sisters of the Holy Family*—S.H.F.

NECROLOGY

(No Deaths)

Diocese of Lexington

Most Reverend

RONALD W. GAINER

Bishop of Lexington; ordained May 19, 1973; appointed Bishop of Lexington December 13, 2002; consecrated February 22, 2003 *Office: The Catholic Center*, 1310 W. Main St., Lexington, KY 40508-2048.

The Catholic Center: 1310 W. Main St., Lexington, KY 40508-2048. Tel: 859-253-1993; Fax: 859-254-6284.

Web: www.cdlex.org

Email: webmaster@cdlex.org

ESTABLISHED MARCH 2, 1988.

Square Miles 16,423.

Comprises the counties of Anderson, Bath, Bell, Bourbon, Boyd, Boyle, Breathitt, Carter, Clark, Clay, Elliott, Estill, Fayette, Floyd, Franklin, Garrard, Greenup, Harlan, Jackson, Jessamine, Johnson, Knott, Knox, Laurel, Lawrence, Lee, Leslie, Letcher, Lincoln, McCreary, Madison, Magoffin, Martin, Menifee, Mercer, Montgomery, Morgan, Nicholas, Owsley, Perry, Pike, Powell, Pulaski, Rockcastle, Rowan, Scott, Wayne, Whitley, Wolfe and Woodford.

Legal Title: For legal titles of parishes and diocesan institutions, consult the Chancellor.

STATISTICAL OVERVIEW

Personnel	
Bishop	1
Retired Bishops	1
Priests: Diocesan Active in Diocese	35
Priests: Diocesan Active Outside Diocese	1
Priests: Retired, Sick or Absent	12
Number of Diocesan Priests	48
Religious Priests in Diocese	23
Total Priests in Diocese	71
Extern Priests in Diocese	1
Ordinations:	
Transitional Deacons	4
Permanent Deacons	33
Permanent Deacons in Diocese	37
Total Brothers	5
Total Sisters	137
Parishes	
Parishes	59
With Resident Pastor:	
Resident Diocesan Priests	35
Resident Religious Priests	9
Without Resident Pastor:	
Administered by Deacons	3
Administered by Professed Religious Men	2
Administered by Religious Women	7
Administered by Lay People	3
Missions	5
Professional Ministry Personnel:	
Brothers	2
Sisters	25
Lay Ministers	38
Welfare	
Catholic Hospitals	7
Total Assisted	1,030,642
Health Care Centers	4
Total Assisted	71,632
Homes for the Aged	1
Total Assisted	82
Special Centers for Social Services	1
Total Assisted	8,025
Educational	
Diocesan Students in Other Seminaries	7
Total Seminarians	7
High Schools, Diocesan and Parish	1
Total Students	880
High Schools, Private	1
Total Students	50
Elementary Schools, Diocesan and Parish	14
Total Students	3,105
Elementary Schools, Private	1
Total Students	189
Catechesis/Religious Education:	
High School Students	755
Elementary Students	2,200
Total Students under Catholic Instruction	7,186
Teachers in the Diocese:	
Priests	1
Sisters	14
Lay Teachers	296
Vital Statistics	
Receptions into the Church:	
Infant Baptism Totals	627
Adult Baptism Totals	472
Received into Full Communion	139
First Communions	874
Confirmations	931
Marriages:	
Catholic	101
Interfaith	147
Total Marriages	248
Deaths	317
Total Catholic Population	45,153
Total Population	1,492,784

Former Bishop—Most Rev. JAMES K. WILLIAMS, D.D., ord. May 25, 1963; appt. Titular Bishop of Catula and Auxiliary Bishop of Covington on April 15, 1984; consecrated June 19, 1984; appt. Bishop of Lexington Jan. 14, 1988; installed March 2, 1988; resigned June 11, 2002.

The Catholic Center—1310 W. Main St., Lexington, 40508-2048. Tel: 859-253-1993; Fax: 859-254-6284. Office Hours: Mon.-Fri. 8:30-4:30

Vicar General—VACANT.

Chancellor—Deacon JIM PARIS.

Vice Chancellor—JANE GUENTERT.

Executive Secretary To The Bishop—SHEILA STEWART.

Finances—Dr. STUART DUBA, Dir., 1310 W. Main St., Lexington, 40508-2048.

Diocesan Consultors—Rev. Msgr. RALPH W. BEITING; Revs. WILLIAM C. BUSH; MICHAEL CHOWNING, O.F.M.; TERENCE HOPPENJANS; DANIEL J. NOLL; FRANK C. OSBURG, 1310 W. Main St., Lexington, 40508-2048.

Regional Councillors—Fayette: Rev. DAN NOLL. Bluegrass West: Rev. WILLIAM BUSH. Bluegrass East: Rev. NORMAN FISCHER. Mountain West: Rev. CHARLES HOWELL II. Mountain East: Rev. MICHAEL CHOWNING, O.F.M. Big Sandy/Licking: Rev. TERENCE HOPPENJANS.

Diocesan Tribunal—1310 W. Main St., Lexington, 40508-2048. Tel: 859-253-1993. RENATA BABICZ-BARRATO, J.U.D., J.C.L., Dir.

Judicial Vicar—Rev. JOHN E. LIST, J.C.L.

Adjutant Judicial Vicar—Rev. JAMES ZUSY, O.P.

Associate Judges—Rev. JAMES AARON, M.Div., M.Ed.; Sr. MARGARET STALLMEYER, C.D.P., J.C.L.

Defenders of the Bond—Revs. THOMAS THAI, Ph.D.; MICHAEL WEGLICKI; PAUL PRABELL; MAURICE RAJKOVICH, J.D.

Case Instructors—CAROLYN SNOWDEN; FRANCES GOODFRIEND.

Promoter of Justice—Rev. PAUL PRABELL.

Notaries—CAROLYN SNOWDEN; FRANCES GOODFRIEND.

Ministry Admissions Board—Most Rev. RONALD W. GAINER.

Priests' Retirement Board—Revs. PATRICK STEWART; DAN NOLL; FRANK OSBURG; CHARLES HOWELL II; CHARLES MCDONALD; Mr. JOHN D. PRICE; WILLIAM TOZER; JOB D. TURNER; STUART DUBA.

Diocesan Offices And Directors

Archives—JIM PARIS, Archivist, 1310 W. Main St., Lexington, 40508-2048. Tel: 859-253-1993, Ext. 236.

Campus Ministry— Newman Center Dir., Contact The Catholic Center, *1310 W. Main St., Lexington, 40508-2048.* Tel: 859-253-1993.

Catholic Scouting—Rev. MICHAEL WEGLICKI, Diocesan Dir. Tel: 859-792-4009.

Catholic Social Service Bureau—Sr. FRANCES MOORE, C.D.P., Dir., Office, 1310 W. Main St., Lexington, 40508-2048. Tel: 859-253-1993.

Communications—THOMAS SHAUGHNESSY, Dir., 1310 W. Main St., Lexington, 40508-2048. Tel: 859-253-1993.

Conciliation, Arbitration Board—CAROL JACKSON, Chm.

Deaf Ministry—Coordinators: CARLENE BUSCHMAN; JOE BUSCHMAN; Rev. JOHN LIST, Chap., 1310 W. Main St., Lexington, 40508-2048. Tel: 859-253-1993; 859-223-2135 (TDD).

Development and Stewardship Office—Deacon BILL WAKEFIELD, 1310 W. Main St., Lexington, 40508-2048. Tel: 859-253-1993, Ext. 252.

Ecumenical Liaison—Mr. ARDEN WOLTERMAN, 3 Lansdowne Estates, Lexington, 40508. Tel: 859-253-1993.

Education—

Secretary of Educational Ministries—Dr. MARGARET RALPH, 1310 W. Main St., Lexington, 40508-2048. Tel: 859-253-1993, Ext. 220.

Director Of Instructional Services—Sr. BERNADETTE MCMANIGAL, B.V.M., 1310 W. Main St., Lexington, 40508-2048. Tel: 859-253-1993, Ext. 219.

Director For Catechetical Services—Mr. PATRICK GUENTERT, 1310 W. Main St., Lexington, 40508-2048. Tel: 859-253-1993, Ext. 221.

Director R.C.I.A., And Evangelization—Dr. MARGARET RALPH, 1310 W. Main St., Lexington, 40508-2048. Tel: 859-253-1993, Ext. 220.

Healthcare—Sr. ELIZABETH WENDELN, S.C.N., Diocesan Coord., 1310 W. Main St., Lexington, 40508-2048. Tel: 859-253-1993.

Hispanic Ministry—Sr. SANDRA DELGADO, O.P., Diocesan Coord.; Rev. WILLIAM SPINE, S.J., Assoc. Dir., 1310 W. Main St., Lexington, 40508-2048. Tel: 859-253-1993.

Buen Pastor - Centro Catolico—1812 Versailles Rd., Lexington, 40504. Tel: 859-254-5507. Staff: ARY BAEZ; RAQUEL APARICIO.

HIV/AIDS Ministry—Rev. JOHN C. CURTIS, Diocesan Coord.

Justice and Peace—Rev. JOHN RAUSCH, G.H.M., Diocesan Coord.

Commission for African American Catholic Concerns—Contacts: Dr. MARIAN SWOPE; Mr. JAMES WEATHERS, P.O. Box 13006, Lexington, 40583-3006. Tel: 859-223-3603.

Rural Life—The Catholic Center, 1310 W. Main St.,

Lexington, 40508-2048. Tel: 859-253-1993, Ext. 244.

Liturgy—KAREN ROOD, Dir., 1310 W. Main St., Lexington, 40508-2048. Tel: 859-253-1993, Ext. 212.

Ministry Formation—Sr. IRIS ANN LEDDEN, S.S.N.D., Dir., 1310 W. Main St., Lexington, 40508-2048. Tel: 859-253-1993, Ext. 248.

Mission Office, Propagation Of The Faith And The Holy Childhood—Deacon BILL WAKEFIELD, Diocesan Dir., 1310 W. Main St., Lexington, 40508-2048. Tel: 859-253-1993, Ext. 245.

Newspaper "Cross Roads"—THOMAS F. SHAUGHNESSY, Editor, 1310 W. Main St., Lexington, 40508-2048. Tel: 859-253-1993, Ext. 258; Fax: 859-259-0951.

Parish Leadership—Sr. ELIZABETH WENDELN, S.C.N., Dir., 1310 W. Main St., Lexington, 40508-2048. Tel: 859-253-1993, Ext. 251.

Pastoral Services—Sr. HELEN MAHER GARVEY, B.V.M., Diocesan Dir., 1310 W. Main St., Lexington, 40508-2048. Tel: 859-253-1993.

Permanent Diaconate—Co-Directors: ARDEN WOLTERMAN; BETTY WOLTERMAN, 3 Lansdowne Estate, Lexington, 40502-3321. Tel: 859-276-4123.

Persons with Disabilities—Mrs. MARY PETTY, 124 Rolling Hills, Danville, 40422. Tel: 859-236-5017.

Priests' Personnel—Rev. LAWRENCE HEHMAN, Dir., 1332 Viley Rd., Lexington, 40504. Tel: 859-252-4259.

Prison Ministry—Rev. DAVID M. SCHILDER, Diocesan Coord., 900 Winchester Ave., Ashland, 41101-7497. Tel: 606-329-1607.

Religious—Sr. HELEN MAHER GARVEY, B.V.M., Dir., 1310 W. Main St., Lexington, 40508-2048. Tel: 859-253-1993, Ext. 236.

Respect Life—JIM PARIS, Diocesan Coord.

Victim Assistance Coordinator—Sr. FRANCES E. MOORE, C.D.P. Tel: 859-253-1993, Ext. 215. Email: fmoore@cdlex.org.

Vocations—Revs. MARK DREVES, Dir.; JOHN MORIARTY, 1310 W. Main St., Lexington, 40508-2048.

Youth and Young Adult Ministries—VACANT, Dir., The Catholic Center, 1310 W. Main St., Lexington, 40508-2048.

CLERGY, PARISHES, MISSIONS AND PAROCHIAL SCHOOLS

CITY OF LEXINGTON
(FAYETTE COUNTY)

1—CATHEDRAL OF CHRIST THE KING (1945), Revs. Paul Prabell, Rector; Patrick Fitzsimons; Joseph Saulino; Sr. Kathy Bilskie, O.S.B, Pastoral Assoc.; Deacons Arden Wolterman; Michael Burns.
Res.: 299 Colony Blvd., 40502. Tel: 859-268-2861; Fax: 859-268-8061.
School—(Grades K-8), 412 Cochran Rd., 40502. Tel: 859-266-5641; Fax: 859-266-4547. Lay Teachers 32; Students 519.
Catechesis/Religious Program—Rita King, D.R.E. Prin.; Kevin Wilson, D.R.E. Students 190.

2—ST. ELIZABETH ANN SETON (1980), Rev. Wilfred J. Fraenzle; Sr. Eileen Golby, O.S.F., Pastoral Assoc.; Deacon Michael Rupinen.
Res.: 1750 Summerhill Dr., 40515. Tel: 859-273-0134.
Parish Center—Tel: 859-273-1318; Fax: 859-272-6988.
Education Office—Tel: 859-273-1318. Candace Dwyer, D.R.E.

3—MARY, QUEEN OF THE HOLY ROSARY (1960), Revs. John Moriarty, Sacramental Min.; Daniel Schwendeman; Mr. William Greenwell, Pastoral Dir.; Deacon Jim Paris.
Church & Res.: 601 Hill'N Dale Rd., 40503. Tel: 859-278-7432; Fax: 859-278-2453.
School—Tel: 859-277-3030; Fax: 859-277-1784. Lay Teachers 35; Students 569.

4—THE NEWMAN CENTER, HOLY SPIRIT (1963),, Parish for Students, Faculty and Staff of the University of Kentucky. Revs. Thomas Farrell; Walter Bado, S.J.
Res.: 320 Rose Ln., 40508. Tel: 859-255-8566; Fax: 859-254-7519.

5—ST. PAUL (1865), [JC] Revs. Daniel Noll; William J. Spine, S.J.; Deacon Thomas Waken; Sr. Clara Fehringer, O.S.U., Pastoral Dir. In Res., Rev. James Zusy, O.P.
Res.: 501 W. Short St., 40507-1254. Tel: 859-252-0738; Fax: 859-225-6127.
School—Inter-Parish Elementary - Sts. Peter and Paul School See St. Peter for details.

6—PAX CHRISTI CATHOLIC CHURCH (1994), Rev. Lawrence W. Hehman; Melissa Holland, Pastoral Assoc.
Res.: 4001 Victoria Way, 40515. Tel: 859-273-9999; Fax: 859-245-8123.

7—ST. PETER (1812), [JC] Rev. Daniel J. Noll, Sacramental Min.; Deacon Bill Wakefield; Lisa Boley, Pastoral Dir. In Res., Revs. Theodore A. Keller (Retired); Henry Kenney, S.J.
Res.: 153 Barr St., 40507. Tel: 859-252-7551; Fax: 859-252-1853.
School—Inter-Parish Elementary - Sts. Peter and Paul School, Tel: 859-254-9257; Fax: 859-254-9050. Lay Teachers 25; Students 386.

8—ST. PETER CLAVER (1887), Rev. James Sichko, Sacramental Min.; Sr. M. Lea Paolucci, S.N.D., Pastoral Dir.
Res.: 410 Jefferson St., 40508-1319. Tel: 859-254-0030; Fax: 859-253-6740.
Catechesis/Religious Program—Tel: 859-257-6802; Fax: 859-253-6740. Michael Elery, D.R.E. Students 50.

OUTSIDE THE CITY OF LEXINGTON

ASHLAND, BOYD CO., HOLY FAMILY (1860), [CEM] Rev. John P. Noe.
Res.: 900 Winchester Ave., 41101-7497. Tel: 606-329-1607; Fax: 606-329-1806.
School—932 Winchester Ave., 41101. Tel: 606-324-7040; Fax: 606-324-6288. Lay Teachers 14; Students 174.
Catechesis/Religious Program—Tel: 606-325-4727. Jane Range, D.R.E. Students 100.
Mission—St. Lawrence Greenup.

BARBOURVILLE, KNOX CO., ST. GREGORY (1910), Rev. Benny Valayath, H.G.N.
Church: 329 N. Sycamore Dr., 40906-1540. Tel: 606-546-4461; Fax: 606-546-4461.

BEATTYVILLE, LEE CO., QUEEN OF ALL SAINTS (1965), Revs. Richard D. Edelen; Charles Savarimuthu, H.G.N.; Sr. Alice Retzner, O.S.F., Pastoral Assoc.
Mailing Address: P.O. Box 563, 41311-0563. Tel: 606-464-8695; Fax: 606-464-3357 (Call First).
Res.: 90 Railroad St., 41311. Tel: 606-464-3357.
Mission—Booneville Catholic Church of the Holy Family (1984), R.R. 2, Box 221, Booneville, Owsley Co. 41314. Tel: 606-593-6948; Fax: 606-593-6999. Sisters Beatrice Herman, O.S.F., Pastoral Assoc.; Karen Linderberger, O.S.F., Pastoral Assoc.
Catechesis/Religious Program—Tel: 606-593-6948; Fax: 606-593-6999. Students 3.
Oratory—St. Therese (1948), P.O. Box 563, Heidelberg, Lee Co. 41311. Tel: 606-464-3357.

BEREA, MADISON CO., ST. CLARE (1950), Rev. John C. Curtis; Vicki Wenz, Pastoral Assoc.
Res.: 622 Chestnut St., 40403. Tel: 859-986-4633; Fax: 859-985-3413.
Mission—St. Paul (1973), P.O. Box 189, McKee, Jackson Co. 40447. Tel: 606-287-7601. Sr. Mary Dormody, C.S.J., Pastoral Assoc.

CARLISLE, NICHOLAS CO., SHRINE OF OUR LADY OF GUADALUPE (1962), Rev. Thomas Vu Minh Thai.
Church: 617 E. Main St., 40311. Tel: 859-289-5502.
Res.: 1007 Main St., Paris, 40361-1709. Tel: 859-987-1571; Fax: 859-987-7367.
Catechesis/Religious Program—Tel: 859-289-5586. Ann Hamon, D.R.E.

CORBIN, KNOX CO., SACRED HEART (1902), Rev. Mark Dreves.
Res.: 703 Masters St., P.O. Box 455, 40702. Tel: 606-528-5222; Fax: 606-523-9901.

CUMBERLAND, HARLAN CO., ST. STEPHEN (1940), Rev. Edward H. Lammert, O.F.M. In Res., Rev. Maynard Tetreault, O.F.M.
Res.: 304 Central St., 40823. Tel: 606-589-5616; Fax: 606-589-4549.
Catechesis/Religious Program—Tel: 606-589-9202. Sr. Margaret Mary Mouch, S.N.D., D.R.E.

DANVILLE, BOYLE CO., SS. PETER & PAUL (1807), Rev. Linh Nguyen; Deacon Jeremiah Noe.
Res.: 117 W. Main St., 40422. Tel: 859-236-2111; Fax: 859-236-2922.
Catechesis/Religious Program—Tel: 859-236-8247. Paula Hill, D.R.E. Students 221.

FRANKFORT, FRANKLIN CO., GOOD SHEPHERD (1845), Revs. Joseph Muench; Albert Fritsch, S.J.; Deacons Joseph Alessic; Thomas Snyder; Miriam Picconi, Dir.
Res.: 310 Wapping St., 40601-2060. Tel: 502-227-4511; Fax: 502-875-9854.
Catechesis/Religious Program—Sr. Mary Clare Windholtz, D.R.E. Students 71.
School—(Grades K-8), 316 Wapping St., 40601. Tel: 502-223-5041; Fax: 502-223-2755. Lay Teachers 25; Students 332.

GEORGETOWN, SCOTT CO., ST. JOHN'S (1869), [CEM] Rev. John E. List, J.C.L.; Deacon John Calancrella.
Res.: 604 E. Main St., 40324. Tel: 502-863-3404; Fax: 502-863-3404.
School—(Grades K-7), 106 Military St., 40324. Tel: 502-863-2607; Fax: 502-863-2259. Religious 2; Lay Teachers 13; Students 172.
Catechesis/Religious Program—Tel: 502-863-7343. Patty Kirchner, D.R.E. Students 98.
Mission—St. Francis de Sales (1794), 4086 Frankfort Pike, White Sulphur, Scott Co. 40324. Tel: 502-863-4516.

GRAYSON, CARTER CO., SS. JOHN & ELIZABETH (1964), Sr. Maria Goretti Browne, O.P., Pastoral Dir.; Revs. Bruce C. Brylinski, G.H.M. (COV); Robert Dalton, G.H.M.
Church: 799 State Hwy. 1947, 41143. Tel: 606-474-9979; Fax: 606-474-9979.
Res.: P.O. Box 341, 41143. Tel: 606-474-9897.
Catechesis/Religious Program—Tel: 606-474-5440. Nancy Kozee, D.R.E. Students 15.

HARLAN, HARLAN CO., HOLY TRINITY (1948), Bro. Mark Ligett, O.F.M., Pastoral Dir.; Rev. Edward H. Lammert, O.F.M., Pastoral Coord.
Res.: 2536 S. U.S. Hwy. 421, 40831-1798 Tel: 606-573-6311; Fax: 606-574-0093.
School—Tel: 606-573-3570. Sisters of Notre Dame 3; Lay Teachers 4; Students 46.
Catechesis/Religious Program—Margie Grieshap, D.R.E. Tel: 606-573-9906. Students 18.

HARRODSBURG, MERCER CO., ST. ANDREW (1858), [CEM] Rev. Joseph Muench.
Res.: 1125 Danville Rd., P.O. Box 648, 40330-0648. Tel: 859-734-4270; Fax: 859-733-9770.
Catechesis/Religious Program—Mary Jane Trimble, D.R.E. Students 75.
Mission—St. Mary (1949), 307 S. Buell St., Perryville, Boyle Co. 40468.

HAZARD, PERRY CO., MOTHER OF GOOD COUNSEL (1913), Rev. Michael Chowning, O.F.M.; Ms. Patricia Riestenberg, Pastoral Assoc.
Res.: 329 Poplar St. & Cedar St., 41701. Tel: 606-436-2533; Fax: 606-435-0171.
Mission—Catholic Church of the Good Shepherd (1987), P.O. Box 742, Campton, Wolfe Co. 41301. Tel: 606-668-3731. Sisters Amy Kistner, O.S.F., Pastoral Assoc.; Noreen McLaughlin, O.S.F., Pastoral Assoc.

JACKSON, BREATHITT CO., HOLY CROSS (1923), Bro. Jerome Beetz, O.F.M., Pastoral Dir.; Rev. Michael Chowning, O.F.M., Pastoral Coord.
Church: 51 Brewers Dr., 41339-9616. Tel: 606-666-7871; Fax: 606-666-7370.

JELLICO, WHITLEY CO., KY & CAMPBELL CO., TN, ST. BONIFACE (1886), [CEM] Revs. Mark Dreves; Thobias Sabariar, H.G.N.; Charles Howell II, Priest Moderator; Deacon Frank Agnoli, Pastoral Dir.
Res.: 76 W. Sycamore St., Williamsburg, 40769. Tel: 606-549-2156.

JENKINS, LETCHER CO., ST. GEORGE (1912), Rev. Edward L. Randall, O.M.I.
Res.: P.O. Box 787, 41537. Tel: 606-832-2409.
Catechesis/Religious Program—Tel: 606-633-2019. Sr. M. Junita, M.C., D.R.E. Students 15.
Mission—Holy Angels (1960), McRoberts, Letcher Co.

LANCASTER, GARRARD CO., ST. WILLIAM (1951), Rev. Michael Weglicki.
Res.: 224 Lexington St., P.O. Box 269, 40444. Tel: 859-792-4009.
Catechesis/Religious Program—Tel: 859-792-4578. Tammy Parsons, D.R.E. Students 22.

LAWRENCEBURG, ANDERSON CO., ST. LAWRENCE (1873), Rev. Charles J. McDonald; Deacon Thomas Rohan.
Res.: 120 Gatewood Ave., 40342. Tel: 502-839-6381; Fax: 502-859-2419.

LONDON, LAUREL CO., ST. WILLIAM (1906), [CEM] Rev. Charles Howell II.
Res.: 521 W. 5th St., 40741. Tel: 606-864-7500; Fax: 606-864-8263.
Catechesis/Religious Program—Sr. Marjorie Manning, C.S.C. Students 74.
Mission—St. Ann (1952), 222 Town Branch Rd., Manchester, Clay Co. 40962-1322. Tel: 606-598-2718; Fax: 606-598-2718.
Oratory—St. Sylvester, East Bernstadt

LOUISA, LAWRENCE CO., ST. JUDE (1982), Rev. Msgr. Ralph Beiting.
Res.: Rt. 5, Box 1083, 41230. Tel: 606-638-0219; Fax: 606-638-0220.
Mission—St. John Neumann (1980), Rte. 292, Hode, Martin Co. 41223. Tel: 606-395-5316.

LYNCH, HARLAN CO., CHURCH OF THE RESURRECTION (1917), Rev. Edward H. Lammert, O.F.M.; Sr. Margaret Mary Mouch, S.N.D., Pastoral Assoc.
Res.: 304 Central St., Cumberland, 40823. Tel: 606-589-5616; Fax: 606-589-4549.

MANCHESTER, CLAY CO., ST. ANN (1952),, Mission to St. William, London. Tel: 606-598-2718; Fax: 606-593-2718.

MIDDLESBORO, BELL CO., ST. JULIAN (1890), Rev. Jerome F. Stern.
Res.: 118 E. Chester Ave., 40965-1256. Tel: 606-248-2068; Fax: 606-248-2068.
School—(Grades K-8), 116 E. Chester Ave., 40965. Tel: 606-248-8309; Fax: 606-248-8307. Sisters 1; Lay Teachers 3; Students 53.
Catechesis/Religious Program—Cheryl Patterson, D.R.E. Tel: 423-869-3348; Barry Tanner, D.R.E. Tel: 423-869-9255. Students 85.
Mission—St. Anthony (1889), P.O. Box 628, Pineville,

Bell Co. 40977-0628. Tel: 606-337-2189.

MONTICELLO, WAYNE CO., ST. PETER (1967), Deacon Thomas Wagner, Pastoral Dir.; Rev. John L. Kieffer, S.J., Sacramental Min.
Office—P.O. Box 669, 42633. Tel: 606-348-9416.
Res.: 311 Michigan Ave., 42633. Tel: 606-348-0086.

MOREHEAD, ROWAN CO., CHURCH OF JESUS OUR SAVIOR (1961), Rev. Joseph Von Handorf; Deacon William T. Buelterman.
Res.: 315 Battson-Oates, P.O. Box 307, 40351. Tel: 606-784-4392; Fax: 606-783-0190.
Catechesis/Religious Program—Sr. Rosemary McCormack, D.R.E. Students 87.
Chapel—Morehead, St. Claire Medical Center, Tel: 606-783-6500.

MT. STERLING, MONTGOMERY CO., ST. PATRICK (1868), [CEM] Revs. Norman Fischer, Sacramental Min.; Lawrence Hehman, Moderator; Sr. Regina M. Baker, CDP, Pastoral Dir.
Office: 7 N. Sycamore St., 40353. Tel: 859-499-1075.

MT. VERNON, ROCKCASTLE CO., OUR LADY OF MT. VERNON (1954), Rev. John C. Curtis.
Res.: 622 Chestnut St., Berea, 40403. Tel: 859-985-8413; Fax: 859-985-8413.

NICHOLASVILLE, JESSAMINE CO., ST. LUKE (1867), Rev. William C. Bush; Deacon Richard Watson, Pastoral Assoc.
Res.: 304 S. Main St., 40356. Tel: 859-885-4892; Fax: 859-885-6762.
Catechesis/Religious Program—Tel: 859--88--489. Theresa Kemp, D.R.E. Students 100.

OTTENHEIM, LINCOLN CO., ST. SYLVESTER (1885), [CEM] Rev. Michael Weglicki.
Res.: 224 Lexington St., P.O. Box 269, Lancaster, 40444. Tel: 859-792-4009.

PAINTSVILLE, JOHNSON CO., ST. MICHAEL CATHOLIC CHURCH (1941), Rev. Terence E. Hoppenjans; Deacon John M. Lewis.
Res.: 720 Washington Ave., 41240. Tel: 606-789-4455; Fax: 606-789-4455.
School—Our Lady of the Mountains, 405 Third St., 41240. Tel: 606-789-3661; Fax: 606-789-3661. Sisters 1; Lay Teachers 5; Students 62.

PARIS, BOURBON CO., ANNUNCIATION OF THE BLESSED VIRGIN MARY (1856), [CEM] Rev. Thomas Vu Minh Thai.
Res.: 1007 Main St., 40361. Tel: 859-987-1571; Fax: 859-987-7367.
School—St. Mary, 1121 Main St., 40361. Tel: 859-987-3815; Fax: 859-987-3815. Lay Teachers 11; Students 123.

PIKEVILLE, PIKE CO., ST. FRANCIS OF ASSISI (1949), Rev. Benny Valayath, H.G.N.; Deacon Robert Boduch.
Res.: 132 Bryan St. (Keel), 41501-6822. Tel: 606-437-6822; Fax: 606-437-4901.
Church: 149 College St., 41501.
School—(Grades K-6), 147 Bryan St., 41501. Tel: 606-437-6117; Fax: 606-437-6192. Lay Teachers 5; Students 73.
Catechesis/Religious Program—Tel: 606-437-0226. Robert Boduch, D.R.E. Students 36.
Mission—St. Joseph the Worker (1985), P.O. Box 55, Elkhorn City, Pike Co. 41522. Tel: 606-754-5225.
Mission—Jesus of the Mountains Catholic Church (1988), 38 Birch Ct., Phelps, Pike Co. 41553. Tel: 606-456-7907. Sr. Grace Pasquarello, S.S.J., Pastoral Min.

PRESTONSBURG, FLOYD CO., ST. MARTHA (1984), Rev. Robert Damron.
Res.: 60 Martha Vineyard, 41653. Tel: 606-874-9526; Fax: 606-874-9526.
Chapel—Martin, Our Lady of the Way Hospital, Tel: 606-285-5181.

RAVENNA, ESTILL CO., ST. ELIZABETH OF HUNGARY (1932), Revs. Richard Edelen, Sacramental Min.; Wilfred Fraenzle; Charles Savarimuthu, H.G.N.; Sr. Diane McGuirt, O.P, Pastoral Dir.
Res.: 314 5th St., 40472-1812. Tel: 606-723-5719; Fax: 606-723-4705.

RICHMOND, MADISON CO., ST. MARK (1867), Rev. Patrick F. Stewart; Deacon Richard Jackson, (Retired).
Res.: 608 W. Main St., 40475. Tel: 859-623-2989; Fax: 859-623-4652.
School—Tel: 859-623-9112; Fax: 859-623-9947. Lay Teachers 15; Students 210.
Mission—St. Stephen the Martyr (1977), 405 University Dr., Madison Co. 40475. Tel: 859-623-9400. Diane Banasiak, Pastoral Assoc. (Eastern Kentucky University, Newman Center)

SALYERSVILLE, MAGOFFIN CO., ST. LUKE (1982), Rev. Robert Damron, Sacramental Min.
1221 Parkway Dr., 41465. Tel: 606-349-5320.
Catechesis/Religious Program—Sr. Mary Catherine Vukmanic, O.S.U., D.R.E. Students 25.

SOMERSET, PULASKI CO., ST. MILDRED (1887), Rev. Michael Ramler; Deacons G. A. Weigel; Vincent E. Cheshire; Larry Cranfill; Carter Ross; John Tohill. 203 S. Central Ave., 42501. Tel: 606-678-5051.

STANTON, POWELL CO., OUR LADY OF THE MOUNTAINS (1984), Revs. Richard Edelen; Wilfred Fraenzle, Moderator; Sr. Kathleen McMullin, O.S.F., Pastoral Dir.
1093 E. College Ave., P.O. Box 727, 40380-2354. Tel: 606-663-5919.
Catechesis/Religious Program—Fax: 606-663-5915. S. Eileen Doherty, D.R.E. Students 9.

VERSAILLES, WOODFORD CO., ST. LEO (1891), Rev. Frank C. Osburg; Sr. Mary Ann Warner, H.M., Pastoral Assoc.
Res.: 213 D. Berry Ave., 40383. Tel: 859-879-8481.
Church: 295 Huntertown Rd., 40383. Tel: 859-873-4573; Fax: 859-873-1495.
School—239 N. Main St., 40383. Tel: 606-873-4591. Sisters of Notre Dame 1; Lay Teachers 14; Students 171.

WEST LIBERTY, MORGAN CO., PRINCE OF PEACE (1963), Rev. Peter Richardson, G.H.M.
Res.: Pine Acres Dr., P.O. Box 393, 41472. Tel: 606-743-4817; Fax: 606-743-3266.
Mission—St. Julie Billiart (1969), P.O. Box 382, Owingsville, Bath Co. 40360. Tel: 606-674-3261. Deacon William R. Grimes.

WHITLEY CITY, MC CREAKY CO., GOOD SHEPHERD CHAPEL (1974), Rev. Michael Ramler; Sr. Nancy Sutton, Int. Pastoral Dir.
Res.: P.O. Box 427, 42653. Tel: 606-376-8728.

WILLIAMSBURG, WHITLEY CO., OUR LADY OF PERPETUAL HELP (1963), Revs. Mark Dreves, Sacramental Min.; Thobias Sabariar, H.G.N.; Charles Howell II; Deacon Frank Agnoli, Pastoral Dir.
Res.: 76 W. Sycamore St., 40769. Tel: 606-549-2156.

WINCHESTER, CLARK CO., ST. JOSEPH (1872), Rev. Norman A. Fischer; Deacon Charles Kennedy.
Office: 248 S. Main St., 40391.
Res.: 254 S. Main St., 40391. Tel: 859-744-4917; Fax: 859-744-0994.
School—St. Agatha Academy, (Grades K-8), 244 S. Main St., 40391. Tel: 859-744-6484; Fax: 859-744-0268. (Montessori) Sisters of Divine Providence of Kentucky 1; Lay Teachers 10; Students 240.
Catechesis/Religious Program—Michael K. Logan, D.R.E. Students 46.

Chaplains of Public Institutions

LEXINGTON. *Federal Medical Center*, 3301 Leestown Rd., 40507. Rev. Arturo Molina, Chap.
Veterans' Administration Hospital, Leestown Pk., 40511. Tel: 859-233-4511. Rev. W. Henry Kenney, S.J. (CHI), Chap.

ASHLAND. *Federal Correctional Institution*. 900 Winchester Dr., Ashland,, 41101-7497. Rev. David M. Schilder, Chap.

MANCHESTER. *Federal Correction Institute*. Rev. David Rabenecker, O.S.B. (IND), Supervisory Chap.

Special Assignment:
Revs.—
Dreves, Mark, 1310 W. Main St., 40508. Vocations Dir.
Fedders, William, (On Administrative Leave)
Johnson, Carl, Federal Bureau of Prisons, Victorville, CA.
Kenney, Henry, S.J., Spiritual Dir., Lexington, KY
Sichko, James, Coord. Campus Min., E.K.U. & Georgetown College

Retired:
Rev. Msgrs.—
Nienaber, Leonard B., Vianney Renewal Center, 6476 Eime Rd., Dittmer, MD 63023.
Rolf, John J., 15 Lemans Dr., Naples, FL 34112.
Revs.—
Blandford, James T., Sacred Heart Village, 2120 Payne St., Rm. 409 A, Louisville, 40206.
Dane, John, 193 Barnsley Rd., Wombwell, Barnsley, South Yorkshire S73 8DR, England.
Imfeld, Thomas J., 200 Red Oak St., Corbin, 40702.
Keller, Theodore, 153 Barr St., 40507.
Nieberding, Robert, 2716 Green Vally Ct., 40511.
Pilger, Joseph J., 260 Pleasant Point Dr., 40517.
Poole, William G., 2724 Green Valley Ct., 40511.
Schmidt, Louis R., Taylor Manor, 300 Berry Ave., Versailles, 40383.
Stratman, Raymond, 2720 Green Valley Ct., 40511.
Trimbur, Lee Francis, Oakmont Nursing Home, 1100 Grandview Dr., Flatwoods, 41139.

Permanent Deacons:
Agnoli, Frank
Alessio, Joseph J.
Barton, James
Boduch, Robert
Buelterman, William
Burns, Michael
Calandrella, John
Cheshire, Vincent
Cox, James H.
Cranfill, Larry
Daukas, Michael R.
Fister, Louis
Flowers, Don K.
Grimes, William R.
Horine, James
Jackson, Richard
Kennedy, Charles
Lackney, Robert R.
Lewis, John M.
Marshall, Boyd
Mellenger, Karl
Noe, Jeremiah, H.
O'Neil, Dennis J.
Paris, Jim
Rohan, Thomas
Ross, Carter, Jr.
Rupinen, Michael
Schueneman, Joseph T.
Snyder, Thomas
Tohill, John J.
Wagner, Thomas
Wakefield, Bill
Waken, Thomas J.
Watson, Richard
Weigel, Gerard A.
Wolterman, Arden J.
Young, Melvin

PARISH PILGRIMAGE SHRINES

CARLISLE. *Our Lady of Guadalupe Shrine*, 617 E. Main St., 40311.

INSTITUTIONS LOCATED IN THE DIOCESE

[A] HIGH SCHOOLS, DIOCESAN

LEXINGTON. *Lexington Catholic High School*, 2250 Clays Mill Rd., 40503. Tel: 859-277-7183; Fax: 859-276-5086. Web: lexingtoncatholic.com. Mr. Bill Glaser, Pres.; Mrs. Sally Stevens, Prin. Sisters 1; Lay Teachers 60; Students 880.

[B] HIGH SCHOOLS, PRIVATE

MARTIN. *The Piarist School*, (Grades 9-12), Rte. 80, P.O. Box 870, 41649. Tel: 606-285-3950; Fax: 606-285-3950. Email: piarist@bellsouth.net. Web: www.geocities.com/piarist. Rev. Thomas R. Carroll, Sch.P., Prin. College Prep High School. Priests 1; Lay Teachers 8; Students 50.

[C] ELEMENTARY SCHOOLS, PRIVATE

CORBIN. *St. Camillus Academy*, (Grades PreK-8), 709 Roy Kidd Ave., 40701. Tel: 606-528-5077; Fax: 606-526-0106. Email: stcam@bellsouth.net. Sisters of Divine Providence of KY, Coed Day School. Sisters 4; Lay Teachers 8; Students 189.

[D] GENERAL HOSPITALS

LEXINGTON. *Continuing Care Hospital, Inc.*, 150 N. Eagle Creek Dr., 40509. Tel: 859-967-5744; Fax: 859-967-5616. Email: hiltonna@sjhlex.org. Neil Hilton, Admin.
St. Joseph Health Care, Inc. dba St. Joseph East , 150 N. Eagle Creek Dr., 40509. Tel: 859-967-5000. Web: www.saintjosephhealthcare.org. Bill Hendrickson, Pres. & CEO; Deacon Thomas Waken, Dir. Chap. Svcs. Bed Capacity 166; Patients Assisted Annually 17,000.
St. Joseph Hospital, One St. Joseph Dr., 40504. Tel: 859-313-1000; Fax: 859-313-3000. Bill Hendrickson, Pres. & CEO; Deacon Thomas Waken, Dir. Chap. Svcs. (Member of Catholic Health Initiatives) Sisters of Charity of Nazareth 7; Bed Capacity 445; Patients Assisted Annually 69,000.

ASHLAND. *Our Lady of Bellefonte Hospital, Inc.*, St. Christopher Dr., 41101. Tel: 606-833-3333; Fax: 606-833-3593. Web: www.olbh.com. Charles W. Neumann, Int. CEO &Vice Pres., Opers. S.E. Div.; Sharon McDonald, Pastoral Care; Rev. John P. Noe, Chap.; Sharon McQuate, Vice Pres., Mission. (Member of Bon Secours Kentucky Health System, Inc.) Bed Capacity 214; Patients Assisted Annually 206,904.

BEREA. *Berea Hospital, Inc.*, 305 Estill St., 40403. Tel: 859-986-3151; Fax: 859-986-6768. Email: angiecarman@catholichealth.net. A member of Catholic Health Initiatives. Bed Capacity 48; Patients Assisted Annually 52,000.

IRVINE. *Marcum and Wallace Memorial Hospital*, 60 Mercy Ct., 40336. Tel: 606-723-2115; Fax: 606-723-2951. Susan Starling, Pres. & CEO. (Member of Mercy Health System, Cincinnati, OH). Bed Capacity 25; Patients Assisted Annually 46,103.

LONDON. *London, Marymount* dba Marymount Medical Center , 310 E. Ninth St., 40741. Tel: 606-878-6520; Fax: 606-877-3707. Email: sleurck@marymount.com. Web: marymount.com. Steve Leurck, Int. CEO; Jim Kaskie, Vice Pres., CHI.

(Member of Catholic Health Initiatives) Bed Capacity 89; Patients Assisted Annually 173,361.

MARTIN. *Our Lady of the Way Hospital, Inc.*, Box 910, 41649. Tel: 606-285-5181; Fax: 606-285-6422. Email: jparsons@olwh.org. Web: www.olwh.org. Ms. Kathy Stumbo, Admin. & CEO; Kevin Lofton, Pres. & CEO. Member of Catholic Health Initiatives Bed Capacity 29; Patients assisted annually: patient visits 60,480.

MOREHEAD. *Saint Claire Medical Center* 40351. Tel: 606-783-6500; Fax: 606-783-6503. Email: mjneff@st-claire.org. Web: st-claire.com. Mr. Mark Neff, Pres. & CEO. Sisters of Notre Dame Sisters 5; Bed Capacity 159; Bassinets 10; Patients Assisted Annually 477,259; Patients with Primary Care Centers 87,403.

[E] PRIMARY HEALTH CARE SERVICES

FRENCHBURG. *Menifee Co. Medical Clinic*, HCR 71, Box 220, Kentucky 36, 40322. Tel: 606-768-2191; Fax: 606-768-6130. Email: craighburrows@st-claire.org. Web: st.claire.org. Craig Burrows, M.D., Clinic & Patient Svcs. Dir. (Div. of St. Claire Medical Center). Patients Assisted Annually 19,000.

OLIVE HILL. *Carter County Medical Clinic*, P.O. Box 1268, 155 Bricklayer St., 41164. Tel: 606-286-4152; Fax: 606-286-2385. Janie Zornes, Clinic Coord. (Div. of St. Claire Medical Center). Patients Assisted Annually 18,936.

OWINGSVILLE. *Bath County Medical Clinic*, 632 Slate Ave., 40360. Tel: 606-674-6386; Fax: 606-674-3096. Email: pgshouse@st-claire.org. Pam Shouse, Clinic Coord. (Div. of St. Claire Medical Center). Patients Assisted Annually 20,000.

SANDY HOOK. *Elliott County Medical Clinic*, P.O. Box 748, 41171. Tel: 606-738-5155; Fax: 606-738-5420. Amy Conley, M.D., Clinic Medical Dir. (Div. of St. Claire Medical Center). Patients Assisted Annually 14,596.

[F] NURSING HOMES

VERSAILLES. *Taylor Manor Nursing Home*, 300 Berry Ave., 40383. Tel: 606-873-4201; Fax: 859-873-4856. Sr. Mary Christina Murray, S.J.W., Admin.; Rev. Frank Sherry, C.P.M., Chap. Sisters of St. Joseph the Worker 7; Patients Assisted Annually 82.

[G] RESIDENCES OF PRIESTS

PRESTONSBURG. *Piarist Fathers*, 99 Martha's Vineyard, 41653. Tel: 606-874-4261. Rev. Thomas R. Carroll, Sch.P. Priests 1.

[H] MONASTERIES FOR SISTERS

MARTIN. *Sisters of St. Benedict-The Dwelling Place Monastery*, 150 Mt. Tabor Rd., 41649. Tel: 606-886-9624; Fax: 606-886-9624. Email: mtabor150@hotmail.com. Web: www.geocities.com/athens/9871. Sr. Eileen Schepers, O.S.B., Prioress. Total number in community perpetually professed 5.

[I] SECULAR INSTITUTES

LEXINGTON. *Society of St. Vincent de Paul*, 4056 Boone Creek Rd., 40509-9711. Tel: 859-264-0979. Email: bernadette.dupont@fhwa.dot.gov. Bernadette Dupont, Pres. District Council of Lexington.

[J] SOCIAL SERVICES

MOUNT VERNON. **Appalachia Science in the Public Interest*, 50 Lair St., 40456. Tel: 606-256-0077; Fax: 606-256-2779. Email: aspi@a-spi.org. Web: www.a-spi.org. Rev. John L. Kieffer, S.J.

[K] RENEWAL CENTERS

HAZARD. *Father Farrell Spiritual Life Center*, 329 Poplar at Cedar, 41701. Tel: 606-436-2533; Fax: 606-435-0171. Email: mike.chowning@mgcce.org. Rev. Michael Chowning, O.F.M., Dir.; Pat Riestenberg, Assoc. Dir.

LANCASTER. *Cliffview Retreat Center*, 789 Bryants Camp Rd., 40444. Tel: 859-792-3333; 877-792-3330; Fax: 859-792-1223. Email: cliffctr@cdlex.org. Web: www.cdlex.org. Deacon Joseph Schueneman, Co-Dir.; Judy Schueneman, Co-Dir.

MARTIN. *Sisters of St. Benedict, Mt. Tabor Retreat Center*, 150 Mt. Tabor Rd., 41649. Tel: 606-886-9624; Fax: 606-886-9624. Email: mtabor150@hotmail.com. Staff Sisters 5.

[L] NEWMAN CENTERS

LEXINGTON. *The Newman Center Holy Spirit Parish University of Kentucky* 320 Rose Ln., 40508. Tel: 859-255-8566; Fax: 859-254-7519. Email: timenewman@aol.com. Revs. Thomas Farrell; Walter Bado, S.J.

BARBOURVILLE. *St. Gregory Church-Union College* 329 N. Sycamore St., 40906-1540. Tel: 606-546-4461; Fax: 606-546-4461. Email: stgreg@barbourville.com. Web: barbourville.catholicweb.com. Rev. Thobias Sabariar, H.G.N.

BEREA. *St. Clare Church-Berea College* 622 Chestnut St., 40403. Tel: 859-986-4633; Fax: 859-985-8413. Email: stclare@zeus.chapel1.com. Rev. John C. Curtis.

MOREHEAD. *Catholic Student Center-Morehead State University* P.O. Box 307, 40351. Tel: 606-784-4392; Fax: 606-783-0190. Email: joscc@adelphia.net. Web: www.cdlex.org/morehead.

RICHMOND. *St. Stephen Newman Center-St. Mark Church* Eastern Kentucky University, 405 University Dr., 40475-2154. Tel: 859-623-9400 (Center); Fax: 859-623-4652. Email: ekunewman@kih.net. Web stmark-richmond.org/newman. Rev. Patrick F. Stewart; Diane Banasiak, Pastoral Assoc.

[M] MISCELLANEOUS

ASHLAND. *Bon Secours Kentucky Health System Foundation, Inc. dba Our Lady of Bellefonte Hospital Foundation*, 1505 Carter Ave., P.O. Box 789, 41105-0789. Tel: 606-833-3655; Fax: 606-324-1186. Email: mstautberg@olbh.com. Web: www.careyoucantrust.com. Mr. Michael D. Stautberg, Vice Pres. External Affairs.

Bon Secours Kentucky Health System, Inc., St. Christopher Dr., 41101. Tel: 606-833-3333; Fax: 606-833-3593. Web: www.olbh.com. Charles W. Neumann, Inc. CEO & Sr. Vice Pres., Opers., SE Div.

WITTENSVILLE. *The Catholic Committee of Appalachia*, P.O. Box 62, 41274. Tel: 606-297-8792; Fax: 606-297-8792. Email: ccappal@foothills.net. Sr. Robbie Pentecost, Contact Person.

RELIGIOUS INSTITUTES OF MEN REPRESENTED IN THE DIOCESE

For further details refer to the corresponding bracketed number in the Religious Institutes of Men or Women section.

[0820]—*Congregation of the Fathers of Mercy*—C.P.M.
[0520]—*Franciscan Friars* (St. John Baptist Prov.)—O.F.M.
[0570]—*Glenmary Home Missioners*—G.H.M.
[]—*Heralds of Good News* (India)—H.G.N.
[0690]—*Jesuit Fathers and Brothers* (Chicago & Detroit Provs.)—S.J.
[0910]—*Oblates of Mary Immaculate* (Eastern American Prov.)—O.M.I.
[0430]—*Order of Preachers*—O.P.
[1040]—*Piarist Fathers* (U.S. Prov.)—Sch.P.

RELIGIOUS INSTITUTES OF WOMEN REPRESENTED IN THE DIOCESE

[0100]—*Adorers of the Blood of Christ* (Ruma, IL)—A.S.C.
[0230]—*Benedictine Sisters of Pontifical Jurisdiction* (Pittsburgh, PA; Covington, KY; Martin, KY)—O.S.B.
[1810]—*Bernardine Sisters of the Third Order of St. Francis*—O.S.F.
[2100]—*Congregation of Humility of Mary*—C.H.M.
[2230]—*Congregation of the Infant Jesus*—C.I.J.
[1920]—*Congregation of the Sisters of the Holy Cross*—C.S.C.
[1730]—*Congregation of the Sisters of the Third Order of St. Francis* (Oldenburg, IN)—O.S.F.
[1780]—*Congregation of the Sisters of the Third Order of St. Francis of Perpetual Adoration* (Eastern Region)—F.S.P.A.
[1070-03]—*Dominican Sisters* (Sinsinawa, WI)—O.P.
[1070-14]—*Dominican Sisters* (Grand Rapids, MI)—O.P.
[1070-13]—*Dominican Sisters* (Adrian, MI)—O.P.
[1440]—*Franciscan Sisters of the Poor*—S.F.P.
[2080]—*Home Mission Sisters of America (Glenmary)*—G.H.M.S.
[2575]—*Institute of the Sisters of Mercy of the Americas* (Charlotte, NC; Philadelphia, PA; West Hartford, CT)—R.S.M.
[2710]—*Missionaries of Charity*—M.C.
[2850]—*Missionary Sisters of the Precious Blood*—C.P.C.
[2070]—*Religious of the Holy Union of the Sacred Hearts*—S.U.S.C.
[2970]—*School Sisters of Notre Dame* (Baltimore)—S.S.N.D.
[1680]—*School Sisters of St. Francis*—O.S.F.
[0430]—*Sisters of Charity of Blessed Virgin Mary* (Dubuque, IA)—B.V.M.
[0440]—*Sisters of Charity of Cincinnati, OH*—S.C.
[0500]—*Sisters of Charity of Nazareth*—S.C.N.
[0580]—*Sisters of Charity of St. Augustine* (Rienfield, OH)—C.S.A.
[1000]—*The Sisters of Divine Providence of Kentucky*—C.D.P.
[]—*Sisters of Mercy* (Ireland)—R.S.M.
[]—*Sisters of Mercy* (South Africa)—R.S.M.
[2560]—*Sisters of Mercy of Detroit* (Farmington Hills, MI)—R.S.M.
[2990]—*Sisters of Notre Dame* (Covington Prov.)—S.N.D.
[3000]—*Sisters of Notre Dame de Namur* (Cincinnati Prov.)—S.N.D.deN.
[3360]—*Sisters of Providence of St. Mary-of-the-Woods, Indiana*—S.P.
[3893]—*Sisters of Saint Joseph of Chestnut Hill, Philadelphia*—S.S.J.
[1540]—*Sisters of St Francis* (Clinton, IA)—O.S.F.
[3750]—*Sisters of St. Chretienne* (Wrentham, MA)—S.S.Ch.
[1650]—*The Sisters of St. Francis of Philadelphia*—O.S.F.
[3830-05]—*Sisters of St. Joseph* (Baden, PA; Brentwood, NY)—C.S.J.
[3830-05]—*Sisters of St. Joseph* (Brentwood, NY)—C.S.J.
[3850]—*Sisters of St. Joseph of Chambery*—C.S.J.
[3920]—*Sisters of St. Joseph the Worker*—S.J.W.
[2110]—*Sisters of the Humility of Mary* (Villa Maria, PA)—H.M.
[1760]—*Sisters of the Third Order of St. Francis of Penance and Charity* (Tiffin, OH)—O.S.F.
[1720]—*Sisters of the Third Order Regular of St. Francis of the Congregation of Our Lady of Lourdes*—O.S.F.
[2150]—*Sisters, Servants of the Immaculate Heart of Mary*—I.H.M.
[4120]—*Ursuline Sisters of Cincinnati*—O.S.U.
[4120-03]—*Ursuline Sisters of the Immaculate Conception* (Louisville, KY)—O.S.U.
[4170]—*Vincentian Sisters of Charity* (Bedford, OH)—V.S.C.

DIOCESAN CEMETERIES

LEXINGTON. *Calvary*
ASHLAND. *Calvary*
MT. STERLING. *St. Thomas*

NECROLOGY

(No Deaths)

Diocese of Lincoln

(Dioecesis Lincolnensis)

Most Reverend

FABIAN W. BRUSKEWITZ, D.D., S.T.D.

Bishop of Lincoln; ordained July 17, 1960; appointed Bishop of Lincoln March 24, 1992; consecrated May 13, 1992. *Mailing Address: P.O. Box 80328, Lincoln, NE 68501-0328.*

Chancery: P.O. Box 80328, Lincoln, NE 68501-0328. Tel: 402-488-0921; Fax: 402-488-3569.

ERECTED AUGUST 2, 1887.

Square Miles 23,844.

Comprises that part of the State of Nebraska south of the Platte River.

Legal Title: "The Catholic Bishop of Lincoln."

For legal titles of parishes and diocesan institutions, consult the Chancery.

STATISTICAL OVERVIEW

Personnel	
Bishop	1
Priests: Diocesan Active in Diocese	117
Priests: Diocesan Active Outside Diocese	8
Priests: Retired, Sick or Absent	23
Number of Diocesan Priests	148
Religious Priests in Diocese	9
Total Priests in Diocese	157
Extern Priests in Diocese	2
Ordinations:	
Diocesan Priests	3
Religious Priests	3
Transitional Deacons	4
Permanent Deacons in Diocese	2
Total Sisters	134
Parishes	
Parishes	136
With Resident Pastor:	
Resident Diocesan Priests	84
Resident Religious Priests	1
Without Resident Pastor:	
Administered by Priests	51
Missions	1
New Parishes Created	1
Professional Ministry Personnel:	
Lay Ministers	2
Welfare	
Catholic Hospitals	3
Total Assisted	210,021
Homes for the Aged	3
Total Assisted	277
Special Centers for Social Services	22
Total Assisted	43,702
Residential Care of Disabled	1
Total Assisted	18
Other Institutions	1
Total Assisted	5,911
Educational	
Seminaries, Diocesan	1
Students from This Diocese	23
Students from Other Diocese	15
Diocesan Students in Other Seminaries	12
Seminaries, Religious	1
Students Religious	56
Total Seminarians	91
High Schools, Diocesan and Parish	6
Total Students	1,779
Elementary Schools, Diocesan and Parish	25
Total Students	5,583
Non-residential Schools for the Disabled	1
Total Students	18
Catechesis/Religious Education:	
High School Students	2,155
Elementary Students	5,400
Total Students under Catholic Instruction	15,026
Teachers in the Diocese:	
Priests	33
Sisters	38
Lay Teachers	506
Vital Statistics	
Receptions into the Church:	
Infant Baptism Totals	1,465
Adult Baptism Totals	157
Received into Full Communion	196
First Communions	1,578
Confirmations	1,793
Marriages:	
Catholic	235
Interfaith	179
Total Marriages	414
Deaths	710
Total Catholic Population	89,431
Total Population	539,402

Former Bishops—Most Revs. THOMAS BONACUM, D.D., Bishop of Lincoln; consecrated Nov. 20, 1887; died Feb. 4, 1911; J. HENRY TIHEN, D.D., consecrated Bishop of Lincoln, July 6, 1911; transferred to the See of Denver, Sept. 21, 1917; died Jan. 14, 1940; CHARLES J. O'REILLY, D.D., consecrated Bishop of Baker City, Aug. 24, 1903; transferred to the See of Lincoln, March 20, 1918; died Feb. 4, 1923; FRANCIS J. L. BECKMAN, S.T.D., consecrated Bishop of Lincoln, May 1, 1924; elevated to the Metropolitan See of Dubuque, Jan. 17, 1930; died Oct. 17, 1948; LOUIS B KUCERA, D.D., consecrated Bishop of Lincoln, Oct. 28, 1930; died May 9, 1957; JAMES V. CASEY, D.D., J.C.D., appt. Auxiliary of Lincoln April 5, 1957; consecrated April 24, 1957; appt. Bishop of Lincoln June 14, 1957; promoted to Archbishop of Denver, Feb. 22, 1967; died March 14, 1986; GLENNON P. FLAVIN, D.D. (Retired), appt. Titular Bishop of Joannina and Auxiliary Bishop of St. Louis April 24, 1957; consecrated May 30, 1957; promoted to See of Lincoln, May 29, 1967; retired March 24, 1992; died Aug. 27, 1995.

Chancery—3400 Sheridan Blvd., Lincoln, 68506. P.O. Box 80328, Lincoln, 68501-0328. Tel: 402-488-0921; Fax: 402-488-3569. Office Hours: 8:30-5

Moderator of the Curia—Rev. Msgr. TIMOTHY J. THORBURN, J.C.L.

Vicar General—Rev. Msgr. TIMOTHY J. THORBURN, J.C.L.

Chancellor—Rev. MARK D. HUBER, J.C.L.

Diocesan Tribunal—3400 Sheridan Blvd., Lincoln, 68506. P.O. Box 80328, Lincoln, 68501-0328.

Officialis—Rev. DANIEL J. SEIKER, J.C.L.

Adjutant Judicial Vicars—Rev. MAURICE H. CURRENT, J.C.L.

Promoters Justitiae—Rev. Msgr. TIMOTHY J. THORBURN, J.C.L.; Rev. MILTON THOMAS, J.C.L.

Defensores Vinculi—Rev. Msgr. TIMOTHY J. THORBURN, J.C.L.; Rev. MILTON THOMAS, J.C.L.

Judges—Revs. MARK D. HUBER, J.C.L.; CRAIG A. DOTY, J.C.L.

Advocates—Revs. THOMAS Y. AU; MICHAEL K. HOULIHAN; JAMES W. COOPER; ANDREW KURZ; DANIEL J. RAYER; ANTHONY O. STAMMITTI; DAVID F. BOUREK; RICHARD A. GYHRA; ANDREW V. MENKE; SCOTT M. COURTNEY; Rev. RAMON E. DECAEN; BRIAN P. KANE; MATTHEW J. VANDEWALLE; JEREL A. SCHOLL; JAMIE S. HOTTOVY; THOMAS S. MACLEAN; Revs. JOSEPH C. BERNARDO; DAVID A. OLDHAM; SEAN M. TIMMERMAN.

Notaries—Very Rev. JOHN T. FOLDA; Rev. CHRISTOPHER L. BARAK; Sr. COLLETTE BRUSKEWITZ, O.S.F.; Mrs. MARILYN L. FRIESEN.

Diocesan Consultors—Rev. Msgrs. ADRIAN HERBEK; TIMOTHY J. THORBURN, J.C.L.; Revs. NICHOLAS BAKER; DAVID HINTZ; DENNIS HUNT; JAMES SCHRADER; DANIEL SEIKER.

Presbyteral Council—Rev. Msgrs. TIMOTHY J. THORBURN, J.C.L.; RAYMOND HAIN; Rev. JAMES SCHRADER; Very Revs. LAWRENCE GYHRA; JOHN FOLDA; BRIAN CONNOR; Rev. DANIEL SEIKER; Very Rev. SEAN REDMOND; Revs. JOHN PERKINTON, M.Div., M.A.; MARK D. HUBER, J.C.L.; Very Revs. ROBERT MAYTA; PHILIP RAUTH; Rev. KARL PIKUS, F.S.S.P.; Very Revs. KENNETH HOESING; JOSEPH NEMEC.

Vicars For Religious—Very Rev. JOHN T. FOLDA; Rev. DANIEL J. SEIKER, J.C.L.

Deaneries and Deans—Rev. Msgrs. MYRON J. PLESKAC, Crete; ADRIAN F. HERBEK, V.F., David City; Very Revs. PAUL E. SHEEHY, Fairbury; ROBERT A. ROH, V.F., Falls City; GREGORY P. PAWLOSKI, Grant; LAWRENCE J. GYHRA, Hastings; NICHOLAS BAKER, Indianola; JAMES C. SCHRADER JR., V.F., Lawrence; PAUL WITT, Lincoln; STEPHEN A. COONEY, Orleans; RONALD E. PATTERSON, Plattsmouth; RUDOLF F. OBORNY, V.F., Wahoo; Rev. Msgr. IVAN F. VAP, York.

Diocesan Offices and Directors

Apostleship of Prayer—Rev. JEREMY L. HAZUKA, Dir.

Apostolate to the Elderly—Revs. JOHN L. COPENHAVER; ANTHONY O. STAMMITTI, Asst.

Apostolate to the Spanish Speaking—Revs. JOHN J. KEEFE, Dir.; BERNARD A. LORENZ, Asst. Dir.; JULIUS TVRDY.

Apostolate of Suffering—Rev. JOSEPH WALSH, Dir.

Archivist—Sr. KATHRYN MANEY, M.S.

Bishop's Lay Committee for Vocations—Rev. ROBERT A. MATYA, Chap.

Bishop's Pastoral Plan for Pro-Life Activities—GREG SCHLEPPENBACH, State Dir., 215 Centennial Mall South, Ste. 410, Lincoln, 68508.

Building Commission—Rev. JOHN PERKINTON, M.Div., M.A., Chm.; Rev. Msgrs. RAYMOND B. HAIN (Retired); ADRIAN F. HERBEK, V.F.; IVAN F. VAP; TIMOTHY J. THORBURN, J.C.L.; Revs. PETER J. GADIENT (Retired); MARK D. HUBER, J.C.L.; JAMIE HOTTOVY.

Catholic Relief Services—Rev. MARK D. HUBER, J.C.L., Dir.

Cemeteries—Rev. DAVID R. HINTZ, Dir.

Censores Librorum—Rev. M. JAMES DIVIS, S.T.L.; Very Rev. JOHN T. FOLDA; Rev. Msgr. TIMOTHY J. THORBURN, J.C.L.

Catholic Social Services—Revs. JOSEPH M. WALSH, Dir.; CHRISTOPHER KUBAT, Asst., Catholic Social Services, 123 N. 25th St., Lincoln, 68503. Tel: 402-474-1600. Administrative Offices & Counseling Services, 8101 "O" St., S-111, Lincoln, 68510. Tel: 402-489-1834. Catholic Social Services, 515 W. 3rd St., Hastings, 68901. Tel: 402-463-2112. Counseling Services, 223 East 14th St., Suite 10, Hastings, 68901. Tel: 402-463-1119.

Clergy Relief Society--The Saint John Vianney Association—Rev. Msgr. TIMOTHY J. THORBURN, J.C.L., Sec. & Treas., Mailing Address, P.O. Box 80328, Lincoln, 68501-0328.

Commission on Alcohol and Drug Abuse—Rev. M. JAMES DIVIS, S.T.L., Dir., 3301 Sheridan Blvd., Lincoln, 68506. Tel: 402-483-1941.

Commission for Sacred Liturgy and Sacred Music—Revs. William D. Grant, Chm.; Christopher L. Barak; Robert K. Barnhill; Maurice H. Current, J.C.L.; M. James Divis, S.T.L.; Matthew Eickhoff; Leo Kosch; Joseph J. Nemec; Sr. Collette Bruskewitz, O.S.F.

Catholic Planned Giving Office—Mr. Michael L. Henkenius, Dir., P.O. Box 80328, Lincoln, 68501-0328. Tel: 402-488-2142.

Catholic Physicians Guild—Very Rev. John Folda, Spiritual Dir., 1301 280th Rd., Seward, 68434-7541. Tel: 402-643-4052.

Office of Religious Education (CCD)—Rev. Christopher L. Barak, Diocesan Dir. Tel: 402-488-2040. Diocesan Area CCD Directors: Revs. Thomas Y. Au; Robert Barnhill; John B. Birkel; Thomas S. Brouillette; John A. Cooper; Maurice H. Current, J.C.L.; William D. Grant; Dennis M. Hunt; Bernard Kimminau; Leo D. Kosch; Troy J. Schweiger; Mark E. Seiker, M.Div.; Michael S. Stec.

Cursillo—Rev. Mark E. Seiker, M.Div.

Deaf Ministry—Revs. Robert K. Barnhill, Dir. Tel: 402-488-2040 (TTY); Michael S. Stec, Asst. Dir.

Diocesan Council of Catholic Women—Mrs. Marilyn Murphy, Pres.; Revs. Peter J. Gadient, Moderator (Retired); Thomas J. Lux, Asst. Spiritual Dir., P.O. Box 4, Bee, 68314.

Diocesan Director of Liturgy—Rev. William D. Grant, P.O. Box 406, Fairbury, 68352.

Bishop Bruskewitz Charity and Stewardship Appeal (DDP)—Rev. Jerry J. Pokorsky, Dir., P.O. Box 80328, Lincoln, 68501-0328.

Diocesan Finance Council—Most Rev. Fabian W. Bruskewitz, D.D., S.T.D.; Rev. Msgr. Timothy J. Thorburn, J.C.L.; Rev. Jerry J. Pokorsky, Finance Officer. Members: Rev. Msgr. Adrian F. Herbek, V.F.; Very Rev. John T. Folda; Rev. Michael G. McCabe.

Diocesan Health Ministries, Inc.—Most Rev. Fabian W. Bruskewitz, D.D., S.T.D., Pres.; Rev. Msgr. Timothy J. Thorburn, J.C.L., Vice Pres.; Very Rev. John T. Folda, Sec., P.O. Box 80328, Lincoln, 68501-0328. Tel: 402-488-0921; Fax: 402-488-3569.

Diocesan Housing Ministries, Inc.—Most Rev. Fabian W. Bruskewitz, D.D., S.T.D., Pres.; Rev. Msgr. Timothy J. Thorburn, J.C.L.; Very Rev. John T. Folda; Revs. Jerry J. Pokorsky; Joseph M. Walsh; Ms. Haton, P.O. Box 80328, Lincoln, 68501-0328. Tel: 402-488-0921.

Ecumenical Affairs, Commission for—Rev. M. James Divis, S.T.L., Chm.; Very Rev. Paul Witt; Rev. Maurice H. Current, J.C.L.

Engaged Encounter—Rev. Matthew F. Eickhoff.

Evangelization Office—Rev. Matthew Eickhoff, Chm.

Evangelization Committee—Rev. Matthew Eickhoff, Chm. Tel: 402-488-2040; Rev. Msgrs. James Dawson; Timothy J. Thorburn, J.C.L.; Very Rev. Paul Witt; Revs. M. James Divis, S.T.L.; Christopher L. Barak; William D. Grant; Joseph J. Nemec.

Family Life Office—Revs. Matthew Eickhoff, Dir.; John R. Sullivan, Asst. Dir., P.O. Box 80328, Lincoln, 68501-0328. Tel: 402-488-2040.

Holy Childhood, Pontifical Association—Rev. K. William Holoubek, Dir., P.O. Box 80328, Lincoln, 68501-0328.

Health Care Facilities—Revs. Paul J. Rutten, 5401 South St., Lincoln, 68506; Edwin L. Stander, Mailing Address, 555 S. 70th St., Lincoln, 68510.

Office of Information and Media—Rev. Kenneth A. Borowiak, Dir., P.O. Box 80329, Lincoln, 68501. Tel: 402-488-0090.

Insurance—Rev. Msgr. Timothy J. Thorburn, J.C.L., Dir.; Mrs. Marsha Morrison, P.O. Box 80328, Lincoln, 68501-0328.

Legion of Mary—Revs. Peter J. Gadient, Spiritual Dir. (Retired); Jeremy L. Hazuka, Asst. Spiritual Dir.; Mrs. Mary Riley, Pres.

Liturgical Ministries—Rev. Mark D. Huber, J.C.L., Diocesan Dir.

Marriage Encounter—Rev. Matthew Eickhoff, Dir.

Missionary Union of the Clergy—Rev. K. William Holoubek.

Natural Family Planning—Rev. Matthew Eickhoff, Diocesan Dir.; Michelle Chambers, Diocesan Coord. Tel: 402-488-2040.

Nebraska Catholic Conference—James R. Cunningham, Exec. Dir., 215 Centennial Mall South, Ste. 410, Lincoln, 68508. Tel: 402-477-7517; Fax: 402-477-1503.

Newman Center University of Nebraska—Rev. Robert A. Matya, Chap., 320 N. 16th St., Lincoln, 68508. Tel: 402-474-7914.

Newspaper—Rev. Kenneth A. Borowiak, Editor, 3336 High St., Lincoln, 68508. Mailing Address, P.O. Box 80329, Lincoln, 68501. Tel: 402-488-0090. "The Southern Nebraska Register"

Office of Diocesan & Social Development—Rev. Liam M. Barr, Delegate, P.O. Box 80328, Lincoln, 68501. Tel: 402-488-0921; Fax: 402-488-3569.

Permanent Deacon Continuing Education Committee—Revs. Mark D. Huber, J.C.L., Dir.; Leo V. Seiker; Douglas D. Dietrich.

PREP—Rev. Matthew F. Eickhoff.

Priests' Continuing Education Committee—Rev. Msgrs. James D. Dawson; Myron J. Pleskac; Timothy J. Thorburn, J.C.L.; Very Rev. John T. Folda; Revs. Christopher L. Barak; Maurice H. Current, J.C.L.; John Perkinton, M.Div., M.A.; Daniel J. Seiker, J.C.L.; Mark D. Huber, J.C.L.; Robert A. Mayta; Jerry J. Pokorsky.

Pro Life—Rev. Msgr. Thomas L. Holoman, Dir. (Retired); Rev. Jeffrey Eickhoff, Asst.

Project Rachel—Catholic Social Services. Tel: 800-964-3787.

Propagation of the Faith—Rev. K. William Holoubek, Dir., P.O. Box 80328, Lincoln, 68501-0328.

Retreat Program—Rev. Lawrence Stoley, Dir., Our Lady of Good Counsel Retreat House. Tel: 402-786-2705.

Rural Life Conference—Rev. David F. Bourek, P.O. Box 80328, Lincoln, 68501-0328. Tel: 402-488-0921.

Serra Club—Rev. Robert A. Matya, Chap. & Spiritual Dir. Tel: 402-474-7914.

Schools—Revs. John Perkinton, M.Div., M.A., Supt.; Lawrence Stoley; Sr. Collette, O.S.F., Asst. Supt., 3400 Sheridan Blvd., Lincoln, 68506. Mailing Address, P.O. Box 80328, Lincoln, 68501-0328.

Scouting—Rev. Robert K. Barnhill.

Society of St. Vincent de Paul - Lincoln Council—Very Rev. Paul Witt, Spiritual Advisor; Thomas Safranek, M.D., Pres.; Joyce Burgess, Council Sec. & Res. Agent, Blessed Sacrament Conference, 1720 Lake St., Lincoln, 68502. Tel: 402-474-4249.

Teens Encounter Christ (TEC)—Rev. John R. Sullivan.

Tridentine Mass Apostolate—Rev. Karl Pikus, F.S.S.P., St. Francis of Assisi Church, 3400 S. 17th St., Lincoln, 68502. Tel: 402-477-5145.

Victim Assistance Coordinator—Rev. Mark D. Huber, J.C.L. Tel: 402-488-0921.

Vocations—Revs. Robert A. Matya, Dir.; Brian Kane, Asst., St. Thomas Aquinas Church, 320 North 16th St., Lincoln, 68508. Tel: 402-474-7914.

CLERGY, PARISHES, MISSIONS AND PAROCHIAL SCHOOLS

CITY OF LINCOLN
(Lancaster County)

1—Cathedral of the Risen Christ (1932), [JC] Revs. Robert G. Tucker; Matthew Vandewalle. In Res., Rev. Mark D. Huber, J.C.L.
Res.: 3500 Sheridan Blvd., 68506. Tel: 402-488-0948; Fax: 402-488-7895.
School—Tel: 402-489-9621. Lay Teachers 22; Students 411.
Catechesis/Religious Program—Tel: 402-489-0949. Students 248.

2—Bishop Bonacum Chancery (1961), Rev. Msgr. Timothy J. Thorburn, J.C.L., Moderator of the Curia.
Res.: 3400 Sheridan Blvd., P.O. Box 80328, 68501. Tel: 402-488-0921; Fax: 402-488-3569.

3—Blessed Sacrament (1922), [JC] Revs. John R. Sullivan; Sean M. Timmerman; Thomas McLean; Thomas S. MacLean.
Res.: 1720 Lake St., 68502. Tel: 402-474-4249; Fax: 402-474-4258.
School—Tel: 402-476-6202; Fax: 402-476-0232. Priests 2; Sisters 2; Lay Teachers 15; Students 215.
Catechesis/Religious Program—Students 110.

4—Christo Rey, Rev. John Keefe.
4245 J St., 68510. Tel: 402-327-2170.

5—Immaculate Heart of Mary (1979), (Vietnamese), Rev. Mark Nguyen Thanh Huynh, C.M.C. (Vietnam).
Res.: 6345 Madison Ave., 68507. Tel: 402-464-0111; Fax: 402-464-0111.
Catechesis/Religious Program—Students 200.

6—St. John the Apostle (1959), [JC] Revs. Lyle Johnson; Jamie Hottovy.
Res.: 731 Sky Way Rd., 68505. Tel: 402-489-1946; Fax: 402-489-2048.
School—Tel: 402-486-1860; Fax: 402-486-4732. Sisters 1; Lay Teachers 22; Students 333.
Catechesis/Religious Program—Students 123.

7—St. Joseph (1976), [JC] Revs. Liam M. Barr; Daniel J. Rayer.
Res.: 7900 Trendwood Dr., 68506. Tel: 402-483-2288; Fax: 402-489-9729.
School—(Grades PreK-8) Tel: 402-489-0341; Fax: 402-489-3260. Sisters 2; Lay Teachers 38; Students 567.
High School—Pius High School Students 197.
Catechesis/Religious Program—Students 265.

8—St. Mary (1867), [JC] Very Rev. Paul Witt; Revs. Christopher Kubat; Joseph C. Bernardo. In Res., Revs. Robert T. McDermott; Joseph P. Finn.
Res.: 1420 K St., 68508. Tel: 402-435-2125.
School—Tel: 402-476-3987; Fax: 402-476-0838. Sisters 1; Lay Teachers 10; Students 166.
Catechesis/Religious Program—Students 31.

9—North American Martyrs (1993), [JC] Rev. Joel Panzer.
Res.: 931 W. Harvest Dr., 68521. Tel: 402-476-8088.
School—1101 Issac Dr., 68521. Tel: 402-476-7373. Priests 1; Sisters 5; Lay Teachers 18; Students 474.
Catechesis/Religious Program—Students 157.

10—St. Patrick's (1893), [JC] Revs. David R. Hintz; David A. Oldham.
Res.: 6126 Morrill Ave., P.O. Box 29106, 68507. Tel: 402-466-2752; Fax: 402-466-3572.
School—Tel: 402-466-3710; Fax: 402-466-3752. Marian Sisters (Waverly, NE) 2; Lay Teachers 12; Students 156.
Catechesis/Religious Program—Students 151.

11—St. Peter (1990), [JC] Revs. Michael R. Christensen; Richard A. Gyhra.
Res.: 4500 Duxhall Dr., 68516. Tel: 402-423-1239; Fax: 402-421-6507.
School—Tel: 402-421-6299. Priests 2; School Sisters of Christ the King 3; Lay Teachers 25; Students 505.
Catechesis/Religious Program—Students 322.

12—Sacred Heart (1919), [JC] Rev. Thomas R. Walsh. In Res. Rev. Anthony O. Stammitti.
Res.: 3128 S St., 68503. Tel: 402-476-2610; Fax: 402-476-2610.
School—Tel: 402-476-1783; Fax: 402-476-3040. Sisters 3; Lay Teachers 10; Students 154.
Catechesis/Religious Program—Students 62.

13—St. Teresa's (1926), [JC] Rev. Joseph J. Nemec; Deacon Stephen T. Kuchar. In Res., Rev. Joseph M. Walsh.
Res.: 735 S. 36th St., 68510. Tel: 402-477-3979.
School—616 S. 36th St., 68510. Tel: 402-477-3358; Fax: 402-477-3361. Sisters 3; Lay Teachers 13; Students 302.
Catechesis/Religious Program—Students 85.

14—St. Thomas Aquinas (1958), [JC] Revs. Robert A. Matya; Brian Kane. In Res., Rev. Christopher Kubat.
Res.: 320 N. 16th St., 68508. Tel: 402-474-7914; Fax: 402-476-2620.

OUTSIDE THE CITY OF LINCOLN

Alma, Harlan Co., St. Joseph's (1909), Rev. John B. Birkel.
Res.: 810 4th, P.O. Box 764, 68920. Tel: 308-928-2575.
Catechesis/Religious Program—Students 27.
Mission—Sacred Heart Bloomington, Franklin Co.
Mission—St. Kathrine Drexel, Harlan Co.

Ashland, Saunders Co., St. Mary's (1900), Rev. Paul York.
Res.: 1625 Adams St., 68003. Tel: 402-944-3554.
Catechesis/Religious Program—Students 95.
Mission—St. Joseph's Greenwood, Cass Co.

Auburn, Nemaha Co., St. Joseph's (1881), [CEM] Rev. Philip J. Rauth.
Res.: 1306 23rd St., P.O. Box 406, 68305. Tel: 402-274-3733.
Catechesis/Religious Program—Tel: 402-274-5364. Students 80.
Mission—St. Clara Peru, Nemaha Co.

Aurora, Hamilton Co., St. Mary's (1888), Rev. Craig A. Doty, J.C.L.
Res.: 1419 10th St., P.O. Box 291, 68818. Tel: 402-694-3427; Fax: 402-694-2455.
Catechesis/Religious Program—Students 166.
Mission—St. Joseph's [CEM] Giltner, Hamilton Co.

Beatrice, Gage Co., St. Joseph's (1869), [CEM] Revs. Mark E. Seiker, M.Div.; Finnian Nwaozor; Andrew V. Menke.
Res.: 612 High St., 68310. Tel: 402-223-2923; Fax: 402-228-0100.
School—Tel: 402-223-5033. Lay Teachers 9; Students 60.
Catechesis/Religious Program—Students 132.

Beaver Crossing, Seward Co., Sacred Heart (1890), Rev. Maurice H. Current, J.C.L.
Res.: 401 Dimery, P.O. Box 208, 68313. Tel: 402-532-2545.
Catechesis/Religious Program—Students 77.
Mission—St. Patrick's [CEM 2] Utica, Seward Co.

Bellwood, Butler Co.

1—St. Peter's (1889), [JC] Rev. Jeremy L. Hazuka.
Res.: 211 Esplanade St., 68624-2402. Tel: 402-538-3135.
Catechesis/Religious Program—Students 99.

Mission—St. Joseph's, Butler Co.
2—PRESENTATION (1874), [JC] Rev. Leo D. Kosch.
Res.: 1291 41 Rd., 68624. Tel: 402-367-3666.
Catechesis/Religious Program—Students 41.
BENKELMAN, DUNDY CO., ST. JOSEPH'S (1911), [CEM] Rev. Bernard Lorenz.
Res.: 817 Cheyenne St., P.O. Box 447, 69021. Tel: 308-423-2329.
Catechesis/Religious Program—Students 55.
Mission—St. Joseph's Stratton, Hitchcock Co.
BRAINARD, BUTLER CO., HOLY TRINITY (1888), [CEM] Rev. Matthew Eickhoff.
Res.: P.O. Box 39, 68626. Tel: 402-545-2691.
Catechesis/Religious Program—Students 92.
BRUNO, BUTLER CO., ST. ANTHONY (1899), [CEM] Rev. James W. Cooper.
Res.: 405 Pine St., 68014. Tel: 402-543-2233.
Catechesis/Religious Program—Tel: 402-543-2465. Students 49.
Mission—SS. Peter and Paul [CEM 2] Abie, Butler Co.
CAMBRIDGE, FURNAS CO., ST. JOHN'S (1880), [CEM] Rev. Robert Barnhill.
Res.: 815 Nelson, P.O. Box F, 69022. Tel: 308-697-3722.
Catechesis/Religious Program—Students 78.
Mission—St. Germanus Arapahoe, Furnas Co.
CAMPBELL, FRANKLIN CO., ST. ANNE (1880), [CEM] Very Rev. James C. Schrader Jr., V.F.
Res.: 518 S. Stewart, P.O. Box 156, 68932-0156. Tel: 402-756-8006.
Catechesis/Religious Program—Students 71.
Mission—Holy Trinity Blue Hill, Webster Co.
CHENEY, LANCASTER CO., ST. MICHAEL (1909), [CEM] Rev. Msgr. James D. Dawson.
Res.: 9230 First St.(Cheney), 68526. Tel: 402-328-8480.
Catechesis/Religious Program—Students 107.
COLON, SAUNDERS CO., ST. JOSEPH'S (1919), [CEM] Rev. Troy Schweiger.
Res.: 111 Cherry St., P.O. Box 58, 68018. Tel: 402-647-4901.
Catechesis/Religious Program—Students 75.
Mission—St. Mary [CEM] Cedar Bluffs, Saunders Co.
CORTLAND, GAGE CO., ST. JAMES (1882), [CEM] Rev. Michael J. Morin.
Res.: 255 W. First, 68331. Tel: 402-798-7335; Fax: 402-798-7336.
Catechesis/Religious Program—Students 94.
CRETE, SALINE CO., SACRED HEART (1873), [CEM] Rev. Julius Turdy.
Res.: 515 E. 14th St., 68333. Tel: 402-826-2044; Fax: 402-826-2318.
School—(Grades K-6) Tel: 402-826-2318. Sisters 2; Lay Teachers 6; Students 93.
Catechesis/Religious Program—Students 137.
CURTIS, FRONTIER CO., ST. JAMES (1914), Rev. Ferdinand Boehme.
Res.: 313 E. 6th St., P.O. Box 144, 69025. Tel: 308-367-4280.
Catechesis/Religious Program—Students 31.
Mission—St. Joseph's Farnam, Dawson Co.
Mission—St. William's Wellfleet, Lincoln Co.
DAVEY, LANCASTER CO., ST. MARY'S (1876), [CEM] Rev. Kenneth F. Hoesing.
Res.: 17630 N. 3rd St., P.O. Box 37, 68336. Tel: 402-785-3445.
Catechesis/Religious Program—Students 83.
DAVID CITY, BUTLER CO.
1—ST. FRANCIS (Center) (1878), [CEM] Rev. Brian P. Connor.
Res.: 3071 P Rd., 68632. Tel: 402-367-4202.
Catechesis/Religious Program—Students 27.
2—ST. MARY'S (1877), [CEM] Rev. Msgr. Adrian F. Herbek, V.F.; Rev. Casey Porada, O.S.
Res.: 580 I St., 68632. Tel: 402-367-3579.
School—(Grades K-5) Tel: 402-367-3669. Priests 1; Sisters 3; Lay Teachers 13; Students 225.
Catechesis/Religious Program—Students 34.
Mission—Assumption (1878),, Butler Co. 68632.
DAWSON, RICHARDSON CO., ST. MARY'S (1873), [CEM] Rev. Bernard Kimminau.
Res.: 312 4th St., P.O. Box 96, 68337. Tel: 402-855-3595.
Catechesis/Religious Program—Students 27.
Mission—St. Anne's [CEM 2] Shubert, Richardson Co.
DENTON, LANCASTER CO., ST. MARY'S (1906), Rev. Msgr. Myron J. Pleskac.
Res.: 7105 Cass, P.O. Box 406, 68339. Tel: 402-797-2105.
Catechesis/Religious Program—Students 75.
DONIPHAN, HALL CO., ST. ANN'S (1888), [CEM] Rev. Steven P. Major.
Res.: 404 Cedar, Box 407, 68832. Tel: 402-845-2707.
Catechesis/Religious Program—Students 44.
DWIGHT, BUTLER CO., ASSUMPTION (1899), [CEM] Rev. Loras K. Grell.
Res.: P.O. Box 70, 68635. Tel: 402-566-2765.
Catechesis/Religious Program—Students 135.

Mission—St. Wenceslaus [CEM] 350 Elm St., Bee, Seward Co. 68314. In Res., Rev. Peter J. Gadient (Retired).
EXETER, FILLMORE CO., ST. STEPHEN'S (1871), [JC] Rev. Kenneth A. Borowiak.
Res.: 207 N. Union Ave., P.O. Box 57, 68351. Tel: 402-266-5581.
Catechesis/Religious Program—Students 86.
FAIRBURY, JEFFERSON CO., ST. MICHAEL'S (1885), [CEM] Rev. William David Grant.
Res.: 807 F St., P.O. Box 406, 68352. Tel: 402-729-2058.
School—(Grades PreK-6) Tel: 402-729-2151; Fax: 402-729-3027. Lay Teachers 4; Students 48.
Catechesis/Religious Program—Students 29.
Mission—St. Mary's 511 Amanda, Alexandria, Thayer Co. 68303.
FALLS CITY, RICHARDSON CO., SS. PETER AND PAUL (1871), [CEM 2] Very Rev. Robert A. Roh, V.F.
Res.: 1820 Fulton St., 68355. Tel: 402-245-3002; Fax: 402-245-3002.
School—(Grades PreK-12) Tel: 402-245-4151; Fax: 402-245-5217. Lay Teachers 23; Students 259.
Catechesis/Religious Program—Students 60.
FRIEND, SALINE CO., ST. JOSEPH'S (1874), [CEM] Rev. David F. Bourek.
Res.: 405 S. Main St., 68359. Tel: 402-947-3651.
Catechesis/Religious Program—Tel: 402-947-3657. Students 73.
Mission—St. Wenceslaus (1874), Milligan, Fillmore Co.
GENEVA, FILLMORE CO., ST. JOSEPH'S (1898), [CEM 2] Rev. Msgr. Ivan F. Vap.
Res.: 831 E St., P.O. Box 383, 68361. Tel: 402-759-3225; Fax: 402-759-3225.
Catechesis/Religious Program—Students 97.
Mission—St. Mary Shickley, Fillmore Co. Tel: 402-627-7395.
GRAFTON, FILLMORE CO., ST. HELENA'S (1877), [CEM] Rev. Mark S. Pfeiffer.
Res.: P.O. Box 65, 68365. Tel: 402-282-7255.
Catechesis/Religious Program—Students 14.
GRANT, PERKINS CO., MOTHER OF SORROWS (1928), Rev. Joseph S. Steele.
Res.: 739 Garfield Ave., P.O. Box 536, 69140. Tel: 308-352-4803.
Catechesis/Religious Program—Students 84.
HARVARD, CLAY CO., ST. JOSEPH'S (1878), Rev. K. William Holoubek.
Res.: 605 N. Kearney, P.O. Box 70, 68944. Tel: 402-772-3511.
Catechesis/Religious Program—Students 50.
HASTINGS, ADAMS CO.
1—ST. CECILIA'S (1878), [JC] Very Rev. Lawrence J. Gyhra; Rev. Ramon E. Decaen. In Res., Revs. James J. Meysenburg; Joseph Van Thanh Nguyen.
Res.: 301 W. 7th St., 68901. Tel: 402-463-1336; Fax: 402-463-1336.
Catechesis/Religious Program—Hastings Catholic Schools, Tel: 402-462-2105; Fax: 402-462-2106. Students 698.
2—ST. MICHAEL'S (1945), [JC] Revs. Michael K. Houlihan; Scott Courtney.
Res.: 715 Creighton Ave., 68901. Tel: 402-463-1023.
Catechesis/Religious Program—Hastings Catholic Schools, 721 Creighton Ave., 68901. Tel: 402-462-6310; Fax: 402-462-6035. Students 698.
HEBRON, THAYER CO., SACRED HEART (1878), [CEM] Very Rev. Paul E. Sheehy.
Res.: 436 N. 3rd St., 68370. Tel: 402-768-6293.
Catechesis/Religious Program—Students 101.
HOLDREGE, PHELPS CO., ALL SAINTS (1902), Very Rev. Stephen A. Cooney.
Res.: 1204 Logan St., 68949. Tel: 308-995-4590; Fax: 308-995-2217.
Catechesis/Religious Program—Tel: 308-995-8931. Students 152.
Mission—St. John's Smithfield, Gosper Co.
IMPERIAL, CHASE CO., ST. PATRICK'S (1903), Very Rev. Gregory P. Pawloski.
Res.: 126 E. 7th St., P.O. Box 96, 69033. Tel: 308-882-4995; Fax: 308-882-3995.
Catechesis/Religious Program—Students 103.
Mission—St. John's [CEM] Wauneta, Chase Co. Tel: 308-394-5440 (Church).
INDIANOLA, RED WILLOW CO., ST. CATHERINE'S (1888), [CEM] Very Rev. Nicholas Baker, V.F.
Res.: 815 D St., P.O. Box 0, 69034. Tel: 308-364-2428.
Catechesis/Religious Program—Students 75.
KENESAW, ADAMS CO., SACRED HEART (1908), Rev. Steven P. Major.
Res.: 404 Cedar, Box 407, Doniphan, 68832. Tel: 402-845-2707 (Pastor).
Catechesis/Religious Program—Tel: 402-752-8149. Students 17.
LAWRENCE, NUCKOLLS CO., SACRED HEART (1893), [CEM 3] Rev. Dennis Hunt.
Res.: P.O. Box 247, 68957. Tel: 402-756-7393.
School—(Grades 1-8) Tel: 402-756-7043. Lay Teachers 4; Students 42.
Catechesis/Religious Program—Students 130.

Mission—Assumption Deweese, Clay Co. Tel: 402-756-7437.
Mission—St. Stephen's, Nuckolls Co.
LOMA, BUTLER CO., ST. LUKE'S CZECH CATHOLIC SHRINE (1912), (Czech), [CEM], Mailing Address: *c/o Rev. Msgr. Myron J. Pleskac*, P.O. Box 406, Denton, 68339. Tel: 402-483-2288; Fax: 402-489-9729.
MANLEY, CASS CO., ST. PATRICK'S (1881), [CEM] Rev. Ronald Patterson.
Res.: 101 N. Broadway, P.O. Box 27, 68403. Tel: 402-234-3595.
Catechesis/Religious Program—Students 148.
Mission—St. Mary's [CEM] Elmwood, Cass Co.
MCCOOK, RED WILLOW CO., ST. PATRICK (1886), [CEM] Revs. Gary G. Brethour; Jerel A. Scholl.
Res.: 612 E. 4th St., P.O. Box 216, 69001. Tel: 308-345-6734; Fax: 308-345-6734.
School—(Grades PreK-8), 401 E. F St., 69001. Tel: 308-345-4546; Fax: 308-345-5542. Priests 2; Lay Teachers 15; Students 120.
Catechesis/Religious Program—Students 198.
Mission—Sacred Heart, Red Willow Co.
Mission—St. Ann's [CEM], Red Willow Co.
MCCOOL JUNCTION, YORK CO., ST. PATRICK'S (1905), [CEM] Rev. Mark S. Pfeiffer.
Res.: P.O. Box 65, Grafton, 68365. Tel: 402-282-7255.
Catechesis/Religious Program—Students 30.
MEAD, SAUNDERS CO., ST. JAMES (1882), [CEM 2] Rev. Charles L. Townsend.
Res.: 213 E. 8th St., P.O. Box 91, 68041. Tel: 402-624-3555.
Catechesis/Religious Program—Students 42.
MINDEN, KEARNEY CO., ST. JOHN'S (1882), Rev. Thomas J. Lux.
Res.: 624 N. Garber Ave., P.O. Box 245, 68959. Tel: 308-832-1245; Fax: 308-832-1626.
Catechesis/Religious Program—Tel: 308-832-1626. Students 115.
Mission—Holy Family Heartwell, Kearney Co.
MORSE BLUFF, SAUNDERS CO., ST. GEORGE (1945), Rev. David Davis.
Res.: 260 Short St., P.O. Box 98, 68648. Tel: 402-666-5280.
Catechesis/Religious Program—Students 21.
Mission—Sacred Heart [CEM] Cedar Hill, Saunders Co.
NEBRASKA CITY, OTOE CO.
1—ST. BENEDICT'S (1856), [CEM] Rev. Mark A. Tasler.
Res.: 411 5th Rue, 68410. Tel: 402-873-3047.
School—Tel: 402-873-6154; Fax: 402-873-3154. (See Lourdes Catholic Schools)
2—ST. MARY'S (1869), [CEM] Revs. Michael G. McCabe; Joseph C. Bernardo.
Res.: 218 N. 6th St., 68410. Tel: 402-873-3024.
Catechesis/Religious Program—Students 61.
NORTH PLATTE, LINCOLN CO,, ST. ELIZABETH ANN SETON (1994), Rev. Thomas Brouillette.
Res.: 3301 Echo Dr., P.O. Box 781, 69101. Tel: 308-534-5461; Fax: 308-534-0914.
Catechesis/Religious Program—Students 43.
ORLEANS, HARLAN CO., ST. MARY'S (1878), [CEM] Rev. Harlan D. P. Waskowiak.
Res.: 109 W. Linn, P.O. Box 446, 68966. Tel: 308-473-3475.
Catechesis/Religious Program—Students 68.
Mission—St. Michael's Oxford, Furnas Co.
OSCEOLA, POLK CO., ST. VINCENT FERRER (1946), Rev. Thomas D. McGuire.
Res.: 751 S. Nance, P.O. Box 212, 68651. Tel: 402-747-3491.
Catechesis/Religious Program—Students 97.
Mission—St. Mary's (1893),, Polk Co.
PALMYRA, OTOE CO., ST. LEO'S (1874), [CEM 2] Rev. Christopher L. Barak.
Res.: 330 W. 8th St., 68418-2537. Tel: 402-780-5535.
Catechesis/Religious Program—Students 27.
Mission—St. Martin's Douglas, Otoe Co.
PAUL, OTOE CO., ST. JOSEPH'S (1871), [CEM] Rev. Sean P. Redmond.
Res.: 5592 O Rd., Nebraska City, 68410. Tel: 402-873-4569.
Catechesis/Religious Program—Students 30.
Mission—St. Bernard's [CEM] Julian, Nemaha Co.
PLATTSMOUTH, CASS CO., CHURCH OF THE HOLY SPIRIT (1862), [CEM] Revs. Patrick J. O'Byrne; Andrew J. Kurz.
Res.: 520 S. 18th St., P.O. Box C, 68048. Tel: 402-296-3139; Fax: 402-296-2408.
School—(Grades K-8) Tel: 402-296-6230. Lay Teachers 14; Students 250.
Catechesis/Religious Program—Students 91.
PRAGUE, SAUNDERS CO., ST. JOHN'S (1901), [CEM] Rev. Ronald G. Homes.
Res.: 122 Center St., P.O. Box 96, 68050. Tel: 402-663-4615.
Catechesis/Religious Program—Students 100.
Mission—SS. Cyril and Methodius [CEM] Plasi, Saunders Co.
RED CLOUD, WEBSTER CO., SACRED HEART (1893), [CEM] Rev. Melvin Rempe.

Res.: 413 N. Seward St., 68970. Tel: 402-746-3750.
Catechesis/Religious Program—Students 32.
Mission—St. Catherine's Riverton, Franklin Co.
Mission—St. Mary Naponee, Franklin Co.

ROSELAND, ADAMS CO., SACRED HEART (1921), Rev. Thomas Y. Au.
Res.: 11818 W. Alexander, P.O. Box 67, 68973. Tel: 402-756-6251.
Catechesis/Religious Program—Students 66.
Mission—Assumption [CEM] Juniata, Adams Co.

RULO, RICHARDSON CO., IMMACULATE CONCEPTION (1863), [CEM] Rev. Thomas B. Dunavan.
Res.: R.R. 1, Box 89C, 68431. Tel: 402-245-4731.
School—Tel: 402-245-4151. Priests 1; Lay Teachers 6; Students 35.
Catechesis/Religious Program—Tel: 402-245-3002. Students 44.
Mission—St. Mary's Arago, Richardson Co.

SEWARD, SEWARD CO., ST. VINCENT DE PAUL (1878), Rev. Brad Zitek.
Res.: 152 Pinewood, 68434. Tel: 402-643-3421; Fax: 402-643-2594.
Catechesis/Religious Program—Tel: 402-643-3521. Students 261.

SHELBY, POLK CO., SACRED HEART (1898), [CEM] Rev. John Rooney.
Res.: 200 S. Walnut St., P.O. Box 340, 68662. Tel: 402-527-5425; Fax: 402-527-5849.
Catechesis/Religious Program—Students 80.

STEINAUER, PAWNEE CO., ST. ANTHONY (1882), [CEM] Rev. Thomas L. Wiedel.
Res.: P.O. Box 98, 68441. Tel: 402-869-2256.
Catechesis/Religious Program—Students 92.
Mission—Sacred Heart [CEM] Burchard, Pawnee Co.

SUPERIOR, NUCKOLLS CO., ST. JOSEPH'S (1934), [CEM] Rev. Philip Luther.
Res.: 1415 California, 68978-1019. Tel: 402-879-3735; Fax: 402-879-4495.
Catechesis/Religious Program—Students 83.
Mission—Sacred Heart Nelson, Nuckolls Co.

SUTTON, CLAY CO., ST. MARY'S, [CEM] Rev. K. William Holoubek.
Res.: 312 S. Saunders Ave., P.O. Box 406, 68979. Tel: 402-773-5346.
Catechesis/Religious Program—Students 84.

SYRACUSE, OTOE CO., ST. PAULINUS (1906), Rev. Michael S. Stec.
Mailing Address: 863 5th St., 68446-9504. Tel: 402-269-3382.
Catechesis/Religious Program—Students 128.
Mission—Holy Trinity [CEM] Avoca, Cass Co.

TECUMSEH, JOHNSON CO., ST. ANDREW'S (1866), [CEM] Rev. John A. Cooper.
Res.: 186 N. 5th St., P.O. Box 656, 68450. Tel: 402-335-3742; Fax: 402-335-2234.
School—(Grades K-6) Tel: 402-335-2234; Fax: 402-335-2234. Marian Sisters 2; Lay Teachers 1; Students 25.
Catechesis/Religious Program—Students 45.
Mission—St. Mary's [CEM] St. Mary, Johnson Co.

TRENTON, HITCHCOCK CO., ST. JAMES (1894), [CEM] Rev. Patrick F. Murphy.
Res.: 117 W. B St., P.O. Box 488, 69044. Tel: 308-334-5328.
Catechesis/Religious Program—Students 33.
Mission—Holy Family Palisade, Hitchcock Co.

ULYSSES, BUTLER CO., IMMACULATE CONCEPTION (1915), [CEM] Rev. Valerian Bartek.
Res.: 205 S. 6th St., P.O. Box 128, 68669. Tel: 402-549-2437.
Catechesis/Religious Program—Students 87.

VALPARAISO, SAUNDERS CO., STS. MARY AND JOSEPH'S (1975), [CEM] Rev. Thomas Kuffel.
Res.: 631 S Iver St., P.O. Box 248, 68065. Tel: 402-784-2511.
Catechesis/Religious Program—Students 120.

WAHOO, SAUNDERS CO., ST. WENCESLAUS (1877), [CEM 2] Very Rev. Rudolf F. Oborny, V.F.; Rev. Thomas M. Bush.
Res.: 214 E. 2nd St., 68066. Tel: 402-443-4235; Fax: 402-443-4275.
School—(Grades K-6) Tel: 402-443-3336; Fax: 402-443-5551. Sisters 1; Lay Teachers 13; Students 296.
Catechesis/Religious Program—Students 50.

WALLACE, LINCOLN CO., ST. MARY'S (1909), Rev. James Benton, Admin.
Res.: 221 N. Commercial Ave., P.O. Box 191 69169. Tel: 308-387-4441.
Catechesis/Religious Program—Students 21.
Mission—Resurrection of Our Lord Elsie, Perkins Co.

WESTON, SAUNDERS CO., ST. JOHN NEPOMUCENE (1885), [CEM 2] Rev. Randall L. Langhorst.
Res.: 110 Front St., P.O. Box 10, 68070. Tel: 402-642-5245.
School—(Grades PreK-6) Tel: 402-642-5231. Lay Teachers 7; Students 98.
Mission—St. Vitus [CEM] Touhy, Saunders Co.

WILBER, SALINE CO., ST. WENCESLAUS (1875), Rev. Douglas Dietrich.
Res.: 501 N Wilson, P.O. Box 706, 68465. Tel: 402-821-2689.
Catechesis/Religious Program—Students 105.
Mission—St. Joseph's Tobias, Saline Co.

WYMORE, GAGE CO., ST. MARY'S (1881), [CEM] Rev. Dennis W. Hetovy.
Res.: 107 N. 11th St., P.O. Box 295, 68466. Tel: 402-645-3051.
Catechesis/Religious Program—Students 65.
Mission—St. Joseph's Barneston, Gage Co.
Mission—St. Mary's [CEM] Odell, Gage Co.

YORK, YORK CO., ST. JOSEPH'S (1878), [CEM] Rev. Leo V. Seiker.
Res.: 505 East Ave., 68467. Tel: 402-362-4565.
School—(Grades K-8) Tel: 402-362-3021; Fax: 402-362-4067. Franciscan Apostolic Sisters 2; Lay Teachers 11; Students 124.
Catechesis/Religious Program—Students 135.

Shrines

CRETE, SALINE CO., SCHOENSTATT SHRINE (2001),
Shrine— 340 Hwy. 103, 68333. Tel: 402-826 4852.

LOMA, BUTLER CO., ST. LUKE'S CZECH CATHOLIC SHRINE,

Chaplains of Public Institutions

LINCOLN. *Nebraska Penal Complex*, 1420 K St., 68508. Tel: 402-742-4421. Revs. John L. Copenhaver, Chap., Anthony O. Stammitti.

DENTON. *U.S. Veterans' Hospital*, 7105 Cass, P.O. Box 406, 68339. Tel: 402-797-2105. Rev. Msgr. Thomas L. Holoman, Chap. (Retired).

On Duty Outside the Diocese:
Rev. Msgrs.—
Fucinaro, Thomas J., Villa Stritch, Via della Nocetta, 63, 00164 Rome, Italy.
Jackels, Michael O., Villa Stritch, Via della Nocetta, 63, 00164 Rome, Italy.
Reinert, James M., Villa Stritch, Via della Nocetta, 63, Rome 00164 Italy.
Revs.—
Gross, Gary, Military Duty, HHC 80, ASE CMR 490, Box 2188, APO 09708 Belgium.
Kalin, William A., 925 Vining St., Milton-Freewater, OR 97862.

Graduate Studies:
Revs.—
Coulter, Gary, Casa Santa Maria, Via dell'Umilta 30, Roma 00187 Italy.
Jansen, Raymond L., Casa Santa Maria, Via dell 'Umilta 30, Roma 00187 Italy.
Mitchell, Peter, Casa Santa Maria, Via dell'Umilta 30, Roma 00187 Italy.

On Sick Leave:
Rev.—
Mika, John M., 5010 S. 41st Ave., Omaha, 68017.

Retired:
Rev. Msgrs.—
Hain, Raymond B., Bonacum House, 3301 Sheridan Blvd., 68506.
Holoman, Thomas L., P.O. Box 91, Mead, 68041.
Kalin, Leonard I., Legacy Terrace, 5706 Fremont #329, 68507.
Keenan, Charles J., Bonacum House, 3301 Sheridan Blvd., 68506.
Pohl, Daniel J., Bonacum House, 3301 Sheridan Blvd., 68506.
Reisdorff, Clarence P., Madonna Hospital, 5401 S. St., 68506.
Revs.—
Danko, Michael S., 201 N. Gregg Rd., Nixa, MO 65714.
Derwinski, Victor A., 806 13th St., P.O. Box 281, Aurora, 68818.
Gadient, Peter J., 380 Elm St., P.O. Box 4, Bee, 68314.
Glaves, John J., Bonacum House, 3301 Sheridan Blvd., 68506.
Hebert, John M., 9 Perralena Ln., Hot Springs, AR 71909.
Kelly, John W., Bonacum House, 3301 Sheridan Blvd., 68506.
Lyons, Patrick J., Bonacum House, 3301 Sheridan Blvd., 68506.
Mroczkowski, Joseph A., P.O. Box 238, Cedar Creek, 68016.
Murphy, Francis J., #1 West End, Millstreet, Co. Cork Ireland.
O'Connor, James M., 2110 30th Ave., #32, Kearney, 68845.
Redmerski, Stanley J., Madonna Rehab. Hospital, 5401 South St., 68506.
Rydz, Zygmund S., 2981 Bluff Rd., Marianna, 68015.
Schieffer, Stanley F., Madonna Hospital, 5401 S. St., 68506.
Zastrow, John A., Bonacum House, 3301 Sheridan Blvd., 68506.

INSTITUTIONS LOCATED IN THE DIOCESE

[A] SEMINARIES, RELIGIOUS OR SCHOLASTICATES

DENTON. *Our Lady of Guadalupe Seminary*, P.O. Box 147, 7880 W. Denton Rd., 68339. Tel: 402-797-7700; Fax: 402-797-7705. Email: seminary@fsst.com. Very Rev. James W. Jackson, F.S.S.P., Rector; Revs. Charles Van Vliet, F.S.S.P., Vice Rector; Calvin R. Goodwin, F.S.S.P.; James B. Buckley, F.S.S.P.; Joseph Terra, F.S.S.P.; Mubarak Amar, F.S.S.P.; Chad Ripperger, F.S.S.P.

SEWARD. *St. Gregory the Great Seminary*, 1301 280th Rd., 68434. Tel: 402-643-4052; Fax: 402-643-6964. Web: www.stgregoryseminary.org. Very Rev. John T. Folda, Rector; Revs. M. James Divis, S.T.L., Spiritual Dir.; Jeffrey Eickhoff; Dr. John D. Thornbrugh, Academic Dean.

[B] ELEMENTARY SCHOOLS, INTERPAROCHIAL

HASTINGS. *St. Michael's Elementary, Hastings Catholic Schools*, 721 Creighton Ave., 68901. Tel: 402-462-6310; Fax: 402-462-6035. Email: smb@esu9.k12.ne.us. Priests 6; Sisters 2; Lay Teachers 23; Students 329.

NEBRASKA CITY. *Lourdes Elementary*, (Grades K-5), 412 2nd Ave., 68410. Tel: 402-873-6154; Fax: 402-873-3154. Lay Teachers 9; Students 138.
Lourdes Primary, (Grades K-3), 411 5th Rue, 68410. Tel: 402-873-3739. Lay Teachers 5; Students 80.

[C] HIGH SCHOOLS, INTERPAROCHIAL

LINCOLN. *Pius X Central High School*, 6000 A St., 68510. Tel: 402-488-0931; Fax: 402-488-1061. Email: webmaster@piusx.net. Web: www.piusx.lincoln.net. Rev. Michael J. Morin, Supt.; Mr. Thomas Seib, Prin.; Mr. Daniel Donohue, Asst. Prin.; Mr. Tom Korta, Asst. Prin.; Mrs. Jan Frayser, Dir. of Guidance; Mr. George O'Boyle, Dir. Activities. Priests 10; Sisters 3; Lay Teachers 51; Students 960.

DAVID CITY. *Aquinas/St. Mary's Schools*, (Grades K-12), 3420 MN Rd., P.O. Box 149, 68632. Tel: 402-367-3175; Fax: 402-367-3176. Email: frbrianconnor@aquinasdc.org. Web: www.aquinas.esu7.org. Rev. Brian P. Connor, Supt.; Mr. David G. McMahon, Prin. (Aquinas High School); Mrs. JoAnn Havlovic, Prin. (St. Mary's); Rev. Leo D. Kosch, Guidance Dir.; Bobbi Schmid, Career Counselor. Priests 5; Sisters 4; Lay Teachers 35; Students 514.

FALLS CITY. *Sacred Heart School*, 1820 Fulton St., 68355. Tel: 402-245-4151; Fax: 402-245-5217. Email: frlarry.stoley@piusx.lincoln.ne.us. Very Rev. Robert A. Roh, V.F., Supt.; Rev. Thomas B. Dunavan, Dir. Guidance; Mr. Douglas Goltz Prin.
High School Priests 3; Lay Teachers 9; Students 86.
Elementary School Priests 3; Lay Teachers 18; Students 142.

HASTINGS. *St. Cecilia's Middle School/High School*, (Grades 6-12), 521 N. Kansas, 68901. Tel: 402-462-2105; Fax: 402-462-2106. Email: mbutler@esu9.org. Web: www.esu9.k12.ne.us/~hcs. Rev. James J. Meysenburg, Supt. Priests 5; Sisters 2; Lay Teachers 32; Students 372.

NEBRASKA CITY. *Lourdes Central Catholic Schools*, (Grades K-12), 412 2nd Ave., 68410. Tel: 402-873-6154; Fax: 402-873-3154. Email: nc606064@navix.net. Rev. Michael G. McCabe, Supt. Priests 5; Sisters 4; Lay Teachers 18; Students 321.

WAHOO. *Bishop Neumann Jr.-Sr. High School*, 202 S. Linden, 68066. Tel: 402-443-4151; Fax: 402-443-5551. Web: bishopneumann.com. Revs. Charles L. Townsend, Supt.; Troy Schweiger, Prin. Priests 6; Sisters 1; Lay Teachers 24; Students 353.

[D] GENERAL HOSPITALS

LINCOLN. *St. Elizabeth Regional Medical Center*, 555 S. 70th St., 68510. Tel: 402-219-8000; Fax: 402-219-8973. Email: blanik@stez.org. Web: www.stez.org. Mr. Robert Lanik, Pres.; Rev. Edwin L. Stander, Chap. Affiliate of Catholic Health Initiatives. Priests 2; Sisters 2; Bed Capacity 204; Patients Assisted Annually 190,796.

NEBRASKA CITY. *St. Mary's Hospital*, 1314 3rd Ave., 68410. Tel: 402-873-3321; Fax: 402-873-9033. Email: dkelly@stez.org. Daniel J. Kelly, CEO, Admin. Affiliate of Catholic Health Initiatives.

Bed Capacity 18; Patients Assisted Annually 26,485.

[E] HOMES FOR AGED

LINCOLN. *Bonacum House*, 3301 Sheridan Blvd., 68506. Tel: 402-483-0391. Rev. Msgrs. Raymond B. Hain (Retired); Charles J. Keenan (Retired); Daniel J. Pohl (Retired); Revs. John J. Glaves (Retired); Patrick J. Lyons (Retired); John W. Kelly (Retired); John A. Zastrow (Retired). Residence for retired priests.

Madonna Rehabilitation Hospital, 5401 South St., 68506. Tel: 402-489-7102; Fax: 402-483-9460. Email: feedback@madonna.org. Web: www.madonna.org. Rev. Paul J. Rutten, Chap. Physical Medicine and Rehabilitation, Outpatient Services, Long-Term Care, Adult Day Care and Supportive Inpatient Hospice, Alzheimers Care. Sisters 8; Bed Capacity 252; Patients Assisted Annually 5,123.

DAVID CITY. *St. Joseph's Court, Inc.*, 646 I St., 68632. Tel: 402-367-4337; Fax: 402-367-4345. Email: stjosephvilla@hotmail.com. Web: saintjosephvilla.org. Assisted Living Residents 26; Total Assisted 28.

St. Joseph's Villa, Inc., 927 7th St., 68632. Tel: 402-367-3045; Fax: 402-367-3730. Email: stjosephsvilla@hotmail.com. Joyce Stewart, Admin. Sisters Adorers of the Blood of Christ (Wichita, KS) Residents 64; Total Assisted 107.

[F] RETREAT HOUSES

WAVERLY. *Our Lady of Good Counsel Retreat House*, 7303 N. 112th St., R.R. No. 1, Box 110, 68462. Tel: 402-786-2705; Fax: 402-786-7211. Email: 9603231@alltel.net. Web: www.goodcounselretreat.com. Rev. Lawrence Stoley, Dir. Private Rooms 50. In Res. Rev. John J. Perkinton.

[G] CONVENTS AND RESIDENCES FOR SISTERS

LINCOLN. *Adoration Convent and Church of Christ the King*, 1040 S. Cotner Blvd., 68510. Tel: 402-489-0765; Fax: 402-489-0864. Sr. Mary Caritas, Supr.; Rev. Joseph J. Nemec, Chap. Sister Servants of the Holy Spirit of Perpetual Adoration Professed Sisters 8.

St. Agnes Convent, 3405 Sheridan Blvd., 68506. Tel: 402-484-7348.

Congregation of Missionary Sisters of the Blessed Virgin Mary, Queen of Mercy, Queen of Mercy Mother, 6400 Nebraska Hwy. 2, 68516. Tel: 402-421-1704; Fax: 402-421-1704. Email: srsqueenmercy@hotmail.com. Professed Sisters 8.

Daughters of the Holy Spirit, Nazareth of the Good Shepherd, Hispanic Apostolate, 110 W. "E" St., 68508-3087. Tel: 402-477-7646; Fax: 402-477-7646. Email: hijasespsto@alltel.net. Sr. Margarita Iturbide, Supr. Sisters 3.

Holy Family Sisters of the Needy - Holy Family Convent, 5720 A St., 68510. Tel: 402-486-3706; Fax: 402-486-3706. Email: holyfamilysister@cs.com. Sr. Petra, Supr.

School Sisters of Christ the King, Villa Regina Motherhouse & Novitiate, 4100 S.W. 56th St., 68522-9201. Tel: 402-477-5232; Fax: 402-477-5232. Email: villaregina@juno.com. Web: www.rc.net/lincoln/schoolsisters. Sr. Joan Paul, C.K., Supr. In Res. Rev. Daniel J. Seiker, J.C.L. Tel: 402-477-1768.

Secular Institute of the Schoenstatt Sisters of Mary, ISSM, P.O. Box 80328, Boulder, CO 80328.

NEBRASKA CITY. *The Franciscan Sisters of the Sorrowful Mother*, 1503 4th Corso, 68410. Tel: 402-873-3052. Email: fs93813@alltel.net. Sr. Ana Maria Solis, O.S.F., Supr.

VALPARAISO. *Carmel of Jesus, Mary, and Joseph*, 9300 Agnew Rd., 68065. Tel: 402-784-0375; Fax: 402-784-0375. Sr. Teresa of Jesus, O.C.D., Prioress.

WAVERLY. *Marian Sisters of the Diocese of Lincoln Motherhouse and Novitiate*, 6765 N. 112th St., 68462-9690. Sr. Bernadette Radek, M.S. Professed 37; Postulants 2.

[H] SPECIAL EDUCATION

LINCOLN. *Villa Marie School and Home for the Educable Mentally Handicapped*, P.O. Box 80328, 68501. Tel: 402-786-3625; Fax: 402-488-6525. Sr. Patricia Stoeckinger, M.S., Prin.; Rev. John J. Perkinton, Dir. Marian Sisters (Waverly, NE) Sisters 3; Students 18.

[I] NEWMAN CENTERS

LINCOLN. *University of Nebraska, Newman Club* 320 N. 16th St., 68508. Tel: 402-474-7914; Fax: 402-476-2620. Email: newmancenter@usa.net. Web: newmancenter.tripod.com. Revs. Robert A. Matya, Vocation Dir.; Brian Kane. See also: St. Thomas Aquinas, Lincoln, NE. In Res. Rev. Christopher Kubat.

[J] FUNDS, FOUNDATIONS AND TRUSTS

LINCOLN. *Chancery*, P.O. Box 80328, 3400 Sheridan Blvd., 68501.
Seminary Burse Fund
Mass Stipends
Food for the Starving
Latin America Fund
Mission Office Fund
Catholic Evangelization Fund
St. Gregory the Great Seminary Fund
The Catholic Foundation of the Diocese of Lincoln, P.O. Box 80328, 68501-0328. Tel: 402-488-0921; Fax: 402-488-3569. Rev. Msgr. Timothy J. Thorburn, J.C.L.

[K] CATHOLIC SOCIAL SERVICES

LINCOLN. *Catholic Social Services*, Administrative Offices, 8101 "O" St., S111, 68510. Tel: 402-489-1834; 800-961-6277 (voice); Fax: 402-489-2046. Email: frjwalsh@csshope.org. Web: csshope.org. Revs. Joseph M. Walsh, Dir.; Christopher Kubat.
Other Addresses:
Apostolate of Suffering, 8101 "O" St., S111, 68510. Tel: 402-489-1834; Fax: 402-489-2046.
123 N. 25th St., 68503. Tel: 402-474-1600; 800-981-8242 (voice); Fax: 402-474-1612. Email: sfeeney@csshope.org.
515 W. Third St., Hastings, 68901. Tel: 402-463-2112; 888-826-9629; Fax: 402-463-2322. Email: tschik@csshope.org.
233 E. 14th St., Hastings, 68901. Tel: 402-463-1119; 888-491-6908 (voice); Fax: 402-463-2770. Email: pgibson@csshope.org.

[L] MISCELLANEOUS LISTINGS

LINCOLN. *Blessed John XXIII Diocesan Center*, Formerly Chancery Annex (Blessed John XXIII Diocesan Center)3700 Sheridan Blvd., 68506. Tel: 402-488-2040; Fax: 402-488-6525.

Calvary Cemetery and Mausoleum, 145 S. 40th St., 68510. Tel: 402-476-8787. Rev. David R. Hintz, Dir. Joint cemetery for Lincoln parishes.

Camp Kateri, P.O. Box 80328, 68501. Rev. Robert Barnhill.

Camp Kateri, P.O. Box 80328, 68501.

Catholic Social Services, 8101 "O" St., S111, 68510. Tel: 402-489-1834; 800-961-6277 (voice); Fax: 402-489-2046. Email: frjwalsh@csshope.org. Web: csshope.org. Rev. Joseph M. Walsh, Dir. St. Thomas Orphanage.

Cristo Rey Catholic Hispanic Center, 4245 J St., 68510. Tel: 402-488-5087.

St. Francis of Assisi Church, 3400 S 17th St., 68502. Tel: 402-477-5145; Fax: 402-477-5159. Rev. Karl A. Pikus, F.S.S.P., Chap.

Holy Family Convent, 5720 A St., 68510. Tel: 402-486-3706.

Magnificat-Lincoln, 917 S. 33rd St., 68510. Tel: 402-476-1880. Email: mharper55@yahoo.com. Mary Harper, Pres.

Pius X Foundation and Pius X Endowment Fund, 6000 A St., 68510. Tel: 402-488-0931; Fax: 402-488-1061. Email: angi.mcandrew@piusx.lincoln.ne.us. Web: www.piusx.lincoln.ne.us. Rev. Michael J. Morin, Sec. & Treas.

CRETE. *Our Lady of the Sacred Heart Shrine*, 340 State Hwy. 103, P.O. Box 276, 68333.

DAVID CITY. *Aquinas High School Endowment Fund*, P.O. Box 149, 68632. Tel: 402-367-3175; Fax: 402-367-3176. Email: fr.brian-connor@aquinasdc.org. Web: aquinas.esu7.org. Rev. Brian P. Connor, Sec. & Treas.

FALLS CITY. *Sacred Heart High School Endowment Fund*, 1820 Fulton St., 68355. Tel: 402-245-4151; Fax: 402-245-3002. Email: rrroh@sentco.net. Very Rev. Robert A. Roh, V.F., Sec. & Treas.

HASTINGS. *St. Cecilia High School Endowment Fund*, 521 N. Kansas, 68901. Tel: 402-462-2105; Fax: 402-462-2106. Email: jmeysenb@esu9.org. Web: www.esu9.k12.ne.us/~hcs. Rev. James J. Meysenburg, Sec. & Treas.

NEBRASKA CITY. *Lourdes Central High School Endowment Fund*, 412 Second Ave., 68410. Tel: 402-873-6154; Fax: 402-873-3154. Email: sm22100@navix.net. Rev. Michael G. McCabe, Sec. & Treas.

WAHOO. *Bishop Neumann High School Endowment Fund*, 202 S. Linden, 68066. Tel: 402-443-4151; Fax: 402-443-5551. Email: ctownsend@bneumann.org. Web: bishopneumann.com. Rev. Charles L. Townsend, Sec. & Treas.

RELIGIOUS INSTITUTES OF MEN REPRESENTED IN THE DIOCESE

For further details refer to the corresponding bracketed number in the Religious Institutes of Men or Women section.

[]—*Congregation of the Mother Coredemptrix* (Vietnamese)—C.M.C.

[1065]—*Priestly Fraternity of St. Peter*—F.S.S.P.

RELIGIOUS INSTITUTES OF WOMEN REPRESENTED IN THE DIOCESE

[0100]—*Adorers of the Blood of Christ*—A.S.C.

[0230]—*Benedictine Sisters of Pontifical Jurisdiction*—O.S.B.

[0420]—*Carmelite Monastery of Jeseu, Mary, and Joseph*—O.C.D.

[]—*Congregation of Missionary Sisters of the Blessed Virgin Mary, Queen of Mercy* (Vietnam)

[0820]—*Daughters of the Holy Spirit, Nazareth of the Good Shepherd*—H.Sp.S.

[1070-01]—*Dominican Sisters*—O.P.

[]—*Franciscan Apostolic Sisters*—F.A.S.

[2575]—*Institute of the Sisters of Mercy of the Americas*—R.S.M.

[2400]—*Marian Sisters of the Diocese of Lincoln*—M.S.

[2960]—*Notre Dame Sisters*—N.D.

[]—*Schoenstatt Sisters of Mary*

[]—*School Sisters of Christ the King*—C.K.

[1680]—*School Sisters of St. Francis*—O.S.F.

[3540]—*Sister Servants of the Holy Spirit of Perpetual Adoration*—S.Sp.S.deA

[1600]—*Sisters of St. Francis of Martyr St. George*—O.S.F.

[1640]—*Sisters of St. Francis of Perpetual Adoration* (Prov. of St. Joseph)—O.S.F.

[4120-05]—*Ursuline Nuns of the Congregation of Paris*—O.S.U.

DIOCESAN CEMETERIES

LINCOLN. *Calvary*, 145 S. 40th St., 68510.

NECROLOGY

† Banach, Walter F., (Retired)—Died Oct. 17, 2003
† Halligan, James, (Retired)—Died March 23, 2003
† Schnoebelen, Kenneth F., (Retired)—Died July 17, 2003

Diocese of Little Rock

(Dioecesis Petriculana)

Most Reverend

JAMES PETER SARTAIN, D.D., S.T.L.

Bishop of Little Rock; ordained July 15, 1978; appointed Bishop of Little Rock January 4, 2000; consecrated and installed March 6, 2000. *Diocese of Little Rock*, 2500 N. Tyler St., P.O. Box 7565, Little Rock, AR 72217. Tel: 501-664-0340; Fax: 501-664-9075.

Chancery: 2500 N. Tyler St., P.O. Box 7565, Little Rock, AR 72217. Tel: 501-664-0340.

Most Reverend

ANDREW J. MCDONALD, D.D., J.C.D.

Bishop Emeritus of Little Rock; ordained May 8, 1948; appointed Bishop of Little Rock July 4, 1972; consecrated September 5, 1972; installed September 7, 1972; retired January 4, 2000. *Res.: St. Joseph's Home for the Elderly*, 80 W. Northwest Hwy., Palatine, IL 60067. Tel: 847-358-5700; Fax: 847-358-5763.

ESTABLISHED NOVEMBER 28, 1843.

Square Miles 53,104.

Comprises the State of Arkansas.

For legal titles of parishes and diocesan institutions, consult the Chancery Office.

STATISTICAL OVERVIEW

Personnel	
Bishop	1
Retired Bishops	1
Abbots	1
Retired Abbots	1
Priests: Diocesan Active in Diocese	57
Priests: Diocesan Active Outside Diocese	1
Priests: Retired, Sick or Absent	16
Number of Diocesan Priests	74
Religious Priests in Diocese	52
Total Priests in Diocese	126
Extern Priests in Diocese	23
Ordinations:	
Diocesan Priests	1
Transitional Deacons	1
Permanent Deacons in Diocese	78
Total Brothers	33
Total Sisters	253
Parishes	
Parishes	88
With Resident Pastor:	
Resident Diocesan Priests	47
Resident Religious Priests	23
Without Resident Pastor:	
Administered by Priests	14
Administered by Deacons	3
Administered by Religious Women	1
Missions	35
Pastoral Centers	5
Professional Ministry Personnel:	
Sisters	26
Lay Ministers	52
Welfare	
Catholic Hospitals	12
Total Assisted	1,123,380
Health Care Centers	6
Total Assisted	29,479
Homes for the Aged	26
Total Assisted	957
Day Care Centers	30
Total Assisted	1,797
Specialized Homes	1
Total Assisted	133
Special Centers for Social Services	2
Total Assisted	1,125
Other Institutions	8
Total Assisted	24,362
Educational	
Diocesan Students in Other Seminaries	15
Total Seminarians	15
High Schools, Diocesan and Parish	4
Total Students	1,001
High Schools, Private	2
Total Students	711
Elementary Schools, Diocesan and Parish	31
Total Students	6,606
Catechesis/Religious Education:	
High School Students	2,705
Elementary Students	6,576
Total Students under Catholic Instruction	17,614
Teachers in the Diocese:	
Priests	8
Brothers	9
Sisters	21
Lay Teachers	640
Vital Statistics	
Receptions into the Church:	
Infant Baptism Totals	2,478
Adult Baptism Totals	269
Received into Full Communion	431
First Communions	2,453
Confirmations	1,626
Marriages:	
Catholic	357
Interfaith	262
Total Marriages	619
Deaths	861
Total Catholic Population	106,051
Total Population	2,710,079

Former Bishops—Rt. Revs. ANDREW BYRNE, D.D., consecrated March 10, 1844; died in Helena, June 10, 1862; EDWARD FITZGERALD, D.D., preconized June 22, 1866; consecrated Feb. 3, 1867; died in Hot Springs, Feb. 21, 1907; Most Revs. JOHN B. MORRIS, D.D., ord. June 11, 1892; consecrated June 11, 1906; died in Little Rock, Oct. 22, 1946; ALBERT L. FLETCHER, D.D. (Retired), ord. June 4, 1920; consecrated April 25, 1940; appt. Bishop of Little Rock Dec. 7, 1946; retired July 3, 1972; died Dec. 6, 1979; ANDREW J. MCDONALD, D.D., J.C.D. (Retired), ord. May 8, 1948; appt. Bishop of Little Rock July 4, 1972; consecrated Sept. 5, 1972; installed Sept. 7, 1972; retired Jan. 4. 2000.

Vicars General—Rev. Msgr. FRANCIS I. MALONE, J.C.L., V.G.; Very Rev. Msgr. J. GASTON HEBERT, V.G., V.F.

Chancery—2500 N. Tyler St., P.O. Box 7565, Little Rock, 72217. Tel: 501-664-0340; Fax: 501-664-9075. Office Hours: Mon.-Fri. 8:30-5

Chancellor for Canonical Affairs—Deacon JOHN M. "BO" MCALLISTER, This office also handles Archives.

Chancellor for Administrative Affairs—Mr. DENNIS P. LEE.

Vice Chancellors—Rev. Msgr. SCOTT L. MARCZUK, J.C.L.; Revs. JOHN K. ANTONY, J.C.L.; GREGORY T. LUYET, J.C.L.

Finance Officer—Mr. GREGORY C. WOLFE, CFO.

Diocesan Tribunal—2500 N. Tyler St., P.O. Box 7565, Little Rock, 72217. Tel: 501-664-0340; Fax: 501-664-9075.

Judicial Vicar—Rev. Msgr. SCOTT L. MARCZUK, J.C.L. Adjutant Judicial Vicars: Revs. JOHN K. ANTONY, J.C.L.; GREGORY T. LUYET, J.C.L.

Judges—Revs. JOHN K. ANTONY, J.C.L.; GREGORY T. LUYET, J.C.L.; Rev. Msgr. SCOTT L. MARCZUK, J.C.L.; Rev. PIUS IWUCHUKWU, J.C.D.; Deacon JOHN M. "BO" MCALLISTER, Assoc. Judge.

Defenders of the Bond—Rev. Msgr. JOHN KORDSMEIER; Mrs. BARBARA ANHALT.

Notaries—Mrs. DEBBIE JOHNSON; JEANNIE MOORE; Mrs. SUZANNE GIOVANELLO.

Minister to Men and Women Religious—Sr. MAXINE VOGAN, D.L.F., St. Francis of Assisi Church, 621 S. Washington, Forrest City, 72335. Tel: 870-633-1665; Fax: 870-633-6307.

Diocesan Consultors—Very Rev. Msgrs. J. GASTON HEBERT, V.G., V.F.; JOHN F. O'DONNELL, V.F.; Rev. Msgrs. BERNARD G. MALONE, V.F.; FRANCIS I. MALONE, J.C.L., V.G.; SCOTT L. MARCZUK, J.C.L.; JACK D. HARRIS, D.Min., V.F.

Deans—Very Rev. Msgrs. C. DAVID LESIEUR, V.F., Central Deanery; JOHN F. O'DONNELL, V.F.; LEO RIEDMUELLER, V.F.; Very Rev. ERNEST HARDESTY, V.F.; Very Rev. Msgr. RICHARD OSWALD, V.F.; Very Rev. CLARENCE EDWIN GRAVES, V.F.; Very Rev. Msgr. JACK D. HARRIS, V.F.; Very Rev. JOSEPH L. PALLO, V.F.; Rev. W. ANDREW SMITH, V.F.; Rt. Rev. JEROME KODELL, O.S.B., V.F.; Very Revs. GREGORY G. HART, V.F.; PHILLIP A. REAVES, V.F.; Rev. H. JON MCDOUGAL, V.F.

Diocesan Offices and Directors

Adoption Services, Inc.—Ms. ANTJE HARRIS, Dir., 2415 N. Tyler St., P.O. Box 7239, Little Rock, 72217. Tel: 501-664-0340; Fax: 501-664-9186.

Diocesan Council for Black Catholics—Rev. WARREN HARVEY, 1516 Parker St., North Little Rock, 72114. Tel: 501-374-7123; Fax: 501-372-2995.

Building Commission—Mr. JIM DRIEDRIC, Exec. Sec., 2500 N. Tyler St., P.O. Box 7565, Little Rock, 72217. Tel: 501-664-0340; Fax: 501-664-9075.

Catholic Social Services—Mrs. SHEILA GOMEZ, Dir. This office also handles: Catholic Relief Services and Catholic Campaign for Human Development. 2415 N. Tyler St., P.O. Box 7239, Little Rock, 72217. Tel: 501-664-0340; Fax: 501-664-9186; Mr. HENRY TUCK, Dir. Human Devel.

Catholic Campus Ministries—Deacon PAUL CRONAN, Dir., St. Thomas Aquinas University Parish, 603 Leverett Ave., Fayetteville, 72701. Tel: 479-444-0223; Fax: 479-442-2633. Email: cronan@uark.edu. Web: www.staup.org.

Catholic Immigration Services - Little Rock Office—Mrs. PAT HOULIHAN, Dir., 2415 N. Tyler St., P.O. Box 7239, Little Rock, 72217. Tel: 501-664-0340; Fax: 501-664-9186.

Catholic Immigration Services - NW Arkansas Office—Mr. FRANK HEAD, Dir., 1677 W. Sunset Ave., Springdale, 72762. Tel: 479-927-1996; Fax: 479-927-2979.

Catholic Women, Diocesan Council of—VACANT, Moderator.

Catholic Youth Ministries—Mr. JOHN HALL, Dir.; Deacon MARCELINO LUNA, Assoc. Dir., 2500 N. Tyler St., P.O. Box 7565, Little Rock, 72217. Tel: 501-664-0340; Fax: 501-664-9075 This office also handles: Scouting.

Cemetery, Greater Little Rock—VACANT, Business Mgr., 2500 N. Tyler St., Little Rock, 72207. Tel: 501-664-0340; Fax: 501-664-9075.

Charismatic Movement, Bishop's Liaison—Rev. Msgr. JAMES E. MANCINI, St. Joseph's Church, P.O. Box 39, 136 Henri de Tonti St., Tontitown, 72770. Tel: 479-361-2612; Fax: 479-361-9271. Email: jamman@mynewroads.com.

Clergy Welfare Board—Rev. Msgr. ROYCE R. THOMAS, J.C.L., Chm., Christ the King Church, 2112 S. Greenwood Ave., Fort Smith, 72901. Tel: 479-783-7745; Fax: 479-783-7075.

Communications Department—VACANT, Dir., P.O. Box 7565, Little Rock, 72217. Tel: 501-664-0340; Fax: 501-664-9075.

Continuing Education for the Clergy—Rev. Msgr. DAVID LESIEUR, V.F., Dir., 2500 N. Tyler St., P.O. Box 7565, Little Rock, 72217. Tel: 501-664-0340; Fax: 501-664-9075.

Cursillo Movement—Rev. Msgr. R. SCOTT FRIEND, Spiritual Dir., Spanish Cursillo Office; Deacon WILLIAM G. BRANDON, Spiritual Dir., English Cursillo Office; Mrs. NANCY CHRISTIAN, Dir. English; Ms. VERONICA VASQUEZ, Dir. Spanish, 2500 N. Tyler St., P.O. Box 7565, Little Rock, 72217. Tel: 501-664-0340; Fax: 501-664-9075.

Information Systems—Rev. Msgr. THOMAS SEBAUGH, Dir., 2500 N. Tyler St., P.O. Box 7565, Little Rock, 72217. Tel: 501-664-0340; Fax: 501-664-9075.

Stewardship and Development Office—Mr. DENNIS P. LEE, Interim Dir., P.O. Box 7565, Little Rock, 72217. Tel: 501-664-0340; Fax: 501-664-9075.

Diaconate Program—Deacon JOHN DUKE, Dir., 2500 N. Tyler St., P.O. Box 7565, Little Rock, 72217. Tel: 501-664-0340; Fax: 501-664-9075.

Ecumenical and Inter-Religious Affairs Office—Deacon JOHN MARSCHEWSKI, Dir., 9 Arles Dr., Little Rock, 72223. Tel: 501-664-0340; Fax: 501-664-9075.

Family Life Office: (Beginning Experience, Pre-Cana, Marriage Encounter, Retrouvaille)—ELIZABETH REHA, Dir., 2500 N. Tyler St., P.O. Box 7565, Little Rock, 72217. Tel: 501-664-0340; Fax: 501-664-9075.

Hispanic Ministry— This office also handles: Radio Hispano. Sr. ESPERANZA MICAELA ESPINOZA, M.C.P., Dir., P.O. Box 7565, Little Rock, 72217. Tel: 501-664-0340; Fax: 501-664-9075.

Hospitals—Rev. Msgr. FRANCIS I. MALONE, J.C.L., V.G., 2500 N. Tyler St., P.O. Box 7565, Little Rock, 72217. Tel: 501-664-0340; Fax: 501-664-9075.

Lay Ministry and Parish Renewal—Deacon JOHN M. "BO" MCALLISTER, Dir., 2500 N. Tyler St., P.O. Box 7565, Little Rock, 72217. Tel: 501-664-0340; Fax: 501-664-9075.

Library—Mrs. TERESA HAYDEN, Librarian, 2500 N. Tyler St., P.O. Box 7565, Little Rock, 72217. Tel: 501-664-0340; Fax: 501-664-9075.

Liturgical Commission—Rev. Msgr. FRANCIS I. MALONE, J.C.L., V.G., Dir., 2500 N. Tyler St., P.O. Box 7565, Little Rock, 72217. Tel: 501-664-0340; Fax: 501-664-9075.

Minister to Priests—Very Rev. Msgr. DAVID LESIEUR, V.F., 2500 N. Tyler St., P.O. Box 7565, Little Rock, 72217. Tel: 501-664-0340; Fax: 501-664-9075.

Newspaper "Arkansas Catholic"—Mrs. MALEA HARGETT, Editor, 2500 N. Tyler St., P.O. Box 7417, Little Rock, 72217. Tel: 501-664-0340; Fax: 501-664-9075.

Presbyteral Council—Rev. Msgr. R. SCOTT FRIEND, Chm., 2500 N. Tyler St., P.O. Box 7565, Little Rock, 72217. Tel: 501-664-0340; Fax: 501-664-9075.

Priests Personnel Board (Diocesan)—Most Rev. J. PETER SARTAIN, D.D., 2500 N. Tyler St., P.O. Box 7565, Little Rock, 72217. Tel: 501-664-0340; Fax: 501-664-9075.

Propagation of the Faith—Mr. DENNIS P. LEE, Dir., 2415 N. Tyler St., P.O. Box 7239, Little Rock, 72217. Tel: 501-664-0340; Fax: 501-664-9186.

Refugee Resettlement Program—Mrs. SHEILA GOMEZ, Dir., 2415 N. Tyler St., P.O. Box 7239, Little Rock, 72217. Tel: 501-664-0340; Fax: 501-664-9075.

Religious Education Department/Christian Initiation—Sr. MARY GLYNN, S.J.C., Dir., 2500 N. Tyler St., P.O. Box 7565, Little Rock, 72217. Tel: 501-664-0340; Fax: 501-664-9075.

Respect Life Office—Mrs. ANNE DIERKS, Dir., 2415 N. Tyler St., P.O. Box 7239, Little Rock, 72217. Tel: 501-664-0340; Fax: 501-664-9186 This office also handles: Project Rachel.

Rural Life Department—VACANT, 2500 N. Tyler St., P.O. Box 7565, Little Rock, 72217. Tel: 501-664-0340; Fax: 501-664-9075.

St. John's Catholic Center/Office Services—Ms. DIANNA GRISWOLD, Mgr., 2500 N. Tyler St., P.O. Box 7565, Little Rock, 72217. Tel: 501-664-0340; Fax: 501-664-9075.

Schools—Mrs. VERNELL BOWEN, Supt., 2500 N. Tyler St., P.O. Box 7565, Little Rock, 72217. Tel: 501-664-0340; Fax: 501-664-9075.

Little Rock Scripture Study—Ms. CACKIE UPCHURCH, Dir.; Ms. LILLY HESS, Assoc. Dir., Administration & Production; Mr. CLIFF YEARY, Assoc. Dir., Devel. of Study Materials, 2500 N. Tyler St., P.O. Box 7565, Little Rock, 72217. Tel: 501-664-0340; Fax: 501-664-9075.

Seminary Endowment Fund (The Msgr. James E. O'Connell Seminary Burse)—Rev. JOHN K. ANTONY, J.C.L., Dir., 2500 N. Tyler St., P.O. Box 7565, Little Rock, 72217. Tel: 501-664-0340; Fax: 501-664-9075.

Social Action Office—Mrs. SHEILA GOMEZ, Dir.; Sr. JOAN PYTLIK, D.C., Legislative Advocate, 2415 N. Tyler St., P.O. Box 7239, Little Rock, 72217. Tel: 501-664-0340; Fax: 501-664-9186 This office also handles: Parish Social Ministry.

Victim Assistance Coordinator—Dr. CAROL SIEMON. Tel: 501-664-0340. Email: csiemon@aristotle.net.

Vocations—Rev. JOHN ANTONY, J.C.L., Dir., 2500 N. Tyler St., P.O. Box 7565, Little Rock, 72217. Tel: 501-664-0340; Fax: 501-664-9075 Also serves as Director of Seminarians.

Westside Free Medical Clinic—Mrs. KAREN DIPIPPA, Dir., 2415 North Tyler St., P.O. Box 7239, Little Rock, 72217. Tel: 501-664-0340; Fax: 501-664-9186.

CLERGY, PARISHES, MISSIONS AND PAROCHIAL SCHOOLS

GREATER LITTLE ROCK
(PULASKI COUNTY)

1—CATHEDRAL OF ST. ANDREW (1845), [JC] Rev. Msgr. Scott L. Marczuk, J.C.L., Rector; Deacons Gary Dollar; B.J. Bowen.
617 Louisiana St., 72201. Tel: 501-374-2794; Fax: 501-375-3292.
Catechesis/Religious Program—Phyllis Rathman, D.R.E. Students 20.

2—ST. ANNE (North Little Rock) (1935), [JC] Revs. John K. Antony, J.C.L.; Salvador Marquez-Munoz; Deacon Ronald F. Stager, Pastoral Admin.
Mailing Address: 6150 Remount Rd., North Little Rock, 72118. Tel: 501-753-3977; Fax: 501-753-3991.
Res.: 801 Sherman St., 72202. Tel: 501-374-5767; Fax: 501-374-5839.
Catechesis/Religious Program—Belinda Kaye Ortner, D.R.E. Students 40.

3—ST. AUGUSTINE (1929), (African American), [JC] Revs. L. Warren Harvey; Oliver Ochieze.
1421 E. Second, North Little Rock, 72114. Tel: 501-375-9617; Fax: 501-375-9617.
Catechesis/Religious Program—Rosalyn G. Pruitt, D.R.E. Students 23.

4—ST. BARTHOLOMEW'S (1907), (African American), Rev. Robert Fisher, S.V.D.; Deacon Kirke Herman.
1622 Marshall St., 72202. Tel: 501-372-4682; Fax: 501-372-1742.

5—CHRIST THE KING (1966), [JC] Rev. Msgr. Francis I. Malone, J.C.L., V.G.; Rev. Jose Uppani; Deacons Bill Hartmann; Bo McAllister; Richard Patterson; Dan Cashman; Don Greenway; Bill Johnson.
4000 N. Rodney Parham Rd., 72212. Tel: 501-225-6774; Fax: 501-225-7169. Web: www.ctkLr.com.
School—Tel: 501-225-7883; Fax: 501-225-1315. Mrs. Kathy House, Prin. Lay Teachers 38; Students 797.
Catechesis/Religious Program—Students 126.
Msgr. Hebert Endowment Fund—Tel: 501-225-7883; Fax: 501-225-1315.

6—ST. EDWARD (1884), [JC] Revs. John K. Antony, J.C.L.; Salvador Marquez-Munoz; Deacons Daniel Hennessey; Marcelino Luna.
815 Sherman St., 72202. Tel: 501-374-5767; Fax: 501-374-5839.
School—E. Ninth & Ferry St., 72202. Tel: 501-374-9166. Theresa Hall, Prin. Lay Teachers 14; Students 175.
Educational Trust Fund for St. Edward School—
Catechesis/Religious Program— Sr. Martha Elena Torres, D.R.E. Students 250.

7—IMMACULATE CONCEPTION (1948), [JC] Rev. James P. West; Deacons William Nolan; John Marschewski.
7000 John F. Kennedy Blvd., North Little Rock, 72116. Tel: 501-835-4323; Fax: 501-834-5598.
School—Tel: 501-835-0771; Fax: 501-834-8652. Marcia Brucks, Prin. Lay Teachers 42; Students 492.
Catechesis/Religious Program—Tel: 501-835-4323, Ext. 30. Brenda Engel, D.R.E. Students 132.
Immaculate Conception School Endowment Fund—Fax: 501-834-0165.

8—IMMACULATE HEART OF MARY (Marche) (1878), (Polish), [CEM] Rev. Robert T. Dienert; Deacon Brunon Strozyk.
7006 Jasna Gora Dr., North Little Rock, 72118. Tel: 501-851-2763; Fax: 501-851-4769.
School—Tel: 501-851-2760; Fax: 501-851-4769. Sr. Rachel Auringer, O.S.U., Prin. Lay Teachers 13; Students 190.
Immaculate Heart of Mary Educational Trust Fund for Immaculate Heart of Mary School—Tel: 501-851-2763.

9—ST. MARY (North Little Rock) (1897), (Polish), Revs. L. Warren Harvey; Oliver Ochieze.
1516 Parker St., North Little Rock, 72114. Tel: 501-374-7123; Fax: 501-372-2995.
School—1518 Parker St., North Little Rock, 72114. Tel: 501-374-5237; Fax: 501-374-5237. Denise Troutman, Prin. Lay Teachers 15; Students 215.
St. Mary's School Endowment Fund—Tel: 501-758-2220; Fax: 501-753-6623.

10—OUR LADY OF GOOD COUNSEL (1894), Revs. Gregory T. Luyet, J.C.L.; Jack Vu; Deacons John Hartnedy; Chuck Farrat.
1321 S. Van Buren St., 72204. Tel: 501-666-5073; Fax: 501-664-1964.
School—1204 S. Jackson St., 72204. Tel: 501-663-7426; Fax: 501-666-2239. Anna Sanders, Prin. Lay Teachers 13; Students 140.
Msgr. Scheper Endowment Fund for Our Lady of Good Counsel Catholic School—Tel: 501-666-5073.
Catechesis/Religious Program—Tel: 501-664-2107. Margaret Zakrzewski, D.R.E. Students 31.

11—OUR LADY OF THE HOLY SOULS (1947), Very Rev. Msgr. David LeSieur, V.F.; Rev. Jose Uppani; Deacons Larry Jegley; Bill Cranford.
Church and Office: 1003 N. Tyler St., 72205. Tel: 501-663-8632; Fax: 501-663-8699.
School—901 N. Tyler St., 72205. Tel: 501-663-4513; Fax: 501-663-1014. Ileana Dobbins, Prin. Lay Teachers 32; Students 540.
Msgr. Allen Trust Fund for Holy Souls School—Students 65.
Catechesis/Religious Program—Anne Thomisee, D.R.E. Students 65.

12—ST. PATRICK'S (1880), [JC] Revs. L. Warren Harvey; Oliver Ochieze; Deacon Peter Stubbs.
211 W. 19th St., North Little Rock, 72114. Tel: 501-758-1155; Fax: 501-753-8251. In Res., Rev. Do Duy Nho.
School—200 West 20th, North Little Rock, 72114. Tel: 501-758-1508; Fax: 501-758-4945. David Grimm, Prin. Lay Teachers 13; Students 105.
Catechesis/Religious Program—Students 6.
St. Patrick's School Endowment Fund—Tel: 501-605-0008; Fax: 501-753-82[illegible].

13—ST. THERESA'S (1954), [JC] Rev. John M. Connell; Deacons Don Francis; Bill R. Wrape II.
6219 Baseline Rd., 72209. Tel: 501-565-9198; Fax: 501-565-3949.
School—Tel: 501-565-3855; Fax: 501-565-9522. Judy Davidson, Prin. Lay Teachers 22; Students 240.
St. Theresa's Catholic School Endowment Fund—
Catechesis/Religious Program—Tel: 501-565-5647. Students 139.

OUTSIDE THE CITY OF LITTLE ROCK

ADONA, CONWAY CO., ST. ELIZABETH'S (Oppelo) (1884), (German), [CEM] Attended by, St. Boniface Church, New Dixie. Rev. Richard P. Davis.
Mailing Address: 20 St. Boniface Dr., Bigelow, 72016. Tel: 501-354-0631; Fax: 501-759-2152.
Catechesis/Religious Program—Students 58.

ALTUS, FRANKLIN CO., ST. MARY (1879), [CEM] Rev. Hilary Filiatreau, O.S.B.; Deacon Matthew Post.
5118 St. Mary's Ln., 72821. Tel: 479-468-2585.
Catechesis/Religious Program—Students 76.

ARKADELPHIA, CLARK CO., ST. MARY'S (1971), Rev. Linus Ukomadu; Deacon E.C. "Bud" Daven.
Church: P.O. Box 26, 71923. Tel: 870-246-7575.

ASHDOWN, LITTLE RIVER CO., ST. ELIZABETH ANN SETON CHURCH, Attended by, St. Edward, Texarkana Very Rev. Phillip A. Reaves, V.F.; Rev. Felix Alaribe (Nigeria).
Mailing Address: P.O. Box 966, 71822. Tel: 870-898-8529; Fax: 870-898-8529.

ATKINS, POPE CO., ASSUMPTION B.V.M. (1878), (German), [CEM] Rev. Vincent Flusche; Deacon Veo J. Condley.
Mailing Address: P.O. Box 337, 72823. Tel: 479-641-7179; Fax: 479-641-9354.
Catechesis/Religious Program—Erma Dunham, D.R.E. Students 59.
Mission—*St. Augustine* 1000 N. 2nd, Dardanelle, Yell Co. 72834. Tel: 479-229-3972.

BALD KNOB, WHITE CO., ST. RICHARD CHURCH,

Attended by, St. James, Searcy Rev. Vincent Ogbuji (Nigeria).
Mailing Address: *c/o St. James*, P.O. Box 172, Searcy, 72145. Tel: 501-268-5252 (Searcy).

BARLING, SEBASTIAN CO., SACRED HEART OF MARY (1902), [CEM] Rev. Henry B. Mischkowiuski.
1301 Frank St., 72923. Tel: 479-452-1795; Fax: 479-452-0571.
Catechesis/Religious Program—Edwina Schwarz, D.R.E.; Dottie Hunter, D.R.E. Students 36.
Mission—SS. Sabina & Mary Church, (See listing under Jenny Lind) , Jenny Lind. Dr. Thomas Bonin, D.R.E.

BATESVILLE, INDEPENDENCE CO., ST. MARY'S (1909), Very Rev. Jon McDougal, V.F.
3800 Harrison St., 72501. Tel: 870-793-7717; 870-793-7464; Fax: 870-793-7717.
Catechesis/Religious Program—Patricia Hinds, D.R.E. Students 90.
Mission—St. Cecilia 2475 Galleria Dr., Newport, Jackson Co. 72112. Tel: 870-523-6542.

BELLA VISTA, BENTON CO., ST. BERNARD (1980), [CEM] Rev. W. Andrew Smith, V.F.
Columbarium: One St. Bernard Ln., 72715. Tel: 479-855-9060; 479-855-9069; Fax: 479-855-9067.
Catechesis/Religious Program—Tel: 479-855-3416. Dan Beshara, D.R.E. Students 45.

BENTON, SALINE CO., OUR LADY OF FATIMA (1942), Rev. Michael E. Bass; Deacons John Duke; Gilbert Morgan.
900 W. Cross St., 72015. Tel: 501-315-5186 (Office); 501-315-1747 (Rectory); Fax: 501-315-1479. Email: olfchurch@up-link.net.
School—Tel: 501-315-3398; Fax: 501-315-1479. Email: holydays@swbell.net. Marguerite Olberts, Prin. Lay Teachers 14; Students 125.
Our Lady of Fatima School Endowment Trust Fund—
Catechesis/Religious Program—Cecelia Fatton, D.R.E. Students 136.
Station—Arkansas Health Center, Tel: 501-860-0500.

BENTONVILLE, BENTON CO., ST. STEPHEN (1989), Rev. Michael Sinkler; Deacon Jerry Becker; Carol M. Patterson, Pastoral Admin.
Mailing Address: 1300 N.E. J St., 72712. Tel: 479-273-1240; Fax: 479-464-0969.
Catechesis/Religious Program—Students 340.
Rectory—1208 N.E. J St., 72712. Tel: 479-273-1240.

BERRYVILLE, CARROLL CO., ST. ANNE (1958), Rev. Thomas Arackal, I.M.S.; Deacon Manny Robles.
614 S. Main, 72616. Tel: 870-423-3927. Mailing Address: P.O. Box 605, 72616. Tel: 870-423-3927.
Res.: 30 Crescent Dr., Eureka Springs, 72632. Tel: 479-253-9853.
Catechesis/Religious Program—Students 85.

BIGELOW, PERRY CO., ST. BONIFACE'S (1879), (German), [CEM] Rev. Richard P. Davis.
20 St. Boniface Dr., 72016. Tel: 501-759-2371; Fax: 501-759-2152.
Catechesis/Religious Program—Students 28.
Mission—St. Francis Little Italy, Pulaski Co.
Mission—St. Elizabeth's Adona, Conway Co.

BLYTHEVILLE, MISSISSIPPI CO., IMMACULATE CONCEPTION (1894), Very Rev. Joseph L. Pallo, V.F.; Deacons William G. Brandon; Kenneth Klinger.
Mailing Address: P.O. Box 747, 72316.
Office: 1301 Main St., 72315. Tel: 870-762-2506; Fax: 870-762-2506.
School—Tel: 870-763-9444; Fax: 870-763-4278. Sharon Warren, Prin. Lay Teachers 8; Students 108.
Catechesis/Religious Program—Tel: 870-561-4120. Sheila Ward, D.R.E. Students 45.

BOONEVILLE, LOGAN CO., CHURCH OF OUR LADY OF THE ASSUMPTION (1953), Rev. Bruno Fuhrmann, O.S.B.
E. 6th & Cherry St., 72927. Tel: 479-675-3371.
Res. & Mailing Address: Subiaco Abbey, Subiaco, 72865. Tel: 479-934-1122.
Catechesis/Religious Program—Students 40.

BRINKLEY, MONROE CO., ST. JOHN THE BAPTIST (1875), [CEM] Rev. Benedict Meyer, O.S.B.
203 W. Ash, 72021-3201. Tel: 870-734-1202.
Catechesis/Religious Program—Tel: 870-734-3392. Carl Frein, D.R.E. Students 5.

CAMDEN, OUACHITA CO., ST. LOUIS (1923), Rev. Wilfred C. Okorochukwu.
Mailing Address: 202 Adams, N.W., 71701. Tel: 870-836-2426.
Res.: 962 Ridgeview, 71701. Tel: 870-836-0036; Fax: 870-352-5037.
Catechesis/Religious Program—Tel: 870-231-6052. Mrs. Tammie Bettis, D.R.E. Students 43.
Mission—Good Shepherd 410 Oak St., P.O. Box 565, Fordyce, Dallas Co. 71742. Tel: 870-352-2328; Fax: 870-352-5037.
Mission—Holy Cross 921 Vine St., P.O. Box 624, Sheridan, Grant Co. 72150-0624. Tel: 870-942-4532.

CARLISLE, LONOKE CO.
1—HOLY TRINITY CHURCH, Attended by, St. Rose, Carlisle Rev. Joseph A. Seiter, C.S.Sp.
Mailing Address: P.O. Box 243, England 72046. Tel: 501-842-2460; Fax: 870-552-3601 (Carlisle).
2—ST. ROSE OF LIMA CHURCH (1895), Rev. Joseph A. Seiter, C.S.Sp.; Deacon William Cunningham Jr.
603 E. Park, P.O. Box M, 72024. Tel: 870-552-3601.
Mission—Holy Trinity, (See listing under England) , England, Lonoke Co.

CENTER RIDGE, CONWAY CO., ST. JOSEPH'S (1881), (Italian), [CEM] Rev. John L. Yates, C.S.Sp.
Mailing Address: 343 Catholic Point Rd., 72027. Tel: 501-893-2887; Fax: 501-893-2887.

CHARLESTON, FRANKLIN CO., SACRED HEART (1879), [CEM] Rev. Peter Sharum, O.S.B.
18 Prairie St., 72933-9403. Tel: 479-965-2432.
Catechesis/Religious Program—Tel: 479-965-2771. Mark Verkamp, D.R.E. Students 114.

CHEROKEE VILLAGE, SHARP CO., ST. MICHAEL'S (1939), Rev. Kevin Atunzu; Deacons Michael Cumnock; Anthony Lucolph; Ray Siwek; Jim Thompson.
Mailing Address: P.O. Box 970, 72525. Tel: 870-257-2850; Fax: 870-257-2200.
Res.: 12 Micanopy Circle, 72529. Tel: 870-257-4456.
Catechesis/Religious Program—Students 47.
Mission—St. Mary of the Mount Church 401 E. Church St., Horseshoe Bend, Izard Co. 72512. Tel: 870-670-5896.
St. Michael Memorial Garden (Columbarium)—Hwy. 62/167 S. Tekakwitha Dr., 72529. Tel: 870-257-2850.

CLARKSVILLE, JOHNSON CO., HOLY REDEEMER (1879), [CEM] Rev. William Wewers, O.S.B.
103 E. Main St., 72830. Tel: 479-754-3610.
Catechesis/Religious Program—Students 235.
Mission—SS. Peter & Paul Church Hwy. 109, Morrison Bluff, Logan Co. Tel: 479-938-2200.

CLINTON, VAN BUREN CO., ST. JUDE CHURCH, Attended by, St. Francis of Assisi, Fairfield Bay Rev. Thomas W. Keller.
Mailing Address: P.O. Box 526, 72031. Tel: 501-745-5716; Fax: 501-745-5716.

CONWAY, FAULKNER CO., ST. JOSEPH'S (1878), [CEM] Revs. Thomas Byrne, C.S.Sp.; Brandon Nguyen, C.S.Sp.; Deacons David Westmoreland; Richard Papini; Richard Bemrich, (Retired); Gerald Harrison.
1115 College Ave., 72032. Tel: 501-327-6568; Fax: 501-329-6305.
Parish Business Office—375 Harkrider, 72032. Tel: 501-327-5528; Fax: 501-327-6607.
School—(Grades K-6) Tel: 501-327-1204; Fax: 501-327-8350. Joe Mallett, Prin.; Terri Seiter, Asst. Prin. (PreK-3); Susie Freyaldenhoven, Asst. Prin. (Grades 4-6). Lay Teachers 23; Students 314.
High School—(Grades 7-12), 502 Front St., 72032. Tel: 501-329-5741; 501-329-5606; Fax: 501-327-8350. Lay Teachers 22; Students 204.
Catechesis/Religious Program—Tel: 501-513-6812. Jean Leffler, D.R.E. Students 514.

CORNING, CLAY CO., ST. JOSEPH CHURCH, Attended by, St. Mary's, Paragould Rev. John E. Marconi.
Mailing Address: c/o CR 186, 72422. Tel: 870-857-6607; Fax: 870-857-6607.

CRAWFORDSVILLE, CRITTENDEN CO., SACRED HEART CHURCH, Attended by, St. Michael, West Memphis Rev. Clayton Gould.
Mailing Address: *c/o St. Michael*, P.O. Box 899, West Memphis, 72303. Tel: 870-733-1212 (West Memphis); Fax: 870-732-4808.

CROSSETT, ASHLEY CO., HOLY CROSS (1954), [JC] Rev. Pius A. Iwuchukwu.
Mailing Address: Box 1245, 71635. Tel: 870-364-4847; Fax: 870-364-4847.
Catechesis/Religious Program—Tel: 870-304-2543. Cheryl Rabalais, D.R.E. Students 23.
Mission— P.O. Box 188, Hamburg, Ashley Co. 71646. Tel: 870-853-8991.

DANVILLE, YELL CO., SAINT ANDREW CHURCH, Attended by, Our Lady of the Lake, Lake Village Rev. Neil Pezzulo, G.H.M.
Mailing Address: c/o P.O. Box 1688, Waldron, 72958. Fax: 479-207-0485.

DARDANELLE, YELL CO., ST. AUGUSTINE (1925),, A mission of the Assumption B.V.M., Atkins.
Res. & Mailing Address: P.O. Box 337, Atkins, 72823. Tel: 501-229-3972.
Church: 1001 N. 2nd., 72834. Tel: 479-641-7179; Fax: 479-641-3354.

DE QUEEN, SEVIER CO., ST. BARBARA'S (1911), [CEM] [JC] Rev. John W. Kerr.
Mailing Address: P.O. Box 86, 71832. Tel: 870-642-2256; Fax: 870-642-3426.
Mission—St. Martin, (See listing under Nashville) , Nashville, Howard Co. Tel: 870-845-1271.

DUMAS, DESHA CO., HOLY CHILD CHURCH, Attended by, Our Lady of the Lake, Lake Village Revs. Erik Pohlmeier; Theophilus Okpara (Nigeria).
Mailing Address: *c/o Our Lady of the Lake*, P.O. Box 272, Lake Village, 71653. Tel: 870-265-5439 (Lake Village); Fax: 870-265-5439.
Res.: 807 E. Waterman St., 71639.

EL DORADO, UNION CO., HOLY REDEEMER (1923), (Spanish), Rev. Gregory Pilcher, O.S.B.
Mailing Address: P.O. Box 10235, 71730-0045.
Church: 440 W. Main St., 71730-5757. Tel: 870-863-3620; Fax: 870-863-7537.
School—Tel: 870-863-8677; Fax: 870-863-7779. Casey Martin, Prin. Lay Teachers 14; Students 90.
Mission—Immaculate Heart of Mary 2114 N. Jackson St., P.O. Box 365, Magnolia, Columbia Co. 71753. Tel: 870-234-2710.
El Dorado Holy Redeemer School Endowment Fund—1103 W. Cedar St., 71730. Tel: 870-863-8677; Fax: 870-863-7779.

ENGELBERG, RANDOLPH CO., ST. JOHN THE BAPTIST (Pocahontas P.O.) (1885), (German), [CEM] Attended by, St. Paul the Apostle, Pocahontas. Revs. Thomas C. Marks; David E. Jacobs, Pastor Emeritus.
4650 Engelberg Rd., Pocahontas, 72455. Tel: 870-892-3780; Fax: 870-892-8127.
Catechesis/Religious Program—Tel: 870-647-2168. Mary M. Weisenbach, D.R.E. Students 48.

EUREKA SPRINGS, CARROLL CO., ST. ELIZABETH OF HUNGARY (1909), Rev. Thomas A. Arackal, I.M.S.
Mailing Address: 232 Passion Play Rd., 72632. Tel: 479-253-2222; Fax: 479-253-6616.
Res.: #30 Crescent Dr., 72632. Tel: 479-253-9853.
Catechesis/Religious Program—Tel: 479-253-6742. Don Barry, D.R.E.; Kathy Tromburg, D.R.E. Students 17.
Mission—St. Anne Hwy. 62, P.O. Box 305, Berryville, Carroll Co. 72616. Tel: 870-423-3927.

FAIRFIELD BAY, VAN BUREN CO., ST. FRANCIS ASSISI (1976), Rev. Thomas W. Keller; Deacon Frank Zanoff.
Res.: 250 Woodlawn Dr., 72088. Tel: 501-884-3349; Fax: 501-884-3349.
Catechesis/Religious Program—Tel: 501-884-7272. Richard Parker, D.R.E. Students 9.
Mission—St. Jude, (See listing under Clinton) , Clinton, Van Buren Co.

FAYETTEVILLE, WASHINGTON CO.
1—ST. JOSEPH'S (1844), [CEM] Rev. Paul Worm; Deacon Bud Baldwin III.
Church and Office: 1722 N. Starr Dr., 72701-2937. Tel: 479-442-0890; Fax: 479-442-7887.
School—Tel: 479-442-4554; Fax: 479-442-7887. Paula Thiessen, Prin. Lay Teachers 27; Students 336.
St. Joseph Endowment and Educational Trust Fund—1722 N. Starr Dr., 72701. Tel: 479-442-4554.
Catechesis/Religious Program—Tel: 479-442-0890, Ext. 254. Janet Fuller, D.R.E. Students 370.
2—ST. THOMAS AQUINAS UNIVERSITY PARISH (1960), Revs. Paul Worm, Sacramental Min.; James Fischer, C.M., Sacramental Min.; Deacon Paul Cronan, Pastoral Admin.
603 N. Leverett Ave., 72701-3220. Tel: 479-444-0223; Fax: 479-444-2633.

FORDYCE, DALLAS CO., GOOD SHEPHERD (1977),, A mission of St. Louis, Camden. Rev. Wilfred C. Okorochukwu.
Mailing Address: P.O. Box 565, 71742-0565. Tel: 870-352-2328; Fax: 870-352-2328.
Catechesis/Religious Program—Jose Castillo, D.R.E. Students 2.

FOREMAN, LITTLE RIVER CO., SACRED HEART CHURCH, Attended by, St. Edward's, Texarkana Very Rev. Phillip A. Reaves, V.F.; Rev. Felix Alaribe (Nigeria).
Mailing Address: P.O. Box 43, 71836. Tel: 870-542-6553; Fax: 870-542-6553.

FORREST CITY, ST. FRANCIS CO., ST. FRANCIS OF ASSISI (1876), [JC] Attended by, St. Peter Church, Wynne Very Rev. Edwin Graves, V.F.; Sr. Maxine Vogan, D.L.F., Pastoral Admin.
621 S. Washington St., P.O. Box 786, 72336-0786. Tel: 870-633-1665; Fax: 870-633-6307.
Catechesis/Religious Program—Students 24.

FORT SMITH, SEBASTIAN CO.
1—ST. BONIFACE (1886), [JC] Rev. William Elser; Deacon Chuck Hankins.
1820 North B St., 72901. Tel: 479-783-6711; Fax: 479-783-7423.
School—201 N. 19th St., 72901. Tel: 479-783-6601; Fax: 479-783-6605. Karen Hollenbeck, Prin. Lay Teachers 11; Students 171.
Catholic Education Endowment Trust of Fort Smith, Arkansas—
Catechesis/Religious Program—Diane Willis, D.R.E. Students 58.
2—CHRIST THE KING (1928), [CEM] [JC] Rev. Msgr. Royce R. Thomas, J.C.L.; Rev. Peter Quang Le.
2112 S. Greenwood Ave., 72901. Tel: 479-783-7745; Fax: 479-783-7075.
School—1918 S. Greenwood, 72901. Tel: 479-782-0614; Fax: 479-782-1098. Pam Byrd, Prin. Lay Teachers 20; Students 268.
Christ the King Catholic School Trust and Endowment Fund—Tel: 479-783-1937.
Catechesis/Religious Program—Tel: 479-783-5305. Shawn Elizabeth Kispert, D.R.E. Students 180.

3—IMMACULATE CONCEPTION (1849), [JC] Very Rev. Msgr. John F. O'Donnell, V.F.; Revs. Philip Panackel (India); Jesus Benjamin Carrillo-Adalpe; Deacons Ramond Brusts; Greg Pair.
Mailing Address: P.O. Box 1866, 72902-1866.
Church: 22 North 13th, 72901. Tel: 479-783-7963; Fax: 479-783-7865.
School—223 South 14th St., 72901. Tel: 479-783-6798; Fax: 479-783-0510. Sharon Blentlinger, Prin. Sisters of Mercy 1; Lay Teachers 32; Students 355.
Immaculate Conception School Educational Trust—
Catechesis/Religious Program—Tel: 479-783-7497. Surennah Werley, D.R.E. Students 420.
Mission—St. Leo's P.O. Box 1866, Hartford, Sebastian Co. 72902.

4—SS. SABINA & MARY CHURCH, Attended by, Sacred Heart of Mary, Barling Rev. Henry B. Mischkowiuski.
Mailing Address: 14304 Old Jenny Loop Rd., 72919. Tel: 479-452-1795 (Barling); Fax: 501-452-0571.

GLENWOOD, PIKE CO., OUR LADY OF GUADALUPE CHURCH, Rev. Jesus Benjamin Carrillo-Aldape.
Mailing Address: P.O. Box 426, 71943. Tel: 870-356-5185; Fax: 870-356-5185.
Res.: *Immaculate Conception*, P.O. Box 1866, Fort Smith, 72902.

GRADY, LINCOLN CO., BLESSED SACRAMENT CHURCH, Attended by, St. Justin, Star City Sr. Kathleen Miles, D.C., Pastoral Admin.
Mailing Address: c/o P.O. Box 128, Star City, 71667.
Res.: 1207 S. Main, 71644. Tel: 870-628-3092; Fax: 870-628-3092.

HAMBURG, ASHLEY CO., HOLY SPIRIT CHURCH (1987), (Hispanic), Attended by, Holy Cross, Crossett. Rev. Pius A. Iwuchukwu.
Mailing Address: c/o Holy Cross Church, P.O. Box 1245, Crossett, 71635. Tel: 870-364-4847; Fax: 870-364-4847.
Church: 110 E. Franklin, 71646. Tel: 870-853-8991.

HARRISON, BOONE CO., MARY, MOTHER OF GOD (1919), Very Rev. Gregory G. Hart, V.F.
Mailing Address: P.O. Box 2150, 72602. Tel: 870-741-5234; Fax: 870-741-4234.
Catechesis/Religious Program—Fax: 870-741-4234. Julie Maguire, D.R.E. Students 93.
Mission—St Andrews Catholic Church, (See listing under Yellville) , Yellville, Marion Co.

HARTFORD, SEBASTIAN CO., ST. LEO'S (1901),, A mission of Immaculate Conception, Fort Smith. Very Rev. Msgr. John F. O'Donnell, V.F.
Mailing Address: P.O. Box 1866, Fort Smith, 72902. Tel: 479-783-7963; Fax: 479-783-7865.

HEBER SPRINGS, CLEBURNE CO., ST. ALBERT CHURCH, Attended by, St. James, Searcy Rev. Vincent Ogbuji (Nigeria).
Mailing Address: 21 Park Rd., 72543. Tel: 501-362-2914; Fax: 501-362-2914.

HELENA, PHILLIPS CO., ST. MARY'S (1858), [CEM] Rev. Joseph Patrick Marconi.
123 Columbia St., 72342. Tel: 870-338-6990; Fax: 870-338-6990.
Catechesis/Religious Program—Students 38.
Mission—St. Andrew 54 W. Tennessee St., P.O. Box 724, Marianna, Lee Co. 72360.

HOPE, HEMPSTEAD CO., OUR LADY OF GOOD HOPE (1875), [CEM] Rev. Msgr. Robert C. Rehkemper (DAL), Admin. (Retired); Deacon Robert V. Regan, (Retired).
Mailing Address: P.O. Box 517, 71801.
Office: 325 S. Walker St., 71802-0517. Tel: 870-777-6156.
Catechesis/Religious Program—Karen Barham, D.R.E.; Sr. Joselina Cedeno, D.R.E. Students 72.

HORSESHOE BEND, IZARD CO., ST. MARY OF THE MOUNT (1974), [CEM] Attended by, St. Michael's, Cherokee Village Rev. Kevin O. Atunzu.
401 Church St., P.O. Box 4012, 72512. Tel: 870-670-5896.
Catechesis/Religious Program—Students 6.

HORSESHOE LAKE, CRITTENDEN CO., ST. MARY OF THE LAKE CHURCH, Attended by, St. Michael, West Memphis Rev. Clayton Gould.
Mailing Address: *c/o St. Michael*, P.O. Box 899, West Memphis, 72303. Tel: 870-733-1212 (West Memphis); Fax: 870-732-4808.

HOT SPRINGS NATIONAL PARK, GARLAND CO.

1—ST. JOHN THE BAPTIST (1907), Revs. William F. Thomas; Jesus Benjamin Carrillo-Aldape; Deacons David Briselden; Frank Sluppick, (Retired); John Connell; Patrick McCruden.
Res.: 589 W. Grand Ave., 71901. Tel: 501-623-6201; Fax: 501-318-0328.
School—583 W. Grand Ave., 71901. Tel: 501-624-3141; Fax: 501-624-3141. Sr. Claudia Ward, Prin. Sisters of Mercy 3; Lay Teachers 10; Students 200.
St. John's School Endowment—Tel: 501-624-3171.

2—ST. MARY OF THE SPRINGS (1869), [JC] Rev. Msgr. Leo A. Riedmueller, V.F.; Deacons Joe Harrison; Lee Leckner.
100 Central Ave., 71901. Tel: 501-623-3233.

HOT SPRINGS VILLAGE, GARLAND CO., SACRED HEART OF JESUS (1979), Rev. Msgr. Bernard G. Malone, V.F.; Deacons Bernard Bauer; Wallace Gieringer; Larry Lipsmeyer; William Friedman.
Rectory—22 Descollar, 71909. Tel: 501-922-4024.
Church: 295 Balearic, 71909. Tel: 501-922-2062; Fax: 501-922-4153.

HUNTSVILLE, MADISON CO., ST. JOHN'S (1963), [JC] Rev. Msgr. James E. Mancini; Anne Beer, Business Mgr.
Church and Mailing Address: 209 Dotson St., 72740. Tel: 479-738-2709.
Catechesis/Religious Program—Tel: 479-232-5790. B. Varner, D.R.E. Students 18.

JACKSONVILLE, PULASKI CO., ST. JUDE THE APOSTLE (1966), Rev. Leslie A. Farley; Deacons James M. Alberson; Max R. Elliott.
2403 McArthur Dr., 72076. Tel: 501-982-4891; Fax: 501-982-0821. In Res., Rev. Francis D. Colavechio.
Catechesis/Religious Program—Tel: 501-843-9467. Brenda Stevens, D.R.E. Students 278.

JONESBORO, CRAIGHEAD CO.

1—BLESSED JOHN NEWMAN UNIVERSITY PARISH, Attended by, Blessed Sacrament, Jonesboro Rev. D. Mark Wood.
Mailing Address: 2800 E. Johnson Ave., 72401. Tel: 870-972-1888; Fax: 870-972-1888 *51.

2—BLESSED SACRAMENT (1885), [CEM] Revs. D. Mark Wood; Martin Osuji (Nigeria); Deacons Victor Stepka; David England.
614 S. Church St., P.O. Box 1735, 72401. Tel: 870-932-2529; Fax: 870-935-4444.
School—Tel: 870-932-3684. Lee Ann Graddy, Prin. Olivetan Benedictine Sisters 2; Lay Teachers 8; Students 133.
Catechesis/Religious Program—Tel: 870-931-7079.
Blessed Sacrament Educational Endowment Fund—Tel: 870-935-2871.

LAKE VILLAGE, CHICOT CO., OUR LADY OF THE LAKE (1869), (Italian), [CEM 2] Revs. Erik Poklmeier; Theophilus Okpara (Nigeria).
Mailing Address: P.O. Box 272, 71653. Tel: 870-265-5439; Fax: 870-265-2162.
School—Tel: 870-265-2921; Fax: 870-265-2921. Kelly Pieroni, Prin. Lay Teachers 6; Students 107.
Mission—Holy Child, (See listing under Dumas) , Dumas, Desha Co.
Mission—St. Mary Church, (See listing under McGehee) , McGehee, Desha Co.
St. Mary's Educational Trust Fund—

LEOLA, GRANT CO., BLESSED JUAN DIEGO CHURCH, Rev. Jesus Benjamin Carrillo-Aldape.
Mailing Address: P.O. Box, 72084. Tel: 501-623-6201; Fax: 501-318-0328 (Hot Springs).

LITTLE ITALY, PULASKI CO., ST. FRANCIS OF ASSISI CHURCH, Attended by, St. Boniface, Bigelow Rev. Richard P. Davis.
Mailing Address: *c/o St. Boniface*, 20 St. Boniface, Bigelow, 72016. Tel: 501-759-2371; Fax: 501-759-2152 (St. Boniface).

MAGNOLIA, COLUMBIA CO., IMMACULATE HEART OF MARY (1946), Attended by, Holy Redeemer Church, El Dorado. Rev. Gregory Pilcher, O.S.B.
Mailing Address: P.O. Box 365, 71754. Tel: 870-234-2710.

MALVERN, HOT SPRING CO., ST. JOHN THE BAPTIST (1949),, A mission of St. John the Baptist, Hot Springs. Rev. Linus Ukomadu.
Mailing Address: P.O. Box 6, 1114 Pine Bluff St., 72104. Tel: 501-332-6244; Fax: 501-332-7100.

MARIANNA, LEE CO., ST. ANDREW, Attended by, St. Mary's, Helena Rev. Joseph Patrick Marconi.
54 W. Tennessee St., P.O. Box 724, 72360. Tel: 870-338-6990; Fax: 870-338-6990.

MARKED TREE, POINSETT CO., ST. NORBERT (1947), Revs. Mark Wood, S.J.; Martin Osuji (Nigeria).
Mailing Address: 42 Frisco St., 72365. Tel: 870-358-2135.
Church: 501 Normandy St., 72365.

MCCRORY, WOODRUFF CO., ST. MARY CHURCH, Attended by, St. Peter, Wynne Very Rev. Edwin Graves, V.F.
Mailing Address: c/o 1695 N. Falls Blvd., P.O. Box 517, Wynne, 72396. Tel: 870-731-0048; Fax: 870-238-2613 (Wynne).

MCGEHEE, DESHA CO., ST. MARY (1906), Attended by, Our Lady of the Lake, Lake Village. Revs. Erik Pohlmeier; Theophilus Okpara (Nigeria).
401 N. 3rd St., 71654. Tel: 870-222-3389; Fax: 870-222-4805.

MENA, POLK CO., ST. AGNES (1896), [CEM] Rev. Norbert F. Rappold.
203 8th St., 71953. Tel: 479-394-1017; Fax: 479-394-2088.
Catechesis/Religious Program—Students 69.
Mission—All Saints, (See listing Mount Ida) , Mount Ida, Montgomery Co.

MONTICELLO, DREW CO., ST. MARK (1975), Rev. Chet Artysiewicz, G.H.M.
Rectory—452 W. Jefferson, 71655. Tel: 870-367-5974.
Church: 1016 N. Hyatt St., 71655. Tel: 870-367-2848.
Catechesis/Religious Program—Tel: 870-460-9919. Rose Ann Adcock, D.R.E. Students 42.
Mission—St. Luke, (See listing under Warren) , Warren, Bradley Co.

MORRILTON, CONWAY CO., SACRED HEART (1879), [CEM] Rev. Charles Thessing; Deacon Oscar Rohlman.
506 E. Broadway, 72110. Tel: 501-354-4181; Fax: 501-354-4181.
Catechesis/Religious Program—Students 54.
School—Tel: 501-354-8113; Fax: 501-354-2001. Lay Teachers 8; Students 128.
High School—106 N. St. Joseph, 72110. Brian Bailey, Prin. Lay Teachers 11; Students 107.
Sacred Heart School Endowment—

MORRISON BLUFF, LOGAN CO., SS. PETER AND PAUL (1878), Attended by, Holy Redeemer, Clarksville. Rev. William Wewers, O.S.B.
Res. & Mailing Address: c/o Holy Redeemer Church, 103 E. Main St., Clarksville, 72830. Tel: 479-754-3610.
Catechesis/Religious Program—Students 35.

MOUNT IDA, MONTGOMERY CO., ALL SAINTS CHURCH, Attended by, St. Agnes, Mena Rev. Norbert F. Rappold.
Mailing Address: P.O. Box 724, 71957. Tel: 479-394-1017; Fax: 479-394-1017 (Mena).

MOUNTAIN HOME, BAXTER CO., ST. PETER THE FISHERMAN (1959), Revs. James M. Fanrak; Stan Swiderski; Deacons John Krug, (Retired); Richard Linstad.
249 Dyer St., P.O. Box 298, 72654. Tel: 870-425-2832; Fax: 870-424-5172.
Catechesis/Religious Program—Rev. James M. Fanrak, D.R.E. Students 155.
Mission—St. Mary Church (1983),, (See listing under Mountain View) , Mountain View, Stone Co.

MOUNTAIN VIEW, STONE CO., ST. MARY CHURCH, Attended by, St. Peter the Fisherman, Mountain Home Revs. James M. Fanrak; Stan Swiderski.
Mailing Address: *c/o Lee Ann Simons*, 1202 Crestridge St., 72560.
Res.: 17170 Hwy. 66 W., 72560. Tel: 870-269-5194; Fax: 870-269-5194.

NASHVILLE, HOWARD CO., ST. MARTIN CHURCH, Attended by, St. Barbara, DeQueen Rev. John W. Kerr.
Mailing Address: 1011 Leslie St., P.O. Box 1039, 71852. Tel: 870-845-1271; Fax: 870-845-1271.

NEWPORT, JACKSON CO., ST. CECILIA'S, Attended by, St. Mary's, Batesville. Very Rev. Jon McDougal, V.F.
2475 Galeria Subdivision: 72112. Tel: 870-793-7464; 870-523-6542.
St. Mary's Church: 3800 Harrison St., Batesville, 72501. Tel: 870-793-7717.
Catechesis/Religious Program—Students 18.

OSCEOLA, MISSISSIPPI CO., ST. MATTHEW'S (1879), Attended by, Immaculate Conception, Blytheville. Very Rev. Joseph L. Pallo, V.F.
Church: P.O. Box 583, 72370. Tel: 870-563-9991.
Res.: 1301 W. Main St., Blytheville, 72315. Tel: 870-762-2506; Fax: 870-762-2506.
Catechesis/Religious Program—800 Betty Lynn, 72370. Tel: 870-563-4889. Mike Schuncke, D.R.E. Students 15.

PARAGOULD, GREENE CO., ST. MARY'S (1883), [CEM] Rev. John E. Marconi; Deacon Rex A. Bouldin.
Rectory—301 W. Highland St., 72450. Tel: 870-236-2568; Fax: 870-236-8674.
Church: 220 N. Second St., 72450. Tel: 870-236-3681.
School—Tel: 870-236-3681; Fax: 870-236-1073. Fran Black, Prin. Lay Teachers 8; Students 84.
Catechesis/Religious Program—Tel: 870-239-3976. Karen Ussery, D.R.E. Students 51.
Mission—Immaculate Heart of Mary, (See listing under Walnut Ridge) , Walnut Ridge, Lawrence Co.
Mission—St. Joseph, (See listing under Corning) , Corning, Clay Co. Tel: 870-857-6607.
St. Mary Educational Trust Fund—

PARIS, LOGAN CO., ST. JOSEPH'S (1879), (German), [CEM] Rev. Eugene Luke, O.S.B.; Deacon Thomas J. Pohlmeier.
15 S. Spruce St., 72855. Tel: 479-963-2131.
School—Tel: 479-963-2119; Fax: 479-963-8039. Elwood Brooks, Prin. Lay Teachers 8; Students 90.
St. Joseph Endowment Fund—Tel: 479-963-2131.

PINE BLUFF, JEFFERSON CO.

1—ST. JOSEPH'S (1858), [CEM 5] [JC] Very Rev. Jack D. Harris, V.F., V.F.; Deacons Tim Massanelli; Robert Johnson; Noel F. "Bud" Bryant.
412 W. 6th Ave., P.O. Box 7434, 71611. Tel: 870-534-4701; Fax: 870-534-4703.
School—St. Joseph's Junior High School, Tel: 870-534-7545; Fax: 870-535-4928. Deacon R. Peter Rivera, Prin. Lay Teachers 10; Students 58.
High School—St. Joseph Catholic Senior High School, 1501 W. 73rd Ave., 71603. Tel: 870-540-0413; Fax: 870-540-0345. Lay Teachers 14; Students 68.
Catechesis/Religious Program—Tel: 870-536-6699.

Brynn Koschel, D.R.E. Students 141.
Mission—St. Mary's P.O. Box 7434, Plum Bayou, Jefferson Co. 71611. Tel: 870-534-4702.
St. Joseph's Education Fund—Tel: 870-879-4217. Gertrude Schimmel, Pres.
Junior High Endowment Fund—
Senior High Trust Fund—

2—ST. PETER'S (1894), (African American), Very Rev. Jack D. Harris, V.F., V.F.; Rev. Donald L. Murrin, S.V.D.
207 E. 16th Ave., 71601. Tel: 870-534-6418; Fax: 870-534-6418.
School—Tel: 870-535-4017; Fax: 870-535-4017. Cynthia Lingo, Prin. Sisters of Notre Dame 3; Lay Teachers 7; Students 153.
Convent—Tel: 870-534-2316.
Mission—St. Raphael's, Jefferson Co.
St. Peter Catholic School Foundation—

PRAIRIE VIEW, LOGAN CO., ST. MEINRAD CHURCH, Attended by, St. Ignatius, Scranton Rev. Denis Soerries, O.S.B.
Mailing Address: 108 Main St., P.O. Box 87, Scranton, 72863.
35 Saint Meinrad Loop, Scranton, 72863. Tel: 479-938-2821; Fax: 479-938-2821 (Scranton).

POCAHONTAS, RANDOLPH CO., ST. PAUL THE APOSTLE (1868), [CEM] Revs. Thomas C. Marks; David E. Jacobs, Pastor Emeritus; Deacon George Edwards.
1002 Convent St., 72455. Tel: 870-892-3319; Fax: 870-892-5199.
School—Tel: 870-892-5639. Olivetan Benedictine Sisters 3; Lay Teachers 6; Students 96.
Catechesis/Religious Program—Tel: 870-892-1990. Sr. Romana Rohmer, D.R.E. Students 90.

RATCLIFF, LOGAN CO., ST. ANTHONY (1879), (German), [CEM] Rev. Harold Heiman, O.S.B.; Deacon Bob Cowie.
Subiaco Abbey: Subiaco, 72865. Tel: 479-934-1000; Fax: 479-934-4328.

ROGERS, BENTON CO., ST. VINCENT DE PAUL (1941), [CEM] Rev. Msgr. Richard S. Oswald, V.F.; Deacons Bill Cook; Clarence Leis; John Pate.
Church: 1416 W. Cypress St., 72758. Tel: 479-636-4020; Fax: 479-631-2548.
School—1315 W. Cypress St., 72758. Tel: 479-636-4421; Fax: 479-631-2548. Kristine Grelle, Prin. Lay Teachers 19; Students 319.
St. Vincent de Paul Endowment Fund—Tel: 479-621-1723; Fax: 479-621-1723.
Catechesis/Religious Program—Students 600.

RUSSELLVILLE, POPE CO.
1—ST. JOHN'S (1950), Very Rev. Ernest L. Hardesty, V.F.
Mailing Address: 1900 W. Main St., P.O. Box 308, 72811. Tel: 479-967-3699; Fax: 479-967-6215.
School—Tel: 479-967-4644; Fax: 479-967-4644 Paula Gallagher, Prin. Benedictine Sisters 2; Lay Teachers 11; Students 77.
Catechesis/Religious Program—Tel: 479-967-3699. Patricia Yucra, D.R.E. (Grades K-5); David Yacko, D.R.E. (Grades 6-12). Students 175.
Mission—St. Leo The Great, (See listing under Jonesboro) ,, Pope Co. Univ. Parish of AR
St. John's Educational Trust—1912 W. Main St., 72801.

2—ST. LEO THE GREAT UNIVERSITY PARISH, Attended by, St. John, Russellville Very Rev. Ernest L. Hardesty, V.F.
Mailing Address: *c/o St. John*, 1900 W. Main, P.O. Box 308, 72802.
509 W. L St., 72801. Tel: 479-967-3699; Fax: 479-967-6215.

ST. VINCENT, CONWAY CO., ST. MARY (1880), [CEM] Rev. Charles Thessing.
11 Kaufman Ln., Hattieville, 72063. Tel: 501-354-3206; Fax: 501-354-4132.
Catechesis/Religious Program—Students 81.

SCRANTON, LOGAN CO., ST. IGNATIUS (1913), (German), [CEM] Rev. Denis Soerries, O.S.B.
Church: P.O. Box 87, 72863. Tel: 479-938-2821.
Catechesis/Religious Program—Tel: 479-938-7474. Susan Johnson, D.R.E. Students 84.
Mission—St. Meinrad, (See listing under Prairie View) , Prairie View, Logan Co.

SEARCY, WHITE CO., ST. JAMES (1915), Rev. Vincent Ogbuji (Nigeria).
1102 Pioneer Rd., P.O. Box 172, 72143. Tel: 501-268-5252 (Office); Fax: 501-268-2388.
Mission—St. Albert, (See listing under Heber Springs) , Heber Springs, Cleburne Co. Deacon Robert Morris.
Mission—St. Richard, (See listing under Bald Knob) , Bald Knob, White Co.

SHERIDAN, GRANT CO., HOLY CROSS (1949),, A mission of St. Louis, Camden. Rev. Wilfred C. Okorochukwu.
Res.: 921 West Vine St., P.O.Box 624, 72150-0624. Tel: 870-942-4532; Fax: 870-352-2328.
Catechesis/Religious Program—Tel: 870-942-8366. Mary Hale, D.R.E. Students 11.

SHOAL CREEK, LOGAN CO., ST. SCHOLASTICA'S (New Blaine) (1878), (German), Rev. Raphael DeSalvo, O.S.B.
288 St. Scholastica Rd., New Blaine, 72851. Tel: 479-938-7565.
Catechesis/Religious Program—Students 10.

SILOAM SPRINGS, BENTON CO., ST. MARY'S (1953), Rev. Richard M. Strock.
Mailing Address: P.O. Box 118, 72761. Tel: 479-524-8526; Fax: 479-524-5677.
Catechesis/Religious Program—Tel: 479-524-3120. Carol Anstart, D.R.E. Students 135.

SLOVAK, PRAIRIE CO., SS. CYRIL AND METHODIUS, [CEM] Attended by, Holy Rosary, Stuttgart Rev. Msgr. John A. Janesko.
Mailing Address: Rte. 1, Box 117, Stuttgart, 72160. Tel: 870-241 3359; Fax: 870-673-6701.
Catechesis/Religious Program—Students 49.

SPRINGDALE, WASHINGTON CO., ST. RAPHAEL'S (1949), [JC] Rev. Msgr. Scott Friend; Rev. Fredy Lozada Lemus; Deacon Chuck Marino.
Church: 1386 S.West End, 72764. Tel: 479-756-6711; Fax: 479-756-8818.
Rectory—1721 West Sunset, 72762. Tel: 479-756-5411.
Catechesis/Religious Program—Students 942.

STAMPS, LAFAYETTE CO., ST. VINCENT DE PAUL, Closed. For inquiries for parish records contact the chancery.

STAR CITY, LINCOLN CO., ST. JUSTIN'S (1986) [CEM] [JC] Sr. Kathleen Miles, D.C., Admin.
Mailing Address: P.O. Box 128, 71667. Tel: 870-628-3092; Fax: 870-628-3092.
Catechesis/Religious Program—Students 14.
Mission—Blessed Sacrament, (See listing under Gary) , Grady, Lincoln Co.

STUTTGART, ARKANSAS CO., HOLY ROSARY (1887), [CEM] Rev. Msgr. John A. Janesko.
1815 S. Prairie St., 72160. Tel: 870-673-8351; Fax: 870-673-6701.
School—Tel: 870-673-3211. Kathy Lorince, Prin. Lay Teachers 6; Students 78.
Catechesis/Religious Program—Students 63.

SUBIACO, LOGAN CO., ST. BENEDICT (1878), [CEM] Rev. Victor Gillespie, O.S.B.
Res.: 81 W. Parish Dr., 72865. Tel: 479-934-4321; Fax: 479-934-4319.
Catechesis/Religious Program—Tel: 479-934-4106. Donna Forst, D.R.E. Students 82.

TEXARKANA, MILLER CO., ST. EDWARD'S (1903), [CEM] Very Rev. Phillip A. Reaves, V.F.; Rev. Felix Alaribe (Nigeria); Deacons Joe Bruick; David Fowler.
Office: P.O. Box 1186, 75504. 410 Beech St., 71854. Tel: 870-772-1115; Fax: 870-773-2890.
Rectory—407 Beech St., P.O. Box 1186, 75504. Tel: 870-772-1115; Fax: 870-773-2890.
Catechesis/Religious Program—Tel: 870-772-7098. Susan Mervish, D.R.E. Students 205.
Mission—St. Elizabeth Ann Seton, (See listing under Ashdown) , Ashdown, Little River Co.
Mission—Sacred Heart, (See listing under Foreman) , Foreman, Little River Co.

TONTITOWN, WASHINGTON CO., ST. JOSEPH'S (1898), (Italian), [CEM] Rev. Msgr. James E. Marconi.
Mailing Address: P.O. Box 39, 72770. Tel: 479-361-2612; Fax: 479-361-9271. 136 Henri de Tonti St., 72770.
Catechesis/Religious Program—Tel: 479-361-2506. Judy Ranalli, D.R.E. Students 188.

VAN BUREN, CRAWFORD CO., ST. MICHAEL'S (1872), Rev. Thomas A. Elliott; Deacon Joe Kramer
1019 Pointer Tr. E., 72956. Tel: 479-471-1211; Fax: 479-471-1219.
Catechesis/Religious Program—Tel: 479-471-1211. Students 187
Mission—Our Lady of the Ozarks Shrine 22741 N. Hwy 71, Winslow, Crawford Co. 72959.

WALDRON, SCOTT CO., ST. JUDE THADDEUS CHURCH, Rev. Neil Pezzulo, G.H.M.
Mailing Address: P.O. Box 1688, 72958. Tel: 479-207-0485; Fax: 479-207-0485.

WALNUT RIDGE LAWRENCE CO., IMMACULATE HEART OF MARY (1925), Attended by, St. Mary, Paragould. Rev. John E. Marconi; Deacon Marlyn Tate.
320 Free St., P.O. Box 70, 72476. Tel: 870-886-2119.
Catechesis/Religious Program—Students 3.

WARREN, BRADLEY CO., ST. LUKE CHURCH, Attended by, St. Mark Monticello Rev. Chet Artysiewicz, G.H.M.
Mailing Address: 508 W. Pine St., 71671. Tel: 870-226-5284. Fax: 870-367-5974 (Monticello).

WEINER, POINSETT CO., ST. ANTHONY'S (1902), [CEM] Revs. Mark Wood, S.J.; Martin Osuji (Nigeria).
Mailing Address: P.O. Box 76, 72479. Tel: 870-684-2656; Fax: 870-684-7506.
407 Kings Hwy., 72479.
Catechesis/Religious Program—Tel: 870-578-4255. Rose Orr, D.R.E. Students 60.
Mission—St. Norbert Church 501 Normandy St., Marked Tree, Poinsett Co. 72365.

WEST MEMPHIS, CRITTENDEN CO., ST. MICHAEL'S (1914), Rev. Clayton Gould.
Mailing Address: P.O. Box 899, 72303.
Res.: 208 W. Cooper Ave., 72301.
Church: 411 Missouri, P.O. Box 899, 72303. Tel: 870-733-1212; 870-735-7983; Fax: 870-732-4808.
School—405 Missouri, P.O. Box 899, 72303. Tel: 870-735-1730. Mr. Steve Coryell, Prin. Olivetan Benedictine Sisters 2; Lay Teachers 10; Students 115.
Catechesis/Religious Program—Students 12.
St. Michael's School Endowment and Charitable Trust—Tel: 870-735-2683. Ken Thomas, CPA.
Mission—Sacred Heart, (See listing under Crawfordsville) , Crawfordsville, Crittenden Co.
Mission—St. Mary's of the Lake, (See listing under Horseshoe Lake) , Horseshoe Lake, Crittenden Co.

WINSLOW, CRAWFORD CO., OUR LADY OF THE OZARKS SHRINE (1946), [CEM] Rev. Thomas A. Elliott; Deacon Dan Daily.
Mailing Address: 22741 N. Hwy. 71, 72959. Tel: 479-634-2181.
Catechesis/Religious Program—1832 Seminole Ct., Fayetteville, 72701. Tel: 479-521-4536.

WYNNE, CROSS CO., ST. PETER'S (1921), Very Rev. Clarence Edwin Graves, V.F.
Mailing Address: P.O. Box 517, 72396. Tel: 870-238-2613; Fax: 870-238-3496.
Mission—St. Mary's, (See listing under McCrory) , McCrory, Woodruff Co.

YELLVILLE, MARION CO., ST. ANDREW CHURCH, Attended by, Mary Mother of God, Harrison Very Rev. Gregory G. Hart, V.F.
Mailing Address: P.O. Box 197, 72687. Tel: 870-449-4850; Fax: 870-741-5234 (Harrison).

Chaplains of Public Institutions

LITTLE ROCK. *John L. McClellan Memorial Hospital, VA Medical Center*, 4300 W. 7th St., 72205. Tel: 501-257-2151; Fax: 501-257-2157. Rev. Victor E. Bertrand, C.S.V., Chap.

FAYETTEVILLE. *U.S. Veterans Administration Hospital*. Attended from St. Joseph Church.

NORTH LITTLE ROCK. *Fort Roots VA Medical Center*, Tel: 501-257-2151; Fax: 501-257-2157. Rev. Victor Bertrand, C.S.V.
Res.: 4801 North Hill Blvd., Apt. 1106, 72116.

On Duty Outside the Diocese:
Rev.—
Gunti, Frederick W., Springhill College, Mobile, AL 33608. Tel: 205-460-2169

On Special or Other Diocesan Assignment:
Rev. Msgr.—
Sebaugh, Thomas, Dir. Information Systems, 2500 N. Tyler St., P.O. Box 7565, 72217. Tel: 501-664-0340; Fax: 501-664-9075

Retired:
Very Rev. Msgr.—
Hebert, J. Gaston, V.G., V.F., 802 Prospect Ave., Hot Springs, 71901.
Rev. Msgrs.—
Kordsmeier, John, St. John's Manor, 2414 N. Tyler, Apt. 306, 72207. Tel: 501-614-8975
Maus, Rudolph E., 210 N. Vancouver, Russellville, 72801.
Revs.—
Barnes, John E., St. John Manor, 2414 N. Tyler St., Apt. 308, 72207. Tel: 501-663-3887
Booth, Earl J., St. John Manor, 2414 N. Tyler St., Apt. 202, 72207. Tel: 501-614-9135
Cheney, Jesse C., St. John Manor, Apt. #201, 2414 N. Tyler St., 72207. Tel: 501-663-7846
Enderlin, Joseph J., One St. Bernard Lane, Bella Vista, 72715.
Esposito, Ralph J., 1503 N. 13th St., Van Buren, 72656.
Hlavacek, John F., St. John Manor, Apt. #307, 2414 N. Tyler St., 72207. Tel: 501-664-0120
Kepple, Robert, 107 Palm, Hot Springs, 71901. Tel: 501-624-1183
Lange, Milton R., P.O. Box 6037, Springdale, 72766.
Oswald, John, St. John Manor, 2414 N. Tyler, Apt. 304, 72207. Tel: 501-663-7472
Preske, Venantius, P.O. Box 4018, Horseshoe Bend, 72512. Tel: 870-670-4771
Rossi, Raymond R., P.O. Box 21817, Hot Springs, 71903.
Savary, James, 6720 Brentwood Rd., 72205. Tel: 501-664-7616
Strassle, H. Paul, Good Shepherd Retirement Center, 2701 Aldersgate Rd., Apt. 219, 72205. Tel: 501-227-4081
Turner, George F., 10631 Gulf Beach Hwy., Pensacola, FL 32507. Tel: 904-492-5741

INSTITUTIONS LOCATED IN THE DIOCESE

[A] SEMINARIES, RELIGIOUS OR SCHOLASTICATES

LITTLE ROCK. *Marylake - Carmelite Novitiate*, 5151 Marylake Dr., 72206. Tel: 501-888-3052; Fax: 501-888-3080. Revs. John Michael Payne, O.C.D., Archivist; Raphael Kitz, O.C.D., Novice Master; Joseph Neilson, O.C.D.; Bonaventure Sauer, O.C.D., Supr. Discalced Carmelite Friars of the Province of St. Therese, Little Rock Priests 4; Brothers 1.

SUBIACO. *Subiaco Monastery* 72865. Tel: 479-934-4295; Fax: 479-934-1000. Revs. Bruno Fuhrmann, O.S.B.; Richard Walz, O.S.B.; Rt. Rev. Jerome Kodell, O.S.B., Abbot; Revs. David Bellinghausen, O.S.B., Prior; Hugh Assenmacher, O.S.B.; Aaron Pirrera, O.S.B.; Andrew Wewer, O.S.B.; Brendan Miller, O.S.B.; Camillus Cooney, O.S.B.; Nicholas Fuhrmann, O.S.B.; Felix Fredeman, O.S.B.; Harold Heiman, O.S.B.; Herbert Vogelpohl, O.S.B.; Leonard Wangler, O.S.B., Novice Master, Formation Dir.; Mark Stengel, O.S.B.; Sebastian Beshoner, O.S.B.; Paul Hoedebeck; Timothy Donnelly, O.S.B.; Eugene Luke, O.S.B. Abbots 1; Monks 60.

[B] HIGH SCHOOLS, DIOCESAN

LITTLE ROCK. *Catholic High School*, 6300 Father Tribou St., 72205. Tel: 501-664-3939; Fax: 501-664-6549. Email: chs@lrchs.org. Dr. Michael M. Rockers, Prin.; Rev. Msgr. Lawrence A. Frederick, Rector.
Legal Title: *Catholic High School of Little Rock, AR* Priests 1; Brothers 1; Lay Teachers 33; Total Staff 35; Students 610.
Catholic High School Foundation, Inc. Tel: 501-664-3939; Fax: 501-664-6549.

CONWAY. *St. Joseph High School*, 502 Front St., 72032-5408. Tel: 501-329-5741; Fax: 501-513-6804. Joe Mallett, Prin.; Susie Freyaldenhoven, Asst. Prin.; Terri Seiter, Asst. Prin. Lay Teachers 18; Students 204.

FORT SMITH. *Trinity Junior High*, 1205 S. Albert Pike, 72903. Tel: 479-782-2451; Fax: 479-782-7263. Email: trinityjh@msn.com. Web: www.trinitycatholicjh.org. Rev. Msgr. Royce R. Thomas, J.C.L., Pastor Representative; Mrs. Ann M. Finch, Prin. Lay Teachers 21; Total Staff 26; Students 277.
Trinity Educational Trust Fund Tel: 479-782-2451; Fax: 479-782-7263.

MORRILTON. *Sacred Heart Catholic School*, 106 N. St. Joseph St., 72110. Tel: 501-354-8113; Fax: 501-354-2001. Email: shcsbailey@cox-internet.com. Mr. Brian Bailey, Prin. Lay Teachers 17; Total Staff 20; Students 234.

PINE BLUFF. *St. Joseph Catholic Senior High School*, 1501 W. 73rd Ave., 71603. Tel: 870-540-0413; Fax: 870-540-0345. Email: stjosephschoolspb@cablelynx.com. Web: www.stjosephschool.cc. Very Rev. Jack D. Harris, V.F., V.F. Total Staff 14; Students 80.

[C] HIGH SCHOOLS, PRIVATE

LITTLE ROCK. *Mount St. Mary Academy* (Girls) , 3224 Kavanaugh Blvd., 72205. Tel: 501-664-8006; Fax: 501-666-4382. Email: pgustafson@mtstmary.edu. Web: www.mtstmary.edu. Sr. Deborah Troillett, R.S.M., Pres.; Rebecca L. Henle, Prin. Priests 1; Sisters of Mercy 5; Lay Teachers 39; Students 546.
Mount St. Mary Academy Endowment and Scholarship Fund Tel: 501-664-8006; Fax: 501-664-4267.

SUBIACO. *Subiaco Academy* (Boys) , 72865. Tel: 479-934-1005; Fax: 479-934-1033. Email: admissions@subi.org. Web: www.subi.org. Rt. Rev. Jerome Kodell, O.S.B., Pres.; Rev. Aaron Pirrera, O.S.B., Headmaster. Priests 6; Brothers 8; Lay Teachers 21; Total Staff 35; Students 165.

[D] DAY CARE CENTERS

LITTLE ROCK. *Little Angel Day Care*, 9111 Auxer Rd., 72209. Tel: 501-568-0694. Sr. Dominica Wise, Dir. Olivetan Benedictine Sisters 2; Students 20.

[E] GENERAL HOSPITALS

LITTLE ROCK. *St. Vincent Doctors Hospital*, 6101 St. Vincent Cir., 72205. Tel: 501-552-3664; Fax: 501-552-8614. Email: kvaughn@stvincenthealth.com. Bed Capacity 282; Total Assisted Annually 65,331; Total Staff 358.
St. Vincent Infirmary Medical Center, No. 2 St. Vincent Circle, 72205. Tel: 501-552-3664; Fax: 501-552-4014. Email: kvaughn@stvincenthealth.com. Rev. Ignatius Gomes, S.F.X., Chap. Catholic Health Initiatives. Sisters 3; Total Staff 1,515; Bed Capacity 691; Patients Assisted Annually 135,314.

FORT SMITH. *St. Edward Mercy Medical Center*, 7301 Rogers Ave., 72917. Tel: 479-314-6000; Fax: 479-314-1770. Web: www.StEdwardMercy.com. Rev. Placidus Eckart, O.S.B., Chap.; John D. Hoffman, M.D., Pres. & CEO. Total Staff 2,016; Bed Capacity 343; Patients Assisted Annually 163,415.
St. Edward Mercy Foundation, 5401 Ellsworth Rd., 72903. Tel: 479-314-1133.
Mercy Northside Clinic, 3202 North 6th, 72904. Tel: 479-314-1456; Fax: 479-782-1462. Email: mheidenfeld@ftsm.mercy.net. Web: www.stedwardmercy.com/services/northside.asp. Operated and sponsored by St. Edward Mercy Medical Center Total Staff 3; Total Assisted 3,260.

HOT SPRINGS NATIONAL PARK. *St. Joseph's Mercy Health Center*, P.O. Box 29001, 71903-9001. Tel: 501-622-1000; Fax: 501-622-1199. Email: tmcvey@htsp.mercy.net. Web: www.saintjosephs.com. Randall J. Fale, Pres. & CEO; Rev. Alan Rosenau, Priest Chap. Total Staff 1,424; Patients Assisted Annually 399,802; Bed Capacity 317.
Sisters of Mercy of St. Joseph Convent of Hot Springs, Arkansas, Inc. Tel: 501-321-1554.

JONESBORO. *St. Bernard's Medical Center*, 225 E. Jackson, 72401. Tel: 870-972-4100; Fax: 870-974-7040. Email: ldalford@sbrmc.org. Web: SBRMC.com. Ben E. Owens, Pres. & CEO. Olivetan Benedictine Sisters 9; Total Staff 1,967; Patients Assisted Annually 141,222; Bed Capacity 375.
St. Bernards Behavioral Health Services, Inc., 2712 E. Johnson Ave., 72401. Tel: 870-932-2800; Fax: 870-268-4126. Email: Lsimpson@sbrmc.org. Ralph Waddell, Legal Counsel. Bed Capacity 60; Staff 110; Patients Assisted Annually 2,342.

MORRILTON. *St. Anthony's Hospital Association*, #4 Hospital Dr., 72110-4510. Tel: 501-977-2300; Fax: 501-354-2830. Email: fgottsponer@stvincenthealth.com. Jonathan S. Davis, Admin.
Legal Title: *St. Anthony's Hospital Association*, Sponsored by St. Vincent Health System, a division of Catholic Health Initiatives. Total Staff 262; Patients Assisted Annually 31,712; Bed Capacity 49.

OZARK. *St. Edward Health Facilities of Franklin County* dba Mercy Hospital/Turner Memorial , 801 W. River St., 72949. Tel: 479-667-4138; Fax: 479-667-4751; 479-667-9778 (Admin.). Email: jmaddox@ftsm.smhs.com. John D. Hoffman, M.D., CEO; Mr. Jim Maddox, Admin. Total Staff 47; Patients Assisted Annually 7,878; Bed Capacity 25.

PARIS. *St. Edward Health Facilities of Logan Co.* dba North Logan Mercy Hospital , 500 E. Academy, 72855. Tel: 479-963-6101; Fax: 479-963-6155. John D. Hoffman, M.D., CEO; Jim L. Maddox, Admin. Tel: 501-963-6101; Fax: 501-963-6155. Total Staff 38; Patients Assisted Annually 8,047; Bed Capacity 16.

ROGERS. *St. Mary-Rogers Memorial Hospital*, 1200 W. Walnut, 72756. Tel: 479-636-0200, Ext. 705; 479-636-2548; Fax: 479-936-2906; 479-936-2903. Email: nking@roge.mercy.net. Web: www.mercyhealthnwa.smhs.com. Rev. Michael Sinkler, Sacramental Min.; Susan Barrett, CEO. Sisters of St. Dominic 6; Total Staff 880; Bed Capacity 165; Patients Assisted Annually 96,897.
St. Mary Hospital Foundation Tel: 479-636-0200; Fax: 479-936-2906.

SHERWOOD. *St. Vincent Medical Center/Sherwood*, 2215 Wildwood Ave., 72120. Tel: 501-552-3664; Fax: 501-660-4014. Email: Kellyv@exchange.svimc.com. Bed Capacity 69; Total Annually Assisted 41,598; Total Staff 206.

WALDRON. *St. Edward Health Facilities of Scott County* dba Mercy Hospital , Hwy. 71 & 80, 865 W. 6th St., 72958. Tel: 479-637-4135; Fax: 479-637-3523. Email: dobara@ftsm.mercy.net. Mr. Jim Maddox, Admin.; Dorothy "Dede" O'Bar, Asst. Admin.; John D. Hoffman, M.D., CEO. Total Staff 56; Patients Assisted Annually 14,164; Bed Capacity 24.

WYNNE. *St. Bernards Community Hospital Corporation* dba Crossridge Community Hospital , 310 S. Falls Blvd., 72396. Tel: 870-238-3300; Fax: 870-238-7432. Email: gsparks@sbrmc.org. Bed Capacity 25; Staff 140; Patients Assisted Annually 18,000.

[F] PROTECTIVE INSTITUTIONS

LITTLE ROCK. *ABBA House, Missionaries of Charity*, 1014 S. Oak St., 72204. Tel: 501-666-9718 (Abba House); 501-663-3596 (convent). Home for expectant mothers, homeless women & children. Missionaries of Charity 4; Weekly food distribution/Total assisted 1,898.

HOT SPRINGS NATIONAL PARK. *St. Michael's School*, 1125 Malvern Ave., 71901. Tel: 501-623-9651; Fax: 501-623-1509. Email: smichael@hotsprings.net. Web: www.LightofMary.org. Sisters Theresa Marie Lalancette, Supr.; Mary Theresa Dionne, Asst. Supr. Sisters of Our Lady of Charity of Refugee (Good Shepherd) 12; Day Care Center 61; Total Staff 18.
Monastery of Our Lady of Charity of Refuge (Good Shepherd), 1125 Malvern Ave., 71901. Tel: 501-623-9651; Fax: 501-623-1509. Email: smichael@hotsprings.net. Web: www.lightofmary.org. Sr. Mary Theresa Dionne, Asst. Supr. Sisters 12; Total Staff 1. In Res. Rev. Benoit Picard, O.F.F.

[G] HOMES FOR AGED

BARLING. *Mercy Crest of Arkansas, Inc.*, 1300 Strozier Ln., 72923. Tel: 479-478-3000; Fax: 479-452-8382. Email: jarnold@ftsm.smns.com. Web: www.mercycrest.com. Jerry Arnold, Admin. Sponsored by the Religious Sisters of Mercy. Total Staff 27; Bed Capacity 102; Independent Living Apartments 32; Patients Assisted Annually 70; Residential Care Facility for the Elderly - number of beds 70.

JONESBORO. *St. Bernard's Village, Inc.*, 1606 Heern Dr., 72401. Tel: 870-932-8141; Fax: 870-933-5563. Web: www.sbrmc.com. Kevin Hodges, Vice Pres., Senior Svcs.; Mr. Brian Rega, Dir. (Affiliated with Olivetan Benedictine Sisters, Inc., Jonesboro, AR) Patients Assisted Annually 175; Total Staff 35.

[H] RESIDENCES FOR PRIESTS

LITTLE ROCK. *St. John Manor*, 2414 N. Tyler St., 72207. Tel: 501-664-0340; Fax: 501-664-9075. Email: dgriswold@dolr.org. Ms. Dianna Griswold, Dir. Facilities; Rev. Msgr. John Kordsmeier. Tel: 501-614-8975; Revs. Jesse C. Cheney (Retired). Tel: 501-663-7846; John F. Hlavacek (Retired). Tel: 501-664-0120; John E. Barnes (Retired). Tel: 501-663-3887; Earl J. Booth (Retired). Tel: 501-614-9135; John Oswald (Retired). Tel: 501-663-7472; Mr. Jinho Zyung, Mgr. Priests 6.

[I] CONVENTS AND RESIDENCES FOR SISTERS

LITTLE ROCK. *Discalced Carmelite Nuns*, 7201 W. 32nd St., 72204-4716. Tel: 501-565-5121; Fax: 501-565-3877. Email: lrcarmel@juno.com. Sr. Joan Monkhouse, O.C.D., Prioress.
Legal Title: *Discalced Carmelite Nuns of Little Rock*, Attended from Catholic High School, Little Rock & Our Lady of Holy Souls, Little Rock. Sisters 15; Nuns with Solemn Vows 15.
Mt. St. Mary's Convent, 3508 Kavanaugh Blvd., 72205. Tel: 501-664-5977; Fax: 501-666-4382. Email: srbkonklerredwine@mtstmary.edu. Sisters 6.

BARLING. *McAuley Convent and Retirement Residence*, 1300 Strozier Ln., 72923. Tel: 479-478-3002; Fax: 479-478-3006. Email: DAllenadm@aol.com. Sisters of Mercy 18; Bed Capacity 30; Number of Persons Served 24.

FORT SMITH. *St. Scholastica Monastery-Motherhouse*, 1301 S. Albert Pike, P.O. Box 3489, 72913. Tel: 479-783-4147; Fax: 479-782-4352. Email: monastery@scholasticafortsmith.org. Web: www.scholasticafortsmith.org. Sisters Cabrini Schmitz, Prioress; Catherine Markey, Archivist; Rev. David McKillin, O.S.B., Chap. Benedictine Professed Sisters 82; Novices 1.
Sisters of Mercy of St. Edward, 2700 S. 74th St., 72903. Tel: 479-312-6098; Fax: 479-312-1760. Email: srsjm@yahoo.com. Sisters of Mercy 6.

HOT SPRINGS. *Monastery of Our Lady of Charity of Refuge (Good Shepherd)*, 1125 Malvern Ave., 71901. Tel: 501-623-9651; Fax: 501-623-1509. Email: smichael@hotsprings.net. Web: www.lightofmary.org. Rev. Benoit Picard, O.F.F., Chap. Sisters 12; Total Staff 1.

JONESBORO. *Holy Angels Convent-Motherhouse* 72403-0130. Tel: 870-935-5810; Fax: 870-935-4210. Email: olivben@olivben.org. Web: www.olivben.org. Sr. Eileen Schneider, O.S.B., Prioress; Rev. Richard Cleary, O.S.B. Olivetan Benedictine Sisters Sisters 44; Novices 3; Postulants 4.

[J] NEWMAN CENTERS

FAYETTEVILLE. *Catholic Campus Ministries* 603 N. Leverett, 72701. Tel: 479-444-0223; Fax: 479-442-2633. Email: ccm@uark.edu. Web: www.staup.org. Deacon Paul Cronan, Dir.; Erin Watson, Admin. Asst.
Arkansas State University, Blessed John Newman University Parish, 2800 E. Johnson St., Jonesboro, 72401. Tel: 870-972-1888; Fax: 870-972-1888. Email: cnc@astate.edu. (Jonesboro)
Campus Ministers: Mary Ruth Staudt, Dir.
Arkansas Tech University, St. Leo the Great University Parish, 509 W. "L" St., Russellville, 72801. Tel:

479-968-8249. Rev. Ernest Hardesty, Sacramental Min.; Pat Buford, Dir. (Russellville)

University of Arkansas at Fort Smith, 10815 Edgewater Rd., Fort Smith, 72903. Tel: 479-638-8685. Deacon Greg Pair, Spiritual Advisor.

Univ. of Arkansas at Little Rock Campus Ministry, 7413 Henderson, 72210. Tel: 501-455-1412; Fax: 501-664-1964. Email: RHanley644@aol.com. Mrs. Diane Hanley, Campus Min.; Deacon Ron Stager, Spiritual Advisor.

University of Arkansas at Monticello, P.O. Box 3460-UAM School of Arts/Humanties, Monticello, 71656. Tel: 870-460-1232. Dr. Linda Webster, Faculty Advisor.

Henderson State Teachers College and Ouchita Baptist University Campus Ministry, P.O. Box 26, Arkadelphia, 71923. Tel: 870-246-7575. Email: teresa@hsnp.com. Rev. Linus Ukomadu, Spiritual Advisor. (Arkadelphia)

University of Central Arkansas & Hendrix College Campus Ministry, 2204 Bruce, Conway, 72032. Tel: 501-336-9091. Email: Catholic@cyberback.com. Deacon Richard Papini, Campus Min. (Conway)

University of Arkansas, St. Thomas Aquinas University Parish, 603 N. Leverett, 72701. Tel: 479-444-0223; Fax: 479-442-2633. Email: ccm@uark.edu. Deacon Paul Cronan, Pastoral Admin.; Revs. Paul Worm, Sacramental Min.; James Fischer, C.M., Sacramental Min.; Erin Watson, Admin. Asst.; T.C. Long, Assoc. Campus Min.; Vera Zawislak, Assoc. Campus Min. (Fayetteville)

Harding University (Searcy) Campus Ministry, 109 Campbell Dr., Beebe, 72012. Tel: 501-882-6299; Fax: 501-882-5465. Email: ffitch@thor.k12.ar.us. Flo Fitch, Campus Min.

University of Ozarks Campus Ministry (Clarksville), Rte. 1, Box 302, Hartman, 72840. Tel: 479-979-1434. Email: mstickl@ozarks.edu. Melodye Stickley, Campus Min.

JONESBORO. *Blessed John Newman University Parish* 2800 E. Johnson Ave., 72401. Tel: 870-972-1888; Fax: 870-972-6294. Email: cnc@astate.edu. Web: www.cit.astate.edu/cnc. Revs. D. Mark Wood; Martin Osuji (Nigeria); Mary Ruth Staudt, Dir.

RUSSELLVILLE. *St. Leo the Great University Parish* 509 W. L St., 72801. Tel: 479-968-8249. Email: stleao@cox-internet.com. Web www.stleoatu.homestead.com/homepage. P.O. Box 308, 72811-0308. Very Rev. Ernest L. Hardesty, V.F., Sacramental Min.; Mrs. Pat Buford, Dir. Campus Ministry.

[K] RETREAT CENTERS

BERRYVILLE. *Little Portion Hermitage* (Integrated Monastery) , 350 CR 248, 72616-8505. Tel: 479-253-7710; Fax: 479-253-6640. Email: Admin@JohnMichaelTalbot.com. Web: www.LittlePortion.org. John Michael Talbot, Gen. Min.; Viola Talbot, B.S.C., Vicar Gen. Min. Legal Title: *Brothers and Sisters of Charity at Little Portion, Inc.*

Little Flower Clinic for the Poor Tel: 479-253-7710; Fax: 479-253-6640.

EUREKA SPRINGS. *Little Portion Retreat and Training Center at More Mt.*, 171 Hummingbird Ln., 72632. Tel: 479-253-7379; Fax: 479-253-8738. Email: retreats@littleportion.org. Web: www.littleportion.org. John Michael Talbot, Exec. Dir.; Mark Shepler, Mgr. Catholic Staff 1.

FORT SMITH. *St. Scholastica Center*, 1205 S. Albert Pike, P.O. Box 3489, 72913. Tel: 479-783-1135; Fax: 479-782-8138. Email: retreatsstscho@hotmail.com. Web: www.scholasticafortsmith.org. Sisters Hilary Decker, O.S.B., Spiritual Dir.; Madeline Bariola, O.S.B., Dir. Maintenance and Hospitality; Macrina Wiederkehr, O.S.B., Retreats & Spiritual Dir. Conducted by Benedictine Sisters 0.

SHOAL CREEK. *Hesychia House of Prayer* Tel: 479-938-7375. Email: hesychia@centurytel.net. Web: www.scholasticafortsmith.org. 204 St. Scholastica Rd., New Blaine, 72851. Sr. Louise Sharum, O.S.B., Dir. Attended from New Subiaco Abbey, Subiaco, AR. Benedictine Sisters 4. Attended from New Subiaco Abbey, Subiaco, AR. Rev. Raphael DeSalvo, O.S.B.

[L] MISCELLANEOUS LISTINGS

LITTLE ROCK. *The "Arkansas Catholic"* Published by Arkansas Catholic, Inc. of the Diocese of Little Rock. , 2500 N. Tyler St., P.O. Box 7417, 72217. Tel: 501-664-0340; 501-664-0125; Fax: 501-664-6572. Email: mhargett@dolr.org. Mrs. Malea Hargett, Editor.

Christopher Homes of Arkansas, Inc., 2417 N. Tyler St., 72207. Tel: 501-664-1881; Fax: 501-664-1631. Email: ddierks@dolr.org. Mr. F.M. Don Dierks Jr., Exec. Dir. Total in Residence 550.

Christopher Homes of Augusta, Inc. Tel: 870-347-2388; Fax: 870-347-2388.

Christopher Homes of Brinkley, Inc. Tel: 870-734-2201; Fax: 870-734-2201.

Christopher Homes of Camden, Inc. Tel: 870-837-1911; Fax: 870-837-1911.

Christopher Homes of Clarendon, Inc. Tel: 870-747-5441; Fax: 870-747-5441.

Christopher Homes of DeQueen, Inc. Tel: 870-642-6211; Fax: 870-642-6211.

Christopher Homes of DeValls Bluff, Inc. Tel: 870-998-7280; Fax: 870-998-7280.

Christopher Homes of Elaine, Inc. Tel: 870-827-3705; Fax: 870-827-3705.

Christopher Homes of El Dorado, Inc. Tel: 870-862-9711; Fax: 870-862-9711.

Christopher Homes of Forrest City, Inc. Tel: 870-633-4804; Fax: 870-633-4804.

Christopher Homes of Horatio, Inc. Tel: 870-832-4014; Fax: 870-832-4014.

Christopher Homes of Hot Springs, Inc. Tel: 501-318-1317; Fax: 501-318-1317.

Christopher Homes of Jonesboro, Inc. Tel: 870-931-9575; Fax: 870-931-9575.

Christopher Homes of Marianna, Inc. Tel: 870-295-6345; Fax: 870-295-6345.

Christopher Homes of Monette, Inc. Tel: 870-486-2748; Fax: 870-486-2748.

Christopher Homes of North Little Rock, Inc. Tel: 501-758-8582; Fax: 501-758-8582.

Christopher Homes of Palestine, Inc. Tel: 870-581-2023; Fax: 870-581-2023.

Christopher Homes of Paragould, Inc. Tel: 870-239-8609; Fax: 870-239-8609.

Christopher Homes of Parkin, Inc. Tel: 870-755-2939; Fax: 870-755-2939.

Christopher Homes of Searcy, Inc. Tel: 501-268-7804; Fax: 501-268-7804.

Christopher Homes of Strong, Inc. Tel: 870-797-7525; Fax: 870-797-7525.

Christopher Homes of West Helena, Inc. Tel: 870-572-9433; Fax: 870-572-9433.

Christopher Homes of Wynne, Inc. Tel: 870-238-3388; Fax: 870-238-3388.

The Guadalupe Prenatal Clinic, 801 Sherman St., 72202. Tel: 501-537-4289; Fax: 501-374-5839. Email: clinic@saintedwards.net. Rev. John K. Antony, J.C.L.; Lilia Hernandez, Clinic Admin.

John Gazzola Trust Estate, P.O. Box 7239, 72217. Tel: 501-664-0340; Fax: 501-664-9186. Mr. Gregory C. Wolfe CFO, Trustee; Mr. Charles Baker, Trustee; Mr. Paul Hiegel, Trustee.

St. John's Seminary, Inc., Endowment Fund, P.O. Box 7565, 72217. Tel: 501-664-0340, Ext. 331 Fax: 501-664-9075. Email: jantony@dolr.org.

Little Rock Scripture Study, 2500 N. Tyler St., P.O Box 7565, 72217. Tel: 501-664-0340; 501-664-6102; Fax: 501-664-9075. Email: lrss@dolr.org. Web: www.littlerockscripture.org. Ms. Cackie Upchurch, Dir.

**Sophia's Center*, 1114 Garland St., 72201-1215. Tel: 501-372-5522; Fax: 501-372-5522. Email: info@sophiacenter.org. Web: www.sophiascenter.org. Sr. Lee Ann McNally, R.S.M., Dir.

St. Thomas More Society of Arkansas, Inc., 320 W. Capitol, Ste. 211, Legal Dept., 72201. Tel: 501-378-3297; Fax: 501-378-3366. Email: fbsewall@arkbluecross.com. David F. Menz, Chm.

BERRYVILLE. *St. Vincent de Paul Thrift Shop*, 1844 Hwy. 62 W., 72616. Tel: 870-423-3572; Fax: 870-423-6779. Mr. T.H. Clement McEnaney, Pres.; Mr. Joe Shaughnessy, Vice Pres. & Treas. Clients Assisted Annually 925.

BLYTHEVILLE. *Immaculate Conception Trust Fund*, 1301 W. Main St., 72315. Tel: 870-762-2506; Fax: 870-762-2506. Very Rev. Joseph L. Pallo, V.F.

DUMAS. *Daughter of Charity Services*, 145 W. Waterman, P.O. Box 158, 71639. Tel: 870-382-4878; Fax: 870-382-4895. Email: pmeeks@dcsark.org. Mr. Paul M. Meeks, Pres. & COO. Patients Assisted Annually 23,877.

Clinics:

St. Elizabeth Health Center, P.O. Drawer 370, Gould, 71643. Tel: 870-263-4317; Fax: 870-263-4782.

DePaul Health Center, P.O. Box 158, 71639. Tel: 870-382-4878; Fax: 870-382-4895.

Wellness Center, Hwy. 65 S., P.O. Box 473, Gould, 71643. Tel: 870-263-4748 Fax: 870-263-4233.

EUREKA SPRINGS. *St. Vincent de Paul Society*, 1471 CR222, 72631. Tel: 479-253-8292. Email: Jimbev@aol.com. Ms. Beverly Anne Wright, Pres. Patients Assisted Annually 91.

JONESBORO. *St. Bernards Healthcare*, 225 E. Jackson Ave., 72401. Tel: 870-972-4284. Mr. Robert S. Jones, Attorney.

Catholic Hispanic Center, 308 W. Monroe, 72401. Tel: 870-931-8853; Fax: 870-931-1884. Email: ewillett@fastdata.net. Rev. Mark Wood, S.J. Tel: 870-931-1884. Sponsored by Blessed Sacrament Church, Jonesboro, AR. Clients Assisted Annually 1,000.

P.O. Box 1735, 72403-1735. Tel: 870-931-3337; Fax: 870-935-4444. Sr. M. Elaine Willett, O.S.B. Pager: 870-930-1177.

P.O. Box 130, 72403. Tel: 870-930-1177 (Pager); Fax: 870-930-4444.

Jonesboro Real Estate Holding Company, Inc., 225 E. Jackson St., 72401. Tel: 870-972-4326; Fax: 870-974-7040. Email: bowens@sbrmc.org. Ralph Waddell, Legal Counsel.

LONSDALE. *Annunzitta, Inc.*, P.O. Box 63, 72087. Tel: 501-939-2060. Email: ajsehgal@up-link.net. Ms. Janice Sehgal, Dir.

MOUNTAIN HOME. *Heart of Mercy Solitude, Inc.*, 116 South St., 72653. Tel: 870-425-5397. Sr. Judith A. Ayers, Dir.

NORTH LITTLE ROCK. *Priestly Fraternity of St. Peter*, 919 W. 47th St., 72118. Tel: 501-812-9155; Fax: 501-812-9225. Email: fssp_arkansas@sbcglobal.net. Web: www.FSSP.org. Revs. William Define, F.S.S.P., Asst. Chap.; Joseph Hearty, F.S.S.P., Asst. Chap.

STUTTGART. *Holy Rosary Catholic School "Vision 2000" Educational Trust Fund*, 1815 S. Prairie St., 72160. Tel: 870-673-8351; Fax: 870-673-6701. Email: HolyRos@IPA.net. Rev. Msgr. John A. Janesko.

RELIGIOUS INSTITUTES OF MEN REPRESENTED IN THE DIOCESE

For further details refer to the corresponding bracketed number in the Religious Institutes of Men or Women section.

[0200]—*Benedictine Monks* (New Subiaco Abbey)—O.S.B.

[1320]—*Clerics of St. Viator*—C.S.V.

[1330]—*Congregation of the Mission*—C.M.

[0260]—*Discalced Carmelite Friars* (St. Therese Prov.)—O.C.D.

[0570]—*Glenmary Home Missioners*—Glmy.

[0650]—*Holy Ghost Fathers* (Western Vice Prov.)—C.S.Sp.

[1065]—*Priestly Fraternity of St. Peter*—F.S.S.P.

[]—*Public Association of the Faithful - Celibate Brotherhood of the Brothers and Sisters of Charity*—B.S.C.

[0420]—*Society of the Divine Word* (Techny, IL)—S.V.D.

RELIGIOUS INSTITUTES OF WOMEN REPRESENTED IN THE DIOCESE

[0230]—*Benedictine Sisters of Pontifical Jurisdiction* (Fort Smith, AR)—O.S.B.

[1855]—*Congregation of the Handmaids of the Holy Child Jesus*—HHCJ

[0470]—*Congregation of the Sisters of Charity of the Incarnate Word, Houston, Texas*—C.C.V.I.

[0760]—*Daughters of Charity of St. Vincent de Paul* (West Central Prov.)—D.C.

[]—*Daughters of Mary of the Cross*—D.M.C.

[]—*Daughters of Our Lady of Fatima*—D.L.F.

[0420]—*Discalced Carmelite Nuns* (Little Rock, AR)—O.C.D.

[1070-10]—*Dominican Sisters*—O.P.

[2575]—*Institute of the Sisters of Mercy of the Americas* (St. Louis, MO)—R.S.M.

[2710]—*Missionaries of Charity*—M.C.

[0390]—*Missionary Carmelites of St. Teresa*—C.M.S.T.

[2860]—*Missionary Sisters of the Sacred Heart*—M.S.C.

[]—*Missioneras Catequestas de los Pobres*—M.C.P.

[3070]—*North American Union Sisters of Our Lady of Charity* (Hot Springs, AR)—N.A.U.-O.L

[0240]—*Olivetan Benedictine Sisters* (Jonesboro, AR)—O.S.B.

[]—*Public Association of the Faithful - Celibate Sisterhood of the Brothers and Sisters of Charity*—B.S.C.

[2940]—*School Sisters of Notre Dame* (Prov. of Dallas)—S.S.N.D.

[0500]—*Sisters of Charity of Nazareth*—S.C.N.

[3860]—*Sisters of St. Joseph of Cluny*—S.J.C.

[0970]—*Sisters of the Divine Compassion*—R.D.C.

[4120-03]—*Ursuline Nuns of the Congregation of Paris*—O.S.U.

CEMETERIES

LITTLE ROCK. *Calvary*

FORT SMITH. *Calvary*

NECROLOGY

† DeClerk, Rev. Msgr. Rainer J., (Retired)—Died Sept. 3, 2003

† Bauer, Ralph, (Retired)—Died Dec. 22, 2002

Archdiocese of Los Angeles

(Archidioecesis Angelorum in California)

His Eminence

ROGER CARDINAL MAHONY, D.D.

Archbishop of Los Angeles; ordained May 1, 1962; appointed Titular Bishop of Tamascani and Auxiliary Bishop of Fresno January 7, 1975; consecrated March 19, 1975; appointed Bishop of Stockton February 26, 1980; installed as the third Bishop of Stockton April 17, 1980; appointed Archbishop of Los Angeles July 16, 1985; installed as the fourth Archbishop of Los Angeles September 5, 1985; Created Cardinal June 28, 1991. *Res.: 555 W. Temple St., Los Angeles, CA 90012. Office: 3424 Wilshire Blvd., Los Angeles, CA 90010-2241.* Tel: 213-637-7261; Fax: 213-637-6510.

Archdiocesan Catholic Center Office: 3424 Wilshire Blvd., Los Angeles, CA 90010-2241. Tel: 213-637-7000; Fax: 213-637-6607.

Web: www.LA-Archdiocese.org

Most Reverend

JOHN J. WARD, D.D., J.C.L., V.G.

Retired Auxiliary Bishop of Los Angeles; ordained May 4, 1946; appointed Titular Bishop of Bria and Auxiliary Bishop of Los Angeles October 16, 1963; consecrated December 12, 1963; Assigned Titular Bishop of California, June 15, 1996; retired July 1, 1996. *Office: 3424 Wilshire Blvd., Los Angeles, CA 90010-2241.*

Most Reverend

JUAN A. ARZUBE, D.D.

Retired Auxiliary Bishop of Los Angeles; ordained May 5, 1954; appointed Titular Bishop of Civitate and Auxiliary Bishop of Los Angeles February 9, 1971; consecrated March 25, 1971; retired June 1, 1993. *Res.: c/o Nazareth House*, 3333 Manning Ave., Los Angeles, CA 90064-4804.

Most Reverend

THOMAS J. CURRY, D.D., PH.D.

Auxiliary Bishop of Los Angeles; ordained June 18, 1967; appointed Titular Bishop of Ceanannus Mor and Auxiliary Bishop of Los Angeles February 8, 1994; ordained Bishop March 19, 1994. *Office: Santa Barbara Pastoral Region*, 3240 Calle Pinon, Santa Barbara, CA 93105.

Most Reverend

JOSEPH M. SARTORIS, D.D., V.G.

Retired Auxiliary Bishop of Los Angeles; ordained May 30, 1953; appointed Titular Bishop of Oliva and Auxiliary Bishop of Los Angeles February 8, 1994; ordained Bishop March 19, 1994; retired December 31, 2002. *1988 Rolling Vista Dr., #21, Lomita, CA 90717.*

Most Reverend

GABINO ZAVALA, D.D., J.C.L., V.G.

Auxiliary Bishop of Los Angeles; ordained May 28, 1977; appointed Titular Bishop of Tamascani and Auxiliary Bishop of Los Angeles February 8, 1994; ordained Bishop March 19, 1994. *Office: San Gabriel Pastoral Region*, 16009 E. Cypress Ave., Irwindale, CA 91706.

Most Reverend

GERALD E. WILKERSON, D.D.

Auxiliary Bishop of Los Angeles; ordained May 1, 1965; appointed Titular Bishop of Vincennes and Auxiliary Bishop of Los Angeles November 5, 1997; ordained Bishop January 21, 1998. *Office: San Fernando Pastoral Region*, 15101 San Fernando Mission Blvd., Mission Hills, CA 91345-1109.

Most Reverend

EDWARD W. CLARK, D.D.

Auxiliary Bishop of Los Angeles; ordained May 27, 1972; appointed Titular Bishop of Gardar and Auxiliary Bishop of Los Angeles January 16, 2001; ordained March 26, 2001. *Office: Regional Bishop, Our Lady of the Angels Pastoral Region*, 2636 S. Mansfield Ave., Los Angeles, CA 90016-3512.

Most Reverend

OSCAR AZARCON SOLIS

Auxiliary Bishop of Los Angeles; ordained April 28, 1979; appointed Titular Bishop of Urci and Auxiliary Bishop of Los Angeles December 11, 2003; installed February 10, 2004. *3424 Wilshire Blvd., Los Angeles, CA 90010-2241.*

Square Miles 8,762.

Diocese Established 1840; an Archbishopric July 11, 1936.

Comprises the Counties of Los Angeles, Santa Barbara and Ventura in the State of California.

Patroness of the Diocese: St. Vibiana.

Legal Title: The Roman Catholic Archbishop of Los Angeles, a Corporation Sole.
Legal Title: *Archdiocese of Los Angeles Education and Welfare Corporation.*
Legal Title: *Our Lady Queen of Angels Seminary.*
Legal Title: *St. John's Seminary College.*
Legal Title: *St. John's Seminary in California.*
Legal Title: *The Cardinal McIntyre Fund for Charity.*
Legal Title: *Catholic Charities of Los Angeles, Inc.*
Legal Title: *Catholic Charities Community Development Corporation.*
Legal Title: *The Tidings.*
Legal Title: *Vida Nueva.*
Legal Title: *For legal titles of parishes and archdiocesan institutions, consult the Chancery Office.*

STATISTICAL OVERVIEW

Personnel	
Cardinals	1
Archbishops	1
Auxiliary Bishops	4
Retired Bishops	3
Abbots	1
Priests: Diocesan Active in Diocese	364
Priests: Diocesan Active Outside Diocese	6
Priests: Diocesan in Foreign Missions	1
Priests: Retired, Sick or Absent	167
Number of Diocesan Priests	538
Religious Priests in Diocese	615
Total Priests in Diocese	1,153
Extern Priests in Diocese	80
Ordinations:	
Diocesan Priests	4
Religious Priests	12
Transitional Deacons	4
Permanent Deacons	21
Permanent Deacons in Diocese	236
Total Brothers	173
Total Sisters	1,765
Parishes	
Parishes	288
With Resident Pastor:	
Resident Diocesan Priests	205
Resident Religious Priests	69
Without Resident Pastor:	
Administered by Priests	10
Administered by Religious Women	1
Administered by Pastoral Teams, etc.	2
Missions	7
Pastoral Centers	3
Professional Ministry Personnel:	
Brothers	4
Sisters	158
Lay Ministers	529
Welfare	
Catholic Hospitals	14
Total Assisted	1,345,630
Health Care Centers	7
Total Assisted	12,906
Homes for the Aged	7
Total Assisted	3,240
Residential Care of Children	2
Total Assisted	598
Day Care Centers	82
Total Assisted	6,340
Specialized Homes	11
Total Assisted	2,724
Special Centers for Social Services	80
Total Assisted	423,260
Residential Care of Disabled	2
Total Assisted	262
Other Institutions	4
Total Assisted	158
Educational	
Seminaries, Diocesan	1
Students from This Diocese	55
Students from Other Diocese	57
Diocesan Students in Other Seminaries	22
Seminaries, Religious	12
Students Religious	48
Total Seminarians	125
Colleges and Universities	5
Total Students	11,845
High Schools, Diocesan and Parish	28
Total Students	16,426
High Schools, Private	22
Total Students	13,793
Elementary Schools, Diocesan and Parish	216
Total Students	62,796
Elementary Schools, Private	9
Total Students	2,627
Catechesis/Religious Education:	
High School Students	32,000
Elementary Students	240,000
Total Students under Catholic Instruction	379,612
Teachers in the Diocese:	
Priests	17
Scholastics	2
Brothers	81

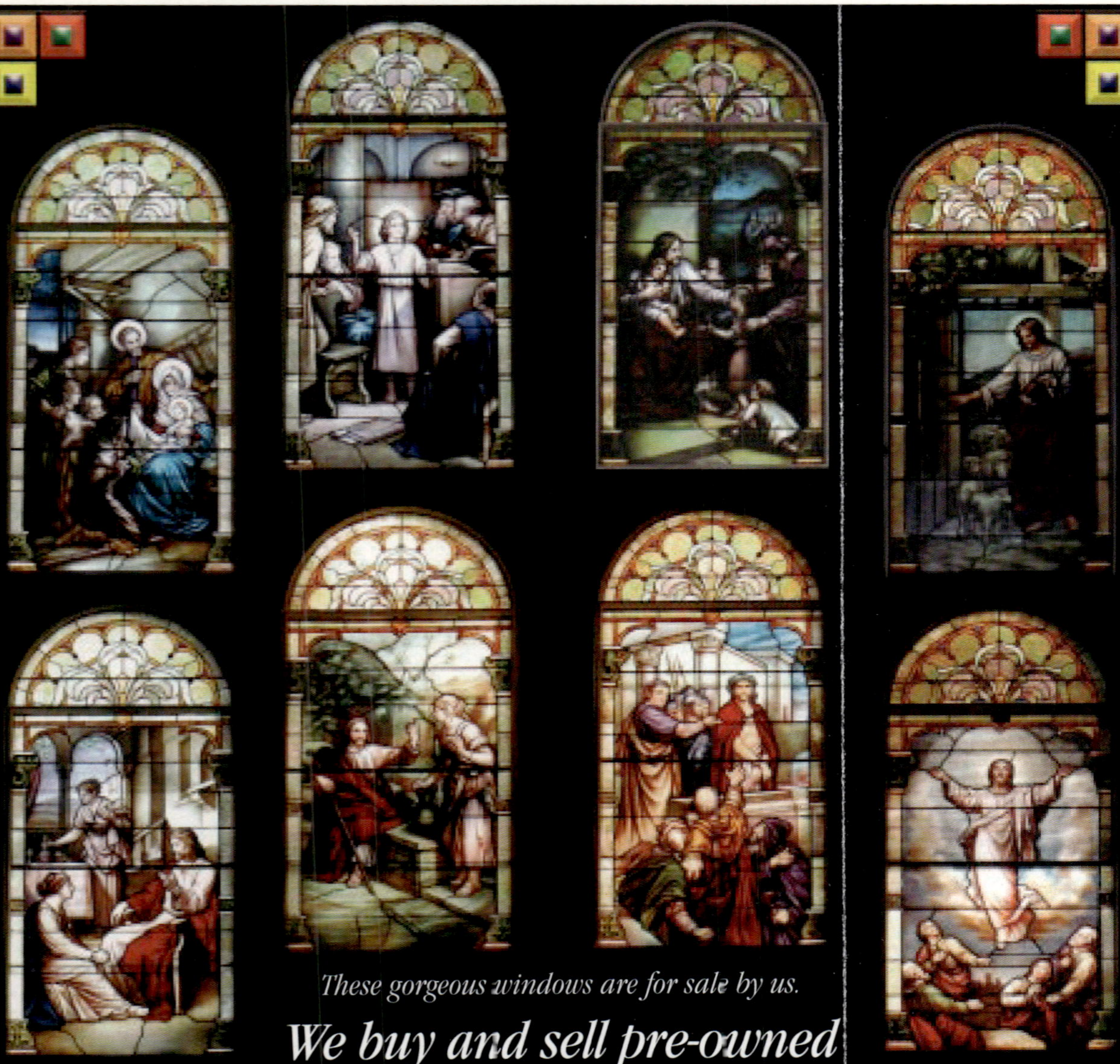

The Mark of Human Hands™
© 2004 Marklin Candle Design. All Rights Reserved
(for Paschals, see page 23F)
Marklin Candle Design
www.marklincandle.com
603-746-2211

Sisters	276
Lay Teachers	4,614
Vital Statistics	
Receptions into the Church:	
Infant Baptism Totals	88,224
Adult Baptism Totals	2,233
Received into Full Communion	2,167
First Communions	56,865
Confirmations	22,056
Marriages:	
Catholic	9,364
Interfaith	1,222
Total Marriages	10,586
Deaths	12,788
Total Catholic Population	4,174,304
Total Population	11,096,200

Former Bishops—Rt. Revs. FRANCIS GARCIA DIEGO Y MORENO, O.F.M., D.D., consecrated Oct. 4, 1840; Bishop of both Californias; died at Santa Barbara, April 30, 1846; JOSEPH SADOC ALEMANY, O.P., D.D., consecrated June 30, 1850; Bishop of Monterey; transferred to San Francisco, July 29, 1853; died in Valencia, Spain, April 14, 1888; THADDEUS AMAT, C.M., D.D., consecrated March 12, 1854; died May 12, 1878; FRANCIS MORA, D.D., consecrated Titular Bishop of Mosynopolis and Coadjutor to Bishop Amat, Aug. 3, 1873; resigned May 6, 1896; died Aug. 3, 1905 in Sarria, Barcelona, Spain; GEORGE MONTGOMERY, D.D., consecrated April 8, 1894, Bishop of Tmul and Coadjutor-Bishop of Monterey and Los Angeles cum jure successionis; succeeded to May 6, 1896; appt. Coadjutor-Archbishop of San Francisco, Jan. 1, 1903; died in San Francisco, Jan. 10, 1907; THOMAS JAMES CONATY, D.D., consecrated Nov. 24, 1901, Titular-Bishop of Samos; appt. Bishop of Monterey and Los Angeles, March 27, 1903; died at Coronado, CA, Sept. 18, 1915; Most Rev. JOHN J. CANTWELL, D.D., LL.D., appt. Bishop of Monterey-Los Angeles, Sept. 21, 1917; consecrated Dec. 5, 1917; appt. Assistant to the Pontifical Throne, Sept. 30, 1929; transferred to Los Angeles, June 1, 1922; elevated to Archepiscopal dignity, July 11, 1936; installed Dec. 3, 1936; died Oct. 30, 1947, at Los Angeles, CA; His Eminence JAMES FRANCIS MCINTYRE, D.D., appt. Auxiliary Bishop of New York, Nov. 16, 1940; consecrated Jan. 8, 1941; promoted to Coadjutor Archbishop, July 20, 1946; appt. Archbishop of Los Angeles, Feb. 7, 1948; installed March 19, 1948; created Cardinal Priest, Jan. 12, 1953; resigned Jan. 21, 1970; died July 16, 1979; TIMOTHY CARDINAL MANNING, D.D., J.C.D. (Retired), appt. Titular Bishop of Lesvi and Auxiliary Bishop of Los Angeles, Aug. 3, 1946; consecrated Oct 15, 1946; installed as first Bishop of Fresno, Dec 15, 1967; appt. Titular Bishop of Capri and Coadjutor Archbishop of Los Angeles, May 26, 1969; appt. Archbishop of Los Angeles, Jan. 21, 1970; created a Cardinal Priest, March 5, 1973; retired Sept. 4, 1985; died June 23, 1989 at Los Angeles, CA.

Archdiocesan Catholic Center Office—3424 Wilshire Blvd., Los Angeles, 90010-2241. Tel: 213-637-7000; Fax: 213-637-6607.

Office of the Cardinal—His Eminence ROGER CARDINAL MAHONY, D.D., 3424 Wilshire Blvd., Los Angeles, 90010-2241. Tel: 213-637-7288; Fax: 213-637-6510.

Priest Secretary/Master of Ceremonies—Rev. Msgr. PAUL M. ALBEE. Tel: 213-637-7261.

Master of Ceremonies for Stational Liturgies—Rev. Msgr. KEVIN KOSTELNIK. Tel: 213-680-5213.

Executive Coordinator—Mrs. EILEEN BONADUCE. Tel: 213-637-7298.

Cardinal's Theologian—Dr. MICHAEL DOWNEY. Tel: 213-637-7447.

Vicar for Canonical Services and Vice Chancellor—Rev. THOMAS ANSLOW, C.M., J.C.L. Tel: 213-637-7888.

Director of Special Services—Sr. MARY JEAN MEIER, R.S.M. Tel: 213-637-7520.

General Counsel—MARGARET G. GRAF. Tel: 213-637-7511.

Chief Financial Officer—RANDOLPH E. STEINER. Tel: 213-637-7218.

Auxiliary Bishops-Vicars General—Most Revs. JOHN J. WARD, D.D., J.C.L., V.G. (Retired), 3424 Wilshire Blvd., Los Angeles, 90010-2241. Tel: 213-637-7265; Fax: 213-637-6265; JUAN A. ARZUBE, D.D. (Retired), Nazareth House, 3333 Manning Ave., Los Angeles, 90064-4804. Tel: 310-839-2361; THOMAS J. CURRY, D.D., Ph.D., Santa Barbara Region, 3240 Calle Pinon, Santa Barbara, 93105-2760. Tel: 805-682-0442; Fax: 805-682-7509; JOSEPH M. SARTORIS, D.D., V.G. (Retired), 3424 Wilshire Blvd., Los Angeles, 90010-2241; GABINO ZAVALA, San Gabriel Pastoral Region, Office, 16009 E. Cypress Ave., Irwindale, 91706-2122. Tel: 626-960-9344; Fax: 626-962-0455; GERALD E. WILKERSON, D.D., San Fernando Pastoral Region, 15101 San Fernando Mission Blvd., San Fernando, 91341-1109. Tel: 818-361-6009; Fax: 818-361-6270; EDWARD W. CLARK, V.G., Our Lady of the Angels Pastoral Region, 2636 S. Mansfield Ave., Los Angeles, 90016-3512. Tel: 323-936-2588; Fax: 323-938-1190.

Moderator of the Curia and Vicar General—Rev. Msgr. ROYALSE M. VADAKIN. Tel: 213-637-7255.

Chancellor—Sr. MARY ELIZABETH GALT, B.V.M. Tel: 213-637-7460.

Vice Chancellor—Rev. Msgr. ALEXANDER SALAZAR. Tel: 213-637-7426.

Archdiocesan Pastoral Regions

Santa Barbara Region—Most Rev. THOMAS J. CURRY, D.D., Ph.D., 3240 Calle Pinon, Santa Barbara, 93105-2760. Tel: 805-682-0442; Fax 805-682-7509.

Deanery 1—Rev. JOHN G. FITZGERALD, V.F. Tel: 805-733-2735.

Deanery 2—Rev. LUIS H. QUIHUIS, S.J., V.F. Tel: 805-963-1734.

Deanery 3—Rev. Msgr. PATRICK J. O'BRIEN, P.A., V.F. Tel: 805-643-4318.

Deanery 4—Rev. Msgr. MICHAEL BUNNY, V.F. Tel: 805-498-3602.

San Fernando Region—Most Rev. GERALD E. WILKERSON, D.D., P.O. Box 7608, Mission Hills, 91346-7608. 15101 San Fernando Mission Blvd., Mission Hills, 91345-2526. Tel: 818-361-6009; Fax: 818-361-6270.

Deanery 5—Rev. Msgr. JAMES C. GEHL, V.F. Tel: 818-341-6534.

Deanery 6—Rev. JOSEPH P. SHEA, V.F. Tel: 818-247-2222.

Deanery 7—Rev. JOHN H. KEESE, V.F. Tel: 818-894-1176.

Deanery 8—Rev. Msgr. EDMOND M. RENEHAN, V.F. Tel: 661-252-3353.

San Gabriel Region—Most Rev. GABINO ZAVALA, 16009 E. Cypress Ave., Irwindale, 91706-2122. Tel: 626-960-9344; Fax: 626-962-0455.

Deanery 9—Rev. JESSE C. GALAZ, V.F. Tel: 323-264-3353.

Deanery 10—Rev. FRANCIS R. COLBORN, V.F., S.T.D. Tel: 626-792-4183.

Deanery 11—Rev. Msgr. MICHAEL MEYERS. Tel: 626-914-3941.

Deanery 12—Rev. Msgr. JAMES J. LOUGHNANE, V.F. Tel: 909-861-7106.

Our Lady of the Angels Pastoral Region—Most Rev. EDWARD W. CLARK, V.G., 2636 S. Mansfield Ave., Los Angeles, 90016. Tel: 323-936-2588 Fax: 323-938-1190.

Deanery 13—Rev. KEVIN L. NOLAN, V.F Tel: 310-838-2477.

Deanery 14—Rev. MICHAEL MANDALA, S.J., V.F. Tel: 323-462-6311.

Deanery 15—Rev. JARLATH CUNNANE, V.F Tel: 323-737-3325.

Deanery 16—Rev. Msgr. TIMOTHY J. DYER, V.F. Tel: 323-759-1562.

San Pedro Pastoral Region—Rev. Msgr. BERNARD LEHENY, E.V., Episcopal Vicar, 3555 St. Pancratius Pl., Lakewood, 90712-1416. Tel: 562-634-0456; Fax: 562-531-4783.

Deanery 17—Rev. Msgr. HENRY GOMEZ, V.F. Tel: 562-927-4495.

Deanery 18—Rev. JOHN WOOLWAY, V.F. Tel: 562-692-3758.

Deanery 19—Rev. Msgr. JOHN BARRY, V.F. Tel: 310-545-5651.

Deanery 20—Rev. Msgr. DOUGLAS W. SAUNDERS, V.F. Tel: 562-425-7459.

Archdiocesan Catholic Center

Unless otherwise listed, all ACC offices are located at: *3424 Wilshire Blvd., Los Angeles, 90010-2241.* Tel: 213-637-7000; Fax: 213-637-6607.

African-American Catholic Center for Evangelization—c/o Verbum Dei High School, 11100 S. Central Ave., Los Angeles, 90059-1199.

Evangelization Center—Tel: 323-357-0523.

AIDS/HIV Ministry—Rev. CHRIS PONNET, Liaison, 1911 Zonal Ave., Los Angeles, 90033. Tel: 213-637-7448 (7HIV); 323-223-9047.

Alcohol and Substance Abuse—Rev. Msgr. T. TERRENCE RICHEY, Dir. Tel: 213-637-7644.

Annual Catholic Appeal—Mr. JOSEPH HINDLEY, Dir. Tel: 213-637-7673; Fax: 213-637-6111.

Apostleship of Prayer—Rev. DOAN HOANG, S.J., Dir., 5322 Franklin Ave., Los Angeles, 90027-1613. Tel: 323-871-1518

Apostleship of the Sea—Rev. Msgr. PATRICK GALLAGHER, Port Chap.; Rev. HENRY HERNANDO, Maritime Chap., 870 W. Eighth St., San Pedro, 90731-3091. Tel: 310-833-3541.

Archives—Rev. Msgr. FRANCIS J. WEBER, Archivist, 15151 San Fernando Mission Blvd., Mission Hills, 91345-2617; Rev. KEVIN FEENEY, Adjunct Archivist. Tel: 818-365-1501; Fax: 818-361-3276.

Brothers Council Religious—Bro. WILLIAM NICK, C.S.C. Tel: 818-933-3610.

Canonical Services, Episcopal Vicar for—Rev. THOMAS ANSLOW, C.M., J.C.L. Tel: 213-637-7888; Fax: 213-637-6178.

Canonical Services Coordinator—Rev. PATRICK HILL, J.C.L. Tel: 213-637-7201.

Dispensations Secretary—NURIA ESCOBAR. Tel: 213-637-7201.

Legal Secretary—ERENDIRA VIRAMONTES. Tel: 213-637-7888.

Cardinal Manning House of Prayer for Priests—Revs. JAMES TORRENS, S.J., Dir. Tel: 213-662-7569; JOHN CLARK, S.J., Assoc. Dir. Tel: 323-662-7966; JOHN D. MCANULTY, S.J., Dir. Emeritus. Tel: 323-662-0044. 3441 Waverly Dr., Los Angeles, 90027-2526. Fax: 323-953-4802 Staffed by: Little Brothers of the Good Shepherd; Bros. MARK HARMUELLER, B.G.S., Admin.; DAVID NICKERSON, B.G.S. Tel: 323-662-0092. Staff Residence, 3445 Waverly Dr., Los Angeles, 90027-2526. Tel: 323-662-3620.

Cardinal McIntyre Fund for Charity—SUSAN VALERIE WEIGHT, Dir. Tel: 213-637-7438; Fax: 213-637-6438.

Catholic Campaign for Human Development—MARIA ELENA PERALES, Dir. Tel: 213-637-7690.

Catholic Charities of Los Angeles—1531 James M. Wood Blvd., P.O. Box 15095, Los Angeles, 90015-0095. Tel: 213-251-3400; Fax: 213-380-4603.

Executive Director—Rev. Msgr. GREGORY A. COX, M.S.W., M.B.A. Tel: 213-251-3464.

Chief Administrative Officer—RONALD G. LOPEZ, M.S.W. Tel: 213-251-3413.

Chief Financial Officer—JAMES E. BATHKER. Tel: 213-251-3410.

Department of Resource Development—ALEXANDRIA "SANDI" ARNOLD, Dir. Tel: 213-251-3495.

Department of Human Resources—JOSEPH W. PAULICIVIC JR., Dir. Tel: 213-251-3414.

Adeste--Child Care Services—ARMINE LALAIAN-SANJAR, Dir. Tel: 213-251-3468.

Central Intake Unit—JOE D. LE, Dir. Tel: 213-251-3445.

C.Y.O. Athletics—TOM DAVIDSON, Prog. Dir. Tel: 213-251-3562.

Immigration and Refugee Services—LOC NAM NGUYEN, Dir. Tel: 213-251-3489; JO MARCEL, Asst. Dir. Tel: 213-251-3470.

Immigration Reception—Tel: 213-251-3411; 213-251-3471; Fax: 213-251-3444.

CCLA Continuous Quality Improvement—Dr. EDWARD NELSON, Dir. Tel: 213-251-3489.

Youth Employment Services—ROBERT GUTIERREZ, Program Dir., 3250 Wilshire Blvd., Ste. 1010, Los Angeles, 90010. Tel: 213-736-5456.

Regional Offices and Community Centers—

Our Lady of the Angels: Metro (Los Angeles Inner City)—JACKIE LAZARUS, Regl. Dir., 4665 Willowbrook Ave., Los Angeles, 90029. Tel: 323-662-1462.

Our Lady of the Angels: Western—JAMES STRATTON, Rgnl. Dir. Tel: 310-392-8701.

San Fernando Pastoral Region—MOEED KHAN, Rgnl. Dir. Tel: 818-883-6015.

San Gabriel Pastoral Region—MARY ROMERO, Rgnl. Dir. Tel: 323-266-3130.

San Pedro Pastoral Region—ANNA R. TOTTA, Rgnl. Dir. Tel: 562-591-1641.

Santa Barbara County—Dr. FRANK BOGNAR, Rgnl. Dir. Tel: 805-965-7045.

Ventura County—ROBERT BAGDAZIAN, Rgnl. Dir. Tel: 805-643-4694.

Catholic Relief Services—MARIA ELENA PERALES, Dir. Tel: 213-637-7690.

Cemeteries, Catholic—Tel: 213-637-7801; Fax: 213-637-6800. JAMES M. TIXIER, Dir. Tel: 213-637-7808.

Pastoral Relations—Deacon SAM FRIAS. Tel: 213-637-7807.

Director of Information Services—BRIAN MCMAHON. Tel: 213-637-7815.

Associate Director of Administration—JOSE OROZCO. Tel: 213-637-7814.

Associate Director of Cemetery Operations—SOFIA SANDRU. Tel: 213-637-7812.

Censores Librorum—Dr. MICHAEL DOWNEY, Coord. Tel: 213-637-7447

Clergy, Vicar for—Rev. Msgrs. CRAIG A. COX, J.C.D., Vicar; GABRIEL GONZALES, Asst. Vicar. Tel: 213-637-7284.

Personnel Board of the Archdiocese—Rev. Msgrs. JAMES J. LOUGHNANE, V.F., Chm.; MICHAEL BUNNY, V.F.; Revs. FREDDIE CHUA; ALEX CHUNG; Rev. Msgr. HENRY GOMEZ, V.F.; Revs. JOHN H. KEESE, V.F.; KEVIN NOLAN, V.F.; NORMAN SUPANCHECK.

Continuing Formation for Clergy—Tel: 213-637-7571.

Construction—Bro. HILARION O'CONNOR, O.S.F., Dir. Tel: 213-637-7852. Construction Project Supervisors:: CECILIA URIBE. Tel: 213-637-7855; RICHARD VILLACORTA. Tel: 213-637-7860; GEORGE HARSCH. Tel: 213-637-7817.

Council of Catholic Women, Archdiocesan—Tel: 213-637-7394.

Cursillo Movement—Rev. Msgr. MODESTO LEWIS PEREZ, J.C.D., Archdiocesan Spiritual Dir. Tel: 805-482-2755, Ext. 1066; Rev. ALBERT CARREON, Spanish Spiritual Advisor. Tel: 323-269-8171; Deacon PETER CHU, Chinese Spiritual Advisor. Tel: 909-598-4710; Rev. JOSE FERNANDO LAMBELHO, Portugese Spiritual Advisor. Tel: 213-637-7482; Rev. Msgr. JUAN MATAS, Assoc. Spanish Spiritual Advisor. Tel: 323-722-5866; Revs. JOHN T. NGHI, Vietnamese Spiritual Advisor. Tel: 909-626-3596; NESTOR REBONG, Filipino Spiritual Advisor. Tel: 626-960-1805; GAEL SULLIVAN, S.D.B., English Spiritual Advisor. Tel: 323-920-7796.

Deacons—Deacon MANUEL J. MARTINEZ, Dir. Tel: 213-637-7734.

Detention Ministry—Co Directors: Rev. GEORGE HORAN. Tel: 213-637-7639; JAVIER E. STAURING. Tel: 213-637-7491.

Development—KEVIN T. O'CONNOR, Chief Devel. Officer; Offertory Program. Tel: 213-637-7617.

Annual Appeal—Mr. JOSEPH HINDLEY, Dir. Tel: 213-637-7673.

Trusts and Estates—H. RICHARD CLOSSON, Dir. Tel: 213-637-7472.

Information Systems—FERDIE NAVALTA, Admin. Tel: 213-637-7393.

Diaconate, Formation Office—Deacon JERRY CELLNER, Dir. Tel: 213-637-7282; Fax: 213-637-5931; Sr. CHRIS MACHADO, S.S.S., Assoc. Dir. Tel: 213-637-7747. Coordinators:: Rev. FRANK FERRANTE, C.M.F. Tel: 213-637-7536; Deacons VALENTIN SAUCEDO. Tel: 213-637-7754; CRIS VEGA. Tel: 213-637-7738.

Ecumenical and Interreligious Affairs—Rev. ALEXEI R. SMITH, Dir., c/o St. Andrew's Church, 538 Concord St., El Segundo, 90245. Tel: 310-322-1892; Fax: 310-322-1919.

Education Foundation—KATHLEEN ANDERSON, Exec. Dir. Tel: 213-637-7282; THERESA FRAGOSA, Program Officer. Tel: 213-637-7694.

Data Financial Records—BONNIE ONKEN. Tel: 213-637-7449.

Ethnic Groups Ministry—16009 E. Cypress Ave., Irwindale, 91706. Tel: 626-960-9344.

Family Life Office—JOAN T. VIENNA, Dir. Tel: 213-637-7227; Fax: 213-637-6681. Email: life@la-archdiocese.org.

Coordinators, Marriage Preparation and Natural Family Planning—CANDY METOYER. Tel: 213-637-7250 (English); GRACIELA VILLALOBOS. Tel: 213-637-7561 (Spanish).

Filipino Ministry—Sr. MARY CHRISTINA SEVILLA, R.G.S., Dir., 4950 Santa Monica Blvd., Los Angeles, 90029-2597. Tel: 323-662-8480.

Financial Services—Information Desk. Tel: 213-637-7500. ADRIAN TAYLOR, C.P.A., Controller. Tel: 213-637-7593; ELISITA LANDRY, Accounts Receivable & Payable. Tel: 213-637-7291; EDNA CRISTOBAL, C.P.A., Investments. Tel: 213-637-7292; SANDRA SMITH, C.P.A., Internal Audit. Tel: 213-637-7622; SANDI PULIDO LENZ, Pension. Tel: 213-637-7544; ROSA R. PADILLA, Payroll. Tel: 213-637-7544; DOREEN RODRIGUEZ, Operations. Tel: 213-637-5456.

Government Funded Programs—LILIA CHAVEZ, Dir., 1543 W. Olympic Blvd., Ste. 424, Los Angeles, 90015-3821. Tel: 213-383-0199; Fax: 213-383-1529.

Pre-School Dir.—ETHEL ANTOINE. Tel: 213-388-1291.

Youth Employment Programs—ROBERT GUTIERREZ, Dir., 3250 Wilshire Blvd., #1010, Los Angeles, 90010. Tel: 213-736-5456.

Health Affairs—Sr. MARY CAROLITA HART, C.S.C., Dir. Tel: 213-637-7531.

Holy Childhood Association— (See Mission Office)

Archdiocesan Union of Holy Name Societies—JESUS MENDEZ, Pres. Tel: 323-721-1786. Mailing Address, 440 S. Fresno St., Los Angeles, 90063.

Moderator—Rev. Msgr. PAUL MONTOYA. Tel: 661-259-2276.

Human Resources/Insurance—WILLIAM HEINEN, Dir. Tel: 213-637-7596; Fax: 213-637-6116; MARGARET M. ANTCZAK, ACC Human Resources Mgr. Tel: 213-637-7625; MARGIE RODRIGUEZ, H.R. Specialist. Tel: 213-637-7371.

Human Resources Representative—Tel: 213-637-7242.

Insurance—LEVONTINE TOMACAN, Assoc. Dir. Tel: 213-637-7279; STEPHEN VAN BUREN, Risk Mgr. Tel: 213-637-7629; HOURIG H. MAZMANIAN, Benefits Admin. Tel: 213-637-7671.

Medical Benefits Consultant—Tel: 213-637-7680.

Information—MARIA P. ACOSTA, ACC Switchboard. Tel: 213-637-7000.

Information Services (Computer Department)—JAMES R. CELONI, Dir. Tel: 213-637-7271.

Insurance— (See Human Resources/Insurance)

Justice and Peace—MARIA ELENA PERALES. Tel: 213-637-7690.

Knights of Columbus—California State Council Office, 10604 Trademark Pkwy. N., Ste. 307, Rancho Cucamonga, 91730-5938. Tel: 909-466-3964; Fax: 909-466-5609.

State Deputy—WILLIAM J. PRZYBYA. Tel: 530-243-3793.

State Chaplain—Rev. MICHAEL NEWMAN. Tel: 530-891-3390.

Ladies of Charity of St. Vincent de Paul—2131 W. Third St., Seton Hall, Los Angeles, 90057-0992. Tel: 213-413-3688.

Lay Mission Helpers— (See Mission Office)

Marriage Encounter—Contacts: CARLOS POBLET; ESTHER POBLET, 15618 Gaymont Dr., La Mirada, 90638. Tel: 714-994-8672. Web: www.wwme.org. Marriage Encounter Weekends are offered in English, Spanish and Korean in the Archdiocese of Los Angeles.

Chaplain—Rev. JAMES GALVIN, C.M., 1964 Las Canoas Rd., Santa Barbara, 93105. Tel: 805-882-1942. Email: galcmwwme@aol.com.

Marriage Tribunal— (See Tribunal)

Media Relations—Mr. TOD TAMBERG, Dir. Tel: 213-637-7215; Fax: 213-385-6586; CAROLINA GUEVARA, Assoc. Dir. Tel: 213-637-7253; CINDY RODRIGUEZ, Sec. Tel: 213-637-7215.

Mission Office—Rev. DAVID JOHN AYOTTE, Dir. Tel: 213-637-7223; Fax: 213-637-6223. Email: missionoffice@la-archdiocese.org.

Holy Childhood Association—Tel: 213-637-7223.

Lay Mission Helpers—Tel: 213-637-7222.

Mission Circles—Tel: 213-637-7223.

Mission Doctors Assoc.—ELISE FREDERICK, Dir. Tel: 213-637-7499.

Propagation of the Faith—Rev. Msgr. TERRANCE FLEMING, S.T.D. Tel: 213-637-7223.

Operations and Building Manager—EILEEN O'BRIEN. Tel: 213-637-7618; HUGO SANDOVAL. Tel: 213-637-7269; DAGOBERTO MEDRANO. Tel: 213-637-7723.

Pastoral Associate Program—Sr. MARY GENINO, R.S.H.M., Coord. Tel: 213-637-7533; MARIA ELENA URIBE. Tel: 213-637-7878.

Priest Pension Plan—LUPE A. GARIBAY. Tel: 213-637-7320.

Project Rachel—Sr. RITA CALLANAN, I.H.M., 1028 N. Lake, Ste. 104, Pasadena, 91104. Tel: 626-398-6100.

Purchasing/Mail Center—SANDY B. VILLAREAL, Purchasing Agent. Tel: 213-637-7535.

Real Estate—MICHAEL DAVITT, Dir. Tel: 213-637-7273; Fax: 213-637-6673.

Escrows—MARIE A. URBACH. Tel: 213-637-7605; Fax: 213-637-6505.

Leases—BEATRIZ VELASQUEZ. Tel: 213-637-7270; Fax: 213-637-6270.

Property Taxes—ALICIA PINKLEY. Tel: 213-637-7516; Fax: 213-637-6516.

Religious Education—Tel: 213-637-7335; Fax: 213-637-6574. Sr. EDITH PRENDERGAST, R.S.C., Dir. Tel: 213-637-7309. Web: ore.la-archdiocese.org.

Adult Education—Rev. DAVID LOFTUS. Tel: 213-637-7654; Dr. ANNE DUNN, I.H.M., Santa Barbara. Tel: 805-569-2779.

Adult Education, Spanish—ALBERTO EMBRY. Tel: 213-637-7355.

Advanced Cathechetical Ministries and Formation—Spanish—LOURDES GONZALES-RUBIO. Tel: 213-637-7344.

Asian-Pacific Perspective—FE MUSGRAVE. Tel: 213-637-7669.

Catechesis in the Black Perspective—SHERYL LANGE. Tel: 213-637-7354.

Confirmation, Junior High and Youth Ministry—MIKE NORMAN. Tel: 213-637-7674; VIKKI SHEPP. Tel: 213-637-7616; DENNIS SANTOS. Tel: 805-682-5500.

Early Childhood—JAN PEDROZA. Tel: 213-637-7352.

Elementary—STEVEN ELLAIR. Tel: 213-637-7410.

Young Adult Ministry—MARTHA NUNEZ, Spanish. Tel: 213-637-7705.

Religious Education Congress—MARY LOU MCGEE, Coord. Tel: 213-637-7332. Web: recongress.org.

ORE Regional Offices—Our Lady of the Angels Region: LANETT REID, 2636 S. Mansfield Ave., Los Angeles, 90016-3512. Tel: 323-931-2875; Fax: 323-938-1190. San Fernando Region: LYNN LANG, San Fernando Pastoral Region, 15101 San Fernando Mission Blvd., Mission Hills, 91345. Tel: 818-365-5123; Fax: 818-361-4133. Mailing Address, P.O. Box 7608, Mission Hills, 91346. San Gabriel Region: EILEEN GATELEY, San Gabriel Pastoral Region, 16009 E. Cypress Ave., Irwindale, 91706. Tel: 626-962-7707; Fax: 626-962-0455. San Pedro Region: PAULETTE SMITH, San Pedro Pastoral Region, 3555 St. Pancratius Pl., Lakewood, 90712. Tel: 562-630-6272; Fax: 562-531-4783. ORE Santa Barbara Region: SUE SPIES, Santa Barbara Pastoral Region, Bishop Garcia Diego Center, 4032 La Colina Rd., Santa Barbara, 93110. Tel: 805-569-1135; Fax: 805-569-2746.

Respect Life Office—Mrs. LICIA NICASSIO, Dir., 42 Chestnut St., Pasadena, 91103-3896. Tel: 626-396-7019. P.O. Box 50328, Pasadena, 91115-0328.

Schools, Department of Catholic—Rev. ALBERT J. DIULIO, S.J., Pres., Los Angeles Archdiocesan Catholic Schools. Tel: 213-637-7313; Fax: 213-637-6140.

Assistant to President and Administrative Coordinator—GUING A. RAMOS. Tel: 213-637-7331.

Superintendent Elementary Schools—PATRICIA LIVINGSTON. Tel: 213-637-7328.

Elementary School Supervisors—NEIL QUINLY. Tel: 213-637-7334; Sr. MONICA QUIGLEY, S.S.L. Tel: 213-637-7334; FRANK MONTEJANO. Tel: 213-637-7317; SANDRA BROSNAHAN. Tel: 213-637-7436; KATHLEEN DAMISCH. Tel: 213-637-7324; MARIE COLLINS. Tel: 213-637-7328.

Director of Elementary School Finances—KATHLEEN DAMISCH. Tel: 213-637-7324.

Director of Personnel (K-8)—LOU ANNE INSPRUCKER. Tel: 213-637-7688.

Director of Curriculum—VACANT. Tel: 213-637-7311.

Director of Professional Resources—NEIL QUINLY. Tel: 213-637-7334.

Superintendent Secondary Schools—Ms. NANCY J. COONIS. Tel: 213-637-7381.

Assistant Superintendent of Secondary Schools—DOROTHY PITTELKAU. Tel: 213-637-7325.

Secondary School Supervisors—ROBERT GEBAUER. Tel: 213-637-7485; DOROTHY PITTELKAU. Tel: 213-637-7325.

Secondary School Finance Director—LOURDES SANTA MARIA. Tel: 213-637-7368.

Coordinator of Religious Formation and Instruction: Secondary Schools—Sr. ANGELA HALLAHAN, C.H.F. Tel: 213-637-7324.

School Accreditation/Assessment—SANDRA BROSNAHAN, Elementary. Tel: 213-637-7436; DOROTHY PITTELKAU, Secondary. Tel: 213-637-7338.

Federal and State Programs—Sr. PATRICIA SUPPLE, C.S.J., Dir. Tel: 213-637-7436.

Scouting, Camp Fire Ministry—JIM SCHIVERS, Chm., 525 N. Fountain Spring Lane, Glendora, 91741-2319. Tel: 626-963-5162. Email: shivers525@aol.com; Deacon WAYNE RASCATI, Chap. Tel: 805-967-5641; SHARON SHELLMAN, Chm. Girls. Tel: 626-967-1815.

Sisters' Council—Tel: 213-637-7559.

Society of St. Vincent de Paul—CHARLES A. MITCHELL, Pres., 210 N. Ave. 21, Los Angeles, 90031-1713. Tel: 323-224-6287; JOSE J. ROSSIER, Exec. Dir. Tel: 800-974-3571.

Synod Implementation—Tel: 213-637-7510. Deacon DAVID ESTRADA, Dir. Tel: 213-637-7474.

Telecommunications—DAVE G. MOORE, Dir. Tel: 213-637-7312. Technical Staff: DAVID SCHMITT, Chief Engineer. Tel: 213-637-7526; FERNANDO DIAZ, Studio Technician. Tel: 213-637-7399.

Theologian, Cardinal's—Dr. MICHAEL DOWNEY. Tel: 213-637-7447.

Theological Commission—Co-Chm.: Dr. MICHAEL DOWNEY; Rev. THOMAS P. RAUSCH, S.J.; Sr. KAREN WILHELMY, C.S.J., Sec. Tel: 661-944-2178.

"The Tidings" (Archdiocesan Newspaper)—Tel: 213-637-7360; Fax: 213-637-6360.

Executive Publisher—Rev. ANTHONY "TONY" T. SCANNELL, O.F.M.Cap. Tel: 213-637-7599.

Editor—MICHAEL NELSON. Tel: 213-637-7543; MARY TRUDEAU-MOTTOLA, Circulation Mgr. Tel: 213-637-7477; JOSE VELASQUEZ, Production Mgr. Tel: 213-637-7380; HERMINE LEES, Directory. Tel: 213-637-7392; CORA LEUTERIO, Finance Officer. Tel: 213-637-7391.

Tribunal—Main Office, 3424 Wilshire Blvd., Los Angeles, 90010-2241. Tel: 213-637-7245; Fax: 213-637-6245. *Santa Barbara/Ventura Branch, P.O. Box 2215, Oxnard, 93034.* Tel: 805-486-6553; Fax: 805-486-3884.

Judicial Vicar—Rev. CHARLES J. CHAFFMAN, J.C.D. Tel: 213-637-7204.

Adjutant Judicial Vicar—Rev. ROBERT V. BIROSCHAK, J.C.L. Tel: 213-637-7220.

Canonical Staff—Sr. ANNE GIBLIN, R.S.C., J.C.L. Tel: 213-637-7211; Rev. PATRICK HILL, J.C.L. Tel: 213-637-7340; Sr. MARGARET ANN MCCAULEY, O.P., J.C.L. Tel: 213-637-7205; Rev. PETER T. NGO, J.C.L. Tel: 213-637-7211; Deacon HAROLD "HAL" PARISH, J.C.D. Tel: 805-486-6553; Sr. MARY ANNE WITTMAN, S.H.F., J.C.L. Tel: 805-486-6553.

Judges—Revs. THOMAS C. ANSLOW, C.M., J.C.D., J.C.L.; ROBERT V. BIROSCHAK, J.C.L.; MICHAEL CARCERANO, J.C.L.; CHARLES J. CHAFFMAN, J.C.D.; JARLATH DOLAN; Rev. Msgr. TERRANCE L. FLEMING, V.G., S.T.D.; Sr. ANNE GIBLIN, R.S.C., J.C.L.; Rev. PATRICK HILL, J.C.L.; Rev. Msgrs. WILLIAM LESER, C.B., S.T.B.; JAMES J. LOUGHNANE, V.F.; Sr. MARGARET ANN MCCAULEY, O.P., J.C.L.; Rev. Msgrs. AUGUST MORETTI; DONAL MULCAHY (Retired); Rev. PETER T. NGO, J.C.L.; Deacon HAROLD "HAL" PARISH, J.C.D.; Rev. MODESTO L. PEREZ, J.C.D.; Sr. MARY ANN WITTMAN, S.H.F., J.C.L.; Rev. WILLIAM P. WOLFE, J.C.L.

Promoters of Justice—Rev. Msgrs. HELMUT A. HEFNER, J.C.L.; FRANCIS T. WALLACE, J.C.L.

Defenders of the Bond—Rev. Msgr. ARNOLD BIEDERMANN; Rev. JEROME A. BOUSKA, M.A.; Rev. Msgr. HELMUT A. HEFNER, J.C.L.; Rev. JAMES SHIFFER, S.S.C., J.C.L.; Rev. Msgr. FRANCIS T. WALLACE, J.C.L.

Advocates and Auditors—MARIA AUEN; HERNAN CAICEDO; CESAR CASTRO; Deacon JAMES HENRY; MARTHA ESTHER LUNA; Deacon JON C. MCPHEETERS; JOAN SUTHERLAND.

Notaries and Other Officials—LETICIA ASCENCIO; SILVIA FERNANDEZ; CLAUDIO FONSECA; RUTH GOMEZ; BOBBIE LOPEZ; LILIA MONROY; ANNA PARISH; MERCED SALCEDO.

Trust and Estate Programs—H. RICHARD CLOSSON, Dir. Tel: 213-637-7472.

Vicar for Canonical Services—Rev. THOMAS C. ANSLOW, C.M., J.C.D., J.C.L. Tel: 213-637-7888.

Vicar for Clergy—Rev. Msgrs. CRAIG A. COX, J.C.D. Tel: 213-637-7284; Fax: 213-637-6289; GABRIEL GONZALES, Asst. Vicar. Tel: 213-637-7284

Director of Deacons—Deacon MANUEL MARTINEZ. Tel: 213-637-6289.

Alcohol and Substance Abuse Ministry—Rev. Msgr. T. TERRENCE RICHEY, Dir. Tel: 213-637-7644.

Ministry to Retired and Ill Priests—Tel: 213-637-7680.

Orientation and Support Programs—LOUIS VELASQUEZ. Tel: 213-637-7575; LUCILLE MILLER, Exec. Asst. Tel: 213-637-7284; MARGARITA FRANCO, Admin. Asst. Tel: 213-637-7573.

Continuing Formation—JANE GRIEP. Tel: 213-637-7571.

Ministry to Recently Ordained Priests—Revs. ALBERT BAHHUTH; EDWARD DOVER; Rev. Msgr. JAMES GEHL; Rev. PAUL HRUBY; Rev. Msgr. ALEXANDER SALAZAR; Revs. JAMES STEHLY; JOHN WOOLWAY.

Vicar for Women Religious—Sr. MARY FAITH CLARKE, S.N.J.M. Tel: 213-637-7592; VACANT, Exec. Sec. Tel: 213-637-7559.

"Vida Nueva" (Archdiocesan Spanish Newspaper)—Tel: 213-637-7360; Fax: 213-637-6360. Rev. Msgr. LLOYD A. TORGERSON, Interim Exec. Publisher. Tel: 213-637-7599; VICTOR ALEMAN, Editor. Tel: 213-637-7310; MARY TRUDEAU-MOTTOLA, Circulation Mgr. Tel: 213-637-7477; JOSE VELASQUEZ, Production Dir. Tel: 213-637-7380.

Vocations—Tel: 213-637-7248. Web: www.vocations.la-archdiocese.org. Sr. KATHLEEN BRYANT, R.S.C., Vocation Dir.. Email: KBryt@aol.com; Revs. ROBERT JUAREZ, Dir. Vocations for Hispanic. Email: Taticbob@aol.com; TRUC NGUYEN, Vietnamese Vocation Liaison. Email: ngtruc@yahoo.com.

Women Religious, Vicar for—Sr. MARY FAITH CLARKE, S.N.J.M. Tel: 213-637-7592.

Worship—Tel: 213-637-7262. Email: worship@la-archdiocese.org. SANDRA DOOLEY, Dir. Tel: 213-637-7513.

Christian Initiation for Adults, (RCIA)—Tel: 213-637-7591.

Hispanic Liturgy and Ministry Coordinator—Rev. MANUEL SANAHUJA, Sch.P. Tel: 213-637-7588

Program Administrator—ELIZABETH OWENS. Tel: 213-637-7586.

Archdiocesan Advisory Boards

Unless otherwise indicated, mailing address for all offices is: *3424 Wilshire Blvd., Los Angeles, 90010-2241.*

Cardinal McIntyre Fund for Charity—His Eminence ROGER CARDINAL MAHONY, D.D., Chm.; Rev. Msgr. ROYALE M. VADAKIN, V.G., Pres.; Rev. FISHER ROBINSON, S.V.D., Vice Pres.; Sr. MARY FAITH CLARKE, S.N.J.M., Sec.; SUSAN VALERIE WEIGHT, Dir. Tel: 213-637-7438; Fax: 213-637-6438. Email: svweight@la-archdiocese.org. Board of Directors:: Revs. THOMAS E. BAKER; STANLEY BOSCH, S.T.; Sr. MARY FAITH CLARKE, S.N.J.M.; Revs. KENNETH DEASY; LARRY S. NEUMEIR; FISHER ROBINSON, S.V.D.; Rev. Msgr. ALEXANDER SALAZAR; Rev. JOSEPH P. SHEA, V.F.

Clergy Misconduct Oversight Board—Judge RICHARD P. BYRNE, Chm.; KRIS TOSTADO, Exec. Sec. Tel: 213-637-7548. Members: JUDI ARNOLD; WILLIAM ARNOLD; ADRIENNE CEDRO-HAMENT; Rev. JARLATH CUNNANE; NANETTE DE FUENTES, PH.D.; Sr. DIANE DONOGHUE, S.S.S.; Rev. JESSE GALAZ; MARK C. HOLSCHER; YVONNE MARIAJIMENEZ; JAMES J. MCGOUGH, M.D.; TERRY SEIDLER; GEORGE K. TAKAHASHI.

Commission for Catholic Life Issues—Rev. Msgr. TIMOTHY O'CONNELL, Chm. Tel: 310-261-1145; Mrs. LICIA NICASSIO, Dir. Respect Life, 42 Chestnut St., Pasadena, 91103. Tel: 626-396-7019. P.O. Box 50328, Pasadena, 91115-0328. Members: WILLIAM ANDERSON, Esq.; PADDY JIM BAGGOT, M.D.; ANDREA BURMAN; MARIAN BURMAN; Rev. THOMAS CUSACK, S.S.C.; VINCENT FORTANASCE, M.D.; Rev. MARCOS GONZALEZ; MARCELLA MELENDEZ; BETTY ODELLO, R.N., M.S.N.; Rev. SAL PILATO; ERNEST SANCHEZ, Esq.; KATHERINE DOWLING SCHLAERTH, M.D.; MARY SHERIDAN; Sr. PAULA VANDEGAER, S.S.S., L.C.S.W.; ENRIQUETA VILLAREAL, M.D.; GERMAINE WENSLEY, R.N.; Ms. MARLENE WILSON, M.S.W., L.C.S.W.

Catholic School Board—RICCI J. RUFFINELLI, Pres.; TERRI MENDOZA, Ph.D., 1st Vice Pres.; RALPH VALENTE, 2nd Vice Pres. Members:: STEVE CHASE; Dr. JOHN A. DAVITT; JOHN R. GUTIERREZ; DELIA JOHNSON; Mrs. ELIZABETH LA DOU; RICHARD L. MORA; PEGGY MORRIS; JOHN QUIGLEY, M.D.; JAMES P. SARNI. Revs. JOSEPH P. SHEA, V.F.; ALBERT J. DIULIO, S.J., Ex Officio.

College of Consultors—Most Revs. EDWARD W. CLARK, V.G.; THOMAS J. CURRY, D.D., Ph.D.; JOSEPH M. SARTORIS D.D., V.G. (Retired); GERALD E. WILKERSON, D.D.; GABINO ZAVALA, D.D., J.C.L., V.G.; Rev. Msgrs. CRAIG A. COX, J.C.D.; CHARLES E. HILL; Revs. MICHAEL JENNETT; ALEXANDER SALAZAR; WILLIAM BONNER; RICHARD VEGA.

Commission for Ecumenical and Interreligious Affairs—Rev. ALEXEI SMITH, Dir., 538 Concord St., El Segundo, 90245. Tel: 310-322-1892; Fax: 310-322-1919. Members: Rev. Msgr. WILLIAM BARRY, P.A.; Sisters MOLUA CONHEADY, S.S.L.; ANNE FIELD, S.S.S.; LAURA GORMLEY, S.S.L.; MONICA HUGHES; Sr. EMILE ANN PALLADINO, S.N.D.; Rev. THOMAS RAUSCH, S.J.; KATHERINE ROUSSEAU.

Council of Deacons—Deacon MANUEL J. MARTINEZ, Dir. Tel: 213-637-7734; BOB SEIDLER, Chm.; JOHN STEELE, Sec.

Regional Representatives—Santa Barbara Pastoral Region: Deacon JOHNNIE HAMMONDS; AMELIA HAMMONDS; TRINO ANDRADE; MARIA ANDRADE. San Fernando Pastoral Region: BOB SEIDLER; PON SEIDLER; JOHN STEELE; KATHELEEN STEELE. San Gabriel Pastoral Region: GARY PATTERSON; MARGE PATTERSON; JIM CROWLEY; ANNETE CROWLEY. Our Lady of the Angels Pastoral Region: ROBERTO VAZQUEZ; VELIA VAZQUEZ; JACK TURNER; JOAN TURNER. San Pedro Pastoral Region: RALPH ULIBARRI; MAXINE ULIBARRI; TOM MOSKE; ENOLA MOSKE.

Continuing Education Committee—Chairpersons: JOSEPH MANION; CAROL MANION.

Spiritual Growth Committee—Mr. MICHAEL MORGAN, Chm.

Council of Priests—His Eminence ROGER CARDINAL MAHONY, D.D., Pres.; Revs. TIMOTHY NICHOLS, Chm. Tel: 213-637-7479; JOHN PROVENZA, Sec.

Elected Members—Santa Barbara Pastoral Region: Rev. Msgrs. MICHAEL BUNNY, V.F.; PETER O'REILLY; Rev. JOSEPH HERNANDEZ. San Fernando Pastoral Region: Rev. Msgrs. JAMES GEHL; PAUL MONTOYA; Rev. ROBERT GALLAGHER. San Gabriel Pastoral Region: Rev. Msgrs. MICHAEL MEYERS; JOHN MORETTA; Rev. TIMOTHY NICHOLS. Our Lady of the Angels Region: Rev. Msgrs. TIMOTHY DYER, V.F.; DAVID O'CONNELL; Rev. RICHARD MARTINI. San Pedro Pastoral Region: Revs. JOHN WOOLWAY, V.F.; JOSEPH BRENNAN; JOHN PROVENZA. Ex Officios: Most Revs. EDWARD W. CLARK, V.G.; THOMAS CURRY, V.G.; Rev. Msgr. BERNARD LEHENY, E.V.; Most Revs. GERALD WILKERSON, V.G.; GABINO ZAVALA, V.G.; Rev. Msgr. ROYALE M. VADAKIN, V.G.

Finance Council—RANDOLPH E. STEINER, CFO Tel: 213-637-7218. Members: His Eminence ROGER CARDINAL MAHONY, D.D., Archbishop of Los Angeles; ALBERT G. ALVARADO, District Dir., U.S. Small Business Admin.; Rev. Msgr. JOHN BARRY, Pastor, American Martyrs Church; KAREN JUAREZ BOYD, Pres., Lumen Financial, Inc.; AVIS CHEUNG, Occidental Petroleum Co.; Rev. Msgr. TIMOTHY DYER, V.F., Pastor, Nativity/St. Columbkille; ROBERT F. ERBURU, Retired Chm. Bd., Times Mirror Co.; Deacon WILLIAM D. HAWKINS, Pres., Hawkins Co.; STEVEN HILTON, Conrad N. Hilton Foundation; THOMAS LARKIN, Pres. & CEO, Trust Co. of the West; JOHN A. MCMAHON, Retired Mng. Dir., Johnson & Higgins/Marsh & McLennan Inc.; Rev. Msgr. PATRICK O'BRIEN, Pastor, San Buenaventura Mission; KENNETH OLSEN, Retired Pres. & CEO, Vons Grocery Co.; Rev. Msgr. EDMOND RENEHAN, V.F., Regl. Dean, Pastor, St. Clare Church, Santa Clarita; ROLAND SEIDLER JR., Chm. & CEO, The Seidler Companies, Inc.; RANDOLPH STEINER, CFO, Archdiocese of Los Angeles; PAUL WATSON, Vice Chm., Wells Fargo Bank; Dr. JOHN T. WHOLIHAN, Dean, College of Business Admin., Loyola Marymount University; Most Rev. GABINO ZAVALA, D.D., J.C.L., San Gabriel Pastoral Region; Rev. Msgr. ROYALE M. VADAKIN, V.G., Ex Officio, Moderator of the Curia & Vicar Gen.

Justice and Peace Commission—GARY SMITH, Chm.; KEN MARTINET, Vice Chm. Tel: 213-637-7690. Members: CATHLEEN A. CRAYTON; Rev. DENNIS GALLO, C.M.F.; ROBERT GARCIA; JUDITH GIRARD; ROBERT GUTIERREZ; Sr. MARY SEAN HODGES, O.P.; ANGELICA SALAS; CAMBRIA SMITH; AQUILINA SORIANO; Deacon JOHN STEELE; CONSUELO VALDEZ; Deacon MANUEL VALENCIA.

Sisters' Council—Tel: 213-637-7559.

Vicar for Women Religious—Sr. MARY FAITH CLARKE, S.N.J.M., Ex Officio.

Secretary—Tel: 213-637-7559.

Members—Sisters PILAR BEDOYA, S.M.; ROBERTA BENNETT, C.S.C.; MONICA BERMISO, M.A.S.T.; BARBARA BOUDREAU, S.N.J.M.; PHILOMENE BREEMANS, I.C.M.; RITA CAMPOS, O.S.F.; MARGE CASHMAN, R.G.S.; INVIOLATA CHANG, I.H.M.M.; MARY ROSE CHINN, J.M.J.; ANTOINETTE CLAY, O.S.F.; MARY PAULINO CRABB, B.V.M.; ALBA DE LA ROSA, H.C.J.S.; MARGARET DEVLIN, S.S.C.; FRANCES MARIE DINARDO, S.N.D.; CARMEL DONOHUE, S.S.L.; BARBARA DUGAN, C.S.J.; SUZANNE DUNN, S.F.C.C.; GERARD EARLS, C.C.V.I.; JOHN BERCHMANNS FLYNN, C.S.N.; MARTHA GARCIA, D.C.; MARY BRIDE GORMLEY, O.S.B.; FRANCES GUSSENHOVEN, R.S.H.M.; FELICITAS HONG, C.S.T.; BARBARINE HOUDEK, O.S.F.; MARY JENSCH, D.M.J.; MARIAN ANNE KELLEY, R.G.S.; TIMOTHY MARIE KENNEDY, O.C.D.; CAROL KENNING, S.N.D.deN.; VERA KRASS, M.M.; RENE LANGENECKER, O.S.F.; GLORIA THERESA LAVIN, O.C.D.; FATIMA LEE, O.P.; JUSTINA LEGARRETA, I.H.M.; MARIJO LYNCH, S.P.; MARY ANNE MARTIN, C.S.J.; M. DIANE MARTIN, O.S.F.; ROSE MARIE MAYOCK, L.S.P.; MARGARET ANN MCCAULEY, O.P., J.C.L.; MARGARET ELLEN MCGRAW, C.S.J.; UNA MCMAHON, R.S.C.; FRANCES MARIE MONSIMER, R.S.C.; MAGDALENE MYUNG, S.K.M.; MARY NGUYEN, L.H.C.; LUKE PARKER, S.J.C.; JEANNINE PERCY, O.S.M.; CLAUDIO ROMERO, O.D.N.; RENA ROMERO, C.S.S.F.; CHRISTO ROSY, M.S.I.; TERESITA SAAVEDRA, S.S.S.; FLORELIA SALAZAR, C.V.D.; IRENE SAN ROMAN, O.S.F.; MARY SCHLEHUBER, O.P.; ROSE SERAPHIM, E.F.M.S.; ELIZABETH ANNE SHEEHEY, C.S.J.P.; MARY JOHN SHIN, D.S.M.; MARY ELIZABETH STRECKER, S.C.L.; MARY SULLIVAN, C.S.C.; MIRIAM JOSEPH TERESI, O.S.F.; MARY TOMASELLA, S.D.S.H.; GUADALUPE VALDEZ, S.S.N.D.; LISA JOSE VETTIKKATT, S.J.C.; LUCY VILLANOVA, S.P.; ROSE MARIE WILSON, O.S.F.; MARY ANNE WITTMAN, S.H.F., J.C.L.; KATHLEEN WOOD, O.S.F.; CARMEL WU, C.S.C.M.; GIULLI ZOBELEIN, O.P.

Spirituality Commission—Rev. JAMES CLARKE, Chm. Tel: 805-482-2755, Ext. 1056. Members: Rev. ALEXEI SMITH; Dr. MICHAEL DOWNEY; STEVEN ELLAIR; Sisters LAURA GORMLEY, S.S.L.; THOMAS BERNARD MACCONNELL, C.S.J.

Theological Commission—Co-Chm.: Dr. MICHAEL DOWNEY; Rev. THOMAS P. RAUSCH, S.J.; Sr. KAREN WILHELMY, C.S.J., M.A., Sec. Tel: 661-944-2178.

Members—Revs. RICHARD B. BENSON, C.M., S.T.D.; JOHN P. BRENNAN, S.M.A., S.T.D.; Most Rev. EDWARD W. CLARK, D.D., S.T.D.; Rev. FRANCIS R. COLBORN, V.F., S.T.D.; Rev. Msgr. CRAIG A. COX, J.C.D.; ELIZABETH ANNE DUNN, Ph.D.; Rev. LUKE DYSINGER, O.S.B., M.D., D.Phil.; PAUL F. FORD, Ph.D.; Rev. Msgr. HELMUT HEFNER, J.C.L., S.T.D.; Sr. MARY MCKAY, C.S.J., Ph.D.

Victim Assistance Coordinator—Sr. SHEILA MCNIFF, S.H.C.J. Tel: 800-355-2545 (Hotline); 213-637-7650 (Office). Email: srsmcniff@la-archdiocese.org.

CLERGY, PARISHES, MISSIONS AND PAROCHIAL SCHOOLS

CITY OF LOS ANGELES
(Los Angeles County)

1—Cathedral of Our Lady of the Angels (2002), His Eminence Roger Cardinal Mahony, K.G.C.H.S.; Rev. Msgrs. Kevin J. Kostelnik; Terrance L. Fleming, V.G., S.T.D.; Rev. Brian Castaneda; Rev. Msgr. Paul M. Albee; Deacon Manny Martinez.
Church: 555 W. Temple St., 90012. Tel: 213-680-5200; Fax: 213-620-1982.

2—St. Agatha (1923), Rev. Ken Deasy.
Res.: 2646 S. Mansfield Ave., 90016. Tel: 323-935-8127; Fax: 323-939-3547.
Catechesis/Religious Program—Tel: 323-933-0963. Students 400.

3—St. Agnes (1903), (Hispanic—Korean), Revs. James Franck, C.PP.S.; John Franck, C.PP.S.; Youngmin Choi, S.J. (SFR).
Res.: 2625 S. Vermont Ave., 90007. Tel: 323-731-2464; Fax: 323-731-6186.
School—Fax: 323-735-7719. Lay Teachers 10; Students 303.
Catechesis/Religious Program—Mrs. Miriam Oliva, D.R.E. Students 410.

4—All Saints (1926), (Hispanic), Revs. Jose L. Vega, O.M.; Gino Vanzillotta, O.M.; Mario Pisano, O.M.; Deacon Pedro Rojas.
Rectory—3431 Portola Ave., 90032-2215. Tel: 323-223-1101; Fax: 323-223-9592.
School—3420 Portola Ave., 90032. Tel: 323-225-7264; Fax: 323-225-1240. Sisters 1; Lay Teachers 9; Students 208.
Catechesis/Religious Program—Tel: 323-225-5193; Fax: 323-225-5193. Students 175.

5—St. Aloysius Gonzaga (1908), (Hispanic), [CEM] Revs. George Aguilera; William J. Delaney, C.PP.S.
Res.: 7814 Crocket Blvd., 90001. Tel: 323-585-4485; Fax: 323-589-8485.
School—Tel: 323-582-4965; Fax: 323-585-4938. Selva Speights, Prin. Lay Teachers 9; Students 306.
Catechesis/Religious Program—2023 E. Nadeau St.. Tel: 323-277-7824. Students 273.

6—St. Alphonsus (1935), (Hispanic), Revs. Jesse C. Galaz, V.F.; Enrique De Los Rios; Hugo R. Neyra.
Res.: 5223 Hastings St., 90022-2625. Tel: 323-264-3353; Fax: 323-264-4858.
School—Tel: 323-268-5165; Fax: 323-268-7784. Lay Teachers 12; Students 266.
Catechesis/Religious Program—552 South Amalia Ave., 90022. Tel: 323-266-0855. Students 585.

7—St. Anastasia (1953), Rev. Thomas F. King; Rev. Msgr. Royale M. Vadakin, V.G In Res., Rev. Msgr. Gregory A. Cox, M.S.W., M.B.A.
Res.: 7390 W. Manchester Ave., 90045. Tel: 310-670-2243; Fax: 310-670-5052.
School—8631 S. Stanmoor Dr., 90045. Tel: 310-645-8816; Fax: 310-645-6923. Mrs. Rosemary Connolly, Prin. Lay Teachers 21; Students 303.
Catechesis/Religious Program—Students 220.

8—St. Ann (1937), Rev. Hugh Crowe; Rev. Msgr. John R. Brosnan, Pastor Emeritus (Retired).
Office:—1365 Blake Ave., 90031. Tel: 323-221-6368.
Res.: 2302 Riverdale Ave., 90031. Fax: 323-222-6871.
Catechesis/Religious Program—Tel: 323-222-9749. Ramona Lopez, D.R.E. Students 125.

9—St. Anselm (1924), Rev. Lawrence Shelton.
Res.: 2222 W. 70th St., 90043. Tel: 323-758-6729; Fax: 323-758-8455.
School—7019 S. Van Ness Ave., 90043. Tel: 323-759-9371; Fax: 323-759-1131. Lay Teachers 7; Students 170.
Catechesis/Religious Program—Students 87.

10—St. Anthony (1910), (Croatian), [CEM] Rev. Mate Bizaca, Admin.; Rev. Msgr. Felix S. Diomartich, Pastor Emeritus (Retired).
Res.: 712 N. Grand Ave., 90012. Tel: 213-628-2938; Fax: 213-628-1635.
Catechesis/Religious Program—Students 90.

11—Ascension (1923), (Hispanic—African American), Rev. David John Ayotte, Admin.
Res.: 517 W. 112th St., 90044. Tel: 323-754-2978; Fax: 323-754-3905.
School—500 W. 111th Pl., 90044. Tel: 323-756-4064; Fax: 323-756-1060. Lisa Cruz, Prin. Lay Teachers 9; Students 264.
Catechesis/Religious Program—Tel: 323-777-6356. Students 475.

12—Assumption (1926), (Hispanic), Rev. Gustavo J. Ramon (Cuba). In Res., Rev. Diosdado Martin.
Res.: 2832 Blanchard St., 90033. Tel: 323-269-8171; Fax: 323-269-0106.
School—3016 Winter St., 90063. Tel: 323-269-4319; Fax: 323-269-2434. Ms. Lydia Ortega, Devel. Dir.; Carolina Gomez, Prin. Lay Teachers 8; Students 182.
Catechesis/Religious Program—Tel: 213-269-5920; Fax: 323-269-7786. Students 182.
Mission—Assumption 414 N. Fresno St., Old Co. 90063.

13—St. Basil's (1920), [CEM] Rev. Msgr. Charles Hill; Rev. Phillip Pak (Korea, South). In Res., Rev. Msgr. Terrence Richey; Rev. Jerome Bouska (Retired).
Res.: 637 S. Kingsley Dr., 90005. Tel: 213-381-6191; Fax: 213-382-5883.
Catechesis/Religious Program—Students 185.

14—St. Bernadette (1947), (African American), Revs. Patrick J. Gorman, Pastor Emeritus; Allan Roberts; Deacon Emile Adams.
Res.: 3825 Don Felipe Dr., 90008. Tel: 323-293-4877; Fax: 323-293-2838.
School—4196 Marlton Ave., 90008. Tel: 323-291-4284; Fax: 323-291-0839. Sr. Joan Mary O'Dwyer, C.S.J., Prin. Sisters 3; Lay Teachers 11; Students 210.
Catechesis/Religious Program—Students 38.

15—St. Bernard (1924), Revs. Gerald McSorley; Armando P. Ibanez, O.P.; Rev. Msgr. Patrick McNulty, Pastor Emeritus. In Res., Rev. John W. Sigler.
Res.: 2500 W. Ave. 33, 90065. Tel: 323-255-6142; Fax: 323-255-2351.
School—Tel: 323-256-4989; Fax: 323-256-4963. Sisters of Charity of the Blessed Virgin Mary 2; Lay Teachers 9; Students 275.
Catechesis/Religious Program—2515 W. Ave. 33, 90065. Tel: 323-256-6242. Students 350.

16—Blessed Sacrament (1924), Revs. Michael J. Mandala, S.J.; John J. Brennan, S.J.; James R. Gallas, S.J.; Thomas F. McCormick, S.J.; Sebastian C. Elanjimannil, S.J. (India); Yolanda Lichtman, Dir. Social Svcs. Tel: 323-871-8042; Fax: 323-464-7796.
Res.: 6657 Sunset Blvd., 90028. Tel: 323-462-6311; Fax: 323-462-0113.
School—6641 Sunset Blvd., 90028. Tel: 323-467-4177; Fax: 323-467-6099. Lay Teachers 14; Students 240.
Catechesis/Religious Program—Tel: 323-463-9820. Sr. Virginia Cipres, E.I.N., D.R.E. Students 330.

17—St. Brendan (1915), Rev. Msgr. Terrance L. Fleming, V.G., S.T.D.; Revs. Albert J. DiUlio, S.J.; Al Diulio, S.J.; Sr. Judy Molosky, C.S.J., Pastoral Admin.
Res.: 310 S. Van Ness Ave., 90020. Tel: 323-936-4656; Fax: 323-936-9058.
School—238 S. Manhatten Pl., 90004. Tel: 213-382-7401; Fax: 213-382-8918. Sisters 1; Lay Teachers 17; Students 315.
Catechesis/Religious Program—Kathy Russell, D.R.E. Students 79.

18—St. Bridget's Chinese Catholic Center (1940), (Chinese), [JC] Rev. Joseph Cheng, S.D.B. (China), Admin.
Res.: 450 Cottage Home St., 90012. Tel: 323-222-5518; Fax: 323-222-0814.
Church: 510 Cottage Home, 90012-1418.
Catechesis/Religious Program—Students 80.

19—St. Brigid's (1920), (African American—Hispanic), Revs. Robert M. Kearns, S.S.J. (BAL); Michael Ume; Deacons Gilbert Lanoix; William Hawkins Jr.; John Turner.
Res.: 5214 S. Western Ave., 90062. Tel: 323-292-0781; Fax: 323-290-1254.
Catechesis/Religious Program—Students 174.

20—St. Camillus De Lellis (1954),, (Center for Pastoral Care). Rev. Christopher D. Ponnet, Dir. & Chap.; His Eminence Roger Cardinal Mahony, K.G.C.H.S.; Rev. Robert J. Jones, C.M., Chap.; Sisters Nancy Bartasavich, S.P., Chap.; Dora Hauchecorne, I.C.M., Chap.; Patricia Krommer, C.S.J., Chap.; Mary Jean Ferry, B.V.M., Chap.; Estelle Marie Kroeger, C.S.J., Chap.; Angela Pacheco, C.S.J., Chap.; Deacon Walter Hanson, Chap.; Rev. James Huang, S.V.D. (PIT), Chap.; Mr. Luis Manuel Torres, Chap.
Res.: 1911 Zonal Ave., 90033-1032. Tel: 323-225-4461; Fax: 323-225-9096.
HIV/AIDS Ministry Center for Archdiocese of Los Angeles—
Catholics Against the Death Penalty Center—Tel: 323-223-9047.

21—St. Casimir (1946), (Lithuanian), Rev. Msgrs. Algirdas Olsaukas, Pastor Emeritus; John A. Kucingis, Pastor Emeritus (Retired); Rev. Stanislovas Anuzis, Admin.
Res.: 2718 St. George St., 90027. Tel: 323-664-4660; Fax: 323-664-8729.
School—2716 St. George St., 90027. Tel: 323-661-9200; Fax: 323-668-1440. Lay Teachers 9; Students 255.
Catechesis/Religious Program—Tel: 818-248-4046. Students 125.

22—Cathedral Chapel (1927), Revs. Charles L. Schwehr; Earl G. Walker, Pastor Emeritus (Retired).
Church: 927 S. La Brea Ave., 90036.
Res.: 922 S. Detroit St., 90036. Tel: 323-935-1128; Fax: 323-935-7308.
School—755 S. Cochran Ave., 90036. Tel: 323-938-9976; Fax: 323-938-9930. Lay Teachers 10; Students 270.
Catechesis/Religious Program—Students 50.

23—St. Cecilia (1909), (African American—Hispanic), Revs. Xavier Colleoni, M.C.C.J.; Francis Abel Modi, M.C.C.J. (Sudan); Robert Kleiner, M.C.C.J.; Paul O'Donnell, M.C.C.J.
Res.: 4230 S. Normandie Ave., 90037. Tel: 323-294-6628; Fax: 323-294-3310.
School—4224 S. Normandie Ave., 90037. Tel: 323-293-4266; Fax: 323-293-5556. Lay Teachers 9; Students 300.
Catechesis/Religious Program—Students 460.

24—Christ the King (1926), Rev. Antonio Cacciapuoti. In Res., Rev. Charles Chaffman.
Res.: 624 N. Rossmore Ave., 90004. Tel: 323-465-7605; Fax: 323-463-4895.
School—617 N. Arden Blvd., 90004. Tel: 323-462-4753; Fax: 323-462-8475. Lay Teachers 9; Students 245.
Catechesis/Religious Program—Tel: 323-465-7084. Students 375.

25—St. Columban (1945), (Filipino), Rev. Colm Rafferty, S.S.C., Admin.; Deacon Felix Dumlao. In Res., Rev. Sean John McGrath, S.S.C.
Res.: 125 S. Loma Dr., 90026. Tel: 213-250-8818; Fax: 213-250-8818.
Catechesis/Religious Program—Students 60.

26—St. Columbkille (1921), (Hispanic—African American), Rev. Msgr. Timothy J. Dyer, V.F.; Rev. Mario Torres. In Res., Rev. James Forsen.
Res.: 6315 S. Main St., 90003. Tel: 323-758-5540; Fax: 323-758-8108.
School—145 W. 64th St., 90003. Tel: 323-758-2284; Fax: 323-750-7141. Sisters 1; Lay Teachers 8; Students 290.
Catechesis/Religious Program—Tel: 323-789-3344. Students 530.

27—Cristo Rey (1954), (Hispanic), [CEM] Revs. Jose Antonio Arias, O.A.R. (Mexico) (NEW); Euben Capacillo, O.A.R. In Res., Rev. Anthony Iroz, O.A.R.
Res.: 4343 Perlita Ave., 90039. Tel: 323-245-4585; Fax: 818-247-8831.
Catechesis/Religious Program—Students 300.

28—Divine Saviour (1907), (Hispanic), Revs. Thomas Boudreau; Miguel Plascencia.
Res.: 610 Cypress Ave., 90065. Tel: 323-225-9181; Fax: 323-225-1099.
School—Tel: 323-222-6077; Fax: 323-225-1099. Lay Teachers 9; Students 277.
Catechesis/Religious Program—Alice Perez, D.R.E. Students 1,300.

29—Dolores Mission (1945), (Hispanic), Rev. Michael E. Kennedy, S.J.; Mr. Eddy Martinez, Business Mgr. In Res., Revs. Robert Dolan, S.J.; Gregory Boyle, S.J.
Res.: 171 S. Gless St., 90033. Tel: 323-881-0039 (Church); Fax: 323-881-0034.
School—Tel: 323-881-0001; Fax: 323-881-0003. Sr. Pat Reinhart, P.B.V.M., Prin. Lay Teachers 9; Students 241.
Catechesis/Religious Program—Sr. Giulii Zobelein, O.P., D.R.E. Students 170.

30—St. Dominic (1921), Very Revs. Raymond Finerty, O.P.; Gerald Buckley, O.P.; Rev. Vincent Foerstier, O.P. (PHX); Bro. Pasquale Manalio, O.P. In Res., Rev. Martin de Porres Walsh, O.P.; Bro. Gregory Lira, O.P.
Res.: 2002 Merton Ave., 90041. Tel: 323-254-2519; Fax: 323-255-3067.
School—Tel: 323-255-5803; Fax: 323-255-2817. Bro. Frederick Narberes, O.P., Prin. Dominican Sisters of San Rafael 1; Lay Teachers 24; Students 445.
Catechesis/Religious Program—Tel: 323-255-6373. Students 184.

31—St. Eugene (1942), (African American), Revs. Sabas N. Mallya; Joseph Barita.
Res.: 9505 Haas Ave., 90047. Tel: 323-757-3121; Fax: 323-757-8872.
School—9521 Haas Ave., 90047. Tel: 323-754-9536; Fax: 323-754-0913. Lay Teachers 11; Students 180.
Catechesis/Religious Program—Students 20.

32—Former Cathedral of St. Vibiana (1876), Closed., For inquiries for Sacramental Records contact 555 W. Temple St., Los Angeles, CA 90012.

33—St. Frances Xavier Cabrini (1946), (African American—Latino), Revs. David O'Connell; Anthony Gonzalez, Pastoral Admin.
Res.: 1440 W. Imperial Hwy., 90047. Tel: 323-757-0271; Fax: 323-757-9267.
School—1428 W. Imperial Hwy., 90047. Tel: 323-756-1354; Fax: 323-756-1157. Sr. Carol Ward, O.P., Prin. Dominican Sisters 3; Lay Teachers 9; Students 260.
Catechesis/Religious Program—Tel: 323-756-8111. Students 664.

34—St. Francis of Assisi (1920), Revs. Daniel Barica, O.F.M.; Alvin Cachola, O.F.M.

Res.: 1523 Golden Gate Ave., 90026. Tel: 323-664-1305; Fax: 323-664-4975.
School—1550 Maltman Ave., 90026. Tel: 323-665-3601; Fax: 323-665-4143. Sisters of Notre Dame 1; Lay Teachers 9; Students 251.
Catechesis/Religious Program—Tel: 323-662-3545. Students 149.

35—ST. GERARD MAJELLA (1952), Revs. Martin Slaughter; Caesar Raffo; Deacon Ricardo Flores. In Res., Rev. Pius Itodo (Nigeria).
Res.: 4439 Inglewood Blvd., 90066 Tel: 310-390-5034; Fax: 310-397-0964.
School—Tel: 310-397-9489; Fax: 310-398-2081. Lay Teachers 8; Students 219.
Catechesis/Religious Program—Tel: 310-391-9637. Students 600; Preschool 10.

36—ST. GREGORY NAZIANZEN (1923), Revs. Edward J. Johnson; Alex Chung.
Res.: 900 S. Bronson Ave., 90019. Tel: 323-935-4224; Fax: 323-934-0016.
School—Tel: 323-936-2542; Fax: 323-936-1690. Zulay Chavez, Prin. Religious 1; Lay Teachers 9; Students 259.
Catechesis/Religious Program—Tel: 323-935-4701. Irene Rodriguez, D.R.E. Students 174.

37—HOLY CROSS (1906), (African American—Hispanic), Revs. Paul O'Donnell, M.C.C.J.; Baltazar Zaratc (Mexico); Bro. Robert Strabla, M.C.C.J. (Italy).
Res.: 4705 S. Main St., 90037. Tel: 323-234-5984; Fax: 323-234-0130.
Catechesis/Religious Program—Tel: 323-235-8360. Students 879.

38—HOLY NAME OF JESUS (1921), (African American), Rev. Gregory C. Chisholm, S.J.; Deacons Hosea Alexander; Alejandro Marin.
Res.: 2190 W. 31st St., 90018. Tel: 323-734-8888; Fax: 323-734-8430.
School—Tel: 323-731-2255; Fax: 323-730-0321. Mrs. Marva Belisle, Prin. Lay Teachers 9; Students 285.
Catechesis/Religious Program—Students 175.

39—HOLY SPIRIT (1926), Rev. Paul A. Sustayta.
Res.: 1425 S. Dunsmuir Ave., 90019-4031. Tel: 323-935-1333; Fax: 323-935-7741.
School—(Grades K-4), 1418 S. Burnside Ave., 90019. Tel: 323-933-7775; Fax: 323-933-7453. Sisters of the Holy Faith 2; Lay Teachers 4; Students 120.
Catechesis/Religious Program—Students 448.

40—HOLY TRINITY (1925), (Filipino—Hispanic), Revs. Thomas Peacha; James E. McElroy; John Daly, Pastor Emeritus; Theodore Jang, Pastoral Assoc.; Deacon Roland Bavtista.
Res.: 3722 Boyce Ave., 90039. Tel: 323-664-4723; Fax: 323-664-2581.
School—3716 Boyce Ave., 90039. Tel: 323-663-2064; Fax: 323-663-0732. Lay Teachers 11; Students 240.
Catechesis/Religious Program—Tel: 626-793-2901. Students 180.

41—ST. IGNATIUS OF LOYOLA (1911), Rev. Arturo Velasco.
Res.: 322 N. Ave. 61, 90042. Tel: 323-256-3041; Fax: 323-256-0105.
School—6025 Monte Vista St., 90042. Tel: 323-255-6456; Fax: 323-255-0959. Dominican Sisters, San Jose Mission 3; Lay Teachers 10; Students 279.
Catechesis/Religious Program—Tel: 323-254-9073; Fax: 323-254-9073. Students 665.

42—IMMACULATE CONCEPTION (1908), (Hispanic), Revs. Pedro E. Amezcua (Mexico); Francisco Alanis; Rafael Ochoa (Mexico); Silvino Torres.
Res.: 1433 James M. Wood Blvd., 90015. Tel: 213-384-1019; Fax: 213-384-0437. Email: dimmaconc@aol.com.
School—830 Green St., 90017. Tel: 213-382-5931; Fax: 213-382-4563. Ms. Mary Ann Murphy, Prin. Lay Teachers 12; Students 295.
Catechesis/Religious Program—832 Green Ave., 90017. Tel: 213-389-7277. Students 218.

43—IMMACULATE HEART OF MARY (1910), Revs. Rodel G. Balagtas; Sergio Renteria Sanchez (Mexico); Deacon George Asmar. In Res., Rev. Mateo Hicarte.
Res.: 4954 Santa Monica Blvd., 90029. Tel: 323-660-0034; Fax: 323-660-0047.
School—1055 N. Alexandria Ave., 90029. Tel: 323-663-4611; Fax: 323-663-6216. Sisters 1; Lay Teachers 9; Students 302.
Catechesis/Religious Program—4954 W. Santa Monica Blvd., 90029. Tel: 323-668-1704. Students 250.

44—ST. JEROME (1949), Rev. Msgr. Norman F. Priebe; Revs. Peter Burns, S.J.; Gaspar J. Mtengetse. In Res., Rev. Abraham Jacob (CHI).
Res.: 5550 Thornburn St., 90045. Tel: 310-348-8212; Fax: 310-417-3577.
School—Tel: 310-670-1678; Fax: 310-670-1678. Sisters of St. Joseph of Carondelet 2; Lay Teachers 14; Students 287.
Catechesis/Religious Program—Tel: 310-645-8318; Fax: 310-645-8318. Students 316.
Convent—5570 Thornburn St., 90045. Tel: 310-670-8838.

45—ST. JOAN OF ARC (1943), (Spanish), Revs. James H. Barnes; Frederick Byaruhanga (Uganda). In Res., Rev. Michael Tang.
Res.: 11534 Gateway Blvd., 90064. Tel: 310-479-5111; Fax: 310-479-2513.
School—11561 Gateway Blvd., 90064. Tel: 310-479-3607; Fax: 310-478-1398. Lay Teachers 9; Students 183.
Catechesis/Religious Program—Tel: 310-479-1490. Students 211.

46—ST. JOHN, THE EVANGELIST (1909), (Hispanic—African American), Revs. Melvin P. James, S.V.D.; Ignacio Estrada, S.V.D.; Deacon Willard Hall. In Res., Rev. Fisher Robinson, S.V.D.; Bro. Richard Morrell, S.V.D.
Res.: 6028 Victoria Ave., 90043. Tel: 323-758-9161; Fax: 323-758-0112.
School—Tel: 323-751-8545; Fax: 323-751-1651. B. Flowers, Prin. Lay Teachers 9; Students 230.
Catechesis/Religious Program—Students 97.

47—ST. JOSEPH (1888), (Hispanic), Rev. Rafael Casillas, Admin.
Res.: 218 E. 12th St., 90015. Tel: 213-748-5394; Fax: 213-748-4793.
School—Tel: 213-749-8894; Fax: 213-749-0424. Sr. Jean Marie Chavez, O.S.F., Prin. Sisters 2; Lay Teachers 10; Students 252.
Catechesis/Religious Program—Tel: 213-748-5394, Ext. 106. Students 285.
Mission—St. Turibius 1524 Essex, Los Angeles Co. 90021. Tel: 213-749-8894; Fax: 213-749-0424.

48—ST. KEVIN (1923), (Hispanic—Filipino), Rev. Leo E. Steinbock. In Res., Rev. Ramon R. Andreu, S.J. (Spain).
Res.: 4072 Beverly Blvd., 90004. Tel: 213-383-8206; Fax: 213-386-4390.
Catechesis/Religious Program—Students 174.

49—ST. LAWRENCE OF BRINDISI (1908), (African American—Hispanic),, Capuchin Franciscan Friary. Revs. Peter Banks, O.F.M.Cap.; James L. Cleary, O.F.M.Cap.; Robert Barbato, O.F.M. Cap.
Res.: 10122 Compton Ave., 90002. Tel: 323-567-1439; Fax: 323-564-4050.
School—10044 Compton Ave., 90002. Tel: 323-564-3051. Sisters of Notre Dame 4; Lay Teachers 9; Students 295.
Catechesis/Religious Program—Tel: 323-567-4698. Students 295.

50—ST. LUCY (1981), (Hispanic), [CEM] Revs. Miguel Mascorro, Sch.P.; Frank Boronat, Sch.P.
Res.: 1419 N. Hazard Ave., 90063. Tel: 323-266-0451; Fax: 323-266-4907.
Catechesis/Religious Program—Tel: 323-266-0456.

51—ST. MALACHY (1926), (Hispanic), Revs. William J. Bonner; Mario Arellano, S.J.
Res.: 1221 E. 82nd St., 90001. Tel: 323-585-1437; Fax: 323-583-5391.
School—1220 E. 81st St., 90001. Tel: 323-582-3112; Fax: 323-582-9340. Lay Teachers 8; Students 261.
Catechesis/Religious Program—Tel: 323-582-0203. Sr. Virginia Sandoval, M.J.C., D.R.E. Students 550.
Convent—Missionaries of Jesus Crucified St. Malachy Convent, 1228 E. 81st St., 90001. Tel: 323-582-2992. Sisters 6.

52—ST. MARCELLINUS (1957), Rev. Jules A. Mayer.
Res.: 2349 Strong Ave., 90040. Tel: 323-269-2733.
Catechesis/Religious Program—Tel: 323-266-4938. Students 185.

53—ST. MARTIN OF TOURS (1946), Rev. Michael S. Grieco, Admin.; Rev. Msgr. Lawrence O'Leary, Pastor Emeritus (Retired); Rev. Donal Keohane (Ireland).
Res.: 11967 Sunset Blvd., 90049. Tel: 310-476-7403; Fax: 310-476-0290.
Church: 11967 Sunset Blvd., 90049.
School—Tel: 310-472-7419; Fax: 310-440-2298. Sisters 1; Lay Teachers 20; Students 248.
Catechesis/Religious Program—Tel: 310-472-1757. Students 74.

54—ST. MARY (1886), Revs. Joseph A. Farias, S.D.B.; Avelino Lorenzo, S.D.B.; Robert Stein, S.D.B.
Res.: 407 S. Chicago St., 90033. Tel: 323-263-7432; Fax: 323-268-8076.
School—(Grades K-8) Tel: 323-262-3395; Fax: 323-262-4738. Daughters of Mary Help of Christians 4; Lay Teachers 10; Students 306.
Catechesis/Religious Program—Tel: 323-268-2351. Students 370.

55—ST. MARY MAGDALEN (1930), Rev. Paul A. Sustagta, Admin., (Retired); Rev. Msgr. Ambrose Nwohu; Rev. Justin Mbonu.
Res.: 1241 Corning St., 90035. Tel: 310-652-2444; Fax: 310-652-4885.
School—Tel: 310-652-4723. Sisters of the Holy Faith 1; Lay Teachers 6; Students 141.
Catechesis/Religious Program—Students 48.

56—MARYKNOLL JAPANESE CATHOLIC CENTER (1921), (Japanese), Revs. David L. Doerner, S.A., Admin.; Ignatius Hideaki Takii, Pastoral Assoc.
Res.: 222 S. Hewitt St., 90012. Tel: 213-626-2279; Fax: 213-628-1757.
Catechesis/Religious Program—Students 65.
Chapel—St. Francis Xavier

57—ST. MICHAEL (1907), (Hispanic—African American), Rev. Msgr. David O'Connell.
Res.: 1016 W. Manchester Ave., 90044. Tel: 323-753-2696; Fax: 323-753-3475.
School—(Grades K-8), 1027 W. 87th St., 90044. Tel: 323-752-6101. Dominican Sisters of Mission San Jose 2; Lay Teachers 8; Students 240.
Catechesis/Religious Program—Tel: 323-753-2976. Students 250.

58—MOTHER OF SORROWS (1923), (Hispanic—African American), Revs. R. Dario Miranda; Martin Eduardo Hernandez Baeza (Mexico).
Res.: 114 W. 87th St., 90003. Tel: 323-758-7697; Fax: 323-758-7853.
School—Tel: 323-758-6204; Fax: 323-758-6203. Sr. Martha Garcia, D.C., Prin. Lay Teachers 12; Students 230.
Catechesis/Religious Program—Tel: 323-789-6316. Alejandra Arenas, D.R.E. Students 587.

59—NATIVITY (1920), (Hispanic—African American), Rev. Msgr. Timothy J. Dyer, V.F.; Rev. Mario Torres.
Res.: 953 W. 57th St., 90037. Tel: 323-759-1562; Fax: 323-759-7716.
School—Tel: 323-752-0720; Fax: 323-752-1945. Lay Teachers 8; Students 320.
Catechesis/Religious Program—Tel: 323-752-1770. Students 1,080.
Loretto Literary & Benevolent Institution—

60—NATIVITY OF BLESSED VIRGIN MARY (1947), (Ukranian—Byzantine), Rev. Myron Mykyta (SD).
Res.: 5154 De Longpre Ave., 90027. Tel: 323-663-6307; Fax: 323-663-0369.

61—ST. ODILIA (1926), (Hispanic—African American), Rev. Francis Eldridge, S.A.
Res.: 5222 Hooper Ave., 90011-4807. Tel: 323-232-8677; Fax: 323-231-9714.
School—5300 S. Hooper Ave., 90011. Tel: 323-232-5449; Fax: 323-233-6154. Ms. Sharon E. Oliver, Prin. Lay Teachers 9; Students 300.
Catechesis/Religious Program—Tel: 323-233-2651. Students 300.
Mission—St. John Bosco 5516 Duarte St., Los Angeles Co. 90058. Tel: 323-581-3345.

62—OUR LADY HELP OF CHRISTIANS (MARIA AUXILIADORA) (1923), (Hispanic), Revs. Miguel Hascorro, Sch.P; Martin Madero, Sch.P.; Romualdo Gonzalez, Sch.P.; Jose Maria Ordorica, Sch.P. In Res., Rev. Manuel Sanahuja.
Res.: 512 S. Ave. 20, 90031. Tel: 323-223-4153; Fax: 323-223-1427.
School—2024 Darwin Ave., 90031. Tel: 323-222-3913; Fax: 323-222-2561. Sr. Esthela Gonzales, M.C., Prin. Poor Clare Missionary Sisters 4; Lay Teachers 7; Students 313.
Catechesis/Religious Program—Tel: 323-225-2846. Students 100.

63—OUR LADY OF GUADALUPE (1923), (Hispanic), Revs. J. Rigoberto Rodriguez; Moises Apolinar.
Res.: 4018 Hammel St., 90063. Tel: 323-261-8051; Fax: 323-261-1259.
School—436 Hazard Ave., 90063. Tel: 323-269-4998; Fax: 323-780-7001. Lay Teachers 12; Students 260.
Catechesis/Religious Program—Tel: 323-262-7957. Students 509.
Mission—San Felipe 738 N. Geraghty Ave., Los Angeles Co. 90063. Tel: 213-266-1433; Fax: 323-261-1259.

64—OUR LADY OF GUADALUPE (Rosehill) (1928), (Hispanic), Revs. Thomas E. Baker; Tulio Maya, S.D.S.; Deacon Miguel Arroyo.
Res.: 4509 Mercury Ave., 90032. Tel: 323-225-4201; Fax: 323-225-3668.
School—4504 Browne Ave., 90032. Tel: 323-221-8187. Missionary Sisters of the Immaculate Heart of Mary 1; Lay Teachers 8; Students 220.
Catechesis/Religious Program—Tel: 323-223-1777. Students 271.

65—OUR LADY OF GUADALUPE SANCTUARY (1929), (Hispanic), Rev. Leslie N. Delgado (Panama).
Res.: 4100 E. Second St., 90063. Tel: 323-261-4365; Fax: 323-261-2735.
Catechesis/Religious Program—Students 317.

66—OUR LADY OF LORETTO (1905), Revs. German Rodriguez Llamas, S.V.D. (Mexico); Dominic Hoan Nguyen, C.M., Vietnamese Ministry.
Res.: 250 N. Union Ave., 90026. Tel: 213-483-3013; Fax: 213-484-0187.
School—258 N. Union Ave., 90026. Tel: 213-483-5251; Fax: 213-463-6709. Lay Teachers 12; Students 260.
Catechesis/Religious Program—Tel: 213-483-8137. Students 300.

67—OUR LADY OF LOURDES (1910), Revs. Eamonn Donnelly, S.V.D.; Richard Casillas, S.V.D.; Gerard O'Doherty, S.V.D.
Res.: 3772 E. Third St., 90063-2408. Tel: 323-526-3800; Fax: 323-526-3807.

School—315 S. Eastman Ave., 90063. Tel: 323-526-3813; Fax: 323-526-3814. Lay Teachers 9; Students 220.
Catechesis/Religious Program—Tel: 323-526-3804. Students 300.

68—OUR LADY OF SOLITUDE (1925), (Hispanic), Revs. Cesar Ibarra, M.S.P.; Alvaro Menino, M.S.P.; Deacon Fernando Aranda Jr.
Res.: 4561 Cesar Chavez Ave., 90022. Tel: 323-269-7248; Fax: 323-269-3600.
School—4545 Dozier St., 90022. Tel: 323-261-1083; Fax: 323-261-5300. Erick von Brockdorff, Prin. Lay Teachers 11; Students 205.
Catechesis/Religious Program—Tel: 323-269-7248, Ext. 22. Students 494.

69—OUR LADY OF THE BRIGHT MOUNT (1925), (Polish), Revs. Edward Mroczynski, S.Chr. (Poland); Bogdan Molenda, S.Chr.
Res.: 3424 W. Adams Blvd., 90018. Tel: 323-734-5249; Fax: 323-734-0046.
Catechesis/Religious Program—Students 160.
Convent—Tel: 323-734-6754. Missionary Sisters of Christ the King (Polonia) 3.

70—OUR LADY OF THE ROSARY OF TALPA (1928), (Spanish), Revs. Francisco Mateos, C.M.; Margarito Severino Martinez; Helios del Cerro, C.M.; Francisco Javier Garcia, C.M. (Mexico).
Res.: 2914 E. Fourth St., 90033. Tel: 323-268-9176; Fax: 323-268-4026.
School—411 S. Evergreen Ave., 90033. Tel: 323-261-0583; Fax: 323-261-0352. Daughters of Charity of St. Vincent de Paul 1; Lay Teachers 9; Students 280.
Catechesis/Religious Program—Tel: 323-264-3345. Students 470.
Convent—427 S. Evergreen St., 90033. Tel: 323-268-7731.
Mission—La Purisima Chapel 3236 Inez St., Los Angeles Co. 90023.

71—OUR LADY OF VICTORY (1966), (Spanish), Rev. Francisco Gomez, S.T.; Bro. Gerardo Oliva Reyna, S.T. In Res., Rev. Norbert Sharon, S.T.
Res.: 1316 S. Herbert Ave., 90023. Tel: 323-268-9502; Fax: 323-780-1719.
Catechesis/Religious Program—1317 S. Herbert Ave., 90023. Tel: 323-262-2101.

72—OUR LADY QUEEN OF MARTYRS, (Armenian), Revs. Raphael Minassian, P.I.A.; Antoine Panossian, P.I.A.
Res.: 1327 Pleasant Ave., 90033. Tel: 323-261-9898; Fax: 323-261-0522.

73—OUR LADY QUEEN OF THE ANGELS (1781), (Spanish), Revs. Dennis G. Gallo, C.M.F.; Steve Niskanen, C.M.F.; Arnold M. Abelardo, C.M.F.; Domingo Zuniga, C.M.F.; Deacon Hernan Ramirez.
Res.: 535 N. Main St., 90012. Tel: 213-629-3101; Fax: 213-629-1951.
Catechesis/Religious Program—Students 455.

74—OUR MOTHER OF GOOD COUNSEL (1925), Revs. Gary E. Sanders, O.S.A.; Walter P. Vogel, O.S.A. In Res., Rev. Thomas W. Behan, O.S.A. (OAK).
Res.: 2060 N. Vermont Ave., 90027. Tel: 323-664-2111; Fax: 323-664-0556.
School—4622 Ambrose Ave., 90027. Tel: 323-664-2131; Fax: 323-664-1906. Mr. Frank D. Crean, Prin. Sisters 1; Lay Teachers 9; Students 284.
Catechesis/Religious Program—Students 370.

75—OUR SAVIOUR CATHOLIC CENTER (1957), Rev. William Messenger.
Res.: 3207 University Ave., 90007. Tel: 213-749-5341; Fax: 213-749-3475.

76—ST. PATRICK (1904), (Hispanic), Rev. Francisco X. Ramirez.
Res.: 1046 E. 34th St., 90011. Tel: 323-234-5963; Fax: 323-234-6725.
Catechesis/Religious Program—Tel: 323-232-5460. Students 610.

77—ST. PAUL (1917), Revs. Gerardo Cabral, M.G.; Antonio Moreno, M.G.
Office—1920 S. Bronson Ave., 90018. Tel: 323-730-9490; Fax: 323-734-5266.
Res.: 4112 W. Washington Blvd., 90018. Tel: 323-730-9491.
School—1908 S. Bronson Ave., 90018. Tel: 213-734-4022; Fax: 323-734-5057. Mrs. Iris Trouillier, Prin.; Sr. Hilda Barrera, Vice Prin. Lay Teachers 8; Students 293.
Catechesis/Religious Program—Tel: 323-731-1784; Fax: 323-731-9157. Students 600.

78—ST. PAUL THE APOSTLE (1928), Revs. Tom Jones, C.S.P., Supr.; Thomas J. Clerkin, C.S.P.; Harold J. Powers, C.S.P.; Paul A. Lannan; Theodore A. Vierra; Edward D. Wrobleski, C.S.P.; Patrick E. Hensy, C.S.P.; James McNulty, C.S.P.; Edward Donovan, C.S.P.; Frank Desiderio, C.S.P.; Brad Schoeberle, C.S.P.; Alan D. Oakes, C.S.P. (AUS); Gregory Apparcel, C.S.P.
Res.: 10750 Ohio Ave., 90024. Tel: 310-474-1527; Fax: 310-474-2897.
School—Tel: 310-474-1588; Fax: 310-474-4272. Daughters of Mary and Joseph 4; Lay Teachers 33; Students 540.
Catechesis/Religious Program—Tel: 310-474-1527, Ext. 241. Students 195.

79—ST. PETER (1904), (Italian), Rev. Giovanni Bizzotto, C.S. In Res., Rev. Guillermo Diaz, C.S.
Res. & Mailing Address: 1039 N. Broadway, 90012-1429. Tel: 323-225-8119; Fax: 323-225-0085.
Mission—San Conrado 1820 Bouett St., Los Angeles Co. 90012. Tel: 323-223-6581.
Scalabrini House of Discernment (Seminary)—Tel: 323-225-4436.
Scalabrini Vocation Center—Tel: 323-225-8027.

80—PRECIOUS BLOOD (1923), Revs. Melchor Villero, M.J., Admin.; Michael Montoya, M.J.
Res.: 435 S. Occidental Blvd., 90057. Tel: 213-389-8439; Fax: 213-389-1951.
School—307 S. Occidental Blvd., 90057. Tel: 213-382-3345; Fax: 213-382-2078. Lay Teachers 12; Students 225.
Catechesis/Religious Program—Tel: 213-382-3906. Students 325.

81—PRESENTATION OF THE MARY (1925), (Hispanic), Revs. Benigno A. Rodriguez; Samuel Crellana; Deacon Valentin Saucedo.
Res.: 6406 Parmelee Ave., 90001. Tel: 323-585-0570; Fax: 323-585-8148.
Catechesis/Religious Program—Students 737.

82—ST. RAPHAEL (1924), (Hispanic—African American), Revs. Tracy O'Sullivan, O.Carm.; Vicente O. Lopez, O.Carm.; Deacon Hernan Ramirez; Mr. Harry Wiley, Dir. African American Ministry.
Res.: 942 W. 70th St., 90044. Tel: 323-758-7100; Fax: 323-758-7134.
School—924 W. 70th St., 90044. Tel: 323-751-2774; Fax: 323-751-1244. Mrs. Barbara Curtis, Prin. Lay Teachers 11; Students 297.
Catechesis/Religious Program—Tel: 213-752-5965; Fax: 323-762-5955. Mrs. Maria Moran, D.R.E. Students 420.

83—RESURRECTION (1923), (Mexican), Rev. Msgr. John T. Moretta; Deacons Richard Fajardo; Hernando Rodriguez.
Res.: 3324 E. Opal St., 90023. Tel: 323-268-1141; Fax: 323-268-1143.
School—3360 E. Opal St., 90023. Tel: 323-261-5750; Fax: 323-261-1463. Carmen O. Hart, Prin. Franciscan Sisters of Mary Immaculate 2; Lay Teachers 10; Students 250.
Catechesis/Religious Program—Tel: 323-264-1963. Students 788.

84—SACRED HEART (1887), (Hispanic), Revs. Alberto Villalobos, Admin.; Robert Victoria; Mr. Fred Flores, Admin. Mgr. In Res., Rev. George Horan.
Res.: 2210 Sichel St., 90031. Tel: 323-221-3179; Fax: 323-221-3613.
School—2109 Sichel St., 90031. Tel: 323-225-4177; Fax: 323-225-2615. Dominican Sisters of Mission San Jose 3; Lay Teachers 9; Students 300.
Catechesis/Religious Program—Tel: 323-223-7571. Students 572.
Convent—2108 Sichel St., 90031. Tel: 323-222-5157.

85—SAN ANTONIO DE PADUA (1926), (Hispanic), Rev. Msgr. Joseph W. Herres.
Res.: 555 N. Fairview Ave., 90033. Tel: 323-225-1301; Fax: 323-225-2534.
School—1500 Bridge St., 90033. Tel: 323-221-6970; Fax: 323-343-9183. Solis Rivas, Prin. Sisters of the Company of Mary 5; Lay Teachers 9; Students 190.
Catechesis/Religious Program—Tel: 323-225-1086. Students 100.

86—SAN CONRADO MISSION (1966),, (See St. Peter, Los Angeles for details.)

87—SAN FRANCISCO CHURCH (1982), (Mexican), [CEM] [JC] Rev. Severiano Castaneda; Deacon Antonio Benjamin Torres.
Res.: 4800 E. Olympic Blvd., 90022. Tel: 323-262-4253; Fax: 323-268-8246.
Catechesis/Religious Program—Tel: 323-261-2447. Students 636.

88—SAN MIGUEL (1927), (Hispanic), Revs. Raul Silva, M.S.C.; Juan Franco, M.S.C. (Mexico) (FRS).
Res.: 2214 E. 108th St., 90059. Tel: 323-569-5951; Fax: 323-567-1850.
School—2270 E. 108th St., 90059. Tel: 323-567-6892; Fax: 323-567-4065. Lay Teachers 8; Students 180.
Catechesis/Religious Program—Students 272.

89—SANTA ISABEL (1948), (Mexican), Revs. Jose Hernandez, M.S.P.; Alvaro Menino, M.S.P.
Res.: 918 S. Soto St., 90023. Tel: 323-268-4065; Fax: 323-268-4180.
School—2424 Whittier Blvd., 90023. Tel: 323-263-3716. School Sisters of Notre Dame 2; Lay Teachers 7; Students 301.
Catechesis/Religious Program—Tel: 323-268-3019; Fax: 323-268-4065. Students 303.
Convent—943 S. Soto St., 90023. Tel: 323-262-1711; 323-264-6556; Fax: 323-526-1655.
Mission—Hermanas Misioneras Servidoras de la Palabra 90023.

90—SANTA TERESITA (1923), (Hispanic), Revs. Miguel Mascorro, Sch.P.; Rafael Lara, Sch.P.
Res.: 2645 Zonal Ave., 90033. Tel: 323-221-2446; Fax: 323-221-2216.
School—(Grades K-8), 2646 Zonal Ave., 90033. Tel: 323-221-1129; Fax: 323-221-6339. Dominican Sisters 3; Lay Teachers 8; Students 263.
Catechesis/Religious Program—Tel: 213-221-2511. Students 249.

91—ST. SEBASTIAN (1924), Rev. Matthew T. Cumberland (JUN).
Res.: 1453 Federal Ave., 90025-2301.
Church: 1425 Federal Ave., 90025.
Parish Center—11607 Ohio Ave., 90025. Tel: 310-478-0136; Fax: 310-479-5121.
School—1430 Federal Ave. W., 90025. Tel: 310-473-3337; Fax: 310-473-3178. Lay Teachers 12; Students 200.
Catechesis/Religious Program—Students 200.

92—ST. STEPHEN (1928), (Hungarian—German), Rev. Hermann-Joseph K. Rettig, O.Praem.
Res.: 3705 Woodlawn Ave., 90011. Tel: 323-234-9246; Fax: 323-234-2455.
Catechesis/Religious Program—Students 231.

93—ST. TERESA OF AVILA (1921), Revs. Alexander Salazar; Engelberto Gammad (Philippines); Thomas W. McLaughlin, Pastor Emeritus (Retired); Deacon Paulino Juarez-Ramirez.
Res.: 2216 Fargo St., 90039. Tel: 323-664-8426; Fax: 323-665-3115.
School—(Grades K-8), 2215 Fargo St., 90039. Tel: 323-662-3777; Fax: 323-662-3420. Lay Teachers 9; Students 300.
Catechesis/Religious Program—Students 215.
Convent—2223 Fargo St., 90039. Tel: 323-661-4284.

94—ST. THOMAS THE APOSTLE (1903), (Hispanic), Revs. Jarlath Cunnane; David Ochoa; Arturo Valadez; Fernando Lopez.
Res.: 1327 S. Mariposa Ave., 90006. Tel: 323-737-3325; Fax: 323-737-2665.
School—Tel: 323-737-4730; Fax: 323-737-6348. Lay Teachers 10; Students 315.
Catechesis/Religious Program—Tel: 323-737-5624; Fax: 323-737-2582. Students 1,136.

95—ST. TIMOTHY (1943), Rev. William J. Brelsford.
Res.: 10425 W. Pico Blvd., 90064. Tel: 310-474-1216; Fax: 310-475-6047.
School—Tel: 310-474-1811; Fax: 310-470-1391. Iselda E. Richmond, Prin. Lay Teachers 13; Students 160.
Catechesis/Religious Program—Students 50.

96—TRANSFIGURATION (1923), (African American), Rev. Richard Martini. In Res., Rev. Michael P. McCullough.
Res.: 2515 W. Martin Luther King Blvd., 90008-2728. Tel: 323-291-1136; Fax: 323-291-8216.
School—4020 Roxton Ave., 90008. Tel: 323-292-3011; Fax: 323-292-1527. Lay Teachers 15; Students 235.
Catechesis/Religious Program—Tel: 323-292-5112. Students 80.

97—ST. VINCENT DE PAUL (1887), (Hispanic), Revs. Antonio Ruiz, C.M.; Michael F. Walsh, C.M.; Johnny Zuluete, C.M.; Bro. Anthony B. Wiedemer, C.M., Admin.
Res.: 621 W. Adams Blvd., 90007. Tel: 213-749-8950; Fax: 213-749-9137.
School—2333 S. Figueroa St., 90007. Tel: 213-748-5367; Fax: 213-748-5347. Sisters 3; Lay Teachers 7; Students 307.
Catechesis/Religious Program—Tel: 213-741-9347. Students 540.
Mission—Santo Nino 601 E. 23rd St., Los Angeles Co. 90011. Tel: 213-748-5246.

98—VISITATION (1943), Rev. Msgr. Timothy O'Connell; Rev. James F. O'Grady, Pastor Emeritus.
Res.: 6561 W. 88th St., 90045. Tel: 310-216-1145; Fax: 310-216-1002.
School—8740 Emerson Ave., 90045. Tel: 310-645-6620; Fax: 310-645-4407. Sisters 1; Lay Teachers 15; Students 257.
Catechesis/Religious Program—Tel: 310-568-9085; Fax: 310-216-4233. Students 200.

OUTSIDE THE CITY OF LOS ANGELES

ALHAMBRA, LOS ANGELES CO.

1—ALL SOULS (1912), Rev. Msgr. William P. O'Toole; Rev. Roberto Jaranilla Jr.
Res.: 17 S. Electric Ave., 91801. Tel: 626-281-0466; Fax: 626-281-2163.
Catechesis/Religious Program—29 S. Electric Ave., 91801. Tel: 626-284-7835. Students 315.

2—ST. THERESE (1924),, (Little Flower) Revs. Matthew Williams, O.C.D.; Jerome Lantry, O.C.D.; Albert Bunsic, O.C.D.
Res.: 510 N. El Molino St., 91801. Tel: 626-282-2744; Fax: 626-282-7560.
School—Tel: 626-289-3364; Fax: 626-284-6700. Lay Teachers 18; Students 315.
Catechesis/Religious Program—Tel: 626-284-0020. Students 75.

3—ST. THOMAS MORE (1948), Revs. Paul F. Menke;

Jeremiah O'Neill, Pastor Emeritus; Mrs. Anna McFee, Business Mgr.; Sisters Margaret Devlin, S.S.C., Pastoral Assoc.; Andrea Johnson, C.S.H., Pastoral Assoc. In Res., Rev. David Loftus.
Res.: 2510 S. Fremont Ave., 91803. Tel: 626-284-8333; Fax: 626-282-4459.
School—Tel: 626-284-5778; Fax: 626-284-3303. Mrs. Judith Jones, Prin.; Mrs. Jennifer Schmidt, Prin. Lay Teachers 13; Students 257.
Catechesis/Religious Program—Tel: 626-457-5302. Mrs. Mary Joslyn, D.R.E. Students 250.

ALTADENA, LOS ANGELES CO.

1—ST. ELIZABETH OF HUNGARY (1918), Revs. Edwin C. Duyshart; Bernard J. Jennings (Retired); Constancio Caberte; Deacon Jose Gallegos; Julliette Marsh-Williams, Pastoral Assoc.
Office:—1879 N. Lake Ave., 91001. Tel: 626-797-1167; Fax: 626-797-9245.
School—1840 N. Lake Ave., 91001. Tel: 626-797-7727; Fax: 626-797-6541. Lay Teachers 15; Students 272.
Catechesis/Religious Program—Students 350.

2—SACRED HEART (1935), Rev. Jerome L. Schmit.
Church: 2889 N. Lincoln Ave., 91001. Tel: 626-794-2046; Fax: 626-794-8315.
Catechesis/Religious Program—Tel: 626-798-6961; Fax: 626-798-2616. Students 600.

ARCADIA, LOS ANGELES CO.

1—ANNUNCIATION (1949), Rev. Eugene Herbert; Deacon Gilbert Chavez. In Res., Rev. Msgr. Roland G. Zimmerman (Retired), Pastor Emeritus; Revs. Ramon Marti, Sch.P.; Michael G. Callahan, M.M. (Retired).
Church Office & Mailing Address: 2701 S. Peck Rd., Monrovia, 91016. Tel: 626-447-6202; Fax: 626-447-9834.
Res.: 1307 E. Longden Ave., 91006.
School—(Grades K-8) Tel: 626-447-8262; Fax: 626-447-3841. Lay Teachers 14; Students 285.
Catechesis/Religious Program—Tel: 626-446-1625. Mrs. Patricia Taylor, D.R.E. Students 214.

2—HOLY ANGELS (1935), Rev. Michael J. Evans; Rev. Msgr. Robert Walsh, Pastor Emeritus; Revs. James J. Kelly; John Hoa Nguyen; Deacon Arnaldo Lopez.
Res.: 370 Campus Dr., 91007. Tel: 626-447-1671; Fax: 626-447-7617.
School—360 Campus Dr., 91007. Tel: 626-447-6312; Fax: 626-447-2843. Lay Teachers 16; Students 325.
Catechesis/Religious Program—Tel: 626-445-2967. Students 450.

ARTESIA, LOS ANGELES CO., HOLY FAMILY (1931), Rev. Msgr. Loreto Gonzales; Revs. Rolly P. Jardiniano; Alex A. Menez (Philippines); Deacon Guadalupe Mejia.
Res.: 18708 S. Clarkdale Ave., 90701. Tel: 562-865-2185; Fax: 562-860-0718.
School—Our Lady of Fatima, 18626 S. Clarkdale Ave., 90701. Tel: 562-865-1621; Fax: 562-860-1091. Lay Teachers 13; Students 260.
Catechesis/Religious Program—Tel: 310-860-5973. Students 836.

AVALON, LOS ANGELES CO., ST. CATHERINE OF ALEXANDRIA (1902), Rev. Paul Alcuin Siebenand.
Res.: Box 735, 90704. Tel: 310-510-0192; Fax: 310-510-8360.
Catechesis/Religious Program—Students 190.

AZUSA, LOS ANGELES CO., ST. FRANCES OF ROME (1908), (Hispanic), [CEM] Revs. David F. Granadino; Michael Sears; Rogue Fernandes.
Res.: 501 E. Foothill Blvd., P.O. Box 637, 91702. Tel: 626-969-1829; Fax: 626-815-2755.
School—734 N. Pasadena Ave., 91702. Tel: 626-334-2018; Fax: 626-815-2760. Lay Teachers 10; Students 226.
Catechesis/Religious Program—508 N. Soldano, 91702. Tel: 626-334-3500. Students 1,295.

BALDWIN PARK, LOS ANGELES CO., ST. JOHN THE BAPTIST (1946), (Hispanic—Filipino), Revs. John G. Montejano; Tony Gomez; Jose A. Ortiz (El Salvador); Eduardo C. Garcia.
Res.: 3848 Stewart Ave., 91706. Tel: 626-960-2795; Fax: 626-960-5085.
School—3870 Stewart Ave., 91706. Tel: 626-337-1421; Fax: 626-337-3733. Sisters of the Love of God 5; Lay Teachers 13; Students 550.
Catechesis/Religious Program—Tel: 626-962-1004. Students 963.
Convent—3963 Baldwin Park Blvd., 91706. Tel: 626-337-0527.

BELL GARDENS, LOS ANGELES CO., ST. GERTRUDE (1938), (Hispanic), Rev. Msgr. Henry Gomez; Rev. Abel Loera; Deacons Chris Vega; Mario Alberto Mejia.
Res.: 7025 Garfield Ave., 90201. Tel: 562-927-4495; Fax: 562-927-5826.
School—6824 Toler Ave., 90201. Tel: 562-927-1216. Salesian Sisters of St. John Bosco 2; Lay Teachers 12; Students 280.
Catechesis/Religious Program—Tel: 562-927-3185. Students 1,256.

BELLFLOWER, LOS ANGELES CO.

1—ST. BERNARD (1923), Revs. Thomas F. Feltz; Philip J. McGrath, Pastor Emeritus; Michael O'Shea (Retired).
Res. 9647 E. Beach St., Box 576, 90706. Tel: 562-867-2337; Fax: 562-867-4863.
School—9626 Park St., 90706. Tel: 562-867-9410; Fax: 310-866-2310. Mrs. Jeanette Cardamone, Prin. Lay Teachers 10; Students 213.
Catechesis/Religious Program—Tel: 562-925-9886. Students 290.

2—ST. DOMINIC SAVIO (1954), Revs. Gael Sullivan, S.D.B.; Zbigniew Baran, S.D.B. (OAK); Ramon Zarate, S.D.B.
Res.: 13400 Bellflower Blvd., 90706. Tel: 562-920-7796; Fax: 562-920-0149.
School—9750 Foster Rd., 90706. Tel: 562-866-3617; Fax: 562-804-6738. Salesian Sisters of St. John Bosco 9; Lay Teachers 11; Students [illegible]69.
Catechesis/Religious Program—Tel: 562-920-7796, Ext. 3[illegible]7. Students 907.

BEVERLY HILLS, LOS ANGELES CO., GOOD SHEPHERD (1924), Rev. Colm O'Ryan. In Res., Rev. George O'Brien.
Res.: 5[illegible]5 N. Bedford Dr., 90210. Tel: 310-285-5425; Fax: 310-285-5433.
School—Tel: 310-275-8601; Fax: 310-275-0366. Terry Miller, Prin. Lay Teachers 10; Students 210.
Catechesis/Religious Program—Tel: 310-271-9745. Students 57.

BURBANK, LOS ANGELES CO.

1—ST. FINBAR (1938), Revs. Albert Bahhuth; Alexander J. Lewis.
Res.: 20[illegible]0 W. Olive Ave., 91506. Tel: 818-846-6251; Fax: 818-846-1703.
School—2120 W. Olive Ave., 91506. Tel: 818-848-0191; Fax: 818-848-4315. Lay Teachers [illegible]0; Students 276.
Catechesis/Religious Program—Tel: 818-846-8715. Students 333.

2—ST. FRANCIS XAVIER (1954), Revs. Richard Albarano; Benny Geroge (India). In Res., Rev. John Murray.
Res.: 380[illegible] Scott Rd., 91504. Tel: 818-504 4400; Fax: 818-767-5096.
School—Tel: 818-504-4422; Fax: 818-504-4424. Lay Teachers 13; Students 309.
Catechesis/Religious Program—Tel: 818-504-4411. Lee Jolly, D.R.E. Students 125.

3—ST. ROBERT BELLARMINE (1907), Rev. Msgrs. Patrick Reilly (Retired); Peter C. Healy (Retired); Rev. Lawrence Signey; Deacon Bruce Sago.
Ministry Center (Offices):—520 E. Orange Grove Ave., 9150[illegible].
Res.: 133 N. Fifth St., 91501. Tel: 818-846-3443; Fax: 818-954-9441.
Church: Fifth St. and E. Orange Grove Ave., 91501.
School—154 N. Fifth St., 91501. Tel: 818-842-5033; Fax: 818-842-9789. Sisters of Providence 1; Lay Teachers 10; Students 342.
Catechesis/Religious Program—Tel: 818-845-3521; Fax: 818-842-3246. Students 471.

CAMARILLO, VENTURA CO.

1—BLESSED JUNIPERO SERRA (1988),, Liturgies celebrated at: Padre Serra Parish, 5205 Upland Rd., Camarillo, CA 93012. Revs. Jarlath Dolan; Varghese Kaitharan; Deacons John Picard; Ludger Gueringer; John Mecozzi; William Spies.
Office & Mailing Address: 5205 Upland Rd. 93012. Tel: 805-482-3417; Fax: 805-987-8100.
Catechesis/Religious Program—Students 533; Preschool 67.

2—ST. MARY MAGDALEN (1940), Rev. James Stehly; Rev. Msgr. John C. Hughes, Pastor Emeritus (Retired); Rev. Alberto Ledesma; Deacons George Bednar; Johnnie Hammonds; Larry Modugno; Eduardo Aguirre. In Res., Rev. John Morgan.
Res.: 2532 Ventura Blvd., 93010. Tel: 805-484-0532; Fax: 805-987-2941.
School—2534 Ventura Blvd., 93010. Tel: 805-482-2611; Fax: 805-987-8211. Lay Teachers 16; Students 302.
Catechesis/Religious Program—Tel: 805-482-1219. Students 325.

CANOGA PARK, LOS ANGELES CO., OUR LADY OF THE VALLEY (1921), Revs. Alden J. Sison; Nelson Trinidad; Sr. Estela del Bando, C.H.S.
Pastoral Center—22021 Gault St., 91303-1804. Tel: 818-592-2880; Fax: 818-592-0299.
School—Tel: 818-592-2894; Fax: 818-592-2896. Lay Teachers 9; Students 260.
Catechesis/Religious Program—Tel: 818-592-2892. Students 695.

CARPINTERIA, SANTA BARBARA CO., ST. JOSEPH (1933), Rev. Adalberto Blanco.
Mailing Address: 5084 El Carro Lane, 93013. Tel: 805-684-2181; Fax: 805-684-0534.
Catechesis/Religious Program—Tel: 805-684-2210. Students 327.
Chapel— 7th & Ash, 93013.

CARSON, LOS ANGELES CO., ST. PHILOMENA (1956), (Filipino), [CEM] Revs. Demetrio Bugayong; Owen de Souza; Doan T. Pham, Carson, CA St. Philomena Church.
Res.: 21900 S. Main St., 90745. Tel: 310-835-7161; Fax: 310-830-5494.
School—Tel: 310-835-4827; Fax: 310-835-1655. Carmelite Sisters 4; Lay Teachers 8; Students 274.
Catechesis/Religious Program—Tel: 310-830-6180; Fax: 310-830-6287. Students 274.
Convent—21832 1/2 S. Main St., 90745. Tel: 310-834-9180.

CHATSWORTH, LOS ANGELES CO., ST. JOHN EUDES (1963), Rev. Msgr. Peter Nugent; Revs. Romeo T. Taguinod; Paul Kottackal (India); Deacon Chet Holly, Admin.
Res.: 10001 Mason Ave., 91311.
Church Office: 9901 Mason Ave., 91311. Tel: 818-341-3680 (Office); Fax: 818-882-4326 (Office).
School—Office, 9925 Mason Ave., 91311. Tel: 818-341-1454; Fax: 818-341-3093. Barbara Danowitz, Prin. Sisters of the Pious Schools 2; Lay Teachers 13; Students 292.
Catechesis/Religious Program—9933 Mason Ave., 91311. Tel: 818-882-9323; Fax: 818-700-5142. Students 897.
Mission—Blessed Alphonsa Catholic Mission, Los Angeles Co.

CLAREMONT, LOS ANGELES CO., OUR LADY OF THE ASSUMPTION (1947), Revs. Thomas Welbers; John Nghi Tran; Paul J. Spellman; Luis Angel Nieto (Mexico); Deacon Arthur Escovedo.
Res.: 435 Berkeley Ave., 91711. Tel: 909-626-3596; Fax: 909-624-3680.
School—Tel: 909-626-7135; Fax: 909-398-1395. Administrators 2; Lay Teachers 22; Students 513.
Catechesis/Religious Program—Tel: 909-624-1360. Students 553; Preschool 40.

COMPTON, LOS ANGELES CO.

1—ST. ALBERT THE GREAT (1949), (Hispanic—African American), [CEM] Rev. Richard Hoynes; Deacons Joseph H. Ledoux; Frank Millholland. In Res., Rev. Cesar Pavon.
Res.: 804 E. Compton Blvd., 90220. Tel: 323-321-0240; 310-329-7548; Fax: 310-329-8462.
School—Tel: 325-770-0984; 310-323-4559; Fax: 310-323-4825. Lay Teachers 17; Students 357.
Catechesis/Religious Program—Tel: 310-323-1599. Arturo Gallardo, D.R.E. Students 480.

2—OUR LADY OF VICTORY (1920), (Hispanic—African American), Revs. Stan Bosch, S.T.; Charles Piatt, S.T.; Roberto Mena, S.T. In Res., Revs. John Seymour, S.T.; Joe Cornely, S.T.
Res.: 519 E. Palmer St., 90221. Tel: 310-631-3233; Fax: 310-886-5681.
School—Tel: 310-631-1320; Fax: 310-631-4280.
Catechesis/Religious Program—Tel: 310-631-1831. Students 500.

3—SAGRADO CORAZON, SACRED HEART (1956), (Hispanic), Revs. Stan Bosch, S.T.; Charles Piatt, S.T.; Roberto Mena, S.T. In Res., Revs. Joseph Cornely, S.T.; John Seymour, S.T.
Res.: 1720 North Culver Ave., 90222. Tel: 310-635-5436; Fax: 310-635-2121.
Catechesis/Religious Program—Tel: 310-635-8483. Students 375.

COVINA, LOS ANGELES CO.

1—ST. LOUISE DE MARILLAC (1963), Rev. Christopher Cunningham; Rev. Msgr. Robert T. Pierce, Pastor Emeritus (Retired); Rev. Lawrence Dowdel Jr.
Mailing Address: 1720 E. Covina Blvd., 91724.
Res.: 1770 E. Covina Blvd., 91724. Tel: 626-915-7873; Fax: 626-332-4431.
School—Tel: 626-966-2317; Fax: 626-967-7947. Lay Teachers 13; Students 308.
Catechesis/Religious Program—Tel: 626-332-5822. Students 715.

2—SACRED HEART (1927), Revs. Brian Cavanagh; Mario Pacheco; Deacons John Horn; Ronald Butler.
Res.: 314 W. Workman St., 91723. Tel: 626-332-3570; Fax: 626-967-4884.
School—360 W. Workman St., 91723. Tel: 626-332-7222; Fax: 626-967-8836. Religious 2; Lay Teachers 15; Students 301.
Catechesis/Religious Program—Tel: 626-331-7914; Fax: 626-966-7165. Students 588.

CUDAHY, LOS ANGELES CO., SAGRADO CORAZON Y SANTA MARIA DE GUADALUPE (1991), (Hispanic), [JC] Revs. Antonio Garnica Lopez, M.S.C.; Hermosillo Lomeli, M.S.C.
4235 Clara St., 90201. Tel: 323-562-3356; Fax: 323-562-3332.
Catechesis/Religious Program—Tel: 323-773-6040.

CULVER CITY, LOS ANGELES CO., ST. AUGUSTINE (1919), Revs. Kevin L. Nolan, V.F.; Ramon Palomera; Richard J. Gleason; Deacon Rafael Victorin. In Res., Rev. Charles Ufomadu (Nigeria).
Res.: 3850 Jasmine Ave., 90232. Tel: 310-838-2477; Fax: 310-838-3070.
School—Tel: 310-838-3144; Fax: 310-838-7479. Daughters of Mary and Joseph 1; Lay Teachers 15; Students 303.

Catechesis/Religious Program—Tel: 310-836-6561; Fax: 310-838-2477. Students 316.

DIAMOND BAR, LOS ANGELES CO., ST. DENIS (1971), Rev. Msgr. James J. Loughnane, V.F.; Revs. Sebastian Vettickal (India); Ikechukuu "I.K." Ikeocha (Nigeria); Deacon Tom Le Donne. In Res., Rev. Donald W. Potthoff, Pastor Emeritus (Retired).
Res.: 2151 S. Diamond Bar Blvd., 91765-2981. Tel: 909-861-7106; Fax: 909-861-2697.
Catechesis/Religious Program—Tel: 909-861-8018. Students 1,311.

DOWNEY, LOS ANGELES CO.
1—OUR LADY OF PERPETUAL HELP (1911), Revs. John Jesus Moloney; Mark Warnstedt; Luis R. Luchetti (Peru); Deacons Charles Denisac; Richard Medina; Carlos Origel.
Res.: 10727 S. Downey Ave., 90241. Tel: 562-923-3246; Fax: 562-862-7020.
School—10441 S. Downey Ave., 90241. Tel: 562-869-9969; Fax: 562-923-0659. Lay Teachers 15; Students 301.
Catechesis/Religious Program—Tel: 562-862-7268; Fax: 562-923-3246. Theresa Nicholas, D.R.E. Students 644.
2—ST. RAYMOND (1956), Revs. Roberto Jaranilla Jr.; John Higgins, Admin.; Donatus Ekenachi (Nigeria); Deacons Ralph Riera; Mario Guerra.
Res.: 12348 Paramount Blvd., 90242. Tel: 562-923-4509; Fax: 562-869-3359.
School—Tel: 562-862-3210; Fax: 562-862-6328. Sisters of Holy Faith 3; Lay Teachers 17; Students 333.
Catechesis/Religious Program—Tel: 562-862-6959. Sr. Paula Strohfus, C.H.F., D.R.E. Students 560.
Mission—Rancho Los Amigos Hospital 7601 Imperial Hwy., Los Angeles Co. 90242. Tel: 562-401-7111.
Mission—Los Padrinos Juvenile Hall 7285 Quill Dr., Los Angeles Co. 90242. Tel: 562-940-8711.

EL MONTE, LOS ANGELES CO.
1—NATIVITY (1923), Revs. Pedro J. Lopez; Guillermo C. Garcia, C.J.; John K. Vo. (Vietnam).
Res.: 3743 N. Tyler Ave., 91731. Tel: 626-444-2511; Fax: 626-443-1417.
School—10907 St. Louis Dr., 91731. Tel: 626-448-2414; Fax: 626-448-2763. Sisters of St. Louis 5; Lay Teachers 8; Students 227.
Catechesis/Religious Program—Tel: 626-448-8895. Students 455.
2—OUR LADY OF GUADALUPE (1973), (Hispanic), Revs. Francisco Vitela; Jesus Castrillo, C.M.F. (Spain).
Res.: 11359 Coffield Ave., 91731. Tel: 626-448-1795; Fax: 626-448-7137.
Catechesis/Religious Program—Tel: 626-448-7131; Fax: 626-448-9507. Students 1,000.

EL SEGUNDO, LOS ANGELES CO.
1—ST. ANDREW (1936), (Russian-Greek), Rev. Alexei R. Smith.
Res.: 538 Concord St., 90245. Tel: 310-322-1892; Fax: 310-322-1919.
Catechesis/Religious Program—Students 15.
2—ST. ANTHONY (1925), Rev. James M. Anguiano; Deacon Richard Pruitt. In Res., Rev. Denis Ssekannyo.
Res.: 710 E. Grand Ave., 90245. Tel: 310-322-4392; Fax: 310-322-0797.
School—233 Lomita St., 90245. Tel: 310-322-4218; Fax: 310-322-2659. Sisters 2; Lay Teachers 10; Students 210.
Catechesis/Religious Program—Tel: 310-615-0766. Students 275.

ENCINO, LOS ANGELES CO.
1—ST. CYRIL (1949), Rev. Msgrs. Carl F. Bell; Cyril Navin, Pastor Emeritus.
Res.: 4601 Firmament Ave., 91436. Tel: 818-986-8234; Fax: 818-986-3310.
School—4548 Haskell Ave., 91436. Tel: 818-501-4155; Fax: 818-501-8480. Lay Teachers 11; Students 303.
Catechesis/Religious Program—Tel: 818-789-5947. Students 130.
2—OUR LADY OF GRACE (1945), Revs. Austin C. Doran; Gilberto Monico. In Res., Rev. Msgr. Craig A. Cox, J.C.D.
Res.: 5011 White Oak Ave., 91316. Tel: 818-342-4686; Fax: 818-342-6579.
School—Tel: 818-344-4126; Fax: 818-344-1736. Sisters 5; Lay Teachers 17; Students 320.
Catechesis/Religious Program—Tel: 818-342-4505; Fax: 818-344-1736. Students 355.

FILLMORE, VENTURA CO., ST. FRANCIS OF ASSISI (1926), [JC] Revs. Joseph Hernandez; George J. Puchekunnel (India); Bernard Gatlin.
Church: 1048 West Ventura St., P.O. Box 757, 93016. Tel: 805-524-1306; Fax: 805-524-0784.
Catechesis/Religious Program—Tel: 805-524-2865. Students 200.
Mission—San Salvador 4039 E. Center St., P.O. Box 508, Piru, Ventura Co. 93040. Tel: 805-521-1077; Fax: 805-521-1077.

GARDENA, LOS ANGELES CO.
1—ST. ANTHONY OF PADUA (1910), Revs. Edward Dover; Lucio Juarez; Deacons Felix Dumlao; Antonio Huerta.
Res.: 1050 W. 163rd St., 90247. Tel: 310-327-5830; Fax: 310-327-6440.
School—1003 W. 163rd St., 90247. Tel: 310-329-7170; Fax: 310-329-9843. Sisters of Providence of St. Mary-of-the-Woods 1; Lay Teachers 14; Students 249.
Catechesis/Religious Program—Tel: 310-323-0860; Fax: 310-323-0860.
2—MARIA REGINA (1956), [CEM] Revs. Miguel Java (Philippines), Admin.; Thomas M. Acton, Pastor Emeritus (Retired); Peter M. Nguyen, Cs.S.R., Chap.; Marco Jeong, O.F.M., Chap.; Deacon Phuoc Van Nguyen.
Res.: 2150 W. 135th St., 90249. Tel: 310-323-0030; Fax: 310-323-8081.
School—Tel: 310-327-9133; Fax: 310-327-2636. Lay Teachers 15; Students 300.
Catechesis/Religious Program—13510 S. VanNess Ave., 90249. Tel: 310-327-4999. Students 960.

GLENDALE, LOS ANGELES CO.
1—CHURCH OF THE INCARNATION (1927), Rev. Paul Hruby; Rev. Msgr. Eugene P. Frilot, Pastor Emeritus (Retired); Rev. Thomas Schweitzer; William Shaules, Pastoral Assoc.; Deacon Restie Noriega.
Res.: 1001 N. Brand Blvd., 91202. Tel: 818-242-2579; Fax: 818-507-4976.
School—Tel: 818-241-2269; Fax: 818-241-4734. Lay Teachers 11; Students 296.
Catechesis/Religious Program—Tel: 818-241-7045. Students 300.
2—HOLY FAMILY (1907), (Hispanic—Filipino), Rev. Joseph Shea; Rev. Msgr. Arthur J. Lirette, P.A., Pastor Emeritus (Retired); Revs. Maurice D. Harrigan; John Kyebasuuta; Deacons Fred Pelletier; John Steele.
Res.: 209 E. Lomita Ave., 91205. Tel: 818-247-2222; Fax: 818-247-4780.
School—(Grades K-8) Tel: 818-243-9239; Fax: 818-243-0976. Sisters 1; Lay Teachers 9; Students 307.
High School—400 E. Lomita Ave., 91205. Tel: 818-241-3178; Fax: 818-241-7753. (Girls) Sisters 3; Lay Teachers 23; Students 300.
Catechesis/Religious Program—400 S. Louise, 91205. Tel: 818-240-6551; Fax: 818-243-2560. Students 561.

GLENDORA, LOS ANGELES CO., ST. DOROTHY (1958), Rev. Msgrs. Michael Meyers; John A. Acton, Pastor Emeritus (Retired); Revs. John Jesus Moloney; Bernard Njeru (Kenya); Deacon William Bolduc.
Res.: 241 S. Valley Center, 91741. Tel: 626-914-3941; Fax: 626-335-0059.
School—215 S. Valley Center, 91741. Tel: 626-335-0772. Sisters 1; Lay Teachers 15; Students 301.
Catechesis/Religious Program—Tel: 626-335-2811. Students 629.

GOLETA, SANTA BARBARA CO., ST. MARK UNIVERSITY PARISH (1966), Revs. Joseph Scott, C.S.P.; Paul Rospond, C.S.P.
Res.: 6550 Picasso Rd., 93117. Tel: 805-968-1078; Fax: 805-968-3965.
Catechesis/Religious Program—Students 30.

GRANADA HILLS, LOS ANGELES CO.
1—ST. EUPHRASIA (1963), Revs. Michael Wakefield; Raymond Saplis, Pastor Emeritus; Deacon Joseph Orth.
Res.: 11766 Shoshone Ave., 91344. Tel: 818-360-4611; Fax: 818-360-2755.
School—Tel: 818-363-5515; Fax: 818-832-6678. Lay Teachers 10; Students 300.
Catechesis/Religious Program—Tel: 818-368-4512. Students 207.
2—ST. JOHN BAPTIST DE LA SALLE (1953), Rev. Robert Milbauer; Rev. Msgr. Peter O'Sullivan, Pastor Emeritus; Rev. Gemnoli Bandivas; Deacon Samuel Frias.
Res.: 10738 Hayvenhurst Ave., 91344. Tel: 818-363-2535; Fax: 818-360-7407.
School—Tel: 818-363-2270; Fax: 818-832-8950. Lay Teachers 23; Students 602.
Catechesis/Religious Program—Tel: 818-368-1514. Students 700.

GUADALUPE, SANTA BARBARA CO., OUR LADY OF GUADALUPE (1867), (Hispanic), [JC] Rev. Abel Suquilvide.
Res.: 1164 Obispo St., P.O. Box 897, 93434. Tel: 805-343-2181; Fax: 805-343-6642.
Catechesis/Religious Program—Tel: 805-343-4404. Students 208.

HACIENDA HEIGHTS, LOS ANGELES CO., ST. JOHN VIANNEY (1965), Revs. Timothy E. Nichols; Christopher Terry, O.P.; Lloyd Ukaegbu (Nigeria); Cyprian Carlo; Deacons Eduardo Delgado; Jesse Martinez; Richard Noon.
Res.: 1345 Turnbull Canyon Rd., 91745. Tel: 626-330-2269; Fax: 626-330-0220.
Catechesis/Religious Program—Students 740.

HAWAIIAN GARDENS, LOS ANGELES CO., ST. PETER CHANEL (1986), (Mexican-Filipino), Revs. Lawrence T. Darnell, O.M.V.; Edward Broom, O.M.V.; Gregory Staab, O.M.V.; John Lyons, O.M.V.
Res.: 21611 Juan Ave., 90716-1117. Tel: 562-924-7591; Fax: 562-402-9411.
Church: 12001 E. 214 St., 90716-1117.
Catechesis/Religious Program—Tel: 562-860-3637; Fax: 562-860-3637. Students 1,623.

HAWTHORNE, LOS ANGELES CO., ST. JOSEPH (1915), Revs. Perry D. Leiker; Eugene Buhr; Raymond Perez; Christopher Bazyouros.
Res.: 11901 Acacia Ave., 90250. Tel: 310-679-1139; Fax: 310-679-3034.
School—11886 Acacia Ave., 90250. Tel: 310-679-1014; Fax: 310-679-1310. Lay Teachers 20; Students 607.
Catechesis/Religious Program—Tel: 310-679-1139, Ext. 114. Students 1,071.

HERMOSA BEACH, LOS ANGELES CO., OUR LADY OF GUADALUPE (1927), Revs. Gary Klauer, O.F.M-.Conv.; Thomas Czeck, O.F.M.Conv.; Deacon Scott Palmer, Business Mgr. In Res., Revs. Alfonso Borgea, O.F.M.Conv.; Peter Mallin, O.F.M.Conv.; Raymond Mallett, O.F.M. Conv.; Bros. James Reiter, O.F.M.Conv.; Christopher Saindon, O.F.M.Conv.
Res.: 320 Massey Ave., 90254. Tel: 310-372-7077; Fax: 310-798-4051.
School—340 Massey Ave., 90254. Tel: 310-372-7486. Mrs. Cheryl Hunt, Prin. Lay Teachers 15; Students 240.
Catechesis/Religious Program—Tel: 310-374-4649. Students 210.

HUNTINGTON PARK, LOS ANGELES CO.
1—ST. MARTHA (1913), (Hispanic), Revs. Antonio Armendariz, M.Sp.S.; Gilberto Rivera Areralo, M.Sp.S.; Guillermo Flores, M.Sp.S.; Bro. Martin Soto, M.Sp.S.
Res.: 6019 Stafford Ave., 90255. Tel: 323-585-5776; Fax: 323-585-4560.
Catechesis/Religious Program—Tel: 323-583-3678; 323-585-4941 (Confirmation). Students 800.
2—ST. MATTHIAS (1913), (Latino), [JC] Revs. Abelardo Bailon; Juan Carlos Diaz; Gustavo Mejia. In Res., Revs. Samuel C. Villegas (Retired); Rody I. Gorman (Retired).
Res.: 7125 Mission Pl., 90255. Tel: 323-588-2134; Fax: 323-588-4519.
School—Tel: 323-588-7253; Fax: 323-588-1136. Lay Teachers 15; Students 275.
Catechesis/Religious Program—7105 Mission Pl., 90255. Tel: 323-277-1188; Fax: 323-277-1192. Students 1,230.

INGLEWOOD, LOS ANGELES CO., ST. JOHN CHRYSOSTOM (1923), (Hispanic), Revs. Stephen Woodland; Javier Altuna, S.J.; Luciano Kamienski, S.D.B.; Deacon Roberto Vasquez.
Res.: 546 E. Florence Ave., 90301. Tel: 310-677-2736; Fax: 310-677-0584.
School—Tel: 310-677-5868; Fax: 310-677-3429. Sisters of St. Joseph of Carondelet 5; Lay Teachers 12; Students 329.
Catechesis/Religious Program—Tel: 310-674-3733. Students 1,300.

IRWINDALE, LOS ANGELES CO., OUR LADY OF GUADALUPE (1964), Rev. Joseph Canna; Deacon Gary Patterson.
Res.: 16025 Cypress St., 91706. Tel: 626-962-3649; Fax: 626-337-3318.
Catechesis/Religious Program—Tel: 626-960-1310. Students 751.

LA CANADA FLINTRIDGE, LOS ANGELES CO., ST. BEDE THE VENERABLE (1951), Rev. Msgr. Francis T. Wallace, J.C.L.; Rev. Kevin A. Kester.
Res.: 215 Foothill Blvd., 91011. Tel: 818-949-4300; Fax: 818-790-9520.
School—(Grades K-8), 4524 Crown Ave., 91011. Tel: 818-790-7884; Fax: 818-790-7887. Lay Teachers 18; Students 280.
Catechesis/Religious Program—Tel: 818-949-4323. Carolyn Polchow, D.R.E.; Marian Macho, D.R.E. Students 707.

LA CRESCENTA, LOS ANGELES CO., ST. JAMES THE LESS (1955), Rev. Msgr. Robert W. Gipson; Deacon Joe Hegenbart.
Res.: 4625 Dunsmore Ave., 91214. Tel: 818-248-3442; Fax: 818-248-9332.
School—4635 Dunsmore Ave., 91214. Tel: 818-248-7778; Fax: 818-248-5242. Sisters 1; Lay Teachers 12; Students 230.
Catechesis/Religious Program—Tel: 818-541-1750. Students 200.

LA MIRADA, LOS ANGELES CO.
1—BEATITUDES OF OUR LORD (1964), Revs. Anthony J. Page; Joseph Visperas (Philippines).
Res.: 13013 S. Santa Gertrudes Ave., 90638. Tel: 562-943-1521; Fax: 562-902-7627.
School—Tel: 562-943-3218; Fax: 562-943-9718. Lay Teachers 14; Students 299.
Catechesis/Religious Program—Tel: 562-943-5678; Fax: 562-943-9419. Students 436.
2—ST. PAUL OF THE CROSS (1956), Revs. Patrick J. Gannon; Joseph Visperas (Philippines); Deacons Arthur Fitzpatrick; Mark Orcutt; Timothy Roberto.
Res.: 14020 Foster Rd., 90638. Tel: 562-921-2914;

Fax: 562-926-1514.
School—14030 Foster Rd., 90638. Tel: 562-921-2118; Fax: 562-802-2048. Lay Teachers 17; Students 256.
Catechesis/Religious Program—Tel: 562-921-4911. Students 290.

LA PUENTE, LOS ANGELES CO.

1—ST. JOSEPH (1919), Rev. Msgr. Patrick J. Staunton; Rev. Guillermo Rodriguez (El Salvador); Deacon Ruben Guerra. In Res., Rev. Eric A. Lewis.
Res.: 550 N. Glendora Ave., 91744. Tel: 626-336-2001; Fax: 626-336-6010.
School—15650 E. Temple Ave., 91744. Tel: 626-336-2821; Fax: 626-369-8921. Carmelite Sisters 5; Lay Teachers 6; Students 246.
Catechesis/Religious Program—15650 E. Temple Ave., 91744. Tel: 626-336-1191; Fax: 626-934-7371. Students 395.

2—ST. LOUIS OF FRANCE (1955), Revs. Lorenzo Miranda; Cesar A. Fernandez; Deacon Oscar Valeriano Jr. In Res., Rev. Msgr. James R. Mulcahy, Pastor Emeritus (Retired).
Res.: 13935 E. Temple, 91746-2098. Tel: 626-918-8314; Fax: 626-917-8413.
School—Tel: 626-918-6210; Fax: 626-918-9549. Sisters of St. Louis 1; Lay Teachers 14; Students 301.
Catechesis/Religious Program—Tel: 626-918-7002. Students 1,307.

LAKEWOOD, LOS ANGELES CO., ST. PANCRATIUS (1953), Rev. Msgr. Joseph F. Greeley; Rev. Hisham Dabaen. In Res., Rev. Thomas Boedy, S.J.
Res.: 3519 St. Pancratius Pl., 90712. Tel: 562-634-6111; Fax: 562-634-7817.
School—3601 St. Pancratius Pl., 90712. Tel: 562-634-6310; Fax: 562-633-0731. Lay Teachers 14; Students 286.
Catechesis/Religious Program—Tel: 562-634-1611; Fax: 562-634-2524. Students 375.

LANCASTER, LOS ANGELES CO.

1—BLESSED JUNIPERO SERRA (Quartz Hill) (1987), Rev. Ernest Candelaria, C.S.J. In Res., Revs. Joseph Scalco, C.S.J.; Mark Withers, C.S.J.; Deacon Edward Caputo.
Res.: 6122 W. Azalea Dr., 93536-3767. Tel: 661-943-4933; Fax: 661-943-6863.
Office—42121 60th St. W., 93536-3767. Tel: 661-943-9314.
Catechesis/Religious Program—Students 990.
Mission—St. Elizabeth P.O. Box 3307, Los Angeles Co. 93586-0307. Tel: 661-724-9911.

2—SACRED HEART (1886), Revs. John J. Vogel; Hung Tran; Deacons John Charters; Ron Routolo; Francisco Gonzalez.
Res.: 45007 N. Cedar Ave., 93534. Tel: 661-942-7122; Fax: 661-945-4255.
School—45002 N. Date Ave., 93534. Tel: 661-948-3613; Fax: 661-945-4235. Lay Teachers 15; Students 324.
Catechesis/Religious Program—45027 N. Cedar Ave., 93534. Tel: 661-948-3011; Fax: 661-948-2697. Students 920.

LOMITA, LOS ANGELES CO., ST. MARGARET MARY ALACOQUE (1937), Rev. Msgr. Patrick Thompson; Revs. Gerard O'Brien; Gustavo Castillo; Deacons Dick Corwin; Craig Siegman; Rick Soria.
Res.: 25429 Eshelman Ave., 90717. Tel: 310-326-3364; Fax: 310-539-1570.
Parish Center—25511 Eshelman Ave., 90717.
Church: 25505 Eshelman Ave., 90717.
School—(Grades K-8), 25515 Eshelman Ave., 90717. Tel: 310-326-9494; Fax: 310-326-2711. Lay Teachers 11; Students 304.
Catechesis/Religious Program—Tel: 310-326-3364, Ext. 11. Students 932.

LOMPOC, SANTA BARBARA CO.

1—LA PURISIMA CONCEPCION (1787), Rev. Richard Vega; Rev. Msgr. Andrew McGrath, Pastor Emeritus; Deacons Tom Edmonds; Charles Hays; Darrell Meter.
Res.: 213 W. Olive Ave., 93436. Tel: 805-735-3068; Fax: 805-735-7649.
School—219 W. Olive Ave., 93436. Tel: 805-736-6210.
Catechesis/Religious Program—Students 215.

2—OUR LADY QUEEN OF ANGELS (1972), Rev. John G. Fitzgerald, V.F.
Res.: 3495 Rucker Rd., 93436. Tel: 805-733-2735; Fax: 805-733-1235.
Catechesis/Religious Program—Tel: 805-733-3155. Students 324.

LONG BEACH, LOS ANGELES CO.

1—ST. ANTHONY (1902), Revs. Richard Krekelberg; Jose L. Magana.
Mailing Address: 600 Olive Ave., 90802.
Res.: 540 Olive Ave., 90802. Tel: 562-590-9229; Fax: 562-590-9048.
School—855 E. 5th St., 90802. Tel: 562-432-5946; Fax: 562-435-8606. Students 298.
High School—620 Olive Ave., 90802. Tel: 562-432-4496; Fax: 562-437-3055. Sisters 4; Lay Teachers 12; Students 338.
Catechesis/Religious Program—Tel: 562-590-9229, Ext. 34. Students 455.
Mission—Our Lady of Mt. Carmel Cambodian Catholic Center 1851 Cerritos Ave., Los Angeles Co. 90806. Tel: 562-591-8477; Fax: 562-591-5367.

2—ST. ATHANASIUS (1933), Rev. William McLean.
Res.: 5390 Linden Ave., 90805. Tel 562-423-7986; Fax: 562-422-0306.
School—5369 Linden Ave., 90805. Tel: 562-428-7422. St. Francis Mission Community 3; Lay Teachers 9; Students 220.
Catechesis/Religious Program—Tel: 562-428-3494. Students 870.

3—ST. BARNABAS (1939), Rev. Msgr. Christopher J. Kennedy, Pastor Emeritus (Retired); Rev. George Reynolds; Sr. Bernice Jordan, C.S.J., Pastoral Assoc. Deacon Alden Bohlig.
Res.: 3955 Orange Ave., 90807. Tel: 562-424-8595; Fax: 562-595-7875.
School—(Grades K-8) Tel: 562-424-7476; Fax: 562-981-3351. Lay Teachers 14; Students 265.
Catechesis/Religious Program—Tel: 562-988-6855; Fax: 562-981-8792. Students 470.

4—ST. BARTHOLOMEW (1937), Rev. Msgr. Sean B. Flanagan.
Res.: 252 Granada Ave., 90803. Tel: 562-438-3826; Fax: 562-438-2227.
Catechesis/Religious Program—Tel: 562-439-1802. Students 270.

5—ST. CORNELIUS (1951), Rev. Michael Reardon, S.D.V.; Rev. Msgr. John Folliard, Pastor Emeritus; Deacon Alexander Lipski.
Res.: 5500 Wardlow Rd., 90808. Tel: 562-421-8966; Fax: 562-421-5096.
School—3330 Bellflower Blvd., 90808. Tel: 562-425-7813; Fax: 562-425-2743. Lay Teachers 11; Students 226.
Catechesis/Religious Program—Tel: 562-420-7613; Fax: 562-420-7613. Students 268.

6—ST. CYPRIAN (1945), Rev. Peter Foran.
Res.: 4714 Clark Ave., 90808. Tel: 562-421-9487; Fax: 562-496-1024.
School—5133 Arbor Rd., 90808. Tel: 562-425-7341; Fax: 562-421-1642. Sisters of St. Louis (Monaghan) 1; Lay Teachers 10; Students 298.
Catechesis/Religious Program—Tel: 562-420-6885; Fax: 562-421-1422. Students 499.

7—HOLY INNOCENTS (1923), (Spanish—Asian), Rev. Antonio P. Astudillo.
Res.: 425 E. 20th St., 90806. Tel: 562-591-6924; Fax: 562-591-2164.
School—2500 Pacific Ave., 90806. Tel: 562-424-1018; Fax: 562-424-4126. Carmelite Sisters of the Most Sacred Heart 5; Lay Teachers 7; Students 240.
Catechesis/Religious Program—Tel: 562-427-8449; Fax: 562-424-3270. Students 240.

8—ST. JOSEPH (1955), Rev. William J. O'Connor; Deacon Don Gath. In Res., Rev. Harold L. Ford (Retired).
Res.: 6220 E. Willow St., 90815. Tel: 562-594-4657; Fax: 562-431-7424.
School—6200 E. Willow St., 90815. Tel: 562-596-6115; Fax: 562-596-6725. Lay Teachers 14; Students 303.
Catechesis/Religious Program—Tel: 562-598-0519. Students 262.

9—ST. LUCY (1944), Rev. Michael Roebert; Rt. Rev. Hoang Dang; Rev. Antonio Rodriguez; Deacons Carlito de los Reyes; Victor Lopez.
Res.: 2344 Cota Ave., 90810. Tel: 562-424-9051; Fax: 562-988-0376.
School—2320 Cota Ave., 90810. Tel: 562-424-9062; Fax: 562-424-3572. Lay Teachers 12; Students 300.
Catechesis/Religious Program—Tel: 562-997-0511. Students 680.

10—ST. MARIA GORETTI (1955), Rev. Msgr. Douglas Wm. Saunders, V.F.
Res.: 3954 Palo Verde Ave., 90808-2298. Tel: 562-425-7459; Fax: 562-421-0475.
School—Tel: 562-425-5112; Fax: 562-425-5672. Lay Teachers 10; Students 240.
Catechesis/Religious Program—3950 Palo Verde Ave., 90808-2298. Tel: 562-420-1321. Students 161.

11—ST. MATTHEW (1920), Revs. Gerald Meisel; Juan Romero.
Mailing Address: P.O. Box 4399, 90804-0399.
Res.: 672 Temple Ave., 90814. Tel: 562-439-0931; Fax: 562-434-7621.
Catechesis/Religious Program—Tel: 562-434-6402. Students 490.

12—OUR LADY OF REFUGE (1948), Rev. Msgr. William J. O'Keeffe; Rev. Alfonso Scott; Deacon Witold Engel.
Res.: 5195 Stearns St., 90815. Tel: 562-498-6641; Fax: 562-498-3314.
School—5210 Los Coyotes Diagonal, 90815. Tel: 562-597-0819; Fax: 562-597-1419. Lay Teachers 11; Students 208.
Catechesis/Religious Program—Tel: 562-597-3102; Fax: 562-494-4381. Students 288.

LOS NIETOS, LOS ANGELES CO., OUR LADY OF PERPETUAL HELP (1958), (Hispanic), Revs. John S. Woolway; Josef Draugialis.
Res.: 8545 S. Norwalk Blvd., 90606. Tel: 562-692-3758; Fax: 562-695-4068.
Catechesis/Religious Program—Tel: 562-463-3389. Students 1,160.

LYNWOOD, LOS ANGELES CO.

1—ST. EMYDIUS (1924), Rev. Msgr. Emigdio Herrera; Revs. W. Ward; Luis Garcia (Mexico); John C. O'Connor; Heriberto J. Palacios (Nicaragua); Samuel Ward; Sr. Margaret Bannan, Pastoral Assoc.
Res.: 10900 California Ave., P.O. Box 100, 90262-2094. Tel: 310-637-7095; Fax: 310-637-3319.
School—10990 California Ave., 90262. Tel: 310-635-7184; Fax: 310-605-3041. Sisters of the Holy Faith 3; Lay Teachers 19; Students 546.
Catechesis/Religious Program—Tel: 310-639-1249. Students 1,102.
Convent—10950 California Ave., 90262. Tel: 310-635-3264. Missionaries of Charity 6.

2—ST. PHILIP NERI (1948), (Hispanic), Rev. Juan Enriguez; Deacon Joe T. Battle. Tel: 310-632-4745.
Res.: 4311 Olanda St., 90262. Tel: 310-632-7179; Fax: 310-632-5119.
Pastoral Center—12435 Cookacre Ave., 90262.
School—12522 Stoneacre Ave., 90262. Tel: 310-638-0341; Fax: 310-638-9805. Lay Teachers 9; Students 322.
Catechesis/Religious Program—Tel: 310-632-7893. Students 1,570.

MALIBU, LOS ANGELES CO., OUR LADY OF MALIBU (1946), Rev. William F. Kerze; Rev. Msgr. John V. Sheridan, Pastor Emeritus (Retired).
Res.: 3625 Winter Canyon Rd., 90265. Tel: 310-456-2361; Fax: 310-456-3942.
School—Tel: 310-456-8071; Fax: 310-456-7767. Lay Teachers 15; Students 145.
Catechesis/Religious Program—Tel: 310-456-8813. Students 130.

MANHATTAN BEACH, LOS ANGELES CO., AMERICAN MARTYRS (1930), Rev. Msgr. John F. Barry; Rev. Steve V. Davoren; Deacon Fred Rose.
Res.: 624 15th St., P.O. Box 3639, 90266. Tel: 310-545-5651; Fax: 310-546-9209.
School—Tel: 310-545-8559; Fax: 310-546-7219. Lay Teachers 18; Students 570.
Catechesis/Religious Program—1701 Laurel Ave., 90266. Tel: 310-546-4734; Fax: 310-546-9104. Students 1,152.

MAYWOOD, LOS ANGELES CO., ST. ROSE OF LIMA (1922), (Hispanic), Revs. David M. Velazquez; Benito Armenta; Edward Soto.
Res.: 4450 E. 60th St., 90270. Tel: 323-560-2381; Fax: 323-560-8537.
School—4422 E. 60th St., 90270. Tel: 323-560-3376; Fax: 323-560-8539. Lay Teachers 12; Students 242.
Catechesis/Religious Program—Tel: 323-560-0187. Students 1,506.

MISSION HILLS, LOS ANGELES CO., SAN FERNANDO REY MISSION (1797), Rev. Msgr. Francis J. Weber, Admin.; Deacon Jack Coplen.
Res.: 15151 San Fernando Mission Blvd., 91345. Tel: 818-361-0186; Fax: 818-361-3276.

MONROVIA, LOS ANGELES CO., IMMACULATE CONCEPTION (1904), Revs. Charles J. Ramirez; Francis Cassidy; Deacons Fred Conrey; Michael Salcido; Neomi H. Torres, Admin.
Res.: 740 S. Shamrock Ave., 91016. Tel: 626-358-1166; Fax: 626-358-6466.
School—726 S. Shamrock Ave., 91016. Tel: 626-358-5129; Fax: 626-358-3933. Religious 1; Lay Teachers 10; Students 189.
Catechesis/Religious Program—Tel: 626-357-3010; Fax: 626-357-5299. Students 1,120.

MONTEBELLO, LOS ANGELES CO.

1—ST. BENEDICT (1906), Revs. Anthony Z. Palos, O.A.R.; James D. McGuire, O.A.R.; Joseph J. Gallardo, O.A.R.; Bro. Anthony J. Torretti, O.A.R.; Deacons James Dillon; David J. Estrada; Alfonso Castillo.
Res.: 1022 W. Cleveland Ave., 90640. Tel: 323-721-1184; Fax: 323-721-5075.
School—Tel: 323-721-3348; Fax: 323-721-8698. Frank Loya, Prin. Lay Teachers 19; Students 597.
Catechesis/Religious Program—1009 W. Madison Ave., 90640. Tel: 323-722-6020, Ext. 10; Fax: 323-722-6006. Mrs. Helen Arvayo, D.R.E. Students 660.

2—OUR LADY OF THE MIRACULOUS MEDAL (1950), Rev. Msgrs. Juan Matas; Robert Howard; Rev. Emile Belletty; Deacons Joseph Spada; Fred Rios. In Res., Rev. Brian Delaney.
Res.: 820 N. Garfield Ave., 90640. Tel: 323-722-5866; Fax: 323-722-2654.
School—Tel: 323-728-5435; Fax: 323-728-8038. Daughters of Charity of St. Vincent de Paul 1; Lay Teachers 20; Aides 10; Students 541.
Catechesis/Religious Program—Tel: 213-725-6962; Fax: 323-722-2654. Carol Lazar, D.R.E. Students 416.

Convent—840 N. Garfield Ave., 90640. Tel: 323-721-4321.

MONTECITO, SANTA BARBARA CO., OUR LADY OF MOUNT CARMEL (1856), Rev. Maurice O'Mahony; Rev. Msgr. Sylvester O'Byrne, Pastor Emeritus; Rev. Carrol O'Sullivan (Retired).
Res.: 1300 E. Valley Rd., Santa Barbara, 93108. Tel: 805-969-6868; Fax: 805-565-5959.
School—530 Hot Springs Rd., 93108. Tel: 805-969-5965; Fax: 805-565-9841. Lay Teachers 16; Students 203.
Catechesis/Religious Program—Tel: 805-969-4868. Students 140.

MONTEREY PARK, LOS ANGELES CO.

1—ST. STEPHEN (1921), Revs. Dennis P. Marrell; Linus Tiala (Indonesia); Sr. Susan M. Slater, S.H.C.J., Pastoral Assoc. In Res., Rev. Jose J. Velasco, S.J.
Res.: 320 W. Garvey Ave., 91754. Tel: 626-573-0427; Fax: 626-288-0260.
School—Tel: 626-573-1716; Fax: 626-573-3251. Lay Teachers 15; Students 345.
Catechesis/Religious Program—Tel: 626-573-4517. Students 185.

2—ST. THOMAS AQUINAS (1960), (Chinese), Rev. Gabriel Lui, Admin.
Res.: 1501 S. Atlantic Blvd., 91754. Tel: 323-264-4447; Fax: 323-264-2524.
Catechesis/Religious Program—Tel: 323-264-1338. Students 235.

MONTROSE, LOS ANGELES CO., HOLY REDEEMER (1925), Revs. John K. Foley; Gabriel E. Kumordji, S.V.D. (Ghana).
Res.: 2411 Montrose Ave., 91020. Tel: 818-249-2008; Fax: 818-249-5642.
School—2361 Del Mar Rd., 91020. Tel: 818-541-9005; Fax: 818-541-9006. Lay Teachers 15; Students 225.
Catechesis/Religious Program—Tel: 818-249-2008, Ext. 443. Students 147.

MOORPARK, VENTURA CO., HOLY CROSS (1982), Rev. Msgr. Joseph Cosgrove; Rev. Michael Sezzi; Deacon Jerry Heyer.
Res.: 13955 Peach Hill, 93021. Tel: 805-529-1397; Fax: 805-529-3939.
Parish Church & Administration Bldg.—13955 Peach Hill Rd., 93021.
Catechesis/Religious Program—Tel: 805-529-0283; Fax: 805-529-3939. Students 929.

NEW CUYAMA, SANTA BARBARA CO., IMMACULATE CONCEPTION (1969), Sr. Mary D. Quinn, C.S.J., Parish Dir.
Res.: 4793 Cebrian St., P.O. Box 265, 93254. Tel: 661-766-2741; Fax: 661-766-2919.
Catechesis/Religious Program—Students 33.

NEWBURY PARK, VENTURA CO., ST. JULIE BILLIART (1969), Rev. Msgr. Michael Bunny; Deacon Louis Henschel.
Church: 2475 Borchard Rd., 91320. Tel: 805-498-3602; Fax: 805-376-2332.
Catechesis/Religious Program—Tel: 805-499-0979. Students 436.

NORTH HOLLYWOOD, LOS ANGELES CO.

1—ST. CHARLES BORROMEO (1921), Rev. Robert J. Gallagher; Rev. Msgr. Thomas Kiefer, Pastor Emeritus; Revs. Peter Ha; Jason Souza. In Res., Rev. Msgr. Gabriel Gonzales; Deacon Walter Hanson.
Res.: 10828 Moorpark St., 91602. Tel: 818-766-3838; Fax: 818-766-2855.
Parish Center—10834 Moorpark St., 91602. Fax: 818-766-5711.
School—10850 Moorpark St., 91602. Tel: 818-508-5359; Fax: 818-508-4511. Sisters 1; Lay Teachers 14; Students 289.
Catechesis/Religious Program—Tel: 818-980-1826. Students 370.

2—ST. JANE FRANCES DE CHANTAL (1948), Rev. Patrick Gavin, O.Carm., Admin.; Bro. Mario Loya, O.Carm.; Deacon Richard Morgan.
Res.: 13001 Victory Blvd., 91606.
Parish Center—12930 Hamlin St., 91606. Tel: 818-985-8600.
School—Tel: 818-766-1714. Mr. Joseph Brown, Prin. Lay Teachers 10; Students 325.
Catechesis/Religious Program—Tel: 818-985-8272. Deacon Richard Morgan, D.R.E. Students 96.

3—ST. PATRICK (1948), Rev. Gregory C. King.
Res. & Office: 6153 Cahuenga Blvd., 91606-5117. Tel: 818-752-3240; Fax: 818-769-6174.
School—10626 Erwin St., 91606. Tel: 818-761-7363; Fax: 818-761-6349. Lay Teachers 14; Students 288.
Catechesis/Religious Program—Tel: 818-769-0263. Students 638.

4—ST. PAUL ASSYRIAN-CHALDEAN (1980), (Assyrian-Chaldean), [JC] Revs. Noel Gorgis; Tomy Tomiekha (SPA).
Res.: 13050 Vanowen St., 91605. Tel: 818-765-3665; Fax: 818-765-0493.

5—SACRED HEART SYRIAC CATHOLIC PARISH (1996),, (Jesus Sacred Heart Antiochene Syrian Catholic Mission, Antiochean Syriac Rite). Rev. Yousif Habach.
10837 Collins St., 91601. Tel: 818-766-7001; Fax: 818-766-7254.

NORTHRIDGE, LOS ANGELES CO., OUR LADY OF LOURDES (1958), Rev. Msgr. Peter C. Moran; Revs. Andrew Diviney, S.J.; Sean Cronin; Deacon Juan Galido.
Church: 18405 Superior St., 91325. Tel: 818-349-1500; Fax: 818-349-2516.
Res.: 9800 Canby Ave., 91325.
School—Tel: 818-349-0245; Fax: 818-349-4156. Lay Teachers 14; Students 314.
Catechesis/Religious Program—Tel: 818-349-1285. Students 440.

NORWALK, LOS ANGELES CO.

1—ST. JOHN OF GOD (1950), Rev. Msgr. Bernard M. Leheny; Revs. Thinh Duc Pham; Jose A. Bautista.
Res.: 13819 S. Pioneer Blvd., 90650. Tel: 562-863-5721; Fax: 562-406-3927.
School—13817 S. Pioneer Blvd., 90650. Tel: 562-863-5721, Ext. 228; Fax: 562-406-3928. Sisters of the Holy Faith 2; Lay Teachers 25; Students 309.
Catechesis/Religious Program—Tel: 562-863-5721, Ext. 231. Students 937.

2—ST. LINUS (1961), Revs. Joseph V. Brennan; Mark M. Martinez; Deacon Chuck Baker.
Res.: 13915 Shoemaker Ave., 90650. Tel: 310-921-6649; Fax: 310-921-5150. In Res., Rev. Paul Vung Le, S.V.D.
School—Tel: 310-921-0336; Fax: 310-921-1666. Lay Teachers 15; Students 321; Sisters of the Holy Faith 1.
Catechesis/Religious Program—Tel: 562-921-5179. Students 462.

OJAI, VENTURA CO., ST. THOMAS AQUINAS (1919), Revs. Patrick J. Keane, O.S.A. (Retired); William V. Olivas, O.S.A.; Michael J. McFadden, O.S.A.; Deacons Allan Doane; Chris Gorman.
Res.: 185 St. Thomas Dr., 93023. Tel: 805-646-4338; Fax: 805-646-5928.
Catechesis/Religious Program—Tel: 805-646-0307. Students 316.

OXNARD, VENTURA CO.

1—ST. ANTHONY (1959), Revs. Gael Sullivan, S.D.B.; Porfirio Alvarez; Deacons James Henry; Jon McPheeters; Oscar Duke.
Res.: 2511 S. C St., P.O. Box 2215, 93034. Tel: 805-486-7301; Fax: 805-486-3142.
School—Tel: 805-487-5317; Fax: 805-486-1537. Lay Teachers 9; Students 209.
Catechesis/Religious Program—2421 S. C St., 93033. Tel: 805-486-0784. Students 1,086.

2—MARY STAR OF THE SEA (1963), (Filipino-Mexican), Revs. Antonio Zabala, O.A.R.; Etelvino Igelsias, O.A.R.; Michael Kenny; Deacon Harold "Hal" Parish, J.C.D.
Res.: 463 W. Pleasant Valley Rd., 93033. Tel: 805-486-6133; Fax: 805-483-6913.
Catechesis/Religious Program—Tel: 805-483-9313. Students 1,105.
Convent—4924 S. F St., 93033. Tel: 805-487-8008.

3—OUR LADY OF GUADALUPE PARISH (1958), (Hispanic), Revs. Enrique Espinosa Ramirez, M.Sp.S.; Conrado Aquino, M.Sp.S.; Jose de Jesus Sanchez, M.Sp.S.; Mario Rodriguez, M.Sp.S.; Deacon Ricardo Barragan.
Res.: 500 N. Juanita Ave., P.O. Box 1091, 93030. Tel: 805-483-0987; 805-483-1481; Fax: 805-486-2434.
School—530 N. Juanita Ave., 93030. Tel: 805-483-5116; Fax: 805-385-7242. Lay Teachers 12; Students 339.
Catechesis/Religious Program—Tel: 805-487-4737; Fax: 805-486-2434. Students 620.
Mission—Christ the King 535 Cooper Rd., Ventura Co. 93030. Tel: 805-483-3499.

4—SANTA CLARA (1904), Rev. Msgr. Charles F. O'Gorman, Senior Priest; Revs. Marco A. Ortiz; John Majarucon; Deacons Milton Rosenberg; John G. Castorena; Fidel Ramirez.
Res.: 323 S. E St., 93030. Tel: 805-487-3891; Fax: 805-487-4733.
School—324 S. E St., 93030. Tel: 805-483-6935; Fax: 805-487-6686. Lay Teachers 16; Students 218.
Catechesis/Religious Program—Tel: 805-487-6742. Students 1,330.
Mission—Santa Clara Chapel 1333 Ventura Blvd., El Rio, Ventura Co. 93030. Tel: 805-485-7335; Fax: 805-981-1183.

PACIFIC PALISADES, LOS ANGELES CO., CORPUS CHRISTI (1950), Rev. Msgr. Liam J. Kidney; Revs. Michael W. Meyer; Frank Desiderio, C.S.P.; Greg Apparcel, C.S.P.; Deacon John P. Allen.
Res.: 880 Toyopa Dr., 90272. Tel: 310-454-1328; Fax: 310-573-5021.
School—Tel: 310-454-9411; Fax: 310-454-3776. Sisters of St. Louis (Monaghan) 2; Lay Teachers 21; Students 289.
Catechesis/Religious Program—890 Toyopa Dr., 90272. Students 80.
Convent—Tel: 310-454-6262.

PACOIMA, LOS ANGELES CO.

1—GUARDIAN ANGEL (1956), (Hispanic), Rev. Steven Guitron, Admin. In Res., Rev. Jose Mejia.
Res.: 10886 Lehigh Ave., 91331. Tel: 818-899-2345; Fax: 818-899-2537.
School—Tel: 818-896-1113; Fax: 818-834-4014. Religious of Jesus and Mary 2; Lay Teachers 7; Students 286.
Catechesis/Religious Program—Tel: 818-899-8907. Students 450.

2—MARY IMMACULATE (1954), (Spanish), Revs. James M. Fee, O.M.I.; Edgar Garcia, O.M.I. (Peru); Leo LeBlanc, O.M.I. (SFD).
Res.: 10390 Remick Ave., 91331. Tel: 818-899-0278; Fax: 818-890-9878.
School—Tel: 818-834-8551; Fax: 818-896-7996. Lay Teachers 15; Students 293.
Catechesis/Religious Program—Tel: 818-899-2111. Students 660.

PALMDALE, LOS ANGELES CO., ST. MARY (1890), Rev. Msgr. Stephen N. Downes; Revs. Dennis Nobleza; Leonel Vargas; Pedro Valdez; Deacon Paul J. Schwerdt. In Res., Rev. Thomas White.
Res.: 1600 E. Ave., R-4, 93550. Tel: 661-947-3306; Fax: 661-947-8687.
School—Tel: 661-273-5555; Fax: 661-273-3845. Carolyn Gries, Prin. Salesian Sisters of St. John Bosco 3; Lay Teachers 12; Students 306.
Catechesis/Religious Program—Tel: 661-273-5554; Fax: 661-273-5525. Students 1,484.
Mission—Our Lady of the Desert Littlerock. 35647 87 St. E., Acton, Los Angeles Co. 93543. Tel: 661-944-1406.

PANORAMA CITY, LOS ANGELES CO., ST. GENEVIEVE (1950), Rev. Msgr. Christian M. Van Liefde; Revs. Jeff J. Deikel; Slawomir Szkredka; Marcial Juan.
Res.: 14061 Roscoe Blvd., 91402. Tel: 818-894-2261; Fax: 818-893-4284.
School—Tel: 818-892-3802; Fax: 818-893-8143. Sisters 2; Lay Teachers 25; Students 626.
High School—13967 Roscoe Blvd., 91402. Tel: 818-894-6417; Fax: 818-892-9853. Sisters 1; Lay Teachers 22; Students 400.
Catechesis/Religious Program—Tel: 818-892-7177. Students 654.

PARAMOUNT, LOS ANGELES CO., OUR LADY OF THE ROSARY (1913), (Hispanic—Tongan), Rev. Edward J. Dober; Rev. Msgr. Bernard O'Reilly (Retired); Rev. Christopher Troxell; Deacon Oscar Corcios.
Res.: 14815 S. Paramount Blvd., 90723. Tel: 562-633-1126; Fax: 562-633-3192.
School—Tel: 562-633-6360; Fax: 562-633-2641. Sisters of the Daughters of Mary and Joseph 4; Lay Teachers 8; Students 268.
Catechesis/Religious Program—Tel: 562-602-0086. Students 1,201.
Mission—Catholic Korean Community of St. Raphael 15946 Downey Ave., Los Angeles Co. 90723. Tel: 562-630-6168. Rev. Mark Choi. (Downey Ave. & Alondra Blvd.)

PASADENA, LOS ANGELES CO.

1—ST. ANDREW (1886), (Hispanic), Rev. Francis Colborn; Rev. Msgr. Tobias P. English, Pastor Emeritus (Retired); Revs. Truc Nguyen; Marcos J. Gonzalez.
Res.: 311 N. Raymond Ave., 91103. Tel: 626-792-4183; Fax: 626-792-4456.
School—(Grades K-8) Tel: 626-796-7697; Fax: 626-796-1931. Sisters of the Holy Names of Jesus and Mary 1; Lay Teachers 9; Students 276.
Catechesis/Religious Program—42 Chestnut St., 91103. Tel: 626-577-1770; Fax: 626-792-4456. Students 750.

2—ASSUMPTION OF THE BLESSED VIRGIN MARY (1950), Rev. Msgr. August Moretti; Rev. Walter Fernando; Deacon Jim J. Crowley.
Res.: 2640 E. Orange Grove Blvd., 91107. Tel: 626-792-1343; Fax: 626-792-0052.
School—2660 E. Orange Grove Blvd., 91107. Tel: 626-793-2089; Fax: 626-793-4070. Mrs. Mary Jo Wynne, Prin. Lay Teachers 18; Students 300.
Catechesis/Religious Program—Tel: 626-792-6844. Elly Dunbar, D.R.E. Students 190.

3—ST. PHILIP THE APOSTLE (1921), Revs. Joseph V. Moniz; John Collins; Deacon William Landa.
Res.: 151 S. Hill Ave., 91106. Tel: 626-793-0693; Fax: 626-793-0733.
School—161 S. Hill Ave., 91106. Tel: 626-795-9691; Fax: 626-795-9946. Lay Teachers 24; Students 450.
Catechesis/Religious Program—Students 486.

PICO RIVERA, LOS ANGELES CO.

1—ST. FRANCIS XAVIER (1939), (Hispanic), Revs. Jorge Penaloza; Victor Ramos; Hernando Barba; Deacon Ben Torres.
Res.: 4245 S. Acacia Ave., 90660. Tel: 562-699-7517; Fax: 562-699-5331.
Catechesis/Religious Program—Tel: 562-699-8527. Students 820.

2—ST. HILARY (1950), Rev. Joshua Peter Lee.
Res.: 5465 Citronell Ave., 90660. Tel: 562-942-7300; Fax: 562-948-3760.
School—Tel: 562-942-7361; Fax: 562-801-9131. School Sisters of Notre Dame 2; Lay Teachers 21; Students 372.

Catechesis/Religious Program—5401 S. Citronell Ave., 90660. Tel: 562-942-7018. Students 676.
Convent—5333 S. Citronell Ave., 90660. Tel: 562-942-7151.

3—ST. MARIANA DE PAREDES (1951), (Hispanic), Revs. Joseph Sebasty; David Gallardo; John Vianney.
Res.: 7922 S. Passons Blvd., 90660. Tel: 562-949-8240; Fax: 562-942-2405.
School—7911 Buhman Ave., 90660. Tel: 562-949-1234; Fax: 562-948-3855. Moises R. Vargas. School Sisters of Notre Dame 1; Lay Teachers 11; Students 283.
Catechesis/Religious Program—Tel: 562-949-5653; Fax: 562-949-9277. Students 407.

POMONA, LOS ANGELES CO.

1—ST. JOSEPH (1886), Revs. Vlatko Poljicak; Jose Alberto Urguizo. In Res., Rev. George El-Far.
Res.: 1150 W. Holt Ave., 91768. Tel: 909-629-4101; Fax: 909-623-0265.
School—Tel: 909-622-3365; Fax: 909-469-5146. Felician Sisters 1; Lay Teachers 12; Students 295.
Catechesis/Religious Program—1200 W. Holt Ave., 91768. Tel: 909-629-1404. Students 1,175.

2—ST. MADELEINE (1963), Rev. Alejandro Aclan; Rev. Msgr. Andrew S. Tseu, Pastor Emeritus (Retired); Deacon Francisco Cuevas.
Res.: 931 E. Kingsley Ave., 91767. Tel: 909-629-9495; Fax: 909-623-7148.
Catechesis/Religious Program—Tel: 909-620-1300. Students 290.

3—SACRED HEART (1935), Revs. Juan Silva; Wayne Noble; Sergio Garcia-Inostroza; Rev. Msgr. Manuel O. Sanchez, Pastor Emeritus (Retired); Deacons Carlos Madigal; Mario Martha.
Res.: 1215 S. Hamilton Blvd., 91766. Tel: 909-622-4553; Fax: 909-623-0841.
Catechesis/Religious Program—Ruth Ibarra, D.R.E. Students 1,100.

RANCHO PALOS VERDES, LOS ANGELES CO., ST. JOHN FISHER (1961), Rev. Msgrs. David A. Sork; Eugene A. Gilb, Pastor Emeritus (Retired); Rev. Freddie T. Chua.
Res.: 5448 Crest Rd., 90275. Tel: 310-377-5571; Fax: 310-377-6303.
School—Tel: 310-377-2800; Fax: 310-377-3863. Sisters 1; Lay Teachers 11; Students 210.
Catechesis/Religious Program—5400 Crest Rd., 90275. Tel: 310-377-4573. Eileen Loughran, D.R.E. Students 900.

REDONDO BEACH, LOS ANGELES CO.

1—ST. JAMES (1892), Revs. Paul K. Fitzpatrick; James F. Kavanagh; Brendan Kearney, S.J.; Deacons Richard Shinkle; Bob Miller. In Res., Rev. Roger Labonte.
Res. and Mailing Address: 415 Vincent St., 90277.
Parish Office:—124 N. Pacific Coast Hwy., 90277. Tel: 310-372-5228; Fax: 310-379-5552.
School—4625 Garnet St., Torrance, 90503. Tel: 310-371-0416; Fax: 310-371-8377. Sisters of St. Joseph of Carondelet 3; Lay Teachers 12; Students 313.
Catechesis/Religious Program—Tel: 310-379-3221. Diana Holly, D.R.E. Students 360.

2—ST. LAWRENCE MARTYR (1955), Rev. Msgrs. Michael Lenihan, V.F., Pastor Emeritus; Paul J. Dotson; Revs. Brian Gabriel Chung; Raymond P. Mallett, O.F.M. Conv.; Deacon Frank Dieter.
Res.: 1900 S. Prospect Ave., 90277-6099. Tel: 310-540-0329; Fax: 310-540-8999.
School—1950 Prospect Ave., 90277-6003. Tel: 310-540-3049; Fax: 310-316-0888. Sisters of St. Joseph of Carondelet 1; Lay Teachers 25; Students 306.
Catechesis/Religious Program—Tel: 310-316-4460. Students 1,100.

RESEDA, LOS ANGELES CO., ST. CATHERINE OF SIENA (1949), Revs. Paul E. Vigil; Raul Cortes; Deacon Pedro Lira.
Res.: 18115 Sherman Way, 91335. Tel: 818-343-2110; Fax: 818-343-1018.
School—18125 Sherman Way, 91335. Tel: 818-343-9880; Fax: 818-343-6851. Lay Teachers 11; Students 256.
Catechesis/Religious Program—Tel: 818-996-4588. Students 710.

ROWLAND HEIGHTS, LOS ANGELES CO., ST. ELIZABETH ANN SETON (1981), Rev. Msgr. Michael F. Killeen; Deacons Steven V. Hillman; Eduardo Delgado; Peter K. Chu.
Church & Mailing Address: 1835 Larkvane Rd., 91748. Tel: 626-964-3629; Fax: 626-913-2209.
Res.: 18090 Via Amorosa, 91748. Tel: 626-964-3629.
Catechesis/Religious Program—Tel: 626-965-5792. Students 768.

SAN DIMAS, LOS ANGELES CO., HOLY NAME OF MARY (1957), Rev. Thomas J. Mullen, SS.CC.; Deacons Marv Estey; Mario Lopez.
Res.: 724 E. Bonita Ave., 91773. Tel: 909-599-1243; Fax: 909-599-4230.
School—Tel: 909-599-1243, Ext. 24; Fax: 909-592-3884. Lay Teachers 18; Students 315.
Catechesis/Religious Program—Tel: 909-599-1243, Ext. 32. Students 369.

SAN FERNANDO, LOS ANGELES CO.

1—ST. FERDINAND (1902), Revs. Paul Nourie, O.M.I.; Manuel "Meme" Villarreal, O.M.I.
Office—1109 Coronel St., 91340. Tel: 818-365-3967; Fax: 818-365-0067.
School—1012 Coronel St., 91340. Tel: 818-361-3264; Fax: 818-361-5894. Sisters of St. Joseph of Carondelet 3; Lay Teachers 10; Students 300.
Catechesis/Religious Program—Tel: 818-361-1813. Students 187.

2—SANTA ROSA (1927), (Hispanic), Revs. Carlos Alarcon, O.M.I.; Harold Fisher, O.M.I. (PMB); Donald Bernard, O.M.I.
Res.: 568 S. Workman St., 91340. Tel: 818-361-4617; Fax: 818-365-8599.
School—1309 Mott St., 91340. Tel: 818-361-5096; Fax: 818-361-2259. Franciscan Missionary Sisters of the Immaculate Conception 6; Lay Teachers 6; Students 269.
Catechesis/Religious Program—Tel: 818-365-5161. Students 460.

SAN GABRIEL, LOS ANGELES CO.

1—ST. ANTHONY (1945), (Hispanic—Filipino), Revs. Michael Gleeson (Ireland); Finbarr Divine; Juan A. Garcia.
Res.: 1901 S. San Gabriel Blvd., 91776. Tel: 626-288-8912; Fax: 626-288-3730.
School—1905 S. San Gabriel Blvd., 91776. Tel: 626-280-7255; Fax: 626-280-3870. Sr. Mirim Mark, S.N.J.M. Prin. Sisters of the Holy Names of Jesus and Mary 1; Lay Teachers 30; Students 428.
Catechesis/Religious Program—Tel: 626-288-5511. Stephanie Ramos, D.R.E. Students 700.
Convent—626 E. Marshall St., 91726. Tel: 626-288-2200.

2—SAN GABRIEL (1771), [CEM], (Old Mission) Revs. Ralph B. Berg, C.M.F.; Manuel A. Diaz, C.M.F.; Arnold Gonzalez, C.M.F.; Mark Clarke, C.M.F. In Res., Revs John Gregory Hencier, C.M.F.; Fernando Vega, C.M.F.
Church and Res.: 428 S. Mission Dr., 91776. Tel: 626-457-3035; Fax: 626-282-5308.
School—415 S. Mission Dr., 91776. Tel: 626-281-2454; Fax: 626-281-4817. Dominican Sisters 1; Lay Teachers 13; Students 253.
High School—254 S. Santa Anita St., 91776. Tel: 626-282-3181; Fax: 626-282-4209. Sisters 3; Lay Teachers 26 Girls 280.
Catechesis/Religious Program—Tel: 626-457-3041. Students 495.
Convent—412 S. Mission Dr., 91776. Tel: 626-284-9585.

SAN MARINO, LOS ANGELES CO., SAINTS FELICITAS AND PERPETUA (1938), Rev. Msgr. Richard A. Loomis; Sr. Mary Anne Martin, C.S.J.
Res.: 1190 Palomar Rd., 91108. Tel: 626-796-0432; Fax: 626-796-0363.
School—2955 Huntington Dr., 91108. Tel: 626-796-8223. Sisters 2; Lay Teachers 13; Students 277.
Catechesis/Religious Program—Students 152.

SAN PEDRO, LOS ANGELES CO.

1—HOLY TRINITY (1924), Revs. Thomas J. Glynn; James Bevacqua; Francis J. Hicks.
Parish Center:—208 N. Hanford Ave., 90732. Tel: 310-548-6535; Fax: 310-833-1134.
Church: 1292 W. Santa Cruz St., 90732.
School—1226 W. Santa Cruz St., 90732. Tel: 310-833-0703; Fax: 310-833-5219. Lay Teachers 26; Students 554.
Catechesis/Religious Program—Tel: 310-833-3500. Students 625.

2—MARY, STAR OF THE SEA (1889), Rev. Msgr. Michael J. Gallagher (SD); Revs. Lorenzo De Domnici (Retired); Gilbert Cruz; Christopher Lawrence; Deacons Nino Crisafulli; William Garcia.
Res.: 870 W. 8th St., 90731. Tel: 310-833-3541; Fax: 310-833-9254.
School—Tel: 310-831-0875; Fax: 310-831-0877. Priests 1; Lay Teachers 10; Students 266.
High School—Tel: 310-547-1138; Fax: 310-547-1827. Priests 5; Lay Teachers 26; Students 461
Catechesis/Religious Program—717 S. Cabrillo Ave., 90731. Tel: 310-833-3933; Fax: 310-832-1257. Students 727.

3—ST. PETER (1965), (Hispanic), Revs. Claudio De Agostini, C.S.J.; Bruno De Santi, C.S.J.; Sylvan Schiavo, C.S.J.
Res.: 338 N. Grand Ave., 90731-2006. Tel: 310-831-5360; Fax: 310-831-0415.
Catechesis/Religious Program—Tel: 310-832-6731. Students 531.

SANTA ANA, ORANGE CO., ST. GEORGE, Rev. Zuhair Toma.
Mailing Address: 4307 W. McFadden, 92704. Tel: 714-531-7760.

SANTA BARBARA, SANTA BARBARA CO.

1—HOLY CROSS (1972), Rev. Ludo DeClippel, C.J. (Belgium); Deacons Nicholas Curran; David Huff; Rick Sanchez. In Res., Revs. Alfred Verstreken, C.J. (Belgium); Thomas J. Elewaut, C.J.
Res.: 1740 Cliff Dr., 93109. Tel: 805-962-0411; Fax: 805-564-6921.
Catechesis/Religious Program—Tel: 805-962-7311. Students 222.

2—OLD MISSION SANTA BARBARA (1786), [CEM] Revs. Richard Juzix, O.F.M. (FRS); Howard Hall, O.F.M.; Deacon Jim Bret.
Res.: 2201 Laguna St., 93105. Tel: 805-682-4713; Fax: 805-687-7841.
Catechesis/Religious Program—Tel: 805-682-4151. Students 51.

3—OUR LADY OF GUADALUPE (1928), (Hispanic), Rev. Rafael Marin-Leon.
Res.: 227 N. Nopal St., 93103. Tel: 805-965-4060; Fax: 805-965-3386.
Catechesis/Religious Program—Tel: 805-962-4441. Students 650.

4—OUR LADY OF SORROWS (1856), Revs. Thomas P. Delaney, S.J.; Martin L. Brewer, S.J., Pastor Emeritus; Luis H. Quihuis, S.J., V.F.; Michael W. Ravencamp, S.J.; Arthur J. Wehr, S.J.; Deacon William Sangster.
Res.: 21 E. Sola St., 93101. Tel: 805-963-1734; Fax: 805-965-6461.
School—Notre Dame, 33 E. Micheltorena St., 93101. Tel: 805-965-1033; Fax: 805-965-1034. Louise MacKenzie, Prin. Lay Teachers 12; Students 245.
Catechesis/Religious Program—Tel: 805-966-4941. Students 525.

5—ST. RAPHAEL (1896), Revs. Bruce Correio; Leo W. Alberg; Deacons Wayne Rascati; Clarke Shea. In Res., Rev. John Fahey.
Res.: 5444 Hollister Ave., 93111. Tel: 805-967-5641; Fax: 805-964-2988.
School—160 St. Joseph St., 93111. Tel: 805-967-2115; Fax: 805-683-9765. Ellen Manning, Prin. Lay Teachers 12; Students 314.
Catechesis/Religious Program—Tel: 805-967-1641. Students 915.

6—SAN ROQUE (1953), [JC] Rev. James M. Ford.
Res.: 325 Argonne Cir., 93105. Tel: 805-687-5215; Fax: 805-682-9778.
Catechesis/Religious Program—Students 175.

SANTA CLARITA, LOS ANGELES CO.

1—BLESSED KATERI TEKAKWITHA (1997), Revs. Michael J. Slattery; Blaise N. Brockman; Deacon Robert O. Seidler.
Mailing Address: P.O. Box 802200, 91380-2200.
Res.: 22508 Copper Hill Dr., 91350. Tel: 661-296-3180; Fax: 661-296-7854.
Catechesis/Religious Program—Tel: 661-296-6945; Fax: 661-296-3723. Students 1,606.

2—ST. CLARE (1977), Rev. Msgr. Edmond M. Renehan, V.F.; Revs. William B. Ustaski, C.R.I.C.; Valentine Zdilla.
Res.: 27341 Camp Plenty Rd., 91351. Tel: 661-252-3353; Fax: 661-252-1539.
Catechesis/Religious Program—Tel: 661-252-6950; Fax: 661-299-6594. Peggy Pigors, D.R.E.; Nancy Fishwick, D.R.E. Students 887.

3—OUR LADY OF PERPETUAL HELP (1944), Rev. Msgr. Paul M. Montoya; Revs. Malcolm Ambrose; Vivian B. Lima; Rainee Herradura, M.F.; Sr. M. Jane Mast, S.H.F., Pastoral Min.; Deacon Richard Karl.
Res.: 23233 Lyons Ave., 91321-2632. Tel: 661-259-2276; Fax: 661-259-1873.
School—Tel: 661-259-1141; Fax: 661-259-8254. Franciscan Sisters of the Immaculate Conception 6; Lay Teachers 8; Students 308.
Catechesis/Religious Program—Tel: 661-259-4266; Fax: 661-259-2084. Students 1,699.
Convent—23719 Rotunda Rd., 91355. Tel: 661-259-5591; Fax: 661-259-6744.

SANTA FE SPRINGS, LOS ANGELES CO., ST. PIUS X (1954), (Hispanic), Revs. Marc V. Trudeau; John McHugh, Pastor Emeritus (Retired); Jose Luis Ochoa, M.G.; Sang V. Tran (Vietnam).
Res.: 10827 Pioneer Blvd., 90670. Tel: 562-863-8734; Fax: 562-868-0051.
School—Tel: 562-864-4818; Fax: 562-864-7120. Lay Teachers 12; Students 310.
Catechesis/Religious Program—Tel: 562-868-2389. Students 800.

SANTA MARIA, SANTA BARBARA CO.

1—ST. JOHN NEUMANN (Santa Barbara) (1986), (Hispanic), Revs. Vaughn Winters; William Escalante; Deacons Chet Bartlett; Ricardo Berumen; Maria A. Rocco, Admin. Asst.
Res.: 966 W. Orchard, 93458-2063. Tel: 805-922-7099; Fax: 805-346-1747.
Catechesis/Religious Program—Tel: 805-922-5288. Students 910.

2—ST. LOUIS DE MONTFORT (Santa Barbara) (1963), [JC] Revs. Charles Hofschulte, C.J.; Mark L. Newman, C.J.; John A. Mayhew, C.J.; Campion W. Aspinall, C.J. (Retired); Deacons Richard Carmody; Douglas Halvorsen; Robert Maciel; Trino Andrade.
Res.: 5075 Harp Rd., 93455. Tel: 805-937-4555; Fax: 805-934-2805.
School—Tel: 805-937-5571; Fax: 805-937-3181. Sisters 1; Lay Teachers 10; Students 269.

Catechesis/Religious Program—Tel: 805-937-8363. Students 730.
Mission—St. Anthony's Church 260 Helena St., Los Alamos, Santa Barbara Co. 93440. Tel: 805-344-1604.

3—St. Mary of the Assumption (1905), [JC] Revs. Riz Carranza; Thomas Cook; Rev. Msgr. James P. Colberg, Pastor Emeritus (Retired); Deacons Francisco Lopez; Zenon Nawrocik.
Res.: 414 E. Church St., 93454. Tel: 805-922-5826; Fax: 805-922-1986.
School—424 E. Cypress St., 93454. Tel: 805-925-6713; Fax: 805-925-3815. Sisters 1; Lay Teachers 11; Students 241.
School—Preschool, 209 S. School St., 93454. Tel: 805-346-6541; Fax: 805-347-7658. Teachers 6; Students 37.
Catechesis/Religious Program—Tel: 805-925-1334; Fax: 805-928-4964. Students 481.

Santa Monica, Los Angeles Co.

1—St. Anne (1951), (Hispanic), Rev. Michael D. Gutierrez.
Res.: 2011 Colorado Ave., 90404. Tel: 310-829-4411; Fax: 310-829-9006.
School—2017 Colorado Ave., 90404. Tel: 310-829-2775; Fax: 310-829-3945. Lay Teachers 9; Students 250.
Catechesis/Religious Program—Tel: 310-829-4040. Students 285.

2—St. Clement (1904), Rev. Tomas A. Elis, Admin.
Res.: 3102 Third St., 90405. Tel: 310-396-2679; Fax: 310-396-4239.
Catechesis/Religious Program—204 Hampton Dr., Venice, 90291. Tel: 310-392-5769. Students 120.

3—St. Monica (1886), Rev. Msgr. Lloyd A. Torgerson; Revs. Ben Le; Willie Raymond, C.S.C.
Church: 725 California Ave., 90403. Tel: 310-393-9287; Fax: 310-319-9758. In Res., Rev. Matthew Tuurosong (Ghana); Deacons Gene McNamara; Frank Vargas.
School—1039 Seventh St., 90403. Tel: 310-451-9801; Fax: 310-394-6001. Lay Teachers 12; Students 280.
High School—1030 Lincoln Blvd., 90403. Tel: 310-394-3701; Fax: 310-458-1353. Sisters 2; Lay Teachers 43; Students 605.
Catechesis/Religious Program—Tel: 310-395-8903. Students 850.

Santa Paula, Ventura Co.

1—Our Lady of Guadalupe (1929), (Hispanic), [CEM] Revs. Pascuale Vuoso, C.R.I.C.; Charles Lueras, C.R.I.C.
Res.: 427 N. Oak St., 93060. Tel: 805-525-3716; Fax: 805-525-3788.
Catechesis/Religious Program—423 N. Oak St., 93060. Tel: 805-525-2225. Students 865.
Convent—432 N. Oak St., 93060. Tel: 805-525-9207.

2—St. Sebastian (1896), Revs. Pasquale Vuoso, C.R.I.C.; Charles Lueras, C.R.I.C.; Thomas J. Dome, C.R.I.C.; Deacon Alfonso A. Guilin.
Res.: 235 N. Ninth St., 93060. Tel: 805-525-2149; Fax: 805-933-5520.
School—325 E. Santa Barbara St., 93060. Tel: 805-525-1575; Fax: 805-525-1576. Lay Teachers 14; Students 183; Preschool 32.
Catechesis/Religious Program—Students 202.

Sepulveda, Los Angeles Co., Our Lady of Peace (1944), Revs. John Keese, Admin.; Francis Ty Bui; Humberto Bernabe; Maria Elena Cardena, Pastoral Assoc.
Res.: 15444 Nordhoff St., North Hills, 91343. Tel: 818-894-1176; Fax: 818-894-3838.
School—9022 Langdon Ave., North Hills, 91343. Tel: 818-894-4059; Fax: 818-894-6759. Lay Teachers 9; Students 285.
Catechesis/Religious Program—Tel: 818-891-3578; Fax: 818-894-5498. Students 745.

Sherman Oaks, Los Angeles Co., St. Francis de Sales (1938), Rev. Kevin J. Larkin. In Res., Rev. Joseph Holguin.
Res.: 13360 Valleyheart Dr., S., 91423. Tel: 818-784-0105; Fax: 818-784-4807.
Church: Moorpark St. at Dixie Canyon Ave., 91423.
School—13368 Valleyheart Dr., 91423. Tel: 818-784-9573; Fax: 818-784-9649. Sr. Ellen Marie McGovern, Prin. Sisters 2; Lay Teachers 18; Students 310.
Catechesis/Religious Program—Tel: 818-782-1907. Students 192.

Sierra Madre, Los Angeles Co., St. Rita (1908), Rev. Msgr. Joseph J. Cokus; Deacon Manuel Valencia.
Res.: 50 E. Alegria Ave., 91024. Tel: 626-355-1292; Fax: 626-355-2290.
School—Tel: 626-355-6114; Fax: 626-355-0713. Lay Teachers 14; Students 304.
Catechesis/Religious Program—Tel: 626-355-3841. Students 190.

Simi Valley, Ventura Co.

1—St. Peter Claver (1972), Rev. Msgr. Gary P. Bauler; Rev. Lawrence Seyer; Deacon Brian Clements.
Res.: 5649 E. Pittman St., 93063. Tel: 805-526-6499; Fax: 805-526-7233.
Catechesis/Religious Program—Tel: 805-526-0680; Fax: 805-526-3658. Students 745.

2—St. Rose of Lima (1921), Revs. Michael J. Carcerano; David Whorton; Deacon Peter Wilson.
Res.: 1305 Royal Ave., 93065. Tel: 805-526-1732; Fax: 805-526-0067.
School—1325 Royal Ave., 93065. Tel: 805-526-5304; Fax: 805-526-0939. Lay Teachers 18; Students 260.
Catechesis/Religious Program—Tel: 805-526-5513; Fax: 805-526-5516. Students 956.

Solvang, Santa Barbara Co., Old Mission Santa Ines (1804), (Spanish), Revs. Michael Mahoney, O.F.M.Cap; Daniel Kabat, O.F.M.Cap.; Bro. Steve Tetreault, O.F.M.Cap.; Rev. Timothy O'Sullivan, O.F.M.Cap.
Res.: 1760 Mission Dr., P.O. Box 408, 93464. Tel: 805-688-4815; Fax: 805-686-4468.
Catechesis/Religious Program—Tel: 805-688-4138. Students 400.

South El Monte, Los Angeles Co., Epiphany (1956), (Hispanic), Revs. Antonio Esteban, Admin.; Luis G. Mejia; Marco Solis; Deacon Doroteo Gonzalez.
Res.: 10911 Michael Hunt Dr., 91733. Tel: 626-442-6262; Fax: 626-575-1738.
School—10915 Michael Hunt Dr., 91733. Tel: 626-442-6264; Fax: 626-442-6074. Religious 1; Lay Teachers 8; Students 205.
Catechesis/Religious Program—Tel: 626-448-3636. Students 1,094.

South Gate, Los Angeles Co., St. Helen (1931), Revs. John F. Provenza; Jorge Guillen.
Res.: 8912 South Gate Ave., 90280. Tel: 323-563-3522; Fax: 323-563-0161.
School—9329 Madison Ave., 90280. Tel: 323-566-5491; Fax: 323-566-2810. Sisters of Notre Dame 1; Lay Teachers 10; Students 360.
Catechesis/Religious Program—9314 Madison Ave., 90280. Tel: 323-569-9550. Students 801.

South Pasadena, Los Angeles Co., Holy Family (1910), Rev. Msgr. Clement J. Connolly; Revs. Daniel A. Fox; Niall O'Leary, Dir. of Spirituality.
Pastoral Center—1527 Fremont Ave., 91030. Tel: 626-799-8908; Fax: 626-799-0423.
School—1301 Rollin St., 91030. Tel: 626-799-4354; Fax: 626-403-6180. Melissa Valenti, Prin. Lay Teachers 16; Students 302.
Catechesis/Religious Program—Tel: 626-403-6118; Fax: 626-403-6199. Students 600.

Sun Valley, Los Angeles Co., Our Lady of the Holy Rosary (1937), Revs. Richard Fanotti, C.S. (Canada); Albert Corradin, C.S.; Joel Cinco, C.S.; Antonio Grasso, C.S.
Res.: 7800 Vineland Ave., 91352. Tel: 818-765-3350; Fax: 818-765-3170.
School—7802 Vineland Ave., 91352. Tel: 818-765-4897; Fax: 818-765-5791. Servant Sisters of the Blessed Sacrament 4; Lay Teachers 7; Students 275.
Catechesis/Religious Program—Tel: 818-982-4248. Diana Cruz, D.R.E. Students 1,300.
Convent—7757 Cleon St., 91352. Tel: 818-764-9857.
Mission—Our Lady of Zapopan 7824 Lankershim Blvd., North Hollywood, Los Angeles Co. 91605. Tel: 818-503-8920.

Sylmar, Los Angeles Co., St. Didacus (1957), Rev. Msgr. Peter L. Amy; Deacons Raymond Camacho; Michael Perez. In Res., Rev. Norman Supan Check.
Res.: 14339 Astoria St., 91342. Tel: 818-367-6181; Fax: 818-367-0604.
School—14325 Astoria St., 91342. Tel: 818-367-5886; Fax: 818-364-5486. Lay Teachers 10; Students 311.
Catechesis/Religious Program—Tel: 818-367-4155. Students 770.

Temple City, Los Angeles Co., St. Luke the Evangelist (1946), Revs. Donald F. Grasha; Joey Buencamino; John Neiman.
Mailing Address: *Parish Administrative Center*, 5605 Cloverly Ave., 91780.
Res.: 9451 E. Broadway, P.O. Box 798, 91780. Tel: 626-291-5900; Fax: 626-287-2332.
School—Tel: 626-291-5959; Fax: 626-285-5367. Lay Teachers 10; Students 272.
Catechesis/Religious Program—Tel: 626-291-5925. Students 418.

Thousand Oaks, Ventura Co., St. Paschal Baylon (1960), Rev. Msgr. David Heney; Rev. Larry Neumeier; Deacon James Robinson.
Res.: 155 E. Janss Rd., 91360. Tel: 805-496-0222; Fax: 805-379-2506.
School—Tel: 805-495-9340; Fax: 805-778-1509. Lay Teachers 16; Students 335.
Catechesis/Religious Program—Tel: 805-496-0222, Ext. 115. Students 747.

Torrance, Los Angeles Co.

1—St. Catherine Laboure (1949), Revs. John O'Byrne; Tovia Lui; J. Kim-Dang Nguyen; Deacon Matilde Magana; Elizabeth Neilson, Admin. In Res., Rev. Sabato Pilato.
Res.: 3846 Redondo Beach Blvd., 90504. Tel: 310-323-8900; Fax: 323-321-0486.
School—Tel: 310-324-8732; Fax: 310-324-2471. Mrs. Kathleen Gorze, Prin. Lay Teachers 21; Students 530.
Catechesis/Religious Program—16831 Ainsworth, 90504. Tel: 310-515-6033; Fax: 310-515-5619. Elaine O'Keefe, D.R.E. Students 677.

2—Nativity (1924), Revs. Alfred Hernandez, Admin.; Patrick J. McHugh, Pastor Emeritus (Retired); Gerhart Habison; Alfonso Borgen-Reithel, O.F.M.Conv.
Res.: 1447 Engracia Ave., 90501-3234. Tel: 310-328-2776; Fax: 310-328-0508.
School—2371 Carson, 90501. Tel: 310-328-5387; Fax: 310-328-5365. Lay Teachers 9; Students 269.
Catechesis/Religious Program—Tel: 310-320-6673. Students 502.

Tujunga, Los Angeles Co., Our Lady of Lourdes (1920), Revs. Mark A. Strader; Damian Fernando; Deacon Paul Chacon.
Res.: 10321 Tujunga Canyon Blvd., 91042. Tel: 818-352-3218; Fax: 818-352-2738.
School—Tel: 818-353-1106; Fax: 818-951-4276. Sisters of Charity of the Blessed Virgin Mary 1; Lay Teachers 12; Students 229.
Catechesis/Religious Program—Tel: 818-353-3053. Students 250.

Valinda, Los Angeles Co., St. Martha (1958), (Hispanic—Filipino), Revs. William T. Easterling; Victor Ruvalcaba; Mauricio O. Goloran (Philippines); Deacon Jacob Favela. In Res., Rev. Msgr. Aidan M. Carroll.
Res.: 444 N. Azusa Ave., 91744-4299. Tel: 626-964-4313; Fax: 626-913-2953.
School—Tel: 626-964-1093; Fax: 626-912-2014. Sisters of the Love of God 4; Lay Teachers 5; Students 269.
Catechesis/Religious Program—Tel: 626-912-2581; Fax: 626-810-5267. Students 1,025.

Van Nuys, Los Angeles Co.

1—St. Bridget of Sweden (1955), Rev. Raymond Morales; Deacon Ramon Rivera.
Res.: 16711 Gault St., 91406. Tel: 818-782-7180; Fax: 818-782-7184.
School—7120 Whitaker, 91406. Tel: 818-785-4422; Fax: 818-785-0490. Lay Teachers 15; Students 300.
Catechesis/Religious Program—Gloria Romono, D.R.E. Students 240.
Convent—16707 Gault St., 91406. Tel: 818-786-1401; Fax: 818-994-5130.

2—St. Elisabeth (1919), (Hispanic), Revs. John Bruno, R.C.J.; Rodolfo D'Agostino, R.C.J.; Jupeter Quinto, R.C.J.; Deacons Wesley Balbuena; Salvador Espana.
Res.: 6635 Tobias Ave., 91405. Tel: 818-779-1756; Fax: 818-785-4492.
School—Tel: 818-779-1766; Fax: 818-779-1768. Lay Teachers 12; Students 272.
Catechesis/Religious Program—Tel: 818-779-1772. Students 500.

Venice, Los Angeles Co., St. Mark (1923), Revs. Michael Rocha; James McPolin, S.J. In Res., Rev. Richard Dimke, S.J.
Res.: 940 Coeur d'Alene Ave., 90291. Tel: 310-821-5058; Fax: 310-821-7031.
School—912 Coeur d'Alene Ave., 90291. Tel: 310-821-6612; Fax: 310-822-6101. Lay Teachers 15; Students 291.
Catechesis/Religious Program—Tel: 310-822-1201. Students 305.

Ventura, Ventura Co.

1—Our Lady of the Assumption (1954), Revs. Michael Jennett; Bobu Gundlapalli; Joseph Dass; Deacons James M. Farley; Rodger Adams; Ed Mlls.
Res.: 3175 Telegraph Rd., 93003-3283. Tel: 805-642-7966; Fax: 805-642-7635.
School—3169 Telegraph Rd., 93003-3282. Tel: 805-642-7198; Fax: 805-642-7110. Sisters 1; Lay Teachers 9; Students 277.
Catechesis/Religious Program—Tel: 805-642-0568. Students 610.

2—Sacred Heart (1966), Rev. Daniel O'Sullivan; Rev. Msgr. Arnold Biedermann, Pastor Emeritus; Rev. Loji C. Pilones.
Res.: 10800 Henderson Rd., 93004. Tel: 805-647-3235; Fax: 805-647-8087.
School—(Grades K-8) Tel: 805-647-6174; Fax: 805-647-2291. Lay Teachers 9; Students 261.
Catechesis/Religious Program—Tel: 805-647-6260. Students 486.

3—San Buenaventura Mission (1782), (Hispanic), Rev. Msgr. Patrick J. O'Brien, P.A., V.F.; Rev. George K. Aziz, S.J. (SJ).
Res.: 211 E. Main St., 93001. Tel: 805-643-4318; Fax: 805-643-7831.
School—Tel: 805-643-1500. Lay Teachers 10; Students 260.
Catechesis/Religious Program—Students 571.

VERNON, LOS ANGELES CO., HOLY ANGELS PARISH OF THE DEAF (1987), Rev. Tom Schweitzer.
Res.: 4433 Santa Fe Ave., 90058. Tel: 323-587-0397 (TDD); 323-587-2096; Fax: 323-587-7193.
Catechesis/Religious Program—Students 60.

WALNUT, LOS ANGELES CO., ST. LORENZO RUIZ (1991), Rev. Michael J. Carroll, C.M. (BRK)
Res.: 747 Meadowpass Rd., 91789. Tel: 909-595-9545; Fax: 909-594-3940.
Catechesis/Religious Program—Tel: 909-595-3400. Students 516.

WEST COVINA, LOS ANGELES CO., ST. CHRISTOPHER (1954), Rev. Nestor D. Rebong; Rev. Msgr. John P. Won; Rev. Roger Marcus Fernando, Admin.; Deacons Douglas Moloney; Loc Nguyen.
Res.: 629 S. Glendora Ave., 91790. Tel: 626-960-1805; Fax: 626-851-0595.
School—900 W. Christopher St., 91790. Tel: 626-960-3079; Fax: 626-338-7910. Mrs. Adela Solis, Prin. Lay Teachers 11; Students 289.
Catechesis/Religious Program—Tel: 626-338-2937. Dolores Zavala, D.R.E. Students 708.
Mission—St. Christopher Korean Catholic Community 833-835 W. Christopher St., Los Angeles Co. 91790. Tel: 626-960-5647.

WEST HOLLYWOOD, LOS ANGELES CO.

1—ST. AMBROSE (1922), Rev. William P. Wolfe, J.C.L. In Res., Rev. Brian Doran.
Res.: 1281 N. Fairfax Ave., 90046. Tel: 323-656-4433; Fax: 323-656-6634.

2—ST. VICTOR (1906), Rev. Msgrs. Jeremiah Murphy, Admin.; George J. Parnassus (Retired).
Res.: 8634 Holloway Dr., 90069. Tel: 310-652-6477; Fax: 310-652-6478.
Catechesis/Religious Program—Students 15.

WESTLAKE VILLAGE, LOS ANGELES CO., ST. JUDE (1970), Rev. Msgr. William J. Leser, C.B.; Rev. Pierre Albalaa, M.L.M.; Deacons Dick Dornan; Joseph Mannion.
Res.: 32032 W. Lindero Canyon Rd., 91361-4270. Tel: 818-889-1279; Fax: 818-889-3405.
School—32036 W. Lindero Canyon Rd., 91361-4270. Tel: 818-889-9483. Lay Teachers 10; Students 315.
Catechesis/Religious Program—32034 W. Lindero Canyon Rd., 91361-4270. Tel: 818-889-0612. Students 370.

WESTLAKE VILLAGE, VENTURA CO., ST. MAXIMILIAN KOLBE (1992), Rev. Msgr. James J. Maher.
Res.: 5801 Kanan Rd., 91362. Tel: 818-991-3915; Fax: 818-991-7152.
Catechesis/Religious Program—Students 770.

WHITTIER, LOS ANGELES CO.

1—ST. BRUNO (1955), Revs. Patrick O'Dwyer; James Bradley, S.D.S.; Deacon P. Michael Freeman.
Res.: 15740 Citrustree Rd., 90603. Tel: 562-947-5637; Fax: 562-943-3193.
School—15700 Citrustree Rd., 90603. Tel: 562-943-8812; Fax: 562-943-2172. Lay Teachers 20; Students 300.
Catechesis/Religious Program—Tel: 562-943-2510; 562-947-5637. Students 998.
Convent—10734 S. Widener Ave., 90603. Tel: 310-947-1177. Sr. Miriam Vu, L.H.C., Supr.

2—ST. GREGORY THE GREAT (1951), Revs. John S. Schiavonne; Robert Folbrecht; Richard Carey; Deacon Servando Patlan.
Res.: 13935 Telegraph Rd., 90604. Tel: 562-941-0115; Fax: 562-941-3785.
School—13925 Telegraph Rd., 90604. Tel: 562-941-0750; Fax: 562-903-7325. Lay Teachers 13; Students 299.
Catechesis/Religious Program—Tel: 562-944-8311; Fax: 562-941-4380. Students 990.

3—ST. MARY OF THE ASSUMPTION (1803), Revs. Arturo Uribe, C.SS.R.; Brian Johnson, C.SS.R.; Charles A. Wehrley Jr., C.SS.R.; Bro. Juan Carlos Garcia, C.SS.R.; Deacon James Fitzgerald, M.D. In Res., Revs. Joseph Elliott, C.SS.R.; Donald Liberty, C.SS.R.; George Dawson, C.SS.R.; Arthur Frost, C.SS.R.; William Adams, C.SS.R.; Enrique Lopez, C.SS.R.
Res.: 7215 S. Newlin Ave., 90602. Tel: 562-698-0107; Fax: 562-696-1617.
School—Tel: 562-698-0253; Fax: 562-698-0206. Lay Teachers 23; Students 500.
Catechesis/Religious Program—Tel: 562-693-3764. Students 700.

WILMINGTON, LOS ANGELES CO.

1—HOLY FAMILY (1929), (Hispanic), Revs. Rafael Marin-Leon; Ramona G. Palomera; Enrique Huerta, S.V.D.; Deacon Ralph Vlibarri.
Pastoral Center—1110 E. Robidoux St., 90744.
Res.: 1220 N. Sanford Ave., P.O. Box 416, 90748. Tel: 310-834-6333; Fax: 310-834-9038.
School—1122 E. Robidoux St., 90748. Tel: 310-518-1440; Fax: 310-518-1257. Miss Hermelinda Oliveros, Prin. Lay Teachers 10; Students 225.
Catechesis/Religious Program—Tel: 310-549-0011. Students 701.

2—SS. PETER AND PAUL'S (1866), Revs. Peter Irving; Roberto Pirrone.
Res.: 515 W. Opp St., 90744. Tel: 310-834-5215; Fax: 310-834-4685.
School—706 Bayview Ave., 90744. Tel: 310-834-5574; Fax: 310-834-1601. Lay Teachers 9; Students 210.
Catechesis/Religious Program—Students 590.

WINNETKA, LOS ANGELES CO., ST. JOSEPH THE WORKER (1956), (Hispanic—Vietnamese), Revs. James C. Gehl; Pedro Cobenas; Huy Nguyen; Mike Stafford, Admin.
Res.: 19808 Cantlay St., 91306. Tel: 818-341-6634; Fax: 818-341-3875.
Parish Center—19808 Cantlay St., 91306.
School—19812 Cantlay St., 91306. Tel: 818-341-6616; Fax: 818-341-1102. Sr. Barbara Joseph Wilson, C.S.J., Prin. Lay Teachers 15; Students 354.
Catechesis/Religious Program—Tel: 818-998-4166. Elizabeth Mattera Hise, D.R.E. Students 556.

WOODLAND HILLS, LOS ANGELES CO.

1—ST. BERNARDINE OF SIENA (1962), Rev. Robert J. McNamara; Rev. Msgr. Richard H. Murray, Pastor Emeritus (Retired); Rev. Alberto Avenido; Deacons Jerry Cellner; Dan McHugh; Dale Taufer.
Res.: 24410 Calvert St., 91367. Tel: 818-888-8200; Fax: 818-888-5046.
School—Tel: 818-340-2130; Fax: 818-340-3417. Lay Teachers 16; Students 326.
Catechesis/Religious Program—6061 Valley Circle Blvd., 91367. Tel: 818-340-1440. Students 450.

2—ST. MEL (1955), Rev. Msgrs. Padraic Loftus; John T. Naughton, Pastor Emeritus (Retired); Michael J. O'Connor, Pastor Emeritus (Retired); Rev. Ramon Valera.
Res.: 20870 Ventura Blvd., 91364. Tel: 818-340-6020; Fax: 818-340-0261.
School—20874 Ventura Blvd., 91364. Tel: 818-340-1924; Fax: 818-347-4426. Sisters of St. Louis 1; Lay Teachers 35; Students 549.
Catechesis/Religious Program—Tel: 818-340-6020, Ext. 1022. Students 273.

Chaplains of Public Institutions
Non-Catholic Hospitals/Institutions

LOS ANGELES. *Cedar Sinai Medical Center*. Rev. Dennis Mongrain, Chap.
8700 Beverly Blvd., Rm. 2508, 90048. Tel: 310-855-5550; Fax: 310-967-0643.
Immigration and Naturalization Service, Tel: 213-251-3509. Rev. Robert W. McChesney, S.J., Coord. Tel: 213-251-3509, Alice Linsmeier, Juvenile Coord. Tel: 213-251-3533, Rev. Peter G. Neeley, S.J. Tel: 310-241-2347.
L.A. City Fire Dept., Tel: 818-894-2261. Rev. Msgr. Sean B. Flanagan. Tel: 562-438-3826.
L.A. County Fire Dept.. Rev. Robert A. Folbrecht, Chap. Tel: 626-960-1136.
L.A. County/University of Southern California Hospital.
Norris Cancer and USC University Hospital, St. Camillus Center for Pastoral Care, 1911 Zonal Ave., 90033. Tel: 323-225-4461; 213-222-9047 (AIDS Center); Fax: 323-225-9096. Revs. Christopher D. Ponnet, Chap., Robert J. Jones, C.M., Chap., Gustavo Lara, Chap., Deacon James Dillon, Chap., Sisters Dora Hauchecorne, I.C.M., Chap., Mary Jean Ferry, B.V.M., Chap., Matilda Ortiz, C.M.S.T., Chap., Angela Pacheco, C.S.J., Chap., Nancy Bartasavich, S.P., Chap., Pat Walsh, O.P., Chap.
L.A. Police Department. Rev. Michael P. McCullough, Chap.
Employee Assistance Unit, 150 N. Los Angeles St., 90012. Tel: 213-485-0703.
Martin Luther King, Jr., Drew Medical Center, 12021 Wilmington Ave., 90059-3019. Rev. Don R. Kribs, Chap. (Retired).
435 S. Occidental, 90057-1598. Tel: 213-388-3742 (Precious Blood Church).
Metropolitan Detention Center. (Federal Institution), 535 N. Alameda St., 90012. Tel: 213-253-9575. Rev. Mark Santo, Chap. (Vacant)

CAMARILLO. *Camarillo State Hospital-Development Center*, P.O. Box 6022-250, 93011. Tel: 805-484-3661, Ext. 4459. Rev. Hippolyte L. Goossens, C.J., Chap.
Youth Correctional Facility, California Youth Authority, 3100 Wright Rd., 93010-8307.

DOWNEY. *Rancho Los Amigos Medical Center*, 7601 E. Imperial Hwy., 90242. Rev. Msgr. John A. Fosselman, Chap. (Retired). Tel: 562-940-7257.

DUARTE. *City of Hope Medical Center*, 1500 E. Duarte Rd., 91010. Tel: 626-359-8911. Rev. Ramon Mart, Sch.P., Chap.

LANCASTER. *Immigration and Naturalization Service*, Mira Loma Facility, 45100 N. 60th St. W., 93536. Tel: 661-949-3811. Deacon Edward E. Caputo, Chap. Tel: 661-949-3848.

LOMPOC. *Lompoc Federal Correctional Institution*, 3600 Guard Rd., 93436-2705. Tel: 805-736-4154, Ext. 725 &. Rev. Michael D. Kirkness, Supvr. & Chap., Deacon John Burke, Chap. Federal Intensive Confinement Center
US Penitentiary, 3901 Klein Rd., 93436. Tel: 805-735-2771, Ext. 450 &. Rev. Michael D. Kirkness, Supvr. & Chap., Deacon John Burke, Chap.
Vandenberg Air Force Base. Rev. David J. Ivey, Chap. Tel: 805-606-5773.
30SW/HC, 587 Utah St., Bldg. 16200, Vandenberg AFB, 93437-6309.

LONG BEACH. *Veterans Affairs Medical Center*. Rev. Leo M. Miller, O.M.I., Chap., Rev. Msgr. Joseph F. Brennan (Retired), USN, Rev. Anselm Deehr, S.T.
5901 E. 7th St., 90822. Tel: 562-494-5418.

NORWALK. *California Youth Authority*. Tom Moletteire, Chap.
Southern Youth Correction Reception, 13200 S. Bloomfield Ave., 90650. Tel: 562-868-9979, Ext. 2467.
Metropolitan State Hospital. Rev. Jerome Stack, C.PP.S., Chap. Tel: 310-863-7011.
11400 S. Norwalk Blvd., 90650. Tel: 562-651-4311.

POINT MUGU. *Naval Air Station*. Rev. Adrian R. Gervacio, LCDR, CHC, USNR.
Bldg. 121, Code NASCG, 93042. Tel: 805-989-7967.

POMONA. *Frank D. Lanterman Developmental Center*, 3530 W. Pomona Blvd., 91768. Tel: 909-595-1221, Ext. 7162. P.O. Box 100, 91769. Tel: 909-444-7162. Sr. Nuala Ryan, S.S.L., Chap. Tel: 909-444-7162.

PORT HUENEME. *Naval Construction Battalion Center*. Rev. Adrian R. Gervacio.
NCBC Code CBCHP, 1000 23rd Ave., 93042. Tel: 805-982-4358.

SAN PEDRO. *Fort MacArthur Annex*. Rev. Michael J. DiRenzo, 61-ABG/HC.
Chaplain's Office, 325 Challenger Way, Ste. 1901, LA AFB, El Segundo, 90245-5677. Tel: 310-363-1956.
Immigration and Naturalization Service, San Pedro Service Processing Center, 2001 Seaside Ave., 90731. Tel: 310-241-2347. Rev. Peter G. Neeley, S.J.

SEPULVEDA. *Veterans Administration Medical Center*. Rev. Patrick O'Hagan, SS.CC. Tel: 818-895-9322.
16111 Plummer St., 91343-2099.

TERMINAL ISLAND. *Federal Correctional Institution*. Rev. Henry L. Hernanco, Contract Chap., 1299 Seaside Ave., San Pedro, 90731. Tel: 626-918-8314.
1299 Seaside Ave., San Pedro, 90731-0207. Tel: 626-918-8314.

TORRANCE. *L.A. County-Harbor-U.C.L.A. Medical Center*, 1000 W. Carson, 90509. Tel: 310-222-2345; 310-222-2167 (Catholic Chap. Office). Rev. Cesar Raffo-Rivasplata, 1000 W. Carson, 90509. Tel: 310-222-2345; 310-222-2167 Catholic Chap. Office.
21900 S. Main St., Carson, 90745. Tel: 310-835-7161 (St. Philomena Parish).

WEST LOS ANGELES. *Veterans Administration Wadsworth Hospital Center*. Rev. Francis Kelly. Tel: 310-824-4312.
Chaplain Service, 11301 Wilshire Blvd. 691/125, 90099-5786. Tel: 310-268-3391.

Detention Ministries

LOS ANGELES. *L.A. Juvenile Detention Facilities*, Central Juvenile Hall, 1605 Eastlake Ave., 90033. Tel: 323-226-8530. Javier E. Stauring, Chap.
MacLaren Hall. (Vacant)
Dorothy Kirby Center. Sr. Claudia L. Romero, O.D.N., Chap. Tel: 818-364-2021.
Los Angeles County Jails in the City of Los Angeles, Adult Facilities, Biscailuz Center, 1060 N. Eastern Ave.. Tel: 323-881-3636. Deacon Thomas E. Brandlin, Chap. Pager: 213-353-6509.
L.A. Men's Central Jail, 441 Bauchet St., 90012. Tel: 213-974-8081. Rev. George Horan, Chap., Deacon Paulino R. Jaurez, Chap., Patricia L. Bartlett, Chap., Ramon Heredia, Chap.
Metropolitan Detention Center, 535 N. Alameda St., 90053. Tel: 213-253-9575. Rev. Mark Santo. (Federal Institution); (Vacant)
Office of Detention Ministry, 3424 Wilshire Blvd., 90010-2241. Tel: 213-637-7639; 213-637-7491; Fax: 213-637-6161. Rev. George Horan, Co-Dir., Javier E. Stauring, Co-Dir.
Twin Towers Correctional Facility I, 450 Bauchet St., 90063. Tel: 213-893-5241; Fax: 213-830-0907. Gerardo F. Gomez, Chap. (Men).

CAMARILLO. *Youth Correctional Facility*, 3100 Wright Rd., 93010. Tel: 805-278-3746.
Twin Towers Correctional Facility II, 450 Bauchet St., 90063. Tel: 213-893-5152; Fax: 213-830-0907. (Women)

DOWNEY. *Los Padrinos Juvenile Hall*, 7285 Quill Dr., 90242. Tel: 562-940-8711; 562-940-8712. Sr. Teresa Doherty, R.S.C.

LANCASTER. *California State Prison, L.A. County*, 44750 60th St. W., 93536-7620. Tel: 805-729-2000, Ext. 6129. Rev. Tomas White, Chap.
Challenger Youth Memorial Center, 5300 West Ave. I, 93536. Tel: 805-940-4165; 805-940-4166. Deacon Edward E. Caputo, Chap.

LYNWOOD. *Century Regional Detention Facility*, 11705 S. Alameda St., 90262. Tel: 323-357-5114. Sixto

Aguirre, Chap.

NORWALK. *Southern Youth Correctional Reception*, 13200 S. Bloomfield Ave., 90650. Tel: 562-868-9979, Ext. 2467. Tom Moletteire, Chap.

OJAI. *Ojai Men's Honor Farm*, 370 W. Baldwin Rd., 93023. Tel: 805-649-6020. Margaret Oberon, Chap. Tel: 805-654-5087.

Ojai Women's Jail Farm, 370 W. Baldwin Rd., 93023. Tel: 805-649-3020. Margaret Oberon, Chap. Tel: 805-654-5087.

SANTA BARBARA. *Los Prietos Boy's Camp*, Star Route, 93105-9722. Tel: 805-898-7008. Marciano Avilla, Chap.

Santa Barbara County Jail, 4436A Calle Real, 93110. Tel: 805-898-7008. Marciano Avilla, Chap.

Santa Barbara Juvenile Hall, 4500 Hollister Avenue, 93111. Tel: 805-681-5334. Marciano Avilla, Chap.

SANTA MARIA. *Juvenile Hall*, 812-B W. Foster Rd., 93454. Tel: 805-681-5334. Eduardo Arnouil, Chap.

SANTA PAULA. *Santa Paula Jail*, 600 S. Todd Rd., 93060. Tel: 805-933-8564. Margaret Oberon, Chap. Tel: 805-654-5087.

SAUGUS. *North County Correctional Facility*, 29340 The Old Road, 91350. Tel: 661-295-7800, Ext. 5217. Gonzalo De Vivero, Chap. Vacant.

Pitchess Detention Center, 29300 The Old Road, 91350.

Medium South. (Closed)

Medium North. Rev. John D. Murray. Tel: 661-295-8840, Ext. 3445.

Maximum East. Patricia R. Bartlett, Chap. Tel: 661-295-8815, Ext. 3337. (Closed)

SYLMAR. *Barry J. Nidorf Juvenile Hall*, 16350 Filbert St., 91342. Tel: 818-364-2021. Sr. Claudia L. Romera, O.D.N., Chap.

THOUSAND OAKS. *East County Jail*, 2101 E. Olsen Rd., 93162. Tel: 805-933-8564. Margaret Oberon, Chap. Tel: 805-654-5087.

VENTURA. *Colston Treatment Center*, 315 N. Hillmont Ave., 93003. Tel: 805-652-5721. Margaret Oberon, Chap.

Ventura County Jail, 800 S. Victoria Ave., 93009. Margaret Oberon, Chap. Tel: 805-654-5087.

Ventura Juvenile Hall-Clifton Tatum Center, 380 N. Hillmont Ave., 93003. Tel: 805-652-5727. Margaret Oberon, Chap. Vacant.

Ventura Juvenile Restitution Project, 381 Hospital Rd., 93003. Tel: 805-652-6594. Margaret Oberon, Chap. Vacant.

WHITTIER. *Fred C. Nelles Correctional Facility*, 11850 E. Whittier Blvd., 90601. Tel: 562-698-6781, Ext. 2532; Fax: 562-696-7485. Rev. P. Jerry Helfrich, S.J., Chap.

Camps

LOS ANGELES. *Juvenile Probation Camps*.

Camp C.B. Afflerbaugh, 6331 N. Stephens Ranch Rd., La Verne, 91750. Tel: 909-596-0686. Connie Arambula, Chap.

Camp Dorothy Kirby Center, 1500 S. McDonnell Ave., 90022. Tel: 213-489-6226. Dwain Miller, Chap.

Camp David Gonzales, 1301 N. Las Virgines Rd., Calabasas, 91302. Tel: 310-821-4126. Bob Strickland, Chap.

Camp Holton, 12653 N. Little Tujunga Canyon Rd., San Fernando, 91342. Tel: 213-637-7554. Janne Shirley, Chap.

Camp Kilpatrick, 427 S. Encinal Canyon Rd., Malibu, 90265. Tel: 818-991-7878. Jim Graham, Chap.

Camp McLaren Children's Center. Closed. , 4024 Durfee Rd., El Monte, 91732. Tel: 213-637-7615. Sr. Claudia L. Romero, O.D.N., Chap.

Camp Kenyon J. Scudder, 287 N. Bouquet Canyon Rd., Saugus, 91350. Tel: 805-268-1564.

Camp Mendenhall, 42230 Lake Hughes Rd., Lake Hughes, 93532. Tel: 661-942-1370. Alfred Miller, Chap.

Camp Miller, 433 S. Encinal Canyon Rd., Malibu, 90265. Tel: 310-458-6621; 310-442-9940. Sandy Belger, Chap.

Camp John Munz, 42220 Lake Hughes Rd., Lake Hughes, 93532. Tel: 805-942-1370. Alfred E. Miller, Chap.

Camp Paige, 6601 N. Stephens Ranch Rd., La Verne, 91750. Tel: 909-596-1676. Frank Cunningham, Chap., Cindy Cunningham, Chap.

Camp Rockey, 1900 N. Sycamore Canyon Rd., San Dimas, 91773. Tel: 909-592-3132. Jim Drolet, Chap.

Camp Routh, 12500 Big Tujunga Rd., Tujunga, 91042. Tel: 213-663-1142. Bro. Kevin Cunniff, Chap.

Camp Scott, 28700 N. Bouquet Canyon Rd., Saugus, 91350. Tel: 805-527-2408. Deacon Pete Wilson, Chap. (Girls)

Camp Kenyon J. Scudder, 287 N. Bouquet Canyon Rd., Saugus, 91350. Tel: 805-268-1564. Maria L. Monica, Chap.

On Duty Outside the Archdiocese:
Rev. Msgr.—
Zak, Steven

Revs.—
Duc Minh, Joseph
Miskella, Richard
Rankin, Robert
Spiteri, Laurence J.
Young, Gerald A.

Foreign Mission:
Rev.—
Joy, Laurence

Military Chaplains:
Revs.—
Llanos, Philip S.
Mayfield, Olin
McNulty, Gerard J.

Graduate Studies:
Revs.—
Forsen, James
Lee, Anthony

Hospital Chaplains:
Revs.—
Comerford, Patrick, Chap., St. John Hospital, Santa Monica
Holguin, Joseph, Chap., Providence St. Joseph, Burbank
Mejia, Jose, Chap. Providence Holy Cross, Mission Hills
Roman, Julio, Chap. St. Vincent Medical Center, Los Angeles
Sigler, John W., Chap. Children's Hospital, Los Angeles

On Sick Leave:
Revs.—
Cavanagh, James
Doran, Brian
Griffin, Noel
LaNier, Michael L.
Lee, Joseph P.
McDonnell, Anthony
Moloney, John
Nuanez, Anthony
Wolkovits, Paul

On Administrative Leave:
Rev. Msgr.—
Van Liefde, Christian M.
Revs.—
Bismonte, Honesto
Granadino, David

Retired:
Most Revs.—
Arzube, Juan A., D.D., Nazareth House, 3333 Manning Ave., 90064-4804.
Sartoris, Joseph M., D.D., V.G., 1988 Rolling Vista Dr., #21, Lomita, 90717.
Ward, John J., 3424 Wilshire Blvd., 90010-2241.

Rev. Msgrs.—
Acton, John A., 627 Avenida Sevilla, Unit C, 90018.
Atwill, William H., St. John of God Hospital, 2035 W. Adams Blvd., 90018.
Barry, William J., P.A., Proto Notary Apostolic, 68 Balboa Coves, Newport Beach, 92663.
Biedermann, Arnold, Sacred Heart, 10800 Henderson Rd., Ventura, 93004-1895.
Brennan, Joseph F., 800 E. Ocean Blvd., Apt. #1205, Long Beach, 90802-5455.
Brosnan, John R., Nazareth House, 3333 Manning Ave., Rm. 162A, 90064-4804.
Clark, Laurence E., 15322 Roselle Ave., Lawndale, 90260.
Clyne, James B., Nazareth House, 3333 Manning Ave., 90064-4804.
Colberg, James P., 208 S. Miller St., Santa Maria, 93454.
Condon, Michael J., Nazareth House, 3333 Manning Ave., 90064-4804.
Diomartich, Felix S., St. Anthony, 712 N. Grand Ave., 90012-2299.
Doherty, John B., Nazareth House, 3333 Manning Ave., 90064.
Donnelly, Lawrence E., 1065 W. Lomita Blvd., Space 411, Harbor City, 90710.
Doyle, Thomas, 3618 Valihi Way, Glendale, 91208.
Duran, George, St. Rose of Lima Church, 4450 E. 60th St., Maywood, 90270.
English, Tobias P., St. Andrew, 311 N. Raymond Ave., Pasadena, 91103-3896.
Escutin, Ciriaco E., 16151 Elgenia St., Covina, 91722.
Folliard, John P., St. Cornelius Church, 5500 E. Wardlow Rd., Long Beach, 90808-3698.
Fosselman, John A., Nazareth House, 3333 Manning Ave., 90064-4804.
Frilot, Eugene P., Incarnation Church, 1001 N. Brand, Glendale, 91202-2979.
George, Alexander C., P.O. Box 2208, Blue Jay, 92317.
George, Joseph, P.O. Box 2208, Blue Jay, 92317.
Gibson, Lawrence J., 2023 Via Mariposa E., Unit A, Laguna Woods, 92653.
Gilb, Eugene A., St. John the Fisher, 5448 Crest Rd., Rancho Palos Verdes, 90274-5097.
Grill, Philip L., Nazareth House, 3333 Manning Ave., 90064-4804.
Healy, Peter C., St. Robert Bellarmine, 133 N. Fifth St., Burbank, 91501-2178.
Holland, Ian, P.O. Box 11475, Marina Del Rey, 90295.
Hughes, John C., St. Mary Magdelen, 2532 Ventura Blvd., Camarillo, 93010-6649.
Kearney, Joseph V., Nazareth House, 3333 Manning Ave., Rm. 109P, 90064-4804.
Kelly, Matthew H., Nazareth House, 3333 Manning Ave., 90064.
Kennedy, Christopher J., 3938 Cerritos Ave., Long Beach, 90807-3799.
Kiefer, Thomas A., St. Charles Borremeo, 10828 Moorpark St., North Hollywood, 91602.
Kucingis, John A., St. Casimir, 2718 St. George St., 90027-3389.
Lenihan, Michael, Proto Notary Apostolic, St. Lawrence Martyr, 1900 S. Prospect Ave., Redondo Beach, 90277-6003.
Lirette, Arthur J., P.A., Proto Notary Apostolic, Holy Family, 209 E. Lomita, Glendale, 91205-1689.
McCabe, Vincent, P.O. Box 30471, Santa Barbara, 93105.
McGovern, Thomas, 564 Bellflower Blvd. #309, Long Beach, 90814.
McGrath, Andrew, 101 South U St. #5, Lompoc, 93436-7299.
McNulty, Patrick, 2501 West Avenue 33, 90065-2892.
Mihan, John A., Maria Prima Retirement Residence, 1501 Selby Ave., 90024.
Mulcahy, Donal, Our Lady of the Assumption, 3175 Telegraph Rd., Ventura, 93003-3283.
Mulcahy, James R., St. Louis of France, 13935 E. Temple Ave., La Puente, 91746-2098.
Murray, Richard H., St. Bernardine of Siena, 24410 Calvert St., Woodland Hills, 91367-1099.
Naughton, John T., St. Mel Church, 20870 Ventura Blvd., Woodland Hills, 91364-2396.
Navin, Cyril, St. Cyril of Jerusalem Church, 4601 Firmament Ave., Encino, 91436-3108.
O'Byrne, Sylvester, Our Lady of Mt. Carmel, 1300 E. Valley Rd., Santa Barbara, 93108-1294.
O'Callaghan, James A., St. John Vianney Church, 1345 Cortez Ave., Hacienda Heights, 91745-2699.
O'Connor, Michael J., St. John of God Hospital, 2035 W. Adams Blvd., 90018.
O'Leary, Lawrence, St. Martin of Tours, 11967 Sunset Blvd., 90049.
O'Reilly, Bernard, 15360 Virginia Ave., Paramount, 90723.
O'Sullivan, Peter, Nazareth House, 3333 Manning Ave., 90064-4804.
Olsauskas, Algirdas, St. Casimir Church, 2718 St. George St., 90027-3389.
Osborne, Francis M., Our Lady of Grace, 5011 White Oak Ave., Encino, 91316-3799.
Parnassus, George J., St. Victor, 8634 Holloway Dr., West Hollywood, 90069-2304.
Pierce, Robert T., St. Louise de Marillac, 1720 E. Covina Blvd., Covina, 91724-1640.
Ravlic, Cornelius C., Nazareth House, 3333 Manning Ave., 90064-4804.
Rawden, John A., St. Francis Medical Center of Santa Barbara, 601 E. Micheltorena, Santa Barbara, 93103.
Reilly, Patrick, St. Robert Bellarmine, 135 N. 5th St., Burbank, 91501-2176.
Royer, Ronald, 40708-B Balch Park Rd., Springville, 93265.
Sheridan, John V., Our Lady of Malibu, 3625 Winter Canyon Rd., Malibu, 90265-4834.
Tseu, Andrew S., St. Madeleine, 931 E. Kingsley Ave., Pomona, 91767-5098.
Von Son, Henry A., 11075 Muirwood, Portland, OR 97225.
Walsh, Michael, Monea, Youghal, County Cork Ireland.
Young, John, 3909 Reche Rd., #116, Fallbrook, 92028.
Zimmerman, Roland G., Annunciation, 1307 E. Longdon Ave., Arcadia, 91006-5597.

Revs.—
Acton, Thomas M., St. Maria Regina Church, 2150 W. 135th St., Gardena, 90249-2498.
Amengual, Miguel, Jeanne Jugan Residence, 2100 S. Western Ave., San Pedro, 90732.
Barone, Fernando, O.F.M.Cap., 8148 Antwerp Ave., 90001.
Bernardo, Emilio A., 2006 Seventh Ave., 90018.
Bouska, Jeroma A., St. Basil, 637 S. Kingsley Dr., 90005-2392.

Bradley, Robert M., 108 Courtside Dr., Butler, PA 16001-2466.
Bray, Kevin, P.O. Box 760, Ojai, 93024.
Brennan, Joseph, O.S.B., St. Andrew Abbey, 31001 N. Valyermo, 93563.
Brincat, George, 37A Mons. Farrugia St. VCT 105 Malta.
Brint, George, 37A Mons. Farrugia St. VCT 105 Malta.
Byrne, Robert P., Nazareth House, 3333 Manning Ave., 90064-4804.
Ciordia, Pedro M., Concejo de Egues #20, 2B, 31016 Mendillorri, Pamplona Navarro, Spain.
Cooley, John E., 31402 Paseo del Mar, Laguna Niguel, 92677-2745.
Coronado, Genero, 2505 W. Foothill Blvd., Apt. 145, San Bernardino, 92410.
Cotter, Patrick J., 1854 Hanscom Dr., South Pasadena, 91030.
Cunningham, John F., 20053 S.W. Rock Bluff, Bend, OR 97702.
Daly, John, Holy Trinity, 3722 Boyce Ave., 90039-1810.
Dao, Nhuong V., 5571 Angelus Ave., San Gabriel, 91776.
DeDominici, Lorenzo, Mary Star of the Sea, 870 W. 8th St., San Pedro, 90731-3091.
Delaney, Matthew S., P.O. Box 2007, Seal Beach, 90745-2998.
Duffy, Eugene J., Bridge St., Louisburgh, County Mayo Ireland.
Fahey, John P., 601 E. Micheltorena St., Santa Barbara, 93103-2216.
Feeney, John J., Nazareth House, 3333 Manning, 90064-4804.
Ferrer, Peter C., 11544 Jerry St., Cerritos, 90703.
Fisher, David S.J., Loyola Marymount University, 7900 Loyola Blvd., 90064-4804.
Fitzgerald, John B., Nazareth House, 3333 Manning Dr., 90064-4804.
Ford, Harold L., St. Joseph, 6220 E. Willow St., Long Beach, 90815-2295.
Fremgen, Edward, 4849 Hersholt Ave., Long Beach, 90808.
Gabriel, Vicente S., 3045 N. Gold Star St., Long Beach, 90810-2708.
Gonzalez, Arnold, C.M.F., San Gabriel Mission, 428 S. Mission Dr., San Gabriel, 91776-1201.
Gorman, Patrick, St. Bernadette, 3825 Don Felipe Dr., 90008-4299.
Gorman, Rody I., St. Matthias, 7125 Mission Pl., Huntington Park, 90255-5299.
Guerrini, Roderic, Nazareth House, 3333 Manning Ave., 90064-4804.
Gutting, John C., St. Athanasius, 5390 Linden Ave., Long Beach, 90805-6062.
Haefeli, Joaquin, St. Ignatius Church, 322 North Ave. 61, 90042.
Halloran, John J., 5255 Stevens Creek, Santa Clara, 95051-6664.
Harman, Charles W., 261 S. Rodeo Dr., Beverly Hills, 90212.
Heery, Stephen, O.Carm., Crespi Carmelite Community, 4966 Alonzo Ave., Encino, 91316.
Hernandez, Stephen, 18277 Barroso St., Rowland Heights, 91748.
Hirte, Mateo, Immaculate Heart of Mary 4950 Santa Monica Blvd., 90029.
Hughes, Patrick M., 2020 Via Mariposa E., Laguna Woods, 92653-2247.
Hunter, William R., St. John of God Hospital, 2035 W. Adams Blvd., 90018.
Iglesias, Fernando, 23505 Evening Snow, Moreno Valley, 92557.
Infuhr, Frank J., St. John of God Nursing Home, 2035 W. Adams, 90018.
Janowski, Rock J., 6964 Dove St., Ventura, 93003.
Jennings, Bernard J., St. Elizabeth, 1849 N. Lake Ave., Altadena, 91001-3097.
Johnson, Henry J., 1211 N. Garden, Covina, 91724.
Johnson, Leo Bede, C.J., Josephite Fathers Novitiate House, 180 Patterson Rd., Santa Maria, 93455.
Kelly, Paul M.
Kolling, James, St. Timothy, 10425 W. Pico Blvd., 90064-2307.
Kribs, Don R., 22221 S. Bloomfield Ave., #21, Cypress, 90630.
Landreau, Edward J., St. Frances of Rome, 501 E. Foothill Blvd., P.O. Box 637, Azusa, 91702-0637.
Luck, Robert O., 388 Thornhill Circle, Henderson, NV 89014.
Madrigal, Ildefonso, 10434 Haldeon Ave., Downey, 90241.
Maechler, Edmund F., 613 California St., Huntington Beach, 92648.
Maechler, Gerald T., 18401 Delaware Ave., Huntington Beach, 92648.
Martin, Arcadio, Dominguez Seminary, 18127 S. Alameda St., Rancho Dominguez, 90220.
Martin, Diosdado, 1808 S. Palm Ave., Alhambra, 91803.
McGee, Peter J., Main St., Miltown Malboy, County Claire Ireland.
McGrath, Philip J., St. Bernard, 9627 E. Beach St., Bellflower, 90706-0576.
McGuire, Kenneth H., C.S.P., 24303 Woolsey Canyon Rd., Apt.#38, West Hills, 91304.
McHugh, John, St. Pius X Church, 10827 S. Pioneer Blvd., Santa Fe Springs, 90670-4298.
McHugh, Patrick J., Nativity, 1447 Engracia Ave., Torrance, 90501-3234.
McLaughlin, Thomas W., St. John of God, 2035 W. Blvd., 90018.
Melley, James, P.O. Box 260424, Encino, 91426.
Merino, Santiago, 959 LaDeney Dr., Ontario, 91762.
Meskill, Patrick A., 63 Ilex Dr., Newbury Park, 91320.
Meskill, Thomas A., 63 Ilex Dr., Newbury Park, 91320.
Miller, George M.
Murphy, Denis J., Our Lady of the Assumption, 3175 Telegraph Rd., Ventura, 93003-3283.
Nocero Pascal F., P.O. Box 279, Oak View, 93022.
O'Grady, James, Glenkeen Louisburgh, County Mayo, Ireland.
O'Grady, James F., Visitation, 6561 W. 88th St., 90045-3716.
O'Leary, Niall F., 1527 Fremont Ave., South Pasadena, 91030-3736.
O'Neill, Jeremiah, 2100 W. Carlos Ave., Alhambra, 91803-4321.
O'Shea, Michael, 9647 Beach St., Bellflower, 90706-5817.
O'Sullivan, Thomas C., Our Lady of Mt. Carmel, 1300 E. Valley Rd., Santa Barbara, 93108-1294.
Parrish, Francis, S.J., Santa Teresita Hospital, 819 Buena Vista St., Duarte, 91010-1703.
Polt, Albert, O.A.R., Nazareth House, 3333 Manning Ave., 90064-4804.
Potthoff, Donald W., St. Denis, 2151 Diamond Bar Blvd., P.O. Box 4096, Diamond Bar, 91765-2860.
Romero, Gilbert, 13220 Southport Ln. #170-E., Seal Beach, 90740-3361.
Rothe, James A., P.O. Box 962, Bridgeport, 93517-0592.
Rucker, Neville, Nazareth House, 3333 Manning Ave., 90064-4804.
Sagardoy, Angel, 11320 Laurel, Canyon Blvd., San Fernando, 91340.
Sanchez, Eliseo, Nazareth House, 3333 Manning Ave., 90064-4804.
Saplis, Raymond A., Mother Gertrude Balcazar Home, 11320 Laurel Canyon Blvd., San Fernando, 91340.
Spada, Rino, C.S., Villa Scalabrini Retirement Center, 10631 Vinedale St., Sun Valley, 91352.
Stehly, Thomas J., 9432 S. Bloomfield Ave., Cypress, 90630.
Sutphin, Carl, 157 Dahlia Way, Ventura, 93004.
Thomas, Sylvester J., Mary Star of the Sea, 870 W. Eighth St., San Pedro, 90731-3091.
Thompson, Jerome H., P.O. Box 4761, Palm Springs, 92263.
Toal, James, 10908 Moorpark St., North Hollywood, 91602.
Torralba, Anatolin B., Sapalicio St., Polangui, Albay Philippines.
Tsang, Peter, St. Elizabeth Ann Seton, 1835 Larkvane Rd., Rowland Hgts., 91748-2501.
Vellucci, Dennis C., St. John Vianney, 1345 Turnbull Canyon Rd., Hacienda Heights, 91745-2699.
Villegas, Samuel C., St. Matthias, 7125 Miss on Pl., Huntington Park, 90255-5299.
Walker, Earl G., Cathedral Chapel, 922 S. Detroit St., 90036-4312.
Walker, Gerald, 2020 Mariposa E., Apt. C, Laguna Woods, 92653-2247.
Walsh, Robert, Santa Teresita Hospital Lourdes Unit, Rm. 110, 1206 Fallen Leaf Ave., 91010.
Weible, Thomas C., 9 Highview Dr., Sandwich, MA 02563.
Ziliotto, Rino, C.S., St. Charles Residence, 10651 Vinedale St., Sun Valley, 91352.

Permanent Deacons:
Acquaviva, Dick, St. Clare, Canyon Country
Adams, Emile, Jr., St. Bernadette, Los Angeles
Adams, J. Rodger, Our Lady of the Assumption Church, Ventura
Adams, James V., Chaminade College Preparatory, West Hills
Aguirre, Eduardo, St. Emydius, Lynwood
Alexander, Hosea, Sr., St. Agatha, Los Angeles
Allen, John P., Corpus Christi, Pacific Palisades
Andrade, Trinidad, St. Louis de Montfort, Santa Maria
Aranda, Fernando, Jr., Our Lady of Solitude, Los Angeles
Arroyo, Miguel, Our Lady of Guadalupe, Los Angeles
Asmar, George, Immaculate Heart of Mary and St. Mary's Coptic Parish, Los Angeles
Auela, Uikirifi, Samoan Catholic Community
Baker, Charles, St. Linus, Norwalk
Balbuena, Wesley M., Jr., St. Elisabeth, Van Nuys
Baragan, Ricardo, Our Lady of Guadalupe, Oxnard
Barragan, Arturo, St. Francis Xavier, Pico Rivera
Barrera, Jose Oscar, St. Patrick, N.Hollywood
Bartlett, Chester, St. John Neumann, Santa Maria
Battle, Joe T., St. Philip Neri, Lynwood
Bautista, Rolando, Holy Trinity, Los Angeles
Bednar, George T., St. Mary Magdalen, Camarillo
Berumen, Ricardo, St. John Neumann, Santa Maria
Bohlig, Alden W., St. Barnabas, Long Beach
Brandlin, Thomas E., Leave of Absence
Bravo, Anthony J., St. Gerard Majela, Los Angeles
Bret, James L., Mission Santa Barbara, Santa Barbara
Burke, John, Federal Penitentiary, Lompoc
Butler, Ronald, Sacred Heart, Covina
Caputo, Edward E., Blessed Junipero Serra, Lancaster
Carmody, Richard, St. Louis de Montford, Santa Maria
Caro, Jose, St. Cecilia, Los Angeles
Castillo, Alfonso, St. Benedict, Montebello
Castorena, John G., Santa Clara, Oxnard
Cellner, Jerry, St. Bernardine of Siena, Woodland Hills
Chacon, Paul, Our Lady of Lourdes, Tujunga
Charters, John, Sacred Heart, Lancaster
Chavez, Gilbert M., Annunciation, Arcadia
Chavez, Manuel, St Anthony, San Gabriel
Chavez, Raul, Guardian Angel, Pacoima
Chu, Peter, St. Elizabeth Ann Seton, Rowland Heights
Clements, Brian, St. Peter Claver, Simi Valley
Clinton, Jack, Holy Name of Mary, San Dimas
Conenen, Jerry, Our Lady of Malibu, Malibu
Conrey, Fred, Immaculate Conception, Monrovia
Coplen, John L., St. Francis de Sales, Sherman Oaks
Corcios, Oscar, Our Lady of the Rosary, Paramount
Corwin, Richard, St. Margaret Mary Alacoque, Lomita
Crisafulli, Nino D., Mary Star of the Sea, San Pedro
Crowley, James, Assumption of the Blessed Virgin Mary, Pasadena
Cuevas, Frank, St. Madeleine, Pomona
Cunneen, Jon, St. Linus, Norwalk
Curran, Nicholas P., Holy Cross, Santa Barbara
De Los Reyes, Carlito, St. Lucy, Long Beach
Delgado, Eduardo T., St. John Vianney, Hacienda Heights
Denisac, Charles M., Jr., Our Lady of Perpetual Help, Downey
Dieter, Frank, St. Lawrence Martyr, Redondo Beach
Dillon, James, St. Benedict, Montebello
Doane, Allan E., St. Thomas Aquinas, Ojai
Dornan, Richard, St. Jude, Westlake Village
Duke, Oscar M., St. Anthony, Oxnard
Dumlao, Felix, St. Columban, Los Angeles
Edmonds, Tom, La Purisima, Lompoc
Elsey, Ken, Santa Rosa, San Fernando
Engel, Witold, Our Lady of Refuge, Long Beach
Escovedo, Arthur, Our Lady of the Assumption, Claremont
Espana, Salvador, St. Elisabeth, Van Nuys
Estey, Marvin, Holy Name of Mary, San Dimas
Estrada, David J., St. Benedict, Montebello
Fajardo, Richard, Resurrection, Los Angeles
Farley, James, Our Lady of the Assumption, Ventura
Favela, Jacobo M., Jr., St. Martha, Valinda
FitzGerald, Gerald M., California City Correctional Facility, California City
Fitzgerald, James, St. Mary of the Assumption, Whittier
Fitzpatrick, Arthur J., St. Paul of the Cross, La Mirada
Freeman, P. Michael, St. Bruno, Whittier
Frias, Sam, St. John the Baptist de la Salle, Granada Hills
Fry, Ralph M., Sacred Heart, Covina
Galido, Juan, Jr., Our Lady of Lourdes, Northridge
Gallegos, Jose, St. Elizabeth, Van Nuys
Garcia, Armando R., St. Matthias, Huntington Park
Garcia, William J., Mary Star of the Sea, San Pedro
Gath, Don, St. Joseph, Long Beach
Gaudin, John, Holy Name of Jesus, Los Angeles
Girard, Joseph, St. Mark, Venice
Gonzales, Francisco, Sacred Heart, Lancaster
Gonzalez, Dorteo, Epiphany, South El Monte
Goodreau, Theodore, St. Anthony, El Segundo
Goodspeed, Lyle, St. John Neumann, Santa Maria
Gorman, Christopher, St. Thomas Aquinas, Ojai
Gueringer, Ludger "Lou" A., Blessed Junipero

Serra, Camarillo
Guerra, Mario, St Raymond, Downey
Guerra, Ruben, St. Joseph, La Puente
Guilin, Alfonso, St. Sebastian, Los Angeles
Gutierrez, Eliseo, Unassigned
Hall, Willard J., Sr., St. John the Evangelist, Los Angeles
Halley, James, St. John's Seminary, Camarillo
Halvorsen, Douglas A., St. Louis de Montfort, Santa Maria
Hammonds, Johnnie, St. John's Seminary, Camarillo
Hammonds, Johnnie, St. Mary Magdalen, Camarillo
Hanson, Walter, St. Charles Borromeo, North Hollywood
Harrison, Russell J., SS Peter and Paul, Wilmington
Hawkins, Bill, St. Brigid, Los Angeles
Hays, Charles D., La Purisima Concepcion, Lompoc
Hegenbart, Joseph, St. James the Less, La Crescenta
Henry, James J., St. Anthony, Oxnard
Henschel, Louis E., St. Julie Billiart, Newbury Park
Heyer, Jerome, Holy Cross, Moorpark
Hillman, Steven V., St. Elizabeth Ann Seton, Rowland Heights
Holly, Chester N. "Chet", St. John Eudes, Chatsworth
Horn, John, Sacred Heart, Covina
Huerta, Antonio, St. Anthony of Padua, Gardena
Huerta, Hipolito, St. Louis of France, La Puenta
Huff, David W., Holy Cross, Santa Barbara
Ito, Mitchell, St. Pascal Baylon, Thousand Oaks
Juarez-Ramirez, Paulino, St. Theresa of Avila, Los Angeles
Karl, Richard J., Our Lady of Perpetual Help, Santa Clarita
Lacy, William S., St. Joseph the Worker, Canoga Park
Lambert, Richard, St. Pancratius, Lakewood
Lambey, Alvin S., Mother of Sorrows, Los Angeles
Landa, William, St. Philip the Apostle, Pasadena
Lanoix, Gilbert, St. Brigid, Los Angeles
Ledonne, Tom, St. Denis, Diamond Bar
Ledoux, Joseph, St. Albert the Great, Compton
Lee, Paul D., St. Bruno, Whittier
Liendo, Manuel, St. John Neumann, Santa Maria
Lim, James, Korean Catholic Center, Canoga Park
Lipski, Alexander, St. Cornelius, Long Beach
Lira, Pedro, St. Catherine of Siena, Reseda
Lopez, Arnaldo, Holy Angels, Arcadia
Lopez, Francisco, La Purisima Concepcion, Lompoc
Lopez, Jose R., (Retired), Our Lady of Lourdes, Los Angeles
Lopez, Mario, Holy Name of Mary, San Dimas
Lopez, Victor, St. Lucy, Long Beach
Macial, Robert, Sr., St. Louis de Montfort, Orcutt
Madrigal, Carlos, Sacred Heart, Pomona
Magana, Matilde, St. Catherine Laboure, Torrance
Magos, Carlos, Precious Blood, Los Angeles
Manion, Joseph, Sr., St. Jude, Westlake Village
Marin, Alejandro, Holy Name of Jesus, Los Angeles
Martha, Mario, Sacred Heart, Pomona
Martinez, Jesse, St. John Vianney, Hacienda Heights
Martinez, Manuel J., Cathedral of Our Lady of the Angels, Los Angeles
Martinez, Randolph M., Santa Clara, Oxnard
Mayfield, Kenneth, Queen of Angels, Lompoc
McHugh, Daniel J., St. Bernardine of Siena, Woodland Hills
McKinley, Braden, Sacred Heart, Ventura
McNamara, Eugene, St. Monica, Santa Monica
McPheeters, Jon C., St. Anthony, Oxnard
Mecozzi, John, Blessed Junipero Serra, Camarillo
Medina, Richard J., Our Lady of Perpetual Help, Downey
Mejia, J. Guadalupe, Holy Family, Artesia
Mejia, Mario, St Gertrude, Bell Gardens
Messer, John, St. Anthony, San Gabriel
Meter, Darrell, La Purisima Concepcion, Lompoc
Miller, Robert, St. James, Redondo Beach
Millholland, Frank O., St. Albert the Great, Compton
Mills, Ed, Our Lady of the Assumption, Ventura
Mimiaga, Guillermo R., St. Raphael, Los Angeles
Mizerski, Joseph R., St. Theresa, Alhambra
Mizerski, Joseph R., St. Therese, Alhambra
Modugno, Larry, St. Mary Madgalen, Camarillo
Moloney, Douglas, St. Christopher, West Covina
Morgan, T. Richard, St. Jane de Chantal, North Hollywood
Moske, Thomas, St. Joseph, Hawthorne
Nawrocik, Zenon L., St. Mary and Marian Medical Center, Santa Maria
Nawrocik, Zenon, Mary of the Assumption, Santa Maria
Nguyen, Loc, St. Christopher, West Covina
Nguyen, Matthew Van, Maria Regina, Gardena
Noon, Richard, St. John Vianney, Hacienda Heights
Noriega, Restie T., Incarnation, Glendale
Nosari, Ernest, (Retired), St. Rita, Sierra Madre
Ochoa, Ruben, Guardian Angel, Pacoima
Orcutt, Mark A., St. Paul of the Cross, La Mirada
Origel, Carlos, Our Lady of Perpetual Help, Downey
Orth, Joseph, St. Euphrasia, Granada Hills
Palmer, William, Our Lady of Guadalupe, Hermosa Beach
Parish, Harold "Hal", J.C.D., Mary Star of the Sea, Oxnard
Patlan, Servando, Sr., St. Gregory the Great, Whittier
Patterson, Gary R., Our Lady of Guadalupe, Irwindale
Patterson, Gregory, Transfiguration
Pelletier, Frederick, Holy Family, Glendale
Pepe, Joseph, Office of the Catholic Chaplain, NCB, Oxnard
Perez, Buenaventura, Mary Star of the Sea, Oxnard
Picard, John B., Blessed Junipero Serra, Camarillo
Pomphrey, Richard, St. Bede the Venerable, La Canada
Poole, Gary, Blessed Junipero Serra, Lancaster
Pruitt, Richard A., St Anthony, El Segundo
Rac, Felix, Christ the King, Los Angeles
Ramirez, Fidel M., Santa Clara, Oxnard
Ramirez, Hernan, St. Raphael, Los Angeles
Rascati, Wayne, St. Raphael, Goleta
Riera, Ralph, St. Raymond, Downey
Rios, Fred, Our Lady of the Miraculous Medal, Montebello
Rivera, Ramon, St. Bridget of Sweden, Van Nuys
Roberto, Timothy, St. Paul of the Cross, La Mirada
Robinson, James M., St. Paschal Baylon, Thousand Oaks
Rodriguez, Hernando, Resurrection, Los Angeles
Rojas, Pedro, All Saints, Los Angeles
Rose, David, Holy Angels Church of the Deaf, Vernon
Rose, Frederick, American Martyrs, Manhattan Beach
Rosenberg, Milton, Santa Clara, Oxnard
Ryan, Jack, Santa Barbara Mission, Santa Barbara
Ryan, Joseph M., St. Raymond, Downey
Sabol, Thomas, St. Timothy, Los Angeles
Sago, Bruce, St. John Bellarmine, Burbank
Salcido, Mike, Immaculate Conception, Monrovia
Sanchez, Enrique R., Holy Cross, Santa Barbara
Sangster, William B., Our Lady of Sorrows, Santa Barbara
Saucedo, Valentin, Presentation of Mary, Los Angeles
Schwerdt, Paul, St. Mary, Palmdale
Sebenius, Wayland "Gus", St. Therese, Alhambra
Seidler, Robert, St. Patrick, North Hollywood
Sevilla, Rodolfo, Our Lady Queen of Angels, (La Placita) Los Angeles
Shea, Clarke, St. Raphael, Goleta
Shinkle, Richard D., St. James, Redondo Beach
Shinn, John, Korean Catholic Center, Canoga Park
Siegman, Craig A., St. Margaret Mary, Lomita
Skupnik, Raymond P., St. Cyprian, Long Beach
Soto, Antonio P., St. Hilary, Pico Rivera
Spada, Joseph D., Our Lady of the Miraculous Medal, Montebello
Spies, William, Blessed Junipero, Serra, Camarillo
Steele, John, Holy Family, Glendale
Suh, Ignatius Jin, St. Mary's Korean Catholic Center, Rowland Heights
Taufer, Wm. Dale., St. Bernardine of Siena, Woodland Hills
Torres, Antonio B., San Francisco, Los Angeles
Torres, Pedro M., Our Lady of Loretto, Los Angeles
Turner, John, Jr., St. Brigid, Los Angeles
Ulibarri, Ralph J., Holy Family, Wilmington
Valencia, Manuel, St. Rita, Sierra Madre
Valeriano, Oscar J., Jr., St. Louis of France, La Puente
Vargas, Frank, St Monica, Santa Monica
Vazquez, Roberto L., St. John Chrysostom, Inglewood
Vega, Cris T., St. Gertrude, Bell Gardens
Vega, Heriberto "Ed", St. Joseph the Worker, Canoga Park
Victorin, Rafael, St. Augustine Church, Culver City
Villacorta, Ricardo, Christ the King, Los Angeles
Wauthy, Guy, St. Rose of Lima, Simi Valley
Wilson, Peter, St. Rose of Lima, Simi Valley
Wu, Jay Jay, St. John's Seminary, Camarillo

INSTITUTIONS LOCATED IN THE ARCHDIOCESE

[A] SEMINARIES, ARCHDIOCESAN

CAMARILLO. *St. John's Seminary*, 5012 Seminary Rd., 93012-2598. Tel: 805-482-2755; Fax: 805-484-4074. Email: Helmut@SJS-SC.ORG. Web: www.stjohnsem.edu. Rev. Msgr. Helmut A. Hefner, J.C.L., Rector & Pres.; Revs. John P. Brennan, S.M.A., S.T.D., Vice Rector; James Clarke, Dir. of Spirtiual Direction; Leon Hutton, Dir. of Human Formation & Evaluations/Div. of Students; Deacon Milton Rosenberg, Dir. Psych.Svcs.; Sisters Regina Robbins, S.S.N.D., Div. of Pastoral Formation & Field Educ.; Mary Milligan, R.S.H.M.; Mary Glennon, R.S.M., Assoc. Dir. Spiritual Formation; Rev. Patrick Mullen, Dir. of Pastoral Formation; Ms. Jacquelein Rotter, Dir. Finance; Mr. Greg Julius, Facilities Mgr.; Mrs. Nanci Braunschweiger, Human Resources; Dr. Mark F. Fischer, Ph.D., Dir. Admissions; Dr. Patricia Lyons Basu, M.L.S., Libraries Dir.; Ms. Esme Takahashi, Registrar; Revs. Richard Benson, C.M., Academic Dean; Peter Albano, C.M.; Eugenio Cardenas, M.Sp.S.; Daniel E. Harris, C.M.; Kevin McCracken, C.M.; Charles E. Miller, C.M.; Binh Nguyen, C.M.; Edward Owens, O.SS.T.; Modesto Perez; Luke Dysinger, O.S.B., M.D. Major Seminary of the Archdiocese of Los Angeles. Priests 15; Sisters 3; Lay Teachers 8; Students 94.

St. John's Seminary College of the Archdiocese of Los Angeles, 5118 Seminary Rd., 93012-2599. Tel: 805-482-2755; Fax: 805-987-5097. Email: recruitment@sjsc.edu. Web: www.sjsc.edu. Revs. Kenneth J. Rudnick, S.J., Pres. & Rector; Gary Landry, C.M., Dean Formation & Vice Rector; Joel Henson, Dir. Students; John D. Stoeger, Dir. of Spiritual Formation; Richard MacDonough, S.S.; Jesus Olivares, C.S.; James Osendorf, C.M., Dir. Liturgy; Sr. Catherine Foley, S.S.L., Dir. of Apostolic Work Program. Staffed by Archdiocesan, Religious Priests and Sisters. Priests 7; Sisters 1; Lay Teachers 9; Students 102.

[B] SEMINARIES, RELIGIOUS OR SCHOLASTICATES

LOS ANGELES. *St. Joseph's Novitiate*, 2468 S. St. Andrews Pl., 90018. Tel: 323-734-0233; Fax: 323-731-5987. Email: usaprov-office@sbcglobal.net. Web: hospitallers.org. Bro. Stephen de la Rosa, O.H., Prov. & Formation Dir. Hospitaller Brothers of St. John of God Brothers 29.

Scalabrini House of Discernment (Seminary) Tel: 323-225-4436.

Scalabrini Vocation Center Tel: 323-225-8027.

ARLETA. *Carmel West Community*, 13600 Wingo St., 91331. Tel: 818-890-6630; Fax: 818-890-6630. Email: thetopwopp@cs.com. Revs. Dominic Savino, O.Carm.; Peter J. Liuzzi, O.Carm. Priests 2.

SANTA MARIA. *St. Joseph Seminary (Josephite Fathers' Novitiate)*, 180 Patterson Rd., 93455. Tel: 805-937-5378; Fax: 805-937-5759. Web: www.josephiteworld.org. Revs. Timothy R. Lane, C.J.; Bede L. Johnson, C.J.; Anthony Runtz, C.J.; John A. Mayhew, C.J.; Frank Guido, C.J.; Edward Jalbert, C.J.; Bro. Thaddeus Haynes, C.J. Priests 5; Brothers 2; Total Staff 7.

SANTA PAULA. *Dom Grea House (House of Formation) Canons Regular of the Immaculate Conception, (C.R.I.C.)*, 984 Monte Vista Dr., 93060-1612. Tel: 805-933-5063; Fax: 805-525-5115. Email: paterthoma@excite.com. Rev. Thomas J. Dome, C.R.I.C., Dir. & Novice Master; Bro. Enrique Vergara, C.R.I.C. Priests 1; Brothers 1; Postulants 1.

Dom Grea House (House of Formation and Novitiate)

SANTA YNEZ. *San Lorenzo Seminary and Prayer Center* Prayer Center: , 1802 Sky Dr., P.O. Box 247, 93460. Tel: 805-688-5630; Fax: 805-686-0775. Web: www.sanlorenzo.org. Revs. Jesus Vela, O.F.M.Cap.; Evangelist Kelly, O.F.M.Cap.; Sebastian Ward, O.F.M.Cap., Chap.; Fintan Whelan, O.F.M.Cap.; Gerald Barron, O.F.M.Cap. (SFR); Jesus Vela, O.F.M.Cap.; Sebastian Ward, O.F.M.Cap.; Evangelist Kelly, O.F.M.Cap.; Fintan Whelan, O.F.M.Cap.; Bros. Pius Higgins, O.F.M.Cap., Vicar; Joseph Slominski, O.F.M.Cap.; Bob Edwards, O.F.M.Cap. Capuchin Fransiscan Friars Priests 5; Brothers 2; Total Staff 7.

[C] COLLEGES AND UNIVERSITIES

LOS ANGELES. *Loyola Marymount University*, One LMU Dr., Ste. 4844, 90045-2659. Tel: 310-338-2700. Web: www.lmu.edu. Revs. Robert B. Lawton, S.J., Pres.; Patrick J. Cahalan, S.J., Chancellor; Dr. Joseph G. Jabbra, Academic Vice Pres.; Sr. Mary Elizabeth Ingham, C.S.J., Assoc. Academic Vice Pres.; Mr. Thomas O. Fleming Jr., Vice Pres. Business & Finance; Mr. Charles Rasberry, Vice Pres. Univ. Rels.; Dr. Lane Bove, Vice Pres. Student Affairs; Revs. Richard A. Robin, S.J., Asst. to the Pres.; Robert V. Caro, S.J., Asst. Pres. Mission & Identity; Dr. Abbie Robinson-Armstrong, Asst. Pres. for Intercultural Affairs; Ms. Lynne Scarboro, Vice Pres. Admin.; Mr. David W. Burcham, Dean Law School; Ms.

Rosenia St. Onge, Assoc. Academic Vice Pres. Records & Registration; Dr. Joseph A. Merante, Assoc. Vice Pres. Academic Affairs; Dr. G. Edward Evans, Assoc. Academic Vice Pres., Library & Info Resources; Dr. Birute Vileisis, Assoc. Vice Pres. for Academic Grants; Ms. Donna Palmer, Dir. Financial Aid; Mr. Frank Montalvo, Asst. Vice Pres. Human Resources; Mr. Fernando D. Moreno, Dir. Campus Ministry; Dr. John T. Wholihan, Dean of Business Admin.; Dr. Gerald S. Jakubowski, Dean of Science & Engineering; Barbara Busse, Acting Dean, Communication & Fine Arts; Ms. Teri Schwartz, Dean of Film & TV; Dr. Kenyon Chan, Dean Liberal Arts; Rev. Albert P. Koppes, O.Carm., Dean, School of Education. Total Enrollment 6,804; Total Staff 783.

Jesuit Community, P.O. Box 45041, 90045-0041. Tel: 310-338-7445; Fax: 310-338-3002. Very Rev. Paul Bernadicou, S.J., Rector; Rev. Terrance L. Mahan, S.J., Min. Priests 48; Brothers 3; Sisters 8; Lay Teachers 339; Total Staff 783; Students 6,804. In Res. Revs. Clinton E. Albertson, S.J.; James Arenz, S.J.; Mark Bandsuch, S.J.; Paul Bernadicou, S.J.; Curtis Bryant, S.J.; Robert I. Burns, S.J.; Patrick J. Cahalan, S.J.; William F. Cain, S.J.; Robert V. Caro, S.J.; Michael Caruso, S.J.; Charles Chilinda, S.J.; Philip J. Chmielewski, S.J. (CHI); John Coleman, S.J.; John P. Daly, S.J.; Sean Dempsey, S.J.; George Dennis, S.J.; Tri M. Dinh, S.J.; Michael E. Engh, S.J.; D. Theodore Fisher, S.J.; James Fredericks; William J. Fulco, S.J.; Fred Heney, S.J.; Thomas P. Higgins, S.J.; Felix Just, S.J.; James H. Keene, S.J.; Albert P. Koppes, O.Carm.; Joseph LaBrie, S.J.; Robert B. Lawton, S.J.; Dorian Llkywelyn, S.J.; Terrance L. Mahan, S.J.; Wayne Negrete, S.J.; Luis Proenca, S.J.; Thomas P. Rausch, S.J.; Richard A. Robin, S.J.; Randall Roche, S.J.; Richard W. Rolfs, S.J.; Herbert J. Ryan, S.J.; Ronald E. Schmidt; Robert W. Scholla, S.J.; Thomas P. Sherman, S.J.; Edward J. Siebert, S.J.; Ernest S. Sweeney, S.J.; Robert H. Taylor, S.J.; Richard P. Vaughan, S.J.; Hanford E. Weckbach, S.J.; Robert J. Welch, S.J.; Mark Zangrando, S.J.; Giuseppe Zito, S.J.; Bros. John Grever, C.F.M.M.; Anthony Smulders, C.F.M.M.; Raymond W. Upton, S.J.

The Sacred Heart of Mary and Sisters of St. Joseph of Orange, One LMU Dr., 90045-2659. Tel: 310-338-2700; 310-641-4682.

Legal Title: *Communities of the Religious of the Sacred Heart of Mary and Sisters of St. Joseph of Orange*

Loyola School of Law, 919 S. Albany St., P.O. Box 15019, 90015. Tel: 213-736-1000. Mr. David W. Burcham, Dean. Students 1,411.

Mount St. Mary's College Tel: 310-954-4010; Fax: 310-954-4019. Email: jpdoud@msmc.la.edu. Web: www.msmc.la.edu. Conducted by the Sisters of St. Joseph of Carondelet, Resident and non-resident students.

Chalon Campus, 12001 Chalon Rd., 90049-1599. Tel: 310-954-4000; Fax: 310-954-4019. Web: www.msmc.la.edu.

Doheny Campus, 10 Chester Pl., 90007. Tel: 213-477-2500; Fax: 213-477-2519. Dr. Jacqueline Powers Doud, Pres.; Dr. Jane Lingua, Vice Pres. Student Affairs; Mr. Larry Smith, Vice Pres. for Info. Support Svcs.; Dr. Mary Boyce, Provost & Academic Vice Pres.; Dr. Lawrence Ryan, Assoc. Academic Vice Pres. & Graduate Dean; Ms. Stephanie Cubba, Vice. Pres.; Mr. Dean Kilgour, Dean of Admissions; Sr. Janet Duffy, Interim Dean of AA Prog. Sisters 6; Priests 2; Lay Teachers 67; Students 2,132.

RANCHO PALOS VERDES. *Marymount College, Palos Verdes, California*, 30800 Palos Verdes Dr., E., 90275-6299. Tel: 310-377-5501; Fax: 310-265-0642. Email: cfausto@marymountpv.edu. Web: www.marymountpv.edu. Dr. Kenneth Rudnick, Pres.; Dr. Robert Matthes, Dean Academic Affairs; Mr. James Reeves, Vice Pres. College Opers. & Student Svcs. An Independent and Catholic Co-Educational Two-Year Liberal Arts College; Resident and Non-Resident. Priests 1; Sisters 1; Lay Teachers 45; Students 745.

ROSEMEAD. *Don Bosco Technical Institute* (Junior College) , 1151 San Gabriel Blvd., 91770-4299. Tel: 626-940-2000; Fax: 626-940-2001. Email: gutierm@boscotech.org. Web: www.boscotech.tec.ca.us. Revs. Carmine Vairo, S.D.B., Pres.; Michael Gergen, S.D.B., Admin. Vice Pres.; Peter Bui, S.D.B.; Timothy Nguyen, S.D.B.; Thinh Nguyen, S.D.B. (SP); Jose Lucero, S.D.B., Campus Youth Min.; Chris Terry; Bros. Patrick Barbariol, S.D.B.; Gene Mylan, S.D.B.; Robert Hennings, S.D.B.; Thien Nguyen, S.D.B. Two-year college program leading to Associate in Science degree in eight technical areas. (Staffed by Salesians of St. John Bosco). Priests 6; Brothers 4; Lay Teachers 79; Students 914; Total Staff 102; Administrators 13.

Don Bosco High School Tel: 626 940-2000; Fax: 626-940-2001. Mr. Memo Gutierrez, Prin. Priests 6; Brothers 4; Lay Teachers 79; Students 914.

SANTA PAULA. *Thomas Aquinas College* 10000 N. Ojai Rd., 93060. Tel: 805-525-4417; Fax 805-525-9342. Email: admissions@thomasaquinas.edu. Web: www.thomasaquinas.edu. Dr. Thomas E. Dillon, Pres.; Dr. Michael F. McLean, Dean; Mr. Peter L. DeLuca III, Vice Pres. Finance & Admin.; Mr. J. Quincy Masteller, Vice Pres. Devel.; Revs. Michael U. Perea, O.Praem., Chap.; Wilfred F. Borden, O.M.I., Chap. Four-year undergraduate program in the Liberal Arts leading to the B.A. Degree; Coeducational. Lay Teachers 32; Students 332.

[D] HIGH SCHOOLS, ARCHDIOCESAN

LOS ANGELES. *Bishop Conaty-Our Lady of Loretto High School* (Girls) , 2900 W. Pico Blvd., 90006-3802. Tel: 323-737-0012; Fax: 323-737-1749. Email: bclhs@earthlink.net. Sisters 4; Lay Teachers 27; Students 480; Total Staff 30.

Bishop Mora Salesian High School (Boys) , 960 S. Soto St., 90023. Tel: 323-261-7124; Fax: 323-261-9474. Email: mdv777@aol.com. Web: salesianmustangs.com. Mr. Manuel Villarreal, Prin.; Mr. Xavier Jimenez, Vice Prin. Salesians of Don Bosco Priests 12; Brothers 2; Sisters 1; Lay Teachers 18; Students 300.

Daniel Murphy Catholic High School (Boys) , 241 S. Detroit St., 90036. Tel: 323-935-1161 Fax: 323-935-1621. Email: dmhs@danielmurphyhs.org. Web: www.danielmurphyhs.org. Denis S. Munoz, Prin. Lay Teachers 19; Students 322; Total Staff 20.

Sacred Heart High School (Girls) , 2111 N. Griffin Ave., 90031. Tel: 323-225-2209; Fax: 323-225-5046. Email: msjmarydiane@hotmail.com. Web: www.shhsla.org. Sr. S. Mary Diane Scott, O.P., Prin. Sisters 3; Lay Teachers 26; Students 326; Total Staff 29.

Verbum Dei High School (Boys) , 11100 S. Central Ave., 90059-1199. Tel: 323-564-6651; Fax: 323-564-9009. Email: jweling@verbumdei.hs. Web: www.verbumdei.hs. Revs. John B. Weing, S.J., Pres.; Scott R. Santarosa, S.J., Vice Pres. Admin.; Jack F. Dullea, S.J., College Counselor; Benjamin F. Callaway Jr., Prin.; Bro. Richard Morrill, S.V.D. Conducted by the Archdiocese of Los Angeles. Priests 3; Brothers 4; Lay Teachers 16; Students 244; Total Staff 23.

Scholastics Revs. Miguelangel Ortiz, S.J.; Jeff Allen, S.J.; Bro. Peter Chai, S.V.D.

Verbum Dei High School WorkStudy, Inc., 11100 S. Central Ave., 90059-1199. Tel: 323-564-6651, Ext. 28; Fax: 323-564-9009. Jeff Bonino-Britsch, Vice Pres. Dir. Corporate Work Study Prog.

BURBANK. *Bellarmine Jefferson High School* (Coed) , 465 E. Olive Ave., 91501. Tel: 818-972-1400 (Main Office); 818-972-1401 (Athletic); 818-972-1402 (Attendance); Fax: 818-559-6387. Email: admissions@bell-jeff.net. Web: www.bell-jeff.net. Sr. Cheryl Milner, Prin. Sisters 2; Brothers 1; Lay Teachers 26; Students 352; Total Staff 29.

DOWNEY. *St. Matthias High School*, 7851 E. Gardendale St., 90242. Tel: 562-861-2271; Fax: 562-869-8652 Email: mryan@stmatthiashs.org. Web: www.stmatthiashs.org. Sisters 2; Lay Teachers 30; Students 500.

GARDENA. *Junipero Serra High School*, 14830 S. Van Ness Ave., 90249. Tel: 310-324-6675; Fax: 310-352-4953. Web: www.SerraHighSchool.com. Rev. Sabato Pilato, Prin.; Mrs. Margaret Shoukry, Vice Prin. Priests 1; Sisters 2; Lay Teachers 31; Students 586; Total Staff 34.

LA PUENTE. *Bishop Amat Memorial High School* (Coed) , 14301 Fairgrove Ave., 91746. Tel: 626-962-2495; Fax: 626-960-0994. Email: president@bishopamat.org. Web: www.bishopamat.org. Rev. Msgr. Aidan M. Carroll, Pres.; Dr. Merritt V. Hemenway, Prin.; Mrs. Kathleen Wiard, Vice Prin.; Ms. Deborah Oswald, Asst. Prin.; Ms. Maria Gover, Asst. Prin.; Ms. Patricia Tereschuk, Asst. Prin. Conducted by the Archdiocese of Los Angeles. Priests 1; Sisters 2; Lay Teachers 76; Students 1,408; Total Staff 82.

LA VERNE. *Damien High School*, 2280 Damien Ave., 91750. Tel: 909-596-1946; Fax: 909-596-1946. Email: dhstravers@hotmail.com. Web: www.damien-hs.edu. Revs. Patrick Travers, SS.CC., Prin.; Peadar Cronin, SS.CC., Vice Prin.; Mr. Sam Pearsall, Asst. Prin. Summer Prog.; Mr. Bob Baiz, Asst. Prin. Academic Affairs; Mr. Thomas Carroll, Asst. Prin. Athletic Activities; Mr. Kenneth Kowalewski, Asst. Prin. & Campus Min.; Rev. Donal McCarthy, SS.CC., Asst. Prin. Guidance.

Legal Title: *Congregation of the Sacred Hearts, Inc.*, Conducted by the Archdiocese of Los Angeles. Faculty Res.: 2150 Damien Ave., 91750. Tel: 909-593-8501. Priests 3; Sisters 1; Lay Teachers 61; Students 1,123; Total Staff 78.

LAKEWOOD. *Saint Joseph High School* (Girls) , 5825 N. Woodruff Ave., 90713. Tel: 562-925-5073; Fax: 562-925-3315. Web: www.sj-jester.org. Terri Mendoza, Ph.D., Prin.; Revs. John Shevlin, S.V.D. (SB); James Henry, S.V.D. Conducted by Archdiocese of Los Angeles. Priests 2; Sisters 6; Lay Teachers 47; Students 825; Total Staff 55.

LANCASTER. *Paraclete High School* (Coed) , 42145 N. 30th St., 93536. Tel: 661-943-3255; Fax: 661-722-9455. Email: janson@paraclete.pvt.k12.ca.us. Web: www.paraclete.pvt.k12.ca.us. John W. Anson, M.Ed., Prin.; Revs. Joseph Scalco, C.S.J.; Mark Withers, C.S.J. Conducted by Archdiocese of Los Angeles. Priests 2; Lay Teachers 42; Students 755.

MISSION HILLS. *Bishop Alemany High School*, 11111 N. Alemany Dr., 91345. Tel: 818-365-3925; Fax: 818-365-2064. Email: principal@alemany.org. Web: www.alemany.org. John C. Monnig, Ed.D., Prin.; Revs. Patrick Argue, SS.CC. (Ireland); Norman Supancheck. Priests 2; Brothers 2; Sisters 4; Lay Teachers 83; Students 1,533; Total Staff 91.

MONTEBELLO. *Cantwell Sacred Heart of Mary High School* (Coed) , 329 N. Garfield Ave., 90640. Tel: 323-887-2066; Fax: 323-724-4332. Email: cshm@cshm.org. Web: www.cshm.org. David Chambers, Prin. Archdiocesan Institution. Sisters 2; Lay Teachers 30; Students 618; Total Staff 32.

OXNARD. *Santa Clara High School*, 2121 Saviers Rd., 93033. Tel: 805-483-9502; Fax: 805-483-1588. Web: www.santaclarahs.org. Mr. Martin Young, Prin.; Mrs. Carmen Lusk, Prin. & WASC Coord.; Ms. Alcia Guerra, Asst. Prin. & Dean of Studies; Mr. Peter Wraith, Campus Min.; Mrs. Natalie Lajoie, Dir. of Activities. Lay Teachers 15; Students 263; Total Staff 20.

PLAYA DEL REY. *St. Bernard High School* (Coed) , 9100 Falmouth Ave., 90293. Tel: 310-823-4651; Fax: 310-827-3365. Email: mcclunejim@hotmail.com. Web: www.stbernardhs.com. Conducted by Archdiocese of Los Angeles. Brothers 2; Sisters 1; Lay Teachers 40; Students 624; Total Staff 43.

POMONA. *Pomona Catholic High School* (Girls) , 533 W. Holt Ave., 91768. Tel: 909-623-5297; Fax: 909-620-6057. Email: principalpchs@verizon.net. Web: www.pomonacatholic.org. Mrs. Kimberlee Gazzolo, Prin.; Mrs. Ann Hardman, Dean of Students. Sisters 3; Lay Teachers 19; Students 270; Total Staff 7.

ROSEMEAD. *Don Bosco Technical Institute* (Boys) , 1151 San Gabriel Blvd., 91770-4299. Tel: 626-940-2000; Fax: 626-940-2001. Email: gutierm@boscotech.org. Web: www.boscotech.tec.ca.us. Rev. Carmine Vairo, S.D.B., Pres.; Mr. Memo Gutierrez, Prin.; Revs. Timothy Nguyen, S.D.B.; Michael Gergen, S.D.B.; Peter Bui, S.D.B.; Thinh Nguyen, S.D.B.; Jose Lucero, S.D.B.; Chris Terry. Secondary Section.; Staffed by Salesians of St. John Bosco. Priests 6; Brothers 4; Lay Teachers 79; Students 914; Total Staff 102; Administrators 13.

SANTA BARBARA. *Bishop Garcia Diego High School* (Coed) , 4000 La Colina Rd., 93110. Tel: 805-967-1266; Fax: 805-964-3178. Email: bishop@bishopdiego.org. Web: www.bishopdiego.org. Revs. Alfred Verstreken, C.J. (Belgium); Thomas J. Elewaut, C.J. Priests 2; Sisters 2; Lay Teachers 22; Students 260; Total Staff 26.

SANTA FE SPRINGS. *St. Paul High School*, 9635 S. Greenleaf Ave., 90670. Tel: 562-698-6246; Fax: 562-696-8396. Email: sphsprincipal@netscape.net. Web: www.stpaulhs.org. Mr. Frank A. Laurenzello, Prin. Conducted by Archdiocese of Los Angeles. Priests 1; Brothers 3; Sisters 2; Lay Teachers 46; Students 740; Total Staff 41.

SANTA MARIA. *St. Joseph High School* (Coed) , 93455. Tel: 805-937-2038; Fax: 805-937-4248. Email: sjhs@sjhsknights.com. Web: www.sjhsknights.com. Revs. Timothy R. Lane, C.J.; Edward Jalbert, C.J. Conducted by Archdiocese of Los Angeles.

180 Patterson Rd., 93455. Tel: 805-937-5378; Fax: 805-937-5759. Priests 2; Sisters 1; Lay Teachers 36; Students 615.

TORRANCE. *Bishop Montgomery High School* (Coed) , 5430 Torrance Blvd., 90503. Tel: 310-540-2021; Fax: 310-543-5102. Email: r_libbon@bmhs.com. Web: www.bmhs.com. Rosemary Libbon, Prin. Conducted by the Archdiocese of Los Angeles. Priests 1; Lay Teachers 76; Students 1,132.

VENTURA. *St. Bonaventure High School* (Coed) , 3167 Telegraph Rd., 93003-3281. Tel: 805-648-6836; Fax: 805-648-4903. Email: office@saintbonaventure.com. Web: www.saintbonaventure.com. Bro. Paulinus Horkan, O.S.F., Prin. Conducted by Archdiocese of Los Angeles. Sisters 1; Brothers 1; Lay Teachers 47; Total Staff 49; Students 740.

[E] HIGH SCHOOLS, PAROCHIAL

High Schools are maintained in the following parishes

(for particulars refer to the individual parishes): Glendale: Holy Family; Long Beach: St. Anthony; San Gabriel: San Gabriel Mission; San Pedro: Mary Star of the Sea; Santa Monica, St. Monica; Van Nuys: St. Genevieve

[F] HIGH SCHOOLS, PRIVATE

LOS ANGELES. *Cathedral High School of Los Angeles, Incorporated* (Boys) , 1253 Bishops Rd., 90012. Tel: 323-225-2438; Fax: 323-222-7223. Email: chsbrjohn@aol.com. Web: www.cathedralhighschool.org. Mr. Martin Farfan, Pres.; Bro. John Montgomery, F.S.C., Prin. Conducted by the Brothers of the Christian Schools Brothers 7; Sisters 1; Lay Teachers 35; Total Staff 43; Students 600.

Immaculate Heart High School (Girls) , 5515 Franklin Ave., 90028. Tel: 323-461-3651; Fax: 323-462-0610. Email: ihhs1@aol.com. Web: www.immaculateheart.org. Conducted by the Immaculate Heart Community Lay Teachers 46; Students 539.

Loyola High School of Los Angeles, 1901 Venice Blvd., 90006. Tel: 213-381-5121; Fax: 213-368-1758. Email: rwalsh@loyolahs.edu. Web: loyolahs.edu. Revs. Robert T. Walsh, S.J., Pres.; John Mitchell, S.J.; Stephen A. Barber, S.J.; J. Philip Conneally, S.J.; Lawrence B. Murphy, S.J.; Louis A. Peinado, S.J.; John Francis Vu, S.J.; John I. Geiszel, S.J.; James V. Schaukowitch, S.J.; Michael Scully, S.J., Min.; John A. Brady, S.J.; John Galvan, S.J.; Jeremiah P. Helfrich, S.J.; Patrick M. Kelly, S.J.; Michael R. Moodie, S.J. (SFR); Bros. Christopher Larsen, S.J., Scholastic; Trung Pham, S.J., Scholastic. Jesuit Community Priests 13; Scholastics 2; Lay Teachers 77; Administrators 27; Total Staff 111; Students 1,212.

Marymount High School (Girls) , 10643 Sunset Blvd., 90077. Tel: 310-472-1205; Fax: 310-476-0910. Email: edutech@mhs-la.org. Web: www.marymount-la.org. Dr. Mary Ellen Gozdecki, Head. Religious of the Sacred Heart of Mary Sisters 1; Lay Teachers 56; Total Staff 90; Students 395.

Notre Dame Academy (Girls) , 2851 Overland Ave., 90064. Tel: 310-839-5289; Fax: 310-839-7957. Email: Ndamp@aol.com. Web: www.ndala.com. Sr. Marie Paul, S.N.D., Prin. Sisters of Notre Dame of Los Angeles 5; Sisters of Providence 1; Lay Teachers 48; Students 470.

ALHAMBRA. *Ramona Convent Secondary School, Ramona Convent of the Holy Names* (Girls Grades 7-12) , 1701 W. Ramona Rd., 91803-3099. Tel: 626-282-4151; Fax: 626-281-0797. Email: ramona@ramona.pvt.k12.ca.us. Web: www.ramona.pvt.k12.ca.us. Ms. Kathleen Pillon, Prin.; Sr. Kathleen Callaway, S.N.J.M., Pres. Sisters of Holy Names of Jesus and Mary 6; Lay Teachers 43; Total Staff 45; Students 551.

BELLFLOWER. *St. John Bosco High School*, 13640 S. Bellflower Blvd., 90706. Tel: 562-920-1734; Fax: 562-867-5322. Email: lbaysinger@bosco.org. Web: www.bosco.org. Revs. Leo Baysinger, S.D.B., Pres.; Anh Le, S.D.B.; John Roche, S.D.B.; Christian H. Woerz, S.D.B. (OAK); Bros. Frank Bracchi, S.D.B.; Al Vu, S.D.B.; Barney Hagus, S.D.B.; Long Mai, S.D.B.; Noel De Bruton, S.D.B. (Boys) Priests 3; Brothers 2; Lay Teachers 65; Students 1,134.

BURBANK. *Providence High School* (Coed) , 511 S. Buena Vista St., 91505. Tel: 818-846-8141; Fax: 818-843-8421. Email: lucille@providencehigh.org. Web: www.providencehigh.org. Sisters Lucille Dean, S.P., Prin.; Una Feeney, S.S.S., Dir. Campus Ministry; Mary Hawkins, S.P., Academic Vice Prin.; C. Victor LeBreton, Vice Prin. Discipline & Student Activities. Sisters 2; Lay Teachers 37; Total Staff 56; Students 550.

CHATSWORTH. *Chaminade College Preparatory*, Office of the President, 10210 Oakdale Ave., 91311-3533. Tel: 818-360-4211; Fax: 818-363-0127. Email: jadams@chaminade.org. Web: www.chaminade.org. James V. Adams, Pres.

Legal Title: *Chaminade College Preparatory*, (Coed Grades 6-8); (Coed Grades 9-12) Sisters 2; Lay Teachers 110; Total Staff 180; Students 1,722.

19800 Devonshire St., 91311. Tel: 818-363-8127; Fax: 818-363-1219. Ms. Christine Hunter, Prin. Chatsworth.

7500 Chaminade Ave., West Hills, 91304. Tel: 818-347-8300; Fax: 818-348-8374. Bro. Thomas Fahy, O.S.F., Prin. West Hills. Priests 3; Sisters 4; Brothers 3; Lay Teachers 114; Students 1,694.

Marianist Community Tel: 818-347-8043; Fax: 818-347-2788. Revs. Edwin Johnson, S.M., Dir.; Theodore Ley, S.M.; Lawrence Mann, S.M.; Thomas Hogan, S.M. Priests 4; Brothers 5.

ENCINO. *Crespi Carmelite High School*, 5031 Alonzo Ave., 91316. Tel: 818-345-1672; Fax: 818-345-6468. Email: jmkocarm@juno.com. Web: www.crespi.org. Rev. John Knoernschild, O.Carm., Pres.; Mr. David Doyle, Prin.; Mr. Jeff Thornton, Vice Prin. & Dean of Men; Ms. Margie Moreno, Treas.; Mr. Daniel Flaherty, Dir. Devel.; Ms. Catherine Scheibe, Academic Vice Prin.; Mr. Richard Fong, Athletic Dir.; Mr. Joseph Schnelldorfer, Campus Min.; Ms. Donna Long, Dir. of Student Activities; Revs. Dominic Savino, O.Carm.; Joseph Fitzgerald, O.Carm., Alumni Relations Dir.; Bro. John Sprissler, O.Carm. Priests 3; Brothers 1; Lay Teachers 37; Students 465. In Res. Revs. Augustine W. Carter, O.Carm.; John Coleman, O.Carm.; Mathias Ewing, O.Carm.; William Heery, O.Carm.; Kevin McBrien, O.Carm., Prior.

GLENDORA. *St. Lucys's Priory High School* (Girls) , 655 W. Sierra Madre Ave., 91741. Tel: 626-335-3322; Fax: 626-335-4373. Email: slphs@aol.com. Sr. Monica Collins, O.S.B., Prin. Conducted by the Benedictine Sisters Sisters 2; Lay Teachers 45; Total Staff 47; Students 865.

INGLEWOOD. *St. Mary's Academy* (Girls) , 701 Grace Ave., 90301. Tel: 310-674-8470; Fax: 310-674-6255. Email: faycsj@aol.com. Web: www.stmarysacademy.org. Sr. Fay Hagen, C.S.J., Prin. Sisters of St. Joseph of Carondelet 11; Lay Teachers 21; Total Staff 14; Students 355.

LA CANADA FLINTRIDGE. *Flintridge Sacred Heart Academy* (Girls) , 440 St. Katherine Dr., 91011. Tel: 626-685-8500; Fax: 626-685-8555. Web: www.fsha.org. Sr. Celeste Marie Botello, Prin.

Legal Title: *Flintridge Sacred Heart Academy, A Corporation* Dominican Sisters of Mission San Jose 4; Lay Teachers 38; Students 400.

St. Francis High School (Boys) , 200 Foothill Blvd., 91011. Tel: 818-790-0325; Fax: 818-790-5542. Web: sfhs.net. Email: elshoffm@sfhs.net. Revs. Matthew Elshoff, O.F.M.Cap., Pres. St. Francis High School; Cris Thiel, O.F.M.Cap.; Anthony Scannel, O.F.M.Cap.; Alejandro Magallanes, O.F.M.Cap. (FRS); Ron Talbott, O.F.M.Cap., Guardian; Gregory Coiro, O.F.M.Cap., Campus Chap.; Bros. Tran Vu, O.F.M.Cap; Bernard McAllister, O.F.M.Cap.; Sr. Barbarine Houdek, O.S.F.

Legal Title: *The Capuchin Franciscan Order of the Western American Province* Priests 5; Brothers 1; Sisters 1; Lay Teachers 49; Total Teachers 45; Total Staff 63; Students 674.

OJAI. *Villanova Preparatory School*, 12096 Ventura Ave., 93023-3999. Tel: 805-646-1464; Fax: 805-646-4430. Email: info@villanovaprep.org. Web: www.villanovaprep.org. Rev. Robert Gavotto, O.S.A., Pres.; Anthony Sabatino, Headmaster.

Legal Title: *Villanova Preparatory School of California* Conducted by Augustinian Fathers (Order of St. Augustine) Priests 1; Sisters 2; Lay Teachers 29; Total Staff 53; Students 289.

PASADENA. *La Salle High School*, 3880 E. Sierra Madre Blvd., 91107. Tel: 626-351-8951; Fax: 626-351-0275. Email: principal@lasallehs.org. Web: lasallehs.org. Mr. Patrick Bonacci, Prin. Priests 2; Brothers 1; Lay Teachers 56; Total Staff 78; Students 745.

Mayfield Senior School of the Holy Child Jesus, 500 Bellefontaine St., 91105-2439. Tel: 626-799-9121; Fax: 626-799-8576. Email: rita.mcbride@mayfieldsenior.org. Web: www.mayfieldsenior.org. Mr. Raymond Valtierra, Business Mgr. Sisters 1; Lay Teachers 38; Students 298.

SHERMAN OAKS. *Notre Dame High School*, 13645 Riverside Dr., 91423. Tel: 818-933-3600; Fax: 818-501-0507. Email: connelly@ndhs.org. Web: www.ndhs.org. Bro. William C. Nick, C.S.C., Pres.; Mrs. Stephanie Connelly, Prin. Priests 1; Brothers 3; Lay Teachers 74; Total Staff 78; Students 1,151.

SIERRA MADRE. *Alverno High School* (Girls) , 200 N. Michillinda Ave., 91024. Tel: 626-355-3463; Fax: 626-355-3153. Web: Alverno-hs.org. Ann M. Gillick, M.S., Prin. Lay Teachers 18; Total Staff 42; Students 275.

THOUSAND OAKS. *La Reina High School* (Girls Grades 7-12) , 106 W. Janss Rd., 91360. Tel: 805-495-6494; Fax: 805-494-4966. Email: lareina@lareina.com. Web: www.lareina.com. Sr. Antoinette Marie Moon, S.N.D., Prin. Sisters of Notre Dame 3; Lay Teachers 40; Total Staff 61; Students 611.

WOODLAND HILLS. *Louisville High School* (Girls) , 22300 Mulholland Dr., 91364. Tel: 818-346-8812; Fax: 818-346-9483. Email: kvercillo@louisvillehs.org. Web: louisvillehs.org. Sr. Kathleen Vercillo, Prin. Sisters 4; Lay Teachers 38; Total Staff 42; Students 507.

[G] ELEMENTARY SCHOOLS, PRIVATE

LOS ANGELES. *Notre Dame Academy (Elementary)*, 2911 Overland Ave., 90064. Tel: 310-287-3895; Fax: 310-838-8983. Sr. Mary LaReina Kelly, S.N.D., Prin. Sisters of Notre Dame of Los Angeles 3; Lay Teachers 11; Total Staff 30; Students 292.

PASADENA. *Mayfield Junior School*, 405 S. Euclid Ave., 91101. Tel: 626-796-2774; Fax: 626-796-5753. Email: mjs@mayfieldjs.org. Web: www.mayfieldjs.org. Lay Teachers 51; Total Staff 70; Students 425.

SANTA BARBARA. *Marymount Academy*, (Grades K-8) , (Coed) , 2130 Mission Ridge Rd., 93103. Tel: 805-569-1811; Fax: 805-682-6892. Email: tmessineo@marymountsb.org. Web: marymountsb.org. Lay Teachers 21; Total Staff 22; Students 235.

[H] ORPHANAGES AND INFANT HOMES

ROSEMEAD, LOS ANGELES. *Maryvale*, 7600 E. Graves Ave., P.O. Box 1039, 91770-1003. Tel: 626-280-6510; 323-283-9311; Fax: 626-288-8903. Email: Maryvale1@aol.com. Sr. Linda Ann Cahill, D.C., Exec. Dir. Daughters of Charity 5; Total Assisted 464; Total Staff 250; Children: Residential Treatment 85; Mental Health Day Treatment 85; Foster Family 6; Day Care 152.

The Los Angeles Orphan Asylum, 7600 E. Graves Ave., 91770. Tel: 626-280-6510; Fax: 626-288-8903.

Los Angeles Orphanage Guild, 7600 E. Graves Ave., 91770. Tel: 626-280-6510; Fax: 626-288-8903.

[I] DAY NURSERIES

LOS ANGELES. *Divine Providence Pre-school and Kindergarten*, 2620 Monmouth St., 90007. Tel: 213-747-3074; Fax: 213-747-3074. Email: odnadems@earthlink.net. Web: www.companyofmary.com. Sr. Guadalupe Hernandez, O.D.N., Dir. Sisters of the Company of Mary 3; Lay Teachers 15; Total Staff 21; Children 175.

St. Jeanne de Lestonnac Kindergarten and Day Nursery, 4001 Venice Blvd., 90019. Tel: 323-737-1217; Fax: 323-737-3672. Sr. Charlotte Turrietta, Supvr. (Formerly Little Flower Kindergarten & Day Nursery) Sisters 3; Lay Teachers 12; Total Staff 18; Children 170.

GARDENA. *St. Anthony's Day Nursery*, 1044 W. 163rd St., 90247. Tel: 310-329-8654. Sr. Soledad Lepez, M.C., Dir. Sisters 10; Total Staff 12; Children 90.

SAN FERNANDO. *Poverello of Assisi Preschool*, 13367 Borden Ave., Sylmar, 91342. Tel: 818-361-5864; Fax: 818-364-8596. Sisters Irene San Roman; Mary Fatima Guevara. Franciscan Missionary Sisters of the Immaculate Conception Sisters 6; Total Staff 16; Children 240.

[J] GENERAL HOSPITALS

LOS ANGELES. *St. Vincent Medical Center*, 2131 W. 3rd St., 90057. Tel: 213-484-7111. Web: www.stvincentmedicalcenter.com. Rev. Julio Roman, Chap. Daughters of Charity Health System.; Sponsored by the Daughters of Charity of St. Vincent de Paul, Province of the West. Bed Capacity 347; Patients Assisted Annually 108,384; Total Staff 1,350.

BURBANK. *Providence Health System* (San Fernando Valley Service Area-Spiritual Care Dept.) Tel: 818-847-4606; Fax: 818-847-4607. Email: jhoffman@phsca.org (Dir.). Arnold Schaffer, CEO; Sr. Colleen Settles, O.P.D. Min., Regional Dir., Mission Leadership. Sponsored by the Sisters of Providence and the Sisters of the Little Company of Mary.

Providence Saint Joseph Medical Center, 501 S. Buena Vista St., 91505. Tel: 818-843-5111; Fax: 818-525-3444. Web: www.providence.org. Jill M. Hoffman, M.Div., Chap. & Dir. Spiritual Care; Sally Kinarthy, Chap.; Sr. Mary Prendergast, Chap.; Jon Arnold, Chap.; Margaret Burdge, Chap. Bed Capacity 427; Sisters 6; Patients Assisted Annually 320,029; Total Staff 2,237.

Providence St. Elizabeth Care Center, 10425 Magnolia Blvd., North Hollywood, 91601. Tel: 818-980-3872; Fax: 818-980-6349. Bed Capacity 52; Patients Assisted Annually 63; Total Staff 53.

Providence Holy Cross Medical Center, 15031 Rinaldi St., P.O. Box 9600, Mission Hills, 91346-9600. Tel: 818-365-8051; Fax: 818-898-4569. Revs. Jose Mejia, Chap.; John De Vries, Chap.; Shawn Kiley, Chap. Bed Capacity 257; Patients Assisted Annually 107,136; Total Staff 1,254.

Providence Saint Joseph Medical Center, 501 S. Buena Vista St., 91505. Tel: 818-843-5111; Fax: 818-525-3444. Revs. John De Vries, Chap.; Joseph Mejia, Chap.; James Toal, Chap. (Retired); Sisters Mary Prendergast, S.S.L., Chap.; Jo Lozano, O.S.F., Chap.; Jill M. Hoffman, M.Div., Dir. & Chap.; Jonathan Tabachnikoff, Chap.; Margaret Burdge, Chap.; Pete Carino, Chap.; Shawn Kiley, Chap. Conducted by the Sisters of Providence Health System Bed Capacity 427; Patients Assisted Annually 320,029; Total Staff 2,237.

DUARTE. *Santa Teresita Hospital*, 819 Buena Vista St., 91010. Tel: 626-359-3243; Fax: 626-357-7166. Email: administration@santa-teresita.org. Web: www.santa-teresita.org. Michael Costello Jr., Pres. & CEO; Rev. Cornelius M. Buckley, S.J., Chap. Bed Capacity 216; Sisters 46; Total Staff 437; Patients Assisted Annually 77,318.

HAWTHORNE. **Hawthorne Community Hospital, Inc.*

dba Robert F. Kennedy Medical Center , Part of Catholic Healthcare West , 4500 W. 116th St., 90250.

Robert F. Kennedy Medical Center, 4500 W. 116th St., 90250-2296. Tel: 310-349-4000; Fax: 310-349-4122. Web: www.robertfkennedymedctr.org. Joan Bero, Pres.; Sr. Michelle Randall, D.C., Vice. Pres. Mission Svcs.; Bro. Christian Demlow, F.S.P., Dir. of Spiritual Care; Rev. John Joseph Sundaram, Chap. Daughters of Charity Health System.; Sponsored by the Daughters of Charity of St. Vincent de Paul, Province of the West.; Sponsored by Daughters of Charity of St. Vincent de Paul. Bed Capacity 246; Patients Assisted Annually 49,996; Total Staff 617; Maternity 15.

INGLEWOOD. *Daniel Freeman Memorial Hospital* Division of Daniel Freeman Hospitals , 333 N. Prairie Ave., 90301. Tel: 310-674-7050; 310-678-0361; Fax: 310-419-8273. Web: www.danielfreeman.org. Joseph W. Dunn, Ph.D., CEO; Nancy J. Lee, R.N., M.S.N., COO; Sr. Regina Clare Salazar, C.S.J., Corp. Vice Pres., Sponsorship & Mission; Daniel J. Ahearn, M.D., Vice Pres. & Medical Dir.; Willard F. Worthen, M.D., Chief of Staff; Rev. Francis X. Chrysostom (Sri Lanka), Chap.; Sisters Loretta Flood, C.S.J., Dir. of Pastoral Care; Kathleen Mary McCarthy, C.S.J., Chm. Sponsored by Sisters of St. Joseph of Carondelet in California. Sisters of St. Joseph of Carondelet 11; Sisters from Other Communities 5; Bed Capacity 364; Patients Assisted Annually 102,115; Total Staff 1,643.

Freeman Hospitals Foundation Tel: 310-419-8292; Fax: 310-419-8248. Sr. Mary Esther McCann, C.S.J., Pres. Emeritus; Brian Gauthier, Vice Pres.; Bernie Sklar, Chm.

LONG BEACH. *St. Mary Medical Center*, 1050 Linden Ave., 90813. Tel: 562-491-9000. Tomi Hadfield, Pres.; Sr. Mary McCluskey, C.C.V.I., Dir. of Spiritual Care. Catholic Healthcare West Southern California Patients Assisted Annually 126,336; Bed Capacity 576; Total Staff 1,896.

St. Mary Medical Center Foundation, P.O. Box 887, 90801. Tel: 562-491-9225; Fax: 562-491-9888. Email: jtwagner@chw.edu. Web: www.stmarymedicalcenter.com/smmc2. Bed Capacity 539; Total Assisted Annually 291,171; Total Staff 1,876.

St. Mary Professional Building, Inc., 1045 Atlantic Ave., 90813. James Riedel, Sec. Tel: 310-491-9010; Tammie McMann Brailsford, Pres.

LYNWOOD. *St. Francis Medical Center*, 3630 E. Imperial Hwy., 90262. Tel: 310-603-6000. Peter Aprato, Pres.; Bro. Richard Hirbe, B.F.C.C., Dir. Spiritual Healthcare Svcs.; Revs. James Cleary, O.F.M., Assoc. Chap.; Boctor Bishara, Assoc. Chap. Sponsored by the Daughters of Charity of St. Vincent de Paul, Province of the West., Daughters of Charity Health System. Patients Assisted Annually 134,668; Bed Capacity 328; Total Staff 1,663.

MARINA DEL REY. *Daniel Freeman Marina Hospital* Division of Daniel Freeman Hospitals, Inc. , 4650 Lincoln Blvd., 90292. Tel: 310-823-8911; Fax: 310-574-7854. Web: www.danielfreeman.org. *c/o Daniel Freeman Hospitals*, 333 N. Prairie Ave., Inglewood, 90301. Joseph W. Dunn, Ph.D., CEO, Daniel Freeman Hospitals; Nancy Lee, R.N., M.S.N., COO; Sr. Regina Clare Salazar, C.S.J., Corp. Vice Pres., Sponsorship & Mission; Daniel J. Ahearn, M.D., Vice Pres. & Medical Dir.; Lawrence J. Cohen, M.D., Chief of Staff; Revs. Lawrence Murphy, S.J.; Jose Mejia; Sisters Joan Hagen, Dir., Pastoral Care; Kathleen Mary McCarthy, C.S.J., Chm. Sponsored by Sisters of St. Joseph of Carondelet in California. Sisters of St. Joseph of Carondelet 1; Sisters from other Communities 1; Total Staff 463; Bed Capacity 166; Patients Assisted Annually 41,170.

OXNARD. *St. John's Regional Medical Center*, 1600 N. Rose Ave., 93030. Tel: 805-988-2500; Fax: 805-981-4440. Web: www.stjohnshealth.com. T. Michael Murray, Pres. Sponsored by Burlingame Regional Community of the Sisters of Mercy Sisters of Mercy 1; Bed Capacity 278; Patients Assisted Annually 92,438; Total Staff 1,251.

St. John's Pleasant Valley Hospital, 2309 Antonio Ave., Camarillo, 93010. Tel: 805-389-5800; Fax: 805-383-7450. Web: www.stjohnshealth.com. T. Michael Murray, Pres. Sponsored by Burlington Regional Community of the Sisters of Mercy Sisters 1; Beds 187; Patients Assisted Annually 51,565; Total Staff 585.

PASADENA. *Catholic Healthcare West Southern California*, Divisional Office, 251 S. Lake Ave., 8th Fl., 91101-4842. Tel: 626-744-2300; Fax: 626-744-2217. Web: www.chwhealth.com. Beth O'Brien, CEO.

Parent Company: Catholic Healthcare West Corporate Office, 1700 Montgomery St., Ste. 300, San Francisco, 94111-1024. Tel: 415-438-5500.

Operating Divisions:

St. John Pleasant Valley Hospital/Camarillo

Robert F. Kennedy Medical Center/Hawthorne Tel: 310-973-1711; Fax: 310-219-3745.

St. Francis Medical Center/Lynwood Tel: 310-900-8900; Fax: 310-604-0864.

St. Mary Medical Center/Long Beach Tel: 562-491-9000 Fax: 562-491-9085.

St. Vincent Medical Center/Los Angeles Tel: 213-484-7111; Fax: 213-484-9304.

St. John Medical Center/Oxnard Tel: 805-988-2500; Fax: 805-981-4440.

St. Francis Hospital/Santa Barbara Tel: 805-962-7661; Fax: 805-568-5704.

Marian Medical Center/Santa Maria Tel: 805-739-3000; Fax: 805-739-3060.

SAN PEDRO. *Little Company of Mary San Pedro Hospital* (Affiliate of Little Company of Mary Health Services) , 1700 W. Seventh St., 90732. Tel: 310-832-3311; Fax: 310-514-5314. Email: bcontratto@providence.org. Web: www.lcmweb.org. Bed Capacity 211; Patients Assisted Annually 40,000; Total Staff 600.

SANTA MARIA. *Marian Medical Center*, 1400 E. Church St., 93454. Tel: 805-739-3000; Fax: 805-739-3060. Charles J. Cova, Pres.; Deacon Zenon L. Nawrocki, Dir. Pastoral Care. Sponsored by Sisters of St. Francis of Penance and Christian Charity Sisters 9; Bed Capacity 167; Patients Assisted Annually 57,977; Total Staff 1,212.

Marian Medical Center Extended Care Facility Tel: 805-739-3650; Fax: 805-922-9067. Skilled Nursing Facility. Beds 95.

Marian Medical Center Day Care Facility for Children Tel: 805-739-3666; Fax: 805-922-9067 Capacity 52.

Marian Residence Retirement Home, 124 S. College Dr., 93454. Tel: 805-922-7731.

Marian Medical Center Foundation, 1405 E. Main St., Ste. E., 93454. Tel: 805-349-9486.

SANTA MONICA. *Saint John's Health Center*, 1328 22nd St., 90404. Tel: 310-829-5511; Fax: 310-315-6134. Web: www.stjohns.org. Sr. Marie Madeleine Shonka, Pres.; Mr. Bruce Lamoureux, CEO; Rev. Patrick Comerford, Chap. Sisters of Charity of Leavenworth Sisters 8; Bed Capacity 233; Patients Assisted Annually 200,000; Total Staff 1,500.

Saint John's Health Center Foundation

The Michael Burke Foundation

The Hope Guild

The Irene Dunne Guild

TORRANCE. *Little Company of Mary Hospital* (Affiliation of the Providence Health System) , 4101 W. Torrance Blvd., 90503. Tel: 310-540-7676; Fax: 310-540-7659. Web: lcmweb.org. Tom Christie, Chm.; Mark Costa, COO; Rev. Joel R. Buchman, M.A., S.T.B., Svc. Area Dir. Spiritual Care; Robert Brunner, Chap.; Sr. Dolores Mikula, S.S.J-T.O.S.F., Chap.; Rev. Jason Cusick, Chap. (Protestant); Revs. Peter Mallin, O.F.M.Conv., Chap.; Chris Onyenobi, Chap. Conducted by: American Province of Little Company of Mary Sisters, Evergreen Park, IL. Total Staff 3,700; Bed Capacity 250; Bassinets 35.

Little Company of Mary Hospital Pavilion 4320 Maricopa St., 90503. Tel: 310-543-5900; Fax: 310-793-0928. Dorothy Girley, Admin. Dir.; Rev. Joel R. Buchman, M.A., S.T.B., Dir. Spiritual Care; Armand Javines, Chap. Pavilion. Skilled nursing facility.; Conducted by: American Province of Little Company of Mary Sisters, Evergreen, IL. Bed Capacity 121.

Little Company of Mary San Pedro Hospital, 1300 W. 7th St., San Pedro, 90732. Tel: 310-832-3311; Fax: 310-514-5314. Web: lcmweb.org. Nancy Carlson, COO; Rev. Joel Buchman, Svc. Area Dir. Spiritual Care; Rev. Frank Gordillo, Chap. (Protestant); Rev. Francis L. Shigo, S.V.D., Chap. (Affiliate of the Providence Health System); Conducted by: American Province of Little Company of Mary Sisters, Evergreen, IL.; Conducted by: American Province of Little Company of Mary Sisters, Evergreen, IL. Bed Capacity 210; Total Staff 889.

Little Company of Mary Community Health Foundation, 4101 Torrance Blvd., 90503. Tel: 310-543-6900; Fax: 310-540-8664. Joseph M. Zanetta, Exec. Dir.

Little Company of Mary Peninsula Diagnostic Center Tel: 310-831-0371; Fax: 310-514-8920.

Little Company of Mary Peninsula Recovery Center Tel: 310-514-5376; Fax: 310-514-5376.

Little Company of Mary San Pedro Peninsula Hospital Pavillion, 1322 W. Sixth St., San Pedro, 90732. Tel: 310-514-5270; Fax: 310-514-5332. Julie Theiring, Admin. Dir.; Rev. Joel R. Buchman, M.A., S.T.B., Dir. Spiritual Care; Rev. Frank Gordillo, Chap. (Protestant); Rev. Francis L. Shigo, S.V.D., Chap. Skilled nursing facility. Bed Capacity 128.

Little Company of Mary Sub-Acute Center-South Bay, 3620 W. Lomita Blvd., 90505. Tel: 310-373-8587; Fax: 310-791-4514. La Verna McMiller, Admin. Dir.; Rev. Joel R. Buchman, M.A., S.T.B., Dir. Spiritual Care; Margaret O'Leary, Chap. Skilled nursing facility.; Conducted by: American Province of Little Company of Mary Sisters, Evergreen, IL. Bed Capacity 212.

WEST COVINA. *Citrus Valley Medical Center, Queen of the Valley Campus*, 1115 S. Sunset Ave., P.O. Box 1980, 91790. Tel: 626-962-4011; Fax: 626-814-2428. Email: catherine@cvhp.com. Web: cvhp.com. Rev. Eric A. Lewis; Mr. James T. Yoshioka, CEO. Bed Capacity 325; Patients Assisted Annually 125,000; Staff 1,500.

[K] SPECIAL HOSPITALS AND SANATORIA FOR INVALIDS

LOS ANGELES. *Franciscan Health Center*, 2859 Glassell St., 90026. Tel: 213-413-1050. Rosie Ortega, Clinic Mgr. Community Clinic Offering Surgical, Medical, OB-GYN, Optometry, Ophthalmology, Pediatrics, & Dental patients. Payment based on ability to pay.; A United Way Agency. Sponsored by Franciscan Sisters of the Sacred Heart. Patients Assisted Annually 5,700.

Knights of Malta Free Clinic, Inc., 2222 W. Ocean View #112, 90057. Tel: 213-384-4323; Fax: 213-384-4097. Email: fremed112@aol.com. David Frelinger, M.D., K.M., Medical Dir.; David Johnson, Admin. Conducted by Knights of Malta Free Clinic, Inc., Primary Health Care for the frail elderly, the working poor and medically underserved children. Medical Encounters 8,670; Total Staff 12; Total Assisted 2,342.

CULVER CITY. *Marycrest Manor, Convalescent Home*, 10664 St. James Dr., 90230-5498. Tel: 310-838-2778; 310-838-0016 (Carmelite Sisters); Fax: 310-838-9647; 310-838-0024 (Carmelite Sisters). Email: marycrest@sbcglobal.net. Sr. Noella, O.C.D., Supr. Dir. Devel.; Mr. Carrey Beers, Admin. Carmelite Sisters of the Most Sacred Heart of Los Angeles., Skilled Nursing Facility attended by priests from Loyola Marymount University and St. Augustine Parish. Carmelite Sisters of the Most Sacred Heart of Los Angeles 4; Pastoral Care Sisters 3; Bed Capacity 57; Residents 57; Total Staff 95; Total Assisted 57.

NEWBURY PARK. *Mary Health of the Sick Convalescent and Nursing Hospital*, 2929 Theresa Dr., 91320. Tel: 805-498-3644; Fax: 805-498-5112. Email: health@ftel.net. Sr. Maritza Arce, S.M., Supr. & Exec. Dir. Sisters Servants of Mary, Skilled Nursing Facility. Sisters 12; Bed Capacity 61; Residents Assisted Annually 89; Total Staff 94.

OJAI. *St. Joseph's Health and Retirement Center*, 2464 E. Ojai Ave., P.O. Box 760, 93024. Tel: 805-646-1466; Fax: 805-646-1013. Email: mayn@ojai.net. Rev. Ignatius Sudol, O.H., Prior; Bro. Gary Hill, O.H., Resident Mgr.; Rev. Carroll Laubacher, S.J. Hospitaller Brothers of St. John of God. Capacity 28; Independent Living 25; Total Staff 48.

[L] HANDICAPPED

SANTA MONICA. *Saint John's Child Study Center, Saint John's Hospital & Health Center*, 1339 20th St., 90404. Tel: 310-829-8921; Fax: 310-829-8455. Rev. Patrick Comerford, Chap.; Rebecca Refuerza, L.C.S.W., Dir. Conducted by Sisters of Charity of Leavenworth, Affiliated with Saint John's Hospital. Children Treated Annually 1,800.

SUNLAND. **Tierra del Sol Foundation*, 9919 Sunland Blvd., 91040. Tel: 818-352-1419; Fax: 818-353-0777. Email: tierradelsol.org. Stephen J. Miller, Exec. Dir.; Nancy Bissonette-Andrew, Clinical Dir. Community Program/Supported Employment for Adults with Developmental Disabilities. Licensed Capacity 304.

VAN NUYS. *Tierra Del Sol West*, 14547 Gilmore St., 91411. Tel: 818-904-9164. Stephen J. Miller, Exec. Dir.; Karen Alitz-Polga, Prog. Dir. Behavior Management Community Program for Adults with Developmental Disabilities. Capacity 50.

[M] CHILD ADOPTION SERVICES

PASADENA. *Holy Family Services, Adoption & Foster Care*, 402 S. Marengo Ave., 91101-3113. Tel: 626-432-5680; Fax: 626-578-7321. Email: hfsadopt@aol.com. Web: www.hfs.org.

Branch Offices:

1403 S. Main St., Santa Ana, 92707-1790. Tel: 714-835-5551; Fax: 714-973-4971.

80 E. Hillcrest Ave., Thousand Oaks, 91360-4219. Tel: 805-374-6797; Fax: 805-379-3088.

1441 N. D St. #201, San Bernardino, 92405-4738. Tel: 909-885-4882; Fax: 909-888-7065.

Holy Family Adoption Foundation, Inc. Tel: 626-432-5680; Fax: 626-578-7321. Auxiliaries of Holy Family Services: Holy Family's Adoptive Parents Organization, Inc., Adoption Guild of Southern Orange County, Angelique Guild, The 200 Associates. Birthparent unplanned pregnancy counseling 217; Foster care families recruited 1; Children placed in adoptive homes 155.

[N] VISITING NURSE SERVICES

LOS ANGELES. *Sisters Servants of Mary, Ministers of the Sick*, 2131 W. 27th St., 90018-3018. Tel: 213-731-5747; Fax: 323-731-4251. Sr. Leticia Rodriguez, S.M., Supr. Sisters 13; Total Assisted 41; Total Staff 7.

[O] PROTECTIVE INSTITUTIONS

LOS ANGELES. *St. Anne's*, 155 N. Occidental Blvd., 90026. Tel: 213-381-2931; Fax: 213-381-7804. Email: stannes@stannes.org. Web: www.stannes.org. Tom Owenson, Pres. & CEO; Rev. William Braud, O.F.M. Sponsored by the Franciscan Sisters of the Sacred Heart, Residential care and community counseling programs for pregnant and parenting adolescents.; St. Anne's also provides counseling to pregnant/parenting young women in their homes and pregnancy prevention (abstinence) classes in schools. Beds Licensed for Children Under 18 years of age 102; Children Served Annually in Residential Care 250.

Support groups include:

St. Anne's Foundation

St. Anne's Guild

St. Anne's Junior Guild

Mabel Mosler Auxiliary

Loretta Young Auxiliary

Sister Winifred Auxiliary Residential 250; Prevention Education 2,000; Total Staff 109.

Convent of the Good Shepherd-Good Shepherd Shelter, Admin. Office: 2561 Venice Blvd., 90019. Tel: 323-737-6111; Fax: 323-737-6113. Email: RGSLA1@aol.com. Conducted by Sisters of the Good Shepherd., Shelter for Battered Women and Their Children. Sisters 10; Women Assisted Annually 24; Children 108.

Little Flower Missionary House, 2434 Gates St., 90031-2824. Tel: 323-221-9248; Fax: 323-221-9831. Email: littleflowercenter@yahoo.com. Web: www.littleflowercenter.org. Sr. Beatriz, O.C.D., Supr. & Admin.; Mrs. Catherine Catano, Dir. & Prin. Attended by Salesian priests.; Child and Kindergarten Care Center. Sisters 7; Lay Teachers 10; Capacity 135; Kindergarten Capacity 40; Total Staff 29.

Missionary Brothers of Charity, 1345 Alvarado Ter., 90006. Tel: 213-251-9707. Day center for homeless youth. Total Assisted Annually 14,000; Total Staff 6.

CHATSWORTH. *Rancho San Antonio*, 21000 Plummer St., 91311. Tel: 818-882-6400; Fax: 818-882-6404. Bro. John Crowe, C.S.C., Exec. Dir. Directed by the Brothers of Holy Cross., Sponsored by Catholic Archdiocese of Los Angeles. Brothers 1; Boys (13-17 yrs.) 168; Total Staff 118; Families Assisted 257.

SANTA BARBARA. *St. Vincent Residence*, 4200 Calle Real, 93110-1454. Tel: 805-683-6381; Fax: 805-967-7508. Email: info@sv-sb.org. Web: www.sv-sb.org. For single moms on welfare and/or very low income. We closed the Probation Program on September 19, 2001 Daughters of Charity of St. Vincent de Paul Sisters 5; Residents 76; Total Assisted 85; Total Staff 46.

St. Vincent's Casa Alegria Children Center, 4200 Calle Real, 93110-1451. Tel: 805-683-6381, Ext. 201; Fax: 805-967-7508. Email: info@sv-sb.org. For infants, toddlers, and preschoolers. Daughters of Charity of St. Vincent de Paul 5; Daycare 53; Total Assisted 59; Total Staff 18.

[P] HOMES FOR AGED

LOS ANGELES. *St. John of God Retirement and Care Center*, 2468 S. St. Andrews Pl., 90018. Tel: 323-731-0641; Fax: 323-731-1452. John Williams, Admin. CFO; Bros. Pablo Lopez, O.H., Prior; Stephen de la Rosa, O.H., Prov. Brothers 10; Bed Capacity 287; SNF 131; Residential Care 105; Patients Assisted Annually 280; Total Staff 200; Independent Living 51.

Supporting Organizations:

Hospitaller Foundation of California, Inc. Tel: 323-731-7141; Fax: 323-731-5717. Bro. Patrick Corr, O.H., Pres.

Women's League of St. John of God, Inc., Helpers Club of St. John of God, Inc. Tel: 323-731-7141; Fax: 323-731-5717.

Nazareth House, 3333 Manning Ave., 90064. Tel: 310-839-2361; Fax: 310-839-4204. Email: naz-la@pacbell.net. Web: www.nazarethouse.org. Sr. Fintan Keaveney, Supr. Conducted by the Poor Sisters of Nazareth. Sisters 8; Retired Priests 18; Total Staff 85; Residents 123.

SAN FERNANDO. *Mother Gertrude Home for Senior Citizens* (Franciscan Missionary Sisters of the Immaculate Conception, Inc.) , 11320 Laurel Canyon Blvd., 91340. Tel: 818-898-1546; Fax: 818-365-3159. Capacity 45; Total Staff 19; Total in Residence 36.

SAN PEDRO. *Little Sisters of the Poor*, Jeanne Jugan Residence, 2100 S. Western Ave., 90732. Tel: 310-548-0625; Fax: 310-548-4504. Email: mslsppd@hotmail.com. Sr. Rose Marie, Supr.

Legal Title: *Little Sisters of the Poor of Los Angeles. A Corporation* Sisters 10; Lay Associates 15; Total Staff 90; Residents 102; Total Assisted Annually 1,260.

SANTA MARIA. *Marian Residence*, 124 S. College Dr., 93454. Tel: 805-922-7731; Fax: 805-922-9834. Email: lmaloney@chw.edu. Conducted by Sisters of St. Francis of Penance and Christian Charity. Sisters 19; Residents 32; Total Staff 42.

SUN VALLEY. *Villa Scalabrini*, 10631 Vinedale St., 91352. Tel: 818-768-6500; Fax: 818-768-0684. Email: villascalabrini.com. Web: www.villascalabrini.com. Rev. Ermete Nazzani, C.S., Exec. Dir. & Admin. Missionary Fathers of St. Charles, Retirement Center and Special Care Unit.; Augustinian Recollect Sisters Bed Capacity 188; Retirement Center 130; Skilled Nursing Unit 58; Total Staff 115.

[Q] MONASTERIES AND RESIDENCES OF PRIESTS AND BROTHERS

LOS ANGELES. *Atonement Friars*, 222 S. Hewitt St., 90012. Tel: 213-626-2279; Fax: 213-628-1757. Rev. David L. Doerner, S.A.

Brothers of John of God, Inc., The, 2425 S. Western Ave., 90018-2608. Tel: 323-734-0233; Fax: 323-731-5987. Email: usaprov-office@sbcglobal.net. Web: www.hospitallers.org. Bro. Stephen de la Rosa, O.H., Prov.

Women's League of St. John of God, Inc., 90002. Tel: 323-731-7141; Fax: 323-731-5717.

Helper's Club, Inc. Tel: 323-731-7141; Fax: 323-731-5717.

St. John of God Retirement & Care Center, 90189. Tel: 323-731-0641; Fax: 323-737-1452.

St. Joseph's Health & Retirement Center Tel: 805-646-1466; Fax: 805-646-1013.

Hospitaller Foundation of California, Inc. Tel: 323-731-7141; Fax: 323-731-5717.

Women's League of St. Joseph's Health & Retirement Center Tel: 805-646-1466; Fax: 805-646-1013.

Grande Apartments-Los Angeles Tel: 323-730-4100; Fax: 323-737-1452.

Hospitaller Brothers Healthcare, Inc. Tel: 805-630-1215; Fax: 805-646-1013.

St. John of God Health Care Services Tel: 760-241-4917; Fax: 760-241-8911.

Brothers of the Good Shepherd, Inc. of California, 3445 Waverly Dr., 90027. Tel: 323-662-3620; 323-662-0092; Fax: 323-662-3619. Email: d_nickerson@hotmail.com. Web: www.lbgs.org. Bros. Mark Harmueller, B.G.S.; David Nickerson, B.G.S.; Rev. Victor Nolan, B.G.S.

Casa Guadalupe, Divine Word Missionaries, 807 N. Fresno St., 90063. Fax: 323-263-1221. Revs. Lukas Bao Teluma, S.V.D. Tel: 323-263-1253; Raymundus Bhia Wea, S.V.D. Tel: 323-267-1121.

Claretian Retreat Center Community, 1119 Westchester Pl., 90019. Tel: 323-731-9329; Fax: 323-733-6201. Email: usawestprov@earthline.net. Very Rev. Roland Lozano, C.M.F., Prov. Supr.; Rev. Frank J. Ferrante, C.M.F., Dir.; Bro. Rene LePage, C.M.F.; Revs. Carlos C. Castillo, C.M.F.; George Whedbee, C.M.F.; John Hampsch, C.M.F.; Theo Fuentes, C.M.F., Admin.; Robert Bishop, C.M.F.; Bernard O'Connor, C.M.F; Bro. Larry Moen, C.M.F., Supr.

Columban Fathers, Procure House, 2600 N. Vermont Ave., 90027-1245. Tel: 323-665-4289; Fax: 323-664-7160. Email: orourkecj@aol.com. Web: www.columban.org. Revs. Charles L. O'Rourke, S.S.C., Supr.; Thomas Cusack, S.S.C.; Paul White, S.S.C.; Anthony Mortell, S.S.C.; Arturo Aguilar, S.S.C.; Jim Shiffer, S.S.C.; Nguyen Xuan Pien, S.S.C.; Peter Kenny, S.S.C.

Columbiere House Formerly Connolly House. , 5322 Franklin Ave., 90027. Tel: 323-466-3723; Fax: 323-466-3826. Email: jclark@colprov.org. Revs. Francis J. Parrish, S.J.; John D. McAnulty, S.J.; John R. LaVecke, S.J.; James S. Torrens, S.J.; Charles Prussing, S.J.; Peter Chu, S.J.; Patrick Connolly, S.J. (Wisconsin); William K. Delaney, S.J.; John W. Clark, S.J.; Doan Hoang, S.J. Jesuit Fathers Priests 9.

Congregation of St. Joseph Casa Nazareth, 2702 Abrigo Ave., 90031. Tel: 213-221-4809. Revs. Giampietro Gasparin, C.S.J.; John Trimaglio, C.S.J., Supr.

Dominic Savio Salesian Residence, 920 Soto St., 90023-1396. Tel: 323-266-6000; Fax: 323-266-3487. Email: sdblosangeles@hotmail.com. Web: www.donboscowest.org. In Res. Revs. Joseph Cheng, S.D.B., St. Bridget's Chinese Catholic Center; Joseph Farias, S.D.B., Pastor St. Mary's & Treas.; Jack Gibson, S.D.B., Dir. Salesian Boys & Girls Club & Family Youth Center; Steve Gomez, S.D.B., Salesian High School; Lucian B. Lomello, S.D.B. (Retired); Avelino Lorenzo, S.D.B., St. Mary's; James Nieblas, S.D.B., Supr. of Community, St. Mary's; William Schafer, S.D.B., Exec. Dir., Salesian Boys' & Girls' Club, Salesian Family Youth Center; Robert Stein, S.D.B., Salesian High School; Richard Voigt, S.D.B., Salesian Boys & Girls Club, Salesian Family Youth Center.

Franciscan Brothers of the Third Order Regular, 4552 Gainsborough Ave., 90027-1227. Tel: 323-644-2740; Fax: 323-644-2977. Email: jhoconnor@yahoo.com. Bro. Hilarion O'Connor, O.S.F., Regl. Supr. Brothers 11.

Guadalupe Missioners Procure, 4714 W. 8th St., 90005. Tel: 323-937-2780; Fax: 323-937-2782. Revs. Santiago G. Lara, M.G., Local Supr.; Abraham R. Garcia, M.G., Asst.

Hospitaller Brothers of St. John of God, 2468 S. St. Andrew's Pl., 90018. Tel: 323-731-0641; Fax: 323-731-5987. Email: usaprov-office@sbcglobal.net. Web: www.hospitallers.org. Bro. Pablo Lopez, O.H., Prior. Brothers 11.

St. John of God Retirement and Care Center, 2035 W. Adams Blvd., 90018. Tel: 323-731-0641; Fax: 323-737-1452. Email: usaprov-office@sbcglobal.net. Web: www.hospitallens.org. Bros. Stephen de la Rosa, O.H., Prov., Chm., & Novice Master; Pablo Lopez, O.H., Local Supr. Brothers 11.

Maryknoll Fathers and Brothers (Catholic Foreign Mission Society of America) , 745 W. Adams Blvd., 90007. Tel: 213-747-9676; Fax: 213-747-8923. Web: www.maryknoll.org.

2701 S. Peck Rd., Monrovia, 91016. Tel: 626-447-6202, Ext. 32. Revs. Roberto Rodriguez, M.M.; John W. Waldrep, M.M.; William M. Boteler, M.M.; Michael G. Callahan, M.M. (Retired).

255 S. Grand Ave., #413, 90012-3017. Tel: 213-625-5702. Rev. James P. Colligan, M.M.

2020 Alaguinas Dr., San Ysidro, 92173. Tel: 619-428-1415, Ext. 12; Fax: 619-428-5626. Rev. Peter L. Ruggere, M.M. Priests 6.

Mill Hill Missionaries Procure (St. Joseph Society for Foreign Missions) , 1841 Camino Palmero, 90046. Tel: 323-876-0505; Fax: 323-876-0508. Email: patmolloy@aol.com. Rev. Patrick J. Molloy, M.H.M. Priests 1.

Minim Fathers, 3431 Portola Ave., 90032. Tel: 323-223-1101; Fax: 323-223-9592. Email: jvega@earthlink.net. Web: home.earthlink.net/~jvega/. Revs. Mario Pisano, O.M., Supr.; Gino Vanzillotta, O.M.; Jose L. Vega, O.M. Priests 3.

Missionaries of Charity Brothers Tel: 213-384-6116.

Casa Teresa, 1316 S. Westlake Ave., 90006. Tel: 213-380-5225. Regional Office; Hospitality for men. Temporary shelter for sick homeless men.

Nuestro Hogar, 1345 Alvarado Terr., 90006. Tel: 213-251-9707. Daycenter for young adults. Total Assisted 85; Total Staff 5.

Missionary Sons of the Immaculate Heart of Mary (Claretian Priests and Brothers) Tel: 323-734-1824; Fax: 323-737-0301. Email: usawestprov@earthlink.net.

Legal Title: *Claretian Missionaries - Western Province, Inc.*

Prov. Headquarters of the Western Prov. of the USA, 1119 Westchester Place, 90019. Tel: 323-734-1824; Fax: 323-737-0301. Very Rev. Roland Lozano, C.M.F., Prov. Supr.; Rev. Dennis G. Gallo, C.M.F., Vice Prov. & Consultor; Bro. Rene LePage, C.M.F., Treas. & Consultor; Revs. Frank J. Ferrante, C.M.F., Consultor; Art Gramaje, C.M.F., Consultor.

Claretian Tape Ministry, Inc. Tel: 323-734-1234; Fax: 323-734-0973.

Dominguez Seminary, Inc., Rancho Dominguez. Tel: 310-631-5981; Fax: 310-631-3518.

Claretian Educational and Renewal Center, Inc. Tel: 323-737-8464; Fax: 323-733-6201. This is a non-profit corporation under the laws of the State of California having as its purpose the support of any Roman Catholic benevolent, charitable, educational or missionary undertakings of the Claretian Missionaries - Western Province, Inc.

Mount Carmel Priory, Carmelite Fathers and Brothers, 801 W. 70th St., 90044. Tel: 213-752-3972. Revs. Augustine W. Carter, O.Carm.; Matt J. Ewing, O.Carm., Prior; Bernard Kangley, O.Carm.; Bro. Stephen Diekemper, O.Carm.

Legal Title: *Fathers of the Order of Mount Carmel, Corporation* Priests 3.

Piarist Fathers, 512 S. Avenue 20, 90031. Tel: 213-223-4153. Revs. Raul Palma, Sch.P.; Francis Boronat, Sch.P., Rector of the Community; Juan Trenchs, Sch.P.; Miguel Campos, Sch.P. Priests 4.

Society of St. Paul (Mexican Province) , 112 Herbert St., 90063. Tel: 323-269-9814. Revs. Valeriano Giachino, S.S.P., Supr.; Gilberto Martinez, S.S.P., Vice Supr.; Tomas Martinez, S.S.P.; Jose R. Lopez; Jesus Antonio Hernandez-Toboada, S.S.P.; Salvadore Ruiz-Armas, S.S.P.; Paulo Cesar Torres Soto, S.S.P., Seminarian; Antonio Francisco

Paredes Monjaras, S.S.P., Seminarian.
Society of the Divine Word, Western Province, Provincial Offices, 2181 W. 25th St., 90018. Tel: 323-735-8130; Fax: 323-735-8122. Email: svdusw@earthlink.net. Office of the Provincial, P.O. Box 7195, 90007. Revs. Joseph A. Miller, S.V.D., Prov. Supr.; Gerard O'Doherty, S.V.D., Prov. Treas.

AZUSA. *Casa Comboni Mission Seminary*, 525 N. Pasadena Ave., 91702. Tel: 626-334-3531; Fax: 626-969-8681. Email: pep44@earthlink.net. Rev. Jose Luis Cuevas, M.C.C.J. (CIN), Supr., Vocation Dir. Priests 2; Students 4. In Res. Rev. Mario Merino, Formation Dir.

BALDWIN PARK. *Vietnamese Redemptorist Mission*, 3452 N. Big Dalton Ave., 91706. Tel: 626-337-7735; Fax: 626-851-1280. Revs. Vu Minh Nghiem, C.Ss.R.; Ngo Dinh Thoa, C.Ss.R.; Dinh Ngoc Que, C.Ss.R.; Nguyen Thanh Son, C.Ss.R.; Pham Quoc Hung, C.Ss.R.; Trinh Duc Hoa, C.SS.R.; Tran Ngoc Bich, C.Ss.R.; Bros. John M. Viet Hien, C.Ss.R.; Martin Nguyen Van Moi, C.Ss.R.
In Residence Elsewhere:
8800 E. 22nd St., Tuscon, AZ 85710. Tel: 602-751-2060. Rev. Dang Phuoc Hoa, C.Ss.R.
22 Stone St., Salinas, 93901. Tel: 408-772-8227. Rev. Tran Dinh Phuc, C.Ss.R.
2458 Atlantic Ave., Long Beach, 90806. Tel: 562-424-2041; Fax: 562-424-2152. Revs. Nguyen Duc Mau, C.Ss.R.; Phan Phat Huon, C.Ss.R.; Ngo Van Dao, C.Ss.R.; Nguyen Ngoc Viet; Doan Trong Son; Nguyen Tat Hai, C.SS.R.; Nguyen Truong Luan; Bro. Vo Thanh Ha, C.Ss.R.
1907 E. Grauwyler Rd., Irving, TX 75061. Tel: 972-438-4082. Revs. Nguyen Duc Thong, C.Ss.R.; Dinh Minh Hai, C.Ss.R.; Bui Quang Tuan, C.Ss.R.; Nguyen Van Phan, C.Ss.R.; Nguyen Phi Long, C.Ss.R.
3417 W. Little York Rd., Houston, TX 77091. Tel: 214-321-9493; Fax: 713-868-4589. Revs. Chau Xuan Bau, C.SS.R.; Le Quang Phung, C.Ss.R.; Nguyen Duc Thanh, C.Ss.R.; Tran Quoc Bao, C.Ss.R.; Nguyen Dinh Trung.
3452 N. Big Dalton Ave., 91706. Tel: 626-939-0357. Priests 26; Brothers 3; Student Clerics 20.

CUDAHY. *Missionaries del Sagrado Corazon y Santa Maria de Guadalupe*, 4235 Clara St., 90201. Tel: 323-562-3356. Tony Vienna Esq., Contact Person. Tel: 213-485-1555; Fax: 213-689-1004.

CULVER CITY. *Ignatius House, The Novitiate of the California Province, Society of Jesus*, P.O. Box 5166, 90231-5166. Tel: 310-815-0166; Fax: 310-815-0170. Email: rfambrini@calprov.org. Web: www.calprov.org.
10775 Deshire Pl., 90230-5017. Tel: 310-815-0166 (Staff); 310-815-0185 (Novices); Fax: 310-815-0170. Revs. Robert A. Fambrini, S.J., Supr. & Dir. of Novices; Thomas J. Reilley, S.J., Asst. Dir. Novices.

LA VERNE. *Congregation of the Sacred Hearts of Jesus and Mary*, 2150 Damien Ave., 91750-5114. Tel: 909-593-5441 (Provinical Office); Fax: 909-593-3971. Email: ssccwest@cpl.net. Web: www.cpl.net/~ssccwest. Revs. Michael W. Barry, SS.CC., Prov.; Peter K. Dennis, SS.CC.; Donal McCarthy, SS.CC.; Patrick Travers, SS.CC.; Peadar Cronin, SS.CC. Priests 5.

MISSION HILLS. *Congregation of the Sacred Hearts*, Alemany High School, 15201 Rinaldi St., 91345. Tel: 818-365-3925; Fax: 818-365-2064. Rev. Patrick Argue, SS.CC. Tel: 818-365-3925; 818-365-3927. Priests 1.

MONTEBELLO. *Vincentian Fathers & Brothers*, 420 Date St.,, 90640. Tel: 323-721-5486; Fax: 323-721-5499. Email: cmwestusa@att.net.
DePaul Evangelization Center, 1105 Bluff Rd., 90640-6198. Tel: 323-721-6060; Fax: 323-887-1765. Revs. Andrew E. Bellisario, C.M., Prov.; James Osendorf, C.M., Supr. & Dir.; Gary Landry, C.M.; Minh J. Pham, C.M. (PHX); Joseph V. Haley, C.M. (SJ); Peter J. Diliberto (Retired); Robert J. Jones, C.M.; Thomas J. McIntyre, C.M. (Retired); Jacques J. Nouws; Bro. Edward D. Graham, C.M. Priests 9; Brothers 1.
St. Mary's Center, 1964 Las Canoas Rd., Santa Barbara, 93105-2351. Tel: 805-966-4829; Fax: 805-564-1662. Revs. Walter Housey, C.M., Supr.; Patrick J. Mullin, C.M., Dir.; Roy A. Persich, C.M., Dir.; James M. Galvin; John V Shine. Priests 5.
Vincent House, 252 F St., Oxnard, 93030. Tel: 805-240-1012; Fax: 805-483-8340. House of Studies Priests 2.
Vincentian Residence, 641 W. Adams Blvd., 90007-2546. Tel: 213-748-9829; Fax: 213-748-9829. Priests 3.
Amat Residence II, 641 W. Adams Blvd., 90007-2546. Tel: 213-748-9829; Fax: 213-748-9829. Revs. Pedro Villarroya, Supr.; Thomas C. Anslow, C.M., J.C.D., J.C.L.; Stafford Poole; Philip A. Van Linden, C.M. Priests 4.
Amat Residence I, 649 W. Adams Blvd., 90007-2596. Tel: 213-747-1227; Fax: 213-749-4504. Email: amathouse@aol.com. Revs. William E. Piletic, C.M.; Hoan N. Nguyen. Priests 2.
Vincentian Fathers and Brothers, 420 Date St., 90640. Tel: 323-721-5486; Fax: 323-721-5499. Email: cmwestusa@att.net. Revs. Andrew E. Bellisario, C.M., Prov.; James Osendorf, C.M., Prov. Treas.; Stafford Poole, Archivist; William R. Piletic, Vocation Dir.
Legal Title: *Congregation of the Mission in California, a Corporation*
Legal Title: *Vincentian Province of the West Suppot Trust Fund*
Legal Title: *Vincentian Foreign Mission Society*
Legal Title: *DePaul Center Corporation*, Province of the West Priests 4.

OXNARD. *St. Augustine Priory O.A.R.*, 400 Sherwood Way, 93033-7510. Tel: 805-486-7433; 805-486-9651 (Vocations); Fax: 805-487-2805. Email: saprovince@yahoo.com. Web: augustinianrecollects.org. Revs. Domingos A. Machado, O.A.R., Prior; Fidel Hernandez, O.A.R., Prefect of Students & Subprior; Eliseo Gonzalez, O.A.R., Vacation Dir. Postulancy Augustinian Recollects & Vocation Center. Total in Residence 14; Students 5. In Res. Revs. Robert Huse, O.A.R.; Francis de la Vega, O.A.R.; Bros. Eric Crelencia, O.A.R.; Raymond Fabrin, O.A.R.; Michael L. Stechmann, O.A.R.; Jorge Valdivia, O.A.R.

PASADENA. *Legionaries of Christ*, 1453 E. California Blvd., 91106. Tel: 626-792-0447; Fax: 626-792-0475. Email: amulcahey@legionaries.org. Web: www.legionofchrist.org. Priests 5; Brothers 3. In Res. Revs. Shawn Aaron, L.C.; Salvador Fernandez, L.C.; Thomas Maher, L.C.; Andrew Mulcahey, L.C.; Juan Rivas, L.C.; Bros. Joseph Freymann, L.C.; Timothy Moran, L.C.; Joseph Ramos, .
Passionist Community, 700 N. Sunnyside Ave., Sierra Madre, 91024. Tel: 626-355-1740; Fax: 626-355-1744. Email: passionistc@yahoo.com.
Passionist Retreat House, 700 N. Sunnyside Ave., Sierra Madre, 91024. Tel: 626-355-7188; Fax: 626-355-0485. Congregation of the Passion, Mater Dolorosa Community
Passionist Residence, 700 N. Sunnyside Ave., Sierra Madre, 91024. Tel: 626-355-1740; Fax: 626-355-1744. Very Rev. Alfred Pooler, C.P., Local Supr.; Revs. Patrick Brennan, C.P., Retreat Dir.; Alan Phillip, C.P., Asst. Supr.; Bros. John Rockenbach, C.P.; Kurt Wernert, C.P. Priests 3; Brothers 1.

RANCHO DOMINGUEZ. *Dominguez Seminary Inc.*, 18127 S. Alameda St., 90220. Tel: 213-636-6020; 310-631-5981; 310-631-8484; Fax: 310-631-3518. Revs. Robert Billett, C.M.F., Supr.; Joseph Daries, C.M.F.; Donald Lavelle, C.M.F., Econome; Diego Barrios, C.M.F., Vicar Supr.; Salvatore Bonano, C.M.F.; Michael Cecere, C.M.F.; John Corominas, C.M.F.; Albert Connors, C.M.F.; Alberto Domingo, C.M.F.; Joseph Gamm, C.M.F.; Isidor Garcia, C.M.F.; James Griffin, C.M.F.; Francis X. Hogan, C.M.F.; Henry Luna, C.M.F.; Patrick McPolin, C.M.F.; Michael Philen, C.M.F.; Frank Pyka, C.M.F.; John Salvador, C.M.F. Congregation of Missionaries Sons of the Immaculate Heart of Mary (Claretian Missionaries), Retirement Center, Ministries Community. Priests 18.

SAN GABRIEL. *Claretian Missionaries (Missionary Sons of the Immaculate Heart of Mary)*, 428 S. Mission Dr., 91776. Tel: 626-457-3035; Fax: 626-282-5308. Email: alsgm1@aol.com. Web: sangabrielmission.org. Revs. Dennis G. Gallo, C.M.F.; Manuel A. Diaz, C.M.F.; John Gregory Hencier, C.M.F.; Arnold J. Gonzalez, C.M.F.; Fernando Vega, C.M.F.; Mark Clarke, C.M.F. Claretians Old Mission Priests 6.

SANTA BARBARA. *St. Anthony's Seminary*, 2300 Garden St., 93105-3696. Tel: 805-682-4720; Fax: 805-682-2870. Email: stanthonys1@home.com. Web: sbfranciscans.org. Rev. Leo Sprietsma, O.F.M., Dir. Priests 2 Brothers 1. In Res. Rev. Nevin Ford, O.F.M.; Bro. Timothy Arthur, O.F.M.
Franciscan Friary, Order of Friars Minor (Old Mission), 2201 Laguna St., 93105. Tel: 805-682-4713; Fax: 805-682-6067. Revs. Alberic Smith, O.F.M., Guardian; Virgil Cordano, O.F.M., Theological Institute; Nevin Ford, O.F.M.; Felipe Baldonado, O.F.M.; Benvenute Bavero, O.F.M.; Virgilio Biasiol O.F.M.; Maurus Kelly, O.F.M.; Richard Juzix (FRS), St. Barbara's; Howard Hall, O.F.M., Hospital Chap.; Leo Sprietsma, O.F.M.; Lucius Grosso, O.F.M. (PHX); Lester Mitchell, O.F.M. (PHX); Pedro Vasquez, O.F.M.; Thomas Messner, O.F.M (MRY); Bros. Timothy Arthur, O.F.M., Prov. Archivist; Joseph Brand, O.F.M.; Gerald Chumik, O.F.M.; Joachim Grant, O.F.M.; Conrado Duran, O.F.M.; Nicholas Heinrich, O.F.M.; Augustine Hootka, O.F.M.; Nevin Janicki, O.F.M.; Philip Morales, O.F.M.; Christian Rogan, O.F.M.; Jan Honchosky, O.F.M.; Ernest LuVisi, O.F.M. Priests 14 Brothers 12.

SANTA PAULA. *Canons Regular of the Immaculate Conception*, Dom Grea House of Formation & Novitiate, 984 Monte Vista Dr., 93060-1612. Tel: 805-933-5063; Fax: 805-525-5115. Email: paterthoma@excite.com. Revs. Pasquale Vuoso, C.R.I.C., Supr. Tel: 805-525-2149; Fax: 805-933-5520; Thomas J. Dome, C.R.I.C., Dir. & Novice Master; Charles R. Lueras, C.R.I.C. Tel: 805-525-2149; Fax: 805-933-5520; James G. Garceau, C.R.I.C. Tel: 805-525-3716; Fax: 805-525-3788; William B. Ustaski, C.R.I.C. Tel: 661-252-3353; Fax: 661-252-1539; Sergio Garcia, C.R.I.C. Tel: 909-622-4553; Fax: 909-623-0841; Bro. Enrique Vergara. Priests 6; Scholastics 1; Postulants 1.

VALYERMO. *St. Andrew's Abbey*, 31001 N. Valyermo Rd., P.O. Box 40, 93563-0040. Tel: 661-944-2178; Fax: 661-944-1076. Email: monks@valyermo.com. Web: www.valyermo.com. Rt. Rev. Francis Benedict, O.S.B., Abbot; Very Rev. Simon O'Donnell, O.S.B., Prior; Revs. John Bosco Stoner, O.S.B., Subprior; Eleutherius Winance, O.S.B.; Werner Papeians de Morchoven, O.S.B.; Bro. Peter Zhou Bang-jiu, O.S.B.; Rev. Philip Edwards, O.S.B.; Bro. Dominic Guillen, O.S.B.; Rev. Gregory Elmer, O.S.B.; Bros. Benedict Dull, O.S.B.; Joseph Iarrobino, O.S.B.; Revs. Luke Dysinger, O.S.B.; Martin Yslas, O.S.B.; Isaac Kalina, O.S.B.; Paul Pluth, O.S.B.; Carlos Lopez, O.S.B.; Bro. Anselmo Taborda, O.S.B.; Rev. Joseph (Dennis) Brennan, O.S.B.; Bros. James Brennan, O.S.B.; Damien Toilolo, O.S.B.; Aelred Niespolo, O.S.B.; Matthew Rios, O.S.B.; Vincent Ng, O.S.B.; Lazarus Tumath, O.S.B.; Herman Kim, O.S.B.; Bartolome Aparicio, O.S.B. Benedictine Monks Priests 13; Brothers 13.

VAN NUYS. *Rogationist Fathers*, 6635 Tobias Ave., 91405. Tel: 818-782-0184; Fax: 818-782-1794. Email: rogdevoff@aol.com. Web: www.rcj.org; www.rogazionisti.it. Revs. Vincenzo Buccheri, R.C.J.; John Bruno, R.C.J.; Rodolfo D'Agostino, R.C.J.
Legal Title: *Congregation of Rogationists, Inc.*

WHITTIER. *Redemptorists of Whittier*, 7215 Newlin Ave., 90602-1266. Tel: 562-698-0107; Fax: 562-696-1617. Web: www.st-maryschurch.org. Revs. Brian Johnson, C.SS.R.; Arturo Uribe, C.SS.R.; Joseph Elliott, C.SS.R.; Charles A. Wehrley Jr., C.SS.R.; Donald Liberty, C.SS.R.; Enrique Lopez, C.SS.R.; George Dawson, C.SS.R.; Arthur Frost, C.SS.R.; William Adams, C.SS.R.; Bro. Juan Carlos Garcia, C.SS.R. Priests 8; Brothers 1.

[R] CONVENTS AND RESIDENCES FOR SISTERS

LOS ANGELES. *California Institute of the Sisters of the Immaculate Heart Mary*, 3431 Waverly Dr., 90027. Tel: 323-664-1124; Fax: 323-664-2215. Email: ritacallanan@aol.com. Web: www.sisters.hmla.org. Sr. Rita Callanan, I.H.M., Supr. Gen.
Legal Title: *California Institute of the Sisters of the Most Holy and Immaculate Heart of the Blessed Virgin Mary* Sisters 17.
Congregation of the Sisters of Nazareth Motherhouse, U.S.A. and Novitiate, 3333 Manning Ave., 90064. Tel: 310-839-2361; 310-839-2362; Fax: 310-839-0648. Email: spflynn@nazarethhouse.org. Web: www.nazarethhouse.org. Sr. John Berchmans, Regl. Supr. Sisters 9.
Eucharistic Franciscan Missionary Sisters, Motherhouse: 943 S. Soto St., 90023. Tel: 213-264-6556; Fax: 213-526-1655. Email: efms@earthlink.net. Sr. Rose Seraphim, E.F.M.S., Supr. Gen. Sisters 25.
Eucharistic Franciscan Missionary Sisters of Los Angeles, Nativity Convent: 1421 Cota Ave., Torrance, 90501. Tel: 310-328-6725; Fax: 310-328-5248.
Guadalupanas Missionaries of the Holy Spirit, 5467 W. 8th St., 90036. Tel: 626-791-4359. Email: ruthagee@juno.com.
Legal Title: *Missionary Guadalupanas of the Holy Spirit* Sisters 7.
Guadalupanas Missionaries of the Holy Spirit, 5467 W. 8th St., 90036. Tel: 323-935-6565; Fax: 323-930-0394. Email: mgspscala@aol.com.
Legal Title: *Missionary Guadalupanas of the Holy Spirit*, Apostolate House. Sisters 5.
Guadalupanas Missionaries of the Holy Spirit Novitiate. , 758 S. Dunsmuir Ave., 90036. Tel: 323-936-0135; Fax: 323-939-8735. Email: niditomgsps@aol.com. Sr. Maria Julia Lozano, Supr.
Lovers of the Holy Cross Sisters, 14700 S. Van Ness Ave., Gardena, 90249.
Mother House & Novitiate, 14700 S. Van Ness Ave., Gardena, 90249. Tel: 310-768-1906; 310-516-0271; Fax: 310-352-6435.
Good Shepherd Center, 267 N. Belmont Ave., 90026. Tel: 213-250-5241; Fax: 213-482-0567.
St. Bruno's Convent, 10734 S. Widener Ave., Whittier, 90603. Tel: 562-947-1177; Fax: 562-947-1177. Total Sisters & Novices 57.
Missionary Benedictines Sisters of Tutzingin in Los

Angeles, Inc., 912 Bronson Ave., 90019-1935. Tel: 323-939-3977; Fax: 323-937-7971. Email: osbgregory@hanmail.net. Sr. Marguerita Choi, O.S.B., Supr. & Contact Person.

Missionary Servants of the Most Blessed Trinity Ascension Missionary Cenacle, 518 W. 111th Pl., 90044. Tel: 213-754-0020.

Missionary Sisters of Christ the King (Poland), 3424 W. Adams Blvd., 90018. Tel: 323-734-5249; Fax: 323-734-0046. Email: plchurchla@earthlink.net. Sisters Gertruda I. Szymanska, Local Supr.; Zofia Turczyn, M.C.H.R., Sacristan Work; Zofia Turczyn, M.C.H.R., Local Supr.; Wiesfana Jamrosik, M.C.H.R., Sec. (Parish Office); Maria Niua, M.C.H.R. Sisters working in Archdiocese of Los Angeles 3.

Monastery of the Angels (Contemplative), 1977 Carmen Ave., 90068. Tel: 323-466-2186; Fax: 323-466-6645. Web: www.op-stjoseph.org/nuns/angels. Sr. Mary Pia, O.P., Prioress; Rev. Armando Ibanez, O.P., Chap. Tel: 323-463-6488. Nuns of the Order of Preachers Professed Cloistered Nuns 23; Professed Extern Sisters 2.

Provincial House of the Sisters of St. Joseph of Carondelet (St. Mary's Provincialate, Carondelet Center) , 11999 Chalon Rd., 90049-1524. Tel: 310-889-2100; Fax: 310-476-8735. Email: provincialate@csjla.org. Web: www.csjla.org. Sisters Maureen O'Connor, Prov. Supr.; Kathleen Kelly, R.S.M., Asst. Prov. Supr.; Ann Patricia O'Connor, Asst. Prov. Supr. Sisters 418.

Sisters of St. Joseph in California Tel: 310-889-2154; Fax: 310-472-5982.

Sisters of St. Joseph Ministerial Services Tel: 310-889-2155; Fax: 310-472-5982.

Sisters of St. Joseph in Arizona Tel: 310-889-2142; Fax: 310-476-8735.

Religious of the Sacred Heart of Mary Formation Community, 2833 Sichel St., 90031. Tel: 323-225-5486; Fax: 323-887-8952. Email: cormariarshm@earthlink.net. Web: www.rshm.org. Sisters 3.

Servants of the Immaculate Child Mary, E.I.N. (Esclavas de la Inmaculada Nina), 5135 Dartmouth Ave., 90032-3323. Tel: 323-225-3279; Fax: 323-269-7786.

350 Boyle Ave., 90033. Tel: 323-264-3232.

Sisters of Our Lady of Perpetual Help, S.O.L.P.H., St. Brendan Convent, 220 S. Manhattan Pl., 90004. Tel: 213-389-6398.

Sisters of Social Service of Los Angeles, General Motherhouse, 2303 S. Figueroa Way, 90007. Tel: 213-746-2117; Fax: 213-747-4499. Email: ssocialser@aol.com. Web: www.socialservicesisters.org. Sr. Michele Walsh, Gen. Dir.

Legal Title: *Sisters of Social Service of Los Angeles, Inc.*

Legal Title: *Sisters of Social Service Support Trust Fund* Sisters 100.

Sisters of Social Service, Formation, 2303 S. Figeroa Way, 90007. Tel: 213-746-2117; Fax: 213-747-4499. Sr. Martha Vega, S.S.S., Team Chair. In Formation 2.

Sisters of St. Joseph of Orange, 8000 Regis Way, 90045. Tel: 310-645-2514; 310-645-0718. Email: regishousela@yahoo.com. Sisters 3.

Sisters of the Company of Mary, 2634 Monmouth Ave., 90007. Tel: 213-747-3542; 213-737-3672; Fax: 213-747-6468. Email: odnadams@earthlink.net. Web: www.companyofmary.com. Sr. Guadalupe Hernandez, O.D.N., Supr. Sisters 5.

Sisters of the Good Shepherd, 2561 Venice Blvd., 90019. Tel: 323-737-6111; Fax: 323-737-6113. Email: rgsla1@aol.com. Sisters 10.

Sisters of the Guardian Angel, 4529 New York St., 90022. Tel: 323-266-4431; Fax: 323-981-0187. Email: rblanco@utla.net.

Sisters of the Immaculate Heart of Mary of Mirinae, I.H.M.M., 423 S. Commonwealth Ave., 90020. Tel: 213-738-1020; Fax: 213-381-6302. Email: laihmm@hanmail.net. Total in Residence 6.

Sisters of the Society Devoted to the Sacred Heart, Local Convent: 628 S. Irving Blvd., 90005. Tel: 323-936-8647; Fax: 323-931-8875. Sr. Frances Kennedy, S.D.S.H., Supr. Sisters 5.

Sisters of the Society Devoted to the Sacred Heart, 869 S. Rimpau Blvd., 90005. Tel: 323-935-2372; Fax: 323-935-5943. Web: www.SDSH.org. Sisters 3.

ALHAMBRA. *Carmel of St. Teresa*, 215 E. Alhambra Rd., 91801. Tel: 626-282-2387; Fax: 626-282-2053. Email: momaria@aol.com. Web: www.carmelites.org/teresacarmel. Sr. Maria, Prioress. Discalced Nuns of the Order of Our Blessed Lady of Mt. Carmel Sisters 16.

Carmelite Sisters of the Most Sacred Heart of Los Angeles, 920 E. Alhambra Rd., 91801-2799. Tel: 626-289-1353; Fax: 626-308-1913. Email: decorcarmeli718@yahoo.com. Web: carmelitegeneralate.homestead.com. Sisters Regina Marie Gorman, O.C.D., Supr. Gen.; Mary Colombiere Welch, O.C.D., Vicar Gen. Total Professed Sisters 132.

Carmelite Sisters of the Most Sacred Heart of Los Angeles Tel: 626-289-1353; Fax: 626-308-1913.

ALTADENA. *Franciscan Sisters of the Sacred Heart*, 579 W. Mariposa St., 91001. Tel: 626-791-4359. Email: ruthagee@juno.com. Sisters 7.

BELLFLOWER. **Sisters of the Korean Martyrs, S.K.M.*, 16272 California Ave., 90706. Tel: 562-461-8100; Fax: 562-461-8864. Email: koreanmartyrs@yahoo.com.

BIG BEAR LAKE. *Sacred Heart Retreat Apostolate*, P.O. Box 1506, 92315. Tel: 909-866-5696. Sisters Susan Blaschke, S.D.S.H., Contact Person; Lucia Tu, S.D.S.H., Corp. Pres. Tel: 818-772-9961.

BONITA. *Sisters Servants of the Blessed Sacrament*, U.S. Provincial House, 3173 Winnetka Dr., 91902. Tel: 619-267-0720; Fax: 619-267-0920. Email: sup@sjs-vicep.org. Sisters in the Vice Province 63.

CULVER CITY. *Daughters of St. Paul*, 3908 Sepulveda Blvd., 90230. Tel: 310-390-4699; Fax: 310-397-8366. Email: fspla@aol.com. Web: pauline.org. Sr. MaryLea Hill, F.S.P., Supr. Sisters 7.

Religious Sisters of Charity, 10668 St. James Dr., 90230. Tel: 310-559-0176; Fax: 310-559-3530. Email: mchcalven@aol.com. Sisters 36.

DOWNEY. *Sisters of the Holy Faith in California*, 12322 S. Paramount Blvd., 90242-3538. Tel: 562-869-6092; Fax: 562-869-4609. Email: shfaith@aol.com. Sisters 40.

ENCINO. *Sisters of St. Louis*, 5001 White Oak Ave., 91316. Tel: 818-344-7825. St. Joseph of CarondoletUrsuline SistersPresentation Sisters Sisters 5.

GARDENA. *Poor Clare Missionary Sisters, Inc.*, 1050 W. 161st St., 90247. Tel: 310-323-9942. Sr. Soledad Lepez, M.C., Supr. Sisters 13.

GLENDORA. *St. Lucy's Priory*, 19045 E. Sierra Madre Ave., 91741. Tel: 626-335-1682; Fax: 626-914-9398. Email: stlucysebrown@aol.com. Web: www.stlucys.com. Sr. Elizabeth Brown, Prioress.

Legal Title: *St. Lucy's Priory of Glendora California, Inc.* Sisters 19.

LONG BEACH. **Little Handmaids of the Most Holy Trinity, M.A.S.T.*, 2495 Earl Ave., 90806. Tel: 562-787-6093. Sr. Monica Bermiso, M.A.S.T., Foundress & Mother Supr.

The Medical Sisters of St. Joseph, 3627 Lemon Ave., 90807. Tel: 562-426-8825; Fax: 562-426-2726. Email: msjnirmala.@aol.com. Web: www.msjnirmala.com. Sr. Dennis Punchakunnel, M.S.J.

MONROVIA. *Convent of the Maryknoll Sisters of St. Dominic*, 340 Norumbega Dr., 91016-2445. Tel: 626-358-1825; Fax: 626-358-1227. Email: parathuzik@juno.com. Sr. Patricia Ann Arathuzik, M.M., Coord. Sisters 32.

Pious Disciples of the Divine Master, 726 S. Shamrock Ave., 91016-3653. Tel: 626-358-1295; Fax: 626-303-1245. Sr. Trinity Taricco. Sisters 7.

MONTEBELLO. *Religious of the Sacred Heart of Mary*, Provincial Center, 441 N. Garfield Ave., 90640-2901. Tel: 323-887-8821; Fax: 323-887-8952. Email: rshmwap@earthlink.net. Web: www.rshm.org.

NORTHRIDGE. *Mother of Mercy Convent*, 9329 Crebs Ave., 91324. Tel: 818-882-4095. Sister of Mercy Burlingame

Sisters of the Society Devoted to the Sacred Heart, Motherhouse: 9814 Sylvia Ave., 91324. Tel: 818-772-9961; Fax: 818-772-2742. Email: mhsdsh2@juno.com. Web: www.SDSH.org. Sr. Lucia Tu, S.D.S.H., Supr. Gen. Sisters 18.

OJAI. *Sisters of Mary Mother of the Church*, 431 Montanna Cir., 93023. Tel: 805-640-1798; Fax: 805-640-1798. Email: SRSMMC@aol.com.

OXNARD. *Sisters Servants of Mary*, 140 North G St., 93030-5214. Tel: 805-486-5502; Fax: 805-486-0663. Sr. Felisa Ripa, S.M., Mistress of Novices. Professed Sisters 17; Novices 8.

PASADENA. *Convent of the Holy Child Jesus*, 460 Shadeland Ave., Drexel Hill, PA 19026. Tel: 626-345-1633; Fax: 610-626-0451. Email: jkelly@shcj.org. Web: www.shcj.org. Corporate Title: Society of the Holy Child Jesus, American Province, Inc.

RANCHO PALOS VERDES. *Daughters of Mary & Joseph, D.M.J.*, Provincial House: 5300 Crest Rd., 90275-5004. Tel: 213-377-9968; 213-541-0784; Fax: 310-541-5967. Email: dmjca@dmjca.org. Web: www.dmjca.org. Sisters 65.

Sisters of Charity of Rolling Hills, 28600 Palos Verdes Dr. E., 90275. Tel: 310-831-4104. Email: svbuchholz@aol.com. Sr. Virginia Buchholz, S.C.R.H., Supr. Gen. Sisters 7.

SAN FERNANDO. *Religious Sisters of Charity*, 1608 Eighth St., 91340. Tel: 818-365-7926; Fax: 818-898-3382. Sisters 2.

SAN PEDRO. *Little Sisters of the Poor*, 2100 S. Western Ave., 90732. Tel: 310-548-0625; Fax: 310-548-4504. Email: mslsppd@hotmail.com. Sr. Rose Marie, Supr. Sisters 10.

SANTA BARBARA. *St. Francis Convent*, 601 E. Micheltorena St., 93103. Tel: 805-962-7661, Ext. 473; Fax: 805-568-5846. Email: sischris72@hotmail.com. Sr. Christine Bowman, O.S.F., Local Leader. Sisters 3.

Monastery of Poor Clares, Cloistered Contemplative Monastery, 215 E. Los Olivos St., 93105. Tel: 805-682-7670; Fax: 805-682-8041. Sr. Mary Clare of Jesus, Abbess. Attended by Franciscan Fathers of the Old Mission Professed 13.

SOLVANG. *Sisters of the Society Devoted to the Sacred Heart*, 1762 Mission Dr., 93463. Tel: 805-688-6158; Fax: 805-688-9247. Email: sdshsol@juno.com. Sr. Elizabeth Normanly, S.D.S.H., Supr. Sisters 3.

SYLMAR. *Franciscan Sisters of the Immaculate Conception*, 13367 Borden Ave., Unit A, 91342. Tel: 818-364-6122; 818-364-5557; Fax: 818-362-7536. Email: prov.stclare@verizon.net.

Legal Title: *Franciscan Missionary Sisters of the Immaculate Conception* Sisters 112; Novices 7; Postulants 3.

Poor Clare Missionary Sisters, P.O. Box 922046, 91392. Tel: 818-361-0591. Sr. Beatriz Aguilar, M.C., Supr. Sisters 5.

THOUSAND OAKS. *Sisters of Notre Dame*, Provincial House, Provincialate, 1776 Hendrix Ave., 91360. Tel: 805-496-3243; Fax: 805-379-3616. Email: kristinsnd@aol.com. Web: www.sndca.org. Sr. Mary Kristin, S.N.D., Supr. Sisters 41.

TORRANCE. *Little Company of Mary Convent*, 20552 Mansel Ave., 90503. Tel: 310-214-3190; Fax: 213-637-6438. Email: cpacini@lcmhs.org. Web: www.lcmweb.org. Sisters 5.

20562 Mansel Ave., 90503. Tel: 310-370-3992; Fax: 310-370-0288. Sisters 2.

VENTURA. *Handmaids of the Sacred Heart of Jesus, Mary and Joseph, + J.M.J.*, P.O. Box 2957, 93002. Tel: 805-653-2379; Fax: 805-653-1383. Email: jmj@anacapa.net. Web: www.anacapa.net/~handmaids/.

Sisters of the Holy Cross, 1931 Poli St., 93001. Tel: 805-641-3206; Fax: 805-653-1354. Email: patrice25@juno.com.

Legal Title: *Sisters of the Holy Cross* Sisters 45.

Sisters of the Holy Cross, Saint Catherine-by-the-Sea, 1931 Poli St., 93001-2360. Tel: 805-652-1700; Fax: 805-653-1354. Rev. James R. Blantz, C.S.C. (FTW); Sr. Patrice McGee, C.S.C., Supr.

Legal Title: *Sisters of the Holy Cross of California*, Residence for Retired Sisters. Sisters 31.

WHITTIER. *Hermanas del Corazon de Jesus Sacramentado*, 11506 Walnut St., 90606. Tel: 310-908-0618; Fax: 760-723-2271. Email: hcjsfbrk@aol.com.

WOODLAND HILLS. *Sisters of St. Louis, Louisville Convent*, 22300 Mulholland Dr., 91364-4933. Tel: 818-883-1678; Fax: 818-346-6109. Email: sslca4@worldnet.att.net. Web: www.st-louis-sisters.org. Sr. Donna Hansen, S.S.L., Regl. Supr. Sisters 15.

[S] SECULAR INSTITUTES

LOS ANGELES. *Society of Our Lady of the Way*, 2339 N. Catalina St., 90027. Tel: 323-665-0333. Email: jllaca27@msn.com. Web: www.ourladyoftheway.com.

Legal Title: *Society of Our Lady of the Way of Southern California, Inc.*

WEST COVINA. *Fr. Kolbe Missionaries of the Immaculata*, 531 E. Merced Ave., 91790. Tel: 626-917-0040; Fax: 626-917-0900. Email: FkMinCAL@aol.com. Web: www.kolbemission.org.

[T] ASSOCIATIONS OF THE FAITHFUL

LOS ANGELES. **Daughters of St. Mary*, 3933 W. 7th St., 90005. Tel: 213-381-2481; Fax: 213-252-0867. Email: daughters-st.mary@att.net. Sr. Mary John Shin, D.S.M.

OJAI. *Trinitas*, P.O. Box 1477, 93024-1477. Tel: 805-659-4158 (English); 805-646-4579 (Spanish).

TUJUNGA. *Community of the Holy Spirit, C.H.S.*, 10358 Las Lunitas Ave., 91042-1812. Tel: 818-951-6002; 213-746-4155.

VENTURA. *Handmaids of the Sacred Heart of Jesus, Mary, and Joseph, + J.M.J.*, P.O. Box 2957, 93002-2957. Tel: 805-653-2379; Fax: 805-653-1383. Email: jmj@anacapa.net. Web: www.anacapa.net/~handmaids.

[U] RESIDENCES FOR WOMEN

LOS ANGELES. *St. Anne's* For further details refer to listing in Special Care Facilities section. , 155 N. Occidental Blvd., 90026. Tel: 213-381-2931; Fax: 213-381-7804. Email: stannes@stannes.org. Web: www.stannes.org. Group Home for pregnant, parenting teens and their babies.

Bethany House, 850 N. Hobart Blvd., 90029. Tel: 323-665-6937; Fax: 323-664-0754. Email: bethany_house@hotmail.com. Sisters 7; Residents 35.

Estrella del Mar, Inc. dba Regis House , 11346 Iowa Ave., 90025. Tel: 310-477-8168; Fax: 310-479-6146. Sisters Albertina Morales, S.S.S., Dir.; Tersuta Sanvedrn, S.S.S., Dir. Sisters of Social Service 2.

Good Shepherd Center for Homeless Women, Languille Emergency Shelter, 267 N. Belmont Ave., 90026. Tel: 213-250-5241; Fax: 213-250-5073. Email: srjuliamary@mail.com. Web: www.thegoodshepherdcenter.com. (A Division of Catholic Charities.) Women in Residence 30; Women Assisted Annually 2,444.

Mother-Child Transitional Residence Administrative Site, 267 N. Belmont Ave., 90026. Tel: 213-469-6540; Fax: 213-469-0370. Mother-Children in Residence 30; Mother-Children Sheltered Annually 150.

Hawkes Residence / Women's Village, 1640 Rockwood St., 90026. Tel: 213-482-0281; Fax: 213-482-0299. Women Sheltered Annually 150.

Angel Guardian Home, 1660 Rockwood St., 90026. Tel: 213-483-6654; Fax: 213-482-0522. Women-Children Sheltered Annually 40.

St. Joseph's Residence, 1124 W. Adams Blvd., 90007. Tel: 213-749-9577; Fax: 213-747-6468. Email: odnadams@earthlink.net. Web: www.companyofmary.com. 16791 E. Main St., Tustin, 92780-4034. Tel: 714-541-3125; Fax: 714-835-0648. Sisters of the Company of Mary Women 65.

[V] RESIDENCES FOR MEN

LOS ANGELES. *"Casa Teresa," Missionaries of Charity Brothers*, 1316 S. Westlake Blvd., 90006. Tel: 213-380-5225. Temporary shelter for sick homeless men. Brothers 7.

Catholic Kolping House, 1225 S. Union Ave., 90015. Tel: 213-388-9438; Fax: 213-388-9438. Email: losangeleskolpinghouse@yahoo.com. Web: www.kolping.org. Rev. Richard J. Russell, Spiritual Dir.; Alma Tamayo, Mgr. Capacity 60.

The Little Brothers of the Good Shepherd, B.G.S., 3445 Waverly Dr., 90027. Tel: 323-662-0092 (Office); 323-662-3620 (Res.); Fax: 323-662-3619. Bros. Mark Harmueller, B.G.S., Admin. House of Prayer; David Nickerson, Asst. Admin. House Prayer. Staff for Cardinal Manning House of Prayer.

Missionaries of Charity Brothers, House of Formation, 1325 S. Westlake Blvd., 90006. Tel: 213-384-6116. Brothers 7.

"Nuestra Hogar" Missionaries of Charity Brothers, 1345 Alvarado Ter., 90006. Tel: 214-251-9707.

[W] RETREAT HOUSES

LOS ANGELES. *Claretian Retreat Center (All Groups)*, 1119 Westchester Pl., 90019. Tel: 323-737-8464; Fax: 323-733-6201. Email: usawestprov@earthlink.net. Very Rev. Roland Lozano, C.M.F., Prov. Supr.; Revs. Frank J. Ferrante, C.M.F., Dir.; Robert Bishop, C.M.F., Admin.; Theo Fuentes, C.M.F.; Bernard Connor, C.M.F.; Carlos C. Castillo, C.M.F.; George Whedbee, C.M.F.; Bros. Larry Moen, C.M.F., Local Supr.; Rene Lepage, C.M.F., Admin.

Immaculate Heart Retreat House (Days of Recollection Only) , 3431 Waverly Dr., 90027-2526. Tel: 323-664-1126; Fax: 323-664-2215. Email: ritacallanan@aol.com. Web: www.retreat@sisters.hm.org. Sr. Margaret Mary, I.H.M., Dir. Conducted by the Sisters of the Immaculate Heart Capacity 48; Sisters 10.

ALHAMBRA. *Retreat House of the Sacred Heart*, 920 E. Alhambra Rd., 91801. Tel: 626-289-1353; Fax: 626-281-3546. Email: shrhrd@pacbell.net. Web: www.shretreathouse.org. Sr. Marisa, O.C.D., Contact Person. Carmelite Sisters of the Most Sacred Heart of Los Angeles, (See Convents) Capacity 89; Sisters 23; Novices 2; Postulants 10.

ENCINO. *Holy Spirit Retreat Center*, 4316 Lanai Rd., 91436. Tel: 818-784-4515; Fax: 818-784-0409. Email: hsrcenter@earthlink.net. Web: www.hsrcenter.com. Sisters of Social Service

MALIBU. *Serra Retreat*, 3401 Serra Rd., P.O. Box 127, 90265. Tel: 310-456-6631; Fax: 310-456-6051. Email: warrenr480@aol.com. Web: sbfranciscans.org. Revs. Warren Rouse, O.F.M., Dir.; Michael Doherty, O.F.M., Vicar; Alex Manville, O.F.M., Guardian; Bros. Samuel Cabot, O.F.M.; Pierre Despres, O.F.M. Franciscan Friars Priests 3; Brothers 2.

MONTEBELLO. *DePaul Evangelization Center*, 1105 Bluff Rd., 90640-6198. Tel: 323-721-6060; Fax: 323-887-0765. Email: DePaulCenter@att.net. Revs. James Osendorf, C.M., Supr. & Dir.; Andrew E. Bellisario, C.M., Prov.; Peter J. Diliberto (Retired); Joseph V. Haley, C.M. (SJ); Robert J. Jones, C.M.; Gary Landry, C.M.; Minh J. Pham, C.M. (PHX); Thomas J. McIntyre, C.M. (Retired); James J. Nouws, C.M. (Retired); Bro. Edward D. Graham, C.M. Formerly St. Vincent's Seminary; Congregation of the Mission (Vincentians); Retreat and Evangelization Center.

RANCHO PALOS VERDES. *Mary and Joseph Retreat Center*, 5300 Crest Rd., 90275-5004. Tel: 310-377-4867; Fax: 310-541-1176. Email: registrar@maryjoseph.org. Web: www.maryjoseph.org. Daughters of Mary and Joseph Retreat Center Capacity 65; Sisters 3.

ROSEMEAD. *St. Joseph's Salesian Youth Renewal Center* (Boys and Girls) , 8301 Arroyo Dr., P.O. Box 1639, 91770. Tel: 626-280-8622 Fax: 626-280-0545. Email: stjosephrc@aol.com. Revs. Paul M. Caporali, S.D.B.; Bill Bolton, S.D.B., Dir. Retreat Center; Ted Montemayor, S.D.B., Dir. & Supr.; Mel Trinidad, S.D.B., Youth Min.; Marc Rougeau, S.D.B. Treas. & Vice Dir.; Bros. Phil Mandile, S.D.B. Larry King, S.D.B. Conducted by Salesians of St. John Bosco Priests 5; Brothers 2.

SAN FERNANDO. *Poverello of Assisi Retreat House*, 1519 Woodworth St., 91340. Tel: 818-365-1071; Fax: 818-361-2751. Email: poverellorthse1@aol.com Sr. Mary Jesus, O.S.F., Dir. Franciscan Missionary Sisters of the Immaculate Conception, For men and women. Marriage Encounter in Korean and Spanish. Other Denominations workshops seminars, staff meetings. Priests and Sisters retreats, assemblies and chapters, one day retreats for Grammar and High Schools. Capacity 112.

SANTA BARBARA. *St. Mary's Seminary Center*, 1964 Las Canoas Rd., 93105. Tel: 805-966-4829; Fax: 805-564-1662. Email: stmarysseminary@cox.net. Revs. Patrick J. Mullin, C.M., Dir; Roy A. Persich, C.M.; James M. Galvin; Walter Housey, C.M.; John Shine, C.M. Priests 5.

SIERRA MADRE. *Mater Dolorosa Retreat Center*, 700 N. Sunnyside Ave., Box 68, 91025. Tel: 626-355-7188; Fax: 626-355-0485. Email: Materdolorosa@compuserve.com. Web: www.materdolorosa.org. Conducted by the Passionist Community, Lay Retreat League for men and women. Specialized Retreats. Priests 2; Brothers 1.
Retreat Team: Rev. Patrick Brennan, C.P. Retreat Dir.; Very Rev. Alfred Pooler, C.P.; Deacon Manuel Valencia; Sr. Judy Rinek, S.N.J.M.; Bro. John Rockenbach C.P.; Mrs. Mary Lou Butler, Admin.

VALYERMO. *St. Andrew's Abbey Retreat Center (All Groups)*, 31001 N. Valyermo Rd., P.O. Box 40, 93563. Tel: 661-944-2178, Ext. 0; Fax: 661-944-1076. Email: retreats@valyermo.com. Web: www.valyermo.com. Revs. Francis Benedict, O.S.B., Retreat Dir. & Abbot. Tel: 661-944-2178; Philip Edwards, O.S.B., Guestmaster. Tel: 661-944-2178, Ext. 0; Bro. Benedict Dull, O.S.B., Guestmaster; Rita Jones, Youth Center Contact Person. Tel: 661-944-2734; Sr. Karen Wilhelmy, C.S.J., Retreat Center Admin. Tel: 661-944-2178, Ext. 102. Conducted by the Benedictine Monks

[X] PERSONAL PRELATURES

LOS ANGELES. *Prelature of the Holy Cross and Opus Dei*, 655 Levering Ave., 90024. Tel: 310-208-0941. Email: office@tildensc.org. Revs. Paul A. Donlan (OAK); John R. Waiss. Tilden Study Center

[Y] CATHOLIC CHARITIES OF CALIFORNIA

LOS ANGELES. *Catholic Charities of Los Angeles, Inc.*, 1531 James M. Wood Blvd., P.O. Box 15095, 90015-0095. Tel: 213-251-3400; Fax: 213-380-4603. Web: catholiccharitiesla.org. His Eminence Roger Cardinal Mahony, K.G.C.H.S.; Rev. Msgr. Gregory A. Cox, M.S.W., M.B.A., Exec. Dir. Tel: 213-251-3464.

Central Administrative Offices, 1531 James M. Wood Blvd., P.O. Box 15095, 90015-0095. Tel: 213-251-3400; Fax: 213-380-4603. Rev. Msgr. Gregory A. Cox, M.S.W., M.B.A., Exec. Dir. Tel: 213-251-3464; Ronald G. Lopez, M.S.W., Chief Admin. Officer. Tel: 213-251-3413; James E. Bathker, CFO. Tel: 213-251-3410; Alexandria "Sandi" Arnold, Dir. Dept. Resource Devel. Tel: 213-251-3495; Joseph W. Paulicivic Jr., Dir. Dept. Human Resources. Tel: 213-251-3414.

ADESTE Child Care Services Tel: 213-251-3463; Fax: 213-251-3510 Armine Lalaian-Sanjar, Quality Improvement Dir. Tel: 213-251-3468.

Archdiocesan Youth Employment Services, 3250 Wilshire Blvd., Ste. 1010, 90010. Tel: 213-736-5456; Fax: 213-736-5654. Robert Gutierrez, Prog. Dir.

CYO Athletics Tel: 213-251-3562; Fax: 213-251-3510 Tom Davidson, Prog. Dir. Tel: 213-251-3562.

Immigration & Refugee Services Tel: 213-251-3489; Fax: 213-251-3444. Loc Nam Nguyen, Prog. Dir. Tel: 213-251-3489; Jo Marcel, Asst. Dir. Tel: 213-251-3470.

Immigration Reception Tel: 213-251-3411; 213-251-3471; Fax: 213-251-3444.

Refugee Resettlement Tel: 213-251-3470.

Central Intake Project Tel: 213-251-3445; Fax: 213-251-3580. Joe Dinh Le, Prog. Dir. Tel: 213-251-3445.

CCLA Continuous Quality Improvement Tel: 213-251-3459; Fax: 213-251-3563. Edward Nelson, Ph.D., Continuous Quality Improvement Dir. Tel: 213-251-3459.

Regional Offices and Community Centers:

OUR LADY OF THE ANGELS METRO REGION, 4665 Willowbrook Ave., 90029. Tel: 323-662-1462; Fax: 323-662-3627. Jackie Lazarus-Warren, Regl. Dir. Tel: 323-662-1462. (Los Angeles Inner City)

ADESTE Child Care, 4665 Willowbrook Ave., 90029. Tel: 323-662-8860; Fax: 323-662-3627.

Community Service Centers:

St. Mary's Center, 4665 Willowbrook Ave., 90029. Tel: 323-662-4391; Fax: 323-662-3627.

St. Catherine of Alexandria Center, 8701 S. Vermont, Unit B, 90044. Tel: 323-752-3786; Fax: 323-752-9763.

El Santo Nino Center, 601 E. 23rd St., 90011. Tel: 213-748-5246; Fax: 213-748-9006.

Shelters & Housing Services:

Angels Flight - Runaway / Homeless Youth Shelter, 357 S. Westlake Ave., 90057. Tel: 213-413-2311; 800-833-2499 (Hotline); Fax: 213-413-5690.

Outreach, 4665 Willowbrook Ave., 90029. Tel: 213-413-2311.

Good Shepherd Center for Homeless Women, 267 N. Belmont Ave., 90026. Tel: 213-250-5241; Fax: 213-250-5073. Sr. Julia Mary Farley, C.S.J., Prog. Dir.

Good Shepherd Mother & Child Center Tel: 323-469-6540; Fax: 323-469-0376.

Good Shepherd Hawkes Transitional Residence, Women's Village, 1650 Rockwood St., 90026. Tel: 213-482-0281; Fax: 213-482-0299.

My Club After School Program, 8701 S. Vermont, Unit A, 90044.

Community United for Meals at Home Tel: 323-662-1462.

OUR LADY OF THE ANGELS WESTERN REGION, 211 Third Ave., Venice, 90291. Tel: 310-392-8701; Fax: 310-399-4097. Jim Stratton, Regl. Dir. (Inglewood, Crenshaw District, Korea Town, West Los Angeles, Malibu & Los Angeles Airport region)

ADESTE Child Care, 211 Third Ave., Venice, 90291. Tel: 310-392-8701; Fax: 310-399-4097.

Community Service Centers:

St. Margaret's Center, 10505 Hawthorne Blvd., Lennox, 90304. Tel: 310-672-2208; Fax: 310-672-1841.

St. Peter Claver Center, 4202 W. Jefferson Blvd., 90016. Tel: 323-737-6036; Fax: 323-737-3649.

St. Robert's Center, 211 Third Ave., Venice, 90291. Tel: 310-392-8701; Fax: 310-399-4097.

Immigration & Refugee Services, St. Margaret's Center, 10505 Hawthorne Blvd., Lennox, 90304. Tel: 310-672-2208.

Psychological Services, 211 Third Ave., Venice, 90291. Tel: 310-399-1451; Fax: 310-399-4097.

St. Margaret's Thrift Store, 10513 Hawthorne Blvd., Inglewood, 90304. Tel: 310-674-9652.

SAN FERNANDO REGION, 21600 Hart St., Canoga Park, 91303. Tel: 818-883-6015; Fax: 818-883-4122. Moeed Khan, Regl. Dir. (Burbank, Glendale, Eagle Rock, Verdugo Hills, Antelope Valley, San Fernando Valley)

ADESTE Child Care, 511 Kalisher St., San Fernando, 91340. Tel: 818-361-5686.

Central Intake Unit, 217 E. Alameda Ave., Stes. 204 & 211, Burbank, 91502. Tel: 818-841-2430.

Community Service Centers:

Glendale Community Services Center, 4322 San Fernando Rd., Glendale, 91204. Tel: 818-409-3080; Fax: 818-244-7579.

Glendale Loaves & Fishes Thrift Store, 423 S. Central Ave., Glendale, 91204. Tel: 818-247-8196.

Temporary Skilled Worker Center, 5101 San Fernando Rd., Glendale, 91204. Tel: 818-548-6495.

Guadalupe Community Center, 21600 Hart St., Canoga Park, 91303. Tel: 818-340-2050.

Loaves and Fishes I, 4322 San Fernando Rd., Glendale, 91204. Tel: 818-409-3080.

Loaves and Fishes II, 14640 Keswick St., Van Nuys, 91405. Tel: 818-997-0943; Fax: 818-497-6980.

Loaves and Fishes III, 511 Kalisher St., San Fernando, 91340. Tel: 818-365-3195.

Loaves and Fishes IV, 21600 Hart St., Canoga Park, 91303. Tel: 818-340-2050.

Santa Rosa Center, 511 Kalisher St., San Fernando, 91340. Tel: 818-365-3194; Fax: 818-365-4645.

Immigration & Refugee Services, 511 Kalisher St., San Fernando, 91340. Tel: 818-365-3194; 818-365-3195.

Immigration & Refugee Services, 4322 San Fernando Rd., Glendale, 91204. Tel: 818-409-3080.

Catholic Psychological Services, 21600 Hart St., Canoga Park, 91303. Tel: 818-883-6015.

Residential Youth Services, Rancho San Antonio, 21000 Plummer St., Chatsworth, 91311. Tel: 818-882-6400; Fax: 818-882-3838. Bro. John Crowe, C.S.C., Dir.

Shelter/Housing Services:

Lancaster Community Shelter, 44611 Yucca Ave.,

Lancaster, 93534. Tel: 661-945-7524.

SAN GABRIEL REGION, 1307 Warren St., 90033. Tel: 323-266-3130; Fax: 323-266-3269. Mary Romero, Regl. Dir. (San Gabriel Valley, Mt. Baldy, Pomona Valley, East Los Angeles)

ADESTE Child Care, 1307 Warren Ave., 90033. Tel: 323-264-4981; Fax: 323-266-3269.

Catholic Psychological Services, 1215 S. Hamilton Blvd., Pomona, 91766. Tel: 909-622-2824.

1910 Huntington Blvd., South Pasadena, 91030. Tel: 818-372-2395.

Central Intake Unit, 11100 Valley Blvd., Stes. 103 & 109, El Monte, 91731. Tel: 626-582-8074; Fax: 626-582-8434.

Community Service Centers:

Brownson House Community Center, 1307 Warren Ave., 90033. Tel: 323-264-8700; Fax: 323-266-3269.

Brother Miguel Center, 315 North Park Ave., Pomona, 91768. Tel: 909-622-3466; Fax: 909-622-4621.

El Monte Community Services Center, 3017 Tyler Ave., #9, El Monte, 91733. Tel: 626-575-7652; Fax: 626-575-1072.

Homeless Collaborative Programs, 415 Glendora Ave., Ste. F, West Covina, 91789. Tel: 626-918-2005.

502 W. Holt, Pomona, 91768. Tel: 909-620-9783.

Immigration & Refugee Services, 3017 Tyler Ave., El Monte, 91731. Tel: 626-575-7633.

9241 E. Valley Blvd., Rosemead, 91770. Tel: 626-286-2846.

SAN PEDRO REGION, 123 E. 14th St., Long Beach, 90813. Tel: 562-591-1641; Fax: 562-591-2481. Anna R. Totta, Regl. Dir. (Long Beach, South Bay, Compton, Rio Hondo, Vernon, Huntington Park, Whittier, Pico Rivera)

ADESTE Child Care, 10441 S. Downey Ave., Downey, 90241. Tel: 562-862-5750.

Central Intake Unit, 3550 Long Beach Blvd., Long Beach, 90807. Tel: 562-981-1399.

Community Service Centers:

Long Beach Community Services, 123 E. 14th St., Long Beach, 90813. Tel: 562-591-1351; Fax: 562-591-2481.

Mahar House Center, 1115 Mahar Ave., Wilmington, 90744. Tel: 310-834-7265; Fax: 310-834-8813.

Family Development Network Tel: 310-834-7265.

Immigration Services Tel: 310-834-7265.

Pico Rivera Family Resource Center, 5014 Passons Rd., Pico Rivera, 90660. Tel: 562-949-0937.

Family Shelter for the Homeless (Elizabeth Ann Seton Residence), 123 E. 14th St., Long Beach, 90813. Tel: 562-591-1351.

Psychological Services, 6505 Rosemead Blvd., Ste. 108, Pico Rivera, 90660. Tel: 562-949-2496; Fax: 562-949-1697.

461 W. 6th St., Ste. 202, San Pedro, 90731. Tel: 310-831-7111.

SANTA BARBARA REGION, 609 E. Haley St., Santa Barbara, 93103. Tel: 805-965-7045; Fax: 805-963-2978. Davida Willis, Regl. Dir. (Lompoc, Santa Maria, Santa Barbara, Carpinteria)

ADESTE Child Care, 609 E. Haley St., Santa Barbara, 93103. Tel: 805-965-7045.

Community Service Centers:

Santa Barbara Community Services, 609 E. Haley St., Santa Barbara, 93103. Tel: 805-965-7045.

Carpinteria Community Services, 941 Walnut St., Carpenteria, 93013. Tel: 805-684-8621; Fax: 805-684-9771.

Lompoc Community Services, 118 N. G, St., Ste. B, P.O. Box 665, Lompoc, 93436. Tel: 805-736-6226; Fax: 805-763-7499.

Santa Maria Community Services, 607 W. Main, Santa Maria, 93458. Tel: 805-922-2059; Fax: 805-925-1979.

Guadalupe Community Services, 4681-11th St., Guadalupe, 93434. Tel: 805-343-1194.

New Cuyama Community Services, 4711 Hwy. 166, New Cuyama, 93254. Tel: 661-766-2469.

Thrift Stores:

St. Vincent de Paul/Catholic Charities Thrift Store, 609 E. Haley St., Santa Barbara, 93103. Tel: 805-966-9659.

Santa Maria Thrift Store, 605 W. Main St., Santa Maria, 93458. Tel: 805-922-4174.

Immigration Services, 609 E. Haley St., Santa Barbara, 93103. Tel: 805-965-7045.

Oasis, 609 E. Haley St., Santa Barbara, 93103. Tel: 805-965-7045.

Psychological Services

609 E. Haley St., Santa Barbara, 93103. Tel: 805-965-7045; Fax: 805-963-2978.

215 E. Fesler St., Santa Maria, 93454. Tel: 805-348-1627; Fax: 805-348-1629.

VENTURA COUNTY REGION, 303 N. Ventura Ave., Ste. A, Ventura, 93001. Tel: 805-643-4694; Fax: 805-643-4781. Robert Bagdazian, L.C.S.W., Regl. Dir. (Camarillo, Moorpark, Oxnard, Thousand Oaks, Simi Valley, Ventura, Conejo Valley)

ADESTE Child Care, 303 N. Ventura Ave., Ste. A, Ventura, 93001. Tel: 805-643-4760.

Community Service Centers:

Ventura Community Services, 303 N. Ventura Ave., Ste. C, Ventura, 93001. Tel: 805-643-4694.

Oxnard Community Services, 402 N. "A" St., Oxnard, 93030. Tel: 805-486-2900.

Moorpark Community Services, 609 Fitch Ave., Moorpark, 93021. Tel: 805-529-0720.

Thousand Oaks Community Services, 80 Hillcrest Dr., #120, Thousand Oaks, 91360. Tel: 805-496-1113.

Handicapables Tel: 805-527-7806; 805-482-4050.

OASIS - Older Adult Services

2532 Ventura Blvd., Camarillo, 93010. Tel: 805-987-2083; Fax: 805-383-1318.

5649 Pittman St., Simi Valley, 93063. Tel: 805-526-3009; Fax: 805-526-4231.

[Z] SUMMER CAMPS

LOS ANGELES. *Scouting and Camp Fire Ministry/ Catholic Youth Camps*, P.O. Box 91764, Long Beach, 90809-1764. Eileen Gallagher, Contact Person. Tel: 652-427-2149; William Leahy, Chm. ACCS. Tel: 661-949-2355; Sharon Shellman, Chm. ACCGS. Tel: 626-792-2076; Rev. James J. Maher, Boy Scout Chap.; Sr. Lucille Coulihan, I.H.M., Girl Scout Chap. Tel: 213-664-1124.

St. Vincent dePaul Ranch Camp, 210 N. Ave. 21st, 90031. Tel: 213-221-9886; Fax: 213-224-6213. (Boys -Ages: 7-13); Sponsored by St. Vincent de Paul Society. Capacity 100.

Camp Mariastella, 1120 Manchester Pl., 90019. Tel: 213-733-1208. (Girls). Coed Program for Developmentally Disabled, Ages 7-Adult.; Owned & Operated by Sisters of Social Service.; Located in Wrightwood. Capacity 140.

Sacred Heart Retreat Camp, 869 S. Rimpau Blvd., 90005. Tel: 213-935-2372. Girls & Boys Sessions, Ages 8-17 years.; Owned and operated by the Sisters of the Society Devoted to the Sacred Heart.; Located at Big Bear Lake.

Camp Office, P.O. Box 1795, Big Bear Lake, 92315. Tel: 909-866-5696; Fax: 909-866-5650. Capacity 150.

Lions Camp at Teresita Pines, P.O. Box 98, Wrightwood, 92397. Fax: 760-249-1063. Email: teresitapines@snowline.net. Web: www.lionswild-camp.com. (Girls), Ages 7-15 years.; Owned & Operated by Lions.; Located in Big Pines Area near Wrightwood. Capacity 125.

St. Nicholas Camp, 1170 Frontier Rd., Frazier Park, 93225. Tel: 805-245-3571; Fax: 805-245-0710. Available for year round camps & rates.

[AA] ST. VINCENT DE PAUL SOCIETY

LOS ANGELES. *Society of St. Vincent de Paul*, 210 N. Avenue 21, 90031. Tel: 323-224-6288; Fax: 323-225-4997. Email: admin@svdpla.org. Web: www.svdpla.org. Jose J. Rossier, Exec. Dir.

St. Vincent de Paul Ranch Camp & Retreat Center, 210 N. Avenue 21, 90031. Tel: 323-224-6213; Fax: 323-225-4997. Ricardo Garcia, Dir.

St. Vincent's Cardinal Manning Center, 231 Winston St., 90013. Tel: 213-229-9963; Fax: 213-620-9141. Joan Sotiros, Dir.

St. Vincent de Paul Stores, 210 N. Avenue 21, 90031. Tel: 323-224-6280; Fax: 323-225-4997.

For Pick Up: 323-224-6280; 800-974-3571. Anthony Terrazas, Store Dir.

[BB] NEWMAN CENTERS

LOS ANGELES. *Campus Ministry c/o Office of the Chancellor* 3424 Wilshire Blvd., 90010-2241. Tel: 213-637-7265; Fax: 213-637-6265.

Loyola Law School, 919 S. Albany St., P.O. Box 15019, 90015. Tel: 213-736-1084; Fax: 213-380-3769. Robert Scholla, S.J., Dir.

Loyola Marymount University, One LMU Blvd., 90045. Tel: 310-338-2860; Fax: 310-338-1845. Mr. Fernando Moreno, Dir.; Revs. Thomas P. Higgins, S.J.; Tri M. Dinh, S.J.; Jose Badenes, S.J.; Mark McGregor, S.J.; Ron Schmidt, S.J.; Sr. Carol Quinlivan, C.S.J.; Mr. John Flaherty.

Mount St. Mary College, Chalon Campus, 12001 Chalon Rd., 90049. Tel: 310-954-4125; Fax: 310-954-4119. Ms. Laura Gomez, Dir.

Mount St. Mary College, Doheny Campus, 10 Chester Pl., 90007-2598. Tel: 213-477-2672, Ext. 2672; Fax: 213-477-2669.

Occidental College, Catholic Campus Ministry, 1600 Campus Rd., 90041. Tel: 323-259-2500, Ext. 3426; Fax: 323-255-3067. Rev. Christopher Terry, O.P., Dir.

University of California, Los Angeles, University Catholic Center, 633 Gayley Ave., 90024. Tel: 310-208-5015; Fax: 310-208-6077. Revs. Bob Sadowski, C.S.P., Dir.; Patrick Hensy, C.S.P.; Ms. Cindy Yoshitomi.

University of Southern California, Our Saviour University Parish, 3207 University Ave., 90007. Tel: 213-749-5341; Fax: 213-749-3475. Mr. Nicholas Stein, Dir.

University of Southern California, Health Sciences Campus, Catholic Campus Ministry, MCH 160, 1333 San Pablo St., 90033. Tel: 323-442-3311; Fax: 626-792-0475.

California Institute of Technology I-88, Pasadena, 91125. Tel: 626-395-6212; Fax: 626-792-0475. Rev. Andrew Mulcahey, L.C., Dir.

Claremont Colleges, McAllister Religious Center, 919 N. Columbia, Claremont, 91711. Tel: 909-621-8825, Ext. 2937; Fax: 909-621-8304. Rev. Wayne Maro, C.PP.S., Dir.

University of California Santa Barbara Tel: 805-968-1078; Fax: 805-968-3965.

St. Mark University Parish: 6550 Picasso Rd., Goleta, 93117. Tel: 805-968-1078; Fax: 805-968-3965. Revs. Paul Rospond, C.S.P.; Joseph Scott, C.S.P.

University of La Verne (La Verne)

Catholic Campus Ministry 1950 Third St., 91750. Tel: 909-593-3511, Ext. 4322; Fax: 909-392-2753. Rev. Kris Offer, M.S.P.

Marymount College (Rancho Palos Verdes)

Campus Ministry 30800 Palos Verdes Dr. E., 90274. Tel: 310-377-4240; Fax: 310-377-6223. Mr. Nassef Girgis, Dir.

Don Bosco Technical Institute (Rosemead)

Campus Ministry 1151 San Gabriel Blvd., 91770. Tel: 626-307-6551; Fax: 626-280-9316. Rudy Herrera, Dir.

Campus Ministry c/o Office of the Chancellor 3424 Wilshire Blvd., 90010-2241. Tel: 213-637-7265; Fax: 213-637-6265.

Loyola Law School, 919 S. Albany St., P.O. Box 15019, 90015. Tel: 213-736-1084; Fax: 213-380-3769. Rev. Robert Scholla, S.J., Dir.; Mr. Fernando Moreno, Dir.; Revs. Thomas P. Higgins, S.J.; Tri M. Dinh, S.J.; Sisters Cecilia Magladry, C.S.J.; Carol Quinlivan, C.S.J.; Rev. Fernando Arizti, S.J.; Mr. John Flaherty; Rabbi Arthur Gross-Schaeffer.

[CC] MISCELLANEOUS LISTINGS

LOS ANGELES. *Association of Christian Therapists*, 1568 Yosemite Dr., Ste.5, 90041-2842. Tel: 323-550-8852; Fax: 626-449-4907. Email: albert-nyland@msn.com. Web: www.actheals.org.

Catholic Big Brothers and Big Sisters, Inc., 3300 W. Temple St., 90026. Tel: 213-251-9800; 213-251-7760 (TTY); Fax: 213-251-9855. Email: info@catholicbigbrothers.org. Web: www.catholicbigbrothers.org. Ken Martinet, Pres. & CEO. Branch offices throughout Los Angeles county.; A mentoring organization for over 70 years, its core program matches adult volunteers with children between the ages of 7 and 14. Volunteer mentors provide role modeling and friendship in a one-to-one relationship. Other programs include group mentoring activities; triangle mentoring among adults-high school youth-elementary children; school based and site based after-school mentoring; juvenile justice mentoring programs at public high schools and community education centers. The agency aslo has a program for deaf and hard-of-hearing children and volunteers.

Catholic Charities Community Development Corporation, Inc., 1531 James M. Wood Blvd., P.O. Box 15095, 90015-0095. Tel: 213-251-3464; Fax: 213-380-4603.

Charisma in Missions, La Porciuncula, 1059 S. Gage Ave., 90023. Fax: 213-260-7221. Catholic Center of Evangelization and renewal ministries. A service for hispanic people through ongoing affirmation and growth seminars and courses; Catholic evangelizers' formation courses; direct evangelization missions; social service programs; prayer hot-line services; television and radio ministries; and a bookstore providing Catholic books, audio and video cassettes.

Collaborative Project for Aging Religious, 2468 S. St. Andrew's Pl., 90018. Tel: 323-735-3625; Fax: 323-737-6320. Email: linkages@cpar.org. Web: www.cpar.org.

Conrad N. Hilton Fund for Sisters, 10100 Santa Monica Blvd. #1000, 90067. Tel: 310-785-0746; Fax: 310-785-0166. Email: hltnsister@aol.com. Web: members.aol.com/hltnsister. Sr. Joyce Meyer, P.B.V.M.

Filipino Pastoral Ministry (Artesia) , 18708 S. Clarkdale Ave., 90701. Tel: 562-402-9226; Fax: 310-860-0178. Email: mac3exodus@aol.com. Rev. Msgr. Loreto Gonzales, Dir.

The Focolare Movement, Men's Branch (California) (Work of Mary), 8016 Cowan Ave., 90045-1405. Tel: 310-670-6736; Fax: 310-670-8036. Email: focolare-mla@sbcglobal.net. Web: www.focolare.org. Mr. Antonio Vallejo, Dir. West Coast. Formation in the Spirituality of Unity.

The Focolare Movement, Women's Branch, 3138 Glendon Ave., 90034-3404. Tel: 310-470-8505; Fax: 310-470-9239. Email: focolare-fla@att.net. Web: focolare.org. Maria A. Pereira, L.I.S.C.W., Co-Dir., Westcoast.

St. Francis Center, 1835 S. Hope St., 90015. Tel: 213-747-5347; Fax: 213-765-8915. Email: stfrasisi@aol.com. His Eminence Roger M. Mahony, Honorary Pres.; Rev. Finian McGinn, O.F.M.

Provincial Definitors of the Province of Saint Barbara Tel: 213-747-5347; 213-765-8915. Eric F. Boyd, Exec. Dir.

Legal Title: *Provincial Definitors of the Province of Saint Barbara Franciscan Friars of California*

Friends of John Paul II Foundation of Southern California, 3424 W. Adams Blvd., 90018. Tel: 626-281-0516; Fax: 626-293-8196. Email: kcybulski@earthlink.net. Stanislaw K. Cybulski, Pres.

Hospitaller Foundation of California, Inc., The, 2468 S. St. Andrew's Pl., 90018. Tel: 323-731-7141; Fax: 323-731-5717. Email: info@hospitallerfoundation.org. Web: www.hospitallerfoundation.org. Bro. Patrick Corr, O.H., Pres., Dir. & Moderator. (Fundraising for St. John of God Retirement and Care Center)

Women's League of St. John of God Tel: 323-731-7141; Fax: 323-731-5717.

Helpers Club of St. John of God Tel: 323-731-7141; Fax: 323-731-5717.

**The Institute for Advanced Catholic Studies*, 3207 University Ave., 90007. Tel: 213-741-1410; Fax: 213-741-1477. Email: iacss@aol.com. Web: www.ifacs.com. Dr. Hugh M. Dempsey, Contact Person.

Korean Catholic Renewal Movement of Southern California, 3422 W. 8th St., 90005.

Luz De Cristo USA Member of Lumen 2000. , 5953 W. 86th Pl., 90045. Tel: 310-641-2000; Fax: 310-641-1127. Email: luzcristo@aol.com. Web: www.luz-de-cristo.org. Non-profit corporation. Spanish evangelism through modern means of communication.

National Catholic Council for Hispanic Ministry, Inc. (NCCHM), 2025 Chickasaw Ave., 90041. Tel: 213-344-9153; Fax: 213-344-9526. Email: NCCHM@aol.com.

St. Peter Claver Center, 4202 W. Jefferson Blvd., 90016-4113. Tel: 323-737-6036; Fax: 323-737-3649.

Salesian Boys & Girls Club of Los Angeles, 3218 Wabash Ave., 90063. Tel: 323-263-7519; Fax: 323-263-8558. Email: Clubinfo@Salesianclubs-la.org. Web: www.salesianclubs-la.org.

Serra Ancillary Care, 3424 Wilshire Blvd., 90010. Tel: 213-637-7531; Fax: 213-637-6531. Sr. M. Carolita Hart, C.S.C., Pres.

Serra Institute, 2060 N. Vermont, 90027. Tel: 323-664-9292. Email: gcrye@aol.com. Web: quantumtheology.org.

Servants of the Immaculate Child Mary, 5135 Dartsmouth Ave., 90032. Tel: 323-225-3279; Fax: 323-225-3279. Email: ImmaculateAL@.com. Sr. Enedina Cuevas, Contact Person.

**South Central Los Angeles Ministry Project AKA South Central Lamp*, 104 W. 47th Pl., 90037. Tel: 323-234-1471; Fax: 323-234-1472. Email: SouthCentralLAMP@juno.com. Web: www.southcentrallamp.org. Mary Hofmann Henriques, M.P.H., Exec. Dir.

Spirituality Center, 2 Chester Pl., 90007. Tel: 213-747-6508; Fax: 213-477-2649. Email: tbernard@msmc.la.edu. Sr. Thomas Bernard MacConnell, C.S.J., Dir.

St. Vincent Senior Citizen Nutrition Program, Inc., 2131 W. Third St., 90057. Tel: 213-484-7778; Fax: 213-484-7276. Sr. Alice Marie Quinn, D.C., Prog. Dir. Meals served daily 2,500.

Vincentians Province of the West, Support Trust Fund, 3663 Martin Luther King Blvd., Lynwood, 90262. Tel: 310-603-6007; Fax: 310-638-0075. Mr. Robert Issai, Contact Person.

AGOURA HILLS

ALHAMBRA. **Carmelite Educational Centers, Inc.*, 920 E. Alhambra Rd., 91801. Tel: 626-289-1353; Fax: 626-308-1913. Email: decorcarmeli718@yahoo.com. Web: www.carmeliteeducationalcenters.com. Sr. Regina Marie Gorman, O.C.D., Dir. Sisters 20.

**Little Flower Center, Inc.*, 920 E. Alhambra Rd., 91801. Tel: 626-289-1353; Fax: 626-308-1913. Email: decorcarmeli718@yahoo.com.

ANAHEIM HILLS. *Equestrian Order of the Holy Sepulchre*, 8141 E. Kaiser Blvd., Ste. 300, 92808. Tel: 714-282-9632; Fax: 714-282-1563. Email: kseifert@khswesternusa.org. Web: www.holysepulchre.net. H.E. Patrick D. Powers, K.C.H.S., K.G.C.H.S. Lt.

3424 Wilshire Blvd., 90010-2241. Tel: 213-637-7000; Fax: 213-637-7691. His Eminence Roger Cardinal Mahony, K.G.C.H.S., Grand Prior.

BALDWIN PARK. *The Redemptorist Vietnamese Mission Corporation*, 3452 N. Big Dalton Ave., 91706. Tel: 626-337-7735; Fax: 626-851-1280. Email: vnmissionc@aol.com. Rev. Vu Minh Nghiem, C.Ss.R., Pres.

BELLFLOWER. *St. John Bosco High School Alumni*, 13640 S. Bellflower Blvd., 90706. Tel: 562-920-1734; Fax: 562-867-5322. Email: kdusserr@bosco.org. Web: www.Bosco.org. Rev. John Itzaina, S.D.B.

World Apostolate of Fatima, Blue Army, USA, Los Angeles Division, 15550 Bellflower Blvd., 90706-3819. Tel: 562-867-8661; Fax: 562-867-8661.

BURBANK. *SCRC (Southern California Renewal Communities)*, 9795 Cabrini Dr., Ste. 105, 91504-1739. Tel: 818-771-1361; Fax: 818-771-1379. Email: spirit@fea.net. Web: www.scrc.org. Dominic Berardino, Pres.; Rev. William Delaney, S.J., Pastoral Coord. Serving Catholic Charismatic Renewal through annual summer convention, pastoral teaching events, healing masses, retreats, book & tape ministry and a bi-monthly publication.

COVINA. *Comboni Mission Center*, 645 S. Aldenville Ave., 91723. Tel: 626-339-1914; Fax: 626-974-4238. Email abmccj@earthlink.net. Web: www.comboni.com. Revs. Angelo G. Biancalana, M.C.C.J. (Italy); Joseph Forlani, M.C.C.J. (Italy); J. Walter Mattiato, M.C.C.J. (Italy); Domenico Pazzaglia, M.C.C.J. (Italy); Tesfaldet Asghedom, M.C.C.J. (Eritrea); Luigi Gasparini, M.C.C.J. (Italy) CHI).

EL MONTE. *Hombre Nuevo*, 12036 Ramona Blvd., 91732. Tel: 626-444-4442; Fax: 626-444-1435. Email: hn@catolico.com. Web: www.catolico.com. Rev. Juan Rivas, L.C.

GLENDALE. **Together in Christ*, 951 N. Louise St., Ste. 109, 91207. Tel: 818-246-5582. Email: TogetherChrist1@aol.com. Nancy Barona, Pres.

LA MIRANDA. *World Wide Marriage Encounter*, 15618 Gaymont Dr., La Mirada, 90638. Tel: 714-994-8672. Email: pobletsce@aol.com. Web: www.wwme.org. Carlos Poblet, Contact; Esther Poblet, Contact.

LA VERNE. *Picpus Charitable Trust*, 2150 Damien Ave., 91750. Tel: 909-596-1946; Fax: 909-596-6112. Email: dastravers@hotmail.com.

LANCASTER. *Our Lady of Charity, Inc.*, P.O. Box 412, 93584. Tel: 805-942-3222; Fax: 661-949-3126. Donald Willey. Tel: 661-946-0125.

LONG BEACH. **Friars of the Sick Poor of Los Angeles, Inc.*, 1276 E. Appleton St., 90802-3632. Tel: 562-432-4770. Email: brrichardhirbe@dochs.org. Bro. Richard A. Hirbe, F.S.P., Contact Person.

St. Mary Catholic Housing Corp., 1050 Linden Ave., 90813. Tel: 562-491-9225; Fax: 562-491-9085.

St. Mary Medical Center Foundation (Catholic Healthcare West) , 1050 Linden Ave., P.O. Box 887, 90801. Tel: 562-491-9225; Fax: 562-491-9888. John T. Wagner, Pres.

LYNWOOD. *Daughters of Charity Ministry Services Corp.*, 3663 Martin Luther King Jr. Blvd., 90262. Tel: 310-603-6007; Fax: 310-638-0075.

Hotel Dieu, Collaro, 90262. Tel: 310-603-6007; Fax: 310-638-0075. Mr. Robert Issai, CFO.

Rosalie Renau, Inc., 1760 Bay Rd., #24, East Palo Alto, 94303. Tel: 650-473-9522. 3663 Martin Luther King Jr. Blvd., 90262. Tel: 310-603-6007; Fax: 310-638-0075. Mr. Robert Issai, CFO

MONTEREY PARK. *Congregation of St. John the Baptist*, 220 S. Ynez Ave., 91754. Tel: 626-280-3430; Fax: 626-280-1590. Email: csjb@gus.net. Web: www2.gus.net/home/c/csjb. Very Rev. Stanislaus Su, C.S.J.B. Contact Person.

Theresian Sisters, 901 W. El Repetto Dr., 91754. Tel: 323-780-1965; Fax: 323-780-1965. Sr. Felicitas M. Hong, C.S.T. Contact Person.

**United Chinese Apostolate Council*, 300 Garfield Ave., Ste. 203, 91754. Tel: 626-280-7721.

OJAI. **International Theological Institute for Studies on Marriage and the Family*, 10882 Creek Rd., 93023. Tel: 805-649-2346; Fax: 805-649-2347. Daniel Grimm, Contact Person.

**St. Joseph's H. & RC Foundation*, 2464 Ojai Ave., P.O. Box 760, 93024-0760. Tel: 805-646-1466; Fax: 805-646-0806. Email: stjosfnd@pacbell.net. Bro. Gary Hill, O.H., Contact Person.

PACIFIC PALISADES. *Paulist Pictures*, P.O. Box 1057, 90272. Tel: 310-454-0688; Fax: 310-454-6549. Email: Paulistmail@paulistproduction.org. Web: www.paulistproductions.org.

Paulist Productions, (Insight) 17575 Pacific Coast Hwy., P.O. Box 1057, 90272. Tel: 310-454-0688; Fax: 310-459-6549. Email: Paulistmail@paulistproduction.org. Web: paulistproductions.org. Rev. Frank Desiderio, C.S.P., Pres.; Enid Sevilla, Gen. Mgr. Financial Officer; Joseph Kim, Vice Pres. Business Affairs; Rev. Greg Apparcel, C.S.P., Vice Pres. Devel.

PASADENA. *Ramona Blvd., Inc.*, 1453 E. California Blvd., 91106. Tel: 626-792-0447; Fax: 626-792-0475.

Territorial Administrative Office, P.O. Box 162, Thornwood, NY 10594. Tel: 914-773-1368; Fax: 914-773-1438. Rev. Juan Sabadell, L.C., Sec. & Treas.

PASADINA. *Franciscan Communications*, 3300 W. Temple St., 90026. Tel: 213-251-9800; Fax: 213-251-9855. Kenneth E. Martinet, Pres. & CEO.

SAN FERNANDO. *Valley Family Center*, 302 S. Brand Blvd., 91340. Tel: 818-365-8588; Fax: 818-898-3382. Email: sistersofcharity@valleyfamilycenter.com. Sisters Una Connolly, R.S.C., Exec. Dir.; Carmel Somers, R.S.C., Dir. of Learning Center. Religious Sisters of Charity, All Services are in English and Spanish. Counseling is available for individual, marriage, family, children/teen, victims of sexual and physical abuse, and adults molested as children (AMAC). Special Programs include School Counseling; Parent Education; anger management; violence prevention; victims and perpetrators of domestic violence; at risk youth. Learning Center Programs include tutorials; basic skill building for children and adults, and opportunities for gifted students.

SAN PEDRO. *Apostleship of the Sea, Catholic Maritime Ministry*, Mary, Star of the Sea Parish, 870 W. 8th St., 90731. Tel: 310-833-3541; Fax: 310-833-9254. Email: marystar2@aol.com. Rev. Msgr. Michael J. Gallagher (SD), Port Chap.; Rev. Henry L. Hernando, Dir. of Chap. Svcs.

Center:, Berth 93A, World Cruise Center, Port of Los Angeles, 90731. Tel: 310-521-1041; Fax: 310-521-1046.

SANTA BARBARA. **The Cause of Blessed Junipero Serra*, Old Mission Santa Barbara, 2201 Laguna St., 93105-3611. Tel: 805-682-4713; Fax: 805-682-6067. Email: FriarTim@aol.com. Bro. Timothy Arthur, O.F.M., Contact Person.

The Franciscan Sisters of the Sacred Heart in CA (A California non-profit corp.) , 65 Chase Dr., 93103. Tel: 805-683-6381, Ext. 106 Work; 805-962-8836 Convent; Fax: 805-967-7508. Sisters Mary Elizabeth Imler, O.S.F., Gen. Supr.; Christine Bowman, O.S.F., Local Community Leader. Franciscan Sisters of the Sacred Heart, (Frankfort, IL)

SANTA MARIA. *Servants and Handmaids of the Sacred Heart of Jesus, Mary and Joseph*, P.O. Box 6164, 93456-6164. Tel: 805-524-5890; 805-739-1922. Email: info@theservantsandhandmaids.net. Web: www.theservantsandhandmaids.net.

STUDIO CITY. **Catholics in Media Associates*, 12400 Ventura Blvd., PMB #228, 91604. Tel: 818-907-2734; Fax: 818-783-8066. Email: cima2734@aol.com. Web: www.catholicsinmedia.org. Barbara Gangi, Pres.

VENICE. *St. Joseph Center*, 204 Hampton Dr., 90291-8633. Tel: 310-396-6468; Fax: 310-392-8402. Email: rmeister@stjosephctr.org. Web: www.stjosephctr.org. Sr. Jill Napier, Contact Person.

VENTURA. *CAREGIVERS: Volunteers Assisting the Elderly*, 1765 Goodyear Ave., #205, 93003. Tel: 805-658-8530; Fax: 805-658-8537. Email: caregivers@vcnet.com. Web: www.vcnet.com/~caregivers.

126 N. 8th St., Santa Paula, 93060. Tel: 805-525-5006.

WEST COVINA. *Federation of Filipino Rosary Groups, Inc.*, 2809 Elena Ave., 91792. Eddie B. De Sagun, Contact. Purpose: To provide evangelization of people, particularly the Filipinos, and to aid in building communities of faith through the propagation of the devotion to the Holy Rosary.

WESTLAKE VILLAGE. *West San Fernando Valley Magnificat Chapter Ministry to Catholic Women*, 32149 Lakemeadow Ln., 91361. Tel: 818-889-8515.

[DD] LEGAL TITLES

LOS ANGELES. *Archdiocesan Catholic Center*, 3424 Wilshire Blvd., 90010-2241. Tel: 213-637-7000; Fax: 213-637-6707. Email: webmaster@la-archdiocese.org. Web: www.la-archdiocese.org. For further information contact the Chancery. Also see Miscellaneous for additional listings.

Recollect Augustinian Fathers & Brothers, Province of St. Augustine, Inc., O.S.A.R., Oxnard Tel: 805-486-7433; Fax: 805-487-2805.

Missionary Oblates of Mary Immaculate, Western Province, Inc., O.M.I., Arleta Tel: 818-891-0579; Fax: 818-893-9819.

School Sisters of Notre Dame de Namur of the California Province, Inc., S.N.D.deN. Tel: 314-544-0455; Fax: 314-544-6754. Various Locations in the Archdiocese

Congregation of the Sacred Heart of Jesus & Mary and of Perpetual Adoration, Inc., SS.CC., LaVerne Tel: 909-593-5441; Fax: 909-593-3971.

Sisters of St. Louis Monaghan, Inc., S.S.L., Woodland Hills Tel: 818-883-1678; Fax: 818-346-6109.

Ursulines of the Western Province, Inc., O.S.U., Encino Tel: 650-346-9897.

RELIGIOUS INSTITUTES OF MEN REPRESENTED IN THE ARCHDIOCESE

For further details refer to the corresponding

bracketed number in the Religious Institutes of Men or Women section.
[0140]—*The Augustinians*—O.S.A.
[0200]—*Benedictine Monks (Congregation of the Annunciation)*—O.S.B.
[0980]—*Brothers of Our Lady Mother of Mercy*—C.F.M.M.
[1350]—*Brothers of St. Francis Xavier*—C.F.X.
[1160]—*Brothers of St. Patrick*—F.S.P.
[0330]—*Brothers of the Christian Schools*—F.S.C.
[]—*Canons Regular of the Immaculate Conception*—C.R.I.C.
[0470]—*The Capuchin Friars* (St. Patrick's Custody)—O.F.M.Cap.
[0270]—*Carmelite Fathers & Brothers* (Prov. of the Most Pure Heart of Mary)—O.Carm.
[0360]—*Claretian Missionaries* (Western Prov.)—C.M.F.
[0380]—*Comboni Missionaries of the Heart of Jesus* (Verona)—M.C.C.J.
[0310]—*Congregation of Christian Brothers*—C.F.C.
[]—*Congregation of St. John the Baptist*—C.S.J.B.
[1150]—*Congregation of St. Joseph*—C.S.J.
[1330]—*Congregation of the Mission* (Prov. of the West)—C.M.
[1210]—*Congregation of the Missionaries of St. Charles*—C.S.
[1000]—*Congregation of the Passion* (Western Prov.)—C.P.
[1140]—*Congregation of the Sacred Hearts of Jesus and Mary*—SS.CC.
[0480]—*Conventual Franciscans* (St. Joseph Cupertino Prov.)—O.F.M.Conv
[0520]—*Franciscan Friars* (St. Barbara Prov.)—O.F.M.
[0530]—*Franciscan Friars of the Atonement*—S.A.
[]—*Guadalupe Missioners* (Mexico)—M.G.
[0650]—*Holy Ghost Fathers*—C.S.Sp.
[0670]—*Hospitaller Brothers of St. John of God*—O.H.
[0690]—*Jesuit Fathers and Brothers* (California Prov.)—S.J.
[0710]—*Josephite Fathers*—C.J.
[0730]—*Legionaries of Christ*—L.C.
[0580]—*Little Brothers of the Good Shepherd*—B.G.S.
[0780]—*Marist Fathers*—S.M.
[0800]—*Maryknoll*—M.M.
[0830]—*Mill Hill Missionaries*—M.H.M.
[]—*Missionaries of Charity Brothers*—M.C.
[]—*Missionaries of Jesus* (Mexico)—M.J.
[0660]—*Missionaries of the Holy Spirit*—M.Sp.S.
[1110]—*Missionaries of the Sacred Heart*—M.S.C.
[0840]—*Missionary Servants of the Most Holy Trinity*—S.T.
[0910]—*Oblates of Mary Immaculate* (Western Prov.)—O.M.I.
[0930]—*Oblates of St. Joseph*—O.S.J.
[0940]—*Oblates of the Virgin Mary*—O.M.V.
[]—*Operarios del Reino de Cristo*—O.R.C.
[0835]—*Order of Minims*—O.M.
[0430]—*Order of Preachers-Dominicans* (Western Prov.)—O.P.
[0150]—*Order of the Augustinian Recollects*—O.A.R.
[1020]—*Pauline Fathers and Brothers, Society of St. Paul*—S.S.P.
[1030]—*Paulist Fathers*—C.S.P.
[1040]—*Piarist Fathers*—Sch.P.
[1050]—*Pontifical Institute for Foreign Missions*—P.I.M.E.
[0610]—*Priests of the Congregation of Holy Cross*—C.S.C.
[1070]—*Redemptorist Fathers* (Oakland Prov.)—C.SS.R.
[1090]—*Rogationist Fathers*—R.C.J.
[1190]—*Salesians of Don Bosco*—S.D.B.
[1240]—*Servites*—O.S.M.
[0110]—*Society of African Missions*—S.M.A.
[1260]—*Society of Christ*—S.Ch.
[0760]—*Society of Mary*—S.M.
[0370]—*Society of St. Columban*—S.S.C.
[0420]—*Society of the Divine Word*—S.V.D.
[1060]—*Society of the Precious Blood*—C.PP.S.
[1290]—*Society of the Priests of St. Sulpice*—S.S.
[0700]—*St. Joseph's Society of the Sacred Heart*—S.S.J.

RELIGIOUS INSTITUTES OF WOMEN REPRESENTED IN THE ARCHDIOCESE

[2120]—*Armenian Sisters of the Immaculate Conception*—C.I.C.
[]—*Augustinian Recollect Sisters*—A.R.
[0230]—*Benedictine Sisters of Pontifical Jurisdiction*—O.S.B.
[1810]—*Bernardine Sisters of the Third Order of St. Francis*—O.S.F.
[]—*Blessed Sacrament Sisters of Charity*
[2930]—*California Institute of the Sisters of the Most Holy and Immaculate Heart of the Blessed Virgin Mary*—I.H.M.
[]—*Caritas Sisters of Miyazaki*
[]—*Carmelitas de San Jose*—C.S.
[0370]—*Carmelite Sisters of the Most Sacred Heart of Los Angeles*—O.C.D.
[]—*Chinese Dominican Sisters*—O.P.
[]—*Congregation of Hermanitas de la Annunciacion*
[]—*Congregation of Kkottongnae Sisters of Jesus*—C.K.S.J.
[2100]—*Congregation of the Humility of Mary*—C.H.M.
[0470]—*Congregation of the Sisters of Charity for the Incarnate Word*—C.C.V.I.
[3242]—*Congregation of the Sisters of Nazareth*—C.S.N.
[3935]—*Congregation of the Sisters of St. Louis, Juilly Monaghan*—S.S.L.
[1920]—*Congregation of the Sisters of the Holy Cross*—C.S.C.
[1940]—*Congregation of the Sisters of the Holy Faith*—C.H.F.
[0760]—*Daughters of Charity of St. Vincent de Paul* (Prov. of the West)—D.C.
[0860]—*Daughters of Mary*—D.M.
[0880]—*Daughters of Mary and Joseph*—D.M.J.
[0850]—*Daughters of Mary Help of Christians*—F.M.A.
[0420]—*Discalced Carmelite Nuns*—O.C.D.
[1050]—*Dominican Comtemplative Nuns (Cloistered)*—O.P.
[1070-03]—*Dominican Sisters*—O.P.
[1070-12]—*Dominican Sisters*—O.P.
[1070-19]—*Dominican Sisters*—O.P.
[1070-21]—*Dominican Sisters*—O.P.
[1070-13]—*Dominican Sisters*—O.P.
[1070-04]—*Dominican Sisters*—O.P.
[]—*Dominican Sisters of Adrian (Pacific West Chapter)*—O.P.
[]—*Dominican Sisters of the Christian Doctrine*—O.P.
[1150]—*Eucharistic Franciscan Missionary Sisters*—E.F.M.S.
[]—*Evangelizadores Eucaristicas de los Pobres*—E.E.P.
[1170]—*Felician Sisters*—C.S.S.F.
[1350]—*Franciscan Missionary Sisters of the Immaculate Conception*—O.S.F.
[1310]—*Franciscan Sisters of Little Falls*—O.S.F.
[1500]—*Franciscan Sisters of Mary Immaculate of the Third Order of St. Francis of Assisi*—F.M.I.
[1780]—*Franciscan Sisters of Perpetual Adoration*—O.S.F.
[1450]—*Franciscan Sisters of the Sacred Heart*—O.S.F.
[1845]—*Guadalupan Missionaries of the Holy Spirit*—M.G.Sp.S.
[]—*Handmaids of the Sacred Heart of Jesus, Mary & Joseph*—J.M.J.
[]—*Hermanas Misioneras Servidoras de la Palabra*—H.M.S.P.
[2575]—*Institute of the Sisters of Mercy of the Americas* (Burlingame, CA)—R.S.M.
[]—*Little Handmaids of the Most Holy Trinity*—M.A.S.T.
[2340]—*Little Sisters of the Poor*—L.S.P.
[2390]—*Lovers of the Holy Cross Sisters*—L.H.C.
[2470]—*Maryknoll Sisters of St. Dominic*—M.M.
[2500]—*Medical Sisters of St. Joseph*—M.S.J.
[]—*Misioneras Eucaristicas De Maria Inmaculada*—M.E.M.I.
[2710]—*Missionaries of Charity*—M.C.
[]—*Missionaries of Jesus Crucified*—M.J.C.
[0210]—*Missionary Benedictine Sisters*—O.S.B.
[0390]—*Missionary Carmelites of St. Theresa*—C.M.S.T.
[2715]—*Missionary Sisters of Christ the King*—M.Chr.
[2880]—*Missionary Sisters of St. Columban*—S.S.C.
[2750]—*Missionary Sisters of the Immaculate Heart of Mary*—I.C.M.
[3530]—*Missionary Sisters Servants of the Holy Spirit*—S.Sp.S.
[]—*Missionary Sisters, Oblates of the Holy Family*—O.H.F.
[0240]—*Olivetan Benedictine Sisters*—O.S.B.
[3760]—*Order of St. Clare*—P.C.C.
[3130]—*Our Lady of Victory Missionary Sisters*—O.L.V.M.
[0980]—*Pious Disciples of the Divine Master*—P.D.D.M.
[0950]—*Pious Society Daughters of St. Paul*—F.S.P.
[2840]—*Poor Clare Missionary Sisters*—M.C.
[0930]—*Religious Daughters of St. Joseph*—F.S.J.
[1145]—*Religious Missionaries of St. Dominic*—O.P.
[3450]—*Religious of Jesus-Mary*—R.J.M.
[3465]—*Religious of the Sacred Heart of Mary*—R.S.H.M.
[3400]—*Religious Sisters of Charity*—R.S.C.
[2970]—*School Sisters of Notre Dame*—S.S.N.D.
[1680]—*School Sisters of St. Francis*—O.S.F.
[3580]—*Servants of Mary (Servite Order)*—O.S.M.
[3499]—*Servants of the Blessed Sacrament*—S.J.S.
[]—*Servants of the Immaculate Child Mary*—E.I.N.
[3615]—*Servants of the Immaculate Child Mary (Esclavas de la Inmaculada Nina)*—E.I.N.
[]—*Sisters for Christian Community*—S.F.C.C.
[0250]—*Sisters of Bethany*—C.V.D.
[0480]—*Sisters of Charity of Leavenworth, Kansas*—S.C.L.
[]—*Sisters of Charity of Rolling Hills*—S.C.R.H.
[0570]—*Sisters of Charity of Seton Hill, Greensburg, Pennsylvania*—S.C.
[0430]—*Sisters of Charity of the Blessed Virgin Mary*—B.V.M.
[]—*Sisters of Little Jesus*—S.L.J.
[2360]—*Sisters of Loretto At the Foot of the Cross* (Southern Prov.)—S.L.
[]—*Sisters of Mary, Mother of the Church*—M.M.C.
[2575]—*Sisters of Mercy* (New York)—R.S.M.
[2990]—*Sisters of Notre Dame* (Prov. of Los Angeles)—S.N.D.
[3000]—*Sisters of Notre Dame de Namur*—S.N.D.deN.
[]—*Sisters of Our Lady of Perpetual Help*—S.O.L.P.H.
[3350]—*Sisters of Providence*—S.P.
[3360]—*Sisters of Providence of Saint Mary-Of-The-Woods, Indiana*—S.P.
[4080]—*Sisters of Social Service of Los Angeles, Inc.*—S.S.S.
[1705]—*Sisters of St. Francis of Assisi*—O.S.F.
[1710]—*Sisters of St. Francis of Joliet*—O.S.F.
[1620]—*Sisters of St. Francis of Millvale, Pennsylvania*—O.S.F.
[1760]—*Sisters of St. Francis of Oldenburg*—O.S.F.
[1630]—*Sisters of St. Francis of Penance and Christian Charity*—O.S.F.
[1650]—*The Sisters of St. Francis of Philadelphia*—O.S.F.
[1530]—*Sisters of St. Francis of Sylvania*—O.S.F.
[3830-03]—*Sisters of St. Joseph*—C.S.J.
[3830-18]—*Sisters of St. Joseph*—C.S.J.
[3860]—*Sisters of St. Joseph Congregation*—S.J.C.
[3840]—*Sisters of St. Joseph of Carondelet*—C.S.J.
[3860]—*Sisters of St. Joseph of Cluny*—S.J.C.
[3830-11]—*Sisters of St. Joseph of Nazareth*—S.S.J.
[3830]—*Sisters of St. Joseph of Orange*—C.S.J.
[3890]—*Sisters of St. Joseph of Peace*—C.S.J.P.
[3930]—*Sisters of St. Joseph to the Third Order of St. Francis*—S.S.J.-T.O
[]—*Sisters of the Blessed Korean Martyrs*—B.K.M.
[0700]—*Sisters of the Company of Mary Our Lady*—O.D.N.
[1830]—*Sisters of the Good Shepherd*—R.G.S.
[1850]—*Sisters of the Guardian Angel*—S.A.C.
[]—*Sisters of the Heart of Jesus in the Blessed Sacrament*—H.C.J.S.
[1960]—*Sisters of the Holy Family*—S.H.F.
[1990]—*Sisters of the Holy Names of Jesus and Mary*—S.N.J.M.
[2120]—*Sisters of the Immaculate Conception*—C.I.C.
[]—*Sisters of the Immaculate Heart of Mary at Mirinae*—I.H.M.M.
[2270]—*Sisters of the Little Company of Mary*—L.C.M.
[]—*Sisters of the Love of God*—R.A.D.
[3200]—*Sisters of the Pious Schools*—Sch.P.
[3320]—*Sisters of the Presentation of the B.V.M.* (San Francisco, CA)—P.B.V.M.
[]—*Sisters of the Sacred Heart of Mary*—C.S.C.M.
[4050]—*Sisters of the Society Devoted to the Sacred Heart*—S.D.S.H.
[4100]—*Sisters of the Sorrowful Mother*—S.S.M.
[1490]—*Sisters of the Third Franciscan Order*—O.S.F.
[3600]—*Sisters Servants of Mary*—S.M.
[4060]—*Society of the Holy Child Jesus*—S.H.C.J.
[1505]—*St. Francis Mission Community*—O.S.F.
[]—*Theresian Sisters*—C.S.T.
[3330]—*Union of Sisters of Presentation of the B.B.M.*—P.B.V.M.
[4110]—*Ursuline Nuns (Roman Union)*—O.S.U.
[]—*Verbum Dei Missionary Fraternity*—V.D.M.F.
[4200]—*Visitation Congregation*—S.V.M.

ARCHDIOCESAN CEMETERIES

LOS ANGELES. *Calvary Cemetery and Mausoleum*, Tel: 323-261-3106. Maria Orozco, Mgr.

CULVER CITY. *Holy Cross Cemetery & Mausoleum &*

Columbarium, Tel: 310-670-7697.

LANCASTER. *Good Shepherd Cemetery & Mausoleum*, Tel: 661-722-0887. Daniel Rejniak, Mgr.

LONG BEACH. *All Souls Cemetery and Mausoleum*, Tel: 562-424-8601. Jesus Castillo, Mgr.

MISSION HILLS. *San Fernando Mission Cemetery & Mausoleum*, Tel: 818-361-7387. Rosalie Castillo, Mgr.

MONTEBELLO. *Resurrection Cemetery & Mausoleum*, Tel: 323-887-2024. Margaret Hunter, Mgr.

OXNARD. *Santa Clara Cemetery & Mausoleum*, Tel: 805-485-5757. Elizabeth Welsh, Mgr.

POMONA. *Holy Cross Cemetery*, Tel: 909-627-3602. Lupe Ramirez, Mgr.

ROWLAND HEIGHTS. *Queen of Heaven Cemetery*, Tel: 626-964-1291. Norberta Orta, Mgr.

SANTA BARBARA. *Calvary Cemetery & Mausoleum*, Tel: 805-687-8811. Gwen Hueston, Mgr.

SIMI. *Assumption Cemetery*, Tel: 805-583-5825. Elizabeth Welsh, Mgr.

NECROLOGY

† Boyer, Rev. Msgr. Leland J., La Canada Flintridge, CA St. Bede the Venerable—Died Jan. 14, 2003

† Caslin, Rev. Msgr. Peter C.—Died Aug. 15, 2003

† Collins, Rev. Msgr. Fachta P., Montrose, CA Holy Redeemer—Died Aug. 12, 2003

† Elder Rev. Msgr. Jerome, St. Anastasia, 7390 W. Manchester Ave., 90045-2340. (Retired)—Died June 30, 2003

† Gualderon, Rev. Msgr. Ernest J.—Died Sept. 29, 2003

† Holland, Rev. Msgr. Ian (Retired)—Died Nov. 26, 2002

† Leuer, Rev. Msgr. Anthony, Rancho Palos Verdes, CA Marymount College—Died Sept. 18, 2003

† Twomey, Rev. Msgr. John P.—Died July 21, 2003

† Chang, Gordan—Died Jan. 9, 2003

† Combs, Regis V., (Retired)—Died June 27, 2003

† Cullen, Francis J., (Retired)—Died Jan. 28, 2003

† Kennedy, John A., (Retired)—Died May 14, 2003

† Lee, Peter, (Retired)—Died June 18, 2003

† Power, Patrick A., Santa Clarita, CA Our Lady of Perpetual Help—Died June 2, 2003

† Sullivan, Patrick H.—Died July 16, 2003

Archdiocese of Louisville

(Archidioecesis Ludovicopolitana)

Most Reverend

THOMAS C. KELLY, O.P., D.D., J.C.D.

Archbishop of Louisville; ordained June 5, 1958; appointed Titular Bishop of Tusuro July 12, 1977; promoted Archbishop of Louisville December 29, 1981. *Office: 212 E. College St., P.O. Box 1073, Louisville, KY 40201.*

Most Reverend

CHARLES G. MALONEY, D.D.

Auxiliary Bishop Emeritus of Louisville; born September 9, 1912; ordained December 8, 1937; appointed Auxiliary December 30, 1954; consecrated February 2, 1955; appointed Titular Bishop of Bardstown February 2, 1995; resigned January 8, 1988. *Res.: 212 E. College St., P.O. Box 1073, Louisville, KY 40201.*

Square Miles 8,124.

Established at Bardstown April 8, 1808; Transferred to Louisville Feb. 13, 1841; created an Archdiocese Dec. 10, 1937.

Comprises the following twenty-four Counties in central Kentucky: Adair, Barren, Bullitt, Casey, Clinton, Cumberland, Green, Hardin, Hart, Henry, Jefferson, Larue, Marion, Meade, Metcalfe, Monroe, Nelson, Oldham, Russell, Shelby, Spencer, Taylor, Trimble and Washington.

For legal titles of parishes and archdiocesan institutions, consult the Chancery.

Chancery: 212 E. College St., P.O. Box 1073, Louisville, KY 40201. Tel: 502-585-3291; Fax: 502-585-2466.

Web: www.archlou.org

Email: chancery@archlou.org

STATISTICAL OVERVIEW

Personnel	
Archbishops	1
Retired Bishops	1
Abbots	1
Retired Abbots	1
Priests: Diocesan Active in Diocese	102
Priests: Diocesan Active Outside Diocese	7
Priests: Diocesan in Foreign Missions	2
Priests: Retired, Sick or Absent	55
Number of Diocesan Priests	166
Religious Priests in Diocese	58
Total Priests in Diocese	224
Ordinations:	
Diocesan Priests	1
Religious Priests	2
Transitional Deacons	4
Permanent Deacons in Diocese	110
Total Brothers	77
Total Sisters	924
Parishes	
Parishes	111
With Resident Pastor:	
Resident Diocesan Priests	87
Resident Religious Priests	11
Without Resident Pastor:	
Administered by Priests	7
Administered by Deacons	3
Administered by Religious Women	2
Administered by Lay People	1
Missions	11
Pastoral Centers	3
Professional Ministry Personnel:	
Brothers	2
Sisters	26
Lay Ministers	164
Welfare	
Catholic Hospitals	2
Total Assisted	185,750
Health Care Centers	1
Total Assisted	2,500
Homes for the Aged	5
Total Assisted	1,154
Residential Care of Children	2
Total Assisted	145
Day Care Centers	1
Total Assisted	150
Special Centers for Social Services	8
Total Assisted	31,000
Educational	
Diocesan Students in Other Seminaries	6
Total Seminarians	6
Colleges and Universities	3
Total Students	4,655
High Schools, Diocesan and Parish	4
Total Students	2,327
High Schools, Private	5
Total Students	3,989
Elementary Schools, Diocesan and Parish	53
Total Students	16,886
Elementary Schools, Private	2
Total Students	488
Non-residential Schools for the Disabled	1
Total Students	52
Catechesis/Religious Education:	
High School Students	1,261
Elementary Students	5,903
Total Students under Catholic Instruction	35,567
Teachers in the Diocese:	
Priests	7
Brothers	7
Sisters	21
Lay Teachers	1,925
Vital Statistics	
Receptions into the Church:	
Infant Baptism Totals	2,570
Adult Baptism Totals	350
Received into Full Communion	485
First Communions	2,966
Confirmations	2,704
Marriages:	
Catholic	571
Interfaith	337
Total Marriages	908
Deaths	1,660
Total Catholic Population	196,888
Total Population	1,119,465

Former Bishops—Rt. Revs. BENEDICT JOSEPH FLAGET, S.S., D.D., consecrated Bishop of Bardstown, Nov. 4, 1810; died Feb. 11, 1850; JOHN B. DAVID, S.S., D.D., Coadjutor; consecrated Aug. 15, 1819; died July 12, 1841; GUY IGNATIUS CHABRAT, S.S., D.D., Coadjutor; consecrated July 20, 1834; died Nov. 21, 1868; MARTIN JOHN SPALDING, D.D., Coadjutor with right of succession; consecrated Sept. 10, 1848; transferred to Baltimore, May 6, 1864; died Feb. 7, 1872; PETER JOSEPH LAVIALLE, D.D., consecrated Sept. 24, 1865; died May 11, 1867; WILLIAM GEORGE MCCLOSKEY, D.D., consecrated May 24, 1868; died Sept. 17, 1909; DENIS O'DONAGHUE, D.D., ord. Sept. 6, 1874; consecrated Titular Bishop of Pomario and Auxiliary of Indianapolis on April 25, 1900; transferred to Louisville, Feb. 7, 1910; transferred to the Titular See of Lebedus, July 26, 1924; died Nov. 7, 1925; Most Revs. JOHN A. FLOERSH, D.D., ord. June 10, 1911; appt. Titular Bishop of Lycopolis and Coadjutor Bishop of Louisville with right of succession, Feb. 6, 1923; consecrated April 8, 1923; succeeded to See July 26, 1924; elevated to Archiepiscopal dignity Dec. 10, 1937; resigned and named to Titular See of Sistroniana, March 1, 1967; died June 11, 1968; THOMAS J. MCDONOUGH, D.D., transferred to Louisville, May 2, 1967; resigned Sept. 29, 1981; died Aug. 4, 1998.

Vicars General—Very Rev. BERNARD J. BREEN; Most Rev. CHARLES G. MALONEY, D.D.

Chancery—212 E. College St., P.O. Box 1073, Louisville, 40201. Tel: 502-585-3291; Fax: 502-585-2466. Office Hours: 8:30-4:30; All applications for dispensations are to be sent to this office.

Chancellor—Dr. BRIAN B. REYNOLDS.

Vice Chancellor—NORMA L. MERRICK.

Secretary to Archbishop—NORMA L. MERRICK.

Archivist—Rev. R. DALE CIESLIK.

Chief Financial Officers—JEROME J. PAKENHAM; PATRICIA J. MEYER.

Metropolitan Tribunal—212 E. College St., P.O. Box 1073, Louisville, 40201. Tel: 502-585-3291.

Judicial Vicar and Director—Very Rev. J. MARK SPALDING.

Adjutant Judicial Vicar—Rev. PHILIP LEE ERICKSON, J.C.L.

Promoter of Justice—Rev. CHARLES C. THOMPSON, J.C.L.

Defenders of the Bond—Revs. DONALD R. GOETZ; JOHN J. STOLTZ; ROBERT E. OSBORNE (Retired); ANTHONY L. CHANDLER, M.A.; PATRICK J. DOLAN, Ph.D., S.T.D.; Deacon WALTON JONES; Dr. ROBERT L. STENGER, S.T.D., J.D.; DONALD M. SWIFT, J.C.D.

Associate Judges—Revs. KENNETH R. FORTENER; THOMAS A. HOMMRICH; T. MICHAEL TOBIN, S.T.L., J.C.B.; Ms. JACQUELINE RAPP, J.D., J.C.L.

Assessor and Tribunal Administrator—PATRICIA A. NORRIS.

Assessor—JO ANN KALB.

Ecclesiastical Notaries—SHARON A. ARCHER; LINDA D. THOMAN; ANN TUMBLIN.

College of Consultors—Most Rev. CHARLES G. MALONEY, D.D.; Very Revs. BERNARD J. BREEN; J. MARK SPALDING; Revs. JOSEPH ATCHER, O.Carm.; JOSEPH RANKIN; CHARLES D. WALKER; THOMAS ANTHONY SMITH; G. NICHOLAS RICE; WILLIAM F. MEDLEY.

Deans—Revs. WILLIAM F. MEDLEY, Bardstown Deanery; GERALD L. BELL, Lebanon Deanery; J. RICHARD SULLIVAN, Elizabethtown Deanery.

Clergy Personnel Commission—Revs. ALBERT L. WILSON (Retired); WILLIAM D. HAMMER; WILLIAM

S. GRINER; GARY T. PADGETT; R. DALE CIESLIK; Deacon BRIAN KARLEY, Dir.

Priests' Council—Most Rev. THOMAS C. KELLY, O.P., D.D., J.C.D., Presider; Rev. G. NICHOLAS RICE, Pres., 508 Breckenridge Lane, Louisville, 40207; NORMA MERRICK, Sec. Ex Officio: Most Rev. CHARLES G. MALONEY, D.D.; Very Revs. BERNARD J. BREEN; J. MARK SPALDING; Revs. BERNARD L. CRAYCROFT (Retired); BERTRAND J. RAPP (Retired); DONALD W. SPRINGMAN; JAMES W. GRAF; JOHN R. BURKE; WILLIAM F. MEDLEY; THOMAS A. SMITH; HARRY J. GELTHAUS; JOSEPH M. RANKIN; CHRISTOPHER M. SCALISE; CHARLES D. WALKER; JAMES R. SCHOOK; WILLIAM M. BOWLING; THOMAS R. CLARK; DANIEL L. LINCOLN; JOSEPH ATCHER, O.Carm.; DANIEL LOBSINGER, C.R.; JOHN CONLEY, C.P.

Archdiocesan Examiners—Very Rev. WILLIAM L. FICHTEMAN; Revs. THOMAS L. BOLAND; GARY T. PADGETT.

Archdiocesan Offices and Directors

Archdiocesan Communications Center—CECELIA PRICE, Chief Communications Officer, Maloney Center, 1200 S. Shelby St., Louisville, 40203. Tel: 502-636-0296; Fax: 502-636-2379.

Byzantine Rite Faithful—Rev. JOHN W. BIRK, Chap., 2914 S. Third St., Louisville, 40208. Tel: 502-637-2058.

Catholic Cemeteries Office—JAVIER FAJARDO, Exec. Dir., 1600 Newburg Rd., P.O. Box 4096, Louisville, 40204. Tel: 502-451-7710; Fax: 502-456-9270.

Catholic Deaf Office—Ms. NANCY REYNOLDS, Dir.; Rev. BRYAN LAMBERSON, Chap., Maloney Center, 1200 S. Shelby St., Louisville, 40203. Tel: 502-636-0296; 502-634-8947 (TTY).

Catholic Charities—Mr. STEVEN E. BOGUS, Exec. Dir., 2911 S. 4th St., Louisville, 40208. Tel: 502-637-9786; Fax: 502-637-9780.

Office of Migration and Refugee Services—Ms. BECKY JORDAN.

Office of Parish Social Ministry—DAVID J. DUTSCHKE.

Respect Life—HELEN ROTHGERBER.

Clergy Personnel Office—Deacon BRIAN KARLEY, Dir., P.O. Box 1073, Louisville, 40201. Tel: 502-585-3291; Fax: 502-585-2466.

Clerical Aid Society—212 E. College St., P.O. Box 1073, Louisville, 40201. Tel: 502-585-3291.

Continuing Education for Clergy-Ministry to Priests—Rev. WILLIAM S. GRINER, Dir., P.O. Box 1073, Louisville, 40201. Tel: 502-585-3291.

Cursillo Movement—Deacon JOSEPH DEW, Spiritual Advisor, Flaget Center, 1935 Lewiston Pl., Louisville, 40216. Tel: 502-448-8581.

Due Process Board—JOHN LAUN, Chm., Kentucky Home Life Building, 239 S. 5th St., Louisville, 40202. Tel: 502-587-0330.

Office of Ecumenical and Interreligious Relations—Rev. WILLIAM D. HAMMER, Dir., Maloney Center, 1200 S. Shelby St., Louisville, 40203. Tel: 502-636-0296.

Catholic Family Center—BARBARA MACDONALD, Dir.; THOMAS D. ROBBINS, Ph.D., Clinical Dir., Maloney Center, 1200 S. Shelby St., Louisville, 40203. Tel: 502-636-0296; Fax: 502-636-2379.

Holy Childhood Association—Deacon ROBERT HALL, Dir., 212 E. College St., Box 1073 Louisville, 40201. Tel: 502-585-3291.

Holy Name Society—MICHAEL HEEB, Pres., 2302 Bradford Dr., Louisville, 40218. Tel: 502-454-7151.

L.A.M.P.— (Louisville Archdiocesan Mission Promoters), Most Revs. THOMAS C. KELLY, O.P., D.D., J.C.D.; CHARLES G. MALONEY, D.D.; Very Rev. BERNARD J. BREEN, 212 E. College St., P.O. Box 1073, Louisville, 40201. Tel: 502-585-3291.

Office of the Diaconate—Deacon ROBERT HALL, Dir., Maloney Center, 1200 S. Shelby St., Louisville, 40203. Tel: 502-636-0296; Fax: 502-636-2379.

Office of Lifelong Formation and Education—Dr. MATTHEW J. HAYES, Exec. Dir., Flaget Center, 1935 Lewiston Pl., Louisville, 40216. Tel: 502-448-8581; Fax: 502-448-5518.

Superintendent of Schools—LEISA SPEER.

Director of Youth Ministry—Dr. CAROLE GOODWIN.

Director of Catechesis—Dr. SUE GRENOUGH.

Office of Ministry and Spirituality—SAL DELLA BELLA, Dir., Maloney Center, 1200 S. Shelby St., Louisville, 40203. Tel: 502-636-0296.

Office of Multicultural Ministry—M. ANNETTE TURNER, Dir., Maloney Center, 1200 S. Shelby St., Louisville, 40203. Tel: 502-636-0296.

Office of Pastoral Care—Rev. PAUL A. SCAGLIONE, Dir., Maloney Center, 1200 S. Shelby St., Louisville, 40203. Tel: 502-636-0296; Fax: 502-636-2379. Email: opc@archlou.org.

Office of Worship—JUDY BULLOCK, Dir., Maloney Center, 1200 S. Shelby St., Louisville, 40203. Tel: 502-636-0296; Fax: 502-636-2379.

Opportunities for Life—LYNDIE RUSCHELL, Dir., 1042 Burlington Lane, Frankfort, 40601. Tel: 502-223-5330; 800-822-5824; Fax: 502-875-2841.

Personnel and Planning—Dr. BRIAN B. REYNOLDS, Dir., 212 E. College, P.O. Box 1073, Louisville, 40201. Tel: 502-585-3291.

Propagation of the Faith— (Missions Office), Deacon ROBERT HALL, Dir., P.O. Box 1073, Louisville, 40201. Tel: 502-585-3291.

Sacred Heart Enthronement Center—Rev. LAWRENCE H. LINDLE, Dir. (Retired), 8191 New Haven Rd., New Haven, 40051. Tel: 502-549-3751.

Stewardship and Development Office—ROSEMARY BISIG SMITH, Dir., 212 E. College St., P.O. Box 1073, Louisville, 40201. Tel: 502-585-3291; Fax: 502-585-2466.

Vicar for Retired Clergy—Rev. KENNETH L. KAMBER (Retired), 4029 Busath Ave., Louisville, 40218. Tel: 502-491-1323.

Victim Assistance Coordinators—BRENDA MARSHALL, M.S.S.W., L.C.S.W., L.F.M.T.; TOM ROBBINS, Ph.D., L.F.M.T. Tel: 502-636-1044. Email: trobbins@archlou.org family@archlou.org.

Vocations—VACANT, Dir.; Mrs. LINDA BANKER, Assoc. Dir., Maloney Center, 1200 S. Shelby St., Louisville, 40203. Tel: 502-636-0296.

CLERGY, PARISHES, MISSIONS AND PAROCHIAL SCHOOLS

CITY OF LOUISVILLE
(JEFFERSON COUNTY)

1—CATHEDRAL OF THE ASSUMPTION, Very Rev. William L. Fichteman; Rev. William D. Hammer; Deacon Joseph P. Wright. In Res., Most Rev. Thomas C. Kelly, O.P.
Res.: 433 S. 5th St., 40202. Tel: 502-582-2971; Fax: 502-582-3919.
Catechesis/Religious Program—Students 71.

2—ST. AGNES, Revs. John Conley, C.P.; Albert Schwer, C.P.; John Hilgert, C.P.
Res.: 1920 Newburg Rd., 40205. Tel: 502-451-2220; Fax: 502-454-8483.
School—1800 Newburg Rd., 40205. Tel: 502-458-2850; Fax: 502-459-5215. Carol Melrose, Prin. Lay Teachers 26; Students 410.
Catechesis/Religious Program—Sheila Linton, D.R.E. Students 26.

3—ST. ALBERT THE GREAT, Revs. Donald M. Hill; Theodore R. Sans; Deacon Vincent (Jim) G. Stanley.
Res.: 1395 Girard Dr., 40222. Tel: 502-425-3940; Fax: 502-394-9896.
School—Tel: 502-425-1804; Fax: 502-394-9896. Jeanne Flowers, Prin. Lay Teachers 37; Students 648.
Catechesis/Religious Program—Tel: 502-423-1590. Students 160.

4—ST. ALOYSIUS, Closed. For inquiries for parish records contact the chancery.

5—ST. ANDREW, Closed. For inquiries for parish records contact the chancery.

6—ST. ANN, Closed. For inquiries for parish records contact the chancery.

7—ST. ANTHONY, Rev. Kent Biergans, O.F.M.Conv. In Res., Revs. John Curran, O.F.M.Conv.; Ken Gering O.F.M.Conv.; Thomas A. Smith, O.F.M.Conv.
Res.: 2222 W. Market St., 40212. Tel: 502-778-7413; Fax: 502-776-3599.

8—ASCENSION OF OUR LORD, Rev. Gary T. Padgett; Deacon Michael Edwards.
Res.: 4600 Lynnbrook Dr., 40220. Tel: 502-451-3860; Fax: 502-458-9782.
School—Tel: 502-451-2535; Fax: 502-451-2535. Maureen Clerkin, Prin. Lay Teachers 28; Students 453.
Catechesis/Religious Program—Tel: 502-451-3860, Ext. 12. Students 22.

9—ST. ATHANASIUS, Rev. Terry L. Bradshaw. In Res., Revs. Robert L. Huber (Retired); James E. Wafzig (Retired).
Res.: 5915 Outer Loop Dr., 40219. Tel: 502-969-3332; Fax: 502-966-8948.
School—(Grades K-8) Tel: 502-969-2345; Fax: 502-969-8974. Diane Arrow, Prin. Lay Teachers 27; Students 442.
Catechesis/Religious Program—Students 83.

10—ST. AUGUSTINE, Rev. Paul A. Scaglione; Deacon John Churchill; Mrs. Genevieve Churchill, Pastoral Assoc.
Res.: 1310 W. Broadway, 40203. Tel: 502-584-4602; Fax: 502-581-0893.
Hines Center—Tel: 502-584-5463.

11—ST. BARNABAS, Revs. Wayne Jenkins; John A. Barker; Deacons James R. Plummer; Robert C. Bryant.
Parish Office—3042 Hikes Ln., 40220. Tel: 502-459-4251; Fax: 502-459-9815.
Res.: 3700 Mic Dale, 40220. Tel: 502-451-0333.
School—3044 Hikes Ln., 40220. Tel: 502-458-4038; Fax: 502-452-1117. Mary Helen Thompson, Prin. Lay Teachers 25; Students 310.
Catechesis/Religious Program—Pat Finck, D.R.E. Students 27.

12—ST. BARTHOLOMEW, Revs. Anthony L. Chandler, M.A.; Bertrand J. Rapp (Retired); Deacon Thomas E. Box; Mrs. Becky Box, Pastoral Assoc.
Parish Office—2042 Buechel Bank Rd., 40218. Tel: 502-499-0883; Fax: 502-499-0877.
Res.: 2040 Buechel Bank Rd., 40218. Tel: 502-499-0876.
School—2036 Buechel Bank Rd., 40218. Tel: 502-499-0421; Fax: 502-499-0421. Doris Swenson, Prin. Lay Teachers 16; Students 254.
Catechesis/Religious Program—Becky Box, D.R.E. Students 30.

13—ST. BASIL, Closed. For inquiries for parish records contact the chancery.

14—ST. BENEDICT, Closed. For inquiries for parish records contact the chancery.

15—ST. BERNARD, Rev. Robert L. Stuempel; Deacon Phillip Hettich.
Res.: 7500 Tangelo Dr., 40228. Tel: 502-239-5178; Fax: 502-239-9025.
School—7501 Tangelo Dr., 40228. Tel: 502-239-5178; Fax: 502-239-9025. Donald Matlock, Prin Lay Teachers 24; Students 395.
Catechesis/Religious Program—Tel: 502-239-5178, Ext. 125. Connie Tobbe, D.R.E. Students 70.

16—ST. BONIFACE, Rev. Timothy A. Hogan.
Parish Office:—531 E. Liberty St., 40202-1107. Tel: 502-584-4279; Fax: 502-584-8659.

17—ST. BRIGID, Revs. Donald R. Goetz; Joseph H. Voor (Retired).
Res.: 1520 Hepburn Ave., 40204. Tel: 502-584-5565; Fax: 502-584-1328.
Catechesis/Religious Program—1826 Edenside, 40204. Tel: 502-451-1420; Fax: 502-451-1429. Students 125.

18—ST. CECILIA, Rev. Joseph M. Fowler.
Res.: 338 N. 25th St. 40212. Tel: 502-772-3694; Fax: 502-772-3695.

19—ST. CHARLES BORROMEO, Closed. For inquiries for parish records contact the chancery.

20—CHRIST THE KING, Rev. John R. Burke.
Res.: 718 S. 44th St., 40211. Tel: 502-778-5055; Fax: 502-776-5120 (Call first).
Catechesis/Religious Program—Tel: 502-772-7851. Loueva Moss, D.R.E. Students 31.

21—ST. CLEMENT, Revs. Harry J. Gelthaus; Thomas E. Donohue (Retired).
Res.: 5431 Johnsontown Rd., 40272-3400. Tel: 502-937-5920; Fax: 502-937-5927.
School—5437 Johnsontown Rd., 40272. Tel: 502-937-1616; Fax: 502-995-3227. John Waldrop, Prin. Lay Teachers 13; Students 158.
Catechesis/Religious Program—Students 35.

22—ST. COLUMBA, Closed. For inquiries for parish records contact the chancery.

23—ST. DENIS, Rev. Donald L. Ryan; Deacon Robert M. Kampschaefer.
Res.: 4205 Cane Run Rd., 40216. Tel: 502-448-2961; Fax: 502-448-3656.
School—4209 Cane Run Rd., 40216. Tel: 502-447-5832; Fax: 502-447-5492. Elaine Wnorowski, Prin. Lay Teachers 10; Students 159.

24—ST. EDWARD, [CEM] Rev. Joseph T. Graffis; Mrs. Betty Deerwester, Pastoral Assoc.
Res.: 9608 Sue Helen Dr., 40299. Tel: 502-267-7494; Fax: 502-267-7495.
School—9610 Sue Helen Dr., 40299. Tel: 502-267-6633; Fax: 502-267-4474. Susan Jones, Prin. Lay Teachers 33; Students 563.
Catechesis/Religious Program—Deborah Grisanti, D.R.E. Students 75.

25—ST. ELIZABETH ANN SETON, Rev. Thomas A. Hommrich; Deacon James C. Olrich; Margee Joseph, Pastoral Assoc.
Res.: 11501 Maple Way, 40229. Tel: 502-969-0004 Parish; 502-966-3164 Rectory; Fax: 502-969-0553.

26—ST. ELIZABETH OF HUNGARY, Revs. J. Roy Stiles; Robert B. Gray (Retired); Herman J. Naber (Retired).
Res.: 1020 E. Burnett Ave., 40217. Tel: 502-636-3706; Fax: 502-636-3707.
School—St. Rose Catholic School, (Grades K-8), 1016 E. Burnett Ave., 40217. Tel: 502-634-1831; Fax: 502-634-0422. Anthony Riegling, Prin. Lay Teachers 9; Aides 2; Students 153.
Catechesis/Religious Program—2931 Pindell Ave., 40217. Tel: 502-635-5813. Students 72.

27—EPIPHANY, Rev. William S. Griner; Deacon Gary E. Becker.
Res.: 914 Old Harrods Creek Rd., 40223. Tel: 502-245-9733; Fax: 502-245-7658.
Catechesis/Religious Program—Students 264.

28—ST. FRANCES OF ROME, Rev. John G. Eifler; Sr.

Carmelita Dunn, S.C.N., Pastoral Assoc.; Deacon William Mullins.
Res.: 2119 Payne St., 40206. Tel: 502-896-8401; Fax: 502-895-0310.
Catechesis/Religious Program—Sr. Mary Jo Gramig, O.S.U., D.R.E. Students 42.

29—ST. FRANCIS OF ASSISI, Rev. Joseph M. Rankin; Deacon Walton G. Jones.
Res.: 1960 Bardstown Rd., 40205-1572. Tel: 502-456-6394; Fax: 502-456-9462.
School—1938 Alfresco Pl., 40205-1876. Tel: 502-459-3088; Fax: 502-456-9462. Katherine Schloemer, Prin. Lay Teachers 15; Students 240.
Catechesis/Religious Program—Tel: 502-456-6394.

30—ST. GABRIEL THE ARCHANGEL, Revs. John J. Stolz; Louis J. Meiman; Deacon William Skeeters.
Res.: 5505 Bardstown Rd., 40291. Tel: 502-239-5481; Fax: 502-239-7717.
School—5503 Bardstown Rd., 40291. Tel: 502-239-5535; Fax: 502-231-1404. Margaret Bowen, Prin. Lay Teachers 36; Students 765.
Catechesis/Religious Program—Gemma Wafzig, D.R.E. Students 117.

31—ST. GEORGE, Closed. For inquiries for parish records contact the chancery.

32—GUARDIAN ANGELS, Rev. Daniel Lobsinger, C.R.
Res.: 6000 Preston Hwy., 40219. Tel: 502-968-5421; Fax: 502-962-1080.
Catechesis/Religious Program—Students 38.

33—ST. HELEN, Rev. Thomas E. Gentile; Sr. Darlene Denton, O.S.U., Pastoral Assoc.
Res.: 4005 Dixie Hwy., 40216. Tel: 502-448-4008; Fax: 502-448-8546.
School—4007 Dixie Hwy., 40216. Tel: 502-447-9671; Fax: 502-447-0940. Diane Smith, Prin. Lay Teachers 12; Students 121.
Catechesis/Religious Program—Students 39.

34—HOLY CROSS, Closed. For inquiries for parish records contact the chancery.

35—HOLY FAMILY, Rev. H. Anthony Olges; Deacon James H. Abell.
Res.: 3926 Poplar Level Rd., 40213. Tel: 502-459-6066; Fax: 502-459-6066 (Call first).
School—3934 Poplar Level Rd., 40213. Tel: 502-458-4531; Fax: 502-456-9188. John Westerfield, Prin. Lay Teachers 17; Students 182.
Catechesis/Religious Program—Students 5.

36—HOLY NAME, Rev. John W. Birk.
Res.: 2914 S. 3rd St., 40208. Tel: 502-637-2058; Fax: 502-634-0819.

37—HOLY SPIRIT, Revs. Thomas A. Smith; Frank B. Grauel (Retired); Jeffrey D. Gatlin; Deacons Joseph A. Raibert; R. James Young.
Res.: 3345 Lexington Rd., 40206. Tel: 502-893-3982; Fax: 502-893-8287.
School—322 Cannons Ln., 40206. Tel: 502-893-7700; Fax: 502-893-8078. Bernadette Ritchey, Prin. Lay Teachers 25; Students 404.
Catechesis/Religious Program—Students 100.

38—HOLY TRINITY, Rev. Charles C. Thompson, J.C.L.
Pastoral Center—501 Cherrywood Rd., 40207. Tel: 502-897-5207; Fax: 502-897-0962.
School—423 Cherrywood Rd., 40207. Tel: 502-897-2785; Fax: 502-896-0990. Mrs. Mary Alice Zettel, Prin. Lay Teachers 40; Students 691.
Catechesis/Religious Program—Tel: 502-897-5207, Ext. 125. Dinah Tichy, D.R.E. Students 104.

39—ST. IGNATIUS, Rev. James R. Schook. In Res., Rev. Gerald L. Timmel (Retired).
Res.: 1816 Rangeland Rd., 40219. Tel: 502-964-5904; Fax: 502-964-5905.
St. Ignatius Child Development Center—1818 Rangeland Rd., 40219. Tel: 502-969-2336. Ms. Mary Lou McGarry, Dir. Lay Teachers 23; Students 96.
Catechesis/Religious Program—Students 35.

40—IMMACULATE HEART OF MARY, Rev. Louis J. Meiman.
Office—1545 S. 34th St., 40211. Tel: 502-774-5772; Fax: 502-774-5899.
Catechesis/Religious Program—Students 3.

41—INCARNATION, Rev. Christian Moore, O.F.M-.Conv.; Deacons Robert Markert; Frank O'Connell.
Res.: 2229 Lower Hunters Trace Rd., 40216. Tel: 502-447-2013; Fax: 502-448-3821.
Catechesis/Religious Program—Bev O'Connell, D.R.E. Students 44.

42—ST. JAMES, Revs. Donald R. Goetz; Joseph H. Voor (Retired).
Res.: 1826 Edenside Ave., 40204. Tel: 502-451-1420; Fax: 502-451-1429.
School—1818 Edenside Ave., 40204. Tel: 502-454-0330; Fax: 502-454-0330. Colette Dumstorf, Prin. Lay Teachers 7; Students 125.
Catechesis/Religious Program—Students 125.

43—ST. JEROME, Revs. Robert E. Ray; Isaac McDaniel; Anthony Chinh N'go; Deacon John Kromer.
Res.: 903 Fairdale Rd., Fairdale, 40118. Tel: 502-363-9929; Fax: 502-363-9960.
Catechesis/Religious Program—Students 75.

44—ST. JOHN, Closed. For inquiries for parish records contact the chancery.

45—ST. JOHN VIANNEY, Revs. Robert E. Ray; Anthony Chinh N'go; Deacon John T. Kromer; Sr. Betty Blandford, S.C.N., Pastoral Assoc.
Res.: 4839 Southside Dr., 40214. Tel: 502-366-5517; Fax: 502-366-3544.
Catechesis/Religious Program—Mr. Tom Morton, D.R.E. Students 114.

46—ST. JOSEPH, Rev. John L. Schindler.
Res.: 1406 E. Washington St., 40206. Tel: 502-583-7401; Fax: 502-589-7465.
Catechesis/Religious Program—Tel: 502-583-0892. Students 40.

47—ST. LAWRENCE, Rev. Jeffrey S. Nicolas; Sr. Ann Marie Howard, O.S.B., Pastoral Assoc.; Deacon David Dalton.
Res.: 1925 Lewiston Dr., 40216. Tel: 502-448-2122; Fax: 502-448-2163.
School—1927 Lewiston Dr., 40216. Tel: 502-447-3155; Fax: 502-448-2163. Bernice Scherr, Prin. Religious 1; Lay Teachers 24; Students 411.
Catechesis/Religious Program— Sr. Ann Marie Howard, O.S.B., D.R.E. Students 40.

48—ST. LEO THE GREAT, Closed. For inquiries for parish records contact the chancery.

49—ST. LEONARD, Rev. R. Dale Cieslik; Sr. Rosella McCormick, O.S.U.
Res.: 440 Zorn Ave., 40206. Tel: 502-897-2595; Fax: 502-896-8259.
School—Tel: 502-897-5265. Tom Schmitt, Prin. Lay Teachers 15; Students 176.
Catechesis/Religious Program—Students 15.

50—ST. LOUIS BERTRAND, Revs. Charles H. O'Brien, O.P.; George G. Christian, O.P.; Robert R. Blais, O.P.; J. Peter Gerhard, O.P.; Joseph C. Burns, O.P.; Francis Ralph, O.P.
Res.: 1104 S. 6th St., 40203. Tel: 502-583-4448; Fax: 502-583-6874.
Shrine—Lourdes Rosary Shrine, Inc., Tel: 502-583-1950; Fax: 502-589-0056.
Shrine—Blessed Margaret Castello Shrine, Tel: 502-583-1950; Fax: 502-589-0056.

51—ST. LUKE, Rev. Richard P. Berding; Deacon Charles Walther.
Res.: 4211 Jim Hawkins Dr., 40229. Tel: 502-969-3291; Fax: 502-969-1718.
Catechesis/Religious Program—Fran Sohl, D.R.E. Students 38.

52—ST. MARGARET MARY, Very Rev. Bernard J. Breen; Revs. R. Paul Beach; William J. Brennan (Retired); Deacon John L. Simpson.
Res.: 7813 Shelbyville Rd., 40222. Tel: 502-426-1588; Fax: 502-426-1503.
School—Tel: 502-426-2635; Fax: 502-426-1304. Charles F. Wittenberg, Prin. Lay Teachers 73; Students 649.
Catechesis/Religious Program—Students 96.

53—ST. MARTHA, Rev. John D. Deatrick; Deacons Ken Ward, Pastoral Assoc.; John P. Maher; Geoffrey Gnau.
Res.: 2825 Klondike Ln., 40218. Tel: 502-491-8535; Fax: 502-491-8536.
School—Tel: 502-491-3171; Fax: 502-495-6107. Sharon Dutton, Prin. Lay Teachers 30; Students 545.
Catechesis/Religious Program— Pamela M. Berry, D.R.E. Students 55.

54—ST. MARTIN, Rev. Dennis Cousens; Deacons Jarvis Jackson; Michael Murphy.
Res.: 639 S. Shelby St., 40202. Tel: 502-582-2827; Fax: 502-582-1780.
Catechesis/Religious Program—Students 90.

55—ST. MARTIN DE PORRES, Consolidated Rev. Michael Huggins; Sr. Dorothy Jackson, S.C.N., Pastoral Assoc.; Deacon James Turner, Pastoral Admin.
Mailing Address: 3112 W. Broadway, 40211. Tel: 502-778-1118; Fax: 502-778-0148. with St. Benedict, Louisville, St. Charles Borromeo, Louisville, and Holy Cross, Louisville, parishes.
Catechesis/Religious Program—Tel: 502-418-3447. Lillian Coleman, D.R.E.; M. Annette Mandley-Turner, D.R.E.; Mary Scott-Jones, D.R.E. Students 113.

56—ST. MARY (Bullitt Co.), Revs. Thomas A. Hommrich; Kenneth R. Fortener; Deacons Paul J. George; Kenneth J. Mitchell.
Res.: 299 Crestwood Ln., 40229. Tel: 502-957-3385; Fax: 502-957-2059.

57—ST. MARY MAGDALEN, , See separate listing under Oratories.

58—ST. MATTHIAS, Rev. Eugene Scheich; Sr. Joan Riedley, O.S.U., Pastoral Assoc.
Res.: 2208 Dixie Hwy., 40210. Tel: 502-776-3250.
Catechesis/Religious Program—Tel: 502-776-3333; Fax: 502-776-3250. Sr. Joan Riedley, D.R.E.; Lorain Kerr; Cindy Kerr; Mike Trainor. Students 21.

59—ST. MICHAEL, Rev. Gary G. Davis; Agnes Tompkins, Pastoral Assoc.; Deacon Martin Brown.
Res.: 12707 Taylorsville Rd., 40299. Tel: 502-266-5611; Fax: 502-267-4272.
School—(Grades PreK-7) Tel: 502-267-6155; Fax: 502-267-4272. Sheila Marstiller, Prin. Lay Teachers 27; Students 419.
Catechesis/Religious Program—Brenda Rickert, D.R.E. Students 165.

60—MOST BLESSED SACRAMENT, Rev. John U. Caskey; Deacons Harry Prestwood; John Simmons.
Res.: 3509 Taylor Blvd., 40215. Tel: 502-361-0149; Fax: 502-375-1076.
School—1128 Berry Blvd., 40215. Tel: 502-361-7103; Fax: 502-367-1513. Fred J. Klausing III, Prin. Sisters 1; Lay Teachers 11; Students 188.
Catechesis/Religious Program—Tel: 502-361-0960. Sandra Blanford, D.R.E. Students 22.

61—MOTHER OF GOOD COUNSEL, Rev. John T. Judie; Deacon Patrick Harris.
Res.: 8509 Westport Rd., 40242. Tel: 502-425-2210; Fax: 502-425-0941.
School—Tel: 502-425-2637; Fax: 502-425-2699. Elizabeth Lueke, Prin. Lay Teachers 27; Students 320.
Catechesis/Religious Program— Judy Keller, D.R.E. Students 78.

62—OUR LADY, Revs. Robert E. Reilly (Retired); Joseph M. Fowler; Deacon William Klump.
Res.: 3511 Rudd Ave., 40212. Tel: 502-776-4666; Fax: 502-776-7746.
Catechesis/Religious Program—Tel: 502-776-3923. Barbara Klump, D.R.E. Students 22.

63—OUR LADY HELP OF CHRISTIANS, Rev. William Joseph Scollard, C.R., Admin.
Res.: 13512 Dixie Hwy., 40272. Tel: 502-937-1818; Fax: 502-937-1818 (Call first).
Catechesis/Religious Program—Tel: 502-937-3675. Catherine Dunn, D.R.E. Students 20.
Mission—St. Patrick Church 1216 Main St., West Point, Hardin Co. 40177.

64—OUR LADY OF CONSOLATION, Rev. Donald W. Springman; Deacons Wayne Thieneman; Charles Beckmann.
Res.: 10801 Deering Rd., 40272. Tel: 502-937-2100; Fax: 502-937-2160.
School—10803 Deering Rd., 40272. Tel: 502-937-7400; Fax: 502-937-6588. Patricia Leonard, Prin. Lay Teachers 10; Students 166.
Catechesis/Religious Program—Students 170.

65—OUR LADY OF LOURDES, Revs. G. Nicholas Rice; William Miller; Deacons Norbert Miller; F. Eugene Waldon. In Res., Rev. Ronald J. Domhoff.
Res.: 508 Breckenridge Ln., 40207. Tel: 502-896-0241; Fax: 502-895-4535.
School—510 Breckenridge Ln., 40207. Tel: 502-895-5122; Fax: 502-893-5051. Laura Glaser, Prin. Lay Teachers 23; Students 462.
Catechesis/Religious Program—Tel: 502-896-0241, Ext. 13; 1. Mary Caroline Marchal, S.C., D.R.E.; Ann Pifer, D.R.E. Students 108.

66—OUR LADY OF MOUNT CARMEL, Revs. Joseph R. Atcher, O.Carm.; Cecil Pickert, O.Carm.
Res.: 5505 New Cut Rd., 40214. Tel: 502-366-5651; Fax: 502-368-9972.
School—5501 New Cut Rd., 40214. Tel: 502-368-8506. Carol Nord, Prin. Lay Teachers 25; Students 486.
Catechesis/Religious Program—Tel: 502-366-5996, Ext. 25. Sharon Schuhmam, D.R.E. Students 60.

67—OUR MOTHER OF SORROWS, Rev. Terry L. Langford.
Res.: 747 Harrison Ave., 40217. Tel: 502-637-7442; Fax: 502-637-3794.
School—(Grades PreK-8), 770 Eastern Pkwy., 40217. Tel: 502-637-7814; Fax: 502-636-0260. Sr. Sharon Marie Blank, O.S.F., Prin. Lay Teachers 14; Students (Grades K-8) 174; Students (Preschool) 9.

68—ST. PATRICK, Rev. Thomas L. Boland; Deacon Jack Conrad.
Res.: 1000 N. Beckley Station Rd., 40245-4550. Tel: 502-244-6083; Fax: 502-244-6083 (Call first).
School—Tel: 502-244-7083; Fax: 502-244-7083 (Call First). Mary Beth Bowling, Prin. Lay Teachers 37; Students 646.
Catechesis/Religious Program—Tel: 502-254-9472. Mary Hynes, D.R.E. Students 100.

69—ST. PAUL, Rev. Maurice Hayes, O.F.M.Conv. In Res., Revs. Simon D. Sauer, O.F.M.Conv.; Raymond Oosdyke, O.F.M.Conv. (GR); Benjamin Knopp, O.F.M.Conv.
Res.: 6901 Dixie Hwy., 40258. Tel: 502-935-1223; Fax: 502-933-7747.
School—Tel: 502-935-5511; Fax: 502-935-5596. Kevin Brever, Prin. Lay Teachers 12; Students 224.
Catechesis/Religious Program—Students 64.

70—ST. PETER CLAVER, Closed. For inquiries for parish records contact the chancery.

71—ST. PHILIP NERI, Closed. For inquiries for parish records contact the chancery.

72—ST. PIUS X, Rev. Charles D. Walker; Sr. Mary Elaine Zehnder, S.C.N., Pastoral Assoc.
Res.: 3521 Goldsmith Ln., 40220. Tel: 502-451-9300 (Office); 502-451-4124 (Rectory); Fax: 502-458-7109.
School—3525 Goldsmith Ln., 40220. Tel: 502-452-1712; Fax: 502-451-2462. Carolyn Zierer, Prin. Lay Teachers 26; Students 385.
Catechesis/Religious Program—Arthur Turner,

D.R.E.; Betsy Walsh, D.R.E. Students 48.

73—St. Polycarp, Rev. William P. Burks; Deacons Jon Hosch; Stephen Smith.
Res.: 7718 Columbine Dr., 40258. Tel: 502-935-4578; Fax: 502-935-4578.
School—7724 Columbine Dr., 40258. Tel: 502-935-4578, Ext. 237; Fax: 502-935-4578. Liz Kenobbie, Prin. Lay Teachers 22; Students 408.
Catechesis/Religious Program—Tel: 502-935-4578, Ext. 245. V. Sharon Cygan, D.R.E. Students 45.

74—St. Raphael the Archangel, Rev. James F. Hackett; Deacon Robert Dever, Pastoral Assoc.
Res.: 2121 Lancashire Ave., 40205. Tel: 502-458-2500.
Parish Offices—2141 Lancashire Ave, 40205. Tel: 502-458-2500; Fax: 502-458-8049.
School—2131 Lancashire Ave., 40205 Tel: 502-456-1541; Fax: 502-451-3632. Paul DeZarn, Prin. Lay Teachers 35; Students 585.
Catechesis/Religious Program—Students 10.

75—Resurrection D.N.J.C., Closed. For inquiries for parish records contact the chancery.

76—St. Rita, Revs. William J. Martin; John W. Curran, O.F.M. Conv.; Thomas A. Smith, O.F.M-.Conv.; Deacon Charles "Mack" Nevitt, Pastoral Assoc.
Res.: 8709 Preston Hwy., 40219. Tel: 502-969-4579; Fax: 502-969-3679.
School—Tel: 502-969-7067; Fax: 502-969-3679. Mary Lee Lanning, Prin. Sisters 1; Lay Teachers 23; Students 402.
Catechesis/Religious Program—Tel: 502-962-7799, Ext. 107. Students 100.

77—SS. Simon and Jude, Rev. William F. Wagner; Sr. Ann Carol Mann, S.C.N., Pastoral Assoc.
Res.: 4335 Hazelwood Ave., 40215. Tel: 502-368-4887; Fax: 502-375-1988.
School—4333 Hazelwood Ave., 40215. Tel: 502-366-2424; Fax: 502-366-0208. Michelle Duvall, Prin. Lay Teachers 15; Students 209.
Catechesis/Religious Program—Students 20.

78—St. Stephen, Martyr, Revs. James J. Lichtefeld (Retired); J. Randall Hubbard; Deacon Sylvester Nitzken.
Res.: 1000 English Ave., 40217. Tel: 502-635-5813; Fax: 502-635-5888.
School—2931 Pindell, 40217. Tel: 502-635-7141. Evelyn Kalbhin, Interim Prin. Lay Teachers 23; Students 352.
Catechesis/Religious Program—Students 30.

79—St. Therese, Revs. J. Roy Stiles; Robert B. Gray (Retired); Herman J. Naber (Retired).
Res.: 1010 Schiller Ave., 40204. Tel: 502-634-3671; Fax: 502-634-3672.
Catechesis/Religious Program—Students 20.

80—St. Thomas More, Rev. James Wayne Murphy; Deacons Michael A. Tolbert; Terry Maguire.
Res.: 6105 S. Third St., 40214. Tel: 502-366-1463; Fax: 502-366-1464.
School—226 Inverness Ave., 40214. Tel: 502-363-3719. Mrs. Donna Sansone, Prin. Lay Teachers 10; Students 198.
Catechesis/Religious Program—Tel: 502-363-3719, Ext. 22. Diane Hoagland, D.R.E. Students 34.

81—St. Timothy, Rev. William Joseph Scollard, C.R.; Deacon Philip Tremblay, C.R.
Res.: 10300 Lower River Rd., 40272. Tel: 502-937-1238; Fax: 502-995-0482.

82—St. Vincent de Paul, , See separate listing under Oratories.

83—St. William, Rev. John R. Burke; Sharan A. Benton, Pastoral Admin.
Res.: 1226 W. Oak St., 40210. Tel: 502-635-6307; Fax: 502-635-6307 (Call first).
Catechesis/Religious Program—Students 31.

OUTSIDE THE CITY OF LOUISVILLE

Albany, Clinton Co., Emmanuel Catholic, Rev. Lawrence J. Gelthaus.
Res.: Hwy. 127 N., P.O. Box 126, 42602. Tel: 606-387-7251.
Catechesis/Religious Program—Students 20
Mission—Holy Cross Catholic 264 Glasgow Rd., P.O. Box 197, Burkesville, Cumberland Co. 42717. Tel: 270-864-4107; Fax: 270-864-4107 (Call First).

Bardstown, Nelson Co.

1—Basilica of St. Joseph Proto-Cathedral, [CEM] Revs. William F. Medley; Brian A. Kenney; Deacons Richard J. Walsh; John Hamilton. In Res., Rev. C. Joseph Batcheldor (Retired).
Res.: P.O. Box 548, 310 W. Stephen Foster Ave., 40004. Tel: 502-348-3126; Fax: 502-349-0941.
School—320 W. Stephen Foster Ave., 40004 Tel: 502-348-5994; Fax: 502-348-4694. Mary Spalding, Prin. Sisters of Charity of Nazareth 2; Lay Teachers 27; Students 415.
High School—Bethlehem High School, 309 W. Stephen Foster Ave., 40004. Tel: 502-348-8594; Fax: 502-349-1247. Religious 1; Lay Teachers 22; Students 288.
Catechesis/Religious Program—Students 154.

2—St. Monica, Rev. Stephen A. Pohl; Deacon Samuel R. Filiatreau, Pastoral Admin.
Res.: 407 S. Third St., 40004. Tel: 502-348-5250; Fax: 502-348-3635.

Brandenburg, Meade Co., St. John the Apostle, [CEM] Rev. Philip L. Erickson; Sr. Justina Heneghan, R.S.M., Pastoral Admin.; Deacon J. Michael Jones.
Res.: 491 E. Broadway, 40108. Tel: 270-422-2196; Fax: 270-422-2471.
School—513 E. Broadway, 40108 Tel: 270-422-2088 Fax: 270-422-5716. Sr. Lucilla Mangion, Prin. Augustinian Sisters, Servants of Jesus and Mary 3; Lay Teachers 6; Students 135.
Catechesis/Religious Program—Monica Lucas, D.R.E. Students 242.

Calvary, Marion Co., Holy Name of Mary, [CEM] Rev. David W. Naylor.
Res.: 3265 Hwy. 208, Lebanon, 40033. Tel: 270-692-2298; Fax: 270-692-5708.
Catechesis/Religious Program—Students 145.
Mission—Our Lady of Fatima Phillipsburg, Marion Co.
Station—Parish Center Lebanon. Tel: 270-692-6491.

Campbellsville, Taylor Co., Our Lady of Perpetual Help, [CEM] Rev. Jeffrey P. Leger; Deacon Joseph Ohnemus.
Office—425 N. Central Ave., 42719. Tel: 270-465-4282; Fax: 270-789-9669.
Catechesis/Religious Program—Linda Ohnemus, D.R.E. Students 58.

Cecilia, Hardin Co., St. Ambrose, Rev. Stanley L. Osborne, Admin.
Res.: c/o 657 St. John Church Rd., Elizabethtown, 42701. Tel: 270-862-9816.
Catechesis/Religious Program—Students 4.

Clementsville, Casey Co., St. Bernard, Rev. Thomas R. Clark.
Res.: 5075 Ky 551, Liberty, 42539. Tel: 606-787-7570.
Catechesis/Religious Program—Tel: 606-787-6600. Sue Goode, D.R.E. Students 46.
Mission—Sacred Heart c/o 5075 KY 551, Liberty, Casey Co. 42539. Tel: 606-787-7324.

Culvertown, Nelson Co., Immaculate Conception, Rev. Lawrence H. Lindle (Retired); Deacon William A. Downs.
Res.: 8191 New Haven Rd., New Haven, 40051-6030. Tel: 502-549-3757; Fax: 502-549-7258.

Edmonton, Metcalfe Co., Christ the Healer, Rev. Kevin J. Bryan, Admin.
Res.: 1610 W. Stockton St., 42129. Tel: 270-432-5024.
Catechesis/Religious Program—Tel: 270-678-6280. Jerry Strange, D.R.E. Students 6.
Mission—Christ the King P.O. Box 518, Tompkinsville, Monroe Co. 42167. Tel: 270-487-8881.

Elizabethtown, Hardin Co., St. James [CEM] Revs. J. Richard Sullivan; Peter Quan Do; Deacons Jay Jenkins; Joseph Chathaparampil; William Clark.
Res.: 307 W. Dixie Ave., 42701. Tel: 270-765-6268; Fax: 270-234-9598.
School—114 N. Miles St., 42701. Tel: 270-765-7011; Fax: 270-769-5745. Sr. Michael Marie Friedman, Prin. Religious Teachers 1; Lay Teachers 27; Students 416.
Catechesis/Religious Program—Margaret Polin, D.R.E.; Cindy McKinley, D.R.E. Students 175.

Fairfield, Nelson Co., St. Michael, [CEM] Revs. Joseph E. Vest; Albert J. Hartlage (Retired).
Res.: P.O. Box 27, 40020. Tel: 502-252-8308.
Catechesis/Religious Program—111 Church St., P.O. Box 20, 40020. Tel: 502-252-8051. Gilly Simpson, D.R.E. Students 97.
Mission—All Saints Church [CEM] 410 W. Main St., P.O. Box 531, Taylorsville, Spencer Co 40071. Tel: 502-477-6676.

Finley, Taylor Co., Our Lady of the Hills, [CEM] Rev. Jeffrey P. Leger.
Office—425 N. Central Ave., Campbellsville, 42718. Tel: 270-465-4282; Fax: 270-789-9669.
Catechesis/Religious Program—Students 70.

Flaherty, Meade Co., St. Martin of Tours, [CEM] Revs. Christopher M. Scalise; Robert N. Mills (Retired); Deacons John R. Whelan; Robert Hall.
Res.: 440 Saint Martin Rd., Vine Grove, 40175. Tel: 270-828-2552; Fax: 270-828-2562.
Catechesis/Religious Program—Tel: 270-828-8484. Sr. Patricia Rae McNamara, O.P., D.R.E. Students 176.

Glasgow, Barren Co., St. Helen, Revs. Joel C. Rogers, C.P.M. Charles Zmudzinski, C.P.M.; Deacon Lee Bidwell.
Res.: 103 W. Brown St., 42141. Tel: 270-651-5263; Fax: 270-651-1373.
Mission—Our Lady of the Caves Church Rte. 31 W., Horse Cave, Hart Co. 42749. Tel: 270-786-1188.

Goshen, Oldham Co., Transfiguration of Our Lord, Rev. Herbert L. Lattis.
Res.: 1620 S. Hwy. 1793, 40026. Tel: 502-228-3665; Fax: 502-228-0355.
Catechesis/Religious Program—Tel: 502-228-3665, Ext. 8305. Robert Sugrue, D.R.E. Students 199.

Greensburg, Green Co., Holy Redeemer, Rev. Jeffrey P. Leger; Deacon Joseph Ohnemus.
Mailing Address: *Office*, 425 N. Central Ave., Campbellsville, 42718-0484. Tel: 270-465-4282; Fax: 270-789-9669.
Church: 110 Industrial Rd., 42743.
Catechesis/Religious Program—Students 4.

Hodgenville, Larue Co., Our Lady of Mercy, [CEM] Rev. James T. Mudd.
Res.: 208 Walters Ave., 42748. Tel: 270-358-4697; Fax: 270-358-3601 (Call First).
Catechesis/Religious Program—Tel: 270-325-3801. Bob Ernst, D.R.E. Students 119.

Holy Cross, Marion Co., Holy Cross, [CEM] Rev. R. Joseph Hemmerle.
Res.: 3560 N. Saint Francis Rd., Loretto, 40037. Tel: 270-865-2521; Fax: 270-865-2071.
Catechesis/Religious Program—Carol Blanford, D.R.E. Students 84.

Howardstown, Nelson Co., St. Ann, [CEM] Rev. James T. Mudd, Admin.
Res.: 7490 Howardstown Rd., 40051. Tel: 502-549-3285.
School—(Grades 1-8) Tel: 502-549-7310. Lois Cecil, Prin. Lay Teachers 4; Students 50.

Jamestown, Russell Co., Holy Spirit, Rev. Daniel L. Lincoln; Sr. Karen Freund, O.P., Pastoral Assoc.
Res.: 406 N. Main St., P.O. Box 247, 42629. Tel: 270-343-3346.
Catechesis/Religious Program—Students 24.
Mission—Good Shepherd P.O. Box 354, Columbia, Adair Co. 42728. Tel: 270-384-4528. Sr. Marilyn Schatz, O.L.M.V., Pastoral Assoc.

LaGrange, Oldham Co., Immaculate Conception, Very Rev. J. Mark Spalding; Rev. John Tran; Deacon Kenneth Carter.
Res.: 502 N. Fifth St., 40031. Tel: 502-222-0255; Fax: 502-225-9844.
School—Tel: 502-222-0671; Fax: 502-222-0604. Gayle Bauch, Prin. Lay Teachers 9; Students 153.
Catechesis/Religious Program—Ms. M. Charlene Davis, D.R.E. Students 259.
Station—Luther Luckett Correctional Center, Tel: 502-222-0363.
Station—Kentucky State Reformatory, Tel: 502-222-9441.
Station—Roederer Farm Prison, Tel: 502-222-0173.
Station—Cedar Lake Lodge, Tel: 502-222-7157.
Station—Tri-County Community Hospital, Tel: 502-222-5388.

Lebanon Junction, Bullitt Co., St. Benedict, Revs. T. Michael Tobin; Ivo E. Cecil (Retired).
Res.: 139 N. Brook St., 40150. Tel: 502-833-4886; Fax: 502-833-4886 (Call first).
Catechesis/Religious Program—Students 37.
Mission—St. Clare [CEM], See separate listing under Oratories.

Lebanon, Marion Co., St. Augustine, [CEM] Revs. Gerald L. Bell; David Sanchez; Deacon Tom Mattingly.
Res.: 235 S. Spalding Ave., 40033. Tel: 270-692-3019; Fax: 270-692-5532.
School—(Grades PreK-8) Tel: 270-692-2063; Fax: 270-692-6597. Sr. Rose Riley, S.C.N., Prin. Lay Teachers 13; Students 199.
Catechesis/Religious Program—Tel: 270-692-9009. Kathy Shannon, D.R.E. Students 253.

Mount Washington, Bullitt Co., St. Francis Xavier, [CEM] Rev. Scott J. Wimsett; Cathy Blandford, Pastoral Assoc.; Deacon Martin J. Brown.
Res.: 155 Stringer Ln., 40047. Tel: 502-538-4933; Fax: 502-955-0449.
Catechesis/Religious Program—Tel: 502-538-0672; Fax: 502-455-0449. Mary Morris, D.R.E. Students 230.

New Haven, Nelson Co., St. Catherine, [CEM] Rev. Clarence J. Howard; Deacon George B. Clark.
Res.: 174 N. Main St., P.O. Box 88, 40051. Tel: 502-549-3152; Fax: 502-549-5410.
School—413 First St., P.O. Box 88, 40051. Tel: 502-549-3680; Fax: 502-549-5410. Eric Hardin, Prin. Lay Teachers 10; Students 213.
Catechesis/Religious Program—George Kaissiah, D.R.E. Students 12.

New Hope, Nelson Co., St. Vincent de Paul, [CEM] Rev. James W. Graf, Admin.; Deacon Edward J. Hutchins.
Mailing Address: 108 Main St., Raywick, 40060. Tel: 270-692-2245; Fax: 270-692-1138.
Church: 101 Church St., 40052.
Catechesis/Religious Program—Students 35.

Payneville, Meade Co., St. Mary Magdalen of Pazzi, [CEM] Rev. Robert M. Abel; Deacon Ernest Singer.
Res.: P.O. Box 110, Hwy. 376, 40157. Tel: 270-496-4333; Fax: 270-496-4790.
Catechesis/Religious Program—Tel: 270-422-3345. Rose Etta Pike, D.R.E. Students 85.

Pewee Valley, Oldham Co., St. Aloysius, [CEM] Revs. John Schwartzlose; John A. Caldwell; Deacon

John W. Dant.
Res.: 212 Mount Mercy Dr., P.O. Box 468, 40056. Tel: 502-241-8452; Fax: 502-243-1740.
School—208 Mt. Mercy Dr., 40056. Tel: 502-241-8516; Fax: 502-243-2241. Rita Yates, Prin. Lay Teachers 29; Students 456.
Catechesis/Religious Program—Tel: 502-241-8452, Ext. 104. Paul Stokell, D.R.E. Students 237.
Station—Kentucky Correctional Institute for Women, Tel: 502-241-8454.
Station—Friendship Manor Nursing Home, Tel: 502-241-8821.

RADCLIFF, HARDIN CO., ST. CHRISTOPHER, [CEM] Rev. Patrick J. Dolan, Ph.D., S.T.D.; Deacon Robert Imel.
Res.: 1225 S. Wilson Rd., 40160. Tel: 270-351-3706; Fax: 270-351-3934.
School—1181 S. Wilson Rd., 40160. Tel: 270-351-3150; Fax: 270-351-3934. Janet Morgan, Prin. Lay Teachers 11; Students 158.
Catechesis/Religious Program—Students 110.

RAYWICK, MARION CO., ST. FRANCIS XAVIER CHURCH, [CEM] Rev. James W. Graf.
Res.: 108 Main St., 40060. Tel: 270-692-2245; Fax: 270-692-1138.
Catechesis/Religious Program—Students 83.

RHODELIA, MEADE CO., ST. THERESA, [CEM] Revs. Robert M. Abel; Albert L. Wilson, Pastor Emeritus (Retired).
Res.: 9245 Rhodelia Rd., Payneville, 40157. Tel: 270-496-4343; Fax: 270-496-4416.
Catechesis/Religious Program—Students 49.
Convent—Sisters of Charity of Nazareth, Tel: 270-496-4314.

ST. FRANCIS, MARION CO., ST. FRANCIS OF ASSISI, [CEM] Rev. R. Joseph Hemmerle.
Res.: 6785 Hwy. 52, 40062. Tel: 270-865-2521; Fax: 270-865-2071.
Catechesis/Religious Program—Students 115.

ST. JOHN, HARDIN CO., ST. JOHN THE BAPTIST, [CEM] Rev. Stanley L. Osborne; Deacon Michael Vessels.
Res.: 657 St. John Church Rd., Elizabethtown, 42701. Tel: 270-862-9816.
Catechesis/Religious Program—Tel: 270-862-3005. Lisa Thomas, D.R.E. Students 95.

ST. JOSEPH, MARION CO., ST. JOSEPH, Closed. For inquiries for parish records contact the chancery.

ST. MARY, MARION CO., ST. CHARLES, [CEM] Rev. Gary Young, C.R.; Sr. Marlene Lehmkuhl, S.C.N., Pastoral Admin.
Res.: 675 Hwy. 327, Lebanon, 40033. Tel: 270-692-4513; Fax: 270-692-6204.
Catechesis/Religious Program—Students 142.

ST. THOMAS, NELSON CO., ST. THOMAS, Rev. Stephen A. Pohl.
Res.: 870 Saint Thomas Ln., Bardstown, 40004. Tel: 502-348-3717; Fax: 502-348-1905.
Catechesis/Religious Program—Students 85.

SAMUELS, NELSON CO., ST. GREGORY, [CEM] Rev. John Schwartzlose; Deacons Joseph E. Livers; Joseph H. Filiatreau.
Parish Office:—330 Samuels Loop, Cox's Creek, 40013. Tel: 502-348-6337; Fax: 502-348-5784.
School—350 Samuel's Loop, Cox's Creek, 40013. Tel: 502-348-9583; Fax: 502-348-9597. Paula Cecil, Prin. Lay Teachers 11; Students 225.
Catechesis/Religious Program—Students 150.

SHELBYVILLE, SHELBY CO., ANNUNCIATION OF THE BLESSED VIRGIN MARY, Rev. William M. Bowling; Deacons John Shoulta; Brendan Kinsella; Charles Brown.
Res.: 105 W. Main St., 40065. Tel: 502-633-1547; Fax: 502-633-1547 (Call first).
Catechesis/Religious Program—Tel: 502-633-1547. Debbie Mudd, D.R.E. Students 135.
Mission—St. John Chrysostom 122 Penn St., Eminence, Henry Co. 40019. Tel: 502-845-7005. Rev. Patrick D. Delahanty.

SHEPHERDSVILLE, BULLITT CO., ST. ALOYSIUS, Revs. T. Michael Tobin; Ivo E. Cecil (Retired).
Res.: 187 Plum St., 40165. Tel: 502-543-5918; 502-955-6370; Fax: 502-955-6370 (Call First).
School—197 Plum St., 40165. Tel: 502-543-6721; Fax: 502-955-1490. Iris Whitney, Prin. Lay Teachers 9; Students 198.
Catechesis/Religious Program—Tel: 502-543-5918; Fax: 502-955-6370. Theresa Secord, D.R.E. Students 22.

SPRINGFIELD, WASHINGTON CO.
1—ST. DOMINIC, [CEM] Rev. Trumie C. Elliott.
Res.: 303 W. Main St., 40069. Tel: 859-336-3569; Fax: 859-336-3549.
School—309 W. Main St., 40069. Tel: 859-336-7165; Fax: 859-336-7169. Pamela Breunig, Prin. Lay Teachers 10; Students 196.
Catechesis/Religious Program—Students 48.
2—HOLY ROSARY, Rev. Charles E. Reteneller; Deacon Ernest Cooper, Pastoral Admin.
Mailing Address: Box 146, 40069. Tel: 859-336-3898; Fax: 859-336-3898 (Call first).
Catechesis/Religious Program—378 Rosary Hgts., 40069. Pamela Grundy, D.R.E.
3—HOLY TRINITY, [CEM] Rev. John Christopher Allegra.
Res.: 306 Fredericktown Rd., 40069. Tel: 859-284-5242.
Catechesis/Religious Program—Tel: 859-284-7894. Jill Clements, D.R.E. Students 120.
Mission—Holy Rosary [CEM] 306 Fredericktown Rd., Manton, Washington Co. 40069.
4—ST. ROSE, [CEM] Revs. Stephen Dominic Hayes, O.P.; Thomas Bernard Smith, O.P.; James Stephen Murray, O.P.
Res.: Hwy. 152, P.O. Box 71, 40069. Tel: 859-336-3121; Fax: 859-336-3841.

VINE GROVE, HARDIN CO., ST. BRIGID, [CEM] Rev. Christopher M. Scalise, Admin.; Deacon Robert Caspar.
Res.: 306 E. Main St., 40175. Tel: 270-877-2461; Fax: 270-877-2523.
School—310 E. Main St., 40175. Tel: 270-877-2451; Fax: 270-877-6864. Wayland Johnston, Prin. Lay Teachers 6; Students 78.
Catechesis/Religious Program—Students 85.

WHITE MILLS, HARDIN CO., ST. IGNATIUS, [CEM] Revs. J. Richard Sullivan; Peter Quan Do; Deacon Jay Jenkins.
Mailing Address: P.O. Box 67, 42788. Tel: 270-369-6279.
Res.: 307 W. Dixie Ave., Elizabethtown, 42701. Tel: 270-765-6268; Fax: 270-737-5661.
Catechesis/Religious Program—Deborah Huffman, D.R.E. Tel: 270-369-9305; Vanessa Huffman, D.R.E. Tel: 270-369-8041. Consolidated with St. James Parish, Elizabethtown, KY.

ORATORIES

LOUISVILLE, JEFFERSON CO.
1—ST. MARY MAGDALEN, Closed. For inquiries for parish records contact the chancery.
2—ST. VINCENT DE PAUL, Closed., For inquiries for parish records contact St. Elizabeth of Hungary, Louisville.

COLESBURG, HARDIN CO., ST. CLARE, Closed., For inquiries for parish records contact St. Benedict, Lebanon Junction.

Chaplains of Public Institutions
For hospitals, contact Office for Pastoral Care, 1200 S. Shelby St., Louisville, KY 40203; Tel: 502-636-0296; Fax: 502-636-2379.

On Duty Outside the Archdiocese:
Revs.—
Branch, Edward B., Catholic Center at Atlanta University Complex, 809 Beckwith St., S.W., Atlanta, GA 30314. Tel: 404-755-2646 Office of Campus Ministry
Dittmeier, Charles R., Maryknoll, P.O.Box 632, Phnom Penh, Cambodia.
Hamilton, Mark M., Sacred Heart Major Seminary, 2701 Chicago Blvd., Detroit, MI 48206.
Hayden, Joseph F., Parroquia Santa Rosa De Lima, Apartado 159, Chimbote, Peru. Tel: 011-51-44-322713
Merkt, Joseph T. (OWN), 515.5 St. Ann St., Owensboro, 42303.

Graduate Studies:
Revs.—
Bromwich, James S., Mundelein Seminary, 1000 E. Maple Ave., Mundelein, IL 60060.
Klotter, Frederick W., North American College, Rome, Italy.

Military Chaplains:
Rev.—
Brown, Benedict J., U.S. Navy

Unassigned:
Revs.—
Mouser, J. Irvin, 515 Nerinx Rd., Loretto, 40049.
Spalding, Francis Larry, 3316 Pinehurst Dr., Holiday, FL 34691.

Retired:
Rev. Msgrs.—
Horrigan, Alfred F., Christopher East Health Care Facility, 4200 Browns Ln., 40220.
O'Bryan, J. A., Sacred Heart Village, 2120 Payne St., 40206.
Revs.—
Batcheldor, C. Joseph, St. Joseph Church, P.O.Box 548, Bardstown, 40004.
Bindner, Charles J., 1723 Parkridge Pkwy., 40214.
Birkel, Robert C., Christopher East Nursing Facility, 4200 Browns Ln., 40220.
Brennan, William J., St. Margaret Mary Church, 7813 Shelbyville Rd., 40222.
Brian, Bertrand J., Nazareth Village II, P.O. Box 2000, #22, Nazareth, 40048.
Brown, Robert A., Sacred Heart Village, 2120 Payne St., 40206.
Butler, John J., 3115 Lexington Rd., 40206.
Cecil, Ivo E., 1080 Optimist Rd., Lebanon Junction, 40150.
Craycroft, Bernard L., 388 University Dr., Radcliff, 40160.
Craycroft, George P., 229 N. Main St., New Haven, 40051.
Dalton, John A., 1176 Castlevale Dr. #4, 40217.
Dawson, Joseph I., 340 Causeway Blvd., Dunedin, FL 34698.
Dentinger, Roy E., 3030 Breckenridge Ln., Bldg. 1, Apt. 501, 40220.
Dentinger, Vincent Paul, Nazareth Village, #8, P.O. Box 2000, Nazareth, 40048.
Dickman, John W., Sacred Heart Village, 2120 Payne St., 40206.
Donohue, Thomas E., 9104 Mahoney Dr., 40258.
Eimer, Frank J., 3426 Pemaquid Rd., 40218.
Flynn, James E., St. Mary Church, P. O. Box 669, Park City, UT 84060.
Gephart, John B., Bishop David Apartments, 5146 Dixie Hwy., 40216.
Grauel, Frank B., Holy Spirit Church, 3345 Lexington Rd., 40206.
Gray, Robert B., St. Elizabeth, 1020 E. Burnett, 40217.
Hanrahan, John W., 1170 Castlevale Dr., #3, 40217.
Hartlage, Albert J., P.O. Box 27, Fairfield, 40020.
Hartlage, William C., Bishop David Apartments, 5146 Dixie Hwy., 40216.
Hendricks, James P., Sacred Heart Village, 2120 Payne St., 40206.
Hendrickson, Frederick, 8021 Edsel Ln., 40291.
Hogan, William E., 3320 Bardstown Rd., Apt. 52, 40218.
Howard, Anthony, 6304 Southside Dr., 40214.
Huber, Robert L., 5915 Outer Loop Dr., 40219.
Jones, John E., 1697 Taylor Wood Rd., Simpsonville, 40067.
Kamber, Kenneth L., 4029 Busath Ave., 40218.
Lenahan, John B., 1286 Parkway Gardens Ct.# 224, 40217.
Lichtefeld, James J., 1278 Parkway Gardens Ct., #227, 40217.
Lindle, Lawrence H., 8191 New Haven Road, New Haven, 40051.
Lyon, Joseph A., Doe Valley Park, 228 Pine Ridge Pk., Brandenburg, 40108.
Magel, John E., Bishop David Apartments, 5146 Dixie Hwy., 40216.
Mills, Robert N., 5500 Hwy. 111, S.E., Elizabeth, IN 47117.
Naber, Herman J., 1020 E. Burnett Ave., 40217.
Nord, Clarence C., 2820 Flora Ave., #15, 40220.
Osborne, Robert E., 3910 Village Green Dr., 40299.
Pank, Julian F., 2832 Pomeroy Dr., 40218.
Rapp, Bertrand J., 2042 Buechel Bank Rd., 40218.
Reilly, Robert E., 3511 Rudd Ave., 40212.
Smith, F. Harold, P. O. Box 15, Versailles, OH 45380.
Spalding, Leon C., P. O. Box 6264, Clearwater, FL 33758.
Stuecker, Henry C., Sacred Heart Village, 2120 Payne St., 40206.
Thompson, James W., Franciscan Health Care Center, 3625 Fern Valley Rd., 40219.
Timmel, Gerald L., 1816 Rangeland Rd., 40219.
Volpert, Robert C., 3004 Aspenwood Way, 40241.
Voor, Joseph H., St. James Church, 1826 Edenside Ave., 40204.
Wafzig, James E., 5915 Outer Loop, 40219.
Wilson, Albert L., 980 Ray Rd., Payneville, 40157.
Zahner, William, Sacred Heart Village, 2120 Payne St., 40206.
Zoeller, Eugene, 3920 Manner Dale Dr., 40220.

Permanent Deacons:
Abell, James H., Holy Family, Louisville
Becker, Gary E., Epiphany
Beckmann, Charles, Our Lady of Consolation, Louisville
Bell, Kenneth, (On Leave)
Benton, James L., (On Leave)
Bidwell, Lee G., St. Helen, Glasgow
Bishop, Joseph C., St. Dominic/Holy Rosary, Springfield
Bissig, Paul F., (On Leave)
Box, Thomas E., St. Bartholomew, Louisville
Brown, Charles K., Annunciation, Shelbyville
Brown, Martin J., St. Michael, Louisville
Bryant, Robert C., St. Barnabas, Louisville; Jefferson County Jail
Burns, Robert L., Central State Hospital, La Grange
Carney, Edward P., Nazareth Home, Louisville
Carter, Kenneth, Immaculate Conception, La Grange
Caspar, Robert J., St. Brigid, Vine Grove
Chathaparampil, Joseph, St. James Church, Elizabethtown
Churchill, John R., St. Augustine, Louisville

Clark, George B., St. Catherine, New Haven
Clark, William V., St. James, Elizabethtown
Collard, Paul J., (Retired)
Conrad, Jack
Cooper, Ernest A., Holy Rosary, Springfield
Cottrell, Francis E., Our Lady Help of Christians, Louisville; Kentucky State Correctional Facility
Dalton, David L., Dismas Charities, St. Lawrence
Dant, John W., St. Aloysius, Pewee Valley
Dant, Joseph R., (Unassigned)
Dever, Robert Glen, St. Raphael, Louisville
Dew, Joseph M., Cursillo
Downs, William A., Immaculate Conception, Culvertown
Edwards, Michael, Ascension, Louisville
Fante, Lamar W., (Retired)
Fargen, J. Jerome, (Retired)
Filiatreau, Joseph H., St. Gregory, Samuels
Filiatreau, Samuel R., St. Monica, Bardstown
Flowers, Donald K., St. Dominic, Springfield
George, Paul J., St. Mary, Louisville
Gnau, William G., St. Martha, Louisville
Hall, Robert, Dir., Permanent Diaconate Office, St. Martin of Tours, Flaherty
Hamilton, John, St. Joseph, Bardstown
Harris, Patrick D., Mother of Good Counsel, Louisville
Hasson, Anthony P., (Retired)
Hettich, Philip, St. Bernard, Louisville; Jefferson County Jail
Higgins, Frederick, (Retired)
Hosch, Jon E., St. Polycarp, Louisville
Houck, Peter L., (Retired)
Hutchins, Joseph E., St. Vincent De Paul, New Hope
Imel, Robert, St. Christopher, Radcliff
Ishmael, Raymond L., (Retired)
Jackson, Jarvis, St. Martin of Tours, Louisville
Jenkins, Jay R., St. James, Elizabethtown
Jones, J. Michael, St. John the Apostle, Brandenburg
Jones, Walton G., St. Francis of Assisi, Louisville
Kampschaefer, Robert M., St. Denis, Louisville
Karley, Brian, Dir., Office of Clergy Personnel
Kinsella, Brendan, Annunciation, Shelbyville
Klump, William R., Church of Our Lady, Louisville
Kromer, John T.
Lincoln, James Bruce, St. Barnabas, Louisville
Livers, Joseph E., St. Gregory, Samuels
Maguire, Terry, St. Thomas More, Louisville
Maher, John P., St. Martha, Louisville
Markert, Clarence Robert, Incarnation, Louisville
Masterson, Donald E., Jefferson County Youth Facility
Mattingly, Thomas, (Retired), St. Augustine, Lebanon
McCulloch, Thomas B., (Retired)
McGinty, David L., (On Leave)
Miller, Norbert F., Our Lady of Lourdes, Louisville
Mitchell, Kenneth J., St. Mary, Louisville
Mullins, William L., St. Francis of Rome, Louisville
Murphy, Michael, St. Martin of Tours, Louisville
Nevitt, Charles, St. Rita, Louisville
Nitzken, Syl J., St. Stephen Martyr, Louisville; Vicar for Senior Deacons
O'Connell, Frank, Incarnation, Louisville
Ohnemus, Joseph, Our Lady of Perpetual Help, Campbellsville
Olrich, James Charles, St. Elizabeth Ann Seton Church, Louisville
Osborne, Kenneth F., (Retired)
Padgett, Joseph E., (Retired)
Patterson, Daniel Eugene, (Retired)
Plummer, James R., St. Barnabas, Louisville
Prestwood, Harry, Most Blessed Sacrament, Louisville
Raibert, Joseph A., Holy Spirit, Louisville
Ratterman, Cletus A., (Retired)
Ronald, Edward R., Jefferson County Department of Corrections, Louisville
Ryan, Thomas, Catholic Deaf Office
Shoulta, John, Annunciation, Shelbyville
Shutts, John F., (Retired), Caritas Medical Center, Louisville
Simmons, John, Most Blessed Sacrament, Louisville
Simpson, John L., St. Margaret Mary, Louisville
Singer, Ernest, St. Mary Magdalen of Pazzi, Paynevville; St. Theresa, Rhodelia
Skeeters, William L., St. Gabriel, Louisville
Smith, Stephen J., St. Polycarp, Louisville
Stanley, Vincent G., St. Albert, Louisville
Steinmetz, Richard Earl, Special Assistant to Bishop Maloney
Sturgeon, James C., Sr., (Retired)
Thieneman, C. Wayne, Our Lady of Consolation, Valley Station
Thomas, William A., (Retired)
Tolbert, Michael A., St. Thomas More, Louisville
Tomes, David R., St. Boniface, Louisville
Tremblay, Philip, St. Timothy, Louisville
Turner, James R., St. Martin de Porres, Louisville
Vessels, Michael, St. John the Baptist, Rineyville; St. Ambrose, Cecelia
Waldon, F. Eugene, Our Lady of Lourdes, Louisville
Walsh, Richard J., St. Joseph, Bardstown
Walther, Charles F., St. Luke, Louisville
Ward, Kenneth M., St. Martha, Louisville
Wheatley, Joseph P., (Unassigned)
Whelan, John R., St. Martin of Tours, Flaherty
Wright, J. Patrick, Cathedral of the Assumption, Louisville
Young, R. James, Holy Spirit, Louisville

INSTITUTIONS LOCATED IN THE ARCHDIOCESE

[A] COLLEGES AND UNIVERSITIES

LOUISVILLE

Administration Officers: Most Rev. Thomas C. Kelly, O.P., Archbishop of Louisville, Chancellor; Revs. Clyde F. Crews; George A. Kilcourse; Dr. Gretchen Anderson, Dean Continuing and Professional Studies; Dr. Dan Bauer, Dean of the Rubel School of Business; Dr. Peter Cimbolic, Ph.D., Provost; Dr. Susan Davis, Dean of the Lansing School of Nursing; Dr. Vince Maniaci, Vice Pres. Institutional Advancement; Dr. Joseph J. McGowan, Pres.; Dr. Maureen Norris, Dean Thornton School of Education; Dr. Fred W. Rhodes, Vice Pres. Student Affairs & Dean of Students; Mr. Tim Sturgeon, Dean of Admissions; Dr. Doris Tegart, Vice Pres. and Exec. Asst. to the President; Dr. Mary Jo Vesper, Dean College of Arts & Sciences; Mr. David Wuinee, Vice Pres. Enrollment Management; Mr. Robert L. Zimlich, Vice Pres. for Business Affairs.

Bellarmine University, 2001 Newburg Rd., 40205-0671. Tel: 502-452-8000; Fax: 502-452-8033. Web: www.bellarmine.edu. Priests 2; Students 2,363.

Spalding University, 851 S. 4th St., 40203. Tel: 502-585-9911; Fax: 502-585-7158. Web: www.spalding.edu. Jo Ann Rooney, L.L.M., J.D., Pres.; Randy Strickland, Vice Pres. Academic Affairs; Sr. Mary Angela Shaughnessy, S.C.N., Vice Pres. for Mission and General Counsel; Dr. Maggie McCullough, Dean College of Business; Dr. Betty Lindsey, Dean College of Education; Bro. Ignatius Perkins, O.P., Dean College of Health and Natural Sciences; Dr. Andy Meyer, Dean, College of Social Sciences and Humanities; Theresa Raidy, Assoc. Vice Pres Univ. Advancement; Audrey Ashton-Savage, Vice Pres., Strategic Initiatives, and Enrollment Management. Priests 1; Sisters 5; Brothers 2; Lay Teachers 62; Students 1,631.

ST. CATHARINE. *St. Catharine College*, 2735 Bardstown Rd., 40061. Tel: 859-336-5082; Fax: 859-336-5031. Email: cosborne@sccky.edu. Web: www.scky.edu. Mr. Bill Huston, Pres.; Dr. David Arnold, Vice Pres. & Academic Dean. Dominican Sisters Priests 1; Sisters 1; Lay Teachers 35; Students 661.

[B] HIGH SCHOOLS, ARCHDIOCESAN

LOUISVILLE. *St. Francis DeSales High School*, 425 Kenwood Dr., 40214. Tel: 502-368-6519; Fax: 502-366-6172. Web: www.desaleshighschool.com. Mr. Tim Keogh, Prin. Priests 1; Lay Teachers 25; Students 314.

The Carmelite Community of The St. Francis De-Sales Priory Tel: 502-368-6553; Fax: 502-366-6172. Revs. Kyrin Caggiano, O.Carm.; Joseph Maisonneuve, O.Carm.

Holy Cross High School, 5144 Dixie Hwy., 40216. Tel: 502-447-4363; Fax: 502-448-1062. Email: holycross@holycrosshs.com. Web: www.holycross.com. Sr. Maryann Tarquinio, O.P., Prin. Sisters 1; Lay Teachers 27; Students 334.

Trinity High School, 4011 Shelbyville Rd., 40207. Tel: 502-895-9427; Fax: 502-895-6337. Email: trinity@thsrock.net. Web: www.thsrock.net. Mr. Robert J. Mullen, Pres.; Mr. David Winkler, Prin.; Rev. David H. Zettel. Priests 1; Lay Teachers 96; Students 1,381.

BARDSTOWN. *Bethlehem High School* 40004. Tel: 502-348-8594; Fax: 502-349-1247. Email: BHS@bethlehemhigh.org. Web: www.bethlehemhigh.org. Tim Weaver, Prin. Sisters of Charity of Nazareth Sisters 1 Lay Teachers 18; Students 298.

[C] HIGH SCHOOLS, PRIVATE

LOUISVILLE. *Academy of Our Lady of Mercy*, 1176 E. Broadway, 40204. Tel: 502-584-4273; Fax: 502-584-9651. Email: mikejohnson@mercyacademy.com. Web: www.mercyacademy.com. Mr. Michael C. Johnson, Pres.; Julie H. Crone, Prin. Sisters of Mercy 1; Lay Teachers 30; Students 413.

Assumption High School, 2170 Tyler Ln., 40205. Tel: 502-458-9551; Fax: 502-454-8411. Email: ahs@iglou.com. Web: www.ashrockets.org. Mary Lee McCoy, Pres.; Mary Ann Steutermann, Prin. Sisters of Mercy Lay Teachers 96; Students 975.

Presentation Academy, 861 S. 4th St., 40203. Tel: 502-583-5935; Fax: 502-583-1342. Email: mbruder@myeroute.com. Web: www.presentationacademy.org. Sisters 2; Lay Teachers 33; Students 356.

Spalding University Leslie Gayle Kaster, Prin.

Sacred Heart Academy, 3175 Lexington Rd., 40206. Tel: 502-897-6097; Fax: 502-893-0120 Email: officesha@sacredheartacad.com. Web: www.sacredheartacad.com. Dr. Beverly McAuliffe, Prin. Ursuline Sisters Sisters 3; Lay Teachers 72; Students 805.

St. Xavier High School, Xaverian Brothers, 1609 Poplar Level Rd., 40217. Tel: 502-637-4712; Fax: 502-634-2171. Email: psangalli@saintx.com. Web: www.saintx.com. Dr. Perry E. Sangall, Pres. Priests 3; Brothers 6; Sisters 1; Lay Teachers 109; Students 1,440.

[D] ELEMENTARY SCHOOLS, PRIVATE

LOUISVILLE. *Holy Angels Academy, Inc.*, 1408 S. Second St., 40208. Tel: 502-634-3223; Fax: 502-634-3223. Joseph M. Norton, Headmaster and Prin., Grade School; Marilyn G. Malone, Prin., High School. Lay Teachers 9; Students 118.

Mercy Montessori School, Inc., 2181 Tyler Ln., 40205. Tel: 502-459-6545; Fax: 502-479-3491. Sr. Mary Alicia McGinty, R.S.M., Dir. Students 48.

Sacred Heart Model School, 3107 Lexington Rd., 40206. Tel: 502-896-3931; Fax: 502-896-3932. Email: wannemuehl@aol.com. Web: ucschools.com/shms. Dr. Sarah Wannemuehler, Prin. Sisters 3; Lay Teachers 44; Students 370.

Ursuline Montessori School, 3105 Lexington Rd., 40206. Tel: 502-896-3941; Fax: 502-896-3966. Web: www.ucschools.com/ums. Linda Otto, Dir. Montessori School Lay Teachers 16; Students 190.

NAZARETH. *Nazareth Montessori Children's Center*, P.O. Box 44, 40048. Tel: 502-348-1540; Fax: 502-331-4050. Email: nmcc@scnazarethky.org. Web: scnazarethky.org/montessori. Mary Cantrell, Dir. Sisters 1; Lay Teachers 6; Students 75.

[E] SPECIAL SCHOOLS

LOUISVILLE. *St. Joseph Child Development Center*, 2823 Frankfort Ave., 40206. Tel: 502-893-0241; Fax: 502-896-2394. Email: sjkids@aol.com. Web: www.sjkids.org. Bronwyn Hudson, Admin. Students 110.

Pitt Academy, 4605 Poplar Level Rd., 40213. Tel: 502-966-6979; Fax: 502-962-8878. Email: pitt@aye.net. Web: www.pitt.com. Ms. Melinda Keiner-Rummel, Prin. Lay Teachers 6; Students 52.

Ursuline Child Development Center, 3105 Lexington Rd., 40206. Tel: 502-895-7798; Fax: 502-212-4639. Email: vfurlow@ucschools.com. Vickie Furlow, Admin.

Ursuline School for the Performing Arts, 3105 Lexington Rd., 40206. Tel: 502-897-1816; Fax: 502-896-3927. Email: apaul@ucschools.com. Web: www.ucschools.com/uspa. Anna Jo Paul, Dir. Students 470.

[F] ORPHANAGES AND INFANT HOMES

LOUISVILLE. *St. Joseph Catholic Orphan Society*, 2823 Frankfort Ave., 40206. Tel: 502-893-0241; Fax: 502-896-2394. Email: sjkids@aol.com. Web: www.sjkids.org. Mr. James Ratterman, Pres. Bd. of Directors.

St. Joseph Children's Home, 2823 Frankfort Ave., 40206. Tel: 502-893-0241; Fax: 502-896-2394. Email: sjkids@aol.com. Web: www.sjkids.org. Mr. William K. Heaton, CEO. Ursuline Sisters 1; Sisters of Charity 1; Children 70.

St. Thomas Orphan Society, Inc., P.O. Box 1073, 40201.

St. Vincent's Orphan Society, Inc., P.O. Box 1073, 40201.

[G] GENERAL HOSPITALS

LOUISVILLE. *Caritas Medical Center*, 1850 Bluegrass Ave., 40215. Tel: 502-361-6000; Fax: 502-361-6799. Web: www.caritas.com. Robert M. Lovell, Pres.; Thomas Gessel, COO. Catholic Health Initiatives Sisters 7; Bed Capacity 331; Patients Assisted Annually 127,000.

BARDSTOWN. *Flaget Memorial Hospital*, 201 Cathedral Manor, 40004. Tel: 502-348-3923, Ext. 4641; Fax: 502-349-4643. Email: taw@flaget.com. Web: www.flaget.com. Bruce Klockars, Pres. & CEO. Catholic Health Initiatives, Attended from St.

Joseph Church. Sisters 4; Bed Capacity 52; Bassinets 8; Patients Assisted Annually 63,974.

[H] SPECIAL HOSPITALS

LOUISVILLE. *Caritas Peace Center*, 2020 Newburg Rd., 40205. Tel: 502-451-3330; Fax: 502-473-1797. Email: michaelahrens@chi-caritas.org. Web: www.caritas.com. Robert M. Lovell, Pres.; JoAnne D. Maamry, Admin. Catholic Health Initiatives, Hospital for Psychiatric Illness. Sisters 2; Bed Capacity 270; Patients assisted annually 2,600.

[I] PROTECTIVE INSTITUTIONS

LOUISVILLE. *Boys' Haven*, 2301 Goldsmith Ln., 40205. Tel: 502-458-1171; Fax: 502-451-2161. Email: vrickert@boyshaven.org. Web: www.boyshaven.org. Mr. Vern Rickert, Exec. Dir. For dependent, neglected, or abused boys, 12 to 18 years of age. Number Assisted 75.

[J] NURSING HOMES

LOUISVILLE. *Franciscan Health Care Center*, 3625 Fern Valley Rd., 40219. Tel: 502-964-3381; Fax: 502-964-3395. Email: srinne@franciscancommunities.com. Web: www.franciscancommunities.com. Suzanne Rinne, Admin. & Exec. Dir.; Rev. Florian Tiel, O.F.M.Conv., Chap.

Legal Title: *Franciscan Communities, Inc. dba Franciscan Health Care Center* Nursing Facility Beds 148; Assisted Living 52; Total Assisted Annually 671.

St. Joseph Home for the Aged, 15 Audubon Plaza Dr., 40217. Tel: 502-636-2300; Fax: 502-636-2239. Sr. Mary Anthony Power, Pres.; Rev. Simon Brzozowski, M.S.F., Chap.

Legal Title: *Home for the Aged of the Little Sisters of the Poor*

Marian Home, 3105 Lexington Rd., 40206. Tel: 502-893-0121; Fax: 502-896-3925. Email: adevine@ursulineslou.org. Sr. Assumpta Devine, O.S.U., Admin.; Rev. Joseph T. Merkt (OWN), Chap. Staff Sisters 2; Residents 69.

Nazareth Home, 2000 Newburg Rd., 40205. Tel: 502-459-9681; Fax: 502-456-9077. Email: mhaynes@nazhome.org. Web: nazhome.org. Mary Neathery Haynes, CEO & Admin.; Revs. Germain Legere, C.P., Chap.; Joseph S. Hall, Chap.; Deacon E. Perry Carney, Chap. Sisters of Charity of Nazareth Staff Sisters 10; Residents 168.

[K] MONASTERIES AND RESIDENCES OF PRIESTS AND BROTHERS

LOUISVILLE. *Bishop David Apartments*, 5146 Dixie Hwy., 40216. Tel: 502-448-7863. Revs. William C. Hartlage (Retired); John E. Magel, Dir. (Retired); John B. Gephart (Retired). Priests 3.

St. Francis of Assisi Friary, 2225 Lower Hunters Trace, 40216. Tel: 502-447-5566; Fax: 502-447-1427. Revs. Christian Moore, O.F.M.Conv.; James Kent, O.F.M.Conv.; Bros. Larry Eberhardt, O.F.M.Conv.; Randall Kin, O.F.M.Conv.

Sacred Heart Retreat, 1924 Newburg Rd., 40205. Tel: 502-451-2330; Fax: 502-451-0192. Email: passky@iglou.com. Web: www.passionist.org. Very Rev. Michael Joseph Stengel, C.P. (CHI), Supr. (Corporate Title: Congregation of the Passion, Sacred Heart Community) Priests 11. In Res. Revs. John Conley, C.P.; Francis W. Cusack, C.P.; James DeManuele, C.P.; Joachim Gemperline, C.P.; John E. Hilgert, C.P.; Walter Kaelin, C.P.; Germain Legere, C.P. (Canada); Forrest Macken, C.P.; Albert Schwer, C.P. (BIR); Bernard Weber, C.P.; Bro. Jerome Milazzo, C.P.

Villa Pacis, Resurrectionist Retirement Home, 4607 Poplar Level Rd., 40213. Tel: 502-968-8010; Fax: 502-969-6375. Email: crvillapacis@aol.com. In Res. Revs. Raymond Hofmann, C.R.; John Lesousky, C.R.; John Miles, C.R.; Charles Schoenbaechler, C.R.

TRAPPIST. *Abbey of Our Lady of Gethsemani, of the Order of Cistercians of the Strict Observance*, 3642 Monks Rd., 40051. Tel: 502-549-3117; Fax: 502-549-8281. Email: getabbot@iglou.com. Rev. Damien Thompson, O.C.S.O., Abbot; Rt. Rev. Timothy Kelly, O.C.S.O., Abbot (Retired); Revs. Bernard Murray, O.C.S.O. (Chile); Roman Ginn, O.C.S.O.; James Conner, O.C.S.O.; Chrysogonus Waddell, O.C.S.O.; Alan Gilmore, O.C.S.O.; Matthew Kelty, O.C.S.O.; Michael Casagram, O.C.S.O.; Carlos Rodriguez, O.C.S.O.; Peter Tong, O.C.S.O.; Bernard Joseph Valoret (ATL) (Retired). Priests 12; Brothers 55.

[L] CONVENTS AND RESIDENCES FOR SISTERS

LOUISVILLE. *St. Catherine Convent*, 1172 E. Broadway, 40204. Tel: 502-583-7641; Fax: 502-584-2752. Email: scathcvt@bellsouth.net. Sr. Mary Quentin Barth, R.S.M., Local Coord. Sisters of Mercy in residence 26.

Monastery of the Discalced Carmelite Nuns, 1740 Newburg Rd., 40205. Tel: 502-451-6796; Fax: 502-458-5272. Sr. Catherine, O.C.D., Prioress. Professed Nuns 10.

Sisters of the Good Shepherd, 204 S. Lyndon Ln., 40222. Tel: 502-412-8001; Fax: 502-412-8002. Email: rglouky@aol.com. Sisters 3.

Ursuline Motherhouse of the Immaculate Conception, 3115 Lexington Rd., 40206. Tel: 502-893-0125; Fax: 502-896-3913. Email: webmaster@ursulineslou.org. Web: www.ursulineslou.org. Sisters Jean Anne Zappa, O.S.U., Pres.; Thomasita Hayes, O.S.U., Coord.; Rev. John J. Butler, Chap. (Retired). Sisters in Motherhouse 47; Total in Congregation 163.

Ursuline Sisters, 1731 Edenside Ave., 40204-1595. Tel: 502-451-8685. Email: eamosu@juno.com. Sr. Amanda Rose Mahoney, Coord. (Mount St. Joseph); Attended from St. James. Sisters 6.

NAZARETH. *Generalate, Motherhouse and Novitiate of the Sisters of Charity of Nazareth*, P.O. Box 172, 40048. Tel: 502-348-1555 (SCN Center & Generalate); 502-348-1500 (Motherhouse); Fax: 502-348-1502. Email: sdsouza@scnazarethky.org. Web: www.scnazarethky.org. Rev. Gary Young, C.R., Chap., Motherhouse. Sisters at Motherhouse 99; Sisters at Russell Hall 18; Sisters at David Hall 13; Sisters at SCN Center 2; Nativity Hall 3; Nazareth Village 8.

NERINX. *Motherhouse and Novitiate of the Sisters of Loretto at the Foot of the Cross*, 515 Nerinx Rd., 40049. Tel: 270-865-5811; Fax: 270-865-2200. Email: maryswain@lorettocommunity.org. Web: www.lorettocommunity.org. Sr. Mary Catherine Rabbitt, S.L., Pres. Sisters in the Motherhouse 98; Total in Congregation 328.

ST. CATHARINE. *St. Catharine of Siena Convent*, 2645 Bardstown Rd., 40061. Tel: 859-336-9303; Fax: 859-336-9306. Email: ttuite@opkentucky.org. Web: www.opkentucky.org. Sr. Joye Gros, O.P., Pres.; Rev. Charles E. Reteneller, Chap. Motherhouse of Dominican Sisters. Sisters in Motherhouse 43; Total in Congregation 230.

Sansbury Care Center, 2625 Bardstown Rd., 40061. Tel: 859-336-3974; Fax: 859-336-1068. Ann Marks, Admin.; Revs. Charles E. Reteneller, Chap.; John Christopher Allegra; James Stephen Murray, O.P. Sisters in Infirmary 54.

[M] HOMES FOR MEN AND WOMEN

LOUISVILLE. *Sacred Heart Village, Inc.* (Rudd-Taylor Memorial) , 2120 Payne St., 40206. Tel: 502-895-9425; Fax: 502-357-5549. Leslie A. Wilson, Pres.; Rev. Joseph S. Hall, Chap.

Legal Title: *Mercy Sacred Heart, Inc.* Sisters of Mercy, Catholic Healthcare Partners, Cincinnati, OH. Sisters 7; Residents 155; Capacity 165; Mercy Assoc. 2.

[N] RETREAT HOUSES

LOUISVILLE. *Catholic Charismatic Renewal*, Maloney Center, 1200 S. Shelby St., 40203. Tel: 502-636-0296; Fax: 502-636-2379. Pat Sloan, Contact Person.

Flaget Center, 1935 Lewiston Dr., 40216. Tel: 502-448-8581; Fax: 502-448-5518. Email: dmc@archlou.org. Donna M. McHugh, Admin.

CRESTWOOD. *Lake St. Joseph Center*, 5800 Old LaGrange Rd., 40014. Tel: 502-241-4469.

NAZARETH. *Catherine Spalding Retreat and Conference Center*, P.O. Box 24, 40048. Tel: 502-348-1515; Fax: 502-348-1518. Email: sreasbeck@scnazarethky.org. Web: www.scnazarethky.org. Suzanne Reasbeck, Dir. Staff Sisters 2; Lay Persons 4.

NERINX. *Knobs Haven*, 515 Nerinx Rd., 40049. Tel: 270-865-2621. Email: knobshaven@yahoo.com. Sr. Mary Gutzwiller, S.L., Co-Dir.; Peg Jacobs, Co-Dir.

NEW HAVEN. *Bethany Spring*, 115 Dee Head Rd., 40051. Tel: 502-549-8277; Fax: 502-549-8270. Email: morningstar@bardstown.com. Mary Luken, Dir.

[O] ST. VINCENT DE PAUL SOCIETY

LOUISVILLE. *Society of St. Vincent de Paul, Council of Louisville*, P.O. Box 17126, 40217-0126. Tel: 502-584-2480; Fax: 502-587-1977. Email: svdplou@win.net. Web: www.svdplou.org. Charles Francesconi, Exec. Dir.; Irvin Lambert, Trustee & Bd. Chm.

De Paul Apartments, 1015-A S. Preston St., 40203. Tel: 502-584-2480; Fax: 502-587-1977. (Transitional Shelter for Homeless Single Parent Families)

De Paul Thrift Stores

1029 S. Preston St., 40203. Tel: 502-589-7837; Fax: 502-587-1977.

248 E. Market St., 40202. Tel: 502-583-1370; Fax: 502-587-1977.

Open Hand Kitchen and Community Center, 1026 S. Jackson St., 40203. Tel: 502-584-2480; Fax: 502-587-1977.

Ozanam Inn, 1034 S. Jackson St., 40203. Tel: 502-584-2480; Fax: 502-587-1977. (Men's Emergency & Transitional Shelter)

Parish Conferences Tel: 502-584-2480; Fax: 502-587-1977.

Roberts Hall, 1032 E. Burnett Ave., 40217. Tel: 502-636-3549; Fax: 502-587-1977. (Women's Housing)

St. Jude Women's Recovery Center, 431 E. St. Catherine St., 40203. Tel: 502-589-6024; Fax: 502-587-1977. (Women's Recovery)

Simon Hall, 1022 S. Jackson St., 40203. Tel: 502-584-2480; Fax: 502-587-1977. (Men's Recovery)

Tranquil House (Housing For Mentally Ill) , 1035 S. Preston St., 40203. Tel: 502-584-2480; Fax: 502-587-1977.

[P] MISCELLANEOUS LISTINGS

LOUISVILLE. *Cathedral Heritage Foundation, Inc.*, 415 W. Muhammad Ali Blvd., Ste. 101, 40202-2334. Tel: 502-583-3100; Fax: 502-583-8524. Email: terry@cathedral-heritage.org. Web: www.cathedral-heritage.org. Terrence A. Taylor, Exec. Dir.

The Franciscan Foundation, Inc., 2220 W. Market St., 40212. Tel: 502-494-3264; Fax: 502-772-5053. Email: thomasa2@juno.com.

Franciscan Shelter House, 748 S. Preston St., 40203. Tel: 502-589-0140; Fax: 502-589-1134. Email: fsh748@aol.com. Web: www.franciscanshelterhouse.com.

Mass of the Air, 508 Breckenridge Ln., 40207. Tel: 502-893-5120; Fax: 502-895-4535. Email: frnick@bellsouth.net. Rev. G. Nick Rice, Dir.

Our Lady's Rosary Makers, 4611 Poplar Level Rd., P.O. Box 37080, 40233. Tel: 502-968-1434; Fax: 502-959-8883. Web: www.olrm.org. Michael Ford, Gen. Mgr.

St. Patrick School Foundation, Inc., 1000 N. Beckley Station Rd., 40245. Tel: 502-244-7083; Fax: 502-244-6083. Web: stpatrick-lou.org. R. Mark Page, Chm.

Perpetual Eucharistic Adoration, P.O. Box 39191, 40233-9191. Tel: 502-637-5309; 502-549-3757; Fax: 502-549-7258. Rev. Lawrence H. Lindle, Spiritual Dir. (Retired).

Publication: "The Record", Maloney Center, 1200 S. Shelby St., 40203-2600. Tel: 502-636-0296; Fax: 502-636-2379. Email: record@archlou.org. Official newspaper of the Archdiocese of Louisville (Weekly).

Office: Archdiocesan Communications Center Joseph E. Duerr, Editor & Gen. Mgr.

Ursuline Campus Schools, Inc., 3105 Lexington Rd., 40206. Tel: 502-896-3910; Fax: 502-895-0989. Email: ucs@ucschools.com. Web: www.ucschools.com. Dr. Cynthia Crabtree, Pres. Sponsored by Ursuline Sisters.

Ursuline Society and Academy of Education, 3105 Lexington Rd., 40206. Tel: 502-897-1811; Fax: 502-896-3913. Email: webmaster@ursulineslou.org. Web: www.ursulineslou.org.

BARDSTOWN. *Flaget Healthcare, Inc.*, 201 Cathedral Manor, 40004. Tel: 502-348-3923; Fax: 502-349-4643. Email: info@flaget.com. Web: flaget.com. Bruce Klockars, Pres. & CEO.

LEBANON. *The Laura*, 1995 Sam Browning Rd., 40033. Tel: 270-692-1790. Email: mking@kyol.net.

LORETTO. *Holy Cross Cemetery Trust, Inc.*, 7945 Loretto Rd., 40037. Tel: 502-348-5404.

NAZARETH. *Nazareth Arts For Life, Inc.*, O'Connell Hall, P.O. Box 14, 40048. Tel: 502-348-1554; Fax: 502-348-1584. Email: nazarts@scnazarethky.org. Web: www.scnazarethky.org/nazarts.

Office of Congregational Advancement, P.O. Box 9, 40048. Tel: 502-348-1578; Fax: 502-348-1587. Email: potoole@scnazarethky.org. Web: www.scnazarethky.org. Sisters of Charity of Nazareth

Sisters of Charity of Nazareth, Inc., P.O. Box 187, Crimmins Hall, 135 West Dr., 40048. Tel: 502-331-4072. Email: gatzscn@scnazarethky.org. Sr. Susan Gatz, S.C.N., Pres.

NERINX. *PROJECT AIMM*, 515 Nerinx Rd., 40049. Tel: 270-865-2332; Fax: 270-699-9995. Email: aaschum@cs.com. Sr. Agnes Ann Schum, S.L., Exec. Dir.

Sisters of Loretto Charitable Trust, 515 Nerinx Rd., 40049-9999. Tel: 270-865-3414; Fax: 270-865-2200. Email: maryswain@lorettocommunity.org. Web: www.lorettocommunity.org. Sr. Mary Swain, S.L., Treas.

NEW HAVEN. *Archdiocesan Marian Committee*, 8191 New Haven Rd., 40051-6030. Tel: 502-549-3757; Fax: 502-549-7258. Rev. Lawrence H. Lindle, Dir. (Retired).

World Apostolate of Fatima (Blue Army), 8191 New

Haven Rd., 40051-6030. Tel: 502-549-3757; Fax: 502-549-7258. Rev. Lawrence H. Lindle, Spiritual Dir. (Retired).

Sacred Heart Apostolate, 8191 New Haven Rd., 40051-6030. Tel: 502-549-3757; Fax: 502-549-7258. Rev. Lawrence H. Lindle, Dir. (Retired).

NEW HOPE. *St. Martin De Porres Lay Dominican Community* 40052. Tel: 270-325-3061; Fax: 270-325-3091. Email: stmdp@newhope-ky.org. Web: www.newhope-ky.org. Mary Frances Musk, T.O.P., T.O.P., Prior.

RELIGIOUS INSTITUTES OF MEN REPRESENTED IN THE ARCHDIOCESE

For further details refer to the corresponding bracketed number in the Religious Institutes of Men or Women section.

[1350]—*Brothers of St. Francis Xavier* (American Central Prov.)—C.F.X.
[0270]—*Carmelite Fathers & Brothers* (Pure Heart of Mary Prov.)—O.Carm.
[0350]—*Cistercians Order of the Strict Observance-Trappists*—O.C.S.O.
[0820]—*Congregation of the Fathers of Mercy*—C.P.M.
[1000]—*Congregation of the Passion* (Holy Cross Prov.)—C.P.
[1080]—*Congregation of the Resurrection* (Rome, Italy)—C.R.
[0480]—*Conventual Franciscans* (Prov. of Our Lady of Consolation)—O.F.M.Conv
[0630]—*Missionaries of the Holy Family*—M.S.F.
[0430]—*Order of Preachers-Dominicans* (St. Joseph Prov.)—O.P.

RELIGIOUS INSTITUTES OF WOMEN REPRESENTED IN THE ARCHDIOCESE

[0230]—*Benedictine Sisters of Pontifical Jurisdiction*—O.S.B.
[2145]—*Congregation of Augustinian Sisters Servants of Jesus and Mary*—O.S.A.
[3830-10]—*Congregation of Sisters of St. Joseph of Tipton*—C.S.J.
[0420]—*Discalced Carmelite Nuns*—O.C.D.
[1070-01]—*Dominican Sisters*—O.P.
[1070-10]—*Dominican Sisters*—O.P.
[1070-13]—*Dominican Sisters*—O.P.
[2575]—*Institute of the Sisters of Mercy of the Americas*—R.S.M.
[2340]—*Little Sisters of the Poor*—L.S.P.
[2470]—*Maryknoll Sisters of St. Dominic*—M.M.
[2490]—*Medical Mission Sisters*—M.M.S.
[0670]—*Order of Trappistines*—O.C.S.O.
[3130]—*Our Lady of Victory Missionary Sisters*—O.L.V.M.
[2970]—*School Sisters of Notre Dame*—S.S.N.D.
[0440]—*Sisters of Charity of Cincinnati, OH*—S.C.
[0500]—*Sisters of Charity of Nazareth*—S.C.N.
[2360]—*Sisters of Loretto At the Foot of the Cross*—S.L.
[3000]—*Sisters of Notre Dame de Namur*—S.N.D.deN.
[3360]—*Sisters of Providence of Saint Mary-of-the-Woods, IN* (St. Gabriel Prov.)—S.P.
[1540]—*Sisters of St. Francis* (Clinton, IA)—O.S.F.
[1630]—*Sisters of St. Francis of Penance and Christian Charity*—O.S.F.
[3830-13]—*Sisters of St. Joseph of Northwest Pennsylvania*—S.S.J.
[1830]—*Sisters of the Good Shepherd*—R.G.S.
[1960]—*Sisters of the Holy Family*
[2150]—*Sisters, Servants of the Immaculate Heart of Mary*—I.H.M.
[4120-03]—*Ursuline Nuns, of the Congregation of Paris*—O.S.U.
[4120-05]—*Ursuline Sisters of Mt. St. Joseph*—O.S.U.

ARCHDIOCESAN CEMETERIES

Offices for all cemeteries: 1600 Newburg Rd., Louisville, KY 40205; Mailing Address: P.O. Box 4096, Louisville, KY 40204. Tel: 502-451-7710; Fax: 502-456-9270.

LOUISVILLE
Calvary, 1600 Newburg Rd., 40205.
St. John, 2601 Duncan St., 40212.
St. Louis, 1215 Barret Ave., 40204.
St. Michael, 1153 Charles St., 40204.

NECROLOGY

† Diersen, William M., (Retired)—Died Nov. 9, 2002
† Hamilton, Joseph K., (Retired)—Died April 9, 2003
† Oyler, George F., (Retired)—Died March 27, 2003

Diocese of Lubbock

Most Reverend

PLACIDO RODRIGUEZ, C.M.F.

Bishop of Lubbock; ordained May 23, 1968; consecrated December 13, 1983; installed Auxiliary Bishop of Chicago; appointed Second Bishop of Lubbock April 5, 1994; installed June 1, 1994 *Res.: 3505 37th St., Lubbock, TX 79413. Office: The Catholic Pastoral Center*, P.O. Box 98700, Lubbock, TX 79499-8700. Fax: 806-792-2953. Email: prodriguez@catholiclubbock.org.

The Catholic Pastoral Center: P.O. Box 98700, Lubbock, TX 79499-8700. Tel: 806-792-3943; Fax: 806-792-8109.

Web: www.catholiclubbock.org

Email: lbehnke@catholiclubbock.org

ESTABLISHED AND CREATED A DIOCESE, JUNE 17, 1983.

Square Miles 23,382.

Comprises the Counties of Bailey, Lamb, Hale, Floyd, Motley, Cottle, Cochran, Hockley, Lubbock, Crosby, Dickens, King, Yoakum, Terry, Lynn, Garza, Kent, Stonewall, Haskell, Gaines, Dawson, Borden, Scurry, Fisher and Jones.

Legal Title: Roman Catholic Diocese of Lubbock.

STATISTICAL OVERVIEW

Personnel	
Bishop	1
Priests: Diocesan Active in Diocese	26
Priests: Diocesan Active Outside Diocese	1
Priests: Retired, Sick or Absent	10
Number of Diocesan Priests	37
Religious Priests in Diocese	8
Total Priests in Diocese	45
Extern Priests in Diocese	10
Ordinations:	
Diocesan Priests	1
Permanent Deacons in Diocese	46
Total Sisters	23
Parishes	
Parishes	62
With Resident Pastor:	
Resident Diocesan Priests	57
Resident Religious Priests	5
Welfare	
Other Institutions	1
Total Assisted	37,000
Educational	
Diocesan Students in Other Seminaries	11
Total Seminarians	11
High Schools, Diocesan and Parish	1
Total Students	18
Elementary Schools, Diocesan and Parish	2
Total Students	363
Catechesis/Religious Education:	
High School Students	3,375
Elementary Students	4,582
Total Students under Catholic Instruction	8,349
Vital Statistics	
Receptions into the Church:	
Infant Baptism Totals	1,604
Adult Baptism Totals	134
Received into Full Communion	201
First Communions	1,139
Confirmations	665
Marriages:	
Catholic	295
Interfaith	45
Total Marriages	340
Deaths	481
Total Catholic Population	80,742
Total Population	486,910

Former Bishops—Most Rev. MICHAEL J. SHEEHAN, S.T.L., J.C.D., ord. July 12, 1964; consecrated and installed as the first Bishop of Lubbock, June 17, 1983; appt. Apostolic Administrator of Santa Fe, April 6, 1993; installed as the 11th Archbishop of Santa Fe, Sept. 21, 1993.

The Catholic Center—4620 Fourth St., Lubbock, 79416. Mailing Address, P.O. Box 98700, Lubbock, 79499-8700. Tel: 806-792-3943; Fax: 806-792-8109; 806-792-2953 (Bishop's Office). Office Hours: Mon.-Fri. 8-5

Chancellor—Rev. NICOLAS RENDON.

Moderator of the Curia—Rev. NICOLAS RENDON.

Bishop's Secretary—JUDY LEOS RODRIGUEZ.

Diocesan Tribunal—P.O. Box 98700, Lubbock, 79499-8700. Tel: 806-792-3943.

Officialis—Very Rev. VICTOR WANJURA.

Administrative Secretary—RITA ORTIZ.

Promoter of Justice—Rev. Msgr. ROLAND BUXKEMPER.

Defender of the Bond—Rev. EUGENE J. DRISCOLL.

Defender of the Bond-Appeal—Rev. EUGENE J. DRISCOLL.

Notaries—RITA ORTIZ; JUDY LEOS RODRIGUEZ; DORA FIERRO.

Presbyteral Council—Very Rev. BEN KASTEEL, V.G.; Rev. NICOLAS RENDON; Very Rev. VICTOR WANJURA; Revs. JOSEPH AUGUSTINE CHORIKAVUNKAL; BRANDON WALSH; MARTIN PINA; PETER D'SOUZA; LEONARDO PAHAMTANG; REYNALDO REYES; EUGENE J. DRISCOLL.

Priests Personnel Board—Most Rev. PLACIDO RODRIGUEZ, C.M.F.; Very Rev. BEN KASTEEL, V.G.; Revs. NICOLAS RENDON; REYNALDO REYES; DAVID R. CRUZ; MARTIN PINA; Deacon CLARKE COCHRAN.

Vicars Forane—Revs. GERARD KENNEY, Plainview Deanery; REYNALDO REYES, Brownfield Deanery; MICHAEL MELCHER, Lubbock Deanery; JOHN CHEROLIKAL, Snyder Deanery.

Superintendent of Schools—ROBERTA MEYER, P.O. Box 98700, Lubbock, 79499; Mrs. CHRISTINE WANJURA, Prin., Christ the King Elementary/Middle School, 4011 54th St., Lubbock, 79413; Mrs. VICTORIA KLOSE, Prin., St. Joseph Elementary School, 20th & W. Division St., Slaton, 79364.

Director of Youth—GREG RAMZINSKI, P.O. Box 98700, Lubbock, 79499.

Campus Ministry, Texas Tech University—MARCEL LEJEUNE, 2305 Main St., Lubbock, 79401. Tel: 806-762-5225.

Director of Scouting—Rev. BILL ANTON, 5802 22nd St., Lubbock, 79407. Tel: 806-799-2649.

Priests' Retirement Board—Most Rev. PLACIDO RODRIGUEZ, C.M.F.; Revs. NICOLAS RENDON; JOHN OHLIG; JESSE CRUZ; Very Rev. VICTOR WANJURA; Revs. JAMES MCCARTNEY; LAWRENCE HEMP; Rev. Msgr. ROLAND BUXKEMPER; Mr. MARK WAGNON; Mr. DON MCCULLOUGH.

Diocesan Building Commission—Very Rev. BEN KASTEEL, V.G.; Mr. MARK CHAPMAN; JOHN CONNORS; Mr. PAUL MEYER; MAX GARZA; Rev. Msgr. ROLAND BUXKEMPER; Mr. LYLE FETTERLY; Mr. PAUL MEYER; Mr. MARK ROBERTI; Mr. BILL HOGGE; Mr. JOSEPH RAPIER.

Diocesan Pastoral Liturgy Commission—Mrs. GLENDA SHAMBURGER, Chm.; Most Rev. PLACIDO RODRIGUEZ, C.M.F.; Rev. JESSE CRUZ, Dir. Office of Worship, P.O. Box 98700, Lubbock, 79499. Tel: 806-792-3943. Email: prodriguez@ catholiclubbock.org; Very Rev. BEN KASTEEL, V.G., 4011 54th St., Lubbock, 79413. Tel: 806-792-6168. Email: bkasteel@ctkcathedral.org; STEPHEN JOHN, Sec., 128 Bowie Lane, Levelland, 79336. Tel: 806-894-9611, Ext. 2210. Email: sjohn@spc.cc.tx.us; GLENDA SHAMBURGER, Chm., P.O. Box 1350, Levelland, 79336. Tel: 806-894-9611, Ext. 2239. Email: gshambur@spc.cc.tx.us; Sr. CELINE THAMES, O.S.F., St. Alice Convent, 1114 Houston, Plainview, 79072-5344. Tel: 806-296-5426; Deacon JOE MARTINEZ, 1308 49th St., Lubbock, 79412. Tel: 806-744-8817. Email: isabell@odsy.net; Rev. MARTIN PINA, P.O. Box 599, Lamesa, 79331. Tel: 806-872-7100.

Office of Christian Formation—Ms. ALICIA ALVAREZ, P.O. Box 98700, Lubbock, 79499. Tel: 806-792-3943.

Delegate of Religious—Sr. MARY JANE ALANIZ, O.S.F., Pres., St. Francis Convent, 4305 54th St., Lubbock, 79413.

Catholic Family Service, Inc.—JEFF MALPIEDE, Dir., 102 Ave. J, Lubbock, 79401. Tel: 806-765-8475.

Director of Hispanic Affairs—VACANT.

Ecumenical Affairs—VACANT.

Diocesan Council of Catholic Women—Rev. GERARD KENNEY, Chap.; MARCY DEMEL, Pres., Rte. 1, Box 144, Sudan, 79371.

Director of Vocations—Rev. GERARD J. KENNEY, Seminarian Formation & Dir. Vocations. Vocation Team Members: Revs. RENE PEREZ; BILL ANTON, P.O. Box 98700, Lubbock, 79499. Tel: 806-792-3943.

Diocesan Attorney—MADISON SOWDER, 1703 Ave. K, Lubbock, 79401. Tel: 806-763-0409.

Diocesan Health Coordinator—VACANT.

Propagation of the Faith—Rev. NICOLAS RENDON, P.O. Box 98700, Lubbock, 79499-8100. Tel: 806-792-3943.

Office of Peace & Justice—VACANT.

Catholic Campaign for Human Development—Catholic Family Service, Inc., 102 Ave. J, Lubbock, 79401. Tel: 806-765-8475. Deacon DARRIS LINDER, 755 S. 20th St., Slaton, 79364. Tel: 806-828-5662.

Director of the Permanent Diaconate—Deacon CLARKE E. COCHRAN, P.O. Box 98700, Lubbock, 79499. Tel: 806-792-3943.

Cursillo Movement—Rev. ANDRES MENDOZA, Spiritual Dir.

Newspaper—Deacon LEROY BEHNKE, Editor, P.O. Box 98700, Lubbock, 79499. Tel: 806-792-3943. "South Plains Catholic"

Director of Communications—Deacon LEROY BEHNKE.

Office of Evangelization—VACANT.

Director of Family Life—Deacon JESSIE ESQUIVEL, P.O. Box 98700, Lubbock, 79499. Tel: 806-792-3943.

Respect Life Office—LAWRENCE D'SOUZA, P.O. Box 98700, Lubbock, 79499. Tel: 806-792-3943.

Diocesan Rural Life Office—Deacon DARRIS LINDER, 1225 Division St., Slaton, 79364.

Victim Assistance Coordinator—Mrs. CHARLOTTE AMATO. Tel: 806-792-6168. Email: camato@ ctkcathedral.org.

CLERGY, PARISHES, MISSIONS AND PAROCHIAL SCHOOLS

CITY OF LUBBOCK
(LUBBOCK COUNTY)

1—CATHEDRAL CHRIST THE KING (1958), Very Rev. Ben Kasteel, V.G.; Rev. Rene Perez.
Res.: 4011 54th St., 79413-4699. Tel: 806-792-6168; Fax: 806-792-1417.
School—Tel: 806-795-8283; Fax: 806-795-9715. Mrs. Christine Wanjura, Prin. Lay Teachers 33; Students 303.
Catechesis/Religious Program—Mrs. Charlotte Amato, D.R.E. Students 304.

2—ST. ELIZABETH UNIVERSITY PARISH (1935), Revs. James O'Connor; Joy Anthony Thachil (India); Deacon Sid Little; Marcel LeJeune, Dir. Campus Min.
Res.: 2305 Main St., 79401-2924. Tel: 806-762-5225; Fax: 806-741-1962.
Catechesis/Religious Program—Tel: 806-747-2230. Sonia Comacho, D.R.E. Students 242.

3—HOLY SPIRIT (1998), Rev. Eugene J. Driscoll.
Mailing Address: 9821 Frankford Ave., 79424. Tel: 806-698-6400; Fax: 806-798-0646.
Res.: 98th St. & Frankford Ave., 79453. Tel: 806-698-6400.
Catechesis/Religious Program—Students 300.

4—ST. JOHN NEUMANN (1979), Very Rev. Victor Wanjura; Rev. William J. Anton; Deacons Thomas F. McCarthy; Richard Wood; Kyle Broderson; Deacon Clarke Cochran.
Res.: 5802 22nd, 79407-1721. Tel: 806-799-2649; Fax: 806-799-0037.
Catechesis/Religious Program—Students 266.

5—ST. JOSEPH'S (1924), (Hispanic), Revs. Michael O'Dwyer, S.A.C.; Brendan J. Walsh, S.A.C.
Res.: 102 N. Ave. P, 79401-1199. Tel: 806-765-9935; Fax: 806-740-0032.
Catechesis/Religious Program—Tel: 806-763-9695. Yolanda Gutierrez, L.M.S.W., D.R.E. Students 470.

6—OUR LADY OF GRACE (1960), (Hispanic), Rev. David Cruz; Deacons Alfredo Jaime; Ernest Hernandez.
Res.: 3111 Erskine St., 79415-1623. Tel: 806-763-4156; Fax: 806-763-2521.
Catechesis/Religious Program—Tel: 806-763-8727. Soyla Castillo, D.R.E.; Sara Garcia, D.R.E. Students 450.

7—OUR LADY OF GUADALUPE (1980), (Mexican), [CEM] Rev. Andres Mendoza.
Res.: 52nd & Ave. L, P.O. Box 3947, 79452-3947. Tel: 806-763-0710; Fax: 806-741-1915.
Catechesis/Religious Program—Tel: 806-763-0732. Elizabeth Trevino, D.R.E. Students 671.

8—ST. PATRICK (1960), (Spanish), Revs. Cornelio C. Ramirez, S.A.C.; Michael Melcher.
Res.: 1603 Cherry Ave., 79403-6099. Tel: 806-765-5123.
Catechesis/Religious Program—Tel: 806-765-6979. Cleta Arrellano, D.R.E. Students 280.
Mission—Our Lady Queen of Apostles Main St. N., New Deal, Lubbock Co. 79403. Tel: 806-735-5123.

9—ST. THERESA'S (1961), (Mexican-American), Rev. William J. Anton.
Res.: 2202 Upland, Rte. 5, Box 285, 79407-9545. Tel: 806-795-2249.
Catechesis/Religious Program—Nancy Sanchez, D.R.E. Students 80.

OUTSIDE THE CITY OF LUBBOCK

ANSON, JONES CO., ST. MICHAEL'S (1960), (Mexican), [JC] Rev. John Cherolikal.
Res.: 2010 County Rd. 477, 79501. Tel: 915-823-2777.
Catechesis/Religious Program—Mrs. Lupe Philips, D.R.E.; Mrs. Joann Flores, D.R.E. Students 98.
Mission—Holy Trinity Hwy. 83, Hamlin, Jones Co. 79520.

BROWNFIELD, TERRY CO., ST. ANTHONY'S (1952), (Hispanic), Rev. Gerald Leatham.
Res.: P.O. Box 671, 79316-0671. Tel: 806-637-6626; Fax: 806-637-6626.
Catechesis/Religious Program—Fax: 806-637-2356. Giovanna Isaacs, D.R.E. Students 200.
Mission—San Francisco de Asis P.O. Box 92, Ropesville, Hockley Co. 79358.

DENVER CITY, YOAKUM CO., ST. WILLIAM (1955), (Hispanic), Rev. Jaime Guerrero.
Res.: 401 Mustang Ave., 79323-2749. Tel: 806-592-2063; Fax: 806-592-2239.
Catechesis/Religious Program—Lidia Ramirez, D.R.E. Students 370.
Mission—Sacred Heart 1305 11th St., Plains, Yoakum Co. 79355. Tel: 806-456-7002.

FLOYDADA, FLOYD CO., ST. MARY MAGDALEN (1928), (Hispanic), [JC] Rev. Arsenio C. Redulla.
Res.: 809 W. Ross, 79235. Tel: 806-983-5878 Fax: 806-983-2601.
Catechesis/Religious Program—Students 95.
Mission—Our Lady of Guadalupe 701 Bundy St., Matador, Motley Co. 79244.
Mission—St. Elizabeth Second St. & Clare St., Paducah, Cottle Co. 79348. Tel: 806-492-3053

HALE CENTER, HALE CO., ST. THERESA'S (1944), (Hispanic), Rev. Raymundo Manriquez Pulido.
Mailing Address: P.O. Box 528, 79041-0528. Tel: 806-839-2310; Fax: 806-839-2308.
Catechesis/Religious Program—Tel: 806-839-9938. Students 75.
Mission—St. Peter, Apostle (1958), P.O. Box 655, Olton, Lamb Co. 79064. Tel: 806-285-2140; Fax: 806-285-2140.

IDALOU, LUBBOCK CO., ST. PHILIP BENIZI (1979), (Spanish), Rev. Msgr. Roland Bunkemper; Deacon Urbano Rodriguez.
Res.: Box 1337, 79329-1337. Tel: 806-892-2743.
Catechesis/Religious Program—Students 236.
Mission—San Lorenzo Jackson & Monroe, Lorenzo, Crosby Co.

LAMESA, DAWSON CO., ST. MARGARET MARY (1929), (Hispanic), [CEM] Rev. Rudolf Craska.
Res.: 908 S. 2nd St., P.O. Box 599, 79331-6104. Tel: 806-872-7100; Fax: 806-872-3630.
Catechesis/Religious Program—Miss Delfina Luna, D.R.E. Students 485.
Mission—Our Lady of Guadalupe P.O. Box 599, Dawson Co. 79331. Fax: 806-872-7100.

LEVELLAND, HOCKLEY CO., ST. MICHAEL'S (1956), Rev. Martin Pina; Deacon Ed King.
Res.: 316 E. Washington St., 79336-2611. Tel: 806-894-2268; Fax: 806-894-9348.
Catechesis/Religious Program—Tel: 806-894-9880. Cathy DeMartino, D.R.E. Students 418.
Mission—San Isidro 1306 S. Slaughter, P.O. Box 764, Sundown, Hockley Co. 79372-0764.

LITTLEFIELD, LAMB CO., SACRED HEART (1921), [CEM] Rev. Patrick Maher.
Res.: Eighth & Sunset, P.O. Box 1347 79339-4234. Tel: 806-385-6043.
Catechesis/Religious Program—Mary Jane Aguirre, D.R.E. Students 190.

MORTON, COCHRAN CO., ST. ANN (1955) [CEM] Rev. Jesse Cruz; Deacon Alfredo Franco.
Res.: 105 N.E. Eighth St., 79346-2719. Tel: 806-266-8693; Fax: 806-266-8692.
Catechesis/Religious Program—Patsy Vasuqez, D.R.E. Students 130.
Mission—St. Philip Neri Fm. Rd., #303, P.O. Box 395, Pep, Hockley Co. 79353. Tel: 806-933-4355.

MULESHOE, BAILEY CO., IMMACULATE CONCEPTION (1956), Hispanic), [CEM 2] [JC] Rev. Joseph Augustine Chorikavunkal (India).
Res.: R.R. 3, Box 247, 79347-2460. Tel: 806-272-4384; Fax: 806-272-4384.
Catechesis/Religious Program—Tel: 806-272-4167. Diane Hernandez, D.R.E. Students 200
Mission—St. Mary Magdalen c/o R.R.3, Box 247, Earth, Lamb Co. 79347.
Catechesis/Religious Program—Irma Olvera, D.R.E. Students 3.

O'DONNELL, LYNN CO., ST. PIUS X (1959), Hispanic), [CEM] Rev. Eduardo Teo.
Res.: Rt. 1, Box 41-A, 79351. Tel: 806-428-3490; Fax: 806-428-3490.
Catechesis/Religious Program—Tel: 806-428-3691; Fax: 806-428-3691. Students 109.
Mission—St. Jude (1951), Tahoka, Lynn Co. Tel: 806-561-4436.

PETERSBURG, HALE CO., SACRED HEART (1959), Rev. Arnold Bravo (Philippines).
Mailing Address: P.O. Box 330, 79250-0330. Tel: 806-667-3733. Mailing Address: R.R. 2, Box 159A, Abernathy, 79311.
Res.: R.R. 2, Box 159A, Abernathy, 79311-9921. Tel: 806-298-4278.
Catechesis/Religious Program—Tel: 806-667-3610. Hermidia Zapata, D.R.E. Students 85.
Mission—St. Isidore 510 S. Ave. D, Abernathy, Hale Co. 79311. Deacon Juan Villanueva, (Retired).
Catechesis/Religious Program—Tel: 806-298-4519. Connie Regma, D.R.E. Students 99.

PLAINVIEW, HALE CO.

1—ST. ALICE (1911), Rev. James McCartney.
Res.: 1114 Houston St., 79072-712-. Tel: 806-293-1903.
Catechesis/Religious Program—Tel: 806-293-2891. Sr. Vianney Martinez, O.S.F., D.R.E. Students 180.
Mission—San Jose 303 S.E. Fourth, Lockney, Floyd Co. 79241. Tel: 806-652-2321. Sr. Sophie Bonelli, O.S.F., Pastoral Assoc.

2—OUR LADY OF GUADALUPE (1946), [CEM] Rev. John M. Ohlig.
Mailing Address: P.O. Box 1269, 79072. Tel: 806-291-0195
Church: 211 W. Seventh St., 79072. Tel: 806-293-0085; Fax: 806-293-4507.
Catechesis/Religious Program—Tel: 806-293-0086. Anna Maria Davila, D.R.E. Students 350.

3—SACRED HEART (1964), (Hispanic), Rev. Gerard J. Kenney.
Res. & Mailing Address: 400 W. 29th St., 79072-2399. Tel: 806-296-2753; Fax: 806-296-6553.
Catechesis/Religious Program—Tel: 806-296-6553. Students 350.

POST, GARZA CO., HOLY CROSS (1955), [JC] Rev. Paul Karieakatt, O.S.B. (India).
Res.: Box 190, 79356-0190. Tel: 806-495-2791.
Catechesis/Religious Program—Paula Valdez, D.R.E.; Nelva Sybertz, D.R.E. Students 66.
Mission—Blessed Sacrament P.O. Box 119, Wilson, Lynn Co. 79381-0119.

RALLS, CROSBY CO., ST. MICHAEL (1959), (Hispanic), [JC] Rev. Leonardo Pahamtang (Philippines).
Mailing Address: P.O. Box 906, 79357-0906. Tel: 806-253-2008; Fax: 806-253-2008.
Catechesis/Religious Program—Tel: 806-253-2242. Students 99.
Mission—St. Joseph P.O. Box 906, Crosbyton, Crosby Co. 79357. Tel: 806-675-7017.

ROTAN, FISHER CO., ST. JOSEPH (1929), Rev. Msgr. Timothy Schwertner; Deacon Saragosa DeLeon.
Res.: 303 E. Lee, 79546-3011. Tel: 325-735-3285; 325-735-2935 (Office); Fax: 325-735-2181.
Catechesis/Religious Program— Rosemary Carrillo, D.R.E.; Frances Zambrano, D.R.E. Students 47.
Mission—Sacred Heart [CEM] Ranchito, Fisher Co.
Mission—St. Mary Aspermont, Stonewall Co.

SEMINOLE, GAINES CO., ST. JAMES (1958), Rev. Reynaldo Reyes.
Res.: P.O. Box 898, 79360-0898. Tel: 915-758-2371.
Catechesis/Religious Program—Maria Hernandez, D.R.E.; Margie Martinez, D.R.E. Students 235.
Mission—St. Paul's P.O. Box 1321, Seagraves, Gaines Co. 79359-1321. Tel: 806-546-2950.

SHALLOWATER, LUBBOCK CO., ST. PHILLIP BENIZI (1967), (Hispanic), [JC] Revs. Nicolas Rendon (Philippines); Philip Pasupil (Philippines); Deacons Nash Revilla, Pastoral Assoc.; Tommy Alvarado, Pastoral Assoc.; Richard Flores, Pastoral Assoc.
Res.: P.O. Box 39, 79363-0039. Tel: 806-832-5915; 806-832-4088.
Catechesis/Religious Program—Tel: 806-832-5576. Richard Flores, D.R.E.; Julia Escobedo, D.R.E. Students 130.
Mission—St. Anthony (1966),

SLATON, LUBBOCK CO.

1—ST. JOSEPH'S (1912), (German), [JC] Rev. Nicolas Rendon (Philippines).
Res.: 205 S. 19th, 79364-3755. Tel: 806-828-3944; Fax: 806-828-4084.
School—20th W. Division, 79364. Tel: 806-828-6761; Fax: 806-828-5396. Victoria "Tori" Klose, Prin. Lay Teachers 9; Students 75.
Catechesis/Religious Program—Students 175.

2—OUR LADY OF GUADALUPE (1952), [JC] Rev. Lawrence A. Hemp; Deacon Phillip Maldonado.
Res.: 705 S. Fourth, 79363-5406. Tel: 806-828-5108 (Office).
Catechesis/Religious Program—Tel: 806-828-4573. Iris Garcia, D.R.E. (Elementary); Billy Gonzales, D.R.E. (High School); Louisa Gonzales, D.R.E. (High School). Students 193.

SNYDER, SCURRY CO.

1—ST. ELIZABETH'S (1952), [CEM] Rev. Roy Badilles.
Res.: 3005 Ave. A, 79549-3909. Tel: 915-573-2590; Fax: 915-573-1553.
Catechesis/Religious Program—Tel: 915-573-8824. Students 119.
Mission—St. John Hwy. 84, Hermeleigh, Scurry Co. 79549.

2—OUR LADY OF GUADALUPE (1945), (Hispanic), [CEM] [JC 2] Rev. Jose Badilles.
Res.: 1311 Ave. K, 79549-9533. Tel: 915-573-3866 (Office); 915-573-1569 (Res.); Fax: 915-573-7142.
Catechesis/Religious Program—Tel: 915-573-7142; Fax: 915-573-7142. Lupe Lopez, D.R.E.; Hope Lopez, D.R.E. Students 182.

SPUR, DICKENS CO., ST. MARY (1948), Rev. Hugh Thekkel, O.S.B.; Deacon Pete Garcia.
Res.: Box 189, 79370-0189. Tel: 806-271-3161; Fax: 806-271-4385.
Catechesis/Religious Program—Students 65.
Mission—Epiphany [JC] Jayton, Kent Co.

STAMFORD, JONES CO., ST. ANN (1952), [CEM] Rev. George Roney.
Res.: 104 New Braunfels, 79553-6415. Tel: 915-773-2659; Fax: 915-773-3622.
Catechesis/Religious Program—Students 78.
Mission—St. George 901 N. 16th St., Haskell, Haskell Co. 79521-3340. Tel: 817-864-3171.
Catechesis/Religious Program—Students 40.

WOLFFORTH, LUBBOCK CO., ST. FRANCIS OF ASSISI MISSION., , See San Ramon, Woodrow for details.

WOODROW, LUBBOCK CO., SAN RAMON (1974), Unassigned.
Church: 15706 Loop 493, 79423. Tel: 806-863-2201.
Catechesis/Religious Program—Tel: 806-863-3435. Students 161.
Mission—St. Francis of Assisi P.O. Box 785, Wolfforth, Lubbock Co. 79382. Tel: 806-866-9007.

Special Assignment:
Rev.—
Anton, William, Dir. Scouting, St. John Newman Church, 5802 22nd St., 79407.

On Duty Outside the Diocese:
Rev.—
Krisman, Ronald, Annunciation Catholic Church, P.O. Box 915887, Longwood, FL 32791-5887.

Retired:
Rev. Msgrs.—
Comiskey, James, 3815 50th, Ste. 70, 79413.
Gonzalez, Antonio, P.O. Box 98255, 79499.
Halfmann, Curtis T., P.O. Box 94722, 79493.
James, Joseph W., Our Lady of Mercy Retreat Center, P.O. Box 744, Slaton, 79364.
Revs.—
Diebel, Thomas, Box 10753, 79408.
Hayden, Johnrose, 428 E. Loyola Dr., Tempe, AZ 85282.
Huber, Clarence, 5062 N. Franks Ln., Monticello, IN 47960.
Judd, Timothy, Sacred Heart Mission, P.O. Box 530, Petersburg, 79250-0530.
Vaze Parampil, Thomas, St. Thomas Priest Home, Desam P.O., Aluva-Kerala 683103, India.

Permanent Deacons:
Acevedo, Miguel, (Retired), St. Mary Magdalen, Earth
Aguilar, Francisco, St. Jude, Tahoka
Almager, Ramon, St. James, Seminole
Alvarado, Tommy, St. Anthony, Anton
Barrera, Salome, Our Lady of Guadalupe, Snyder
Behnke, Leroy, St. Phillip Benizi, Shallowater
Brito, Benny, Our Lady of Grace, Lubbock
Broderson, Kyle, St. John Neumann, Lubbock
Bustamante, Juan, St. Ann, Stamford
Canale, Randy, Christ the King, Lubbock
Cantu, Agustin, Sacred Heart, Plainview
Castro, Daniel L., St. Patrick, Lubbock
Cavazos, Jesus Z., On Duty Outside the Diocese
Cochran, Clarke E., St. John Neumann, Lubbock
DeLeon, Saragosa, (Retired), St. Joseph, Rotan
Esquivel, Jessie, St. William, Denver City.
Estrada, Julian, St. George, Haskell
Flores, Antonio B., St. Michael's, Ralls
Flores, Richard, St. John Neumann, Lubbock
Franco, Alfredo, St. Ann, Morton
Garcia, Doroteo, Sacred Heart, Littlefield
Garcia, Pedro, St. Michael's, Ralls
Gracia, Pedro, St. Mary, Spur
Guerrero, Jesus, Our Lady of Grace, Lubbock
Hernandez, Ernesto, Our Lady of Grace, Lubbock
Jaime, Alfredo B., Our Lady of Grace, Lubbock
Juarez, Pedro, Sacred Heart, Littlefield
King, Edward, St. Michael, Levelland
Linder, Darris D., St. Joseph's, Slaton
Little, Sidney R., St. Elizabeth's, Lubbock
Maldonado, Phillip, Our Lady of Guadalupe, Slaton
Martinez, Joe, Our Lady of Guadalupe, Lubbock
Martinez, Nasario, (Retired), St. Mary's, Sudan
McCarthy, Thomas E., St. John Neumann, Lubbock
McDonald, Isaac, St. Michael, Levelland
Mireles, Ted, (Retired)
Ortegon, Frank, Our Lady of Guadalupe, Snyder
Peralez, Catarino, (Retired), St. Philip Benizi, Idalou
Ramirez, Robert, Our Lady of Guadalupe, Snyder
Rendon, Dario, (Retired), St. Patrick's, Lubbock
Revilla, Nash, St. Phillip Benizi, Shallowater
Richard, Joseph N., St. John Newmann, Lubbock
Rodriguez, Simon, Christ the King, Lubbock
Rodriguez, Urbano, Outside the Diocese
Serna, Ray, Sacred Heart, Littlefield
Thompson, Richard, Sacred Heart, Littlefield
Valenzuela, Daniel, St. Margaret Mary, Lamesa
Vasquez, Enrique, St. Mary Magdalen, Floydada
Villanueva, Juan, St. Isidore, Abernathy
Wood, Richard, St. John Neumann, Lubbock

INSTITUTIONS LOCATED IN THE DIOCESE

[A] CHRISTIAN RENEWAL CENTERS

LUBBOCK. *Christian Renewal Center*, P.O. Box 98700, 79499-8700. Tel: 806-792-1105; Fax: 806-792-5613. Alicia Alvarez, Center Dir. Total Staff 3.

Office for Cursillo Movement, P.O. Box 98303, 79499-8296. Tel: 806-792-4308. Rev. Andrew Mendoza, Spiritual Dir.

[B] RETREAT HOUSES

SLATON. *Our Lady of Mercy Retreat Center*, 605 S. 19th St., P.O. Box 744, 79364-0744. Tel: 806-828-6428; Fax: 806-828-3856. Email: mercy@door.net. Web: www.catholiclubbock.org/mercycenter. Rev. Msgr. Joseph W. James, Dir. Emeritus (Retired); Deacon Darris D. Linder, Exec. Dir. Total in Residence 6; Total Staff 10.

[C] CONVENTS AND RESIDENCES FOR SISTERS

LUBBOCK. *St. Mary Convent*, 3820 24th St., 79410. Tel: 806-725-6000; Fax: 806-725-4379. Email: colivier@covhs.org. Covenant Hospital Convent.

Our Lady of Grace Convent, 3101 Erskine, 79415. Tel: 806-747-7472. Missionary Catechists of the Sacred Hearts of Jesus and Mary 3.

PLAINVIEW. *St. Alice Convent*, 1114 Houston, 79072. Tel: 806-296-5426; Fax: 806-296-5426. St. Francis Mission Community Sisters 3.

WOLFFORTH. *St. Francis Mission Sisters* (1981), Our Lady of the Angels Motherhouse, 8202 CR 7700, 79382. Tel: 806-863-4904; Fax: 806-863-4906. Email: franciscan@door.net. St. Francis Mission Community 7.

[D] MISCELLANEOUS LISTINGS

LUBBOCK. *Catholic Foundation of the Diocese of Lubbock, Inc.*, P.O. Box 98700, 79499-8700. Tel: 806-792-3943; Fax: 806-792-2953. Email: nptomey@catholiclubbock.org. Web: www.catholiclubbock.org.

Christ the King Cathedral School Foundation, 4011 54th St., 79413. Tel: 806-795-6477; Fax: 806-795-9715. Email: ccason@CTKCathederal.org. Web: www.CTKCathederal.org. Art Chavez, Chm. Total Staff 16.

RELIGIOUS INSTITUTES OF WOMEN REPRESENTED IN THE DIOCESE

For further details refer to the corresponding bracketed number in the Religious Institutes of Men or Women section.

[]—*Dominican Sisters*—O.P.

[2700]—*Missionary Cathechists of the Sacred Hearts of Jesus and Mary*—M.C.SS.CC.

[2575]—*Sisters of Mercy of the Americas*—R.S.M.

[1620]—*Sisters of Saint Francis of Millvale, PA*—O.S.F.

[3830]—*Sisters of St. Joseph of Orange*—C.S.J.

[]—*St. Francis Mission Community* (Amarillo, TX)—O.S.F.

NECROLOGY

† Bach, James To Duc, (Retired)—Died March 31, 2003

Diocese of Madison

(Dioecesis Madisonensis)

Most Reverend

ROBERT C. MORLINO

Bishop of Madison; ordained June 1, 1974; appointed Bishop of Helena July 6, 1999; consecrated and installed September 21, 1999; appointed Bishop of Madison May 23, 2003; installed August 1, 2003. *Chancery: Bishop O'Connor Catholic Pastoral Center*, 702 S. High Point Rd., P.O. Box 44983, Madison, WI 53744-4983.

Chancery: Bishop O'Connor Catholic Pastoral Center, 702 S. High Point Rd., P.O. Box 44983, Madison, WI 53744-4983. Tel: 608-821-3000; Fax: 608-821-3013.

Web: www.madisondiocese.org

Email: diocese@madisondiocese.org

Most Reverend

WILLIAM H. BULLOCK, D.D., ED.S.

Retired Bishop of Madison; ordained June 7, 1952; appointed Auxiliary Bishop of St. Paul and Minneapolis and Titular Bishop of Natchez June 3, 1980; consecrated August 12, 1980; appointed Bishop of Des Moines February 10, 1987; installed April 2, 1987; appointed Bishop of Madison April 13, 1993; installed June 14, 1993; retired May 23, 2003.

Most Reverend

GEORGE O. WIRZ, D.D., S.T.L.

Retired Auxiliary Bishop of Madison; ordained May 31, 1952; appointed Auxiliary Bishop of Madison and Titular Bishop of Municipa December 20, 1977; consecrated March 9, 1978; retired February 10, 2004. *Chancery: Bishop O'Connor Center*, 3577 S. High Point Rd., Madison, WI 53719-4999.

ESTABLISHED 1946.

Square Miles 8,070.

Corporate Title: "Roman Catholic Diocese of Madison."

Comprises the Counties of Columbia, Dane, Grant, Green, Green Lake, Iowa, Jefferson, Lafayette, Marquette, Rock and Sauk in the State of Wisconsin.

Legal Title: For legal titles of parishes and diocesan institutions, consult the Chancery.

STATISTICAL OVERVIEW

Personnel	
Bishop	1
Auxiliary Bishops	1
Retired Bishops	1
Priests: Diocesan Active in Diocese	99
Priests: Diocesan Active Outside Diocese	1
Priests: Retired, Sick or Absent	49
Number of Diocesan Priests	149
Religious Priests in Diocese	13
Total Priests in Diocese	162
Extern Priests in Diocese	2
Ordinations:	
Diocesan Priests	3
Permanent Deacons	2
Permanent Deacons in Diocese	2
Total Brothers	6
Total Sisters	298
Parishes	
Parishes	135
With Resident Pastor:	
Resident Diocesan Priests	84
Resident Religious Priests	1
Without Resident Pastor:	
Administered by Priests	45
Professional Ministry Personnel:	
Brothers	6
Sisters	27
Lay Ministers	131
Welfare	
Catholic Hospitals	4
Total Assisted	335,305
Health Care Centers	2
Total Assisted	668
Homes for the Aged	4
Total Assisted	956
Day Care Centers	18
Total Assisted	988
Special Centers for Social Services	7
Total Assisted	36,120
Residential Care of Disabled	1
Total Assisted	375
Educational	
Diocesan Students in Other Seminaries	6
Total Seminarians	6
Colleges and Universities	1
Total Students	2,400
High Schools, Private	1
Total Students	664
Elementary Schools, Diocesan and Parish	44
Total Students	6,878
Elementary Schools, Private	1
Total Students	306
Catechesis/Religious Education:	
High School Students	8,445
Elementary Students	15,654
Total Students under Catholic Instruction	34,353
Teachers in the Diocese:	
Brothers	2
Sisters	27
Lay Teachers	831
Vital Statistics	
Receptions into the Church:	
Infant Baptism Totals	3,058
Adult Baptism Totals	128
Received into Full Communion	282
First Communions	2,813
Confirmations	2,249
Marriages:	
Catholic	628
Interfaith	396
Total Marriages	1,024
Deaths	1,753
Total Catholic Population	269,556
Total Population	947,699

Former Bishops—Most Revs. WILLIAM P. O'CONNOR, D.D., Ph.D., ord. March 10, 1912; appt. Bishop of Superior, Dec. 31, 1941; consecrated March 7, 1942; transferred to as first Bishop of Madison, Feb. 22, 1946; resigned Feb. 22, 1967; died July 13, 1973; CLETUS F. O'DONNELL, D.D., J.C.D., ord. May 3, 1941; appt. Titular Bishop of Abrittum and Auxiliary of Chicago, Oct. 26, 1960; consecrated Dec. 21, 1960; promoted to Bishop of Madison, Feb. 22, 1967; resigned April 18, 1992; died Aug. 31, 1992; WILLIAM H. BULLOCK, D.D., ED.S. (Retired), ordained June 7, 1952; appointed Auxiliary Bishop of St. Paul and Minneapolis and Titular Bishop of Natchez June 3, 1980; consecrated Aug. 12, 1980; appointed Bishop of Des Moines Feb. 10, 1987; installed April 2, 1987; appointed Bishop of Madison April 13, 1993; installed June 14, 1993; retired May 23, 2003.

Vicar-General—Most Rev. GEORGE O. WIRZ, D.D., S.T.L.; Rev. Msgr. PAUL J. SWAIN, J.D.

Chancery—Bishop O'Connor Catholic Pastoral Center, 702 S. High Point Rd., P.O. Box 44983, Madison, 53744-4983. Office Hours: Mon.-Fri. 8-4:30

Chancellor—Mr. JAY CONZEMIUS, J.C.L.

Director of Finance—GREGORY J. KELLER. Tel: 608-821-3021.

Diocesan Tribunal—Bishop O'Connor Catholic Pastoral Center, 702 S. High Point Rd., P.O. Box 44983, Madison, 53744-4983. Tel: 608-821-3060; Fax: 608-821-3067. Email: tribunal@straphael.org.

Judicial Vicar—Rev. Msgr. MICHAEL E. HIPPEE, J.C.L.

Director of the Tribunal—JAY CONZEMIUS, J.C.L.

Judges—Rev. JAMES W. HINNEN, J.C.L.; Rev. Msgr. MICHAEL E. HIPPEE, J.C.L.; Ms. ADELA MARIA KIM, J.C.L.; Mr. JAY CONZEMIUS, J.C.L.

Defender of the Bond—Mr. JAY CONZEMIUS, J.C.L.

Auditor/Advocate—VACANT.

Notary—SUSAN STACK.

Diocesan Consultors—Most Rev. GEORGE O. WIRZ, D.D., S.T.L.; Rev. Msgrs. JOSEPH P. HIGGINS, Sec. (Retired); PAUL J. SWAIN, J.D.; DANIEL T. GANSHERT; JAMES L. GUNN; Revs. JOHN H. HEDRICK; DAVID H. RUNDE (Retired).

Presbyteral Council—Most Revs. ROBERT C. MORLINO, Pres.; GEORGE O. WIRZ, D.D., S.T.L., Ex Officio. Elected: Rev. Msgr. JAMES L. GUNN; Revs. JOHN R. AUBY; KENNETH J. KLINK; Rev. Msgr. JAMES UPPENA; Revs. JOHN H. HEDRICK; ROGER H. TAYLOR; JOHN M. MEINHOLZ; STEPHEN J. UMHOEFER; D. CHARLES SCHLUTER; GARY L. KRAHENBUHL; STEVEN J. KORTENDICK; PATRICK NORRIS, O.P.; DALE W. GRUBBA; JASON E. HESSELING. Appointed: Rev. Msgrs. MICHAEL L. BURKE; DANIEL T. GANSHERT; PAUL J. SWAIN, J.D.; Revs. TODD VAN NATTA; DAVID A. WANISH.

Personnel Board—Revs. MICHAEL A. RESOP; MICHAEL C. RICHEL; WILLIAM J. SEIPP; Rev. Msgrs. DOUGLAS L. DUSHACK; PAUL J. SWAIN, J.D.; GERARD M. HEALY.

Vicar for Religious—Sr. LUCILLE MARIE FROST, O.P., 1000 Edgewood College Dr., Madison, 53711.

Deaneries—Revs. RAYMOND J. DISCHLER, Columbia Deanery; MICHAEL C. RICHEL, East Dane Deanery; VACANT, Grant Deanery; VACANT, Iowa Deanery; Revs. THOMAS P. MARR, Jefferson Deanery; RANDY J. BUONDE, Lafayette Deanery; Rev. Msgr. KENNETH J. FIEDLER, Madison Deanery; Rev. DALE W. GRUBBA, Marquette-Green Lake Deanery; Rev. Msgr. RAYMOND N. KERTZ, Rock-Green Deanery; Revs. GERALD P. VOSEN, Sauk Deanery; THOMAS L. KELLEY, West Dane Deanery.

Diocesan Offices and Directors

Apostolate to the Handicapped—Rev. Msgr. THOMAS F. CAMPION, P.O. Box 443, Monroe, 53566. Tel: 608-324-1000.

Apostolate to the Deaf—VACANT.

Archives—VACANT, Archivist, Bishop O'Connor Catholic Pastoral Center, 702 S. High Point Rd.,

P.O. Box 44983, Madison, 53744-4983. Tel: 608-821-3000; Fax: 608-821-3013.

Catholic Committee on Scouting—Mr. THOMAS LEONARD, Chm., 533 Blanche Dr., Apt. #3, Milton, 53563. Tel: 608-868-6116.

Building Commission—Rev. Msgrs. THOMAS F. BAXTER; MICHAEL E. HIPPEE, J.C.L.; DUANE R. MOELLENBERNDT; Rev. DONALD J. HEIAR; Dr. PATRICK GORMAN; Mr. PAUL BROWN; Mr. ARTHUR MCCLURE; Mrs. SABINA MIRABELLI-CONZEMIUS; Mr. TONY PAWLOWSKY, Chm.; Rev. Msgr. PAUL J. SWAIN, J.D.

Camp Gray—PHILIP C. DELONG, Dir., E10213 Shady Lane Rd., Reedsburg, 53959. Tel: 608-356-8200; Fax: 608-356-5855. Email: bigfun@campgray.com.

Catholic Relief Services—Rev. Msgr. PAUL J. SWAIN, J.D.

Cemeteries—THOMAS B. HANLON JR., Diocesan Dir., Central Office, 2705 Regent St., Madison, 53705. Tel: 608-238-5561; Fax: 608-238-5768.

Charities--Catholic Charities of the Diocese of Madison, Inc.—Bishop O'Connor Catholic Pastoral Center, 702 S. High Point Rd., P.O. Box 46550, Madison, 53744-6550. Tel: 608-821-3100. BRIAN CAIN, Dir. Fax: 608-821-3125. Madison Area Offices, 30 S. Franklin St., Madison, 53703. Tel: 608-256-2358. 426 S. Yellowstone Dr., Ste. 100, Madison, 53719. Tel: 608-833-4800. Beloit District Office, 3311 Prairie Ave., Beloit, 53511. Tel: 608-365-3665. Janesville District Office, 2020 E. Milwaukee St., Ste. 208, Janesville, 53545. Tel: 608-752-4906.

Office for the Continuing Education of Priests—Most Rev. GEORGE O. WIRZ, D.D., S.T.L., Bishop O'Connor Catholic Pastoral Center, 702 S. High Point Rd., P.O. Box 44983, Madison, 53744-4983. Tel: 608-821-3000.

Education—VACANT, Dir., Religious Educ., Bishop O'Connor Catholic Pastoral Center, 702 S. High Point Rd., P.O. Box 44983, Madison, 53744-4983. Tel: 608-821-3160; JACK MCBRIDE, Assoc. Dir., Adult & Special Educ.; BEN WEISSE, Assoc. Dir., Youth Ministries & Child Catechetics; JAMES R. SILVER, Ed.D., Supt., Schools. Tel: 608-821-3180; JUDY L. PEPPARD, Asst. Supt., Bishop O'Connor Catholic Pastoral Center, 702 S. High Point Rd., P.O. Box 44983, Madison, 53744-4983.

Saint Raphael Society Clergy Retirement Plan—Rev. Msgr. PAUL J. SWAIN, J.D., Bishop O'Connor Catholic Pastoral Center, 702 S. High Point Rd., P.O. Box 44983, Madison, 53744-4983. Tel: 608-821-3015.

Council of Catholic Women—Rev. Msgr. DUANE R. MOELLENBERNDT, Moderator, Sacred Hearts of Jesus & Mary, 221 Columbus St., Sun Prairie, 53590-2297. Tel: 608-837-7381; Rev. LORIN M. BOWENS, Co-Moderator, St. Boniface Parish, P.O. Box 60, Lime Ridge, 53942. Tel: 608-986-2101.

Director of Communications—WILLIAM K. BROPHY. Tel: 608-821-3033.

Holy Childhood, Pontifical Association—Rev. Msgr. DELBERT L. SCHMELZER, Dir. (Retired), Bishop O'Connor Catholic Pastoral Center, 702 S. High Point Rd., P.O. Box 44983, Madison, 53744-4983. Tel: 608-821-3052.

Information—Rev. Msgr. PAUL J. SWAIN, J.D., P.O. Box 44983, Madison, 53744-4983.

Office of Worship—Dr. PATRICK GORMAN, Bishop O'Connor Catholic Pastoral Center, 702 S. High Point Rd., P.O. Box 44983, Madison, 53744-4983. Tel: 608-821-3080.

Office of Family Ministry—VACANT, Dir.; BEVERLY HARTBERG, Assoc. Dir., Bishop O'Connor Catholic Pastoral Center, 702 S. High Point Rd., P.O. Box 44983, Madison, 53744-4983. Tel: 608-821-3168.

Office for Justice and Peace—J. MARK BRINKMOELLER, Dir., Bishop O'Connor Catholic Pastoral Center, 702 S. High Point Rd., P.O. Box 44983, Madison, 53744-4983. Tel: 608-821-3086.

St. Martin House—Catholic Multicultural Center, 1862 Beld St., Madison, 53713. Tel: 608-255-1287.

Newman Apostolate—Madison: Rev. RANDY J. TIMMERMAN, Dir., St. Paul Univ. Catholic Center, 723 State St., Madison, 53703. Tel: 608-258-3140. Platteville: Rev. JAMES H. MURPHY, St. Augustine Newman Center, 135 S. Hickory St., Platteville, 53818. Tel: 608-348-7530.

Newspaper—MARY UHLER, Editor, Bishop O'Connor Catholic Pastoral Center, 702 S. High Point Rd., P.O. Box 44983, Madison, 53744-4983. Tel: 608-821-3070. "Catholic Herald, Madison Edition"

Office of Hispanic Ministry—VACANT, Dir., Bishop O'Connor Catholic Pastoral Center, 702 S. High Point Rd., P.O. Box 44983, Madison, 53744-4983. Tel: 608-821-3092.

Centro Pastoral Guadalupano—ROMILIA SCHLUETER, Coord., Catholic Multicultural Center, 1862 Beld St., Madison, 53725-9226. Tel: 608-255-8471.

Office of Pastoral Services—KATE WISKUS, Dir., Bishop O'Connor Catholic Pastoral Center, 702 S. High Point Rd., P.O. Box 44983, Madison, 53744-4983. Tel: 608-821-3083.

Propagation of the Faith—Rev. Msgr. DELBERT L. SCHMELZER, Dir. (Retired), Bishop O'Connor Catholic Pastoral Center, 702 S. High Point Rd., P.O. Box 44983, Madison, 53744-4983. Tel: 608-821-3052.

St. Vincent de Paul Society—Rev. FRANCIS J. STEFFEN, 305 W. Main St., P.O. Box 429, Dickeyville, 53808-0429. Tel: 608-568-7519.

Serra Clubs—Madison: Rev. JAMES R. BARTYLLA. Janesville: Rev. JOHN R. AUBY. Beloit: Rev. GARY L. KRAHENBUHL.

Vigilance Council— (The Very Rev. Deans)

Vocations—Bishop O'Connor Catholic Pastoral Center, 702 S. High Point Rd., P.O. Box 44983, Madison, 53744-4983. Tel: 608-821-3088.

Wisconsin Catholic Conference—JOHN HUEBSCHER, Exec. Sec., 131 W. Wilson St., Ste. 1105, Madison, 53703. Tel: 608-257-0004.

Office of Human Resources—JOHN MILLER, Dir., Bishop O'Connor Catholic Pastoral Center, 702 S. High Point Rd., P.O. Box 44983, Madison, 53744-4983. Tel: 608-821-3047.

Office of Stewardship and Development—Mr. JAY CONZEMIUS, J.C.L., Dir., Bishop O'Connor Catholic Pastoral Center, 702 S. High Point Rd., P.O. Box 44983, Madison, 53744-4983. Tel: 608-821-3040.

CLERGY, PARISHES, MISSIONS AND PAROCHIAL SCHOOLS

CITY OF MADISON
(DANE COUNTY)

1—ST. RAPHAEL CATHEDRAL, [JC], (Linked with Holy Redeemer, Madison) Rev. Msgr. Paul J. Swain, J.D., Rector; Rev. Michael E. Moon, Hispanic Min.
Res.: 222 W. Main St., 53703. Tel: 608-256-5614; Fax: 608-256-5842.
Holy Redeemer: 120 W. Johnson St., 53703-2297. Tel: 608-255-1658; Fax: 608-225-5386.

2—ST. BERNARD, [JC] Rev. Msgr. Michael E. Hippee, J.C.L.
Res.: 2450 Atwood Ave., 53704. Tel: 608-249-9256; Fax: 608-244-3773.
Catechesis/Religious Program—2438 Atwood Ave., 53704. Students 135.

3—BLESSED SACRAMENT, [JC] Revs. Patrick F. Norris, O.P. (CHI); Ronald G. Kreul, O.P. In Res., Revs. Benjamin J. Russell, O.P.; John Vincent Blake, O.P.; Bros. Vincent Dirienzo; Gilbert Hensley; Dominic Rothering.
Res.: 2131 Rowley Ave., 53726. Tel: 608-238-3471; Fax: 608-238-4220.
School—2112 Hollister Ave., 53726. Tel: 608-233-6155. Lay Teachers 23; Students 337.
Catechesis/Religious Program—Students 192.

4—ST. DENNIS, [JC] Revs. Kent A. Schmitt; Tait C. Shroeder.
Res.: 313 Dempsey Rd., 53714. Tel: 608-246-5124; Fax: 608-246-5138.
School—Tel: 608-246-5121. Dominican Sisters Sinsinawa 4; Lay Teachers 14; Students 201.
Catechesis/Religious Program—Tel: 608-246-5123; Fax: 608-246-5138. Judy Hronek, D.R.E. (PreK-3); Ann Esser, D.R.E. (4-8); David Hendrickson, D.R.E. (H.S.). Students 855.

5—HOLY REDEEMER, , (Linked with St. Raphael Cathedral) Rev. Michael E. Moon; Rev. Msgr. Paul J. Swain, J.D.
Res.: 120 W. Johnson St., 53703. Tel: 608-255-1658; Fax: 608-255-5386.
St. Raphael Cathedral: 222 W. Main St., 53703-3197. Tel: 608-256-5614; Fax: 608-256-5842.
Catechesis/Religious Program—Tel: 608-277-7675. Milton Pozo, D.R.E.; Mercedes Pozo, D.R.E. Students 90.

6—IMMACULATE HEART OF MARY, [JC] Rev. John M. Meinholz.
Res.: 5101 Schofield Ave., 53716. Tel: 608-221-1521; Fax: 608-221-1794.
School—4913 Schofield Ave., 53716. Tel: 608-222-8831; Fax: 608-221-4492. Lay Teachers 16; Students 122.
Catechesis/Religious Program—Students 194.

7—ST. JAMES, [JC] Rev. Msgr. Thomas F. Baxter.
Res.: 1128 St. James Ct., 53715. Tel: 608-255-1656; Fax: 608-255-6311.
School—1204 St. James Ct., 53715. Tel: 608-256-3095; Fax: 608-256-6311. Lay Teachers 17; Students 160.

8—SAINT JOSEPH, Merged, with All Saint, Rev. Msgr. Kenneth J. Fiedler, Admin.; Jack McBride, D.R.E.
Res.: 1905 W. Beltline Hwy., 53713. Tel: 608-271-5771; Fax: 608-271-9366.
Catechesis/Religious Program—Tel: 608-821-3161; Fax: 608-821-3181. Students 70.

9—ST. MARIA GORETTI, [JC] Rev. Msgr. Michael L. Burke; Rev. James M. Poster.
Res.: 10 Maria Pl., 53711. Tel: 608-271-7421; Fax: 608-275-6621.
Church: 5313 Flad Ave., 53711.
School—5405 Flad Ave., 53711. Tel: 608-271-7551; Fax: 608-275-6625. Lay Teachers 26; Students 340.
Catechesis/Religious Program—Tel: 608-271-8081. Students 600.

10—OUR LADY, QUEEN OF PEACE, [JC] Rev. Msgr. Kenneth J. Fiedler; Revs. Todd Van Natta; Brian J. Wilk; Sr. Sue Hetebrueg, S.S.N.D., Pastoral Assoc.
Res. and Parish Center: 401 S. Owen Dr., 53711. Tel: 608-231-4600; Fax: 608-213-4606.
School—418 Holly Ave., 53711. Tel: 608-231-4580. Lay Teachers 28; Students 484.
Catechesis/Religious Program—Tel: 608-231-4610. Mary Jo Trapani, D.R.E. Students 380.

11—ST. PATRICK, [JC] Rev. William J. Seipp.
Res.: 404 E. Main St., 53703. Tel: 608-257-5000; Fax: 608-257-5565.

12—ST. PAUL UNIVERSITY PARISH, [JC] Revs. Randy J. Timmerman; David A. Wanish; Faye A. Darnall, M.Div.; Steven W. Dressel, J.D., Dir. of Liturgical Ministries.
Office—723 State St., 53703. Tel: 608-258-3140; Fax: 608-258-3141.

13—ST. PETER, [JC] Rev. Roger G. Nilles.
Res.: 5001 N. Sherman Ave., 53704. Tel: 608-249-6651; Fax: 608-249-6651.
Catechesis/Religious Program—Students 271.

14—ST. THOMAS AQUINAS, [JC] Rev. Msgr. Terrence Connors.
Res.: 602 Everglade Dr., 53717. Tel: 608-833-2600; Fax: 608-833-1129.
Catechesis/Religious Program—Tel: 608-833-2606. Holly Irving, D.R.E.; Kay Schachte, D.R.E. Students 479.

OUTSIDE THE CITY OF MADISON

ALBANY, GREEN CO., ST. PATRICK, [CEM] Rev. Donn Joseph Heiar Jr.
Res.: 1005 W. 2nd Ave., Brodhead, 53520-1406. Tel: 608-897-2666; Fax: 608-897-4614.

ARGYLE, LAFAYETTE CO., ST. JOSEPH, [CEM 2] Rev. Thomas H. Schroeder.
Res.: 313 N. Lafayette St., P.O. Box 76, 53504. Tel: 608-543-3631.
Catechesis/Religious Program—Tel: 608-543-3053. Ms. Marie Isely, D.R.E. Students 52.

ASHTON, DANE CO., ST. PETER'S, [CEM] Rev. Eugene F. Hollfelder.
Res.: 7121 Co. Trunk K, Middleton, 53562. Tel: 608-831-4843; Fax: 608-831-5377.
School—Tel: 608-831-4846; Fax: 608-831-5377. Lay Teachers 6; Students 40.
Catechesis/Religious Program—Students 133.

AVOCA, IOWA CO., ST. JOSEPH, [CEM] Rev. Roger H. Taylor.
Res.: 341 N. Wisconsin Ave., P.O. Box 35, Muscoda, 53573. Tel: 608-739-3391; Fax: 608-739-9195.

BARABOO, SAUK CO., ST. JOSEPH, [CEM] Rev. Gerald P. Vosen.
Res.: P.O. Box 70, 53913. Tel: 608-356-4773; Fax: 608-356-4024.
School—Lay Teachers 11; Students 152.
Catechesis/Religious Program—Tel: 608-356-5353; Fax: 608-356-4024. Sr. Rose Marie Dischler, O.P., D.R.E. (Grade 1-5); Becky Thompson, D.R.E. (Grade 6-12). Students 337.

BARNEVELD, IOWA CO., IMMACULATE CONCEPTION, [CEM] [JC] Rev. Donald F. Lange.
Res.: 803 W. Main St., Ridgeway, 53582. Tel: 608-924-2441.
Catechesis/Religious Program—111 E. Main St., Ridgeway, 53582. Tel: 608-924-1650. Students 88.

BELLEVILLE, DANE CO., ST. MARY OF LOURDES, [CEM] Rev. Kenneth J. Klink.
Res.: 221 Frederick St., P.O. Box 349, 53508. Tel: 608-424-3681.
Catechesis/Religious Program—Tel: 608-527-2153. Kay Parish, D.R.E.; Dorothy Love, D.R.E. Students 640.

BELMONT, LAFAYETTE CO., ST. PHILOMENA, [CEM] Rev. Monte E. Robinson.
Res.: 338 Chestnut St., Box 345, 53510. Tel: 608-762-5446.
Catechesis/Religious Program— Also serves these Missions: St. Michael's at Calamine, WI & Immaculate Conception at Truman, WI Students 114.

BELOIT, ROCK CO.

1—ST. JUDE, [JC] Rev. Steven J. Kontendick.
Res.: 747 Hackett St., 53511. Tel: 608-364-2820; Fax: 608-364-2822.
School—Brother Dutton School, 717 Hackett St., 53511. Tel: 608-364-2825; Fax: 608-364-2827. Lay Teachers 13; Students 103.
Catechesis/Religious Program—Students 208.

2—Our Lady of the Assumption, [JC] Rev. Gary L. Krahenbuhl.
Res.: 2222 Shopiere Rd., 53511. Tel: 608-362-9066; Fax: 608-368-2820.
School—Lay Teachers 14; Students 156.
Catechesis/Religious Program—Tel: 608-362-1231. Christine Scallon, D.R.E.; Sandy Blevins, Youth Min. Students 273.
3—St. Paul, Closed., 1988. For inquiries for parish records contact St. Thomas the Apostle, Beloit.
4—St. Thomas the Apostle, Rev. James G. Kuhn.
Res.: 822 E. Grand Ave., P.O. Box 933, 53512. Tel: 608-362-1034; Fax: 608-363-9931.
Catechesis/Religious Program—Ruth Kolpack, D.R.E. Students 194.

Benton, Lafayette Co., St. Patrick, [CEM] Rev. Cyril O. Weisensel.
Res.: P.O. Box 3, 53803. Tel: 608-759-2131.
Catechesis/Religious Program—Students 119.

Berlin, Green Lake Co.
1—All Saints, [CEM 2] Rev. Jerome J. Maksvytis.
Church & Res.: 167 N. Wisconsin 54923. Tel: 920-361-2354; Fax: 920-361-9781.
Catechesis/Religious Program— 54923. Tel: 920-361-1391. Students 280.
2—St. Joseph, Merged, with St. Michael, Berlin and St. Stanislaus, Berlin to form All Saints, Berlin.
3—St. Michael, Merged, with St. Joseph, Berlin and St. Stanislaus, Berlin to form All Saints, Berlin.
4—St. Stanislaus, Merged, with St. Joseph, Berlin and St. Michael, Berlin to form All Saints, Berlin.

Blanchardville, Lafayette Co., Immaculate Conception, [CEM] Rev. Sanctus K. Ibe.
Res.: P.O. Box 37, Hollandale, 53544. Tel: 608-967-2344; Fax: 608-967-2344.
Catechesis/Religious Program—P.O. Box 33, 53516. Students 24.

Bloomington, Grant Co., St. Mary, [CEM 2] Rev. Eric H. Nielsen.
Res.: 535 Congress St., P.O. Box 35, 53804-0035. Tel: 608-994-2526; Fax: 608-994-2530.
School—Lay Teachers 6; Students 70.
Catechesis/Religious Program—P.O. Box 33, Blanchardville, 53516. Students 186.

Boscobel, Grant Co., Immaculate Conception, Rev. Robert J. Butz.
Res.: 405 E. LeGrand St., 53805. Tel: 608-375-4257; Fax: 608-375-4256.
Catechesis/Religious Program—Tel: 608-375-2422; 605--. Sue Weigel, D.R.E.; Jan Miller, D.R.E. Students 161.

Briggsville, Marquette Co., St. Mary Help of Christians, [CEM] Revs. John H. Hedrick; Jason E. Hesseling.
Res.: N565 Hwy. A, Box 127, 53920-0127. Tel: 608-981-2282.

Brodhead, Green Co., St. Rose, [JC] Rev. Donn Joseph Heiar Jr.
Res.: 1005 W. 2nd Ave., 53520-1406. Tel: 608-897-2666; Fax: 608-897-4614.

Buffalo, Buffalo Co., St. Andrew, [CEM] Revs. John H. Hedrick; Jason E. Hesseling.
Mailing Address: 318 S. Main St., Pardeeville, 53954. Tel: 608-429-3030; Fax: 608-429-3129.

Calamine, Lafayette Co., St. Michael, [CEM] Rev. Monte E. Robinson.
Res.: 338 Chestnut St., Box 345, Belmont, 53510. Tel: 608-762-5446.

Cambridge, Dane Co., St. Pius X, Rev. Daniel P. Volkert.
Res.: 701 W. Water St., P.O. Box 110, 53523. Tel: 608-423-3015.
Catechesis/Religious Program—Tel: 608-423-4699. Michele Bacsik, D.R.E.; Berdie Daggett, D.R.E. Students 96.

Cassville, Grant Co., St. Charles Borromeo, [CEM 2] Rev. John Norder.
Res.: 605 E. Dewey St., 53806. Tel: 608-725-5595; Fax: 608-725-2343.
School—521 E. Dewey St., 53806. Tel: 608-725-5173; Fax: 608-725-5179. School Sisters of St. Francis 1; Lay Teachers 8; Students 86.
Catechesis/Religious Program—Tel: 608-725-2330. Patricia Ballweg, D.R.E. Students 70.

Castle Rock, Grant Co., St. John Nepomucene, [CEM] Rev. Robert J. Butz.
Res.: 405 E. LeGrand St., Boscobel, 53805. Tel: 608-375-4257; Fax: 608-375-4256.

Clinton, Rock Co., St. Stephen, Rev. J. Thomas Fitzgerald.
Res.: Box 399, 53525. Tel: 608-676-2241; Fax: 608-676-4981.

Clyde, Dodge Co., St. Malachy, [CEM] Rev. Michael A. Resop.
Res.: 1240 Nachreiner Ave., Plain, 53577-0023. Tel: 608-546-2482; Fax: 608-546-2616.

Columbus, Columbia Co., St. Jerome, [CEM] Rev. Bruce M. Hennington.
Parish Office—1550 Farnham St., 53925. Tel: 920-623-3753; Fax: 920-623-1115.
Res.: 329 Folsom St., 53925. Tel: 920-623-2720.
School—Tel: 920-623-5780. Sisters 1; Lay Teachers 13; Students 165.

Cottage Grove, Dane Co., St. Patrick, [CEM] Rev. Msgr. Raymond N. Kertz.
Res.: 434 N. Main St., P.O. Box 400, 53527-0400. Tel: 608-251-7857; Fax: 608-839-3593.
Catechesis/Religious Program—Sandra Dunn, D.R.E.; Lenny Komorowski, Youth Min. Students 330.

Cross Plains, Dane Co., St. Francis Xavier, [CEM] Rev. Thomas L. Kelley.
Res.: 2947 Thinnes St., P.O. Box 35, 53528. Tel: 608-798-3491; Fax: 608-798-2976.
School—Lay Teachers 14; Students 198.
Catechesis/Religious Program—Tel: 608-798-4824. Peggy Liginski, D.R.E.; Cindy Ballweg, D.R.E. Students 267.

Cuba City, Grant Co., St. Rose of Lima, [CEM] Rev. David J. Flanagan.
Res.: 519 W. Roosevelt, 53807. Tel: 608-744-2010; Fax: 608-744-3709.
School—Dominican Sisters Sinsinawa, WI 1; Lay Teachers 10; Students 148.
Catechesis/Religious Program—Students 152.

Dane, Dane Co., St. Michael, [CEM] Rev. Nicholas S. Okere (Nigeria), Admin.
Res.: 53529. Tel: 608-849-5610; Fax: 608-850-5610.
School—Tel: 608-848-5619. Lay Teachers 6; Students 30.

Darlington, Lafayette Co., Holy Rosary, [CEM 2] Rev. Randy J. Budnar.
Res.: 104 E. Harriet St., P.O. Box 208, 53530. Tel: 608-776-2251; Fax: 608-776-4059.
School—Lay Teachers 7; Students 56.
Catechesis/Religious Program—730 Wells St., 53530. Students 389.

Dayton, Green Co., St. James, [CEM] Rev. Kenneth J. Klink.
Res.: 221 Frederick St., P.O. Box 349, Belleville, 53508. Tel: 608-424-3681.

De Forest, Dane Co., St. Olaf, [CEM] Rev. Gary A. Wankerl.
Res.: 623 Jefferson St., 53532. Tel: 608-846-3812.
Catechesis/Religious Program—Tel: 608-846-5726. David Fuccillo, D.R.E. Students 466.

Dickeyville, Grant Co., Holy Ghost, [CEM] Revs. Francis J. Steffen; Francis Xavier Ekwugha.
Res.: 305 W. Main St., 53808. Tel: 608-568-7519; Fax: 608-568-3872.
School—Tel: 608-568-7790; Fax: 608-568-3872. Lay Teachers 7; Students 103.
Catechesis/Religious Program—Mary Cecelia Meyer, D.R.E., (Grade School). Tel: 563-582-5000; Diane Kieler, D.R.E., (High School). Tel: 608-568-3493. Students 95.

Dodgeville, Iowa Co., St. Joseph, [CEM 3] Rev. Paul Ugo Arinze.
Res.: 405 S. Dacotah St., 53533-1799. Tel: 608-930-3392; Fax: 608-930-1722.
School—305 E. Walnut St., 53533. Lay Teachers 13; Students 240.
Catechesis/Religious Program—Students 230.

Doylestown, Columbia Co., St. Patrick, [CEM] Rev. Bruce M. Hennington.
Res.: N4085 Bruce St., P.O. Box 40, 53928. Tel: 920-992-3343; Fax: 920-623-1115.

Durward's Glen, Columbia Co., St. Camillus, [CEM] Rev. Louis Lussier, O.S.Cam.
Res.: W. 11876 McLeish Rd., Baraboo, 53913. Tel: 608-356-8113.
Catechesis/Religious Program—Fax: 608-356-5530. Students 31.

East Bristol, Dane Co., St. Joseph, [CEM] Rev. Gary A. Wankerl.
Res.: 623 Jefferson St., DeForest, 53532. Tel: 608-846-3812.
Catechesis/Religious Program—1935 Highway V, Sun Prairie, 53590. Students 129.

Edgerton, Rock Co., St. Joseph, [CEM 2] Rev. William J. Hower.
Res.: 590 S. St. Joseph's Cir., 53534-1242. Tel: 608-884-3038; Fax: 608-884-3298.
Catechesis/Religious Program—Tel: 608-884-6231. Students 260.

Elk Grove, Lafayette Co., St. Peter, [CEM] Rev. James R. Lins.
Res.: Rfd. 1, Shullsburg, 53586. Tel: 608-965-4518.

Evansville, Rock Co., St. Paul, [CEM] Rev. Donn Joseph Heiar Jr.
Res.: 35 Garfield Ave., 53536. Tel: 608-882-4138; Fax: 608-882-0690.
Catechesis/Religious Program—Students 187.

Fennimore, Grant Co., St. Mary, [CEM] Rev. George B. Horath.
Res.: 930 Jefferson St., 53809. Tel: 608-822-6425.
Catechesis/Religious Program—Tel: 608-822-3520. Students 208.

Footville, Rock Co., St. Augustine, Rev. Donn Joseph Heiar Jr., Admin.
Church: P.O. Box 325, 53537. Tel: 608-876-6252; Fax: 608-876-6252.
Res.: 1005 W. 2nd Ave., Brodhead, 53520.
Catechesis/Religious Program—1438 N. Cty. H, Janesville, 53547. Tel: 608-876-6311. Students 84.

Fort Atkinson, Jefferson Co., St. Joseph, [CEM] Rev. William A. Nolan; Sr. Gemma Therese Harvey, S.S.N.D., Pastoral Assoc.
Res.: 11 N. 3rd St., 53538. Tel: 920-563-3029; Fax: 920-563-3150.
School—310 N. Main St., 53538. Mr. Leonard Bannon, Prin. Lay Teachers 14; Students 102.
Catechesis/Religious Program—Tel: 920-563-4778. Carol Ann Dzwinel, D.R.E.; Lois Fritz, D.R.E. Students 326.

Glen Haven, Grant Co., St. Mary Help of Christians, [CEM 2] Rev. John Norder.
Res.: 605 E. Dewey St., Cassville, 53806. Tel: 608-725-5595; Fax: 608-725-2343.
School—521 E. Dewey St., Cassville, 53806. Tel: 608-725-5173; Fax: 608-725-5179. School Sisters of St. Francis 1; Lay Teachers 8; Students 86.

Gratiot, Lafayette Co., St. Joseph, [CEM] Rev. David J. Flanagan, Admin.
Res.: Box 37, 53541. Tel: 608-922-6456.
Catechesis/Religious Program—Students 38.

Green Lake, Green Lake Co., Our Lady of the Lake, Rev. Philip J. Krogman.
Res.: 530 Ruth St., P.O. Box 215, 54941. Tel: 920-294-6440; Fax: 920-294-6550.
Catechesis/Religious Program—Lawrence D. Behlen, D.R.E. Students 78.

Hazel Green, Grant Co., St. Francis de Sales, [CEM] Rev. Cyril O. Weisensel.
Res.: 2630 N. Main St., 53811-9681. Tel: 608-854-2392.
Catechesis/Religious Program—Students 286.

Highland, Iowa Co., SS. Anthony and Philip, [CEM 2] Rev. Kenneth J. Frisch.
Res.: 726 Main St., P.O. Box 306, 53543. Tel: 608-929-7490; Fax: 608-929-7701.
Catechesis/Religious Program—Tel: 608-929-7701. Mary Kay Brown, D.R.E. Students 158.

Hollandale, Iowa Co., St. Patrick, [CEM] Rev. Sanctus K. Ibe.
Res.: P.O. Box 37, 53544. Tel: 608-967-2344; Fax: 608-967-2344.
Catechesis/Religious Program—Students 59.

Janesville, Rock Co.
1—St. John Vianney, [JC] Rev. Michael J. Doro.
Res.: 1245 Clark St., 53545. Tel: 608-752-8708; Fax: 608-752-1970.
School—Lay Teachers 19; Students 262.
Catechesis/Religious Program—1238 E. Racine St., 53545. Tel: 608-755-1476; Fax: 608-758-3321. JoEllen Bigelow, D.R.E. Students 456.
2—Nativity of St. Mary, [JC] Rev. Stephen Umhoefer.
Res.: 313 E. Wall St., 53545. Tel: 608-752-7861; Fax: 608-758-0720.
School—Tel: 608-754-5221. Lay Teachers 17; Students 188.
Catechesis/Religious Program—117 N. Wisconsin St., 53545. Students 140.
3—St. Patrick, [JC] Rev. J. Daryl Furlong.
Res.: 315 Cherry St., 53545. Tel: 608-754-8193; Fax: 608-754-0357.
School—Lay Teachers 13; Students 124.
Catechesis/Religious Program—Tel: 608-754-0531. Kathleen Fritz, D.R.E. Students 156.
4—St. William, [JC] Rev. John R. Auby.
Res.: 1815 Ravine St., 53545. Tel: 608-755-5180; Fax: 608-755-5190.
School—1822 Ravine St., 53545. Tel: 608-755-5184; Fax: 608-755-5182. Lay Teachers 12; Students 217.
Catechesis/Religious Program—Tel: 608-755-5183. Greg Bergenske, D.R.E. Students 167.

Jefferson, Jefferson Co.
1—St. John the Baptist, [CEM] Rev. Thomas J. Coyle.
Res.: 214 N. Sanborn Ave., 53549. Tel: 920-674-2025; Fax: 920-674-2521.
School—Lay Teachers 11; Students 143.
Catechesis/Religious Program—Julie Endl, D.R.E.; Jennifer Ludtke, D.R.E. Students 225.
2—St. Lawrence, [CEM] Rev. Thomas J. Coyle.
Res.: W. 4926 Hwy. 18, 53549. Tel: 920-674-3217.
Catechesis/Religious Program—W4975 Hwy. 18, 53549. Tel: 920-674-2822. Students 75.

Johnson Creek, Jefferson Co., St. Mary Magdalene, [CEM] Rev. Robert W. Hughes.
Res.: 602 College St., P.O. Box 16, Lake Mills, 53551. Tel: 920-648-2468; Fax: 920-648-2468.
Catechesis/Religious Program—Tel: 920-699-2913. Carol Hunn, D.R.E. Students 49.

Kieler, Grant Co., Immaculate Conception, [CEM] Revs. Francis J. Steffen, Admin.; Francis Xavier Ekwugha.
Res.: Box 57, 53812. Tel: 608-568-7530.
School—Tel: 608-568-7220. Lay Teachers 7; Students 87.
Catechesis/Religious Program—3685 County HHH. Students 97.

KINGSTON, GREENLAKE CO., ST. MARY, [CEM] Rev. Richard D. Lesniak.
Res.: 45 St. Joseph St., P.O. Box 370, Markesan, 53946-0370. Tel: 920-398-3146; Fax: 920-398-3146.

LA VALLE, SAUK CO., HOLY FAMILY, [CEM 2] Rev. Lorin M. Bowens.
Res.: Lime Ridge, 53942. Tel: 608-986-2101.
Catechesis/Religious Program—Tel: 608-985-7915. Nora Durst, D.R.E. Students 52.

LAKE MILLS, JEFFERSON CO., ST. FRANCIS XAVIER, Rev. Robert W. Hughes.
Res.: 602 College St., P.O. Box 16, 53551. Tel: 920-648-2468; Fax: 920-648-2468.
Catechesis/Religious Program—Students 166.

LANCASTER, GRANT CO., ST. CLEMENT, [CEM 2] Rev. Msgr. Daniel T. Ganshert.
Res.: 135 S. Washington St., 53813. Tel: 608-723-4990.
School—Sisters 3; Lay Teachers 6; Students 97.
Catechesis/Religious Program—Tel: 608-723-7425. Kitty Mumm, D.R.E.; Michelle Strobush, D.R.E. Students 261.

LIME RIDGE, SAUK CO., ST. BONIFACE, [CEM] Rev. Lorin M. Bowens.
Res.: 105 Church St., P.O. Box 60, 53942. Tel: 608-986-2101.
Catechesis/Religious Program—Tel: 608-983-2763. Students 59.

LODI, COLUMBIA CO., ST. PATRICK, [CEM] Rev. Nicholas S. Okere (Nigeria), Admin.
Res.: 515 Fair St., 53555. Tel: 608-592-4510; Fax: 608-592-2078.
Catechesis/Religious Program—Tel: 608-592-5711. Cynthia S. Fischer, D.R.E. Students 409.

LORETO, MANITOWOC CO., ST. PATRICK, [CEM 2] Rev. Michael A. Resop.
Res.: 105 Church St., Lime Ridge, 53942. Tel: 608-986-2101.

MARKESAN, GREEN LAKE CO., ST. JOSEPH, Rev. Richard D. Lesniak.
Res.: 45 St. Joseph St., P.O. Box 370, 53946-0370. Tel: 920-398-3146; Fax: 920-398-3147.
Catechesis/Religious Program—Roland Salter, D.R.E. Students 72.

MARSHALL, DANE CO., ST. MARY'S OF THE NATIVITY, [CEM] Rev. Thomas E. Gillespie.
Res.: P.O. Box 250, 53559-0250. Tel: 608-655-3708.
Catechesis/Religious Program—Tel: 920-478-3232. Eileen Bender, D.R.E. Students 202.

MARTINSVILLE, DANE CO., ST. MARTIN, [CEM] Rev. Francis J. Schmidt.
Res.: 5959 St. Martin Cir., Cross Plains, 53528-9312. Tel: 608-798-2815.
Catechesis/Religious Program—Tel: 608-798-2328. Sharon Helt, D.R.E. Students 138.

MAZOMANIE, DANE CO., ST. BARNABAS, [CEM] Rev. Kevin F. Dooley.
Res.: 113 E. Division St., P.O. Box 68, 53560-0068. Tel: 608-795-2480.
Catechesis/Religious Program—Students 159.

MCFARLAND, DANE CO., CHRIST THE KING, Rev. D. Stephen Smith.
Res.: P.O. Box 524, 53558. Tel: 608-838-8776; Fax: 608-838-6449.
Catechesis/Religious Program—Students 288.

MERRIMAC, SAUK CO., ST. MARY, HEALTH OF THE SICK, Rev. Louis Lussier, O.S.Cam.
Res.: W. 11876 McLeish Rd., Baraboo, 53913. Tel: 608-356-8113.

MIDDLETON, DANE CO., ST. BERNARD, [CEM] Rev. Msgr. Douglas L. Dushack.
Res.: 2015 Parmenter St., P.O. Box 620187, 53562-0187. Tel: 608-831-6531; Fax: 608-831-8101.
Catechesis/Religious Program—Students 666.

MILL CREEK, ST. JOHN THE BAPTIST, Rev. Kevin F. Dooley.
Res.: 113 E. Division St., P.O. Box 68, Mazomanie, 53560-0068. Tel: 608-795-9918.

MILTON, ROCK CO., ST. MARY, [CEM] Rev. Msgr. James J. Uppena.
Res.: 837 Parkview Dr., 53563. Tel: 608-868-3338; Fax: 608-868-3337.
Catechesis/Religious Program—Tel: 608-868-3336. Mary Kapheim, D.R.E.; Sabrina Elsen, Youth Min. Students 706.

MINERAL POINT, IOWA CO., CONGREGATION OF ST. MARY-ST. PAUL, [JC 2] Rev. James W. Hinnen, J.C.L.
Res.: 224 Davis St., 53565. Tel: 608-987-2026; Fax: 608-987-3361.
Catechesis/Religious Program—Tel: 608-987-3361. Students 264.

MONROE, GREEN CO., ST. VICTOR, [CEM] Rev. Michael E. Klarer.
Res.: 1760 14th St., 53566. Tel: 608-325-9506; Fax: 608-325-3115.
School—Tel: 608-325-3444. Lay Teachers 10; Students 85.
Catechesis/Religious Program—Students 280.

MONTELLO, MARQUETTE CO., ST. JOHN THE BAPTIST, [CEM] Rev. Richard M. Heilman.
Res.: 277 E. Montello St., 53949. Tel: 608-297-2217; Fax: 608-297-8047.
Catechesis/Religious Program—Tel: 608-297-7423. Students 107.

MONTFORT, GRANT CO., ST. THOMAS, [CEM] Rev. Kenneth J. Frisch.
Res.: Box 68, 53569. Tel: 608-943-6944; Fax: 608-943-6944.
Catechesis/Religious Program—Anne Adams, D.R.E. Students 212.

MOUNT HOPE, GRANT CO., ST. LAWRENCE O'TOOLE, [CEM] Rev. George B. Horath.
Res.: 930 Jefferson St., Fennimore, 53809. Tel: 608-822-6425.

MOUNT HOREB, DANE CO., ST. IGNATIUS, [CEM] Rev. James R. Bartylla.
Res.: 111 S. Sixth St., 53572. Tel: 608-437-5195; Fax: 608-437-7691.
Catechesis/Religious Program—Tel: 608-437-5348. Jan Haasl, D.R.E. Students 321.

MUSCODA, GRANT CO., ST. JOHN THE BAPTIST, [CEM] Rev. Roger H. Taylor.
Res.: 341 N. Wisconsin Ave., P.O. Box 35, 53573. Tel: 608-739-3391; Fax: 608-739-9195.
Catechesis/Religious Program—Students 203.

NESHKORO, MARQUETTE CO., ST. JAMES, [CEM] Rev. Dale W. Grubba.
Church: 315 N. Main St., 54960. Tel: 920-293-4211; Fax: 920-293-4211.
Res.: 1211 W. Main St., Princeton, 54968.

OREGON, DANE CO., HOLY MOTHER OF CONSOLATION, [CEM] Rev. William R. Connell.
Res.: 651 N. Main St., 53575. Tel: 608-835-5763; Fax: 608-835-5764.
Catechesis/Religious Program—Tel: 608-835-5764. Students 916.

PALMYRA, JEFFERSON CO., ST. MARY, [CEM] Rev. Msgr. John H. Hebl.
Res.: 919 W. Main St., P.O. Box P, 53156. Tel: 262-495-2395; Fax: 262-593-5450.
Catechesis/Religious Program—Tel: 262-495-2533; Fax: 262-593-5450. Dolores Van Duzor, D.R.E. Students 37.

PAOLI, DANE CO., ST. WILLIAM, [CEM] Rev. David W. Timmerman.
Res.: 301 W. Main St., P.O. Box 930070, Verona, 53593. Tel: 608-845-7323; Fax: 608-848-4293.

PARDEEVILLE, COLUMBIA CO., ST. MARY, Revs. John H. Hedrick; Jason E. Hesseling.
Res.: 309 W. Cook St., P.O. Box 216, Portage, 53901. Tel: 608-429-3030.
Catechesis/Religious Program—Students 130.
Education Center & Hall—Fax: 608-429-3129.

PATCH GROVE, GRANT CO., ST. JOHN, [CEM] Rev. Eric H. Nielsen.
Res.: P.O. Box 35, Bloomington, 53804. Tel: 608-994-2526; Fax: 608-994-2530.

PERRY, DANE CO., HOLY REDEEMER, [CEM] Rev. Sanctus K. Ibe.
Res.: 601 Grover St., P.O. Box 37, Hollandale, 53544. Tel: 608-967-2344; Fax: 608-967-2344.
Catechesis/Religious Program—111 S. Sixth St., Mount Horeb, 53572. Tel: 608-437-5195; Fax: 608-437-7691.

PINE BLUFF, DANE CO., ST. MARY OF PINE BLUFF, [CEM] [JC] Rev. James R. Bartylla.
Res.: 111 S. 6th St., Mount Horeb, 53572. Tel: 608-798-2111; Fax: 608-798-2112.
Catechesis/Religious Program—Tel: 608-798-2115. Valerie Bennett, D.R.E. Students 139.

PLAIN, SAUK CO., ST. LUKE, [CEM 2] [JC 2] Rev. Michael A. Resop; Sr. Jean Ferstl, O.P., Pastoral Assoc.
Res.: 1240 Nachreiner Ave., 53577. Tel: 608-546-2482; Fax: 608-546-2616.
School—Lay Teachers 9; Students 124.

PLATTEVILLE, GRANT CO.

1—ST. AUGUSTINE UNIVERSITY PARISH, Rev. James H. Murphy.
Res.: 135 S. Hickory St., 53818. Tel: 608-348-7530; Fax: 608-348-7530.

2—ST. MARY, [CEM] Rev. O. Charles Schluter.
Res.: 130 W. Cedar St., 53818. Tel: 608-348-9735; Fax: 608-348-9920.
School—Tel: 608-348-5806; Fax: 608-348-7883. Lay Teachers 12; Students 110.
Catechesis/Religious Program—Tel: 608-348-5806; Fax: 608-348-9883. Students 214.

PORTAGE, COLUMBIA CO., ST. MARY OF THE IMMACULATE CONCEPTION, [CEM] Revs. John H. Hedrick; Jason E. Hesseling.
Res.: 309 W. Cook St., P.O. Box 216, 53901-0216. Tel: 608-742-6998; Fax: 608-747-1039.
School—315 W. Cook St., 53901. Tel: 608-742-4998. Lay Teachers 13; Students 136.
Catechesis/Religious Program—Pat Niles, D.R.E. Students 302.

POYNETTE, COLUMBIA CO., ST. THOMAS, [JC] Rev. Raymond J. Dischler.
Res.: 655 S. Main, P.O. Box 310, 53955-0310. Tel: 608-635-4326.
Catechesis/Religious Program—Tel: 608-635-8375. Julie Cross, D.R.E.; Gerald Peterson, D.R.E. Students 124.

PRINCETON, GREEN LAKE CO., ST. JOHN THE BAPTIST, [CEM] Rev. Dale W. Grubba.
Res.: 1211 W. Main, 54968. Tel: 920-295-6209; Fax: 920-295-0231.
School—Lay Teachers 10; Students 92.
Catechesis/Religious Program—Students 86.

REEDSBURG, SAUK CO., SACRED HEART, [CEM 3] Rev. Thomas J. Monaghan.
Res.: 624 N. Willow St., 53959. Tel: 608-524-2412; Fax: 608-524-3831.
School—545 N. Oak St., 53959. Tel: 608-524-3611. Lay Teachers 12; Students 183.
Catechesis/Religious Program—Mary Ann Polcyn, D.R.E. Students 350.

RIDGEWAY, IOWA CO., ST. BRIDGET, [CEM] [JC] Rev. Donald F. Lange.
Res.: 803 W. Main, 53582. Tel: 608-924-2441.
Catechesis/Religious Program—5230 U.S. Hwy. 151, Platteville, 53818. Tel: 608-348-2924. Students 120.

RIO, COLUMBIA CO., ST. JOSEPH, [CEM] Rev. Raymond J. Dischler.
Res.: 655 S. Main St., P.O. Box 310, Poynette, 53955-0310. Tel: 608-635-4326.

ROXBURY, DANE CO., ST. NORBERT, [CEM] Rev. Laverne G. Meier.
Res.: 8944 County Rd. Y, Sauk City, 53583-9510. Tel: 608-643-3661.
Catechesis/Religious Program—Tel: 608-643-8108; 622--. Juanita Wipper Furth, D.R.E.; Ethel Kippley, D.R.E. Students 249.

SAUK CITY, SAUK CO., ST. ALOYSIUS, [CEM 2] Rev. Kevin D. Holmes.
Res.: 115 Madison St., 53583. Tel: 608-643-2449; Fax: 608-643-2440.
School—Tel: 608-643-6868. Lay Teachers 8; Students 139.
Catechesis/Religious Program—Tel: 608-643-4062. Jason Simon, D.R.E. Students 314.

SEYMOUR, LAFAYETTE CO., OUR LADY OF HOPE, [CEM] Rev. James R. Lins.
Res.: Rte. 1, Shullsburg, 53586. Tel: 608-965-4518.

SHULLSBURG, LAFAYETTE CO., ST. MATTHEW, [CEM 2] [JC 2] Rev. James R. Lins.
Res.: 344 Judgment St., 53586. Tel: 608-965-4518.

SINSINAWA, GRANT CO., ST. JOSEPH, [CEM 2] Revs. Francis J. Steffen, Admin.; Francis Xavier Ekwugha.
Res.: 780 Hwy. Z, Hazel Green, 53811. Tel: 608-748-4528.
School—Tel: 608-748-4442. Lay Teachers 5; Students 58.

SOUTH WAYNE, LAFAYETTE CO., ST. JOHN, [CEM] Rev. David J. Flanagan, Admin.
Res.: Box 37, Gratiot, 53541. Tel: 608-922-6456.
Catechesis/Religious Program—Students 32.

SPRING GREEN, SAUK CO., ST. JOHN THE EVANGELIST, [CEM] Rev. Michael A. Resop.
Res.: 1240 Nachreiner Ave., Plain, 53577-0023. Tel: 608-546-2482; Fax: 608-546-2616.
School—Lay Teachers 6; Students 75.
Catechesis/Religious Program—Tel: 608-546-6436; Fax: 608-588-9372. Students 153.

STOUGHTON, DANE CO., ST. ANN, [CEM] Rev. Msgr. Gerard M. Healy; Sr. Mary Ann Schroedl, O.S.F., Pastoral Assoc.
Res.: 320 N. Harrison St., 53589. Tel: 608-873-7633; Fax: 608-873-6425.
School—Tel: 608-873-3343. Poor Sisters of Nazareth of Stoughton, Inc. 1; Students 178.

SULLIVAN, JEFFERSON CO., ST. MARY HELP OF CHRISTIANS, [CEM] Rev. Msgr. John H. Hebl.
Res.: W. 856 Hwy. 18, 53178. Tel: 262-593-2250; Fax: 262-593-5450.
Catechesis/Religious Program—Tel: 262-593-5450. Dolores Van Duzor, D.R.E. Students 65.

SUN PRAIRIE, DANE CO.

1—ST. ALBERT THE GREAT, Rev. Michael C. Richel.
Res.: 2420 St. Albert Dr., 53590. Tel: 608-837-3798; Fax: 608-837-8576.
Catechesis/Religious Program—Sr. Joan Meyer, D.R.E. Students 778.

2—SACRED HEARTS OF JESUS AND MARY, [CEM] Rev. Msgr. Duane R. Moellenberndt; Rev. Bart D. Timmerman; Sr. Anne Raymond Gasser, S.S.N.D., Pastoral Assoc.
Res.: 221 Columbus St., 53590. Tel: 608-837-7381; Fax: 608-825-9585.
School—Tel: 608-837-8508. Lay Teachers 28; Students 443.
Catechesis/Religious Program—Students 302.

TENNYSON-POTOSI, GRANT CO., SS. ANDREW AND THOMAS, [CEM 2] Rev. Richard J. Leffler.
Res.: 101 Church St., Potosi, 53820. Tel: 608-763-2671.
School—100 Hwy. 61 N., P.O. Box 160, Potosi, 53820. Tel: 608-763-2120; Fax: 608-763-2120. Lay Teachers 7; Students 71.
Catechesis/Religious Program—Tel: 608-763-2527

(1-8); 205-- (H.S.). Beth Flesch, D.R.E. (1-8); Kathy Schink, D.R.E. (High School). Students 155.

TRUMAN, LAFAYETTE CO., IMMACULATE CONCEPTION, [CEM] Rev. Monte E. Robinson.
Res.: 338 Chestnut St., Box 345, Belmont, 53510. Tel: 608-762-5446.

VERONA, DANE CO., ST. ANDREW, [CEM] Rev. David W. Timmerman.
Res.: P.O. Box 930070, 53593. Tel: 608-845-7323; Fax: 608-848-4293.
Catechesis/Religious Program—Tel: 608-845-9757. Greg Blatz, D.R.E. Students 469.

WATERLOO, JEFFERSON CO., ST. JOSEPH, [CEM] Rev. Thomas E. Gillespie.
Res.: 205 W. Milwaukee Ave., 53594-1329. Tel: 920-478-2032.
School—Lay Teachers 4; Students 76.
Catechesis/Religious Program—Tel: 920-478-3232. Eileen Bender, D.R.E. Students 127.

WATERTOWN, JEFFERSON CO.
1—ST. BERNARD, [CEM] Rev. Thomas P. Marr; Sr. Virginia Brunner, S.S.S.F., Pastoral Assoc.
Res.: 114 S. Church St., 53094-4399. Tel: 920-261-5133; Fax: 920-261-8371.
School—Lay Teachers 14; Students 180.
Catechesis/Religious Program—111 S. Montgomery St., 53094. Tel: 920-261-2582; Fax: 920-261-7215. Students 336.
2—ST. HENRY, [CEM] Rev. Bernard E. Rott.
Res.: 412 N. 4th St., 53094. Tel: 920-261-7273; Fax: 920-261-3681.
School—300 Cady St., 53094. Tel: 920-261-2586. Lay Teachers 13; Students 154.
Catechesis/Religious Program—Tel: 920-261-6332. Todd Weissenborn, D.R.E. Students 230.

WAUNAKEE, DANE CO., ST. JOHN THE BAPTIST, [CEM] Rev. Msgr. James L. Gunn; Rev. Diego O. Cuevas.
Res.: 209 South St., 53597. Tel: 608-849-5121; Fax: 608-849-5866.
School—Tel: 608-849-5325; Fax: 608-849-5342. Lay Teachers 19; Students 270.
Catechesis/Religious Program—Fax: 608-850-6225. Students 580.

WESTFIELD, MARQUETTE CO., GOOD SHEPHERD, Rev. Richard M. Heilman; Darlene Duley, D.R.E.
Res.: 277 E. Montello St., Montello, 53949. Tel: 608-297-2217; Fax: 608-297-8047.
Catechesis/Religious Program—241 E. 6th St., 53964. Tel: 608-296-3631; Fax: 608-296-3631. Students 93.

WESTPORT, DANE CO., ST. MARY OF THE LAKE, [CEM] Rev. Daniel P. Finnane.
Res.: 5460 Marylake Rd., Waunakee, 53597-9121. Tel: 608-849-4116; Fax: 608-849-4122.
Catechesis/Religious Program—Tel: 608-849-4376. Mary Gartland, D.R.E. Students 87.

WISCONSIN DELLS, COLUMBIA CO., ST. CECILIA, [CEM] Rev. Felix G. Oehrlein.
Res.: 604 Oak St., P.O. Box 436, 53965. Tel: 608-254-8381; Fax: 608-254-8382.
Catechesis/Religious Program—Tel: 608-253-5621. Students 231.

YELLOWSTONE, LAFAYETTE CO., ST. MICHAEL, [CEM] Rev. Thomas H. Schroeder.
Res.: 313 N. Lafayette St., P.O. Box 76, Argyle, 53504. Tel: 608-543-3631.

Chaplains of Public Institutions

MADISON. *Columbia County Institution.* Attended from St. Mary's Church, Portage.
Dane County Institution. Attended from St. Andrew, Verona.
Grant County Institution. Attended from St. Clement Church, Lancaster.
Green County Institution. Attended from St. Victor Church, Monroe.
Iowa County Institution. Attended from St. Joseph Church, Dodgeville.
Madison-Meriter General Hospital. Attended from St. Raphael Cathedral.
Mendota State Hospital. Vacant.
University Hospitals. Rev. Lawrence M. Bakke, Chap. 5079 Sheboygan Ave., # 201, 53705.

JANESVILLE. *Jefferson County Institution.* Attended from St. John the Baptist Church, Jefferson.
LaFayette County Institution. Attended from Holy Rosary Church, Darlington.
Mercy Hospital. Attended from Janesville Parishes, Janesville.
Rock County Institution. Attended from Janesville Parishes, Janesville.
Sauk County Institution. Attended from St. Boniface Church, Lime Ridge.
Wisconsin State School for the Blind. Attended from St. Patrick's Church, Janesville.

Leave of Absence:
Revs.—
Clauder, J. Gibbs
Steele, Steven G.
Stillmank, John G.

Absent on Sick Leave:
Revs.—
Adams, Archie H.
Doherty, Patrick J.
Dutchoff, C. Robert
Runde, Raymond E.
Sosinski Thomas P.

Retired:
Rev. Msgrs.—
DeBock, William A., Bishop O'Connor Catholic Pastoral Center, 702 S. High Point Rd., P.O. Box 44983, 53744-4983.
Dietzel, Elmer J., Bishop O'Connor Catholic Pastoral Center, 702 S. High Point Rd., P.O. Box 44983, 53744-4983.
Doherty, Francis E., Rte. 3 W., 11031 Lakeview Dr., Lodi, 53555.
Erbe, Edward J., Bishop O'Connor Catholic Pastoral Center, 702 S. High Point Rd., P.O. Box 44983, 53744-4983.
Hastrich, George M., 501 Bram St., 53713.
Higgins, Joseph P., 3424 Maple Grove Rd., 53719.
Klass, Raymond E., c/o St. Mary of the Nativity Church, 112 S. Begbg St., Box 250, Marshall, 53559-0250.
Kramer, James G., Bishop O'Connor Catholic Pastoral Center, 702 S. High Point Rd., P.O. Box 44983, 53744-4983.
Schmelzer, Delbert L., 7575 Pioneer Pl., Verona, 53593.
Stack, William E., 706 Jefferson, Sauk City, 53583.
Revs.—
Bauhs, Eugene J., 6205 Mineral Point Rd., #216, 53705.
Brickl, Joseph M., 760 E. Verona Ave., Verona, 53593.
Browne, Vincent T., 19 Moygannon Ct., Warren Point, Ireland.
Buenzil, August H., 6165 Mineral Point Rd., 53705.
Buholzer, Robert E., 300 Silverado Dr., Apt. 204, Stoughton, 53589-5472.
Cassidy, Kevin W., P.O. Box 391, Mauston, 53948.
Conlon, Philip J., 306 Michael Ave., P.O. Box 326, Hollister, MO 65672.
Cox, Joseph C., 2515 Deerfield St., Portage, 53901-1081.
Deitelhoff, Bernard H., 204 Buell St., 53704.
Doheny, Thomas R., 28851 Bermuda Lago Ct., # 102, Bonita Springs, FL 34134.
Dominic, Francis J., 2029 Brennan Ct., Cuba City, 53807.
Fox, George W., 1850 Beld St., Apt. 2, 53713.
Grasso, Philip A., P.O. Box 29, Dickeyville, 58808-0429.
Heindl, Arthur W., N. 7157 Cottage Dr., Westboro, 54490.
Kalscheuer, Henry N., 1017 S. Holiday Dr., Waunakee, 53597.
Kieffer, Lawrence J., 2500 Overlook Ter., Rm. B 1061, 53705-2286.
Klink, Delbert D., S 7612 AW Grandview Ave., Merrimac, 53561.
Koth, Arthur R., 1626 Wheeler Rd., #103, 53704.
Mattucci, James J., 43285 Polo Cir., Sterling Heights, MI 48313.
McEnery, James G., 5001 N. Sherman Ave., 53704-1499.
Murray, Donald J., 8541 Greenway Blvd., #302, Middleton, 53562.
Pickarts, Bernard J., River House, Co Hwy Y- # 10126, Mazomanie, 53560.
Pierick, Bernard E., Bishop O'Connor Catholic Pastoral Center, 702 S. High Point Rd., P.O. Box 44983, 53744-4983.
Rank, Ronald G., 436 Farnham St., Apt. # 3, Marshall, 53599.
Runde, David H., 2649 Stanbrook St., Fitchburg, 53711.
Schubiger, Albert B., 185 Fuchsia Pl., Ventura, CA 93004.
Schumacher, Anthony J., 2976 Chapel Valley, #103, 53711.
Schuster, Wilfred J., Bishop O'Connor Catholic Pastoral Center, 702 S. High Point Rd., P.O. Box 44983, 53744-4983.
Turner, Jerome R., 5711 NE Fox Glove Ln., Poulsbo, WA 98370-8934.
Walsh, John B., Bishop O'Connor Catholic Pastoral Center, 702 S. High Point Rd., P.O. Box 44983, 53744-4983.
Wiecki, Donald J., 506 Bassett St., De Forest, 53532.
Young, Anthony J., 5784 Chapel Valley Rd., Fitchburg, 53719.

INSTITUTIONS LOCATED IN THE DIOCESE

[A] SEMINARIES, RELIGIOUS OR SCHOLASTICATES

BARABOO. *St. Camillus Monastery and Retreat Center*, W 11876 McLeish Rd., 53913. Tel: 608-356-8113; Fax: 608-356-5530. Rev. Louis Lussier, O.S.Cam. Priests 1.

[B] COLLEGES

MADISON. *Edgewood College*, 1000 Edgewood College Dr., 53711. Tel: 608-663-4861; Fax: 608-663-6717. Email: juselman@edgewood.edu. Web: www.edgewood.edu. Dr. James A. Ebben, Pres.; Sisters Maureen McDonnell, O.P., Campus Min.; Margaret Hopkins, O.P., Dir., Office of Dominican Mission; Stephen Bullock, Campus Ministry; Rev. Ronald Kreul, O.P., Chap. Dominican Sisters, Sinsinawa, WI Sisters 13; Lay Teachers 230; Students 2,400.

[C] HIGH SCHOOLS, PRIVATE

MADISON. *Edgewood High School*, 2219 Monroe St., 53711. Tel: 608-257-1023; Fax: 608-257-9133. Web: www.edgewoodhs.org. K. Michele Clarke, Pres.; Mr. Robert Growney, Prin. Dominican Sisters, Sinsinawa Lay Teachers 58; Students 615.

[D] ELEMENTARY SCHOOLS, PRIVATE

MADISON. *Edgewood Campus Grade School*, 829 Edgewood College Dr., 53711. Tel: 608-663-4100; Fax: 608-663-4101. Web: www.campus-school.edgewood.edu. Connie Irlbeck, Pres. & Prin. Dominican Sisters, Sinsinawa Sisters 1; Brothers 1; Lay Teachers 21; Students 307.

[E] GENERAL HOSPITALS

MADISON. *St. Marys Hospital Medical Center*, 707 S. Mills St., 53715. Tel: 608-251-6100; Fax: 608-258-6731. Email: paula_mckenzie@ssmhc.com. Mr. Gerald W. Lefert, Pres. Franciscan Sisters of Mary (St. Louis, MO), Member of SSM Health Care. Sisters 2; Staffed 295; Capacity 440; Patients Assisted Annually 105,190.
Pastoral Care Department Chaplains: Revs. Caroline Heath, Religious Science International; Gary Hein, Lutheran Min., Evangelical Lutheran Church of America; Garrett Keegstra, O.F.M.Cap.; Rev. Ted Lindquist, Lutheran Min., Evangelical Lutheran Church of America; Revs. David Smith, Church of God in Christ; Kenneth Smits, O.F.M.Cap.; Sisters Mary Ellen Lewis, F.S.M.; Pamela Moehring, S.S.N.D.; Clement Sabol, V.S.C.; Sandra Schmitz, O.P.; Liz Allen; Paula McKenzie, Dir.; Julia Weaver, United Church of Christ.

BARABOO. *St. Clare Hospital and Health Services*, 707 14th St., 53913. Tel: 608-356-1400; Fax: 608-356-1367. Web: www.stclare.com. Sandra L. Anderson, Pres.; Rev. William Beers, Ph.D. Member of the SSM Health Care. Franciscan Sisters of Mary (St. Louis, MO) 3; Bed Capacity 100; Patients Assisted Annually 55,615; Staff 365.

MONROE. *The Monroe Clinic, Inc.*, 515 22nd Ave., 53566. Tel: 608-324-1000; Fax: 608-324-1114. Email: mike_sanders@themonroeclinic.org. Web: www.themonroeclinic.org/. Michael B. Sanders, Pres. & CEO; Rev. Msgr. Thomas F. Campion, Chap.; Julie Wilke, CFO, Contact Person. Sisters of the Congregation of St. Agnes Bed Capacity 100; Nurses 175; Patients Assisted Annually 245,000; Staff 945.

PORTAGE. *Divine Savior Healthcare, Inc.*, 2817 New Pinery Rd., 53901. Tel: 608-742-4131; Fax: 608-742-6098. Email: mdnelson@dshealthcare.com. Web: dshealthcare.com. Mr. Michael Decker, Pres. & CEO; Levonne Tappa, Dir. Spiritual Care & Chap.; Monica Holden, Chap. Sisters of the Divine Savior Sisters 3; Bed Capacity 49; Patients Assisted Annually 84,000; Total Staff 463.

[F] HOMES FOR THE AGED

MADISON. *St. Marys Care Center*, 1347 Fish Hatchery Rd., 53715. Tel: 608-257-0781; Fax: 608-257-9420. William Bender, Admin.; P. Norton, Contact Person. Member of SSM Health Care. Total Assisted 625; Total Staff 260.

BARABOO. *St. Clare Meadows Care Center*, 1414 Jefferson St., 53913. Tel: 608-356-5764; Fax: 608-356-5441. Web: www.stclare.com. Ronnie E. Schaetzl, Admin. Member of SSM Health Care. Total Assisted 19; Total Staff 116.

JANESVILLE. *St. Elizabeth Home*, 502 St. Lawrence

Ave., 53545. Tel: 608-752-6709; Fax: 608-752-1724. Email: scmc@inwave.com. Rev. Timothy Gericke. Aged Residents 43.

PORTAGE. *Divine Savior Nursing Home*, 2817 New Pinery Rd., P.O. Box 387, 53901-0387. Tel: 608-742-4131; Fax: 608-742-3463. (See Divine Savior Hospital, Portage.) Aged Residents 100; Bed Capacity 110.

STOUGHTON. *Nazareth House*, 814 Jackson St., 53589. Tel: 608-873-6448; Fax: 608-873-0829. Email: nazareth@nazhouse.com. Sr. Margaret Brody, C.S.N., Supr. Sisters of Nazareth of Stoughton, Inc. Sisters 5; Aged Residents 99.

[G] MONASTERIES AND RESIDENCES OF PRIESTS

MADISON. *Bishop O'Connor Catholic Pastoral Center*, 702 S. High Point Rd., P. O. Box 44983, 53744-4983. Tel: 608-821-3000; Fax: 608-821-3013. Email: o'connorcenter@straphael.org. Web: www.madisondiocese.org. In Res. Most Revs. William H. Bullock, D.D., ED.S. (Retired); George O. Wirz, D.D., S.T.L.; Rev. Msgrs. William A. DeBock (Retired); Elmer Dietzel; Edward J. Erbe (Retired); James G. Kramer (Retired); Revs. Bernard J. Pierick; Wilfred J. Schuster (Retired); John B. Walsh (Retired).

EDGERTON. *Koshkonong Pastoral Center*, 432 Liquori Rd., 53534. Tel: 608-884-3425; Fax: 608-884-9231. Revs. Thomas Moylan, L.C., Supr., Contact Person; Fergus O'Carroll, L.C., Chap.; Bros. Scott Murphy, L.C.; Robert DeCesare, L.C.; James Brooks, L.C.; Timothy Wysocki, L.C.; Juan Pablo Avina, L.C.

[H] CONVENTS AND RESIDENCES FOR SISTERS

MADISON. *Franciscan Sisters of Mary, St. Joseph of the Lake Community*, 919 Erin St., 53715-1841. Tel: 608-255-1510; Fax: 608-258-6731. Email: melpw@charter.net. Web: www.fsmonline.org. Sisters 2.

Monastery of Saint Benedict Center, P.O. Box 5070, 53705-0070. Tel: 608-836-1631; Fax: 608-836-5586. Email: mwalgenbach@sbcenter.org. Web: www.sbcenter.org. Sr. Mary David Walgenbach, O.S.B., Prioress. Monastery of the Sisters of Saint Benedict Sisters 5.

Secular Institute of Schoenstatt Sisters of Mary, 5901 Cottage Grove Rd., 53718-1397. Tel: 608-222-7208; Fax: 608-222-0430. Email: schoenstattheights@schsrsmary.org. Sr. M. Erlinda Pimo, Supr. Sisters 5.

BARABOO. *Franciscan Sisters of Mary*, 1021 Ash St., 53913-2163. Tel: 608-356-8641. Sr. Claire M. Borst, S.F.M., Contact Person. Sisters 3.

BELOIT. *Blessed Sacrament Convent*, 916 Bluff St., 53511. Tel: 608-362-3326. Sr. Pauline Labrecque, A.B.S., Supr. Gen. Motherhouse of the Auxiliaries of the Blessed Sacrament. Sisters in Residence 4.

PRAIRIE DU SAC. *Valley of Our Lady Monastery* 53578-9737. Tel: 608-643-3520; 608-643-7986 (Altar Breads); Fax: 608-643-0684. Email: volocist@chorus.net. Web: www.nunocist.org. Sr. M. Paula Hannah, O.Cist., Prioress, Contact Person. Cistercian Nuns Solemnly Professed 11; Simply Professed 2; Novice 1.

SINSINAWA. *Dominican Motherhouse*, 585 County Rd. Z, 53824-9700. Tel: 608-748-4411; Fax: 608-748-4491. Email: toniharrisop@aol.com. Web: www.sinsinawa.org. Sisters Toni Harris, O.P., Prioress of the Congregation; Mary Ellen Green, O.P., Eastern Prov.; Christa Cunningham, O.P., Southern Prov.; Mary Ann Nelson, O.P., Western Prov.; Jane Boland, O.P.; Revs. John C. Risley, O.P., Chap.; John Gerlach, O.P., Chap.; Sisters Joris Binder, O.P., Prioress Team; Patricia Gallagher, O.P., Prioress Team; Sharon Casey, O.P., Prioress Team. Sinsinawa Dominican Congregation of the Most Holy Rosary Sisters in the Congregation 753; Sisters 190; Dominican Novitiate: Novices 1.

[I] CHARITABLE INSTITUTIONS

MADISON. *Catholic Charities, Inc.* Diocese of Madison , Administrative Center, 702 S. High Point Rd., P.O. Box 46550, 53744-6550. Tel: 608-821-3100; Fax: 608-821-3125. Email: cathcharities@straphael.org. Web: www.ccmdsn.org. Brian Cain, Dir.

Central City Counseling Services, 30 S. Franklin St., 53703. Tel: 608-256-2358; Fax: 608-256-2350.

Beloit District Office, 3311 Prairie Ave., Beloit, 53511. Tel: 608-365-3665; Fax: 608-365-1279.

Janesville District Office, 2020 E. Milwaukee St., Janesville, 53545. Tel: 608-752-4906; Fax: 608-752-9699.

Yellowstone Office, 426 S. Yellowstone Dr., Ste. 100, 53719. Tel: 608-833-4800; Fax: 608-833-7897.

DiocesanCouncil of Madison, 1109 Jonathan Dr., 53713-3230. Tel: 608-278-4550; Fax: 608-278-2926. Edward O'Neill, Council Pres.

Saint Martin House Saint Martin House , 1862 Beld St., 53713. Tel: 608-255-1287; Fax: 608-441-7598. Email: smaurice@straphael.org. Rev. George M. Hastrich, Spiritual Dir. Volunteer Staff; Steve Maurice, Coord.

Society of St. Vincent de Paul (District Council of Madison, Inc.) , 1109 Jonathon Dr., 53713-3230. Tel: 608-278-4550; Fax: 608-278-2926. Email: svdpmad@svdpmadison.org. Web: www.svdpmadison.org. Edward O'Neill, Council Pres.

JEFFERSON. *St. Coletta of Wisconsin, Inc.*, W4955 Hwy. 18, 53549. Tel: 920-674-4330; Fax: 920-674-4603. Web: www.stcolettawi.org. Robert Stearns, Pres. & CEO. Sponsored by the Sisters of St. Francis of Assisi. Milwaukee Sisters 3; Brothers 1; Residents 375; Lay Staff 425.

[J] RETREAT HOUSES

MADISON. *Saint Benedict Center, Ecumenical Retreat and Conference Center*, P.O. Box 5070, 53705-0070. Tel: 608-836-1631; Fax: 608-831-9312. Email: mwalgenbach@sbcenter.org. Web: www.sbcenter.org. Sr. Mary David Walgenbach, O.S.B. Sisters 7.

[K] MISCELLANEOUS

MADISON. *Catholic Health Association of Wisconsin, Inc.*, 5721 Odana Rd., 53719-1222. Tel: 608-274-5588; Fax: 608-274-8554. Web: www.wha.org/chaw. Sr. Jomary Trstensky, O.S.F., Chairperson of the Board.

Edgewood Incorporated, 1000 Edgewood College Dr., 53711. Tel: 608-663-4861; Fax: 608-663-6717. Email: ebben@edgewood.edu. Web: www.edgewood.edu. Dr. James A. Ebben, Pres. Sponsored by Sinsinawa Dominican Sisters of Sinsinawa, WI.; Purpose: The education of individuals in such subjects as are usually taught in high schools, academies, and colleges.

St. Marys Hospital and Care Center Foundation, Inc., 707 S. Mills St., 53715. Tel: 608-258-5600; Fax: 608-258-5711. Email: steve_sparks@ssmhc.com. Web: www.stmarysmadison.com. Steven Sparks, Contact Person; Mr. Bernard C. Huger, Contact Person & Attorney. Sponsored by the Franciscan Sisters of Mary., Purpose: To solicit, manage, invest and expend endowment funds and other gifts, grants and bequests primarily for the maintenance and benefit of St. Mary's Hospital Medical Center and St. Mary's Care Center of Madison, WI; to support other medical research, educational or charitable programs or activities in the Madison, WI area. Member of SSM Health Care.

San Damiano Friary, 4123 Monona Dr., 53716. Tel: 608-222-6238; Fax: 608-222-6766. Revs. Rupert Dorn, O.F.M.Cap; Garrett Keegstra, O.F.M.Cap.; Loran Miller, O.F.M.Cap.; Bro. Edward Hagman, O.F.M.Cap. Capuchin Order-Province of St. Joseph, House of Healing and Hospitality.

SSM Health Care of Wisconsin, Inc., 2901 Landmark Pl., Ste. 300, 53713. Tel: 608-258-6120; Fax: 608-258-6218. Email: msharrison@ssmhc.com. Mary Starmann-Harrison, CEO, Contact Person. Sponsored by: Franciscan Sisters of Mary, Purpose: To provide either directly or in conjunction with other persons or organizations health care, health education and related facilities and services. Member of SSM Health Care.

University of Wisconsin - Madison Roman Catholic Foundation Inc., 723 State St., 53703-1087. Tel: 608-258-3140; Fax: 608-258-3141. Email: info@stpaulscc.org. Web: www.stpaulscc.org. Most Rev. Robert C. Morlino, Pres.; Cathie Hanlon, Treas.; Thomas Bellavia, Sec.; Juan Colaas, Chiar.; Rev. Randy J. Timmerman.

BARABOO. *St. Clare Health Care Foundation, Inc.*, 707 14th St., 53913. Tel: 608-356-1449; Fax: 608-356-1367. Email: keri_olson@ssmhc.com. Web: www.stclare.com. Sposored by The Franciscan Sisters of Mary., Purpose: to solicit, manage, invest and expend endowment funds and other gifts, grants and bequests primarily for the maintenance and benefit of St. Clare Hospital & Health Services and St. Clare Meadows Care Center of Baraboo, WI; to support other medical research, educational or charitable programs or activities in the Baraboo, Wisconsin Dells and Lake Delton, Wisconsin Area. Member SSM Health Care

Saint Vincent de Paul Society-Baraboo (District Council of Baraboo) , 408 8th St., 53913. Tel: 608-356-8549; Fax: 608-356-2018. Email: trikes@merr.com. Roger LaMasney, Council Pres., Contact Person. Sponsored by: Saint Vincent de Paul Society, Purpose: To help the poor and needy in a Vincentian spirit and manner.

EDGERTON. *Oaklawn Academy*, 432 Liguori Rd., 53534. Tel: 608-884-3425; Fax: 608-884-8175. Email: oaklawnusa@aol.com. Web: www.oaklawnusa.com. Mr. Javier Valenzuela, Contact Person.

Oaklawn Incorporated, 432 Liguori Rd., 53534. Tel: 608-884-3425; Fax: 608-884-8175. Email: oaklawnusa@aol.com. Web: www.oaklawnusa.com. Revs. Thomas Moylan, L.C., Chap.; Fergus O'Carroll, L.C., Chap.; Mr. Javier Valenzuela, Prin., Contact Person.

PLATTEVILLE. *St. Augustine Newman Center*, 135 S. Hickory, 53818. Tel: 608-348-7530; Fax: 608-348-7530. Email: newmanclub@uwplatt.edu. Web: www.uwplatt.edu/~newmanclub/. Rev. James H. Murphy, Contact Person. Please refer to St. Augustine University Parish, Platteville.

PRAIRIE DU SAC. *Society of Saint Vincent de Paul, Sauk-Prairie/Roxbury Area*, 815 19th St., 53578. Tel: 608-643-8905; Fax: 608-643-8905. Email: stvdppdc@chorus.net. Jim Vande Hey, Pres. Sponsored by: Saint Vincent de Paul Society., Purpose: To help the poor and needy in a Vincentian spirit and manner.

SINSINAWA. *Mother Samuel Coughlin Charitable Trust*, 585 County Rd. Z, 53824-9700. Tel: 608-748-4411; Fax: 608-748-5501. Email: toniharrisop@aol.com. Web: www.sinsinawa.org. Sr. Jane Boland, O.P., Contact Person. Sponsored by: Sinsinawa Dominicans, Purpose: To provide financial support to the aged, infirm or disabled vowed members of the Sinsinawa Dominicans.

Sinsinawa Housing, Inc., 585 County Rd. Z, 53824-9700. Tel: 608-748-4411; Fax: 608-748-4491. Email: toniharrisop@aol.com. Web: www.sinsinawa.org. Sr. Jane Boland, O.P., Contact Person. Sponsored by the Sinsinawa Dominicans, Purpose: To provide low- to moderate-income housing for senior residents of southwestern Wisconsin.

Sinsinawa Nursing, Inc., 585 County Rd. Z, 53824-9701. Tel: 608-748-4111; Fax: 608-748-4491. Email: toniharrisop@aol.com. Web: www.sinsinawa.org. Sr. Jane Boland, O.P., Contact Person. Sponsored by the Sinsinawa Dominicans., To organize, construct, operate and maintain a care center in southwestern Wisconsin for the elderly and infirm.

RELIGIOUS INSTITUTES OF MEN REPRESENTED IN THE DIOCESE

For further details refer to the corresponding bracketed number in the Religious Institutes of Men or Women section.

[0470]—*The Capuchin Fathers*—O.F.M., Ca

[0730]—*Legionaires of Christ*—L.C.

[0430]—*Order of Preachers-Dominicans* (Prov. of St. Albert the Great)—O.P.

[0240]—*Order of St. Camillus*—O.S.Cam.

RELIGIOUS INSTITUTES OF WOMEN REPRESENTED IN THE DIOCESE

[]—*Auxiliaries of the Blessed Sacrament*—A.B.S.

[0230]—*Benedictine Sisters of Pontifical Jurisdiction* (Yorktown, Watertown, SD)—O.S.B.

[0680]—*Cistercian Nuns*—O.Cist.

[]—*Congregation of the Handmaids of the Holy Child Jesus* (Nigeria, Africa)—H.H.C.J.

[3710]—*Congregation of the Sisters of Saint Agnes*—C.S.A.

[1070-03]—*Dominican Sisters*—O.P.

[1070-09]—*Dominican Sisters*—O.P.

[1230]—*Franciscan Sisters of Christian Charity*—O.S.F.

[1415]—*Franciscan Sisters of Mary*—F.S.M.

[2575]—*Institute of the Sisters of Mercy of the Americas*—R.S.M.

[2970]—*School Sisters of Notre Dame*—S.S.N.D.

[1680]—*School Sisters of St. Francis*—O.S.F.

[]—*Secular Institute of Schoenstatt Sisters of Mary*

[3020]—*Sisters Oblates to the Blessed Trinity*

[0530]—*Sisters of Charity of Our Lady, Mother of the Church*—S.C.M.C.

[3930]—*Sisters of St. Joseph of the Third Order of St. Francis* (Prov. of St. Joseph)—S.S.J.-T.O

[1030]—*Sisters of the Divine Savior*—S.D.S.

[1705]—*Sisters of the Third Order of St. Francis of Assisi*—O.S.F.

DIOCESAN CEMETERIES

MADISON. *Resurrection*, 2705 Regent St., 53705. Tel: 608-238-5561.

BELOIT. *Calvary*, 1827 N. Washington, Janesville, 53545. Tel: 608-754-3472.

Mount Thabor, 1827 N. Washington, Janesville, 53545. Tel: 608-754-3472.

JANESVILLE. *Mount Olivet*, 1827 N. Washington St., 53545. Tel: 608-754-3472.

NECROLOGY

† Henry, Rev. Msgr. Joseph L., (Retired)—Died Oct. 20, 2003

† Niglis, Rev. Msgr. Joseph C., (Retired)—Died March 6, 2003

† Fitzpatrick, Jerold F., Gratiot, WI St. Joseph; South Wayne, WI St. John—Died May 5, 2003

† Turner, Wayne A., (Retired)—Died Nov. 24, 2003

Diocese of Manchester

(Dioecesis Manchesteriensis)

Most Reverend

JOHN B. McCORMACK, D.D.

Bishop of Manchester; ordained February 2, 1960; consecrated December 27, 1995; installed September 22, 1998. *Res.: 657 N. River Rd., Manchester, NH 03104.*

Most Reverend

ODORE J. GENDRON, D.D.

Retired Bishop of Manchester; ordained May 31, 1947; appointed December 12, 1974; consecrated February 3, 1975. *Res.: St. Joseph Cathedral*, 145 Lowell St., Manchester, NH 03104-6135.

Most Reverend

FRANCIS J. CHRISTIAN, Ph.D.

Auxiliary Bishop of Manchester; ordained June 29, 1968; appointed April 2, 1996; consecrated May 14, 1996. *Res.: St. Joseph Cathedral*, 145 Lowell St., Manchester, NH 03104-6135.

ESTABLISHED 1884.

Square Miles 9,305.

Comprises the State of New Hampshire.

For legal titles of parishes and diocesan institutions, consult the Chancery Office.

Chancery Office: 153 Ash St., P.O. Box 310, Manchester, NH 03105. Tel: 603-669-3100; Fax: 603-669-0377.

Web: www.catholicchurchnh.org

Email: webmaster@rcbm.org

STATISTICAL OVERVIEW

Personnel	
Bishop	1
Auxiliary Bishops	1
Retired Bishops	1
Abbots	1
Priests: Diocesan Active in Diocese	114
Priests: Diocesan Active Outside Diocese	5
Priests: Retired, Sick or Absent	97
Number of Diocesan Priests	216
Religious Priests in Diocese	60
Total Priests in Diocese	276
Extern Priests in Diocese	7
Ordinations:	
Diocesan Priests	5
Religious Priests	1
Transitional Deacons	1
Permanent Deacons in Diocese	51
Total Brothers	32
Total Sisters	608
Parishes	
Parishes	120
With Resident Pastor:	
Resident Diocesan Priests	110
Resident Religious Priests	10
Missions	24
New Parishes Created	1
Closed Parishes	3
Professional Ministry Personnel:	
Sisters	35
Lay Ministers	331
Welfare	
Catholic Hospitals	2
Total Assisted	272,857
Health Care Centers	9
Total Assisted	545
Residential Care of Children	2
Total Assisted	44
Day Care Centers	111
Total Assisted	610
Specialized Homes	2
Special Centers for Social Services	12
Total Assisted	40,500
Educational	
Diocesan Students in Other Seminaries	11
Seminaries, Religious	2
Students Religious	2
Total Seminarians	13
Colleges and Universities	4
Total Students	4,302
High Schools, Diocesan and Parish	3
Total Students	1,668
High Schools, Private	1
Total Students	846
Elementary Schools, Diocesan and Parish	22
Total Students	5,333
Elementary Schools, Private	3
Total Students	959
Catechesis/Religious Education:	
High School Students	5,399
Elementary Students	26,711
Total Students under Catholic Instruction	45,231
Teachers in the Diocese:	
Priests	6
Brothers	15
Sisters	75
Lay Teachers	1,144
Vital Statistics	
Receptions into the Church:	
Infant Baptism Totals	4,275
Adult Baptism Totals	312
Received into Full Communion	440
First Communions	5,029
Confirmations	3,392
Marriages:	
Catholic	764
Interfaith	308
Total Marriages	1,072
Deaths	2,965
Total Catholic Population	327,353
Total Population	1,275,000

Former Bishops—Rt. Revs. DENIS M. BRADLEY, D.D., first Bishop of Manchester; consecrated June 11, 1884; died Dec. 13, 1903; JOHN B. DELANY, D.D., consecrated Sept. 8, 1904; died June 11, 1906; Most Revs. GEORGE ALBERT GUERTIN, D.D., consecrated March 19, 1907; died Aug. 6, 1931; JOHN B. PETERSON, D.D., consecrated Auxiliary Bishop of Boston, Nov. 10, 1927; transferred to See, May 13, 1932; died March 15, 1944; MATTHEW F. BRADY, D.D., consecrated Oct. 26, 1938; transferred to See, Nov. 11, 1944; died Sept. 20, 1959; ERNEST J. PRIMEAU, S.T.D., S.T.D., appt. Nov. 27, 1959; resigned Jan. 30, 1974; died June 15, 1989; ODORE J. GENDRON, D.D., ord. May 31, 1947; appt. Dec. 12, 1974; consecrated Feb. 3, 1975; LEO E. O'NEIL, D.D., ord. June 4, 1955; appt. Coadjutor Oct. 17, 1989; succeeded to See June 12, 1990; died Nov. 30, 1997.

Vicar General—Most Rev. FRANCIS J. CHRISTIAN, Ph.D., D.D., 153 Ash St., P.O. Box 310, Manchester, 03105-0310. Tel: 603-669-3100.

Vicar for Clergy—Most Rev. FRANCIS J. CHRISTIAN, Ph.D., D.D.

Canonical Services and Tribunal—153 Ash St., P.O. Box 310, Manchester, 03105-0310. Tel: 603-669-3101; Fax: 603-669-3102.

Judicial Vicar—Rev. JOHN J. MAHONEY JR., J.C.L.

Associate Judicial Vicars—Revs. RICHARD P. TETU, J.C.L.; MICHAEL S. TAYLOR, J.C.L.

Promoter of Justice—Rev. Msgr. PAUL L. BOUCHARD, V.F., S.T.L., J.C.L.

Advocates—Revs. ROGER H. CROTEAU; MICHAEL E. GENDRON; MICHAEL KERPER; ANDRE THIBODEAU.

Defenders of the Bond—Rev. Msgrs. PAUL L. BOUCHARD, V.F., S.T.L., J.C.L.; DONALD J. GILBERT, J.C.L.

Diocesan Judges—Revs. FRANCIS L. DEMERS, O.M.I., J.C.D.; JOHN J. MAHONEY JR., J.C.L.; RICHARD P. TETU, J.C.L.; MICHAEL S. TAYLOR, J.C.L.

Auditors—WENDY MCGRATH; Rev. MICHAEL R. MONETTE; Sr. KELLY CONNORS.

Notaries—KATHLEEN MASSE; SHIRLEY PEDRICK; MONIQUE KAMINSKI.

Council of Priests—Most Rev. JOHN B. MCCORMACK, D.D., Pres.; Revs. GERALD R. BELANGER, Chm.; ROBERT E. GORSKI, V.F.; STEVEN G. MONTESANTI; Most Rev. FRANCIS J. CHRISTIAN, Ph.D., D.D.; Rev. EDWARD J. ARSENAULT, S.T.L.; Very Rev. WILFRED H. DESCHAMPS; Rev. C. PETER DUMONT; Rev. Msgrs. JOHN E. MOLAN; JOHN P. QUINN; Very Rev. ROGER P. BILODEAU, V.F. (Retired); Revs. BERNARD CAMPBELL, O.F.M.Cap.; JOHN R. FORTIN, O.S.B.; GILLES GENEST, M.S.; MARC F. GUILLEMETTE; DENNIS J. AUDET; PAUL F. RUZZO; ALBERT J. TREMBLOY; FREDERICK J. PENNETT JR.; JOHN F. MULLIN, S.J.; RICHARD H. DION; PATRICK N. GILBERT; Rev. Msgrs. PAUL L. BOUCHARD, V.F., S.T.L., J.C.L.; THOMAS J. HANNIGAN.

College of Consultors—Most Rev. FRANCIS J. CHRISTIAN, Ph.D., D.D.; Rev. EDWARD J. ARSENAULT, S.T.L.; Very Rev. WILFRED H. DESCHAMPS; Revs. C. PETER DUMONT; ROBERT E. GORSKI, V.F.; Rev. Msgrs. JOHN E. MOLAN; JOHN P. QUINN.

Diocesan Pastoral Council—Most Revs. JOHN B. MCCORMACK, D.D.; FRANCIS J. CHRISTIAN, Ph.D., D.D.; Sr. MARGARET CROSBY, S.N.D.deN., Ex Officio; Mr. MICHAEL ANGIULO; Mr. GEOFFREY ASHMAN; Sr. ROSINA BECHARD, F.C.S.C.J.; Mr. THOMAS BRYANT; Mrs. JOANN FENTON; Sr. MARIE HENAULT, P.M.; Ms. SUSAN HOLDEN; Mr. ROBERT DUNN JR., Esq.; Ms. JANET LEROUX; Ms. LORI LEWIS; Mr. DE PHAM; Mr. ALFRED PILLARELLI; Sr. ELLEN KURTZ, R.S.M.; Mrs. MARILYN RIEL; Mrs. SUSAN SMITH; Mr. SHAWN MCDONOUGH; Deacon GREGORY MCGINN; Ms. MARIE STADTMILLER; Ms. MAGALIE ROWE.

Diocesan Finance Council—Most Rev. JOHN B. MCCORMACK, D.D., Chm.; Rev. Msgr. JOHN P. QUINN, Sec. for Finance & Real Estate; HAROLD ACRES; FRANK O. BUHL; DORIS M. DESAUTEL; RUSSELL GRADY; STEPHEN J. KANEB; STEVEN R.

MCMANIS; RONALD J. RIOUX; FRANK YANCO.

Clergy Personnel Board—Most Revs. JOHN B. MCCORMACK, D.D.; FRANCIS J. CHRISTIAN, Ph.D., D.D., Ex Officio; Rev. Msgr. THOMAS J. HANNIGAN, Ex Officio; Revs. DENNIS J. AUDET; RICHARD B. THOMPSON; PAUL L. GREGOIRE; ROBERT G. BIRON; STEVEN G. MONTESANTI; Rev. Msgr. JOHN E. MOLAN; Revs. C. PETER DUMONT, V.F.; COLIN A. MACDONALD; Rev. Msgr. ANTHONY R. FRONTIERO.

Masters of Ceremonies—Revs. JOSEPH M. COOPER; MARC F. GUILLEMETTE.

Cabinet Secretary for Administration—Rev. EDWARD J. ARSENAULT, S.T.L.. Email: earsenault@rcbm.org.

Cabinet Secretary for Education and Formation—Sr. MARY ELIZABETH WHALEN, S.N.D.deN.. Email: mwhalen@rcbm.org.

Cabinet Secretary for Community Services—Sr. MARGARET CROSBY, S.N.D.deN.. Email: pcrosby@rcbm.org.

Cabinet Secretary for Finance & Real Estate—Rev. Msgr. JOHN P. QUINN. Email: jquinn@rcbm.org.

Cabinet Secretary for Human Services—Sr. PATRICIA SULLIVAN, R.S.M.. Email: psullivan@catholiccharitiesnh.org.

Cabinet Secretary for Pastoral Services—Rev. MARC F. GUILLEMETTE. Email: mguillemette@rcbm.org.

Chancellor—Rev. EDWARD J. ARSENAULT S.T.L., 153 Ash St., P.O. Box 310, Manchester, 03105-0310. Tel: 603-669-3100.

Secretary to Bishop—JAYE GIBSON.

Secretary to the Auxiliary Bishop—FRANCEEN M. MORASSE.

Secretariat for Administration—

Communications Office—VACANT, Dir.

Development Office—VACANT, Dir.

Office of the Delegate for Ministerial Conduct—Rev. EDWARD J. ARSENAULT, S.T.L., Delegate; JOSEPH P. NAFF, L.I.C.S.W., Asst. to Delegate for Pastoral Care; DIANE M. QUINLAN, Asst. to Delegate for Policy Administration.

Diocesan Review Board—DAVID BULMER, M.D.; PETER FAVREAU; Rev. Msgr. DONALD J. GILBERT, J.C.L.; J. MICHAEL MCDONOUGH, Esq.; CHRISTINE TREMBLAY; Rev. GAYLE WHITTEMORE, MICHAEL DURETTE; MONIQUE IERARDI.

Diocesan Museum—JUDITH FOSHER, Archivist, 140 Laurel St., Manchester, 03103. Tel: 603-624-1729.

Personnel Officer—Rev. EDWARD J. ARSENAULT, S.T.L.

Legal Affairs Office—Rev. EDWARD J. ARSENAULT, S.T.L., Sec.

Operations & Information Systems—Sr. SHEILA GARVEY, R.S.M., Dir.

Risk Management and Insurance Office—MARTHA KIPP, Dir.

Secretariat for Education and Formation—Sr. MARY ELIZABETH WHALEN, S.N.D.deN.

Department of Catholic Schools—Rev. DENNIS J. AUDET; Sr. ELAINE POITRAS, C.S.C., Assoc. Supt.

Department of Faith Development—

Adult Education—PATRICIA GABREE, Dir.

Catechetics—PATRICIA GABREE, Dir.

Office of the Catechumenate including Re-Membering Church and Small Church Communities—Sr. MARY ELIZABETH WHALEN, S.N.D.deN., Dir.

Spiritual Renewal Services—Sr. MARY ELIZABETH WHALEN, S.N.D.deN.

Charismatic Renewal & Cursillo Movement—Very Rev. PAUL D. MONTMINY, V.F.; Revs. RICHARD E. ST. LOUIS; MARC B. DROUIN, Liaison; STEPHEN DUFFLEY.

Marian Ministries—Liaisons: Revs. A. STEPHEN MARCOUX; ROBERT COUTO.

Kairos Prison Ministry—Deacon MICHAEL C. SHAULIS, Spiritual Dir.

Men of St. Joseph—Rev. Msgr. MARC F. GUILLEMETTE.

Youth Programs—

Catholic Scouting Office—Rev. RAYMOND A. BALL, Dir.

Youth Adult Ministry and Youth Ministry—PAT GABREE, Dir.

Catholic Youth Organization Office—THERESA ROOT, Dir.

Diocesan Camps—GUS PLANCHET, Dir., P.O. Box 206, Gilmanton Iron Works, 03837-0206. Tel: 603-364-5851; Fax: 603-364-5038.

Secretariat for Community Services—

Diocesan Public Policy Office—Co Directors: Sr. MARGARET J. CROSBY, S.N.D.deN.; Deacon ROBERT J. ANDERSON JR.

Institutional Ministries Office—Deacon ROBERT J. ANDERSON JR., Dir.

Ecumenical and Interreligious Affairs—Rev. ROBERT G. BIRON, Dir., Our Lady of Fatima, 724 Main St., New London, 03257-4609. Tel: 603-526-4484.

Sacrament of Matrimony Office—Sr. MARGARET J. CROSBY, S.N.D.deN., Dir.

Multi-Cultural Ministries Office—Sr MARGARET CROSBY, S.N.D.deN., Dir.

African Apostolate—Rev. ANTHONY SUNDAY OGUNLEYE, St. Anne Rectory, 231 Merrimack St., Manchester, 03103. Tel: 603-623-8809. St. Augustine Rectory, 383 Beech St., Manchester, 03103. Tel: 603-625-5655.

Brazilian Apostolate—Rev. JOHN MAZZEI; ANA GOEDERT, Infant Jesus Rectory, 121 Allds St., Nashua, 03060-6395. Tel: 603-598-2622.

Hispanic Apostolate—Rev. JOHN M. GALLAGHER, O.F.M.Cap., J.C.L.; Sr. MARIA LUZ CERVANTES, M.S.C., St. Anne Rectory, 231 Merrimack St., Manchester, 03103. Tel: 603-623-8809. St. Augustine Rectory, 383 Beech St., Manchester, 03101. Tel: 603-625-5655; Revs. RICHARD H. DION, St. Aloysius Rectory, 48 W. Hollis St., Nashua, 03060-3286. Tel: 603-882-4362; LOURDES ULLOA. Tel: 603-882-4362; Sisters MARTHA RICO HERNANDEZ, H.S.M.P.; ELIZABETH GONZALES, H.S.M.P.; GUADALUPE GRANDO, H.S.M.P., 5 Green St., Nashua, 03064. Tel: 603-882-0893.

Indonesia Apostolate—Rev. JOHN TAN, St. Leo Rectory, 59 Main St., Gonic, 03839-5220. Tel: 603-332-1624.

Korean Apostolate—Merrimack College, Andover, MA.

Vietnamese Apostolate—Rev. JOSEPH NGUYEN, St. Anne Rectory, 231 Merrimack St., Manchester, 03103. Tel: 603-623-8809. St. Christopher Church 601 Manchester St., Nashua, 03064. Tel: 603-882-0632. St. Augustine Rectory, 383 Beech St., Manchester, 03103-5397. Tel 603-625-5655. St. Joseph Parish, 150 Central Ave., Dover, 03820-4090. Tel: 603-742-4837.

NH Diocesan Council of Catholic Women—Sr. MARGARET CROSBY, S.N.D.deN., Moderator.

Office of Priestly Life and Ministry—Rev. Msgr. ANTHONY R. FRONTERIO, Dir.

Pastoral Ministries Office—Sr. MARY ELIZABETH WHALEN, S.N.D.deN., Dir.

Respect Life Office—Deacon ROBERT J. ANDERSON JR., Dir.

Vocations Office—Directors: Revs. MARC F. GUILLEMETTE; MARC R. MONTMINY, V.F.

Secretariat for Finance and Real Estate—

Finance Officer—Rev. Msgr. JOHN P. QUINN.

Controller—MAURICE PRATTE.

Real Estate Office—PAUL HARRINGTON, Dir. Facilities Mgmt.; RAY CLEMENT, Dir. Cemeteries.

Propagation of the Faith—Rev. GERARD A. BOUCHER, Diocesan Dir. (Retired).

Catholic Campaign for Human Development / Operation Rice Bowl—Sr. MARGARET CROSBY, S.N.D.deN., Dir.

Catholic Relief Services—Rev. Msgr. JOHN P. QUINN, Dir.

Manchester Mission—CLAIRE AUCOIN, R.N., Dir.

Liaison for Religious Congregations—Sr. MARY ELIZABETH WHALEN, S.N.D.deN., Liaison.

Corpus Christi Food Pantry—KAY GOLDEN, New Hampshire Catholic Charities, 43 Franklin St., Nashua, 03064.

Diocesan Cemetery Office—RAYMOND P. CLEMENT, Dir., 153 Ash St., P.O. Box 310, Manchester, 03105.

Secretariat for Human Services—

New Hampshire Catholic Charities, Inc.—215 Myrtle St., Manchester, 03104. Tel: 603-669-3030; Fax: 603-626-1252.

Family Services Office—VACANT.

Diocesan Consultation and Counseling Services—JOSEPH P. NAFF, L.I.C.S.W., Clinical Dir.

Elderly Services—Sr. MARY ROSE ORLANDO, R.S.M., Social Worker.

Adoption and Maternity Services—ELAINE C. LANGTON, Social Worker.

Project Rachel—ROBERT P. CLOHOSEY, A.C.S.W., Coord.

Our Place—ROBERT P. CLOHOSEY, A.C.S.W., Program Dir.

Parish Social Ministry Office—RICHARD J. SHANNON, Dir.

Office of Persons with Disabilities—Sr. PAULINE LOFOND, P.M., Program Coord.

Deaf Ministry—Sr. PAULINE LOFOND, P.M.; Very Rev. THOMAS L. DUSTON, V.F., Pastoral Contact.

Immigration and Refugee Services—Sr. MARGARET CROSBY, S.N.D.deN., Dir.; LAN TRUONG, BIA Accredited Rep. (Level 1); KIMBERLY GEORGE, Immigration Attorney; MARIA EVELETH, BIA Fully Accredited Rep. Tel: 603-893-1971.

Diocesan Bureau of Housing—CAROL A. HAEBLER, Housing Coord., 323 Franklin St., Manchester, 03101. Tel: 603-625-5422; Fax: 603-625-1014.

Secretariat for Pastoral Services—

Office of the Permanent Diaconate—Rev. MARC F. GUILLEMETTE, Dir.

Office for Worship—Rev. JOSEPH M. COOPER, Dir.

Censor Librorum—Most Rev. FRANCIS J. CHRISTIAN, Ph.D., D.D.

Society of Saint Vincent de Paul—RAYMOND RIOUX, Pres., NH State Council, 8 Maplewood Ave., Manchester, 03102. Tel: 603-622-1036. Email: riouxr@nationwide.com.

Victim Assistance Coordinator—JOSEPH P. NAFF, L.I.C.S.W. Tel: 603-668-0014; 800-475-5585 (NH). Email: jnaff@catholiccharitiesnh.org.

CLERGY, PARISHES, MISSIONS AND PAROCHIAL SCHOOLS

CITY OF MANCHESTER
(HILLSBOROUGH COUNTY)

1—ST. JOSEPH CATHEDRAL (1869), [CEM] Rev. Joseph M. Cooper, Rector; Joan Poro, Pastoral Assoc. In Res., Most Revs. Francis J. Christian, Ph.D., D.D.; Odore J. Gendron, D.D.; Rev. Msgr. Colin A. MacDonald (Retired); Revs. Dennis J. Audet; Edward J. Arsenault, S.T.L.; Deacon Robert Potvin.
Res.: 145 Lowell St., 03104-6135. Tel: 603-622-6404; Fax: 603-626-4415.
Chapel—St. Joseph Cathedral Chapel, Formerly St. Joseph Eucharistic
Chapel—Convent, Tel: 603-624-6897.
Catechesis / Religious Program—Joan Poro, P.A., D.R.E.

2—ST. ANNE (1848), Rev. John M. Gallagher, O.F.M.Cap., J.C.L.; Sr. Maria Luz Cervantes, M.S.C., Pastoral Assoc. In Res., Rev. Bernard J. Campbell, O.F.M.Cap; Shirley Brien; Deacon Ramon Andrade.
Office & Mailing Address: 383 Beech St., 03103-5397.
Res.: 231 Merrimack St., 03103. Tel: 603-623-8809; Fax: 603-626-1517.
Church: 447 Union St..
Catechesis / Religious Program—Tel: 603-623-8800.

3—ST. ANTHONY OF PADUA (1899), (French), Rev. Charles E. DesRuisseaux; Dr. Elise B. Tougas, Pastoral Assoc. In Res., Rev. Normand A. Fillion, O.M.I.; Rev. Msgr. Leo L. St. Pierre (Retired); Very Rev. Roger E. Bilodeau, V.F. (Retired); Rev. William J. Hamilton, S.J.
Res.: 172 Belmont St., 03103-4452. Tel: 603-625-6409; Fax: 603-625-0099.
School—(Grades K-6), 148 Belmont St., 03103. Tel: 603-622-0414; Fax: 603-669-5212. Constance Bilodeau, Prin.

4—ST. AUGUSTIN (1871), (French), [CEM] Rev. John M. Gallagher, O.F.M.Cap., J.C.L. In Res. Revs. John J. Mahoney Jr., J.C.L.; Thomas Faiola, O.F.M. Cap. (NY); Deacon Ramon Andrade.
Office—383 Beech St., 03103-5397. Tel: 603-625-5655; Fax: 603-626-1517.
St. Anne Rectory: 231 Merrimack St., 03103

5—BLESSED SACRAMENT (1907), Rev. John Bavaro, O.F.M. In Res., Rev. Dennis Arambasick, O.F.M. (PRT).
Res.: 14 Elm St., 03103-7297. Tel: 603-622-5445; Fax: 603-627-5983.

6—ST. CATHERINE (1954), Rev. Msgr. Thomas J. Hannigan; Rev. Robert Gorski; Sr. Jeannette Landreville, C.S.C., Pastoral Min. In Res., Rev. Richard F. Vickery (Retired).
Res.: 207 Hemlock St., 03104-3299. Tel: 603-622-4966; Fax: 603-622-0236.
School—(Grades K-6), 206 N. St., 03104. Tel: 603-622-1711; Fax: 603-624-4935. Sr. Janet Belcourt, C.S.C., Prin. & D.R.E.

7—ST. EDMUND (1914), (French), Merged, in 2002 and became Transfiguration, Manchester.

8—ST. GEORGE (1890), (French), Closed., Merged with St. Joseph Cathedral in 2002.

9—ST. HEDWIG (1902), [CEM] Rev. Msgr. Alfred Daniszewski.
Res.: 147 Walnut St., 03104-4225. Tel: 603-623-4835.
School—St. Casimir, (Grades K-8), 456 Union St., 03103. Tel: 603-623-6411. Sr. Mary Lawrence Lojko, C.S.S.F., Prin. Felician Sisters 4; Students 231.

10—ST. JOHN THE BAPTIST (1914), (French), Merged, in 2002 to form Transfiguration, Manchester.

11—ST. MARIE (1880), [CEM 2] Revs. Marc R. Montminy, V.F.; John M. Grace; Sr. Doris Bernier, P.M., P.A., Pastoral Assoc.; Deacon Frank Gallinaro. In Res., Revs. Richard P. Tetu, J.C.L.; Wilfred Demers.
Res.: 378 Notre Dame Ave., 03102-3793. Tel: 603-622-4615; Fax: 603-666-4732.
Catechesis / Religious Program—Terry Boldue, D.R.E.
Chapel—Joseph House, Formerly Joseph House Chapel 279 Cartier St., 03102. Tel: 603-627-9493.
Chapel—Chapel of North American Martyrs
Chapel—St. Joan of Arc
Chapel—Eucharist Adoration Chapel
Convent—Sisters of the Presentation of Mary, 133 Wayne St., 03102-3793. Tel: 603-623-0815.

12—OUR LADY OF PERPETUAL HELP (1911), (English), Rev. Marcel M. Allard.
Res.: 266 Cypress St., 03103-3700. Tel: 603-622-2535; Fax: 603-668-0356.
Catechesis/Religious Program—Tel: 603-668-3985. Linda M. Lambert, D.R.E.
13—ST. PATRICK (1898), (Irish), [CEM] Rev. Nicholas P. Rogers; Deacon Harry Kram.
Res.: 138 Coolidge Ave., 03102-3298. Tel: 603-624-4115; Fax: 603-621-9616.
14—ST. PIUS X (1955), Rev. Msgrs. Anthony R. Frontiero; John E. Molan; Rev. Humbert Oliviera (Retired); Deacon Mark F. Hobson.
Res.: 575 Candia Rd., 03109-4708. Tel: 603-622-6510; Fax: 603-626-1323.
Catechesis/Religious Program—Mary Nedder, D.R.E.
15—ST. RAPHAEL (1888), [CEM] Rev. Jerome J. Day, O.S.B.
Res.: 103 Walker St., 03102-4534. Tel: 603-623-2604; Fax: 603-623-2604 (call ahead).
Catechesis/Religious Program—Tel: 603-647-2283. Therese Dame, D.R.E.
16—SACRED HEART OF JESUS (1911), (French), Revs. Marc R. Montminy, V.F.; John M. Grace; Deacon Frank Gallinaro.
Mailing Address & Office: 247 S. Main St., 03102-4890.
Church: 265 S. Main St., 03102. Tel: 603-625-9525; Fax: 603-666-4732.
Catechesis/Religious Program—Tel: 603-622-3312. Karen Hettrick, D.R.E.
17—ST. THERESA, Rev. John Bavaro, O.F.M., Admin.; Sr. Olivia Kidney, R.S.M., Pastoral Assoc.
Res.: 140 Mitchell St., 03103-6599. Tel: 603-623-5055; Fax: 603-622-6138.
Catechesis/Religious Program—Blessed Sacrament Parish, Tel: 603-622-5445.
18—TRANSFIGURATION (2002), Rev. Msgr. Paul L. Bouchard, V.F., S.T.L., J.C.L.; Sr. Pauline Maurier, C.S.C., P.A., Pastoral Assoc.; Deacon Richard J. Shannon. In Res., Rev. Msgr. James J. Markham (Retired); Revs. Leonard R. Foisy (Retired); Andre L. Bedard (Retired); Jean Lemay.
Res.: 107 Alsace St., 03102-3006. Tel: 603-623-4715; Fax: 603-623-4715.
Catechesis/Religious Program—Tel: 603-625-6025. Anita H. Plourde, D.R.E.

OUTSIDE THE CITY OF MANCHESTER

ALTON, BELKNAP CO.
1—ST. JOAN OF ARC (1961), Merged, in 2003 to form St. Katharine Drexel, Alton.
2—ST. KATHARINE DREXEL (2003), Rev. George E. Ham.
Mailing Address: P.O. Box 180, Wolfeboro, 03894-0180. Tel: 603-569-2548; 603-875-7191; Fax: 603-569-6659.
ASHLAND, GRAFTON CO., ST. AGNES, Revs. Eddy N. Bisson; John B. Loughnane Jr.
Res.: 6 Hill St., P.O. Box 1166, 03217-1166. Tel: 603-968-4433; Fax: 603-968-9870.
AUBURN, ROCKINGHAM CO., ST. PETER (1948), Rev. C. Peter Dumont. In Res., Rev. Msgr. John E. Molan; Rev. Marc F. Guillemette.
Res. & Church: 567 Manchester Rd., 03032-3123. Tel: 603-623-5429; Fax: 603-669-5598.
Catechesis/Religious Program—Tel: 603-669-5134.
BEDFORD, HILLSBOROUGH CO., ST. ELIZABETH SETON (1964), Rev. Msgr. John P. Quinn.
Res.: 190 Meetinghouse Rd., 03110-6027. Tel: 603-669-7444; Fax: 603-644-5371.
Catechesis/Religious Program—Mary Danielson; Deacons Joseph Mazzuchelli; Maurice Jeffrey.
BELMONT, BELKNAP CO., ST. JOSEPH (1949), Rev. Albert J. Tremblay Jr.; Deacon Thomas J. Oetinger.
Res.: 6 High St., P.O. Box 285, 03220-0285. Tel: 603-267-8174; Fax: 603-267-1170.
Catechesis/Religious Program—Kathy Loiacono, D.R.E.
BENNINGTON, HILLSBOROUGH CO., ST. PATRICK (1936), [CEM] Rev. Richard A. Smith.
Res.: 10 Greenfield Rd., P.O. Box 147, 03442-0147. Tel: 603-588-2180; Fax: 603-588-4917.
Catechesis/Religious Program—Tel: 603-547-2670; Fax: 603-547-3620. Brenda Wesoly, D.R.E.
BERLIN, COOS CO.
1—ST. ANNE (1885), (French), Consolidated, For inquiries for parish records contact Good Shepherd Parish, Berlin.
2—GOOD SHEPHERD (2000), Revs. Richard A. Roberge; John B. MacKenzie; Patrick N. Gilbert; Sr. Monique Therriault, R.S.M., P.A., Pastoral Assoc.; Deacon Merle Albert.
Office—151 Emery St., P.O. Box 570, 03570-0570. Tel: 603-752-2880; Fax: 603-752-1855.
Res.: 162 Madison Ave., 03570-0570.
Catechesis/Religious Program—Tel: 603-752-5443; Fax: 603-752-1743. Cecile Labbe, D.R.E. Students 457.
3—GUARDIAN ANGEL (1917), Merged, in 2002 to form Good Shepherd, Berlin.
4—ST. JOSEPH (1943), (French), Merged, in 2000 to form Good Shepherd, Berlin.
5—ST. KIERAN (1894), Consolidated, Merged to form Good Shepherd, Berlin.
BRISTOL, GRAFTON CO., ST. TIMOTHY (1953), Rev. Eddy N. Bisson; Deacon Christopher R. Clark.
Res.: 111 School St., P.O. Box 37, 03222-0037. Tel: 603-744-2700; Fax: 603-744-2782.
Mission—Our Lady of Grace 2 W. Shore Rd., Newfound Lake, Grafton Co. 03222.
CANDIA, ROCKINGHAM CO., ST. PAUL (1971), Rev. Daniel F. Szopa, Admin.; Lorette Nault, Pastoral Min.
Res.: 54 Main St., P.O. Box 276, 03034-0276. Tel: 603-483-8481; Fax: 603-483-8481.
Catechesis/Religious Program—Tel: 603-483-5516.
Station—St. Jerome Chester.
CASCADE, COOS CO., ST. BENEDICT, Closed., For Sacramental records contact Good Shepherd, Berlin.
CENTER OSSIPEE, CARROLL CO., ST. JOSEPH (1965), Rev. Edmund A. Babicz; Deacon William Rich.
Res.: 23 Moultonville Rd., P.O. Box 248, 03814-0248. Tel: 603-539-5036; Fax: 603-539-6295.
Catechesis/Religious Program—Pat Scannell, D.R.E.
CHARLESTOWN, SULLIVAN CO., ST. CATHERINE, Rev. Michael E. Gendron; Sisters Bernadette Ann Bozak, O.S.F., Pastoral Min.; Sylvia Pavlochin, O.S.F., Pastoral Min.
Res.: 285 Main St., Box 332, 03603-0332. Tel: 603-826-3359; Fax: 603-826-5875.
Catechesis/Religious Program—Debra Piletz, D.R.E.
CLAREMONT, SULLIVAN CO.
1—ST. JOSEPH (1920), (Polish), Rev. Stanley J. Piwowar.
Res.: 58 Elm St., P.O. Box 824, 03743-0824. Tel: 603-542-5732; Fax: 603-543-3673.
Catechesis/Religious Program—46 Elm St., 03743. Tel: 603-542-9933.
2—ST. MARY (1823), [CEM] Rev. Shawn M. Therrien; Deacon Paul R. Boucher.
Res.: 32 Pearl St., 03743-2552. Tel: 603-542-9518; Fax: 603-542-9614.
School—(Grades PreK-8), 18 Central St., 03743. Tel: 603-542-6341; Fax: 603-542-5260. Leanne K. Mortell, Prin. (Grades K-8). Lay Teachers 13; Students 171.
Mission—Old St. Mary Old Church Rd., West Clairmont, Sullivan Co.
COLEBROOK, COOS CO., ST. BRENDAN (1953), [CEM] Rev. Albert A. Bellefeuille.
Res.: 28 Pleasant St., P.O. Box 65, 03576-0065. Tel: 603-237-4342; Fax: 603-237-8580.
Catechesis/Religious Program—Sr. Annette Levasseur, F.C.S.C.J.
Mission—St. Pius X [CEM] P.O. Box 65, Errol, Coos Co. 03576.
Chapel—St. William of York Dixville.
CONCORD, MERRIMACK CO.
1—IMMACULATE HEART OF MARY (1956), Rev. Paul M. Gousse.
Res.: 180 Loudon Rd., 03301-6028. Tel: 603-224-4393; Fax: 603-224-6229.
Catechesis/Religious Program—Tel: 603-225-2026. Nancy Theroux, D.R.E.
2—ST. JOHN THE EVANGELIST (1865), Rev. Steven Montesanti.
Res. & Church: 72 S. Main St., 03301-4887. Tel: 603-224-2328; Fax: 603-224-2625.
Catechesis/Religious Program—Tel: 603-224-2062; 603-410-6438. Nancy Pare, D.R.E.
3—ST. PETER (1946), Revs. Francis X. Maguire, C.M.; Stephen J. Minkiel, C.M.
Res.: 135 N. State St., 03301. Tel: 603-225-2131; Fax: 603-228-4580.
Catechesis/Religious Program—Michael L. Morison, D.R.E.
4—SACRED HEART (1892), (French), Rev. Michael E. Sevigny, O.F.M.Cap.
Res.: 52 Pleasant St., 03301-3925. Tel: 603-225-6942; Fax: 603-225-3526.
Catechesis/Religious Program—Margaret Pince, D.R.E.
DERRY, ROCKINGHAM CO.
1—HOLY CROSS (1989), Rev. Roger H. Croteau.
Church & Office: 187 Hampstead Rd., 03038-4835.
Res.: 4 Belle Brook Ln., 03038. Tel: 603-437-9544; Fax: 603-537-1208.
Catechesis/Religious Program—Tel: 603-437-7550. George Strout, D.R.E.
2—ST. THOMAS AQUINAS (1888), Revs. Joseph F. Lorenzo, O.F.M.; Thomas Washburn, O.F.M.; Deacon George Long.
Res.: 26 Crystal Ave., 03038-1799. Tel: 603-432-5000; Fax: 603-434-0518.
School—(Grades K-8), 3 Moody St., 03038. Tel: 603-432-2712; Fax: 603-432-2179. Sr. Jacqueline Brodeur, C.S.C., Prin. Sisters 3; Lay Teachers 11; Students 304.
DOVER, STRAFFORD CO.
1—ST. CHARLES (1893), (French), [CEM] Unassigned. Rev. Paul L. Gregoire.
Res. & Church: 577 Central Ave., 03820-3464. Tel: 603-742-1354; Fax: 603-743-3360.
Catechesis/Religious Program—Tel: 603-742-8868. Nancy Watkins, D.R.E. Tel: 603-742-8868.
2—ST. JOSEPH (1945), Revs. Robert F. Cole; Paul F. Ruzzo; Deacon Robert J. Gagnon.
Res.: 150 Central Ave., 03820-4090. Tel: 603-742-4837; Fax: 603-749-6779.
Catechesis/Religious Program—Tel: 603-742-8868. Nancy Gurick, D.R.E.; Nancy Watkins, D.R.E.
Mission—Chapel of the Nativity Rte. 9, P.O. Box 163, Barrington, Strafford Co. 03825. Tel: 603-664-9336; Fax: 603-664-2310. Sr. Lorraine G. Choiniere, C.S.C., Pastoral Assoc.
3—ST. MARY (1833), Revs. Fritz J. Cerullo, O.S.A.; Albert G. Baillargeon (Retired); Arthur Burt, Pastoral Min.
Res.: 25 Third St., 03820-3385. Tel: 603-742-2619; Fax: 603-742-7166.
Catechesis/Religious Program—Nancy Watkins, D.R.E.; Nancy Gurick, D.R.E.
DURHAM, STRAFFORD CO., ST. THOMAS MORE, Rev. Daniel A. St. Laurent; Amy E. Cady, Pastoral Min.; Mary Beth Nazzaro, Pastoral Min.; Deacon Arnold J. Gustafson.
Office, Res. & Church: 6 Madbury Rd., Box 620, 03824-0620. Tel: 603-868-2666 (Office); Fax: 603-868-3765.
Catechesis/Religious Program—Ann Kimball, D.R.E.
ENFIELD, GRAFTON CO., ST. HELENA (1899), Rev. Thomas Huhn, M.S.; Deacon John St. George.
Res.: 36 Shaker Hill Rd., 03748-3524. Tel: 603-632-4263; Fax: 603-632-7874.
Catechesis/Religious Program—
Mission—St. Mary Rte. 4, Canaan, Grafton Co. 03741. Tel: 603-523-9955 (Hall).
EPPING, ROCKINGHAM CO., ST. JOSEPH (1898), [CEM] Rev. Michael S. Taylor, J.C.L.
Res.: Rte. 27 208 Pleasant St., 03042. Tel: 603-679-8805; Fax: 603-679-5192.
Catechesis/Religious Program—Debi Bennis, D.R.E.
EXETER, ROCKINGHAM CO., ST. MICHAEL (1859), Revs. Marc B. Drouin; Volney J. DeRosia; Joyce LaPointe, Pastoral Min.
Res.: 9 Lincoln St., 03833-3297. Tel: 603-772-2494; Fax: 603-778-1629.
Church: Front St., 03833-3297.
Catechesis/Religious Program—Catherine Smith, D.R.E.
FARMINGTON, STRAFFORD CO., ST. PETER (1920), Rev. W. Pierre Baker; Deacon Richard A. Falardeau.
Res.: 90 Central St., P.O. Box 565, 03835-0565. Tel: 603-755-2280; Fax: 603-755-9124.
Catechesis/Religious Program—Madonna M. Kling.
FRANKLIN, MERRIMACK CO., ST. PAUL (1884), [CEM] Rev. William E. Babineau; George L. Desautel, Pastoral Assoc.
Res.: 108 School St., P.O. Box 490, 03235-0490. Tel: 603-934-5013; Fax: 603-934-3469.
Catechesis/Religious Program—Mary Ellen Shaw, D.R.E.
GOFFSTOWN, HILLSBOROUGH CO., ST. LAWRENCE (1955), Rev. Donald F. Gauthier Jr.
Res.: 51 Main St., 03045-1644. Tel: 603-497-2651; Fax: 603-497-3668.
Catechesis/Religious Program—Tel: 603-497-4093. Phyllis Hanavan, D.R.E.
GONIC, STRAFFORD CO., ST. LEO (1892), [CEM] Very Rev. Paul D. Montminy, V.F.; Rev. Jason Y. Jalbert; Sr. Lucille Monette, S.A.S.V., Pastoral Min.
Res.: 59 Main St., 03839-5220. Tel: 603-332-1624; Fax: 603-332-7623.
Catechesis/Religious Program—Tel: 603-332-1863; Fax: 603-330-0365. Gabrielle Gagne, C.S.C., D.R.E.; Shirley Felker, D.R.E.
GORHAM, COOS CO., HOLY FAMILY, [CEM] Rev. Richard A. Roberge; Deacon Merle M. Albert.
Res.: 5 Church St., 03581-1695. Tel: 603-466-2335; Fax: 603-466-3490.
GREENVILLE, HILLSBOROUGH CO., SACRED HEART (1888), (French), [CEM] Rev. Anthony Di Russo.
Res.: 15 High St., 03048-3121. Tel: 603-878-1121; Fax: 603-878-4657.
Catechesis/Religious Program—Tel: 603-878-2274. Lynne Saucier, D.R.E.
GROVETON, COOS CO., ST. FRANCIS XAVIER (1899), (French), [CEM] Revs. Daniel R. Deveau; Craig Cheney; Sisters Helen Georges, S.G.M., Pastoral Min.; Marie Mansfield, S.G.M., Pastoral Min.
Res.: 10 State St., Box 72, 03582-0072. Tel: 603-636-1047; Fax: 603-636-2549.
HAMPSTEAD, ROCKINGHAM CO., ST. ANNE (1979), Rev. Frederick J. Pennett Jr.; Deacon William E. Mullen.
Res.: 26 Emerson Ave., P.O. Box 339, 03841-0339. Tel: 603-329-5886; Fax: 603-329-4468.
Catechesis/Religious Program—Jeanne Pinard, D.R.E.; Genivieve Sedensky, D.R.E., Youth Min.
HAMPTON BEACH, ROCKINGHAM CO., ST. PATRICK, , Open in summer months. For all records contact

O.L.M.M. Parish, Hampton Tel: 603-926-2206.
HAMPTON, ROCKINGHAM CO., OUR LADY OF THE MIRACULOUS MEDAL (1949), Revs. Maurice R. Larochelle; Philip J. Enrico; Michael J. Griffin (Retired); Deacons Dennis M. Jacobs; Paul E. Testa; Sisters Doris Ouelette, C.S.C., Pastoral Min.; Theresa Malouin, C.S.C., Pastoral Min.
Res.: 289 Lafayette Rd., 03842-2109. Tel: 603-926-2206; Fax: 603-926-8602.
School—Sacred Heart School, (Grades PreK-8) Tel: 603-926-3254; Fax: 603-929-1109. Sr. Mary Joan Walsh, O.L.L., Prin. Sisters 4; Lay Teachers 21; Students 449.
Catechesis/Religious Program—Tel: 603-926-5573. Claudette Dachowski, D.R.E.
Mission—St. Elizabeth's of Hungary, Formerly St. Elizabeth's Rte. 1-A, Seabrook Beach, Rockingham Co. 03874. Tel: 603-474-3839.
HANOVER, GRAFTON CO., ST. DENIS (1907), Rev. Kevin T. Connor.
Res.: 8 Sanborn Rd., 03755-2182. Tel: 603-643-2166; Fax: 603-643-9881.
Catechesis/Religious Program—Mary St. Germain, D.R.E.
HARRISVILLE, CHESHIRE CO., ST. DENIS, Attended by, Sacred Heart, Marlborough.
HENNIKER, MERRIMACK CO., ST. THERESA (1945), Closed. For inquiries for parish records contact the chancery. Rev. Mark E. Dollard; Deacon Winton P. DeRosia.
Mailing Address: P.O. Box 729, 03242-0729. Fax: 603-428-4479.
Mission—St. Mary Contoocook, Merrimack Co. 03229. P.O. Box 557, 03242.
HILLSBORO, HILLSBOROUGH CO., ST. MARY (1892), [CEM] [JC] Rev. Andre M. Thibodeau.
Res.: 38 Church St., P.O. Box 907, 03244-0907. Tel: 603-464-5565; Fax: 603-464-5565.
Catechesis/Religious Program—Gina Erickson, D.R.E.
Parish Hall—Tel: 603-464-6021.
HINSDALE, CHESHIRE CO., ST. JOSEPH (1884), [CEM] Rev. Raymond J. Potvin.
Res.: P.O. Box 46, 12 Prospect St., 03451. Tel: 603-336-5414; Fax: 603-336-7314.
Catechesis/Religious Program—Ann Whittle, D.R.E.
HOOKSETT, MERRIMACK CO., HOLY ROSARY (1886), [CEM] Rev. Edmund G. Crowley; Deacon David J. Shrader.
Res.: 21 Main St., 03106-1630. Tel: 603-485-3523; Fax: 603-485-8435.
Catechesis/Religious Program—Tel: 603-485-8567. Donna McCormack, D.R.E.
HUDSON, HILLSBOROUGH CO.
1—ST. JOHN THE EVANGELIST (1949), Rev. John C. Horan; Deacon Raymond V. Marcotte. In Res., Rev. Msgr. Joseph E. Desmond (Retired); Rev. Norman J. Simoneau (Retired).
Res.: 27 Library St., 03051-4239. Tel: 603-882-3603; Fax: 603-594-0813.
Catechesis/Religious Program—23 Library St., 03051. Tel: 603-882-6541. Mrs. Kathleen Cox, D.R.E.
2—ST. KATHRYN (1968), Rev. Gary J. Belliveau; Deacon Robert J. Anderson Jr.
Mailing Address & Church: 4 Dracut Rd., 03051-5006. Tel: 603-882-7793; Fax: 603-595-1465.
Catechesis/Religious Program—Marianne Hutchins, D.R.E.
JAFFREY, CHESHIRE CO., ST. PATRICK (1885), [CEM] Rev. Wilfred Deschamps.
Res.: 87 Main St., 03452-6139. Tel: 603-532-6634; Fax: 603-532-6633.
Church: 89 Main St., 03452-6139.
School—(Grades K-8), 70 Main St., 03452. Tel: 603-532-7676; Fax: 603-532-7476. William Collins, Prin. Sisters 2; Lay Teachers 14; Students 147.
Catechesis/Religious Program—Suzanne Sullivan, D.R.E.
KEENE, CHESHIRE CO.
1—ST. BERNARD (1862), [CEM] Revs. Daniel O. Lamothe; Eric T. Delisle.
Res.: 173 Main St., 03431-3790. Tel: 603-352-3525; Fax: 603-352-7472.
Church: 185 Main St., 03431-3790.
Catechesis/Religious Program—St. Joseph School, 92 Wilson St., 03431. Tel: 603-352-2720; Fax: 603-358-5465. Joy Davis, D.R.E. Students 143.
2—ST. MARGARET MARY (1955), Rev. Gerard L. Bertin.
Res.: 35 Arch St., 03431-2297. Tel: 603-352-1311; Fax: 603-358-5250.
Catechesis/Religious Program—Tel: 603-357-3781. Maribeth Boss, D.R.E.
Mission—Our Lady of the Lake 754 B, Rte. 63, Chesterfield, Cheshire Co. 03443. Tel: 603-363-4834.
LACONIA, BELKNAP CO.
1—ST. JOSEPH (1871), [CEM] Rev. Gary J. Kosmowski; Deacon Michael C. Shaulis.
Res.: 30 Church St., 03246-3401. Tel: 603-524-1442; Fax: 603-527-3534.
Catechesis/Religious Program—Tel: 603-524-4196. Kathryn Canfield, D.R.E.
2—SACRED HEART (1891), (French-Canadian), [CEM] Rev. Adrien R. Longchamps.
Res. 291 Union Ave., 03246-3125. Tel: 603-524-9609; Fax: 603-527-2617.
Catechesis/Religious Program—Tel: 603-524-4155. Daniel Bean, D.R.E.
LAKEPORT, BELKNAP CO., OUR LADY OF THE LAKES, Rev. George J. Soberick; Deacon William McCarty.
Res.: 50 Washington St., 03246-2339. Tel: 603-524-1357; Fax: 603-524-4524.
Catechesis/Religious Program—Margaret Gibbs, D.R.E.
Mission—St. Helena Weirs Beach, Belknap Co.
LANCASTER, COOS CO., ALL SAINTS (1856), [CEM] Rev. Raymond Ball.
Res.: 163 Main St., 03584-1723. Tel: 603-788-2083; Fax: 603-788-5553.
Catechesis/Religious Program—Marion Dunham, D.R.E.
Mission—St. Agnes Rte. 2, Jefferson, Coos Co. 03583.
LEBANON, GRAFTON CO., SACRED HEART (1876), (French), Rev. Gilles Genest, M.S., Admin. In Res., Revs. John F. Mullin, S.J.; Rene Parent.
Res.: 2 Hough St., P.O. Box 482, 03766-0482. Tel: 603-448-1262; Fax: 603-448-3754.
Catechesis/Religious Program—Karen R. Boucher, D.R.E.
LINCOLN, GRAFTON CO., ST. JOSEPH (1902), Very Rev. Roger P. Bilodeau, V.F. (Retired).
Res.: Church St., P.O. Box 128, 03251-0128. Tel: 603-745-2266; Fax: 603-745-2888.
Catechesis/Religious Program—Barbara Vitale, D.R.E.
LISBON, GRAFTON CO., ST. CATHERINE OF SIENA (1956), Rev. Daniel J. Sinibaldi.
Res.: c/o 21 Pine St., Woodsville, 03785-1215. Tel: 603-747-2038; Fax: 603-747-8071.
Church: 28 Highland Ave.. Tel: 603-838 2852.
Catechesis/Religious Program—Sandy Perry, D.R.E.
LITCHFIELD, HILLSBOROUGH CO., ST. FRANCIS OF ASSISI (1953), Rev. Dennis A. Broussard.
Parish Office—9 St. Francis Way, 03052-8050. Tel: 603-424-3456; Fax: 603-424-8603.
School—(Grades K-6), .. Tel: 603-424-3312; Fax: 603-424-9128. Sisters of Mercy 1; Lay Teachers 9; Students 151.
Catechesis/Religious Program—Tel: 603-424-9061.
LITTLETON, GRAFTON CO., ST. ROSE OF LIMA (1882), [CEM] Rev. Joseph S. Klatka.
Res.: 77 Clay St., 03561-1205. Tel: 603-444-2593; Fax: 603-444-3126.
Mission—Christ the King Main St., Bethlehem, Grafton Co. 03574.
Mission—Our Lady of the Snows Main St., Franconia, Grafton Co. 03580.
LONDONDERRY, ROCKINGHAM CO.
1—ST. JUDE (1962), Rev. Robert Couto; Deacon Marc G. Poyeur; Sr. Janice Rooney, S.N.D.deN., Pastoral Assoc.
Res.: 435 Mammoth Rd., 03053-2304. Tel: 603-432-3333; Fax: 603-432-1639.
Catechesis/Religious Program—Tel: 603-437-7026. Margaret A. Donahue-Turner, P.A., D.R.E.
2—ST. MARK THE EVANGELIST (1981), Very Rev. Thomas L. Duston, V.F.; Deacon Lee Abbott, P.A.
Res.: One South Rd., 03053-3814. Tel: 603-432-8711; Fax: 603-434-6748.
Catechesis/Religious Program—Marilynn P. Heitman, D.R.E.
MARLBOROUGH, CHESHIRE CO., SACRED HEART (1886), [CEM] Rev. James P. Walsh.
Res.: 9 Ling St., P.O. Box 517, 03455-0517. Tel: 603-876-3804 Fax: 603-876-4327.
MEREDITH, BELKNAP CO., ST. CHARLES (1946), Rev. Richard B. Thompson; Sr. Harriet Cutting, S.N.D.deN., P.A., Pastoral Assoc. In Res., Rev. Gerard A. Boucher (Retired).
Res.: 300 Rte 25, P.O. Box 327, 03253-0237. Tel: 603-279-4403; Fax: 603-279-9924.
MERRIMACK, HILLSBOROUGH CO.
1—ST. JOHN NEUMANN (1982), Rev. Agapit H. Jean Jr.; Deacon Richard A. Cloutier.
Res.: 208 Naticook Rd., 03054-4612.
Church: 708 Milford Rd. (Rte. 101A), 03054-4612. Tel: 603-880-4689; Fax: 603-881-9668.
Catechesis/Religious Program—Tel: 603-880-0825. Michelle Marrone.
2—OUR LADY OF MERCY (1954), Revs. Leo A. LeBlanc; Paul T. Gilbert; Christine Patterson, Pastoral Assoc.; Deacon James E. Patterson.
Res.: 16 Baboosic Lake Rd., 03054-3603. Tel: 603-424-3757; Fax: 603-424-1780.
Catechesis/Religious Program—14 Baboosic Lake Rd., 03054. Tel: 603-424-4477. Elizabeth Lochman, D.R.E.
MILFORD, HILLSBOROUGH CO., ST. PATRICK (1895), [CEM] Rev. Andrew W. Cryans; Patti Sigvardson, P.A., Pastoral Assoc.; Dolores S. Ahlgren, P.A., Pastoral Assoc.
Res.: 34 Amherst St., P.O. Box 27, 03055-0027. Tel: 603-673-1311; Fax: 603-673-3687.
Share Program—Tel: 603-673-9898. Mrs. Mariette Facques, Co. Dir.; Carolyn Momenee, Co. Dir. (A non-denominational outreach program for the local needy).
Mission—Infant Jesus P.O. Box 27, Brookline, Hillsborough Co. 03055.
NASHUA, HILLSBOROUGH CO.
1—ST. ALOYSIUS (1871), [CEM 3] Rev. Richard H. Dion; Deacon David Hamel. In Res., Rev. Alfred Bouchard.
Res.: 48 W. Hollis St., 03060-3286. Tel: 603-882-4362; Fax: 603-886-8923.
Chapel—Corpus Christi Chapel 43 Franklin St., 03064.
Catechesis/Religious Program—Giselle North, D.R.E.
2—ST. CASIMIR, Closed., in 2002 to form St. Patrick, Nashua.
3—ST. CHRISTOPHER (1950), Rev. Richard J. Kelley; Sr. M. Leon Pennell, R.S.M., P.A., Pastoral Assoc.
Mailing Address: 60 Manchester St., 03064-6296. In Res., Rev. Bruce W. Collard.
Res.: 62 Manchester St., 03064-6296. Tel: 603-882-0632; Fax: 603-881-8728.
School—(Grades K-6), 20 Cushing Ave., 03060. Tel: 603-882-7442; Fax: 603-594-9253. Sr. Joan Marie Messier, R.S.M., Prin. Students 377.
Catechesis/Religious Program—Mary Roy, D.R.E.
4—ST. FRANCIS XAVIER (1885), [CEM] Merged, in 2003 to form St. Aloysius, Nashua.
5—IMMACULATE CONCEPTION (1968), Rev. Marc R. Gagne; Deacon James P. Daly; Stephen Kimbell, D.R.E.
Res.: 216 E. Dunstable Dr., 03062-2344. Tel: 603-888-0321; Fax: 603-888-8407.
Parish Hall—Tel: 603-888-0608.
Catechesis/Religious Program—Eileen Bowes, D.R.E.
6—INFANT JESUS (1909), (French), Revs. Raymond E. Gagnon; John C. Mazzei (Brazil). In Res., Rev. Andre L. Bedard (Retired).
Res.: 121 Allds St., 03060-6395. Tel: 603-882-2462; Fax: 603-882-7104.
School—(Grades K-6), 3 Crown St., 03060-6366. Tel: 603-889-2649; Fax: 603-594-9117. Sr. Marie Henault, P.M., Prin.
Convent—Sisters of the Holy Cross, Tel: 603-882-0553.
Catechesis/Religious Program—Tel: 603-886-9725. Mary Jane Nichols, D.R.E.
7—ST. JOSEPH (1955), Most Rev. Francis J. Christian, Ph.D., D.D., Admin.; Deacon Alfred A. LaBonte Jr.
Res.: 777 W. Hollis St., 03062-3553. Tel: 603-883-0757; Fax: 603-883-8057.
Catechesis/Religious Program—Janice Mercure, D.R.E.
8—ST. PATRICK (1855), [CEM 2] Rev. Martin T. Kelly. In Res., Rev. John E. Healey.
Res.: 29 Spring St., 03060-3490. Tel: 603-882-2262; Fax: 603-577-9817.
9—RESURRECTION (1970), Rev. Stephen Marcoux III; Ann M. Cormier, Pastoral Min.
Pastoral Center—449 Broad St., 03063-3412. Tel: 603-882-0925; Fax: 603-881-3561.
Catechesis/Religious Program—Tel: 603-889-0012. Terry Root, Co. Coord.; Charlene Tabat, Co. Coord.
10—ST. STANISLAUS (1908), (Polish), Closed., For inquires for parish records please see St. Aloysius of Gonzaga.
NEW LONDON, MERRIMACK CO., OUR LADY OF FATIMA (1952), Rev. Robert G. Biron; Deacon Gregory R. McGinn; Cheryl Fitzgerald, P.A., Pastoral Assoc.
Res. & Church: 724 Main St., 03257-4609. Tel: 603-526-4484; Fax: 603-526-8055.
Mission—Immaculate Conception Church St., Potter Place, Merrimack Co. 03216. Tel: 603-735-5821.
NEWMARKET, ROCKINGHAM CO., ST. MARY (1878), [CEM] Rev. John B. Finnigan.
Res.: 182 Main St., P.O. Box 337, 03857-0337. Tel: 603-659-3643; Fax: 603-659-8924.
Catechesis/Religious Program—Cheryl Miller, D.R.E.
Mission—Sacred Heart 52 Main St., Newfields, Rockingham Co. 03856.
NEWPORT, SULLIVAN CO., ST. PATRICK (1902), [CEM] Rev. Richard E. St.Louis Jr.
Res.: 32 Beech St., 03773-1416. Tel: 603-863-1422; Fax: 603-863-7898.
Catechesis/Religious Program—Claire Donohue, D.R.E.
Mission—St. Joachim Rte. 11, Sunapee, Sullivan Co. 03782. Tel: 603-763-5940.
NEWTON, ROCKINGHAM CO., MARY, MOTHER OF THE CHURCH (1967), Rev. Michael R. Monette.
Res.: 12 Amesbury Rd., 03858-3200. Tel: 603-382-6566; Fax: 603-382-5102.
Catechesis/Religious Program—Tel: 603-642-8885;

Fax: 603-642-7446. Sisters Mary Malone, C.S.J., D.R.E.; Mildred Malone, C.S.J., D.R.E.
Mission—St. Frederick 3 New Boston Rd., Kingston, Rockingham Co. 03848.

NORTH CONWAY, CARROLL CO., OUR LADY OF THE MOUNTAINS (1902), [CEM 2] Revs. Ronald R. Goupil; Louis A. Soucey (Retired); Eusebio F. Silva, Admin.; Deacon John Carey.
Office, Res. & Church: 2905 White Mountain Hwy., P.O. Box 1199, Intervale, 03845. Tel: 603-356-2535.
Catechesis/Religious Program—Gloria Theophelakes, D.R.E.

NORTH STRATFORD, COOS CO., SACRED HEART (1888), (French), [CEM 2] Revs. Daniel R. Deveau; Craig Cheney; Sisters Marie Mansfield, S.G.M., Pastoral Assoc.; Helene Georges, S.G.M., Pastoral Assoc.
Church: 121 Main St., P.O. Box C, 03590-0227. Tel: 603-922-3360; Fax: 603-636-2549.
St. Francis Xavier Rectory: Groveton, 03582. Tel: 603-636-1047.

NORTH WALPOLE, CHESHIRE CO., ST. PETER (1878), [CEM] Rev. Michael E. Gendron; Sisters Bernadette Ann Bozak, O.S.F., Pastoral Min.; Sylvia Pavlochin, O.S.F., Pastoral Min.
Church: 38 Church St., 03609-1715. Tel: 603-445-5304; Fax: 603-445-2115.
St. Catherine of Siena Rectory: P.O. Box 332, Charlestown, 03603-0332. Tel: 603-826-3359.
Catechesis/Religious Program—Maria Castellano, D.R.E.
Mission—St. Joseph Elm St., Walpole, Cheshire Co. 03608. Tel: 603-756-3444.

PELHAM, HILLSBOROUGH CO., ST. PATRICK (1946), Rev. Robert G. Guillemette; Deacon John F. Ross.
Res. & Church: 12 Main St., 03076-3724. Tel: 603-635-3525; Fax: 603-635-3919.
School—(Grades K-8), 16 Main St., 03076. Tel: 603-635-2941; Fax: 603-635-9800. Roger Dumont, Prin. Lay Teachers 13; Students 235.
Catechesis/Religious Program—Tel: 603-635-1447. Donna Delanty, D.R.E.

PENACOOK, MERRIMACK CO., IMMACULATE CONCEPTION (1880), [CEM] Rev. W. Timothy Thibeault.
Res.: 9 Bonney St., 03303-1654. Tel: 603-753-4413; Fax: 603-753-4071.
Catechesis/Religious Program—Jesus Guzman, D.R.E.

PETERBOROUGH, HILLSBOROUGH CO., ST. PETER (1900), [CEM] Rev. William J. Kelley.
Res.: 18 Vine St., 03458-2403. Tel: 603-924-3819; 603-924-7647 (Office); Fax: 603-924-8365.
Catechesis/Religious Program—Tel: 603-924-3811. Mary Pat Farr-Szep, D.R.E.

PITTSFIELD, MERRIMACK CO., OUR LADY OF LOURDES (1889), Rev. Georges F. de Laire; Deacon Robert Esposito.
Res.: 20 River Rd., 03263-3314. Tel: 603-435-6242; Fax: 603-435-8840.
Catechesis/Religious Program—Tel: 603-942-8716. Katrina Allan, D.R.E.
Mission—St. Joseph [CEM] 20 River Rd., Northwood, Rockingham Co. 03263. Tel: 603-435-6242.

PLAISTOW, ROCKINGHAM CO., HOLY ANGELS (1892), [CEM] Rev. Marcel Martel; Deacon George J. Borkush.
Res.: 8 Atkinson Depot Rd., Rte. 121, 03865-3103. Tel: 603-382-8324; Fax: 603-382-1113.
Catechesis/Religious Program—Tel: 603-382-8824. Thomas Griffin Sr.

PLYMOUTH, GRAFTON CO., ST. MATTHEW (1916), Revs. Eddy N. Bisson, Admin.; John B. Loughnane Jr., Assoc. Pastor.
Res.: 46 Langdon St., 03264-1438. Tel: 603-536-4700; Fax: 603-536-4709.

PORTSMOUTH, ROCKINGHAM CO.
1—ST. CATHERINE OF SIENA (1951), Rev. Msgr. Lawrence E. Burns.
Res.: 845 Woodbury Ave., 03801-3294. Tel: 603-436-0344; Fax: 603-334-3393.
Catechesis/Religious Program—Sr. Bernadette Whitney, O.L.L.; Dianne Shannon, D.R.E.
2—IMMACULATE CONCEPTION (1851), [CEM 2] Rev. Edward J. Kelley; Beverly De Matteo, Pastoral Assoc.; Sr. Bernadette Whitney, O.L.L., Youth Min. In Res., Rev. Timothy R. O'Donnell (Retired).
Res.: 98 Summer St., 03801-4398. Tel: 603-436-0048; Fax: 603-436-8848.
Catechesis/Religious Program—Rita Lena, D.R.E.
3—ST. JAMES (1958), [JC] Rev. Michael Kerper.
Res.: 2075 Lafayette Rd., 03801-5697. Tel: 603-436-4555; Fax: 603-433-4401.
Church: 2079 Lafayette Rd., 03801-5697.

ROCHESTER, STRAFFORD CO.
1—HOLY ROSARY (1883), (French), [CEM] Very Rev. Paul D. Montminy, V.F.; Rev. Jason Y. Jalbert; Shirley Felker, Pastoral Min.
Res. & Church: 189 N. Main St., 03867-1299. Tel: 603-436-4555; Fax: 603-330-0865.
Catechesis/Religious Program—16 Bridge St., 03867. Tel: 603-332-3026; Fax: 603-332-2915.
2—ST. MARY (1872), [CEM] Revs. W. Pierre Baker; Maurice W. Lampron (Retired); Mary Ann Gilmore, Pastoral Min.; Sr. Lucie Ducas, C.S.C., P.A., Pastoral Assoc.; Deacon Richard A. Falardeau.
Res.: 71 Lowell St., 03867-5002. Tel: 603-332-1869; Fax: 603-332-2040.
Catechesis/Religious Program—Judy Jordan, D.R.E.; Anna Ingram, D.R.E.

ROLLINSFORD, STRAFFORD CO., ST. MARY (1856), [CEM] Rev. Thomas Coover.
Mailing Address: P.O. Box 350, Somersworth, 03878-0350.
Holy Trinity Rectory: 404 High St., Somersworth, 03878. Tel: 603-692-4367; Fax: 603-692-4454.
Catechesis/Religious Program—Tel: 603-749-1666. Laura Ingle, D.R.E.

RYE BEACH, ROCKINGHAM CO., ST. THERESA (1979), Rev. Maurice D. Lavigne.
Res.: 815 Central Rd., P.O. Box 482, 03871-0482. Tel: 603-964-6440; Fax: 603-964-4139.
Catechesis/Religious Program—Tel: 603-964-9878. Sr. M. Gregory Pickford, R.S.M., D.R.E.

SALEM, ROCKINGHAM CO.
1—ST. JOSEPH (1910), Revs. Gerald R. Belanger; Ray J. Labrie; Deacon David Costello, Pastoral Min. In Res., Rev. Thomas J. Bresnahan (Retired).
Res. & Church: 33 Main St., 03079-1922. Tel: 603-898-4933; Fax: 603-893-9236.
Catechesis/Religious Program—Tel: 603-893-9692. Jerry Bergeron, D.R.E.
2—MARY, QUEEN OF PEACE (1966), Rev. John W. Fleming; Sr. Rachel M. Jette, C.S.C., P.A., Pastoral Assoc.; Deacon Leonard B. Albis.
Res.: 200 Lawrence Rd., 03079-3978. Tel: 603-893-8661; Fax: 603-890-0292.
Catechesis/Religious Program—Marie Mullen, D.R.E.

SANBORNVILLE, CARROLL CO., ST. ANTHONY (1908), [CEM] Rev. Edmund A. Babicz; Mary Sullivan, Pastoral Min.
Res.: 239 Meadow St., P.O. Box 490, 03872-0490. Tel: 603-522-3304; Fax: 603-522-8273.
Catechesis/Religious Program—William Banks, D.R.E.

SOMERSWORTH, STRAFFORD CO.
1—HOLY TRINITY (1857), [CEM] Rev. Thomas Coover; Sr. Mary Judith Mountain, R.S.M., Pastoral Min.
Res.: 404 High St., P.O. Box 350, 03878-0350. Tel: 603-692-4367; Fax: 603-692-4454.
Catechesis/Religious Program—Tel: 603-692-5403. Gary Hodsdon, D.R.E.
2—ST. MARTIN (1882), (French), [CEM] Rev. Aaron J. Pfaff.
Res.: 120 Maple St. Ext., 03878-1999. Tel: 603-692-2172; Fax: 603-692-2499.
Catechesis/Religious Program—Janet Jacobson, D.R.E.

SUNCOOK, MERRIMACK CO., ST. JOHN THE BAPTIST (1873), [CEM 2] Rev. Donald J. Clinton.
Res. & Church: 10 School St., 03275-1817. Tel: 603-485-3113; Fax: 603-485-2113.
Catechesis/Religious Program—Tel: 603-485-3972. Muriel Previe, D.R.E.

TILTON, BELKNAP CO., ST. MARY OF THE ASSUMPTION (1894), [CEM] Rev. Richard M. Giroux.
Res.: 16 Chestnut St., 03276-5546. Tel: 603-286-4445; Fax: 603-286-4663.
Catechesis/Religious Program—Tel: 603-286-4554. Mary Tilton, D.R.E.

TROY, CHESHIRE CO., IMMACULATE CONCEPTION, [CEM] Rev. James P. Walsh.
Office & Mailing Address: c/o Sacred Heart Rectory, 9 Ling St., P.O. Box 517, Marlborough, 03455-0517. Tel: 603-876-3804; Fax: 603-876-4327.

WEST LEBANON, GRAFTON CO., HOLY REDEEMER (1953), Merged, in 2003 to form Sacred Heart, Lebanon.

WEST STEWARTSTOWN, COOS CO., ST. ALBERT (1926), [CEM] Revs. Daniel Deveau; Craig Cheney.
Mailing Address: P.O. Box 176, Beecher Falls, VT 05902-0176.
Res. & Church: 10 Church St., 03597. Tel: 603-246-8829; Fax: 603-246-7167.
Station—Coos County House of Corrections

WEST SWANZEY, CHESHIRE CO., ST. ANTHONY (1958), Revs. Daniel O. Lamothe; Eric T. Delisle.
Mailing Address: *St. Bernard Church*, 185 Main St., Keene, 03431-3790.
Church: 50 S. Winchester St., 03469-0117. Tel: 603-352-3525; Fax: 603-352-7472.
Catechesis/Religious Program—Jeanne Symonds, D.R.E.

WHITEFIELD, COOS CO., ST. MATTHEW (1886), [CEM 2] Rev. George Majka; Deacon Joseph A. Polcari.
Res.: 9 Jefferson Rd., 03598-3101. Tel: 603-837-2558; Fax: 603-837-2558.
Mission—St. Patrick Twin Mountain. Rte. 3 & 302, Carroll, Coos Co. 03595.
Shrine—Brenton Woods, Our Lady of the Mountains Bretton Woods.

WILTON, HILLSBOROUGH CO., SACRED HEART (1882), [CEM] Rev. Anthony Di Russo.
Res. & Mailing Address: c/o Sacred Heart Rectory, 15 High St., Greenville, 03048-3121. Tel: 603-654-6554 (Parish); 603-878-1121 (Res.); Fax: 603-878-4657.
Church: 49 Maple St., 03086. Tel: 603-878-2991.

WINCHESTER, CHESHIRE CO., ST. STANISLAUS (1962), (Polish), Rev. Raymond J. Potvin.
Res. & Mailing Address: c/o St. Joseph Rectory, 12 Prospect St., P.O. Box 14, Hinsdale, 03451-0014.
Church: 80 Richmond St., 03470. Tel: 603-239-4312.
Catechesis/Religious Program—Elaine Ellis, D.R.E.

WINDHAM, ROCKINGHAM CO., ST. MATTHEW (1962), [JC] Rev. Msgr. Donald J. Gilbert, J.C.L.; Deacon Clarence R. Cummins.
Res.: 2 Searles Rd., 03087-1298. Tel: 603-893-3336; Fax: 603-898-4008.
Catechesis/Religious Program—Wendy Statdmiller, D.R.E.; Margaret O'Brien, D.R.E.

WOLFEBORO, CARROLL CO., ST. CECILIA, Merged Rev. George E. Ham. to form St. Katherine Drexel, Alton.
Res.: 205 S. Main St., P.O. Box 180, 03894-0180. Tel: 603-569-2548; Fax: 603-569-6659.
Catechesis/Religious Program—Robert Simoneau, D.R.E.

WOODSVILLE, GRAFTON CO., ST. JOSEPH (1896), [CEM] Revs. Daniel J. Sinibaldi; Philip Brody.
Res.: 21 Pine St., 03785-1215. Tel: 603-747-2038; Fax: 603-747-8071.
Catechesis/Religious Program—Sandy Perry, D.R.E.

Chaplains of Public Institutions

MANCHESTER. *Catholic Medical Center*. Revs. Bernard Campbell, O.F.M., Donald E. Lafond (Retired), Sr. Andrea McDonald, Dir. Pastoral Care.
Elliott Hospital. Revs. Paul Gilbert, William J. Hamilton, S.J.
Hillsborough County Jail. Sisters Marguerite Gravel, Chap., Andrienne Gordon, P.M.
Veterans Administration Medical Center. Revs. Maurice R. Lacroix (Retired), William J. Hamilton, S.J.
Youth Development Center. Vacant.

BERLIN. *Androscoggin Valley Hospital*. Sr. Monique Therriault, R.S.M., Chap.

BOSCAWEN. *Merrimack County House of Corrections*. Rev. W. Timothy Thibeault.

BRENTWOOD. *Rockingham County House of Corrections*. Rev. Michael Kerper.

CLAREMONT. *Sullivan County House of Corrections*. Revs. Stanley J. Piwowar, Shawn M. Therrien.

CONCORD. *Concord Hospital*. Sharon Martin, Chap.
N.H. State Prison. Deacon Michael C. Shaulis.
New Hampshire Hospital. Rev. Michael E. Sevigny, O.F.M.Cap.
State Prison for Men. Deacon Michael Shaulis, Chap.

DOVER. *Strafford County House of Corrections*. Vacant

GOFFSTOWN. *New Hampshire State Prison for Women*. Rev. Msgr. John E. Molan.

LACONIA. *Lakes Region Prison Facility*. Michael Shaulis, Chap.

LEBANON. *Dartmouth-Hitchcock Medical Center*. Revs. John F. Mullin, S.J., Christopher Chukwu.

NASHUA. *St. Joseph Hospital*. Rev. John C. Mazzei (Brazil), Deacon John Martin, Chap.
Southern N.H. Regional Medical Center and Nursing Homes. Sr. Doris Gagnon, P.M., Chap., Rev. John C. Mazzei (Brazil), Chap.

NORTH HAVERHILL. *Grafton County House of Corrections*. Rev. Daniel J. Sinibaldi.

OSSIPEE. *Carroll County House of Correction*. Rev. Edmund A. Babicz.

WEST STEWARTSTOWN. *Coos County House of Corrections*. Rev. Craig Cheney.

WESTMORELAND. *Cheshire County House of Corrections*. Rev. Gerard L. Bertin.

On Duty Outside the Diocese:
Revs.—
Coyne, Emmett A., 201 S.E. 11 Terr., #207, Dania, FL 33004.
Polito, Victor V.J., St. Mary Rectory, 156 E. Main St., Amsterdam, NY 12010-4899. Tel: 518-842-4500

Military Chaplains:
Revs.—
Cody, Kevin W., Major, P.S.C. 5 Box 804, Apo, AE 09050.
Decker, James D., Major, 6715 Forest Haven, San Antonio, TX 78240.
Glasgow, Robert K., CH, Major, USA, 293rd BSB, Unit 29901, Box 24, Apo, AE 09086-9901.

Absent on Sick Leave:
Revs.—
Goupil, Ronald R.
Rundzio, Mark A.
St. Louis, Scott J.

Absent on Leave:
Revs.—
Desmarais, Gerard R.
Kucharski, Steven M.
Lamy, Raymond J.

Retired:
Rev. Msgrs.—
Blair, Raymond O., 1 Harborside Dr., #4201, Delroy Beach, FL 33483-5157.
Crosby, Charles E., 793 Ocean Blvd., Hampton, 03842.
Curran, Francis L., Bishop Peterson Residence, 221 Orange St., 03104-4324.
Desmond, Joseph E., St. John the Evangelist Rectory, 27 Library St., Hudson, 03051.
Kenney, Philip J., Bishop Peterson Residence, 221 Orange St., 03108-4324.
MacDonald, Colin A., St. Joseph Cathedral, 145 Lowell St., 03104-6135.
Markham, James J., Parish of The Transfiguration, 107 Alsace St., 03102.
McDonough, T. Joseph, Bishop Peterson Residence, 221 Orange St., 03108-4324.
Molan, John E., St. Peter Rectory, 567 Manchester Rd., Auburn, 03032-3123.
Murphy, Eugene, Bishop Peterson Residence, 221 Orange St., 03108-4324.
Paradis, Wilfrid H., Bishop Peterson Residence, 221 Orange St., 03104-4324.
Pichette, Fernand L., 164 Boutwell St., 03102.
St. Pierre, Leo L., St. Anthony Parish, 172 Belmont St., 03103.
Very Rev.—
Bilodeau, Roger P., V.F., St. Anthony Parish, 172 Belmont St., 03103-4452.
Revs.—
Auger, Gerald E., 235 Alsace St., 03102-3008.
Baillargeon, Albert G., 12 Jacobs Dr., Rochester, 03867-2453.
Bedard, Andre L., Infant Jesus, 121 Allds St., Nashua, 03060-6395. Tel: 603-882-3832
Blais, Roland O., Bishop Peterson Residence, 221 Orange St., 03104-4324.
Boisvert, Robert G., 6 Faith Ln., Center Barnstead, 03225.
Boucher, Gerard A., St. Charles Rectory, 281A Daniel Webster Hwy., P.O. Box 237, Meredith, 03253-0237.
Bracq, Edward E., 14 Oldfield Rd., Nashau, 03060-5067.
Bresnahan, Thomas J., St. Joseph, 33 Main St., Salem, 03079-1922. Tel: 603-898-0044
Bryson, John H., Bishop Peterson Residence, 221 Orange St., 03104-4324.
Clifford, Francis M., 399 Pleasant St., South Weymouth, MA 02190-2647.
Demers, Raymond A., Mt. Carmel Healthcare Center, 235 Myrtle St., 03104-4399.
Demers, Wilfred G., St. Marie Rectory, 378 Norte Dame Ave., 03102-3760.
Desjardins, George A., 6 Pleasant St., E-3, Hocksett, 03106-1421.
Desjardins, Raymond S., Bishop Gendron Apartments, 195 Dover Point Rd., Dover, 03820-4693.
Dunn, Gerald R., P.O. Box 1390, Wolfeiboro, 03894-1390. Tel: 603-569-5058
Foisy, Leonard R., Parish of The Transfiguration, 107 Alsace St., 03102-3006.
Frechette, Leo L., P.O. Box 68, West Nottingham, 03291-0068.
Gagnon, Leo G., 13002 E. Coal Hopper Ln, #1A, Midlothian, VA 23113-4603.
Gallant, Rodrigue J., P.O. Box 428, Belmont, 03220-0428.
Goggin, Cornelius J., 96 River Rd., 03104. Tel: 603-644-5150
Goodwin, Robert T., 4851 W. Gancy Blvd., #8-40, Tampa, FL 33611-3039.
Griffin, Michael J., Our Lady of The Miraculous Medal Parish, 289 Layfayette Rd., Hampton, 03842-2109.
Griffin, Robert F., Bishop Peterson Residence, 221 Orange St., 03104-4324.
Horan, Denis F., 3 Oak Hill Ln., #309, Nashua, 03062-4639.
Hughes, Lawrence J., 2601 N.E. 14th St. #536, Pompano Beach, FL 33062-8319.
Irwin, Patrick F., 71 Israel Head RD #17, Ogunquit, ME 03907.
Keenan, Thomas E., 679 Lemoine Beach Rd., Lemoine, ME 04605.
Kelso, Francis E., 774 Dana Hill Rd., New Hampton, 03256.
Kemmery, Robert J., 18 Gull Ln., Orleans, MA 02653-3003.
Lacroix, Maurice R., 704 Bridge St., 03104-5447.
Lafond, Donald E., 3010 Brown Ave., #1, 03103.
Lampron, Maurice W., P.O. Box 717, Wolfeboro Falls, 03896-0717.
Lefebvre Leo P., Bishop Apartments, St. Theresa Health Care Center, 519 Bridge St., 03104-5396.
Marchand, Robert A., 419 Coolidge Ave., 03102-3214.
McHugh, Paul F., P.O. Box 3352, Concord, 03301-3352.
Montplaisir, Roland A., 2950 Palm-Aire Dr., Apt. 502, Pompano Beach, FL 33069-3441.
Moran, John V., Hillcrest Estates, 24 Tura Terrace, Portsmouth, Portsmouth 03801-6009.
O'Connor, Francis J., 15 Pilgrim Cir. Apt. D, Methuen, MA 01844.
O'Connor, J. Kieran, Bishop Peterson Residence, 221 Orange St., 03104-4324.
O'Donnell, Timothy R., Immaculate Conception, 98 Summer St., Portsmouth, 03801-4398. Tel: 603-433-1819
Oliviera, Humbert, 9 Hollis St., Cambridge, MD 02140.
Savage, Thomas J., P.O. Box 5531, 03108.
Shields, Joseph E., St. Mary Rectory, 182 Main St., P.O. Box 337, Newmarket, 03857-0337.
Simoneau, Norman J., St. John The Evangelist, 27 Library St., Hudson, 03051-4239.
Soucey, Louis A., 141 Lamplighters Park #16, North Conway, 03860-5174.
Tremblay, Jean A., 110 Cilley Rd., 03103-5638.
Turgeon, Armand A., Winchester Arms, 53 New Rochester Rd. #12, Dover, 03820-2158.
Vickery, Richard F., St. Catherine, 207 Hemlock St., 03104-3299.
Wegman, Richard H., 70 Taylor Dr. Back Bay, Wolfeboro, 03894-4356.
Wright, John A., 13 Brandon Ave., Goffstown, 03045.

Permanent Deacons:
Abbott, Leon, St. Mark Parish, Londonderry
Albert, Merle M., Good Shepherd and Holy Family, Gorham
Albis, Leonard B., (Retired)
Anderson, Robert J., Jr., St. Kathryn, Hudson
Andrade, Ramon, St. Anne and St. Augustine, Manchester
Borkush, George J., Holy Angels, Plaistow
Boucher, Paul R., St. Mary, Claremont
Carey, John J., Our Lady of The Mountains, N. Conway
Clarke, Christopher R., St. Timothy, Bristol
Cloutier, Richard A., St. John Neumann, Merrimack
Costello, David T., St. Joseph, Salem
Cummins, Clarence R., St. Matthew, Windham
Daly, James P., Immaculate Conception, Nashua
DeRosia, Winton P., St. Theresa, Henniker
Esposito, Robert, Our Lady of Lourdes, Pittsfield
Falardeau, Richard A., St. Mary, Rochester and St. Peter, Farmington
Fitzpatrick, T. Kelly, Piermont, NH
Ford, Thomas J., Waldoboro, ME
Gagnon, Robert J., St. Joseph, Dover
Gallinaro, Frank, St. Mary and Sacred Heart, Manchester
Gustafson, Arnold J., St. Thomas More, Durham
Hamel, David, St. Aloysius, Nashua
Hilston, Edmund C.
Hobson, Mark F., St. Pius X, Manchester
Jacobs, Dennis M., Our Lady of the Miraculous Medal, Hampton
Kayser, Charles Douglas, (On Leave of Absence)
Kram, Harry A., St. Patrick, Manchester
LaBonte, Alfred A., Jr., St. Joseph, Nashua
LaFleur, William Carl, Jr., Westerly, R.I.
Long, George H. (Gary), Jr., St. Thomas Aquinas, Derry
Marcotte, Raymond V., St. John the Evangelist, Hudson
Martin, John J., St. Joseph Hospital, Nashua
Mazzuchelli, Joseph, St. Elizabeth, Bedford
McCarty, William, Our Lady of the Lakes, Lakeport
McGinn, Gregory R., Our Lady of Fatima
Mullen, William E., St. Anne, Hampstead
Oetinger, Thomas J., St. Joseph, Belmont
Patterson, James E., Our Lady of Mercy, Merrimack
Payeur, Marc G., St. Jude, Londonderry
Polcari, Joseph A., St. Matthew, Whitefield
Potvin, Robert R., St. Joseph and St. George, Manchester
Rich, William, St. Joseph, Center Ossipee
Ross, John F., St. Patrick, Pelham
Schladenhauffen, Charles D., Sick leave
Shannon, Richard J., Parish of the Transfiguration
Shaulis, Michael C., St. Joseph, Laconia
Shrader, David J., Holy Rosary,
St. George, John H., St. Helena Parish, Enfield
St. Laurent, Lionel A., (Retired)
Testa, Paul E., Our Lady of the Miraculous Medal, Hampton
Tumulty, Peter J., Sun City Center, FL (Retired)

INSTITUTIONS LOCATED IN THE DIOCESE

[A] SEMINARIES, RELIGIOUS OR SCHOLASTICATES

MANCHESTER. *St. Anselm Abbey Seminary*, 100 St. Anselm Dr., 03102. Tel: 603-641-7000; Fax: 603-641-7116. Email: wsulliva@anselm.edu. Web: www.anselm.edu. Rev. William J. Sullivan, O.S.B., Dir. Studies. Order of St. Benedict Faculty 4; Students 2.

CENTER HARBOR. *Immaculate Conception Apostolic School*, Plymouth St., P.O. Box 936, 03226. Tel: 603-253-7728; Fax: 603-253-8740. 1109 Dane Rd., 03226. Revs. David Steffy, L.C., Prin.; James Perez, L.C. (HRT), Vice Prin.; Steven Liscinsky, L.C.; Victor Franco, L.C.; Bros. Thanh Nguyen, L.C.; David Kovaks, L.C.; Kevin Leahy, L.C.; Thomas Vendetti, L.C. Priests 4; Brothers 4; Lay Teachers 10; Students 131.

[B] COLLEGES AND UNIVERSITIES

MANCHESTER. *Saint Anselm College* 03102. Tel: 603-641-7000; Fax: 603-641-7284. Email: jdefelic@anselm.edu. Web: www.anselm.edu. Rt. Rev. Matthew K. Leavy, O.S.B., Ph.D., Chancellor; Rev. Jonathan P. DeFelice, O.S.B., J.C.L., Pres. Admin & Faculty. Order of St. Benedict Priests 4; Brothers 2; Sisters 3; Lay Teachers 120; Students 2,016.

MERRIMACK. *The Thomas More College of Liberal Arts*, 6 Manchester St., 03054. Tel: 603-880-8308; Fax: 603-880-9280. Email: tmc@thomasmoorecollege.edu. Web: www.thomasmorecollege.edu. Peter V. Sampo, Pres. Students 91; Total Staff 10.

NASHUA. *Rivier College* 03060-5086. Tel: 603-888-1311; Fax: 603-897-8812. Web: www.rivier.edu. William J. Farrell, Pres.; Rev. Paul R. Demers, S.C., Chap. Sisters of the Presentation of Mary Presentation Sisters 21; Teaching Sisters 6; Teaching Priests 1; Lay Teachers 197; Students 2,331.

WARNER. *Magdalen College*, 511 Kearsarge Mountain Rd., 03278-9206. Tel: 603-456-2656; Fax: 603-456-2660. Email: administration@magdalen.edu. Web: www.magdalen.edu. Jeffrey J. Karls, Pres.; Teresa K. Rudkins, Dean of Students; Dr. Patrick Powers, Academic Dean; Rev. Joseph Simburger, Chap. Lay Teachers 8; Students 73; Total Staff 22.

[C] HIGH SCHOOLS, DIOCESAN

MANCHESTER. *Trinity High School*, 581 Bridge St., 03104-5395. Tel: 603-668-2910; Fax: 603-668-2913. Email: webmaster@trinity-hs.org. Web: www.trinity-hs.org Mr. Denis Mailloux, Prin.; Edward McMonagle, Asst. Prin.; Patrick D. Smith, Dean of Students; Rev. Raymond A. Ball, Chap.; Karen Courser, Campus Min. Lay Teachers 27; Students 518; Total Staff 50.

CONCORD. *Bishop Brady High School*, 25 Columbus Ave., 03301. Tel: 603-224-7418; Fax: 603-228-6664. Email: info@bishopbrady.edu. Web: www.bishopbrady.edu. Jean Barker, Prin.; Joy Degnan, Asst. Prin. Sisters of Mercy Lay Teachers 31; Students 450.

DOVER. *St. Thomas Aquinas High School*, 197 Dover Point Rd., 03820. Tel: 603-742-3206; Fax: 603-749-7822. Email: sta@stalux.org. Web: www.stalux.org. Mr. Jeffrey A. Quinn, Prin. Sisters 2; Lay Teachers 47; Students 700.

[D] HIGH SCHOOLS, PRIVATE

NASHUA. *Bishop Guertin High School*, 194 Lund Rd., 03060. Tel: 603-889-4107; Fax: 603-889-0701. Email: brmark@bghs.org. Web: www.bghs.org. Bro. Mark E. Hilton, S.C., Contact Person, Pres.; Edward Quinn, Prin.; Bro. Paul Demers, S.C., Chap. Brothers of the Sacred Heart, (Coed) Brothers 7; Lay Teachers 57; Students 846.

[E] REGIONAL ELEMENTARY SCHOOLS

MANCHESTER. *St. Anthony School*, (Grades K-6), 148 Belmont St., 03103. Tel: 603-622-0414; Fax: 603-669-5212. Email: info@stanthonyschool-nh.com. Web: www.stanthonyschool-nh.com. Ms. Constance A. Bilodeau, Prin.; Sandy Major, Contact Person. Sisters 3; Lay Teachers 24; Boys 188; Girls 191.

St. Benedict Academy, Formerly West Side Catholic Regional School, (Grades K-6), 85 Third St., 03102. Tel: 603-669-3932. Email: wscr@comcast.net. Web: stbenedictacademy.org. Sr. Maria Rosa, P.M., Prin. Sisters 2; Lay Teachers 14; Students 158.

St. Casimir School, (Grades K-8), 456 Union St.,

03103. Tel: 603-623-6411; Fax: 603-623-6411. Email: smlcssf@yahoo.com. Web: www.stcasimirnh.org. Sr. Mary Lawrence Lojko, C.S.S.F., Prin. Sisters 2; Lay Teachers 7; Students 157.

St. Catherine School, (Grades K-6), 206 North St., 03104. Tel: 603-622-1711; Fax: 603-624-4935. Email: stcatherinenh@mediaone.net. Web: stcatherines.org. Sr. Janet Belcourt, C.S.C., Prin. Sisters 2; Lay Teachers 22; Students 401.

St. Francis of Assisi School, 9 St. Francis Way, Litchfield, 03052-8050. Tel: 603-424-3312; Fax: 603-424-9128. Email: shogan@stfranisschool.org. Susan Hogan, Prin. & Contact Person. Lay Teachers 8; Students 154.

St. Joseph Regional Junior High, (Grades 7-8), 460 Pine St., 03104-6102. Tel: 603-624-4811; Fax: 603-624-6670. Email: bmclean650@aol.com. Web: members.aol.com/stjoesjrhs. Sr. Barbara McLean, R.S.M., Prin. Lay Teachers 22; Students 323.

BERLIN. *St. Michael School* (Berlin Regional Catholic School) , 140 Blanchard St., 03570. Tel: 603-752-7413; Fax: 603-752-1743. Email: smichael@ncia.net. Karen Wood, Prin. & Contact. Lay Teachers 7; Students 80.

CLAREMONT. *St. Mary School*, (Grades PreK-8), 18 Central St., 03743. Tel: 603-542-6341; Fax: 603-542-5260. Leanne K. Mortell, Prin. & Contact. Lay Teachers 9; Students 144.

CONCORD. *St. John Regional School*, 61 S. State St., 03301. Tel: 603-225-3222; Fax: 603-225-0195. Email: fthrfoot@aol.com. Sr. Irene Turgeon, S.N.D., Prin. Sisters 4; Lay Teachers 10; Students 254.

DERRY. *St. Thomas Aquinas School*, (Grades K-8), 3 Moody St., 03038. Tel: 603-432-2712; Fax: 603-432-2179. Email: srjackie@comcast.net. Web: www.staderry.com. Sr. Jacqueline Brodeur, C.S.C., Prin. & Contact. Sisters 4; Lay Teachers 10; Students 257.

DOVER. *St. Mary Academy*, 222 Central Ave., 03820. Tel: 603-742-3299; Fax: 603-743-3483. Email: reese@saintmaryacademy.org. Web: www.saintmaryacademy.org. Rosemary S. Reese, Prin. Sisters 2; Lay Teachers 24; Students 465.

HAMPTON. *Sacred Heart School*, (Grades PreK-8), 289 Lafayette Rd., 03842. Tel: 603-926-3254; Fax: 603-929-1109. Email: smjwalsh@shshampton.org. Web: www.OLMMparish.org. Sr. Mary Joan Walsh, O.L.L., Prin. Sisters 4; Lay Teachers 28; Students 395.

JAFFREY. *St. Patrick School*, (Grades K-8), 70 Main St., 03452. Tel: 603-532-7676; Fax: 603-532-7476. Email: faculty@stpats.mv.com. Web: www.saintpatschool.org. William E. Collins, Prin.; Theresa Wyatt, Adm. Asst. Sisters 2; Lay Teachers 13; Students 150.

KEENE. *St. Joseph School*, (Grades PreK-8), 92 Wilson St., 03431. Tel: 603-352-2720; Fax: 603-358-5465. Email: ldellasanta@hotmail.com. Web: stjosephkeene.org. Sr. Laura Della Santa, Prin. & Contact. Lay Teachers 14; Students 135; Total Staff 20.

LACONIA. *Holy Trinity*, (Grades K-8), 50 Church St., 03246. Tel: 603-524-3156; Fax: 603-527-3534. Email: jfortier@holytrinity.pvt.k12.nh.us. Web: holytrinity.pvt.k12.nh.us. Mr. Jack Fortier, Prin. Lay Teachers 11; Students 158; Total Staff 21.

NASHUA. *St. Christopher School*, (Grades K-6), 20 Cushing Ave., 03064. Tel: 603-882-7442; Fax: 603-594-9253. Email: principal@stchrisschoolnh.org. Web: www.stchrisschoolnh.org. Sr. Joan Marie Messier, R.S.M., Prin. Lay Teachers 19; Students 344.

Infant Jesus School, (Grades K-6), 3 Crown St., 03060. Tel: 603-889-2649; Fax: 603-594-9117. Email: school@infantjesus.mv.com. Web: www.infantjesusparish.org/ijs. Sr. Marie Henault, P.M., Prin. Sisters 1; Lay Teachers 21; Students 338.

Nashua Catholic Regional Junior High, (Grades 7-9), 6 Bartlett Ave., 03064-1602. Tel: 603-883-6707; 603-882-7011; Fax: 603-594-8955. Email: sandra.hillyard@comcast.net. Web: www//ncrjhs.org. Ms. Sandra J. Clay-Hillyard, Prin. Lay Teachers 23; Students 342.

PELHAM. *St. Patrick School*, (Grades K-8), 16 Main St., 03076. Tel: 603-635-2941; Fax: 603-635-9800. Email: stpatsk8@hotmail.com. Web: ultranet.com/~stpats. Roger Dumont, Prin. & Contact. Lay Teachers 20; Students 235.

PORTSMOUTH. *St. Patrick*, (Grades PreK-8), 125 Austin St., 03801. Tel: 604-436-0739; Fax: 604-436-1569. Web: www.stpatsschool.com. Janet DiNatale, Prin. & Contact. Lay Teachers 15; Students 175.

ROCHESTER. *St. Elizabeth Seton School*, (Grades K-8), 16 Bridge St., 03867. Tel: 603-332-4803; Fax: 603-332-2915. Email: stbrochester@metrocast.net. Suzanne T. Boutin, Prin. Sisters 2; Lay Teachers 20; Students 285.

SALEM. *St. Joseph Regional Catholic School*, Formerly St. Joseph Regional School, (Grades K-8), 40 Main St., 03079. Tel: 603-893-6811; Fax: 603-893-6811. Email: sjrcs@comcast.net. Web: sjrcs.com. Ms. Pauline A. Boulanger, Prin. Lay Teachers 28; Total Staff 47; Religious Teacher 1; Students 329.

Kindergarten Lay Teachers 2; Students 52.

[F] ELEMENTARY SCHOOLS, PRIVATE

MANCHESTER. *St. Augustin Pre-School*, 251 Merrimack St., 03103. Tel: 603-669-1864; Fax: 603-626-1517. Mrs. Mary Tremblay, Dir. Lay Teachers 3; Boys 14; Girls 18.

Holy Cross Early Childhood Center, 357 Island Pond Rd., 03109-4811. Tel: 603-668-0510. Sr. Yvette M. Robert, C.S.C., Prin. & Admin. Sisters 2; Lay Teachers 1; Students 27.

Mt. St. Mary Academy, (Grades PreK-6), 2291 Elm St., 03104. Tel: 603-623-3155; Fax: 603-621-9254. Email: principal@mtstmary.org. Web: www.mtstmary.org. Sr. Gloria Morin, R.S.M., Prin.; Kelly Flynn, Contact Person. Sisters 2; Lay Teachers 12; Students 164.

GOFFSTOWN. *Villa Augustina School*, (Grades PreK-8), 208 S. Mast St., 03045. Tel: 603-497-2361; Fax: 603-497-5981. Email: villaaugustina@netscape.net. Web: www.villaaugustina.org. Sr. Cecile Provost, C.S.C., Prin. Sisters 4; Lay Teachers 27; Students 322.

HUDSON. *Presentation of Mary Academy*, (Grades K-8), 182 Lowell Rd., 03051. Tel: 603-889-6054; Fax: 603-595-8504. Web: www.pmaschool.org. Paul Raikey, Prin. Sisters of the Presentation of Mary Sisters 6; Lay Teachers 36; Students 473.

[G] CATHOLIC CHARITIES

MANCHESTER. *Catholic Charities Administration*, 215 Myrtle St., 03104. Tel: 603-669-3030; Fax: 603-626-1252. Web: catholiccharitiesnh.org. Sr. Patricia Sullivan, R.S.M., Diocesan Dir.; Mrs. Dominque Rust, Dir. Admin. Svcs.; Robert P. Clohosey, A.C.S.W., Dir. Family Svcs.; Mrs. Theresa Chabot, Cons.; Sr. Peggy Crosby, S.N.D.deN., Dir. Social Concerns; Mr. Jeffrey J. Martin, Dir. Health Care Svcs.; Mr. Richard J. Shannon, Dir. Parish Social Ministry; Mrs. Kathy St. Onge, Dir. Supportive Svcs.; Mrs. Melanie Gosselin, Dir. of N.H. Food Bank.

District Offices:

P.O. Box 182, 633 Third Ave.,, Berlin, 03570. Tel: 603-752-1325; Fax: 603-752-6174. Nicole Plourde, Parish Outreach Coord.

176 Loudon Rd., Concord, 03301. Tel: 603-228-1108; Fax: 603-228-6025. Sr. Rosemary Crowley, Parish Outreach Coord.

222 West St., Suite 24, Keene, 03431. Tel: 603-357-3093; Fax: 603-357-7810. Barnes Peterson, Admin. Mgr. & LCMH Clin. Sup.; Sr. Kathleen Haight, R.C.D., P.A., Parish Outreach Coord.

17 Gilford Ave, Laconia, 03246. Tel: 603-528-3035; Fax: 603-524-7153. Mary A. Kenison, Admin. Mgr., LICSW, Clin. Sup.

24 Hanover St., #8, Lebanon, 03766. Tel: 603-448-5151; Fax: 603-448-5155. Marc Cousineau, Admin. Mgr.

P.O. Box 323, 41 Cottage St., Littleton, 03561. Tel: 603-444-7727; Fax: 603-444-7728. Anthony Poekert, Admin. Mgr.

325 Franklin St., 03101. Tel: 603-624-4717; Fax: 603-624-4736. Debra McMahon, Admin. Mgr.

261 Lake St., Nashua, 03060. Tel: 603-889-9431; Fax: 603-880-4643. Mary A. Kenison, Admin. Mgr.

23 Grant St., Rochester, 03867. Tel: 603-332-7701; Fax: 603-332-9629. Janet O'Connell, Admin. Mgr.

23 Searles Rd., Windham, 03087. Tel: 603-893-1971; Fax: 603-898-8661. Janet O'Connell, Admin. Mgr.

Other Programs:

Diocesan Consultation & Counseling Services, 593 Maple St., 03104. Tel: 603-668-0014; Fax: 603-623-7676. Joseph Naff, Dir.

Diocesan Bureau of Housing, 323 Franklin St., 03101. Tel: 603-625-5422; Fax: 603-625-1014. Email: dbhinc@grolen.com. Carol A. Haebler, Mgr.

Healthcare Services, 16 Oak St., 03104. Tel: 603-641-0577; Fax: 603-641-6210. Email: nhcc@nrmail.com. Mr. Jeffrey J. Martin, Dir.

Immigration and Refugee Services, 23 Searles Rd., Windham, 03087. Tel: 603-893-1971; Fax: 603-898-8661. Sr. Peggy Crosby, S.N.D.DeN., Dir. Legal and case management services for immigrants and refugees.

New Hampshire Food Bank, 62 W. Brook St., 03101. Tel: 603-669-9725; Fax: 603-669-0270. Mrs. Melanie Gosselin, Exec. Dir. Statewide food distribution to soup kitchens, food pantries and direct service programs.

Our Place, 282 Concord St., 03104. Tel: 603-647-2244; Fax: 603-647-9933. Robert P. Clohosey, A.C.S.W., Dir. Family Svcs.; Nancy M. Ryan, Admin. Mgr. Services for pregnant and parenting teens.

St. Charles Children's Home, 19 Grant St., Rochester, 03867. Tel: 603-332-4768; Fax: 603-332-3948. Email: spm@notrocast.net. Sr. Paul Marie Santa Lucia, S.C.M.C., Admin. Residential services for children who have been removed from unsafe home environments. Total Staff 18; Total Assisted 25.

Bishop Peterson Residence, 221 Orange St., 03104-4324. Tel: 603-641-6277; Fax: 603-641-0385.

[H] CHILD CARE INSTITUTIONS

MANCHESTER. *St. Peter's Home*, 300 Kelley St., 03102-3093. Tel: 603-625-9313; Fax: 603-625-1910. Sr. Florence Therrien, S.C.S.H., Dir.; Mrs. Donna M. Vachon, Asst. Dir.; Sr. Rita Beaulieu, S.C.S.H., Treas. Sisters of Charity (Grey Nuns) 4; Children 309; Total Staff 75.

ALLENSTOWN. *Pine Haven Boys Center*, River Rd., P.O. Suncook, 03275. Tel: 603-485-7141; Fax: 603-485-7142. Email: phbc@comcast.net. Revs. John Vitali, C.R.S., M.Ed., Dir.; Paul Riva, C.R.S.; Remo Zanatta, C.R.S. Somascan Fathers Children 20; Total Staff 38.

ROCHESTER. *St. Charles Children's Home*, 19 Grant St., 03867-3099. Tel: 603-332-4768; Fax: 603-332-3948. Email: stcharles@metrocast.net. Sisters Paul Marie, Admin.; Santa Lucia, S.C.M.C., Admin. Sisters of Charity of Our Lady, Mother of The Church, New Hampshire Catholic Charities. Sisters 6; Dependent Children 24.

[I] GENERAL HOSPITALS

MANCHESTER. *Catholic Medical Center of Manchester, NH, Inc.*, 100 McGregor St., 03102. Tel: 603-668-3545; Fax: 603-663-6850. Web: www.catholicmedicalcenter.org. Alyson Pitman Giles, Pres. & CEO. Sisters 8; Bed Capacity 330; Inpatient Admissions 9,042; Outpatient Admissions 82,831.

NASHUA. *St. Joseph Hospital*, 172 Kinsley St., 03061. Tel: 603-882-3000; Fax: 603-598-2483. Email: cdescoteaux@sjh_nh.org. Web: www.stjosephhospital.com. Peter B. Davis, Pres. & CEO; Sr. Carol J. Descoteaux, C.S.C., Ph.D., Vice Pres. Mission Integration & Ethics; Deacon John Martin, Staff Chap. Bed Capacity 208; Patients Assisted Annually 6,000; Total Staff 1,720.

Rivier-St. Joseph School of Nursing Fax: 603-897-8813.

[J] HEALTH CARE FACILITIES

MANCHESTER. *Carpenter Center, Inc.*, 323 Franklin St., 03101. Tel: 603-625-5422; Fax: 603-625-1014. Email: dbhinc@grolen.com. Carol Haebler, Mgr. Apartments 96.

DBH Shelter, Inc. Tel: 603-625-5422; Fax: 603-625-1014.

DBH Shelter II, Inc. Group Home 8.

DBH Shelter III, Inc. Apartments 28.

DBH Management, Inc. Total Staff 8; Total Assisted 112.

St. Joseph Residence, Office of Development, 495 Mammoth Rd., 03104. Tel: 603-668-6011; Fax: 603-644-1276. Email: mjmakowski@presmarynh.org. Marlene Makowski, Contact. Sponsored by the Mary Sisters., New Hampshire Catholic Charities

Mt. Carmel Healthcare Center, 235 Myrtle St., 03104-4399. Tel: 603-627-3811; Fax: 603-626-4696. Email: mtcadmin@metro2000.net. Ted Purdy, Admin. & Contact; Rev. Maurice Lagueux, Chap. New Hampshire Catholic Charities. Residents 120.

St. Teresa Heathcare Center, Formerly St. Teresa's Heathcare Center, 519 Bridge St., 03104-5396. Tel: 603-668-2373; Fax: 603-668-0059. Email: Linda@xtol.com. Monique Dosogne, Admin. & Contact; Rev. Leo P. Lefebvre (Retired). New Hampshire Catholic Charities Total Staff 62; Aged Residents 51.

Bishop Primeau Apartments Tel: 603-668-7703; Fax: 603-668-0059. Linda Illg, Apartment Mgr. Total Staff 3; Apartments 25.

BERLIN. *St. Vincent de Paul Healthcare Center*, 29 Providence Ave., 03570-3199. Tel: 603-752-1820; Fax: 603-752-7149. Email: stvdp@ncia.net. Louise Marquis, Admin. New Hampshire Catholic Charities. Residents 80; Total Staff 112.

DOVER. *St. Ann Healthcare Center*, 195 Dover Point Rd., 03820-4693. Tel: 603-742-2612; Fax: 603-743-3055. Email: kjp@netway.com. Karyn Partin, Admin. New Hampshire Catholic Charities. Residents 54; Total Staff 76.

Bishop Gendron Apartments Tel: 603-742-2612; Fax: 603-743-3055. Cathy Meattey-Stawarz, Apartment Mgr. Total Staff 1; Apartments 31.

JAFFREY. *Good Shepherd Healthcare Center*, 20 Plantation Dr., 03452-1935. Tel: 603-532-8762; Fax: 603-532-6057. Ann Nunn, Admin. & Contact. New Hampshire Catholic Charities. Total Staff 115; Total Assisted 83.

LACONIA. *Bishop Bradley Apartments*, 406 Court St., 03246. Tel: 603-524-0466; Fax: 603-527-0884. Email: fay444@aol.com. Mrs. Julieann R. Fay, Contact. Apartments 25; Total Staff 2.

St. Francis Healthcare Center, 406 Court St., 03246-3000. Tel: 603-524-0466; Fax: 603-527-0884. Email: fay444@aol.com. Mrs. Julieann R. Fay, Admin.; Rev. Andre J. Gagnon, Chap. New Hampshire Catholic Charities. Residents 51; Total Staff 70.

Bishop Bradley Apartments Total Staff 2; Apartments 25.

NASHUA. *Marguerite's Place*, 87 Palm St., 03060. Tel: 603-598-1582; Fax: 603-598-7574. Email: margplace@aol.com. Sr. Mary Sharon Walsh, G.N.S.H., CEO. Total Assisted 265; Total Staff 15; Total in Residence 25.

WINDHAM. *Warde Health Center*, 21 Searles Rd., 03087-1297. Tel: 603-890-1290; Fax: 603-890-1293. Email: wardehealth@aol.com. Sr. Janice Turner, R.S.M., Admin. & Contact. Sisters of Mercy, Managed by New Hampshire Catholic Charities. Residents 28; Total Assisted 36; Total Staff 68.

[K] MONASTERIES AND RESIDENCES OF PRIESTS AND BROTHERS

MANCHESTER. *St. Anselm Abbey* Of the Order of St. Benedict and St. Anselm College, including Seminary and Formation Program. , 100 St. Anselm Dr., 03102-1310. Tel: 603-641-7000; Fax: 603-641-7267. Email: webmaster@anselm.edu. Web: www.anselm.edu/abbey/index.html. Rt. Rev. Matthew K. Leavy, O.S.B., Ph.D., Abbot & Chancellor; Rev. William J. Sullivan, O.S.B., Prior; Very Rev. Peter J. Guerin, O.S.B , Subprior; Revs. Aquinas F. Cafarelli, O.S.B.; Bede G. Camera, O.S.B.; James G. Cassidy, O.S.B.; Mark A. Cooper, O.S.B.; Michael H. Custer, O.S.B.; Jerome J. Day, O.S.B.; Jonathan P. DeFelice, O.S.B., J.C.L.; Daniel G. Dempski, O.S.B.; Cecil J. Donahue, O.S.B.; Mathias D. Durette, O.S.B.; John R. Fortin, O.S.B.; Jude J. Gray, O.S.B.; Benedict M. Guevin, O.S.B.; Augustine G. Kelly, O.S.B.; Iain G. MacLellan, O.S.B.; Finbar P. O'Mahony, O.S.B.; Benet C. Phillips, O.S.B.; Placidus H. Riley, O.S.B.; Lawrence Schlegel, O.S.B.; Patrick M. Sullivan, O.S.B.; Bros. Armand Huppe, O.S.B.; Thomas Laur, O.S.B.; Malachy R. McCarthy, O.S.B.; Issac T. Murphy, O.S.B.; Bernard Disco, O.S.B.; Anselm Smedile, O.S.B.; Andrew Thornton, O.S.B. Priests 23; Brothers 7; Joan of Arc Sisters 8; Benedictine Sisters 2.

COLEBROOK. *Shrine of Our Lady of Grace* 03576. Tel: 603-237-5511; Fax: 603-237-8998. Revs. Robert G. Levesque, O.M.I., Supr.; Henri A. DeLisle, O.M.I. (NOR); Bro. Maurice Violette, O.M.I. Oblates of Mary Immaculate (United States Province) Priests 2; Brothers 1.

ENFIELD. *Shrine of Our Lady of La Salette*, 410 NH Rte. 4A, P.O. Box 420, 03748-0420. Tel: 603-632-4301 (Gift Shop); 603-632-7087 (Business); Fax: 603-632-7648. Email: djcarigone@yahoo.com. Revs. Robert Campbell, M.S., Dir.; Donald Jeffrey, M.S.; Leo Maxfield, M.S., Chap.; Joseph Ross, M.S., Chap.; Bros. Andre Bolduc, M.S., Chap.; Emile Morin, M.S., Chap.; Robert Roy, M.S., Chap.; Claude Rheaume, M.S., Chap.; David Carignan, M.S., Chap.

Legal Title: *La Salette of Enfield, Inc.* Priests 4; Brothers 6; Total Staff 13.

NASHUA. *Brothers of the Sacred Heart*, 28 Berkeley St., 03064. Tel: 603-595-2712. Bro. Raymond Hetu, S.C., Dir. Brothers 6.

194 Lund Rd., 03060. Tel: 603-883-3683. Bro. Roger Lemoyne, S.C., Dir. Brothers 5.

[L] CONVENTS AND RESIDENCES OF SISTERS

MANCHESTER. *Cathedral Rectory*, 145 Lowell St., 03101-6135. Tel: 603-622-6404; Fax: 603-626-4415. Sr. Lucille Brunette, P.S.S.F., Supr. Little Sisters of the Holy Family in charge of domestic department Sisters 3.

St. George Manor, 357 Island Pond Rd., 03109. Tel: 603-624-4557; Fax: 603-645-1516. Sr. Lorraine Paille, C.S.C., Local Adm.; Rev. Bruce W. Collard, Chap. (Non-residential). Sisters 69.

Monastery of the Precious Blood, 700 Bridge St., 03104. Tel: 603-623-4264; Fax: 603-647-8385. Sr. Mary Agnes, Supr.; Rev. Maurice R. Lacroix, Chap. (Retired). Sisters Adorers of the Precious Blood Sisters 29.

Missionary Rosebushes of St. Theresa, 700 Bridge St., 03104.

Regional Office of the Sisters of Holy Cross, 377 Island Pond Rd., 03109. Tel: 603-622-9504; Fax: 603-622-9782. Email: elmcsc@holycross.com. Web: sistersoftheholycross.org. Sr. Elaine Marquis, C.S.C., Regl. Rep. Total Staff 6.

Sisters of the Presentation of Mary Provincial House, 495 Mammoth Rd., 03104-5494. Tel: 603-669-1080; Fax: 603-622-4953. Email: provincialhouse@presmarynh.org. Web: www.presentationofmary.com. Sisters Suzanne Bourret, P.M., Prov. Supr.; Lorraine Trottier, Contact Person. Sisters in the Diocese 168; Sisters of the Presentation of Mary 183.

St. Joseph Residence, 495 Mammoth Rd., 03104-5494. Tel: 603-627-5831; 603-668-6011.

St. Marie Residence, 495 Mammoth Rd., 03104-5494. Tel: 603-623-0671.

Bethany House, 25 Garmon St., 03104. Tel: 603-625-1957

Presentation of Mary Academy, 182 Lowell Rd., Hudson, 03051-4987. Tel: 603-883-8192; 603-889-6362; Fax: 603-883-8054.

Presentation of Mary Novitiate, 180 Lowell Rd., Hudson, 03051-4987. Tel: 603-880-8186; Fax: 603-880-0298.

Trinity House, 186 Lowell Rd., Hudson, 03051-4908. Tel: 603-882-1347.

Presentation of Mary Convent, 638 Third Ave., Berlin 03570. Tel: 603-752-1176; Fax: 603-752-4115.

Our Lady of Hope House of Prayer, 400 Temple Rd., New Ipswich, 03071. Tel: 603-878-2346; Fax: 603-878-4552.

Holy Angels Convent, 6 Atkinson Depot Rd., Rte 121, Plaistow, 03865. Tel: 603-382-2744.

Emmaus Convent, 664 Central St., 03103. Tel: 603-647-4083.

Presentation of Mary Convent, 135 Ash St., Nashua, 03060. Tel: 603-882-9824.

CONCORD. *Monastery of Discalced Carmelites*, 275 Pleasant St., 03301-2590. Tel: 603-225-5791; Fax: 603-223-9670. Sr. Emmanuel Sacke, O.C.D., Prioress. Rev. Michael E. Sevigny, O.F.M.Cap, Chap. Professed Sisters 10.

GOFFSTOWN. *St. Joseph Mission Center*, Formerly Villa Augustina Convent, 135 Dremer St., 03112-4121. Tel: 603-232-4107; Fax: 603-497-4030. Email: RoselineMarcoux@yahoo.com. Sisters Michelle Authier, R.J.M., Supr.; Roseline Marcoux, R.S.M., Supr. Religious of Jesus and Mary 19.

LITTLETON. *Provincial House of Daughters of the Charity of the Sacred Heart of Jesus*, Mount Sacred Heart, 226 Grove St., 03561. Tel: 603-444-5346; Fax: 603-444-5348. Email: sjrpro@nh.aol.net. Sisters Theresa Fournier, Local Supr.; Jeannette Roy, Prov. Supr. Sisters 36.

LONDONDERRY. *Sisters of Holy Cross*, Londonderry House, 68 Mammoth Rd., 03053-4024. Tel: 603-432-2430. Louise A. Auclair.

NEW IPSWICH. *Our Lady of Hope, House of Prayer*, 400 Temple Rd., 03071. Tel: 603-878-2346; Fax: 603-878-4552. Email: jmleblanc@earthlink.net. Web: presentationofmary.com. Sr. Jacqueline LeBlanc, P.M., Supr. & Dir. Sisters 6.

PORTSMOUTH. *Our Lady of Lourdes Convent*, 125 Austin St., #2, 03801. Tel: 603-436-6612; Fax: 603-436-7429. Email: lourdesll@comcast.net. Sr. Mary Joan Walsh, O.L.L., Supr. Sisters of Our Lady of Lourdes (S.L.L.) Sisters 2.

WINDHAM. *Sisters of Mercy of the Americas* Tel: 603-893-6550; Fax: 603-893-2413. Email: nhsistersofmercy@worldnet.att.net. Sisters of Mercy of New Hampshire

Motherhouse of the Sisters of Mercy, Inc., Regional Community of New Hampshire, 21 Searles Rd., 03087-1297. Tel: 603-893-6550 (Admin. Office); Fax: 603-893-2413. Sr. Ellen Kurtz, R.S.M., Regl. Community Pres. Sisters 152.

Mount Saint Mary Corporation of the Sisters of Mercy, Inc., Nashua. Tel: 603-883-7874; Fax: 603-594-4178.

Manchester Convent of the Sisters of Mercy Tel: 603-893-6550 Fax: 603-893-2413.

Warde Health Center, Inc. Tel: 603-890-1290; Fax: 603-890-1293

Mount St. Mary Academy, Inc. Tel: 603-623-3155; Fax: 603-621-9254.

Frances Warde House Tel: 603-893-6550; Fax: 603-893-2413.

[M] RETREAT HOUSES

ENFIELD. *La Salette Shrine and Center of Enfield*, 417 N.H. Rte. 4A, P.O. Box 420, 03748. Tel: 603-632-7087 (Business); 603-632-4301 (Gift Shop); Fax: 603-632-7648. Revs. Donald Jeffrey, M.S., Supr.; Robert Campbell, M.S., Shrine Dir.; Leo Maxfield, M.S., Chap.; Joseph Ross, M.S., Chap.; Bro. David J. Carignon, M.S. Priests 4; Deacons 1; Brothers 6; Total Staff 13.

[N] CAMPUS MINISTRY AND NEWMAN CENTERS

DURHAM. *St. Thomas More Catholic Student Center at the University of New Hampshire* 6 Madbury Rd., P.O. Box 620, 03824-0620. Tel: 603-862-1310; Fax: 603-868-3765. Email: stmdurham@aol.com. Rev. Daniel A. St. Laurent, Chap.; Deacon Arnold J. Gustafson; Venizie Gonga, Admin. Asst.; Mary Beth Nazzaro, Assoc. Chap.

HANOVER. *The Catholic Student Center at Dartmouth, Aquinas House, Aquinas at Dartmouth, Inc.* 2 Occom Ridge, P.O. Box 147, 03755. Tel: 603-643-2154; Fax: 603-643-9411. Web: www.dartmouth.edu/~aquinas. Rev. Brendon Buckley, O.F.M., Dir.; Anna Mae Mayer, Assoc. Chap.; Christal Costello, Assoc. Campus Min. Total in Residence 1; Total Staff 3.

KEENE. *Keene State College, Catholic Newman Center* 232 Main St., P.O. Box 491, 03431. Tel: 603-352-7785; 603-358-2100. Mary Ann Damato, Campus Min.

PLYMOUTH. *Plymouth State University Campus Ministry*, Formerly Plymouth State College Campus Ministry Plymouth State University, Ste. A6, 03264. Tel: 603-535-2673. Email: mewargo@mail.plymouth.edu. Mary Ellen Wargo, Catholic Campus Min. Tel: 603-535-2673.

RINDGE. *Franklin Pierce College Newman Center* Keene State College, 232 Main St., P.O. Box 60, 03461. Tel: 603-352-7785.

[O] MISCELLANEOUS

MANCHESTER. *CMC Healthcare System*, 100 McGregor St., 03102. Tel: 603-669-3100; Fax: 603-669-0377. Email: carsenault@rcbm.org. Rev. Edward J. Arsenault, S.T.L., Chair; Alyson Pitman Giles, Pres.

Catholic Medical Center

Catholic Medical Center Physician Practice Associates (CMCPPA), 100 McGregor St., 03102. Tel: 603-668-3545; Fax: 603-663-6850. Alyson Pitman Giles, Pres. & CEO.

Alliance Ambulatory Services, Inc., 100 McGregor St., 03102. Tel: 603-668-3545; Fax: 603-663-6850. Alyson Pitman Giles, Pres. & CEO.

Alliance Resources Inc, 100 McGregor St., 03102. Tel: 603-668-3545; 608-663-6850. Alyson Pitman Giles, Pres. & CEO.

Hillcrest Terrace Inc., 200 Alliance Way, 03103. Tel: 603-645-6500; Fax: 603-626-7724. Alyson Pitman Giles, Pres. & CEO.

Diocesan Cemetery Office, 153 Ash St., P.O. Box 310, 03105. Raymond P. Clement, Dir.

St. Patrick Cemetery, Amherst, 03031.
St. Joseph Cemetery, Bartlett, 03812.
St. Joseph Cemetery, Bath, 03740.
St. Joseph Cemetery, Bedford, 03110.
St. Hedwig Cemetery, Bedford, 03110.
Mount Calvary Cemetery, Bennington, 03442.
Calvary Cemetery, Berlin, 03570.
St. Anne Cemetery, Berlin, 03570.
St. Kieran Cemetery, Berlin, 03570.
Mount Calvary Cemetery, Berlin, 03570.
St. Margaret Cemetery, Carroll, 03598.
St. Catherine Cemetery, Charlestown, 03603.
St. Mary Cemetery, Claremont, 03743.
St. Brendan, Colebrook, 03576.
St. Charles Cemetery, Dover, 03822.
St. Mary Cemetery, Dover, 03822.
St. Peter Cemetery, Drewsville, 03604.
St. Joseph Cemetery, Epping, 03042.
St. Pius Forest Lawn Cemetery, Errol, 03579.
Holy Cross Cemetery, Franklin, 03235.
Mount Calvary Cemetery, (Gonic), Rochester, 03839.
Holy Family Cemetery, Gorham, 03581.
St. Francis Xavier Cemetery, Groveton, 03582.
St. Denis, Harrisville, 03450.
St. Joseph Cemetery, Hinsdale, 03451.
Holy Rosary Cemetery, Hooksett, 03106.
Holy Cross Cemetery, Hudson, 03051.
St. Patrick Cemetery, Hudson, 03051.
St. Patrick Cemetery, Jaffrey, 03452.
St. Joseph Cemetery, Keene, 03435.
Sacred Heart Cemetery, Laconia, 03247.
St. Lambert's Cemetery, Laconia, 03247.
All Saints Cemetery, Lancaster, 03584.
Calvary Cemetery, Lancaster, 03584.
St. Rose of Lima Cemetery, Littleton, 03561.
Holy Cross Cemetery, Londonderry, 03053.
St. Augustine Cemetery, 03111.
Mount Calvary Cemetery, 03111.
Mount Calvary Cemetery, Marlborough, 03455.
St. Louis Cemetery, Nashua, 03064.
St. Francis Xavier Cemetery, Nashua, 03064.
St. Stanislaus Cemetery, Nashua, 03064.
Sacred Heart of Jesus Cemetery, New Ipswich, 03071.
Calvary Cemetery, Newmarket, 03857.
St. Patrick Cemetery, Newport, 03773.
Our Lady of the Mountains Cemetery, North Conway, 03860.
Sacred Heart Cemetery, North Stratford, 03590.
Calvary Cemetery, Penacook, 03303.
St. Peter Cemetery (old), Peterborough, 03458.
St. Peter Cemetery (new), Peterborough, 03458.
Mount Calvary Cemetery, Pittsfield, 03263.
Holy Angels Cemetery, Plaistow, 03865.
Calvary Cemetery, Portsmouth, 03804.
St. Mary Cemetery, Portsmouth, 03804.

Holy Rosary Cemetery, Rochester, 03839.
St. Mary's Cemetery, Rochester, 03839.
St. Patrick Cemetery, Rollinsford, 03805.
Mount Calvary Cemetery, Sanbornville, 03872.
Holy Trinity Cemetery, Somersworth, 03878.
Mount Calvary Cemetery, Somersworth, 03878.
St. John the Baptist Cemetery, Suncook, 03275.
St. John the Baptist Old Cemetery, Suncook, 03275.
St. John's Cemetery, Tilton, 03299.
Mount Carmel Cemetery, Troy, 03465.
St. Margaret Cemetery, Twin Mountain, 03595.
St. Peter Cemetery, Walpole, 03608.
St. Albert Cemetery, West Stewartstown, 03597.
St. Matthew Cemetery, Whitefield, 03598.
Mount Calvary Cemetery

Holy Cross Health Center, Inc., 357 Island Pond Rd., 03109-4811. Tel: 603-628-3550; Fax: 603-626-6270. Email: hchcjudy@banet.net. Bonnie McMahon, N.H.A., Admin. Nursing home for women religious.

CENTER HARBOR. *L.C. Center Harbor, Inc.*, Plymouth St., P.O. Box 936, 03226. Tel: 603-253-7728; Fax: 603-253-8740. Rev. David Steffy, L.C.

GILFORD. *The Missionary Servants of Pope John Paul I*, 22 Boyd Hill Rd., 03249. Tel: 603-524-4740; Fax: 603-524-4740. The Missionary Servants of Pope John Paul I is a lay missionary association founded to aid established missionaries. Help is mainly given to Mother Teresa's missions in Haiti; however, shipments have also been made to Honduras, the Sudan, British Columbia, areas of the U.S. and to the local poor.

NASHUA. *Holy Infant Jesus Convent*, 3 Crown St., 03060-6366. Tel: 603-934-4874; 603-837-2835. Shirley Brien, Exec. Dir.; Fran Miller, H.C.A., Sec.

[P] SPECIAL APOSTOLATE CENTERS

LACONIA. *Christian Life Center*, Box 306, 03247. Tel: 603-524-7503. Janet Leroux, Coord.

SWANZEY. *Catholic Faith Formation Center*, Formerly Christian Life Center c/o St. Anthony Parish50 S. Winchester St., 03446-3211. Tel: 603-352-7662; Fax: 603-352-7662. Email: sisterjoan3@juno.com.

[Q] CAMPS AND COMMUNITY CENTERS

CENTER OSSIPEE. *Camp Marist*, Rte. 25 E., 03814. Tel: 603-539-4552; Fax: 603-539-8318. Email: marist@ix.netcom.com. Web: www.campmarist.org. Bro. Jim Halliday, Dir. Total Staff 100; Total Assisted 250.

GILMANTON IRON WORKS. *Camp Bernadette (Girls) Camp Fatima (Boys)*, Formerly Camp Bernadette (Girls) , Winter Business Office, P.O. Box 206, 03837-0206. Tel: 603-364-5851; 603-669-3100; Fax: 603-364-5038; 603-669-0377. Email: info@diocamps.org. Web: www.diocamps.org. Most Rev. John B. McCormack, D.D., Chmn. of the Bd.; Sr. Mary Elizabeth Whalen, S.N.D.deN., Pres.; Mr. Gus Planchet, Dir. Total Assisted Annually 1,000; Total Staff 80.

Summer Business Office for Camp Bernadette, Formerly Summer Business Office 83 Richards Rd., Wolfeboro, 03894. Tel: 603-569-1692. Total Staff 80; Total Assisted 1,080.

Camp Fatima (Boys) , Business Office, P.O. Box 206, 03837-0206. Tel: 603-364-5851; Fax: 603-364-5038. Email: info@diocamps.org. Web: www.diocamps.org. Total Assisted 1,100; Total Staff 80.

RELIGIOUS INSTITUTES OF MEN REPRESENTED IN THE DIOCESE

For further details refer to the corresponding bracketed number in the Religious Institutes of Men or Women section.

[0190]—*Basilian Salvatorian Fathers*—B.S.O.
[0200]—*Benedictine Monks* (Corpus Christi Abbey)—O.S.B.
[0200]—*Benedictine Monks* (St. Anselm Abbey)—O.S.B.
[1100]—*Brothers of the Sacred Heart* (New England Prov.)—S.C.
[1320]—*Clerics of St. Viator*—C.S.V.
[]—*Congregation of Holy Cross*—C.S.C.
[1330]—*Congregation of the Mission* (New England Prov.)—C.M.
[1330]—*Congregation of the Mission* (Eastern Prov.)—C.M.
[0520]—*Franciscan Friars* (Province of the Immaculate Conception)—O.F.M.
[0690]—*Jesuit Fathers and Brothers* (New England Prov.)—S.J.
[0730]—*Legionaries of Christ*—L.C.
[0770]—*Marist Brothers of the Schools* (Esopus Prov.)—F.M.S.
[0720]—*The Missionaries of Our Lady of La Salette* (Immaculate Heart of Mary & Our Lady of Seven Dolors Provinces)—M.S.
[0910]—*Oblates of Mary Immaculate*—O.M.I.
[0760]—*Society of Mary*—S.M.
[0370]—*Society of St. Columban*—S.S.C.
[1250]—*Somascan Fathers*—C.R.S.
[0410]—*Sons of Divine Providence, Inc.*—F.D.P.
[0140]—*The Augustinians*—O.S.A.
[0470]—*The Capuchin Friars*—O.F.M.Cap.

RELIGIOUS INSTITUTES OF WOMEN REPRESENTED IN THE DIOCESE

[0200]—*Benedictine Sisters*—O.S.B.
[1000]—*Congregation of Divine Providence of Kentucky*—C.D.P.
[2410]—*Congregation of the Marianites of Holy Cross*—M.S.C.
[3815]—*Congregation of the Sisters of St. Joan of Arc*—S.J.A.
[1150]—*Congregation of the Sisters of St. Joseph of Boston*—C.S.J.
[1990]—*Congregation of the Sisters of the Holy Names of Jesus and Mary - New York*—S.N.J.M.
[0750]—*Daughters of the Charity of the Sacred Heart of Jesus*—F.C.S.C.J.
[0420]—*Discalced Carmelites Nuns*—O.C.D.
[]—*Dominican Sisters of Hope*—O.P.
[1170]—*Felician Sisters*—C.S.S.F.
[1310]—*Franciscan Sisters of Little Falls, MN*—O.S.F.
[1840]—*Grey Nuns of the Sacred Heart*—G.N.S.H.
[2575]—*Institute of the Sisters of Mercy of the Americas* (Manchester, NH)—R.S.M.
[2320]—*The Little Sisters of the Holy Family*—P.S.S.F.
[]—*Little Sisters of St. Francis*—O.S.F.
[2410]—*Marianites of Holy Cross*—M.S.C.
[2470]—*Maryknoll Sisters of St. Dominic*—M.M.
[2480]—*Medical Missionaries of Mary*—M.M.M.
[3450]—*Religious of Jesus and Mary*—R.J.M.
[2970]—*School Sisters of Notre Dame*—S.S.N.D.
[1680]—*School Sisters of St. Francis*—O.S.F.
[0110]—*The Sisters Adorers of the Precious Blood*—A.P.B.
[0490]—*Sisters of Charity of Montreal (Grey Nuns)*—S.G.M.
[0530]—*Sisters of Charity of Our Lady, Mother of the Church*—S.C.M.C.
[0610]—*Sisters of Charity of St. Hyacinthe (Grey Nuns)*—S.C.S.H.
[0640]—*Sisters of Charity of St. Vincent De Paul, Halifax*—S.C.
[1930]—*Sisters of Holy Cross*—C.S.C.
[3000]—*Sisters of Notre Dame de Namur - Boston Province*—S.N.D.deN.
[3000]—*Sisters of Notre Dame de Namur - Ipswich Province*—S.N.D.deN.
[3080]—*Sisters of Our Lady of Christian Doctrine*—R.C.D.
[]—*Sisters of Our Lady of Lourdes (Pius Association of the Faithful)*—O.L.L.
[3350]—*Sisters of Providence* (Montreal)—S.P.
[3360]—*Sisters of Providence of Saint Mary-of-the-Woods, IN*—S.P.
[3718]—*Sisters of St. Ann*—S.S.A.
[3750]—*Sisters of St. Chretienne*—S.S.C.h.
[0150]—*Sisters of the Assumption*—S.A.S.V.
[3310]—*Sisters of the Presentation of Mary*—P.M.
[3320]—*Sisters of the Presentation of the B.V.M.*—P.B.V.M.
[]—*Society of Sisters for the Church*—S.S.C.

NECROLOGY

† Watson, Rev. Msgr. James P., (Retired)—Died June 18, 2003
† Boulanger, Maurice R., (Retired)—Died April 26, 2003
† Houde, Arthur O., (Retired)—Died Aug. 1, 2003
† Knott, Edward J., (Retired)—Died Jan. 2, 2003
† Laforest, Conrad—Died May 21, 2003
† Quirk, William L., (Retired)—Died Aug. 2, 2003

Diocese of Marquette

(Dioecesis Marquettensis)

Most Reverend

JAMES H. GARLAND, M.A., M.S.W., D.D.

Bishop of Marquette; ordained 1959 appointed Titular Bishop of Garriana and Auxiliary Bishop of Cincinnati June 2, 1984; consecrated July 25 1984; appointed Bishop of Marquette October 6, 1992 installed November 11, 1992. *Res.: 300 Rock St., P.O. Box 550, Marquette, MI 49855.* Tel: 906-225-1141.

Most Reverend

MARK F. SCHMITT, D.D.

Retired Bishop of Marquette; ordained May 22, 1948; appointed Titular Bishop of Kells and Auxiliary of Green Bay May 5, 1970; consecrated June 24, 1970; appointed to Marquette March 21, 1978; installed May 8, 1978; retired November 11, 1992. *Res.: HCO1 Box 159, Marquette, MI 49855.*

VICARIATE-APOSTOLIC JULY 29, 1853; DIOCESE 1857.

Square Miles 16,281.

Comprises the Upper Peninsula of the State of Michigan.

Legal Title: For legal titles of parishes and diocesan institutions, consult the Pastoral Office.

Chancery Office: 444 S. Fourth St., P.O. Box 550, Marquette, MI 49855. Tel: 906-225-1141; Fax: 906-225-0437.

Email: asample@dioceseofmarquette.org

STATISTICAL OVERVIEW

Personnel	
Bishop	1
Retired Bishops	1
Priests: Diocesan Active in Diocese	48
Priests: Diocesan Active Outside Diocese	4
Priests: Retired, Sick or Absent	36
Number of Diocesan Priests	88
Religious Priests in Diocese	11
Total Priests in Diocese	99
Extern Priests in Diocese	10
Ordinations:	
Diocesan Priests	1
Transitional Deacons	2
Permanent Deacons	4
Permanent Deacons in Diocese	29
Total Sisters	59
Parishes	
Parishes	74
With Resident Pastor:	
Resident Diocesan Priests	50
Resident Religious Priests	8
Without Resident Pastor:	
Administered by Priests	13
Administered by Religious Women	3
Missions	23
Professional Ministry Personnel:	
Sisters	11
Lay Ministers	18
Welfare	
Catholic Hospitals	1
Total Assisted	87,300
Homes for the Aged	1
Total Assisted	123
Special Centers for Social Services	6
Total Assisted	2,856
Educational	
Diocesan Students in Other Seminaries	14
Total Seminarians	14
Elementary Schools, Diocesan and Parish	10
Total Students	1,508
Catechesis/Religious Education:	
High School Students	2,791
Elementary Students	5,194
Total Students under Catholic Instruction	9,507
Teachers in the Diocese:	
Sisters	3
Lay Teachers	115
Vital Statistics	
Receptions into the Church:	
Infant Baptism Totals	786
Adult Baptism Totals	91
Received into Full Communion	107
First Communions	957
Confirmations	2,878
Marriages:	
Catholic	290
Interfaith	175
Total Marriages	465
Deaths	1,141
Total Catholic Population	68,360
Total Population	317,616

Former Bishops—Most Revs. FREDERIC BARAGA, D.D., first Bishop; consecrated Nov. 1, 1853; died Jan. 19, 1868; IGNATIUS MRAK, D.D., consecrated Feb. 7, 1869; resigned 1878; transferred to Antinoe 1879; died Jan. 2, 1901; JOHN VERTIN, D.D., consecrated Sept. 14, 1879; died Feb. 26, 1899; FREDERICK EIS, D.D., consecrated Aug. 24, 1899; made Asst. at the Pontifical Throne July 13, 1922;; resigned July 8, 1922; appt. Titular Bishop of Bita; died May 5, 1926; PAUL JOSEPH NUSSBAUM, D.D., consecrated Bishop of Corpus Christi May 20, 1913; resigned March 26, 1920; appt. Bishop of Marquette Nov. 14, 1922; died June 24, 1935; JOSEPH CASIMIR PLAGENS, D.D., LL.D., consecrated Sept. 30, 1924, Auxiliary Bishop of Detroit; Titular Bishop of Rhodiopolis;; appt. to See of Marquette Nov. 16, 1935; transferred to the See of Grand Rapids Dec. 16, 1940; died March 31, 1943; FRANCIS J. MAGNER, D.D., appt. Dec. 21, 1940; consecrated Feb. 24, 1941; died June 13, 1947; THOMAS L. NOA, D.D. (Retired), consecrated March 19, 1946; Titular Bishop of Salona and Coadjutor Bishop of Sioux City; appt. Bishop of Marquette Aug. 20, 1947; retired March 25, 1968; died March 13, 1977; CHARLES A. SALATKA, D.D., appt. Titular Bishop of Cariana and Auxiliary of Grand Rapids Dec. 9, 1961; consecrated March 6, 1962; appt. Bishop of Marquette Jan. 10, 1968; installed March 25, 1968; appt. Archbishop of Oklahoma City Oct. 11, 1977; MARK F. SCHMITT, D.D. (Retired), appt. Titular Bishop of Kells and Auxiliary of Green Bay May 5, 1970; consecrated June 24, 1970; appt. Bishop of Marquette March 21, 1978; installed May 8, 1978; retired November 11, 1992.

Chancery Office—444 S. Fourth St., P.O. Box 550, Marquette, 49855. Tel: 906-225-1141; Fax: 906-225-0437. Office Hours: June-Aug. Mon.-Fri. 8-4; Sept.-May Mon.-Fri. 9-5

Vicar General—Rev. Msgr. JOHN E. PATRICK, V.G.

Chancellor—Rev. ALEXANDER K. SAMPLE.

Secretary to the Bishop—Mrs. PATRICIA A. PETERSON. Tel: 906-227-9115.

Diocesan Tribunal—444 S. Fourth St., P.O. Box 550, Marquette, 49855. Tel: 906-227-9111.

Judicial Vicar—Rev. Msgr. PETER OBERTO, J.C.L.

Adjutant Judicial Vicar—Rev. BENEDETTO J. PARIS, J.C.L.

Diocesan Judges—Rev. Msgr. PETER OBERTO J.C.L.; Rev. BENEDETTO J. PARIS, J.C.L.

Defensore Vinculi—Revs. JOHN J. SHIVERSKI; ALEX K. SAMPLE, J.C.L.

Advocates—Revs. FRANCIS J. DEGROOT; JAMES M. ROETZER.

Notary—MARY C. JESKE.

Priests' Council—

Executive Board—Revs. JAMES P. CHALLANCIN, Chm.; WAYNE E. MARCOTTE, Vice Chm.; GLENN J. THEORET, Sec.

Deans—Revs. JOHN J. SHIVERSKI, Marquette; MARTIN T. SCHAEFER, Escanaba; WAYNE E. MARCOTTE, Houghton; Rev. Msgr. JAMES A. KACZMAREK, Iron Mountain; Revs. DARRYL J. PEPIN, Ironwood; MATHEW PERUMPALLY, Menominee; VACANT, Sault Ste. Marie; Revs. GEORGE J. KUPPAYIL, M.S.T., Iron River; GLENN J. THEORET, Manistique.

Consultors—Revs. CHRISTOPHER B. GARDINER; JOHN F. MCARDLE (Retired); RAYMOND J. ZEUGNER; NORMAN A. CLISCH; WAYNE E. MARCOTTE; Rev. Msgr. JOHN E. PATRICK, V.G.; Rev. ALEXANDER K. SAMPLE.

Diocesan Offices and Directors

Administration & Finance, Dept. of—RICHARD R. SCHAEFER, C.P.A., Dir.; CAROL J. PARKER, Accountant & Computer Information Coord., 444 S. Fourth St., P.O. Box 550, Marquette, 49855. Tel: 906-227-9105; Fax: 906-225-0437.

Archives—Rev. ALEX K. SAMPLE, J.C.L., Chancellor; ELIZABETH DELENE, Archivist, 347 Rock St., Marquette, 49855. Tel: 906-227-9117; Fax: 906-228-2469.

Development, Office of—TERRI GADZINSKI, Dir., 444 S. Fourth St., P.O. Box 550, Marquette, 49855. Tel: 906-227-9138; Fax: 906-225-0437.

Catholic Social Services, Dept. of—LARRY ZIOMKOWSKI, Dir., 347 Rock St., Marquette, 49855. Tel: 906-227-9119; Fax: 906-228-2469 Branch Offices: Houghton, Escanaba, Iron Mountain, Sault Ste., Marie, Ironwood.

Communication Services, Dept. of—LOREENE ZENO KOSKEY, Dir., 347 Rock St., P.O. Box 548, Marquette, 49855. Tel: 906-227-9129; Fax: 906-226-6941.

Faith Formation & Education, Dept. of—GLORIA KALBFLEISCH, Dir. & Supt. of Schools; VACANT, Pres., Bd. of Educ.; VACANT, Vice Pres., Bd. of Educ.; GREG GOSTOMSKI, Coord. Intergenerational Faith Formation. Tel: 906-227-9125; DENISE FOYE, Coord. Catechist Svcs. & Program Devel. Tel: 906-227-9130. 347 Rock St., P.O. Box 280, Marquette, 49855. Tel: 906-227-9127; Fax: 906-228-1522.

Newspaper "The U.P. Catholic"—JOSEPH ZYBLE, Editor, 347 Rock St., P.O. Box 548, Marquette, 49855. Tel: 906-227-9131; Fax: 906-226-6941.

Ministry Personnel Services, Dept. of—Rev. ALEXANDER K. SAMPLE, Dir., 444 S. Fourth St., P.O. Box 550, Marquette, 49855. Tel: 906-227-9111; Fax: 906-225-0437.

Priests' Personnel, Office of—STEPHEN LYNOTT, M.S.W., Mgr. Clergy Support Svcs., 615 S. Fourth St., P.O. Box 550, Marquette, 49855. Tel: 906-228-0229; Fax: 906-228-0280.

Apostleship of the Sea—Rev. TED BRODEUR, Chap., Holy Name of Mary Parish, 377 Maple St., Sault Ste. Marie, 49783. Tel: 906-632-3381.

Bishop Baraga Association Inc.— An international organization to promote the Cause of the Beatification of the Most Rev. Frederic Baraga. *347 Rock St., P.O. Box 548, Marquette, 49855*. Tel: 906-227-9117; Fax: 906-228-2469. Revs. ALEX K. SAMPLE, J.C.L., Exec. Dir., Treas. & Vice-Postulator; PAOLO LOMBARDO, O.F.M., Postulator; ELIZABETH J. DELENE, Archivist & Editor of the Baraga Bulletin.

Building Commission, Diocese of Marquette—RICHARD R. SCHAEFER, C.P.A., Sec., P.O. Box 550, Marquette, 49855. Tel: 906-227-9108.

Catholic Relief Services—Rev. LAWRENCE T. GAUTHIER, Dir. (Retired), P.O. Box 550, Marquette, 49855.

Cemeteries—RICHARD R. SCHAEFER, C.P.A., Bishop's Rep. for Catholic Cemeteries, 444 S. Fourth St., P.O. Box 550, Marquette, 49855. Tel: 906-227-9102.

Charismatic Prayer Groups—Rev. MICHAEL J. STEBER, Diocesan Liaison, St. Anne Parish, 817 S. Lincoln Rd., Escanaba, 49829. Tel: 906-786-1421.

Clergy Continuing Education—Rev. GLENN J. THEORET, Dir., St. Francis de Sales Parish, 330 Oak St., Manistique, 49854. Tel: 906-341-5355.

Council of Catholic Women—Sr. DYONNE FINN, S.S.N.D., 5563 "F" Rd., Bark River, 49807. Tel: 906-466-2127.

Cursillo—Rev. Msgr. TIMOTHY H. DESROCHERS, Diocesan Moderator, Marygrove, P.O. Box 38, Garden, 49835. Tel: 906-644-2771.

Ecumenical Officer—GREGORY DeZIEL, St. Joseph & St. Patrick Parish, 709 First Ave. S., Escanaba, 49829. Tel: 906-789-6244.

Family Life Ministry—623 Ludington St., Ste. 200, Escanaba, 49829. Tel: 906-789-2604.

Holy Childhood Association—Rev. LAWRENCE T. GAUTHIER, Dir. (Retired), P.O. Box 550, Marquette, 49855. Tel: 906-227-9106.

Knights of Columbus—Rev. ALEX K. SAMPLE, J.C.L., Diocesan Chap., P.O. Box 550, Marquette, 49855. Tel: 906-227-9111.

Panama Mission Fund—Rev. PAUL G. MANDERFIELD, 444 S. Fourth St., Marquette, 49855. Tel: 906-225-1141.

Permanent Diaconate Formation Program—Deacon SCOTT JAMIESON, Dir., P.O. Box 550, Marquette, 49855. Tel: 906-227-9103.

Planning, Office of—Deacon ROBERT LACOSSE, 444 S. Fourth St., P.O. Box 550, Marquette, 49855. Tel: 906-227-9112; Fax: 906-225-0437.

Propagation of the Faith—Rev. LAWRENCE T. GAUTHIER, Diocesan Dir. (Retired), P.O. Box 550, Marquette, 49855. Tel: 906-227-9106.

Retreats—Rev. Msgr. TIMOTHY H. DESROCHERS, Dir., Marygrove Retreat Center, Garden, 49835. Tel: 906-644-2771.

Victim Assistance Coordinator—ROSALYN GROVES, 623 Ludington St., Ste. 200, Escanaba, 49829. Tel: 906-233-9306. Email: regroves@uplogon.com.

St. Joseph Association— An Association of the Priests of the Diocese to provide Retirement Benefits. Rev. RICK L. COURIER, Pres., St. Thomas the Apostle Parish, 1820 9th Ave. N., Escanaba, 49829. Tel: 906-786-4627.

U.P. Catholic Services Appeal—RICHARD R. SCHAEFER, C.P.A., Coord., 444 S. Fourth St., P.O. Box 796, Marquette, 49855. Tel: 906-227-9101.

Vocation Office—Rev. JAMES C. ZIMINSKI, Dir., St. Ann Parish, 318 Lyons St., Baraga, 49908. Tel: 906-353-6565; Fax: 906-353-6568.

Women Religious—Sr. DYONNE FINN, S.S.N.D., P.O. Box 550, Marquette, 49855. Tel: 906-466-2127.

CLERGY, PARISHES, MISSIONS AND PAROCHIAL SCHOOLS

CITY OF MARQUETTE
(MARQUETTE COUNTY)

1—ST. PETER CATHEDRAL, Revs. Louis C. Cappo; Allen P. Mott; Deacons Scott A. Jamieson; Donald Thoren. In Res., Rev. Alexander K. Sample.
Res.: 311 Baraga Ave., 49855. Tel: 906-226-6548; Fax: 906-226-8683.
School—Father Marquette Catholic Central Schools System See Elementary Interparochial Schools under Institutions Located in the Diocese.
Catechesis/Religious Program—Tel: 906-226-6548, Ext. 207. Dan Rydholm, D.R.E. Students 215.
Mission—St. Mary Big Bay, Marquette Co.

2—ST. CHRISTOPHER, Rev. Alexander K. Sample; Sr. Colleen Sweeting, O.S.F., Pastoral Coord.
Res.: 2372 Badger St., 49855. Tel: 906-226-2265; Fax: 906-226-8678.

3—ST. JOHN THE BAPTIST, Closed., 1986. For inquiries for parish records, contact St. Peter's Cathedral.

4—ST. LOUIS (Harvey), Rev. Benedetto J. Paris, J.C.L.; Deacon David P. Adler.
Res.: 264 Silver Creek Rd., 49855. Tel: 906-249-1438; Fax: 906-249-3428.
School—Father Marquette Catholic Central Schools System See Elementary Interparochial Schools under Institutions Located in the Diocese.

5—ST. MICHAEL, Rev. Msgr. John E. Patrick, V.G.
Res.: 401 W. Kaye Ave., 49855. Tel: 906-228-8180; Fax: 906-228-5502.
School—Father Marquette Catholic Central Schools System See Elementary Interparochial Schools under Institutions Located in the Diocese.
Catechesis/Religious Program—Sally Luft, D.R.E. Students 190.

OUTSIDE THE CITY OF MARQUETTE

AHMEEK, KEWEENAW CO., OUR LADY OF PEACE, , (Keweenaw Catholic Missions) Rev. Sebastian Ettolil, M.C.B.S. (India).
Mailing Address: Box 517, Mohawk, 49950. Tel: 906-337-1966; Fax: 906-337-1966.
Mission—Holy Redeemer Eagle Harbor, Keweenaw Co.
Mission—Our Lady of the Pines Copper Harbor, Keweenaw Co.

ALPHA, IRON CO., ST. EDWARD, Closed. For inquiries for parish records contact the chancery.

ASSININS, BARAGA CO., THE MOST HOLY NAME OF JESUS-BLESSED KATERI TEKAKWITHA, Revs. James C. Ziminski; Gregory R. Heikkala.
Res.: 318 Lyons St., Baraga, 49908. Tel: 906-353-6836.

BARAGA, BARAGA CO., ST. ANN, Rev. James C. Ziminski; Deacon Robert L. Wahmhoff.
Res.: 318 Lyons St., 49908. Tel: 906-353-6565; Fax: 906-353-6568.

BARBEAU, CHIPPEWA CO,, HOLY FAMILY MISSION, Rev. John S. Hascall, O.F.M.Cap.
Res.: 1529 Marquette Ave., Sault Sainte Marie, 49783. Tel: 906-632-3213; Fax: 906-632-8490.
Catechesis/Religious Program—Tel: 906-647-7202. Lisa Cryderman, D.R.E. Students 33.

BARK RIVER, DELTA CO., ST. ELIZABETH ANN SETON, , Formerly St. George, Bark River; Sacred Heart of Jesus, Schaffer; & St. Michael, Perronville. Rev. Christopher B. Gardiner.
Res.: 1216 12th Rd., P.O. Box 187, 49807. Tel: 906-466-9938; Fax: 906-466-0194.
Catechesis/Religious Program—Darlene Vandermissen, D.R.E. Students 148.

BESSEMER, GOGEBIC CO., ST. SEBASTIAN, Rev. James M. Roetzer.
Res.: 210 E. Iron St., 49911. Tel: 906-667-0952; Fax: 906-667-0952.
School—Tel: 906-667-0322. Lay Teachers 7; Students 42.

BRIMLEY, CHIPPEWA CO., ST. FRANCIS XAVIER, Rev. Peter H. Fosu (Ghana); Deacon Joseph A. LaPlante.
Mailing Address: P.O. Box 429, 49715. Tel: 906-248-3443.
Catechesis/Religious Program—Tel: 906-248-5386. Marian Newland, D.R.E. Students 63.
Mission—Blessed Kateri Tekakwitha Bay Mills, Chippewa Co. Fax: 906-248-3443. (Formerly St. Catherine)

CALUMET, HOUGHTON CO.

1—ST. PAUL THE APOSTLE, Rev. Sebastian Ettolil, M.C.B.S. (India).
Res.: 301 Eighth St., 49913. Tel: 906-337-2044; Fax: 906-337-2058.

2—SACRED HEART, Rev. Abraham J. Mupparathara, M.C.B.S. (India).
Mailing Address: P.O. Box 546, 49913. Tel: 906-337-0810; Fax: 906-337-6424.

CASPIAN, IRON CO., ST. CECILIA, Rev. Norman A. Clisch; Deacon Robert J. Kostka.
Mailing Address: P.O. Box 517, 49915. Tel: 906-265-3777; Fax: 906-265-3224.

CHAMPION, MARQUETTE CO., SACRED HEART, Rev. Msgr. Peter Oberto, Canonical Pastor; Sisters Margey Schmelzle, O.S.F., Pastoral Coord.; Lois Risch, O.S.F., Pastoral Coord.
Mailing Address: P.O. Box 99, 49879. Tel: 906-376-8475; Fax: 906-376-8475.
Catechesis/Religious Program—Students 15.

CHANNING, DICKINSON CO., ST. ROSE, Rev. George J. Kuppayil, M.S.T. (India).
Mailing Address: P.O. Box 235, 49815. Tel: 906-542-3215; Fax: 906-542-9084.
Catechesis/Religious Program—Tel: 906-542-6341. Edith Raffin, D.R.E. Students 52.
Mission—St. Joseph Foster City, Dickinson Co. Tel: 906-246-3490.

CHASSELL, HOUGHTON CO., ST. ANNE, Rev. Larry P. VanDamme.
Mailing Address: P.O. Box 407, 49916. Tel: 906-523-4912; Fax: 906-523-4904.
Mission—Sacred Heart Painesdale, Houghton Co. Closed. For inquiries for parish records contact Holy Family, South Range.
Mission—Immaculate Heart of Mary Donken, Houghton Co. Closed. For inquiries for parish records contact Holy Family, South Range.

COOKS, SCHOOLCRAFT CO., ST. MARY MAGDALENE, [CEM] Rev. Thomas Joseph Varickamackal (India).
Mailing Address: P.O. Box 68, Garden, 49835. Tel: 906-644-2626; Fax: 906-644-2626.

CRYSTAL FALLS, IRON CO., GUARDIAN ANGELS, Rev. Dino F. Silvestrini; Deacon Bernard Kut.
Res.: 412 Crystal Ave., 49920. Tel: 906-875-3019; Fax: 906-875-1034.
Catechesis/Religious Program—Jeanne Brown, D.R.E. Students 123.

DAGGETT, MENOMINEE CO., ST. FREDERICK, Closed., For inquiries for parish records contact Precious Blood Parish, Stephenson.

DETOUR, CHIPPEWA CO., SACRED HEART, Revs. Sebastian Kavumkal, M.S.T. (India); Jerome A. Nowacki; Deacon Ronald P. Andrzejewski.
Mailing Address: P.O. Box 8, 49725. Tel: 906-297-3781; Fax: 906-297-5108.
Mission—St. Florence Drummond Island, Chippewa Co.

ENGADINE, MACKINAC CO., OUR LADY OF LOURDES, Rev. Timothy W. Hruska.
Mailing Address: P.O. Box 123, 49827. Tel: 906-477-6223; Fax: 906-477-6731.
Mission—St. Stephen Naubinway, Mackinac Co.
Mission—Divine Infant of Prague Gulliver, Schoolcraft Co. Deacon Gilbert G. Sablack.

ESCANABA, DELTA CO.

1—ST. ANNE, Revs. Michael J. Steber; George S. Maki; Deacons Lewis Vailliencourt; Michael LeBeau.
Res.: 817 S. Lincoln Rd., 49829. Tel: 906-786-1421; Fax: 906-786-9346.
School—Holy Name Central Grade School See Elementary Inter-Parochial Schools under Institutions Located in the Diocese.

2—ST. JOSEPH & ST. PATRICK, Merged, (Formerly St. Joseph, Escanaba; Formerly St. Patrick, Escanaba). Rev. Francis G. Dobrzenski; Deacon William D. Hemes.
Res.: 709 First Ave. S., 49829. Tel: 906-789-6244; Fax: 906-789-1213.
School—Holy Name Central Grade School See Elementary Inter-Parochial Schools under Institutions Located in the Diocese.
Catechesis/Religious Program—Tel: 906-789-1010. Janice Dubord, D.R.E. Students 264.

3—ST. THOMAS THE APOSTLE, Rev. Rick L. Courier.
Res.: 1820 Ninth Ave. N., 49829. Tel: 906-786-4627; Fax: 906-789-5558.
School—Holy Name Central Grade School See Elementary Inter-Parochial Schools under Institutions Located in the Diocese.
Catechesis/Religious Program—Tel: 906-786-3506. Rev. Diane Talford, D.R.E. Students 66.

EWEN, ONTONAGON CO., SACRED HEART, Rev. George Kallarackal Joseph, M.C.B.S. (India).
Mailing Address: P.O. Box 169, 49925. Tel: 906-988-2310; Fax: 906-988-2631.
Catechesis/Religious Program—Nina Humphrey, D.R.E. Tel: 906-988-2578; Bette Rigoni, D.R.E. Tel: 906-988-2398. Students 30.
Mission—St. Francis Xavier Sidnaw, Houghton Co.
Catechesis/Religious Program—Donna Johnson, D.R.E. Students 1.

GARDEN, DELTA CO., ST. JOHN THE BAPTIST, Rev. Thomas Joseph Varickamackal (India); Deacon Rodney Groleau.
Mailing Address: P.O. Box 68, 49835. Tel: 906-644-2626; Fax: 906-644-2626.

GLADSTONE, DELTA CO.

1—ALL SAINTS, Rev. Arnold J. Grambow.
Res.: 715 Wisconsin Ave., P.O. Box 392, 49837. Tel: 906-428-3199; Fax: 906-428-2829.

2—HOLY FAMILY, Rev. Frank M. Lenz.

Res.: 4011 CO 416-20th Rd., 49837. Tel: 906-786-1209; Fax: 906-786-0846.

GOETZVILLE, CHIPPEWA CO., ST. STANISLAUS KOSTKA, [CEM] Revs. Sebastian Kavumkal, M.S.T. (India); Jerome A. Nowacki.
Mailing Address: 12841 E. Traynor Rd., 49736. Tel: 906-297-5211; Fax: 906-297-5108.
Mission—Our Lady of the Snows Hessel, Mackinac Co. Tel: 906-484-3825; 906-484-2773 (Parish House).

GRAND MARAIS, ALGER CO., HOLY ROSARY CHURCH, [CEM] Rev. Joy Joseph Adimakkeel (India).
Mailing Address: P.O. Box 424, 49839. Tel: 906-494-2589; Fax: 906-494-2589.
Mission—St. Therese Germfask, Schoolcraft Co.
Mission—St. Timothy Curtis, Mackinac Co.

GWINN, MARQUETTE CO., ST. ANTHONY, Rev. Ronald K. Timock.
Res.: 320 Iron St., P.O. Box 1358, 49841. Tel: 906-346-5312; Fax: 906-346-3040.
Catechesis/Religious Program—Tel: 906-346-6645. Cindy Wedig, D.R.E. Students 44.
Mission—St. Joseph Northland, Marquette Co. Tel: 906-238-4444.

HANCOCK, HOUGHTON CO., RESURRECTION, [CEM] Rev. Wayne E. Marcotte.
Res.: 900 Quincy St., 49930. Tel: 906-482-0215; Fax: 906-482-5268.
Catechesis/Religious Program—Tel: 906-482-1175. Julie Lancour, D.R.E. Students 203.
Mission—St. Francis of Assisi Dollar Bay, Houghton Co. Tel: 906-482-6489.

HERMANSVILLE, MENOMINEE CO., ST. JOHN NEUMANN, , (Formerly St. Mary, Hermansville; St. Francis Xavier, Spalding). Rev. Michael T. Vichich.
Res.: P.O. Box 125, 49847. Tel: 906-498-7730; 906-497-5800 (Spalding); Fax: 906-497-5800.
Catechesis/Religious Program—Lana Scott, D.R.E. Students 175.

HOUGHTON, HOUGHTON CO.
1—ST. ALBERT THE GREAT UNIVERSITY PARISH, , (Michigan Technological University) Rev. Larry P. VanDamme.
Res.: 411 MacInnes Dr., 49931. Tel: 906-482-5530; Fax: 906-482-4828.
2—ST. IGNATIUS LOYOLA, Rev. John E. Martignon.
Res.: 305 Portage St., 49931. Tel: 906-482-0212; Fax: 906-482-8110.
Mission—St. Mary Atlantic Mine, Houghton Co. Closed. For inquiries for parish records contact St. Ignatius Loyola, Houghton.

HUBBELL, HOUGHTON CO., ST. CECILIA, Rev. Eric E. Olson.
Mailing Address: c/o 701 Calumet St., Lake Linden, 49945. Tel: 906-296-6851.

IRON MOUNTAIN, DICKINSON CO.
1—IMMACULATE CONCEPTION OF THE BLESSED VIRGIN MARY, Rev. Msgr. James A. Kaczmarek.
Res.: 500 E. Blaine St., 49801-1840. Tel: 906-774-0511; Fax: 906-779-9953.
School—Dickinson Area Catholic School System See Elementary Inter-Parochial Schools under Institutions Located in the Diocese.
Catechesis/Religious Program—Students 279.
2—ST. MARY AND ST. JOSEPH, Rev. Daniel S. Zaloga; Deacon Donald R. Christy.
Res.: 411 W. B St., 49801. Tel: 906-774-2046; Fax: 906-774-6015.
School—Dickinson Area Catholic School System See Elementary Inter-Parochial Schools under Institutions Located in the Diocese.

IRON RIVER, IRON CO., ST. AGNES, Rev. Norman A. Clisch; Deacon Robert J. Kostka.
Res.: 702 N. Fourth St., 49935. Tel: 906-265-4557; Fax: 906-265-7155.
Catechesis/Religious Program—Jean Zielinski, D.R.E. Students 262.

IRONWOOD, GOGEBIC CO.
1—ST. AMBROSE, Consolidated, with Holy Trinity & St. Michael to form Our Lady of Peace Parish, 1986.
2—ST. MICHAEL, Consolidated, with St. Ambrose & Holy Trinity to form Our Lady of Peace Parish, 1986.
3—OUR LADY OF PEACE, Consolidated, from Holy Trinity, St. Ambrose & St. Michael, 1986. Rev. Darryl J. Pepin; Deacon Robert A. Hamen.
Res.: 108 S. Marquette St., 49938. Tel: 906-932-0174; Fax: 906-932-1019.
School—Tel: 906-932-3200. Lay Teachers 8; Students 73.
Catechesis/Religious Program—Tel: 906-932-1708. Patricia Niksich, D.R.E. Students 282.

ISHPEMING, MARQUETTE CO.
1—ST. JOHN THE EVANGELIST, Rev. Msgr. Peter Oberto.
Res.: 325 S. Pine, 49849. Tel: 906-486-6212; Fax: 906-486-4244.
Religious Education Center—335 S. Pine St., 49849. Tel: 906-486-9361. Betty Lou Bosio, Admin.
2—ST. JOSEPH, Rev. James Challancin.
Office (All Mail):—1889 Prairie Avenue,, 49849-1045.
Res.: 1890 Prairie Ave., 49849-1044. Tel: 906-485-4200; Fax: 906-485-4185.
3—ST. PIUS X, Closed., For inquiries for parish records contact St. Joseph Church, 1889 Prairie Ave., Ishpeming, MI 49849.

KINGSFORD, DICKINSON CO.
1—AMERICAN MARTYRS, Rev. Joseph O. Gouin.
Res.: 908 W. Sagola Ave., 49802. Tel: 906-774-0630; Fax: 906-774-4417.
2—ST. MARY QUEEN OF PEACE, Rev. Michael A. Woempner.
Res.: 600 Marquette Blvd., 49802. Tel: 906-774-6122; Fax: 906-774-2349.
Catechesis/Religious Program—Mary Beth Casanova, D.R.E. Students 124.

L'ANSE BARAGA CO., SACRED HEART, Rev. Gregory R. Heikkala.
Res.: 16 S. Sixth St., 49946. Tel: 906-524-6424; Fax: 906-524-6422.
School—433 E. Baraga Ave., 49946. Tel: 906-524-5157; Fax: 906-524-5154. Lay Teachers 6; Students 73.
Catechesis/Religious Program—Tel: 906-524-7585. Sr. Phyllis Kernz, S.S.N.D., D.R.E. Students 110.

LAKE LINDEN, HOUGHTON CO., ST. JOSEPH, Rev. Eric E. Olson.
Res.: 701 Calumet St., 49945. Tel: 906-296-6851.

MACKINAC ISLAND, MACKINAC CO., STE. ANNE DE MICHILIMACKINAC (1695), Rev. James M. Williams.
Mailing Address: P.O. Box 537, 49757. Tel: 906-847-3507; Fax: 906-847-0361.

MANISTIQUE, SCHOOLCRAFT CO., ST. FRANCIS DE SALES, Rev. Glenn J. Theoret; Deacons Gilbert G. Sablack; Robert M. Cross.
Res.: 330 Oak St., 49854. Tel: 906-341-5355; Fax: 906-341-3984.
School—Tel: 906-341-5512. Sisters 6; Lay Teachers 7; Students 109.
Catechesis/Religious Program—Tel: 906-341-8151. Patricia Peck-Faketty, D.R.E. Students 200.

MENOMINEE, MENOMINEE CO.
1—HOLY REDEEMER (Birch Creek), Rev. Ronald J. Skufca; Deacon Roland Chaltry.
Res.: W-5541 Birch Creek Rd. No. 6, 49858. Tel: 906-863-3920; Fax: 906-863-7303.
School—Menominee Catholic Central See Elementary Inter-Parochial Schools under Institutions Located in the Diocese.
2—HOLY SPIRIT, Rev. S. Patrick Wisneske.
Res.: 1016 10th Ave., 49858. Tel: 906-863-5239; Fax: 906-863-2249.
School—Menominee Catholic Central See Elementary Inter-Parochial Schools under Institutions Located in the Diocese.
Catechesis/Religious Program—Tel: 906-863-2249. Marlene Varady, D.R.E. Students 130.
3—RESURRECTION, Rev. Francis J. DeGroot; Deacon Vincent W. Beckley.
Res.: 2607 18th St., 49858. Tel: 906-863-3405; Fax: 906-863-9090.
School—Menominee Catholic Central See Elementary Inter-Parochial Schools under Institutions Located in the Diocese.
Catechesis/Religious Program—Students 201.

MORAN, MACKINAC CO., IMMACULATE CONCEPTION, [CEM] Rev. C. Michael Rhoades.
Res.: 120 Church St., St. Ignace, 49781. Tel: 906-643-7671; Fax: 906-643-7755.

MUNISING, ALGER CO., SACRED HEART OF JESUS, Rev. Dennis L. Lorca; Deacon James E. Anderson.
Office—110 W. Jewell St., P.O. Box 99, 49862. Tel: 906-387-4900; Fax: 906-387-4422.
Catechesis/Religious Program—Tel: 906-387-4901. Barbara Fellhusen, D.R.E. Students 104.

NADEAU, MENOMINEE CO., ST. BRUNO, Rev. Mathew Perumpally (India).
Res.: P.O. Box 95, 49863. Tel: 906-639-2388; Fax: 906-639-3207.
Catechesis/Religious Program—Tel: 906-639-2150. Cindy Mellen, D.R.E. Students 46.

NAHMA, DELTA CO., ST. ANDREW, Rev. Thomas Joseph Varickamackal (India); Deacon Rodney Groleau.
Mailing Address: P.O. Box 68, Garden, 49834. Tel: 906-644-2626; Fax: 906-644-2626.

NEGAUNEE, MARQUETTE CO., ST. PAUL, Revs. John J. Shiverski; Mathew Antony Kadavil (India).
Res.: 202 W. Case St., 49866. Tel: 906-475-9969; Fax: 906-475-9987.
Catechesis/Religious Program—Tel: 906-475-5245. Sr. Annette Marie Johnson, D.R.E. Students 280.
Mission—Our Lady Perpetual Help Palmer Marquette Co. Tel: 906-475-4630.

NEWBERRY, LUCE CO., ST. GREGORY, Rev. Paul P. Karottekunnel, M.S.T. (India).
Office—212 W. Harrie St., 49868. Tel: 906-293-5511; Fax: 906-293-5575.
Res.: 111 W. Harrie St., 49868. Tel: 906-293-5001.
Mission—Our Lady of Victory Paradise, Chippewa Co.

NORWAY, DICKINSON CO., ST. MARY, Rev. Mark A. McQuesten; Deacon Ronald J. LeMire Sr.
Res.: 401 Main St., 49870. Tel: 906-563-9845; Fax: 906-563-7623.
School—Holy Spirit Central Grade School See Elementary Inter-Parochial Schools under Institutions Located in the Diocese.

ONTONAGON, ONTONAGON CO., HOLY FAMILY, [CEM] Rev. Abraham Kazhunadiyil (India).
Res.: 515 Pine St., 49953. Tel: 906-884-2569; Fax: 906-884-6030.

PERKINS, DELTA CO., ST. JOSEPH, Rev. Jacek S. Wtyklo.
Res.: 5803 Hwy. M-35, P.O. Box 99,, 49872. Tel: 906-359-4701; Fax: 906-359-4701.

PERRONVILLE, MENOMINEE CO., ST. ELIZABETH ANN SETON, , (Formerly St. Michael. See Bark River.)

QUINNESEC, DICKINSON CO., ST. MARY, Closed., For inquiries for parish records contact St. Mary Parish, Norway, MI.

RAMSAY, GOGEBIC CO., CHRIST THE KING, Closed., For inquiries for parish records contact St. Sebastian, Bessemer.

RAPID RIVER, DELTA CO., ST. CHARLES BORROMEO, Rev. David W. Sedlock; Deacon William Green.
Mailing Address: P.O. Box 247, 49878. Tel: 906-474-6606; Fax: 906-474-9087.

REPUBLIC, MARQUETTE CO., ST. AUGUSTINE, [CEM] Rev. Msgr. Peter Oberto, Canonical Pastor; Rev. James Challancin; Sr. Margey Schmelzle, O.S.F., Pastoral Coord.
Mailing Address: Rte. 1, Box 670, 49879. Tel: 906-376-8475; Fax: 906-376-8475.
Catechesis/Religious Program—Sr. Lois Risch, O.S.F., D.R.E. Students 15.

ROCKLAND, ONTONAGON CO., ST. MARY, Rev. Abraham Kazhunadiyil (India); Deacon Karl L. Wadman.
Mailing Address: Holy Family Parish, 515 Pine St., Ontonagon, 49953. Tel: 906-884-2569; Fax: 906-884-6030.

RUDYARD, CHIPPEWA CO., ST. JOSEPH, Rev. Cyriac Kottayarikil, M.C.B.S. (India).
Mailing Address: P.O. Box 150, 49780. Tel: 906-478-4331; Fax: 906-478-4331.
Catechesis/Religious Program—Brenda Coffey, D.R.E. Students 69.
Mission—St. Mary Trout Lake, Chippewa Co.
Station—Kinross Correctional Facility Kincheloe.
Station—Chippewa Correctional Facility Kincheloe.
Station—Chippewa Regional Facility Kincheloe.
Station—Hiawatha Correctional Facility Kincheloe.

ST. IGNACE, MACKINAC CO., ST. IGNATIUS LOYOLA, [CEM] Rev. C. Michael Rhoades; Deacon Donald F. Olmstead.
Res.: 120 Church St., 49781. Tel: 906-643-7671; Fax: 906-643-7755.
Catechesis/Religious Program—Tel: 906-643-8887. Betty Springsteen, D.R.E.; Mary Beth Fochtman, D.R.E. Students 169.

SAULT SAINTE MARIE, CHIPPEWA CO.
1—HOLY NAME OF MARY, Rev. Theodore J. Brodeur.
Res.: 377 Maple St., 49783. Tel: 906-632-3381; Fax: 906-632-0741.
School—Tel: 906-635-6141. Sisters 1; Lay Teachers 8; Students 143.
Mission—Sacred Heart Sugar Island, Chippewa Co.
2—ST. ISAAC JOGUES MISSION, Rev. John S. Hascall, O.F.M.Cap.
Res.: 1529 Marquette Ave., 49783. Tel: 906-632-3213; Fax: 906-632-8490.
Catechesis/Religious Program—Tel: 906-632-2856. Patti Oshelski, D.R.E. Students 34.
3—ST. JOSEPH, Rev. Pawel J. Mecwel; Deacon William J. Piche.
Res.: 606 E. Fourth Ave., 49783. Tel: 906-632-9625; Fax: 906-632-9625.
Catechesis/Religious Program—Tel: 906-632-9625, Ext. 13. Renee Theut, D.R.E. Students 130.
4—NATIVITY OF OUR LORD, Closed., For inquiries for parish records contact St. Joseph, Sault Sainte Marie.

SCHAFFER, DELTA CO., ST. ELIZABETH ANN SETON, , (Formerly Sacred Heart of Jesus. See Bark River)

SOUTH RANGE, HOUGHTON CO., HOLY FAMILY, Rev. John E. Martignon; Deacon Paul D. Lucchesi.
Mailing Address: Box 369, 49963. Tel: 906-482-0684; Fax: 906-482-6824.

SPALDING, MENOMINEE CO., ST. FRANCIS XAVIER, Merged, with St. Mary, Hermansville to form St. John Neumann, Hermansville. P.O. Box 125, Hermansville, MI 49847.

STEPHENSON, MENOMINEE CO., PRECIOUS BLOOD CHURCH, Rev. Mathew Perumpally (India).
Res.: S. 304 Bluff St., 49887. Tel: 906-753-2562; Fax: 906-753-2811.
Catechesis/Religious Program—Tel: 906-753-4771. Mary Oczus, D.R.E. Students 167.

TRENARY, ALGER CO., ST. RITA, Rev. Thomas J. Thekkel, M.S.T. (India).
Mailing Address: P.O. Box 207, 49891. Tel: 906-446-3350; Fax: 906-446-3523.

Catechesis/Religious Program—Tel: 906-439-5696. Jewell Hoy, D.R.E. Students 43.
Mission—St. Therese Autrain, Alger Co. Tel: 906-892-8189.

VULCAN, DICKINSON CO., ST. BARBARA, Rev. William P. Callari.
Mailing Address: P.O. Box 493, 49892. Tel: 906-563-9834; Fax: 906-563-7664.
School—Holy Spirit Central Grade School, Norway See Elementary Inter-Parochial Schools under Institutions Located in the Diocese.

WAKEFIELD, GOGEBIC CO., IMMACULATE CONCEPTION OF THE BLESSED VIRGIN MARY, Rev. Chacko D. Kakaniyil (India).
Res.: 407 Ascherman St., 49968. Tel: 906-224-7851; Fax: 906-224-9118.
Mission—St. Catherine Marenisco, Gogebic Co. Tel: 906-787-2258. In Res., Rev. Raymond F. Moncher (Retired).

WATERSMEET, GOGEBIC CO., IMMACULATE CONCEPTION, Rev. George Kallarackal Joseph, M.C.B.S. (India).
Mailing Address: E23933 D Ave., P.O. Box 398, 49969. Tel: 906-358-4607. In Res., Rev. Aloysius J. Hasenberg (Retired).
Catechesis/Religious Program—Tel: 906-472-2664. Jerry Berezik, D.R.E. Students 40.

WELLS, DELTA CO., ST. ANTHONY, Rev. Martin T. Schaefer (WIN).
Mailing Address: 6576 N. Third St., 49894. Tel: 906-786-5002; Fax: 906-786-8992.
School—Holy Name Central Grade School, Escanaba See Elementary Inter-Parochial Schools under Institutions Located in the Diocese.
Catechesis/Religious Program—Dorothy Boden, D.R.E. Students 106.

WHITE PINE, ONTONAGON CO., ST. JUDE, Rev. Thomas Ettolil (India).
Mailing Address: 8 Cedar St., P.O. Box 427, 49971. Tel: 906-885-5763; Fax: 906-885-5332.
Mission—St. Ann Bergland, Ontonagon Co.

ZEBA, BARAGA CO., THE MOST HOLY NAME OF JESUS-BLESSED KATERI TEKAKWITHA, , (See Assinins)

Indian Missions

ASSININS, BARAGA CO., THE MOST HOLY NAME OF JESUS-BLESSED KATERI TEKAKWITHA, , Indian Mission Revs. James C. Ziminski; Gregory R. Heikkala, Co-Pastor.
Res.: 318 Lyons St., Baraga, 49908.

BAY MILLS, CHIPPEWA CO., BLESSED KATERI TEKAKWITHA, Rev. Peter H. Fosu (Ghana).
Mailing Address: P.O. Box 429,, Brimley, 49715.

SAULT SAINTE MARIE, CHIPPEWA CO., ST. ISAAC JOGUES, Rev. John S. Hascall, O.F.M.Cap.
1529 Marquette Ave., 49783.

SUGAR ISLAND, CHIPPEWA CO., SACRED HEART, , Indian Missionaries, East. Rev. Theodore J. Brodeur.
377 Maple St., Sault Sainte Marie, 49783.

WATERSMEET, GOGEBIC CO., LAC VIEUX DESERT RESERVATION, Rev. George Kallarackal Joseph, M.C.B.S. (India).
Mailing Address: P.O. Box 398, 49969.

ZEBA, BARAGA CO., THE MOST HOLY NAME OF JESUS-BLESSED KATERI TEKAKWITHA, , (See Assinins)

Chaplains of Public Institutions

MARQUETTE. *Marquette General Hospital*, Tel: 906-228-9440. Rev. Jeff G. Johnson.

On Duty Outside the Diocese:
Revs.—
Longbucco, John L., 1001-761 St., Tank Battalion Ave., Fort Hood, TX 76541-5017.
Murphy, Patrick E., 5500 Armstrong Rd. (118c), Battle Creek, 49016. Dept. of Veterans Affairs Medical Center
Oniskiewicz, Mieczyslaw T., St. Mary Parish, P.O. Box 68, Kinde, 48455-0068.
Wantland, Thomas, 21505 August Ave., No. 4, Port Charlotte, FL 33952.

Special Assignment:
Revs.—
Sample, Alexander K., Chancellor & Dir., Dept. of Ministry Personnel Svc.
Schmied, Thomas, O.F.M.Cap., P.O. Box 368, Ahmeek, 49901.

Leave of Absence:
Rev.—
Erno, Shaun A.

Retired:
Rev. Msgr.—
LaViolette, Matt H., P.O. Box 1068, Escanaba, 49829.
Revs.—
Andary, Thomas M., 18765 Caminito Cantilena, Apt. 101, San Diego, CA 92128.
Bracket, Louis P., 307 Eddy St., Wakefield, 49968.
Brewer, Gervase, P.O. Box 158, 49855.
Gauthier, Lawrence T., P.O. Box 550, 49855.
Goerner, Basil S., 29 High Bluff Villa 2005, Hilton Head, SC 29926.
Gondek, Joseph A., Iron County Medicare Facility, 1523 Hwy US2, Crystal Falls, 49920.
Harris, David T., P.O. Box 88, Rockland, 49960.
Hasenberg, Aloysius J., E23933 "D" Ave., P.O. Box 398, Watersmeet, 49969.
Hollenbach, Frank A., 9255 E. Pueblo, Mesa, AZ 85208.
Kichak, Joseph A., Keen Agers, 303 Brotherton St., Wakefield, 49968.
Landreville, Norbert B., 131 Mackinac Hts. Dr., St. Ignace, 49781.
Manderfield, R.P. Geraldo, Apartado 2810, Managua, Nicaragua.
Mayotte, Allan J., 405 'C' St., Wakefield, 49968.
McArdle, John F., 4305 Sixth St., Menominee, 49858.
Menapace, James L., 703 N. Corbridge Rd., Gulliver, 49840.
Minelli, Peter A., 117 Savage, Gwinn, 49841.
Moncher, Raymond F., P.O. Box 175, Marenisco, 49947.
Neurohr, Gilbert N., Bishop Noa Home, 2916 Third Ave., S., Escanaba, 49829.
Nomellini, Paul J., HC2 Box 978-I, Florence, WI 54121.
Olivier, John H., S.S., St. Charles Villa, 603 Maiden Choice Ln., Baltimore, MD 21228.
Parrotta, Arthur J., St. Francis Hospital, 3401 Ludington St., Escanaba, 49829.
Poisson, Thomas L., P.O. Box 37, L'Anse, 49946.
Polakowski, Joseph, 1869 E. Shore Dr., Green Bay, 54302.
Ryan, John, 1600 N. 19th St., Escanaba, 49829.
Sartorelli, Otto, 113 Lundin St., Iron River, 49935.
Schiska, Paul A., 1490 15.5 Rd., Bark River, 49807.
Shiroda, Donald L., 807 W. 28th Ave., Apt. 4B, Sault Sainte Marie, 49783.
Smith, Neil B., Box 451, Ramsay, 49959.
Strelick, Charles J., 4420 Devonshire Ave., Spring Hill, FL 34609.
Valerio, Raymond A., 831 E. Grant, Iron Mountain, 49801.
Vanitvelt, Milton H., 1524 Seventh St., Menominee, 49858.
Wenzel, Edward J., Rte. 1, Box 491, Baraga, 49908.

Permanent Deacons:
Adler, David, St. Louis the King, Marquette
Anderson, James, Sacred Heart of Jesus, Munising
Andrzejewski, Ronald P., St. Stanislaus Kostka, Goetzville; Our Lady of Snows Mission, Hessel: Sacred Heart, DeTour; St. Florence Mission, Drummond Island
Beckley, Vincent W., Resurrection, Menominee
Bygrave, Roger A., St. Joseph, Rudyard & St. Mary Mission, Trout Lake
Chaltry, Roland, Holy Redeemer, Menominee
Christy, Donald R., St. Mary-St. Joseph, Iron Mountain
Cross, Robert M., St. Francis de Sales, Manistique (Incardinated in Diocese of Sioux Falls, South Dakota)
Giesen, Donald, (Retired), St. Barbara, Vulcan
Green, William, St. Charles Borromeo, Rapid River
Groleau, Rodney R., Garden Area Churches, Garden
Hamen, Robert, Our Lady of Peace, Ironwood
Hemes, Dr. Bill D., St. Joseph & St. Patrick, Escanaba
Hermann, Dean, Traverse City
Jamieson, Scott A., St. Peter Cathedral, Marquette
Kostka, Robert J., St. Cecilia, Caspian; St. Agnes, Iron River
Kut, Bernard, Guardian Angels, Crystal Falls (Incardinated in Archdiocese of Chicago, IL)
LaCosse, Robert, Chancery Office and St. Michael, Marquette (Incardinated in Archdiocese of Chicago, IL)
LaPlante, Joseph A., St. Francis Xavier, Brimley & Mission of Blessed Kateri Tekakwitha, Bay Mills (Incardinated in Diocese of Rockford, IL)
LeBeau, Michael, St. Anne, Escanaba
LeMire, Ronald J., Sr., St. Mary, Norway
Lucchessi, Paul, Holy Family, South Range
Olmstead, Donald F., St. Ignatius Loyola, St. Ignace
Piche, William J., St. Joseph, Sault Ste. Marie
Sablack, Gilbert G., Engadine Cathloic Missions & St. Francis de Sales, Manistique
Thoren, Donald W., St. Peter Cathedral, Marquette
Vailliencourt, Lewis, St. Anne, Escanaba
Wadman, Karl L., St. Mary, Rockland
Wahmhoff, Robert L., St. Ann, Baraga

INSTITUTIONS LOCATED IN THE DIOCESE

[A] ELEMENTARY INTERPAROCHIAL SCHOOLS

MARQUETTE. *Fr. Marquette Catholic Central Schools System*, 500 S. Fourth St., 49855. Tel: 906-225-1129; Fax: 906-225-1987. Judy Hanson, C.A.O. Serving the following parishes: St. Peter's Cathedral; St. Louis; St. Michael; St. Christopher. Lay Teachers 21; Students 352.

ESCANABA. *Holy Name Central Grade School*, 409 S. 22nd St., 49829. Tel: 906-786-7550; Fax: 906-786-7582. Email: holynameschool@hotmail.com. Barbara Mead, Prin. Lay Teachers 19; Students 320.

IRON MOUNTAIN. *Dickinson Area Catholic School System*, 406 W. B St., 49801. Tel: 906-774-2277; Fax: 906-774-8704. Patricia Covitz, Prin. Lay Teachers 10; Students 156.

MENOMINEE. *Menominee Catholic Central*, 1406 10th Ave., 49858. Tel: 906-863-3190; Fax: 906-863-3990. Email: ewmcc@marinet. Eric Weydt, Prin. Lay Teachers 13; Students 176.

NORWAY. *Holy Spirit Central School*, 201 Saginaw St., 49870. Tel: 906-563-8817; Fax: 906-563-8854. Barbara L. Heiser, Prin. Lay Teachers 12; Students 72.

[B] ENDOWMENT FUNDS

MARQUETTE. *Endowment Foundation of the Diocese of Marquette*, 444 S. Fourth St., P.O. Box 550, 49855. Tel: 906-227-9138; Fax: 906-225-0437. Email: tgadzins@dioceseofmarquette.org. Web: dioceseofmarquette.org. Terri Gadzinski, Devel. Dir.
St. John's Memorial Scholarship Committee, 1300 Kimber, 49855. Tel: 906-225-1936. Joylyn Wahla, Pres.
Marquette Area Catholic Education Fund, P.O. Box 550, 49855. Tel: 906-225-1141.

BESSEMER. *St. Sebastian School Endowment Fund*, 210 E. Iron St., 49911. Tel: 906-667-0952; Fax: 906-667-0952. Rev. James M. Roetzer.

ESCANABA. *Holy Name Central Endowment Fund*, 409 S. 22nd St., 49829. Tel: 906-786-7550.
Holy Name Scholarship Foundation, 409 S. 22nd St., 49829. Tel: 906-786-7550.

IRON MOUNTAIN. *Dickinson Area Catholic School Education Foundation*, 406 W. B St., 49801. Tel: 906-774-2277; Fax: 906-774-8704.

IRONWOOD. *Our Lady of Peace School Educational Fund*, 106 S. Marquette St., 49938. Tel: 906-932-3200; Fax: 906-932-1019. Rev. Darryl J. Pepin.

L'ANSE. *Sacred Heart School Endowment Fund*, 16 S. 6th St., 49946. Tel: 906-524-6424; Fax: 906-524-6422. Web: www.sacredheartlanse.com. Rev. Gregory Heikkala.

MANISTIQUE. *St. Francis de Sales Education Foundation, Inc.*, 330 Oak St., 49854. Tel: 906-341-5355; Fax: 906-341-3984.

MENOMINEE. *Menominee Catholic Education Fund*, 1406 Tenth Ave., 49858-2604. Tel: 906-863-2723; Fax: 906-341-3984. Kim M. Duffrin, Office Mgr.

NEGAUNEE. *Negaunee St. Paul Endowment Fund*, 202 W. Case St., 49866. Tel: 906-475-9969. Rev. John Shiverski.

NORWAY. *Holy Spirit Central School Educational Fund*, 201 Saginaw, 49870. Tel: 906-563-8817; Fax: 908-563-8854.

SAULT SAINTE MARIE. *Holy Family School Endowment Fund, Inc.*, 377 Maple St., 49783. Tel: 906-632-3381; Fax: 906-632-0741.

[C] GENERAL HOSPITALS

ESCANABA. *O.S.F. St. Francis Hospital* O.S.F. Healthcare System. , 3401 Ludington, 49829. Tel: 906-786-3311; Fax: 906-786-4004. Rev. Arthur J. Parrotta, Chap. (Retired); Mr. Roger Burgess, Admin. Sisters 2; Patients Assisted Annually 87,300; Bed Capacity 110.

[D] HOMES FOR THE AGED

ESCANABA. *Bishop Noa Home for Senior Citizens*, 2900 3rd Ave. S., 49829. Tel: 906-786-5810; Fax: 906-786-5372. Sisters of St. Paul de Chartres Sisters 6; Residents 123. In Res. Rev. Gilbert N. Neurohr, Chap. (Retired).

[E] CONVENTS AND RESIDENCES OF SISTERS

MARQUETTE. *Provincialate of the Sisters of St. Paul de*

Chartres, 1300 County Rd. 492, 49855. Tel: 906-226-3932; Fax: 906-226-8734. Sr. Gloria Schultz, Dist. Supr. Sisters 17.

IRON MOUNTAIN. *Monastery of the Holy Cross*, N4028 Hwy. U.S. 2, P.O. Box 397, 49801. Tel: 906-774-0561. Sr. Maria of Jesus, O.C.D., Prioress; Rev. Leonard Cornelius, O.F.M., Chap. Discalced Carmelite Nuns Cloistered Nuns: Professed 14; Extern Professed Sisters 2; Temporary Professed Sister 1; Novices 1.

[F] RETREAT HOUSES

GARDEN. *Marygrove Retreat Center*, P.O. Box 38, 49835. Tel: 906-644-2771; Fax: 908-644-2463. Email: mgc@up.net. Web: www.marygrove.org. Rev. Msgr. Timothy H. Desrochers, Dir. Retreats and workshops for priests, religious and laity.

[G] NEWMAN CLUBS

MARQUETTE. *Catholic Campus Ministry-Northern Michigan University* 1200 Hebard Ct , 49855. Tel: 906-228-3302; Fax: 906-228-9938. Email: ccm@nmu.edu. Web: www.dioceseofmarquette.org/nmu; www.ccmnmu.org/. Rev. Antony Kadavil, Chap.; B. Kim Dolan, Dir.

HOUGHTON. *St. Albert the Great, University Parish* 411 MacInnes Dr., 49931. Tel: 906-482-5530; Fax: 906-482-4828. Email: stalbert@chartermi.net. Web: www.sos.mtu.edu/stalbert. Rev. Larry P. VanDamme, Dir.

SAULT SAINTE MARIE. *Lake Superior State University, Newman Center* 517 W. Easterday, 49783.

[H] MISCELLANEOUS

MARQUETTE. *St. Vincent De Paul Society*, 2119 Presque Isle Ave., 49855. Tel: 906-226-2311; Fax: 906-226-4599. Email: stvin@portup.com.

MENOMINEE. *Missionaries of the Liturgy*, 302 E. Margaret St., Iron Mountain, 49801. Tel: 906-779-0599 Email: sismaria@sault.com. Web: www.missionariesoftheliturgy.com. Sr. Maria Volp, Supr.

RELIGIOUS INSTITUTES OF MEN REPRESENTED IN THE DIOCESE

For further details refer to the corresponding bracketed number in the Religious Institutes of Men or Women section.

[0470]—*The Capuchin Friars* (Detroit, MI)—O.F.M.Cap.

[0520]—*Franciscan Friars* (Cincinnati, OH)—O.F.M.

RELIGIOUS INSTITUTES OF WOMEN REPRESENTED IN THE DIOCESE

[3710]—*Congregation of the Sisters of Saint Agnes*—C.S.A.

[0420]—*Discalced Carmelite Nuns*—O.C.D.

[1070-09]—*Dominican Sisters*—O.P.

[1070-13]—*Dominican Sisters*—O.P.

[]—*Franciscan Clarist Congregation* (India)—F.C.C.

[1630]—*Franciscan Sisters of Christian Charity*—O.S.F.

[2380]—*Institute of the Blessed Virgin Mary (Sisters of Loretto)*—I.B.V.M.

[2970]—*School Sisters of Notre Dame*—S.S.N.D.

[3840]—*Sisters of St. Joseph of Carondelet*—C.S.J.

[3980]—*Sisters of St. Paul of Chartres*—S.P.C.

[2180]—*Sisters of the Immaculate Heart of Mary*—I.H.M.

[3260]—*Sisters of the Precious Blood*—C.PP.S.

[1770]—*Sisters of the Third Order of St. Francis* (Peoria, Illinois)—O.S.F.

DIOCESAN CEMETERIES

MARQUETTE. *Holy Cross*

ESCANABA. *Holy Cross*

NECROLOGY

† Spelgatti, Rev. Msgr. David P., (Retired)—Died Jan. 22, 2003

† Beyer, Emil J., (Retired)—Died Aug. 10, 2003

Diocese of Memphis

(Memphitana in Tennesia)

Most Reverend

J. TERRY STEIB, S.V.D., D.D.

Bishop of Memphis; ordained January 6, 1967; appointed Titular Bishop of Fallaba and Auxiliary Bishop of St. Louis December 6, 1983; consecrated February 10, 1984; appointed Bishop of Memphis March 23, 1993; installed May 5, 1993

Catholic Center: P.O. Box 341669, Memphis, TN 38184-1669. Tel: 901-373-1200; Fax: 901-373-1269.

Web: www.cdom.org

ESTABLISHED JANUARY 6, 1971.

Square Miles 10,682.

Comprises the Counties of Benton, Carroll, Chester, Crockett, Decatur, Dyer, Fayette, Gibson, Hardeman, Hardin, Haywood, Henderson, Henry, Lake, Lauderdale, McNairy, Madison, Obion, Shelby, Tipton and Weakley in the State of Tennessee.

Legal Title: For legal titles of parishes and diocesan institutions, consult the Chancery Office.

STATISTICAL OVERVIEW

Personnel	
Bishop	1
Priests: Diocesan Active in Diocese	48
Priests: Diocesan Active Outside Diocese	2
Priests: Retired, Sick or Absent	14
Number of Diocesan Priests	64
Religious Priests in Diocese	12
Total Priests in Diocese	76
Extern Priests in Diocese	7
Permanent Deacons in Diocese	51
Total Brothers	42
Total Sisters	86
Parishes	
Parishes	42
With Resident Pastor:	
Resident Diocesan Priests	35
Resident Religious Priests	5
Without Resident Pastor:	
Administered by Deacons	2
Missions	5
Pastoral Centers	1
Professional Ministry Personnel:	
Sisters	13
Lay Ministers	42
Welfare	
Homes for the Aged	2
Total Assisted	300
Specialized Homes	3
Total Assisted	400
Special Centers for Social Services	1
Total Assisted	18,000
Educational	
Diocesan Students in Other Seminaries	9
Total Seminarians	9
Colleges and Universities	1
Total Students	2,030
High Schools, Diocesan and Parish	4
Total Students	1,097
High Schools, Private	2
Total Students	1,191
Elementary Schools, Diocesan and Parish	19
Total Students	4,646
Elementary Schools, Private	2
Total Students	358
Non-residential Schools for the Disabled	3
Total Students	176
Catechesis/Religious Education:	
High School Students	850
Elementary Students	3,753
Total Students under Catholic Instruction	14,110
Teachers in the Diocese:	
Priests	2
Brothers	9
Sisters	21
Lay Teachers	575
Vital Statistics	
Receptions into the Church:	
Infant Baptism Totals	950
Adult Baptism Totals	474
Received into Full Communion	283
First Communions	1,273
Confirmations	1,083
Marriages:	
Catholic	175
Interfaith	154
Total Marriages	329
Deaths	426
Total Catholic Population	63,820
Total Population	1,455,808

Former Bishops—Most Revs. CARROLL T. DOZIER, D.D. (Retired), ord. March 19, 1937; appt. Nov. 17, 1970; consecrated Jan. 6, 1971; retired July 27, 1982; died Dec. 7, 1985; J. FRANCIS STAFFORD, D.D., ord. Dec. 15, 1957; consecrated Bishop Feb. 29, 1976; appt. Nov. 16, 1982; appt. to Archdiocese of Denver, June 3, 1986; DANIEL M. BUECHLEIN, O.S.B., D.D., ord. May 3, 1964; appt. Jan. 20, 1987; appt. to Archdiocese of Indianapolis, July 14, 1992.

Vicar General and Moderator of the Curia—Rev. Msgr. PETER P. BUCHIGNANI, V.G., St. Francis of Assisi, 8151 Chimney Rock, Cordova, 38018. Tel: 901-756-1213.

Catholic Center Offices—Mailing Address, P.O. Box 341669, Memphis, 38184-1669. Tel: 901-373-1200; Fax: 901-373-1269. *5825 Shelby Oaks Dr., Memphis, 38134.* Office Hours: Mon.-Fri. 7:45-4:45

Chancery

Chancellor and Executive Director of the Catholic Center—Deacon CHARLES R. WELLS, P.O. Box 341669, Memphis, 38184-1669. Tel: 901-373-1200.

Notaries—MARIANNA RAMPERSAD; M. TERESA WILTCHER.

Senior Director of Technology—Mr. DAVID MASTERSON.

Catholic Public Policy Commission of Tennessee—P.O. Box 341669, Memphis, 38184-1669.

Office of Ecumenism—Rev. VALENTINE N. HANDWERKER, Dir., 6529 Stage Rd., Memphis, 38134. Tel: 901-373-6011.

Clergy Personnel Board—Revs. JOSEPH PAOLOZZI; MICHAEL L. STEWART; Rev. Msgr. PETER BUCHIGNANI.

Continuing Education for the Clergy—Rev. BRYAN P. TIMBY, Dir., 4851 Park Ave., Memphis, 38117. Tel: 901-767-6949.

Victim Assistance Coordinator—Mr. RON AMBUEHL. Tel: 901-276-9002.

Presbyteral Council and College of Consultors—Revs. BRYAN TIMBY, Vice Chm. Tel: 901-767-6949; CHARLES A. BAUER; Rev. Msgr. PETER P. BUCHIGNANI, V.G.; Revs. VICTOR P. CIARAMITARO; J. EDWIN CREARY; RICHARD M. GANTERT; VALENTINE N. HANDWERKER; JIM J. MARTELL; JOHN B. MCARTHUR; JAMES K. MCCARVER; ROBERT D. PONTICELLO; J. KEITH STEWART; JIM WIESNER, C.S.P.

Permanent Deacons Community—Deacon RICHARD GRIFFITH, 5825 Shelby Oaks Dr., Memphis, 38134. Tel: 901-373-1216.

Dean of the Jackson Deanery—Rev. VICTOR CIARAMITARO, Holy Cross Church, 1210 E. Wood St., Paris, 38242. Tel: 901-642-4681.

Director of Seminarians—Rev. J. KEITH STEWART.

Director of Vocations—Rev. J. KEITH STEWART.

Tribunal

Judicial Vicar—Rev. JOSEPH L. TAGG III.

Adjutant Judicial Vicar—Rev. Msgr. PETER P. BUCHIGNANI, V.G.

Defender of the Bond—Rev. ROBERT D. PONTICELLO.

Promoter of Justice—Rev. ROBERT D. PONTICELLO.

Auditor—Rev. GABRIEL DIFEDERICO.

Notary—Mrs. TERESA WILTCHER, Ecclesiastical Notary.

Department of Financial Administration

Secretary—CRAIG HOFER, P.O. Box 341669, Memphis, 38184-1669. Tel: 901-373-1200.

Calvary Cemeteries and All Saints Cemetery—RICHARD B. SMITH, Supt., 1663 Elvis Presley Blvd., Memphis, 38106. Tel: 901-948-1529.

Controller—EDDIE WALDRUP.

Data Processing—BETTY FURR.

Employee Benefits—MAY LOPEZ.

Facilities and Risk Management—Deacon WILLIAM F. HERBERS.

Maintenance—ROBERT PELT.

Department of Education

Secretary—Dr. MARY MCDONALD, P.O. Box 341669, Memphis, 38184-1669. Tel: 901-373-1200.

Office of Catechetical Ministry—Mr. MARLON DELATORRE, Dir.

Office of Catholic Schools—Dr. MARY MCDONALD, Supt.; JANET M. DONATO, Assoc. Supt.; Mrs. SALLY HERMSDORFER, Asst. Supt.; Sr. MARIE DEMONTFORT, Asst. Supt.; SONDRA MORRIS, Dir. Diocesan Athletics; JOHN HENRY, Diocesan Schools Finance Coord.; DEBRA SLAWSON, Dir. Food Service; CATHY BIRD, Dir. Inclusion & Special Needs; SHARON MASTERSON, Media Liaison.

Department Of Associated Catholic Charities

Secretary—EILEEN HIVNER, Exec. Dir., 1325 Jefferson Ave., P.O. Box 41705, Memphis, 38174-1705. Tel: 901-722-4777.

Catholic Charities, Inc.—VACANT, Dir.; CHANDRA TUGGLE, Communication Dir.; JAMES ABERNATHY, Finance Dir.

Community Outreach Services—JOSEPH PFEIFFER, Dir.; ERICA THOMAS, Parish Liaison.

Parish Social Ministry—VACANT.

Genesis House—CLIFTON HARRIS, Dir., Transitional shelter for homeless.

Refugee Resettlement Unit—CAROLYN TISDALE, Dir.

Day Care Services—VIRGINIA DAVENPORT, Dir.

St. Ann-Bartlett Extended Care Program—KAREN OTTS, Site Supvr.

St. Benedict at Auburndale Extended Care—PAMELA O'BRYAN, Site Supvr.

St. Louis Extended Care—LORI TUCKER, Site Supvr.

St. Peter Home Day Care Center—ANNE WOOD, Dir.

St. Michael Extended Care—Mrs. AMY DE LA TORRES, Dir.
Extended Care Programs— (After-School Care) VACANT.
Diocese of Memphis Housing Corporation—Mr. DAVID FIELD, Exec. Dir.
St. Peter Villa Nursing Home—KAE WERKHOVEN, Admin.
St. Peter Home for Children—Sr. BETTY FRACCHIA, Admin.
Mid South Caring, Inc.—EILEEN HIVNER, 1325 Jefferson Ave., P.O. Box 41705, Memphis, 38174-1705.

Department for Worship and Spiritual Life

Secretary—Rev. R. BRUCE CINQUEGRANI, P.O. Box 341669, Memphis, 38184-1669. Tel: 901-373-1200.
Office of Rites and Sacraments—Mrs. JUDY GRAY, Dir.
Office of Liturgical Music—Sr. MAUREEN GRINER, O.S.U., Dir.
Office of Spiritual Formation—Sr. EILEEN FUCITO, C.P., Dir.
Cursillo Movement—Spiritual Advisors: Rev. R. BRUCE CINQUEGRANI; Sr. EILEEN FUCITO, C.P.
Liturgical Ministry Institute—Sr. MAUREEN GRINER, O.S.U., Dir.
Charismatic Renewal—Rev. RICHARD MICKEY, Diocesan Liaison.

Department for Development and Communications

Secretary—VACANT, P.O. Box 341669, Memphis, 38184-1669. Tel: 901-373-1200.
Planned Giving and Major Donors—DAVID CREMERIUS, Dir.
Communications—JOHN E. MORRIS, Dir.; PAM FLYNN, Assoc. Dir.
Newspaper—*5825 Shelby Oaks Dr., Memphis, 38134. "West Tennessee Catholic"*

Department of Evangelization and Pastoral Services

Secretary—Deacon RICHARD GRIFFITH, P.O. Box 341669, Memphis, 38184-1669. Tel: 901-373-1200.
Resource Library—MARY BETH BOLTON
Professional Ministry Enrichment Programs—Deacon RICHARD GRIFFITH.
Parish Pastoral Councils—Deacon RICHARD GRIFFITH.
Prison Ministries—Deacons RICHARD GRIFFITH. Tel: 901-373-1245; BILL DAVIS, Chair. Tel: 901-373-1299.
Office of Family Ministries—PATRICIA PERRY, Dir.
Committee for Separated, Divorced, Widowed—PAT PERRY.
Marriage Encounter—DAVID HUNT; SHEILA HUNT.
Retrouvaille—Coordinators: JIM CISSELL; ANN CISSELL.
Natural Family Training Center—MARY PAT VAN EPPS, Dir. Tel: 901-373-1200.
Programs for the Engaged—PAT PERRY
Project Rachel/Rachel's Vineyard—Coordinators: LORI SOLAAS; MARY CRONE.

Office of Youth and Young Adult Ministries—CATHERINE MENSI, Dir.
Search Program—Rev. MICHAEL WERKHOVEN.
Scouting—Rev. WAYNE ARNOLD.
Campus Ministry—Memphis: Deacon RICHARD GRIFFITH, Dir.; Rev. ARTHUR KIRWIN, Campus Minister. Martin: Rev. JOSEPH PAOLOZZI, Dir. Christian Brothers University: Sr. DOLORES MONTINI, C.S.P., Dir.
Office of Multicultural & African American Catholic Ministries—Rev. ANTHONY CLARK, S.V.D., Dir.
Office of Hispanic Ministry—Rev. ANTHONY CLARK, S.V.D.
Office of Community Health Ministries—ALMA ABUELOUF, Dir. Tel: 901-373-1200.
Comunidad Hispana Catolica de Memphis—Rev. RICHARD CORTESE, Spiritual Advisor.
Council for African American Catholic Ministry—Deacon ROBERT ATKINS, Chm.
Native American Ministry—RUTH ALLEN, Coord.
Polish Catholic Ministries—Mrs. BARBARA WALKOWC. Tel: 901-754-1649.
Vietnamese Community—Rev. JOSEPH DAO VU, S.V.D. Tel: 901-726-1891; Sr. MARY PHUC, O.P., Sacred Heart.
Sudanese Community—Mr. STEPHEN BIEL. Tel: 901-454-0492.
Filipino Catholic Ministry—Dr. FRED DONATO.
Korean Catholic Ministry—Rev. BENEDICT KIM, S.V.D. Tel: 901-754-1204. Coordinators: Deacon JOHN KANG; Mrs. JOHN KANG.

CLERGY, PARISHES, MISSIONS AND PAROCHIAL SCHOOLS

CITY OF MEMPHIS
(SHELBY COUNTY)

1—CATHEDRAL OF THE IMMACULATE CONCEPTION (1921), Revs. Valentine N. Handwerker, Rector; J. Keith Stewart; Deacons Dick Powelson; Frank Williams.
Offices: 1695 Central Ave., 38104. Tel: 901-725-2700; Fax: 901-725-2709.
School—1669 Central Ave., 38104. Tel: 901-725-2710; Fax: 901-725-2715. Gail Fox, Prin. Priests 2; Lay Teachers 20; Students 256.
High School— See separate category.
Catechesis/Religious Program—Tel: 901-314-5329. Eric Thomas, D.R.E. Students 63.

2—ST. ANN (Bartlett) (1950), Revs. R. Bruce Cinquegrani; Joseph Thinh Duc Nguyen; Joel P. Schultz; Deacons Nick Bonaiuto; Chip Jones.
Res.: 6529 Stage Rd., Bartlett, 38134. Tel: 901-373-6011; Fax: 901-373-9030.
School—Tel: 901-386-3328; Fax: 901-386-1030. Sisters 1; Lay Teachers 42; Students 655.

3—ST. ANNE'S (1933), Rev. James L. Pugh; Deacons Jack Chitwood; Charles O'Bryant.
Res.: 706 S. Highland St., 38111. Tel: 901-323-3817; Fax: 901-323-3151.
School—670 S. Highland St., 38111. Tel: 901-323-1344; Fax: 901-458-5215. Lay Teachers 16; Students 164.
Catechesis/Religious Program—Tel: 901-382-5223. Mark McKnett, D.R.E. Students 10.

4—ST. AUGUSTINE (1937), (African American), Rev. John J. Geaney, C.S.P.; Deacons Robert Atkins; Andrew Terry.
Church: 1169 Kerr Ave., 38106. Tel: 901-774-2297; Fax: 901-774-3067.
Catechesis/Religious Program—Tel: 901-774-2298. Deacon Robert Atkins, D.R.E. Students 60.

5—BLESSED SACRAMENT (1912), Rev. Michael A. Morgera.
Church: 2564 Hale Ave., 38112. Tel: 901-452-1543; Fax: 901-452-1592.

6—ST. BRIGID (1992), Rev. Michael L. Stewart.
Church: 7801 Lowrance Rd., 38125-2825. Tel: 901-758-0128; Fax: 901-758-8862.
Res.: 4200 Thunderstone Cir. W., 38125-3108. Tel: 901-759-9628.
Catechesis/Religious Program—Barbara Bailey, D.R.E. Students 60.

7—CHURCH OF THE ASCENSION (1974), Rev. Richard L. Mickey; Deacons John T. Oates; Harvey Stewart.
Res.: 3680 Ramill Rd., 38128. Tel: 901-372-1364; Fax: 901-372-9411.
Catechesis/Religious Program—Tel: 901-372-1364, Ext. 103. Shelly Beer, D.R.E.; Amparo Parker, D.R.E. Students 100.

8—CHURCH OF THE NATIVITY (1979), Rev. Robert D. Ponticello; Deacon Franklin O. Larker.
Res.: 5955 St. Elmo, Barlett, 38135. Tel: 901-382-2504; Fax: 901-382-3644.
Catechesis/Religious Program—Peter Voss, D.R.E. Students 109.

9—CHURCH OF THE RESURRECTION (1973), Rev. Ernie DeBlasio.
Res.: 5475 Newberry, 38115-3629. Tel: 901-794-8970; Fax: 901-794-8806.
Catechesis/Religious Program—Tel: 901-794-8971. Jacky Becker, D.R.E. Students 144.

10—ST. FRANCIS OF ASSISI (1985), Rev. Msgr. Peter P. Buchignani, V.G.; Revs. Kevin W. Braswata; Charles A. Bauer; Deacons Max Saller; Chuck Lightcap; Mick Hovanec.
Res.: 8217 Chimneyrock Blvd., Cordova, 38016. Tel: 901-753-1494; Fax: 901-755-2168.
Church: 8151 Chimneyrock Blvd., Cordova, 38016. Tel: 901 756-1213.
Catechesis/Religious Program—Mrs. Terry Harvey, D.R.E. Students 481.

11—HOLY NAMES OF JESUS AND MARY (1939), Rev. Joseph Dao Vu, S.V.D.; Deacon Charles R. Wells, Pastoral Admin.
Res.: 697 Keel Ave., 38107-2599. Tel: 901-525-9870; Fax: 901 527-7436.
Catechesis/Religious Program—Tel: 901-526-5456. Students 77.

12—HOLY ROSARY (1955), Revs. Bryan P. Timby; Gabriel DiFederico; Deacons Kenneth McCarver; Fred Brunner; Rev. Msgr. Edward Odell Heymer (Retired).
Church, Res. & Office: 4851 Park Ave., 38117. Tel: 901-767-6949; Fax: 901-767-8504.
School—4841 Park Ave., 38117. Tel: 901-685-1231; Fax: 901-818-0335. Sisters 1; Students 465.

13—HOLY SPIRIT (1975), Revs. Albert E. Kirk; Alphonso Carew (Sierra Leone) (WDC); Deacons Ned Turner; Richard Griffith; Bill Nourse; Werner Rose.
Church: 2300 Hickory Crest, 38119. Tel 901-754-7146; Fax: 901-754-0102.
Catechesis/Religious Program—Tel: 901-754-7146, Ext. 104. Agnes Kovacs, D.R.E. Students 303.

14—INCARNATION (1978), Revs. William J. Parham; Wayne Arnold; Deacon Miles Merwin.
Office & Res.: 360 Bray Station Rd., Collierville, 38017. Tel: 901-853-7468; Fax: 901-854-0536.
School—(Grades PreK-6) Tel: 901-853-7804; Fax: 901-854-0536. Mrs. Karen Stimart, Pres.; Mrs. Trena Kilp, Sec.
Catechesis/Religious Program—Tel: 901-853-0135. Martha Drennan, D.R.E. Students 550.

15—ST. JAMES (1956), Rev. Patrick F. Heenan.
Res.: 4180 LeRoy, 38108. Tel: 901-767-8672; Fax: 901-767-8672.

16—ST. JOHN'S (1947), Rev. Joseph L. Tagg III.
Res.: 2742 Lamar Ave., 38114. Tel: 901-743-4551; Fax: 901-743-5944.

17—ST. JOSEPH'S (1878), Rev. Anthony P. Clark, S.V.D.
Res.: 3825 Neely Rd., 38109. Tel: 901-396-9996; Fax: 901-332-8691.

18—ST. LOUIS (1957), Revs. John B. McArthur; Richard Cortese; John C. Pecoraro; Mathew Joseph; Deacon Ralph Donati.
Office:—203 S. White Station Rd., 38117. Tel: 901-682-6606; Fax: 901-680-0571.
School—5192 Shady Grove Rd., 38117. Tel: 901-328-9798. Lay Teachers 27; Aides 3; Students 509.
Catechesis/Religious Program—Libby Pretti, D.R.E. Students 140.

19—ST. MARY'S (1860), Rev. Eric Peterson.
Church and Office: 155 Market St., 38105. Tel: 901-522-9420; Fax: 901-522-8314.

20—ST. MICHAEL'S (1951), Revs. John V. Atkinson; Paul Wangaih; Deacon Joseph Mensi.
Office—3848 Forrest Ave., 38122. Tel: 901-323-0896; 901-324-6411; Fax: 901-323-3557.
Res.: 3867 Summer Ave., 38122. Tel: 901-454-1349; 901-452-6036.
School—3880 Forrest Ave., 38122. Tel: 901-323-2162; Fax: 901-323-3557. Lay Teachers 15; Students 135.

21—OUR LADY OF PERPETUAL HELP (1952), Revs. J. Edwin Creary; Michael E. Werkhoven; Chima Nwamadi; Benedict Kim, S.V.D.; Deacons Paul Hamblen; William Herbers; John Kang. In Res., Rev. Edward C. Elliott (Retired).
Res.: 8151 Poplar, Germantown, 38138. Tel: 901-754-1204; Fax: 901-754-0969.
School—(Grades PreK-5), 8151 Poplar, Germantown, 38138. Tel: 901-753-1181, Ext. 200; Fax: 901-754-1475. Mrs. Patricia Wyckott, Prin.; Mrs. Toni Pollet, Sec.
Catechesis/Religious Program—Mrs. Gretchen K. Kirk, D.R.E. Students 562.

22—OUR LADY OF SORROWS (1926), Rev. James Martell; Deacon Donald A. Bennis.
Res.: 3700 Thomas St., 38127. Tel: 901-353-1530; Fax: 901-353-1052.
School—3690 Thomas St., 38127. Tel: 901-358-7431. Lay Teachers 11; Students 141.
Catechesis/Religious Program—Brenda Plessinger, D.R.E. Students 51.

23—ST. PATRICK'S (1866), Revs. James F. Wiesner, C.S.P.; Bruce Nieli, C.S.P.; John S. Geaney, C.S.P.; Deacons James Calicott; Eugene Champion; Eddie Ramsey.
Res.: 277 S. Fourth St., 38126. Tel: 901-527-2542; Fax: 901-525-1147.
School—Sr. Noelita McDermott, S.M.S.M., Prin. See separate listing under the Institutions Located in the Diocese.

24—ST. PAUL THE APOSTLE (1944), Revs. Richard M. Gantert; Ruben Villanueva.
Res.: 1425 E. Shelby Dr., 38116. Tel: 901-346-2380; Fax: 901-346-2385.
School—Tel: 901-346-0862; Fax: 901-396-2677. Sisters 3; Lay Teachers 25; Students 296.
Catechesis/Religious Program—Tel: 901-794-2441; Fax: 901-346-2385. Joseph Giannino, D.R.E. Students 64.

25—ST. PETER'S (1840), Revs. Edward E. Everitt, O.P.; Bertrand E. Ebben, O.P.; Arthur R. Kirwin, O.P.; Deacon Harold Yarbrough.
Res.: 190 Adams Ave., 38103. Tel: 901-527-8282; Fax: 901-526-6882.

26—SACRED HEART (1899), Revs. Joseph Dao Vu, S.V.D.; Frank Drzaic, S.V.D.; Miguel Ruiz, S.V.D.; Dominic Dung Nguyen, S.V.D.
Res.: 1324 Jefferson Ave., 38104. Tel: 901-726-1891; Fax: 901-726-9272.

27—ST. THERESE OF THE INFANT JESUS (1930), Rev. Richard D. Coy; Deacon James P. Schmall.
Res.: 1644 Jackson Ave., 38107. Tel: 901-276-1412; Fax: 901-274-4476.
Catechesis/Religious Program—Mrs. Claire Hyrka, D.R.E. Students 25.

28—ST. WILLIAM (1951), Rev. William F. Burke; Deacon John W. Hivner.
Res.: 4932 Easley Ave., Millington, 38053. Tel: 901-872-4099; 901-872-2279; Fax: 901-872-8920.
Catechesis/Religious Program—Maureen Kennedy,

O.P., D.R.E. Students 117.

OUTSIDE SHELBY COUNTY

BOLIVAR, HARDEMAN CO., ST. MARY (1950), Rev. Carl J. Hood.
Res.: 223 Mecklinberg Dr., 38008-1736. Tel: 731-658-4627; Fax: 731-658-4627.

BROWNSVILLE, HAYWOOD CO., ST. JOHN (1949), Rev. James K. McCarver.
Church: 901 N. Washington Ave., Box 872, 38012. Tel: 731-668-2596.

CAMDEN, BENTON CO., ST. MARY CHURCH (1981), Rev. Edward K. Fisher.
Res.: 220 W. Main St., 38320. Tel: 901-584-6459; Fax: 901-584-6446.
Mission—Holy Family Church 265 Cotham Dr., Huntingdon, Carroll Co. 38344. Tel: 901-986-2817.

COVINGTON, TIPTON CO., ST. ALPHONSUS (1952), Rev. William J. DeVries.
Res.: 1512 Evergreen, 38019. Tel: 901-476-0374; Fax: 901-476-9650.
Church: 1225 Hwy. 51 S., P.O. Box 430, 38019. Tel: 901-476-8140.
Mission—Ave Maria 664 S. Washington, Ripley, Lauderdale Co. 38063. Tel: 901-635-8800.

DYERSBURG, DYER CO., HOLY ANGELS (1940), Rev. Elbert Callis.
Res.: 535 Tucker St., P.O. Box 1929, 38025-1929. Tel: 731-287-8000; Fax: 731-287-7632.
Catechesis/Religious Program—Peggy Holley, D.R.E. (PreK-6). Tel: 731-696-5004; Tom Grueser, D.R.E. (7-12). Tel: 731-286-2584. Students 97.

HUMBOLDT, GIBSON & CROCKETT CO., SACRED HEART (1872), Rev. Robert W. Marshall Jr.
Res.: P.O. Box 660, 38343. Tel: 901-784-3904; Fax: 901-784-5048.
Mission— 9060 Telecom, Milan, Northern Gibson Co. 38358. Tel: 731-686-8686.

JACKSON, MADISON CO., ST. MARY'S (1867), Rev. James McCarver; Deacons Dr. William Lafont; James Cooley.
Res.: 1665 Hwy. 45 Byp., 38305. Tel: 731-668-2596; Fax: 731-668-9809.
School—Tel: 731-668-2525; Fax: 731-668-1164. Sisters 4; Lay Teachers 18; Students 381.
Catechesis/Religious Program—Kathleen Hicks, D.R.E. Students 199.
Mission—St. John Church P.O. Box 872, Brownsville, Haywood Co. 38012. Tel: 731-772-3514.

LEXINGTON, HENDERSON CO., ST. ANDREW (1981), Rev. J. David Graham.
Church: 895 N. Broad St., 38351. Tel: 731-968-6393; Fax: 731-967-1228.
Res.: 311 Elizabeth Circle, 38351. Tel: 731-968-7949; Fax: 731-967-1228.
Catechesis/Religious Program—Tel: 731-847-2054; Fax: 731-847-2054. Sr. Janet Delperdang, D.R.E. Students 50.
Mission—St. Regina 108 Skyline Ln., Parsons, Decatur Co. 38361. Tel: 731-847-2054.
Catechesis/Religious Program—Sr. Janet Delperdang, D.R.E. Students 34.

MARTIN, WEAKLEY CO., ST. JUDE'S (1968), Rev. Joseph L. Paolozzi.
Church and Mailing Address: 435 Moody St., 38237. Tel: 731-587-9777; Fax: 731-587-9778.
Res.: 110 Hannings Ln., 38237. Tel: 731-588-5675.

MILAN, GIBSON CO., ST. MATTHEW MISSION (1977), Rev. Robert W. Marshall Jr.
Mailing Address: *c/o Sacred Heart Church*, P.O. Box 660, Humboldt, 38343. Tel: 731-784-3904; Fax: 731-784-5048.

PARIS, HENRY CO., HOLY CROSS (1921), Rev. Victor P. Ciaramitaro; Deacons Michael Gore; Rodney Seyller.
Res.: 1210 E. Wood St., 38242. Tel: 731-642-4681; Fax: 731-644-9668.
Catechesis/Religious Program—Students 75.

SAVANNAH, HARDIN CO., ST. MARY'S (1948), Rev. Thomas Kirk.
Church & Res.: 835 Clifton, 38372. Tel: 731-925-4852; Fax: 731-925-9612.
Catechesis/Religious Program—Tel: 731-925-8139. Students 40.
Catechesis/Religious Program—Tel: 731-689-3971. Brenda Caperton, D.R.E. Students 9.
Mission—Our Lady of the Lake Pickwick, Hardin Co. Tel: 731-689-5301.

SELMER, MCNAIRY CO., ST. JUDE (1982), Rev. Carl J. Hood; Deacons Jim Gray; Jim Tucker.
Res.: P.O. Box 342, 38375. Tel: 731-645-4188; Fax: 731-645-4188.

SOMERVILLE, FAYETTE CO., ST. PHILIP THE APOSTLE (1981), Deacon Bill Davis, ., Pastoral Admin.
Church: 11710 Hwy. 64, 38068. Tel: 731-465-8685; Fax: 731-466-1645.

UNION CITY, OBION CO., IMMACULATE CONCEPTION (1891), Rev. Herman J. Lattus.
Res.: 1303 E. Reelfoot Ave., 38261. Tel: 731-885-0963; Fax: 731-885-9960.
Catechesis/Religious Program—Teresa Vallee, D.R.E.; Karen Buehlman, D.R.E. Students 65.

Chaplains of Public Institutions

MEMPHIS. *Federal Correctional Institute at Memphis.* Rev. Faustino Maramot, Chap.

On Duty Outside the Diocese:
Revs.—
Kelly, Edward, St. Louis University, St. Louis, MO.
Moore, Dan, S.S., St. Mary's Seminary and University, Baltimore, MD.
Nobile, Angelo

Military Chaplains:
Rev.—
Danner, James L., US. Pacific fleet-Code NOIC, 250 Makalapa Dr., Pearl Harbor, HI 96860.

Retired:
Rev. Msgrs.—
Batson, John R., c/o The Catholic Center, Office of the Bishop, 5826 Shelby Oaks Dr., 37134.
Davis, William F., 745 Loeb St., 38111.
Heymer, Edward Odell, 941 Ivy Rd., 38117. Tel: 901-722-8228
Revs.—
Elliott, Edward C., Our Lady of Perpetual Church, 8151 Poplar Ave., Germantown, 38138. Tel: 901-754-1204
Foley, David M., c/o The Catholic Center, Office of the Bishop, 5825 Shelby Oaks Dr., 37134.
Knight, David B., c/o His Way Spiritual Growth Ctr., 1306 Dellwood Ave., 38127. Tel: 901-357-6662
Murphy, James W., 950 Cherry Rd.,# 210, 38117.
Oglesby, J. Leonard, 263 Shadow Grove Cove, Cordova, 38018.
St. Charles, Paul W., 122 Tallwood Dr., Nashville, 37211-2711.

Permanent Deacons:
Atkins, Robert
Bennis, Donald
Bonaiuto, Nick
Brunner, Fred
Calicott, James
Champion, Eugene
Champion, James
Chitwood, Jack
Cooley, Jim
Cranford, William R.
Davis, Bill
Donati, Ralph
Finnegan, William
Gore, Michael
Gray, Jim
Griffith, Richard
Hamblen, Paul
Herbers, Bill
Herbers, Jerome E.
Hicks, Joseph
Hivner, John
Hovanec, Mick
Howell, Larry
Johnson, Eldon
Jones, Chip
Kang, John
Lafont, Bill
Larker, Frank
Lightcap, Charles
McCarver, Kenneth
Mensi, Joseph
Merwin, Miles
Miller, James
Nourse, Bill
O'Bryant, Charles
Oates, John
Powelson, Richard
Ramsey, Eddie
Rose, Werner
Saller, Max
Schmall, James
Seyller, Rod
Stewart, Harvey
Talley, Curtiss
Terry, Andrew, Jr.
Tucker, Jim
Turner, Ned
Van Tassel, Everell E.
Wells, Charles
Williams, Frank
Yarbrough, Harold

INSTITUTIONS LOCATED IN THE DIOCESE

[A] COLLEGES AND UNIVERSITIES

MEMPHIS. **Christian Brothers University* (1871), (Coed) , 650 E. Parkway S., 38104. Tel: 901-321-3000; Fax: 901-321-3290. Bros. Stanislaus Sobczyk, F.S.C., Pres.; Louis Althaus, F.S.C., Vice Pres. Academic Affairs; John Edward Doody, F.S.C., Dir. Grants & Proposals; Sr. Dolores Montini, C.S.J., Ministry; Mr. Dan Wortham, Finance; Mr. Nick Scully, Vice Pres. Institutional Advance & Affairs; Ms. Betty McWillie, Dir. Career Devel. & Placement; Mr. Thomas Cochran, Controller; John Kerr, Dir. Communications & Mktg.
Legal Title: *Christian Brothers Univ. (of Memphis, Tenn.)*, Four-Year University with Schools of Business, Engineering, Arts, and Sciences. Graduate programs in Business, and Engineering, and Education. Brothers 32; Sisters 3; Lay Teachers 166; Students 2,027.

[B] DIOCESAN SCHOOLS

MEMPHIS. *St. Augustine School*, 1169 Kerr Ave., 38106. Tel: 901-942-8002; Fax: 901-942-4564. Email: saes@bellsouth.net. Sr. Marie Demontfort Breaux, Prin. Sisters 1; Lay Teachers 9; Students 96.

Bishop Byrne High School (1965), 1475 E. Shelby Dr., 38116. Tel: 901-346-3060; Fax: 901-346-9488. Email: membbhs@gaggle.net. Dr. Donald Edwards, Prin. Sisters 2; Lay Teachers 23; Students 230.

De La Salle School at Blessed Sacrament, 2540 Hale Ave., 38112. Tel: 901-866-9084; Fax: 901-866-9086. Email: sdelasal@midsouth.rr.com. Web: www.cbhs.org/delasalle. Bro. Mark Snodgrass, F.S.C., Prin. Brothers 1; Lay Teachers 4; Students 62.

Holy Names Elementary, 709 Keel Ave., 38107. Tel: 901-507-1503; Fax: 901-507-1507. Email: daur@holynamesmemphis.org. Mr. Didier de Carvalho Aur, Prin.; Mrs. Francine Washington, Sec. Lay Teachers 4; Students 65.

St. John School, 2718 Lamar Ave., 38114. Tel: 901-743-6700; Fax: 901-743-6720. Email: sstjohns@midsouth.rr.com. Teddi Niedzwiedz, Prin.

St. Joseph School, 3851 Neely Rd., 38109. Tel: 901-344-0021; Fax: 901-348-0787. Email: eperiod99@aol.com. Mr. Jim Rigg, Prin.

Little Flower School, 1666 Jackson Ave., 38107. Tel: 901-725-9900; Fax: 901-725-5779. Sr. Trudy Foster, Prin. Sisters 1; Lay Teachers 4; Students 68.

Memphis Catholic High School and Middle School, 61 N. McLean Blvd., 38104. Tel: 901-276-1221; Fax: 901-725-1447. Email: dredwards@mcath.com. Mr. Jim Polhman, Prin. Sisters 1; Lay Teachers 26; Students 327.

St. Patrick School, 277 S. Fourth St., 38126. Tel: 901-527-2542; Fax: 901-525-1147. Email: vsmsmdak@aol.com. Sr. Noelita McDermott, S.M.S.M., Prin.

CORDOVA. *St. Benedict at Auburndale School*, (Grades 9-12), 8250 Varnavas Dr., 38016. Tel: 901-388-7321; Fax: 901-388-8201. Email: valadieg@sbaeagles.org. Web: www.sbaeagle.org. Mr. George Valadie, Pres. of Campus & Prin. (Grades 9-12); Mr. Doug Workman, Prin. (Grades PreK-8); Mrs. Cathy Bird, Prin.(Plus Prog.), Asst. High School Prin. Special programs for gifted and learning disabled. Lay Teachers 95; Students 1,191.

[C] HIGH SCHOOLS, PRIVATE AND PAROCHIAL

MEMPHIS. *St. Agnes Academy* (1851), (Grades PreK-12), 4830 Walnut Grove Rd., 38117. Tel: 901-767-1356; Fax: 901-435-5866. Email: bdaush@saa-sds.org. Web: www.saa-sds.org. Barbara Daush, Pres.; Joy Maness, Dean of Upper School. Sisters of St. Dominic (St. Catharine, KY), Title of Incorporation: St. Agnes Academy-St. Dominic School, Inc. Lay Teachers 35; Students 358.

**Christian Brothers High School*, 5900 Walnut Grove Rd., 38120-2174. Tel: 901-682-7801; Fax: 901-682-7815. Email: info@cbhs.org. Web: www.cbhs.org. Bros. Christopher Englert, F.S.C., Prin.; Joel McGraw, Dir. Brothers' Community. Title of Incorporation: Christian Brothers (LaSalle) High School. Brothers 8; Lay Teachers 60; Students 834.

Immaculate Conception High School (1950), 1725 Central Ave., 38104. Tel: 901-276-6341; Fax: 901-726-0141. Mindy Chalmers, Prin.; Rev. Valentine Handwerker. Lay Teachers 24; Students 159.

CORDOVA. *Sr. Ruth Ann Program* (Special Education) , 8151 Chimneyrock, 38016. Tel: 901-765-1213; 901-388-7321 (admin. office); Fax: 901-388-8201. Mr. George Valadie, Admin.; Mrs. Michele Cervetti Spears, Dir. & Educator; Mrs. Susan Fetz, Admin. Asst.

[D] ELEMENTARY SCHOOLS, PRIVATE

MEMPHIS. *St. Agnes Academy*, (Grades PreK-12), 4830 Walnut Grove Rd., 38117. Tel: 901-767-1377; Fax: 901-684-5316. Email: bdaush@Saa-sds.org. Web: www.saa-sds.org. Barbara Daush, Pres.; Kathy Toes, Dean of Lower School. Sisters of St. Dominic. (St. Catharine, KY) Lay Teachers 16; Students 273.

St. Dominic Boys School, 30 Avon Rd., 38117. Tel: 901-682-3011; Fax: 901-681-0047. Email: jmurphy@saa-sds.org. Web: www.saa.sds.org. Mrs. Barbara Daush, Pres.; Mr. John Murphy, Dean. Sisters of St. Dominic. (St. Catharine, KY) Lay Teachers 16; Students 247.

GERMANTOWN. *Madonna Learning Center*, 7007 Poplar, 38138. Tel: 901-752-5767; Fax: 901-752-5039. Email: jhinkle@madonna-learnig.org. Mrs. Clara Kirchner, Prin.; Mrs. Carolyn Jordan, Sec.; Mrs. Jo Ann M. Hinkle, Exec. Dir.

[E] CHILD-CARING INSTITUTIONS

MEMPHIS. *St. Peter Home for Children* (1852), 3060 Baskin St., 38127-7799. Tel: 901-354-6300; Fax: 901-354-6343.

[F] DAYCARE CENTERS

MEMPHIS. *St. Louis Extended*, 5192 Shady Grove Rd., 38117. Tel: 901-682-9692. Ms. Lori Tucker, Site Supvr. Children 100.

St. Michael Extended, 3880 Forrest Ave., 38122. Tel: 901-324-6662; Fax: 901-323-0481 Amy Dela Torre, Dir. Children 100.

CORDOVA. *St. Benedict at Auburndale Extended*, 2100 N. Germantown Rd., 38018. Tel: 901-381-2595. Ms. Pamela O'Bryan, Dir. Children 142.

[G] ADULT RESIDENCES & HOMES FOR AGED

MEMPHIS. *Diocese of Memphis Housing Corp.*, P.O. Box 41705, 38174-1705. Tel: 901-722-4761; 901-722-4772; Fax: 901-722-4732. Email: dfield@cathchar.org. Web: www.cathchar.org. Mr. David Field, Dir. of Housing.

St. Peter Manor, 108 N. Auburndale, 38104. Tel: 901-278-8200; Fax: 901-278-8210. Email: mtwig@mecca32.mecca.org. Mrs. Karen F. Brown, Mgr.

St. Peter Chapel & Activity Center Tel: 901-278-8200; Fax: 901-278-8210.

St. Peter Villa, 141 N. McLean, 38104-2644. Tel: 901-276-2021; Fax: 901-725-3564. Email: kae@cathchar.org. Mrs. Kae Werkhoven, Admin. Diocesan Nursing Home.

DYERSBURG. *St. Joseph Manor*, 885 Hwy. 51, Byp. W., 38024. Tel: 901-285-8560; Fax: 901-285-8562. Email: beverlybates@bellsouth.net. Beverly Bates, Mgr.

St. Joseph Village, 885 Hwy. 51 Byp. W, 38024. Tel: 901-285-8560; Fax: 901-285-8562. Email: beverlybates@bellsouth.net. Beverly Bates, Mgr.

HUMBOLDT. *St. Matthew Manor*, 2575 Viking Dr., 38343. Tel: 731-784-7229; 731-784-9309. Mrs. Amber M. Kee, Mgr.

St. Matthew Manor - West, 2575 Viking Dr., 38343. Tel: 731-824-3793; Fax: 731-784-9303. Mrs. Amber M. Kee, Mgr.

JACKSON. *St. Mary Manor*, 1771 Hwy. 45 By-Pass, 38305. Tel: 731-668-5633; Fax: 731-668-9252. Email: stmary1@aeneas.net. Anne M. Sain, Mgr. Total Staff 10; Independent Living Apartments 149.

MOSCOW. *St. Mark Village Apartments*, 85 St. Mark Cove, 38057. Tel: 901-877-3456. Ms. Georgia Laughter, Mgr.

[H] CATHOLIC CHARITIES

MEMPHIS. *St. Ann-Bartlett Extended Care*, 6529 Stage Rd., 38134. Tel: 901-382-3370. Ms. Karen Otts, Site Supvr.

[I] RESIDENCES OF PRIESTS AND BROTHERS

MEMPHIS. *Brothers Of The Christian Schools (Mid-West Prov.)*, Christian Brothers University, 650 E. Parkway S., 38104. Tel: 901-321-3000. Fax: 901-321-3290. Web: www.cbu.edu.

Christian Brothers High School, 5900 Walnut Grove Rd., 38119. Tel: 901-682-4704; Fax: 901-682-7815. Email: bstan@cbu.edu. Web: www.cbhs.org. Brothers 41.

The Dominican Friars of Memphis, Inc., 190 Adams Ave., 38103. Tel: 901-527-8282; Fax: 901-526-6882. Revs. Edward E. Everitt, O.P., Chm. & Pres.; Bertrand Ebben, O.P.

Order Of Preachers (Southern Dominican Prov.), 190 Adams Ave., 38103. Tel: 901-527-8282; Fax: 901-526-6882. Email: eeveritt@opsouth.org. Revs. Bertrand E. Ebben, O.P.; Edward E. Everitt, O.P.; Arthur R. Kirwin, O.P.

Society of the Divine Word (Chicago Province), 1254 S. Lauderdale, 38106. Tel: 901-774-8191; Fax: 901-774-8192. Email: vusvd@hotmail.com. Revs. Joseph Dao Vu, S.V.D.; Frank Drzaic, S.V.D.; Benedict Kim, S.V.D.; Anthony Clark, S.V.D.; Miguel Ruiz, S.V.D.; Dominic Dung Nguyen, S.V.D.

JACKSON. *Brothers of St. Francis Xavier (Xaverians)*, 611 Burkett St., 38301. Tel: 731-424-5003. Email: dobrien@aeneas.net. Web: www.stmarys.tn.org. Bro Dan O'Brien, C.F.X.

[J] CONVENTS AND RESIDENCES FOR SISTERS

MEMPHIS. *Dominican Sisters, Congregation of St. Cecilia*, 1488 Maurine Dr., 38116. Tel: 901-346-0251; Fax: 901-346-0333. Email: www.nashvilledominican.org.

Legal Title: *Dominican Sisters, Congregation of St. Cecilia (Nashville, TN), St. Paul Convent* Sisters 8.

The House of the Good Shepherd of Memphis, 3911 Mallard Point Dr., 38128. Tel: 901-387-0513; Fax: 901-379-0483. Sr. Michael Maguire, Supr. & Admin. Sisters 5.

Missionaries of Charity, 700 N. 7th St., 38107. Tel: 901-527-4947. Sisters 4.

Shelter Tel: 901-526-5456. Sr. M. Salvina, M.C., Supr. Sisters 5.

Missionary Sisters Of The Society Of Mary (Waltham, MA) S.M.S.M., 60 S. Auburndale, 38104. Tel: 901-272-2808; Fax: 901-272-2808. Email: smsm60au@aol.com. Sisters 4.

Monastery Of St. Clare O.S.C., 1310 Dellwood Ave., 38127. Tel: 901-357-6662; Fax: 901-353-3783. Email: stclare@mem.net. Web: www.poorclare.org/memphis. Sr. Mary Helen Kelley, O.S.C., Abbess. Sisters 6; Huehuetenango, Guatemala 3.

Sisters Of Charity Of The Blessed Virgin Mary (Dubuque, IA) B.V.M., 437 N. Dickinson, 38112. Tel: 901-274-9015. Email: memphisbvm@aol.com. Sr. Jacquelyn Cramer, B.V.M., Community Representative. Sisters 2.

Sisters Of St. Joseph Of Pennsylvania (Erie, PA) S.S.J., 931 Ivy, 38117. Tel: 901-821-9907.

HUNTINGDON. *Franciscan Sisters of Little Falls (Little Falls, MN)*, 257 Cotham Dr., 38344-1401. Tel: 731-986-2481; 731-986-4944; Fax: 731-986-4944. Sisters 3.

[K] NEWMAN CENTERS

MEMPHIS. *Campus Ministry, University of Memphis, Rhodes College, UT - Memphis* 3625 Mynders Ave., 38111. Tel: 901-323-3051; Fax: 901-323-0925. Email: ucc@cdom.org. Deacon Richard Griffith, Dir. of Campus Ministry; Brenda Kindelan, Campus Minister.

MARTIN. *Cooperative Ministries Interfaith Center* 312 Lovelace Ave., 38237. Tel: 901-587-2603. Rev. Joseph L. Paolozzi.

[L] MISCELLANEOUS

MEMPHIS. *Catholic Charities, Inc.*, 1325 Jefferson Ave., 38104-2097. Tel: 901-722-4700; Fax: 901-722-4791. Web: www.cathchar.org. P.O. Box 41705, 38174-1705.

Charismatic Prayer Groups, Tel: 901-332-1364. Rev. Richard Mickey.

DeNeuville Learning Center, 840 Dickinson Ave., 38107. Tel: 901-726-5902; Fax: 901-726-0010. Email: lnap5902@bellsouth.net. Web: www.deneuvillecenter.org. Sr. Lakshmie Napagoda, R.G.S., Prog. Dir. Operated by the House of the Good Shepherd of Memphis.

Diocesan Council of Catholic Women, 3369 Luci Bill Rd, 38116. Tel: 901-346-8882. Ms. Gilda Lewis.

House of the Good Shepherd of Memphis DeNeuville Learning Center, 840 Dickinson St., 38107. Tel: 901-726-5902; Fax: 901-726-0010. Email: lnap5902@bellsouth.net. Web: www.deneuvillecenter.org. Sr. Lakshmie Napagoda, Dir.

House of the Good Shepherd of Memphis, Casa Maria, 4083 Hemingway St., 38128. Tel: 901-373-7456; Fax: 901-379-0483. Email: Lindargs@hotmail.com. Sr. Linda Larkman, R.G.S., Prog. Dir.

Knights of St. Peter Claver (St. Benedict the Black Council No. 188) and Assembly 26 Bishop James P., 5600 Santa Barbara, 38116. Tel: 901-396-8315. Mr. Joseph Randolph, Grand Knight & Faithful Comptroller.

Ladies of Charity of Memphis, P.O. Box 17699, 38187-0699. Tel: 901-681-0221. Web: www.famvin.org/lcwsa. Mrs. Wilma Moore, Pres.

**Madonna Circle, Inc.* (Catholic Women's Service Organization), 8890 Darby Dan Lane, Germantown, 38138-8259. Tel: 901-748-4000. Mimi Roy, Pres.

Marriage Preparation Program, The Catholic Center, 5825 Shelby Oaks Dr., 38134. Tel: 901-373-1235; Fax: 901-373-1269. Email: pperry@cdom.org. Web: www.cdom.org. Mrs. Patricia A. Perry, Coord.

St. Martin de Porres Shrine & Institute, 190 Adams Ave., 38103. Tel: 901-527-8282.

St. Patrick's Center, 277 S. Fourth St., 38126. Tel: 901-527-2542; Fax: 901-525-1147. Email: jwiesner@stpatsmemphis.org. Web: www.stpatsmemphis.org. Rev. James F. Wiesner, C.S.P., Dir.

CAMDEN. *Good Samaritan Village*, 192A Post Oak Ave., 38320. Tel: 731-584-1300; Fax: 731-584-1344. Email: gsrff@bellsouth.net. Mrs. Amber Kee, Mgr.

COLLIERVILLE. *Cenacle Retreat League*, 1404 Glen Oaks Dr., 38119-5906. Tel: 901-685-6055. Jean Deacon, Pres.

Serra Club of Memphis, 2760 Halle Pkwy., 38017. Mike Watermeier, Pres. Tel: 901-726-5296; Rev. John B. McArthur, Chap.

CORDOVA. *Society of St. Vincent DePaul*, 8634 Ashley Glen Cir., N., 38018. Tel: 901-751-3765, Ext. 312; Fax: 901-409-8021. Mr. Vince Thompson, Dist. Council Pres.; Rev. Michael A. Morgera, Spiritual Advisor.

RELIGIOUS INSTITUTES OF MEN REPRESENTED IN THE DIOCESE

For further details refer to the corresponding bracketed number in the Religious Institutes of Men or Women section.

[1350]—*Brothers of St. Francis Xavier*—C.F.X.

[0330]—*Brothers of the Christian Schools* (St. Louis Prov.)—F.S.C.

[1000]—*Brothers of the Cross and Passion*—C.P.

[]—*Missionary Congregation of the Blessed Sacrament*—M.C.B.S.

[0430]—*Order of Preachers (Dominicans)*—O.P.

[1030]—*Paulist Fathers*—C.S.P.

[0420]—*Society of Divine Word*—S.V.D.

RELIGIOUS INSTITUTES OF WOMEN REPRESENTED IN THE DIOCESE

[1950]—*Congregation of the Sisters of the Holy Family*—S.S.F.

[1070-01]—*Dominican Sisters*—O.P.

[1070-03]—*Dominican Sisters*—O.P.

[1070-07]—*Dominican Sisters*—O.P.

[1310]—*Franciscan Sisters of Little Falls, Minnesota*—O.S.F.

[2070]—*Holy Union Sisters*—S.U.S.C.

[2420]—*Marist Missionary Sisters*—S.M.S.M.

[2710]—*Missionaries of Charity*—M.C.

[3530]—*Missionary Sisters Servants of the Holy Spirit*—S.Sp.S.

[3760]—*Order of St. Clare* (Memphis, TN)—O.S.C.

[0440]—*Sisters of Charity of Cincinnati, Ohio*—S.C.

[0500]—*Sisters of Charity of Nazareth*—S.C.N.

[]—*Sisters of Charity of St. Charles Borromeo*—C.B.

[0430]—*Sisters of Charity of the Blessed Virgin Mary*—B.V.M.

[]—*Sisters of Mercy* (Ireland)—R.S.M.

[2575]—*Sisters of Mercy of the Americas*—R.S.M.

[3710]—*Sisters of St. Agnes*—C.S.A.

[3830-09]—*Sisters of St. Joseph* (Erie)—S.S.J.

[3830-13]—*Sisters of St. Joseph* (Pittsburgh, Baden)—C.S.J.

[3180]—*Sisters of the Cross and Passion*—C.P.

[1830]—*Sisters of the Good Shepherd* (St. Louis Prov.)—R.G.S.

[4120-05]—*Ursuline Nuns of the Congregation of Paris* (Owensboro, KY)—O.S.U.

DIOCESAN CEMETERIES

MEMPHIS. *All Saints*, c/o Calvary Cemetery, 1663 Elvis Presley Blvd., 38106. Tel: 901-948-1529.

Calvary, 1663 Elvis Presley Blvd., 38106. Tel: 901-948-1529.

JACKSON. *Calvary*

NECROLOGY

† Lynch, Rev. Msgr. Patrick J., (Retired)—Died Aug. 8, 2003

† Gaffney, James, (Retired)—Died 2003

† Stelling, William F., Memphis, TN St. Joseph's—Died July 22, 2003

Diocese of Metuchen

Most Reverend

PAUL G. BOOTKOSKI, D.D.

Bishop of Metuchen; ordained May 28, 1966; appointed Titular Bishop of Zarna and Auxiliary Bishop of Newark July 8, 1997; ordained September 5, 1997; appointed Fourth Bishop of Metuchen January 4, 2002; installed March 19, 2002 *Res.: 10 Library Pl., Metuchen, NJ 08840.*

Most Reverend

EDWARD T. HUGHES, D.D.

Bishop Emeritus of Metuchen; ordained May 31, 1947; appointed Auxiliary to Archbishop of Philadelphia and Titular Bishop of Segia June 14, 1976; consecrated July 21, 1976; appointed Second Bishop of Metuchen December 16, 1986; installed February 5, 1987; retired September 8, 1997 *Res.: Bethany Ridge*, 914 Milford-Warren Glen Rd., Milford, NJ 08848.

ESTABLISHED NOVEMBER 19, 1981.

Square Miles 1,425.

Legal Corporate Title: The Diocese of Metuchen.

Comprises the Counties of Warren, Hunterdon, Somerset and Middlesex in the State of New Jersey.

The Diocesan Center: P.O. Box 191, Metuchen, NJ 08840. Tel: 732-562-1990; Fax: 732-562-1427.

Web: www.diometuchen.org

STATISTICAL OVERVIEW

Personnel	
Bishop	1
Retired Bishops	1
Priests: Diocesan Active in Diocese	151
Priests: Diocesan Active Outside Diocese	21
Priests: Retired, Sick or Absent	38
Number of Diocesan Priests	210
Religious Priests in Diocese	52
Total Priests in Diocese	262
Extern Priests in Diocese	23
Ordinations:	
Diocesan Priests	1
Transitional Deacons	3
Permanent Deacons in Diocese	141
Total Brothers	18
Total Sisters	397
Parishes	
Parishes	108
With Resident Pastor:	
Resident Diocesan Priests	98
Resident Religious Priests	5
Professional Ministry Personnel:	
Brothers	1
Sisters	47
Lay Ministers	116
Welfare	
Catholic Hospitals	1
Total Assisted	284,933
Health Care Centers	2
Total Assisted	4,569
Homes for the Aged	2
Total Assisted	610
Day Care Centers	3
Total Assisted	209
Specialized Homes	6
Total Assisted	241
Special Centers for Social Services	9
Total Assisted	18,862
Educational	
Diocesan Students in Other Seminaries	13
Total Seminarians	13
High Schools, Diocesan and Parish	4
Total Students	2,443
High Schools, Private	2
Total Students	1,207
Elementary Schools, Diocesan and Parish	42
Total Students	12,888
Non-residential Schools for the Disabled	1
Total Students	50
Catechesis/Religious Education:	
High School Students	2,324
Elementary Students	43,319
Total Students under Catholic Instruction	63,244
Teachers in the Diocese:	
Brothers	10
Sisters	87
Lay Teachers	1,008
Vital Statistics	
Receptions into the Church:	
Infant Baptism Totals	6,508
Adult Baptism Totals	140
Received into Full Communion	259
First Communions	7,390
Confirmations	6,282
Marriages:	
Catholic	1,120
Interfaith	307
Total Marriages	1,427
Deaths	4,048
Total Catholic Population	556,682
Total Population	1,325,432

Former Bishops—Most Revs. THEODORE E. MCCARRICK, ord. May 31, 1958; appt. Titular Bishop of Rusibisir and Auxiliary to the Archbishop of New York, May 24, 1977; consecrated June 29, 1977; appt. first Bishop of Metuchen, Nov. 19, 1981; installed Jan. 31, 1982; promoted to the Archdiocese of Newark, June 3, 1986; installed July 25, 1986; EDWARD T. HUGHES (Retired), ord. May 31, 1947; appt. Titular Bishop of Segia and Auxiliary to the Archbishop of Philadelphia, June 14, 1976; consecrated July 21, 1976; appt. second Bishop of Metuchen, Dec. 16, 1986; installed Feb. 5, 1987; retired Sept. 8, 1997; VINCENT DEPAUL BREEN, D.D., ord. July 15, 1962; appt. Third Bishop of Metuchen July 8, 1997; consecrated and installed Sept. 8, 1997; retired Jan. 4, 2002; died March 30, 2003.

The Diocesan Center—P.O. Box 191, Metuchen, 08840. Tel: 732-562-1990; Fax: 732-562-1427.

Vicars General—Rev. Msgrs. WILLIAM BENWELL, J.C.L., V.G.; JOHN B. SZYMANSKI, V.G.

Episcopal Vicars—Very Revs. DANIEL J. HERLIHY; LOUIS F. STINGEL; Rev. Msgr. MICHAEL J. CORONA; Very Rev. ANDREW L. SZAROLETA; Rev. Msgr. ROBERT J. ZAMORSKI.

Assistant to the Bishop—Rev. MICHAEL A. MAKARA.

The Diocesan Curia

Moderator—Rev. Msgr. WILLIAM BENWELL, J.C.L., V.G.

The Chancery

Chancellor—LORI BROWER, J.C.L.

Vice Chancellors—CAROL M. MACDERMOTT; Rev. ROBERT W. MEDLEY.

The Tribunal

The Diocesan Center—P.O. Box 191, Metuchen, 08840. Tel: 732-562-1990; Fax: 732-562-1193.

Judicial Vicar—Rev. RICHARD J. LYONS, J.C.L.

Canonical Staff—Rev. Msgr. WILLIAM BENWELL, J.C.L., V.G.; LORI BROWER, J.C.L.; Revs. NEIL W. DAVIN, C.P., J.C.L.; CHESTER H. CARINA, J.C.L.; ROBERT V. MEYERS, J.C.L.; GEORGE M. PISANELLO, J.C.L.

Auditors—Sr. MARY A. KERWIN, R.S.M.; CAROL M. MACDERMOTT; BARBARA J. REAVEY.

Psychological Consultants—MARY ANN SODROSKI, E.D.S.; Rev. RICHARD MUCOWSKI, O.F.M., Ed.D., Ph.D.; MICHAEL W. MILLARD, Ph.D.

Notary—Sr. M. WILLIAM WASIELEWSKI, C.S.S.F.

Office of Child and Youth Protection—LAWRENCE V. NAGLE, Dir.

Department for Administrative Services

General Secretary for Administrative and Legal Services—RONALD C. RAK, Esq.

Office of Finance—THOMAS G. TOOLAN, Dir.

Department of Insurance and Pensions—VACANT.

Department of Cemeteries—RUSSELL B. DEMKOVITZ, Dir.

Department of Information Systems—LEONARDO G. CORTELEZZI, Dir.

Department of Property and Facilities Management—MONICA P. DEMKOVITZ, Dir.

Office of the Missions—Rev. Msgr. RICHARD A. BEHL, Dir.; PATRICIA HUMMEL, Asst. Dir.

Office of Personnel Management—RUTH E. MELCHIORRE, Dir. CEBS.

Commission on Building—VACANT.

Commission for Sites and Boundaries—VACANT.

Department for Planning & Development

Planning & Development—Rev. Msgr. JOHN B. SZYMANSKI, V.G.

Office of Stewardship—Rev. SYLVESTER J. CRONIN, Dir.

Office of Development—VINCENT STAHL, Dir.

Department of Education

Department of Education—Rev. Msgr. MICHAEL CORONA, Exec. Dir.

Office of the Schools—Dr. THOMAS E. HART, Ph.D., Supt. Assistant Superintendents: Dr. FRANCIS X. HEELAN, Ed.D.; Ms. MARY BOYLE; Dr. NANCY GILROY, Ed.D.

Office of Religious Education—MARY KAY CULLINAN, Dir.; MARY MORRELL, Assoc. Dir. Rel. Educ.

Office of Youth and Young Adult Ministry—KEVIN EARLEY, Dir.

Office of Communications and Public Relations—JOANNE WARD, Dir.; ALBERT F. FEMIA, Broadcast Media.

"The Catholic Spirit"—RAYANNE DAMIANO, Editor-in-Chief.

Department of Personnel in Ministry

Department of Personnel in Ministry—Very Rev. TERRANCE M. LAWLER, Exec. Dir.

Office of Ministry to Priests—Rev. CHARLES W. CICERALE, Dir.

Office of Priest Personnel—Very Rev. TERRANCE M. LAWLER, Dir.

Office of the Diaconate—Deacon JOEL R. LIVINGSTON JR., Dir.

Office for Religious—Sr. JULIA JAMINK, S.J.H., Delegate.

Office of Vocations—Rev. JOSEPH G. CELANO, Dir.; Very Rev. PETER CEBULKA, C.O.; Bro. ROBERT ZIOBRO, S.C.

Board for Seminary Education—Rev. ROBERT W. MEDLEY, Chm.

Victim Assistance Coordinator—Sr. ELIZABETH O'HARA, R.S.M. Tel: 908-722-1881. Email: eohara@ccdom.org.

Department of Pastoral Life

Pastoral Life—Very Rev. RAYMOND L. COLE, Exec. Dir.

Office of Worship—Rev. Msgr. MICHAEL J. ALLIEGRO, Dir.

Office of Family Life Ministry—JUDITH A. PSOTA, Dir.

Office for Multicultural Ministries—Rev. GLENN J. COMANDINI, S.T.D., Dir.

Office of Parish Leadership Formation—Sr. JOANNA KERWIN, G.N.S.H., Dir.

Commission for African-American Catholic Ministry—JOSEPH J. POWELL, Chm.

Commission for Ecumenical and Interreligious Affairs—Rev. JEROME A. JOHNSON, Chm.

Commission for the Filipino Apostolate—Rev. EDGARDO D. ABANO, Chm.

Commission for Hispanic Ministry—Rev. JOHN B. GORDON, Chm.

Chinese Apostolate—Rev. VINCENT P. CHEN, Chap.

Korean Apostolate—Rev. ANDREW YOUNG-MIN IM, Chap.

Portuguese Apostolate—Rev. LAURO C. SEDLMAYER, Chap.

Eastern European Commission—Rev. JOHN STEC, Chm.

Commission for Pro-Life Action—Rev. Msgr. RICHARD A. BEHL, Chm.

Commission for Ministry for People with Disabilities—Ms. VENUS MAJEWSKI, Chm.

Vietnamese Apostolate—Rev. JOSEPH OANH DANG, S.V.D., Chap.

Diocesan Organizations, Movements and Moderators

Catholic Relief Services—Rev. JOSEPH KERRIGAN, Dir.

Catholic Scouting Movement—Rev. Msgr. MICHAEL J. CORONA, Moderator.

Charismatic Movement—DORIS BRENNAN, Moderator.

Diocesan Council of Catholic Women—Rev. EDWARD M. O'NEILL, Moderator.

Diocesan Eucharistic League—Rev. LOPE D. PASCUAL, Dir.

Diocesan Holy Name Society—Rev. JOSEPH HOLUP, Moderator.

Diocesan Home School Association—Rev. Msgr. MICHAEL J. CORONA, Moderator.

Legion of Mary—Rev. A. PAUL DA SILVA, Moderator.

St. Vincent de Paul Societies—Mr. JOSEPH D. FLANNIGAN, Pres.

Department of Catholic Social Services—MARIANNE MAJEWSKI, L.C.S.W., Exec. Dir., (See category for Catholic Charities under Institutions Located in the Diocese for the full listing).

Consultative Bodies

College of Consultors—Rev. Msgrs. JOHN B. SZYMANSKI, V.G.; ANTHONY J. LUISINI; WILLIAM BENWELL, V.G.; SEAMUS F. BRENNAN; GEORGE M. BREMBOS, Ed.D.; Rev. GLENN J. COMANDINI, S.T.D.; Very Revs. MICHAEL G. KRULL; TERRANCE M. LAWLER; Rev. CHARLES T. O'CONNOR, Sec.

Deans—Very Rev. JOHN PAUL ALVARADO, Cathedral Deanery; Rev. EDWARD C. PULEO, Arthur Kill Deanery; Very Revs. ROBERT J. LYNAM, Forsgate Deanery; DAVID J. PEKOLA, Morris Canal Deanery; STANLEY G. GROMADZKI, Raritan Bay Deanery; RAYMOND L. COLE, County Seat Deanery; JOHN J. CASEY, Somerset Hills Deanery; J. WILLIAM MICKIEWICZ, Round Valley Deanery; MARCO A. CACERES, New Brunswick Deanery; THOMAS F. RYAN, Perth Amboy Deanery.

Presbyteral Council—Most Rev. PAUL G. BOOTKOSKI, D.D., Pres.

Theological Commission—Rev. GLENN J. COMANDINI, S.T.D., Chm.

Diocesan Pastoral Council—Most Rev. PAUL G. BOOTKOSKI, D.D.

Episcopal Council—Most Rev. PAUL G. BOOTKOSKI, D.D.; LORI BROWER, J.C.L.; Rev. Msgr. WILLIAM BENWELL, J.C.L., V.G.; Very Revs. RAYMOND L. COLE; ANDREW L. SZAROLETA; DANIEL J. HERLIHY; TERRANCE M. LAWLER; Revs. RICHARD J. LYONS, J.C.L.; MICHAEL A. MAKARA; MARIANNE MAJEWSKI, L.C.S.W.; Very Rev. LOUIS F. STINGEL; RONALD C. RAK, Esq.; Rev. Msgrs. JOHN B. SZYMANSKI, V.G.; ROBERT J. ZAMORSKI; MICHAEL J. CORONA.

CLERGY, PARISHES, MISSIONS AND PAROCHIAL SCHOOLS

BOROUGH OF METUCHEN
(MIDDLESEX COUNTY)

CATHEDRAL OF ST. FRANCIS (1871), Rev. Msgr. Richard A. Behl, Rector; Revs. John C. Grimes; John C. Gloss; Deacons Frank J. Cammarano; Cornelius S. Smoyak; Paul G. Licameli; Guido J. Brossoni.
Res.: 32 Elm Ave., 08840. Tel: 732-548-0100; Fax: 732-549-1033.
School—528 Main St., 08840. Tel: 732-548-3107; Fax: 732-548-5760. Sisters of Christian Charity 2; Lay Teachers 25; Students 435.

OUTSIDE THE BOROUGH OF METUCHEN

ALPHA, WARREN CO., ST. MARY (1902), Rev. Msgr. Anthony J. Luisini; Rev. Jonathan S. Toborowsky.
Res.: 830 Fifth Ave., 08865. Tel: 908-454-0444; Fax: 908-454-7745.

AVENEL, MIDDLESEX CO., ST. ANDREW (1920), Rev. David B. Kosmoski, O.M.V.
Res.: 244 Avenel St., 07001. Tel: 732-634-4355; Fax: 732-750-5905.
Station—Woodbridge State School
Station—Woodbridge Emergency Reception Center 07001. Tel: 732-636-4261.

BAPTISTOWN, HUNTERDON CO., OUR LADY OF VICTORIES (1973), Revs. David I. Fulton, S.T.D., J.C.L.; Edward J. Nester, Pastor Emeritus (Retired); Deacon John T. Monahan.
Res.: P.O. Box 127, 08803. Tel: 908-996-2068; Fax: 908-996-3525.

BASKING RIDGE, SOMERSET CO., ST. JAMES (1864), Rev. Msgr. William J. Capik; Rev. Sean W. Kenney; Deacons James S. Bell; Luke J. Hally.
Res.: 184 S. Finley Ave., P.O. Box 310, 07920. Tel: 908-766-0888; Fax: 908-766-1815.
School—200 S. Finley Ave., P.O. Box 310, 07920. Tel: 908-766-4774; Fax: 908-766-4432. Lay Teachers 20; Students 372.

BELVIDERE, WARREN CO., ST. PATRICK (1892), Rev. Richard Rusk; Deacon John F. Dumschat.
Res.: 327 Greenwich St., 07823. Tel: 908-475-2559; Fax: 908-475-1943.

BERNARDSVILLE, SOMERSET CO., OUR LADY OF PERPETUAL HELP (1898), [CEM] Rev. John N. Fell; Rev. Msgr. John R. Torney, P.A., Pastor Emeritus (Retired); Rev. Daniel Gomez; Deacons Joseph E. O'Keefe; Joel R. Livingston; Benigno Ruiz-Diaz.
Res.: 111 Claremont Rd., 07924. Tel: 908-766-0079; Fax: 908-766-1185.
School—School of St. Elizabeth, Seney Dr., 07924. Tel: 908-766-0244; Fax: 908-766-5372. Sisters of Christian Charity 1; Lay Teachers 11; Students 233.
Chapel—Bernardsville, Sacred Heart (Chapel of Convenience) Bernards Ave., 07924.

BLAIRSTOWN, WARREN CO., ST. JUDE (1945), Rev. Ronald L. Jandernoa.
Res.: 7 Eisenhower Rd., P.O. Box N, 07825. Tel: 908-362-6444; Fax: 908-362-6862.

BLOOMSBURY, HUNTERDON CO., CHURCH OF THE ANNUNCIATION (1948), Rev. Roberto Coruna.
Res.: 80 Main St., P.O. Box 136, 08804-0136. Tel: 908-479-4905.

BOUND BROOK, SOMERSET CO.

1—ST. JOSEPH (1876), [CEM] Revs. Charles T. O'Connor; John Peter Nyaga, I.M.C.; Deacons George D. Coleman; Gustavo Sandoval.
Office—124 E. Second St., P.O. Box 72, 08805. Tel: 732-356-0027; Fax: 732-356-8092.
Res.: 304 John St., 08805. Tel: 732-356-8936.

2—ST. MARY OF CZESTOCHOWA (1914), (Polish), Revs. Leon S. Aniszczyk; Marian Drozd.
Res.: 193 W. High St., 08805. Tel: 732-356-0358; Fax: 732-356-1338.

BRIDGEWATER, SOMERSET CO.

1—ST. BERNARD (1843), [CEM] Revs. Joseph G. Celano; John Barbella; Deacons Patrick J. Cline; Paul L. Anderson; Gerard C. Sims.
Res.: 500 Rte. 22, 08807. Tel: 908-526-6859; 725-055- (Office); Fax: 908-237-9789; 725-452- (Office).

2—HOLY TRINITY (1948), Rev. John R. Pringle; Deacon Michael A. Forrestall.
Res.: 60 Maple St., 08807. Tel: 908-526-2394; Fax: 908-526-5837.

CALIFON, HUNTERDON CO., ST. JOHN NEUMANN (1982), Very Rev. J. William Mickiewicz; Deacon Thomas J. Gilheany.
Res.: P.O. Box 455, 07830. Tel: 908-832-2513; Fax: 908-832-7618.

CARTERET, MIDDLESEX CO.

1—ST. ELIZABETH OF HUNGARY (1914), (Hungarian), Rev. Patrick H. Barrett.
Res.: 119 Washington Ave., 07008. Tel: 732-541-5202.

2—HOLY FAMILY (1907), (Polish), Rev. Edmund J. Shallow.
Res.: 213 Pershing Ave., 07008. Tel: 732-541-5768; Fax: 732-541-5871.

3—ST. JOSEPH (1893), Rev. Edward C. Puleo; Rev. Msgr. Donald M. Endebrock (Retired); Deacons Philip Fiore; Ramon L. Torres.
Res.: 7 Locust St., 07008. Tel: 732-541-8946; Fax: 732-541-0500.
School—865 Roosevelt Ave., 07008. Tel: 732-541-7111; Fax: 732-541-0676. Lay Teachers 14; Students 246.

4—SACRED HEART (1910), (Slovak), Rev. Gerald Browne.
Res.: 67 Fitch St., 07008. Tel: 732-541-5410.

CLINTON, HUNTERDON CO., IMMACULATE CONCEPTION (1864), [CEM] Very Rev. Andrew L. Szaroleta; Rev. Krzysztof Kaczynski; Deacon William R. Bauer.
Res.: Rte. 633, Old Allerton Rd., P.O. Box 5400, 08809-0400. Tel: 908-735-7319; Fax: 908-735-4552.
School—Immaculate Conception School, P.O. Box 5400, 08809. Tel: 908-735-6334; Fax: 908-238-0724. Anna Marie Reilly, Prin. Religious 2; Lay Teachers 24; Students 466.
Station—Edna Mahan Correctional Facility for Women. Tel: 908-735-7111; Fax: 908-735-5246.
Station—Hunterdon Developmental Center, Tel: 908-735-4031; Fax: 908-730-1311.

COLONIA, MIDDLESEX CO., ST. JOHN VIANNEY (1959), Revs. Edward M. O'Neill; Joseph V. Szoke; Jeffrey R. Willingham; Deacon Joseph D. Ragucci. In Res., Rev. John D. Murphy.
Res.: 420 Inman Ave., 07067. Tel: 732-574-0150; Fax: 732-574-0050.
School—420 Inman Ave., 07067. Tel: 732-388-1662; Fax: 732-388-1003. Bernardine Sisters 2; Lay Teachers 34; Students 820.

CRANBURY, MIDDLESEX CO., NATIVITY OF OUR LORD (1992), Rev. Edward R. Flanagan; Deacons Michel G. Morend; Gregory R. D'Angelo.
Res.: 185 Applegarth Rd., Monroe Township, 08831. Tel: 609-371-0499.

DUNELLEN, MIDDLESEX CO., ST. JOHN THE EVANGELIST (1879), Rev. Richard J. Lyons, J.C.L.
Res.: 317 First St., 08812. Tel: 732-968-2621; Fax: 732-968-2588.

EAST BRUNSWICK, MIDDLESEX CO., ST. BARTHOLOMEW (1959), Rev. Msgr. Michael J. Alliegro; Revs. Patrick J. Kuffner; Joseph J. Kerrigan; Deacons John F. Kenny; Anthony J. Gostkowski; John P. McShane.
Res.: 460 Ryders Ln., 08816. Tel: 732-257-7722; Fax: 732-257-7723.
School—470 Ryders Ln., 08816. Tel: 732-254-7105. Lay Teachers 24; Students 384.

EDISON, MIDDLESEX CO.

1—GUARDIAN ANGELS (1959), Rev. Msgr. James P. Moran.
Res.: 37 Plainfield Ave., P.O. Box 1216, 08817-1216. Tel: 732-985-7565; Fax: 732-985-0970.
Mission—St. Margaret Mary Alacoque Woodbridge Ave., Bonhamtown, Middlesex Co. 08817.

2—ST. HELENA (1965), Rev. Msgr. Armando J. Perini; Revs. Salvatore J. Rossetti, O.P.; Joseph Lukose, C.M. (India) (NY).
Res.: 950 Grove Ave., 08820. Tel: 732-494-3399; Fax: 732-494-2076.
School—930 Grove Ave., 08820. Tel: 732-549-6234. Felician Sisters 3; Lay Teachers 25; Students 350.
Convent—882 Grove Ave., 08820. Tel: 732-321-1462.

3—ST. MATTHEW (1952), Revs. James W. McLaughlin; A. Gregory Uhrig; Deacons Barry C. Demarest; Eric S. Massimei; Bernard A. Cribbin. In Res., Revs. Neil W. Davin, C.P., J.C.L.; Thomas Myladil, O.C.D.
Res.: 81 Seymour Ave., 08817. Tel: 732-985-5063; Fax: 732-985-9104.
School—Tel: 732-985-6633; Fax: 732-985-7748. Sisters of Mercy 2; Lay Teachers 20; Students 360.

FAR HILLS, SOMERSET CO., ST. ELIZABETH (1906), Rev. Msgr. George M. Brembos, Ed.D.; Deacon Lawrence Duffy.
Res.: Peapack Rd., Box 37, 07931. Tel: 908-234-0079; Fax: 908-234-2923.
Mission—St. Brigid Main St., Peapack, Somerset Co. 07977. Tel: 908-234-1265; Fax: 908-234-2923.

FLEMINGTON, HUNTERDON CO., ST. MAGDALEN DE PAZZI (1864), [CEM] Revs. Timothy Christy, Admin.; Joey R. Cervantes; R. David Chalackal; Deacons John H. Purdy; Thaddeus Wislinski.
Res.: 105 Mine St., 08822. Tel: 908-782-2922; Fax: 908-782-0952.

FORDS, MIDDLESEX CO., OUR LADY OF PEACE (1919), Rev. Msgr. Robert J. Zamorski; Rev. Michael

Gromadzki; Deacons Joseph S. Petrovich; Salvatore J. Gagliano; William B. McGann; Alexander G. Mendoza.
Res.: 26 Maple Ave., P.O. Box 69, 08863. Tel: 732-738-7940; Fax: 732-738-3848.
School—Amboy Ave., 08863. Tel: 732-738-7464; Fax: 732-738-0026. Dominican Sisters of Divine Providence 1; Lay Teachers 24; Students 350.

GREAT MEADOWS, WARREN CO., SS. PETER AND PAUL (1921), (Polish), Revs. Ignatius H. Kuziemski; Stanislaw Lewinski, O.Carm.
Res.: 360 Rte. 46, P.O. Box 156, 07838. Tel: 908-637-4269; Fax: 908-637-6896.

HACKETTSTOWN, WARREN CO., ASSUMPTION OF THE BLESSED VIRGIN MARY (1864), Very Rev. David J. Pekola; Rev. Msgr. Stephen A. Bielen, Pastor Emeritus (Retired).
Res.: 305 High St., P.O. Box 547, 07840-0547. Tel: 908-852-3320; Fax: 908-852-3662.
School—Cook & Liberty Sts., 07840. Tel: 908-852-4791; Fax: 908-852-4180. Sisters of Christian Charity 1; Lay Teachers 10; Students 224.

HAMPTON, HUNTERDON CO., ST. ANN (1859), [CEM] Rev. Michael C. Saharic; Deacon Joseph J. Foldvary.
Res.: 6 Church St., P.O. Box 405, 08827. Tel: 908-537-2221; Fax: 908-537-1158.
Station—NJ State Hospital for Geriatrics Glen Gardner.

HELMETTA, MIDDLESEX CO., HOLY TRINITY (1911), (Polish), [CEM] Rev. Stanley Jarosz.
Res.: 100 Main St., 08828. Tel: 732-521-0172; Fax: 732-521-0824.

HIGH BRIDGE, HUNTERDON CO., ST. JOSEPH (1880), Rev. Maurice T. Carlton; Deacon Charles A. Paolino.
Res.: 59 Main St., 08829. Tel: 908-638-6211; Fax: 908-638-5802.

HIGHLAND PARK, MIDDLESEX CO., ST. PAUL THE APOSTLE (1912), Rev. Robert V. Meyers, J.C.L.; Deacon Edward Krupa.
Res.: 502 Raritan Ave., 08904. Tel: 732-572-0977; Fax: 732-572-7497.
Convent—Sisters of St. Joseph of Chesnut Hill, PA, 20 S. 6th Ave., 08904. Tel: 732-572-2485.

HILLSBOROUGH, SOMERSET CO.

1—ST. JOSEPH (Millstone Borough) (1883), Very Rev. Raymond L. Cole; Deacons George D. LaPolice; Joseph C. Moscinski; John Craig.
Church: 34 Yorktown Rd., 08844.
Res.: Livingston Ave., East Millstone, 08875. Tel: 908-874-3141; Fax: 908-874-7040.

2—MARY, MOTHER OF GOD (1948), Rev. Liam A. Minogue.
Res.: 157 S. Triangle Rd., 08844. Tel: 908-874-8220; Fax: 908-874-4183.
School—Teachers 2; (PreK) 63.

HOPELAWN, MIDDLESEX CO., OUR LADY OF THE MOST HOLY ROSARY (1904), (Italian), Rev. Glenn J. Comandini, S.T.D.
Res.: 625 Florida Grove Rd., 08861. Tel: 732-826-2771; Fax: 732-826-0320.

ISELIN, MIDDLESEX CO., ST. CECELIA (1923), Revs. Jerome A. Johnson; Francis F. Vaz; George Targonski; Deacons Belardino A. Lupini; Jack Gimblett.
Res.: 45 Wilus Way, 08830. Tel: 732-283-2300; Fax: 732-283-3326.
School—Tel: 732-283-2824. Religious Teachers Filippini 4; Lay Teachers 20; Students 347.
Station—NJ State Home for Disabled Veterans Edison.
Station—Roosevelt Care Center Edison.

JAMESBURG, MIDDLESEX CO., ST. JAMES THE LESS (1878), [CEM] Very Rev. Louis F. Stingel; Rev. Charles P. Scillieri.
Res.: 36 Lincoln Ave., 08831. Tel: 732-521-0100; Fax: 732-521-8287.
Station—State Home for Boys Monroe Township. Tel: 732-521-0030.

KENDALL PARK, MIDDLESEX CO., ST. AUGUSTINE OF CANTERBURY (1952), Very Rev. Robert G. Lynam; Deacon Richard McCarron.
Res.: 51 Henderson Rd., 08824. Tel: 732-297-3000; Fax: 732-940-1746.
School—45 Henderson Rd., 08824. Tel: 732-297-6042; Fax: 732-297-7062. Brothers of Sacred Heart 1; Lay Teachers 30; Students 415; Preschool 70.

LAMBERTVILLE, HUNTERDON CO., ST. JOHN THE EVANGELIST (1843), [CEM] Revs. Leon J. Kasprzyk; Louis Mattina; Deacon Joseph J. Masterson.
Res.: 44 Bridge St., 08530. Tel: 609-397-3350; Fax: 609-397-8713.
Mission—St. Agnes Main St., Stockton, Hunterdon Co. 08559.

LAURENCE HARBOR, MIDDLESEX CO., ST. LAWRENCE (1943), Rev. Joseph Szulwach; Deacon Stephen J. Gajewski.
Res.: 109 Laurence Pkwy., 08879. Tel: 732-566-1093; Fax: 732-765-9311.

MANVILLE, SOMERSET CO.

1—CHRIST THE KING (1948), Rev. Daniel Sloan; Deacon Donald J. De Lorenzo.
Res.: 211 Louis St., 08835. Tel: 908-231-1330; Fax: 908-231-1645.
School—99 N. 13th Ave., 08835. Tel: 908-526-1339; Fax: 908-526-3541. Lay Teachers 15; Students 183.

2—SACRED HEART OF JESUS (1919), (Polish), [CEM] Revs. Boguslaw Adam Augustyn, C.SS.R.; Jan Kwiecien; Radoslaw Jaszczuk, C.SS.R.
Res.: 136 S. Main St., P.O. Box 924, 08835. Tel: 908-725-0072; Fax: 908-685-3029.

MARTINSVILLE, SOMERSET CO., BLESSED SACRAMENT (1968), Rev. Msgr. Eugene Prus; Rev. Allen Abadines.
Res.: 852 Newmans Ln., P.O. Box 563, 08836. Tel: 732-356-4442; Fax: 732-356-5172.

MIDDLESEX, MIDDLESEX CO., OUR LADY OF MOUNT VIRGIN (1943), Revs. Blaise R. Baran; John Szczepanik; Deacon John R. Tietjen.
Res.: 600 Harris Ave., 08846. Tel: 732-356-2149; Fax: 732-356-1302.
School—450 Drake Ave., 08846. Tel: 732-356-6560; Fax: 732-356-7860. Lay Teachers 13; Students 267.

MILFORD, HUNTERDON CO., ST. EDWARD THE CONFESSOR (1944), Rev. Michael E. Crummy; Deacon James W. Hendrix.
Res.: 61 Mill St., P.O. Box 522, 08848. Tel: 908-995-4723; Fax: 908-995-9353.

MILLTOWN, MIDDLESEX CO., OUR LADY OF LOURDES (1921), Revs. Thomas V. Perunilam; Edward A. Czarcinski.
Res.: 233 N. Main St., 08850. Tel: 732-828-0011; Fax: 732-828-3133.
School—43 Cleveland Ave., 08850. Tel: 732-828-1951; Fax: 732-828-7871. Little Servant Sisters of the Immaculate Conception 5; Lay Teachers 11; Students 200.

MONMOUTH JUNCTION, MIDDLESEX CO., ST. CECILIA (1982), Rev. Sylvester Cronin.
Office—10 Kingston Ln., 08852. Tel: 732-329-2893; Fax: 732-329-4693.
Res.: 46 Kingston Ln., 08852. Tel: 732-438-9483.

NEW BRUNSWICK, MIDDLESEX CO.

1—ST. JOHN THE BAPTIST (1867), (German—Spanish), [CEM] Very Rev. Marco A. Caceres; Deacon Luis F. Moral.
Res.: 29 Abeel St., 08901. Tel: 732-545-5267; Fax: 732-545-0446.
Church: Neilson and Carman Sts., 08901.

2—ST. JOSEPH (1924), (Polish), Rev. Joseph A. Krajewski, Admin.
Res.: 15 Maple St., 08901. Tel: 732-545-2195.

3—ST. LADISLAUS (1904), (Hungarian), Revs. Capistran L. Polgar, O.F.M.; L. Stephen Galambos, O.F.M.
Res.: 215 Somerset St., 08901. Tel: 732-545-1427; Fax: 732-545-8501.

4—ST. MARY OF MOUNT VIRGIN (1904), (Italian), Rev. Robert L. Santa Barbara.
Res.: 190 Sandford St., 08901. Tel: 732-545-5090; Fax: 732-937-9290.
School—192 Sandford St., 08901. Tel: 732-249-7753; Fax: 732-448-1517. Sisters 4; Lay Teachers 11; Students 137.
Mission—St. Theresa of the Infant Jesus Fox Rd., Edison, Middlesex Co. 08817. Fax: 732-937-9240.

5—OUR LADY OF MT. CARMEL (1977), (Hispanic), Revs. Raymond L. Nacarino; Antonio M. Alvarez.
Res.: 86 New St., 08901. Tel: 732-846-5873; Fax: 732-846-5397.
Church: 75 Morris St., 08901. Tel: 732-246-9826.

6—ST. PETER APOSTLE (1829), [CEM] Rev. Joseph M. Curry; Deacon Thaddeus C. Raczkowski.
Res.: 94 Somerset St., 08901. Tel: 732-545-6820; Fax: 732-545-4069.
School—165 Somerset St., 08901. Tel: 732-545-1473; Fax: 732-545-2508. Sisters 1; Lay Teachers 20; Students 205.
High School—175 Somerset St., 08901. Tel: 732-846-8046; Fax: 732-220-9560. Sisters 1; Lay Teachers 20; Students 180.

7—SACRED HEART (1883), Rev. James McGuffey, Admin.; Deacon Richard R. Kaseta.
Res.: 56 Throop Ave., 08901. Tel: 732-545-1681; Fax: 732-545-5059.

NORTH BRUNSWICK, MIDDLESEX CO., OUR LADY OF PEACE (1969), Rev. John V. Polyak.
Res.: 277 Washington Pl., 08902. Tel: 732-297-9680; Fax: 732-297-1024.

NORTH PLAINFIELD, SOMERSET CO.

1—ST. JOSEPH (1882), Very Rev. John J. Casey.
Res.: 41 Manning Ave., 07060. Tel: 908-756-3383; Fax: 908-756-1155.
School—101 Westervelt Ave., 07060. Tel: 908-756-9539. Sisters of Mercy 3; Lay Teachers 12; Students 162.

2—ST. LUKE (1965), Rev. John C. Giordano; Deacons Albert C. Parenti; Dann C. Rossi.
Res.: 300 Clinton Ave., 07063. Tel: 908-754-8811; Fax: 908-754-0120.

OLD BRIDGE, MIDDLESEX CO.

1—ST. AMBROSE (1961), Revs. Charles F. Kelly; Virgilio Tolentino; Frank W. Fellrath; Deacons Charles J. Damian; Andrew J. Strus.
Res.: 96 Throckmorton Ln., 08857. Tel: 732-679-5666; Fax: 732-679-0853.
School—Tel: 732-679-4700; Fax: 732-679-6062. Sisters of St. Joseph (Chestnut Hill) 3; Lay Teachers 36; Students 475.
Convent—94 Throckmorton Ln., 08857. Tel: 732-679-5509.

2—MOST HOLY REDEEMER (1983), Rev. Chester H. Carina, J.C.L., Admin.; Deacons Robert T. McGovern; A. Keith Berg; Frank C. D'Auguste.
Res.: 133 Amboy Rd., Old Bridge Township, Matawan, 07747. Tel: 732-566-9334; Fax: 732-566-2245.

3—ST. THOMAS THE APOSTLE (1921), Rev. Msgr. John B. Szymanski, V.G.; Revs. Randall J. Vashon; Kevin M. Casey, C.P.; Deacons John J. Fitzsimmons; Paul E. Featherman; Robert Bonfante Sr.
Res.: One St. Thomas Plaza, 08857. Tel: 732-251-4000; Fax: 732-251-4946.
School—333 Hwy. 18, 08857. Tel: 732-251-4812; Fax: 732-251-5315. Lay Teachers 21; Students 453.

OXFORD, WARREN CO., ST. ROSE OF LIMA (1864), [CEM] Rev. Richard Rusk.
Res.: Academy St., P.O. Box 88, 07863. Tel: 908-453-2034; Fax: 908-453-4425.

PARLIN, MIDDLESEX CO., ST. BERNADETTE (1956), Revs. James W. Hagerman; Kenneth R. Kolibas; Deacons Nicholas J. Thornton; Samuel Rutch; Donald Zampella.
Res.: 20 Villanova Rd., 08859. Tel: 732-721-2772; Fax: 732-727-5188.

PERTH AMBOY, MIDDLESEX CO.

1—HOLY SPIRIT (1944), Rev. Robert G. Gorman; Deacon Sam Costantino. In Res., Rev. Sean Winters.
Res.: 580 Hazel Ave., 08861. Tel: 732-826-4859; Fax: 732-826-6078.

2—HOLY TRINITY (1899), (Slovak—Hispanic), [CEM] Very Rev. Thomas F. Ryan; Deacon Jose M. Martinez.
Res.: 474 Penn St., 08861. Tel: 732-826-0439; Fax: 732-826-2758.

3—LA ASUNCION (1981), (Hispanic), Revs. John B. Gordon; Nicholas Norena; Deacons Enrique Garcia; Corpus V. Perez; Noe Cortez.
Mailing Address: 777 Cortlandt St., P.O. Box 1335, 08862. Tel: 732-826-4991; Fax: 732-826-6951.

4—ST. MARY (1845), Rev. Michael P. Scott; Deacons Basilio D. Perez; Antonio Bezares.
Res.: 104 Center St., 08861. Tel: 732-442-0039; Fax: 732-324-4383.

5—OUR LADY OF FATIMA (1960), (Hispanic), Revs. Frank Iacona, C.M.F. (ATL); Benjamin Martinez, C.M.F.; Kenneth Oguejiofor, C.M.F.; Ruben Matute, C.M.F.; Deacons Angel P. Perez; Herminio Rivera; Pablo Bencosme.
Res.: 380 Smith St., 08861. Tel: 732-442-6634; Fax: 732-826-0958.

6—OUR LADY OF HUNGARY (1902), (Hungarian), [CEM] Very Rev. Thomas F. Ryan, Admin.
Res.: 697 Cortlandt St., 08861. Tel: 732-442-0512; Fax: 732-442-3037.

7—OUR LADY OF THE ROSARY OF FATIMA (1981), (Portuguese), Rev. Lauro C. Sedlmayer (Brazil), Admin.
Res.: 188 Wayne St., 08861. Tel: 732-826-4350.

8—ST. STEPHEN (1892), (Polish), [CEM] Revs. John Stec; Wladyslaw Wiktorek, C.SS.R.
Res.: 490 State St., 08861. Tel: 732-826-1395; Fax: 732-826-4217.

PHILLIPSBURG, WARREN CO.

1—SS. PETER AND PAUL (1913), (Slovak), Closed., Records at St. Philip & St. James, Phillipsburg

2—ST. PHILIP & ST. JAMES (1860), [CEM] Rev. Msgr. Michael J. Corona; Revs. Vincent P. Chen (Taiwan); Mark Kehoe; James McGuffey; Deacons John T. Flynn; Enock Berluche Sr.; George Frank.
Res.: 430 S. Main St., 08865-3094. Tel: 908-454-0112; Fax: 908-454-0125.
Mission—St. Christopher New Village, Warren Co.

PISCATAWAY, MIDDLESEX CO.

1—ST. FRANCES CABRINI (1961), Revs. Edgardo D. Abano; Danilo A. Canceran; Deacons James O'Neill; Roger Ladao. In Res., Rev. Msgr. Reynaldo Nunez.
Res.: 208 Bound Brook Ave., 08854-4097. Tel: 732-885-5313; Fax: 732-885-9031.
School—2300 Cooper St., 08854. Tel: 732-885-1066; Fax: 732-885-5252. Sisters of Mercy 1; Lay Teachers 17; Students 222.

2—OUR LADY OF FATIMA (1948), Revs. Herbert J. Stab; Paul daSilva; Jose M. Marcelo; Deacons Stanley J. Lorenc; Lawrence P. Reilly.
Res.: 501 New Market Rd., 08854. Tel: 732-968-5555; Fax: 732-968-5959.
School—499 New Market Rd., 08854. Tel: 732-968-5017; Fax: 732-968-9259. Lay Teachers 14; Students 113; Preschool 40.

PITTSTOWN, HUNTERDON CO., ST. CATHERINE OF SIENA (1992), Rev. Peter Suhaka; Deacon Dennis K. Webster.
Res.: P.O. Box 245, 08867-0245. Tel: 908-735-4024; Fax: 908-735-0355.
Catechesis/Religious Program—Students 407.

PLAINSBORO, MIDDLESEX CO., QUEENSHIP OF MARY (1982), Rev. Robert W. Medley.

Res.: P.O. Box 759, 08536. Tel: 609-799-7511; Fax: 609-799-8904.

PORT MURRAY, WARREN CO., ST. THEODORE (1983), Rev. Anthony M. Siranni, Admin.
Res.: P.O. Box 146, 07865. Tel: 908-689-8318; Fax: 908-689-9242.

PORT READING, MIDDLESEX CO., ST. ANTHONY OF PADUA (1906), Rev. William J. smith, Admin.; Deacon Albert Coppola.
Res.: 436 Port Reading Ave., 07064. Tel: 732-634-1403; Fax: 732-602-0119.

RARITAN, SOMERSET CO.

1—ST. ANN (1903), (Italian), Rev. Kenneth D. Brighenti; Deacon John R. Pacifico.
Res.: 45 Anderson St., 08869. Tel: 908-725-1008; Fax: 908-707-1915.
School—29 Second Ave., 08869. Tel: 908-725-7787. Religious Teachers Filippini 2; Lay Teachers 13; Students 246.

2—ST. JOSEPH (1912), (Slovak), Rev. Kevin A. Kaminski. In Res., Rev. Charles W. Cicerale. Tel: 908-725-5775.
Res.: 16 E. Somerset St., 08869. Tel: 908-725-0163.

SAYREVILLE, MIDDLESEX CO.

1—OUR LADY OF VICTORIES (1885), Very Rev. Michael G. Krull; Revs. Joseph D. Kraus; Roberto Coruna.
Mailing Address: 42 Main St., 08872.
Res.: 24 Main St., 08872. Tel: 732-257-0077; Fax: 732-651-1898.
School—36 Main St., 08872. Tel: 732-254-1676; Fax: 732-254-5066. Lay Teachers 24; Students 326.

2—ST. STANISLAUS KOSTKA (1914), (Polish), [CEM] Revs. Kenneth R. Murphy; Andrzej Wielczko.
Res.: 225 MacArthur Ave., 08872. Tel: 732-254-0212; Fax: 732-390-2989.
School—MacArthur Ave., 08872. Tel: 732-254-5819; Fax: 732-257-2903. Lay Teachers 13; Students 209.

SKILLMAN, SOMERSET CO., ST. CHARLES BORROMEO (1982), Rev. Gregory E. S. Malovetz; Deacon Thomas J. Giacobbe.
Res.: 376 Burnt Hill Rd., 08558. Tel: 609-466-0300; Fax: 609-466-0602.

SOMERSET, SOMERSET CO., ST. MATTHIAS (1962), Revs. Douglas J. Haefner; John Brundage; Deacons Stephen J. Holzinger II; Ronald J. Caimi; John M. Radvanski.
Mailing Address: 168 J.F. Kennedy Blvd., 08873. Tel: 732-828-1400; Fax: 732-828-0866.
Res.: 166 J.F. Kennedy Blvd., 08873.
School—170 J.F. Kennedy Blvd., 08873. Sisters 4; Lay Teachers 28; Students 613.

SOMERVILLE, SOMERSET CO., IMMACULATE CONCEPTION (1882), [CEM] Rev. Msgr. Seamus F. Brennan; Revs. Alexander J. Carles; James S. Convery; Deacons John B. Ivers; Arnold J. De Marco; Frank J. Quinn; Luis E. Vindas.
Res.: 35 Mountain Ave., 08876. Tel: 908-725-1112; Fax: 908-725-6269.
School—Tel: 908-725-6516; Fax: 908-725-3172. Sisters 4; Lay Teachers 23; Preschool 30; Students 529.
High School—Tel: 908-722-0200; Fax: 908-218-7765. Sisters 13; Lay Teachers 68; Students 883.
Convent—Sisters, Servants of the Immaculate Heart of Mary, 230 Mountain Ave., 08876. Tel: 908-722-6894.

SOUTH AMBOY, MIDDLESEX CO.

1—ST. MARY (1864), [CEM] Rev. Dennis R. Weezorak; Deacons Stephen N. Laikowski; Richard O'Brien.
Res.: 256 Augusta St., 08879. Tel: 732-721-0179; Fax: 732-721-0360.
School—Second St., 08879. Tel: 732-721-1514; Fax: 732-721-9666. Lay Teachers 14; Students 200.

2—SACRED HEART (1895), (Polish), [CEM] Rev. Joseph V. Romanoski.
Res.: 224 N. Feltus St., 08879. Tel: 732-721-0040; Fax: 732-721-4448.
School—Tel: 732-721-0834; 732-721-1446 (Preschool); Fax: 732-316-0326. Sisters of St. Francis of the Martyr St. George 2; Lay Teachers 15; Students 200.

SOUTH BOUND BROOK, SOMERSET CO., OUR LADY OF MERCY (1949), Very Rev. Daniel J. Herlihy.
Res.: 122 High St., 08880. Tel: 732-356-1037; Fax: 732-356-1318.

SOUTH PLAINFIELD, MIDDLESEX CO.

1—OUR LADY OF CZESTOCHOWA (1943), (Polish), Rev. J. Maciej Melaniuk.
Res.: 120 Kosciusko Ave., 07080. Tel: 908-756-1333; Fax: 908-756-4501.

2—SACRED HEART (1906), [CEM] Revs. John Paul Alvarado; John J. Werner; Deacon Joseph J. Stanczak.
Res.: 149 S. Plainfield Ave., 07080. Tel: 908-756-0633; Fax: 908-757-5655.
School—Tel: 908-756-0632. Sisters 2; Lay Teachers 22; Students 278.

SOUTH RIVER, MIDDLESEX CO.

1—CORPUS CHRISTI (1944), Revs. Kevin P. Duggan; Timothy J. Lambert.
Res.: 100 James St., 08882. Tel: 732-254-1800; Fax: 732-254-8063.
School—80 David St., 08882. Tel: 732-257-5200; Fax: 732-257-6390. Lay Teachers 13; Students 178.

2—ST. MARY OF OSTRABRAMA (1903), (Polish), [CEM] Very Rev. Stanely G. Gromadzki; Rev. Stanislaw Kolano.
Res.: 30 Jackson St., 08882. Tel: 732-254-2220; Fax: 732-651-8182.

3—ST. STEPHEN PROTOMARTYR (1907), (Hungarian), Rev. George M. Pisanello, J.C.L., Admin.
Res.: 20 William St., 08882. Tel: 732-257-0100; Fax: 732-257-4646.

SPOTSWOOD, MIDDLESEX CO., IMMACULATE CONCEPTION (1946), Revs. Harold L. Hirsch; John Primich; Andrzej Gajewski; Deacon John H. McGuire.
Res.: 18 South St., 08884. Tel: 732-251-3110; Fax: 732-251-2407.
School—23 Manalapan Rd., 08884. Tel: 732-251-3090; Fax: 732-251-8270. Felician Sisters 2; Lay Teachers 30; Students 350.
Convent—Tel: 732-251-3446.

THREE BRIDGES, HUNTERDON CO., ST. ELIZABETH ANN SETON (1984), Rev. Thomas J. Serafin; Deacon Paul Santella.
Mailing Address: 105 Summer Road, 08887.
Res.: 7 Forest Hill Dr., 08887. Tel: 908-782-1475; Fax: 908-782-6230.

WARREN, SOMERSET CO., OUR LADY OF THE MOUNT (1911), Very Rev. Terrance M. Lawler; Rev. James Considine; Deacons Walter S. Maksimik; Thomas Sicola.
Res.: 167 Mount Bethel Rd., 07059. Tel: 908-647-1075; Fax: 908-647-7885.

WASHINGTON, WARREN CO., ST. JOSEPH (1872), [CEM] Rev. Robert J. Ascolese.
Res.: 200 Carlton Ave., 07882. Tel: 908-689-0058; Fax: 908-689-3436.

WATCHUNG, SOMERSET CO., ST. MARY-STONY HILL (1847), [CEM] Rev. Brian J. Nolan; Deacon Arthur J. Wise, Emeritus.
Res.: 225 Mountain Blvd., 07069. Tel: 908-756-6524; Fax: 908-756-2111.

WHITEHOUSE STATION, HUNTERDON CO., OUR LADY OF LOURDES (1923), Rev. Leonard F.A. Rusay; Deacon Samuel J. Damiano.
Res.: 390 Country Rd. 523, 08889. Tel: 908-534-2319; Fax: 908-534-5670.

WOODBRIDGE, MIDDLESEX CO.

1—ST. JAMES (1860), [CEM] Rev. Charles W. Cicerale, Temp. Admin.; Deacon Carl E. Psota. In Res., Revs. Sebastian D. Kaithackal, C.M.I.; Jerome Kim, S.S.T.; Joseph Oahn Dang, S.V.D.
Res.: 145 Grove St., 07095. Tel: 732-634-0500; Fax: 732-602-1487.
School—341 Amboy Ave., 07095. Tel: 732-634-2090. Bernadine Franciscan Sisters 1; Lay Teachers 17; Students 331.
Convent—Tel: 732-634-0176.

2—OUR LADY OF MOUNT CARMEL (1921), (Hungarian), Revs. Vincent C. Cornejo; Michael M. Vincze, Pastor Emeritus (Retired).
Res.: 267 Smith St., 07095. Tel: 732-634-1438; Fax: 732-634-5368.

Chaplains of Public Institutions

ANNANDALE. *Mountainview Youth Correctional Facility* 08801. Tel: 732-741-6208. Attended by Immaculate Conception, Clinton

AVENEL. *Woodbridge State School*. Attended by St. Andrew the Apostle.

BELLE MEAD. *Carrier Clinic*. Rev. Norman R. St. John, S.V.D.

BELVIDERE. *Warren Correctional Center*. Attended by St. Patrick, Belvidere.

CLINTON. *Edna Mahan Correctional Facility for Women*. Tel: 908-735-7319. Attended by Immaculate Conception, Clinton.
Hunterdon Developmental Center. Very Rev. Andrew L. Szaroleta, Chap. Attended by Immaculate Conception, Clinton.

EDISON. *John F. Kennedy Medical Center*. Revs. John D. Murphy, Chap., Pauly Thekkan, C.M.I.

FLEMINGTON. *Hunterdon Medical Center*. Attended by St. Magdalen de Pazzi.

GLEN GARDNER. *N.J. State Hospital for Geriatrics*. Attended by St. Ann, Hampton.

HACKETTSTOWN. *Hackettstown Community Hospital*. Attended by Assumption of the Blessed Virgin Mary.

JAMESBURG. *N.J. State Training School for Boys*. Attended by St. James the Less.

LYONS. *U.S. Veterans Medical Center*. Revs. George F. Kelly, C.Ss.R., William Warman (BAL), Joseph C. Chacko.

MENLO PARK. *Roosevelt State Hospital*. Attended by St. Cecelia, Iselin.

NEW BRUNSWICK. *Robert Wood Johnson University Hospital*. Rev. Gregorio Neri.

NORTH BRUNSWICK. *Middlesex County Adult Detention Center*. Attended by Our Lady of Peace.

OLD BRIDGE. *Old Bridge Regional Hospital*. Attended by St. Ambrose.

PERTH AMBOY. *Raritan Bay Medical Center*, Tel: 732-826-2771. Revs. Sean Winters, Sebastian D. Kaithackal, C.M.I.

PHILLIPSBURG. *Warren Hospital*, Tel: 908-454-0112. Rev. Vincent P. Chen (Taiwan).

RAHWAY. *East Jersey State Prison*, Tel: 732-634-4355. Attended from St. Andrew the Apostle Church, Avenel.

SKILLMAN. *NJ State Neuropsychiatric Institute*. Attended by St. Charles Borromeo.

SOMERVILLE. *Somerset Medical Center*, Tel: 908-526-2394. Rev. Radoslaw Jaszczuk, C.SS.R.

SOUTH AMBOY. *South Amboy Memorial Hospital*. Attended by St. Mary and Sacred Heart.

On Duty Outside the Diocese:
Revs.—
Albaladejo, Juan A., Society of Jesus Christ the Priest
Bihuniak, Michael J.
Bochnak, Zenon A., Military
Carpena, Octavio R., Society of Jesus Christ the Priest, Murcia, Spain
Dandry, Anthony M. (Retired)
Desmond, Joseph L., Tennessee
Escribano, Peter E., Society of Jesus Christ the Priest, Murcia, Spain
Fitzgerald, Garrett J.
Haddad, Wayne M., Military
Jones, Kevin C.
Kochon, Michael A.
Kottar, Michael T., Diocese of Charlotte
Leonard, William F.
Marin, John L., Society of Jesus Christ the Priest, Guayaquil, Ecuador
Marincioni, Raniero A., Society of Jesus Christ the Priest, Ecuador
McCord, Kent G., Bremerton, MA
Moore, Thomas G.
Moya, Peter O., Society of Jesus Christ the Priest Murcia, Spain
Oterino, Francis L., Society of Jesus Christ the Priest, Guayaquil, Ecuador
Pepel, Clement
Prats, Charles R., Society of Jesus Christ the Priest, Murcia, Spain
Ruiz, Faustino C., Society of Jesus Christ the Priest, Chile
Scarcella, Philip J., 6300 Woodbend Dr., Apt. N, Charlotte, NC 28212-2039.
Shaner, Edward G., Pauline Fathers, Doylestown, PA
Venditti, J. Michael, Eparchy of Passaic, NJ

Retired:
Rev. Msgrs.—
Bielen, Stephen A.
Endebrock, Donald M.
Gambino, Anthony J.
Haughney, William J.
Kennedy, J. Nevin
Torney, John R., P.A.
Revs.—
Abramowicz, Richard B.
Attanasio, Raymond V.
Avery, Raymond
Crowley, R. Kevin
Dandry, Anthony M.
Driscoll, Michael A.
Egierd, Henry A.
Ewing, Richard A.
Hemmerling, Henry L.
Hogan, Joseph F.
Holup, Joseph M.
Kearns, Edward A.
Miller, Robert J.
Muccilli, Robert L.
Nebus, Vincent J.
Nester, Edward J.
Przechacki, Casimir J.
Roca, Albert L.
Schellberg, Eugene
Skwara, John M.
Struzik, Edward J.
Thul, Joseph T.
Vadakkskara, J. Philip
Vielgus, Thaddeus A.
Vincze, Michael M.
Walega, Stanley J.

Permanent Deacons:
Albert, Henry F.
Alexander, Russell C., (Retired)
Anderson, Paul L.
Bauer, William R.
Bell, James S.
Bencosme, Pablo
Berg, Albert K.

Berluche, Enock, Sr.
Bezares, Antonio
Bolash, George L.
Bonfante, Robert, Sr.
Brossoni, Guido J.
Caimi, Ronald J.
Cammarano, Frank J.
Clementi, Leo F.
Cline, Patrick J., Brooklyn
Coleman, George D.
Coppola, Albert
Cortex, Noe
Cortez, Noe
Costantino, Samuel J.
Cribbin, Bernard A.
Czekaj, John R.
D'Angelo, Gregory
D'Auguste, Frank C.
Daley, James M., (Retired)
Damian, Charles J.
Damiano, Samuel J.
De Blasio, Anthony A., On Leave
De Frange, David A.
De Lorenzo, Donald J.
De Marco, Arnold J.
Demarest, Barry C.
Dominiecki, Thomas F.
Duffy, Lawrence J.
Dumschat, John F.
Featherman, Paul E.
Fierst, Henry, Jr.
Fiore, Philip
Fitzsimmons, John J.
Flynn, John T.
Foldvary, Joseph J.
Forrestall, Michael J.
Frank, George A.
Gagliano, Salvatore J.
Gajewski, Stephen J.
Garcia, Enrique
Gellentien, Robert P.
Giacobbe, Thomas J.
Gilheany, Thomas J., Newark
Gimblett, John
Gleason, Michael P.
Gleason, Michael P.
Gostkowski, Anthony J.
Hally, Luke J.
Hanna, John H.
Heissenbuttel, Thomas A., On Leave
Hendrix, James W.
Hewitt, James, III
Holowienka, Edward
Holzinger, Stephen J., II
Ibern, Jose
Ivers, John B.
Kaseta, Richard R.
Kenny, John F.
Klein, Robert J.
Koy, Martin L.
Krupa, Edward
La Police, George D.
Ladao, Rogelio
Laikowski, Stephen N.
Licameli, Paul G.
Livingston, Joel R.
Long, James A.
Lorenc, Stanley J.
Lupini, Belardino A.
Maksimik, Walter S.
Marano, Francis J., (Retired)
Martinez, Jose M.
Massimei, Eric S.
Masterson, Joseph J.
Maurer, Joseph S., (Retired)
McCarron, Richard
McCarthy, Keith M.
McGann, William B.
McGovern, Robert T.
McGrath, James G., On Leave
McGreevy, Robert A., On Leave
McGuire, John H.
McShane, John P.
Mendoza, Alexander
Monahan, John T.
Moral, Luis S.
Morend, Michel G., Newark
Moscinski, Joseph C.
Mulroy, Martin B., Brooklyn
Murtha, Michael P., On Leave
Nardi, Samuel, On Leave
Nemeth, Stephen F.
O'Brien, Richard
O'Keefe, Joseph E.
O'Neill, James
Pacifico, John R.
Page, Warren C., Syracuse
Paolino, Charles
Parenti, Albert C.
Payne, Alfred C., Jr.
Perez, Angel P.
Perez, Basilio A., Dominican Republic
Perez, Corpus V.
Petrovich, Joseph S.
Psota, Carl E.
Purdy, John H., II
Quinn, Frank J.
Raczkowski, Thaddeus C.
Radvanski, John M.
Ragucci, Joseph D.
Reilly, Lawrence P.
Rivera, Herminio
Rossi, Dann P.
Ruiz-Diaz, Benigno I.
Rutch, Samuel
Sandoval, Gustavo
Santella, Paul
Sheridan, John T.
Sicola, Thomas
Sims, Gerard C.
Smoyak, Cornelius S.
Stanczak, Joseph J.
Strus, Andrew J.
Sullivan, Michael J., Jr.
Suswal, Carl S., (Retired)
Thornton, Nicholas J.
Tietjen, John R.
Torres, Ramon L.
Van Haute, John
Vanzino, William C.
Villegas, Felix
Vindas, Luis E.
Vivona, Joseph A.
Webster, Dennis K.
Wise, Arthur J.
Wislinski, Thaddeus
Zampella, Donald

INSTITUTIONS LOCATED IN THE DIOCESE

[A] HIGH SCHOOLS, DIOCESAN

EDISON. *Bishop Ahr High School*, One Tingley Ln., 08820. Tel: 732-549-1108; Fax: 732-494-2229. Email: 5bgaed@diometuchen.org. Web: www.bgahs.com. Sr. Donna Marie Trukowski, C.S.S.F., Prin. Felician Sisters 2; Lay Teachers 57; Students 913.

SOUTH AMBOY. *Cardinal McCarrick High School*, 310 Augusta St., 08879. Tel: 732-721-0748; Fax: 732-727-7018. Dr. Frank J. Ianniruberto, Prin.; Revs. Michael Scott, Chap.; John Gordon, Chap. Sisters 5; Lay Teachers 24; Students 472.

[B] HIGH SCHOOLS, PRIVATE

METUCHEN. *St. Joseph High School*, 145 Plainfield Ave., 08840-1099. Tel: 732-549-7600; Fax: 732-549-0664. Web: www.stjoes.org. Bros. Dennis Wermert, S.C., Pres.; Matthew Scanlon, S.C., D.R.E.; Peter Murphy, S.C., Chap.; Mr. Lawrence N. Walsh, Prin. Brothers of the Sacred Heart 10; Sisters of St. Joseph (Philadelphia) 3; Lay Teachers 49; Boys 844.

WATCHUNG. *Mount St. Mary Academy* 07069. Tel: 908-757-0108; Fax: 908-756-5751. Email: lgambacorto@mountsaintmary.org. Web: www.mountsaintmary.org. Sr. Lisa D. Gambacorto, R.S.M., E.D.S.; Rev. William T. Morris (NEW), Chap. Day school for girls. College preparatory only. Sisters of Mercy 6; Lay Teachers 41; Girls 366.

[C] INTER-PAROCHIAL ELEMENTARY SCHOOLS

BOUND BROOK. *Holy Family Academy*, St. Joseph Campus, 120 E. Second St., 08805. Tel: 732-356-1151; Fax: 732-356-6884. Email: 4hfabbsj@diometuchen.org. Web: www.hfawildcats.com. Mrs. Donna Kanowitz, Prin. Teachers 15; Students 222.

PERTH AMBOY. *Perth Amboy Catholic Elementary School*, (Grades PreK-2), Brace & Carlock Aves., 08861. Tel: 732-826-5747; Fax: 732-826-6096. Lay Teachers 9; Students 172.

Perth Amboy Catholic Intermediate School, (Grades 3-5), 500 State St., 08861. Tel: 732-826-1598; Fax: 732-826-7063. Email: rpiatek@diometuchen.org. Lay Teachers 6; Students 128.

Perth Amboy Catholic School - Main Central Office, 583 McKeon St., 08862. Tel: 732-442-9533; Fax: 732-442-2887. Sr. Jeanette DeSena, M.P.F., Admin.

Perth Amboy Middle School, (Grades 6-8), 680 Catherine St., 08861. Tel: 732-442-1713. Sisters 2; Lay Teachers 8; Students 143.

PHILLIPSBURG. *Saints Philip & James School*, 137 Roseberry St., 08865. Tel: 908-859-1244; Fax: 908-859-1202. Email: isena@diometuchen.org. Web: www.catholic-church.org/sspj/. Mrs. Irene D. Sena, Prin. Sisters 4; Lay Teachers 21; Students 367.

WASHINGTON. *St. Joseph Catholic Academy*, 200 Carlton Ave., 07882. Tel: 908-689-0093; Fax: 908-689-6811. Dr. Julia P. Healey. Lay Teachers 19; Students 81; Preschool 58.

[D] SPECIAL SCHOOLS, PRIVATE

WATCHUNG. *McAuley School for Exceptional Children*, 1633 U.S. Hwy. 22, 07069. Tel: 908-754-4114; Fax: 908-754-3312. Email: mcaschool@aol.com. Sr. Lee Ann Amico, R.S.M., Dir. Sisters 3; Lay Teachers 20; Students 50.

[E] CATHOLIC CHARITIES

BRIDGEWATER. *Bridgewater Family Service Center*, 540 U.S. Rte. 22 E., 08807. Tel: 908-722-1881; Fax: 908-704-0215. Email: jcotc@ccdom.org. Web: ccdom.org. Julio Coto.

Somerset County Services, 540-550 U.S. Rte. 22 E., 08807. Tel: 908-722-1881; Fax: 908-704-0215. Web: www.ccdom.org. Suzanne Silverio, L.C.S.W., C.A.D.C., Division Dir.

EAST BRUNSWICK. *East Brunswick Family Service Center*, Formerly Mental Health Center, 288 Rues Ln., 08816. Tel: 732-257-6100; Fax: 732-257-6929. Email: jcoto@ccdom.org. Web: www.ccdom.org.

EDISON. *Family Service Center*, 26 Safran Ave., 08837. Tel: 732-738-1323; Fax: 732-738-3896. Web: www.ccdom.org. Jean Beil, L.C.S.W., Div. Dir. Housing & Social Concerns.

FLEMINGTON. *Flemington Family Service Center*, Formerly Hunterdon County Services, 6 Park Ave., 08822. Tel: 908-782-7905; Fax: 908-782-5934. Web: www.ccdom.org.

PERTH AMBOY. *Catholic Charities Central Office*, 319 Maple St., 08861. Tel: 732-324-8200; Fax: 732-826-3549. Web: www.ccdom.org. Marianne Majewski, L.C.S.W., Exec. Dir.; Larry Wenger, M.S.W., Assoc. Exec. Dir.; Joan Lorah, L.C.S.W., Asst. Exec. Dir.; Christine Benitez, M.B.A., C.P.A., CFO; Annie Lachs, M.Ed., Dir. Communications; Douglas J. Suson, J.D., Dir. Compliance; R. Susan Tillman, M.A., Dir. Human Resources.

Trinity Health & Family Services of Catholic Charities, Formerly Trinity Health & Community Services Center Catholic Charities, 271 Smith St., 08861. Tel: 732-826-9160; Fax: 732-826-8342. Email: ervoir@ccdom.org. Ernest Revoir, Div. Dir.

PHILLIPSBURG. *Phillipsburg Family Service Center*, Formerly Family Service Office, 700 Sayre Ave., 08865. Tel: 908-454-2074; Fax: 908-454-9871. Email: dromero@ccdom.org. Web: www.ccdom.org.

Social Service Center, 372 S. Main St., 08865. Tel: 908-859-5447; Fax: 908-859-6375. Email: mpopovice@ccdom.org. Sr. M. Michaelita Popovice, R.S.M., Prog. Dir.

Warren County Office, 700 Sayre Ave., 08865. Tel: 908-454-2074; Fax: 908-454-9871. Web: www.ccdom.org.

[F] GENERAL HOSPITALS

NEW BRUNSWICK. *Saint Peter's University Hospital*, 254 Easton Ave., P.O. Box 591, 08903-0591. Tel: 732-745-8600; Fax: 732-247-9888. Email: jbrady@saintpetersuh.com. Web: www.saintpetersuh.com. Revs. Cecilio E. Sipaco (Philippines), Chap.; Raynard Smith, Chap.; Lazaro Perez (Philippines), Chap.; Sisters Breda Boyle, C.S.J.P., Chap.; Barbara Ortmann, O.P., Chap.; Jerome Herauf, M.A., Dir. Pastoral Care. Bed Capacity 422; Bassinets 77; Neonatal Intensive Care Bassinetts 35; Intermediate Care Bassinetts 19; Patients assisted annually 284,933.

[G] HOMES FOR AGED

NORTH PLAINFIELD. *Villa Maria Sanitarium*, 641 Somerset St., 07060-4909. Tel: 908-757-3050; Fax: 908-754-4939. Rev. Severin Dietrich, O.F.M.Conv., Chap. Tel: 908-757-3050. Administration: Franciscan Sisters, Home for the aged. Patients and Residents 16.

SOMERSET. *McCarrick Care Center*, 15 Dellwood Ln., 08873. Tel: 732-545-4200; Fax: 732-846-1089. James F. Caron, Admin.; Rev. Thomas P. Ganley, Chap. Patients Assisted Annually 160. In Res. Revs. Vincent T. Calderwood (Retired); John M. Skwara (Retired); Joseph T. Thul (Retired).

WOODBRIDGE. *St. Joseph Assisted Living Residence*, One St. Joseph Terr., 07095. Tel: 732-634-0004; Fax: 732-634-4586. Email: cierpinska@aol.com. Sr. Mary Louise, L.S.I.C., Admin. Little Servant Sisters 18; Residents 60.

[H] MONASTERIES AND RESIDENCES FOR PRIESTS AND BROTHERS

METUCHEN. *Brothers of the Sacred Heart*, 145 Plainfield Ave., 08840. Tel: 732-548-2292; Fax: 732-548-3101. Email: cairns@castle.org. Bro. Ronald Cairns, S.C., Supr. Brothers 9.

ASBURY. *Lanteri House*, 668 Mountain View Rd., 08802. Tel: 908-689-5242.

PRINCETON. *Vincentian Residence*, 65 Mapleton Rd., 08540-9614. Tel: 609-452-2144; Fax: 609-452-7242. Web: www.sjseminary.org. Revs. Joseph A. Morris, C.M.; Charles F. Krieg, C.M.; Joseph P. McClain, C.M.; John G. Nugent, C.M.; Hydo Emerick, C.M.; John T. Maher, C.M.; Richard Kehoe, C.M.; Aidan Rooney, C.M.; Francis W. Sacks, C.M. (PH); Bros. Carmen Ciardullo, C.M.; Frank Mallaghan, C.M.

RARITAN. *Clairvaux House*, 52 W. Somerset St., 08869. Tel: 908-526-6232. Web: www.arch-angel.net/shrine. Rev. Juan A. Albaladejo.

SOMERSET. *Consolata Society for Foreign Missions*, Provincial Headquarters, 2301 Rt. 27, P.O. Box 5550, 08875. Tel: 732-297-9191; Fax: 732-940-3121. Email: supreus@ismico.org. Web: www.consolata.org. Very Rev. Leonard DePasquale, I.M.C., Prov. Supr.; Revs. Michele Brizio, I.M.C.; Herman Crespi, I.M.C.; David Kamau Gikonyo, I.M.C. (WDC); Aventino Oliveira, I.M.C.; Van Allen Hager, I.M.C.; Paul Stefanowich, I.M.C.

Maria Regina Residence, 5 Dellwood Ln., 08873. Tel: 732-828-6800; Fax: 732-828-7206. Rev. Thomas P. Ganley, Chap.; Sr. M. Carista Born, F.S.G.M., Dir.; Rev. John C. Giordano, Admin.; Rev. Msgrs. John R. Torney, P.A. (Retired); William J. Haughney (Retired); J. Nevin Kennedy (Retired); Stephen A. Bielen (Retired); Anthony J. Gambino (Retired); Revs. Raymond Avery; Edward J. Nester (Retired); Joseph M. Holup (Retired); Edward J. Struzik (Retired). Retirement home for Diocesan priests.

The Metuchen Oratory, Congregation of the Oratory of St. Philip Neri, 2301 Hwy. 27, P.O. Box 6078, 08875. Tel: 732-297-6401; Fax: 732-297-6403. Email: Oratorymet@aol.com. Very Rev. Peter R. Cebulka, C.O., Provost; Revs. Thomas J. Walsh, C.O., Vicar; Thomas A. Odorizzi, C.O., Treas. Priests 3; Brothers 1.

SOUTH RIVER. *Passionist Provincial Office*, 80 David St., 08882. Tel: 732-257-7177; Fax: 732-257-0042. Email: terry@cpprov.org. Very Rev. Terence Kristofak, C.P. Priests 5.

Consultors: Revs. Gerald Laba, C.P.; Joseph Jones, C.P.; Melvin Shorter, C.P.; Francis Finnigan, C.P.

St. Gabriel's Monastery, 650 Sheppard Ave. E., Willowdale ON M2K 1B7 Canada. Tel: 416-221-8866; Fax: 416-221-8893. Rev. Stephen Dunn, C.P.

84 Clarinda Dr., Toronto ON M2K 1V3 Canada. Tel: 416-229-9690; Fax: 416-225-5445. Revs. Paul Cusack, C.P.; Luigi Malorzo, C.P.; Bernard McEachern, C.P.

Religious of the Province in Residences Not Listed Elsewhere:

Mercy Medical Center, P.O. Box 6009, Redding, CA 90099. Tel: 530-225-6000. Rev. Michael Brennan, C.P.

St. Thomas the Apostle, One St. Thomas Plaza, Old Bridge, 08857. Tel: 732-251-4000; Fax: 732-251-4946. Rev. Kevin Casey, C.P.

St. Mathew's Rectory, 81 Seymour Ave., Edison, 08817. Tel: 732-985-5063; 732-283-3800 (Office). Rev. Neil W. Davin, C.P., J.C.L.

Georgian Institution, 391-D Picardy Court, Lakewood, 08701. Tel: 732-367-4543. Rev. Norman Demeck, C.P.

St. Ursula Rectory, 8801 Harford Rd., Baltimore, MD 21234. Tel: 410-665-2111; Fax: 410-665-0758. Rev. Gerald Hynes, C.P.

P.O. Box 1800, Orlando, FL 32802-1800. Tel: 407-246-4800; Fax: 407-246-4941. Bro. Augustine Paul Lowe, C.P.

15 McBride Ave., White Plains, NY 10603. Tel: 914-761-5439. Rev. Gerard A. Orlando, C.P.

5859 Nottingham St., St. Louis, MO 63109. Tel: 314-977-3149; Fax: 314-377-3696. Rev. Theodore Vitali, C.P.

204 N. Church St., Dublin, GA 31021.

316 N. 6th St., Apt. 101, Leavenworth, KS 66048. Tel: 913-651-2647. Rev. Carrol W. Thorne, C.P.

4301-A Four Farms Rd., Greensboro, NC 27410. Tel: 336-282-8236; Fax: 336-252-3164. Rev. Thomas Berry, C.P.

578 Marcy Ave., Brooklyn, NY 11206. Tel: 718-388-5196; Fax: 718-388-5153. Rev. James (Jim) O'Shea, C.P.

Curia Generalizia Dei Passionisti, Piazza SS Giovanni E Paolo 13, Rome 00184 Italy. Tel: 39-060-772-711; Fax: 39-06-700-8454. Rev. Lawrence Rywalt, C.P.

Visitation of the B.V.M. Parish: 98 Richards St., Brooklyn, NY 11231. Tel: 718-624-1572; Fax: 718-722-7748. Rev. Neil Tiedemann, C.P.

St. Mary's Seminary 5400 Roland Ave., Baltimore, MD 21210-1994. Tel: 410-864-4279; Fax: 410-864-4278. Rev. Paul Zilonka, C.P.

Paul VI Pastoral Center, 667 Stone & Shannon Rd., Wheeling, WV 26003-6742. Rev. Jerome McKenna, C.P.

Assumption of the BVM: 200 Chestnut St., Centereach, NY 11720. Tel: 631-585-8760; Fax: 631-585-3601. Rev. Peter O'Rourke, C.P.

Church of the Annunciation: 470 Westchester Ave., Crestwood, NY 10707. Rev. Salvatore Riccardi, C.P.

St. John's Seminary, 127 Lake St., Brighton, MA 02135. Rev. Robin Ryan, C.P.

St. Theresa Parish: 24 N. Main St., Windham, NY 12496. Rev. James Schiffer.

319 Grayson Hwy., Lawrenceville, GA 30045. Tel: 678-377-5498. Rev. Joseph Fahy, C.P. (ATL).

St. Therese Residence, 200 S. Meade St., Wilkes-Barre, PA 18702. Tel: 570-823-6131. Rev. James McHugh, C.P.

Rev. Alphonsus Coen, C.P. (SCR).

8433-A Dempster St., Niles, IL 60714. Tel: 847-384-0134. Rev. James Barry, C.P. (CHI).

5110 S. Kenwood Ave., Apt. 706, Chicago, IL 60615. Tel: 773 575-1380. Rev. David Monaco, C.P. (CHI).

4 Chateau Way, Naples, FL 34112. Tel: 239-732-6471. Rev. John Cashman, C.P.

Visitation Monastery, 200 E. 2nd St., Frederick, MD 21701. Tel: 301-662-3322. Rev. Jerome Vereb, C.P. (BAL).

STEWARTSVILLE. *Society of Jesus Christ the Priest*, P.O. Box 157 08886. Tel: 908-213-1447; Fax: 908-859-5210. Email: meadwater@direcway.com. Rev. Lope D. Pascual, Dir.

[I] CONVENTS AND RESIDENCES FOR SISTERS

BELLE MEAD. *Religious of the Sacred Heart*, 209 Lancaster Ct., 08502. Tel: 908-874-9937; Fax: 609-497-0784. Email: fdelachapelle@rscj.org.

BOUND BROOK. *Sisters of Jesus Our Hope*, 514 Church St., 08805. Tel: 732-271-5777; Fax: 732-271-8067. Email: sjh@sistersofjesusourhope.org. Web: www.sistersofjesusourhope.org. Sisters 7.

EAST BRUNSWICK. *DePaul House*, 528 Ryders Ln., 08816. Tel: 732-238-3638. Email: dcebnj@comcast.net. Web: www.dc-northeast.org. Sr. Margaret Palmer, D.C., Local Supr. Sisters 4.

EDISON. *St. Thomas Aquinas Convent*, 15 Wren Ct., 08820. Tel: 732-321-0137; Fax: 732-549-9050. Email: aquinasis@aol.com. Sr. Donna Marie Trukowski, C.S.S.F., Local Min. Sisters 3.

FLEMINGTON. *The Carmel of Mary Immaculate and St. Mary Magdalen*, 26 Harmony School Rd., 08822. Tel: 908-782-4802. Web: www.carmelitehermitage.com/flemingtoncarmel.htm. Rev. Paul N. Lonappan, C.M.I., Chap. Nuns professed with solemn vows 12; Novices 4.

HAMPTON. *Sisters of Jesus Our Hope*, 32 Main St., 08827. Tel: 908-537-6583. Email: sjh@sistersofjesusourhope.org. Web: www.sistersofjesusourhope.org. Sisters 3.

NEW BRUNSWICK. *Sisters of St. Joseph of Peace*, 61 Jefferson Ave., 08901. Tel: 732-249-5644. Email: jrusch@saintpetersuh.com. Sisters 2.

NORTH PLAINFIELD. *Servants of the Holy Child Jesus Regional House*, 641 Somerset St., 07060-4909. Tel: 908-757-3050; 756-418-; Fax: 908-754-9190. Email: scominic1@aol.com. Sr. M. Dominic Ritter, O.S.F., Regl. Supr.; Rev. Severin Dietrich, O.F.M.Conv., Chap. Regional House for Congregation of the Servants of the Holy Child of Jesus. Sisters 24.

PISCATAWAY. *St. Joseph of Chestnut Hill*, 137 Metlars Ln., 08854. Tel: 732-393-9640 Email: metlarslane@yahoo.com. Sisters 6.

SOMERSET. *St. Elizabeth Convent*, 13 Renfro Rd., 08873. Tel: 732-247-3697. Email: altonfranciscans@piasanet.com. Sr. M. Carista Born, F.S.G.M., Supr. Sisters 2.

SOUTH AMBOY. *Sacred Heart Convent*, P.O. Box 3005, 08879-3005. Tel: 732-727-2094. Sr. M. Kateri, S.F.M.G., Supr. Sisters 6.

WATCHUNG. *McAuley Hall Inc.*, Health Care Center, 1633 U.S. Hwy 22, 07060. Tel: 908-754-3663; Fax: 908-754-3502. Rev. Paul Varga, O.F.M.Conv. Retired Sisters 54.

Mount St. Mary, 1645 U.S. Hwy. 22 W., 07069-6587. Tel: 908-756-0994; Fax: 908-754-0_64. Web: www.newjerseymercy.org. Sr. Diane Szubrowski, R.S.M., Pres., Regl. Com.; Rev. Edward M. Edwards (CHI), Chap. Sisters of Mercy of the Americas Regional Community of New Jersey Professed Sisters 270.

WOODBRIDGE. *St. Joseph Convent*, 184 Amboy Ave., 07095. Tel: 732-634-0807; Fax: 732-634-7888. Email: lucylsic@aol.com. Sr. Lucy Szczepek, L.S.I.C., Supr. Sisters 9.

[J] RETREAT HOUSES

BELVIDERE. *Sacred Heart Renewal Center*, P.O. Box 68, 07823. Tel: 908-475-4694. Bros. Eric Gougen, S.C., Dir. Thomas Woods, S.C., Assoc. Dir.; Julian Przytulski, S.C.; Austin Kazalski, S.C.; James Mullen. Brothers 5.

FLEMINGTON. *Our Lady of Providence*, 31 Britton Dr., 08822. Tel: 908-782-4495. Sr. Jean, L.S.P., Dir. Little Sisters of the Poor

MILFORD. *Bethany Ridge*, 914 Milford-Warren Glen Rd., 08848. Tel: 908-995-9758; Fax: 908-995-7299. Rev. Peter Suhaka, Dir. Spirituality Center for Priests.

PERTH AMBOY. *Emmaus House*, 101 Center St., 08861. Tel: 732-442-7688; Fax: 732-442-5510. Email: smcgrath@diometuchen.org. Web: www.emmaushousenj.com. Sr. Susan McGrath, S.M.G., Dir. Sisters 3.

PRINCETON. *Vincentian Renewal Center*, 75 Mapleton Rd., 08540-9614. Tel: 609-520-9626; Fax: 609-520-0593. Email: vre@vincetianfamilycenter.com. Web: www.vincentianfamilycenter.com. Rev. Joseph A. Morris, C.M., Dir.; Sr. Mary Frate, D.C., Asst. Dir.

WATCHUNG. *Mt. St. Mary House of Prayer*, 1651 U.S. Hwy. 22, 07069-6587. Tel: 908-753-2091; Fax: 908-757-0792. Email: msmhope@juno.com. Web: www.msmhope.com. Sisters Theresina Flannery, R.S.M., Dir.; Eileen P. Smith, R.S.M., Dir.; Mary Jo Kearns, R.S.M., Dir. Sisters 3.

[K] SHRINES AND PUBLIC ORATORIES

BERNARDSVILLE. *Sacred Heart Chapel* , (Chapel of Convenience) , Bernards Ave., 07924. Fax: 908-766-1185. Rev. John N. Fell, Pastor.

RARITAN. *Shrine Chapel of the Blessed Sacrament* 50 W. Somerset St., 08869. Tel: 908-722-1489; Fax: 908-526-6232. Email: blessedsacrament.shrine@verizon.net. Web: www.arch-angel.net/shrine. Rev. Lope D. Pascual, Rector.

WASHINGTON. *Blue Army Shrine of the Immaculate Heart of Mary* 674-675 Mountainview Rd., P.O. Box 976, 07882. Tel: 908-213-2223; Fax: 908-213-2263. Email: bluearmy@ix.netcom.com. Web: www.bluearmy.com.

[L] PRIVATE ASSOCIATIONS OF THE FAITHFUL

WASHINGTON. *Handmaids of Mary Immaculate*, Holy House Convent, Mountain View Rd., P.O. Box 976, 07882. Tel: 908-689-7330; Fax: 908-689-0972. Email: smami1@juno.com. Sr. Mary John, A.M.I., Supr. Sisters 8.

[M] PUBLIC ASSOCIATIONS OF THE FAITHFUL

BOUND BROOK. *Sisters of Jesus Our Hope*, 514 Church St., 08805. Tel: 732-271-5777; Fax: 732-271-8067. Email: sjh@sistersofjesusourhope.org. Web: www.sistersofjesusourhope.org. Sr. Julia Jamink, S.J.H., Community Sister Servant. Sisters 15.

FLEMINGTON. *Sisters of Jesus Our Hope*, 83 Bonnell St., 08822. Tel: 908-806-3332. Email: sjh@sistersofjesusourhope.org. Web: www.sistersofjesusourhope.org. Sr. Patricia Vayda, S.J.H., Sister Servant. Sisters 5.

PHILLIPSBURG. *The Anawim Community*, 82 Summit Ave., 08865. Tel: 908-859-2049; Fax: 908-213-9032. Email: phillipsburg@anawim.com. Web: www.anawim.com. Revs. Francis J. Marino, S.M., Founder; Daniel H. Healy, Dir.; Charles A. Sabella, Vocation Dir.; Richard M. Rusk, Missions Dir.

SOUTH AMBOY. *Dominican Sisters of Divine Providence*, 265 Augusta St., 08879. Tel: 732-721-0354; Fax: 732-721-7686. Email: smmichele698@aol.com. Sr. Maria Michele Armato, O.P., Supr. Sisters 6.

SOUTH PLAINFIELD. *Religious of the Virgin Mary*, 200 Randolph Ave., 07080. Tel: 908-756-0631; Fax: 908-757-5655. Email: cramirez@diometuchen.org. Sr. Maria Cornelia Ramirez, R.V.M. Sisters 3.

[N] CAMPUS MINISTRY

NEW BRUNSWICK. *Catholic Center at Rutgers University* 17 Mine St., 08901-1111. Tel: 732-545-6663; Fax: 732-545-3495. Email: coldon@rci.rutgers.edu. Web: www.catholic-center.rutgers.edu. Revs. Thomas J. Walsh, C.O., Dir. & Chap.; Peter Cebulka, C.O., Chap.; Thomas Odorizzi, C.O., Chap.; Jean-Marie Dimeeh-Juchniewicz, M.A., Chap.

[O] MISCELLANEOUS LISTINGS

METUCHEN. *The Foundation for Catholic Education*, P.O. Box 191, 08840. Most Rev. Paul G. Bootkoski, D.D.

The Fund for the Future, Inc., P.O. Box 191, 08840. Most Rev. Paul G. Bootkoski, D.D.

The Priestly Education Fund, Inc., P.O. Box 191, 08840. Most Rev. Paul G. Bootkoski, D.D.

EDISON. *The Ozanam Shelter for Families and Single Women*, 89 Truman Dr., 08817. Tel: 732-985-0327; Fax: 732-985-2449. Carmen Fernandez, Admin.

Pauline Books and Media, Wick Plaza, 561 Rte. 1 S., 08817. Tel: 732-572-1200; Fax: 732-572-5427. Email: edison@pauline.org. Web: www.pauline.org.

JACKSON. *Nicholas House*, 384 Vath St., 08527. Tel: 732-408-0298; Fax: 732-408-1821. Web: www.ccdom.org. Adrian Martinez, Contact Person. Residential Services.

LAMBERTVILLE. *The Jesus School*, (Church of St. John the Evangelist), 44 Bridge St., 08530. Tel: 609-397-0593; Fax: 609-397-8713. Email: mconaughton@diometuchen.org. Sr. Marie Conaughton, Prin. Students 48.

NEW BRUNSWICK. *Catholic Charities Ozanam Inn*, 20-22 Abeel St., 08901. Tel: 732-729-0850; Fax: 732-729-0794. Email: wsmoore@usa.net. Web: www.ccdom.org. Wesley R. Moore, Prog. Dir.

St. John's Health & Family Service Center, Formerly St. John of God Community Health Center24 Abeel St., 08901. Tel: 732-745-9800; Fax: 732-745-9107. Web: www.ccdom.org. Steven J. Levin, M.D., Medical Dir.; Sharon Oshatz, M.T. (A.S.C.P.), Asst. Dir.

OLD BRIDGE. *Community House at St. Thomas*, 124 Bentley Ave., 08857. Tel: 732-251-1786; Fax: 732-826-8342. Email: erevoir@ccdom.org. Judith Cusumano, Dir.

PEAPACK. *Msgr. George E. Everitt Academy*, Main St., P.O. Box 440, 07977. Tel: 908-234-1524; Fax: 908-234-9435. Email: everitta@bellatlantic.net. Rev. Msgr. George M. Brembos, Ed.D.; Sr. Madeline Sarli, S.S.J., Prin. Relig. Teacher 1; Lay Teachers 8; Students 116.

PERTH AMBOY. *Metuchen Community Services Corporation*, 319 Maple St., 08861. Tel: 732-826-5142; Fax: 732-826-3549. Email: dsusan@ccdom.org. Doug Susan, Acting Exec. Dir.

Nazareth House, 156 Wayne St., 08861. Tel: 732-324-0437; Fax: 732-442-7930. Web: www.ccdom.org. Dominic Romero, Div. Dir.

Poor Servants of the Mother of God, Regional Office, 101 Center St., 08861. Tel: 732-442-7783; Fax: 732-442-7793. Sr. Teresa Twomey, S.M.G., Regl. Supr.

PHILLIPSBURG. *St. Peter and Paul House*, 702 Sayre Ave., 08865. Tel: 908-454-0912; Fax: 908-454-3085. Dominic Romero, Div. Dir.

SOMERSET. *Mission International, Inc.*, 2301 Hwy. 27, 08873. Tel: 732-297-9191; Fax: 732-940-3121. Rev. Leonard DePasquale, I.M.C., Chm.

SOMERVILLE. *The Center for Great Expectations, Inc.*, 88 West End Ave., 08876. Tel: 908-218-0570; Fax: 908-218-1772. Email: pwright@thecenterforgreatexpectations.org. Web: www.thecenterforgreatexpectations.org. Mrs. Peg Wright, Pres., CEO. Residence and comprehensive program for homeless pregnant women and adolescents.

SOUTH RIVER. **Friends of Mandeville, Inc.*, c/o The Passionists Province Pastoral, 80 David St., 08882. Tel: 732-257-7177; Fax: 732-257-0042. Email: jjonescp@aol.com.

WASHINGTON. *Blue Army of Our Lady of Fatima, U.S.A., Inc.*, P.O. Box 976, 07882. Tel: 908-213-2223; Fax: 908-213-2263. Email: bluearmy@ix.net.com. Web: www.bluearmy.com.

WOODBRIDGE. *Mt. Carmel Home Nursing Service*, 184 Amboy Ave., 07095. Tel: 732-634-0807. Sr. Maria Wojcek, L.S.I.C., Dir.

RELIGIOUS INSTITUTES OF MEN REPRESENTED IN THE DIOCESE

For further details refer to the corresponding bracketed number in the Religious Institutes of Men or Women section.

[1100]—*Brothers of the Sacred Heart*—S.C.
[0470]—*The Capuchin Friars*—O.F.M.Cap.
[0275]—*Carmelites of Mary Immaculate*—C.M.I.
[0360]—*Claretian Missionaries* (Eastern Prov.)—C.M.F.
[0310]—*Congregation of Christian Brothers*—C.F.C.
[1330]—*Congregation of the Mission*—C.M.
[1000]—*Congregation of the Passion*—C.P.
[0390]—*Consolata Missionaries*—I.M.C.
[0520]—*Franciscan Friars* (Custody of St. John Capistran)—O.F.M.
[0650]—*Holy Ghost Fathers*—C.S.Sp.
[1110]—*Missionaries of the Sacred Heart*—M.S.C.
[0940]—*Oblates of the Virgin Mary*—O.M.V.
[0950]—*Oratorians*—C.O.
[0480]—*Order Friars Minor Conventual*—O.F.M. Con
[0430]—*Order of Preachers (Dominicans)* (Prov. of St. Joseph)—O.P.
[1070]—*Redemptorist Fathers*—C.SS.R.
[1190]—*Salesians of Don Bosco*—S.D.B.
[1240]—*Servites*—O.S.M.
[0420]—*Society of the Divine Word*—S.V.D.

RELIGIOUS INSTITUTES OF WOMEN REPRESENTED IN THE DIOCESE

[0130]—*Apostles of the Sacred Heart of Jesus*—A.S.C.J.
[1810]—*Bernardine Sisters of the Third Order of St. Francis*—O.S.F.
[3110]—*Congregation of Our Lady of the Retreat in the Cenacle*—R.C.
[0760]—*Daughters of Charity of St. Vincent De Paul* (Albany Prov.)—D.C.
[0790]—*Daughters of Divine Charity* (Prov. of St. Joseph)—F.D.C.
[0420]—*Discalced Carmelite Nuns*—O.C.D.
[1070-18]—*Dominican Sisters* (Caldwell)—O.P.
[1070-15]—*Dominican Sisters* (Blauvelt, N.Y.)—O.P.
[1070-06]—*Dominican Sisters of Hope* (Ossining, N.Y.)—O.P.
[1170]—*Felician Sisters* (Immaculate Conception Prov.)—C.S.S.F.
[1180]—*Franciscan Sisters of Allegany, New York*—O.S.F.
[2575]—*Institute of the Sisters of Mercy of the Americas* (New Jersey)—R.S.M.
[2300]—*Little Servant Sisters of the Immaculate Conception*—L.S.I.C.
[2340]—*Little Sisters of the Poor* (Brooklyn Prov.)—L.S.P.
[2700]—*Missionary Catechists of the Sacred Hearts of Jesus and Mary*—M.C.
[2810]—*Missionary Sisters of the Mother of God* (Byzantine-Ukrainian)—M.S.M.G.
[0950]—*Pious Society Daughters of St. Paul*—F.S.P.
[3640]—*Poor Servants of the Mother of God*—S.M.G.
[3320]—*Presentation of the Blessed Virgin Mary* (New Windsor, NY)—P.B.V.M.
[]—*Religious of the Blessed Virgin Mary*—R.V.M.
[3430]—*Religious Teachers Filippini* (St. Lucy Prov.)—M.P.F.
[1700]—*School Sisters of the Third Order of St. Francis*—O.S.F.
[1980]—*Servants of the Holy Child of Jesus*—O.S.F.
[3630]—*Servants of the Most Sacred Heart of Jesus*—S.S.C.J.
[0590]—*Sisters of Charity of Saint Elizabeth, Convent Station*—S.C.
[0660]—*Sisters of Christian Charity* (North American Eastern Prov.)—S.C.C.
[3893]—*Sisters of Saint Joseph of Chestnut Hill, Philadelphia*—S.S.J.
[1650]—*Sisters of St. Francis of Philadelphia*—O.S.F.
[1600]—*Sisters of St. Francis of the Martyr St. George*—F.S.G.M.
[3890]—*Sisters of St. Joseph of Peace*—C.S.J.P.
[1190]—*Sisters of the Atonement* (Graymoor)—S.A.
[2170]—*Sisters Servants of the Immaculate Heart of Mary*—I.H.M.
[2170]—*Sisters Servants of the Immaculate Heart of Mary* (Scranton)—I.H.M.

DIOCESAN CEMETERIES

JAMESBURG. *Holy Cross Burial Park*, 840 Cranbury Rd., 08816. Tel: 800-943-8400.

PISCATAWAY. *Resurrection Burial Park*, 899 Lincoln Ave., P.O. Box 189, 08854. Tel: 732-463-1424.

NECROLOGY

✠ Breen, Most Rev. Vincent De Paul, Bishop Emeritus of Metuchen—Died March 30, 2003
† Cashioli, Lawrence J., (Retired)—Died July 21, 2001
† Gall, Florian J., Whitehouse Station, NJ Our Lady of Lourdes—Died June 28, 2003
† Hewitt, William, (Retired)—Died Feb. 22, 2003
† Labonte, Louis Roger, Edison, NJ St. Helena—Died March 25, 2003
† Smith, Lawrence H.F., Parlin, NJ St. Bernadette—Died Aug. 15, 2003

Archdiocese of Miami

(Archidioecesis Miamiensis)

Most Reverend

JOHN C. FAVALORA, D.D.

Archbishop of Miami; ordained December 20, 1961; appointed Bishop of Alexandria June 16, 1986; ordained and installed July 29, 1986; appointed Third Bishop of St. Petersburg March 7, 1989; installed May 16, 1989; appointed Third Bishop of Miami November 3, 1994; installed December 20, 1994. *Office: 9401 Biscayne Blvd., Miami, FL 33138.*

Pastoral Center: 9401 Biscayne Blvd., Miami, FL 33138. Tel: 305-757-6241; Fax: 305-754-1897 (Chancery); 305-751-6227 (Communications Office).

Web: www.archdioceseofmiami.org

Email: information@miamiarch.org

Most Reverend

EDWARD A. MCCARTHY, D.D., S.T.D., J.C.D.

Retired Archbishop of Miami; ordained May 29, 1943; appointed Titular Bishop of Tamascani and Auxiliary of Cincinnati April 21, 1965; Transferred to Phoenix August 25, 1969; installed December 2, 1969; appointed Coadjutor Archbishop of Miami September 17, 1976; succeeded to Archbishop of Miami July 26, 1977; retired November 3, 1994. *Office: 9401 Biscayne Blvd., Miami Shores, FL 33138.*

Most Reverend

AGUSTIN A. ROMAN, D.D., V.G.

Retired Auxiliary Bishop of Miami; ordained July 5, 1959; appointed Titular Bishop of Sertei and Auxiliary of Miami February 6, 1979; consecrated March 24, 1979; retired June 7, 2003.

Most Reverend

GILBERTO FERNANDEZ, D.D.

Retired Auxiliary Bishop of Miami; ordained May 17, 1959; appointed Titular Bishop of Irina and Auxiliary of Miami June 24, 1997; consecrated September 3, 1997; retired December 10, 2002. *Res.: 5260 N.E. 7th Ave., Miami, FL 33137.*

Most Reverend

FELIPE DEJESUS ESTEVEZ

Auxiliary Bishop of Miami; ordained May 30, 1970; appointed Titular Bishop of Kearney and Auxiliary Bishop of Miami November 21, 2003; consecrated January 7, 2004. *Res.: 5260 N.E. 7th Ave., Miami, FL 33137.*

ESTABLISHED AUGUST 13, 1958.

Square Miles 4,958.

Created an Archbishopric, June 13, 1968.

Comprises the Counties in the southern part of the State of Florida, namely, Broward, Miami-Dade and Monroe.

For legal titles of Parishes and Archdiocesan institutions, consult the Pastoral Center.

STATISTICAL OVERVIEW

Personnel	
Archbishops	1
Retired Archbishops	1
Auxiliary Bishops	1
Retired Bishops	2
Priests: Diocesan Active in Diocese	180
Priests: Diocesan Active Outside Diocese	7
Priests: Diocesan in Foreign Missions	1
Priests: Retired, Sick or Absent	75
Number of Diocesan Priests	263
Religious Priests in Diocese	123
Total Priests in Diocese	386
Extern Priests in Diocese	80
Ordinations:	
Diocesan Priests	6
Transitional Deacons	4
Permanent Deacons	1
Permanent Deacons in Diocese	144
Total Brothers	58
Total Sisters	316
Parishes	
Parishes	112
With Resident Pastor:	
Resident Diocesan Priests	101
Resident Religious Priests	10
Missions	7
Pastoral Centers	3
New Parishes Created	1
Professional Ministry Personnel:	
Brothers	3
Sisters	37
Lay Ministers	138
Welfare	
Catholic Hospitals	2
Total Assisted	691,992
Health Care Centers	3
Total Assisted	16,227
Homes for the Aged	5
Total Assisted	5,368
Residential Care of Children	6
Total Assisted	343
Day Care Centers	7
Total Assisted	2,545
Specialized Homes	6
Total Assisted	25,869
Special Centers for Social Services	45
Total Assisted	1,439,815
Residential Care of Disabled	1
Total Assisted	145
Other Institutions	13
Total Assisted	2,425
Educational	
Seminaries, Diocesan	1
Students from This Diocese	22
Students from Other Diocese	25
Diocesan Students in Other Seminaries	31
Students Religious	5
Total Seminarians	58
Colleges and Universities	2
Total Students	12,020
High Schools, Diocesan and Parish	9
Total Students	9,576
High Schools, Private	4
Total Students	3,016
Elementary Schools, Diocesan and Parish	57
Total Students	24,235
Elementary Schools, Private	2
Total Students	937
Non-residential Schools for the Disabled	2
Total Students	11,665
Catechesis/Religious Education:	
High School Students	5,013
Elementary Students	41,473
Total Students under Catholic Instruction	107,993
Teachers in the Diocese:	
Priests	15
Brothers	20
Sisters	29
Lay Teachers	2,225
Vital Statistics	
Receptions into the Church:	
Infant Baptism Totals	16,952
Adult Baptism Totals	793
Received into Full Communion	717
First Communions	14,807
Confirmations	9,041
Marriages:	
Catholic	2,343
Interfaith	337
Total Marriages	2,680
Deaths	5,122
Total Catholic Population	856,783
Total Population	4,036,799

Former Archbishops—Most Revs. COLEMAN F. CARROLL, D.D., ord. June 15, 1930; appt. Titular Bishop of Pitanae and Auxiliary Bishop of Pittsburgh, Aug. 25, 1953; consecrated Nov. 10, 1953; appt. first Bishop of Miami, Aug. 13, 1958; installed Oct. 7, 1958; appt. Archbishop of Miami, March 13, 1968; died July 26, 1977; EDWARD A. MCCARTHY, D.D., S.T.D., J.C.D. (Retired), ord. May 29, 1943; appt. Coadjutor Archbishop of Miami "cum jure successionis," Sept. 17, 1976; appt. Archbishop of Miami, July 26, 1977; retired Nov. 3, 1994.

Pastoral Center—9401 Biscayne Blvd., Miami Shores, 33138. Tel: 305-757-6241; Fax: 305-754-1897 (Chancery Office); 305-751-6227 (Communications Office).

Vicars General—Most Rev. FELIPE J. ESTEVEZ, D.D., S.T.D., V.G.; Rev. Msgr. WILLIAM J. HENNESSEY, V.G.

Chancellor—Rev. Msgr. MICHAEL A. SOUCKAR, J.C.D. (Cand.). Email: chancellor@miamiarch.org.

Moderator of the Curia—Rev. Msgr. WILLIAM J. HENNESSEY, V.G.

Secretary to the Archbishop—Rev. Msgr. MICHAEL SOUCKAR, J.C.L.. Email: secretary@miamiarch.org.

Metropolitan Tribunal— Address all Rogatory commissions and matrimonial matters to the Tribunal, *9401 Biscayne Blvd., Miami Shores, 33138.* Tel: 305-762-1161; Fax: 305-762-1178.

Judicial Vicar—Rev. Msgr. ANDREW L. ANDERSON, J.C.D.

Adjutant Judicial Vicar—Very Rev. KENNETH SCHWANGER, J.C.D., V.F.

Judges—Rev. Msgrs. MICHAEL A. SOUCKAR, J.C.D. (Cand.); MICHAEL THOMAS, J.C.D.; Revs. JOSE BIAIN, O.F.M.; FERNANDO HERIA, J.C.L.; ERNESTO MOLANO (Retired); ALVARO PINZON; Sisters DEBORA CERULLO, J.C.L.; JEANNE-MARGARET MCNALLY, J.C.L., Ph.D.; Dr. STEFANO BENIGNI, J.C.L.; MARIA PAZ RAMOS, J.C.L.

Promoters of Justice—Rev. CARL MORRISON, J.C.L.; Rev. Msgr. TOMAS MARIN, J.C.L., (non-matrimonial cases); Very Rev. KENNETH SCHWANGER, J.C.D., V.F., (non-matrimonial cases).

Defenders of the Bond—Revs. CARL MORRISON, J.C.L.; RONALD PUSAK (Retired).

Notaries—Ms. KATIA ARRIAZA; KATHLEEN CHERRIS, C.P.S.; LILLIAN HUMARA; VIRGINIA MARTIN; Mrs. JOAN MATELIS.

Assessors—Deacon ANTONIO MACEO; Sr. ISABEL MAZARREDO, O.P.; ROSARIO BERGOUIGNAN; DEE DUGGAN.

Counsel-Assistant to the Tribunal—Mr. J. PATRICK FITZGERALD, Esq.

Consultors—Most Rev. FELIPE J. ESTEVEZ, D.D., S.T.D., V.G.; Rev. Msgrs. WILLIAM J. HENNESSEY, V.G.; VINCENT T. KELLY; JOHN NOONAN; PABLO NAVARRO; MICHAEL A. SOUCKAR, J.C.D. (Cand.); Rev. GUSTAVO MIYARES.

Deans and Deaneries—Very Rev. KENNETH SCHWANGER, J.C.D., V.F., (Northeast Broward); Rev. Msgr. NOEL FOGARTY, P.A., V.F., (Northwest Broward); Very Rev. THOMAS O'DWYER, V.F., (South Broward); Rev. JOSE L. HERNANDO, (East Dade); Very Revs. SEAMUS DOYLE, V.F., (Northeast Dade); PEDRO LUIS PEREZ, V.F., (Northwest Dade); JAMES FETSCHER, V.F., (South Dade); BERNARD KIRLIN, V.F., (West Dade); GERALD MORRIS, V.F., (Monroe).

Incardination Committee—Most Revs. JOHN C. FAVALORA, D.D.; FELIPE J. ESTEVEZ, D.D., S.T.D., V.G.; Rev. Msgrs. WILLIAM J. HENNESSEY, V.G.; PABLO A. NAVARRO; VINCENT T. KELLY; MICHAEL A. SOUCKAR, J.C.D. (Cand.); Rev. JAMES MURPHY.

Presbyteral Council—Most Rev. JOHN C. FAVALORA, D.D., Pres.; Very Rev. THOMAS O'DWYER, V.F., Vice Pres.; Rev. MICHAEL HOYER, Sec.

Priests' Personnel Board—Rev. Msgr. PABLO NAVARRO, Chm. Consultants: Most Rev. FELIPE J. ESTEVEZ, D.D., S.T.D., V.G.; Rev. Msgrs. WILLIAM J. HENNESSEY, V.G.; MICHAEL A. SOUCKAR, J.C.D. (Cand.). Members: Rev. Msgr. JOHN NOONAN; Very Rev. PEDRO LUIS PEREZ, V.F.; Rev. ANTHONY MULDERRY.

Ministry Of General Services

Executive Director—Rev. Msgr. WILLIAM J. HENNESSEY, V.G.

Chancellor's Office—Rev. Msgr. MICHAEL A. SOUCKAR, J.C.D. (Cand.), Chancellor; MARIA E. GALINDO, Vice Chancellor.

Coordinator of Special Projects—Rev. PATRICK O'NEILL.

Legal Services—PATRICK FITZGERALD, 110 Merrick Way, Ste. 3-B, Coral Gables, 33134. Tel: 305-443-9162; Fax: 305-443-6613.

Communications Dept.—MARY ROSS AGOSTA, Dir.; MELISSA VISCOUNT, Coord.; MIRIAM MIRANDA, Admin. Asst.

Public and Media Relations—MARY ROSS AGOSTA, Dir.

Community Information—MARY ROSS AGOSTA, Dir., Mailing Address (for Communications, Public and Media Relations and Community Information), 9401 Biscayne Blvd., Miami, 33138. Tel: 305-762-1043; 305-762-1045; Fax: 305-751-6227.

Television and Radio Center—MARY ROSS AGOSTA, Dir.; ERNESTO GONZALEZ, Production Mgr.; TERESA MARTINEZ, Producer; CARLOS MENENDEZ, Staff Dir.; Revs. PEDRO CORCES, Producer & TV Mass Coord. (Spanish); KRIS BARTOS, TV Mass Producer (English), Mailing Address, 9920 N.E. 2nd Ave., Miami, 33138. Tel: 305-751-0990.

Newspapers—MARY ROSS AGOSTA, Dir., Mailing Address for Newspapers, 9401 Biscayne Blvd., Miami, 33138.

"The Florida Catholic"—ANA RODRIGUEZ-SOTO, Editor (English). Tel: 305-762-1131.

"La Voz Catolica"—Ms. DORA AMADOR, Exec. Editor (Spanish). Tel: 305-762-1125; Fax: 305-762-1223.

Pax Catholic Communications—Very Rev. JOSE LUIS HERNANDO, V.F., Pres. Tel: 305-638-9729; Fax: 305-636-4571. Web: www.paxcc.org.

Radio Peace - WAXY, 790 AM—Rev. ALBERTO CUTIE, Gen. Dir., 1779 N.W. 28th St., Miami, 33142. Tel: 305-253-3101; SCOTT KALDAHL, Programming Coord.

Radio Paz - WACC, 830 AM—Rev. ALBERTO CUTIE, Dir.; IVETTE ACOSTA, Admin. & Office Mgr., 1779 N.W. 28 St., North Miami, 33142. Tel: 305-638-9729; Fax: 305-636-3976; MARITE ALFONSO, Programming Dir.

Radio Ke Poze - WLQY, 1320 AM—Rev. ALBERTO CUTIE, Dir., 1779 N.W. 28 St., Miami, 33142. Tel: 305-638-9729; HANS MARDY, Programming Coord.

PaxNet—1779 N.W. 28 St., Miami, 33142. Tel: 305-638-9729; Fax: 305-638-9944. GONZALO PENAGOS, Operations Dir.

Catholic Office for Inter-Faith Activities and Catholic-Jewish Relations Commission—Rev. PATRICK H. O'NEILL, Exec. Dir., 9401 Biscayne Blvd., Miami Shores, 33138. Tel: 305-762-1254; Fax: 305-754-1897.

Christian Unity Commission—Rev. PATRICK H. O'NEILL, Ecumenical Officer, 9401 Biscayne Blvd., Miami Shores, 33138. Tel: 305-762-1254; Fax: 305-754-1897.

Ministry Of Christian Formation

Executive Director—Rev. Msgr. VINCENT T. KELLY.

Department of Schools—Rev. Msgr. VINCENT T. KELLY, Vicar, Christian Formation; Bro. RICHARD DE MARIA, C.F.C., Supt.; KRISTEN HUGHES; JOSEPHINE KENNA; Bro. ANGELO PALMIERI, F.M.S.; LYNN VANDER WYDE.

Department of Religious Education—Sr. ROSA MONIQUE PENA, O.P., Dir.; SILVIA DE LA PENA, Exec. Asst.; YVONNE TUMA, Certification Sec. Consultants: FLORANGEL GONZALEZ; ELIZABETH LEVITZ; MARIA JOSE MITSOULIS.

Archdiocesan Media Center—MARIA JOSE MITSOULIS, Mgr.

Archdiocese of Miami Education Endowment Fund, Inc.—CHRISTOPHER SAILSBURY, Exec. Dir.

Archdiocesan Safe Environment Program—Bro. JOSEPH TESTON, F.M.S., Coord.; VICKI KAUFMANN, M.A., M.P.S.T., Victim Assistance Coord.

Catholic Charities of the Archdiocese of Miami, Inc.—Rev. Msgr. WILLIAM J. HENNESSEY, V.G., Interim Pres.; RICHARD TURCOTTE, Ph.D., C.E.O.; Rev. ROBERTO GARZA, Dir. Mission Effectiveness; RONALD A. HASSELL, Chief Admin. Officer; VICKY KAUFMAN, Chief Operating Officer; ORLANDO LOPEZ, C.F.O., 9401 Biscayne Blvd., Miami Shores, 33138. Tel: 305-762-1306; Fax: 305-754-6649. Web: catholiccharitiesadm.org; BRIAN STEVENS, Dir. Social Advocacy, 9401 Biscayne Blvd., Miami Shores, 33138. Tel: 305-762-1338.

Behavioral Health Care Division—Dr. JULIAN SERRANO, Dir., 7707 N.W. 2nd Ave., Miami, 33150. Tel: 305-795-0077; Fax: 305-795-0030.

Catholic Campaign for Human Development—9401 Biscayne Blvd., Miami Shores, 33138. Tel: 305-762-1323; Fax: 305-762-1344.

Catholic Commission for Social Advocacy—9401 Biscayne Blvd., Miami Shores, 33138. Tel: 305-762-1323; Fax: 305-762-1344.

Catholic Relief Services—9401 Biscayne Blvd., Miami Shores, 33138. Tel: 305-762-1323; Fax: 305-762-1344.

Genesis Programs, Inc.—ANGELA MACHADO-VALDEZ, Dir., 3675 S. Miami Ave., Miami, 33133. Tel: 305-856-1043; Fax: 305-856-1633.

Family and Individual Counseling—

Dade— Perrine, South Miami, Hialeah, Miami.

Broward—For Appointments, call:. Tel: 866-758-0025. Hollywood, Wilton Manors, Deerfield Beach.

School Counseling—

Dade— St. Monica, St. Lawrence, St. Theresa, St. James.

Broward— Annunciation, St. Bonaventure, Nativity, St. Helen.

Abstinence Education—130 N.E. 62 St., 2nd Fl., Miami, 33138. Tel: 305-756-6968. Email: abstinence@catholiccharitiesadm.org.

Healthy Start—9615 Sterling Dr., Miami, 33157. Tel: 305-238-2381; Fax: 305-232-5421. Email: healthystart@catholiccharitiesadm.org.

Substance Abuse—

St. Luke's Addiction Center—7707 N.W. 2nd Ave., Miami, 33150. Tel: 305-795-0077; Fax: 305-795-0030. Email: stlukes@catholiccharitiesadm.org.

Child Care Division—LUCIA VICENCIO, Dir., 970 S.W. First St., Ste. 305, Miami, 33130. Tel: 305-324-4226; Fax: 305-324-0460. Email: childcareadm@catholiccharitiesadm.org.

Centro Hispano Catolico Child Care Center—144 N.W. 26 St., Miami, 33125. Tel: 305-576-3461; Fax: 305-576-6446. Email: centrohispano@catholiccharitiesadm.org.

Centro Mater Child Care Center—418 S.W. 4th Ave., Miami, 33130. Tel: 305-545-0760; Fax: 305-324-6162. Email: centromater1@catholiccharitiesadm.org.

Centro Mater West Child Care Center—8298 N.W. 103 St., Hialeah Gardens, 33016. Tel: 305-827-4040; Fax: 305-827-4033. Email: centrowest2@catholiccharitiesadm.org.

Good Shepherd Child Care Center—18601 S.W. 97 Ave., Perrine, 33157. Tel: 305-235-1756; Fax: 305-255-2788. Email: goodshepherd@catholiccharitiesadm.org.

Notre Dame Child Care Center—130 N.E. 62 St., Miami, 33138. Tel: 305-751-6778; Fax: 305-751-6959. Email: notredame@catholiccharitiesadm.org.

Sagrada Familia Child Care Center—970 S.W. 1st St., Miami, 33130. Tel: 305-324-5424; Fax: 305-325-0642. Email: sagradafam@catholiccharitiesadm.org.

South Dade Child Care Center—28520 S.W. 148 Ave., Leisure City, 33033. Tel: 305-245-0979; Fax: 305-242-8796. Email: southdade@catholiccharitiesadm.org.

Child Care Food Program—970 S.W. First St., Ste. 305, Miami, 33130. Tel: 305-324-4226; Fax: 305-324-0460. Email: foodprogram@catholiccharitiesadm.org.

Child Welfare Division—Dr. JULIAN SERRANO, Dir., 9615 Sterling Dr., Perrine, 33157. Tel: 305-238-2381; Fax: 305-232-5421.

Catholic Home for Children—9615 Sterling Dr., Perrine, 33157. Tel: 305-238-2381; Fax: 305-232-5421. Email: catholichome@catholiccharitiesadm.org. Bethany House, Cowgill House, Walsh House.

Foster Care and Adoption—9615 Sterling Dr., Perrine, 33157. Tel: 305-238-2381; Fax: 305-232-5421. Email: adoption@catholiccharitiesadm.org.

Unaccompanied Minors Program—ANITA GAWOR, 11400 S.W. 137 Ave., Miami, 33186. Tel: 305-380-0141; Fax: 305-385-8301. Email: umpadm@catholiccharitiesadm.org.

Victim Assistance Coordinator—VICKI KAUFMANN, M.A., M.P.S.T. Tel: 866-802-2873. Email: vkaufmann@catholiccharitiesadm.org.

Community Services Division—FRANKLIN MONJARREZ, Dir., 7900 N.E. 2nd Ave., 7th Fl., Miami, Fl 33138. Tel: 305-751-2456; Fax: 305-751-2188.

Refugee Resettlement and Employment Services—60 E. 3rd St., Ste. 206, Hialeah, 33010. Tel: 305-883-4555; Fax: 305-883-4498. Email: refugee2@catholiccharitiesadm.org.

Pierre Toussaint Haitian Social Services Center—130 N.E. 62 St., Miami, 33138. Tel: 305-795-3050; Fax: 305-754-7423. Email: pierretoussaint@catholiccharitiesadm.org. Neighborhood Revitalization, Elderly Refugee Services, Creole Literacy and Acculturation.

Haitian Job Development—1105 N.W. 6 Ave., Fort Lauderdale, 33311. Tel: 954-524-4122. Email: haitiancenter@catholiccharitiesadm.org. Emergency Rent, Utility and Food Assistance.

Catholic Charities Legal Services—RANDOLPH P. MCGRORTY, Supervising Attorney.

Miami Office—7101 Biscayne Blvd., Miami, 33138. Tel: 305-758-3301; Fax: 305-756-6435.

Hialeah Office—60 E. 3rd St., Ste. 206, Hialeah, 33010. Tel: 305-887-8333; Fax: 305-887-8813.

Broward Office—1210 N.W. 6th Ave., Pompano Beach, 33060. Tel: 954-783-3434.

Catholic Hospice, Inc.—TONY PALUMBO, CEO, 14100 Palmetto Frontage Rd., Miami Lakes, 33016. Tel: 305-822-2380; Fax: 305-824-0665.

One Stop Employment Center/Little Haiti—7900 N.E. 2nd Ave., Ste. 700, Miami, 33138. Tel: 305-251-2456; Fax: 305-758-8216.

Elderly Services Division—MIRANDA SGOUROS, Dir., 1505 N.E. 26 St., Wilton Manors, 33305. Tel: 954-630-9404; Fax: 954-566-6026.

Adult Day Care Programs—

Central West—6915 Stirling Rd., Davie, 33134. Tel: 954-583-6446.

St. Elizabeth—801 N.E. 33 St., Pompano Beach, 33064. Tel: 954-781-0461.

Wilton Manors—1503 N.E. 26 St., Wilton Manors, 33305. Tel: 954-630-9501; Fax: 954-566-6026. Email: adultcareadm@catholiccharitiesadm.org.

Nutrition and Socialization Programs—Carroll Senior Center, 9900 N.E. 2 Ave., Miami, 33138. Tel: 305-751-5203. *Gesu Church, 118 N.E. 2 St., Miami, 33132. Malcom Ross Senior Center, 1800 N.W. 28 St., Miami, 33128.* Tel: 305-633-0462. *Marian Towers, 17505 N. Bay Rd., Miami Beach, 33160. Palmer House, 1225 S.W. 107 Ave., Miami, 33174. St. Mary's, 7525 N.W. 2 Ave., Miami, 33138. McCarthy Residence, 13201 N.W. 28 Ave., Opa Locka, 33054.*

Elder Care Management Senior Solutions—1505 N.E. 26 St., Wilton Manors, 33305. Tel: 954-630-9404; Fax: 954-566-6026.

Housing Division—ANITA GAWOR, Dir., 9401 Biscayne Blvd., Miami Shores, 33138. Tel: 305-754-2444; Fax: 305-754-6649.

Dade—

Project Emmanuel—3620 N.W. First Ave., Miami, 33127. Tel: 305-573-3333.

New Life Family Center—3620 N.W. First Ave., Miami, 33127. Tel: 305-573-3333; Fax: 305-576-5111. Email: newlifeadm@catholiccharitiesadm.org.

Special Housing Initiative—6660 Biscayne Blvd., Miami, 33138. Tel: 305-758-2462.

Broward—

Providence Place—1299 E. Oakland Park Blvd., Fort Lauderdale, 33334. Tel: 954-568-6610. Email: providenceplace@catholiccharitiesadm.org.

Angelica House—1077 S.E. 22 Ave., Pompano Beach, 33062. Tel: 954-943-7060.

Monroe—

Theresa House—1621 Spaulding Ct., Key West, 33040. Tel: 305-292-9790.

Homeless Drop-In Center—2700 Flagler St., Key West, 33048. Tel: 305-292-9790.

Ministries Division—

HIV/AIDS Ministry—

Dade—1050 N.E. 129 St., North Miami, 33161. Tel: 305-899-0446; Fax: 305-899-7984. Email: counseling@cathloicharitiesadm.org.

Broward—1505 N.E. 26 St., Wilton Manors, 33305. Tel: 954-630-9404; Fax: 954-566-6026. Email:

fdr252@catholiccharitiesadm.org.

Catholic Charities Endowment Trust—VACANT, Exec. Dir., 9401 Biscayne Blvd., Miami, 33138. Tel: 305-762-1323; Fax: 305-762-1344.

Ascending Life—HUGH CLEAR, U.S. Rep., 9401 Biscayne Blvd., Miami Shores, 33138. Tel: 305-762-1229; Fax: 305-762-1249.

Ministry of Catholic Health Services

Catholic Health Services, Inc.—JOSEPH CATANIA, Pres. & CEO; JAMES A. BALL, C.O.O., 4790 N. State Rd. 7, Lauderdale Lakes, 33319. Tel: 954-484-1515.

Catholic Housing for the Elderly and Handicapped, Inc.—

Catholic Housing Management—TERE SPRING, Vice Pres. Elderly Housing Services, 11440 N. Kendall Dr., Ste. E-209, Miami, 33176. Tel: 305-757-2824.

Archbishop Carroll Manor—MARIO YANES, Mgr., 3667 S. Miami Ave., Miami, 33133. Tel: 305-854-8953.

Archbishop Hurley Hall—ALEJA PAGAN, Mgr., 632 N.W. 1st St., Hallandale, 33009. Tel: 954-454-0855.

Marian Towers—FAUSTO FERNANDEZ, Mgr., 17505 N. Bay Rd., Miami Beach, 33160. Tel: 305-932-1300.

Archbishop McCarthy Residence—ROSLYN WILLIAMS, Mgr., 13201 N.W. 28 Ave., Opa Locka, 33054. Tel: 305-688-2700.

Palmer House—NOEMI DIAZ-MONTORO, Mgr., 1225 S.W. 107 Ave., Miami, 33174. Tel: 305-221-9566.

St. Andrew Towers—CAROL NICHOLS, Mgr., 2700 N.W. 99 Ave., Coral Springs, 33065. Tel: 954-752-3960.

St. Dominic Gardens—MARIO YANES, Mgr., 5849 N.W. 7th St., Miami, 33126. Tel: 305-262-0962.

St. Elizabeth Gardens—JOHN CAMERON, Mgr., 801 N.E. 33rd St., Pompano Beach, 33064. Tel: 954-941-4597.

St. Joseph Towers—DEBRA HAMELRATH, Mgr., 3475 N.W. 30th St., Lauderdale Lakes, 33311. Tel: 954-485-5150.

St. Mary Towers—FAUSTO FERNANDEZ, Mgr., 7615 N.W. 2nd Ave., Miami, 33150. Tel: 305-757-3190.

Stella Maris—ANN H. SMITH, Mgr., 8638 Harding Ave., Miami Beach, 33141. Tel: 305-865-6841.

St. Anne's Gardens—MERCEDES PUJALS, Mgr., 11800 Quail Roost Dr., Miami, 33177. Tel: 305-234-1994.

St. Boniface Gardens—8200 Johnson St., Pembroke Pines, 33024. Tel: 305-433-3899. ALEJA PAGAN, Mgr.

St. Vincent de Paul Gardens—2000 N.W. 103 St., Miami, 33147. Tel: 305-757-2824.

Nursing and Retirement Centers—

BROWARD:

St. Joseph Residence, Inc., RON BONAVITA, Admin., 3485 N.W. 30 St., Lauderdale Lakes, 33311. Tel: 954-739-1483. *St. John's Rehabilitation Hospital and Nursing Center, Inc.*, dba St. John's Nursing Center DIANE DUBE, Exec. Dir., 3075 N.W. 35 Ave., Lauderdale Lakes, 33311. Tel: 954-739-6233. *St. John's Rehabilitation Hospital and Nursing Center, Inc.*, dba St. Anthony's Rehabilitation Hospital LINDA MOTTE, Admin., 3075 N.W. 35 Ave., Lauderdale Lakes, 33319. Tel: 954-739-6233. *Catholic Hospice of Broward, Inc., 4790 N. State Rd. 7, Lauderdale Lakes, 33319.* Tel: 954-484-1515. *Catholic Home Health Medicare Services, Inc., 4790 N. State Rd. 7, Lauderdale Lakes, 33319.* Tel: 954-484-1515. *Catholic Home Health Services, Inc., 4790 N. State Rd. 7, Lauderdale Lakes, 33319.* Tel: 954-484-1515. *Catholic Home Health Services of Broward, Inc.*, JOAN BUDDI, Admin., 3075 N.W. 35 Ave., Lauderdale Lakes, 33311. Tel: 954-486-3660.

DADE:

St. Anne's Nursing Center, St. Anne's Residence, Inc., TIMOTHY REARDON, Exec. Dir., 11855 Quail Roost Dr., Miami, 33177. Tel: 305-252-4000. *Miami-Dade Nursing Center, Inc., c/o 4790 N. State Rd. 7, Lauderdale Lakes, 33319.* Tel: 954-484-1515. *Villa Maria Nursing and Rehabilitation Center, Inc.*, dba Villa Maria Nursing Center MR. JAMES REISS, Exec. Dir., 1050 N.E. 125 St., North Miami, 33161. Tel: 305-891-8850. *Villa Maria Nursing and Rehabilitation Center, Inc.*, dba St. Catherine Rehabilitation Hospital GINGER IRVING, Admin., 1050 N.E. 125 St., North Miami, 33161. Tel: 305-357-1735. *Villa Maria Health Care Services, Inc.*, dba Catholic Home Health Services of Miami Dade CAROL HYLTON, Admin., 1050 N.E. 125 St., North Miami, 33161. Tel: 305-899-0400. *Villa Maria Adult Day Care*, GWEN DUNCAN, Dir., 20855 N.W. 9 Ct., Box R-2, North Miami, 33169. Tel: 305-651-0034. *Villa Maria Foundation, Inc., 1050 N.E. 125 St., North Miami, 33161.* Tel: 305-891-8850. *Special Education*, THOMAS HORAN, Ed.D., Exec. Dir., 15701 N.W. 37 Ave., Opa Locka, 33054. Tel: 305-625-8354; Fax: 305-625-0744. (Developmentally handicapped and mentally retarded) Marian Center Services.

Catholic Cemeteries of the Archdiocese of Miami, Inc.—PAUL JOHNSON, Vice Pres. Cemetery Services, 11411 N.W. 25th St., Miami, 33172. Tel: 305-592-0521.

Archdiocesan Cemeteries—Our Lady of Mercy Cemetery, 11411 N.W. 25th St., Miami, 33172. Tel: 305-592-0521. *Our Lady Queen of Heaven Cemetery, 1500 S. State Rd. 7, North Lauderdale, 33068.* Tel: 954-972-1234.

Catholic Elderly Services, Inc.— dba Catholic Health Services Foundation *4790 N. State Rd. 7, Lauderdale Lakes, 33319.* Tel: 954-484-1515.

Ministry of Pastoral Services

Ministry of Pastoral Services—Most Rev. FELIPE J. ESTEVEZ, D.D., S.T.D., V.G., Exec. Dir., 9401 Biscayne Blvd., Miami, 33138. Tel: 305-762-1096.

Campus Ministry—PATRICIA STOCKTON, M.A., M.S.W., Dir., 9401 Biscayne Blvd., Miami, 33138. Tel: 305-762-1096.

Barry University—Sr. ARLENE SCOTT, O.P., Asst. Vice Pres. Mission & Ministry; Rev. SCOTT O'BRIEN, O.P., Chap.; ALEX SCHLICH, Campus Min.; MICHELLE BROWN, Admin. Asst., 11300 N.E. 2nd Ave., Miami Shores, 33161. Tel: 305-899-3650.

FIU-North Miami—MAMONNE ONELIEN, Campus Min., 3000 N.E. 151st St. & Biscayne Blvd., North Miami, 33181. Tel: 305-919-5247.

FIU-University Park—Revs. ROLANDO GARCIA, Dir.; ALEXANDER EKECHUKWU, Assoc. Dir.; RIGOBERTO VEGA, Campus Min., St. Agatha Church, 1111 S.W. 107th Ave., Miami, 33174. Tel: 305-222-1506; 305-348-3900.

Miami Dade CC-South—Rev. MICHAEL KISH, Chap.; CARMEN VILLAFANE, Campus Min., 7270 S.W. 120 St., Miami, 33156. Tel: 305-238-7562.

Florida Memorial College—PATRICIA STOCKTON, M.A., M.S.W., Campus Min., 9401 Biscayne Blvd., Miami, 33138. Tel: 305-762-1096.

St. Thomas University—Revs. WARREN HALL, Acting Dir.; EDWARD BLACKWELL JR., Ed.D., Dir. Community Outreach; KATHRYN ANGOLD, Grad. Asst.; MARIA PEREZ-RUDISILL, Liturgical Choir Dir.; ANGELA SIMS, Admin. Asst., 16400 N.W. 32nd Ave., Miami, 33054. Tel: 305-628-6525.

University of Miami—Very Rev. BERNARD KIRLIN, V.F., University Chap.; Rev. MIGUEL SEPULVEDA, Assoc. Chap.; SILVIA TARAFA, Campus Min., St. Augustine Church, 1400 Miller Rd., Coral Gables, 33146. Tel: 305-661-1648.

Miami Dade CC-North—CARMEN VILLAFANE, Campus Min.

Miami Dade CC-Wolfson Campus—Rev. THOMAS MADDEN, S.J., Chap.; CARMEN VILLAFANE, Campus Min.; Dr. PAUL GEORGE Faculty Advisor, Gesu Church, 118 N.E. 2 St., Miami, 33132. Tel: 305-379-1424; 305-347-3000.

Broward CC-Central and NOVA University—RIGOBERTO VEGA, Campus Min., Pastoral Center, 9401 Biscayne Blvd., Miami, 33138. Tel: 305-762-1013 (Dade); 305-525-5157, Ext. 1013 (Broward).

Catholic Daughters of America—Court 634, Regent: NORMA FARALDO. Vice-Regent:: VIOLET PITA, St. Mary Star of the Sea Church, 1010 Windsor Ln., Key West, 33040. Tel: 305-294-1018. Local Chaplain:: Rev. FRANCISCO J. HERNANDEZ.

Family Life Ministry—ELAINE M. SYFERT, Dir. & Coord. Hispanic Ministry; JEAN VALDES-FAULI DUDA, Coord., Divorced & Separated; DOT HERING, Coord. Ministry to Engaged & Married Couples, 9401 Biscayne Blvd., Miami, 33138. Tel 305-762-1157; Fax: 305-762-1144.

Lay Apostolic Movements and Associations—

Agrupacion Catolica Universitaria (ACU)—Rev. AMANDO LLORENTE, S.J., Spiritual Dir., 720 N.E. 27 St., Miami, 33137. Tel: 305-573-1418; 305-576-2748

St. Martin de Porres Assoc.—LEONA COOPER, Pres., Mailing Address, P.O. Box 330102, Miami, 33133. Tel: 305-443-9466; Fax: 305-461-8669.

Archdiocesan Council of Catholic Women—Rev. Msgr. ANDREW ANDERSON, Moderator, 9401 Biscayne Blvd., Miami Shores, 33138. Tel: 305-762-1158 VIRGINIA BENEDUCE, Pres., 317 Jackson St., Hollywood, 33019. Tel: 954-920-5034. Email: ducebene@aol.com. Spiritual Moderators: Very Rev. GERALD MORRIS, V.F., (Monroe District); Revs. GABRIEL VIGUES, (North Broward District); FRANCIS MCCARTHY, (South Broward District); MICHAEL GREER, (South Dade District); WILLIAM ELBERT, (North Dade District).

Camino (Spanish)—Deacon JORGE GONZALEZ, Dir., P.O. Box 524160, Miami, 33152-4160. Tel: 305-226-4664

Catholic Charismatic Services--Archdiocese of Miami—VACANT, Archdiocesan Liaison, 3600 S.W. 32 Blvd., Hollywood, 33023; Rev. DANIEL DOYLE, S.M., Assoc. Archdiocesan Liaison, Charismatic Services: P.O. Box 816128, Hollywood, 33081-0128. Tel: 954-961-1856; Fax: 954-961-3662. Spanish: Deacon RAFAEL DE LOS REYES, Spiritual Dir.; JOSE FUENTES, Coord., Centro Carismatico Catolico: 500 N.W. 22 Ave., Miami, 33125. Tel: 305-631-0007; Fax: 305-642-0006. Email: rcch@bellsouth.net.

Ministry to Cultural Groups (Non-Hispanic Ethnicities)—Rev. JEAN PIERRE, Dir. Tel: 305-762-1228.

African Apostolate—Rev. ALEXANDER EKECHUKWU, C.S.Sp., St. Agatha Parish, 1111 S.W. 107th Ave., Miami, 33174. Tel: 305-222-1500; Fax: 305-222-1505.

Brazilian and Portuguese Apostolate—O.L. Aparecida Roman Catholic Mission, 1618 Polk St., Hollywood, 33020. Tel: 954-920-1070; Fax: 954-920-0776. Rev. CARLOS ANKLAN, C.S., Coord.

Chinese Apostolate—Deacon ALEX LAM, 7270 S.W. 120 St., Miami, 33156. Tel: 350-238-7562.

Croatian Apostolate—Tel: 305-762-1323; Fax: 305-762-1344.

Filipino Apostolate—Ms. JANET MACASERO, 6320 Plunkett St., Hollywood, 33023. Tel: 954-981-7843.

French-Canadians—Tel: 305-762-1323; Fax: 305-762-1344.

Haitians—Rev. JEAN PIERRE, Apostolate Dir., Haitian Apostolate, 9401 Biscayne Blvd., Miami, 33138. Tel: 305-762-1228; Fax: 305-762-1344 Notre Dame d'Haiti Mission,; Rev. Msgr. GERARD DARBOUZE, 110 N.E. 62 St., Miami, 33138. Tel: 305-751-6289 St. Joseph Haitian Catholic Mission; Revs. MARY KIDNEY ST. JEAN, 1210 N.W. 6th Ave., Pompano Beach, 33060. Tel: 954-941-3095 Divine Mercy Haitian Catholic Mission; FRANKY JEAN, 1105 N.W. 6th Ave., Fort Lauderdale, 33311. Tel: 954-764-8519.

Hispanic—Most Rev. FELIPE J. ESTEVEZ, D.D., S.T.D., V.G., Dir.

Hungarians—Deacon MIKLOS A. BEREGSZASZI, St. Catherine of Siena Parish, 9200 S.W. 107th Ave., Miami, 33176. Tel: 305-274-6333; Fax: 305-274-6337.

Indians—Rev. JAMES PARAPPALLY, Chap. (India) Our Lady of Mercy Parish, 5201 N. Military Trail, Pompano Beach, 33064. Tel: 954-421-3246; Fax: 954-421-1973.

Italian—Rev. CHRISTOPHER MARINO, Visitation Parish, 19100 N. Miami Ave., Miami, 33169. Tel: 305-652-3624; Fax: 305-652-5207.

Jamaican—Mrs. JUNE CHIN, 11534 SW 127 Ct., Miami, 33186. Tel: 305-387-0442; Fax: 305-382-8466.

Native Americans—Rev. JEAN PIERRE, Dir. Tel: 305-762-1228.

Korean—Rev. DANIEL HEE-MOON YANG, 14344 S. Cove Cir., Davie, 33325. Tel: 954-474-9091; KEVIN KIM, Asst. Tel: 954-336-0178 (Cell).

Polish - (Our Lady of Czestochowa)—Rev. CZESLAW RYBACHI, S.Ch., Dir., 2400 N.E. 12 St., Pompano Beach, 33062. Tel: 954-946-6347; Fax: 954-946-0512.

Vietnamese—Rev. ISIDORE BAKY, Coord., St. Helen Church, 3033 N.W. 33 Ave., Fort Lauderdale, 33311. Tel: 954-714-9860; Fax: 954-739-9632.

Christian Family Movement— Spanish: Rev. ANGEL VILLARONGA, O.F.M., Spiritual Dir., Casa Cana, 480 E. 8 St., Hialeah, 33010. Tel: 305-888-4819.

Cofradia Nuestra Senora de la Caridad (Spanish)—Most Rev. AGUSTIN A. ROMAN, D.D., V.G., Dir. (Retired), 3609 S. Miami Ave., Miami, 33133. Tel: 305-854-2404; Fax: 305-854-8022.

Ministry to the Deaf and Disabled—Sisters MARGARET JOHNSON, O.P., Exec. Dir.; CONLETH BRANNAN, C.S.J., Dir. Schott Center Programs, Co-Founder; NERY RODRIGUEZ, Dir. Schott Center Svcs. & Interpreter; MARY ROUKAS, Dir. Residences & Counselor; PATTY SACCO, Dir. Devel.; AUDREY BROWN, Dir. Human Resources, Schott Memorial Center, 6591 S. Flamingo Rd., Cooper City, 33330. Tel: 954-434-3306; Fax: 954-434-3307.

Comunidad de Vida Cristiana (CVX) Regina Mundi—Rev. VICTOR HERNANDEZ, S.J., Spiritual Dir., Belen Jesuit Prep. School, 500 S.W. 127 Ave., Miami, 33184. Tel: 305-223-8600.

Cursillo—VACANT. Assoc. Directors: Deacons ROBERT BINDER; THOMAS J. DAWSON, Spanish:; Rev. SANTIAGO MATHEU, Spiritual Dir., Casa Emaus, 16250 S.W. 112 Ave., Miami, 33157. Tel: 305-235-7160; 305-235-4215; Fax: 305-235-7392.

Encuentros Familiares (Spanish)—Rev. FLORENTINO AZCOITIA, S.J., Dir.; IGNACIO GARCIA DE OSUNA, Coord.; NELLY GARCIA DE OSUNA, Coord., Casa Manresa, P.O. Box 651512, Miami, 33265. Tel: 305-596-0001; Fax: 305-596-9655. Email: manresa@bellsouth.net. Web: efjc.com.

Encuentros Juveniles (Spanish)—Sr. CLAUDIA ORTEGA, R.M.I., Spiritual Dir., Youth Center, 3333 S. Miami Ave., Miami, 33133. Tel: 305-856-3404; Fax: 305-854-8888.

Impacto (Spanish)—Deacon HENRY GONZALEZ, P.O. Box 440973, Tamiami Station, Miami, 33144. Tel: 305-571-7111.

Knights of Columbus (English and Spanish)—Rev. Msgr. EMILIO VALLINA, Archdiocesan Chap., St. John Bosco Parish, 1301 W. Flagler St., Miami, 33125. Tel: 305-649-5464.

La Nueva Jerusalen - Comunidad de Alianza—WILLIAM F. BROWN JR., Head Coord., P.O. Box 65-1702, Miami, 33265-1702. Tel: 305-273-7460; Fax: 305-273-7467.

Legion of Mary (English Speaking)—Rev. RICHARD SOULLIERE, Dir. (Retired), P.O. Box 221937, Hollywood, 33022. Tel: 954-961-6740 (Spanish Speaking); ADOLFINA VAZQUEZ, Pres. Tel: 305-824-3060.

Marian Movements & Devotions—Rev. RICHARD SOULLIERE, Coord. (Retired), P.O. Box 221937, Hollywood, 33022. Tel: 954-961-6740.

Apostleship of the Sea— (serving Seafarers) Rev. JOSE M. PAZ, Archdiocesan Dir. & Chap., Port of Miami; Mrs. ANGELA GREGORIO, Dir. Port of Miami, Stella Maris Seamen's Center, 1275 S. America Way, Miami, 33132. Tel: 305-371-6272; Mr. ISABEL ROSIGNOLI, Dir., Stella Maris Seamen's Center, 2550 Eisenhower Blvd., Amman Bldg. No. 7, Port Everglades, 33316. Tel: 954-527-0467; Fax: 954-527-0471.

Prison Ministry—SAMUEL DIAZ, Dir.; MYRIAM NIEVES, Assoc. Dir., 9401 Biscayne Blvd., Miami, 33138. Tel: 305-762-1093; 305-762-1108. Email: detention@miamiarch.org.

Respect Life Office—Rev. JORDI RIVERO, Dir.; JOAN CROWN, Assoc. Dir., 18340 N.W. 12 Ave., Miami, 33169. Tel: 305-653-2921; Fax: 305-653-1001. Email: ilovlife@bellsouth.net.

Project Rachel—Tel: 877-908-1212.

Respect Life Branch Offices-Emergency Pregnancy Services—

N. Dade Central Office, 18340 N.W. 12 Ave., Miami, 33169. Tel: 305-653-2921.

North Broward Office, 5115 Coconut Creek Pkwy., Margate, 33063. Tel: 954-977-7769.

Hialeah Office, 2024 E. 4th Ave., Hialeah, 33011. Tel: 305-883-2229.

Hollywood Office (S. Broward), 6151 Washington St., Hollywood, 33023. Tel: 954-963-2229.

Ft. Lauderdale Office, 2909 N. Andrews Ave., Wilton Manors, 33311. Tel: 954-565-8506.

Sunset Office, 9642 Sunset Dr., Miami, 33173. Tel: 305-273-8507.

Rural Life Ministry—Rev. PEDRO GARCIA, Dir.

Everglades Community Assoc.—Everglades Villas, 19200 S.W. 380th St., Florida City, 33030. South Dade Ctr., 31248 S.W. 134 Ave., Homestead, 33033. Redlands Camp, US 1 & 298 St., Homestead, 33030.

St. Ann Mission—

Naranja and Migrant Ministry—13875 SW 264 St., Naranja, 33032. Mailing Address, P.O. Box 322278, Naranja, 33032. Tel: 305-258-3968; 305-258-9682; Fax: 305-258-3591.

Youth and Young Adult Ministry—Sr. ONDINA CORTES, R.M.I., Dir., Pastoral Center, 9401 Biscayne Blvd., Miami Shores, 33138. Tel: 305-762-1101.

Scouting—Sr. ONDINA CORTES, R.M.I., Rel. Advisor; Deacon THOMAS FRANKLIN, Chap., 9401 Biscayne Blvd., Miami, 33138.

Ministry of Temporalities

Executive Director—Rev. Msgr. JOHN J. VAUGHAN, Vicar Temporalities.

Business Office—MICHAEL CASCIATO, Archdiocesan Financial Admin.; JOSEPH CATANIA, Treas.

Building Commission—ROBERT A. BROWN, Dir.; Rev. Msgr. JOHN J. VAUGHAN; Revs. FREDERICK J. BRICE; GABRIEL O'REILLY; EDMOND WHYTE; EMILIO MARTIN; GUSTAVO MIYARES; JAMES DETRICK.

Archdiocesan Fund-Raising & Assessments Committee—Rev. Msgrs. WILLIAM J. HENNESSEY, V.G.; JOHN J. VAUGHAN; Very Rev. TERENCE HOGAN, S.L.D.; Revs. GABRIEL O'REILLY; GUSTAVO MIYARES; JEAN PIERRE; EDMOND WHYTE; WILLIAM ELBERT; ARNALDO LOPEZ; JOSEPH CATANIA; MICHAEL CASCIATO.

Finance Council—Rev. Msgrs. JOHN J. VAUGHAN; WILLIAM J. HENNESSEY, V.G.; Rev. ANTHONY MULDERRY; Mr. J. PATRICK FITZGERALD, Esq.; MICHAEL CASCIATO; RAUL MASVIDAL; THOMAS PENNEKAMP; FRANK BUTTACAVOLI; MIRIAM LOPEZ; PEDRO GARCIA; JOSEPH CATANIA.

Lay Personnel—ABBIE MEHLER.

Archdiocese of Miami Health Plan Trust—Rev. Msgr. TOMAS M. MARIN, Chm.; Ms. SUSAN WADDELL, Acting Admin.; Ms. DIANNE TRILLO, Human Resources.

Pension—Most Rev. JOHN C. FAVALORA, D.D., Chm.; Rev. Msgr. NOEL FOGARTY, Vice Chm.

Real Estate Board—Rev. Msgr. JOHN J. VAUGHAN, Dir.; Revs. FREDERICK J. BRICE; ANTHONY MULDERRY; HENRY BEZOLD.

Plant Operations—ROBERT BROWN.

Ministry of Worship and Spiritual Life

Executive Director—Very Rev. TERENCE HOGAN, S.L.D.; CATALINA PRADO, Admin. Asst.

Worship & Spiritual Life Commission—Rev. MICHAEL GREER, Chm.

Celebration and Rite Committee—Very Rev. TERENCE HOGAN, S.L.D., Chm.

Spiritual Life Committee—SUSAN LORETTA.

Sacred Art & Architecture—Rev. PAUL V. VUTURO.

Liturgical Music—SUZANNE ARSENAULT.

Committee on Popular Piety—Rev. JUAN J. SOSA.

Ministry of Persons

Ministry of Persons—VACANT, Exec. Dir.

Vocations—Rev. PEDRO M. CORCES, Dir., 9401 Biscayne Blvd., Miami, 33138. Tel: 305-762-1137.

Archdiocesan Vocations Review Board—Rev. Msgr. JOHN NOONAN, Rector, St. John Vianney College Seminary, Miami; Rev. GUSTAVO MIYARES; Very Rev. THOMAS O'DWYER, V.F.; Revs. JAMES MURPHY; PEDRO CORCES; MICHAEL CARRUTHERS; JUAN SOSA; KENNETH SCHWANGER; JEAN PIERRE; FEDERICO CAPDEPON; ENRIQUE J. ESTRADA; Sisters ONDINA CORTES, R.M.I.; ANN MCDERMOTT, O.S.F.; Ms. PAT STOCKTON; BOB MORGAN; Dr. MANUEL ALVAREZ.

Office for Religious—Rev. JOHN R. MADIGAN, O.M.I., Dir.; MARIA CANO, Sec.

Priestly Life and Ministry—Rev. Msgr. JOHN NOONAN, Dir., St. John Vianney College Seminary, 2900 S.W. 87 Ave., Miami, 33165. Tel: 305-223-4561, Ext. 12; Fax: 305-223-0650.

Permanent Diaconate—Most Rev. JOHN C. FAVALORA, D.D., Dir.; Very Rev. KENNETH SCHWANGER, J.C.D., V.F., Chm. Advisory Board; Deacons IAN TAYLOR, Exec. Dir.; BERNARDO PITA, Dir. Formation.

Lay Ministry—Sr. ANN E. MCDERMOTT, O.S.F., Dir.; ADELE GONZALEZ, D.Min., Asst. Dir. Educators & Consultants: ZOILA L. DIAZ, D.Min.; ROGELIO ZELADA, M.A.; MARIA HORTENSIA SAN PELAYO, Admin. Asst.

Continuing Education for the Clergy—Rev. Msgr. JOHN NOONAN, Dir., St. John Vianney College Seminary, 2900 S.W. 87 Ave., Miami, 33165. Tel: 305-223-4561, Ext. 12; Fax: 305-223-0650.

Priests' Sabbaticals—Rev. Msgr. JOHN NOONAN, Chm.

Retired Priests' Committee—Very Rev. SEAMUS DOYLE, V.F., Chm.; Rev. Msgrs. JOHN J. VAUGHAN; VINCENT T. KELLY; Revs. MICHAEL HOYER; MARTIN CASSIDY; PATRICK FITZGERALD, (Legal).

Ministry to Professional Groups—

Catholic Educators' Guild—VACANT, Chap.

Catholic Funeral Directors' Guild—Rev. Msgr. ANDREW ANDERSON, Chap.

Catholic Lawyers' Guild—Rev. Msgr. ANDREW ANDERSON, Chap.

Catholic Physicians' and Dentists' Guild—Rev. Msgr. TOMAS M. MARIN, Chap., Dade & Broward.

Catholic Law Enforcement Ministry—Police Chaplains: Rev. Msgr. JOHN J. VAUGHAN, (Miami Beach Police); Rev. MICHAEL KISH, (City of Miami Police); VACANT, (Florida Highway Patrol, Troop K).

Catholic Fire Service Ministry—Rev. MICHAEL LYNCH, Fire Chap. (City of Coral Gables, Margate).

Special Apostolates

Amor En Accion--(Love in Action)—P.O. Box 141523, Coral Gables, 33114. Tel: 305-762-1236. ALICIA MARRILL, Pres.; TERESITA GONZALEZ, Dir. & Coord. Tel: 305-762-1226.

Archbishop Hurley Scholarship Fund—Rev. Msgr. VINCENT T. KELLY, Vicar, Christian Formation, 9401 Biscayne Blvd., Miami, 33138. Tel: 305-762-1076.

Catholic Alumni Club of South Florida—VACANT.

Downtown Senior Citizens' Community Center at Gesu Church—Sr. MARIA ISABEL RINCON, O.P., 118 N.E. 2nd St., Miami, 33132. Tel: 305-374-6099.

Pontifical Mission Societies—Rev. JEAN PIERRE, Dir.

Society for the Propagation of the Faith—

Holy Childhood Association—

The Society of St. Peter Apostle—

Missionary Union of Priests and Religious—

Priests Purgatorial Society—

Serra Club—

Miami—Dr. IDALIA LASTRA, Pres., 2498 S.W. 3rd Ave., Miami, 33129. Tel: 305-856-7180; 305-854-3795.

Broward—Mr. THOMAS J. METZGER SR., Pres., 2811 N.E. 53rd Ct., Lighthouse Point, 33064. Tel: 954-803-1001.

Chaplains--Dade County - Serra Club—Rev. EMIL FARDELLONE. N. Broward Co.: VACANT.

The St. Vincent De Paul Society, Archdiocesan Council of Miami, Inc.—P.O. Box 934334, Margate, 33093-4334. Tel: 954-974-7121. Mr. VINCENT MURPHY, Pres. & Trustee; Revs. WILLIAM ELBERT, Dade Co. Chap.; FREDERICK BRICE, Broward County Chap.

CLERGY, PARISHES, MISSIONS AND PAROCHIAL SCHOOLS

CITY OF MIAMI
(DADE COUNTY)

1—ST. MARY'S CATHEDRAL (1930), Very Rev. Terence Hogan, S.L.D., Rector; Rev. Pierre-Louis Joseph (Haiti). In Res., Rev. Alvaro Pinzon (Colombia); Deacon Ian Taylor.
Res.: 7525 N.W. 2nd Ave., Miami, 33150. Tel: 305-759-4531; 305-759-4532; Fax: 305-757-7456.
School—Tel: 305-795-2000; Fax: 305-795-2013. Sr. Jane Stoecker, S.S.J., Prin. Sisters of St. Joseph of St. Augustine 7; Lay Teachers 14; Students 321.
Catechesis/Religious Program—Tel: 305-795-2016; Fax: 305-757-6870. Students 321.

2—ST. AGATHA (1971), Revs. Rolando G. Garcia; Cristobal J. Puertas (Colombia); Alexander Ekechukwu, C.S.Sp.; Deacons Pedro Calvo; Angel Pintado.
Res.: 1111 S.W. 107th Ave., Miami, 33174. Tel: 305-222-1500; Fax: 305-222-1505.
School—Tel: 305-222-8751; Fax: 305-222-1517. Mrs. Maria Glass, Prin.; Susana Del Riego, Asst. Prin. Lay Teachers 47; Students 681.
Catechesis/Religious Program—Tel: 305-222-8067; Fax: 305-222-8078. Mrs. Matilde Menendez, D.R.E.; Mrs. Maria Gonzalez, Asst. D.R.E. Students 627.

3—ST. BRENDAN (1954), Revs. Fernando Heria, J.C.L.; Charles Peterman; Raul Soutuyo; Francisco Calderon, O.P.; Jose Alvarez; Deacons Jose P. Alonso; Eduardo Blanco; Billy Lannon Jr.
Res.: 8725 S.W. 32 St., Miami, 33165. Tel: 305-221-0881; Fax: 305-226-6249.
School—Tel: 305-221-2722; Fax: 305-554-6726. Mrs. Emma A. Ventura. Lay Teachers 37; Students 673.
Catechesis/Religious Program—Tel: 305-226-2628; 305-221-2861. Esperanza Ginoris, D.R.E.; Rosmery Ortega, D.R.E. Students 638.

4—ST. CATHERINE OF SIENA (1968), Revs. Juan J. Sosa; Rafael Cos (Cuba); Deacons Miklos A. Bereg-szaszi; Vicente Moreno.
Res.: 9200 S.W. 107 Ave., Miami, 33176. Tel: 305-274-6333; Fax: 305-274-6337.
Catechesis/Religious Program—Tel: 305-274-6333, Ext. 26. Lydia Mayorga, D.R.E. Students 579.

5—CHRIST THE KING (1961), Revs. James Joseph Flavin, O.M.I.; Raymond Crowe, O.M.I.; John Gordon, O.M.I. In Res., Rev. Charles Clements; Deacons Max Colastin; George Gibson.
Res.: 16000 S.W. 112th Ave., Miami, 33157. Tel: 305-238-2485; Fax: 305-254-0330.
Catechesis/Religious Program—Tel: 305-235-0293. Students 144.

6—CORPUS CHRISTI (1941), Revs. Jose L. Menendez; Jorge L. Saenz; Jose Maria Herreras, S.J. (Spain).
Res.: 3220 N.W. 7th Ave., Miami, 33127. Tel: 305-635-1331; Fax: 305-635-2031.
School—Tel: 305-635-8571; Fax: 305-636-4421. Ms. Beatriz Perez, Prin. Lay Teachers 21; Students 235.
Catechesis/Religious Program—Sr. Carmen Alvarez, M.R.I. Tel: 305-633-5824. Students 667.
Mission—San Francisco y Santa Clara 402 N.E. 29 St., Miami, 33137.
Mission—San Juan Bautista 3116 N.W. 2nd Ave., Miami, 33127.
Mission—Nuestra Senora de Altagracia 1779 N.W. 28th St., Miami, 33142.
Mission—La Milagrosa 1860 N.W. 18th Ter., Miami, 33125.

7—ST. DOMINIC (1962), Revs. Alberto Rodriguez, O.P.; Restituto Perez, O.P.; Desiderio Eguino, O.P.; Bro. Jose D. Padilla, O.P. In Res., Revs. Mark Wedig, O.P.; Scott O'Brien, O.P.; Bro. David G. Caron, O.P.; Rev. Jorge Presmanes, O.P.
Res.: 5909 N.W. 7th St., Miami, 33126. Tel: 305-264-0181; Fax: 305-262-4685.
Catechesis/Religious Program—Tel: 305-264-3372. Students 269.

8—EPIPHANY (1951), Rev. Msgr. Jude O'Doherty; Rev. Jesus Alberto Bohorquez; Deacons Jose Carrion; Donald Livingston; Paul H. Munter; Norman Ruiz-Castaneda.
Res.: 8081 S.W. 54 Ct., Miami, 33143. Tel: 305-667-4911; Fax: 305-667-8067.
School—Tel: 305-667-5251; Fax: 305-667-6828. Sr. Mary Henrich, I.H.M., Prin. Sisters Servants of the Immaculate Heart of Mary 3; Lay Teachers 68; Students 1,087.
Catechesis/Religious Program—Tel: 305-665-0037.

Students 356.

9—St. Francis Xavier (1927), Rev. John Madigan, O.M.I.
Mailing Address: P.O. Box 01-1901, Miami, 33101-1901. Fax: 305-624-6641.
Res.: 1698 N.W. 4th Ave., Miami, 33136. Tel: 305-576-2957; Fax: 305-576-3120.
School—Tel: 305-573-8532; Fax: 305-573-0263. Lay Teachers 16; Students 170.
Catechesis/Religious Program—Tel: 305-754-3442. Students 42.

10—Gesu (1896), Revs. William J. Mayer, S.J.; Sergio Figueredo, S.J.; Fernando Lopez, S.J.; Thomas A. Griffin, S.J.; William Kidwell, S.J.; Leo Leise, S.J. In Res., Rev. E. Matthew Turk, S.J. (MO); Deacon Thomas Franklin.
Res.: 118 N.E. 2nd St., Miami, 33132. Tel: 305-379-1424; Fax: 305-372-9544.
Catechesis/Religious Program—Tel: 305-374-6099. Students 75.

11—Good Shepherd (1977), Revs. Michael Greer; Eduardo Jimenez; Andrew Dowgiert (Poland); Deacons Michael Plummer; Jorge Prieto; Santos Rodriguez; Julio Zayas.
Res. & Church: 14187 S.W. 72nd St., Miami, 33183. Tel: 305-385-4320; Fax: 305-386-2407.
School—(Grades PreK-8) Tel: 305-385-7002; Fax: 305-385-7026. Dr. Maria Elena Lopez, Prin. Lay Teachers 35; Students 330.
Catechesis/Religious Program—Tel: 305-388-9877; Fax: 305-388-5272. Maria Changsut, D.R.E.; Sr. Rosa Garcia, O.P., D.R.E. Students 950.

12—Holy Redeemer (1950), Rev. Gari Ruthenberg, O.M.I.
Church: 1301 N.W. 71st St., Miami, 33147. Tel: 305-691-1701; Fax: 305-691-7074.
Catechesis/Religious Program—Students 53.

13—St. James (1952), Rev. Jean Pierre. In Res., Revs. Martin Adu; Jude Nwabugwu (Nigeria); Christian E. Plancher, S.M.M.
Res.: 540 N.W. 132nd St., Miami, 33168. Tel: 305-681-7428; Fax: 305-685-0631.
School—Tel: 305-681-3822; Fax: 305-681-6435. Religious 3; Lay Teachers 13; Students 270.
Catechesis/Religious Program—Tel: 305-681-2676. Students 140.

14—St. Joachim (1972), Rev. Jesus J. Arias. In Res., Rev. Raul Moretto (Argentina); Deacon Bernardo Pita.
Rectory—11720 S.W. 192nd St., Miami, 33177.
Church: 19150 S.W. 117th Ave., Miami, 33177.
Catechesis/Religious Program—Students 584.

15—St. John Bosco (1962), Rev. Msgr. Emilio Vallina; Revs. Jorge I. Perales; Wilfredo Contreras.
Mailing Address: P.O. Box 993, Miami, 33125. In Res., Revs. Leopoldo Leon (Venezuela); Francisco P. Villaverde, O.P.; Deacons Rodolfo Baez; Diego Chavez; Rodolfo Padron.
Res.: 1301 W. Flagler St., Miami, 33135. Tel: 305-649-5464; 305-649-5465; Fax: 305-541-0988.
Catechesis/Religious Program—Tel: 305-649-5466. Angela Esparraguera, D.R.E. Students 809.

16—St. John Neumann (1982), Rev. Msgr. Pablo Navarro; Revs. Albert Lahens; Jose N. Alfaro; Deacons Thomas Aguilu; Robert Binder; Ralph Gazitua; Charles Murphy.
Res.: 12125 S.W. 107th Ave., Miami, 33176. Tel: 305-255-6642; Fax: 305-233-3742.
School—Tel: 305-255-7315; 305-255-7316; Fax: 305-255-7316. Mrs. Maria M. Fernandez, Prin. Lay Teachers 28; Aides 5; Students 355.
Catechesis/Religious Program—Tel: 305-253-3081. Marian Blessing, D.R.E. Students 1,477.

17—St. Kevin (1963), Revs. Jesus Saldana; Jose Garcia; Ernest Biriruka (Burundi) (Ngozi); Deacon Robert B. Dinsmore.
Res.: 12525 S.W. 42 St., Miami, 33175. Tel: 305-223-0633; Fax: 305-554-9950.
School—4001 S.W. 127 Ave., Miami, 33175. Tel: 305-227-7571; Fax: 305-227-7574. Dr. Yolanda Minagorri, Prin.; Mrs. Maria C. Carreras, Asst. Prin. Lay Teachers 55; Students 645.
Catechesis/Religious Program—Tel: 305-223-2469. Mrs. Maggie Enjamio, D.R.E. Students 975.

18—St. Kieran (1967), Revs. John Masiello, S.D.B.; Albino Simonetti, S.D.B.; Antonio Altarejos, S.D.B. (Spain). In Res., Revs. Emil Fardelone, S.D.B.; Bruce Craig, S.D.B.
Res.: 3605 S. Miami Ave., Miami, 33133. Tel: 305-854-1521; Fax: 305-854-5986.
Catechesis/Religious Program—Tel: 786-357-4685. Students 130.

19—St. Louis (1963), Revs. James F. Fetscher; Michael A. Kish; Wallace A. McGowan; Jaime Acevedo; Deacons John Green; Thomas Hanlon; Alex Lam; Vincent McInerney; John Peremenis; Jeffrey J. Reyes; James R. Tomonto; Robert Yglesias.
Res.: 7270 S.W. 120th St., Pinecrest, 33156. Tel: 305-238-7562; Fax: 305-238-6844.
School—Fax: 305-238-4286. Christine Mathisen, Prin. Lay Teachers 23; Students 303.
Catechesis/Religious Program—Tel: 305-238-7461. Peggy Santella, D.R.E. Students 950.

20—St. Michael the Archangel (1947), Revs. Jose M. Paz; Eduardo Pastor; Ronald Noguera (Retired); Deacon Ernesto Rodriguez.
Res.: 2987 W. Flagler St., Miami, 33135. Tel: 305-649-1811; Fax: 305-642-6815.
School—300 N.W. 28 Ave., Miami, 33125. Tel: 305-642 6732; Fax: 305-649-5867. Sr. Alicia Velazquez, R.A., Prin. Sisters 7; Lay Teachers 33; Students 400.
Catechesis/Religious Program—Tel: 305-643-4661; Fax: 305-642-8574. George Briz, D.R.E. Students 630.

21—Mother of Christ (1983), Revs. Raul Angulo; Joaquin Perez-Pupo (Cuba); Deacons Jose Leroy Martinez; Manuel Saavedra; Lazaro Ulloa.
Rectory—2390 S.W. 139th Pl., Miami, 33175. Tel: 305-551-7046 (Office).
Church: 14141 S.W. 26th St., Miami, 33175. Tel: 305-559-3111; Fax: 305-551-7047.
School—(Grades PreK-4) Tel: 305-559-6047.
Catechesis/Religious Program—Tel: 305-559-0163. Students 929.

22—Mother of Our Redeemer (1988), Rev. Fernando Compaired (Spain); Deacon Jose Manuel Gordillo.
Res.: 18928 N.W. 80th Ct., Miami, 33015.
Church: 8445 N.W. 186 St., Miami, 33015. Tel: 305-829-3141; Fax: 305-829-3059.
Catechesis/Religious Program—Tel: 305-829-3988; Fax: 305 829-3019. Students 778.

23—Notre Dame d'Haiti (1981), Rev. Msgr. Gerard Darbouze; Rev. Reginald Jean-Mary.
Res.: 110 N.E. 62nd St., Miami, 33138. Tel: 305-751-6289; Fax: 305-756-6470.
Catechesis/Religious Program—Tel: 305-758-5560; Fax: 305-395-1851. Sr. Yamile Saieh, D.R.E. Students 400.

24—Our Lady of Divine Providence (1973), Revs. Luis Rivera; Fermin Solana (Cuba); Deacon Eduardo Panellas.
Church & Mailing Address: 10205 W. Flagler St., Miami, 33174. Tel: 305-551-8113; 305-551-8114; Fax: 305-220-3164.
Res.: 10420 S.W. 4th St., Miami, 33174. Tel: 305-226-5058.
Catechesis/Religious Program—Tel: 305-551-8113, Ext. 18. Students 116.

25—Our Lady of Guadalupe (2001), Rev. Msgr. Tomas M. Marin.
Mailing Address: 3900 N.W. 79th Ave., Ste. 731, Miami, 33166. Tel: 305-593-6123; Fax: 305-593-6130.
Catechesis/Religious Program—Students 280.

26—Our Lady of Lourdes (1985), Rev. Fernando Isern. In Res., Rev. Michael Davis.
Res.: 10452 S.W. 134 Pl., Miami, 33186. Tel: 305-380-7673.
Church: 11291 S.W. 142 Ave., Miami, 33186. Tel: 305-386-4121; Fax: 305-386-6881.
School—Tel: 305-386-8446; Fax: 305-386-6694. Dr. Maria Arellar-Fleming, Prin.; Marilyn Bimonte, Asst. Prin. Lay Teachers 43; Students 565.
Catechesis/Religious Program—Tel: 305-386-4894; Fax: 305-386-6670. Mrs. Bobbi Loeos, D.R.E. Students 1,205.

27—Our Lady of the Holy Rosary (1959), Revs. Luis A. Perez; Edmund Ogbonna (Nigeria) (FAR); Deacons Steve W. Apodaca; William H. Barrenberg.
Res.: 9500 S.W. 184th St., Miami, 33157. Tel: 305-235-5135; Fax: 305-254-9045.
School—Tel: 305-235-5442; Fax: 305-235-5670. Bernadette Kraich, Prin. Lay Teachers 26; Students 474.
Catechesis/Religious Program—Tel: 305-235-5135, Ext. 110. Students 330.

28—SS. Peter and Paul (1938), Revs. Juan M. Lopez; Juan Luis Sanchez.
Res.: 900 S.W. 26th Rd., Miami, 33129. Tel: 305-858-2621; Fax: 305-858-8073.
School—Tel: 305-858-3722; Fax: 305-856-4322. Lay Teachers 38; Students 625.
Catechesis/Religious Program—Students 365.

29—Prince of Peace (1987), Rev. Francisco G. Diaz; Deacon Francisco Estrada. In Res., Rev. Pedro Corces.
Church & Res.: 12800 N.W. 6th St., Miami, 33182. Tel: 305-559-3171; Fax: 305-559-3172.
Catechesis/Religious Program—Maggie Pernas, D.R.E. Students 695.

30—St. Raymond (1969), Rev. Msgr. Armando Balado; Rev. Sergio Cabrera.
Res.: 3475 S.W. 17 St., Miami, 33145. Tel: 305-446-2427; Fax: 305-445-0472.
Catechesis/Religious Program—Tel: 305-446-5108. Students 83.

31—St. Richard (1969), Rev. Stephen J. Hilley. In Res., Rev. Sylvester D'Cruz (India); Deacon Robert F. O'Malley Jr.
Res.: 7500 S.W. 152 St., Miami, 33157. Tel: 305-233-8711; Fax: 305-254-2756.
Catechesis/Religious Program—Tel: 305-233-8755. Students 550.

32—St. Robert Bellarmine (1968), Rev. Omar A. Huesca.
Res.: 3405 N.W. 27th Ave., Miami, 33142. Tel: 305-633-6009; Fax: 305-638-9480.
Catechesis/Religious Program—Flor Maria Matamoros, D.R.E. Students 177.

33—St. Thomas the Apostle (1959), Revs. Daniel I. Kubala; Anibal Morales; Philip Fabiano, O.F.M.Cap.; Alvaro Huertas (Colombia); Deacon Angel L. Cuesta.
Res.: 7377 S.W. 64 St., Miami, 33143. Tel: 305-665-5600; Fax: 305-662-9034.
School—Tel: 305-661-8591; Fax: 305-661-2181. Nuria Baldor, Prin. Lay Teachers 71; Students 746.
Catechesis/Religious Program—Tel: 305-665-6862. Students 298.

34—St. Timothy (1960), Revs. Rolando Castillo; Isidro Perez (Cuba); Jose Somoza, O.F.M.; Deacons Fernando Bestard; Manuel Buigas; Manuel Canovaca; Henri Gonzalez; Benito Loyola; Roberto Ochoa. In Res., Rev. Armando Alonso.
Office—5400 S.W. 102 Ave., Miami, 33165. Tel: 305-274-8224; Fax: 305-598-1159.
School—Tel: 305-274-8229; Fax: 305-598-7107. Mrs. Jo-Ann Leskanic, Prin. Lay Teachers 41; Students 657.
School—Sister Carolyn Learning Center, Tel: 305-598-3184; Fax: 305-412-6650. Eugenia Bulnes, D.R.E. (PreK & 2-3) Lay Teachers 8; Students 80.
Catechesis/Religious Program—Tel: 305-274-8225. Sr. Mary Carolyn Meehan, O.P., D.R.E. Students 665.

35—St. Vincent De Paul (1962), Rev. Hector Gonzalez-Abreu. In Res., Rev. Marc Presume, C.S.C. (Haiti).
Res.: 2000 N.W. 103rd St., Miami, 33147. Tel: 305-691-0771; 305-693-0529; Fax: 305-691-3352.
Catechesis/Religious Program—Tel: 305-266-6485. Students 95.

36—Visitation (1956), Rev. Christopher Marino.
Res.: 19100 N. Miami Ave., Miami, 33169. Tel: 305-652-3624; Fax: 305-652-5207.
Catechesis/Religious Program—100 N.E. 191 St., Miami, 33169. Tel: 305-651-7044. Students 140.

METROPOLITAN DADE COUNTY

Coconut Grove, St. Hugh (1959), Revs. George Garcia; Jose I. Bardino (Cuba).
Res.: 3460 Royal Rd., 33133. Tel: 305-444-8363; Fax: 305-444-4312.
School—Tel: 305-448-5602; Fax: 305-444-4299. Sr. Kathleen Donnelly, O.P., Prin. Sisters 2; Lay Teachers 22; Students 296.
Catechesis/Religious Program—Students 137.

Coral Gables

1—St. Augustine (1969), Very Rev. Bernard G. Kirlin, V.F.; Rev. Miguel A. Sepulveda; Deacon Victor M. Pimentel.
Res.: 1400 Miller Rd., 33146. Tel: 305-661-1648; Fax: 305-661-6392.
Catechesis/Religious Program—Students 281.

2—Little Flower (1926), Revs. Arthur Dennison; Alfredo Rolon Ortiz; Juan Carlos Paguaga; Deacon Miguel Parlade. In Res., Rev. Sean O'Sullivan.
Office—2711 Indian Mound Tr., 33134. Tel: 305-446-9950; Fax: 305-446-7624.
Res.: 1270 Anastasia Ave., 33134. Tel: 305-529-5475.
School—2701 Indian Mound Tr., 33134. Tel: 305-446-1738; Fax: 305-446-2877. Sisters 3; Lay Teachers 58; Students 973.
Catechesis/Religious Program—Tel: 305-446-5540. Students 420.

Hialeah

1—St. Benedict (1973), Rev. Jose L. Paniagua (Spain).
Res.: 650 W. 80th St., 33014. Tel: 305-556-3278; Fax: 305-558-3705.
Church: 701 W. 77th St., 33014. Tel: 305-558-2150.
Catechesis/Religious Program—Tel: 305-557-2511. Maria de la Fe, D.R.E. Students 470.

2—St. Cecilia (1971), Rev. Msgr. Emiliano Ordax; Rev. Luis Garcia; Deacon Jesus Tosco.
Res.: 1040 W. 29th St., 33012. Tel: 305-885-4614; 305-885-4615; Fax: 305-885-2327.
Catechesis/Religious Program—Tel: 305-885-5504. Students 380.

3—Immaculate Conception (1954), Revs. Gustavo J. Miyares; Jorge Noda. In Res., Rev. Michael Carruthers; Deacons Abelardo DeGuzman; Manuel Alfonso.
Res.: 4497 W. First Ave., 33012. Tel: 305-822-2011; Fax: 305-821-3481.
School—Tel: 305-822-6461; Fax: 305-822-0289. Mr. Eddy Garcia, Prin. Lay Teachers 47; Students 1,008.
Catechesis/Religious Program—Tel: 305-823-9563; Fax: 305-822-7868. Nubia Stanley, D.R.E. Students 795.

4—St. John the Apostle (1945), Revs. Emilio Martin; Jose Lopez; George Christopher Healy. In Res., Revs. George Cardona (Retired); Ignacio

Morras (Retired); Sergio Carrillo (Retired); Deacon Julke Llorens.
Res.: 475 E. 4th St., 33010. Tel: 305-888-9769; Fax: 305-888-9341.
School—Tel: 305-888-6819; Fax: 305-887-1256. Ms. Elizabeth Furmanick, Prin. Lay Teachers 26; Students 441.
Catechesis/Religious Program—Students 608.

5—San Lazaro (1982), Very Rev. Pedro Luis Perez, V.F.; Revs. Carlos Perez (Cuba); Jorge Bez-Chabebe (Cuba).
Res.: 4400 W. 18th Ave., 33012. Tel: 305-556-1717; Fax: 305-556-8918.
Catechesis/Religious Program—Tel: 305-558-4078. Sr. Gloria Plasencia, D.R.E. Students 580.

Hialeah Gardens, Santa Barbara (1987), Revs. Miguel Gomez; Rolando Medina; Deacon Pablo A. Fernandez.
Mailing Address: 6801 W. 30 Ave., 33018. Tel: 305-556-4442; Fax: 305-558-7256. In Res., Rev. Fabio Arango (Colombia).
Res.: 3004 W. 68 Pl., 33018. Tel: 305-827-1110.
Catechesis/Religious Program—Tel: 305-556-4442, Ext. 106. Students 530.

Homestead, Sacred Heart (1929), Revs. James McCreanor; Robes C. Charles.
Mailing Address: P.O. Box 901248, 33090-1248.
Church & Res.: 106 S.E. 1st Dr., 33030. Tel: 305-247-4405; Fax: 305-245-3002.
School—300 S.E. 1st Dr., 33030. Tel: 305-245-2678; Fax: 305-247-6317. Mary Preston, Prin. Lay Teachers 15; Students 212.
Catechesis/Religious Program—Tel: 305-247-0760. Students 395.

Key Biscayne, St. Agnes (1954), Revs. Jose L. Hernando; Manuel Francisco Alvarez; Deacon Miguel M. Gonzalez.
Res.: 100 Harbor Dr., 33149. Tel: 305-361-2351; 305-361-2451; Fax: 305-361-8514.
School—122 Harbor Dr., 33149. Tel: 305-361-3245; Fax: 305-361-6329. Mrs. Sheila Cruse, Prin. Lay Teachers 45; Students 394.
Catechesis/Religious Program—Tel: 305-361-1378. Nery Quintela, D.R.E. Students 442.

Leisure City, St. Martin de Porres Church (1990), Rev. Carlos Vega; Deacons Blas Gonzalez; Feliciano Sierra.
Mailing Address: 14881 S.W. 288 St., 33033. Tel: 305-248-5355; Fax: 305-245-3047.
Catechesis/Religious Program—Students 199.

Miami Beach

1—St. Francis de Sales (1964), Revs. Alvaro Guichard; Luis Efrain Mojica (Colombia); Deacon Jose Irizarry.
Res.: 621 Alton Rd., 33139. Tel: 305-672-0093; Fax: 305-673-8559.
Catechesis/Religious Program—Students 60.

2—St. Joseph (1942), Rev. Enrique J. Estrada. In Res, Rev. Noel I. Bennett (Retired).
Res.: 8670 Byron Ave., 33141. Tel: 305-866-6567; Fax: 305-864-1069.
School—Tel: 305-866-1471; Fax: 305-866-3175. Mrs. Jill Bishop, Prin. Lay Teachers 16; Students 220.
Catechesis/Religious Program—Fax: 305-864-1049. Students 270.

3—St. Patrick (1926), Rev. Msgr. John J. Vaughan; Rev. Manuel A. Soler. In Res., Rev. Msgr. Francis Dunleavy (Retired).
Office—3716 Garden Ave., 33140. Tel: 305-531-1124; Fax: 305-538-3203.
Res.: 3700 Meridian Ave., 33140.
School—Tel: 305-534-4616; Fax: 305-538-5463. Bertha Moro, Prin. Lay Teachers 20; Students 233.
Catechesis/Religious Program—Students 219.

Miami Lakes, Our Lady of the Lakes (1967), Revs. James Murphy; Carlos Miyares. In Res., Rev. Oscar Brantome; Deacons Orlando Aguayo; Roger Currier; Albert Mindel.
Res.: 15801 N.W. 67 Ave., 33014. Tel: 305-558-2202; Fax: 305-558-2631.
School—6600 Miami Lakeway N., 33014. Tel: 305-362-5315. Shelly Sweeney, Prin. Lay Teachers 36; Students 570.
Catechesis/Religious Program—Anita Brown, D.R.E.; Diane Leahy, D.R.E. Students 980.

Miami Shores

1—St. Martha (1970), Rev. Federico Capdepon. In Res., Rev. Carl T. Morrison.
Res.: 9221 Biscayne Blvd., 33138. Tel: 305-751-0005; Fax: 305-754-6930.
Catechesis/Religious Program—Tel: 305-751-8759. Students 163.

2—St. Rose of Lima (1946), Very Rev. Seamus Doyle, V.F.; Rev. Jorge Rodriguez.
Res.: 415 N.E. 105 St., 33138. Tel: 305-758-0539; Fax: 305-751-8398.
School—Tel: 305-751-4257; Fax: 305-751-5034. Sr. Nancy Kindelan, I.H.M., Prin. Sisters 5; Lay Teachers 39; Students 594.
Catechesis/Religious Program—Tel: 305-757-6434. Students 150.

Miami Springs, Blessed Trinity (1952), Revs. Joseph T. Carney; Joaquin Rodriguez; Andrew Chan-A-Sue; Deacon Dennis E. Jordan.
Res.: 4020 Curtiss Pkwy., 33166. Tel: 305-871-5780; Fax: 305-871-5781.
School—Tel: 305-871-5766. Mrs. Maria Teresa Perez, Prin. Lay Teachers 18; Students 277.
Catechesis/Religious Program—Tel: 305-876-1749. Students 225.

Naranja, St. Ann Mission (1960), Rev. Pedro Garcia.
Res.: 13875 S.W. 264 St., P.O. Box 322278, 33032-1505. Tel: 305-258-3968; 305-258-9682; Fax: 305-258-3591.
Catechesis/Religious Program—Tel: 305-248-3735; Fax: 305-247-0755. Students 690.

North Miami, Holy Family (1950), Revs. Jordi S. Rivero; Ferry Brutus (Haiti); Mark Thomas Reeves.
Res.: 14500 N.E. 11 Ave., 33161. Tel: 305-947-5043; 305-947-1471; Fax: 305-949-5591.
School—Tel: 305-947-6535; Fax: 305-947-1826. Mrs. Lori St. Thomas, Prin. Lay Teachers 15; Students 261.
Catechesis/Religious Program—Tel: 305-947-7739; Fax: 305-947-1417. Students 355.

North Miami Beach, St. Lawrence (1956), Rev. William Elbert.
Res.: 2200 N.E. 191 St., 33180. Tel: 305-932-3560; Fax: 305-936-8050.
School—Tel: 305-932-4912; Fax: 305-932-7898. Mrs. Dian Hyatt, Prin. Lay Teachers 11; Students 180.
School—Child Care Center, Tel: 305-932-5366. Lay Teachers 10; Students 90.
Catechesis/Religious Program—Tel: 305-931-6650. Kelly Lee, D.R.E.; Joanne Lambert, D.R.E. Students 450.

Opa Locka

1—St. Monica (1959), Revs. Leo Dionne, O.M.I.; Marek Stroba, O.M.I.
Res.: 3490 N.W. 191 St., 33056. Tel: 305-621-9846; Fax: 305-621-5608.
School—Tel: 305-621-2356; Fax: 305-621-2356. Lay Teachers 21; Students 352.
Catechesis/Religious Program—Tel: 305-621-6093. Students 178.

2—Our Lady of Perpetual Help Church (1954), Rev. Marcos A. Somarriba.
Church & Res.: 13401 N.W. 28 Ave., 33054. Tel: 305-688-9663; 305-688-9664; Fax: 305-685-8031.
Catechesis/Religious Program—Tel: 305-685-5354. Students 319.

3—St. Philip (1953), Rev. John Madigan, O.M.I.
Res.: 15700 N.W. 20 Ave. Rd., 33054. Tel: 305-624-6641; Fax: 305-624-8119.
Catechesis/Religious Program—Students 72.

Sunny Isles Beach, St. Mary Magdalen (1955), Rev. Thomas G. Honold.
Res.: 17775 N. Bay Rd., 33160. Tel: 305-931-0600; Fax: 305-931-0601.
Catechesis/Religious Program—Students 103.

OUTSIDE METROPOLITAN DADE COUNTY

Big Pine Key, Monroe Co., St. Peter (1962), Rev. Thomas Mullane.
Res.: 31300 Overseas Hwy., P.O. Box 430657, 33043-0657. Tel: 305-872-2537; Fax: 305-872-0122.
Catechesis/Religious Program—Students 115.
Mission—Sugarloaf Firehouse Sugarloaf Shores, 33042.

Coconut Creek, Broward Co., St. Luke (1985), Rev. John Paszko.
Res.: 2370 Hammock Blvd., 33063. Tel: 954-977-0427; Fax: 954-978-1902.
Catechesis/Religious Program—Tel: 954-974-1863. Students 205.

Coral Springs, Broward Co.

1—St. Andrew (1969), Revs. George Puthusseril; Damian Flanagan; Cristobal De Paula; Matthew Thundathil (India); Deacons Mario Lopez; Denis Mieyal.
Res.: 9950 N.W. 29 St., 33065-6103. Tel: 954-752-3950; Fax: 954-752-3986.
School—Tel: 954-753-1280; Fax: 954-753-1933. Mrs. Sonia Rodriguez, Prin. Lay Teachers 33; Students 522.
Catechesis/Religious Program—Tel: 954-752-3988. Zoraida Perez, D.R.E. Students 6,455.

2—St. Elizabeth Ann Seton (1985), Rev. Edward M. Kelly; Deacon John Friel.
Res.: 1401 Coral Ridge Dr., 33071. Tel: 954-753-3330; Fax: 954-753-8442.
Catechesis/Religious Program—Tel: 954-345-7071. Students 1,279.

3—Our Lady of Health Catholic Church, , (St. Thomas Syro-Malabar Diocese of Chicago) Rev. John Melepuram (India).
Mailing Address: 201 N. University Dr., 33071. Tel: 954-726-2525; Fax: 954-726-0822.

Dania, Broward Co., Church of the Resurrection (1958), Revs. Anthony Tomasulo, O.S.A.; James G. Glennon, O.S.A. In Res., Rev. James Ryan, O.S.A.
Res.: 441 N.E. Second St., 33004. Tel: 954-923-2806; Fax: 954-923-1018.
Catechesis/Religious Program—Students 27.

Davie, Broward Co., St. David (1974), Revs. Gabriel O'Reilly; Patrick J. Naughton (Scranton); Deacon Donald Cronin.
Res.: 3900 S. University Dr., 33328. Tel: 954-475-8046; Fax: 954-370-0819.
School—Tel: 954-472-7086; Fax: 954-452-8243. Mrs. Mariann Kiar, Prin. Lay Teachers 43; Students 656.
Catechesis/Religious Program—Tel: 954-475-1521. Pam McMillan, D.R.E. Students 682.

Deerfield Beach, Broward Co.

1—St. Ambrose (1962), Revs. John Bryan Dalton; James Connaughton, Pastor Emeritus; Michael Lynch; John L. McCullen (TOL) (Retired).
Res.: P.O. Box 999, 33443. Tel: 954-427-2225; Fax: 954-421-1638.
School—Tel: 954-427-2226; Fax: 954-427-4293. Ms. Anita Gentile, Prin. Lay Teachers 20; Students 286.
Catechesis/Religious Program—Students 238.

2—Our Lady of Mercy (1974), Rev. James Parappally (India).
Parish Center and Office—5201 N. Military Tr., Pompano Beach, 33064. Tel: 954-421-3246; Fax: 954-421-1973.
Catechesis/Religious Program—Tel: 954-426-3197. Students 35.

Fort Lauderdale, Broward Co.

1—St. Anthony (1921), Revs. Timothy G. Hannon; Jeremiah Singleton.
Res.: 901 N.E. 2nd St., 33301. Tel: 954-463-4614; Fax: 954-527-5411.
School—820 N.E. Third St., 33301. Tel: 954-467-7747; Fax: 954-467-9908. Mrs. Suzanne Sandelier, Prin. Lay Teachers 25; Students 333.
Catechesis/Religious Program—Tel: 954-467-7749. Students 225.

2—Blessed Sacrament (1961), Rev. Michael P. Sullivan; Deacon Michael Leon.
Res.: 1701 E. Oakland Park Blvd., 33334. Tel: 954-564-1010; Fax: 954-566-0301.
Catechesis/Religious Program—Students 75.

3—St. Bonaventure (1985), Rev. Edmond Prendergast; Deacons Arthur DeNunzio; Joseph M. Pearce.
Res.: 1301 S.W. 136th Ave., Davie, 33325-4300. Tel: 954-424-9504; 954-424-9505; Fax: 954-424-9505.
Catechesis/Religious Program—Tel: 954-476-5204; Fax: 954-476-5203. Mariela Brink, D.R.E.; Susan McCrea, D.R.E. Students 1,820.

4—St. Clement (1954), Revs. Peter Lambert; Henry Mullin, C.S.Sp.; Samuel Muodiaju, C.S.Sp.
Res.: 2975 N. Andrews Ave., 33311. Tel: 954-563-1183; Fax: 954-564-6628.
School—Tel: 954-563-5608; Fax: 954-563-1355. Ms. Mary Ellen McKinney, Prin. Lay Teachers 15; Students 248.
Catechesis/Religious Program—Tel: 954-561-4641. Sr. Colette O'Rourke, D.R.E. Students 310.

5—Divine Mercy Mission (1980), Rev. Franky Jean, Admin.
1105 N.W. 6th Ave., 33311. Tel: 954-764-8519; Fax: 954-764-8583.
Catechesis/Religious Program—Students 60.

6—St. George (1964), Rev. Robert F. Tywoniak; Deacon Daniel C. Blaha.
Res.: 3640 N.W. 8th St., 33311. Tel: 954-583-5892; Fax: 954-583-0725.
Catechesis/Religious Program—Students 36.

7—St. Helen (1968), Rev. Msgr. William Dever; Revs. Joseph Kalariparampil; Isidore Baky; William Muniz; Anthony O'Brien. In Res., Rev. Msgr. John W. Delaney (Retired).
Res.: 3033 N.W. 33rd Ave., 33311. Tel: 954-731-7314; Fax: 954-739-9632.
School—Tel: 954-739-7094; Fax: 954-739-0797. Ms. Antonia Ruiberriz, Prin. Lay Teachers 20; Students 261.
Catechesis/Religious Program—Tel: 954-484-3036. Students 230.

8—St. Jerome (1960), Rev. Kenneth K. Schwanger. In Res., Rev. Francis X. McCarthy (Retired); Deacon Frank B. O'Gorman.
Res.: 2533 S.W. 9th Ave., 33315. Tel: 954-525-4133; Fax: 954-525-0964.
School—Tel: 954-524-1990; Fax: 954-524-7439. Sr. Vivian Gomez, R.F., Prin. Sisters of St. Philip Neri 4; Lay Teachers 19; Students 298.
Catechesis/Religious Program—2601 S.W. 9th Ave., 33315. Students 80.

9—St. John the Baptist (1969), Rev. Msgr. Vincent T. Kelly; Revs. James F. Daly, C.S.Sp.; Paul Frank, O.M.I.
Res.: 4595 Bayview Dr., 33308. Tel: 954-771-8950; Fax: 954-771-4178.
Catechesis/Religious Program—Students 206.

10—St. Mark (1985), Revs. Edmond F. Whyte; Octavio Guillermo Colominas; Thomas Mannix Stack; Deacons Vincent Farinato; John Lorenzo.
Res.: 5601 S. Flamingo Rd., Southwest Ranches, 33330. Tel: 954-434-3777; Fax: 954-434-3125.

School—Tel: 954-434-3887; Fax: 954-434-3595. Shirley Sandusky, Prin. Students 692.
Catechesis/Religious Program—Tel: 954-252-9899. Susan Mikluscak, D.R.E. Students 1,278.

11—ST. MAURICE (1970), Rev. Roger Holoubek; Deacon Norman Carroll.
Res.: 2851 Stirling Rd., Dania Beach, 33312. Tel: 954-961-7777; Fax: 954-961-4358.
Catechesis/Religious Program—Tel: 954-983-5267. Students 180.

12—OUR LADY QUEEN OF MARTYRS (1956), Revs. Michael Hoyer; Armando Perez; Roman J. Schaefer (NU) (Retired).
Res.: 2731 S.W. 11 Ct. (Haddy Hoyer Street), 33312. Tel: 954-583-8725; Fax: 954-583-9315.
School—Tel: 954-583-8112; Fax: 954-797-4984. Mrs. Althea Mossop, Prin. Lay Teachers 25; Students 350.
Catechesis/Religious Program—Tel: 954-583-3307. Students 239.

13—ST. PIUS X (1959), Revs. Patrick C. Slevin; Harry Ringenberger; Deacon George P. Sutcavage.
Res.: 2500 N.E. 33rd Ave., 33305. Tel: 954-564-1763; Fax: 954-568-2212.
Church: 2511 N. Ocean Blvd. (A1A), 33308.
Catechesis/Religious Program—Students 49.

14—ST. SEBASTIAN (1959), Rev. Msgr. Patrick McDonnell; Rev. William F. Mylchreest.
Res.: 2518 Barbara Dr., 33316. Tel: 954-524-9344; Fax: 954-524-9347.
Catechesis/Religious Program—Students 30.

HALLANDALE, BROWARD CO.

1—ST. CHARLES BORROMEO (1968), Rev. Sean Mulcahy.
Res.: 123 N.W. 6 Ave., 33009. Tel: 954-458-1914; Fax: 954-458-8770.
Catechesis/Religious Program—Students 30.

2—ST. MATTHEW (1959), Revs. James A. Quinn; James Nero, O.F.M.
Res.: 542 Blue Heron Dr., 33009. Tel: 954-458-1590; Fax: 954-458-0612.
Catechesis/Religious Program—Tel: 954-458-3600. Students 60.

HOLLYWOOD, BROWARD CO.

1—ST. BERNADETTE (1959), Revs. Brendan Dalton; Andrzej Pietraszko.
Res.: 7450 Stirling Rd., 33024. Tel: 954-432-5313; Fax: 954-432-5344.
School—Tel: 954-432-7022; Fax: 954-443-8030. Mrs. Mary Ellen Letvinchuk, Prin. Lay Teachers 25; Students 353.
Catechesis/Religious Program—Tel: 954-432-6300; Fax: 954-432-7089. Students 355.

2—LITTLE FLOWER (1924), Very Rev. Thomas O'Dwyer, V.F.; Revs. Patrick O'Shea; Jorge L. Bello; Deacons Walter Keough; William A. Watkins.
Res.: 1805 Pierce St., 33020. Tel: 954-922-3517; Fax: 954-922-6634.
School—Tel: 954-922-1217; Fax: 954-927-8962. Mrs. Maureen McNulty, Prin. Lay Teachers 18; Students 247.
Catechesis/Religious Program—Tel: 954-923-7634. Students 104.

3—NATIVITY (1960), Revs. Patrick J. Murnane; Michael Grady; Abraham Joseph Pallivathuckal (India); Victor Babin, S.S.C.
Res.: 5220 Johnson St., 33021. Tel: 954-987-3300; Fax: 954-987-3044.
School—Tel: 954-987-3300, Ext. 221. Mrs. Elena Ortiz, Prin.; Ms. Judy Skehan, Vice Prin. Lay Teachers 36; Students 857.
Catechesis/Religious Program—Tel: 954-987-3300, Ext. 214. Students 385.

4—OUR LADY APARECIDA MISSION (1996), Revs. Horecio Carlos Anklan, C.S. (NY); Tiziano Paolazzi, C.S. 1618 Polk St., 33020. Tel: 954-920-1070; Fax: 954-920-0776.
Catechesis/Religious Program—Students 322.

KEY LARGO, MONROE CO., ST. JUSTIN MARTYR (1973), Rev. Enrique Delgado.
Res.: 105500 Overseas Hwy., 33037. Tel: 305-451-1316; Fax: 305-451-4633.
School—St. Justin Marine Academy, Tel: 305-451-6415; Fax: 305-451-6416. Students 105.
Catechesis/Religious Program—Tel: 305-451-6406. Students 120.

KEY WEST, MONROE CO., ST. MARY, STAR OF THE SEA (1846), Revs. Francisco J. Hernandez; David Dueppen; Deacon Peter Batty.
Res.: 1010 Windsor Ln., 33040. Tel: 305-294-1018; Fax: 305-292-8096.
School—Tel: 305-294-1031; Fax: 305-294-2095. Sisters 2; Brothers 1; Deacons 1; Lay Teachers 17; Students 197.
Catechesis/Religious Program—Tel: 305-295-0306. Students 214.

LIGHTHOUSE POINT, BROWARD CO., ST. PAUL THE APOSTLE (1968), Rev. Frederick J. Brice.
Res.: 2700 N.E. 36th St., 33064. Tel: 954-943-9154; 954-943-9155; Fax: 954-943-1954.
Catechesis/Religious Program—Students 111.

MARATHON, MONROE CO., SAN PABLO (1958), Very Rev. Gerald R. Morris, V.F.
Res.: 550 122nd St. Ocean, 33050. Tel: 305-289-0636; Fax: 305-743-8192.
Catechesis/Religious Program—Students 60.

MARGATE, BROWARD CO., ST. VINCENT (1960), Revs. Neil Doherty; Joseph Maroor (India); Deacon Allen Asselin. In Res., Rev. Joseph Angelini (Retired).
Res.: 6350 N.W. 18th St., 33063. Tel: 954-972-0434; Fax: 954-971-9411.
Catechesis/Religious Program—Tel: 954-972-7708. Students 121.

MIRAMAR, BROWARD CO.

1—ST. BARTHOLOMEW (1962), Revs. Paul Vuturo; Yves Jocelyn (Haiti); Deacons Humberto Brizuela; Montas Onelien; Perry Vitale.
Res.: 8005 Miramar Pkwy., 33025. Tel: 954-431-3600; Fax: 954-435-9591.
School—Tel: 954-431-5253; Fax: 954-431-3385. Myriam Rodriguez, Prin. Lay Teachers 18; Students 322.
Catechesis/Religious Program—Students 470.

2—BLESSED JOHN XXIII CHURCH, Rev. Joseph Kottayil; Deacon Louis Phang Sang.
Res.: P.O. Box 278528, 33027. Tel: 954-874-1641; Fax: 954-874-1642.
Catechesis/Religious Program—Students 200.

3—ST. STEPHEN (1956), Revs. Stephen Conserva, O.M.I.; James Allen, O.M.I.; Paul M. Ouellette, O.M.I.; Deacon Jose Solorzano.
Res.: 6044 S.W. 19th St., 33023. Tel: 954-987-1100; Fax: 954-966-9881.
School—Tel: 954-983-2636; Fax: 954-986-8557. Sisters of St. Joseph of St. Augustine 1; Lay Teachers 17; Students 239.
Catechesis/Religious Program—Tel: 954-962-2112; 954-962-3801. Students 628.

NORTH LAUDERDALE, BROWARD CO., OUR LADY QUEEN OF HEAVEN (1974), Rev. Julio R. Solano; Deacon Joseph G. Soucy.
Res. & Church: 1400 S. State Rd. 7, 33068. Tel: 954-971-5400; Fax: 954-972-4008.
Catechesis/Religious Program—Tel: 954-973-3406. Students 385.

PARKLAND, BROWARD CO., MARY HELP OF CHRISTIANS CHURCH (1989), Rev. Thomas Wisniewski; Deacons Vincent Eberling Jr.; William H. Cresswell.
Church: 5980 University Dr., 33067. Tel: 954-323-8012; Fax: 954-323-8011.
Catechesis/Religious Program—Tel: 954-340-2872; 954-323-8027. Students 915.

PEMBROKE PINES, BROWARD CO.

1—ST. BONIFACE (1971), Rev. Antonio R. Silio. In Res., Rev. Kris Bartos.
Res.: 8330 Johnson St., 33024. Tel: 954-432-2750; Fax: 954-432-2756.
Catechesis/Religious Program—Tel: 954-437-3215. Students 340.

2—ST. EDWARD (1995), Rev. Msgr. Michael Eivers; Rev. Oscar Sarmiento; Deacon Arnold J. DeLuca.
Res. & Church Address: 19000 Pines Blvd., 33029. Tel: 954-436-7944; Fax: 954-436-7506.
Catechesis/Religious Program—Tel: 954-430-4107. Students 1,600.

3—ST. MAXIMILIAN KOLBE (1983), Revs. Jeffrey McCormick; Edel Lozano, O.C.D. (Cuba); Deacons Edward J. Breitfelder; Carl Carieri; John Chinelly Sr.; Victor Lopez; David Smith.
Res.: 11051 N.W. 16th St., 33026. Tel: 954-432-8289. Church: 701 N. Hiatus Rd., 33026. Tel: 954-432-0206; Fax: 954-432-0775.
Catechesis/Religious Program—Tel: 954-435-3000. Students 823.

PLANTATION, BROWARD CO., ST. GREGORY (1959), Rev. Msgr. Noel Fogarty, P.A.; Rev. John C. Baker (PRO).
Res.: 200 N. University Dr., 33324. Tel: 954-473-6261; Fax: 954-473-4599.
School—Tel: 954-473-8169; Fax: 954-472-1638. Ms. Barbara Rosini, Prin.; Ms. Brenda Cummings, Asst. Prin. Sisters 1; Lay Teachers 52; Students 864.
Catechesis/Religious Program—Tel: 954-473-8321. Students 411.

POMPANO BEACH, BROWARD CO.

1—ASSUMPTION (1951), Revs. Martin J. Cassidy; John Handrahan, S.J.
Res.: 2001 S. Ocean Blvd., Lauderdale-by-the-Sea, 33062. Tel: 954-941-7647; Fax: 954-941-9620.
Catechesis/Religious Program—

2—ST. COLEMAN (1959), Revs. Thomas F. Foudy; Pedro Leo; James E. Quinn (Retired).
Res.: 1200 S. Federal Hwy., 33062. Tel: 954-942-3533; Fax: 954-942-7869.
School—Tel: 954-942-3500; Fax: 954-785-0603. Lay Teachers 37; Aides 6; Students 589.
Catechesis/Religious Program—1285 S.E. 22nd Ave., 33062. Tel: 954-782-1461. Students 350.

3—ST. ELIZABETH OF HUNGARY CATHOLIC CHURCH (1959), Revs. Gabriel Vigues; Paul Kane; Deacons Willie Harris Sr.; Daniel Moretti.
Res.: 3331 N.E. 10 Ter., 33064-5298. Tel: 954-941-8117; Fax: 954-941-0999.
School—901 N.E. 33rd. St., 33064. Tel: 954-942-2161; Fax: 954-942-7551. Mrs. Rita A. O'Leary, Prin. Sisters 1; Lay Teachers 27; Students 456.
Catechesis/Religious Program—Tel: 954-943-6801. Students 317.

4—ST. GABRIEL (1967), Rev. Sean Hyland.
Res.: 731 N. Ocean Blvd., 33062. Tel: 954-943-3684; Fax: 954-943-3656.
Catechesis/Religious Program—

5—ST. HENRY (1969), Rev. Msgrs. James B. Reynolds; Arthur T. Geoghegan (Retired); Rev. Francis Akwue, C.S.Sp.
Res.: 1500 S. Andrews Ave., 33069. Tel: 954-785-2450; Fax: 954-785-6958.
Catechesis/Religious Program—Students 75.

6—ST. JOSEPH MISSION (1981), Rev. M. Kidney St. Jean.
1210 N.W. 6th Ave., 33060. Tel: 954-941-3095; Fax: 954-941-3115.
Catechesis/Religious Program—Students 98.

7—OUR LADY OF CZESTOCHOWA MISSION (1997), (Polish), Rev. Czeslaw Rybacki, S.Ch. (SFR).
2400 N.E. 12th St., 33062. Tel: 954-946-6347; Fax: 954-946-0512.
Catechesis/Religious Program—Students 82.

8—SAN ISIDRO (1970), Revs. Ricardo C. Castellanos; Alberto Cutie; Roberto Garza; Maximo Leoz, Sch.P.; Gustavo Gutierrez (Colombia).
Res.: 2310 Martin Luther King Blvd., 33069-1591. Tel: 954-971-8780; 954-940-8719 (Dade); Fax: 954-972-3607.
Catechesis/Religious Program—Students 400.

SUNRISE, BROWARD CO.

1—ALL SAINTS (1982), Rev. Anthony J. Mulderry; Deacons David Bloom; Richard Bouker; Angelo Gervasi; Randall O. Musselman; Vincent Tola.
Office—10900 W. Oakland Park Blvd., 33351. Tel: 954-742-2666; Fax: 954-741-7238.
School—Tel: 954-742-4842; Fax: 954-742-4870. Mrs. Antoinette McNamara, Prin. Students 300.
Catechesis/Religious Program—Tel: 954-742-7742. Students 910.

2—ST. BERNARD (1971), Rev. Michael Hourigan.
Res.: 8279 Sunset Strip, 33322. Tel: 954-741-7800; Fax: 954-742-4558.
Catechesis/Religious Program—Tel: 954-741-0275. Students 149.

TAMARAC, BROWARD CO., ST. MALACHY (1973), Revs. Dominick O'Dwyer; Daniel Cernauskas (Bahamas); Deacons Nicholas Costea; Joseph Sommovigo.
Res.: 6200 John Horan Terr., 33321. Tel: 954-726-1237; Fax: 954-726-0822.
Catechesis/Religious Program—Tel: 954-721-5337. Concetta Sobkowski, D.R.E. Students 190.

TAVERNIER, MONROE CO., SAN PEDRO (1954), Rev. John P. Peloso.
Res.: 89500 Overseas Hwy., Plantation, 33388. Tel: 305-852-5372; Fax: 305-852-3315.
Catechesis/Religious Program—Students 100.

WEST HOLLYWOOD, BROWARD CO., ANNUNCIATION (1959), Rev. Michael Quilligan; Deacon Mitchell C. Abdallah.
Res.: 3781 S.W. 39th St., 33023. Tel: 954-989-0606; Fax: 954-989-0660.
School—Tel: 954-989-8287. Sr. Josephine Sherry, R.S.M., Prin. Sisters 2; Lay Teachers 18; Students 323.
Catechesis/Religious Program—Students 70.

WESTON, BROWARD CO., ST. KATHARINE DREXEL (2001), Rev. Paul Edwards; Deacons Paul Brancheau; Luis Gonzalez.
Mailing Address: P.O. Box 268477, 33326. Tel: 954-389-5003; Fax: 954-389-1228.
Office: 2700 Glades Cir., #200, 33327.
Catechesis/Religious Program—Tel: 954-389-1219. Students 500.

Special Assignment:
Rev. Msgrs.—
Anderson, Andrew L., J.C.D., Judicial Vicar
Souckar, Michael A., J.C.D. (Cand.), Chancellor
Revs.—
Acevedo, Anthony
Adu, Martin K., Jackson Memorial Hospital
Clements, Charles, Health Care Coordinator, South Dade
Fink, John, Broward General Hospital
Fishwick, Joseph, Baptist Hospital & South Miami Hospital, Miami
O'Neill, Patrick H., Coord. Special Projects, Ministry of General Services
Smith, David, Jackson Memorial Hospital

On Duty Outside the Archdiocese:
Revs.—
Barajas, Abel, Mexico
Espino, Jose, Guantanamo,Cuba
O'Hala, Stephen, Boynton Beach (St. Vincent de

Paul Seminary) (West Palm Beach)
O'Leary, John, Peru
Quijano, Jose Juan, S.T.L.
Scheiding, Philip, Mexico

Military Chaplains:
Rev.—
Gubbins, John

Higher Studies:
Revs.—
Alonso, Armando, Miami, FL
Carruthers, Michael, Miami, FL
Cioffi, Alfred, Layfayette, IN
Quijano, Jose Juan, S.T.L., Rome, Italy

Absent on Sick Leave:
Revs.—
Brantome, Oscar
Montoya, Juan
Puerta, Jorge
Reiser, John

Absent on Leave:
Revs.—
Christman, Robert
Cinesi, Joseph
Fenger, Guy
Grogan, Brendan
Keener, Michael
Kiddy, Curtis
Kudlo, Frank
Malicki, Jan
Piano, Timothy
Powers, Charles

Retired:
Most Revs.—
McCarthy, Edward A., D.D., S.T.D., J.C.D.
Fernandez, Gilberto, D.D.
Roman, Agustin A., D.D., V.G.
Rev. Msgrs.—
Fazzalaro, Francis J.
Glorie, John W.
Morras, Xavier
Revs.—
Angelini, Joseph
Bennett, Noel I.
Blasco, Ignacio
Boned, Enrique
Brohammer, Ronald
Cahill, Frank
Carbajales, Ignacio
Cardona, George
Carrillo, Sergio
Casabon, Luis
Connaughton, James
Conway, Laurence
Coucelo, Andres
Duffy, George
Dunleavy, Francis J.
Engbers, Thomas
Escala, Rafael
Fernandez, Miguel A.
Fernandez, Nelson
Garcia-Miro, Sergio
Gunther, William
Hampton, James
Huck, Joseph
Hudak, Cyril
Ireland, Donald
Kent, Daniel
Lucking, Aloysius
Lyons, Francis
Lyons, Lawrence
Massi, Anthony
McGowan, Wallace
McGrath, Gerald
McGrath, John
McLaughlin, John
Melley, James J.
Mercieca, Anthony
Mitchell, Walter
Molano, Ernesto
Morras, Ignacio
Noguera, Ronald
O'Sullivan, Sean
Olszewski, Edward T.
Pedroso, Rafael
Planas, Salvador
Puisis, Leonard
Pusak, Ronald
Quinlan, Eugene
Quinn, James E.
Rivas, Romeo
Russell, David
Scherer, Richard
Shannon, Brendan
Smith, Trevor
Soulliere, Richard
Valoret, Joseph
Vann, John C.
Villegas, Hernando
Whittaker, Kenneth

Permanent Deacons:
Abdallah, Mitchell C.
Aguayo, Orlando
Aguilu, Thomas
Alfonso, Manuel
Alonso, Jose P.
Apodaca, Steve W.
Asselin, Allen
Avery, John, Outside the Archdiocese
Baez, Rodolfo
Batty, Peter
Benavides, Luis, (PT)
Beregszaszi, Miklos A.
Bestard, Fernando
Binder, Robert
Blaha, Daniel C.
Blanco, Eduardo
Bloom, David
Bouker, Richard
Brancheau, Paul
Breitfelder, Edward J.
Brizuela, Humberto
Buigas, Manuel
Calvo, Pedro P.
Camacho, Vidal, (NY)
Canovaca, Manuel
Carieri, Carl
Carrion, Jose
Carroll, Norman
Chavez, Diego
Chinelly, John, Sr.
Colastin, Max
Coniglio, Philip, Outside the Archdiocese
Costea, Nicholas
Crawford, Jr. Frederick, Outside the Archdiocese
Cresswell, William H.
Cronin, Donald
Cuesta, Angel L.
Currier, Roger
Dawson, Thomas
DeGuzman, Abelardo
DeLuca, Arnold J.
DeNunzio, Arthur
Diehl, William, Outside the Archdiocese
Dinsmore, Robert B.
Donates, Rafael
Draughon, Woodworth R., Jr., Outside the Archdiocese
Dugan, Richard, Outside the Archdiocese
Eberling, Vincent, Jr.
Estrada, Francisco
Fallon, Martin, (Retired)
Farinato, Vincent
Fathauer, Ronald, Outside the Archdiocese
Fernandez, Pablo A.
Fiore, Charles, Outside the Archdiocese
Franklin, Thomas
Friel, John
Fuentes, Rafael
Galard, John, Outside the Archdiocese
Galvez, Rene, (ARL)
Gazitua, Ralph
Gervasi, Angelo
Gibson, George
Gonzalez, Blas
Gonzalez, Henri
Gonzalez, Jorge G.
Gonzalez, Luis
Gonzalez, Miguel A.
Gordillo, Jose Manuel
Green, John F.
Hanlon, Thomas F.
Harris, Willie, Sr.
Hubbell, Carl, Outside the Archdiocese
Irizarry, Jose
Jordan, Dennis E.
Karrenberg, William H.
Keough, Walter
Knox, Terrence, Outside the Archdiocese
Lam, Alex S.
Lannon, Billy, Jr.
Leon, Michael
Livingstone, Donald
Llaneza, Oscar, (NEW)
Llorens, Julke
Lopez, Mario
Lopez, Pedro
Lopez, Victor
Lorenzo, John
Loyola, Benito
Maceo, Antonio J.
Martinez, Jose
McClain, Kirby, (Retired)
McInerney, Vincent
Mickwee, George, Outside the Archdiocese
Mieyal, Denis
Mindel, Albert
Moreno, Vicente
Moretti, Daniel
Morillo, Felix, (NY)
Munter, Paul H.
Murphy, Charles
Murray, Paul, Outside the Archdiocese
Musselman, Randall O.
Nerys, Jose A., (SJN)
O'Gorman, Frank B.
O'Malley, Robert F., Jr.
Onelien, Montas
Ortega, Ray
Padron, Rodolfo
Panellas, Eduardo
Parlade, Miguel
Pearce, Joseph M.
Peremenis, John
Perez, Manuel
Phang Sang, Louis
Pimentel, Victor M.
Pintado, Angel
Pita, Bernardo
Plummer, Joseph, Outside the Archdiocese
Plummer, Michael
Polcari, Joseph A., Outside the Archdiocese
Prieto, Jorge
Raymond, Donald, Outside the Archdiocese
Reyes, Jeffrey J.
Reyes, Rafael de los
Rodriguez, Ernesto
Rodriguez, Jorge, On Duty Outside the Archdiocese
Rodriguez, Santos
Romero, Alberto, (NEW)
Rosado, Jose, (NEW)
Ruiz-Castaneda, Norman
Saavedra, Manuel
Smith, David
Solorzano, Jose
Sommovigo, Joseph
Soucy, Joseph O.
Starzinski, Louis
Sutcavage, George P.
Taylor, Ian
Taylor, Timm, Outside the Archdiocese
Teolis, Matthew
Thesing, John
Tola, Vincent
Tomonto, James R.
Tosco, Jesus
Ulloa, Lazaro
Venezia, Richard
Vitale, Perry
Waldman, Gerald, Outside the Archdiocese
Watkins, William A.
Yglesias, Robert
Zayas, Julio
Zayas, Luis, On Duty Outside the Archdiocese

INSTITUTIONS LOCATED IN THE ARCHDIOCESE

[A] SEMINARIES, ARCHDIOCESAN

MIAMI. *St. John Vianney College Seminary*, 2900 S.W. 87th Ave., 33165. Tel: 305-223-4561; 305-223-4562; Fax: 305-223-0650. Email: noonan@sjvcs.edu. Web: www.sjvcs.edu. Rev. Msgr. John Noonan, Rector; Bro. Edward Van Merrienboer, O.P., Academic Dean; Maria Rodriguez, Librarian; Revs. Kenneth Malley, S.P., Vice Rector, Dean of Students; Robert Vallee; Lesly Jean. Priests 5; Brothers 1; Lay Teachers 5; Total Staff 20; Students 52. In Res. Rev. Liam Quinn.

[B] COLLEGES AND UNIVERSITIES

MIAMI. *Barry University* President's Office , 11300 N.E. 2nd Ave., 33161. Tel: 305-899-3010; Fax: 305-899-3018. Email: jolaughlin@mail.barry.edu. Web: www.barry.edu. Sisters Jeanne O'Laughlin, O.P., Ph.D., Pres.; Peggy Albert, O.P., Ph.D., Exec. Vice Pres.; Dr. J. Patrick Lee, Ph.D., Provost & Senior Vice Pres. Academic Affairs; Sr. Arlene Scott, O.P., Asst. Vice Pres. for Mission & Ministry; Ms. Debra Weyman, Registrar; Mr. Timothy H. Czerniec, Senior Vice Pres. Business & Finance; Dr. Michael Griffin, Ph.D., Vice Pres. Student Svcs.; Dr. Carol-Rae Sodano, Dean School of Adult & Continuing Education; Dr. Eileen McDonough, Assoc. Vice Pres. Student Svcs.; Maria Luisa Alvarez, Assoc. Vice Pres. for Student Svcs.; Revs. Mark Wedig, O.P.; Daniel P. Madden, O.P.; Pedro A. Suarez, S.J.; John F. O'Grady, S.S.D., S.T.D. (ALB); Scott O'Brien, O.P.; Victor LaRoche, O.P.; David Caron, O.P.; Sisters Evelyn Piche, O.P., Ph.D., Dean of School of Education; John Karen Frei, O.P., Ph.D., Assoc. Vice Pres. Research &

Dean School of Natural & Health Science; Chester A. Evans, D.P.M., Assoc. Vice Pres. & Dean, School of Podiatric Medicine; Jack Scarborough, Ph.D., Dean School of Business; Linda Peterson, Ph.D., Interim Dean School of Arts & Sciences; Estrella Iglesias, Dir., Library; Pegge Bell, Ph.D., Dean School of Nursing; Stephen M. Holloway, Ph.D., Assoc. Vice Pres. Graduate Studies & Dean School of Social Work; William Fenton, Vice Pres., Institutional Advancement & Chm. Capital Campaign; Sr. Sarah Cavanaugh, O.P., M.S., Assoc. Vice Pres. Institutional Advancement; G. Jean Cerra, Ph.D., Dean School of Human Performance; Sr. Candace Introcaso, C.D.P., Vice Pres. for Planning & Assessment. Sisters of St. Dominic (Adrian, MI) Priests 6; Sisters 32; Lay Teachers 324; Students 8,469.

OPA LOCKA. *St. Thomas University* (Coed) , 16400 N.W. 32nd Ave., 33054. Tel: 305-625-6000; Fax: 305-628-6511. Email: signup@stu.edu. Web: www.stu.edu. Clergy and Religious Full-time Faculty: Priests 4; Lay Teachers 242; Students 3,551.

Board of Trustees: Rev. Msgr. William J. Hennessey, V.G.; Bro. Richard J. DeMaria; Pamela Adams; Elio Boccitto; Carl Buccellato; Jorge De Cespedes; Bob Dickinson; Thomas J. Flood; Arthur J. Furia Esq.; Diane Saulney Gaines Esq.; Robert C. Hudson; Cyrus M. Jollivette; Raul P. Masvidal; James McDonald Esq.; Robert J. McKee Esq.; Uriel Mendieta; Dr. Emmanuel Nwadike; Alicio Pina; Carlos Planas; Dr. P. Alan Smurfit, Trustee Emeritus; Gregory T. Swienton; Stanley G. Tate.

The Member: Most Rev. John Clement Favalora.

Of Counsel: Mr. J. Patrick Fitzgerald, Esq.

Administration: Rev. Msgr. Franklyn M. Casale, Pres.; Rev. Edward A. Blackwell, Dir. of Campus Ministry; Beverly Bachrach, Vice Pres. Univ. Advancement; Mr. Norman Blair, Vice Pres. for Admin. & Treas.; Robert Butterworth, Dean of the School of Law; Gregory Chan, Vice Pres. for Academic Affairs; Dr. Fred Holman, Dean of Adult & Continuing Education; Dr. Joseph Iannone, Dean of the School of Graduate Studies; Dr. Sarah Shumate, Vice Pres. Student Affairs.

Clergy and Religious Full-Time Faculty: Revs. Warren R. Hall (NEW); Daniel Kent (Retired); James L. MacDougall, O.S.A.; Jorge Sardinas.

[C] HIGH SCHOOLS, ARCHDIOCESAN

MIAMI. *Archbishop Coleman Carroll High School*, 10300 S.W. 167 Ave., 33196. Tel: 305-388-6700; Fax: 305-388-4371. Email: colemancarroll@colemancarroll.org. Web: www.colemancarroll.org. Rev. Michael Davis, Supervising Prin.; Richard Fenchak, Prin. Lay Teachers 29; Total Staff 52; Students 668.

Archbishop Curley-Notre Dame High School, 4949 N.E. 2nd Ave., 33137-3199. Tel: 305-751-8367; Fax: 305-751-3517. Email: acavet@acnd.net. Web: www.acnd.net. Bro. Anthony K. Cavet, C.F.C., Prin.; Ms. Beatriz Rodriguez, Asst. Prin. Emerita; Mr. Michael Gates, Asst. Prin. Brothers 5; Sisters 1; Lay Teachers 30; Students 469.

St. Brendan High School, 2950 S.W. 87 Ave., 33165. Tel: 305-223-5181; Fax: 305-220-7434. Email: sabres@stbhs.org. Web: www.stbhs.org. Bro. Felix A. Elardo, F.M.S., Prin.; Rev. Fernando Heria, J.C.L., Supervising Prin.; Dr. Carmen Castello, Asst. Prin.; Mrs. Isabel Lopez-Healy, Asst. Prin.; Ms. Barbara Behnke, Dean of Students. Brothers 4; Lay Teachers 68; Counselors 5; Students 1,175.

La Salle High School, 3601 S. Miami Ave., 33133. Tel: 305-854-2334; Fax: 305-858-5971. Email: principal@lasallehighschool.com. Web: www.lasallehighschool.com. Sr. Patricia Roche, F.M.A., Prin.; Mr. Erik Shane, Asst. Prin. for Student Affairs; Mrs. Luisa Serratore, Asst. Prin. for Curriculum; Ms. Ana Torres, Financial Admin.; Mr. Christopher Crotty, Athletic Dir.; Ms. Carmen Hoyos, Activities Dir. Priests 1; Sisters 3; Lay Teachers 43; Students 629.

Msgr. Edward Pace High School, 15600 Spartan Blvd., N.W. 32 Ave., 33054. Tel: 305-624-8534; Fax: 305-521-0185. Email: bami@msgrpace.com. Web: www.msgr-pace.com. Bro. Anthony M. Iazzetti, F.M.S., Prin.; Revs. Gustavo J. Miyares, Supervising Prin.; Cyril J. Smith, O.S.A., Academic Dean; Bro. Vincent Moriarty, F.M.S., Asst. Prin. for Academics; Mrs. Ana Garcia, Asst. Prin. Curriculum Instruction; Bro. Ken Ward, Dean of Students (Grades 9 & 12); Mr. Samuel Lilly, Dean of Students (Grades 10-11). Priests 2; Brothers 5; Lay Teachers 62; Students 1,219.

Our Lady of Lourdes Academy, 5525 S.W. 84th St., 33143. Tel: 305-667-1623; Fax: 305-663-3121. Email: principal@olla.org. Web: www.olla.org. Sr. M. Sheila Foy, I.H.M., Prin. Servants of the Immaculate Heart of Mary 4; Lay Teachers 56; Students 839.

FORT LAUDERDALE. *Archbishop Edward A. McCarthy High School*, 5451 S. Flamingo Rd., 33330. Tel: 954-434-8280; Fax: 954-680-4835. Email: maverick@mccarthyhigh.org. Web: www.mccarthyhigh.org. Rev. Edmond F. Whyte, Supervising Prin.; Dr. Richard Pechla, Prin. Priests 2; Lay Teachers 63; Students 1,200.

Cardinal Gibbons High School, 2900 N.E. 47th St., 33308. Tel: 954-491-2900; Fax: 954-772-1025. Email: cghs@cghsfl.org. Web: www.cghsfl.org. Sr. Marie Schramko, O.S.F., Asst. Prin.; Mr. Paul D. Ott, Prin.; Revs. Oscar Alonso, Sch.P.; Charles Newburn, Sch.P.; John Callan, Sch.P.; Bros. Grant R. Ferris, O.S.F.S.; Michael Brickmann, C.S.C. Priests 3; Brothers 2; Sisters of St. Francis 2; Lay Teachers 63; Students 1,203.

St. Thomas Aquinas High School, 2801 S.W. 12 St., 33312. Tel: 954-581-2127; 954-581-0700; Fax: 954-581-8263. Email: tjones@aquinas-sta.org. Web: www.aquinas-sta.org. Rev. Msgr. Vincent T. Kelly, Supervising Prin.; Mrs. Tina Jones, Prin.; Dr. Robert Mulder, Asst. Prin.; Denise Aloma, Asst. Prin.; Mr. Victor Penn, Dept. Chair, Theology; Sr. Peggy Manning, O.P., Campus Min.; Mr. Paul Gomulinski, Dean of Students. Priests 1; Sisters 3; Lay Teachers 109; Students 2,139.

[D] HIGH SCHOOLS, PRIVATE

MIAMI. *Belen Jesuit Preparatory School*, 500 S.W. 127 Ave., 33184. Tel: 305-223-8600; Fax: 305-227-2565. Email: webmaster@belenjesuit.org. Web: www.belenjesuit.org. Revs. Marcelino Garcia, S.J., Pres, Prin. & Contact; Jorge Sardina, S.J.; Juan Manuel Dorta, S.J.; Eduardo Alvarez, S.J.; Jorge Munguia, S.J.; Francisco Perez-Lerena, S.J.; Victor M. Hernandez, S.J., Supr.; Guillermo Garcia-Tunon, S.J.; Eduardo Barrios, S.J.; Pedro Cartaya, S.J.; Nelson Garcia, S.J. Our Lady of Belen Jesuit Foundation, Inc. Priests 11; Sisters 1; Lay Teachers 75; Students 1,145.

Carrollton School of the Sacred Heart, 3747 Main Hwy., 33133. Tel: 305-446-5673; Fax: 305-529-6533. Email: scooke@carrollton.org. Web: www.carrollton.org. Sr. Suzanne Cooke, R.S.C.J., Headmistress. Religious of the Sacred Heart 4; Lay Teachers 63; Students 670.

Christopher Columbus High School, 3000 S.W. 87 Ave., 33165. Tel: 305-223-5650; Fax: 305-559-4306. Email: www.columbushs.com. Web: www.columbushs.com. Christopher Columbus High School Endowment Trust Marist Brothers 14; Lay Teachers 68; Students 1,300.

Campus Ministers: Rev. Liam Quinn; Bros. Michael Brady, F.M.S., Admissions Dir.; Kevin Handibode, F.M.S., Pres.; Patrick McNamara, F.M.S., Prin.; Mrs. Patricia Call, Asst. Prin. (Academic Dean); Mr. Juan Gomez, Dean of Students; Mr. Christopher McKeon, Dean of Students; Edmund Sheehan, F.M.S., Librarian.

HOLLYWOOD. *Chaminade-Madonna College Preparatory*, 500 Chaminade Dr., 33021-5800. Tel: 954-989-5150; Fax: 954-983-4663. Email: info@chaminade-madonna.org. Web: www.chaminade-madonna.org. Rev. John F. Thompson, S.M., Pres.; M. Gloria Ramos, Prin. Marianist Priest 1; Marianist Brothers 6; Lay Teachers 56; Students 873.

[E] ELEMENTARY SCHOOLS, PRIVATE

KEY WEST. *Mary Immaculate Star of the Sea*, 700 Truman Ave., 33040. Tel: 305-294-1031; Fax: 305-294-2095. Email: seastar@key4ez.com. Web: www.maryimmaculate.cc. Brothers 1; Sisters 2; Lay Teachers 13; Students 186.

[F] SHELTERS

MIAMI. *Camillus House, Inc.*, P.O. Box 11829, 33101-1829. Email: savio@camillus.org. Web: www.camillus.org. Provides services to the homeless: emergency services, substance abuse rehabilitation, transitional housing

336 N.W. 5th St., 33128. Tel: 305-374-1065; Fax: 305-372-1402. Bro. Savio Charron, B.G.S., Pres., Contact

Camillus Health Concern, Inc., P.O. Box 12408, 33101-2408. Email: jdiaz@hcnetwork.org. Provides medical and social services to the homeless and indigent.

336 N.W. 5th St., 33128. Tel: 305-577-4840; Fax: 305-373-7431.

Charity Unlimited of Florida, Inc. Tel: 305-374-1065; Fax: 305-530-1851. Provides buildings and grounds for charitable works.

Brothers of the Good Shepherd, Inc. Tel: 305-759-8206; Fax: 305-756-8349. Web: www.bgs.org. A religious congregation Brothers 4; Grand Total Assisted 526,460; Total Staff 150.

Brothers of the Good Shepherd of Haiti, Inc. Tel: 305-756-8349; Fax: 305-756-8349. Provides aid and assistance to orphanages and schools operated in Haiti by the Brothers of Good Shepherd

MIAMI, DADE CO.. *Gift of Hope, Missionaries of Charity*, 724 N.W. 17 St., 33136. Tel: 305-326-0032. Sr. Nirmala, Supr. Gen.

Women's and Children's Shelter Tel: 305-326-0032. Total Women Assisted 352; Total Children Assisted 90.

Soup Kitchen for Men Tel: 305-326-0032. Total Assisted 55,461; Total Staff 6.

[G] GENERAL HOSPITALS

MIAMI. *Mercy Hospital*, 3663 S. Miami Ave., 33133. Tel: 305-854-4400; Fax: 305-285-2114. Email: sisterliz@mercymiami.com. Web: www.mercymiami.com. Sisters Elizabeth Anne Worley, S.S.J., Chm. of the Bd. of Trustees & Contact; Edith Gonzalez, S.S.J., Vice Pres., Mission and Ministry. Sponsored by the Sisters of St. Joseph of St. Augustine, FL

Mercy Mission Services (Subsidiaries of Mercy Hospital)

Mercy Outpatient Services, Inc. Tel: 305-285-2121; Fax: 305-285-2114. Revs. Carl T. Morrison, Chap.; Joseph Fishwick, Chap.; Fabio Arango, Chap.; Anthony Acevedo, Chap.; Julio Estada, Chap. Sisters 9; Bed Capacity 512; Patients Assisted Annually 262,489; Total Staff 1,926.

FORT LAUDERDALE. *Holy Cross Hospital*, 4725 N. Federal Hwy., 33308. Tel: 954-771-8000; Fax: 954-351-5947. Email: john.johnson@holy-cross.com. Web: www.holy-cross.com. John C. Johnson, Pres. & CEO; Sr. Rita Levasseur, R.S.M., Co-Dir. & Chap., Dir. of Spirituality; Ms. Barbara Ouellette, Dir. & Chap., Dir. Clinical Pastoral Services; Revs. William Muniz, Chap.; Robert Monti, Chap.; John Mullet, Chap.; James Nero, O.F.M., Chap.; Gary Wiesmann (Jamaica); Sisters Ann Driscoll, R.S.M., Chap.; Margaret Ritchie, R.S.M., Chap.; Claudia Steger, O.S.F., Chap.; Mary Louise Simon, R.S.M., Chap.; Rosemary Petrie, R.S.M., Chap.; Deacon Matthew Teolis, Chap.; Mr. Alex Garvey, Chap. Sisters of Mercy 11; Sisters of St. Francis 1; Total Staff 2,650; Bed Capacity 577; Patients Assisted Annually 567,648.

Holy Cross Health Ministries, Inc. Tel: 954-492-5796; Fax: 954-351-5947.

Holy Cross Hospital, Inc. Tel: 954-492-5796; Fax: 954-351-5947.

Holy Cross Long Term Care, Inc. Tel: 954-492-5796; Fax: 954-351-5947.

[H] MONASTERIES AND RESIDENCES OF PRIESTS AND BROTHERS

MIAMI. *Casa San Lorenzo*, 16400 N.W. 32 Ave., 33054. Tel: 305-624-0775; Fax: 305-625-4529. Revs. Cyril J. Smith, O.S.A.; James L. MacDougall, O.S.A., Prior, Contact; John J. Kelly, O.S.A.; Thomas R. Cook, O.S.A.; Edward Doherty, O.S.A.; Richard Mullen, O.S.A. Augustinian Fathers Total in Residence 6.

Dominican Fathers of Miami, Inc., 5909 N.W. 7th St., 33126-3199. Tel: 305-264-0181, Ext. 22; Fax: 305-262-4685. Email: mwedig@mail.barry.edu. Web: www.opsouth.org. Revs. Restituto Perez, O.P.; Desiderio Eguino, O.P.; Mark Weidig, O.P.; Scott O'Brien, O.P.; Jorge Presmanes, O.P.; David Caron, O.P.; Alberto Rodriguez, O.P. House of Religious Men 1; Total in Residence 8.

Franciscan Fathers' Residence, 2044 S.W. 22nd Ter., 33145. Tel: 305-856-5257. Revs. Jose Biain, O.F.M.; Angel Villaronga, O.F.M.

Marist Brothers Residences, 8230 S.W. 136th St., 33156. Tel: 305-251-6484; Fax: 305-378-2081. Email: maristsw@bellsouth.com. Bros. Charles Filiatraut, F.M.S., Contact; Damian Galligan, F.M.S.; Fabian Mayor, F.M.S.; Simeon Ouellet, F.M.S.; Robert Ryan, F.M.S.; Vincent Dinnean, F.M.S.; Paul Ambrose, F.M.S.

2790 S.W. 89 Ave., 33165. Tel: 305-223-5570. Bros. Bernard Nolan, F.M.S.; Michael Brady, F.M.S.; Joseph Teston, F.M.S.; Vincent J. Dougherty, F.M.S.; Thomas Delaney, F.M.S.

Marcellin House, 8850 S.W. 154th Ter., 33157. Tel: 305-232-1264; Fax: 305-232-2106. Bros. Chanel L. Lambert, F.M.S.; Paul Ambrose, F.M.S.; Thomas Edward, F.M.S.; Kenneth Marino, F.M.S.

Villa Javier Belen Jesuit Fathers, Inc. , 12725 S.W. 6th St., 33184-1305. Tel: 305-559-9066; Fax: 305-222-1256. Email: belensj@aol.com. Revs. Eduardo Alvarez, S.J.; Guillermo Arias, S.J.; Florentino Azcoitia, S.J.; Marcelino Garcia, S.J.; Guillermo Garcia-Tunon, S.J.; Victor M. Hernandez, S.J.; Francisco Perez-Lerena, S.J., Supr.; Jorge Sardina, S.J.; Juan M. Dorta, S.J.; Jorge Munguia, S.J.; Eduardo Barrios, S.J.; Pedro Cartaya, S.J.; Gerardo Freire, S.J.; Pedro Suarez; Oscar Mendez, S.J.; Nelson Garcia, S.J.

Belen Jesuit Alumni Association Tel: 305-661-6180; Fax: 305-661-9639. Rev. Juan Manuel Dorta, S.J., Moderator.

BAL HARBOUR. *Dominican Friars Residence*, 50 Park Dr., Apt. 3, 33154-1345. Tel: 305-864-6593; Fax: 305-899-3385. Email: dmadden@mail.barry.edu.

Web: www.barry.edu/artsci/theology/madden/danspg96.htm. Rev. Daniel P. Madden, O.P.

HIALEAH. *Franciscan Friars of the Holy Name Province*, 1125 W. 35th St., 33012. Tel: 305-822-4367; Fax: 305-698-0479. Email: rapofm@bellsouth.net. Web: www.franmow.org. Revs. John Anglin, O.F.M.; Martin Bednar, O.F.M.; Roderic Petrie, O.F.M., Contact Person; Charles Steen, O.F.M.

[I] CONVENTS AND RESIDENCES FOR SISTERS

MIAMI. *Daughters of Charity of St. Vincent de Paul* (Santurce, P.R.), Mision San Vicente de Paul. , 500 N.W. 63rd Ave., 33126. Tel: 305-266-6485; Fax: 305-265-9671. Email: caridad@gate.net. Web: www.gate.net/~caridad. Asociacion Hijas de la Caridad de San Vicente de Paul del Estado de la Florida, Inc.

Ermita Nacional de Nuestra Senora de la Caridad, 3609 S. Miami Ave., P.O. Box 330555, 33133. Tel: 305-854-2404; Fax: 305-854-8022. Sr. Eva Perez-Puelles, Contact.

Daughters of St. Paul Convent, 11117 S.W. 2nd St., 33174. Tel: 305-554-0175; Fax: 305-220-1639. Email: miami@pauline.org. Web: www.pauline.org. Sr. Maria Elizabeth Borovia, F.S.P., Supr., Contact. Houses of Religious Women 1; Total in Residence 6.

Guadalupan Missionaries of the Holy Spirit, 2483 S.W. 4 St., 33135-2907. Tel: 305-642-9544; Fax: 305-649-2422. Email: mgspsus@aol.com.
Legal Title: *Missionary Guadalupanas of the Holy Spirit, Inc.*, U.S. Delegation Headquarters In Residence 8.

House of Studies, 8670 SW 28th St., 33155. Tel: 305-552-0650. In Res. 5.

Handmaids of the Sacred Heart of Jesus A.C.J. St. Rafaela's Faith Community , 1615 N.E. 108 St., 33161. Tel: 305-891-9161; Fax: 305-891-8791. Email: miamihandmaids@netzero.net. Web: www.acjusa.org. Sisters 4.

Missionaries of Charity, 727 N.W. 17th St., 33136. Tel: 305-545-5699. Sr. Clara, M.C., Supr. (Contact). Houses of Religious Women 1; Total in Residence 6; Total Assisted 2,612.

Monastery of the Most Holy Trinity, (Discalced Carmelite Nuns), 6901 S.W. 66th St., 33143. Tel: 305-668-8663; Fax: 305-665-1175. Sr. Teresa Lucia del Inmaculado Corazon, O.C.D., Prioress.

CORAL GABLES. *Congregation of the French-Cuban Dominican Sisters of Holy Rosary, Inc.*, 600 S.W. 45th Ave., 33134. Tel: 305-441-9488. Email: maria56k@excite.com. Sr. Mary Cecilia Alonso, Pres., Treas. & Contact. Houses of Religious Women 1; Total in Residence 4.

MIAMI SHORES. *Franciscan Sisters of Allegany*
138 N.E. 111 St., 33161. Tel: 305-751-3093; Fax: 305-757-5147. Total in Residence 3.

St. Francis Medical and Health Care Services, Inc.
Allegany Franciscan Foundation, Dade County, Inc.

St. Francis Hospital, Inc. (dba Franciscan Sisters of Allegany Ministries).

[J] RETREAT HOUSES

MIAMI. *Dominican Retreat House, Mary Queen of Apostles*, 7275 S.W. 124 St., 33156. Tel: 305-238-2711; Fax: 305-238-2717. Email: drhmia@bellsouth.net. Sr. June Fitzgerald, O.P., Contact. Dominican Sisters of St. Catherine de Ricci (Motherhouse-Elkins Park, PA) Sisters 6; Capacity for Overnight Retreat Programs 60; Retreat Center 1; Total in Residence 5; Staff 11.

John Paul II Retreat House, 720 N.E. 27th St., 33137-4697. Tel: 305-576-2748; 305-573-1418; Fax: 305-576-2748. Email: webmaster@acu-adsum.org. Web: www.acu-adsum.org. Rev. Amando Llorente, S.J., Spiritual Dir., Contact. Total in Residence 2; Total Staff 8.

Agrupacion Catolica Universitaria, Inc. Tel: 305-573-1418; Fax: 305-576-2748.

Jesuit Fathers of the Province of the Antilles, Inc.

[K] CENTERS

MIAMI. *National Shrine of Our Lady of Charity*, 3609 S. Miami Ave., P.O. Box 330555, 33133. Tel: 305-854-2404; Fax: 305-854-8022. Email: ermita@compusource.net. Most Rev. Agustin Roman, V.G., V.G., Rector Emeritus; Very Rev. Oscar Castaneda, Rector; Revs. Francisco Santana, Assoc. Rector; Jose Carlos Piedra (Cuba), Assoc. Rector; Deacon Manuel Perez. Sisters 3; Houses of Religious Women 1; Total in Residence 4.

Pauline Book & Media Center, 145 S.W. 107th Ave., 33174. Tel: 305-559-6715; 305-559-6716; Fax: 305-559-6717. Email: miami@pauline.org. Web: www.pauline.org. Sr. Maria Elizabeth Borovia, F.S.P., Supr. Daughters of St. Paul 6; Houses of Religious Women 1; Total in Residence 6; Pauline Book & Media Center 1; Staff 12.

Paulinas Spanish Distribution Center Tel: 305-225-2513; Fax: 305-225-4189. Web: www.paulinasusa.org (Spanish).

Respect Life Office, 18340 N.W. 12 Ave., 33169. Tel: 305-653-2921; Fax: 305-653-1001. Email: ilovlife@bellsouth.net. Web: www.respectlifemiami.com. Rev. Jordi S. Rivero, Dir.; Mrs. Joan Crown, Assoc. Dir. Special Centers for Social Services 6; Total Assisted 7,261; Staff 7.

Southeast Pastoral Institute, 7700 S.W. 56th St., 33155. Tel: 305-279-2333; Fax: 305-279-0925. Email: sepimiami@aol.com. Web: socrates.barry.edu/lib-poneill/sepi.htm. Rev. Mario B. Vizcaino, Sch.P., Dir., Contact; Lydia Menocal, Dir. Asst., Sepi Exec. Sec. & Registrar; Zulima Marin, Admin. Asst. & Office Mgr.

Southeast Regional Office for Hispanic Ministry, Inc.: 7700 S.W. 56th St., 33155. Tel: 305-279-2333; Fax: 305-279-0925. Email: sepimiami@aol.com. Web: www.socrates.barry.edu/lib-poneill/sepi.htm. Rev. Mario B. Vizcaino, Sch.P., Regl. Dir. & Contact; Lydia Menocal, Dir. Asst., Sepi Exec. Sec. & Registrar; Zulima Marin, Admin. Asst. & Office Mgr.

MIAMI SHORES. *Family Life Ministry*, 9401 Biscayne Blvd., 33138. Tel: 305-762-1140; Fax: 305-762-1144. Email: dirfec@miamiarch.org. Web: www.miamiarch.org/main. Mrs. Elaine Syfert, Dir.

[L] PERSONAL PRELATURE

MIAMI. *Prelature of the Holy Cross and Opus Dei*, 4415 S.W. 88th Ave., 33165. Tel: 305-551-7956; Fax: 305-551-7957. Revs. Salvador Serrano-Vahi, Contact Person; Orestes Gonzalez.

[M] MISCELLANEOUS LISTINGS

MIAMI. *Alumni Association of the Apostolate of Cuba (in Exile), Inc.*, P.O. Box 650721, 33265-0721. Tel: 305-271-4151. Web: www.geocities.com/aaapostolado. Mercedes F. Perez, Pres.; Maria Antonia Pena, Treas. Tel: 305-271-4151; Teresita G. Garcia, Sec.

Alumni of Apostolate Charity Foundation, Inc., P.O. Box 650721, 33265-0721. Tel: 305-271-4151. Web: www.geocities.com/aaapostolado. Berta San Pedro, Pres. Tel: 305-445-8900; Maria Antonia D. Pena, Treas., Contact. Tel: 305-271-4151.

Claretian Missions, Inc., 7080 S.W. 99 Ave., 33173. Tel: 305-274-6148; Fax: 305-274-5695. Email: ondina@claretiansisters.org. Web: www.claretiansisters.org. Sr. Ondina Cortes, Supr. (Contact).
Legal Title: *Claretian Missionary Sisters of Florida, Inc.* Sisters 10; Houses of Religious Women 4; Total in Residence 15.

Discalced Carmelite Friars of Miami, Inc. Our Lady of Mt. Carmel Spiritual Life Center. , 18330 N.W. 12 Ave., 33169. Tel: 305-654-9760; Fax: 305-654-9345. Email: eugona46@hotmail.com. Web: carmelitesmiami.com. Revs. Eusebio Gomez, O.C.D., Pres., Contact; Lucio del Burgo, O.C.D., Vice Pres.; Denis William Read, O.C.D. Retreat Center 1; Total in Residence 3; Staff 6.

Federacion de Institutos Pastorales, Inc., 7700 S.W. 56th St., 33155. Tel: 305-279-2333; Fax: 305-279-0925. Rev. Mario B. Vizcaino, Sch.P., Pres.

Foundation of the Cuban Association of the S.M.O. of Malta, Inc., Grand Bay Plaza, Ste. 200, 2665 S. Bayshore Dr., 33133. Tel: 305-285-0800; Fax: 305-285-0837. Email: jon@abogadosfla.com. Fernando Garcia-Chacon, Pres.; Juan T. O'Naghten, Vice Pres.; Jose Fernandez Penichet, Treas.; Lodovico Blanc, Dir.

St. Luke's Center, Inc., 7707 N.W. 2nd Ave., 33150. Tel: 305-795-0077; Fax: 305-795-2022. Email: stlukes@catholiccharitiesadm.org. Web: www.catholiccharitiesadm.org/stluke. Sharon Crippen, Admin.; Dr. Julian Serrano, Division Dir. Total in Residence 50; Total Staff 35.

Addiction Recovery Center

Peruvian Mission, Inc. (A Florida Not-for-Profit Corporation) , P.O. Box 432745, 33143. Tel: 305-596-6738; Fax: 305-596-6738. Email: perumision@aol.com. Most Revs. Miguel Irizar, C.P., Bishop of Callao, Pres.; Luis Bambaren, S.J., Bishop of Chimbote, Vice Pres.; Maria Delia Salazar, Dir., Sec. & Contact Person.

SEPI Evangelization and Education Foundation, Inc., 7700 S.W. 56th St., 33155. Tel: 305-279-2333; Fax: 305-279-0925. Email: sepimiami@aol.com. Rev. Mario B. Vizcaino, Sch.P., Exec. Dir., Sec., Contact.

Teresian Institute, Inc. (Rome, Italy), Teresian Institute of Florida, Inc. An International Association of the Faithful. , 3400 S.W. 99 Ave., 33165. Tel: 305-553-8567; 305-221-1037; Fax: 305-553-8567. Email: portillr@earthlink.net. Web: www.instituciontersiana.org. Ela Alvarado, Contact. Total in Residence 3; Total Staff 5.

Center of Activities, National Headquarters

Theatine Sisters of the Immaculate Conception, Co. aka Religiosas Teatinas de la Immaculada Concepci, 12261 S.W. 6th St., 33184. Tel: 305-223-2512; Fax: 305-227-6951. Email: teatinas@aol.com. Sr. Mercedes Exposito, Supr.

COOPER CITY. *Schott Memorial Center Foundation, Inc. dba Schott Communities* (A Florida Not-for-Profit Corporation) , 6591 S. Flamingo Rd., 33330. Tel: 954-434-3306; Fax: 954-434-3307. Email: mjohnson@schottcommunities.org. Web: www.schottcommunities.org. Margaret Johnson, O.P., Ed.D., Exec. Dir., Contact. Programs and services for persons who are deaf or disabled. Total Assisted 11,520; Total Staff 10.

CORAL GABLES. *House of the Divine Will, Inc. dba Casa de la Divina Voluntad*, 5900 Leonardo St., 33146-3332. Tel: 305-667-5714; Fax: 305-667-7173. Email: casadivinavoluntad@msn.com. Web: www.casadeladivinavoluntad.org. Rev. Carlos Antonio Massieu Avila, Pres. & Chm.; Marianela Perez, Treas. & Contact Person.

Magnificat, Inc., 5031 Maggiore St., 33146. Tel: 305-661-9833; Fax: 305-663-0629. Cristina Beato, Bd. of Directors; Valli Leoni, Bd. of Directors; Rory Lombana, Bd. of Directors; Susy Alverez, Bd. of Directors; Maria Monzon, Bd. of Directors.

HIALEAH. *Dominicas de la Inmaculada Concepcion*, 571 W. 33 Pl., 33012. Tel: 305-823-3282. Email: dominimiami@hotmail.com. Sisters Enith Montero, Supr.; Maria Ines Siguenza; Carmen Aguilar. Houses of Religous Women 1; Total in Residence 3.

HOLLYWOOD. *Catholic Charismatic Services of the Archdiocese of Miami, Inc.*, P.O. Box 816128, 33081-0128. Tel: 954-961-1856; Fax: 954-961-3662. Email: ccs112@juno.com. Web: www.garg.com/ccc/directory/north_america/usa/florida/aofm.html. Emery Horvath, Dir.; Mary Horvath, Co-Dir.

KEY LARGO. *Mass Times Trust*, 67 N. Bounty Ln., 33037. Tel: 305-852-4530; Fax: 305-852-1582. Email: masstimes@aol.com. Web: www.masstimes.org. Robert A. Hummel, Trustee; Phyliss H. Hummel, Sec.; Jerry Early, Trustee. Toll telephone listing of local Catholic Churches with Mass times to assist travelers in finding Mass schedules is 410-676-6000

MARGATE. *Word & Life Catholic Ministry, Inc.*, 541 State Rd., Ste. 13, 33068. Tel: 954-970-7766; Fax: 954-969-7879. Email: info@wordandlife.org. Web: www.wordandlife.org. P.O. Box 5150, 33093. Revs. Ricardo C. Castellanos, Founder; Roberto Garza, Pres.

MIAMI SHORES. *Archdiocese of Miami Millennium Appeal, Inc.*, 9401 Biscayne Blvd., 33138. Tel: 305-757-6241; Fax: 305-758-5261. Most Rev. John C. Favalora, D.D., Pres.; Rev. Msgrs. William J. Hennessey, V.G., Vice Pres.; John J. Vaughan, Treas.; Michael A. Souckar, J.C.D. (Cand.), Sec.

Archdiocese of Miami, Inc., 9401 Biscayne Blvd., 33138. Tel: 305-757-6241; Fax: 305-758-5261. Most Rev. John C. Favalora, D.D., Pres.; Rev. Msgrs. William J. Hennessey, V.G., Vice. Pres.; John J. Vaughan, Treas.; Michael A. Souckar, J.C.D. (Cand.), Sec.

Bahamas Mission of Florida, Inc., Archdiocese of Miami, 9401 Biscayne Blvd., 33138. Tel: 305-762-1220. Email: tmarin@adom.us.

Bishops' Indemnity Corporation, 9401 Biscayne Blvd., 33138. Tel: 305-757-6241.

Catholic Community Foundation, Inc., 9401 Biscayne Blvd., 33138. Tel: 305-762-1080; Fax: 305-762-1257. Email: aef@miamiarch.org. Michael Bienes, Pres.; Roger Shay, Vice Pres.; Rev. Msgr. Vincent Kelly, Sec. & Treas.

DOM, Inc., 9401 Biscayne Blvd., 33138. Tel: 305-757-6241; Fax: 305-758-5261.

Francis Realty Corporation, 9401 Biscayne Blvd., 33138. Tel: 305-757-6241; Fax: 305-758-5261.

Marbella Condominium 207 Association, Inc., 9401 Biscayne Blvd., 33138. Tel: 305-757-6241; Fax: 305-758-5261.

P.O.M., Inc., 9401 Biscayne Blvd., 33138. Tel: 305-757-6241; Fax: 305-758-5261.

Pooled Income Trust Fund, 9401 Biscayne Blvd., 33138. Tel: 305-757-6241; Fax: 305-758-5261.

Provincial Realty Associates, Inc. (A Florida Not-for-Profit Corporation) , 9401 Biscayne Blvd., 33138. Tel: 305-757-6241; Fax: 305-758-5261. Land Holding Corporation.

R. A. Sanchez Family Foundation, Inc., 9401 Biscayne Blvd., 33138. Tel: 305-670-4343; Fax: 305-666-8602. Email: rsanchezfl@aol.com.

Stella Maris Seaman Center, Inc., 9401 Biscayne Blvd., 33138. Tel: 305-649-1811; Fax: 305-642-6815. Rev. Jose M. Paz, Sec.

POMPANO BEACH. *Indian Catholic Association of Florida, Inc.*, 731 N. Ocean Blvd., 33062. Tel: 954-943-3684; Fax: 954-943-3656. Email: frjpedathua@aol.com. Web: www.indiacatholic.com. Rev. James Parappally (India), Chap.

Ministerio Catolico Verbo y Vida, Inc., P.O. Box

1057, 33061. Tel: 954-969-7909; Fax: 954-969-7879. Email: info@verboyvida.org. Web: www.verboyvida.org. Rev. Roberto Garza, Pres.

SWEETWATER. *Asociacion Nacional de Diaconos Hispanos, Inc.*, 50 S.W. 103rd Avenue, 33174. Tel: 305-223-2065. Email: ppcalvo@bellsouth.net. Deacons Alfredo Vasquez, Pres.; John Munoz, Vice Pres.; Pedro Calvo, Treas.; George Benavente, Treas.; Fernando Bestar, Sec.

TALLAHASSEE. *Florida Catholic Conference*, 313 S. Calhoun St., 32301-1807. Tel: 850-222-3803; Fax: 850-681-9548. Email: flacathconf@flacathconf.org. Web: www.flacathconf.org. D. Michael McCarron, Ph.D., Exec. Dir.

RELIGIOUS INSTITUTES OF MEN REPRESENTED IN THE ARCHDIOCESE

For further details refer to the corresponding bracketed number in the Religious Institutes of Men or Women section.

[0140]—*The Augustinians* (St. Thomas of Villanova Prov.)—O.S.A.
[0600]—*Brothers of the Congregation of Holy Cross*—C.S.C.
[0580]—*Brothers of the Good Shepherd*—B.G.S.
[0470]—*Capuchin Friars* White Plains, NY—O.F.M.Cap.
[0270]—*Carmelite Fathers & Brothers*—O.Carm.
[0310]—*Congregation of Christian Brothers* (Eastern Prov.)—C.F.C.
[1330]—*Congregation of the Mission*—C.M.
[1080]—*Congregation of the Resurrection*—C.R.
[1140]—*Congregation of the Sacred Hearts of Jesus and Mary*—SS.CC.
[0260]—*Discalced Carmelite Friars*—O.C.D.
[0520]—*Franciscan Friars* (Most Holy Name & San Sebastion Provs.)—O.F.M.
[0650]—*Holy Ghost Fathers*—C.S.Sp.
[0690]—*Jesuit Fathers and Brothers* (Antilles, New Orleans and New England Provs.)—S.J.
[0770]—*The Marist Brothers* (Bayonne, N.J. & Poughkeepsie Provs.)—F.M.S.
[0800]—*Maryknoll Fathers & Brothers*—M.M.
[1210]—*Missionaries of St. Charles-Scalabrinians*—C.S.
[0910]—*Oblates of Mary Immaculate*—O.M.I.
[0920]—*Oblates of St. Francis de Sales*—O.S.F.S.
[0430]—*Order of Preachers (Dominican)* (St. Joseph & Southern Provs.)—O.P.
[1020]—*Pauline Fathers & Brothers*—S.S.P.
[1040]—*Piarist Fathers*—Sch.P.
[0610]—*Priests of the Congregation of the Holy Cross*—C.S.C.
[1190]—*Salesians of Don Bosco*—S.D.B.
[1260]—*Society of Christ*—S.Ch.
[0760]—*Society of Mary (Marianists)*—S.M.
[0370]—*Society of St. Columban*—S.S.C.
[1060]—*Society of the Precious Blood*—C.PP.S.

RELIGIOUS INSTITUTES OF WOMEN REPRESENTED IN THE ARCHDIOCESE

[0370]—*Carmelite Sisters of the Most Sacred Heart of Los Angeles*—O.C.D.
[0685]—*Claretian Missionary Sisters*—R.M.I.
[0270]—*Congregation of Bon Secours*—C.B.S.
[1710]—*Congregation of the Third Order of St. Francis of Mary Immaculate, Joliet, IL*—O.S.F.
[0760]—*Daughters of Charity of St. Vincent de Paul*—D.C.
[0790]—*Daughters of Divine Charity*—F.D.C.
[0850]—*Daughters of Mary Help of Christians*—F.M.A.
[]—*Daughters of Mary, Mother of Mercy (Nigeria)*—D.M.M.M.
[0420]—*Discalced Carmelite Nuns*—O.C.D.
[1070-13]—*Dominican Sisters (Adrian)*—O.P.
[1070-17]—*Dominican Sisters (Elkins Park)*—O.P.
[1070-06]—*Dominican Sisters (Newburgh)*—O.P.
[]—*Dominican Sisters of Our Lady of the Most Holy Rosary (Colombia)*—O.P.
[]—*Dominicas de la Inmaculada Concepcion (Ecuador)*
[1340]—*Franciscan Missionary Sisters of the Divine Child*—F.M.D.C.
[1180]—*Franciscan Sisters of Allegany, New York*—O.S.F.
[1845]—*Guadalupan Missionaries of the Holy Spirit* (Mexico)—M.G.Sp.S.
[1870]—*Handmaids of the Sacred Heart of Jesus*—A.C.J.
[2575]—*Institute of the Sisters of Mercy of the Americas* (Pittsburgh, PA; Rochester, NY; Clogher, Ireland; Newfoundland, Canada)—R.S.M.
[]—*Marianites* (Santa Mariana de Jesus Institute, Inc.)—R.M.
[2710]—*Missionaries of Charity*—M.C.
[3040]—*Oblate Sisters of Providence*—O.S.P.
[3130]—*Our Lady of Victory Missionary Sisters*—O.L.V.M.
[0950]—*Pious Society Daughters of St. Paul*—F.S.P.
[3380]—*Religious of the Apostolate of the Sacred Heart*—F.A.
[3390]—*Religious of the Assumption*—R.A.
[2970]—*School Sisters of Notre Dame* (Baltimore, MD; Chicago, IL)—S.S.N.D.
[0430]—*Sisters of Charity of the Blessed Virgin Mary* (Davenport, IA)—B.V.M.
[]—*Sisters of Jesus the Saviour* (Nigeria)—S.J.S.
[2540]—*Sisters of Mercy* (Clogher, Northern Ireland)—R.S.M.
[2575]—*Sisters of Mercy* (Pittsburg, Pa)—R.S.M.
[2519]—*Sisters of Mercy* (St. John's, New foundland, Canada)—R.S.M.
[3000]—*Sisters of Notre Dame de Namur (Baltimore, MA)*—S.N.D.deN.
[3350]—*Sisters of Providence*—S.P.
[4090]—*Sisters of Social Service*—S.S.S.
[3740]—*Sisters of St. Casimir*—S.S.C.
[1620]—*Sisters of St. Francis of Millvale, Pennsylvania*—O.S.F.
[1630]—*Sisters of St. Francis of Penance and Christian Charity*—O.S.F.
[3830-13]—*Sisters of St. Joseph (Baden, PA)*—C.S.J.
[]—*Sisters of St. Joseph Benedict Cottolengo*—S.S.J.C.
[3830-09]—*Sisters of St. Joseph (Erie, PA)*—S.S.J.
[3840]—*Sisters of St. Joseph of Carondelet* (St. Louis, MO)—C.S.J.
[3850]—*Sisters of St. Joseph of Chambery* (Hartford, CT)—C.S.J.
[3900]—*Sisters of St. Joseph of St. Augustine, Florida*—S.S.J.
[]—*Sisters of St. Philip Neri Missionary Teachers*—R.F.
[2180]—*Sisters of the Immaculate Heart of Mary*—I.H.M.
[1490]—*Sisters of the Third Franciscan Order*—O.S.F.
[2150]—*Sisters, Servants of the Immaculate Heart of Mary* (Monroe, MI)—I.H.M.
[2180]—*Sisters, Servants of the Immaculate Heart of Mary* (Clewiston, FL)
[2160]—*Sisters, Servants of the Immaculate Heart of Mary* (Scranton, PA)—I.H.M.
[2170]—*Sisters, Servants of the Immaculate Heart of Mary* (Immaculata, PA)—I.H.M.
[2460]—*Society of Mary Reparatrix*—S.M.R.
[4020]—*Society of St. Teresa of Jesus*—S.T.J.
[4070]—*Society of the Sacred Heart*—R.S.C.J.
[]—*Theatine Sisters of the Immaculate Conception (Religiosas Teatinas de la Inmaculada Concepcion)*—R.T.

NECROLOGY

† McKeever, Rev. Msgr. William F., Miami, FL St. John Bosco—Died Aug. 13, 2003

Archdiocese for the Military Services, U.S.A.

Military Ordinariate

Most Reverend

EDWIN F. O'BRIEN, S.T.D.

Archbishop for the Military Services; ordained May 29, 1965; appointed Titular Bishop of Tizica and Auxiliary Bishop of New York March 25, 1996; appointed Coadjutor April 8, 1997; succeeded as Ordinary to the Military Services August 12, 1997.

Chancery: P.O. Box 4469, Washington, DC 20017-0469. Tel: 202-269-9100; Fax: 202-269-9022.

Web: www.milarch.org

Email: info@milarch.org

Most Reverend

JOHN J. KAISING, D.D.

Auxiliary Bishop for the Military Services; ordained December 22, 1962; appointed Titular Bishop for Orrea Celia and Auxiliary Bishop of the Archdiocese of the Military Services February 21, 2000; ordained Bishop April 11, 2000.

Most Reverend

JOSEPH T. DIMINO, D.D.

Former Archbishop for the Military Services; ordained June 4, 1949; appointed Titular Bishop of Carini and Auxiliary Bishop to the Military Vicar March 29, 1983; consecrated May 10, 1983; appointed Ordinary to the Military Services May 13, 1991; resigned August 12, 1997.

Most Reverend

FRANCIS X. ROQUE, D.D.

Auxiliary Bishop for the Military Services; ordained September 19, 1953; appointed Titular Bishop of Bagai and Auxiliary Bishop to the Military Vicar March 29, 1983; consecrated May 10, 1983.

Most Reverend

JOSEPH J. MADERA, M.SP.S., D.D.

Auxiliary Bishop for the Military Services; ordained June 15, 1957; appointed Coadjutor Bishop of Fresno with the right of succession December 18, 1979; consecrated March 4, 1980; succeeded to See July 1, 1980; appointed Titular Bishop of Orte and Auxiliary Bishop of the Archdiocese of the Military Services May 28, 1991.

Most Reverend

JOHN J. GLYNN, D.D.

Retired Auxiliary Bishop for the Military Services; ordained April 11, 1951; appointed Titular Bishop of Monteverde and Auxiliary Bishop of the Archdiocese for the Military Services December 10, 1991; ordained Bishop January 6, 1992; retired August 13, 2002.

Established as Military Vicariate of the United States September 8, 1957 created Archdiocese For The Military Services, U.S.A. (Ordinariatus Castrensis) March 25, 1985.

Serving U.S. Catholics of the Army, Navy, Air Force, Marine Corps, Coast Guard, Department of Veterans Affairs and those in Government Service overseas.

STATISTICAL OVERVIEW

Personnel	
Archbishop	1
Retired Archbishop	1
Auxiliary Bishops	3
Retired Bishops	1
Priest Chaplains are on loan from their diocese or religious community. Deacons who assist at chapels are volunteers from the local diocese.	
Educational	
Catechesis/Religious Education:	
High School Students	21,000
Elementary Students	44,200
Total Students under Catholic Instruction	65,200
Religious Education Teachers:	
Sisters	12
Lay Teachers	220
Total	232
Vital Statistics	
Receptions into the Church:	
Infant Baptism Totals	3,978
Adult Baptism Totals	747
Received into Full Communion	323
First Communions	2,662
Confirmations	2,302
Marriages:	
Catholic	465
Interfaith	313
Total Marriages	778
Catholics, Active Duty Military	375,000
Family Members	737,500
Reserve/Guard Catholic Personnel	204,000
Catholic Residents, VA facilities	29,000
Civilian Catholic Overseas	66,000
Total Population	1,411,500

Former Military Vicars—His Eminence PATRICK CARDINAL HAYES, consecrated Titular Bishop of Tagaste, Oct. 28, 1914; appt. "Bishop Ordinary of U.S. Army and Navy Chaplains," Nov. 24, 1917; appt. Archbishop of New York, March 10, 1919; created Cardinal, March 24, 1924; died Sept. 4, 1938; FRANCIS CARDINAL SPELLMAN, consecrated Auxiliary Bishop of Boston, Sept. 8, 1932; appt. Archbishop of New York, April 15, 1939; appt. "Military Vicar for the Armed Forces of U.S.," Dec. 11, 1939; created Cardinal, Feb. 18, 1946; died Dec. 2, 1967; TERENCE CARDINAL COOKE, consecrated Auxiliary Bishop of New York, Dec. 13, 1965; appt. Archbishop of New York, March 2, 1968; appt. "Military Vicar of U.S. Armed Forces," April 4, 1968; created Cardinal, April 28, 1969; died Oct. 6, 1983; Most Revs. JOSEPH T. RYAN (Retired), appt. first Archbishop of Anchorage, Feb. 7, 1966; consecrated March 25, 1966; appt. Titular Archbishop of Gabi and Coadjutor (Archbishop) of the Military Vicar, Oct. 24, 1975; installed first Ordinary of the Archdiocese for the Military Services March, 25, 1985; retired May 13, 1991; died Oct. 9, 2000; JOSEPH T. DIMINO, D.D. (Retired), appt. Auxiliary Bishop of Military Vicar and Titular Bishop of Carini, March 29, 1983; consecrated May 10, 1983; appt. second Ordinary for the Military Services, May 13, 1991; retired Aug. 12, 1997.

Vicar General—Rev. Msgr. ALOYSIUS R. CALLAGHAN, S.T.L., J.C.D.

Archdiocese Offices

Chancery—P.O. Box 4469, Washington, 20017. Tel: 202-269-9100; Fax: 202-269-9022. Email: info@milarch.org. Web: www.milarch.org.

Moderator of the Curia—Rev. Msgr. ALOYSIUS R. CALLAGHAN, S.T.L., J.C.D.

Chancellor—Rev. JAMES R. DIXON.

Vice Chancellors—Very Rev. JOSEPH A. HOWARTH, J.C.L., S.T.B.; DAVID LEVITE.

Office of Chaplain Personnel—

Vicar for Chaplains and Seminarians—Most Rev. JOHN J. KAISING, D.D.

Director—Mrs. MARGARET SCUDERI.

Pastoral Support, Community Concerns—Most Rev. JOSEPH J. MADERA, M.Sp.S., D.D.

Veterans Concerns—Most Rev. FRANCIS X. ROQUE, D.D.

Assistant to the Archbishop—Sr. CATHERINE MARIE CHONG, R.S.M.

Director of Administration—Mrs. JO ANN REDMOND.

Director of Sacramental Records—Mr. FRANK CALANDRA.

Director of Development—Mr. DAVID LEVITE.

Archivist—Mrs. PATRICIA THACKER.

Tribunal—

Judicial Vicar—Very Rev. JOSEPH A. HOWARTH, J.C.L., S.T.B.

Adjutant Judicial Vicar—Rev. Msgr. ALOYSIUS R. CALLAGHAN, S.T.L., J.C.D.

Judges—Rev. Msgr. THOMAS F. SHREVE, J.C.L.; Revs. WAYNE L. BALL, J.C.D.; ROBERT R. CANNON, J.C.D. (Cand.); JOSEPH C. DIECKHAUS, J.C.L.; FREDERICK J. FEUSAHRENS, J.C.L.; EMMETT J. GAVIN, O.Carm., J.C.L.; G. PAUL HERBERT, J.C.L.; ROBERT M. HERBST, O.F.M., J.C.L.; ROBERT L. KINCL, J.C.L.; EDUARDO G. MONTERO, J.C.L.; EDMOND PRENDIVILLE, J.C.L.; GILBERT J. SEITZ, J.C.L.; JOHN B. WARD, J.C.L.; Dr. ALEJANDRO A. CAMPOS, J.C.L., J.D.; Ms. JACQUELINE E. HANNEM, J.C.L.; Ms. MELISSA L. SCHOOLS, J.C.L.

Defenders of the Bond—Revs. DAVID F. O'CONNOR, S.T., J.C.D.; ANTHONY MCLAUGHLIN, J.C.L.

Promoter of Justice—Rev. JOHN B. WARD, J.C.L.

Procurator-Advocate—Most Rev. FRANCIS X. ROQUE, D.D.

Notary—Miss PATRICIA HUTCHISON.

Presbyteral Council—Most Revs. EDWIN F. O'BRIEN, D.D., S.T.D.; FRANCIS X. ROQUE, D.D.; JOSEPH J. MADERA, M.Sp.S., D.D.; JOHN J. KAISING, D.D.; Rev. Msgr. ALOYSIUS R. CALLAGHAN, S.T.L., J.C.D., Exec. Sec.; Rev. JAMES R. DIXON; Very Rev. JOSEPH A. HOWARTH, J.C.L., S.T.B.; Rev. Msgr. JEROME A. HABEREK; Revs. F. RICHARD SPENCER; LOUIS IASIELLO; LEWIS BROWN; JOSEPH WALLROTH; CARLO MONTECALVO; WILLIAM VANDER HAYDEN; PAUL S. HOLT.

Military Council of Catholic Women—Most Rev. JOSEPH J. MADERA, M.Sp.S., D.D., Episcopal Moderator.

Areas of Service

Armed Forces Active Duty

The Archdiocese for the Military Services is responsible for the pastoral care of the Catholic men and women who serve on active duty in the five branches of the U.S. Armed Forces. It is also responsible for the dependents of these persons. Included also are the cadets and resident personnel of the three military academies (West Point--the U.S. Military Academy, the U.S. Air Force Academy at Colorado Springs, the U.S. Naval Academy at Annapolis) and the U.S. Coast Guard Academy at New London as well as the U.S. Merchant Marine Academy at Kings Point, NY. Pastoral care is provided by priest chaplains on loan from their dioceses or religious communities to serve as chaplains for the Military and Department of Veterans Affairs. Members of the Marines and Coast Guard are served by Navy Chaplains. ; Armed Forces, Reserves, National Guard: In addition to the personnel on active duty in the Armed Forces, there is a considerable reserve component. Some of these personnel serve a number of days each year on active duty with a branch of the service; some serve on extended tours of active duty; all are subject to recall to active duty in a national emergency. In addition to the reserve components of the Army, Air Force, Navy and

Coast Guard, there are also the Air National Guard and the Army National Guard, which are organized on a state-by-state basis. ; Department of Veterans Affairs: The Archdiocese for the Military Services is responsible for the spiritual care of Catholics at V.A. medical facilities. Chaplaincy services are provided by full- and part-time priests, many of whom are retired military chaplains. ; U.S. Government Civilian Employees Abroad: U.S. citizens in government service abroad (and their family members living with them) are subjects of the Archdiocese for the Military Services. ; There is only one full-time Catholic chaplain conducting pastoral programs for the embassy: in Moscow. The Embassy in Moscow has a program conducted by the Augustinians of the Assumption and is separate from the Archdiocese; it serves Catholics in the Foreign Service of other countries as well as Americans. ; Civil Air Patrol: The Civil Air Patrol, as an auxiliary of the Air Force, is under the jurisdiction of the Archdiocese for the Military Services. The jurisdiction applies to its chaplains and members only when participating in exercises on a military installation.

UNITED STATES ARMY CHAPLAINS

Regular Army Chaplains:

Rev. Msgrs.—
Burns, Vincent P. (PH)
Goudreau, Joseph L. (PRT)
Hill, Philip W. (NY)
Spiegel, Robert H. (DAV)

Revs.—
Albano, Alwyn M. (Philippines)
Albertson, Eric J. (ARL)
Amano, Antonio A. (Philippines)
Amezcua, Mario M., L.C.
Angotti, Joseph A. (GRY)
Arflack, Gregory A. (OWN)
Arnoldt, David M. (WIN)
Bendorf, Richard, O.F.M. (STL)
Besinga, Dino J. (Philippines)
Bleboo, Lawrence T. (Ghana)
Bluett, James K. (PT)
Bolton, Paul J. (PRO)
Bomba, Paul M. (WOR)
Briganti, Philip J. (PAT)
Buckon, Neal J. (CLV)
Calasara, Mansuelo T. (Philippines)
Carey, William F. (BGP)
Carlson, Kenneth F. (CHI)
Carlson, Steven V. (R)
Cerrone, Michael J. (SAV)
Chilen, Michael D. (CC)
Coindreau, James M., L.C.
Connelly, Christian T. (ARL)
Czech, Edward M. (CLV)
D'Emma, Gregory J. (NEW)
D'Silva, Joseph R. (India)
Denig, Philip P. (DEN)
Deponai, Joseph J. (NY)
DiGregorio, Joseph L. (PH)
Dormer, David J. (SCR)
Dynek, Wieslaw A. (Poland)
Ehrhart, Charles M. (RVC)
Fleury, Joseph M., S.M. (WDC)
Fukes, Gary M. (SY)
Fuller, Orland R. (Philippines)
Glasgow, Robert K. (WIL)
Goellen, Richard M. (FAR)
Gonzalez, George G. (SAT)
Gross, Gary L. (LIN)
Haberak, Jerome A. (PRO)
Halka, Frantisek (ALT)
Hannon, Joseph F., S.D.B.
Heninger, Michael B. (ATL)
Herrera, Jose G. (STV)
Herron, John B. (FAR)
Higgins, Richard B. (SAC)
Honor, Michael P. (Philippines)
Hubbs, Timothy L. (CAM)
Hurley, Paul K. (BO)
Inghilterra, Vincent J. (TR)
Irizarry, Alan M. (ARE)
Jones, James W., O.F.M.Cap. (NY)
Kazarnowicz, Anthony S. (WOR)
Kelley, Edward J. (PRO)
Kenehan, David A., O.S.F.S.
Kincl, Robert L., J.C.L. (AUS)
Kirchhoefer, Thomas A. (STL)
Kirk, David R. (TOL)
Kokeram, Sudash J. (NEW)
Kopec, Krzysztof A. (WIL)
Kopec, Rajmund (NEW)
Lanuevo, Victor (HON)
Lawrence, Andrew F. (DUB)
Longbucco, John L. (MAR)
Lorenc, Henryk (Poland)
Madden, James J., O.Praem.
Madej, Paul D. (SY)
Madu, Ferdinand E. (Nigeria)
Majkut, Tadeusz (Paraguay)
McLain, John J., S.J. (R)
Minch, Richard (SAV)
Niemeier, Dennis A. (CIN)
O'Grady, J. Frank (PAT)
O'Keefe, Joseph L. (ALB)
O'Neal, James E. (STA)
Obeng-Kyeremeh, Simon (STV)
Ohm, Edward U. (PEO)
Pagan, Alberto, O.P. (SJN)
Passamonti, Paul G. (WDC)
Patton, Patrick G. (HEL)
Pawlikowski, Matthew (NEW)
Perez, John C. (SJN)
Ratigan, Patrick A. (OG)
Reyes, Armando I. (Philippines)
Roetzel, Robert E., C.S.C. (FTW)
Rohen, Patrick J. (TOL)
Rutherford, Donald L. (ALB)
Rzasowski, Jerzy (Poland)
Santry, Robert (HON)
Sheil, James (CLV)
Spencer, F. Richard (BAL)
Stahl, Allen M. (ORL)
Stodola, Francis (LAR)
Studniewski, Gary R. (WDC)
Sykes, Gregory P. (OG)
Tadeo, Victor C. (Philippines)
Tellez, Jairo A. (SAT)
Torm, Agustin (CHR)
Travaglione, Michael, O.F.M. (BO)
Ugwuanya, Valentine C. (NEW)
Uhde, Peter M. (NEW)
Vakoc, Henry T. (STP)
Valentine, Timothy S., S.J. (NY)
Van Alstyne, Donald J., M.I.C.
Wilk, Mitchell S. (SPC)
Willett, William D. (OWN)
Wydeven, John L. (OAK)
Yoakam, Lee R., O.S.B. (GBG)

Army National Guard Chaplains:

Rev. Msgrs.—
Bill, Ronald C. (SY) (Retired)
Coyle, Edward J. (ALN)
Engelbrecht, Henry H. (NO)
Herzog, Ronald P. (BLX)
Madus, Peter P. (SCR)
Thomas, Royce R., J.C.L. (LR)

Revs.—
Abreau, Felix, C.S.Sp.
Acevedo, Edward (MGZ)
Albrecht, Louis H. (BAK)
Bain, John K. (RNO)
Bilodeau, Leopold J. (BUR)
Bowe, John F. (PH)
Brando, Joseph J. (KNX)
Brennan, Brian C. (NY)
Brennan, Eugene P. (STL)
Carmody, James F. (WOR)
Castillejo-Llusia, Jorge J. (Spain) (SJN)
Cavanaugh, Kevin P. (HRT)
Chavez, Johnny Lee (SFE)
Converse, Brian J. (NOR)
Corneille, Cecil C. (STV)
Derrane, Mark G. (BO)
Diacetis, Anthony C. (ALB)
Dolan, Patrick J., Ph.D., S.T.D. (L)

Very Rev.—
Donohoe, Richard E. (BIR)

Revs.—
Farley, Daniel H. (LC)
Fehn, Jerome W. (STP)
Feltz, John G. (BUR)
Foster, Thomas J. (DUL)
Giese, Samuel C. (WDC)
Gonzalez, Julio Angel (MGZ)
Hebert, Donald J. (SY)
Holzhauser, John J. (SFS)
Janecek, James E. (CC)
Jaramillo, Peter (AMA)
Kilmurray, Fintan J. (BLX)
Kozen, Bert S. (SCR)
Lang, James Paul (Y)
Leone, William B. (ROC)
Lindsay, Michael P. (LSC)
Lippstock, Paul Eldon (DUB)
Lomax, Mark (NO)
Machnik, Theodore F. (COL)
McGinnis, James J. (PH)
McHugh, Donald (P) (Retired)
McShane, James J. (BUR)
Metzdorf, William C. (WDC)
Mink, John J. (WIL)
Moran, Michael F. (MIL)
Murphy, David F. (WIL)
Nash, James (WIL)
Neuman, Eugene C. (MIL)
Operts, David P. (SUP)
Pelletier, George C. (PRT)
Repenning, Robert B. (NY)
Rivera-Saez, Adalin (PCE)
Roberson, Henry (OKL)
Rubiano, Cesar A., C.J.M.
Russo, Ricardo, O.F.M. (SFE)

Very Rev.—
Safko, Gerard F., V.F. (SCR)

Revs.—
Sanchez-Munoz, Alejandro (STV)
Skufca, Ronald J. (MAR)
Smith, Gabriel J. (CHR)
Sparks, Kenneth A. (PIT)
Stang, William J., C.PP.S. (LFT)
Steiner, John W. (LC)
Tamalis, John J. (SCR)
Tetreault, Raymond A. (PRO)
Thompson, Richard B. (MAN)
Vigil, Michael A. (GLP)
Worster, John R. (B)
Kane, Brian P.

Army Reserve Chaplains:

Most Rev.—
Listecki, Jerome E. (CHI)

Rev. Msgrs.—
Giordani, Mark J. (PAT)
Midura, Francis S., M.Div., J.C.D. (RVC)
Molloy, Thomas E. (RVC)

Revs.—
Arens, John F. (BO)
Augustyn, Boguslaw Adam, C.SS.R. (MET)
Betz, James F. (CAM)
Bucon, Raymond H. (DET)
Darling, William G. (ROC)
De Guzman, Dennis (OM)
De Rouchey, Gary K. (SFS)
Denemark, Emil J., S.J.
DeSanctis, Peter A. (BRK)
Desmond, David A. (SFS)
Dinello, John E. (PIT)
Dolbec, Jacques D., S.O.L.T.
Dziedzic, Gerald H. (HRT)
Fitzgibbons, Peter L. (CHL)
Grice, Edward M. (NO)
Hudak, Thomas R. (SCR)
Kane, Edward R. (BRK)
Kean, james F. (DET)
Kinnane, James F. (HRT)
Kneemiller, William C. (DAV)
Krische, James J. (BRK)
Lambert, Theodore (Sri Lanka)
Larche, James M. (OG)
Lee, Sang Yil (AUS)
Mahalic, Philip A. (LFT)
McCabe, Edward D. (BO)
McConville, James P. (STP)
Medairos, Anthony J. (BO)
Morse, Jonathan K. (STF)
Ndubuisi, John (GAL)
Nolan, Kevin L., V.F. (LA)
Orlandi, Joseph J. (PAT)
Pamula, Robert (Poland)
Pfeiffer, Carl, O.SS.T. (BAL)
Pilsner, Peter R. (NY)
Piontkowski, Richard L., Jr., S.T.L., J.C.L. (GI)
Plaushin, Mark, O.S.F.S. (PH)
Posey, Thaddeus J., O.S.F.S.
Rodriguez, Rafael A. (CGS)
Rossetti, Mark T. (SCR)
Scully, Richard D. (AMA)
Silva, Luis (CR)
Sousa, Peter E., C.SS.R. (VEN)
Sta.Maria, Nicanor, aaa

Very Rev.—
Staszewski, Joseph P., V.F. (E)

Revs.—
Tyhovych, Ivan (STF)
Wagner, William C. (CIN)
Ziemkiewicz, Frank, O.S.B. (E)

UNITED STATES AIR FORCE CHAPLAINS

Regular Air Force Chaplains:

Rev. Msgrs.—
Cusack, John J. (PAT)
McCahon, Joseph F.S. (SP)
Montecalvo, Carlo F. (PRO)

Revs.—
Abbot, Kerry M., O.F.M.Conv.
Adversario, Efran F. (AGN)
Angelo, Thomas M. (NOR)
Bailey, J. Lawrence (SEA)
Bartoul, William (SAM)
Beale, Kenneth R. (NEW)
Beck, R. Patrick (BEA)
Berthelette, Ernest H. (PRO)
Biewend, Michael, C.J. (SAT)
Blazek, Eugene (HON)
Bochnak, Zenon A. (MET)
Booth, Stephen R., M.M. (NY)
Breig, Gary R. (STL)
Bruno, Robert A., O.F.M.
Butler, Timothy A. (BO)
Charbonneau, William R. (HRT)

Cody, Kevin W. (MAN)
Cote, David P. (PRT)
Czartorynski, David F. (ALN)
Decker, James D. (MAN)
Deichert, Joseph (BIS)
Del Toro, Jose L., T.O.R.
Diab, Thomas P. (SAN)
Diphe, Juan M. (HEL)
Dunn, Richard B. (SY)
Erickson, Richard M. (BO)
Fadallan, Elbert A. (LUB)
Fey, Thomas J. (LUB)
Fitz-Patrick, David M. (WDC)
Fitzgerald, Richard M. (R)
Fletcher, Patrick (PCE)
Gallagher, Robert A. (STU)
Garcia, Gildardo (Colombia)
George, George C. (AUS)
Gills, Thomas (BAL)
Glaros, Matthew J. (CLV)
Gosselin, Lawrence (NTN)
Guico, Maual R. (SJF)
Hall, Douglas C. (OM)
Hamel, James A. (NEW)
Hanley, Dennis P. (HRT)
Hanrahan, William P. (NEW)
Harbour, Linn S. (MOB)
Higginbotham, Robert (BLX)
Hochreiter, Robert S. (SCR)
Ippolito, Robert F., M.S. (HRT)
Jarman, Glenn M., C.P.M.
King, Martin (P)
Kinney, John M. (LFT)
Kovalcin, John A. (STL)
Kruse, David B. (BAL)
Kuan, Joseph S. (Philippines)
Kurzak, John F. (SC)
Lambert, Peter S. (DUL)
Lim, Joseph D. (Philippines)
Linsky, Gary S. (CHR)
Llanos, Phillip S. (LA)
Ludwikoski, James E. (KCK)
McManus, Gerald D. (PH)
Mikalofsky, Hilarion A. (MIL)
Monagle, Robert J. (BO)
Moreno, Antonio O., O.F.M.Conv.
Motsay, Joseph R. (SCR)
Mueller, Jerome D., O.F.M.
Munsell, Richard F. (GF)
Nolan, John (SFD)
Novotny, Richard (RC)
O'Neill, Michael F. (NO)
Omana, Max B. (Philippines)
Pieczara, Stanislaw (Poland)
Raux, Redmond P. (BO)
Reeson, David G. (OM)
Rigonan, Antonio R. (Philippines)
Roberts, Randall, O.F.M. (GB)
Rowan, Mark P. (RVC)
Salditos, Ricardito P. (Philippines)
Sanchez, Albert N. (Philippines)
Sanchez, Raul N. (GLP)
Schnipke, Eugene H., C.PP.S. (CIN)
Srode, John S., C.PP.S. (CIN)
Strzadala, Wieslaw P., S.D.S.
Theisen, Eugene J. (STP)
Thomas, James P. (ALN)
Toledo, Nelson T. (Philippines)
Torres-Graciana, Ivan J. (SJN)
Tran, Joseph J. (RIC)
Underwood, Gary E. (TUC)
Vitaliano, Dominic J. (PEO)
Voelker, David A. (BEL)
Volmi, Dennis G. (WIL)
Voyt, Stephen A. (PT)
Vu, J.P. Minh (TLS)
Wallroth, Joseph R., O.Carm. (JOL)
Weber, Michael J., O.Praem. (GB)
Zeller, Leonard H. (BAL)
Zielinski, Chad W. (GAY)
Zygadlo, Mitchell (ROC)

Air National Guard Chaplains:
Revs.—
Amora, Edito D. (Phil)
Barnhill, Robert K. (LIN)
Barry, Robert L., O.P. (CHI)
Belanger, Gerald R. (MAN)
Bergbower, Daniel J. (SFD)
Very Rev.—
Brubaker, George J., J.C.L. (WIL)
Revs.—
Butler, Michael T. (STL)
Casaleggio, David E. (LAV)
Collins, Thomas E. (NY)
Cooney, Patrick, O.S.B. (IND)
Crowley, Edmund G. (MAN)
De La Rosa, Jose Luis (SAT)
Decker, Douglas A. (OG)
Echert, John P., S.S.L. (STP)
Evans, James L. (AUS)
Fitzgerald, John P. (PIT)
Fuller, Timothy (OKL)
Gomez, Walter (ARE)
Henke, Donald E. (STL)
Humenay, Robert L. (E)
Jackson, Robert H. (CLV)
Jeselnick, Stephen E. (E)
Keller, Robert J. (DET)
Kinney, Thomas E., J.C.L. (NO)
Laible, Jeffrey G. (PEO)
LaMorte, Joseph P. (NY)
Ludwig, Thomas (KC)
Marciano, Robert L. (PRO)
Martinez, Michael (TUC)
Mathis, Raymond P. (SY)
McGuire, Stephen J. (NYC)
McKenna, Timothy (SEA)
Mizeur, Thomas (PEO)
Moenkedick, Leo (SCL)
Moran, Edward (RIC)
Nguyen, Joseph D. (NOR)
Ortiz, Gary (SFE)
Pleiness, Gregg A. (LAN)
Ross, Joseph R. (OKL)
Schaff, Tyrone J. (SPK)
Shea, Michael J. (SFE)
Silva, Caesar (HT)
Sirianni, Richard D. (P)
Stephenson, Alfonse J. (PAT)
Stevens, David E. (SFS)
Sutton, Stephen (BAL)
Tirado, Ramon Orlando, C.M. (SJN)
Vialpando, Kenneth L. (SLC)
Weber, Joseph A. (STL)

Air Force Reserve Chaplains:
Revs.—
Bailey, Douglas S., S.D.S. (ORL)
Baratelli, David J., Ed.D. (NEW)
Beers, John Michael, Ph.D. (ALN)
Blair, Stephen N. (England)
Brosk, Steven J. (NEW)
Caggianelli, Gregg (VEN)
Very Rev.—
Cannon, Robert R., J.C.L., M.Th. (VEN)
Revs.—
Chimiak, Karl A. (WDC)
Coogan, Roch A., O.F.M. (SP)
Cordery, Robert J. (BOS)
Coulthard, Gregory, S.D.S. (GB)
Very Rev.—
Crotty, Desmond G., V.F. (NO)
Revs.—
Cuevas, Randy M., S.T.L. (BR)
Dean, James N. (MOB)
Dinh, Van (OAK)
Drabek, Howard E. (GAL)
Fernandes, Stephen A. (FR)
Fischer, Richard O. (BAK)
Fitzpatrick, Robert M. (OM)
Fredericks, Michael (SB)
Gaglione, John R. (BUF)
Gallagher, John P. (DAV)
Garcia, Millan (SFE)
Herbert, G. Paul, J.C.L. (WDC)
Hewes, Robert S. (RVC)
Hirten, Timothy (BRK)
Hoffmann, Christopher (ORL)
Jaeger, James P. (ROC)
Johnson, James B. (SP)
Jones, Michael T. (WDC)
Kadera, Thomas (CHY)
Kahlich, Daniel P. (SAT)
Kaim, Phillip (RCK)
Kaszczak, Ivan (STF)
Kayatta, Francis P. (PRO)
Kelleher, Mark A. (WIL)
Kelly, Thomas D. (DEN)
Kowalik, Jacek (VEN)
Kuczborski, Joseph M. (PMB)
Laroche, Christopher J. (PRT)
Lilly, Thomas C. (ANC)
Lordemann, Francis W. (OM)
Lowe, Francis E. (SB)
Mack, John P. (BUF)
Maikowski, Thomas R. (GLP)
Malloy, Francis X. (MIL)
McDonald, G. Malcom (PIT)
McDowell, Leo G. (GF)
McGrade, Kevin M. (BO)
McGuill, Martin F. (ARL)
McGuine, Peter M. (SD)
McHugh, Brian J. (BO)
McNamara, Brian J. (RVC)
Medas, Michael B. (BO)
Mescher, Michael J. (DUB)
Mockler, Patrick J. (BLX)
Moore, William C. (STO)
Morrow, Michael J. (NY)
O'Hara, Daniel J. (SY)
Osinski, Ronald V. (ALT)
Padazinski, Michael C., J.C.D. (SFR)
Parker, Paul R. (BOS)
Randall, Kevin S. (NOR)
Richtsteig, Erik John (SLC)
Robbins, Thomas P. (COV)
Sable, Robert M. (DET)
Schultz, Charles F., S.T.D. (SB)
Sewell, Jack (ORG)
Sickler, Robert, M.S.A. (NOR)
Stakem, Ward G., O.F.M.Cap. (PIT)
Stewart, Paul (PT)
Sweeney, Daniel, S.J. (MD)
Tero, Richard D. (ANC)
Tomasiewicz, Mark A. (OM)
Tran, Luan Quach (P)
Travers, Patrick J., J.C.L., J.D. (JUN)
Urnick, Charles B. (NEW)
Valko, George J. (ALT)
Vaverek, Hayden J. (CHR)
Wedeking, Patrick (GLP)
Willette, Donald C. (DEN)
Wulinski, Stanley F. (BRK)
Zalewski, Peter Lawrence (PT)

UNITED STATES NAVY CHAPLAINS

Regular Navy Chaplains:
Rev. Msgr.—
Gomulka, Eugene T. (HON)
Revs.—
Aguilera, Salvador (ELP)
Bargola, Cerino O. (Philippines)
Barrett, Miles J. (SC)
Biala, Romeo B. (SEA)
Borger, Marvin G., J.C.L. (TOL)
Borzych, Alexander J. (GI)
Boucher, Roger R. (WOR)
Boyle, Dennis P. (PH)
Brown, Benedict J. (L)
Brown, Lewis E. (ROC)
Brown, Shaun S. (NTN)
Brzek, Jon J. (PIT)
Burnette, John C. (SFD)
Caiazzo, Gregory G. (RIC)
Cain, Robert K.C. (TLS)
Carlos, Joseph, O.F.M. (STL)
Coffey, Joseph L. (PH)
Concha, Alfonso J. (PH)
Connolly, James M.T. (ALN)
Cowan, Steven (RIC)
Coyle, Robert (RVC)
Creider, Philip B. (OKL)
Cuddy, William F. (BO)
Cunha, Egionor (NEW)
Cusick, Kevin M. (WDC)
D'Souza, Matthew F. (India)
Dang, Chin Van (RIC)
Danner, James L. (MEM)
Dansak, Thomas E. (PIT)
Deeley, Kevin J. (BO)
Delis, Robert, S.D.B. (SFR)
Dermott, William R. (ALN)
Diaz, Michael (SD)
Dillon, Jerome V. (OM)
Dory, Michael (GB)
Enriquez, Rean F. (Philippines)
Erestain, Alfonso E. (Philippines)
Estabrook, Joseph (ALB)
Everett, Willis E. (COL)
Evers, Paul H. (HON)
Falkenthal, Thomas W. (CHI)
Ferretti, Sam (CAM)
Finley, James F. (BRK)
Fix, Donald P. (PIT)
Foley, Francis P. (PH)
Fremont-Smith, Peter, S.O.L.T.
Fronk, Christopher S., S.J. (BAL)
Fry, James Q. (ORG)
Gardocki, Patrick M., O.F.M.
Garvey, Michael (Y)
Gay, James A. (BGP)
Gegotek, Tadeusz (BEL)
Geinzer, John A. (PIT)
Gergel, Stephen J. (ALT)
Gervacio, Adrian R. (HON)
Gwudz, John S. (NOR)
Haddad, Wayne M. (MET)
Hall, Thomas P., C.S.P. (NY)
Hannigan, John T. (CHI)
Hellwig, Lee W. (HRT)
Hoedl, John D. (FAR)
Hogan, Timothy D. (DET)
Hoke, John R. (HBG)
Hoog, Eric R., C.SS.R.
House, Richard M. (YAK)
Ianucci, Thomas (RIC)
Iasiello, Louis V., O.F.M. (NY)
Janning, Timothy J. (CIN)
Jennings, Tommie (SD)
Johnson, Charles W., O.Praem.
Johnson, Lawrence P. (DUL)
Joslyn, James W. (CHI)
Kanicki, Philip A. (RIC)
Karava, Norbert, O.F.M.Cap. (PAT)
Kaul, John L. (DET)

Kawcznski, Ronald L. (FAR)
Keane, Robert L., S.J. (BO)
Kelly, Brian F. (SCR)
Kennedy, William M. (BO)
Kersten, Jay J. (LAN)
Kienzle, Jerome C. (MIL)
Klepacki, Michael S. (CHL)
Kloak, David G. (CHI)
Koch, Joseph A., C.V.
Koester, Timothy J. (BUF)
Kuss, Allen R. (BIS)
Lamonde, Joseph R. (PIT)
Lee, John T.M. (WDC)
Lesak, William P. (NEW)
Lindblad, Karl-Albert (NY)
Linehan, Stephen J. (BO)
Logan, Aidan Archur H., O.C.S.O. (WOR)
Lopes, Richard, O.F.M.Cap. (SFR)
Lott, Lawrence M. (MOB)
Lyle, John W., O.S.F.S. (WIL)
Malene, Robert (E)
Mandato, Kieran (NY)
Mayfield, Olin (LA)
McClanahan, Robert P., Jr. (PT)
McCord, Kent G. (MET)
McCormick, Patrick J. (ATL)
McGeory, Peter (NY)
McKenzie, John H., O.S.B.
McLaughlin, Paul F. (VEN)
Medve, Kenneth A. (ALN)
Mensah, Gabriel (VIC)
Merris, Christopher (SD)
Mikstay, Michael (Y)
Moss, Donald G. (AUS)
Mudd, David A. (WDC)
Mueller, Michael (ORL)
Muhm, William M. (NY)
Mulkerin, Terrence J. (BRK)
Neis, William P. (LC)
Nguyen, An Binh Joseph (Vietnam)
Nielson, Karl, O.S.B. (P)
Onuh, William I. (Nigeria)
Osuju, Samuel D. (Nigeria)
Parisi, Michael (PAT)
Petruska, William M. (SCR)
Pimental, Joseph W., O.P.
Reardon, Joseph D. (KC)
Remy, David P. (DUB)
Rendon, Matthias, O.F.M.
Rock, Stephen B. (BO)
Rodes, Kenneth J.
Russo, Lawrence J. (BO)
Salamoni, Vincent, M.S.A. (NOR)
Scordo, Joseph Anthony, O.P. (NY)
Shaughnessy, Paul J., S.J. (BAL)
Shimotsu, John M. (ORG)
Shuley, Keith J. (CC)
Simpson, Brian L. (CHI)
Smith, S. Douglas, C.S.C. (FTW)
Soto, Charles, O.F.M. (NY)
Spencer, Robert A. (CHR)
St. George, Peter T. (CIN)
Stake, Ronald P. (CHI)
Steed, Donald R., M.M. (NY)
Suellentrop, Anthony J. (DOD)
Sweeney, Kevin (ORG)
Tiongson, Joselito S. (Philippines)
Tran, Philip P. (NY)
Trapani, Anthony M. (RVC)
Travers, Alan (NY)
Ubalde, Ulysses L. (NEW)
Vanden Boogard, Richard J., O.Praem.
Vidrine, Richard (LAF)
Walsh, Francis E. (SPR)
Welch, Bernard J. (PRT)
Wheatley, R. Carroll (OWN)
Yagesh, Richard C. (PIT)
Zuffoletto, Michael P. (BUF)

Navy Reserve Chaplains:
Most Rev.—
Seminack, Richard S., D.D. (STN)
Rev. Msgr.—
Keenan, Patrick J. (NY)
Revs.—
Baggetta, Joseph J. (BO)
Barber, Michael C., S.J. (SFR)
Barch, Howard C. (PEO)
Bergner, David J., S.D.S. (WDC)
Bishop, Marc J. (BO)
Bower, Lawrence C. (BAK)
Brighenti, Kenneth D. (MET)
Calderone, Joseph D., O.S.A. (PH)
Camarda, Ronald A. (STA)
Cannon, Richard E. (BO)
Carrington, Richard J. (NEW)
Cheney, James W. (FAR)
Cienik, Kenneth, S.A. (WDC)
Clark, Robert J., O.S.B.
Clovis, Stephen M. (P)
Condon, William G., C.S.C. (FR)
Cricchio, Santo, O.F.M.Conv.
D'Aurora, Joseph (RIC)
DeSocio, John A. (ROC)
Dhein, William A. (LC)
Donohoe, Stephen S. (BO)
Very Rev.—
Donohue, Michael T. (NOR)
Revs.—
Doyle, Michael J. (BO)
Duesterhaus, Michael R. (ARL)
Emechete, Innocent (Nigeria) (SAC)
Ethen, Jeffrey D. (SCL)
Foote, Job, O.S.B. (ALT)
Gayton, John J., M.I.C.
Glassmire, David Richard (BUF)
Griffin, Thomas, O.S.A. (CHI)
Hamaday, Ronald A., O.S.A. (CAM)
Hernandez, Henry L. (LA)
Hussey, Daniel C. (GLP)
Johnson, Patrick D., C.S.P.
Judge, Timothy M. (PH)
Kantor, Robert Joseph (VEN)
Kehoe, James P. (CHI)
Kilian, Waldemar Aleksander (CHI)
Klarer, Michael E. (MAD)
Kucharczyk, Dennis H. (SAG)
Labo, Timothy P. (ORL)
Ladniak, Lawrence J. (CHI)
Langan, William J.P. (SCR)
Lavastida, Jose I., S.T.D., S.T.L. (NO)
Legaspi, Alex L. (SFR)
Madey, Louis (LAN)
McCandless, William T., O.S.F.S. (WIL)
McCann, Thomas M. (NO)
Mode, Daniel L. (ARL)
Morris, Michael P. (NY)
Murray, Gerald E. (NY)
Neitzke, Eon P. (JOL)
Nenneau, Thomas D. (LAN)
Nguyen, Van T. (NO)
O'Brien, Sean Patrick (SY)
O'Connell, Terry J. (P)
O'Neill, John J. (SFR)
Parenti, Thomas M. (SFR)
Peek, Joseph (ATL)
Porpiglia, Joseph D. (BUF)
Reamer, Mark G., O.F.M. (R)
Reilly, Mark R. (OG)
Reitmeyer, Todd (SFS)
Robichaud, Paul G., C.S.P.
Rogers, Patrick W. (COL)
Seminack, Richard S. (PHI)
Sera, Enrique J. (ORG)
Slowinski, Thomas F. (DET)
Smith, Lawrence C., S.J. (BO)
Smith, Lawrence H. (MET)
Stefula, Salvator M., aaa
Very Rev.—
Sullivan, Robert J. (BIR)
Revs.—
Sweeney, Luke M. (NY)
Thorne, Thomas P. (BGP)
Wallace, Richard (P)
Weise, Thomas J. (JUN)
Winters, Darvin E. (IND)

AUXILIARY CHAPLAINS CONTRACT CHAPLAINS:
Most Rev.—
Listecki, Jerome E. (CHI)
Rev. Msgrs.—
Hallisey, James T. (B)
Metsy, Norman G. (PRO) (Retired)
O'Keeffe, Richard W. (TUC)
Sego, Arthur (LFT)
Smith, Thomas H., V.F. (HBG)
Revs.—
Ahern, John J. (CHI)
Anderson, James W., M.S.A.
Arminio, Alfonse (NEW)
Ashe, Michael B. (CC)
Ashkar, Dominic (SAM)
Bauer, John J., C.SS.R.
Borger, Theodore R. (DAV) (Retired)
Boyle, Patrick J., S.J., Ph.D. (CHI)
Cervinski, Paul L. (BIS)
Chong, Young-Ku (Korea, South)
Covarrubias, Raul R. (B)
Cowart, Conrad (STA)
Crandall, Thomas (PT)
Cuneo, James J. (DEN) (Retired)
Dillman, Alan M. (ATL) (Retired)
Dorney, James J. (NY)
Drury, Michael P., C.O. (MRY)
Very Rev.—
Dunham, Larry C., O.F.M. (SFE)
Revs.—
Edwards, R. Dale (FWT)
Farias, Joseph G. (PAT)
Ferrer, Gonzalo, T.O.R. (AUS)
Freidl, Thomas (CR)
Gaeta, David (SLC)
Gagliardo, Anthony F. (BUF) (Retired)
Gnall, Joseph, O.S.B.
Goellen, Richard M. (FAR)
Gribbon, Joseph, C.SS.R. (ALB)
Grothjan, James K., C.PP.S.
Habenight, James F., M.M.
Hacker, Louis, O.S.B.
Hamilton, Thomas M., S.M. (SFR)
Hickey, Dennis W., C.S.P. (NY)
Intranuovo, Ralph, S.C.J. (GAL)
Jacobi, Joseph A. (OKL)
Jelinek, Anthony J. (CHI)
Kearney, Thomas L., O.P.
Kelley, Thomas W., O.S.F.S.
Kelley, William J., S.V.D.
Kelty, Edward J., O.S. (PCE)
Kettle, Laurence, O.F.M. (Ireland)
Kieffer, Thomas, C.O.
Krick, Howard (PHI)
Kucera, Edward J., O.S.B. (JOL)
Kuchar, Matthew, O.S.B.
Kukucka, Joseph G. (PBL) (Retired)
Labo, Timothy P. (ORL)
Lamendola, Salvatore R., M.Div. (GBG)
Lane, Timothy R., C.J. (LA)
Langston, Micheas, O.S.B. (IND)
Lawson, Ronald (Canada)
Lenihan, Michael (CC)
Loftus, Conrad W., O.F.M. (NY)
Lombard, Richard J. (SHP)
Maddineni, Ananda Prasad, M.S.F. (India) (ATL)
Majerus, Daniel (SCL) (Retired)
Malnar, Matthew (MIL)
Mandock, Patrick H. (GBG)
Marcantonio, Clement (PBL) (Retired)
Marsh, John, C.SS.R.
Martin, Michael, O.S.B.
Martinez-Navarro, Modesto, T.C.
Martire, Leonardo (Argentina)
Massoth, Charles, O.S.B.
McCormick, Thomas, S.J.
McGrath, John R. (BLX)
McGrath, Thomas (BLX)
McLeod, David H. (PAT)
Merfeld, Vincent (DUB)
Messaro, Michael A., M.SS.CC. (HBG)
Metzbower, Francis X., S.J. (BAL)
Middendorf, Cyril G., S.M. (CIN)
Morley, John M. (NEW) (Retired)
Morris, John J. (NEW) (Retired)
Mulhern, Joseph P., O.P.
Nakireru, Omoviekobwa A. (Nigeria)
O'Loughlin, Michael, S.S.C.
O'Meara, Henry R., C.SS.R.
O'Neill, Joseph, M.M.
O'Shea, Gerard D. (STA)
Olson, Benedict, O.P.
Ondo, Michael A. (LFT)
Perumpilly, Marcel (Bahrain)
Phillips, Christopher (SA)
Phillips, Randall (DET)
Picard, Norman, C.I.C.M.
Piskura, Joseph (CLV) (Retired)
Potter, Gerald L. (FAR)
Power, Bernard, C.SS.R. (ALB)
Quinlivan, Francis L., C.S.C.
Regan, John J. (BO) (Retired)
Reigel, William A., C.S.B.
Richardson, Edward, S.M.A. (NEW)
Rimmele, Leo, O.S.B. (P)
Roberson, Ronald G., C.P.
Rokusek, Robert J. (DET)
Sanders, Peter, C.O.
Saucci, Robert R., M.M.
Schmidt, Raymond F. (BRK)
Schreiber, Gerard, C.SS.R.
Shay, Michael, S.D.S. (TUC)
Shay, Robert M., S.T.
Simonelli, Bruno, O.F.M.Cap.
Smith, Ignatius E., O.F.M. (NY)
Sousa, Peter E., C.SS.R. (VEN)
Spiteri, Joseph (Panama)
St. Pierre, Romeo A. (PRT) (Retired)
Stadmueller, Roman, S.D.S.
Succi, Vincento, O.F.M.Cap.
Sueper, Alban, S.S.C. (OM)
Sullivan, Alan, O.F.M. (NY)
Thelen, Robert (BRK)
Thomas, Donald (HON) (Retired)
Thorne, Carroll W., C.P.
Tomas, Francisco
Vaz, Rock I., S.J.
Waite, Patrick J. (SC) (Retired)
Walljasper, Mark A. (LC) (Retired)
Wood, Michael (SA)
Woster, Michael B. (RC)
Zinzer, Walter W. (STL) (Retired)
Friar—
Victor, Gerard, O.F.M.

DEPARTMENT OF VETERANS AFFAIRS HOSPITALS AND CHAPLAINS Rev. Paul S. Holt, Assoc. Dir., National VA Chap. Svc. & Special Liaison of

Military Archdiocese to VA.
ALABAMA
Birmingham Vacant (GB).
Montgomery Rev. David J. Tokarz (MOB).
Tuscaloosa Vacant (GB).
Tuskegee Rev. David J. Tokarz (MOB).
ARIZONA
Phoenix Revs. Mathias J. Crehan, O.F.M., Kenneth R. Kleiber (CHI).
Prescott Rev. Gerald Caffrey, C.M.F. (PHX).
Tucson Rev. David H. Reinders (TUC).
ARKANSAS
Fayetteville Vacant (GB).
North Little Rock Rev. Victor E. Bertrand, C.S.V. (LR).
CALIFORNIA
Fresno Vacant (GB).
Loma Linda Rev. Leonard J. Mestas (BWN).
Martinez Rev. William Johnson (OAK).
Palo Alto Revs. John Kenneth Coleman (SFR), Augustine Koilparampil (India) (OAK), James M. Stump, O.F.M.Cap. (SFR).
San Diego Revs. Patrick J. Durkin, C.S.V., Charles R. Eis (SPK) (Retired), Theodore Gryga (SY), Jerry Hamperzonian (PSC).
San Francisco Rev. Richard C. Bain (SFR).
Sepulveda Vacant (GB).
West Los Angeles Rev. Max Ernesto M. Saldua (Philippines).
COLORADO
Denver Rev. Roland P. Freeman (DEN).
Fort Lyon Vacant (GB).
Grand Junction Vacant (GB). **CONNECTICUT**
Newington Vacant (GB).
West Haven Rev. Daniel Scott, M.S.
DELAWARE
Wilmington Revs. Sean P. Connery, O.S.F.S. (WIL), William B. Kauffman (WIL).
DISTRICT OF COLUMBIA
Washington, D.C. Rev. Jonathan D. Lao (Philippines) (WDC).
FLORIDA
Bay Pines Rev. Thomas M. Dieter (JOL).
Gainesville Rev. Dennis M. Young (STA).
Lake City Vacant (GB).
Miami Revs. Rinaldo Damian (WOR), E. Matthew Turk, S.J.
Tampa Rev. Edward Lamp (SP).
West Palm Beach Rev. Joseph B. Westfall (LFT).
GEORGIA
Augusta Revs. Allan J. McDonald (SAV), Thomas J. Peyton (SAV).
Decatur Vacant (GB).
Dublin Vacant (GB).
IDAHO
Boise Vacant (GB).
ILLINOIS
Chicago-Lakeside Rev. Christopher P. Myers, S.O.L.T.
Chicago-West Side Rev. Robert J. Borre (MAD).
Danville Rev. John Schultz (LFT).
Hines Rev. James Burnett (DAV).
Marion Vacant (GB).
North Chicago Rev. William F. Vander Heyden (GB). **INDIANA**
Fort Wayne Rev. Daniel R. Leeuw (FTW).
Indianapolis Revs. Joseph Kiene, O.F.M.Conv., Gordon P. Wagoner (LFT).
Marion Rev. Joseph W. Grace (FTW).
IOWA
Des Moines Rev. Samuel I. Palmer (DM) (Retired).
Iowa City Revs. Rudolph C. Berndt (DAV), Louis J. Leonhart (DAV), Brian J. Shepley (DAV).
Knoxville Rev. Mark P. Spring (DAV). **KANSAS**
Leavenworth Rev. Carrol W. Thorne, C.P. (MET).
Topeka Rev. James Moster, O.F.M.Cap. (KCK).
Wichita Rev. H. Patrick Malone (WCH).
KENTUCKY
Lexington Rev. Wilton Henry Kenney, S.J.
Louisville Rev. Simon D. Sauer, O.F.M.Conv. (L).
LOUISIANA
Alexandria Revs. Stephen J. Brandow (ALX), Christudas A. Nayak (India).
New Orleans Rev. Edmund Akordor (Ghana).
Shreveport Rev. Philip Michiels (ALX).
MAINE
Togus Rev. Raymond R. Lagace, O.F.M. (PRT).
MARYLAND
Baltimore Revs. Paul J. Henry (ORL), Edward T. Hill (BAL) (Retired), William J. Moorman, O.SS.T.
Loch Raven Rev. Conan H. Timoney, C.P. (BAL).
Perry Point Revs. Keith A. Brehob, S.J. (BAL), Paul Henry (BAL), Jeffrie S. Reynolds (BIR).
MASSACHUSETTS
Bedford Revs. Philip A. Cabasino, C.SS.R. (BO), Joseph P. Robinson (BO), Sebastian A. Ugochukwu (Nigeria).
Boston Rev. Philip Salois (FR).
Brockton Revs. Avelino R. Garcia (SP), Henry P. Nichols (BO).
Northhampton Rev. Lionel E. Bonneville (SPR).
MICHIGAN
Ann Arbor Revs. Darin T. Robert (LAN), Quang Minh Tran (SAV), Vincent VanDoan (LAN).
Battle Creek Rev. Patrick E. Murphy (MAR).
Detroit Rev. Joseph Duc Vu (Vietnam).
Iron Mountain Vacant (GB).
Saginaw Revs. Richard E. Jozwiak (SAG), Joseph A. Schabel (SAG) (Retired).
MINNESOTA
Minneapolis Revs. Joseph Safraniec (STU), Gerald F. (Damien) Schill (FAR).
St. Cloud Rev. Alfred E. Stangl (SCL).
MISSISSIPPI
Biloxi Revs. Joseph A. Dilettuso (BLX), Anthony Menz, O.C.S.O. (SPC).
Jackson Rev. Daniel N. Gallagher (JKS).
MISSOURI
Columbia Rev. Edwin J. Cole (JC).
Kansas City Rev. Ambrose G. Karels (KC) (Retired).
Poplar Bluff Rev. Michael V. McDevitt, M.A. (SPC).
St. Louis Revs. George P. Brennan (STL), Patrick J. Christopher (STL), John H. Schneider (STL).
MONTANA
Fort Harrison Vacant (GB).
Miles City Vacant (GB).
NEBRASKA
Grand Island Revs. Donald O'Brien (GI), Walter M. Phelan (GI) (Retired).
Omaha Rev. Msgr. Richard A. Wolbach (OM) (Retired).
NEVADA
Las Vegas Rev. Gerard J. McNulty (LA).
Reno Vacant (GB).
NEW HAMPSHIRE
Manchester Revs. William J. Hamilton, S.J. (MAN), Maurice R. Lacroix (MAN) (Retired).
NEW JERSEY
East Orange Revs. Mathew Eraly (India), George F. Kelly, C.SS.R.
Lyons Revs. Joseph C. Chacko, William Warman (BAL).
NEW MEXICO
Albuquerque Rev. David O. Klein, C.S.B.
NEW YORK
Albany Revs. John Minkler (ALB), Dominick Ntsiful-Amissah (ALB), Charles S. San Fratello, O.F.M.
Batavia Rev. Ivan R. Trujillo (BUF).
Bath Rev. Martin D. Smith (STU).
Bronx Revs. Roland P. LaFontant (France), Gregory Lyttle (NY), Rev. Msgr. Joseph J. Zammit (NY).
Brooklyn Revs. Thomas J. Mullin (NY), Stephen Shubiak (STF), Andrew Sioleti, i.v.dei., Rev. Msgr. Vito Tiboni (NEW).
Buffalo Rev. Richard F. Sowinski (BUF).
Canandaigua Revs. William J. Cosgrove (ROC), Martin D. Smith (STU).
Castle Point Revs. Uldarico De la Pena (Philippines), Raymond A. Pavlick (PAT).
Montrose Revs. John W. Hickey (NY), Robert D. Tracy, O.Carm. (NY).
New York City Revs. Pasquale V. Laghezza, SS.CC. (NY), Andrew Sioleti, i.v.dei.
Northport Revs. John S. Malone, C.S.Sp., John A. Rich, M.M. (NY).
Syracuse Rev. Msgr. Wilfred F. Evans (SY), Rev. David J. James (SY).
NORTH CAROLINA
Asheville Rev. Frank J. Seabo (CHL).
Durham Vacant (GB).
Fayetteville Vacant (GB).
Salisbury Rev. Thomas P. Clements (CHL) (Retired).
NORTH DAKOTA
Fargo Vacant (GB).
OHIO
Chillicothe Revs. Richard F. Engle (COL) (Retired), Joseph O. Vazhupadickal, S.A.C. (COL).
Cincinnati Revs. Luke U. Odor (Nigeria), Warren Zeisler, O.F.M. (CIN).
Cleveland Revs. John Bolan, C.PP.S. (CIN), L. David Mani (India).
Dayton Revs. John J. Butler (HON), George V. Uralikunnel (India).
OKLAHOMA
Muskogee Vacant (GB).
Oklahoma City Vacant (GB).
OREGON
Portland Rev. William E. Wickham, C.S.C. (P).
Roseburg Vacant (GB).
White City Revs. Donald H. Salisbury, O.P., Joseph E. Shirey, S.J. (P).
PENNSYLVANIA
Altoona Rev. David R. Becker (ALT).
Butler Revs. Marvin L. Justi, O.F.M.Cap. (PIT), William J. Ritzert (PIT).
Coatesville Revs. Lawrence Gould, S.A.C., Joseph S. Hasieber (ALX).
Erie Revs. Robert G. Craig (E) (Retired), Thomas M. Fialkowski (E).
Lebanon Rev. James N. Drucker (PSC).
Philadelphia Revs. Edward V. Griffin, O.S.A. (PH), James E. King (NTN) (Retired), Michael A. Lipareli (NY).
Pittsburgh-Highland Drive Revs. Frank A. Mitolo (PIT), Emett J. Schuler, O.F.M.Cap. (PIT).
Pittsburgh-University Drive Revs. Robert N. Craig, O.F.M.Cap. (PIT), Mark W. Glasgow (PIT).
Wilkes-Barre Rev. Stephen J. Stavoy (SCR).
RHODE ISLAND
Providence Rev. Francis J. Crowley (BO).
SOUTH CAROLINA
Charleston Rev. William C. Burn (CHR) (Retired).
Columbia Vacant (GB).
SOUTH DAKOTA
Fort Meade Rev. Paul Dahms (RC).
Hot Springs Rev. Thomas J. Tierney, S.J. (RC).
Sioux Falls Rev. Kenneth J. Koster (SFS).
TENNESSEE
Memphis Vacant (GB).
Mountain Home Vacant (GB).
Murfreesboro Vacant (GB).
Nashville Rev. James Norman Miller (NSH).
TEXAS
Amarillo Vacant (GB).
Big Spring Rev. Richard J. Regan (SAN).
Bonham Rev. Felix F. Vistal (DAL).
Dallas Rev. Timothy A. Gollob (DAL).
Houston Rev. Clarito Z. Rara, (Tagbilaran, PI).
Kerrville Rev. Michael J. Boulette (SAT).
Marlin Vacant (GB).
San Antonio Revs. Robert M. Chukwu (Nigeria), Marian A. Piekarczyk, S.D.S. (Poland) (SAT), Edward P. Walsh (BIR).
Temple Rev. Richard J. Beyer (DAV).
Waco Rev. Thomas Niemira (JKS).
UTAH
Salt Lake City Rev. Gebran Bou-Merhi (OLL).
VERMONT
White River Junction Revs. Adrien Pelletier, S.M., Ronald Saunders, S.M.
VIRGINIA
Hampton Revs. Donald J. Cavey (RIC), Lloyd F. Stephenson (RIC) (Retired).
Richmond Rev. Msgr. Walter C. Barrett (RIC).
Salem Rev. Constantine L. Silayo (RIC).
WASHINGTON
Seattle Rev. Thomas R. Park, O.S.B. (SEA).
Spokane Vacant (GB).
Tacoma Rev. Leo R. Rimmele, O.S.B. (SEA).
Walla Walla Vacant (GB).
WEST VIRGINIA
Beckley Vacant (GB).
Clarksburg Rev. Peter A. Giannamore (WH).
Huntington Vacant (GB).
Martinsburg Revs. Donald B. Conroy, S.T.L., Ph.D. (GBG), T. Matthew Rowgh (WH).
WISCONSIN
Madison Vacant (GB).
Milwaukee Revs. Edward E. Lisowski (MIL), Norman Oswald (MIL).
Tomah Rev. George Thekkedam (LUB).
WYOMING
Cheyenne Rev. James Doudican (CHY) (Retired).
Sheridan Vacant (GB).
PUERTO RICO
San Juan Rev. Luis A. Lopez-Alvarado (CGS).
CIVIL AIR PATROL:
Most Rev.—
Hurley, Francis T., D.D. (ANC) (Retired)
Rev. Msgr.—
McGuire, Richard J. (E)
Revs.—
Birk, John G. (SPK)
Caron, Edward J., C.SS.P.
DeCrans, Joseph J. (CR)
DeMuro, Salvatore (HRT)
Dupuis, George H. (BUR)
Friederick, John J. (DUB)
Goeser, Peter J., O.S.B.
King, James E. (NEW)
Kovarik, James, O.S.Cam. (MIL)
Lamitie, Robert O. (OG) (Retired)
Obin, Arthur T., O.M.I.
Parker, James (CHR)
Reiter, James (E)
Shortt, David J. (PBR)
Sommer, Allan J. (MIL)
Van Sickler, Robert (BAK)
Wolesky, John A. (SAL)

PERMANENT DEACONS SERVING IN THE ARCHDIOCESE FOR THE MILITARY

AMS Chancery:
Vacant (GB)

Air Force:
Deacons—
Bautista, Teofilo, Jr.
Bonanno, Frederick R.
Crockette, Alvin
Dineen, Terry P.
Elliott, Max R.
Ellis, Billy Joe
Frankenfield, Thomas H.
Henn, Thomas W.
Henry, Lawrence B.
Jachimowicz, John J.
Kieffer, William A.
Kwon, Peter H., Ph.D.
Lopez, Demetrio
Macey, James R.
Manning, Richard M.
McAtee, Ralph H.
McLaughlin, Richard B.
Moragas, Lucien F., Jr.
Murello, Andrew
Neville, Richard F., Jr.
Perry, Robert W.
Pfleger, James W.
Richardson, Walter H.
Scarbo, David B.
Schwerdt, Paul J.
Sekinger, Eugene E.
Sliger, Douglas R.
Yarawsky, William S.

Army:
Deacons—
Barnard, Robert
Bowles, Richard J.
Cardona, David M.
Dew, Joseph M.
Foster, George H.
Jones, Frederick B., Jr.
Marchek, Michael V.
Medrano, Efren
Miller, Larry L.
Plowman, Kent M.
Rienzi, Thomas M.
Rowland, Robert
Schoebel, James
Shuffer, George M.

Navy:
Deacons—
Ditewig, William
Ladouceur, Gerald J.
Nartowicz, Edward C.
Pellosie, John C.
Rauen, Michael J.
Starr, Robert, Sr.
Stigall, Donald R.
Wurm, Eugene L.

Marines:
Deacon—
Hernandez, Nieves J.

Veterans Administration:
Deacons—
Abler, Donald J.
Dixon, Louis
Hare, Martin
Lauer, Paul
Luft, Dennis M.
Martino, Anthony
Miller, Jerome A.
Mills, Hugh H., Jr.
Montgomery, David
Moreira, Adelson
Moseley, Cyrus P.
Salchert, John J.
Stenbeck, John H.

DIOCESES WITH PRIESTS SERVING IN THE ARCHDIOCESE FOR THE MILITARY SERVICES

Albany.
Alexandria.
Allentown.
Altoona-Johnstown.
Arlington.
Atlanta.
Austin.
Baltimore.
Baton Rouge.
Beaumont.
Belleville.
Biloxi.
Birmingham.
Bismarck.
Boston.
Bridgeport.
Brooklyn.
Brownsville.
Buffalo.
Caguas, Puerto Rico.
Camden.
Caroline Islands.
Charleston.
Charlotte.
Cheyenne.
Chicago.
Cincinnati.
Cleveland.
Columbus.
Corpus Christi.
Dallas.
Davenport.
Denver.
Des Moines
Detroit.
Dodge City.
Dubuque.
Duluth.
El Paso.
Erie.
Fargo.
Fort Wayne-South Bend.
Gallup.
Gary.
Gaylord.
Grand Island.
Great Falls-Billings.
Green Bay.
Greensburg.
Harrisburg
Hartford.
Helena.
Honolulu.
Jackson.
Jefferson City.
Joliet.
Kansas City.
Kansas City-St. Joseph.
Knoxville.
LaCrosse.
Lafayette, IN.
Lafayette, LA.
Lansing.
Lincoln.
Los Angeles.
Louisville.
Lubbock.
Madison.
Manchester.
Marquette.
Mayaguez, PR.
Memphis.
Metuchen.
Milwaukee
Mobile.
Nashville.
Newark.
New Orleans.
Newton (Melkite Rite).
New York.
Norwich.
Oakland.
Ogdensburg.
Oklahoma City.
Omaha.
Orange.
Orlando.
Owensboro.
Passaic (Byzantine).
Paterson.
Pensacola-Tallahassee.
Peoria.
Philadelphia.
Pittsburgh
Ponce, Puerto Rico.
Portland, ME.
Portland, OR.
Providence.
Raleigh.
Rapid City.
Reno.
Richmond.
Rochester.
Rockford.
Rockville Centre.
Sacramento.
Saginaw.
St. Augustine.
St. Cloud.
St. Louis.
St. Maron
St. Paul-Minneapolis.
St. Petersburg.
Salt Lake City.
San Angelo.
San Antonio.
San Bernardino.
San Diego.
San Francisco.
San Juan, Puerto Rico.
Savannah.
Scranton.
Seattle.
Sioux City.
Sioux Falls.
Spokane.
Springfield-Cape Girardeau.
Springfield, IL.
Springfield, MA.
Stamford (Ukrainian).
Steubenville.
Superior.
Syracuse.
Toledo.
Trenton.
Tucson.
Tulsa.
Venice.
Victoria.
Washington, D.C..
Wheeling-Charleston.
Wichita.
Wilmington.
Winona.
Worcester.
Yakima.
Youngstown.

COUNTRIES WITH PRIESTS SERVING IN THE ARCHDIOCESE FOR THE MILITARY SERVICES

Africa.
Canada.
Colombia.
Czechoslovakia.
Ecuador.
France.
Ghana.
India.
Nigeria.
Pakistan.
Paraguay.
Peru.
Philippines.
Poland.
United Kingdom.
Vietnam.

RELIGIOUS INSTITUTES WITH PRIESTS SERVING IN THE ARCHDIOCESE FOR THE MILITARY SERVICES

Vincentian Fathers—C.M.
Claretian Missionaries—C.M.F.
Congregation of the Passion—C.P.
Congregation of the Fathers of Mercy—C.P.M.
Society of the Precious Blood—C.PP.S.
Basilian Fathers—C.S.B.
Congregation of the Holy Cross—C.S.C.
Paulist Fathers—C.S.P.
Holy Ghost Fathers—C.S.Sp.
Redemptorist Fathers—C.SS.R.
Viatorian Fathers—C.SS.R.
Legionaries of Christ—L.C.
Congregation of Marians of the Immaculate Conception—M.I.C.
Maryknoll Missioners—M.M.
Missionaries of Our Lady of LaSalette—M.S.
Missionaries of the Holy Apostles—M.S.A.
Missionaries of the Sacred Heart—M.S.C.
Carmelite Fathers—O.Carm.
Cistercians of the Strict Observance—O.C.S.O.
Franciscan Fathers—O.F.M.
Cap. Capuchins—O.F.M.
Conv. Conventual Franciscans—O.F.M.
Order of Preachers—O.P.
Premonstratensian Fathers—O.Praem.
The Augustinians—O.S.A.
Benedictine Fathers—O.Praem.
Oblates of St. Francis de Sales—O.S.F.S.
Trinitarian Fathers—O.SS.T.
Society of the Catholic Apostolate—S.A.C.
Salensian Fathers—S.D.B.
Society of Divine Savior—S.D.S.
Jesuit Fathers—S.J.
Marist Fathers—S.M.
Society of Our Lady of the Most Holy Trinity—S.O.L.T.
Fathers of the Sacred Hearts—SS.CC.
Congregation of the Blessed Sacrament—S.S.S.
Third Order Regular of St. Francis—T.O.R.

ASSOCIATIONS SUPPORTING THE MISSION OF THE ARCHDIOCESE

21st Century Centurions.
The Chaplains Aid Association.
National Conference of Veterans Affairs Catholic Chaplains, Inc.. Most Rev. Francis X. Roque, D.D., (Episcopal Advisor), Rev. William F. Vander Heyden (GB) President 2004Tel: 847-688-1900, Ext. 83163.
Catholic War Veterans, USA, Inc., 441 North Lee St., Alexandria, VA 22314-2301. Tel: 703-549-3622.

Archdiocese of Milwaukee

(Archidioecesis Milvauchiensis)

Most Reverend

TIMOTHY M. DOLAN

Archbishop of Milwaukee; ordained June 19, 1976; appointed Auxiliary Bishop of St. Louis June 19, 2001; installed August 15, 2001; appointed Archbishop of Milwaukee June 25, 2002; installed as Tenth Archbishop August 28, 2002. *Res.: 3303 S. Lake Dr., Milwaukee, WI 53235-3703. All official communications to the Most Rev. Archbishop should be addressed to: Archbishop Cousins Catholic Center,* 3501 S. Lake Dr., P.O. Box 070912, Milwaukee, WI 53207-0912.

Chancery Office: Archbishop Cousins Catholic Center, 3501 S. Lake Dr., P.O. Box 070912, Milwaukee, WI 53207-0912. Tel: 414-769-3340; Fax: 414-769-3408.

Web: www.archmil.org

Email: information@archmil.org

Most Reverend

REMBERT G. WEAKLAND, O.S.B., D.D.

Archbishop Emeritus of Milwaukee; ordained June 24, 1951; appointed Archbishop of Milwaukee September 20, 1977; consecrated and installed as Ninth Archbishop November 8, 1977; retired May 24, 2002. *Res.: 3501 S. Lake Dr., Apt. E-101, St. Francis, WI 53235.*

Most Reverend

RICHARD J. SKLBA, D.D.

Auxiliary Bishop of Milwaukee; ordained December 20, 1959; appointed Auxiliary Bishop of Milwaukee and Titular Bishop of Castro November 6, 1979; consecrated December 19, 1979. *Res.: 2491 N. Murray Ave., Milwaukee, WI 53211.* Tel: 414-962-3941. *All official communications should be addressed to: Archbishop Cousins Catholic Center,* 3501 S. Lake Dr., P.O. Box 070912, Milwaukee, WI 53207-0912. Tel: 414-769-3486.

Square Miles 4,758.

Established November 28, 1843; Created Archbishopric February 12, 1875.

Corporate Title: Archdiocese of Milwaukee.

Comprises the Counties of Dodge, Fond du Lac, Kenosha, Milwaukee, Ozaukee, Racine, Sheboygan, Walworth, Washington and Waukesha in the State of Wisconsin.

For legal titles of parishes and archdiocesan institutions, consult the Chancery Office.

STATISTICAL OVERVIEW

Personnel	
Archbishops	1
Retired Archbishops	1
Auxiliary Bishops	1
Abbots	1
Retired Abbots	2
Priests: Diocesan Active in Diocese	232
Priests: Diocesan Active Outside Diocese	16
Priests: Diocesan in Foreign Missions	1
Priests: Retired, Sick or Absent	165
Number of Diocesan Priests	414
Religious Priests in Diocese	345
Total Priests in Diocese	759
Extern Priests in Diocese	31
Ordinations:	
Diocesan Priests	2
Transitional Deacons	2
Permanent Deacons in Diocese	151
Total Brothers	63
Total Sisters	2,290
Parishes	
Parishes	219
With Resident Pastor:	
Resident Diocesan Priests	167
Resident Religious Priests	21
Without Resident Pastor:	
Administered by Priests	24
Administered by Deacons	1
Administered by Lay People	6
Pastoral Centers	14
New Parishes Created	4
Closed Parishes	9
Professional Ministry Personnel:	
Brothers	1
Sisters	54
Lay Ministers	358
Welfare	
Catholic Hospitals	11
Total Assisted	2,053,387
Health Care Centers	1
Total Assisted	10,876
Homes for the Aged	25
Total Assisted	5,052
Day Care Centers	4
Total Assisted	544
Specialized Homes	5
Total Assisted	4,012
Special Centers for Social Services	22
Total Assisted	244,827
Residential Care of Disabled	4
Total Assisted	164
Educational	
Seminaries, Diocesan	1
Students from This Diocese	21
Diocesan Students in Other Seminaries	1
Seminaries, Religious	1
Students Religious	19
Total Seminarians	41
Colleges and Universities	5
Total Students	26,308
High Schools, Diocesan and Parish	7
Total Students	4,070
High Schools, Private	6
Total Students	2,980
Elementary Schools, Diocesan and Parish	120
Total Students	29,168
Elementary Schools, Private	3
Total Students	180
Non-residential Schools for the Disabled	1
Total Students	9
Catechesis/Religious Education:	
High School Students	17,262
Elementary Students	52,880
Total Students under Catholic Instruction	132,898
Teachers in the Diocese:	
Priests	42
Scholastics	1
Brothers	8
Sisters	110
Lay Teachers	3,397
Vital Statistics	
Receptions into the Church:	
Infant Baptism Totals	9,322
Adult Baptism Totals	488
Received into Full Communion	686
First Communions	8,947
Confirmations	6,427
Marriages:	
Catholic	2,018
Interfaith	794
Total Marriages	2,812
Deaths	5,677
Total Catholic Population	731,516
Total Population	2,261,397

Former Bishops—Most Revs. JOHN MARTIN HENNI, D.D., consecrated March 19, 1844; created Archbishop, Feb. 11, 1875; died Sept. 7, 1881; MICHAEL HEISS, D.D., consecrated Bishop of La Crosse, Sept. 6, 1868; appt. Coadjutor of Milwaukee and Titular Archbishop of Adrianople, March 14, 1880; succeeded to Archbishop Henni in 1881; died March 26, 1890; FREDERICK XAVIER KATZER, D.D., consecrated Sept. 21, 1886; Bishop of Green Bay; transferred to Milwaukee and raised to the Archiepiscopal Dignity, Jan. 30, 1891; died July 20, 1903; SEBASTIAN GEBHARD MESSMER, D.D., D.C.L., ord. July 23, 1871; consecrated March 27, 1892; Bishop of Green Bay; transferred to Milwaukee and raised to the Archiepiscopal dignity Dec. 10, 1903; made assistant at the Pontifical Throne, Nov. 16, 1906; died Aug. 4, 1930; His Eminence SAMUEL ALPHONSUS STRITCH, D.D., ord. May 21, 1910; consecrated Nov. 30, 1921; Bishop of Toledo; transferred to Milwaukee and raised to the Archiepiscopal dignity, Aug. 26, 1930; transferred to Chicago, Dec. 27, 1939; created Cardinal, Feb. 18, 1946; died May 27, 1958; Most Rev. MOSES E. KILEY, S.T.D., appt. Bishop of Trenton, Feb. 10, 1934; consecrated March 17, 1934; appt. Archbishop of Milwaukee, Jan. 1, 1940; died April 15, 1953; His Eminence ALBERT G. MEYER, S.T.D., S.S.L., ord. July 11, 1926; consecrated Bishop of Superior, April 11. 1946; appt. Archbishop of Milwaukee, July 21, 1953; transferred to Chicago, Sept. 24, 1958; created Cardinal, Dec. 14, 1959; died Apr. 9, 1965; Most Revs. WILLIAM E. COUSINS, D.D. (Retired), ord. April 23, 1927; appt. Titular Bishop of Forma and Auxiliary Bishop of Chicago Dec. 17, 1948; consecrated March 7, 1949; appt. Bishop of Peoria, May 19, 1952; installed July 2, 1952; appt. Archbishop of Milwaukee, Dec. 18, 1958; installed Jan. 27, 1959; retired Sept. 20, 1977; died Sept. 14, 1988; REMBERT G. WEAKLAND, O.S.B. (Retired), ord. June 24, 1951; appt. Archbishop of Milwaukee, Sept. 20, 1977; consecrated and installed as Ninth Archbishop, Nov. 8, 1977; retired May 24, 2002.

Archbishop Cousins Catholic Center—3501 S. Lake Dr., P.O. Box 070912, Milwaukee, 53207-0912. Tel: 414-769-3300; Fax: 414-769-3408. All Archdiocesan Offices are located at this address unless otherwise noted.

Vicars General—Most Rev. Richard J. Sklba, S.S.L., S.T.D.; Very Rev. Joseph F. Hornacek.

Deans—Very Revs. Michael T. Newman, District 1; John R. Kern, District 2; John D. Hemsing, District 3; Revs. Jerome M. Hudziak, District 4; John P. Schreiter, District 5; Gerald W. Brittain, District 6; Very Revs. Charles H. Wester, District 7; Patrick E. Heppe, District 8; Rev. Eugene Neuman, District 9; Very Revs. Michael Barrett, District 10; Kenneth P. Knippel, District 11; Ralph C. Gross, District 12; Rev. Dennis A. Dirkx, District 13; Very Rev. James L. Dammeir, District 14; Rev. Ronald J. Gramza, District 15; Very Rev. Kenneth E. Omernick, District 16.

Chancery—Tel: 414-769-3340. Email: chancery@archmil.org.

Chancellor—Barbara Anne Cusack. Tel: 414-769-3341.

Vice Chancellor—Rev. James C. Connell, J.C.D. Tel: 414-769-3338.

Archivist—Timothy D. Cary. Tel: 414-769-3407. Email: archives@archmil.org.

Vice Chancellor—Rev. James C. Connell, J.C.D. Tel: 414-769-3338.

Archivist—Timothy D. Cary. Tel: 414-769-3407. Email: archives@archmil.org.

Secretary to Archbishop—Rev. Jerome G. Herda. Tel: 414-769-3496; Fax: 414-769-3430. Email: herdaj@archmil.org.

Victim Assistance Coordinator—Barbara Reinke, Ph.D. Tel: 414-769-3436. Email: reinkeb@archmil.org.

Metropolitan Tribunal Archbishop Cousins Catholic Center—3501 S. Lake Dr., P.O. Box 070912, Milwaukee, 53207-0912. Tel: 414-769-3300; Fax: 414-769-3310. Email: tribunal@archmil.org. Please direct all Rogatory Commissions to Defenders of the Bond: Mr. Jesus Cabrera, J.C.L.

Judicial Vicar—Very Rev. Paul B.R. Hartmann, M.Div., J.C.L.

Associate Director of the Tribunal—Ms. Zabrina Decker, J.C.L.

Office Manager—Mr. Maurice C. Thompson.

Judges for First Instance—Rev. Thomas T. Brundage; Very Rev. Paul B.R. Hartmann, M.Div., J.C.L.; Rev. Thomas Olsczyk, J.C.L.; Ms. Zabrina Decker, J.C.L.; Mr. Eduardo Huerta, J.C.L.

Judges for Second Instance—Revs. Thomas T. Brundage; John Cella, O.F.M.; James E. Connell; Barbara Anne Cusack; Revs. Curt J. Frederick; Thomas Olsczyk, J.C.L.; Thomas Olsczyk, J.C.L.; Very Rev. Paul B.R. Hartmann, M.Div., J.C.L.; Revs. James J. Jarumbo, J.C.L.; Dennis C. Klemme (Retired); Very Rev. Michael T. Newman; Revs. Bernard S. Sippel; Philip D. Reifenberg, J.C.L.; Mr. Eduardo Huerta, J.C.L.; Ms. Zabrina Decker, J.C.L.

Defenders of the Bond Second Instance—Rev. John D. Aiello; Mr. Jesus Cabrera, J.C.L.

Psychological Expert—Thomas R. Budde, M.S.

Procurator Advocates—Andrew Vaughn, M.A.; Stephen Harvey.

Promoters of Justice—Revs. Robert G. Sampon (Retired); Philip D. Reifenberg, J.C.L.

Notaries—Rev. John D. Aiello; Mr. Maurice C. Thompson; Mary Chris Ellison; Joyce Hryniewicki; Alice Prier.

Office for Marital Reconciliation-Separation—Very Rev. Paul B.R. Hartmann, M.Div., J.C.L., Delegate.

Archdiocesan Court of Equity—Very Rev. Paul B.R. Hartmann, M.Div., J.C.L.; Rev. Thomas Olsczyk, J.C.L.; Ms. Zabrina Decker, J.C.L.; Mr. Eduardo Huerta, J.C.L.

Archdiocesan Consultors—Most Rev. Richard J. Sklba, S.S.L., S.T.D.; Revs. Dennis Ackeret; Richard J. Cerpich; William P. Callahan, O.F.M.Conv.; Rev. Msgr. T. George Gajdos; Very Rev. Ralph C. Gross; Rev. Jeffrey R. Haines; Very Rev. Joseph F. Hornacek; Rev. Jerome M. Hudziak.

Archdiocesan Council of Priests—Rev. Jeffrey R. Haines, Moderator. Tel: 414-769-3452.

Archdiocesan Pastoral Council—Tel: 414-769-3449.

Department for Ministerial Formation

Saint Francis Seminary—Very Rev. Michael G. Witczak, M.Div., S.L.D., Rector, 3257 S. Lake Dr., St. Francis, 53235. Tel: 414-747-6400; Fax: 414-747-6442. Email: mwitczak@sfs.edu.

Continuing Formation of Clergy—Vacant, Dir. Tel: 414-747-6417; Fax: 414-747-6442.

Vocations Office—Rev. Robert X. Stiefvater, Dir., 3257 S. Lake Dr., St. Francis, 53235. Tel: 414-747-6437; Fax: 414-747-6442. Email: rxs@sfs.edu.

College Program—Rev. Joseph J. Juknialis, Dir., 2479 N. Murray Ave., Milwaukee, 53211. Tel: 414-964-6970; Fax: 414-962-8183. Email: jjuknial@sfs.edu.

Department for Clergy

Department for Clergy—Tel: 414-769-34[illegible]4. Email: clergy@archmil.org.

Vicar for Clergy—Very Rev. Joseph F. Hornacek. Tel: 414-769-3490.

Associate Vicar for Clergy—Rev. William E. Kohler. Tel: 414-769-3458.

Services for Senior Priests—Rev. Thomas J. Walker. Tel: 414-769-3345.

Minister to Priests—Rev. Richard P. Abert, S.J. Tel: 414-481-4340.

Deacon Services—Deacon David L. Zimprich, Coord. Tel: 414-769-3409.

Department for Communication

Department for Communication—Tel: 414-769-3453. Email: communication@archmil.org.

Archbishop's Delegate for Communication—Jerry Topczewski. Tel: 414-769-3517.

Associate Director for Communication—Jean Mulloolly. Tel: 414-769-3461.

Communication Coordinator—Kathleen Hohl. Tel: 414-769-3494.

Coordinator of Publications—Mary Conarchy. Tel: 414-769-3460.

"Catholic Herald"--Newspaper—P.O. Box 070913, Milwaukee, 53207-0913. Tel: 414-769-3500; Fax: 414-769-3468. Email: chn@execpc.com. Most Rev. Timothy M. Dolan, Publisher; Maryangela Layman-Roman, Editor. Tel: 414-769-3476.

Department for Community Services

Department for Community Services—Tel: 414-769-3425. Email: socialconcerns@archmil.org.

Archbishop's Delegate for Community Services—Celia Jackson. Tel: 414-769-3389. Email: jacksonc@archmil.org.

Ecumenical and Interfaith Concerns—Judith Longdin, Dir. Tel: 414-769-3483. Email: longdinj@archmil.org.

Social Concerns Office—Celia Jackson, Dir. Tel: 414-769-3389 Email: jacksonc@archmil.org Marjorie Morgan, Assoc. Dir. Tel: 414-769-3402. Email: morganm@archmil.org.

Catholic Campaign for Human Development—Celia Jackson, Dir. Tel: 414-769-3389. Email jacksonc@archmil.org.

Office for World Mission—Frances Cunningham, O.S.F., Dir. Tel: 414-769-3404 Email: cunninghamf@archmil.org; Sr. Rosemary Huddleston, O.P., International Mission Coord. Tel: 414-769-3405. Email: huddlestonr@archmil.org.

Rural Life Office—Marjorie Morgan, Dir. Tel: 414-769-3402 Email: morganm@archmil.org.

Catholic Charities—Diane M. Knight, Exec. Dir. Tel: 414-769-3417; Fax: 414-769-3428 Email: dknight@ccmke.org; Gary Howley, Assoc. Dir. Tel: 414-769-3416; Fax: 414-769-3428. Email: ghowley@ccmke.org. (Legal Title: Catholic Charities of the Archdiocese of Milwaukee, Inc.); Matthew R. Lemke, C.F.O. Tel: 414-769-3516; Fax: 414-769-3428. Email: mlemke@ccmke.org; Anthony Kiesler, Dir. Human Resource. Tel: 414-769-3351 Fax: 414-769-3428. Email: akiesler@ccmke.org.

Catholic Charities Residential Programs for Developmentally Disabled— (Persons with Disabilities Ministries) Richard Kohl, Dir. Tel: 414-769-3401; Fax: 414-769-3428. Email: rkohl@ccmke.org.

Ministry on Aging—William Leon. Tel: 414-769-3412; Fax: 414-769-3428. Email: bleon@ccmke.org.

Persons of Diverse Cultures Ministries—

Child Welfare Ministries—Nancy Irizarry, Dir. Tel: 262-637-8888; Fax: 262-637-0695. Email: nirizarry@ccmke.org.

Family & Children's Ministries—

Hope & Healing Ministries—John Nesseth, Dir. Tel: 262-547-2463; Fax: 262-547-8002. Email: jnesseth@ccmke.org.

Older Adult Minsitries—Cathy Young, Dir. Tel: 414-771-2881; Fax: 414-771-1674. Email: cyoung@ccmke.org.

Social Ministries—Ron Spitz, Dir. Tel: 414-769-3419; Fax: 414-769-3428. Email: rspitz@ccmke.org.

Department for Development

Department for Development—Tel: 414-769-3457; Fax: 414-769-3388. Email: development@archmil.org.

Archbishop's Delegate for Development—Joan Feiereisen. Tel: 414-769-3320. Email: feiereisenj@archmil.org.

Catholic Stewardship Appeal—Debra Lethlean, Dir. Tel: 414-769-3322. Email: lethleand@archmil.org.

Parish Stewardship and School Development—Pamela Mueller, Dir. Tel: 414-769-3185. Email: muellerp@archmil.org; Julie Pach, Assoc. Dir. Tel: 414-769-3331. Email: pachj@archmil.org.

Major and Planned Giving—Mary Ann Vance, Dir. Tel: 414-769-3583. Email: vancem@archmil.org.

Catholic Charities Development—Carol Bergmann, Dir. Tel: 414-769-3524. Email: cbergmann@ccmke.org.

Department for Finance and Administration

Department for Archdiocesan Finance and Administration—Tel: 414-769-3326. Email: finance@archmil.org.

Archbishop's Delegate for Archdiocesan Finance and Administration—Wayne A. Schneider. Tel: 414-769-3319. Email: schneiderw@archmil.org.

Consultant for Legal Counsel—Wayne A. Schneider. Tel: 414-769-3319.

Office for Archdiocesan Finance and Administrative Services—Wayne A. Schneider, Dir. & Controller.

Office for Information Services—Jerry Schulz, Dir. Tel: 414-769-3530. Email: schulzj@archmil.org.

Webmaster/Coordinator Electronic Communication—Mark Barthel. Tel: 414-769-3454. Email: barthelm@archmil.org.

Office for Parish Finances—Katie Hoeller, Dir. Tel: 414-769-3377. Email: hoellerk@archmil.org.

Office for Cemeteries and Mausoleums—Vacant, Dir., 7301 W. Nash St., Milwaukee, 53216. Tel: 414-438-4430.

Office for Building Services—William Kreitzer, Dir. Tel: 414-769-3491. Email: kreitzerw@archmil.org.

Office for Printing Services—Thomas Wal, Dir. Tel: 414-769-3487. Email: waltom@archmil.org.

Department for Human Resources

Department for Human Resources—Tel: 414-769-3329. Email: humanresources@archmil.org.

Archbishop's Delegate for Human Resources—Richard J. Tank. Tel: 414-769-3370. Email: tankr@archmil.org.

Office for Human Resources, Central Offices and Agencies—Susan Gorski, Dir. Tel: 414-769-3328. Email: gorskis@archmil.org.

Office for Parish and School Personnel—Richard J. Tank, Dir.; Maureen Siwula, Assoc. Dir. Tel: 414-769-3336. Email: siwulam@archmil.org.

Office for Consecrated Life—Rev. Alan D. Veik, O.F.M.Cap., Dir. Tel: 414-769-3375. Email: veika@archmil.org.

Archdiocesan Office for Women—Thelma Walker, Dir. Tel: 414-769-3434. Email: women@archmil.org.

Department for Parishes

Department for Parishes—Tel: 414-769-3449. Email: parishes@archmil.org.

Archbishop's Delegate for Parishes—Maureen Gallagher, Ph.D. Tel: 414-769-3450. Email: gallagherm@archmil.org.

Office for Multi-Cultural Concerns—Schauneille Allen, Multi-Cultural Consultant & Dir. African-American Ministry. Tel: 414-769-3411. Email: africanamericanministry@archmil.org; Pedro Martinez, Multi-Cultural Consultant & Dir. Hispanic Ministry. Tel: 414-769-3393. Email: hispanicministry@archmil.org; Rev. Paul Fliss, Multi-Cultural Consultant, Asian Ministry. Tel: 414-769-3376. Email: asianministry@archmil.org.

Parish Consultants—Tel: 414-769-3539. Email: parishconsultants@archmil.org. Districts 1, 2, 3: Valerie Keller. Tel: 414-769-3395. Districts 4, 5, 10, 11, 12, 13: Catherine O'Neill. Tel: 414-769-3372. Districts 6, 15, 16: Mark Peters. Tel: 414-769-3392. Districts 7, 8, 9: Gail Kraig. Tel: 414-769-3394. Districts 10, 11, 12, 13: Eva J. Diaz. Tel: 414-769-3397. District 14 (Milwaukee Near Southside and Parishes of the Archdiocese with Hispanic Ministry): Roberto Cortes. Tel: 414-769-3371.

Office for Parish Councils and Planning—Noreen Welte, Dir. Tel: 414-769-3352. Email: parishcouncils@archmil.org; Robert Melcher, Assoc. Dir., Planning. Tel: 414-769-3381. Email: planning@archmil.org.

Office for Human Concerns/Respect Life—Peg Flahive, Dir. Tel: 414-769-3426. Email: humanconcerns@archmil.org.

Office for Prayer and Worship—Dean Daniels, Dir. Tel: 414-769-3348. Email: oremus@archmil.org; James Wickman, Assoc. Dir. Tel: 414-769-3350.

Office for Adult and Family Ministry—Tel: 414-769-3439.

Marriage and Family Ministry—Randy Nohl, Dir. Tel: 414-769-3440. Email: nohlr@archmil.org.

Engaged Programs—Marie Grevsmuehl, Coord. Tel: 414-769-3441. Email: grevsmuehlm@archmil.org.

Campus Ministry—Milwaukee: Constance M. Popp. Email: poppc@archmil.org; Rev. Robert J. Lotz. Tel: 414-964-6640. Email: lotzr@archmil.org. Kenosha/Racine: Edith Padgett. Tel: 262-654-3630. Email: padgette@archmil.org. Whitewater: Brian Zanin. Tel: 262-473-5555. Email: zaninb@archmil.org.

Special Needs—Tel: 414-769-3439.
Ministry to Special Needs and Deaf and Hard of Hearing Ministry—PAMELA SOMMERS, Assoc. Dir. Tel: 414-769-3455 (V/TTY). Email: sommersp@archmil.org.
Office for Schools, Child and Youth Ministries—Tel: 414-769-3363.
Director of Catholic Education—DAVID PROTHERO. Tel: 414-769-3357. Email: protherod@archmil.org.
Administrative Services—JOHN T. NORRIS, Ph.D., Dir. Tel: 414-769-3366. Email: norrisj@archmil.org.
Student Activities & Services—W. SCOTT WEYDA, Assoc. Dir. Tel: 414-769-3359. Email: weydas@archmil.org.
Curriculum & Instruction—SUE NELSON, Assoc. Dir. Tel: 414-769-3358. Email: nelsons@archmil.org.
Youth & Young Adult Ministry—LAURIE KISH, Assoc. Dir. Tel: 414-769-3361. Email: kishl@archmil.org.
Catechetics to Children—KATHIE AMIDEI, Assoc. Dir. Tel: 414-769-3373. Email: amideik@archmil.org.
Early Adolescent Ministry—LISA MARIE CALDERONE-STEWART, Assoc. Dir. Tel: 414-769-3360. Email: calderonel@archmil.org.
Technology and Communication—MORT ZAYDEL, Assoc. Dir. Tel: 414-769-3313. Email: zaydelm@archmil.org.

CLERGY, PARISHES, MISSIONS AND PAROCHIAL SCHOOLS

CITY OF MILWAUKEE
(MILWAUKEE COUNTY)

1—CATHEDRAL OF ST. JOHN THE EVANGELIST (1847), Very Rev. Carl A. Last, Rector; Rev. Carl E. Diederichs.
Mailing Address: 831 N. Van Buren St., 53202.
Res.: 802 N. Jackson St., 53202. Tel: 414-276-9814; Fax: 414-276-8285.
Catechesis/Religious Program—Tel: 414-263-8230. Students 21.

2—ST. ADALBERT (1908), (Polish—Hispanic), Revs. Thomas Lemieux, Temp. Admin.; Eleazar Perez Rodriguez.
Office—1854 W. Windlake, 53215. Tel: 414-645-4773; Fax: 414-645-5622.
School—1913 W. Becher St., 53215-2688. Tel: 414-645-5450; Fax: 414-645-5510. Ms. Julia Hutchinson, Prin. Lay Teachers 15; Students 262.
Catechesis/Religious Program—Students 80.

3—ST. AGNES, Closed., For sacramental records, contact Archdiocese of Milwaukee Archives Office. Tel.: 414-769-3407.

4—ST. ALBERT, Closed., For sacramental records, contact Archdiocese of Milwaukee Archives Office. Tel.: 414-769-3407.

5—ST. ALEXANDER (1926), (Polish), Rev. Robert W. Nawrocki.
Res.: 3373 S. 15th Pl., 53215. Tel: 414-645-9820; Fax: 414-385-9250.
School—Holy Wisdom Academy West See listing in the Consolidated Elementary Schools section. Tel: 414-383-3453; Fax: 414-672-2645. Mr. Richard Mason, Prin.
Catechesis/Religious Program— Twinned with St. Helen, Milwaukee , 3307 S. 10th St.. Tel: 414-744-3695; Fax: 414-744-2874.

6—ALL SAINTS (1994), (African American), Rev. Dennis A. Dirkx; Deacon Edward Blaze.
Office—4060 N. 26th St., 53209-6695. Tel: 414-444-5610; Fax: 414-444-5709.
Catechesis/Religious Program—Students 107.
Mission—St. John's Chapel 3717 W. Keefe, Milwaukee Co. 53216.

7—ST ANNE, Closed., For sacramental records, contact Archdiocese of Milwaukee Archives Office. Tel.: 414-769-3407.

8—ST. ANTHONY (1872), Revs. Anthony Cirignani, O.F.M.; Robert Kose, O.F.M.Cap. In Res., Revs. Robert F. Mueller (Retired); Robert Konkel, O.F.M., School Chap.
Res.: 1711 S. 9th St., 53204. Tel: 414-645-1455; Fax: 414-645-1456.
School—1747 S. 9th St., 53204. Tel: 414-384-1730; Fax: 414-384-1733. Jeffrey Johnson, Prin. Sisters 1; Lay Teachers 45; Students 600.
Catechesis/Religious Program—Bro. Jose Gonzalez, O.F.M., D.R.E. Students 350.

9—ST. ANTHONY OF PADUA (1923), Closed., For sacramental records, contact St. Vincent Pallotti, Milwaukee. Tel.: 414-453-4225.

10—ST. AUGUSTINE (1888), (German), Rev. Thomas F. Wittliff; Ms. Chiara Sainer, Pastoral Assoc.
Res.: 2530 S. Howell Ave., 53207. Tel: 414-744-0808; Fax: 414-744-1231.
School—St. Elizabeth Ann Seton Academy, 1051 E. Russell Ave., 53207. Tel: 414-482-8996; Fax: 414-747-9219. Lay Teachers 13; Students 152.
Catechesis/Religious Program—Students 79.

11—ST. BARBARA, Closed., For sacramental records, contact Archdiocese of Milwaukee Archives Office. Tel.: 414-769-3407

12—BASILICA OF ST. JOSAPHAT (1888), (Polish), Revs. William P. Callahan, O.F.M.Conv., Rector; Robert Joseph Switanowski, O.F.M.Conv., Vicar; Michael Glastetter, O.F.M.Conv., Vicar.
Res.: 2333 S. 6th St., 53215. Tel: 414-645-5623; Fax: 414-645-0912.
School—801 W. Lincoln Ave., 53215. Tel: 414-645-4378; Fax: 414-645-1978. Mrs. Carolyn Trawitzki. Lay Teachers 12; Students 205; School Sisters of St. Francis 6; School Sisters of Notre Dame 2.
Catechesis/Religious Program—Parish Center, 2322 S. 7th St., 53215. Tel: 414-671-3938. Students 56.

13—ST. BENEDICT THE MOOR (1908), Rev. John Celichowski, O.F.M.Cap.; Deacon John I. Champagne. In Res., Rev. Michael Crosby, O.F.M-.Cap.; Bros. Jerome Smith, O.F.M.Cap.; David Schwab, O.F.M.Cap.
Res.: 1015 N. 9th St., 53233. Tel: 414-271-0135; Fax: 414-271-0637.
Catechesis/Religious Program—Students 23.

14—ST. BERNADETTE (1958), Rev. Lawrence Sepich; Deacon John A. Ebel.
Res.: 8200 W. Denver Ave., 53223. Tel: 414-358-4600; Fax: 414-358-1478.
School—8202 W. Denver Ave., 53223. Tel: 414-358-4603; Fax: 414-760-1037. Mary Lorusso, Prin. Lay Teachers 10; Students 190.
Catechesis/Religious Program—Tel: 414-358-4600, Ext. 157. Students 65.

15—BLESSED SACRAMENT (1927), (Polish), Rev. Robert D. Turner; Deacon Richard M. Flynn.
Res.: 3100 S. 41st St., 53215. Tel: 414-649-4720; Fax: 414-649-4727.
Church: S. 41st St. and W. Oklahoma Ave., 53215.
School—3126 S. 41st St., 53215. Tel: 414-649-4730; Fax: 414-649-4726. Sr. Rene Kuban, S.F.C.C., Prin. Lay Teachers 12; Students 211.
Catechesis/Religious Program—Tel: 414-649-4735. Students 130.

16—BLESSED VIRGIN OF POMPEI, Closed., For sacramental records, contact Three Holy Women, Milwaukee. Tel.: 414-271-2165.

17—ST. BONIFACE, Closed., For sacramental records, contact Archdiocese of Milwaukee Archives Office. Tel.: 414-769-3407

18—ST. CASIMIR (1894), (Polish—Spanish), Merged, with St. Mary Czestochowa, Milwaukee to form Our Lady of Divine Mercy, Milwaukee

19—ST. CATHERINE (1922), Rev. Romanus N. Nwaru; Deacon Ralph W. Kornburger Jr. In Res., Rev. Santhiagu John Kennedy (India).
Res.: 5101 W. Center St., 53210. Tel: 414-445-5115; Fax: 414-445-5198.
School—2647 N. 51st St., 53210. Tel: 414-445-2846; Fax: 414-445-0448. Deborah Zabinski, Prin. Lay Teachers 23; Students 228.
Catechesis/Religious Program—Students 76.

20—ST. CATHERINE (Granville) (1855), [CEM] Rev. Jeffery A. Prasser.
Res.: 8661 N. 76th Pl., 53223. Tel: 414-365-2039; 365-202- (Office); Fax: 414-365-2021 (Office).
School—8660 N. 76th Pl., 53223. Tel: 414-365-2030; Fax: 414-365-2021. Mr. Michael Howell, Prin. Sisters 1; Lay Teachers 12; Students 168.
Catechesis/Religious Program—Tel: 414-365-2025. Dennie De Broux, Coord. Students 155.

21—ST. CHARLES BORROMEO (1960), Rev. Anthony J. Zimmer.
Res.: 5571 S. Marilyn Ave., 53221. Tel: 414-281-8115; Fax: 414-281-8150.
School—3100 W. Parnell Ave., 53221. Tel: 414-282-0767; Fax: 414-817-9605. Lay Teachers 15; Students 155.
Catechesis/Religious Program—Tel: 414-281-8115, Ext. 24. Students 178.

22—CONGREGATION OF THE BLESSED TRINITY (1991), Rev. Brian M. Beno, Temp. Admin.
Pastoral Offices—4717 N. 38th St., 53209. Tel: 414-463-6921; Fax: 414-463-0349.
Catechesis/Religious Program—Students 28.

23—CONGREGATION OF THE GREAT SPIRIT (1989), (Native American), Rev. Edward J. Cook.
Res. & Mailing Address: 1050 W. Lapham St., 53204. Tel: 414-672-6989; Fax: 414-643-5688.
Catechesis/Religious Program—Students 30.

24—CORPUS CHRISTI (1958), Rev. Michael D. Strachota; Deacon James L. Aschenbrener.
Parish Center—8607 W. Villard Ave., 53225. Tel: 414-464-5033; Fax: 414-464-0079.
School—8545 W. Villard Ave., 53225. Tel: 414-464-5775; Fax: 414-464-5775. Roger A. Baehr, Prin. Lay Teachers 14; Students 160.
Catechesis/Religious Program—Students 67.

25—SS. CYRIL AND METHODIUS (1893), (Polish), Revs. Andrzej Galant, S.Ch.; Eleazar Perez Rodriguez.
Office—2427 S. 15th St., 53215. Tel: 414-645-4773; Fax: 414-645-5622.

26—ST. ELIZABETH, Closed., For sacramental records, contact Archdiocese of Milwaukee Archives Office. Tel.: 414-769-3407.

27—ST. EMERIC (1919), (Hungarian), Closed., For sacramental records, contact Sacred Heart, Milwaukee. Tel.: 414-774-9418.

28—ST. FLORIAN (1911), (German—Austrian), Revs. Leonard R. Copeland, O.C.D.; Timothy McGough, O.C.D. In Res., Revs. William Healy, O.C.D.; Phillip Thomas, O.C.D.; Jude Peters, O.C.D.; Ralph Elias-Haddix, O.C.D.; Fred Alexander, O.C.D.; Bro. Bonaventure Potter, O.C.D.
Res.: 1233 S. 45th St., 53214. Tel: 414-383-3565; Fax: 414-383-2708.
School—1215 S. 45th St., 53214. Tel: 414-383-4204; Fax: 414-383-4281. Lay Teachers 11; Students 89.
Catechesis/Religious Program—Students 95.

29—ST. FRANCIS OF ASSISI (1871), (Hispanic—African American), Revs. Paul Koenig, O.F.M.Cap.; Robert Kose, O.F.M.Cap. In Res., Revs. Robert Wheelock, O.F.M.Cap.; Myron Kowalsky, O.F.M.Cap.; Michael Zuelke, O.F.M.Cap.; Bro. Isidore Herriges, O.F.M.Cap.
Res.: 1927 N. 4th St., 53212. Tel: 414-374-5750; Fax: 414-374-5553.

30—ST. GABRIEL (1913), (Lithuanian), Closed., For sacramental records, contact Archdiocese of Milwaukee Archives Office. Tel.: 414-769-3407.

31—ST. GALL, Closed., For sacramental records, contact Archdiocese of Milwaukee Archives Office. Tel.: 414-769-3407.

32—ST. GERARD (1925), Closed., For sacramental records, contact Archdiocese of Milwaukee Archives Office. Tel.: 414-769-3407.

33—GESU PARISH (1893), Revs. Peter J. Etzel, S.J.; John D. Campbell, S.J.; Kenneth J. Herian, S.J.; Patrick E. Walsh, S.J.; Larry Jonas, S.J.; Jeffrey R. Loebl, S.J.; James P. McDermott, S.J.
Res.: 1210 W. Michigan St., P.O. Box 495, 53201-0495. Tel: 414-288-7101; Fax: 414-288-5339.
Catechesis/Religious Program—Students 130.

34—ST. GREGORY THE GREAT (1955), Very Rev. Kenneth E. Omernick; Rev. Steven Dunn.
Office—3160 S. 63rd St., 53219. Tel: 414-543-8292; Fax: 414-328-3881.
Res.: 3129 S. 63rd St., 53219.
School—3132 S. 63rd St., 53219. Tel: 414-321-1350. Lay Teachers 24; Students 403.
Catechesis/Religious Program—Tel: 414-543-8292. Students 245.

35—ST. HEDWIG (1871), (Polish), Closed., For sacramental records, contact Three Holy Women, Milwaukee. Tel.: 414-271-2165.

36—ST. HELEN (1925), (Polish), Rev. Michael A. Ignaszak.
Res.: 3307 S. 10th St., 53215. Tel: 414-744-3695; 414-744-8292; Fax: 414-744-2874.
School—Holy Wisdom Academy: East Site See listing in the Consolidated Elementary Schools section. Tel: 414-744-7188; Fax: 414-744-8370. Mr. Richard Mason, Prin.
Catechesis/Religious Program—Fax: 414-744-2874. Students 41.

37—HOLY ANGELS, Closed., For sacramental records, contact Archdiocese of Milwaukee Archives Office. Tel.: 414-769-3407.

38—HOLY CROSS (1879), Closed., For sacramental records, contact St. Vincent Pallotti, Milwaukee. Tel.: 414-453-4225.

39—HOLY REDEEMER, Closed., For sacramental records, contact Archdiocese of Milwaukee Archives Office. Tel.: 414-769-3407.

40—HOLY ROSARY (1885), (Irish), Closed., For sacramental records, contact Three Holy Women, Milwaukee. Tel.: 414-271-2165

41—HOLY SPIRIT (1902), (German), Closed., For sacramental records, contact Archdiocese of Milwaukee Archives Office. Tel.: 414-769-3407

42—HOLY TRINITY-OUR LADY OF GUADALUPE (1849), (Hispanic), Closed., For sacramental records, contact Our Lady of Guadalupe, Milwaukee. Tel.: 414-271-6181

43—ST. HYACINTH (1883), (Polish—Hispanic), Revs. Ronald E. Kotecki; Eleazar Perez Rodriguez.
Res.: 1414 W. Becher St., 53215. Tel: 414-383-4010; Fax: 414-383-3252.
Catechesis/Religious Program—Students 245.

44—ST. IGNATIUS LOYOLA, Closed., For sacramental records, contact Archdiocese of Milwaukee Archives Office. Tel.: 414-769-3407.

45—IMMACULATE CONCEPTION (1870), Rev. Dennis M. Witz; Deacon John R. Wargin.
Res.: 1023 E. Russell Ave., 53207. Tel: 414-769-2480.
School—St. Elizabeth Ann Seton Academy Consolidated School. Parish Sponsors: Immaculate Conception and St. Augustine. , 1051 E. Russell Ave.,

53207. Tel: 414-482-8996; Fax: 414-747-9219. Lay Teachers 9; Students 145.
Catechesis/Religious Program—Tel: 414-769-2488. Students 35.

46—ST. JOHN DE NEPOMUC, Closed., For sacramental records, contact Archdiocese of Milwaukee Archives Office. Tel.: 414-769-3407.

47—ST. JOHN KANTY (1907), (Polish), Rev. Carl M. Kazmierczak.
Res.: 966 W. Dakota St., 53215. Tel: 414-744-5885; Fax: 414-744-1393.
School—2840 S. 10th St., 53215. Tel: 414-483-8780; 414-744-1846; Fax: 414-744-1846. Beth Eichman, Prin. Lay Teachers 14; Students 140.
Catechesis/Religious Program—Tel: 414-483-1906. Students 25.

48—ST. JOSEPH, Closed., For sacramental records, contact St. Joseph, Wauwatosa. Tel.: 414-771-4626.

49—ST. LAWRENCE (1888), Closed., For sacramental records, contact Archdiocese of Milwaukee Archives Office. Tel.: 414-769-3407.

50—ST. LEO, Closed., For sacramental records, contact Archdiocese of Milwaukee Archives Office. Tel.: 414-769-3407.

51—ST. MARGARET MARY (1955), Very Rev. Ralph C. Gross. Tel: 414-536-8720; Rev. Joseph Wolf. Tel: 414-358-1629; Deacon Michael R. Rooney.
Rectory Office: 3930 N. 92nd St., 53222-2588. Tel: 414-461-6073; Fax: 414-461-5590.
School—3950 N. 92nd St., 53222-2587. Tel: 414-463-8760; Fax: 414-463-2373. Brenda White, Prin. Sisters of St. Agnes 1; Lay Teachers 25; Students 410.
Catechesis/Religious Program—Tel: 414-462-9660. Students 360.

52—ST. MARTIN DE PORRES (1994), (African American), Rev. Brian Braun, O.F.M.Cap.
Office—128 W. Burleigh St., 53212-2046. Tel: 414-372-3090; Fax: 414-372-0356.
Catechesis/Religious Program—Students 50.

53—ST. MARY MAGDALEN (1925), (Polish), Rev. Thomas Lemieux.
Res.: 1854 W. Windlake Ave., 53215. Tel: 414-645-4773; Fax: 414-645-5622.

54—ST. MARY OF CZESTOCHOWA (1907), (Polish), Merged, with St. Casimir, Milwaukee to form Our Lady of Divine Providence, Milwaukee.

55—MARY, QUEEN OF MARTYRS (2001),, (Merger of Mother of Perpetual Help and St. Stephen Martyr). Rev. Mark Molling.
Res.: 5409 W. Villard Ave., 53218-4222. Tel: 414-438-0669; Fax: 414-438-9265.
School—5140 N. 55th St., 53218. Tel: 414-438-2745; Fax: 414-438-9330. Barbara O'Donnell, Prin. Sisters 1; Lay Teachers 21; Students 234.
Catechesis/Religious Program—Tel: 414-438-2993. Students 10.

56—ST. MATTHEW (1892), Closed., For sacramental records, contact Archdiocese of Milwaukee Archives Office. Tel.: 414-769-3407.

57—ST. MATTHIAS (1851), [CEM] Revs. David E. Cooper; Joseph A. Aufdermauer; Deacon David W. Sommers.
9306 W. Beloit Rd., 53227. Tel: 414-321-0893; Fax: 414-321-1330.
School—Tel: 414-321-0894; Fax: 414-321-9228. Sisters 1; Lay Teachers 29; Students 525.
Catechesis/Religious Program—Students 476.

58—ST. MAXIMILIAN KOLBE, Rev. Andrzej Galant, S.Ch.
Res.: 2427 S. 15th St., 53215. Tel: 414-383-3974.

59—ST. MICHAEL (1883), Very Rev. Dennis J. Lewis, Admin.; Deacon Carl H. Thelin, Laotian Pastoral Ministry & Pastoral Assoc.; Sr. Maria Herlinda, Hispanic Pastoral Ministry & Pastoral Assoc.; Deacon Blong P. Yang, Hmong Pastoral Ministry & Pastoral Assoc.; Shanedra Johnson, Youth Dir. & Pastoral Assoc.
Res.: 1445 N. 24th St., 53205. Tel: 414-933-3143; Fax: 414-933-1915.
Catechesis/Religious Program—Tel: 414-342-2678. Students 260.

60—MOTHER OF GOOD COUNSEL (1925), Rev. Carey T. Lahrs, S.D.S.; Deacons Dean J. Collins; Andrew Meuler.
Church: 6924 W. Lisbon Ave., 53210-1259. Tel: 414-442-7600; Fax: 414-444-0408.
School—3001 N. 68th St., 53210-1299. Fax: 414-442-0664. Regina Shaw, Prin. Lay Teachers 26; Students 335.
Catechesis/Religious Program—Tel: 414-442-7600, Ext. 127. Students 80.

61—MOTHER OF PERPETUAL HELP (1941), Closed., For sacramental records, contact Archdiocese of Milwaukee Archives Office. Tel.: 414-769-3407

62—ST. NICHOLAS, Closed., For sacramental records, contact Archdiocese of Milwaukee Archives Office. Tel.: 414-769-3407.

63—OLD ST. MARY (1846), (Bavarian—German), Rev. George M. Rebatzki.
Res.: 836 N. Broadway, 53202. Tel: 414-271-6180; Fax: 414-271-7782.
Catechesis/Religious Program—Students 47.

64—OUR LADY OF DIVINE PROVIDENCE (2003), [CEM] Rev. Gerald Hessel.
Res.: 3055 N. Fratney St., 53212. Tel: 414-264-0049; Fax: 414-264-7177.
Catechesis/Religious Program—924 E. Clarke St., 53212. Tel: 414-263-8230; Fax: 414-263-8222. Students 13.

65—OUR LADY OF GOOD HOPE (1952), Rev. Donald Hying; Deacons Michael E. Cesarec; Joseph H. Kastenholz. In Res., Rev. John R. Kolarko.
Office—7152 N. 41st St., 53209. Tel: 414-352-1148; Fax: 414-352-3042.
School—7140 N. 41st St., 53209. Tel: 414-352-7980; Fax: 414-352-7358. Yolande Lasky, Prin. Lay Teachers 12; Students 144.
Catechesis/Religious Program—Tel: 414-352-8140. Barbara Krieger, D.R.E. Students 160.

66—OUR LADY OF GUADALUPE PARISH (2000), (Hispanic), Rev. Vincent F. Kobia; Deacons Jose H. Gutierrez; Juan A. Molina Sr.
Res.: 613 S. 4th St., 53204. Tel: 414-271-6181; Fax: 414-278-6090.
Catechesis/Religious Program—Tel: 414-271-6543. Students 215.

67—OUR LADY OF LOURDES (1958), Rev. Michael Savio; Deacon John P. Monday; Mrs. Judith Bialk, Pastoral Assoc.
Office—3722 S. 58th St., 53220. Tel: 414-545-4316; Fax: 414-541-2251.
Catechesis/Religious Program—Tel: 414-541-9470. Students 298.

68—OUR LADY OF SORROWS (1955), Rev. Gregory A. Chycinski.
Res.: 4063 N. 64th St., 53216. Tel: 414-463-3180; Fax: 414-463-3668.
School—4059 N. 64th St., 53216. Tel: 414-463-3878; Fax: 414-535-9265. Miss Patricia Wilkum, Prin. Lay Teachers 12; Students 145.
Catechesis/Religious Program—Tel: 414-438-2993; Fax: 414-438-9265. Sr. Kathy Kreie, D.R.E. Students 10.

69—OUR LADY, QUEEN OF PEACE (1948), Rev. Gregory M. Spitz.
Res.: 3222 S. 29th St., 53215. Tel: 414-672-0313; Fax: 414-672-0441.
School—2733 W. Euclid Ave., 53215. Tel: 414-672-6660; Fax: 414-672-2739. Janet Orlowski, Prin. Sisters 1. Lay Teachers 14; Students 180.
Catechesis/Religious Program—Students 22.

70—ST. PATRICK (1876), (Hispanic), [CEM] Revs. Jose Luis Moreno, S.J.; David M. Shields, S.J.; William J. Brennan, S.J.
Res.: 723 W. Washington St., 53204. Tel: 414-645-7624; Fax: 414-645-3733.

71—ST. PAUL (1920), Rev. Andrew L. Nelson; Daryl Olszewski, Parish Dir.
Res.: 1720 E. Norwich Ave., 53207. Tel: 414-482-3510; Fax: 414-482-1031.
School—3945 S. Kansas Ave., 53207. Tel: 414-482-4790; Fax: 414-482-2983. Lay Teachers 8; Students 107.
Catechesis/Religious Program—Tel: 414-482-3911. Students 92.

72—SS. PETER AND PAUL (1889), (German), Revs. Thomas T. Brundage; Joseph J. Juknialis. In Res., Most Rev. Richard J. Sklba.
Res.: 2491 N. Murray Ave., 53211. Tel: 414-962-2443; Fax: 414-962-8183.
School—Catholic East Elementary, Tel: 414-964-1770; Fax: 414-964-6578. See Catholic East School, Inc. listing in the Consolidated Elementary Schools section.
Catechesis/Religious Program—East Side Child & Youth Ministry Consolidated from the following parishes: SS. Peter & Paul, St. Casimir, St. Mary Czestochowa, Cathedral of St. John the Evangelist, Three Holy Women, and Old St. Mary. , 924 E. Clarke St., 53212. Tel: 414-263-8230; Fax: 414-962-2443. Students 81.

73—ST. PHILIP NERI (1956), Rev. David J. Meinholz, Temp. Admin.
Res.: 5566 N. 69th St., 53218. Tel: 414-464-6721; Fax: 414-464-8504.
School—5501 N. 68th St., 53218. Tel: 414-466-0470; Fax: 414-466-3740. Mr. Michael Brown, Prin. Lay Teachers 16; Students 178.
Catechesis/Religious Program—Ms. Mary Evangelista, D.R.E. Students 26.

74—PRINCE OF PEACE/PRINCIPE DE PAZ (1999), Very Rev. James L. Dammeir; Rev. Ricardo Martin Pinillos
Office—1138 S. 25th St., 53204-1940. Tel: 414-645-8786; Fax: 414-645-8918.
School—(25th St. Campus), 1114 S. 25th St., 53204. Tel: 414-383-2157; Fax: 414-383-1181.
School—(22nd St. Campus), 1646 S. 22nd St., 53204. Tel: 414-645-4922; Fax: 414-645-4940. Ms. Donna Schmidt, Prin.; Mr. Norbert Smurawa, Assoc. Prin. Religious 3; Lay Teachers 23; Students 384.
Catechesis/Religious Program—Students 501.

75—ST. RAFAEL THE ARCHANGEL (1999), (Hispanic), Rev. James Kimla; Deacon William A. Banach.
Res.: 2059 S. 33rd St., 53215. Tel: 414-645-9172; Fax: 414-645-4732.
School—Tel: 414-645-1300; Fax: 414-645-1415. Mrs. Carolyn Ettlie, Prin. Lay Teachers 13; Students 220.
Catechesis/Religious Program—Tel: 414-645-5414. Students 53.

76—ST. RITA (1936), (Italian), Closed., For sacramental records, contact Three Holy Women, Milwaukee. Tel.: 414-271-2165.

77—ST. ROBERT (1912), Revs. John J. Pulice; Russel J. Stommel; Deacon Daniel T. Zozakiewicz; Mary Schroedl, Business Mgr.
Res.: 4019 N. Farwell Ave., 53211. Tel: 414-332-1164; Fax: 414-332-2599.
School—2200 E. Capital Dr., 53211. Tel: 414-332-1164, Ext. 3018; Fax: 414-332-7355. Mary Miller, Prin. Lay Teachers 26; Students 325.
Catechesis/Religious Program—Tel: 414-332-1164, Ext. 3012. Sr. Ruth Brings, S.S.S.F., D.R.E.(K-6). Students 205.

78—ST. ROMAN (1956), (Polish), Revs. William C. Burkert; Todd Budde.
Res.: 1710 W. Bolivar Ave., 53221. Tel: 414-282-9063; Fax: 414-282-6464.
School—1810 W. Bolivar Ave., 53221. Tel: 414-282-7970; Fax: 414-282-5140. Lay Teachers 21; Students 385.
Catechesis/Religious Program—Students 289.

79—ST. ROSE (1888), Very Rev. Dennis J. Lewis; Deacon Julio Lopez.
Res.: 528 N. 31st St., 53208. Tel: 414-342-1778; Fax: 414-342-7510.
School— See Elementary Schools, Archdiocesan, Catholic Urban Academies. Tel: 414-933-6070; Fax: 414-933-6071.
Catechesis/Religious Program—Students 30.

80—SACRED HEART (1917), (Croatian), Rev. Paul Maslach, O.F.M. (Croatia).
Res.: 917 N. 49th St., 53208. Tel: 414-774-9418; Fax: 414-774-7406.
Catechesis/Religious Program—Students 10.

81—ST. SEBASTIAN (1911), Rev. Charles H. Schramm; Deacon Warren D. Braun, (Retired). In Res., Rev. David J. Meinholz.
Res.: 5400 W. Washington Blvd., 53208. Tel: 414-453-1061; Fax: 414-453-9449.
School—1747 N. 54th St., 53208. Tel: 414-453-5830. Lay Teachers 29; Students 400.
Catechesis/Religious Program—Tel: 414-453-7150. Students 266.

82—ST. STANISLAUS (1866), (Polish—Hispanic), Revs. Ronald E. Kotecki, Admin.; Eleazar Perez Rodriguez.
Res.: 524 W. Mitchell St., 53204. Tel: 414-645-8170; Fax: 414-645-8170.
Catechesis/Religious Program—Tel: 414-383-4010; Fax: 414-383-3252. Students 25.

83—ST. STEPHEN (Airport) (1847), (German), [CEM 2] Rev. Richard A. Liska; Anita H. Kowalski, Pastoral Assoc.
Office—5880 S. Howell Ave., 53207. Tel: 414-483-2685; Fax: 414-483-3160.
Catechesis/Religious Program—Tel: 414-483-2658. Lay Teachers 8; Religious 1; Students 201.

84—ST. STEPHEN, MARTYR (1907), (Slovak), Closed., For sacramental records, contact Archdiocese of Milwaukee Archives Office. Tel.: 414-769-3407

85—ST. THERESE (1954), Dr. Alexandra Guliano, Parish Dir.; Jim Beuscher, Pastoral Assoc.; Judy Wargin, Pastoral Assoc.
Res.: 9525 W. Bluemound Rd., 53226. Tel: 414-771-2500; Fax: 414-771-2410.
Catechesis/Religious Program—Tel: 414-476-5580. Students 140.

86—ST. THOMAS AQUINAS, Closed., For sacramental records, contact Archdiocese of Milwaukee Archives Office. Tel.: 414-769-3407.

87—THREE HOLY WOMEN (2000), [CEM] Rev. Timothy L. Kitzke.
Res.: 1716 N. Humboldt Ave., 53202. Tel: 414-271-2165; Fax: 414-271-7988.
Catechesis/Religious Program— (Collaborative-Catholic East) , 924 E. Clarke St., 53212. Tel: 414-263-8230; Fax: 414-263-8222. Students 22.

88—ST. VERONICA (1925), Revs. Mark Payne; Ronald Engel; Deacon John R. Dziennik.
Mailing Address: 353 E. Norwich St., 53207. Tel: 414-482-2920.
School—341 E. Norwich St., 53207. Tel: 414-744-1214; Fax: 414-482-3025. Sr. Marie Estelle Kuczynski, Prin. Sisters 2; Lay Teachers 21; Students 370.
Catechesis/Religious Program—Tel: 414-481-0777. Students 175.

89—ST. VINCENT DE PAUL (1888), (Polish), [CEM] Rev. Vincent F. Kobia; Deacon Jorge Benavente.
Res.: 2114 W. Michell St., 53204. Tel: 414-645-3400;

Fax: 414-645-3450.
Catechesis/Religious Program—Students 134.
90—ST. VINCENT PALLOTTI (1998), Rev. Joseph Koyickal, S.A.C. (India).
Res.: 201 N. 76th St., 53213. Tel: 414-453-5344, Ext. 102; Fax: 414-453-4225.
School—West Site, Tel: 414-258-4165; Fax: 414-258-9844. Julie Palkowski, Prin. Religious 2; Lay Teachers 14; Students 124.
Catechesis/Religious Program—Tel: 414-453-5344, Ext. 103. Students 58.
91—ST. WENCESLAUS (1883), (Hispanic), Closed., For sacramental records, contact Our Lady of Guadalupe, Milwaukee. Tel.: 414-271-6181.

OUTSIDE THE CITY OF MILWAUKEE

ADELL, SHEBOYGAN CO., ST. PATRICK (1853), (Irish), Closed., For sacramental records, contact Our Lady of the Lakes, Random Lake. Tel.: 920-994-4380.
ALLENTON, WASHINGTON CO.
1—ST. ANTHONY (1851), Closed., For sacramental records, contact Resurrection, Allenton. Tel.: 262-629-5240
2—RESURRECTION (1997), [CEM 3], Consolidation of Sacred Heart, Allenton; St. Anthony, Allenton; and Ss. Peter and Paul, Nenno. Rev. Richard C. Breitbach; Sr. Mary Arnold Franz, S.S.N.D., Pastoral Assoc.
Parish Office—215 Main St., P.O. Box 96, 53002. Tel: 262-629-5240; Fax: 262-629-4152.
Church: 209 Main St., 53002.
Catechesis/Religious Program—Tel: 262-629-1500. Students 157.
Convent—School Sisters of Notre Dame, 632 Church St., P.O. Box 356, 53002. Tel: 262-629-5342.
3—SACRED HEART (1917), Closed., For sacramental records, contact Resurrection, Allenton. Tel.: 262-629-5240.
ARMSTRONG, FOND DU LAC CO., OUR LADY OF ANGELS (1856), (Irish), Closed., For sacramental records, contact Good Shepherd, 303 E. Main St., P.O. Box 128, Eden. Tel.: 920-477-3201; Fax: 920-477-3030
ASHFORD, FOND DU LAC CO., ST. MARTIN (1847), [CEM] Rev. Neil G. Zinthefer.
Mailing Address: P.O. Box 740, Campbellsport, 53010. Tel: 920-533-4441; Fax: 920-533-5280. In Res., Rev. Wayne J. Barta (Retired).
Catechesis/Religious Program— Included with St. Matthew , 419 Mill St., P.O. Box 740, Campbellsport, 53010.
AUBURN, FOND DU LAC CO., ST. MATTHIAS (1863), (German), Closed., For sacramental records, contact Holy Trinity, Kewaskum. Tel.: 262-626-2860.
BEAVER DAM, DODGE CO.
1—ST. KATHARINE DREXEL (2003), [CEM] Revs. William W. Key; Emmanuel Udo.
Res.: 131 W. Maple Ave., 53916. Tel: 920-887-2082; Fax: 920-885-7602.
Catechesis/Religious Program—Students 481.
2—ST. MICHAEL (1893), Merged, with St. Patrick, Beaver Dam & St. Peter, Beaver Dam to form St. Katharine Drexel, Beaver Dam
3—ST. PATRICK (1860), Merged, with St. Michael, Beaver Dam & St. Peter, Beaver Dam to form St. Katharine Drexel, Beaver Dam
4—ST. PETER (1855), Merged, with St. Michael, Beaver Dam & St. Patrick, Beaver Dam to form St. Katharine Drexel, Beaver Dam
BELGIUM, OZAUKEE CO., ST. MARY (1848), (German—Luxembourg), [CEM] Rev. James P. Vojtik.
Res.: 6092 Lake Church Rd., 53004. Tel: 262-285-3040; Fax: 262-285-4104.
School—Tel: 262-285-3532; Fax: 262-285-3532. JoAnn Karpin, Prin. Lay Teachers 3; Students 45.
Catechesis/Religious Program—Tel: 920-980-0660; Fax: 262-285-3040. Students 143.
BIG BEND, WAUKESHA CO., ST. JOSEPH (1920), Rev. Richard J. Robinson.
Res.: S89 W22650 Milwaukee Ave., 53103. Tel: 262-662-2832; Fax: 262-662-0783.
School—W227 S8930 St. Joseph Dr., 53103. Tel: 262-662-2737; Fax: 262-662-2684. Susan Holman, Prin. Lay Teachers 14; Students 209.
Catechesis/Religious Program—Tel: 262-662-3317. Mary L. Kozlik, D.R.E.; Rev. David J. Braun, D.R.E. (Retired). Students 416.
BRANDON, FOND DU LAC CO., ST. BRENDAN (1921), (German), [CEM], Also serves St. Joseph, Waupun and St. Mary, Springvale. Rev. Michael F. Moran.
Mailing Address: 118 W. Main St., Waupun, 53963. Tel: 920-324-5400; Fax: 920-324-1040.
Catechesis/Religious Program—Tel: 920-346-5110. Students 25.
BRIGHTON, KENOSHA CO., ST. FRANCIS XAVIER (1838), (German), [CEM] Rev. James T. Volkert; Cheryl Theigs, Pastoral Assoc.
Res.: 1704 240th Ave., Kansasville, 53139. Tel: 262-878-2267; Fax: 262-878-3683.
School—Providence Catholic School Consolidated with St. John the Baptist, 1481-172 N. Ave., Paris, Union Grove, WI 53182, Tel.: 262-878-2713. , 1714 240th Ave., Kansasville, 53139. Tel: 262-878-2713; Fax: 262-878-3299. Deacon Wilson A. Shierk, Prin. Sisters 1; Lay Teachers 7; Students 65.
Catechesis/Religious Program—Students 77.
BRISTOL, KENOSHA CO., ST. SCHOLASTICA (1945), [CEM] Rev. Roger Savage.
Res.: 18700 116th St., 53104. Tel: 262-857-2068.
Catechesis/Religious Program—Tel: 262-857-9032. Students 147.
BROOKFIELD, WAUKESHA CO.
1—ST. DOMINIC (1866), [CEM] Revs. Curt J. Frederick; Paul A. Stanosz; Deacon Larry LaFond; Patrick J. Russell, Ph.D., Adult & Family Min.; Susan Petersen, Pastoral Assoc.
Res.: 18255 W. Capitol Dr., 53045-1422. Tel: 262-781-3480; Fax: 262-781-3283.
School—18105 W. Capitol Dr., 53045-1425. Tel: 262-783-7565. Ms. Joyce Steffan, Prin. Lay Teachers 24; Students 434.
Catechesis/Religious Program—Kathleen Beuscher, D.R.E.; Debbie Olla, D.R.E. Students 725.
2—ST. JOHN VIANNEY (1956), Revs. Leonard S. Van Vlaenderen; Gerald J. Dominiak; Deacon Terry Starns.
Office—1755 N. Calhoun Rd., 53005-5036. Tel: 262-796-3940; Fax: 262-796-3958.
School—17500 W. Gebhardt Rd., 53045-5096. Tel: 262-796-3942; Fax: 262-796-3953. Colleen Terry, Prin. Lay Teachers 26; Students 476.
Catechesis/Religious Program—Tel: 262-796-3944. Students 938.
3—ST. LUKE (1956), Rev. Francis X. Malloy.
Res.: 1300 San Lucas Dr., 53045. Tel: 262-782-0032; Fax: 262-782-6057.
School—Fax: 262-782-5852. Mary Laidlaw-Otto, Prin. Lay Teachers 16; Students 210.
Catechesis/Religious Program—Jan Grosshadl, D.R.E. Students 300.
Convent—1305 Davidson Rd., 53045.
BURLINGTON, RACINE CO.
1—ST. CHARLES (1908), [CEM] Rev. Jan M. Kieliszewski.
Res.: 456 Kendall St., 53105. Tel: 262-763-2260; Fax: 262-763-9171.
School—449 Conkey St., 53105. Tel: 262-763-2848; 262-762-2637 (Grade School); Fax: 262-763-3818. Email: parishoffice@stmarysburlingtonwi.org. Sr. Margaret Pietsch, Prin. Lay Teachers 16; Students 223.
Catechesis/Religious Program—Tel: 262-763-1505; Fax: 262-763-4229. Email: parishoffice@stmarysburlingtonwi.org. Students 213.
2—IMMACULATE CONCEPTION (1838), [CEM] Very Rev. David H. Reith; Rev. Joseph E. Debski.
Res.: 108 McHenry St., 53105. Tel: 262-763-1500; Fax: 262-763-1680. Email: parishoffice@stmarysburlingtonwi.org.
School—225 W. State St., 53105. Tel: 262-763-1515; Fax: 262-763-1508. Email: parishoffice@stmarysburlingtonwi.org. Priests 2; Lay Teachers 17; Students 336.
Catechesis/Religious Program—Tel: 262-763-1505. Email: parishoffice@stmarysburlingtonwi.org. Mary Spiegelhoff, D.R.E. Students 361.
Chapel—Powers Lake, St. Theresa
BUTLER, WAUKESHA CO., ST. AGNES (1915), Rev. Timothy C. Bickel; Deacon Raymond Waitrovich.
Office—12801 W. Fairmount Ave., 53007. Tel: 262-781-9521; Fax: 262-781-3512.
School—Tel: 262-781-4996. Mrs. Jayme Hartmann, Prin. Sisters 1; Lay Teachers 14; Students 209.
Catechesis/Religious Program—Tel: 262-781-6998. Students 155.
BYRON, FOND DU LAC CO.
1—ST. JOHN (1847), Closed., For sacramental records contact Sons of Zebedee: Saints James and John, Byron. Tel.: 920-922-1167
2—SONS OF ZEBEDEE: SAINTS JAMES AND JOHN (2000), [CEM] Rev. James B. Posanski.
Mailing Address: W5882 Church Rd., Fond du Lac, 54937-8602. Tel: 920-922-1167; Fax: 920-922-1924.
Catechesis/Religious Program—Students 150.
CALEDONIA, RACINE CO., ST. LOUIS (1846), [CEM] Rev. Mark J. Danczyk; Deacon Jim Zdeb.
Parish Office—13207 Hwy. G, 53108-9533. Tel: 262-835-4533; Fax: 262-835-0421.
School—13125 Hwy. G, 53108-9533. Tel: 262-835-2166. Sr. Kathryn Dean Strandell, Prin. Lay Teachers 7; Students 49.
Catechesis/Religious Program—Students 217.
CAMPBELLSPORT, FOND DU LAC CO., ST. MATTHEW (1864), [CEM] Rev. Neil G. Zinthefer; Deacon Robert J. Fazen.
Parish Center—419 Mill St., P.O. Box 740, 53010. Tel: 920-533-4441; Fax: 920-533-5280.
School—Tel: 920-533-4103; Fax: 920-533-8078. Joan M. Wuest, Prin. Lay Teachers 11; Students 130.
Catechesis/Religious Program—Students 170.
CASCADE, SHEBOYGAN CO., ST. MARY- CASCADE (1852), Closed., For sacramental records, contact Our Lady of the Lakes, Random Lake. Tel.: 920-994-4380.
CEDARBURG, OZAUKEE CO.
1—DIVINE WORD (1970), Closed., For sacramental records, contact St. Francis Borgia, Cedarburg. Tel.: 262-377-1070
2—ST. FRANCIS BORGIA (1844), [CEM] Rev. Thomas Eichenberger.
Res.: 1375 Covered Bridge Rd., 53012. Tel: 262-377-1070; Fax: 262-377-6898.
School—N43 W6005 Hamilton Rd., 53012. Tel: 262-377-2050; Fax: 262-377-4099. Sue Brandley, Co-Prin.; Kelly Swietlik, Co-Prin. Lay Teachers 34; Students 395.
Catechesis/Religious Program—Pauline Underhill, D.R.E. Students 700.
CLYMAN, DODGE CO., ST. JOHN (1900), (German—Irish), [CEM 2], Also serves Holy Family, Reeseville & St. Columbkille, Elba. Rev. Patrick Wendt, Admin.
Mailing Address: P.O. Box 277, Reeseville, 53579-0277. Tel: 920-696-3430; 920-927-3102.
Catechesis/Religious Program—Students 15.
CUDAHY, MILWAUKEE CO.
1—ST. FREDERICK (1896), Closed., For sacramental records, contact Nativity of the Lord, Cudahy. Tel.: 414-744-6622
2—HOLY FAMILY (1900), Closed., For sacramental records, contact Nativity of the Lord, Cudahy. Tel.: 414-744-6622.
3—ST. JOSEPH (1909), (Slovak—Moravian), Closed., For sacramental records, contact Nativity of the Lord, Cudahy. Tel.: 414-744-6622.
4—NATIVITY OF THE LORD PARISH (2000), [JC] Rev. Philip D. Reifenberg, J.C.L.; Bryan Martin, Dir. Admin. Svcs.
Res.: 4611 S. Kirkwood Ave., 53110. Tel: 414-744-6622; Fax: 414-483-4599.
School—(Grades K-8), 3776 E. Hammond Ave., 53110. Tel: 414-481-0939; Fax: 414-481-2636. Barbara S. Lee, Prin. Religious 3; Lay Teachers 6; Students 80.
Catechesis/Religious Program—3658 E. Plankinton Ave., 53110. Tel: 414-481-6880. Students 60.
DACADA, SHEBOYGAN CO., ST. NICHOLAS (1848), (Luxembourgian), Closed., For sacramental records, contact Our Lady of the Lakes, Random Lake. Tel.: 920-994-4380.
DELAFIELD, WAUKESHA CO., ST. JOAN OF ARC (1923), [CEM] Rev. James P. Loehr.
Res.: 120 Nashotah Rd., Nashotah, 53058. Tel: 262-646-8078; Fax: 262-646-8079.
School—Tel: 262-646-5821; Fax: 262-646-5861. Mary Ann Rudella, Prin. Lay Teachers 9; Students 116.
Catechesis/Religious Program—Tel: 262-646-5979. Students 464.
DELAVAN, WALWORTH CO., ST. ANDREW (1848), [CEM] Rev. Brian Holbus.
Res.: 714 E. Walworth Ave., 53115. Tel: 262-728-5922; Fax: 262-728-5878.
School—Tel: 262-728-6211; Fax: 262-728-3683. Julie Supernaw, Prin. Lay Teachers 14; Students 171.
Catechesis/Religious Program—Tel: 262-728-2792. Mrs. Kathy Zambito, D.R.E. Students 252.
DOTYVILLE, FOND DU LAC CO., ST. MICHAEL (1853), (German), Closed., For sacramental records, contact Good Shepherd, 303 E. Main St., P.O. Box 128, Eden. Tel.: 920-477-3201; Fax: 920-477-3030
DOUSMAN, WAUKESHA CO., ST. BRUNO (1850), [CEM] Rev. John P. Schreiter; Deacons Tom Filipiak; Gordon J. Snyder; Jorge Benavente.
Res.: 266 W. Ottawa Ave., 53118. Tel: 262-965-2332; Fax: 262-965-4749.
School—Tel: 262-965-2291; Fax: 262-965-2249. Judith Hoeppner, Prin. Lay Teachers 10; Students 97.
Catechesis/Religious Program—Tel: 262-965-4200. Students 195.
EAGLE, WAUKESHA CO., ST. THERESA (1852), [CEM 2] Rev. Dennis Ackeret, Admin.
Office—136 W. Waukesha Rd., 53119-2026. Tel: 262-594-5200; Fax: 262-594-5201.
Catechesis/Religious Program—Tel: 262-594-5201. Students 240.
EAST TROY, WALWORTH CO., ST. PETER (1854), (Irish—German), [CEM] Rev. Lawrence J. Chapman; Deacon Donald Kuban.
Res.: 1975 Beulah Ave., 53120. Tel: 262-642-7225; Fax: 262-642-7228.
School—3001 Elm St., 53120. Tel: 262-642-5533; Fax: 262-642-5633. Randolph Kress, Prin. Lay Teachers 11; Students 138.
Catechesis/Religious Program—Tel: 262-642-3634. Students 248.
EDEN, FOND DU LAC CO.
1—ST. MARY (1888), (Irish), Closed., For sacramental records, contact Good Shepherd, 303 E. Main St., P.O. Box 128, Eden. Tel.: 920-477-3201; Fax: 920-477-3030
2—SHEPHERD OF THE HILLS (GOOD SHEPHERD) (2001), [JC 6] Rev. Kevin J. Wester.
Res.: 303 E. Main St., P.O. Box 128, 53019. Tel: 920-477-3201; Fax: 920-477-3030.
School—303 E. Main St., 53019. Tel: 920-477-3551;

Fax: 920-477-7211. Roselyn Baker, Prin. Lay Teachers 12; Students 76.
Catechesis/Religious Program—Tel: 920-477-3741. Mary Borgen, D.R.E. Students 260.
Mission—St. Michael Chapel Cascade. Scenic Dr., Mitchell, Sheboygan Co. 53011.

ELBA, DODGE CO., ST. COLUMBKILLE (1843), (Irish), [CEM], Also serves Holy Family, Reeseville and St. John the Baptist, Clyman. Rev. Patrick Wendt, Admin.
Mailing Address: P.O. Box 277, Reeseville, 53579-0277. Tel: 920-623-3989; 920-927-3102.
Catechesis/Religious Program—Students 8.

ELDORADO, FOND DU LAC CO.
1—ST. MARY, Closed., For sacramental records, contact Our Risen Savior, Eldorado. Tel.: 920-922-2412.
2—OUR RISEN SAVIOR (1998), [CEM 2] Rev. John Simon.
Church: W8272 Forest Avenue Rd., 54932-9631. Tel: 920-922-2412.
Catechesis/Religious Program—Students 125.

ELKHART LAKE, SHEBOYGAN CO.
1—ST. GEORGE (1896), Closed., For sacramental records, contact St. Thomas Aquinas, Elkhart Lake. Tel.: 920-876-2457
2—ST. THOMAS AQUINAS (2001), [CEM 2], (Merger of St. George, Elkhart Lake and St. Fridolin, Glenbeulah). Rev. Daniel J. Lasecki.
Res.: 94 N. Lincoln St., P.O. Box T, 53020-0396. Tel: 920-876-2457; Fax: 920-876-2036.
Catechesis/Religious Program—Students 213.

ELKHORN, WALWORTH CO., ST. PATRICK (1878), (Irish—German), [CEM] Rev. Michael Benham; Sr. Mary Lou Fischbach, Pastoral Assoc.
Res.: 107 W. Walworth St., 53121. Tel: 262-723-5565; Fax: 262-723-7856.
School—534 Sunset Dr., 53121. Tel: 262-734-4258; Fax: 262-723-8793. Mrs. Carol Degen, Prin. Lay Teachers 16; Students 149.
Catechesis/Religious Program—Tel: 262-203-1826. Students 328.

ELM GROVE, WAUKESHA CO., ST. MARY (1848), [CEM] Revs. Daniel J. Pakenham; Charles Conley; Deacons Charles J. Kustner; Richard T. Piontek; Richard D. Niggemann.
Res.: 1260 Church St., 53122. Tel: 262-782-4575; Fax: 262-782-0677.
School—Tel: 262-782-7057; Fax: 262-782-3035. Lynn Ann Reesman, Prin. Sisters 3; Lay Teachers 24; Students 466.
Catechesis/Religious Program—Tel: 262-782-9470. Students 194.

FARMINGTON, WASHINGTON CO., ST. JOHN OF GOD (1859), (Irish), Closed., For sacramental records, contact St. Michael Parish, St. Michael. Tel.: 262-334-5270.

FOND DU LAC, FOND DU LAC CO.
1—HOLY FAMILY (2000), Very Rev. Patrick E. Heppe, Team Moderator; Revs. Dennis G. Budka; Victor R. Capriolo; John J. Radetski.
Church: 26 W. Follett St., 54935. Tel: 920-921-0580; Fax: 920-921-6708.
Catechesis/Religious Program—Fax: 920-922-4866. Students 1,848.
2—ST. JOSEPH (1871), Closed., For sacramental records through June 12, 1967, contact Archdiocese of Milwaukee Archives Office. Tel.: 414-769-3407; For records after June 12, 1967, contact Holy Family, Fond du Lac. Tel.: 920-921-0580.
3—ST. LOUIS (1847), (French), Closed., For sacramental records through September 19, 1959, contact Archdiocese of Milwaukee Archives Office. Tel.: 414-769-3407; For records after September 19, 1959, contact Holy Family, Fond du Lac. Tel.: 920-921-0580.
4—ST. MARY (1866), (German), Closed., For sacramental records through 1975, contact Archdiocese of Milwaukee Archives Office. Tel.: 414-769-3407; For records after 1975, contact Holy Family, Fond du Lac. Tel.: 920-921-0580.
5—ST. PATRICK (1855), Closed., For sacramental records through September 18, 1960, contact Archdiocese of Milwaukee Archives Office. Tel.: 414-769-3407; For records after September 18, 1960, contact Holy Family, Fond du Lac. Tel.: 920-921-0580.
6—SACRED HEART (1957), (German), Closed., For sacramental records through November 1970, contact Archdiocese of Milwaukee Archives Office. Tel.: 414-769-3407; For records after November 1970, contact Holy Family, Fond du Lac. Tel.: 920-921-0580.

FONTANA, WALWORTH CO., ST. BENEDICT (1912), [JC] Rev. Daniel J. Sanders.
Res.: 137 Dewey Ave., 53125. Tel: 262-275-2480; Fax: 262-275-6426.
Catechesis/Religious Program—Tel: 262-275-2993. Patricia J. Donovan, D.R.E. (Grades 1-6); Edward Konieczka, D.R.E. (Grades 7-11). Students 255.

FOX LAKE, DODGE CO.
1—ANNUNCIATION (1998), [CEM 3] Rev. Michael L. Wild.
Res.: 305 W. Green St., 53933-9472. Tel: 920-928-3513; Fax: 920-928-6334.
Catechesis/Religious Program—Tel: 920-928-6022. Sr. Rose Marie Buscemi, O.S.F., D.R.E.; Linda Lentz, D.R.E. Students 105.
2—ST. MARY (1850), (Irish), Closed., For sacramental records, contact Annunciation, Fox Lake. Tel.: 920-928-3513.

FOX POINT, MILWAUKEE CO., ST. EUGENE (1957), Very Rev. Kenneth P. Knippel; Sr. Kathy Slesar, O.P., Pastoral Assoc.
Res.: 7600 N. Port Washington Rd., 53217. Tel: 414-918-1100; Fax: 414-918-1111.
School—Tel: 414-918-1120; Fax: 414-918-1122. Mr. Michael Taylor, Prin. Lay Teachers 2[illegible]; Students 274.
Catechesis/Religious Program—Tel: 414-918-1130. Ms. Jeanette Lambrecht, D.R.E. (Child Ministry); Mike Heimbach, D.R.E. (Youth Ministry). Students 328.

FRANKLIN, MILWAUKEE CO.
1—ST. JAMES (1857), [CEM] Rev. Kenneth J. Augustine.
Office—7219 S. 27th St., 53132. Tel: 414-761-0480; Fax: 414 761-2208.
Catechesis/Religious Program—Fax 414-761-0480. Students 180.
2—ST. MARTIN OF TOURS (1998), [CEM] Rev. Anthony P. Russo, S.C.J. In Res., Rev. John Nitzki, S.C.J.
Res.: 7963 S. 116th St., 53132. Tel: 414-425-1114; Fax: 414 425-2527.
School—7933 S. 116th St., 53132. Tel: 414-425-9200. Jeanne Johnson, Prin. Lay Teachers 11; Students 173.
Catechesis/Religious Program—Students 240.
3—SACRED HEARTS OF JESUS AND MARY (1858), Closed., For sacramental records, contact St. Martin of Tours, Franklin. Tel.: 414-425-1114.

FREDONIA, OZAUKEE CO.
1—HOLY ROSARY (2001), [CEM 4], (Merger of St. Rose of Lima, Fredonia; Mother of Sorrows, Little Kohler and Holy Cross, Holy Cross). Rev. Richard J. Fleischman.
Res.: 305 Fredonia Ave., P.O. Box 250, 53021-0250. Tel: 262-692-9994; Fax: 262-692-3085.
School—*Rosemary Catholic* 53021. Tel: 262-692-2141. Lay Teachers 7; Students 99.
Catechesis/Religious Program—Students 210.
2—ST. ROSE OF LIMA (1909), Closed., For sacramental records, contact Holy Rosary, Fredonia. Tel.: 262-692-9994

GENESEE DEPOT, WAUKESHA CO., ST. PAUL (1863), [CEM] Very Rev. Robert D. Gosma; Deacon Larry E. Normann; Len Grassmann, Pastoral Assoc.
Mailing Address: P.O. Box 95, 53127.
Res.: 53127. Tel: 262-968-3865; Fax: 262-968-5546.
School—Tel: 262-968-3175; Fax: 262-968-3867. Linda Cooney, Prin. Lay Teachers 11; Students 189.
Catechesis/Religious Program—Tel: 262-968-2276. Janet Shanahan, D.R.E. (Grades K-12); Mariangela Fledl, D.R.E. (Adult); Juan Armenta, Youth Min. (Grades 6-12). Students 600.

GERMANTOWN, WASHINGTON CO., ST. BONIFACE (1845), [CEM] Rev. Bernard S. Sippel.
Res.: W204 N11940 Goldendale Rd., 53022. Tel: 262-628-2040; Fax: 262-628-2076.
School—W204 N11968 Goldendale Rd., 53022. Tel: 262-628-1955; Fax: 262-628-1689. Lay Teachers 15; Students 295.
Catechesis/Religious Program—Tel: 262-628-8143. Students 631.

GLENBEULAH, SHEBOYGAN CO., ST. FRIDOLIN (1878), Closed., For sacramental records, contact St. Thomas Aquinas, Elkhart Lake. Tel.: 920-876-2457

GRAFTON, OZAUKEE CO., ST. JOSEPH (1849), [CEM] Rev. Michael G. Barrett; Deacon Richard J. Govek.
Pastoral Center—1619 Washington St., 53024. Tel: 262-375-6500; Fax: 262-375-6509.
School—1210 16th Ave., 53024. Tel: 262-375-6505. Lay Teachers 13; Students 193.
Catechesis/Religious Program—Students 442.

GREENDALE, MILWAUKEE CO., ST. ALPHONSUS (1938), Revs. Richard J. Aiken; Walter J. Vogel; Deacon Theodore A. Gurzynski.
Res.: 5960 W. Loomis Rd., 53129. Tel: 414-421-2442; Fax: 414-421-8744.
School—6000 W. Loomis Rd., 53129. Tel: 414-421-1760. Margaret Roushar, Prin. Lay Teachers 28; Students 350.
Catechesis/Religious Program—Tel: 414-421-0690. Students 854.

GREENFIELD, MILWAUKEE CO., ST. JOHN THE EVANGELIST (1916), Revs. Richard J. Talaska; Richard R. Verberg.
Res.: 8500 W. Cold Spring Rd., 53228. Tel: 414-321-1965; Fax: 414-321-4407.
School— 53228. Tel: 414-321-8540. Maria Schram, Prin. Lay Teachers 13; Students 208.
Catechesis/Religious Program—Tel: 414-321-8922; Fax: 414-321-8922. Debbie Melian, D.R.E. Tel: 414-321-4450. Students 202.

HALES CORNERS, MILWAUKEE CO., ST. MARY (1842), [CEM] Revs. Arthur G. Heinze; Gary D. Nowicki; Mary Matestic, Pastoral Assoc.
Res.: 9520 W. Forest Home Ave., 53130. Tel: 414-425-2174; Fax: 414-425-9432.
School—9553 W. Edgerton Ave., 53130. Tel: 414-425-3100; Fax: 414-425-6270. Jeanne Siegenthaler, Prin. Lay Teachers 30; Students 409.
Catechesis/Religious Program—Tel: 414-425-3101; Fax: 414-425-9432. Joanne Prei, D.R.E. (Children); Timothy Winters, D.R.E. (Young Adult). Students 1,273.

HARTFORD, WASHINGTON CO., ST. KILIAN (1863), [CEM 4] Rev. Michael J. Petrie. Tel: 262-673-4831, Ext. 401; Sr. Helen Hurley, Pastoral Assoc. Tel: 262-673-4831, Ext. 402.
Res.: 428 First St., 53027. Tel: 262-673-4831; Fax: 262-673-4872.
School—245 High St., 53027. Tel: 262-673-3081; Fax: 262-673-0412. Beverly Miller, Prin. Tel: 262-673-3081, Ext. 116. Lay Teachers 17; Students 220.
Catechesis/Religious Program—Tel: 262-673-3746. June Strobel, D.R.E. Tel: 262-673-4831, Ext. 406. Students 324.

HARTLAND, WAUKESHA CO., ST. CHARLES (1906), [CEM] Rev. Thomas P. Demse.
Office—313 Circle Dr., 53029-1824. Tel: 262-367-0800; Fax: 262-367-6960.
Res.: 521 Renson Rd., 53029. Tel: 262-367-9936.
School—Tel: 262-367-2040. Douglas Dunlop, Prin. Lay Teachers 15; Students 204.
Catechesis/Religious Program—Tel: 262-367-3277. Students 895.

HOLY CROSS, OZAUKEE CO., HOLY CROSS (1845), (Luxembourgian), Closed., For sacramental records, contact Holy Rosary, Fredonia. Tel.: 262-692-9994

HOLY HILL, WASHINGTON CO., ST. MARY OF THE HILL (1860), (German—Irish), [CEM] [JC] Rev. Mark Develis, O.C.D.
Res.: 1525 Carmel Rd., Hubertus, 53033. Tel: 262-628-3606; 262-673-7505; Fax: 262-673-7568.
Catechesis/Religious Program—Tel: 262-628-3606, Ext. 4. Sue Krebs, D.R.E. Students 158.

HORICON, DODGE CO.
1—ST. MALACHY (1856), Closed., For sacramental records, contact Sacred Heart, Horicon. Tel.: 920-485-2427
2—SACRED HEART (2001), [CEM 2], (Merger of St. Malachy, Horicon and Immaculate Conception, Juneau) Rev. M. Eugene Kinney.
Parish Center—113 Valley St., 53032. Tel: 920-485-2427; Fax: 920-485-2427.
Res.: 319 N. Main St., Juneau, 53039. Tel: 920-386-4964.
Catechesis/Religious Program—Tel: 920-485-2708. Students 267.

HUBERTUS, WASHINGTON CO.
1—ST. GABRIEL (2002), [CEM] [JC 3] Rev. Charles T. Hanel.
Res.: 3727 Hubertus Rd., 53033. Tel: 262-628-1141; Fax: 262-628-1911.
School—3733 Hubertus Rd., 53033. Tel: 262-628-1711; Fax: 262-628-0280. Lay Teachers 14; Students 138.
Catechesis/Religious Program—Tel: 262-628-2840. Students 348.
2—ST. HUBERT (1846), Merged, with St. Columba, Lake Five and St. Mary, Richfield to from St. Gabriel, Hubertus. Tel.: 262-628-1141

JOHNSBURG, FOND DU LAC CO., ST. JOHN THE BAPTIST (1840), [CEM] Rev. Joseph H. Coerber.
Res.: N9288 County W, Fond du Lac, 54935. Tel: 920-795-4316; Fax: 920-898-9002.
School—(Grades 3-6) Tel: 920-795-4222. Sharon Allen, Coord.
School—Consolidated Parochial Elementary School See Holy Cross, Mount Calvary. Tel: 920-753-4811.
Catechesis/Religious Program—Tel: 920-898-4040. Students 146.

JUNEAU, DODGE CO., IMMACULATE CONCEPTION (1875), Closed., For sacramental records, contact Sacred Heart, Horicon. Tel.: 920-485-2427

KANSASVILLE, RACINE CO., ST. MARY-DOVER (1869), [CEM] Rev. James B. Cera.
Mailing Address: P.O. Box 126, 53139.
Res.: 23211 Church Rd., 53139. Tel: 262-878-1762.
Catechesis/Religious Program—Tel: 262-878-4943. Students 85.

KENOSHA, KENOSHA CO.
1—ST. ANTHONY (1910), (Slovak), [JC] Rev. Paul L. Raczynski.
Mailing Address: 2223 51st St., 53140. Tel: 262-652-1844; Fax: 262-605-8262.
Catechesis/Religious Program—Students 17.
2—ST. CASIMIR (1901), Closed., For sacramental records, contact Archdiocese of Milwaukee Archives Office. Tel.: 414-769-3407
3—ST. ELIZABETH (2000), (Polish—German), [CEM 2] Rev. Roman Stikel.
Res.: 4816 7th Ave., 53140-3347. Tel: 262-657-6875.

Catechesis/Religious Program—Tel: 262-657-1156, Ext. 110; Fax: 262-657-1495. Students 43.
4—ST. GEORGE (1851), (German), Closed., For sacramental records, contact Archdiocese of Milwaukee Archives Office. Tel.: 414-769-3407.
5—ST. JAMES (1845), (Irish), [CEM] Rev. Frederick A. Heuser.
Res.: 5804 Sheridan Rd., 53140. Tel: 262-658-8071; Fax: 262-658-2490.
Catechesis/Religious Program—Students 52.
6—ST. MARK (1924), Very Rev. Kenneth J. Metz; Rev. Carlos A. Florez Ardila; Deacons Patrick H. Frye; Gregorio M. Lebron; Alvaro Dominguez; Charles Short, Business Mgr.; Karen Metallo, Pastoral Assoc.
Res.: 7117 14th Ave., 53143. Tel: 262-656-7373; Fax: 262-656-7375.
School—7207 14th Ave., 53143. Tel: 262-656-7360. Frank Germinaro, Prin. School Sisters of St. Francis 1; Lay Teachers 12; Students 180.
Junior Academy— (Preschool) Tel: 262-656-7363. Lay Teachers 2; Students 30.
Catechesis/Religious Program—Tel: 262-656-7362. Colleen A. Reddy, D.R.E. Students 430.
Latin American Center—1320 73rd St., 53143-5459. Tel: 262-656-7370.
7—ST. MARY (1929), Very Rev. Michael T. Newman; Rev. Mark J. Niehaus; Deacons Ronald F. Lesjak; James S. Francois; Wilson A. Shierk.
Res.: 7307 40th Ave., 53142. Tel: 262-694-6018; Fax: 262-694-6048.
School—7400 39th Ave., 53142. Tel: 262-694-6018, Ext. 130; Fax: 262-694-6740. Sandra Wiercinski, Prin. Lay Teachers 20; Students 326.
Catechesis/Religious Program—Jane Delfield, D.R.E.; Sandy Slivon, D.R.E.; Edith Padgett, Youth Min. Students 784.
8—OUR LADY OF MOUNT CARMEL (1904), (Italian), Rev. John J. Richetta.
Res.: 1919 54th St., 53140. Tel: 262-652-7660; 262-652-7683; Fax: 262-652-2542.
School—5400 19th Ave., 53140. Tel: 262-652-7660. Paul Cera, Prin. Lay Teachers 8; Students 145.
Catechesis/Religious Program—Tel: 262-652-5057. Students 260.
9—OUR LADY OF THE HOLY ROSARY (1904), (Italian), Revs. Allen J. Bratkowski; Thunkuchan Steve Varghese, S.A.C.
Res.: 2224 45th St., 53140. Tel: 262-652-2771; Fax: 262-652-0183.
School—4400 22nd Ave., 53140. Tel: 262-652-5950; Fax: 262-652-6179. Sr. M. Bertina, F.S.S.J., Prin. Franciscan Sisters of St. Joseph (Hamburg, NY) 7; Lay Teachers 13; Students 338.
Catechesis/Religious Program—Fax: 262-652-1083. Mrs. Emily Selovich, D.R.E. Students 283.
10—ST. PETER (1903), Revs. William Hayward, M.I.C.; Pete Cibulskis, M.I.C.; Deacon Terrance A. Maack.
Res.: 2224 30th Ave., 53144. Tel: 262-551-9004; Fax: 262-552-7004.
School—Tel: 262-551-8383; Fax: 262-551-9833. Rev. John R. Kolanko, Prin. Lay Teachers 8; Students 102.
Catechesis/Religious Program—Tel: 262-897-2602. Students 300.
11—ST. THERESE (1953), Rev. Michael E. Nowak.
Res.: 9005 22nd Ave., 53143-6699. Tel: 262-694-4695; Fax: 262-694-7284.
School—2020 91st St., 53143. Tel: 262-694-8080. Mrs. Jean Kuklenski, Prin. Lay Teachers 10; Students 121.
Catechesis/Religious Program—Tel: 262-694-0118. Students 209.
12—ST. THOMAS AQUINAS (1911), Closed., For sacramental records, contact Archdiocese of Milwaukee Archives Office. Tel.: 414-769-3407
KEWASKUM, WASHINGTON CO., HOLY TRINITY (1861), [CEM 2] [JC 3] Rev. Mark R. Jones.
Res.: 331 Main St., P.O. Box 461, 53040. Tel: 262-626-2860; Fax: 262-626-2301.
School—305 Main St., 53040. Tel: 262-626-2603; Fax: 262-626-8863. Mrs. June Gauvin, Prin. Lay Teachers 15; Students 169.
Catechesis/Religious Program—Tel: 262-626-2650. Mrs. Sharon Warsh, D.R.E. Students 272.
KOHLER, SHEBOYGAN CO., ST. JOHN EVANGELIST (1927), Rev. Thomas F. Lijewski.
Res.: 600 Green Tree Rd., 53044. Tel: 920-452-9623; Fax: 920-452-9633.
Catechesis/Religious Program—Tel: 920-458-9931. Students 219.
LAKE FIVE, WASHINGTON CO., ST. COLUMBA (1843), Merged, with St Hubert, Hubertus and St. Mary, Richfield to from St. Gabriel, Hubertus. Tel.: 262-628-1141
LAKE GENEVA, WALWORTH CO., ST. FRANCIS DE SALES (1842), [CEM] Revs. Terrance J. Huebner; Julio Mirables Drago.
Res.: 148 W. Main St., 53147. Tel: 262-248-8524; Fax: 262-248-5302.
School—130 Main St., 53147. Tel: 262-248-2778; Fax: 262-248-7860. Lay Teachers 9; Students 190.
Catechesis/Religious Program—Tel: 262-248-8526. Mrs. Rita Leahy, D.R.E. Students 247.
LE ROY, DODGE CO., ST. ANDREW (1849), [CEM], Also serves St. Mary, Mayville. Very Rev. Charles H. Wester.
Res.: W3081 County Tr. Y, Lomira, 53048. Tel: 920-583-4125; 920-387-2470; Fax: 920-387-1121.
Catechesis/Religious Program—Students 49.
LIMA, SHEBOYGAN CO., ST. ROSE (1860), Closed., For sacramental records, contact Blessed Trinity, Sheboygan Falls. Tel.: 920-467-4616
LITTLE KOHLER, OZAUKEE CO., MOTHER OF SORROWS, Closed., For sacramental records, contact Holy Rosary, Fredonia. Tel.: 262-692-9994
LOMIRA, DODGE CO., ST. MARY (1870), (German), [CEM] Rev. Kevin J. Kowalske.
Res.: 699 Milwaukee St., 53048. Tel: 920-269-4429; Fax: 920-269-7359.
School—(Grades 4-8), 705 Milwaukee St., 53048. Tel: 920-269-4326. Dorothy Zitlow, Prin. Consolidated with St. Theresa to form Consolidated Catholic School of Lomira-Theresa. Lay Teachers 8; Students 81.
Catechesis/Religious Program—Tel: 920-269-7273. Gail Stephany, D.R.E. Students 176.
LOST LAKE, DODGE CO., ST. MARY (1893), Closed., For sacramental records, contact Annunciation, Fox Lake. Tel.: 920-928-3513.
LYONS, WALWORTH CO.
1—ST. JOSEPH (1870), (German), [CEM 2] Daniel L. Hull, Parish Dir.
Res.: 1540 Mill St., Box 60, 53148-0060. Tel: 262-763-2050; Fax: 262-763-9377.
Catechesis/Religious Program—Students 88.
2—ST. KILIAN, Closed., For sacramental records, contact St. Joseph, Lyons. Tel.: 262-763-2050.
MAPLETON, WAUKESHA CO., ST. CATHERINE (1847), (Irish), [CEM] Rev. David A. Verhasselt.
Res.: W359 N8512 Brown St., Oconomowoc, 53066. Tel: 920-474-7000; 877-871-8489 (Toll Free); Fax: 920-474-4661.
Catechesis/Religious Program—Fax: 920-474-4461. Students 227.
MARYTOWN, FOND DU LAC CO., ST. MARY (1849), [CEM] Rev. Joseph H. Coerber.
Res.: N10232 Hwy. 149, New Holstein, 53061. Tel: 920-898-4040; Fax: 920-898-9002.
School— See Holy Cross, Mt. Calvary for details. Tel: 920-753-4811.
Catechesis/Religious Program—Students 60.
MAYVILLE, DODGE CO., ST. MARY (1856), [CEM], Also serves St. Andrew, LeRoy. Very Rev. Charles H. Wester; Deacon Willis Heideman.
Res.: 112 S. German St., P.O. Box 22, 53050-0022. Tel: 920-387-2470; 920-387-3130 (Parish Center); Fax: 920-387-1121.
School—(Grades PreK-2), W. 3018 City Hwy. Y, Lomira, 53048. Tel: 920-583-4286.
School—(Grades 3-8), 28 Naber St., 53050. Tel: 920-387-2920. Lay Teachers 13; Students 153.
Catechesis/Religious Program—Fax: 920-387-0362. Students 269.
MENOMONEE FALLS, WAUKESHA CO.
1—ST. ANTHONY (1846), [CEM] Rev. Jerry Repenshek; Deacon Robert A. Wodushek.
Res.: N74 W13604 Appleton Ave., 53051. Tel: 262-251-5910; Fax: 262-251-6564.
School—N74 W13646 Appleton Ave., 53051. Tel: 262-251-4390; Fax: 262-251-2412. Anne Schramka, Prin. Lay Teachers 18; Students 215.
Catechesis/Religious Program—Tel: 262-251-8868. Marian Lamoureux, Dir. Youth and Adult & Family Min.; Chris Meier, Dir. Child Min. Students 493.
2—GOOD SHEPHERD (1957), Rev. Kenneth A. Mich; Deacon Eugene M. Christensen; Joseph Strazishar, Dir. of Admin. Svcs.; Jane Clare Ishiguro, Pastoral Assoc.
Church & Office: N88 W17658 Christman Rd., 53051-2630. Tel: 262-255-2035; Fax: 262-255-2020.
Catechesis/Religious Program—Matthew Hakes, D.R.E.; Jean Newman, D.R.E. Students 680.
3—ST. JAMES (1847), [CEM] Rev. Eugene J. Doda Jr.; Patricia Knuth, Pastoral Assoc.
Res.: W 220-N 6588 Town Line Rd., 53051. Tel: 262-251-3944; Fax: 262-250-2679.
Catechesis/Religious Program—Tel: 262-251-0897. Sr. Carol Ann Jaeger, D.R.E. (Adult Min.); Dorothy Grantham, D.R.E. (Youth Min.); Vicki Lopez-Kaley, D.R.E. (Child Min.). Students 824.
4—ST. MARY (1905), [CEM] Revs. Gregory J. Greiten; Quintin T. Heck; Sr. Jane Mary Lorbiecki, S.S.N.D., Pastoral Assoc.; Deacons Robert H. Buth; Thomas H. Wuchterl.
Res.: N89W 16297 Cleveland Ave., 53051. Tel: 262-251-0220; Fax: 262-251-6948.
School—N. 89 W. 16215 Cleveland Ave., 53051. Tel: 262-251-1050; Fax: 262-502-1671. Christopher Montezon, Prin. Lay Teachers 26; Students 420.
Catechesis/Religious Program—Tel: 262-251-1154. Students 299.
MEQUON, OZAUKEE CO., ST. JAMES (1851), (German), [CEM] Rev. Thomas D. DeVries. Tel: 262-242-7967; Deacons Clif Perryman. Tel: 262-512-1460; Anthony Monfre. Tel: 262-241-4719.
Res.: 11300 N. St. James Ln.,, 53092. Tel: 262-242-7967; Fax: 262-242-7970.
School—*SS. Cecilia and James*, (Grades PreK-8) Tel: 262-242-7960; Fax: 262-512-8986. Mr. Richard Goeden, Prin. Consolidated with St. Cecilia, Thiensville. Sisters 2; Lay Teachers 38; Students 556.
Catechesis/Religious Program—Tel: 262-512-8983; Fax: 262-242-7970. Vicki Clark, D.R.E. (Youth); Terri Schiller, D.R.E. (Child); Jeff Wenzler, Dir. Teen Formation. Consolidated program with St. Cecilia, Thiensville Students 720.
MITCHELL, SHEBOYGAN CO., ST. MICHAEL (1852), Closed., For sacramental records, contact Good Shepherd, 303 E. Main St., P.O. Box 128, Eden. Tel.: 920-477-3201; Fax: 920-477-3030
MONCHES, WAUKESHA CO., ST. JOHN (1843), [CEM] Rev. Anthony T. McCarthy.
Mailing Address: c/o St. Clare, P.O. Box 68, North Lake, 53064. Tel: 262-966-2191; Fax: 262-966-1829.
Catechesis/Religious Program— Clustered with St. Clare, North Lake. Tel: 262-966-7010. Students 67.
MOUNT CALVARY, FOND DU LAC CO., HOLY CROSS (1849), [CEM] Rev. Peter P. Kutch, O.F.M.Cap.
Res.: P.O. Box 176, 53057. Tel: 920-753-3311; Fax: 920-753-2130.
School—(Grades 1-8), 100 Notre Dame St., 53057. Tel: 920-753-4811; Fax: 920-753-2411. Consolidated Parochial Elementary School Mount Calvary (CPES): St. John the Baptist, Johnsburg; St. Mary, Marytown; Holy Cross, Mount Calvary; St. Cloud, St. Cloud. Lay Teachers 15; Students 151.
Catechesis/Religious Program—Students 125.
MUKWONAGO, WAUKESHA CO., ST. JAMES (1896), Rev. Robert J. Drutowski.
Res.: 830 Hwy. NN East, 53149. Tel: 262-363-7615; Fax: 262-363-2416.
School—Tel: 262-363-8152. Jeanne Caldwell, Prin. Lay Teachers 12; Students 188.
Catechesis/Religious Program—Tel: 262-363-5529. Students 653.
MUSKEGO, WAUKESHA CO., ST. LEONARD CONGREGATION (1957), Rev. Jerome A. Rinzel; Deacon Ralph Wisniewski; Carlene S. Larson, Pastoral Assoc.
Res.: W173 S7743 Westwood Dr., 53150. Tel: 262-679-1773; Fax: 262-679-4210.
School—Tel: 262-679-0451; Fax: 262-679-8519. Richard Bagemihl, Prin. Lay Teachers 14; Students 229.
Catechesis/Religious Program—Tel: 262-679-0880; Fax: 262-679-8502. Judee Weber, D.R.E. Students 951.
NABOB, WASHINGTON CO., ST. MATTHIAS (1848), Closed., For sacramental records, contact St. Lawrence Parish, St. Lawrence. Tel.: 262-644-5701.
NENNO, WASHINGTON CO.
1—ST. ANTHONY, Closed., For sacramental records, contact Resurrection, Allenton. Tel.: 262-629-5240.
2—SS. PETER AND PAUL (1848), Closed., For sacramental records, contact Resurrection, Allenton. Tel.: 262-629-5240.
NEOSHO, DODGE CO., ST. MATTHEW (1857), (German), [CEM], Also serves St. Mary, Woodland & St. John, Rubicon. Rev. Alois Van Beek.
Res.: 148 W. Lehman St., P.O. Box 45, 53059. Tel: 920-625-3144; Fax: 920-625-2143.
Catechesis/Religious Program—Tel: 920-625-3092. Students 117.
Mission—St. Mary Woodland, Dodge Co. 53099.
NEW BERLIN, WAUKESHA CO.
1—ST. ELIZABETH ANN SETON (1981), Rev. Steven J. Amann; Deacon John D'Alessio.
Church & Office: 12700 W. Howard Ave., 53151. Tel: 262-782-6760; Fax: 262-782-4763.
Catechesis/Religious Program—Tel: 262-782-8982. Marilyn Zwick, D.R.E. Students 648.
2—HOLY APOSTLES (1855), [CEM] Revs. David C. Filut; Joseph G. Anderson.
Res.: 16000 W. National Ave., 53151. Tel: 262-786-7330; Fax: 262-786-0425.
School—Tel: 262-786-7331. Gregory Dehli-Young, Prin. Sisters 1; Lay Teachers 24; Students 499.
Catechesis/Religious Program—Tel: 262-786-2035. Students 578.
NEW MUNSTER, KENOSHA CO., ST. ALPHONSUS (1849), (German), [CEM] Rev. Thomas E. Biersack.
Res.: 6301 344th Ave., P.O. Box 767, 53152. Tel: 262-537-4370; Fax: 262-537-4370.
School—Tel: 262-537-4379; Fax: 262-537-3527. Lay Teachers 7; Students 84.
Catechesis/Religious Program—Tel: 262-537-4359. Students 192.
NEWBURG, WASHINGTON CO., HOLY TRINITY (1859), (German), [CEM 3] Rev. Guy Gurath; Deacon Steven J. Przedpelski.
Res.: Box 16, 53060-0016. Tel: 262-675-6256. Email: htrinity@execpc.com.
Catechesis/Religious Program—Tel: 262-675-6933.

Students 86.
Station—St. Augustine (1857), Trenton.
Station—St. Peter (1855), Farmington.

NORTH FOND DU LAC, FOND DU LAC CO., PRESENTATION OF THE BLESSED VIRGIN (1902), [JC] Rev. John Simon; Deacon Paul S. Monzel.
Res.: 705 Michigan Ave., 54937. Tel: 920-921-9383; Fax: 920-921-1309.
Catechesis/Religious Program—Tel: 920-921-5873. Email: htrinity@execpc.com. Alice Newton, D.R.E. Students 256.

NORTH LAKE, WAUKESHA CO., ST. CLARE (1916), [CEM] Rev. Anthony T. McCarthy.
Res.: P.O. Box 68, 53064. Tel: 262-966-2191; Fax: 262-966-1829.
Catechesis/Religious Program—Tel: 262-966-7010. Email: htrinity@execpc.com. Students 429.

OAK CREEK, MILWAUKEE CO., ST. MATTHEW (1841), [CEM] Rev. William L. Stanfield; Alice Hatzenbeller, Pastoral Assoc.
Res.: 9303 S. Chicago Rd., 53154. Tel: 414-762-4200; Fax: 414-571-9973.
School—9329 S. Chicago Rd., 53154. Tel: 414-762-6820; Fax: 414-762-3686. Email: htrinity@execpc.com. Lay Teachers 12; Students 230.
Catechesis/Religious Program—Tel: 414-762-6847. Email: htrinity@execpc.com. Students 311.

OAKFIELD, FOND DU LAC CO., ST. JAMES (1909), Closed., For sacramental records, contact Sons of Zebedee: Saints James and John, Byron. Tel.: 920-583-4376.

OCONOMOWOC, WAUKESHA CO., ST. JEROME (1860), [CEM] Rev. John G. Yockey.
Res.: 211 S. Main St., 53066. Tel: 262-569-3020; Fax: 262-569-3022.
School—110 Third St., 53066. Tel: 262-569-3030; Fax: 262-569-3023. Email: htrinity@execpc.com. Third Order Schoenstatt 1; Lay Teachers 23; Students 291.
Catechesis/Religious Program—Tel: 262-569-3025. Email: htrinity@execpc.com. Students 445.

PARIS, KENOSHA CO., ST. JOHN THE BAPTIST (1859), [CEM] Rev. James T. Volkert; Cheryl Theigs, Pastoral Assoc.
Parish Office—1501 172nd Ave., Union Grove, 53182. Tel: 262-859-2484; Fax: 262-859-2684.
School—Providence Catholic School Consolidated with St. Francis Xavier, Brighton. , 1481 172nd Ave., Union Grove, 53182. Tel: 262-859-2007; 262-878-2713; Fax: 262-859-2604. Email: htrinity@execpc.com. Deacon Wilson A. Shierk, Prin. Religious 1; Lay Teachers 7; Students 65.
Catechesis/Religious Program—Email: htrinity@execpc.com. Students 83.

PELL LAKE, WALWORTH CO., ST. MARY (1928), [JC] Rev. Dennis D. Callahan; Marilyn Kingston, Parish Coord.
Res.: Box 34, 53157. Tel: 262-279-6295.
Catechesis/Religious Program—Email: htrinity@execpc.com. Students 107.

PEWAUKEE, WAUKESHA CO.
1—ST. ANTHONY (1918), Rev. R. Thomas Venne; Margaret Horner, Pastoral Assoc.
Res.: W 280 N 2101 Hwy. SS., 53072. Fax: 262-691-2063. Email: htrinity@execpc.com.
School—Tel: 262-691-0460; 262-691-1173 (Parish Center); Fax: 262-691-7376. Email: htrinity@execpc.com. Lay Teachers 18; Students 184.
Catechesis/Religious Program—Tel: 262-691-9170. Email: htrinity@execpc.com. Ann Fons, D.R.E.; Debbie Rusch, D.R.E.; Clare Peiffer, D.R.E.; Jon Metz, D.R.E. Students 830.
2—ST. MARY (1858), Closed., For sacramental records, contact Queen of Apostles, Pewaukee. Tel.: 262-691-1535
3—SS. PETER AND PAUL (1848), Closed., For sacramental records, contact Queen of Apostles, Pewaukee. Tel.: 262-691-1535.
4—QUEEN OF APOSTLES (1997), [CEM 2], Consolidation of St. Mary's, Pewaukee and Ss. Peter and Paul, Pewaukee. Rev. R. Michael Grellinger.
Mailing Address: P.O. Box 220, 53072. Tel: 262-691-1535; Fax: 262-691-9219.
School—449 W. Wisconsin Ave.. Tel: 262-691-2120; Fax: 262-691-8606. Email: htrinity@execpc.com. Pamela Kalaczynski, Prin. Tel: 262-691-2120. Lay Teachers 9; Students 186.
Catechesis/Religious Program—Tel: 262-691-2878. Lynn Famularo, D.R.E.; Bill Eder, D.R.E. Students 510.

PLEASANT PRAIRIE, KENOSHA CO., ST. ANNE (1998), Rev. Donald H. Thimm.
Mailing Address: 8550 88th Ave., 53158-2016. Tel: 262-942-8300; Fax: 262-942-8472.
Catechesis/Religious Program—Email: htrinity@execpc.com. Students 280.

PLYMOUTH, SHEBOYGAN CO., ST. JOHN THE BAPTIST (1861), [CEM] Rev. Dennis E. Van Beek.
Res.: 115 Plymouth St., 53073. Tel: 920-892-4006; Fax: 920-893-8444.
School—116 Pleasant St., 53073. Tel: 920-893-5961; Fax: 920-893-3160. Mary Jo Sizonen, Prin. Lay Teachers 17; Students 291.
Catechesis/Religious Program—Tel: 920-892-6015. Email: htrinity@exepc.com. Students 391.

PORT WASHINGTON, OZAUKEE CO.
1—ST. MARY (1853), [CEM] Rev. Allan J. Sommer.
Office—430 N. Johnson St., 53074. Tel: 262-284-5771; Fax: 262-284-4112.
School— Consolidated with St. Peter of Alcantara to form Port Washington Catholic School, Inc. , 1802 N. Wisconsin St., 53074. Tel: 262-284-2441 (PreK-4); 262-284-2682 (Grades 5-8); Fax: 262-284-4216. Email: htrinity@execpc.com. School Sisters of Notre Dame 1; Lay Teachers 21; Students 276.
Catechesis/Religious Program— Consolidated with St. Peter of Alcantara, Port Washington. Tel: 262-284-6472. Sr. Mary Hornung, C.S.A., D.R.E. (Grades K-6); Maureen Kavanaugh, D.R.E. (Grades 7-11). Tel: 262-284-2102. Students 350.
2—ST. PETER OF ALCANTARA (1966), Rev. Joseph H. Haas; Deacon Thomas J. Surges.
Res.: 1800 N. Wisconsin St., 53074. Tel: 262-284-4266; Fax: 262-284-4216.
School—Port Washington Catholic School See St. Mary for details. Tel: 262-284-2382; Fax: 262-284-4168.
Catechesis/Religious Program— Clustered with St. Mary, Port Washington. Tel: 262-284-6472 (Child Ministry ; 262-284-2102 (Youth Ministry). Sr. Mary Hornung, C.S.A., D.R.E. (Grades K-6); Maureen Kavanaugh, D.R.E. (Grades 7-12). Students 282.

RACINE, RACINE CO.
1—ST. CASIMIR (1913), (Lithuanian), Closed., For sacramental records, contact Archdiocese of Milwaukee Archives Office. Tel.: 414-769-3407.
2—CRISTO REY (1980), (Hispanic), Rev Robert J. McGlinn (CHI), Admin.
Res.: 800 Wisconsin Ave., 53403. Tel: 262-632-3151; Fax: 262-886-6167.
Catechesis/Religious Program—Students 210.
3—ST. EDWARD (1919), Rev. Richard J. Molter.
Office and Res.: 1401 Grove Ave., 53405. Tel: 262-636-3040; 262-636-8049 (Res); Fax: 262-636-8052. Email: htrinity@execpc.com.
School—1435 Grove Ave., 53405. Tel: 262-636-8044; Fax: 262-636-8046. Email: htrinity@execpc.com. Joseph Majowski, Prin. Dominican Sisters (Racine) 1; Lay Teachers 21; Students 390.
Catechesis/Religious Program—Tel: 262-636-8042. Students 155.
4—HOLY NAME, Closed., For sacramental records, contact Archdiocese of Milwaukee Archives Office. Tel.: 417-769-3407.
5—HOLY NAME (1884), (German), Closed , For sacramental records, contact Archdiocese of Milwaukee Archives Office. Tel.: 414-769-3407.
6—HOLY TRINITY (1914), Closed., For sacramental records, contact Archdiocese of Milwaukee Archives Office. Tel.: 414-769-3407
7—ST. JOHN NEPOMUK (1896), [JC] Mrs. Sande K. Jensen, Parish Dir.
Res.: 700 English St., 53402. Tel: 262-634-5647; Fax: 262-637-1436.
School—1923 Green St., 53402. Tel: 262-637-9349; Fax: 262-637-0711. Email: htrinity@execpc.com. School Sisters of St. Francis 1; Lay Teachers 12; Students 120.
Catechesis/Religious Program—Email: htrinity@execpc.com. Students 44.
8—ST. JOSEPH (1875), (German), [JC 4] Rev. John D. Aiello.
Office—1532 N. Wisconsin St., 53402. Tel: 262-633-8284; Fax: 262-633-8285. Email: htrinity@execpc.com.
Res.: 1526 Erie St., 53402. Tel: 262-632-6487.
School—1525 Erie St., 53402. Tel: 262-633-2403. Email: htrinity@execpc.com. Charles T. Cooper, Prin. Lay Teachers 18; Students 240.
Catechesis/Religious Program—Tel: 262-633-9005. Email: htrinity@execpc.com. Susan Gehrig, D.R.E. Students 222.
9—ST. LUCY (1958), Rev. Jeffrey M. Thielen.
Res.: 3101 Drexel Ave., 53403. Tel: 262-554-1801; Fax: 262-554-2009.
School—3035 Drexel, 53403. Fax: 262-554-7618. Email: htrinity@execpc.com. Lay Teachers 14; Students 289.
Catechesis/Religious Program—Email: htrinity@execpc.com. Sandra Gottfredsen, D.R.E. Students 277.
10—ST. MARY BY THE LAKE (1852), [JC] Rev. Stephen J. Stracinger, Admin.; Deacon James E. Devona.
Mailing Address: P.O. Box 044200, 53404-7004. Tel: 262-639-3616; Fax: 262-639-1999.
Church: 7605 Lakeshore Dr., 53402.
Catechesis/Religious Program—Tel: 262-639-4493. Students 126.
11—ST. PATRICK (1856), (Hispanic), [JC 4] Rev. Oriol Regales, Admin.; Deacon Emilio Coca.
Res.: 1100 Erie St., 53402. Tel: 262-632-8808; Fax: 262-637-1536.
Catechesis/Religious Program—Email: htrinity@execpc.com. Students 90.
12—ST. PAUL THE APOSTLE (1965), [JC] Rev. Paul M. Esser; Deacon Willard M. Widmar.
Res.: 6400 Spring St., 53406. Tel: 262-886-0530; Fax: 262-886-0737.
Catechesis/Religious Program—Tel: 262-886-0531. Carol Badzinski, D.R.E.; Pat Jorgenson, Adult & Family Coord. Students 189.
13—ST. RICHARD OF CHICHESTER (1998), [JC] Very Rev. John R. Kern; Deacon Howard J. Wirtz.
Res.: 1509 Grand Ave., 53403. Tel: 262-637-8374; Fax: 262-635-2426.
School—1510 Villa St., 53403. Tel: 262-637-7673; Fax: 262-637-6364. Charles Leonard, Prin. Lay Teachers 11; Students 200.
Catechesis/Religious Program—Students 130.
14—ST. RITA (1925), [CEM] Revs. Joseph G. Stobba, O.S.A.; John T. Shirley, O.S.A.; Deacon Dan Burmeister. In Res., Revs. Eugene DelConte, O.S.A.; Alvin P. Metzger, O.S.A.; Raymond R. Ryan, O.S.A.; Henry Maibusch, O.S.A.; Bro. Robert J. Schurman, O.S.A.
Res.: 4339 Douglas Ave., 53402. Tel: 262-639-3223; Fax: 262-639-3602.
School—Tel: 262-639-3333. Lay Teachers 15; Students 239.
Catechesis/Religious Program—Tel: 262-639-6280. Leticia Gutierrez-Kenny, D.R.E. Students 230.
15—ST. ROSE (1886), Closed., For sacramental records, contact Archdiocese of Milwaukee Archives Office. Tel.: 414-769-3407.
16—SACRED HEART CONGREGATION (1916), [CEM 4] [JC 4] Rev. Ronald O. Crewe.
Res.: 2201 Northwestern Ave., 53404. Tel: 262-634-5526; Fax: 262-634-5767.
School—2023 Northwestern Ave., 53404. Tel: 262-637-2012; Fax: 262-637-5130. Dr. Kimberly Strike, Prin. Lay Teachers 17.
Catechesis/Religious Program—Tel: 262-634-3607. Mrs. Donna Joas, D.R.E. Students 249.
17—ST. STANISLAUS (1904), (Polish), Closed., For sacramental records, contact Archdiocese of Milwaukee Archives Office. Tel.: 414-769-3407.

RANDOLPH, COLUMBIA CO., ST. GABRIEL, Closed., For sacramental records, contact Annunciation, Fox Lake. Tel.: 920-928-3513.

RANDOM LAKE, SHEBOYGAN CO.
1—ST. MARY (1855), Closed., For sacramental records, contact Our Lady of the Lakes, Random Lake. Tel.: 920-944-4380.
2—OUR LADY OF THE LAKES (1998), [CEM 4] Rev. Richard J. Cerpich.
Mailing Address: 230 Butler St., 53075-1710. Tel: 920-994-4380; Fax: 920-994-2605.
School—306 Butler St., 53075-1712. Tel: 920-994-9962; Fax: 920-994-2499. Catherine Pohl, Prin. Lay Teachers 7.
Catechesis/Religious Program—Tel: 920-994-8033. Students 208.
Chapel—St. Mary 230 Butler St..
Chapel—St. Nicholas W4274 Hwy. K.
Chapel—St. Patrick W4690 Hwy. A, Adell.
Chapel—St. Mary 111 Madison Ave., Cascade.

REESEVILLE, DODGE CO., HOLY FAMILY (1901), (German), [CEM], Also serves St. Columbkille, Elba and St. John the Baptist, Clyman. Rev. Patrick Wendt, Admin.
Res.: 302 Prairie St., P.O. Box 277, 53579-0277. Tel: 920-927-3102.
Catechesis/Religious Program—Students 46.

RICHFIELD, WASHINGTON CO., ST. MARY (1854), (German), Merged, with St. Hubert, Hubertus and St. Columba, Lake Five to from St. Gabriel, Hubertus. Tel.: 262-628-1141

RIPON, FOND DU LAC CO.
1—ST. PATRICK (1858), [CEM] Rev. Robert A. Fictum.
Mailing Address: 218 Blossom St., 54971-1560. Tel: 920-748-2345.
Res.: 411 E. Fond du La St., 54971. Tel: 920-748-2325.
School—222 Blossom St., 54971. Fax: 920-748-3760. Cheryl McCarthy, Prin. Lay Teachers 5; Students 54.
Catechesis/Religious Program—Tel: 920-748-9503. Students 139.
2—ST. WENCESLAUS (1896), (Polish), [JC] Rev. Robert A. Fictum.
Res.: 411 E. Fond du Lac St., 54971-1591. Tel: 920-748-2325; Fax: 920-748-8218.
Catechesis/Religious Program—Tel: 920-748-3826. Students 173.

RUBICON, DODGE CO., ST. JOHN (1870), (German), [CEM] [JC], Also serves St. Matthew, Neosho and St. Mary, Woodland. Rev. Alois Van Beek.
Mailing Address: W1170 Rome Rd., 53078. Tel: 262-673-3380; Fax: 920-625-2143.
Res.: 148 W. Lehman, Neosho, 53059. Tel:

920-625-3144.
Church: W1170 Rome Rd., P.O. Box 17, 53078. Tel: 262-673-3380.
Catechesis/Religious Program—Tel: 262-673-4397. Students 158.

ST. CLOUD, FOND DU LAC CO., ST. CLOUD (1870), (German), [CEM] Rev. Peter P. Kutch, O.F.M.Cap.
Res.: 924 Main St., P.O. Box 138, 53079. Tel: 920-999-2011; Fax: 920-753-2130.
School—(Grades 6-8), 920 Main St., Box 89, 53079-0138. Tel: 920-999-2411; Fax: 920-753-2411. Mrs. Jeanette Jankowski, Bldg. Coord. Consolidated Parochial Elementary School. See Holy Cross, Mount Calvary.
Catechesis/Religious Program—Tel: 920-753-3311. Students 111.

ST. FRANCIS, MILWAUKEE CO., SACRED HEART OF JESUS (1868), [CEM] Rev. Robert F. Surges.
Office—3635 S. Kinnickinnic Ave., 53235-3741. Tel: 414-481-2330; Fax: 414-744-7222.
School—Tel: 414-744-2483. Julie Ann Robinson, Prin. Lay Teachers 4; Students 61.
Catechesis/Religious Program—Tel: 414-486-3945. Students 68.

ST. GEORGE, SHEBOYGAN CO., ST. GEORGE (1860), Closed., For sacramental records, contact Blessed Trinity, Sheboygan Falls. Tel.: 920-467-4616

ST. JOE, FOND DU LAC CO., ST. JOSEPH (1858), (German), [CEM] Rev. Peter P. Kutch, O.F.M.Cap.
Res.: W620 County G, P.O. Box 138, St. Cloud, 53079-0138. Tel: 920-999-3131; Fax: 920-753-2130.
Catechesis/Religious Program—Tel: 920-753-3311. Students 47.

ST. KILIAN, FOND DU LAC CO., ST. KILIAN (1848), [CEM] Rev. Neil G. Zinthefer.
419 Mill St., P.O. Box 470, Campbellsport, 53010. Tel: 920-533-4441; Fax: 920-533-5280.

ST. LAWRENCE, WASHINGTON CO., ST. LAWRENCE (1846), (German), [CEM] Rev. Charles Wheatley.
Res.: 4886 Hwy. 175, Hartford, 53027. Tel: 262-644-5701; Fax: 262-644-5701.
Catechesis/Religious Program—Tel: 262-644-0011. Students 237.

ST. MARTIN, MILWAUKEE CO., HOLY ASSUMPTION, Closed., For sacramental records through 1990, contact St. Mary, Hales Corners. Tel.: 414-425-2174; For sacramental records after 1990, contact St. Martin of Tours, Franklin. Tel.: 414-425-1114.

ST. MICHAEL, WASHINGTON CO., ST. MICHAEL (1846), (German—Irish), [CEM] [JC 2] Rev. Robert J. Artmann.
Res.: 8877 Forestview Rd., Kewaskum, 53040. Tel: 262-334-5270; Fax: 262-334-5233.
Catechesis/Religious Program—Tel: 262-334-4195. Mrs. Sharon Warsh, D.R.E. Students 101.

ST. PETER, FOND DU LAC CO., ST. PETER (1867), (German), Closed., For sacramental records through 1952, contact Archdiocese of Milwaukee Archives Office. Tel.: 414-769-3407; For records after 1952, contact Holy Family, Fond du Lac. Tel.: 920-921-0580.

SAUKVILLE, OZAUKEE CO., IMMACULATE CONCEPTION (1858), [CEM] Rev. Karl H. Acker.
Res.: 145 W. Church St., 53080. Tel: 262-284-0276; Fax: 262-284-3090.
Catechesis/Religious Program—Tel: 262-284-0277. Students 157.

SHARON, WALWORTH CO., ST. CATHERINE (1854), [CEM] Rev. Richard R. Dolezal; Mr. Thomas McKenna, Parish Dir.
Mailing Address: P.O. Box 502, 53585. Tel: 262-736-4615.
Res.: Tel: 815-569-2530.
Catechesis/Religious Program—Students 13.

SHEBOYGAN FALLS, SHEBOYGAN CO.

1—BLESSED TRINITY (2001), (German), [CEM] [JC 3], (Merger of St. Mary, Sheboygan Falls; St. Rose, Lima; and St. George, St. George) Rev. Eugene Neuman.
Rectory:: 327 Giddings Ave., 53085-1598. Tel: 920-467-4616; Fax: 920-467-4290.
Catechesis/Religious Program—Tel: 920-467-6282. Students 340.

2—ST. MARY (1896), (German), Closed., For sacramental records, contact Blessed Trinity, Sheboygan Falls. Tel.: 920-467-4616

SHEBOYGAN, SHEBOYGAN CO.

1—ST. CLEMENT (1914), [JC] Revs. James E. Connell; Edward F. Monroe, C.SS.R.; Deacon Baleriano O. Gonzalez.
Res.: 522 New York Ave., 53081. Tel: 920-457-4629; Fax: 920-452-2417.
Catechesis/Religious Program—Tel: 920-452-5256. High School collaborated with St. Dominic. Students 159.

2—SS. CYRIL AND METHODIUS (1910), (Slovenian), [CEM] Rev. Glenn E. Powers.
Mailing Address: 2705 S. 14th St., 53081-6707.
Res.: 822 New Jersey Ave., 53081. Tel: 920-457-7110; Fax: 920-457-5885.
Catechesis/Religious Program—Tel: 920-457-8422; Fax: 920-457-4001. Students 103.

3—ST. DOMINIC (1927), (German—Dutch), [JC] Rev. James J. Jarumbo, J.C.L.; Deacon Donald J. Lydolph; Joseph Zenk, Pastoral Assoc.
Res.: 2133 N. 22nd St., 53081. Tel: 920-458-8787; Fax: 920-458-3280.
School—2108 N. 21st St., 53081. Tel: 920-452-8747; Fax: 920-458-4809. Peggy Henseler, Prin. Lay Teachers 14; Students 162.
Catechesis/Religious Program—Tel: 920-458-5390. Students 397.

4—HOLY NAME (1845), (German), [JC] Revs. James E. Connell; Edward F. Monroe, C.SS.R.
Res.: 807 Superior Ave., 53081. Tel: 920-458-7721; Fax: 920-459-9108.
School—814 Superior Ave., 53081. Tel: 920-452-1571; Fax: 920-208-4371. Kay Miller, Prin. Lay Teachers 15; Students 199.
Catechesis/Religious Program—Tel: 920-452-0129. Mary Ann Zoch, D.R.E.; Sue Seymour, D.R.E. Students 205.

5—IMMACULATE CONCEPTION (1903), (Lithuanian), [CEM] Rev. Glenn E. Powers.
Res.: 2705 S. 14 St., 53081. Tel: 920-457-3967; Fax: 920-457-5885.
School—Christ Child Academy, 1449 S. 12th St., 53081. Tel: 920-459-2663.
School—Christ Child Academy, 2722 Henry St., 53081. Tel: 920-459-2660. George Streeck, Prin. Lay Teachers 18; Students 185.
Catechesis/Religious Program—Tel: 920-208-7922. Sally Schenk, D.R.E. Students 165.

6—ST. PETER CLAVER (1888), (German), [CEM] Rev. Stephen J. Lampe, M.Div., S.S.L., S.T.D.; Deacon Michael F. Burch; Sr. Marilyn Brodd, O.S.F., Pastoral Assoc.
Res.: 1444 S. Eleventh St., 53081. Tel: 920-457-9408; Fax: 920-457-5290.
School—Christ Child Academy, (Grades PreK-5) , See Immaculate Conception for Details. Tel: 920-459-2663; Fax: 920-457-5885.
Catechesis/Religious Program—Tel: 920-452-2759. Barbara Leonhardt, D.R.E. Students 97.

SLINGER, WASHINGTON CO., ST. PETER (1856), (German), [CEM 2] Rev. Richard J. Stoffel; Deacon Bernard J. Wendt.
Res.: 202 E. Washington St., 53086. Tel: 262-644-8083; Fax: 262-644-7951.
School—Tel: 262-644-8325. Ms. Virginia Miller, Prin. Lay Teachers 12; Students 111.
Catechesis/Religious Program—Jennifer Funk, D.R.E. Students 532.

SOUTH MILWAUKEE, MILWAUKEE CO.

1—ST. ADALBERT (1898), Merged, with St. John, South Milwaukee, St. Mary, South Milwaukee & St. Sylvester, South Milwaukee to form Divine Mercy, South Milwaukee

2—DIVINE MERCY (2003), [JC] Very Rev. Ronald Gramza, Team Moderator; Rev. Robert Betz, Team Member; Deacon James Leggett.
Office and Church: 1304 Manitoba, 53172. Tel: 414-762-6810; Fax: 414-762-8326.
School—16th Ave., 1800 16th Ave., 53172. Tel: 414-762-0064. Judy Kalinowski, Prin. Aides 1; Lay Teachers 13; Students 149.
School—College Ave., 695 College Ave., 53172. Tel: 414-764-4360. Thomas Hage, Prin. Tutor 1; Lay Teachers 14; Students 196.
Catechesis/Religious Program—Students 726.

3—ST. JOHN (1893), (Irish), Merged, with St. Adalbert, South Milwaukee, St. Mary, South Milwaukee & St. Sylvester, South Milwaukee to form Divine Mercy, South Milwaukee

4—ST. MARY (1893), Merged, with St. Adalbert, South Milwaukee, St. John, South Milwaukee & St. Sylvester, South Milwaukee to form Divine Mercy, South Milwaukee

5—ST. SYLVESTER (1962), (Polish—Irish), Merged, with St. Adalbert, South Milwaukee, St. John, South Milwaukee & St. Mary, South Milwaukee to form Divine Mercy, South Milwaukee

SPRINGVALE, ST. MARY (1858), (Irish), [CEM], See Immaculate Conception for Details. Rev. Michael F. Moran.
Mailing Address: 118 W. Main St., Waupun, 53963-1453. Tel: 920-324-5400; Fax: 920-324-1040.
Catechesis/Religious Program—Tel: 920-346-5110. Students 5.

STURTEVANT, RACINE CO., ST. SEBASTIAN (1906), Rev. James Kendzierski, O.F.M.; Deacon DeSales Wisniewski, O.F.M., Pastoral Assoc.
Res.: 3126 95th St., 53177. Tel: 262-886-4398; Fax: 262-886-2055.
School—3030 95th St., 53177. Tel: 262-886-2806. Diane Davis, Prin. Lay Teachers 10; Students 159.
Catechesis/Religious Program—Tel: 262-886-4420. Students 90.

THERESA, DODGE CO., ST. THERESA (1849), [CEM] Rev. Kevin J. Kowalske.
102 Church St., St. Theresa, 53091. Tel: 920-269-4429; Fax: 920-269-7359. Mailing Address: 699 Milwaukee St., Lomira, 53048. Tel: 920-269-4429; Fax: 920-269-7359.
School—Consolidated Catholic School of Lomira-Theresa, (Grades PreK-3), 105 W. Rock River St., 53091. Tel: 920-488-4543. Dorothy Zitlow, Prin.
Catechesis/Religious Program—Tel: 920-269-7273. Gail Stephany, D.R.E. Students 76.

THIENSVILLE, OZAUKEE CO., ST. CECILIA (1919), Rev. Dennis Andrews; Deacon Joseph P. Wenzler.
Parish Office—138 W. Buntrock Ave., 53092. Tel: 262-512-8980; Fax: 262-242-7977.
Res.: 101 Ellenbecker Rd., 53092.
School—(Grades PreK-3) , Consolidated with St. James, Mequon to form SS. Cecilia and James. , 116 N. Orchard, 53092. Tel: 262-242-7965; Fax: 262-242-7976. Mr. Richard Goeden, Prin. Lay Teachers 50; Students 554.
Catechesis/Religious Program— Program consolidated with St. James, Mequon. Tel: 262-242-7963. Vicki Clark, D.R.E. Students 222.

THOMPSON, WASHINGTON CO., ST. PATRICK (Tn. Erin) (1855), (Irish), Closed., For sacramental records, contact St. Kilian, Hartford. Tel.: 262-673-4831.

TWIN LAKES, KENOSHA CO., ST. JOHN (1932), [CEM] Rev. Michael J. Erwin; Deacon Stanley Cebrzynski.
Res.: 701 N. Lake Ave., 53181. Tel: 262-877-2557; Fax: 262-877-2431.
Catechesis/Religious Program—Tel: 262-877-3033. Students 97.

UNION GROVE, RACINE CO., ST. ROBERT BELLARMINE (1965), [CEM] Rev. Howard G. Haase.
Res.: 3320 S. Colony Ave., 53182. Tel: 262-878-3476; Fax: 262-878-0194.
Catechesis/Religious Program—Michelle Heeren, D.R.E. Students 290.

WATERFORD, RACINE CO., ST. THOMAS AQUINAS (1851), [CEM] Rev. Edwin M. Kornath; Deacons Carl A. Mahnke; Joseph H. Hying.
Res.: 305 First St., 53185. Tel: 414-534-2255; Fax: 414-534-2929.
School—Tel: 262-534-2265; Fax: 262-534-5549. Lay Teachers 15; Students 224.
Catechesis/Religious Program—Students 415.

WAUKESHA, WAUKESHA CO.

1—ST. JOHN NEUMANN (1981), Rev. Donald F. Zerkel, Interim Pastor (Retired); Deacon Michael J. Finley; June Wessa, Pastoral Assoc.
Mailing Address: 2400 W. State Hwy. 59, 53189-6323. Tel: 262-549-0223; 262-549-0898; Fax: 262-549-0444.
School—Waukesha Catholic School System, (Grades PreK-8) Tel: 262-896-2920 (St. William); 262-896-2930 (St. Joseph); 262-896-2932 (St. Mary); Fax: 262-896-2925.
Catechesis/Religious Program—Tel: 262-549-2223. Sr. Dolores Pertzborn, D.R.E. (Grades K-6); Marilyn Lieske, D.R.E. (Grades 7-12). Students 455.

2—ST. JOSEPH (1844), (Hispanic), Revs. Michael F. Michalski; Aurelio Perez; Deacons Luiz Pena; Aristeo Ortiz.
Parish Office—818 N. East Ave., 53186. Tel: 262-542-2589; Fax: 262-542-2570.
Res.: 822 N. East Ave., 53186. Tel: 262-542-5487.
School—Waukesha Catholic School System, (Grades 6-8), 841 Martin St., 53186. Tel: 262-896-2930; Fax: 262-896-2935. Mrs. Kathleen Rempe, Prin.
Catechesis/Religious Program—Tel: 262-542-2589, Ext. 211. Sr. Julie Weckwerth, C.S.S.F., Pastoral Assoc. Christian Formation; Ruth Weiss, D.R.E.; Manuel Maldonado, D.R.E. Students 371.

3—ST. MARY (1950), Rev. Brian G. Mason.
Res.: 225 S. Hartwell Ave., 53186-6400. Tel: 262-547-6555; Fax: 262-547-6714.
School— School is a campus of the Waukesha Catholic School System. Tel: 262-896-2932; Fax: 262-896-2931. Mrs. Carolyn Caruso, Prin. Sisters 2; Lay Teachers 15; Students 360.
Catechesis/Religious Program—Phyllis Hamann, D.R.E. Students 329.

4—ST. WILLIAM (1957), [JC] Rev. Leonard M. Barbian.
Res.: 440 N. Moreland Blvd., 53188. Tel: 262-542-0456; Fax: 262-547-3616.
School—Waukesha Catholic School System, (Grades PreK-5), 444 N. Moreland Blvd., 53188. Tel: 262-896-2920; Fax: 262-896-2925. Robert Radomski, Campus Prin. Students 186.
Catechesis/Religious Program—Tel: 262-547-2763. Kay Hokans, D.R.E.; Barb Gawlik, D.R.E.; Joe Nettesheim, D.R.E. Students 711.

WAUPUN, FOND DU LAC CO., ST. JOSEPH (1866), (Irish), [CEM], Also serves St. Brendan, Brandon & St. Mary, Springvale. Rev. Michael F. Moran.
Office—118 W. Main St., 53963. Tel: 920-324-5400; Fax: 920-324-1040.
Catechesis/Religious Program—Tel: 920-324-3891. Pat Essmann, D.R.E. Students 184.

WAUWATOSA, MILWAUKEE CO.

1—ST. BERNARD (1911), (Irish), Rev. Peter C. Drenzek.
Res.: 7474 Harwood Ave., 53213. Tel: 414-258-4320; Fax: 414-258-9972.
School—1500 Wauwatosa Ave., 53213. Tel: 414-258-9977. Mary Kopp, Prin. Religious 1; Lay Teachers

12; Students 200.
Catechesis / Religious Program—Students 125.

2—CHRIST KING (1939), Rev. Msgr. T. George Gajdos; Deacon Arthur C. Dallman.
Res.: 2604 Swan Blvd., 53226. Tel: 414-258-2604; Fax: 414-258-1993.
School—2646 N. Swan Blvd., 53226. Tel: 414-258-4160. Sr. Janet Neureuther, Prin. Lay Teachers 25; Students 445.
Catechesis / Religious Program—Tel: 414-258-0916. Barbara Schveidler, D.R.E. Students 260.

3—ST. JOSEPH CONGREGATION (1855), Rev. Jerome M. Hudziak; Deacons Jose Gonzales; Peter LoCoco.
Mailing Address: 12130 W. Center St., 53222-4096. Tel: 414-771-4626; Fax: 414-771-4311.
Res.: 12130 W. Hadley St., 53222-4097. Tel: 414-771-4627.
School—2750 N. 122nd St., 53222. Fax: 414-771-9826. Shirley Hubbard, Prin. Lay Teachers 17; Students 229.
Catechesis / Religious Program—Students 360.

4—ST. JUDE THE APOSTLE (1928), Rev. Peter P. Carek; Sr. Mary La Von Lauer, O.S.F., Pastoral Assoc.; Deacon Donald A. Borkowski; Gary Heun, Pastoral Assoc. In Res., Rev. Joseph Uko (Nigeria).
Res.: 734 Glenview Ave., 53213. Tel: 414-258-8821; Fax: 414-258-7371.
School—800 Glenview Ave., 53213. Tel: 414-771-1520; Fax: 414-771-3748. Catherine LaDien, Prin. Sisters 2; Lay Teachers 26; Students 380.
Catechesis / Religious Program—Tel: 414-259-0950. Gary Heun, D.R.E. Students 207.

5—ST. PIUS X (1952), Rev. Bob Marsicek, S.D.S.
Res.: 2506 Wauwatosa Ave., 53213. Tel: 414-453-3875; Fax: 414-453-7570.
School—2520 Wauwatosa Ave., 53213. Tel: 414-778-0880. Lay Teachers 12; Students 139.
Catechesis / Religious Program—Tel: 414-453-1153. Students 174.

WAYNE, WASHINGTON CO., ST. BRIDGET, Closed., For sacramental records, contact Holy Trinity, Kewaskum. Tel.: 262-626-2860.

WEST ALLIS, MILWAUKEE CO.

1—ST. ALOYSIUS (1920), Rev. John H. Baumgartner.
Res.: 1414 S. 93rd St., 53214. Tel: 414-476-3803; Fax: 414-774-7727.
School—1435 S. 92nd St., 53214. Tel: 414-476-0751; Fax: 414-259-9285. Gail Kowalsky, Prin. Lay Teachers 14; Students 122.
Catechesis / Religious Program—Tel: 414-257-3088. Sr. Angela Keil, O.S.F., D.R.E. Students 148.

2—ST. AUGUSTINE (1928), (Croatian), [CEM] Rev. Lawrence Frankovich, O.F.M.
Res.: 6762 W. Rogers St., 53219. Tel: 414-541-5207; Fax: 414-541-0273.
School—6763 W. Rogers St., 53219. Tel: 414-545-2120. Sisters 4; Lay Teachers 4; Students 72.
Catechesis / Religious Program—Students 50.

3—HOLY ASSUMPTION (1902), Rev. Robert E. Massey; Deacons George P. Sherman; Claude V. Kennedy.
Res.: 1525 S. 71st St., 53214. Tel: 414-774-3010; Fax: 414-774-3735.
School—Tel: 414-383-4204; Fax: 414-383-4281. School Sisters of Notre Dame 1; Lay Teachers 12; Students 88.
Catechesis / Religious Program—Students 109.

4—IMMACULATE HEART OF MARY (1948), Rev. Karl J. Schneider; Deacons Dennis E. Fietz; Walter Henry.
Res.: 1121 S. 116th St., 53214. Tel: 414-453-5192; Fax: 414-453-0137.
Catechesis / Religious Program—Tel: 414-453-0300.

5—ST. JOSEPH (1909), (Polish), Closed., For sacramental records, contact Archdiocese of Milwaukee Archives Office. Tel.: 414-769-3407.

6—ST. MARY, HELP OF CHRISTIANS (1907), (Slovenian), [CEM] Rev. Denis P. Weis.
Res.: 1210 S. 61st St., 53214. Tel: 414-771-8313.
Catechesis / Religious Program—Tel: 262-238-9040. Students 12.

7—MARY, QUEEN OF HEAVEN (1958), Rev. Michael F. Merkt.
Office—2322 S. 106th St., 53227. Tel: 414-328-5566; Fax: 414-328-5561.
School—2360 S. 106th St., 53227. Tel: 414-328-5577; Fax: 414-328-5573. Mrs. Marilyn Marzolf, Prin. Lay Teachers 12; Students 138.
Catechesis / Religious Program—Tel: 414-328-5570. Nicholas Balducci, D.R.E. Students 265.

8—OUR LADY OF MT. CARMEL (1938), (Italian), Closed., For sacramental records, contact Archdiocese of Milwaukee Archives Office. Tel.: 414-769-3407.

9—ST. RITA (1924), Revs. Richard E. Mirsberger; Robert Katorski.
Res.: 2318 S. 61st St., 53219. Tel: 414-541-7515; Fax: 414-541-7568.
School—6021 W. Lincoln Ave., 53219. Tel: 414-327-5020; Fax: 414-327-7308. Sr. Joyce Wagner, S.S.S.F., Prin. Sisters 4; Lay Teachers 14; Students 170.
Catechesis / Religious Program—Tel: 414-541-7515. Karen Barczak, D.R.E. Students 157.

WEST BEND, WASHINGTON CO.

1—ST. FRANCES CABRINI (1955), Revs. Jeffrey R. Haines; Michael Petersen; Deacon Michael S. Koebel; Michael Sepersky, Dir. of Admin. Svcs.
Parish Office—1025 S. 7th Ave., 53095. Tel: 262-338-2366; Fax: 262-338-2348.
School—529 Hawthorn Dr., 53095. Tel: 262-334-7142; Fax: 262-334-8168. Mark Quinn, Prin. Lay Teachers 36; Students 426.
Catechesis / Religious Program—Tel: 262-334-9511. Judy Schroeder, D.R.E. Students 522.

2—HOLY ANGELS (1852), [CEM] Revs. Gerald W. Brittain; John Wutscheck.
Res.: 135 N. 8th Ave., 53095. Tel: 262-334-3038; Fax: 262 334-3088.
School—230 N. 8th Ave., 53095. Tel: 262-338-1148; Fax: 262-334-1334. Mike Sternig, Prin. Lay Teachers 21; Students 412.
Catechesis / Religious Program—Tel: 414-334-9393. Nan Jacoby, D.R.E. Students 366.

3—IMMACULATE CONCEPTION (1857), [CEM] Revs. Mark R. Jones; Robert Bales; Richard Harter, Parish Dir.
Res.: 406 Jefferson St., 53090. Tel: 262-338-5600; Fax: 262-335-2475.
School—Tel: 262-338-5602. Lay Teachers 14; Students 172.
Catechesis / Religious Program—Tel: 262-338-5605. Mary Abel, D.R.E.; Marge Schinker, D.R.E. Students 296.

WHITEFISH BAY, MILWAUKEE CO.

1—HOLY FAMILY (1949), Rev. Laurin J. Wenig.
Office—4[illegible]25 N. Wildwood Ave., 53217. Tel: 414-332-9220; Fax: 414-961-7396.
School—[illegible]849 N. Wildwood Ave., 53217. Tel: 414-332-8175 Fax: 414-961-7196. Rebecca Jones, Prin. Lay Teachers 20; Students 269.
Catechesis / Religious Program—Tel: 414-332-8156. Barbara O'Neil, D.R.E. Students 435.

2—ST. MONICA (1923), Rev. Alan F. Jurkus; Deacon Eugene E. Van Garsse. In Res., Rev. John R. Paczesny (Retired).
Res.: 160 E. Silver Spring Dr., 53217. Tel: 414-332-1576; 414-332-1577; Fax: 414-332-2462.
School—Tel: 414-332-3660; Fax: 414-332-8649. Karen Rambadt, Prin. Lay Teachers 29; Students 405.
Catechesis / Religious Program—Tel: 414-964-8780; Fax: 414-964-2493. Heidi Russell, D.R.E. Students 245.

WHITEWATER, WALWORTH CO., ST. PATRICK (1853), [CEM] Rev. Thomas Suriano.
Office—1225 W. Main St., 53190-1620. Tel: 262-473-3143; Fax: 262-473-3052.
Catechesis / Religious Program—Tel: 262-473-8834. Katie DeBruin, D.R.E. (Grades 1-6); Angela Alesci, D.R.E. (Grades 7-12). Students 196.

WILMOT, KENOSHA CO., HOLY NAME OF JESUS (1856), [CEM] Rev. Roger Savage.
Res.: 301[illegible]0 Wilmot Rd., P.O. Box 188, 53192. Tel: 262-862-6466; Fax: 262-862-7244.
Catechesis / Religious Program—Tel: 262 862-2361. Students 166.

WIND LAKE, RACINE CO., ST. CLARE (1965) Very Rev. John D. Hemsing; Deacon Richard E. Milbauer.
Res. & Mailing Address:: Parish Office, 7616 Fritz St., 53185. Tel: 262-895-2729; Fax: 262-895-3601.
Catechesis / Religious Program—Tel: 262-895-2797. Ms. Carleen Schendzielos, D.R.E. Students 299.

WOODHULL, FOND DU LAC CO., ST. JOHN THE BAPTIST, Closed., For sacramental records, contact Our Risen Savior, Eldorado. Tel.: 920-922-2412.

WOODLAND, DODGE N CO., ST. MARY, (German), [CEM], Also serves St. Matthew, Neosho & St. John, Rubicon. Rev. Alois VanBeek.
Mailing Address: 148 W. Lehman St, P.O. Box 45, Neosho, 53059. Tel: 920-625-3144; Fax: 920-625-2143.
Catechesis / Religious Program—Tel: 920-625-3092. Students 48.

Chaplains of Public Institutions

MILWAUKEE. *St. Luke's Medical Center*, 2900 W. Oklahoma Ave., 53215. Rev. Ray Mateljan, Chap.
Milwaukee County House of Correction. Attended by St. James Franklin.
Milwaukee County Jail. Bro. Jerome Smith, O.F.M.Cap., Chap.

JUNEAU. *Dodge County Center.* Attended by Sacred Heart, Horicon.

KENOSHA. *Kenosha Hospital and Medical Center*, 6308 8th Ave., 53143-5082. Vacant.

WALES. *Ethan Allen School for Boys*, P.O. Box 900, 53183-0900. Tel: 414-646-3341. (Vacant)

WAUWATOSA. *Froedtert Memorial Lutheran Hospital*, 9200 W. Wisconsin Ave., 53226. Rev. Robert J. Gloudeman, Chap.

WEST ALLIS. *West Allis Memorial Hospital*, 8901 W. Lincoln Ave., 53227. Tel: 414-328-6000. Rev. Charles G. Zabler, Chap.

WOOD. *Veterans Administration Medical Center*, P.O., 53193. Tel: 414-384-2000. Revs. James Kovarik, O.S.Cam., Chap., Edward E. Lisowski, Chap., Norman R. Oswald, Chief, Chap. Svc.

Special Assignment:

Most Rev.—
Sklba, Richard J., Auxiliary Bishop, 3501 S. Lake Dr., P.O. Box 070912, 53207-0912.

Very Revs.—
Hartmann, Paul B.R., M.Div., J.C.L., Metropolitan Tribunal, 3501 S. Lake Dr., P.O. Box 070912, 53207-0912.
Hornacek, Joseph F., Vicar Gen. & Vicar for Clergy Personnel, 3501 S. Lake Dr., P.O. Box 070912, 53207-0912. Tel: 414-769-3490
Witczak, Michael G., M.Div., S.L.D., Rector, Saint Francis Seminary, 3257 S. Lake Dr., St. Francis, 53235.

Revs.—
Avella, Steven M., Faculty, Marquette University, 3222 S. 29th St., 53215.
Beno, Brian M., Coord. Min., Health Care Facilities, 3827 N. 66th St., 53216.
Brundage, Thomas T., Interim Assoc. Publisher/Exec. Editor, Catholic Herald, 3501 S. Lake Dr., P.O. Box 070913, 53207-0913. Tel: 414-769-3300
Cane-Gombau, Pere, Missionary Community of St. Paul, 2512 Westwood Dr., Racine, 53404.
Connell, James E., Vice Chancellor, Archdiocese of Milwaukee, 3501 S. Lake Dr., P.O. Box 07912, 53207-0912. Tel: 414-769-3338
Dietzler, William J., Chap., St. Mary's Medical Center, 3801 Spring St., Racine, 53405-1617.
Duffy, James H., Madonna House, Combermere ON K0J 1L0 Canada.
Fliss, Paul, Asian Ministry Office, P.O. Box 070912, 53207-0912.
Gaberle, Jiri, Ministry to Healthcare Facilities, 5937 N. 35th St. #4, 53209-4062.
Gloudeman, Robert J., Chap., Froedert Memorial Lutheran Hospital, 9200 W. Wisconsin Ave., 53226.
Hammer, Michael J., Coord. Catholic AIDS Ministry, 802 N. Jackson St., 53202-3879.
Herda, Jerome G., Archbishop Sec., 3501 S. Lake Dr., P.O. Box 070912, 53207-0912.
Keefe, Charles R., Pastoral Care Dir., Milwaukee Catholic Home, 2462 N. Prospect Ave., 53211-4462.
Knoebel, Thomas L., Sacred Heart School of Theology Faculty, P.O. Box 429, Hales Corner, 53130-0429.
Kohler, William E., Assoc. Vicar, Clergy, Priests' Placement Board, 3501 S. Lake Dr., P.O. Box 07912, 53207-0912. Tel: 414-769-3458
Lampe, Stephen J., M.Div., S.S.L., S.T.D., Saint Francis Seminary, 3257 S. Lake Dr., St. Francis, 53235. (Faculty)
Lazarski, Marvin I., Arch. Cemetery System, 7301 W. Nash St., 53321. Tel: 414-438-4430
Lisowski, Edward E., Chap., Zablocki VA Medical Center, 5000 W. National Ave., 53295.
Lobacz, James E., Campus Ministry, Cardinal Stritch University, 6801 N. Yates Rd. # 388, 53217-3985.
Lotz, Robert J., Chap., Newman Center, UW-Milwaukee, 3001 N. Downer Ave., 53211.
Massingale, Bryan N., Saint Francis Seminary, 3257 S. Lake Dr., St. Francis, 53235. (Faculty)
Michalski, Melvin E., Ph.L., Th.D., Vice Rector & Faculty, Saint Francis Seminary, 3257 S. Lake Dr., St. Francis, 53235.
Murphy, Daniel T., Chap., Clement Manor, 3939 S. 92nd St., Greenfield, 53228-2140.
Nelson, Andrew L., Saint Francis Seminary, 3257 S. Lake Dr., St. Francis, 53235.
O'Brien, Timothy J., Faculty, Marquette University, 8521 Kenyon Ave., Wauwatosa, 53226.
Oswald, Norman R., Chief Chap., Veterans Administrative Medical Center, 5000 W. National Ave., 53295.
Pocernich, Eugene, Chap., St. Mary Hospital, 2323 N. Lake Dr., 53211.
Roetzer, Russell G., Faculty, St. Catherine High School, 1200 Park Ave., Racine, 53403.
Schuerman, James T., Saint Francis Seminary, 3257 S. Lake Dr., St. Francis, 53235. (Faculty)
Shecterle, Ross A., Dir. Counseling, North American College 00120 Vatican City State.
Slodowski, Bruno, Chap., St. Joseph Home for the Aged, 9244-29th Ave., Kenosha, 53143-6646.
Stiefvater, Robert X., Dir. Office of Vocations, 3257 S. Lake Dr., St. Francis, 53235. Tel: 414-747-6437
Sturm, Michael O., Coord., Detention Ministries, W192 N16330 Lea Fon Cir., Jackson, 53037. Tel: 262-677-8390
Tikalsky, Russell F., Chap., 7804 St. Anne Ct., Wauwatosa, 53213.
Walker, Thomas J., Coord. Services for Senior Priests, 3501 S. Lake Dr., P.O. Box 070912, 53207-0912. Tel: 414-769-3345
Wheatley, Charles, 2821 S. Superior St., WI 53207.

Zabler, Charles G., Chap., West Allis Memorial Hospital, 8901 W. Lincoln Ave., West Allis, 53227.

On Duty Outside the Archdiocese:
Rev. Msgr.—
Malloy, David J., USCCB, 3211 4th St. NE, Washington, DC 20017-1194.
Revs.—
Brophy, John L., St. Antoninus, Box 93, Deloraine, Manitoba R0M0M0 Canada.
Colom, Marti, La Sagrada Familia, Apartado 53, Azua, Dominican Republic.
Dolezal, Richard R., 5053 N. Ridgeway, Chicago, IL 60625-6021.
Konkel, Eugene J., S.S., Vatican II Institute, 320 Middlefield Rd., Menlo Park, CA 94025.
Kowalski, Ronald, St. John the Baptist, 513 State Rd., Rib Lake, 54470.
Lamb, Matthew L., Faculty, Boston College, Horizon East 411, 125 Coolidge Ave., Watertown, MA 02172.
Marek, Dean V., Chap., Box 1332, Rochester, MN 55903-1332. Rochester Methodist Hospital
McDermott, Robert T., St. Joseph, 7607 Trendwood Dr., Lincoln, NE 68506-6544.
Schwartz, Norman R., Chap., Veterans Hospital, Ann Arbor, MI 48104.
Shmauz, Donald A., 301 Troy Dr., Madison, 53704.
Tino, Robert F., Western State Hospital, 9601 Steilacoom Blvd., S.W., Tacoma, WA 98498-7213.
Van Abel, John W., W5431 Hwy. 106 E., R.R. #2, Fort Atkinson, 53538-9616.

Military Chaplains:
Revs.—
Kienzle, Jerome C.
Mikalofsky, Hilarion A.
Richter, Robert J.

Graduate Studies:
Revs.—
Bustos, Javier, Pontifical Academy Alfonsianum 00120 Vatican City State.
Dunn, Steven
Olszyk, Thomas P.
Stanosz, Paul A.

On Leave:
Revs.—
DeLeers, Stephen V.
Dulek, Lawrence V.
O'Loughlin, Patrick J.
Pacheo-Sanchez, Luis

Personal Leave:
Revs.—
Bittner, Wayne W.
Clapp, Kenneth
Graczyk, Glen
Lee, Roy

Sick Leave:
Rev.—
Hdubowicz, Vincent B.

Retired:
Most Rev.—
Weakland, Rembert G., O.S.B.
Rev. Msgrs.—
Donovan, John T., Cousins Center, P.O. Box 070912, 53207-0912.
Murphy, John F., 5510 N. Lake Dr., Oconomowoc, 53066.
Schmit, Ralph R., Alexian Village, 7979 W. Glenbrook Rd., #5012, 53223.
Revs.—
Amrhein, Peter T., St. Camillus Health Center, 10101 W. Wisconsin Ave., #104A, Wauwatosa, 53226.
Andre, Leonard J., Alexian Village, 7979 Glenbrook Rd. # 4021, 53223.
Arciszewski, Gilbert, 9151 S. Aspen Dr. # 9, Oak Creek, 53154.
Baran, Joseph L., 2022 N. 86th St., Wauwatosa, 53226-2745.
Baranowski, Stanley A., W782 County Rd. A, Randolph, 53956.
Barta, Wayne J., N1271 Minnie Lane, Campbellsport, 53010.
Beck, Richard P., 5606 Cynthia Ln., Sarasota, FL 34235.
Beitzinger, George J., 4139 Los Altos Ct., Naples, FL 34109.
Belda, Leo W., Camillus Court East, #321, 10100 W. Bluemound Rd., Wauwatosa, 53226.
Berghammer, Robert J., 201 A-J Ct., Theresa, 53091.
Brady, James J., Cousins Center, P.O. Box 070912, 53207-0912.
Brahm, Harvey, San Camillo # 725, 10200 W. Bluemound Rd., Wauwatosa, 53226.
Braun, David J., 1250 Wisconsin St. #108B, Lake Geneva, 53147.
Braun, Donald B., 108 Lakeshore Terr., Beaver Dam, 53916.
Braun, Edgar F., W6895 Lost Lake Rd., Pearson, 54462-8009.
Breit, Melvin, 9002 W. Lisbon Ave. # 303, 53222.
Brey, Lawrence S., 1705 County Rd. 137, Waite Park, MN 56387.
Bryl, Thaddeus J., 3920 N. Green Bay Rd., Racine, 53404.
Carroll, Edward E., 15000 W. Cleveland Ave., #226, New Berlin, 53151-3766.
Cox, William E., 4816 Westway Ave., Racine, 53406-3634.
Cunningham, Joseph L., W 369 S10450 Shearer Rd., Eagle, 53119.
Daniels, Paul A., 1216 N. Sunnyslope Dr., #103, Racine, 53406.
Darnieder, Donald A., Camillus Court East # 317, 10100 W. Bluemound Rd., Wauwatosa, 53226.
Derfus, Kenneth J., 3501 S. Lake Dr., St. Francis, 53235.
Dineen, Michael P., 435 N. Ave., Sheboygan, 53083.
Dionne, Earl J., Cousins Center, P.O. Box 070912, 53207-0912.
Dreher, Ernest O., 310 E. 11th St., Fond du Lac, 54935.
Endejan, John, 9410 W. Loomis Rd. # 5, Franklin, 53132.
Enders, Robert F., 238 S. Hartwell Ave., Waukesha, 53186-6403.
Ernster, James M., 570 Hwy. D, Belgium, 53004.
Eschweiler, Edward R., Cousins Center, P.O. Box 070912, 53207-0912.
Fleischmann, George R., Cousins Center, P.O. Box 070912, 53207-0912.
Frederick, Joseph B., 237 Southtowne Pl., #BB212, South Milwaukee, 53172.
Gehl, Walter N., St. Francis Home, 33 Everett, Fond du Lac, 54935.
Glass, Rolland T., St. Francis Home, 365 Gillett St., #7, Fond du Lac, 54935.
Grebasch, Richard L., E6118 Snowtrasse, Bessemer, MI 49911.
Hanauska, Joseph F., 1001 S. Pine St., Pine Brook Pointe, Burlington, 53105.
Hauser, Gerald B., Cousins Center, P.O. Box 070912, 53207-0912.
Heck, Roger C., 172 N. Brookfield Rd., Brookfield, 53045.
Heffron, William M., Meyer Hall, 3253 S. Lake Dr. # 101, St. Francis, 53235.
Hentzner, John T., 3501 S. Lake Dr., St. Francis, 53235.
Herkowski, Arthur M., 1299 Flora Glen Dr., Sparks, NV 89434-0742.
Hess, James W., c/o William Sonneburg, 601 Center Ave., Sheboygan, 53081.
Hmircik, Donald A., 104 St. Franciscus St., P.O. Box 64, Mount Calvary, 53057-0064.
Huber, George L., 3253 S. Lake Dr., St. Francis, 53235.
Hussli, Edward J., HCR1, Box 81, Clam Lake, 54517.
Janette, Paul, 929 N. Astor St., #203, 53202-3435.
Jautz, Martin L., Camillus Health Center, #155, 10101 W. Wisconsin Ave., Wauwatosa, 53226.
Johnson, Howard J., W6332 Lake Ellen Dr., Cascade, 53011.
Jordan, Francis W., 2527 Ole Davidson Rd., Racine, 53405-1442.
Kasten, Edward F., 7979 W. Glenbrook Rd., #6002, 53223.
Kemmer, Victor A., N30 W29497 Hillcrest Dr., Pewaukee, 53072-3237.
Klauck, Stanley B., 12621 E. Laurel Ln., Scottsdale, AZ 85259.
Klemme, Dennis C., W267 N2517 Meadowbrook Rd., Pewaukee, 53072.
Klink, Anthony G., P.O. Box 93, Berlin, 54923.
Kolanko, John R., 7164 N. 42nd St., #2, 53209.
Kowalski, Leo S., 3441 S. 10th St., 53215-5117.
Kurkiewicz, Raymond J., Camillus Terrace, 530 N. 103rd St., Wauwatosa, 53226.
Lambert, Leo M., Camillus Court East # 321, 10100 W. Bluemound Rd., Wauwatosa, 53226.
Le Mieux, Thomas A., P.O. Box 510306, 53203-0051.
Leack, Lawrence J., Camillus Court West # 12, 530 N. 103rd St., Wauwatosa, 53226.
Lippert, Paul R., Box 238, Plainfield, 54966-0238.
Loehr, Charles D., W1452 Hwy. T, Mount Calvary, 53057.
Lukaszewicz, John C., 3257 S. Lake Dr., St. Francis, 53235.
Luljak, Louis P., 918 St. Andrew's Rd., Waterford, 53185.
Mackin, William H., Cousins Center, P.O. Box 070912, 53207-0912.
Macoskie, Melvin H., Cousins Center, P.O. Box 070912, 53207-0912.
Maney, Robert L., 9431 W. Beloit Rd., 53227.
Matt, Erwin H., 3253 S. Lake Dr., St. Francis, 53235.
McLaughlin, Owen F., 6079 Thornapple Dr., Greendale, 53129.
Morgan, Walter N., 523 W. 11th St., Fond du Lac, 54935.
Mueller, Robert F., 524 W. Historic Mitchell St., 53204-3599.
Murphy, John M., Cousins Center, P.O. Box 070912, 53207-0912.
Murray, William F., 3253 S. Lake Dr., St. Francis, 53235-3705.
Musinski, Donald T., Camillus Court East, #309, 10100 W. Bluemound, Wauwatosa, 53226.
Myszel, George G., 26503 Angelica Rd., Punta Gorda, FL 33955-1408.
Novotny, Robert J., Meyer Hall # 402, 3253 S. Lake Dr., St. Francis, 53235.
Okopinski, Louis S., Meyer Hall, 3253 S. Lake Dr., St. Francis, 53235.
Orzechowski, Walter B., N8180 Lakeview Rd., Fond du Lac, 54935.
Paczesny, John R., 160 E. Silver Spring Dr., Whitefish Bay, 53217.
Palermo, Albert A., 1524 Arthur Ave., Racine, 53405.
Quartana, Donald F., 8500 W. Coldspring Rd., Greenfield, 53228.
Rausch, John W., Box 475, Eagle, 53119.
Rodriguez, Robert, 502 Amber Horizon St., Henderson, NV 89015.
Roensch, Frederick J., P.O. Box 210, Nashotah, 53058.
Roscioli, Dominic J., 5412 23rd Ave., Kenosha, 53140-3505.
Rykowski, Valerian J., 1411 Winfield, Swartz Creek, MI 48473.
Safiejko, Edward M., 10420 Plum Tree Cir., Hales Corners, 53130.
Sampon, Robert G., 3800 N. 92nd St., 53222.
Sanfelippo, Frank J., P.O. Box 1504, 53201-1504.
Santo, Mark Charles, 2114 W. Mitchell St., 53204.
Schaefer, Verne B., 412 Oak Lodge Rd., Waterford, 53185.
Scheuerell, Charles A., P.O. Box 211, Nashotah, 53058.
Schlenker, Richard J., Cousins Center, P.O. Box 070912, 53207-0912.
Schmelzer, Linus L., Cousins Center, P.O. Box 070912, 53207-0912.
Schmidt, Donald, Meyer Hall # 205, 3257 S. Lake Dr., St. Francis, 53235.
Schmitt, Warren J., 9115 S. Cactus Ln., Sun Lakes, AZ 85248-6903.
Schmitz, Gerald P., 806 Lake Ave. # 3, Racine, 53403.
Schmitz, John A., 1011 Berlin Rd., Ripon, 54971.
Schubert, Herbert, 5104 S. Hidden Dr. # 21, Greenfield, 53221.
Schwinn, Joseph F., Camillus Court West # 22, 530 N. 103rd St., Wauwatosa, 53226.
Seramur, Leo J., 3253 S. Lake Dr., St. Francis, 53235.
Sippel, Edward F., 519 W. 11th St., Fond du Lac, 54935.
Skeris, Robert A., 722 Dillingham Ave., Sheboygan, 53081.
Sowinski, Albin F., St. Camillus Health Center, #226, 10101 W. Wisconsin Ave., Wauwatosa, 53226.
Stangel, Mark J., Cousins Center, P.O. Box 070912, 53207-0912.
Strenski, Joseph A., Cousins Center, P.O. Box 070912, 53207-0912.
Strupp, James A., 580 S. 18th Ave., West Bend, 53095-3755.
Sukup, Joseph G., 1104 Park Ave., #4, South Milwaukee, 53172.
Thanh Hung, John B., 5250 Gasmer Dr., Houston, TX 77035.
Theisen, John J., 536 Lake Dr., Random Lake, 53075.
Twomey, John E., 2885 Klovar Ln., #3, East Troy, 53120.
Uhen, Cletus V., 1100 Fountain Dr., #208A, Racine, 53406-3767.
Van Beck, Alfred F., 2009 Elevada St., Oceanside, CA 92054.
Verhalen, Charles J., 3253 S. Lake Dr., St. Francis, 53235.
Wallaik, William H., 3222 S. 29th St., 53215.
Walter, John F., Camillus Court East # 316, 10100 W. Bluemound Rd., Wauwatosa, 53226.
Wawiorka, Ray W., P.O. Box 578, Kenosha, 53141.
Wawrzyniakowski, Edwrd J., N7594 Sandy Beach Rd., Fond du Lac, 54937.
Weber, Donald N., Brookfield Highlands, #1006, 20950 George Hunt Cir., Waukesha, 53186.
Weber, Gordon A., Brookfield Highlands, #1006,

20950 George Hunt Cir., Waukesha, 53186.
Weishar, Paul M., N110 W16973 Ashbury Cir., #6, Germantown, 53022.
Whalen, William, W3327 Orchard Ave., Green Lake, 54941.
Wieland, Edward R., Cousins Center, P.O. Box 070912, 53207-0912.
Wilimek, Louis, 1833 Northwood Ct., Sheboygan, 53081.
Winkler, Eugene, 3253 S. Lake Dr. # 301, St. Francis, 53235.
Witon, Russell F., 11515 W. Cleveland Ave. # 303A, West Allis, 53227.
Wolf, Robert J., Cousins Center, P.O. Box 070912, 53207-0912.
Yaniak, Frank J., 3501 S. Lake Dr., St. Francis, 53235.
Zeihen, Joseph N., Cousins Center, P.O. Box 070912, 53207-0912.
Zens, Roger A., 2620 S. 30th St., 53215.
Zerkel, Donald F., W15519 McKinley Ln., Athelstane, 54104.
Zwaska, Victor L., 1201 Hughitt Ave., Box 969, Superior, 54880.

Permanent Deacons:
Acosta, Carlos R., (Retired)
Anderson, Dennis D., St. Anthony, Pewaukee
Aschenbrener, James L., Corpus Christi, Milwaukee
Banach, William A., St. Rafael the Archangel, Milwaukee
Benavente, Jorge, St. Joseph, Waukesha
Blas, Francisco, Cristo Rey, Racine
Blaze, Edward, All Saints, Milwaukee
Borkowski, Donald A., St. Jude the Apostle, Wauwatosa
Brah, Eugene D., St. James, Mukwonago
Braun, Warren D., (Retired)
Brousseau, Gerald A., Out of Archdiocese
Brown, Richard J., St. Rita, West Allis
Burch, Michael F., SS. Cyril & Methodius, Sheboygan
Burmeister, Dan, St. Rita, Racine
Burns, John R., St. Mary, Hales Corners
Buth, Robert H., St. Mary's, Menomonee Falls
Buyck, Gerald W., Out of Archdiocese
Castaneda, Claudio C., Leave of Absence
Cebrzynski, Stanley, (Retired)
Cesarec, Michael E., (Retired)
Champagne, John I., St. Benedict the Moor, Milwaukee
Chrisien, James, St. Boniface, Germantown
Christensen, Eugene M., Good Shepherd, Menomonee Falls
Coca, Emilio, St. Patrick, Racine
Cody, Edward F., St. Katharine Drexel, Beaver Dam
Colainni, Arthur R., Awaiting Assignment
Collins, Dean J., Mother of Good Counsel, Milwaukee
Connors, Joseph, (Retired)
Cornejo, Carlos, St. Anthony, Milwaukee
Corsten, Dale, Leave of Absence
D'Alessio, John, St. Elizabeth Ann Seton, New Berlin
Dahlen, Clarence J., (Retired)
Dallman, Arthur C., (Retired)
Devona, James E., St. Mary, Racine
Dineen, Terry, Divine Mercy, South Milwaukee
Doerr, George J., Out of Archdiocese
Dominguez, Alvaro, St. Mark, Kenosha
Dziennik, John R., St. Veronica, Milwaukee
Ebel, John A., St. Bernadette, Milwaukee
Fazen, Robert J., St. Matthew, Campbellsport
Ference, Dennis H., (Retired)
Fietz, Dennis E., Immaculate Heart of Mary, West Allis
Filipiak, Thomas P., St. Bruno, Dousman
Finley, Michael J., St. John Neumann, Waukesha
Flynn, Richard M., Blessed Sacrament, Milwaukee
Francois James S., St. Mary, Kenosha
Fricano, John A., St. Luke, Brookfield
Frye, Patrick H., St. Mark, Kenosha
Fuentes, Roberto, Cristo Rey, Racine
Gamez, Antonio U., Leave of Absence
Gates, Joseph, (On Duty Outside of the Archdiocese)
Gliniecki, Harry F., (Retired)
Gonzales, Jose U., St. Joseph, Wauwatosa
Gonzalez, Baleriano O., St. Clement, Sheboygan
Goodman, Robert E., Three Holy Women, Milwaukee
Goulding, William, St. Mary, Hales Corners
Govek, Richard J., St. Joseph, Grafton
Gramza, Richard G., (Retired)
Griffiths, Joseph J., Out of Archdiocese
Grimyser, Peter G., Leave of Absence
Gurzynski, Theodore A., St. Alphonsus, Greendale
Guttierrez, Jose H., Our Lady of Guadalupe, Milwaukee
Guzman, Armindo, Out of Archdiocese
Heideman, Willis, St. Mary, Mayville
Henry, Walter, Immaculate Heart of Mary, West Allis
Hiller, Richard D., (Retired)
Horner, Ralph E., Immaculate Conception, West Bend
Huber, Paul, St. Francis Borgia, Cedarburg
Hughes, Larry L., Holy Family, Fond du Lac
Hughes, Wayne W., (Retired)
Hunt, Thomas N., SS. Peter & Paul, Milwaukee
Hying, Joseph H., St. Thomas Aquinas, Waterford
Janasik, Ralph R., Personal Leave
Jens, William T., Blessed Trinity, Sheboygan Falls
Kabara, Donald F., (Retired)
Kaczmarek, Raymond J., (Retired)
Kastenholz, Joseph H., (Retired)
Kehrer, Daniel F., St.Elizabeth, Kenosha
Kempka, Eugene A., St. Joseph, Waukesha; Queen of Peace, Pewaukee
Kennedy, Claude V., Holy Assumption, West Allis
Kennedy, David L., Out of Archdiocese
Klinkhammer, Phillip H., (Retired)
Koebel, Michael S., St. Frances Cabrini, West Bend
Kornburger, Ralph W., Jr., St. Catherine, Milwaukee
Kuban, Donald J., St. Peter, East Troy
Kustner, Charles J., St. Mary, Elm Grove
La Fond, M. Larry, Jr., St. Dominic, Brookfield
Lauer, David A., (Personal Leave)
Lazaga, Alfred C., Out of Archdiocese
Lebron, Gregorio M., (Retired)
Leggett, A. James, Divine Mercy, South Milwaukee
Lesjak, Ronald F., St. Mary, Kenosha
Libecki, John K., (Retired)
Lo Coco, Peter L., (Awaiting Assignment)
Lopez, Julio, Sts. Rose, Michael and Francis of Assisi, Milwaukee
Losiniecki, Thomas, (Retired)
Lowe, Stanley, St. Charles Borromeo, Milwaukee
Lukacevich, William J., (Retired)
Lupo, Samuel J., (Retired)
Lydolph, Donald J., St. Dominic, Sheboygan
Maack, Terrance A., St. Peter, Kenosha
Macias, Rogelio, St. Patrick and St. Rafael the Archangel, Milwaukee
Mahnke, Carl A., St. Thomas Aquinas, Waterford
Majewski, Edward H., (Retired)
Major, Troy, St. Francis of Assisi, Milwaukee
Malischke, Carl J., Leave of Absence
Malueg, Gerald D., Holy Rosary, Fredonia
Mandujano, J. Eufemio, Leave of Absence
Martino, Anthony, (Awaiting Assignment)
McGuine, Thomas W., (On Duty Outside of the Archdiocese)
Mensah, Anthony J., (Retired)
Merten, Arthur H., (Retired)
Meuler, Andrew, Mother of Good Counsel, Milwaukee
Milbauer, Richard E., St. Clare, Wind Lake
Miller, Kenneth J., (Retired)
Missureli, Russell A., St. Edward, Racine
Moczydlowski, Chester A., (Retired)
Molina, Juan A., Sr., Our Lady of Gualdalupe, Milwaukee
Monday, John P., Our Lady of Lourdes, Milwaukee
Monday, Thomas C., (On Duty Outside of the Archdiocese)
Monfre, Anthony, St. James, Mequon
Monzel, Paul S., Presentation, North Fond du Lac
Munoz, Ricardo, Holy Family, Fond du Lac
Nawrocik, Zenon L., Out of Archdiocese
Nguyen, Bruno Long H., St. Anthony, Milwaukee
Nicholas, Keith P., Leave of Absence
Niggemann, Richard D., St. Mary, Elm Grove
Normann, Larry E., St. Paul, Genesee Depot
Nowicki, Edward J., (Retired)
Ode, LeRoy, Sacred Heart of Jesus, St. Francis
Oelke, Gordon R., Leave of Absence
Ortiz, Aristeo, St. Joseph, Waukesha
Pemper, Frank, Out of Archdiocese
Pena, Luiz, St. Joseph, Waukesh
Perryman, Clif, St. James, Mequon
Peterson, James J., St. Sebastian, Milwaukee
Pettey, Lawrence C., (Retired)
Piontek, Richard T., St. Mary, Elm Grove
Pollak, David R., St. Charles Borromeo, Milwaukee
Ponec, Gerald R., Nativity of the Lord, Cudahy
Price, Gregory R., St. James, Mukwonago
Przedpelski, Steven J., Corpus Christi, Milwaukee
Ramirez-Murphy, Eugenio, Our Lady of Divine Providence, Milwaukee
Regan, Sylvester R., (Retired)
Rick, Wayne W., Leave of Absence
Rodriguez, Virgilio, Out of Archdiocese
Rooney, Michael R., St. Margaret Mary, Milwaukee
Rosado, Salvador, Sts. Francis of Assisi, Michael, Rose, Milwaukee
Salazar, Roberto, (On Duty Outside of the Archdiocese)
Schieffer, Robert M., (On Duty Outside of the Archdiocese)
Schimmels, Thomas J., (Retired)
Schopper, Eugene E., (Retired)
Sherman, George P., (Retired)
Shierk, Wilson A., St. Mary, Kenosha
Snyder, Gordon J., St. Bruno, Dousman
Sommers, David W., St. Matthias, Milwaukee
Starns, Terry, St. John Vianney, Brookfield
Stodola, John, Nativity of the Lord, Cudahy
Surges, Thomas J., St. Peter of Alcantara, Port Washington
Thoresen, Norman, (Retired)
Treichel, Robert B., Out of Archdiocese
Truttschel, Robert A., St. Katharine Drexel, Beaver Dam
Van Garsse, Eugene E., St. Monica, Whitefish Bay
Waitrovich, Raymond, St. Agnes, Butler
Wargin, John R., Immaculate Conception, Milwaukee
Weber, C. Edward, (Retired)
Wells, Randal S., St. Katharine Drexel, Beaver Dam
Wendt, Bernard J., St. Peter, Slinger
Wenzler, Joseph P., St. Cecilia, Thiensville
Widmar, Willard M., St. Paul the Apostle, Racine
Winkowski, Richard, St. Mary, Waukesha
Wirtz, Howard J., St. Richard, Racine
Wisniewski, DeSales, O.F.M., St. Sebastian, Sturtevant
Wisniewski, Ralph, St. Leonard, Muskego
Wodushek, Robert A., St. Anthony, Menomonee Falls
Wolf, Kenneth W., (Retired)
Wuchterl, Thomas H., St. Mary, Menomonee Falls
Yang, Blong P., St. Michael (Hmong Community), Milwaukee
Zalewski, Leon J., Our Lady of the Holy Rosary, Kenosha
Zimprich, David L., St. William, Waukesha
Zozakiewicz, Daniel T., St. Robert, Shorewood

INSTITUTIONS LOCATED IN THE DIOCESE

[A] SEMINARIES, ARCHDIOCESAN

ST. FRANCIS. *Saint Francis Seminary*, 3257 S. Lake Dr., 53235. Tel: 414-747-6400; Fax: 414-747-6442. Email: bjanczak@sfs.edu. Web: www.sfs.edu. Very Rev. Michael G. Witczak, M.Div., S.L.D., Rector; Rev. Melvin E. Michalski, Ph.L., Th.D., Vice Rector; Dr. David A. Stosur, Ph.D., Academic Dean; Ms. Mary Karr, M.A., MAPS, Registrar; Rev. James T. Schuerman, Mag. Theol., D.Min., Spiritual Dir.; Mr. Gary Pokorny, M.Div., D.Min. (Cand.), Dir. Lay Formation; Dr. Barbara V. Schauer, D.Min., Dir. Pastoral Formation; Rev. Stephen E. Malkiewicz, O.F.M., M.A., Dir. Worship; Cynthia Rapacke, M.A., Liturgical Music Dir.; Ms. Colleen O'Connor, M.Div., Dir. Salzmann Library; Ms. Mary E. Carian, M.A., M.S., Assoc. Dir. of Salzmann Library; Rev. David E. Windsor, C.M., Psy.D., Dir. Admissions; Mr. Timothy Charek, M.Div., M.B.A., Dir. Certificate Division; Deacon John A. Ebel, Assoc. Dir. Certificate Division; Ms. Maria Borda-Wiesner, M.A.P.S., C.N.A., Coord., Cert. Division's Hispanic/Latino Component; Rev. Niles J. Kauffman, O.F.M.Cap., M.A., Assoc. Dir., Pastoral Formation Certificate Programs; Sr. Callista Robinson, O.S.F., M.Ed., Coordinator Certificate Division African American Component; Ms. Sarita Herrera, Information System Admin.; Ms. Patricia Young Wesialowski, M.A.P.S., Advancement Dir.; Revs. Joseph J. Juknialis, Dir. Preaching Institute; Stephen J. Lampe, M.Div., S.S.L., S.T.D.; Bryan N. Massingale; Melvin E. Michalski, Ph.L., Th.D.; David E. Windsor, C.M., Psy.D.; Dr. Steven C. Kuhl, Ph.D.; Dr. Daniel J. Scholz, Ph.D.; Dr. Jane E. Linahan, Ph.D.; Dr. Dennis D. Sylva, Ph.D. Administration & Faculty 26; Priests 9; Sisters 1; Lay Staff 16; Seminarians 22; Lay Graduate Students 81; Certificate Lay Students 25; Certificate Deacon Students 18; Certificate Spanish Lay Students 18; Certificate Spanish Deacon Students 6.

College Formation Program, SS. Peter and Paul Residence, 2479 N. Murray Ave., 53211. Tel: 414-964-6982; Fax: 414-962-8183. Rev. Joseph J. Juknialis, Dir. Tel: 414-964-6970. Priests 1; Students 7.

[B] SEMINARIES, RELIGIOUS OR SCHOLASTICATES

FRANKLIN. *Xaverian Missionary Fathers College Seminary*, 4500 Xavier Dr., 53132. Tel: 414-421-0831; Fax: 414-421-9108. Email: xavmissionswi@

hotmail.com. Web: www.xaviermissionaries.org. Very Rev. Alfredo Turco, S.X. (Italy); Revs. Lawrence Crosara, S.X.; Victor Mosele, S.X. (Italy); Dominic Caldognetto, S.X. (Italy). Priests 4.

HALES CORNERS. *Sacred Heart School of Theology*, 7335 S. Highway 100, P.O. Box 429, 53130-0429. Tel: 414-425-8300; Fax: 414-529-6999. Email: rector@shst.edu. Web: www.shst.edu. Very Rev. James D. Brackin, S.C.J., M.Div., J.D., Pres. Rector; Revs. Raul Gomez, S.D.S., M.Div., M.P.A., Ph.D., Vice Rector; Thomas L. Knoebel, Academic Dean & Dir. Recruitment/Admissions & M.A. Program; Robert W. Schiavone, M.A., Dir. Pastoral Formation; Martin Barnum, D.Min., M.A., M.Div., Dir. Spiritual Formation; Ms. Margaret E. Boyles, M.E.P.D., Dir. Public Rels.; Mr. Michael Erato, Dir. Plant Operations; Ms. Kathleen M. Harty, M.R., M.A.L.S., Dir. Library; Ms. Rose Stinefast, M.A., Registrar & Asst. to Academic Dean; Dir. Continuing Educ.; Ms. Sally Smits, M.B.A., Vice Pres. Finance & Personnel; Revs. Otto N. Bucher, O.F.M.Cap., Prof. Emeritus; John T. O'Connor, S.C.J., J.C.L., S.T.D., Prof. Emeritus; Joseph Gole, S.T.D. (Slovenia), Prof. Emeritus; Sr. Martine Hundelt, S.S.S.F., Ph.D., Prof. Emerita.
Full-Time Faculty: Revs. Hugh G. Birdsall, S.D.S., M.A., M.S.; Charles Bisgrove, S.C.J.; Jan de Jong, S.C.J., S.T.D., S.T.L.; Paul Grizzelle-Reid, S.C.J., M.S., M.Div.; Jerome Higgins, O.F.M.Cap., M.Ed., M.A.S., D.Min.; Donald Krebs, M.A.; Thomas M. McLernon, M.Ed.; Vincent McNally, Ph.D. (Canada); Andre Papineau, S.D.S., M.A.; C. Michael Weldon, O.F.M., M.Div.; Sisters Mary C. Carroll, S.S.S.F., M.A., D.Min.; Marilyn Cowser, O.S.F., M.A.; Lucille Flores, S.S.M., M.P.S.; Joan Koehler, S.S.S.F., M.Ed., M.A.; Roseann Wagner, S.S.S.F., B.M., M.T.S.; Ms. Mary Brittnacher, M.L.S.; Dr. John Gallam, Ph.D.; Dr. Robert Gotcher, Ph.D.; Dr. Richard Lux, Ph.D.; Dr. Bruce Malchow, Ph.D.; Dr. Steven Shippee, Ph.D.; Mr. C. Christian Rich, B.A., M.M.; Ms. Ruth MacKechnie, M.Ed., Ph.D. (Cand.); Ms. Brooke Haley, M.A.
Part-Time Faculty: Revs. Charles Brown, S.C.J.; Thomas Brundage, J.C.L., M.Div.; John Cella, O.F.M.; Michael Van Der Peet, S.C.J.; Marc Berkson, D.H.L., M.H.L., Rabbi; Ms. Mary DeSantis, B.A.; Eva J. Diaz; Ms. Jennifer Laske, M.A.; Ms. Brigid O'Donnell, M.A.; Ms. Barbara Scherrer, B.A., M.S.T.

MOUNT CALVARY. *St. Felix Friary*, W1754 State Hwy. 149, 53057. Tel: 920-753-3111; Fax: 920-753-2306. Email: harmoniken@juno.com. Revs. Oliver Bambenek, O.F.M.Cap.; Kenneth R. Casper, O.F.M.Cap., Local Min., Novitiate Team; Simeon Keogh, O.F.M.Cap.; Martin Curtin, Novice Dir. Novitiate House of the Capuchin Province of St. Joseph, St. Mary and Mary Mother of the Good Shepherd Priests 4.

St. Lawrence Seminary 53057. Tel: 920-753-7500; Fax: 920-753-7507. Web: stlawrence.edu. Revs. Dennis Druggan, O.F.M.Cap., Rector & Pres.; Oliver Bambenek, O.F.M.Cap.; Gary Wegner, O.F.M.Cap.; Keith Clark, O.F.M.Cap., Local Min.; Elroy Pesch, O.F.M.Cap.; Thomas Zelinski, O.F.M.Cap.; Bros. Douglas Bode, O.F.M.Cap.; Neal Plale, O.F.M.Cap.; John Willger, O.F.M.Cap.; Jerome Johnson, O.F.M.Cap.; Jerome Campbell, O.F.M.Cap.; John Scherer, O.F.M.Cap.; Carl Schaefer, O.F.M.Cap.; Mr. Dennis Holm, Dean of Students; Mr. David Bartel, Academic Dean; Mr. Harlan Swift, Business Mgr. High School Seminary and Ministry Program Priests 6; Brothers 7; Sisters 1; Lay Teachers 15; Non-teaching Lay Staff 41; Students 205; Total Staff 69.

[C] COLLEGES AND UNIVERSITIES

MILWAUKEE. *Alverno College*, 3400 S. 43rd St., P.O. Box 343922, 53234-3922. Tel: 414-382-6000; Fax: 414-362-6354. Web: www.alverno.edu. Gary P. Grunau, Chm., Bd. of Trustees; Sr. Kathleen O'Brien, O.S.F., Interim Pres. & Sr. Vice Pres. Academic Affairs; Mr. James Oppermann, Sr. Vice Pres. Finance & Mgmt. Svcs. Sisters 7; Lay Teachers 98; Students 2,160; Total Staff 243.

Cardinal Stritch University, 6801 N. Yates Rd., 53217. Tel: 414-410-4000; Fax: 414-410-4239. Email: admityou@stritch.edu. Web: www.stritch.edu. Sr. Mary Lea Schneider, O.S.F., Pres.; Dr. Marna Boyle, Vice Pres. Academic Affairs; Revs. James E. Lobacz, Office of Campus Ministry; Trinette McCray, Office of Campus Ministry. Conducted by Sisters of St. Francis of Assisi Sisters 15; Lay Teachers 129; Students 5,855; Total Staff 290.

**Marquette University* (1881), P.O. Box 1881, 53201-1881. Tel: 414-288-7250. Email: webquestions@marquette.edu. Web: www.marquette.edu.
Legal Title: *Marquette University*, Conducted under the auspices of the Society of Jesus.
Major University Officers: Rev. Robert A. Wild, S.J., Pres.; Mr. John C. Lamb, Vice Pres. Finance; Ms. Cynthia M. Bauer, Vice Pres. & Gen. Counsel; Ms. Rana Altenburg, Vice Pres. Public Affairs; Mr. Gregory J. Kliebhan, Senior Vice Pres.; Rev. Andrew J. Thon, S.J., Vice Pres. Student Affairs; Ms. Julie Tolan, Vice Pres. Univ. Advancement; Dr. Madeline Wake, Provost; Dr. Thomas H. Wenzel, Vice Provost Undergraduate Programs & Teaching; Dr. T. Daniel Griffiths, Vice Provost Research & Graduate Programs; Ms. Stephanie Russell, Exec. Dir. Univ. Mission & Identity; Mr. Arthur F. Scheuber, Vice Pres. Admin.
Deans: Dr. Michael A. McKinney, Dean, College of Arts & Science; Dr. David L. Shrock, Dean College of Business Admin.; Dr. William R. Elliott, Dean College of Communication; Dr. William K. Lobb, Dean School of Dentistry; Dr. John J. Augenstein, Dean School of Education; Dr. Stanley V. Jaskolski, Dean College of Engineering; Dr. Jack C. Brooks, Dean College of Health Sciences; Dr. Nicholas C. Burckel, Dean Libraries; Dr. Lea Acord, Dean College of Nursing; Dr. Robert J. Deahl, Dean College of Professional Studies.
Additional Department Heads: Revs. D. Edward Mathie, S.J., Dir. Univ. Ministry; John D. Laurance, S.J., Acting Chair Dept.of Theology.

Mount Mary College, 2900 N. Menomonee River Pkwy., 53222-4545. Tel: 414-258-4810; Fax: 414-256-1224. Web: www.mtmary.edu. Patricia D. O'Donoghue, Pres. Sponsored by the School Sisters of Notre Dame Sisters 29; Lay Teachers 67; Students 1,610; Total Staff 356.

FOND DU LAC. *Marian College of Fond du Lac*, 45 S. National Ave., 54935. Tel: 920-923-7600; Fax: 920-923-8087. Email: admissions@mariancollege.edu. Web: www.mariancollege.edu. Dr. Richard I. Ridenour, Pres.; Sheryl Ayala, Vice Pres. Academic Affairs; Sr. Marie Scott, C.S.A., Campus Min. Sisters of the Congregation of St. Agnes 4; Lay Teachers 71; Students 2,672; Total Staff 280.

[D] HIGH SCHOOLS, ARCHDIOCESAN AND PAROCHIAL

MILWAUKEE. **Messmer High School*, 742 W. Capitol Dr., 53206. Tel: 414-264-5440; Fax: 414-264-0674. Email: jmonday@messmerhigh.com. Web: messmerhigh.com. Bro. Bob Smith, Pres.; Jeff Monday, Prin. Lay Teachers 49; Students 550.

Pius XI High School, 135 N. 76th St., 53213. Tel: 414-290-7000; Fax: 414-290-7001. Email: piusxi@piusxi.org. Web: www.piusxi.org. Very Rev. Robert V. Carney, S.A.C.; Rev. Richard J. Gunderman, S.A.C. School Sisters of St. Francis 5; Lay Teachers 115; Students 1,390.

Thomas More High School, 2601 E. Morgan Ave., 53207. Tel: 414-481-8370; Fax: 414-481-3382. Email: ljanick@tmore.org. Web: www.tmore.org. Mr. Joel Eul, Prin. (Coed) Sisters 1; Lay Teachers 36; Students 573; Total Staff 43.

BURLINGTON. *Catholic Central High School*, 148 McHenry St., 53105. Tel: 262-763-1510; Fax: 262-763-1509. Email: rlynch@cchsnet.org. Web: www.cchsnet.org. Ralph J. Lynch Jr.; Rev. Lawrence J. Chapman, Chap. Priests 1; Lay Teachers 18; Students 181.

FOND DU LAC. *St. Mary's Springs High School*, 255 County Rd. K, 54935. Tel: 920-921-4870; Fax: 920-921-2786. Email: rjensen@springs.k12.wi.us. Web: www.springs.k12.wi.us. Robb W. Jensen, CEO & Pres. Sisters 1; Lay Teachers 21; Students 240; Total Staff 22.

KENOSHA. *St. Joseph High School*, 2401 69th St., 53143. Tel: 262-654-8651; Fax: 262-654-1615. Email: rfreund@kenoshastjoseph.com. Web: stjosephhs.com. Mr. Robert Freund, Prin. Sisters 2; Lay Teachers 32; Students 316; Total Staff 34.

WAUKESHA. *Catholic Memorial High School*, 601 E. College Ave., 53186-5598. Tel: 262-542-7101; Fax: 262-542-1633. Email: jdavenport@catholicmemorial.net. Web: www.cathmem.org. Jay E. Davenport, Pres.; Kathleen A. Cepelka, Ph.D., Prin.; J. Patrick Farrell, Asst. to the Pres. for Operations/Vice Prin.; Elizabeth A. Dolan, Dir. of Devel. Lay Teachers 60; Students 820; Total Staff 76.

[E] HIGH SCHOOLS, PRIVATE

MILWAUKEE. *Divine Savior Holy Angels High School, Inc.* (Girls). , 4257 N. 100th St., 53222. Tel: 414-462-3742; Fax: 414-466-0590. Email: dsha@dsha.k12.wi.us. Web: www.dsha.k12.wi.us. Ellen Bartel, Pres.; Sr. Virginia Honish, S.D.S., Prin. Sponsored by the Sisters of the Divine Savior Sisters 3; Lay Teachers 54; Students 631; Total Staff 85.

St. Joan Antida High School, Inc. (Girls). , 1341 N. Cass St., 53202. Tel: 414-272-8423; Fax: 414-272-3135. Email: siouxhenzig@hotmail.com. Web: www.saintjoanantida.org. Sr. Monica Fumo, S.C.S.J.A., Pres.; Susan Henzig, Prin. Sisters of Charity of St. Joan Antida 7; Lay Teachers 25; Students 323; Total Staff 53.

Marquette University High School (Boys). , 3401 W. Wisconsin Ave., 53208. Tel: 414-933-7220; Fax: 414-937-8588. Email: muhs.edu. Web: www.muhs.edu. Revs. Thomas C. Manahan, S.J., Pres.; Robert J. Kroll, S.J.; Terrence M. Brennan, S.J.; John M. Belmonte, S.J.; Thomas M. Doyle, S.J.; Michael R. Kolb, S.J.; Charles L. Stang, S.J. (See separate listing for resident information). Priests 7; Scholastics 1; Lay Teachers 64; Students 1,039; Total Staff 72.

RACINE. *St. Catherine's High School*, 1200 Park Ave., 53403. Tel: 262-632-2785; Fax: 262-632-5144. Email: bmiller5@stcatherines.k12.wi.us. Web: stcatherines.k12.wi.us. Mr. Thomas Knitter, Pres.; Mr. Robert Miller, Prin.; Sr. Jane Weiss, Asst. Prin. Dominican Sisters (Racine) 5; Lay Teachers 34; Students 430.

WHITEFISH BAY. *Dominican High School*, 120 E. Silver Spring Dr., 53217. Tel: 414-332-1170; Fax: 414-332-4101. Email: dhs@dominicanhighschool.com. Web: dominicanhighschool.com. Paul M. McInerny, Ph.D., Pres.; James G. Piatt, Prin.; April Holland, Dean Academic Affairs; Jane McAuliffe, Chm. Religion Dept. Sponsored by Sinsinawa Dominicans Dominican Sisters of the Congregation of the Most Holy Rosary, Sinsinawa, WI 1; Admin. 4; Lay Teachers 30; Students 352.

[F] ELEMENTARY SCHOOLS, ARCHDIOCESAN

MILWAUKEE. *St. Leo Catholic Urban Academy*, 2458 W. Locust St., 53206. Tel: 414-442-1100; Fax: 414-873-0119. Email: birlemj@archmil.org. Sponsored and accredited by the Archdiocese of Milwaukee. Lay Teachers 14; Students 185; Total Staff 22.

St. Rose Catholic Urban Academy, 514 N. 31st St., 53208. Tel: 414-933-6070; Fax: 414-933-3071. Email: polczynskm@archmil.org. Web: www.archmil.org/schools. Sponsored and accredited by the Archdiocese of Milwaukee. Lay Teachers 14; Students 204; Total Staff 19.

[G] ELEMENTARY SCHOOLS, PRIVATE

MILWAUKEE. *St. Coletta Day School of Milwaukee*, 1740 N. 55th St., 53208. Tel: 414-453-1850; Fax: 414-453-9449. William A. Koehn, Prin. & Admin. For Exceptional Children Lay Teachers 2; Students 9.

Nativity Jesuit Middle School, Inc. (Boys). , 1115 S. Seventh St., 53204. Tel: 414-645-1060; Fax: 414-645-0505. Email: nativity@njms.org. Web: www.njms.org. Rev. William T. Johnson, S.J., Pres.; Ms. Rosario Sanchez, Prin. Wisconsin Province of the Society of Jesus Priests 1; Sisters 1; Lay Teachers 8; Students 54; Total Staff 16.

Notre Dame Middle School, Inc., 1420 W. Scott St., 53204. Tel: 414-671-3000; Fax: 414-671-3170. Email: ndmswi@aol.com. Alvaro Garcia-Velez, Pres.; Mary Garcia-Valez, Prin. Sponsored by: School Sisters of Notre Dame. Sisters 3; Lay Teachers 5; Volunteers 3; Students 96.

RACINE. *San Juan Diego Middle School, Inc.*, 1101 Douglas Ave., 53402. Tel: 262-619-0402; Fax: 262-898-9524. Email: mfrontier@wi.rr.com. Web: www.sjdms.org. Kenneth Leonard, Contact Person.

[H] CONSOLIDATED ELEMENTARY SCHOOLS

MILWAUKEE. *All Saints Catholic East School System, Inc.*, 2491 N. Murry Ave., 53211. Tel: 414-964-1770; Fax: 414-964-6578. Email: pattersonl@archmil.org. Rev. Gerald Hessel, Bd. Chm. Sponsored by the following Milwaukee parishes: Cathedral of St. John the Evangelist; Our Lady of Divine Providence; Old St. Mary's; Ss. Peter and Paul; Three Holy Women Catholic Parish. Lay Teachers 15; Students 147.

Catholic East Elementary, (Grades K-8), 2461 N. Murray Ave., 53211. Tel: 414-964-1770; Fax: 414-964-6578. Email: pattersonl@archmil.org. Mr. Larry Patterson, Prin. Members: SS. Peter and Paul, St. Mary of Czestochowa, Old St. Mary, St. Casimir, Cathedral of St. John the Evangelist, Three Holy Women. Lay Teachers 15; Students 147.

St. Elizabeth Ann Seton Academy, Ltd., 1051 E. Russell Ave., 53207. Tel: 414-482-8996; Fax: 414-747-9219. Email: seton@execpc.com. Ellen Knippel, Prin. School sponsored by Immaculate Conception and St. Augustine parishes, Milwaukee. Students 147.

Holy Wisdom Academy, c/o St. Alexander Congregation 3373 S. 15th Pl., 53215-5039. Tel: 414-383-3453; Fax: 414-672-2645. Rev. Michael A. Ignaszak, Contact. Sponsored by St. Alexander and St. Helen Parishes, Milwaukee.

BEAVER DAM. *Unified Catholic Parish Schools of*

Beaver Dam, 503 S. Spring St., 53916-2598. Tel: 920-885-5558; Fax: 920-885-7610. Email: ucpsbeaverdam.org. Web: www.archmil.org/schools/main.asp. Barbara M. Haase, Prin. Members: St. Katharine Drexel. Lay Teachers 23; Students 346.

FOND DU LAC. *Fond du Lac Area Catholic Education System (FACES)*, 26 W. Follett St., P.O. Box 2138, 54936-2138. Tel: 920-924-0993; Fax: 920-922-7849. Email: facesl@faces.k12.wi.us. Web: www.faces.k12.wi.us. Susan L. Zacherl, System Admin. Members: Holy Family, Fond du Lac; Presentation of the Blessed Virgin; North Fond du Lac

Faces Primary Campus, 95 E. Second St., 54935. Tel: 920-921-5300; Fax: 920-921-5908. Sr. Susan Zacherl, Prin. Lay Teachers 14; Students 233.

Faces Intermediate and Middle School, 63 E. Merrill St., 54935. Tel: 920-921-9610; Fax: 920-921-0457. Ms. Cheryl Jaeger, Prin. Lay Teachers 19; Students 293.

LOMIRA. *Consolidated Catholic School, Lomira-Theresa*, 705 Milwaukee St., 53048-9520. Tel: 920-269-4326; Fax: 920-269-7342. Email: cclt@dotnet.com. Dorothy Zitlow, Prin. Members: St. Mary, Lomira; St. Theresa, Theresa. Lay Teachers 8; Students 81.

MEQUON. *Ss. Cecilia and James School*, 11300 N. St. James Ln., #28 W, 53092. Tel: 262-242-7960; Fax: 262-242-7976. Email: rlg@stscj.org. Web: www.stscj.org. Mr. Richard Goeden, Prin. Members: St. Cecilia, Thiensville; St. James, Mequon. Lay Teachers 40; Students 542.

St. Cecilia Campus:: 116 W. Orchard St., Thiensville, 53092. Tel: 262-242-7965; Fax: 262-242-7976.

St. James Campus:: 11300 N. St. James Ln., 53092. Tel: 262-242-7960; Fax: 262-512-8986.

MOUNT CALVARY. *Consolidated Parochial Elementary School*, 100 Notre Dame St., 53057. Tel: 920-753-4811; Fax: 920-753-2411. Email: cpes@charter.com. Mary Beth Leonard, Prin. & Admin. Members: St. John the Baptist, Johnsburg; St. Mary, Marytown; Holy Cross, Mount Calvary; St. Cloud, St. Cloud. Sisters 1; Lay Teachers 14; Students 155.

WAUKESHA. *Waukesha Catholic School System, Inc.*, 440 N. Moreland Blvd., 53188. Tel: 262-896-2920; Fax: 262-896-2925. Email: business@waukeshacatholicschoolsystem.org. Rev. Michael F. Michalski, Pastor Liaison. Tel: 262-542-2589. Members: St. Joseph, St. Mary, St. John Neumann, St. William.

St. Joseph Campus, 818 N. East Ave., 53186. Tel: 262-896-2930; Fax: 262-896-2935. Mrs. Kathleen Rempe, Prin. Lay Teachers 19; Students 227.

St. Mary Campus, 520 N. Newhall Ave., 53186. Tel: 262-896-2932; Fax: 262-896-2931. Mrs. Carolyn Caruso, Prin. Sisters 2; Lay Teachers 17; Students 364.

St. William Campus, 444 N. Moreland Blvd., 53188. Tel: 262-896-2920; Fax: 262-896-2925. Robert Radomski, Prin. Sisters 1; Lay Teachers 11; Students 167.

[I] CHILD CARE CENTERS

MILWAUKEE. *Child Development Center of St. Joseph*, 1600 W. Oklahoma Ave., 53215. Tel: 414-645-5337; Fax: 414-645-5329. Web: www.childdevctr-stjoes.org. Sr. Mary Ramona Dombrowski, C.S.S.F., Pres. Felician Sisters 7; Lay Teachers 31; Children 245; Total Staff 51; Other Sisters 2; Other Staff 11.

Guardian Angel Learning Center, Inc., 1540 N. Jefferson, 53202. Tel: 414-277-9474; Fax: 414-277-9482. Email: gscholl1@wi.rr.com. Web: www.scsja.org. Sr. Marie Louise Balistrieri, S.C.S.J.A., Admin. Sisters of Charity of St. Joan Antida., The center is licensed for ages 6 weeks to 11 years with a school age program. Sisters of Charity of St. Joan Antida 4; Lay Teachers 18; Students 80.

Seton Children's School, Inc., 8647 N. Port Washington Rd., 53217. Tel: 414-352-6115. Email: amarquar@columbia_stmarys.org. Operated by the Ascension Health System. A licensed center for comprehensive early childhood educational programs and day care Lay Teachers 10; Children 83.

Other Locations:

2330 N. Prospect Ave., 53211. Tel: 414-220-8494. Lay Teachers 7; Children 52.

13133 N. Port Washington Rd., Mequon, 53097. Tel: 414-243-7318. Lay Teachers 3; Children 34.

SOUTH MILWAUKEE. *Franciscan Villa Child Day Care Center*, 3601 S. Chicago Ave., 53172. Tel: 414-570-5410; Fax: 414-764-0706. Email: dawnmariewester@catholichealth.net. Web: www.franciscanvilla.com. Affiliate of Catholic Health Initiatives. Lay Teachers 5; Children 50.

WAUWATOSA. *Carmelite Home, Inc.*, 1214 Kavanaugh Pl., 53213. Tel: 414-258-4791; Fax: 414-258-8464. Email: brobin1148@aol.com. Sr. Mary Petra, Admin.; James E. Lewis, M.S.W., ICSW, Treatment Dir. Residential Treatment Center for Adolescent Boys Sisters 3; Social Workers 3; Residents 30; Lay Teachers 3.

[J] GENERAL HOSPITALS

MILWAUKEE. *St. Francis Hospital*, 3237 S. 16th St., 53215. Tel: 414-647-5000; Fax: 414-647-5565. Email: mworley@covhealth.org. Web: www.stfrancishospital.net. Debra K. Standridge, Pres. & CEO; Rev. Joseph L. Bisoffi, O.S.Cam., Chap. Sponsored by the Congregation of the Sisters of St. Felix of Cantalice of the United States of America, Chicago Province (Felician Sisters). Sisters 7; Chaplains 6; Bed Capacity 260; Patients Assisted Annually 202,430; Total Staff 1,435.

St. Joseph Regional Medical Center, Inc., 5000 W. Chambers St., 53210. Tel: 414-447-2000; Fax: 414-874-4393. Web: www.covhealth.org. Daniel J. Bonk, Pres.; Trisha Crissman, Interim Regl. Dir. Franciscan Sisters, Daughters of the Sacred Hearts of Jesus and Mary (Wheaton, IL) 8; Bed Capacity 567; Patients Assisted Annually 316,224; Total Staff 2,592.

St. Mary's Hospital of Milwaukee, 2323 N. Lake Dr., P.O. Box 503, 53201-0503. Tel: 414-291-1000; Fax: 414-291-1444. Email: tpandl@columbia-stmarys.org. Web: www.columbia-stmarys.org. Therese Pandl, Exec. Vice Pres.; Revs. Russell F. Tikalsky Chap.; Eugene Pocernich, Chap.; Rev. Vicki Watkins, Chap.; Sisters Rosalynn Dzikonski, O.S.F., Chap.; Margaret Ann Arnold, S.S.S.F., Chap.; Margaret Wenzel, Chap. Corporate Title: St. Mary's Hospital of Milwaukee.; Ascension Health System Bed Capacity 294; Patients Assisted Annually 411,266; Total Staff 2,417.

St. Michael Hospital of Franciscan Sisters of Milwaukee, Inc., 2400 W. Villard Ave., 53209. Tel: 414-527-3000; Fax: 414-527-8461. Web: www.covhealth.org. Mr. R. Bruce James, Pres.; Trisha Crissman, Regl. Dir. Spiritual Care. Franciscan Sisters, Daughters of the Sacred Hearts of Jesus and Mary (Wheaton, IL) 6; Bed Capacity 405; Patients Assisted Annually 207,871; Total Staff 1,242.

Ministry Health Care, Inc., 11925 W. Lake Park Dr., 53224. Tel: 414-359-1060; Fax: 414-359-1656. Email: info@ministryhealth.org. Web: www.ministryhealth.org. Nicholas Desien, Pres. & CEO.

Subsidiaries and Affiliated Hospitals located throughout Wisconsin:

Door County Memorial Hospital, Sturgeon Bay. Tel: 920-743-5566; Fax: 920-743-8165.

Mercy Medical Center of Oshkosh, Inc., Oshkosh. Tel: 920-223-2000; Fax: 920-223-0508.

Ministry Behavioral Health of St. Michael's Hospital, Inc., Stevens Point. Tel: 715-344-4611; Fax: 715-344-8127.

Ministry Home Care, Inc, Marshfield. Tel: 715-389-3802; Fax: 715-387-9950.

Saints, Inc, Rhinelander. Tel: 715-369-6400; Fax: 715-369-6441.

Sacred Heart-Saint Mary's Hospitals, Inc. Tomahawk and Rhinelander, WI Tel: 715-369-6600; Fax: 715-369-6441.

Saint Elizabeth's Hospital's of Wabasha, Inc., Wabasha, MN. Tel: 651-565-4531; Fax: 651-565-2482.

Saint Joseph's Hospital of Marshfield, Inc., Marshfield. Tel: 715-387-1713; Fax: 715-387-5601.

Saint Clair's Hospital of Weston, Inc., Wausau.

St. Michael's Hospital of Stevens Point, Inc., Stevens Point. Tel: 715-346-5000; Fax: 715-346-5088.

Victory Medical Center, Inc., Stanley. Tel: 715-644-5571; Fax: 715-644-6221.

Dr. Kate Newcomb Convalescent Center Inc., Woodruff. Tel: 715-356-8888; Fax: 715-356-3861.

Eagle River Memorial Hospital, Incorporated, Eagle River. Tel: 715-479-7411; Fax: 715-479-2748.

The Howard Young Medical Center, Inc, Woodruff. Tel: 715-356-8000; Fax: 715-356-6097.

Howard Young Health Care, Inc., Woodruff. Tel: 715-356-8000; Fax: 715-356-6097.

Affinity Health System, Oshkosh. Tel: 920-720-1700; Fax: 920-720-1907.

Agape Community Center of Milwaukee, Inc. Tel: 414-464-4440; Fax: 414-464-9420.

Ministry Medical Group, Inc. Tel: 414-359-1060; Fax: 414-359-1656.

BROOKFIELD. *Elmbrook Memorial Hospital, Inc.*, 19333 W. North Ave., 53045. Tel: 262-785-2000; Fax: 262-785-2444. Web: www.covhealth.org. Kimry A. Johnsrud, Pres.; Trisha Crissman, Interim Regl. Dir. Franciscan Sisters, Daughters of the Sacred Hearts of Jesus and Mary (Wheaton, IL) Bed Capacity 166; Patients Assisted Annually 91,661; Total Staff 978.

FOND DU LAC. *Agnesian Health Care* dba St. Agnes Hospital , 430 E. Division St., 54935. Tel: 920-929-2300; Fax: 920-926-4866. Email: fale@agnesian.com. Web: www.agnesian.com. Mr. Robert A. Fale, Pres. & CEO. Sisters 7; Bed Capacity 190, (18 TCU) 0; Patients Assisted Annually 189,910; Total Staff 1,250.

KENOSHA. *St. Catherine's Hospital*, 6308 Eighth Ave., 53143. Tel: 262-656-2011; Fax: 414-656-2124. Richard O. Schmidt Jr., Pres. & CEO. Sponsored by Franciscan Sisters and Daughters of the Sacred Hearts of Jesus and Mary, Wheaton, IL

MEQUON. *St. Mary's Hospital Ozaukee, Inc.*, 13111 N. Port Washington Rd., 53097. Tel: 414-243-7300; 800-848-2844; Fax: 414-243-7416. Email: tpandl@columbia-stmarys.org. Web: www.columbia-stmarys.org. Therese Pandl, Exec. Vice Pres. & COO; Rev. John R. Paczesny, Chap. (Retired); Sr. Angela Spence, Chap. Ascension Health System Bed Capacity 106; Patients Assisted Annually 218,092; Total Staff 980.

RACINE. *All Saints Medical Center, Inc.*, 3801 Spring St., 53405. Tel: 262-687-4011; Fax: 262-687-8039. Email: kbuser@allsaintshealthcare.org. Web: allsaintshealth.com. Kenneth R. Buser, Pres. & CEO; Rev. William J. Dietzler, Dir. Pastoral Care & Chap. Bed Capacity 325; Patients Assisted Annually 381,316; Total Staff 2,665.

Ambulatory Clinics Tel: 262-687-4011; Fax: 262-687-8039. Patients Assisted Annually 404,560; Total Staff 804.

All Saints Medical Group-Northwestern Campus, 2405 Northwestern Ave., 53404. Tel: 262-687-6000; Fax: 262-687-6422.

All Saints Medical Group-Spring St. Campus, 3807 Spring St., 53405. Tel: 262-687-2011; Fax: 262-687-8089.

All Saints Medical Group- Union Grove Campus, 1120 Main St., Union Grove, 53182. Tel: 262-878-4424; Fax: 262-687-8591.

All Saints Medical Group- Northside, 2408 Four Mile Rd.. Tel: 262-687-5900; Fax: 262-687-5950.

SHEBOYGAN. *St. Nicholas Hospital*, 1601 N. Taylor Dr., 53081. Tel: 920-459-8300; Fax: 920-452-8336. Email: mbrasseaux@sns.hshs.org. Web: www.stnicholashospital.org. Mary T. Brasseaux, Exec. Vice Pres. & Admin.; Sr. Renelle Brueggemann, O.S.F., Rel. Coord.; Barbara Mulcahy, Dir. Spiritual & Pastoral Support Svcs. Hospital Sisters of the Third Order of St. Francis 2; Bed Capacity 185; Patients Assisted Annually 90,172; Total Staff 583.

WAUPUN. *Waupun Memorial Hospital*, 620 W. Brown St., 53963. Tel: 920-324-5581; Fax: 920-324-2085. Web: www.agnesian.com. James E. Baer, Pres. & CEO. Corporate Title: Waupun Memorial Hospital, Inc. Bed Capacity 29; Patients Assisted Annually 34,617; Staff 200.

[K] SPECIAL HOSPITALS AND SANATORIA

MILWAUKEE. *Sacred Heart Rehabilitation Institute, Inc.*, 2350 N. Lake Dr., 53211. Tel: 414-298-6700; Fax: 414-298-6712. Therese Pandl, Exec. Vice Pres.; Sr. Margaret Ann Arnold, S.S.S.F. Ascension Health System Sisters 1; Bed Capacity 67; Patients Assisted Annually 10,876; Total Staff 153.

Satellite Locations:

St. Mary's Hospital of Milwaukee, 53211. Tel: 414-298-6700; Fax: 414-298-6712.

Sacred Heart Rehabilitation Institute, Memorial Hosp. at Oconomowoc, 791 E. Summit Ave., Oconomowoc, 53066. Tel: 414-569-0640; Fax: 414-569-0653.

[L] PROTECTIVE INSTITUTIONS

MILWAUKEE. *St. Charles Youth and Family Services, Inc.*, 151 S. 84th St., 53214. Tel: 414-476-3710; Fax: 414-778-5985. Email: k.grimes@stcharlesinc.org. Web: www.stcharlesinc.org. Ms. Cathy Connolly, Pres. Residents 78; Total Assisted 950; Total Staff 430.

Daystar, Inc., P.O. Box 2130, 53201-2130. Tel: 414-385-0334; Fax: 414-385-0336. Email: daystar@daystarinc.org. Web: www.daystarinc.org. Transitional living program for formerly battered women without children, for up to two years. Residents 10; Total Staff 8; Total Assisted 25.

Rosalie Manor Community & Family Services, Inc., 4803 W. Burleigh St., 53210. Tel: 414-449-2868; Fax: 414-449-2870. Email: rosaliemanor@aeronet. Web: www.rosaliemanor.org. Marilyn Lange, Interim Exec. Dir. Community Programs for Single and First-Time Parents and an abstinence-based pregnancy prevention program for youth.; Sponsored by the Archdiocese of Milwaukee Total Assisted 2,957; Total Staff 64.

MOUNT CALVARY. *Cristo Rey Ranch, Inc.*, N8102 Calvary St., 53057. Tel: 920-753-2026; 920-753-3211; Fax: 920-753-3100. Email: villasisters@netscape.net. Sister Servant of Christ the King, Provides weekend respite services to families caring for emotionally/behaviorally challenged children and adolescents. Program emphasis on pet therapy. Some day and evening programs thru County Social Services Department. Total Assisted 290; Total Staff 5.

[M] HOMES FOR AGED AND NURSING HOMES

MILWAUKEE. *Alexian Village of Milwaukee, Inc.*, 9301 N. 76th St., 53223. Tel: 414-355-9300; Fax: 414-357-5106. Email: gmohn@abhses.com. Web: www.alexianvillage.org. Gary Mohn, CEO; Rev. Joe Jagodensky, S.D.S., Chap.; Sr. Mary Kainz, S.C.S.J.A. Congregation of Alexian Brothers, Immaculate Conception Province, Continuing Care Retirement Community. Units 290; Residents 501; Brothers 3; Total Assisted 80; Total Staff 280.

St. Ann Center for Intergenerational Care, Inc., 2801 E. Morgan Ave., 53207. Tel: 414-977-5000; Fax: 414-977-5050. Sr. Edna Lonergan, O.S.F., Pres. Sisters of St. Francis of Assisi, St. Francis, WI Total Assisted 700; Total Staff 110.

St. Ann Rest Home, 2020 S. Muskego Ave., 53204-3522. Tel: 414-383-2642; Fax: 414-383-2642. Email: stann2@execpc.com. Rev. Cantius J. Kobak, O.F.M., Pastoral Care Min.; Sr. M. Columba, O.P., Admin. Conducted by the Dominican Sisters (Congregation of the Immaculate Conception) Sisters 9; Residents 50; Total Staff 47.

St. Anne's Salvatorian Campus, 3800 N. 92nd St., 53222. Tel: 414-463-7570; Fax: 414-463-2311. Email: lvogt@wi.rr.com. Web: www.wahsa.org/st.anne/index.html. Ms. Lynn Vogt, Admin.; Rev. Neil Durham, S.D.S., Chap. Sisters of the Divine Savior Assisted Living Apartments 25; Residents 107; Total Staff 194.

Catholic Charities Adult Day Services and Resource Center, 1919 N. 60th St., 53208. Tel: 414-771-2881, Ext. 162; Fax: 414-771-9115. Email: catholiccharities@ccmke.org. Web: www.ccmke.org. Cathy Young, Contact Person. Total Assisted 150; Total Staff 16.

Catholic Charities Adult Day Services, New Hope Center, 4033 W. Good Hope Rd., 53209. Tel: 414-228-7740; Fax: 414-352-3042. Sponsored by Catholic Charities of the Archdiocese of Milwaukee

Catholic Charities Adult Day Services, 13700 W. National Ave., New Berlin, 53151. Tel: 262-782-0740; Fax: 262-782-0024. National Regency

**Marian Franciscan Center, Inc.*, 9632 W. Appleton Ave., 53225. Tel: 414-461-8850; Fax: 414-461-9570. Web: www.covhealth.org. James D. Gresham, Pres. Franciscan Sisters, Daughters of the Sacred Hearts of Jesus and Mary, Wheaton, IL Residents 305; Total Staff 428.

**Milwaukee Catholic Home*, 2462 N. Prospect Ave., 53211-4462. Tel: 414-224-9700; Fax: 414-224-1666. Email: info@milwaukeecatholichome.org. Web: milwaukeecatholichome.org. Mr. Paul J. Connolly, N.H.A., Exec. Dir.; Rev. Charles R. Keefe, Dir. Pastoral Care. Corporate Title: Milwaukee Catholic Home, Inc. Retirement Home Residents 138; Retirement Home Total Staff 67; Nursing Home Residents 122; Nursing Home Total Staff 200; Day Care (Adult) 17; Assisted Living 29.

Mount Carmel Health and Rehabilitation Center (Mount Carmel, LLC), 5700 W. Layton Ave., 53220. Tel: 414-281-7200; Fax: 414-281-0744. Email: mike.berry@bhshealth.org. Michael W. Berry, N.H.A., Admin. Patients Assisted Annually 828; Total Staff 585.

The Terrace at St. Francis, Inc., 3200 S. 20th St., 53215. Tel: 414-389-3200; Fax: 414-389-3300. James D. Gresham, Pres. Member of Covenant Healthcare. Sponsored by the Felician Sisters and the Wheaton Franciscan Sisters, Skilled Nursing Facility for Transitional & Extended Subacute Care. Bed Capacity 81; Total Staff 120.

Villa St. Francis, Inc., 1910 W. Ohio Ave., 53215. Tel: 414-649-2888; Fax: 414-649-2880. Web: www.villastfrancis.org. Sr. Mary Ramona Dombrowski, C.S.S.F., Pres. Sponsored by the Congregation of the Sisters of St. Felix of Cantalice of the United States of America, Inc. Chicago Province (Felician Sisters), Independent & Assisted Living Facility Resident Apartments 139; Total Assisted 172; Total Staff 63.

FOND DU LAC. *St. Francis Home for Aged*, 33 Everett St., 54935. Tel: 920-923-7980; Fax: 920-923-7995. Douglas Trost, Admin.; Rev. Joachim Strupp, O.F.M.Cap., Chap. Sisters of St. Agnes, C.S.A. Sisters 3; Residents 107.

St. Clare Terrace Tel: 920-923-7996; Fax: 920-923-7995. Residents 33; Independent Elderly Apartments 30; Total Staff 3.

St. Francis Terrace Tel: 920-923-7980; Fax: 920-923-7995. Residents 13; Assisted Living Units 13; Total Staff 5.

Nazareth Center-Nazareth Court, 375 Gillett St., 54935. Tel: 920-923-7993; Fax: 920-907-6800. Email: lccsa@ticon.net. Douglas Trost, Admin. Retirement Home Sponsored by the Congregation of Sisters of St. Agnes. Sisters 72.

GREENFIELD. *Clement Manor Health Center*, 3939 S. 92nd St., 53228. Tel: 414-321-1800; Fax: 414-546-7357. Web: www.clementmanor.com. Richard Rau, Pres. & CEO; Mr. Dennis Ferger, Admin.; Rev. Daniel T. Murphy, Chap. Sponsored by School Sisters of St. Francis, Corporate Title: Clement Manor, Inc. Sisters 4; Residents 166; Adult Day Care 35; Child Day Care 30.

Clement Manor Retirement Community, 9339 W. Howard, 53228. Tel: 414-546-7374; Fax: 414-546-7357. Web: www.clementmanor.com. Mr. Greg Szpak; Rev. Daniel T. Murphy, Chap. Corporate Title: Clement Manor, Inc. Sponsored by the School Sisters of St. Francis. Sisters 4; Residents 235; Apartments 130; Assisted Living Apartments 71.

KENOSHA. *St. Joseph's Adult Day Care Center, Inc.*, 9244 29th Ave., 53144. Tel: 262-694-6000; Fax: 262-694-0148. Email: sjoseph@acronet.net. Web: www.stjoseph.com. Ms. Joyce Mitchell, Dir. Sponsored by: Carmelite Sisters of the Divine Heart of Jesus Total Assisted 140; Total Staff 17.

St. Joseph's Home for the Aged, 9244 29th Ave., 53143. Tel: 262-694-0080; Fax: 262-694-7325. Email: st.josephs1@wi.rr.com. Web: www.stjosephs.com. Sisters Mary Emmanuel Apanites, D.C.J., Admin.; M. Jacinta Cusumano, D.C.J., Supr.; Rev. Bronislaw Slodowski. Corporate Title: Carmelite Sisters of the Divine Heart of Jesus.; St. Joseph's Villa, Independent living units Sisters 5; Residents 93; Adult Day Care 45; Total Staff 150; Apartments 44.

MOUNT CALVARY. *Villa Loretto Nursing Home*, N8114 Calvary St., 53057. Tel: 920-753-3211; Fax: 920-753-3100. Email: villasisters@netscape.net. Sr. Mary Rose, Supr. Corporate Title: Sister Servants of Christ the King, Inc. dba Villa Loretto. Sisters 6; Residents 52; Total Assisted 63; Total Staff 78.

RACINE. *Marian Housing Center, Inc.*, 4105 Spring St., 53405. Tel: 262-633-5807; Fax: 262-633-9780. Email: www.wfs-inc.org. Total Assisted 38; Total Staff 2.

St. Monica's Senior Citizens Home, Inc., 3920 N. Green Bay Rd., 53404. Tel: 262-639-5050; Fax: 262-639-5673. Email: srirene@clmail.com. Sr. Irene Hanika, O.S.A., Supr. & Admin.; Rev. Thaddeus J. Bryl (Retired). Non-Profit Corp. Sisters of St. Rita 7; Residents 110; Total Staff 45.

ST. FRANCIS. *Canticle Court, Inc.*, 3201 S. Lake Dr., 53235. Tel: 414-744-9959; Fax: 414-744-7636. Email: jcpres@seii.com. An Apartment building sponsored by the Sisters of St. Francis of Assisi funded by HUD for low income elderly persons who can live independently Units 48; Total in Residence 49; Total Staff 2.

Juniper Court, Inc., 3209 S. Lake Dr., 53235-3702. Tel: 414-744-5878; Fax: 414-744-7636. Email: jcpres@seii.com. Mrs. Carol Keen, Pres. An apartment building with congregate meal site for persons of low to moderate income who can live independently.; Sponsored by the Sisters of St. Francis of Assisi, St. Francis, WI. Total in Residence 55; Total Units 53; Total Staff 2.

SOUTH MILWAUKEE. *Franciscan Villa of South Milwaukee, Inc.*, 3601 S. Chicago Ave., 53172. Tel: 414-764-4100; Fax: 414-764-0706. Email: susangoelz@catholichealth.net. Web: www.franciscanvilla.org. Roger L. DeMark, Admin. & CEO. Catholic Health Initiatives Residents 150; Alzheimer's Assisted Living 64; Adult Day Care 30; Child Day Care 36.
Residential Care Apartment Complex:

WAUWATOSA. *St. Camillus Health Center, Inc.*, 10101 W. Wisconsin Ave., 53226. Tel: 414-258-1814; Fax: 414-259-4987. Email: rljohnson@stcam.com. Web: www.stcam.com. Rev. Louis Lussier, O.S.Cam.; Very Rev. Richard O'Donnell, O.S.Cam., Prov.; Rick Johnson, Pres. & CEO; Rev. Carlo Notaro, O.S.Cam., Chap.; Deacon Albert Schempp, O.S.Cam., Chap.; Bro. Mario Crivello, O.S.Cam., Chap.; Ms. Sally Redmond, Chap. Order of the Servants of the Sick (Order of St. Camillus), Skilled Nursing Home Patients Assisted Annually 190; Total Staff 550. In Res. Revs. Peter T. Amrhein (Retired); Victor Bartelt; Leo Belda; Robert P. Hart, S.J.; Vincent Holubowicz; Leo M. Lambert (Retired); Lawrence J. Leack (Retired); Owen McLaughlin; Donald Musinski; Jerome E. Rohrer, S.J.; Joe Schwinn; Thomas Simcox; Albin F. Sowinski (Retired); John F. Walter (Retired); Deacon Thomas N. Hunt.

San Camillo, Inc., 10200 W. Blue Mound Rd., 53226. Tel: 414-259-6300. Rev. Louis Lussier, O.S.Cam.; Very Rev. Richard O'Donnell, O.S.Cam., Prov.; Marie D'Amico, Vice Pres. Housing. Order of the Servants of the Sick (Order of St. Camillus), Independent living facilities for older adults. Residents 340; Total Assisted 118; Total Staff 550.

[N] PERSONAL PRELATURES

BROOKFIELD. *Prelature of the Holy Cross and Opus Dei.*, 12900 W. North Ave., 53005. Tel: 262-784-1523; Fax: 262-782-5283. Email: info@opusdei.org. Revs. Timothy J. Uhen; John C. Kubeck. Layton Study Center for men

[O] MONASTERIES AND RESIDENCES FOR PRIESTS AND BROTHERS

MILWAUKEE. *Alexian Brothers Community* Immaculate Conception Province , 7979 W. Glenbrook Rd., 53223. Tel: 414-355-9300; Fax: 414-357-5290. Email: jhoward31331@core.com. Bros. Robert Petersen, C.F.A.; John Howard, C.F.A.; Richard Remetch, C.F.A. Brothers 3.

Arrupe House Jesuit Community, 831 N. 13th St., 53233-1706. Tel: 414-288-5855; Fax: 414-288-5852. Revs. John M. Paul, S.J., Supr.; Philip J. Rossi, S.J.; Thomas N. Brennan, S.J.; Michael A. Fahey, S.J.; D. Thomas Hughson, S.J.; Eugene F. Merz, S.J.; Douglas J. Leonhardt, S.J.; Warren J. Sazama, S.J.; Very Rev. James E. Grummer, S.J.; Revs. Cyprianus Kuntoro Adi, S.J. (Indonesia); Hugo Alexis Moreno, S.J. (Colombia); Willard J. Dressel, S.J.; Gregory N.P. Konz, S.J.; Aloysius F. Schmitz, S.J.; Bro. Lee A. McNamee, S.J. Society of Jesus, Wisconsin Prov. Priests 14; Brothers 1.

St. Conrad Friary, 3138 N. 2nd St., 53212. Tel: 414-372-3620. Revs. Brian Braun, O.F.M.Cap.; Otto N. Bucher, O.F.M.Cap.; Richard Hart, O.F.M.Cap.; Niles J. Kauffman, O.F.M.Cap., M.A.; Timon W. Costello. Capuchin Friars, Province of St. Joseph Priests 5; Total in Residence 5.

Jesuit Community at Marquette University, 1404 W. Wisconsin Ave., 53233. Tel: 414-288-5000; Fax: 414-288-1758. Revs. G. Thomas Krettek, S.J., Rector; Robert W. Leiweke, S.J., Asst. Rector; James J. Gladstone, S.J., Min.; Philip Abraham, S.J. (India); Joseph Oduor Afulo, S.J.; Richard H. Ahler, S.J.; Emmanuel Arockiam, S.J. (India); Charles R. Baumann, S.J.; John M. Belmonte, S.J.; Ronald R. Bieganowski, S.J.; Harold C. Bradley, S.J.; Thaddeus J. Burch, S.J.; Francis J. Burke, S.J.; Peter N. Bwanal, S.J. (Zambia); Thomas Caldwell, S.J.; Michael D. Class, S.J.; David Coffey (Australia); Keith D'Souza, S.J. (India); John P. Donnelly, S.J.; Patrick J. Dorsey, S.J.; Robert L. Faricy, S.J.; James E. Fitzgerald (BUF); James P. Flaherty, S.J.; Grant S. Garringer, S.J.; Raymond T. Gawronski, S.J.; Robert J. Joda, S.J.; William J. Kelly, S.J.; Daniel J. Kenney, S.J.; William J. Kidd, S.J.; James M. Kubicki, S.J.; Michael D. Kurimay, S.J.; William S. Kurz, S.J.; Robert W. Lambeck, S.J.; John D. Laurance, S.J.; Frank A. Majka, S.J.; D. Edward Mathie, S.J.; Donald R. Matthys, S.J.; James E. Mauel, S.J.; James P. McDermott, S.J.; Richard A. McGarrity, S.J.; Michael G. Morrison, S.J.; Joseph G. Mueller, S.J. (DET); John E. Naus, S.J.; James J. Padinjareknra, S.J. (India); Sang-Hun Pak, S.J. (Korea, South); William F. Prospero, S.J.; Francis Paul Prucha, S.J.; John H. Rainaldo, S.J.; David G. Schultenover, S.J.; Richard F. Sherburne, S.J.; James J. Spillane, S.J. (Indonesia); Paul B. Steinmetz, S.J.; Walter J. Stohrer, S.J.; Roland J. Teske, S.J.; Andrew J. Thon, S.J.; Ranjit Tigga, S.J. (India); Norbert J. Tracy, S.J.; Robert A. Wild, S.J.; Frederick P. Zagone, S.J.; Michael J. Zeps, S.J. Marquette Jesuit Associates, Inc. Priests 59.

Jesuit Provincial Office, Wisconsin Province, P.O. Box 080288, 53208-0288. Tel: 414-937-6949; Fax: 414-937-6950. Email: wisprov@marquette.edu. Web: www.jesuitswisprov.org. Very Rev. James E. Grummer, S.J., Prov.; Revs. John M. Paul, S.J., Asst. Prov.; Eugene M. Dutkiewicz, S.J., Asst. for Finance; Richard A. McGarrity, S.J., Pres., Jesuit Partnership; Eugene L. Donahue, S.J., Retreat Min. Corporate Title: Wisconsin Province of the Society of Jesus. Priests 5.
Priests of the Province Serving Abroad:

Curia of the Society of Jesus, C.P. 6139, 00195 Rome-Prati, Italy. Tel: 3906-689-77-433; Fax: 3906-686-8214. Rev. Nicholas F. Pope, S.J.

Pontifical Gregorian University, Piazza della Pilotta 4, Rome, Italy. Tel: 011-39-06-6701-5498. Rev. Daniel C. McDonald, S.J.

Pontifical Biblical Institute, Via della Pilotta 25, 00187 Rome, Italy. Tel: 3906-695-26-6119; Fax: 3906-695-26-6151. Rev. Frederick E. Brenk, S.J.

Mwangaza Jesuit Spirituality Center, P.O. Box 15057, Langata Nairobi, Kenya. Rev. James J. Strzok.

Arrupe International Residence, P.O. Box 216, U.P. Post Office, 1144 Quezon City, Philippines. Tel: 632-8426-5911; Fax: 632-8426-5964. Rev. John D. Mace, S.J.

Casa Cural, Yoro 23101, Honduras. Tel: 504-671-2154. Rev. Philip E. Pick, S.J.

Centro Loyola, Barrio Palmira, Apdo 676, Tegucigalpa, Honduras. Tel: 504-32-5467. Rev. Nicholas E. Schiel, S.J.

Iglesia San Jose Obrero: Juan Larrea 1161, 4400 Salta, Argentina. Tel: 54387 423-5519. Rev. John R. Schak, S.J.

P.O. Box 7300, Kampala, Uganda. Tel: 25641-510-340; Fax: 25641-268-149. Rev. Anthony J. Wach, S.J.

Xavier House, Nsambya Hill, P.O. Box 7300, Kampala, Uganda. Tel: 25641-510-340; Fax: 25641-268-149. Rev. James A. Egan, S.J.

St. Francis Xavier, P.O. Box 266, Mwanza, Tanzania. Rev. Jonathan Haschka, S.J.

Priests of the Province Not Otherwise Listed:

Southern Illinois University, Black American Studies Dept., 2003 W. Freeman St., Carbondale, IL 62901-2109. Tel: 618-453-7147. Rev. Joseph A. Brown, S.J.

9455 Watertown Plank Rd., 53226. Rev. William R. Duffey, S.J.

Presentation Heights, 1500 N. 2nd St., Aberdeen, SD 57401-1238. Tel: 605-229-8402. Rev. Oscar L. Benzinger, S.J.

13338 Del Monte Dr., #3-K, Seal Beach, CA 90740-5411. Tel: 562-430-7801; Fax: 562-493-0922. Rev. George A. Maloney, S.J.

7626 Callaghan, Apt. 2201, San Antonio, TX 78229-2722. Tel: 210-308-8742. Rev. William J. Ellos, S.J.

Georgetown Court, #211, 5820 E. River Rd., Minneapolis, MN 55432-5338. Tel: 612-571-5955. Rev. James M. Radde, S.J.

5998 Alcala Park Unit 7181, San Diego, CA 92110-2486. Tel: 619-260-2955. Rev. James J. O'Leary, S.J.

550 N. Pantano Rd. # 151, Tucson, AZ 85710-2355. Tel: 520-321-0041. Rev. Timothy J. Howard, S.J.

Priests of the Province Engaged in Higher Studies:

Loyola House, 87 Eglinton Rd., Dublin 4, Ireland. Rev. James M. Pribek, S.J.

Pontifical Biblical Institute, Via della Pilotta 25, Rome, Italy. Tel: 011-39-06-69526-6123. Rev. Thomas S. Anderson, S.J.

La Salette Fathers Missionaries of Our Lady of La Salette , 1607 E. Howard Ave., 53207. Tel: 414-769-7113; Fax: 414-769-1057. Bro. Gerald Buraczewski, M.S. Brothers 1; Total in Residence 1.

Miguel Pro Jesuit Community, 1037 S. 10th St., 53204-1340. Tel: 414-672-9690. Revs. Eugene L. Donahue, S.J., Supr.; Richard P. Abert, S.J.; William J. Brennan, S.J.; William T. Johnson, S.J.; Jose Moreno, S.J. (Mexico); Gregory J. O'Meara, S.J.; Cletus H. Pfab, S.J.; David M. Shields, S.J.; Thomas P. Sweetser, S.J.; Bro. James D. Holub, S.J. Society of Jesus, Wisconsin Province Priests 9; Brothers 1.

Pallotti House, 5424 W. Bluemound Rd., 53208. Tel: 414-258-0653 (Provincial Offices); Fax: 414-258-9314. Email: mdprov@dias.net. Web: www.pallotti.net. Very Rev. Robert V. Carney, S.A.C., Prov. Supr.; Revs. Jerome A. Hapka, S.A.C.; Leon J. Martin, S.A.C.; William E. Lemanski, S.A.C.; Robert J. Albers, S.A.C.; Gregory P. Serwa, S.A.C., Supr., Pallotti House; Bruce J. Schute, S.A.C.; Thomas Kuttiyanickal, S.A.C.; Joseph Dominic Elukunnel, S.A.C.; Stephen Kaichiramattathil, S.A.C.; Bro. James Scarpace. Residence of Fathers and Brothers and Offices of Mother of God Province of the Society of the Catholic Apostolate also, Formation House: Novitiate Priests 9; Brothers 1.

Pere Marquette House Jesuit Community, 726 N. 34th. St., 53208-3301. Tel: 414-342-7503; Fax: 414-937-8588. Revs. Michael R. Kolb, S.J., Supr.; Terrence M. Brennan, S.J.; Thomas M. Doyle, S.J.; Robert J. Kroll, S.J.; Thomas C. Manahan, S.J.; Charles L. Stang, S.J.; Mr. Richard H. Ralphson, S.J. Society of Jesus, Wisconsin Province Priests 6; Scholastics 1.

Provincial Offices - Discalced Carmelites, 1233 S. 45th St., 53214-3693. Tel: 414-672-7212; Fax: 414-672-3138. Email: juderj@juno.com. Rev. Jude Peters, O.C.D., Prov.; Sr. Beth Lyman, S.S.S.F., Prov. Admin. Asst.

Serving abroad: Revs. Thomas Martin, O.C.D., Philippines; Alan J. Rieger, O.C.D., Philippines; Ignacio Read, O.C.D., Philippines; Arnold Boehme, O.C.D., Philippines; Reginald Foster, O.C.D., Rome; Dennis Geng, O.C.D. (Kenya); Eugene C. Wehner, O.C.D. (Kenya).

Priests of the Province not otherwise listed: Revs. Daniel McCauley, O.C.D.; William McNamara, O.C.D.; Salvatore Sciurba, O.C.D.; Stephen-Joseph Ross, O.C.D.

Salvatorian Provincial Residence, 1735 N. Hi-Mount Blvd., 53208-1720. Tel: 414-258-1735; Fax: 414-258-1934. Email: sds@salvatorians.com. Web: salvatorians.com. Society of the Divine Savior

USA Provincial Council: Revs. Peter Schuessler, S.D.S., Prov.; Joseph Rodrigues, S.D.S., Vicar Prov. & Dir. Initial Formation; John Gorman, S.D.S., Dir. Personnel & Consultor; Bro. Sean McLaughlin, S.D.S., Consultor.

9 Serpentine Ct., Silver Spring, MD 20904-5336. Tel: 301-933-3451; Fax: 301-933-3330. Revs. Keith Brennan, S.D.S., Dir. Mission & Ongoing Formation; David Bergner, S.D.S.

3809 Foxfield Ct., Richmond, VA 23233-1000. Revs. Joseph Lubrano, S.D.S., Dir. Candidates & Vocations; Scott Wallenfelsz, S.D.S., International Dir. Finance Bruce Brentrup, S.D.S.; Michael Henseler, S.D.S.; Karl LeClaire, S.D.S.

Priests at Residences Not Listed Elsewhere:

7811 W. Center St., 53222-4920. Tel: 414-476-9261. Revs. Raphael Birringer, S.D.S.; Michael Hoffman, S.D.S.

P.O. Box 574, Racine, 53401-0574. Tel: 262-633-0210. Rev. Bruce Clanton, S.D.S.

Calle la Guairita 16-16, Chuao, Caracas 1061, Venezuela. Rev. Richard Driscoll, S.D.S.

W2754 St. Charles Rd., Chilton, 53014-9625. Tel: 920-849-4175. Rev. Cyril Dickrell, S.D.S.

3477 N. Crystal Hill Ave., Tucson, AZ 85745-7103. Tel: 520-313-0134. Rev. Michael Kendall, S.D.S.

St. Anne Church: 7724 24th St., Sacramento, CA 95832-1329. Tel: 916-428-5422. Rev. John Kouba, S.D.S.

995 E. Baseline Rd. #1086, Tempe, AZ 85283-1333. Tel: 480-777-7686. Rev. Joseph Wambach, S.D.S.

Priests of the USA Province serving at the Generalate in Rome, Italy: Very Rev. Dennis D. Thiessen, S.D.S., Generalate; Rev. Joseph Henn S.D.S.

St. Joseph's Salvatorian Community (Novitiate), 3221-C S. Lake Dr., St. Francis, 53235-3702. Tel: 414-744-2402. Revs. Joseph Rodrigues, S.D.S., Dir. Novices; Raul Gomez, S.D.S., M.Div., M.P.A., Ph.D., Dir. Initial Formation.

St. Mary's Home for the Aged, 2005 Division St., Manitowoc, 54220-5699. Tel: 920-684-7171. Rev. James McKenna, S.D.S.

Salvatorian House of Studies, 255 Lee St., Oakland, CA 94610-4238. Rev. Salvatore Ragusa, S.D.S., Dir.

Salvatorians - Jordan Hall, 3800 N. 92nd St., 53222-2504. Tel: 414-463-6733. Email: hchonney@aol.com. Bro. John Hauenstein, S.D.S.; Revs. Thomas Novak, S.D.S.; Patrick Ritter, S.D.S.; Eric Middlecamp, S.D.S.; Bro. Roger Pelky, S.D.S. Fathers & Brothers of the Society of the Divine Savior Priests 3; Brothers 2.

St. Anne's Home for the Elderly, 3800 N. 92 St., 53222-2589. Tel: 414-463-7570. Bros. Arthur Studt, S.D.S.; Boniface Papke, S.D.S.; Florian Schueth, S.D.S. Brothers 3.

SCJ Community, 937 N. 37th St., 53208. Tel: 414-344-0710; Fax: 414-937-6665. Revs. Charles Brown S.C.J.; Thomas Cassidy, S.C.J.; Paul Kelly, S.C.J.; John Klingler, S.C.J.; Terence Langley, S.C.J.; Richard MacDonald, S.C.J., Prov. Supr.; Yvon Sheehy, S.C.J.; Bros. Lyle Hennen, S.C.J.; Benedict Humpfer, S.C.J. Priests of the Sacred Heart Priests 7; Brothers 2.

St. Vincent Community, 145 S. 76th St., 53214. Tel: 414-476-3211. Web: www.pallotti.net. Revs. Richard J. Gunderman, S.A.C.; Francis Hueller, S.A.C. Rector; Eugene H. Jarosch, S.A.C.; Richard J. Lorenz, S.A.C.

BENET LAKE. *St. Benedict's Abbey*, 12605 224th Ave., 53102 Tel: 262-396-4311; Fax: 262-396-4365. Email info@BenetLake.org. Web: www.BenetLake.org. Rev. Edmund J. Boyce, O.S.B., Abbot; Rt. Revs. Andrew V. Garber, O.S.B., Resigned Abbot; Robert C. Schoofs, O.S.B., Resigned Abbot; Leo M. Ryska, O.S.B., Resigned Abbot Very Rev. Henry V. Nurre, O.S.B., Prior; Revs. Kevin J. Murphy, O.S.B.; Jaime Velasco Rivera, O.S.B. Priests 7; Brothers 10.

BURLINGTON. *St. Francis Friary*, 503 S. Browns Lake Dr., 53105. Tel: 262-763-3600; Fax: 262-763-4229. In Res. Revs. Duane Brown, O.F.M.; Linus Kopczewski, O.F.M.; Michael Kalan, O.F.M.; Colman Majchrzak, O.F.M.; Jerome Zawada, O.F.M.

Queen of Peace Friary, 523 S. Brown's Lake Dr., P.O. Box 40, 53104-0040. Tel: 262-763-3241; Fax: 262-763-3326. Revs. Albin Miklaszewski, O.F.M.; Herbert Silko, O.F.M.; Paschal Grigus, O.F.M.; George Dubowski; Raymond Zsoczai; Anthony Chojnacki; Campion Kluczynski; Bros. Brendan Kowalski, O.F.M.; Joseph Krymkowski, O.F.M.; Joseph Molinari, O.F.M., Guardian; Edward Makowiecki, O.F.M.; Gregory Havel, O.F.M. Franciscan Friars of the Assumption B.V.M. Province, Retirement Home for Franciscan Friars Priests 7; Brothers 5.

EAST TROY. *Divine Word Missionaries*, Box 107, 53120. Tel: 262-642-3300; Fax: 262-642-7754. Email: etsvc@centurytel.net. Revs. John F. Fincutter, S.V.D.; Bernard Fisher, S.V.D.; Lucien Gaudreault, S.V.D.; Vincent Ohlinger, S.V.D.; Raymond Weisenberger, S.V.D.; Jerome Ziliak, S.V.D.; Patrick Fincutter, S.V.D.; William Halvey, S.V.D.; Robert Mertes, S.V.D.; Lawrence Wagner, S.V.D.; Bros. Bernard Scherger, S.V.D.; Raymond Albers, S.V.D.; William Morgan, S.V.D. Society of the Divine Word Priests 10; Brothers 3; Total in Residence 13.

FRANKLIN. *Dehon Study Center*, 10731 W. Rawson Ave., 53132. Tel: 414-425-3768; Fax: 414-425-8768. Email: mcguirescj@aol.com. Web: www.scj.org. Rev. Paul J. McGuire, S.C.J. Priests of the Sacred Heart

Francis and Clare Friary, 9230 W. Highland Park Ave., 53132. Tel: 414-525-9402; Fax: 414-525-9289. Email: province@ofm-abvm.org.org. Web: www.ofm-abvm.org.

Provincial Offices Tel: 414-525-9253; Fax: 414-525-9289. Revs. Paul Reczek, O.F.M.; Stephen E. Malkiewicz, O.F.M., M.A.; Roch Niemier, O.F.M.; Thomas Luczak, O.F.M., Prov. Min.; John Cella, O.F.M., Treas.; Michael Weldon, O.F.M.; Eliot Bacia, O.F.M., Sec.; Deacon Jerry Tokarz, O.F.M., Dir. of Communications. Priests 7; Brothers 1.

St. Francis Residence, 12001 W. Woods Rd., 53132. Tel: 414-529-0332; Fax: 414-529-8777. Revs. Jan de Jong, S.C.J., S.T.D., S.T.L.; Anthony P. Russo, S.C.J.; Bro. Frank Presto, S.C.J.

St. Martin of Tours, 7963 S. 116th St., 53132. Tel: 414-425-1114; Fax: 414-425-2527. Rev. John Nitzki, S.C.J.

Dehon Study Center, 10731 W. Rawson Ave., 53132. Tel: 414-425-3768; Fax: 414-425-8768. Email: mcguirescj@aol.com. Rev. Paul J. McGuire, S.C.J. Priests 4.

Villa Maria, 7330 S. Lovers Lane Rd., 53132. Tel: 414-425-5968; 425-598-; Fax: 414-425-0268. Web: www.scj.org. Revs. Jim Alexander, S.C.J.; George Balderrama, S.C.J.; Donald Barnd, S.C.J.; Paul Casper, S.C.J.; Edward Griesemer, S.C.J.; Joseph Haselbauer, S.C.J.; Kevin McInnis, S.C.J.; Howard Melzer, S.C.J.; Lawrence Rucker, S.C.J.; Leonard Tadyszak, S.C.J.; Michael Van Der Peet, S.C.J.; Stephen Wiese, S.C.J.; Bro. Steve Cyr, S.C.J.; Deacon Lawrence Gauthier, S.C.J.; Bro. Matthew Miles, S.C.J., Supr. Priests 12; Brothers 3.

GREENDALE. *Salvatorian Community*, 7100 W. Old Loomis Rd., 53129-2761. Tel: 414-427-8352. Revs. Hugh G. Birdsall, S.D.S., M.A., M.S.; Gerald Sirois, S.D.S.; Bro. Wayne Madala, S.D.S.; Mr. Michael Burns, S.D.S., Scholastic. Society of the Divine Savior Priests 2; Brothers 1; Scholastics 1.

HALES CORNERS. *Priests of the Sacred Heart*, 6871 S. Lovers Lane Rd., P.O. Box 289, 53130-0289. Tel: 414-425-6910; Fax: 414-425-2938. Email: provsec@poshusa.org. Web: www.scj.org. Revs. Richard MacDonald, S.C.J., Prov. Supr.; Bernard J. Rosinski, S.C.J., Prov. Sec.; Brian McCullough, S.C.J., Prov. Treas. & Mission Procurator; Edward Kilianski, S.C.J., Dir. Justice & Peace; Yvon Sheehy, S.C.J., Dir. Formation & Vocations; John Klingler, S.C.J., Dir. Ministries & Ministers; Anthony P. Russo, S.C.J., Dir. Dehonian Affiliates; Joseph Dean, S.C.J., Dir. Admissions; Stephen Wiese, S.C.J., Dir. Senior Life.

Priests of the Province Serving Abroad:

10 Park Ln., Port Elizabeth 6001 South Africa. Tel: 27-41-373-4734; Fax: 27-41-373-6141. Most Rev. Evert Baaij, S.C.J.

Priests of the Sacred Heart, 12001 W. Woods Rd., 53132. Tel: 414-529-0332; Fax: 414-529-8777. Revs. Jan de Jong, S.C.J., S.T.D., S.T.L.; Anthony P. Russo, S.C.J.; Bro. Frank Presto, S.C.J.

Attached to the Province but Living Elsewhere:

c/o Provincialate Offices, P.O. Box 289, 53130-0289. Tel: 414-425-6910; Fax: 414-425-2938.

5463 Dempsey, St. Louis, MO 63110. Tel: 314-771-5867. Rev. Jerome Clifford, S.C.J.

P.O. Box 220, Dittmer, MO 63023. Tel: 636-285-1733. Rev. Bryan Benoit, S.C.J.

P.O. Box 960, Occidental, CA 95465. Tel: 707-874-1483; Fax: 707-874-1433. Rev. Edward Kilianski, S.C.J.

St. Paul's, P.O. Box 1475, Valparaiso, IN 46364. Tel: 219-464-4831; Fax: 219-464-4833. Rev. Robert Naglich, S.C.J.

5375 Kenrick Parke Dr. N. #305, St. Louis, MO 63119. Tel: 314-968-3765; Fax: 314-647-3688. Rev. James Schroeder, S.C.J.

2833 Moland St., #3, Madison, 53704. Bro. Bernard Taube, S.C.J.

Sacred Heart Monastery, 7335 S. Lovers Lane, P.O. Box 566, 53130. Tel: 414-425-8300; Fax: 414-529-6988. Email: preid@shst.edu. Web: www.scj.org.

Priests of the Sacred Heart, 7335 S. Lovers Ln., P.O. Box 566, 53130-0566. Tel: 414-425-5323; Fax: 414-529-6988. Rev. Charles Bisgrove, S.C.J.; Very Rev. James D. Brackin, S.C.J., M.Div., J.D.; Revs. Paul Grizzelle-Reid, S.C.J., M.S., M.Div., Supr.; Joseph Gole, S.T.D. (Slovenia); Justin Guiltnane, S.C.J.; Wayne Jenkins, S.C.J.; Brian McCullough, S.C.J.; John T. O'Connor, S.C.J., J.C.L., S.T.D.;

Bernard J. Rosinski, S.C.J.; Bro. James Willis, S.C.J. Priests 9; Brothers 1.

HOLY HILL. *Discalced Carmelite Monastery - Holy Hill National Shrine of Mary Help of Christians*, 1525 Carmel Rd., Hubertus, 53033. Tel: 262-628-1838; 262-673-3540; Fax: 262-628-0170. Email: pfohlinocd@yahoo.com. Web: www.holyhill.com. Revs. Jude Peters, O.C.D., Prov. Supr.; Paul Fohlin, O.C.D., Prior; Matthias Montgomery, O.C.D., Dir. Novices; David Centner, O.C.D.; Larry Daniels, O.C.D.; Patrick J. Farrell, O.C.D.; Joseph-Mary Flanery, O.C.D.; Michael Griffin, O.C.D.; Cyril Guise, O.C.D., Shrine Dir. & Subprior; Ernest Unverdorben, O.C.D.; Redemptus Short, O.C.D.; Mark Develis, O.C.D.; Donald Brick, O.C.D.; Dominic Scheerer, O.C.D.; Bros. Martin Murphy, O.C.D.; Frank Salamone, O.C.D. Priests 15; Brothers 2.

Retreat Center, 1525 Carmel Rd., Hubertus, 53033. Tel: 262-628-1838; Fax: 262-628-4294.

KENOSHA. *Order of Preachers, Province of St. Albert the Great* Friends of God, A Dominican Ashram , 720 35th St., 53140. Tel: 262-658-1062. Email: ashram@dominicans.org. Revs. Donald J. Goergen, O.P.; Stanley A. Drongowski, O.P.

MOUNT CALVARY. *St. Lawrence Friary*, 301 Church St., 53057. Tel: 920-753-7500; Fax: 920-753-7507. Email: frkeith@stlawrence.edu. Web: stlawrence.edu. Revs. Keith Clark, O.F.M.Cap., Supr.; Gary Wegner, O.F.M.Cap.; Joachim Strupp, O.F.M.Cap.; Dennis Druggan, O.F.M.Cap.; Ronald Jansch, O.F.M.Cap.; Elroy Pesch, O.F.M.Cap.; Kenan Siegel, O.F.M.Cap.; Anthony Will, O.F.M.Cap.; Vernon Wagner, O.F.M.Cap.; Eugene Wolf, O.F.M.Cap.; Paul Yaroch, O.F.M.Cap.; Thomas Zelinski, O.F.M.Cap.; Bros. Douglas Bode, O.F.M.Cap.; Jerome Campbell, O.F.M.Cap.; Jerome Johnson, O.F.M.Cap.; Neal Plale, O.F.M.Cap.; Mark Rehlinger, O.F.M.Cap.; Carl Schaefer, O.F.M.Cap.; John Scherer, O.F.M.Cap., Vicar; Dismas Seward, O.F.M.Cap.; John Willger, O.F.M.Cap. Priests 12; Brothers 9.

OCONOMOWOC. *Austin Hall, Tolentine Center*, 20300 Governors Hwy., Olympia Fields, IL 60461-1081. Augustinians/Province of Our Mother of Good Counsel, Olympia Fields, IL
954 Dousman Rd., 53066. Tel: 262-965-4640.

RACINE. *Augustinian Novitiate*, 4335 Douglas Ave., 53402-2956. Tel: 262-681-3221; Fax: 262-681-0628. Email: racineosa@juno.com. Revs. Eugene A. Del Conte, O.S.A., Prior; Raymond R. Ryan, O.S.A., Novice Dir.; Alvin P. Metzger, O.S.A., Treas. Priests 3; Novices 1.

ST. FRANCIS. *St. Camillus Formation Community*, 3661 S. Kinnickinnic Ave., 53235. Tel: 414-481-3696; Fax: 414-481-8044. Web: www.camillians.org. Rev. Louis Lussier, O.S.Cam.; Very Rev. Richard O'Donnell, O.S.Cam., Prov.; Deacons Scott Binet, O.S.Cam.; Albert Schempp, O.S.Cam.; Bros. Mario Crivello, O.S.Cam.; Allan Gidley, O.S.Cam. Priests 2; Deacons 2; Brothers 2.

St. Camillus Provincialate, 3661 S. Kinnickinnic Ave., 53235. Tel: 414-481-3696; Fax: 414-481-8044. Very Rev. Richard O'Donnell, O.S.Cam., Prov.; Revs. Bernard Blasich; Stephen Braddock; William Burt; Joseph L. Bisoffi, O.S.Cam., Prov. Counselor; Louis Lussier, O.S.Cam., Prov. Counselor; James Kovarik; Bros. Mario Crivello, O.S.Cam., Prov. Counselor; Nelson DeLoria, O.S.Cam., Prov. Counselor. Provincial offices for the North American Province of the Order of the Servants of the Sick (Order of Saint Camillus) Priests 7; Brothers 2.

TWIN LAKES. *La Salette Missionaries Shrine*, Box 777, 53181. Tel: 262-877-3111. Email: lasalette@techeadnet.com. Web: www.members.techeadnet.com/lasalette. Revs. Thaddeus Galuszka, M.S.; Gerald Lebanowski, M.S.; Henry Wojtunik, M.S.; Bros. Adam Mateja, M.S.; Anthony Sepanik, M.S. Priests 3; Brothers 2.

WAUWATOSA. *St. Camillus Community House*, 10213 W. Wisconsin Ave., 53226. Tel: 414-774-5634. Email: jimcamk@execpc.com. Revs. William Cronin; Richard Korzinek, O.S.Cam.; Joseph L. Bisoffi, O.S.Cam.; Carlo Notaro, O.S.Cam.; Bros. Nelson DeLoria, O.S.Cam., Supr.; Herman Moellenhoff, O.S.Cam.; Roland Wild, O.S.Cam. Priests 4; Brothers 3.

Jesuit Community at St. Camillus, 10100 W. Bluemound Rd., 53226-4386. Tel: 414-259-3784 (Court East); 414-258-1814 (Skilled Care); Fax: 414-259-4950. Revs. Eugene M. Dutkiewicz, S.J., Supr.; Anthony L. Dagelen, S.J., Asst. Supr.; Orville J. Catuso, S.J.; William E. Dooley, S.J.; Joseph C. Gill, S.J.; George J. Guenther, S.J.; Walter H. Halloran, S.J.; Robert P. Hart, S.J.; J. Cletus Healy, S.J.; Lawrence C. Helmueller, S.J.; Robert E. Hoene, S.J.; John G. Holbrook, S.J.; Lawrence D. Kelly, S.J.; Charles L. Kerr, S.J.; James P. Kramper, S.J.; Earl J. Kurth, S.J.; Norbert J. Lemke, S.J.; William J. Mehok, S.J.; Robert P. Neenan, S.J.; Robert G. North, S.J.; Robert C. Ostertag, S.J.; Richard L. Porter, S.J.; Bernard J. Portz, S.J.; Robert F. Purcell, S.J.; Leon S. Rausch, S.J., Min.; Jerome E. Rohrer, S.J.; John M. Scott, S.J.; James P. Scull, S.J.; Paul G. Stockhausen, S.J.; William A. Van Roo, S.J.; Kenneth T. Walleman, S.J.; Theodore F. Zuern, S.J.; Bros. Paul J. Kempker, S.J.; Gerald E. McKeever, S.J.; James R. Zuercher, S.J. Society of Jesus, Wisconsin Province Priests 31; Brothers 3.

[P] CONVENTS AND RESIDENCES FOR SISTERS

MILWAUKEE. *Ancilla Convent* Inter-Community living for religious women.
3601 S. 41st St., 53221. Tel: 414-384-6535. Sr. Barbarina Jantsch, Dir. Sisters 20.

St. Clare Convent, 3276 S. 16th St., 53215. Tel: 414-647-2437. Sr. M. Samuel Holowacz, Local Min. Felician Sisters Sisters 3.

St. Dominic Center, 1727 S. 9th St., 53204. Tel: 414-384-4873; Fax: 414-384-0246. Web: www.nutudaminh.org. Sr. Maria Theresa Kim Hong Nguyen, O.P., Supr. Vietnamese Dominican Sisters Sisters 3; Postulants 9.

St. Felix Convent, 3159 S. 17th St., 53215. Tel: 414-389-9803. Sr. M. Jeanette Skornia, C.S.S.F., Local Min. Felician Sisters Sisters 3.

St. Francis Convent, 3170 S. 17th St., 53215. Tel: 414-643-6387; Fax: 414-647-5372. Email: beatricecssf@hormail.com. Sr. M. Beatrice Knipple, Local Min. Felician Sisters Sisters 4.

St. Joseph Convent, General Motherhouse of the School Sisters of St. Francis, 1501 S. Layton Blvd., 53215. Tel: 414-384-4105; Fax: 414-944-6060. Email: generalate@sssf.org. Web: www.sssf.org. Sisters Joan Puls, O.S.F., Pres.; Alida Lopez, 1st Vice Pres.; Toni Anne Gradisnik, Vice Pres.; Barbara Kraemer, O.S.F., Prov.
Legal Title: *School Sisters of St. Francis, Inc.* Sisters 53; Total in Congregation 1,266.

Mercedes Molina - Instituto Santa Mariana de Jesus, 1234 N. 24th Pl., 53205. Tel: 414-931-7163; Fax: 414-931-7887. Email: GPGarzon@aol.com. Sr. Gloria Piedad Garzon, Supr. Corporate Title: Mercedes Molina, Inc. Sisters 4.

Monastery of the Perpetual Rosary, 217 N. 68th St., 53213. Tel: 414-258-0579; Fax: 414-258-0226. Email: frannl@aol.com. Web: www.dsopr.org. Sr. Miriam Leonard, O.P., Prioress. Cloistered Dominican Sisters of the Perpetual Rosary Professed Sisters 12.

Sacred Heart Center, 1545 S. Layton Blvd., 53215. Tel: 414-383-9038; Fax: 414-647-4889. S. Joann Riesterer, O.S.F., Coord. of Health & Housing Svcs.; Sisters Therese Thoenen, O.S.F., Coord. Sisters Living Group; Mary Louise Reinke, O.S.F., Facility Dir. Home for retired and infirm School Sisters of St. Francis Sisters 47.

San Damiano Convent, 2008 E. Euclid Ave., 53207. Tel: 414-489-9195; Fax: 414-483-5861. Email: smclarette@fs-inc.net. Sr. Mary Ramona Dombrowski, C.S.S.F., Local Min. Felician Sisters 3.

Sisters of Charity of St. Joan Antida Tel: 414-276-5153. Email: stritas@scsja.org.

St. Rita Convent, 1621 N. Cass St., 53202. Tel: 414-276-5153. Sr. Monica Fumo, S.C.S.J.A., Supr. Sisters 5.

Sisters of Charity of St. Joan Antida Convent (Presentation), 1329 N. Cass St., 53202. Tel: 414-276-4173. Email: present@scsja.org. Sr. Anne Marie Baemmert, S.C.S.J.A., Supr. Sisters 7.

Sisters of Charity of St. Joan Antida Convent (St. Charles Community), 3214 W. Parnell Ave., 53221. Tel: 414-282-9627. Email: stchas@scsja.org. Sr. Marie Grohall, S.C.S.J.A., Supr. Sisters 7.

Sisters of Charity of St. Joan Antida Regina Mundi Provincial House and Novitiate, 8560 N. 76th Pl., 53223. Tel: 414-354-9233; Fax: 414-355-6463. Email: sisters@scsja.org. Web: www.scsja.org. Sr. Jennifer L. Daul, S.C.S.J.A., Prov. Sisters 3; Total in Community 42.

Sisters of the Divine Savior, 4311 N. 100th St., 53222-1393. Tel: 414-466-0810; Fax: 414-466-4335. Email: schoedlJ@dsha.k12.wi.us. Web: www.sdssisters.org. Provincial Administration Provincial Team: Sisters Marion Etzel, S.D.S., Prov. Leader; Carol Thresher, S.D.S., Vicaress; Jeanette Clarke, S.D.S., Treas.

Salvatorian Sisters Residence, 3810 N. 92nd St., 53222. Tel: 414-760-7900; Fax: 414-358-9906. Sr. Deanna Schroeder, S.D.S., Coord. Sisters 32.

United States Province, 1515 S. Layton Blvd., 53215. Tel: 414-384-1515; Fax: 414-384-1950. Email: info@sssf.org. Web: www.sssf.org. Sisters Barbara Kraemer, O.S.F., Prov. Team; Elizabeth Heese, O.S.F., Prov. Team; Maureen McCarthy, O.S.F., Prov. Team. School Sisters of St. Francis., Corporate Title: The School Sisters of St. Francis of St. Joseph's Convent, Milwaukee, Wisconsin, Inc.; Corporate Title: Congregational Support Charitable Trust. Total in U.S. Province 800.

BROWN DEER. *Sisters of the Sorrowful Mother-Generalate, Inc.*, 9056 N. Deerbrook Tr., 53223-2474. Tel: 414-357-8940; Fax: 414-357-8950. Email: ssmintl@aol.com. Web: ssmfranciscans.org. Sr. M. Helen Malolepsy, Gen. Supr.

CAMPBELLSPORT. *St. Joseph Convent*, 526 Mill St., 53010. Tel: 920-533-8351; Fax: 920-533-5394. Sisters Joanne Armatowski, S.S.N.D., Facility Dir.; Dorothy McKeague, O.S.F., Living Group Coord.; Rita Clare Johnson, O.S.F., Dir. Pastoral Svcs. School Sisters of St. Francis, Retirement Home/Health Care Center Sisters 183.

CEDAR GROVE. *Sacred Heart of the Lake Chalet*, Box 46A, 53013. Tel: 262-285-3084. *St. Mary's Home*, 2005 Division St., Manitowoc, 54220. Sr. Mary Carlotta Myszka, Contact Person. Recreation Home for Felician Sisters of the Mother of Good Counsel Province.

DELAVAN. *Villa Celine*, 3127 S. Shore Dr., 53115. Tel: 773-792-6363; Fax: 773-792-9590. 7432 W. Talcott Ave., Chicago, IL 60631. Sr. M. Barbara Sniegowski, C.R., Prov. Supr. & Contact Person. Summer Rest Home for Sisters of the Resurrection

ELM GROVE. *Notre Dame of Elm Grove*, 13105 Watertown Plank Rd., 53122-2291. Tel: 262-782-1450; Fax: 262-782-2349. Email: ezettel@ssnd-milw.org. Web: www.ssnd-milw.org. Sr. Elise Zettel, S.S.N.D., Admin. Leader. The School Sisters of Notre Dame, Milwaukee Province, Inc., S.S.N.D. Assisted Care, Independent Living. Total in Residence 124; Total Staff 82.

School Sisters of Notre Dame, Provincial Offices, 13105 Watertown Plank Rd., 53122-2291. Tel: 262-782-9850; Fax: 262-782-5725. Email: mkesler@ssnd-milw.org. Web: www.ssnd-milw.org. Sr. Marilyn Kesler, S.S.N.D., Prov. Leader.
Legal Title: *School Sisters of Notre Dame, Milwaukee Province, Inc.*
Legal Title: *School Sisters of Notre Dame at Milwaukee, Wisconsin, Inc. Charitable Trust* Total in Milwaukee Province 484; Total Staff 38.

FOND DU LAC. *Convent of the Sisters of St. Agnes* Motherhouse. , 320 County Rd. K, 54935-8958. Tel: 920-907-2300; Fax: 920-923-3194. Email: csaadm@csasisters.org. Web: www.csasisters.org. Sr. Mary Christine Fellerhoff, C.S.A., Gen. Supr.
Legal Title: *Congregation of Sisters of St. Agnes of Fond du Lac, Wisconsin, Inc.* Sisters 23; Total in Community 347.

KENOSHA. *Kenosha Dominicans*, P.O. Box 1288, 53141-1288. Tel: 262-694-2067; Fax: 262-694-6542. Email: kenoshaop@aol.com. Sr. Susan Anne Snyder, O.P., Prioress. Congregation of the Dominican Sisters of St. Catherine of Siena of Kenosha Total Religious in Community 18.

MANITOWOC. *Sisters of Saint Elizabeth, Inc.*, 2005 Division St., 54220-5699. Tel: 920-684-7171, Ext. 268 (St. Mary's Home). Sr. Mary Rita Amrhein, S.S.E., Mother Gen. Sisters of St. Elizabeth Sisters 5.

MEQUON. *Sisters of the Sorrowful Mother, Novitiate House*, 4823 W. Bonniwell Rd., 53097-2202. Tel: 262-242-5770; Fax: 262-236-0174. Email: ssmfarm@aol.com. Web: ssmfranciscans.org. Sisters 3.

MOUNT CALVARY. *Loretto Convent*, N8114 Calvary St., 53057. Tel: 920-753-3211; Fax: 920-753-3100. Email: sisters@netscape.net. Sr. Mary Rose, Supr. General Motherhouse of Sister-Servants of Christ the King; Corporate Title: Congregation of Sister Servants of Christ the King, Inc. Sisters 6.

Our Lady of Mt. Carmel Convent 53057. Tel: 920-753-2131; 920-753-2036; Fax: 920-753-2116. Email: msrnka@ssnd-mil.org. Sr. Mary Ann Srnka, S.S.N.D., Leadership. Home for Retired Sisters. School Sisters of Notre Dame 36.

OCONOMOWOC. *St. Joseph Convent*, 2653 Mill Rd., 53066. Tel: 414-646-2707. Web: www.childdevctr-stjoes.org. Sr. M. Margaret Narloch, C.S.S.F., Local Min. Sponsored by the Congregation of the Sisters of St. Felix of Cantalice of the United States of America, Inc. Chicago Province. Sisters 3.

PEWAUKEE. *Carmel of the Mother of God*, W267 N2517 Meadowbrook Rd., 53072. Tel: 262-691-0336; Fax: 262-691-0336. Email: pewaukeecarmel@aol.com. Web: www.geocities.com/pewaukeecarmel. Sr. Mary Agnes Kramer, O.C.D., Prioress; Rev. Dennis C. Klemme, Chap. (Retired). Discalced Carmelite Nuns Professed Sisters 8; Postulants 2.

RACINE. *Convent of St. Catherine of Siena* Tel: 262-639-4100; Fax: 262-639-9702. Email: sienactr3@miliserv.net. Web: www.racinedominicans.org. Motherhouse of the Sisters of St. Dominic

(Congregation of St. Catherine of Siena), Corporate Title: Sisters of St. Dominic.
Siena Center, 5635 Erie St., 53402. Tel: 262-639-4100; Fax: 262-639-9702. Web: www.racinedominicans.org. Sr. Carol Wester, O.P., Pres. Sisters 90; Total Religious in Community 214.

ST. FRANCIS. *St. Francis Convent, Motherhouse of the Sisters of St. Francis of Assisi*, 3221 S. Lake Dr., 53235-3799. Tel: 414-744-1160; Fax: 414-744-7193. Email: lakeosfs@lakeosfs.org. Web: www.lakeosfs.org. Sisters Marcia Lunz, O.S.F., Dir. of the Congregation; Kathleen Hurley, O.S.F., Assoc. Dir.; Linda Tan, O.S.F., Assoc. Dir.
Legal Title: *The Sisters of St. Francis of Assisi, Inc.*
Legal Title: *The Ongoing Community Support Trust of the Sisters of St. Francis of Assisi*, Corporate Title: The Sisters of St. Francis of Assisi, Milwaukee, Wis. Total in Community 340.

SHEBOYGAN. *Hospital Sisters of the Third Order of St. Francis*, 1907 N. 29th St., 53081. Tel: 920-459-8785; Fax: 920-208-0237. Web: www.springfieldfranciscans.org.
1907 N. 29th St., 53081. Tel: 920-459-8785. Hospital Sisters of the Third Order of St. Francis 2.

WAUWATOSA. *Provincial Motherhouse of the Carmelite Sisters of the Divine Heart of Jesus*, 1230 Kavanaugh Pl., 53213. Tel: 414-453-4040; Fax: 414-453-5603. Email: carmelwau@aol.com. Web: carmelitedejnorth.org. Sr. Maria Giuseppe, Prov. Supr. Corporate Title: Carmelite Sisters of the Divine Heart of Jesus, Milwaukee, Wisconsin. Sisters 8; Total Religious in Province 25; Total Assisted 185; Total Staff 93.

WEST ALLIS. *Missionary Sisters of the Holy Family* (Poland). , 1665 S. 64th St., 53214. Tel: 414-327-4068; Fax: 414-543-4740. Email: hofasi@wi.net. Sr. Danuta Kujalowicz, M.S.F., Supr. Sisters 9.
Sisters of Charity of St. Joan Antida Convent (Regina Coeli), 2716 Root River Pkwy., 53227. Tel: 414-545-2917. Email: rcoeli@scsja.org. Sr. Kathleen M. Lundwall, S.C.S.J.A., Supr. Sisters 3.

[Q] HERMITAGES

SLINGER. *Carmelite Hermit of the Trinity - CHT*, Mount Carmel Hermitage, 4270 Cedar Creek Rd., 53086-9795. Email: sisterjm@carmelitehermit.org. Web: carmelitehermit.homestead.com. Rev. James M. Tambornino, S.O.L.T.; Sr. Joseph Marie, Carmelite Hermit of the Trinity.

[R] RETREAT HOUSES

MILWAUKEE. *Archdiocesan Retreat Center at Archbishop Cousins Catholic Center*, 3501 S. Lake Dr., P.O. Box 070912, 53207-0912. Tel: 414-769-3491; Fax: 414-769-3408. Email: kreitzerw@archmil.org. Web: www.archmil.org. William Kreitzer, Dir. Bldg. Svcs. Total Staff 2.
The Dwelling Place, 1704 E. Norwich St., 53207. Tel: 414-489-9444. Email: jskap@hotmail.com. Revs. Francis J. Dombrowski, O.F.M.Cap.; Jerome Schroeder, O.F.M.Cap.; Mary Klotz, Team Member. Priests 2; Total in Residence 3; Total Staff 3.

ELKHORN. *St. Vincent Pallotti Center* Pallotine Fathers , N. 6409 Bowers Rd., 53121. Tel: 262-723-2108; Fax: 262-723-8608. Email: vpallelk@elknet.net. Web: www.elknet.net/vpallelk. Retreat and Christian formation Center Lay Staff 2.

OCONOMOWOC. *The Redemptorist Retreat Center*, 1800 N. Timber Trail Ln., 53066-4897. Tel: 262-567-6900; Fax: 262-567-0134. Email: rrc@edemptoristrstrest.org. Web: www.redemptoristretreat.org. Revs. Charles Beierwaltes, C.Ss.R.; Edward F. Monroe, C.SS.R.; James White, C.Ss.R.; Stephen Benden, C.Ss.R.; Deacon Daniel Korn, C.Ss.R.; Bro. Gerard Patin, C.Ss.R. Priests 4; Total in Residence 6; Brothers 2.

RACINE. *Racine Dominican Ministries, Inc. - Racine Dominican Retreat Program*, 5635 Erie St., 53402-1900. Tel: 262-639-4100; Fax: 262-639-9702. Email: rdrp@miliserv.net. Web: www.racinedominicans.org. Sr. Rita Lui, O.P., Dir.

WAUKESHA. *Schoenstatt Retreat Center*, W284 N698 Cherry Ln., 53188-9402. Tel: 262-547-7733; Fax: 262-547-7749. Email: intlcenter@schsrsmary.org. Web: www.schsrsmary.org. Sr. M. Jacinta Brunner, Supr. Sisters 9; Total Staff 2.

[S] SECULAR INSTITUTES

MILWAUKEE. *Secular Institute of the Schoenstatt Sisters of Mary*, 5310 W. Wisconsin Ave., 53208-3061. Tel: 414-774-0520; Fax: 414-774-2911. Sr. Ellen-Marie Baranek, Supr. Sisters 8.

WAUKESHA. *Secular Institute of Schoenstatt Fathers*, Tel: 262-548-9061; Fax: 262-548-9593. Email: frgerold@hotmail.com.
Schoenstatt Fathers, W284 N746 Cherry Ln., 53188. Tel: 262-548-9061; Fax: 262-548-9593. Revs. Gerold M. Langsch, Supr.; Dietrich A. Haas; Jonathan J. Niehaus; Mark J. Niehaus. Priests 6; Total in Residence 4.
Attached to the house but living elsewhere: Revs. Hector R. Vega, C.C.; Christian Christensen, C.C.
Secular Institute of the Schoenstatt Sisters of Mary, W284 N404 Cherry Ln., 53188-9416. Tel: 262-542-4384; 262-542-1544; Fax: 262-542-5730. Email: schoenstattsisters@schsrsmary.org. Web: www.schsrsmary.org. Sisters M. Virginia Riedl, Prov. Supr.; M. Elizabeth Dingbaum, Supr. Sisters 30.

[T] ASSOCIATIONS OF THE FAITHFUL

BELOIT. *Franciscan Sisters of Our Lady*, 2110 Bootmaker Dr., 53511. Tel: 608-365-7257. Sr. Mary Timothy Geenen, F.S.O.L., Supr. Sisters 4.

FRANKLIN. *Franciscan Sisters of Saint Clare, Inc.*, 7732 S. 51st St., 53132. Tel: 414-421-8257; Fax: 414-421-7869. Email: smcfssc@execpc.com. Web: fssclare.org. Sr. Mary Celine Stein, F.S.S.C., Supr. Gen. Non-Cloistered Contemplative Community. Professed Sisters 2; Associate Sisters 2; Lay Affiliates 61; Candidates 1.

[U] MISSIONARY ACTIVITIES

MILWAUKEE. *St. Boniface Mission League, Inc.*, 3501 S. Lake Dr., P.O. Box 070912, 53207-0912. Tel: 414-769-3406; Fax: 414-769-3408. Email: wmo@archmil.org. Web: archmil.org/dept/wmo. Frances Cunningham, O.S.F., Pres. Partners in World Mission formerly known as St. Boniface Mission League, Inc.; Furnishes aid to home and foreign missions since 1913, with a special focus on the archdiocesan sister parish in the Dominican Republic.
Milwaukee Archdiocesan Office for World Mission (Formerly Latin American Office) , 3501 S. Lake Dr., P.O. Box 070912, 53207-0912. Tel: 414-769-3406; Fax: 414-769-3408. Email: wmo@archmil.org. Web: archmil.org/dept/wmo. Frances Cunningham, O.S.F., Dir.; Sr. Rosemary Huddleston, O.P., International Mission Coord. Sends priests and supports laity in overseas mission. Educates and raises funds for worldwide mission. Promotes parish twinning between archdiocese and other countries.
Missionary Association of Catholic Women, 3501 S. Lake Dr., P.O. Box 070912, 53207-0912. Tel: 414-769-3406; Fax: 414-769-3408. Email: wmo@archmil.org. Web: archmil.org/dept/wmo. Frances Cunningham, O.S.F., Dir. Office for World Mission. Provides aid to home and foreign missions
Our Blessed Lady of Victory Mission, Inc., 5430 W. Vliet St., 53208-2175. Tel: 414-774-3128. Revs. Lawrence J. Leack, Chap. (Retired); Leslie A. Stelter (Fgm); Agnes J. Ryan, Pres.
Society for the Propagation of the Faith, Holy Childhood Association (Pontifical Mission Aid Societies) Tel: 414-769-3406; Fax: 414-769-3408. Email: wmo@archmil.org. Web: archmil.org/dept/wmo. Raises funds and educates for worldwide mission, under papal auspices
3501 S. Lake Dr., P.O. Box 070912, 53207-0912. Tel: 414-769-3406; Fax: 414-769-3408. Frances Cunningham, O.S.F., Dir.; Sr. Rosemary Huddleston, O.P., International Mission Coord.

ELM GROVE. *Family Unity International, Inc.*, 12750 Stephen Pl., 53122-1964. Tel: 414-784-7448; Fax: 414-769-3408. Email: wmo@archmil.org. Web: archmil.org/dept/wmo. Patricia J. Parks, Pres. Raises and distributes funds to the missions of the Working Boys' Center. Organization is under the supervision of the Director of the Milwaukee Archdiocesan Office for World Mission

GREENDALE. *Volunteer Missionary Movement (VMM)*, 5980 W. Loomis Rd., 53129. Tel 414-423-8660; Fax: 414-423-8964. Email: vmm@vmmusa.org. Web: www.vmmusa.org. Sandra A. McCabe, Exec. Dir. Recruits, trains, and sends Christian men and women to areas of need in the world

[V] SOCIETIES

MILWAUKEE. **Christ Child Society, Inc. - Milwaukee Chapter*, 4040 N. 66th St., 53216. Tel: 414-535-0018; 414-352-4642. Email: child@milwpc.com. Nancy Lucey, Pres.
Milwaukee Archdiocesan Council of Catholic Women, 3501 South Lake Dr., P.O. Box 070912, 53207-0912. Tel: 414-769-3501; Fax: 414-769-3408. Email: walkert@archmil.org. Rev. Ronald O. Crewe, Moderator.
Priests' Purgatorial Society, 3501 S. Lake Dr., P.O. Box 070912, 53207-0912. Tel: 414-769-3340; Fax: 414-769-3908. Email: cusackb@archmil.org. Web: archmil.org. Barbara Anne Cusack, Sec.
St. Vincent de Paul Society, 9601 W. Silver Spring Dr. 53225. Tel: 414-462-7837; Fax: 414-462-5458. Email: svdpco@ameritech.net. Web: www.svdpmilw.org. Mr. Gerald H. Felsecker, Exec. Dir., Milwaukee Archdiocesan Council.
Council of Racine, 926 LaSalle St., Racine, 53404. Tel: 262-633-6468; Fax: 262-633-6408.
Council of Kenosha, 6201 14th Ave., Kenosha, 53143. Tel: 262-657-6366; Fax: 262-657-5790.
Council of Fond du Lac, 401 N. Hickory, Fond du Lac, 54935. Tel: 920-922-3650; Fax: 920-322-9120.
Council of Sheboygan, 4215 Hwy. 42 N., Sheboygan, 53083. Tel: 920-457-4844; Fax: 920-457-4750.
Council of Waukesha, 305 E. Main St., Waukesha, 53186. Tel: 262-547-3281; Fax: 262-522-9048.
Council of Beaver Dam, 316 S. Spring St., Beaver Dam, 53916. Tel: 920-885-6971.
Council of Washington County, 420 River Rd., West Bend, 53095. Tel: 262-334-7291; Fax: 262-334-9191.
Council of Ozaukee County, P.O. Box 59, Port Washington, 53074. Tel: 262-284-4637; Fax: 262-284-6703. Total Assisted 30,000; Total Staff 5,000.

FOND DU LAC. *Christ Child Society - Fond du Lac Chapter*, Fahey School, 247 Doty St., 54935. Tel: 920-923-6490. Mailing Address: P.O. Box 418, Butte Des Morts, 54927. Sue Neumann, Pres. N6461 Danny Ln., 54935. Tel: 920-923-6490.

HORICON. *Legion of Mary*, 113 Valley St., 53032. Tel: 920-485-2427; Fax: 920-485-2427. Email: mekinneymalachy@ameritech.net. Rev. M. Eugene Kinney, Spiritual Dir.; Ms. Virginia Wojtanowski, Pres.

RACINE. *Cursillos in Christianity*, 5110 Charles St., 53402. Tel: 262-639-6576. Email: clardweb@yahoo.com. Web: www.cursillo.org/milwaukee. Rev. William W. Key, Spiritual Dir., English Speaking Secretariat; Clarence Weber, Lay Dir. Tel: 262-639-6576. Total Staff 7.

WAUWATOSA. *Milwaukee Archdiocesan Holy Name Union*, 2431 N. 63rd St., 53213. Tel: 414-258-1310; Fax: 414-258-1310. Email: swedemilw@juno.com. Mr. Steve Lazarczyk, Pres.; Rev. Edward Griesemer, S.C.J.

[W] NEWMAN CENTERS

MILWAUKEE. *Marquette University Ministry* Tel: 414-288-6873; Fax: 414-288-3696. Email: susan.niemi@marquette.edu. Web: www.mu.edu/um.
Alumni Memorial Union 236, P.O. Box 1881, 53201-1881. Tel: 414-288-6873; Fax: 414-288-3696. Revs. Frank A. Majka, S.J., Assoc. Dir.; D. Edward Mathie, S.J., Dir.
Milwaukee Archdiocesan Campus Ministry P.O. Box 070912, 53207-0912. Tel: 414-769-3440; Fax: 414-769-3408. Email: nohlr@archmil.org.
Legal Title: *Campus Ministry of the Archdiocese of Milwaukee*
University of Wisconsin - Milwaukee, Newman Center, 3001 N. Downer Ave., 53211. Tel: 414-964-6640; Fax: 414-964-3608. Email: cmfp@csd.uwm.edu; rjlotz@execpc.com. Constance M. Popp; Rev. Robert J. Lotz.
U.W. Parkside and Carthage College, 6203-54th. Ave., Kenosha, 53142. Tel: 262-654-7416; Fax: 262-694-6048. Email: edith@wi.rr.com. Edith Padgett.
Whitewater Campus Ministry (Whitewater), 344 N. Prairie St., Whitewater, 53190. Tel: 262-473-5555; Fax: 262-473-5855. Email: bzanin@ticon.com.

[X] MISCELLANEOUS

MILWAUKEE. *Agape Community Center of Milwaukee, Inc.*, Tel: 414-464-4440; Fax: 414-464-9420. Email: msluzalis@agape-center.org. Web: www.ministryhealth.org. Corporate Sponsor: Ministry Health Care, Inc. (Milwaukee, WI); Sponsored by Sisters of the Sorrowful Mother.
6100 N. 42nd St., 53209. Tel: 414-464-4440; Fax: 414-464-9420. Maria Sluzalis, Exec. Dir.
Alexian Elderly Services, Inc., 9301 N. 76th St., 53233. Tel: 414-355-9300; 312-755-2562; Fax: 414-357-5106. Email: gmohn@abhses.com. Gary Mohn, Contact Person.
Alternative Residential Arrangements, Inc., P.O. Box 070912, 53207-0912. Tel: 414-769-3400; Fax: 414-769-3428. Email: catholiccharities@ccmke.org. Web: www.ccmke.org. Group Homes for Developmentally disabled adults
Other Locations:
6609 N. 53rd St., 53223. Tel: 414-358-0852; Fax: 414-358-0669. Richard Kohl, Dir. Tel: 414-769-3401.
5255 S. 18th St., 53221. Tel: 414-282-6366; Fax: 414-282-3205.
St. Ann Center Supporting Fund, Inc., 2801 E. Morgan Ave., 53207. Tel: 414-744-1160; Fax: 414-977-5050. Email: jpglaser@stanncenter.org. Web: www.stanncenter.org. John P. Glaser, CFO.
Apostle of Prayer, 3211 S. Lake Dr., Ste. 216, 53235. Tel: 414-486-1152; 800-214-8908; Fax: 414-486-1159. Email: aposprayer@aol.com. Web: www.apostlesofprayer.org. Rev. James M. Kubicki, S.J., Contact.

Apostleship of the Sea, 3501 S. Lake Dr., P.O. Box 070912, 53207-0912.

Archdiocesan Marian Shrine, 141 N. 68th St., 53213. Tel: 414-257-0155. Rev. Anthony S. Trenier, Dir.

**Archdiocese of Milwaukee Supporting Fund, Inc.*, 125 S. 84th St., Ste. 110, 53214. Tel: 414-607-6040; Fax: 414-607-6045. Erica P. John, CEO.

Assisi Homes - Jefferson Court, Inc., 415 E. Knapp St., 53202. Tel: 414-271-5370; Fax: 414-271-5988. Web: www.wfs-inc.org.

Assisi Homes of Milwaukee, Inc., 3345 W. Highland St., 53210. Tel: 262-271-5370; Fax: 262-271-5988. Web: www.wfs-inc.org. Franciscan Sisters, Daughters of the Sacred Hearts of Jesus and Mary (Wheaton, IL), Purpose: To acquire, or develop and operate housing projects for low income families and elderly persons and to provide for human and other charitable services required by the residents

Association of Franciscan Colleges and Universities, Inc., 6801 N. Yates Rd., P.O. Box 334, 53217. Tel: 414-410-4109; Fax: 414-410-4120. Email: gkowalski@stritch.edu. Web: www.franciscancollegesuniversities.org. Sr. Gabrielle Kowalski, Exec. Dir.

St. Benedict Community Meal (Province of St. Joseph of the Capuchin Order, Inc.). , 1015 North 9th St., 53233. Tel: 414-271-0135; Fax: 414-271-0637. Email: stbens@execpc.com. Mr. Tom Plakut, Dir. Provides a free evening meal Sunday through Friday to those in need. Total Assisted 110,000; Total Staff 8.

Capuchin Franciscan Volunteer Corps, Inc., 1015 N. 9th St., 53233-1468. Tel: 414-271-0135; Fax: 414-271-0637. Email: capcorps@juno.com. Web: www.capuchinfranciscans.org/capcorps.htm. Bro. David Schwab, O.F.M.Cap., Dir. Purpose: To serve as a religious organization which recruits, places, and supports Christian volunteers in service to people in need. Total Assisted 10,000; Total Staff 1.

Casa Romero Renewal Center, Inc., 423 W. Bruce St., 53204. Tel: 414-224-7564; Fax: 414-270-9817. Email: casaromero@wi.rr.com. Rev. David M. Shields, S.J., Exec. Dir.

Cathedral Preservation Foundation, Inc., 831 N. Van Buren, 53202. Tel: 414-276-9814; Fax: 414-276-8285. Email: carllast@stjohncathedral.org. Web: stjohncathedral.org. Very Rev. Carl A. Last, Pres.

St. Catherine Residence, Inc., 1032 E. Knapp St., 53202. Tel: 414-272-8470; Fax: 414-272-7579. Web: www.stcatherineresidence.org. Lynne J. Oehlke, M.S.W., Exec. Dir.
Legal Title: *St. Catherine Residence, Inc.*, Affordable house serving women in transition, and those who will benefit from an environment where women support, encourage and network with eachother. Includes a Right Start Program for first-time, single, pregnant women over the age of 17. Sisters 1; Residents 150.

The Catholic Charismatic Renewal Office of Southeastern Wisconsin, Inc., P.O. Box 070912, 53207-0912. Tel: 414-482-1727; Fax: 414-482-3616. Email: ccr@archmil.org. Deacon Patrick H. Frye, Liaison; Rosalita Villa, Office Mgr.

Catholic Charities Foundation, Inc., 3501 S. Lake Dr., P.O. Box 070912, 53207-0912. Tel: 414-769-3400; Fax: 414-769-3428. Email: Catholiccharities@ccmke.org. Web: www.ccmke.org. Diane M. Knight, Registered Agent.

Catholic Charities of the Archdiocese of Milwaukee, Inc., 3501 S. Lake Dr., P.O. Box 070912, 53207-0912. Tel: 414-769-3400; Fax: 414-769-3428. Email: catholiccharities@ccmke.org. Web: www.ccmke.org. Diane M. Knight, Exec. Dir.; Gary Howley, Assoc. Dir.
Area Offices:
2021 N. 60th St., 53208. Tel: 414-771-2881; Fax: 414-771-1674. Catherine Young, Contact.
2711 19th St., Racine, 53403. Tel: 262-637-8888; Fax: 262-637-0695. Nancy Irizarry, Contact.
503 Wisconsin Ave., Sheboygan, 53081. Tel: 920-458-5726; Fax: 920-458-5826. Kristin Blanchard, Contact.
741 N. Grand Ave., Suite 210, Waukesha, 53186. Tel: 262-547-2463; Fax: 262-547-8002. John Nesseth, Contact.
6202 25th Ave., Kenosha, 53140. Tel: 262-658-2088; Fax: 262-658-0841. Nancy Irizarry, Contact.
191 S. Main St., Fond du Lac, 54935. Tel: 920-923-2550; Fax: 920-923-1777. Kristin Blanchard, Contact.

Adult Day Services & Resource Center, 1919 N. 60th St., 53208. Tel: 414-771-2881; Fax: 414-771-9115. Lisa Davis, Contact Person.

Adult Day Services - New Hope Center, 4033 W. Good Hope Rd., 53209. Tel: 414-228-7740; Fax: 414-352-3042. Susan Yee, Contact Person.

Adult Day Sevices - National Regency Center, 13700 W. National Ave., New Berlin, 53151. Tel: 262-782-0740; Fax: 262-782-0024. Valerie Ruppel, Contact Person. Other Offices: Beaver Dam, Brookfield, Burlington, Lake Geneva, Menomonee Falls, Milwaukee South, Milwaukee Southwest, Port Washington, West Bend. Total Assisted Annually 28,000.

St. Clare Management, Inc., 1545 S. Layton Blvd., 53215. Tel: 414-643-6501; Fax: 414-643-4474. Email: stclaremgt@aol.com. Philip Aggen, Pres. & CEO. Sponsored by the School Sisters of St. Francis, Housing management organization committed to providing quality residential services to low income elderly and/or persons with disabilities

Clare Towers II, Inc. dba Clare Woods, 3576 S. 43rd St., 53220. Tel: 414-643-6501; Fax: 414-643-4474. Sponsored by School Sisters of St. Francis, Housing Facility for physically disabled to live independently Apartments 32.

Clare Towers, Inc., 1546 S. 29th St., 53215. Tel: 414-643-6501; Fax: 414-643-4474. Sponsored by School Sisters of St. Francis, Housing facility for physically disabled to live independently Apartments 25.

Convergence, Inc., 1501 S. Layton Blvd., 53215. Tel: 414-384-4105; Fax: 414-944-6060. Email: cfoxho@sssf.org. Sisters Jeanne Schweickert, S.S.S.F., Pres. & Exec. Dir.; Anne Beitzinger, Vice Pres.; Charlita Foxhoven, Bd. Members; Frances Brenner, Bd. Members; Anne Beitzinger, Bd. Members.

**Covenant Healthcare System, Inc.*, 1126 S. 70th St., Ste. 306, P.O. Box 14970, 53214-0970. Tel: 414-456-2300; Fax: 414-456-2363. Web: www.covhealth.org. Paul Dell Uomo, Pres. & CEO. Franciscan Sisters, Daughters of the Sacred Hearts of Jesus and Mary, Wheaton, IL

Covenant Home Health and Hospice, Inc., 9688 W. Appleton Ave., 53225. Tel: 414-535-6900; Fax: 414-535-6902. Web: www.covhealth.org. James D. Gresham, Pres. Franciscan Sisters, Daughters of the Sacred Hearts of Jesus and Mary, Wheaton, IL Total Served 6,701; Total Staff 269.

**Covenant Medical Group, Inc.*, 1126 S. 70th St., Ste. 306, P.O. Box 14970, 53214-0970. Tel: 414-456-2300; Fax: 414-456-2363. Email: psboard@covhealth.org. Web: www.covhealth.org. Patrick Board, Pres.

DISMAS Ministry, P.O. Box 070363, 53207. Tel: 414-977-5064; Fax: 414-481-6764. Email: dismasmin@aol.com. Web: www.dismasministry.org. Ronald Zeilinger, Contact Person. A Catholic outreach to inmates, victims, their families, and the community.

Dominican Center for Women, Inc., 2470 W. Locust St., 53206-1134. Tel: 414-444-9930; Fax: 414-444-4041. Email: amhalloran@aol.com. Sr. Ann Halloran, O.P., Dir. & Contact Person.

Eastside Senior Services, 2717 E. Hampshire, 53211. Tel: 414-961-0661; Fax: 414-961-2290. Marylou Parthum, Dir. Corporate Title: Eastside Senior Services, Inc. - an Interfaith Outreach Program.; Sponsored by SS. Peter and Paul, Lake Park Lutheran Church, ELCA, St. Mark's Episcopal Church, Plymouth Church United Church of Christ, Our Lady of Divine Providence, and Three Holy Women, Milwaukee. Total Assisted 700; Total Staff 2.

**St. Francis Foundation of Milwaukee, Inc.*, 3237 S. 16th St., 53215. Tel: 414-647-5515; Fax: 414-647-5686. Email: jhodnik@covhealth.org. Web: www.stfrancishospital.net. Sponsored by the Felician Sisters., Fund development for St. Francis Hospital, Villa St. Francis, The Terrace at St. Francis, Child Development Center of St. Joseph and Community Outreach Efforts of the Felician Sisters.

Franciscan Peacemakers, Inc., Milwaukee, 1938 N. 4th St., 53212. Tel: 414-562-4780; Fax: 414-562-4790. Email: franpax2001@yahoo.com. Web: www.franpax.org. Deacon Steven J. Przedpelski, Exec. Dir. Total Assisted 37,000; Total Staff 3.

Franciscan Shared Laboratory, Inc., 1126 S. 70th St., Ste. S306, 53214. Tel: 414-456-2300. Web: www.covhealth.org. Alicia Modjeska, Chair. Sponsored by Franciscan Sisters, Daughters of the Sacred Hearts of Jesus and Mary (Wheaton, IL), Medical Laboratory Serving Healthcare Institutions.

House of Peace, 1702 W. Walnut St., 53205-1616. Tel: 414-933-1300; Fax: 414-933-0395. Email: markdcarico@juno.com. Web: www.houseofpeacemilwaukee.org. Mark Carrico, O.F.M.Cap., Dir.; Rev. Matthew Gottschalk, O.F.M.Cap., Spiritual Dir. In Res. Rev. Alan D. Veik, O.F.M.Cap.
Affiliates: Rev. Michael Fountain, O.F.M.Cap.; Deacon TL Michael Auman, O.F.M. Cap.

The Jesuit Partnership, P.O. Box 080287, 53208-0287. Tel: 414-937-6955; Fax: 414-937-6950. Revs. Eugene M. Dutkiewicz, S.J., Treas.; Richard A. McGarrity, S.J., Pres.

**St. Joan Antida High School Foundation, Ltd.*, 1341 N. Cass St., 53202. Tel: 414-354-9233; Fax: 414-355-6463. 8560 N. 76th Pl., 53223. Sr. Kathleen M. Lundwall, S.C.S.J.A., Contact Person.

**St. Josaphat Basilica Foundation, Inc.*, 620 W. Lincoln Ave., 53215-3220. Tel: 414-385-3263; Fax: 414-385-3269. Email: basilica@execpc.com. Web: www.thebasilica.org. Mr. Michael J. Murry, Chm.; Mr. Richard C. Thomas, Exec. Dir.

St. Joseph Regional Medical Center Foundation, Inc., 5000 W. Chambers St., 53210. Tel: 414-447-2844; Fax: 414-874-4399. Web: www.covhealth.org. William Johnson, Exec. Dir. Sponsored by Franciscan Sisters, Daughters of the Sacred Hearts of Jesus and Mary, Wheaton, IL

The Korean Catholic Community of Milwaukee, 1842 W. Windlake Ave., 53215. Tel: 414-672-6416; Fax: 414-672-6416. Email: psheenc@catholic.or.kr. Rev. Immanuel Pyo.

**LaFarge Lifelong Learning Institute, Inc.*, 1501 S. Layton Blvd., 53215. Tel: 414-944-6023; Fax: 414-944-6060. Email: cfoxho@sssf.org. Sr. Charlita Foxhoven, Treas. Continuing Education Program for older adults

Layton Blvd. West Neighbors, Inc., 1545 S. Layton Blvd., 53215. Tel: 414-383-9038; Fax: 414-647-4886. Email: lbwn@execpc.com. Web: www.lbwn.org. Charlotte John-Gomez, Exec. Dir. Sponsored by The School Sisters of St. Francis of St. Joseph's Convent, Milwaukee, WI, Inc., Purpose: To stabilize and revitalize the area of the city known as Layton Blvd. West Neighbors by building partnerships which achieve shared responsibility for the Neighborhood

MAREDA Archdiocese of Milwaukee, Office for Schools, Child and Youth Ministry. OSCYM/Dept. Parishes. , 3501 S. Lake Dr., P.O. Box 070912, 53207-0912. Tel: 414-769-3385; Fax: 414-769-3408. Email: amideik@archmil.org. Web: www.archmil.org. Jeff Montoya, Treas.

St. Mary's Hospital, Milwaukee Foundation, Inc., 2320 N. Lake Dr., 53202. Tel: 414-291-1425; Fax: 414-291-1441. Email: rglick@columbia-stmarys.org. Web: www.stmarysfoundation-milwaukee.org. Tim Frautchie, Chm. Sponsored by Ascension Health System.

St. Michael Hospital Community Foundation, Inc., 2400 W. Villard Ave., 53209. Tel: 414-527-8205; Fax: 414-527-8461. Email: bjmurray@covhealth.org. Web: www.covhealth.org. Bradley Murray, Exec. Dir. Franciscan Sisters, Daughters of the Sacred Hearts of Jesus and Mary, Wheaton, IL.

Milwaukee Achiever Literacy Services, Inc., 1512 W. Pierce St., 53204. Tel: 414-643-5108, Ext. 101; Fax: 414-643-8804. Email: ppalmer@milwaukeeachiever.org. Web: www.milwaukeeachiever.org. Dennis J. Purtell Esq., Legal Counsel. Founded by the School Sisters of St. Francis; Sisters of St. Francis of Assisi; School Sisters of Notre Dame, Purpose: To provide adult literacy education to economically and educationally disadvantaged adults in the Greater Milwaukee area. Total Assisted Annually 650; Total Staff 20.

Milwaukee Archdiocesan Council of Deacons, Tel: 414-769-3409. Email: zimprichd@archmil.org.
Advisory/Governing Board of Deacons
P.O. Box 070912, 53207-0912. Tel: 414-769-3409; Fax: 414-769-3408. Deacon Eugene M. Christensen.

Milwaukee Archdiocesan Elementary Principals' Association (MAEPA), P.O. Box 070912, 53207-0912. Tel: 414-769-3363; Fax: 414-769-3408. Email: mark@stfcabrini.com. Mark Quinn, Treas. Tel: 262-334-7142; Paul Hohl, Chairperson. Tel: 414-453-5830. Archdiocese of Milwaukee, Office for Schools, Child and Youth Ministry

Milwaukee Archdiocesan Secondary Principals' Association (MASPA), 3501 S. Lake Dr., P.O. Box 070912, 53207-0912. Tel: 414-769-3373; Fax: 414-769-3408. Email: scheeln@archmil.org. Mr. Robert Miller, Pres.; Bro. Nivard Scheel, C.F.X., Asst. to the Supt. of Schools & Contact Person.

Milwaukee Catholic Press Apostolate, 3501 S. Lake Dr., P.O. Box 070913, 53207-0913. Tel: 414-769-3468. Email: chnonline@archmil.org. Rev. Thomas T. Brundage, Interim Assoc. Publisher & Exec. Dir.

Ministry Health Care, Inc., 11925 W. Lake Park Dr., 53224. Tel: 414-359-1060; Fax: 414-359-1656. Email: info@ministryhealth.org. Web: www.ministryhealth.org. Nicholas Desien, Pres. & CEO.

**Ministry Medical Group, Inc.*, 11925 W. Lake Park Dr., 53224. Tel: 414-359-1060; Fax: 414-359-1656. Email: info@ministryhealth.org. Web:

www.ministrymedicalgroup.org. Michael Kryda, M.D., Pres.

National Association of Catholic Chaplains, 3501 S. Lake Dr., P.O. Box 070473, 53207-0473. Tel: 414-483-4898; Fax: 414-483-6712. Email: nacc@nacc.org. Web: www.nacc.org. Rev. Joseph J. Driscoll (BO), Pres. & CEO.

National Office of Post-Abortion Reconciliation and Healing, Inc., 3501 S. Lake Dr., P.O. Box 070477, 53207-0477. Tel: 414-483-4141; Fax: 414-483-7376. Email: noparh@juno.com. Web: www.noparh.org. Victoria M. Thorn, Pres. Total Assisted 4,500; Total Staff 3.

Novus Group, 3160 S. 63rd St., 53219-4113. Tel: 414-328-3892; Fax: 414-328-3881. Email: Kohalc@archmil.org. Christine Kohal, Devel. Dir. (An Alliance of Southwest Side Catholic Schools)

O.S.F. Services, Inc., 1126 S. 70th St., Ste. S306, P.O. Box 14970, 53214-0970. Tel: 414-456-2300. John D. Oliverio, Pres. Sponsored by Franciscan Sisters, Daughters of the Sacred Hearts of Jesus and Mary, Wheaton, IL.

Pallottine Fathers and Brothers, Inc., Disability Trust, 5424 W. Bluemound Rd., 53208. Tel: 414-259-0688; Fax: 414-258-9314. Email: mdprov@dias.net. Web: www.pallotti.net. Very Rev. Robert V. Carney, S.A.C., Pres.; Rev. Richard J. Gunderman, S.A.C., Treas.

Pallottine Fathers and Brothers, Inc., Educational and Apostolic Ministry Trust, 5424 W. Bluemound Rd., 53208. Tel: 414-259-0688; Fax: 414-258-9314. Email: mdprov@dias.net. Web: www.pallotti.net. Very Rev. Robert V. Carney, S.A.C., Prov.; Rev. Richard J. Gunderman, S.A.C., Treas.

**Region 6 Development Association*, 3100 W. Parnell Ave., 53221. Tel: 262-512-4171; Fax: 262-512-9893. Email: Fayview@aol.com. 6753 West Rogers, West Allis, 53219. Mrs. Carolyn Ettlie, Chairperson. Purpose: To build a community of educators with new resiliency in Catholic education, emphasizing the critical importance of on-going professional development.

S.E.T. Ministry, Inc., 2977 N. 50th St., 53210. Tel: 414-449-2680; Fax: 414-442-1770. Sr. Lucina Halbur, C.S.A., Pres. & CEO. Wheaton Franciscan Services, Inc., Corporate Sponsor, Joint Sponsored by 18 Religious Congregations., Health and Human Services Outreach Programs. Total Assisted 4,200.

S.I.S. (Sisters Interacting with Seniors), 222 N. 33rd St., #913, 53208. Tel: 414-933-2270. Sr. Julius Voelz, R.S.M., Coord. Total Assisted 250; Total Staff 2.

Santa Fe Communications, Inc. Heart of the Nation a.k.a. Lightning Bug Flix , 1126 S. 70th. St., Ste. S216A, 53214. Tel: 414-475-4444; Fax: 414-475-3621. Email: Bruno1@aol.com. Web: www.heartofthenation.org. Dr. William Thorn, Pres.; Mr. Jon Pray, Treas. Total Staff 4.

The School Sisters of Saint Francis of St. Joseph's Convent Congregational Support Charitable Trust, 1515 S. Layton Blvd., 53215. Tel: 414-384-1515; Fax: 414-384-1950. Email: info@sssf.org. Web: www.sssf.org. Sr. Helen Butzler, O.S.F., Trustee. Corporate Title: Congregational Support Charitable Trust

Seton Health Corporation of Wisconsin, 2320 N. Lake Dr., 53211. Tel: 414-291-1000; Fax: 414-291-1444. Email: amarquar@columbia-stmarys.org. Robert Henkel, Chm. Operated by Ascension Health System.

Society of the Divine Savior Ongoing Community Support Trust, 1735 N. Hi Mount Blvd., 53208-1720. Tel: 414-258-1735; Fax: 414-258-1934. Email: sds@salvatorians.com. Web: salvatorians.com.

St. Stephen's League (of the Archdiocesan Council of Deacons). , P.O. Box 070912, 53207-0912. Tel: 414-769-3409; Fax: 414-769-3408. Email: zimprichd@archmil.org. Deacon David L. Zimprich.

Telos, Inc. dba Clare Heights, Clare Meadows, Clare Lakes, Clare Court, Clare Place and Clare Central Tel: 414-643-6501; Fax: 414-643-4474. Sponsored by the School Sisters of St. Francis, Housing for physically disabled to live independently
1545 S. Layton Blvd., 53215. Tel: 414-643-6501; Fax: 414-643-4474. Apartments 107.

Theological Studies, Inc., Marquette University, 100 Coughlin Hall, P.O. Box 1881, 53201-1881. Tel: 414-288-3164; Fax: 414-288-1413. Email: Michael.Fahey@Marquette.edu. Web: www.ts.mu.edu. Revs. Michael A. Fahey, S.J., Editor; David G. Schultenover, S.J., Book Review Editor. Publisher of the quarterly Theological Studies

St. Thomas More Lawyers Society, 3501 S. Lake Dr., P.O. Box 07912, 53207-0912. Tel: 414-769-3312; Fax: 414-769-3310. Email: webmaster@stthomasmorewi.org. Web: www.stthomasmorewi.org. Very Rev. Paul B.R. Hartmann, M.Div., J.C.L., Chap.; Rev. James E. Connell, Chap.

Wisconsin Association of Principals of Catholic Secondary Schools Archdiocese of Milwaukee, Office for Schools, Child and Youth , P.O. Box 070912, 53207-0912. Tel: 414-769-3368; Fax: 414-769-3408. Email: norrisj@archmil.org. John T. Norris, Ph.D., Contact.

Young Christian Workers of Milwaukee, Inc., 2223 W. Sunbury Ct., 53215-4547. Tel: 414-672-0186; Fax: 414-672-0186. Email: jrdonat@hotmail.com. John R. Donat, Pres.

BRISTOL. *Mercy Retreat Center*, 12009 221st Ave., 53104. Tel: 262-862-6648. Sr. Timothy Matthews, R.S.M., Contact Person. Tel: 630-365-0828. Sisters of Mercy of the Americas, Regional Community of Chicago

BROOKFIELD. **Elmbrook Memorial Healthcare Foundation, Inc.*, 19333 W. North Ave., 53045-4198. Tel: 262-785-2000. Email: pvkessenich@covhealth.org. Web: www.covhealth.org. Patrick V. Kessenich, Exec. Dir.

BROWN DEER. *Sisters of the Sorrowful Mother Charitable Trust*, 9056 N. Deerbrook Tr., 53223-2474. Tel: 414-357-8940; Fax: 414-357-8950. Email: ssmintl@aol.com. Web: ssmfranciscans.org. Sr. M. Helen Malolepsy, Gen. Supr. To help provide for the needs of the aged and infirm members of the Sisters of the Sorrowful Mother

Sisters of the Sorrowful Mother International Finance, Inc., 9056 N. Deerbrook Tr., 53223-2474. Tel: 414-357-8940; Fax: 414-357-8950. Email: ssmintl@aol.com. Web: ssmfranciscans.org. Sr. M. Helen Malolepsy, Chairperson & Pres.

BURLINGTON. *Misioneras Franciscanas de la Juventud, Inc.*, 456 Kendall St., 53105. Tel: 262-767-2630; 262-769-3300; Fax: 262-763-9171. Email: emtunu@yahoo.com. Sr. Lilia G. Paredes, M.F.J., Contact Person.

FOND DU LAC. *St. Francis Home Foundation, Inc.*, 33 Everett St., 54935. Tel: 920-923-7980; Fax: 920-923-7995. Douglas Trost, Pres. Sponsored by the Congregation of Sisters of St. Agnes

Hazotte Ministries, Inc., 320 County Rd. K, 54935-8958. Tel: 920-907-2300; Fax: 920-923-3194. Sr. Hertha Longo, C.S.A., Pres. Sponsored by the Congregation of Sisters of St. Agnes

FRANKLIN. *Congregation of the Priests of the Sacred Heart Support and Maintenance Trust*, 6871 S. Lovers Lane Rd., 53132. Tel: 414-425-6910; Fax: 414-425-2938. Email: provsec@poshusa.org. Web: www.scj.org. Revs. Terence Langley, S.C.J., Trustee; Joseph Dean, S.C.J., Trustee; Bro. Peter Mankins, S.C.J., Trustee.

Franciscan Pilgrimage Programs, Inc., P.O. Box 321490, 53132. Tel: 414-427-0570; Fax: 414-427-0590. Email: info@franciscanpilgrimages.com. Web: www.franciscanpilgrimages.com. Revs. Roch Niemier, O.F.M., Pres.; John Celia, O.F.M., Vice Pres. Operate a Catholic Franciscan Pilgrimage Program for religious men and women, leaders in Franciscan based institutions, members of the Secular Franciscan Order and others who desire to deepen their Franciscan values and spirituality.

Friends of Theophane, P.O. Box 320101, 53132. Tel: 414-481-6739; Fax: 414-481-6764. Ronald Zeilinger, Contact Person. To collect information and promote knowledge of the reputation for holiness of the late Frater Theophane Prenderville, S.C.J.

GREENDALE. *COURAGE Association* P.O. Box 193, 53129-0193. Tel: 262-514-4212. Email: CourageMKE@excite.com. Web: couragerc.org. Rev. Michael Harrer; Peter Caprise, Dir.

HALES CORNERS. *Development Office* Sacred Heart Monastery-Priests of the Sacred Heart-Reign of the Sacred Heart, Inc. , 6889 S. Lovers Lane Rd., P.O. Box 900, 53130. Tel: 414-425-3383; Fax: 414-425-5719. Web: www.scj.org. Mr. Patrick R. Thompson, Pres. U.S. Province of the Priests of the Sacred Heart

KENOSHA. *Assisi Homes - Kenosha, Inc.* Independent Housing for Low Income Elderly , 1860 27th Ave., 53140. Tel: 262-551-9821; Fax: 262-551-9843. Web: www.wfs-inc.org. 26 West 171 Roosevelt Rd., Wheaton, IL 60189.

Assisi Homes - Saxony, Inc. Independent Housing for Low Income Elderly. , 1876 22nd Ave., 53140. Tel: 262-551-9005; Fax: 262-551-7586. Web: www.wfs-inc.org.

Catholic Woman's Club, c/o PPG Management Consultants, LLC, 5525 Green Bay Rd., 53144. Tel: 262-657-2060; Fax: 262-657-2080. Email: osterj@ppgmanagement.net. Lillian DeFazio, Pres. & Contact Person.

Franciscan Seniors, Kenosha, Inc., 1920 27th Ave., 53140. Tel: 630-462-9271; 262-551-0989; Fax: 262-551-8683. Web: www.wfs-inc.org.

St. Mark Latin American Center, 1320 73rd St., 53143-5459. Tel: 262-656-7370; Fax: 262-656-7375. Email: stmark@acronet.net. Web: www.stmark-kenosha.org. Rev. Carlos Florez; Deacons Gregorio M. Lebron; Roberto Salazar; Alvaro Dominquez; Betty Regalado, Coord. of Human Resources; Peggy Avila, Sec.; Irene Santos, Volunteer. Total Assisted 2,500; Total Staff 5.

MANITOWOC. *Sisters of St. Elizabeth, Inc., Congregational Support Charitable Trust*, 2005 Division St., 54220-5699. Tel: 920-684-7171. 3800 W. Peterson Ave., Chicago, IL 60659-3116. Sr. M. Barbara Ann Bosch, S.S.E., Trustee.

MEQUON. *St. Mary's Foundation Ozaukee, Inc.*, 13111 N. Port Washington Rd., 53097. Tel: 262-243-7472; Fax: 262-243-7416. Email: rheuerma@columbia-stmarys.org. Web: www.stmarysfoundation-ozaukee.org. Donald Levy, Chm. Sponsored by Ascension Health System

PLEASANT PRAIRIE. *The Women's Health Center Foundation, Inc.*, 9956 76th St., 53158. Tel: 262-656-2587; Fax: 262-653-5554. Email: lynn.westlund@uhsi.org. Web: www.acronet.net/~stcath. *United Hospital System, c/o Breast Imaging Ctr. - Kmcc*, 6308 8th Ave., Kenosha, 53143. Lynn Westlund, Contact Person. Sponsored by the Wheaton Franciscan Services, Inc.

RACINE. *All Saints Healthcare Foundation, Inc.*, 1320 Wisconsin Ave., 53403. Tel: 262-687-2293; Fax: 262-687-2674. Email: kbuser@allsaintshealthcare.org. Web: allsaintshealth.com. Kenneth R. Buser, Pres. Franciscan Sisters, Daughters of the Sacred Hearts of Jesus and Mary, Wheaton, IL

**All Saints Healthcare System, Inc.*, 3801 Spring St., 53405. Tel: 262-687-4011; Fax: 262-687-4540. Email: kbuser@allsaintshealthcare.org. Web: allsaintshealth.com. Kenneth R. Buser, Pres. & CEO. Franciscan Sisters, Daughters of the Sacred Hearts of Jesus and Mary, Wheaton, IL

Catherine Marian Housing, Inc., 5635 Erie St., 53402. Tel: 262-639-4100; Fax: 262-639-9702. Web: www.racinedominicans.org. Racine Dominican Ministries, Inc. and Franciscan Ministries, Inc.

St. Catherine's High School Corporation, 1200 Park Ave., 53403. Tel: 262-632-2785; Fax: 262-632-5144. Gary Meier, Chap.

St. Catherine's High School of Racine, Inc., 5635 Erie St, 53402. Tel: 262-639-4100; Fax: 262-639-9702. Sr. Carol Wester, O.P., Pres.

St. Catherine's Infirmary, Inc., 5635 Erie St., 53402. Tel: 262-639-4100; Fax: 262-639-9702. Sr. Carol Wester, O.P., Pres.

Dominican College of Racine, Inc., 5635 Erie St., 53402. Tel: 262-639-4100; Fax: 262-639-9702. Sr. Carol Wester, O.P., Pres.

Missionary Community of St. Paul the Apostle and Mary, Mother of the Church, Inc. An international Public Association of Christian Faithful, comprised of clergy and laity. It is present in Africa, Europe, North and South America. It fosters pastoral activities and human development initiatives, while promoting mission awareness internationally. , 2512 Westwood Dr., 53404. Tel: 262-634-2666; Fax: 262-635-1910. Email: 0mcsp@aol.com. Revs. Pere Cane, Pres.; Marti Colom, Sec.; Oriol Regales, Treas.; Ricardo Martin.

Racine Area Catholic Foundation/Education Association, 3710 Foxwood Rd., 53405. Tel: 262-554-0779. Margaret M. Tuscany, Sec.

Racine Dominican Ministries, Inc- Racine Dominican Retreat Program, 5635 Erie St., 53402-1900. Tel: 262-639-4100; Fax: 262-639-9702. Email: rdrp@miliserv.net. Web: www.racinedominicans.org. Sr. Rita Lui, O.P., Dir. & Contact Person.

Racine Dominican Ministries, Inc., 5635 Erie St., 53402. Tel: 262-639-4100; Fax: 262-639-9702. Web: www.racinedominicans.org. Sr. Carol Wester, O.P., Pres.

Racine Dominican Ministries, Inc. Senior Companion Program , 5635 Erie St., 53402. Tel: 262-639-4100; Fax: 262-639-9702. Web: www.racinedominicans.org. Gloria Stedman Brown, Dir.

Racine Dominican Ministries, Inc.- Adult Learning Program, 5635 Erie St., 53402-1900. Tel: 262-639-4100; Fax: 262-639-9702. Email: alpsc@miliserv.net. Web: www.racinedominicans.org. Sr. Joyce Quintana, O.P., Dir.

Racine Elementary Association for Development, 3035 Drexel Ave., 53403. Tel: 262-554-4491. Corinne LeRose, Devel. Dir.

Villa St. Anna, Inc., 5737 Erie St., 53402. Tel: 262-639-9757; Fax: 262-639-9744. Web: www.wfs-inc.org. To provide assisted living for the elderly of low and moderated income Residents 70.

ST. FRANCIS. *Archdiocese of Milwaukee Catholic Community Foundation, Inc.*, 3501 S. Lake Dr., 53235. Tel: 414-769-3443; Fax: 414-769-3438. Web:

legaciesoffaith.org. Ms. Mary Ellen Markowski, Contact.

St. Camillus Communities, Inc., 3661 S. Kinnickinnic Ave., 53235. Tel: 414-259-4511. Rev. Louis Lussier, O.S.Cam.; Very Rev. Richard O'Donnell, O.S.Cam., Prov.; Deacons Scott Binet, O.S.Cam.; Albert Schempp, O.S.Cam.; Bros. Mario Crivello, O.S.Cam.; Allan Gidley, O.S.Cam. Students 3; Total in Residence 6.

Foundation for Religious Retirement, Inc., 3221 S. Lake Dr., 53235. Tel: 414-483-9128; Fax: 414-744-7193. Email: jparrott@lakeosfs.org. Jan Parrott, Exec. Dir. Raises funds to fulfill the needs of retired women religious in the Milwaukee Archdiocese

USCCB Commission on Certification and Accreditation, 3211 S. Lake Dr., Ste. 317, 53235-3702. Tel: 414-486-0139; Fax: 414-489-0006. Jean Marie Weber, Contact Person.

SHEBOYGAN. *St. Thomas More High School, Inc.*, 522 New York Ave., 53081. Tel: 920-457-4629. A fund to provide youth and adult religious education programs within the county.

STONE BANK. **Tyme Out Youth Ministry Center, Inc.*, Tel: 262-966-1800; Fax: 262-966-1815. Email: youth@tymeout.org. Web: www.tymeout.org. W332 N6786 County Rd. C, Nashotah, 53058-9737. Tel: 262-966-1800. Sr. Kieran Sawyer, S.S.N.D., Dir. Total in Residence 3; Total Staff 16.

WATERFORD. *General Secretariat of the Franciscan Missions, Inc.*, P.O. Box 130, 53185. Tel: 262-534-5470; Fax: 262-534-4342. Email: framis@wi.net. Web: franciscanmissions.org. Revs. Sereno Baiardi, O.F.M., Dir.; Sante De Angelis, O.F.M., Assoc. Dir. General Secretariat of the Franciscan Missions, Inc. Missionaries 5,400.

WAUWATOSA. *St. Camillus Health System, Inc.*, 10101 W. Wisconsin Ave., 53226. Tel: 414-258-1814. Very Rev. Richard O'Donnell, O.S.Cam., Pres. & Prov.; Rev. Louis Lussier, O.S.Cam., Treas.; Bro. Nelson DeLoria, O.S.Cam., Vice Pres. Management Corporation. Order of the Servants of the Sick (Order of St. Camillus) Total Assisted 596.

St. Camillus Ministries, Inc., 10101 W. Wisconsin Ave., 53226. Tel: 414-258-1814. Rev. Louis Lussier, O.S.Cam., Treas.; Very Rev. Richard O'Donnell, O.S.Cam., Prov. & Pres.; Nelson Deleria, O.S.Cam., Vice Pres. St. Camillus Ministries, Inc operates under the auspices of the Order of St. Camillus and sponsors Durward's Glen Retreat and Conference Center and all social concerns ministry of the Order. Total Served 300; Total Staff 6.

Friends of Calvary Cemetery, Inc., 2515 N. 66th St., 53213. Tel: 414-778-1187; Fax: 414-778-1187. Email: swerk@juno.com. Mr. Keith Schultz, Pres. Purpose: To raise funds in connection with the restoration of Calvary Chapel located at Calvary Cemetery, 5503 West Bluemound Rd., Milwaukee, WI and overseeing such restoration.

Order of St. Camillus Foundation, Inc., 10200 W. Bluemound Rd., 53226. Tel: 414-259-8335; Fax: 414-259-4590. David Kremer, Exec. Dir. & Contact Person.

WEST BEND. *Visitation Rural Ministries, Inc.*, 7660 Townline Rd., 53090. Tel: 262-629-4154; Fax: 262-629-5034. Email: mmbub@juno.com. Mary Bub, Co-Dir., CEO & Pres.; Sr. Bernita Marie Bittner, S.S.N.D., Co-Dir.

WHITEFISH BAY. *Association of Ladies of Charity of Milwaukee, Wisconsin*, 4825 N. Wildwood Ave., 53217. Tel: 414-962-2462. Email: djscws50@aol.com. 2806 E. Locust Ave., 53211. Rev. Matthew Gottschalk, O.F.M.Cap., Archdiocesan Spiritual Advisor.

[Y] CLOSED PARISHES

MILWAUKEE. *St. Agnes* For sacramental records, contact Archives, Archdiocese of Milwaukee, P.O. Box 070912, Milwaukee, 53207-0912. Tel.: 414-769-3407; Fax: 414-769-3408

St. Albert For sacramental records, contact Archives, Archdiocese of Milwaukee, P.O. Box 070912, Milwaukee, 53207-0912. Tel.: 414-769-3407; Fax: 414-769-3408

St. Anne For sacramental records, contact Archives, Archdiocese of Milwaukee, P.O. Box 070912, Milwaukee, 53207-0912. Tel.: 414-769-3407; Fax: 414-769-3408

St. Anthony of Padua For sacramental records, contact St. Vincent Pallotti Parish, 7622 W. Stevenson St., Milwaukee, 53223. Tel.: 414-453-5344; Fax: 414-453-4225

St. Barbara For sacramental records, contact Archives, Archdiocese of Milwaukee, P.O. Box 070912, Milwaukee, 53207-0912. Tel.: 414-769-3407; Fax: 414-769-3408

Blessed Virgin of Pompeii For sacramental records, contact Three Holy Women Parish, 1716 N. Humboldt Ave., Milwaukee, 53202-1623. Tel.: 414-271-2165; Fax: 414-271-7988

St. Boniface For sacramental records, contact Archives, Archdiocese of Milwaukee, P.O. Box 070912, Milwaukee, 53207-0912. Tel.: 414-769-3407; Fax: 414-769-3408

St. Elizabeth For sacramental records, contact Archives, Archdiocese of Milwaukee, P.O. Box 070912, Milwaukee, 53207-0912. Tel.: 414-769-3407; Fax: 414-769-3408

St. Emeric For sacramental records, contact Sacred Heart Parish, 917 N. 49th St., Milwaukee, 53208. Tel.: 414-774-9418; Fax: 414-774-7406

St. Gabriel For sacramental records, contact Archives, Archdiocese of Milwaukee, P.O. Box 070912, Milwaukee, 53207-0912. Tel.: 414-769-3407; Fax: 414-769-3408

St. Gall For sacramental records, contact Archives, Archdiocese of Milwaukee, P.O. Box 070912, Milwaukee, 53207-0912. Tel.: 414-769-3407; Fax: 414-769-3408

St. Gerard For sacramental records, contact Archives, Archdiocese of Milwaukee, P.O. Box 070912, Milwaukee, 53207-0912. Tel.: 414-769-3407; Fax: 414-769-3408

St. Hedwig For sacramental records, contact Three Holy Women Parish, 1716 N. Humboldt Ave., Milwaukee, 53202-1623. Tel.: 414-271-2165; Fax: 414-271-7988

Holy Angels For sacramental records, contact Archives, Archdiocese of Milwaukee, P.O. Box 070912, Milwaukee, 53207-0912. Tel.: 414-769-3407; Fax: 414-769-3408

Holy Cross For sacramental records, contact St. Vincent Pallotti Parish, 7622 W. Stevenson St., Milwaukee. Tel.: 414-453-5344; Fax: 414-453-4225

Holy Redeemer For sacramental records, contact Archives, Archdiocese of Milwaukee, P.O. Box 070912, Milwaukee, 53207-0912. Tel.: 414-769-3407; Fax: 414-769-3408

Holy Rosary For sacramental records, contact Three Holy Women Parish, 1716 N. Humboldt Ave., Milwaukee, 53202-1623. Tel.: 414-271-2165; Fax: 414-271-7988

Holy Spirit For sacramental records, contact Archives, Archdiocese of Milwaukee, P.O. Box 070912, Milwaukee, 53207-0912. Tel.: 414-769-3407; Fax: 414-769-3408

Holy Trinity-Our Lady of Guadalupe For sacramental records, contact Our Lady of Guadalupe Parish, 613 S. 4th St., Milwaukee, 53204. Tel.: 414-271-6181; Fax: 414-278-6090

St. Ignatius For sacramental records, contact Archives, Archdiocese of Milwaukee, P.O. Box 070912, Milwaukee, 53207-0912. Tel.: 414-769-3407; Fax: 414-769-3408

St. John de Nepomuc For sacramental records, contact Archives, Archdiocese of Milwaukee, P.O. Box 070912, Milwaukee, 53207-0912. Tel.: 414-769-3407; Fax: 414-769-3408

St. Joseph For sacramental records, contact St. Joseph Parish, 12130 Center St., Wauwatosa, 53222-4096. Tel.: 414-771-4626; Fax: 414-771-4311

St. Lawrence For sacramental records, contact Archives, Archdiocese of Milwaukee, P.O. Box 070912, Milwaukee, 53207-0912. Tel.: 414-769-3407; Fax: 414-769-3408

St. Leo For sacramental records, contact Archives, Archdiocese of Milwaukee, P.O. Box 070912, Milwaukee, 53207-0912. Tel.: 414-769-3407; Fax: 414-769-3408

St. Matthew For sacramental records, contact Archives, Archdiocese of Milwaukee, P.O. Box 070912, Milwaukee, 53207-0912. Tel.: 414-769-3407; Fax: 414-769-3408

St. Michael For sacramental records, contact Good Shepherd Parish, W762 Armstrong Rd., Campbellsport, 53010-1400. Tel.: 920-477-3201 Fax: 920-477-3030

Mother of Perpetual Help For sacramental records, contact Archives, Archdiocese of Milwaukee, P.O. Box 070912, Milwaukee, 53207-0912. Tel.: 414-769-3407; Fax: 414-769-3408

St. Nicholas For sacramental records, contact Archives, Archdiocese of Milwaukee, P.O. Box 070912, Milwaukee, 53207-0912. Tel.: 414-769-3407; Fax: 414-769-3408

St. Rita For sacramental records, contact Three Holy Women Parish, 1716 N. Humboldt Ave., Milwaukee, 53202-1623. Tel.: 414-271-2165; Fax: 414-271-7988

St. Stephen Martyr For sacramental records, contact Archives, Archdiocese of Milwaukee, P.O. Box 070912, Milwaukee, 53207-0912. Tel.: 414-769-3407; Fax: 414-769-3408

St. Thomas Aquinas For sacramental records, contact Archives, Archdiocese of Milwaukee, P.O. Box 070912, Milwaukee, 53207-0912. Tel.: 414-769-3407; Fax: 414-769-3408

St. Wenceslaus For sacramental records, contact Three Holy Women Parish, 1716 N. Humboldt Ave., Milwaukee, 53202-1623. Tel.: 414-271-2165; Fax: 414-271-7988

ADELL. *St. Patrick* For sacramental records, contact Our Lady of the Lakes Parish, 230 Butler St., Random Lake, 53075-1710. Tel.: 920-994-4380; Fax: 920-994-2605

ALLENTON. *Sacred Heart* For sacramental records, contact Resurrection Parish, P.O. Box 96, Allenton, 53002-0096. Tel.: 262-629-5240

ARMSTRONG. *Our Lady of Angels* For sacramental records, contact Good Shepherd, 303 E. Main St., P.O. Box 128, Eden. Tel.: 920-477-3201; Fax: 920-477-3030

AUBURN. *St. Matthias* For sacramental records, contact Resurrection Parish, P.O. Box 96, Allenton, 53002-0096. Tel.: 262-629-5240

BYRON. *St. John* For sacramental records, contact Sons of Zebedee: Saints James and John Parish W5882 Church Rd., Fond du Lac, 54937-8602. Tel.: 920-922-1167

CASCADE. *St. Mary* For sacramental records, contact Our Lady of the Lakes Parish, 230 Butler St., Random Lake, 53075-1710. Tel.: 920-994-4380; Fax: 920-994-2605

CEDARBURG. *Divine Word* For sacramental records, contact St. Francis Borgia Parish, 1375 Covered Bridge Rd., Cedarburg, 53012. Tel.: 262-377-1070; Fax: 262-377-6898

COLGATE. *St. Columba* For sacramental records, contact St. Francis Borgia Parish, 1375 Covered Bridge Rd., Cedarburg, 53012. Tel.: 262-377-1070; Fax: 262-377-6898

CUDAHY. *St. Frederick* For sacramental records, contact Nativity of the Lord Parish, 4611 S. Kirkwood Ave., Cudahy, 53110. Tel.: 414-744-6622

Holy Family For sacramental records, contact Nativity of the Lord Parish, 4611 S. Kirkwood Ave., Cudahy, 53110. Tel.: 414-744-6622

St. Joseph For sacramental records, contact Nativity of the Lord Parish, 4611 S. Kirkwood Ave., Cudahy, 53110. Tel.: 414-744-6622

DACADA. *St. Nicholas* For sacramental records, contact Our Lady of the Lakes Parish, 230 Butler St., Random Lake, 53075-1710. Tel.: 920-994-4380; Fax: 920-994-2605

DOTYVILLE. *St. Michael* For sacramental records, contact Good Shepherd, 303 E. Main St., P.O. Box 128, Eden. Tel.: 920-477-3201; Fax: 920-477-3030

EDEN. *St. Mary* For sacramental records, contact Good Shepherd, 303 E. Main St., P.O. Box 128, Eden. Tel.: 920-477-3201; Fax: 920-477-3030

ELDORADO. *St. Mary* For sacramental records, contact Our Risen Savior Parish, W8272 Forest Avenue Rd., Eldorado, 54932-9801. Tel.: 920-922-2412

ELKHART LAKE. *St. George* For sacramental records, contact St. Thomas Aquinas Parish, P.O. Box T, Elkhart Lake, 53020-0396. Tel.: 920-876-2457

FARMINGTON. *St. John of God* For sacramental records, contact St. Michael Parish, 8877 Forestview Rd., Kewaskum, 53040. Tel.: 262-334-5270; Fax: 262-334-5233

FOND DU LAC. *St. Joseph* For sacramental records prior to June 12, 1967, contact Archdiocese of Milwaukee Archives. Tel.: 414-769-3407; For records after June 12, 1967, contact Holy Family Parish, 26 W. Follett St., Fond du Lac, 54935. Tel.: 920-921-0580.

St. Louis For sacramental records prior to Sept. 20, 1959, contact Archdiocese of Milwaukee Archives. Tel.: 414-769-3407; For records after Sept. 20, 1959, contact Holy Family Parish, 26 W. Follett St., Fond du Lac, 54935. Tel.: 920-921-0580

St. Mary For sacramental records through 1975, contact Archdiocese of Milwaukee Archives. Tel.: 414-769-3407; For records after 1975 contact Holy Family Parish, 26 W. Follett St., Fond du Lac, 54935. Tel.: 920-921-0580.

St. Patrick For sacramental records prior to September 19, 1960, contact Archdiocese of Milwaukee Archives. Tel.: 414-769-3407; For records after September 19, 1960, contact Holy Family Parish, 26 W. Follett St., Fond du Lac, 54935. Tel.: 920-921-0580 For sacramental records prior to September 19, 1960, contact Archdiocese of Milwaukee Archives. Tel.: 414-769-3407; For records after September 19, 1960, contact Holy Family Parish, 26 W. Follett St., Fond du Lac, 54935. Tel.: 920-921-0580

Sacred Heart For sacramental records prior to December 1970, contact Archdiocese of Milwaukee Archives. Tel.: 414-769-3407; For records after November 1970, contact Holy Family Parish, 26 W. Follett St., Fond du Lac, 54935. Tel.: 920-921-0580

FOX LAKE. *St. Mary* For sacramental records, contact Annunciation Parish, 305 Green St., P.O. Box 85, Fox Lake, 53933-0085. Tel.: 920-928-3513; Fax: 920-928-6334

FRANKLIN. *Sacred Hearts of Jesus and Mary* For

sacramental records, contact St. Martin of Tours, 7963 S. 116th St., Franklin, 53132. Tel.: 414-425-1114; Fax: 414-425-2527

FREDONIA. *St. Rose of Lima* For sacramental records, contact Holy Rosary Parish, 305 Fredonia Ave., P.O. Box 250, Fredonia, 53021-0250. Tel.: 262-692-9994; Fax: 262-692-3085

GLENBEULAH. *St. Fridolin* For sacramental records, contact St. Thomas Aquinas Parish, P.O. Box T, Elkhart Lake, 53020-0396. Tel.: 920-876-2457

HOLY CROSS. *Holy Cross* For sacramental records, contact Holy Rosary Parish, 305 Fredonia Ave., P.O. Box 250, Fredonia, 53021-0250. Tel.: 262-692-9994; Fax: 262-692-3085

HORICON. *St. Malachy* For sacramental records, contact Sacred Heart Parish, 113 Valley St., Horicon, 53032. Tel.: 920-485-2427

HUBERTUS. *St. Hubert* For sacramental records, contact St. Gabrial, 3727 Hubertus Rd., Hubertus, 53033. Tel.: 262-628-1141

JUNEAU. *Immaculate Conception* For sacramental records, contact Sacred Heart Parish, 113 Valley St., Horicon, 53032. Tel.: 920-485-2427

KENOSHA. *St. Casmir* For sacramental records, contact the Archdiocese of Milwaukee Archives. Tel.: 414-769-3407

St. George For sacramental records, contact the Archdiocese of Milwaukee Archives. Tel.: 414-769-3407

St. Thomas Aquinas For sacramental records, contact St. Mary Parish, 7307 40th Ave., Kenosha, 53142-4325. Tel.: 262-694-6018; Fax: 262-694-6048

LIMA. *St. Rose of Lima* For sacramental records, contact Blessed Trinity Parish, 327 Giddings Ave., Sheboygan Falls, 53085. Tel.: 920-467-4616; Fax: 920-467-4290

LITTLE KOHLER. *Mother of Sorrows* For sacramental records, contact Holy Rosary Parish, 305 Fredonia Ave., P.O. Box 250, Fredonia, 53021-0250. Tel.: 262-692-9994; Fax: 262-692-3085

LOST LAKE. *St. Mary* For sacramental records, contact Annunciation Parish, 305 Green St., P.O. Box 85, Fox Lake, 53933-0085. Tel.: 920-928-3513; Fax: 920-928-6334

LYONS. *St. Kilian* For sacramental records, contact St. Joseph Parish, 1540 Mill St., P.O. Box 60, Lyons, 53148-0060. Tel.: 262-763-2050; Fax: 262-763-9377

MITCHELL. *St. Michael* For sacramental records, contact Good Shepherd, 303 E. Main St., P.O. Box 128, Eden. Tel.: 920-477-3201; Fax: 920-477-3030

NABOB. *St. Matthias* For sacramental records, contact St. Lawrence Parish, 4886 Hwy. 175, Hartford, 53027. Tel: 262-644-5701

NENNO. *St. Anthony* For sacramental records, contact Resurrection Parish, P.O. Box 96, Allenton, 53002-0096. Tel.: 262-629-5240

SS. Peter and Paul For sacramental records, contact Resurrection Parish, P.O. Box 96, Allenton, 53002-0096. Tel.: 262-629-5240

OAKFIELD. *St. James* For sacramental records, contact Sons of Zebedee: Saints James and John Parish, W5882 Church Rd., Fond du Lac, 54937-8602. Tel.: 920-922-1167

PEWAUKEE. *St. Mary* For sacramental records, contact Queen of Apostles Parish, W280 N2101 Hwy. SS, Pewaukee, 53072. Tel.: 262-691-1535; Fax: 262-691-7376

SS. Peter and Paul For sacramental records, contact Queen of Apostles Parish, W280 N2101 Hwy. SS, Pewaukee, 53072. Tel.: 262-691-1535; Fax: 262-691-7376

RACINE. *St. Casimir* For sacramental records, contact Archives, Archdiocese of Milwaukee, P.O. Box 070912, Milwaukee, 53207-0912. Tel.: 262-769-3407; Fax: 262-769-3408

Holy Name For sacramental records, contact Archives, Archdiocese of Milwaukee, P.O. Box 070912, Milwaukee, 53207-0912. Tel.: 262-769-3407; Fax: 262-769-3408

Holy Trinity For sacramental records, contact Archives, Archdiocese of Milwaukee, P.O. Box 070912, Milwaukee, 53207-0912. Tel.: 262-769-3407; Fax: 262-769-3408

St. Rose For sacramental records, contact Archives, Archdiocese of Milwaukee, P.O. Box 070912, Milwaukee, 53207-0912. Tel.: 262-769-3407; Fax: 262-769-3408

St. Stanislaus For sacramental records, contact Archives, Archdiocese of Milwaukee, P.O. Box 070912, Milwaukee, 53207-0912. Tel.: 262-769-3407; Fax: 262-769-3408

RANDOLPH. *St. Gabriel* For sacramental records, contact Annunciation Parish, 305 Green St., P.O. Box 85, Fox Lake, 53933-0085. Tel.: 920-928-3513; Fax: 920-928-6334

St. Mary For sacramental records, contact Annunciation, 305 Green St., P.O. Box 85, Fox Lake 53933-0085. Tel.: 920-928-3513; Fax: 920-928-6334

RANDOM LAKE. *St. Mary* For sacramental records, contact Our Lady of the Lakes Parish, 230 Butler St., Random Lake, 53075-1710. Tel.: 920-994-4380; Fax: 920-994-2605

RICHFIELD. *St. Mary* For sacramental records, contact St. Gabriel, 3727 Hubertus Rd., Hubertus, 53033. Tel.: 262-628-1141

ST. GEORGE. *St. George* For sacramental records, contact Blessed Trinity Parish, 327 Giddings Ave., Sheboygan Falls, 53085. Tel.: 920-467-4616; Fax: 920-467-4290

ST. MARTIN. *Holy Assumption* For sacramental records through 1990, contact St. Mary Parish, 9520 W. Forest Home Ave., Hales Corners, 53130. Tel.: 414-425-2174; Fax: 414-425-9432. For records after 1990, contact St. Martin of Tours Parish, 7963 S. 116th St., Franklin, 53132. Tel.: 414-425-1114; Fax: 414-425-1114

ST. PETER. *St. Peter* For sacramental records prior to 1953, contact Archdiocese of Milwaukee Archives. Tel.: 414-769-3407; For records after 1952, contact Holy Family Parish, 26 W. Follett St., Fond du Lac, 54935. Tel.: 920-921-0580

THOMPSON. *St. Patrick* (Erin) For sacramental records contact St. Kilian Parish, 264 W. State St., Hartford, 53027. Tel.: 262-673-4831

WAYNE. *St. Bridget* For sacramental records, contact Holy Trinity Parish, 331 Main St., P.O. Box 461, Kewaskum, 53040. Tel.: 262-626-2860; Fax: 262-626-2301

WEST ALLIS. *St. Joseph* For sacramental records, contact Archives, Archdiocese of Milwaukee, P.O. Box 070912, Milwaukee, 53207-0912. Tel.: 414-769-3407; Fax: 414-769-3408

Our Lady of Mount Carmel For sacramental records, contact Archives, Archdiocese of Milwaukee, P.O. Box 070912, Milwaukee, 53207-0912. Tel.: 414-769-3407; Fax: 414-769-3408

WOODHULL. *St. John the Baptist* For sacramental records, contact Our Risen Savior Parish, W8272 Forest Avenue Rd., Eldorado, 54932-9801. Tel.: 920-922-2412

RELIGIOUS INSTITUTES OF MEN REPRESENTED IN THE ARCHDIOCESE

For further details refer to the corresponding bracketed number in the Religious Institutes of Men or Women section.

[0120]—*Alexian Brothers* (Immaculate Conception Prov.)—C.F.A.
[0140]—*The Augustinians* (Mother of Good Counsel Prov.)—O.S.A.
[0200]—*Benedictine Monks*—O.S.B.
[0600]—*Brothers of the Congregation of Holy Cross* (Midwest Prov.)—C.S.C.
[0470]—*The Capuchin Friars* (Prov. of St. Joseph)—O.F.M.Cap.
[0740]—*Congregation of Marians of the Immaculate Conception*—M.I.C.
[1130]—*Congregation of the Priests of the Sacred Heart*—S.C.J.
[0480]—*Conventual Franciscans* (St. Bonaventure, Prov. of Our Lady of Consolation)—O.F.M.Conv
[0260]—*Discalced Carmelite Friars* (Prov. of the Immaculate Heart of Mary)—O.C.D.
[0520]—*Franciscan Friars*—O.F.M.
[0690]—*Jesuit Fathers and Brothers*—S.J.
[0720]—*The Missionaries of Our Lady of La Salette* (Prov. of Mary, Queen of Peace)—M.S.
[0430]—*Order of Preachers* (Province of St. Albert the Great)—O.P.
[0240]—*Order of St. Camillus-Camillian Fathers and Brothers*—O.S.Cam.
[1070]—*Redemptorist Fathers* (St Louis Prov.)—C.SS.R.
[0990]—*Society of the Catholic Apostolate* (Mater Dei Prov.)—S.A.C.
[1200]—*Society of the Divine Savior* (American Prov.)—S.D.S.
[0420]—*Society of the Divine Word* (Northern Prov.)—S.V.D.
[1360]—*Xaverian Missionary Fathers*—S.X.

RELIGIOUS INSTITUTES OF WOMEN REPRESENTED IN THE ARCHDIOCESE

[0230]—*Benedictine Sisters of Pontifical Jurisdiction* (Erie, PA)—O.S.B.
[0360]—*Carmelite Sisters of the Divine Heart of Jesus*—Carmel.D.C
[]—*The Christian Sisters (Pious Union)*—C.S.
[]—*Congregation of Institutio Santa Mariana de Jesus*
[3710]—*Congregation of the Sisters of Saint Agnes*—C.S.A.
[1780]—*Congregation of the Sisters of the Third Order of St. Francis of Perpetual Adoration* (Eastern Region)—F.S.P.A.
[0760]—*Daughters of Charity of St. Vincent De Paul*—D.C.
[0790]—*Daughters of Divine Charity*—F.D.C.
[0420]—*Discalced Carmelite Nuns*—O.C.D.
[1060]—*Dominican Contemplative Sisters*—O.P.
[1070-03]—*Dominican Sisters*—O.P.
[]—*Dominican Sisters* (Vietnam)
[1070-09]—*Dominican Sisters*—O.P.
[1070-27]—*Dominican Sisters*—O.P.
[1070-25]—*Dominican Sisters*—O.P.
[1170]—*Felician Sisters*—C.S.S.F.
[1230]—*Franciscan Sisters of Christian Charity*—O.S.F.
[1310]—*Franciscan Sisters of Little Falls, MN*—O.S.F.
[1415]—*Franciscan Sisters of Mary*—F.S.M.
[1430]—*Franciscan Sisters of Our Lady of Perpetual Help*—O.S.F.
[]—*Franciscan Sisters of Our Lady (Pious Union)*—F.S.O.L.
[]—*Franciscan Sisters of St. Clare (Pious Union)*—F.S.S.C.
[1470]—*Franciscan Sisters of St. Joseph*—F.S.S.J.
[1240]—*Franciscan Sisters, Daughters of the Sacred Hearts of Jesus and Mary*—O.S.F.
[]—*Hermitage of the Trinity*
[1820]—*Hospital Sisters of the Third Order of St. Francis*—O.S.F.
[]—*Missionary Sisters of the Holy Family*—M.S.F.
[3230]—*Poor Handmaids of Jesus Christ*—P.H.J.C.
[2970]—*School Sisters of Notre Dame*—S.S.N.D.
[1680]—*School Sisters of St. Francis*—O.S.F.
[]—*Secular Institute of Schoenstatt Sisters of Mary*—I.S.S.M.
[0600]—*Sisters of Charity of St. Joan Antida*—S.C.S.J.A.
[0430]—*Sisters of Charity of the Blessed Virgin Mary*—B.V.M.
[2575]—*Sisters of Mercy of the Americas*—R.S.M.
[3800]—*Sisters of St. Elizabeth*—S.S.E.
[1705]—*The Sisters of St. Francis of Assisi*—O.S.F.
[1520]—*Sisters of St. Francis of Christ the King*—O.S.F.
[3930]—*Sisters of St. Joseph of the Third Order of St. Francis*—S.S.J.-T.O
[4020]—*Sisters of St. Rita*—O.S.A.
[1030]—*Sisters of the Divine Savior*—S.D.S.
[4100]—*Sisters of the Sorrowful Mother (Third Order of St. Francis)*—S.S.M.
[3510]—*Sisters Servants of Christ the King*—S.S.C.K.

ARCHDIOCESAN CEMETERIES

MILWAUKEE. *St. Adalbert*
Calvary
Holy Cross
Holy Trinity
Mount Olivet

FRANKLIN. *All Souls*

KENOSHA. *All Saints*

MEQUON. *Resurrection*

SOUTH MILWAUKEE. *Holy Sepulcher*, 675 College Ave., 53172-1252. Tel: 414-762-6800. Gregg F. Apostoloff, Archdiocesan Dir.

TAYCHEEDAH. *St. Charles Cemetery*, Tel: 920-921-0347. (See St. Patrick Parish, Fond du Lac)

WAUKESHA. *St. Joseph*

NECROLOGY

† Etzel, George A., (Retired)—Died April 11, 2003
† Goebel, Nicholas L., (Retired)—Died May 10, 2003
† Hanley, John P., (Retired)—Died March 31, 2003
† Ide, Harold J., (Retired)—Died May 15, 2003
† McCormick, Robert J., (Retired)—Died July 10, 2003
† Mueller, Joseph J., (Retired)—Died Feb. 26, 2003
† Thompson, Jerome F., Azua, Dominican Republic LaSagrada Familia Church—Died May 17, 2003

Archdiocese of Mobile

(Archidioecesis Mobiliensis)

Most Reverend

OSCAR H. LIPSCOMB, D.D., PH.D.

Archbishop of Mobile; ordained July 15, 1956; appointed July 29, 1980; consecrated November 16, 1980. *Res.: 400 Government St., P.O. Box 1966, Mobile, AL 36633.* Tel: 251-434-1585.

Chancery Office: 400 Government St., P.O. Box 1966, Mobile, AL 36633. Tel: 251-434-1585; Fax: 251-434-1588.

Email: aom_chan@bellsouth.net

Square Miles 22,969.

Established as Vicariate-Apostolic of Alabama and the Floridas, 1825; Diocese of Mobile, May 15, 1829; Name changed to Diocese of Mobile-Birmingham, July 9, 1954; Redesignated, June 28, 1969. Raised to rank of Archdiocese November 16, 1980.

Comprises the lower 28 Counties of the State of Alabama, namely: Choctaw, Clarke, Wilcox, Dallas, Autauga, Elmore, Lee, Russell, Macon, Montgomery, Lowndes, Barbour, Bullock, Pike, Crenshaw, Butler, Monroe, Conecuh, Escambia, Covington, Coffee, Geneva, Dale, Henry, Houston, Washington, Baldwin and Mobile.

For legal titles of parishes and archdiocesan institutions consult the Chancery Office.

STATISTICAL OVERVIEW

Personnel	
Archbishops	1
Priests: Diocesan Active in Diocese	73
Priests: Diocesan Active Outside Diocese	6
Priests: Retired, Sick or Absent	29
Number of Diocesan Priests	108
Religious Priests in Diocese	32
Total Priests in Diocese	140
Extern Priests in Diocese	8
Ordinations:	
Transitional Deacons	2
Permanent Deacons in Diocese	61
Total Brothers	10
Total Sisters	156
Parishes	
Parishes	76
With Resident Pastor:	
Resident Diocesan Priests	57
Resident Religious Priests	13
Without Resident Pastor:	
Administered by Priests	5
Administered by Deacons	1
Missions	11
Pastoral Centers	3
Professional Ministry Personnel:	
Brothers	4
Sisters	14
Lay Ministers	31
Welfare	
Catholic Hospitals	1
Total Assisted	172,769
Health Care Centers	2
Total Assisted	4,800
Homes for the Aged	3
Total Assisted	299
Residential Care of Children	1
Total Assisted	130
Day Care Centers	4
Total Assisted	403
Special Centers for Social Services	11
Total Assisted	87,528
Residential Care of Disabled	3
Total Assisted	130
Other Institutions	2
Total Assisted	263
Educational	
Diocesan Students in Other Seminaries	10
Total Seminarians	10
Colleges and Universities	1
Total Students	1,735
High Schools, Diocesan and Parish	3
Total Students	1,463
Elementary Schools, Diocesan and Parish	19
Total Students	5,433
Catechesis/Religious Education:	
High School Students	1,186
Elementary Students	3,731
Total Students under Catholic Instruction	13,558
Teachers in the Diocese:	
Priests	11
Brothers	4
Sisters	14
Lay Teachers	553
Vital Statistics	
Receptions into the Church:	
Infant Baptism Totals	1,095
Adult Baptism Totals	163
Received into Full Communion	334
First Communions	1,140
Confirmations	962
Marriages:	
Catholic	171
Interfaith	146
Total Marriages	317
Deaths	548
Total Catholic Population	65,588
Total Population	1,652,398

Former Prelates—Rt. Revs. MICHAEL PORTIER, D.D., First Bishop; consecrated Nov. 5, 1826; died May 14, 1859; JOHN QUINLAN, D.D., consecrated Dec. 4, 1859; died March 9, 1883; DOMINIC MANUCY, D.D., appt. Vicar Apostolic of Brownsville and cons. Bishop of Dulma Dec. 8, 1874; transferred to Mobile March 9, 1884, but resigned in the same year; died at Mobile, Dec. 4, 1885; JEREMIAH O'SULLIVAN, D.D., consecrated Sept. 20, 1885; died Aug. 10, 1896; E. P. ALLEN, consecrated May 16, 1897; died Oct. 21, 1926; Most Revs. THOMAS J. TOOLEN, D.D., consecrated May 4, 1927; appt. Archbishop "ad personam," May 27, 1954; resigned Oct. 8, 1969; died Dec. 4, 1976; JOHN L. MAY, D.D., ord. May 3, 1947; appt. Titular Bishop of Tagarbala and Auxiliary Bishop of Chicago, June 21, 1967; consecrated Aug. 24, 1967; transferred to Mobile, Oct. 8, 1969; installed Dec. 10, 1969; appt. to Saint Louis, Jan. 29, 1980; died March 24, 1994.

Vicar General—Rev. Msgr. JOHN AHERNE, V.G., Holy Name of Jesus Church, P.O. Box 557, Semmes, 36575. Tel: 251-694-4794.

Regional Episcopal Vicars—Rev. Msgrs. F. CHARLES TRONCALE, Holy Spirit Church, 8570 Vaughn Rd., Montgomery, 36117. Tel: 334-277-5631; TIMOTHY DEASY, Christ the King Church, P.O. Box 549, Daphne, 36526. Tel: 251-626-2343; Very Rev. PATRICK GALLAGHER, St. Columba Church, 2700 W. Main St.,, Dothan, 36301. Tel: 334-793-5802.

Archivist—Mr. RICHARD CHASTANG.

Chancery Office—400 Government St., P.O. Box 1966, Mobile, 36633. Tel: 251-434-1585; Fax: 251-434-1588. Email: aomchan2@bellsouth.net.

Chancellor—Very Rev. MICHAEL L. FARMER, S.T.L.

Metropolitan Tribunal—14 S. Franklin St., P.O. Box 2405, Mobile, 36652. Tel: 251-432-4609; Fax: 251-432-4647. Please address all rogatory commissions and matrimonial matters to the Office of the Tribunal.

Judicial Vicar—Rev. Msgr. ANTHONY MCDEVITT, J.C.D., S.T.L.; Rev. JAMES S. KEE, S.T.L., J.C.L.

Associate Judges—Rev. Msgr. KENNETH J. KLEPAC, J.C.L.; Mrs. KATHERINE S. WEBER; Mr. VICTOR WHELAN.

Judicial Consultant—Rev. Msgr. ANTHONY MCDEVITT, J.C.D., S.T.L.

Defenders of the Bond—Deacon HENRY F. O'BRIEN; Mrs. KATHARINE S. WEBER, M.S. (Th), J.C.L.

Advocate—Mr. VICTOR WHELAN, S.T.M.

Court Clerk and Notary—Mrs. DANICE ENTREKIN, M.Ed.

Notary—Rev. JAMES MONTINI-COLEMAN, M.Div.

Notaries and Secretaries—Mrs. SHARON B. CUSIMANO; Mrs. PATRICIA K. CONNER.

Archdiocesan Consultors—Rev. Msgr. JOHN AHERNE, V.G.; Revs. PETER J. CUNNINGHAM; FRANCIS V. CUSACK; PATRICK MAHER; WILLIAM J. SKONEKI; Rev. Msgr. G. WARREN WALL.

Vicars for Religious—Mobile District-Baldwin Escambia Deanery: Rev. ROBERT B. RIMES, S.J., Spring Hill College, 4000 Dauphin St., Mobile, 36608. Tel: 251-460-2175. Montgomery-Dothan Deaneries: Rev. Msgr. WILLIAM R. JAMES, P.O. Drawer 1367, Robertsdale, 36567. Tel: 251-947-5054.

Secretary for Education—Miss GWENDOLYN P. BYRD, P.O. Box 129, Mobile, 36601. Tel: 251-438-4611.

Vicar for Ministry to Persons with Disabilities and the Deaf—Rev. PATRICK J. MADDEN, 4350 Moffett Rd., Mobile, 36618. Tel: 251-342-6449.

Vicar for Vietnamese Affairs—Rev. CU MINH DUONG, St. Monica Parish, 1131 Dauphin Island Pkwy., Mobile, 36605. Tel: 251-479-7360.

Archdiocesan Offices and Directors

Apostleship of Prayer—Very Rev. MICHAEL L. FARMER, S.T.L., P.O. Box 1966, Mobile, 36633. Tel: 251-434-1585.

Apostleship of the Sea—Rev. PRIMITIVO MARAVILLA, Port Chap.; Deacon JOSEPH V. CONNICK III, Dir., Catholic Maritime Club, 261 Dauphin St., Mobile, 36602. Tel: 251-432-7339; Fax: 251-433-4618.

Apostolate for Aging—Deacon STEVE SEYMOUR, 5305 Woodline Dr. S., Mobile, 36693. Tel: 251-666-9916.

Archdiocese of Mobile Cursillo Center—Rev. DAVID J. TOKARZ, Spiritual Dir., St. Bede Catholic Church, 3870 Atlanta Hwy., Montgomery, 36109. Tel: 334-272-3463; Fax: 334-272-3492; Mr. LEE EILERS, 4228 Todd Blvd., Mobile, 36619. Tel: 251-443-5419. Email: lee4228@aol.com.

Archdiocesan Council of Catholic Women (ACCW)—Mrs. RITA TURNER, Pres.; Mrs. MARIE D. MARTIN, Pres., Priests' Burse Club, 400 Government St., Mobile, 36602.

Boy Scouts—Rev. STEVEN WILLIAMS, St. Mary Church, 106 Providence St., Mobile, 36604. Tel: 251-432-8678.

Campaign for Human Development—Rev. WILLIAM J. SKONEKI, Dir. Funding Office for charitable and other works of Archdiocese 356 Government St., P.O. Box 230, Mobile, 36601. Tel: 251-438-9668; Fax: 251-434-1547.

Catholic Charities Appeal Office—Deacon ROBERT E. KIRBY JR., Dir., 356 Government St., P.O. Box 230, Mobile, 36601. Tel: 251-438-9668; Fax: 251-434-1547 Funding Office for charitable and other works of Archdiocese,.

Catholic Housing of Mobile, Inc.—Most Rev. OSCAR H. LIPSCOMB, D.D., Ph.D., Pres.; Very Rev. MICHAEL L. FARMER, S.T.L., Vice Pres., Sec. & Treas., Office, P.O. Box 1966, Mobile, 36633. Tel:

251-434-1585 Nonprofit Corp. of the State of Alabama,.

Catholic Housing Authority of Montgomery, Inc.—Rev. Msgr. F. CHARLES TRONCALE, Pres.; BILL PEARSON, Vice Pres.

Catholic Publishing Co., Inc.— Publisher of the Archdiocesan Newspaper "The Catholic Week" LARRY WAHL, Editor, P.O. Box 349, Mobile, 36601. Tel: 251-432-3529.

Catholic University, Friends of—Rev. RUSSELL BIVEN, Our Savior Church, 1801 Cody Rd. S., Mobile, 36695. Tel: 251-633-6762.

Catholic Youth Organization—PAUL CRANE, Exec. Dir., P.O. Box 6955, Mobile, 36660. Tel: 251-471-0062.

Catholic Youth Ministry—Rev. TIMOTHY EVANS, Dir., 1413 Old Shell Rd., Seton Center, Mobile, 36604. Tel: 251-433-4138.

Cemeteries—Very Rev. MICHAEL L. FARMER, S.T.L., P.O. Box 1966, Mobile, 36633. Tel: 251-434-1585; Mr. ROBERT OVERMEYER, Mgr., 1700 Dr. Martin Luther King Jr. Ave., Mobile, 36617. Tel: 251-479-5305. P.O. Box 230, Mobile, 36601.

Censor Librorum—Very Rev. MICHAEL L. FARMER, S.T.L., Chancery Office, P.O. Box 1966, Mobile, 36633. Tel: 251-434-1585; Fax: 251-434-1588.

Charismatic Movement—Deacon JAMES LABADIE, Our Lady Queen of Mercy, 4421 Narrow Lane Rd., Montgomery, 36116. Tel: 334-288-2850; Fax: 334-281-7884.

Charities— (Listing under Catholic Social Services)

Clergy Retirement Association—Rev. WILLIAM J. SKONEKI, Fiscal Management Office, P.O. Box 230, Mobile, 36601. Tel: 251-432-2737; Fax: 251-434-1547.

Archdiocesan Coordinator of Health Affairs—Mr. CLARK P. CHRISTIANSON, Pres. & CEO, Providence Hospital, 6801 Airport Blvd., P.O. Box 850429, Mobile, 36685. Tel: 251-633-1000.

Ecumenical Commission—Very Rev. MICHAEL L. FARMER, S.T.L., Chm., Cathedral of the Immaculate Conception, P.O. Box 1966, Mobile, 36633. Tel: 251-434-1565; Fax: 251-434-1588.

Family Life Director—Mr. TOM MCDONALD; Mrs. CAROLINE MCDONALD, Catholic Social Services, P.O. Box 7591, Mobile, 36601. Tel: 251-434-1550.

Handicapped, Apostolate to the—Rev. PATRICK MADDEN, Dir., 4350 Moffett Rd., Mobile, 36618. Tel: 251-342-6449.

Hispanic Apostolate—Rev. CHRISTOPHER VISCARDI, S.J., Dir., Spring Hill College, 4000 Dauphin St., Mobile, 36608. Tel: 251-380-3085.

Hispanic Pastoral Ministry—Rev. CHRISTOPHER VISCARDI, S.J., 712 Dauphin Island Pkwy., Mobile, 36606. Tel: 251-478-3737.

Holy Childhood Association—Rev. LEO BLANCHET, Dir., St Bridget Church, P.O. Box 13357, Whistler, 36612. Tel: 251-457-6847.

Holy Name Society—Deacon JOSEPH V. CONNICK III, 261 Dauphin St., Mobile, 36602. Tel: 251-432-7339.

Liturgical Commission—Very Rev. MICHAEL L. FARMER, S.T.L., Chm., P.O. Box 1966, Mobile, 36633.

McGill Institute, A Corporation—P.O. Box 1966, Mobile, 36633.

McGill-Toolen Foundation, The—Mrs. MONDE DONALDSON, Dir., Devel., 1501 Old Shell Rd., Mobile, 36604. Tel: 251-432-0788, Ext. 48.

Office of Ministry to the Deaf—4350 Moffett Rd., Mobile, 36618. Tel: 251-342-6449.

Mobile Provincial Conference of Bishops and Priests' Council—P.O. Box 1966, Mobile, 36633. Tel: 251-434-1585.

Newspaper "The Catholic Week"—LARRY WAHL, Editor, 356 Government St., P.O. Box 349, Mobile, 36601. Tel: 251-432-3529; 251-432-3520.

Pastoral Council—MARY NELL PECOT, Chm., 4604 Virginia Loop Rd., Apt. 3148-C, Montgomery, 36116. Tel: 334-281-5020.

Permanent Diaconate Program—Co-Dirs.: Rev. Msgr. JOHN AHERNE; Very Rev. MICHAEL L. FARMER, S.T.L.; Rev. PAUL G. ZOGHBY, Holy Name of Jesus Church, P.O. Box 557, Semmes, 36575. Tel: 251-649-4794.

Planned Giving—Deacon WILLIAM R. DOLAN, Dir., P.O. Box 230, Mobile, 36601. Tel: 251-432 1369.

Priests' Council—Most Rev. OSCAR H. LIPSCOMB, D.D., Ph.D., Pres. Officers: Rev. Msgr. JOHN AHERNE, Chm.; Revs. PETER CUNNINGHAM, Vice Chm.; JAMES MONTINI-COLEMAN, M.Div., Treas.; Very Rev. MICHAEL L. FARMER, S.T.L., Record. Sec.; Rev. JAMES A. HAVENS, Corresponding Sec.

Ex Officio Members—Rev. Msgrs. TIMOTHY DEASY, Baldwin Dean; F. CHARLES TRONCALE, Montgomery Dean; JOHN P. AHERNE, V.G.; Very Revs. PATRICK GALLAGHER, Dothan Dean; MICHAEL L. FARMER, S.T.L., Chancellor. Consultors: Rev. Msgr. G. WARREN WALL; Rev. PETER CUNNINGHAM; Rev. Msgr. JOHN AHERNE; Rev. WILLIAM SKONEKI.

Appointed Member & Consultor—Rev. Msgr. G. WARREN WALL.

Elected Members—Group I: Revs. L. RUSSELL BIVEN; PETER J. CUNNINGHAM; FRANK CUSACK. Group II: Revs. JAMES A. HAVENS; WILLIAM GORMAN; JAMES ZOGHBY. Group III: Revs. MARK I. NESKE; J. FRANCIS SOFIE JR.; DAVID CARUCCI. Group IV: Revs. PAUL HALLADAY; JAMES MONTINI-COLEMAN, M.Div.; ERNEST HYNDMAN.

Religious—Revs. HENRY E. DICKSON, S.S.J.; CARROLL W. PLOURDE, S.S.E.

Priests' Eucharistic League—Rev. MICHAEL D. IRWIN JR., St. Pius X Church, 217 S. Sage Ave., Mobile, 36606. Tel: 251-471-2449.

Priests' Personnel Board—Rev. JAMES F. ZOGHBY, Chm., Corpus Christi Church, 6300 McKenna Dr., Mobile, 36608. Tel: 251-342-1852.

Priests' Retirement Fund—Rev. WILLIAM J. SKONEKI, P.O. Box 230, Mobile, 36601. Tel: 251-432-2737.

Propagation of the Faith—Rev. LEO BLANCHET, St. Bridget Church, P.O. Box 13357, Whistler, 36613. Tel: 251-457-6847.

Radio and Television Communications—c/o Chancery Office, P.O. Box 1966, Mobile, 36633. Tel: 251-434-1585.

School Education Department—Miss GWEN BYRD, Supt., P.O. Box 129, Mobile, 36601. Tel: 251-438-4611.

Office of Religious Education—14 S. Franklin St., P.O. Box 2405, Mobile, 36652. Tel: 251-433-6991. Mrs. REBECCA TITFORD, Dir., 14 S. Franklin St., P.O. Box 2405, Mobile, 36652; Sr. PENNY SMITH, O.P., Dir., Rte. 3, Box 50, Ozark, 36360. Tel: 334-299-6671.

Serra Club of Mobile—Mr. JON GREEN, Pres.

Serra Club of Montgomery—Mr. LAWRENCE RUSSO.

Serra Club of Dothan—Dr. NICK E. BARRECA.

Serra Club of Daphne—Mr. JAMES M. FELSMAN.

Seton Haven Management Corporation—Dr. JIM LAROSE, Pres., 3721 Wares Ferry Rd., Montgomery, 36193. Tel: 334-272-4000.

Toolen Institute for Parish Services (TIPS)—Dr. AIDAN LICARI, Dir., P.O. Box 2405, Mobile, 36652. Tel: 251-438-6121.

Victim Assistance Coordinator—Rev. JAMES J. CINK, Dir., P.O. Box 230, Mobile, 36601. Tel: 800-856-4184 (Sexual Abuse Helpline); 251-432-2737 (Office). Email: childprotection@bellsouth.net.

Vocations—Revs. ALEJANDRO E. VALLADARES, Dir., 4156 Burma Rd., Mobile, 36693. Tel: 251-343-3662; DAVID SHOEMAKER, Asst. Dir., Holy Redeemer Church, 515 W. Broad St., Eufaula, 36027.

CLERGY, PARISHES, MISSIONS AND PAROCHIAL SCHOOLS

CITY OF MOBILE
(MOBILE COUNTY)

1—CATHEDRAL OF THE IMMACULATE CONCEPTION (1704), Most Rev. Oscar H. Lipscomb, D.D., Ph.D.; Very Rev. Michael L. Farmer, S.T.L., Rector; Rev. Primitivo Maravilla. In Res., Rev. James S. Kee, S.T.L., J.C.L.; Deacons Joseph V. Connick III; Charles H. Kenny.
Cathedral & Rectory—400 Government St., P.O. Box 1966, 36633. Tel: 251-434-1565; Fax: 251-434-1588.

2—ST. CATHERINE OF SIENA (1913), Rev. Edwin P. Beachum.
Res.: 2605 Springhill Ave., 36607. Tel: 251-473-1415; 251-473-1427; Fax: 251-473-6307.
Catechesis/Religious Program—Students 47.
Novitiate, Josephite Fathers—2609 Spring Hill Ave., 36607. Tel: 251-473-5130.

3—CORPUS CHRISTI (1958), Revs. James F. Zoghby; John S. Boudreaux (LAF); Deacon Arthur W. Robbins.
Res.: 6300 McKenna Dr., 36608. Tel: 251-342-1852; Fax: 251-342-6313.
School—Tel: 251-342-5474; Fax: 251-380-0325. Mrs. Joan T. McMullen, Prin. Lay Teachers 26; Students 566; Aides 13.
Catechesis/Religious Program—Tel: 251-342-5474, Ext. 2. Students 185.

4—ST. DOMINIC (1958), Revs. William J. Skoneki; William Patrick Saucier; Deacons Edward Connick; Robert Kirby. In Res., Rev. Msgr. Francis C. Murphy (Ireland); Rev. Alejandro Valladares.
Res.: 4156 Burma Rd., 36693. Tel: 251-661-5130; Fax: 251-661-0469.
School—4160 Burma Rd., 36693. Tel: 251-661-5226; Fax: 251-660-2242. Mrs. Ann Zimlich, Prin. Sisters of Mercy 1; Lay Teachers 31; Students 541.
Catechesis/Religious Program—Students 100.
Convent—Tel: 251-661-3229.

5—ST. FRANCIS XAVIER (1867), (African American), Rev. Anietie Akama Ukanide, M.S.P. (Nigeria); Deacon Alexander Moore, Pastoral Assoc.
Res.: 2034 St. Stephens Rd., 36617. Tel: 251-473-4975; Fax: 251-473-4940.
Catechesis/Religious Program—Students 34.

6—HOLY FAMILY (1959), Rev. Ernest R. Hyndman; Deacon Patrick Kelly.
Res.: 1304 Garland St., 36618. Tel: 251-344-0271; Fax: 251-344-0296.
School—Tel: 251-344-1781; Fax: 251-344-0769. Ms. Maureen Glavey Goodwin, Prin. Lay Teachers 14; Students 163.

7—ST. IGNATIUS (Spring Hill) (1947), Rev. Msgr. G. Warren Wall; Revs. James Montini Coleman; Paul A. Halladay; Deacons Charles J. Fontana; Marvin C. Johns; Abraham Lopez.
Res.: 3704 Springhill Ave., 36608. Tel: 251-342-9221; Fax: 251-341-1481.
School—Tel: 251-342-5442; Fax: 251-344-0944. Miss Janet Murray, Prin. Lay Teachers 22; Students 482.
School—Preschool, Tel: 251-345-1090. Jan Murray, Dir.; Jackie S. Mills, Coord. Lay Teachers 8; Students 120.
Catechesis/Religious Program—Students 340.

8—ST. JOAN OF ARC (1920), Rev. Msgr. Kenneth J. Klepac, J.C.L.
Res.: 1260 Elmira St., 36604. Tel: 251-432-3505.

9—ST. JOSEPH (1857), Rev. E. J. Jacques, S.J.
Res.: 808 Springhill Ave., 36602. Tel: 251-432-4218.

10—ST. JOSEPH (Maysville) (1944), (African American), Rev. Jeremiah A. Brady, S.S.J.; Deacon Ronnie A. Hathorne Sr.
Res.: 1703 Dublin St., 36605. Tel: 251-473-3761.
Convent—1701 Dublin St., 36605. Tel: 251-478-3292.

11—LITTLE FLOWER (1928), Revs. David P. Carucci; Jose Mudavankunnel.
Res.: 2053 Government St., 36606. Tel: 251-478-3381; Fax: 251-478-3381.
School—2103 Government St., 36606. Tel: 251-479-5761; Fax: 251-476-4064. Sr. Mary Joyce Bringer, C.S.J., Prin. Lay Teachers 10; Students 175.
Catechesis/Religious Program—Students 29.
Convent—411 Little Flower Ave., 36606. Tel: 251-479-1198.

12—ST. MARY (1867), Revs. Peter J. Cunningham; W. Bry Shields; Sr. M. Magdalena Langlois, C.S.A., Pastoral Assoc.; Deacons Ernest J. Johnson Jr.; William Dolan.
Mailing Address: 106 Providence St., 36604. In Res., Rev. Steven T. Williams.
Res.: 1453 Old Shell Rd., 36604. Tel: 251-432-8678; Fax: 251-432-1009.
School—Tel: 251-433-9904; Fax: 251-438-9069. Mrs. Debbie Ollis, Prin. Lay Teachers 16; Students 250.
Catechesis/Religious Program—Tel: 251-432-0929. Students 50.

13—ST. MATTHEW (1904), Rev. Joseph M. Bolling.
Res.: 906 Garrity St., 36605-4699. Tel: 251-432-4784.

14—ST. MONICA (1950), Rev. Cu Minh Duong; Deacons James C. Burns; Truat Van Nguyen.
Res.: 1131 Dauphin Island Pkwy., 36605. Tel: 251-479-7360.

15—MOST PURE HEART OF MARY (1899), (African American), Rev. Stephen Brett, S.S.J.; Deacon James D. Bryant.
Residence & Mailing Address: 304 Sengstak St., 36603. Tel: 251-432-3344; Fax: 251-432-1192.
School—Most Pure Heart of Mary, Tel: 251-432-5270; Fax: 251-432-5271. Sr. Nancy Crossen, O.S.F., Prin.
Catechesis/Religious Program—Students 28.
Convent—310 Sengstak St., 36603. Tel: 251-433-6519.

16—OUR LADY OF LOURDES (1949), Rev. Francis V. Cusack; Deacons Gordon Kenny; Raymond Vrazel.
Res.: 1621 Boykin Blvd., 36605. Tel: 251-479-9885; Fax: 251-479-9892.
School—Tel: 251-479-4007; 251-479-2367; Fax: 251-479-7977. Mrs. Martha Mundine, Prin. Lay Teachers 13; Students 117.
Catechesis/Religious Program—Students 50.

17—OUR SAVIOR (1977), Rev. Louis Russell Biven; Deacon Stephen R. Seymour.
Office:—1801 Cody Rd. S., 36695. Tel: 251-633-6762; Fax: 251-633-7790.
Catechesis/Religious Program—Students 146.

18—ST. PIUS X (1954), Revs. Matthew O'Connor; Michael Dennis Irwin; Deacon William L. Tew.
Res.: 217 S. Sage Ave., 36606. Tel: 251-471-2449; Fax: 251-471-2441.
School—Tel: 251-473-5004; Fax: 251-473-5008. Mrs. Lauren Alvarez, Prin. Sisters 1; Lay Teachers 27;

Students 398.
Catechesis/Religious Program—Tel: 251-473-4381. Students 31.
19—PRINCE OF PEACE (1970), (African American), Rev. Jeremiah D. Brady, S.S.J.
Res.: 454 Charleston St., 36603. Tel: 251-432-2364; Fax: 251-432-2372.
Catechesis/Religious Program—Tel: 251-433-1494. Students 15.

OUTSIDE THE CITY OF MOBILE

ANDALUSIA, COVINGTON CO., CHRIST THE KING (1933), Rev. John L. Holleman, Admin.
Res.: 504 Sanford Rd., P.O. Drawer 1546, 36420. Tel: 334-222-4808; Fax: 334-222-4808.
Catechesis/Religious Program—Students 38.

ATMORE, ESCAMBIA CO., ST. ROBERT BELLARMINE (1943), Rev. Jan Zagorski.
Res.: 600 S. Main St., 36502-2825. Tel: 251-368-3615; Fax: 251-368-3615.
Catechesis/Religious Program—Students 15.

AUBURN, LEE CO., ST. MICHAEL (1965), Revs. J. Francis Sofie Jr.; Todd Kreitinger, Campus Min.; Deacon John Read Haughery.
Res.: 302 E. Magnolia Ave., 36830. Tel: 334-887-5540; 334-887-5573; Fax: 334-887-5572.
Catechesis/Religious Program—Students 252.
Joyland Child Development Center—Tel: 334-821-7624; Fax: 334-821-5583.
Chaplaincy—Tel: 334-887-5380. Auburn University, Auburn University Chapel, Catholic Student's Association.

BAY MINETTE, BALDWIN CO., ST. AGATHA CHURCH (1951), Rev. James E. Dane.
Church: 1001 Hand Ave., 36507. Tel: 251-937-2026; 251-580-3194 (Res.).
Mission—St. John Bromley, AL, Baldwin Co.

BAYOU LABATRE, MOBILE CO., ST. MARGARET (1880), [CEM] Revs. Timothy Evans; John Trung Nguyen.
Res.: P.O. Box 365, 36509. Tel: 251-824-2415; Fax: 251-824-4114.
Catechesis/Religious Program—Students 100.

BELLE FONTAINE, MOBILE CO., ST. PHILIP NERI (1908), Rev. Fergus J. Prendergast, Admin.; Deacon James L. Scott.
Res.: 9101 Dauphin Island Pkwy., 36582. Tel: 251-973-2096.
Catechesis/Religious Program—Students 48.

BREWTON, ESCAMBIA CO., ST. MAURICE (1948), Rev. Adrian L. Cook.
Res.: 202 E. Jackson St., P.O. Box 206, 36427-0206. Tel: 251-867-5189.

BUTLER, CHOCTAW CO., ST. JOHN THE EVANGELIST (1958), Rev. Austin Conry.
Res.: 401 E. Pushmataha St., P.O. Box 456, 36904. Tel: 205-459-3129.
Mission—St. Paul Chatom, 36518. P.O. Box 456, Washington Co. 36904.

CAMDEN, WILCOX CO., ST. JOSEPH, Rev. Patrick Madden, Admin.
Res.: 490 Whiskey Run Rd., 36767.
Mission—Mission of Annunciation Parish P.O. Box 883, Monroeville, Dallas Co. 36461. Tel: 251-575-2644.

CHASTANG, MOBILE CO., ST. PETER THE APOSTLE (1860), [CEM] Rev. Andrew Toyinbo, M.S.P.
Mailing Address: P.O. Box 456, Mount Vernon, 36560. Tel: 251-829-5134; Fax: 251-829-6874.
Catechesis/Religious Program—Students 30.
Mission—Our Lady of Sorrows Fairford, Washington Co.

CHICKASAW, MOBILE CO., ST. THOMAS THE APOSTLE (1947), Rev. John Lynes; Sr. Anne Matisek, C.S.A., Pastoral Assoc.; Deacon Tony LePiane.
Res.: 251 N. Craft Hwy., P.O. Box 11061, 36611. Tel: 251-456-7931; Fax: 251-452-9837.
Parish Center—253 N. Craft Hwy., 36611. Tel: 251-452-9837.

CITRONELLE, MOBILE CO., ST. THOMAS (1913), Rev. John Coghlan.
Res.: 8025 State St., P.O. Box 61, 36522. Tel: 251-866-7505.
Mission—St. Theresa West Mount Vernon, Mobile Co. Tel: 251-829-6900.

DAPHNE, BALDWIN CO.
1—CHRIST THE KING (1896), [CEM] Rev. Msgr. Timothy Deasy; Rev. James F. Carlsen; Deacons Malcolm Zellner; Walter Crimmins; Holcombe Pryor; Sr. Joan O'Donovan, Pastoral Assoc.
Res.: 715 College Ave., P.O. Box 549, 36526. Tel: 251-626-2343; 251-626-3740; Fax: 251-621-1640.
School—Tel: 251-626-1692; Fax: 251-626-9976. Sr. Maureen Nolan, Prin. Presentation Sisters 2; Lay Teachers 30; Students 500.
Catechesis/Religious Program—Tel: 251-626-5963. Students 340.
Convent—1500 Main St., P.O. Box 901, 36526. Tel: 251-626-2431. Presentation Sisters 3.
2—SHRINE OF THE HOLY CROSS (1950), Rev. John J. Stryjewski.
Res.: 612 Main St., 36526. Tel: 251-621-0012; Fax: 251-621-0012.

DAUPHIN ISLAND, MOBILE CO., ST. EDMUND-BY-THE-SEA, [CEM] Rev. William N. Gorman. In Res., Rev. Louis Suffredini.
Res.: P.O. Box 6, 36528. Tel: 251-861-2352.
Church: Cadillac Ave..

DOTHAN, HOUSTON CO., ST. COLUMBA (1943), Very Rev. Patrick J. Gallagher; Revs. Erik T.A. Walters; David Becherer, Hispanic Min.; Deacons W. Harold Grant; Rick Risher.
Res.: 2700 W. Main St., 36301. Tel: 334-793-5802; Fax: 334-792-2816.
Catechesis/Religious Program—Tel: 334-792-3065. Students 297.

ELBERTA, BALDWIN CO., ST. BARTHOLOMEW (1911), (German), [CEM] Rev. Howard R. Moussier, O.S.B.; Deacon Kenneth J. Kaiser Sr.
Res.: P.O. Drawer 280, 36530. Tel: 251-986-8142; Fax: 251-987-5251.
School—St. Benedict's, Tel: 251-986-8143; Fax: 251-986-8144. Mrs. Claudia Adam, Prin. Lay Teachers 15; Students 230; Aides 4.
Catechesis/Religious Program—Students 50.

ENTERPRISE, COFFEE CO., ST. JOHN (1959), Rev. Joseph S. Wadas; Deacons Gary Rasponi; Karl Lukas.
Church: 123 Heath St. P.O. Box 311066, 36331-1066. Tel: 334-347-6751.
Res.: 614 Alberta, 36331. Tel: 334-347-7345.
Catechesis/Religious Program—Students 210.
Mission—St. Mary 100 S. Commerce, Geneva, Geneva Co. 36340.

EUFAULA, BARBOUR CO., HOLY REDEEMER (1859), Rev. David M. Shoemaker.
Res.: 515 W. Broad St., 36027. Tel: 334-687-3716; Fax: 334-687-3766.
Catechesis/Religious Program—Students 19.
Mission—St. Pius X 308 Kennon St., Union Springs, Bullock Co. 36089.
Mission—Bullock County Correctional Facility P.O. Box 5107, Union Springs, Bullock Co. 36089. Tel: 334-738-5625.
Mission—Ventress Correctional Facility P.O. Box 769, Clayton, Barbour Co. 36016. Tel: 334-775-3331.

FAIRHOPE, BALDWIN CO., ST. LAWRENCE (1961), Revs. Gordon Milsted; Johnny Savoie; Deacon George W. Yeend Jr.
Res.: 370 S. Section St., 36532. Tel: 251-928-5931; Fax: 251-928-5938.
Catechesis/Religious Program—Students 225.
Chapel—Battles Wharf, Baldwin Co., Sacred Heart

FOLEY, BALDWIN CO., ST. MARGARET QUEEN OF SCOTLAND (1951), [CEM] Rev. Msgr. Michael D. Kelly; Rev. Paul G. Zoghby; Deacons William Scarboro Jr.; Christopher Surek.
Res.: 601 W. Laurel Ave., 36535. Tel: 251-943-4009; 251-943-3528 (Rectory); Fax: 251-943-4010.

GRAND BAY, MOBILE CO., ST. JOHN BAPTIST (1924), Rev. Msgr. Hugh Maguire.
Res.: P.O. Box 417, 36541. Tel: 251-865-6902; Fax: 251-865-1412.
Church: 12450 Hwy. 188, 36541.

GREENVILLE, BUTLER CO., ST. ELIZABETH (1894), Rev. Gary G. Williams, Admin.
Res.: 407 E. Walnut St., 36037. Tel: 334-382-6203.

GROVE HILL, CLARKE CO., SACRED HEART (1944), Rev. James Havens. In Res., Rev. Francis Messing.
Res.: Hwy. 43 N., P.O. Box 70, 36451. Tel: 251-275-3665.
Mission—Visitation 135 W. Clinton St., Jackson, Clarke Co. 36545.
Mission—St. Joseph W. Front St., Thomasville, Clarke Co. 36784.

GULF SHORES, BALDWIN CO., OUR LADY OF THE GULF (1952), Rev. Robert W. Fulton.
Res.: 308 E. 22nd Ave., P.O. Box 515, 36547-0515. Tel: 251-968-7062.
Catechesis/Religious Program—322 Magnolia Dr.. Tel: 251-974-5706. Barbara Shamblin, D.R.E. Students 53.

HERON BAY, MOBILE CO., ST. MICHAEL THE ARCHANGEL (1880), Rev. Timothy Evans.
Mailing Address: 15872 Heron Bay Loop Rd. E., Coden, 36523. Tel: 251-873-4719.

HOLY TRINITY, RUSSELL CO., ST. JOSEPH (1925), Rev. Dennis Berry, S.T. In Res., Bro. David Sommer, S.T.
Church: 1444 Hwy. 165, Fort Mitchell, 36856. Tel: 334-855-3148; Fax: 334-855-3115.

LILLIAN, BALDWIN CO., ST. JOSEPH (1941), [JC] Rev. Edward P. Markley, O.S.B.; Deacon Richard M. Sullivan.
Res.: 34290 U.S. Hwy. 98, 36549. Tel: 251-962-2049; Fax: 251-962-3649.

MAGNOLIA SPRINGS, BALDWIN CO., ST. JOHN THE BAPTIST (1881), [CEM] [JC 2] Rev. Msgr. Guido Calleja.
Res.: 10797 St. John's Ln., P.O. Box 206, 36555. Tel: 251-965-7719.
Mission—Our Lady of Bon Secour Bon Secour, Baldwin Co.

MILLBROOK, ELMORE CO., ST. ELIZABETH ANN SETON (1978), Rev. Albert P. Kelly.
Mailing Address: P.O. Box 585, 36054.
Church: 4831 Hwy. 14, 36054-0585. Tel: 334-285-7000.
Res.: 109 Crossgate Dr., Elmore, 36025.
Mission—St. Mark's Wetumpka, Elmore Co.

MON LUIS ISLAND, MOBILE CO., ST. ROSE OF LIMA (1853), [CEM] Rev. Patrick Maher.
Res.: 2951 Durette Ave. (Mon Luis Island), Coden, 36523. Tel: 251-973-2592.

MONROEVILLE, MONROE CO., ANNUNCIATION (1982), Rev. Patrick J. Madden.
Res.: 565 Whetstone St., P.O. Box 883, 36460. Tel: 251-575-2644.
Catechesis/Religious Program—Students 43.
Mission—St. Joseph 490 Whiskey Run Rd., Camden, Wilcox Co. 36767.

MONTGOMERY, MONTGOMERY CO.
1—ST. ANDREW (1910), Rev. Wilbur T. Kissell.
Mailing Address: P.O. Box 241303, 36124.
Res.: 433 Clayton St., 36124. Tel: 334-262-3241.
2—ST. BEDE (1925), Revs. David J. Tokarz; Bieu Van Nguyen; Deacons Charles Gulley; Arnold Brewer; Joseph Phung.
Office—3870 Atlanta Hwy., 36109. Tel: 334-272-3463; Fax: 334-272-3492.
School—3850 Atlanta Hwy., 36109. Tel: 334-272-3033; Fax: 334-272-9394. Mrs. Eleanor McCormack, Prin. Lay Teachers 28; Students 428.
Catechesis/Religious Program—Students 138.
Child's Development Center—, Formerly Children's Center, 3840 Atlanta Hwy., 36109. Tel: 334-277-8551; Fax: 334-213-2347.
3—CHURCH OF THE HOLY SPIRIT (1977), Rev. Msgr. F. Charles Troncale; Rev. Michael William Labadie; Deacon Eugene Wadas.
Res.: 8570 Vaughn Rd., 36117. Tel: 334-277-5631; Fax: 334-272-1008.
Catechesis/Religious Program—Tel: 334-277-1989; Fax: 334-277-2895. Students 313.
4—ST. JOHN THE BAPTIST (1908), Rev. Wilbur Kissell.
Res.: 553 S. Union St., 36104. Tel: 334-264-6274; Fax: 334-262-3012.
5—ST. JUDE (1934), (African American), Rev. James Holden; Deacons Fred J. Briers; Leo McMeans. In Res., Rev. Robert Kieltyka (Retired).
Res.: 2048 W. Fairview Ave., St. Jude, 36108. Tel: 334-265-1390; Fax: 334-265-1399.
High School—Tel: 334-264-5376; Fax: 334-264-6669. Mr. Leon Robinson, Prin. Lay Teachers 17; Students 139.
Catechesis/Religious Program—Students 139.
6—OUR LADY, QUEEN OF MERCY (1954), Revs. James N. Dean; Michael J. Sreboth; Deacon James R. Labadie.
Res.: 4421 Narrow Lane Rd., 36116. Tel: 334-288-2850; Fax: 334-281-7884.
School—Tel: 334-288-5334; Fax: 334-288-5395. Mrs. Mary Kaye McCooey, Prin. Lay Teachers 12; Students 131.
Catechesis/Religious Program—Tel: 334-288-5342. Students 7.
Child Development Center—Tel: 334-613-0340.
7—ST. PETER (1834), [CEM] Revs. Stephen E. Martin; Jose Paillacho, Hispanic Min.
Res.: 219 Adams Ave., P.O. Box 114, 36101. Tel: 334-262-7304; Fax: 334-262-9735.
8—RESURRECTION CATHOLIC CHURCH (1943), Rev. Manuel Williams, C.R. In Res., Rev. Casimir J. Wilczynski, C.R.; Bros. Christopher Trimpe, C.R.; Fred Briers, C.R.; Deacon Clarence L. Mears Jr.
Res.: 2815 Forbes Rd., 36110. Tel: 334-269-1770; Fax: 334-265-8081.
School—Resurrection Catholic School, Tel: 334-265-4615; Fax: 334-265-4568. Rosalyn O. King, Prin. Religious 3; Lay Teachers 16; Students 184.
Mission—Resurrection Catholic Mission 2815 Forbes Rd., Montgomery Co. 36110. Tel: 334-263-4221; Fax: 334-263-4999. Rev. Manuel Williams, C.R., Dir.

MOUNT VERNON, MOBILE CO., ST. CECILIA (1929), [CEM] Rev. Matthew Sindik.
Res.: 1315 Military Rd., P.O. Box 847, 36560. Tel: 251-829-9531.

OPELIKA, LEE CO., ST. MARY OF THE MISSION (1910), Rev. John E. Kane, C.M.; Deacon Donald Canonica.
Res.: 1000 4th Ave., 36801. Tel: 334-749-8359; Fax: 334-749-6312.
Catechesis/Religious Program—Tel: 334-745-3432. Students 34.

ORANGE BEACH, BALDWIN CO., ST. THOMAS BY THE SEA (1991), Rev. Mark I. Neske; Deacon Henry Pouliot.
Mailing Address: P.O. Box 1190, 36561. Tel: 251-981-8132; Fax: 251-981-1981.

ORRVILLE, DALLAS CO., IMMACULATE CONCEPTION, Rev. Carroll W. Plourde, S.S.E.
Church: 13663 Alabama Hwy. 22 W., 36767.
Res.: 309 Washington St., Selma, 36703. Tel: 334-874-8931; Fax: 334-874-8976.

OZARK, DALE CO., ST. JOHN (1963), [JC] Rev. Charles J. McCabe; Deacon John Ross Jr.

Res.: 475 Camilla Ave., P.O. Box 1008, 36361-1008. Tel: 334-774-6826; Fax: 334-774-8675.
Catechesis/Religious Program—Students 28.

PHENIX CITY, RUSSELL CO.

1—MOTHER MARY PARISH (1940), Rev. Thomas D. Weise, Admin.
Res.: 318 Seale Rd., 36869. Tel: 334-298-9025; Fax: 334-298-9233.
School—Tel: 334-298-6371; Fax: 334-298-7934. Sr. M. Cecelia Harrison, F.M.S., Prin. Sisters 2; Lay Teachers 12; Students 160.
Catechesis/Religious Program—Students 46.
Convent—Franciscan Missionary Sisters of Our Lady of Perpetual Help of Jamaica, Tel: 334-291-0122. Franciscan Missionaries Sisters 2.

2—ST. PATRICK (1911), Rev. Thomas D. Weise.
Res.: 1502 Broad St., P.O. Box 147, 36868-0147. Tel: 334-298-9025; Fax: 334-298-9233.
School—3910 Lakewood Dr., P.O. Box 1614, 36868. Tel: 334-298-3408; Fax: 334-298-3352. Mrs. Ginger Morris, Prin. Lay Teachers 11; Students 84; Aides 3.
Catechesis/Religious Program—Students 110.
Convent—St. Patrick's Missionary Cenacle, 2701 40th St., 36867. Tel: 334-298-0708. Missionary Servants of the Most Blessed Trinity 3.

PLATEAU, MOBILE CO., OUR MOTHER OF MERCY (1926), (African American), Rev. Anietie Akama Ukanide, M.S.P. (Nigeria).
Mailing Address: P.O. Box 10306, Prichard, 36610. Tel: 251-473-4975; Fax: 251-473-4940.
Res.: 805 East St., 36610.

PRATTVILLE, AUTAUGA CO., ST. JOSEPH CHURCH (1963), Rev. Philip McKenna; Deacons Samuel Shippen; Mario Quintero.
Res.: 511 N. Memorial Dr., 36067-2133. Tel: 334-365-8680; Fax: 334-365-2267.
Catechesis/Religious Program—Students 347.

PRICHARD, MOBILE CO.

1—ST. JAMES MAJOR (1925), (African American), Rev. Henry E. Dickson, S.S.J.
Res.: 714 S. College St., 36610. Tel: 251-456-6842; Fax: 251-456-6843.
School—Tel: 251-452-1883. Mrs. Louise West, Prin. Lay Teachers 9; Students 131.
Catechesis/Religious Program—Students 73.
Convent—927 W. Prichard Ave., 36610. Tel: 251-457-9396.

2—OUR LADY OF FATIMA (1949), Closed. For inquiries for parish records contact the chancery.

ROBERTSDALE, BALDWIN CO., ST. PATRICK (1974), Rev. Msgr. William R. James.
Res.: P.O. Box 1367, 36567. Tel: 251-947-5054; Fax: 251-947-3860.
School—(Grades K-8), P.O. Drawer 609, 36567. Tel: 251-947-7395. Sr. Margaret Harte, P.B.V.M., Prin. Presentation Sisters 1; Lay Teachers 13; Students 194.
Catechesis/Religious Program—Students 55.
Convent—P.O. Box 609, 36567. Tel: 251-947-7396; Fax: 251-947-3860.

SELMA, DALLAS CO., OUR LADY QUEEN OF PEACE (1850), Rev. Carroll W. Plourde, S.S.E.
Office—309 Washington St., 36703. Tel: 334-874-8931 (Office & Res.); Fax: 334-874-8976.
Res.: 2511 Summer Field Rd., 36701. Tel: 334-874-8475.
Catechesis/Religious Program—Students 48.

SEMMES, MOBILE CO., HOLY NAME OF JESUS (1977), Rev. Msgr. John Aherne, V.G.; Deacons Frank Lee; Joseph Gottstine.
Res.: 2275 Snow Rd., P.O. Box 557, 36575. Tel: 251-649-4794.
Catechesis/Religious Program—Students 77.

TALLASSEE, ELMORE CO., ST. VINCENT DE PAUL (1955), [JC] Rev. Francis A. Lynch, C.M.; Deacon Frank May.
Res.: 620 Gilmer Ave., P.O. Box 780487, 36078-0487. Tel: 334-283-2169; Fax: 334-283-8500.

TILLMAN'S CORNER, MOBILE CO., ST. VINCENT DE PAUL (1971), Rev. James Cink; Deacon Robert Nouwen.
Res.: 5023 Camelot Dr., 36619. Tel: 251-661-3908; Fax: 251-665-4956.
School—Tel: 251-666-8022; Fax: 251-666-8022. Amy Heim, Prin. Lay Teachers 10; Students 127.
Catechesis/Religious Program—Tel: 251-661-3908. Students 40.

TROY, PIKE CO., ST. MARTIN OF TOURS (1915), Rev. Cecil R. Spotswood.
Res.: 725 Elba Hwy., 36079. Tel: 334-566-2630.
Catechesis/Religious Program—Students 51.

TUSKEGEE INSTITUTE, MACON CO., ST. JOSEPH (1940), Deacon Stanley Maxwell, Admin.
Res.: 2007 Montgomery Rd., 36088. Tel: 334-727-2710.
School—(Grades K-8), 2009 Montgomery Rd., 36088. Tel: 334-727-0620; 334-727-0642. Sr. Geraldine O'Meara, O.P., Prin. Sinsinawa Dominicans 2; Lay Teachers 8; Students 100.

WHISTLER, MOBILE CO., ST. BRIDGET (1864), Rev. Leo Blanchet.
Res.: 3625 W. Main St., P.O. Box 13357, 36613. Tel: 251-457-6847.

Chaplains of Public Institutions

CLAYTON. *Ventress Correctional Institution*. Rev. David M. Shoemaker.
515 W. Broad St., Eufaula, 36027. Tel: 334-687-3716; Fax: 334-687-3766.

UNION SPRINGS. *Bullock County Correctional Facility*. Rev. David M. Shoemaker.
515 W. Broad St., Eufaula, 36027. Tel: 334-687-3716; Fax: 334-687-3766.

On Leave from the Archdiocese:
Rev. Msgr.—
Amos, John R.
Revs.—
Dalton, Peadar
Fields, William
Harbour, Linn S.
Lemming, Patrick W.
Lott, Lawrence M.
McGuiness, David
Miley, Eamon
Nicholson, Patrick
Phan, Vincent Huo
Reskey, George A.
Robinson, Jerome
Smith, Edward E.
Staff, Stephen M.
Tipton, Paul S.
Trosch, David

Absent on Sick Leave:
Rev. Msgr.—
Kelly, Michael D.

On Administrative Leave:
Rev.—
Schrenger, Arthur C.

Retired:
Rev. Msgrs.—
Aucoin, Charles
Cullen, Thomas J.
Jennings, Joseph
McGuinness, Michael
Murphy, Francis
Shields, Maurice L.
Revs.—
Becherer, David
Desmond, Barry
Dorrill, James F., Ph.D.
Folsom, William P., Jr.
Hay, Theodore H., S.T.L.
Keller, Brendan
Kieltyka, Robert
Robinson, John C.
Stauter, Andrew
Suffredini, Louis

Permanent Deacons:
Brewer, Arnold L.
Briers, Fred J.
Bryant, James D.
Burns, James C.
Canonica, Donald A.
Connick, Edward G.
Connick, Joseph V., III
Crimmins, Walter J., Jr.
Diaz-Rivera, Alfonso
Dolan, William R.
Fontana, Charles J.
Gottstine, Joseph G.
Grant, Harold
Gulley, Charles
Hamilton, John B., On Leave
Hathorne, Ronnie A., Sr.
Haughery, John Read
Johns, Marvin C.
Johnson, Ernest
Kaiser, Kenneth J., Sr.
Kelly, Patrick
Kenny, Charles H.
Kenny, Gordon
King, A. B., On Leave
Kirby, Robert E., Jr.
Labadie, James
LePiane, Tony
Lee, Frank A.
Lopez, Abraham
Lukas, Karl L.
Maxwell, Stanley B.
May, Frank J.
McGonagle, Joseph P.
McMeans, Leo
Mears, Clarence L., Jr.
Moore, Alexander
Nguyen, Truat Van
Nouwen, Robert
O'Brien, Henry F.
Phung, Joseph H.
Pouliot, Henry
Pry, Jackie T., (Retired)
Pryor, William Holcombe
Quintero, Mario
Rasponi, Gary A.
Risher, Rick
Robbins, Arthur
Ross, John
Scarboro, William, Jr.
Scott, James L.
Seymour, Stephen R.
Sheldon, Paul
Shippen, Samuel
Sullivan, Richard M.
Surek, Christopher
Tew, William L.
Vrazel, Raymond
Wadas, Eugene
Yeend, George W., Jr.
Zellner, Malcolm

INSTITUTIONS LOCATED IN THE ARCHDIOCESE

[A] COLLEGES AND UNIVERSITIES

MOBILE. *Spring Hill College* (1830), 4000 Dauphin St., 36608. Tel: 251-380-4000; Fax: 251-460-2195. Web: www.shc.edu. Revs. Stephen Campbell, S.J., Rector; Gregory Lucey, S.J., Pres.; Frederick W. Gunti (LR); David Borbridge, S.J.; Gerald T. Regan, S.J. (Wisconsin); Gerald T. Hughes, S.J.; Robert B. Rimes, S.J.; Michael A. Williams, S.J. (Maryland); Christopher J. Viscardi, S.J.; Bro. Ferrell Blank. Priests of Faculty 5; Brothers 1; Lay Teachers 61; Students 1,735.

[B] HIGH SCHOOLS, ARCHDIOCESAN

MOBILE. *McGill-Toolen Catholic High School*, 1501 Old Shell Rd., 36604. Tel: 251-432-0784; Fax: 251-433-8356. Email: shieldsb@mcgill.pvt.k12.al.us. Web: www.mcgill.pvt.k12.al.us. Revs. W. Bry Shields, Pres.; Steven T. Williams, Chap. Priests 2; Brothers of the Sacred Heart 3; Sisters of Loretto 1; Lay Teachers 88; Students 1,059.

MONTGOMERY. *St. Jude Educational Institute*, 2048 W. Fairview Ave., 36108. Tel: 334-264-5376; Fax: 334-264-6669. Email: lrobiinson@yahoo.com. Web: www.saintjudeschool.com. Leon Robinson, Prin. Lay Teachers 17; Students 143.

Montgomery Catholic Preparatory School, 5350 Vaughn Rd., 36116. Tel: 334-272-7220; Fax: 334-272-2440. Email: F_Weber@knights.pvt.k12.al.us. Web: www.knights.pvt.k12.al.us. Mr. Faustin N. Weber, Pres. Priests 3; Lay Teachers 58; Total Enrollment 820.

Our Lady Queen of Mercy Campus (Grades K-6), 4437 Narrow Lane Rd., 36116. Tel: 334-288-5334; Fax: 334-288-5395. Mrs. Mary Kaye McCooey, Prin. Teachers 12; Students 131.

St. Bede Campus (Grades K-6), 3850 Atlanta Hwy., 36109. Tel: 334-272-3033; Fax: 334-272-9394. Mrs. Eleanor McCormack, Prin. Teachers 28; Students 428.

High School Campus (Grades 9-12) Email: d-jones@knights.pvt.k12.al.us. Mr. Douglas E. Jones, Prin. Teachers 18; Students 261.

Middle School Campus (Grades 7-8), 5350 Vaughn Rd., 36116. Tel: 334-272-7220; Fax: 334-272-2440.

[C] CHILDREN'S HOMES

MOBILE. *St. Mary's Home*, 4350 Moffat Rd., 36618. Tel: 251-344-7733. Mr. Phillip A. Wynne, Admin. Dependent Children 48.

[D] GENERAL HOSPITALS

MOBILE. *Providence Foundation*, 6701 Airport Blvd., B. 227, P.O. Box 850429, 36608. Tel: 251-639-2050; Fax: 251-639-2052. Beth McFadden Rouse, Chm. of the Bd.; Lawrence J. McKinney, Vice Chm.; Caroline Brown Vella, Sec.; John L. McCarron, Treas. Patients Assisted Annually 172,769; Total Staff 1,901; Nurses 535; Bed Capacity 349.

Providence Healthcare Services, 6801 Airport Blvd., P.O. Box 850429, 36685. Tel: 251-633-1000; Fax: 251-633-1679. Mr. Clark P. Christianson, Pres., CEO & Chm. Patients Assisted Annually 172,769; Nurses 535; Total Staff 1,901.

Providence Hospital, 6801 Airport Blvd., P.O. Box 850429, 36608. Tel: 251-633-1000; Fax: 251-633-1679. Web: www.providencehospital.org. Mr. Clark P. Christianson, Pres. & CEO; Sr. Mary Frances Loftin, D.C., Chm.; Rev. Leo Weishaar, Chap. Daughters of Charity of St. Vincent de Paul 10; Bed Capacity 349; Patients Assisted Annually

172,769; Nurses 535; Total Staff 1,901.

Seton Health Corp. of South Alabama, 6801 Airport Blvd., P.O. Box 850429, 36608. Tel: 251-633-1660; Fax: 251-633-1679. Web: providencehospital.org. Mr. Clark P. Christianson, Pres., CEO & Chm.; Sr. Elise Boudreaux, D.C., Sec. Patients Assisted Annually 172,769; Nurses 535; Total Staff 1,901.

Seton Medical Management, Inc., 6701 Airport Blvd., Suite D-439, 36608. Tel: 251-639-2660; Fax: 251-639-2664. Mr. Clark P. Christianson, Chm.; Dr. James L. Walker, Pres. & Vice Chair; Vince N. Formica, Sec. & Treas. Patients Assisted Annually 172,769; Nurses 535; Total Staff 1,901; Bed Capacity 349.

[E] SPECIAL HOSPITALS, SCHOOLS AND HOMES FOR THE AGED

MOBILE. *Allen Memorial Home Skilled Nursing Facility*, 735 S. Washington Ave., 36603. Tel: 251-433-2642; Fax: 251-431-6044. Email: allenmhome@aol.com. Cheryl Robinson, Admin. Bed Capacity 119; Patients Assisted Annually 154; Total Staff 130.

Little Sisters of the Poor, Home For the Aged, Inc., Sacred Heart Residence, 1655 McGill Ave., 36604. Tel: 251-476-6335; Fax: 251-478-6519. Sr. Marcel Joseph McCanless, Supr.; Rev. Michael Finbar Desmond; Rev. Msgr. Michael D. Kelly. Sisters 10; Residents 84.

DAPHNE. *Mercy Medical*, P.O. Box 1090, 36526. Tel: 251-626-2694; Fax: 251-626-0315. Email: theresam@sa-mercymedical.org. Web: www.mercymedical.com. Sr. Mary Eileen Wilhelm, R.S.M., Pres/CEO; Rev. Msgr. Maurice L. Shields, Chap. (Retired). A Corporation.; Acute Rehabilitation Hospital, Hospice, Home Health, Long Term Care, Skilled Nursing Facility, Alzheimer's Care.

Carroll Place Tel: 251-928-5555; Fax: 251-990-2620. (Assisted living community.)

Catherine Place Tel: 251-626-9000; Fax: 251-626-7981. (Assisted living community.)

The Hamlet Tel: 251-928-5413; Fax: 251-990-8427. (Life care retirement community.)

McAuley Place Tel: 251-344-3866; Fax: 251-304-3035. (Assisted living community.)

Portier Place Tel: 251-343-4449; Fax: 251-304-3143. (Life care retirement community.) Sisters of Mercy 5; Professional Nurses 169; Bed Capacity 162; Patients/Residents assisted annually 4,800; Residential Care Units 260.

MARBURY. *Resurrection Catholic Nursing Home* Skilled Nursing Facility. , 165 County Rd. 20 E., P.O. Box 89, 36051-0089. Tel: 334-775-1139; Fax: 334-755-1461. Rev. Manuel Williams, C.R., Dir. Registered Nurses 4; Licensed Practical Nurses 10; Bed Capacity 65; In-Patients 61.

MONTGOMERY. *St. Bede Child Development Center*, 3840 Atlanta Hwy., 36109. Tel: 334-277-8551; Fax: 334-213-2347. Email: ahanks@school.stbede.org. Alisha Hanks, Dir. Total Students 125; Total Staff 25.

City of St. Jude, Inc., The, 2048 W. Fairview Ave., 36108. Tel: 334-265-6791; Fax: 334-269-1988. Rev. James T. Holden, Dir.; Mr. Michael G. McCormack, Exec. Dir.

Father Purcell Memorial Exceptional Children's Center Tel: 334-834-5590; Fax: 334-834-5592. Patients Assisted Annually 58; Total Staff 117.

St. Jude Administration Building Tel: 334-265-6791; Fax: 334-269-1988.

St. Jude Church and Rectory: Tel: 334-265-1390; Fax: 334-265-1399.

St. Jude Educational Institute Tel: 334-263-6121 (Mid.); 334-264-5376 (H.S.); Fax: 334-265-8847 (Mid.); 334-264-6669 (H.S.). Students 139; Staff 28.

St. Jude Head Start Tel: 334-262-6197. Students 65; Staff 10.

St. Jude Social Services Center Tel: 334-269-1983; Fax: 334-269-1988. Persons assisted annually 13,809; Staff 3.

Vincentian Sisters' Convent Tel: 334-269-5933.

The Old Convent Tel: 334-263-0129.

Central Alabama Laubach Literacy Tel: 334-264-1239; Fax: 334-264-1239 (call before faxing). Students 250; Staff 5.

St. Jude Apartments Tel: 334-265-8356; Fax: 334-265-1908. Units 96; Staff 4.

City of Jude Administration, Maintenance and Appeals Total Staff 10.

Father Purcell Memorial Exceptional Children Center, 2048 W. Fairview Ave., 36108. Tel: 334-834-5590; Fax: 334-834-5592. Web: www.mnw.net/fpm. Mr. Sam Palomaria, Admin. Bed Capacity 58; Patients Assisted Annually 58.

Father Walter Memorial Center for Handicapped Children, 2815 Forbes Dr., 36199. Tel: 334-262-6421; Fax: 334-262-2265. Rev. Manuel Williams, C.R., Dir.; Mrs. Betty A. Thomas, Admin.; Kim K. Johnson, Asst. Admin. A skilled nursing facility for the mentally and physically handicapped child. Operated by The Resurrection Catholic Missions. R.N. 8; L.P.N. 13; Bed Capacity 54; Patients Assisted Annually 54; Total Staff 82.

Resurrection Early Childhood Center, 2815 Forbes Dr., 36110. Tel: 334-265-4615; Fax: 334-265-4568. Sr. Rita Washington, S.F.C.C., Prin. Licensed by Alabama State Dept. of Human Resources for 45 Students, Ages 2 1/2 to 5 years.

[F] HOUSING FOR THE ELDERLY

MOBILE. *Cathedral Place*, 351 Conti St., 36602. Tel: 251-434-1590; Fax: 251-434-1562. Email: marie.dismukes@royalmgmt.com. Web: www.royalmgmt.com. Marie Dismukes, Acting Mgr.; Jimmie Fay Roberts, Leasing Agt. Residents 157; Total Staff 8.

MONTGOMERY. *Seton Haven*, 3721 Wares Ferry Rd., 36109. Tel: 334-272-4000; Fax: 334-272-1788. Email: sh36109@aol.com. Sr. A. Ann Alosi, Admin. Residents 106; Total Staff 14.

[G] MONASTERIES AND RESIDENCES OF PRIESTS AND BROTHERS

MOBILE. *Brothers of the Sacred Heart*, 60 N. Catherine St., 36604. Tel: 251-438-3812. Email: leebarkersc@hotmail.com. Bros. Lee Barker, S.C., Dir.; Celestine Algero, S.C., Sub. Dir.; Paul Mulligan, S.C.; John Moore, S.C.; Malcolm Melcher. Brothers 5.

SELMA. *Edmundite Fathers*, Edmundite Missions House, 1401 Broad St., 36701. Tel: 334-872-6221; Fax: 334-872-8123. Email: RogerLac@aol.com. Web: www.edmunditemissions.com. Revs. Carroll W. Plourde, S.S.E., Supr.; Roger J. LaCharite, S.S.E., Missions Dir.; Francis A. Donnellan, S.S.E.; Robert J. Sheehey, S.S.E.; Maurice F. Ouellet, S.S.E. (VEN); James F. Ryan, S.S.E.; Paul I. Plouffe, S.S.E.; Bros. Peter J. Stanfield, S.S.E., Prog. Dir.; Francis J. Hagerty, S.S.E.

Legal Title: *Fathers of St. Edmund Southern Missions, Inc.* Priests 7; Brothers 2; Total Assisted 133,188; Total Staff 60.

[H] CONVENTS AND RESIDENCES OF SISTERS

MOBILE. *Blessed Trinity Missionary Cenacle*, 604 Barksdale Dr. W., 36606. Tel: 251-476-4803. Missionary Servants 5.

Convent of the Sisters of Mercy of the Americas Baltimore Regional Community, 101 Wimbledon Dr. W., 36608. Tel: 251-344-1377; Fax: 251-344-1617. Email: coberkirch@aol.com. Web: www.mercysistersbalt.com. Sr. Carolyn Oberkirch, R.S.M., Admin. Sisters 24; Total Staff 11.

Other Residences:

4301 Bit & Spur Rd., 36608. Tel: 251-343-3674.

606 Bay Bluff East, Daphne, 36526. Tel: 251-626-0130.

2902 Brierwood Dr., 36606. Tel: 251-476-4605.

172 N. Lafayette St., 36604. Tel: 251-432-3178.

Portier Place, 4363 Old Shell Rd., 36608. Tel: 251-304-3150; Fax: 251-304-3143. Sisters Marilyn Graf, Admin.; Ruth Handren, Asst. Admin.

Huntleigh Woods, Apt. N-205, 375 Hillcrest Rd., 36608. Tel: 251-344-9388.

3700 Whispering Pines, Apt. 47C, 36608-1149. Tel: 251-343-4435.

Convent of the Sisters of St. Agnes, 1701 Dublin St., 36605. Tel: 251-478-3292; Fax: 251-434-1509. Email: smitscsa@aol.com. Web: www.csasisters.org. Sisters 4.

Monastery of Discalced Carmelite Nuns, 716 Dauphin Island Pkwy., 36606. Sr. Marie Therese, O.C.D., Prioress. Solemnly Professed 4.

Sisters of Loretto, 1408 Old Shell Rd., 36604-2244. Tel: 251-431-6735; Fax: 251-690-9367. Email: ardoyns@mcgill.pvt.k12.al.us. Sr. Sandra Ardoyno, S.L.

Visitation Monastery and Retreat House, 2300 Spring Hill Ave., 36607. Tel: 251-473-2321; Fax: 251-476-9761. Web: visitationmonasterymobile.org. Sr. Jane de Chantal Word, Supr. Sisters 6; Total Staff 3.

ALBERTA. *Alberta Health Center*, P.O. Box 97, 36720. Tel: 334-573-2493.

CAMDEN. *Sisters of St. Joseph*, 490 Whiskey Run Rd., 36726. Tel: 334-682-4144. Email: roseannecook@yahoo.com.

HOLY TRINITY. *Blessed Trinity Shrine Retreat and Cenacle*, 107 Holy Trinity Rd., 36859. Tel: 334-855-4474; Fax: 334-855-4525. Email: btsr107@juno.com. Sisters Theresa Mary Finan, M.S.B.T., Co-Dir.; Geraldine Whelan, M.S.B.T., Co-Dir. Missionary Servants of the Most Blessed Trinity 6; Retreat House Capacity 40.

MARBURY. *Dominican Monastery of St. Jude (St. Jude Monastery)*, P.O. Box 170, 36051. Tel: 205-755-1322; Fax: 205-755-9847. Email: stjudemonastery@juno.com. Web: www.opsouth.org/marburynuns. Sr. Mary Joseph, O.P., Prioress. Cloistered Dominican Nuns of Perpetual Adoration and Rosary Professed Sisters 7; Postulants 1.

MONTGOMERY. *Mater Dei Missionary Cenacle*, 784 Spring Valley Rd., 36116. Tel: 334-288-4544; Fax: 334-288-9322. Email: nagle@cssalabama.org. Web: cssalabama.org. Missionary Servants of the Most Blessed Trinity 3.

OZARK. *Sinsinawa Dominican Sisters*, 375 County Rd. 404, 36360. Tel: 334-299-6671; Fax: 334-299-0171. Email: psmithop@charter.net. Sr. Penny Smith, O.P.

PHENIX CITY. *St. Patrick's Missionary Cenacle*, 2701 Fortieth St., 36867. Tel: 334-298-0708. Missionary Servants of the Most Blessed Trinity 4.

PINE APPLE. *Sisters of St. Joseph of Rochester*, 702 County Rd. 59, 36768. Tel: 334-746-2584. Email: ssjpineapple@juno.com. Web: www.ssjvolunteers.org. Sisters 4.

SELMA. *Sisters Residence*, 911 Mabry St., 36701. Tel: 334-874-6536. Email: ellennp@aol.com. Sisters 7.

VREDENBURGH. *Emmanuel Community*, P.O. Box 365, 36481. Tel: 334-337-4484.

[I] ARCHDIOCESAN SOCIAL SERVICES

MOBILE. *Catholic Social Services, Archdiocese of Mobile*, P.O. Box 759, 36601.

400 Government St., 36602. Tel: 251-434-1550; Fax: 251-434-1549. Sr. Frances Louise Sheridan, M.S.B.T., Archdiocesan Dir.; Marilyn Davis King, Dir. Total Assisted 46,102.

Branch Offices:

4455 Narrow Lane Rd., Montgomery, 36116. Tel: 334-288-8890; Fax: 334-288-9322. Susan Meehan, Dir. Total Assisted 5,433.

P.O. Box 870, Robertsdale, 36567. Tel: 251-947-2293; Fax: 251-947-4058. Mrs. Michele Prockup, Dir. Total Assited 7,585.

P.O. Box 1105, Chatom, 36518. Tel: 251-847-2708. Mrs. Joyce Yocum, Dir. Total Assisted 3,732.

P.O. Box 6184, Dothan, 36302. Tel: 334-793-3601. Vickie Alleman, Dir. Total Assisted 5,799.

P.O. Box 85, Jackson, 36545. Tel: 251-246-0131; Fax: 251-246-4414. Shiela Smith, Dir. Total Assisted 2,300.

Refugee Resettlement, 211 S. Catherine St., 36604. Tel: 251-471-1305; Fax: 251-476-5319. Jana Curran, Dir. Total Assisted 1,100.

2-B Crisis Pregnancy Center, 100 S. University Blvd., 36608. Tel: 251-343-4636. Jerry Bodden, Dir. Total Assisted 568.

610 Railroad Ave., Bay Minette, 36507. Tel: 251-937-7858. Buffy Long Marston, Dir. Total Assisted 1,000.

To Be Crisis Pregnancy, 730 S. Section St., P.O. Box 783, Fairhope, 36532. Tel: 251-928-8661. Sonja Brueck, Dir. Total Assisted 100.

Service Center of Catholic Social Services, 555 Dauphin St., 36602. Tel: 251-434-1500; Fax: 251-434-1509. Email: cscadmin@mobilecan.org. Web: www.mobilecan.org. Sr. Judith Smits, C.S.A., Dir. Total Assisted 46,102; Total Staff 26.

CHATOM. *Chatom Office of Catholic Social Services*, P.O. Box 1105, 36518. Tel: 251-847-2708; Fax: 251-847-3788. Joyce Yocum, Supvr. Total Assisted 3,732; Total Staff 2.

DOTHAN. *Dothan Office of Catholic Social Services*, P.O. Box 6184, 36302. Tel: 334-793-3601; Fax: 334-702-0825. Email: vaua@aol.com. Total Assisted 5,799; Total Staff 3.

MONTGOMERY. *Catholic Social Services of Montgomery*, 4455 Narrow Lane Rd., 36116-2953. Tel: 334-288-8890; Fax: 334-288-9322. Email: meehan@cssalabama.org. Web: cssalabama.org. Susan W. Meehan, Dir. Total Assisted 5,433; Total Staff 18.

ROBERTSDALE. *Robertsdale Office of Catholic Social Services*, P.O. Box 870, 36567. Tel: 251-947-2293; Fax: 251-947-4058. Email: cssbald@gulftel.com. Ms. Michele Prockup, Dir. Total Assisted 7,585; Total Staff 8.

[J] NEWMAN CENTERS

MOBILE. *Spring Hill College Campus Ministry* 4000 Dauphin St., 36608-1791. Tel: 251-380-3495; Fax: 251-460-2174. Email: dentac@shc.edu. Web: www.shc.edu. Rev. Stephen Campbell, S.J.

University of South Alabama Newman Center Catholic Student Center, 6051 Old Shell Rd., 36608. Tel: 251-343-3662. Email: usacsc@minsdspring.com. Rev. Alejandro E. Valladares; Salvatore M. Ballacchino, S.T.L., Dir. & Asst. Campus Min.

AUBURN. *Auburn University Newman Center* 302 E. Magnolia Ave., 36830. Tel: 334-887-5380; Fax: 334-887-5572. Web: www.auburn.edu/~stmcso1. Rev. Todd Kreitinger.

DOTHAN. *George C. Wallace Jr. Community College Newman Center* 2700 W. Main St., 36301. Tel:

334-793-5802; Fax: 334-792-2816. Email: saintcolumba@ala.net. Very Rev. Patrick J. Gallagher.

MONROEVILLE. *Alabama Southern Community College Newman Center* P.O. Box 883, 36460-0883. Tel: 251-575-2644. Email: annuneat@frontiernet.net. Rev. Patrick Madden.

MONTGOMERY. *Alabama State University Newman Center* 553 S. Union St., 36104. Tel: 334-264-6274. Rev. Wilbur T. Kissell.

Huntington College Newman Center 4421 Narrow Lane Rd., 36116. Tel: 334-288-2850; Fax: 334-281-7884. Email: fatherdean@olqm.org. Web: www.olqm.org. Rev. James N. Dean.

SELMA. *Marion Institute Newman Center* 309 Washington St., 36703. Tel: 334-874-8931; Fax: 334-874-8976. Rev. Carroll W. Plourde, S.S.E. Students 52.

TROY. *Troy State University Newman Center* 725 Elba Hwy., 36079. Tel: 334-566-2630; Fax: 334-566-2630. Rev. Cecil R. Spotswood.

TUSKEGEE INSTITUTE. *Tuskegee University Newman Center* 2007 Montgomery Rd., 36088. Tel: 334-727-2710. Deacon Stanley B. Maxwell. Total Staff 1.

[K] MISCELLANEOUS LISTINGS

MOBILE. *Apostleship of Prayer*, P.O. Box 1966, 36633. Tel: 251-434-1585. Very Rev. Michael L. Farmer, S.T.L.

Catholic High Schools Alumni Association of Mobile, 1501 Old Shell Rd., 36604. Tel: 251-441-0809; Fax: 251-433-8356. Email: wattsm@mcgill.pvt.k12.al.us. Web: www.mcgill.pvt.k12.al.us. Marian Watts, Alumni Dir.

St. Ignatius Child Care - Mobile, 3953-B Springhill Ave., 36608. Tel: 251-342-3322; Fax: 251-342-3530. Jackie S. Mills, Dir.

L'Arche, 151 S. Ann St., 36604. Tel: 251-438-2094; Fax: 251-438-2094. Email: larchmob@hotmail.com. Web: http://bellsouthpwp.net/l/a/larchmob/. Dennis O'Keefe, Dir. Christian non-profit organization-community where persons with developmental disabilities and non-disabled persons share their lives together in a home. Handicapped People 18; Assistants 12.

Ladies of Charity, P.O. Box 6987, 36630-0987. Tel: 251-661-9448.

**Providence Building Corporation*, P.O. Box 850429, 36685. Tel: 251-633-1600; Fax: 251-633-1679. Web: providencehospital.org. 6801 Airport Blvd., 36608. Tel: 251-633-1000; Fax: 251-633-1679. Sisters Marilyn Moore, D.C., Chm.; Betty Gunselman, D.C., Sec. & Treas.

Society of St. Vincent de Paul, 411 S. Broad St., 36603. Tel: 251-432-5173. Wendy Makin, Pres.

DOTHAN. *St. Columba Preschool*, 2700 W. Main St., 36301. Tel: 334-793-6742; Fax: 334-792-2816. Email: cdstc@alanet.com. Mrs. Cathy Dedmon, Dir.

HURTSBORO. *John XXIII Center*, P.O. Box 117, 36860. Tel: 334-667-7770; Fax: 334-667-0798. Email: blessedjohnXXIIIcenter@earthlink.net. Rev. Dennis Berry, S.T., Admin.

MONTGOMERY. *The City of St. Jude, Inc.*, 2048 W. Fairview Ave., 36108. Tel: 334-265-6791; Fax: 334-269-1988. Rev. James T. Holden, Dir.; Mr. Michael G. McCormack, Exec. Dir.

St. Margaret's Services, 4455 Narrow Lane Rd., 36116. Tel: 334-288-0005; Fax: 334-288-9322. Email: meehan@cassalabama.org. Susan Meehan, Dir.; Carol Herron, SMS Program Coord. Care for the poor, frail elderly and homebound disabled through Elderly Outreach and Interfaith Volunteer Caregivers. Missionary Servants of the Most Blessed Trinity 1.

SELMA. *Edmundite Guild* Society of St. Edmund, Inc. , P.O. Drawer 490, 36701. Tel: 888-540-7722; Fax: 334-875-8189. Email: Rogerlac27@aol.com. Rev. Roger J. La charite, S.S.E., Exec. Dir. Priests 7; Lay Person 1.

RELIGIOUS INSTITUTES OF MEN REPRESENTED IN THE ARCHDIOCESE

For further details refer to the corresponding bracketed number in the Religious Institutes of Men or Women section.

[0200]—*Benedictine Monks*—O.S.B.
[1100]—*Brothers of the Sacred Heart* (New Orleans Prov.)—S.C.
[1330]—*Congregation of the Mission* (Eastern Prov.)—C.M.
[1080]—*Congregation of the Resurrection* (Chicago Prov.)—C.R.
[0690]—*Jesuit Fathers and Brothers* (New Orleans Prov.)—S.J.
[0840]—*Missionary Servants of the Most Holy Trinity*—S.T.
[0440]—*Society of Saint Edmund* (Selma, AL)—S.S.E.
[0700]—*St. Joseph's Society of the Sacred Heart* (Baltimore, MD)—S.S.J.

RELIGIOUS INSTITUTES OF WOMEN REPRESENTED IN THE ARCHDIOCESE

[3710]—*Congregation of the Sisters of Saint Agnes*—C.S.A.
[1780]—*Congregation of the Sisters of the Third Order of St. Francis of Perpetual Adoration*—F.S.P.A.
[0760]—*Daughters of Charity of St. Vincent de Paul*—D.C.
[]—*Daughters of Mary Mother of Mercy*—D.M.M.M.
[0820]—*Daughters of the Holy Spirit*—D.H.S.
[0960]—*Daughters of Wisdom*—D.W.
[0420]—*Discalced Carmelite Nuns*—O.C.D.
[1050]—*Dominican Contemplative Nuns*—O.P.
[1070-03]—*Dominican Sisters*—O.P.
[1070-13]—*Dominican Sisters*—O.P.
[1070-18]—*Dominican Sisters*—O.P.
[]—*Franciscan Missionary Sisters* (Jamaica)—F.M.S.
[2575]—*Institute of the Sisters of Mercy of the Americas*—R.S.M.
[2340]—*Little Sisters of the Poor*—L.S.P.
[2790]—*Missionary Servants of the Most Blessed Trinity*—M.S.B.T.
[3040]—*Oblate Sisters of Providence*—O.S.P.
[]—*Order of St. Benedict*—O.S.B.
[]—*Sisters for Christian Community*—S.F.C.C
[0430]—*Sisters of Charity of the Blessed Virgin Mary*—B.V.M.
[2360]—*Sisters of Loretto At the Foot of the Cross*—S.L.
[2550]—*Sisters of Mercy*—R.S.M.
[3360]—*Sisters of Providence of Saint Mary-of-the-Woods, Indiana*—S.P.
[1650]—*Sisters of St. Francis of Philadelphia*—O.S.F.
[3830-14]—*Sisters of St. Joseph*—S.S.J.
[3830-15]—*Sisters of St. Joseph*—C.S.J.
[3840]—*Sisters of St. Joseph of Carondelet*—C.S.J.
[3850]—*Sisters of St. Joseph of Chambery*—C.S.J.
[1970]—*Sisters of the Holy Family of Nazareth*—C.S.F.N.
[3480]—*Sisters of the Resurrection*—C.R.
[2150]—*Sisters, Servants of the Immaculate Heart of Mary*—I.H.M.
[3330]—*Union of the Sisters of the Presentation of the Blessed Virgin Mary*—P.B.V.M.
[4170]—*Vincentian Sisters of Charity* (Perryville, PA)—V.S.C.
[4190]—*Visitation Nuns*—V.H.M.

NECROLOGY

† Stuardi, Rev. Msgr. J. Edwin, Daphne, AL Mercy Medical—Died Aug. 21, 2003
† McDonnell, Vincent M., (Retired)—Died Nov. 5, 2003

Diocese of Monterey in California

(Montereyensis in California)

Most Reverend

SYLVESTER D. RYAN, D.D.

Bishop of Monterey; ordained May 3, 1957; appointed Auxiliary Bishop of Los Angeles and Titular Bishop of Remesiana February 17, 1990; ordained Bishop on May 31, 1990; appointed Bishop of Monterey January 28, 1992; installed March 19, 1992. Email: SDRB@dioceseofmonterey.org.

Pastoral Office: 631 Abrego St., Monterey, CA 93940. Tel: 831-373-4345; Fax: 831-373-1175. *Mailing Address: P.O. Box 2048, Monterey, CA 93942-2048.*

Web: www.dioceseofmonterey.org

Email: diocese@dioceseofmonterey.org

Square Miles 21,916.

Established November 20, 1849. Re-established December 14, 1967. Formerly Diocese of Monterey-Fresno.

Comprises the Counties of Monterey, San Benito, San Luis Obispo and Santa Cruz in the State of California.

Legal Titles:
Diocese of Monterey in California.
The Diocese of Monterey Education and Welfare Corporation.
The Roman Catholic Bishop of Monterey, California, a Corporation Sole.
The Bishop Harry A. Clinch Endowment Fund of the Diocese of Monterey.
Catholic Charities of the Diocese of Monterey (Corporation).
Villa Serra Corporation.
Ave Maria Convalescent Hospital, Inc.
St. Francis Central Coast Catholic High School, Inc.

For legal titles of parishes and diocesan institutions, consult the Pastoral Office.

STATISTICAL OVERVIEW

Personnel	
Bishop	1
Priests: Diocesan Active in Diocese	52
Priests: Diocesan Active Outside Diocese	1
Priests: Retired, Sick or Absent	30
Number of Diocesan Priests	83
Religious Priests in Diocese	28
Total Priests in Diocese	111
Extern Priests in Diocese	10
Permanent Deacons in Diocese	3
Total Brothers	35
Total Sisters	135
Parishes	
Parishes	46
With Resident Pastor:	
Resident Diocesan Priests	36
Resident Religious Priests	5
Without Resident Pastor:	
Administered by Priests	4
Administered by Deacons	1
Professional Ministry Personnel:	
Brothers	1
Sisters	15
Lay Ministers	41
Welfare	
Catholic Hospitals	1
Total Assisted	143,892
Homes for the Aged	3
Total Assisted	448
Educational	
Diocesan Students in Other Seminaries	11
Students Religious	4
Total Seminarians	15
High Schools, Diocesan and Parish	2
Total Students	672
High Schools, Private	3
Total Students	1,039
Elementary Schools, Diocesan and Parish	10
Total Students	2,766
Elementary Schools, Private	3
Total Students	747
Catechesis/Religious Education:	
High School Students	2,411
Elementary Students	11,393
Total Students under Catholic Instruction	19,043
Teachers in the Diocese:	
Priests	3
Brothers	4
Sisters	15
Lay Teachers	330
Vital Statistics	
Receptions into the Church:	
Infant Baptism Totals	6,330
Adult Baptism Totals	217
Received into Full Communion	154
First Communions	4,381
Confirmations	1,530
Marriages:	
Catholic	754
Interfaith	167
Total Marriages	921
Deaths	1,120
Total Catholic Population	193,598
Total Population	967,992

Former Prelates of the Diocese of Monterey—Rt. Rev. THOMAS JAMES CONATY, D.D., consecrated Nov. 24, 1901; Titular Bishop of Samos; appt. Bishop of Monterey-Los Angeles, March 27, 1903; died Sept. 18, 1915; Most Revs. HARRY ANSELM CLINCH, D.D., ord. June 6, 1936; appt. Titular Bishop of Badiae and Auxiliary to the Bishop of Monterey-Fresno, Dec. 5, 1956; consecrated Feb. 27, 1957; installed as first Bishop of Monterey in California, Dec. 14, 1967; retired Jan. 19, 1982; died March 8, 2003; THADDEUS SHUBSDA, D.D., Fourth Bishop of Monterey, ord. April 26, 1950; Titular Bishop of Trau and Auxiliary Bishop of Los Angeles; Episcopal Ordination; appt. Feb. 19, 1977; named Bishop of Monterey in California, June 1, 1982; installed as second Bishop of Monterey, July 1, 1982; died April 26, 1991; Rev. Msgr. CHARLES G. FATOOH, V.G., appt. Administrator of the Diocese of Monterey, April 26, 1991 - March 19, 1992.

Vicar General—Rev. PETER A. CRIVELLO, V.G., 631 Abrego St., Monterey, 93940. Mailing Address, P.O. Box 2048, Monterey, 93942-2048. Tel: 831-373-4345; Fax: 831-373-1175. Email: pcrivellovg@dioceseofmonterey.org.

Chancellor—Sr. PATRICIA MURTAGH, I.M., Chancellor & Dir. Protection of Children & Young People, 631 Abrego St., Monterey, 93940. Mailing Address, P.O. Box 2048, Monterey, 93942-2048. Tel: 831-373-4345; Fax: 831-373-5765. Email: srpmurtagh@dioceseofmonterey.org.

Episcopal Vicar—Rev. JAMES HENRY, V.F., 298 S. Thompson, Nipomo, 93444. Tel: 805-929-1922; Fax: 805-929-2662. Email: nipomostjo@aol.com.

Vicar General—Rev. Msgr. D. DECLAN MURPHY, V.G. (Retired), P.O. Box 2048, Monterey, 93942-2048.

Vicar for Clergy—Rev. JERRY MCCORMICK, St. Angela's Church, 146 8th St., Pacific Grove, 93950. Tel: 831-655-4160; Fax: 831-372-5026.

Vicar for Religious—Sr. GABRIELA COVI-MAFFEI, I.M., 15785 Alto Way, Salinas, 93907. Tel: 831-663-3675; Fax: 831-663-3749.

Pastoral Office—Administrative Assistants: DONA LOGEMAN ACUFF. Email: DAcuff@dioceseofmonterey.org; IRENE CASAS. Email: ICasas@dioceseofmonterey.org; PATRICIA GRAB. Email: PGrab@dioceseofmonterey.org; Sr. MAUREEN ROONEY, C.S.C.. Email: SrMRooney@dioceseofmonterey.org; AIKO SOKOLOWSKI. Email: asokolowski@dioceseofmonterey.org; 631 Abrego St., Monterey, 93940. Mailing Address, P.O. Box 2048, Monterey, 93942-2048. Tel: 831-373-4345; Fax: 831-373-1175. Email: diocese@dioceseofmonterey.org.

Pastoral Office, Ecclesiastical Notaries—DONA LOGEMAN ACUFF; IRENE CASAS; PATRICIA GRAB; Sr. MAUREEN ROONEY.

Deans—Very Revs. JOHN C. GRIFFIN, V.U., Monterey; PETER CRIVELLO, V.G., Santa Cruz; LARRY KAMTITSCH, V.F., Salinas; Rev. JAMES HENRY, V.F., San Luis Obispo.

Diocesan Consultors—Rev. Msgr. D. DECLAN MURPHY, V.G. (Retired); Very Rev. JOHN C. GRIFFIN, V.U.; Rev. PETER CRIVELLO, V.G.; Very Rev. LARRY KAMBITSCH, V.F.; Rev. JAMES HENRY, V.F.

Diocesan Departments, Directors and Offices

Archivist—Bro. LAWRENCE SCRIVANI, S.M., 580 Fremont St., Monterey, 93940. Tel: 831-373-2127; Fax: 831-373-3534. Email: Archives@dioceseofmonterey.org; P.O. Box 2048, Monterey, 93942-2048.

Office of Legal Counsel—

Attorneys—SUSAN A. MAYER, Esq., 631 Abrego St., Monterey, 93940. Email: smayer@dioceseofmonterey.org; Mailing Address, P.O. Box 2048, Monterey, 93942-2048. Tel: 831-373-4345; Fax: 831-373-5765; ALBERT S. HAM, Esq., 485 Church St., Monterey, 93940. Email: AHam@dioceseofmonterey.org; Mailing Address, P.O. Box 2048, Monterey, 93942-2048. Tel: 831-373-4345; Fax: 831-373-5765.

Finance Officer—THOMAS H. RIORDAN, 631 Abrego St., Monterey, 93940. Tel: 831-373-4345; Fax: 831-373-1175. Email: TRiordan@dioceseofmonterey.org; Mailing Address, P.O. Box 2048, Monterey, 93942-2048.

Communication—Most Rev. SYLVESTER D. RYAN, D.D., Publisher. "The Observer"

Monterey Office

KEVIN J. DRABINSKI, Editor & Dir. Communications, 485 Church St., Monterey, 93940. Mailing Address, P.O. Box 2079, Monterey, 93942-2079. Tel: 831-373-2919; Fax: 831-373-1175. Email: observer@dioceseofmonterey.org; San Luis Obispo Office: 2146 Parker St., Ste. B-4, San Luis Obispo, 93401. Tel: 805-541-5963; Fax: 805-541-5964.

Curator—Sir RICHARD MENN, G.C.St.G.G., c/o 3080 Rio Rd., Carmel, 93923. Tel: 831-624-3600; Fax: 831-624-0658. Email: SIRRJM@aol.com.

Finance Office—WILLIAM J. COAKER II, Controller & Chief Investment Officer. Email: BCoaker@dioceseofmonterey.org; ANNE M. MCGUIRE, Computer Services/Parish Business Outreach, Technical Support and Web Site Mgr.. Email: AMcGuire@dioceseofmonterey.org; ANDREA OLSEN, Accounting Mgr.. Email: AOlsen@dioceseofmonterey.org; 485 Church St., Monterey, 93940. Mailing Address, P.O. Box 2048, Monterey, 93942-2048. Tel: 831-373-4666; Fax: 831-373-2831.

Health Care Coordinator—Sr. JEANNE BURNS, O.P., Dominican Santa Cruz Hospital, 1555 Soquel Dr., Santa Cruz, 95060. Tel: 831-462-7670; Fax: 831-462-7555.

Human Resources—SUSAN A. MAYER, Esq., Dir.;

STEFANIE OLSEN, Human Resources Assoc. Dir., 631 Abrego St., Monterey, 93940. Mailing Address, P.O. Box 2048, Monterey, 93942-2048. Tel: 831-373-4345; Fax: 831-373-5765. Email: humanres@dioceseofmonterey.org.

Catholic Schools Department—435 Church St., Monterey, 93940. Mailing Address, P.O. Box 350, Monterey, 93942-0350. Tel: 831-373-1608; Fax: 831-373-0173. Sr. MARY CATHERINE EVANS, O.P., Supt.; MARY MARCHI, Assoc. Admin.; MIRIAM "MIMI" SCHWERTFEGER, Asst. Dir.. Email: schools@dioceseofmonterey.org.

Cemeteries—CLANCY D'ANGELO, Dir., Administrative Office, 485 Church St., Monterey, 93940. Mailing Address, P.O. Box 2048, Monterey, 93942-2048. Tel: 831-373-4345; Fax: 831-373-6761. Email: cdangelo@dioceseofmonterey.org.

Diocesan Tribunal—485 Church St., Monterey, 93940. Mailing Address, P.O. Box 350, Monterey, 93942-0350. Tel: 831-373-1833; Fax: 831-373-6761. Email: Tribunal@dioceseofmonterey.org.

Judicial Vicar—Rev. KENNETH J. LAVERONE, O.F.M., M.A.; FRAYLNE SAN FILIPPO, Admin.; IRENE CASAS, Admin. Asst.; Rev. DAVID H. SCHUYLER, S.M., S.T.L., J.C.D., Adjutant Judicial Vicar.

Judges—Revs. KENNETH J. LAVERONE, O.F.M., M.A.; DAVID SCHUYLER, S.M., J.C.D.; Sr. ELIZABETH McDONOUGH, O.P., J.C.D., S.T.L.

Defenders of the Bond—Sr. LILIANA BONELLO, I.M., J.C.L.; Revs. PATRICK DOOLING; EMIL ROBU, O.F.M.Conv.; PAUL K. VALDEZ.

Advocates—Very Rev. JOHN C. GRIFFIN, V.U.; Revs. MICHAEL MARINI (Retired); EUGENIO ARAMBURO; HEIBAR CASTANDA.

Promoter of Justice—Rev. EMIL ROBU, O.F.M.Conv.

Notaries—IRENE CASAS; FRAYLNE SAN FILIPPO.

Divine Worship Department—Sr. BARBARA ANN LONG, O.P., Dir.; SUSAN SASO, Admin. Asst., 126 High St., Santa Cruz, 95060. Tel: 831-423-4973; Fax: 831-423-4973. Email: worship@dioceseofmonterey.org.

Pastoral Response Coordinator—MARTINA O'SULLIVAN, Dir., 631 Abrego St., Monterey, 93940. Tel: 831-373-4345, Ext. 285; 800-321-5220; Fax: 831-373-5765. Email: mosullivan@dioceseofmonterey.org; P.O. Box 2048, Monterey, 93942-2048.

Protection of Children and Young People—Sr. PATRICIA MURTAGH, I.M., Dir., 631 Abrego St., Monterey, 93940. Tel: 831-373-4345, Ext. 221; Fax: 831-373-1175. Email: srpmurtagh@dioceseofmonterey.org; P.O. Box 2048, Monterey, 93942-2048.

Priestly Life & Ministry—Rev. MARK STETZ, Holy Cross Church, 126 High St., Santa Cruz, 95060. Tel: 831-423-4182; Fax: 831-423-1043.

Safety Coordinator—KEVIN DRABINSKI, Diocesan Safety Coord., P.O. Box 2048, Monterey, 93942-2048. Tel: 831-373-2919; Fax: 831-373-1175. Email: observer@dioceseofmonterey.org.

Stewardship—Sr. LAURA GOEDKEN, O.P., Dir.. Email: lgoedken@dioceseofmonterey.org; THERESA ALLION, Administrative Asst.. Email: tallion@dioceseofmonterey.org; 485 Church St., Monterey, 93940. Mailing Address, P.O. Box 2048, Monterey, 93942-2048. Tel: 831-373-4345; Fax: 831-373-0302. Email: Stewardship@dioceseofmonterey.org.

Office of Faith Formation—Rev. ROY SHELLY, S.D.B., Dir., 485 Church St., Monterey, 93940. Tel: 831-373-4345; Fax: 831-373-6761. Email: FrRShelly@dioceseofmonterey.org; Mailing Address, P.O. Box 2048, Monterey, 93942-2048.

Campus Ministry Department—Revs. ROY SHELLY, S.D.B., Dir., 485 Church St., Monterey, 93940. Tel: 831-373-4345; Fax: 831-373-6761. Email: FrRShelly@dioceseofmonterey.org; Mailing Address, P.O. Box 2048, Monterey, 93942-2048; ROLAND BUNDA, S.M., Dir. Campus Ministry Santa Cruz, California State University at Monterey Bay, 285 Meder St., Santa Cruz, 95060. Tel: 831-423-9400; Fax: 831-423-8163. Email: newmanslug@aol.com. Web: www.newmanite.org; JOHN ULRICH, S.M., Dir.. Email: frjohn@slonewman.org; KEVIN DUGGAN, S.M., Assoc. Dir., 1472 Foothill Blvd., San Luis Obispo, 93401. Tel: 805-543-4105; Fax: 831-543-5671.

Catechetical Ministries Department—22 Stone St., Salinas, 93901. Tel: 831-424-4076, Ext. 23; Fax: 831-424-5221. *Mailing Address, P.O. Box 4727, Salinas, 93912-4727.* TISH SCARGILL, Dir.; OLGA FLORES, Admin. Asst. Tel: 831-424-4076, Ext. 23; Fax: 831-754-2474; SALLY EQUINOA, Consultant, San Luis Obispo Deanery, 221 Daly Ave., San Luis Obispo, 93405. Tel: 805-541-1441. Email: ssequonia@dioceseofmonterey.org.

Hispanic Ministry Department—Sr. LYDIA SCHNEIDER, I.M., Dir.; ALICIA CORDOVA, Administrative Asst.; BEATRIZ MUNOZ, Sec., 22 Stone St., Salinas, 93901. Tel: 831-424-4076; Fax: 831-424-5221. Email: Hispanic@dioceseofmonterey.org.

Migrant Ministry Coord.—MARINA OCAMPO, 22 Stone St., Salinas, 93901. Tel: 831-424-4076; Fax: 831-424-5221.

Parish Life Ministry—Sr. MOLLY NEVILLE, S.N.J.M., Dir.; MARIA OROZCO, Admin. Asst., 405 Palma Dr., Salinas, 93901-1822. Tel: 831-796-0136; Fax: 831-796-0138. Email: vocations@dioceseofmonterey.org.

Permanent Diaconate—Rev. ROY SHELLY, S.D.B., Dir.; Ms. CHERIE MICHAELSON, Assoc. Dir., 485 Church St., Monterey, 93940. P.O. Box 2048, Monterey, 93942-2048. Tel: 831-373-4345; Fax: 831-373-6761. Email: formation@dioceseofmonterey.org.

Respect Life/Family Life Ministry—Rev. ROY SHELLY, S.D.B., Dir. Office Assistants: JULIA ALIOTO; NOREEN BRIDGE, 642 Trigo Lane, Paso Robles, 93446. Tel: 805-237-1905; Fax: 805-237-1854. Email: respectlife@tcsn.net.

Youth and Young Adult Ministry—PATRICK MOONEY, Dir.; MARIA OROZCO, Admin. Asst., 405 Palma Dr., Salinas, 93901-1822. Tel: 831-796-0136; Fax: 831-796-0138. Email: youth@dioceseofmonterey.org.

Scouting—PATRICK MOONEY, Chap., 405 Palma Dr., Salinas, 93901-1822. Tel: 831-796-0136; Fax: 831-796-0138. Email: youth@dioceseofmonterey.org.

Vocations Director—Sr. MOLLY NEVILLE, S.N.J.M., Dir.; MARIA OROZCO, Admin. Asst., 405 Palma Dr., Salinas, 93901-1822. Tel: 831-796-0136; Fax: 831-796-0138. Email: Vocations@dioceseofmonterey.org; Revs. ANTONIO SANCHEZ, Asst. Dir., Our Lady of the Assumption Church, 100 Salinas Rd., Watsonville, 95076. Tel: 831-722-1104; Fax: 831-722-1931; MICHAEL VOLK, Asst. Dir., St. Theodore's Church, P.O Drawer B, Gonzales, 93926. Tel: 831-675-3648; Fax: 831-675-8360.

Cursillo—Revs. MIKE MILLER, Spiritual Dir., Sacred Heart Church, 22 Stone St., Salinas, 93901. Tel: 831-424-1959; Fax: 831-424-0788. Email: scrhrt@aol.com; MICHAEL L. VOLK, Spiritual Dir., St. Theodore's Church, Drawer B, Gonzales, 93926. Tel: 831-675-3648; Fax: 831-675-8360.

Ecumenism—Rev. SCOTT (CORNELIUS) McCARTHY, Dir., Our Lady of Mt. Carmel Church, P.O. Box 195, Carmel Valley, 93924. Tel: 831-659-2224; Fax: 831-659-9186. Email: mtcarmel@value.net.

Holy Childhood Association—PATRICIA GRAB, Coord., Diocese of Monterey, 631 Abrego St., Monterey, 93940. Tel: 831-373-4345; Fax: 831-373-1175. Email: PGrab@dioceseofmonterey.org; Mailing Address, P.O. Box 2048, Monterey, 93942-2048.

Native American Ministry—Rev. SCOTT (CORNELIUS) McCARTHY, Dir., Our Lady of Mt. Carmel Church, P.O. Box 195, Carmel Valley, 93924. Tel: 831-659-2224; Fax: 831-659-9186. Email: mtcarmel@value.net.

Pontifical Mission Societies—PATRICIA GRAB, Coord., Diocese of Monterey, 631 Abrego St., Monterey, 93940. Tel: 831-373-4345; Fax: 831-373-1175. Email: PGrab@dioceseofmonterey.org; Mailing Address, P.O. Box 2048, Monterey, 93942-2048.

St. Joseph's Conference Center—485 Church St., Monterey, 93940.

St. Vincent De Paul—Rev. RICHARD BONJEAN, Dir., 1651 Little River Dr., Salinas, 93906. Tel: 831-449-1149.

Catholic Charities of the Diocese of Monterey—

Administrative Office—MARTINA S. O'SULLIVAN, Exec. Dir.. Email: mosullivan@dioceseofmonterey.org; CYNTHIA WEIGLE, Administration & Operations Mgr., 922 Hilby Ave., Ste. C, Seaside, 93955. Tel: 831-393-3110; Fax: 831-393-3115. Email: charities@dioceseofmonterey.org cweigle@dioceseofmonterey.org.

Catholic Charities - Salinas Office—Buckley Hall, St. Mary of the Nativity Church, 1702 2nd Ave., Salinas, 93905. Tel: 831-422-0602; 831-393-3113 (Counseling); 831-393-3110 (Family Supportive Svcs.); 831-422-0602 (Immigration & Citizenship Svcs.); Fax: 831-422-0759.

Catholic Charities - San Luis Obispo Office—Mission San Luis Obispo, 715 Palm Ave., San Luis Obispo, 93401. Tel: 805-541-9110; Fax: 805-541-9121.

Catholic Charities - Watsonville Office—55 Brennan St., Watsonville, 95076. Tel: 831-722-2675 (Family Supportive Svcs.); 831-722-2791 (Counseling); 831-722-2675 (Immigration & Citizenship Svcs.); Fax: 831-722-9921.

Campaign for Human Development—Sr. LAURA GOEDKEN, O.P., Dir., 485 Church St., Monterey, 93940. Tel: 831-393-4345; Fax: 831-373-0302. Email: lgoedken@dioceseofmonterey.org; P.O. Box 2048, Monterey, 93942-2048.

Catholic Relief Service—Sr. LAURA GOEDKEN, O.P., Dir., 485 Church St., Monterey, 93940. Tel: 831-373-4345; Fax: 831-373-0302. Email: lgoedken@dioceseofmonterey.org; P.O. Box 2048, Monterey, 93942-2048.

Boards, Commissions, Committees and Councils

Administrative Committee Priests' Pension Plan—Most Rev. SYLVESTER D. RYAN, D.D.; Revs. EUGENIO ARAMBURO; JOSEPH L. OCCHIUTO; GREG SANDMAN; MICHAEL L. CROSS, Chm.; PAUL K. VALDEZ.

Ave Maria Board—Sisters M. CONSTANCE PETRUCELLI, O.S.F., Pres.; M. ROSANNA PELTIER, O.S.F., Sec.; CLANCY D'ANGELO, Vice Pres.; THOMAS H. RIORDAN, Treas.; Most Rev. SYLVESTER D. RYAN, D.D., Chm.

Bishop Harry A. Clinch Endowment Fund, The Bishop Sylvester D. Ryan Continuing Education Fund— The Bishop Shubsda Memorial Seminary Endowment Burse and The Cemetery Endowment Burse Most Rev. SYLVESTER D. RYAN, D.D.; Rev. CHARLES TILLY, S.J.; ROBERT SEMAS; ELIZABETH HELFRICH; MICHAEL MORRIS; RONALD PASQUINELLI; LARRY SAGE, Chm.; LEAH DUNCAN; THOMAS H. RIORDAN, Ex Officio, Finance Officer; Sr. LAURA GOEDKEN, O.P., Dir. Stewardship; LEON GRADCOLAS; JOE PEZZINI.

Building Commission—Contact Persons: Very Rev. JOHN GRIFFIN, V.F., Carmel Mission, P.O. Box 2235, Carmel, 93921-2235. Tel: 831-624-1271; Fax: 831-624-8050; THOMAS H. RIORDAN, Diocese of Monterey, 631 Abrego St., P.O. Box 2048, Monterey, 93942-2048. Tel: 831-373-4345; Fax: 831-373-1175.

Catholic Charities Board—Most Rev. SYLVESTER D. RYAN, D.D., Chm.; Very Rev. PETER A. CRIVELLO, V.G.; BILL SLEZAK, Pres.; Rev. JERRY McCORMICK, Sec.; LARRY SAGE, Treas.; GEORGETTE DUFRESNE; LUCY PIAZRRO; DIANE SAIGN; CELIA ORGANISTA; MADELEINE WRIGHT; JUAN URANGA; MARTINA O'SULLIVAN, Exec. Dir.; THOMAS H. RIORDAN, Finance Officer; CYNTHIA WEIGLE, Recording Sec.

Diocesan Consultors—Rev. Msgr. D. DECLAN MURPHY, V.G. (Retired); Very Revs. JOHN C. GRIFFIN, V.U.; PETER CRIVELLO, V.G.; LARRY KAMBITSCH, V.F.; Rev. JAMES HENRY, V.F.

Ecumenical Commission—Revs. IGNATIUS MARTINEZ; GIL MACELLI; SCOTT McCARTHY, Chm.; Bro. TONY YOUNG.

Emergency Preparedness Task Force—VIC COLLINS; KEVIN DRABINSKI; Sr. MARY CATHERINE EVANS, O.P.; SUSAN A. MAYER, Esq.; Sr. PATRICIA MURTAGH, I.M.; JACK McGILVRAY, Chm.; Chief TERRY MEDINA; MARTINA O'SULLIVAN; THOMAS H. RIORDAN; Most Rev. SYLVESTER D. RYAN, D.D.; Sr. MAUREEN ROONEY, C.S.C., Recording Sec.

Evangelization Board—Very Rev. PETER A. CRIVELLO, V.G.; SHEILAH LYNCH; DANIEL WEBER; JONDELLE WRIGHT; ESPERANZA TORRES; IMELDA VIDALES; ROSARIO ZARAGOZA.

Finance Council—RICHARD FALGE; TOD SANCHEZ; Sr. JOANNE WIMMER, O.P.; Rev. WALTER ESPINOZA; Deacon DAVE LEACH; Very Rev. PETER A. CRIVELLO, V.G.; Sr. CARLOTTA O'DONNELL; RONALD PASQUINELLI; Most Rev. SYLVESTER D. RYAN, D.D.; Rev. PAUL K. VALDEZ. Ex Officio: THOMAS H. RIORDAN, Finance Officer; DONA LOGEMAN ACUFF, Recording Sec.

Historical Review Committee—Sir RICHARD MENN, G.C.St.G.G., Diocesan Curator; Bro. LAWRENCE SCRIVANI, S.M., Diocesan Archivist; ELIZABETH HILLEARY; Sir LEWIS CHARLES SCOTT; SUSAN A. MAYER, Esq.; Chief JOHN J. McGILVRAY (RETIRED).

Insurance Committee—Deacon DAVE LEACH; SUSAN A. MAYER, Esq.; THOMAS H. RIORDAN; Rev. PAUL K. VALDEZ.

Lay Employees Non-Qualified Pension Committee—THOMAS H. RIORDAN, Chm.; TONY KARACHALE, Consultant.

Lay Employee Pension Plan Committee—WILLIAM COAKER, Chm.; SUSAN A. MAYER, Esq.; CLANCY D'ANGELO; RONALD PASQUINELLI; THOMAS H. RIORDAN, Ex Officio; TOD D. SANCHEZ; TONY KARACHALE, Consultant; AIKO SOKOLOWSKI, Recording Sec.

Observer Advisory Board—Sr. LYDIA SCHNEIDER, I.M., Chm.; TOM RIORDAN; BUDD STUBBS; KEVIN J. DRABINSKI, Dir. Communications; DONA LOGEMAN ACUFF, Recording Sec.; LLOYD GRAFF; KATIE KRIEGER; Bro. LARRY SCRIVANI, S.M.

Permanent Diaconate Advisory Board—Rev. ROY SHELLY, S.D.B.; Ms. CHERIE MICHAELSON; Deacons STEVE MICHAELSON; DAVID LEACH; HAROLD MILLER; Revs. MICHAEL CICINATO; RON GREEN; ROBERTO VERA; Sisters LAURA GOEDKEN, O.P.; MOLLY NEVILLE, S.N.J.M.; Mr. RUSS BROWN.

Presbyteral Council—Very Revs. PETER A. CRIVELLO, V.G.; JOHN C. GRIFFIN, V.U.; Rev. JAMES R. HENRY, V.F.; Very Rev. LARRY KAMBITSCH, V.F.; Revs. PATRICK DOOLING; JOSEPH BUTTERS; MIGUEL GRAJEDA; JAMES NISBET; EUGENIO ARAMBURO; MARK STETZ; GREGORY SANDMAN; RON SHIRLEY; JERRY McCORMICK; Most Rev. SYLVESTER D. RYAN,

D.D.; PATRICIA GRAB, Recording Sec.

Priestly Life and Ministry Board—Revs. ENRIQUE HERRERA; SCOTT MCCARTHY; EUGENIO ARAMBURO; Sr. MOLLY NEVILLE, S.N.J.M.; Most Rev. SYLVESTER D. RYAN, D.D.; Revs. RON SHIRLEY; PAUL P. MURPHY; MARK STETZ, Chm.; JONDELL DEVEAUX WRIGHT; Rev. ALBERTO VASQUEZ-MARTINEZ.

Priest's Personnel Board—Very Rev. JOHN C. GRIFFIN, V.U.; Rev. JAMES HENRY, V.F.; Very Revs. LARRY KAMBITSCH, V.F.; PETER CRIVELLO, V.G.; Revs. JERRY MCCORMICK; RON SHIRLEY; Most Rev. SYLVESTER D. RYAN, D.D.; Rev. ANTONIO SANCHEZ.

Parish Life Ministry—Advisory Committee: Rev. MICHAEL MILLER; Sisters MOLLY NEVILLE, S.N.J.M., Dir.; PATRICIA MURTAGH, I.M.; JONDELL DEVEAUX WRIGHT; PATRICK CONWAY.

Safety Committee—KEVIN DRABINSKI; CLANCY D'ANGELO; Sr. MARY CATHERINE EVANS, O.P.; SUSAN A. MAYER, Esq.; JACK MCGILVRAY; ANNE MCGUIRE; RON O'ROURKE; THOMAS H. RIORDAN; Rev. PAUL K. VALDEZ, Chm.; KAREN VICTORINO; MIRIAM "MIMI" SCHWERTFEGER, Recording Sec.; PATRICK MOONEY; Sr. PATRICIA MURTAGH, I.M.; TISH SCARGILL.

St. Francis Central Coast Catholic High School, Inc.—Most Rev. SYLVESTER D. RYAN, D.D.; Rev. DAVID PURDY, S.D.B.; Very Rev. PETER A. CRIVELLO, V.G.; Rev. RICHARD PRESENTI, S.D.B.; THOMAS H. RIORDAN; Rev. NICHOLAS REINA, S.D.B.

Villa Serra Board—Most Rev. SYLVESTER D. RYAN, D.D.; RICHARD FALGE; ROGER HITE; RICK HARRON; Sr. JULIE HYER, O.P.; THOMAS H. RIORDAN.

Vocations Board—Revs. ROLAND BUNDA, S.M.; ANTONIO CORTES; RON GREEN; Sisters MOLLY NEVILLE, S.N.J.M., Dir. Core Team; ROSEANGELA FILIPPINI, I.M.; Most Rev. SYLVESTER D. RYAN, D.D.; NICK PASULLI; MARIA FLORES; Revs. ANTONIO SANCHEZ, Asst. Dir. Core Team; MICHAEL A. VOLK, Asst. Dir. Core Team; MARIA OROZCO, Recording Sec.

Web Site Development Committee—MARIO FEDERICO; Sr. LAURA GOEDKEN, O.P.; ANNE MCGUIRE; TOM RIORDAN; KEVIN J. DRABINSKI; PATRICK MOONEY; Rev. EMIL ROBU, O.F.M.Conv.

CLERGY, PARISHES, MISSIONS AND PAROCHIAL SCHOOLS

CITY OF MONTEREY
(MONTEREY COUNTY)

CATHEDRAL OF SAN CARLOS BORROMEO (1770), Revs. Joseph L. Occhiuto, Rector; Alberto Cabrera; Deacon Harold Miller, Pastoral Assoc.
Mailing Address: 500 Church St., 93940. Tel: 831-373-2628; Fax: 831-373-0518.
Res.: 550 Church St., 93940.
School—450 Church St., 93940. Tel: 831-375-1324; Fax: 831-375-9736. Dr. Jack Marchi, PhD. Lay Teachers 32; Students 288.
Catechesis/Religious Program—Tel: 831-373-4101. Students 103.

OUTSIDE THE CITY OF MONTEREY

APTOS, SANTA CRUZ CO., RESURRECTION (1968), Rev. Peter A. Crivello, V.G.
Res.: 7600 Soquel Dr., P.O. Box 87, 95001. Tel: 831-688-4300; Fax: 831-688-6921.
School—Good Shepherd School (Inter-Parish), (Grades PreK-8) Tel: 831-429-1018; Fax: 831-429-5832. See Star of the Sea Parish, Santa Cruz.
Catechesis/Religious Program—Tel: 831-688-4300; Fax: 831-688-6921. Students 100.

ARROYO GRANDE, SAN LUIS OBISPO CO., ST. PATRICK (1886), Revs. Joseph Butters; Jose Alberto Vasquez-Martinez.
Res.: 501 Fair Oaks Ave., P.O. Box 860, 93421. Tel: 805-489-2680; Fax: 805-489-1316.
School—(Grades K-8), 900 W. Branch St., 93420. Tel: 805-489-1210; Fax: 805-489-7662. Kathy Tyree, Prin. Sisters of Mercy 3; Lay Teachers 13; Students 324.
Catechesis/Religious Program—Tel: 805-481-2990. Students 384.
Mission—St. Francis of Assisi 17th & Beach, Oceano, San Luis Obispo Co. 93445.
Shamrock Thrift Shop—924 Grand Ave., Grover City, 93433. Tel: 805-481-0612. Alana Owen.

ATASCADERO, SAN LUIS OBISPO CO., ST. WILLIAM'S (1948), [JC] Rev. Joseph R. Hercek, V.F.
Mailing Address: P.O. Box 2230, 93423. Tel: 805-466-0849; Fax: 805-461-0743.
Res.: 6410 Santa Lucia Rd., 93422.
Catechesis/Religious Program—Students 250.

BOULDER CREEK, SANTA CRUZ CO., ST. MICHAEL (1921), Rev. Paul K. Valdez.
Res.: 13005 Pine St., 95006. Tel: 831-338-6112; Fax: 831-338-7522.
Catechesis/Religious Program—Students 30.

CAMBRIA, SAN LUIS OBISPO CO., SANTA ROSA (1961), [CEM] Rev. Dennis Gilbert.
Res.: 1174 Main St., 93428. Tel: 805-927-4816; Fax: 805-927-2880.
Catechesis/Religious Program—Tel: 805-924-1728. Students 125.

CAPITOLA, SANTA CRUZ CO., ST. JOSEPH (1904), [JC] Rev. Patrick Dooling; Sr. Joan Derry, S.H.F., Pastoral Assoc.; Tom McNamara, Pastoral Assoc. & Business Mgr.
Res.: 435 Monterey Ave., 95010. Tel: 831-475-8211; Fax: 831-475-2601.
School—Good Shepherd School (Inter-Parish), (Grades K-8) , See Star of the Sea Parish, Santa Cruz and Resurrection Church, Aptos. Tel: 831-476-4000; Fax: 831-476-0948.
Catechesis/Religious Program—Tel: 831-475-9510; Fax: 831-475-2601. Students 191.

CARMEL VALLEY, MONTEREY CO., OUR LADY OF MT. CARMEL (1953), Rev. Cornelius Scott McCarthy.
Res.: 9 El Caminito, P.O. Box 195, 93924. Tel: 831-659-2224; Fax: 831-659-9186.
Catechesis/Religious Program—Students 52.

CARMEL, MONTEREY CO., SAN CARLOS BORROMEO BASILICA (1771), [CEM], (Carmel Mission) Very Rev. John C. Griffin, V.U.; Rev. Emil Robu, O.F.M.Conv.
Res.: Rio Rd. and Lasuen Dr., P.O. Box 2235, 93921. Tel: 831-624-1271; Fax: 831-624-8050.
School—Junipero Serra School, (Grades K-8), 2992 Lasuen Dr., 93923. Tel: 831-624-8322; Fax: 831-624-8311. Dr. Virginia Higgins, Ed.D., Prin. Lay Teachers 14; Students 163.
Catechesis/Religious Program—Tel: 831-624-6846; Fax: 831-624-6846. Students 305.
Mission—St. Francis of the Redwoods Hwy. 1, Big Sur, Monterey Co. 93920.
Chapel—Blessed Sacrament

CASTROVILLE, MONTEREY CO., OUR LADY OF REFUGE (1869), [JC] Revs. Eugenio Aramburo; Roberto Vera Vasquez.
Res.: 11140 Preston St., 95012. Tel: 831-633-4015; Fax: 831-633-4653.
Catechesis/Religious Program—Tel: 831-633-4016. Students 510.

CAYUCOS, SAN LUIS OBISPO CO., ST. JOSEPH (1905), Rev. Anthony Gurnell, Admin.
Res.: 360 Park Ave., P.O. Box 437, 93430. Tel: 805-995-3243; Fax: 805-995-2838.
Catechesis/Religious Program—Tel: 805-995-2137. Students 9.

CORRALITOS, SANTA CRUZ CO., HOLY EUCHARIST (1969), Rev. Paul P. Murphy.
Res.: 527 Corralitos Rd., 95076. Tel: 831-722-5490; Fax: 831-722-5421.
Catechesis/Religious Program—Students 145.

DAVENPORT, SANTA CRUZ CO., ST. VINCENT DE PAUL (1935), Rev. Brian Crawford, O.S.J. (SAC), Admin.
Res.: 544 W. Cliff Drive, Santa Cruz, 95060. Tel: 831-471-1702; 831-429-1426; Fax: 831-457-1317.
Catechesis/Religious Program—123 Marine View Ave., 95017. Tel: 831-423-5373. Students 9.

FELTON, SANTA CRUZ CO., ST. JOHN'S (1952), Rev. Michael L. Cross.
Res.: Russell at Hwy. 9, P.O. Box M-1, 95018. Tel: 831-335-4657; Fax: 831-335-4648.
Catechesis/Religious Program—Tel: 831-335-4667; Fax: 831-335-4679. Students 51.

GONZALES, MONTEREY CO., ST. THEODORE (1892), [JC] Revs. Michael Volk; Dominic Joseph Castro, O.F.M.Conv.
Office:—125 S. Center St., 93926.
Res.: 120 First St., P.O. Drawer B, 93926. Tel: 831-675-3648; Fax: 831-675-8360.
Catechesis/Religious Program—Tel: 831-675-2100; Fax: 831-675-2975. Students 810.
Mission—Chualar Mission Scott & Grant Sts., Chualar, Monterey Co. 93925. Tel: 831-679-2981.

GREENFIELD, MONTEREY CO., HOLY TRINITY (1951), (Mexican—Italian), Rev. Antonio Cortes.
Res.: 803 Elm Ave., Box 276, 93927. Tel: 831-674-5428; Fax: 831-674-5285.
Catechesis/Religious Program—Tel: 831-674-3695. Evelia Ayala, D.R.E. Students 251.

HOLLISTER, SAN BENITO CO, ST. BENEDICT, Merged, with Sacred Heart, Hollister to form Sacred Heart/St. Benedict Catholic Community, Hollister.

HOLLISTER, SAN BENITO CO.

1—SACRED HEART (1877), Merged, with St. Benedict, Hollister to form Sacred Heart/St. Benedict Catholic Community, Hollister.

2—SACRED HEART/ST. BENEDICT CATHOLIC COMMUNITY (1877), [CEM] Revs. Rudy Ruiz; Claudio Cabrera Carranza. In Res., Rev. Fabian Vela (Retired).
Res.: 540 College St., P.O. Box 1040, 95024. Tel: 831-637-9212; Fax: 831-637-7299.
St. Benedict: 1200 Fairview Rd., 95023. Tel: 831-637-6600.
Pastoral Center—680 College St., P.O. Box 1040, 95023.
School—(Grades K-8), 670 College St., 95023. Tel: 831-637-4157; Fax: 831-637-4164. Kathleen O'Donnell, Prin. Lay Teachers 24; Students 522.
Catechesis/Religious Program—Tel: 831-637-8291. Tish Scargill, D.R.E. Students 894.

JOLON, MONTEREY CO., SAN ANTONIO MISSION (1771), Rev. John E. Gini, O.F.M. In Res., Rev. Anthony F. Lavorin, O.F.M.; Bro. Kevin Dunne, O.F.M.
Res.: Box 803, 93928. Tel: 831-385-4478; Fax: 831-386-9332.
Mission—South Shore of Lake San Antonio, Monterey Co.
Catechesis/Religious Program—Students 10.

KING CITY, MONTEREY CO., ST. JOHN THE BAPTIST (1891), (Hispanic), Rev. Ronald L. Green.
Res.: 504 N. Third St., 93930. Tel: 831-385-3377; Fax: 831-385-3317.
Catechesis/Religious Program—Tel: 831-385-3464. Kay Paz, D.R.E. Students 481.
Mission—St. Luke Main St., San Lucas, Monterey Co. 93954.

LOS GATOS, SANTA CRUZ CO., CHRIST CHILD (1983), Revs. Marvin J. Steffes, C.PP.S. (OAK); Paul K. Valdez, Admin. In Res., Rev. Frank J. Muscolino.
Res.: 23230 Summit Rd., 95033. Tel: 408-353-2210; Fax: 408-353-8680.
Catechesis/Religious Program—Students 21.

LOS OSOS, SAN LUIS OBISPO CO., ST. ELIZABETH ANN SETON (1984), Rev. Joel J. Almendras; Deacon David P. Leach.
Res.: 2050 Palisades Ave., 93402. Tel: 805-528-5319; Fax: 805-528-8893.
Catechesis/Religious Program—Students 88.

MARINA, MONTEREY CO., ST. JUDE PARISH COMMUNITY (1963), (Filipino—Korean), Rev. Ronald Shirley.
Res.: 303 Hillcrest Ave., 93933-3599. Tel: 831-384-5434; Fax: 831-384-7011.
Catechesis/Religious Program—Tel: 831-384-8268. Students 245.

MORRO BAY, SAN LUIS OBISPO CO., ST. TIMOTHY (1950), Rev. Edward J. Holterhoff; Rev. Msgr. Cornelius Sweeney, Pastor Emeritus.
Mailing Address: 962 Piney Way, 93442. Tel: 805-772-2840; Fax: 805-772-3184.
Catechesis/Religious Program—Tel: 805-772-9272. Students 93.

NIPOMO, SAN LUIS OBISPO CO., ST. JOSEPH (1968), Revs. James Henry; Jose Alberto Vazquez-Martinez.
Res.: 298 S. Thompson, 93444. Tel: 805-929-1922; Fax: 805-929-2662.
Catechesis/Religious Program—Tel: 805-929-3730. Students 276.

PACIFIC GROVE, MONTEREY CO., ST. ANGELA (1928), [CEM] Revs. Anthony Phuc, C.SS.R., Assoc. Pastor; Jerry McCormick.
Res.: 161 Ninth St., 93950. Tel: 831-655-4160; Fax: 831-372-5026.
Office:—146 Eighth St., 93950.
School—Preschool, 136 Eighth St., 93950. Tel: 831-372-3555; Fax: 831-372-1965. Virginia Ziomek, Prin.
Catechesis/Religious Program—Tel: 831-373-6311. Students 135.

PASO ROBLES, SAN LUIS OBISPO CO., ST. ROSE (1922), [CEM] [JC] Revs. Derek Hughes (Ireland); Efrain Medina Ruiz (Mexico); Sr. Maris Stella O'Loghlen, Pastoral Assoc.
Office—642 Trigo Ln., P.O. Box 790, 93447. Tel: 805-238-2218; Fax: 805-238-2762.
Res.: 820 Creston Rd., P.O. Box 790, 93447. Tel: 805-238-2218; Fax: 805-238-2762.
School—(Grades PreK-8), 900 Tucker Ave., 93446. Tel: 805-238-0304; Fax: 805-238-7393. James Brescia, Prin. Lay Teachers 18; Students 286.
Catechesis/Religious Program—Tel: 805-239-2412; Fax: 805-238-2762. Students 418.

PISMO BEACH, SAN LUIS OBISPO CO., ST. PAUL THE APOSTLE (1930), [JC] Revs. Ronald Rocky, O.F.M-.Conv.; Charles Kozanecki, O.F.M.Conv. In Res., Rev. Peter Parchem, O.F.M.Conv., Pastor Emeritus.
Res.: 800 Bello St., 93449. Tel: 805-773-2219; Fax: 805-773-8617.
Catechesis/Religious Program—Tel: 805-773-3185. Students 98.

SALINAS, MONTEREY CO.

1—CHRIST THE KING (1995), (Hispanic), Rev. Miguel A. Grajeda.
Res.: 240 Calle Cebu, 93901. Tel: 831-422-6543; Fax: 831-422-7218.
Religious Education Office—Tel: 831-422-6722.
Catechesis/Religious Program—Students 550.

2—MADONNA DEL SASSO (1960), Very Rev. Larry Kambitsch, V.F.; Revs. Robert Murrin; Michael A. Bethancourt, Regl. Chap. Hospitals & Jails; Sr. Angela Milioto, R.S.H.M., Pastoral Assoc.
Res.: 320 E. Laurel Dr., 93906. Tel: 831-422-5323; Fax: 831-422-0536.
School—(Grades PreK-8), 20 Santa Teresa Way, 93906. Tel: 831-424-7813; Fax: 831-424-3359. Dr.

Charles E. White, Ed.D., Prin. Sisters of Notre Dame 1; Lay Teachers 14; Students 330.
Catechesis/Religious Program—Students 415.
3—ST. MARY OF THE NATIVITY (1947), (Hispanic), Rev. Enrique Herrera.
Res.: 1702 Second Ave., 93905. Tel: 831-758-1669; Fax: 831-758-4715.
Catechesis/Religious Program—Tel: 831-422-9964. Ms. Edith Sanchez, D.R.E. Students 950.
4—SACRED HEART (1877), Revs. Michael J. Miller; Pedro Espinoza. In Res., Rev. Eleutherio Sanz (Retired).
Res.: 22 Stone St., 93901-2643. Tel: 831-424-1959; Fax: 831-424-0788.
School—(Grades K-8), 123 W. Market St., 93901. Tel: 831-771-1310; Fax: 831-771-1314. Sr. Paulette Tiefenbrunn, S.S.N.D., Prin. Sisters 5; Lay Teachers 10; Students 294.
Catechesis/Religious Program—Tel: 831-772-8232. Mary Scattini, D.R.E. Students 554.
SAN JUAN BAUTISTA, SAN BENITO CO., SAN JUAN BAUTISTA (1797), (Hispanic), [CEM], (Old Mission) Rev. Edward Fitz-Henry.
Res.: 406 Second St., P.O. Box 400, 95045. Tel: 831-623-2127; Fax: 831-623-2433.
Catechesis/Religious Program—Tel: 831-623-4178. Students 152.
SAN LUIS OBISPO, SAN LUIS OBISPO CO.
1—NATIVITY OF OUR LADY (1964), Rev. Michael Cicinato.
Res.: 221 Daly Ave., 93405-1099. Tel: 805-544-2357; Fax: 805-544-6756.
Catechesis/Religious Program—Students 73.
2—SAN LUIS OBISPO (1772),, (Old Mission) Revs. Jerry Maher; Charles J. Tilley, S.J., Prin.; John Arul; Walter Espinoza.
Res.: 751 Palm St., 93401. Tel: 805-781-8220; Fax: 805-781-8214.
School—Preschool, 221 Daly Ave., 93401. Tel: 805-549-8819. Teri Stegman, Prin.
School—(Grades PreK-8), 761 Broad St., 93401. Tel: 805-543-6019; Fax: 805-543-6246. Teri Stegman, Prin. Lay Teachers 23; Students 370.
Catechesis/Religious Program—Tel: 805-781-8220, Ext. 18. Students 237.
SAN MIGUEL, SAN LUIS OBISPO CO., SAN MIGUEL (1797), (Hispanic—Filipino), [CEM], (Old Mission) Rev. Raymond Tintle, O.F.M.; Sr. Loretta Guevarra, S.A., Pastoral Assoc.
Res.: 775 Mission St., P.O. Box 69, 93451.
Parish—Tel: 805-467-2131; Fax: 805-467-2141.
Catechesis/Religious Program—Tel: 805-467-2325. Students 82.
Mission—Our Lady of Ransom San Ardo, Monterey Co.
Mission—Our Lady of Guadalupe Bradley, Monterey Co.
Station—Heritage Ranch Paso Robles.
SANTA CRUZ, SANTA CRUZ CO.
1—HOLY CROSS (1791), [CEM 3] [JC 2] Rev. Mark Stetz. In Res., Rev. Cyprian Consiglio, O.S.B.Cam.
Res.: 126 High St., 95060. Tel: 831-423-4182; Fax: 831-423-1043.
School—(Grades PreK-8), 150 Emmet St., 95060. Tel: 831-423-4447; Fax: 831-423-0752. Sr. Jean Williams, Prin. Lay Teachers 20; Students 221.
Catechesis/Religious Program—Tel: 831-458-3041; Fax: 831-458-1043. Students 213.
2—STAR OF THE SEA (1947), Revs. Hector Cruz, S.M.; Patrick Scully, S.M.
Res.: 515 Frederick St., 95062. Tel: 831-429-1018; Fax: 831-429-5832.
School—Good Shepherd Preschool, 2727 Mattison Ln., 95062. Tel: 831-476-4000; Fax: 831-476-0948. Sr. Deanna Young, Prin. (Inter-Parish) Students 140.
Catechesis/Religious Program—Ivonne Mansnerus, D.R.E. Students 335.
Chapel—Villa Maria del Mar, Tel: 831-475-1236; Fax: 831-475-8867.
SANTA MARGARITA, SAN LUIS OBISPO CO., SANTA MARGARITA DE CORTONA (1934), [JC] Rev. James J. Frerkes.
Res.: 5073 Meadowlark Ln., Paso Robles, 93446. Tel: 805-239-2720; 805-438-5383; Fax: 805-438-4313.
Catechesis/Religious Program—Tel: 805-239-3769. Students 40.
Mission—St. James Mission P.O. Box 3055, Carrissa Plains, San Luis Obispo Co. 93453. Tel: 805-475-2222.
SCOTTS VALLEY, SANTA CRUZ CO., SAN AGUSTIN (1969), Rev. Matthew Pennington.
Res.: 257 Glenwood Dr., 95066. Tel: 831-438-3633; Fax: 831-438-0973.
Catechesis/Religious Program—Students 225.
SEASIDE, MONTEREY CO., ST. FRANCIS XAVIER (1950), Rev. Heibar Castaneda, Admin. In Res., Rev. Msgr. Charles G. Fatooh, V.G.
Res.: 1475 LaSalle Ave., P.O. Box 247, 93955. Tel: 831-394-8546; Fax: 831-394-5414.
Catechesis/Religious Program—Students 562.
SOLEDAD, MONTEREY CO., OUR LADY OF SOLITUDE (1933), (Spanish), [CEM] [JC] Revs. Ignacio Martinez; Dominic Joseph Castro, O.F.M.Conv.
Res.: 235 Main St., 93960. Tel: 831-678-2731; Fax: 831-678-2968.
Catechesis/Religious Program—Tel: 831-678-1277. Sr. Liza Raphael, D.R.E. Students 851.
Mission—Nuestra Senora de la Soledad Rte. 1, Box 72, Monterey Co. 93960. Tel: 408-678-2586.
SPRECKELS, MONTEREY CO., ST. JOSEPH (1969), Rev. Jim Nisbet.
Res.: One Railroad Ave., P.O. Box 7153, 93962. Tel: 831-455-2249; Fax: 831-455-9357.
Catechesis/Religious Program—St. Joseph's Religion Center, 15 First St., P.O. Box 7153, 93962. Tel: 831-455-8720; Fax: 831-455-9357. Bro. Dennis J. Peterson, C.F.C., D.R.E. Students 386.
TRES PINOS, SAN BENITO CO., IMMACULATE CONCEPTION (1904), Rev. Richard D. Clark.
Res.: 7290 Airline Hwy., P.O. Box 247, 95075. Tel: 831-628-3216; 831-628-3060 (Hall); Fax: 831-628-3602.
Catechesis/Religious Program—Alice Farnham, D.R.E. Students 82.
WATSONVILLE, SANTA CRUZ CO.
1—OUR LADY HELP OF CHRISTIANS (1854), (Portuguese—Spanish), Revs. Harry V. Rasmussen, S.D.B.; Justo V. Davila, S.D.B.; David Purdy, S.D.B. In Res., Revs. John T. Itzaina, S.D.B.; Joseph Nguyen, O.S.B.; Bro. Jerry V. Weirich, S.D.B.
Res.: 2401 E. Lake Ave., 95076. Tel: 831-722-2665; Fax: 831-722-8305. Rev. John T. Itzaina, S.D.B.; Bro. Jerry V. Weirich, S.D.B.
Catechesis/Religious Program—Tel: 831-728-5518; Fax: 831-728-0273. Students 173.
2—OUR LADY OF THE ASSUMPTION (1953), (Hispanic), [CEM] Revs. J. Antonio Sanchez; Miguel Gomez Ortiz.
Res.: 100 Salinas Rd., 95076. Tel: 831-722-1104; Fax: 831-722-1931.
Catechesis/Religious Program—Tel: 831-722-9938. Cristofina Carrillo, D.R.E. Students 647.
3—ST. PATRICK (1861), Revs. Gregory Sandman; Jose Chavez; Victor Manuel Prado Cerda.
Res.: 721 Main St., 95076. Tel: 831-724-1317; Fax: 831-724-1627.
Catechesis/Religious Program—Tel: 831-724-2141. Sylvia Rosales, D.R.E. (English & Spanish). Students 1,095.

Shrines

SANTA CRUZ, SANTA CRUZ CO., SHRINE OF ST. JOSEPH GUARDIAN OF THE REDEEMER (1952), Res.: 544 W. Cliff Dr., 95060-6147. Tel: 831-471-0442; Fax: 831-457-1317. Rev. Brian Crawford, O.S.J. (SAC).
Guardian of the Redeemer Bookstore—Tel: 831-471-1700; Fax: 831-457-1317.

Chaplains of Public Institutions

ATASCADERO. *Atascadero State Hospital*. Rev. Richard Mickella.
PASO ROBLES. *El Paso de Robles School*. Mr. Jose Domingo Ojeyda. Dept. of the Youth Authority.
SAN LUIS OBISPO. *California Men's Colony East*.
California Men's Colony West. Rev. Michael T. Bell.
SOLEDAD. *Correctional Training Facility*. Sr. Maryann Cantlon, C.S.J., Chap. (Vacant)
Salinas Valley State Prison. (Vacant)

Special Assignment:
Very Rev.—
Crivello, Peter, V.G., Pastoral Office, 631 Abrego St., P.O. Box 2048, 93942-2048. Tel: 831-373-4345; Fax: 831-373-1175
Revs.—
Henry, James, V.F., Episcopal Vicar, 298 S. Thompson, Nipomo, 93444. Tel: 805-929-1922; Fax: 805-929-2662
Bethancourt, Michael A., Madonna del Sasso, 320 E. Laurel Dr., Salinas, 93906. Tel: 831-422-5323
Hill, Scott F., O.M.I., Catholic Chap., Dominican Santa Cruz Hospital, 1555 Soquel Ave., Santa Cruz, 95065. Tel: 831-462-7707; Fax: 831-462-7558
Laverone, Kenneth J., O.F.M., M.A., Judicial Vicar, Diocesan Tribunal, 485 Church St., 93940.
Sanchez, Antonio, Asst. Dir. of Vocations, Our Lady of the Assumption, 100 Salinas Rd., Watsonville, 95076. Tel: 831-722-1104; Fax: 831-722-1254
Volk, Michael, Asst. Dir. Vocations, St. Theodore's Church, P.O. Drawer B, Gonzales, 93926. Tel: 831-675-3648

On Leave:
Rev. Msgr.—
Fatooh, Charles G., V.G., P.O. Box 2048, 93942-2048. Tel: 831-373-4345; Fax: 831-373-1175
Rev.—
Faria, Carl M.D.

Retired:
Rev. Msgrs.—
MacMahon, Eamon, 24631 Guadalupe St., Carmel, 93923. Tel: 831-624-2275
Morgan, Thomas, New Bethany, 1441 Berkeley Dr., Los Banos, 93635. Tel: 209-829-0333
Murphy, D. Declan, V.G., Ceann Mhara, Myrtleville, County Cork, Ireland. Tel: 011-353-4831-566
Stieger, Joseph, c/o 161 Broad St., San Luis Obispo, 93405. Tel: 805-543-3284
Sweeney, Cornelius, 962 Piney Way, Morro Bay, 93442.
Revs.—
Adams, Michael T., Mary Star of the Sea Church, 870 8th St., San Pedro, 90731. Tel: 310-833-3541
Betrozoff, Larry, 528-B Sixth St., Hollister, 95023-3818. Tel: 831-636-7844. P.O. Box 1136, Tres Pinos, 95075-1136.
Bonjean, Richard, 1651 River Dr., Salinas, 93906. Tel: 831-449-1149
Cadera, James R., 2411 N. Boxwood St., Santa Maria, 93458-9031. Tel: 702-882-1968
Canal, Manuel, El Ferrol, 3-13a-la, Madrid, Spain.
Carvajal, Raul H.
Cowan, Vincent, P.O. Box 993, Fort Stockton, TX 79735. Tel: 510-623-0409
Freiermuth, Harry, P.O. Box 6923, Salinas, 93912-6923. Tel: 831-757-6656
Grech, Joseph, 49 Main Gate St., Victoria-Gozo 103 Malta.
Hall, Henry, P.O. Box 462312, Escondido, 92046-2312. Tel: 760-737-9001
Marini, Michael, 518 King St., Santa Cruz, 95060. Tel: 831-457-8628
Matz, Leo, Avila Gardens, 1171 Encanto Pkwy., Duarte, 91610. Tel: 626-359-5617
McDonald, Martin, 2 Huband Meys, Stephens Ln., Dublin 2, Ireland. Cell: 011-35-387-969-0117. Email: martinjmcdonald@hotmail.com
McSweeney, John, 1320 Padre Dr., Salinas, 93901. Tel: 831-422-4584
Migliazzo, Felix, 1249 Josselyn Canyon Rd., P.O. Box 88, 93942. Tel: 831-373-9120
O'Halloran, Richard, New Bethany, 1441 Berkeley Dr., Los Banos, 93635. Tel: 209-828-6077
O'Sullivan, Michael, 2247 Idylwild Pl., Arroyo Grande, 93420. Tel: 805-489-9160
Santamaria, Max, Cr. de Arizala 7, 31178 Abaruza, Navarra, Spain. Tel: 011-344-452-0021
Sanz, Eleutherio, Sacred Heart Church, 22 Stone St., Salinas, 93901. Tel: 831-424-1959
Schwarz, Robert, 4103 Golden Oaks Ln., 93940. Tel: 831-372-8848
Soares, Bernaro Manuel, P.O. Box 211, San Juan Bautista, 95045. Tel: 831-623-2056; Fax: 831-623-4169
Sweeney, James, 194 Island St., Morro Bay, 93442. Tel: 805-773-4108
Toan, Francis, 2034 N. Main St., Salinas, 93906. Tel: 831-449-0449
Vela, Fabian

Permanent Deacons:
Leach, David, St. Elizabeth Ann Seton Parish, 2050 Palisades Ave., Los Osos, 93402. Tel: 805-528-5319; Fax: 805-528-8893
Michaelson, Steve, 465 Golden Meadow Dr., Paso Robles. Tel: 805-434-2090
Miller, Harold, 121 Robin Dr., Marina, 93933. Tel: 831-883-2601

INSTITUTIONS LOCATED IN THE DIOCESE

[A] HIGH SCHOOLS, PRIVATE

MONTEREY. *Santa Catalina Upper School* (Girls) , 1500 Mark Thomas Dr., 93940-5291. Tel: 831-655-9315; Fax: 831-649-3056. Email: sister_claire@santacatalina.org. Web: www.santacatalina.org. Sr. Claire, Head of School. Lay Teachers 44; Total Enrollment (Grades 9-12) 295.

SALINAS. *Christian Brothers Institute of California, Inc. dba Palma High School* (Boys) , 919 Iverson St., 93901-1898. Tel: 831-422-6391; Fax: 831-422-5065. Email: dunne@palmahs.org. Web: www.palmahs.org. Bro. Patrick D. Dunne, C.F.C., Prin. Congregation of Christian Brothers Brothers 2; Lay Teachers 36; Boys (Jr. High) 161; Boys (Total) 632; Total Staff 38.
Congregation of Christian Brothers Residence, 935 Iverson St., 93901-1816. Tel: 831-758-2127; Fax: 831-422-5065. Bro. Bernard S. Samp, C.F.C., Community Leader. Brothers 5.

[B] HIGH SCHOOLS, DIOCESAN

SALINAS. *Notre Dame High School*, 455 Palma Dr., 93901. Tel: 831-751-1850; Fax: 831-757-5749. Email: info@nd-spirits.org. Web: www.notredamesalinas.org. Fabienne M. Esparza, Prin. Sisters 1; Lay Teachers 36; Girls 420.

SAN LUIS OBISPO. *Mission College Preparatory Catholic High School*, 682 Palm St., 93401. Tel: 805-543-2131; Fax: 805-543-4359. Email: info@missionprep.org. Web: www.missionprep.org. Rev. Charles J. Tilley, S.J., Prin. Sisters 1; Lay Teachers 19; Students 256; Total Staff 32.

WATSONVILLE. *St. Francis Central Coast Catholic High School*, 2400 E. Lake Ave., P.O. Box 2649, 95077-2649. Tel: 831-724-5933; Fax: 831-724-5995. Email: info@stfrancishigh.net. Web: www.stfrancishigh.net. Rev. John MRY, S.D.B., Pres.; Bro. Michael Touchstone, S.D.B., Prin. Joint High School between Diocese of Monterey and Salesians of St. John Bosco. Priests 2; Brothers 1; Sisters 2; Lay Teachers 6; Total Enrollment 115; Total Staff 15.

Moreland Notre Dame School, 133 Brennan St., 95076. Tel: 831-728-2051; Fax: 831-728-2052. Email: morelandnd@aol.com.

Sisters of Notre Dame de Namur Tel: 831-728-2051; Fax: 831-728-9205. Email: morelandnd@aol.com. Web: sndden.org. Christine Grul, Prin. Sisters 2; Lay Teachers 9; Students 275.

[C] ELEMENTARY SCHOOLS, PRIVATE

MONTEREY. *Santa Catalina Lower School*, (Grades PreK-8) , (Coed) , 1500 Mark Thomas Dr., 93940. Tel: 831-655-9324; Fax: 831-655-9303. Email: christy_pollacci@santacatalina.org. Web: www.santacatalina.org. Mrs. Linda Mutty, Div. Head, Grades 5-8; Christy Pollacci, Div. Head, PreK-4; Mary Coleman, Sec.; Linda Hughes, Sec. Lay Teachers 25; (Grades Pre-K-8) 266.

CORRALITOS. *Salesian Elementary & Jr. High School: Mary Help of Christians Youth Center*, (Grades K-8), 605 Enos Ln., 95076. Tel: 831-728-5518; Fax: 831-728-0273. Email: salesiansc@aol.com. Sr. Charlotte Greer, F.M.A. Sisters 8; Lay Teachers 10; Students 203; Total Staff 12.

WATSONVILLE. *St. Francis Youth Center*, 2401 E. Lake Ave., 95076. Tel: 831-722-3274. St. Francis Youth Center supports youth activities at parish summer camp and school level. Priests 2; Brothers 3; Total Staff 5.

[D] GENERAL HOSPITALS

SANTA CRUZ. *Dominican Hospital* dba Catholic Healthcare West , 1555 Soquel Dr., 95065. Tel: 831-462-7700; Fax: 831-462-7555. Web: www.dominicanhospital.org. Sr. Julie Hyer, O.P., Pres. & CEO. Sponsored by Sisters of St. Dominic, Congregation of the Most Holy Rosary, Adrian, MI Beds 402; Total Assisted 143,892; Total Staff 1,469.

[E] SPECIAL HOSPITALS AND SANATORIA ACUTE CARE HOSPITAL

MONTEREY. *Ave Maria Convalescent Hospital*, 1249 Josselyn Canyon Rd., 93940. Tel: 831-373-1216; Fax: 831-373-2238. Email: gjamch@aol.com. Rev. Felix Migliazzo, Chap. (Retired). Franciscan Sisters of the Immaculate Conception 4; Bed Capacity 31; Patients Assisted Annually 60; Total Staff 46.

[F] MONASTERIES AND RESIDENCES OF PRIESTS AND BROTHERS

MONTEREY. *Oratorian Community-Congregation of the Oratory of Pontifical Right*, 302 High St., P.O. Box 1688, 93942-1688. Tel: 831-373-0476; Fax: 831-373-1718. Very Rev. Peter C. Sanders, C.O., Provost. Tel: 831-375-9769; Revs. Thomas A. Kieffer, C.O., Vicar & Sec. Tel: 831-372-1325; Michael P. Drury, C.O. Tel: 831-646-8278 Leave of Absence. Priests 3.

Society of Mary (Marianists), P.O. Box 2048, 93942-2048. Tel: 831-373-2127; Fax: 831-373-3534. Email: lscrivani@dioceseofmonterey.org. Bro. Lawrence Scrivani, S.M., Contact.

ARROYO GRANDE. *St. Joseph Cupertino Friary*, 1352 Dale Ave., P.O. Box 820, 93421-0820. Tel: 805-473-2256; Fax: 805-489-8303. Revs. Roch Bartman, O.F.M.Conv. (Retired); Gregory Kareta, O.F.M. Conv. (Retired); Alphonse Van Guilder, O.F.M.Conv.; Charles Shelton, O.F.M. Conv.; Viktor Perez, O.F.M. Conv.; Bros. Dario Garcia, O.F.M.Conv.; Gerard Villanueva, O.F.M. Conv.; Casimir Roland, O.F.M.Conv., Guardian; Raphael Drew, O.F.M. Conv. Priests 5; Brothers 4; Friars 9.

St. Joseph Cupertino Province, Provincial Center, P.O. Box 820, 93421. Tel: 805-489-1012; Fax: 805-489-8303. Email: cldeitz@earthlink.net. Revs. Christopher L. Deitz, Min. Prov.; Ronald Rocky, Vicar Prov. & Prov. Sec.; Bros. Casimir Roland, O.F.M.Conv., Prov. Econom; George Cherrie, O.F.M.Conv., Prov. Exactor.

Attached to the Province but outside friaries: Rev. Kerry Abbott, O.F.M.Conv., Chap. Cpt., (U.S.A.F.).

BIG SUR. *New Camaldoli Hermitage*, 62475 Coast Hwy. # 1, 93920-9656. Tel: 831-667-2456; Fax: 831-667-0209. Email: monks@contemplation.com. Web: www.contemplation.com. Very Rev. Raniero Hoffman, O.S.B.Cam., Prior; Revs. Bruno Barnhardt, O.S.B.Cam.; Peter Damian Belisle, O.S.B.Cam.; Joseph Diemer, O.S.B.Cam.; Romuald Duscher, O.S.B.Cam.; Michael Fish, C.S.S.R.; Daniel Manger, O.S.B.Cam.; Bernard Massicotte, O.S.B.Cam.; Zacchaeus Maria Naegele, O.S.B.Cam.; Isaiah Teichert, O.S.B.Cam.; Joseph Wong, O.S.B.Cam. Professed Monks (including 17 priests) 25; Brothers 10.

On Special Assignment:

Incarnation Monastery, 1369 La Loma Ave., Berkeley, 94708. Tel: 510-845-0601; Fax: 510-548-6439. Revs. Andrew Colnaghi, O.S.B.Cam., Supr., Incarnation; Arthur Poulin, O.S.B.Cam.; Robert Hale, O.S.B.Cam.

On Leave: Revs. Cyprian Consiglio, O.S.B.Cam.; Robert John Powell, O.S.B.Cam.

SALINAS. *Palma Community*, 935 Iverson St., 93901. Tel: 831-758-2127; Fax: 831-422-5065. Email: brosamp@palmahs.org. Web: palmahs.org. Bros. B. Sebastian Samp, C.F.C.; Patrick D. Dunne, C.F.C.; Anthony C. O'Grady, C.F.C.; Gerard F. Murray, C.F.C.; Dennis J. Peterson, C.F.C.; Daniel L. Oehrle, C.F.C. Congregation of Christian Brothers Brothers 6.

SAN JUAN BAUTISTA. *Franciscan Friars*, P.O. Box 970, 95045-0970. Tel: 831-623-4234; Fax: 831-623-9046. Email: info@stfrancisretreat.com. Web: www.stfrancisretreat.com.

SAN LUIS OBISPO. *Monastery of the Risen Christ*, P.O. Box 3931, 93403. Tel: 805-544-1810; Fax: 805-544-1810. Email: monrc87@aol.com. Web: www.daily-word-of-life.com/monastery.htm.

Men's Residence, 2308 O'Connor Way, 93405. Tel: 805-544-1810; Fax: 805-544-1810. Rt. Rev. David Geraets, O.S.B., Supr.; Revs. Raymond V. Roh, O.S.B.; Stephen Odenbrett, O.S.B.; Albert Meyer, O.S.B.; Bro. Steve Coffey, O.S.B.; Rev. Raymond Greco, O.S.B. (Retired). Total Staff 4; Total in Residence 5.

Society of Mary (Marists)-S.M., 210 Lincoln St., 93405-2330. Tel: 805-541-4954. Rev. John Ulrich, S.M. (PHX), Contact.

SAN MIGUEL. *Franciscan Friars, O.F.M.* (Province of St. Barbara, Old Mission) , P.O. Box 69, 93451. Tel: 805-467-3256; Fax: 805-467-2248. Revs. Jerome Ahles, O.F.M.; Clifford Herle, O.F.M.; Thomas Messner, O.F.M.; Raymond Tintle, O.F.M.; Joseph Zermeno, O.F.M.; Bros. William Short, O.F.M., Guardian; Arturo Noyes, O.F.M., Vicar; Regan Chapman, O.F.M; Victor Hunter, O.F.M.; Bartholomew Mitchell, O.F.M.; Quentin Watson, O.F.M. Total Staff 3; Total in Residence 11.

Novitiate House for the Franciscan Friars, O.F.M. (Province of St. Barbara) , P.O. Box 69, 93451. Tel: 805-467-2801; Fax: 805-467-2448. Bro. Regan Chapman, O.F.M, Master of Novices; Rev. Clifford Herle, O.F.M., Asst.; Bro. William Short, O.F.M., Instructor. Novices 4; Total in Residence 7.

SANTA CRUZ. *Oblates of St. Joseph Provincial House and Shrine*, 544 W. Cliff Dr., 95060. Tel: 831-457-1868; Fax: 831-457-1317. Email: provincial@osjoseph.org. Web: www.osjoseph.org.

Legal Title: *Oblates of St. Joseph, Provincial House and Shrine of St. Joseph, Guardian of the Redeemer*

Religious Community Tel: 831-471-1702; Fax: 831-457-1317.

Provincial Tel: 831-457-1868; Fax: 831-457-1317.

Shrine of St. Joseph Tel: 831-471-0442; Fax: 831-457-1317. Revs. Aldo Grasso, O.S.J. (Italy); Bronius Kaunas, O.S.J. (Lithuania); Thomas Russo, O.S.J.; Brian Crawford, O.S.J., Prov. Supr. & Rector; Bros. Duain O'Mara, O.S.J.; Marcello DiNardo, O.S.J. Priests 4; Brothers 2; Total in Residence 6.

Religious Community Tel: 831-471-1702; Fax: 831-457-1317.

Society of Mary, Marianists, 285 Meder St., 95060. Tel: 831-423-9400; Fax: 831-423-8163. Email: RolBunda@aol.com. Web: www.newmanite.org. Rev. Roland Bunda, S.M., Dir.; Bro. Anthony Young, S.M. Total Staff 2; Total in Residence 2.

Society of Mary, Marists, Marist Community, 436 Effey St., 95062-2640. Tel: 831-425-5202; Fax: 831-429-5832. Email: hectorcsm3@aol.com. Revs. Percy Kimble, S.M.; Hector J. Cruz, S.M.; Scully S. Patrick, S.M. Total in Residence 3.

WATSONVILLE. *Salesians of St. John Bosco*

Saint Francis Salesian Community, 2401 East Lake Ave., 95076-2670. Tel: 831-763-4487; Fax: 831-722-8305. Web: www.donboscowest.org. Revs. Joseph Nguyen, S.D.B.; Harry Rasmussen, S.D.B., Vice Dir.; Justo Davila, S.D.B.; Roy Shelly, S.D.B., Diocesan Office; John Itzaina, S.D.B., Dir.; Bros. Michael Touchstone, S.D.B., Prin.; Michael Herbers, S.D.B., Treas.; Jerry Weirich, S.D.B., Business Mgr. In Res. Bro. Abel Zanella, S.D.B.

[G] CONVENTS AND RESIDENCES FOR SISTERS

MONTEREY. *Ave Maria Convent*, 1249 Josselyn Canyon Rd., P.O. Box 1977, 93942-1977. Tel: 831-373-1216; 831-375-8680; Fax: 831-373-2238. Sr. Constance, Supr.; Rev. Felix Migliazzo, Chap. (Retired). Motherhouse of the Franciscan Sisters of the Immaculate Conception and St. Joseph for the Dying Sisters 5.

Congregation of the Most Holy Rosary Sinsinawa Dominican Sisters, O.P. , c/o P.O. Box 2048, 93942-2048. Tel: 831-373-4345; Fax: 831-373-0302. Email: lgoedken@dioceseofmonterey.org.

APTOS. *St. Joseph's Monastery of the Poor Clares (Colettines)*, 1671 Pleasant Valley Rd., P.O. Box 160, 95001-0160. Tel: 831-761-9659; 831-761-9481; Fax: 831-761-9481. Sr. Mary Clare, P.C.C., Abbess. Poor Clares of California, Inc. Professed Sisters (Cloistered) 12; Extern 2; Postulants 1.

AROMAS. *Daughters of Charity of St. Vincent de Paul*, 829 Rebecca Cir., 95004-9019. Tel: 831-726-7176. Email: docaromas4@aol.com.

ARROYO GRANDE. *Sisters of Mercy*, 900 W. Branch St., 93420. Tel: 805-489-1438; Fax: 805-489-4367.

CAMBRIA. *Sisters of Charity of the Infant Mary*, 328 Warwick, 93428. Tel: 805-927-2943.

CARMEL. *Carmelite Monastery of Our Lady and St. Therese*, 27601 Hwy. 1, 93923-9612. Tel: 831-624-3043; Fax: 831-624-5495. Email: olmediatrix-st@carmelite-nuns.org. Sr. Mercedes of Mary Immaculate, O.C.D., Prioress. Professed Nuns 14.

Sisters of Notre Dame de Namur, 27951 Hwy. 1, 93921. Tel: 831-624-9416; Fax: 831-624-4865. Email: carmelhop@aol.com.

CORRALITOS. *Daughters of Mary Help of Christians*, 605 Enos Ln., 95076. Tel: 831-728-4700; Fax: 831-728-5802. Email: fmasuocor@aol.com. Sr. Theresa Sironi, F.M.A., Supr. Sisters 8.

FREEDOM. *Sisters of the Divinie Savior (Salvatorians)-S.D.S.*, 2030 Pajaro Ln, #3202, 95019. Tel: 831-724-9678. Email: srjeanschafer@aol.com. Sr. Jean Schafer, S.D.S., Contact.

GONZALES. *Sisters of Charity of the Infant Mary Capitanio Convent*, 512 Fairview Dr., Box 178, 93926. Tel: 831-675-2975; Fax: 831-675-2974. Email: sistersmb@aol.com. Sr. Rosangela Filippini, I.M., Supr. Residents 4.

MORRO BAY. *Immaculate Heart of Mary*, P.O. Box 695, 93443-0695. Tel: 805-772-8146. Sr. Moira Lyons, I.H.M., Contact Person.

PISMO BEACH. *Franciscan Sisters of the Atonement (Graymoor)*, 344 Pomeroy Ave., 93449. Tel: 805-773-3427.

SALINAS. *Bethany*, 15785 Alto Way, 93907. Tel: 831-663-3675; Fax: 831-663-3749. Email: virgennina@aol.com. Sr. Patricia Murtagh, I.M., Supr. Sisters of Charity of the Infant Mary Residents 4.

Sisters of Notre Dame, 56 Talbot St., 93901. Tel: 831-424-4370. Email: bmatasci@aol.com. Residents 2.

Sisters of St. Joseph of Carondolet, 1335 Byron Dr., 93901. Tel: 831-758-0931; Fax: 831-758-1318. Email: mmscsj@hotmail.com. Web: www.csjla.org. Rev. Richard O'Halloran, Chap. Madonna Manor Sisters 3.

SAN JUAN BAUTISTA. *Franciscan Sisters of the Atonement*, P.O. Box 1094, 95045. Tel: 831-623-4267; Fax: 831-623-4359. Franciscan Sisters of Atonement 4.

SAN LUIS OBISPO. *Monastery of the Risen Christ* (Women's Residence) , P.O. Box 3931, 9340--393. Tel: 805-544-7808; Fax: 805-544-1810. Email: monrc87@aol.com. Web: www.daily-word-of-life.com/monastery.htm. 2304 O'Connor Way, 93405. Tel: 805-544-7808; Fax: 805-554-1810. Connie Mayrhofer, O.S.B., O.B.L.

SAN MIGUEL. *Franciscan Sisters of the Atonement (Graymoor)*, P.O. Box 238, 93451. Tel: 805-467-0022.

SANTA CRUZ. *Franciscan Hospitaller Sisters of the Immaculate Conception*, 907 Columbia St., 95060. Tel: 831-426-5035. Sr. Elisa Santos, F.H.I.C., Local Supr. Total Residents 3.

Immaculate Heart of Mary, Holy Cross Church, 126 High St., 95060. Tel: 831-423-4182; Fax: 831-423-1043. Email: bpedrazzi@compuserve.com.

Sisters of the Holy Names of Jesus and Mary, Villa Maria del Mar, 2-1918 East Cliff Dr., 95062. Tel: 831-475-1236; Fax: 831-475-8867. Email: jmvillasc@earthlink.net. Provincial Admin., P.O. Box 907, Los Gatos, 95031. Sisters also living in Aptos, Hollisten, Salinas and Watsonville. Sisters 4.

SOQUEL. *St. Clare's Retreat*, 2381 Laurel Glen Rd., 95073. Tel: 831-423-8093; Fax: 831-423-1541. Email: stclaresretreat@juno.com. Web: www.infoteam.com/nonprofit/stclaresretreat/index.html. Sr. Mary Frances Coleman, R.S.M., Supr. Total Staff 8; Total Residents 6.

WATSONVILLE. *Congregation of the Most Holy Rosary (San Rafael Dominican Sisters) O.P.*, 26-B Kilburn St., 95076. Tel: 831-776-6877. Sr. Cathy Murray, O.P., Contact Person.

Moreland Notre Dame Convent, 656 Main St., 95076. Tel: 831-724-7696; 831-724-3670; Fax: 831-768-9828. Email: watsonsnd@aol.com. Web: sndden-ca.org. Sr. Denis Marie Harney, S.N.D., Coord. Sisters of Notre Dame de Namur Residents 7.

Sisters of the Holy Names of Jesus and Mary, Watsonville Community, 26 Kilburn St., 95076. Tel: 831-728-4063. Sisters 3.

[H] RETREAT HOUSES

APTOS. *Camp St. Francis*, 2320 Sumner Ave., 95003. Tel: 831-684-1439; Fax: 831-662-2454. Bro. Michael Herbers, S.D.B., Dir. Conducted by Salesians of St. John Bosco.; Summer Camp for Boys 8-17, Meeting Center for large groups and Retreat Center for large groups of youth and adults.

BIG SUR. *New Camaldoli Hermitage*, 62475 Coast Hwy. #1, 93920-9656. Tel: 831-667-2456; Fax: 831-667-0209. Email: monks@contemplation.com. Web: www.contemplation.com. Very Rev. Raniero Hoffman, O.S.B.Cam., Prior. Camaldolese Hermitage and retreat house. Total in Residence 24.

SAN JUAN BAUTISTA. *St. Francis Retreat Center* Conducted by Franciscan Friars. Province of St. Barbara. , P.O. Box 970, 95045. Tel: 831-623-4234; Fax: 831-623-9046. Email: info@stfrancisretreat.com. Web: www.stfrancisretreat.com. Deacon Angelo Cardinalli, O.F.M.; Rev. Richard McManus, O.F.M., Dir. & Local Guardian; Deacon Fabian Walker, O.F.M.; Rev. Gavin Griffith, O.F.M. Retreats for men, women, singles, married couples, A.A. and 12-step. Programs include Spiritual Growth, Ecumenical, Spanish. Priests 2; Brothers 2; Total in Residence 10; Total Staff 18.

SAN MIGUEL. *San Miguel Retreat House*, P.O. Box 69, 93451. Tel: 805-467-3256; Fax: 805-467-2448. Bro. Bill Short, O.F.M., Supr. Total Staff 2.

SANTA CRUZ. *Villa Maria del Mar*, 2-1918 E. Cliff Dr., 95062. Tel: 831-475-1236; Fax: 831-475-8867. Email: villamariadelmar@earthlink.net. Provincial Admin., P.O. Box 907, Los Gatos, 95031. Sr. Patricia Doyle, S.N.J.M., Admin. Sisters of the Holy Names of Jesus and Mary Sisters 7; Lay Staff 12; Total Staff 19.

SOQUEL. *St. Clare's Retreat House*, 2381 Laurel Glen Rd., 95073. Tel: 831-423-8093; Fax: 831-423-1541. Email: stclaresretreat@juno.com. Web: www.infoteam.com/nonprofit/stclaresretreat/index.html. Sr. Mary Frances Coleman, R.S.M., Retreat Dir.; Rev. William Hallahan, O.M.I. (OAK), Chap. Franciscan Missionary Sisters of Our Lady of Sorrows 6; Total Staff 8.

[I] NEWMAN CHAPLAINS AND CENTERS

MONTEREY. *Department of Campus Ministry* P.O. Box 2048, 93942-2048. Tel: 831-373-4345, Ext. 299; Fax: 831-373-6761. Email: frrshelly@dioceseofmonterey.org. Web: www.dioceseofmonterey.org. Rev. Roy Shelly, S.D.B., Dir. Total in Residence 1; Total Staff 15.

California State Polytechnic Institute/Cuesta College, Newman Catholic Center, 1472 Foothill Blvd., San Luis Obispo, 93405-1416. Tel: 805-543-4105; Fax: 805-543-5671. Email: ncc@slonewman.org. Web: www.slonewman.org. Sisters Theresa Harpin, C.S.J., Dir.; Mary Pat White, R.S.C.J., Assoc. Dir.; Linda Garcia-Inchausti, Dir. of Admin.; David Maichrowicz, Student Asst.; Tom Scortino, Student Asst.

Cabrillo College, Santa Cruz, 95064. Tel: 831-479-6100; Fax: 831-423-8163. Rev. Roland Bunda, S.M., Dir. Campus Ministry, Newman Catholic Community, (Marianist); Bro. Anthony Young, S.M., Outreach & Ecumenical Min., (Marianist); Ann Brown, Lay Volunteer, (Marist).

University of California at Santa Cruz, 285 Meder St., Santa Cruz, 95060. Tel: 831-423-9400; Fax: 831-423-8163. Web: www.newmanite.org. Rev. Roland Bunda, S.M., Chap. & Dir. Campus Ministry, Newman Catholic Community, (Marianist); Bro. Anthony Young, S.M., Outreach & Ecumenical Min., (Marianist); Ann Brown, (Marist Lay Volunteer).

California State University of Monterey Bay Tel: 831-423-9400; Fax: 831-423-8163. Rev. Roland Bunda S.M., Dir. Campus Ministry, Newman Catholic Community, (Marianist); Bro. Anthony Young, S.M., Outreach & Ecumenical Min., (Marianist); Ann Brown, (Marist Lay Volunteer). 285 Meder St., Santa Cruz, 95060. Tel: 831-423-9400; Fax: 831-423-8163.

[J] SENIOR RESIDENCES

SALINAS. *Villa Serra Corporation*, 1320 Padre Dr., 93901. Tel: 831-754-5532; Fax: 831-754-5609. Email villaserra2@emeritus.com. Sponsored by the Diocese of Monterey and Dominican Santa Cruz Hospital. Total in Residence 149; Total Staff 65.

SANTA CRUZ. *Dominican Oaks Corporation*, 3400 Paul Sweet Rd., 95062. Tel: 831-462-6257; Fax: 831-462-6742. Email: droutley@chw.edu. Web: www.dominicanoaks.com. Sponsored by the Dominican Santa Cruz Hospital. Total in Residence 228; Total Staff 80.

[K] MISCELLANEOUS

MONTEREY. *Newman Institute for Historical and Religious Studies*, Domus Patris Foundation, P.O. Box 748, 93942. Tel: 831-373-0477. Rev. Thomas A. Kieffer, Orat., Admin.

SALINAS. *Villa Serra Corporation*, 1320 Padre Dr., 93901. Tel: 831-754-5532; Fax: 831-754-5609. Email: villaserra2@emeritus.com Total in Residence 161; Total Staff 62.

WATSONVILLE. *Magnificat the Monterey Bay Chapter*, 120 Enos Ln., 95076. Tel: 831-724-6933. Maureen Roach, Coord.; Patricia Probert, Treas.; Gayle Stenstrom, Sec.; Rev. Patrick Dooling, Spiritual Advisor. A Ministry to Catholic Women

St. Thomas More Society, c/o 262 E. Lake Ave., 95076. Tel: 831-722-2456; Fax 831-722-0414. Raymond A. AmRhein, Pres.

RELIGIOUS INSTITUTES OF MEN REPRESENTED IN THE DIOCESE

For further details refer to the corresponding bracketed number in the Religious Institutes of Men or Women section.

[]—*Camaldolesi Hermits*—O.S.B.Cam.
[0310]—*Congregation of Christian Brothers* (Western U.S. Prov., Joliet, IL)—C.F.C.
[0480]—*Conventual Franciscans*—O.F.M.Conv
[0520]—*Franciscan Friars* (Santa Barbara Prov.)—O.F.M.
[0910]—*Oblates of Mary Immaculate*—O.M.I.
[0930]—*Oblates of St. Joseph* (Asti, Italy)—O.S.J.
[0950]—*Oratorians*—Orat.
[0200]—*Order of St. Benedict* (Monastery of the Risen Christ)—O.S.B.
[1070]—*Redemptorist Fathers*—C.SS.R.
[1190]—*Salesians of Don Bosco (Turin, Italy)*—S.D.B.
[0690]—*Society of Jesus*—S.J.
[0760]—*Society of Mary, Marianists*—S.M.
[]—*Society of Mary, Marist*—S.M.

RELIGIOUS INSTITUTES OF WOMEN REPRESENTED IN THE DIOCESE

[]—*Congregation of the Most Holy Rosary* (San Rafael Dominican Sisters)—O.P.
[1070-13]—*Congregation of the Most Holy Rosary - Adrian Dominican Sisters*—O.P.
[1070-03]—*Congregation of the Most Holy Rosary - Sinsinawa Dominican Sisters*—O.P.
[1920]—*Congregation of the Sisters of the Holy Cross* (Western Region)—C.S.C.
[0760]—*Daughters of Charity of St. Vincent de Paul*—D.C.
[0880]—*Daughters of Mary & Joseph*—D.M.J.
[0850]—*Daughters of Mary of Help of Christians*—F.M.A.
[0420]—*Discalced Carmelite Nuns*—O.C.D.
[1270]—*Franciscan Hospitaller Sisters of the Immaculate Conception*—F.H.I.C.
[1390]—*Franciscan Missionary Sisters of Our Lady of Sorrows*—O.S.F.
[1190]—*Franciscan Sisters of the Atonement*—S.A.
[1300]—*Franciscan Sisters of the Immaculate Conception and St. Joseph for the Dying*—O.S.F.
[]—*Immaculate Heart of Mary*—I.H.M.
[3760]—*Order of St. Clare*—P.C.C.
[3465]—*Religious of the Sacred Heart of Mary*—R.S.H.M.
[]—*Salesian Sisters of St. John Bosco*
[2970]—*School Sisters of Notre Dame*—S.S.N.D.
[]—*Sisters of Charity of the Infant Mary*—I.M.
[2575]—*Sisters of Mercy* (Irish American Prov.)—R.S.M.
[3000]—*Sisters of Notre Dame de Namur*—S.N.D.deN.
[]—*Sisters of St. Benedict* (Monastery of the Risen Christ)—O.S.B.
[]—*Sisters of St. Benedict*—O.S.B.
[3840]—*Sisters of St. Joseph of Carondelet*—C.S.J.
[]—*Sisters of St. Joseph of Carondelet*
[1030]—*Sisters of the Divine Savior* (Salvatorians)—S.D.S
[]—*Sisters of the Holy Cross*
[1990]—*Sisters of the Holy Name of Jesus and Mary*—S.N.J.M.

DIOCESAN CEMETERIES

MONTEREY. *Diocesan Cemeteries Office*, P.O. Box 2048, 93942-2048. 485 Church St., 93940. Tel: 831-373-4345; Fax: 831-373-6761. Email: cemeteries@dioceseofmonterey.org. Mr. Clancy D'Angelo, Dir.

San Carlos, Tel: 831-372-0327; Fax: 831-372-8726.

CAMBRIA. *Old Santa Rosa*, Tel: 805-541-0584; Fax: 805-541-2127.

HOLLISTER. *Sacred Heart/Calvary*, Tel: 831-637-0131; Fax: 831-637-2980.

SALINAS. *Queen of Heaven*, Tel: 831-449-5890; Fax: 831-449-6928.

SAN LUIS OBISPO. *Old Mission*, Tel: 805-541-0584; Fax: 805-541-2127.

SANTA CRUZ. *Holy Cross*, Tel: 831-475-3222; Fax: 831-475-6132.

NECROLOGY

✠ Clinch, Most Rev. Harry Anselm, Retired Bishop of Monterey in California—Died March 8, 2003
† Marron, Rev. Msgr. James, (Retired)—Died March 8, 2003
† Degan, Siro Dal—Died Nov. 28, 2002
† Leonard, Joseph, (Retired)—Died Nov. 1, 2003

Diocese of Nashville

(Dioecesis Nashvillensis)

Most Reverend

EDWARD U. KMIEC, D.D., S.T.L.

Bishop of Nashville; ordained December 20, 1961; appointed Titular Bishop of Simidicca and Auxiliary Bishop of Trenton August 26, 1982; consecrated November 3, 1982; appointed Bishop of Nashville October 13, 1992; installed December 3, 1992 *Office: The Catholic Center*, 2400 21st Ave., S., Nashville, TN 37212. Tel: 615-383-6393.

Most Reverend

JAMES D. NIEDERGESES, D.D.

Retired Bishop of Nashville; ordained May 20, 1944; appointed April 8, 1975; consecrated May 20, 1975; retired October 13, 1992 *Res.: 239 Cana Cir., Nashville, TN 37205.*

ESTABLISHED JULY 28, 1837.

Square Miles 16,302.

Comprises the Counties of Bedford, Cannon, Cheatham, Clay, Coffee, Davidson, DeKalb, Dickson, Franklin, Giles, Grundy, Hickman, Houston, Humphreys, Jackson, Lawrence, Lewis, Lincoln, Macon, Marshall, Maury, Montgomery, Moore, Overton, Perry, Putnam, Robertson, Rutherford, Smith, Stewart, Sumner, Trousdale, VanBuren, Warren, Wayne, White, Williamson and Wilson in the State of Tennessee.

Legal Title: For legal titles of parishes and diocesan institutions, consult the Chancery Office.

Chancery Office: 2400 21st Ave., S., Nashville, TN 37212. Tel: 615-383-6393; Fax: 615-292-8411.

Web: www.serve.com/DIOCNASH/

Email: nashdio@aol.com

STATISTICAL OVERVIEW

Personnel	
Bishop	1
Retired Bishops	1
Priests: Diocesan Active in Diocese	34
Priests: Diocesan Active Outside Diocese	3
Priests: Retired, Sick or Absent	12
Number of Diocesan Priests	49
Religious Priests in Diocese	28
Total Priests in Diocese	77
Extern Priests in Diocese	8
Permanent Deacons in Diocese	52
Total Brothers	1
Total Sisters	183
Parishes	
Parishes	51
With Resident Pastor:	
Resident Diocesan Priests	27
Resident Religious Priests	13
Without Resident Pastor:	
Administered by Priests	11
Missions	3
Pastoral Centers	2
Professional Ministry Personnel:	
Brothers	1
Sisters	5
Lay Ministers	37
Welfare	
Catholic Hospitals	1
Total Assisted	57,451
Health Care Centers	4
Total Assisted	190,561
Homes for the Aged	1
Total Assisted	110
Day Care Centers	3
Total Assisted	770
Special Centers for Social Services	9
Total Assisted	64,500
Educational	
Diocesan Students in Other Seminaries	10
Total Seminarians	10
Colleges and Universities	1
Total Students	863
High Schools, Diocesan and Parish	2
Total Students	1,345
High Schools, Private	1
Total Students	273
Elementary Schools, Diocesan and Parish	17
Total Students	3,915
Elementary Schools, Private	2
Total Students	653
Catechesis/Religious Education:	
High School Students	1,672
Elementary Students	5,648
Total Students under Catholic Instruction	14,379
Teachers in the Diocese:	
Priests	1
Sisters	34
Lay Teachers	481
Vital Statistics	
Receptions into the Church:	
Infant Baptism Totals	1,879
Adult Baptism Totals	203
Received into Full Communion	333
First Communions	1,443
Confirmations	1,271
Marriages:	
Catholic	252
Interfaith	194
Total Marriages	446
Deaths	410
Total Catholic Population	71,188
Total Population	2,105,161

Former Bishops—Rt. Revs. RICHARD PIUS MILES, O.P., D.D., consecrated Sept. 16, 1838; died Feb. 21, 1860; JAMES WHELAN, O.P., D.D., consecrated May, 1859; resigned May, 1863; died Feb. 18, 1878; P. A. FEEHAN, consecrated Nov. 1, 1865; created first Archbishop of Chicago, Sept. 10, 1880; died July 12, 1902; JOSEPH RADEMACHER, D.D., consecrated June 24, 1883; transferred to Ft. Wayne, July 13, 1893; died Jan. 12, 1900; THOMAS S. BYRNE, D.D., consecrated July 25, 1894; died Sept. 4, 1923; Most Revs. ALPHONSE J. SMITH, D.D., consecrated March 25, 1924; died Dec. 16, 1935; WILLIAM L. ADRIAN, D.D., consecrated April 16, 1936; died Feb. 13, 1972; JOSEPH A. DURICK, D.D. (Retired), consecrated March 24, 1955; retired April 8, 1975; died June 26, 1994; JAMES D. NIEDERGESES, D.D. (Retired), consecrated May 20, 1975; retired Oct. 13, 1992.

Vicars General—Revs. J. PATRICK CONNOR, V.G., 3019 Cayce Ln., Columbia, 38401; DAVID R. PERKIN, J.C.L., V.G., 2400 21st Ave., S., Nashville, 37212.

Moderator of the Curia and Vicar General—Rev. DAVID R. PERKIN, J.C.L., V.G., The Catholic Center, 2400 21st Ave., S., Nashville, 37212.

Deans—Revs. W. BERNARD NIEDERGESES, Central Deanery; DAVID R. CHOBY, Northeast Deanery; EDWARD STEINER, Northwest Deanery; DEXTER S. BREWER, J.C.L., Southeast Deanery; RICHARD G. BUCHIGNANI, Southwest Deanery.

Vicar for Catholic Charities—Rev. PHILIP M. BREEN, 5101 Charlotte Ave., Nashville, 37209.

Chancery Office—2400 21st Ave. S., Nashville, 37212. Tel: 615-383-6393; Fax: 615-292-8411. Office Hours: Mon.-Fri. 8-4:30; All Official business should be directed to this office.

Chancellor—Deacon HANS M. TOECKER.

Assistant Chancellor—MARY MARGARET LAMBERT.

Accounting Systems—Mr. MICHAEL F. NOLAN, Chief Fin. Officer; Ms. ELAINE FLICK, Controller; TERESA OSBORNE, Asst. Controller, Central Accounting.

General Counsel—Rev. JAMES K. MALLETT.

Diocesan Tribunal—2400 21st Ave. S., Nashville, 37212. Tel: 615-383-6393; Fax: 615-292-8411.

Judicial Vicar—Rev. DEXTER S. BREWER, J.C.L.

Adjutant Judicial Vicar—Rev. DAVID R. PERKIN, J.C.L., V.G.

Promoter of Justice—Ms. JANETTE BUCHANAN.

Defenders of the Bond—Most Rev. JAMES D. NIEDERGESES, D.D. (Retired); Revs. JOHN C. HENRICK; JOHN SIMS BAKER; JANETTE BUCHANAN, J.C.L.

Advocates—Ms. JANETTE BUCHANAN; Mrs. PATRICIA BURNS; Mrs. JULIE CONNOLLY; Mrs. LINDA NELSON.

Judges—Revs. DEXTER S. BREWER, J.C.L.; DAVID R. CHOBY; RICHARD G. BUCHIGNANI; WILLIAM S. BEVINGTON; JAMES K. MALLETT; DAVID R. PERKIN, J.C.L., V.G.

Assessors—Mrs. LINDA NELSON; Mrs. PATRICIA BURNS.

Formal Case Instructor—Mrs. JULIE CONNOLLY.

Documentary Case Instructor—Mrs. LINDA NELSON.

Auditors— All priests and deacons assigned in the Nashville and Knoxville dioceses

Secretary-Notaries—Mrs. PATRICIA BURNS; Mrs. JULIE CONNOLLY; Mrs. LINDA NELSON; Mrs. ANN H. KANENGIETER.

Presbyteral Council and College of Consultors—Most Rev. EDWARD U. KMIEC, D.D., S.T.L.; Revs. THOMAS BIELAWA, S.D.S.; JOSEPH DESMOND; WIATT A. FUNK; JOHN C. HENRICK; ZACHARIAS PAYIKAT, C.M.I.; JOHN SAPPENFIELD; EDWARD T. ALBERTS; EDWARD F. STEINER III; JAMES K. MALLETT; JAMES ARMOUR; DAVID R. PERKIN, J.C.L., V.G.

Diocesan Finance Board—Most Rev. EDWARD U. KMIEC, D.D., S.T.L.; Revs. STEPHEN A. KLASEK; JAMES K. MALLETT; DAVID R. PERKIN, J.C.L., V.G.; DAVID R. CHOBY; Mr. MICHAEL F. NOLAN; Mr. DENNIS DONOVAN; Mr. L. GINO MARCHETTI; Mr.

JOE IMORDE; Mr. MICHAEL J. KANE; Mr. WILLIAM HILL; Ms. SHEILA JACKSON PRIEBEL; Mr. KEVIN MARCHETTI; Mr. EDWARD STACK; Mr. WILLIAM P. VARLEY; Mr. DON TURK; Dr. JAMES WILSON; Mr. PAT WATSON.

DIONASH— A Partnership acting as Nominee for marketable securities for the Diocese of Nashville

Diocesan Offices and Directors

The following offices and agencies are located at the Chancery unless otherwise indicated.

Archives and Records—Deacon HANS M. TOECKER.

Campaign for Human Development—Mr. WILLIAM P. SINCLAIR, A.C.S.W., Dir., St. Mary Villa, 30 White Bridge Rd., Nashville, 37205.

Campus Ministries—Rev. RICHARD GROSS, S.J., Diocesan Coord.

Vanderbilt—Rev. RICHARD GROSS, S.J., Vanderbilt Catholic Community, Box 6311, Station B, Nashville, 37235. Tel: 615-322-0104.

Korean—Rev. JOSEPH AN, Dir., Korean Catholic Community, 512 Old Hickory Blvd., Nashville, 37209. Tel: 615-353-5730.

MTSU-Murfreesboro—Rev. WIATT A. FUNK, St. Rose of Lima Church, 1601 N. Tennessee Blvd., Murfreesboro, 37130. Tel: 615-893-1843.

Austin Peay-Clarksville—Rev. EDWARD STEINER, Immaculate Conception, 709 Franklin St., Clarksville, 37040. Tel: 931-645-6275.

Tenn. Tech-Cookeville—Rev. DONALD LOSKOT, S.D.S., St. Thomas Aquinas Church, 401 N. Washington Ave., Cookeville, 38501. Tel: 931-565-2575.

Fisk-Meharry-Tennessee State University Campus Ministries—KAREN MTSHALI, St. Vincent de Paul Church, 1700 Heiman St., Nashville, 37208. Tel: 615-320-0695.

Univ. of South-Sewanee—Rev. DEXTER S. BREWER, J.C.L., Good Shepherd Church, 2021 Decherd Blvd., Decherd, 37324. Tel: 931-967-0961.

Catholic Charismatic Renewal—Rev. JOHN KIRK, Bishop's Liaison; Mrs. TERESA SEIBERT, Assoc. Liaison.

Catholic Charities of Tennessee, Inc.—Mr. WILLIAM P. SINCLAIR A.C.S.W., Dir., St. Mary Villa, 30 White Bridge Rd., Nashville, 37205. Tel: 615-352-3087; Fax: 615-352-8591.

Catholic Public Policy Commission of TN—Exec. Secretaries: JENNFIER MURPHY; MICHAEL MURPHY.

Catholic Relief Services—Deacon HANS M. TOECKER, Dir.

Catholic Social Services of Nashville—Ms. EILEEN BEEHAN Dept. Dir., St. Mary Villa, 30 White Bridge Rd., Nashville, 37205. Tel: 615-352-3087.

Catholic Youth Office and Search Program—Rev. MARK BECKMAN, 2011 West End Ave., Nashville, 37203. Tel: 615-327-0674.

Cemeteries—Mr. MICHAEL F. NOLAN, Dir.

Censor Librorum—Rev. JAMES K. MALLETT.

Clergy Benefit Foundation—Most Rev. EDWARD U. KMIEC, D.D., S.T.L., Pres.; Revs. EDWARD F. STEINER III, Chm.; CHARLEY GIACOSA; WYATT FUNK; DEXTER BREWER; STEVE WOLF; Mr. MICHAEL F. NOLAN, Admin.

Clergy Personnel Board—Most Rev. EDWARD U. KMIEC, D.D., S.T.L.; Revs. STEPHEN A. KLASEK; MARK BECKMAN; DAVID R. PERKIN, J.C.L., V.G.

Continuing Education of Clergy—Rev. EDWARD STEINER, Dir.

Cursillo—DAN HOLDEN, Lay Dir.; Deacon MARTIN DESCHENES, Assoc. Spiritual Advisor

Permanent Diaconate Office—Deacon JAMES W. MCKENZIE, Dir.

Diocesan Communications Director—RICK MUSSACHIO.

Diocesan Planning—Rev. STEPHEN A. KLASEK, Dir.

Ecumenical and Interreligious Relations—Deacon WILLIAM J. DICKSON, Dir.

Hispanic Ministry—Rev. RICHARD GAGNON, S.D.S., Dir.; Mrs. ANABELL C. TREVINO, Asst. Dir.

Korean Catholic Community of St. Joseph—Rev. JOSEPH AN, Dir., 5565 Pettus Rd., Antioch, 37013. Tel: 615-727-1225. Email: koreancc@comcast.net.

Holy Childhood Association—Deacon HANS M. TOECKER, Dir.

Human Resources—TERRY ROBINSON, Dir.

Lay Retirement Administrative Board—Mr. MICHAEL F. NOLAN; JACK SMITHWICK, Chm.; ROBERT TRUE; JAN LAWRENCE; TERRY ROBINSON.

Liturgical Life—Rev. EDWARD T. ALBERTS, Dir.

Ministry Formation Services—Ms. JOCELINE LEMAIRE, Dir., Contact this office for the following concerns: Religious Education, Family Ministry, Youth Ministry, Pastoral Services, Liturgy, Parish Councils, Leadership Training, Lay Ministry, Rite of Christian Initiation of Adults, Pro-Life Education Evangelization, Peace & Justice.

Newspaper—RICK MUSACCHIO, Editor. "The Tennessee Register"

Prison Ministry—TERRANCE HORGAN, Ph.D., Criminal Justice Advocacy.

Pontifical Mission Societies—Deacon HANS M. TOECKER, Dir.

Catholic Charities Refugee Resettlement Program—HOLLY JOHNSON, Dir., 10 S. 6th St., Nashville, 37206. Tel: 615-259-3567; Fax: 615-259-2851.

Schools Office—THERESE WILLIAMS, Supt., 30 White Bridge Rd., Nashville, 37205. Tel: 615-352-3087.

Stewardship and Development—MARK BERLYN, Dir.

Victim Assistance Coordinator—Deacon HANS M. TOECKER, 2400 21st Ave., S., Nashville, 37212. Tel: 615-783-0765; Fax: 615-292-8411. Email: hans.toecker@dioceseofnashville.com.

Vietnamese Ministry—Rev. PETER DO QUANG CHOU, P.O. Box 55, Ashland City, 37015. Tel: 615-792-4255.

Vocations—Rev. STEPHEN J. WOLF, Dir. Vocation Formation, 14544 Lebanon Rd., Old Hickory, 37138.

CLERGY, PARISHES, MISSIONS AND PAROCHIAL SCHOOLS

CITY OF NASHVILLE
(DAVIDSON COUNTY)

1—CATHEDRAL OF THE INCARNATION (1909), Revs. Patrick J. Kibby; James E. Armour. In Res., Most Rev. Edward U. Kmiec; Deacons Mark Faulkner; John G. Krenson.
Church: 2015 W. End Ave., 37203. Tel: 615-327-2330; Fax: 615-320-5650.
Catechesis/Religious Program—Tel: 615-327-0919. Suzanne Southworth, D.R.E. Students 295.

2—ST. ANN (1921), Rev. Philip M. Breen; Deacons John P. Casey; William J. Dickson.
Church: 5101 Charlotte Ave., 37209. Tel: 615-298-1782; Fax: 615-297-4326.
School—Tel: 615-269-0568; Fax: 615-297-1383. Mr. John Foreman, Prin. Lay Teachers 13; Students 180.
Catechesis/Religious Program—Martin Mulloy, D.R.E.; Stephanie Keller, D.R.E. Students 70.

3—ASSUMPTION (1859), Attended by, St. Pius X Church, Nashville. Revs. W. Bernard Niedergeses; Joseph Shepherd, C.M.I.
Church: 1227 Seventh Ave. N., 37208. Tel: 615-256-2729; Fax: 615-256-0987.

4—CHRIST THE KING (1937), Rev. James K. Mallett; Deacons Andrew D. McKenzie; James E. Stanford; Robert H. True.
Church: 3001 Belmont Blvd., 37212. Tel: 615-292-2884; Fax: 615-383-0026.
School—Tel: 615-292-9465; Fax: 615-292-2477. Mrs. Christine Caron Gebhardt, Prin. Lay Teachers 20; Students 242.
Catechesis/Religious Program—Tel: 615-292-2884, Ext. 302. David Lovell, D.R.E. Students 75.

5—CHURCH OF THE MOST HOLY NAME (1857), Rev. Joseph A. Sanches (ATL), Admin.; Deacon Robert L. Mahoney.
Church: 521 Woodland St., 37206. Tel: 615-254-8847; Fax: 615-254-1106.
Catechesis/Religious Program—Tom Cook, D.R.E. Students 43.

6—ST. EDWARD (1952), Rev. Joseph P. Breen; Deacons Gary D. Altman; Brian Edwards; Milton Von Mann.
Church: 188 Thompson Ln., 37211. Tel: 615-833-5520; Fax: 615-833-3738.
School—Tel: 615-833-5770; Fax: 615-833-9739. Brian Knoop, Prin. Lay Teachers 31; Students 474.
Catechesis/Religious Program—Sr. Louise Shoulta, R.S.M., D.R.E. Students 275.

7—ST. HENRY (1958), Revs. Michael O. Johnston; Charley Giacosa; Deacons Jack Srouji; Martin Deschenes.
Church: 6401 Harding Rd., 37205. Tel: 615-352-2259; Fax: 615-356-6321.
School—Tel: 615-352-1328; Fax: 615-356-9293. Sr. Mary Anne Zuberbueler, O.P., Prin. Dominican Sisters of St. Cecilia Congregation 4; Lay Teachers 45; Students 676.
Catechesis/Religious Program—Tel: 615-353-0668. Sr. Suzanne Stalm, R.S.M., D.R.E. Students 269.

8—HOLY ROSARY (1954), Rev. Stephen A. Klasek; Deacons Gilbert P. Huhlein; Kenneth Steinbrecher; Wayne Gregory.
Church: 190 Graylynn Dr., 37214. Tel: 615-889-4065; Fax: 615-889-3421.
School—Tel: 615-883-1108; Fax: 615-885-5100. Peggy Walker, Prin. Lay Teachers 31; Students 528.
Catechesis/Religious Program—Students 77.

9—ST. MARY OF THE SEVEN SORROWS (1847), Rev. James Norman Miller.
Mailing Address: P.O. Box 190606, 37219.
Res.: 2823 Hazelwood Dr., #4, 37212. Tel: 615-297-3310.
Church: 330 Fifth Ave. N., 37219. Tel: 615-256-1704; Fax: 615-256-7307.

10—MARY QUEEN OF ANGELS PARISH COMMUNITY (1982), Rev. Msgr. Steven P. Rohlfs, S.T.D., V.G. (PEO); Deacon Harold McBrayer.
Church: 34 White Bridge Rd., 37205. Tel: 615-352-3087; Fax: 615-352-8591.

11—ST. PATRICK (1891), Rev. Joseph A. Sanches (ATL), Admin.
Church: 1219 2nd Ave. S., 37210. Tel: 615-256-6498; Fax: 615-256-6476.
Catechesis/Religious Program—Bruce Shahan, D.R.E.; Barbara Shahan, D.R.E. Students 24.

12—ST. PIUS X (1958), Revs. W. Bernard Niedergeses; Joseph Shepherd, C.M.I.
Church: 2800 Tucker Rd., 37218. Tel: 615-244-4093; Fax: 615-256-0987.
School—Tel: 615-255-2049; Fax 615-255-2049. Sr. Mary Johanna Mellody, O.P., Prin. Dominican Sisters of St. Cecilia Congregation 4; Lay Teachers 9; Students 140.
Catechesis/Religious Program—Allison Bernhardt, D.R.E. Students 6.

13—ST. VINCENT DE PAUL (1932), Revs. Frank Coens, O.F.M.; Pio Jackson, O.F.M.
Church: 1700 Heiman St., 37208. Tel: 615-320-0695; Fax: 615-320-0698.
School—Tel: 615-320-1374; Fax: 615-320-0722. Sr. Joanne Cozzi, D.C., Prin. Lay Teachers 13; Students 155.

OUTSIDE THE CITY OF NASHVILLE

ANTIOCH, DAVIDSON CO., ST. IGNATIUS OF ANTIOCH (1976), Rev. John C. Henrick; Deacons Jack Nulty; P. J. Hoefler; Edwin Rodgers; Doug Shafer.
Church: 601 Bell Rd., 37013. Tel: 615-367-0085; Fax: 615-367-1712.
Catechesis/Religious Program—Kathryn Skinner, D.R.E. Students 210.

ASHLAND CITY, CHEATHAM CO., ST. MARTHA (1975), Rev. Peter Quang Chau Do.
Mailing Address: P.O. Box 55, 37015.
Church: 1331 Bell St., 37015. Tel: 615-792-4255; Fax: 615-792-4255.
Catechesis/Religious Program—Bernard Arndz, D.R.E. Students 94.

BRENTWOOD, WILLIAMSON CO., HOLY FAMILY (1989), Rev. Edward T. Alberts.
Church & Mailing Address: 9100 Crockett Rd., 37027. Tel: 615-373-4696; Fax: 615-377-3823.
Catechesis/Religious Program—Tel: 615-373-4351. Catherine Birdwell, D.R.E. Students 1,050.

CENTERVILLE, HICKMAN CO., CHRIST THE REDEEMER (1983), Attended by, Holy Trinity, Hohenwald. Rev. Joseph Kevin Dowling.
Mailing Address: P.O. Box 323, 37033. Tel: 931-796-3738.
Church: 1515 Woodland Dr., 37033. Tel: 931-729-4669.
Catechesis/Religious Program—Susan Barr, D.R.E.

CLARKSVILLE, MONTGOMERY CO., IMMACULATE CONCEPTION (1845), Revs. Edward F. Steiner III; Wieslaw Burakowski; Deacons Dominick Azzara; Robert Berberich; Timothy Winters. In Res., Rev. Jean Baptiste Kyabuta.
Res.: 709 Franklin St., 37040. Tel: 931-645-6275; Fax: 931-552-0331.
School—St. Mary's School, 1901 Madison St., 37043. Tel: 931-645-1865; Fax: 931-645-1160. Denise Tucker, Prin. Lay Teachers 11; Students 145.
Catechesis/Religious Program—Students 532.

COLUMBIA, MAURY CO., ST. CATHERINE (1843), Rev. J. Patrick Connor, V.G.; Deacon Price Keller.
Church & Mailing Address:: 3019 Cayce Ln., 38401. Tel: 931-388-3803; Fax: 931-381-8837.
Church: 5018 Hays Dr., 38401. Tel: 931-540-0056.
Catechesis/Religious Program—Tel: 931-381-6784. Candice Barton, D.R.E. Students 256.

COOKEVILLE, PUTNAM CO., ST. THOMAS AQUINAS (1951), Rev. Peter Coffey, S.D.S. In Res., Rev. Donald Loskot, S.D.S.
Church: 421 N. Washington Ave., 38501. Tel: 931-526-2575; Fax: 931-526-5869.
Catechesis/Religious Program—Tel: 931-526-4411. Valerie Richardson, D.R.E. Students 164.
Mission—Divine Savior Celina, Clay Co.

DECHERD, FRANKLIN CO., GOOD SHEPHERD (1900), Rev. Dexter S. Brewer, J.C.L.; Ms. Janet Johnson, Pastoral Assoc.
Church: 2021 Decherd Blvd., 37324. Tel: 931-967-0961; Fax: 931-967-3569.
School—2037 Decherd Blvd., 37324. Tel: 931-967-5673. Diane Jernigan, Prin. Lay Teachers 9; Students 77.
Catechesis/Religious Program—Tel: 931-967-1067. Brigid Stewart, D.R.E. Students 48.

Mission—St. Margaret Mary 9458 Old Alto Hwy., Alto, Franklin Co. 37324. Tel: 931-962-2144.

DICKSON, DICKSON CO., ST. CHRISTOPHER (1951), Rev. Stephen Gideon.
Church: 713 W. College St., 37055. Tel: 615-446-3927; Fax: 615-446-7339.
Catechesis/Religious Program—Tel: 615-446-1969. Debbie Allsbrook, D.R.E. Students 123.

DOVER, STEWART CO., ST. FRANCIS OF ASSISI (1982), Rev. Davis Chackaleckel, M.S.F.S.
Mailing Address: P.O. Box 307, 37058-0307.
Church: 417 Spring St.. Tel: 931-232-6982.
Catechesis/Religious Program—Tel: 931-232-4605. Ellen Grooms, D.R.E.; Florence Heath, D.R.E. Students 38.

FAYETTEVILLE, LINCOLN CO., ST. ANTHONY (1983), Rev. Francois Pellissier, G.H.M.
Church: 1900 Huntsville Hwy., 37334. Tel: 931-433-6525; Fax: 931-433-6283.
Catechesis/Religious Program—Theresa Puemmeler, D.R.E. Students 70.

FRANKLIN, WILLIAMSON CO.
1—ST. MATTHEW (1979), Revs. Mark Beckman; Mark Hunt; Deacon James Walsh.
Church: 535 Sneed Rd., 37069. Tel: 615-646-0378; Fax: 615-646-5230.
School—Tel: 615-662-4044; Fax: 615-662-6822. Barby Magness, Prin. Lay Teachers 12; Students 195.
Catechesis/Religious Program—Tel: 615-646-9938, Ext. 13. Sr. Lauren Cole, R.S.M., D.R.E. Students 256.
2—ST. PHILIP (1843), Revs. Edward C. Arnold; John L. Kirk.
Church: 113 2nd Ave. S., 37064. Tel: 615-794-4236; Fax: 615-794-3083.
Catechesis/Religious Program—Tel: 615-794-8588. Lorraine Blank, D.R.E.; Kimberlie Leisinger, D.R.E. Students 784.

GALLATIN, SUMNER CO., ST. JOHN VIANNEY (1929), Revs. David R. Choby; John Sappenfield.
Church: 449 N. Water St., 37066. Tel: 615-452-2977; Fax: 615-452-0323.
School—Tel: 615-230-7048; Fax: 615-206-9839. Sr. Louise Busby, D.C., Prin. Lay Teachers 8; Students 105.
Catechesis/Religious Program—Students 145.

HENDERSONVILLE, SUMNER CO., OUR LADY OF THE LAKE (1969), Revs. William S. Bevington; Tomy Pullyanampatta, M.S.F.S.; Sr. Maria Edwards, R.S.M., Pastoral Assoc.; Deacon James F. Carr.
Mailing Address: Box 279, 37077.
Church: 1739 Stop Thirty Road, 37075. Tel: 615-824-3276; Fax: 615-824-7989.
Catechesis/Religious Program—Cyndi Sabatino, D.R.E. Students 358.

HOHENWALD, LEWIS CO., HOLY TRINITY (1983), Rev. Joseph Kevin Dowling.
Church: 610 Kimmins St., 38462. Tel: 931-796-3738; Fax: 931-796-3738.
Catechesis/Religious Program—Darie McCarthy, D.R.E. Students 35.

JOELTON, DAVIDSON CO., ST. LAWRENCE'S (1885), [CEM] Rev. Thomas Bielawa, S.D.S.
Church: 5655 Clarksville Hwy., 37080. Tel: 615-876-2127; Fax: 615-876-7923.

LAFAYETTE, MACON CO., HOLY FAMILY (1982), Rev. Dennis Holly, G.H.M. (OWN).
Church: 901 Vinson Rd., 37083. Tel: 615-666-6466; Fax: 615-444-3704.
Catechesis/Religious Program—Donna Kirby, D.R.E. Students 17.

LAWRENCEBURG, LAWRENCE CO., SACRED HEART (1870), [CEM] Rev. Richard G. Buchignani.
Mailing Address: P.O. Box 708, 38464.
Church: 206 Berger St., 38464. Tel: 931-762-3183; Fax: 931-762-5128.
School—220 Berger St., 38464. Tel: 931-762-6125; Fax: 931-762-6125. Mrs. Bonnie Thigpen, Prin. Lay Teachers 8; Students 74.
Catechesis/Religious Program—Connie Hollman, D.R.E. Students 48.

LEBANON, WILSON CO., ST. FRANCES CABRINI (1953), Rev. Zacharias Payikat, C.M.I.; Deacon Donald E. Climer.
Church: 300 S. Tarver Ave., 37087. Tel: 615-444-0524; Fax: 615-444-3704.
Catechesis/Religious Program—Roger Hutto, D.R.E.; Regina Santana, D.R.E. Students 150.
Station—Smith & Trousdale counties

LEWISBURG, MARSHALL CO., ST. JOHN THE EVANGELIST (1982), Rev. Thomas Perrin, S.D.S.
Church: 1061 S. Ellington, 37091. Tel: 931-359-5017; Fax: 931-359-9844.
Catechesis/Religious Program—Sara Keller, D.R.E. Students 64.

LORETTO, LAWRENCE CO., SACRED HEART (1872), [CEM] Rev. Matthew Cheeramkuzhy; Deacon Samuel Beckman.
Mailing Address: P.O. Box 86, 38469.
Church: 300 Church St., 38469. Tel: 931-853-4370; Fax: 931-853-4373.
School—307 Church St., 38469. Tel: 931-853-4388. Mrs. Catherine N. Bradley, Prin. Lay Teachers 5; Students 57.
Catechesis/Religious Program—Nancy Whitsett, D.R.E. Students 110.

MADISON, DAVIDSON CO., ST. JOSEPH (1953), Rev. Joseph V. McMahon; Deacons Gordon W. McBride Sr.; Theodore B. Welsh.
Church: 1225 Gallatin Rd. S., 37115. Tel: 615-865-1071; Fax: 615-868-4900.
School—Tel: 615-865-1491; Fax: 615-612-0228. Sr. Patrick Stephen, O.P., Prin. Dominican Sisters of St. Cecilia Congregation 3; Lay Teachers 25; Students 430.
Catechesis/Religious Program—Jackie Baltz, D.R.E. Students 146.

MANCHESTER, COFFEE CO., ST. MARK (2001), Rev. William M. Kelly.
Mailing Address: P.O. Box 1095, 37349. Tel: 931-723-4107; Fax: 931-723-4123.
Res.: 304 W. Gizzard St., Tullahoma, 37388. Tel: 931-455-3060; Fax: 931-455-8298.
Church: 2941 McMinnville Hwy., 37349.
Catechesis/Religious Program—Students 50.

MCEWEN, HUMPHREYS CO., ST. PATRICK (1855), [CEM] Rev. John Sims Baker.
Mailing Address: 175 St. Patrick St., 37101.
Church: 123 St. Patrick St., 37101. Tel: 931-582-3493; Fax: 931-582-6386.
School—Tel: 931-582-3493. Sr. Ann Hyacinth, O.P., Prin. Dominican Sisters of St. Cecilia Congregation 3; Lay Teachers 7; Students 77.
Catechesis/Religious Program—Ellen Bourke, D.R.E. Students 36.

MCMINNVILLE, WARREN CO., ST. CATHERINE (1958), Rev. James J. Bretl, S.D.S. In Res., Rev. Barry Griffin, S.D.S.; Deacon Robert L. Graham.
Church: 1024 Faulkner Spring Rd., 37110. Tel: 931-473-4932; Fax: 931-473-0799.
Catechesis/Religious Program—Tel: 931-473-2435. Rachel McGee, D.R.E. Students 68.
Station—Van Buren Co.

MURFREESBORO, RUTHERFORD CO., ST. ROSE OF LIMA (1929), Rev. Wiatt A. Funk; Deacons Bernard J. Casey; Thomas McGrane.
Church & Res.: 1601 N. Tennessee Blvd., 37130. Tel: 615-893-1843; Fax: 615-895-1150.
School—Tel: 615-898-0555; Fax: 615-898-0497. Sr. Ann Marie Karlovic, O.P., Prin. Sisters 4; Teachers 16; Students 224.
Catechesis/Religious Program—Tel: 615-895-1150. Robert Carney, D.R.E. Students 573.

OLD HICKORY, WILSON CO., ST. STEPHEN (1952), Rev. Stephen J. Wolf; Deacons Gordon S. Rose; Hans Toecker; Fred Bourland.
Church: 14544 Lebanon Rd., 37138. Tel: 615-758-2424; 615-754-4454; Fax: 615-754-0043.
Catechesis/Religious Program—Mary Craven, D.R.E.; Teresa Bosio, D.R.E. Students 373.

PULASKI, GILES CO., IMMACULATE CONCEPTION (1941), Rev. Jose Karimadam, C.M.I.; Kathleen M. O'Brien, Parish Coord.
Mailing Address: Box 363, 38478.
Church: Elkton Hwy. South. Tel: 931-363-5776; Fax: 931-363-6953.
Catechesis/Religious Program—Jo Anne Beam, D.R.E. Students 26.

SAINT JOSEPH, LAWRENCE CO., ST. JOSEPH (1872), Attended by, Sacred Heart, Loretto. Rev. Matthew Cheeramkuzhy, C.M.I.
Mailing Address: P.O. Box 86, Loretto, 38469. Tel: 931-853-4370; Fax: 931-853-4373.
Church: American Blvd., St. Joseph, 38481.

SHELBYVILLE, BEDFORD CO., ST. WILLIAM (1941), Rev. Paul J. Portland, S.D.S.
Church: 719 N. Main St., 37160. Tel: 931-684-8745; Fax: 931-684-6154.
Catechesis/Religious Program—Bro. Van Todd, S.D.S., D.R.E. Students 55.

SMITHVILLE, DEKALB CO., ST. GREGORY (1982), Attended by, St. Catherine, McMinnville. Rev. James J. Bretl, S.D.S.
Mailing Address: P.O. Box 712, 37166.
Church: 712 Main St.. Tel: 931-473-4932; Fax: 931-473-0799.
Catechesis/Religious Program—Maureen Nokes, D.R.E. Students 26.

SMYRNA, RUTHERFORD CO., ST. LUKE (1982), Revs. Richard Gagnon, S.D.S.; Augustine Lucca, S.D.S.; Deacons Ken Levinson; Simeon Panagatos.
Mailing Address: P.O. Box 907, 37167-0907.
Church: 10682 Nashville Hwy., 37167. Tel: 615-459-9672; Fax: 615-459-3989.
Catechesis/Religious Program—Denise M. Leaver, D.R.E. Students 240.

SPARTA, WHITE CO., ST. ANDREW (1982), Rev. Fred J. Schmit, S.D.S.
Church: 829 Valley View Dr., 38583. Tel: 931-738-2140; Fax: 931-738-2592.
Catechesis/Religious Program—Students 40.

SPRINGFIELD, ROBERTSON CO., OUR LADY OF LOURDES (1946), [CEM] Rev. Joseph Desmond; Deacon W. Michael Hume.
Church: 103 Golf Club Ln., 37172. Tel: 615-384-6200; Fax: 615-384-5837.
Catechesis/Religious Program—Carol Twork, D.R.E. Students 102.
Mission—St. Michael [CEM] Cedar Hill, Robertson Co.

TENNESSEE RIDGE, HOUSTON CO., ST. ELIZABETH ANN SETON (1977), Attended by, St. Patrick, McEwen. Rev. John Sims Baker.
Mailing Address: P.O. Box 85, 37178. Tel: 931-721-3769; Fax: 931-582-6366.
Church: 755 State Rte. 49, 37178.
Catechesis/Religious Program—Tel: 931-289-4932. Travis Gerlach, D.R.E. Students 36.

TULLAHOMA, COFFEE CO., ST. PAUL THE APOSTLE (1954), Rev. William M. Kelly, S.D.S. (BIR).
Church: 304 W. Grizzard St., 37388. Tel: 931-455-3050; Fax: 931-455-8298.
School—Tel: 931-455-4221. Sr. Suzanne Miller, F.M.A., Prin. Lay Teachers 17; Students 142.
Catechesis/Religious Program—Students 75.
Station—Manchester, Coffee Co.

WAYNESBORO, WAYNE CO., ST. CECILIA (1982), Attended by, Holy Trinity, Hohenwald. Rev. Joseph Kevin Dowling.
Mailing Address: *Holy Trinity Church*, 610 Kimmins St., Hohenwald, 38462.
Church: 526 Hwy. 64 E., 38485. Tel: 931-796-3738; Fax: 931-796-3738.
Catechesis/Religious Program—Sandy Bell, D.R.E. Students 8.

On Special Assignment:
Rev.—
Perkin, David, Moderator of the Curia & Vicar Gen.

On Duty Outside the Diocese:
Revs.—
Campion, Owen F., Our Sunday Visitor, 200 Noll Plaza, Huntington, IN 46750.
McMurry, John E., S.S., St. Mary's Spiritual Center, 600 N. Paca St., Baltimore, MD 21201-1995.
McMurry, Vincent deP., S.S., St. Mary's Seminary, 5400 Roland Ave., Baltimore, MD 21210.

Retired:
Rev. Msgr.—
Hitchcock, James, 5837 Happy Hollow Ln., Joelton, 37080.
Revs.—
Baltz, John P., Jr., 2146 Oakland St., 37210.
Clements, Daniel A., 924 Rose Petal Ln., Knoxville, 37938.
Doyle, Thomas, S.S., 1248 Brentwood Pointe, Brentwood, 37027.
Julius, Joseph W., St. Francis of Assisi, 7715 River Rd., Townsend, 37882.
Murray, James B., St. Paul the Apostle, 1425 E. Shelby Dr., Memphis, 38116.
Nolan, William N., 2258 Lebanon Rd., #25, 37214.
Rudisill, James A., 3216 S. Waynoka Cir., Memphis, 38111-3615.

Permanent Deacons:
Altman, Gary D., St. Edward, Nashville
Azzara, Dominic D., Immaculate Conception, Clarksville
Bainbridge, Frank, Prison Ministry, Nashville
Batcheldor, James M., Jr., (Retired)
Bauman, Frank, (Retired)
Beckman, Samuel C., Sacred Heart, Loretto
Berberich, Robert R., Immaculate Conception, Clarksville
Bourland, Fred, St. Stephen, Old Hickory
Carr, James F., Our Lady of the Lake, Hendersonville
Carroll, John B., (Retired)
Casey, Bernard J., St. Rose of Lima, Murfreesboro
Casey, John P., St. Ann, Nashville
Climer, Donald E., St. Frances Cabrini, Lebanon
Coen, Joseph, Sr., (Retired)
Deschenes, Martin, St. Henry, Cursillo, Nashville
Dickson, William J., St. Ann, Nashville; Diocesan Ecumenical Dir.
Edwards, Brian, St. Edward, Nashville
Faulkner, Mark C., Cathedral of the Incarnation, Nashville
Francescon, Samuel A., (Retired)
Graham, Robert L., St. Catherine, McMinnville
Gregory, L. Wayne, Holy Rosary, Nashville
Henry, James R., (Retired)
Hoefler, Paul J., St. Ignatius, Antioch
Huhlein, Gilbert P., Holy Rosary, Nashville
Hume, W. Michael, Our Lady of Lourdes, Springfield

Keller, I. Price, St. Catherine, Nashville
Krenson, John G., Cathedral of the Incarnation, Nashville
Laws, Donald A., (Unassigned)
Levinson, Ken, St. Luke, Smyrna
Mahoney, Robert L., Holy Name, Nashville
McBrayer, J. Harold, Jr., Mary Queen of Angels Catholic Community, Nashville
McBride, Gordon W., Sr., St. Joseph, Madison
McGinn, George P., (Retired)
McGrane, Thomas J., St. Rose Lima, Murfreesboro
McKenzie, Andrew D., Christ the King, Nashville
McKenzie, James W., Vanderbilt Catholic Community, Nashville
Montini, Robert A., (Unassigned)
Nulty, Jack, St. Ignatius, Antioch
Panagatos, Simeon W., St. Luke, Smyrna
Randall, Ralph, (Retired)
Rodgers, Edwin C., St. Ignatius of Antioch, Antioch
Rose, Gordon, St. Stephen, Old Hickory
Shafer, L. Douglas, St. Ignatius of Antioch, Antioch
Srouji, Jack, St. Henry, Nashville
Stanford, James E., Christ the King, Nashville
Steinbrecher, Kenneth, Holy Rosary, Nashville
Steltemeier, William, Jr., (Unassigned)
Toecker, Hans M., St. Stephen, Old Hickory
True, Robert H., Christ the King, Nashville
Von Mann, Milton, Prison Ministry, St. Edward, Nashville
Welsh, Theodore B., St. Joseph, Madison
Winters, Timothy F., Immaculate Conception, Clarksville
Walsh, James F., Jr., St. Matthew, Franklin

INSTITUTIONS LOCATED IN THE DIOCESE

[A] COLLEGES

NASHVILLE. *Aquinas College*, 4210 Harding Rd., 37205. Tel: 615-297-7545; Fax: 615-297-3892. Email: admissions@aquinas-tn.edu. Web: www.aquinas-tn.edu. Sisters Rose Marie Masserano, O.P., Chm.; Thomas Aquinas Halbmaier, O.P., Pres.; Mary Justin Haltom, Vice Pres., Academic Affairs. Dominican Sisters of St. Cecilia Congregation Sisters 5; Lay Teachers 28; Students 863.

[B] HIGH SCHOOLS, DIOCESAN

NASHVILLE. *Father Ryan High School* (1925), Corporate Title: Father Ryan High School, Inc. , 700 Norwood Dr., 37204. Tel: 615-383-4200; Fax: 615-383-9056. Email: postmaster@FATHERRYAN.org. Web: www.FATHERRYAN.org. Mr. John J. Langton, Prin.; Rev. Mark Hunt, Assoc. Prin. Pastoral Affairs. Priests 1; Lay Teachers 79; Students 954.

Father Ryan Board of Trust, Devel. & Alumni Office, 770 Norwood Dr., 37204. Tel: 615-269-7926.

HENDERSONVILLE. *Pope John Paul II High School, Inc.*, 117 Caldwell Ln., 37075. Tel: 615-822-2375; Fax: 615-822-6226. Email: info@jp2hs.org. Web: www.jp2hs.org. Hans Broekman, Prin. Priests 1; Lay Teachers 40; Students 391.

[C] HIGH SCHOOLS, PRIVATE

NASHVILLE. *St. Cecilia Academy* (1860), The Dominican Campus, 4210 Harding Rd., 37205. Tel: 615-298-4525; Fax: 615-783-0561. Email: coteg@stcecilia.edu. Web: www.stcecilia.edu. Sr. Mary Charles Sterne, O.P., Prin.

Legal Title: *St. Cecilia Academy.* Conducted by the St. Cecilia Congregation of Dominican Sisters Sisters 8; Lay Teachers 30; Students 273.

[D] ELEMENTARY SCHOOLS, PRIVATE

NASHVILLE. **St. Bernard Academy*, 2020 24th Ave. S., 37212-4202. Tel: 615-385-0440; Fax: 615-783-0241. Email: mhonick@stbernard.org. Web: www.stbernard.org. Sr. Catherine Warwick, Acting Dir.

Legal Title: *Saint Bernard Academy Corporation.* Sisters 3; Lay Teachers 22; Students 323.

Overbrook School, 4210 Harding Rd., 37205. Tel: 615-292-5134; Fax: 615-783-0560. Web: www.overbrook.edu. Sr. Mary Cecilia Goodrum, O.P., Prin.; Jennifer Ford, Office Mgr. The St. Cecilia Congregation of Dominican Sisters Lay Teachers 24; Students 330.

[E] CHILD-CARING INSTITUTIONS

NASHVILLE. **St. Bernard After School Program*, 2020 24th Ave. S., 37212. Tel: 615-298-1298; Fax: 615-783-0241. Brenda Dye, Dir. Lay Staff 17; Students 120.

St. Mary Villa Child Development Center, 30 White Bridge Rd., 37205. Tel: 615-356-6336; Fax: 615-356-6421. Email: joanne@stmaryvilla.org. Joanne Chase, Exec. Dir. Staff 45; Children 370.

St. Mary Villa, Inc., 30 White Bridge Rd., 37205. Tel: 615-356-6336; Fax: 615-356-6421.

[F] GENERAL HOSPITALS

NASHVILLE. *St. Thomas Hospital* (1898), 4220 Harding Rd., 37205. Tel: 615-222-2111; Fax: 615-222-6502. Email: nshlsthl.stthomas.org. Web: www.saintthomas.org. Deborah German, M.D., Pres. & CEO; Sr. Janet Keim, D.C., Supr.

Legal Title: *St. Thomas Hospital.* Daughters of Charity of St. Vincent de Paul, (East Central Prov., Evansville, IN) Sisters 3; Lay Staff 3,542; Bed Capacity 541; Chaplains 8.

Saint Thomas Foundation Tel: 615-222-6800; Fax: 615-222-6159.

St. Thomas Health Services Tel: 615-222-2111; Fax: 615-222-6502.

Covenant Care, Inc. Tel: 615-222-2111; Fax: 615-222-6502.

Seton Corporation (2001), 4220 Harding Rd., 37205. Tel: 615-252-3286; Fax: 615-252-6386. Email: jhardcastle@boultcummings.com. Web: www.stthomas.org. Jay Hardcastle, Attorney.

[G] HOMES FOR THE AGED

NASHVILLE. *Villa Maria Manor, Inc.* dba Villa Maria Manor , 32 White Bridge Rd., 37205. Tel: 615-352-3084; Fax: 615-352-0553. Email thevilla@bellsouth.net. Mr. David Glascoe, Mng. Agent. Residents 230.

[H] MONASTERIES AND RESIDENCES OF PRIESTS AND BROTHERS

NASHVILLE. *Franciscan Friars*, 1608 Tynewood Dr., 37215-4214. Tel: 615-665-7313; Fax: 615-320-0698. Email: friarfc@aol.com. Revs. Frank Coens, O.F.M. Pio Jackson, O.F.M.; Albert Merz, O.F.M.; Deacon Steve Suding, O.F.M.

Glenmary Home Missioners, 1307 6th Ave. N., 37208. Tel: 615-242-1885; Fax: 615-256-1902. Email: Bhare95@aol.com. Web: www.glenmary.org. Revs. Robert Hare; Wilfred Steinbacher; Robert Dalton.

[I] CONVENTS AND RESIDENCES FOR SISTERS

NASHVILLE. *St. Cecilia Convent* Motherhouse and Novitiate of St. Cecilia Congregation of Dominican Sisters. , 801 Dominican Dr., 37228-1909. Tel: 615-256-5486; Fax: 615-726-1333. Web: www.nashvilledominican.org. Sisters Rose Marie Masserano, O.P., Prioress Gen.; Mary George Barrett, O.P., Prioress. Sisters in Residence 130; Novices 13; Postulants 11.

Mercy Convent, 2629 Pennington Bend Rd., 37214. Tel: 615-885-1863; Fax: 615-885-4304. Sr. Mary Judith Coode, R.S.M., Dir.; Rev. Stephen Stolewski, Chap.

Legal Title: *Sisters of Mercy of Nashville, TN, Inc.* Sisters 15.

[J] CAMPS AND COMMUNITY CENTERS

FAIRVIEW. *Camp Marymount* Catholic summer camp for boys and girls. , 1318 Fairview Blvd., 37062. Tel: 615-799-0410; Fax: 615-799-2261. Email: Thagey@campmarymount.com. Web: www.campmarymount.com. Tommy Hagey, Dir.

[K] RENEWAL CENTERS

LIBERTY. *Carmel Center of Spirituality*, 610 Bluff Rd., 37095. Tel: 615-536-5177; Fax: 615-536-5499. Email: carmliberty@yahoo.com. Web: www.saintfrancescabrinichurch.org. P.O. Box 117, 37095. Revs. Zachary Payikat, C.M.I., Dir.; Matthew Cheeramkuzhy; Jose Kariamadam, C.M.I.; George Thadathil, C.M.I., Adjunct Priest for Sacramental Svcs.; Jos Shepherd Edakkulathoor, C.M.I.

[L] MISCELLANEOUS

NASHVILLE. *Catholic Foundation of Tennessee, Inc.*, 2400 21st Ave. S., 37212. Tel: 615-783-0278; Fax: 615-292-8411. Mark Berlyn, Devel. Dir. Email: markberlyn@dioceseofnashville.com.

**Catholic Media Productions*, 700 Harpeth Knoll Ct., 37221. Tel: 615-646-4041; Fax: 615-662-7454. Email: cmp.inc@home.com. Web: www.catholicmediapro.com. James F. Walsh Jr., Pres.

Diocesan Council of Catholic Women, 2400 21st Ave. S., 37212. Tel: 615-889-4065; Fax: 615-889-3421. Email: merve8371@aol.com. Rev. Kevin Dowling, Dir.

Diocesan Properties, Inc. dba Marina Manor East Apartments, 2400 21st Ave. S., 37212. Tel: 615-383-6393; Fax: 615-292-8411. Mr. Michael F. Nolan, Sec. & Treas.

Dominican Campus, 4210 Harding Rd., 37205. Tel: 615-279-3841; Fax: 615-383-2196. Email: sparks@dominicancampus.org. John Sparks, C.F.O.

Endowment for the Advancement of Catholic Schools, Trust, Formerly Roman Catholic Diocese of Nashville Endowment for the Advancement of Catholic Schools Trust2400 21st Ave. S., 37212. Tel: 615-383-6393; Fax: 615-292-8411. Most Rev. Edward U. Kmiec, Trustee.

Families First Partners, Inc., 10 S. 6th St., 37206. Tel: 615-259-3567; Fax: 615-259-3567. Email: ff@cctennessee.org. Ms. Elaine Flick, Sec. & Treas.

Glenmary Department of Pastoral Services A national center serving parishes and other ministries staffed by Glenmary Home Missioners. , 1312 5th Ave. N., 37208. Tel: 615-256-1900; Fax: 615-256-1902. Email: dps@glenmary.org. Web: www.glenmary.org/dps/. Rev. Michael Langell, Dir. Pastoral Svcs.

Glenmary Berson Office, 1312 5th Ave. N., 37208. Tel: 615-256-1900, Ext. 120; Fax: 615-256-1902. Rev. Robert Hare, Facilities Mgr.

Glenmary Office of Pastoral Coordinators, 1312 5th Ave. N., 37208. Tel: 615-256-4384; Fax: 615-256-1902. Rev. Robert Dalton. A project for establishing new missions with lay persons.

Glenmary Reserch Center, 1312 5th Ave., N., 37208. Tel: 615-256-1905; Fax: 615-251-1472. Dr. Ken Sanchagrin, Dir. Applied research for the ecumenical and rural apostolate.

Growing in Faith for Tomorrow Capital Campaign Trust, Inc., 2400 21st Ave., S., 37212. Tel: 615-783-0284; Fax: 615-292-8411. Mr. Edward Stack, Pres.

**St. Henry Property Development, Inc. dba The Cloister*, 30 White Bridge Rd., 37205. Tel: 615-760-4424; Fax: 615-352-8591. Email: david@maryqueenofangels.com. David Glacoe, Exec. Dir.

Holy Name Loaves and Fishes Community Meal, 521 Woodland St., 37206. Tel: 615-256-7256; Fax: 615-256-4763. Web: sites.jaffy.com/holyname. William Barry, Exec. Dir.

Ladies of Charity of Nashville, Inc., 2216 State St., 37203. Tel: 615-327-3453; 615-327-3430; Fax: 615-321-3312. Affiliated with the Ladies of Charity of the United States of America, LCUSA, and the Association of International Charities, AIC.

Ladies of Charity Welfare Agency, Inc., 2212 State St., 37203. Tel: 615-327-3430; Fax: 615-321-3312. Mrs. Terri Puma, Exec. Dir.; Rev. Phillip Breen, Moderator; Rev. Msgr. Steven P. Rohlfs, S.T.D., V.G. (PEO), Moderator, Emeritus.

Mary, Queen of Angels. Inc., 30 White Bridge Rd., 37205. Tel: 615-760-4424; Fax: 615-352-8591. Email: david@maryqueenofangels.com. Web: www.maryqueenofangels.com. Mr. David Glascoe, CEO.

Mid-Tennessee Rural Outreach Association, 30 White Bridge Rd., 37205. Tel: 615-352-3087.

Legal Title: *Mid-Tennessee Rural Outreach Association; Assumption-St. Vincent North Nashville Outreach Association.*

Parish Twinning Program of the Americas, 208 Leake Ave., 37205. Tel: 615-356-5999; Fax: 615-352-5114. Web: www.parishprogram.org. Theresa Patterson, Exec. Dir.

HENDERSONVILLE. *Legion of Mary*, Tel: 615-824-3276; Fax: 615-824-7989. Email: WSBev@aol.com. Web: www.catholic-church.org/OLOL. P.O. Box 279, 37077-0279. Rev. William S. Bevington, Dir.

Priests Eucharistic League, Tel: 615-824-3276; Fax: 615-824-7989. Email: WSBev@aol.com. Web: www.catholic-church.org/OLOL. P.O. Box 279, 37077-0729. Rev. William S. Bevington, Dir.

RELIGIOUS INSTITUTES OF MEN REPRESENTED IN THE DIOCESE

For further details refer to the corresponding bracketed number in the Religious Institutes of Men or Women section.

[0275]—*Carmelites of Mary Immaculate*—C.M.I.
[0520]—*Franciscan Friars* (Prov. of Sacred Heart)—O.F.M.
[0570]—*Glenmary Home Missioners*—G.H.M.
[0690]—*Jesuit Fathers and Brothers*—S.J.
[]—*Missionaries of St. Francis de Sales* (Annecy, France)—M.S.F.S.
[0430]—*Order of Preachers-Dominicans* (Southern Prov.)—O.P.
[1200]—*Society of the Divine Savior* (Milwaukee, WI)—S.D.S.

RELIGIOUS INSTITUTES OF WOMEN REPRESENTED IN THE DIOCESE

[0760]—*Daughters of Charity of St. Vincent de Paul* (East Central Prov., Evansville, IN)—D.C.
[1070-03]—*Dominican Sisters*—O.P.
[1070-07]—*Dominican Sisters*—O.P.
[1070-09]—*Dominican Sisters*—O.P.
[2575]—*Institute of the Sisters of Mercy of the Americas* (Baltimore, MD; Cincinnati, OH)—R.S.M.

[]—*Sacred Heart Congregation* (Mexico)

[]—*Sacred Heart Congregation (India)*—S.H.

[1680]—*School Sisters of St. Francis*—S.S.S.F. -

[]—*Sisters for Christian Community* (St. Louis)—S.F.C.C.

[0990]—*Sisters of Divine Providence* (St. Louis Prov.)—C.D.P.

[1705]—*Sisters of St. Francis of Assisi*—O.S.F.

[3270]—*Sisters of the Most Precious Blood*—C.PP.S.

DIOCESAN CEMETERIES

NASHVILLE. *Calvary Cemetery*, 1001 Lebanon Rd., 37210.

NECROLOGY

† Schnupp, Luzerne A., (Retired)—Died Feb. 1, 2003

Archdiocese of Newark

(Archidioecesis Novarcensis)

Most Reverend

JOHN J. MYERS, J.C.D., D.D.

Archbishop of Newark; ordained December 17, 1966; appointed Coadjutor Bishop of Peoria July 14, 1987; Episcopal ordination September 3, 1987; succeeded to See of Peoria January 23, 1990; appointed Fifth Archbishop of Newark July 24, 2001; installed October 9, 2001; Pallium conferred June 29, 2002. *Res.: Cathedral Basilica of the Sacred Heart*, 89 Ridge St., Newark, NJ 07104 Tel: 973-484-4600; Fax: 973-497-4018.

Archdiocesan Center: 171 Clifton Ave., P.O. Box 9500, Newark NJ 07104-9500. Tel: 973-497-4000; Fax: 973-497-4033.

Web: www.rcan.org

Email: webmaster@rcan.org

Most Reverend

PETER LEO GERETY, D.D.

Archbishop Emeritus of Newark; ordained June 29, 1939; appointed Coadjutor Bishop of Portland March 4, 1966; Episcopal ordination June 1, 1966; appointed Apostolic Administrator February 18, 1967; succeeded to See September 15, 1969; appointed Archbishop of Newark April 2, 1974; installed June 28, 1974; Pallium conferred December 12, 1974; retired June 1, 1986. *Res.: 60 Home Ave., Rutherford, NJ 07070.* Tel: 201-460-1369; Fax: 201-842-0724.

Most Reverend

DOMINIC A. MARCONI, D.D.

Retired Auxiliary Bishop of Newark; ordained May 30, 1953; appointed Titular Bishop of Bure and Auxiliary Bishop of Newark May 3, 1976; Episcopal ordination June 25, 1976; retired July 1, 2002. *Res.: 71 Washington Ave., Chatham, NJ 07928-2014.* Tel: 973-635-8777; Fax: 973-635-8647.

Most Reverend

ARTHUR J. SERRATELLI, S.S.L., S.T.D., D.D.

Auxiliary Bishop of Newark; ordained December 20, 1968; appointed Titular Bishop of Enera and Auxiliary Bishop of Newark July 3, 2000; Episcopal ordination September 8, 2000. *Res.: Cathedral Basilica of the Sacred Heart*, 89 Ridge St., Newark, NJ 07104. Tel: 973-484-4600; Fax: 973-497-4018.

Most Reverend

DAVID ARIAS, O.A.R., D.D.

Auxiliary Bishop of Newark; ordained May 31, 1952; appointed Titular Bishop of Badie and Auxiliary Bishop of Newark January 25, 1983; Episcopal ordination April 7, 1983. *Res.: St. Joseph of the Palisades Rectory*, 6401 Palisade Ave., West New York, NJ 07093. Tel: 201-861-6644; Fax: 201-861-7799.

Most Reverend

CHARLES J. McDONNELL, D.D.

Auxiliary Bishop of Newark; ordained May 29, 1954; appointed Titular Bishop of Pocofelto and Auxiliary Bishop of Newark March 15, 1994; Episcopal ordination May 12, 1994. *Res.: Holy Trinity Rectory*, 34 Maple Ave., Hackensack, NJ 07601. Tel: 201-343-5170; Fax: 201-343-5067.

Most Reverend

EDGAR M. DA CUNHA, S.D.V.

Auxiliary Bishop of Newark; ordained March 27, 1982; appointed Titular See of Ucres and Auxiliary Bishop of Newark June 27, 2003; Episcopal ordination September 3, 2003. *Res.: 170 Broad St., Newark, NJ 07104.* Tel: 973-482-8619; Fax: 973-497-4555.

Square Miles 513.

Diocese Established, 1853; Erected an Archdiocese, December 10, 1937.

Comprises Four Counties in the State of New Jersey, viz.: Bergen, Hudson, Essex and Union.

For legal titles of parishes and archdiocesan institutions, consult the Chancery Office.

STATISTICAL OVERVIEW

Personnel	
Archbishops	1
Retired Archbishops	1
Auxiliary Bishops	4
Retired Bishops	1
Abbots	1
Priests: Diocesan Active in Diocese	489
Priests: Diocesan Active Outside Diocese	52
Priests: Diocesan in Foreign Missions	8
Priests: Retired, Sick or Absent	196
Number of Diocesan Priests	745
Religious Priests in Diocese	228
Total Priests in Diocese	973
Extern Priests in Diocese	84
Ordinations:	
Diocesan Priests	9
Religious Priests	2
Transitional Deacons	14
Permanent Deacons	18
Permanent Deacons in Diocese	201
Total Brothers	85
Total Sisters	1,264
Parishes	
Parishes	234
With Resident Pastor:	
Resident Diocesan Priests	206
Resident Religious Priests	28
Without Resident Pastor:	
Administered by Priests	17
Pastoral Centers	137
Professional Ministry Personnel:	
Brothers	9
Sisters	112
Lay Ministers	267
Welfare	
Catholic Hospitals	11
Total Assisted	1,489,585
Health Care Centers	13
Total Assisted	5,214
Homes for the Aged	6
Total Assisted	697
Day Care Centers	147
Total Assisted	5,338
Specialized Homes	6
Total Assisted	988
Special Centers for Social Services	34
Total Assisted	67,436
Residential Care of Disabled	2
Total Assisted	38
Other Institutions	11
Total Assisted	2,342
Educational	
Seminaries, Diocesan	3
Students from This Diocese	97
Students from Other Diocese	45
Diocesan Students in Other Seminaries	5
Seminaries, Religious	1
Students Religious	20
Total Seminarians	122
Colleges and Universities	4
Total Students	17,450
High Schools, Diocesan and Parish	16
Total Students	8,361
High Schools, Private	20
Total Students	8,345
Elementary Schools, Diocesan and Parish	120
Total Students	34,327
Elementary Schools, Private	7
Total Students	1,612
Non-residential Schools for the Disabled	5
Total Students	183
Catechesis/Religious Education:	
High School Students	2,637
Elementary Students	50,307
Total Students under Catholic Instruction	123,344
Teachers in the Diocese:	
Priests	128
Brothers	36
Sisters	238
Lay Teachers	3,935
Vital Statistics	
Receptions into the Church:	
Infant Baptism Totals	16,967
Adult Baptism Totals	435
Received into Full Communion	598
First Communions	14,581
Confirmations	11,381
Marriages:	
Catholic	3,761
Interfaith	543
Total Marriages	4,304
Deaths	11,554
Total Catholic Population	1,319,558
Total Population	2,835,594

Former Bishops—Most Revs. JAMES ROOSEVELT BAYLEY, D.D., consecrated Oct. 30, 1853; promoted to the Archiepiscopal See of Baltimore, July 30, 1872; died Oct. 3, 1877; MICHAEL AUGUSTINE CORRIGAN, D.D., consecrated May 4, 1873; promoted to the Archiepiscopal See of Petra, Oct. 1, 1880; succeeded to the Archiepiscopal See of New York, Oct. 10, 1885; died May 5, 1902; WINAND MICHAEL WIGGER, D.D., consecrated Oct. 18, 1881; died Jan. 5, 1901; JOHN JOSEPH O'CONNOR, D.D., ord. Dec. 22, 1877; consecrated July 25, 1901; died May 20, 1927; THOMAS J. WALSH, S.T.D., J.C.D., ord. Jan. 27, 1900; appt. Bishop of Trenton, May 10, 1918; consecrated July 25, 1918; made Assistant at the Pontifical Throne March 13, 1922; transferred to the See of Newark, March 2, 1928; appt. First Archbishop of Newark, Dec. 10, 1937; Pallium conferred, Dec. 18, 1937; installed April 27, 1938; died June 6, 1952; THOMAS A. BOLAND, S.T.D., LL.D. (Retired), ord. Dec. 23, 1922; appt. Titular Bishop of Hirina and Auxiliary to the Archbishop of Newark, May 21, 1940; consecrated July 25, 1940; transferred to Paterson, June 21, 1947; appt. Second Archbishop of Newark, Nov. 15, 1952; installed Jan. 14, 1953; Assistant at the Pontifical Throne, May 6, 1965; retired April 2, 1974; died March 16, 1979; PETER LEO GERETY, D.D. (Retired), ord. June 29, 1939; appt. Coadjutor Bishop of Portland, March 4, 1966; consecrated June 1, 1966; succeeded to See, Sept. 15, 1969; appt. Third Archbishop of Newark, April 2, 1974; installed June 28, 1974; retired June 1, 1986; THEODORE E. McCARRICK, Ph.D., ord. May 31, 1958; appt. Auxiliary Bishop of New York and Titular Bishop of Rusibisir, May 24, 1977; Episcopal ordination June 29, 1977; appt. First Bishop of Metuchen, Nov. 19, 1981; appt. Fourth Archbishop of Newark, May 30, 1986; Pallium conferred June 29, 1986; installed July 25, 1986; appt. to See of Washington, D.C., Nov. 21, 2000; installed Jan. 3, 2001.

Chancery—Archdiocesan Center, 171 Clifton Ave., P.O. Box 9500, Newark, 07104-0500. Tel: 973-497-4000; Fax: 973-497-4033. Email: webmaster@rcan.org. Open Mon.-Fri. 8:45-4:45. (Dispensation Requests or Questions regarding Canonical Matters can be directed to: Rev. Msgr. Frank G. Del Prete, J.C.D., Judicial Vicar, at P.O. Box 9500, Newark, NJ 07104-0500. Tel: 973-497-4145; Fax 973-497-4138; Email delprefr@rcan.org). All offices are in the Archdiocesan Center unless otherwise noted.

Vicar General and Moderator of Curia—Most Rev. ARTHUR J. SERRATELLI, S.T.D., D.D., S.S.L. Tel: 973-497-4002; Fax: 973-497-4018.

Chancellor—Ms. SHERI A. RICKERT, Esq. Tel: 973-497-4010; Fax: 973-497-4018.

Archdiocesan Archivist—Rev. Msgr. FRANCIS R. SEYMOUR, Walsh Library, Seton Hall University, 400 South Orange Ave., South Orange, 07079. Tel: 973-761-9126; Fax: 973-761-9550.

Secretary to the Archbishop and Vice Chancellor—Rev. JAMES M. SHEEHAN, J.C.L. Tel: 973-497-4005; Fax: 973-497-4018.

Executive Assistant to the Archbishop—Ms. ROSEANN BIASI-VASQUEZ. Tel: 973-497-4006.

Vice Chancellor—Rev. ROBERT E. EMERY, J.C.L. Tel: 973-497-4011; Fax: 973-497-4018.

Vice Chancellor for Administration—Deacon JOSEPH A. DWYER JR. Tel: 973-497-4559; Fax: 973-497-4031.

Judicial Vicar Archdiocesan Metropolitan Tribunal—Rev. Msgr. FRANK G. DEL PRETE, J.C.D. Tel: 973-497-4149; Fax: 973-497-4138.

Delegate for Religious—Sr. MARGARET THOMAS MCGOVERN, O.P. Tel: 973-497-4582; Fax: 973-497-4018.

Minister for Priests—Rev. Msgr. JAMES J. FINNERTY, St. John Rectory, 22 Mulberry St., Newark, 07102. Tel: 973-799-0201; Fax: 973-623-6804.

Executive Director for Priest Personnel—Rev. ROBERT E. TEMPLETON. Tel: 973-497-4222; Fax: 973-497-4219.

Vicar for Permanent Deacons—Rev. Msgr. THOMAS M. O'LEARY (Retired), 700 Wyckoff Ave., Wyckoff, 07481. Tel: 201-891-1122; Fax: 201-847-8518.

Director of Vocations—Rev. BRIAN G. PLATE. Tel: 973-497-4367; Fax: 973-497-4369.

Secretary for Education—Sr. DOMINICA ROCCHIO, S.C., Ed.D. Tel: 973-497-4250; Fax: 973-497-4249.

Vicar for Pastoral Life—Rev. Msgr. RICHARD J. ARNHOLS. Tel: 973-497-4321; Fax: 973-497-4555.

Secretary for Temporal Administration and Chief Financial Officer—Ms. CAROL PURCELL, C.P.A. Tel: 973-497-4050; Fax: 973-497-4033.

Cathedral Healthcare—Rev. Msgr. JOSEPH T. SLINGER, Liaison to the Archbishop.

Catholic Community Services (CCS)—Rev. Msgr. RONALD J. ROZNIAK, V.G., Liaison to the Archbishop.

Regional Bishops and Regional Vicars

Regional Bishops and Regional Vicars—Most Revs. CHARLES J. MCDONNELL, D.D., Regl. Bishop - Bergen County; DAVID ARIAS, O.A.R., D.D., Regl. Bishop - Hudson County & Vicar, Hispanic Affairs; Rev. EDGAR DA CUNHA, S.D.V., D.D., Regl. Bishop - Essex County; Very Rev. SEAN R. CUNNEEN, V.E., Regl. Vicar - Union County.

Deans

Deans—

BERGEN COUNTY—Northwest Bergen Region Deanery 1: Very Rev. JOHN R. O'CONNELL, V.F., Nativity, 315 Prospect St., Midland Park, 07432. Tel: 201-444-6362; Fax: 201-444-5056. Northeast Bergen Region Deanery 2: Very Rev. CHARLES P. GRANDSTRAND, V.F., Our Lady of Mercy, 2 Fremont Ave., Park Ridge, 07656. Tel: 201-391-5315; Fax: 201-391-5614. Central Bergen Region Deanery 3: Very Rev. ROBERT G. LAFERRARA, V.F., St. Mary, 280 Washington Ave., Dumont, 07628. Tel: 201-384-0557; Fax: 201-384-4986. Southwest Bergen Region Deanery 4: Rev. Msgr. PAUL L. BOCHICCHIO, V.F., Our Lady of Mt. Virgin, 188 MacArthur Ave., Garfield, 07026. Tel: 973-772-2295; Fax: 973-478-4389. South Central Bergen Deanery 5: Rev. PATRICK W. DONOHUE, V.F., Holy Trinity Parish, 34 Maple Ave., Hackensack, 07601. Tel: 201-343-5170; Fax: 201-343-5067. Southeast Bergen Region Deanery 6: Very Rev. DONALD DIPASQUALE, Church of the Epiphany, 247 Knox Ave., Cliffside Park, 07010. Tel: 201-943-7320; Fax: 201-943-1779. South Bergen Region Deanery 7: Very Rev. CHARLES J. MILLER, V.F., Sacred Heart Rectory, 324 Ridge Rd., Lyndhurst, 07071. Tel: 201-438-1137; Fax: 201-507-5861.

HUDSON COUNTY—North Hudson Deanery 8: Rev. CARLO FORTUNIO, O.P., St. Mary's, Help of Christians, 6502 Jackson St., West New York, 07093. Tel: 201-868-9444; Fax: 201-868-6451. Central Hudson Region Deanery 9: Rev. KENNETH J. HERBSTER, V.F., Our Lady of Grace, 400 Willow Ave., Hoboken, 07030. Tel: 201-659-0369; Fax: 201-659-5833. Jersey City North Region Deanery 10: Very Rev. KEVIN E. CARTER, V.F., St. Nicholas Rectory, 122 Ferry St., Jersey City, 07037. Tel: 201-659-5354; Fax: 201-798-6868. Jersey City Downtown Deanery 11: Very Rev. GREGORY J. STUDERUS, V.F., Parish of the Resurrection, 370 Montgomery St., P.O. Box 467, Jersey City, 07302-0407. Tel: 201-434-8500; Fax: 201-333-1816. Jersey City South Deanery 12: Very Rev. ROBERT A. ANTCZAK, V.F., St. Paul the Apostle Parish, 14 Greenville Ave., Jersey City, 07305. Tel: 201-433-8500; Fax: 201-433-9886. Bayonne Deanery 13: Very Rev. ANTHONY J. KULIG, V.F., Our Lady of Mt. Carmel Rectory, 39 E. 22nd St., Bayonne, 07002. Tel: 201-339-2070; Fax: 201-339-3676. West Hudson Region Deanery 14: Very Rev. MICHAEL G. WARD, St. Cecilia Parish, 120 Kearny Ave., Kearny, 07032-2316. Tel: 201-991-1116; Fax: 201-998-4437.

ESSEX COUNTY—West Essex Deanery 15: Rev. ALBERT J. BERNER, B.A., S.T.B., M.A., V.F., Monclair State University, 894 Valley Rd., Upper Montclair, 07043. Tel: 973-746-2323; Fax: 973-783-3313. North Essex Deanery 16: Rev. Msgr. ROBERT M. CHABAK, V.F., St. Valentine Parish, 125 N. Spring St., Bloomfield, 07003. Tel: 973-743-0220; Fax: 973-743-2041. Central Essex Deanery 17: Very Rev. MICHAEL M. WALTERS, V.F., J.C.L., Holy Spirit/Help of Christians, 17 N. Clinton St., East Orange, 07017. Tel: 973-673-1077; Fax: 973-676-6494. South Essex Deanery 18: Rev. THEODORE W. OSBAHR, V.F., St. Paul the Apostle, 954 Stuyvesant Ave., Irvington, 07111. Tel: 973-375-8568; Fax: 973-375-7040. North Newark Essex Deanery 19: Rev. Msgr. JOSEPH P. PLUNKETT, Our Lady of Good Counsel, 654 Summer Ave., Newark, 07104. Tel: 973-482-1274; Fax: 973-482-8257. Central Newark Deanery 20: Very Rev. PHILIP J. WATERS, O.S.B., V.F., St. Mary of the Immaculate Conception, 528 Martin Luther King Blvd., Newark, 07102-1314. Tel: 973-792-5793; Fax: 973-643-6922. Ironbound Deanery 21: Very Rev. JOSEPH F. AMBROSIO, V.F., Our Lady of Mt. Carmel, 259 Oliver St., Newark, 07105. Tel: 973-589-2090; Fax: 973-589-2662.

UNION COUNTY—Union Northwest Deanery 22: Very Rev. STEPHEN S. FEEHAN, V.F., Little Flower Parish, 110 Roosevelt Ave., Berkeley Heights, 07922. Tel: 908-464-1585; Fax: 908-464-6342. Union North Deanery 23: Very Rev. MATHIAS T. CONVA, V.F., St. Michael Parish, 1212 Kelly St., Union, 07083. Tel: 908-688-1232; Fax: 908-810-1076. Union County Southeast Deanery 24: Very Rev. BENEDICT M. WORRY, O.S.B., V.F., St. Elizabeth of Hungary, 179 Hussa St., Linden, 07036. Tel: 908-486-2514; Fax: 908-486-1757. Elizabeth Deanery 25: Very Rev. JOHN E. WASSELL, V.F., Holy Rosary/St. Michael, 52 Smith St., Elizabeth, 07201. Tel: 908-354-2454; Fax: 908-354-3207. Union County Southwest Deanery 26: Rev. Msgr. JOSEPH P. MASIELLO, V.F., Holy Trinity, 315 First St., Westfield, 07090. Tel: 908-232-8137; Fax: 908-654-8780.

Advisory Bodies

College of Consultors—Most Rev. JOHN J. MYERS, J.C.D., D.D., Pres.; Rev. Msgr. RONALD J. ROZNIAK, V.G., Sec.; Most Revs. DAVID ARIAS, O.A.R., D.D.; CHARLES J. MCDONNELL, D.D.; ARTHUR J. SERRATELLI, S.T.D., D.D., S.S.L.; EDGAR M. DA CUNHA, S.D.V., D.D.; Rev. Msgrs. EDWARD J. CIUBA; JOHN E. DORAN, V.E.; Very Rev. SEAN CUNNEEN, V.E.; Rev. Msgr. JOHN J. GILCHRIST; Rev. JOSEPH S. BEJGROWICZ, V.F.; Rev. Msgr. PAUL L. BOCHICCHIO, V.F.; Revs. RENATO GRASSELLI; KENNETH J. HERBSTER, V.F.

Presbyteral Council—Most Rev. JOHN J. MYERS, J.C.D., D.D., Pres.; Rev. KENNETH J. HERBSTER, V.F., Exec. Sec. Members: Most Revs. DAVID ARIAS, O.A.R., D.D.; CHARLES J. MCDONNELL, D.D.; ARTHUR J. SERRATELLI, S.T.D., D.D., S.S.L.; EDGAR M. DA CUNHA, S.D.V., D.D.; Very Rev. SEAN R. CUNNEEN, V.E.; Rev. Msgrs. JOHN E. DORAN, V.E.; PAUL L. BOCHICCHIO, V.F.; JAMES BOUFFARD; WILLIAM HARMS; RAYMOND J. POLLARD (Retired); RONALD J. ROZNIAK, V.G.; PETER J. ZACCARDO; Very Rev. JOSEPH F. AMBROSIO, V.F.; Revs. ANTHONY BICO; JAMES M. CAFONE, S.T.D.; JOHN J. CRYAN, V.F., M.Div.; LAWRENCE J. FAMA; NICHOLAS S. GENGARO, S.T.D.; RENATO GRASELLI; GERALD GREAVES; FERNANDO GUILLEN; KEVIN HANBURY; VICTOR P. KENNEDY, V.F.; ATTILIO MORELLI; BRIAN G. PLATE; WILLIAM SHERIDAN; ROBERT E. TEMPLETON.

Priest Personnel Policy Board—Rev. ROBERT E. TEMPLETON, Archbishop's Liaison; Rev. Msgr. WILLIAM J. FADROWSKI, Archbishop's Delegate. Ex Officio Members: Revs. EDWARD G. BRADLEY, S.T.L., M.A.; VENANTIUS FERNANDO; Rev. Msgrs. JOHN W. FLESEY, S.T.D.; THOMAS A. MCCARTHY. Elected Members: Rev. JOSEPH A. D'AMICO; Rev. Msgr. PAUL L. BOCHICCHIO, V.F.; Rev. JOHN J. CRYAN, V.F., M.Div.; Rev. Msgrs. THOMAS A. DONATO; PHILIP D. MORRIS, S.T.D.; RAYMOND J. POLLARD (Retired).

Diaconate Executive Committee—Deacons JOSEPH YANDOLI, Chm.; MICHAEL MAIONE, Vice Chm. Tel: 973-497-4223.

Archdiocesan Incardination Board—Most Rev. CHARLES J. MCDONNELL, D.D.; Rev. Msgr. FRANK G. DEL PRETE, J.C.D.; Revs. ROBERT E. TEMPLETON; VENANTIUS FERNANDO.

Archdiocesan Stewardship Advisory Committee—Staff: ANDREW KACZYNSKI; Rev. Msgrs. PAUL L. BOCHICCHIO, V.F. Tel: 973-497-4015; CHARLES GUSMER, S.T.D.; WILLIAM HARMS; Revs. JOHN CRYAN, V.F.; JOHN D. GABRIEL; LARRY EVANS; MICHAEL J. KREDER; Deacon NICHOLAS J. DELUCCA; Sr. AGNES BERNARD; Mr. MICHAEL BURCK; Ms. MARIKEL FAJARDO; Ms. EVEY JOHNSON; Ms. MARICELA QUINTANA. Tel: 973-497-4332.

Priestly Vocation Board—Rev. Msgr. DONALD E. GUENTHER, Chm.; Most Rev. ARTHUR J. SERRATELLI, S.T.D., D.D., S.S.L.; Revs. BRIAN G. PLATE; ANTHONY BICO; RICARD CORBETT; Very Rev. JOSEPH DOYLE; Revs. JOSEPH D'AMICO; RENATO GRASSELLI; DOMINICK J. LENOCI; GERARD H. MCCARREN, S.T.D.; MARK O'MALLEY; JOSEPH REILLY; JAMES O. SHEERIN (Retired).

Archdiocesan Pro-Life Commission—JAMES SONDEY, Chm. Members: Most Rev. JOHN J. MYERS, J.C.D., D.D.; Rev. Msgrs. RICHARD ARNHOLS; RICHARD M. MCGUINNESS; TRAUDE BARBIERO; DAN KRAFT; BONNIE LUDWIG; BRIAN LUDWIG; DAMON OWENS; MELANIE OWENS; THOMAS RUSSO; JUAN RYAN, Esq.; Dr. LEONIE WATSON; Dr. RICHARD WATSON.

Archdiocesan Finance Council—JOHN W. CULLIGAN, Chm. Members: CHARLES C. CARELLA; LAWRENCE R. CODEY; Mr. DONALD M. DANIELS; ANNE EVANS ESTABROOK; ADRIAN M. FOLEY JR., Esq.; ALBERT R. GAMPER JR.; LESLIE A. HYNES; BRIAN D. MCAULEY; W. PETER MCBRIDE; JOSEPH L. MUSCARELLE JR.; EDWARD F. RYAN; GARRY J. SCHEURING.

Archdiocesan Women's Commission—Ms. SHERI A. RICKERT, Esq., Chm. Members: ANN BURGMEYER; MARTA CABRERA; MARY ELAINE CONNELL; JOANNE DEPASQUALE PARENT; LINDA ENGLISH; Dr. ZENI FOX; ANNA GROVES; ANA LOPO; Sr. MARGARET T. MCGOVERN, O.P.; PAULA METZGER; SHARON MUSCARELLE; LOIS PAGNOZZI.

Archdiocesan Theological Commission—Rev. Msgr. ROBERT J. WISTER, Chm.; Revs. JAMES M. CAFONE, S.T.D.; JOHN CHADWICK; LAWRENCE FRIZZELL, D.Phil.; THOMAS G. GUARINO, S.T.D.; PAUL HOLMES, S.T.D.; Rev. Msgr. THOMAS MCCARTHY, Ph.D.; Rev. LAWRENCE PORTER, Ph.D.; Sr. MARGARET THOMAS MCGOVERN, O.P.; Rev. C. ANTHONY ZICCARDI, S.T.L., S.S.L.

Censors of Books—Rev. Msgrs. EDWARD CIUBA, S.T.L., S.S.L.; CHARLES GUSMER, S.T.D.; THOMAS P. IVORY, S.T.D.; Revs. DONALD BLUMENFELD, Ph.D.; JAMES M. CAFONE, S.T.D.; THOMAS G. GUARINO, S.T.D.; GERARD H. MCCARREN, S.T.D.; LAWRENCE B. PORTER, O.P., Ph.D.; JOSEPH R. REILLY, S.T.L., Ph.D.; ANTHONY FIGUEREIDO, S.T.D.; C. ANTHONY ZICCARDI, S.T.L., S.S.L.

Archdiocesan Pastoral Council—BLANCHE BISHOP, Chm.; OTTO PAYONZECK, Vice Chm.; GEORGEANNA CAMERON, Sec.; Sr. VIRGINIA STANTON, S.S.J., Staff. Tel: 973-497-4350.

Archdiocesan Commission on Justice and Peace—Deacon WILLIAM TOTH, Ph.D., Chm.; KAY FURLANI, Exec. Sec. Tel: 973-497-4341.

Archdiocesan Commission for Christain Unity—Revs. LUKE A. EDELEN, O.S.B., Chm.; PHILIP F. LATRONICO, Exec. Sec., Newark Abbey, 528 Martin Luther King Blvd., Newark, 07102. Tel: 973-643-4800.

Archdiocesan Commission for Interreligious Affairs—Rev. Msgr. JOHN GILCHRIST, Chm.; Rev. PHILIP F. LATRONICO, Exec. Sec. Tel: 973-497-4321.

Archdiocesan Liturgical Commission—Rev. ROBERT G. LAFERRERA, Chm. Tel: 973-497-4345; ANITA FOLEY, Sec.

Metropolitan Tribunal of the Archdiocese of Newark

Metropolitan Tribunal of the Archdiocese of Newark—Archdiocesan Center, 171 Clifton Ave., P.O. Box 9500, Newark, 07104-0500. Tel: 973-497-4145; Fax: 973-497-4138. Email: delprefr@rcan.org.

Judicial Vicar—Rev. Msgr. FRANK G. DEL PRETE, J.C.D.

Full-time Staff—Sr. CATHERINE MARY RAYMOND, J.C.L.; Rev. JOHN F. CONNOR, S.T.B.

Archdiocesan Judges—Rev. Msgr. JAMES P. MCMENEMIE, S.T.L. (Retired); Revs. JOHN J. CRYAN, V.F., M.Div.; ROBERT E. EMERY, J.C.L.; Rev. Msgr. ROBERT J. HARRINGTON, M.Div.; Revs. NORBERT F. LASKOWSKI, B.A.; ROBERT G. MCBRIDE, J.C.L.; BERNARD N. MOHAN, B.S. (Retired); JOHN S. OLSZEWSKI (Retired); JAMES M. SHEEHAN, J.C.L.; Rev. Msgr. GEORGE R. TRABOLD, J.C.L.; Very Rev. MICHAEL M. WALTERS, V.F., J.C.L.; Deacon EDWARD CAMPANELLA.

Part-time Staff—Rev. Msgr. FRANCIS HOUGHTON; Revs. JOSEPH A. D'AMICO; GERALD GEAVES; THOMAS KENNA; JEREMIAH MCGINLEY, O.F.M.; WILLIAM A. MAHON; Deacon VINCENT E. MESSINA; Sr. RUTHE

MORGAN, R.S.M.; Revs. JAMES M. SHEEHAN, J.C.L.; THOMAS ORIANS, S.A.; FRANK ROSE.

Promoter of Justice—Rev. Msgr. ROBERT F. COLEMAN, J.C.D.

Defenders of the Bond—Rev. Msgr. VINCENT J. DOYLE, J.C.L.; Rev. ROBERT S. MEYER, S.T.L., J.D., J.C.L.

Notaries—NANCY NUNEZ; MARGARET RUSSO; SANDRA PERRINI; JOHN WALSH.

Vicar General and Moderator of the Curia

Vicar General and Moderator of the Curia—Most Rev. ARTHUR J. SERRATELLI, S.T.D., D.D., S.S.L., Archdiocesan Center, P.O. Box 9500, 171 Clifton Ave., Newark, 07104-0500. Tel: 973-497-4002; Fax: 973-497-4018 All Offices are at the Archdiocesan Center unless otherwise noted.

Office of Archdiocesan Counsel— Carella, Byrne, Bain, Gilfillan, Cheechi, Stewart & Oldstein liaison to the following: CHARLES M. CARELLA, Counsellor-at-Law, 6 Becker Farm Rd., Roseland, 07068-1739. Tel: 973-994-1700; 973-497-4302; Fax: 973-497-4310.

Propagation of the Faith—Rev. Msgr. ROBERT J. FUHRMAN, Dir. Tel: 973-497-4375; Fax: 973-497-4371.

Holy Childhood Association—Sr. ARLINE ZURICH, O.S.B., Mission Coord. Tel: 973-497-4376; Fax: 973-497-4371.

Vocations Office—Rev. BRIAN G. PLATE, Dir. Tel: 973-497-4365; Fax: 973-497-4369.

Office of Communications and Public Relations—JAMES GOODNESS, Dir. Tel: 973-497-4190; Fax: 973-497-4185.

"The Catholic Advocate", Archdiocesan Newspaper—GREGORY TOBIN, Editor & Assoc. Publisher. Tel: 973-497-4193; Fax: 973-497-4192. Email: tobingre@rcan.org.

Office of the Chancellor

Chancellor—Ms. SHERI A. RICKERT, Esq. Tel: 973-497-4010; Fax: 973-497-4018. Email: rickersh@rcan.org.

Vice Chancellors—Revs. JAMES M. SHEEHAN, J.C.L.; ROBERT E. EMERY, J.C.L.. Email: sheehaja@rcan.org emeryrob@rcan.org.

Archdiocesan Offices and Ministries

All offices are in the Archdiocesan Center unless otherwise noted.

Office of Clergy Personnel

Office of Clergy Personnel—Rev. ROBERT E. TEMPLETON, Exec. Dir. Tel: 973-497-4220; Fax: 973-497-4219.

Diocesan Priest Personnel and Clergy/Religious Healthcare Personnel—Rev. ROBERT E. TEMPLETON, Dir.; CRISTINA PARDO, Admin. Asst. Tel: 973-497-4220; Fax: 973-497-4219.

Adjunct Clergy Personnel—Rev. VENANTIUS FERNANDO, Dir.; Ms. FRANCES DOWNING, Admin. Asst. Tel: 973-497-4225; Fax: 973-497-4180.

Ministry to Retired Priests—Rev. EDWARD G. BRADLEY, S.T.L., M.A., Dir. Tel: 973-497-4226; Fax: 973-497-4219.

Retired Priests' Residences—

St. John Vianney Priests' Residence—Rev. Msgr. EDWARD F. KAVIN, Dir. (Retired); CAROL HUBBA, Admin., 60 Home Ave., Rutherford, 07070. Tel: 201-933-5155. *St. John Vianney Annex, 64 Home Ave., Rutherford, 07070.* Tel: 201-933-5155. *Rev. Msgr. James F. Kelley Residence*, Rev. GEORGE MADER, Dir.; JOAN STEVENS, Admin., 247 Bloomfield Ave., Caldwell, 07006. Tel: 973-364-1121.

Continuing Education of Priests—Rev. Msgr. THOMAS A. MCCARTHY, Dir. Tel: 973-497-4221.

Continuing Formation of Priests—Rev. Msgr. JOHN W. FLESEY, S.T.D., Dir. Tel: 973-497-4225.

Permanent Diaconate—Deacons EDWARD W. PORTER, Dir. Tel: 973-497-4223; DANIEL RAVELO, Coord. of Spanish-Speaking.

Office of Hospital Ministry—Rev. Msgr. MANUEL CRUZ, Dir., St. Michael's Medical Center, 306 Martin Luther King Blvd., Newark, 07104. Tel: 973-877-2606; Rev. ALAN F. GUGLIELMO, Coord. Pastoral Care.

Bergen County Hospitals—

Bergen Regional Medical Center—230 E. Ridgewood Ave., Paramus, 07652. Tel: 201-967-4000. Deacon VICTOR PETERSON, Hospital Minister. Chaplains: Revs. JOSEPH BUZZERIO; SEBASTIAN FERNANDO; MARCELLINUS UWANDU.

Englewood Hospital & Medical Center—350 Engle St., Englewood, 07631. Tel: 201-894-3000. Rev. MATHEW CHANDRANKUNNEL, Chap.

Hackensack University Medical Center Hospital—30 Prospect St., Hackensack, 07601. Tel: 201-996-2000. Chaplains: Revs. ALPHONSUS EZEOKE; PETER IGWILO; ANTHONY UDOGU.

Holy Name Hospital—718 Teaneck Rd., Teaneck, 07666. Tel: 201-833-3000. Sr. LOIS JABLONSKI, S.S.J., M.Div., Pastoral Staff. Chaplains: Revs. PATERNO GOROSPE; THOMAS THARAYIL. Hospital Ministers: Deacons WILLY MALARCHER; EDGAR CACERES.

Pascack Valley Hospital—250 Old Hook Rd., Westwood, 07675. Tel: 201-358-3000 Chaplains: Revs. THOMAS NORTON; NOEL MORALES.

The Valley Hospital—223 N. Van Dien Ave., Ridgewood, 07450. Tel: 201-447-8000. Chaplains Revs. MERT CORDERO; NOEL MORALES.

Essex County Hospitals—

Newark Beth Israel Medical Center—201 Lyons Ave., Newark, 07112. Tel: 973-926-7000. Chaplains: Revs. THOMAS MCLAUGHLIN; CHRISTOPHER ANYANWU.

Clara Maass Medical Center—One Clara Maass Dr., Belleville, 07109. Tel: 973-450-2000. Chaplains: Revs. GEORGE JOSEPH; JOHN DONOHUE.

Columbus Hospital—495 N. 13th St., Newark, 07107. Tel: 973-268-1400. Rev. ROBERT TOOMAN, Chap.

Essex County Hospital Center—125 Fairview Ave., Cedar Grove, 07009. Tel: 973-228-8000. Rev. POLYCARP NNAJIOFIR.

Hospital Center at Orange—188 S. Essex St., Orange, 07051. Tel: 973-266-2000. Rev. FELIX UGWUOZAR, Chap.

Kessler Institute for Rehabilitation—1199 Pleasant Valley Way, West Orange, 07052. Tel: 973-731-3600. Rev. LOUIS PAMBELLO, Chap.

Mountainside Hospital—One Bay Ave., Montclair, 07042. Tel: 973-429-6000. Chaplains: Revs. WILLIAM GYURE; BERNARD FERNANDO.

Pope John Paul II Pavilion—135 S. Centre St., Orange, 07050. Tel: 973-266-3000. Rev. FELIX UGWUOZAR, Chap.

St. Barnabas Medical Center—94 Old Short Hills Rd., Livingston, 07039. Tel: 973-533-5015. Chaplains: Revs. RICHARD CHILMARK; PETER VINH Q. NGUYEN.

St. James Hospital—155 Jefferson St., Newark, 07105. Tel: 973-589-1300. Rev. AROKIASAMY IRUDAYANATHAN, Chap.; Sr. DOLORES CERVI, Pastoral Staff.

St. Michael's Medical Center—306 Martin Luther King Blvd., Newark, 07102. Tel: 973-877-5000. Sr. MARY ARCHANGEL DUDZINSKA, C.S.S.F., Pastoral Staff. Chaplains: Rev. Msgr. MANUEL CRUZ; Rev. ALAN F. GUGLIELMO Hospital Ministers: Deacons EDWARD MCFADDEN; RAFAEL VARGAS; JOSE M. CLASS.

UMDNJ University Hospital—100 Bergen St., Newark, 07103. Tel: 973-972-4300. Rev. EUSTACE EDOMOBI, Chap. Hospital Ministers: Deacons LEO MONTINI; CESAR A. ORTEGA-ESCOBAR.

Veterans Administration Hospital—Tremont Ave. & Centre St., East Orange, 07019. Tel: 973-676-1000. Rev. GEORGE KELLY, C.SS.R.

Hudson County Hospitals—

Bayonne Medical Center—29 E. 29th St., Bayonne, 07002. Tel: 201-858-5000. Rev. J. M. PATRICIUS, Chap.

Christ Hospital—176 Palisades Ave., Jersey City, 07304. Tel: 201-795-8200. Rev. ALOYSIUS EZENWATA, Chap.

Jersey City Medical Center—50 Baldwin Ave., Jersey City, 07304. Tel: 201-915-2000. Rev. Msgr. EDMUNDO A. SURBAN, Chap.

Palisades Medical Center—7600 River Rd., North Bergen, 07047. Tel: 201-854-5000. Rev. JOHN T. MICHALCZAK, Chap.

St. Mary's Hospital—308 Willow Ave., Hoboken, 07030. Tel: 201-418-1000. Rev. MICHAEL ONYEKWELE, Chap.

West Hudson Hospital—206 Bergen Ave., Kearny, 07032. Tel: 201-955-7000. Rev. JOSEPH KHAI VU, Chap.

Union County Hospitals—

Trinitas Hospital—225 Williamson St., Elizabeth, 07202. Tel: 908-994-5000. Chaplains: Revs. BRENDAN QUINN; EDWARD A. HABER (Retired). Pastoral Staff: Sisters MARY CORRIGAN; MARIE TANSEY; DOROTHY APPRICH, S.S.J.

Runnells Specialized Hospital—40 Watchung Way, Berkeley Heights, 07922. Tel: 908-771-5700. Rev. CHARLES I. ANEMELU, Chap.

Muhlenberg Regional Medical Center—Park Ave. & Randolph Rd., Plainfield, 07061. Tel: 908-668-2000. Rev. JOHN PALADINO, Chap.; Deacon ROBERT GURSKE, Hospital Minister.

Overlook Hospital—99 Beauvoir Ave., Summit, 07902. Tel: 908-522-2000. Rev. JOHN P. HOLIAN, Chap.; Sr. PATRICIA MURPHY, Pastoral Staff.

Rahway Hospital—865 Stone St., Rahway, 07065. Tel: 732-381-4200. Rev. WILLIAM REED, Chap.; Deacon J. WILLIAM COURTNEY, Hospital Minister.

Union Hospital—1000 Galloping Hill Rd., Union, 07083. Tel: 908-687-1900. Rev. GEORGE M. KEATING, Chap. (Retired).

Office of Prison Ministry—Deacon DAVID LOMAN, Dir. Tel: 973-497-4223; 201-310-7690; Fax: 973-497-4019.

Bergen County Prison Ministry—

Bergen County Jail—160 S. River Rd., Hackensack, 07601. Tel: 201-527-3000. Rev. JOSEPH BUZZERIO, Chap.

Bergen County Juvenile Detention Center—296 E. Ridgewood Ave., Paramus, 07652. Tel: 201-599-6185. Deacon MICHAEL J. CECHONY, Prison Minister.

Essex County Prison Ministry—

CURA (Community United to Rehabilitate Addicts)—P.O. Box 180, Newark, 07101-0180. Tel: 973-622-3570. Chaplains: Revs. ANTHONY BICO; ROBERT J. CORMIER.

Delaney Hall Assessment Center—451 Doremus Ave., Newark, 07105. Tel: 908-289-6768. Rev. PAUL J. NOLAN, Chap.; Mr. MICHAEL YORK, Pastoral Staff.

Essex County Jail—60 Nelson Pl., Newark, 07104. Tel: 973-621-5163; 973-621-5162. Rev. PAUL J. NOLAN, Chap.; Deacon CESAR A. ORTEGA-ESCOBAR, Prison Minister; GREGORY QUINN, Pastoral Staff.

Essex County Jail Annex—45 Elm Rd., Caldwell, 07006. Tel: 973-364-5341. Rev. PAUL J. NOLAN, Chap.

Essex County Juvenile Detention Center—208 Sussex Ave., Newark, 07103. Tel: 973-497-4720; 973-497-4735. Rev. ANTHONY BICO, Chap.

Northern State Prison—168 Frontage Rd., P.O. Box 2300, Newark, 07114. Tel: 973-465-0068, Ext. 4505. Mr. EDWARD BOYLE, Pastoral Staff. Chaplains: Revs. ROBERT J. CORMIER; THOMAS C. ROBERTS. Prison Ministers: Deacons DAVID B. LOMAN; THOMAS M. SMITH.

Hudson County Prison Ministry—

Hudson County Correctional Center—35 Hackensack Ave., Kearny, 07032. Tel: 973-491-5500. Rev. STEPHEN J. TOTH, Chap. Prison Ministers: Deacons JOSEPH J. DELMONTE; WILFRID LECONTE; JUAN B. SUAREZ.

Hudson County Juvenile Detention Center—635 County Ave., Secaucus, 07094. Tel: 201-319-3750. Rev. GIORDANO BELANICH, Chap. Pastoral Staff: Sr. ANTONELLE CHUNKA; Bro. THOMAS COREY.

Talbot Hall Assessment Center—100-140 Lincoln Hwy., Kearny, 07032. Tel: 973-589-1114. Rev. STEPHEN J. TOTH, Chap.; Deacon EDWARD A. CAMPANELLA, Prison Minister.

Union County Prison Ministry—

Union County Jail—15 Elizabethtown Plaza, Elizabeth, 07207. Tel: 908-558-2600; 908-558-2636. Rev. PAUL J. NOLAN, Chap.; Deacon MICHAEL DEROBERTS, Prison Minister.

Elizabeth Detention Center (Federal)—625 Evans St., Elizabeth, 07201. Tel: 908-352-3776. Rev. GEORGE F. SHARP, Chap.

Vice Chancellor for Administration—Deacon JOSEPH A. DWYER JR., Vice Chancellor. Tel: 973-497-4128; Fax: 973-497-4031; LYNN SKALKO, Exec. Asst. Tel: 973-497-4559.

Office of Development—Deacon JOSEPH A. DWYER JR., Exec. Dir. Tel: 973-497-4128; Fax: 973-497-4031.

Archbishop's Annual Appeal & Special Events—Ms. CARLA GONZALEZ, Dir. Tel: 973-497-4127; THERESA LYNCH, Office Asst. & Donor Rels. Tel: 973-497-4042; RAYMOND QUINTANA, AAA Asst. Operations Mgr. Tel: 973-497-4130; RAMONA FLORES, Asst. Dir., Special Events & Grants. Tel: 973-497-4026; 973-497-4127 General Inquiries; 973-497-4126 Archbishop's Annual Appeal Inquiries.

Office of Research and Planning/Planned Giving and Stewardship—JOSEPH A. VANCIO, M.A., Dir. Tel: 973-497-4024; ANDREW KACZYNSKI, Coord. Stewardship & Planned Giving. Tel: 973-497-4332; MARIA DEPAULA, Asst., Data Management. Tel: 973-497-4027; Fax: 973-497-4028.

Cooperative Supply Services, Inc.— (Cooperative Purchasing Network (CPN)-centralized purchasing organization for the five NJ dioceses) Tel: 800-275-6474 Member Toll Free Number; Fax: 866-FAX2CPN. *Central Jersey Office.* Tel: 732-562-1990, Ext. 1825. *Southern Jersey Office.* Tel: 609-601-0200. STEPHEN E. MICHALEK JR., Exec. Dir. Tel: 973-497-4170; Fax: 973-497-4174.

Office of Computing Services—ROBERT J. KENNELLY, Dir. Tel: 973-497-4161; Fax: 973-497-4277; ELGIO MARIANO, Asst. Dir. Tel: 973-497-4162.

Office of Human Resources—Deacon JOHN MCKENNA, Dir. Tel: 973-497-4125; LEAN PAGLIUCA, Exec. Asst. Tel: 973-497-4135; Fax: 973-497-4103; DOUG MCGUIRK, Assoc. Dir. Tel: 973-497-4095; SERENA JOHNSON, Benefits Mgr. Tel: 973-497-4092.

Office of Plant Services—Mr. STEVEN BELLOISE, Dir. Property Management Administration. Tel: 973-497-4118; Fax: 973-497-4362; THEODORE DEC, Dir. Engineering & Architecture. Tel: 973-497-4110;

Fax: 973-497-4362; JAMES RUFF, Environmental Coord. Tel: 973-497-4114; BEVERLY POCHTAR, Office Mgr. Tel: 973-497-4116.

Office of Security—THOMAS MCCUE, Dir. Tel: 973-497-4113; Fax: 973-497-4033.

Secretary for Temporal Administration

Secretary for Temporal Administration—CAROL PURCELL, C.P.A., CFO. Tel: 973-497-4051; Fax: 973-497-4033.

Counsel to Temporal Administration—JANICE FALIVENA, Esq., Counsellor-at-Law. Tel: 973-497-4330.

Risk Management/Insurance Services—JOSEPH A. FRANK, Dir. Tel: 973-497-4040; Fax: 973-497-4031.

Office of Finance—GEORGE PERALTA, Dir. Tel: 973-497-4055; Fax: 973-497-4031.

Office of Banking and Investments—MATTHEW PHELAN, Mgr. Tel: 973-497-4070; Fax: 973-497-4031.

Office Services/Mailroom—ELIZABETH MATOS, Supvr. Tel: 973-497-4035; Fax: 973-497-4037.

Office of Catholic Cemeteries—Rev. Msgr. WILLIAM NAEDELE, Dir.; ANDREW P. SCHAEFER, Exec. Dir., 171 Clifton Ave., P.O. Box 9500, Newark, 07104-0500. Tel: 973-497-7981 (Cemeteries); 973-497-7988 (Mausoleums); Fax: 973-497-7984.

Office of Parish Internal Audit—NANCY F. LYSTASH, Dir. Tel: 973-497-4074; Fax: 973-497-4031.

Secretariat for Education

Secretariat for Education—Sisters DOMINICA ROCCHIO, S.C., Ed.D., Sec. Educ./Supt. Schools; CATHERINE ROCHE, S.S.J., Admin. Asst. Tel: 973-497-4260; Fax: 973-497-4249.

Catechetical Office—Mr. RONALD L. PIHOKKER, M.A., Dir. Tel: 973-497-4285; Fax: 973-497-4249. Associate Directors: Sr. DELPHINE CROFT, O.P., Parish Catechetics in Catholic Schools. Tel: 973-497-4295; Ms. ROBERT MURPHY, M.A., Parish Catechetics. Tel: 973-497-4296; Dr. EUGENE TOZZI, Ph.D., Adults and Families Catechesis. Tel: 973-497-4289; Ms. ELIZABETH FOER, Certification/Enrichment. Tel: 973-497-4297; Dr. JOSE PLANAS, Catechesis with Families. Tel: 973-497-4290; Mrs. CAROL HENDERSON, Technology Resource Consultant. Tel: 973-497-4292.

Scholarship Fund for Inner City Children—KEVIN P. MORIARTY, Exec. Dir. Tel: 973-497-4281; Fax: 973-497-4279.

Office of the Superintendent of Schools—Sr. DOMINICA ROCCHIO, S.C., Ed.D., Supt. Tel: 973-497-4260; Bro. RALPH DARMENTO, F.S.C., Deputy Supt. Schools. Assoc. Superintendents: Rev. JOHN CONNOLLY, S.D.B., Education Technology; Sr. PATRICIA BUTLER, S.C., M.A., Elementary School Admin.; Mr. JOHN O'NEIL, M.A., Secondary Schools. Asst. Superintendents for Elementary Schools: Sisters JOAN AMELIA FERRUGGIARO, S.S.J., M.A.; MARIE GAGLIANO, M.P.F., M.A.; LOUISE CABABE, O.P., Ph.D., Curriculum & Testing. Directors: Sr. ANNE KAVANAGH, R.D.C., Personnel & Events Mgr.; Mrs. GRACE PIETROPINTO, B.S., Finance; Ms. KATHLEEN CIRAULO, Marketing; GLORIA CASTUCCI, M.A., Early Childhood Education; Mrs. ANN MCNIERNEY, M.S., Govt. Programs; Sr. LORETTA HOGAN, S.S.J., M.A., Elementary School Finance.

NJ Alliance for Catholic School Families—MARY MCELROY, Esq.

Personnel and Events—Sr. ANNE KAVANAUGH, R.D.C.

Vicariate for Pastoral Life

Vicar for Pastoral Life—Rev. Msgr. RICHARD J. ARNHOLS; Mrs. LINDA ROBINSON, Admin. Asst. Tel: 973-497-4321; Fax: 973-497-4555.

Multi Cultural Affairs—

Hispanic Apostolate—Ms. MARICELA QUINTANA. Tel: 201-497-4335 Centro Guadalupe:; Revs. JOSE RODRIGALVAREZ, O.A.R., Dir.; JUAN L. CALDERON, O.A.R., Asst. Dir., 545 35th St., Union City, 07087. Tel: 201-348-8400; Fax: 201-348-1809. Email: njcentroguadalupe@hotmail.com.

Office of Black Catholic Affairs—Mr. TRACEY BATTLES, Dir. Tel: 973-497-4340; Fax: 973-497-4317.

Council for Multi-Cultural Concerns—Rev. Msgr. WILLIAM J. REILLY, Chm. Tel: 973-497-4321.

Brazilian Apostolate—Rev. CLEMENT M. KRUG, C.SS.R., Coord., St. James Parish, 143 Madison St., Newark, 07105. Tel: 973-344-8322.

Chinese Apostolate—Rev. Msgr. JOSEPH CHIANG, Coord., Holy Rosary Rectory, 344 6th St., Jersey City, 07302. Tel: 973-795-0210.

Indian Apostolate—Rev. THOMAS THOTTUNGAL, Coord., 691 West Side Ave., Jersey City, 07304. Tel: 201-433-6365.

Filipino Apostolate—Rev. Msgr. JEREMIAS REBANAL, Coord., 800 Bergen Ave., Jersey City, 07306. Tel: 201-433-6800.

Haitian Apostolate—VACANT, Coord. Tel: 973-497-4321.

Liaison to the Irish Community—Rev. Msgr. MICHAEL E. KELLY, M.A., Seton Hall Prep, 120 Northfield Ave., West Orange, 07052. Tel: 973-325-6624.

Italian Apostolate—Very Rev. JOSEPH F. AMBROSIO, V.F., Coord., Our Lady of Mt. Carmel, 259 Oliver St., Newark, 07105. Tel: 973-589-2090.

Korean Apostolate—Rev. Msgr. AUGUSTIN PARK, Coord., St. Andrew Kim Parish, 257 Central Ave., Orange, 07050. Tel: 973-673-1366.

Nigerian IGBO Catholic Community—Rev. ANSELM NWAORGU, Blessed Sacrament/St. Charles, 15 Van Ness Pl., Newark, 07108. Tel: 973-824-6548.

Polish Apostolate—Rev. THADDEUS STASIK, Coord., St. Ann, 291 St. Paul Ave., Jersey City, 07306. Tel: 201-656-4018.

Portugese Apostolate—Rev. Msgr. JOHN S. ANTAO, Coord., 403 Spring St., Elizabeth, 07201. Tel: 908-355-3810.

Vietnamese Apostolate—Rev. JOSEPH TRI MINH NGUYEN, Coord., St. Michael Rectory, 252 Ninth St., Jersey City, 07302. Tel: 201-434-8500.

Chaplain to the India Catholic Association (Syro-Malabar Rite)—Rev. SEBASTIAN KUNNATH, Coord., Our Lady of the Visitation, 234 Fairview Ave., Paramus, 07652. Tel: 201-444-0272.

Department of Human Concerns—KAY FURLANI, Dir. Tel: 973-497-4341; Fax: 973-497-4317.

Parish Pastoral Councils— (Contact Office of Research and Planning) Tel: 973-497-4024; 973-497-4027; Fax: 973-497-4028.

Ministerial Development Center—Sr. VIRGINIA STANTON, S.S.J., Dir. Tel: 973-497-4350.

Worship Office—Sr. SANDRA DE MASI, S.S.J., Dir. Tel: 973-497-4345; Fax: 973-497-4348; Revs. MICHAEL J. SHEEHAN, Dir. RCIA; THOMAS B. IWANOWSKI, Assoc Dir. for Parish Life; THOMAS A. DENTE, Assoc. Dir. of Liturgical Formation; Rev. Msgrs. RICHARD F. GRONCKI, Archdiocesan Ceremonies; CHARLES W. GUSMER, V.E., S.T.D., Consultant for Liturgy; Very Rev. CHARLES PINYAN, Word on Worship.

Music Ministry—JOHN MILLER.

Respect Life Office—Rev. Msgr. RICHARD M. MCGUINNESS, 1805 Penbrook Ter., Linden, 07036. Tel: 732-388-8211.

Campus Ministry—Rev. JOHN B. BARON, Ph.D., Dir., Newman Center, 45 Bleeker St., Newark, 07112. Tel: 973-642-1613; Fax: 973-642-2061.

Family Life Ministries—Ms. JUDITH MILLER, M.A., Dir.

Pre-Cana Reservations—NANCY DELLISANTI. Tel: 973-497-4328.

Ministry with Separated, Divorced and Widowed Catholics—JANET MCCORMICK, Assoc. Dir.; Revs. ROBERT EMERY, Chap., Separated and Divorced; THOMAS ARMINIO, Chap., Widows and Widowers. Tel: 973-497-4327.

Hispanic Family Life Ministries—REINA BASUALDO, Assoc. Dir. Tel: 973-497-4326.

Couples for Christ—Rev. PAUL J. LEHMAN, Chap. (Retired). Tel: 973-623-0258; DANNY RODRIGUEZ, Coord., 26 Golf Rd., East Brunswick, 08816. Tel: 732-562-2636.

Families for Nazareth—PETER DOWNING, Pres., 812 N. Wood Ave., Ste. 101, Linden, 07036. Tel: 908-486-3366; Fax: 908-486-0398.

Focolare Movement (East Coast Regional Directors)—HORTENSIA LOPEZ, 2615 Schurz Ave., Bronx, NY 10465. Tel: 718-828-1969; Fax: 718-892-0419; CARLOS BAJAS, 167 Commonwealth Ave., Mt. Vernon, NY 10552. Tel: 914-667-5916; Fax: 914-667-5939. Local Coordinators: JIM MILWAY; MARY JANE MILWAY. Tel: 973-726-6224.

Engaged Encounter—Rev. PETER K. FUNESTI, Chap., 60 Byrd Ave., Bloomfield, 07003. Tel: 201-338-9190.

Marriage Encounter Resources—Very Rev. MICHAEL M. WALTERS, V.F., J.C.L., Priest Coord. Tel: 973-673-1077. Area Coordinators: PATRICIA DETURA; JAMES DETURA, 114 E. Clinton Ave., Bergenfield, 07621. Tel: 201-384-8497. *Registration/Information*, Tel: 800-823-LOVE.

Pastoral & Matrimonial Renewal Center—Rev. CHARLES GALLAGHER, Dir., 67 Prince St., Elizabeth, 07209. Tel: 908-353-8640.

Natural Family Planning—Rev. THOMAS NYDEGGER, Chap. & Coord. Chaircouple: KAREN DOYLE; KEVIN J. DOYLE, Holy Name Hospital, Teaneck, 07666. Tel: 201-833-3121.

Remarriage Ministry—Rev. RICHARD G. FRANCESCO, Chap. Coordinators: CAROLE MAZZUCCO; THOMAS MAZZUCCO, 28 Sherwood Downs, Park Ridge, 07656. Tel: 201-391-1331.

CYO Youth and Young Adult Ministries—Youth Center, 499 Belgrove Ave., Kearny, 07032. Tel: 201-998-0088. Rev. RICHARD R. CORBETT, Exec. Dir. Directors Youth Ministry: ALBERT FORSYTHE; KERRY O'CONNELL.

CYO Retreat Center—499 Belgrove Dr., Kearny, 07032. Fax: 201-998-9606. GLORIA O'NEILL, Facility Coord. Tel: 201-998-0088, Ext. 814. Email: oneill@rcan.org; RICH DONOVAN, Summer Camp Program. Tel: 201-998-0088, Ext. 816; CORY ROBINSON, Dir. Athletics. Tel: 201-998-0088, Ext. 811; BETTY WHITE, Receptionist. Tel: 201-998-0088, Ext. 810; REBECCA PACE, Dir. Food Svcs. Tel: 201-998-9607.

Boy Scouts of America/Catholic Committee on Scouting—499 Belgrove Dr., Kearny, 07032. Tel: 201-998-0088. GABRIEL D. FELTZ, Dir. Tel: 201-998-0088, Ext. 812. Email: feltzgab@rcan.org; ANNETTE B. FELTZ, Sec.; Rev. VICTOR P. KENNEDY, V.F., Chap. Tel: 201-656-2490; Very Rev. MICHAEL M. WALTERS, V.F., J.C.L., Asst. Chap. Tel: 973-673-1077; Revs. EUGENE J. FIELD, Area Chap. Tel: 201-641-6464; KEVIN A. GUGLIOTTA, Area Chap. Tel: 973-379-3912; JOSEPH A. MANCINI, Area Chap. Tel: 201-998-3314; DONALD HUMMEL, NCCA Assoc. Chap. Tel: 908-322-5192; ROSE MARIE MOSCHETTA, Committee Chm. Tel: 908-273-6076. Bergen County: KEVIN O'BOYLE. Tel: 201-385-2261. Essex County: GREGORY NIPKOWSKI. Tel: 973-338-1974. Hudson County: JUDY VERHEYEN; RON VERHEYEN. Tel: 201-433-0128. Union County: CHARLES GYECSEK. Tel: 908-245-1950.

Archdiocesan Girl Scouts—171 Clifton Ave., P.O. Box 9500, Newark, 07104-0500. Tel: 973-497-4512. TERESA STACZEWICZ, Archdiocesan Coord.. Email: staczete@rcan.org; Rev. DONALD K. HUMMEL, Chap.

The Vicar General and Moderator of the Curia is the Archbishop's liaison to the following apostolates:

Archdiocesan Council of Catholic Women (N.C.C.W.)—171 Clifton Ave., P.O. Box 9500, Newark, 07104-0500. Tel: 973-497-4356; Fax: 973-497-4317. D. JEAN SCHNEIDER, Pres., 178 Bay Ave., Glen Ridge, 07028. Email: schneije@rcan.org; Rev. DANIEL DANIK, Moderator, 2046 Ingalls Ave., Linden, 07076. Tel: 908-587-9144; FRANCES DONNELLY, First Vice Pres.; FLORENCE HORGAN, Second Vice Pres.; IDA MIZEL, Third Vice Pres.; AUDREY CALLIGY, Treas.; CLARINDA BRUECK, Recording Sec.; MILDRED LOUGHLIN, Corresponding Sec.

District Moderators

District Moderators—Essex-Suburban: VACANT; ETTA RIZZUTO, Pres. Tel: 973-676-4725. Union-Westfield: Rev. DANIEL A. DANIK (Retired); JOAN MACCHIA, Pres. Tel: 973-322-6987. South Hudson: Rev. HENRY M. NADDEO; MARY ELAINE CONNELL, Pres. Tel: 201-434-7235. North Hudson: VACANT; AUDRY CALLIGY, Contact. Tel: 201-659-5723. Union-Elizabeth: VACANT; IDA MIZEL, Pres. Tel: 908-352-9685. Bergen-Hackensack: Deacon NICHOLAS SIMONELLI; ADELE CICCONE, Pres. Tel: 201-939-7639. Bergen-Paramus: Rev. MICHAEL A. SAPORITO; MARY R. LOFTUS, Pres. Tel: 201-265-2048. Essex-Montclair: VACANT; MILDRED LOUGHLIN, Pres. Tel: 973-338-0699. Essex-Newark: VACANT; JUNE PICILLO, Representative. Tel: 201-998-1303.

Charismatic Renewal—Rev. PHILIP J. ROTUNNO, Coord. English and Multi-Cultural Prayer Groups, 5808 Kennedy Blvd., West New York, 07093. Tel: 201-867-5535.

The Community of God's Love—70 W. Passaic Ave., Rutherford, 07070. Tel: 201-935-0344. LES WILLIAMS, Dir.; Rev. PHILIP F. LATRONICO, Chap. Tel: 201-935-6492.

Bukas-Loob Sa Diyos Community (B.L.D.) (Open to the Spirit of God)—321 Millburn Ave., Ste. 2, Millburn, 07041. Tel: 973-376-4880; Fax: 973-912-9331. Secretaries: EMIL CARLOS; BOBY CARLOS; Rev. PAUL J. LEHMAN, Chap. (Retired). District Council of Stewards: ROGER SANTIAGO; IRMA SANTIAGO; WINSTON ALCRUZ; EVE ALCRUZ; RICHARD DE LA FUENTE; LEE DE LA FUENTA; DONNIE DEVERA; NINGING DEVERA; NOEL TRILLANA; LETTY TRILLANA.

Commission for the Men's Apostolate—Rev. Msgr. WILLIAM C. HATCHER, Chm., 60 Byrd Ave., Bloomfield, 07003. Tel: 973-338-9190.

Cursillo Movement—Rev. THOMAS P. LIPNICKI, Spiritual Dir., Our Lady of Perpetual Help, 25 Perdue Ave., Oakland, 07436; RAY FALCON, Lay Dir. Tel: 201-573-8587; LINDA ARMONAITIS, Cursillo Sec. Tel: 973-249-0049.

Sacred Heart Institute—P.O. Box 985, West Caldwell, 07007-0985. Tel: 973-226-7077. Email: sacredheartinst@worldnet.att.net. Rev. GERALD P. RUANE, Dir.

Catholic Community Services— Affiliated Agencies: Associated Catholic Charities, Mt. Carmel Guild, New Jersey Boystown, The Guild Social Service Center. Tel: 973-266-7960. PHILLIP FRESE, Ph.D., C.P.A., Exec. Dir., 37 Evergreen Pl., East Orange, 07018. Tel: 973-266-7998; Fax: 973-675-7385; Bro.

Benedict Lo Balbo, F.M.S., Dir. Bd. Affairs, 37 Evergreen Pl., East Orange, 07018. Tel: 973-266-7994; Fax: 973-266-7990; John Westervelt, B.A., C.F.O. & Assoc. Exec. Dir. Finance, Plant Svcs. Risk Management & Grants, 499 Belgrove Dr., Kearny, 07032. Tel: 201-246-7259; Fax: 201-991-4726.

Communications—Christina Crovetto, M.S., Dir., 37 Evergreen Pl., East Orange, 07018. Tel: 973-266-7965; Fax: 973-675-8641.

Development—Michelle Pignatello, A.B., Dir., 37 Evergreen Pl., East Orange, 07018. Tel: 973-266-7988; Fax: 973-266-7950.

Human Resources—37 Evergreen Pl., East Orange, 07018. Tel: 973-266-7979; Fax: 973-675-7809. Raymond Quintana. Tel: 973-497-4130.

Information Technology—Sal Cerruto, Chief Information Officer, 1160 Raymond Blvd., Newark, 07102. Tel: 973-596-5109; Fax: 973-623-2679.

Grants—Paul Steffens, M.A., Dir., 37 Evergreen Pl., East Orange, 07018. Tel: 973-266-7968; Fax: 973-675-8641.

General Counsel—Alexander Sharnoff, Esq., 37 Evergreen Pl., East Orange, 07018. Tel: 973-266-7997; Fax: 973-266-7940.

Internal Audit—Alice Fenney, M.P.F., Dir., 37 Evergreen Pl., East Orange, 07018. Tel: 973-266-7995; Fax: 973-266-7940.

Risk Management—Marissa Feldman, M.S.P.H., Dir., 37 Evergreen Pl., East Orange, 07018. Tel: 973-266-7983; Fax: 973-266-7970.

Behavioral Healthcare Division—1160 Raymond Blvd., Newark, 07102. Tel: 973-596-4100. *Behavioral Healthcare Access*. Tel: 800-227-7705. Michael Leitzes, M.B.A., Administrative Dir. Healthcare, 1160 Raymond Blvd., Newark, 07102. Tel: 973-639-5026; Fax: 973-596-4105; Mark Alvarado, M.D., Medical Dir., 1160 Raymond Blvd., Newark, 07102. Tel: 973-596-3857; Margery Grimm DeFranco, L.C.S.W., M.A., Rgnl. Dir. Union County, 108 Alden St., Cranford, 07016. Tel: 908-497-3975; Fax: 908-272-9268; Nuzhat Iqbal, Rgnl. Dir. Essex County, 1160 Raymond Blvd., Newark, 07102. Tel: 973-596-3971; Fax: 973-642-7412; Michael Zavada, L.C.S.W., Rgnl. Dir. Hudson County, 249 Virginia Ave., Jersey City, 07304. Tel: 201-395-5403; Fax: 201-434-4386.

Addictions Treatment Services - Cranford—505 South Ave. E., Cranford, 07016. Tel: 908-497-3923; 800-227-7705; Fax: 908-709-9612.

Addictions Treatment Services - Newark—1160 Raymond Blvd., Newark, 07102. Tel: 973-596-3858; 800-227-7705.

Addictions Treatment Services - Jersey City—249 Virginia Ave., Jersey City, 07304. Tel: 201-395-5400; 800-227-7705.

Ambulatory Detoxification Program—1160 Raymond Blvd., Newark, 07102. Tel: 973-596-3858; 800-227-7705.

Medication Monitoring - Newark—1160 Raymond Blvd., Newark, 07102. Tel: 800-227-7705.

Medication Monitoring - Jersey City—249 Virginia Ave., Jersey City, 07304. Tel: 201-395-5400; 800-227-7705.

Clinical Services Division—Rosemarie Pratt, L.C.S.W., Dir., 37 Evergreen Pl., East Orange, 07018. Tel: 973-266-7991; Fax: 973-266-7950.

Day Treatment Center—Christine Muscadin, M.A., 285 Magnolia Ave., Jersey City, 07306. Tel: 201-395-4812; Fax: 201-434-4386.

Guild Halfway House—Gail Phillips, 56 Freeman St., Newark, 07105. Tel: 973-344-0067; Fax: 973-344-6750.

Intensive Family Support Services—Iskra Gomez, 3040 Kennedy Blvd., Jersey City, 07306. Tel: 201-798-9924; Fax: 201-656-1707.

Integrated Case Management Services-Essex County—Roman Z. Mykyta, L.C.S.W., Program Mgr., 273 Oliver St., Newark, 07105. Tel: 973-522-2100; 800-607-8245.

Integrated Case Management Services-Union County—Angela Romano-Lucky, L.C.S.W., Program Mgr., 77 Central Ave., Clark, 07066. Tel: 732-669-3521.

Intensive In-Home Family Counseling—Jane Nash, 3040 Kennedy Blvd., Jersey City, 07306. Tel: 201-798-9900; Fax: 201-656-1707.

MICA (Mentally ILL Chemical Abusers)—285 Magnolia Ave., Jersey City, 07306. Tel: 201-395-5453; 800-227-7705; Fax: 201-435-9580.

Outpatient Services - Cranford—505 South Ave. E., Cranford, 07016. Tel: 908-497-3925; 800-227-7705.

Outpatient Services - Newark—1160 Raymond Blvd., Newark, 07102. 1160 Raymond Blvd., Newark, 07102. Tel: 973-596-4190; 800-227-7705.

Outpatient Services - Jersey City—249 Virginia Ave., Jersey City, 07304. Tel: 201-395-5400; 800-227-7705.

Outpatient Services - Union City—2201 Bergenline Ave., Union City, 07087. Tel: 201-558-3700; 800-227-7705.

PACT Program—Thomas Patitucci, M.S.W., Program Mgr., 269 Oliver St., Newark, 07105. Tel: 973-466-1348; 888-MCG-PACT.

Project Home (Group Home)—Gina DeMarco, Program Mgr., 249 Virginia Ave., Jersey City, 07304. Tel: 201-332-4365; 800-227-7705.

Supported Employment and Early Employment Initiative—Janice Stubbs, 103-110 Third St., Elizabeth, 07206. Tel: 908-282-4630; Fax: 908-353-5632.

Therapeutic Nursery-Cranford—Dr. Ellen Clark, 505 South Ave. E., Cranford, 07016. Tel: 908-497-3925.

Therapeutic Nursery-Newark—Dr. Ellen Clark, 1160 Raymond Blvd., Newark, 07102. Tel: 800-227-7705.

Education Division—William Shlala, M.A., M.S., Dir., 505 South Ave. E., Cranford, 07016. Tel: 908-497-9328; Fax: 908-709-9735.

Mt. Carmel Guild School—Enoch Peters, Prin., 25 N. 7th St., Belleville, 07109. Tel: 973-844-3700.

Mt. Carmel Guild Preschool—Katharine Thornton, M.P.A., Prin., 10 Commerce Ct., Newark, 07102. Tel: 973-639-6622; Fax: 973-639-6626.

St. Anthony's School—Patricia Kling, Prin., 100 Linden Ave., Irvington, 07111. Tel: 973-351-2811; Fax: 973-351-9714.

St. Leo's Center—Anne Boyd-Hinton, M.A., Prin., 100 Linden Ave., Irvington, 07111. Tel: 973-351-2800; Fax: 973-351-1591.

St. Patrick's School—Meg Herman, Acting Prin., 100 Valley Way, West Orange, 07052. Tel: 973-325-4400.

Early Childhood Programs—Elizabeth Driscoll, Program Dir., 103-110 Third St., Elizabeth, 07206. Tel: 908-282-4610; Fax: 908-282-4600.

The Little Schoolhouse Preschool/Toddler Center (Day Care)—Jodi Calice, Program Mgr., 103-110 Third St., Elizabeth, 07206. Tel: 908-282-4610; Fax: 908-282-4600.

CCS Cares Child Development Center (Day Care)—Merna LaRue, Program Mgr., 87 Park Ave., Newark, 07104. Tel: 973-483-9387; Fax: 973-268-2359.

School Social Work Program—Rosa Faria-Flosa, Dir., 1160 Raymond Blvd., Newark, 07102. Tel: 973-639-6542; Fax: 973-824-5498.

Social Services Division—Elizabeth McClendon, L.C.S.W., Dir., 37 Evergreen Pl., East Orange, 07018. Tel: 973-266-7992; Fax: 973-266-7950.

Canaan House (HIV/AIDS)—Cleveland Young, 389 Bergen Ave., Jersey City, 07304. Tel: 201-434-3919; Fax: 201-432-4223.

Edna McLaughlin Residence (Women)—Vacant, 162 Bidwell Ave., Jersey City, 07305. Tel: 201-413-1556; Fax: 201-413-0825.

Franciska Residence (HIV/AIDS)—Thomas Crestilli, 615 Grove St., Jersey City, 07310. Tel: 201-656-7201; Fax: 201-656-0412.

Hope House (Women & Children)—Nancy Melendez, 246 2nd St., Jersey City, 07302. Tel: 201-420-1070; Fax: 201-420-1825.

St. Jude's Oasis—Kathleen Eadwan, Program Mgr., 612, 614, 616, 618 & 620 Grove St., Jersey City, 07310. Tel: 201-656-5771; Fax: 201-656-0412.

St. Lucy's Single Person Shelter (Men and Women)—Brenda Pulaski, Program Mgr., 619 Grove St., Jersey City, 07310. Tel: 201-656-7201; Fax: 201-656-0412.

St. Rocco's Family Residence (Women and Children)—Donna Smith, Program Mgr., 368 S. 7th St., Newark, 07103. Tel: 973-286-4175; Fax: 973-242-4854.

Adult Services Division—Clare Elton, L.C.S.W., L.S.W., Dir., 505 South Ave. E., Cranford, 07016. Tel: 908-497-3938; Fax: 908-709-9580.

Adult Protective Services—Susan Harrigan Fowles, L.C.S.W., 505 South Ave. E., Cranford, 07016. Tel: 908-497-3900; Fax: 908-709-9583.

Care Management for Older Adults, Information and Assistance Program, Telephone Conferencing—Diane McTigue, 540 Hudson St., Hackensack, 07601. Tel: 201-440-7077.

Engel Center (Adult Day Care)—Hazel Garlic, 505 South Ave. E., Cranford, 07016. Tel: 908-497-3900; Fax: 908-709-9583.

SAFE Advocacy Center— Telephone Reassurance, Home Shopping Services, Hispanic Older Adult Information and Referral Guadalupe Salamanca, 505 South Ave. E., Cranford, 07016. Tel: 908-497-3900; Fax: 908-709-9583.

Senior Health Insurance Program (SHIP)—Vacant, 505 South Ave. E., Cranford, 07016. Tel: 908-497-3948; Fax: 908-709-9583.

Visually Impaired Seniors Program—Addy Nunes, 505 South Ave. E., Cranford, 07016. Tel: 908-497-3900; Fax: 908-709-9583.

Good Shepherd (HIV/AIDS Support Services)—Bro. Joseph McAlister, M.A., 404 University Ave., Newark, 07102. Tel: 973-799-0484; Fax: 973-799-0486.

HIV Follow-Up and Outreach Program—Perry Bonds, 505 South Ave. E., Cranford, 07016. Tel: 908-497-3900; Fax: 908-709-9580.

Queen's Angels Drop-In Center—Treva Young, 88 Irving Turner Blvd., Newark, 07102. Tel: 973-848-2381; Fax: 973-623-8790.

St. Bridget's Residence AIDS/HIV Support/Outreach Center—Bro. Joseph McAlister, M.A., 404 University Ave., Newark, 07102. Tel: 973-799-0484; Fax: 973-799-0486.

Hudson County Prison Project (Men and Women)—Vacant, 75 Greenville Ave., Jersey City, 07305. Tel: 201-369-5580; Fax: 201-946-1202.

Ryan White HIV Program—Sidsel Vengel, 540 Hudson St., Hackensack, 07601. Tel: 201-440-7083.

Union County Substance Abuse Program (Women)—Marilyn McCusker, 505 South Ave. E., Cranford, 07016. Tel: 908-497-3900; Fax: 908-709-9583.

Immigration Assistance and Refugee Resettlement Division—Clare Elton, L.C.S.W., L.S.W., Dir., 505 South Ave. E., Cranford, 07016. Tel: 908-497-3938; Fax: 908-709-9580.

Immigration Assistance Program—Meaghan Tuohey-Kay, Esq., Mng. Attorney, 976 Broad St., Newark, 07102. Tel: 973-733-3516; Fax: 973-733-9631.

Refugee Resettlement, Project Haven—Sawson Sorial, 220 Msgr. Kemezis Pl., Elizabeth, 07206. Tel: 908-351-2141; Fax: 908-351-5745.

Targeted Assistance for Cuban and Haitian Refugees—Marta Isaza, 400 38th St., Union City, 07087. Tel: 201-553-1308; Fax: 201-553-1376.

Workforce Development Division—Kristin Retlin, Dir., 321 Central Ave., Newark, 07102. Tel: 973-268-3160; Fax: 973-350-0790.

Hope VI Family Self-Sufficiency—Rita Veiga, 220 Msgr. Kemezis Pl., Elizabeth, 07206. Tel: 908-351-9301; Fax: 908-527-6209.

Sunrise House—Vacant, 185 Parkhurst Ave., Newark, 07105. Tel: 973-624-9478.

Transportation—Will Aviles, 505 South Ave. E., Cranford, 07016. Tel: 908-497-3915; Fax: 908-276-2999.

Vocational Rehabilitation and Training, Development Disabilities Program—Michael Myers, M.A., 321 Central Ave., Newark, 07102. Tel: 973-268-3163; Fax: 973-350-0790.

Workforce Development - Hudson County—Vacant, 400 38th St., Union City, 07087. Tel: 201-325-4824; Fax: 201-601-4090.

Children and Family Services Division—Lesley Moore, L.C.S.W., Dir., 3040 Kennedy Blvd., Jersey City, 07306. Tel: 201-798-9957; Fax: 201-656-1707.

Family and Adoption Services—Patricia Chiarello, M.S.W., 499 Belgrove Dr., Kearny, 07032. Tel: 201-246-7378; Fax: 201-991-7306.

Family Crisis Intervention—Lela Keels, 114 Clifton Pl., Jersey City, 07305. Tel: 201-915-1202; Fax: 201-985-2343.

Family Resource Center—Jane Nash, 3040 Kennedy Blvd., Jersey City, 07306. Tel: 201-798-9900; Fax: 201-656-1707.

In-Home Hispanic Family Services, Child Protective Services—Jane Nash, 505 South Ave. E., Cranford, 07016. Tel: 201-798-9900; Fax: 201-656-1707.

Newark Youth Leadership Project—Vanessa Hughes, 1160 Raymond Blvd., Newark, 07102. Tel: 973-596-5113; Fax: 973-424-9556.

PRIDE Mentor Program—Gilma Garcia, 3040 Kennedy Blvd., Jersey City, 07306. Tel: 201-798-9920; Fax: 201-798-2644.

Project Intercept—Taleasia McCants, 540 Hudson St., Hackensack, 07601. Tel: 201-440-7077.

Providence Malta Prep, Project PAYBACC—Taleasia McCants, 75 Greenville Ave., Jersey City, 07305. Tel: 201-369-5580; Fax: 201-451-5198.

Pastoral and Social Ministry Division and Project HEAL—Catherine L'Insalata, M.S., C.S.W., Dir., 1160 Raymond Blvd., Newark, 07102. Tel: 973-596-5119; Fax: 973-596-3836.

Project HEAL (9/11 Relief and Recovery Services)—1160 Raymond Blvd., Newark, 07102. Tel: 973-596-4066.

Apostolate with The Deaf and Ministry with the Deaf—Thomas Smith, B.A., C.S.W., Dir., 1160 Raymond Blvd., Newark, 07102. Tel: 973-596-5121; 973-824-5568 (TTY); Fax: 973-596-3836.

Apostolate and Ministry with the Developmentally Disabled—Sr. Eileen Byrne, O.P., M.A., 1160

Raymond Blvd., Newark, 07102. Tel: 973-596-5130; Fax: 973-596-3836.

Emergency Food and Nutrition Network—SHARON REILLY-TOBIN, B.A., C.S.W., Dir., 1160 Raymond Blvd., Newark, 07102. Tel: 973-596-5128; Fax: 973-824-5602.

HIV/AIDS Ministry—1160 Raymond Blvd., Newark, 07102. Tel: 973-596-5119.

New Day Community—VINCENT MCMAHON, Ed.D., Dir. Tel: 201-998-8235; 973-763-6430.

Parish Access Centers— Information and Referral Tel: 800-227-7413.

Parish Access Center - Bergen County—KRISTINE BEIRNE, 54 Hudson St., Hackensack, 07601. Tel: 201-440-7086; Fax: 201-641-2823.

Parish Access Center - Essex County—ROSAIRE DIEGUE, 160 E. Passaic St., Bloomfield, 07003. Tel: 973-743-5304; Fax: 973-743-5289.

Parish Access Center - Hudson County—CARMEL GALASSO, 3040 Kennedy Blvd., Jersey City, 07306. Tel: 201-798-9958; Fax: 201-659-6216.

Parish Access Center - Union County—GLORIA WIERZALIS, 505 South Ave. E., Cranford, 07016. Tel: 908-497-3966; Fax: 908-276-7185.

Catholic Campaign for Human Development—Sr. CATHERINE DALY, O.P., M.S., C.S.W., 1160 Raymond Blvd., Newark, 07102. Tel: 973-596-5116; Fax: 973-424-9859.

Archdiocesan Housing Office (Domus Corporation)—CHRIS GARLIN, Dir., 1160 Raymond Blvd., Newark, 07102. Tel: 973-596-5115; Fax: 973-424-9559.

Programs Managed by CCS—

Archdiocesan Housing Office (Domus Corporation)—CHRIS GARLIN, 494 Broad St., Newark, 07102. Tel: 973-297-1425; Fax: 973-424-9559.

Miscellaneous

Affirmative Action Council—CHARLES M. CARELLA, Counselor-at-Law, Archdiocesan Center, 171 Clifton Ave., Newark, 07104. Tel: 973-497-4302.

Apostleship of Prayer—Rev. Msgr. ROBERT J. FUHRMAN, Dir., 171 Clifton Ave., P.O. Box 9500, Newark, 07104-0500. Tel: 973-497-4375; Fax: 973-497-4033.

Association of St. Philomena's Helpers to the Suffering and the Poor—Rev. GEORGE KEATING, Dir., P.O. Box 393, Union, 07083-0393. Tel: 908-687-7205.

Blue Army—VACANT. Tel: 973-497-4011.

Catholic Relief Services—Rev. THOMAS P. NYDEGGER, M.Div., Dir., 171 Clifton Ave., Newark, 07104. Tel: 973-761-9575.

Archdiocesan School Advisory Board—Mr. FRANCIS X. FALCICCHIO, Pres.; Mrs. KATHLEEN MASKER, Vice Pres.; Mrs. MARY D. BAIER, Sec.; Mrs. DONNA J. BABOULIS; Ms. CATHERINE M. COWLEY; Ms. PATRICIA CAREY-FITZPATRICK; Ms. KAY GRUSENSKI; Dr. MADELYN M. HEALY; Mrs. KERRY E. LOW; Ms. JOANN MATHEWS; Mr. ROBERT RINGLEY; Ms. PAULA FRANGESE-ROSELLA; Ms. ANN MARIE SKOWRONSKI; Mr. ROBERT J. WISCHUSEN; Bro. RALPH DARMENTO, School Office Liaison. Tel: 973-497-4260.

Scholarship Fund for Inner-City Children—RONALD J. MOUNT, Pres., Bd. of Trustees; JOHN C. WALCOTT, Sec.; JOHN T. SHANAHAN, C.P.A., Treas.; KEVIN P. MORIARTY, Exec. Dir., Archdiocesan Center, 171 Clifton Ave., Newark, 07104. Tel: 973-497-4279.

The New Jersey Alliance of Catholic School Families & Supporters—Bro. RALPH DARMENTO, Coord. Tel: 973-497-4260.

Holy Name Federation—Rev. Msgr. RICHARD M. MCGUINNESS, Archdiocesan Dir. County Dirs.: Revs. JOHN LAFERRARA, Essex-West Hudson; RICHARD J. CARRINGTON, Hudson; VACANT, Bergen; Rev. JOSEPH G. SHEEHAN, Union (Retired), 1805 Penbrook Ter., Linden, 07036. Tel: 908-486-6363.

Legion of Mary—Newark Comitum: Rev. CHARLES H. MCTAGUE (Retired), 16 Church Square, Harrison, 07029. Tel: 973-484-5678. Bergen County Curia: Rev. RINO LAVARONI, Dir., 2 Fremont Ave., Park Ridge, 07656. Tel: 201-391-5315. Maria Immaculata of Hudson County: Rev. JAMES W. MCFARLAND, Dir. (Retired), 21 Skillman Ave., Jersey City, 07306. Tel: 201-963-7640. Hispanic Curia of Hudson County: Rev. FELIPE LOPEZ, Dir., 3900 New York Ave., Union City, 07087. Tel: 201-863-0233. Hispanic Curia of Essex and Union: Rev. MICHAEL A. FUINO, Dir. (Retired), 60 Home Ave., Rutherford, 07070. Tel: 973-804-2750. Korean/Our Lady Mother of God Curia: Rev. Msgr. AUGUSTIN PARK, 595 Saddle River Rd., Saddle River, 07663. Tel: 201-703-0080. Korean/Mary Most Humble Curia: Rev. DOMINIC AHN, 280 County Rd., Demarest, 07627. Tel: 201-767-1954. Our Lady, Gate of Heaven Curia (Korean): Rev. Msgr. AUGUSTIN PARK, Dir., 257 Central Ave., Orange, 07050. Tel: 973-672-6650.

Seton Hall University Archives—Rev. Msgr. FRANCIS R. SEYMOUR, Archdiocesan Archivist, Seton Hall University Archives, Walsh Library, 400 South Orange Ave., South Orange, 07079. Tel: 973-761-9126. Email: seymour@shu.edu.

New Jersey Catholic Historical Records Commission—Most Rev. DOMINIC A. MARCONI, D.D., Chm.; JOSEPH F. MAHONEY, Ph.D., Dir., Seton Hall University, Fahy Hall, 400 South Orange Ave., South Orange, 07079. Tel: 973-275-2773.

Our Lady of Fatima First Saturday Club—Revs. PAUL BOCHICCHIO, Chap., 188 MacArthur Ave., Garfield, 07026. Tel: 201-772-2295; KEVIN E. CARTER, Chap., 122 Ferry St., Jersey City, 07307. Tel: 201-659-5354.

Propagation of the Faith; Society of St. Peter the Apostle Missionary Union of Priests/Religious—Rev. Msgr. ROBERT J. FUHRMAN, Dir., Archdiocesan Center, 171 Clifton Ave., Newark, 07104. Tel: 973-497-4375.

Priests' Eucharistic League—60 Home Ave., Rutherford, 07070. Tel: 201-939-8138.

Serra Clubs—Dr. AGNES M. MORSE, L.H.S., Regl. Representative (NJ, PA & DE), 137 Bergen Ct., Ridgewood, 07450-4603. Tel: 201-444-0710; ALFRED G. MORSE, K.H.S., Deputy Regl. Representative, 137 Bergen Court, Ridgewood, 07450-4603. Tel: 201-444-0710; RICHARD R. MARGERM, Governor-District 22, 71 Dale Dr., Summit, 07901. Tel: 908-522-1496; Revs. GEORGE M. REILLY, Serra Club of Bergen County East, Chap., 105 Harrison St., New Milford, 07646. Tel: 201-261-0148; JOSEPH M. QUINLAN, Serra Club of Bergen County South, Chap. (Retired), 786 Kearny Ave., Kearny, 07032. Tel: 201-998-6056; Rev. Msgr. CARL HINRICHSEN, Serra Club of Bergen County West, Chap., 137 Bergen Ct., Ridgewood, 07450-4603. Tel: 201-444-0710; Revs. THOMAS P. NYDEGGER, M.Div., Serra Club of the Oranges, Chap., Seton Hall University, South Orange, 07079. Tel: 973-761-9126; JOSEPH DERBYSHIRE, Serra Club of Union County West, 325 2nd Ave., Garwood, 07027. Tel: 908-789-0280; DANIEL A. DANIK, Serra Club of West Essex, Chap. (Retired), 2046 Ingalls Ave., Linden, 07036. Tel: 908-486-9155.

Mothers of Priests Apostolate of Prayer—Mrs. ROSALIE D'ANDREA, Contact, Archdiocese of Newark Chapter, 14 Gerard Rd., Nutley, 07110. Tel: 973-667-5674.

Victim Assistance Coordinator—Ms. SHERI A. RICKERT, Esq. Tel: 973-497-4009. Email: rickersh@rcan.org.

CLERGY, PARISHES, MISSIONS AND PAROCHIAL SCHOOLS

CITY OF NEWARK

1—CATHEDRAL BASILICA OF THE SACRED HEART (1889), Rev. Msgr. Richard Groncki, Rector; Rev. Luis O. Gonzalez. In Res., Most Revs. Arthur J. Serratelli, S.T.D., D.D., S.S.L.; John J. Myers, J.C.D.; Revs. James M. Sheehan, J.C.L.; Brian Plate.
Res.: 89 Ridge St., 07104. Tel: 973-484-4600; Fax: 973-483-8253.

2—ST. ALOYSIUS (1877), (Hispanic), Rev. Javier Losarcos.
Res.: 66 Fleming Ave., 07105. Tel: 973-344-4736; Fax: 973-522-1169.
Catechesis/Religious Program—Students 105.

3—ST. ANN (1886), Rev. William Halbing, Admin.; Deacon Cesar A. Ortega Escobar.
Church Office: 337 South Orange Ave., 07103.
Res.: Tel: 973-642-4217; Fax: 973-623-0694.

4—ST. ANTONINUS (1875), Revs. William J. Halbing; Eustace Edomobi (Nigeria). In Res., Rev. Robert Tooman.
Res.: 337 South Orange Ave., 07103. Tel: 973-623-0258; Fax: 973-623-0694.
Catechesis/Religious Program—Students 46.

5—ST. AUGUSTINE'S (1874), (German), Rev. Neil J. Mahoney, Admin.; Deacons Vicente Rodriquez; Daniel Mendez.
Church Office: P.O. Box 1390, 07101-1390. Tel: 973-482-1817; Fax: 973-482-5475.
Convent—Sisters Missionaries of Charity, 168 Sussex Ave., 07103. Tel: 973-483-0165.
Women's Shelter Queen of Peace—170 Sussex Ave., 07103. Tel: 973-481-9056.

6—ST. BENEDICT'S (1854), Revs. Armand Mantia; Rene Lima; Sisters Philomena McCartney, O.P., Pastoral Assoc.; Ann Jerome Kociolek, O.P., Pastoral Assoc.
Res.: 65 Barbara St., 07105. Tel: 973-589-7930; Fax: 973-589-3665.
School—124 Niagara St., 07105. Tel: 973-589-7295; Fax: 973-589-2968. Mrs. Patricia Whelan, Prin. Lay Teachers 11; Students 235.
Catechesis/Religious Program—Students 244.

7—BLESSED SACRAMENT/ST. CHARLES BORROMEO (1905), (African American), Revs. Anselm I. Nwaorgu; Valentine C. Ugwuanya; Pius Ejrofor (Nigeria), Pastoral Assoc.
Res.: 15 Van Ness Pl., 07108. Tel: 973-824-6548; Fax: 973-624-6030.
School—600 Clinton Ave., 07108. Tel: 973-824-5859; Fax: 973-824-2304. O.M.M.M. 1; Lay Teachers 17; Students 232.
Catechesis/Religious Program—Students 36.
Convent—Tel: 201-824-8475.

8—ST. BRIDGET'S (1887), Merged, with St. Patrick's Pro-Cathedral. Records located at St. Patrick's, Newark. Tel: 973-623-0497.

9—ST. CASIMIR'S (1908), (Polish), Revs. Gerald Bajek; Stanley Kostrzomb.
Res.: 164 Nichols St., 07105-2596. Tel: 973-344-2743; Fax: 973-344-8182.
School— (1910), 380 E. Kinney St., 07105. Tel: 973-589-0108; Fax: 973-589-0239. Mrs. Lorraine Novak, Prin. Lay Teachers 11; Students 211.
Catechesis/Religious Program—Tel: 973-596-4500, Ext. 3674. Students 50.

10—ST. CHARLES BORROMEO'S (1910), Merged, with Blessed Sacrament. Records located at Blessed Sacrament, Newark. Tel.: 973-824-6548.

11—ST. COLUMBA'S (1869), (Hispanic), Rev. Yves-Michel Touzin, C.S. (Haiti).
Res.: 25 Thomas St., 07114. Tel: 973-622-7712; Fax: 973-621-2021.
Catechesis/Religious Program—Students 215.
Convent—Tel: 973-622-7325.

12—ST. FRANCIS XAVIER (1914), [JC] Revs. Jan Sasin; Frederick A. Pfeifer; Giovanni Rizzo.
Res.: 243 Abington Ave., 07107-2598. Tel: 973-482-8410; Fax: 973-485-7471.
School— (1924), 594 N. Seventh St., 07107. Tel: 973-482-9410; Fax: 973-482-2466. Maestre Pie Filippini (Religious Teachers Filippini) 2; Lay Teachers 12; Students 237.
Catechesis/Religious Program—Sr. Clare Ricciardelli, M.P.F., D.R.E. Students 268.
Convent—Tel: 973-484-5200.

13—HOLY TRINITY (1901), (Lithuanian), Merged, with Epiphany, Newark. Sacramental records located at Holy Trinity - Epiphany, Newark.

14—HOLY TRINITY - EPIPHANY (1992), (Portuguese), Rev. Msgr. George C. Lutz; Rev. Roman Ceglarski.
Holy Trinity Rectory: 207 Adams St., 07105. Tel: 973-491-9761; Fax: 973-344-5641.
Catechesis/Religious Program—Students 100.

15—IMMACULATE CONCEPTION (1925), (Italian), Rev. Anthony J. Lionelli. In Res., Rev. John F. O'Connor, S.T.B.
Res.: 390 Woodside Ave., 07104. Tel: 973-482-0619; Fax: 973-482-9456.

16—IMMACULATE HEART OF MARY (1926), (Spanish), Revs. Gregorio Mateu, T.O.R. (Spain), Local Supr.; Bernardo Cloquell, T.O.R. (Spain); Deacons Escolastico Mejias; Miguel Loperena.
Res.: 114 Prospect St., 07105. Tel: 973-589-8249; Fax: 973-589-1858.
Catechesis/Religious Program—Tel: 973-589-5794; Fax: 973-589-0154. Students 398.
Convent—121 Congress St., 07105. Missionary Sisters of the Blessed Sacrament and Mary Immaculate 4.

17—ST. JAMES (1854), (Brazilian—Portuguese), Revs. Clement Krug, C.SS.R., Admin.; Luis Marques, C.SS.R.; Marcos Just, C.SS.R.; Sr. Hilaria Oliveira, O.S.F., Pastoral Assoc.
Res.: 143 Madison St., 07105. Tel: 973-344-8322; Fax: 973-344-6158.
Catechesis/Religious Program—Students 53.

18—ST. JOHN'S (1826), Rev. Msgr. James J. Finnerty.
Res.: 22 Mulberry St., 07102. Tel: 973-623-0822; Fax: 973-623-6804.
Chapel—St. John's Chapel Gateway I, 07102.

19—ST. JOSEPH'S (1850), Closed., Records located at Seton Hall University Archives, South Orange. Tel.: 973-761-9476; Fax: 973-761-9550.

20—ST. LUCY'S (1891), (Italian), Rev. Msgr. Joseph J. Granato; Revs. Joseph S. Nativo; Anthony Forte.
Res.: 118 Seventh Ave., 07104. Tel: 973-482-6663; Fax: 973-482-6575.
School— (1904), 12 Amity Pl., 07104. Tel: 973-482-4756; Fax: 973-482-7992. Sisters 6; Lay Teachers 5; Students 225.
Catechesis/Religious Program—Tel: 973-482-6663; Fax: 973-482-6575. Students 200.

21—ST. MARY MAGDALENE (1893), Closed., Records located at Seton Hall University Archives, South Orange. Tel.: 973-761-9476; Fax: 973-761-9550.

22—ST. MARY'S (1842),, (Newark Abbey Church) Very Rev. Philip J. Waters, O.S.B., V.F.; Rev. Linus V. Edogwo (Nigeria); Sr. Linda Klaiss, S.S.J., Pastoral Assoc.
Res.: 528 Martin Luther King, Jr. Blvd., 07102. Tel: 973-792-5793; Fax: 973-643-6922.
School—180 William St., 07103. Tel: 973-286-3870; Fax: 973-286-3873. Sisters of St. Joseph of Chestnut Hill 3; Lay Teachers 16; Students 260.

Catechesis / Religious Program—Tel: 973-792-5790. Students 260.
Convent—Tel: 973-824-8475.

23—ST. MICHAEL'S (1878), Revs. Antonio da Silva, S.D.V.; James Butts, S.D.V.; Lorenzo Gomez, S.D.V.; Deacons Alberto Gomez; Daniel Ravelo; Restituto Quintana; Juan Suarez; Cecilio S. Polanco; Miguel Figueroa; Jose A. Negron.
Res.: 25 Crittenden St., 07104. Tel: 973-484-7100; Fax: 973-482-7209.
School— (1881), 27 Crittenden St., 07104. Tel: 973-482-7400; Fax: 973-482-1833. Sisters of St. Martha 3; Sisters of Charity of Ottawa 2; Lay Teachers 24; Students 629.
School—Perpetual Help Day Nursery, 170 Broad St., 07104. Tel: 973-484-3535; Fax: 973-484-2526. Vocationist Sisters 7; Lay Teachers 13; Children 140.
Catechesis / Religious Program—Tel: 973-482-1109. Students 455.
Convent—Tel: 973-484-5261.

24—OUR LADY OF FATIMA (1956), (Portuguese), Revs. Mario Nunes, Admin.; Anthony Bico; Antonio F. da Silva.
Res.: 82 Congress St., 07105. Tel: 973-589-8433; Fax: 973-589-2611.
School—Day Nursery, 79 Jefferson St., 07105. Tel: 973-589-1639.
Catechesis / Religious Program—Students 4.

25—OUR LADY OF GOOD COUNSEL (1902), Rev. Msgr. Joseph P. Plunkett; Rev. Marcos Sequeira (Costa Rica); Deacons Ramon Villeda; Oscar Rivera; Jose Rodriguez.
Res.: 654 Summer Ave., 07104. Tel: 973-482-1274; Fax: 973-482-8257.
School— (1913), 239 Woodside Ave., 07104. Tel: 973-482-1241. Sisters of Charity 1; Lay Teachers 8; Students 181.
High School— (1922),Tel: 973-482-1209; Fax: 973-482-4321. Dominican 1; Lay Teachers 15; Students 210.
Catechesis / Religious Program—Students 243.

26—OUR LADY OF MT. CARMEL (1889), (Italian), Rev. Joseph Ambrosio. In Res., Revs. Joseph Kikeram; Eugene Bernas (Philippines).
Res.: 259 Oliver St., 07105. Tel: 973-589-2090; Fax: 973-589-2662.

27—OUR LADY OF THE ROSARY (1918), (Italian), Closed., For inquiries for parish records contact Our Lady of Mt. Carmel, Newark. Tel: 973-589-2090

28—ST. PATRICK'S PRO-CATHEDRAL (1848), Rev. Msgr. Neil J. Mahoney; Rev. Joseph Kabali. In Res., Rev. Joseph Khai Vu.
Res.: 91 Washington St., 07102. Tel: 973-623-0497; Fax: 973-623-2030.

29—ST. PETER'S (1864), Closed., For inquiries for parish records contact Seton Hall University Archives, South Orange. Tel: 973-761-9476; Fax 973-761-9550.

30—ST. PHILIP NERI (1887), Closed., For inquiries for parish records contact Seton Hall University Archives, South Orange. Tel: 973-761-9476; 973-761-9550.

31—QUEEN OF ANGELS (1930), (African American), Rev. James J. McConnell, S.M.A.; Deacons Robert Botts, (Retired); Edward Botts, (Retired); Willie E. Moore Jr.; Tracey G. Battles, Pastoral Assoc.
Res.: 44 Irvine Turner Blvd., 07103. Tel: 973-642-1610; Fax: 973-642-0755.
School—40 Irvine Turner Blvd., 07103. Tel: 973-642-1531; Fax: 973-622-0472. Mrs. Everlyn V. Hay, Prin.; Mrs. Sharon Massey, Vice Prin. Lay Teachers 11; Students 266.
Catechesis / Religious Program—Tel: 973-372-4992; Fax: 973-642-1610. Students 16.

32—ST. ROCCO'S (1899),, (National Historic Landmark) Rev. Josephat Kato Kalema, O.C.S.O. (Uganda), Admin.
Res.: 208 Hunterdon St., 07103. Tel: 973-824-1652; Fax: 973-824-4944.

33—ST. ROSE OF LIMA (1888), Rev. Msgr. William J. Linder; Deacon Robert Cormier.
Res.: 11 Gray St., 07107. Tel: 973-482-0682; Fax: 973-482-2137.
School— (1892), 540 Orange St., 07107. Tel: 973-481-5582; Fax: 973-481-3398. Arthur L. Wilson, Prin. Sisters 2; Lay Teachers 15; Students 311.
Catechesis / Religious Program—Students 311.
Convent—Tel: 973-481-6566.

34—SACRED HEART (Vailsburg) (1892), Revs. Andrew Prachar, Admin.; John B. Martin; Deacon Cesar Torres.
Res.: 481 Sanford Ave., 07106. Tel: 973-373-9790; Fax: 973-374-4047.
School—(Grades PreK-8), 24 Hazelwood Ave., 07106. Tel: 973-372-4441; Fax: 973-372-4157. Bro. Patrick Byrne, O.A.R., Prin. Religious 12; Lay Teachers 42; Students 650.
Catechesis / Religious Program—Students 30.
Convent—Tel: 973-374-2730; Fax: 973-374-4656.

35—ST. STANISLAUS (1889), (Polish), Rev. Bogumil Chrusciel.
Res.: 146 Irvine Turner Blvd., 07103. Tel: 973-642-7961; Fax: 973-642-2295.

36—ST. STEPHEN'S (1902), Closed., For inquiries for parish records contact Seton Hall University Archives, South Orange. Tel: 973-761-9476; Fax: 973-761-9550.

37—ST. THOMAS AQUINAS (1957), (Hispanic), Revs. Raul E.L. Comesanas; Miguel A. Loredo, O.F.M., Weekend Asst.; Deacons Jose A. Rodriguez; Mario Eschavarria.
Res.: 40 Ludlow St., 07114. Tel: 973-242-6703; Fax: 973-242-7143.
Catechesis / Religious Program—Students 65.

OUTSIDE THE CITY OF NEWARK

ALLENDALE, BERGEN CO., GUARDIAN ANGEL (1954), Very Rev. Charles Pinyan.
Res.: 320 Franklin Turnpike, 07401. Tel: 201-327-4359; Fax: 201-327-6478.
School—St. Thomas More Interparochial School, Tel: 201-447-3088. See Nativity Parish, Midland Park for details.
Catechesis / Religious Program—Tel: 201-327-0352. Students 398.

BAYONNE, HUDSON CO.

1—ST. ANDREW'S (1914), Rev. John R. Doherty; Rev. Msgr. Edward F. Wojtycha, Pastor Emeritus (Retired); Rev. Gary Ward; Deacon Raymond Sanderson. In Res., Revs. Thomas M. Foye (Retired); Michael J. O'Grady (Retired).
Res.: 125 Broadway, 07002. Tel: 201-437-0833; Fax: 201-858-3477.
School—124 Broadway, 07002. Tel: 973-437-0139. Sisters of St. Joseph 1; Lay Teachers 9; Students 200.
Catechesis / Religious Program—Tel: 201-437-9062. Students 400.

2—ST. HENRY'S (1889), Rev. Msgr. Edward J. Hajduk, S.T.L., M.S.S.; Rev. Paul A. Cannariato; Rev. Msgr. Peter Cheplic.
Res.: 82 W. 29th St., 07002. Tel: 201-436-0857; Fax: 201-823-4611.
Catechesis / Religious Program—Avenue C & 28 St., 07002. Tel: 201-339-0319. Miss Marie Pope. Students 440.

3—ST. JOSEPH'S (1888), (Slovak), Rev. Msgr. Edward M. Matash.
Res. 317 Ave. E, 07002. Tel: 201-339-1122; Fax: 201-339-1009.
Catechesis / Religious Program—Students 50.

4—ST MARY STAR OF THE SEA (1861), Revs. Lawrence J. Miller; Thomas P. Conheeney; Tobias Rodriguez; Sr. Jane Veronica Walsh, S.S.J., Pastoral Assoc.
Res.: 326 Avenue C, 07002. Tel: 201-437-4090; Fax: 201-437-0388.
School— (1879), 19 W. 13th St., 07002. Tel: 201-437-2888; Fax: 201-437-6084. Lay Teachers 17; Students 248.
Catechesis / Religious Program—Tel: 201-437-0010. Students 170.

5—ST. MICHAEL'S (1907), (Lithuanian), Revs. John J. Gibbons, M.Div., Pastor Emeritus (Retired); Gerard M. Lombardo. In Res., Revs. J. M. Patricius, Hospital Chap.; Thomas C. Roberts, Chap.
Res.: 15 E. 23rd St., 07002-3737. Tel: 201-436-1412; Fax: 201-436-5979.
Catechesis / Religious Program—Students 50.

6—MT. CARMEL (1898), (Polish), Very Rev. Anthony J. Kulig, V.F.; Rev. Msgr. Joseph A. Marjanczyk, Pastor Emeritus (Retired); Revs. Kazimierz Kuczynski; Robert A. Pachana; Andrew Puchalski (Poland).
Res.: 39 E. 22nd St., 07002. Tel: 201-339-2070; Fax: 201-339-3676.
School— (1902), 19 E. 22nd St., 07002. Tel: 201-339-1839; Fax: 201-339-2238. Lay Teachers 13; Students 215.
Catechesis / Religious Program—Nichalas Winkel, D.R.E. Students 130.

7—OUR LADY OF THE ASSUMPTION (1902), (Italian), Revs. Joseph F. Barbone; Francisco Javier Cabezas; Deacon William Giordano.
Res.: 531 Ave. C, 07002. Tel: 201-436-8160; Fax: 201-436-4135.
Church: 91 W. 23rd St., 07002. Fax: 201-436-3145.
Catechesis / Religious Program—Tel: 201-437-1867; Fax: 201-436-4897. Nordie M. Pacheco, M.A. Students 350.

8—ST. VINCENT DE PAUL (1894), Revs. Peter P. Galdon; Camilo Lopez. In Res., Rev. Carl Arico; Deacon Ralph Savo, Business Mgr.
Res.: 979 Ave. C, 07002. Tel 201-436-2222; Fax: 201-437-5235.
School— (1920), 80 W. 47th St., 07002. Tel: 201-339-4438; Fax: 201-339-3058. Lay Teachers 14; Students 226.
Catechesis / Religious Program—Tel: 201-823-0184. Kathleen DiMartino, D.R.E. Students 325.

BELLEVILLE, ESSEX CO.

1—ST. ANTHONY'S (1901), (Italian), Revs. Joseph A. Ferraro; Joseph J. Cestaro, Pastor Emeritus (Retired); Edito Gamallo; Paul Prevosto; Deacons Louis Acocella, Ed.D.; Richard B. Searls.
Res.: 750 N. Seventh St., 07107. Tel: 973-481-1991; Fax: 973-481-1993.
Church: 63 Franklin Ave., 07109.
Catechesis / Religious Program—25 N. 7th St., 07109. Tel: 973-751-0549. Students 179.

2—ST. PETER'S (1837), (Spanish), [CEM] Revs. Joseph D. Girone; Patrick R. Flannery; Mark A. O'Connell; Deacons William Valladares; Julio Roig.
Res.: 155 William St., 07109. Tel: 973-751-2002; Fax: 973-751-6201.
School— (1854), 152 William St., 07109. Tel: 973-759-3143; Fax: 973-759-4160. Sisters of Charity 1; Lay Teachers 19; Students 310.
Catechesis / Religious Program—Tel: 973-751-4290. Students 300.
Convent—Tel: 973-759-2432.

BERGENFIELD, BERGEN CO., ST. JOHN THE EVANGELIST (1905), Rev. Msgrs. Richard J. Arnhols; Joseph J. Donovan, Pastor Emeritus, (Retired); Revs. Ernesto Tibay; Raymond R. Filipski; Jose E. Marquez; Jacek Marchewka; Deacon Patrick Miney.
Res.: 29 N. Washington Ave., 07621. Tel: 201-384-0101; Fax: 201-384-2055.
School— (1921), 10 Bradley Ave., 07621. Tel: 201-384-3627; Fax: 201-384-0293. Sisters 1; Lay Teachers 20; Students 344.
Catechesis / Religious Program—15 N. Washington Ave., 07621. Tel: 201-384-3601; Fax: 201-384-9306. Students 998.

BERKELEY HEIGHTS, UNION CO., CHURCH OF THE LITTLE FLOWER (1955), Very Rev. Stephen S. Feehan, V.F.; Revs. Joseph P. Fagan, Pastor Emeritus (Retired); Brian F. McFadden; Edmund G. Bernauer (Retired). In Res., Rev. Charles Anemelu.
Res.: 110 Roosevelt Ave., 07922. Fax: 908-464-6342.
Church: 310 Plainfield Ave., 07922. Tel: 908-464-1585.
Catechesis / Religious Program—Tel: 908-464-7444. Students 725.

BLOOMFIELD, ESSEX CO.

1—CHURCH OF ST. THOMAS THE APOSTLE (1939), Rev. Msgrs. William C. Hatcher; Vincent P. Coburn, Pastor Emeritus (Retired); Revs. Peter K. Funesti; Jose Amante Abalon; Mr. Robert Miller, Pastoral Assoc.; Jenny Juntwait, Youth Minister. In Res., Rev. John Connolly, S.D.B.
Res.: 60 Byrd Ave., 07003. Tel: 973-338-9190; Fax: 973-338-4224.
School— (1939),(Grades PreK-8), 50 Byrd Ave., 07003. Tel: 973-338-8505; Fax: 973-338-9565. Sisters 3; Lay Teachers 28; Students 415.
Catechesis / Religious Program—Tel: 973-338-7400. Students 782.
Convent—Tel: 973-338-9118; Fax: 973-338-6495.

2—SACRED HEART (1878), [CEM] Revs. Richard P. Kwiatkowski; Daniel A. Danik, Pastor Emeritus (Retired); Paul Aleria; Jaroslaw Zaniewski, (Adjunct).
Res.: 76 Broad St., 07003. Tel: 973-748-1800; Fax: 973-748-2028.
School— (1879), 683 Bloomfield Ave., 07003. Tel: 973-743-4015; Fax: 973-743-0723. Sisters 2; Lay Teachers 17; Students 375.
Convent—Tel: 973-743-0838; Fax: 973-743-4167.
Catechesis / Religious Program—Tel: 973-743-4061. Students 212.

3—ST. VALENTINE (1899), (Polish), Rev. Msgr. Robert M. Chabak, V.F.; Rev. Juancho G. DeLeon. In Res., Revs. Alan F. Guglielmo; John J. Donohue.
Res.: 125 N. Spring St., 07003. Tel: 973-743-0220; Fax: 973-743-2041.
Catechesis / Religious Program—Tel: 973-743-6122. Mrs. Patricia Hope, D.R.E. Students 215.

BOGOTA, BERGEN CO., ST. JOSEPH'S (1929), Revs. Terrence Cyr, O.Carm.; Richard Supple, O.Carm.; Sr. Catherine McDermott, C.N.D., Pastoral Assoc.; Deacons Walter Lynn; Michael Fitzgerald. In Res., Revs. Gregory Battafarano, O.Carm.; Clement Laurendeau, O.Carm.
Res.: 115 E. Fort Lee Rd., 07603. Tel: 201-342-6300; Fax: 201-883-9392.
School— (1925), 131 E. Fort Lee Rd., 07603. Tel: 201-487-8641; Fax: 201-487-7405. Sr. Regina Miriam, F.S.P., Prin. Franciscan Sisters of Peace 2; Lay Teachers 9; Students 241.
Catechesis / Religious Program—Tel: 201-343-4316. Students 445.
Convent—Tel: 201-342-4684.

CALDWELL, ESSEX CO., ST. ALOYSIUS (1892), Revs. John J. Laferrera; Nigel Mohammed; Joseph A. Scarangella; Deacon William J. McDermott. In Res., Rev. Msgr. Benjamin A. Piazza (Retired).
Res.: 219 Bloomfield Ave., 07006. Tel: 973-226-0221; Fax: 973-226-2204.
School— (1991), 235 Bloomfield Ave., 07006. Tel: 973-226-3386; Fax: 973-226-6548. (Co-Sponsored) Trinity Academy Sisters 3; Lay Teachers 30; PreK-8 551.
Catechesis / Religious Program—Tel: 973-226-0209;

Fax: 973-226-0923. Students 769.
CEDAR GROVE, ESSEX CO., ST. CATHERINE OF SIENA (1949), Rev. Msgr. Charles W. Gusmer, V.E., S.T.D.; Revs. James Redstone; Robert K. Suszko.
Res.: 339 Pompton Ave., 07009. Tel: 973-239-7960; Fax: 973-239-1008.
School— (1958), 39 E. Bradford Ave., 07009. Tel: 973-239-6968. Sisters of St. Dominic 1; Lay Teachers 20; Students 294.
Catechesis/Religious Program—Tel: 973-239-3332. Students 400.
Convent—Tel: 973-239-3362.
CLARK, UNION CO., ST. AGNES (1961), Rev. Msgr. James A. Choma; Rev. John Chadwick.
Res.: 332 Madison Hill Rd., 07066. Tel: 732-388-7852; Fax: 732-388-7064.
School— (1963), 342 Madison Hill Rd., 07066. Tel: 732-381-0850; Fax: 732-381-1745. Lay Teachers 11; Students 198.
Catechesis/Religious Program—Tel: 732-388-2560. Students 530.
CLIFFSIDE PARK, BERGEN CO., EPIPHANY (1916), Revs. Donald J. Di Pasquale; Carlos Viego; Jungsoo Kim.
Res.: 247 Knox Ave., 07010. Tel: 201-943-7320; Fax: 201-943-1779.
School— (1930), 263 Lafayette Ave., 07010. Tel: 201-945-1194; Fax: 201-224-8721. Lay Teachers 9; Students 192; Religious 2.
Catechesis/Religious Program—Tel: 201-945-1164; Fax: 201-943-2255. Students 255.
Convent—228 Knox Ave., 07010. Tel: 201-943-2660.
CLOSTER, BERGEN CO., ST. MARY (1912), Rev. James T. McKenna.
Res.: 20 Legion Pl., 07624. Tel: 201-768-7565; Fax: 201-784-5814.
School—300 High St., 07624. Tel: 201-768-2627; Fax: 201-768-6660. Sisters 5; Lay Teachers 13; Students 130.
Catechesis/Religious Program—Tel: 201-767-8247. Students 121.
CRANFORD, UNION CO., ST. MICHAEL'S (1872), Revs. John P. McGovern; Krzysztof Maslowski; Edgardo P. Jocson; Sr. Mary Small, S.S.J., Pastoral Assoc.; Deacon Daniel Wilverding; Leonard A. Minichino, Business Mgr.
Res.: 40 Alden St., 07016. Tel: 908-276-0360; Fax: 908-272-0273.
School— (1929), Alden and Miln Sts., 07016. Tel: 908-276-9425; Fax: 908-276-4391. Lay Teachers 42; Students 400.
Catechesis/Religious Program—100 Alden St., 07016. Tel: 908-276-2050. Lynda Furey, D.R.E. Students 1,352.
CRESSKILL, BERGEN CO., ST. THERESE OF LISIEUX (1931), Revs. Joseph O'Brien, O.Carm.; Samuel Citero, O.Carm.; Sr. Marian Bandille, M.F.I.C., Pastoral Assoc. In Res., Rev. Paul T. Hoban, O.Carm.
Res.: 120 Monroe Ave., 07626. Tel: 201-567-2528; Fax: 201-567-6759.
School—220 Jefferson Ave., 07626. Tel: 201-568-4296; Fax: 201-568-3179. Lay Teachers 18; Students 205.
Catechesis/Religious Program—200 Jefferson Ave., 07627. Tel: 201-567-4781; Fax: 201-541-1269. Students 641.
DEMAREST, BERGEN CO.
1—ST. JOSEPH (1998), (Korean), Revs. Dominic G. An (Korea, South); Yong-Jae Kim, Admin.
Res.: 274 County Rd., 07627. Tel: 201-767-1954; Fax: 201-767-1854.
Catechesis/Religious Program—279 County Rd., 07627. Fax: 201-767-8874. Students 368.
2—ST. JOSEPH'S (1931), Rev. William O'Malley, O.Carm.; Deacon James Puliatte.
Res.: 280 County Rd., 07627. Tel: 201-768-2371; Fax: 201-768-2466.
School—St. Joseph, Sacred Heart Interparochial School, 573 Piermont Rd., 07627. Tel: 201-768-5534; Fax: 201-768-2620. Lay Teachers 17; Students 125.
Catechesis/Religious Program—Tel: 201-768-6886; Fax: 201-768-4128. Students 250.
DUMONT, BERGEN CO., ST. MARY'S (1914), Revs. Robert G. Laferrera; Edward C. Thompson; John M. McCrone; Sr. Elizabeth Mullen, C.S.J., Pastoral Assoc. In Res., Revs. Mathew Chandrankunnel (India); Theodore A. Szelest (Retired).
Res.: 280 Washington Ave., 07628. Tel: 201-384-0557; Fax: 201-384-4986.
School— (1951), 21-31 New Milford Ave., 07628. Tel: 201-384-0512; Fax: 201-384-0819. Sisters 2; Lay Teachers 15; Students 320.
Catechesis/Religious Program—Tel: 201-384-3062. Students 795.
EAST NEWARK, HUDSON CO., ST. ANTHONY'S (1901), (Italian), Rev. Anthony F. Granato. In Res., Rev. Francis T. Maione.
Res.: 409 N. Second St., 07029. Tel: 973-483-4680; Fax: 973-483-2396.
Catechesis/Religious Program—Students 130.

EAST ORANGE, ESSEX CO.
1—HOLY NAME OF JESUS (1910), Revs. William G. Cook; Jerome S. Arthasseril (India); Deacons Leo Woodruff; Thomas J. Bulgia.
Res.: 184 Midland Ave., 07017. Fax: 973-675-5901.
Parish Center—200 Midland Ave., P.O. Box 5244, 07017-1855. Tel: 973-675-4444; Fax: 973-674-1767.
2—HOLY SPIRIT-OUR LADY HELP OF CHRISTIANS (1882), (African American—Haitian), Very Rev. Michael M. Walters, V.F., J.C.L.; Rev. Beaubrun Ardouin; Deacon Sidney Huff. In Res., Rev. George Kelly, C.SS.R.
Res.: 17 N. Clinton St., 07017. Tel: 973-673-1077; Fax: 973-676-6494.
School— (1883), 23 N. Clinton St., 07017. Tel: 973-677-1546; Fax: 973-677-3939. Lay Teachers 17; Students 529.
Catechesis/Religious Program—Students 100.
3—ST. JOSEPH'S (1916), Rev. William A. Mahon; Deacons Joseph Fiore, (Retired); Alonzo C. Jackson.
Res.: 110 Telford St., 07018. Tel: 973-678-4030; Fax: 973-677-7875.
School—115 Telford St., 07018. Tel: 973-674-2326; Fax: 973-674-7718. Religious Teachers Filippini 2; Lay Teachers 17; Students 428.
Catechesis/Religious Program—Students 428.
Convent—Tel: 201-677-0812.
4—OUR LADY OF ALL SOULS (1914), Closed., For inquiries for parish records contact Seton Hall University Archives, South Orange. Tel: 973-761-9476; Fax: 973-761-9550
5—OUR LADY OF THE MOST BLESSED SACRAMENT (1916), Closed., For inquiries for parish records contact Seton Hall University Archives, South Orange. Tel: 973-761-9476; Fax: 973-761-9550
EAST RUTHERFORD, BERGEN CO., ST. JOSEPH'S (1872), [CEM] Revs. Francis Gunn, O.F.M.; Edward J. Donohue, O.F.M.; Brian Linehan, O.F.M.; Sr. Marigene Kennedy, O.S.F., Pastoral Min. Tel: 201-507-8842; Edward J. Chaudron, Business Mgr. In Res., Rev. Daniel Lanahan, O.F.M.
Res.: 120 Hoboken Rd., 07073. Tel: 201-939-0457; Fax: 201-939-4196.
School— (1879), 20 Hackensack St., 07073. Tel: 201-939-3193; Fax: 201-939-1913. Mrs. Frances Alberta, Prin. Lay Teachers 13; Students 194.
Catechesis/Religious Program—Tel: 201-939-3441. Ms. Verna Paiotti, D.R.E. Students 424.
Convent—Tel: 201-460-4961.
EDGEWATER, BERGEN CO., HOLY ROSARY (1906), Rev. George Ruane; Deacons Robert E. Thomson; Michael A. Lydon. In Res., Rev. William M. Giblin (Retired).
Res.: 365 Undercliff Ave., 07020. Tel: 201-945-6329 (Parish Center); Fax: 201-945-6599.
Catechesis/Religious Program—Students 88.
ELIZABETH, UNION CO.
1—ST. ADALBERT'S (1905), (Polish), [CEM] Rev. Msgr. Ronald J. Marczewski; Rev. Krzysztof Szczotka, S.D.S. (Poland); Deacons Joseph J. Lubas; Philip Rejrat.
Res.: 250 E. Jersey St., 07206. Tel: 908-352-2791; Fax: 908-354-2828.
Catechesis/Religious Program—Students 60.
2—ST. ANTHONY'S (1895), (Italian), Revs. Donald Delaney, S.D.B.; Vincent Paczkowski, S.D.B.; Gennaro J. Sesto, S.D.B.; Joseph Santa-Bibiana, S.D.B.; Bro. David Iovacchini, S.D.B.
Res.: 853 Third Ave., 07202. Tel: 908-351-3300; Fax: 908-351-3609.
School—227 Centre St., 07202. Tel: 908-352-7419. Sisters of Charity of Convent Station 2; Lay Teachers 13; Students 240.
Catechesis/Religious Program—Students 240.
Convent—Tel: 908-354-0825.
3—BLESSED SACRAMENT (1922), Revs. Fernando Guillen; Leonardo Jaramillo; Deacons Jose R. Fernandez; Eliut Casanova; Cristina Pardo, Pastoral Assoc. In Res., Rev. Thomas McLaughlin.
Res.: 1096 North Ave., 07201. Tel: 908-352-0338; Fax: 908-352-4553.
School— (1926), 1086 North Ave., 07201. Tel: 908-352-8629; Fax: 908-352-7934. Lay Teachers 9; Students 270.
Catechesis/Religious Program—Students 211.
4—ST. GENEVIEVE'S (1920), Rev. Msgr. Hugh A. O'Donnell; Revs. Roy James DeLeo; Arnel Tadeo (Philippines).
Res.: 200 Monmouth Rd., 07208. Tel: 908-351-4444; Fax: 908-351-5454.
School— (1929), 209 Princeton Rd., 07208. Tel: 908-355-3355; Fax: 908-355-1460. Lay Teachers 24; Students 395.
Catechesis/Religious Program—Tel: 908-355-1584. Students 254.
Convent—Tel: 908-353-0736.
5—ST. HEDWIG'S (1925), (Polish), Revs. Henry P. Marciniak (Retired); Thomas J. Lewczak; Wojciech Kowalski, S.D.S.; Andrew Zmarlicki.
Res.: 716 Clarkson Ave., 07202. Tel: 908-352-1448; Fax: 908-352-8389.
Religious Education Center—717 Polonia Ave., 07202. Tel: 908-355-8409.

Catechesis/Religious Program—Students 278.
6—HOLY ROSARY (1886), Merged, Records at Our Lady of Most Holy Rosary/St. Michael, Elizabeth. Tel: 908-354-2454; Fax: 908-354-3207.
7—IMMACULATE CONCEPTION (1907), Revs. Jorge Chacon; Aurelio Yanez (Colombia).
Pastoral Center: 424 Westminister Ave., 07208. Tel: 908-352-6662.
Res.: 425 Union Ave., 07208. Tel: 908-352-6662; Fax: 908-352-8484.
Catechesis/Religious Program—417 Union Ave., 07208. Tel: 908-351-4242. Students 292.
8—IMMACULATE HEART OF MARY (1947), (Hispanic), Revs. Fabio Brenes-Chavez; Wojciech Jaskowiak.
Res.: 215 Court St., 07206. Tel: 908-354-0023; Fax: 908-355-0926.
Catechesis/Religious Program—Tel: 908-354-8388; Fax: 908-354-8288. Students 95.
Convent—Tel: 908-354-8388.
9—ST. JOSEPH'S (1911), (Slovak), Closed., Records at Holy Family, Linden. Tel: 908-862-1060.
10—ST. MARY OF THE ASSUMPTION (1844), [CEM] Rev. Msgr. Robert J. Harrington, M.Div.; Revs. Jose Saltarin; Pawel Molewski; Deacon Luis Carlos Lorza; Sisters Ruth Morgan, R.S.M., Pastoral Assoc.; Elaine Maguire, F.S.P., Pastoral Assoc.; Maria Castillo-Lorza, Pastoral Assoc. In Res., Rev. Edward Haber.
Res.: 155 Washington Ave., 07202. Tel: 908-352-5154; Fax: 908-352-0350.
School— (1868), 237 S. Broad St., 07202. Tel: 908-355-0717. Lay Teachers 10; Students 221.
High School—Tel: 908-352-4350; Fax: 908-352-2359. Sisters 2; Lay Teachers 20; Students 320.
School—Child Care Center, Tel: 908-355-8723. Students 68.
Catechesis/Religious Program—Tel: 908-352-0926. Students 526.
Convent—Tel: 908-352-1455.
11—OUR LADY OF FATIMA (1973), (Portuguese), Rev. Msgr. John S. Antao; Rev. Jose Manuel Fernandes (Portugal).
Res.: 403 Spring St., 07201. Tel: 908-355-3810; Fax: 908-355-4791.
Catechesis/Religious Program—Tel: 908-352-7185. Students 698.
12—OUR LADY OF MOST HOLY ROSARY/ST. MICHAEL (1886/1852), [JC] Very Rev. John E. Wassell, V.F.; Revs. Romane St. Vil, M.M.; Leonardo Caceres. In Res., Rev. William C. Reed.
Res.: 52 Smith St., 07201. Tel: 908-354-2454; Fax: 908-354-3207.
Catechesis/Religious Program—Students 150.
13—ST. PATRICK'S (1858), (Hispanic), [CEM] Rev. Fabio Brenes-Chavez; Deacon Nestor Charriez.
Res.: 215 Court St., 07206. Tel: 908-354-0023; Fax: 908-355-0926.
School— (1863), 227 Court St., 07206. Tel: 908-351-2188; Fax: 908-351-6086. See Elizabethport Catholic School.
High School— (1863), 221 Court St., 07206. Tel: 908-353-5220; Fax: 908-629-1123. Brothers 1; Sisters 1; Lay Teachers 15; Students 233.
Catechesis/Religious Program—Students 140.
14—SS. PETER AND PAUL'S (1895), (Lithuanian), Revs. Alfred Zemeikis; Peter M. Aquino.
Res.: 211 Ripley Pl., 07206. Tel: 908-352-2271; Fax: 908-353-2851.
15—SACRED HEART (1871), Merged, Records at Our Lady of Fatima Parish, Elizabeth. Tel: 908-355-3810.
ELMWOOD PARK, BERGEN CO., ST. LEO'S (1931), Revs. Kevin J. Mullen, O.F.M.; Richard P. Biasiatto, O.F.M.; Theodore F. Lehr, O.F.M.; Bro. Ray Selker, O.F.M.
Res.: 324 Market St., 07407. Tel: 201-796-3521; Fax: 201-703-8408.
School— (1912), 300 Market St., 07407. Tel: 201-796-5156. Franciscan Sisters of Peace 3; Lay Teachers 15; Students 417.
Catechesis/Religious Program—Students 200.
Convent—Tel: 201-797-6993.
EMERSON, BERGEN CO., CHURCH OF THE ASSUMPTION (1947), Revs. Eugene J. Hazewski; Michael Hansen; James T. Brown; Deacons John E. Hogan; James Tobin.
Res.: 29 Jefferson Ave., 07630. Tel: 201-262-1122; Fax: 201-262-7855.
School—35 Jefferson Ave., 07630. Tel: 201-262-0300; Fax: 201-262-5910. Sisters 3; Lay Teachers 19; Students 260.
Catechesis/Religious Program—Tel: 201-986-0970. Students 260.
ENGLEWOOD, BERGEN CO., ST. CECILIA'S (1866), [JC] Revs. Robert A. Wolfe, O.Carm. (Retired); Robert Boley, O.Carm.; Hilary Milton, O.Carm.; Bro. David McGinnis, O.Carm., Pastoral Assoc. In Res., Revs. Noel Ahrens, O.Carm.; Ellis Reinert, O.Carm.; Anthony Palo, O.Carm.; Carl Pfister, O.Carm.
Res.: 55 Demarest Ave., 07631. Tel: 201-568-0364; Fax: 201-568-0654.

School—St. Cecilia Interparochial School (1874), 85 W. Demarest Ave., 07631. Tel: 201-568-2615; Fax: 201-768-7734. Lay Teachers 11; Students 163.
Catechesis/Religious Program—Tel: 201-568-7882. Students 170.

FAIR LAWN, BERGEN CO., ST. ANNE'S (1909), Revs. Ronald J. Pecci, O.F.M.; Jeremiah V. McGinley, O.F.M.; Evan Banks, O.F.M.; Bernadine C. Kessing, O.F.M.; Deacon Richard McGarry. In Res., Rev. Anthony R. Fedell, O.F.M.
Res.: 15-05 Saint Anne St., 07410. Tel: 201-791-1616; Fax: 201-791-1871.
School— (1950), 1-30 Summit Ave., 07410. Tel: 201-796-3353; Fax: 201-796-9058. Lay Teachers 17; Students 300.
Catechesis/Religious Program—Tel: 201-791-2331. Students 799.

FAIRFIELD, ESSEX CO., ST. THOMAS MORE (1962), Revs. John D. Gabriel; Eugene Gniewyk; Sisters Agnes Bernard, O.P., Pastoral Assoc.; Catherine Reilly, O.P., Pastoral Assoc.; Deacons P. Aidan King; Dominick Messina; Frank Campione.
Res.: 210 Horseneck Rd., 07004. Tel: 973-227-0055; Fax: 973-227-2495.
Catechesis/Religious Program—(Grades K-8), 12 Hollywood Ave., 07004. Tel: 973-227-3607; Fax: 973-808-9032. Cabrina Kinslow, D.R.E. Students 490.

FAIRVIEW, BERGEN CO.

1—ST. JOHN THE BAPTIST (1873), Revs. Michael E. Gubernat; James J. Carroll; Giordano Belanich; Deacon Anton Tarabokija.
Res.: 239 Anderson Ave., 07022. Tel: 201-945-4865; Fax: 201-945-8171.
Catechesis/Religious Program—Students 170.

2—OUR LADY OF GRACE (1913), (Italian), Revs. Peter T. Sticco, S.A.C.; Pompeo Luciani, S.A.C.
Res.: 395 Delano Pl., 07022. Tel: 201-943-0904; Fax: 201-313-5616. Rev. Francis M. Gaetano, S.A.C.
School—400 Kamena St., 07022. Tel: 201-945-8300; Fax: 201-945-4580. Lay Teachers 15; Students 342.
Catechesis/Religious Program—Tel: 201-945-1201. Students 225.

FORT LEE, BERGEN CO.

1—HOLY TRINITY (1906), Revs. Steven Conner; Paul Lee (Korea, South); Deacon Leandro C. Centenera; Paul Reiser, Music Minister; Joanna Kowalska, Music Minister.
Res.: 2367 Lemoine Ave., 07024-6269. Tel: 201-947-1216; Fax: 201-947-1217.
School—Christ the Teacher Interparochial School, Tel: 201-944-0421. Co-Sponsored. (See Madonna Parish, Fort Lee)
Catechesis/Religious Program—Tel: 201-947-1216. Sr. Rose O'Brien, C.B.S., D.R.E. Students 181.
Convent—Tel: 201-944-2911.

2—MADONNA (1858), [CEM] Revs. John P. Ryan; Stanley Lobo; Ulysses L. Ubalde; Theesmas Pankiraj. In Res., Rev. John M. Shih (Retired).
Res.: 340 Main St., 07024. Tel: 201-944-2727; Fax: 201-944-5986.
School— (1991), 359 Whiteman St., 07024. Tel: 201-944-0421. Christ the Teacher Interparochial School Sisters 3; Lay Teachers 19; Students 260.
Catechesis/Religious Program—Madonna Religious Education Center, Tel: 201-944-4266. Students 195.

FRANKLIN LAKES, BERGEN CO., MOST BLESSED SACRAMENT (1961), Rev. Msgr. Thomas J. McDade; Rev. Peter J. Palmisano.
Res.: 787 Franklin Lake Rd., 07417. Tel: 201-891-4200; Fax: 201-891-4243.
School— (1963), 785 Franklin Lake Rd., 07417. Tel: 201-891-4250; Fax: 201-847-9227. Lay Teachers 25; Students 229.
Catechesis/Religious Program—Tel: 201-891-8390. Students 552.
Convent—Tel: 201-891-4292.

GARFIELD, BERGEN CO.

1—CHURCH OF OUR LADY OF SORROWS (1917), Revs. John K. Gurski; Michael Guba.
Res.: 69 Market St., 07026. Tel: 973-772-7889; Fax: 973-772-7806.
School—Garfield Catholic Academy, (Grades PreK-8), 200 MacArthur Ave., 07026. Tel: 973-772-0416; Fax: 973-772-3301.
School—(Grades K-8), 208 Lanza Ave., 07026.
Catechesis/Religious Program—Students 80.

2—HOLY NAME (1911), (Hispanic), Rev. Msgr. William J. Reilly; Deacons Edgar Caceres; Cesar Torres.
Res.: 99 Marsellus Pl., 07026. Tel: 973-340-0032; Fax: 973-340-1618.
School—Garfield Catholic Academy, (Grades PreK-8), 200 MacArthur Ave., 07026. Tel: 973-772-0416; Fax: 973-772-3301.
Catechesis/Religious Program—Students 162.

3—OUR LADY OF MT. VIRGIN (1901), (Italian), Rev. Msgr. Paul L. Bochicchio, V.F.; Rev. Alfonso Picone (Italy); Deacon Dominic Riccio.
Res.: 188 MacArthur Ave., 07026. Tel: 973-772-2295; Fax: 973-478-4389.
School—Garfield Catholic Academy (1951),(Grades PreK-8), 200 MacArthur Ave., 07026. Tel: 973-772-0416; Fax: 973-772-3301. Ms. Terri Suchocki, Prin. Religious Teachers Filippini 1; Lay Teachers 10.
Catechesis/Religious Program—Tel: 973-253-1399. Sr. Jo Ann Jankowski, M.P.F., D.R.E. Students 175.
Convent—410 Maywood Ave., Maywood 07607. Tel: 201-845-9568.

4—ST. STANISLAUS KOSTKA (1917), (Polish), Revs. Edward P. Szpiech; Wladyslaw Gorak; Marek Wiorkiewicz, S.D.S.
Res.: 184 Ray St., 07026. Tel: 973-772-7922; Fax: 973-772-4178.
Catechesis/Religious Program—Tel: 201-794-0620. Students 268.
Convent—Tel: 973-772-4644.

GARWOOD, UNION CO., CHURCH OF ST. ANNE (1925), Rev. Msgr. John Philip O'Connor. In Res., Rev. Eugene Marcone.
Res.: 325 Second Ave., 07027. Tel: 908-789-0280; Fax: 908-789-3099.
Catechesis/Religious Program—Tel: 908-789-4745. Students 360.

GLEN ROCK, BERGEN CO., ST. CATHARINE (1953), Rev. Dennis J. Cohan; Rev. Msgr. Richard J. Holmes, Pastor Emeritus (Retired); Rev. Dominick J. Lenoci; Christine Thielke, Pastoral Assoc.; Pat Vest, Pastoral Assoc.; Roberta Maguire, Pastoral Assoc.; Jeanne Pond, Pastoral Assoc.; Deacons Leonard A. Mnichino, Pastoral Assoc.; James Mueller, Pastoral Assoc.; John Sarno, Pastoral Assoc.; Paul Schnieder, Pastoral Assoc. In Res., Rev. Sebastian M. Fernando.
Res.: 905 S. Maple Ave., 07452. Tel: 201-445-3703; Fax: 201-670-7149.
School—Academy of Our Lady, 180 Rodney St., 07452. Tel: 201-445-0622; Fax: 201-445-8345. Mrs. Patricia Keenaghan, Prin. Lay Teachers 33; Students 492.
Catechesis/Religious Program—Tel. 201-444-5690. Students 1,017.

GUTTENBERG, HUDSON CO., ST. JOHN NEPOMUCENE (1910), (Slovak), Rev. Richard D. Carlson.
Res. 7007 Polk St., 07093. Tel: 201-869-6834; Fax: 201-369-2408.
School—7111 Polk St., North Bergen, 07047. Tel: 201-869-5404; Fax: 201-869-5418. Sisters of St. Francis 2; Lay Teachers 15; Students 178; Franciscan Miss. 1.
Catechesis/Religious Program—Students 55.
Convent—Tel: 201-869-2099.

HACKENSACK, BERGEN CO.

1—CHURCH OF ST. FRANCIS OF ASSISI (1917), (Italian—Hispanic), Revs. Brian Tomlinson, O.F.M.Cap.; Paschal Caccavalle, O.F.M.Cap.; Eduardo Alzpide, O.P.; Bro. Jose Rojas, O.F.M.Cap.; Deacon Alejandro Polanco.
Res.: 50 Lodi St., 07601. Tel: 201-343-6243; Fax: 201-343-0854.
School—100 S. Main St., 07601. Tel: 201-488-8862; Fax: 201-525-0498. Lay Teachers 17; Students 290.
Catechesis/Religious Program—Tel: 201-488-2614. Students 275.

2—HOLY TRINITY (1861), [CEM] Most Rev. Charles J. McDonnell, D.D.; Revs. Patrick W. Donohue, V.F.; J. Orlando Rengifo; Robert Wolfe; Joseph Cheng; Deacon Amilgar Prado; Sr. Emily Marie Walsh, Parish Min.
Res.: 34 Maple Ave., 07601. Tel: 201-343-5170; Fax: 201-343-5067.
School— (1869), 43 Maple Ave., 07601. Tel: 201-489-6870; Fax: 201-489-2981. Franciscan 1; Sisters of Charity 3; Lay Teachers 19; Students 265.
Catechesis/Religious Program—Mrs. Carol Thee, D.R.E. Students 350.
Convent—Tel: 201-342-1996; Fax: 201-968-0035.

3—IMMACULATE CONCEPTION (1891), Rev. Gerard J. Graziano.
Res.: 49 Vreeland Ave., 07601. Tel: 201-440-2798; Fax: 201-440-6756.
Catechesis/Religious Program—Students 117.

4—ST. JOSEPH'S (1909), (Polish), Rev. Marian Spanier.
Res.: 460 Hudson St., 07601. Tel: 201-440-3224; Fax: 201-440-3224.

HARRINGTON PARK, BERGEN CO., OUR LADY OF VICTORIES (1910), Rev. John F. Renard; Deacon Al McLaughlin. In Res., Rev. Msgr. Roger A. Reynolds (Retired).
Res.: 81 Lynn St., 07640-1831. Tel: 201-768-1706; Fax: 201-768-3962.
School—Holy Family Interparochial School, Norwood, Tel: 201-768-1605; Fax: 201-768-0796. (See Immaculate Conception, Norwood)
Catechesis/Religious Program—(Grades K-8), 155 The Parkway, 07640-1820. Tel: 201-768-1400. Sr. Bernard Mary Herlihy, M.S.B.T., D.R.E. Students 350.
Convent—145 The Parkway 07640-1820. Tel: 201-768-1705.

HARRISON, HUDSON CO.

1—HOLY CROSS (1865), Rev. Msgr. John J. Gilchrist; Rev. Paulo Frade. In Res., Rev. Charles McTague (Retired); Sisters Doris DeLotto, S.S.C., Pastoral Assoc.; Barbara Graziadei, S.S.C.
Res.: 16 Church Sq., 07029. Tel: 973-484-5678; Fax: 973-484-0906.
School— (1871), 15 S. F.E. Rodgers Blvd., 07029. Tel: 973-481-0340; Fax: 973-481-0488. Lay Teachers 10; Students 182.
Catechesis/Religious Program—Students 180.
Convent—Holy Cross Convent, Tel: 973-485-2632.

2—OUR LADY OF CZESTOCHOWA (1908), (Polish), Rev. Rudolf Zubik.
Res.: 115 S. Third St., 07029. Tel: 973-483-2255; Fax: 973-483-4688.
Catechesis/Religious Program—Students 64.

HASBROUCK HEIGHTS, BERGEN CO., CORPUS CHRISTI (1897), Revs. Lewis V. Papera; Raymond M. Holmes; Rev. Msgr. Rodrigo San Pedro; Rev. James P. Whelan; Jennifer Jinks, Youth Minister; Douglas Duca, Music Minister.
Parish Offices & Center—218 Washington Pl., 07604. Tel: 201-288-4844; Fax: 201-288-0237.
School— (1928), 215 Kipp Ave., 07604. Tel: 201-288-0614; Fax: 201-288-5956. Lay Teachers 29; Students 415.
Catechesis/Religious Program—Tel: 201-288-5133; Fax: 201-288-0137. Flora Hand, D.R.E. Students 610.

HAWORTH, BERGEN CO., SACRED HEART (1914), Rev. Msgr. James F. Bouffard; Rev. Joseph W. Nealon, Pastor Emeritus (Retired).
Res.: 123 Maple St., P.O. Box S, 07641. Tel: 201-387-0080; Fax: 201-439-1395.
School—St. Joseph's Interparochial School (See St. Joseph, Demarest. Tel: 201-768-5534)
Catechesis/Religious Program—102 Park St., 07641. Tel: 201-384-6454. Students 200.

HILLSDALE, BERGEN CO., ST. JOHN THE BAPTIST (1925), Rev. Msgr. Philip D. Morris, S.T.D.; Revs. Michael J. Moran, M.Div. (Retired); Thomas A. Dente; Sisters Kathryn A. Malone, S.S.J., M.A., Pastoral Assoc.; Thomas Therese, S.S.J., Pastoral Assoc.
Res.: 69 Valley St., 07642. Tel: 201-664-3131; Fax: 201-664-0772.
School—St. John's Academy (1955), 460 Hillsdale Ave., 07642. Tel: 201-664-6364; Fax: 201-664-8096. Sisters 1; Lay Teachers 27; Students 488.
Catechesis/Religious Program—Faith Formation Center, Tel: 201-666-2707. Students 803.

HILLSIDE, UNION CO.

1—ST. CATHERINE OF SIENA (1912), Rev. Richard A. Villanova; Deacon Osiris Molina.
Res.: 19 King St., 07205. Tel: 908-351-1515; Fax: 908-351-2139.
School— (1920), 1003 N. Broad St., Elizabeth, 07208. Tel: 908-352-8029; Fax: 908-352-3677. Lay Teachers 15; Students 190.
Catechesis/Religious Program—Elizabeth. Tel: 908-352-8068. Students 85.

2—CHRIST THE KING (1948), Revs. Venantius M. Fernando; Romeo J. Axalan (Philippines).
Res.: 411 Rutgers Ave., 07205. Tel: 908-686-0722; Fax: 908-686-2504.
School— (1953), 397 Columbia Ave., 07205. Tel: 908-686-6740; Fax: 908-686-3819. Sisters 1; Lay Teachers 17; Students 215.
Catechesis/Religious Program—Tel: 908-686-0234. Students 100.

HOBOKEN, HUDSON CO.

1—ST. ANN'S (1900), (Italian), Revs. Francis Sariego, O.F.M.Cap.; Thomas A. Crangle, O.F.M.Cap.
Res.: 704 Jefferson St., 07030. Tel: 201-659-1114; Fax: 201-659-1416.
School—Hoboken Catholic Academy (1999), 555 Seventh St., 07030. Tel: 201-963-9535; Fax: 201-963-1256. Michael Massone, Prin. (Conducted by the parishes of Deanery 9) Lay Teachers 19.
Catechesis/Religious Program—Students 43.

2—ST. FRANCIS (1888), (Italian), Revs. Michael V. Guglielmelli; James F. Muntz.
Res.: 308 Jefferson St., 07030. Tel: 201-659-1772; Fax: 201-222-7975.
School—Hoboken Catholic Academy, Tel: 201-963-9535; Fax: 201-963-1256. See separate listing under St. Ann's, Hoboken.
Catechesis/Religious Program—Students 54.

3—ST. JOSEPH'S (1871), Revs. Kenneth J. Herbster, V.F., Admin.; Gerardo Gallo; Deacon Luis Montanez.
Res.: c/o Our Lady of Grace, 400 Willow Ave., 07030. Tel: 201-659-0369; Fax: 201-659-5833.
School—Hoboken Catholic Academy See separate listing under St. Ann's, Hoboken.

4—OUR LADY OF GRACE (1851), Revs. Kenneth J. Herbster, V.F.; Gerardo Gallo; Sr. Maria Iglesias, S.C. In Res., Rev. Msgr. Frederick M. Eid (Retired); Rev. Michael Onyekwele.
Res.: 400 Willow Ave., 07030. Tel: 201-659-0369; Fax: 201-659-5833.
School—Hoboken Catholic Academy See separate listing under St. Ann's, Hoboken.

Catechesis/Religious Program—Students 95.
5—SS. PETER AND PAUL'S (1889), Rev. Msgr. Frank G. Del Prete, J.C.D.; Rev. Joseph D'Amico; Sisters Susan DiDomemicantonio, I.C.M., Pastoral Assoc.; Patricia Wormann, O.P., Pastoral Assoc.; Deacon Primitivo Cruz.
Res.: 404 Hudson St., 07030. Tel: 201-659-2276; Fax: 201-659-5062. Web: www.spphoboken.com.
School—Hoboken Catholic Academy See separate listing under St. Ann's, Hoboken.
Catechesis/Religious Program—Catherine Walsh Haehle, D.R.E. Students 95.
HOHOKUS, BERGEN CO., ST. LUKE'S (1864), [CEM] Revs. James J. Weiner, Admin.; MinHyun Cho; Calin Cionca; Paschal Tsiquaye; Deacon John McKeon. In Res., Rev. Msgr. Richard J. Holmes, Pastor Emeritus (Retired).
Res.: 340 N. Franklin Tpke., 07423. Tel: 201-444-0272; Fax: 201-652-7044.
School—St. Thomas More Interparochial School, Tel: 201-447-3088. Serving the Parish Communities of St. Luke's, Nativity and Guardian Angel. (See Nativity Parish, Midland Park)
Catechesis/Religious Program—Tel: 201-447-2779. Miss Bridget Sarkowicz, D.R.E. Students 745.
IRVINGTON, ESSEX CO.
1—ASSUMPTION OF THE BLESSED VIRGIN MARY (1907), (Hungarian), Closed., For inquiries for parish records contact Seton Hall University Archives, South Orange. Tel: 973-596-9476
2—ST. LEO'S (1878), Revs. Thomas M. Cembor; Denis R. McKenna, Pastor Emeritus (Retired); Max Osias; Octavio Gonzalez; Deacon Victor Reyes.
Res.: 103 Myrtle Ave., 07111. Tel: 973-372-1272; Fax: 973-416-8819.
School—St. Leo's/Sacred Heart School See Sacred Heart of Jesus, Irvington.
Catechesis/Religious Program—Students 140.
Convent—Tel: 973-374-6397.
3—ST. PAUL THE APOSTLE (1948), Revs. Theodore W. Osbahr, V.F.; Robert Cio.
Res.: 954 Stuyvesant Ave., 07111. Tel: 973-375-8568; Fax: 973-375-7040.
School— (1950), 285 Nesbit Ter., 07111. Tel: 973-375-0659; Fax: 973-373-4882. Sisters of St. Dominic 1; Students 195.
Catechesis/Religious Program—Tel: 973-375-2688. Students 210.
Convent—972 Stuyvesant Ave., 07111. Tel: 973-374-2277.
4—SACRED HEART OF JESUS (1925), (Polish), Revs. Tadeusz Trela; Andrew Ostaszewski.
Res.: 537 Grove St., 07111. Tel: 973-373-2232; Fax: 973-373-5935.
School—St. Leo's/Sacred Heart School, 123 Myrtle Ave., 07111. Tel: 973-372-7555; Fax: 973-351-7601. Mr. Paulo Sociedade, Prin. Lay Teachers 22; Students 435.
Catechesis/Religious Program—Students 92.
JERSEY CITY, HUDSON CO.
1—ST. AEDAN'S (1912), Rev. Msgr. Jeremias R. Rebanal, J.C.D., Ph.D.; Rev. Henry M. Naddeo.
Res.: 800 Bergen Ave., 07306. Tel: 201-433-6800; Fax: 201-433-1222.
School— (1913), 41 Tuers Ave., 07306. Tel: 201-435-6528; Fax: 201-985-8975. Sisters 4; Lay Teachers 18; Students 325.
Convent—Tel: 201-451-8109.
2—ST. ALOYSIUS (1897), Revs. Richard J. Kelly; Thomas Thottungal; Jose Monte De Oca; Sr. Georgette A. Gavioli, S.S.J., Pastoral Assoc.; Deacons Stephen Liptak; Miguel A. Franco; Alfredo Zapata. In Res., Rev. Msgr. Martin Kelly (Retired); Revs. Edward S. Malkiewicz (Retired); James Delaney, C.S.Sp.
Res.: 691 West Side Ave., 07304. Tel: 201-433-6365; Fax: 201-451-6438.
School— (1897), 721 West Side Ave., 07306. Tel: 201-433-4270; Fax: 201-433-6916. Sisters of Charity 2; Lay Teachers 29; Students 430.
High School—Tel: 201-435-9240; Fax: 201-435-2115. Lay Teachers 22; Students 325.
Catechesis/Religious Program—Students 755.
Convent—Tel: 201-433-5759.
3—ST. ANN'S (1910), (Lithuanian), Closed., For inquiries for parish records contact Seton Hall University Archives, South Orange. Tel: 201-761-9476, Fax: 201-761-9550
4—ST. ANN'S (1911), (Polish), Revs. Thaddeus Stasik; George Idzik.
Res.: 291 St. Paul's Ave., 07306-5008. Tel: 201-656-4018; Fax: 201-656-0741.
Catechesis/Religious Program—Students 27.
5—ST. ANNE'S (1903), Revs. Victor P. Kennedy, V.F.; Julio I. Roman. In Res., Revs. John F. X. Bauman; Kevin P. Ashe.
Res.: 3545 John F. Kennedy Blvd., 07307. Tel: 201-656-2490; Fax: 201-795-3817.
School— (1904), 255 Congress St., 07307. Tel: 201-659-0450. Mrs. Marlene Bartram, Prin. Lay Teachers 11; Students 238.
Catechesis/Religious Program—Tel: 201-659-1794. Sr. Alberta Manzo, F.S.R., D.R.E. Students 135.
Convent—Tel: 201-963-0998.
6—ST. ANTHONY OF PADUA (1884), (Polish), Revs. Joseph Urban, Admin.; Andrzej Ostaszewski; Sr. Reginald Zajac, O.S.F., Pastoral Assoc.
Res.: 330 Sixth St., 07302. Tel: 201-653-0343; Fax: 201-653-0005.
Catechesis/Religious Program—Students 5.
7—ASSUMPTION/ALL SAINTS (1896), Revs. Eugene P. Squeo, J.D., Admin.; Stanley Rousseau (Haiti); Francis E. Schiller; Deacons Joseph Del Monte; Jesus Reyes.
Res.: 492 Bramhall Ave., 07304. Tel: 201-332-8600; Fax: 201-216-1600.
School—301 Whiton St., 07304. Tel: 201-433-6087. Sisters of Charity 2; Lay Teachers 20; Students 200.
Catechesis/Religious Program—Anne Marie Padillo, D.R.E. Students 75.
Convent—Tel: 201-451-2765.
8—ST. BONIFACE'S (1863), Merged, with St. Bridget, St. Mary, St. Michael and St. Peter to form Parish of the Resurrection, June 1997. For inquiries for parish records call Tel: 201-434-8500.
9—ST. BRIDGET'S (1869), Merged, with St. Boniface, St. Mary, St. Michael and St. Peter to form Parish of the Resurrection, June 1997. For inquiries for parish records call Tel: 201-434-8500.
10—CHRIST, THE KING (1930), (African American), Rev. John Edmunds, S.T.; Deacons Leon Johnson; Keith McKnight.
Res.: 768 Ocean Ave., 07304. Tel: 201-333-4862; Fax: 201-433-6352.
Catechesis/Religious Program—Students 62.
11—CHURCH OF OUR LADY OF SORROWS (1914), Rev. John Cryan, V.F., Admin.; Sisters Alice McCoy, O.P., Pastoral Assoc.; Elise Reomerski, O.P., Pastoral Assoc.
Res.: 93-95 Clerk St., 07305. Tel: 201-433-0626; Fax: 201-433-2928.
Catechesis/Religious Program—Students 48.
12—HOLY ROSARY (1885), (Italian), Rev. Rino Lavaroni; Rev. Msgr. Gerard M. Santora, Pastor Emeritus (Retired); Deacon Aart Markenstein. In Res., Rev. Brendan Quinn.
Res.: 344 Sixth St., 07302. Tel: 201-795-0120; Fax: 201-610-1389.
13—ST. JOHN THE BAPTIST (1884), Rev. Msgrs. Charles G. Stengel; Joseph A. Beggans, Pastor Emeritus (Retired); Rev. Peter H. Tran. In Res., Rev. Lawrence Correa, S.V.D. (India).
Res.: 3026 John F. Kennedy Blvd., 07306. Tel: 201-653-8814; Fax: 201-653-3771.
School—Visitation School, Formerly Saints John and Ann School (1886),(Grades PreK-8), 3044 John F. Kennedy Blvd., 07306. Tel: 201-653-4416; Fax: 201-653-7452. Co-Sponsored. Saints John and Ann School. Lay Teachers 13; Students 288.
Catechesis/Religious Program—Students 30.
Mission—St. Thomas Malankara, Hudson Co.
14—ST. JOSEPH'S (1856), Revs. James V. Pagnotta; Francisco Ponce.
Res.: 511 Pavonia Ave., 07306. Tel: 201-653-0392; Fax: 201-222-6481.
Church: Baldwin Ave., 07306.
School— (1876), 509 Pavonia Ave., 07306. Tel: 201-653-0128; Fax: 201-222-5324. Lay Teachers 11; Students 200.
Catechesis/Religious Program—Tel: 201-659-5929. Students 141.
Convent—Tel: 201-963-1428.
15—ST. LUCY'S (1884), Closed., For inquiries for parish records contact Parish of the Resurrection. Tel: 201-434-8500.
16—ST. MARY'S (1854), (Hispanic—Filipino), Merged, with St. Boniface, St. Bridget, St. Michael, and St. Peter, to form Parish of the Resurrection, June 1997. For inquiries for parish records call Tel: 201-434-8500.
17—ST. MICHAEL'S (1867), Merged, with St. Boniface, St. Bridget, St. Mary and St. Peter to form Parish of the Resurrection, June 1997. For inquiries for parish records call Tel: 201-434-8500.
18—ST. NICHOLAS (1886), (German), Rev. Kevin E. Carter; Rev. Msgr. Joseph C. Manz, Pastor Emeritus (Retired); Rev. Alex Ver (Philippines). In Res., Rev. Aloysius Ezenwata (Nigeria); Deacons Robert A. Baker Sr.; Wilson Cordbro.
Res.: 122 Ferry St., 07307. Tel: 201-659-5354; Fax: 201-798-1069.
School— (1886), 118 Ferry St., 07307. Tel: 201-659-5948. Sisters of Christian Charity 3; Lay Teachers 16; Students 291.
Catechesis/Religious Program—Tel: 201-659-5354. Students 82.
Convent—Tel: 201-659-5644.
19—OUR LADY OF CZESTOCHOWA (1911), (Polish), Rev. Thomas B. Iwanowski. In Res., Rev. Alexander M. Santora.
Res.: 120 Sussex St., 07302. Tel: 201-434-0798; 333-041- (Sisters Res.); Fax: 201-985-0918.
School— (1911), Marin Blvd. & York St., 07302. Tel: 201-434-2405; Fax: 201-434-6068. Lay Teachers 13; Students 210.
Catechesis/Religious Program—Students 10.
20—OUR LADY OF MERCY (1963), (Filipino), Revs. John J. Cryan, V.F., M.Div.; Martin Borbon Jacinto; Donato Cobardo Jr.; Deacon Nicholas Fargo.
Res.: 40 Sullivan Dr., 07305. Tel: 201-434-7500; Fax: 201-432-2885.
School—254 Bartholdi Ave., 07305. Tel: 201-434-4091; Fax: 201-434-8405. Lay Teachers 30; Students 525.
Convent—Tel: 201-451-4615.
Catechesis/Religious Program—Students 185.
21—OUR LADY OF MT. CARMEL (1905), (Italian), Revs. Michael C. Santoro; John Galeano. In Res., Rev. Walter L. Genzlinger (Retired).
Res.: 99 Broadway, 07306. Tel: 201-435-7080; Fax: 201-432-4476.
School— See Visitation School at St. John the Baptist Parish.
Catechesis/Religious Program—Mrs. Joyce Bowen, D.R.E. Students 72.
22—OUR LADY OF VICTORIES (1917), Revs. Victor E. Paloma; Walter J.F. Swenson, Pastor Emeritus (Retired); William Yabao (Philippines); Francisco Nicolas P. Magnaye Jr., C.M. (Philippines). In Res., Rev. James Tortora, Ph.D.
Res.: 2217 John F. Kennedy Blvd., 07304-1497. Tel: 201-433-4152; Fax: 201-433-0705.
School— (1930),Tel: 201-434-4040; Fax: 201-434-5356. Lay Teachers 13; Students 276.
Catechesis/Religious Program—Students 35.
23—PARISH OF THE RESURRECTION (1997),, (Formerly Parishes of St. Boniface, St. Bridget, St. Mary, St. Michael and St. Peter) Very Rev. Gregory J. Studerus, V.F.; Revs. Peter O'Brien, S.J.; Edgardo P. Jocson; Vincent B. Sullivan, S.J.; Bro. Louis N. Mauro, S.J., Business Mgr.; Deacons Pedro Gonzalez; Jaime Ortiz; Leopoldo Polanco; Sisters Mercedes Salinas, S.C., Pastoral Assoc.; Jean Young, S.C., Pastoral Assoc.; Ms. Roxanne Clark, Pastoral Assoc.; Ms. Elizabeth Hopf, Pastoral Assoc.
Mailing Address & Parish Office: 370 Montgomery St., 07302. Tel: 201-434-8500; Fax: 201-333-1816.
St. Boniface: 262 First St., 07302.
St. Bridget: 372 Montgomery St., 07302.
St. Michael: 252 Ninth St., 07302. (Shrine of St. Jude Perpetual Novena)
St. Mary: 219 Third St., 07302.
St. Peter: 144 Grand Street, 07302.
School—Resurrection, St. Bridget Campus (1873), 372 Montgomery St., 07302. Tel: 201-432-3588; Fax: 201-432-7978. Sr. Barbara Nesbihal, S.C., Prin.
High School—St. Mary, 209 Third St., 07302. Tel: 201-656-8008; Fax: 201-653-4518. Sr. Jacqueline Carey, S.C., Prin.
Catechesis/Religious Program—Tel: 201-795-3426. Sr. Mary Lynch, S.S.N.D., D.R.E. Students 415.
24—ST. PATRICK'S (1869), Revs. Eugene P. Squeo, J.D.; Francis E. Schiller; Stanley Rousseau (Haiti); Deacon Christopher Isinta. In Res., Rev. Edward J. Kearney (Retired).
Res.: 492 Bramhall Ave., 07304. Tel: 201-332-8600; Fax: 201-324-3919.
School— (1909),Tel: 201-433-4664. Sisters of Charity of St. Elizabeth 4; Lay Teachers 32; Students 519.
Catechesis/Religious Program—Fax: 201-216-1600. Students 49.
Convent—345 Pacific Ave., 07304. Tel: 201-451-2765.
25—ST. PAUL OF THE CROSS (1868), Revs. Andres J. Reyes; Nigel Mohammed; Melvin Oseguera.
Res.: 156 Hancock Ave., 07307. Tel: 201-798-7900; Fax: 201-798-7902.
School— (1869), 211 Sherman Ave., 07307. Tel: 201-659-6919; Fax: 201-610-0875. Lay Teachers 9; Students 133.
Catechesis/Religious Program—Students 230.
Convent—Tel: 201-659-1414.
26—ST. PAUL'S (1861), Revs. Robert Antczak; Jose Gamba; Stephen J. Toth; Sr. Rosanna Quinn, O.P., Pastoral Assoc. In Res., Rev. Raymond T. McKeon (Retired).
Res.: 14 Greenville Ave., 07305. Tel: 201-433-8500; Fax: 201-433-9886.
Catechesis/Religious Program—Tel: 201-433-1054. Students 150.
Convent—Tel: 201-434-2962.
27—ST. PETER'S (1831), (Hispanic), Merged, with St. Boniface, St. Bridget, St. Mary and St. Michael to form Parish of the Resurrection, June 1997. For parish inquiries call Tel: 201-434-8500.
28—SACRED HEART (1905), Very Rev. Peter Martin Batts, O.P.; Rev. David C. Adiletta, O.P.; Sr. Elaine Keenan, O.P., Pastoral Assoc.
Res.: 183 Bayview Ave., 07305. Tel: 201-332-6771 (Parish); 201-332-6773 (Priory); Fax: 201-332-5831(Parish)

School— (1913),Tel: 201-332-7111; Fax: 201-332-7160. Sr. Frances Salemi, S.C., Prin. Sisters of Charity 4; Sisters of St. Joseph of Peace 2; Lay Teachers 16; Students 375.
Sacred Heart Priory—Tel: 201-332-8667; Fax: 201-332-8375. Very Rev. Peter M. Batts, O.P., Prior; Rev. Gerard Lessard, O.P.; Sr. Gerard Maley, O.P.; Revs. Hugh D. Burns, O.P.; Ralph V. Townsend, O.P.; Henry Camacho, O.P.; Val La France, O.P.; Bro. John Jude Locchetto, O.P.

KEARNY, HUDSON CO.

1—ST. CECILIA'S (1893), Revs. Michael Ward; Alphonse De Condorpusa. In Res., Rev. Msgr. Francis R. Seymour.
Res.: 120 Kearny Ave., 07032. Tel: 201-991-1116; Fax: 201-998-4437.
Catechesis/Religious Program—Students 370.

2—OUR LADY OF SORROWS (1915), (Lithuanian), Revs. James J. Reilly, Admin.; Patrick R.C. Wilhelm; Deacon Leonard J. Mackesy.
Res.: 136 Davis Ave., 07032. Tel: 201-998-4616; Fax: 201-997-8659.
Catechesis/Religious Program—Students 94.

3—ST. STEPHEN'S (1904), Rev. Msgr. Michael J. Desmond; Revs. Joseph A. Mancini; Bryan F.J. Adamcik; Deacons Herbert R. Gimbel; Earl W. White; Patricia Sherwen, Youth Minister; Robert Maidhof, Music Minister.
Res.: 141 Washington Ave., 07032. Tel: 201-998-3314; Fax: 201-998-4924.
School— (1904), 131 Midland Ave., 07032. Tel: 201-991-3217; Fax: 201-991-7829. Madeline O'Sullivan, Prin. Lay Teachers 15; Students 325.
Catechesis/Religious Program—Tel: 201-991-0236. Sr. Rita Kearney, S.S.J., D.R.E. Students 460.

KENILWORTH, UNION CO., ST. THERESA'S (1949), Rev. Joseph S. Bejgrowicz, V.F.; Richard Donovan, Youth Minister. Tel: 908-709-1930. In Res., Revs. George M. Keating (Retired); Jose Erlito Ebron (Philippines); Al Kowalski (Retired); Henry P. Marciniak (Retired).
Res.: 541 Washington Ave., 07033. Tel: 908-272-4444; Fax: 908-272-2252.
School—540 Washington Ave., 07033. Tel: 908-276-7220; Fax: 908-709-1103. Sr. Marisa De Rose, F.M.A. Salesian Sisters 4; Lay Teachers 17; Students 309.
Catechesis/Religious Program—Tel: 908-276-4881. Maureen Madden, D.R.E. Students 550.
Convent—Tel: 908-276-5028.

LEONIA, BERGEN CO., ST. JOHN THE EVANGELIST'S (1912), Revs. Robert Traudt, O.Carm.; Roy Ontiveros, O.Carm.; Sr. Patricia McDermott, F.S.P., Pastoral Assoc.; Deacon Joseph Yandoli, Business Mgr. In Res., Rev. James Boyce, O.Carm.
Res.: 235 Harrison St., 07605. Tel: 201-947-4545; Fax: 201-947-3891.
School—260 Harrison St., 07605. Tel: 201-944-4361; Fax: 201-944-2195. School Sisters of Notre Dame 3; Lay Teachers 12; Students 234.
Catechesis/Religious Program—Tel 201-944-4346. Gerri Bianchi, D.R.E. Students 279.
Convent—Tel: 201-944-4362.

LINDEN, UNION CO.

1—ST. ELIZABETH'S (1909), Very Rev. Benedict Michael Worry, O.S.B., V.F.; Revs. Donal R. Fox, O.S.B.; Damian Breen, O.S.B.; Alexander Cruz.
Res.: 179 Hussa St., 07036. Tel: 908-486-2514; Fax: 908-486-1757.
School—Sts. Mary & Elizabeth Academy (1873), 170 Hussa St., 07036. Tel: 908-486-2507; Fax: 908-486-4032. Attended by St. Mary's, Rahway. Dominican Sisters of Caldwell 1; Lay Teachers 10; Students 266.
Convent—Tel: 908-486-2737.
Catechesis/Religious Program—170 Hussa St.. Tel: 908-486-2509; Fax: 908-487-1757. Students 259.

2—HOLY FAMILY (Tremley Point) (1955), (Slovak), [CEM] Rev. Eugene Diurczak; Rev. Msgr. Michael A. Komar, Pastor Emeritus (Retired).
Res.: 210 Monroe St., 07036. Tel: 908-862-1060; Fax: 908-862-1060.
Church: 2709 Parkway Ave., 07036. Fax: 908-862-1060.
Catechesis/Religious Program—Students 36.

3—ST. JOHN THE APOSTLE (1948), Rev. Msgr. Richard M. McGuinness; Revs. Joseph A. Meagher; Luke Tran; Philip F. Latronico, Youth Minister; Deacons George Ross; Edward A. Campanella; Guy Paredes, (Retired). In Res., Rev. Joseph G. Sheehan (Retired).
Res.: 1805 Penbrook Ter., 07036. Tel: 908-486-6363; Fax: 908-486-5345.
School— (1950), Valley Rd., Clark, 07066. Tel: 732-388-1360; Fax: 732-388-0775. Sister of St. Dominic 2; Lay Teachers 22; Students 469.
Catechesis/Religious Program—Tel: 732-388-1253; Fax: 732-388-8221. Amy Giglio, D.R.E. Students 605.
Convent—1731 Valley Rd., 07036. Tel: 908-486-3701.

4—ST. THERESA OF THE CHILD JESUS (1925), (Polish), Rev. Msgr. Bronislaw Wielgus; Revs. Marek Chachlowski (Poland); Miroslaw K. Krol; Deacon Alexander Czerepka.
Res.: 122 Liberty St., 07036. Tel: 908-862-1116; Fax: 908-862-2930.
Church: 131 E. Edgar Rd., 07036.
School— (1930), 705 Clinton St., 07036. Tel: 908-862-7551; Fax: 908-862-5982. Lay Teachers 10; Students 215.
Catechesis/Religious Program—Tel: 908-862-1388. Students 442.
Convent—18 Liberty Ave., 07036. Tel: 908-862-4820.

LITTLE FERRY, BERGEN CO., ST. MARGARET OF CORTONA (1912), Revs. Arthur Frank Humphrey, S.T.M., M.A.; William A. Lusik.
Res.: 31 Chamberlain Ave., 07643-1898. Tel: 201-641-2988; Fax: 201-641-0664.
Catechesis/Religious Program—Tel: 201-641-3937. Sr. Dorothy A. Donovan, S.S.J., D.R.E. Students 345.

LIVINGSTON, ESSEX CO.

1—ST. PHILOMENA (1927), Rev. Msgrs. Owen J. Hendry; Thomas J. Daly (BO), Pastor Emeritus (Retired); Revs. Stephen A. Kopacz; Ernest G. Rush; Deacons Joseph Francione; Fred Smith. In Res., Rev. Msgr. Robert T. Lennon (Retired).
Res.: 386 S. Livingston Ave., 07039. Tel: 973-992-0994; Fax: 973-992-0970.
School—Aquinas Academy (1952), 388 S. Livingston Ave., 07039. Tel: 973-992-1587; Fax: 973-992-1742. Sr. Patricia Tavis, Prin. Dominican Sisters of Caldwell 1; Lay Teachers 25; Students 247.
School—Early Childhood Center, Tel: 973-992-5181; Fax: 973-992-2652. Lay Teachers 12; Students 75.
Catechesis/Religious Program—Tel: 973-992-4466. Students 435.
Convent—Tel: 973-992-1581.

2—ST. RAPHAEL (1961), Rev. Msgr. Ronald A. Newland; Brenda Mansheim, Youth Minister; K. Rives Casses, Music Minister. In Res., Rev. John E. O'Brien (Retired).
Res.: 346 E. Mt. Pleasant Ave., 07039. Tel: 973-992-9490; Fax: 973-740-0236.
Catechesis/Religious Program—Yolanda Cifarelli, D.R.E. Students 550.

LODI, BERGEN CO.

1—ST. FRANCIS DE SALES (1854), [CEM] Rev. Timothy G. Graff; Sr. Martine M. Pijanowski, C.S.S.F., R.N. In Res., Rev. John B. Baron, Ph.D.
Res.: 125 Union St., 07644. Tel: 973-779-4330; Fax: 973-779-8842.
Catechesis/Religious Program—Tel 973-779-3949. Students 176.
Convent—Tel: 973-773-4366.

2—ST. JOSEPH'S (1917), (Italian), Revs. Hector DiNardo, C.R.M.; Americo Salvi, C.R.M.; Jason S. Caganap, C.R.M.; Gabriel M. Lucarelli, C.R.M.
Res. 40 Spring St., 07644. Tel: 973-779-0643; Fax: 973-471-1442.
Catechesis/Religious Program—Tel: 973-779-8275; Fax: 973-779-0490. Students 300.

LYNDHURST, BERGEN CO.

1—ST MICHAEL'S (1912), (Polish), Rev. Joseph Szklarski; Deacon Vincent Serzan. In Res., Rev. Msgr. James Mc Menemie.
Res.: 624 Page Ave., 07071. Tel: 201-939-1161; Fax: 201-939-7571.
School— (1951),Tel: 201-939-0350; Fax: 201-438-6189. Lay Teachers 11; Students 185.
Catechesis/Religious Program—Tel: 201-438-8316. Students 169.
Convent—Tel: 201-438-1882.

2—OUR LADY OF MOUNT CARMEL (1966), (Italian), Revs. Nazareno Orandi; Thomas J. Kenna.
Res.: 197 Kingsland Ave., 07071. Tel: 201-935-1177; Fax: 201-935-5675.
Catechesis/Religious Program—146 Copeland Ave., 07071. Tel: 201-935-5467. Students 263.

3—SACRED HEART (1905), [CEM] Very Rev. Charles J. Miller, V.F.; Revs. Marek Wysocki; Salvatore DiStefano; Deacon Brett Moore.
Res.: 324 Ridge Rd., 07071. Tel: 201-438-1147; Fax: 201-507-5861.
School—620 Valley Brook Ave., 07071. Tel: 201-939-4277. Sisters 1; Lay Teachers 23; Students 400.
Catechesis/Religious Program—Tel: 201-935-3094. Students 350.

MAHWAH, BERGEN CO.

1—IMMACULATE CONCEPTION (1930), Rev. M. Christen Beirne. In Res., Rev. James R. White.
Res.: 900 Darlington Ave., 07430. Tel: 201-327-1276; Fax: 201-327-0185.
School—St. Paul's Interparochial School, Tel: 201-327-1108; Fax: 201-327-6197.
Catechesis/Religious Program—Tel: 201-825-0333. Mr. James Crosson, D.R.E. Students 396.

2—IMMACULATE HEART OF MARY (1915), (Polish), Revs. Floyd Rotunno; Marek Bakota.
Res.: 47 Island Rd., 07430. Tel: 201-529-3517; Fax: 201-529-4401.
School—St. Paul's Interparochial School (1991), (See St. Paul's, Ramsey. Tel: 201-327-1108; Fax: 201-327-6197) Sisters of Charity 2; Lay Teachers 12; Students 255.
Catechesis/Religious Program—Tel: 201-529-2294. Students 130.

MAPLEWOOD, ESSEX CO.

1—IMMACULATE HEART OF MARY (1954), Rev. Frank J. Rocchi.
Res.: 280 Parker Ave., 07040. Tel: 973-763-5019; Fax: 973-763-9010.
School— (1957), 276 Parker Ave., 07040. Tel: 973-763-0031; Fax: 973-763-3622. Lay Teachers 14; Students 150; Preschool 12.
Catechesis/Religious Program—Students 90.

2—ST. JOSEPH'S (1914), Revs. John A. Quill; Manolo Punzalan. In Res., Rev. Msgr. William B. Naedele.
Res.: 767 Prospect St., 07040. Tel: 973-761-5933; Fax: 973-761-6705.
School— (1930), 240 Franklin Ave., 07040. Tel: 973-761-4033; Fax: 973-761-0473. Lay Teachers 24; Students 370.
Catechesis/Religious Program—Students 226.

MAYWOOD, BERGEN CO., OUR LADY QUEEN OF PEACE (1950), Revs. Stephen J. Cinque; Paul B. Sretenovic; Sr. Louise DelCarpine, Pastoral Assoc.; Deacon Anthony Balistieri.
Res.: 400 Maywood Ave., 07607. Tel: 201-845-9566; Fax: 201-845-3742.
Catechesis/Religious Program—Tel: 201-845-9545. Students 360.
Convent—Tel: 201-845-9568.

MIDLAND PARK, BERGEN CO., NATIVITY (1955), Very Rev. John R. O'Connell, V.F. In Res., Rev. Marcellinus Uwandu.
Res.: 315 Prospect St., 07432. Tel: 201-444-6362; Fax: 201-444-5056.
School—St. Thomas More Interparochial School, 321 Prospect St., 07432. Tel: 201-447-3088; Fax: 201-447-4145. Lay Teachers 12; Students 183.
Catechesis/Religious Program—Tel: 201-447-1776. Students 478.

MONTCLAIR, ESSEX CO.

1—IMMACULATE CONCEPTION (1864), [CEM] Rev. Msgr. Timothy J. Shugrue; Revs. Frank J. Burla; William P. Sheridan; Sr. Cora Marie McGuire, M.S.B.T., Pastoral Assoc. In Res., Rev. Louis M. Pambello.
Res.: 30 N. Fullerton Ave., 07042. Tel: 973-744-1005; Fax: 973-744-7936.
Parish Center:—1 Munn St., 07042. Tel: 973-509-1111; Fax: 973-744-7936.
School—Preschool (1997), Tegakwita Academy, 1 Munn St., 07042. Tel: 973-744-5650. Lay Teachers 2; Students 17.
High School— (1919), 33 Cottage Pl., 07042. Tel: 973-744-7445; Fax: 973-744-3926. Sisters 5; Lay Teachers 30; Students 310.
Catechesis/Religious Program—Students 355.

2—OUR LADY OF MT. CARMEL (1907), (Italian), Revs. Thomas J. Petrillo; Peter Phong Vo. In Res., Rev. Thomas C. Roberts.
Res.: 94 Pine St., 07042. Tel: 973-744-1074; Fax: 973-744-0205.
Catechesis/Religious Program—Tel: 973-744-6935. Students 115.

3—ST. PETER CLAVER (1931), (African American), Revs. John P. Nickas; Dominic G. Fuccile, Temp. Admin.; Deacons John Coffey; Wilfrid Leconte.
Res.: 56 Elmwood Ave., 07042. Tel: 973-783-4852; Fax: 973-783-3261.
Catechesis/Religious Program—Students 105.

MOONACHIE, BERGEN CO., ST. ANTHONY (1931), Closed., For inquiries for parish records contact Seton Hall University Archives: South Orange. Tel.: 973-761-9476; Fax: 973-761-9550

MOUNTAINSIDE, UNION CO., OUR LADY OF LOURDES (1958), Revs. John M. McCrone; Piotr Michota; Jae Hwa Kim; Rev. Msgr. Raymond J. Pollard (Retired).
Res.: 300 Central Ave., 07092. Tel: 908-232-1162; Fax: 908-232-0776.
School—Holy Trinity Interparochial School Mountainside Campus (1991),(Grades PreK-8), 304 Central Ave., 07092. Tel: 908-233-1899; Fax: 908-233-2109. Leslie Lewis, Dir. (Westfield Campus Tel: 908-233-0484) Lay Teachers 15; Students 312.
Catechesis/Religious Program—Tel: 908-233-1777. Students 357.

NEW MILFORD, BERGEN CO., ASCENSION (1953), Revs. David W. Milliken; Joy Alappat; Arcadio Munoz (Philippines); Deacons Harold Bates; Paul Kliauga.
Res.: 256 Azalea Dr., 07646. Tel: 201-836-8961; Fax: 201-836-5896.
School—1092 Carnation Dr., 07646. Tel: 201-836-7074; Fax: 201-836-4475. Students 229.
Catechesis/Religious Program—Tel: 201-836-3085. Students 393.

NEW PROVIDENCE, UNION CO., OUR LADY OF PEACE (1942), Very Rev. Sean Cunneen, V.E.; Rev. Msgr. Paul J. Hayes, Pastor Emeritus (Retired); Revs.

Francis A. Heinen; Thomas Pendrick.
Res.: 111 South St., 07974. Tel: 908-464-7600; Fax: 908-508-1845.
School—99 South St., 07974. Tel: 908-464-8657; Fax: 908-464-3377. Lay Teachers 18; Students 225.
Catechesis/Religious Program—Tel: 908-464-8156. Students 691.
Convent—Tel: 908-464-8223.

NORTH ARLINGTON, BERGEN CO., QUEEN OF PEACE (1922), Rev. Msgrs. William J. Fadrowski; Thomas G. Madden, Pastor Emeritus (Retired); Revs. Scott Attanasio; Walter D. Lucey; Brian Keenan Muzas; Deacons William R. Benedetto; William H. Myers; George Schlitt, Business Mgr.; Anthony Tabish, Music Minister.
Res.: 10 Franklin Pl., 07031. Tel: 201-997-0700; Fax: 201-997-6214.
School— (1925), 21 Church Pl., 07031. Tel: 201-998-8222; Fax: 201-997-7930. Sisters of St. Joseph of Chestnut Hill 2; Lay Teachers 20; Students 495.
High School— (1930), 191 Rutherford Pl., 07031. Tel: 201-998-8227; Fax: 201-998-3040. Sisters 5; Lay Teachers 50; Students 720.
Catechesis/Religious Program—Tel: 201-998-0901. Mary Fleischbein, D.R.E. Students 515.
Convent—Tel: 201-997-2141.

NORTH BERGEN, HUDSON CO.

1—ST. BRIGID (1900), Revs. Manuel D. Rios, Admin.; Cresencio Balino.
Res.: 4501 Liberty Ave., 07047. Tel: 201-863-0160; Fax: 201-863-3877.
Catechesis/Religious Program—Students 58.

2—OUR LADY OF FATIMA (1963), Rev. John J. Korbelak.
Res.: 8016 Kennedy Blvd., 07047. Tel: 201-869-7244; Fax: 201-869-0940.
Catechesis/Religious Program—Tel: 201-869-0506. Students 206.

3—SACRED HEART (1917), (Polish), Rev. Anthony G. Robak.
Mailing Address: Box 9007, 07047.
Res.: 246 Hudson Pl., Cliffside Park, 07010. Tel: 201-943-0305; Fax: 201-943-2676.
Catechesis/Religious Program—Students 40.

NORTH CALDWELL, ESSEX CO., NOTRE DAME (1962), Rev. Msgr. Edward J. Ciuba; Rev. Anthony J. Randazzo; Sr. Carol Jaruszewski, R.S.M., Pastoral Assoc.
Res.: 359 Central Ave., 07006. Tel: 973-226-0979; Fax: 973-226-4118.
Catechesis/Religious Program—Tel: 973-228-3338. Students 590.

NORTHVALE, BERGEN CO., ST. ANTHONY'S (1890), Rev. Jerry Hahn. In Res., Revs. Thomas Norton; Robert J. Halliwell (Retired); Benedict P. Militello (Retired).
Res.: 199 Walnut St., 07647. Tel: 201-768-1177; Fax: 201-768-2522.
School—Holy Family School, Tel: 201-768-1605; Fax: 201-768-8006. (See Immaculate Conception, Norwood)
Catechesis/Religious Program—Tel: 201-768-5945. Students 248.

NORWOOD, BERGEN CO., IMMACULATE CONCEPTION (1921), Rev. Charles B. Urnick; Sr. Elizabeth Heller, S.C., Pastoral Assoc.
Res.: 211 Summit St., 07648. Tel: 201-768-1600; Fax: 201-768-8006.
School—Holy Family Interparochial School (1991), 200 Summit St., 07648. Tel: 201-768-1605; Fax: 201-768-0796. Miss Patricia Bliss., Prin. Sisters 1; Lay Teachers 26; Students 450.
Catechesis/Religious Program—Tel: 201-768-1771. Sr. Susanne Reynolds, S.S.J. Students 300.

NUTLEY, ESSEX CO.

1—HOLY FAMILY (1909), (Italian), Rev. Msgr. Peter J. Zaccardo; Rev. Michael A. Andreano; Sisters Eileen Hubbert, S.S.J., Pastoral Assoc.; Anita Canale, M.P.F., Pastoral Assoc. In Res., Rev. Alex Barbieto (Philippines).
Res.: 28 Brookline Ave., 07110. Tel: 973-667-0026; Fax: 973-661-1714.
School—Good Shepherd Academy (1992), 24 Brookline Ave., 07110. Tel: 973-667-2049; Fax: 973-661-9259. Co-sponsored by 3 area churches. Religious Teachers Filippini 5; Lay Teachers 22; Students 346.
Catechesis/Religious Program—Tel: 973-667-6018. Sr. Angelina DelVecchio, M.P.F., D.R.E. Students 750.
Convent—Tel: 973-667-2050.

2—ST. MARY'S (1876), Revs. David C. Hubba; Matthew Kunnath; George Sharp; Henry Schreitmueller (Retired); Sr. Alicia Cavanaugh, C.S.J.P., Pastoral Assoc. In Res., Rev. Bernard Fernando.
Res.: 17 Msgr. Owens Pl., 07110. Tel: 973-235-1100; Fax: 973-661-0233.
School—Good Shepherd Academy, Tel: 973-667-0026; Fax: 973-661-1714. (See Holy Family, Nutley. Tel: 973-667-2049)
Catechesis/Religious Program—Tel: 973-667-8239; Fax: 973-661-0233. Brian Lynch, D.R.E. Students 750.

3—OUR LADY OF MOUNT CARMEL (1925), (Polish), Revs. Thomas J. Ciba, M.P.A.; Emmanuel A. Soriso (Philippines); Deacon Aldo P. Antola; Sr. Arlene Oswald, O.P. In Res., Rev. William Gyure.
Res.: 120 Prospect St., 07110. Tel: 973-667-2580; Fax: 973-667-0648.
School—Good Shepherd Academy, Tel: 973-667-2049. (See Holy Family, Nutley)
Catechesis/Religious Program—Students 175.

OAKLAND, BERGEN CO., OUR LADY OF PERPETUAL HELP (1960), Rev. Thomas P. Lipnicki.
25 Purdue Ave., 07436. Tel: 201-337-7596; Fax: 201-337-7810.
Catechesis/Religious Program—Tel: 201-337-5537. Students 570.
Convent—Tel: 201-337-5364.

OLD TAPPAN, BERGEN CO., ST. PIUS X (1954), Rev. Patrick M. Mulewski; Deacons Richard G. Hodges; John J. McKenna.
Res.: 268 Old Tappan Rd., 07675. Tel: 201-664-0913; Fax: 201-664-1013.
School—Holy Family Interparochial School, Fax: 201-768-0796. (See Immaculate Conception, Norwood. Tel: 201-768-1605)
Catechesis/Religious Program—Tel: 201-664-0927. Students 450.

ORADELL, BERGEN CO., ST. JOSEPH'S (1903), Revs. George M. Reilly; Peter G. Wehrle; Richard J. Mroz.
Res.: 105 Harrison St., New Milford, 07646. Tel: 201-261-0148; Fax: 201-261-0369.
School— (1939), 305 Elm St., 07649. Tel: 201-261-2388; Fax: 201-261-0830. Sisters 3; Lay Teachers 23; Students 525.
Catechesis/Religious Program—300 Elm St., 07649. Tel: 201-265-8880; Fax: 201-634-0640. Annette Ziegler, D.R.E. Students 820.

ORANGE, ESSEX CO.

1—ST. ANDREW KIM (1972), (Korean), Rev. Yong Il Park (Korea, South). In Res., Rev. Msgr. Augustin C. Park, Coord. Korean Apostolate; Revs. Luis Kim (Korea, South); Sae Wan Oh (Korea, South).
Res.: 257 Central Ave., 07050. Tel: 973-673-1366; 973-672-6650; Fax: 973-673-2030.
Catechesis/Religious Program—Students 245.
Convent—Tel: 973-674-1618.

2—HOLY SPIRIT (1931), Merged, For inquiries for parish records contact Holy Spirit-Our Lady Help of Christians, East Orange. Tel: 201-673-1077.

3—ST. JOHN'S (1851), (Hispanic), [CEM] Rev. George Faour; Rev. Msgr. Ricardo Gonzalez, Pastor Emeritus (Retired); Rev. Jose Fernandez; Deacon Jerry Romero.
Res.: 94 Ridge St., 07050. Tel: 973-674-0110; Fax: 973-674-3965.
School— (1855), 455 White St., 07050. Tel: 973-674-8951; Fax: 973-674-6126. Sisters of Charity 4; Lay Teachers 12; Students 368.
Catechesis/Religious Program—Students 340.
Convent—Tel: 973-673-1263.

4—MT. CARMEL (1896), (Italian), Revs. David E. Aguilar (Philippines); John Perricone, Admin.
Res.: 103 S. Center St., 07050. Tel: 973-674-2052; Fax: 973-675-1342.
Catechesis/Religious Program—Students 8.
Center—264 Capuchin Way, 07050.

5—OUR LADY OF THE VALLEY (1873), Rev. George Hanna, S.D.B.
Res.: 510 Valley St., 07050. Tel: 973-674-7500; Fax: 973-672-8341.
Catechesis/Religious Program—Tel: 973-674-4272. Students 75.

6—ST. VENANTIUS (1886), Merged, For inquiries for parish records contact St. Andrew Kim Parish, Orange. Tel: 973-673-1366.

PALISADES PARK, BERGEN CO.

1—ST. MICHAEL'S (1912), Revs. James F. Reilly; Michael T. Mickelson.
Res.: 19 E. Central Blvd., 07650-1799. Tel: 201-944-1061; Fax: 201-947-1798.
School—Notre Dame Interparochial, Elementary Division (1991),(Grades 2-8), 312 First St., 07650. Tel: 201-947-5262; Fax: 201-945-3796.
School—Primary Division (1991),(Grades PreK-1), 555 Prospect Ave., Ridgefield, 07657. Tel: 201-943-5757; Fax: 201-947-8319. Sr. Ellen McMahon, Prin.
Catechesis/Religious Program—324 First St., 07650. Tel: 201-944-0070; Fax: 201-947-1798. Margaret M. Manley, D.R.E. Students 120.

2—ST. NICHOLAS (1923), (Italian—Brazilian), Revs. Armando M. Palmieri, S.D.V. (Italy), Admin.; Castrese Muoio, S.D.V. (Italy). In Res., Rev. Robert Vass, S.D.V.
Res.: 442 E. Brinkerhoff Ave., 07650. Tel: 201-944-1154; Fax: 201-944-9510.
School—Notre Dame Interparochial School (1991), (See St. Matthew, Ridgefield for Primary Division. Tel: 201-943-4747) (See St. Michael, Palisades Park for Elementary Division. Tel: 201-947-5262)
Catechesis/Religious Program—Tel: 201-944-1138. Rev. Armando M. Palmieri, S.D.V. (Italy). Students 107.

PARAMUS, BERGEN CO.

1—ANNUNCIATION (1953), Revs. Michael J. Sheehan; William Crum; Deacons Joseph Niland; William D. Joyce.
Res.: 50 W. Midland Ave., 07652. Tel: 201-261-6322; Fax: 201-261-6227.
Parish Center & Mailing Address: 49 Demarest Rd., 07652.
School— (1991),Tel: 201-262-6067; Fax: 201-261-4613. (See Visitation Academy, Our Lady of the Visitation Parish, Paramus)
Catechesis/Religious Program—Mary Ann Cassidy, D.R.E. Students 500.

2—CARMELITE CHAPEL OF ST. THERESE (1970), Revs. Brice E. Riordan, O.Carm., Dir.; Daniel Smith, O.Carm., Dir.; Guy McPartland, O.Carm.
Res.: 135 Gertrude Ave., 07652-2515. Tel: 201-845-6392.
Church: Bergen Mall, 07652. Tel: 201-845-6115.

3—OUR LADY OF THE VISITATION (1952), Rev. Msgr. Joseph T. Slinger; Revs. Dennis Reiff; Sebastian Kunnath; Joseph J. Astarita.
Res.: 234 Farview Ave., 07652. Tel: 201-261-6080; Fax: 201-261-2995.
School—Visitation Academy (1991), 222 Farview Ave., 07652. Tel: 201-262-6067; Fax: 201-261-4613. Sr. Rene Donohue, S.C., Prin. Co-Sponsored. Sisters 3; Lay Teachers 22; Students 412.
Catechesis/Religious Program—Tel: 201-265-3812. Mrs. Barbara D'Arrigo, D.R.E. Students 587.

PARK RIDGE, BERGEN CO., OUR LADY OF MERCY (1902), Revs. Charles P. Granstrand; Robert T. Ulak; Rev. Msgr. James C. Turro, Ph.D., Weekend Asst. (Retired). In Res., Rev. Msgr. Carl D. Hinrichsen (Retired).
Res.: 2 Fremont Ave., 07656. Tel: 201-391-5315; Fax: 201-391-5614.
School—Our Lady of Mercy Interparochial School (1950), 25 Fremont Ave., 07656. Tel: 201-391-3838; Fax: 201-391-3838. Lay Teachers 28; Students 431.
Catechesis/Religious Program—50 Pascack Rd., 07656. Tel: 201-391-3590; Fax: 201-802-1771. Students 639.

PLAINFIELD, UNION CO.

1—ST. BERNARD'S (1921), Revs. Frank Rose; Jan Krzystof Lebdowicz (Poland).
Office:—368 Sumner Ave., P.O. Box 2844, 07062. Tel: 908-756-3393; Fax: 908-756-3059.
Rectory: 368 Sumner Ave., 07062.
Catechesis/Religious Program—Students 121.

2—ST. MARY (1851), [CEM] Revs. Kenneth Jones; Sean Manson; Deacons Martin P. Macaluso, S.F.O.; Pedro Nieves. In Res., Rev. Ken St. Amand.
Res.: 516 W. Sixth St., 07060. Tel: 908-756-0085; Fax: 908-756-1658.
Catechesis/Religious Program—Tel: 908-561-7143. Students 306.
Convent—Missionaries of Charity, (Contemplative), 513 Liberty St., 07060. Tel: 908-754-1978. Sisters 6.

3—ST. STANISLAUS KOSTKA (1919), (Polish), Revs. Frank Rose, Admin.; Jan Krzystof Lebdowicz (Poland).
Mailing Address: 368 Sumner Ave., P.O. Box 2844, 07062. Tel: 908-756-3393; Fax: 908-756-3059. (For Churches in North Plainfield and South Plainfield, please see the Diocese of Metuchen.)
Church: 1020 W. Seventh St., 07063. Tel: 908-756-9900.

RAHWAY, UNION CO.

1—ST. MARK'S (1871), (German), Rev. William T. Morris.
Res.: 287 Hamilton St., 07065. Tel: 732-499-9230; Fax: 732-388-7036.
Catechesis/Religious Program—Tel: 732-388-7036. Students 100.

2—ST. MARY'S (1854), [CEM] Revs. Michael J. Feketie; Donald B. Ransom, Pastoral Assoc.; Peter Vo, Pastoral Assoc.; Reinerio Agaloos, Pastoral Assoc.; Deacons J. William Courtney; Robert Fencik.
Res. & Office: 232 Central Ave., 07065. Tel: 732-388-0082; Fax: 732-388-0020.
School—Sts. Mary & Elizabeth Academy See St. Elizabeth's, Linden, Tel: 908-486-2507.
Catechesis/Religious Program—Tel: 732-382-0004; Fax: 732-382-4784. Students 323.

RAMSEY, BERGEN CO., ST. PAUL (1939), Rev. Msgr. Lawrence W. Cull; Rev. James M. Manos.
Res.: 200 Wyckoff Ave., 07446. Tel: 201-327-0976; Fax: 201-327-6197.
School—St. Paul's Interparochial School, 187 Wyckoff Ave., 07446. Tel: 201-327-1108; Fax: 201-236-1318. Lay Teachers 27; Students 300.
Catechesis/Religious Program—Tel: 201-327-8010. Students 1,570.

RIDGEFIELD PARK, BERGEN CO., ST. FRANCIS OF ASSISI (1890), Revs. Joseph C. Doyle; Eugene J. Field; Deacon Nicholas Simonelli; Constance Sheehan, Pastoral Assoc.

Res.: 114 Mt. Vernon St., 07660. Tel: 201-641-6464; Fax: 201-641-2282.
School— (1915), 110 Mt. Vernon St., 07660. Tel: 201-641-9159; Fax: 201-641-4091. Sr. Patricia Meidhof, Prin. Sisters 1; Lay Teachers 18; Students 273.
Catechesis/Religious Program—Students 370.

RIDGEFIELD, BERGEN CO., ST. MATTHEW'S (1899), Revs. Donald P. Sheehan; William A. Lusik; Deacon Drew Dickson. In Res., Rev. Msgr. William J. Koplik (Retired).
Res.: 555 Prospect Ave., 07657. Tel: 201-945-3500; Fax: 201-945-3796.
School—Notre Dame Interparochial Primary Division (1991),(Grades PreK-1), Edgewater Ave., 07657. Tel: 201-943-5757; Fax: 201-943-4209; 201-947-8319. Sisters 2; Lay Teachers 6; Students 167.
Catechesis/Religious Program—Students 346.

RIDGEWOOD, BERGEN CO., OUR LADY OF MOUNT CARMEL (1889), Rev. Msgr. Ronald J. Rozniak, V.G.; Revs. Robert G. Gibney, Pastor Emeritus; Ivan Sciberras; Hongshik Don Bosco Park; Deacons Robert V. Thomann; Nicholas De Lucca; Sr. Rose Vincent, S.C., Pastoral Assoc.; Mrs. Linda English, Pastoral Assoc.; Mr. Peter Sicko, Music Minister; Ms. Kathryn Sullivan, Youth Minister. In Res., Rev. Mert Cordero.
Res.: 1 Passaic St., 07450-4309. Tel: 201-444-2000; Fax: 201-444-2002.
School—Academy of Our Lady, Tel: 201-445-0622.
Catechesis/Religious Program—Tel: 201-444-0211; Fax: 201-444-4421. Paula Metzger, D.R.E. Students 1,486.
Convent—Tel: 201-445-2077.

RIVER EDGE, BERGEN CO., ST. PETER THE APOSTLE (1948), Rev. Robert H. Slipe; Rev. Msgr. David J. Casazza, Pastor Emeritus (Retired); Revs. Michael J. German; George Klybus; Deacon Edward Bowen.
Res.: 445 Fifth Ave., 07661. Tel: 201-261-3366; Fax: 201-261-0117.
School—St. Peter Academy (1952), 431 Fifth Ave., 07661. Tel: 201-261-3468; Fax: 201-261-4316. Sisters 2; Lay Teachers 16; Students 240.
Catechesis/Religious Program—Tel: 201-265-6019. Students 677.
Convent—Tel: 201-845-9568.

ROCHELLE PARK, BERGEN CO., SACRED HEART (1917), Revs. Norbert Laskowski; William O'Brien.
Res.: 12 Terrace Ave., 07662. Tel: 201-843-1722; Fax: 201-843-3542.
School— (1991),Tel: 201-262-6067. Co-Sponsored. (See Visitation Academy, Our Lady of Visitation Parish, Paramus)
Catechesis/Religious Program—Tel: 201-843-1077. Karl Patterman, D.R.E. Students 305.

ROSELAND, ESSEX CO., OUR LADY OF THE BLESSED SACRAMENT (1955), Rev. Msgr. Louis F. Fimiani; Rev. Stephen A. Carey; Deacon Pat Quagliana; Sisters Rie Crowley, S.S.J., Pastoral Assoc. (Sick and Homebound Parish Outreach); Regina Suplick, S.C., Pastoral Assoc. (Baptismal Ministry); Joseph Wozniak, Pastoral Assoc. (Liturgical Music). In Res., Rev. James B. Sullivan (Retired).
Res.: 28 Livingston Ave., 07068. Tel: 973-226-7288; Fax: 973-226-4893.
Catechesis/Religious Program—Tel: 973-226-5251; Fax: 973-403-8871. Maurica Doyle, D.R.E. Students 625.

ROSELLE PARK, UNION CO., THE ASSUMPTION (1907), (Italian), Rev. Ken Evans, Admin.
Res.: 113 Chiego Pl., 07204. Tel: 908-245-1107; Fax: 908-245-2789.
Catechesis/Religious Program—110 Chiego Pl., 07204. Tel: 908-245-6572. Students 560.

ROSELLE, UNION CO., CHURCH OF ST. JOSEPH THE CARPENTER (1895), Revs. George D. Gillen; John Spino; Nerva Dugue; Deacon Vincent Belluscio. Sisters of St. Joseph, Chestnut Hill
Res.: 157 E. Fourth Ave., 07203. Tel: 908-241-1250; Fax: 908-241-6311.
School— (1913), 150 E. Third Ave., 07203. Tel: 908-245-6560. Sisters 1; Lay Teachers 24; Students 390.
Catechesis/Religious Program—Tel: 908-245-2119. Students 52.
Convent—135 E. Fourth Ave., 07203. Tel: 908-245-1594.

RUTHERFORD, BERGEN CO., ST. MARY'S (1908), Revs. Michael J. Kreder; Charles W. Hartling; Deacons John Di Meo; Michael Matthews.
Res.: 91 Home Ave., 07070. Tel: 201-438-2200; Fax: 201-438-1098.
School— (1916), 72 Chestnut St., 07070. Tel: 201-933-8410; Fax: 201-531-9020. Lay Teachers 20; Students 290.
High School— (1928), 64 Chestnut St., 07070. Tel: 201-933-5220; Fax: 201-933-0834. Lay Teachers 37; Students 363.
Catechesis/Religious Program—Tel: 201-438-2476. Students 563.
Convent—Tel: 201-933-2910.

SADDLE BROOK, BERGEN CO.

1—KOREAN MARTYRS (1998), (Korean), Revs. John Hee Dong Park (Korea, South); Deog-Su Han, Admin.
Res.: 585 Saddle River Rd., 07663. Tel: 201-703-0002; Fax: 201-703-7111.

2—ST. PHILIP THE APOSTLE (1953), Revs. Robert G. McBride, J.C.L.; Matthew Fonseka; Thomas J. Kenna; Deacons Philip Salerno; Joseph Mantinzo.
Res.: 488 Saddle River Rd., 07663. Tel: 201-843-1888; Fax: 201-368-9161.
Catechesis/Religious Program—Tel: 201-843-2240. Students 520.

SADDLE RIVER BOROUGH, BERGEN CO., ST. GABRIEL THE ARCHANGEL (1952), Rev. Msgr. Robert J. Fuhrman; Rev. Stephen J. Fichter.
Res.: 3 W. Church Rd., 07458. Tel: 201-327-5663; Fax: 201-327-7063.
School—St. John's Academy, Tel: 201-664-6364; Fax: 201-664-8096. (See St. John's Parish, Hillsdale)
Catechesis/Religious Program—Tel: 201-825-0275. Students 295.

SCOTCH PLAINS, UNION CO.

1—ST. BARTHOLOMEW (1948), Revs. Donald K. Hummel; John J. Lester; Antonio Kuizon (Philippines); Joy Alookaran (India). In Res., Rev. John Paladino.
Res.: 2032 Westfield Ave., 07076. Tel: 908-322-5192; Fax: 908-322-2598.
School—St. Bartholomew Interparochial (1950),Tel: 908-322-4265. Religious Teachers Filippini 4; Lay Teachers 15; Students 239.
Catechesis/Religious Program—Tel: 908-322-2359. Students 467.
Convent—Tel: 908-322-5619.

2—IMMACULATE HEART OF MARY (1964), Very Rev. John F. Kennedy, V.F.; Rev. Charles Alookaran (India); Most Rev. Michael Pateta; Rev. Robert Patterson (Retired).
Res.: 1571 S. Martine Ave., 07076. Tel: 908-889-2100 Fax: 908-889-9477.
Catechesis/Religious Program—Jeanne Fox, D.R.E.; Sr. Elizabeth Cahill, S.C., D.R.E. Students 790.

SECAUCUS, HUDSON CO., IMMACULATE CONCEPTION (1903), Revs. Joseph P. Pietropinto; Jose M. Abalon.
Res. 1219 Paterson Plank Rd., 07094. Tel: 201-863-4840; Fax: 201-863-3537.
School— (1949), 760 Post Pl., 07094. Tel: 201-864-9346; Fax: 201-864-0245. Lay Teachers 8; Students 194.
Catechesis/Religious Program—Tel: 201-863-4840, Ext 28. Students 600.

SHORT HILLS, ESSEX CO., ST. ROSE OF LIMA (1852), [CEM] Rev. Msgr. George R. Trabold, J.C.L.; Revs. Edmund G. Bernauer (Retired); Kevin A. Gugliotta; Richard Cabezas; Deacons Joseph M. Persinger; Daniel G. McCarren Jr. In Res., Rev. Msgr. Vincent P. Coburn (Retired).
Res.: 50 Short Hills Ave., 07078. Tel: 973-379-3912; Fax: 973-379-6157.
School— (1869), 52 Short Hills Ave., 07078. Tel: 973-379-3973; Fax: 973-379-3722. Lay Teachers 35 Students 331.
Catechesis/Religious Program—52 Short Hills Ave., 07078. Tel: 973-376-1960; Fax: 973-376-3818. Students 722.

SOUTH ORANGE, ESSEX CO., OUR LADY OF SORROWS (1887), Rev. Msgr. John E. Doran, V.E.; Revs. Marc A. Vicari; James M. Moran.
Res.: 217 Prospect St., 07079. Tel: 973-763-5454; Fax: 973-763-9506.
School— (1890), 172 Academy St., 07079. Tel: 973-763-5169; Fax: 973-378-9781. Lay Teachers 24; Religious 1; Students 394.
Catechesis/Religious Program—Students 394.

SPRINGFIELD, UNION CO., ST. JAMES (1923), Revs. Robert B. Stagg; James Worth; Sr. Roseann M. Treston, S.S.J., Pastoral Assoc.; Deacons Jerry Bongiovanni; Michael DeRoberts; Daniel O'Neill.
Res.: 45 S. Springfield Ave., 07081. Tel: 973-376-3044; Fax: 973-376-0560.
School—41 S. Springfield Ave., 07081. Tel: 973-376-5194. Ms. Patricia Dolansky. Lay Teachers 12; Students 200.
Catechesis/Religious Program—Tel: 973-376-2061. Ms. Diane McGee, D.R.E. Students 530.

SUMMIT, UNION CO., ST. TERESA'S (1863), [CEM] Rev. Msgr. Robert E. Harahan; Revs. Thomas F. Blind; Bruce E. Harger; Sr. Winifred Tormey, S.S.J., Pastoral Assoc.; Mr. David O'Brien, Pastoral Assoc.; Deacons Charles Cederroth; Frank Gisoldi; Alcides Vega. In Res., Rev. Frank McNulty.
Res.: 306 Morris Ave., 07901. Tel: 908-277-3700; Fax: 908-273-5909.
Catechesis/Religious Program—Tel: 908-273-6975; Fax: 908-273-1770. Students 1,361.

TEANECK, BERGEN CO., ST. ANASTASIA'S (1908), Revs. Daniel O'Neill, O.Carm.; Peter McGarry, O.Carm.; Gerard Heinen, O.Carm.; Deacon Roland Bianchi.
Res.: 1095 Teaneck Rd., 07666. Tel: 201-837-3354; Fax: 201-837-3360.
School—St. Cecilia's Interparochial School (See St. Cecilia, Englewood. Tel: 201-568-2615)
Catechesis/Religious Program—Tel: 201-837-3356. Sr. Adrienne Bradley, S.S.J., D.R.E. Students 259.
Convent—Tel: 201-837-3153.

TENAFLY, BERGEN CO., OUR LADY OF MOUNT CARMEL (1873), Revs. Ashley Harrington, O.Carm.; Peter Byrth, O.Carm.
Res.: 10 County Rd., 07670. Tel: 201-568-0545; Fax: 201-568-3215.
School— (1879),Tel: 201-567-6491. Lay Teachers 16; Students 234.
Catechesis/Religious Program—Tel: 201-871-4662. Students 444.

UNION CITY, HUDSON CO.

1—ST. ANTHONY OF PADUA (1899), (Italian), Revs. Ilario Crepaz (Italy); Fabio Venturini; Carlos Flor.
Res.: 615 Eighth St., 07087. Tel: 201-867-3818; Fax: 201-867-8859.
School—700 Central Ave., 07087. Tel: 201-864-5605; Fax: 201-223-1101. Religious Teachers Filippini 2; Lay Teachers 12; Students 210.
Catechesis/Religious Program—Students 275.

2—ST. AUGUSTINE'S (1886), Revs. Pedro Navarro, Admin.; Felipe Lopez; Deacons John McCarthy; Edwardo Pons; Eduardo Donoso.
Res.: 3900 New York Ave., 07087. Tel: 201-863-0233.
School— (1891), 3920 New York Ave., 07087. Tel: 201-865-5319; Fax: 201-865-2567. Sisters of Charity 4; Lay Teachers 18; Students 370.
Catechesis/Religious Program—Tel: 201-863-0233; Fax: 201-863-1341. Students 1,000.
Convent—312 39th St., 07083. Tel: 201-348-0527.

3—HOLY FAMILY (1857), Revs. Francisco J. Legarra, O.A.R.; Alberto Fuente, O.A.R. (Spain), Vicar.
Res.: 530 35th St., 07087. Tel: 201-867-6535; Fax: 201-867-1357.
Catechesis/Religious Program—Miss Carol Stronach, D.R.E.

4—STS. JOSEPH AND MICHAEL (1887; 1851), Revs. Fernando Carranza, Admin.; Robert Santamaria; Deacons Thomas Barrett; Asterio Velasco; Ricardo Flores.
Res.: 1314 Central Ave., 07087. Tel: 201-865-2325; Fax: 201-348-4412.
School—Mother Seton Grammar School, 1501 New York Ave., 07087. Tel: 201-863-8433; Fax: 201-863-8145. Lay Teachers 9; Students 200.
Catechesis/Religious Program—Tel: 201-863-8145. Students 350.

5—ST. ROCCO'S (1912), Revs. Manuel D. Rios, Admin.; Cresencio Balino.
Res.: 4206 Kennedy Blvd., 07087. Tel: 201-863-1427; Fax: 201-863-3877.
Catechesis/Religious Program—Students 59.
Mission House—4214 Kennedy Blvd., 07087. Tel: 201-863-5727.

UNION, UNION CO.

1—HOLY SPIRIT (1963), Rev. Msgrs. Vincent J. Doyle, J.C.L.; John H. Koenig, Pastor Emeritus (Retired); Revs. Edward G. Furrevig; James M. Manos; John M. Ballweg, Weekend Asst. (Retired).
Res.: 971 Suburban Rd., 07083. Tel: 908-687-3327; Fax: 908-687-1312.
School—Morris Ave. & Suburban Rd., 07083. Tel: 908-687-8415. Lay Teachers 14; Students 218.
Catechesis/Religious Program—984 Suburban Rd., 07083. Tel: 908-964-7533. Students 665.

2—ST. MICHAEL'S (1928), Revs. Matthias T. Conva; Charles B. McDermott; Anthony Onyekwelu; Bartley Baker; Sr. Ann Dominic, O.P., Pastoral Assoc. for Social Concerns; Joan Conlon, Business Mgr.
Res.: 1212 Kelly St., 07083. Tel: 908-688-1232; Fax: 908-810-1076.
School— (1931), 1211 Orange Ave., 07083. Tel: 908-688-1063; Fax: 908-687-7927. Mrs. Adele Ellis. Sisters of St. Dominic 1; Lay Teachers 23; Students 320.
Catechesis/Religious Program—Tel: 908-964-0965. Carol Skrocki, D.R.E. Students 1,025.
Convent—Tel: 908-686-3839.

UPPER MONTCLAIR, ESSEX CO., ST. CASSIAN (1895), Revs. John G. Judge; Robert M. Brennan.
Res.: 187 Bellevue Ave., 07043. Tel: 973-744-2850; Fax: 973-744-6187.
School—190 Lorraine Ave., 07043. Tel: 973-746-1636; Fax: 973-746-3271. Lay Teachers 15; Students 210.
Catechesis/Religious Program—Students 450.

UPPER SADDLE RIVER, BERGEN CO., CHURCH OF THE PRESENTATION (1961), Rev. Msgr. Thomas Ivory; Rev. Larry Evans II.
Office—271 W. Saddle River Rd., 07458. Tel: 201-327-1313; Fax: 201-818-0722.
Res.: 41 Riverview Ter., 07458.
School—St. Paul's Interparochial School (1990),Tel: 201-327-1108; Fax: 201-327-6197. (See St. Paul, Ramsey)
Catechesis/Religious Program—Tel: 201-327-3055; Fax: 201-327-8430. Students 1,373.

VERONA, ESSEX CO., OUR LADY OF THE LAKE (1923),

Revs. Michael A. Hanly; James V. Teti; Deacons Pat Vuolo; Michael Maione.
Res.: 32 Lakeside Ave., 07044. Tel: 973-239-5696; Fax: 973-239-7190.
School— (1924), 22 Lakeside Ave., 07044. Tel: 973-239-1160; Fax: 973-239-6496. Sr. Mary Agnes Sullivan, O.P., Prin. Sisters 2; Lay Teachers 10; Students 253.
*Catechesis/Religious Program—*Tel: 973-239-7643. Students 744.

WALLINGTON, BERGEN CO., MOST SACRED HEART OF JESUS (1942), (Polish), [CEM] Very Rev. Canon Felix R. Marciniak; Revs. Stephen D. D'Andrea; Henryk Wiecek.
Res.: 127 Paterson Ave., 07057. Tel: 973-778-7405; Fax: 973-778-7750.
School— (1943), 6 Bond St., 07057. Tel: 973-777-4817; Fax: 973-777-4982. Sisters 3; Lay Teachers 14; Students 175.
*Catechesis/Religious Program—*Tel: 973-777-9505; Fax: 973-778-7750; 973-777-4982. Students 361.

WASHINGTON TOWNSHIP, BERGEN CO., OUR LADY OF GOOD COUNSEL (1959), Rev. Msgr. Thomas A. McCarthy; Rev. Stephen J. Duffe; Sr. Joseph Miriam Blackwell, M.S.B.T., Pastoral Assoc.
Res.: 668 Ridgewood Rd., 07676. Tel: 201-664-6624; Fax: 201-664-0095.
School—Our Lady of Mercy Interparochial School (See Our Lady of Mercy, Park Ridge. Tel: 201-391-3838; Fax: 201-391-5614)
*Catechesis/Religious Program—*Tel: 201-664-1679. Sr. Brenda E. Rowe, R.S.M., D.R.E. Students 338.

WEEHAWKEN, HUDSON CO., ST. LAWRENCE'S (1887), Rev. Robert E. Emery, J.C.L.
Res.: 22 Hackensack Ave., 07086. Tel: 201-863-6464; Fax: 201-863-6656.
School—Hoboken Catholic Academy See separate listing under St. Ann's, Hoboken.
*Catechesis/Religious Program—*Students 150.

WEST NEW YORK, HUDSON CO.

1—ST. JOSEPH OF THE PALISADES (1875), (Hispanic), Bro. David Arias, O.A.R., D.D.; Revs. Richard J. Carrington, Admin.; Agustin Pedrosa, S.M. (Spain); Ordanico De La Pena; Robert J. Cid; Randy Guillen.
Res.: 6401 Palisade Ave., 07093. Tel: 201-854-7006; Fax: 201-861-7799.
School— (1872), 6408 Palisade Ave., 07093. Tel: 201-861-3227; Fax: 201-861-5744. Franciscan Missionary Sisters of the Sacred Heart 3; Lay Teachers 20; Students 420.
*High School—*5400 Broadway, 07093. Tel: 201-864-9700. Priests 3; Sisters 2; Lay Teachers 22; Students 300.
*Catechesis/Religious Program—*Students 900.
Chapel—North Bergen, Immaculate Heart of Mary Chapel—Cor Jesu
*Convent—*Tel: 201-861-3337.

2—ST. MARY HELP OF CHRISTIANS (1895), Rev. Carlo Fortunio, O.P. (Italy), Admin. In Res., Rev. Angelo Pachetti.
Res.: 6502 Jackson St., 07093. Tel: 201-868-9444; Fax: 201-868-6451.
*Catechesis/Religious Program—*Students 200.

3—OUR LADY OF LIBERA (1902), (Italian), Rev. Philip J. Rotunno; Deacon Rosendo Abreu.
Res.: 5808 John F. Kennedy Memorial Blvd., 07093. Tel: 201-867-2642.
*School—*5800 John F. Kennedy Memorial Blvd., 07093. Tel: 201-864-5557. Sisters 3; Lay Teachers 14; Students 385.
Convent—Religious Teachers Filippini, Tel: 201-868-6113.
*Catechesis/Religious Program—*Students 150.

WEST ORANGE, ESSEX CO.

1—ST. JOSEPH'S (1934), Revs. Richard G. Francesco; Kevin J. Schott; Deacons Luis Velo; Richard O'Hara. In Res., Rev. Msgr. Thomas J. Daly (BO) (Retired).
Res.: 44 Benvenue Ave., 07052. Tel: 973-669-3221; Fax: 973-669-0385.
School— (1956), 8 St. Cloud Pl., 07052. Tel: 973-731-3503; Fax: 973-731-2117. Lay Teachers 11; Students 145.
*Catechesis/Religious Program—*Pauline Alger, Pastoral Assoc. & D.R.E. Students 330.

2—OUR LADY OF LOURDES (1914), Revs. Joseph A. Petrillo; James N. Chern.
Res.: 1 Eagle Rock Ave., 07052. Tel: 973-325-0110; Fax: 973-325-9105.
School— (1925), 100 Valley Way, 07052. Tel: 973-325-0555; Fax: 973-243-1480. Mary Cassels, Prin. Sisters of Charity 1; Lay Teachers 8; Students 200.
*Catechesis/Religious Program—*Tel: 973-325-0029. Sr. Ann Sweeney, O.P., D.R.E. Students 183.
*Convent—*Tel: 973-325-0318; Fax: 973-325-0691.

WESTFIELD, UNION CO.

1—ST. HELEN (1968), Rev. Msgr. William C. Harms; Revs. Donald E. McLaughlin; Lawrence J. Fama.
Res.: 1600 Rahway Ave., 07090. Tel: 908-232-1214; Fax: 908-317-5459.
School—Holy Trinity Interparochial School (1991),Tel: 908-233-0484; Fax: 908-233-6204. Co-Sponsored. (See Holy Trinity Parish, Westfield)
*Catechesis/Religious Program—*Tel: 908-233-8757. Students 1,715.

2—HOLY TRINITY (1872), Rev. Msgr. Joseph P. Masiello, V.F.; Rev. Donald F. Cialone; Sr. Joan Connelly, S.S.N.D., Pastoral Assoc.; Deacon Thomas A. Pluta.
Res.: 315 First St., 07090. Tel: 908-232-8137; Fax: 908-654-8780.
School— (1991),(Grades PreK-8), 336 First St., 07090. Tel: 908-233-0484; 908-233-1899 Mountainside Campus; Fax: 908-233-6204. Co-Sponsored, Holy Trinity Interparochial School. Lay Teachers 28; Students 470.
*Catechesis/Religious Program—*Tel: 908-233-7455. Sr. Kathleen J. Burton, S.S.J., D.R.E. Students 775.

WESTWOOD, BERGEN CO., ST. ANDREW'S (1889), [CEM] Revs. Ward P. Moore; Gerald T. Hahn; Deacons Joseph J. Paulillo; Robert S. Pontillo; Mary Jean Conroy, Pastoral Assoc., Child Catechesis; Barbara Stewart, Pastoral Assoc., Parish Ministries; Alan Pitman, Pastoral Assoc., Teens.
Res.: 120 Washington Ave., 07675. Tel: 201-666-1100; Fax: 201-722-1432.
School—St. John's Academy (See St. John the Baptist, Hillsdale. Tel: 201-664-6364; Fax: 201-664-8096)
*Catechesis/Religious Program—*Tel: 201-664-6777. Students 722.

WOOD-RIDGE, BERGEN CO., OUR LADY OF THE ASSUMPTION (1926), Revs. Brian Cullinane, O.F.M.; Paul Sinnema, O.F.M.; Thomas Kelly, O.F.M.
Res.: 143 First St., Wood Ridge, 07075. Tel: 201-438-5555; Fax: 201-438-6747.
*School—*151 First St., Wood Ridge, 07075. Tel: 201-933-0239; Fax: 201-438-6408. Lay Teachers 21; Students 272.
Catechesis/Religious Program—Hayes Center, 142 Second St.. Tel: 201-933-6118. Students 425.
*Convent—*Tel: 201-939-4274.

WOODCLIFF LAKE, BERGEN CO., OUR LADY MOTHER OF THE CHURCH (1967), Rev. Msgr. Cajetan P. Salemi; Rev. Thomas G. Arminio, Pastor Emeritus. In Res., Rev. Msgr. Joseph C. Manz (Retired).
Church: 209 Woodcliff Ave., 07675. Tel: 201-391-2826; Fax: 201-391-7101.
*Rectory—*130 Apple Ridge, 07675.
School—St. John the Baptist Interparochial School, Tel: 201-664-3131; Fax: 201-664-0772. (See St. John the Baptist, Hillsdale)
*Catechesis/Religious Program—*Tel: 201-391-7400. Students 281.

WYCKOFF, BERGEN CO., ST. ELIZABETH (1902), Rev. Msgr. Donald E. Guenther; Rev. Michael A. Saporito; Deacons Robert Kratchman; Joseph De Maria; William J. Toth.
Res.: 700 Wyckoff Ave., 07481. Tel: 201-891-1122; Fax: 201-847-8518.
*School—*Greenwood Ave., 07481. Tel: 201-891-1481; Fax: 201-891-3147. Lay Teachers 25; Students 274.
*Catechesis/Religious Program—*Tel: 201-891-3262; Fax: 201-891-3708. Marlene Malenda, D.R.E. Students 1,177.

Hospital Chaplaincy

NEWARK. *Office of Health Care Personnel.* Revs. Manuel Cruz, Archdiocesan Dir., St. Michael's Medical Center, 306 Martin Luther King Blvd., 07104. Tel: 973-877-2572, Alan F. Guglielmo, Coord. Health Care Apostolate Cont. Ed., 306 Martin Luther King Blvd., 07104. Tel: 973-743-0220.
Coordinator for Health Care Apostolate Continuing Education, St. Michael's Medical Center: 306 Martin Luther King Blvd., 07104. Tel: 973-743-0220. Rev. Alan Euglielmo.

Bergen County

ENGLEWOOD. *Englewood Hospital & Medical Center,* Formerly Englewood Hospital350 Engle St., 07631. Tel: 201-894-3000. Revs. Mathew Chandrankunnel, Chap. (Adjunct), John E. Komar, Chap.

HACKENSACK. *Hackensack University Medical Center,* 30 Prospect St., 07601. Tel: 201-996-2000; 201-996-2345. Revs. Alphonsus Ezeoke, Chap. (Adjunct), Peter Igwilo, Chap. (Adjunct), Anthony Udogu, Chap. (Adjunct).

PARAMUS. *Bergen Regional Medical Center,* 230 E. Ridgewood Ave., 07652. Tel: 201-967-4177; Fax: 201-967-4277. Revs. Joseph Buzzerio, Chap., Sebastian Fernando, Chap. (Adjunct), Marcellinis Uwandu, Chap. (Adjunct), Deacon Victor Peterson, Hospital Min.

RIDGEWOOD. *Valley Hospital,* 223 N. Van Dien Ave., 07450. Tel: 201-447-8150. Revs. Mert Cordero, Chap., Noel Morales, Dir. & Chap.

TEANECK. *Holy Name Hospital,* 718 Teaneck Rd., 07666. Tel: 201-833-3000; 201-833-3243 (Pastoral Care). Sr. Lois Jablonski, S.S.J., M.Div., Pastoral Staff, Revs. Thomas Tharayil, Chap. (Adjunct), Paterno Gorospe, Chap., Deacons Willy Malarcher, Chap., Edward Caceres, Chap.

WESTWOOD. *Pascack Valley Hospital,* 250 Old Hook Rd., 07675. Tel: 201-358-3000. Revs. Thomas Norton, Chap., Noel Morales, Chap.

Essex County

NEWARK. *Columbus Hospital,* 495 N. 13th St., 07107. Tel: 201-268-1400. Rev. Robert Tooman, Chap.
Beth Israel Medical Center, Formerly Beth Israel Hospital201 Lyons Ave., 07112. Tel: 973-926-7000; 973-926-7178 (Pastoral Care). Revs. Thomas R. McLaughlin, Chap., Christopher Anyanwu, (Adjunct).
St. James Hospital, 155 Jefferson St., 07105. Tel: 973-589-1300. Sr. Dolores Cervi, Pastoral Staff. Tel: 973-465-2671, Rev. Arokiasamy Irudayanathan, Chap.
St. Michael Medical Center, 306 Martin Luther King Blvd., 07102. Tel: 973-877-5467. Rev. Msgr. Jose Agan, Chap., Revs. John F. X. Bauman, Chap., Manuel Cruz, Chap., Deacons Edward McFadden, Chap., Rafael Vargas, Chap.
University of Medicine & Dentistry (UMDNJ), 100 Bergen St., 07103. Tel: 973-972-4300. Rev. Eustace Edomobi, Chap. (Adjunct), Deacons Leo Montini, Hospital Min., Cesar A. Ortega-Escobar, Hospital Min.

BELLEVILLE. *Clara Maass Medical Center,* Formerly Clara Maass HospitalOne Clara Maass Dr., 07109. Tel: 973-450-2000. Revs. John Donohue, Chap. (Adjunct), George Joseph, Chap.

CEDAR GROVE. *Essex County Hospital Center,* 125 Fairview Ave., 07009. Tel: 973-228-8000. Rev. Polycarp Nnajiofir, Chap. (Adjunct).
St. Vincent Nursing Home, 315 E. Lindsley Rd., 07009. Tel: 973-754-4800. Sr. Elizabeth Ann Noonan, S.C., Chap.

EAST ORANGE. *Veterans Administration Hospital,* Tremont Ave. & Center St., 07019. Tel: 973-676-1000; 973-972-5688 (Pastoral Care). Rev. George Kelly, C.SS.R.

LIVINGSTON. *St. Barnabas Medical Center,* 94 Old Short Hills Rd., 07039. Tel: 973-533-5015. Revs. Richard Chilmark, Chap., Peter Vinh Q. Nguyen, Chap.

MONTCLAIR. *Mountainside Hospital,* One Bay Ave., 07042. Tel: 973-429-6000; 973-429-6047 (Pastoral Care). Revs. Bernard Fernando, Chap., William Gyure, Chap.

ORANGE. *Hospital Center at Orange,* 188 S. Essex St., 07051. Tel: 973-266-2000. Rev. Felix Ugwuozor, Chap. (Adjunct).
Pope John Paul II Pavilion, Formerly Pope John Paul II Pavilion at St. Mary's135 S. Centre St., 07050. Tel: 973-266-3000. Rev. Felix Ugwuozar, Chap.

WEST ORANGE. *Kessler Institute for Rehabilitation,* 1199 Pleasant Valley Way, 07052. Tel: 973-731-3600. Rev. Louis Pambello, Chap.

Hudson County

BAYONNE. *Bayonne Medical Center,* Formerly Bayonne Hospital29 E. 29th St., 07002. Tel: 201-858-5000. Rev. J. M. Patricius.

HOBOKEN. *St. Mary's Hospital,* 308 Willow Dr., 07030. Tel: 201-418-1000. Rev. Michael Onyekwele.

JERSEY CITY. *Christ Hospital,* 176 Palisades Ave., 07304. Tel: 201-795-8200. Rev. Aloysius Ezenwata, Sr. Nancy Krug.
Jersey City Medical Center, 50 Baldwin Ave., 07304. Tel: 201-915-2000. Rev. Msgr. Edmundo A. Surban.

KEARNY. *West Hudson Hospital,* 206 Bergen Ave., 07032. Tel: 201-955-7000. Rev. Joseph Khai Vu.

NORTH BERGEN. *Palisades Medical Center,* Formerly Palisades General Hospital7600 River Rd., 07047. Tel: 201-854-5000. John T. Michalczak.

Union County

BERKELEY HEIGHTS. *Runnells Specialized Hospital,* Formerly Runnells County Hospital40 Watchung Ave., 07922. Tel: 908-771-5700. Rev. Charles I. Anemelu.

ELIZABETH. *Trinitas Hospital,* 225 Williamson St., 07202. Tel: 201-418-1000. Revs. Brendan Quinn, Edward A. Haber (Retired), Sr. Mary Corrigan, Pastoral Staff.

PLAINFIELD. *Muhlenberg Regional Medical Center,* Formerly Muhlenberg Medical CenterPark Ave. & Randolph Rd., 07061. Tel: 908-668-2000. Rev. John Paladino, Deacon Robert Gurske, Hospital Min.

RAHWAY. *Rahway Hospital,* 865 Stone St., 07065. Tel: 732-381-4200. Rev. William Reed, Deacon J. William Courtney, Hospital Min.

SUMMIT. *Overlook Hospital,* 99 Beauvoir Ave., 07902. Tel: 908-522-2000. Rev. John P. Holian, Pastoral Staff, Sr. Patricia Murphy, S.S.J., Dir.

UNION. *Union Hospital,* 1000 Galloping Hill Rd., 07083. Tel: 908-687-1900. Rev. George M. Keating (Retired).

Prison Ministry

NEWARK. *Office of Prison Ministry*, P.O. Box 9500, 07104. Tel: 973-497-4223; Fax: 973-497-4219. Deacon David B. Loman, Dir.

Bergen County

HACKENSACK. *Bergen County Jail*, 160 S. River Rd., 07601. Tel: 201-527-3000. Rev. Joseph Buzzerio.

PARAMUS. *Bergen County Juvenile Detention Center*, 296 E. Ridgewood Ave., 07652. Tel: 201-599-6185. Deacon Michael J. Cechony.

Essex County

NEWARK. *Cura (Community United to Rehabilitate Addicts)*, P.O. Box 180, 07101-0180. Tel: 973-622-3570. Revs. Anthony Bico, Robert J. Cormier, Bro. Thomas Corey.

Essex County Jail, 60 Nelson Pl., 07104. Tel: 973-621-5163. Rev. Paul J. Nolan, Prison Min., Deacon Ceasear Ortega, Pastoral Staff, Gregory Quinn, Pastoral Staff.

Essex County Juvenile Detention Center, Formerly Essex County Juvenile Correctional Center208 Sussex Ave., 07103. Tel: 973-497-4735. Rev. Anthony Bico.

Northern State Prison, 168 Frontage Rd., 07114. Tel: 973-465-0068, Ext. 4505. Revs. Thomas C. Roberts, Robert Cormier, Deacons Thomas M. Smith, Prison Min., David Loman, Mr. Edward Boyle.

CALDWELL. *Essex County Jail Annex*, 45 Elm Rd., 07006. Tel: 973-364-5341. Rev. Paul J. Nolan.

Hudson County

SECAUCUS. *Hudson County Juvenile Correctional Center*, Formerly Hudson County Youth Juvenile Correctional Center635 County Ave., 07094. Tel: 201-319-3750 (Promise/Outreach Ministry). Rev. Giordano Belanich, Sr. Antonelle Chunka, Pastoral Staff, Bro. Thomas Corey, Pastoral Staff.

SOUTH KEARNY. *Hudson County Correctional Center*, 35 Hackensack Ave., 07032. Tel: 973-491-5500. Rev. Stephen J. Toth, Deacons Joseph Del Monte, Prison Min., Wilfred LeConte, Prison Min., Juan Suarez, Prison Min.

Talbot Hall Assessment Center, Tel: 201-491-5500. Rev. Stephen J. Toth, Deacon Edward A. Campanella, Prison Min.

Union County

NEWARK. *Delaney Hall Assessment Center*, Formerly Delaney Hall451 Doremus Ave., 07105. Tel: 908-289-6768. Rev. Paul Nolan, Mr. Michael York.

ELIZABETH. *Elizabeth Federal Detention Center*, 625 Evans St., 07201. Tel: 908-352-3776. Rev. George F. Sharp.

Union County Jail, 15 Elizabethtown Plaza, 07207. Tel: 908-558-2636. Rev. Paul Nolan, Prison Min., Deacon Michael DeRoberts.

Special Assignment in the Archdiocese:

Rev. Msgr.—

Kleissler, Thomas A., Dir. Renew International

Revs.—

Ashe, Kevin P., Exec. Dir. Park Theatre Performing Arts Center, Inc.

Randl, Ewald, Neo-Catechumenate Communities

On Duty Outside the Archdiocese:

Rev. Msgrs.—

Casale, Franklyn M., 16500 Collins Ave., North Miami Beach, FL 33160.

Radano, John A., Villa Stritch, Via Della Nocetta 63, Rome 00164 Italy.

Tiboni, Vito, Veterans' Hospital, 800 Poly Pl., Apt. 15W, Brooklyn, NY 11209.

Revs.—

Acosta, Jorge E.

Alfaro, Gustavo A., SS. Peter & Paul Rooma Katoliku Kirik, Vene tn 18, Tallinn 10123 Estonia.

Arata, Miguel A., Tartu P. Neitsi Maarja Kogudus, Veski TN 1-1A, EE2400, Tartu, Estonia.

Arvay, Alfred S., 5128 Mentmore Ave., Spring Hill, FL 34606.

Baldacchino, Peter, Chancellor, R.C. Mission, OL of Divine Providence, Leeward Hwy., P.O. Box 340, Grand Turks Islands, Turks and Caicos Islands.

Barrow, Joseph A., Our Lady of Lourdes Church, 4423 Lasalle Ave., New Orleans, LA 70115.

Basile, Gioacchino, Parroquia San Jose, Apartado 25, Penuelas, PR 00624.

Bornhauser, Emmanuel, Holy Cross Mission, P.O. Box 70, Turks and Caicos Islands.

Carraro, Francesco, St. Raphael Parish, 162 Oak St., Bridgeport, CT 06604.

Ciriaco, Dominic G. (WDC), Oblates of St. Francis de Sales, De Sales Hall, Washington, DC 20017.

De La Pena, Jose Manuel, Our Lady of the Assumption, 404 Summer St., Boston, MA 02128.

DiGiovanni, Alfonso, SS. Peter & Paul R.K. Kirik, Vene TN 18, 10123, Tallin, Estonia.

Donini, Leone, Paroisse Notre Dame de Routes, 648 Chemin de Rigoumel, Toulon 83200 France.

Gonzalez, Luis P., Parish of Our Lady of Sorrows, 1006 Larch Ave., Takoma Park, MD 20912.

Gordon, John F.

Hall, Warren R., St. Elizabeth, 809 S. Broom St., Wilmington, DE 19805.

Ince, Owen F., Our Lady of Assumption, 404 Summer St., Boston, MA 02128.

Katompa, Zephyrin, St. Roseline Church, 409 Edouard Herriot Escallion, Toulon 83200 France.

Kirchner, James A., Cathedral Healthcare Partnership of NJ, 760 Alexander Rd., Princeton, 08543.

Koch, Eugene, St. Crispin's Friary, 420 E. 156th St., Bronx, NY 10455.

Kukura, Joseph W., Center for Ethics & Ministry, 935 Allwood Rd., Clifton, 07012.

Kunze, Robert W., St. Andrew's, 120 United States Ave., Gibbsboro, 08026.

Lee, David Seungyoon, Divine Word College, 1025 Michigan Ave., N.E., Washington, DC 20017.

Ligonde, Jean-Marie F., St. Charles Borromeo Church, 21505 Augusta Ave., Port Charlotte, FL 33952.

Livolsi, Sylvester J., Sanctuary of Mary, 252 Wantage Ave., Branchville, 07826.

Martin, Oscar, Our Lady of Divine Providence RC Mission, Leeward Hwy., P.O. Box 340, Turks and Caicos Islands.

Merdinger, Philip E., Brotherhood of Hope, 194 Summer Ave., Sumerville, MA 02143.

Miller, Frederick L., Pontifical North American College, 00120 Vatican City, Italy

Morelli, Attilip, St. Philomena Parish, 3300 N. Twelve Oaks Dr., Peoria, IL 61604.

Oddo Peter A., P.O. Box 11, Swartswood, 07877.

Papalia, Pasquale A., St. James, 94 Broad St., Red Bank, 07701.

Passant, Paul A.

Prindiville, Gerald T., Pastor, Our Lady of the Annunciation, 25 Donovan Ave., Maroubra, NSW 2035 Australia.

Regula, Ronald R., 14A Gramercy Lane, Manchester Township, 08759.

Russo, Michael A. (OAK), St. Mary College, Box 5136, Moraga, CA 94575.

Scaramella, Renzo L., Pastor, Our Lady of Providence, R.C. Mission, Leeward Hwy., P.O. Box 340, Turks & Caicos Islands, Turks and Caicos Islands.

Schute, Arthur B., 276 Orlando Blvd., Port Charlotte, FL 33954.

Starasinich, James E., Redemptoris Mater Seminary, 130 Chalan Seminariu, Yona, Guam, GU 96915.

West, Peter, Priests for Life, 128 Targee St., Staten Island, NY 10304.

Wilson, William P., Nativity of the Blessed Virgin Mary, 99 E. Tioga St., Tunkhannock, PA 18657.

Zaniewski, Jaroslaw, SS. Cyril & Methodius Seminary, 3535 Indian Trail, Orchard Lake, MI 48324.

Military Chaplains:

Revs.—

Beale, Kenneth R., Capt., 48FW/HC, Apo, AE 09464.

Berchmanz, Anthony, Chap., NCAS Miramar, P.O. Box 452013, San Diego, CA 92145.

Brosk, Steven J., 57 Sandy Stone Rd., Orangeville, PA 17859.

Cunha, Egionor, Lt., CHC USNR, Naval Support Facility, PSC 466 Box 18, Diego Garcia, AP 96595.

D'Emma, Gregory J., 4356 Varney Ave., Fort George Meade, MD 20755-5065.

Hamel, James A., PSC Box 3835, Apo, AP 96266.

Hanrahan, William P., Chap., 8413 Metzger #A, Elmendorf AFB, AK 99506.

Kokeram, Sudash J., O.L. of Mt. Carmel, 259 Oliver St., 07105.

Kopec, Rajmund, Capt., 428 Fourth St., Carlstadt, 07072.

Lesak, William P., 5904 Mount Eagle Dr., Alexandria, VA 22303.

Pawlikowski, Matthew, Capt., HSC ISB Unit 31520, North Camp, Apo, AE 09832.

Ubalde, Ulyssesl, Our Lady of Lourdes, 300 Central Ave., Mountainside, 07092.

Ugwuanya, Valentine C., P.O. Box 25592, Fayetteville, NC 28314.

Uhde, Peter (OG), 9920A Saratoga Rd., Fort Drum, NY 13602.

Retired:

Most Rev.—

Marconi, Dominic A., 238 E Blancke St., Linden, 07036.

Rev. Msgrs.—

Alba, Jose M., 9 Delgado St., Iloilo City 5000 Philippines.

Beggans, Joseph A., St. Catherine of Siena, Inc., F Ryerson Ave., Caldwell, 07006.

Bonelli, Theodore V., 120-B Ironwood Plaza, Monroe Twp., 08831.

Burke, James A., Nativity Church, 315 Prospect St., Midland Park, 07432.

Burns, G. Thomas, 1639 Kingsdown Rd., Sarasota, FL 34240.

Capozzelli, Emmanuel M., Rev. Msgr. James F. Kelley Residence, 247 Bloomfield Ave., Caldwell, 07006.

Casazza, David J., 426 Jefferson Ave., Avon-by-the-Sea, 07717.

Chiang, Joseph, St. John Vianney Residence, 60 Home Ave., Rutherford, 07070.

Coburn, Vincent P., 1802 Ravine Dr., Forked River, 08731.

Daly, Thomas J. (BO), St. Joseph's Rectory, 44 Benvenue Ave., West Orange, 07052.

Donovan, Joseph J., 1 Kensington Court, Jackson, 08527.

Duffy, Robert E., Alterra Wynwood, 520 Prospect Ave., West Orange, 07052.

Eid, Frederick M., Our Lady of Grace, 400 Willow Ave., Hoboken, 07030.

Fleming, Edward J., Immaculate Conception Seminary, Seton Hall University, South Orange, 07079.

Flusk, Joseph F., P.O. Box 66, Beachwood, 08722.

Gonzalez, Ricardo, 116 New Jersey Ave., Point Pleasant, 08742.

Hayes, Paul J., 197 Riverside Dr. N., Bricktown, 08724.

Hinrichsen, Carl D., Our Lady of Mercy Rectory, 2 Fremont Ave., Park Ridge, 07656.

Holmes, Richard J., Allendale Nursing Home, 85 Harreton Rd., Allendale, 07401.

Houghton, Francis J., 2316 Blue Jay Tr., Point Pleasant, 08742.

Hourihan, John P., 5 Johnson St., Monmouth Beach, 07750.

Johnson, James, St. John Vianney Residence, 60 Home Ave., Rutherford, 07070.

Kavin, Edward F., St. John Vianney Residence, 60 Home Ave., Rutherford, 07070.

Kelly, Martin, St. Aloysius Parish, 691 Westside Ave., 07304.

Koenig, John H., Msgr. James Kelly Residence, 247 Bloomfield Ave., Caldwell, 07006.

Komar, Michael A., 188 W. 31st Street, Bayonne, 07002.

Koplik, William J., St. Matthew, 555 Prospect Ave., Ridgefield, 07657.

Lennon, Robert T., St. Philomena's Church, 386 S. Livingston Ave., Livingston, 07039.

LoBianco, Francis R., 32 Woodland Ave., Jamaica Plain, MA 02130.

Madden, Thomas G., St. John Vianney Residence, 60 Home Ave., Rutherford, 07070.

Manz, Joseph C., Our Lady Mother of the Church, 209 Woodcliff Ave., Woodcliff Lake, 07675.

Marjanczyk, Joseph A., P.O. Box 456, Point Pleasant, 08742.

McMenemie, James P., S.T.L., St. Michael the Archangel, 624 Page Ave., Lyndhurst, 07071.

Murray, Harold A., 50 Willow Way, Manasquan, 08736.

O'Brien, Martin F., 13 Hedden Ter., North Arlington, 07031.

O'Leary, Thomas M., St. John the Baptist, 69 Valley St., Hillsdale, 07642.

Piazza, Benjamin A., St. Aloysius, 219 Bloomfield Ave., Caldwell, 07006.

Pollard, Raymond J., 2316 Blue Jay Tr., Point Pleasant, 08742.

Reynolds, Roger A., Our Lady of Victories, 81 Lynn St., Harrington Park, 07640.

Santora, Gerard M., St. John Vianney Residence, 60 Home Ave., Rutherford, 07070.

Sullivan, Edwin V., St. Catherine of Siena, 7 Ryerson Ave., Caldwell, 07006.

Turro, James C., Ph.D., Immaculate Conception Seminary, Seton Hall University, South Orange, 07079.

Wojtycha, Edward F., 1800 S.E. St. Lucie Blvd., 2202, Stuart, FL 34996.

Revs.—

Anta, Antonio, Plaza del Maiz, N. 3, Celanova-Orense, (Galicia) 328000 Spain.

Arminio, Alfonse M., Wharfside Manor Condo, 172 Park Rd., Apt. 17, Monmouth Beach, 07750.

Arminio, Thomas, 1057 Trent Pl., Union, 07083.

Ayamanathil, Mathew, Msgr. James F. Kelley Residence, 247 Bloomfield Ave., Caldwell, 07006.

Ballance, Harvey, 92 Edgemont Rd., Montclair, 07043.

Ballweg, John M., P.O. Box 202, Monmouth Beach, 07750.

Batista, George L., Palm Road W., West Palm Beach, FL 33406.

Bergeur, John X., Allendale Nursing Home, 85 Harreton Rd., Allendale, 07401.

Bernauer, Edmund G., St. Rose of Lima, 50 Short Hills Ave., Short Hills, 07078.

Borowik, John, St. John Vianney Residence, 60 Home Ave., Rutherford, 07070.

Carney, Aloysius S., JFK Hartwyck Nursing Home, 1340 Park Ave., Plainfield, 07060.
Cassidy, Joseph L., St. John Vianney Annex, 64 Home Ave., Rutherford, 07070.
Celiano, Alfred V., Ph.D., Seton Hall University, 400 South Orange Ave., South Orange, 07079.
Cestaro, Joseph J., St. John Vianney Residence, 60 Home Ave., Rutherford, 07070.
Coda, Joseph F., St. John Vianney Residence, 60 Home Ave., Rutherford, 07070.
Collins, Neil J., 135 Montgomery St., Jersey City, 07302.
Connors, Robert A., 330 Lincoln Ave., Avon-by-the-Sea, 07717.
Cooper, Donald A., 3220 Keith Ln., P.O. Box 3, Lavallette, 08735.
Cozzini, Robert P., Msgr. James F. Kelley Residence, 247 Bloomfield Ave., Caldwell, 07006.
Daly, Robert L. (MET), Immaculate Conception Rectory, 18 South St., Spotswood, 08884.
Danik, Daniel A., 2046 Ingalls Ave., Linden, 07036.
De Rosa, Arnold P., Ph.D., Seton Hall University, 400 South Orange Ave., South Orange, 07079.
Debold, Walter A., M.A., Seton Hall University, 400 South Orange Ave., South Orange, 07079.
Derbyshire, Joseph V., Runnels County Hospital, 40 Watchung Way, Berkeley Heights, 07922.
DiGirolamo, Dante, Eucharistic Shrine of the Adorable Face of Jesus, P.O. Box 455, Kearny, 07032.
DiPeri, Joseph B., Leisure Ridge, 303 Devon St., Lakehurst, 08733.
Dowling, John C., 585 Bloomfield Ave., Apt. 35, West Caldwell, 07006.
Driscoll, William D., 51 Monterey Ave., Teaneck, 07666.
Duffy, Stephen F., 422 Ocean Blvd., Unit 5J, Long Branch, 07740.
Fagan, Joseph P., Waterford Glen, 2021 Highway 35, Wall, 07719.
Farley, Leo O., Rev. Msgr. James F. Kelley Residence, 247 Bloomfield Ave., Caldwell, 07006.
Ferrazoli, Henry R., 149 Orlando Blvd., Toms River, 08757.
Finn, Francis J., 26 Kent Dr., Bricktown, 08723.
Fiorino, Dominic J., Msgr. James F. Kelley Residence, 247 Bloomfield Ave., Caldwell, 07006.
Foye, Thomas M., St. Andrew, 125 Broadway, Bayonne, 07002.
Frank, Joseph A., Rev. Msgr. James F. Kelley Residence, 247 Bloomfield Ave., Caldwell, 07006.
French, Walter V., 26 Rogerene Way, Landing, 07850.
Fu, Joseph, St. Bridget Chinese Catholic Center, 510 Cottage Home St., Los Angeles, CA 90012.
Fuino, Michael A., St. John Vianney Residence, 60 Home Ave., Rutherford, 07070.
Garoffolo, Vincent, Ashbrook Nursing Home, 1610 Raritan Rd., Scotch Plains, 07076.
Genzlinger, Walter L., Mt. Carmel, 99 Broadway, Jersey City, 07306.
Gibbons, John J., M.Div., 626 Aviary Way, Toms River, 08755.
Giblin, William M., Msgr. James F. Kelley Residence, 247 Bloomfield Ave., Caldwell, 07006.
Gibney, Robert G., Msgr. James F. Kelley Residence, 247 Bloomfield Ave., Caldwell, 07006.
Haber, Edward A., St. Mary's Church, 155 Washington Ave., 07202.
Halliwell, Robert J., St. Anthony's Church, 199 Walnut St., Northvale, 07647.
Hermanns, Harold T., St. John Vianney Residence, 60 Home Ave., Rutherford, 07070.
Herr, Charles W., St. John Vianney Residence, 60 Home Ave., Rutherford, 07070.
Heyndricks, Eugene P., 48A Stoneybrook Rd., Whiting, 08759.
Horgan, Timothy J., 102 Barbuda St., P.O. Box 3453, Toms River, 08756-3453.
Iaquinto, Robert, 41 Juniper St., Jersey City, 07305.
Jacunski, Robert D., Msgr. James F. Kelley Residence, 247 Bloomfield Ave., Caldwell, 07006.
Kasper, Eugene J., c/o Dr. & Mrs. Mitchell Kasper, 1 Oak Hill Drive, Bridgeton, 08003.
Kearney, Edward J., St. Patrick, 492 Bramhall Ave., Jersey City, 07304.
Keating, George M., St. Theresa, 541 Washington Ave., Kenilworth, 07033.
Kenny, Thomas A., 24 Chesapeake Ct., Barnegat, 08005.
Koerner, Frederick C., St. John Vianney Residence, 60 Home Ave., Rutherford, 07070.
Kowalski, Alfred J., St. Theresa, 541 Washington Ave., Kenilworth, 07033.
Krozser, John J., 1616 Georgetowne Blvd., Sarasota, FL 34232.
Langdon, Robert H., John Vianney Annex, 64 Home Ave., Rutherford, 07070.
Laudati, Joseph J., 5 Nostrand Dr., Toms River, 08757.
Lehman, Paul J., P.O. Box 499, Branchville, 07826.
Lennon, Peter F., Seton Hall University, 400 South Orange Ave., South Orange, 07079.
Leonard, Patrick J.
Looney, Mathew D., 3411 Seaview Rd., Lavallette, 08735.
Lukenda, Raymond T., 133 Liberty Ave., Linden, 07036.
Lynch, Thomas F., Allendale Nursing Home, 85 Harreton Rd., Allendale, 07401.
Macho, George S., 1825 Buttonwood Ave., Toms River, 08755.
Madden, John J., 60 Home Ave., Rutherford, 07070.
Mader, George L., Msgr. James F. Kelley Residence, 247 Bloomfield Ave., Caldwell, 07006.
Malanga, Salvatore T., Allendale Nursing Home, 85 Harreton Rd., Allendale, 07401.
Malkiewicz, Edward S., St. Aloysius, 691 Westside Ave., Jersey City, 07304.
Marchand, Gerald A., P.O. Box 3102, Point Pleasant, 08742.
Marciniak, Henry P.
Marcone, Eugene F., St. Anne's Church, 325 Second Ave., Garwood, 07027.
Marotta, Robert G., 600 County Ave., Apt. 108, Secaucus, 07094.
McFarland, James W., St. John Vianney Residence, 60 Home Ave., Rutherford, 07070.
McKenna, Denis R., McAuley Health Care Center, 1633 Hwy. 22, Watchung, 07069.
McKeon, Raymond T., St. Paul the Apostle, 14 Greenville Ave., Jersey City, 07305.
McNulty, Francis J., St. Teresa's, 306 Morris Ave., Summit, 07901.
McTague, Charles H., Holy Cross, 16 Church Sq., P.O. Box 73, Harrison, 07029.
Merzena, Carl J., Allendale Nursing Home, 85 Harreton Rd., Allendale, 07401.
Militello, Benedict P., St. Anthony, 199 Walnut St., Northvale, 07647.
Miller, Ferdinand B., 20 Buena Vista Dr., Brick, 08723-1530.
Miodowski, Leonard A., St. John Vianney Residence, 60 Home Ave., Rutherford, 07070.
Mohan, Bernard N., B.S., 409 Earl Dr., Brick, 08723.
Moran, Michael J., M.Div., 1833 Starboard Court, Toms River, 08753.
Morel, John J., 381 Park Ave., Apt. 2L, Scotch Plains, 07076.
Morley, John M., 1819 Boat Point Dr., Point Pleasant, 08742.
Morris, John J., 5424 Keystone Pl., Virginia Beach, VA 23464.
Mukalel, Joseph V., 2 Amherst Ct., Maplewood, 07040.
Mulvey, John J., 4424 Tatum St., Port Charlotte, FL 33948.
Murphy, Joseph H., 175 Mount Nebo Rd, Milford, 08848.
Myers, J. Edward, 432 Bethel Village Circle, Lehigh Acres, FL 33936.
Nardone, Richard M., Seton Hall University, 400 South Orange Ave., South Orange, 07079.
Nealon, Joseph W., 3360 Canoe Creek Ter., Palm City, FL 34990.
Netta, John G., P.O. Box 864, Oakhurst, 07755.
O'Brien, John E., 346 Mt. Pleasant Ave., Livingston, 07039.
O'Brien, Michael J., Romana Sacerdotalis, Via della Trasponhina, 18, Rome 00193 Italy.
O'Grady, Michael J., St. Andrew's Church, 125 Broadway, Bayonne, 07002.
O'Keefe, Maurice L., Allendale Nursing Home, 85 Harreton Rd., Allendale, 07401.
O'Leary, Robert A., 252 Genes Dr., Toms River, 08753.
Olsen, Thomas F., 26 E. 3rd St., Bayonne, 07002.
Olszewski, John S., Holy Spirit Church, 971 Suburban Rd., Union, 07083.
Osorio, Rudolfo B., 2438 Fruit Ave., S.E., Port Lucie, FL 34952.
Palasits, John A.
Patterson, Robert, P.O. Box 334, Waretown, 08758.
Pikula, Zygmunt, Holy Trinity-Epiphany, 207 Adams St., 07105.
Provinzano, Rocco, 16 Main St., Matawan, 07747.
Quinlan, Joseph M., 18 Ellsworth Ct., Red Bank, 07701.
Reinbold, Charles, Mt. St. Francis, 250 South St., Peekskill, NY 10566.
Revuelto, Manuel, Calle Julio Romero de Torres, 5 Urbanizacion Casablanca Marbella, Malaga 29600 Spain.
Rischmann, Edward, 146 Skyline Drive, Brick, 08724.
Rischmann, Robert J., 2805 68th St., Circle West, Bradenton, FL 34209.
Rock, John J., 200 Springfield Ave., Apt. 5023, Springfield, 07081.
Sapeta, Joseph S., St. Hedwig, 1062 Dewey Pl., 07202.
Scanlan, Charles V., Allendale Nursing Home, 85 Harreton Rd., Allendale, 07401.
Scherer, Donald R., P.O. Box 764, Robert, LA 70455.
Schreitmueller, Henry, 8 Poinsettia Ct., Kinnelon, 07405.
Schulte, William P., Brester's Guest House, 477 Mt. Prospect Ave., 07104.
Sheehan, Joseph G., St. John the Apostle, 1805 Penbrook Ter., Linden, 07036.
Sheerin, James O., St. John Vianney Residence, 60 Home Ave., Rutherford, 07070.
Shih, John M., Madonna Church, 340 Main St., Fort Lee, 07024.
Smith, Donald C., M.A., Seton Hall University, 400 South Orange Ave., South Orange, 07079.
Stulb, Joseph A., 100 Clinton St., #2C, Hoboken, 07030-2574.
Sullivan, James B., O.L. of the Blessed Sacrament, 28 Livingston Ave., Roseland, 07068.
Sweeney, John D., Allendale Nursing HOme, 85 Harreton Rd., Allendale, 07401.
Swenson, Walter J.F., 72 Windsor Pl., Kenilworth, 07033.
Swierzbinski, Edward, P.O. Box 342, Normandy Beach, 08739.
Szelest, Theodore A., Church of St. Mary, 280 Washington Ave., Dumont, 07628.
Theobald, Charles, 602 Bloomfield Ave., Montclair, 07042.
Waldron, John R., Allendale Nursing Home, 85 Harreton Rd., Allendale, 07401.
Wightman, John H., 1215 Windlass Dr., Manahawkin, 08050.
Wortmann, Joseph F., M.A., Seton Hall University, 400 South Orange Ave., South Orange, 07079.
Yeo, Wilfred, 4 Sumutka Ct., Carteret, 07008.
Zuber, Thaddeus F., St. John Vianney Residence, 60 Home Ave., Rutherford, 07070.

Permanent Deacons:
Coyle, Thomas J. (MAD), St. Thomas, Bloomfield
Abad, Ernesto, Our Lady of Lourdes, West Orange
Abreu, Rosendo, Our Lady of Libera, West New York
Accardi, Vincent, St. Mary's, Elizabeth
Acocella, Louis, St. Francis, Newark
Andrews, Marshall, Our Ladly of the Valley, Orange
Antola, Aldo P., Our Lady of Mt. Carmel, Nutley
Aristy, Jesus D., Our Lady of Libera, West New York
Baker, Robert A., Sr., St. Nicholas, Jersey City
Balestrieri, Anthony A., Our Lady of the Visitation, Paramus
Baltus, John M., St. Theresa, Kenilworth
Barrett, Thomas J., St. Joseph's and St. Michael's, Union City
Basch, Peter J., St. Ann, Hoboken
Bates, Harold L., Ascension, New Milford
Bellascio, Vincent, St. Joseph the Carpenter, Roselle
Benedetto, William R., Queen of Peace, North Arlington
Besida, Dennis J., St. Thomas, Bloomfield
Bongiovanni, Jerome C., St. James, Springfield
Bowen, Edward J., St. Peter the Apostle, River Edge
Bulgia, Thomas, Holy Name, East Orange
Byrnes, Richard, Our Lady of Good Counsel, Washington Township
Caceres, Edgar, Most Holy Name, Garfield
Campanella, Edward, St. John the Apostle, Linden
Campione, Frank J., St. Thomas More, Fairfield
Caporaso, Joseph, St. Anthony, Elizabeth
Carr, Patrick V., Community Hospital, Montclair
Casanova, Eliot, St. Aloysius, Jersey City
Cauceglia, Arthur J., Assumption, Wood-Ridge
Centenera, Leandro, Holy Trinity, Fort Lee
Charriez, Nestor, St. Patrick, Elizabeth
Chechony, Michael J., St. Joseph, Oradell
Class, Jose M., St. Augustine, Newark
Coffey, John J., St. Peter Claver, Montclair
Collins, Thomas F., Bergen Pines Hospital
Connelly, Earle S., Jr., Immaculate Conception, Secaucus
Cook, William R., On Duty Outside the Archdiocese
Cordero, Juan A., St. Nicholas, Jersey City
Courtney, J. William, St. Mary's, Rahway
Cruz, Primitivo, Sts. Peter & Paul, Hoboken
Daher, Paul D., Inactive
Daniele, Paul, St. John's, Newark
DeBenedictis, Thomas, Cathedral Basilica of the Sacred Heart, Newark
Degnon, Robert F., On Duty Outside the Archdiocese
Del Monte, Joseph J., Assumption-All Saints, Jersey City
DeLucca, Nicholas J., Our Lady of Mt. Carmel, Ridgewood
DeMaria, Joseph, Jr., St. Elizabeth, Wyckoff

DeRoberts, Michael, St. James the Apostle, Springfield
Di Meo, John J., St. Mary, Rutherford
Diaz-Rojas, Andres, (Retired)
Dickson, Joseph A., St. Matthew, Ridgefield
Donosso, Edward G., St. Augustine, Union City
Dwyer, Joseph A., Jr., Archdiocesan Center, Newark
Echevarria, Mario, St. Thomas Aquinas, Newark
Fargo, Nicholas C., Our Lady of Mercy, Jersey City
Fedison, Stanley F., Our Lady Mother of the Church, Woodcliff Lake
Fencik, Robert, St. Mary, Rahway
Fernandez, Jose R., Blessed Sacrament, Elizabeth
Ferraiuola, Lex, Our Lady of Mt. Carmel, Tenafly
Figueroa, Miguel, St. Michael, Newark
Fitzgerald, Michael J., St. Joseph, Bayonne
Flores, Ricardo, SS. Joseph & Michael, Union City
Francione, Joseph, St. Philomena, Livingston
Franco, Miguel A., St. Aloysius, Jersey City
Freeman, Gerald, St. Paul, Irvington
Garcia, David, Our Lady of the Lake, Verona
Gimbel, Herbert, St. Stephen, Kearny
Giordano, William J., Our Lady of Assumption, Bayonne
Gisoldi, Frank A., St. Teresa of Avila, Summit
Glasner, Robert, Our Lady of Good Counsel, Washington Township
Gomez, Alberto, St. Michael's, Newark
Gonzalez, Frank, St. Paul the Apostle, Jersey City
Gonzalez, Pedro, St. Boniface, Jersey City
Gray, John A., St. John the Baptist, Hillsdale
Grieder, Gustave, (Retired)
Gurske, Robert, St. Bartholomew, Scotch Plains
Haas, Henry W., Our Lady of Mt. Carmel, Montclair
Hemberger, Martin R., Holy Name Hospital, Teaneck; St. Michael, Palisades Park
Higgins, Leonard F., Our Lady of Mercy, Park Ridge
Hodges, Richard G., St. Pius X, Old Tappan
Hoefling, Edward J., On Duty Outside the Archdiocese
Hogan, John E., Church of the Assumption, Emerson
Huff, Sidney E., Holy Spirit-Help of Christians, East Orange
Inguaggiato, John M., Our Lady of Sorrows, South Orange
Jackson, Alonzo, St. Joseph, East Orange
Johnson, Leon, Christ the King, Jersey City
Joyce, William, Annunciation, Paramus
Kautz, Frederick, Immaculate Conception, Mahwah
Keturwitis, Henry J., Sts. Peter & Paul, Elizabeth
Kim, Joseph, Church of Korean Martyrs, Saddle Brook
King, Aidan P., St. Thomas More, Fairfield
Kliauga, Paul, Ascension, New Milford
Kratchman, Robert M., St. Elizabeth, Wyckoff
Langlois, Jose, St. Anthony of Padua, Union City
Leary, Gerald, St. Mary, Closter
LeConte, Wilfrid, St. Peter Claver, Montclair
Liptak, Stephen J., St. Aloysius, Jersey City
Loman, David B., Our Lady of Mt. Carmel, Tenafly
Loperena, Miguel A., Immaculate Heart of Mary, Newark
Lopez, Sixto, University Hospital, Newark
Lorza, Louis C., St. Mary of the Assumption, Elizabeth
Lubas, Joseph, St. Adalbert, Elizabeth
Lydon, Michael A., Holy Rosary, Edgewater
Lynch, John W., St. Helen, Westfield
Lynn, Walter, St. Joseph, Bogota
Macaluso, Martin P., S.F.O., St. Mary, Plainfield
Mackesy, Leonard J., Our Lady of Sorrows, Kearny
Maione, Michael, Our Lady of the Lake, Verona
Malanga, Joseph J., St. Valentine, Bloomfield
Malarcher, Willy J., Holy Name Hospital, Teaneck
Mantineo, Joseph L., St. Philip the Apostle, Saddle Brook
Marcelo, David S., Parish of the Resurrection, Jersey City
Marchese, Stephen, St. Joseph, Lodi
Markenstein, Aart, Holy Rosary, Jersey City
Marques, Albino P., Our Lady of Fatima, Newark
Martinez, Jose, St. Columba, Newark
Matos, William, Jr., St. Columba, Newark
Matthews, Michael, St. Mary, Rutherford
McCarren, Daniel G., Jr., St. Rose of Lima, Short Hills
McCarthy, John T., St. Augustine's, Union City
McDermott, William, St. Aloysius, Caldwell
McFadden, Edward, St. Michael's Hospital, Newark
McGarry, Richard M., St. Anne's, Fairlawn
McKenna, John J., Archdiocesan Center, Newark
McKeon, John W., St. Luke, Hohokus
McKnight, Keith, Christ the King, Jersey City
McLaughlin, Albert, Our Lady of Victory, Harrington Park
Mejias, Escolastico, Immaculate Heart of Mary, Newark
Mendez, Daniel, St. Augustine's, Newark
Messina, Dominic S., St. Thomas More, Fairfield
Messina, Vincent, Holy Trinity, Hackensack
Miner, Patrick F., St. John's, Bergenfield
Minichino, Leonard A., St. Catharine's, Glen Rock
Mohr Richard, Our Lady of Perpetual Help, Oakland
Molina, Osiris, St. Catherine, Hillside
Montanez, Luis, St. Joseph, Hoboken
Montemurro, Michael V., Little Flower, Berkeley Heights
Moore, Brett O., Sacred Heart, Lyndhurst
Moore, Willie, Blessed Sacrament; St. Charles Barromeo, Newark
Mueller, James A., St. Catherine, Glen Rock
Myers, William, Queen of Peace, North Arlington
Negron, Jose A., St. Michael, Newark
Nieves, Pedro, St. Mary, Plainfield
Niland, Joseph, Annunciation, Paramus
Nunez, Ernesto, Parish of the Resurrection, Jersey City
O'Connell, Brian, On Duty Outside the Archdiocese
O'Hara, Richard, St. Joseph, West Orange
O'Neill, Daniel, St. James, Springfield
Ortega, Cesar, St. Ann, Newark
Ortiz, Jaime, Parish of the Resurection, Jersey City
Osborne, Charles E., St. Rocco, Union City
Paulillo, Joseph J., St. Andrew's, Westwood
Persinger, Joseph M., St. Rose of Lima, Short Hills
Peterson, Victor, Bergen County Institutions
Petrozelli, James, St. Lawrence, Weehawken
Pluta, Thomas A, Holy Trinity, Westfield
Polanco, Cecilio S., St. Michael, Newark
Polanco, Leopoldo, St. Francis, Hackendack
Pons, Eduardo, St. Augustine, Union City
Pontillo, Robert, St. Andrew, Westwood
Porter, Edward W., St. Teresa, Summit; Permanent Diaconate Office
Puliatte, James, St. Joseph, Demarest
Quigliana, Pat, Our Lady of the Blessed Sacrament, Roseland
Quintana, Restituto, St. Michael's, Newark
Ramirez, Nelson, St. Leo, Irvington
Ramos-Villeda, Ramon, Our Lady of Good Counsel, Newark
Ravelo, Daniel, St. Michael's, Newark
Raymundo, Ranulfo, St. Michael's Hospital, Newark
Rehse, Jeremiah, St. Paul, Ramsey
Rejrat, Philip J., St. Adalbert, Elizabeth
Reyes, Jesus, Assumption/All Saints, Jersey City
Reyes, Victor, St. Leo, Irvington
Riccio, Dominick, Our Lady of Mount Virgin, Garfield
Rice, George F., Mt. Carmel, Ridgewood
Rivera, Oscar, Our Lady of Good Counsel, Newark
Rodack, Stephen, Most Sacred of Jesus, Wallington
Rodriguez, Jose A., St. Thomas Aquinas, Newark
Rodriguez, Justo, St. Rocco, Newark
Rodriguez, Vicente, St. Augustine's, Newark
Roig, Julio, St. Peter, Belleville
Romero, Alberto, St. Joseph of the Palisades, West New York
Romero, Jerry, St. John, Orange
Rosado, Jose F., Immaculate Conception, Elizabeth
Ross, George A., St. John the Apostle, Linden
Salerno, Philip, St. Philip, Saddle Brook
Sanchez, Orlando, Holy Rosary; St. Michael, Elizabeth
Sanderson, Raymond, St. Andrew's, Bayonne
Sarno, John A., St. Catherine, Glen Rock
Savo, Ralph, St. Vincent, Bayonne
Scalzo, Anthony, St. Rose of Lima, Short Hills
Schneider, Paul, (Retired)
Searls, Richard, St. Anthony, Belleville
Serzan, Vincent C., St. Michael's, Lyndhurst
Simonelli, Nicholas, St. Francis, Ridgefield Park
Smith, John F., St. Philomena, Livingston
Smith, Thomas M., Catholic Community Services, Newark
Soto, Anibal, Holy Trinity, Hackensack
Stumbar, James P., Little Flower, Berkeley Heights
Suarez, Juan B., St. Michael, Newark
Tankard, Gary, Ascension Church, New Milford
Tarabokija, Anton, St. John's, Fairview
Thomann, Robert V., Mt. Carmel, Ridgewood
Thomson, Robert E., Holy Rosary, Edgewater
Tizzano, Albert H., St. Thomas, Bloomfield
Tobin, James, Church of the Assumption, Emerson
Torres, Cesar Augusto, Sacred Heart, Newark (Vailsburg)
Toth, William, St. Elizabeth, Wyckoff
Valentin, Carlos, Our Lady of Good Counsel, Newark
Valladares, Guillermo, St. Peter's, Belleville
Vargas, Rafael, St. Michael's Medical Center, Newark
Vega, Alcides, St. Teresa, Summit
Velasco, Asterio, SS. Joseph & Michael, Union City
Velo, Luis, St. Joseph, West Orange
Ventola, Samuel, Northern State Prison, Newark
Vitale, Incoronato M., (Retired)
Vrindten, Joseph G., St. Francis, Hackensack
Vuolo, Pasquale, Our Lady of the Lake, Verona
White, Earl, St. Stephens, Kearny
Wilverding, Daniel J., St. Michael, Cranford
Woodruff, Leo A., Holy Name, East Orange
Yandoli, Joseph, St. John, Leonia
Zaparta, Alfredo, St. Aloysius, Jersey City

INSTITUTIONS LOCATED IN THE ARCHDIOCESE

[A] SEMINARIES, ARCHDIOCESAN

KEARNY. *Redemptoris Mater*, 672 Passaic Ave., 07032. Tel: 201-997-3220; Fax: 201-997-5552. Email: secretary@rmnewark.org. Revs. Jose Matias Diaz, Rector; Renato Grasselli, Vice Rector; Neil X. O'Donoghue, Prefect of Studies; Raymond Labranche, Spiritual Dir. Priests 4; Students 57.

SOUTH ORANGE. *Immaculate Conception Seminary*, 400 South Orange Ave., 07079. Tel: 973-761-9575; Fax: 973-761-9577. Email: theology@shu.edu. Web: www.shu.edu.

Administration Officers: Rev. Msgrs. Robert T. Sheeran, S.T.D., Pres.; Robert F. Coleman, J.C.D., Rector & Dean; Revs. Joseph R. Chapel, S.T.D., Assoc. Dean; Thomas P. Nydegger, M.Div., Vice Rector & Business Mgr.; Dr. Dianne Traflet, S.T.D., Asst. Dean; Rev. Msgrs. Andrew T. Cusack, Ph.D. (BGP), Staff Psychologist; Thomas A. Donato, Spiritual Dir.; James C. Turro, Ph.D., Library Svcs. (Retired); Rev. Donald F. Blumenfeld, Ph.D., Dir. Field Education; Margaret Smolin, Student Svcs. Asst.

Full-Time Faculty: Revs. W. Jerome Bracken, C.P., Ph.D.; Joseph R. Chapel, S.T.D.; Anthony J. Figueiredo, S.T.D.; Thomas G. Guarino, S.T.D.; Gerard H. McCarren, S.T.D.; Rev. Msgr. Robert J. Wister, D.Eccl.Hist.; Revs. Lawrence B. Porter, O.P., Ph.D., Ph.D.; John F. Russell, O.Carm., M.A., S.T.L., S.T.D., (on leave for service to the Church); Anthony Ziccardi, S.S.L.; Deacon William J. Toth; Zeni V. Fox, Ph.D.; Gregory Glazov, D.Phil.; Steve M. Vlasac, Dir. Devel.

Darlington Fund Tel: 973-761-9552; Fax: 973-761-9577. Development Agency for Immaculate Conception Seminary. Priests 14; Sisters 2; Lay Teachers 4; Deacons 1; Total Staff 20; Total Enrollment 233.

Seton Hall University College Seminary, St. Andrew Hall, 07079. Tel: 973-761-9420; Fax: 973-761-9421. Email: reillyjr@shu.ed. Rev. Msgr. Robert T. Sheeran, S.T.D., Pres.; Revs. Joseph R. Reilly, S.T.L., Ph.D., Rector; James Spera, Vice Rector; Stanley Gomes, Spiritual Dir. Priests 3; Total Enrollment 19.

[B] COLLEGES AND UNIVERSITIES

CALDWELL. *Caldwell College* Incorporated under the laws of the State of New Jersey with full power to confer degrees. , 9 Ryerson Ave., 07006. Tel: 973-618-3000; Fax: 973-618-3600. Email: admissions@caldwell.edu. Web: www.caldwell.edu. Priests 9; Sisters 8; Sisters of St. Dominic 7; Lay Teachers 167; Students 2,219.

College Faculty: Sr. Patrice Werner, O.P., Ph.D., Pres.; Dr. Paul R. Douillard, Ph.D., Vice Pres., Dean for Academic Affairs; Rev. Thomas Orians, S.A., Coord. of Campus Ministry.

JERSEY CITY. *Saint Peter's College*, 2641 Kennedy Blvd., 07306-5997. Tel: 201-915-9000; Fax: 201-451-0036. Email: nieves_l@spc.edu. Web: www.spc.edu. Rev. James N. Loughran, S.J., Pres.; Eileen L. Poiani, Vice Pres. Student Affairs; Dr. Eugene Cornacchia, Acting Academic Vice Pres. & Provost; Mr. Joseph Hartnett, Vice Pres. Office of Finance & Business; Dr. Richard Petriello, Academic Dean Day Session; Ms. Mildred Broccoli, Dean of Freshmen & Asst. Academic Dean, Day Session; Dr. Theresa Lewis, Dean School of Professional & Continuing Education; Mr. William Morrison, Dean of Upper Classmen; Mr. Joe Giglio, Dir. Admissions; Mr. Ben Scholz, Dir. Enrollment, Research, & Technology; Ms. Susan E. Nelson, Registrar & Dir. Enrollment Svcs.; Mary Sue Callan-Farley, Dir. Campus Ministry. Priests 31.

St. Peter's College Jesuit Community, Gothic Towers, 50 Glenwood Ave., 07306-4606. Fax: 201-432-7397. Priests 11; Lay Teachers 99; Students 4,000.

Jesuit Center, St. Peter Hall, 2652 Kennedy Blvd., 07306. Tel: 201-433-2527; 201-433-2528 (Rector's Office); Fax: 201-433-7139. Revs. Thomas C. Blessin, S.J.; Edward W. Brande, S.J.; John M. Buckley,

S.J.; Laurence L. Cassidy, S.J.; James A. Catalano, S.J.; Mark T. DeStephano, S.J.; Juan Diaz Vilar; Leo J. Daly, S.J.; Bro. Patrick T. Flanagan, S.J.; Revs. Charles A. Gallagher, S.J.; Edward J. Heavey, S.J.; Robert E. Kennedy, S.J.; James N. Loughran, S.J.; T. Patrick Lynch, S.J.; Donal T. MacVeigh, S.J.; Oscar G. Magnan; William F.X. Maher, S.J.; Edmund W. Majewski, S.J.; Robert E. McCarty, S.J.; William A. McKenna, S.J.; Joseph A. Novak, S.J.; Joseph J. Papaj, S.J.; John P. Ruane, S.J.; John P. St. George, S.J.; Raymond A. Schroth, S.J.; Brendan Scott, S.J.; David X. Stump, S.J.; Thomas L. Sheridan, S.J.; John P. Wrynn.

LODI. *Felician College* Tel: 201-559-6000; Fax: 201-559-6188. Email: admissions@inet.felician.edu. Web: www.felician.edu.
Lodi Campus:
262 Main St., 07644. Tel: 201-559-6000; Fax: 201-559-6188.
Rutherford Campus:
223 Montross Ave., Rutherford, 07070. Tel: 201-559-3563; Fax: 201-559-3578. Sr. Theresa Mary Martin, C.S.S.F., Pres.; Dr. Charles J. Rooney, Exec. Vice Pres. for Admin. & Finance; R. David Chancey, Exec. Vice Pres. & Rutherford Campus Admin.; Sisters Patricia A. Morris, O.P., Vice Pres. for Academic Affairs; Mary Tarcilia Juchniewicz, C.S.S.F., Vice Pres. for Student Affairs; Marc J. Chalfin, Vice Pres. & CFO; Susan M. Chaflin, Vice Pres. Enrollment Mgmt.; Sr. Mary Firmina Lajewski, C.S.S.F., Coord. Planning; Dr. Donna M. Barron, Dean Div. of Teacher Education; Dr. Muriel M. Shore, Dean Div. of Health Sciences; Dr. Gerard P. O'Sullivan, Dean Div. of Arts & Sciences; Dr. William B. Morgan, Dean of Div. of Business Mgmt.; Revs. Damian Colicchio, Dir. Campus Ministry; John P. O'Neill, Assoc. Dir. Campus Ministry; Sr. Marie Teresa Soltys, Assoc. Dir. Campus Ministry; Cynthia Sievewright, Dir. Undergraduate Admission; Elizabeth A. Griffin, Dir. Adult & Graduate Admission; June Finn, Registrar; Norma Betz, Dir. Financial Aid. Priests 2; Brothers 1; Sisters 1; Lay Teachers 67; Total Staff 107; Total Enrollment 1,524.

SOUTH ORANGE. *Seton Hall University* (1856), 400 South Orange Ave., 07079. Tel: 973-761-9000; Fax: 973-275-2361. Web: shu.edu. Rev. Msgr. Robert T. Sheeran, S.T.D., Pres. Priests 50; Lay Teachers 350; Students 9,760.
Officers of University: Mary Meehan, Exec. Vice Pres. Admin.; Mel J. Shay, Provost & Exec. Vice Pres. Academic Affairs; Laura A. Wankel, Ed.D., Vice Pres. Student Affairs; Dennis Garbini, M.B.A., Vice Pres. Finance & Technology; Catherine Kiernan, J.D., Vice Pres. & Univ. Counsel; Deborah Raikes-Colbert, Assoc. Vice Pres. Human Resources; Joseph Sandoron, Vice Pres. for Univ. Advancement.
Administrators: Tracy Gottlieb, Dean Freshman Studies; Richard Stern, Acting Dean; Robert DeMartino, Ph.D., Dir. Grants & Contracts; Jeff Fogelson, Dir. University Athletics; Revs. James M. Cafone, S.T.D., Min. to Priest Community; James F. Spera, M.Div., Dir. Campus Ministry; Robert S. Meyer, S.T.L., J.D., J.C.L., Assoc. Vice Pres. Student Affairs; Rev. Msgr. Andrew T. Cusack, Ph.D., Dir. National Institute for Clergy Formation.
College of Arts and Sciences Molly Smith, Ph.D., Dean. Tel: 973-761-9022.
School of Business Karen E. Boroff, Ph.D., Dean. Tel: 973-761-9013.
College of Education and Human Services Joseph De Pierro, Dean. Tel: 973-761-9025.
College of Nursing Phyllis Hansell, Ed.D., Dean. Tel: 973-761-9014.
School of Law Patrick E. Hobbs, J.D., L.L.M., Dean. One Newark Center, 07102. Tel: 973-642-8750.
School of Theology Rev. Msgr. Robert F. Coleman, J.C.D., Rector & Dean. Tel: 973-761-9016.
School of Graduate Medical Education David L. Felton, Ph.D., Dean. Tel: 973-761-9710.
College Seminary Rev. Msgr. Robert F. Coleman, J.C.D.
School of Diplomacy and Intl. Rels. Clay Constantinou, J.D., L.L.M., Dean. Tel: 973-375-2515.
Priest Community: Rev. John F. Morley, Ph.D.; Rev. Msgrs. Robert F. Coleman, J.C.D.; Andrew T. Cusack, Ph.D.; Edward J. Fleming (Retired); John W. Flesey, S.T.D.; Richard M. Liddy, Ph.D.; Dennis Mahon; Robert T. Sheeran, S.T.D.; James C. Turro, Ph.D. (Retired); Robert J. Wister; Revs. Donald Blumenfeld; Ian Boyd; W. Jerome Bracken, C.P., Ph.D.; Alfred V. Celiano, Ph.D. (Retired); Christopher Ciccarino; Gabriel B. Costa, Ph.D.; Eugene J. Cotter, D.Lett; Walter A. Debold, M.A. (Retired); John D. Dennehy; Arnold P. De Rosa, Ph.D. (Retired); Rev. Msgr. Thomas A. Donato; Revs. Anthony Figueiredo; Lawrence E. Frizzell, D.Phil.; Nicholas S. Gengaro, S.T.D.; Stanley Gomes; Thomas G. Guarino, S.T.D.; Kevin M. Hanbury, Ed.D.; Paul A. Holmes, S.T.D., Vice Pres. for Mission & Ministry; Christopher J. Hynes, Ed.S.; S. David Lee; Peter F. Lennon (Retired); Gerald H. McCarren, S.T.D.; Robert S. Meyer, S.T.L., J.D., J.C.L.; John F. Morley, Ph.D.; Richard M. Nardone (Retired); Robert P. Nestor, Ed.D.; Lawrence B. Porter, O.P., Ph.D.; John J. Ranieri, Ph.D.; Joseph Reilly; Donald C. Smith, M.A. (Retired); James F. Spera, M.Div.; C. Anthony Ziccardi, S.T.L., S.S.L. In Res. Revs. Joseph R. Chapel, S.T.D.; Douglas J. Milewski, S.T.L.; Thomas P. Nydegger, M.Div.; Joseph F. Wortmann, M.A. (Retired).

[C] HIGH SCHOOLS, PRIVATE

NEWARK. *St. Benedict's Preparatory School*, (Grades 7-12), 520 Dr. Martin Luther King, Jr. Blvd., 07102-1314. Tel: 973-792-5800; Fax: 973-643-6922. Email: graybee@sbp.org. Web: www.sbp.org. Revs. Edwin D. Leahy, O.S.B., Headmaster; Paul E. Thornton, Vice Pres. Devel. & Finance. Tel: 973-792-5775; Fax: 973-643-6922. Benedictine Monks of Newark Abbey 11; Priests 8; Brothers 3; Lay Teachers 58; Boys 580.
St. Vincent Academy (Girls) , 228 W. Market St., 07103. Tel: 973-622-1613; Fax: 973-622-1128. Email: sisterjunefavata@ba_dsg.net. Web: www.svanewark.org. Sr. June Favata, Admin. Dir. Sisters 8; Lay Teachers 24; Students 324.

BAYONNE. *Holy Family Academy*, 239 Ave. A, 07002. Tel: 201-339-7341; Fax: 201-339-9295. Email: hfa@bayonne.net. Web: www.hfa.bayonne.net. Sr. Mary Ellen Ford, S.S.J., Prin. Sisters of St. Joseph of Chestnut Hill, Philadelphia, PA Sisters 8; Lay Teachers 22; Girls 280.
Marist High School (Coed) , 1241 Kennedy Blvd., 07002. Tel: 201-437-4544; Fax: 201-437-6013. Email: mhsfms@aol.com. Web: www.marist.org. Bros. Joseph Matthews, F.M.S., Pres.; Steve Schlitte, F.M.S., Prin.; Joseph Sacino, F.M.S., Acting Prin.; Stephen Kappes, F.M.S.; Robert Warren, F.M.S.; William Maske, F.M.S.; John Healy, F.M.S.; Francis Farrell, F.M.S. Marist Brothers Brothers 8; Sisters 2; Lay Teachers 36; Students 486.

CALDWELL. *Mount St. Dominic Academy* (Girls) , 3 Ryerson Ave., 07006-6196. Tel: 973-226-0660; Fax: 973-226-2693. Email: msda@academy.org. Web: www.msdacademy.org. Sr. Francis Sullivan, O.P., Prin. Sisters of St. Dominic of Caldwell Sisters 8; Lay Teachers 32; Girls 312.

DEMAREST. *Academy of the Holy Angels* (Girls) , 315 Hillside Ave., 07627. Tel: 201-768-7822; Fax: 201-768-6362. Web: www.holyangels.org. Mary Farrell, Pres. Conducted by School Sisters of Notre Dame Sisters 7; Lay Teachers 46; (Girls) 540.

ELIZABETH. *Benedictine Academy*, 840 N. Broad St., 07208-2508. Tel: 908-352-0670; Fax: 908-352-0698. Web: www.benedictineacad.org. Adele Kosinski, Prin. Benedictine Sisters of Elizabeth, NJ, College Preparatory High School (Girls) Sisters 5; Lay Teachers 17; Total Staff 27; Girls 185.

HOBOKEN. *Academy of the Sacred Heart* (Girls) , 713 Washington St., 07030. Tel: 201-659-7139; Fax: 201-659-8027. Email: arnew32102@connectinc.com. Sr. Mary Fallon, S.C., Prin. Sisters of Charity of St. Elizabeth Sisters 4; Lay Teachers 18; Girls 143.

JERSEY CITY. *Academy of St. Aloysius* (Girls: Grades 9-12) , 2495 John F. Kennedy Memorial Blvd., 07304. Tel: 201-433-8877; Fax: 201-433-8839. Email: arnew32103@connectinc.com. Web: www.academyofstaloysius.org. Mrs. Tara Brunt, Prin. Sisters of Charity of St. Elizabeth Sisters 4; Lay Teachers 19; Total Staff 23; Students 170.
St. Anthony High School, 175 Eighth St., 07302. Tel: 201-653-5143; Fax: 201-653-8120. Email: www.stanthonysfriars.com. Sr. Mary Felicia, C.S.S.F., Prin. Conducted by Felician Sisters Brothers 1; Sisters 3; Lay Teachers 26; Total Staff 6; Students 239.
St. Dominic Academy (Girls) , 2572 John F. Kennedy Memorial Blvd., 07304. Tel: 201-434-5938; Fax: 201-434-2603. Email: stdominicacad@hotmail.com. Web: www.stdominicacad.com. Sr. Vivien Jennings, O.P., Ph.D. Dominican Sisters of Caldwell Sisters 9; Lay Teachers 39; Total Staff 52; Students 493.
St. Peter's Preparatory School, 144 Grand St., 07302. Tel: 201-434-4400; Fax: 201-547-6421. Web: www.stpetersprep.org. Revs. Vincent B. Sullivan, S.J., Rector; James F. Keenan, S.J., Pres.; Mr. John R. Raslowsky, Prin.; Mr. Patrick Reidy, Vice Prin.; Mr. James Horan, Vice Pres. External Affairs; Mr. James Collins, Dean of Students; Mr. John M. Corcoran, Treas.; Mr. Kenneth Dandorph, Asst. Prin., Student Affairs; Revs. Charles F.X. Dolan, S.J., Vice Pres. Alumni Affairs; Anthony J. Azzarto, S.J., Chap.; Raymond J. Balduf, S.J., College Admissions; Erwin G. Beck, S.J.; Bro. Ralph Cilia, S.J.; Revs. Daniel A. Degnan, S.J.; John A. Dinneen, S.J. (NY); Francis X. McFarland, S.J.; Michael R. Hoag, S.J.; Sean J. McCann, S.J.; Thomas F. McManus, S.J.; Thomas V. O'Connor, S.J.; Harold J. Oppido, S.J.; Enrico Raulli, S.J. Priests 18; Brothers 4; Scholastics 1; Sisters 1; Lay Teachers 68; Students 927.
Res.: 220 W. 98th St., Apt. 4E, New York, NY 10025. In Res. Revs. Michael E. Browne, S.J.; Peter F. O'Brien, S.J.; John J. Rohr, S.J.; Edward P. Sheehy, S.J.; Joseph T. Watson, S.J.; Bros. Joseph J. Griffin, S.J.; Louis N. Mauro, S.J.

LODI. *Immaculate Conception High School*, 258 S. Main St., 07644. Tel: 973-773-2400; 973-773-2401; Fax: 973-614-0893. Email: aadametz@ichslodi.com. Web: www.ichslodi.com. Sr. Mary Alicia Adametz, C.S.S.F., Prin. Sisters 5; Lay Teachers 18; Lay Staff 10; Girls 197.

ORADELL. *Bergen Catholic* (Boys) , 1040 Oradell Ave., 07649. Tel: 201-261-1844; Fax: 201-599-9507. Email: brmurphy@bergencatholic.org. Web: www.bergencatholic.org. Rev. James R. White, Chap.; Bro. Lawrence T. Murphy, C.F.C., Pres.; Dr. Joseph S. Fusco, Prin. Congregation of Christian Brothers Priests 1; Brothers 7; Lay Teachers 50; Total Staff 58; Boys 861.

RAMSEY. *Don Bosco Preparatory High School*, 492 N. Franklin Tpke., 07446. Tel: 201-327-8003; Fax: 201-327-3397. Web: donboscoprep.com. Revs. Steven Shafran, S.D.B., Dir. & Pres.; Brendan K. Kilroy, S.P.S.; Peter Sella, S.D.B.; Louis Konopelski, S.D.B.; Stephen Leake, S.D.B.; Richard Rosin, S.D.B.; John Serio, S.D.B.; Joseph Bajorek, S.D.B.; Eugene Palumbo, S.D.B.; Jerzy Schneider, S.D.B.; Alfred Sokol, S.D.B.; Albert Sofia, S.D.B.; Anthony A. Spano, S.D.B.; Bros. Frank Tilton, S.D.B.; James Wiegand, S.D.B. Salesians of St. John Bosco Priests 13; Brothers 2; Sisters 1; Lay Teachers 48; Students 840.

SOUTH ORANGE. *Marylawn of the Oranges, High School for Girls*, 445 Scotland Rd., 07079. Tel: 973-762-9222. Email: arnew22106@impresso.com. Sisters 4; Lay Teachers 13; Girls 183.

SUMMIT. *Oak Knoll School of the Holy Child Upper School*, (Grades 7-12) , (Girls) , 44 Blackburn Rd., 07901. Tel: 908-522-8100 (Main); 908-522-8130; Fax: 908-273-4616. Email: tina.hummerstone@oakknoll.org. Web: www.oakknoll.org. Mrs. Bettina Hummerstone, Head of School; Sr. Mary Sciarrillo, Prin. Conducted by the Sisters of the Holy Child Jesus Lay Teachers 42; Total Staff 44; Students 300.

UPPER MONTCLAIR. *Lacordaire Academy, Secondary Division*, 155 Lorraine Ave., 07043. Tel: 973-744-1156; Fax: 973-783-9521. Web: www.lacordaire.net. Sr. Suzanne McCaffrey, O.P. Sisters of St. Dominic Priests 1; Sisters 6; Lay Teachers 15; Total Staff 32; Girls 140.

WEST ORANGE. *Seton Hall Preparatory School*, 120 Northfield Ave., 07052. Tel: 973-325-6624; Fax: 973-325-6652. Email: mkelly@shp.org. Web: www.shp.org. Rev. Msgr. Michael E. Kelly, M.A., Headmaster. Priests 6; Lay Instructors 84; Students 959.
Resident Faculty: Revs. Edward G. Bradley, S.T.L., M.A.; Bruce G. Janiga, M.A.; Stephen M. Kilcarr, B.A.; William J. Melillo, M.A., M.Div.; Kevin Murphy, Chap.

[D] HIGH SCHOOLS, ARCHDIOCESAN

CLARK. *Mother Seton (Girls) Regional High School*, Valley Rd., 07066. Tel: 732-382-1952; Fax: 732-382-4725. Email: srriginamartin@motherseton.org. Web: www.motherseton.org. Sr. Regina Martin, S.C., Prin. Sisters of Charity of St. Elizabeth Sisters 8; Lay Teachers 32; Girls 430.

JERSEY CITY. *Hudson Catholic High School*, 790 Bergen Ave., 07306. Tel: 201-332-5970; Fax: 201-332-6373. Email: hudsoncath@aol.com. Web: members.aol.com/hudsoncath/ppl.htm. Bro. Tim Ahern, F.S.C., Prin. Brothers of the Christian Schools Brothers 12; Sisters 1; Lay Teachers 28; Total Staff 51; Boys 575.

MONTVALE. *St. Joseph Regional High School* (Boys) , 40 Chestnut Ridge Rd., 07645. Tel: 201-391-3300; Fax: 201-391-8073. Web: www.saintjosephregional.org. John R. Job, Prin. Brothers 2; Sisters 1; Lay Teachers 31; Boys 470.

PARAMUS. *Paramus Catholic High School* (Coed) , 425 Paramus Rd., 07652. Tel: 201-445-4466; Fax: 201-445-6440. Email: jvail@paramus-catholic.org. Web: www.paramus-catholic.org. James P. Vail, Pres.; Joseph P. Agostino, Prin.; Leonard Lewandoski, Vice Prin.; Stephanie Macaluso, Vice Prin.; Rev. Leo J. Butler, Chap. Priests 1; Sisters 1; Deacons 1; Lay Teachers 97; Total Staff 100; Students 1,430.

ROSELLE. *Roselle Catholic High School* (Coed) , Raritan Rd., 07203. Tel: 908-245-2350; Fax: 908-241-3869. Email: rchs3@injersey.com. Web: www.rosellecatholic.org. Bro. Owen Ormsby, F.M.S., Prin. Marist Brothers Brothers 6; Sisters

1; Lay Teachers 48; Total Staff 55; Students 784.

SCOTCH PLAINS. *Union Catholic Regional High School* (Coed) , 1600 Martine Ave., 07076. Tel: 908-889-1600; Fax: 908-889-7867. Email: mainoffice@unioncatholic.org. Web: www.unioncatholic.org. Sr. Percylee Hart, R.S.M., Prin. Lay Teachers 49; Total Staff 66; Students 805.

SUMMIT. *The Oratory Catholic Preparatory School*, (Grades 7-12), 1 Beverly Rd., 07901. Tel: 908-273-1084; Fax: 908-273-5505. Email: brothrrobert@oratoryprep.org. Web: oratoryprep.org. Bro. Robert Wickman, F.S.C., Headmaster; Revs. Nicholas G. Figurelli; Paul R. Manning. Priests 2; Lay Teachers 28; Total Staff 31; Students 255. In Res. Rev. Edmund G. Bernauer (Retired).
Res.: 14 Bedford Rd.. Tel: 908-273-7563.

WASHINGTON TOWNSHIP. *Immaculate Heart Academy* (Girls) , 500 Van Emburgh Ave., 07676. Tel: 201-445-6800; Fax: 201-445-7416. Email: teachername@ihahs.com. Web: www.ihahs.com. Sr. Ellen Cronan, A.S.C.J., Prin. Apostles of the Sacred Heart Sisters 4; Lay Teachers 60; Total Staff 64; Girls 848.

[E] ELEMENTARY SCHOOLS, PRIVATE

NEWARK. *Link Community School, Inc.*, 120 Livingston St., 07103. Tel: 973-642-0529; 973-642-8510; Fax: 973-642-1978. Email: linkcs@linkschool.org. Web: www.linkschool.org. William Kurtz, Prin. Dominican Sisters of Caldwell Sisters 1; Lay Teachers 14; Jesuit Volunteer 1; Students 128.

St. Lucy Filippini Academy, 142 Jefferson St., 07105. Tel: 973-344-4806; Fax: 973-344-8424. Email: principal@slfa.org. Web: www.slfa.org. Sr. Mary Rose Conforto, M.P.F., Prin. Sisters 2; Lay Teachers 15; Students 200.

ELIZABETH. *Bender Memorial Academy*, 416 Linden Ave., 07202. Tel: 908-352-4406; Fax: 908-352-7308. Email: sister416@aol.com. Sr. Marie Therese Hayes, O.S.B., Prin. Sisters of St. Benedict Sisters 6; Lay Teachers 12; Total Staff 13; Students 175.

Elizabethport Catholic School, 227 Court St., 07206. Tel: 908-351-2188; Fax: 908-351-6086. Web: www.rcan.org/eport/index. Dr. Theodore Kadela, Prin. Lay Teachers 12; Total Staff 13; Total Enrollment 182.

JERSEY CITY. *St. Joseph's School for the Blind*, 253 Baldwin Ave., 07306. Tel: 201-653-0578; Fax: 201-653-4087. Email: stjosschbl@aol.com. Web: www.sjsb.net. Mr. Herbert Miller, Admin.; Dennis Cruz, Prin. School for visually impaired, multi-disabled children; non-graded; Early Intervention Program, 5-day Residential Program, Outreach Services. Lay Teachers 12; Students 103; Total Staff 12.

KEARNY. *Sacred Heart School*, 22 Wilson Ave., 07032. Tel: 201-991-0628; Fax: 201-991-0226. Email: parlati@aol.com. Web: www.shskearny.com. Sisters of the Catholic Apostolate Sisters 3; Lay Teachers 14; Total Staff 11; Students 220.

Day Care Center Tel: 201-991-6600. Lay Teachers 3; Students 30.

LODI. *The Felician School for Exceptional Children*, 260 S. Main St., P.O. Box 530, 07644. Tel: 973-777-5355; Fax: 973-777-0725. Email: fsecinlodi@aol.com. Web: www.fsec.org. Sr. Mary Ramona, C.S.S.F., Dir. Sisters 6; Lay Teachers 21; Total Staff 4; Children 138.

Day Program Tel: 973-777-5355, Ext. 12. Capacity 150.

SUMMIT. *Oak Knoll School of The Holy Child, Lower School*, (Grades K-6) , (Coed) , 44 Blackburn Rd., 07901. Tel: 908-522-8120; 908-522-8100 (Main); Fax: 908-598-9757. Email: tina.hummerstone@oakknoll.org. Web: www.oakknoll.org. Mrs. Bettina Hummerstone, Head of School; Mrs. Joanne L. Ainsworth, Prin.; Ms. Carla DiOrio, Guidance Counselor. Conducted by the Sisters of the Holy Child of Jesus Lay Teachers 27; Total Staff 27; Students 240.

UNION CITY. *St. Francis Academy*, 1601 Central Ave., 07087. Tel: 201-863-4112; Fax: 201-601-5905. Email: lucy@stfrancisacademy.com. Web: www.stfrancisacademy.com. Sr. Dora Sartino, O.S.F., Prin. Missionary Franciscan Sisters of the Immaculate Conception Sisters 6; Lay Teachers 18; Students 268.

Holy Rosary Academy, 501 15th St., 07087. Tel: 201-864-0332; Fax: 201-864-5586. Email: hraes1@yahoo.com. Web: www.holyrosaryacademyunioncity.com. Martha C. Velez, Prin. Sisters of the Catholic Apostolate (Pallottine) 5; Lay Teachers 10; Students 145.

UPPER MONTCLAIR. *Lacordaire Academy-Elementary Division*, 153 Lorraine Ave., 07043. Tel: 973-746-2660; Fax: 973-783-6804. Email: lacordaire2b@home.com. Web: www.lacordaireacademy.net. Mrs. Mary Anne Ford, Prin. Dominican Sisters of Caldwell Lay Teachers 15; Students 145; Total Staff 15.

[F] CATHEDRAL HEALTHCARE SYSTEM OF ARCHDIOCESE OF NEWARK

NEWARK. *Cathedral Healthcare System, Inc.*, 219 Chestnut St., 07105. Tel: 973-690-3600; Fax: 973-690-3601. Email: dond@cathedral-health.org. Web: www.cathedral-health.org. Mr. Donald M. Daniels, Chm. & CEO.

Catholic Health New Jersey, Inc. Tel: 973-690-3600; Fax: 973-690-3601. Catholic Health New Jersey is the sole corporate member of Cathedral Healthcare System.

Cathedral Health Services, Inc. Hospitals:

St. Michael's Medical Center Division, Newark Tel: 973-877-5411; Fax: 973-877-5672.

St. James Hospital Division, Newark Tel: 973-465-2707; Fax: 973-465-2801.

St. Mary's Life Center Inc.-Pope John Paul II Pavilion, Orange Tel: 973-266-3200; Fax: 973-266-3302.

Columbus Hospital, Newark Tel: 973-268-1475; Fax: 973-268-1523.

The Hospital Center of Orange, Orange Tel: 973-266-2211; Fax: 973-414-4951.

Montclair Community Hospital, Montclair Tel: 973-690-3606; Fax: 973-690-3601.

Cathedral Healthcare Affiliated Agencies: Tel: 973-690-3606; Fax: 973-690-3601.

219 Chestnut St., 07105-1558. Tel: 973-690-3606; Fax: 973-690-3601. Anita Holland, Vice Pres. & Corp. Sec.

Cathedral/Columbus Group, Newark Tel: 973-690-3606; Fax: 973-690-3601.

Cathedral Affiliated Group at Orange Inc., Newark Tel: 973-690-3606; Fax: 973-690-3601.

Orange Mountain Healthcare, Inc., Newark Tel: 973-690-3606; Fax: 973-690-3601.

Cathedral Affiliated Group at Montclair, Newark Tel: 973-690-3606; Fax: 973-690-3601.

Cathedral Foundation, Inc., 219 Chestnut St., 07105. Tel: 973-690-3606; Fax: 973-690-3601.

[G] GENERAL HOSPITALS

NEWARK. *Cathedral Affiliated Group at Orange, Inc., Newark*, 219 Chestnut St., 07105-1558. Tel: 973-690-3606; Fax: 973-690-3601. Parent Corporation: Cathedral Healthcare System, Inc.

Cathedral Health Services, Inc., 219 Chestnut St., 07105.

Catholic Community Services (C.C.S.) Mt. Carmel Guild Hospital, 494 Broad St., 07102. Tel: 973-596-4084. Web: www.ccsnewark.org. Rev. Msgr. Ronald J. Rozniak, V.G., Exec. Dir., C.C.S.; Ronald Finch, Ed.D., Dir. Healthcare. Bed Capacity 20; Staff 29; Patients Assisted Annually 352.

Columbus Hospital, 495 N. 13th St., 07107. Tel: 973-268-1475; Fax: 973-268-1523. Email: rgiorgino@columbushospital. Parent Institution: Cathedral Healthcare System, Inc. Bed Capacity 210; Total Staff 900; Admission 9,575.

St. James Hospital, 155 Jefferson St., 07105. Tel: 973-589-1300; Fax: 973-465-2861. Email: stjames@cathedralhealthcare.org. Ceu Cirne-Neves, Admin.; Colleen Aurori, Vice Pres. Operations; Sr. Dolores Cervi, Chap.; Rev. Arokiasamy Irudayanathan; Martin Estok Jr., M.D., Pres. Medical Staff; Mary Fuhro, Vice Pres. Nursing & Patient Svcs. Parent Corporation: Cathedral Healthcare System, Inc. Bed Capacity 186; Bassinets 12; Staff 615; Patients Assisted Annually 50,469.

Saint Michael's Medical Center, a Division of Cathedral Health Services, Inc., 268 Dr. Martin Luther King. Jr. Blvd., 07102-9850. Tel: 973-877-5411; Fax: 973-877-5672. Email: BarbaraB@cathedralhealth.org. Barbara J. Loughney, Admin.; Rev. Msgr. Manuel Cruz, Mgr. Pastoral Care; Dr. Frederick Weisbrot, Pres. Medical Staff. Parent Corporation: Cathedral Healthcare System, Inc. Bed Capacity 337; Sisters 3; Admissions 10,711; Outpatient Visits 182,230; Total Staff 1,560.

**Orange Mountain Healthcare, Inc.*, 219 Chestnut St., 07105. Tel: 973-690-3606; Fax: 973-690-3601. Parent Corporation: Cathedral Healthcare System, Inc.

ELIZABETH. *Trinitas Hospital*, Jersey Street Campus, 925 E. Jersey St., 07201. Tel: 908-994-8600; Fax: 908-994-5756. Web: www.trinitashospital.com. Gary Horan, Pres.; Sr. Dorothy Apprich, S.S.J., Dir. Mission Effectiveness. Sisters of Charity of Saint Elizabeth Sisters 11; Total Staff 3,086; Bed Capacity 812; Bassinets 9; Patients Assisted Annually 410,642.

Trinitas Hospital, Williamson Street Campus, 225 Williamson St., 07207.

Trinitas Hospital, New Point Campus, 655 E. Jersey St., 07206.

**Marillac Corp.*, 240 Williamson St., 07207. Tel: 908-994-5756; Fax: 908-994-5520. Gary Horan, Pres.

ORANGE. **The Hospital Center of Orange*, 188 S. Essex Ave., 07050. Tel: 973-266-2211; Fax: 973-414-4951. Email: marke@cathedralhealth.org. Parent Corporation: Cathedral Healthcare System, Inc. Bed Capacity 270; Total Staff 800; Admissions 5,275.

Saint Mary Life Center, Inc. - Pope John Paul II Pavilion Skilled nursing facility, comprehensive personal care. , 135 S. Center St., 07050. Tel: 973-266-3000; Fax: 973-266-3202. Frank Infante, Admin. Bed Capacity 190; Total Staff 190; Admissions 234.

TEANECK. *Holy Name Hospital*, 718 Teaneck Rd., 07666. Tel: 201-833-3000; Fax: 201-833-3230. Web: www.holyname.org. Michael Maron, Pres. & CEO. Sisters of St. Joseph of Peace Bed Capacity 318; Bassinets 36; Total Staff 1,445.

School of Nursing Tel: 201-833-3002. Sr. Clare Tynan, C.S.J.P., Senior Vice Pres. Sisters 4.

Pastoral Care: Sisters Lois Jablonski, S.S.J., M.Div., Dir.; Nora Molyneux, C.S.J.P., Vice Pres. Mission; Revs. Paterno Gorospe, Chap.; Thomas Tharayil, Chap.; Deacons Edgar Caceres, Chap.; Willy Malarcher, Chap.

[H] HOMES FOR AGED

CALDWELL. *St. Catherine of Siena, Inc.*, 7 Ryerson Ave., 07006. Tel: 973-226-1577; Fax: 973-226-5058. Email: auhlop@hotmail.com. Web: www.caldwellop.org. Sisters Joan Doyle, Pres.; Alice Uhl, O.P., Vice Pres.; Arlene Antczak, O.P., Sec.; Patricia McKearney, O.P., Treas.; Mrs. Lucy Grygorcewicz, Admin. Total Assisted Annually 12; Total Staff 51.

CEDAR GROVE. *St. Vincent's Nursing Home* (Div. of St. Joseph's Regional Medical Center) , 315 E. Lindsley Rd., 07009. Tel: 973-754-4800; Fax: 973-812-4491. Email: kenny@sjhmc.org. Thomas Kenny, Admin.; Sr. Elizabeth Noonan, Chap. Conducted by Sisters of Charity of St. Elizabeth Sisters 4; Capacity: Long term care beds 151; Patients Assisted Annually 220; Total Staff 175.

JERSEY CITY. *St. Ann's Home for the Aged*, 198 Old Bergen Rd., 07305. Tel: 201-433-0950; Fax: 201-433-6554. Email: paix2@aol.com. Web: www.saintannshome.com. Sr. Norah Clarke, C.S.J.P., LNHA Admin.; Henry Wojtowicz, Pastoral Care. Sisters of St. Joseph of Peace 6; Total Staff 200; Under Care (Male & Female) 120; Adult Medical Day Care Clients 50.

PARAMUS. *Mount St. Andrew Villa*, 55 W. Midland Ave., 07652. Tel: 201-261-5950. Sr. JoAnn Bromley, S.C. Sisters of Charity of St. Elizabeth 2; Residents 55.

SADDLE RIVER. *Villa Marie Claire* Residence for retired, independent men & women. , 12 W. Saddle River Rd., 07458. Tel: 201-327-1325; Fax: 201-327-6647. Email: vcmoshea@aol.com. Sisters of St. Joseph of Peace 13; Total Staff 12; Residents 19.

[I] HOMES FOR THE BLIND

JERSEY CITY. *St. Joseph's Home for the Blind*, 537 Pavonia Ave., 07306. Tel: 201-653-8300; Fax: 201-653-7705. Email: ataylor@sjhb.com. Sr. Ann Taylor, C.S.J.P., Admin.; Rev. William R. O'Leary, S.J. Sisters of St. Joseph of Peace Sisters 5; Total Staff 158; Nursing Home Patients 139.

[J] DAY NURSERIES

NEWARK. *Perpetual Help Day Nursery*, 170 Broad St., 07104. Tel: 973-484-3535; Fax: 973-497-2526. Email: perhelp@yahoo.com. Vocationist Sisters Sisters 10; Lay Teachers 10; Total Staff 21; Children 161.

ELIZABETH. *Immaculate Heart of Mary Nursery, School & Kindergarten*, 205 E. Jersey St., 07206. Tel: 201-354-8388. Sr. Marianna Perrella, M.P.F., Prin. Religious Teachers Filippini 4; Children 111.

JERSEY CITY. *St. Elizabeth's Child Care Center*, 129 Garrison Ave., 07306. Tel: 201-795-1443; Fax: 201-795-4121. Email: sisterrose@comcast.net. Sr. Romilda Chiga, Supr. Franciscan Sisters of St. Elizabeth Sisters 11; Total Staff 32; Children 270.

NUTLEY. *Holy Family Day Nursery and Convent*, 174 Franklin Ave., 07110. Tel: 973-235-1170; Fax: 973-235-1940. Sr. Mary Clare Chungath, F.S.S.E., Supr. Franciscan Sisters of St. Elizabeth Sisters 9; Children 80.

RAMSEY. *St. Joseph Pre-School*, 372 Wyckoff Ave., 07430. Tel: 201-825-8386. Sr. Liberina De Pari, Supr. Franciscan Sisters of St. Elizabeth Sisters 4; Children 25.

[K] PROTECTIVE INSTITUTIONS

NEWARK. *Missionaries of Charity, Queen of Peace Women's Shelter & Soup Kitchen*, 60 Jay St., 07103. Tel: 973-481-9056; 973-483-0165.

Missionaries of Charity Total Staff 6; Total Assisted (Shelter) 300; Total Assisted (Soup Kitchen) 34,200.

HOBOKEN. *Good Counsel, Inc. (St. Francis Home)*, 303 Madison St., 07030. Tel: 201-798-9059; 201-795-0637; 800-723-8331 (Hotline); Fax: 201-795-0809. Email: cxbell@aol.com. Web: www.goodcounselhomes.org. Rev. Benedict J. Groeschel, C.F.R., Chm.; Christopher R. Bell, Exec. Dir. Housing, counseling and referrals for single women who are pregnant or single mothers with children.

Good Counsel, Inc., P.O. Box 6068, 07030. Rev. Benedict J. Groeschel, C.F.R., Chm.; Christopher R. Bell, Exec. Dir. Residences for single mothers and children. Women & Children Assisted Annually 380; Total Staff 60; Total Assisted Annually 2,380.

JERSEY CITY. *St. Joseph's Home*, 81 York St., 07302. Tel: 201-413-9280; Fax: 201-451-0952. Sr. Rosemary Coffey, Dir. Transitional housing for homeless women and children. Total Staff 14; Total Assisted 89.

The Nurturing Place Tel: 201-451-1982. Sr. Barbara Moran, C.S.J.P., Dir. Tel: 201-413-1982. A developmental child care center for disadvantaged youngsters. Total Staff 18; Total Assisted 112.

KEARNY. *New Jersey Boystown* Family Counseling Services. , 499 Belgrove Dr., 07032. Tel: 201-991-3770. Janis Orlafsky, Dir.; Rev. Francis T. Malone, Clients Rights Advocate & Pastoral Care Coord. Tel: 973-297-4749.

[L] HOMES FOR WOMEN

JERSEY CITY. *St. Mary's Residence for Business and Professional Women*, 240 Washington St., 07302-3806. Tel: 201-432-6289; Fax: 201-451-0952. Sr. Harriet Hamilton, O.S.F., Admin. Sisters of St. Joseph of Peace Total Staff 6; Total Assisted 40.

[M] PERSONAL PRELATURES

SOUTH ORANGE. *Prelature of the Holy Cross and Opus Dei*, 170 Montrose Ave., 07079. Tel: 973-763-8397; Fax: 973-762-1794. Web: www.opusdei.org. Rev. Robert A. O'Connor.

[N] MONASTERIES AND RESIDENCES OF PRIESTS AND BROTHERS

NEWARK. *Newark Abbey*, 528 Dr. Martin Luther King, Jr. Blvd., 07102. Tel: 973-792-5800; Fax: 973-643-6922. Email: newarkabbey@sbp.org. Web: www.newarkabbey.org. Rt. Rev. Melvin J. Valvano, O.S.B., Abbot; Very Rev. Mark M. Payne, O.S.B., Prior; Revs. Matthew S. Wotelko, O.S.B., Subprior; Albert T. Holtz, O.S.B., Novice Master; John T. Browne, O.S.B.; Bro. Maximillian Buonocore, O.S.B.; Revs. Declan J. Cunniff, O.S.B.; Augustine J. Curley, O.S.B.; Luke A. Edelen, O.S.B.; Francis Flood, O.S.B.; Bro. Mark Hayden, O.S.B.; Revs. Edwin D. Leahy, O.S.B.; Malachy M. McPadden, O.S.B.; Maynard G. Nagengast, O.S.B.; Bro. Gereon J. Reuter, O.S.B.; Rev. Boniface J. Treanor, O.S.B.; Very Rev. Philip J. Waters, O.S.B., V.F.; Bro. Patrick Winbush, O.S.B.

St. Maur Priory Very Rev. Charles W. Henry, O.S.B.; Bros. Francis Dachs, O.S.B.; Anthony Streit, O.S.B. Priests 15; Non-Clerical Brothers 6.

BAYONNE. *Marist Brothers*, Champagnat Residence, 1241 Kennedy Blvd., 07002. Tel: 201-437-4115. Bro. John Dunning, F.M.S., Dir. Brothers 6.

CALDWELL. *The Rev. Msgr. James F. Kelley Residence for Retired Priests*, 247 Bloomfield Ave., 07006. Tel: 973-364-1121; Fax: 973-364-9873. Email: rcan445@intac.com. Mrs. Joan Stevens, Admin.; Rev. Msgrs. Emmanuel M. Capozzelli (Retired); John H. Koenig (Retired); Revs. Mathew Ayamanthil; Robert P. Cozzini (Retired); Leo O. Farley (Retired); Dominic J. Fiorino (Retired); Joseph A. Frank (Retired); Robert G. Gibney; Robert D. Jacunski (Retired); George L. Mader, Dir. (Retired).

CLIFFSIDE PARK. *St. Patrick's Missionary Society*, 70 Edgewater Rd., P.O. Box 3080, 07010. Tel: 201-943-6575; Fax: 201-943-2946. Email: mission@stpatrickfathers.org. Web: www.stpatrickfathers.org. Revs. Patrick Cullen, S.P.S.; Brendan K. Kilroy, S.P.S.; Michael Morris, S.P.S.; John McLaughlin; Edward Walsh, S.P.S.; Patrick Cullen, S.P.S.

EAST RUTHERFORD. *Sacred Heart Friary*, 4 Jersey St., 07073. Tel: 973-778-1915; Fax: 973-778-0053. Email: WGFOFM3@aol.com. Bro. William G. Fitzgerald, O.F.M., Dir. AIDS Residential Ministry of Holy Name Province, Franciscan Friars: Housing for six men with HIV/AIDS

HOBOKEN. *F.A.I.T.H. Services.*, 307 Willow Ave., 07030. Tel: 201-792-6161; 201-420-1554 (Brothers Residence). Bro. Robert J. Reinke, C.F.P. Brothers of the Poor of St. Francis (C.F.P.) Total Staff 22; Total Assisted 2,298.

HOHOKUS. *St. Anthony of Padua*, 67 Arbor Dr., P.O. Box 40, 07423. Tel: 201-612-9763; Fax: 201-612-9869. Email: kevofm229@aol.com. Web: www.franmow.org. Revs. Daniel Lanahan, O.F.M., Guardian; Kevin Cronin, O.F.M., Guardian; Claude Lenehan, O.F.M. In Res. Rev. Daniel Lanahan, O.F.M.

JERSEY CITY. *Brothers of the Christian Schools* Hudson Catholic Brothers' Residence , 790 Bergen Ave., 07306-4535. Tel: 201-332-0971; Fax: 201-332-6373. Email: hudsoncath@aol.com. Web: members.aol.com/hudsoncath/pp1.htm. Bro. Carl Clayton, F.S.C. Brothers 13.

Jesuit Community of St. Peter's Prep, Inc., 144 Grand St., 07302. Tel: 201-434-4400; Fax: 201-547-6476. Revs. Vincent B. Sullivan, S.J., Rector; Anthony Aracich, S.J.; Anthony J. Azzarto, S.J.; Raymond J. Balduf, S.J.; Erwin G. Beck, S.J.; Michael E. Browne, S.J.; Daniel A. Degnan, S.J.; John A. Dinneen, S.J. (NY); Michael R. Hoag, S.J.; James F. Keenan, S.J.; Sean J. McCann, S.J.; Thomas F. McManus, S.J.; Daniel A. O'Brien, S.J.; Peter F. O'Brien, S.J.; Thomas V. O'Connor, S.J.; William R. O'Leary, S.J.; Harold J. Oppido, S.J.; John J. Rohr, S.J.; Joseph T. Watson, S.J.; Bros. Ralph Cilia, S.J.; Louis N. Mauro, S.J.; Rev. Edward P. Sheehy, S.J. Total in Residence 22.

Jesuits of Saint Peter's College, Inc., 50 Glenwood Ave., 07306-4606. Tel: 201-432-6288; Fax: 201-432-7397. Email: novak_j@spc.edu. Revs. Joseph A. Novak, S.J., Rector; Thomas C. Blessin, S.J.; Edward W. Brande, S.J.; John M. Buckley, S.J.; Laurence L. Cassidy, S.J.; James A. Catalano, S.J.; Leo J. Daly, S.J.; Mark T. DeStephano, S.J.; J. Juan Diaz Vilar, S.J. (Spain); Bro. Patrick T. Flanagan, S.J.; Revs. Charles A. Gallagher, S.J.; Edward J. Heavey, S.J.; Robert E. Kennedy, S.J.; James N. Loughran, S.J.; T. Patrick Lynch, S.J.; Donal T. MacVeigh, S.J.; Oscar G. Magnan; William F.X. Maher, S.J.; Edmund W. Majewski, S.J.; Robert E. McCarty, S.J.; William A. McKenna, S.J.; Joseph J. Papaj, S.J.; John P. Ruane, S.J.; John P. St. George, S.J.; Raymond A. Schroth, S.J.; Brendan T. Scott, S.J.; Thomas L. Sheridan, S.J.; David X. Stump, S.J.; John F. Wrynn, S.J. Total Staff 29; Total in Residence 29.

MAHWAH. *Paulist Fathers - Paulist Press*, 997 MacArthur Blvd., 07430. Tel: 201-825-7300; Fax: 201-825-8345. Email: info@paulistpress.com. Web: www.paulistpress.com. Revs. Lawrence Boadt, C.S.P., Supr.; Kevin A. Lynch, C.S.P.

MONTCLAIR. *Comboni Missionaries of the Heart of Jesus (Verona Fathers)*, 88 High St., P.O. Box 138, 07042-0138. Tel: 973-744-8080; Fax: 973-744-8919. Email: comboninj@igc.apc.org. Revs. Pasquino Panato, M.C.C.J., Supr.; Paul Ewers, M.C.C.J., Bursar. Total Staff 5; Total in Residence 3. In Res. Rev. Sergio Contran, M.C.C.J. (CIN).

MONTVALE. *Xaverian Brothers*, Xaverian Brothers' Residence, 40 Chestnut Ridge Rd., 07645. Tel: 201-391-8071; Fax: 201-391-8073. Brothers 1.

NORTH ARLINGTON. *DeLaSalle Brothers of the Christian Schools*, Christian Brothers' Residence, 200 Ridge Rd., 07031. Tel: 973-991-0235. Email: arnew12103@connectinc.com. Web: www.qphs.org. Brothers 12.

ORADELL. *Congregation of Christian Brothers*, Bergen Catholic Brothers' Residence, 1040 Oradell Ave., 07649. Tel: 201-261-1816; Fax: 201-599-9507. Brothers 7.

ORANGE. *The Salesian Community*, Don Bosco Residence, 518-B Valley St., 07050. Tel: 973-674-2400; Fax: 973-674-7051. Email: sdbonj@aol.com. Bro. Steve Ryan, S.D.B., Dir.; Revs. Gus Baek, S.D.B., Vice Dir.; Mario Balbi, S.D.B.; David Moreno, S.D.B.; Bros. Steven Aldorasi, S.D.B.; Kevin Connolly, S.D.B.; Cristiano Cotrim, S.D.B.; Robert DiPede, S.D.B.; Manuel Gallo, S.D.B.; Michael Lee, S.D.B. Total in Residence 12; Candidates 3; Total in Residence 24.

RAMSEY. *Don Bosco Prep Salesian Residence*, 429 Franklin Tpke., 07446-2811. Tel: 201-327-8100; Fax: 201-327-8174. Revs. Joseph Bajorek, S.D.B.; Louis Konopelski, S.D.B.; Stephen Leake, S.D.B.; Eugene Palumbo, S.D.B.; Richard Rosin, S.D.B.; Jerzy Schneider, S.D.B.; Peter Sella, S.D.B.; John Serio, S.D.B.; Steven Shafran, S.D.B., Dir.; Albert Sofia, S.D.B.; Alfred Sokol, S.D.B.; Anthony A. Spano, S.D.B.; Bros. Frank Tilton, S.D.B.; James Wiegand, S.D.B. Total in Residence 14.

ROSELLE. *Marist Brothers Residence*, Roselle Catholic High School, 1 Raritan Rd., 07203. Tel: 908-245-3574; Fax: 908-620-9507. Brothers 9.

RUTHERFORD. *St. John Vianney Residence for Priests*, 60 Home Ave., 07070. Tel: 201-933-5155; Fax: 201-933-4467. Carol Hubba, Admin.; Rev. Msgr. Edward F. Kavin, Dir. (Retired). Total in Residence 22; Total Staff 14. In Res. Most Rev. Peter L. Gerety, Archbishop Emeritus; Rev. Msgrs. Joseph Chiang (Retired); James Johnson (Retired); Thomas G. Madden (Retired); Gerard M. Santora (Retired); Revs. John Borowik; Joseph L. Cassidy (Retired); Joseph J. Cestaro (Retired); Joseph F. Coda (Retired); Joseph Derbyshire; Michael Fuino; Harold T. Hermanns (Retired); Charles W.A. Herr; Frederick C. Koerner (Retired); Robert H. Langdon (Retired); John Madden; James W. McFarland (Retired); Leonard Midowski; Joseph Rice; James O. Sheerin (Retired); Thaddeus F. Zuber (Retired).

SOUTH ORANGE. *Pallottine Fathers & Brothers*, 204 Raymond Ave., P.O. Box 979, 07079-0979. Tel: 973-762-2683; Fax: 973-762-2939. Very Rev. Frank Amato, S.A.C., Prov.; Bro. Francis Meo, S.A.C., Admin.

Salesian House, 315 Self Pl., 07079. Tel: 973-761-4475; Fax: 973-763-9330. Email: salvoc@aol.com. Web: www.salesians.org. Bros. Steve Ryan, S.D.B.; Piedad Francisco Pinto, S.D.B.

TENAFLY. *Society of African Missions, Provincialate, S.M.A. Fathers*, 23 Bliss Ave., 07670. Tel: 201-567-0450; 201-567-9085; Fax: 201-541-1280; 201-567-7156. Email: SMAUSA-C@smafathers.org. Web: www.smafathers.org. Very Rev. Thomas W. Wright, S.M.A., Prov. Supr.; Revs. Thomas E. Hayden, S.M.A., Vice Prov.; James Gessler, S.M.A., Prov. Councillor; Brendan Darcy, S.M.A., Local Supr.; Michael Moran, S.M.A. (WDC), Local Supr.; Edward J. Biggane, S.M.A.; Daniel Cullen, S.M.A.; Terrance Doherty, S.M.A.; John Feeney, S.M.A. (Retired); Joseph Foley, S.M.A. (Retired); Edward Galvin, S.M.A. (Retired); Francis Gilfether, S.M.A.; John Guiney, S.M.A. (Retired); James Harrold, S.M.A. (Retired); James C. Hickey, S.M.A. (Retired); George Landry, S.M.A. (Retired); John Francis Murray, S.M.A.; James J. McConnell, S.M.A.; James Perrone, S.M.A. (Retired); Edward Richardson, S.M.A.; Eugene Riordan, S.M.A. (Retired); John Sheehan, S.M.A. (Retired); James H. Sullivan, S.M.A.

UNION CITY. *Augustinian Recollects, St. Nicholas of Tolentine Monastery*, Formerly Augustinian Recollects Prov. of St. Nicholas of Tolentine. , 3201 Central Ave., 07087. Tel: 201-433-7550; Fax: 201-422-7570. Email: plegarra@hotmail.com. Rev. Francisco Legarra, O.A.R. (NY), Supr.

Capuchin Friars - Province of the Sacred Stigmata of St. Francis, P.O. Box 809, 07087. Tel: 201-865-0611; Fax: 201-866-7035. Email: VFortucap@aol.com. Very Rev. Vincent Fortunato, O.F.M.Cap., Prov. Min.; Rev. Thomas A. Crangle, O.F.M.Cap., Vicar Prov.; Very Rev. Jude Duffy, O.F.M.Cap., Councillor; Prov. Sec.; Revs. Cyprian Rosen, O.F.M.Cap. (WIL), Councillor; Brian Tomlinson, O.F.M.Cap. (PAT), Councilor; Very Rev. Vincent Fortunato, O.F.M.Cap., Dir. Missionary Activity; Rev. Thomas A. Crangle, O.F.M.Cap., Dir. Devel.; Margaret Milizzo, Sec.

Congregation of the Passion (Passionists)-St. Michael's Residence, 526 Monastery Pl., 07087. Tel: 201-864-0018; Fax: 201-867-8651. Email: vhoagland@cpprov.org. Web: www.cptryon.org. Rev. Sebastian Kolinovsky, C.P., Mission Procurator.

Development Office Tel: 201-867-6400; Fax: 201-867-7596. John DeGraaf, Dir.

Special Gifts & Special Events Tel: 201-867-0235; Fax: 201-867-8857. Rev. Paul Wierichs, C.P.; Monica Sharp, Dir. Mgr.

Passionist Press, Inc. Tel: 201-867-6400; Fax: 201-867-8651. Email: crossplace@cpprov.org.

"Compassion" Magazine Tel: 201-867-6400; Fax: 201-864-1337. Revs. Victor Hoagland, C.P., Dir., Editor & Supr. Dir. Tel: 201-864-0018; Xavier Vitacolonna, C.P. Tel: 201-864-0018; Mr. James Fitzgerald, Lay Assoc. Tel: 201-864-0018.

Financial Office Tel: 201-867-7479; Fax: 201-867-0357. Sr. Mary Ann Tierney, S.C., CFO. Tel: 201-867-6400.

Passionist Archives Tel: 201-867-6400; Fax: 201-617-7011. Rev. Robert Carbonneau, C.P., Dir. Archives & Province Historian; Miss Anita Lewis, Archivist. Tel: 201-867-6400.

VERONA. *The Salvatorian Fathers* (Polish Mission House) , 23 Crestmont Rd., 07044. Tel: 973-746-8770; Fax: 973-857-7789. Email: salvatorianie@salvator.org. Web: www.salvator.org. Revs. Tadeusz Majcher, S.D.S., Supr.; Palka Bogdan, S.D.S.; Jacek Zebrowski, S.D.S.; Andrzej Kielkowski, S.D.S., Konsultor; Wojciech Kowalski, S.D.S.; Jan J. Mysliwiec, S.D.S.; Krzysztof Szczotka, S.D.S. (Poland), Treas.; Tadeusz Pieniazek, S.D.S.; Strzadala Wieslaw, S.D.S.; Marek Wiorkiewicz, S.D.S.; Bros. Piotr Bogawski, S.D.S.; Damian Marek, S.D.S.; Revs. Damian Tomiczek, S.D.S., Vice Supr.; Dariusz Ziebowicz, S.D.S., Konsultor; Andrzej Waszczenko, S.D.S.

WEST ORANGE. *Augustinian Recollects* Prov. Res., Monastery of St. Cloud , 29 Ridgeway Ave., 07052. Tel: 973-731-0616; Fax: 973-731-1033. Email: SAprovince@yahoo.com. Web: www.augustinianrecollects.org. Very Rev. John A.

Gruben, O.A.R., Prior Prov.; Revs. Charles Huse, O.A.R.; Francis Cregan, O.A.R. (LA). Priests 3.

[O] CONVENTS AND RESIDENCES FOR SISTERS

NEWARK. *Hermanas Misioneras del Corazon de Jesus (HMCJ)* Parish Ministry. , Sacred Heart Convent, 109 Parker St., 07104. Tel: 973-484-1516; Fax: 973-484-9701. Email: misionerascj@aol.com. Sr. Ana Josefa Fiajardo, Supr. Sisters 4.

St. Michael's Convent, 182 Broadway, 07104. Tel: 973-497-0614; 973-482-7400 (School); Fax: 973-497-0486; 973-482-1433 (School). Email: flodem@yahoo.com. Sisters of St. Francis of the Providence of God Sisters of Charity of Ottawa 2; Sisters of St. Martha 2; Total in Residence 3.

Missionaries of Charity - St. Augustine Convent, 168 Sussex Ave., 07103. Tel: 973-483-0165. Sisters 6.

Missionary Sisters of the Most Blessed Sacrament and Mary Immaculate Day Care Center. , 121 Congress St., 07105. Tel: 973-589-5794; Fax: 973-589-0154. Email: grande815@msn.com. Sr. Guadalupe Grande, Supr. Sisters 4.

Sisters of St. Joseph of Chestnut Hill, Thea House, 39 Bleeker St., 07102. Tel: 973-622-7056. Email: ssjthea@aol.com. Total in Residence 3.

Vocationist Sisters (Our Lady of Perpetual Help Center). Perpetual Help Day Nursery. , 172 Broad St., 07104. Tel: 973-484-3535; Fax: 973-484-2526. Email: perhelp@yahoo.com. Sisters 7; Total Assisted 160; Total Staff 21.

BAYONNE. *Sisters of St. Francis of Millvale*, 130 W. 49th St., 07002. Tel: 201-451-1177; Fax: 201-451-0952. Web: www.millvalefranciscans.org.

BLOOMFIELD. *Sisters of the Divine Compassion (RDC)*, Formerly Religious of the Divine Compassion (RDC), 21 Spring St., Apt. 2, 07003. Tel: 973-748-6559. Email: skavan6578@aol.com. Sisters 2.

CALDWELL. *Motherhouse and Novitiate of Sisters of St. Dominic*, 1 Ryerson Ave., 07006. Tel: 973-403-3331; Fax: 973-228-9611. Email: auhlop@hotmail.com. Web: www.caldwellop.org. Sr. Joan Doyle, Prioress. Sisters in Community 184; Sisters in Diocese 157.

DEMAREST. *Missionary Benedictine Sisters of Norfolk - St. Joseph Convent*, 274 County Rd., 07627. Tel: 201-767-3114. Sisters 4.

ELIZABETH. *Franciscan Sisters of the Immaculate Heart of Mary*, 212 Princeton Rd., 07208. Tel: 908-353-0736. Email: immaculateamerica@hotmail.com. Sisters 4.

Sisters of St. Francis of the Providence of God - SS. Peter & Paul Convent, 214 Ripley Pl., 07206. Tel: 908-289-6024; Fax: 908-289-3988. Sisters 2.

St. Walburga Monastery, 851 N. Broad St., 07208-2593. Tel: 908-352-4278; Fax: 908-352-6331. Email: Bensisnj@aol.com. Web: www.catholic-forum.com/bensisnj. Benedictine Sisters of Elizabeth, NJ Sisters In Archdiocese 49; Professed Sisters 55.

ENGLEWOOD CLIFFS. *St. Joseph Province Shalom Center*, 399 Hudson Terrace, 07632. Tel: 201-568-6348; Fax: 201-568-3764. Web: www.csjp.org/sjp. Sisters Mary Rattigan, C.S.J.P., Prov. Leader; Nora Molyneux, C.S.J.P., Asst. Prove Leader; Theresette Hunting, C.S.J.P., Archivist. Congregation of Sisters of St. Joseph of Peace, Provincial Office for St. Joseph's Province of the Sisters of St. Joseph of Peace. Sisters in Community 130.

St. Ann's Home for the Aged Tel: 201-433-0950; Fax: 201-433-6554. Total Staff 190; Total in Residence 116.

St. Ann Day Care Tel: 201-433-0950; Fax: 201-985-9638. Staff 10; Adults 50.

St. Joseph Home for the Blind Tel: 201-653-8300; Fax: 201-963-4346. Total Staff 120; Total in Residence 129.

St. Joseph School for the Blind Tel: 201-653-0578; Fax: 201-653-4087. Total Staff 99; Total in Residence 52.

St. Joseph Home Tel: 201-413-9280. Total Staff 14; Total in Residence 47.

St. Mary's Residence Tel: 201-432-6289. Total Staff 7; Total in Residence 38.

Villa Marie Claire Tel: 201-327-1325; Fax: 201-327-6647. Total Staff 11; Total in Residence 29.

Nurturing Place Day Care Tel: 201-413-1982. Child Development Center Staff 19; Children 43.

The Kenmare School Tel: 201-451-1177; Fax: 201-451-0952. Staff 13; Students 39.

The York Street Project Tel: 201-451-9838; Fax: 201-451-0952. Total Staff 9.

Stella Maris Retreat Center Tel: 732-229-0602; Fax: 732-229-8960. Total Staff 8; Total in Residence 2.

Waterspirit Ministry Tel: 732-923-9788; Fax: 732-229-8960. Total Staff 2.

St. Joseph Messenger Office Tel: 201-798-4141. Total Staff 3.

St. Michael Villa, 399 Hudson Ter., 07632. Tel: 201-871-1620; Fax: 201-871-7313. Email: sck.world@verizon.net. Sr. Cecilia King, C.S.J.P., Admin.; Rev. Walter Cron, Chap. Sisters of St. Joseph of Peace, Senior Sisters Residence and Infirmary for St. Joseph Province. Sisters 38; Total Staff 45; Total in Residence 38.

FORT LEE. *Holy Trinity Convent*, 199 Myrtle Ave., 07024. Tel: 201-944-2911. Sisters 24.

IRVINGTON. *Immaculate Conception Convent*, 121 Myrtle Ave., 07111. Tel: 201-374-6397. Augustinian Recollect Sisters (Cloistered) 10.

JERSEY CITY. *Dominican Sisters of St. Catherine of Siena (Philippines) - St. Aedan Convent*, 39 Tuers Ave., 07306. Tel: 201-451-8109; Fax: 201-985-8975. Email: fgomezop@aol.com. Web: www.saintaedan.com. Sisters Maria Fatima Gomez, O.P., Supr.; Seldita Tiorosio O.P., Prin. Sisters 4.

Holy Rosary Convent, 189 Brunswick St., 07302. Religious Teachers of St. Lucy Filippini 9.

St. Nicholas Convent, 115 Ferry St., 07307. Tel: 201-659-5644; Fax: 201-798-6868. Email: smarcelener@juno.com. Sr. Marcelene Riggin, S.C.C., Supr.

Sisters of St. Joseph of Peace, 25 Reservoir Ave., 07307. Tel: 201-656-7928.

KEARNY. *Sacred Heart Convent - Pallottine Sisters (Sisters of the Catholic Apostolate)*, 22 Wilson Ave., 07032. Tel: 201-991-0529; Fax: 201-991-0226. Email: parlati@aol.com. Web: www.shskearny.com. Sisters 7.

LODI. *Immaculate Conception Convent*, 260 S. Main St., 07644-2196. Tel: 973-473-7447; Fax: 973-473-7126. Email: felicianslodi@hotmail.com. Web: www.feliciansisters.org. Revs. Sebastian Kus, O.F.M., Chap.; Damian Colicchio, Chap.; Placid Stroik, O.F.M., Chap. Provincial House, Novitiate and Infirmary of the Felician Sisters. Sisters in Community 198.

NUTLEY. *Sisters of St. Joseph of Brentwood*, 28 Brookline Ave., 07110. Tel: 973-662-0445. Palisades Park

PLAINFIELD. *Contemplative Convent of the Missionaries of Charity*, 513 Liberty St., 07060. Tel: 908-754-1978. Sr. Mary Lourdes, M.C., Supr. Total in Residence 22.

Vocationist Sisters, 218 14th St., Palisades Park, 07650. Tel: 201-944-2413. Sr. Antonietta Cioce, S.D.V. Sisters 4.

RIDGEFIELD. *Pallottine Sisters - St. Vincent Pallotti Convent*, 545 Victory Ave., 07567. Tel: 201-941-4552. Email: sralicemarie@lycos.com. Sisters 3.

SADDLE BROOK. *Miyazaki Caritas Sisters (Korea) - Caritas Sisters Convent*, 9 Jamros Ter., 07663. Tel: 201-398-0199.

SCOTCH PLAINS. *Union Catholic Convent*, 1600 Martine Ave., 07076. Tel: 908-889-5813. Sisters of Mercy of New Jersey (R.S.M.) and Sisters of St. Joseph (S.S.J.) Total in Residence 7.

SOUTH ORANGE. *Marylawn of the Oranges Convent*, 425 Scotland Rd., 07079. Tel: 973-762-7218; Fax: 973-762-6513. Email: mloconvent@yahoo.com. Sisters 10.

SPRINGFIELD. *St. James Convent*, 35 S. Springfield Ave., 07081. Tel: 973-376-7596. Sisters of St. Joseph, Chestnut Hill, Philadelphia Total in Residence 9.

SUMMIT. *Monastery of Our Lady of the Rosary*, Morris Ave. & Springfield Ave., 07901. Tel: 908-273-1228; Fax: 908-273-6511. Email: nunsopsummit@att.net. Web: www.op.org/nunsopsummit. Sr. Mary Martin Jacobs, O.P., Prioress.

Legal Title: *Monastery of Our Lady of the Rosary, Dominican Nuns of the Perpetual Rosary* Professed Sisters 16.

TENAFLY. *Convent of Our Lady of the Angels*, 253 Knickerbocker Rd., 07670. Tel: 201-568-2171; Fax: 201-568-2352. Email: OLABetty@aol.com. Sr. Elizabeth Mannion, M.F.I.C., Supr. Missionary Franciscan Sisters of the Immaculate Conception, Attended by Carmelite Fathers from Tenafly. Sisters 61.

UNION. *Sisters of St. Francis of the Providence of God*, 1137 Burnet Ave., 07083. Tel: 908-206-1136. Sisters 2.

UNION CITY. *Holy Rosary Convent*, 1514 Central Ave., 07087. Tel: 201-617-4638; Fax: 201-617-4366. Email: holyrosaryconv@att.net. Sisters of the Catholic Apostolate (Pallottines) Sisters 6.

Holy Rosary Academy, 501 15th St., 07087. Tel: 201-864-0332; Fax: 201-864-5586.

Monastery of the Dominican Nuns of the Perpetual Rosary (Contemplative) , 605 14th St. and West St., 07087-3199. Sr. Mary Clare, O.P., Prioress. Professed Sisters 8; Total Staff 2; Total in Residence 8.

[P] RETREAT HOUSES

KEARNY. *CYO Retreat Center* Archdiocesan Youth Center and Retreat House. Retreats for groups, parishes, days of prayer recollection, workshops, seminars for laity, priests, and religious. Rooms for overnight and food service. , 499 Belgrove Dr., 07032. Tel: 201-998-0088, Ext. 814.

MAHWAH. *Carmel Retreat*, Formerly Carmel Retreat House Carmelite Community and House of Prayer. Retreats (groups, directed, private), Days of prayer, rentals, meetings, seminars. , 1071 Ramapo Valley Rd., 07430. Tel: 201-327-7090; Fax: 201-327-9133. Email: mail@carmelretreat.com. Web: www.carmelretreat.com. Revs. Michael Wastag, O.Carm., Dir.; Paul Schweizer, O.Carm., Prior; Leonard Gilman, O.Carm.; Bro. Robert Murphy, O.Carm. Priests 3; Brothers 1; Sisters 1; Total Staff 9; Total in Residence 4.

[Q] CAMPUS MINISTRY

NEWARK. *Archdiocesan Campus Ministry* 45 Bleeker St., 07102. Tel: 973-642-1613; Fax: 973-642-2601. Email: newmancenter@optonline.net. Web: www.catholiccampusministry.org. Rev. John B. Baron, Ph.D., Dir.; Sr. Jennifer Tunnicliffe, Coord. for Admin. & Devel. Total Staff 2.

The Newman Catholic Center at University Heights (Rutgers/Newark/NJIT), Formerly Essex County College, Rutgers University/Newark/NJIT 45 Bleeker St., 07102. Tel: 973-642-1613; Fax: 973-642-2601. Email: NewmanCenter@optonline.net. Web: www.catholiccampusministry.org. Rev. Mark Francis O'Malley, Campus Min. & Chap.; Maureen Madigan, Campus Min.; Sr. Jennifer Tunnicliffe, Coord. for Admin. & Devel. Serving Essex County College, Rutgers University/Newark Campus, New Jersey Institute of Technology Total Staff 3.

BLOOMFIELD. *Bloomfield College* 12 Austin Pl., 07003Web: www.catholiccampusministry.org. Rev. James J. Reilly, Chap. & Campus Min.

CRANFORD. *Union County College* 1033 Springfield Ave., 07016Web: www.catholiccampusministry.org.

HOBOKEN. *Stevens Institute of Technology* Castle Point on the Hudson, 07030. Tel: 201-659-2276. Web: www.catholiccampusministry.org. Sr. Patricia Wormann, O.P., Campus Min. & Chap.; Debra Sheridan, Campus Min. Total Staff 1.

JERSEY CITY. *New Jersey City University, Gilligan Student Center*, Formerly Jersey City State College 2039 Kennedy Blvd., Rm. 319, 07305. Tel: 201-200-2565; Fax: 201-200-2329. Web: www.catholiccampusministry.org. Rev. Luke A. Edelen, O.S.B., Chap. & Campus Min. Total Staff 1.

MAHWAH. *Ramapo College* 505 Ramapo Valley Rd., Room SC207, 07430. Tel: 201-684-7251; Fax: 201-825-0276. Email: rstanley@ramapo.edu. Rev. Ronald Stanley, O.P., Chap. & Campus Min. Total Staff 1; Students 5,200.

TEANECK. *Fairleigh Dickinson Univ.-Teaneck Campus* 1000 River Rd., 07666. Tel: 201-692-2406; Fax: 201-692-2769. Email: jbbaron@verizon.net. Rev. John B. Baron, Ph.D., Campus Min. Total Staff 1.

UNION. *Kean University* Catholic Campus Ministry, 1000 Morris Ave., 07083-7131. Tel: 908-737-4585; Fax: 201-985-0918. Email: padrealex@yahoo.com. Rev. Alexander M. Santora, Campus Min.

UPPER MONTCLAIR. *Montclair State University* Newman Catholic Center, 894 Valley Rd., 07043-2116. Tel: 973-746-2323; Fax: 973-783-3313. Email: berner@mail.montclair.edu. Rev. Albert J. Berner, B.A., S.T.B., M.A., V.F., Campus Min. & Chap.; Mrs. Mary Lou Vinges, Admin. Asst. Total Staff 2.

[R] SHRINES

KEARNY. *Eucharistic Shrine of the Adorable Face of Jesus* 672 Passaic Ave., 07032-1305. Tel: 201-997-1270; Fax: 201-997-5552.

[S] MISCELLANEOUS LISTINGS

NEWARK. *Alexian Brothers of New Jersey, Inc., Archdiocese of Newark*, P.O. Box 9500, 07104-0500. Tel: 847-640-7550; Fax: 847-981-5561.

Catholic Health and Human Services Corporation, 1160 Raymond Blvd., 07102. Tel: 973-690-3607; Fax: 973-690-3601. Mr. Donald M. Daniels, CEO & Chm. Bd.; Henry J. Amoroso, Esq, COO, & Vice Chm. Bd.; Leslie A. Hynes, Sec.; Bro. Benedict LoBalbo, F.M.S., Asst. Sec.

CatholiCare, Inc., 171 Clifton Ave., P.O. Box 9500, 07104-0500. Tel: 973-497-4002; Fax: 973-497-4018. Most Rev. Arthur J. Serratelli, S.T.D., D.D., S.S.L., Vicar Gen. & Moderator of Curia.

Deacon St. Lawrence Welfare Fund, Office of Permanent Diaconate, 171 Clifton Ave., P.O. Box 9500, 07104-9500. Tel: 973-497-4223; Fax: 973-497-4219. Email: portered@rcan.org. Deacon Ed Porter.

Diaconate Executive Committee, Archdiocesan Center, 171 Clifton Ave., P.O. Box 9500, 07104-9500. Tel: 973-497-4223; Fax: 973-497-4219.

Email: portered@rcan.org. Deacon Edward Porter.
New Ark of Hope Foundation, Inc., 494 Broad St., 07102. Tel: 973-596-4180; Fax: 973-623-2415. Richard Suszek, Exec. Vice Pres.; Bro. Benedict LoBalbo, Sec.
New Jersey Caritas Corporation, Inc., 1160 Raymond Blvd., 12th Fl., 07102. Tel: 973-497-4002; Fax: 973-497-4018. Most Rev. Paul G. Bootkoski, D.D. (MET).
CCS Holding Corporation, Inc. Tel: 973-596-3835; Fax: 973-596-3836. Catholic Community Services (See Curia Section, Vicariate for Human Services).
Domus Corporation, Inc., 494 Broad St., 07102. Tel: 973-596-5115; Fax: 973-424-9596.
Canaan House, Inc., 494 Broad St., 07102. Tel: 973-596-5115; Fax: 973-424-9596.
Sunrise House, 185 Parkhurst St., 07114. Tel: 973-624-9478; Fax: 973-424-9596.
Carmel House of Jersey City, Inc., 494 Broad St., 07102. Tel: 973-596-5115; Fax: 973-424-9596.

BAYONNE. *The Gregoire Trust*, 1241 Kennedy Blvd., 07002. Tel: 201-823-1115; Fax: 201-823-2232. Email: maristpto@aol.com. Bros. Benedict LoBalbo, F.M.S. Trustee; Edward Breslin; Lawrence Lavallee, F.M.S.; Ken Hogan.
Marist Brothers Support Trust, 1241 Kennedy Blvd., 07002. Tel: 201-823-1115; Fax: 201-823-2232. Email: maristpto@aol.com. Bros. Stephen Martin, F.M.S.; Benedict Lo Balbo, F.M.S. Congregation of the Marist Brothers

ELIZABETH. *St. Joseph's Social Service Center*, 118 Division St., 07201. Tel: 908-352-2989; 908-352-2966; Fax: 908-354-1433. Sr. Jacinta Fernandes, O.S.B., Dir. Total Staff 5; Total Assisted 4,550.

EMERSON. *Magnificat: A Ministry to Catholic Women*, 160 Jefferson Ave., 07630. Tel: 201-265-2738. Email: grand174@aol.com.
Glen Rock NJ-Handmaid of the Lord Chapter Service Team Elizabeth Tobin, Coord.; Cheryl Sarno, Asst. Coord.; Patricia Patterman, Treas.; Joanne Gurske, Sec.; Peggy O'Neil, Historian; Rev. Gerald Lombardo, Spiritual Advisor.

HOBOKEN. *F.A.I.T.H. Services Inc.*, 307 Willow Ave., 07030. Tel: 201-792-6161; Fax: 201-792-8595. Email: jlorenzo@fhsnj.org. Web: www.faithservices.org. Deacon John Lorenzo; Sr. Renee Zinciuk, C.S.W., L.C.S.W., Dir. Clinical Svcs. & Referrals for Svcs. Extends the religious apostolate of charitable services of the Franciscan Sisters of the Poor, a religious congregation of the Roman Catholic Church by fulfilling the specific purposes set forth as follows: To provide community-based case management, education, counseling and other social support services for HIV/AIDS persons, their significant others and caregivers. Total Staff 25; Total Assisted 2,188.

JERSEY CITY. *Bon Secours & Canterbury Partnership for Care*, 25 McWilliams Pl., 07302. Tel: 201-418-2047; Fax: 201-418-2286. Joan Quigley, Vice Pres. External Affairs & Contact Person.
St. Francis Hospital, 25 McWilliams Pl., 07302. Tel: 201-418-2047; Fax: 201-418-2286. Michael Sniffen, Interim CEO; Richard Evans, Vice Pres., Mission; Rev. Michael Onyekwere, Chap.; Janet Freed, Dir. Pastoral Care & Chap.; John E. Hopkins, Chap.; Marjorie Boyden-Edmonds, Chap. Bed Capacity 238; Patients Assisted Annually 52,000.
St. Mary Hospital, 308 Willow Ave., Hoboken, 07030. Tel: 201-418-1045; Fax: 201-418-1011. Michael Sniffen, Interim CEO; Richard Evans, Vice Pres., Mission; Rev. Michael Onyekwere, Chap.; Janet Freed, Dir. Pastoral Care & Chap.; John E. Hopkins, Chap.; Marjorie Boyden-Edmonds, Chap. Franciscan Sisters of the Poor 2; Bed Capacity 328; Patients Assisted Annually 105,000.
Ministry Resource Center for Women Religious, 41 Emory St., 07304. Tel: 201-332-3240. Email: minconn@earthlink.net. Web: www.ministryconnect.org. Susan Whitsell, C.S.J.P., Dir. Total Staff 1; Total Assisted 200.
St. Patrick's Housing Corp., 492 Bramhall Ave., 07304. Tel: 201-332-8600. Christopher Garlin, Dir.

KEARNY. *The Family of Nazareth, Inc.*, 672 Passaic Ave., 07032. Tel: 201-997-3220; Fax: 201-997-5552. Email: fnazareth@rmnewark.org. Fred Canlas, Pres. A foundation to support the work of the Redemptoris Mater Missionary Seminary and for the new evangelization.
New Jersey Boystown, 499 Belgrove Dr., 07032. Tel: 201-246-7378; Fax: 201-991-7306.

LODI. **The Promise Outreach, Inc.* We visit, correspond with, and provide opportunity for spirituality and other basic needs to teens in programs, correctional institutions and centers of rehabilation. , 260 S. Main St., 07644. Tel: 973-460-3229; Fax: 973-473-7126. Email: felicianpromise@aol.com. Total Staff 20.

MAHWAH. *Paulist Press*, 997 MacArthur Blvd., 07430. Tel: 201-825-7300; Fax: 201-825-8345. Email: info@paulistpress.com. Web: www.paulistpress.com. Revs. Kevin A. Lynch, C.S.P.; Lawrence Boadt, C.S.P.; Michael J. Hunt, C.S.P. Total Staff 80.

ORANGE. *Mee Joo Catholic Inc.*, Formerly Mee Joo Catholic Publishing257 Central Ave., 07050. Tel: 973-672-6650; Fax: 973-673-6720. Email: augpark@yahoo.com. Web: www.koreancatholic.org. Rev. Msgr. Augustin C. Park.

PLAINFIELD. *RENEW International*, 1232 George St., 07062-1717. Tel: 908-769-5400; Fax: 908-769-5660. Email: Renew@renewintl.org. Web: www.renewintl.org; www.ParishLife.com. Rev. Msgr. Thomas A. Kleissler, Pres.; Michael Brough, Dir.; Deirdre Trabert Malacrea, Asst. Dir.; Mary Beth Oria, Asst. Dir.
Coordinators: Eric Dill, Human Resources; Sr. Cheryl Erb, R.S.M., RENEW Services; Peter Glen, Finance Mgr.; Deacon Michael Hanly, RENEW Services; Jose Hernandez, Development; Sisters Mary McGuinness, O.P., Special Projects; Theresa Rickard, O.P., Controller; Theresa Rickard, O.P., Small Community Svcs.
RENEW International Service Team: Sr. Louise Alff, F.M.D.C.; Dr. Irma Chavez; Sisters Maureen Colleary, F.S.P.; Sue Seltenright DeFerrari; Alma Garcia; Dolly Bandura, Campus RENEW; Manuel Hernandez; Lynn Hull; Mary Ann Jeselson; Greg Kremer; Sr. Barbara Ann Sgro, O.P.; Lee Thomas, Renew/Young Adult Ministry; Anthony Visocchi; Sr. Joanne Wallace, I.H.M.
Operations and Administrative Staff: Susan Capurso; Clara Chernes; Regina Crowley; Sean Donahue; Josephine Hutchins; Julie Jones; Carolyn Newkirk; Sonia Pena; C. William Reilly; Sandra Schroyer; Sr. Alice Yohe, S.S.J.

RUTHERFORD. *The Community of God's Love* Catholic Charismatic Community , 70 W. Passaic Ave., 07070. Tel: 201-935-0344; Fax: 201-804-8279. Email: theCGL@aol.com. Rev. P. Latronico, Chap.; Leslie T. Williams, Community Dir.

SHORT HILLS. *Friends of the Newark Monastery, Inc.*, 9 Grosvenor Rd., 07078. Email: aluzarraga@shearman.com. Alberto Luzarraga, Pres. & Contact Person.

SOUTH ORANGE. *The Pallottines of South Orange, Inc.*, 204 Raymond Ave., 07079-2305. Tel: 973-763-5591. Bro. Francis Meo, S.A.C., Supr.
Salesians of Don Bosco, Salesians House, 315 Self Pl., 07079. Tel: 973-761-0201; Fax: 973-763-9330. Email: salvoc@aol.com salymeast@aol.com. Web: www.salesians.org.
Offices of Vocation and Youth Ministry Tel: 973-761-0102; Fax: 973-763-9330. Email: salvoc@aol.com. Revs. Steve Ryan, S.D.B., Vocation Dir. & Prov. Councillor for Youth Ministry; P. Francis Pinto, S.D.B. Total in Residence 2.
U.S. Catholic China Bureau, Seton Hall University, 07079-2689. Tel: 973-763-1131; Fax: 973-763-1543. Email: chinabur@shu.edu. Web: www.usccb.net. Eugene Theroux Esq., Chm., Bd. of Directors; C. Douglas Lovejoy, Exec. Dir.; Sr. Janet Carroll, M.M., Outreach Prog. Assoc.; Barbara McCarthy, Admin. Asst. & Prog. Assoc. Exists to foster communication and friendship with the people of China through sharing the values of the Gospel of Jesus Christ. It promotes understanding among American Catholics about the Catholic Church and the situation of Catholic communities in China. It fosters re-engagement of the U.S. Catholic Church in a new missionary partnership with the Catholic Church in China. USCCB publishes the "China Church Quarterly", sponsors National Catholic China Conference, religious study tours to China and other activities to sustain a shared commitment to mission with the Catholic Church in China. Total Staff 3.

TEANECK. *Holy Name Health Care Foundation*, 718 Teaneck Rd., 07666. Tel: 201-833-3187; Fax: 201-227-6230. Email: masio@mailholyname.org. Web: www.holyname.org. Michael Maron, Pres. Sisters of St. Joseph of Peace

UNION. *The Association of St. Philomena's Helpers to the Suffering & Poor*, P.O. Box 393, 07083-0393. Tel: 908-851-7205; Fax: 908-687-4209. Rev. George M. Keating, Spiritual Moderator (Retired).

UNION CITY. *Park Performing Arts, Inc.* (Home of America's oldest Passion Play) , 560 32nd St., 07087. Tel: 201-865-6980; Fax: 201-865-5339. Email: parkpac/@aol.com. Web: www.passionplayusa.org; www.parkpac.org. Rev. Kevin P. Ashe, Exec. Dir. Total Staff 7.

RELIGIOUS INSTITUTES OF MEN REPRESENTED IN THE ARCHDIOCESE

For further details refer to the corresponding bracketed number in the Religious Institutes of Men or Women section.

[0100]—*Adorno Fathers*—C.R.M.
[0200]—*Benedictine Monks* (Newark Abbey; St. Mary Abbey)—O.S.B.
[0330]—*Brothers of Christian Schools* (Baltimore Prov.; Long Island/New England Prov.; New York Prov.)—F.S.C.
[1350]—*Brothers of St. Francis Xavier*—C.F.X.
[0470]—*The Capuchin Friars* (Prov. of the Stigmata)—O.F.M.Cap.
[0270]—*Carmelite Fathers & Brothers* (American Prov.)—O.Carm.
[0380]—*Comboni Missionaries of the Heart of Jesus (Verona)*—M.C.C.J.
[0310]—*Congregation of Christian Brothers*—C.F.C.
[1000]—*Congregation of the Passion* (Eastern Prov.)—C.P.
[0520]—*Franciscan Friars* (Prov. of Most Holy Name; Prov. of the Assumption)—O.F.M.
[0530]—*Franciscan Friars of the Atonement*—S.A.
[0535]—*Franciscan Friars of the Renewal*—C.F.R.
[0690]—*Jesuit Fathers and Brothers* (Prov. of New York).—S.J.
[0770]—*The Marist Brothers*—F.M.S.
[1210]—*Missionaries of St. Charles (Scalabrinians)*—C.S.
[0840]—*Missionary Servants of the Most Holy Trinity*—S.T.
[0430]—*Order of Preachers-Dominicans* (Prov. of St. Joseph, Eastern Dominican Prov.)—O.P.
[0150]—*Order of the Augustinian Recollects* (Prov. of St. Augustine)—O.A.R.
[0150]—*Order of the Augustinian Recollects* (Prov. of St. Nicholas of Tolentine)—O.A.R.
[1030]—*Paulist Fathers*—C.S.P.
[]—*Province of the Immaculate Conception*
[1070]—*Redemptorist Fathers* (Byzantine Ukrainians)—C.Ss.R.
[1070]—*Redemptorist Fathers* (Prov. of Campo Grande, Brazil)—C.Ss.R.
[1190]—*Salesians of Don Bosco*—S.D.B.
[0110]—*Society of African Missions*—S.M.A.
[0990]—*Society of the Catholic Apostolate* (Prov. of the Immaculate Conception)—S.A.C.
[1200]—*Society of the Divine Savior*—S.D.S.
[1170]—*St. Patrick Missionary Society*—S.P.S.
[0560]—*Third Order Regular of Saint Francis* (U.S.A. Commissarate of the Spanish Prov.)—T.O.R.
[]—*Union Lumen Dei*—L.D.
[1340]—*Vocationist Fathers*—S.D.V.

RELIGIOUS INSTITUTES OF WOMEN REPRESENTED IN THE ARCHDIOCESE

[0130]—*Apostles of the Sacred Heart of Jesus*—A.S.C.J.
[]—*Augustinian Recollect Sisters* (Mexico)—O.A.R.
[0230]—*Benedictine Sisters of Pontifical Jurisdiction-Newark* (Benedictine Sisters of Baltimore; Benedictine Sisters of Elizabeth)—O.S.B.
[1810]—*Bernardine Franciscan Sisters*—O.S.F.
[]—*Congregation of Kkottongnae Sisters of Jesus*—C.K.S.J.
[0850]—*Daughters of Mary Help of Christians*—F.M.A.
[]—*Daughters of Mary, Mothers of Mercy* (Nigeria)—D.M.M.M.
[1050]—*Dominican Contemplative Nuns (Cloistered)*—O.P.
[1070-11]—*Dominican Sisters* (Sparkill, NY)—O.P.
[1070-18]—*Dominican Sisters* (Caldwell, NJ)—O.P.
[1070-15]—*Dominican Sisters* (Blauvelt, NY)—O.P.
[1070-06]—*Dominican Sisters of Hope* (Newburgh, NY)—O.P.
[1070-09]—*Dominican Sisters of St. Catherine of Siena (Philippines)*
[1170]—*Felician Sisters*—C.S.S.F.
[1400]—*Franciscan Missionary Sister of the Sacred Heart*—F.M.S.C.
[1180]—*Franciscan Sisters of Allegany, New York*—O.S.F.
[1425]—*Franciscan Sisters of Peace*—F.S.P.
[1460]—*Franciscan Sisters of St. Elizabeth*—F.S.S.E.
[1190]—*Franciscan Sisters of the Atonement*—S.A.
[]—*Franciscan Sisters of the Immaculate Heart of Mary (India)*—F.I.H.M.
[1440]—*Franciscan Sisters of the Poor*—S.F.P.
[]—*Hermanas Missionaras del Corazon de Jesus* (Dominican Republic)—H.M.C.J.
[3790]—*Institute of the Sisters of St. Dorothy*—S.S.D.
[2300]—*Little Servant Sisters of the Immaculate Conception*—L.S.I.C.
[]—*Maryknoll Sisters of St. Dominic*—M.M.
[2710]—*Missionaries of Charity* (Active and Contemplative)—M.C.
[0210]—*Missionary Benedictine Sisters of Tutzing* (Korean Mission)—O.S.B.
[1360]—*Missionary Franciscan Sisters of the*

Immaculate Conception—M.F.I.C.
[2790]—*Missionary Servants of the Most Blessed Trinity*—M.S.B.T.
[2760]—*Missionary Sisters of the Immaculate Conception of the Mother of God*—S.M.I.C.
[2780]—*Missionary Sisters of the Most Blessed Sacrament and Mary Immaculate*—M.SS.M.I.
[]—*Miyazaki Caritas Sisters* (Japan/Korea)—C.S.M.
[3430]—*Religious Teachers Filippini*—M.P.F.
[2970]—*School Sisters of Notre Dame*—S.S.N.D.
[1700]—*School Sisters of the Third Order of St. Francis* (Bethlehem, PA)—O.S.F.
[0540]—*Sisters of Charity of Ottawa*—S.C.O.
[0590]—*Sisters of Charity of Saint Elizabeth, Convent Station*—S.C.
[0650]—*Sisters of Charity of St. Vincent de Paul of New York*—S.C.
[0660]—*Sisters of Christian Charity*—S.C.C.
[2575]—*Sisters of Mercy of the Americas* (New Jersey)—R.S.M.
[1620]—*Sisters of Saint Francis of Millvale, Pennsylvania*—O.S.F.
[3893]—*Sisters of Saint Joseph of Chestnut Hill, Philadelphia*—S.S.J.
[1650]—*Sisters of St. Francis of Philadelphia*—O.S.F.
[1660]—*Sisters of St. Francis of Providence of God*—O.S.F.
[3820]—*Sisters of St. John the Baptist*—C.S.J.B.
[3890]—*Sisters of St. Joseph of Peace*—C.S.J.P.
[3830-05]—*Sisters of St. Joseph of Rockville Centre, Brentwood*—C.S.J.
[3937]—*Sisters of St. Martha of Antigonish, N.S.*—C.S.M.
[3140]—*Sisters of the Catholic Apostolate (Pallottine)*—C.S.A.C.
[2980]—*Sisters of the Congregation of Notre Dame*—C.N.D.
[0970]—*Sisters of the Divine Compassion*—R.D.C.
[1490]—*Sisters of the Third Franciscan Order*—O.S.F.
[3610]—*Sisters Servants of Mary Immaculate*—S.S.M.I.
[2160]—*Sisters, Servants of the Immaculate Heart of Mary (Scranton)*—I.H.M.
[4060]—*Society of the Holy Child Jesus*—S.H.C.J.
[1650]—*The Sisters of St. Francis of Philadelphia*—O.S.F.
[]—*Union Lumen Dei*—L.D.
[4210]—*Vocationist Sisters*—S.D.V.

ARCHDIOCESAN CEMETERIES

COLONIA. *St. Gertrude*
DARLINGTON. *Maryrest*
EAST HANOVER. *Gate of Heaven*
EAST ORANGE. *Holy Sepulchre*
St. Mary
FRANKLIN LAKES. *Christ the King*
JERSEY CITY. *Holy Name*
Saint Peter
NORTH ARLINGTON. *Holy Cross*
RIVER VALE. *St. Andrew*

PAROCHIAL CEMETERIES

NEWARK. *Mount Olivet*
BELLEVILLE. *St. Peter's*
BLOOMFIELD. *Mount Olivet*
CLARK. *St. Mary's*
FORT LEE. *Madonna*
HACKENSACK. *St. Joseph's*
HOHOKUS. *St. Luke's*
LINDEN. *Mount Calvary*
LYNDHURST. *St. Joseph's*
ORANGE. *St. John's*
PLAINFIELD. *St. Mary's*
RIVER VALE. *St. Andrew's*
SHORT HILLS. *St. Rose of Lima*
SUMMIT. *St. Teresa's*
TENAFLY. *Mount Carmel*
UPPER MONTCLAIR. *Immaculate Conception*

NECROLOGY

† Abramowicz, Rev. Msgr. Sylvester, (Retired)—Died Feb. 1, 2003
† Jarvais, Rev. Msgr. Walter G., (Retired)—Died Feb. 3, 2003
† Orrico, Rev. Msgr. Caesar G., Pastor Emeritus—Died Aug. 1, 2003
† Price, Rev. Msgr. Edward G.—Died Nov. 20, 2003
† Clyde, George A., (Retired)—Died Oct. 20, 2003
† Czachorowski, Richard C., Lyndhurst, NJ St. Michael—Died July 21, 2003
† DiCesare, Giosue Scotto, Newark, NJ St. Michael's—Died 2003
† Doyle, John F., (Retired)—Died Nov. 27, 2003
† Drexler, George D., (Retired)—Died Oct. 15, 2003
† Hart, William T., (Retired)—Died July 5, 2003
† Hill, James, Tenafly, NJ Society of African Missions, Provincialate—Died 2003
† Holick, Rev. Robert
† McGuinness, Lester A., (Retired)—Died Dec. 9, 2003
† O'Neill, James R., (Retired)—Died April 27, 2003
† Rutkowski, Stephen C., (Retired)—Died March 2, 2003
† Sogliuzzo, W. Gerard—Died Oct. 3, 2003

Archdiocese of New Orleans

(Archidioecesis Novae Aureliae)

Most Reverend

ALFRED C. HUGHES, S.T.D.

Archbishop of New Orleans; ordained December 15, 1957; appointed Auxiliary Bishop of Boston July 21, 1981; ordained Auxiliary Bishop of Boston September 14, 1981; appointed Bishop of Baton Rouge September 7, 1993; installed Bishop of Baton Rouge November 4, 1993; appointed Coadjutor Archbishop of New Orleans February 16, 2001; appointed Archbishop of New Orleans January 3, 2002 *Office: 7887 Walmsley Ave., New Orleans, LA 70125*. Tel: 504-861-9521.

Archdiocesan Administration Building: 7887 Walmsley Ave., New Orleans, LA 70125-3496. Tel: 504-861-9521; Fax: 504-866-2906.

Web: www.archdiocese-no.org

Most Reverend

FRANCIS B. SCHULTE, D.D.

Former Archbishop of New Orleans; ordained May 10, 1952; appointed Titular Bishop of Afufenia and Auxiliary Bishop of Philadelphia June 27, 1981; ordained to the episcopacy August 12, 1981; appointed Sixth Bishop of Wheeling-Charleston June 4, 1985; promoted to Metropolitan See of New Orleans December 13, 1988; installed February 14, 1989; retired January 3, 2002

Most Reverend

PHILIP M. HANNAN, D.D., J.C.D., S.T.L.

Former Archbishop of New Orleans; ordained December 8, 1939; appointed Titular Bishop of Hieropolis and Auxiliary Bishop of Washington June 16, 1956; consecrated August 28, 1956; promoted to Archbishop of New Orleans September 29, 1965; installed October 13, 1965; retired February 14, 1989 *106 Metairie Lawn Dr., Metairie, LA 70001*. Tel: 504-840-9898.

Most Reverend

ROGER P. MORIN

Auxiliary Bishop of New Orleans; ordained April 15, 1971; appointed Titular Bishop of Aulona and Auxiliary Bishop of New Orleans February 11, 2003; consecrated April 22, 2003 *Office: 7887 Walmsley Ave., New Orleans, LA 70125-3496*.

Most Reverend

DOMINIC CARMON, S.V.D., D.D., V.G.

Auxiliary Bishop of New Orleans; ordained February 2, 1960; appointed Auxiliary Bishop of New Orleans and Titular Bishop of Rusicade December 16, 1992; consecrated February 11, 1993 *Office: P.O. Box 641000, Kenner, LA 70064-1000*. Tel: 504-468-1441; Fax: 504-468-3305.

Most Reverend

NICHOLAS D'ANTONIO, O.F.M., D.D.

ordained June 7, 1942; appointed Prelate Nullius, Ordinary of Olancho, Honduras, C.A. December 31, 1963; consecrated July 25, 1966; appointed Vicar for Spanish-Speaking, New Orleans August 22, 1977; retired July 10, 1991 *Res.: 2820 Burdette St., New Orleans, LA 70125-2596*. Tel: 504-866-2741.

Square Miles 4,208.

Established April 25, 1793; Archdiocese July 19, 1850.

Comprises the following Parishes of Louisiana: Orleans, St. Bernard, Plaquemines, Jefferson, St. Charles, St. John the Baptist, St. Tammany and Washington.

Legal Title: For legal titles of parishes and archdiocesan institutions, consult the Chancery Office.

STATISTICAL OVERVIEW

Personnel	
Archbishops	1
Retired Archbishops	2
Auxiliary Bishops	2
Retired Bishops	1
Abbots	1
Priests: Diocesan Active in Diocese	154
Priests: Diocesan Active Outside Diocese	13
Priests: Diocesan in Foreign Missions	1
Priests: Retired, Sick or Absent	52
Number of Diocesan Priests	220
Religious Priests in Diocese	190
Total Priests in Diocese	410
Extern Priests in Diocese	26
Ordinations:	
Diocesan Priests	3
Religious Priests	2
Transitional Deacons	3
Permanent Deacons in Diocese	190
Total Brothers	111
Total Sisters	739
Parishes	
Parishes	142
With Resident Pastor:	
Resident Diocesan Priests	101
Resident Religious Priests	35
Without Resident Pastor:	
Administered by Priests	6
Missions	8
Pastoral Centers	1
Welfare	
Health Care Centers	4
Total Assisted	194,610
Homes for the Aged	25
Total Assisted	2,908
Residential Care of Children	2
Total Assisted	331
Day Care Centers	16
Total Assisted	1,441
Specialized Homes	3
Total Assisted	4,143
Special Centers for Social Services	63
Total Assisted	114,229
Residential Care of Disabled	10
Total Assisted	180
Other Institutions	6
Total Assisted	1,413
Educational	
Seminaries, Diocesan	2
Students from This Diocese	23
Students from Other Diocese	133
Seminaries, Religious	2
Students Religious	37
Total Seminarians	60
Colleges and Universities	3
Total Students	11,185
High Schools, Diocesan and Parish	10
Total Students	6,014
High Schools, Private	13
Total Students	10,608
Elementary Schools, Diocesan and Parish	72
Total Students	31,778
Elementary Schools, Private	10
Total Students	1,898
Non-residential Schools for the Disabled	1
Total Students	225
Catechesis/Religious Education:	
High School Students	4,118
Elementary Students	14,972
Total Students under Catholic Instruction	80,858
Teachers in the Diocese:	
Priests	77
Brothers	29
Sisters	136
Lay Teachers	4,341
Vital Statistics	
Receptions into the Church:	
Infant Baptism Totals	5,790
Adult Baptism Totals	658
Received into Full Communion	533
First Communions	5,999
Confirmations	5,532
Marriages:	
Catholic	1,502
Interfaith	480
Total Marriages	1,982
Deaths	4,396
Total Catholic Population	488,004
Total Population	1,359,136

Former Bishops and Archbishops—Rt. Revs. LUIS PENALVER Y CARDENAS, D.D. (Retired), consecrated in 1793; transferred to Guatemala, in 1801; resigned in 1806; retired to Havana, Cuba; died in Havana, July 17, 1810; Under the administration of the Archbishop of Baltimore from 1805-1815.; FRANCIS PORRO Bishop-elect; LOUIS WILLIAM DUBOURG, S.S., D.D., consecrated Sept. 24, 1815; died Archbishop of Besancon, Dec. 1833; JOSEPH ROSATI, C.M., D.D., consecrated March 25, 1824; Bishop of Tanagre and coadjutor; transferred to St. Louis, March 20, 1827; died Sept. 25, 1843; LEO DE NECKERE, C.M., D.D., consecrated Aug. 4, 1829; died Sept. 4, 1833; Most Revs. ANTOINE BLANC, first Archbishop; consecrated Nov. 22, 1835; Archbishop, July 19, 1850; died June 20, 1860; JEAN MARIE ODIN, C.M., D.D., consecrated Bishop of Claudiopolis and Vicar-Apostolic of Texas, March 6, 1842; transferred to Galveston, 1847; promoted to New Orleans in 1861; died at Ambierle, France, May 25, 1870; NAPOLEON J. PERCHE, consecrated Bishop of Abdera and coadjutor, March 21, 1870; promoted to the See of New Orleans, May 25, 1870; died Dec. 1883; F. X. LERAY, D.D., consecrated Bishop of Natchitoches, April 22, 1877; appt. coadjutor of New Orleans, and Bishop of Janopolis, Oct. 23, 1879; promoted to the See of New Orleans, Dec., 1883; died at Chateaugiron, France, Sept. 23, 1887; FRANCIS JANSSENS, D.D., consecrated Bishop of Natchez, MS, May 1, 1881; promoted to the Archiepiscopal See of New Orleans, Aug. 7, 1888; died June 9, 1897; PLACIDE LOUIS CHAPELLE, D.D., Apostolic Delegate Extraordinary for Cuba and Puerto Rico; Archbishop of New Orleans; appt. Bishop of Arabissus and Coadjutor of Santa Fe cum jure successionis, Aug. 21, 1891; consecrated Nov. 1, 1891; promoted to the Titular Archiepiscopal See of Sebaste May 10, 1893; Archbishop of Santa Fe, Jan. 9, 1894; appt. to New Orleans, Dec. 1, 1897; died Aug. 9, 1905; JAMES H. BLENK, S.M., D.D., appt. Bishop of Puerto Rico, June 12, 1899; consecrated July 2, 1899; promoted to the See of New Orleans, April 20, 1906; died April 20, 1917; JOHN W. SHAW, D.D., appt. Coadjutor Bishop of San Antonio, Feb. 7, 1910; consecrated Titular Bishop of Castabala, April 14, 1910; succeeded to the See of San Antonio, March 11, 1911; made assistant at the Pontifical Throne, Sept., 1916;; promoted to the See of New Orleans, Jan. 25, 1918; died Nov. 2, 1934; JOSEPH FRANCIS RUMMEL, D.D., ord. May 24, 1902; appt. Bishop of Omaha, March 30, 1928; consecrated May 29, 1928; appt. Archbishop of New Orleans, Mar. 9, 1935; died Nov. 8, 1964; His Eminence JOHN CARDINAL CODY, D.D., consecrated July 2, 1947; promoted to Coadjutor cum jure successionis of New Orleans, Aug. 10, 1961; acceded to the See, Nov. 8, 1964; transferred to Chicago, June 16, 1965; created

Cardinal, June 26, 1967; died April 25, 1982; Most Revs. Philip M. Hannan, D.D., J.C.D., S.T.L. (Retired), Archbishop of New Orleans; ord. Dec. 8, 1939; appt. Titular Bishop of Hieropolis and Auxiliary Bishop of Washington, June 16, 1956; consecrated Aug. 28, 1956; promoted to Archbishop of New Orleans, Sept. 29, 1965; retired Feb. 14, 1989; Francis B. Schulte, D.D. (Retired), Archbishop of New Orleans; ord. May 10, 1952; appt. Titular Bishop of Afufenia and Auxiliary Bishop of Philadelphia, June 27, 1981; appt. Sixth Bishop of Wheeling-Charleston, June 4, 1985; appt. Archbishop of New Orleans, Dec. 13, 1988; installed Feb. 14, 1989; Pallium conferred by Pope John Paul II at the Vatican, June 29, 1989;; retired Jan. 3, 2002.

Vicars General—Most Rev. Dominic Carmon, S.V.D., P.O. Box 641000, Kenner, 70064-1000. Tel: 504-468-1441; Fax: 504-468-3305; Rev. Msgr. Roger P. Morin, V.G., 7887 Walmsley Ave., New Orleans, 70125-3496. Tel: 504-861-6262; 504-861-9521; Fax: 504-861-6312; 504-866-2906.

Moderator of the Curia—Rev. Msgr. Roger P. Morin, V.G.

Chancellor—Rev. Gerald L. Seiler Jr., M.Div., J.C.L., 7887 Walmsley Ave., New Orleans, 70125-3496. Tel: 504-861-6256; 504-861-9521; Fax: 504-866-2906.

Financial and Administrative Services—Mr. John L. Eckholdt.

Archdiocesan Administration Building—7887 Walmsley Ave., New Orleans, 70125-3496. Tel: 504-861-9521; Fax: 504-866-2906. Office Hours: Mon.-Fri. 9-5

Metropolitan Tribunal—Very Rev. Raymond C. Finn, O.P., Judicial Vicar All rogatorial commissions should be sent to this address c/o: 7887 Walmsley Ave., New Orleans, 70125-3496. Tel: 504-861-6291; Fax: 504-866-2906. Email: tribunal@archdiocese-no.org.

Court of First Instance—

Adjutant Judicial Vicar—Rev. Msgr. Clinton J. Doskey, J.C.L.

Coordinator (Court of First Instance)—Sr. Waldia Ann Warden, O.P., J.C.L.

Court of Second Instance— Reviews all marriage cases from the six dioceses of Louisiana.

Adjutant Judicial Vicar—Rev. Gerald L. Seiler Jr., M.Div., J.C.L., 7887 Walmsley Ave., New Orleans, 70125-3496. Tel: 504-861-6256; Fax: 504-866-2906.

Coordinator (Court of Second Instance)—Deacon A. David Warriner Jr.

Judges—Rev. William J. O'Donnell, J.C.L.; Rev. Msgr. L. Earl Gauthreaux, J.C.L., V.F.; Revs. Thomas E. Kinney, J.C.L.; Vien The Nguyen, J.C.L.; Rev. Msgr. Andrew C. Taormina, J.D.

Associate Judges—Deacons Peter E. Duffy, J.D.; Frans Labranche Jr., J.D.; Paul A. Nalty; Sr. Esther Redmann, O.S.U., J.C.L.

Defenders of the Bond—Revs. Benjamin Piovan; Lee J. Saloy, M.Div.; Sr. Waldia Ann Warden, O.P., J.C.L.

Approved Advocates— Priests and Deacons of the Archdiocese.

Appointed Special Advocates—Deacons Andrea Capaci; Gerard Fasullo Sr.; Arthur Kingsmill; A. David Warriner Jr.; Sr. M. Judene Lillie, O.P.

Court Experts—Octavia Kennedy, Ph.D.; Sr. Carmelita Centanni, M.S.C., Ph.D.

Secretaries/Ecclesiastical Notaries (Court of First Instance)—Ms. Olivia George; Mrs. Elena Graf-Gonzalez; Ms. Louann Hood; Mrs. Rosalina Nunez-Nguyen; Mrs. Lynn R. Strander, (Court of Second Instance).

Archdiocesan Consultors—Most Rev. Dominic Carmon, S.V.D., D.D., V.G.; Rev. Msgrs. Clinton J. Doskey, J.C.L.; Ray P. Hebert (Retired); Crosby W. Kern; Very Rev. Neal W. McDermott, O.P.; Rev. Msgr. Roger P. Morin, V.G.

Deans—Very Revs. Michael P. Jacques, S.S.E., V.F., Cathedral Deanery I; James A. Tarantino, V.F., City Park-Gentilly Deanery II; Desmond G. Crotty, V.F., Uptown Deanery III; Michel R. Boutot, C.S.Sp., V.F., Inner City Deanery IV; Rev. Msgrs. Frank J. Giroir, V.F., East Jefferson Deanery V; Henry J. Bugler, V.F., St. John-St. Charles Deanery VI; Very Revs. William O'Riordan, V.F., West Bank Deanery VII; Patrick B. Sanders, V.F., Algiers-Placquemines Deanery VIII; Mark Lomax, V.F., St. Bernard Deanery IX; Ronald L. Calkins, V.F., West St. Tammany-Washington Deanery X; Rev. Msgrs. L. Earl Gauthreaux, J.C.L., V.F., New Orleans East Deanery XI; Lanaux J. Rareshide, V.F., East St. Tammany-Washington Deanery XII.

Archdiocesan Administrative Council—Most Rev. Alfred C. Hughes, S.T.D., Chm.; Rev. Msgr. Roger P. Morin, V.G., Vice Chm.; Very Rev. Joseph S. Palermo Jr., Sec. Members of the Board: Most Rev. Dominic Carmon, S.V.D., D.D., V.G.; Very Rev. Neal W. McDermott, O.P.; Rev. Gerald L. Seiler Jr., M.Div., J.C.L.; Sisters Anthony Barczykowski, D.C.; Suellen Tennyson, M.S.C.; Rev. Msgr. Terry B. Becnel, V.F.; Mr. John L. Eckholdt.

Priests Council—Most Rev. Alfred C. Hughes, S.T.D., Pres.; Rev. Msgr. Andrew C. Taormina, J.D., Chm.

Archdiocesan Finance Council—Most Rev. Alfred C. Hughes, S.T.D., Chm.; Rev. Msgr. Roger P. Morin, V.G., Vice Chm.

Censores Librorum—Rev. Gerald L. Seiler Jr., M.Div., J.C.L., Coord.

Louisiana Catholic Conference—Mr. Daniel J. Loar, Dir., 3423 Hundred Oaks Ave., Baton Rouge, 70808-1548. Tel: 225-344-7120; Fax: 225-383-9591. Email: lacathconf@cox.net.

Office of the Vicar General and Moderator of the Curia

Vicar General and Moderator of the Curia—Rev. Msgr. Roger P. Morin, V.G., 7887 Walmsley Ave., New Orleans, 70125-3496. Tel: 504-861-6262; Fax: 504-861-6312; 504-866-2906.

Archives (Archdiocesan)—Dr. Charles E. Nolan, 1100 Chartres St., New Orleans, 70116-2596. Tel: 504-529-2651; Fax: 504-529-3075.

Canonical Permissions and Dispensations—Rev. Gerald L. Seiler Jr., M.Div., J.C.L., 7887 Walmsley Ave., New Orleans, 70125-3496. Tel: 504-861-6256; 504-861-9521; Fax: 504-866-2906.

Catholic Foundation for the Archdiocese of New Orleans, Inc.—Mr. Peter R. Quirk, Exec. Dir., 1000 Howard Ave., Ste. 700, New Orleans, 70113-1903. Tel: 504-596-3045; Fax: 504-596-3068.

Communications—Rev. William F. Maestri, M.Div., M.A., Dir., 1000 Howard Ave., Ste. 400, New Orleans, 70113-1903. Tel: 504-596-3023; Fax: 504-596-3020.

Development Office—Mr. Peter R. Quirk, Exec. Dir., 1000 Howard Ave., Ste. 700, New Orleans, 70113-1903. Tel: 504-596-3045; Fax: 504-596-3068.

Legal Services—Rev. Msgr. Roger P. Morin, V.G.; Charles I. Denechaud III; Otto Schoenfeld; Edward Denechaud; Richard Bordelon; F. Evans Schmidt; Ralph J. Aucoin, 210 Baronne St., Ste. 1207, New Orleans, 70112-4100. Tel: 504-522-4756; Fax: 504-568-0783.

Newspaper— Newspaper of the Archdiocese of New Orleans. Published by Clarion Herald Publishing Co., Inc., Rev. Msgr. Crosby W. Kern, Moderator; Peter P. Finney Jr., Gen. Mgr. & Exec. Editor, 1000 Howard Ave., Ste. 400, New Orleans, 70113-1903. Tel: 504-596-3035; Fax: 504-596-3020. "Clarion Herald"

Old Ursuline Convent—Rev. Msgr. Crosby W. Kern, Admin., 1100 Chartres St., New Orleans, 70116-2596. Tel: 504-529-3040; Fax 504-529-2001.

Victim Assistance Coordinator—Sr. Carmelita Centanni, M.S.C., Ph.D., 7887 Walmsley Ave., New Orleans, 70125-3496. Tel: 504 861-6253; Fax: 504-866-2906. Email: srcarmelita@archdiocese-no.org.

Department of Christian Formation

Executive Director—Very Rev. Neal W. McDermott, O.P., 7887 Walmsley Ave., New Orleans, 70125-3496. Tel: 504-861-6228; Fax: 504-861-6260.

Campus Ministry—Very Rev. Neal W. McDermott, O.P., 7887 Walmsley Ave., New Orleans, 70125-3496. Tel: 504-861-6228; Fax: 504-861-6260.

Catholic Schools Office—Dr. J. Rene Coman, Supt. Assoc. Superintendents: Mr. Vincent Scozzari; Mr. Joseph R. Rosolino; Dr. Thomas Becker; Dr. Judy Mulla; Sr. Leona Bruner, S.S.F.; Mr. William McSweeney, C.P.A., Finances & Planning; Mr. Joseph R. Rosolino, Coord. Personnel Svcs.; Sr. Mary Hilary Simpson, O.P., Dir. Instrumental Music; Mrs. Carolyn Morvant, Dir. Spec. Educ.; Ms. Nancy Baird, Government Programs Dir. Mktg. & Pub. Rels., 7887 Walmsley Ave., New Orleans, 70125-3496. Tel: 504-861-9521; Fax: 504-861-6260.

Catholic Youth Organization and Youth Ministry Office—Mr. John Smestad Jr., Dir., 2241 Mendez St., New Orleans, 70122-5276. Tel: 504-286-3959; Fax: 504-286-1440.

Youth Retreats— Youth Retreats: Contact CYO-Youth Ministry Office. *2241 Mendez St., New Orleans, 70122-5276.* Tel: 504-286-3959.

Ministry of Evangelization & Spiritual Renewal—Rev. Msgr. Robert I. Guste, 1908 Short St., Kenner, 70062-7599. Tel: 504-464-0413; Fax: 504-465-0930.

Religious Education—Bro. Edward Kiefer, S.M., Dir., 7887 Walmsley Ave., New Orleans, 70125-3496. Tel: 504-861-6270; 504-861-9521; Fax: 504-866-2906.

Pontifical Mission Societies—

Pontifical Mission Societies/Holy Childhood Association— Propagation of the Faith, St. Peter the Apostle, Missionary Union, Mission Outreach Programs. ; Acompano, Sotuta Mission, Bridge Builders, Christ the Healer and Christ the Builder. Rev. Wayne C. Paysse, Dir.; Sr. Judith Gomila, M.S.C., M.R.E., Assoc. Dir., Mailing Address, 7887 Walmsley Ave., New Orleans, 70125. 6340-B Pines Blvd., New Orleans, 70126. Tel: 504-241-7533; Fax: 504-241-7507.

Department of Clergy

Executive Director—Rev. Msgr. Terry B. Becnel, V.F., 7887 Walmsley Ave., New Orleans, 70125-3496.

Continuing Formation for Priests—Rev. Msgr. Douglas A. Doussan, Dir.

Permanent Diaconate—Deacon James W. Swiler, Dir., 7887 Walmsley Ave., New Orleans, 70125-3496. Tel: 504-861-6265; 504-861-9521; Fax: 504-866-2906.

Priest Personnel Office—Rev. Msgrs. Douglas A. Doussan, Dir.; Roger P. Morin, V.G., Bd. Directors, 7887 Walmsley Ave., New Orleans, 70125-3496. Tel: 504-861-6269; Fax: 504-866-2906.

Ministry to Retired Priests—Rev. Msgr. Ignatius Roppolo, Coord. Tel: 504-865-9251.

Ministry to Sick Priests—Rev. Douglas Brougher, Coord. Tel: 504-945-5878.

Psychological Services—Mr. Glenn LeBoeuf, C.L.C.S.W., B.C.D., Coord. Tel: 504-861-6269; 504-885-4611.

Vocation Office—Rev. Msgr. Henry J. Bugler, V.F., Dir., 7887 Walmsley Ave., New Orleans, 70125-3496. Tel: 504-861-6298; 504-861-9521; Fax: 504-866-2906.

Liaison with Conference of Major Superiors of Men and Retired Priests—Vacant.

Department of Community Services

Executive Director—Sr. Anthony Barczykowski, D.C., 1000 Howard Ave., Ste. 800, New Orleans, 70113-1900. Tel: 504-596-3090; Fax: 504-596-3098.

Archconfraternity of St. Ann—4920 Loveland St., Metairie, 70006.

Confraternity of the Holy Face—1050 Robert Blvd., Slidell, 70458.

Apostleship of the Sea—Deacon Ernest Elfer, Port Chap., Stella Maris Maritime Center, 4219 Constance St., New Orleans, 70115-1440. Tel: 504-891-6677; Fax: 504-891-1237.

Archbishop's Community Appeal (Philmat, Inc.)—Mr. Gordon R. Wadge, Exec. Dir., 1000 Howard Ave., Ste. 700, New Orleans, 70113-1900. Tel: 504-596-3083; Fax: 504-596-3098.

Catholic Campaign for Human Development—Mr. Thomas M. Costanza, 1000 Howard Ave., Ste. 800, New Orleans, 70113-1900. Tel: 504-596-3085; Fax: 504-596-3098.

Catholic Human Relations Committee—Rev. Msgr. Roger P. Morin, V.G., Dir., 7887 Walmsley Ave., New Orleans, 70125-3496. Tel: 504-861-6262; Fax: 504-861-6312.

Christopher Homes, Inc.—Ms. Alonda Harrison, Exec. Dir., 1000 Howard Ave., Ste. 100, New Orleans, 70113-1903. Tel: 504-596-3460; Fax: 504-596-3466.

Disaster Relief—Sr. Anthony Barczykowski, D.C., Dir., 1000 Howard Ave., Ste. 800, New Orleans, 70113-1900. Tel: 504-596-3090; Fax: 504-596-3098.

Charities--Catholic Charities Archdiocese of New Orleans—Mr. James R. Kelly, CEO, Catholic Charities Archdiocese of New Orleans, 1000 Howard Ave., Ste. 1000, New Orleans, 70113-1942. Tel: 504-523-3755; Fax: 504-523-2789; Mr. Wayne Plaisance, CFO; Mr. Orville Duggan, Chief Admin. Officer. Div. Directors: Ms. Jane Brewer; Ms. Anne Byrne; Ms. Pashena Casimire.

AIDS Housing/Shelter:—Ms. Lois Falk.

AIDS Peer Counseling—Ms. Fleta Garsaud.

Beyond Shelter—Ms. Vallarie Burriss.

Bridges to Self Sufficiency—Ms. Helen Evans.

Ciara Community Services—Ms. Monetta Clark, Ciara House, Ciara Independent Living Program.

Hope Haven Center—Mr. Robert Guasco, Hope Haven-Madonna Manor; St. Elizabeth's.

Padua Adult Residential Program— Ocean Avenue Community Home, St. Catherine of Siena, St. Jude the Apostle, Sts. Mary and Elizabeth, St. Peter the Fisherman, St. Rosalie, Supervised Apartments. Ms. Beanca Williams, Admin.

Padua Pediatric Residential Program—Ms. Ronna Trager.

Adult Day Health Care Centers—Ms. Pashena Casimire, Alpha House, New Directions, Greenwalt Center for Alzheimer's Day Care & Research.

Children's Head Start Centers—Ms. Gloria Cabrera, El Yo Yo Head Start, Flint Goodridge Early Head Start, Florida Head Start, Leslie Early Head Start, Louise Head Start, St. Anthony Head Start.

Maternity and Adoption Services—Ms. JANE BREWER, ACCESS Pregnancy/Referral Centers; Adoption Services; St. Vincent Maternity Clinic; Second Glance Resale Shoppe.
Immigration and Refugee Services—Dr. SUSAN WEISHAR, Refugee Health Screening; Legal/ Resettlement Services; Social Services; Immigrant Domestic Violence Prevention/ Outreach; ESL Program.
Independent Living Skills Program—Ms. JUDY POTTER.
Gert Town Community Center—Ms. SHARON ALEXIS.
CARE Centers—Ms. CONNIE ANDRY, CARE Center; Jefferson CARE Center; Baronne Street Transitional Housing.
Counseling Solutions—Ms. JANE BREWER, Metairie & New Orleans Office, 433 Metairie Rd., Ste. 106, Metairie, 70005-4324. Tel: 504-835-5007.
St. Tammany Branch Office—Ms. RENE RIVETTE, 1925-C Corporate Sq. Blvd., Slidell, 70458-3165. Tel: 985-641-8120.
St. Charles Branch Office—Mr. PETER YUSLUM, P.O. Box 60, Hahnville, 70057-6000. Tel: 985-783-2906.
St. John Branch Office—Ms. ANDREA KENT STEIMKAMP, 1706 Cannes Dr., LaPlace, 70068-2407. Tel: 985-652-4330.
St. Bernard Branch Office—Ms. BARBARA LAUGHLIN, 2626 Charles Dr., Chalmette, 70043-3773. Tel: 504-279-7636.
Westbank Branch Office—781 Berhman Hwy., Ste. 102, Gretna, 70056-3049. Tel: 504-391-0370. Ms. REBECCA HENLEY, 781 Berhman Hwy., Ste. 102, Gretna, 70056-3049. Tel: 504-391-0370.
Crescent House—Ms. MARY CLAIRE LANDRY.
Deaf Action Center of Greater New Orleans—Ms. MARY CLAIRE LANDRY.
Information and Referral—Mr. MICHAEL PIZZOLATO.
Family Preservation—Ms. MAMIE HALL-LANDRY.
Ciara Permanent Housing Program—Ms. LOLA LEWIS-DAVIS.
Job Search—Ms. NELLIE PERRY.
Development and Communications—ANN LACOUR, M.S.C.
PACE New Orleans—Ms. ANNE WITMER, Exec. Dir., 2317 Burgundy St., New Orleans, 70117. Tel: 504-945-1531.
PACE Louisiana—1000 Howard Ave., Ste. 800, New Orleans, 70113.
Senior Citizens Groups—Sr. ANNE BYRNE.
Project S.A.V.E. (Spouse Abuse Victim Empowerment)—Ms. THERESA MARCHESE.
Therapeutic Family Services—Mr. JEFFERY SWEATT.
Transportation Assistance Program—Ms. IMELDA MOLTEN.
Foster Grandparents—Ms. DORIS LALA.
Volunteer Department—Ms. AUDREY FONTANA.

Social Apostolate Office (PHILMAT, Inc.)—Most Rev. ALFRED C. HUGHES, S.T.D., Pres.; Mr. GORDON R. WADGE, Exec. Dir., 1000 Howard Ave., Ste. 800, New Orleans, 70113-1900. Tel: 504-596-3080; Fax: 504-596-3098.
Dignity of Work—Mr. STEVE LENAHAN.
Food for Families/Food for Seniors—Mr. TIMOTHY ROBERTSON, Exec. Dir., 8326 Apricot St., New Orleans, 70118-3198. Tel: 504-861-3555; Fax: 504-861-1435.
IMATT (Integrated Mobile Assessment and Treatment Team)—VACANT.
Head Start Centers—Mrs. CORAL ROBINSON, Incarnate Word Head Start Program, St. John the Baptist Head Start Program, St. Philip Head Start Center.
**Second Harvesters Food Bank of Greater New Orleans, Inc.*—Mr. S. BRIAN GREENE, Dir., 1201 Sams Ave., Harahan, 70123-2236. Tel: 504-734-1322; Fax: 504-733-8336.
Summer Witness Program—1000 Howard Ave., Ste. 800, New Orleans, 70113-1903. Tel: 504-596-3086; Fax: 504-596-3098.

COMMUNITY CENTERS:
Incarnate Word Center—Ms. SHIRLEY LACHMANN, Dir., 8326 Apricot St., New Orleans, 70118-3198. Tel: 504-866-8918; Fax: 504-864-9922.
Our Lady of Lourdes Center—Mrs. JANET M. ROUSSO, Dir., 2401 Jena St., New Orleans, 70115-5998. Tel: 504-895-0216; Fax: 504-895-0629.
St. John the Baptist—Mr. DOUG ANDERSON, Dir., 1920 Clio St., New Orleans, 70113-1214. Tel: 504-581-4987; Fax: 504-581-4991.
St. Mary of the Angels—Mr. STEVE LENAHAN, Dir., 2301 Gallier St., New Orleans, 70117-5833. Tel: 504-949-1506; Fax: 504-945-9115.
St. Philip Community Center—Ms. SYBIL DUPRE, Dir., 3333 Clouet St., New Orleans, 70126-5700. Tel: 504-944-8848; Fax: 504-945-4648.

Department of Financial and Administrative Services

Officers—Mr. JOHN L. ECKHOLDT, CFO; Mr. LEON W. MATHES JR., Chief Admin. Officer, 7887 Walmsley Ave., New Orleans, 70125-3496. Tel: 504-861-6252; 504-861-9521; Fax: 504-866-2906.
Accounting Office—Mrs. KIM O. RAMSEY, Controller, 7887 Walmsley Ave., New Orleans, 70125-3496. Tel: 504-861-6236; 504-861-9521; Fax: 504-866-2906.
Building Office—Mr. ANDRE L. VILLERE JR., Dir., 7887 Walmsley Ave., New Orleans, 70125-3496. Tel: 504-861-6210; 504-861-9521; Fax: 504-866-2906.
Human Resources—Ms. BETH TINTO, Dir., 1000 Howard Ave., Ste. 1200, New Orleans, 70113. Tel: 504-310-8792; Fax: 504-568-1699.
Insurance Office—Ms. CHERYL HARPER, Operations Mgr.; Mrs. CYNTHIA MITCHELL, Risk & Claims Mgr., 6340-A Pines Blvd., New Orleans, 70126-2629. Tel: 504-241-2211; Fax: 504-241-2285.
Internal Audit Office—Mr. JEFFREY J. ENTWISLE, Financial Review Officer, 7887 Walmsley Ave., New Orleans, 70125-3496. Tel: 504-861-6203; Fax: 504-866-2906.
Internet Services—Mr. KEN BEASLEY, Interim Dir., 1000 Howard Ave., Ste. 700, New Orleans, 70113-1903. Tel: 504-596-3064; Fax: 504-566-9718.
New Orleans Archdiocesan Cemeteries and New Orleans Cemeteries Trust—Mr. MICHAEL D. BOUDREAUX, Dir., 1000 Howard Ave., Ste. 500, New Orleans, 70113-1903. Tel: 504-596-3050; Fax: 504-596-3055.
Property and Building Management—Mr. LAWRENCE J. ECUYER, Dir., 1000 Howard Ave., Ste. 107, New Orleans, 70113-1903. Tel: 504-596-3070; Fax: 504-596-3073.
Parish Sites & Boundaries Committee—Rev. Msgrs. FRANK J. GIROIR, V.F., Chm.; ROGER P. MORIN, V.G., Coord., 7887 Walmsley Ave., New Orleans, 70125-3496. Tel: 504-861-6262; 504-861-9521; Fax: 504-861-6312.
Property Records Office—Mrs. EMILY MORRIS, 7887 Walmsley Ave., New Orleans, 70125-3496. Tel: 504-861-6323; Fax: 504-866-2906.
School Food Services—Mrs. PATRICIA H. FARRIS, Dir., 1000 Howard Ave., Ste. 300, New Orleans, 70113-1925. Tel: 504-596-3434; Fax: 504-596-3459.

Department of Pastoral Services

Executive Director—Very Rev. JOSEPH S. PALERMO JR., 7887 Walmsley Ave., New Orleans, 70125-3496. Tel: 504-861-6294; 504-861-9521; Fax: 504-866-2906.
Ave Maria Retreat House—Rev. WILLIAM J. AXE, O.SS.T., Dir., 8089 Barataria Blvd., Crown Point, 70072-7556. Tel: 504-689-3837; Fax: 504-689-2785.
Black Catholics Ministries—Deacon DAN VINCENT, 7887 Walmsley Ave., New Orleans, 70125-3496. Tel: 504-861-6207; 504-861-9521; Fax: 504-866-2906.
Center of Jesus the Lord—Rev. JOHN M. CAPUCI, Dir., 1236 N. Rampart St., New Orleans, 70116-2497. Tel: 504-529-1636; Fax: 504-529-5003.
Charismatic Renewal—Liaisons: Mr. AL MANSFIELD; Mrs. PATTI MANSFIELD, 3000 26th St., Ste. 200, Metairie, 70002-6002. Tel: 504-828-1368; Fax: 504-828-2133.
Ecumenical Officer—Very Rev. JAMES A. TARANTINO, V.F., Chm., 1322 Moss St., New Orleans, 70119-2998. Tel: 504-488-2659; Fax: 504-488-6741.
Family Life Apostolate—Mrs. PAULA D'ALBOR STUCKART, Dir., 7887 Walmsley Ave., New Orleans, 70125-3496. Tel: 504-861-6243; 504-861-9521; Fax: 504-866-2906.
Commission for Persons with Disabilities—Mrs. PAULA D'ALBOR STUCKART, 7887 Walmsley Ave., New Orleans, 70125-3496. Tel: 504-861-6243; Fax: 504-866-2906.
Filipino Catholic Ministry—Rev. DANILO C. DIGAL, Coord., 2320 Paris Rd., Chalmette, 70043-5098. Tel: 504-271-3441.
Hanmaum Korean Catholic Chapel—Rev. YONG HWAN SON, Chap., 4812 W. Napoleon Ave., Metairie, 70001-2364. Tel: 504-888-8772; Fax: 504-888-2366.
Hispanic Apostolate—Mr. MARTIN GUTIERREZ, Exec. Dir., 4309 Williams Blvd., Kenner, 70063. P.O. Box 640249, Kenner, 70064. Tel: 504-464-5478; Fax: 504-464-6267.
Mensaje, Inc.—Rev. PEDRO NUNEZ, 2241 Mendez St., 2nd Fl., New Orleans, 70122-5276. Tel: 504-283-0659; Fax: 504-283-0537.
Prisons Apostolate—Deacon LOUIS STALL, Archdiocesan Dir., P.O. Box 388, Gretna, 70054-0388. Tel: 504-374-7709.
Renovacion Carismatica Catolica Hispana—Deacon RODOLFO J. MARTINEZ; Mr. ENRIQUE OBANDO, Coord., P.O. Box 640057, Kenner, 70064. Tel: 504-348-2959; Fax: 504-464-6267.
Vietnamese Catholics Office—VACANT, Dir., 5069 Willowbrook Dr., New Orleans, 70129-0745. Tel: 504-254-5660; Fax: 504-254-9250. P.O. Box 29745, New Orleans, 70189-0745.
Worship Office—Deacon RONALD J. GUIDRY, Dir., 7887 Walmsley Ave., New Orleans, 70125-3496. Tel: 504-861-6300; 504-861-9521; Fax: 504-866-2906.
Liturgical Commission—Deacon RONALD J. GUIDRY, Coord., 7887 Walmsley Ave., New Orleans, 70125-3496. Tel: 504-861-6300; 504-861-9521; Fax: 504-866-2906.
Master of Ceremonies—Deacon RONALD GUIDRY, 7887 Walmsley Ave., New Orleans, 70125-3496. Tel: 504-861-6300; 504-861-9521; Fax: 504-866-2906.

Department of Religious

Executive Director—Sr. SUELLEN TENNYSON, M.S.C. Liaison with Leadership Conference of Women Religious, Religious Institutes of Brothers and Sisters and Secular Institutes. 7887 Walmsley Ave., New Orleans, 70125-3496. Tel: 504-861-6281; 504-861-9521; Fax: 504-866-2906.

Archdiocesan Offices and Corporations

Bernard A. Grehan Trust—7887 Walmsley Ave., New Orleans, 70125-3496. Tel: 504-861-9521.
Catholic Charities Children's Day Care Centers Inc.—Registered Office, 1000 Howard Ave., Ste. 1000, New Orleans, 70113-1942.
Mental Health Association Development Corporation—7887 Walmsley Ave., New Orleans, 70125-3496. Tel: 504-861-9521.
St. Elizabeth's Home Registered Office—1000 Howard Ave., Ste. 1000, New Orleans, 70113-1942.
St. Gertrude's Retirement Center—Most Rev. ALFRED C. HUGHES, S.T.D., Pres., 7887 Walmsley Ave., New Orleans, 70125-3496.
St. Mary's Catholic Orphan Boys' Asylum Board—1000 Howard Ave., Ste. 1000, New Orleans, 70113-1942.
St. Vincent's Infant and Maternity Home Registered Office—1000 Howard Ave., Ste. 1000, New Orleans, 70113-1942.

Catholic Organizations

Apostles of Divine Mercy, New Orleans—Mrs. MARGARET BIESER, Dir., 6968 Gen. Diaz St., New Orleans, 70124-3436. Tel: 504-283-3070.
Beginning Experience—Ms. DEANNE CAMPO, Pres., P.O. Box 74345, Metairie, 70033-4345. Tel: 504-467-4338.
Blessed Brother Andre Acadians Prayer Group—Deacon IRVING J. DAIGLE, Spiritual Moderator, 529 S. Telemachus St., New Orleans, 70119-7043. Tel: 504-486-7190.
Blue Army of Our Lady of Fatima—Rev. DENZIL M. PERERA, Spiritual Dir. (Retired), 1342 Moss St., New Orleans, 70119-2998. Tel: 504-488-4535; Fax: 504-488-6741.
Catholic Charities Association Inc.—Mr. RONALD K. ARCHER, Pres., 1000 Howard Ave., Ste. 1000, New Orleans, 70113-1942. Tel: 504-581-BALL.
Catholic Knights of America—Rev. BENJAMIN PIOVAN, Spiritual Dir., 799 Fairway Dr., LaPlace, 70068-2007. Tel: 504-652-2615; Fax: 504-652-7291.
Catholic Order of Foresters—Mr. EDWIN HADLEY, State Chief Ranger, 4701 Stephen Girard Ave., New Orleans, 70126-4757. Tel: 504-282-5432.
Catholic Physicians Guild of New Orleans—Dr. BRIAN BARKEMEYER, Pres., 6075 Argonne Blvd., New Orleans, 70124. Tel: 504-568-4421; Fax: 504-568-7532.
Chateau de Notre Dame Guild—Most Rev. NICHOLAS D'ANTONIO, O.F.M., Spiritual Dir., 2920 Burdette St., Apt. 416, New Orleans, 70125-2596. Tel: 504-314-6907.
Closer Walk Ministries—Rev. M. JEFFERY BAYHI, Dir., P.O. Box 50860, New Orleans, 70150-0860. Tel: 504-472-6050; Fax: 504-472-6046.
Come, Lord Jesus Program of Prayer and Scripture—Mrs. LORETTA ARCENEAUX, Coord., 1913 Idaho St., Kenner, 70062. Tel: 504-466-7368.
Community of John the Evangelist—Ms. VIVIEN MICHALS, Contact, 2639 DeSoto St., New Orleans, 70119. Tel: 504-944-4000.
Council of Catholic Men—Mr. BEN RAPHAEL, Dir., 7887 Walmsley Ave., New Orleans, 70125-3496. Tel: 504-283-5427.
Council of Catholic School Cooperative Clubs—Rev. H. WILLIAM REED, Spiritual Moderator, 3500 Ames Blvd., Marrero, 70072-5699. Tel: 504-347-2203; Fax: 504-347-2223.
Council of Catholic Women—Rev. H. WILLIAM REED, Spiritual Dir., 3500 Ames Blvd., Marrero, 70072-5699. Tel: 504-347-2203; Fax: 504-347-2223; Mrs. IDA C. LEWIS, Pres.
Cursillo—Mr. BILLY APP, Lay Dir., 19 Yellowstone Dr., New Orleans, 70131. Tel: 504-464-0181, Ext. 111.
Engaged Encounter—Executive Couples: TY SALVANT; DERRICK SALVANT; Mr. PAUL VLOSICH; Mrs. STEPHANIE VLOSICH.
Eucharistic Adoration Society—Mrs. NOVA LACOMBE, Pres., 6232 Milne Blvd., New Orleans, 70124-2016. Tel: 504-482-9632.
Holy Name Societies—Mr. BEN RAPHAEL, Exec. Sec.,

7887 Walmsley Ave., New Orleans, 70125-3496. Tel: 504-283-5427; Fax: 504-866-2906.

Jesus Caritas Fraternity of Priests—Rev. Msgr. ROBERT I. GUSTE, 1908 Short St., Kenner, 70062-7599. Tel: 504-464-0413; Fax: 504-465-0930.

Junior Catholic Charities Association—Ms. EMMA ECUYER, Pres., 1000 Howard Ave., Ste. 1000, New Orleans, 70113-1942. Tel: 504-523-3755.

Knights of Columbus—Rev. FRANCIS J. CARABELLO, Archdiocesan Chap., 610 6th St., Gretna, 70053-6098. Tel: 504-368-1313; Fax: 504-368-6841.

Ladies of Charity of the Archdiocese—Rev. HAROLD DICHARRY, C.M., Spiritual Dir., 1025 Napoleon Ave., New Orleans, 70115-2898. Tel: 504-899-1378; Fax: 504-899-0480.

Ladies of Madonna—Ms. SHIRLEY OSTER, Pres., 500 Papworth Ave., Metairie, 70005. Tel: 504-828-3157.

Lay Carmelites of Our Lady of Mount Carmel—420 Robert E. Lee Blvd., New Orleans, 70124-2596. Tel: 504-288-8553.

Legion of Mary—Deacon J. VERNON INSLEY, Spiritual Dir., New Orleans Comitium, 315 Desoto Dr., Luling, 70070. Tel: 985-785-8491.

Living Waters Program (Radio Ministry)—Rev. Msgr. ROBERT I. GUSTE, Dir., 1908 Short St., Kenner, 70062. Tel: 504-464-0413; Fax: 504-465-0930.

Magnificat, Ministry to Catholic Women—Mrs. PETER QUIRK, Pres. Central Svc. Team, 1201 Beverly Garden Dr., Metairie, 70002. Tel: 504-834-0057.

Marians of New Orleans—Mrs. GAIL VETERS, Pres., 4708 Carthage St., Metairie, 70002. Tel: 504-455-2194.

Marians of Metairie—Mrs. FLORENCE O. ONSTAD, Pres., 102 Tara Ct., Pearl River, 70452.

Marriage Encounter—MARK DELAUNE; CHERI DELAUNE. Tel: 985-447-6720.

Maryknoll Mission Education Center (Promotion of Missionary Work)—Mr. MATT ROUSSO, Dir., 7730 Walmsley Ave., New Orleans, 70125. Tel: 504-866-8516.

Mary's Children—Mrs. NORA LAMBERT, Pres., 631 St. Charles Ave., New Orleans, 70130-3411. Tel: 504-288-4408.

Mary's Helpers (Medjugorje Information)—Mrs. MARGARET TROSCLAIR, Dir., P.O. Box 1853, Marrero 70073-1853. Tel: 504-348-7729.

Medjugorje Star—Rev. CHARLES SELLARS, O.M.I., Spiritual Dir. Directors: HUBIE MULE; KAY MULE, 2627 David Dr., Metairie, 70003-4599. Tel: 504-889-1713; Fax: 504-889-1714.

MIR Group (Medjugorje Information Center)—Ms. MIMI KELLY, 1 Galleria Blvd., Ste. 744, Metairie, 70001-2081. Tel: 504-849-2570; Fax: 504-849-2574.

Missionaries of St. Therese—Rev. WAYNE C. PAYSSE, Spiritual Moderator, 6300 Pines Blvd., New Orleans, 70126-2697. Tel: 504-242-6900; Fax: 504-242-6901.

Naim Conference—Mr. JOHN ROBERT, 1800 High Ave., Metairie, 70001-2239. Tel: 504-888-4417.

National Council of Catholic Men—Mr. BEN RAPHAEL, Dir., 7887 Walmsley Ave., New Orleans, 70125-3496. Tel: 504-283-5427.

National Council of Catholic Women—Rev. H. WILLIAM REED, Spiritual Moderator 3500 Ames Blvd., Marrero, 70072-5699. Tel: 504-347-2203; Fax: 504-347-2223.

Pax Christi New Orleans—Chairpersons: Mr. TOM EGAN; Mrs. JEANNIE EGAN, P.O. Box 50304, New Orleans, 70150-0304. Tel: 504-522-3751.

Priests for Life—Rev. Msgr. ROGER A. SWENSON, Coord., 105 Bonnabel Blvd., Metairie, 70005-3798. Tel: 504-835-9343; Fax: 504-835-1525.

Retrouvaille/Rediscovery—JUDI DIEDLING; MIKE DIEDLING. Tel: 985-641-3802.

Rosary Congress Committee—Very Rev. NEAL W. MCDERMOTT, O.P., Spiritual Dir., 775 Harrison Ave., New Orleans, 70124-3192. Tel: 504-482-4156.

St. Elizabeth's Guild—Mrs. ROBERT E. WINN, Pres., 1101 Barataria Blvd., Marrero, 70072.

St. Margaret's Daughters—Mrs. AUGUSTINE MOLL, Pres., 5220 Chartres St., New Orleans, 70117. Tel: 504-276-4411.

St. Thomas More Catholic Lawyers Association—Very Rev. JOSEPH S. PALERMO JR., 7887 Walmsley Ave., New Orleans, 70125-3496. Tel: 504-861-6294; Fax: 504-866-2906.

St. Vincent de Paul Society—Mrs. SANTOS ARSENAULT, Pres.; Ms. ANN LAICHE, Exec. Sec., 2601 Canal St., New Orleans, 70119-6498. Tel: 504-822-9288; Fax: 504-822-1964.

St. Vincent Infant and Maternity Home Guild—1000 Howard Ave., Ste. 1000, New Orleans, 70113-1942. Tel: 504-523-3755.

Scouting—Deacon DANIEL FLYNN, Chap., Boy Scouts, 251 Halsey Dr., Harahan, 70123-4401. Tel: 504-737-8370; Mrs. COLLEEN R. LAROCCA, Chm., Girl Scouts, 25 Brentwood Dr., Metairie, 70003-3831. Tel: 504-734-8527.

Serra Clubs—

Serra Club of New Orleans—Rev. Msgr. HENRY J. BUGLER, V.F., Chap., 7887 Walmsley Ave., New Orleans, 70125-3496. Tel: 504-861-6298; Fax: 504-866-2906.

Serra Club of Downtown New Orleans—Rev. Msgr. ANDREW C. TAORMINA, J.D., Chap., 448 Metairie Rd., Metairie, 70005-4371. Tel: 504-834-0340.

Serra Club of East Jefferson—Mr. THOMAS RIDGLEY, Pres. Tel: 504-888-5557.

Serra Club of St. Bernard—Rev. WAYNE C. PAYSSE, Chap., 6300 Pines Blvd., New Orleans, 70126-2697. Tel: 504-242-6900.

Serra Club of West St. Tammany—Very Rev. RONALD L. CALKINS, V.F., Chap., 1501 W. Causeway Approach, Mandeville, 70471-3047; Mr. JOHN FAHERTY, Pres. Tel: 985-893-0526 Serra Club of West Bank.

Serra Club of West Bank—Mr. ADOLPH BOUDREAUX, Pres. Tel: 504-361-0923.

The Theresians—Mrs. SALLY DUPLANTIER, Co-Pres., Crescent City, 5601 Charlotte Dr., New Orleans, 70122-2609. Tel: 504-288-1897; Mrs. LIZ RARESHIDE, Co-Pres., Crescent City, 3840 Napoleon Ave., New Orleans, 70125. Tel: 504-861-8673.

Woman's New Life Center—Ms. SUSAN M. MIRE, M.A., Founder & Dir.; Ms. SHARON NORMAND, M.Ed., N.B.C.C., Counselor, 2613 Napoleon Ave., New Orleans, 70115. Tel: 504-269-8186; Fax: 504-269-9260. Email: smire@wnlc.coxmail.com. Web: www.womansnewlife.com.

CLERGY, PARISHES, MISSIONS AND PAROCHIAL SCHOOLS

CITY OF NEW ORLEANS
(ORLEANS CIVIL PARISH)

1—ST. LOUIS CATHEDRAL (1720),, (A Minor Basilica) Rev. Msgr. Crosby W. Kern, Rector; Deacons Ron Guidry; Richard Brady; David Warriner; Francis M. Minor. In Res., Revs. Frank Montalbano, O.M.I., S.T.L., S.S.L.; Gerald L. Seiler Jr., M.Div., J.C.L.
Res.: 615 Pere Antoine Alley, 70116-3291. Tel: 504-525-9585; Fax: 504-525-9583.
School—820 Dauphine St., 70116-3089. Tel: 504-525-3860; Fax: 504-525-3193. Ms. Vanessa Chavis, Prin. Lay Teachers 11; Students 170.
Mission—Our Lady of Guadalupe, Orleans Civil Parish. Tel: 504-525-1551; Fax: 504-525-1827.
Shrine—International Shrine of St. Jude Revs. Joseph Ferraioli, O.M.I.; Michael J. Amesse, O.M.I.; Sr. Christopher Foy, S.S.F., Pastoral Assoc.
Res.: 411 N. Rampart St., 70112-3594.
St. Jude Community Center—400 N. Rampart St., 70112-3594. Tel: 504-522-8290; Fax: 504-522-8830.

2—ALL SAINTS (1919), (African American), Rev. Peter C. Weiss, S.S.J.; Deacon Larry L. Calvin; Sr. M. Letitia Senegal, S.S.J., Pastoral Asst.
Res.: 1441 Teche St., 70114-5899. Tel: 504-361-8835; Fax: 504-361-9802.
School—1415 Teche St., 70114-5898. Tel: 504-362-0741; Fax: 504-362-0732. Francine M. Collins, Prin. Lay Teachers 13; Students 200.
Catechesis/Religious Program—Students 75.

3—ST. ALPHONSUS (1847), (Irish), Revs. Gerard B. LaPorte, C.SS.R.; Scott Katzenberger, C.SS.R.; Luong Uong, C.SS.R.; Byron J. Miller, C.SS.R.; Sr. Jane Briseno, R.S.M., Pastoral Assoc.; Bro. Andrew Lawson, C.SS.R.; Deacon Maurice J. Hartson III.
Res.: 2030 Constance St., 70130-5099. Tel: 504-522-6748; Fax: 504-523-3734.
School—2001 Constance St., 70130-5094. Tel: 504-523-6594. Sr. Monica Ellerbusch, R.S.M., Prin. Sisters 2; Lay Teachers 24; Students 320.

4—ST. ANDREW THE APOSTLE (1952), Revs. Paul S. Hart; Michael J. Kettenring; Deacons Chris J. DiGrado; Tom Stallings.
Res.: 3101 Eton St., 70131-5399. Tel: 504-393-2334; Fax: 504-392-0635.
School—Tel: 504-394-4171; Fax: 504-391-3627. Sisters 2; Lay Teachers 36; Students 767.
Catechesis/Religious Program—Tel: 504-393-0140; Fax: 504-393-0334. Students 112.

5—ANNUNCIATION (1844), Merged, with St. Cecilia, St. Gerard, SS. Peter & Paul & St. Vincent de Paul to form Blessed Francis Xavier Seelos, New Orleans

6—ST. ANTHONY OF PADUA (1915), Revs. Ian Bordenave; Juan Torres, O.P.; John B. Norton, O.P.; Ronald Henery, O.P.; Very Rev. Carl B. Trutter, O.P.; Revs. Henry B. Groover, O.P.; Jeffery Ott, O.P. (SAT); Richard Archer, O.P.; Paul D Watkins, O.P.; Very Rev. Emiliano Zapata, O.P.; Bros. Timothy Wrinn, O.P.; Richard Bontempo, O.P.; Herman Johnson, O.P.
Res.: 4640 Canal St., 70119-5892 Tel: 504-488-2651 Fax: 504-488-1842.
School—4601 Cleveland Ave., 70119-5893. Tel: 504-488-4426; 504-482-3672; Fax: 504-488-5373. Sr. Ruth Angelette, O.P., Prin. Sisters of St. Dominic 2; Lay Teachers 25; Students 384.
Catechesis/Religious Program—Tel: 504-488-2651, Ext. 251. Students 30.

7—ST. AUGUSTINE (1841), (African American), Rev. Jerome LeDoux, S.V.D.; Deacon Lloyd S. Glapion.
Res. 1210 Gov. Nicholls St., 70116-2324. Tel: 504-525-5934; Fax: 504-523-2473.
Catechesis/Religious Program—Students 30.

8—BLESSED FRANCIS XAVIER SEELOS (2001), [CEM] Rev. Joseph A. Benson; Deacons Jesse Watley; Jose A. Sierra; Arthine T. Vicks, Pastoral Assoc.
Res.: 3053 Dauphine St., 70117-6794. Tel: 504-943-5566; Fax: 504-943-5501.
Catechesis/Religious Program—Students 64.

9—BLESSED SACRAMENT (1915), (African American), Rev Howard W. Byrd, S.S.J., Admin. In Res., Rev. Joseph E. Okoro, C.M.F. (Nigeria)
Res.: 5018 Constance St., 70115-1798. Tel: 504-897-0955; Fax: 504-897-0950.
Catechesis/Religious Program—Students 6.

10—ST. BRIGID (1977), Rev. Msgr. T. Gaspard Glasgow; Deacon Joseph G. Casanova
Res.: 13435 Granville St., P.O. Box 29626, 70129-1210. Tel: 504-254-3538; Fax: 504-254-3520.
Catechesis/Religious Program—Tel: 504-254-5115. Mary Kittles, D.R.E. Students 65

11—ST. CECILIA (1897), Merged, with Annunciation, St. Gerard, SS. Peter & Paul & St. Vincent de Paul to form Blessed Francis Xavier Seelos, New Orleans

12—CORPUS CHRISTI (1916), (African American), Revs. Ray P. Bomberger, S.S.J.; Darren Hazeur, S.S.J.; Bro. Louis Tomasso, S.S.J.; Deacon Alfred D. White Jr.
Res.: 2022 St. Bernard Ave., 70116-1388. Tel: 504-945-8931; Fax: 504-947-5347.
School—Tel: 504-943-6131; Fax: 504-947-7736. Mrs. Tanya Netter-Wilson, Prin. Sisters 3; Lay Teachers 17; Students 375.
Catechesis/Religious Program—Students 112.

13—ST. DAVID (1937), (African American), Rev. Joseph J. Campion, S.S.J.; Deacon Irvin Williams.
Res.: 5617 St. Claude Ave., 70117-2533. Tel: 504-947-2853; Fax: 504-948-7852.
School—Tel: 504-943-1523; Fax: 504-943-1533. Mrs. Julie LaRoche, Prin. Sisters 3; Lay Teachers 14; Students 265.
Catechesis/Religious Program—Mrs. Iris Labeaud, D.R.E. Students 65.

14—ST. DOMINIC (1924), Rev. Donald Dvorak, O.P.; Very Rev. Martin J. Gleeson, O.P.; Revs. Victor Brown, O.P.; Dominic Tamburello, O.P.; Eduardo Gabriel, O.P.; Very Rev. Val A. McInnes, O.P.; Revs. John I. Reardon, O.P. (Retired); Daniel Shanahan, O.P.; Bros. Roger Shondel, O.P.; John Dominic Sims, O.P.; Deacon John Pippenger.
Res.: 775 Harrison Ave., 70124-3192. Tel: 504-482-4156; Fax: 504-488-0906; 504-488-3409 (Prior).
School—Tel: 504-482-4123; Fax: 504-486-3870. Sisters 1; Lay Teachers 46; Students 657.
Catechesis/Religious Program—Tel: 504-486-9731. Students 111.

15—EPIPHANY (1948), (African American), Revs. Ray P. Bomberger, S.S.J.; Darren S. Hazeur, S.S.J.; Deacon Reginald J. Seymour.
Res.: 1949 Duels St., 70119-1198. Tel: 504-944-2646; Fax: 504-945-5251.
Catechesis/Religious Program—Tel: 504-944-1679. Students 71.

16—ST. FRANCES XAVIER CABRINI (1952), Rev. Burnick J. Terrebonne; Deacons Gerald J. Martinez; Peter C. Rizzo.
Res.: 5500 Paris Ave., 70122-2699. Tel: 504-288-4224; Fax: 504-288-2152.
School—1500 Prentiss Ave., 70122-2098. Tel: 504-288-4249; Fax: 504-283-8161. Lay Teachers 17; Students 292.
Catechesis/Religious Program—Students 360.

17—ST. FRANCIS DE SALES (1870), (African American), Rev. Victor H. Cohea. In Res., Rev. John V. Muweesi (Uganda).
Res.: 2203 Second St., 70113-2545. Tel: 504-895-7749; Fax: 504-899-0434.
Catechesis/Religious Program—Tel: 504-891-9544. Students 81.

18—ST. FRANCIS OF ASSISI (1890), Very Rev. Desmond G. Crotty, V.F.
Res.: 631 State St., 70118-5899. Tel: 504-891-4479; Fax: 504-891-4470.
Catechesis/Religious Program—Students 7.

19—ST. GABRIEL THE ARCHANGEL (1954), (African

American), Rev. Msgr. Douglas A. Doussan.
Office—4700 Pineda St., 70126-3599. Tel: 504-282-0296; Fax: 504-288-8585.
Catechesis/Religious Program—Tel: 504-288-7914. Students 74.

20—St. Gerard (1971), Merged, with Annunciation, St. Cecilia, SS. Peter & Paul & St. Vincent de Paul to form Blessed Francis Xavier Seelos, New Orleans

21—St. Henry (1856), Rev. Msgr. Henry H. Engelbrecht; Deacons Henry A. Garon; Earl Wilson Jr.
Res.: 812 General Pershing St., 70115-2797. Tel: 504-891-6359; Fax: 504-895-0486.
Catechesis/Religious Program—Students 19.

22—Holy Ghost (1915), (African American), Very Rev. Michel R. Boutot, C.S.Sp., V.F. In Res., Rev. O. Hugh Stout.
Res.: 2015 Louisiana Ave., 70115-5294. Tel: 504-891-3172; Fax: 504-891-9284.
School—2035 Toledano St., 70115-5295. Tel: 504-899-6782; Fax: 504-899-6782. Sr. Angela Smith, S.S.F., Prin. Sisters 4; Lay Teachers 6; Students 310.

23—Holy Name of Jesus (1892), Revs. Paul Schott, S.J.; Donald A. Hawkins, S.J.; Clair M. Cazayoux, S.J.
Res.: 6220 LaSalle Pl., 70118-6236. Tel: 504-865-7430; Fax: 504-866-3391.
School—6325 Cromwell Pl., 70118-6299. Tel: 504-861-1466; Fax: 504-861-1480. Courtney Wolbrette, Prin. Sisters of Mercy 5; Lay Teachers 50; Students 485.
Catechesis/Religious Program—Tel: 504-572-2469. Students 61.

24—Holy Name of Mary (Algiers) (1848), [CEM 2] [JC 2] Rev. John C. Arnone; Deacon Ernest C. Elfer Jr.
Res.: 500 Eliza St., 70114-1098. Tel: 504-362-5511; Fax: 504-367-3504.
School—502 Olivier St., 70114-1099. Tel: 504-361-4004; Fax: 504-361-4044. Mrs. Betty J. Sierra, Prin. Lay Teachers 13; Students 232.
Catechesis/Religious Program—Students 17.

25—Holy Spirit (1972), Rev. Msgr. Allen J. Roy; Deacon Thomas Guntherberg, Pastoral Assoc.
Res.: 6201 Stratford Pl., 70131-7397. Tel: 504-394-5492; Fax: 504-398-0901.
Catechesis/Religious Program—Marcia Hubbard, D.R.E. Students 76.

26—Holy Trinity, Closed. For inquiries for parish records contact the chancery.

27—Immaculate Conception (1851), Revs. James C. Carter, S.J.; James Herbert Mead, S.J.; Edgar J. Tiblier, S.J. (GAL); Bro. Walter A. Eckler, S.J.
Res.: 130 Baronne St., 70112-2304. Tel: 504-529-1477; 504-529-1478; Fax: 504-524-0155.

28—Immaculate Heart Of Mary (1954), (African American), Rev. Wayne C. Paysse.
Res.: 6300 Pines Blvd., 70126. Tel: 504-242-6900; Fax: 504-242-6901.
School—6360 Pines Blvd., 70126. Tel: 504-242-6151; Fax: 504-242-6805. Mrs. Eleanor Davis, Prin. Lay Teachers 25; Students 365.
Catechesis/Religious Program—Regina Pirolozzi, D.R.E.; Diane Calamia, D.R.E. Students 35.

29—Incarnate Word (1922), Rev. Francis Ferrie.
Res.: 8316 Apricot St., 70118-3199. Tel: 504-866-3679; Fax: 504-866-0722.
Catechesis/Religious Program— Clustered with St. Rita, New Orleans. Students 7.

30—St. James Major (1920), Rev. Leo A. Meyer. In Res., Rev. Douglas C. Brougher.
Res.: 3736 Gentilly Blvd., 70122-6199. Tel: 504-945-2165; Fax: 504-945-9899.
School—Day Care Center, 3800 Gentilly Blvd., 70122-6130. Tel: 504-949-1680. Mrs. Peggy Frey, Dir. Staff 8; Students 58.
Catechesis/Religious Program—Students 77.

31—St. Joan of Arc (1909), (African American), Rev. Henry J. Davis, S.S.J.; Deacon Irvin Stewart Sr.
Res.: 8321 Burthe St., 70118-1195. Tel: 504-866-7330; Fax: 504-866-1319.
School—Tel: 504-861-2887; Fax: 504-866-9588. Sisters of Holy Family 3; Lay Teachers 15; Students 270.
Catechesis/Religious Program—Students 65.

32—St. John the Baptist (1851), (Irish), Very Rev. Perry Henry, C.M., V.F.; Rev. Mark Ford, C.M.
Mailing Address: 1802 Tulane Ave., 70112. Tel: 504-522-3186; Fax: 504-522-3171.
Res.: 1139 Oretha Castle Haley Blvd., 70113-1215. Tel: 504-525-1726; Fax: 504-524-4090.

33—St. Joseph (1844), Very Rev. Perry F. Henry, C.M., V.F.; Rev. Mark Ford, C.M.; Deacon Adrian G. Schwartzmann II.
Legal Title: *(Legal Title: St. Joseph Roman Catholic)*
Res.: 1802 Tulane Ave., 70112-2246. Tel: 504-522-3186; Fax: 504-522-3171.
Catechesis/Religious Program—Students 5.

34—St. Julian Eymard (1952), Rev. William H. Blank; Deacons Harold Vincent; Cesar C. Carrillo.
Res.: 2701 Lawrence St., 70114-3099. Tel: 504-367-7730; Fax: 504-367-2603.

35—St. Leo the Great (1920), (African American), Rev. John Cisewski; Deacon Arthur G. Kingsmill. In Res., Rev. Cyprian Devold.
Res.: 2916 Paris Ave., 70119-1840. Tel: 504-945-8750; Fax: 504-949-8899.
School—1501 Abundance St., 70119-2098. Tel: 504-943-1482; Fax: 504-944-5895. Dominican Sisters (Cabra, Ireland) 2; Lay Teachers 18; Students 323.
Catechesis/Religious Program—Students 44.

36—St. Maria Goretti (1965), Rev. Msgr. L. Earl Gauthreaux, J.C.L., V.F.; Rev. Robustiano D. Morgia (Philippines); Deacons Peter E. Duffy, J.D.; Ildefonso R. DeLeon; Terrel J. Broussard.
Mailing Address: 7300 Crowder Blvd., 70127-1599. Tel: 504-242-7554; Fax: 504-242-0755.
School—(Grades PreK-PreK) Tel: 504-242-1313; Fax: 504-242-4126. Lay Teachers 2; Students 26.
Catechesis/Religious Program—Students 170.

37—St. Mary of the Angels (1925), (African American), Revs. Bart Pax, O.F.M.; Anthony Walter, O.F.M.; Luis Aponte-Merced, O.F.M. In Res., Bro. Martin Humphreys, O.F.M.
Res.: 3501 N. Miro St., 70117-5899. Tel: 504-945-3186; Fax: 504-945-9115.
School—2225 Congress St., 70117-5898. Tel: 504-943-5687; Fax: 504-943-6673. Sr. Beatrice P. Stanley, Prin. Lay Teachers 17; Students 280.
Catechesis/Religious Program—Students 50.

38—Mary, Queen of Vietnam (1983), (Vietnamese), [JC] Revs. Vien The Nguyen, J.C.L.; Michael Nam Hoang Nguyen; Deacon Joseph Hiep Pham.
Res.: 5069 Willowbrook Dr., P.O. Box 29745, 70129-1047. Tel: 504-254-5660; Fax: 504-254-9250.
Catechesis/Religious Program—Tel: 504-254-5247. Students 915.
Mission—Our Lady of La Vang 6054 Vermillion Blvd., Orleans Civil Parish 70122-4296. Tel: 504-283-0559; Fax: 504-286-1937. Rev. Dominic Huyen Duc Nguyen.
Chapel—Vietnamese Martyrs 14400 Peltier Dr., New Orleans East, 70129-1713. Tel: 504-254-5660.

39—Mater Dolorosa (1848), Rev. John T. Hinton; Deacons Walter Beyer; Richard E. Deichmann; Dr. Marian O'Neil, Pastoral Assoc. In Res., Rev. David A. Boileau.
Res.: 8128 Plum St., 70118-2012. Tel: 504-866-3669; Fax: 504-866-2349.
Catechesis/Religious Program—Tel: 504-866-5641. Dr. Marian O'Neil, D.R.E. Students 50.

40—St. Matthias (1920), (African American), Rev. Eliseus Ibeh, M.S.P.; Deacon Raymond Lewis.
Res.: 4230 S. Broad St., 70125-3699. Tel: 504-822-3394; Fax: 504-822-3397.
Catechesis/Religious Program—Students 20.

41—St. Maurice (1852), Rev. Michael Roberson; Deacon Elliot Arendt Sr.
Res.: 605 St. Maurice Ave., 70117-1598. Tel: 504-279-5231; Fax: 504-279-0543.
Catechesis/Religious Program—Tel: 504-271-8923. Students 58.

42—St. Monica (1924), (African American), [CEM] Rev. John Asare-Dankwah (Ghana); Deacon Herman Williams.
Res.: 2327 S. Galvez St., 70125-3198. Tel: 504-821-9500; Fax: 504-821-9502.
School—2323 Galvez St., 70125-3101. Tel: 504-821-3321; Fax: 504-821-5631.
Catechesis/Religious Program—Students 189.

43—St. Nicholas of Myra (1971), [CEM] Rev. Arthur J. Ginart.
Res.: Rte. 6, Box 146-BE, 70129-9799. Tel: 504-662-5339; Fax: 504-662-5339.
Catechesis/Religious Program—Students 21.

44—Our Lady of Good Counsel (1887), Revs. Patrick Collum; Carroll Heffner; Deacon Raymond (Kevie) Richardson.
Res.: 1307 Louisiana Ave., 70115-2494. Tel: 504-891-1906; Fax: 504-895-5871.

45—Our Lady of Guadalupe /International Shrine of St. Jude (1826), (African American),, (Quasi Parish) Revs. Michael J. Amesse, O.M.I.; Anthony Rigoli, O.M.I.; Bro. Danna Gauthreaux, O.M.I.
Res.: 411 N. Rampart St., 70112. Tel: 504-525-1551; Fax: 504-525-1827.
Catechesis/Religious Program—Tel: 504-522-8546. Students 78.

46—Our Lady of Lourdes (1905), (African American), Rev. Raphael Ezeh, M.S.P.
Res.: 4423 La Salle St., 70115-5909. Tel: 504-891-4401; Fax: 504-891-5503.
School—2437 Jena St., 70115-5998. Tel: 504-897-0154; Fax: 504-897-0155. Lay Teachers 18; Students 298.
Catechesis/Religious Program—Students 18.

47—Our Lady of The Rosary (1907), Very Rev. James A. Tarantino, V.F., V.F.; Rev. Denzil M. Perera (Retired); Deacons James Bialas; John David Hamm; Henry Nuss.
1322 Moss St., 70119-2998. Tel: 504-488-2659; Fax: 504-488-6741. In Res., Very Rev. Neal W. McDermott, O.P.
Catechesis/Religious Program—Students 30.

48—Our Lady Star of The Sea (1911), Rev. Rodney A. Ricard; Deacons Uriel A. Durr; Melvin C. Jones Sr.
Res.: 1835 St. Roch Ave., 70117-8199. Tel: 504-944-0166; Fax: 504-948-9555.
Catechesis/Religious Program—Students 69.

49—St. Patrick (1833), (Irish), Rev. Stanley P. Klores. In Res., Rev. Randy P. Roux.
Res.: 724 Camp St., 70130-3757. Tel: 504-525-4413; Fax: 504-568-1324.

50—St. Paul the Apostle (1947), (African American), [CEM] Rev. Bernard Kwame Assenyoh, S.V.D.; Deacon Daniel P. Vincent.
Res.: 6828 Chef Menteur Hwy., 70126-5297. Tel: 504-242-7934; Fax: 504-242-1777.
School—Tel: 504-242-5962. Lay Teachers 12; Students 206.
Catechesis/Religious Program—Students 95.

51—SS. Peter and Paul (1848), Merged, with Annunciation, St. Cecilia, St. Gerard & St. Vincent de Paul to form Blessed Francis Xavier Seelos, New Orleans

52—St. Peter Claver (1920), (African American), Very Rev. Michael P. Jacques, S.S.E., V.F.; Deacons Rudolph Rayfield; Allen Stevens, Pastoral Assoc.; Pearl Dupart, Pastoral Assoc.; Wanda Brooks, Office Mgr.
Office—1923 St. Philip St., 70116-2199. Tel: 504-822-8059; Fax: 504-822-9251.
School—1020 N. Prieur St., 70116-2194. Tel: 504-822-8191; Fax: 504-822-1679. Mr. Walter Bonum, Prin. Lay Teachers 16; Students 302.
Catechesis/Religious Program—Tel: 504-822-8176. Alena Boucree, D.R.E. Students 188.

53—St. Philip the Apostle (1949), (African American), Rev. Rodney Anthony Ricard; Deacon Allen Stevens.
Res.: 3304 Metropolitan St., 70126-5799. Tel: 504-945-2122; Fax: 504-945-2128.
Catechesis/Religious Program—Students 45.

54—St. Pius X (1953), Rev. Msgr. Clinton J. Doskey, J.C.L.; Most Rev. Philip M. Hannan; Deacon William A. Glennon.
Res.: 6666 Spanish Fort Blvd., 70124-4398. Tel: 504-282-3332; Fax: 504-283-8984.
School—Tel: 504-282-2811; Fax: 504-282-3043. Lay Teachers 30; Students 449.
Catechesis/Religious Program—Students 85.

55—St. Raphael the Archangel (1947), Rev. Horace L. Brignac Jr.; Deacon Norbert Gubert. In Res., Rev. Pedro Nunez.
Res.: 2212 Prentiss Ave., 70122-5399. Tel: 504-282-6494; Fax: 504-282-2955.
Catechesis/Religious Program—Students 49.

56—St. Raymond (1927), (African American), Rev. John E. O'Hallaran, S.S.J.; Deacons John B. Williams; Dwight Alexander.
Res.: 3738 Paris Ave., 70122-2399. Tel: 504-288-1272; Fax: 504-283-3069.
School—Tel: 504-282-5563; Fax: 504-282-2344. Sr. Patricia Ann Williams, S.S.F., Prin. Sisters of the Holy Family 3; Lay Teachers 20; Students 285.
Catechesis/Religious Program—Students 84.

57—The Resurrection Of Our Lord (1963), Rev. Michael Joseph Vinh Ngoc Nguyen; Deacon Samuel P. Hull III.
Res.: 9701 Hammond St., 70127-3519. Tel: 504-242-8669; Fax: 504-242-8767.
School—4861 Rosalia Dr., 70127-3598. Tel: 504-242-6222; Fax: 504-241-7363. Dr. Si Nguyen, Prin. Lay Teachers 25; Students 343.
Catechesis/Religious Program—Students 39.

58—St. Rita (1921), Rev. James Richard Day; Deacons Wilbur A. Toups; Paul Cimino. In Res., Rev. Wilfred F. Meridier; Rev. Msgr. Ignatius M. Roppolo (Retired); Very Rev. Joseph S. Palermo Jr.
Res.: 2729 Lowerline St., 70125-3599. Tel: 504-866-3621; Fax: 504-861-0338.
School—65 Fontainebleau Dr., 70125-3495. Tel: 504-866-1777; Fax: 504-861-8512. Marianites of Holy Cross 7; Lay Teachers 12; Students 269.
Catechesis/Religious Program—Students 8.

59—St. Rose of Lima (1857), Very Rev. James A. Tarantino, V.F., Admin.
Office & Res.: 1322 Moss St., 70119-2998. Tel: 504-488-2659; Fax: 504-488-6741.
Church: 2545 Bayou Rd., 70119-2398.
Catechesis/Religious Program—Students 31.

60—Sacred Heart of Jesus (1879), [CEM] Rev. Robert J. Brennan, C.S.C.; Deacons Irving J. Daigle; Walfredo Corral. In Res., Revs. James Denn, C.S.C.; Thomas E. Chambers, C.S.C.; Bros. Richard Kelly, C.S.C.; Walter Gluhm, C.S.C.
Res.: 139 S. Lopez St., 70119-6284. Tel: 504-827-1481; Fax: 504-821-5109.
Catechesis/Religious Program—Students 75.

61—St. Simon Peter (1986), (African American), Rev. Quentin E. Moody.

Office:—7600 Gannon Rd., 70128. Tel: 504-243-9214; Fax: 504-243-9251.
School—Tel: 504-243-9241. Mrs. Camille Treaudo, Prin.
Catechesis/Religious Program—Tel: 504-244-6758. Sr. Vianney Moore, S.L.W., D.R.E. Students 48.

62—ST. STEPHEN (1849), Revs. George Weber; Harold E. Dicharry, C.M. (Retired); Deacon Bertrand Scalise Jr. In Res., Very Rev. Perry F. Henry, C.M., V.F.; Bro. James Steinbach, C.M.
Res.: 1025 Napoleon St., 70115-2898. Tel: 504-899-1378; Fax: 504-899-0480.
School—1027 Napoleon Ave., 70115-2899. Tel: 504-891-1927; Fax: 504-891-1928. Mrs. Suzette Cochiara, Prin.; Sr. Juanita Chenevert, D.C., Pres. Daughters of Charity of St. Vincent de Paul 2; Lay Teachers 14; Students 266.

63—ST. THERESA OF AVILA (1848), Revs. Teodoro Agudo, O.F.M.Cap. (Spain); Eutiquiano Miguel, O.F.M.Cap.; Deacon Francis J. Fleischer.
Res.: 1404 Erato St., 70130-4387. Tel: 504-525-4226; Fax: 504-525-6014.
Catechesis/Religious Program—Students 12.

64—ST. THERESA OF THE CHILD JESUS (1929), (African American), Rev. Francis Ferrie. In Res., Deacons Rodrigo A. Fonseca; Lawrence Keller.
Res.: 3810 Leonidas St., 70118-4698. Tel: 504-482-1668; Fax: 504-486-8179.
Catechesis/Religious Program—Mrs. Sheila Fonseca, D.R.E. Students 20.

65—ST. THOMAS MORE (1970),, (The Community of St. Thomas More for Tulane Univ.) Very Rev. Carl B. Trutter, O.P.; Rev. Paul D. Watkins, O.P., Campus Minister; Deacon Joseph R. Rosato.
Res.: 1037 Audubon St., 70118-5294. Tel: 504-866-0984; Fax: 504-865-1914.
Catechesis/Religious Program—Students 85.

66—ST. THOMAS THE APOSTLE (1974),, (University of New Orleans) Rev. Thomas W. Hoffman, S.J.; Deacon Eric Gamble.
Res.: UNO Newman Center, 70148-0001. Tel: 504-288-6336; Fax: 504-288-6344.

67—ST. VINCENT DE PAUL (1838), Merged, with Annunciation, St. Cecilia, St. Gerard & SS. Peter & Paul to form Blessed Francis Xavier Seelos, New Orleans

OUTSIDE THE CITY OF NEW ORLEANS

ABITA SPRINGS, ST. TAMMANY PARISH, ST. JANE DE CHANTAL (1887), [JC] Rev. Robert C. Cavalier; Deacons Frans Labranche Jr.; Don Bourgeois.
Res.: 22122 Main St., P.O. Box 1870, 70420-0187. Tel: 985-892-1439; Fax: 985-871-9547.
Catechesis/Religious Program—72049 Hickory St., 70420-3931. Tel: 985-893-3914. Students 325.
Mission—St. Michael the Archangel Hwy. 41, Bush, St. Tammany Parish 70431. Tel: 985-886-3868; Fax: 985-886-0687.

AMA, ST. CHARLES PARISH, ST. MARK (1974), Rev. John M. Perino.
Res.: P.O. Box 556, 70031-0556. Tel: 504-431-8505; Fax: 504-431-8506.
Catechesis/Religious Program—Tel: 504-431-8507. Joyce King, D.R.E. Students 56.

ARABI, ST. BERNARD PARISH

1—ST. LOUISE DE MARILLAC (1954), Rev. Dennis J. Hayes III; Deacons Alvin C. Miester Jr.; Alex J. Seruntine Jr.
Res.: 6800 Patricia St., 70032-1496. Tel: 504-271-4671; Fax: 504-271-7727.
School—Tel: 504-271-1678; Fax: 504-276-3002. Edward Kavanagh, Prin. Congregation of the Most Holy Sacrament Sister 1; Daughters of Our Lady of the Holy Rosary 1; Lay Teachers 13; Students 225.
Catechesis/Religious Program—Students 133.

2—ST. ROBERT BELLARMINE (1964), Rev. Lich Van Nguyen; Deacon Curles P. Reeson.
Res.: 408 Cougar Dr., 70032-2098. Tel: 504-279-8215; Fax: 504-277-7656.
School—815 Badger Dr., 70032-1996. Tel: 504-279-6466; Fax: 504-279-2259. Lay Teachers 27; Students 493.
Catechesis/Religious Program—Students 112.

AVONDALE, JEFFERSON PARISH, ST. BONAVENTURE (1965), Rev. Peter Nam Van Tran; Deacon J. Vernon Insley.
Res.: 329 S. Jamie Blvd., 70094-2821. Tel: 504-436-1279; Fax: 504-436-1300.
Catechesis/Religious Program—Tel: 504-436-0744. Maxine Authement, D.R.E. Students 130.

BELLE CHASSE, PLAQUEMINES PARISH, OUR LADY OF PERPETUAL HELP (1928), [CEM] Very Rev. Patrick B. Sanders, V.F.; Deacons Leslie D. Vincent; Robert Beaumont.
Res.: 8968 Hwy. 23, 70037-2296. Tel: 504-394-0314; Fax: 504-394-0376.
School—Tel: 504-394-0757; Fax: 504-394-1627. Sr. Elizabeth Hebert, S.L.W., Prin. Sisters 2; Lay Teachers 17; Students 293.
Catechesis/Religious Program—Nanette Carpenter, D.R.E. Students 346.

BOGALUSA, WASHINGTON PARISH, ANNUNCIATION B.V.M. (1906), [JC 3] Rev. Lawrence J. Phelps O.S.B.
Res.: 517 Avenue B, 70427-3723. Tel: 985-732-4280; Fax: 985-735-1042.
School—511 Avenue C, 70427-3797. Tel: 985-735-6643; Fax: 985-735-6119. Lay Teachers 15; Students 231.
Catechesis/Religious Program—Tel: 985-735-8167. Students 231.

BRIDGE CITY, JEFFERSON PARISH, HOLY GUARDIAN ANGELS (1963), Rev. Msgr. J. Anthony Luminais.
Res.: 1701 Bridge City Ave., P.O. Box 9069, 70094-9069. Tel: 504-436-4712; Fax: 504-436-4070.
Catechesis/Religious Program—Tel: 504-436-9376. Students 120.

BURAS, PLAQUEMINES PARISH, OUR LADY OF GOOD HARBOR (1864), [CEM] Rev. Joseph Man Tran.
Mailing Address: 240 Buras River Rd. 70041-9188. Tel: 985-657-9873; Fax: 985-657-9878.
Catechesis/Religious Program—Students 155.
Mission—St. Ann Empire, Plaquemines Parish.
Mission—St. Anthony Venice, Plaquemines Parish.

CHALMETTE, ST. BERNARD PARISH

1—ST. MARK (1964), Revs. Mark Lomax Hoang Minh Tuong; Deacons Raymond Rivere; Albert A. Levy III; Kenneth Madere.
Res.: 3024 Charles Dr., 70043-3798. Tel: 504-279-6073; Fax: 504-279-9403.
School—Tel: 504-271-1694; Fax: 504-277-7195. Sharon Coll, Prin. Daughters of Divine Providence 2; Lay Teachers 26; Students 395.
Catechesis/Religious Program—Tel: 504-277-2584; Fax: 504-277-2584. Sr. Pier Carla, F.D.P., D.R.E. Students 504.
Convent—Daughters of Divine Providence, 3100 Mumphrey Rd., 70043-3735. Tel: 504-279-4617; Fax: 504-279-3002.

2—OUR LADY OF PROMPT SUCCOR (1951), Revs. Danilo C. Digal; Mark S. Raphael; Deacons Henry A. Casson Jr.; Julius T. Zimmer; Fallon H. Lorenz.
Res.: 2320 Paris Rd., 70043-5098. Tel: 504-271-3441; Fax: 504-271-2927.
School—2305 Fenelon St., 70043-4951. Tel: 504-271-2953; Fax: 504-271-1490. Evelyn Kingston, Prin. School Sisters of Notre Dame 1; Lay Teachers 37; Students 616.
Catechesis/Religious Program—Tel: 504-271-1217. Brenda Tromatore, D.R.E. Students 302.
Mission—Chapel of St. Lawrence St. Bernard Parish Prison, St. Bernard Parish 70043. Tel: 504-278-7645; Fax: 504-278-7785.

3—PRINCE OF PEACE (1977), Rev. Paul V. Tung Nguyen; Deacon Frank W. Rhodes Jr.
Res.: 3700 Jean Lafitte Pkwy., 70043-1199. Tel: 504-271-1664; Fax: 504-279-8023.
Catechesis/Religious Program—Tel: 504-277-6070. Yvette Caillouet, D.R.E. Students 138.

COVINGTON, ST. TAMMANY PARISH, ST. PETER (1843), Revs. William J. McGough; Thomas M. McCann; Deacons Charles Heine; Charles Read.
Res.: 125 E. 19th St., 70433-3195. Tel: 985-892-2422; Fax: 985-898-1998.
School—Tel: 985-892-1831; Fax: 985-898-2185. Miss Lana O'Dwyer, Prin. Lay Teachers 35; Students 723.
Catechesis/Religious Program—Tel: 985-893-2446; Fax: 985-892-7567. Students 364.

CROWN POINT, JEFFERSON PARISH, ST. PIUS X (1971), Rev. G. Amaldoss.
Res.: 8151 Barataria Blvd., 70072. Tel: 504-689-2381; Fax: 504-689-7417.
Catechesis/Religious Program—Students 89.

DES ALLEMANDS, ST. CHARLES PARISH, ST. GERTRUDE (1955), [CEM] Rev. James Nguyen Bach; Deacon Landry Matherne.
Res.: P.O. Box 767, 70030-0767. Tel: 985-758-7542; Fax: 985-758-7591.
Catechesis/Religious Program—Tel: 985-758-1332. Mrs. Nellie Matherne, D.R.E. Students 183.

DESTREHAN, ST. CHARLES PARISH, ST. CHARLES BORROMEO (1723), (German), [CEM] Rev. Msgr. Henry J. Bugler, V.F.; Deacons Harry Schexnayder; Theodore Roussel; Michael Stohlman. In Res., Rev. Luke Hungdung Nguyen.
Res.: 13396 River Rd., P.O. Box 428, 70047-0428. Tel: 985-764-6383; Fax: 985-764-6948.
School—Tel: 985-764-9232; Fax: 985-764-3726. Lay Teachers 37; Students 468; Preschool Students 74
Catechesis/Religious Program—Students 602.

DIAMOND, PLAQUEMINES PARISH, ST. JUDE (1981), Rev. John C. Hegarty, C.S.Sp.
Res.: P.O. Box 36, Port Sulphur 70083-0036. Tel: 985-564-2182; Fax: 985-564-2077.
Catechesis/Religious Program—Students 11.

EDGARD, ST. JOHN THE BAPTIST PARISH, ST. JOHN THE BAPTIST (1770), (African American), [CEM] Rev. Joel P. Cantones.
Res.: 2361 Hwy. 18, 70049-9101. Tel: 985-497-3412; 985-497-8470; Fax: 985-497-3965.
Catechesis/Religious Program—Students 157.

FLORISSANT, ST. BERNARD PARISH, SAN PEDRO PESCADOR (1966), (Islenos), Rev. Herbert J. Kiff Jr.
Res.: 205 Florissant Hwy., St. Bernard, 70085-9703. Church: P.O. Box 457, St. Bernard, 70085-0457. Tel: 504-676-3719; Fax: 504-676-9996.
Catechesis/Religious Program—Tel: 504-676-3565. Students 98.

FOLSOM, ST. TAMMANY PARISH, ST. JOHN THE BAPTIST (1921), Rev. Jonathan M. DeFrange, O.S.B.; Deacon Clayton J. Guitterrez.
Res.: 11345 St. John Church Rd., 70437-7155. Tel: 985-796-9214; Fax: 985-790-9554.
Office—Tel: 985-796-3806; Fax: 985-796-9554.
Catechesis/Religious Program—Tel: 985-796-5507. Students 161.

FRANKLINTON, WASHINGTON PARISH, HOLY FAMILY (1982), Revs. William H. Blank; Peter E. Hammett, O.S.B.
Res.: 1213 14th Ave., 70438. Tel: 985-839-4040; Fax: 985-839-2429.
Catechesis/Religious Program—Students 64.

GARYVILLE, ST. JOHN THE BAPTIST PARISH, ST. HUBERT (1907), Rev. Charles J. Caluda; Deacon Garland J. Roussel Jr.
Res.: P.O. Box K, 70051-0851. Tel: 985-535-2828; Fax: 985-535-1849.
Catechesis/Religious Program—Students 50.

GRETNA, JEFFERSON PARISH

1—ST. ANTHONY (1920), Revs. Patrick Gannon; Patrick J.R. Kennedy (Retired).
Res.: 924 Monroe St., 70053-2299. Tel: 504-368-6161; Fax: 504-362-7811.
School—Tel: 504-367-0689; Fax: 504-361-0054. Mrs. Marie K. Cannon, Prin. Sisters of the Living Word 2; Lay Teachers 9; Students 251.
Catechesis/Religious Program—Students 35.

2—ST. CLETUS (1965), Rev. Eugene F. Jacques; Deacon Louis W. Stall.
Res.: 3600 Claire Ave., 70053-7699. Tel: 504-367-7951; Fax: 504-367-7928.
School—Tel: 504-366-3538; Fax: 504-366-0011. Mr. Paul Gauthe, Prin. Lay Teachers 40; Students 581.
Catechesis/Religious Program—Tel: 504-361-4805. Students 230.

3—ST. JOSEPH (1857), Rev. Francis J. Carabello.
Res.: 610 Sixth St., 70053-6098. Tel: 504-368-1313; Fax: 504-368-6841.
Catechesis/Religious Program—Students 5.

HAHNVILLE, ST. CHARLES PARISH, OUR LADY OF THE HOLY ROSARY (1877), [CEM] Rev. Bernard C. Francis.
Res.: #1 Rectory Ln., 70057. Tel: 985-783-1199; Fax: 985-783-1974.

HARAHAN, JEFFERSON PARISH, ST. RITA (1950), Rev. Msgr. Frank J. Giroir, V.F.; Revs. Vinh Dinh Luu; Callons Cuccia; Deacons Nolen J. LeBlanc; Nicholas L. Mistretta; Danny Flynn.
Mailing Address: 7100 Jefferson Hwy., 70123-4928. Fax: 504-737-2921.
Res.: 160 Imperial Woods Dr., 70123-4998. Tel: 504-737-2915; Fax: 504-737-2921.
School—194 Ravan Ave., 70123-4999. Tel: 504-737-0744; Fax: 504-738-2184. Dr. Melanie B. Verges, Prin. Lay Teachers 26; Students 546.
Catechesis/Religious Program—Mrs. Beth Lomax, D.R.E. Students 84.

HARVEY, JEFFERSON PARISH

1—INFANT JESUS OF PRAGUE (1969), Rev. Peter Nam Van Tran; Deacon Cesar Carrillo.
Res.: 700 Maple St., 70058-4008. Tel: 504-368-1397; Fax: 504-368-0662.
Catechesis/Religious Program—Students 90.

2—ST. JOHN BOSCO (1983), Rev. Sidney Figlia, S.D.B.; Deacon Milton G. Webre.
Res.: 2114 Oakmere Dr., 70058-2275. Tel: 504-340-0444; Fax: 504-340-9521.
Catechesis/Religious Program—Brenda C. Baker, D.R.E. Students 50.

3—ST. MARTHA (1973), Very Rev. William O'Riordan, V.F.; Deacon Gerard L. Labadot.
Res.: 2555 Apollo Dr., 70058-5813. Tel: 504-366-1604; Fax: 504-366-1100.
Catechesis/Religious Program—Tel: 504-366-4142. Students 84.

4—ST. ROSALIE (1949), Revs. Thomas E. Ruekert, S.D.B.; James Curran, S.D.B.
Parish Offices—600 2nd Ave., 70058-2728. Tel: 504-340-1962; Fax: 504-340-1546.
Res.: 608 1st Ave., 70058-2799. Tel: 504-341-5656.
School—Elementary School, 617 Second Ave., 70058-2798. Tel: 504-341-4342; Fax: 504-347-0271.
School—Middle School, 2115 Oakmere Dr., 70058-2276. Tel: 504-348-9330; Fax: 504-348-9331. Mary C. Wenzel, Prin. Lay Teachers 60; Students 1,200.
Catechesis/Religious Program—Tel: 504-349-7896. Students 73.

JEFFERSON, JEFFERSON PARISH, ST. AGNES (1931), Revs. Peter O'Grady; Samuel Oracion; Deacon Piero Caserta.
Res.: 3310 Jefferson Hwy., 70121-2699. Tel: 504-833-3366; Fax: 504-834-1532.

School—Tel: 504-835-6486; Fax: 504-835-4295. Lay Teachers 17; Students 251.
Catechesis/Religious Program—Students 278.

KENNER, JEFFERSON PARISH

1—ST. ELIZABETH ANN SETON (1981), Most Rev. Dominic Carmon, S.V.D., V.G.; Rev. Luis F. Rodriguez; Deacons Andrea Capaci; Noel W. Martinsen; Garland Bourgeois.
Parish Office:—4121 St. Elizabeth Dr., P.O. Box 641000, 70064-1000. Tel: 504-468-1441; Fax: 504-468-3305.
School—Tel: 504-468-3524. Lay Teachers 27; Students 532.
Catechesis/Religious Program—Tel: 504-468-3233. Students 154.

2—ST. JEROME (1963), Rev. Alberto Bermudez, Temp. Admin.; Deacons Daniel J. Cordes; Luis Campuzano Sr.; Ernesto Morales; Santiago R. Angeli. In Res., Rev. Donald M. Byrnes (Retired).
Res.: 2400 33rd St., 70065-3899. Tel: 504-443-3174; Fax: 504-443-5499.
Catechesis/Religious Program—Gail Bordelon, D.R.E. Students 144.

3—NATIVITY OF OUR LORD (1977), Revs. Dean L. Robins; Curtis Thomas; Deacons John LeDoux; Roberto Mendieta; David E. Caldero.
Office—3325 Loyola Dr., 70065-2567. Tel: 504-466-5016; Fax: 504-467-8575.
Catechesis/Religious Program—Tel: 504-464-9664. Mrs. Donna Schloegel, D.R.E. Students 310.

4—OUR LADY OF PERPETUAL HELP (1869), Rev. Richard M. Miles; Rev. Msgr. Robert I. Guste. Tel: 504-464-0413; Deacons Edgar P. Dragon; Greg A. Gross.
Res.: 1908 Short St., 70062-7599. Tel: 504-464-0361; Fax: 504-465-0930.
School—Tel: 504-464-0531; Fax: 504-464-0725. Michael Orkus, Prin. Sisters of Mercy 2; Lay Teachers 26; Students 350.
Catechesis/Religious Program—Tel: 504-464-0147. Students 145.

LA PLACE, ST. JOHN THE BAPTIST PARISH

1—ASCENSION OF OUR LORD (1979), Rev. Benjamin Piovan; Deacon Thomas J. St. Pierre.
Res.: 799 Fairway Dr., 70068-2007. Tel: 985-652-2615; Fax: 985-652-7291.
School—1809 Greenwood Dr., 70068-2098. Tel: 985-652-4532; Fax: 985-651-5151. Lay Teachers 27; Students 405.
Catechesis/Religious Program—Fax: 504-652-2791. Students 90.

2—ST. JOAN OF ARC (1947), [JC] Rev. Joseph Dan Van Nguyen; Deacon Dominic J. Arcuri.
Res.: P.O. Box 490, 70069-0490. Tel: 985-652-9100; Fax: 985-651-2920.
School—412 Fir St., 70068-4310. Tel: 985-652-6310; Fax: 985-652-6390. Mr. Larry J. Bourgeois Jr., Prin. Sisters of St. Dominic 2; Lay Teachers 40; Students 743.
Catechesis/Religious Program—Tel: 985-651-0894. Mrs. Connie Cambre, D.R.E. Students 179.

LACOMBE, ST. TAMMANY PARISH

1—ST. JOHN OF THE CROSS (1984), Rev. Gilmer Martin; Deacon Joseph LeRose.
Res.: 61051 Brier Lake Dr., 70445-2911. Tel: 985-882-3779; Fax: 985-882-9282.
Catechesis/Religious Program—Tel: 985-882-6225. Students 87.

2—SACRED HEART (1890), Rev. William J. O'Donnell, J.C.L.; Deacon William P. Curry Jr.
Res.: P.O. Box 1080, 70445-1080. Tel: 985-882-5229; Fax: 985-882-9034.
Catechesis/Religious Program—Tel: 985-882-8041. Students 120.

LAFITTE, JEFFERSON PARISH, ST. ANTHONY (1936), [CEM] Rev. John Ryan; Deacon Brian Joseph Klause. In Res., Rev. Donald Duffy (Retired).
Res.: 2653 Jean Lafitte Blvd., 70067. Tel: 504-689-4101; Fax: 504-689-4102.
Catechesis/Religious Program—Tel: 504-689-2451. Mrs. Patricia Klause, D.R.E. Students 320.

LULING, ST. CHARLES PARISH

1—ST. ANTHONY OF PADUA (1961), Rev. Joseph Duc Dzien; Deacon Paul J. Donnaud.
Res.: 234 Angus Dr., 70070-4427. Tel: 985-785-8885; Fax: 985-785-8882.
Catechesis/Religious Program—Tel: 504-785-0050. Students 121.

2—HOLY FAMILY (1980), Rev. John P. Finn; Deacon Coy Landry.
Res.: 155 Holy Family Ln., 70070-6103. Tel: 985-785-8585; Fax: 985-785-1167.
Catechesis/Religious Program—Tel: 985-331-9100. Diane Faucheux, D.R.E. (High School); Marlene Savoie, D.R.E. Students 521.

MADISONVILLE, ST. TAMMANY PARISH, ST. ANSELM (1962), Very Rev. Alan R. Weseman, V.F.; Deacons John Glover; Louis Mire.
Res.: P.O. Box 40, 70447-0040. Tel: 985-845-7342; Fax: 985-845-3076.
Catechesis/Religious Program—Tel: 985-845-7912. Celie Clark, D.R.E. Students 500.

MANDEVILLE, ST. TAMMANY PARISH

1—MARY QUEEN OF PEACE (1988), Very Rev. Ronald L. Calkins, V.F.; Deacons Anthony J. Ferretti; John J. Finn.
Res.: 1501 W. Causeway Approach, 70471-3047. Tel: 985-626-6977; Fax: 985-626-6971.
School—1515 W. Causeway Approach, 70471. Tel: 985-674-2466; Fax: 985-674-1441. Dr. Jan Lancaster, Prin. Students 219.
Catechesis/Religious Program—Tel: 985-674-9794. Students 617.

2—OUR LADY OF THE LAKE (1850), [JC] Rev. Rhenne A. Cervantes; Rev. Msgr. Joseph L. Chotin, Pastor Emeritus; Deacons Joseph Lazo; Ed Kelly; Sr. Joycelin Staempfli, M.S.C., Chief Admin. Officer.
Res.: 312 Lafitte St., 70448-5827. Tel: 985-626-5671; Fax: 985-626-5422.
School—Tel: 985-626-5678; Fax: 985-626-4337. Janet B. Buras, Prin. Lay Teachers 41; Students 740.
Catechesis/Religious Program—Tel: 985-626-7901. Karin Wheeler, D.R.E. Students 988.

MARRERO, JEFFERSON PARISH

1—ST. AGNES LE THI THANH (1995), (Vietnamese), [JC], (Personal Parish for Southeast Asians) Rev. J.B Han Vu.
Mailing Address, Office & Rectory: 1000 Westwood Dr., 70072-2415. Tel: 504-347-4725; Fax: 504-340-2476.
Church: 6851 St. Le Thi Thanh St., 70072-2556.
Mission—Assumption of Mary 172 Noel Dr., Avondale, Jefferson Civil Parish 70094-2900. Rev. Andrew Tran Cao Tuong, Admin.
Mission—St. Joseph 6450 Kathy Ct., Orleans Civil Parish 70131-7515. Rev. Joseph Pham Van Tue, Admin.
Catechesis/Religious Program—Students 921.

2—IMMACULATE CONCEPTION (1924), (Hispanic), Revs. Warren L. Cooper; John F. Talamo; Deacons Wilfred Robichaux Jr.; Rodolfo Martinez. In Res., Rev. Denver B. Pentecost.
Res.: 4401 7th St., 70072-2099. Tel: 504-341-9516; Fax: 504-341-9517.
School—601 Avenue C, 70072-2098. Tel: 504-347-4409; Fax: 504-341-2766. Sr. Lise Parent, F.M.A., Prin. Salesian Sisters 2; Lay Teachers 43; Students 881.
High School—Immaculata, 537 Avenue D, 70072-2027. Tel: 504-341-6217; Fax: 504-341-6229. Sr. Maria Colombos, F.M.A., Prin. Sisters 3; Lay Teachers 33; Students 405.
Catechesis/Religious Program—Students 119.

3—ST. JOACHIM (1985), Rev. Harry J. Adams.
Res.: 5505 Barataria Blvd., 70072-6660. Tel: 504-341-9226; Fax: 504-348-0093.
Catechesis/Religious Program—Cynthia Dulte, D.R.E. Students 158.

4—ST. JOSEPH THE WORKER (1955), (African American), Rev. Paul G. McQuillen, S.S.E.
Res.: 455 Ames Blvd., 70072-1599. Tel: 504-347-8438; Fax: 504-340-9538.
School—Tel: 504-347-3704; Fax: 504-347-0852. Lay Teachers 25; Students 212.
Catechesis/Religious Program—Tel: 504-348-4784. Students 112.

5—THE VISITATION OF OUR LADY (1963), Very Rev. Michael B. Fraser, V.F.; Rev. H. William Reed; Deacons Larry Murphy; Ferris Duet Jr.
Res.: 3500 Ames Blvd., 70072-5699. Tel: 504-347-2203; Fax: 504-347-2223.
School—3520 Ames Blvd., 70072-5698. Tel: 504-347-3377; Fax: 504-341-5378. Mrs. Carolyn Levet, Prin. Lay Teachers 39; Students 773.
Catechesis/Religious Program—Tel: 504-341-4499. Cheryl Tourelle, D.R.E. Students 126.

METAIRIE, JEFFERSON PARISH

1—ST. ANGELA MERICI (1964), Rev. Msgr. Kenneth J. Hedrick; Deacons Gilbert R. Schmidt; Nicholas Chetta.
Res.: 901 Beverly Garden Dr., 70002-5085. Tel: 504-835-0324; Fax: 504-834-9709.
School—835 Melody Dr., 70002-5095. Tel: 504-835-8491; Fax: 504-835-4463. Mrs. Colleen Remont, Prin. Lay Teachers 27; Students 465.
Catechesis/Religious Program—Tel: 504-837-9347. Students 56.

2—ST. ANN CHURCH AND SHRINE (1971), Revs. Michael J. Scheneller; Frank Candalisa; Deacons Phillip E. Doolen; Raymond J. Bertin.
Res.: 4920 Loveland St., 70006-4099. Tel: 504-455-7071; Fax: 504-455-7076.
School—4921 Meadowdale St., 70006-4098. Tel: 504-455-8383; Fax: 504-455-9572. Lay Teachers 60; Students 1,085.
Catechesis/Religious Program—Tel: 504-455-7809; Fax: 504-455-7837. Students 106.

3—ST. BENILDE (1964), Revs. Patrick B. Wattigny; John P. Grenham; Deacons Biaggio DiGiovanni; Clifford S. Wright.
Res.: 1901 Division St., 70001-2798. Tel: 504-834-4980; Fax: 504-831-5810.
School—1801 Division St., 70001-2799. Tel: 504-833-9894; Fax: 504-834-4380. Mrs. Vicky G. Helmsetter, Prin. Lay Teachers 31; Students 546.
Catechesis/Religious Program—Students 69.

4—ST. CATHERINE OF SIENA (1921), Rev. Msgr. Roger A. Swenson; Deacons Michael Coney; Jere Crago; Don M. Richard.
Res.: 105 Bonnabel Blvd., 70005-3736. Tel: 504-835-9343; Fax: 504-835-1525.
School—400 Codifer Blvd., 70005-3797. Tel: 504-831-1166; Fax: 504-833-8982. Sr. Imelda Moriarty, Prin. Sisters of Charity of the Incarnate Word 3; Lay Teachers 61; Students 1,002.
Catechesis/Religious Program—Tel: 504-835-6648. Students 59.

5—ST. CHRISTOPHER THE MARTYR (1947), Revs. Kenneth Harney; Michael M. Thanh Ngoc Nguyen; Deacons Charles Duke; Rodney A. Trahan Sr. In Res., Rev. Charles L. Mueller.
Res.: 309 Manson Ave., 70001-4898. Tel: 504-837-8214; Fax: 504-837-8303.
School—(Grades PreK-8), 3900 Derbigny St., 70001-4999. Tel: 504-837-6871; Fax: 504-834-0522. Ruth Meche, Prin. Lay Teachers 41; Students: (PreK) 141; (K-8) 765.
Catechesis/Religious Program—Tel: 504-831-7691. Doris Marse, D.R.E. Students 80.

6—ST. CLEMENT OF ROME (1965), Rev. Msgr. Ralph E. Carroll; Rev. Joseph M. Krafft; Deacons Kenneth Boe; Ed Dorvin; Frank Minor.
Res.: 4317 Richland Ave., 70002-3097. Tel: 504-887-7821; Fax: 504-454-3906.
School—3978 W. Esplanade Ave., 70002-3099. Tel: 504-888-0386; Fax: 504-885-8273. Susan Perry, Prin. Lay Teachers 27; Students 514.
Catechesis/Religious Program—Students 140.

7—ST. EDWARD THE CONFESSOR (1964), Revs. Philip G. Landry; Clayton Charbonnet; Deacons Gerard J. Fasullo Sr.; August Mendel.
Parish Office:—4921 W. Metairie Ave., 70001-4466. Tel: 504-888-0703; Fax: 504-455-5443.
School—Tel: 504-888-6353; Fax: 504-456-0960. Sr. Mary de Lourdes Charbonnet, S.L.W., Prin. & D.R.E. Sisters of the Living Word 2; Lay Teachers 26; Students 567.
Catechesis/Religious Program—Students 46.

8—ST. FRANCIS XAVIER (1924), Rev. Msgr. Andrew C. Taormina, J.D.; Deacons Paul Nalty; Charles E. Coudrain Jr. In Res., Rev. Thomas Kinney (Retired).
Res.: 448 Metairie Rd., 70005-4371. Tel: 504-834-0340; 504-837-4733; Fax: 504-837-8735.
School—215 Betz Ave., 70005-4167. Tel: 504-833-1471; Fax: 504-833-1498. Stephen R. Labranche, Prin. Lay Teachers 25; Students 475.
Catechesis/Religious Program—444 Metairie Rd., 70005-4307. Tel: 504-834-0348. Students 140.

9—ST. LAWRENCE THE MARTYR (1958), Rev. Richard N. Maughan; Deacons Sterling Ohlmeyer; Ray Richardson.
Res.: 2525 Maine Ave., 70003-5446. Tel: 504-466-6236; Fax: 504-467-4945.
Catechesis/Religious Program—Tel: 504-469-5262. Students 35.

10—ST. LOUIS KING OF FRANCE (1947), Rev. Msgr. Joseph O. Lorio; Revs. Ronald Braud; Otis W. Young Jr.; Deacon Wilbur Martinez.
Res.: 1609 Carrollton Ave., 70005-1498. Tel: 504-834-9977; Fax: 504-834-9979.
School—1600 Lake Ave., 70005-1499. Tel: 504-833-8224; Fax: 504-838-9938. Dr. Thomas Spranley, Prin. Lay Teachers 32; Students 486.
Catechesis/Religious Program—Students 26.

11—ST. MARY MAGDALEN (1955), Rev. Msgr. Robert D. Massett; Rev. Joseph Thang Dinh Tran; Deacon Angeles Robin.
Res.: 6425 W. Metairie Ave., 70003-4327. Tel: 504-733-0922; Fax: 504-733-0869.
School—6421 W. Metairie Ave., 70003-4395. Tel: 504-733-1433; Fax: 504-736-0727. Mrs. Bonnie Gaspard, Prin. Teresians Sisters 1; Lay Teachers 28; Students 659.
Catechesis/Religious Program—Tel: 504-733-8980. Linda Earle, D.R.E. Students 154.

12—OUR LADY OF DIVINE PROVIDENCE (1965), Revs. David W. Dufour; Minh Cong Phan; Deacons Fred C. Memleb Jr.; Barry Campeaux.
Res.: 1000 N. Starrett Rd., 70003-5899. Tel: 504-466-4511; Fax: 504-466-4858.
School—917 N. Atlanta St., 70003-5898. Tel: 504-466-0591; Fax: 504-466-0671. Mrs. Elvina DiBartolo, Prin. Lay Teachers 36; Students 505.
Catechesis/Religious Program—Mrs. Nancy Campeaux, D.R.E. Students 310.

13—ST. PHILIP NERI (1960), Revs. Lee John Saloy; David J. Robicheaux; Deacons Jerry L. Harrison; Charles Hausknecht Sr.; Edward R. Cannon; Jerry L. Harrison; Justin Lazarre Jr., Business Mgr.
Res.: 6500 Kawanee Ave., 70003-3298. Tel: 504-887-5535; Fax: 504-885-6259.
School—6600 Kawanee Ave., 70003-3199. Tel: 504-887-5600; Fax: 504-456-6857. Dr. Carol Stack,

Prin. Lay Teachers 35; Students 636.
Catechesis/Religious Program—Tel: 504-889-0089. Holly Caffarel, D.R.E. Students 162.

NORCO, ST. CHARLES PARISH, SACRED HEART OF JESUS (1959), Rev. Terence Hayden (Ireland).
Res.: 401 Spruce St., P.O. Box 515, 70079-2197. Tel: 985-764-6503; Fax: 985-725-0512.
School—Tel: 985-764-9958; Fax: 985-764-0041. Cheryl Orillion, Prin. Lay Teachers 17; Students 189.
Catechesis/Religious Program—Students 215.

PARADIS, ST. CHARLES PARISH, ST. JOHN THE BAPTIST (1971), Rev. Msgr. James C. Moragne.
Res.: P.O. Box 1498, 70080-1498. Tel: 985-758-2668; Fax: 985-758-2901.
Catechesis/Religious Program—Tel: 985-758-1593. Students 175.

PEARL RIVER, ST. TAMMANY PARISH, SS. PETER AND PAUL (1970), Rev. Bac-Hai Viet Tran; Deacons John F. Howard Jr.; John Patrick Downey; Francis W. Drake.
Res.: 66192 St. Mary Dr., 70452-5705. Tel: 985-863-7935; Fax: 985-863-5431.
Catechesis/Religious Program—Students 136.

POINTE A LA HACHE, PLAQUEMINES PARISH, ST. THOMAS (1844), [CEM 2] Rev. Raymond Joseph Guillot, Parochial Admin.
Res.: P.O. Box 98, 70082-0098. Tel: 985-333-4465; Fax: 985-333-9933.
Mission—Assumption of the Blessed Virgin 6951 Hwy. 39, Braithwaite, Plaquemines Parish 70040-0063. Tel: 504-682-5607; Fax: 504-682-5617.

PORT SULPHUR, PLAQUEMINES PARISH, ST. PATRICK (1870), [CEM] Rev. Gerard P. Stapleton.
Res.: 28698 Hwy. 23, 70083-9623. Tel: 985-564-3284; Fax: 985-564-3108.
Catechesis/Religious Program—Tel: 985-564-2803. Students 100.
Mission—St. Joseph Potash, Plaquemines Parish.

RESERVE, ST. JOHN THE BAPTIST PARISH
1—OUR LADY OF GRACE (1937), (African American), Rev. Joseph C. Rodney Jr., S.S.J.; Deacon Joseph Mamou.
Mailing Address: P.O. Box 464, 70084-0464.
Res.: 772 Hwy. 44, 70084-0464. Tel: 985-536-2613; Fax: 985-536-1819.
School—Tel: 985-536-4291; Fax: 985-536-4250. Mrs. Stephanie Watkins, Prin. Lay Teachers 9; Students 175.
Catechesis/Religious Program—Tel: 985-536-2028. Myrtle Ann Lucas, D.R.E. Students 50.
2—ST. PETER (1864), [CEM] Rev. Tuan Anh Pham.
Res.: 1550 Hwy. 44, P.O. Box 435, 70084-0435. Tel: 985-536-2887; Fax: 985-536-7078.
School—Tel: 985-536-4296; Fax: 985-536-4305. C. J. Tastet, Prin. Lay Teachers 18; Students 223.
Catechesis/Religious Program—Tel: 985-536-2886. Students 213.

RIVER RIDGE, JEFFERSON PARISH, ST. MATTHEW THE APOSTLE (1959), Revs. Nghiem Van Nguyen; Callons Cuccia; Vinh Dinh Luu; Deacons Russell LeBlanc; Dan Dorsey; Roland Bienvenu.
Res.: 10021 Jefferson Hwy., 70123-2498. Tel: 504-737-4537; Fax: 504-737-4033.
School—Tel: 504-737-4604; Fax: 504-738-7985. Lay Teachers 32; Students 591.
Catechesis/Religious Program—Students 90.

ST. BENEDICT, ST. TAMMANY PARISH, ST. BENEDICT (1970), Rev. Marian E. Larmann, O.S.B.; Deacon Nelvin Luke.
Res.: Smith-Stafford Rd., 70457-9999. Tel: 985-892-1216; Fax: 985-892-4211.
Catechesis/Religious Program—Tel: 985-809-7752; Fax: 985-867-2270. Students 193.

ST. BERNARD, ST. BERNARD PARISH, ST. BERNARD (1787), [CEM] Rev. Herbert J. Kiff Jr., Parochial Admin.
Mailing Address: P.O. Box 220, 70085-0220.
Res.: 2805 Bayou Rd., 70085-9748. Tel: 504-682-5493; 504-682-3709; Fax: 504-682-8915.
Catechesis/Religious Program—Tel: 504-676-3565. Students 126.

SLIDELL, ST. TAMMANY PARISH
1—ST. GENEVIEVE (1968), Rev. Jose Roel G. Lungay; Deacons George Menges; Daniel Haggerty Jr.; Paul Mumme Sr.
Res. and Mailing Address: 58203 Hwy. 433, 70460-3121. Tel: 985-643-3832; Fax: 985-649-5294.
Catechesis/Religious Program—Tel: 985-641-5220; Fax: 985-641-5220. Students 265.
2—ST. LUKE THE EVANGELIST (1982), Revs. Rodney P. Bourg; Elberto T. Vasquez; Deacons Robert Binney; Harold Burke-Sivers; Robert Trainor. In Res., Rev. Gerard P. Kinane.
Office:—910 Cross Gates Blvd., 70461-8414. Tel: 985-641-6429; Fax: 985-847-0742.
Catechesis/Religious Program—Tel: 985-641-2570; Fax: 985-641-6570. Students 651.
3—ST. MARGARET MARY (1965), Rev. Msgr. Lanaux J. Rareshide, V.F.; Revs. Thomas Kilisara; Luis Henao (BAL); Deacons Richard W. Calkins; John C. Weber; Carlos A. Ramirez.
Res.: 1050 Robert Blvd., 70458-2098. Tel: 985-643-6124; Fax: 985-643-6126.
School—Tel: 985-643-4612; Fax: 985-643-4659. Mr. Bobby Ohler, Prin. Lay Teachers 40; Students 698.
Catechesis/Religious Program—Tel: 985-649-3055. Students 445.
4—OUR LADY OF LOURDES (1890), [CEM] Rev. Adrian B. Hall; Deacons Charles B. Faler Jr.; George H. Frilot II.
Res.: 3924 Berkley St., 70458-5198. Tel: 985-643-4137; Fax: 985-643-1675.
School—345 Westchester Pl., 70458-5299. Tel: 985-643-3230; Fax: 985-645-0648. Mr. Robert V. Kiefer Jr., Prin. Sisters 1; Lay Teachers 31; Students 595.
Catechesis/Religious Program—Tel: 985-643-1742. Mrs. Patricia S. Andrews, D.R.E. Students 359.

TERRYTOWN, JEFFERSON PARISH, CHRIST THE KING (1963), Rev. Jose Ladra; Rev. Msgr. Joseph Bourgeois; Deacons Dean D. Herrick; James W. Swiler.
Res.: 535 Deerfield Rd., 70056-2899. Tel: 504-361-1500; Fax: 504-361-0632.
School—Tel: 504-367-3601; Fax: 504-367-3679. Lay Teachers 28; Students 419.
Catechesis/Religious Program—Students 80.

VIOLET, ST. BERNARD PARISH, OUR LADY OF LOURDES (1916), Rev. Msgr. Frank J. Lipps; Rev. Kyle V. Dave; Deacon William Chiappetta.
Res.: 6305 E. St. Bernard Hwy., 70092-9506. Tel: 504-682-3046; Fax: 504-682-4470.
Church: 2621 Colonial Blvd., 70092.
Catechesis/Religious Program—6413 E. St. Bernard Hwy., 70092-9508. Tel: 504-682-0919. Students 193.

WAGGAMAN, JEFFERSON PARISH, OUR LADY OF THE ANGELS (1978), [CEM] Rev. Raul V. Lobo; Deacon Gilbert Smith.
Res.: 139 Herman St., 70094-2404. Tel: 504-436-4459; Fax: 504-436-4459.
Catechesis/Religious Program—Students 105.

WESTWEGO, JEFFERSON PARISH, OUR LADY OF PROMPT SUCCOR (1920), [CEM] [JC] Rev. David L. Rabe.
Res.: 146 Fourth St., 70094-4297. Tel: 504-341-9522; Fax: 504-341-5957.
School—531 Avenue A, 70094-4294. Tel: 504-341-9505; Fax: 504-341-9508. Sr. Rita Fantin, F.M.A., Prin. & Supr. Sisters 3; Lay Teachers 22; Students 354.
Catechesis/Religious Program—Students 95.

Non-Parochial Churches & Chapels

MANDEVILLE, ST. TAMMANY PARISH, ST. DYMPHNA CATHOLIC CENTER AND CHAPEL (1971), Rev. Raphael Barousse, O.S.B., Chap.; Deacons Pat Downey, Chap.; Chris Bertucci, Chap.
Southeast Louisiana Hospital, P.O. Box 3850, 70470-3850. Tel: 504-626-6317.

NEW ORLEANS, ORLEANS PARISH
1—CHAPEL OF THE VIETNAMESE MARTYRS (1978), (Vietnamese),
Church: 14400 Peltier Dr., 70129-1713. Tel: 504-254-5660; Fax: 504-254-9250.
2—HANMAUM KOREAN CATHOLIC CHAPEL, Rev. Jung-Rae Cho.
1812 W. Napoleon Ave., Metairie, 70001-2364. Tel: 504-888-8772; Fax: 504-888-2366.
3—ST JOSEPH CHAPEL (1895),, Mailing Address: 1000 Howard Ave, Ste. 500, 70113-1903. Tel: 504-596-3050; Fax: 504-596-3055. St. Joseph Cemetery, 2220 Washington Ave., 70113-2647. Tel: 504-895-2507.
4—ST. MARY CHURCH (1845),, (Shrine of St. Lazarus of Jerusalem) Rev. Msgr. Crosby W. Kern, Rector.
Mailing Address: 615 Pere Antoine Ally, 70116. In Res., Rev. Msgr. Terry B. Becnel, V.F.
Church: 1116 Chartes St., 70116-2596. Tel: 504-529-3040; Fax: 504-529-2001.
5—ST. MARY'S ASSUMPTION (1858) (German), Rev. Luong Uong, C.SS.R.
Church: 2030 Constance St., 70130-5099. Tel: 504-522-6748; Fax: 504-523-3734
6—ST. MARY'S CHAPEL, Rev. Luong Uong, C.SS.R. 1516 Jackson Ave., 70130. Tel: 504-522-6748.
7—NATIONAL SHRINE OF BLESSED FRANCIS XAVIER SEELOS (2000), Rev. Byron J. Miller, C.SS.R., Dir. 2030 Constance St., 70130-5099. Tel: 504-525-2495; Fax: 504-581-9181.
8—OUR LADY OF PROMPT SUCCOR NATIONAL SHRINE (1926), Sr. Ann Barrett, Shrine Admin.
Mailing Address: 2734 Nashville Ave., 70115.
Church: 2701 State St., 70118-6399. Tel: 504-866-0200; Fax: 504-866-8300.
9—ST. ROCH CHAPEL, , St. Roch Cemetery, St. Roch Ave. & Music St., 70117-8223. Tel: 504-945-5961.

Pilgrimage Shrines

METAIRIE, JEFFERSON PARISH, ST. ANN NATIONAL SHRINE (1971), Rev. Michael J. Schneller.
Church: 4920 Loveland, 70002-4099. Tel: 504-455-7071; Fax: 504-455-7076.
Catechesis/Religious Program—Tel: 504-455-7809; Fax: 504-455-7837. Students 106.

NEW ORLEANS, ORLEANS PARISH
1—OUR LADY OF PROMPT SUCCOR NATIONAL SHRINE (1926), Sr. Ann Barrett, Shrine Admin.
Res.: 2701 State St., 70118-6399. Tel: 504-866-0200; Fax: 504-866-8300.
2—SHRINE OF ST. JUDE THADDEUS (1826), (African American), Revs. Michael Amesse, O.M.I., Dir.; Anthony Rigoli, O.M.I., Assoc. Dir.
411 N. Rampart St., 70112-3594. Tel: 504-525-1551; Fax: 504-525-1827.
Catechesis/Religious Program—Tel: 504-522-8546. Students 78.
3—SHRINE OF ST. LAZARUS OF JERUSALEM, Rev. Msgr. Alvin J. O'Reilly, Rector (Retired).
Mailing Address: 615 Pere Antoine Alley, 70116.
Church: 1116 Chartres St., 70116-2596. Tel: 504-529-2651; Fax: 504-529-2001.

Non-Parochial Community

NEW ORLEANS, ORLEANS PARISH, BYZANTINE CATHOLIC MISSION (1978),, Ruthenian Rite Jurisdiction. Rev. Ellis L. DePriest, S.M. Ruthenian Rite Jurisdiction.
Church: 2437 S. Carrollton Ave., 70118. Tel: 504-524-5192; Fax: 504-524-9796.

Chaplains of Public Institutions
Hospitals

NEW ORLEANS. *Charity Hospital*, 1532 Tulane Ave., 70140-1015. Tel: 504-679-9204. Rev. Eutiquiano Miguel, O.F.M.Cap., Chap.
Children's Hospital, 200 Henry Clay Ave., 70118. Tel: 504-899-9511. Deacons Roland Bienvenu, Chap., Charles J. Smith Jr., Chap.
DePaul Hospital, 1040 Calhoun St., 70118. Tel: 504-899-8282. Deacon Richard E. Deichmann, Chap.
Jo Ellen Smith Nursing Facility, 4502 General Meyer Ave., 70114-3531. Tel: 504-361-7923. Deacon Robert G. Beaumont Sr.
Kindred Hospital, 3601 Coliseum St., 70115-3687. Tel: 504-899-1555; Fax: 504-899-1509. Deacons Richard E. Deichmann, Chap., William A. Glennon, Chap.
Memorial Medical Center, 301 N. Jefferson Davis Pkwy., 70119-5397. Tel: 504-483-5248. Rev. Msgr. William Bilinsky, Chap., Deacon Thomas Guntherberg, Chap. Mercy Campus
Memorial Medical Center, 2700 Napoleon Ave., 70115-6996. Tel: 504-899-9311. Rev. Kofi Adzaku, Pastoral Assoc., Deacon Thomas J. Guntherberg. Baptist Campus
Methodist Hospital, 5620 Read Rd., 70127-0103. Tel: 504-244-5719. Deacon Joseph R. Rosato.
Touro Infirmary, 1401 Foucher St., 70115-3593. Tel: 504-897-7011. Rev. Douglas C. Brougher, Chap. Tel: 504-897-7011; 504-945-5878.
United Medical Center, 3419 St. Claude Ave., 70117-6198. Tel: 504-948-8200. Attended from Blessed Francis Xavier Seelos Parish.
University Hospital, 2021 Perdido St., 70112-1396. Tel: 504-588-3000. Rev. Vincent Bechamps, O.SS.T., Chap. Tel: 504-588-3175.
Veterans Affairs Medical Center, 1601 Perdido St., 70146-2000. Tel: 504-568-0811. Rev. Edmund Akordor.

CHALMETTE. *Chalmette Medical Centers*, 9001 Patricia St., 70043-1799. Tel: 504-277-8011.
801 Virtue St., 70043-1298. Tel: 504-277-7711. Deacon Alex Serantine, Chap.

COVINGTON. *Lakeview Regional Medical Center*, 95 E. Fairway Dr., 70433. Tel: 504-867-3800. Deacon Louis Mire, Chap. (Vacant)
St. Tammany Hospital, 1202 S. Tyler St., 70433. Tel: 504-898-4000. (Vacant)

GRETNA. *Meadowcrest Hospital*, 2500 Belle Chasse Hwy., 70056-7127. Tel: 504-392-3131. Deacons Thomas Stallings, Chap., Leslie D. Vincent, Dir. Pastoral Care.

JEFFERSON. *Elmwood Partners*, 1221 S. Clearview Pkwy., 70121-1029. Tel: 504-734-1900. Rev. Lawrence Pandolfo, O.P., Chap.
Ochsner Foundation Hospital, 1516 S. Clearview Pkwy., 70121-2484. Tel: 504-842-3000. Rev. Wilfred F. Meridier, Chap. Tel: 504-866-7713.

MANDEVILLE. *Southeast Louisiana Hospital*, P.O. Box 3850, 70470-3850. Tel: 504-626-6317; Fax: 504-626-6658. Rev. Raphael Barousse, O.S.B., Deacons John Patrick Downey, Chris Bertucci, Chap., Reginald J. Seymour, Chap.

MARRERO. *West Jefferson General Hospital*, 4500 11th St., 70072-3191. Tel: 504-347-5511. Rev. Denver B. Pentecost, Chap.
Wynhoven Health Care Center, 1050 Medical Center Blvd., 70072-3170. Tel: 504-347-0777. Rev. Denver B. Pentecost, Chap.

METAIRIE. *Doctors Hospital of Jefferson*, 4320 Houma Blvd., 70002-2973. Tel: 504-849-8684. Deacon Charles Duke, Chap.
East Jefferson General Hospital, 4200 Houma Blvd., 70002-2970. Tel: 504-454-4000. Rev. Charles L. Mueller, Chap., Deacons Charles Hauseknecht Sr.,

Chap., Raymond E. Heap, Assoc. Chap.
Lakeside Hospital, 4700 S.1-10 Service Rd. West, 70001. Tel: 504-780-8282. Deacon August Mendel, Chap.
SLIDELL. *Greenbriar Nursing & Convalescent Home*, 505 Robert Rd., 70458-1699. Tel: 985-643-6900. Rev. Msgr. Lanaux J. Rareshide, V.F., Chap. Tel: 504-643-6124, Rev. Thomas Kilisara, Chap.
Guest House of Slidell Nursing Home, 1051 Robert Rd., 70458-2011. Tel: 985-643-5630. Rev. Msgr. Lanaux J. Rareshide, V.F., Chap. Tel: 504-643-6124, Rev. Thomas Kilisara, Chap.
Live Oak Village Assisted Living Community, 2200 Gause Blvd. E., 70461-8414. Tel: 985-781-4545. Chaplain: Priests and Deacons of St. Luke the Evengelist
North Shore Living Center, 106 Medical Center Dr., 70461-7833. Tel: 985-643-0307. Attended by St. Luke the Evangelist, Slidell.
North Shore Regional Medical Center, 100 Medical Center Dr., 70461-7833. Tel: 985-649-7070. Attended by St. Luke the Evangelist, Slidell.
Slidell Memorial Hospital, 1001 Gause Blvd., 70458-2987. Tel: 985-643-2200. Deacons Richard W. Calkins, Francis W. Drake. Attended by St. Margaret Mary, Slidell.
Trinity Neurologic Rehabilitation Center at Slidell, 1400 W. Lindberg Dr., 70458-3193. Tel: 985-641-4985. Rev. Msgr. Lanaux J. Rareshide, V.F., Chap. Tel: 985-643-6124, Rev. Thomas Kilisara, Chap.

Colleges and Universities

NEW ORLEANS. *Delgado College*, 615 City Park Ave., 70119. Tel: 504-288-6336. Revs. Thomas W. Hoffman, S.J., Chap., Ronald Henery, O.P., Chap., Deacon Eric Gamble, Assoc. Chap.
Delgado Community College, School of Nursing, 4133 Banks St., 70119-6883. Tel: 504-568-6411. Rev. Louis E. Meyers, S.J., Chap.
Louisiana State University Medical Center, 4133 Banks St., 70119-6883. Tel: 504-568-6411. Rev. Thomas W. Hoffman, S.J., Chap.
Southern University in New Orleans, UNO Newman Center, 70148-0001. Tel: 504-288-6336. Rev. Thomas W. Hoffman, S.J., Chap.
Tulane-Newcomb, 1037 Audubon St., 70118-5294. Tel: 504-866-0984. Very Rev. Carl B. Trutter, O.P.
University of New Orleans, UNO Newman Center, 70148-0001. Tel: 504-288-6336. Rev. Thomas W. Hoffman, S.J., Chap.

Prisons

NEW ORLEANS. *Orleans Parish Correctional Center*, 521 S. Broad St., 70119-7490. Tel: 504-822-8000. Rev. Theodore M. Kalamaja, S.J., Chap., Deacons Jose A. Sierra, Chap., Rodrigo Alonso Fonseca, Chap., George H. Frilot II, Chap., Rodney A. Trahan Sr., Chap., Garland Bourgeois Jr., Chap., David Caldero, Chap., Larry Calvin, Chap., Clifford S. Wright, Chap., Uriel Durr, Chap., Sam Hull, Chap., Noel Martinsen, Chap.
Orleans Parish House of Detention, 2735 Perdido St., 70119-7390. Tel: 504-822-8000. Sisters Lilianne Flavin, O.P., Pastoral Min., Victor Allain, R.S.M., Pastoral Min.
ANGIE. *Washington Correctional Institute*, 27268 Hwy. 21, 70426-3030. Tel: 985-848-5232. Deacon Charles Hartman, Chap.
ANGOLA. *Louisiana State Penitentiary*. Deacon Joseph Mamou, Chap.
P.O. Box 169, Garyville, 70051-0169. Tel: 985-535-3682.
CHALMETTE. *St. Bernard Parish Prison*, St. Bernard Courthouse, 70043-4793. Tel: 504-279-8823. Deacon Alex J. Seruntine Jr., Chap.
GRETNA. *Jefferson Parish Correctional Center*, P.O. Box 388, 70054-0388. Tel: 504-374-7700, Ext. 3109. Rev. Robert J. Ratchford, S.J., Chap., Deacons Louis Stall, Chap., Ralph Fray, Chap., Brian J. Klause, Chap., Gerard L. Labadot, Chap.
HARVEY. *Rivarde Juvenile Detention Home*, 1525 Manhattan Blvd., 70058-3405. Tel: 504-392-2097. Deacons Ralph Fray, Chap., Gerard L. Labadot.
MANDEVILLE. *St. Tammany Parish Prison*, Tel: 985-892-8324. Deacon Charles Read Jr.

On Duty Outside the Archdiocese:
Rev. Msgr.—
Calkins, Arthur B., Villa Stritch, Via della Nocetta, 63, 00164, Rome, Italy.
Revs.—
Calamari, Paul, P.O. Box 4640, Harrisburg, PA 17111.
deWater, Joseph M., Steenschuur 19, 2311 ES, Leiden, The Netherlands.
Fernandez, Luis J., VA Medical Center, 6863 S.W. 16th St., Miami, FL 33155-1709.
Highfill, H. Brian (LAV), 1271 Mound House St., Las Vegas, NV 89110-5900.
Jeanfreau, James J., Jr.
Nalty, Christopher, Congregation for the Clergy, Rome, Italy.
Picado, Rodrigo, 50 Vs E. Cortel, Curridabat, San Jose, Costa Rica, CA.
Planea, John (Philippines), Cardinal Rosales Pastoral Center, Patria Bldg. J. Avelino St., Calbayog City, 6710 Philippines.

Graduate Studies:
Revs.—
Payne, John J., Jr., Canon Law
Pericone, Nicholas P., Canon Law

Military Chaplains:
Revs.—
Austin, Walter J.
Dixon, James R.
Grice, Edward M.
Lavastida, Jose I., S.T.D., S.T.L.
O'Neill, Michael F., 100 ARW/HC, Unit 4905, Box 230, APO, AE 09459-5230. U.S.A.F.

Unassigned:
Rev.—
Duffy, Stephen

On Medical Leave of Absence:
Revs.—
Berner, Francis
Mongeon, Peter M.

Retired:
Most Rev.—
D'Antonio, Nicholas, O.F.M., D.D., Chateau de Notre Dame, 70125.
Rev. Msgrs.—
Boeshans, Francis G., P.O. Box 6328, Diamondhead, MS 39525-6000.
Byrnes, Donald M., St. Jerome, 2400 33rd St., Kenner, 70065.
Carroll, Richard L., 9811 Ana Hula, Bay, St. Louis, MS 39520.
Duke, Charles J., 3513 Lemon St., Metairie, 70006.
Hebert, Ray P., St. John Vianney Villa, 4701 Wichers Dr., Apt. D, Marrero, 70072.
Hecker, Lawrence A., St. John Vianney Villa, 4701 Wichers Dr., Marrero, 70072.
O'Reilly, Alvin J.
Poche, Gerard W., Our Lady of Wisdom Healthcare Center, 5600 Gen. DeGaulle Dr., 70131.
Reisch, Milton L., St. John Vianney Villa, 4701 Wichers Dr., Apt. A, Marrero, 70072.
Roeten, Winus, 9512 Kuepferle Ct., River Ridge, 70123.
Roppolo, Ignatius M., St. Rita, 2729 Lowerline St., 70125-3599.
Schutten, Marion F., P.O. Box 3174, Covington, 70434.
Sontheimer, W. Wendell
Tomasovich, John A., 69 Lake Lynn Dr., Harvey, 70058.
Van der Werff, Martin, 3609 Lake des Allemands, Harvey, 70058.
Vincent, Robert G., P.O. Box 459, LaPlace, 70069-0459.
Revs.—
Barattini, John H., Casella Postale 79, 16043, Chiavari, Italy.
Dabria, Jerry J., 401 S. Gatehouse Dr., Apt. G, Metairie, 70001-2039.
Davidson, Carl J., 517 Central Ave., Houma, 70364.
De La Pinera, Fernando, Casa Sacerdotal, de la Catedral S/N, Almeria 04001 Spain.
DeMaria, Lawrence A., 8 Mesa St., Kenner, 70065.
Desrosiers, Paul H., St. John Vianney Villa, 4701 Wichers Dr., Marrero, 70072.
Dicharry, Harold E., C.M., St. Stephen, 1025 Napoleon Ave., 70115-2898.
Duffy, Donald, 2653 Jean Lafitte Blvd., Lafitte, 70067.
Ernst, Albert C., P.O. Box 640400, Kenner, 70064-0400.
Kennedy, Patrick J. R., 924 Monroe St., Gretna, 70053-2299.
Mele, Rudolph, 2832 Burdette St., 70125.
Mitchell, Royce, 1512 Gardena Dr., 70122.
Monzillo, Oneil, 532 Indian Bluff, Las Vegas, NV 89128.
Moore, Matthias, C.S.Sp.
Morgan, Brendan P., P.O. Box 73128, Metairie, 70033.
Mosely, Stan D., O.S.B., St. Joseph Abbey, St. Benedict, 70457-9999.
Perera, Denzil M., 1322 Moss St., 70119-2998.
Perkovic, Anton, 444 Adair St., 70448.
Persac, Louis A., 4201 Woodland Dr., 70131-7398.
Pieris, Timothy, 6564 Fleur de Lis St., Apt. 9, 70124.
Pijoan, L. Adrian M. Figuerola, St. Augustine Home, 2345 W. 86th St., Indianapolis, IN 46260.
Qui, Vincent, 421 Pat Dr., Avondale, 70094.
Schmaltz, Bernard, 500 Prentiss Rd., Pass Christian, MS 39571.
Schott, James E., 4744 Marigny St., 70122.
Serio, Anthony, 3809 Hudson St., Metairie, 70006.
Texada, David Ker, 1923 Salem St., Alexandria, 71301-3840.
Tranchina, Joseph, 2820 Burdette St., 70125.
Trinchard, Paul, 446 Crystal St., 70124.
Vitte, Jules, 38 Grande Rue, 25300, Les Fourges, France.
Walsh, Laurence, Lyrattin, Ballinamult, Co. Waterford, Ireland.
White, Anthony J., St. John Vianney Villa, 4701 Wichers Dr., Marrero.
Young, Bernard L., 1405 Ingleside Dr., Fayetteville, SC 28314.

Permanent Deacons:
Alexander, Dwight, St. Raymond, New Orleans
Angeli, Santiago Roberto, Chap., Ozanam Inn, New Orleans; St. Jerome, Kenner
Arcuri, Dominic Joseph, Chap., Stella Maris Maritime Center, New Orleans; St. Joan of Arc, LaPlace
Arendt, Elliott, Sr., Maurice, New Orleans
Armshaw, Cornelius, St. Anthony, Gretna
Attaway, Charles, (On Leave)
Balderas, Robert, Sr., Diocese of Lafayette
Beaumont, Robert G., Sr., Our Lady of Perpetual Help, Belle Chasse; Chaplain, Jo Ellen Smith Nursing Facility
Beckendorf, Edward, (On Duty Outside the Archdiocese)
Bertin, Raymond J., St. Ann, Metairie
Bertucci, Chris, Chap., Southeast Louisiana State Hospital, Mandeville
Beyer, Walter L., (Retired), Mater Dolorosa, New Orleans
Bialas, James, Our Lady of the Rosary, St. Rose of Lima, New Orleans
Bienvenu, Roland, St. Matthew the Apostle, River Ridge; Children's Hospital, New Orleans
Binney, Robert, St. Luke the Evangelist, Slidell
Blanchard, John, On Leave
Boe, Kenneth, Chap., Jefferson Parish Sheriff's Office; St. Clement of Rome, Metairie
Bourgeois, Don, St. Jane de Chantal, Abita Springs
Bourgeois, Garland, St. Elizabeth Ann Seton, Kenner; Chaplain, Orleans Parish Correctional Center
Brady, Richard, St. Loius Cathedral
Broussard, Terrel J., St. Maria Goretti, New Orleans
Burke-Sivers, Harold, St. Luke the Evangelist, Slidell
Caffery, Thomas E., Jr., Assoc. Dir. Permanent Dioconate, Our Lady of the Lake, Mandeville
Calamia, S.J., (Retired)
Caldero, Davis Eugenio, Chap., Orleans Parish Correctional Center, New Orleans; Nativity of Our Lord, Kenner
Calkins, Richard W., Chap., Slidell Memorial Hospital & St. Margaret Mary, Slidell
Calvin, Larry Lee, Chap., Orleans Parish Correctional Center, New Orleans; All Saints, New Orleans
Campeaux, Barry G., Our Lady of Divine Providence, Metairie
Campuzano, Luis A., St. Jerome, Kenner
Cannon, Edward, St. Philip Neri, Metairie
Capaci, Andrea, Assoc. Dir., Family Life Apostolate, St. Elizabeth Ann Seton, Kenner; Appointed Special Advocate, Metropolitan Tribunal
Carrillo, Cesar Cornelio, Chap., Infant Jesus of Prague, Harvey
Casanova, Joseph Glen, Chap., Ozanam Inn, New Orleans; St. Brigid, New Orleans
Caserta, Piero, St. Agnes, Jefferson; Covenant House, New Orleans
Cassou, Henry A., Jr., Our Lady of Prompt Succor, Chalmette
Chetta, Nick, St. Angela Merici, Metairie
Cimino, Paul, St. Rita, New Orleans
Coney, Michael, St. Catherine of Siena, Metairie
Cordes, Daniel J., St. Jerome, Kenner
Corral, Walfredo, Chap., Ozanam Inn, New Orleans; Sacred Heart, New Orleans
Coudrain, Charles E., Jr., Our Lady of Prompt Succor Shrine, New Orleans; St. Francis Xavier, Metairie
Crago, Jere, St. Catherine of Siena, Metairie
Curry, William P., Jr., Sacred Heart, Lacombe
Daigle, Irving J., Sacred Heart of Jesus, New Orleans
Deichmann, Richard, Mater Dolorosa, Kindred & DePaul Hospitals, New Orleans
DeLeon, Ildefonso R., St. Maria Goretti, New Orleans
DiGiovanni, Biaggio, St. Benilde, Metairie; Ozanam Inn, New Orleans
DiGrado, Chris, St. Andrew the Apostle, New Orleans
Donnaud, Paul J., St. Anthony of Padua, Luling

Doolen, Philip E., St. Ann, Metairie
Dorsey, Dan, St. Matthew the Apostle, River Ridge; Chaplain, Archdiocesan Spirituality Center
Dorvin, Edwin, St. Clement of Rome, Metairie
Downey, John Patrick, Chap., Ss. Peter and Paul, Pearl River; Southeast Lousiana State Hospital, Mandeville
Dragon, Edgar P., Our Lady of Perpetual Help, Kenner
Drake, Francis W., SS. Peter and Paul, Pearl River; Slidell Memorial Hospital, Slidell
Duet, Ferris J., Jr., Visitation of Our Lady, Marrero
Duffy, Peter E., J.D., St. Maria Goretti, New Orleans; Assoc. Judge, Metropolitan Tribunal
Duke, Charles, St. Christopher the Martyr; Doctors Hospital of Jefferson, Metairie
Duplechain, Raphael, Jr., Assoc. Dir., Permanent Diaconate
Durbin, Oscar A., (Retired)
Durr, Uriel Andrew, Chap., Orleans Parish Correctional Center, New Orleans; Our Lady Star of the Sea, New Orleans
Elfer, Ernest C., Jr., Stella Maris Maritime Center, New Orleans; Holy Name of Mary, (Algiers), New Orleans
Engel, Randall L., Duty Outside
Fandal, Wendolen, Jr., (Retired)
Farinelli, David W., Assoc. Dir., Family Life Apostolate
Fariss, Jeffrey, Leave of Absence
Fasullo, Gerard, Sr., St. Edward the Confessor, Metairie; Appointed Special Advocate, Metropolitan Tribunal
Ferretti, Anthony J., Mary Queen of Peace, Mandeville
Finn, John Joseph, Chap., Forest Manor Nursing Home, Mandeville; Mary Queen of Peace, Mandeville
Fleischer, Francis J., St. Theresa of Avila & Center of Jesus the Lord, New Orleans
Flynn, Dan, St. Rita, Harahan, Catholic Committee on Boy Scouting
Fonseca, Rodrigo Alonso, Chap., St. Theresa of the Child Jesus & Orleans Parish Correctional Center, New Orleans
Fray, Ralph, Jefferson Parish Correctional Center, Gretna; Rivarde Juvenile Detention Home, Harvey
Frilot, George H., II, On Leave
Gaiennie, Richard M., Our Lady of the Rosary, New Orleans
Gamble, Eric, St. Thomas the Apostle, UNO & Byzantine Catholic Mission, New Orleans
Garon, Henry A., St. Henry & Ozanam Inn, New Orleans
Glapion, Lloyd St. Clair, (Retired) St. Augustine, New Orleans
Glennon, William A., Jr., St. Pius X & Kindred Hospital, New Orleans
Glover, John A., St. Anselm, Madisonville
Gross, Greg Andrew Nicholas, Our Lady of Perpetual Help, Kenner; Chaplain, Ozanam Inn
Gubert, Norbert, St. Raphael the Archangel, New Orleans
Guidry, Ronald, Dir., Office of Worship, St. Louis Cathedral, New Orleans
Guitterrez, Clayton J., St. John the Baptist, Folsom
Guntherberg, Thomas James, Chap., Memorial Medical Center, Baptist Campus, New Orleans; Holy Spirit, New Orleans
Haggerty, Daniel, Jr., Chap., F.B.I. & Slidell Police Dept., St. Genevieve, Slidell
Hamm, John David, Our Lady of the Rosary and St. Rose of Lima, New Orleans
Harrison, Jerry, St. Philip Neri, Metairie; Kenner Police Dept., Kenner
Hartman, Charles, (Retired)
Hartson, Maurice, III, St. Alphonsus
Hauseknecht, Charles B., St. Philip Neri & East Jefferson General Hospital, Metairie
Heap, Raymond E., East Jefferson Hospital, Metairie
Heine, Charles, St. Peter, Covington
Herrick, Dean D., Christ the King, Terrytown
Howard, John, Sts. Peter & Paul, Pearl River
Hull, Samuel Petrus, III, Chap., Orleans Parish Correctional Center, New Orleans; Resurrection of Our Lord, New Orleans
Insley, J. Vernon, St. Bonaventure, Avondale
Johnson, Dwight J., St. Clement of Rome, Metairie
Jones, Melvin C., Sr., Our Lady Star of the Sea, New Orleans
Keller, Lawrence, St. Theresa of the Child Jesus, New Orleans
Kelley, Edward Francis, Our Lady of the Lake, Mandeville
Kingsmill, Arthur George, St. Leo the Great & Archdiocesan Metropolitan Tribunal, New Orleans
Klause Brian Joseph, Chap., St. Anthony, Lafitte; Jefferson Parish Correctional Center, Gretna
Labadot, Gerard L., Chap., St. Martha, Harvey; Jefferson Parish Correctional Center, Gretna; Rivarde Juvenile Detention Center
Labranche, Frans, Jr., St. Jane de Chantal, Abita Springs; Assoc. Judge, Metropolitan Tribunal
Landry, Coy, Holy Family, Luling
Lazo, Joseph, Our Lady of the Lake Mandeville
LeBlanc, Ames P., Jr., (On Leave)
LeBlanc, Nolen J., St. Rita, Harahan
LeBlanc, Russell T., (Retired), St. Matthew the Apostle, River Ridge
LeDoux, John, Nativity of Our Lord, Kenner
LeRose, Joseph R., St. John of the Cross, Lacombe
Levy, Albert A., III, St. Mark, Chalmette
Lewis Raymond, St. Matthias, New Orleans
Lorenz, Fallon Herbert, Chap., Our Lady of Prompt Succor & Chalmette Medical Center, Chalmette
Luke, Nelvin, St. Benedict Church, St. Benedict
Madere, Kenneth P., St. Mark, Chalmette
Mallerich, Walton J., (On Leave)
Mamcu, Joseph, Our Lady of Grace, Reserve; Chap., Louisiana State Penitentiary, Angola
Martinez, Gerald J., Dir. of Stewardship, St. Frances Xavier Cabrini, New Orleans
Martinez, Rodolfo J., Assoc. Dir., Permanent Diaconate, Immaculate Conception, Marrero; Renovacion Carismatic Catolica Hispana
Martinez, Wilbur, St. Louis King of France, Metairie
Martinsen, Noel W., St. Elizabeth Ann Seton, Kenner; Chaplain, Orleans Parish Correctional Center
Matherne, Landry, St. Gertrude, Des Allemands
Mathews, Michael Schmid, (On Duty Outside the Archdiocese)
Mendleb, Fred C., Jr., Our Lady of Divine Providence, Metairie
Mendel, August B., Chap., St. Edward the Confessor & Lakeside Hospital, Metairie
Mendieta, Roberto, Nativity of Our Lord, Kenner
Menges, George, St. Genevieve, Slidell
Miester, Alvin C., Jr., St. Louise de Marillac, Arabi
Minor, Francis M., St. Clement of Rome, Metairie
Mire, Louis N., Chap., St. Anselm, Madisonville; Lakeview Reg. Medical Center
Missretta, Nicholas L., St. Rita, Harahan
Moragas, Lucien, (On Duty Outside the Archdiocese)
Morales, G. Ernesto, St. Jerome, Kenner
Mumme, Paul, Sr., St. Genevieve, Slidell
Murphy, Larry, Assoc. Dir., Permanent Diaconate Office, Visitation of Our Lady, Marrero
Nalty, Paul A., Chap., St. Francis Xavier, Metairie; Malta Park Assisted Living Residence, New Orleans; Assoc. Judge, Metropolitan Tribunal
Nunez, Charles R., Sr., (Retired)
Nuss, Henry, Our Lady of the Rosary and St. Rose of Lima, New Orleans
Ohlmeyer, Sterling, St. Lawrence the Martyr, Metairie
Perez, Jose D., (Duty Outside)
Pham, Joseph Hiep, Mary Queen of Vietnam, New Orleans
Pippenger, John, St. Dominic, New Orleans
Ramirez, Carlos Alfredo, St. Margaret Mary, Slidell
Rayfield, Rudolph J., Sr., Assoc Dir., Permanent Diaconate, St. Peter Claver , New Orleans
Read, Charles, Jr., St. Peter, Covington; St. Tammany Prison, Mandeville
Reeson, Curles P., St. Robert Bellarmine, Arabi
Rhodes, Frank W., Jr., Prince of Peace, Chalmette
Richard, Don Michael, St. Catherine of Siena, Metairie
Richardson, Ray, St. Lawrence the Martyr, Metairie
Rivere, Raymond H., Chap., St. Mark & Chalmette Medical Facility, Chalmette
Rizzo, Peter C., St. Frances Xavier Cabrini , New Orleans
Robicheaux, Wilfred, Jr., Immaculate Conception, Marrero
Robin, Angelas, St. Mary Magdalen & Jefferson Parish Sheriff's Office, Metairie
Rosato, Joseph R., St. Thomas More & Christ the Healer Prog., New Orleans
Rougelot, Sidney, (Retired)
Roussel, Garland Joseph, Jr., St. Hubert, Garyville
Roussel, Theodore, St. Charles Borromeo, Destrehan
Sandman, Arthur, Sr., (On Leave)
Scalise Jr., Bertrand, St. Stephen, New Orleans; Chaplain, Ozanam Inn
Schexnayder, Harry, St. Charles Borromeo, Destrehan
Schlette, Peter B., (On Duty Outside the Archdiocese)
Schmidt, Gilbert R., Assoc. Dir., Permanent Diaconate, St. Angela Merici, Metairie
Schwartzmann, Adrian Gustave, II, Chap., Ozanam Inn, New Orleans; St. Joseph, New Orleans
Seruntine, Alex J., Jr., St. Louise de Marillac, Arabi; Chaplain, St. Bernard Parish Prison and Chalmette Medical Center, Chalmette
Seymour, Reginald John, Chap., Southeast Louisiana State University Hospital, Mandeville; Epiphany, New Orleans
Shelly, Ceaser, (On Leave)
Sierra, Jose A., Chap., Blessed Francis Xavier Seelos, New Orleans
Smith, Charles J., Children's Hospital & St. Stephen, New Orleans
Smith, Gilbert, Our Lady of Angels, Waggaman
Sorensen, George A., Jr., (Retired)
St. Pierre, Thomas Joseph, Chap., Stella Maris Maritime Center, Destrehan; Ascension of Our Lord, LaPlace
Stall, Louis W., Dir., Prisons Apostolate; Dir. Jefferson Parish Correctional Ctr., Gretna
Stallings, Thomas Ray, Chap., Meadowcrest Hospital, Gretna; St. Andrew the Apostle, New Orleans
Stevens, Allen, St. Philip the Apostle, New Orleans
Stewart, Irvin, Sr., St. Joan of Arc, New Orleans
Stohlman, Michael H., St. Charles Borromeo, Destrehan
Strahan, Douglas H., St. Bernard, St. Bernard; Chaplain St. Bernard Parish Prison and Chalmette Medical Center, Chalmette
Swiler, James W., Dir. Office of Permanent Diaconate, Christ the King, Terrytown
Toups, Wilbur A., St. Rita, New Orleans
Trahan Sr., Rodney A., Chap., St. Christopher, Metairie; Orleans Parish Correctional Center, New Orleans
Trainor, Robert, St. Luke the Evangelist, Slidell
Vicknair, Percy, (Retired)
Vicroy, Clarence, (Retired)
Vincent, Dan, Dir. Black Catholic Ministries, St. Paul the Apostle, New Orleans
Vincent, Harold, St. Julian Eymard, New Orleans
Vincent, Leslie D., Chap., Our Lady of Perpetual Help, Belle Chasse & Meadowcrest Hospital, Gretna
Warriner, David A, St. Louis Cathedral; Metropolitan Tribunal
Watley, Jesse A., Assoc. Dir., Permanent Diaconate, Blessed Francis Xavier Seelos, New Orleans
Weber, John C., St. Margaret Mary, Slidell
Webre, Milton G., St. John Bosco, Harvey
White, Alfred, Corpus Christi, New Orleans
Williams, Everett, Our Lady of Lourdes, New Orleans
Williams, Herman, St. Monica, New Orleans
Williams, Irvin, (Retired), St. David, New Orleans
Williams, John B., St. Raymond, New Orleans
Wilson, Earl McMahon, Jr., St. Henry, New Orleans
Wong, Peter, (On Duty Outside the Archdiocese)
Wright, Clifford S., Chap., St. Benilde, Metairie; Orleans Parish Correctional Center
Zeringue, Alfred, (On Duty Outside the Archdiocese)
Zimmer, Julius T., Our Lady of Prompt Succor, Chalmette
Zornman, Raymond L., (On Leave)

INSTITUTIONS LOCATED IN THE ARCHDIOCESE

[A] SEMINARIES, ARCHDIOCESAN

NEW ORLEANS. *Notre Dame Seminary Graduate School of Theology* (1923), 2901 S. Carrollton Ave., 70118-4391. Tel: 504-866-7426; Fax: 504-866-3119. Email: pjw@nds.edu. Web: www.nds.edu. Priests 14; Laymen 8; Laywomen 7; Rabbis 1; Women Religious 5; Seminarians 114.

Administration: Revs. Lance J. Campo, S.T.L., Dir. of Spiritual Formation; F. Hampton Davis, M.Div., Dir. Field Education; Jose I. Lavastida, S.T.D., S.T.L., Academic Dean; Clarence C. Menard, O.M.I., H.E.L., H.E.D., Spiritual Dir.; Very Rev. Patrick J. Williams, M.Div., M.S., Pres. & Rector; Mrs. Margaret Ann Breaux, B.A., Registrar; Dr. John A. Brun, Ph.D., Psychological Counselor; Mr. George Dansker, M.P.H., M.L.I.S., Librarian; Ms. Natalie E. Finnegan, B.A., Dir. of Development; Mrs. Gayle A. Golden, Dir. of Facilities & Student Services; Ms. Michelle W. Klein, Business Mgr.

Faculty: Rev. Msgr. Terry T. Tekippe, M.A., S.T.L., Ph.D.; Revs. Paul Counce, M.A., M.C.L.; Stanley Klores, M.A., M.Div., S.T.L., S.T.D.; Glenn David LeCompte, M.Div., S.T.L. (HT); William F. Maestri, M.Div., M.A.; Donald Martin, S.J., M.A., Ph.D.; Frank Montalbano, O.M.I., S.T.L., S.S.L.; Gregory S. Ross, O.C.D., M.Div., S.T.L.; Gerald L. Seiler Jr., M.Div., J.C.L.; Sisters Janet Bodin, M.S.C., M.A., Ph.D.; Elizabeth Fitzpatrick, O.Carm., M.A.; Judith Gomila, M.S.C., M.R.E.; Noel Toomey, O.P.,

M.A.; Elizabeth Willems, S.S.N.D., M.A., Ph.D.; Rabbi Edward Cohn, M.A.H.L., D.D., D.Min.; Dr. Basil Davis, M.A., Ph.D.; Mr. Bruce Dinwiddie, B.A.; Judith Farrelly, M.A.; Ms. Jennifer Golden, M.A.; Dr. James M. Jacobs, M.A., Ph.D.; Dr. Sara M. Lavastida, Ph.D., M.A., M.Ed.; Dr. David Liberto, M.A., Ph.D.; Mr. Dreux Montegut, M.Mus.; Dr. Charles Nolan, H.E.D., M.Ed.

ST. BENEDICT. *St. Joseph Seminary College* (1890), 70457-9999. Tel: 504-892-1800; Fax: 504-867-2270. Email: rector@sjasc.edu. Web: www.sjasc.edu. Very Rev. Gregory M. Boquet, O.S.B., M.A., Rector & Pres.; Rev. Justin Brown, O.S.B., Abbot; Friar Vincent Dufresne, S.T.L.; Revs. Aelred Kavanagh, O.S.B., M.T.S., S.T.M., S.T.D., Vice Rector; Scott J. Underwood, O.S.B., M.T.S., M.Ed.; Charles Benoit, O.S.B., M.A.Th., Dean of Students; Adam Begnaud, O.S.B., M.S.; Timothy J. Burnett, O.S.B.; Matthew R. Clark, O.S.B., M.A.; Augustine E. Foley, O.S.B., M.A.Th.; Thomas L. Gwozdz, S.B.D., Ph.D.; Ken Ramon-Landry (BLX); Thomas C. Ranzino (BR); James Vanderholt (AUS); Patricia Oman, M.Ed., Vice Pres. for Admin.; Dr. Russ Pottle, Ph.D., Academic Dean; Glen Huacuja, Business Officer; Bros. Mark Allen, O.S.B.; Bernard Boudreaux, O.S.B.; Becket Ghioto, O.S.B.; Bede Roselli, O.S.B.; Simon Stubbs, O.S.B. Benedictine Monks. Conducted by Provinces of New Orleans and Mobile and Monks of St. Joseph's Abbey Priests 14; Brothers 5; Sisters 1; Lay Teachers 30; Seminarians 82; Total Enrollment 171; Lay Staff 14.

Faculty: Revs. Charles J. Benoit, O.S.B.; Justin Brown, O.S.B., B.A., M.A., Abbot; Matthew R. Clark, O.S.B., M.A.; Augustine E. Foley, O.S.B., M.A.Th.; Thomas L. Gwozdz, S.B.D., Ph.D.; Aelred Kavanagh, O.S.B., M.T.S., S.T.M., S.T.D.; Kenneth Ramon-Landry, O.S.B., B.A., B.S., M.Div.; James Vanderholt (AUS); Sr. Jeanne d'Arc Kernion, O.S.B.; Merle Albers; Ms. Josette Beaulieu-Grace, M.A.; Jeffrey Bell, Ph.D.; Peggy Caruthers, M.L.S.; Al Dragmuet Jr., M.A.; Peter M. Emerson, Ph.D.; Ralph M. Forestieri, Ph.D.; Eva Gold, Ph.D.; Michael Greene, M.S.; Agnieszka Gutthy, Ph.D.; John E. Hebert, Ph.D.; John V. Hoover Jr., M.Ed.; Linda Jackson, M.A.; Nancy McKeand; Harry McMurray, Ph.D.; Aileen Mootoo; Ann K. Nauman, Ph.D.; Karen Perry; Russ Pottle, Ph.D.; Francie Rich; Kathryn K. Rombs, Ph.D.; Ronnie J. Rombs, Ph.D.; Andrew Traver, Ph.D.

Religious Studies Institute: Rev. Thomas C. Ranzino (BR); Friar Vincent Dufresne, S.T.L.; Brenda Atkinson, M.A.; Elizabeth Bourgeois, M.R.E.; Thomas Eldringhoff, M.A.; Charles Jumonville, M.R.E.; Ronnie J. Rombs, Ph.D.; Mr. Kenneth J. Thevenet, M.Mus.

Diaconate Program: Charles Jumonville, M.R.E.; Kathryn K. Rombs, Ph.D.; Ronnie J. Rombs, Ph.D.

Professional Lay Staff: Claudette Arcement, Alumni Sec.; Jim Beck, Dir. Institute Technology; Carol Bryant, Academic Sec.; Betty Ann Burns, Dir. Financial Aid; Betty Dominguez, Sec. to President-Rector; Ann Dubroc, Treasurer; Pamela Egan, R.N., N.P., Dir. of Student Health Services; Julie King, Devel. Sec.; Beverly Krieger, Sec.; Adrienne Laborde, Dir. Devel.; Sabrina Sterling, Library Asst.

[B] SEMINARIES, RELIGIOUS OR SCHOLASTICATES

NEW ORLEANS. *St. John of the Cross, Discalced Carmelite House of Studies*, 2925 S. Carrollton Ave., 70118-4301. Tel: 504-861-9102; Fax: 504-865-1751. Rev. Gregory S. Ross, O.C.D., M.Div., S.T.L. Priests 1; Religious Seminarians 2.

Josephite House of Studies, 2000 St. Bernard Ave., 70116-1390. Tel: 504-945-1359; Fax: 504-948-3049. Email: trfatjhf@bellsouth.net. Priest Candidates 1.

METAIRIE. *Congregation of the Mother Coredemptrix Formation House*, 112 Lilac St., 70005-1817. Tel: 504-835-9746; Fax: 504-835-9746. Email: cmcneworleans@hotmail.com. Rev. Hilary Tran Cong Ly, C.M.C. (FWT), Dir. Priests 1; Brothers 13.

[C] COLLEGES AND UNIVERSITIES

NEW ORLEANS. *Loyola University New Orleans* (1912), 6363 St. Charles Ave., 70118-6195. Tel: 504-865-2011; Fax: 504-865-3851. Email: ramagos@loyno.edu. Web: www.loyno.edu. Revs. Bernard P. Knoth, S.J., Pres.; Simon J. Hendry, S.J., Jesuit Center Dir.; Walter Harris Jr., Interim Provost/Vice Pres. for Academic Affairs; Revs. James P. Bradley, S.J., Rector; Edward B. Arroyo, S.J.; Stephen Duffy, S.T.D.; Gerald M. Fagin, S.J.; Ernest Ferlita, S.J.; Alvin J. Holloway, S.J.; Theodore M. Kalamaja, S.J.; Marvin C. Kitten, S.J.; Lawrence Moore, S.J.; Leo A. Nicoll, S.J.; Peter S. Rogers, S.J.; Edward B. Arroyo, S.J., Min.; Peter J. Bernardi, S.J.; Very Rev. Alfred C. Kammer, S.J., Prov.; Revs. Edward P. Buvens, S.J.; James M. Deshotels, S.J.; Robert S. Gerlich, S.J.; Stephen C. Rowntree, S.J.; Charles E. O'Neill, S.J.; Edwin L. Gros, S.J.; Bros. Gebhard R.M. Frohlich, (Retired); Lawrence J. Lundin, S.J.; Francis J. Riedinger, S.J., (Retired); Revs. James M. Caime, S.J.; David A. Boileau; Kenneth P. Keulman; Dr. Frank Scully, Dean College of Arts and Sciences; Dr. Edward Kvet, Dean College of Music; Dr. J. Patrick O'Brien, Dean College of Business Admin.; Dr. Marcel Dumestre, Dean City College; Brian Bromberger, Dean Law School. Priests 26; Brothers 3; Lay Teachers 515; Students 5,842.

Our Lady of Holy Cross College, 4123 Woodland Dr., 70131-7399. Tel: 504-394-7744; Fax: 504-391-2421. Email: smcneely@olhcc.edu. Web: www.olhcc.edu. Carol A. Jobe, Ph.D., Pres.; Dr. Edward Dupuy, Vice Pres. Academic Affairs; Mr. David Logsder, Vice Pres. Business Affairs; Michael Ferguson, Registrar. Priests 1; Brothers 1; Congregation of the Sisters Marianites of Holy Cross 6; Sisters 2; Lay Teachers 36; Students 1,431; Total Staff 160.

Xavier University of Louisiana (Coed) , One Drexel Dr., 70125-1098. Tel: 504-486-7411; Fax: 504-485-7904. Email: apply@xula.edu. Web: www.xula.edu. Dr. Norman C. Francis, Pres.; Dr. Deidre Labat, Vice Pres. Academic Affairs; Mrs. Lisa Lewis McClain, Dir. Office of Campus Ministry. Priests 1; Brothers 1; Sisters of the Blessed Sacrament 8; Lay Teachers 226; Students 3,912.

[D] HIGH SCHOOLS, ARCHDIOCESAN

NEW ORLEANS. *Redeemer-Seton High School*, 1453 Crescent Dr., 70122-2099. Tel: 504-288-1494; Fax: 504-288-1499. Email: redeemerseton@archdiocese-no.org. Web: www.redeemerseton.org. Mr. Arthur L. Schmitt, Pres.; Joan G. Johnson, Prin. School Sisters of Notre Dame 1; Daughters of Charity 2; Lay Teachers 30; Students 341.

COVINGTON. *St. Scholastica Academy*, P.O. Box 1210, 70434-1210. Tel: 985-892-2540; Fax: 985-893-5256. Email: mcelestin@ssacad.com. Web: www.ssacad.com. Mrs. Marguerite S. Celestin, Prin. Sisters 2; Lay Teachers 48; Students 667.

GRETNA. *Archbishop Blenk High School*, 17 Gretna Blvd., 70053-4989. Tel: 504-367-2626; Fax: 504-367-7128. Email: abhs@blenkhs.org. Web: www.blenkhs.org. Mr. David Pooley, Prin. Priests 1; Lay Teachers 46; Students 605.

LA PLACE. *St. Charles Catholic High School*, 100 Dominican Dr., 70068-3499. Tel: 985-652-3809; Fax: 985-652-2609. Email: stcharlescath@archdiocese-no.org. Web: www.scc-comets.com. Mr. Andrew C. Cupit, Prin. Lay Teachers 32; Students 424.

MARRERO. *Archbishop Shaw High School*, 1000 Barataria Blvd., 70072-3052. Tel: 504-340-6727; Fax: 504-347-9883. Email: arnoshaw@archdiocese.org. Web: www.archbishopshaw.org. Revs. James McKenna, S.D.B. (PMB), Dir.; Michael Conway, S.D.B., Prin.; Mr. John Corb, Financial Admin.; Revs. Paul Aronica, S.D.B.; Joseph Vien Hoang, S.D.B.; James P. Horan, S.D.B.; Thomas McGahee, S.D.B.; Bros. Joseph Tortorici; Dave Verrett. Salesians of St. John Bosco Priests 6; Brothers 2; Lay Teachers 34; Boys 526.

MERAUX. *Archbishop Hannan High School*, 2501 Archbishop Philip M. Hannan Blvd., 70075-2630. Tel: 504-279-1921; Fax: 504-279-0200. Email: archhannan@archdiocese-no.org. Mr. John Serio, Prin. Priests 2; Lay Teachers 42; Students 520.

METAIRIE. *Archbishop Chapelle High School*, 8800 Veterans Blvd., 70003-5235. Tel: 504-467-3105; Fax: 504-466-3191. Email: achs@archbishopchapelle.org. Web: www.archbishopchapelle.org. Miss Beth Johnson, Pres.; Mrs. Mary Beth Drez, Prin.; Catherine Vanhuss, Asst. Prin. Priests 1; Lay Teachers 80; Girls 1,100.

Archbishop Rummel High School, P.O. Box 663, 70004-0663. Tel: 504-834-5592; Fax: 504-832-4016. Web: www.rummelraiders.com. 1901 Severn Ave., 70001-2893. Mr. David J. Hardin, Pres.; Mr. Michael Begg, Prin. Lay Teachers 90; Boys 1,335.

Rummel Alumni Association, Inc. Tel: 504-833-9625; Fax: 504-833-2232. Members 10,275.

SLIDELL. *Pope John Paul II Catholic High School*, 1901 Jaguar Dr., 70461-9098. Tel: 985-649-0914; Fax: 985-649-5494. Email: pjp@pjp.org. Web: www.slidell.com/schools/pjp. Mr. Richard Berkowitz, Prin. Lay Teachers 24; Students 300.

[E] HIGH SCHOOLS, PAROCHIAL

MARRERO. *Immaculata High School*, 537 Avenue D, 70072-2027. Tel: 504-341-6217; Fax: 504-341-6229. Email: immaculataha@archdiocese-no.org. Web: www.immaculatahigh.org. Sr. Maria Colombo, F.M.A., Prin. Sisters 2; Lay Teachers 34; Girls 422.

[F] HIGH SCHOOLS, PRIVATE

NEW ORLEANS. *Academy of the Sacred Heart "The Rosary"* (1887), (Grades 9-12), 4521 St. Charles Ave., 70115-9990. Tel: 504-891-1943; Fax: 504-891-9744. Email: sacredheart@ashrosary.org. Web: www.ashrosary.org. Dr. Timothy Burns; Sr. Lynne Lieux, R.S.C.J., Prin. Religious of the Sacred Heart 2; Carmelite 1; Lay Teachers 36; Girls 267.

St. Augustine High School (1951), (Grades 10-12), 2600 A.P. Tureaud Ave., 70119-1299. Tel: 504-944-2424; Fax: 504-947-7712. Email: staughs@archdiocese-no.org. Web: purpleknights.com. Rev. Joseph M. Doyle, S.S.J., Pres.; Mr. Reginald Delecia, Prin. Josephite Community, (See Separate Listing for Residence.) Priests 5; Lay Teachers 38; Boys 592.

Brother Martin High School (1869), (Grades 8-12), 4401 Elysian Fields Ave., 70122-3898. Tel: 504-283-1561; Fax: 504-286-8462. Email: gtullier@wwlmail.com. Web: brothermartin.com. Mr. John J. Devlin III, Pres.; Mr. Gerald E. Tullier, Prin. Sisters 2; Brothers of the Sacred Heart 9; Lay Teachers 107; Boys 1,554.

Cabrini High School, 1400 Moss St., 70119-2997. Tel: 504-482-1193; Fax: 504-483-8671. Mrs. Frances Dee Tarantino, Pres.; Mrs. Yvonne L. Hrapmann, Prin. Missionary Sisters of the Sacred Heart 3; Lay Teachers 43; Girls 515.

Cabrini High School, Inc. Tel: 504-482-1193; Fax: 504-483-8673.

De La Salle Senior High School (1949), (Grades 10-12) , (Coed) , 5300 St. Charles Ave., 70115-4999. Tel: 504-895-5717; Fax: 504-895-1300. Email: delasalle@delasallenola.com. Web: www.delasallenola.com. Mr. Kenneth Tedesco, Pres.; Gina Hall, Prin. Brothers of the Christian Schools 4; Sisters 1; Lay Teachers 65; Students 750.

Holy Cross School (1879), (Grades 5-12), 4950 Dauphine St., 70117-4399. Tel: 504-942-3100; Fax: 504-943-7676. Email: contactus@holycrosstigers.com. Web: www.HolyCrossTigers.com. Dr. James Lipovsky, Headmaster. Brothers of the Congregation of Holy Cross, Southwest Province 1; Lay Teachers 66; Boys 940.

Jesuit High School (1847), (Boys) , 4133 Banks St., 70119-6883. Tel: 504-486-6631; Fax: 504-483-3816. Email: principal@jesuitnola.org. Web: www.jesuitnola.org. Rev. Anthony F. McGinn, S.J., Rector; Mr. Michael Giambelluca, Prin.; Revs. Claude P. Boudreaux, S.J.; Richard T. Hermes, S.J.; Norman B. O'Neal, S.J.; Nicholas T. Schiro, S.J. Priests 5; Brothers 1; Lay Teachers 91; Boys 1,180. In Res. Revs. Paul Deutsch, S.J.; Louis E. Meyers, S.J.; Thomas H. Stahel, S.J. Tel: 504-483-3900.

Office, 500 Jefferson Davis Pkwy., 70119. Tel: 504-821-0334. Priests 7; Brothers 1; Lay Teachers 85; Boys 1,191.

St. Mary's Academy of the Holy Family, Mailing Address:: 6905 Chef Menteur Hwy., 70126-5291. Tel: 504-245-0200; Fax: 504-245-8732. Email: smaoffice@archdiocese-no.org. Web: www.smaneworleans.com. Sr. Jennie Jones, S.S.F., Prin.

St. Mary's Dominican High School, 7701 Walmsley Ave., 70125-3494. Tel: 504-865-9401; Fax: 504-866-5958. Email: president@stmarysdominican.org. Web: www.stmarysdominican.org. Sr. Cynthia A. Thomas, Pres.; Dr. Nancy P. Autin, Prin. Priests 1; Sisters 3; Brothers 1; Lay Teachers 80; Students 1,065.

Mount Carmel Academy, 7027 Milne Blvd., 70124-2395. Tel: 504-288-7626; Fax: 504-288-7629. Email: mca@mcacubs.org. Web: www.mtcarmelcubs.org. Sr. Camille Anne Campbell, O.Carm., Pres. & Prin. Congregation of Our Lady of Mount Carmel Sisters 7; Lay Teachers 114; Girls 1,226.

Ursuline Academy Secondary Dept. Day School College Prep. , 2635 State St., 70118-6399. Tel: 504-861-9150; Fax: 504-861-9159. Email: ursulinehs@archdiocese-no.org. Web: www.ursulineneworleans.org. Marcia M. Abide, Ph.D., Pres.; Nancy M. Hernandez, Prin. Sisters 1; Lay Teachers 38; Girls 445.

Xavier Prep School, 5116 Magazine St., 70115-1899. Tel: 504-899-6061; Fax: 504-891-8766. Email: xavierprep@archdiocese-no.org. Web: www.xavierprep.com. Mrs. Carolyn Dubre, Prin. Sisters 6; Lay Teachers 39; Girls 448.

COVINGTON. *The St. Paul's School* (1911), (Grades 8-12), P.O. Box 928, 70434-0928. Tel: 985-892-3200; Fax: 985-892-4048. Email: stpauls@stpauls.com. Web: www.stpauls.com. Bro. Raymond Bulliard, F.S.C., Prin. Day School for Young Men Brothers of the Christian Schools of the New Orleans-Santa Fe Province 6; Lay Teachers 50; Boys 700.

[G] ELEMENTARY SCHOOLS, ARCHDIOCESAN

NEW ORLEANS. *Joseph Central Catholic Elementary School*, (Grades PreK-5), 3774 Gentilly Blvd., 70122. Tel: 504-945-1015; Fax: 504-954-1050. Email: stjosephcen@archdiocese-no.org. Dr. Geralyn Dell, Prin. Sisters 1; Lay Teachers 17; Students 360.

Marian Central Catholic Middle School, 2221 Mendez St., 70122-5267. Tel: 504-288-1411; Fax: 504-286-0209. Email: mariancentral@archdiocese-no.org. Web: www.mariancentral.org. Sr. Maeve McMahon, O.P., Pres. & Prin. Sisters 6; Lay Teachers 23; Students 432.

MARRERO. *Archbishop Shaw Junior High School*, (Grades 8-9), 1000 Barataria Blvd., 70072-3052. Tel: 504-340-6727; Fax: 504-347-9883. Email: arnoshaw@archdiocese-no.org. Web: www.archbishopshaw.org. Rev. James McKenna, S.D.B. (PMB), Dir.; Jim Callow, Prin. Priests 6; Brothers 2; Lay Teachers 30; Students 161.

METAIRIE. *Archbishop Rummel Junior High School*, (Grades 8-9), 1901 Severn Ave., 70001-2893. Tel: 504-834-5592; Fax: 504-832-4016. Email: archrummel@archdiocese-no.org. Web: www.rummelraiders.com. Michael Scalco, Asst. Prin. Lay Teachers 47; Boys 455.

[H] ELEMENTARY SCHOOLS, PRIVATE

NEW ORLEANS. *Academy of the Sacred Heart*, (Grades PreK-8), 4521 St. Charles Ave., 70115-9990. Tel: 504-891-1943; Fax: 504-891-9939. Email: sacredheart@ashrosary.org. Web: www.ashrosary.org. Dr. Timothy Burns, Headmaster. Religious of the Sacred Heart 2; Lay Teachers 63; Girls 553.

St. Augustine High School, (Grades 8-8), 2600 A.P. Tureaud Ave., 70119-1299. Tel: 504-944-2424; Fax: 504-947-7712. Email: staughs@archdiocese-no.org. Web: purpleknights.com. Rev. Joseph M. Doyle, S.S.J., Pres.; Mr. John C. Charles Jr., Prin. Priests 2; Lay Teachers 21; Boys 274.

St. Benedict the Moor School, (Grades PreK-4), 5010 Piety Dr., 70126. Tel: 504-288-2745; Fax: 504-282-9386. Email: stbenmoor@archdiocese-no.org. Phyllis M. Benoit, Prin. Lay Teachers 6; Students 89.

Brother Martin High School (Grade 8) , 4401 Elysian Fields Ave., 70122-3898. Tel: 504-283-1561; Fax: 504-286-8462. Email: gtullier@wwlmail.com. Web: brothermartin.com. Michael Baricos, Prin. Lay Teachers 24; Boys 229.

Cabrini High School, (Grades 8-12), 1400 Moss St., 70119-2997. Tel: 504-482-1193; Fax: 504-483-8671. Web: cabrinihigh.com. Mrs. Frances Dee Tarantino, Pres.; Mrs. Yvonne L. Hrapmann, Prin. Sisters 1; Lay Teachers 39; Students 509.

Christian Brothers School, (Grades 5-7), City Park, #8 Fredericks Ave., 70124-4602. Tel: 504-486-6770; Fax: 504-486-1053. Email: school@cbs-no.org. Web: www.homework-central.com/schools/christian. Bro. Edward Scanlan, F.S.C., Pres.; Mr. Joey M. Scaffidi, Prin. Brothers 7; Lay Teachers 14; Boys 273.

De La Salle Junior High School, (Grades 8-9) , (Coed) , 5300 St. Charles Ave., 70115-4999. Tel: 504-895-5717; Fax: 504-895-1300. Email: peggys@delasallenola.com. Web: www.delasallenola.com. Mr. Kenneth Tedesco, Pres.; Peggy St. John, Prin. Brothers 1; Lay Teachers 29; Students 203.

Henriette Delille Middle School, Inc., 4700 Pineda St., 70126. Tel: 504-288-1644; Fax: 504-288-0224. Email: hdelille@archdiocese-no.org. Sr. Carmen Marie Bertrand, S.S.F., Pres. Sisters 1; Lay Teachers 4; Students 35.

Holy Cross School, (Grades 5-12), 4950 Dauphine St., 70117-4399. Tel: 504-942-3100; Fax: 504-943-7676. Email: contactus@holycrosstigers.com. Web: www.HolyCrossTigers.com. Dr. James Lipovsky, Headmaster. Brothers of the Congregation of Holy Cross 1; Lay Teachers 65; Boys 926.

House of the Holy Family School, (Grades 1-3), 7100 Chef Menteur Hwy., 70126-5220. Tel: 504-242-1810; Fax: 504-241-5082. Email: househlyfam@archdiocese-no.org. Sr. Elizabeth Ann Holmes, S.S.F., Admin. Sisters 6; Lay Teachers 1; Children 30.

Jesuit High School, (Grades 8-8), 4133 Banks St., 70119-6883. Tel: 504-486-6631; Fax: 504-483-3816. Email: principal@jesuitnola.org. Web: www.jesuitnola.org. Rev. Anthony F. McGinn, S.J., Pres.; Mr. Michael A. Giambelluca, Prin. Priests 1; Lay Teachers 20; Boys 256.

St. Mary's Academy, (Grades 7-8), 6905 Chef Menteur Hwy., 70126-5291. Tel: 504-245-0200; Fax: 504-245-8732. Email: smaoffice@archdiocese-no.org. Web: www.smaneworleans.com. Sr. Jennie Jones, S.S.F., Prin. Priests 1; Sisters of the Holy Family 12; Lay Teachers 32; Girls 178.

St. Mary's Dominican High School, 7701 Walmsley Ave., 70125-3494. Tel: 504-865-9401; Fax: 504-866-5958. Email: president@stmarysdominican.org. Web: www.stmarysdominican.org. Ms. Cynthia A. Thomas Pres.; Dr. Nancy P. Autin, Prin. Priests 1; Brothers 1; Sisters 3; Lay Teachers 80; Girls 1,065.

Stuart Hall School for Boys, 2032 S. Carrollton Ave., 70182. Tel: 504-861-1954; Fax: 504-861-5389. Email: claforge@stuarthall.org. Mrs. Cissy LaForge, Prin.

Ursuline Academy, (Grades Toddler-7) 2635 State St., 70118-6399. Tel: 504-866-5260; Fax: 504-866-5293. Email: ursulineelem@archdiocese-no.org. Web: www.ursulineneworleans.org. Marcia M. Abide, Ph.D., Pres.; Kimberly H. Shankle, Prin. Sisters 1; Lay Teachers 35; Students 283.

COVINGTON. *The St. Paul's School*, (Grades 8-12), P.O. Box 928, 70434-0928. Tel: 985-892-3200; Fax: 985-892-4048. Email: stpauls@stpauls.com. Web: www.stpauls.com. Bro. Raymond Bulliard, F.S.C., Prin.; John Morvant, Asst. Prin. Brothers of the Christian Schools, (See St. Paul's School under High Schools, Private) Brothers 6; Lay Teachers 54; Boys 750.

[I] SPECIAL EDUCATION

NEW ORLEANS. *Bishop Perry Middle School* (Boys) , 1941 Dauphine St., 70116-1609. Tel: 504-943-3734; Fax: 504-943-1320. Email: bpms@bpms.org. Web: www.bpms.org. Revs. Paul G. McQuillen, S.S.E., Pres.; David J. Theroux, S.S.E., Prin. Society of St. Edmund 2; Priests 2; Lay Teachers 8; Boys 59.

St. Gerard Majella Alternative School, 5500 Paris Ave., 70122-2699. Tel: 504-288-2789; Fax: 504-288-2789. Email: majellaalt@archdiocese-no.org. Sr. Rose Elaine Kessler, S.S.N.D., Prin. Sisters 1; Lay Teachers 4; Students 25.

Good Shepherd Nativity School, 353 Baronne St., 70112-1628. Tel: 504-598-9399; Fax 504-598-9346. Email: www.kenneth@thegoodshepherdschool.org. Web: www.thegoodshepherdschool.org. Mrs. Karen Ranatza, Prin. Lay Teachers 4; Total Staff 14; Students 50.

Holy Rosary Academy, 3368 Esplanade Ave., 70119-3132. Tel: 504-482-7173; Fax: 504-482-7229. Email: holyrosaryaca@archdiocese-no.org. Michael J. Finder, Prin. Sisters 2; Lay Teachers 23; Students 134.

St. Michael Special School, 1522 Chippewa St.. Tel: 504-524-7285; Fax: 504-524-5883. Email: stmichspecial@archdiocese-no.org. Jane Silva, Prin. Religious 3; Lay Teachers 21 Students 225.

MARRERO. *Hope Haven Center*, 1101 Barataria Blvd., 70072-3085. Tel: 504-347-5581; Fax: 504-340-2075. Lay Teachers 14; Students 99.

[J] DAY CARE CENTERS, CAMPS AND PRESCHOOLS

NEW ORLEANS. *St. Anthony Head Start*, 5407 Dauphine St., 70117-3023. Tel: 504-943-6952; Fax: 504-943-6813. Ms. Melba Hart, Prog. Dir.

Carmel in the Business District (Carmelite Ministries, Inc.), 246 Loyola Ave. 70112. Tel: 504-529-8856; Fax: 504-529-8861. Email: grillote@bellsouth.net. Web: mountcarmel.home.mindspring.com/cbd. Sisters Alice Abate, O.Carm., Exec. Dir.; Gwen Grillot, O.Carm., Prog. Dir.; Elizabeth Coe, Child Care & Preschool Dir.

Cub Corner (Carmelite Ministires, Inc.), 420 Robert E. Lee Blvd., 70124. Tel: 504-283-9499; Fax: 504-283-9483. Web: www.mountcarmel.home.minspring.com. Sr. Alice Abate, O.Carm., Executive Dir.

El Yo Yo Head Start Center, 735 Gen. Pershing St., 70115-1448. Tel: 504-899-6165; Fax: 504-899-5409. Ms. Gaynell Anderson, Prog. Dir. Total Assisted 100; Total Staff 14.

Flint Goodridge Early Head Start Center, 3306 Freret St., 70115-6029. Tel: 504-895-3487; Fax: 504-895-9830. Ms. Susie Foucher, Prog. Dir.

Florida Head Start, 2631 Alvar St., 70117-3364. Tel: 504-945-8115; Fax: 504-943-6813. Eve Pleasant, Prog. Dir. Total Assisted 66; Total Staff 13.

Incarnate Word Head Start Program, Formerly Incarnate Word Preschool Program, 8326 Apricot St., 70118-3198. Tel: 504-866-2309; Fax: 504-861-1435. Ms. Gloria Crassons, Supvr.

St. James Major Day Care Center, 3800 Gentilly Blvd., 70122-6130. Tel: 504-949-1680; Fax: 504-949-5765. Mrs. Peggy Frey, Dir. Staff 9; Average Daily Enrollment 59.

St John Berchmans Child Development Center, 2710 Gentilly Blvd., P.O. Box 8623, 70182-3098. Tel: 504-943-5060; Fax: 504-943-5063. Email: st.johnberchmanscdc@netzero.com. P.O. Box 8623, 70182-8623. Tel: 504-943-5060; Fax: 504-943-5063. Sisters 3; Lay Staff 18; Children 130; Total Assisted 1,125.

Lafon Child Development Center, 7024 Chef Menteur Hwy., 70126-5295. Tel: 504-242-2431; Fax: 504-242-2434. Email: lefon242@earthlink.net. Sr. Mary Laurita Oliver, Admin. Sisters 3; Children (Daily Average) 110; Total Staff 16.

Leslie Early Head Start Center, 2126 Constance St., 70130-5044. Tel: 504-522-2725. Irma Cavalier, Prog. Dir. Total Staff 5.

Louise Early Head Start Center, 1205 Louisiana Ave., 70115-2488. Tel: 504-891-2871; Fax: 504-895-3129. Ms. Irma Cavalier, Prog. Dir.

St. Philip Head Start Program, Formerly St. Philip Preschool, 3333 Clouet St., 70126-5700. Tel: 504-944-2640; Fax: 504-944-4450. Email: blavigne@archdiocese-no.org. Ms. Shirley Lachman, Supvr. Staff 14; Children (Daily Average) 94.

Rosary Child Development Center, 5100 Willow Brook Dr., 70129-1047. Tel: 504-254-1528; Fax: 504-254-1531. Email: rosarycdc@yahoo.com. Sr. Thu-Ha Nguyen, F.M.S.R., Dir. Staff 15; Children (Daily Average) 95.

St. John the Baptist Head Start Program, Formerly St. John the Baptist Pre-School Program, 1920 Clio St., 70113-1214. Tel: 504-529-2557 (Preschool); Fax: 504-581-2028 (Center). Email: sjbcc@archdiocese-no.org. Mr. Doug Anderson, Dir.; Esperanza Martinez, Preschool Supvr. Lay Staff 11; Children 57.

CHALMETTE. *Our Lady of Prompt Succor Child Care Center*, 2217 Fenelon St., 70043-4991. Tel: 504-271-3491; Fax: 504-271-0268. Mrs. Cynthia Dazet, Dir.

ST. BENEDICT. *Abbey Youth Camp, Inc.*, St. Joseph Abbey, 70457. Tel: 985-892-3600; Fax: 985-867-2270. Email: abo@sjasc.edu. Rev. Matthew R. Clark, O.S.B., M.A., Dir.

[K] HOMES FOR CHILDREN AND YOUTH

NEW ORLEANS. *Boys Hope Girls Hope* Group Homes for Boys and Girls. , 4128 Baudin St., 70119-6815. Tel: 504-486-6030; Fax: 504-484-6120. Web: www.boyshopegirlshope.org. Cory J. Howat, Dir. Total Staff 6; Boys 5; Girls 4.

**Covenant House* Home for Runaway, Abused & Homeless Youth , 611 N. Rampart St., 70112-3540. Tel: 504-584-1111; 800-999-9999 (Hotline); Fax: 504-584-1171. Email: dlouque@covenanthouse.org. Web: covenanthouseno.org. Stacy Horn Koch, Exec. Dir. Total Assisted 1,300; Total Staff 100.

BELLE CHASSE. *Padua Pediatric Residential Program* Residential Facility for Severely-Profoundly Retarded and Multihandicapped Children , 200 Beta St., 70037-1499. Tel: 504-392-0502; Fax: 504-392-5411. Ms. Beanca Williams, Admin.

MARRERO. *Hope Haven Center* (1925), Residential Treatment Center and School , 1101 Barataria Blvd., 70072-3085. Tel: 504-347-5581; Fax: 504-340-2075. Mr. Robert Guasco, Dir.

[L] RESIDENCES, ADULT

NEW ORLEANS. *CARE CENTER*, 4222 S. Broad St., 70125-3660. Tel: 504-822-3751; Fax: 504-822-3761. Mrs. Connie Andry, Admin.; Kathleen Kennedy, Prog. Dir. Temporary Residence for Homeless Women and their Children

Baronne Street Transitional Housing, 2407 Baronne St., 70113-1621. Tel: 504-269-9311. Ms. Michell Brown, Prog. Dir.; Connie Andry, Admin.

Ciara House, 1131 St. Andrew St., 70130-5124. Tel: 504-524-8394; Fax: 504-524-0224. Ms. Monetta Clark, Admin.

Crescent House, Formerly Crescent House I and II Temporary residence for abused women and their children Tel: 504-866-9554 (crisis line); Fax: 504-865-0050. Email: mclandry@archdiocese-no.org. *Office*, 1000 Howard Ave., 70113-1916. Tel: 504-865-0057; Fax: 504-865-0050. Ms. Mary Claire Landry, Admin. Total Staff 13; Total Assisted 438.

Ozanam Inn Shelter for Homeless Men , 843 Camp St., 70130-3751. Tel: 504-523-1184; Fax: 504-523-1187. Deacon Biaggio DiGiovanni, Admin. Sponsored by Society of St. Vincent de Paul

Project Lazarus Residential Program for Persons with AIDS , P.O. Box 3906, 70177-3906. Tel: 504-949-3609; Fax: 504-944-7944. Ms. Susan Banks, Exec. Dir. Total in Residence 24; Total Staff 32.

GRETNA. *St. Jude the Apostle*, 1430 Claire Ave., 70053-7436. Tel: 504-361-8457; Fax: 504-367-6952. Residential Facility for Developmentally Disabled Adults

Ocean Avenue Community Home, 361 Ocean Ave., 70053-4726. Tel: 504-361-0674; Fax: 504-367-6952. Residential Facility for Developmentally Disabled Adults

St. Rosalie, 119 Kass St., 70053-3828. Tel: 504-361-8320; Fax: 504-367-6952. Padua Adult Residential Program for Developmentally Disabled Adults

Supervised Apartments, 1430 Claire Ave., 70053-7436. Tel: 504-367-1465; Fax: 504-367-6952.

Supervised Apartments for Developmentally Disabled Adults

HARVEY. *St. Catherine of Siena Supervised Apartment,* 3021 Sienna Dr., 70058-2180. Tel: 504-347-6069; Fax: 504-367-6952. Ms. Beanca Williams, Admin. Residential Program for Developmentally Disabled Adults

MARRERO. *Jefferson CARE Center,* 1108 Barataria Blvd., 70072-3025. Tel: 504-347-0772; Fax: 504-371-8783. Ms. Earline Perique, Prog. Dir. Temporary Residence for Homeless Families

METAIRIE. *Ss. Mary & Elizabeth,* 720 N. Elm St., 70003-6022. Tel: 504-738-6959; Fax: 504-738-8320. Residential Facility for Developmentally Disabled Adults

SLIDELL. *St. Peter the Fisherman,* 62269 Airport Rd., 70460-5242. Tel: 985-641-4914; Fax: 985-641-7575. Ms. Beanca Williams, Admin. Residential Facility for Developmentally Disabled Adults

[M] DAY CARE CENTERS (ADULT)

NEW ORLEANS. *New Directions Adult Day Health Care Center,* 1523 N. Dorgenois St., 70119-2419. Tel: 504-943-9418; Fax: 504-948-3633. Kim Pierre, Prog. Dir.

People Program, 1200 Mirabeau Ave., 70122-1886. Tel: 504-288-3171; Fax: 504-288-3503. Email: info@peopleprogram.org. Web: www.peopleprogram.org. Ms. Mary Catherine Lombard, Dir.

COVINGTON. *Alpha House Adult Day Health Care Center,* 20127 Hwy. 36, 70433-8658. Tel: 985-892-7074; Fax: 985-893-1962. Ms. Theresa Jones, Prog. Dir.

KENNER. *The Greenwalt Center for Alzheimer's Day Care and Research,* 1926 18th St., 70062-6208. Tel: 504-461-5889; Fax: 504-461-5795. Ms. Linda Greenwalt, Asst. Admin.

NORCO. *Norco Adult Day Care,* 425 Spruce St., 70079-8464. Tel: 504-764-9084; Fax: 504-764-0041. Ms. Kathleen Landry, R.N., Dir.

[N] HOMES AND RESIDENCES FOR FAMILIES AND SENIOR CITIZENS

NEW ORLEANS. *The 1540 House,* 1540 N. Johnson St., 70116-1721. Tel: 504-945-0253. Ms. Pam Callahan, Community Mgr. Residents 12.

Annunciation Inn Residence for Elderly , 1220 Spain St., 70117-8369. Tel: 504-944-0512; Fax: 504-944-0514. Mrs. Mercedes White, Community Mgr. Units 106; Total Staff 8; Residents 111.

Chateau de Notre Dame Residence and Nursing Home , 2832 Burdette St., 70125-2596. Tel: 504-866-2741; Fax: 504-866-6769. Email: jtieperman@archdiocese-no.org. Web: cdnd.org. Mr. John Tieperman, Exec. Dir.; Most Rev. Nicholas D'Antonio, O.F.M., Chap. Residential Units 56; Nursing Beds 175; Residential units with assistance 54; Priests 1; Sisters 2; Lay Staff 210.

Christopher Inn Apts. Private Nonprofit Residence for Senior Citizens Sponsored by the Archdiocese , 2110 Royal St., 70116-1693. Tel: 504-949-0312; Fax: 504-945-2634. Mrs. Mercedes White, Asst. Community Mgr. Residents 144; Total Staff 6.

DeLille Inn, 6924 Chef Menteur Hwy., 70126-5260. Tel: 504-241-4877; Fax: 504-241-1828. Email: srtekawitha@christopherhomesinc.org. Sr. M. Tekakwitha Vega, S.S.F., Community Mgr. Total Staff 5; Residents 51.

Haydel Heights Apartments, 6649 Ransom St., 70126-4052. Tel: 504-242-4438; Fax: 504-242-4061. Ms. Linda Chapman, Admin. Units 65; Total Assisted 225; Total Staff 2.

St. John Berchmans Manor, 3400 St. Anthony St., 70122-3098. Tel: 504-943-9343; Fax: 504-947-6090. Email: srmary@christopherhomesinc.org. Sr. M. de Chantal St. Julien, S.S.F., Admin.; Rev. Thaddeus Boucree, S.V.D., Chap. Tel: 504-948-4425. Units 150; Residents 158; Total Staff 11.

Lafon Nursing Facility of the Holy Family, 6900 Chef Menteur Hwy., 70126-5296. Tel: 504-246-1100; Fax: 504-241-6672. Email: admin@lafoninocoxmail.com. Sr. Augustine McDaniel, S.S.F., Admin. Sisters of the Holy Family Sisters 6; Residents 155; Total Staff 145.

St. Margaret's, 6220 Chartres St., 70117-1595. Tel: 504-279-6414; Fax: 504-277-1834. Email: stmargaretsl.org. Web: www.stmargaretsno.org. Mr. Larry Stansberry, CEO. Residents 115; Total Staff 109; Total Assisted 139.

St. Martin Manor, 1501 N. Johnson St., 70116-1720. Tel: 504-945-7728; Fax: 504-945-7726. Email: mveal@christopherhomesinc.org. Sr. M. Camillus Durald, S.S.F., Admin. Residential Units 140; Total Staff 8; Total in Residence 145.

Mary-Joseph Residence for the Elderly (1868), 4201 Woodland Dr., 70131-7398. Tel: 504-394-2200; Fax: 504-391-3347. Email: msneworlsp@earthlink.net. Sr. Rosemary Rese, L.S.P., Supr.; Rev. Francis Whatley, O.SS.T., Chap. Sisters 10; Total Staff 133; Residents 83; Independent Living 19.

Nazareth II, 9640 Hayne Blvd., 70127-4725. Tel: 504-246-9640; Fax: 504-240-6686. Email: bschoust@christopherhomesinc.org. Ms. Sharline O'Brien, Asst. Community Mgr. Apartments 120; Total Staff 5; Total in Residence 120.

Nazareth Inn, 9630 Hayne Blvd., 70127-1260. Tel: 504-241-9630; Fax: 504-241-9631. Email: aharrisonjr@christopherhomesinc.org. Mr. Alvin C. Harrison Jr., Community Manager.
Legal Title: *Nazareth Manor, Inc.* Apartments 150; Total Staff 9; Total in Residence 158.

Our Lady of Wisdom Health Care Center (Inter-Community Health Care, Inc.) , 5600 Gen. deGaulle Dr., 70131. Tel: 504-394-5991; Fax: 504-304-5421. Email: ourladyofwisdom@netscape.net. Web: www.olwhealth.org. Sr. Marjorie Hebert, M.S.C., Exec. Dir.; Wendy Locco, Admin. Inter-community healthcare facility for Archdiocesan clergy and Religious Men: Order of Preachers, Society of Jesus, Society of Mary (Marists), Vincentian, Christian Brothers and Brothers of the Sacred Heart; Religious Women: Sisters of St. Joseph of Medaille, Sisters of Mercy, Sisters of the Living Word, Eucharistic Missionaries of St. Dominic, Sisters of the Immaculate Conception, Marianites of the Holy Cross, Sisters of Mount Carmel, Order of Saint Clare (Poor Clares) and Daughters of Charity. Total Staff 170; Bed Capacity 138.

Villa St. Maurice Residence for Senior Citizens & Handicapped , 500 St. Maurice Ave., 70117-1568. Tel: 504-277-8477; Fax: 504-277-8493. Email: jmoore@christopherhomesinc.org. Mrs. Gaynell McKee, Community Mgr. Residential Units 110; Residents 193; Total Staff 5.

Villa St. Maurice II (Villa Additions) Residence for Senior Citizens & Handicapped. , 6101 Douglas St., 70117-2100. Tel: 504-277-8731; Fax: 504-277-8493. Mrs. Gaynell McKee, Community Mgr. Residential Units 75; Residents 80; Total Staff 2.

LA PLACE. *Place Dubourg, Inc.,* 201 Rue Dubourg, 70068-2433. Tel: 985-652-1981; Fax: 985-651-6147. Email: chpalmisano@christopherhomesinc.org. Ms. Christine Palmisano, Admin. Units 115; Total Staff 8; Total in Residence 116.

MANDEVILLE. *Roquette III,* 4300 Hwy. 22, 70448-2824. Tel: 985-626-5217; Fax: 985-626-9226. Residential Units 67; Staff 3.

Rouquette Lodge St. Tammany Manor, Inc. ; Residence for Senior Citizens , 4300 Hwy. 22, 70448-2824. Tel: 985-626-5217; Fax: 985-626-9226. Bro. Harold Ehlinger, C.S.C., Admin. Residential Units 119; Total in Residence 119; Total Staff 7.

Rouquette II, 4300 Hwy. 22, 70448-2824. Tel: 985-626-5217; Fax: 985-626-9226. Residential Units 51; Total in Residence 51; Total Staff 3.

MARRERO. *Villa D'Ames Apartments,* 6305 Fourth St., 70072-1513. Tel: 504-347-0474; Fax: 504-347-0451. Email: chroussell@christopherhomesinc.org. Charlotte Roussell, Community Mgr. Total Staff 7; Units 200; Total Assisted 200.

Wynhoven Apartments and Wynhoven II Private Non-Profit Residence for Senior Citizens Sponsored by the Archdiocese , 4600-10th St., 70072-3048. Tel: 504-347-8442; Fax: 504-340-6076. Email: jjones@christopherhomesinc.org. Joannette Jones, Community Mgr.; Erin Schieffler, Asst. Community Mgr. Residents 381; Total Staff 15.

Wynhoven Health Care Center, 1050 Medical Center Blvd., 70072-3170. Tel: 504-347-0777; Fax: 504-341-7240. Email: wynhoven@wynhoven.org. Jane Fockler, Admin.; John Tieperman, Exec. Dir. Total Assisted 190; Total Staff 173.

MERAUX. *St. Bernard Manor, St. Bernard II, and St. Bernard III,* 2400 Archbishop Hannan Blvd., 70075-2640. Tel: 504-277-2441; Fax: 504-277-6300. Email: bschouest@christopherhomesinc.org. Brenda Schouest, Community Mgr. Residents 230; Total Staff 11.

METAIRIE. *Metairie Manor, Metairie II, and Metairie III,* 4929 York St., 70001-1013. Tel: 504-456-1467; Fax: 504-887-3718. Mr. Tommy Dale, Asst. Community Mgr.; Ms. Lynn Richard, Asst. Community Mgr.; Rev. John A. Powers, O.P., Chap. Residential Units 369.

[O] CATHOLIC HEALTH SERVICES

NEW ORLEANS. *Daughters of Charity Services of New Orleans,* 3900 S. Carrollton Ave., 70118-4712. Tel: 504-482-2080; Fax: 504-483-6016. Email: dward@dcsno.org. Mr. David J. Ward, Pres. & CEO.

Daughters of Charity Health Center at Carrollton, 3900 S. Carrollton Ave., 70118-4712. Tel: 504-482-0084; Fax: 504-483-6018. Email: dsimpson@dcsno.org. Dolly M. Simpson, Exec. Dir.

Daughters of Charity Neighborhood Health Partnership, 8326 Apricot St., 70118-3198. Tel: 504-866-4978; Fax: 504-866-4676. Email: rarnaud@dcsno.org jdesh@loyno.edu. Ms. Roslyn Arnaud, Assoc. Dir.; Rev. James M. Deshotels, S.J., Assoc. Dir.

Seton Resource Center for Child Development, 4310 Chestnut St., 70115. Tel: 504-896-8235; Fax: 504-899-4083. Email: src@bellsouth.net. Dr. Irene Schulz, Dir.

Vincentian Ministries, 8326 Apricot St., 70118-3198. Tel: 504-866-4978; Fax: 504-866-4676. Email: kflahert@dcsno.org. Sr. Mary Louise Hoeller, D.C., Dir.

METAIRIE. *Sisters of Mercy Ministries* dba Mercy Family Center , Psychological and psychiatric evaluation and counseling. , 110 Veterans Memorial Blvd., Ste. 425, 70005. Tel: 504-838-8283; Fax: 504-838-9799. Email: sjc181@aol.com.
839 Heavens Dr., Mandeville, 70471. Tel: 985-792-1833; Fax: 985-792-1051. Mr. Bernard A. Duco, Pres.; Stewart J. Clark, Ph.D., Exec. Dir. Total Assisted 11,500; Staff 16.

[P] MONASTERIES AND RESIDENCES OF PRIESTS AND BROTHERS

NEW ORLEANS. *Brothers of the Sacred Heart* Tel: 504-282-5693; Fax: 504-288-9920. Email: bileblanc@hotmail.com. *Provincial Office, New Orleans Province,* 4540 Elysian Fields Ave., 70122-3826. Tel: 504-282-5693; Fax: 504-288-9920. Bro. Ivy LeBlanc, S.C., Prov.

Brothers of the Sacred Heart Foundation of the New Orleans Province, Inc., 4540 Elysian Fields Ave., 70122. Tel: 504-282-5693; Fax: 504-288-9920.

Hospitality Center/Volunteer Service Community, 4600 Elysian Fields Ave., 70122-3938. Tel: 504-282-5631. Bro. Henry Gaither, S.C., Dir.

Formation Center, 1156 City Park Ave., 70119-3736. Tel: 504-488-1353. Bro. Matthias Amos, S.C., Dir.
4671 Painters St., 70122-5001. Tel: 504-283-6448. Bro. Alan Drain, S.C., Dir. Total Brothers 16.
Ordained Brothers:
1156 City Park Ave., 70119. Tel: 504-488-1353. Bro. Louis Couvillon, S.C.
175 St. Joseph St., Thibodaux, 70360. Tel: 985-447-4354. Bro. Carl Evans, S.C.
4540 Elysian Fields Ave., 70122-3937. Tel: 504-282-5693. Bro. Albert Guarino, S.C., (Retired).

St. Anne's Mission Unit 50, HC58, Box 90, Ganado, AZ 86505. Tel: 928-652-2631. Bro. William McCue, S.C.
Piazza Del Sacro Cuore, #3, Rome 00151 Italy. Bro. Ray Hebert, S.C.

Dominican Friars, Southern Dominican Province of St. Martin de Porres Tel: 504-837-2129; Fax: 504-837-6604. Email: provincial@opsouth.org. Web: www.opsouth.org. *Provincial Headquarters,* 1421 N. Causeway Blvd., Ste. 200, Metairie, 70001-4144. Very Revs. Martin J. Gleeson, O.P., Prov.; Emiliano Zapata, O.P., Socius & Vicar Prov.; Joseph J. Konkel, O.P., Steward; R. B. Williams, O.P., Promoter of Permanent Formation; Rev. Henry B. Groover, O.P., Promoter of Vocations. Priests in the Archdiocese 25; Brothers in the Archdiocese 3.
Assigned but working elsewhere: Revs. Bryan Fontenot, O.P., (On Sabbatical); Armando Ibanez, O.P., Producer Dir., CA; Bro. Francis Dinet, O.P., Cherry Valley, CA.
Working Abroad:

Home for the Clergy, Fleur de Lys BRK 09 Malta. Tel: 498-166 (011-35-6). Rev. Emanuel M. Camilleri, O.P.

Provincia Dominicana de San Juan Bautista del Peru, Apartado 4169, Lima 1, Peru. Tel: 427-7426 (011-51-1); Fax: 427-6791 (011-51-1). Rev. James Linus Dolan, O.P.

Parroquia de Santiago Apostol, Av. Varsovia Malta-California Sur, Apdo. 76176, Caracas 1070 Venezuela. Tel: 272-7254 (011-58-02). Rev. Jesus de Vianney Guerra, O.P.

Convento Santa Sabrina, Piazza Pietro d' Illiria, 1 (Aventino), Rome 00153 Italy. Tel: 57-94-0546 (011-39-06); Fax: 579-41 (011-39-06). Rev. Michael O'Rourke, O.P.

San Juan de Letran, Calle 19, #258, Entre JEI, Vedado D.P. 104, La Habana, Cuba. Tel: 53-7327329. Rev. Rafael Proenza, O.P.
Iglesia La Dolorosa: Apartado 10,002, San Jose 1000 Costa Rica. Rev. Luis Roberto Aguilar Leal, O.P.

Universita San Tommaso, Largo Angelicum 1, Rome 00184 Italy. Tel: 670-2226 (011-39-06); Fax: 679-0407 (001-39-06). Rev. Alfred W. Wilder, O.P.

Dominican Vocation Sponsors, 1421 N. Causeway Blvd., Ste. 200, Metairie, 70001-4144. Tel: 504-837-2129; Fax: 504-837-6604.

Southern Dominican Foundation, 1421 N. Causeway Blvd., Ste. 200, Metairie, 70001-4144. Tel: 504-837-2129; Fax: 504-837-6604. Very Revs. Martin J. Gleeson, O.P., Pres.; Emiliano Zapata, O.P., Vice Pres. & Sec.; Joseph J. Konkel, O.P., Treas.; Raymond C. Finn, O.P., Promoter of Devel.; Nora P. Fine, Dir. of Devel.

Southern Dominican Global Missions, P.O. Box

3111, Memphis, TN 38173. Tel: 901-529-1255; Fax: 901-526-6882. Bro. Herman Johnson, O.P., Co-Dir.; Rev. Brian J. Pierce, O.P., Co-Dir.

St. Martin de Porres Shrine 1421 N. Causeway Blvd., Ste. 200, Metairie, 70001-4144. Tel: 901-529-1255; Fax: 901-526-6882. Rev. Thomas Condon, O.P., Dir. Total in Residence 29.

Ignatius Residence, 6321 Stratford Pl., 70131-7325. Tel: 504-394-2411; Fax: 504-433-2882. Email: ratchfrd@loyno.edu. Revs. John H. Edwards, S.J., Supr.; Robert L. Anderson, S.J.; Eugene T. Bannin, S.J.; John J. Capelle, S.J.; Thomas D. Culley, S.J.; Claude R. Daly; John P. Driscoll, S.J.; Walter L. Furman, S.J. (MOB); Richard G. Hartnett, S.J.; Very Rev. Wayne D. Herpin, S.J.; Revs. John H. Kaack, S.J.; Michael F. Kennelly, S.J. (SP); Rodney T. Kissinger, S.J.; Henry R. Montecino, S.J.; Vincent A. Orlando, S.J.; Austin N. Park, S.J.; Donald Pearce, S.J.; Herve P. Racivitch, S.J.; Robert J. Ratchford, S.J.; Norman J. Rogge, S.J.; Edward W. Schott, S.J.; Roy W. Vollenweider, S.J.; Bros. Charles J. Blouin, S.J.; Anthony S. Coco, S.J.; C. Robert Doherty, S.J.; H. Francis Hinze, S.J. Priests 21; Brothers 4.

Jesuit Provincial Office New Orleans Province , 500 S. Jefferson Davis Pkwy., 70119-7192. Tel: 504-821-0334; Fax: 504-822-5322. Email: noprovsj@norprov.org. Very Rev. Alfred C. Kammer, S.J., Prov.; Revs. Thomas H. Stahel, S.J., Socius; Paul Deutsch, S.J., Prov. Asst. Secondary Ed. and Formation; James L. Lambert, S.J., Asst. for Pastoral and Retreat Min.; Bro. Lawrence J. Lundin, S.J., Treas.

Legal Title: *Catholic Society of Religious and Literary Education* Priests 4; Brothers 1.

Priests of the Province Abroad:

Casa Parroquial, Santa Rosa (Misiones), Paraguay. Tel: 595-858-221; Fax: 595-858-221. Rev. Charles B. Thibodeaux, S.J.

Ave. Rio de Janiero 327, Campinas, SP 13031-340 Brazil. Tel: 55-19-3871-3422; Fax: 55-19-3871-0164. Rev. Edward J. Dougherty, S.J.

CP 3910, Teresina, PI 64.051-971 Brazil. Tel: 55-86-237-0666; Fax: 55-51-590-4895. Rev. Edward G. Benya, S.J.

Villa Kostka C.P. 9, Indaiatuba, SP 13330-970 Brazil. Tel: 55-193-894-8555; Fax: 55-19-3894-8866. Rev. Gerard Fineran, S.J.

CP 3937 Noviciado Ir. Vincente Canas, Manaus-AM 69085-970 Brazil. Tel: 011-55-92-682-2033. Rev. David H. Romero, S.J.

C.P. 6139 Prati, Rome 00195 Italy. Tel: 39-06-689-77215; Fax: 39-06-689-77663. Rev. Mark Lewis, S.J.

POB MP 320, Mt. Pleasant, Harare, Zimbabwe. Tel: 2634-745-411; Fax: 263-4-745-904. Rev. Patrick S. Madigan, S.J.

Campion Hall, Oxford OX1 1QS England. Tel: 44-1865-286126. Rev. Michael A. Bouzigard, S.J.

POB MP 320, Mt. Pleasant, Harare, Zimbabwe. Tel: 2634-745-411; Fax: 2634-745-904. Rev. John R. Stacer, S.J.

Curia, Society of Jesus, CP 6139, Prati, Rome 00195 Italy. Tel: 39-06-6897-7253; Fax: 39-06-687-9283. Rev. Joseph A. Tetlow, S.J.

Pontifical Gregorian Univ., Piazza della Pilotta 4, Rome 00187 Italy. Tel: 39-06-6701-5376; Fax: 39-06-6701-5413. Rev. Joseph A. Carola, S.J.

P/Box "Inigo", UlLevitana 38,630051, Novosibirsk, Russia. Tel: 7383277-20-13; Fax: 7383277-14-13. Rev. Anthony J. Corcoran, S.J.

P.O. Box 30652, Lusaka, Zambia. Tel: 260-1-230-585; Fax: 260-1-293-763. Rev. Roland J. Lesseps, S.J.

Luwisha House, Plot 5880 Great East Road, Lusaka, Zambia. Tel: 260-1-291606; Fax: 260-1-290912. Rev. Michael S. Gallagher, S.J.

Parroquia San Bartolome, Arcatao Barrio Centro, Chalatenango, El Salvador, CA. Tel: 503-354-8009. Rev. Donald G. Bahlinger, S.J.

Campion Hall, Oxford OXI IQS England. Tel: 44 1865 286 135. Rev. David A. Brown, S.J.

Residenza del Gesu, Via degli Astalli 16, Rome 00186 Italy. Tel: 06 069700 242; Fax: 06 69700 319.

Jesuit Health Trust Tel: 504-821-0334; Fax: 504-822-5322. Rev. Eugene M. Dutkiewicz, S.J., Chm.; Bro. Lawrence J. Lundin, S.J., Sec.

Jesuits of Pohnpei, P.O. Box 160, Pohnpei, FM 96941-0160. Tel: 691-320-2317. Rev. David L. Andrus, S.J.

Arrupe International Residence, P.O. Box 216 UP 1144, Quezon City, Philippines. Tel: 632-426-5911; Fax: 632-426-5964. Rev. William J. Farge, S.J.

Josephite Fathers and Brothers Tel: 504-943-6593. (See Separate Listing for School)

The Josephite Faculty House of St. Augustine High School, 1911 Law St., 70119-1397. Tel: 504-943-6593; Fax: 504-947-7712. Very Rev. Wilbur J. Atwood, S.S.J., Rector; Bro. Laurence E. Price, S.S.J., Vice Rector; Rev. Robert Bowen, S.S.J.; Very Rev. Joseph Doyle, S.S.J.

Marist Fathers, 1706 Jackson Ave., 70113. Tel: 504-524-5192; Fax: 504-524-9796. Revs. Peter R. Blanchard, S.M.; Ellis L. DePriest, S.M.; Edwin L. Keel, S.M.; Joseph P. Mullin, S.M.; Raymond J. Carr, S.M.; Leonard P. Kellerman, S.M.; Edward J. Templeton, S.M.; Bro. Albert Thiffault, S.M.

School Sisters of Notre Dame, Formerly Franciscan Fraternity *Tau House*, 1029 Gov. Nicholls St., 70116-2432. Tel: 504-529-3569. Email: roddysnd@aol.com margmary27@hotmail.com. Sisters Ann Roddy, S.S.N.D; Margaret Mary Frieserhahn, S.S.N.D. Center for the Spiritual Empowerment of those infected with or affected by the HIV/AIDS. Total in Residence 2; Total Staff 3

Vincentian Fathers Tel: 504-897-3976; Fax: 504-899-7603. *DePaul Residence*, 812 Constantinople St., 70115-2726. Tel: 504-897-3976; Fax: 504-899-7603; 504-899-3603. Rev. Robert E. Lamy, C.M.; Very Rev. Perry Henry, C.M., V.F.; Revs. Dennis Martin; Raul Garza.

ST. BENEDICT. *St. Joseph Abbey* (1890), 70457-9999. Tel: 985-892-1800; Fax: 985-867-2270. Web: www.stjosephabbey.org. Rev. Justin Brown, O.S.B., Abbot; Rt. Rev. Patrick Regan, O.S.B. (Retired); Revs. Raphael Barousse, O.S.B.; Hugh Baumann, O.S.B.; Adam Begnaud, O.S.B., M.S.; Charles J. Benoit, O.S.B.; Very Rev. Gregory M. Boquet, O.S.B., M.A.; Revs. Dominic R. Braud, O.S.B.; Timothy J. Burnett, O.S.B.; Basil David Burns, O.S.B.; Matthew R. Clark, O.S.B., M.A.; Jonathan M. DeFrange, O.S.B.; Sean B. Duggan, O.S.B.; James D. Foley (BO); Peter E. Hammett, O.S.B.; Michael Jung, O.S.B.; Aelred Kavanagh, O.S.B., M.T.S., S.T.M., S.T.D.; Marian E. Larmann, O.S.B.; William J. MacCandless, O.S.B.; Paul Miranne, O.S.B.; Stan Moseley, O.S.B.; Thomas E. Perrier, O.S.B.; Lawrence J. Phelps, O.S.B.; Francis Sander, O.S.B.; Scott J. Underwood, O.S.B., M.T.S., M.Ed.; Ambrose G. Wathen, O.S.B. Priests 26; Brothers 24; Novices 2.

[Q] CONVENTS AND RESIDENCES FOR SISTERS

NEW ORLEANS. *St. Clare's Monastery of the Blessed Sacrament, O.S.C.* (1885), 720 Henry Clay Ave., 70118-5891. Tel: 504-895-2019; Fax: 504-899-6218. Email: elizmortell@juno.com. Web: www.poorclarenuns.com. Sr. Elizabeth Mortell, O.S.C., Abbess. Nuns of the Order of St. Clare Solemn Professed Nuns 9.

Congregation of Divine Providence, C.D.P., 504 Fern, 70118-3830. Tel: 504-861-0284. Web: www.cdptexas.org.

Congregation of the Sisters of the Holy Faith, C.H.F., 2741 St. Anthony St., 70119-1298. Tel: 504-943-7203. Email: EpiphanyCHF@aol.com. Web: www.holyfaithsisters.net. Total Sisters in Archdiocese 3.

Daughters of Charity of St. Vincent de Paul, D.C., Sisters' Residence, 2718 Cambronne St., 70118-3140. Tel: 504-866-0968. Email: sranthony@archdiocese-no.org. Sr. Anthony Barczykowski, D.C., Sister Servant. Total Sisters in Archdiocese 37.

Daughters of Our Lady of the Holy Rosary Provincial House, F.M.S.R., 1492 Moss St., 70119-2904. Tel: 504-486-0039; Fax: 504-483-7910. Sr. M John Bosco Dinh Thi Kim Thanh, F.M.S.R., Prov. Supr. Total Sisters in Archdiocese 48.

Dominican Sisters (Cabra, Ireland) O.P., 6315 Caldwell Dr., 70122-2850. Tel: 504-283-5768; Fax: 504-282-3264. Email: mmmpres@aol.com. Web: www.cabraop.org. Sr. Maeve Mc Mahon, O.P., Prioress. Total Sisters in Archdiocese 9.

Eucharistic Missionaries of St. Dominic, O.P., 3801 Canal St., Ste. 400, 70119-6048. Tel: 504-486-1133; Fax: 504-486-6547. Email srdotop@aol.com. Web: www.emdsisters.org. Total Sisters in Archdiocese 20.

Generalate of the Dominican Sisters, O.P., Congregation of St. Mary, 7300 St. Charles Ave., 70118-3809. Tel: 504-861-8183; Fax: 504-861-8184. Email: jordanoplang@aol.com. Web: www.dominican-sisters.net/stmarys/. Sr. Angeline Magro, O.P., Prioress. Generalate Staff Sisters 3; Total Sisters in Archdiocese 41.

Little Sisters of the Poor, L.S.P., 4201 Woodland Dr., 70131-7398. Tel: 504-394-2200; Fax: 504-391-3347. Email: msneworlsp@earthlink.net. Sisters 10.

Marianites of Holy Cross, M.S.C. (1841), 1011 Gallier St., 70117-6111. Tel: 504-945-1620; Fax: 504-944-0756. Email: mscsec@marianites.org. Web: www.marianites.org. Sr. Mary Kay Kinberger, Congregational Leader. Total Sisters in Archdiocese 93.

Missionary Sisters of the Sacred Heart (Cabrini) M.S.C., 3443 Esplanade Ave., 70119. Tel: 504-822-5553; Fax: 504-822-5559. Total Sisters in Archdiocese 3.

Presentation Sisters of the Blessed Virgin Mary, 1920 Robert E. Lee Blvd., 70122-3512. Tel: 504-283-3352. Email: presis6@cs.com. Web: www.gnofn.org/~presis.

Legal Title: *Union of Sisters of the Presentation of the Blessed Virgin Mary (United States Prov.)*

Religious of the Good Shepherd, R.G.S., 4934 Hauck Dr., 70127. Tel: 504-244-0034; Fax: 504-244-3202. Good Shepherd Services. After school program for girls and adult counseling. Total Sisters in Archdiocese 3.

Religious of the Sacred Heart, R.S.C.J., 1837 Milan St., 70115. Tel: 504-899-3037; Fax: 504-899-6210. Web: www.nscj.org. Sisters 3.

4600 Carondelet St., 70115-4822. Tel: 504-891-0412. Sr. Mary Blish, R.S.C.J., Dir. Sisters 3; Sisters 4; Total Sisters in Archdiocese 10.

School Sisters of Notre Dame (Dallas, TX), S.S.N.D., Redeemer Convent, 7010 Milne Blvd., 70124-2343. Tel: 504-288-5002. Email: redeem3@bellsouth.net. Web: www.ssnd.org. Total Sisters in Archdiocese 21.

Sinsinawa Dominican Congregation of the Most Holy Rosary, O.P., 3727 Gentilly Blvd., 70122. Tel: 504-282-9138; Fax: 504-282-9138. Web: www.sinsinawa.org. Sr. Elayne Hill, O.P. Sisters 4.

Sisters of Mercy of the Americas, R.S.M., 6024 Freret St., 70118. Tel: 504-891-4639; Fax: 504-838-9799. Email: drducey@aol.com. (St. Louis Regional Community) Total Sisters in Archdiocese 42.

Sisters of St. Joseph of Medaille, New Orleans, C.S.J., 1200 Mirabeau Ave., 70122-1997. Tel: 504-283-9493; Fax: 504-288-4044. Email: gracelyncsj@juno.com. Web: www.sistersofstjoseph.org. Sr. Gracelyn Soignet, C.S.J., Coord. of Complex. Total Sisters in Archdiocese 60.

People Program, Inc., 1200 Mirabeau Ave., 70122-1997. Tel: 504-288-3171; Fax: 504-288-3503. Sr. Carolyn Brady, C.S.J., Pres.; Ms. Mary Catherine Lombard, Dir.

Sisters of the Blessed Sacrament, S.B.S., 3812 Pine St., 70125-1105. Tel: 504-488-5325.

Xavier University Convent, 3812 Pine St., 70125. Tel: 504-482-0917; Fax: 504-482-6219.

5116 Magazine St., 70115. Tel: 504-897-0235.

5014 Howard Ave., 70125. Tel: 504-486-2474. Total Sisters in the Archdiocese 25.

Sisters of the Holy Family Motherhouse and Novitiate, S.S.F. (1842), 6901 Chef Menteur Hwy., 70126-5290. Tel: 504-242-8315; 504-241-5400; Fax: 504-241-3957. Email: sylviathib@aol.com. Web: www.sistersoftheholyfamily.org. Sr. Sylvia Thibodeaux, S.S.F., Supr. Gen.; Rev. Jerome Robinson. Tel: 504-241-5400, Ext. 37. Total Sisters in Archdiocese 129.

Sisters of the Holy Family Development Office, 6901 Chef Menteur Hwy., 70126. Tel: 504-244-4445; Fax: 504-244-0445.

Sisters, Servants of Mary, S.M., 5001 Perlita St., 70122-1999. Tel: 504-282-5549; Fax: 504-282-5550. Sr. Josefina Torres, S.M., Supr. Total Home Nursing Sisters in Archdiocese 17.

Ursuline Sisters of the Roman Union, O.S.U. (1727), 2734 Nashville Ave., 70115-7008. Tel: 504-866-1472; Fax: 504-866-8300. Email: cdolce@bellsouth.net. Sr. Carla Dolce, O.S.U., Prioress. Total Sisters in Archdiocese 15.

CHALMETTE. *Daughters of Divine Providence, F.D.P.*, 3100 Mumphrey Rd., 70043-3735. Tel: 504-279-4617; Fax: 504-279-3002. Email: chalmette@fdpusa.net. Total Sisters in Archdiocese 5.

COVINGTON. *Carmelite Nuns, Discalced, O.C.D., Monastery of St. Joseph and St. Theresa* (1877), 73530 River Rd., 70435-2206. Tel: 504-898-0923; Fax: 504-871-9333. Email: covingtoncarmel@aol.com. Web: www.ettinger.net/carmelcov. Professed Nuns 6; Novices 2.

Teresian Sisters (Society of St. Teresa of Jesus), S.T.J., Provincial House, 18080 St. Joseph's Way, 70435-5623. Tel: 985-893-1470; Fax: 985-893-2476. Email: teresians@aol.com. Web: www.teresians.org. Sr. Maria Isabel Ordono, S.T.J., Prov. Sisters 22.

Formation House, 18158 St. Joseph's Way, 70435-5624. Tel: 985-893-1557; Fax: 985-871-0724. Sr. Dolores Rodriguez, S.T.J., Supr.

GRETNA. *Sisters of the Living Word, S.L.W.*, 901 Hancock St., 70053-2227. Tel: 504-366-5358. Email: sjdslw2@msn.com. Web: www.slw.org. Sisters 2; Total Sisters in Archdiocese 12.

LACOMBE. *Congregation of Our Lady of Mount Carmel, O.Carm.* (1833), Generalate, P.O. Box 476, 70445-0476. Tel: 985-882-7577; 504-524-2398; Fax: 504-524-5011. Email: mountcarmel@mindspring.com. Web: mountcarmel.home.mindspring.com. Sr. M. Ursula Diasselliss, O.Carm., Pres. Sisters 93.

Mount Carmel Development Office, P.O. Box 1160, 70445-1160. Tel: 985-882-7577; 504-524-2398; Fax: 504-524-5011.

Child Care Center: Carmel in the Business District Tel: 504-529-8856; Fax: 504-529-8933; Fax: 504-529-8861. Sr. Alice Abate, O.Carm., Dir. Total Staff 11; Total Enrolled 52.

Cub Corner Tel: 504-283-9499; Fax: 504-283-9483. Sr. Mary Ellen Wheelahan, O.Carm., Dir. Total Staff 18; Total Enrolled 90.

Carmelite Spirituality Center, P.O. Box 476, 70445-0476. Tel: 985-882-7577; Fax: 504-524-5011.

MANDEVILLE. *St. Gertrude's Convent, Benedictine Sisters*, c/o Prieto & Prieto, Attorneys, 2900 E. Causeway Approach, Ste. D, 70448-3597.

MARRERO. *Salesian Sisters (Daughters of Mary Help of Christians) F.M.A.*, Immaculate Conception Convent, 612 Avenue B, 70072-2016. Tel: 504-347-8449; Fax: 504-347-8440. Email: fmamarrero@aol.com. Web: www.salesiansisters.org. Sisters in Archdiocese 4.

METAIRIE. *Daughters of St. Paul Convent, F.S.P.*, Pauline Book & Media Center, 4403 Veterans Memorial Blvd., 70006-5321. Tel: 504-887-7631; Fax: 504-887-1357. Email: neworleans@pauline.org. Total Sisters in Archdiocese 5.

Incarnate Word Sisters, C.C.V.I., 400 Codifer Blvd., 70005-3797. Tel: 504-835-6648; Fax: 504-833-8982. Total Sisters in Archdiocese 4.

Religious of Our Lady of the Retreat in the Cenacle, R.C., The Cenacle Retreat House, 5500 St. Mary St., P.O. Box 8115, 70011-8115. Tel: 504-887-1420; Fax: 504-887-6624. Email: cenacle2@aol.com. Web: www.cenaclesisters.org/metairie.htm. Sr. Evelyn Jegen, R.C., Supr. Sisters 6; Total Staff 26.

Sisters of the Most Holy Sacrament, M.H.S., 422 Bonnabel Blvd., 70005-3240. Tel: 504-832-0513. Total Sisters in Archdiocese 4.

[R] RETREAT HOUSES

NEW ORLEANS. *Archdiocesan Spirituality Center*, 2901 S. Carrollton Ave., 70118-4391. Tel: 504-861-3254. Sr. Noel Toomey, O.P., Dir.

Center of Jesus the Lord, 1236 N. Rampart St., 70116-2497. Tel: 504-529-1636; Fax: 504-529-5003. Email: CCRCNO@aol.com. Web: www.centerofjesusthelord.org. Total Assisted 314; Total Staff 4; Total in Residence 4.

Dominican Conference Center, 540 Broadway, 70118-3593. Tel: 504-861-8711; Fax: 504-861-8718. Email: dcc15@juno.com. Sr. Joel Gubler, O.P., Dir. Total in Residence 4; Total Staff 3.

Sophie Barat House, 1719 Napoleon Ave., 70115-4809. Tel: 504-899-6027; Fax: 504-899-6210. Email: jmckinlay@rscj.org. Sisters Mary Blish, R.S.C.J.; Margaret Hoffman, R.S.C.J.; Jane McKinlay, R.S.C.J. Total Staff 3; Total in Residence 4.

CROWN POINT. *Ave Maria Retreat House*, 8089 Barataria Blvd, 70072. Tel: 504-689-3837; Fax: 504-689-2785. Email: avemariarh@cox.net. Rev. William J. Axe, O.SS.T., Dir. Total Staff 6; Total in Residence 1.

METAIRIE. *Cenacle Retreat House*, 5500 St. Mary St., P.O. Box 8115, 70011-8115. Tel: 504-887-1420; Fax: 504-887-6624. Email: cenacle2@aol.com. Web: www.cenaclesisters.org/metairie.htm. Sr. JoAnn Viviano, R.C., Retreat House Admin. Religious 6; Total Staff 26.

PONCHATOULA. *Magnificat Center of the Holy Spirit*, 23629 Faith Rd., 70454. Tel: 985-386-5815; 800-531-9710; Fax: 504-200-7771. Rev. John M. Capuci, Dir. Total in Residence 90; Total Staff 4.

ST. BENEDICT. *Abbey Christian Life Center*, St. Joseph Abbey, 70457-9999. Tel: 985-892-3473; 985-892-1800; Fax: 985-892-3448. Rev. Thomas E. Perrier, O.S.B., Dir. Conducted by Benedictine Monks

[S] MISCELLANEOUS

NEW ORLEANS. *Christian Brothers Foundation*, 8 Friederichs Ave., 70124-4602. Tel: 504-486-1053; Fax: 504-488-2802. Email: cbfoundation@yahoo.com.

Jesuit Seminary and Mission Fund, 500 S. Jefferson Davis Pkwy., 70119-7192. Tel: 504-827-4043; Fax: 504-827-9931. Email: jsmb@norprov.org. Mr. Vincent Liberto, Exec. Officer.

MCA Foundation, 420 Robert E. Lee Blvd., 70124-2596. Tel: 504-524-2398; Fax: 504-524-2398. Email: mountcarmel@mindspring.com. Web: mountcarmel.home.mindspring.com. Sr. Rose Marie Penouilh, O.Carm., Pres.

**Pan African Roman Catholic Clergy Conference*, 2203 Second St., 70113-2535. Tel: 504-895-9020; 504-895-7749; Fax: 504-899-0434. Most Rev. Leonard J. Olivier, S.V.D., D.D. (WDC), Episcopal Mod.; Rev. Clarence Williams, Exec. Dir.

The Patrons of the Vatican Museums in the South, Inc., 775 Harrison Ave., 70124-3192. Tel: 504-482-4158; Fax: 504-485-0906. Email: vmcinnes@opsouth.org. Very Rev. Val A. McInnes, O.P., Founder & Pres. Emeritus; Mr. John J. Kelly, Pres.

Pierre Toussaint Foundation of New Orleans, Inc., 2600 A.P. Tureaud Ave., 70119-1299. Tel: 504-949-3113; Fax: 504-945-4134. Email: josmdoyle@netscape.net. Rev. Joseph M. Doyle, S.S.J., Pres.

**Second Harvesters Food Bank of Greater New Orleans*, 1201 Sams Ave., 70123-2236. Tel: 504-734-1322; Fax: 504-733-8336. Email: bgreen@secondharvest.org. Web: www.secondharvestersfoodbank.org.

Stella Roman Foundation, Inc., 210 Baronne St. Suite 1207, 70112-4100. Tel: 504-522-4756; Fax: 504-568-0783. Email: cidlaw@bellsouth.net. Rev. Msgr. Francis G. Boeshans, Pres. (Retired).

METAIRIE. *Equestrian Order of the Holy Sepulchre* (of Jerusalem, Southeastern Lieutenancy of the U.S.) , 2955 Ridgelake Dr., Ste. 205, 70002. Tel: 504-832-0892; Fax: 504-832-1929. Email: office@sleohs.com. Lt. Robert B. Acomb Jr., K.G.C.H.S.

**Focus Worldwide TV Network*, 106 Metairie Lawn Dr., 70001. Tel: 504-840-9898; Fax: 504-840-9818. Email: focus@focustv.org. Web: www.focusvideos.com. Most Rev. Philip M. Hannan, Pres. & Board of Trustees.

International Dominican Foundation, One Galleria Blvd., Ste. 710-B, 70001. Tel: 504-836-8180; Fax: 504-836-8189. Email: info@idfaf.org. Most Rev. Timothy M. Dolan, Chmn. of the Bd.; Very Revs. Val A. McInnes, O.P., Pres.; Neal W. McDermott, O.P., Sec.; Edmund C. Nantes, O.P., Treas.

Southern Dominican Foundation, 1421 N. Causeway Blvd., Ste. 200, 70001-4144. Tel: 504-837-2129; Fax: 504-837-6604. Email: provincial@opsouth.org. Web: www.opsouth.org. Very Revs. Martin J. Gleeson, O.P., Pres.; Emiliano Zapata, O.P., Vice Pres. & Sec.; Joseph J. Konkel, O.P., Treas.; Raymond C. Finn, O.P., Promoter Devel.

Southern Dominican Global Missions, 1421 N. Causeway Blvd., Ste. 200, 70001-4144. Tel: 210-738-6688; Fax: 210-738-1755. Rev. Brian J. Pierce, O.P., Co-Dir.; Bro. Herman Johnson, O.P., Co-Dir.

**Willwoods Community*, 3330 N. Causeway Blvd., Ste. 345, 70002. Tel: 504-830-3700; Fax: 504-840-9838. Email: Willwoods@wlae.psb.org. Rev. Thomas E. Chambers, C.S.C., Pres.

**WLAE-TV, Educational Broadcasting Foundation, Inc.*, 3330 N. Causeway Blvd., Ste. 345, 70002. Tel: 504-866-7411; Fax: 504-840-9838. Email: info@wlae.pbs.org. Web: www.wlae.org.

SLIDELL. **S.A.V.E., Inc. (Suffering Abortion Victims Embraced)*, 770 Gause Blvd., Ste. B, 70458. Tel: 859-428-0901; Fax: 859-428-3090. Mrs. Linda Jefferson, Pres.

SECULAR INSTITUTES

NEW ORLEANS. *Society of Our Lady of the Way*, 6044 Louis XIV St., 70124-2919. Tel: 504-486-2506.

ABITA SPRINGS. *Caritas*, Administration Center, P.O. Box 308, 70420-0308. Tel: 985-892-4345. Email: caritas11@juno.com.

Daraja House, P.O. Box 524, Covington, 70434. Tel: 985-893-2261.

RELIGIOUS INSTITUTES OF MEN REPRESENTED IN THE ARCHDIOCESE

For further details refer to the corresponding bracketed number in the Religious Institutes of Men or Women section.

[0200]—*Benedictine Monks*—O.S.B.
[0330]—*Brothers of the Christian Schools* (New Orleans Prov.)—F.S.C.
[0600]—*Brothers of the Congregation of Holy Cross* (Midwest; Southwest Provs.)—C.S.C.
[0470]—*The Capuchin Friars*—O.F.M.Cap.
[0220]—*Congregation of the Blessed Sacrament*—S.S.S.
[1330]—*Congregation of the Mission of St. Vincent de Paul Fathers & Brothers* (Southern Prov.)—C.M.
[]—*Congregation of the Mother Coredemptrix*—C.M.C.
[0260]—*Discalced Carmelite Friars*—O.C.D.
[0520]—*Franciscan Friars*—O.F.M.
[0650]—*Holy Ghost Fathers* (Western Vice Prov.; Ireland)—C.S.Sp.
[]—*Incarnational Consecration*—I.C.
[0690]—*Jesuit Fathers and Brothers* (New Orleans)—S.J.
[0780]—*Marist Fathers and Brothers* (Washington Prov.)—S.M.
[0840]—*Missionary Servants of the Most Holy Trinity*—S.T.
[]—*Missionary Society of St. Paul*—M.S.P.
[0910]—*Oblates of Mary Immaculate* (Southern American Prov.)—O.M.I.
[0430]—*Order of Preacher-Dominicans* (Southern Prov.)—O.P.
[1310]—*Order of the Most Holy Trinity*—O.SS.T.
[1100]—*Priests and Brothers of the Sacred Heart* (Metuchen, NJ)—S.C.
[0610]—*Priests of the Congregation of Holy Cross* (Southern Prov.; Indiana Prov.)—C.S.C.
[1070]—*Redemptorist Fathers and Brothers* (New Orleans)—C.SS.R.
[1190]—*Salesians of Don Bosco*—S.D.B.
[0760]—*Society of Mary* St. Louis Province—S.M.
[0440]—*Society of St. Edmund*—S.S.E.
[0420]—*Society of the Divine Word* (St. Augustine Prov.)—S.V.D.
[0700]—*St. Joseph's Society of the Sacred Heart* (Baltimore, MD)—S.S.J.
[1170]—*St. Patrick Missionary Society*—S.P.S.

RELIGIOUS INSTITUTES OF WOMEN REPRESENTED IN THE ARCHDIOCESE

[0230]—*Benedictine Sisters of Pontifical Jurisdiction* (Colorado)—O.S.B.
[0400]—*Congregation of Our Lady of Mount Carmel*—O.Carm.
[3110]—*Congregation of Our Lady of the Retreat in the Cenacle*—R.C.
[1940]—*Congregation of Sisters of the Holy Faith*—C.H.F.
[2410]—*Congregation of the Marianites of Holy Cross*—M.S.C.
[0460]—*Congregation of the Sisters of Charity of the Incarnate Word*—C.C.V.I.
[1950]—*Congregation of the Sisters of the Holy Family*—S.S.F.
[]—*Daughters of Divine Love*—D.D.L.
[0800]—*Daughters of Divine Providence*—F.D.P.
[0850]—*Daughters of Mary Help of Christians*—F.M.A.
[0895]—*Daughters of Our Lady of the Holy Rosary*—F.M.S.R.
[0760]—*Daughters of St. Vincent de Paul*—D.C.
[0420]—*Discalced Carmelite Nuns*—O.C.D.
[1110]—*Dominican Sisters of Our Lady of the Rosary and of Saint Catherine of Siena, Cabra, Ireland*—O.P.
[1070-08]—*Dominican Sisters, Congregation of St. Mary*—O.P.
[1070-13]—*Dominican Sisters, Congregation of the Most Holy Rosary*—O.P.
[1140]—*Eucharistic Missionaries of St. Dominic*—O.P.
[1430]—*Franciscan Sisters of Our Lady of Perpetual Help*—O.S.F.
[]—*Handmaids of the Holy Child of Jesus*—H.H.C.J.
[2340]—*Little Sisters of the Poor*—L.S.P.
[]—*Lovers of the Holy Cross Sisters at Cho Quan*—L.H.C.
[2860]—*Missionary Sisters of the Sacred Heart*—M.S.C.
[0950]—*Pious Society Daughters of St. Paul*—F.S.P.
[3760]—*Poor Clare Nuns, Order of St. Clare*—O.S.C.
[2970]—*School Sisters of Notre Dame* (Dallas & Mankato)—S.S.N.D.
[]—*Sisters for Christian Community*—S.F.C.C.
[0440]—*Sisters of Charity of Cincinnati, Ohio*—S.C.
[0660]—*Sisters of Christian Charity* (Wilmette, IL)—S.C.C.
[1010]—*Sisters of Divine Providence of San Antonio, Texas*—C.D.P.
[2575]—*Sisters of Mercy of the Americas* (Brooklyn; St. Louis)—R.S.M.
[2630]—*Sisters of Mercy of the Holy Cross*—S.C.S.C.
[1640]—*Sisters of St. Francis of Perpetual Adoration*—O.S.F.
[]—*Sisters of St. Francis of Philadelphia*—O.S.F.
[1670]—*Sisters of St. Francis of Savannah*—O.S.F.
[1530]—*Sisters of St. Francis of the Congregation of Our Lady of Lourdes, Sylvania, Ohio*—O.S.F.
[3880]—*Sisters of St. Joseph of Medaille*—C.S.J.
[3830-11]—*Sisters of St. Joseph, Kalamazoo*—S.S.J.
[0260]—*Sisters of the Blessed Sacrament for Indians and Colored People*—S.B.S.
[1830]—*Sisters of the Good Shepherd*—R.G.S.
[2050]—*Sisters of the Holy Spirit and Mary Immaculate*—S.H.Sp.
[2120]—*Sisters of the Immaculate Conception*—C.I.C.
[2350]—*Sisters of the Living Word*—S.L.W.
[2940]—*Sisters of the Most Holy Sacrament*—M.H.S.
[3600]—*Sisters Servants of Mary*—S.M.
[4020]—*Society of St. Teresa of Jesus*—S.T.J.
[4060]—*Society of the Holy Child Jesus*—S.H.C.J.
[4070]—*Society of the Sacred Heart*—R.S.C.J.
[3330]—*Union of the Sisters of the Presentation of the Blessed Virgin Mary*—P.B.V.M.
[4110]—*Ursuline Nuns*—O.S.U.

NECROLOGY

† Grennan, Thomas J. (Retired)—Died Oct. 22, 2003
† Grennan, Thomas J. (Retired), (Retired)—Died Oct. 22, 2003

Diocese of New Ulm

(Dioecesis Novae Ulmae)

Most Reverend

JOHN C. NIENSTEDT

Bishop of New Ulm; ordained July 27, 1974; appointed Auxiliary Bishop of Detroit June 12, 1996; ordained July 9, 1996; appointed Bishop of New Ulm June 12, 2001; installed August 6, 2001

Diocesan Pastoral Center: 1400 6th St., N., New Ulm, MN 56073-2099. Tel: 507-359-2966; Fax: 507-354-3667.

Web: www.dnu.org

Email: dnu@dnu.org

ESTABLISHED NOVEMBER 18, 1957.

Square Miles 9,863.

Comprises the Counties of Big Stone, Brown, Chippewa, Kandiyohi, Lac Qui Parle, Lincoln, Lyon, McLeod, Meeker, Nicollet, Redwood, Renville, Sibley, Swift and Yellow Medicine in the State of Minnesota.

Legal Title: For legal titles of parishes and diocesan institutions, consult the Diocesan Pastoral Center.

STATISTICAL OVERVIEW

Personnel	
Bishop	1
Priests: Diocesan Active in Diocese	44
Priests: Diocesan Active Outside Diocese	5
Priests: Diocesan in Foreign Missions	2
Priests: Retired, Sick or Absent	25
Number of Diocesan Priests	76
Religious Priests in Diocese	1
Total Priests in Diocese	77
Extern Priests in Diocese	2
Ordinations:	
Transitional Deacons	1
Permanent Deacons in Diocese	4
Total Sisters	68
Parishes	
Parishes	80
With Resident Pastor:	
Resident Diocesan Priests	42
Without Resident Pastor:	
Administered by Priests	20
Administered by Deacons	1
Administered by Religious Women	17
Administered by Lay People	2
Missions	2
Professional Ministry Personnel:	
Sisters	23
Lay Ministers	43
Welfare	
Catholic Hospitals	2
Total Assisted	17,351
Homes for the Aged	6
Total Assisted	299
Residential Care of Disabled	2
Total Assisted	1,725
Other Institutions	1
Total Assisted	100
Educational	
Diocesan Students in Other Seminaries	6
Total Seminarians	6
High Schools, Diocesan and Parish	3
Total Students	470
Elementary Schools, Diocesan and Parish	17
Total Students	2,771
Catechesis/Religious Education:	
High School Students	3,800
Elementary Students	7,033
Total Students under Catholic Instruction	14,080
Teachers in the Diocese:	
Sisters	4
Vital Statistics	
Receptions into the Church:	
Infant Baptism Totals	1,008
Adult Baptism Totals	46
Received into Full Communion	109
First Communions	1,032
Confirmations	1,197
Marriages:	
Catholic	200
Interfaith	163
Total Marriages	363
Deaths	767
Total Catholic Population	69,503
Total Population	285,061

Former Bishops—Most Revs. ALPHONSE J. SCHLADWEILER, D.D. (Retired), ord. June 9, 1929; appt. Nov. 28, 1957; consecrated Jan. 29, 1958; installed Jan. 30, 1958; retired Dec. 23, 1975; died April 3, 1996; RAYMOND A. LUCKER, S.T.D., ord. June 7, 1952; appt. Titular Bishop of Meta July 12, 1971; consecrated Sept. 8, 1971; appt. Bishop of New Ulm, Dec. 23, 1975; installed Feb. 19, 1976; retired Nov. 17, 2000; died Sept. 19, 2001.

Diocesan Officials

Diocesan Pastoral Center—Most Rev. JOHN C. NIENSTEDT, S.T.D., 1400 6th St. N., New Ulm, 56073-2099. Tel: 507-359-2966, Ext. 306; Fax: 507-354-3667.

Vicar General—Rev. DOUGLAS L. GRAMS, Diocesan Pastoral Center, 1400 6th St. N., New Ulm, 56073-2099. Tel: 507-359-2966, Ext. 303; Fax: 507-354-3667.

Chancellor—Rev. MARK S. MALLAK, Diocesan Pastoral Center, 1400 6th St. N., New Ulm, 56073-2099. Tel: 507-359-2966, Ext. 315; Fax: 507-354-3667.

Vice-Chancellor—Rev. JOHN G. BERGER, Church of St. Gregory the Great, 440 6th St., P.O. Box 5, Lafayette, 56054-0005. Tel: 507-228-8298.

Diocesan Tribunal—

Judicial Vicar (Officialis)—Rev. JOHN G. BERGER, Church of St. Gregory the Great, 440 6th St., P.O. Box 5, Lafayette, 56054-0005. Tel: 507-228-8298.

Moderator—VACANT, Diocesan Pastoral Center, 1400 6th St. N., New Ulm, 56073-2099. Tel: 507-359-2966, Ext. 329; Fax: 507-354-3667.

Associate Judges—Revs. EUGENE L. LOZINSKI; PAUL L. WOLF; DOUGLAS L. GRAMS.

Defender of the Bond—Rev. MARK S. MALLAK.

Office Manager—JANELLE DREXLER. Tel: 507-359-2966, Ext. 319.

Notaries—JANELLE DREXLER; SHERI JOHNSON.

Diocesan Boards and Councils

Building Committee—Revs. GEORGE V. SCHMIT JR., Chm., Church of St. Mary, 220 S. 10th St., P.O. Box 500, Bird Island, 55310-0500. Tel: 320-365-3593; Fax: 320-365-3142; MICHAEL M. DOYLE; Mr. RICHARD GREENE; KAY OSBORNE; Mr. JOE EIKMEIER; Mr. RAYMOND MARTIN.

College of Consultors—Revs. DOUGLAS L. GRAMS; BRIAN L. MANDEL; FRANCIS J. GARVEY; STEVEN J. VERHELST; ROBERT J. WYFFELS; JOSEPH A. STEINBEISSER; JOHN G. BERGER; GERMAIN P. RADEMACHER; EUGENE M. BROWN.

Committee on Parishes—NANCY HANNA, Chm.; JUNE BRUST, Vice Chm.; Revs. WILLIAM A. SPRIGLER; ANTHONY J. STUBEDA; DOUGLAS L. GRAMS; BRIAN L. MANDEL; FRANCIS J. GARVEY; Sisters RUTH ANN TAKES, P.B.V.M.; BETTY LARSON, O.S.B.; LAETITIA LARIVIERE, I.H.M.; RAYMOND TRAEN; DOLORES BERG; MARK C. KEMMETER, Staff Liaison.

Corporate Board—Most Rev. JOHN C. NIENSTEDT, S.T.D.; Rev. MARK S. MALLAK; Mr. WILLIAM T. O'CONNOR; Mr. PAUL A. ZIMS; Rev. DOUGLAS L. GRAMS.

Diocesan Pastoral Council—DOLORES BERG, Chm., 20449 U.S. Hwy. 71, Sanborn, 56083-3018. Tel: 507-648-3550; Fax: 507-648-3640; PAULETTE SVOBODA, Vice Chm.; RICHARD HESSE, Sec. Members: MARY ANN KRAMER; STEVE SCHREIBER; Sisters MONICA WAGNER, S.S.N.D.; CARMEN SONNEK, O.S.F.; NANCY O'LEARY; PAULETTE COLLINS; MARY ANN HESSE; WAYNE CARLSON, Member at Large; SUE FLEEGEL; Rev. FRANCIS J. GARVEY; ROSEMARY DITTRICH; ALEJANDRO MORENE; JAMES GUNTER; GERALDINE PEHRSON; DOREEN KROMBACK; SANDY SCHLOSSER; MARK C. KEMMETER, Staff Liaison.

Finance Council—Revs. JOHN A. RICHTER; PATRICK L. CASEY; Sr. SHARON NOHNER, O.S.B; DAVID CZECH; NANCY O'LEARY; DONNA SANDERS; DAVID LYNN; THOMAS J. HOLZER, Staff Liaison.

Priests' Council—Revs. JOSEPH A. STEINBEISSER, Chm., Church of St. Mary, 713 12th St., S.W., Willmar, 56201-3099. Tel: 320-235-0118; Fax: 320-235-0153; FRANCIS J. GARVEY, Vice Chm.; EUGENE M. BROWN, Sec.; ROBERT J. WYFFELS, Treas.; DOUGLAS L. GRAMS; STEVEN J. VERHELST; JOHN G. BERGER; GERMAIN P. RADEMACHER.

Sisters' Council—Executive Committee: Sisters SUE TORGERSEN, C.S.J., Pres.; NANCY TRAEGER, S.S.N.D., Vice Pres.; JEANETTE HOMAN, O.S.F., Sec. & Treas.; BETTY LARSON, O.S.B., Staff Liaison.

Diocesan Pastoral Center

Coordinator of Diocesan Staff—MARK C. KEMMETER, Diocesan Pastoral Center, 1400 6th St. N., New Ulm, 56073-2099. Tel: 507-359-2966, Ext. 322; Fax: 507-354-3667. Email: mkemmeter@dnu.org.

Office of Finance—THOMAS J. HOLZER, Dir., Diocesan Pastoral Center, 1400 6th St. N., New Ulm, 56073-2099. Tel: 507-359-2966, Ext. 309; Fax: 507-354-3667. Email: tomholzer@dnu.org.

Office of Development—VACANT, Dir., Diocesan Pastoral Center, 1400 6th St. N., New Ulm, 56073-2099. Tel: 507-359-2966; Fax: 507-354-3667.

Evangelization and Catechesis—

Religious Education/Adult Religious Education—JOANN BORCHERT, Dir., Diocesan Pastoral Center, 1400 6th St. N., New Ulm, 56073-2099. Tel: 507-359-2966, Ext. 324; Fax: 507-354-3667. Email: jborchert@dnu.org.

Catholic Schools—Sr. BETTY LARSON, O.S.B., Dir., Schools, Diocesan Pastoral Center, 1400 6th St. N., New Ulm, 56073-2099. Tel: 507-359-2966, Ext. 323; Fax: 507-354-3667. Email: blarson@dnu.org.

Youth & Young Adult Ministry—Sr. SUE TORGERSEN, C.S.J., Dir., Diocesan Pastoral Center, 1400 6th

St. N., New Ulm, 56073-2099. Tel: 507-359-2966, Ext. 327; Fax: 507-354-3667. Email: storgersen@dnu.org.

Riverbend TEC (Adult/Teens Encounter Christ)—Rev. DENNIS C. LABAT, Coord., Church of St. Raphael, 112 W. Van Dusen, Springfield, 56087-1396. Tel: 507-723-4141. Email: dlabat@springfield-sanborn.net. Web: www.riverbendtec.org.

Communications—Sr. MARY CHARLES MAYER, R.S.M., Assoc. Dir., Diocesan Pastoral Center, 1400 6th St. N., New Ulm, 56073-2099. Tel: 507-359-2966, Ext. 333; Fax: 507-354-3667. Email: mcharlesmayer@dnu.org.

"Prairie Catholic"—Co Editors: Sr. MARY CHARLES MAYER, R.S.M., Editor. Tel: 507-359-2966, Ext. 333. Email: mcharlesmayer.com; CHRISTINE CLANCY, Editor, Diocesan Pastoral Center, 1400 6th St. N., New Ulm, 56073-2099. Tel: 507-359-2966, Ext. 332; Fax: 507-354-3667. Email: cclancy@dnu.org.

Committee for Evangelization & Catechesis—Sr. LOUISE BAUER, O.S.F., Chm.; Rev. TODD J. PETERSEN; Sr. SHARON NOHNER, O.S.B; LYNN SCHUELLER; ROGER OSBORNE; SUE FLEEGEL; DON CLASEMANN.

Office of Worship and Spiritual Life—VACANT, Dir., Diocesan Pastoral Center, 1400 6th St. N., New Ulm, 56073-2099. Tel: 507-359-2966, Ext. 320; Fax: 507-354-3667.

Worship Committee—VACANT, 1400 6th St. N., New Ulm, 56073-2099. Tel: 507-359-2966, Ext. 320; Fax: 507-354-3667. Members: KAY OSBORNE, Chm.; Revs. GERALD S. MEIDL; ANTHONY R. HESSE; RONALD V. HUBERTY; JEFFREY P. HOREJSI; Sr. MONICA WAGNER, S.S.N.D.; JOANN BORCHERT; KATY HENRICH; MARY BOLEK; BEV SULLIVAN; DELLA CONROY.

RCIA Network—VACANT, Diocesan Pastoral Center, 1400 6th St. N., New Ulm, 56073-2099. Tel: 507-359-2966, Ext. 320; Fax: 507-354-3667.

Charismatic Renewal—JAN CROWE, Diocesan Liaison, 21907 705th Ave., Dassel, 55325. Tel: 320-275-2424. Email: jancro@ll.net.

Liturgical Guidelines Committee—Revs. JEFFREY P. HOREJSI, Chm.; GEORGE V. SCHMIT JR.; Sr. MONICA WAGNER, S.S.N.D.; Rev. DENNIS C. LABAT, Staff Liaison.

Ecumenical Director—Deacon RICHARD A. CRONICAN, 400 Cedar St., P.O. Box 117, Milroy, 56263-0117. Tel: 507-336-2505. Email: deacdick@means.net.

Office of Social Concerns and Family Life—CHRISTOPHER A. LOETSCHER, Dir., Diocesan Pastoral Center, 1400 6th St. N., New Ulm, 56073-2099. Tel: 507-359-2966, Ext. 338; Fax: 507-354-3667. Email: cloetscher@dnu.org.

Social Concerns Committee—Rev. BRIAN L. MANDEL; SANDY SCHLOSSER; CHARLES PRATT; Sr. RITA VON HOLTUM, S.S.N.D.; CHRISTOPHER A. LOETSCHER, Staff Liaison.

Family Life—CHRISTOPHER A. LOETSCHER, Dir., Diocesan Pastoral Center, 1400 6th St. N., New Ulm, 56073-2099. Tel: 507-359-2966, Ext. 338; Fax: 507-354-3667. Email: cloetscher@dnu.org. Marriage Preparation, Natural Family Planning, Resources & Referral for Marriage & Family Concerns, Divorced/Separated.

Retrouvaille—Tel: 800-470-2230.

AIDS Ministry—Rev. PAUL A. SCHUMACHER, Church of St. Catherine, 900 E. Flynn, P.O. Box 383, Redwood Falls, 56283-0383. Tel: 507-644-2278; Fax: 507-644-2643.

Propagation of the Faith/Holy Childhood Association—Rev. PHILIP M. SCHOTZKO, Diocesan Pastoral Center, 1400 6th St. N., New Ulm, 56073-2099. Tel: 507-359-2966; Fax: 507-354-3667.

San Lucas Mission Office—Rev. Msgr. GREGORY T. SCHAFFER; KATHY HUEBERT, Diocesan Pastoral Center, 1400 6th St. N., New Ulm, 56073-2099. Tel: 507-359-2966, Ext. 304; Fax: 507-354-3667. Email: khuebert@dnu.org.

Hispanic Ministry—Rev. ANTHONY J. STUBEDA, Dir., Diocesan Pastoral Center, 1400 6th St. N., New Ulm, 56073-2099. Tel: 507-359-2966, Ext. 327; Fax: 507-354-3667. Email: tstubeda@dnu.org.

Office of Personnel—

Priest Personnel—Rev. DOUGLAS L. GRAMS, Dir., Diocesan Pastoral Center, 1400 6th St. N., New Ulm, 56073-2099. Tel: 507-359-2966, Ext. 303; Fax: 507-354-3667.

Priest Personnel Board—Revs. DOUGLAS L. GRAMS, Exec. Dir.; DENNIS C. LABAT; GERALD S. MEIDL; MARK S. MALLAK; EUGENE L. LOZINSKI; PAUL A. SCHUMACHER; TODD J. PETERSEN; JOHN A. RICHTER.

Pastoral Administrators—Rev. DENNIS C. LABAT, Supvr., Diocesan Pastoral Center, 1400 6th St. N., New Ulm, 56073-2099. Tel: 507-359-2966, Ext. 316; Fax: 507-354-3667. Email: dlabat@springfield-sanborn.net.

Bishop's Delegate in Matters Pertaining to Sexual Misconduct—Rev. DOUGLAS L. GRAMS, Diocesan Pastoral Center, 1400 6th St. N., New Ulm, 56073-2099. Tel: 507-359-2966, Ext. 303; Fax: 507-354-3667.

Office of Conciliation—MARK C. KEMMETER, Dir., 1400 6th St. N., New Ulm, 56073-2099. Tel: 507-359-2966, Ext. 322; Fax: 507-354-3667. Email: mkemmeter@dnu.org.

Vocations Team—Most Rev. JOHN C. NIENSTEDT, S.T.D., Team Chm.; Revs. TODD J. PETERSEN, Dir., Diocesan Pastoral Center, 1400 6th St. N., New Ulm, 56073-2099. Tel: 507-359-2966; 507-233-5328; 507-794-6974, Ext. 328. Email: toddpetersen@mac.com; FRANCIS J. GARVEY, Seminary, Internship Supvr. Tel: 320-693-8900; BRIAN W. OESTREICH, Website Supvr. Tel: 507-794-4171; Sr. SUE TORGERSEN, C.S.J., Coord., Vocation Fairs & Other Program Events, Diocesan Pastoral Center, 1400 6th St. N., New Ulm, 56073-2099. Tel: 507-359-2966; 507-233-5327, Ext. 327; Fax: 507-354-3667.

Continuing Education of Clergy—Sr. MARY DANIELLE JOHNSON, R.S.M., Dir., Diocesan Pastoral Center, 1400 6th St. N., New Ulm, 56073-2099. Tel: 507-359-2966; 507-233-5310, Ext. 310; Fax: 507-354-3667. Email: mdaniellejohnson@dnu.org.

Committee for Continuing Education of Clergy—Revs. PHILIP M. SCHOTZKO; MARK S. MALLAK; JOHN G. BERGER; JEFFREY P. HOREJSI; Sr. DONNA WERMUS, S.S.N.D.; KATHLEEN LANDREVILLE; Sr. MARY DANIELLE JOHNSON, R.S.M., Staff Liaison.

Board of Trustees for Pension Plan for Priests—Revs. DOUGLAS L. GRAMS; MARK S. MALLAK; HARRY P. BEHAN; JOHN H. BRUNNER; DONALD GUGGEMOS JR.; KATHY FRANCISCUS; MICHAEL SCHWARTZ; THOMAS J. HOLZER, Staff Liaison.

Vicar for Retired Priests—Rev. FRANCIS J. GARVEY, 57482 CSAH 3, Grove City, 56243-9786. Tel: 320-693-8900; Fax: 320-693-8900. Email: frgarvey@meltel.net.

Victim Assistance Coordinator—CHRISTOPHER A. LOETSCHER. Tel: 507-359-2966, Ext. 338. Email: cloetscher@dnu.org.

Organizations in the Diocese of New Ulm

Diocesan Council of Catholic Women—ELLEN NESTER, Pres., 505 Galles Dr., Redwood Falls, 56283. Tel: 507-637-8879; Rev. EUGENE L. LOZINSKI, Diocesan Moderator.

Girl Scouts—MARY HAUSER, 1608 17th Ave., N.W., Willmar, 56201. Tel: 320-235-3471.

Boy Scouts—Rev. ANDREW J. MICHELS, Church of St. Edward, 409 N. Adams St., Minneota, 56264-9801. Tel: 507-872-6346; Fax: 507-872-5263.

Marriage Encounter—WAYNE CARLSON; DEB CARLSON, R.R.2, Box 22, Hanley Falls, 56245. Tel: 507-423-6328.

CLERGY, PARISHES, MISSIONS AND PAROCHIAL SCHOOLS

CITY OF NEW ULM
(BROWN COUNTY)

1—CATHEDRAL OF THE HOLY TRINITY (1856), [CEM] [JC], Clustered with Searles; St. Mary's, New Ulm; Lafayette, West Newtown Township. Revs. John A. Richter; Samuel Perez Tax. In Res., Rev. Msgr. Antony J. Leifeld (Retired). Tel: 507-359-9848; Rev. Mark S. Steffl.
Res. and Mailing Address: 605 N. State St., 56073-1898. Tel: 507-354-4158; Fax: 507-354-2563. Email: newulmcathedral@hotmail.com. Web: cathedralht.org.
School—New Ulm Area Catholic Schools, Tel: 507-354-2719; Fax: 507-354-7071. See separate listing under the Institutions for further explanation and statistics.
Catechesis/Religious Program—Students 293.

2—ST. MARY (1911), [JC], Clustered with Cathedral, New Ulm; Searles; Lafayette, West Newton Township. Revs. Douglas L. Grams; Edward J. Ardolf. Tel: 507-232-3857.
Res.: 417 S. Minnesota St., 56073-2120. Tel: 507-233-9500; Fax: 507-354-8414.
School—New Ulm Area Catholic Schools, Tel: 507-354-2719; Fax: 507-354-7071. See separate listing under the Institutions for further explanation and statistics.
Catechesis/Religious Program—Tel: 507-233-9505; Fax: 507-354-8414. Students 313.

OUTSIDE THE CITY OF NEW ULM

APPLETON, SWIFT CO., ST. JOHN (1880), [CEM 2] [JC 2] Rev. Michael M. Doyle.
Mailing & Res. Address: 450 S. Gaulke St., 56208-1516. Tel: 320-289-1146 (Office); 320-289-1211 (Rectory); Fax: 320-289-1146.
Church: 350 S. Edquist St., 56208-1516.
Catechesis/Religious Program—Tel: 320-289-1146. Students 81.

ARLINGTON, SIBLEY CO., ST. MARY (1864), [CEM], Clustered with Gaylord. Rev. Jerry E. Paulson.
Res.: 504 7th Ave., N.W., P.O. Box 392, 55307-0392. Tel: 507-964-5413; Fax: 507-964-5425. Email: stmararl@frontiernet.net.
Catechesis/Religious Program—Tel: 507-964-5425. Students 163.

BARRY, BIG STONE CO., ST. BARNABAS, Closed., For sacramental records contact Holy Rosary, Graceville.

BEARDSLEY, BIG STONE CO., ST. MARY (1884), [CEM], Clustered with Graceville Sr. Marlene Konrady, O.S.B., Pastoral Admin.
Res. & Mailing Address: 518 S. Forest St., P.O. Box 299, 56211-0299. Tel: 320-265-6916 (Church); 320-265-6113 (Rectory).
Church: 510 S. Forest St., 56211.
Catechesis/Religious Program—Students 109.

BECHYN, RENVILLE CO., ST. MARY, Closed., For sacramental records contact St. Aloysius, Olivia.

BELGRADE, NICOLLET CO., ST. MICHAEL, Closed., For sacramental records contact St. Paul, Nicollet.

BENSON, SWIFT CO., ST. FRANCIS (1881),, Clustered with Clontarf, Danvers, De Graff & Murdock. Rev. Steven J. Verhelst. Tel: 320-843-2342. Area Pastoral Leaders:, Sisters Laetitia Lariviere, I.H.M., Pastoral Admin. Tel: 320-875-2246 (Murdock & DeGraff); Louise Bauer, O.S.F., Pastoral Min. Tel: 320-843-2026 (Clontarf); Christine Ahles, Pastoral Min. Tel: 320-843-3883 (DeGraff).
Area Office—Tel: 320-842-4271; Fax: 320-843-2264. Email: stfran@willmar.com. Web: www.catholicareaparishes.org.
Church: 508 13th St. N., 56215-1228.
Catechesis/Religious Program—Students 271.

BIRCH COOLIE, RENVILLE CO., ST. PATRICK, Closed., For sacramental records contact Sacred Heart, Franklin. Earlier records located at St. John, Morton.

BIRD ISLAND, RENVILLE CO., ST. MARY (1879), [CEM], Clustered with Hector, Oliva, Renville. Rev. George V. Schmit Jr.
Res.: 220 S. 10th St., P.O. Box 500, 55310-0500. Tel: 320-365-3593; Fax: 320-365-3142. Email: stmarybi@willmar.com.
School—(Grades K-8), 140 S. 10th St., P.O. Box 500, 55310-0500. Tel: 320-365-3693. Web: www.st-marysschoolbirdisland.com. Sr. Patricia McCusker, S.S.N.D., Prin. Sisters 1; Lay Teachers 12; Students 165.
Catechesis/Religious Program—Students 122.

CANBY, YELLOW MEDICINE CO., ST. PETER (1897), [CEM], Clustered with St. Leo. Rev. Anthony R. Hesse.
Res.: 307 W. 4th St., 56220-1211. Tel: 507-223-7304; Fax: 507-223-5776.
School—(Grades K-6), 410 Ring Ave. N., 56220-1237. Tel: 507-223-7729; Fax: 507-223-7178. Ms. Sandra Kollar, Prin. Lay Teachers 6; Students 57.
Catechesis/Religious Program—(Grades PreK-12) Students 198.

CLARA CITY, CHIPPEWA CO., ST. CLARA (1890),, Clustered with Granite Falls & Montevideo. Sr. Ruth Ann Takes, P.B.V.M., Pastoral Admin. Area Pastoral Leaders:, Rev. James W. Devorak. Tel: 320-269-5954 (Montevideo).
Church: 414 N. Main St., P.O. Box 310, 56222-0310. Tel: 320-847-2256. Email: stclara@hcinet.net.
Catechesis/Religious Program—Tel: 320-847-2445. Students 104.

CLARKFIELD, YELLOW MEDICINE CO., ST. ISIDORE, Closed., For sacramental records contact St. Joseph, Montevideo.

CLEMENTS, REDWOOD CO., ST. JOSEPH (1902), [CEM], Clustered with Morgan. Sr. Judi Angst, O.S.F., Pastoral Admin.
120 Ash St., P.O. Box 56, 56224-0056. Tel: 507-692-2181. Email: frans2@redred.com.
Catechesis/Religious Program—Students 20.

CLONTARF, SWIFT CO., ST. MALACHY (1878), Rev. Steven J. Verhelst. Tel: 320-567-2342 (Benson). Clustered with Benson, Danvers, De Graff & Murdock. Area Pastoral Leaders:, Sr. Laetitia Lariviere, I.H.M., Pastoral Admin. Int. Tel: 320-875-2246 (Murdock & DeGraff); Christine Ahles, Pastoral Min. Tel: 320-875-2246 (De Graff); Sr. Louise Bauer, O.S.F., Pastoral Min. Tel: 320-843-2026 (Clontarf).
Mailing Office: P.O. Box 218, 56226-0218. Tel: 320-843-2026; 320-843-2514 (Parish Hall); Fax: 320-843-2264. Email: stfran@willmar.com. Web: catholicareaparishes.org.
Church Address: 300 Armagh St. S.W., 56226. Tel: 320-842-4271 (area office).

Catechesis/Religious Program—Tel: 320-843-2026. Students 49.

COMFREY, BROWN CO., ST. PAUL (1900), [CEM], Clustered with Leavenworth. Sr. Sharon Nohner, O.S.B., Pastoral Admin.
Res. & Mailing Address: 209 N. Field St., P.O. Box 277, 56019-0277. Tel: 507-877-2361; Fax: 507-877-2361. Email: stpcomfrey@yahoo.com.
Catechesis/Religious Program—Tel: 507-877-9800. Students 90.

COTTONWOOD, LYON CO., ST. MARY (1902), [CEM], Clustered with Green Valley & Marshall. Rev. Paul J. Hadusek.
Res. & Mailing Address: 255 W. 4th St. S., P.O. Box 228, 56229-0228. Tel: 507-423-5220; Fax: 507-423-5275.
Catechesis/Religious Program—Students 170.

DANVERS, SWIFT CO., CHURCH OF THE VISITATION (1885),, Clustered with Benson, Clontarf, De Graff & Murdock. Rev. Steven J. Verhelst. Tel: 320-843-4271; Fax: 320-843-2264 (Benson).
Mailing Address: 508 13th St. N., Benson, 56215-1228. Area Pastoral Leaders:, Sr. Laetitia Lariviere, I.H.M., Pastoral Admin. Int. Tel: 320-875-2246 (Murdock & DeGraff); Christine Ahles, Pastoral Min. Tel: 320-843-3883 (DeGraff); Christine Ahles, Pastoral Min. Tel: 320-843-3883 (De Graff); Sr. Louise Bauer, O.S.F., Pastoral Min. Tel: 320-843-2026 (Clontarf).
Rectory—Rectory Address: 201 Washington Ave., P.O. Box 18, 56231.
Church: 201 County Rd. 14, 56231-0018. Email: stfran@willmar.com. Web: catholicareaparishes.org.
Area Office—Tel: 320-842-4271; Fax: 320-843-2264.
Catechesis/Religious Program—Students 22.

DARWIN, MEEKER CO., ST. JOHN (1861), [CEM], Clustered with Forest City. Rev. Patrick L. Casey.
Res. & Mailing: 106 N. 4th St., 55324-6016. Tel: 320-275-2915; 320-693-6878; Fax: 320-275-0198. Email: stjncath@hutchtel.net. Web: www.stjohnscatholic-darwin.com.
Catechesis/Religious Program—Tel: 320-286-2800. Students 163.

DAWSON, LAC QUI PARLE CO., ST. JAMES (1898), [CEM], Clustered with Madison. Sr. Vivian Petersen, O.S.B., Pastoral Admin.
Res. & Mailing Address: 10th & Locust, P.O. Box 270, 56232-0270. Tel: 320-769-4465.
Catechesis/Religious Program—Students 92.

DE GRAFF, SWIFT CO., ST. BRIDGET (1876),, Clustered with Benson, Clontarf, Danvers & Murdock. Rev. Steven J. Verhelst. Tel: 320-843-2342 (Benson). Area Pastoral Leaders:, Sisters Laetitia Lariviere, I.H.M., Pastoral Admin. Int. Tel: 320-567-2278 (Murdock & DeGraff); Louise Bauer, O.S.F., Pastoral Min. Tel: 320-843-2026 (Clontarf); Louise, Pastoral Min.; Christine Ahles, Pastoral Min. Tel: 320-843-3883 (DeGraff).
Church & Mailing Address: 501 3rd St. S., 56271. Tel: 320-843-3883; Fax: 320-843-2264. Email: stfran@willmar.com. Web: www.catholicareaparishes.org.
Area Office—Tel: 320-842-4271; Fax: 320-843-2264.
Catechesis/Religious Program—St. Bridget Activity Center, 405 5th St. S., DeGraff, 56233. Tel: 320-843-2005. Students 38.

EDEN VALLEY, MEEKER CO., ST. PETER (1903), Closed., For inquiries for parish records contact Assumption Church, Eden Valley, Diocese of St. Cloud.

FAIRFAX, RENVILLE CO., ST. ANDREW (1871), [CEM], Clustered with Franklin, Gibbon & Winthrop. Rev. Ronald V. Huberty. Tel: 507-834-6461.
Res & Mailing Address: 15 S.E. First St., P.O. Box C, 55332-0903. Tel: 507-426-7125; Fax: 507-426-7125. Email: standfx@praire.lakes.com.
Catechesis/Religious Program—Students 110.

FAXON TOWNSHIP, SIBLEY CO., ST. JOHN-ASSUMPTION (1859), [CEM 2], Clustered with Green Isle, Henderson & Jessenland. Sr. Donna Wermus, S.S.N.D., Pastoral Admin.
Res. & Mailing Address: 26523 200th St., Belle Plaine, 56011-9302. Tel: 952-873-4390.
Catechesis/Religious Program—Tel: 952-873-4390. Students 88.

FOREST CITY, MEEKER CO., ST. GERTRUDE (1857), [CEM], Clustered with Darwin. Rev. Patrick L. Casey. Tel: 320-693-6878 (Darwin); Kathleen Landreville, Pastoral Admin. Int.
Res. & Mailing Address: 31626 650th Ave., Litchfield, 55355-9998. Tel: 320-693-7801; Fax: 320-693-5877. Email: stgert@hutchtel.net. Web: www.forministry.com/55355cosg.
Church: 31608 650th Ave., Litchfield, 55355-9998. Tel: 320-693-5877.
Catechesis/Religious Program—Students 63.

FRANKLIN, RENVILLE CO., SACRED HEART (1898), [CEM 2], Clustered with Fairfax, Gibbon, & Winthrop. Rev. Ronald V. Huberty. Tel: 507-834-6461.
Res. & Mailing Address: 15 S.E. First St., P.O. Box C, Fairfax, 55332-0903. Tel: 507-426-7125.
Church E. Main St., 55333-0175. Tel: 507-557-2759.
Catechesis/Religious Program—Students 64.

GAYLORD, SIBLEY CO., ST. MICHAEL (1882),, Clustered with Arlington. Rev. Jerome E. Paulson. Tel: 507-964-5413; Fax: 507-964-5425 (Arlington).
Res. & Mailing Address: 411 Court Ave., P.O. Box 357, 55334-0357. Tel: 507-237-2851; Fax: 507-237-5300.
Catechesis/Religious Program—P.O. Box 357, 55334. Ann Whalen, D.R.E.; Marie Engleby, D.R.E. Students 156.

GHENT, LYON CO., ST. ELOI (1883), [CEM], Clustered with Minneota & Taunton. Charles Pratt, Pastoral Admin.
Church: 306 W. McQuestion, 56239-9750. Tel: 507-428-3285; Fax: 507-872-5263. Email: steloi@starpoint.net.
Catechesis/Religious Program—Students 106.

GIBBON, SIBLEY CO., ST. WILLIBRORD (1886), [CEM] Rev. Ronald V. Huberty. Tel: 507-426-7125 (Fairfax).
Res. & Mailing Address: 1032 Ash Ave., P.O. Box 187, 55335-0187. Tel: 507-834-6461; Fax: 507-426-7125.
Catechesis/Religious Program—Tel: 507-834-6659. Students 85.

GLENCOE, MCLEOD CO.
1—ST. GEORGE, Closed., For sacramental records, contact St. Pius X, Glencoe.
2—SS. PETER AND PAUL, Closed., For sacramental records, contact St. Pius X, Glencoe.
3—ST. PIUS X (1983), [CEM] Rev. Eugene L. Lozinski.
Res., Church & Mailing Address: 1014 Knight Ave., 55336-2300. Tel: 320-864-5162; 320-864-2963 (Rectory); Fax: 320-864-5163. Email: stpius@earthlink.net.
School—(Grades PreK-6), 1103 E. 10th St., 55336-2399. Tel: 320-864-3214. Joanne Pohland, Prin. Lay Teachers 8; Students 118.
Catechesis/Religious Program—Tel: 320-864-5162. Students 157.

GRACEVILLE, BIG STONE CO., HOLY ROSARY (1878), [JC], Clustered with Beardsley. Rev. John A. Nordick; Deacon Art D. Abel. Tel: 320-748-7573 (Home).
Res & Mailing Address: 511 Studdart Ave., P.O. Box 7, 56240-0007. Tel: 320-748-7313.
Catechesis/Religious Program—517 Studdart Ave., 56240. Tel: 320-748-7501. Students 178.

GRANITE FALLS, YELLOW MEDICINE CO., ST. ANDREW (1885), [CEM], Clustered with Montevideo & Clara City. Rev. James Devorak. Tel: 320-269-5954; Fax: 320-269-7555 (Montevideo).
Mailing Address: 1094 Granite St., 56241-1355. Tel. 320-564-2335; Fax: 320-564-2335 (Call before sending). Email: standrew@kilowatt.net.
Res.: 512 Black Oak Ave., Montevideo, 56241.
Catechesis/Religious Program—1056 Fourth St., 56241. Tel: 320-564-2336. Students 174.

GREEN ISLE, SIBLEY CO., ST. BRENDAN (1854), [CEM], Clustered with Faxon Township, Henderson & Jessenland. Rev. Bernard J. Stenner.
Res. & Mailing Address: 221 McGrann St., S., P.O. Box 85, 55338-0085. Tel: 507-326-5111.
Catechesis/Religious Program—Students 36.

GREEN VALLEY, LYON CO., ST. CLOTILDE (1912), [CEM], Clustered with Cottonwood & Marshall. Rev. Paul J. Hadusek. Tel: 507-423-5220 (Cottonwood).
Church: R.R., Marshall, 56258.
Res. & Mailing Address: 255 W. 4th St. S., P.O. Box 228, Cottonwood, 56229-0228. Tel: 507-423-5220; Fax: 507-423-5275.
Catechesis/Religious Program—Tel: 507-532-6141. Students 61.

GREENLEAF, MEEKER CO., ST. COLUMBAN, Closed., For inquiries for sacramental records contact St. Philip, Litchfield.

HECTOR, RENVILLE CO., CHURCH OF ST. JOHN (1878), [CEM], Clustered with Bird Island, Olivia, & Renville. Donald A. Clasemann, Pastoral Admin.
Church: 301 Cedar Ave. E., P.O. Box 295, 55342-0295. Tel: 320-848-6437; Fax: 320-848-2407. Email: stjohnshec@yahoo.com.
Catechesis/Religious Program—Students 86.

HEGBERT, SWIFT CO., ST. AGNES, Closed., For sacramental records, contact St. John, Appleton.

HENDERSON, SIBLEY CO., ST. JOSEPH (1859), [CEM], Clustered with Faxon Township, Green Isle & Jessenland. Sr. Jovann Irrgang, S.S.N.D., Pastoral Admin.
Res. & Mailing Address: 213 S. 6th St., P.O. Box 427, 56044-0427. Tel: 507-248-3550.
Catechesis/Religious Program—Students 64.
Mission—St. Thomas 31624 Scenic Byway Rd., Jessenland, Sibley Co. 56144-0427.

HOLLOWAY, SWIFT CO., ST. JOSEPH, Closed., For sacramental records, contact St. John, Appleton.

HUTCHINSON, MCLEOD CO., CHURCH OF ST. ANASTASIA (1866), [CEM], Clustered with Stewart. Rev. William A. Sprigler.
Mailing Address: 460 Lake St. S.W., 55350-2349.
Church: 400 Lake St., S.W., 55350-2349.
Res.: 1016 Roe Ave., 55350-2117. Tel: 320-587-6507; Fax: 320-234-6756.
School—(Grades PreK-6) Tel: 320-587-2490. Karla Cross, Prin.. Email: kcross@stranastasia.net. Lay Teachers 13; Students 231.
Catechesis/Religious Program—Tel: 320-234-6129. Students 493.

IVANHOE, LINCOLN CO., SS. PETER & PAUL (1900), [CEM], Clustered with Wilno. Rev. David L. Breu; Sr. M. Ellen Hoemberg, I.S.S.M., Pastoral Assoc. Tel: 507-694-1225 (Wilno).
Res. & Mailing Address: 111 N. Sherwood, P.O. Box 49, 56142-0049. Tel: 507-694-1402; Fax: 507-694-1437.
Catechesis/Religious Program—3069 Kowno St., 56142. Tel: 507-694-1225; Fax: 507-694-1548. Students 86.

JESSENLAND, SIBLEY CO., ST. THOMAS (MISSION) (1856), [CEM], Clustered with Faxon Township, Green Isle, & Henderson. Sr. Jovann Irrgang, S.S.N.D., Pastoral Admin.
Res. & Mailing address: 213 S. Sixth St., P.O. Box 427, Henderson, 56044-0427. Tel: 507-248-3550.
Church: 31624 Scenic Byway Rd., Henderson, 56044.
Catechesis/Religious Program—Students 23.

KANDIYOHI, KANDIYOHI CO., ST. PATRICK (1868), [CEM], Clustered with Lake Lillian. Rev. William H. Bowles.
Mailing Address: P.O. Box 164, 56251-0164.
Res. & Mailing Address: 245 N. 2nd St., P.O. Box 164, 56251-0164. Tel: 320-382-6424.
Catechesis/Religious Program—Students 87.

LAFAYETTE, NICOLLET CO., ST. GREGORY THE GREAT (1942), [CEM], Clustered with West Newton Township. Rev. John G. Berger.
Res. & Mailing Address: 440 6th St., P.O. Box 5, 56054-0005. Tel: 507-228-8298.
Catechesis/Religious Program—Students 128.

LAKE BENTON, LINCOLN CO., ST. GENEVIEVE (1897), [CEM], Clustered with Tyler. Rev. Harry P. Behan.
Res. & Mailing Address: 213 Linwood St., Box P.O. 310, Tyler, 56178. Tel: 507-247-3464; Fax: 507-247-3286.
Church: 119 S. Sherman St., 56149. Tel: 507-368-4232.
Catechesis/Religious Program—Fax: 507-247-3286. Students 81.

LAKE LILLIAN, KANDIYOHI CO., ST. THOMAS MORE (1934),, Clustered with Kandiyohi. Rev. William H. Bowles. Tel: 320-382-6424 (Kandiyohi).
Res. & Mailing Address: 245 3rd St. E., P.O. Box 164, Kandiyohi, 56251-0164. Tel: 320-382-4810.
Church: 840 Second St. E., 56253. Tel: 320-664-4810.
Catechesis/Religious Program—Students 36.

LAMBERTON, REDWOOD CO., ST. JOSEPH (1895), [CEM], Clustered with Walnut Grove & Tracy. Sr. Marian Kemper, O.S.B., Pastoral Admin.
Res. & Mailing Address: 400 W. 2nd Ave., P.O. Box 458, 56152-0458. Tel: 507-752-7269. Email: joe@rrcnet.org.
Catechesis/Religious Program—Students 73.

LEAVENWORTH, BROWN CO., CHURCH OF THE JAPANESE MARTYRS (1867), [CEM], Clustered with Comfrey, Sleepy Eye. Rev. Todd J. Petersen.
Res. & Mailing Address: 30881 County Rd. 24, Sleepy Eye, 56085-4361. Tel: 507-794-6974; Fax: 507-794-6972. Email: jmartyrs@sleepyeyetel.net.
Catechesis/Religious Program—Tel: 507-794-6460. Students 38.

LESTER PRAIRIE, MCLEOD CO., ST. CONRAD, Closed., Incorporated but never organized. No sacramental records.

LITCHFIELD, MEEKER CO., ST. PHILIP (1859), [CEM] Rev. Mark S. Mallak.
Res.: 306 N. Holcombe Ave., 55355-2223. Tel: 320-693-3313; Fax: 320-693-2247. Email: stphilip@hutchtel.net. Web: www.litch.com/churches/stphilip.
School—(Grades K-5), 225 E. 3rd St.. Tel: 320-693-6283. Dania M. Carney, Prin. Lay Teachers 7; Students 72.
Catechesis/Religious Program—225 E. Third St., 55355. Students 246.

LUCAN, REDWOOD CO., OUR LADY OF VICTORY (1889), (German), [CEM], Clustered with Wabasso, Seaforth and Wanda. Sr. Michelle McGurran, O.S.B., Pastoral Admin.
Res. & Mailing Address: P.O. Box 96, 56255-0096. Tel: 507-747-2231; Fax: 507-747-2233.
Church: 303-3rd St., 56255.
Catechesis/Religious Program—Students 26.

MADISON, LAC QUI PARLE CO., ST. MICHAEL (1884), [CEM], Clustered with Dawson. Rev. Jeffrey P. Horejsi.
Res.: 412 3rd St., 56256-1494. Tel: 320-598-3690; Fax: 320-598-3619. Email: stmike2@frontiernet.net.
Catechesis/Religious Program—Students 106.

MANANNAH, MEEKER CO., CHURCH OF OUR LADY (1876), Rev. Francis J. Garvey.

Res.: 57482 CSAH 3, Grove City, 56243-9786. Tel: 320-693-8900; Fax: 320-693-8900.
Catechesis/Religious Program—Students 104.

MARSHALL, LYON CO., HOLY REDEEMER (1883), [CEM], Clustered with Cottonwood & Green Valley. Revs. Gerald S. Meidl; Eugene M. Brown; Craig A. Timmerman.
Res. & Mailing Address: 503 W. Lyon St., 56258-1390. Tel: 507-532-5711; Fax: 507-532-3262. Web: www.holy-redeemer.com.
School—(Grades K-8), 501 S. Whitney. Tel: 507-532-6642; Fax: 507-532-2636. Carol J. DeSmet, Prin.. Email: cdsmet@holy-redeemer.com. Lay Teachers 26; Students 384.
Catechesis/Religious Program—503 S. Whitney St., 56258. Tel: 507-532-3602. Patti Watkins, D.R.E. (Grades K-6). Students 580.

MIDDLE LAKE, NICOLLET CO., ST. NICHOLAS, Closed., For sacramental records, contact St. Paul's, Nicollet.

MILROY, REDWOOD CO., ST. MICHAEL (1904), [CEM], Clustered with Marshall. Deacon Richard A. Cronican, Pastoral Admin.
Res. & Mailing Address: 400 Cedar St; P.O. Box 117, 56263-0117. Tel: 507-336-2505. Email: deacdick@means.net.
Catechesis/Religious Program—Students 112.

MINNEOTA, LYON CO., ST. EDWARD (1880), [CEM], Clustered with Ghent & Taunton. Rev. Andrew J. Michels.
Church & Res.: 409 N. Adams St., 56264-9801. Tel: 507-872-6346; Fax: 507-872-6346. Email: stedwardchurch@mvtvwireless.com.
School—(Grades 1-8), 210 W. 4th St.. Tel: 507-872-6391; Fax: 507-872-5263. Kathleen Fjedheim, Prin. Lay Teachers 12; Students 116.
Catechesis/Religious Program—Tel: 507-428-3285. Students 146.

MONTEVIDEO, CHIPPEWA CO., ST. JOSEPH (1882), [CEM], Clustered with Granite Falls & Clara City. Rev. James W. Devorak.
Res. & Mailing Address: 521 Eureka Ave., 56265-1899. Tel: 320-269-8623.
Church: 512 Black Oak Ave., 56265-1874. Tel: 320-269-5954; Fax: 320-269-7555.
Catechesis/Religious Program—Students 190.

MORGAN, REDWOOD CO., ST. MICHAEL (1890), [CEM], Clustered with Clements. Rev. Robert J. Wyffels.
Res. & Mailing Address: 510 W. 3rd St., P.O. Box 459, 56266-0459. Tel: 507-249-3643; Fax: 507-249-2557. Email: stmichaels@redred.com.
Church: 514 W. 3rd St..
School—(Grades PreK-6), 612 W. 3rd St., P.O. Box 459, 56266-0459. Tel: 507-249-3192. Patty McCauley, Prin. Lay Teachers 7; Students 65.
Catechesis/Religious Program—Tel: 507-692-2181. Students 68.

MORTON, RENVILLE CO., ST. JOHN (1873), [CEM], Clustered with Redwood Falls. Sr. JoAnne Backes, O.S.B., Pastoral Admin.
Res. & Mailing Address: 341 W. 3rd St., P.O. Box 88, 56270-0088. Tel: 507-697-6120.
Catechesis/Religious Program—Students 28.

MURDOCK, SWIFT CO., CHURCH OF THE SACRED HEART (1879),, Clustered with Benson, Clontarf, Danvers & De Graff. Rev. Steven J. Verhelst. Tel: 320-843-2342 (Benson); Sisters Laetitia Lariviere, I.H.M., Pastoral Admin. Int., (Murdock & DeGraff); Louise Bauer, O.S.F., Pastoral Min. Tel: 320-843-2026 (Clontarf); Christine Ahles, Pastoral Min. Tel: 320-875-2246 (De Graff).
Res. & Mailing Address: 201 Orleans, P.O. Box 9, 56271-0009. Tel: 320-875-2451; 320-842-4271 (Area Office); Fax: 320-843-2264. Email: stfran@willmar.com. Web: www.catholicareaparishes.org.
Catechesis/Religious Program—Tel: 320-875-2451. Students 99.

NASSAU, LAC QUI PARLE CO., ST. JAMES (1902), [CEM], Clustered with Ortonville and Rosen. Rev. Robert P. Goblirsch, (Ortonville).
Res. & Mailing Address: 421 Madison Ave., Ortonville, 56278-2713. Tel: 320-839-2772; Fax: 320-839-2873.

NICOLLET, NICOLLET CO., ST. PAUL (1907), [CEM 4] Rev. Edward J. Ardolf.
Res. & Mailing Address: 411 5th St., P.O. Box 248, 56074-0248. Tel: 507-232-3857.
Catechesis/Religious Program—Students 89.

NORTH MANKATO, NICOLLET CO., HOLY ROSARY (1924), Rev. Peter C. Nosbush.
Res. & Mailing Address: 525 Grant Ave., 56003-2939. Tel: 507-387-6501; Fax: 507-388-2017.
School—546 Grant Ave., 56003-2937. Tel: 507-345-6765. Sr. Katherine DuVal, S.S.N.D., Supt. School is part of Mankato Area Catholic Schools, Diocese of Winona. Numbers are reported by the Winona Diocese.
Catechesis/Religious Program—Students 301.

OLIVIA, RENVILLE CO., ST. ALOYSIUS (1888), [CEM 2] [JC], Clustered with Renville, Hector, Bird Island. Rev. Paul H. van de Crommert.
Mailing Address: 301 S. 10th St., 56277-1288.
Church: 302 S. 10th St., 56277-1288. Tel: 320-523-2030 (Office); 320-523-1271 (Rectory).
Catechesis/Religious Program—Tel: 320-523-2030. Students 164.

ORTONVILLE, BIG STONE CO., ST. JOHN (1879),, Clustered with Nassau & Rosen. Rev. Robert P. Goblirsch.
Res.: 421 Madison Ave., 56278-2713. Tel: 320-839-2772; Fax: 320-839-2873.
Catechesis/Religious Program—Tel: 320-839-2873. Students 144.

RAYMOND, KANDIYOHI CO., SACRED HEART, Closed., For sacramental records, contact St. Clara, Clara City.

REDWOOD FALLS, REDWOOD CO., ST. CATHERINE (1870), [CEM], Clustered with Morton. Rev. Paul A. Schumacher.
Church & Mailing Address: 900 E. Flynn St., P.O. Box 383, 56283-0383. Tel: 507-644-2278; Fax: 507-644-2643. Email: stcath@redred.com.
Res.: 904 E. Flynn St., P.O. Box 383, 56283-0383. Tel: 507-644-8114.
Catechesis/Religious Program—Students 282.

REGAL, KANDIYOHI CO., ST. ANTHONY (MISSION) (1933), [CEM], Clustered with Spicer. Rev. Frederick T. Fink. Tel: 320-796-5664 (Spicer).
Res. & Mailing Address: 13722 Hwy. 23 N.E., Spicer, 56288-9659. Tel: 320-796-5664.
Church: 293rd Ave. & 145th St., Spicer, 56288.
Catechesis/Religious Program—Tel: 320-243-7290. Students 25.

RENVILLE, RENVILLE CO., HOLY REDEEMER (1891), [CEM], Clustered with Olivia, Bird Island, Hector. Rev. Paul H. van de Crommert; Deacon Michael Rajcich, Pastoral Assoc.
Church & Mailing Address: 106 S.E. 3rd St., P.O. Box 401, 56284-0401. Tel: 320-329-3884; Fax: 320-329-3884. Email: hrchurch@midstate.tds.net.
Catechesis/Religious Program—Tel: 320-329-8219. Students 136.

ROSEN, LAC QUI PARLE CO., ST. JOSEPH (1885), [CEM], Clustered with Nassau & Ortonville Rev. Robert P. Goblirsch. Tel: 320-839-2772 (Ortonville).
Mailing Address: 421 Madison Ave., Ortonville, 56278-2713. Tel: 320-839-2772; Fax: 320-839-2873.
Catechesis/Religious Program—Tel: 320-568-2428. Students 57.

ST. LEO, YELLOW MEDICINE CO., ST. LEO (1881), [CEM], Clustered with Canby. Rev. Anthony R. Hesse. Tel: 507-223-7304 (Canby).
Church & Mailing Address: 202 W. Church St., 56264. Tel: 507-224-2289.
Catechesis/Religious Program—Tel: 507-223-7729. Students 5.

ST. PETER, NICOLLET CO.

1—IMMACULATE CONCEPTION, Closed., For sacramental records, contact St. Peter's, St. Peter.

2—ST. PETER (1856), [CEM] Rev. Philip M. Schotzko; Sr. Ramona Fallon, O.S.B., Pastoral Assoc.; Kay Osborne, Pastoral Assoc.
Mailing Address: 1801 W. Broadway, P.O. Box 522, 56082-0522. Tel: 507-931-1628; Fax: 507-931-2977. Email: office@churchofstpeter.org. Web: www.churchofstpeter.org.
School—John Ireland School, (Grades K-6) Tel: 507-931-2810; Fax: 507-931-9179. Email: ramona.fallon@churchofstpeter.org. Sr. Ramona Fallon, O.S.B., Prin. Lay Teachers 12; Students 99.
Catechesis/Religious Program—Tel: 507-931-3662. Teresa Guillemette, D.R.E. Students 328.

SANBORN, REDWOOD CO., ST. THOMAS (1902),, Clustered with Springfield. Sr. Jeanette Homan, O.S.F., Pastoral Admin.
Res. and Mailing Address: 301 E. Winona St., P.O. Box 176, 56083-0176. Tel: 507-648-3754.
Catechesis/Religious Program—Students 27.

SEAFORTH, REDWOOD CO., ST. MARY (1880), [CEM 2] [JC 2], Clustered with Wabasso, Lucan & Wanda. Rev. John A. Pearson, (Wabasso).
Mailing Address: P.O. Box 239, Wabasso, 56293-0239. Tel: 507-342-5190 (Office); 507-342-5155 (Rectory); 507-984-5421 (Church Hall); Fax: 507-342-5156.
Catechesis/Religious Program—Students 30.

SEARLES, BROWN CO., ST. JOHN THE BAPTIST (1905), [CEM], Clustered with Cathedral, New Ulm; St. Mary's, New Ulm; Lafayette; West Newton Township. Sr. Monica Wagner, S.S.N.D., Pastoral Admin.
Res. & Mailing Address: 18241 First Ave. S., 56073-5171. Tel: 507-359-4244; Fax: 507-359-4244.
School—New Ulm Area Catholic Schools., Tel: 507-354-2719; Fax: 507-354-7071. See separate listing for details
Catechesis/Religious Program—Tel: 507-354-4158; Fax: 507-354-2563. Students 36.

SILVER LAKE, MCLEOD CO.

1—ST. ADALBERT, Closed., For sacramental records, contact Holy Family, Silver Lake.

2—CHURCH OF THE HOLY FAMILY (1993), [CEM 4] [JC 4] Rev. Robert J. Mraz.
Res. & Mailing Address: 720 W. Main St., P.O. Box 326, 55381-0326. Tel: 320-327-2261; Fax: 320-327-2261.
School—(Grades PreK-6), 700 W. Main St., P.O. Box 346, 55381-0346. Tel: 320-327-2356; Fax: 320-327-2356 (Call First). Email: hfcsprincipal@earthlink.net. William Berning, Prin. Lay Teachers 7; Students 75.
Catechesis/Religious Program—Tel: 320-327-2931; Fax: 320-327-2931. Students 165.

3—ST. JOSEPH, Closed., For sacramental records, contact Holy Family, Silver Lake.

SLEEPY EYE, BROWN CO., ST. MARY (1876), [CEM] Revs. Brian W. Oestreich; Celestine C. Pistulka (Retired); Deacon Mark D. Kober. Tel: 507-794-4682.
Res.: 636 First Ave. N., 56085-1004. Tel: 507-794-4171; Fax: 507-794-5871. Email: stmarys@sleepyetel.net. Web: www.stmarys-sleepyeye.com.
School—(Grades PreK-6), 104 W. St. Mary St.. Tel: 507-794-6141; Fax: 507-794-4841. Mr. Wayne Pelzel, Prin. Lay Teachers 20; Students 315.
High School—(Grades 7-12) Tel: 507-794-4121. Mr. Jerry Neubauer, Prin. Lay Teachers 21; Students 259.
Catechesis/Religious Program—Tel: 507-794-4067; Fax: 507-794-5871. Students 116.

SPICER, KANDIYOHI CO., OUR LADY OF THE LAKES (1962), [CEM], Clustered with Regal. Rev. Frederick T. Fink.
Res.: 6680-153rd Ave., N.E., 56288-9659. Tel: 320-796-5664. Email: ourlady@wecnet.com. Web: www.ourladyofthelakeschurch.com.
Catechesis/Religious Program—Tel: 320-796-5968. Students 319.
Mission—St. Anthony

SPRINGFIELD, BROWN CO., ST. RAPHAEL (1874), [CEM], Clustered with Sanborn. Rev. Dennis C. Labat.
Res.: 112 W. Van Dusen St., 56087-1396. Tel: 507-723-4137 (Office); 507-723-4141 (Rectory).
School—(Grades K-6), 20 W. VanDusen. Tel: 507-723-4315; Fax: 507-723-5409. Email: strays@springfield-sanborn.net. Sr. Therese Collison, S.S.N.D., Prin. Tel: 507-723-4136. Sisters 2; Lay Teachers 7; Students 58.
Catechesis/Religious Program—Tel: 507-723-4138. Students 255.

STEWART, MCLEOD CO., CHURCH OF ST. BONIFACE (1877), [CEM], Clustered with Hutchinson. Rev. William A. Sprigler. Tel: 320-587-6507 (Hutchinson).
Mailing Address: 551 Main St., P.O. Box 202, 55385-0202.
Catechesis/Religious Program—Students 81.

SWAN LAKE, NICOLLET CO.

1—THE CHURCH OF THE VISITATION, Closed., For sacramental records, contact St. Paul, Nicollet.

2—VISITATION, Closed., For sacramental records, contact St. Paul, Nicollet.

TAUNTON, LYON CO., SS. CYRIL AND METHODIUS (1895), [CEM 2], Clustered with Ghent & Minneota. Rev. Andrew J. Michels. Tel: 507-872-6346.
Res. & Mailing Address: 101 N. Lincoln St., P.O. Box 368, 56291-0368. Tel: 507-872-5150.

TRACY, LYON CO., ST. MARY (1880), [CEM], Clustered with Walnut Grove & Lamberton. Rev. Brian L. Mandel.
Res. & Mailing Address: 249 6th St., 56175-1114. Tel: 507-629-4075; Fax: 507-629-3227 (Rectory); 507-629-3667 (Office).
Church: 285 6th St., 56175. Tel: 507-629-3841 (Church Hall).
School—(Grades K-6), 225 6th. St., 56175-1114. Tel: 507-629-3270. Email: smschool@iw.net. Mrs. Lisa Schaar, Prin. Lay Teachers 7; Students 60.
Catechesis/Religious Program—Tel: 507-629-3667. Students 145.

TYLER, LINCOLN CO., ST. DIONYSIUS (1880), [CEM], Clustered with Lake Benton. Rev. Harry P. Behan.
Parish Office and Mailing Address: 213 Linwood St., P.O. Box 310, 56178-0310.
Res.: 213 Linwood St., 56178-0310. Tel: 507-247-5807 (Church); 507-247-3464 (Office); Fax: 507-247-3286.
Church: 203 Linwood St., 56178.
Catechesis/Religious Program—Students 145.

VESTA, REDWOOD CO., HOLY NAME, Closed., For sacramental records, contact St. Catherine's, Redwood Falls.

WABASSO, REDWOOD CO., ST. ANNE (1900), [CEM] [JC], Clustered with Lucan, Wanda, Seaforth. Rev. John A. Pearson.
Mailing Address: 1052 Cedar St., P.O. Box 239, 56293-0239.
Church Address: 950 North St., 56293-0239. Tel: 507-342-5190 (Office); 507-342-5155 (Rectory); Fax: 507-342-5156.
School—(Grades K-6), 1054 Cedar St., 56293-0239. Tel: 507-345-5389; Fax: 507-342-5156. Email: stannes@redred.com. Lisa Dudgeon, Prin. Lay

Teachers 9; Students 97.
Catechesis/Religious Program—Tel: 507-342-5190. Students 127.

WALNUT GROVE, REDWOOD CO., ST. PAUL (1902), [CEM] Rev. Brian L. Mandel. Tel: 507-629-3227 (Tracy).
Mailing Address: P.O. Box 236, 56180-0236. Tel: 507-859-2164; Fax: 507-859-2153. Clustered with Tracy & Lamberton.
Catechesis/Religious Program—Tel: 507-629-4075; Fax: 507-629-3667. Students 18.

WANDA, REDWOOD CO., ST. MATHIAS (1871), [CEM], Clustered with Seaforth, Lucan, Wabasso. Rev. John A. Pearson, (Wabasso).
Mailing Address: P.O. Box 239, Wabasso, 56293.
Church: 308 St. Mathias Blvd., 56293. Tel: 507-342-5190 (Office); 507-342-5155 (Rectory); Fax: 507-342-5156.
Catechesis/Religious Program—Students 56.

WATKINS, MEEKER CO., CHURCH OF ST. ANTHONY (1889), [CEM] Rev. John H. Brunner.
Res. & Mailing Address: 171 Central Ave. S., P.O. Box 409, 55389-0409. Tel: 320-764-2755; Fax: 320-764-2755.
Church: 201 Central Ave. S., 55389.
Catechesis/Religious Program—Tel: 320-764-5722. Students 196.

WEST NEWTON TOWNSHIP, NICOLLET CO., ST. GEORGE (1857), [CEM], Clustered with Lafayette; Searles; Cathedral-NewUlm; St. Mary's-New Ulm. Rev. John G. Berger. Tel: 507-228-8298 (Lafayette).
Mailing Address: 440 6th St., P.O. Box 5, Lafayette, 56054-0005. Tel: 507-228-8298; 507-359-9013.
Church: Hwy. 16 & County Rd. 5. Tel: 507-359-9553.
Catechesis/Religious Program—Students 7.

WILLMAR, KANDIYOHI CO., ST. MARY (1871), [CEM] Revs. Joseph A. Steinbeisser; Anthony J. Stubeda.
Church & Mailing Address: 713 12th St., S.W., 56201-3099. Tel: 320-235-0118; Fax: 320-235-0153.
Catechesis/Religious Program—Tel: 320-235-3982. Students 801.

WILNO, LINCOLN CO., ST. JOHN CANTIUS (1883), [CEM], Clustered with Cantius Ivanhoe. Rev. David L. Breu. Tel: 507-694-1402 (Ivanhoe).
Mailing Address: P.O. Box 49, Ivanhoe, 56142-0049. Tel: 507-694-1402; Fax: 507-694-1437.
Catechesis/Religious Program—Tel: 507-694-1225; Fax: 507-694-1548. Students 116.

WINSTED, MCLEOD CO., HOLY TRINITY (1869), [CEM 2] Rev. Paul L. Wolf.
Res. & Mailing Address: 111 Winsted Ave. W., P.O. Box 9, 55395-0009. Tel: 320-485-4421; Fax: 320-485-4283.
School—(Grades PreK-6), 211 2nd St. N., P.O. Box 38, 55395-0038. Tel: 320-485-2314. Email: htprincipal@mchsi.com. Todd Stejskal, Prin. Lay Teachers 10; Students 187.
High School—(Grades 7-12), 110 Winsted Ave., P.O. Box 38, 55395-0038. Tel: 320-485-2182. Email: htprincipal@mchsi.com. Rev. Paul L. Wolf, Supt.; Todd Stejskal, Prin. Lay Teachers 17; Students 141.
Catechesis/Religious Program—Tel: 320-485-3752; Fax: 320-485-4283. Students 162.

WINTHROP, SIBLEY CO., ST. FRANCIS DE SALES (1906),, Clustered with Gaylord, Fairfax, Franklin. Rev. Ronald V. Huberty. Tel: 507-426-7125 (Fairfax).
Church & Mailing Address: 510 N. Brown St., P.O. Box 447, 55396-0447. Tel: 507-237-2851.
Catechesis/Religious Program—P.O. Box F, 55396. Tel: 507-647-5894; Fax: 507-647-7070. Ms. Pamela Osborne, D.R.E. Students 41.

Chaplains of Public Institutions

APPLETON. *Prairie Correctional Facility*. Rev. Michael M. Doyle, Chap.

IVANHOE. *Divine Providence Hospital & Home*. Rev. Marion G. Casey, Chap. (Retired).

ST. PETER. *St. Peter Regional Treatment Center*. Rev. John G. Berger, Chap.

WILLMAR. *Regional Treatment Center*. Rev. William H. Bowles, Chap., Sisters Cecile Schueller, SS.ND., Chap., Nadine Touhey, SS.ND., Chap.

WINSTED. *St. Mary's Care Center*. Rev. Martin F. Rath, O.S.B., Chap.

On Special or Other Diocesan Assignment:
Revs.—
Grams, Douglas L.
Labat, Dennis C.
Mallak, Mark S.
Petersen, Todd J.
Schotzko, Philip M.
Stubeda, Anthony J.

On Duty Outside the Diocese:
Rev. Msgr.—
Schaffer, Gregory T., Parroquia San Lucas Toliman, Depto. Solola 07013, Guatemala. Tel: 011-502-722-0112; Fax: 011-502-722-0112
Revs.—
Goggin, John T., Parroquia San Lucas Toliman, Depto. Solola 07013 Guatemala. Tel: 011-502-722-0112; Fax: 011-502-722-0112
Hansen, Lawrence H., St. Mary Medical Center, Langhorne & Newtown Rd., Langhorne, PA 19047. Tel: 215-750-5140
Martinka, Stanley V., San Alfonso Mission, 1218 Lonewood, El Paso, TX 79925. Tel: 915-598-0900
Mead, Leland C., 22295 Lakewood Dr., Madison Lake, 56063-9706. Tel: 507-243-3868

Military Chaplains:
Rev.—
Wagner, John M., Lt. Col. (Retired), 117 E. Summit Ave., San Antonio, TX 78212-2953. Tel: 210-738-3481

Retired:
Rev. Msgrs.—
Leifeld, Antony J., 605 N. State St., 56073-1898. Tel: 507-359-9848
Ward, John C., Leo C. Byrne Residence, 60 S. Mississippi Blvd. Apt. 225, St. Paul, 55105-1052. Tel: 651-698-8175
Revs.—
Adrian, Stephen J., 10410 E. Twilight Dr., Sun Lakes, AZ 85248. Tel: 602-895-0465
Barry, James D., Raven Hill Apt., 109-13000 Harriet Ave., So., Burnsville, 55337. Tel: 952-846-0551
Becker, Dennis E., 11208 Co. Rd. 12 NW, Garfield, 56332. Tel: 320-834-2100
Bonin, Richard G., Leo C. Bryne Residence, 60 S. Mississippi Blvd., Apt. 314, St. Paul, 55105-1052. Tel: 651-699-0535
Brandes, John F. (STP), Parroquia San Lucas Toliman, Depto. Solola 07013, Guatemala. Tel: 011-502-722-0112; Fax: 011-502-722-0112
Casey, Marion G., Divine Providence Health Center, 312 E. George, Box 136, Ivanhoe, 56142-0136. Tel: 507-694-1414
Fleming, John R., Marian Center of St. Paul, 200 Earl St., Rm. 510, St. Paul, 55106. Tel: 651-793-4308
Gross, Richard C., P.O. Box 6, Watkins, 55389. Tel: 320-764-2856
Irrgang, Kenneth E., 740 14th St. S. Apt. 13, St. Cloud, 56301-5518. Tel: 320-654-1008
Jenniges, Leonard J. (STP), 18760 Co. Hwy. 17, Sanborn, 56083-3038. Tel: 507-342-5134
Krystosek, Robert H. (GI), P.O. Box 425, Clara City, 56222-0425. Tel: 320-847-2615
McGowan, Myles P., Leo C. Byrne Residence, 60 S. Mississippi River Blvd., Apt. 223, St. Paul, 55105-1052. Tel: 651-690-9002
Monnens, Merle W., 225 Lakeview Dr., Spicer, 56288. Tel: 320-796-4541
O'Connor, Michael F., Church of St. Joseph, 23945 Nicolai Ave. E., Hastings, 55033-9650. Tel: 651-437-3526
Pistulka, Celestine C., Lake Villa Maria Apartments, 702 Third Ave., N.W., Rm. 201, Sleepy Eye, 56085-1099. Tel: 507-794-5688
Plathe, Anthony H., 1381 Mission Hills Blvd., Clearwater, FL 33759-2767. Tel: 727-510-5491
Schaefer, Roman J., Church of Our Lady Queen of Martyrs, 2731 Happy Hoyer St., Fort Lauderdale, FL 33312-2901. Tel: 305-583-8725
Schreiner, Bernard P., The Watkins House, 341 4th St. N., P.O. Box 246, Watkins, 55389-0246. Tel: 320-764-2894
Siebenand, Ambrose F., Benedict Village, 2000 15th Ave., S.E., Apt. 313, St. Cloud, 56304-2423. Tel: 320-654-2376
Siebenand, John N., Benedict Court, 1980 15th Ave., S.E., Apt. 5, St. Cloud, 56304. Tel: 320-253-2655
Wojtowicz, Edward L., Leo C. Byrne Residence, 60 S. Mississippi River Blvd., Apt. 310, St. Paul, 55105-1052. Tel: 651-698-6926

INSTITUTIONS LOCATED IN THE DIOCESE

[A] NEW ULM AREA CATHOLIC SCHOOLS

NEW ULM. *New Ulm Area Catholic Schools*, 515 N. State St., 56073-1897. Tel: 507-354-2719; Fax: 507-354-7071. Mary Ellen Domeier, Exec. Officer. Consolidated: The three schools consolidated under the above title are as follows:
St. Anthony Elementary School (Grades PreK-4), 514 N. Washington St., 56073. Tel: 507-354-2928; Fax: 507-359-7029. Christine Olson, Prin., (Grades Pre K-4). Elementary: Lay Teachers 31; Students 406.
Holy Trinity Middle School, 515 N. State St., 56073-1897. Tel: 507-354-4311; Fax: 507-354-7071. Email: chris.olson@nuacs.com. Christine Olson, Prin., (Grades 5-8).
Cathedral High School, 600 N. Washington St., 56073-1897. Tel: 507-354-4511; Fax: 507-354-5711. Shelly Bauer, Prin., (Grades 9-12). High School: Sisters 1; Lay Teachers 19; Students 206; Lay Teachers 31; Students 406.

[B] GENERAL HOSPITALS

GRACEVILLE. *Graceville Health Center* dba Holy Trinity Hospital and Grace Home , 115 W. 2nd St., 56240-0157. Tel: 320-748-7223; Fax: 320-748-7225. Email: hjorve@ghealth.net. Bed Capacity 15; Inpatients 403; Outpatients 7,069; Clinic Patients 6,942; Total Staff 112; Health Home Visits 2,187.

IVANHOE. *Divine Providence Health Center*, 312 E. George St., P.O. Box 136, 56142-0136. Tel: 507-694-1414; Fax: 507-694-1191. Web: www.dphc.com. Mark Vortherms, Admin.; Rev. Marion G. Casey, Chap. (Retired). Schoenstatt Sisters of Mary (Waukesha, WI) Sisters 2; Aged Residents 35; Bed Capacity 43.

[C] HOMES FOR AGED

CLINTON. *Clinton Providence Center*, Hwy. 322 County Rd. 6, P.O. Box 379, 56225-0379. Tel: 320-325-5414; Fax: 320-325-5416. Email: clinprovcen@yahoo.com. Sr. Pia Rottinghaus, O.S.B., Pres. Bed Capacity 32; Patients Assisted Annually 41; Staff 51.

GRACEVILLE. *Graceville Health Center* dba Trinity Hospital and Grace Hospital , 116 W. 2nd St., 56240-0157. Tel: 320-748-7261; Fax: 320-748-7225. Email: hjorve@ghealth.net. Bed Capacity 55; Patients Assisted Annually 49; Total Staff 57.

SLEEPY EYE. *Divine Providence Community Home & Lake Villa Maria Senior Apts.*, 700 3rd Ave. N.W., 56085-1099. Tel: 507-794-3011; 507-794-5333; Fax: 507-794-3020. Email: divine@sleepyeyetel.net. Sisters Bernardine Kauffmann, D.S.M.P., Supr.; Linda Willette, Admin. Daughters of St. Mary of Providence Sisters 6; Lay Workers 95; Aged Residents 58; Tenants 21.

WINSTED. *St. Mary's Care Center*, 551 4th St., N, P.O. Box 750, 55395-0750. Tel: 320-485-2151; Fax: 320-485-4241. Email: dhschwartz@bhshealth.org. Web: www.bhshealth.org. Rev. Martin Rath, O.S.B., Chap.; Darrel H. Schwartz, Admin. & CEO. Subsidiary of the Benedictine Health System. Bed Capacity 80; Staff 150.

[D] RETREAT HOUSES

NEW ULM. *St. Alphonsus Retreat House*, 1400 6th St. N , 56073-2099. Tel: 507-359-2966; Fax: 507-354-3667. Email: dnu@dnu.org. Mark C. Kemmeter, Staff Coord.

SLEEPY EYE. *Schoenstatt Sisters of Mary (Secular Institute)*, 27762 County Rd. 27, 56085-9801. Tel: 507-794-7727; 507-794-5622; Fax: 507-794-7727. Email: schoenstattsisters@schsrsmary.org. Web: schoenstattsisters@schsrsmary.org. Sisters M. Angela Macari, Supr.; M. Emily Kenkel, Youth Min.; M. Alice Kunz, Librarian; M. Deanne Niehaus, Retreat House Mgr.; M. Ellen Hoemberg, I.S.S.M., D.R.E.; Maripaula Flaig, Chap. Coord.,; M. Candace Fier, R.N., N.F.P. Educ. Total Staff 7.

[E] YOUTH CENTERS

RENVILLE. *Center for Youth Ministry*, c/o Catholic Pastoral Center, 1400 6th St. N., 56073-2099. Tel: 507-359-2966; Fax: 507-354-3667. Sr. Sue Torgersen, C.S.J., Dir. Youth Ministry.

[F] MISCELLANEOUS

APPLETON. *Prairie Correctional Facility*, 445 S. Munsterman St., 56208. Tel: 320-289-2052; Fax: 320-289-2059. Rev. Michael M. Doyle, Chap. Patients Assisted Annually 100; Maximum Capacity 1,400.

ST. PETER. *St. Peter Regional Treatment Center*, 100 Freeman Dr., 56082-1599. Tel: 507-931-7100; Fax: 507-931-7711. Revs. John G. Berger, Chap.; Gordon Long, (Protestant) Chap. Mental Health and Chemical Dependency: Patients Assisted Annually 825; Bed Capacity 530; Total Staff 1,256.

WILLMAR. *Willmar Regional Treatment Center*, 1550 Hwy. 71 N.E., 56201-1128. Tel: 320-231-5100; Fax: 320-231-5329. Sr. Cecile Schueller, S.S.N.D., Chap.; Rev. William Bowles, Chap.; Sr. Nadine Touhey, Chap. Mental Health and Chemical Dependency: Patients Assisted Annually 900; Bed Capacity 114; Total Staff 430.

RELIGIOUS INSTITUTES OF MEN REPRESENTED IN THE DIOCESE

For further details refer to the corresponding bracketed number in the Religious Institutes of Men or Women section.

[0200]—*Benedictine Monks* (Collegeville, MN)—O.S.B.

RELIGIOUS INSTITUTES OF WOMEN REPRESENTED IN THE DIOCESE

[0230]—*Benedictine Sisters of Pontifical Jurisdiction* (Federation of St. Benedict, St. Joseph, MN; Federation of St. Gertrude, Crookston, MN; Mother of Go—O.S.B.

[0940]—*Daughters of St. Mary of Providence* (Immaculate Conception Province, Chicago, IL)—D.S.M.P.

[1310]—*Francisan Sisters of Little Falls, Minnesota* (Little Falls, MN)—O.S.F.

[0210]—*Missionary Benedictine Sisters of Pontifical Jurisdiction* (Norfolk, NE)—O.S.B.

[]—*Religious Sisters of Mercy* (Alma,MI)—R.S.M.

[]—*Schoenstatt Sisters of Mary* (Waukesha, WI)

[2970]—*School Sisters of Notre Dame* (Mankato Province, Mankato, MN; Milwaukee Province, Elm Grove, WI)—S.S.N.D.

[1680]—*School Sisters of St. Francis* (Milwaukee, WI)—O.S.F.

[1570]—*Sisters of St. Francis of the Holy Family* (Dubuque, IA)—O.S.F.

[3840]—*Sisters of St. Joseph of Carondelet* (St. Paul, MN)—C.S.J.

[]—*Sisters of St. Joseph of La Grange* (La Grange Park, IL)—C.S.J.

[3830-03]—*Sisters of St. Joseph of Orange* (Orange, CA)—C.S.J.

[3320]—*Sisters of the Presentation of the B.V.M.* (Dubuque, IA)—P.B.V.M.

[1720]—*Sisters of the Third Order Regular of St. Francis of the Congregation of Our Lady of Lourdes* (Rochester, MN)—O.S.F.

[2150]—*Sisters, Servants of the Immaculate Heart of Mary* (Monroe, MI)—I.H.M.

NECROLOGY

† Berg, Rev. Msgr. Arnold J.—Died 2003
† Hillesheim, Gerald A., Gibbon, MN St. Willebrord; Franklin, MN Sacred Heart; Fairfax, MN St. Andrew—Died March 27, 2003
† Kasel, Joseph M., (Retired)—Died Oct. 11, 2003
† Merth, Robert J., (Retired)—Died Oct. 27, 2003
† Roney, David A., (On Duty Outside the Diocese)—Died Jan. 27, 2003

Archdiocese of New York

(Archidioecesis Neo-Eboracensis)

Most Reverend

PATRICK V. AHERN, D.D.

Retired Auxiliary Bishop of New York; ordained January 27, 1945; appointed Titular Bishop of Najiera and Auxiliary Bishop of New York February 3, 1970; consecrated March 19, 1970; retired April 26, 1994. *Res.: St. Thomas More*, 65 E. 89th St., New York, NY 10128.

Most Reverend

ROBERT A. BRUCATO, D.D.

Auxiliary Bishop of New York; ordained June 1, 1957; appointed Titular Bishop of Temuniana and Auxiliary Bishop of New York July 1, 1997; consecrated August 25, 1997. *Res.: St. John The Evangelist*, 348 E. 55 St., New York, NY 10022.

Most Reverend

FRANCISCO GARMENDIA, D.D.

Retired Auxiliary Bishop of New York; ordained June 28, 1947; appointed Titular Bishop of Limisa and Auxiliary Bishop of New York May 24, 1977; consecrated June 29, 1977; retired October 30, 2001. *Res.: St. Vincent de Paul*, 900 Intervale Ave., Bronx, NY 10459.

Most Reverend

JOSU IRIONDO, D.D.

Auxiliary Bishop of New York; ordained December 23, 1962; appointed Titular Bishop of Alton and Auxiliary Bishop of New York October 30, 2001; consecrated December 12, 2001. *Res.: St. Anthony of Padua*, 832 E. 166 St., Bronx, NY 10459.

Most Reverend

DOMINICK J. LAGONEGRO, D.D.

Auxiliary Bishop of New York; ordained May 31, 1969; appointed Titular Bishop of Modrus and Auxiliary Bishop of New York October 30, 2001; consecrated December 12, 2001. *Res.: Sacred Heart*, 301 Ann St., Newburgh, NY 12550.

His Eminence

EDWARD CARDINAL EGAN, J.C.D., D.D.

Archbishop of New York; ordained December 15, 1957; appointed Titular Bishop of Allegheny and Auxiliary Bishop of New York April 1, 1985; consecrated May 22, 1985; appointed Bishop of Bridgeport November 8, 1988; installed December 14, 1988; appointed Archbishop of New York May 11, 2000; installed June 19, 2000; elevated to Cardinal February 21, 2001. *Res.: 452 Madison Ave., New York, NY 10022.*

Chancery: 1011 First Ave., New York, NY 10022. Tel: 212-371-1000; Fax: 212-813-9538.

Web: www.ny-archdiocese.org

Most Reverend

JAMES F. McCARTHY, D.D.

Retired Auxiliary Bishop of New York; ordained June 1, 1969; appointed Titular Bishop of Verrona and Auxiliary Bishop of New York May 11, 1999; consecrated June 29, 1999; retired June 15, 2002.

Most Reverend

WILLIAM J. McCORMACK, D.D.

Retired Auxiliary Bishop of New York; ordained February 21, 1959; appointed Titular Bishop of Nicives and Auxiliary Bishop of New York December 23, 1986; consecrated January 6, 1987; retired October 30, 2001. *Res.: 142 E. 29th St., New York, NY 10016.*

Most Reverend

ANTHONY F. MESTICE, D.D.

Retired Auxiliary Bishop of New York; ordained June 4, 1949; appointed Titular Bishop of Villanova and Auxiliary Bishop of New York March 5, 1973; consecrated April 27, 1973; retired October 30, 2001. *Res.: Resurrection*, 910 Boston Post Rd., Rye, NY 10580.

Most Reverend

PATRICK J. SHERIDAN, D.D.

Retired Auxiliary Bishop of New York; ordained March 1, 1947; appointed Titular Bishop of Curzola and Auxiliary Bishop of New York October 30, 1990; consecrated December 12, 1990; retired January 15, 2001. *John Cardinal O'Connor Residence*, 5655 Arlington Ave., Bronx, NY 10470.

SEE ERECTED APRIL 8, 1808.

Square Miles 4,683.

Created an Archdiocese July 19, 1850.

Comprises the Boroughs of Manhattan, Bronx, and Richmond of the City of New York, and the Counties of Dutchess, Orange, Putnam, Rockland, Sullivan, Ulster and Westchester in the State of New York.

Legal Title: Archdiocese of New York.

STATISTICAL OVERVIEW

Personnel	
Cardinals	1
Auxiliary Bishops	4
Retired Bishops	6
Priests: Diocesan Active in Diocese	522
Priests: Diocesan Active Outside Diocese	37
Priests: Retired, Sick or Absent	140
Number of Diocesan Priests	699
Religious Priests in Diocese	913
Total Priests in Diocese	1,612
Extern Priests in Diocese	241
Ordinations:	
Diocesan Priests	4
Transitional Deacons	14
Permanent Deacons	10
Permanent Deacons in Diocese	359
Total Brothers	454
Total Sisters	3,153
Parishes	
Parishes	409
With Resident Pastor:	
Resident Diocesan Priests	312
Resident Religious Priests	76
Without Resident Pastor:	
Administered by Priests	20
Administered by Deacons	1
Closed Parishes	3
Professional Ministry Personnel:	
Brothers	12
Sisters	141
Lay Ministers	1,112
Welfare	
Catholic Hospitals	14
Total Assisted	2,060,587
Health Care Centers	3
Total Assisted	172,607
Homes for the Aged	17
Total Assisted	22,508
Residential Care of Children	65
Total Assisted	2,304
Day Care Centers	115
Total Assisted	3,533
Specialized Homes	39
Total Assisted	21,387
Special Centers for Social Services	838
Total Assisted	336,920
Residential Care of Disabled	67
Total Assisted	1,967
Other Institutions	480
Total Assisted	31,403
Educational	
Seminaries, Diocesan	2
Students from This Diocese	48
Students from Other Diocese	24
Seminaries, Religious	5
Students Religious	52
Total Seminarians	100
Colleges and Universities	11
Total Students	54,853
High Schools, Diocesan and Parish	23
Total Students	14,150
High Schools, Private	29
Total Students	15,497
Elementary Schools, Diocesan and Parish	217
Total Students	79,159
Elementary Schools, Private	19
Total Students	3,060
Non-residential Schools for the Disabled	6
Total Students	311
Catechesis/Religious Education:	
High School Students	3,027
Elementary Students	105,934
Total Students under Catholic Instruction	276,091
Teachers in the Diocese:	
Priests	80
Brothers	106
Sisters	451
Lay Teachers	5,147
Vital Statistics	
Receptions into the Church:	
Infant Baptism Totals	28,557
Adult Baptism Totals	1,673
Received into Full Communion	894
First Communions	26,217
Confirmations	20,998
Marriages:	
Catholic	4,854
Interfaith	1,265
Total Marriages	6,119
Deaths	15,041
Total Catholic Population	2,521,087
Total Population	5,602,418

Succession of Prelates—Most Rev. R. LUKE CONCANEN, O.P., D.D., first Bishop; consecrated April 24, 1808; died June 19, 1810; Rt. Revs. JOHN CONNOLLY, O.P., D.D., second Bishop; consecrated Nov. 6, 1814; died Feb. 6, 1825; JOHN DUBOIS, S.S., D.D., third Bishop; consecrated Oct. 29, 1826; died Dec. 20, 1842; Most Rev. JOHN HUGHES, D.D., consecrated Titular Bishop of Basileopolis and coadjutor to the Bishop of New York, Jan. 7, 1838; succeeded to the See of New York, Dec. 20, 1842; created first Archbishop, July 19, 1850; died Jan. 3, 1864; His Eminence JOHN CARDINAL McCLOSKEY, second Archbishop; consecrated Titular Bishop of Axiere, and coadjutor to the Bishop of New York, March 10, 1844; translated to the See of Albany, May 21, 1847; promoted to the See of New York, May 6, 1864; created first U.S. Cardinal, Cardinal Priest of the Holy Roman Church, March 15, 1875 under the title of Sancta Maria Supra Minervam; died Oct. 10, 1885; Most Rev. MICHAEL AUGUSTINE CORRIGAN, D.D., third Archbishop; consecrated Bishop of Newark, NJ May 4, 1873; promoted to the Archiepiscopal See of Petra and made coadjutor to His Eminence

Cardinal McCloskey, Archbishop of New York, with the right of succession, Oct. 1, 1880; succeeded to the See of New York, Oct. 10, 1885; made Assistant at the Pontifical Throne, April 19, 1887; died May 5, 1902; His Eminence JOHN CARDINAL FARLEY, fourth Archbishop of New York; ord. June 11, 1870; consecrated Titular Bishop of Zeugma and Auxiliary to the Archbishop of New York, Dec. 21, 1895; promoted to this See, Sept. 15, 1902; preconized June 22, 1903; made Assistant at the Pontifical Throne, Dec. 4, 1904; created Cardinal Priest of the Holy Roman Church under the Title of Sancta Maria Supra Minervam, Nov. 27, 1911; died Sept. 17, 1918; PATRICK CARDINAL HAYES, fifth Archbishop of New York; ord. Sept. 8, 1892; appt. Auxiliary to the Archbishop of New York, July 3, 1914; consecrated Titular Bishop of Tagaste, Oct. 28, 1914; appt. Bishop Ordinary of U.S. Army and Navy Chaplains by the Holy See, Nov. 24, 1917; promoted to the See of New York, March 10, 1919; created Cardinal Priest of the Holy Roman Church under the title of Sancta Maria in Via, March 24, 1924; died Sept. 4, 1938; FRANCIS CARDINAL SPELLMAN, sixth Archbishop of New York; ord. May 14, 1916; appt. Auxiliary Bishop of Boston, July 30, 1932; consecrated Sept. 8, 1932; appt. to the See of New York, April 15, 1939; appt. Military Vicar for the Armed Forces of the United States, Dec. 11, 1939; created and proclaimed Cardinal Priest under the title of SS. John and Paul in the Consistory, Feb. 18, 1946; died Dec. 2, 1967; TERENCE CARDINAL COOKE, seventh Archbishop of New York; ord. Dec. 1, 1945; appt. Auxiliary Bishop of New York, Sept. 15, 1965; consecrated Dec. 13, 1965; appt. to the See of New York, March 8, 1968; installed and appt. Military Vicar of the United States Armed Forces, April 4, 1968; created and proclaimed Cardinal Priest under the title of SS. John and Paul in the Consistory, April 28, 1969; died Oct. 6, 1983; JOHN CARDINAL O'CONNOR, eighth Archbishop of New York; ord. Dec. 15, 1945; appt. Titular Bishop of Curzola and Auxiliary Bishop to the Military Vicar, April 24, 1979; consecrated May 27, 1979; appt. Bishop of Scranton, May 10, 1983; installed June 29, 1983; appt. Archbishop of New York, Jan. 31, 1984; installed March 19, 1984; created Cardinal Priest, May 25, 1985; died May 3, 2000.

Vicars General—Most Revs. ROBERT A. BRUCATO, D.D., V.G.; TIMOTHY A. MCDONNELL, D.D., V.G. Fax: 212-826-6020.

Retired Bishops—Most Revs. PATRICK V. AHERN, D.D.; FRANCISCO GARMENDIA, D.D.; JAMES F. MCCARTHY, D.D.; WILLIAM J. MCCORMACK, D.D.; ANTHONY F. MESTICE, D.D.; PATRICK J. SHERIDAN, D.D. (Retired).

Episcopal Vicars of the Archdiocese—

South Bronx—Most Rev. JOSU IRIONDO, D.D., Church of St. Anthony of Padua, 832 E. 166 St., Bronx, 10459. Tel: 718-542-7293.

Orange—Most Rev. DOMINICK J. LAGONEGRO, D.D., Church of the Sacred Heart, 301 Ann St., Newburgh, 12550. Tel: 845-561-2264.

Regional Vicars of the Archdiocese—

Manhattan (West)—Rev. Msgr. THOMAS P. LEONARD, Holy Trinity Church, 213 W. 82nd St., New York, 10024. Tel: 212-787-0634.

Manhattan (North)—Rev. Msgr. GERALD T. WALSH, St. Elizabeth Church, 268 Wadsworth Ave., New York, 10033. Tel: 212-568-8803.

Manhattan (South)—Rev. KEVIN J. NELAN, Our Lady of Guadalupe/St. Bernard Church, 328 W. 14th St., New York, 10014. Tel: 212-243-0265.

Manhattan (East)—Rev. Msgrs. JOHN G. WOOLSEY, Co-Vicar, St. John the Martyr Church, 259 E. 71st St., New York, 10021. Tel: 212-744-4880; THOMAS A. MODUGNO, Co-Vicar, St. Monica Church, 413 E. 79th St., New York, 10021. Tel: 212-288-6250.

Manhattan (Central Harlem)—Rev. Msgr. WALLACE HARRIS, Church of St. Charles Borromeo, 211 W. 141st St., New York, 10030. Tel: 212-281-2100.

Bronx (Northwest)—Rev. ROBERT T. RITCHIE, Church of Our Lady of Angels, 2860 Webb Ave., Bronx, 10468. Tel: 718-548-3005.

Bronx (Northeast)—Rev. Msgr. EDWARD BARRY, St. Barnabas Church, 409 E. 241st St., Bronx, 10470. Tel: 718-324-1478.

Bronx (East)—Rev. DONALD M. DWYER, Our Lady of the Assumption Church, 1634 Mahan Ave., Bronx, 10461. Tel: 718-824-5454.

Staten Island—Rev. Msgr. JAMES J. DORNEY, St. Peter's Church, 53 St. Mark's Pl., New Brighton, Staten Island, 10301. Tel: 718-727-2672.

Central Westchester—Rev. Msgr. PATRICK J. BOYLE, Church of the Resurrection, 910 Post Rd., Rye, 10508. Tel: 914-967-0142.

Northern Westchester and Putnam—Rev. Msgr. GEORGE P. THOMPSON, St. Patrick Church, State Rd., Bedford, 10506. Tel: 914-234-3668.

Westchester (Yonkers)—Rev. Msgr. HUGH CORRIGAN, Immaculate Conception Church, 103 S. Broadway, Yonkers, 10701. Tel: 914-963-0156.

Westchester (South Shore)—Rev. Msgr. HOWARD W. CALKINS, Sacred Heart Church, 115 Sharp Blvd., Mt. Vernon, 10550. Tel: 914-668-7440.

Orange—Rev. Msgr. GEORGE J. VALASTRO, Co-Vicar, St. Joseph Church, 149 Cottage St., Middletown, 10940. Tel: 845-343-6013.

Rockland—Rev. EDWARD J. WEBER, St. Francis of Assisi Church, 128 Parrott Rd., West Nyack, 10994. Tel: 845-634-4957.

Dutchess—Rev. Msgr. WILLIAM J. BELFORD, Church of Bl. Kateri Tekakwitha, 1925 Rte. 82, Lagrangeville, 12540. Tel: 845-227-8380.

Ulster—Rev. Msgr. WILLIAM E. WILLIAMS, St. John the Evangelist Church, 915 Rte. 212, Saugerties, 12754. Tel: 914-246-9581.

Sullivan—Rev. Msgr. EDWARD F. STRAUB, St. Peter's Church, 264 N. Main St., Liberty, 12748. Tel: 845-292-4525.

Vicar for Development—Rev. Msgr. GERALD T. WALSH, 1011 First Ave., New York, 10022. Tel: 212-371-1000, Ext. 3320.

Vicars for Religious—Rev. BARTHOLOMEW DALY, M.H.M.; Sr. HELEN COLDRICK, 1011 First Ave., New York, 10022. Tel: 212-371-1000, Ext. 2575.

Vicar for Hispanic Affairs— (Vicario, Asuntos Hispanos), Most Rev. JOSU IRIONDO, D.D., 1011 First Ave., New York, 10022. Tel: 212-371-1000, Ext. 2982.

Archbishopric of New York—1011 First Ave., New York, 10022. Tel: 212-371-1000. (Cable Address: Curia New York).

Chancery—1011 First Ave., New York, 10022. Tel: 212-371-1000; Fax: 212-813-9380.

Chancellor—Rev. Msgr. THOMAS E. GILLEECE.

Vice-Chancellors—Rev. Msgr. GREGORY MUSTACIUOLO; Rev. DOUGLAS J. MATHERS, J.C.D.; Sr. EILEEN CLIFFORD, O.P.

Secretary to the Archbishop—Rev. Msgr. GREGORY MUSTACIUOLO.

Archbishop's Delegate for Administration and Finance—Mr. BERNARD E. REIDY.

Archbishop's Delegate for Healthcare—KARL P. ADLER, M.D.

Chief Financial Officer—Mr. WILLIAM E. WHISTON.

General Counsel—JAMES P. MCCABE, J.D.

Canon 1742 Panel of Pastors—Rev. Msgrs. EDWARD BARRY; PATRICK CARNEY; GERARDO COLACICCO; LAWRENCE CONNAUGHTON; JAMES DOYLE; JOHN FARLEY; RICHARD GUASTELLA; LESLIE IVERS; ROBERT LARKIN; JOSEPH MARTIN; DESMOND O'CONNOR; ROBERT TRAINOR.

Archdiocesan Consultors—Most Revs. ROBERT A. BRUCATO, D.D., V.G.; DOMINICK LAGONEGRO; PATRICK SHERIDAN; Rev. Msgrs. THOMAS J. BERGIN; PETER FINN; THOMAS GILLEECE; LESLIE IVERS; GREGORY MUSTACIUOLO; EDWARD O'DONNELL; GERALD WALSH; Rev. CARLOS RODRIGUEZ.

Metropolitan Tribunal—

Judicial Vicar—Rev. Msgr. DESMOND J. VELLA, J.C.D., S.T.L., M.S.

Vice Judicial Vicars—Revs. WILLIAM S. ELDER, J.C.D.; JOHN A. VIGILANTI, J.C.L., Ph.D.

Judges—Rev. Msgr. OSCAR AQUINO, LL.D.; Revs. JOHN J. DELANEY, J.D.; ALBERT DELUCA, M.S.; VINCENT B. GROGAN, O.F.M., J.C.D.; JOHN F. LAURI, J.C.L.; Sr. AMADEUS MCKEVITT, O.S.U., J.C.L.; Revs. JOSE G. MARABE, J.C.D.; GEORGE OONNOONNY, J.C.L.; KENNETH SMITH, M.A., S.T.B.; RICHARD L. WELCH, C.SS.R., J.C.D.; MAREK SUCHOCKI, J.C.D.; Ms. SILVANA USANDIVARAS, J.D.

Defender of the Bond—Rev. ALBERT DE LUCA, M.S.

Promoter of Justice—Rev. RICHARD L. WELCH, C.SS.R., J.C.D.

Tribunal Assessors-Auditors—Sr. MARY DANIEL BAUER, F.S.P., B.A.; Ms. SILVANA USANDIVARAS, J.D.

Canonical Consultants—Ms. CATHERINE A. BARRETT; Rev. RAFAEL G. CORNIEL, J.C.L., M.A.; Sr. DORIS HEINLEIN, S.C., M.S.; Ms. LYDIA MARTINEZ; Ms. INGRID PENA.

Regional Offices—

Mt. Kisco Office—Rev. JOHN A. VIGILANTI, J.C.L., Ph.D., 12 Green St., Mt. Kisco, 10549. Tel: 914-666-2583.

Poughkeepsie Office—240 Church St., Poughkeepsie, 12601. Tel: 845-452-1400; Fax: 845-452-2227. Auditors: Rev. JOHN A. BIDA, J.C.L.; Sr. ANNE CONNELLY, O.P., M.A.; Rev. BRIAN E. MCWEENEY, M.S., D.Min.

Interdiocesan Tribunal of New York State—201 Seminary Ave., Yonkers, 10704. Tel: 914-968-4301.

Judicial Vicar—Rev. Msgr. WALTER F. KENNY, S.T.D.

Censors Librorum—Rev. Msgrs. FRANCIS MCAREE; WILLIAM SMITH; Revs. DONALD HAGGERTY; MICHAEL F. HULL, S.T.D.

Archdiocesan Offices and Directors

Apostleship of Prayer—Rev. JAMES J. TUBRIDY (Retired), Cardinal O'Connor Residence, 5655 Arlington Ave., Bronx, 10471.

Apostleship of the Sea—Rev. KEVIN J. NELAN, Dir., Stella Maris Maritime Center for Seamen, Pier 52, New York, 10019. Tel: 212-265-5020.

Archivist—Sr. MARGUERITA SMITH, St. Joseph's Seminary, 201 Seminary Ave., Yonkers, 10704. Tel: 914-476-6333.

Bishops' Resettlement Committee for Refugees—Mr. PAUL MARTIN, Dir., 1011 First Ave., New York, 10022. Tel: 212-371-1000.

Black Ministry, Office of—Bro. TYRONE DAVIS, C.F.C., Dir., 1011 First Ave., New York, 10022. Tel: 212-371-1000.

Building Commission—St. Joseph's Seminary, 201 Seminary Ave., Yonkers, 10704. Tel: 914-476-1058.

Director—Mr. WILLIAM J. O'CONNOR.

Business Manager—Mr. STEVEN BELLOISE.

Consultants—Mr. ANDREW J. CRYAN; Deacon JOHN LARKIN; Mr. LAURENCE J. RICE.

Cardinal's Archdiocesan Appeal—Ms. CATHERINE CALLAGY, 1011 First Ave., New York, 10022. Tel: 212-371-1000.

Cardinal's Committee of the Laity—Mr. JACK DUNNE, Dir., 1011 First Ave., New York, 10022. Tel: 212-371-1000.

Cardinal's Fund for Charity and Education—1011 First Ave., New York, 10022.

Catechetical Office—Sr. JOAN CURTIN, C.N.D. Tel: 212-371-1000, Ext. 2849.

Catechumenate, Office of—VACANT, Dir. Tel: 212-371-1000, Ext. 2690.

Catholic Charismatic Center— (Centro Carismatico Catolico) Most Rev. JOSU IRIONDO, D.D., Center Dir., 826 E. 166th St., Bronx, 10460. Tel: 212-378-1734.

Catholic Charities—Rev. Msgr. KEVIN SULLIVAN, Exec. Dir., 1011 First Ave., New York, 10022. Tel: 212-371-1000 (Consult separate listing.).

Catholic Health Care System—KARL P. ADLER, M.D., Chm. Bd. Trustees, 155 E. 56 St., New York, 10022. Tel: 212-752-7300; Fax: 212-752-7547.

Catholic Health Care Foundation of the Archdiocese of New York, Inc.—KARL P. ADLER, M.D., Pres., 155 E. 56th St., New York, 10022. Tel: 212-752-7300; Fax: 212-752-7547.

Catholic High School Association—1011 First Ave., New York, 10022.

Catholic New York— (See Ecclesiastical Communications Corp.), JOHN WOODS, Editor; ARTHUR L. MCKENNA, Gen. Mgr., 1011 First Ave., New York, 10022. Tel: 212-688-2399.

Catholic World Wide Web Corporation—1011 Frist Ave., New York, 10022.

Cemeteries— (The Trustees of St. Patrick's Cathedral in the City of New York, Inc.) Mr. ANTHONY V. ROINA, Exec. Dir., 1011 First Ave., New York, 10022. Tel: 212-753-4883.

Center for Spiritual Development—ANN MARIE WALLACE, Ph.D., Dir., 96 Milton Rd., Rye, 10580. Tel: 914-967-7328.

Central Services—1011 First Ave., New York, 10022. Tel: 212-371-1000. Archdiocese of New York,

Charismatic Renewal Office—Rev. WILLIAM B. COSGROVE; Sr. PAULINE CINQUINI, S.C., 194 Gaylor Rd., Scarsdale, 10583. Tel: 914-725-1773; Fax: 914-725-5227. Email: charismny@juno.com.

Communications Office (Bureau of Information for the Media)—Mr. JOSEPH ZWILLING, Dir.; Rev. PAUL KEENAN, Asst. Dir., Radio Min.; Ms. WANDA VASQUEZ, Asst. Dir., Spanish Communications, 1011 First Ave., New York, 10022. Tel: 212-371-1000, Ext. 2990.

Conciliation and Arbitration, Office of—Rev. DOUGLAS MATHERS, Dir., 1011 First Ave., New York, 10022. Tel: 212-371-1000.

Coordinator for Special Ministries—Revs. ROBERT AUFIERI; EMILE FRISCHE, M.H.M., 1011 First Ave., New York, 10022. Tel: 212-371-1000.

Coordinator of Priest Retiree Affairs—Deacon DONALD QUIGLEY; Mrs. MARY LYNCH, R.N., St. Joseph's Seminary, 201 Seminary Ave., Yonkers, 10704. Tel: 914-968-6200, Ext. 8107.

Criminal Justice, Office of—Mr. KENNETH HOFFARTH, Dir., 1011 First Ave., New York, 10022. Tel: 212-371-1000, Ext. 3166.

Data Systems Center and Telecommunication Office—Mr. ANDREW J. DONNELLY, Dir., 1011 First Ave., New York, 10022. Tel: 212-371-1000.

Deaf, Catholic Center for—Rev. Msgr. PATRICK P. MCCAHILL, Dir., 1011 First Ave., New York, 10022. Tel: 212-988-8563.

Development, Archdiocesan Office of—Rev. Msgr. GERALD T. WALSH, Vicar; HELEN T. LOWE, Exec. Dir., 1011 First Ave., New York, 10022. Tel: 212-371-1000.

Disabilities, Office of Persons with—Rev. ROBERT PAGLIARI C.SS.R., Dir.

Ecclesiastical Assistance Corporation—1011 First Ave., New York, 10022. Tel: 212-371-1000.

Ecclesiastical Communications Corp.—1011 First Ave., New York, 10022. Tel: 212-371-1000.

Ecclesiastical Maintenance Services, Inc.—Mr. EDWARD WOODS, Gen. Mgr. Area Supvrs.: Mr. FRANK ORTIZ; Mr. ROBERT SCULLY, 1011 First Ave., New York, 10022. Tel: 212-371-1000.

Ecclesiastical Properties Corporation—1011 First Ave., New York, 10022.

Office of Ecumenical and Interreligious Affairs—Rev. ROBERT AUFIERI, Dir., 1011 First Ave., New York, 10022.

Educational Services of the Archdiocese of New York, Inc.—1011 First Ave., New York, 10022.

Education, Dept. of, Archdiocese of New York—1011 First Ave., New York, 10022. Tel: 212-371-1000. (Consult separate listing.)

Education, Secretary for—Dr. CATHERINE HICKEY, Sec., 1011 First Ave., New York, 10022. (Consult separate listing.).

Family Life/Respect Life Office—Sisters MARY ELIZABETH, S.V., Dir.; MARY GRACE, S.V., Asst. Dir. & Dir. Respect Life Activities; Mr. EDWARD MECHEMANN, Esq., Asst. Dir., 1011 First Ave., New York, 10022. Tel: 212-371-1000 (Consult separate listing.).

Hispanic Affairs, Vicar— (Vicario, Asuntos Hispanos), Most Rev. JOSU IRIONDO, D.D.; Mr. PEDRO CALDRON, Sec., 1011 First Ave., New York, 10022. Tel: 212-371-1000, Ext. 2982.

Holy Childhood Pontifical Association—Rev. Msgr. MICHAEL CRIMMINS, Dir.; Sr. PAULINE CHURCHIRILLO, P.B.V.M., Mission Educ. Dir., 1011 First Ave., New York, 10022. Tel: 212-371-1000.

Holy Name Society Archdiocesan Union of New York—Rev. JAMES P. CONNOLLY, Dir.; Mr. ANTHONY J. MEROLLA, Exec. Sec., 1011 First Ave., New York, 10022. Tel: 212-931-9239.

Information, Bureau of and Radio-T.V. Communications— See Communications

Inner City Scholarship Fund, Inc.—1011 First Ave., New York, 10022. Tel: 212-371-1000.

Institutional Commodity Services Corporation—Mr. VINCENT HEINTZ, Gen. Mgr.; ROBERT SCHIAVI, Dept. Mgr.; NANETTE MELERA, Food Serv. Dir., 1011 First Ave., New York, 10022. Tel: 212-371-1000.

Intercultural Institute—Most Rev. JOSU IRIONDO, D.D., Dir. Tel: 212-371-1000, Ext. 2982.

Instructional T.V. Communications Center—Mr. MICHAEL LAVERY, Dir., St. Joseph's Seminary, 201 Seminary Ave., Yonkers, 10704. Tel: 914-968-7800.

Insurance Division—DANNY HOLTSCLAW, Oper. Mgr., 1011 First Ave., New York, 10022. Tel: 212-371-1000, Ext. 3024.

Inter-Parish Financing, Commission for—Rev. Msgr. DENNIS P. KEANE, Ph.D., Chm.; ROBERT J. CUDDY, Dir., 1011 First Ave., New York, 10022. Tel: 212-371-1000.

Italian Apostolate, Office of the—Rev. ROBERT AUFIERI, Dir., 1011 First Ave., New York, 10022. Tel: 212-371-1000, Ext. 3055.

Justice and Peace, Archdiocesan Office of—1011 First Ave., New York, 10022. Tel: 212-371-1000. Mr. GEORGE HORTON, Dir., 1011 First Ave., New York, 10022. Tel: 212-371-1000.

Legal Affairs, Office of—JAMES P. MCCABE, J.D., Gen. Counsel; RODERICK J. CASSIDY, J.D., Assoc. Gen. Counsel, 1011 First Ave., New York, 10022. Tel: 212-371-1000, Ext. 2440; Fax: 212-826-8795.

Language Institute— Class Schedule: Wed. 4-7 pm Cardinal Hayes High School EVELYN ZINGONE, Supvr., 1011 First Ave., New York, 10022. Tel: 212-371-1000, Ext. 2982.

Legion of Mary—Rev. GERALD MURRAY, Dir., 1011 First Ave., New York, 10022.

Light and Life Evangelization Program— (Luz y Vida) *St. Joseph's Cursillo Center, 523 W. 142nd St., New York, 10031.* Tel: 212-926-7433.

Liturgical Commission, Archdiocesan—Sr. JANET BAXENDALE, S.C., St. Joseph's Seminary, 201 Seminary Ave., Yonkers, 10704.

**The Malta Human Services Foundation, 1011 First Ave., Rm. 1350, New York, 10022.* Tel: 212-371-1522. Email: jshine@maltausa.org. Web: www.maltausa.org. Mr. JOHN SHINE, Exec. Dir. & Contact Person.

Mary Help of Christians Ev. Community—(Auxiliadora) Deacon LUIS FONTANEZ, Asst. Dir., 328 W. 14th St., New York, 10014.

Palante-Con-Cristo Evangelization and Prayer Movement—Rev. JOHN OLDFIELD, O.A.R., Spiritual Dir.; Deacons LUIS FONTANEZ, Asst. Spiritual Dir., Tagaste Monastery, Suffern, 10901. Tel: 914-357-0067; EDMUNDO RAMOS. Tel: 718-204-0816.

Pastoral Council, Archdiocesan—VACANT, Chm.; Rev. ROBERT AUFIERI, Exec. Sec.

Pastoral Life Conference—Rev. Msgr. DESMOND O'CONNOR, 1011 First Ave., New York, 10022. Tel: 212-371-1000.

Pastoral Services, Archdiocese of New York—1011 First Ave., New York, 10022. Tel: 212-371 1000.

Pension Office, Archdiocesan—Mr. ARTHUR MONTEGARI, Exec. Sec., 1011 First Ave., New York, 10022. Tel: 212-371-1000.

Permanent Diaconate Formation Program—(Programa de Formacion para Diaconos) Deacon ANTHONY CASSANETO, Dir., St. Joseph's Seminary, 201 Seminary Ave., Yonkers, 10704. Tel: 914-968-6200, Ext. 8269.

Personnel—Mrs. EILEEN F. EGAN, Dir., 1011 First Ave., New York, 10022. Tel: 212-371-1000, Ext. 2906; Fax: 212-838-0637.

Personnel Board, Archdiocesan—Rev. Msgr. DESMOND O'CONNOR, Dir., 1011 First Ave., New York, 10022. Tel: 212-371-1000.

Priests Council of the Archdiocese of New York—Rev. Msgrs. WALLACE A. HARRIS, Chm.; GREGORY MUSTACIUOLO, Sec., 1011 First Ave., New York, 10022. Tel: 212-371-1000.

Prison Apostolate—Rev. Msgr. LESLIE J. IVERS, Dir., St. Frances de Chantal, 190 Hollywood Ave., Bronx, 10465. Tel: 718-792-5500.

Propagation of the Faith, Society for the—Archdiocesan Office, Rev. Msgr. MICHAEL CRIMMINS, Archdiocesan Dir.; Sr. PAULINE CHURCHIRILLO, P.B.V.M., Mission Educ. Coord., 1011 First Ave., New York, 10022. Tel: 212-371-1000, Ext. 2700.

Propagation of the Faith, National Office—Rev. JOHN KOZAR, Natl. Dir., 366 Fifth Ave., New York, 10001. Tel: 212-563-8700. National Office,

Retirement Plan for Priests—Rev. Msgr. PATRICK J. BOYLE, Chm., 1011 First Ave., New York, 10022. Tel: 212-371-1000, Ext. 2934.

Safe Environment Program—PAUL E. WARD, Ed.D., Dir.; Ms. JENNIFER MCLAUGHLIN, Admin. Asst., 1011 First Ave., New York, 10022. Tel: 212-371-1000, Ext. 2810.

St. Joseph's Cursillo Center—Rev. FRANK PELUSO, O.A.R., Dir., 275 West 230th St., Bronx, 10463. Tel: 718-796-4340.

Schools, Superintendent of—Dr. CATHERINE HICKEY, Supt.; Ms. JENNIFER MCLAUGHLIN, Admin. Asst., 1011 First Ave., New York, 10022. Tel: 212-371-1000 (Consult separate listing.).

**Sovereign Military Hospitaller Order of Saint John of Jerusalem of Rhodes and of Malta* American Association, U.S.A. *1011 First Ave., Rm. 1350, New York, 10022.* Tel: 212-371-1522. Web: www.maltausa.org. Email: jshine@maltausa.org. Mr. JOHN SHINE, Exec. Dir. & Contact Person.

Spiritual Development, Office of—Rev. EUGENE J. FULTON, Dir., One Pryer Manor Rd., Larchmont, 10538. Tel: 914-235-6839.

Trustees of St. Patrick's Cathedral in the City of New York, Inc.—Rev. Msgr. JAMES K. VAUGHEY, Exec. Dir., Cemeteries; Mr. ANTHONY V. ROINA, Asst. Exec. Dir., Cemeteries.

Victim Assistance Coordinators—Sr. EILEEN CLIFFORD, O.P. Tel: 212-371-1000, Ext. 2949; Rev. Msgr. DESMOND O'CONNOR. Tel: 212-371-1000, Ext. 2931. Email: victimsassistance@archny.org.

CLERGY, PARISHES, MISSIONS AND PAROCHIAL SCHOOLS

NEW YORK CITY
BOROUGH OF MANHATTAN

1—CATHEDRAL OF ST. PATRICK (Old, 1809; New, 1879), Rev. Msgrs. Eugene V. Clark, P.A., Rector; John T. Ferry, Assoc. Rector; Revs. John Fraser; Jose Marabe (Philippines); J. Michael Rajendram (Sri Lanka); Deacon Edmundo Ramos.
Rectory—460 Madison Ave., 10022. Tel: 212-753-2261; Fax: 212-755-4128.
Res.: 452 Madison Ave., 10022. His Eminence Edward Cardinal Egan; Most Rev. Timothy A. McDonnell, Vicar Gen.; Rev. Msgrs. Thomas E. Gilleece, Chancellor; Gregory Mustaciuolo, Cardinal's Sec.
Chapel—New York, Sts. Faith, Hope and Charity, Records at St. Patrick Cathedral.

2—ST. AGNES (1873), Revs. Richard Adams; Matthew Farrelly, C.S.Sp.; Venant LeLonde, O.F.M.; Kasimierz A. Kowalski; William M. Shelley (Retired). In Res., Revs. William Kennedy (Retired); Octavio Ramos (Philippines).
Res.: 143 E. 43rd St., 10017. Tel: 212-682-5722; Fax: 212-370-5791.

3—ST. ALBERT (1916), Closed., Parochial records at Sacred Heart.

4—ALL SAINTS (1879), (African American), Rev. Neil J. O'Connell, O.F.M., Admin.& Campus Min. In Res., Rev. Christopher B. Keenan, O.F.M., Chap., Fire Deptartment of NY; Bros. Charles F. Gilmartin, O.F.M., Pastoral Assoc., St. Francis of Assisi Parish; Daniel P. Sulmasy, O.F.M., Physician & Charir of Bio-Medical Ethics, St. Vincent's Hospital.
Res.: 47 E. 129th St., 10035. Tel: 212-534-3535; Fax: 212-987-1930.
School— (1900), 52 E. 130th St., 10037. Tel: 212-534-0558; Fax: 212-831-6343. Anthony Georges, Prin. Lay Teachers 12; Students 262.
Catechesis/Religious Program—Students 35.

5—ST. ALOYSIUS (1899), Revs. Kenneth J. Boller, S.J.; Thomas P. Green, S.J.
Res.: 219 W. 132nd St., 10027. Tel: 212-234-2848; Fax: 212-234-6495.
School— (1940), 223 W. 132nd St., 10027. Tel: 212-283-0821; Fax: 212-234-4198. Richard Burke, Prin.; Laurel D. Senger, Pres. Priests 1; Lay Teachers 20; Students 300; Religious 3.
Catechesis/Religious Program—Students 46.

6—ST. ALPHONSUS (1847), Closed., Records at St. Anthony of Padua.

7—ST. AMBROSE (CHAPEL CENTRO MARIA) (1897), Closed., Records at Sacred Heart Church.

8—ST. ANDREW (1842), Revs. James Hayes, S.S.S.; Thomas McKeon, S.S.S., New York Infirmary Beekman Downtown Hospital. Blessed Sacrament Fathers and Brothers In Res., Rev. John Kamas, S.S.S. (CIV); Bros. Stanley Kolwaski, S.S.S.; Thomas Mello, S.S.S.; Michael Perez, S.S.S.
Res.: 20 Cardinal Hayes Pl., 10007. Tel: 212-962-3972; 212-962-3973; Fax: 212-962-1012
Catechesis/Religious Program—Tel: 212-509-8999, Ext. 213. Students 70.
Station—New York Infirmary Beekman Downtown Hospital 170 William St., 10007. Tel: 212-312-5000.
Station—St. Margaret's House 49 Fulton St., 10007. Tel: 212-766-8122.

9—ST. ANN (1911), (Spanish), Revs. Victor Muzzin, F.D.P. (Italy); Pasquale Ruggieri, F.D.P. (Italy).
Res.: 312 E. 110th St., 10029. Tel: 212-534-3856; Fax: 212-831-3395.
School— (1926), 314-318 E. 110th St., 10029. Tel: 212-722-1295. Sr. Josephine Cioffi, Prin. Priests 2; Sisters, Servants of the Immaculate Heart of Mary 1; Lay Teachers 12; Students 320.
Catechesis/Religious Program—Students 95.
Chapel—St. Ann's Convent 319 E. 109 St., 10029. Tel: 212-534-8321.

10—ST. ANN'S ARMENIAN CATHOLIC CATHEDRAL (1983), (Armenian), Most Rev. Manuel Batakian; Rev. Antoine Noradounghian.
Res.: 110 E. 12th St., 10003. Tel: 212-477-2030; Fax: 212-477-2185.

11—ST. ANN'S ROMAN CATHOLIC CHURCH (1852), Rev. Joy Mampilly, Admin.
110 E. 12th St., 10003. Administered from Immaculate Conception Church.

12—ANNUNCIATION (1853), Revs. Felix Jimenez, Sch.P. (Spain); Jose M. Clavero, Sch.P. (Spain); Felix Ganuza, Sch.P. (Spain).
Res.: 88 Convent Ave., 10027. Tel: 212-234-1919; Fax: 212-281-7205.
School— (1858), 461 W. 131st St., 10027. Tel: 212-281-7174; Fax: 212-281-1732. David Smithers, Prin. Lay Teachers 13; Students 240.
Catechesis/Religious Program—Students 246.

13—ST. ANTHONY OF PADUA (Org. 1859; Re-org. 1866), (Italian), Revs. Simeon C. Distefano, O.F.M.; Rashid Peter Francis, O.F.M.; Bro. Dominic Poirier, O.F.M.
Res. & Chapel: 154 Sullivan St., 10012. Tel: 212-777-2755; Fax: 212-673-6684.
School— (1874), 60 MacDougal St., 10012. Tel: 212-477-1297; Fax: 212-529-2018. Franciscan Sisters of Allegany 2; Lay Teachers 9; Students 170.
Catechesis/Religious Program—Tel: 212-477-5792. Sisters Eileen Lambert, O.S.F., D.R.E.; Annette Seiter, O.S.F., D.R.E. Students 30.

14—ASCENSION (1895), (Hispanic), Revs. John P. Duffell; Sixto Quezada (Dominican Republic); Sean McCaughley (Ireland); Deacon Constancio Soto.
Res.: 221 W. 107th St., 10025. Tel: 212-222-0666; Fax: 212-961-1086.
School— (1912), 220 W. 108th St., 10025. Tel: 212-222-5161; Fax: 212-280-4690. Lay Teachers 13; Students 281.
Catechesis/Religious Program—Tel: 212-749-5938; Fax: 212-749-8658. Students 450.
Chapel—C.Y.O. Grace Ministry 218 W. 108th St., 10025. Tel: 212-666-6598.
Chapel—Riverside Study Center 330 Riverside Dr., 10025. Tel: 212-222-3285; Fax: 212-316-3629. (Opus Dei)

15—ASSUMPTION (1858), Closed., Records at Sacred Heart Church.

16—ST. BENEDICT THE MOOR (1883), (Spanish), Attended by, Sacred Heart of Jesus, New York Rev. Msgr. Joachim B. Beaumont, Admin.
Res.: 457 W. 51st St., 10019. Tel: 212-265-5020; Fax: 212-977-4116.

17—ST. BERNARD (1868), Rev. Kevin J. Nelan.
Res.: 328 W. 14th St., 10014. Tel: 212-243-0265; Fax: 212-255-8466.
School— (1916), 327 W. 13th St., 10014. Tel: 212-243-6368.
Catechesis/Religious Program—Students 46.

18—BLESSED SACRAMENT (1887), Revs. Robert B. O'Connor; Alfredo Balinong, S.J. (Philippines); Rev. Msgr. William J. Toohy; Rev. Alexis Bastidas (Venezuela).
Res.: 152 W. 71st St., 10023. Tel: 212-877-3111; Fax: 212-799-6233.
School— (1902), 147-152 W. 70th St., 10023. Tel: 212-724-7561; Fax: 212-724-7561. Elmeda Engel, Prin. Lay Teachers 11; Students 276.
Catechesis/Religious Program—Students 156.
Chapel—Convent of Blessed Sacrament 133 W. 70th St., 10023. Tel: 212-877-8076.
Chapel—St. Agnes' Home 237 W. 74th St., 10023. Tel: 212-874-9203.
Chapel—Archdiocese Teachers Residence 22 W. 70th St., 10023.

19—ST. BONIFACE (1858), Closed., Records at Holy Family Church.

20—ST. BRIGID (1848; 1955), Revs. Michael J. Conway, O.SS.T., Admin.; Joseph C. Gidaro, O.SS.T.; Deacon Rafael Bello. In Res., Rev. Aaron M. Dowdell, O.SS.T.
Res.: 119 Avenue B, 10009. Tel: 212-228-5400; Fax: 212-254-0334.
School—185 E. Seventh St., 10009. Tel: 212-677-5210; Fax: 212-260-2262. Sisters 1; Lay Teachers 15; Students 215.
Catechesis/Religious Program—Students 125.

21—ST. CATHERINE OF GENOA (1887), Rev. David E. Nolan.
Res.: 506 W. 153rd St., 10031. Tel: 212-862-6130; Fax: 212-491-6272.
School— (1910), 508-510 W. 153rd St., 10031. Tel: 212-926-0252. Lay Teachers 10; Students 330.
Catechesis/Religious Program—Students 460.

22—ST. CATHERINE OF SIENA (1897), Very Rev. Edmund M. Gorman, O.P., Prior; Revs. Robert Philip Fitzsimmons, O.P.; John Thaddeus Murphy, O.P.; Carl Louis Mason, O.P. (L); Stephen Francis Carmody, O.P.; C. Antoninus Niemiec, O.P.; Carlos-Bartolome Quijano, O.P.; Sr. Margaret Oettinger, O.P., Hospital Chap.
Res.: 411 E. 68th St., 10021. Tel: 212-988-8300; Fax: 212-988-6918.

23—ST. CECILIA (1873), Revs. Francis G. Skelly, C.SS.R.; William Jacob, C.SS.R.; John K. Graham, C.SS.R.; Karl Krauser, C.SS.R.; Senen Javier, C.SS.R.; Blas Caceres, C.SS.R.; Leo Armada, C.SS.R.; Bro. Francis Alfone, C.SS.R. Sisters of the Atonement
Res.: 125 E. 105th St., 10029. Tel: 212-534-1350; Fax: 212-410-6177.
School—Day Nursery, 118 E. 106 St., 10029. Tel: 212-534-8423; Fax: 212-534-5757.
Catechesis/Religious Program—Tel: 212-534-8423. Students 200.

24—ST. CHARLES BORROMEO (1888), (African American), Rev. Msgr. Wallace A. Harris.
Res.: 211 W. 141st St., 10030. Tel: 212-281-2100; Fax: 212-862-1881.
School— (1904), 214 W. 142 St., 10030. Tel: 212-368-6666; Fax: 212-281-1323. Sr. Marianne Poole, S.B.S., Prin. Sisters of the Blessed Sacrament 3; Lay Teachers 18; Students 520.
Catechesis/Religious Program—Students 61.

25—THE CHURCH OF ST. GABRIEL (1867), Closed., Records at Church of Sacred Hearts of Jesus and Mary.

26—ST. CLARE (1903), Closed., Records at St. Raphael's Church.

27—ST. CLEMENS MARY (1909), Closed., Records at Holy Cross Church, Manhattan.

28—ST. COLUMBA (1845), Rev. Frank Scanlon, Admin. In Res., Rev. Joseph Hien.
Res.: 343 W. 25th St., 10001. Tel: 212-807-8876.
School— (1847), 331-333 W. 25th St., 10001. Sisters of Congregation of Notre Dame 2; Lay Teachers 9; Students 243.
Chapel—Sisters of Congregation of Notre Dame 329 W. 25th St., 10001.

29—CORPUS CHRISTI (1906), Rev. Raymond M. Rafferty; Rev. Msgr. Myles M. Bourke, Pastor Emeritus (Retired). In Res., Rev. Msgr. Kevin L. Sullivan; Rev. Randall Renter, C.S.C.
Res.: 529 W. 121st St., 10027. Tel: 212-666-9350; Fax: 212-531-2487.
School— (1907), 535 W. 121st St., 10027. Tel: 212-662-9344; Fax: 212-662-2725. Sr. Mary Tyler, O.P., Prin. Lay Teachers 11; Students 224.
Catechesis/Religious Program—Students 35.

30—ST. CYRIL (1916), (Slovenian), Rev. Krizolog Cimerman, O.F.M.
Res.: 62 St. Mark's Pl., 10003. Tel: 212-674-3442; Fax: 212-674-3442.

31—SS. CYRIL AND METHODIUS - ST. RAPHAEL (1913; 1886), (Croatian), Revs. Ivica Majstorovic, O.F.M.; Ante Bekavac.
Res.: 502 W. 41st St., 10036. Tel: 212-563-3395; Fax: 212-868-1203.

32—ST. ELIZABETH (1869), Rev. Msgr. Gerald T. Walsh; Revs. Jose Serrano; Luis Saldana.
Res.: 268 Wadsworth Ave., 10033. Tel: 212-568-8803; Fax: 212-781-2754.
School— (1936), 612 W. 187th St., 10033. Tel: 212-568-7291; Fax: 212-928-2515. Sisters 3; Lay Teachers 18; Students 525.
Catechesis/Religious Program—Tel: 212-923-4900. Students 426.
Chapel—Sisters Residence 612 W. 187th St., 10033.
Chapel—Cabrini Chapel 701 Ft. Washington Ave., 10040. Tel: 212-923-3536; Fax: 212-923-1871.
Isabella Geriatric Center—515 Audubon Ave., 10040. Tel: 212-342-9245.

33—ST. ELIZABETH OF HUNGARY (1891), (Slovak),, Ministry for deaf persons. Rev. Msgr. Patrick P. McCahill.
Res.: 211 E. 83rd St., 10028-2854. Tel: 212-734-5747; 212-988-1903 (TTY); Fax: 212-988-1903.
Catechesis/Religious Program—Students 28.

34—ST. EMERIC (1949), Rev. Msgr. Joachim B. Beaumont.
Res.: 185 Avenue D, 10009. Tel: 212-228-4494; Fax: 212-375-1163.
Catechesis/Religious Program—Students 306.

35—EPIPHANY (1868), (Irish), Rev. Msgrs. Walter J. Niebrzydowski; George J. Cascelli; Rev. Paul Baffuor-Awuah; Sisters Doris Sayhonne, R.C.D., Pastoral Assoc.; Christine Gates, R.G.S., Social Worker.
141 E. 28th St., 10016. Tel: 212-473-4496; Fax: 212-473-4537.
Res.: 239 E. 21st St., 10010. Tel: 212-475-1966; Fax: 212-477-0537.
School— (1869), 234 E. 22nd St., 10010. Tel: 212-473-4128; Fax: 212-473-4392. Sisters 1; Lay Teachers 35; Students 550.
Catechesis/Religious Program—Students 112.

36—ST. FRANCES XAVIER CABRINI (1973), Rev. Peter A. Miqueli.
Res.: 555 Main St., Roosevelt Island, 10044. Tel: 212-832-6778 (office).
Catechesis/Religious Program—Students 75.

37—ST. FRANCIS DE SALES (1894), Rev. Msgr. Oscar Aquino, J.C.D.; Rev. Charles Murr; William Ramos, Pastoral Assoc.
Res.: 135 A E. 96th St., 10128. Tel: 212-289-0425; Fax: 212-996-2028.
School—St. Francis de Sales & St. Lucy Academy (1993), 116-120 E. 97th St. & 340 E. 104th St., 10029. Tel: 212-289-0680; 212-534-4021; Fax: 212-534-4130. Bro. Terence M. Connolly, C.F.C., Prin. Congregation of Christian Brothers 3; Lay Teachers 31; Students 651.
Catechesis/Religious Program—Students 651.

38—ST. FRANCIS OF ASSISI (1844), (Franciscan), Rev. Peter Brophy, O.F.M., Guardian & Pastor; Bro. Thomas Cole, O.F.M. (For priests and brothers not listed here, see St. Francis Monastery under Monasteries and Residences of Priests and Brothers.) In Res., Revs. Alcuin Coyle, O.F.M.; John M. Felice, O.F.M.; Brennan Fitzgerald, O.F.M.; Benjamin J. Foerch, O.F.M.; Robert A. Gavin, O.F.M.; Bro. Charles F. Gilmartin, O.F.M.; Revs. Vincent B. Grogan, O.F.M., J.C.D.; Joseph M. Hertel, O.F.M.; Brian Jordan, O.F.M.; Joseph Juracek, O.F.M.; Francis Kim, O.F.M.; Vincent A. Laviano, O.F.M.; Miguel A. Loredo, O.F.M.; Bro. William Mann, O.F.M.; Revs. Michael McDonnell, O.F.M.; Felix P. McGrath, O.F.M.; Cassian Miles, O.F.M.; Bro. Timothy Miskowski, O.F.M.; Revs. John J. McVean, O.F.M.; James R. O'Connell, O.F.M.; Timothy J. Shreenan, O.F.M.; Bros. Daniel P. Sulmasy, O.F.M.; Sebastian Tobin, O.F.M.; Revs. Kevin Tortorelli, O.F.M.; Lambert F. Valentine, O.F.M.; Allan G. Von Kobs, O.F.M.; Rayner F. Williams, O.F.M.; Dennis M. Wilson, O.F.M.
Res.: 135 W. 31st St., 10001. Tel: 212-736-8500; Fax: 212-736-8545.

39—ST. FRANCIS XAVIER (1847), Rev. Edward J. Coughlin, S.J.; Mr. Thomas Kocherry, Business Mgr.; Ms. Lesley Ann Woo, Pastoral Assoc.
Office—55 W. 15th St., 10011. Tel: 212-627-2100; Fax: 212-675-6997.

40—GOOD SHEPHERD (1912), (Dominican—Irish), Revs. Marcos Zamora, C.S.P.; Lionel A. de Silva, C.S.P.; Kevin A. Devine, C.S.P.; Sr. Acela Rodriguez, H.C.C.S.; Deacon Rafael Then. In Res., Rev. Lawrence E. Boadt, C.S.P.
Res.: 608 Isham St., 10034. Tel: 212-567-1300; Fax: 212-567-1476.
School— (1925), Cooper St. & Isham St., 10034. Tel: 212-567-5800; Fax: 212-567-5839. Sisters of Mercy of the Union 3; Lay Teachers 29; Students 600.
Catechesis/Religious Program—Students 275.
Chapel—Convent of Sisters of Mercy 630 Isham St., 10034. Tel: 212-567-1600. (Private)

41—ST. GREGORY (1907), Revs. Joseph Darbouze; Donald C. Baker.
Res.: 144 W. 90th St., 10024. Tel: 212-724-9766; 212-724-9767; Fax: 212-579-3380.
School— (1913), 138 W. 90th St., 10024. Tel: 212-362-5410; Fax: 212-362-5062. Ms. Deborah Hurd, Prin. Lay Teachers 9; Students 254.
Catechesis/Religious Program—Students 254.

42—GUARDIAN ANGEL (1888), Rev. Richard Carbo, Admin. In Res., Revs. Philip Phan; Abraham Lotha (India).
Res.: 193 Tenth Ave., 10011. Tel: 212-929-5966.
School— (1911),Tel: 212-989-8280. Maureen McElduff, Prin. Sisters of St. Dominic 1; Lay Teachers 9; Students 260.
Chapel—Sisters of St. Dominic & Franciscan Sisters 407 W. 21st St., 10011. Tel: 212-243-2266.

43—ST. HEDWIG (1934), Closed., Parochial records at St. Stanislaus Church.

44—HOLY AGONY (1930), (Spanish), Revs. Victor Elia, C.M.; Candido Arrizurieta, C.M.; Venancio Goyeneche, C.M.
Res.: 1834 Third Ave., 10029. Tel: 212-289-5589; Fax: 212-289-8321.

45—HOLY CROSS (1852), Revs. Peter M. Colapietro; Thomas Del Valle; Deacon Lawrence C. McNeill; Mr. Edward Green, LAMP Min.
Res.: 329 W. 42nd St., 10036. Tel: 212-246-4732; Fax: 212-307-5033.
School— (1864), 332 W. 43rd St., 10036. Tel: 212-246-0923; Fax: 212-246-0923. Sr. Mary Theresa Dixon, O.P., Prin. Sisters of St. Dominic of Blauvelt 1; Lay Teachers 16; Students 400.
Convent—Dominican Convent, 460 W. 44th St., 10036. Tel: 212-246-9768.
Chapel—St. Joseph's Home 425 W. 44th St., 10036. Tel: 212-246-5363.

46—HOLY FAMILY (1924), Revs. Robert J. Robbins; George Perera, O.M.I.; Emile Frische, M.H.M.
Res.: 315 E. 47th St., 10017-2318. Tel: 212-753-3401; Fax: 212-753-3428. Email: churchhf@aol.com.
Catechesis/Religious Program—Students 15.

47—HOLY INNOCENTS (1866), Rev. Msgr. Donald Sakano; Rev. William J. Delaney.
Res.: 128 W. 37th St., 10018. Tel: 212-279-5861; Fax: 212-714-9313.

48—HOLY NAME OF JESUS (1868), Revs. Jerome Massimino, O.F.M.; Michael Tyson, O.F.M.; Richard Trezza, O.F.M.; Hugh Hines, O.F.M. In Res., Rev. Francis J. DiSpigno, O.F.M.; Bro. Francis Edward Coughlin, O.F.M.
Res.: 207 W. 96th St., 10025. Tel: 212-749-0276; Fax: 212-749-2045.
School— (1905), Amsterdam Ave. & 97th St., 10025. Tel: 212-749-1240; Fax: 212-663-1939. Bro. Richard Grieco, F.S.C., Prin. Brothers 2; Lay Teachers 20; Students 620.
Catechesis/Religious Program—Tel: 212-749-0276, Ext. 250. Students 180.

49—HOLY ROSARY (1884), (Augustinian), Revs. Angel Dulanto, O.S.A.; Abel Alvarez, O.S.A.
Res.: 444 E. 119th St., 10035. Tel: 212-534-0740; Fax: 212-534-7572.
School— (1949), 371 Pleasant Ave., 10035. Tel: 212-876-7555; Fax: 212-876-0152. Lay Teachers 10; Students 226.
Catechesis/Religious Program—Students 40.

50—HOLY TRINITY (1898), Rev. Msgr. Thomas P. Leonard; Revs. Kenneth J. Smith; Andrew M. O'Connor. In Res., Rev. William R. Dailey, C.S.C.
Res.: 213 W. 82nd St., 10024. Tel: 212-787-0634; Fax: 212-787-4917.
Catechesis/Religious Program—Students 115.
Chapel—Chinese Catholic Information Center 86 Riverside Dr., 10024. Tel: 212-787-6969; Fax: 212-787-0351.

51—ST. IGNATIUS LOYOLA (1851), Revs. Walter F. Modrys, S.J.; William J. Bergen, S.J.; Mark C. Hallinan, S.J.; Joseph T. Browne, S.J.; Ms. Joanne F. Cunneen, M.A., M.S., Pastoral Assoc.; Ms. Mary Naughton, M.A., Pastoral Assoc.
Res.: 980 Park Ave., 10028. Tel: 212-288-3588; Fax: 212-734-3671.
School— (1854), 50 E. 84th St., 10028. Tel: 212-861-3820; Fax: 212-879-8248. Lay Teachers 21; Students 567.
School—Day Nursery, 240 E. 84th St., 10028. Tel: 212-734-6427; Fax: 212-734-6972. Lay Assistants 15; Capacity 107.
Catechesis/Religious Program—Tel: 212-861-4764. Ms. Joanne Cunneen, M.A., D.R.E. Students 525.
High School—Regis High School, 55 E. 84th St., 10028. Tel: 212-288-1100; Fax: 212-794-1221.
School—Loyola School, Tel: 212-288-3522; Fax: 212-861-1021.
School—Marymount School, 1028 Fifth Ave., 10028.

Tel: 212-744-4486; Fax: 212-744-0163.

52—IMMACULATE CONCEPTION (1855), Revs. Joy Mampilly; Francis X. Buu; Richard J. Neuhaus; Misael Bacleon (Philippines). In Res., Rev. Msgr. Desmond J. Vella, J.C.D., S.T.L., M.S.; Revs. Edwin J. Conlin; John J. Delaney, J.D.; John P. Moore.
Res.: 414 E. 14th St., 10009. Tel: 212-254-0200; Fax: 212-505-7610.
School— (1864), 419 E. 13th St., 10009. Tel: 212-475-2590; Fax: 212-777-2818. Sisters 1; Lay Teachers 14; Students 360.
Catechesis/Religious Program—Students 95.

53—INCARNATION (1908), (Hispanic), Revs. Gabriel La Paz; Felino Reyes Nin; Antonio Almonte; Aroldo Guerra; Evaristus Ohuche.
Res.: 1290 St. Nicholas Ave., 10033. Tel: 212-927-7474; Fax: 212-928-0315.
School— (1910), 568-570 W. 175th St., 10033. Tel: 212-795-1030; Fax: 212-795-1564. Lay Teachers 22; Students 596.
Catechesis/Religious Program—Maria Minaya, D.R.E. Students 709.

54—ST. JAMES (1827), Revs. Robert J. Poveromo; Jesus P. Enojo; Joseph Chao.
Res.: 23 Oliver St., 10038. Tel: 212-233-0161.
School— (1854), 37 St. James Place, 10038. Tel: 212-267-9289. Sr. Josefa Marie Curcio, C.S.J.B., Prin. Sisters of St. John the Baptist 4; Lay Teachers 8; Students 210.
Chapel—St. James Convent 21 Oliver St., 10038. Tel: 212-962-0840.

55—ST. JEAN BAPTISTE (1882), Revs. Anthony Schueller, S.S.S.; Ernest R. Falardeau, S.S.S., Supr.; Bernard J. Camire, S.S.S., Lenox Hill Chaplaincy; Deacon Richard Russo, Pastoral Assoc. In Res., Revs. Eugene LaVerdiere, S.S.S.; Thomas McKeon, S.S.S.; Rt. Rev. Leo M. Ryska, O.S.B.
Res.: 184 E. 76th St., 10021. Tel: 212-288-5082; Fax: 212-717-8397.
High School—173 E. 75th St., 10021. Tel: 212-288-1645; Fax: 212-288-6540. Sisters of the Congregation of Notre Dame 3; Lay Teachers 36; Students 385.
Catechesis/Religious Program—Tel: 212-472-2853, Ext. 6; Fax: 212-717-8397. Students 25.
Chapel—Sisters' Convent, Tel: 212-472-1230 (Apt. A); 212-472-8821 (Apt. B); Fax: 212-396-2025.

56—ST. JOACHIM (1888), (Italian), Closed., Parochial records are at Church of St. Joseph.

57—ST. JOHN NEPOMUCENE (1895), (Slovak), Rev. Martin Svitan.
Res.: 411 E. 66th St., 10021. Tel: 212-734-4613; 212-734-4370; Fax: 212-734-2483.
Chapel—Sisters' Convent 320 E. 66th St., 10021. Tel: 212-734-6640; Fax: 212-734-2483.

58—ST. JOHN THE BAPTIST (1840), (German),, (Capuchin-Franciscan Friars) Revs. Bernard M. Maloney, O.F.M.Cap., Guardian & Pastor; James Gavin, O.F.M.Cap.; Gavin Reilly, O.F.M.Cap.; Bros. Salvatore Patricoia, O.F.M.Cap.; Luke Benbrook, O.F.M.Cap., Pastoral Assoc. In Res., Revs. John Clermont, O.F.M.Cap., Part-time Honduras, CA; Armand Dasseville, O.F.M.Cap. (Retired); Andrew Drew, O.F.M.Cap. (Retired); Francis Gasparik, O.F.M.Cap., Dir. Office of Mission & Devel.; Leonard Glavin, O.F.M.Cap. (Retired); Thomas Houle, O.F.M.Cap., Chap.; Bro. George McCloskey, O.F.M.Cap., Dir. Communications; Rev. Matthias Wesnofske, O.F.M.Cap., Spiritual Asst. of Secular Order of St. Francis.
Res.: 210 W. 31st St., 10001-2876. Tel: 212-564-9070; Fax: 212-564-3964.

59—ST. JOHN THE EVANGELIST (1840), [CEM] Most Rev. Robert A. Brucato, D.D., V.G.; Revs. James P. Connolly; Robert Aufieri; Rev. Msgr. George A. Kelly (Retired); Rev. Bernal Stainwall.
Res.: 348 E. 55th St., 10022. Tel: 212-753-8418; Fax: 212-826-1848.

60—ST. JOHN THE MARTYR (1903), Rev. Msgr. John G. Woolsey; Rev. Joseph W. Baker. In Res., Rev. Msgr. Desmond O'Connor.
Res.: 259 E. 71st St., 10021-4596. Tel: 212-744-4880; 212-744-4881; Fax: 212-628-6662.
Catechesis/Religious Program— Regional. See St. Ignatius Loyola, New York.

61—ST. JOSEPH (1829), Revs. Aldo J. Tos; Owen J. Lafferty; Sr. Anne Tahaney, O.P., Pastoral Assoc.; Deacon Thomas Johnson; Alvin Donius, Parish Mgr. In Res., Rev. Michael C. Crimmins.
Res.: 371 Sixth Ave., 10014. Tel: 212-741-1274; Fax: 212-741-2147.
School—111 Washington Pl., 10014. Tel: 212-929-5134; Fax: 212-929-5105. Lay Teachers 10; Students 132.
Catechesis/Religious Program—Patricia Flanagan, D.R.E. Students 25.

62—ST. JOSEPH (1924), (Italian—Chinese), Revs. Lydio F. Tomasi, C.S.; Paul Dao (China), (Chinese Apostolate).
Res.: 5 Monroe St., 10002. Tel: 212-267-8376; Fax: 212-267-4357.
School— (1926), One Monroe St., 10002. Tel: 212-233-5152. Apostles of the Sacred Heart of Jesus 4; Lay Teachers 11; Students 235.
Catechesis/Religious Program—Students 1[illegible].
Convent—83 Madison St., 10002. Tel: 212-233-5670. Apostles of the Sacred Heart of Jesus 4.

63—ST. JOSEPH (1873), (German), Rev. Msgr. Lawrence M. Connaughton; Revs. Emmanuel Nartey; Matthew Yatkauskas.
Res.: 404 E. 87th St., 10128. Tel: 212-289-6030; Fax: 212-348-8075.
School— (1880), 420 E. 87th St., 10128. Tel: 212-289-3057; Fax: 212-289-7239. Sisters 1; Lay Teachers 13; Students 271.
Catechesis/Religious Program—Tel: 212-861-4764; Fax: 212-734-3671. Regional. See St. Ignatius Loyola, New York. Students 14.

64—ST. JOSEPH OF THE HOLY FAMILY (1860), Revs. Philip J. Kelly, Admin.; Victor Emuwen; Jose L. Mesa, S.J. (Dominican Republic) (STA); Deacon Domingo Lopez.
Res.: 405 W. 125th St., 10027. Tel: 212-662-9125.
School— (1862), 168 Morningside Ave., 10027. Tel: 212-662-1736; Fax: 212-662-1490. Daughters of Charity of St. Vincent de Paul 4; Lay Teachers 7; Students 250.
Catechesis/Religious Program—Students 170.
Convent—4[illegible]0 W. 126th St., 10027. Tel: 212-678-0585.

65—ST. JUDE (1949), (Spanish), Revs. Elias Isla; Rodrigo Ortega; Deacon Porfirio Rodriguez.
Res.: 431 W. 204th St., 10034. Tel: 212-569-3000; Fax: 212-304-4545.
School— (1953), 433 W. 204th St., 10034. Tel: 212-569-3400; Fax: 212-304-4479. Lay Teachers 16; Students 400.
Catechesis/Religious Program—Tel: 212-569-3002. Students 5[illegible]0.
Chapel—New York, St. Jude Convent

66—ST. LEO (1880), Closed., Parochial records at St. Stephen's Church.

67—ST. LUCY (1900), (Hispanic), William Rivera, Pastoral Assoc.; Revs. Esviardo Palomino, Pastor Emeritus; Charles Murr, Admin.
Res.: 344 E. 104th St., 10029. Tel: 212-534-1470.
School— (1942), 340 E. 104th St., 10029. Tel: 212-534-4021; Fax: 212-354-4130. Bro. Paul Beaudin, C.F.C., Prin. Consolidated with St. Francis de Sales School to form St. Francis de Sales-St. Lucy Academy (1993).

68—ST. MALACHY'S (1902),, (The Actors' Chapel) Revs. Ern[illegible] Diaz; Joseph A. Kelly, S.J.; Joy Paswa, Parish Mgr.
Res.: 239 W. 49th St., 10019. Tel: 212-489-1340; Fax: 212-262-6224.
Encore Community Services—Tel: 212-581-2910; Fax: 212-757-0244. Sisters Elizabeth Hasselt, O.P., Exec. Dir.; Bernadette Gayor, S.H.C.J., Finance Dir.
Encore Community Center & Programs—Tel: 212-581-2910. Sr. Lillian McNamara, O.P., Dir.
Encore 49 Residence—Tel: 212-246-0880; 212-581-3490 (Social Svc.); Fax: 212-541-7697.
Catechesis/Religious Program—Students 8.

69—ST. MARK THE EVANGELIST (1907), (African American), Revs. Thomas P. Tunney, C.S.Sp.; Freddy Washington, C.S.Sp.
Res.: 65 W. 138th St., 10037. Tel: 212-281-4931; Fax: 212-491-6803.
School— (1912), 55 W. 138th St., 10037. Tel: 212-283-4848; Fax: 212-926-0419. Sr. Catherine Hagan, D.C., Prin. Daughters of Charity of St. Vincent de Paul 1; Lay Teachers 14; Students 258.
Catechesis/Religious Program—Students 33.
Chapel—St. Mark's Convent, Tel: 212-283-4966.

70—ST. MARY (1826), Rev. Msgr. Neil A. Connolly; Revs. Robert J. O'Neil, M.H.M.; Peter Ma, (Chinese Apostolate), (Retired).
Res.: 28 Attorney St., 10002. Tel: 212-674-3266; Fax: 212-539-0216.
Catechesis/Religious Program—Students 310.

71—MARY HELP OF CHRISTIANS (1908), (Spanish), Revs. John P. Blanco, S.D.B.; Frank Santana. In Res., Very Rev. James Heuser, S.D.B.; Bro. Gerald Warner, S.D.B.
Res.: 440 E. 12th St., 10009. Tel: 212-254-0058; Fax: 212-505-3769.
School—435-437 E. 11th St., 10009. Tel: 212-254-3596; Fax: 212-505-5037. Daughters of Mary Help of Christians 4; Lay Teachers 11; Students 210.
Catechesis/Religious Program—Students 198.
Convent—429 E. 12 St., 10009. Tel: 212-254-2537.

72—ST. MARY MAGDALEN (1873), (German), Closed., Parochial records at Immaculate Conception Church.

73—ST. MATTHEW (1902), Closed., Parochial records at Blessed Sacrament Church.

74—ST. MICHAEL (1857), Rev. Msgr. Marc A. Filacchione. In Res., Rev. Msgr. James Reinert; Rev. Robert Aufieri.
Res.: 424 W. 34th St., 10001. Tel: 212-563-2575; Fax: 212-563-4087.
High School— (1866-1874), 425 W. 33rd St., 10001. Tel: 212-563-2547. Sr. Kathleen Cusak, P.B.V.M., Prin. Sisters of the Presentation 7; Lay Teachers 28; Girls 425.
Catechesis/Religious Program—Students 420.
Chapel—Sacred Heart 419 W. 33rd St., 10001. Tel: 212-947-7668.

75—ST. MICHAEL CHAPEL (1936), (Russian), Rev. Juan Soles; Deacon Christopher LiGreci.
Res.: 266 Mulberry St., 10012. Tel: 212-226-2644; Fax: 718-788-9144.
Catechesis/Religious Program—Students 11.

76—ST. MONICA (1879), Rev. Msgr. Thomas A. Modugno; Revs. Joseph A. Francis, O.P.; Thomas M. Mulvanerty. In Res., Rev. Francis Abaya; Deacon Victor Taylor.
Res.: 413 E. 79th St., 10021. Tel: 212-288-6250; Fax: 212-570-1562.
Chapel—St. Monica Convent 404 E. 80th St., 10021. Tel: 212-288-1986.

77—MOST HOLY CRUCIFIX (1925), (Italian), Rev. Thomas Kallumady.
Res.: 378 Broome St., 10013. Tel: 212-226-2556.

78—MOST HOLY REDEEMER (1844), Revs. Lenin Delgado; Jerome Holland, C.SS.R.; Arthur G. Wendel, C.SS.R.
Res.: 173 E. Third St., 10009. Tel: 212-673-4224; Fax: 212-472-4097.
Catechesis/Religious Program—Students 162.

79—MOST PRECIOUS BLOOD (1891), (Italian), [CEM] Rev. Fabian Grifone, O.F.M.
Res.: 109 Mulberry St., 10013. Tel: 212-226-6427; Fax: 212-226-1837.

80—NATIVITY (1842), (Hispanic),, (Jesuit) Rev. Donald C. Gannon, S.J. In Res., Revs. Michael J. Lynch, S.J.; George M. Anderson, S.J.; Robert E. Reiser, S.J.; Vincent P. De Cola, S.J.; Bro. Christopher Derby, S.J., Supr.; Andrzej Kowalski, S.J., Supr.
Res.: 44 Second Ave., 10003. Tel: 212-674-8590; Fax: 212-674-8789.
Nativity Mission Center—204 Forsyth St., 10002. Tel: 212-477-2472; Fax: 212-473-0538.
Catechesis/Religious Program—Students 50.

81—ST. NICHOLAS (1833), (German), Closed., Parochial records at Most Holy Redeemer Church.

82—NOTRE DAME (1910), Revs. Andrzej J. Fornal, O.P.; Jacek Buda, O.P., Vicar; Lukasz Kubiak, O.P., Vicar.
Res.: 405 W. 114th St., 10025. Tel: 212-866-1500; Fax: 212-222-5704.
Catechesis/Religious Program—Students 12.
St. Luke's Hospital Amsterdam House—Tel: 212-523-2017.
Amsterdam Nursing Home—Tel: 212-678-2600.

83—OUR LADY OF ESPERANZA (1912), (Spanish), Rev. Msgr. Peter C. O'Donnell.
Res.: 624 W. 156th St., 10032. Tel: 212-283-4340; Fax: 212-283-4388.
Catechesis/Religious Program—Students 350.

84—OUR LADY OF GOOD COUNSEL (1886), Rev. Msgr. Dennis P. Keane, Ph.D.; Revs. Arthur Leone; Richard Terga.
Res.: 230 E. 90th St., 10128. Tel: 212-289-1742; Fax: 212-427-5643.
School— (1904), 323-329 E. 91st St., 10128. Tel: 212-289-6730. Mr. Donald Kramer, Prin. Lay Teachers 10; Students 230.

85—OUR LADY OF GRACE (Stanton St.) (1907), Closed., Parochial records at Church of the Nativity.

86—OUR LADY OF GUADALUPE (1902), (Spanish), Revs. Kevin Nelan; J. Oscar Munoz; Salvatore Sportino; Deacon Rene Garcia.
Res.: 328 W. 14th St., 10014. Tel: 212-243-0265; Fax: 212-255-8466.
Catechesis/Religious Program—Tel: 202-242-8224. Students 112.

87—OUR LADY OF LORETO (1891), (Sicilian), Rev. Msgr. John B. Ahern.
Res.: 309 Elizabeth St., 10012. Tel: 212-431-9840; Fax: 212-625-9096.
Holy Name Centre for Homeless Men—Tel: 212-226-5848.

88—OUR LADY OF LOURDES (1901), Revs. Joseph J. Tyrrell, Parish Admin.; Millard S. Cook; Deacon Pedro O'Brien. In Res., Rev. Lawrence E. Lucas.
. Tel: 212-862-4380, Ext. 10; Fax: 212-862-4126.
School— (1903), 462-468 W. 143rd St., 10031. Tel: 212-926-5820, Ext. 11; Fax: 212-491-6034. Cathy M. Hufnagel, Prin. Lay Teachers 23; Students 200.
Catechesis/Religious Program—Tel: 212-862-4380, Ext. 10; Fax: 212-862-4126. Students 250.
Chapel—Convent of Our Lady of Lourdes 463 W. 142nd St., 10031. Tel: 212-926-1150; Fax: 212-862-4126.

89—OUR LADY OF MT. CARMEL (1884), (Italian), Revs. Peter J. Rofrano, S.A.C.; Severino Dominicis, S.A.C.; Anthony Kelly, S.A.C.; Girolamo D'Ambrosi, S.A.C.; Chris Salvatori, S.A.C.
Res.: 448 E. 116th St., 10029-0614. Tel: 212-534-0681; Fax: 212-534-0629.
School—Mt. Carmel-Holy Rosary, 371 Pleasant

Ave., 10035. Tel: 212-876-7555; Fax: 212-876-0152. Sisters 1; Lay Teachers 10; Students 180.
Catechesis/Religious Program—Students 300.
Convent—456 E. 116th St., 10029-0614. Tel: 212-427-2381. Sisters of Charity 8.

90—OUR LADY OF PEACE (1918), (Italian), Rev. Bartholomew Daly, M.H.M., Admin. In Res., Rev. Paul A. Keenan.
Res.: 237 E. 62nd St., 10021. Tel: 212-838-3189; Fax: 212-308-4819.
Catechesis/Religious Program—Students 20.

91—OUR LADY OF PERPETUAL HELP (1887), Closed., Sacramental records at Our Lady of Peace.

92—OUR LADY OF POMPEII (1892), (Italian), Revs. Joseph A. Cogo, C.S.; Bernabe Sison (Philippines); Bro. Michael La Mantia, C.S. In Res., Rev. Ruben Camayo (Philippines).
Res.: 25 Carmine St., 10014. Tel: 212-989-6805; Fax: 212-727-3139.
School— (1930), 240 Bleecker St., 10014. Tel: 212-242-4147; Fax: 212-691-2361. Apostles of the Sacred Heart of Jesus 5; Lay Teachers 13; Students 233.
Catechesis/Religious Program—Students 23.

93—OUR LADY OF SORROWS (1867), (English—Spanish), Rev. Joseph Gurdak, O.F.M.Cap.; Bro. Robert Gerdin, O.F.M.Cap.; Deacons Eusebio Maldonado; Wallace Zambrana. In Res., Bro. James Wieland, O.F.M.Cap.
Res.: 213 Stanton St., 10002-1898. Tel: 212-475-2321; Fax: 212-475-2452.
Church: 103 Pitt St., 10002. Tel: 212-673-0900; Fax: 212-982-0166.
School— (1867), 219 Stanton St., 10002. Tel: 212-473-0320; Fax: 212-420-0285. Lay Teachers 12; Students 165.
Catechesis/Religious Program—Tel: 212-673-0900, Ext. 306. Students 132.

94—OUR LADY OF THE MIRACULOUS MEDAL (1926), Closed., Records at Holy Agony.

95—OUR LADY OF THE ROSARY (1883),, Shrine of St. Elizabeth Ann Seton, Rev. Peter Meehan; Rev. Msgr. Timothy Collins, Pastor Emeritus; Revs. Joseph O'Meara; Edward G. Zogby, S.J. In Res., Rev. Vincent Euk.
Res.: 7 State St., 10004. Tel: 212-269-6865; Fax: 212-809-6850.

96—OUR LADY OF THE SCAPULAR/ST. STEPHEN (1889; 1848), Revs. Sean R. Harlow, O.Carm.; John Canning, O.Carm., Pastoral Assoc.; Roberto Perez, O.Carm., Pastoral Assoc. In Res., Most Rev. William J. McCormack, D.D.
Res.: 142 E. 29th St., 10016. Tel: 212-683-1675; Fax: 212-683-7921.
Catechesis/Religious Program—Students 90.
Chapel—Bellevue Hospital, Chapel of Our Lady Helper of the Sick, Tel: 212-561-4440. Revs. John Logan, O.Carm.; Philip Marani, O.Carm.

97—OUR LADY OF VICTORY (1944), Rev. Msgr. Edward J. Mitty, P.A.; Revs. George E. Baker; Joseph Lukose, C.M. (India); Joseph D'Souza, O.C.D. (Tanzania). In Res., Revs. John E. Fanning; Thomas J. Darby (Retired).
Res.: 60 William St., 10005. Tel: 212-422-5535; Fax: 212-509-5336.

98—OUR LADY OF VILNIUS (1905), (Lithuanian), Rev. Eugene A. Sawicki, R.N., J.C.L., Admin.
Res.: 32 Dominick St., 10013. Tel: 212-255-2648; Fax: 212-924-6210.
Church: 570 Broome St., 10013.

99—OUR LADY QUEEN OF ANGELS (1886), (German), Rev. Gerard Mulvey, O.F.M.Cap.; Bros. Pius Blandino, O.F.M.Cap., Guardian; Christopher Varley, O.F.M.Cap. In Res., Revs. Gregory Noel, O.F.M-.Cap.; Philip Romano, O.F.M.Cap.; Patrick Sullivan, O.F.M.Cap.; Peter Vettikanakudy, O.F.M.Cap. (India); Deacon Luis Martinez.
Res.: 226 E. 113th St., 10029. Tel: 212-369-9088 (Friary); Fax: 212-427-8261.
School— (1886 and 1955), 229-231 E. 112th St., 10029. Tel: 212-722-9277; Fax: 212-987-8837. Brothers 2; Lay Teachers 14; Students 286.
Catechesis/Religious Program—Tel: 212-860-7618; Fax: 212-828-0506. Students 50.
Chapel—Parish Center 232 E. 113th St., 10029. Tel: 212-860-7618; Fax: 212-828-0506.

100—OUR LADY QUEEN OF MARTYRS (1927), Revs. Daniel S. Kearney; Jose Miranda; Manuel Feliz (Dominican Republic); Deacons Narciso Hernandez; Manuel Cespedes; Luis Feliz; Delio Fernandez. In Res., Rev. Donald Johnston, Chap., Columbia Presbyterian Hospital.
Res.: 91 Arden St., 10040. Tel: 212-567-2637; Fax: 212-567-1305.
School— (1932), 71 Arden St., 10040. Tel: 212-567-3190; Fax: 212-304-8587. Andrew Woods, Prin. Lay Teachers 14; Students 386.
Catechesis/Religious Program—Students 602.

101—OUR SAVIOUR (1955), Revs. George W. Rutler; Koshy George Chirayath (India); Patrick Ettampola (Sri Lanka). In Res., Revs. Douglas J. Mathers, J.C.D.; John P. Larkin (Retired).
Res.: 59 Park Ave., 10016. Tel: 212-679-8166; Fax: 212-213-0352.

102—ST. PATRICK OLD CATHEDRAL (1809), Rev. Thomas Kallumady; Rev. Msgr. Nicholas Marinacci, Pastor Emeritus; Rev. Andrew Thi.
32-38 Prince St., 10012. Tel: 212-226-4799. In Res., Rev. John E. Kozar.
Res.: 263 Mulberry St., 10012. Tel: 212-226-8075; Fax: 212-226-1219.
School—Boys & Girls Depts. (1817), 233-239 Mott St., 10012. Tel: 212-226-3984; Fax: 212-226-4469. Lay Teachers 10; Students 231.
Catechesis/Religious Program—Students 49.
Chapel—St. Michael (Russian—Other), [JC] 266 Mulberry St., 10012. Tel: 212-226-2644; Fax: 212-226-1219.

103—ST. PAUL (1834), Revs. Walter D. Mallo, I.V.E.; Pablo Waldmann, I.V.E. (Argentina); Deacon Miguel Granda. In Res., Rev. Jose Otero (Argentina).
Res.: 113 E. 117th St., 10035. Tel: 212-534-4422; Fax: 212-996-5588.
School— (1870), 114-122 E. 118th St., 10035. Tel: 212-534-0619; Fax: 212-534-3990. Lay Teachers 14; Students 267.
Catechesis/Religious Program—Tel: 212-534-4481. Students 230.
Convent—Exodus House, 149 E. 117th St., 10035.

104—ST. PAUL THE APOSTLE (1858), Revs. Robert A. O'Donnell, C.S.P.; Ronald Franco, C.S.P., Pastoral Assoc.; Timothy F. Sullivan, C.S.P., Pastoral Assoc. Mailing Address: 405 W. 59th, 10019. Tel: 212-265-3495; Fax: 212-262-9239. In Res., Revs. Stephen J. Connor, C.S.P., Dir. Vocations; Thomas P. Ryan, C.S.P., Office of Ecumenism; Joseph F. Mahon, C.S.P., Missions; Rudolph T. Vorisek, C.S.P., Hospital Chap.; James F. McQuade, C.S.P., Hospital Chap.; Robert J. O'Donnell, C.S.P.; James B. Lloyd, C.S.P.; John C. Reynolds, C.S.P.; Rev. Msgr. Richard J. Walsh, C.S.P.; Revs. Joseph P. Flynn, C.S.P.; Francis X. Diskin, C.S.P.; John E. Collins, C.S.P., Missions; Donal F. Forrester, C.S.P.; Kevin A. Lynch, C.S.P.; Michael J. Hunt, C.S.P. (NEW); Timothy P. Tighe, C.S.P.; Patrick Traynor, C.S.P.; Dennis W. Hickey, C.S.P.; Thomas A. Tavella, C.S.P., Missions; Joseph J. Scott, C.S.P., Paulist Press; Brett Hoover, C.S.P.
Catechesis/Religious Program—Students 114.
Chapel—Oblates of Jesus the Priest, Tel: 212-265-3209; Fax: 212-265-4154.

105—ST. PETER (1785), Rev. Msgr. Wallace A. Harris, Admin.; Revs. Kevin Madigan; Michael B. Dibble; Donald T. Fussner; James J. Halligan.
Res.: 16 Barclay St., 10007. Tel: 212-233-8355; Fax: 212-285-0497.
Chapel—St. Joseph's Chapel 385 South End Ave., 10280. Tel: 212-466-0131. In Res., Rev. Msgr. Joseph J. Zammit, Chap., N.Y.C. Police Dept.

106—ST. RAPHAEL (1886), Closed., See Sts. Cyril and Methodius.

107—RESURRECTION (1907), (African American—Hispanic), Rev. Msgr. Wallace A. Harris, Admin.; Deacons Kenneth Radcliff; Miguel Granda.
Res.: 276 W. 151st St., 10039. Tel: 212-690-7555; Fax: 212-690-6590.
School— (1910), 282 W. 151 St., 10039. Tel: 212-690-7524; Fax: 212-690-2346. Lay Teachers 9; Students 215.
Catechesis/Religious Program—Students 45.

108—ST. ROSE (1868), Closed., Parochial records at St. Mary Church.

109—ST. ROSE OF LIMA (1902), Revs. Manuel Machado; Eusebio Mana-Ay. In Res., Rev. Frederick Carrigan.
Res.: 510 W. 165th St., 10032. Tel: 212-568-0091.
School— (1924), 517 W. 164th St., 10032. Sisters 2; Lay Teachers 10; Students 310.
Chapel—St. Rose of Lima Convent 509 W. 164th St., 10032.
Medical Centre—

110—SACRED HEART OF JESUS (1876), (Spanish), Rev. Msgr. Joachim B. Beaumont.
Res.: 457 W. 51st, 10019. Tel: 212-265-5020; Fax: 212-977-4116.
School— (1892), 456 52nd St., 10019. Tel: 212-246-4784; Fax: 212-707-8382. Congregation of Christian Brothers 1; Lay Teachers 12; Students 187.
Chapel—Centro Maria 539 W. 54th St., 10019. Tel: 212-757-6989; Fax: 212-307-5687.
Chapel—Convent of Sacred Heart 450 W. 51st St., 10019. Tel: 212-397-1396; Fax: 212-397-1397.
Catechesis/Religious Program—Tel: 212-247-3264. Students 180.

111—SACRED HEARTS OF JESUS AND MARY (1914), (Italian), Rev. Msgr. Donald Sakano, Admin.; Revs. Francise Kolencherry (India); Albert De Luca, Pastor Emeritus; Deacon Lawrence P. Mulligan. In Res., Rev. Anthony Nwachukwu (Nigeria).
Res.: 307 E. 33rd St., 10016. Tel: 212-889-2133; Fax: 212-481-2924.
Chapel—Convent of the Sacred Heart of Jesus and Mary 325 E. 33rd St., 10016. Tel: 212-889-3886.
Station—N.Y.U. Rehabilitation Hospital, Tel: 212-889-3886.

112—ST. SEBASTIAN (1915), Closed., Parochial records at Epiphany Church.

113—ST. STANISLAUS (1872), (Polish), Revs. Lucius Tyrasinski, O.S.P.; Bogdan Kolmaga, O.S.P.
Res.: 101 E. Seventh St., 10009. Tel: 212-475-4576; Fax: 212-674-4894.

114—ST. STEPHEN (1848), Consolidated, in 1990. See Our Lady of Scapular/St. Stephen for details.

115—ST. STEPHEN OF HUNGARY (1902), (Hungarian), Revs. Angelus Gambatese, O.F.M., Guardian Franciscan Community; Dominic Csorba, O.F.M. (Hungary); Vianney M. Devlin, O.F.M.; Sr. Natalie M. Runfola, R.S.C.J., Pastoral Assoc. In Res., Revs. Russell C. Becker, O.F.M.; Anthony M. Carrozzo, O.F.M.; Francis de Paul Kealy, O.F.M.; Ronald P. Stark, O.F.M.; John Coughlin, O.F.M.; Xavier Suebert, O.F.M.; Bros. Gregory P. Day, O.F.M.; Glenn Humphrey, O.F.M.
Res.: 414 E. 82nd St., 10028. Tel: 212-861-8500; Fax: 212-535-9221.
School— (1918), 408 E. 82nd St., 10028. Tel: 212-288-1989; Fax: 212-517-5877. Carol O'Connor, Prin. Religious Teachers 1; Lay Teachers 8; Students 169.
Cooke Center for Learning and Development—Tel: 212-472-7209; Fax: 212-280-4473. Lay Teachers 8; Students 21.
Catechesis/Religious Program—Interparish Religious Education Program, c/o St. Ignatius of Loyola, 980 Park Ave., 10028. Tel: 212-861-4764; Fax: 212-734-3671. Students 15.
Dewitt Nursing Home—211 E. 79th St., 10021. Tel: 212-879-1600.

116—ST. TERESA (1863), Rev. Donald C. Baker; Sr. Diane Olmstead, M.S.C., Pastoral Assoc.
Res.: 141 Henry St., 10002. Tel: 212-233-0233; Fax: 212-619-4538.
Church: 16 & 18 Rutgers St., 10002. Tel: 212-233-0233; Fax: 212-619-4538.
Catechesis/Religious Program—Students 176.

117—ST. THOMAS MORE (1950), Revs. John A. Boehning; John E. Halborg. In Res., Most Rev. Patrick V. Ahern; Rev. Msgr. Thomas J. Shelley.
Res.: 65 E. 89th St., 10128. Tel: 212-876-7718; Fax: 212-831-5756.
Catechesis/Religious Program—Narnia Clubs, F.D.R. Station, P.O. Box 967, 10150. Tel: 212-535-9329; Fax: 212-628-8409. Students 185.
Chapel—Convent of Sacred Heart and Academy 1 E. 91st St., 10022. Tel: 212-722-4745; Fax: 212-996-1784.

118—ST. THOMAS THE APOSTLE (1889), (African American), [CEM] Rev. Paul Grauls, S.D.B., Admin.; Bro. Anthony Ambrogio, S.D.B.
Res.: 262 W. 118th St., 10026. Tel: 212-662-2693; Fax: 212-662-4560.
Don Bosco Harlem Association, Inc.—262 W. 118th St., 10026. Tel: 212-662-9228.
Catechesis/Religious Program—Students 127.

119—TRANSFIGURATION (1827), (Chinese-English), Rev. Raymond J. Nobiletti, M.M.
Res.: 29 Mott St., 10013. Tel: 212-962-5157; Fax: 212-962-5217.
School— (1853),Tel: 212-962-5265; Fax: 212-964-8965. Mr. Kevin Scanlon, Prin. Lay Teachers 12; Students 278.
Catechesis/Religious Program—Students 106.

120—ST. VERONICA (1887), Rev. Kevin J. Nelan, Admin.
Res.: 328 W. 14th St., 10014. Tel: 212-243-0265; Fax: 212-255-8466.
Church: 149-155 Christopher St., 10014. Tel: 212-924-5628.
Mission—Gift of Love 657 Washington St., New York Co. 10014. Tel: 212-645-0587.

121—ST. VINCENT DE PAUL (1841), (French), Rev. Gerald E. Murray. In Res., Revs. Robert J. Poveromo; John F. Harvey, O.S.F.S.; Harry Tiercelin (Retired); Gerard Messier, A.A.
Res.: 116 W. 24th St., 10011. Tel: 212-243-4727; Fax: 212-675-0528.
Church: 123 W. 23rd St., 10011.
Catechesis/Religious Program—Students 310.

122—ST. VINCENT FERRER (1867), Very Rev. Kevin Dominic Robb, O.P., Prior; Revs. Bernard Lawrence Keitz, O.P.; Kevin Anthony McGrath, O.P.; Bro. Damian McCarthy, O.P.
Res.: 869 Lexington Ave., 10021-6680. Tel: 212-744-2080; Fax: 212-327-3011.
High School—151 E. 65th St., 10021. Tel: 212-535-4680; Fax: 212-988-3455. Sr. Gail Morgan, O.P., Prin. Sisters of St. Dominic, Columbus, OH 6; Lay Teachers 29; Girls 488.
Catechesis/Religious Program—Students 60.
Chapel—Sisters of St. Dominic 152 E. 66th St., 10021. Tel: 212-744-2375; Fax: 212-249-5355.
Chapel—Dominican Academy 44 E. 68th St., 10021. Tel: 212-744-0195; Fax: 212-744-0375.

BOROUGH OF BRONX

1—St. Adalbert (1898), (Polish), Closed. For inquiries for parish records contact the chancery.

2—St. Angela Merici (1899), Revs. Peter Mushi, A.J.; John Kalungi, A.J.; Deacon Felipe Sin.
Res.: 917 Morris Ave., Bronx, 10451. Tel: 718-293-0984; Fax: 718-293-7325.
Church: E. 163rd St., Bronx, 10451.
School— (1917), Morris Ave. & 163rd St., Bronx, 10451. Tel: 718-293-3365; Fax: 718-293-6617. Lay Teachers 24; Students 527.
Catechesis/Religious Program—Fax: 718-293-0984. Students 400.

3—St. Ann (1927), Rev. Msgr. Robert M. Trainor; Rev. Christopher Opara (Nigeria). In Res., Revs. Matthew Azhakath (India); Misael Bacleon (Philippines).
Res.: 3519 Bainbridge Ave., Bronx, 10467. Tel: 718-547-9350; Fax: 718-547-1718.
School— (1928), Bainbridge Ave. & Gun Hill Rd., Bronx, 10467. Tel: 718-655-3449; Fax: 718-547-4020. Miss L. DiJusto, Prin. Students 280.
Catechesis/Religious Program—Tel: 718-655-3449; Fax: 718-547-2020. Students 135.

4—St. Anselm (1892), Revs. Francisco J. Legarra, O.A.R. (NEW); Antonio Palacios, O.A.R.
Res.: 685 Tinton Ave., Bronx, 10455. Tel: 718-585-8666; Fax: 718-401-6686.
School— (1908),Tel: 718-993-9464; Fax: 718-292-3496. Ms. Teresa M. Lopes, Prin. Lay Teachers 23; Students 630.
Catechesis/Religious Program—Tel: 718-585-8542. Students 720.

5—St. Anthony (1908), (Hispanic), Revs. Joseph J. Kelly; John J. Piderit, S.J. In Res., Rev. Michael J. Allessandro.
Res.: 1496 Commonwealth Ave., Bronx, 10460. Tel: 718-931-4040; 718-931-4041; Fax: 718-863-0202.
School— (1931), St. Lawrence Ave. & Mansion St., Bronx, 10460. Tel: 718-892-1244; Fax: 718-892-4656. Lay Teachers 9; Students 230.
Catechesis/Religious Program—Students 227.

6—St. Anthony (1919), (Italian), Rev. Nicholas F. Milazzo (Retired).
Res.: 4505 Richardson Ave., Bronx, 10470. Tel: 718-324-8787; Fax: 718-324-6354.
School— (1953), 4520 Matilda Ave., Bronx, 10470. Tel: 718-324-5104. Mrs. Roma Barone, Prin. Lay Teachers 12; Students 167.
Convent—4500 Matilda Ave., Bronx, 10470.

7—St. Anthony of Padua (1903), (African American—Hispanic), [CEM] Most Rev. Josu Iriondo; Rev. Hugo Martinez (Ecuador).
Res.: 832 E. 166th St., Bronx, 10459. Tel: 718-542-7293; Fax: 718-378-1819.
Catechesis/Religious Program—Students 146.

8—St. Athanasius (1907), Rev. Msgr. William J. Smith; Rev. Pompilio Alvarez (Spain); Deacon Alejandro Rosado.
Res.: 878 Tiffany St., Bronx, 10459. Tel: 718-328-2558; Fax: 718-328-3121.
School— (1913), 830 Southern Blvd., Bronx, 10459. Tel: 718-542-5161; Fax: 718-542-7584. Marianne Kraft, Prin. Sisters 2; Lay Teachers 13; Students 370.
Catechesis/Religious Program—Students 380.

9—St. Augustine (1849), Rev. Thomas B. Fenlon. In Res., Revs. Edmund Okere (Nigeria); John Gilvey, O.S.F.S.
Res.: 1183 Franklin Ave., Bronx, 10456. Tel: 718-893-0072; Fax: 718-861-3080.
Church: E. 167th St., Bronx, 10456.
School— (1887), 1176 Franklin Ave., Bronx, 10456. Tel: 718-542-3633; Fax: 718-542-7871. Cathryn Trapp, Prin. Lay Teachers 9; Students 245.
Catechesis/Religious Program—1176 Franklin Ave., Bronx, 10456. Tel: 718-617-4191; Fax: 718-617-4191.

10—St. Barnabas (1910), Revs. Donald M. Dwyer, Vicar; Rees W. Doughty; John Francis Antony (India); Cyprian Onyeihe (Nigeria); Deacons Vincent Laurato; Cornelius Manning.
Res.: 409 E. 241st St., Bronx, 10470. Tel: 718-324-1478; Fax: 718-324-1479.
School— (1912), 415 E. 241st St., Bronx, 10470. Tel: 718-324-1088; Fax: 718-324-2397. Lay Teachers 24; Students 750.
High School—High School for Girls (1924), 425 E. 240th St., Bronx, 10470. Tel: 718-325-8800; Fax: 718-325-8820. Sisters 5; Lay Teachers 23; Students 260.
Catechesis/Religious Program—Tel: 718-324-0865. Students 250.
Chapel—Annunciation 1033 McLean Ave., Yonkers, 10704.

11—St. Benedict (1923), Rev. Msgr. Edmund J. Whalen, S.T.D.; Rev. Eric Raaser; Rev. Msgr. John J. Gillen (Retired); Deacons John Simpson; Joseph Forte.
Res.: 2969 Otis Ave., Bronx, 10465-2198. Tel: 718-828-3403; Fax: 718-829-1304.
School— (1923), 1016 Edison Ave., Bronx, 10465. Tel: 718-829-9557. Sisters 1; Lay Teachers 16; Students 395.
Catechesis/Religious Program—Tel: 718-829-1200. Students 400.
Chapel—St. John 1082 Edison Ave., Bronx, 10465.

12—Blessed Sacrament (1927), Rev. Msgr. James E. White; Rev. Alejandro Lopez-Cardinale; Deacon Epi Portalatin.
Res.: 1170 Beach Ave., Bronx, 10472. Tel: 718-892-3214; Fax: 718-892-3907.
School— (1929), 1160 Beach Ave. & 1141 Taylor Ave., Bronx, 10472. Tel: 718-892-0433; Fax: 718-892-3337. Grace Chemi, Prin. Lay Teachers 23; Students 475.
Catechesis/Religious Program—Tel: 718-863-4620. Students 190.

13—St. Brendan (1908), Revs. Patrick D. Hennessy; Michael J. Morrow; Antoni S. Szewczyk. In Res., Rev. Paul Baffour (Ghana).
Res.: 333 E. 206th St., Bronx, 10467. Tel: 718-547-6655; Fax: 718-547-6579.
School— (1912), 268 E. 207th St., Bronx, 10467. Tel: 718-653-2293; Fax: 718-653-3234. Mrs. Patricia Gatti, Prin. Sisters of St. Dominic (Sparkill, NY) 1; Lay Teachers 20; Students 625.
Catechesis/Religious Program—Tel: 718-654-6424. Students 395.
Chapel—Dominican Sisters 260 E. 207th St., Bronx, 10467. Tel: 718-798-2460.

14—Christ the King (1926), (Hispanic—African American), Revs. Fernando A. Hernandez; Aaron Gyamfi-Appiah, C.SS.P. In Res., Rev. George Oonnooney.
Res.: 141 Marcy Pl., Bronx, 10452. Tel: 718-538-5546; Fax: 718-538-3081.
School—Tel: 718-538-5959; Fax: 718-538-6369. Lay Teachers 26; Students 584.
Catechesis/Religious Program—Tel: 718-538-5959. Students 616.

15—St. Clare of Assisi (1929), (Italian), Revs. Richard Guarnieri; John J. Voglio.
Res.: 1918 Paulding Ave., Bronx, 10462. Tel: 718-863-8974; Fax: 718-931-6909.
Church: 1027 Rhinelander Ave., Bronx, 10462.
School— (1951), 1911 Hone Ave., Bronx, 10461. Tel: 718-892-4480; Fax: 718-239-1007. Janice Desmond, Prin. Sisters 3; Lay Teachers 21; Students 583.
Catechesis/Religious Program—Tel: 718-829-9624. Students 210.
Chapel—Bronx, Morningside House Chapel, Tel: 718-409-8200.

16—St. Dominic (1924), (Italian), Revs. John Knapp, Admin.; Carlos Mullins; Deacon Reynaldo Rosado.
Res.: 1739 Unionport Rd., Bronx, 10462. Tel: 718-828-2424; Fax: 718-823-4450.
School— (1953), 1684 White Plains Rd., Bronx, 10462. Tel: 718-829-4837; Fax: 718-792-6912. Sr. Josefa Curcio, C.S.J.B., Prin. Sisters of St. John Baptist 7; Lay Teachers 21; Students 525.
Catechesis/Religious Program—Tel: 718-823-9044. Students 100.
Convent—1710 Unionport Rd., Bronx, 10462. Tel: 718-824-2580. Sisters 9.

17—St. Frances de Chantal (1927), Rev. Msgrs. Leslie J. Ivers; Joseph M. Devlin, Pastor Emeritus (Retired); Revs. Floyd A. Grace; Epifanio Marcaida (Philippines); Deacon John Murphy.
Res.: 190 Hollywood Ave., Bronx, 10465. Tel: 718-792-5500; Fax: 718-792-1824.
School— (1929), 2962 Harding Ave., Bronx, 10465. Tel: 718-892-5359; Fax: 718-892-6937. Michael Houlihan, Prin. Lay Teachers 30; Students 720.
Catechesis/Religious Program—Students 207.
Convent—Convent of Sisters of Life, 198 Hollywood Ave., Bronx, 10465. Tel: 718-863-2264.
Chapel—House of the Holy Family 2780 Schurz Ave., Bronx, 10465. Tel: 718-863-9134.

18—St. Frances of Rome (1898), Revs. Francis J. Corry; John P. Sheehan; Sr. Ellen Kublitz, O.P., Pastoral Assoc. In Res., Rev. John Uko.
Res.: 4307 Barnes Ave., Bronx, 10466. Tel: 718-324-5340; 718-324-5341; Fax: 718-324-5373.
Church: Moore Plaza & E. 236 St., Bronx, 10466.
School— (1926), 4321 Barnes Ave., Bronx, 10466. Tel: 718-324-7360; Fax: 718-994-3694. Dina Monti, Prin.; Sr. M. Gregory West, P.B.V.M., D.R.E. Sisters of the Presentation 2; Lay Teachers 12; Students 210.
Catechesis/Religious Program—Tel: 718-994-3694. Students 120.

19—St. Francis of Assisi (1928), Rev. Michael Sepp, Admin.
1544 Shakespeare Ave., Bronx, 10452. Tel: 718-731-6840; 718-731-6841. Mailing Address: P.O. Box 520013, Bronx, 10452. Fax: 718-731-6841.
Catechesis/Religious Program—Students 190.

20—St. Francis of Assisi (1949), Revs. Michael P. Morris; James P. Clark (Retired).
Res.: 4343 Baychester Ave., Bronx, 10466. Tel: 718-994-8736; Fax: 718-994-9460.
Church: 4300 Baychester Ave., Bronx, 10466.
School—Tel: 718-994-4650; Fax: 718-994-6990. Dr. Patrick Taharally, Prin. Lay Teachers 12; Students 348.

21—St. Francis Xavier (1928), Revs. Arthur T. Welton; Peter D. Gibbons (Ireland); Francis Gayam (India).
Res.: 1703 Lurting Ave., Bronx, 10461. Tel: 718-892-3330; Fax: 718-931-6890.
School— (1930), 1711 Haight Ave., Bronx, 10461. Tel: 718-863-0531; Fax: 718-319-1152. Mrs. Angela Deegan, Prin. Lay Teachers 25; Students 415.
Catechesis/Religious Program—Students 70.
Chapel—St. Francis Xavier Convent 1661 Haight Ave., Bronx, 10461. Tel: 718-892-9466; Fax: 718-829-1488.

22—St. Gabriel (1939), Rev. Thomas R. Kelly; Rev. Msgrs. Charles J. McManus (Retired); John T. Doherty, Pastor Emeritus (Retired); Revs. Millard S. Cook; Myles P. Murphy; Silas N. Onuoha; Deacon Eugene Burke.
Res.: 3250 Arlington Ave., Bronx, 10463. Tel: 718-548-4470; Fax: 718-548-6451.
Church: 235th & Netherland Ave., Bronx, 10463. Fax: 718-548-0444.
School—590 W. 235th St., Bronx, 10463. Tel: 718-548-0444; Fax: 718-796-2638. Sr. Claire Dandeneau, R.J.M., Prin. Lay Teachers 11; Students 261.
Catechesis/Religious Program—Tel: 718-548-6585. Mr. Glenn A. McCarthy, D.R.E. Students 100.

23—St. Helena (1940), Rev. Msgr. Thomas B. Derivan; Revs. Edmundo Gomez; Anthony Sebamalai (Sri Lanka); Joseph Ligory (Sri Lanka); Charles Szivos.
Res.: 1315 Olmstead Ave., Bronx, 10462. Tel: 718-892-3232; Fax: 718-892-3078.
School— (1941), 2050 Benedict Ave., Bronx, 10462. Tel: 718-892-3234; Fax: 718-892-3924. Richard Meller, Prin. Sisters of St. Dominic (Sparkill, NY) 1; Lay Teachers 24; Students 626.
High School—Msgr. Scanlan High School (1949), 915 Hutchinson River Pkwy., Bronx, 10465. Tel: 718-430-0100; Fax: 718-892-8845. Sr. Marie O'Donnell, O.P., Prin. (Coed) Sisters of St. Dominic (Sparkill, NY) 8; Lay Teachers 35; Students 650.
Catechesis/Religious Program—Tel: 718-892-5557. Students 121.

24—Holy Cross (1921), Revs. Aubrey McNeil, O.F.M.; Matthew A. Pravetz, O.F.M.; Thadeus M. Sapio, O.F.M.; Charles Miller, O.F.M., Formation Dir.; Brennan Connelley, O.F.M.; Bros. Daniel Murray, O.F.M., Vicar; Peter Alheim, O.F.M.; William Herbst, O.F.M.; Deacons Jaime A. Bello; Richard Bragg; Juan Rodriguez.
Res.: 600 Soundview Ave., Bronx, 10473. Tel: 718-893-5550; Fax: 718-378-3655.
School— (1923 and 1955), Randall Ave. & Thieriot Ave., Bronx, 10473. Tel: 718-842-4492; Fax: 718-842-4052. Franciscan Sisters of Allegany, NY 1; Lay Teachers 25; Students 525.
Catechesis/Religious Program—Tel: 718-328-1054. Students 205.
Chapel—Franciscan Sisters of Allegany 620 Thieriot Ave., Bronx, 10473. Tel: 718-842-2615.

25—Holy Family (1896), Rev. James D. Flanagan; Deacon Dhoel Canals.
Res.: 2158 Watson Ave., Bronx, 10472. Tel: 718-863-9156; Fax: 718-597-5560.
School— (1913), 2169 Blackrock Ave., Bronx, 10472. Tel: 718-863-7280; Fax: 718-931-8690. Sisters of St. Agnes 1; Lay Teachers 32; Students 716.
Catechesis/Religious Program—2169 Black Rock Ave., Bronx, 10472. Tel: 718-822-8030. Students 210.
Chapel—Sisters of St. Agnes 2155 Blackrock Ave., Bronx, 10472. Tel: 718-828-4488.

26—Holy Rosary (1925), Revs. Robert A. Quarato; Levelt Germain; Raul G. Miguez (Italy); Florin Bejenaru (Romania); Deacons Joseph Solanto; Joseph D'Aiello.
Res.: 1510 Adee Ave., Bronx, 10469. Tel: 718-379-4432; 718-379-4654; Fax: 718-379-9028.
School— (1927; 1955), 1500 Arnow Ave., Bronx, 10469. Tel: 718-652-1838; Fax: 718-515-9872. Mrs. Ann Marie Fusco, Contact Person. Sisters 1; Lay Teachers 21; Students 600.
Catechesis/Religious Program—Tel: 718-654-9381. Students 75.
Chapel—Holy Rosary Convent 2755 Woodhull Ave., Bronx, 10469. Tel: 718-798-6435.

27—Holy Spirit (1901), (Spanish), Revs. Joseph Vijayan (India); Carlos Mesa (Colombia).
Res.: 1940 University Ave., Bronx, 10453. Tel: 718-583-0120; Fax: 718-583-1444.
School— (1913), 1960 University Ave., Bronx, 10453. Tel: 718-583-1570; Fax: 718-583-3378. Lay Teachers 12; Students 357.
Catechesis/Religious Program—Students 305.

28—Immaculate Conception (1853), (German), Very Rev. Ronald E. Bonneau, C.SS.R.; Revs. John Olcnick, C.SS.R.; Thomas (Martin) Deely, C.Ss.R.; William Gaffney, C.Ss.R.; Daniel Francis, C.Ss.R.;

Francis Gargani, C.Ss.R.; Bro. Stephen Lendvay, C.Ss.R.; Deacon Cristobal Rodriguez.
Res.: 389 E. 150th St., Bronx, 10455. Tel: 718-292-6970; Fax: 718-292-4603.
Perpetual Help Center—294 E. 150th St., Bronx, 10455. Tel: 718-585-3678; Fax: 718-993-5870.
School— (1854), 378 E. 151st St., Bronx, 10455. Tel: 718-585-4843; Fax: 718-585-6846. Sisters of Christian Charity 5; Lay Teachers 22; Students 570.
Catechesis / Religious Program—Tel: 718-292-6780. Oscar Cruz, D.R.E. Students 175.
Chapel—Sisters of Christian Charity 365 E. 150th St., Bronx, 10455. Tel: 718-585-8981.

29—IMMACULATE CONCEPTION (1903), Revs. John Lo Sasso, O.F.M.Cap.; Peter Napoli, O.F.M.Cap.; Nicholas Mormando, O.F.M.Cap.; Francis Maurice, O.F.M-.Cap.; Bro. Jesu Perez, O.F.M.Cap., Pastoral Assoc.; Deacon Carlos Mercado, Pastoral Assoc.
Capuchin Friary: 754 E. Gun Hill Rd., Bronx, 10467. Tel: 718-653-2200; Fax: 718-882-0054.
School—Tel: 718-547-3346; Fax: 718-547-5505. Sr. Latecia Aviles, O.B.T., Prin. Priests 4; Brothers 2; Oblates to the Blessed Trinity 4; Franciscan Missionary Sisters 2; Missionary Sisters of the Catechism 4; Lay Teachers 13; Students 895.

30—ST. JEROME'S (1869), Revs. John Grange; Carmelo Amantegui, S.J.
Res.: 230 Alexander Ave., Bronx, 10454. Tel: 718-665-5533.
School— (1871), 222 Alexander Ave., Bronx, 10454. Lay Teachers 10; Students 267.
Catechesis / Religious Program—Sr. Josephin Stabile, D.R.E.; Dina Monti, D.R.E. Students 150.

31—ST. JOAN OF ARC (1949), Revs. Paul J. LeBlanc; Carlos A. Ruiz; Deacon Ismael Camacho.
Res.: 1372 Stratford Ave., Bronx, 10472. Tel: 718-842-2233; Fax: 718-842-4720.
Catechesis / Religious Program—Students 270.

32—ST. JOHN CHRYSOSTOM'S (1899), Rev. Carlos Rodriguez; Deacon Victor Pino.
Res.: 985 E. 167th St., Bronx, 10459. Tel: 718-542-6164; Fax: 718-542-0448.
School— (1914), 1144 Hoe Ave., Bronx, 10459. Tel: 718-328-7226; Fax: 718-378-5368. Sr. Mary Elizabeth Mooney, O.P., Prin. Sisters of St. Dominic (Sparkill, NY) 11; Lay Teachers 19; Students 611.
Catechesis / Religious Program—Tel: 718-328-3580. Students 367.

33—ST JOHN NAM (1989), (Korean), Rev. Simon Nam.
Res.: 3663 White Plains Rd., Bronx, 10467. Tel: 718-231-2414; Fax: 718-405-0053.

34—ST. JOHN VIANNEY, CURE OF ARS (1960), Revs. Jesus M. Mena, O.A.R.; Blas Montenegro, O.A.R.; Deacons Al Leasiolagi; Andes Almanzar; Edwin Cruz.
Res.: 715 Castle Hill Ave., Bronx, 10473. Tel: 212-863-4411; Fax: 917-463-3837.
School—2141 Seward Ave., Bronx, 10473. Tel: 718-892-4400. Lay Teachers 9; Students 280.

35—ST. JOHN'S (1886), (Hispanic), Revs. Fredric Abiera; Edward J. Fagan, O.A.R.; Deacon Andrew Rivera. In Res., Rev. Jose Luis Martinez, O.A.R. (LA); Bro. Mario Alvarez, O.A.R.
Res.: 3021 Kingsbridge Ave., Bronx, 10463. Tel: 718-548-1221; Fax: 718-548-7774.
School— (1903), 3143 Kingsbridge Ave., Bronx, 10463. Tel: 718-548-0255; Fax: 718-548-0864. Mr. Ray Vitiello, Prin. Sisters 2; Lay Teachers 12; Students 315.
Catechesis / Religious Program—Tel: 718-884-2627. Students 210.
Convent—Religious of Jesus and Mary, 3029 Godwin Ter., Bronx, 10463. Tel: 718-548-4902; 718-543-2454.

36—ST. JOSEPH (1873), (Spanish—African American), Rev. Rufino Lecumberri.
Res.: 1949 Bathgate Ave., Bronx, 10457. Tel: 718-731-2504; Fax: 718-731-0478.
School— (1922), 1946 Bathgate Ave., Bronx, 10457. Tel: 718-583-9432; Fax: 718-299-0780. Janine A. Hughes, Prin. Lay Teachers 16; Students 400.
Catechesis / Religious Program—Students 35.

37—ST. LUCY (1927), Revs. Robert J. Norris; Neil Kelly; Michael Holleran; Deacons Wilfredo Miranda; William Bebert. In Res., Rev. Msgr. Frederick J. Becker.
Church: 833 Mace Ave., Bronx, 10467. Tel: 718-882-0710; Fax: 718-882-8876.
School— (1955), 830 Mace Ave., Bronx, 10467. Tel: 718-882-2203; Fax: 718-547-8351. Dr. Peter A. Mutarelli, Prin. Lay Teachers 24; Students 600.
Catechesis / Religious Program—Tel: 718-652-0295. Students 259.

38—ST. LUKE (1897), (Hispanic—African American), Rev. Msgr. Gerald J. Ryan; Mary Kay Louchart, Pastoral Assoc.; Sharon Joslyn, Pastoral Assoc.
Res.: 623 E. 138th St., Bronx, 10454. Tel: 718-665-6677; Fax: 718-665-0898.
School— (1910), 608 E. 139th St., Bronx, 10454. Tel: 718-585-0380; Fax: 718-665-3407. Sisters of St. Dominic (Blauvelt) 3; Lay Teachers 16; Students 387.
Catechesis / Religious Program—Tel: 718-665-8956. Students 300.
Chapel—St. Luke Convent 621 E. 138th St., Bronx, 10454. Tel: 718-292-3016.

39—ST. MARGARET MARY (1923), Revs. Robert P. Arce; Alonso Escobar (Colombia); Jose Ambooken (India). In Res., Rev. Robert A. Jeffers.
Res.: 1914 Morris Ave., Bronx, 10453-5904. Tel: 718-299-4233; Fax: 718-583-3726.
School— (1923), 121 E. 177th St., Bronx, 10453. Tel: 718-731-5905; Fax: 718-731-8924. Sisters of Mercy of the Americas 2; Lay Teachers 13; Students 370.
Catechesis / Religious Program—Students 600.

40—ST. MARGARET OF CORTONA (1887), Rev. Msgrs. John J. Farley; Daniel A. Peake, Pastor Emeritus (Retired); Revs. Terrence J. Lee, M.H.M.; John P. McDonagh. In Res., Rev. Msgr. Michael J. Wrenn.
Res.: 6000 Riverdale Ave., Bronx, 10471. Tel: 718-549-8053; Fax: 718-543-3432.
School— (1926), 452 W. 260th St., Bronx, 10471. Tel: 718-549-8580; Fax: 718-884-3298. Sr. Dorothy DeYoung, Prin. Sisters 1; Lay Teachers 18; Students 338.
Catechesis / Religious Program—Tel: 718-884-9777. Sr. Teresa Sheehan, D.R.E. Students 212.
Chapel—Bronx, Our Lady of Grace

41—ST. MARTIN OF TOURS (1897), Revs. John C. Flynn; Benito A. Liriano; Deacons Frankie Vazques; Frankie Lopez; Jose A. Mojica. In Res., Rev. Msgr. Thomas McGarry (Retired).
Res.: 664 Grote St., Bronx, 10457. Tel: 718-295-0913.
School— (1926), E. 182nd St. & Crotona Ave., Bronx, 10457. Tel: 718-733-0347; Fax: 718-733-5142. Dominican Sisters (Sparkill, NY) 2; Lay Teachers 9; Students 290.
Catechesis / Religious Program—Ana Delia Mojica, D.R.E. Students 220.
Chapel—Dominican Convent 695 E. 182nd St., Bronx, 10457.

42—ST. MARY (1866), Rev. John B. Sullivan.
Res.: 650 E. 226th St., Bronx, 10466. Tel: 718-547-8000; Fax: 718-547-8001.
Church: White Plains Rd., Bronx, 10466.
School— (1950), 3956 Carpenter Ave., Bronx, 10466. Tel: 718-547-0500; Fax: 718-547-0530. Lay Teachers 14; Students 310.
Catechesis / Religious Program—Tel: 718-231-2569. Students 110.
Chapel—Convent 3961 Carpenter Ave., Bronx, 10466. Tel: 718-652-2873.
School Chapel—E. 224th St., Bronx, 10466.

43—ST. MARY STAR OF THE SEA (1887), Revs. Robert J. Moore; Alexander N. Iheonunekwu (Nigeria); Eugene Sudath (Sri Lanka); Deacon William J. Mueller; Sr. Bernadette Hannanay, O.S.U., Pastoral Assoc.
Res.: 595 Minneford Ave., Bronx, 10464-1118. Tel: 718-885-1440; Fax: 718-885-9498.
Church: 600 City Island Ave., Bronx, 10464.
School— (1931), 580 Minneford Ave., Bronx, 10464. Tel: 718-885-1527; Fax: 718-885-1552. Dominican Sisters of Blauvelt 2; Lay Teachers 9; Students 255.
Catechesis / Religious Program—Students 215.
Chapel—Dominican Sisters 176 Kilroe St., Bronx, 10464. Tel: 718-885-0849.

44—ST. MICHAEL (1969), Rev. William J. Luciano.
Res.: 765 Co-Op City Boulevard, Bronx, 10475-1601. Tel: 718-671-8050; Fax: 718-320-3776.
Catechesis / Religious Program—Students 81.

45—NATIVITY OF OUR BLESSED LADY (1924), Rev. Jaime H. Duenas (Retired).
Rectory: 1531 E. 233rd St., Bronx, 10466. Tel: 718-324-3531; Fax: 718-798-0628.
School— (1953), 3893 Dyre Ave., Bronx, 10466. Tel: 718-324-2188; Fax: 718-324-1128. Lay Teachers 20; Students 326.
Catechesis / Religious Program—Students 30.
Convent—1534 E. 233rd St., Bronx, 10466.

46—ST. NICHOLAS OF TOLENTINE (1906), Revs. John F. Dello Russo, O.S.A.; Joseph Tran; Robert Terranova, O.S.A. In Res., Revs. William J. Wallace, O.S.A.; Russell Ortega, O.S.A.; Jesus Guzman, O.S.A. (Mexico); Bro. Michael Duffy, O.S.A.
Res.: 2345 University Ave., Bronx, 10468. Tel: 718-295-6800; Fax: 718-367-7411.
School— (1907), 2336 Andrews Ave., Bronx, 10468. Tel: 718-364-5110; Fax: 718-561-3964. Sisters of St. Dominic of Blauvelt 1; Dominican Sisters of Sparkill 1; Lay Teachers 14; Students 430.
Catechesis / Religious Program—Tel: 718-295-6770. Mrs. Gregoria Gomez, D.R.E. Students 700.
Chapel—Convent of St. Nicholas of Tolentine 2341 University Ave., Bronx, 10468. Tel: 718-367-3102.

47—OUR LADY OF ANGELS (1924), Revs. Robert T. Ritchie; Antonio Aldana (Mexico); Fabian Lopez; Deacon Luis Delgado.
Res.: 2860 Webb Ave., Bronx, 10468. Tel: 718-548-3005; Fax: 718-884-2450.
Church: 2860 Sedgwick Ave., Bronx, 10468.
School— (1928), 2865 Claflin Ave., Bronx, 10468. Tel: 718-549-3503. Sr. Mary Ann Cleary, S.C., Prin. Sisters of Charity of St. Vincent de Paul 2; Lay Teachers 18; Students 470.
Catechesis / Religious Program—Students 340.

48—OUR LADY OF GOOD COUNSEL (1969), (Albanian), [CEM] Revs. Peter Popovich, Admin.; Andrew Nargaj, O.F.M.
Albanian Roman Catholic Center: 4221 Park Ave., Bronx, 10457. Tel: 718-294-6981.

49—OUR LADY OF GRACE (1924), Revs. Walter A. Birkle; Philip J. Caruso; Jose L. Soto, M.D.R. (Colombia).
Res.: 3985 Bronxwood Ave., Bronx, 10466. Tel: 718-652-4817; Fax: 718-652-2996.
School—Tel: 718-547-9918; Fax: 718-547-7602. Denise Rigano, Prin. Lay Teachers 18; Students 430.

50—OUR LADY OF MERCY (Fordham) (1852-1892), Revs. Ambiorix Rodriguez; John Rueda (Colombia); Pablo Rentino (Philippines); Deacon Rolando Nolasco.
Res.: 2496 Marion Ave., Bronx, 10458. Tel: 718-933-4400.
School— (1907), 2512 Marion Ave., Bronx, 10458. Tel: 718-367-0237. Lay Teachers 18; Students 310.
Catechesis / Religious Program—Students 250.
Chapel—Convent 2473 Valentine Ave., Bronx, 10458. Tel: 718-367-5558.

51—OUR LADY OF MT. CARMEL (1906), (Italian), Rev. Msgr. John A. Ruvo. In Res., Revs. Nicholas F. Basile (Retired); Anthony D'Antonio.
Res.: 627 E. 187th St., Bronx, 10458. Tel: 718-295-3770; Fax: 718-367-2240.
School— (1925), 189th St. & Bathgate Ave., Bronx, 10458. Tel: 718-295-6080; Fax: 718-329-1269. Susan L. Cotronei, Prin. Lay Teachers 13; Students 268.
Catechesis / Religious Program—Students 264.
Convent—Suore Missionarie del Catechismo, 2410 Hughes Ave., Bronx, 10458. Tel: 718-329-0390; Fax: 718-329-0390. Sisters 5.

52—OUR LADY OF PITY (1908), (Hispanic), Rev. Matthew Morreale, O.F.M., Guardian & Pastor; Bro. Dominic Poirier, O.F.M.
Res.: 276 E. 151st St., Bronx, 10451. Tel: 718-665-3880.

53—OUR LADY OF REFUGE (1923), [JC] Rev. Msgr. John J. Jenik.
Res.: 290 E. 196th St., Bronx, 10458. Tel: 718-367-4690; Fax: 718-365-7644.
School— (1923), 2708 Briggs Ave., Bronx, 10458. Tel: 718-367-3081; Fax: 718-367-0741. Lay Teachers 11; Students 345.
Catechesis / Religious Program—Tel: 718-367-3384. Students 315.

54—OUR LADY OF SOLACE (1903), Revs. John M. Knapp; Francisco Imperial (Philippines); Thomas Seraphin Parambi, C.S.T. (India).
Res.: 731 Morris Park Ave., Bronx, 10462. Tel: 718-863-3282; Fax: 718-792-4950.
School— (1916), 1804 Holland Ave., Bronx, 10462. Tel: 718-792-9947; Fax: 718-597-2482. Religious of the Presentation 2; Lay Teachers 8; Students 324.
Catechesis / Religious Program—Tel: 718-823-9044. Students 327.

55—OUR LADY OF THE ASSUMPTION (1923), Revs. Donald M. Dwyer; James F. Pilsner; Deacon Howard Banker. In Res., Rev. Aloysius Thumma, S.T.D.
Res.: 1634 Mahan Ave., Bronx, 10461. Tel: 718-824-5454; Fax: 718-824-5456.
School— (1928), 1617 Parkview Ave., Bronx, 10461. Tel: 718-829-1706. Barbara S. Kavanagh, Prin. Sisters 1; Lay Teachers 20; Students 590.
Catechesis / Religious Program—Tel: 718-904-8464. Patricia Gregory, D.R.E. Students 415.
Chapel—Convent 1639 Parkview Ave., Bronx, 10461. Tel: 718-829-7980.

56—OUR LADY OF VICTORY (1909), Rev. Peter Gavigan.
Res.: 1512 Webster Ave., Bronx, 10457. Tel: 718-583-4044; Fax: 718-583-4764.
Catechesis / Religious Program—Students 185.

57—OUR SAVIOUR (1912), (Hispanic), Revs. Jose Gabriel Piedrahita, M.X.Y.; Orlando Corrales; Jorge I. Fernandez, M.X.Y.
Res.: 2317 Washington Ave., Bronx, 10458. Tel: 718-295-9600; Fax: 718-295-9607.
Catechesis / Religious Program—Students 170.

58—ST. PETER AND ST. PAUL (1897), Rev. Luis Alberto Ordejon.
Res.: 833 St. Ann's Ave., Bronx, 10456. Tel: 718-665-3924; Fax: 718-292-5159.
School— (1911), 838 Brook Ave., Bronx, 10456. Tel: 718-665-2056. Sisters 5; Lay Teachers 14; Students 496.
Catechesis / Religious Program—Students 82.

59—SS. PHILIP AND JAMES (1949), Rev. Pat F. Rossi, Ph.D.; Deacons Albert V. Welhous; Robert Santana. In Res., Rev. Bededict Paul.
Res.: 1160 E. 213th St., Bronx, 10469. Tel: 718-547-2203; Fax: 718-231-8160.

School— (1953), 1160 E. 213th St., Bronx, 10469. Tel: 718-882-4576; Fax: 718-653-6167. Sisters of St. Dominic (Blauvelt) 1; Lay Teachers 9; Students 300.
Catechesis/Religious Program—Students 60.
Chapel—Dominican Sisters Convent 1180 E. 214th St., Bronx, 10469.

60—ST. PHILIP NERI (1898), Revs. John Bonnici; Philip Ibasco; Carlos Mullins; Hyacinth Njoku. In Res., Rev. Martin Onyebuchi (Nigeria).
Res.: 3025 Grand Concourse, Bronx, 10468. Tel: 718-733-3200; Fax: 718-733-4390.
School— (1913), 3031 Grand Concourse, Bronx, 10468. Tel: 718-365-8806. Bro. John Casey. Christian Brothers 1; Ursuline Sisters 2; Lay Teachers 23; Students 670.
Catechesis/Religious Program—Students 240.
Chapel—Convent of Mount St. Ursula Marion Ave. & 200th St., Bronx, 10468. Tel: 718-365-7410.
Chapel—Kolping Residence Kolping Society, 2916 Grand Concourse, Bronx, 10468. Tel: 718-733-6119.
Chapel—Ursuline Residence 2850 Marion Ave., Bronx, 10468. Tel: 718-295-6094.
St. Mary's Hall—323 E. 198th St., Bronx, 10468. Tel: 718-933-9894. (Ursuline)

61—ST. PIUS V (1907), Revs. Edward Russell; Adolfo Romero-Rios (Argentina); Deacons Raul Padron; Luis Torres.
Res.: 420 E. 145th St., Bronx, 10454. Tel: 718-665-6642; Fax: 718-665-4007.
School— (1913), 413 E. 144th St., Bronx, 10454. Tel: 718-665-5075; Fax: 718-665-2987. Lay Teachers 15; Students 400.
High School—500 Courtlandt Ave., Bronx, 10454. Tel: 718-292-3636; Fax: 718-402-1704. Lay Teachers 14; Students 210.
Catechesis/Religious Program—Students 190.

62—ST. RAYMOND (1842), [CEM 2] Rev. Msgr. Thomas Bergin, Admin.; Revs. George R. Stewart; George H. Hill; Eugene Cahavet, O.P.; Deacons Aldo Preti; Miguel Sepulveda. In Res., Rev. Cyril I. Akalonu (Nigeria); Rev. Msgr. Charles Chiew (Malaysia); Rev. Zacharia Samjumi (Nigeria).
Res.: 1759 Castle Hill Ave., Bronx, 10462. Tel: 718-792-4044; Fax: 718-863-8509.
School— (1909), 2380 E. Tremont Ave., Bronx, 10462. Tel: 718-597-3232; Fax: 718-892-4449. Ms. Jennifer Ciavirella, Prin. Sisters 1; Lay Teachers 24; Students 562.
High School— (Boys) , 2151 St. Raymond Ave., Bronx, 10462. Tel: 718-824-5050; Fax: 718-863-8808. Bro. Daniel J. Brenner, F.S.C., Prin. Brothers of the Christian Schools 4; Lay Teachers 56; Students 841.
High School— (Girls) Tel: 718-824-4220; Fax: 718-829-3571. Sr. Mary Ann D'Antonio, S.C., Prin. Sisters 5; Lay Teachers 19; Students 282.
Catechesis/Religious Program—Tel: 718-792-4044, Ext. 238. Mrs. Ann O'Keefe, D.R.E. Students 420.
Family Outreach Program—1720 Metropolitan Ave., Bronx, 10462. Tel: 718-792-2087. Ms. Regina Piazza, Dir.
Chapel—Brothers Residence 1754 Castle Hill Ave., Bronx, 10462. Tel: 718-829-1417; Fax: 718-863-8392. Brothers of the Christian Schools 8.

63—ST. RITA OF CASCIA SHRINE CHURCH (1900), (Spanish), Revs. Antonio Morales; Jose Gregorio Gutierrez.
Res.: 448 College Ave., Bronx, 10451. Tel: 718-585-5900; Fax: 718-585-5901.
Catechesis/Religious Program—452 College Ave..

64—ST. ROCH (1899), (Spanish), Rev. Francisco Oviedo, O.A.R., Admin.
Res.: 525 Wales Ave., Bronx, 10455. Tel: 718-292-3834; Fax: 718-292-3834.

65—SACRED HEART (1875), Revs. Michael Sepp; Mario A. Portella; Fabio E. Jaramillo (Colombia); Deacon Alfonso Ramos.
Res.: 1253 Shakespeare Ave., Bronx, 10452. Tel: 718-293-2766; Fax: 718-293-1581.
School—Primary Division (1950), 95 W. 168th St., Bronx, 10452. Tel: 718-293-4288; Fax: 718-293-4886. Kevin Smith, Prin. Lay Teachers 15; Students 440.
School—Middle School (1926), 1248 Nelson Ave., Bronx, 10452. Tel: 718-293-6040. Lay Teachers 16; Students 440.
Catechesis/Religious Program— Sr. Christina Dougherty, P.B.V.M., D.R.E. Students 340.

66—SANTA MARIA (1926), Revs. Fernando Real, M.Id., Ph.D.; Antimo Fiorillo, Pastor Emeritus; Cristobal Martin, M.Id., Ph.D.
Res.: 2352 St. Raymond Ave., Bronx, 10462. Tel: 718-828-2380; Fax: 718-828-4296.
School— (1951), 1510 Zerega Ave., Bronx, 10462. Tel: 718-823-3636; Fax: 718-823-7008. Sr. Ellen O,Connor, A.S.C.J., Prin. Sisters Apostles of the Sacred Heart 3; Lay Teachers 12; Students 250.
Catechesis/Religious Program—Students 76.
Chapel—Santa Maria Convent 1460 Zerega Ave., Bronx, 10462.

67—ST. SIMON STOCK (1919), Revs. Michael Kissane, O.Carm.; David Kearns, O.Carm. In Res., Rev. Andrew Skotnicki, O.Carm.
Res.: 2191 Valentine Ave., Bronx, 10457. Tel: 718-367-1251; Fax: 718-933-8822.
Church: East 182nd St. & Ryer Ave., Bronx 10457.
School—182nd St. & Valentine Ave., Bronx 10457. Tel: 718-367-0453; Fax: 718-733-1441. Lay Teachers 20; Students 640.
Catechesis/Religious Program—Students 275.

68—ST. THERESA OF THE INFANT JESUS (1927), (Italian), Revs. Robert F. Grippo; Christopher Monturo; Robert Imbelli (Vatican City State); Deacon Anthony P. Cassaneto. In Res., Rev. Msgr. Joseph Devlin; Rev. John Lauri.
Res.: 2855 St. Theresa Ave., Bronx, 10461. Tel: 718-892-1900; Fax: 718-892-1146.
School— (1954), 2872 St. Theresa Ave., Bronx, 10461. Tel: 718-792-3688; Fax: 718-892-9441. Ms. Ann M. Gevlin, Prin. Lay Teachers 25; Students 550.
Catechesis/Religious Program—Tel: 718-792-8434. Sr. Martha Otterstedt, D.R.E. Students 114.

69—ST. THOMAS AQUINAS (1890), Most Rev. Francisco Garmendia, D.D., Pastor Emeritus, Admin.; Revs. Fortunato Romero; Lorenzo Ato.
Res.: 1900 Crotona Pkwy., Bronx, 10460. Tel: 718-589-5235; Fax: 718-893-0498.
School— (1907), 1909 Daly Ave., Bronx, 10460. Tel: 718-893-7600; Fax: 718-378-5531. Lay Teachers 23; Students 540.
Convent—1899 Daly Ave., Bronx, 10460.

70—ST. VALENTINE (1891), (Polish), Unassigned.
Res.: 810 E. 221st St., Bronx, 10467. Tel: 718-652-3197.

71—VISITATION (1928), Rev. Msgr. Robert W. Larkin; Rev. Viliam Litavec (Slovakia); Deacon George McGowan.
Res.: 160 Van Cortlandt Park S., Bronx, 10463. Tel: 718-548-1455; Fax: 718-548-0289.
School— (1932), Putnam Ave. & W. 239th St., Bronx, 10463. Tel: 718-543-2250; Fax: 718-543-3665. Priests 2; Sisters 3; Lay Teachers 7; Students 240.
Catechesis/Religious Program—Students 120.

BOROUGH OF RICHMOND STATEN ISLAND

1—ST. ADALBERT (Elm Park) (1901), (Polish), Rev. Eugene J. Carrella; Deacon Joseph J. Rentkowski. In Res., Rev. Msgr. John D. Burke (Retired).
Res.: 337 Morningstar Rd., 10303. Tel: 718-442-8476; Fax: 718-727-1241.
School— (1905), 355 Morningstar Rd., Elm Park, 10303. Tel: 718-442-2020; Fax: 718-447-2012. Priests 1; Lay Teachers 9; Students 370.
Catechesis/Religious Program—Students 100.

2—ST. ANN (1914), Rev. Lawrence T. Quinn; Rev. Msgr. Vincent F. Clyne, Pastor Emeritus (Retired); Revs. Pancrose Kalist (India); Mathew Eraly (India); Terence O'Rourke, O.S.A.
Res.: 101 Cromwell Ave., 10304. Tel: 718-351-0270; Fax: 718-980-4731.
School— (1955), 125 Cromwell Ave., 10304. Tel: 718-351-4343. Presentation Nuns 1; Lay Teachers 12; Students 349.
Catechesis/Religious Program—Michael A. Mazella, D.R.E. Students 471.

3—ST. ANTHONY (1908), Rev. John J. Wroblewski.
Res.: 24 Shelly Ave., 10314. Tel: 718-761-6660; Fax: 718-761-1029.
Church: Victory Blvd., 10314.
Catechesis/Religious Program—Students 177.

4—ASSUMPTION (1922), (Italian), Rev. CanonJohn A. Pintabone, K.H.S.
Res.: 15 Webster Ave., 10301. Tel: 718-727-4594; Fax: 718-981-2098.

5—ST. BENEDICTA (1925), Closed., For inquiries for parish records contact Our Lady of Mount Carmel.

6—BLESSED SACRAMENT (1910), Rev. Msgr. Francis V. Boyle; Revs. Stephen M. Ryan; Joseph Victor Arenas (Philippines); Michael R. Paradela (Philippines).
Res.: 30 Manor Rd., 10310. Tel: 718-442-1581; Fax: 718-442-1398.
Church: Manor Rd. & Forest Ave., 10310.
School— (1917), 830 Delafield Ave., 10310. Tel: 718-442-3090; Fax: 718-442-9654. Mrs. Linda Magnusson, Prin. Sisters, Servants of the Immaculate Heart of Mary 3; Lay Teachers 20; Students 698.
Catechesis/Religious Program—Tel: 718-448-0378. Students 333.

7—ST CHARLES (1960), Rev. Msgr. Thomas J. Gaffney (Retired); Revs. Robert W. Dillon; Albin Roby; Deacons Vincent Brigande; Michael Calafiore; Lawrence Droge.
Res.: 644 Clawson St., 10306. Tel: 718-987-2670; Fax: 718-987-7950.
School—Tel: 718-987-0200. Sisters of St. Dominic (Blauvelt) 1; Lay Teachers 24; Students 827.
Catechesis/Religious Program—Tel: 718-979-6800. Students 520.

8—ST. CHRISTOPHER (1926), (Italian—Irish), Rev. Msgr. Kenneth A. Gerathy; Revs. Michael Arputham Arockiam (India); Pawel P. Sochacki (Poland).
Res.: 130 Midland Ave., 10306. Tel: 718-351-2452; Fax: 718-351-1174.
School— (1930), 15 Lisbon Pl., 10306. Tel: 718-351-0902; Fax: 718-351-0975. Catherine Mizzi-Gili, Prin. Lay Teachers 14; Students 299.
Catechesis/Religious Program—Students 140.

9—ST. CLARE (1921), Rev. Msgr. Joseph P. Murphy; Revs. Joseph Karikunnel; Michael Panful; Matthew J. Furey; Deacons Richard Mitchell; Nunzio Sorrentino.
Res.: 110 Nelson Ave., 10308. Tel: 718-984-7873; Fax: 718-966-8420.
School—151 Lindenwood Rd., 10308. Tel: 718-984-7091. Sr. Rosemary Ward, Prin. Sisters Religious of the Presentation 2; Lay Teachers 20; Students 679.
Catechesis/Religious Program—Tel: 718-948-4829. Mrs. Virginia Tannacore, D.R.E. Students 1,785.

10—ST. CLEMENT (1910), Rev. Msgr. Nicholas J. Soares; Rev. Manuel I. Rojas (Peru).
Res.: 207 Harbor Rd., 10303. Tel: 718-442-1688; Fax: 718-442-4689.
Church: 126 Van Pelt Ave., 10303.
Catechesis/Religious Program—Tel: 718-727-6442. Students 430.

11—HOLY CHILD (1966), Revs. Thomas P. Devery; John S. Kostek; Basil Akut; Romeo Castillo; Deacon Alfred Thompson; Sr. Jean Wagner, P.B.V.M., Pastoral Assoc.; Joseph Giammanco, Youth Min.; Ann Lukasiewicz.
Res.: 4747 Amboy Rd., 10312. Tel: 718-356-5890; Fax: 718-356-5995.
Preschool Office—4747 Amboy Rd., 10312. Tel: 718-356-5159; Fax: 718-356-1933.
School—School of Religion, Tel: 718-356-5277; Fax: 718-227-0898. Marie Ferro, D.R.E. Lay Teachers 112; Students 1,200.

12—HOLY FAMILY (1966), [JC] Revs. Austin E. Titus; Albert Pucci; Patrick N. Nsionu; Rev. Msgr. Francis J. Glynn, Pastor Emeritus (Retired).
Mailing Address: 366 Watchogue Rd., 10314. Tel: 718-761-6663; Fax: 718-982-0287.
School—School of Religion (1967), 330 Watchogue Rd., 10314. Tel: 718-761-1598. (Elementary & High School) Sisters 2; Lay Teachers 54; Students 540.
Catechesis/Religious Program—Students 550.
Convent—85 Delmore St., 10314. Tel: 718-698-3118.

13—HOLY ROSARY (1927), Rev. Msgr. Richard J. Guastella; Revs. Eduardo Amora (Philippines); Stephen G. Challman; Deacon Rosario Tirella. In Res., Rev. John P. DeLora, Dir. Pastoral Care, Staten Island University Hospital.
Res.: 80 Jerome Ave., 10305. Tel: 718-727-3360; Fax: 718-876-6183.
School— (1955),(Grades PreK-8), 100 Jerome Ave., 10305. Tel: 718-447-1195; Fax: 718-815-5862. Diane R. Murphy, Prin.; Joanne DelGeorge, Asst. Prin. Lay Teachers 23; Students 630.
Catechesis/Religious Program—Tel: 718-273-6695. Sr. Catherine Shanahan, S.N.D.deN., D.R.E. Students 345.

14—IMMACULATE CONCEPTION (1887), Rev. Peter J. Byrne. In Res., Rev. Peter J. West.
Res.: 128 Targee St., 10304. Tel: 718-447-2165; Fax: 718-447-4835.
School— (1908), 104 Gordon St., 10304. Tel: 718-447-7018; Fax: 718-447-4365. Ms. Kathleen Curatolo, Prin. Sisters 1; Lay Staff 15; Students 192.
Catechesis/Religious Program—Students 180.
Chapel—Bayley Seton Hospital Bay St., 10304. Tel: 718-390-6000.

15—ST. JOHN NEUMANN (1982), Revs. James Malley; Mario Ramirez, M.S.C.
Res.: 1380 Arthur Kill Rd., 10312. Tel: 718-984-8535; Fax: 718-689-6948.
Catechesis/Religious Program—Tel: 718-966-7327. Students 401.

16—ST. JOHN THE BAPTIST DE LA SALLE (1900), Rev. Peter J. Byrne, Admin. In Res., Rev. Thomas Mullin.
Res.: 128 Targee St., 10304. Tel: 718-447-2165; Fax: 718-447-4835.
Church: 76 Jackson St., 10304.

17—ST. JOSEPH (1902), (Italian), Rev. Msgr. John T. Servodidio (Retired).
Parish Office—463 Tompkins Ave., 10305. Tel: 718-816-0047; Fax: 718-816-4529.
Res.: 171 St. Mary's Ave., 10305.
Church: 466 Tompkins Ave., 10305.
School—139 St. Mary's Ave., 10305. Tel: 718-447-7686; Fax: 718-447-7687. Linda Bilotti, Prin. Lay Teachers 12; Students 271.
Catechesis/Religious Program—Students 88.

18—ST. JOSEPH, ST. THOMAS (1848), [CEM] Revs. Michael W. Cichon; Richard Veras; Evangelio R.

Suaybaguio; Mario R. Valle (Philippines).
Res.: 6135 Amboy Rd., 10309. Tel: 718-984-4572; Fax: 718-948-3885.
School—Tel: 718-356-3344; Fax: 718-227-9531. JoAnn Gaal, Prin. Lay Teachers 11; Students 342.
Catechesis/Religious Program—Tel: 718-984-1156. Students 1,319.

19—ST. MARGARET MARY (1926), Rev. Robert J. Navins.
Res.: 560 Lincoln Ave., 10306. Tel: 718-351-2612; Fax: 718-987-0446.
School— (1925), 556 Lincoln Ave., 10306. Tel: 718-351-4778; Fax: 718-351-3786. Sr. Barbara Heclo, Prin. Sisters, Religious of the Presentation 1; Lay Teachers 8; Students 232.
Catechesis/Religious Program—Tel: 718-987-4388. Students 141.

20—ST. MARY (1852), [CEM] Rev. Victor J. Buebendorf.
Res.: 1101 Bay St., 10305. Tel: 718-727-0671; Fax: 718-815-7393.
School— (1853), 1124 Bay St., 10305. Tel: 718-447-1842; Fax: 718-447-0986. Virginia Savarese, Prin. Lay Teachers 10; Students 220.
Catechesis/Religious Program—Students 129.

21—ST. MARY OF THE ASSUMPTION (1853), [CEM] Rev. D. Michael Flynn, S.J., Admin.; Deacon James Stahldecker.
Res.: 2230 Richmond Ter., 10302. Tel: 718-442-6372; Fax: 718-448-2159.
Catechesis/Religious Program—Students 241.
Mission—Christ the King 182 Park Ave., Richmond Co. 10302.

22—ST. MICHAEL (1922), Rev. Msgr. Nicholas J. Soares; Rev. Manuel I. Rojas (Peru).
Res.: 207 Harbor Rd., 10303. Tel: 718-442-1688; Fax: 718-442-4689.
Church: 211-213 Harbor Rd., 10303.
Catechesis/Religious Program—Tel: 718-727-6442. Students 430.

23—OUR LADY HELP OF CHRISTIANS (1898), Revs. Jarlath Quinn; John Tran; Deacons Edward J. Wetherall; John Singler; Richard Salhany.
Res.: 7396 Amboy Rd., 10307. Tel: 718-317-9772; Fax: 718-317-0038.
School— (1910 and 1955), 23 Summit St., 10307. Tel: 718-984-1360; Fax: 718-966-9356. Mrs. N. Fresca, Prin. Lay Teachers 10; Students 190.
Catechesis/Religious Program—Tel: 718-356-3888. Students 850.

24—OUR LADY OF GOOD COUNSEL (1898), Revs. Francis A. Sirolli, O.S.A., Pastor; Luis M. Madera, O.S.A.; Augustus C. Sandmann, O.S.A., Acting Prior; Deacon Arthur W. Eccleston.
Res.: 10 Austin Pl., 10304. Tel: 718-447-1503; Fax: 718-447-7361.
School— (1923), 42 Austin Pl., 10304. Tel: 718-447-7260; Fax: 718-815-7262. Mrs. Frances Santangelo, Prin. Lay Teachers 13; Students 285.
Catechesis/Religious Program—Tel: 718-816-0542. Patricia Odessa, D.R.E. Students 217.

25—OUR LADY OF MT. CARMEL-ST. BENEDICTA (1913), (Irish—Italian), Revs. Thomas N. Cerulo, O.SS.T.; Daniel Houde, O.SS.T. In Res., Rev. Joseph F. Lupo, O.SS.T.
Res.: 1265 Castleton Ave., 10310. Tel: 718-442-3411; Fax: 718-442-3997.
School—285 Clove Rd., 10310. Tel: 718-981-5131; Fax: 718-981-0027.
Catechesis/Religious Program—Students 275.

26—OUR LADY OF PITY (1923), (Italian), Rev. Msgr. Philip J. Franceschini; Rev. John E. Mercer; Sr. Eugene Sanita, Pastoral Assoc.; Rev. Msgr. Robert R. Mazziotta, Pastor Emeritus (Retired).
Res.: 1616 Richmond Ave., 10314. Tel: 718-761-5421; Fax: 718-983-6225.
Catechesis/Religious Program—Tel: 718-477-5999. Carmen Iacobelli, D.R.E. Students 414.

27—OUR LADY STAR OF THE SEA (1916), Rev. Msgr. Jeffrey Conway; Rev. Eric Rapaglia; Sr. Ann Marie Perugini, Pastoral Assoc.; Mrs. Debra Emigholz, Business Mgr.
Res.: 5371 Amboy Rd., Huguenot Park, 10312. Tel: 718-984-0593; Fax: 718-984-5203.
School— (1958), 5411 Amboy Rd., 10312. Tel: 718-984-5750. Sisters 1; Lay Teachers 27; Students 960.
Catechesis/Religious Program—5411 Amboy Rd., 10312. Tel: 718-984-1885. Mrs. Cathy Alegre, D.R.E. Students 1,225.

28—OUR LADY, QUEEN OF PEACE (1922), Revs. Robert I. Gannon; John A. DeBellis; John J. Sheehan; Deacon Ross Calimano. In Res., Rev. James Garisto.
Res.: 90 Third St., 10306. Tel: 718-351-1093.
School— (1924), 22 Steele Ave., 10306. Tel: 718-351-0370. Sr. Mary Regina Gibbons, Prin. Sisters of the Presentation 1; Lay Teachers 17; Students 600.
Catechesis/Religious Program—Tel: 718-979-0989. Students 570.
Mission—Our Lady of Lourdes Cedar Grove Ave., New Dorp Beach, Richmond Co. 10306.
Chapel—St. Therese of the Child Jesus 62 Cloister Pl., 10306. Tel: 718-351-0209.

29—ST. PATRICK (1862), Rev. Msgr. John M. McCarthy; Revs. Mark G. Vaillancourt; Francisco H. Lanzaderad; Deacon Joseph Hooghuis.
Parish Office:—3560 Richmond Rd., 10306. Tel: 718-979-4227; Fax: 718-979-7637.
Res.: 53 St. Patrick's Pl., 10306. Tel: 718-351-0044; Fax: 718-351-0824.
School— (1919), 3560 Richmond Rd., 10306. Tel: 718-979-8815; Fax: 718-979-4984. Sr. Mary Ferro, S.S.D., Prin. Sisters 1; Lay Teachers 22; Students 601.
Catechesis/Religious Program—Tel: 718-979-1272. Students 378.

30—ST. PAUL (1924), Revs. Vincent Bartley; Ignatius Vu.
Res. & Mailing Address: 145 Clinton Ave., 10301. Tel: 718-447-6362; Fax: 718-720-0106.
School— (1954), 129 Clinton Ave., 10301. Tel: 718-447-5774; Fax: 718-447-5881. Ms. Mary Chiapperino, Prin. Lay Teachers 9; Students 250.
Catechesis/Religious Program—Students 50.
Christian Brothers Residence—148 Cassidy Pl., 10301.

31—ST. PETER (1839), [CEM] Rev. Msgr. James J. Dorney.
Res.: 53 St. Mark's Pl., 10301. Tel: 718-727-2672; Fax: 718-720-9269.
School—300 Richmond Ter., 10301. Tel: 718-447-1796; Fax: 718-447-4240. Mrs. Lisa Moudatsos, Prin. Lay Teachers 12; Students 277.
High School—Boys High School, 200 Clinton Ave., 10301. Tel: 718-447-1676; Fax: 718-447-4027. Mr. John Fodera, Prin.; Bro. James Kelly, F.S.C., Pres. Sisters 2; Brothers of the Christian Schools 4; Lay Teachers 34; Students 781.
High School—Girls High School, Tel: 718-447-0304; Fax: 718-447-0832. Miss Florence Bricker, Prin. Lay Teachers 18; Students 261.
St. Joseph, Brothers' House—Tel: 718-447-2815.
Catechesis/Religious Program—Students 42.

32—ST. RITA (1921), Revs. Austin E. Titus; John F. Reardon.
Res.: 281 Bradley Ave., 10314. Tel: 718-698-3746; Fax: 718-698-3791.
School— (1922), 30 Wellbrook Ave., 10314. Tel: 718-961-2504. Sisters 2; Lay Teachers 18; Students 560.
Catechesis/Religious Program—Students 470.
Chapel—Dominican Sisters 61 Wellbrook Ave., 10314. Tel: 718-761-1171. (Roman Congregation of St. Dominic)

33—ST. ROCH (1922), Rev. Leo R. Prince, Ph.D. In Res., Rev. G. David Sears, M.S., C.S.W. (SY).
Res.: 602 Port Richmond Ave., 10302. Tel: 718-442-4755; Fax: 718-981-4455.
School—465 Villa Ave., 10302. Tel: 718-448-2424. Sr. Mary Patricia, Prin. Sisters of St. John the Baptist 5; Lay Teachers 9; Students 297.
Catechesis/Religious Program—Students 120.

34—SACRED HEART (1875), Rev. Louis Jerome; Rev. Msgr. Andrew F. Quinn, Pastor Emeritus (Retired); Rev. Charles Oduro.
Res.: 981 Castleton Ave., 10310. Tel: 718-442-0058; Fax: 718-816-8006.
School— (1875), 301 N. Burgher Ave., 10310. Tel: 718-442-0347; Fax: 718-440-6978. Jacqueline DiSanto, Prin. Lay Teachers 23; Students 522.
Catechesis/Religious Program—Tel: 718-448-1536. Students 522.

35—ST. STANISLAUS KOSTKA (1923), (Polish), Revs. Marek Suchocki, J.C.D., M.Th. (Poland); Jacek Wozny (Poland).
Res.: 109 York Ave., 10301. Tel: 718-447-3937; Fax: 718-815-5733.
Catechesis/Religious Program—Students 69.

36—ST. SYLVESTER (1921), (Irish—Italian), Rev. Arthur A. Golino.
Res.: 854 Targee St., 10304-4517. Tel: 718-727-4639; Fax: 718-273-2950.
School— (1930), 884 Targee St., 10304. Tel: 718-442-4938; Fax: 718-442-8177. Nancy Bushman, Prin. Lay Teachers 10; Students 297.
Catechesis/Religious Program—Tel: 718-442-1374. Students 90.

37—ST. TERESA (1926), (Irish—Italian), Revs. William J. Boldt, Pastor Emeritus (Retired); John J. O'Hara; James Miara.
Res.: 1634 Victory Blvd., 10314. Tel: 718-442-5412; Fax: 718-442-9041.
School— (1955), 1632 Victory Blvd., 10314. Tel: 718-448-9650. Lay Teachers 22; Students 605.
Catechesis/Religious Program—Tel: 718-981-2632; Fax: 718-981-0026. Students 271.
Mission—St. Nicholas Northern Blvd., Staten Island Co. 10301.
Chapel—St. Nicholas La Bau Ave. & Northern Blvd., 10314.

OUTSIDE THE CITY OF NEW YORK

AMENIA, DUTCHESS CO., IMMACULATE CONCEPTION (1868), [CEM] Rev. John L. Durkin; Deacon David Weinstein; Rev. Abraham A. Berko (Ghana).
Res.: 4 Lavelle Rd., Box 109, 12501. Tel: 845-373-8193; Fax: 845-373-8194.
Catechesis/Religious Program—Students 150.
Mission—St. Patrick [CEM] Church St., Millerton, Dutchess Co. 12546.

ARDSLEY, WESTCHESTER CO., OUR LADY OF PERPETUAL HELP (1929), Revs. Philip J. Gagliano; Robert J. Duane, Pastor Emeritus (Retired).
Res.: One Cross Rd., 10502. Tel: 914-693-0030; Fax: 914-693-5332.
Catechesis/Religious Program—Tel: 914-693-0037. Students 394.

ARMONK, WESTCHESTER CO., ST. PATRICK (1966), Rev. John F. Quinn; Rev. Msgr. Walter L. Schroeder, Pastor Emeritus (Retired).
Res.: 29 Cox Ave., P.O. Box 6, 10504. Tel: 914-273-9724.
Catechesis/Religious Program—Tel: 914-273-8226. Mrs. Ann O'Sullivan, D.R.E. Students 420.

BANGALL, DUTCHESS CO., IMMACULATE CONCEPTION (1919), [CEM] Unassigned.
Res.: Hunns Lake Rd., P.O. Box 623, 12506. Tel: 914-868-1923; Fax: 914-868-1593.
Catechesis/Religious Program—Students 28.
Mission—St. Joseph (1883), Clinton Corners, Dutchess Co. 12514.

BARRYTOWN, DUTCHESS CO., SACRED HEART, Closed., Parochial records at St. Christopher, Red Hook.

BEACON, DUTCHESS CO.

1—ST. JOACHIM (1853), [CEM 2] Revs. Joseph F. Bisignano, Admin.; John Lynch.
Res.: 31 Willow St., 12508. Tel: 845-831-0422; Fax: 845-831-1009.
Church: 57 Leonard St., 12508. Tel: 845-831-0377; Fax: 845-831-9504.
Catechesis/Religious Program—Tel: 845-838-5376. Students 102.

2—ST. JOHN EVANGELIST (1887), Revs. Joseph J. Bisignano; Tomas Bobadilla (Mexico); Thaddeus Obba (Nigeria).
Res.: 31 Willow St., P.O. Box 549, 12508. Tel: 845-831-0422; Fax: 845-831-1009.
Catechesis/Religious Program—Tel: 914-838-5376; Fax: 914-831-1009. Students 545.

BEDFORD, WESTCHESTER CO., ST. PATRICK (1929), Rev. Msgrs. George P. Thompson; John B. Kauta (Uganda).
Res.: 7 Pound Ridge Rd., 10506. Tel: 914-234-3668; Fax: 914-234-9126.
School— (1956), State Rd., 10506. Tel: 914-234-7914; Fax: 914-234-0773. Mrs. Elizabeth Frangella, Prin. Lay Teachers 12; Students 189.
Catechesis/Religious Program—Tel: 914-234-3775; Fax: 914-234-0579. Students 510.

BLAUVELT, ROCKLAND CO., ST. CATHARINE (1868), [CEM] Rev. Msgr. Emmet R. Nevin; Revs. Herbert P. Degaris; Abraham Vallayil, C.M.I.; Deacon John C. Kelleher.
Res.: 523 Western Hwy., 10913. Tel: 845-359-0542; Fax: 845-365-2387.
School— (1957), 517 Western Hwy., 10913. Tel: 845-359-4330. Ms. Sharon Goodman, Prin. Sisters of St. Dominic of Blauvelt 1; Lay Teachers 10; Students 275.
Catechesis/Religious Program—Tel: 845-359-4014. Mrs. Audrey Angelini, D.R.E. Students 283.

BREWSTER, PUTNAM CO., ST. LAWRENCE O'TOOLE (1878), [CEM] Revs. Robert J. DeJulio; Paul Yeboah; Andrew Gyabbah; Deacons Mark Shkreli; John Baffa.
Res.: 31 Prospect St., 10509. Tel: 845-279-2021; Fax: 845-279-7441.
School— (1928), 11 Eastview Ave., 10509. Tel: 845-279-5164; Fax: 845-279-8165. Mrs. Sharyn O'Leary, Prin. Lay Teachers 13; Students 260.
Catechesis/Religious Program—Tel: 845-279-6098; Fax: 845-279-6098. Mrs. Nancy Breznicky, D.R.E. Students 675.

BRIARCLIFF MANOR, WESTCHESTER CO., ST. THERESA (1926), Rev. Msgr. James K. Vaughey; Rev. L. Praxid DeSilva (Sri Lanka).
Res.: 1394 Pleasantville Rd., 10510. Tel: 914-941-1646; Fax: 914-944-9503.
School—Tel: 914-762-1050; Fax: 914-941-9483. Lay Teachers 10; Students 200.
Catechesis/Religious Program—Tel: 914-923-3286. Students 500.
Mission—Our Lady of the Wayside Rte. 100, Millwood, Westchester Co. 10546.

BRONXVILLE, WESTCHESTER CO., ST. JOSEPH (1922), Rev. Msgrs. James F. Doyle; Guy Vinci; James Sullivan; Rev. William A. Kelleher (Retired). In Res., Revs. Dawson Ambosta (India); Irvdayam Antony (India).
Res.: 15 Cedar St., 10708. Tel: 914-337-1660; Fax: 914-337-1342.
School— (1951), 30 Meadow Ave., 10708. Tel: 914-337-0261; Fax: 914-395-1192. Nancy Langehennig, Prin. Lay Teachers 25; Students 265.
Catechesis/Religious Program—28 Meadow Ave.,

10708. Tel: 914-337-6383; Fax: 914-337-1342. Students 550.

BUCHANAN, WESTCHESTER CO., ST. CHRISTOPHER (1929), Rev. Msgr. Donald W. Hendricks; Rev. Leonard J. DiNola; Deacon Ronald J. Schlitt.
Res.: 94 Albany Post Rd., 10511. Tel: 914-737-1046; Fax: 914-737-9320.
Catechesis / Religious Program—Students 370.

CALLICOON, SULLIVAN CO., HOLY CROSS (1870), [CEM] [JC 2] Rev. Ignatius E. Smith, O.F.M.
Res.: 9719 Rte. 97, P.O. Box 246, 12723. Tel: 845-887-5450; Fax: 845-887-5873.
Catechesis / Religious Program—Students 104.
Mission—St. Patrick c/o P.O. Box 246, Long Eddy, Sullivan Co. 12723.
Chapel—Callicoon, Holy Cross Rectory

CARMEL, PUTNAM CO., ST. JAMES THE APOSTLE (1913), Revs. Joseph J. Faraone; Anthony D. Sorgi; Vincent dePaul Howley; Peter Alade (Nigeria); Deacons James Attridge; Charles T. Borsavage; Tony Gruerio; Gerard Cartwright; Anthony Gruerio.
Res.: 14 Gleneida Ave., 10512. Tel: 914-225-2079; Fax: 914-225-5566.
School— (1954),Tel: 914-225-9365; Fax: 914-228-2859. Lay Teachers 16; Students 302.
Catechesis / Religious Program—Tel: 914-225-6504. Students 1,429.
Mission—Our Lady of the Lake [JC] Noonan Dr., Lake Carmel, Putnam Co. 10512. Tel: 914-228-1235.

CENTERVILLE, ULSTER CO., ST. JOHN THE EVANGELIST (1886), Rev. Msgr. William E. Williams; Deacon Edwin R. Topple. In Res., Rev. James W. Derrenbacher (Retired).
Res.: 915 Rte. 212, Saugerties, 12477. Tel: 845-246-9581; Fax: 845-246-9582.
Office—Tel: 845-246-9581.
Catechesis / Religious Program—Students 202.

CHAPPAQUA, WESTCHESTER CO., ST. JOHN AND ST. MARY (1922), Rev. Msgr. Charles S. Kelly; Deacons Louis Santore; Charles Devlin; Mrs. Joan Ferroni, Pastoral Assoc. In Res., Rev. John A. Vigilanti, J.C.L., Ph.D.
Res.: 15 St. John's Pl., 10514. Tel: 914-238-3274; Fax: 914-238-3354.
Catechesis / Religious Program—30 Poillon Rd., 10514. Tel: 914-238-3696. Sr. Margaret Breslin, O.P., D.R.E. Students 635.

CHESTER, ORANGE CO., ST. COLUMBA (1875), [CEM] Revs. Thomas J. Curley; Salvatore Paterno; Joseph Doran; Waclaw Swierzbiolek.
Res.: 27 High St., 10918. Tel: 845-469-2108; Fax: 845-469-6165.
Catechesis / Religious Program—Tel: 914-469-9503. Students 228.
Station—Camp La Guardia Greycourt. Tel: 914-469-6200. (NYC Homeless Shelter).

COLD SPRING-ON-HUDSON, PUTNAM CO., OUR LADY OF LORETTO (1833), Revs. Brian T. McSweeney; Nicholas Addison (Ghana).
Res.: 24 Fair St., 10516. Tel: 845-265-3718; Fax: 845-265-4309.
Catechesis / Religious Program—Tel: 845-265-2594. Sr. Ann Teresa Nagy, S.A., D.R.E. Students 281.
Mission—St. Joseph's Chapel Garrison, Putnam Co. 10524.

CONGERS, ROCKLAND CO., ST. PAUL (1896), [CEM] Revs. Arthur Mastrolia; Niranjan Rodrigo, S.S.S.; Deacons Dominic Buonocore; John W. McSherry; James Gorman.
Res.: 82 Lake Rd. W., 10920. Tel: 845-268-4464; Fax: 845-268-6790.
School—365 Kings Hwy., Valley Cottage, 10989. Tel: 914-268-6506; Fax: 914-268-1809. Sr. Stephen Gerard, O.P., Prin. Sisters 3; Lay Teachers 16; Students 397.
Catechesis / Religious Program—Tel: 845-268-5442. Students 803.
Chapel—Congers, Sisters' Convent and School

CORNWALL-ON-HUDSON, ORANGE CO., ST. THOMAS OF CANTERBURY (1870), [CEM] Revs. Bernard P. Heter; Richard J. Caplice, S.J.
Res.: 10 Second St., 12520. Tel: 914-534-2547; Fax: 914-534-1357.
School— (1913), Hudson St., 12520. Tel: 914-534-2019. Mrs. Agnes Maleakas, Prin. Lay Teachers 9; Students 253.
Catechesis / Religious Program—Tel: 914-534-9393. Mrs. Judy Valentine, D.R.E. Students 675.

CORTLANDT MANOR, WESTCHESTER CO.
1—ST. COLUMBANUS (Van Cortlandtville) (1950), Rev. Msgr. Patrick J. Keenan; Rev. John Nicholas Muthusamy (India); Deacon John J. Coppola.
Res.: 122 Oregon Rd., 10567. Tel: 914-737-4705; Fax: 914-736-7476.
School—122 Oregon Rd., 10567. Tel: 914-739-1200; Fax: 914-739-1109. Lay Teachers 11; Students 254.
Catechesis / Religious Program—Tel: 914-739-2441. Students 595.
Mission—North American Martyrs Putnam Valley. 55 Oscawana Lake Rd., Lake Peekskill, Putnam Co. 10579. Tel: 914-528-6433.
2—HOLY SPIRIT (1966), Rev. Thomas P. Kiely; Rev. Msgr. William J. McMahon, Ph.D. (Retired); Deacons Ray Parchen; Eddy Beckendorf.
Res.: 1969 Crompond Rd., 10567-4113. Tel: 914-737-2316; Fax: 914-737-6882.
Catechesis / Religious Program—Tel: 914-734-9243. Students 650.
Chapel—Cortlandt Manor

CRESTWOOD, WESTCHESTER CO., CHURCH OF THE ANNUNCIATION (1931), Rev. Msgr. Dennis P. Keane, Ph.D.; Rev. William J. Damroth III. In Res., Rev. Msgr. Harry C. Barrett.
Res.: 470 Westchester Ave., 10707. Tel: 914-779-7345; 914-779-7542; Fax: 914-961-5688.
School— (1943), 465 Westchester Ave., 10707. Tel: 914-337-8760; Fax: 914-337-8878. Sr. Anne Massell, P.B.V.M., Prin. Sisters 5; Lay Teachers 25; Students 525.
Catechesis / Religious Program—Tel: 914-779-2374. Students 72.

CROTON FALLS, WESTCHESTER CO., ST. JOSEPH (1845), Rev. Msgr. James R. Moore; Revs. Jude Aquwa (Nigeria); George T. M. Hafemann; Jerome Ofoegbu (Nigeria).
Res.: 10 Croton Falls Rd., 10519. Tel: 914-277-3765; 914-277-3877; Fax: 914-277-1823.
School— (1949),(Grades K-8) Tel: 914-277-3783; Fax: 914-277-3238. Lay Teachers 10; Students 165.
Catechesis / Religious Program—14 Croton Falls Rd., 10519. Tel: 914-276-1067. Catherine Garnsey, D.R.E. Students 1,100.
Mission—St. Michael Park Ave., Goldens Bridge, Westchester Co. 10526.
Mission—St. John [CEM] Rte. 116, North Salem, Westchester Co. 10560.

CROTON-ON-HUDSON, WESTCHESTER CO., HOLY NAME OF MARY (1874), Revs. Michael Keane, Admin.; Loyola Amalraj; Deacon Albert Mazza. In Res., Rev. Henry Tanto.
Res.: 110 Grand St., 10520. Tel: 914-271-4797; Fax: 914-271-6841.
School—Tel: 914-271-5182.
Catechesis / Religious Program—114 Grand St., 10520. Tel: 914-271-4254; Fax: 914-271-6841. Students 408.
Mission—Church of the Good Shepherd Benedict Blvd. and Young Ave., Harmon, Westchester Co. 10520.

DOBBS FERRY, WESTCHESTER CO.
1—OUR LADY OF POMPEII (1922), (Italian), Rev. Charles Glavina; Deacon N. Anthony Barbieri.
Res.: 95 Palisade St., 10522. Tel: 914-693-1839; Fax: 914-693-8660.
Catechesis / Religious Program—Students 74.
2—SACRED HEART (1862), Rev. Timothy J. Scannell, Ph.D.; Deacon Patrick D. Troy; Sr. Connie Koch, O.P., Pastoral Assoc.
Res.: 18 Bellewood Ave., 10522. Tel: 914-693-0119; Fax: 914-693-3408.
Church: Broadway and Ashford Ave., 10522.
Catechesis / Religious Program—Tel: 914-479-1045. Mrs. Mary Perillo, D.R.E. Students 353.

DOVER PLAINS, DUTCHESS CO., ST. CHARLES BORROMEO (1859), [CEM] Rev. Msgr. Edward Barry.
Res.: P.O. Box 9, 83 Mill St., 12522. Tel: 845-877-9934; Fax: 845-877-9936.
Catechesis / Religious Program—Tel: 845-832-6989; Fax: 845-832-6989. Students 359.
Mission—Our Lady of Solace Mission Wingdale, Dutchess Co.

EAST KINGSTON, ULSTER CO., ST. COLMAN (1904), Rev. Luke W. McCann, Ph.D. In Res., Rev. John C. McGuire (Retired).
Res.: 18 Brigham St., Kingston, 12401. Tel: 914-336-8237; Fax: 914-382-1488.
Catechesis / Religious Program—Students 80.

ELLENVILLE, ULSTER CO., ST. MARY AND ST. ANDREW (1850), Rev. Msgr. Robert P. Hickey
Res.: 137 S. Main St., 12428. Tel: 914-647-6080.
Mission—Our Lady of Lourdes Kerhonkson, Ulster Co. 12446.

ELMSFORD, WESTCHESTER CO., OUR LADY OF MT. CARMEL (1904), Rev. Thomas P. D'Angelo.
Res.: 59 E. Main St., 10523. Tel: 914-592-6789; Fax: 914-592-3898.
School— (1929), E. Main St., 10523. Tel: 914-592-7575; Fax: 914-345-1591. Sisters of Divine Compassion 4; Lay Teachers 7; Students 211.
Catechesis / Religious Program—Tel: 914-592-4280. Students 109.

FISHKILL, DUTCHESS CO., CHURCH OF ST. MARY, MOTHER OF THE CHURCH (1953), Rev. Msgr. Joseph A. Martin; Rev. Kent Wilson; Deacon Martin Kazimir.
Res.: 103 Jackson St., P.O. Box L, 12524-0499. Tel: 845-896-6400; Fax: 845-896-4575
School— (1955),Tel: 845-896-9561; Fax: 845-896-8477. Mrs. Elizabeth Carufe. Lay Teachers 9; Students 350.
Catechesis / Religious Program—Tel: 845-896-6430; Fax: 845-896-6764. Students 950.

FLORIDA, ORANGE CO., ST. JOSEPH (1895), (Polish), [CEM] Rev. Joseph M. Tokarczyk, Admin.
Res.: 14 Glenmere Ave., 10921. Tel: 845-651-7792; Fax: 845-651-7793.
School— (1915), 21 Glenmere Ave., 10921. Tel: 845-651-7873. Sisters 1; Lay Teachers 12; Students 200.
Catechesis / Religious Program—Tel: 845-651-4240. Students 181.
Mission—St. Andrew Bobola Maple Ave., (Pellets Island), New Hampton, Orange Co. 10958.

FORESTBURGH, SULLIVAN CO., ST. THOMAS AQUINAS (1900), [CEM] Rev. Ivan L. Csete; Deacon Paul A. Rausch.
Res.: One Forestburgh Rd., 12777. Tel: 914-791-7400; Fax: 914-791-7700.

GARDINER, ULSTER CO., ST. CHARLES BORROMEO (1883), (Irish—Italian), [CEM] Rev. Robert M. Panek; Deacons Harold N. Carroll; Joseph N. Guglielmo.
Res.: 2212 Rte. 44/55, 12525. Tel: 845-255-1374; Fax: 845-256-9050.
Catechesis / Religious Program—Tel: 845-564-1153. Students 145.

GARNERVILLE, ROCKLAND CO., ST. GREGORY BARBARIGO (1961), Revs. John J. Backes; John J. Higgins; Deacons Augustine A. Pappalardo; Roland Dowen.
Res.: 21 Cinder Rd., 10923. Tel: 845-947-1873; Fax: 845-947-8256.
School—Tel: 845-947-1330; Fax: 845-947-4392. Sr. Kathleen Gorres, O.P., Prin. Sisters of St. Dominic (Sparkill) 2; Lay Teachers 9; Students 275.
Catechesis / Religious Program—Tel: 845-429-2775. Marie Kiely, D.R.E. Students 1,051.

GLASCO, ULSTER CO., ST. JOSEPH (1921), (Italian—Irish), Rev. Charles F. Zanotti.
Res.: Glasco Tpke., Box 208, 12432. Tel: 845-246-5453; Fax: 845-247-9343.
A-Villa St. Dominic—Tel: 914-246-8941. Rest House for Ladies. Dominican Sisters (Sparkill). Also Known as Corazon Center.
Catechesis / Religious Program—Tel: 845-246-4598. Students 150.

GOSHEN, ORANGE CO., ST. JOHN THE EVANGELIST (1837), [CEM] Revs. Thomas Dicks; Frank Bassett; Trevor Nicholls; Deacons Luis Baerga; Vincent Cookingham; James McGarry.
Res.: 71 Murray Ave., 10924. Tel: 845-294-5328; Fax: 845-294-2577.
School—77 Murray Ave., 10924. Tel: 845-294-6434; Fax: 845-294-7303. Sr. Barbara Werner, O.P., Prin. Sisters 2; Lay Teachers 8; Students 232.
Catechesis / Religious Program—Tel: 914-294-6847. Students 865.
Chapel—Immaculate Conception Convent 73 Murray Ave., 10924. Tel: 845-294-8620.
Chapel—Presentation Sisters Convent Fletcher St., 10924.
Chapel—John S. Burke H. S. Chapel; Our Lady of the Blessed Sacrament Broadlea, 10924. Tel: 845-294-5481.
Station—Orange County Home and Infirmary, Tel: 845-294-7971.
Station—Orange County Jail, Tel: 845-294-6166.
Station—Campbell Hall Nursing Facility Orange. Tel: 845-294-8154.
Station—Arden Hill Life-Care Center, Tel: 845-294-9797.
Arden Hill Hospital—Tel: 845-294-5441.

GREENBURGH, WESTCHESTER CO., CHURCH OF OUR LADY OF SHKODRA (1989), (Albanian), [CEM] Rev. Peter Popovich.
Res.: 361 W. Hartsdale Ave., Hartsdale, 10530. Tel: 914-761-3523; Fax: 914-949-2690.

GREENWOOD LAKE, ORANGE CO., HOLY ROSARY (1954), Rev. Robert J. Sweeney; Deacon Ralph D. Longo.
Res.: 41 Windermere Ave., 10925-2105. Tel: 914-477-8378; Fax: 914-477-7238.
Catechesis / Religious Program—Tel: 918-477-0906. Students 210.

HARRIMAN, ORANGE CO., ST. ANASTASIA (1899), [CEM] Rev. Joseph F. Reynolds; Deacons Eugene E. Bormann; James Faulkner. In Res., Rev. Lawrence X. McCaffrey, S.J.
Res.: 21 N. Main St., 10926. Tel: 845-783-3571; Fax: 845-783-0881.
Catechesis / Religious Program—Tel: 845-782-5099. Students 410.

HARRISON, WESTCHESTER CO., ST. GREGORY THE GREAT (1911), Rev. Msgrs. Francis J. McAree, S.T.D.; Daniel V. Flynn, J.C.D., Senior Priest; Joseph J. Raimondo, Senior Priest (Retired).
Res.: 215 Halstead Ave., 10528. Tel: 914-835-0677; Fax: 914-835-5152.
Catechesis / Religious Program—94 Broadway, 10528. Tel: 914-835-1278; Fax: 914-835-2070. Students 630.

HARTSDALE, WESTCHESTER CO., SACRED HEART (1926), Rev. Patrick J. Carney; Rev. Msgr. John V. Wilkinson, Pastor Emeritus; Rev. Divya Paul (India); Deacon Benjamin D'Arconte.

Res.: 10 Lawton Ave., 10530. Tel: 914-949-0028; Fax: 914-289-0398.
School— (1953), 59 Wilson St., 10530. Tel: 914-946-7242; Fax: 914-946-7323. Mrs. Virginia Salamone, Prin. Sisters 2; Lay Teachers 18; Students 266.
Catechesis/Religious Program—Tel: 914-428-5043. Students 172.
Convent—11 Lawton Ave., 10530. Tel: 914-946-2581.

HASTINGS-ON-HUDSON, WESTCHESTER CO.
1—ST. MATTHEW (1892), Rev. Msgr. Edward J. McCorry; Rev. James Smyth.
Res.: 616 Warburton Ave., 10706. Tel: 914-478-2822; Fax: 914-478-3681.
School— (1911),Tel: 914-478-3343; Fax: 914-478-0670. Lay Teachers 9; Students 170.
Catechesis/Religious Program—Tel: 914-478-1092. Students 170.
Mission—Andrus Nursing Home, Westchester Co.
2—ST. STANISLAUS KOSTKA (1912), (Polish), Rev. Msgr. Edward J. McCorry.
Res.: 616 Warburton Ave., 10706. Tel: 914-478-2822; Fax: 914-478-3681.
Church: 52 Main St., 10706.

HAVERSTRAW, ROCKLAND CO.
1—ST. MARY (1899), (Slovak), Rev. Msgr. Robert J. McCabe, Admin.
Res.: 46 Conklin Ave., 10927. Tel: 845-429-2245; Fax: 845-429-1350.
Catechesis/Religious Program—Students 65.
2—ST. PETER (1848), [CEM] [JC] Revs. Thomas Madden, Admin.; Richard Smith; Miguel Castillo.
Res.: 115 Broadway, 10927. Tel: 914-429-2196; Fax: 914-947-4564.
School— (1884), Ridge St., 10927. Tel: 914-429-5311. Mrs. Margaret Hamilton, Prin. Lay Teachers 10; Students 230.
Catechesis/Religious Program—21 Ridge St., 10927. Tel: 914-429-8824. Students 594.
Station—Helen Hayes Hospital West Haverstraw. Tel: 914-947-3000.
Station—Senior Citizen Apts. Walnut Hill. Tel: 914-429-3033.
Station—Green Hills Home, Tel: 914-429-8411.
Station—Northern Riverview Health Care Center, Tel: 914-429-5381.

HAWTHORNE, WESTCHESTER CO., HOLY ROSARY (1901), Revs. Anthony J. Giuliano; T. Augustine Badgley, P.V.
Res.: 170 Bradhurst, 10532. Tel: 914-769-0030; Fax: 914-769-3326.
School— (1955), 180 Bradhurst Ave., 10532. Tel: 914-769-4549; Fax: 914-769-2768. Lay Teachers 10; Students 187.
Catechesis/Religious Program—Tel: 914-769-3338. Deacon Richard McLoughlin. Students 639.

HIGHLAND FALLS, ORANGE CO., SACRED HEART OF JESUS (1870), [CEM] Rev. Jack Arlotta.
Res.: 353 Main St., 10928. Tel: 845-446-4609; Fax: 845-446-2343.
School— (1930), 7 Cozzens Ave., 10928. Tel: 845-446-2674; Fax: 845-446-3713. Lay Teachers 12; Students 250.
Catechesis/Religious Program—Tel: 845-446-2071; Fax: 845-446-4610. Maryann Brigham, D.R.E. Students 200.
Mission—Blessed Sacrament Rte 9W, Fort Montgomery, Orange Co. 10922.

HIGHLAND MILLS, ORANGE CO., ST. PATRICK (1957), Revs. Gerard P. Travers; Thomas Njarackel, V.C. (India); Deacon Paul Weireter.
Res.: 26 Hunter St., 10930. Tel: 845-928-6027; Fax: 845-928-2982.
Catechesis/Religious Program—Tel: 845-928-6688; Fax: 845-928-3189. Students 873.

HIGHLAND, ULSTER CO., ST. AUGUSTINE (1899), Revs. Eugene Keane; Thomas Lutz.
Res.: 55 Main St., 12528. Tel: 845-691-7673; Fax: 845-691-6680.
School— (1958), Phillips Ave. and Elting Pl., 12528. Tel: 845-691-2338; Fax: 845-691-2338. Mrs. Laurette McKercher, Prin. Lay Teachers 10; Students 214.
Catechesis/Religious Program—Students 289.

HOPEWELL JUNCTION, DUTCHESS CO.
1—ST. COLUMBA (1992), Rev. Msgr. Gerardo J. Colacicco; Revs. Andrew J. Walsh; Thomas L. Kreiser; Deacons William Alvarado; John Reilly; Warren Testa.
Res.: 835 Rte. 82, P.O. Box 428, 12533. Tel: 845-227-8380; Fax: 845-227-8390.
School—St. Denis-St. Columba, Tel: 845-227-7777; Fax: 845-226-8470. Sr. Anne Daniel, Prin. Sisters 1; Lay Teachers 16; Students 509.
Catechesis/Religious Program—P.O. Box 368, Hopewell Jct., 12533. Tel: 845-221-4900. Mrs. Jo Ann Griffin, D.R.E. Students 2,145.
2—ST. DENIS (1899), [CEM] Revs. William B. Cosgrove; Philip T. Persico; Deacons Walter Dauerer; Stanley Aviles.
Res. & Office: 602 Beekman Rd., P.O. Box 10, 12533. Tel: 845-227-8382; Fax: 845-227-3951.
School—The Ark and The Dove Preschool:, Tel: 845-227-5232; Fax: 845-227-0435.
School—St. Denis-St. Columba See St. Columba for details. Tel: 845-227-7777; Fax: 845-226-8470. See St. Columba for details.
Catechesis/Religious Program—P.O. Box 1139, 12533. Tel: 845-227-3949; Fax: 845-227-0435. Students 525.

HYDE PARK, DUTCHESS CO., REGINA COELI (1863), Revs. John A. Bida, J.C.L.; Augustine Twum-Obuor (Ghana); Deacons William E. Biskup; Frank J. Gohl; Gerald Lindley; Mark O'Sullivan. In Res., Rev. James J. LeBar.
Res.: 2 Harvey St., 12538. Tel: 845-229-2134; Fax: 845-229-1668.
School— (1955), Albany Post Rd., 12538. Tel: 845-229-8589; Fax: 845-229-1388. Lay Teachers 15; Students 215.
Catechesis/Religious Program—Tel: 845-229-9139; Fax: 845-229-1668. Students 235.
Mission—St. Paul (1851), Mulford Ave., Staatsburg, Dutchess Co. 12580.

IRVINGTON-ON-THE-HUDSON, WESTCHESTER CO., IMMACULATE CONCEPTION (1873), Revs. Raymond J. Byrne; John Nambusseril, C.M.I.; Jacob Joseph, C.M.I.
Res.: 16 N. Broadway, 10533. Tel: 914-591-7480; Fax: 914-591-7806.
School— (1908),Tel: 914-591-9330; Fax: 914-591-8639. Lay Teachers 10; Students 142.
Catechesis/Religious Program—Tel: 914-591-7740. Students 380.

JEFFERSONVILLE, SULLIVAN CO.
1—ST. GEORGE (1963), [CEM] Merged, with St. Francis of Assisi to form St. George-St. Francis, Jeffersonville
Res.: 12748. Tel: 845-482-4640; Fax: 845-482-3276.
Catechesis/Religious Program—Students 110.
2—ST. GEORGE-ST. FRANCIS, Rev. Paul J. Osborne, O.F.M.
P.O. Box 128, 12748. Tel: 845-482-4640; Fax: 845-482-3276.
Catechesis/Religious Program—Students 110.

KATONAH, WESTCHESTER CO., ST. MARY OF THE ASSUMPTION (1908), Revs. Edmund P. Connors; Paul M. Waddell, Admin.
Res.: 117 Valley Rd., 10536. Tel: 914-232-3356; Fax: 914-232-5736.
Catechesis/Religious Program—99 Valley Rd., 10536. Tel: 914-232-4648. Deacon Robert Esposito, D.R.E. Students 700.
Mission—St. Matthias (1909), Babbitt Rd., Bedford Hills, Westchester Co. 10507.
Mission—South Salem Presbyterian Church Spring St., South Salem, Westchester Co. 10590.

KINGSTON, ULSTER CO.
1—HOLY NAME OF JESUS (1884), Closed.
2—IMMACULATE CONCEPTION (1896), (Polish), [CEM] Rev. John W. Borzuchowski (Poland).
Res.: 467 Delaware Ave., 12401. Tel: 845-331-0846; Fax: 845-331-7647.
Catechesis/Religious Program—Tel: 847-331-7352. Students 60.
3—ST. JOSEPH (1868), Revs. Frank J. Damis; Sergio Millares; Rick De La Pena; Deacons Donald Droulette; Richard Frohmiller; Robert Winrow; John Peters; Joseph Doherty. In Res., Rev. Msgr. James V. Keating (Retired).
Res.: 242 Wall St., 12401. Tel: 845-338-1554; Fax: 845-340-1961.
School— (1869), Wall & Pearl Sts., 12401. Tel: 845-339-4390; Fax: 845-339-7001. Lay Teachers 16; Students 380.
Catechesis/Religious Program—Tel: 845-339-4391; Fax: 845-339-4391. Students 355.
Chapel—St. Joseph Mission Zandhoeck Rd., Hurley, 12443. Tel: 845-338-7121.
4—ST. MARY (1842), [CEM] Rev. Edmund M. Burke.
Res.: 160 Broadway, 12401. Tel: 845-331-0301; Fax: 845-339-6165.
School—Kingston Catholic School (1867), 159 Broadway, 12401. Tel: 845-331-9318; Fax: 845-331-2674. Jill Albert, Prin. Lay Teachers 12; Students 215.
Catechesis/Religious Program—Students 250.
5—ST. PETER (1858), (German), [CEM] Rev. Edmund Burke, Admin. In Res., Rev. Marc K. Oliver.
Res.: 93 Wurts St., 12401. Tel: 914-331-0436; Fax: 914-331-7149.

LAGRANGEVILLE, DUTCHESS CO., BLESSED KATERI TEKAKWITHA (2002), Rev. Msgr. William J. Belford.
Res.: 1810 Rt 82, 12540. Tel: 845-227-1710; Fax: 845-227-1734.
Catechesis/Religious Program—Tel: 845-223-3767; Fax: 845-226-6150. Students 565.

LAKE KATRINE, ULSTER CO., ST. CATHERINE LABOURE (1957), Rev. John T. Kearney; Deacon John M. Sullivan.
Res.: Tuytenbridge Rd., P.O. Box 271, 12449. Tel: 914-382-1133; Fax: 914-382-1051.
Catechesis/Religious Program—Students 166.

LARCHMONT, WESTCHESTER CO.
1—ST. AUGUSTINE (1892), Rev. Msgr. Walter F. Kenny. In Res., Revs. Joseph A. DeSanto; Antony Gutt.
Res.: 18 Cherry Ave., 10538. Tel: 914-834-1220; Fax: 914-833-2130.
Catechesis/Religious Program—Tel: 914-834-9523. Students 455.
2—SS. JOHN AND PAUL (1949), Rev. Msgrs. Dennis J. Sullivan; Lamont R. Hamilton; Deacon James Brown.
Res.: 280 Weaver St., 10538. Tel: 914-834-5458; Fax: 914-833-5081.
School— (1952),Tel: 914-834-6332; Fax: 914-834-6332. Anne A. Menno, Prin. Lay Teachers 18; Students 311.
Catechesis/Religious Program—Tel: 914-834-4597; Fax: 914-834-7493. Students 473.

LIBERTY, SULLIVAN CO., ST. PETER (1894), [CEM] Rev. Msgr. Edward F. Straub; Deacon John Riley.
Res.: 264 N. Main St., 12754. Tel: 914-292-4525; Fax: 914-292-1627.
Catechesis/Religious Program—Students 192.

LIVINGSTON MANOR, SULLIVAN CO., ST. ALOYSIUS (1899), [CEM] Rev. William J. Collins.
Res.: Church St., Box 206, 12758. Tel: 914-439-5625; Fax: 914-439-5188.
Mission—Sacred Heart (1906), P.O. Box 206, De Bruce, Sullivan Co. 12758.
Mission—Gate of Heaven (1901), Highland Ave., Roscoe, Sullivan Co. 12776.
Catechesis/Religious Program—Students 25.

MAHOPAC, PUTNAM CO., ST. JOHN THE EVANGELIST (1889), Revs. Brian C. Brennan; William F. Woodruff; Andrew Bielak (Poland); Francis Borkowski; Deacons John Armo; Robert Esposito; Bernard Moran; John Scarfi.
Res.: 221 E. Lake Blvd., 10541. Tel: 845-628-2006; Fax: 845-628-5970.
School— (1955),Tel: 845-628-6464; Fax: 845-628-6469. Religious of the Divine Compassion 1; Lay Teachers 10; Students 232.
Catechesis/Religious Program—Students 1,972.
Chapel—Convent of Religious of the Divine Compassion, Tel: 914-628-6497.

MAMARONECK, WESTCHESTER CO.
1—HOLY TRINITY (1874), Revs. Joseph F. Irwin; Joseph Kahumburu (Kenya).
Res.: 320 E. Post Rd., 10543. Tel: 914-698-5944; Fax: 914-698-5274.
Catechesis/Religious Program—Tel: 914-698-1868. Students 196.
2—ST. VITO (1911), (Italian), Revs. James F. Healy; Edward O'Neil; Colbert DaSilva, S.D.B.; Sr. Catherine Duignan, O.P.
Res.: 816 Underhill Ave., 10543. Tel: 914-698-2648; Fax: 914-698-6081.
Catechesis/Religious Program—826 Underhill Ave., Mamaronek, 10543. Tel: 914-698-2949. Students 350.

MARLBORO, ULSTER CO., ST. MARY (1900), [CEM] Revs. Edward Bader; Jing Shan Xu; Deacons Vincent Porcelli, Pastoral Team; John T. Repke, Pastoral Team; Thomas Cornell, Pastoral Team.
Res.: 71 Grand St., P.O. Box 730, 12542. Tel: 914-236-4340; Fax: 914-236-3183.
Catechesis/Religious Program—Tel: 845-236-7791; Fax: 845-236-3183. Sr. Joan Mary Gleason, P.B.V.M., D.R.E. Students 540.
Mission—Our Lady of Mercy River Rd., Roseton, Orange Co. 12550.

MAYBROOK, ORANGE CO., ASSUMPTION (1907), Rev. Daniel M. O'Hare; Deacon Edward M. Grosso.
Res.: 211 Homestead Ave., 12543. Tel: 845-427-2046; Fax: 845-427-7005.
Catechesis/Religious Program—Tel: 845-427-5318. Students 134.

MIDDLETOWN, ORANGE CO.
1—HOLY CROSS (1999), Rev. Robert Porpora.
Res.: 626 County Rte. 22, 10940. Tel: 845-355-4439; Fax: 845-355-4709.
Catechesis/Religious Program—Tel: 845-355-6255. Students 520.
Mission—Our Lady of the Scapular 125 Main St., Unionville, Orange Co. 10988. Tel: 845-726-3222.
2—ST. JOSEPH (1865), (Irish—Italian), [CEM] Rev. Msgr. George J. Valastro; Revs. Dennis Nikolic; Rafael Laiton (Colombia); Ludovico Angella (Italy); Deacons Richard Trapani; Albert Loeffler.
Res.: 149 Cottage St., 10940. Tel: 914-343-6013; Fax: 914-344-4735.
School— (1889), 113 Cottage St., 10940. Tel: 914-343-3139; Fax: 914-346-4647. Richard Jackson, Prin. Lay Teachers 14; Students 245.
Catechesis/Religious Program—Tel: 914-343-4415. Students 652.
3—OUR LADY OF MT. CARMEL (1912), Revs. Francis F. Dixon, O.Carm.; Roberto Perez, O.Carm., Pastoral Assoc.; Raymond Bagdonis, O.Carm., Pastoral Assoc.; Patrick McGuigan, O.Carm., Pastoral Assoc.; Deacons Edward Woods, Pastoral Assoc.; John

Frohbose, Pastoral Assoc. In Res., Revs. James Sidoti, O.Carm.; Alfred Isacsson, O.Carm.; Robert Greco, O.Carm.
Res.: 90 Euclid Ave., 10940. Tel: 845-343-4121; Fax: 845-343-4433.
School—205 Wawayanda Ave., 10940. Tel: 845-343-8836; Fax: 845-342-1404. Lay Teachers 16; Students 261.
Catechesis/Religious Program—Tel: 845-342-1510. Students 380.
Mission—Our Lady of the Assumption P.O. Box 216, Bloomingburgh, Sullivan Co. 12721. Tel: 845-733-1477; Fax: 845-733-6691.
Mission—St. Paul Rte. 17K, Bullville, Orange Co. 10915. Tel: 845-361-3107; Fax: 845-361-4201.

MILLBROOK, DUTCHESS CO., ST. JOSEPH (1890), [CEM] Revs. James T. O'Connor; William Kyere.
Res.: North Ave., 12545. Tel: 845-677-3422; Fax: 845-677-3423.
School— (1957),Tel: 845-677-3670. Lay Teachers 10; Students 285.
Catechesis/Religious Program—Tel: 845-677-3273. Students 332.
Chapel—Millbrook, Cardinal Hayes Home for Children
Station—Green Briar Home, Tel: 845-677-9997.

MILTON, ULSTER CO., ST. JAMES (1874), (Italian), Rev. Fred Kempfirl.
Res.: State Rd., 12547. Tel: 914-795-2255; Fax: 914-795-1008.

MONROE, ORANGE CO., SACRED HEART CHURCH (1957), Revs. Carl D. Johnson; George Pulparayil (India); Vincent dePaul Howley; Deacons Peter Brockmann; James Burns; Richard McCarthy; Angelo Corsaro; Robert Duncan.
Res.: 26 Still Rd., 10950. Tel: 914-782-8510; Fax: 914-782-3593.
School— (1964),Tel: 914-783-0365; Fax: 914-782-0354. Cynthia Reimer, Prin. Sisters 1; Lay Teachers 11; Students 226.
Catechesis/Religious Program—(Grades PreK-8) Tel: 914-782-7420. Sr. Rose O'Rourke, D.R.E. Students 1,422.
Convent—Still Rd., 10950.
Chapel— Stage Rd., 10950.

MONTGOMERY, ORANGE CO., HOLY NAME OF MARY (1868), [CEM] Rev. Joseph D. Sullivan.
Res.: 89 Union St., 12549. Tel: 845-457-5276; Fax: 845-457-3072.
Catechesis/Religious Program—Tel: 845-457-1738. Sr. Grace Mary McGuire, D.R.E. Students 330.

MONTICELLO, SULLIVAN CO., ST. PETER (1874), [CEM] Revs. Robert J. Ginel; John Tran. In Res., Rev. Stanislaus Ogbonna, C.S.Sp. (Nigeria).
Res.: 10 Liberty St., 12701. Tel: 914-794-5577; Fax: 914-791-1210.
Catechesis/Religious Program—Tel: 914-791-7172. Students 375.
Mission—St. Joseph Mongaup Valley, Sullivan Co.
Mission—St. Anne White Lake, Sullivan Co.

MT. KISCO, WESTCHESTER CO., ST. FRANCIS OF ASSISI (1871), [CEM] Revs. Ralph A. Villani; William P. Dalton (Retired).
Res.: 2 Green St., 10549. Tel: 914-666-5986; Fax: 914-666-3859.
Catechesis/Religious Program—Tel: 914-666-3161; Fax: 914-666-5474. Students 315.

MT. VERNON, WESTCHESTER CO.

1—ST. MARY (1894), Rev. John T. Meehan.
Res.: 23 S. High St., 10550. Tel: 914-664-5855; Fax: 914-663-6097.
Catechesis/Religious Program—Students 134.

2—OUR LADY OF MOUNT CARMEL (1897), (Italian), Rev. Lawrence Quinn; Deacon Vincent T. Piro.
Res.: 10550. Tel: 914-668-3540; Fax: 914-668-4393.

3—OUR LADY OF VICTORY (1871), Revs. Vincenzo L. Ronchi, C.S.; Amarilho Checon, S.J. In Res., Rev. Ademir Guerrini, C.S.
Res.: 28 W. Sidney Ave., 10550. Tel: 914-668-5861; Fax: 914-668-0161.
School— (1898), 38 N. Fifth Ave., 10550. Tel: 914-667-4063; Fax: 914-665-3135. Janet Heed, Prin. Lay Teachers 15; Students 290.
Catechesis/Religious Program—Tel: 914-668-5953. Students 93.

4—SS. PETER AND PAUL (1929), (Italian), Rev. Msgr. Patrick J. Barry; Deacon Robert F. Schimpf. In Res., Rev. Msgr. Thomas F. Scanlon.
Res.: 129 Birch St., 10552. Tel: 914-668-9815; Fax: 914-668-6052.
School—Tel: 914-664-1321; Fax: 914-664-2951. Sisters 1; Lay Teachers 12; Students 240.
Catechesis/Religious Program—Tel: 914-668-9880. Students 100.

5—SACRED HEART (1872), Rev. Msgr. Howard W. Calkins.
Res.: 115 S. Fifth Ave., 10550. Tel: 914-668-7440; Fax: 914-668-1177.
School— (1895), Second St. & S. Fifth Ave., 10550. Tel: 914-667-1734; Fax: 914-667-1497. Sisters of Mercy 1; Lay Teachers 9; Students 265.
Chapel—Sacred Heart Convent 67 S. Fifth Ave., 10550. Tel: 914-668-5349.

6—ST. URSULA (1908), Rev. John T. McLoughlin; Deacons Thomas J. Abbamont; Carl Degenhardt. In Res., Rev. Patrick Okafor (Nigeria).
Res.: 214 E. Lincoln Ave., 10552. Tel: 914-668-0085; Fax: 914-668-4228.
Saint Ursula's Learning Center For the Learning Disabled—133 Rich Ave., 10552. Tel: 914-664-6656; Fax: 914-668-0592.
Catechesis/Religious Program—Tel: 914-699-7964. Sr. Margaret Hoban, C.R., D.R.E. Students 95.

NANUET, ROCKLAND CO., ST. ANTHONY (1897), [CEM] Revs. William V. Reynolds; Michael Martine; Ferdinando Caindec; Deacon John Maloney.
Res.: 36 West Nyack Rd., 10954. Tel: 914-623-2138; Fax: 914-623-5556.
School— (1953), 32-34 West Nyack Rd., 10954. Tel: 914-623-2311; Fax: 914-623-2406. Bridget Browne, Prin. Sisters 5; Lay Teachers 18; Students 463.
Catechesis/Religious Program—Tel: 914-624-2230. Ms. Ann Malloy, D.R.E. Students 875.

NARROWSBURG, SULLIVAN CO., ST. FRANCIS XAVIER (1862), [CEM 2] Rev. Thomas Jones, O.F.M.
Res.: 151 Bridge St., 12764. Tel: 845-252-6581; Fax: 845-252-6519.
Catechesis/Religious Program—Students 52.
Mission—Our Lady of the Lake Rte. 52, Lake Huntington, Sullivan Co. 12752. Tel: 845-252-6681.

NEW CITY, ROCKLAND CO., ST. AUGUSTINE (1957), Rev. Msgr. William J. Foley; Revs. Francis J. Samoylo; Varghese I. Chethipuzha; Deacons Michael G. McCabe; Lawrence O'Toole.
Res.: 140 Maple Ave., 10956. Tel: 845-634-3641; Fax: 845-639-6118.
School—Tel: 845-634-7060; Fax: 845-634-8725. Katharine Murphy, Prin. Lay Teachers 11; Students 236.
Catechesis/Religious Program—Tel: 845-634-8462. Students 750.

NEW PALTZ, ULSTER CO., ST. JOSEPH (1894), Revs. Maurice Moreau, O.F.M.Cap.; Barnabas Keck, O.F.M.Cap.; John Mellitt, O.F.M.Cap., Chap.; Bro. Timothy Jones, O.F.M.Cap., Vocation Min. Coord. In Res., Bro. Walter Puhal, O.F.M.Cap.
Res.: 34 S. Chestnut St., 12561. Tel: 845-255-5635; Fax: 845-255-5679.
Catechesis/Religious Program—Tel: 845-255-0237; Fax: 845-256-0687. Sisters Francene Van Eck, O.S.B., D.R.E.; Mary Glaser, O.S.B., D.R.E. Students 500.
Station—Lake Mohonk

NEW ROCHELLE, WESTCHESTER CO.

1—BLESSED SACRAMENT (1848), [CEM] Rev. Msgr. William J. Bradley; Revs. Charles Imokhai (Nigeria); Lawrence Maria Singarayer (India); Deacons Charles Rizzo; Frank Orlando.
Res.: 15 Shea Pl., 10801. Tel: 914-632-3700; Fax: 914-632-0732.
School—New Rochelle Catholic Elementary (1866), 24 Maple Ave., 10801. Tel: 914-632-0511; Fax: 914-632-3762. George Pitula, Prin. Lay Teachers 16; Students 240.
High School—24 Shea Pl., 10801. Tel: 914-632-2595; Fax: 914-632-3321. Edward Sullivan, Prin. (Coed) Congregation of Christian Brothers 1; Sisters 2; Lay Teachers 25; Students 532.
Catechesis/Religious Program—Tel: 914-235-7311. Mrs. Judith Anastasio, D.R.E. Students 562.

2—ST. GABRIEL (1893), (Hispanic), Rev. Patrick V. McNamara.
Res.: 120 Division St., 10801. Tel: 914-632-0211; Fax: 914-637-8991.

3—HOLY FAMILY (1913), Rev. Msgr. Ferdinando D. Berardi; Revs. Gary Mead; George K. Nedumaruthumchalil; Deacon Arthur Hull Hayes Jr.
Res.: 83 Clove Rd., 10801. Tel: 914-632-0673; Fax: 914-576-8556.
Church: Mayflower Ave. & Mt. Joy Pl., 10801. Tel: 914-632-0573.
School— (1921), Mayflower Ave., 10801. Tel: 914-632-3810; Fax: 914-636-6758. Lay Teachers 10; Students 130.
Catechesis/Religious Program—Tel: 914-636-6758; Fax: 914-636-6758. Students 367.
Chapel—Ursuline Sisters 1352 N. Ave., 10804. Tel: 914-636-3456; Fax: 914-576-2620.
Chapel—Iona Grammar and Preparatory Schools 173 Stratton Rd., 10804. Tel: 914-633-7744; 914-632-2727; Fax: 914-235-6338.
Chapel—Iona College 715 N. Ave., 10801. Tel: 914-633-2000; Fax: 800-633-2329.
Chapel—New Rochelle, St. Patrick Prov. 30 Montgomery Circle, 10801. Tel: 914-633-6851; Fax: 914-633-5579.
Chapel—New Rochelle, St. Joseph Chapel, Tel: 914-632-6592; Fax: 914-533-4264.
Chapel—Edmond Rice Hall 33 Prier Ter., 10804. Tel: 914-636-6194; Fax: 914-636-0021.
Chapel—Opus Dei 99 Overlook Cir., 10804. Tel: 914-235-1201; Fax: 914-235-7805.
Chapel—Holy Cross Brothers Provincialate 85 Overlook Cir., 10804. Tel: 914-632-1951; Fax: 914-632-2490.

4—HOLY NAME OF JESUS (1929), Revs. Martin J. Biglin; Joy Mankulam Devassy (India); Deacons Carmine DeMarco; Robert Gontcharuk.
Res.: 75 Lispenard Ave., 10801. Tel: 914-636-4856; Fax: 914-636-8474.
Church: Petersville Rd. and Halligan St., 10801.
School— (1954), 70 Petersville Rd., 10801. Tel: 914-576-6672; Fax: 914-576-6676. Mr. Albert D'Angelo, Prin. Sisters 1; Lay Teachers 9; Students 203.
Catechesis/Religious Program—Tel: 914-576-6038. Students 182.
Chapel—Sisters of Charity Convent 78 Petersville Rd., 10801. Tel: 914-636-4354.

5—ST. JOSEPH (1901), (Italian), Rev. Philip J. Caruso.
Res.: 280 Washington Ave., 10801. Tel: 914-632-0675; Fax: 914-633-4264.
Catechesis/Religious Program—Tel: 914-646-6368. Students 180.

NEW WINDSOR, ORANGE CO., ST. JOSEPH (1962), Rev. Robert G. Hilfiker; Deacons Joseph Lieby; Anthony Ferraiuolo.
Res.: 4 St. Joseph Pl., 12553. Tel: 845-561-8467; Fax: 845-562-3269.
School—148 Windsor Hwy., 12553. Tel: 845-565-5110; Fax: 845-565-6321. Sisters 1; Lay Teachers 9; Students 204.
Catechesis/Religious Program—Tel: 845-561-8475. Students 305.

NEWBURGH, ORANGE CO.

1—ST. FRANCIS OF ASSISI (1909), (Polish), [CEM] Rev. John J. Vondras; Deacon Jack Seymour.
Res.: 145 Benkard Ave., 12550. Tel: 845-561-1317; Fax: 845-561-1337.
School—Now Sacred Heart-St. Francis of Assisi School. Merged in Sept. 1992. , 24 S. Robinson Ave., 12550. Tel: 845-561-1433.
Catechesis/Religious Program—Tel: 845-561-6697. Students 420.
Chapel—St. Francis Convent (1955), 153 Benkard Ave., 12550. Tel: 845-561-5914; Fax: 845-561-1123.

2—ST. MARY (1875), Rev. William A. Scafidi, M.Ss.A.; Deacon John Buckley.
Res.: 180 South St., 12550. Tel: 845-562-0862; Fax: 845-562-0876.

3—ST. PATRICK (1836), [CEM 2] Rev. Msgr. John J. Budwick; Rev. Louis Van Thanh; Deacons Fred Steup; Donald Halter; Frank Russell; William Glover; Sisters Virginia Wilkinson, Adult Formation; Yliana Hernandez, Spanish Apostolate; Helen Raynor, Spanish Apostolate.
Res.: 55 Grand St., 12550. Tel: 914-561-0885; Fax: 914-561-8629.
Catechesis/Religious Program—Tel: 914-561-6470. Ms. Mary Jane Newman, D.R.E. Students 620.
Mission—Our Lady of the Lake Lakeside & Rte. 52, Orange Lake, Orange Co. 12550. Tel: 914-561-9537.

4—SACRED HEART (1912), (Italian), Most Rev. Dominick J. Lagonegro; Revs. Alfred Pizzuto; Luke M. Sweeney; Deacons Dominick Casadone; Peter Haight; Lawrence Kawula.
Res.: 301 Ann St., 12550. Tel: 914-561-2264; Fax: 914-562-7144.
School— (1951), 24 S. Robinson Ave., 12550. Tel: 914-561-1433; Fax: 914-561-4383. Religious 3; Lay Teachers 9; Students 248.
Catechesis/Religious Program—Tel: 914-561-2589. Students 501.

NORTH TARRYTOWN, WESTCHESTER CO., HOLY CROSS (1921), (Slovak—Polish), Rev. Francis P. Gorman; Rev. Msgr. Cyril J. Potocek, Pastor Emeritus (Retired).
Res.: 118 Beekman Ave., 10591. Tel: 914-631-1493.

NYACK, ROCKLAND CO., ST. ANN (1869), Revs. Robert P. Henry; Emil Bettley; Cresus Fernando (Sri Lanka); Joseph Domfeh-Boateng (Ghana); Deacons Alan Hudson; Thomas Luke Conroy; John Scott.
Res.: 16 Jefferson St., 10960. Tel: 845-358-4707; Fax: 845-358-3246.
School— (1892),Tel: 845-358-0125; Fax: 845-358-7911. Mrs. Dana Spicer, Prin. Lay Teachers 5; Students 70.
Catechesis/Religious Program—33 Jefferson St., 10960. Tel: 845-358-3758. Ms. Julie LePore, D.R.E. Students 230.
Convent—150 Third Ave., 10960. Tel: 845-358-2697.

OBERNBURG, SULLIVAN CO., ST. MARY (1854), (German), [CEM] Rev. John M. Richardson, O.F.M.; Deacon Lawrence Knack.
Res.: 12767. Tel: 914-482-5541; Fax: 914-482-9340.

OSSINING, WESTCHESTER CO.

1—ST. ANN (1927), Rev. Edward G. Byrne; Sr. Eileen Finnerty, Pastoral Assoc.; Rev. Carlos Zapata; Deacon Jose DeJesus. In Res., Rev. Arthur Aldin.
Res.: 25 Eastern Ave., 10562. Tel: 914-941-2556; Fax: 914-923-9239.
School—16 Elizabeth St., 10562. Tel: 914-941-0312; Fax: 914-941-3514. Mrs. Dorethea Muccigrosso,

Prin. Lay Teachers 15; Students 385.
Catechesis/Religious Program—Tel: 914-941-2420. Students 360.
Convent—10 Elizabeth St., 10562.
2—ST. AUGUSTINE (1853), [CEM] Rev. Msgr. Hilary Franco; Rev. Robert M. Dunn.
Res.: Eagle Park Rte. 9, 10562. Tel: 914-941-0067; Fax: 914-944-0828.
School— (1893),Tel: 914-941-3849; Fax: 914-941-4342. Sr. Mary Elizabeth Donoghue, Prin. Priests 2; Sisters of St. Dominic (Columbus) 1; Lay Teachers 25; Students 555.
OTISVILLE, ORANGE CO., HOLY NAME (1969), [CEM] Rev. Peter Tran Van Phat, Admin.
Res.: P.O. Box 597, 10963. Tel: 845-386-1320; Fax: 845-386-6105.
Catechesis/Religious Program—Tel: 845-386-2327. Mrs. Annette Ford, D.R.E. Students 254.
PATTERSON, PUTNAM CO., SACRED HEART (1957), Revs. James P. Flynn, Pastor Emeritus (Retired); Robert F. McKeon, Admin.
Res.: 414 Haviland Dr., 12563. Tel: 845-279-4832; Fax: 845-278-0432.
Catechesis/Religious Program—Mrs. Tee Vozzella, D.R.E. Students 417.
PAWLING, DUTCHESS CO., ST. JOHN THE EVANGELIST (1848), [CEM] Rev. John J. Duff.
Res.: 31 E. Main St., 12564. Tel: 845-855-5488; Fax: 845-855-1273.
Catechesis/Religious Program—Tel: 845-855-9408. Students 420.
PEARL RIVER, ROCKLAND CO.
1—ST. AEDAN (1966), Rev. Msgr. Joseph P. Penna; Rev. John Bosco Durai Samy; Deacon James F. Maher.
Res.: 23 Reld Dr., 10965. Tel: 845-735-7405; Fax: 845-735-4125.
Catechesis/Religious Program—Tel: 845-735-2531. Students 825.
2—ST. MARGARET (1923), Rev. Msgr. Rudolph Eisler; Revs. Angelo Palermo, S.A.C.; Antonio Ong (Philippines); Rev. Msgr. John Harrington (Retired); Deacons William Donovan; William Tobin.
Res.: 33 N. Magnolia St., 10965. Tel: 845-735-4746; Fax: 845-735-4744.
School— (1953), 34 N. Magnolia St., 10965. Tel: 914-735-2855; Fax: 914-735-0131. Mrs. Patricia O'Connor, Prin. Lay Teachers 13; Students 350.
Catechesis/Religious Program—Tel: 914-735-5489. Mrs. Ellen Fanelli, D.R.E. Students 700.
PEEKSKILL, WESTCHESTER CO., ASSUMPTION (1859), (Indian—Hispanic), [CEM] Rev. Msgr. Francis J. Ansbro; Revs. Arthur R. Leo; Steven E. Clark; Vernon P. Wickrematunge; Deacon James F. Roberts.
Res.: 131 Union Ave., 10566. Tel: 914-737-2071; Fax: 914-737-1633.
School— (1907), S. Division & First St., 10566. Tel: 914-737-0680; Fax: 914-737-1322. Sisters 3; Lay Teachers 10; Students 209.
Catechesis/Religious Program—Tel: 914-737-2231; Fax: 914-737-2353. Students 220.
Chapel—St. Joseph Home, Tel: 914-737-3373; Fax: 914-736-9614.
PELHAM MANOR, WESTCHESTER CO., OUR LADY OF PERPETUAL HELP (1954), Rev. Msgr. Hugh D. Curran; Rev. James E. Burke; Deacon Guy Pellegrini.
Res.: 559 Pelham Manor Rd., 10803. Tel: 914-738-1449; Fax: 914-738-9454.
School— (1957), 575 Fowler Ave., 10803. Tel: 914-738-5158. Sr. Marie Morris, S.C., Prin. Sisters 1; Lay Teachers 11; Students 225.
Catechesis/Religious Program—Tel: 914-738-0670. Students 600.
PELHAM, WESTCHESTER CO., ST. CATHARINE (1896), Rev. Peter F. Bannan.
Res.: 25 Second Ave., 10803. Tel: 914-738-1491; Fax: 914-738-0398.
Catechesis/Religious Program—Tel: 914-738-1332. Students 270.
PHOENICIA, ULSTER CO., ST. FRANCIS DE SALES (1902), [CEM] Rev. Christopher H. Berean.
Res.: Main St., P.O. Box 25, 12464. Tel: 845-688-5617; Fax: 845-688-5630.
Catechesis/Religious Program—Students 84.
Mission—Our Lady of Lourdes Rte. 28, Allaben, Ulster Co. 12480.
Mission—Our Lady of La Salette Rte. 28, Boiceville, Ulster Co. 12412.
PIERMONT, ROCKLAND CO., ST. JOHN (1852), Rev. Msgr. John T. Mulligan.
Res.: 895 Piermont Ave., 10968. Tel: 845-359-0078; Fax: 845-359-2976.
Catechesis/Religious Program—Tel: 845-359-7444. Students 97.
PINE BUSH, ORANGE CO., THE INFANT SAVIOUR (1951), Rev. William Young, Admin.
Res.: 22 Holland Ave., 12566. Tel: 845-744-2391; Fax: 845-744-5938.
Catechesis/Religious Program—Tel: 845-744-9944. Students 425.
Mission—Our Lady of the Valley Walker Valley, Ulster Co. 12588.
PINE ISLAND, ORANGE CO., ST. STANISLAUS (1912), (Polish), [CEM] Rev. Joaquim J. Olendzki.
Res.: 17 Pulaski Hwy., P.O. Box 248, 10969. Tel: 845-258-4426; Fax: 845-258-5526.
Catechesis/Religious Program—Students 230.
PINE PLAINS, DUTCHESS CO., ST. ANTHONY (1958), Rev. William A. White; Deacon Jerome F. Stuetzle.
Res.: 68 Poplar Ave., 12567-5531. Tel: 518-398-7115; Fax: 518-398-9146.
Catechesis/Religious Program—Students 82.
PLATTEKILL, ULSTER CO., OUR LADY OF FATIMA (1960), Rev. John Jaume, C.R.
Res.: P.O. Box 77, 12568. Tel: 845-564-4972; Fax: 845-566-1954.
Catechesis/Religious Program—Students 200.
PLEASANT VALLEY, DUTCHESS CO., ST. STANISLAUS KOSTKA (1903), Revs. Charles P. Quinn; Charles Owenja (Africa); Deacon John Dunn.
Res.: 1598 Main St., P.O. Box 558, 12569. Tel: 845-635-1700; Fax: 845-635-8675.
Catechesis/Religious Program—Tel: 845-635-8611. Students 520.
PLEASANTVILLE, WESTCHESTER CO., HOLY INNOCENTS (1894), [CEM] Revs. Joseph Payne, O.P.; Daniel Davies, O.P.; Terrance Quinn; Sr. Kathleen O'Hanlon, O.P., Pastoral Assoc.
Res.: 431 Bedford Rd., 10570. Tel: 914-769-0025; Fax: 914-747-2476.
Catechesis/Religious Program—Tel: 914-769-3297. Sr. Clare Kelleher, F.S.P., D.R.E. Students 724.
Mission—Our Lady of Pompeii Saragota and Garrigan, Pleasantville Park, Westchester Co. 10570.
PORT CHESTER, WESTCHESTER CO.
1—CORPUS CHRISTI (1925), (Italian), [CEM] Revs. James Marra, S.D.B.; Peter Granzotto, S.D.B.; John Blanco; Deacons John B. Munnick Jr.; Dan Ciccone.
Res.: 136 S. Regent St., 10573. Tel: 914-939-3169; Fax: 914-939-7249.
School—135 S. Regent St., 10573. Tel: 914-937-4407; Fax: 914-937-6904. Sisters, Daughters of Mary Help of Christians 3; Lay Teachers 18; Students 380.
Catechesis/Religious Program—Students 230.
2—OUR LADY OF MERCY (1854), [CEM] Revs. Ralph V. Curcio; Joe Braganza; Sr. Lorraine Dougherty, P.B.V.M., Pastoral Assoc.; Deacon Robert A. Fien.
Res.: 260 Westchester Ave., 10573. Tel: 914-939-0612; Fax: 914-939-2807.
Catechesis/Religious Program—Tel: 914-937-5288. Mrs. Kathleen McCarthy, D.R.E. Students 240.
Chapel—Sister of Charity 18 Spring St., 10573. Tel: 914-937-2440.
3—OUR LADY OF THE ROSARY (1904), (Italian), Revs. Timothy C. Ploch, S.D.B.; Tarcisio Dos Santos, S.D.B. (Brazil); Timothy Zak, S.D.B.; Julio Soto, S.D.B. (Dominican Republic); Deacons William Vaccaro; Frank Del Campo.
Church & Mailing Address: 22 Don Bosco Pl., 10573. Tel: 914-939-0547; Fax: 914-937-0692.
Res.: 23 Nicola Pl., 10573. Tel: 914-937-5532.
School— (1945), Central Ave., 10573. Tel: 914-939-1021; Fax: 914-939-7127. Mrs. Mary Norelli, Prin. Lay Teachers 7; Students 165.
Catechesis/Religious Program—Students 250.
Chapel—Adoration Chapel, Tel: 914-939-4456.
4—SACRED HEART OF JESUS (1917), Rev. Peter Gelsomino.
Res.: 229 Willett Ave., 10573. Tel: 914-939-1497.
PORT EWEN, ULSTER CO., PRESENTATION OF THE VIRGIN MARY (1874), Rev. Peter J. Vianney, Ph.D.
Res.: Fr. Kelley Dr., 12466. Tel: 845-331-0053; Fax: 845-331-3836.
Catechesis/Religious Program—Students 200.
Mission—Sacred Heart [JC] P.O. Box 219, Esopus, Ulster Co. 12429. Tel: 914-384-6828; Fax: 845-384-6234. Rev. Eugene J. Grohe, C.SS.R.
PORT JERVIS, ORANGE CO.
1—IMMACULATE CONCEPTION (1851), [CEM] Rev. Denis M. Dinan; Mary Ellen Hubbard, Ph.D., Pastoral Assoc.; RoseMary Conklin, Office Admin.
Res.: 46 Ball St., Box 712, 12771. Tel: 845-856-8212; Fax: 845-858-8375.
Catechesis/Religious Program—Students 213.
2—MOST SACRED HEART (1899), Rev. David A. De Simone.
Res.: 12 McAllister St., 12771. Tel: 914-856-1331; Fax: 914-858-0687.
POUGHKEEPSIE, DUTCHESS CO.
1—HOLY TRINITY (1921), Rev. Joseph P. LaMorte; Deacon Andrew J. Daubman. In Res., Rev. Gamini E. Fernando (Sri Lanka), Chap., Green Haven Correctional Facility.
Res.: 775 Main St., 12603. Tel: 845-452-1863; Fax: 845-485-7569.
School— (1952), 20 Springside Ave., 12603. Tel: 845-471-0520; Fax: 845-471-0520. Mrs. Mary Ann McGivney, Prin. Sister Servants of the Immaculate Heart of Mary 2; Lay Teachers 8; Students 263.
Catechesis/Religious Program—Tel: 845-471-5838; Fax: 845-471-0309. Mrs. Linda Fitzsimmons, D.R.E. Students 354.
Chapel—Holy Trinity Convent 769 Main St., 12603. Tel: 914-454-2160.
2—ST. JOHN THE BAPTIST (1923), (Slovak), Rev. Peter J. Kihm, Admin.
Res.: 1 Grand St., 12601. Tel: 914-454-0340.
3—ST. JOSEPH (1901), (Polish), Rev. Zdzislaw Nawrocki, S.CHP. (PAT).
Res.: 9 Lafayette Pl., 12601. Tel: 914-452-2333; Fax: 914-452-6686.
Chapel—Poughkeepsie, Rectory
Chapel—Cemetery Chapel Evergreen Ave., 12601.
4—ST. MARTIN DE PORRES (1962), [CEM] Revs. Brian E. McWeeney, M.S., D.Min.; James B. Hynes, M.Div., S.T.B.; Thomas D'Albro, S.T.D.; Deacons Robert Jarmick, Pastoral Assoc.; Franklin Hung, Pastoral Assoc.; Victor Salamone, Pastoral Assoc.; Patrick Hogan, Pastoral Assoc.
Res.: 118 Cedar Valley Rd., 12603. Tel: 845-473-4222; Fax: 845-473-4223.
School—122 Cedar Valley Rd., 12603. Tel: 914-452-4428. Mrs. Mary Jane Daley, Prin. Lay Teachers 11; Students 284.
Catechesis/Religious Program—Tel: 845-471-8728. Eileen Andros, D.R.E. Students 908.
5—ST. MARY (1873), Revs. John J. Brinn, M.A.; John J. Hunter, M.S. (Retired). In Res., Rev. Eusebio Mana-Ay, Chap., Vassar Bros. Medical Center.
Res.: 231 Church St., 12601-4114. Tel: 845-452-8250; Fax: 845-452-8266.
Catechesis/Religious Program—Tel: 845-471-4747; Fax: 845-471-4747. Students 156.
6—OUR LADY OF MT. CARMEL (1910), (Italian), Rev. Peter J. Kihm; Deacon George F. Cacchione.
Res.: 11 Mt. Carmel Pl., 12601. Tel: 845-454-0340; Fax: 845-486-8154.
School—Tel: 845-471-2460; Fax: 845-471-2699. Mr. Gabriel F. Ponte, Prin. Lay Teachers 11; Students 230.
Catechesis/Religious Program—Students 169.
7—ST. PETER (1837), [CEM] Rev. James A. Garisto; Deacons James R. Hayes; Albert J. Klein.
Res.: 6 Father Cody Plaza, Hyde Park, 12601. Tel: 914-452-8580; Fax: 914-483-0189.
Church: 147 Salt Point Rd., 12601. Tel: 845-471-4800.
School— (1844),Tel: 914-471-6600. Sisters of Charity of St. Vincent de Paul 2; Lay Teachers 12; Students 270.
Catechesis/Religious Program—Tel: 845-452-8580, Ext. 205. Students 301.
Chapel—Poughkeepsie, Convent of St. Peter, Tel: 845-471-7664.
Chapel—Poughkeepsie, Hudson River Psychiatric Center, Our Lady of the Holy Rosary, Tel: 845-452-4163.
RED HOOK, DUTCHESS CO., ST. CHRISTOPHER (1875), [CEM] Revs. Charles P. Coen; Xavier S. Santiago (India).
Res.: 7411 S. Broadway, 12571. Tel: 845-758-3732; Fax: 845-758-1214.
Catechesis/Religious Program—Tel: 845-758-5506; Fax: 845-758-5682. Students 352.
RHINEBECK, DUTCHESS CO., THE GOOD SHEPHERD (1901), [CEM] Revs. Jeffrey R. Galens; Lawrence Xavier.
Res.: 3 Mulberry St., 12572. Tel: 914-876-4583; Fax: 914-876-7884.
Catechesis/Religious Program—Tel: 845-876-7298. Students 300.
Mission—St. Joseph Church St., Rhinecliff, Dutchess Co. 12574.
Chapel—Astor Home for Children, Tel: 845-876-4081; Fax: 845-876-2020.
Rhinebeck, Ferncliff Nursing Home—Tel: 845-876-2011; Fax: 845-876-4810.
Rhinebeck, Sisters of St. Ursula, Linwood Retreat House—Tel: 845-876-4178; Fax: 845-876-6544.
ROSENDALE, ULSTER CO., ST. PETER (1855), [CEM] Rev. Andrew Florez.
Res.: 1017 Keator Ave., P.O. Box 471, 12472. Tel: 845-658-3117; Fax: 845-658-3540.
Catechesis/Religious Program—Tel: 845-658-8911. Deborah Ferry, D.R.E. Students 233.
Mission—Our Lady Help of Christians J.F.K. Ln., High Falls, Ulster Co. 12440.
RYE, WESTCHESTER CO., RESURRECTION (1880), Rev. Msgr. Patrick Boyle; Revs. Daniel O'Reilly; Zacharias Nadackal, C.M.I. (India); Rev. Msgr. John Mescall, Pastor Emeritus. In Res., Rev. Msgr. Edward O'Donnell.
Res.: 910 Boston Post Rd., 10580. Tel: 914-967-0142; 914-967-0254; Fax: 914-967-6494.
School— (1906), 116 Milton Rd., 10580. Tel: 914-967-1218; Fax: 914-967-0295. Lay Teachers 37; Students 569.
Catechesis/Religious Program—Tel: 914-967-1270. Students 981.
Chapel—Seton Hall Convent of the Sisters of

Charity, Tel: 914-967-7085.
SAUGERTIES, ULSTER CO., ST. MARY OF THE SNOW (1833), [CEM] Rev. Hugh R. Grace; Deacons Perry Bunyar; Donald Trees; Karl Pietkiewicz; Arnie Hyland; Hank Smith.
Res.: 36 Cedar St., 12477. Tel: 914-246-4913; Fax: 914-246-4996.
School— (1881), 25 Cedar St., 12477. Tel: 914-246-6381. Miss Christine M. Molinelli, Prin. Lay Teachers 10; Students 139; Preschool 39.
Chapel—Saugerties, Parish Center
Catechesis/Religious Program—Tel: 845-246-7534. Students 157.
SCARSDALE, WESTCHESTER CO.
1—IMMACULATE HEART OF MARY (1912), Rev. Robert J. Verrigni; Rev. Msgrs. John J. Scanlon, Pastor Emeritus; Edward M. Connors, Pastor Emeritus (Retired); Revs. Matthew F. Fernan; Richard Seagraves; Deacons Ernest F. Salomone; Robert di Targiani.
Res.: 8 Carman Rd., 10583. Tel: 914-723-0276; Fax: 914-722-0628.
School— (1928), 201 Boulevard, 10583. Tel: 914-723-5608; Fax: 914-723-8004. Robert W. Billings, Prin. Lay Teachers 19; Students 273.
Catechesis/Religious Program—Tel: 914-723-7593; Fax: 914-723-7209. Students 850.
2—OUR LADY OF FATIMA (1948), Rev. Msgr. Hugh F. McManus; Deacons Michael J. Fox; John J. Kollar; Irene Ingham Kollar, Pastoral Assoc.
Res.: 5 Strathmore Rd., 10583. Tel: 914-723-7421; Fax: 914-723-7229.
School— (1950),Tel: 914-723-0460. Mrs. Janice Arcaro, Prin. Lay Teachers 10; Students 219.
Catechesis/Religious Program—Tel: 914-472-6604; Fax: 914-472-6679. Students 184.
3—ST. PIUS X (1954), Revs. John P. O'Brien; Sebastian F. Bacatan (Philippines); Deacons Theodore A. Gaskin; William J. Hill.
Res.: 91 Secor Rd., 10583. Tel: 914-725-2755; Fax: 914-725-2782.
School— (1957), 85 Palmer Ave., 10583. Tel: 914-725-0541. Lay Teachers 14; Students 115.
Catechesis/Religious Program—Tel: 914-472-5594. Students 170.
SHRUB OAK, WESTCHESTER CO., SAINT ELIZABETH ANN SETON (1963), Rev. Msgr. Thomas P. Sandi; Revs. George C. Lodi; S. Kulandairajan; Deacons Gaspare F. Bruno; Michael Wilson.
Res.: Main St., 10588. Tel: 914-528-3547; Fax: 914-528-4216.
School—Tel: 914-528-3563; Fax: 914-528-0341. Sr. Gabriel Miriam, S.C., Prin. Sisters 1; Lay Teachers 25; Students 485.
Catechesis/Religious Program—Tel: 914-528-8553; Fax: 914-528-1047. Elizabeth Rust, D.R.E. Students 1,290.
SLEEPY HOLLOW, WESTCHESTER CO.
1—IMMACULATE CONCEPTION (1917), (Italian), Rev. Louis J. Mazza.
Res.: 199 N. Broadway, 10591. Tel: 914-631-0446; Fax: 914-631-4157.
2—THE MAGDALENE (1894), Rev. Msgr. Donald J. Pryor, Pastor Emeritus; Revs. Joseph S. Dietz; Theodore M. Nnaji (Nigeria). In Res., Rev. Msgr. Walter L. Schroeder (Retired).
Res.: 525 Bedford Rd., Pocantico Hills, 10591-1216. Tel: 914-631-0529; Fax: 914-332-7958.
Catechesis/Religious Program—Students 150.
3—ST. TERESA OF AVILA (1853), (Spanish—Portuguese), Revs. Francis P. Gorman; Jude Egbeji.
Res.: 130 Beekman Ave., 10591. Tel: 914-631-0720; Fax: 914-366-6459.
Catechesis/Religious Program—Tel: 914-631-1831. Students 249.
SLOATSBURG, ROCKLAND CO., ST. JOAN OF ARC (1966), (Italian—Irish), Rev. D. Francis Dias, Admin.
Res.: 32 Eagle Valley Rd., 10974. Tel: 845-753-5239; Fax: 845-753-5341.
Catechesis/Religious Program—Tel: 845-753-5193. Students 185.
SPRING VALLEY, ROCKLAND CO., ST. JOSEPH (1894), Rev. Rudolph F. Gonzalez; Rev. Msgr. Carl Sansaricq (Retired). In Res., Revs. Joseph Kazhuvidayil; Felix Kumai; Alder Valon; Patrick Adekola.
Res.: 333 Sneden Pl. W., 10977. Tel: 914-356-0311; Fax: 914-352-8126.
School— (1927), 245 N. Main St., 10977. Tel: 914-356-0054; Fax: 914-356-9654. Mrs. Dorothy Kelly, Prin. Lay Teachers 11; Students 200.
Catechesis/Religious Program—Tel: 914-356-9654; Fax: 914-352-5686. Students 600.
STONY POINT, ROCKLAND CO., IMMACULATE CONCEPTION (1889), Revs. Robert J. Staar; Joseph Soysa (Sri Lanka); Deacons Philip Marino; John Crapanzano. In Res., Rev. Abraham Drapankal.
Res.: 26 John St., 10980. Tel: 845-786-2742; Fax: 845-942-2614.
School— (1902), Main St., 10980. Tel: 845-786-5245; Fax: 845-786-3416. Lay Teachers 10; Students 197.
Catechesis/Religious Program—Tel: 914-786-5298. Students 195.
SUFFERN, ROCKLAND CO., SACRED HEART (1868), Rev. Msgr. Joseph P. Meehan; Revs. Andrew P. Carrozza; Clement O. Oyafemi (Nigeria); Deacons John Baterbury; Robert J. Johnson, Business Mgr.; Joseph A. Witt; Robert C. Keller.
Res.: 125 Lafayette, 10901. Tel: 845-357-0035; Fax: 845-368-0393.
School— (1909), 60 Washington Ave., 10901. Tel: 845-357-1684; Fax: 845-357-0318. Sr. Rose Andrew, O.P., Prin. Sisters 3; Lay Teachers 25; Students 476.
Catechesis/Religious Program—Tel: 845-357-6044. Mary Ann von Doehren, D.R.E. Students 648.
Chapel—Good Samaritan Hospital, Tel: 845-368-5000.
Chapel—Tagaste Monastery, Tel: 845-357-0067; Fax: 845-369-0625.
TAPPAN, ROCKLAND CO., OUR LADY OF THE SACRED HEART (1952), Rev. John F. Dwyer.
Res.: 120 King's Hwy., 10983. Tel: 845-359-1230.
Catechesis/Religious Program—Tel: 845-359-1230. Students 376.
TARRYTOWN, WESTCHESTER CO., TRANSFIGURATION (1896), Rev. Lucian W. Beltzner, O.Carm. In Res., Revs. Robert D. Tracy, O.Carm.; Richard Champigny, O.Carm.
Res.: 268 S. Broadway, 10591. Tel: 914-631-1672; Fax: 914-524-9352.
School— (1949), 40 Prospect Ave., 10591. Tel: 914-631-3737; Fax: 914-631-6640. Mary Margaret Henshaw, Prin. Lay Teachers 15; Students 251.
Catechesis/Religious Program—Tel: 914-631-2380. Students 225.
TIVOLI, DUTCHESS CO., ST. SYLVIA (1890), [CEM] Rev. H. Theriault, M.Div.
Res.: 104 Broadway, P.O. Box 95, 12583-0095. Tel: 845-757-2442; Fax: 845-757-3553.
Catechesis/Religious Program—Tel: 845-757-3501; Fax: 845-757-3553. Students 96.
TUCKAHOE, WESTCHESTER CO.
1—ASSUMPTION (1911), (Italian), Rev. Msgr. Francis E. Oliverio; Revs. Patrick A. Walsh, S.M.A.; Joseph Fallon; Joseph Emmanuel; Deacon Anthony Viola.
Res.: 53 Winterhill Rd., 10707. Tel: 914-961-3643; Fax: 914-961-0283.
Church: 100 Pleasant Ave., 10707.
Catechesis/Religious Program— Clustered with Immaculate Conception, Tuckahoe.
2—IMMACULATE CONCEPTION (1853), [CEM] [JC] Rev. Msgr. Francis E. Oliverio; Revs. Patrick A. Walsh, S.M.A.; Joseph Fallon; Joseph Emmanuel (Sri Lanka); Deacon Anthony Viola.
Res.: 53 Winterhill Rd., 10707. Tel: 914-961-3643; Fax: 914-961-0283.
School— (1913),Tel: 914-961-3785; Fax: 914-961-6054. Dr. Elaine Farrell, Prin. Sisters 2; Lay Teachers 26; Students 393.
Catechesis/Religious Program—Tel: 914-961-1076; Fax: 914-961-4765. Lynn Callahan, D.R.E. Students 823.
Chapel—Sisters Convent, Tel: 914-961-3970.
TUXEDO, ORANGE CO., OUR LADY OF MT. CARMEL (1895), Rev. John F.X. Smith.
Res.: Rte. 17, P.O. Box 697, 10987. Tel: 914-351-5284; Fax: 914-351-4866.
Catechesis/Religious Program—Students 87.
VALHALLA, WESTCHESTER CO., HOLY NAME OF JESUS (1896), Revs. Joseph A. Blenkle; Michael J. O'Leary (Ireland).
Res.: Two Broadway, 10595. Tel: 914-949-2323; Fax: 914-686-6325.
School—Tel: 914-948-1744; Fax: 914-686-1749. Judith Foster, Prin. Lay Teachers 12; Students 174.
Catechesis/Religious Program—Tel: 914-949-1422. Students 510.
VERPLANCK, WESTCHESTER CO., ST. PATRICK (1843), (Irish—Italian), [CEM] Rev. Andrew E. Kurzyna.
Res.: 240 11th St., 10596. Tel: 914-737-0635; Fax: 914-788-0584.
Catechesis/Religious Program—Tel: 914-737-1348. Students 152.
Chapel—Convent Seventh St., 10596. Tel: 914-737-1373.
WALDEN, ORANGE CO., MOST PRECIOUS BLOOD (1894), Rev. Kenneth M. Loughman.
Res.: 42 Walnut St., 12586. Tel: 845-778-5719; Fax: 845-778-3785.
School—Tel: 845-778-3028. Sisters of St. Dominic (Sparkill) 1; Lay Teachers 9; Students 213.
Catechesis/Religious Program—Tel: 914-778-7081. Students 398.
Mission—St. Benedict Wallkill, Ulster Co. 12589.
WAPPINGERS FALLS, DUTCHESS CO., ST MARY (1850), [CEM Rev. Msgr. Francis P. Bellew; Rev. Robert B. Repenning.
Res.: 11 Clinton St., 12590. Tel: 845-297-6261; 845-297-6262; Fax: 845-297-3227.
School— (1890 and 1955), Convent Ave., 12590. Tel: 914-297-7500. Mrs. Mary Ellen LaRose, Prin. Lay Teachers 18; Students 216.
Catechesis/Religious Program—Tel: 845-297-7586. Patricia Manuli, D.R.E. Students 510.
Chapel—Mt. Carmel, St. Mary Convent
WARWICK, ORANGE CO., ST. STEPHEN (1865), [CEM] Rev. Michael P. McLoughlin; Rev. Msgr. Bernard J. Corrigan, Pastor Emeritus (Retired); Rev. Thomas Byrnes; Deacons Authur J. Cuccia; Thomas MacDougall; Emmet Noonan.
Res.: 75 Sanfordville Rd., 10990. Tel: 845-986-4028; Fax: 845-986-4109.
School—Tel: 845-986-3533; Fax: 845-986-7023. Lay Teachers 13; Students 300.
Catechesis/Religious Program—Tel: 845-986-2231; Fax: 845-986-2231. Students 1,162.
Mission—St. Edward (1881), Main St., Florida, Orange Co. 10921.
WASHINGTONVILLE, ORANGE CO., ST. MARY (1902), [CEM] Revs. John J. Keaveney; Paul DMoch; Deacon John Shepard.
Res.: 2 Fr. Tierney Cir., 10992. Tel: 914-496-3730; Fax: 914-496-3159.
Catechesis/Religious Program—Tel: 845-496-4101. Students 1,750.
WESLEY HILLS, ROCKLAND CO., ST. BONIFACE (1966), Rev. Robert D. Saccoman.
Res.: 5 Willow Tree Rd., 10952. Tel: 845-354-7307; Fax: 914-354-9046.
Catechesis/Religious Program—Tel: 845-354-7039. Students 437.
WEST HURLEY-WOODSTOCK, ULSTER CO., ST. JOHN (Woodstock) (1860), Rev. George W. Hommel.
Res.: 12 Holly Hills Dr., Woodstock, 12498. Tel: 914-679-7696; Fax: 914-679-8393.
Catechesis/Religious Program—Tel: 914-679-2869. Students 305.
Mission—St. Augustine Watson Hollow Rd., West Shokan, Ulster Co. 12494. Tel: 914-657-2190.
WEST NYACK, ROCKLAND CO., ST. FRANCIS OF ASSISI (1964), Rev. Edward J. Weber. In Res., Rev. Gerard F. Rafferty, S.S.L.
Res.: 128 Parrott Rd., 10994. Tel: 845-634-4957; Fax: 845-639-6629.
Catechesis/Religious Program—Tel: 845-638-4215. Students 955.
WEST POINT, ORANGE CO., CATHOLIC CHAPEL OF THE MOST HOLY TRINITY (1899),, Most Holy Trinity is being served under the Archdiocese for Military Services. For inquiries for sacramental records before Jan. 1, 1999, please contact Sacred Heart, Highland Falls.
WHITE PLAINS, WESTCHESTER CO.
1—ST. ANTHONY (1952), Rev. Msgr. Rudolph Eisler; Rev. Peter C. Scaramuzzo.
Res.: 85 Harrison St., West Harrison, 10604. Tel: 914-948-1480; Fax: 914-948-0488.
School— (1957), Gainsborg Ave., West Harrison, 10604. Tel: 914-949-6986; Fax: 914-328-1981. Sisters of Divine Compassion 3; Students 185.
Catechesis/Religious Program—Tel: 914-949-0212. Students 500.
2—ST. BERNARD (1926), Revs. Edward M. Roos; Jose Vilaplana, S.J. (Spain); Benedict J. Kuolt (Retired); Paul Appiah-Sekyere (Ghana); Deacons Robert Whiteman; Daniel Pellegrin.
Res.: 51 Prospect St., 10606. Tel: 914-949-2111; Fax: 914-949-6044.
Catechesis/Religious Program—Students 511.
3—ST. JOHN THE EVANGELIST (1868), [CEM] Rev. Msgrs. Neil Graham; William B. Delaney, Pastor Emeritus (Retired); Revs. Christopher H. Daly; Thomas J. Joyce; Donald V. O'Brien, S.J.; Thomas Kalarickal, C.M.I. (India).
Res.: 148 Hamilton Ave., 10601. Tel: 914-949-0439; Fax: 914-421-1202.
School— (1890), 146 Hamilton Ave., 10601. Tel: 914-949-4374. Lay Teachers 12.
Catechesis/Religious Program—Tel: 914-997-7137. Students 270.
4—OUR LADY OF MT. CARMEL (1902), (Italian), Rev. Albert Azrak, C.S.S. In Res., Revs. Leonard DellaBadia, C.S.S.; Phillip Pornchoi, C.S.S.; Peter C. Pramote, C.S.S.
Res.: 92 S. Lexington Ave., 10606. Tel: 914-948-5909; Fax: 914-428-2676.
Catechesis/Religious Program—Tel: 914-428-2676. Students 130.
5—OUR LADY OF SORROWS (1929), Revs. Patrick J. Dunne; Carmine J. Rita; Rev. Msgr. John K. Daly, Pastor Emeritus.
Res.: 920 Mamaroneck Ave., 10605. Tel: 914-949-9819; Fax: 914-949-4148.
School— (1957),Tel: 914-761-0124; Fax: 914-761-0176. Sr. Marie Cecile, Prin. Lay Teachers 14; Students 210.
Catechesis/Religious Program—Tel: 914-761-5257. Students 353.
WOODBOURNE, SULLIVAN CO., IMMACULATE CONCEPTION (1957), [CEM] Rev. John J. Lynch.
Res.: P.O. Box 66, 12788. Tel: 845-434-7643; Fax: 845-436-7370.

Catechesis/Religious Program—Tel: 845-436-7370. Students 142.

WURTSBORO, SULLIVAN CO., ST. JOSEPH (1880), [CEM] Rev. Peter J. Madori.
Res.: 180 Sullivan St., P.O. Box 277, 12790. Tel: 845-888-4522; Fax: 845-888-5072.
Catechesis/Religious Program—Students 99.

YONKERS, WESTCHESTER CO.

1—ST. ANN (1947), Revs. John A. De Bellis; John Carson; Thaddeus Obba (Nigeria).
Res.: 854 Midland Ave., 10704. Tel: 914-965-1555; 914-965-5584; Fax: 914-965-0678.
School—40 Brewster Ave., 10704. Tel: 914-965-4333; Fax: 914-965-1778. Mrs. Lisa Lanni, Prin. Lay Teachers 18; Students 284.
Catechesis/Religious Program—Students 120.

2—ST. ANTHONY (Nepera Park) (1923), Revs. Karl A. Bauer; Robert Ashman.
Res.: 10 Squire Ave., 10703. Tel: 914-965-2733; Fax: 914-963-2285.
Church: 1405 Nepperhan Ave., 10703.
School—Tel: 914-476-8489; Fax: 914-965-7939. Mrs. Elizabeth Carney, Prin. Lay Teachers 11; Students 260.
Catechesis/Religious Program—Tel: 914-965-5535. Students 90.

3—ST. ANTHONY (Willow St.), Closed., For inquiries for parish records contact Our Lady of Mt. Carmel, Yonkers.

4—ST. BARTHOLOMEW (1911), Rev. Brian P. McCarthy; Rev. Msgr. Charles J. McManus, Pastor Emeritus (Retired); Deacons Robert A. Clemens; Anthony Mercandetti.
Res.: 15 Palmer Rd., 10701. Tel: 914-965-0566; Fax: 914-965-9046.
School— (1958), 278 Saw Mill River Rd., 10701. Tel: 914-476-7949; Fax: 914-476-7957. Sr. Ann Marie McMahon, P.B.V.M., Prin. Sisters 2; Lay Teachers 13; Students 300.
Catechesis/Religious Program—Tel: 914-476-6676. Students 150.

5—ST. CASIMIR (1899), (Polish), Revs. Jerzy Maj, O.S.P.; Krzysztof Drybka, O.S.P., 94; Deacon John Radzilowicz.
Res.: 239 Nepperhan Ave., 10701. Tel: 914-963-1254; Fax: 914-969-5204.
School— (1906), 259 Nepperhan Ave., 10701-3461. Tel: 914-965-2730; Fax: 914-965-3347. Mr. Christopher Coyne, Prin. Lay Teachers 12; Students 197.

6—CHRIST THE KING (1927), Rev. Msgr. A. Francis Burns; Rev. Abraham Chacko (India). In Res., Rev. Leo D. Lefebure (CHI).
Res.: 740 N. Broadway, 10701. Tel: 914-963-7474; 914-963-7564; Fax: 914-963-7548.
School— (1955), 750 N. Broadway, 10701. Tel: 914-476-1711; Fax: 914-423-4101. Bro. Robert Falcone, C.S.C., Prin. Sisters 2; Lay Teachers 12; Students 209.
Catechesis/Religious Program—Tel: 914-964-5324. Students 151.

7—ST. DENIS (1910), Revs. Edward P. O'Halloran; Michael Challinor.
Res.: 470 Van Cortlandt Park Ave., 10705. Tel: 914-963-8468; Fax: 914-963-7354.
School— (1928), McLean Ave. & Lawrence St., 10705. Tel: 914-963-3438. Mrs. Dorothy O'Neill-Williams, Prin. Lay Teachers 10; Students 202.
Catechesis/Religious Program—Tel: 914-476-8077. Rev. Edward P. O'Halloran, D.R.E. Students 100.

8—ST. EUGENE (1949), Rev. Leonard F. Villa, Admin. In Res., Revs. Richard Seagrams; P.J. Thawale; Deacon Donald M. Quigley, Pastoral Assoc.
Res.: 32 Massitoa Rd., 10710. Tel: 914-779-5460; Fax: 914-793-8913.
School— (1951), 707 Tuckahoe Rd., 10710. Tel: 914-779-2956; Fax: 914-779-7668. Sisters 2; Lay Teachers 21; Students 500.
Catechesis/Religious Program—Tel: 914-793-2158; Fax: 914-337-9868. Students 165.
Chapel—Yonkers, Franciscan Sisters Convent, Tel: 914-779-7379.

9—IMMACULATE CONCEPTION (1848), (Spanish—Arabic), [CEM] Rev. Msgr. Hugh J. Corrigan; Revs. Sami Totah (Jordan); Virgilio Compentente (Philippines).
Res.: 103 S. Broadway, 10701. Tel: 914-963-0156; Fax: 914-963-1803.
School— (1857), 15 St. Mary's St., 10701. Tel: 914-965-7048; Fax: 914-423-2826. Mr. Eugene T. Hewitt, Prin. Sisters 1; Lay Teachers 9; Students 204.
Catechesis/Religious Program—Tel: 914-963-1053. Students 245.
Chapel—Sisters of Charity, St. Mary Convent 4 St. Mary's St., 10701. Tel: 914-963-1449.
Good Shepherd Arabic Community of St. Mary—Rev. Sami Totah (Jordan), Dir.

10—ST. JOHN THE BAPTIST (1903), (Italian—Irish), Rev. Msgr. J. Christopher Maloney; Revs. Thomas Valenti; Daniel Ulloa, O.P. (Mexico); Lino Gonsalves; Deacon Martin J. Olivieri; Vacant (GB).
Res.: 670 Yonkers Ave., 10704. Tel: 914-963-1486; Fax: 914-375-1115.
School— (1954),Tel: 914-965-2356. Sisters 3; Lay Teachers 8; Students 360.
Catechesis/Religious Program—Tel: 914-965-2338. Anne Yedowitz, D.R.E. Students 129.
Chapel—Convent 176 Sweetfield Circle, 10704. Tel: 914-965-1837.

11—ST. JOSEPH (1871), (Hispanic), [CEM] Revs. George J. Kuhn; Paul V. Sullivan (Retired); Deacon Abraham Santiago.
Res.: 141 Ashburton Ave., 10701. Tel: 914-963-0730; Fax: 914-964-5833.
Catechesis/Religious Program—Students 175.
Convent—Sisters of Charity, Tel: 914-423-1351. Sisters 7.

12—ST. MARGARET OF HUNGARY (1928), Rev. Gabriel Kiss, S.J. (Hungary), Admin.; Deacon Louis JuHasz.
Res.: 76 Locust Hill Ave., 10701. Tel: 914-423-2211.

13—MOST HOLY TRINITY (1894), (Slovak), Rev. Anthony J. Pleho.
Res.: 18 Trinity Pl., 10701. Tel: 914-963-0720; Fax: 914-709-0224.
Chapel—Franciscan Friars of the Renewal 15 Trinity Pl., 10701. Tel: 914-476-7279; Fax: 914-476-5033. Rev. Glenn Sudano, C.F.R.

14—OUR LADY OF FATIMA (1977), (Portuguese), Rev. Osvaldo Franklin, J.C.D., Admin.; William Farren, Business Mgr.
Portuguese R.C. Center: 355 S. Broadway, P.O. Box 283, 10705. Tel: 914-423-9688; Fax: 914-423-8271.

15—OUR LADY OF MT. CARMEL (1913), (Italian), Revs. Terzo Vinci, S.A.C.; Chris Salvatori, S.A.C.; Deacons Alfred R. Impallomeni; Nick A. Mazzei Jr.
Res.: 70 Park Hill Ave., 10701. Tel: 914-963-4766; Fax: 914-375-1069; 914-963-4766.
School—Mt. Carmel-St. Anthony, 85 Linden St., 10701. Tel: 914-476-8888; Fax: 914-375-1069. Mrs. Teresita Fajardo. Lay Teachers 10; Students 140.
Catechesis/Religious Program—Tel: 914-423-8848. Students 215.

16—OUR LADY OF THE ROSARY (1907), (Portuguese), Rev. Thomas Gumprecht, S.A.; Bro. John Baptist Hildreth, S.A., Pastoral Min.; Deacon Joaquim Pereira.
Res.: 226 Warburton Ave., 10701. Tel: 914-963-0806; Fax: 914-963-3958.
Catechesis/Religious Program—Students 35.

17—ST. PAUL THE APOSTLE (1923), Rev. Msgr. John A. Gallagher; Sr. Eileen Treanor, Parish Ministry; Deacons James Hamilton; Rudolfo Teng.
Res.: 602 McLean Ave., 10705. Tel: 914-963-7330; Fax: 914-963-1952.
Church: Lincoln Park, 10705.
School— (1949), 77 Lee Ave., 10705. Tel: 914-965-2165; Fax: 914-965-5792. Grace Mallardi, Prin. Lay Teachers 10; Students 312.
Catechesis/Religious Program—Students 84.

18—ST. PETER (1894), Revs. Antonio Almonte; Jose L. Mena; Deacons Pedro Irizarry; Randy Velez.
Res.: 91 Ludlow St., 10705. Tel: 914-963-0822; Fax: 914-968-9305.
School— (1894 and 1955), 204 Hawthorne Ave., 10705. Tel: 914-963-2314; Fax: 914-966-8822. Lay Teachers 10; Students 230.
Catechesis/Religious Program—Tel: 914-476-7946. Students 476.

19—SACRED HEART (1891), Revs. Theodosius Corley, O.F.M.Cap.; Christopher Dietrich, O.F.M.Cap.; Raynold Thibodeau, O.F.M.Cap., Chap.; Thomas Murphy, O.F.M.Cap., Chap.; John B. Riordan, O.F.M.Cap., Guardian; Bros. Roger Deguire, O.F.M-.Cap.; Robert Falcone, C.S.C.
Res.: 110 Shonnard Pl., 10703. Tel: 914-963-4205; Fax: 914-476-4960.
School— (1893),Tel: 914-963-5318. Lay Teachers 16; Students 311.
High School—34 Convent Ave., 10703. Tel: 914-965-3114; Fax: 914-965-4510. Lay Teachers 25; Students 394.
Sacred Heart Parish High School Foundation, Inc.—34 Convent Ave., 10703. Tel: 914-963-4205; Fax: 914-476-4960. Rev. John B. Riordan, O.F.M.Cap., Pres.
Catechesis/Religious Program—Students 90.
Convent—27 Convent Ave., 10703. Tel: 914-476-4602.

YORKTOWN HEIGHTS, WESTCHESTER CO., ST. PATRICK (1898), Rev. Msgr. Dermot R. Brennan; Revs. Joseph McLafferty; James Hauver.
Res.: 137 Moseman Rd., 10598. Tel: 914-962-5050; 914-962-5051; Fax: 914-962-0595.
School— (1953), 117 Moseman Rd., 10598. Tel: 914-962-2211; Fax: 914-243-4814. Sisters 2; Lay Teachers 22; Students 400.
Catechesis/Religious Program—Tel: 914-962-5586; Fax: 914-962-3207. Students 2,216.

YOUNGSVILLE, SULLIVAN CO., ST. FRANCIS OF ASSISI (1963), Merged, with St. George, Jeffersonville to form St. George-St. Francis, Jeffersonville

YULAN, SULLIVAN CO., ST. ANTHONY OF PADUA (1907), (Irish—German), [CEM] Rev. Anthony F. Moore, O.F.M.
Res.: 12792. Tel: 845-557-8512; Fax: 845-557-3527.
Catechesis/Religious Program—Students 83.
Mission—Sacred Heart Berme Church Rd., Pond Eddy, Sullivan Co. 12770. Tel: 845-557-8122.

Chaplains of Public Institutions
Military Installations

NEW YORK. *National Catholic Community Service*, 487 Park Ave., 10022. Rev. Msgr. Richard Cahill, Dir. (Cardinal Spellman Servicemen's Club)
New York City Veterans Administration Hospital, 406 First Ave., 10022. Rev. Edmund McCaffrey, O.Carm.

BRONX. *Veterans Administration Hospital*, 130 W. Kingsbridge Rd., 10460. Rev. Edward A. Kozlowski, Rev. Msgr. Charles P. Boccio.

MONTROSE. *Franklin D. Roosevelt Hospital*. Revs. Daniel F. Lynch, O.Carm., Albert Daly, O.Carm.

WEST POINT. *Stewart Field*. Rev. Nash P. Geany.
West Point.
U.S. Military Academy 10966. Vacant.

Societies

NEW YORK. *Marine and Aviation Department*. Vacant.
New York Fire Department. Rev. Msgr. Marc A. Filacchione.
New York Police Department. Rev. Msgr. Joseph J. Zammit.
New York Postal Service.
New York Sanitation Department. Rev. Peter M. Colapietro.

YONKERS. *Yonkers Fire Department*.
Yonkers Police Department.

Prisons

CITY. *Adolescent Remand & Detention Center*. Sr. Margaret McCabe.
11-11 Hazen St., East Elmhurst, 11370. Tel: 718-546-7223.
Anna M. Kross Center. Revs. George J. Dash, O.F.M.Cap., Charles Keeney.
18-18 Hazen St., East Elmhurst, 11370. Tel: 718-546-3654.
Correctional Institution for Men. Sr. Mary O'Connor, Rev. Thomas Houle, O.F.M.Cap.
10-10 Hazen St., East Elmhurst, 11370. Tel: 718-546-5796.
George M. Motchan Detention Center. Revs. Joseph P. Kane, S.J., Thomas Mestriparampil.
15-15 Hazen St., East Elmhurst, 11370. Tel: 718-546-4543.
George Vierno Center. Rev. Thomas Hoyle, O.F.M., Chap., Sr. Marie Hermann.
09-09 Hazen St., East Elmhurst, 11370. Tel: 718-204-5079, Ext. 2254.
Manhattan Detention Center. Rev. Reginald John. 125 White St., 10013. Tel: 212-225-1367.
North Infirmary Command. Rev. Lawrence E. Lucas, Sr. Amy Henry.
15-00 Hazen St., East Elmhurst, 11370. Tel: 718-546-1256.
Otis Bantum Correctional Center. Revs. Lawrence E. Lucas, Thomas Mestriparampil.
16-00 Hazen St., East Elmhurst, 11370. Tel: 718-546-6617.
Rose M. Singer Center. Rev. Joseph P. Kane, S.J. Tel: 718-546-7498, Sr. Marion Defeis.
19-19 Hazen St., East Elmhurst, 11370.
Spofford Juvenile Center. Vacant.
1221 Spofford Ave., Bronx, 10474. Tel: 718-579-0100.
VCBC. Rev. Vincent P. McNamara, Deacon Kenneth Radcliff.
1 Halleck, Bronx, 10474. Tel: 718-579-4371.
West Facility.
16-06 Hazen St., East Elmhurst, 11370. Tel: 718-546-4495.

COUNTY. *Dutchess County Jail*, Poughkeepsie, 12601. Tel: 845-297-5706. Rev. Ernest D'Onofrio, O.F.M.
Orange County Jail. Attended from St. John, Goshen. Tel.: 845-294-5328.
Putnam County Jail. Attended by St. James, Carmel. Tel.: 845-225-2079.
Rockland County Jail. Attended by St. Augustine, New City. Tel.: 845-634-3641.
Sullivan County Jail. Attended by St. Peter, Monticello. Tel.: 845-794-5577.
Ulster County Jail, Kingston, 12401. Tel: 845-338-1554. Deacon John Bellacicco.
Westchester County Jail. Revs. Paul Tolve, O.F.M-.Cap., Joseph Dietz.
Box 389, Valhalla, 10595. Tel: 914-347-6132.

FEDERAL. *Federal Correctional Institution*. Rev. David Baary, 78.
Otisville, 10963. Tel: 845-386-5855, Ext. 291.
Metropolitan Correctional Center. Revs. Juan Soles, Michael O'Hara, O.M.I.
150 Park Row, 10007-1779. Tel: 212-240-9656, Ext. 6454.

STATE. *Arthur Kill Correctional Facility*. Rev. Frank Naccarato.

2911 Arthur Kill Rd., Staten Island, 10309-1197. Tel: 718-356-7333.

Bayview Correctional Facility. Rev. Charles Keeney. 550 W. 20th St., 10011-2878. Tel: 212-255-7590.

Beacon Correctional Facility. Rev. Arecio Dormido, Deacon John O'Reilly.

Box 780, Beacon, 12508-0780. Tel: 845-831-4200.

Bedford Hills Correctional Facility. Rev. Michael O'Shea, Sr. Elaine Roulet.

247 Harris Rd., Bedford Hills, 10507-2499. Tel: 914-241-3100.

Downstate Correctional Facility. Rev. Arecio Dormido, Deacons Frank Gohl, Anthony Gruerio.

Box 445, Fishkill, 12524-0445. Tel: 845-831-6600.

Eastern Correctional Facility. Rev. Paul Thymootil, C.M.I., Deacon Franklyn Russell.

Napanoch, 12458-0338. Tel: 845-647-7400.

Edgecombe Correctional Facility. Deacon Nicholas Mazzei.

611 Edgecombe Ave., 10032-4398. Tel: 212-923-2575.

Fishkill Correctional Facility. Revs. Nimal Mendis, C.H.S., George J. Dash, O.F.M.Cap.

Box 307, Beacon, 12508. Tel: 845-831-4800.

Fulton Correctional Facility. Deacon Nicholas Mazzei.

1511 Fulton Ave., Bronx, 10457-8398. Tel: 718-583-8000.

Green Haven Correctional Facility. Rev. Gamini E. Fernando (Sri Lanka), Deacon David Weinstein.

Stormville, 12582. Tel: 845-221-2711.

Lincoln Correctional Facility. Deacon Nicholas Mazzei.

31-33 W. 110 St., 10026-4398. Tel: 212-860-9400.

Mid-Orange Correctional Facility. Deacon Ricardo Rosado, Rev. Augustine Graap, O.Carm.

Warwick, 10990-0990. Tel: 845-986-2291.

Otisville Correctional Facility. Rev. Augustine Graap, O.Carm., Deacon Eugene Bormann.

Box 8, Otisville, 10963-0008. Tel: 845-386-1490, Ext. 4830.

Shawangunk Correctional Facility. Rev. Paul Thymootil, C.M.I., Deacon Joseph Doherty.

Box 750, Wallkill, 12589-0750. Tel: 845-895-2081, Ext. 4821.

Sing Sing Correctional Facility. Rev. Ronald J. Lemmert.

354 Hunter St., Ossining, 10562-5442. Tel: 914-941-0108, Ext. 4810.

Sullivan Correctional Facility. Rev. Stanislaus Ogbonna, C.S.Sp. (Nigeria).

P.O. Box AG, Fallsburg, 12733-0116. Tel: 845-434-2080.

Taconic Correctional Facility. Sr. Antonia Maguire.

250 Harris Rd., Bedford Hills, 10507-2498. Tel: 914-241-3010.

Ulster Correctional Facility. Rev. Paul Thymootil, C.M.I., Deacon Angel Lamberty.

Berme Rd., P.O. Box 800, Napanoch, 12458. Tel: 914-647-1670, Ext. 4800.

Wallkill Correctional Facility. Rev. Paul Thymootil, C.M.I., Deacon Angelo Cosaro.

Box G, Wallkill, 12589-0286. Tel: 845-895-2021.

Woodbourne Correctional Facility. Rev. Matthias Ndylaka.

Pouch 1, Woodbourne, 12788. Tel: 845-434-7730.

Hospitals

BEACON. *Craig House Hospital*, Tel: 914-831-1200. Serviced by St. Joachim, Beacon.

BRONX. *St. Barnabas Hospital*, Tel: 718-960-9000. Rev. Msgr. Thomas McGarry (Retired), Sr. Miriam Hanratty, O.P., Deacon Victor Pino.

Bronx Municipal Hospital Center, Abraham Jacobi Hospital, Nathan B. VanEtten Hospital. Revs. Sancho G. Garrote, Robert Holick, M.H.M. Tel: 718-918-5254.

Bronx Psychiatric Center, Tel: 718-931-0600.

Bronx-Lebanon Hospital Center, Tel: 718-590-1800; 718-518-5059. Revs. Robert A. Jeffers, Ruben Cammayo, Deacon Alfonso Ramos.

Calvary Hospital, Tel: 718-518-2114. Ms. Eileen M. Pesek, Asst. Admin. & Dir. Pastoral Ministries.

Lincoln Medical and Mental Health Center, Tel: 718-579-5000; 718-579-5059. Rev. Abel Alvarez, O.S.U.

Montefiore Medical Center, Tel: 718-920-4997. Revs. Matthew Azakath, Mark Oquamanam.

North Central Bronx Hospital, Tel: 718-519-5000. Serviced by Jacobi Medical Chaplain.

Our Lady of Mercy Medical Center. Rev. Msgr. Frederick J. Becker, Vice Pres. Pastoral Svcs., Rev. John Ulko, Sr. Cathanne McVicar, S.M.

Pelham Bay Division, Tel: 718-920-9086; 920-900-. Serviced by priests and chaplains from Our Lady of Mercy Medical Center.

U.S.V.A. Medical Center. Rev. Msgr. Joseph J. Zammit, Revs. Roland LaFontant (France), Gregory Little, Eugene O'Hara, Stephen Shubiak. Tel: 718-584-9000.

Union Hospital, Tel: 718-200-2020. Serviced by St. Barnabas Hospital.

Westchester Square Hospital, Tel: 718-828-2380. Serviced by Santa Maria Parish.

BRONXVILLE. *Lawrence Hospital*. Rev. Paul Vezhaparambil, C.M.I. (India), Sr. Agnes Regina Hughes. Tel: 914-787-1000.

CALLICOON. *Community General Hospital*, Tel: 845-887-5530. Serviced by St. Peter, Monticello.

CARMEL. *Putnam Hospital Center*, Tel: 845-279-5711. Rev. Robert J. Ginel. Serviced by St. James the Apostle, Carmel.

CASTLE POINT. *Veterans Administration Medical Center*, Tel 845-831-2000, Ext. 5453. Revs. Raymond A. Pavlick, Robert Brennan, Richard DeLaPena, Brennan Egan, O.F.M.

COLD SPRING. *Julia L. Butterfield Memorial Hospital*, Tel: 914-265-3642. Serviced by Our Lady of Loretto, Cold Spring.

CORNWALL. *The Cornwall Hospital*, Tel: 845-534-2547. Serviced by St. Thomas of Canterbury, Cornwall-on-Hudson.

DOBBS FERRY. *St. Cabrini Nursing Home*, Tel: 914-693-6800. Sr. Mary Jo Lyons, O.S.B., Rev. Edwin F.D. Robinson, O.F.M.

Community Hospital of Dobbs Ferry, Tel: 914-693-0700. Serviced by Sacred Heart, Dobbs Ferry.

ELLENVILLE. *Ellenville Community Hospital*, Tel: 845-647-6080. Serviced by the Church of St. Mary & St. Andrew, Ellenville.

GOSHEN. *Arden Hill Hospital*, Tel: 914-294-5441. Serviced by St. John, Goshen.

HARRIS. *Community General Hospital of Sullivan County*, Tel: 845-292-4525. Serviced by St. Peter, Monticello.

HARRISON. *St. Vincent Hospital and Medical Center of New York*, Tel: 914-967-6500. Rev. Joseph F. Cavoto, S.A., Dir. Pastoral Care.

HAWTHORNE. *Rosary Hill Home*, Tel: 914-769-0114. Rev. John Mahoney, O.F.M.Cap.

KINGSTON. *Benedictine Hospital*, Tel: 845-338-2500. Sisters M. Dorothy Huggard, O.S.B., Dir Pastoral Care, Mary Feehan, O.S.B., Revs. Louis Yaya, Stephen Achi.

Kingston City Hospital, Tel: 845-331-3131. Rev. John Didam.

MANHATTAN. *Bellevue Hospital*. Revs. John Logan, O.Carm., Philip Marani, O.Carm.

Beth Israel Medical Center, Tel: 212-420-2759, Ext. 3. Revs. Edmund O'Kere, Reynaldo Domagas.

Bird S. Coler Memorial Hospital and Home, Tel: 212-838-8155. Revs. Harold F.X. O'Donnell, S.J., Peter Murray, S.J.

Cabrini Medical Center, Tel: 212-995-6056. Revs. Andrew Sioleti, O.F.M., Supvr., C.P.E., Daniel B. Morey, O.F.M.Cap., Raymond G. Pierini, M.M., Chap., Rafael R. Macaranas, Chap., Sisters Sofia Unneta Wood, R.S.C.J., Chap., Stephanie Kabacinksi, M.S.C., Chap., Consolata Demma, M.S.C., Chap.

St. Clare's Hospital & Health Center, Tel: 212-586-1500. Rev. John J. Donahue, C.S.C., Sr. Pascal Conforti, O.S.U.

Columbia Presbyterian Medical Center, Tel: 212-305-3101. Rev. Donald Johnson.

Allen Pavilion. Rev. Thomas McDonald.

Goldwater Memorial Hospital, Tel: 212-318-8000; 212-318-4738. Rev. Timothy A. Healey, S.J., Chap., Mrs. Margaret Karwoski, Chap.

Gouverneur Hospital, Tel: 212-374-4000. Rev. Msgr. Dennis J. Sullivan.

Gracie Square, Tel: 212-988-4400. Serviced by St. Jean Baptiste.

Harlem Hospital, Tel: 212-281-4931. Rev. Freddy Washington, C.S.Sp. Serviced by St. Mark.

Hospital for Special Surgery, Tel: 212-606-1757. Sr. Margaret Oettinger, O.P.

Lenox Hill Hospital, Tel: 212-439-2547. Revs. John Bucchino, O.F.M. Tel: 212-434-2000; 212-434-2545, Bernard Camire, S.S.S.

St. Luke's-Roosevelt Hospital Center, Tel: 212-523-4000.

Roosevelt Site. Rev. James F. McQuade, C.S.P.

St. Luke's Site. Rev. Msgr. Christopher Maloney, Revs. Thomas Valenti, Daniel Ulloa, C.P. (Mexico).

Manhattan Eye, Ear & Throat Hospital, Tel: 212-838-9200. Serviced by St. Vincent Ferrer.

Manhattan Psychiatric Center, Tel: 212-369-0500, Ext. 2530. Rev. Andrew Cuu Nguyen.

Medical Arts Center Hospital, Tel: 212-755-0200. Serviced by St. Patrick Cathedral.

Memorial Sloan Kettering Cancer Center. Tel: 212-639-5982. Revs. William Robert Gannon, O.P., Stephen Carmody, O.P.

Metropolitan Hospital. Rev. Michael J. Sala, S.J.

Mount Sinai Medical Center. Revs. Philip Romano, O.F.M.Cap., Francisco Abaya.

New York Downtown Hospital - New York Infirmary, Tel: 212-312-5000; 212-233-5300. Revs. Thomas McKeon, S.S.S., Peter Ma.

New York Eye & Ear Infirmary, Tel: 212-673-3480. Vacant.

New York Presbyterian Hospital, Tel: 212-746-4690. Revs. David A. Butler, O.P., Philip Fitzsimmons, O.P., Sr. Margaret T. Oettinger, O.P.

New York University Medical Center, Tel: 212-263-7300. Revs. Vincent Euk, Francis Ogofa.

Hospital for Joint Disease. Serviced by Mary Help of Christians, 212-254-0058.

North General Hospital, Tel: 212-862-4380; 212-423-4511. Rev. Lawrence E. Lucas. Serviced by All Saints.

Rockefeller University, Tel: 212-570-8000. Serviced by St. Catherine of Siena.

Terence Cardinal Cooke Health Care Center, Tel: 212-360-3993. Revs. Ronald Green, Benedict J. D'Alessandro, O.F.M., Sisters Lorraine Cooper, S.C., Maryanne Daly, S.C., Dir. Pastoral Care.

U.S.V.A. Medical Center, Tel: 212-686-7500. Revs. Edmund McCaffrey, O.Carm., Francis C. Morgan, SS.CC., Pasquale V. Laghezza, SS.CC., Andrew Sioleti, O.F.M.

St. Vincent Hospital, Tel: 212-604-7858. Revs. James O'Connell, O.F.M., Jefferson Hammer, Sisters Elizabeth Butler, S.C., Alberta Jerewicz.

MIDDLETOWN. *Horton Memorial Hospital*, Tel: 845-343-2424. Serviced by St. Joseph, Middletown.

Middletown Psychiatric Center, Tel: 845-342-5511. Rev. Robert D. Tracy, O.Carm.

MONTROSE. *FDR DVA Hospital*. Vacant.

MOUNT KISCO. *Northern Westchester Hospital*, Tel: 914-666-1200. Serviced by St. Francis, Mt. Kisco.

MOUNT VERNON. *Mount Vernon Hospital*, Tel: 914-664-8000. Rev. Isaac Aganbi.

NEW HAMPTON. *MID Hudson Psychiatric Center*. Rev. John Eyrrick, Senior Chap. Tel: 845-374-3171.

NEW ROCHELLE. *Sound Shore Medical Center*, Tel: 914-632-5000. Rev. Vethamuther Emmanuel.

NEWBURGH. *St. Luke Hospital*, Tel: 845-561-4400. Serviced by St. Patrick, Newsburgh.

NORTH TARRYTOWN. *Phelps Memorial Hospital*, Tel: 914-631-0720. Serviced by St. Theresa's, Sleepy Hollow.

NYACK. *Nyack Hospital*, Tel: 845-358-6200. Shirley Blair, Dir. Pastoral Care. Serviced By St. Ann, Nyack.

ORANGEBURG. *Rockland Psychiatric Center*. Rev. Donald T. Driscoll. Tel: 845-359-1000.

OSSINING. *Stony Lodge Hospital*, Tel: 914-941-7400. Serviced by St. Augustine, Ossining.

PEEKSKILL. *Hudson Valley Hospital Center*, Tel: 914-737-9000. Serviced by Holy Spirit, Cortlandt Manor.

POMONA. *Dr. Robert L. Yeager Health Center*. Susan Osborne, Pastoral Care. Tel: 845-364-2889.

PORT CHESTER. *United Hospital*, Tel: 914-939-0612. Serviced by Our Lady of Mercy, Port Chester.

PORT JERVIS. *Bon Secours Community Hospital*, Tel: 845-856-5351. Deacon Albert W. Perroult, Dir. Pastoral Care, Rev. Bernard McDonald, Deacon John Nash.

POUGHKEEPSIE. *St. Francis Hospital*, Tel: 845-471-2000. Rev. Thomas A. Heffernon, Dir. Pastoral Care Assoc., Sisters Mary Ellen Smith, O.S.F., Pastoral Care Assoc., Marie Colette, O.S.F., Pastoral Care Assoc., Patricia Nugent, Pastoral Care Assoc., Alice Howley, Pastoral Care Assoc.

Hudson River Psychiatric Center, Tel: 845-452-7378. Rev. James J. LeBar.

Vassar Brothers Hospital, Tel: 845-454-8500. Rev. Anthony S. Marian.

RHINEBECK. *Northern Dutchess Hospital*, Tel: 845-876-4583. Serviced by Good Shepherd, Rhinebeck.

RYE. *Rye Psychiatric Hospital Center*, Tel: 914-967-4567. Serviced by Church of the Resurrection, Rye.

STATEN ISLAND. *Bayley Seton Hospital*, Tel: 718-354-6000. Rev. Edward J. Datty, S.A., Dir. Pastoral Care, Sr. Claire Marian Barton, S.C., Chap., Bro. Kieran Cullen, S.A., Chap.

Doctor's Hospital of Staten Island, Tel: 718-727-4639. Serviced by St. Sylvester.

Seaview Hospital and Home, Tel: 718-371-3000, Ext. 3284. Rev. Blase B. Kardos, O.F.M.Conv.

Staten Island University Hospital North. Rev. John DeLora, Deacon Rosario J. Tirella.

Staten Island University Hospital South, Tel: 718-260-2000. Rev. Deo Linago, Pastoral Care.

St. Vincent's Medical Center of Richmond, Tel: 718-876-2062. Rev. Ralph Dawis, Chap., Sr. Mary Alice Duggan, O.S.U.

SUFFERN. *Good Samaritan Hospital*, Tel: 914-357-3300. Sisters Sheila Mullins, O.P., Margaret Strouch, S.S.N.D., Mgr. of Pastoral Care, Revs. Brian Coffey, M.H.M., Chap., Frank Wilder, O.A.R., Chap., Sr. Sheila Mullins, O.P., Chap.

TUXEDO PARK. *Tuxedo Memorial Health Care Center*, Tel: 914-351-4751. Vacant.

VALHALLA. *Blythdale Children's Hospital*, Tel: 914-592-7555. Serviced by Holy Name of Jesus.

Westchester County Medical Center, Tel: 914-347-7000. Rev. Cyril Owambo.

WARWICK. *St. Anthony Community Hospital*, Tel: 845-986-2276. Rev. Joseph P. McAndrew, O.F.M.

WASSAIC. *Taconic, D.D.S.O.*. Rev. John Durkin. Serviced by Immaculate Conception Armenia.

WEST HAVERSTRAW. *Helen Hayes Hospital*, Tel: 845-947-2200. Serviced by Marion Shrine, Salesians

WHITE PLAINS. *St. Agnes Hospital*, Tel: 914-681-4500. Sisters Mary Virginia Brady, R.D.C., Dir. Pastoral Care, Mary Vogl, Pastoral Assoc., Rev. James Larkin, M.SS.A., Chap., Sr. Mary Lusk, P.B.V.M.

Burke Rehabilitation Center, Tel: 914-948-0050. Rev. Patrick J. Dunne, Pastor, Sr. Laura Morgan, F.M.S.C.

New York Hospital - Cornell Medical Center, Tel: 914-949-9819. Served by Our Lady of Sorrows, Mamaroneck, NY

White Plains Hospital, Tel: 914-681-0600. Rev. Benedict J. Kuolt (Retired).

YONKERS. *St. John Hospital*, Tel: 914-964-4444. Rev. Raymond Thibodeau, O.F.M.Cap. (Night Call-Christ the King, Yonkers, 914-963-7474)

St. Joseph Hospital, Tel: 914-378-7000. Sisters Carolyn Parker, R.S.M., Dir., Dolores Doyle, P.B.V.M., Pastoral Care Assoc., Rev. Thomas Murphy, O.F.M-.Cap., Sr. Margaret Kelly, S.C., Deacon John Treiling.

Yonkers General Hospital, Tel: 914-964-7300. Rev. Josef Krajnak.

On Special or Other Archdiocesan Assignment:
Rev. Msgr.—
Barrett, Harry C., New York Medical College, Valhalla, 10595.

On Duty Outside the Archdiocese:
Rev. Msgrs.—
Balvo, Charles D., Apostolic Nunciatura, Estonia/Latvia, Lithuania.
Brown, Charles, Congregation Pro, Doctrina Fidei
Cassidy, James
Irwin, Kevin W., Catholic University of America, Washington, DC.
Meier, John P., Notre Dame Univ., South Bend, IN.
Murnion, Philip J., National Pastoral Life Conference
Shelley, Thomas J.
Stern, Robert L., Catholic Near East Welfare Association, 1011 First Ave., 10022-4195.
Revs.—
Connell, Mark, St. Mary College, Newburgh, 12550.
DeSanto, John, Iona College, New Rochelle, 10810.
Dillon, Richard J., Fordham University, Fordham Rd., Bronx, 10458.
Hartley, Christopher
Hartmann, Edward J. (FBK), Archdiocese of Fairbanks, Fairbanks, AK 99701.
Imbelli, Robert, Boston College, Boston, MA.
Kang, Paul, Holy Spirit Parish, Inchon Shi, Korea, South.
Kennedy, Robert T., Catholic University of America, Washington, DC.
Komonchak, Joseph A., Catholic University of America, Washington, DC 20006.
Marino, Umberto J.
Martin, William F., P.O. Box 65, Warren, VT 05674.
McDonald, Thomas M., Fordam University, Lincoln Center.
Petrillo, Thomas, Apostolic Nunclature, Washington, DC.
Quinn, John L., Christian Foundation for Children and Aging, Fort Lauderdale, FL.
Serra, Dominic
Smarsh, Charles F.
Tou, John, Holy Family.
Whitson, Robley E., United Institute, Bethelem, CT.

Graduate Studies:
Revs.—
O'Reilly, Kevin
Saldana, Luis

Military Chaplains:
Rev. Msgr.—
Hill, Philip W., Office of the Chief of Chaplains, 2700 Army Pentagon, Washington, DC.
Revs.—
Borkowski, Francis, 1901 Saratoga Dr., Fort Lee, VA. U.S.A.
Deponai, Joseph J., 548 Winnans Rd., West Point. U.S.A.
Lindblad, Karl-Albert, Merchant Marine Academy, Kings Point, 11024. U.S.N.
Mandato, Kieran, 231 Melinda Way, Oceanside, CA 92057. U.S.N.
McGeory, Peter, COMNAVACTUK (AO4) PSC821, Box 1, Fpo, AE 09421-0001. U.S.N.
Muhm, William M., USS Wasp (LHD-1), Fpo, AE 09556-1660.
O'Reilly, Edward M. (Retired)
Pugliese, Francis A., 5835 Edgewater Cove #7, Memphis, TN 38134.
Tran, Philip P., PSC 567, Box 6813, 95384-6813.
Travers, Alan, Chaplain's Office, USS Essex (LHD-Z), Fpo, AP 96643-1661.

Awaiting Assignment:
Rev.—
Garabedian, Thomas

Absent on Sick leave:
Revs.—
Bida, John
Brendan, Ross
Fennessey, Keith
O'Brien, William
Sandstrom, Philip

On Leave of Absence:
Revs.—
Harder, William
Outlaw, Keith
Peluso, Michael
Quinn, James

Retired:
Most Revs.—
Ahern, Patrick, St. Thomas More, 65 E. 89th St., 10128.
McCormack, William J., D.D., St. Stephen / O.L. of the Scapalar, 142 E. 29, 10016.
Sheridan, Patrick J., D.D., Cardinal's Res., 452 Madison Ave., 10022.
Rev. Msgrs.—
Alessandro, Michael J., 1496 Commonwealth Ave., Bronx, 10460.
Bourke, Myles M., Portsmouth Abbey School, Portsmouth, RI.
Burke, John, St. Adalbert, 337 Morningstar Rd., Staten Island, 10303.
Byrne, Harry J., 222 E. 93rd St., Apt. 39E, 10128.
Clyne, Vincent F., 376 Baden Pl., Staten Island, 10306.
Collins, Timothy, 40 Cove Rd., Lyme, CT 06371.
Connors, Edward M., Stepinac Archbishop Residence, 950 Mamaroneck Ave., White Plains, 10605.
Corrigan, Bernard J., St. Stephen, 75 Sanfordville Rd., Warwick, 10990.
Costello, Francis M., 1743 Village Blvd., Apt. 108, West Palm Beach, FL 33409.
Cox, James, 999 Shapley Rd., Bainbridge, 13733.
Daly, John, 14309 A Canalview Dr., Delray Beach, FL 33484.
Delaney, William B., 43 W. Orland Rd., Milford, CT 06460.
Devlin, Joseph M., St. Theresa, 2855 St. Theresa Ave., Bronx, 10461.
DiBlasi, Augustine J., Archbishop Stepinac Residence, 950 Mamaroneck, White Plains, 10605.
Doherty, John T., Stepinac Residence, 950 Mamaroneck Ave., White Plains, 10605.
Donovan, Edward, 40 Rutland St., Box 342, Mt. Kisco, 10549.
Duffy, Francis X., 1083 Washington Green, New Windsor, 12553.
Dunne, Joseph A., Our Lady of Consolation Residence, 3103 Arlington Ave., Bronx, 10463.
Dwyer, Michael F., 3121 Ninth Ave. N., St. Petersburg, FL 33713.
Ford, Robert, St. John the Evangelist, 895 Piermont Ave., Piermont, 10968.
Fowler, Eugene A., Hearts Content Rd., Roundtop, 12474.
Gallagher, Thomas V., Our Lady of Consolation, 3103 Arlington Ave., Bronx, 10463.
Geissler, Robert, 196 Azalea Cir., Jackson, NJ 08527.
Gillen, John J., St. Benedict, 2969 Otis Ave., Bronx, 10465.
Glynn, Francis J., Archbishop Stepinac Residence, 950 Mamaroneck Ave., White Plains, 10605.
Gorman, James T., Our Lady of Consolation Residence, 3103 Arlington Ave., Bronx, 10463.
Guido, William F., 121 Egbert Ave., Staten Island.
Hammer, Edmond, Bethel Nursing Home, Ossining, 10562.
Jeffers, Vincent W., St. Patrick's Home, 66 Van Cortland Parks, Bronx, 10463.
Keating, James V., St. Joseph, 242 Wall St., Kingston, 12401.
Keehan, Daniel J., Frances Schervier Home, 2975 Independence, Bronx, 10463.
Kelly, George A., 107-10 Shore Front Pkwy., Rockaway Beach, 11694.
Marinacci, Nicholas, St. Patrick's Old Cathedral, 263 Mulberry St., 10012.
Mazziotta, Robert R., P.O. Box 705, Philmont, 12565.
McCormack, Robert, Convent of St. Brigitta, 4 Runkenhage Rd., Danien, CT 06830.
McMahon, William J., Ph.D., Holy Spirit, 1969 Crompond Rd., Cortland Manor, 10566.
Montano, Edward J., 4 Fiero Rd., P.O. Box 152, Malden-on-Hudson, 12453.
Narkun, Peter P., Cardinal Hayes High School, 650 Grand Concourse, Bronx, 10451.
O'Brien, William, 142 Garth Rd., Apt. 4T, Scarsdale, 10583.
Peake, Daniel A., Stepinac Residence, White Plains, 10605.
Plo, John, St. Joseph Parish, 141 Ashburton Ave., 10701.
Potocek, Cyril J., Holy Cross, 142 Beekman Ave. N., Sleepy Hollow, 10591.
Quinn, Andrew F., Sacred Heart, 981 Castleton Ave., Staten Island, 10310.
Quinn, John J., St. Joseph's Seminary, 10704.
Quinn, Joseph J., Our Lady of Consolation Residence, 3103 Arlington Ave., Bronx, 10463.
Raimondo, Joseph J., St. Gregory the Great, 215 Halstead Ave., Harrison, 10528.
Rigney, Raymond P., Archbishop Stepinac Residence, 950 Mamaroneck Ave., White Plains, 10605.
Rossbach, George F.
Scanlon, Thomas, Sts. Peter & Paul, 129 Birch St., Mt. Vernon, 10552.
Schroeder, Walter L., 525 Bedford Rd., Sleepy Hollow, 10591.
Wilkinson, John, Archbishop Stepinac Residence, 950 Mamaroneck Ave., White Plains, 10605.
Revs.—
Arold, Richard J., 1851 Madison Rd., Brooklyn, 11229.
Basile, Nicholas F., Our Lady of Mt. Carmel, 627 E. 187 St., Bronx, 10458.
Boldt, William J., 115 Windsor Rd., Staten Island, 10304.
Brennan, Robert J., St. Lawrence Friary, 182 Sargent Ave., Beacon, 12508.
Buttinelli, Anthony, Via Valle della Storta 75, Rome 00123 Italy.
Carroll, Patrick, Our Lady of Loreto, 309 Elizabeth St., 10012.
Cavanaugh, John L., Our Lady of Consolation Residence, 3103 Arlington Ave., Bronx, 10463.
Chiang, John B. (China), 16 Ling Jiang Rd., Shashi, Huber 434000 China.
Cholette, John B., 7209 Hopkins Rd., Richmond, VA 23237.
Ciarvalo, Ronald, 213 Fairview Ave., Box 898, Montauk, 11954.
Conlin, Edwin, Immaculate Conception, 414 E. 14th St., 10009.
Conte, James W., 2555 Willow St., San Diego, CA 92106.
Conti, John P., 537 Third St., Brooklyn, 11215.
Crotty, John M., 660 Americana Dr., Annapolis, MD 21403.
Cusma, Joseph S., 255 Bronx River Rd., Apt. 8N, 10704.
d'Anjou, Henry G., Archbishop Stepinac Residence, 950 Mamaroneck Ave., White Plains, 10605.
D'Antonio, Anthony, Our Lady of Mt. Carmel, 627 E. 187th St., Bronx, 10458.
D'Auriol, Vincent, Sts. Peter & Paul Parish, 833 St. Ann Ave., Bronx, 10456.
Darby, Thomas J., Our Lady of Victory, 60 William St., 10005.
Dardis, Hugh A., 235 Revere Ave., Bronx, 10465.
DeLuca, Albert J., Sacred Hearts of Jesus & Mary, 307 E. 33 St., 10016.
Derrenbacher, James W., St. John Evangelist, 915 Rte. 212, Woodstock Rd., Saugerties, 12477.
Dibble, Michael, Christ the King, 99 Brandon Rd., Pleasant Hill, CA 94523.
DiSenso, Gerald, 8000 Shore Front Pkwy., Apt. 114, Rockaway Beach, 11693.
Doyle, Philip R., Box 1088, Carmel, 10512.
Duane, Robert J., 8000 Shore Front Pkwy., Rockaway Beach, 11693.
Dumpson, Roland J., Franciscans Handmaids of Mary Convent, 15 W. 124th St., 10027.
Fazio, Cosimo, Box 1895, New Smyina Beach, FL 32170.
Fiorillo, Antimo, Santa Maria Parish, 2352 St. Raymond's Ave., Bronx, 10462.
Fleming, John F., 1083 Washington Green, New Windsor, 12553.
Flynn, James P., 1310 Stoneybrook Ave., Mamaronek, 10543.
Fogarty, Daniel, 6333 Rancho Mission Rd., San Diego, CA 92108.
Gallagher, Eugene P., 118 Pine St., Apt. 3, Maybrook.
Geissler, Robert, 196 Azalea Cir., Jackson, NJ 08527.
Gibney, Laurence, Box 437, Salisbury, 12577.
Gilhooley, James, 112 Patchett Way, Montgomery, 12549.
Gollinge, Donald, 37401 Chancey Rd., Zephrhills, FL 33541.

Griffin, James, 8440 - B Pebble Circle, Tampa, FL 33615.
Gussoni, Lino, Via Rodini Tedeschi 19, Piacenza 29100 Italy.
Halligan, James, 2130 E. Tremont Ave., Bronx, 10462.
Holihan, John W., Our Lady Queen of Peace, 90 3rd Ave., Staten Island, 10306.
Jenko, Aloysius, Our Lady of Consolation Residence, 3103 Arlington Ave., Bronx, 10463.
Kelly, William E., Our Lady of Consolation, 3103 Arlington Ave., Bronx, 10463.
Kennedy, William J., St. Agnes, 143 E. 43 St., 10017.
Kuolt, Benedict J., St. Bernard, 51 Prospect St., White Plains, 10606.
Lancelloti, Vincent, Stepinac Residence, 950 Mamaroneck Ave., White Plains, 10605.
Larkin, John P., Our Savior, 59 Park Ave, 10016.
Maher, John J., O. L. of Consolation Residence, 3103 Arlington Ave., Bronx, 10463.
McHale, Charles P., 266 Near Rd., Red Hook, 12571.
McKay, Francis, 333 W. 86 St., 10024.
McKenna, John J., St. Joan of Arc, 32 Eagle Valley Rd., Sloatsburg, 10974.
McMahon, Bernard, 301 E. 63 St., 10021.
Meade, John F., Archbishop Stepinac Residence, 950 Mamaroneck Ave., White Plains, 10605.
Miller, Frederick J., 56 Sprague Ave., Staten Island, 10307.
Minielli, Anthony, St. Augustine, 116 Sixth Ave., Brooklyn, 11217.
Moore, John, Immaculate Conception, 414 E. 14 St., 10009.
Mulloy, Matthew, Our Lady of Consolation Residence, 3103 Arlington Ave., Bronx, 10463.
Neilson, Richard J., P.O. Box 999, South Orleans, MA 02662.
O'Connor, Maurice, c/o Mrs. Bruckner, 356 Saxony, Kings Point, Delray Beach, FL 33446.
O'Hara, Eugene R., Our Lady of Consolation Residence, 3103 Arlington Ave., Bronx, 10463.
O'Keefe, Thomas E., Stepinac High School, 950 Mamaroneck Ave., White Plains, 10605.
O'Reilly, Edward M., 503 Lafayette Blvd., Long Beach, 11561.
O'Shea, Gerard, 2610 State Rd., Apt. 920, Atlantic Beach, FL 32233.
O'Shea, Joseph J., St. Helena, 1315 Olmstead Ave., Bronx, 10462.
Palomino, Edwardo, St. Lucy, 344 E. 104 St., 10029.
Pane, Andrew, 9 Pasadena Rd., Bronxville, 10708.
Parsons, Harold J., Our Lady of Consolation Geriatric Care Center, 111 Beach Dr., West Islip, 11795.
Pryor, Donald, P.O. Box 342, Ashley Falls, MA 01222.
Pucci, Alfred, Holy Family, 366 Watchogue Rd., Staten Island, 10314.
Sheridan, Eugene, P.O. Box 653, Woodbourne, 12788.
Smolinski, Joseph J., 11 Dale Ave., Apt. 21, Highland Falls, 10928.
Smyth, James, St. Matthew, 616 Warburton Ave., Hastings-on-Hudson, 10706.
Sullivan, Frederick
Sullivan, Paul V., St. Joseph, 141 Ashburton Ave., 10701.
Thenen, James, St. Peter's, 53 St. Marks Pl., Staten Island, 10301.
Tiercelin, Harry, St. Vincent de Paul Rectory, 116 W. 24 St., 10011.
Tolentino, Thomas J., O.L. of Consolation, 3103 Arlington Ave., Bronx, 10463.
Tubridy, James J., 12H Springdale Rd., Croton-on-Hudson, 10520.
Vala, John B., O.L. of Consolation Residence, 3103 Arlington Ave, Bronx, 10463.
Walsh, Ronald J., Star Crest, Sand Lake, 12153.

Permanent Deacons:
Abbamont, Thomas J., St. Ursula, Mount Vernon
Abels, Gregory
Aglietti, Richard, St. Mary's, Mt. Vernon
Almanzar, Andres A., St. John Vianney, Bronx
Alvarado, William, St. Columba, Hopewell Junction
Armo, John, St. John Evangelist, Mahopac
Attridge, James C., St. James the Apostle, Carmel
Aviles, Stanley, St. Denis, Hopewell Junction
Baerga, Luis, St. John the Evangelist, Goshen
Baffa, John, St. Lawrence O'Toole, Brewster
Banker, Howard A., Our Lady of Assumption, Bronx
Barbieri, Nicola A., Our Lady of Pompeii, Dobbs Ferry
Baterbury, John J., Sacred Heart of Jesus, Suffern
Battersby, William L., St. Mary, Mount Vernon
Beckford, Rodney, St. Charles Borromeo, NYC
Bellacicco, John A., St. Augustine, Highland
Bello, James, Holy Cross, Bronx
Bello, Rafael J., St. Brigid, Manhattan
Bernal, Enrique, Our Lady of Guadalupe, South Manhattan
Biasotti, John C.
Biskup, William E., Regina Coeli, Hyde Park
Blake, George W., Block Island, RI
Blood, Jerome, Transfiguration, Tarrytown
Bormann, Eugene, St. Anastasia, Harriman
Borsavage, Charles T., St. James the Apostle, Carmel
Bouwmans, Philip R., Immaculate Conception, Port Jervis
Bragg, Richard, Holy Cross, Bronx
Brigande, Vincent G., St. Charles, Staten Island
Brockmann, Peter, Sacred Heart, Monroe
Brown, James A., SS. John & Paul, Larchmont
Bruno, Gaspare F., St. Elizabeth Ann Seton, Shrub Oak
Buckley, John, St. Mary, Newburgh
Bunyar, Perry A., St. Mary of the Snow, Saugerties
Buonocore, Dominic A., St. Paul, Congers
Burke, Eugene F., St. Gabriel, Bronx
Burnett, Robert V.
Burns, James T., Sacred Heart, Monroe
Cacchione, George F., Our Lady of Mt. Carmel, Poughkeepsie
Calafiore, Michael R., St. Charles, Staten Island
Calimano, Ross J., Our Lady Queen of Peace, Staten Island
Camacho, Ismael, St. Joan of Arc, Bronx
Camacho, Vidal J., St. Elizabeth of Hungary, Pompano Beach, FL
Canals, Dioel M., Holy Family, Bronx
Carlino, Frank R., St. Columba, Chester
Carnajal, Rafael, Christ the King, Bronx
Carroll, Harold N., St. Charles Borromeo, Gardiner
Casadone, Dominic G., Sacred Heart, Newburgh
Cassaneto Anthony P., St. Theresa of the Child Jesus, Bronx
Charlesworth, Myles J., Our Lady of Lourdes Parish, Raleigh, NC
Check, Raymond P., St. Gregory the Great, Virginia Beach, VA
Ciccone, Daniel J., Corpus Christi, Port Chester
Clemens, Robert A., St. Bartholomew, Yonkers
Collins, George J., St. Thomas More Boynton Beach, FL
Colton, Thomas, St. Boniface, Wesley Hills
Conner, Albert C., Annunciation, Crestwood
Conroy, Luke, St. Ann, Nyack, NY
Cookingham, Vincent, St. John the Evangelist, Goshen NY
Coppola, John J., St. Columbanus, Peekskill
Corsaro, Angelo, Sacred Heart, Monroe
Cosme, Felix
Cotto, Angel L., Caguas, Puerto Rico
Crapanzano, John, Immaculate Conception, Stony Point, NY
Cruz, Edwin J., St. John Vianney, Bronx
D'Aiello, Joseph, Our Lady of Grace, Bronx
D'Arconte, Benjamin
Darlestin, Leones J., Holy Name of Jesus, Manhattan
Daubman, Andrew, Holy Trinity, Poughkeepsie
Dauerer, Walter P., St. Denis, Hopewell Junction
De Jesus, Jose L., St. Ann, Ossining
De Los Santos, German
De Maio, Donald J., Venice, FL
De Marco, Carmine J., Holy Name of Jesus, New Rochelle
De Meis, John, Our Lady of Grace, Staten Island
Degenhardt, Carl, St. Ursula, Mount Vernon
Del Campo, Francis, Our Lady Rosary Port Chester
Delgado Luis, Our Lady of Angels, Bronx
Deschler, Bernard M., St. Thomas More; St. Edmund, Rockaway Pt.
Devlin, Charles, St. John & St. Mary, Chappaqua
Di Targiani, Robert, Immaculate Heart of Mary, Scarsdale
Dingee, Richard D., Port St. Lucy, FL
Doherty Joseph, St. Joseph, Kingston
Donovan, William, St. Margaret, Pearl River
Dowen, Roland, St. Gregory, Garnerville
Dringus, William L., Holy Spirit, E. Greenbush
Droge, Lawrence, St. Charles, SI
Drouletle, Donald L., St. Joseph, Kingston
Duncan, Robert, Sacred Heart, Monroe
Dunn, John, St. Stanislaus, Pleasant Valley, NY
Duran, Nelson, St. Anthony of Padua, Bronx
Eccleston, Arthur W., Our Lady of Good Counsel, Staten Island
Edgerton, John M., St. Luke the Evangelist, Palm Harbor, FL
Esposito, Robert A., St. John the Evangelist, Mahopac
Estela, Jorge, St. Peter's, Haverstraw
Fama, Arthur, St. Joseph-St. Thomas, Staten Island
Feliz, Luis J., Our Lady Queen of Martyrs, NYC
Fernandez, Roberto, St. Raymond, Bronx
Ferraiuolo, Anthony P., St. Joseph, New Windsor
Fien, Robert A., Our Lady of Mercy, Port Chester
Fontanez, Luis
Forte, Joseph, St. Benedict, Bronx
Fox, Michael J., Our Lady of Fatima, Scarsdale
Francis, James, Sts. Peter and Paul, Bronx
Frohbose, John M., Our Lady of Mt. Carmel, Middletown
Frohmiller, Richard J., St. Joseph, Kingston
Gallagher, Daniel J., Boynton Beach, FL
Garcia, Rene, Our Lady of Guadalupe, New York
Gaskin, Theodore A., St. Pius X, Scarsdale
Gilbert, John, St. Paul, Leesburgh, FL
Glover, William, St. Patrick, Newburgh
Gohl, Frank, Regina Coeli, Hyde Park
Gontcharuk, Robert, Holy Name of Jesus, New Rochelle
Gonzalez, Faustino, Santiago de Compostella, Spain
Gonzalez, Ismael, Caguas, Puerto Rico
Gorman, James, St. Paul, Congers
Gorzka, Stephen S.
Graham, Patrick, St. Margaret Mary, SI
Granda, Miguel E., Resurrection, NYC
Griffin, Francis J., Our Lady of Fatima, Scarsdale
Grosso, Edward, Assumption, Maybrook
Gruerio, Anthony G., St. James, Carmel
Hafemann, Joseph R., St. Mary, Fishkill
Haight, Peter R., Sacred Heart, Newburgh
Halter, Donald, St. Patrick, Newburgh
Hamilton, Eugene R., St. Peter, Haverstraw
Hamilton, James J., St. Paul the Apostle,Yonkers
Hanson, Lee, Conifer Park & Sanatoga Hospital Nursing Home, Albany
Hayes, James R., St. Peter, Poughkeepsie
Hernandez, Narcisco, Our Lady Queen of Martyrs, Manhattan
Hill, William J., St. Pius X, Scarsdale
Hodges, Raymond, Our Savior, Pine Bush
Hogan, Patrick J., St. Martin de Porres, Poughkeepsie
Hooghuis, Joseph, St. Patrick, Staten Island
Hopkins, Farrell J., St. Charles Borromeo, Dover Plains
Horvath, Robert J., St. Thomas More Parish, Sarasota, FL
Hudson, Alan A.
Hung, Franklin, St. Martin dePorreas, Poughkeepsie
Hyland, Arnold, St. Mary of the Snow, Saugerties
Impallomeni, Alfred R., Our Lady of Mount Carmel, Yonkers
Irizarry, Pedro, St. Peter, Yonkers
Jarmick, Robert E., St. Martin de Porres, Poughkeepsie
Jean-Gilles, Gabriel, Miami, FL
Johnson, Robert, Sacred Heart, Suffern
Johnson, Thomas R., St. Joseph, Greenwich Village
Juhasz, Lajos, St. Margaret of Hungary, Yonkers
Kawula, Lawrence, Sacred Heart, Newburgh
Kazimir, Martin, St. Mary, Fishkill
Kelleher, John C., St. Catharine, Blauvelt
Klein, Albert J., St. Peter, Poughkeepsie
Klein, John P., St. William, Ward, SC
Knack, Lawrence F., St. Mary, Obernberg
Knight, Charles C., Marysville, OH
Koch, George J., Our Lady of Lourdes, Sun City West, AZ
Kollar, John J., Our Lady of Fatima, Scarsdale
Lagotta, Anthony A., Our Lady of Mt. Carmel & St. Benedicta, Staten Island
Lamberty, Angel, Sts. Mary & Andrew, Ellenville, NY
Larkin, John J., St. Peter, Rosendale
Laurato, Vincent I., St. Barnabas, Bronx
Lawlor, James, St. Charles Borromeo, Dover Plains, NY
Le Blanc, Vincent F., Westchester Medical Center
Leasiolagi, Taulafoga, St. John Vianney, Bronx
Li Greci, Christopher, St. Michael Chapel, Manhattan
Lieby, Joseph, St. Joseph, New Windsor
Liegey, Gabriel, Brewster, MA
Liggan, John J., St. Peter, Rosendale
Lindley, Gerard, Regina Coeli, Hyde Park
Loeffler, Albert, St. Joseph, Middletown
Longo, Ralph D., Holy Rosary, Greenwood Lake
Lopez, Domingo, Springfield, OH
Lopez, Francisco, St. Martin of Tours, Bronx
Lugo, Alejandro, St. Cecilia, Manhattan
Mac Dougall, Thomas, St. Stephen The Marty R, Warwick, NY
Maher, James, St. Aedans, Pearl River
Maldonado, Eusebio, Our Lady of Sorrows, Manhattan
Maloney, John R., St. Anthony, Nanuet
Manning, Cornelius J., St. Barnabas, Bronx
Manzione, Arthur, St. Anthony of Padua, West Harrison

Marino, Philip A., Immaculate Conception, Stony Point
Maroon, Phillip J., St. Rita, Staten Island
Martinez, Luis A., Our Lady Queen of Angels, Manhattan
Martinez, Rafael, Caguas, Puerto Rico
Mazza, Albert, Holy Name of Mary, Croton-on-Hudson
Mazzei, Nicholas A., Our Lady of Mt. Carmel, Yonkers
McCabe, Michael G., St. Augustine, New City
McCarthy, Richard, Sacred Heart, Monroe
McCormick, Daniel F., St. Mark, Virginia Beach, VA
McGarry, James, St. John the Evangelist, Goshen
McGowan, George J., Visitation B.V.M., Bronx
McLaughlin, Richard, Holy Rosary, Hawthorne
McNeill, Lawrence C., Holy Cross, Manhattan
McSherry, John W., St. Paul, Congers
Meier, Anthony C., St. Bernadette, Fuquay Varina, NC
Mercado, Carlos V., Immaculate Conception, Bronx
Mercandetti, Anthony, St. Bartholomew, Yonkers
Miranda, Wilfredo, St. Lucy, Bronx
Mitchell, Richard F., St. Clare, Staten Island
Mo, Jose, St. Martin of Tours, Bronx
Monegro, Juan, Incarnation, Manhattan
Moran, Bernard, St. Clare's, Bronx
Morillo, Felix M., Miramar, FL
Morrette, Thomas, St. Mary, Katonah
Mueller, William J., St. Mary Star of the Sea, Bronx
Mulryan, W. Joseph, Our Lady of Grace, Bronx
Munnick, John B., Jr., Corpus Christi, Port Chester
Munoz, John, Prison Chap., Scranton, PA
Murphy, John G., St. Frances de Chantal, Bronx
Nash, John J., Mercy Hospital, Port Jervis
Nolasco, Rolando, Our Lady of Mercy, Bronx
Noonan, Emmet, St. Stephen the Martyr, Warwick, NY
Nunez, Acadio, Puerto Rico
O'Brien, Donald F., St. Francis of Assisi, West Nyack
O'Brien, Henry F., St. Lawrence, Fairhope, AL
O'Brien, Pedro Lambert, Our Lady of Lourdes, Manhattan
O'Connor, Gerard R., Albany County Nursing Home
O'Reilly, John F., Our Lady of Loretto, Cold Spring
O'Sullivan, Mark, Regina Coeli, Hyde Park
O'Toole, Lawrence, St. Augustine, New York
Ocasio, Roberto, St. Catherine of Siena, Kissimmee, FL
Olivieri, Martin J., St. John the Baptist, Yonkers
Orlando, Francis B., Blessed Sacrament, New Rochelle
Ortiz, Louis, Ponce, Puerto Rico
Ortiz, Pablo, Puerto Rico
Ottaviano, Frank S., St. Augustine, Highland
Pacheco, Angel, St. Isaac Jogues Parish, Orlando, FL
Padron, Jose R., St. Pius V, Bronx
Palladino, Joseph, St. Joseph, New Paltz
Pappalardo, Augustine A., St. Gregory Barbarigo, Garnerville
Parchen, Raymond, Holy Spirit, Peekskill
Patricola, Salvatore P., St. John the Baptist, NYC
Pelella, John V., St. Thomas of Canterbury, Cornwall-on-Hudson
Pellegrin, Daniel, St. Bernard, White Plains
Pellegrini, Guy A., Our Lady Perpetual Help, Pelham
Pereira, Joaquim, Our Lady of the Rosary, Yonkers
Perez, Primitivo, Queen of Peace, Oscala, FL
Peters, John, St. Joseph, Kingston
Pietkiewicz, Karl J., St. Mary of the Snow, Saugerties
Pino, Victor M., St. John Chrysostom, Bronx
Pipher, Jesse E., Our Lady Queen of Martyrs, Sarasota, FL
Piro, Vincent T., Our Lady of Mt. Carmel, Mt. Vernon
Pollick, Donald F., Westchester Medical Center Hospital, Valhalla
Porcel, Carlos M., Holy Rosary, NYC
Porcelli, Vincent, St. Mary, Marlboro, NY
Portalatin, Epimegnio, Blessed Sacrament, Bronx
Preti, Aldo, St. Raymond, Bronx
Quigley, Donald M., St. Eugene, Yonkers
Radcliffe, Kenneth L., Resurrection, Central Harlem
Radzilowicz, John, St. Casimir, Yonkers
Ramos, Alfonso, Sacred Heart, Bronx
Ramos, Edmundo A., St. Patrick's Cathedral, Manhattan
Ramos, Epifanio, Altamonte Springs, FL
Ramos, Rafael, St. John Vianney, Bronx
Rausch, Paul A., St. Thomas Aquinas, Forestburg
Reilly, John P., St. Columba, Hopewell Junction
Rentkowski, Joseph, St. Adalbert, Staten Island
Repke, John W., St. Mary, Marlboro
Rescildo, Ralph J., St. Teresa, Woodbury, CT
Rettino, P. Robert
Reynolds, Peter E., Our Lady of Mt. Carmel, Elmsford
Riley, John M., St. Peter, Liberty
Rivera, Andrew A., St. John, Kingsbridge Ave., Bronx
Rivera, Jose A., Aquas Buenas, Puerto Rico
Rizzo, Charles A., Blessed Sacrament, New Rochelle
Roberts, James F., Our Lady of the Assumption, Peekskill
Rodriguez, Arnaldo, Nativity, Manhattan
Rodriguez, Cristobal, Immaculate Conception, Bronx
Rodriguez, Hector, St. John Fisher, Richmond, TX
Rodriguez, Jacinto, San Antonio, Guayama, PR
Rodriguez, Jesus, Guayanilla, Puerto Rico
Rodriguez, Juan J., Holy Cross, Bronx
Rodriguez, Porfirio, St. Jude, Manhattan
Romagosa, Guillermo P.
Rosado, Alejandro, St. Athanasius, Bronx
Rosado, Odalis R.
Rosado, Reynaldo, St. Dominic, Bronx
Rosado, Ricardo, Mid-Orange Correctional Facility, Warwick
Rush, James J.
Russell, Franklyn R., St. Patrick, Newburgh
Russo, Richard J., St. Jean Baptist, Manhattan
Sakowitz, Albert, Christ the King, Yonkers
Salamone, Victor A., St. Martin de Porres, Poughkeepsie
Salomone, Ernest F., Immaculate Heart of Mary, Scarsdale
Sanchez, Oscar, Taujillo Alto, Puerto Rico
Santana, Richard, Albany, NY
Santana, Robert, SS. Philip & James, Bronx
Santiago, Abraham, St. Joseph, Yonkers
Santore, Louis, St. John & St. Mary, Chappaqua
Scarfi, John, St. John the Evangelist, Mahopac
Schimpf, Robert, Sts. Peter & Paul, Mt. Vernon
Schlitt, Ronald, St. Christopher, Buchanan
Scott, John, St. Benedict, Bronx
Sepulveda, Miguel A., St. Raymond, Bronx
Sequeira, Ronald, O.L. of Refuge, Bronx
Serrano, Jose I., O.L. of Grace, Bronx
Seymour, John L., St. Francis of Assisi, Newburgh
Sheeley, Robert B., Holy Name of Jesus, Kingston
Shepard, John, St. Mary, Washingtonville
Shiel, Thomas P., Corpus Christi, Temple Terrace, FL
Shkreli, Marash, St. Lawrence O'Toole, Brewster
Simpson, John J., St. Benedict, Bronx
Sin-Garciga, Felipe, St. Angela Merici, Bronx
Singler, John A., Our Lady Help of Christians, Staten Island
Slominski, Timothy, St. Augustine, Ossining, NY
Smith, Henry, St. Mary of the Snow, Saugerties
Smith, John A., St. Edmond, Rehoboth Beach, DE
Solanto, Joseph P., Holy Rosary, Bronx
Sorrentino, Nunzio, St. Clare, Staten Island
Soto, Constancio, Ascension, Manhattan
Stafford, William, St. Thomas of Canterbury, Cornwall on Hudson, NY
Stahlnecker, James J., St. Mary of the Assumption, Staten Island
Steup, Fredrick C., St. Patrick, Newburgh
Stewart, George, St. Columba, Hopewell Junction
Stuetzle, Jerome, St. Anthony, Pine Plains
Suarez, Israel, Guaynabo, Puerto Rico
Sullivan, John D., Holy Trinity, West Harwich, MA
Sullivan, John M., St. Mary, Kingston
Sweeney, Walter F., Our Lady of Good Counsel, Staten Island
Tayco, Renato, St. John the Baptist, Manhattan
Taylon, Victor, St. Monica, NYC
Teng, Rudolph, St. Paul the Apostle, Yonkers
Testa, Warren, St. Columba, Hopewell Junction
Then, Rafael, Good Shepherd, Manhattan
Thompson, Alfred, Holy Child, SI
Tirella, Rosario J., Holy Rosary, Staten Island
Tobin, William D., St. Margaret, Pearl River
Tola, Vincente, Sunrise, FL
Topple, Edwin R., St. John the Evangelist, Centerville
Torres, Gilberto, St. Clare, Deltona, FL
Torres, Luis, Mayaguez, Puerto Rico
Torres, Luis A., St. Pius V., Bronx
Trapani, Richard, St. Joseph, Middletown, NY
Trees, Donald F., St. Mary of the Snow, Saugerties
Treiling, John F., St. Joseph Home & Hospital, Yonkers
Troy, Patrick D., Sacred Heart, Dobbs Ferry
Vaccaro, William N., Our Lady of the Rosary, Port Chester
Vargas, Thomas A.
Vasquez, Domingo, St. Thomas Aquinas, Bronx
Vazquez, Juan F., St. Martin of Tours, Bronx
Velez, Randy, St. Peter, Yonkers
Venezia, Ignatius
Verboys, Joseph, Our Lady of Peace, Hewitt
Viola, Anthony, Immaculate Conception, Tuckahoe
Wallace, Benjamin S., St. Lawrence O'Toole, Brewster
Weinstein, David, Immaculate Conception, Amenia
Weir, John E., Southberry, CT
Weireter, Paul J., St. Patrick, Highland Mills
Weiss, Robert W., St. Augustine, Highland
Welhous, Albert V., SS. Philip & James, Bronx
Wetherall, Edward J., Our Lady Help of Christians, Staten Island
Whiteman, Robert, St. Bernard, White Plains, NY
Wilson, Michael, St. Elizabert Ann Seton, Shrub Oak, NY
Winrow, Robert P., St. Joseph, Kingston
Witt, Joseph A., Sacred Heart, Suffern
Woods, Edward J., Our Lady of Mt. Carmel, Middletown
Wyka, Stanley A., St. Columba, Hopewell Jct.
Zambrana, Wallace, O.L. of Sorrows, NYC
Zatarga, Michael, St. Thomas, Boynton Beach, FL

INSTITUTIONS LOCATED IN THE ARCHDIOCESE

[A] SEMINARIES, ARCHDIOCESAN

NEW YORK. *Cathedral Preparatory Seminary Formation Program* Tel: 914-968-6200, Ext. 8182; Fax: 914-376-2019. Email: frlynchprep@aol.com. Web: www.cathedralprep.com.

Archdiocesan Preparatory Seminary, 201 Seminary Ave., Yonkers, 10704. Tel: 914-968-6200; Fax: 914-966-1490. Rev. Thomas A. Lynch, Dean. Priests 1; Students 21.

Dunwoodie, Yonkers, 10704. Tel: 914-968-6200; 914-968-8182; Fax: 914-376-2019.

YONKERS. *St. John Neumann Residence and Hall*, 201 Seminary Ave., 10704-1896. Tel: 914-964-3025; Fax: 914-968-6671. Email: sjnrh@archny.org. Web: www.archny.org. Revs. Michael F. Hull, S.T.D., Dean; Pascual Cervera, Spiritual Dir. Priests 3. In Res. Rev. Thomas M. Tierney (WOR), Vocation Dir.

St. Joseph's Seminary, Archdiocesan Major Seminary, 201 Seminary Ave., 10704-1896. Tel: 914-968-6200; Fax: 914-376-2019. Web: www.ny-archdiocese.org/pastoral/seminary.cfm. Rev. Msgrs. Peter G. Finn, M.Div., M.S., M.Ed.; William B. Smith, S.T.D., Academic Dean; Kevin O'Brien, Spiritual Dir.; Revs. Donald F. Haggerty, S.T.D., Asst. Spiritual Dir.; Joseph P. Tierney, M.Div., Vocation Dir.; Andrew R. King, S.T.L.; Michael F. Hull, S.T.D., (cand.); Thomas Lynch, Ph.D., (Cand.); Joseph R. Giandurco, J.C.D., Dean of Admissions & Dean of Students; Sr. Sara Butler, M.S.B.T., Ph.D. Non-Resident Faculty: Priests 21; Sisters 7; Lay Teachers 1; Students 67.
Non-Resident Faculty: His Eminence Avery Dulles, S.J.; Rev. Msgrs. Edmund J. Whalen, S.T.D.; James C. Turro, Ph.D. (NEW) (Retired); Revs. Joseph T. Lienhard, S.J.; Richard Baker; Andrew D. Apostoli, C.F.R., M.S.; Benedict J. Groeschel, C.F.R.; James M. Sullivan, O.P.; Gerard F. Rafferty, S.S.L.; Robert G. Kelly, S.J., M.A.T.; Christopher Walsh; Peter J. Cameron, O.P.; Dr. Philip Cristantiello, Ph.D.; Dr. Stephen Buglione, Ph.D.; Sisters Janet Baxendale, S.C., M.A.; Marie Pappas, C.R., M.A.; Monica Wood, S.C., Dir. Library Svcs.; Mary Frances Mills, O.S.F., Registrar.

[B] SEMINARIES, RELIGIOUS OR SCHOLASTICATES

NEW YORK. *Society of St. Paul*, 2187 Victory Blvd., 10314. Tel: 718-761-0047; Fax: 718-761-0057. Email: sspsiny@aol.com. Web: www.albahouse.org. Rev. Anthony C. Warren, S.S.P., Supr. & Dir. Alba House Publications; Bros. Kevin J. Cahill, S.S.P., Book Store Coord.; Augustine Condon, S.S.P., Book Store Coord.; Lawrence H. Schubert, S.S.P., Bursar, Book Store Coord.; Revs. Edmund C. Lane, S.S.P., Book Store Coord.; Ernesto Tigreros, S.S.P., Book Store Coord.; Victor L. Viberti, S.S.P., Book Store Coord.; Ignatius Staniszewski, S.S.P., Book Store Coord. Priests 5; Brothers 12; Lay Teachers 8.

BEACON. *St. Lawrence of Brindisi Friary*, Province of the Stigmata of St. Francis, 182 Sargent Ave., 12508-3993. Tel: 845-831-0394; 845-838-0759 (Infirmary); Fax: 845-831-0918; 845-838-1352 (Infirmary). Bros. Bernard Frey, O.F.M.Cap.; Julius Tkaczyk, O.F.M.Cap., Vicar; Efrain Sosa, O.F.M.Cap.; Douglas Soik, O.F.M.Cap.; Peter Reilly, O.F.M. Cap.; Tom Burns, C.S.C.; Matthew Defamio, O.F.M.Cap.; Amtopnine Lizama, O.F.M.Cap.; Antonine Lizama, O.F.M.Cap.; Revs. Gerard De Leonardis, O.F.M.Cap.; Sylvester Catallo, O.F.M.Cap.; Robert Brennan; Anthony Giudice, O.F.M.Cap.; Alexander Davis,

O.F.M.Cap.; Bernard Smith, O.F.M.Cap., Guardian; Joseph Mezzanote, O.F.M.Cap. (NEW); John Mahoney, O.F.M.Cap.; Luke GuasTella, O.F.M.Cap.; Gabriel Msassaro, O.F.M.Cap.; John Langweld, O.F.M.Cap. (Friary and Infirmary) Priests 11; Brothers 9; Lay Staff 11.

BRONX. *Ciszek Hall* Residence for Jesuit Scholastics and Brothers engaged in Philosophy and Theology Studies at Fordham University. , 2502 Belmont Ave., 10458-6282. Tel: 718-365-8752; Fax: 718-365-3166. Revs. Thomas H. Feely, S.J., Rector; Henry J. Bertels, S.J., Spiritual Dir.; Steven C. Dillard, S.J. (P), Asst. Rector, Minister. Scholastics 22.

MARYKNOLL. *Center for Mission Research and Study at Maryknoll*, P.O. Box 305, 10545-0305. Tel: 914-941-7590; Fax: 914-941-5753. Email: cmrsm@maryknoll.org. Web: www.maryknoll.org/society/cmrsm. Thomas Bamat, Exec. Dir.; Rev. William D. McCarthy, M.M., Mission History Consultant; Anne Reissner, Dir. of Study; Jean Paul Weist, Senior Researcher; Mary Ann Cejka, Assoc. Researcher; Rev. Carl P. Mevlemms, M.H., Coord. of Society History; Diane Pella, Dir. Library. Purpose: To investigate the contexts, trends and challenges of Christian Mission among Christians and peoples of other living faiths, and to foster reflection on the practical implications of these investigations. Priests 1; Lay Persons 5.

SUFFERN. *Tagaste Monastery* Major Seminary of the Province of St. Augustine of the Augustinian Recollect Fathers & Brothers. , 220 Lafayette Ave., 10901. Tel: 845-357-0067; Fax: 845-369-0625. Email: tagaste@optonline.net. Web: www.augustinianrecollects.org. Revs. Frank T. Wilder, O.A.R., Prior; Marlon Beof, O.A.R., Subprior & Prefect of Students; Francis Moriones, O.A.R. (Spain); George Mattioni, O.A.R.; J. Michael Rafferty, O.A.R.; Bros. Joseph Joly, O.A.R.; Paul Rodriguez, O.A.R.; Ramiro Munoz, O.A.R. Priests 5; Brothers 3; Simple Professed 3; Solemn Professed Clerics 1.

[C] COLLEGES AND UNIVERSITIES

NEW YORK. *College of Mount Saint Vincent* (Coed) ; Founded by the Sisters of Charity of Saint Vincent de Paul. Chartered by the University of the State of New York. , 6301 Riverdale Ave., 10471-1093. Tel: 718-405-3200; Fax: 718-549-2603. Email: cfinegan@mountsaintvincent.edu. Web: www.mountsaintvincent.edu. Charles L. Flynn Jr., Ph.D., Pres.; Eleanor Green, Ph.D., Vice Pres., Academic Affairs; Lenore Mott, Vice Pres. Institutional Advancement and College Relations. Priests 1; Brothers 1; Sisters 7; Lay Faculty 62; Total Enrollment 1,633.

Marymount Manhattan College Chartered by the Univ. of the State of NY. , 221 E. 71st St., 10021. Tel: 212-517-0400. Email: vdorgan@mmm.edu. Web: www.mmm.edu. Dr. Judson Shaver, Pres.; Dawn Webber, Vice Pres. Academic Affairs; Christy Gaiti, Vice Pres. Student Affairs (Acting); Paul Ciraulo, Vice Pres. Business & Financial Affairs; Mary Kay Demetry-Jeynes, Dean Courses for Adults; Jeanne Evans, Dir. College Rels. & Institutional Advancement; Sr. Virginia Dorgan, R.S.H.M., Campus Min. Sisters 3; Students 2,330.

BRONX. **Fordham University* (1841), Second campus and Branch campus at Lincoln Center, New York, NY 10023 and Marymount College, Tarrytown, NY 10591. Chartered by the Legislature of the State of New York. , Fordham Rd., 10458. Tel: 718-817-3040; Fax: 718-817-3050. Web: www.fordham.edu. Rev. Joseph A. O'Hare, S.J., Pres.; Mr. John J. Lordnn, Senior Vice Pres., CFO & Treas.; Dr. John C. Hollwitz, Vice Pres. Academic Affairs; Mr. Bruno M. Santonocito, Vice Pres. Devel. & Univ. Rels.; Mr. Charles H. Hodulik, Vice Pres. Lincoln Center; Mr. Jeffrey L. Gray, Vice Pres. Students Affairs; Dr. Brian Byrne, Vice Pres. Admin.; Dr. Peter Stace, Vice Pres. for Enrollment; Dr. Nancy Busch, Dean of Graduate School of Arts & Sciences; Rev. Jeffrey Von Arx, S.J., Dean of Fordham College at Rose Hill; Dr. Sharon Smith, Dean, College of Business Admin. & Interim Dean, Graduate School of Business Adm; Dr. Ernest Scalberg, Dean of Graduate School of Business Admin.; Dr. Regis D. Bernhadt, Dean of Graduate School of Education; John D. Feerick, L.L.B., Dean of School of Law; Dr. Peter B. Vaughan, Dean of Graduate School of Social Service; Rev. Robert R. Grimes, S.J., Dean of Fordham College at Lincoln Center; Dr. Michael Gillan, Dean of Fordham College of Liberal Studies; Rev. Vincent M. Novak, S.J., Dean of Graduate School of Religion and Religious Education. Priests 30; Sisters 5; Lay Teachers 600; Total Staff 635; Total Enrollment 13,800.

Manhattan College, Manhattan College Pkwy., 10471. Tel: 718-862-7200; 800-622-9235; Fax: 718-862-8019. Email: admit@manhattan.edu. Web: www.manhattan.edu. Bro. Thomas Scanlan, F.S.C., Pres. Priests 2; Brothers 4; Sisters 3; Lay Staff 162; Total Staff 171; Total Enrollment 2,881.

MT. KISCO. *Legion of Christ College, Inc.*, 773 Armonk Rd., 10549. Tel: 914-773-1368; Fax: 914-773-1438. Rev. Alexander Kim, Contact Person.

NEW ROCHELLE. **The College of New Rochelle*, Formerly College of New Rochelle Founded in 1904 by the Religious of the Order of St. Ursula. Chartered by the Regents of the University of the State of New York. The College is composed of four schools. School of Arts and Sciences (Women); Graduate School; School of New Resources; School of Nursing (Coed). , 29 Castle Pl., 10805. Tel: 914-654-5000; Fax: 914-654-5980. Email: info@cnr.edu. Web: www.cnr.edu. Dr. Stephen J. Sweeny, Ph.D., Pres. Tel: 914-654-5430; Fax: 914-654-5980; Dr. Ellen Curry Damato, Exec. Vice Pres.; Dr. Joan Bailey, Senior Vice Pres. Academic Affairs; Dr. Rose Marie Hurrell, Dean School of Arts & Sciences; Dr. Nancy Brown, Dean Graduate School; Dr. Donna Demarest, Dean School of Nursing; Ms. Elza Dinwiddie-Boyd, Dean of School of New Resources; Judith Huntington, Vice Pres. Financial Affairs; Rev. J. Joseph Flynn, O.F.M.Cap., Chap.; Mr. Terence McCorry, Dir., Campus Ministry. Sisters 6; Lay Teachers 590; Students 6,980.

Iona College (Coed) ; Education in the tradition of the Christian Brothers. Independent College. , 715 North Ave., 10801. Tel: 914-633-2000. Email: webmaster@iona.edu. Web: www.iona.edu. Priests 3; Brothers 27; Sisters 11; Lay Teachers 468; Students 4,897.

Branch Orangeburg Campus, One Dutch Hill Rd., Orangeburg, 10962. Tel: 914-359-2252.

Branch Manhattan Campus, St. Michael High School, 425 W. 33rd St., 10001. Tel: 212-630-0270. Bro. James A. Liguori, Ed.D., Pres.; Dr. Judson R. Shaver, Vice Pres. for Academic Affairs & Provost; Mr. John Braunstein, Vice Provost for Enrollment Management; Dr. Michael McGrath, Vice Provost for Student Devel.; Ms. Dixie K. Norris, Vice Pres. Finance & Admin.; Mr. James Link, Vice Pres. for Advancement; Dr. Warren Rosenberg, Dean of School of Arts & Sciences; Dr. Nicholas Beutell, Dean of the Hagan School of Business; Ms. Joy Collins, Dir. of Libraries.

NEWBURGH. *Mt. St. Mary College* (195-), (Coed) , Leslie Reggero, 12550. Tel: 914-561-0800; Fax: 914-562 6762. Email: williams@msmc.edu. Web: www.msmc.edu. Sisters Ann Sakac, O.P., Pres.; Agnes Foyle, O.P., Academic Dean; Gerald Jilbert, Registrar; Patricia Kobes, Registrar Rev. Mark Connell, Chap. Divisions: Arts & Letters; Education; Business; Nursing; Natural Sciences; Mathematics & Computer Science; Philosophy & Religious Studies; Social Sciences. Sisters 4; Lay Teachers 62; Students 2,559.

ORANGEBURG. *Dominican College* Chartered by University of the State of New York. , 470 Western Hwy., 10962. Tel: 845-359-7800; Fax: 845-359-2313. Email: admissions@dc.edu. Web: www.dc.edu. Sisters Mary Eileen O'Brien, O.P., Pres.; Kathleen Sullivan, O.P., Chancellor; Dr. Leigh Holt, Vice Pres. Academic Affairs & Academic Dean; Dohn Harshbarger, Vice Pres. Student Devel. & Dean of Students; Cathleen Kenny, Vice Pres. Financial Affairs & Chief Fiscal Officer; Dorothy Filoramo, Vice Pres. Institutional Advancement; Brian Fernandes, Vice Pres. Enrollment Mgmt.; Sr. M. Noel Dwyer, O.P., Registrar; Dr. Lance Angell, Institutional Research; Mr. Joseph Clinton, Athletics; Sr. Barbara McEneany, Campus Min. Sisters 16; Lay Teachers 124; Students 1,700.

Divisions: Dr. Beryl Herdt, Allied Health; Dr. William Hurst, Arts & Sciences; Mr John Spillner, Business Admin.; Dr. Maureen Creegan, Nursing; Dr. Barbara Socor, Social Sciences; Dr. Marie Pagliaro, Education Teacher.

SPARKILL. *St. Thomas Aquinas College* 10976. Tel: 845-398-4000; Fax: 845-359-8136. Web: www.stac.edu. Sr. Margaret M. Fitzpatrick, S.C., Ed.D., Pres.; Dr. L. John Duvney, Vice Pres. Academic Affairs. Founded by Dominican Sisters of Sparkill in 1952. Senior coed college, chartered by Univ. of the State of New York Sisters 6; Lay Professors 66; Students 2,200.

STATEN ISLAND. *St. John's University Staten Island Campus*, 300 Howard Ave., 10301. Tel: 718-390-4545; Fax: 718-816-4520. Very Rev. Donald J. Harrington, C.M., Pres.; Rev. James F. Kiernan, C.M., Senior Vice Pres., Staten Island; Sr. Margaret John Kelly, D.C., Academic Dean & Dean of Faculty St. John's College; Donna Narducci, Asst. Dean & Dir. Programs Colleges of Business; Kathleen MacDonald, Dean St. Vincent's College; Dr. Stephen Kuntz, Asst. Dean, School of Education, Graduate Div.; Mr. James R. Guilbert, Dean, Office of Student Life. Vincentian Community

TARRYTOWN. *Marymount College of Fordham University*, Formerly Marymount College Founded by the Religious of the Sacred Heart of Mary. Women Resident and non-resident. , 10591. Tel: 914-631-3200. Email: admiss@mmt.marymt.edu. Web: www.marymt.edu. Revs. Joseph A. McShane, S.J., Pres.; Gerard Reedy, S.J., Dean. Sisters 3; Lay Teachers 56; Students 886.

[D] DEPARTMENT OF EDUCATION

NEW YORK. *Department of Education*, 1011 First Ave., 10022. Tel: 212-371-1000, Ext. 2800; Fax: 212-317-9236. Email: secretary@adnyschools.org. Web: www.nycatholicschools.org. Dr. Catherine Hickey, Sec. Education & Supt.

Office of Finance Tel: 212-371-1011, Ext. 2819; Fax: 212-371-1011. Mr. John Coyne, Exec. Dir.; Mr. John D. Poling, Consultant.

Vocations Office, 1011 First Ave., 10022. Tel: 212-371-1011, Ext. 2803; Fax: 212-758-3018. Sr. Deanna Sabetta, C.N.D., Vocations Dir. for Rel. Life.

University Apostolate, University Apostolate, 1011 First Ave., 10022. Tel: 212-371-1011, Ext. 2803; Fax: 212-758-3018. Sr. Deanna Sabetta, C.N.D., Dir.

Division of Elementary and Secondary Education, 1011 First Ave., 10022. Tel: 212-371-1000, Ext. 2801; Fax: 212-371-9236. Dr. Catherine Hickey, Supt. of Schools & Sec.; Dr. Mary Jane Krebbs, Assoc. Sec.; Sr. Marie Pappas, C.R., Assoc. Sec.

Associate Superintendents: Sr. Patricia Anastasio, P.V.B.M., Personnel; Mr. Michael Ramos, Professional Recruitment; Mr. James Mahoney, Publicly Assisted Programs; Bro. Thomas Schady, F.M.S., Secondary Educ.; Mrs. Nora Murphy, Communications Mktg.

Assistant Superintendents: Sisters Mary Kilmartin, S.C., Curriculum; Winifred Lyons, S.C., Pro-Life Coord., Parent Volunteer Prog.; Mrs. Catherine Mendrzycki, Teacher Staff Devel.; Theresa Simmonds, R.Ed.; Ms. Barbara Heaney, Gov. Staff Devel.

Directors: Mr. Hugh Keenan, Admin.; Sr. Alice Kirk, O.P., Dir., Technology Staff Devel.; Dorothea Muccigrosso, Early Childhood Consultant; Joanne DeMizio, Math Curriculum; Ms. Ann Maschin, Admin. Asst.

District Superintendents: Mr. Paul Beaudin, Bronx; Mrs. Zoilita Herrera, Staten Island; Sisters Helen Doyehak, O.P., Rockland, Orange, Sullivan, Duchess, & Ulster; June Clare Tracy, O.P., Manhattan; Mr. Philip Gorrasi, Westchester/Putnam.

Archdiocesan Drug Abuse Prevention Program, 2789 Schurz Ave., 10465. Tel: 718-904-1333; Fax: 718-823-2177. Mrs. Frances Maturo, Dir.

Child Nutrition and School Management Service, 323 E. 91st St., 10128. Tel: 212-722-0111; Fax: 212-722-5252. Mr. Edward Albano.

Head Start Program, 1720 Metropolitan Ave., Bronx, 10462. Tel: 718-409-1277; Fax: 718-409-3219. Dr. Nora Feury.

Cooke Center for Learning and Development, 475 Riverside Dr., Ste. 730, 10115. Tel: 212-280-4477. Dr. Michael Termini.

Seton Foundation for Learning, 104 Gordon St., 10304. Tel: 718-447-1750; Fax: 718-447-8022. Mrs. Diane Cunningham, Education Dir.

Catholic Special Education Elementary Program in the Bronx, 1725 Castle Hill Ave., Bronx, 10462. Tel: 212-792-9669; Fax: 212-792-9669. Mrs. Patricia Alberti.

St. Ursula Learning Center, 183 Rich Ave., Mt. Vernon, 10550. Tel: 914-664-6656; Fax: 914-663-7948. Mrs. Barbara Stefaniki, Education Dir.

Cooke Inclusive Academy Special Needs High School Program, 1725 Castle Hill Ave., Bronx, 10462. Tel: 212-792-9669; Fax: 212-792-9669. Mr. James A. Simone, Dir.

Joan Ann Kennedy Memorial Preschool, 26 Sharpe Ave., Staten Island, 10302. Tel: 718-876-0939; Fax: 718-816-6507. Dr. Kathryn Meyer, Education Dir.

Bishop Patrick V. Ahern High School, 315 Arlene St., Staten Island, 10314. Tel: 718-982-5084; Fax: 718-982-5114. Ms. Diane Cunningham, Exec. Dir.

Family Life/Respect Life Office, 1011 First Ave., 10022. Tel: 212-371-1000, Ext. 3186; Fax: 212-371-3382. Rev. John S. Bonnici, S.T.D., Dir.; Mr. Edward Mechmann, Asst. Dir. & Coord. of Marriage Preparation Programs; Vera V. Galeas, Coord. Respect Life & Spanish Programs; Dana Larson-Super, Coord. Wedding Anniversary Awards Ceremony; Mr. Stefano Galluzzo, Asst. Coord. Respect Life; Mrs. Nancy Rizzi, Coord. Marriage Enrichment; Mrs. Lisa Dunleavy-Jenning, Asst. Coord. Marriage Preparation Programs; Mrs. Eileen Murphy, Coord., Education for Parenting; Mr. Mizraim Cordero, Asst. Coord. Separated & Divorced Ministry; Mrs. Mary Kay King, Coord. Bereavement Ministry; John & Laura Weidner,

Coord. Couple, Engaged Encounter. Tel: 845-298-4772; Jim & Nancy Rizzi, Coord. Couple, Marriage Encounter. Tel: 718-317-5881.

Archdiocesan Catechetical Office, 1011 First Ave., 10022. Tel: 212-371-1000, Ext. 2849; Fax: 212-371-1011. Sr. Joan Curtin, C.N.D., Archdiocesan Dir.; Ms. Mary T. Burke, Asst. to Dir. Tel: 212-371-1000, Ext. 2859; Sisters Mary Elizabeth Kelleher, O.P., Dir. Catechist Formation. Tel: 212-371-1000, Ext. 2861; Teresita Morse, R.J.M., Dir. Formation of Directors & Coordinators. Tel: 212-371-1000, Ext. 2858; Bro. Francis Zaglauer, F.M.S., Dir. Adult Catechesis. Tel: 212-371-1000, Ext. 2851; Sr. Loretta DeDomenicis, F.M.A., Dir. Adolescent Catechesis. Tel: 212-371-1000, Ext. 2864; Mrs. Linda Sgammato, Dir. Special Rel. Education. Tel: 212-371-1000, Ext. 2852.

Catechetical Regional Offices

Bronx Tel: 718-367-0420; Fax: 718-367-7880. Sr. Jeannette Chishibanji, X.M.M., Dir.
323 E. 198th St., Bronx, 10458.

Manhattan: Tel: 212-923-0950; Fax: 212-923-0950. Sr. Catherine Ryan, F.S.P., Dir.
c/o Mother Cabrini High School, 701 Fort Washington Ave., 10040.

Staten Island Tel: 718-273-3833; Fax: 718-273-9602. Mrs. Frances DeFrange, Dir.
203 Sand Ln., Staten Island, 10305.

Dutchess County Tel: 845-471-5427; Fax: 845-471-5427. Sr. Miriam Eugene Fenton, S.C.
26 S. Hamilton Ave., Poughkeepsie, 12601-2599.

Ulster County Tel: 845-338-3222; Fax: 845-338-3222. Sr. Miriam Eugene Fenton, S.C., Dir.
157 Broadway, Kingston, 12401.

Central & Southern Westchester County Tel: 914-921-2678; Fax: 914-921-2678. Mrs. Linda DeMarkey, Dir.
910 Boston Post Rd., Rye, 10580.

Orange County Tel: 845-294-6428; Fax: 845-294-6428. Sr. Kevin John Shields, O.P., Dir.

John S. Burke Catholic High School, Fletcher St., P.O. Box 114, Goshen, 10924.

Rockland County, No. Westchester, Putnam Tel: 845-627-1236; Fax: 845-624-3190. Mrs. Marilyn Hilpert, Dir.
798 Rte 304 & Germonds Rd., P.O. Box 9162, Bardonia, 10954-1694.

Sullivan County Tel: 845-292-9100; Fax: 845-292-9100. Sr. Kevin John Shields, O.P., Dir.

Blessed Kateri Tekakwitha Center, P.O. Box 1011, Liberty, 12754.

Center for Spiritual Development Tel: 914-967-7328; Fax: 914-967-7387. Anne Marie Wallace, Ph.D., Dir.
96 Milton Rd., Rye, 10580.

Instructional Television Tel: 914-968-7800; Fax: 914-968-2075. Mr. Michael Lavery, Admin. Dir.
215 Seminary Ave., Yonkers, 10704. Elementary School: Full-Time Sisters 280; Part-Time Sisters 81; Full-Time Brothers 30; Part-Time Brothers 8; Full-Time Order Priests 8; Part-Time Order Priests 9; Full-Time Lay Teachers 3,358; Part-Time Lay Teachers 681; Total Parish Enrollment 76,387; Total Inter-Parish Enrollment 1,709; Total Private Enrollment 4,250; High School: Full-Time Sisters 161; Part-Time Sisters 45; Full-Time Brothers 76; Part-Time Brothers 31; Full-Time Order Priests 46; Part-Time Order Priests 16; Full-Time Diocesan Priests 26; Full-Time Lay Teachers 1,763; Part-Time Lay Teachers 130; Total Diocesan Enrollment 10,588; Parish Enrollment 4,664; Private Enrollment 12,359.

[E] HIGH SCHOOLS, ARCHDIOCESAN

NEW YORK. *Cardinal Hayes High School* (Boys). , 650 Grand Concourse, 10451. Tel: 718-292-6100; Fax: 718-292-5607. Email: jgraham@cardinalhayes.org. Web: www.cardinalhayes.org. Rev. Msgr. John K. Graham, Pres.; Revs. Harry Burke; Alfred D'Incecco; Robert Harrison; Rev. Msgrs. Victor C. Pavis (Retired); Harold Robertson (Retired). Priests 6; Brothers 4; Sisters 2; Lay Teachers 60; Students 1,053. In Res. Rev. Msgr. Peter P. Narkun (Retired).

Cardinal Spellman High School Tel: 718-881-8000; Fax: 718-515-6615. Email: spellman@adnysch.org. Web: www.cardinalspellman.org. One Cardinal Spellman Pl., Bronx, 10466. Tel: 718-881-8000; Fax: 718-515-6615. Rev. Msgr. James P. Sullivan, Pres.; Revs. John R. Kraljic; John T. Monaghan; James J. O'Shaughnessy; Peter R. Pilsner; Francis J. Principe. Priests 8; Sisters 3; Lay Teachers 79; Students 1,400. In Res. Revs. Walter C. Adams; Richard F. Gorman.

Cathedral High School (Girls) , 350 E. 56th St., 10022. Tel: 212-688-1545; Fax: 212-754-2024. Email: egraham@cathedralhs.org. Web: cathedralhs.org. Sr. Elizabeth Graham, O.P., Prin.; Revs. Robert J. Poveromo; John Scarangello. Priests 2; Sisters 10; Lay Teachers 53; Students 925.

Monsignor Farrell High School, 2900 Amboy Rd., 10306. Tel: 718-987-2900; Fax: 718-987-4241. Web: www.msgrfarrellhs.org. Revs. John N. Paddack, Prin.; John P. Comiskey; Robert G. Macchietto; John Pedulla; John Lagiovane. Priests 5; Brothers 2; Sisters 3; Lay Teachers 70; Students 1,200.

Moore Catholic High School, 100 Merrill Ave., 10314. Tel: 212-761-9200; Fax: 718-982-7779. Revs. Robert I. Gannon; Edmund P. Connors. Priests 1; Sisters of the Presentation 1; Lay Teachers 48; Students 880.

GOSHEN. *John S. Burke Catholic High School*, 80 Fletcher St., 10924. Tel: 845-294-5481; Fax: 845-294-0817. Email: eagles@burkecatholic.org. Web: www.burkecatholic.org. Rev. James T. Byrnes, Ph.D., Prin.; Miss Karen DeCrosta, Asst. Prin. for Academics; Mr. Kevin Canty, Asst. Prin. for Student Affairs; Mr. John Dolan, Asst. Prin. for Operations; Mrs. Roberta Huntington, Asst. Prin. for Finance. Priests 1; Sisters 1; Lay Teachers 43; Students 630.

HARTSDALE. *Maria Regina High School*, 500 W. Hartsdale Ave., 10530. Tel: 914-761-3300; Fax: 914-761-0860. Email: mariaregina@cloud9.net. Web: mariaregina.org. Sr. Danielle M. Baran, C.R., Prin. & Supr. Sisters of the Resurrection, Franciscan Sisters, Dominican Sisters Sisters 9; Lay Teachers 35; Students 550.

HURLEY. *John A. Coleman Catholic High School*, 430 Hurley Ave., 12443. Tel: 845-338-2750; Fax: 845-388-0250. Email: finance@colemanlives.com. Web: www.colemanlives.com. Mr. John Traverse, Prin. Lay Teachers 23; Students 156.

POUGHKEEPSIE. *Our Lady of Lourdes High School*, 131 Boardman Rd., 12603. Tel: 845-463-0400; Fax: 845-463-0174. Email: lourdes@adnyschools.org. Web: www.ollhs.org. Bros. Robert LeClerc, F.M.S.; Michael Mullin, F.M.S., Prin.; Larry Gordon, F.M.S., Asst. Prin., Academics; Todd Patenaude, Campus Ministry; Henry Sawicki, F.M.S.; Gregory DelaNoy, F.M.S., Dir. of Guidance; James Stevens, F.M.S.; Mr. James Lyons, Dean of Men; Mrs. Ellen Anderson, Dean of Women; Catherine Masterson, Dean of Admissions; Sr. Lois Dee, O.P., Asst. Prin., Faculty. Brothers 7; Sisters 1; Lay Teachers 55; Students 913.

SOMERS. *John F. Kennedy High School*, 54 Rte. 138, 10589. Tel: 914-232-5061; Fax: 914-232-3416. Email: jfkadmin@dbestweb.net. Rev. Msgr. Anthony D. Marchitelli, Prin.; Mr. Stephen Schmidt, Asst. Prin. & Academic Dean; Rev. James Teague; Sr. Barbara Heil, R.D.C., Treas.; Mr. David Concepicon, Dean of Students. Sisters of Divine Compassion, Sisters of St. Francis Priests 2; Sisters 8; Lay Teachers 35; Students 614.

WHITE PLAINS. *Archbishop Stepinac High School*, 950 Mamaroneck Ave., 10605. Tel: 914-946-4800; Fax: 914-686-3615. Email: stepinac50@aol.com. Web: www.stepinac.org. Rev. Msgr. John J. O'Keefe, Pres.; Mr. Steven E. Murphy, Prin.; Deacon Al Impallomen Jr., Admin. Asst. & Dean of Students; Rev. Thomas E. Collins, Assoc. Dean of Students. Priests 4; Sisters 3; Lay Teachers 42; Students 640.

Staff of School: Revs. Patrick M. Carroll; Philip J. Quealy In Res. Rev. Msgrs. George F. Bardes (Retired); Edward M. Connors (Retired); Augustine J. DiBlasi (Retired); John T. Doherty (Retired); Raymond P. Rigney (Retired); John Wilkinson (Retired); Revs. Henry G. d'Anjou (Retired); Thomas E. O'Keefe (Retired).

[F] HIGH SCHOOLS, PRIVATE

NEW YORK. *Academy of Mount St. Ursula* (Girls) , 330 Bedford Park Blvd., 10458. Tel: 718-364-5353; Fax: 718-364-2354. Email: mread@amsu.org. Web: www.amsu.org. Sr. Mary Beth Read, O.S.U., Prin. Ursuline Nuns Sisters 4; Lay Teachers 32; Students 460.

St. Agnes Boys High School, 555 West End Ave., 10024-2795. Tel: 212-873-9100; Fax: 212-873-9292. Bro. Emil D. Denworth, Prin. Brothers 3; Lay Teachers 20; Total Enrollment 350.

All Hallows Institute (also known as All Hallows High School). ; (Boys) , 111 E. 164th St., 10452. Tel: 718-293-4545; Fax: 718-293-8634. Web: www.allhallows.org. Mr. Sean J. Sullivan, Prin.; Mr. Paul Krebbs, Pres. Congregation of Christian Brothers 4; Lay Teachers 31; Students 510.

Aquinas High School (Girls) Tel: 718-367-2113; Fax: 718-295-5864. Email: administration@mail2.aquinashs.org. Web: aqhs@aol.com. 685 E. 182nd St., Bronx, 10457. Sisters Margaret Ryan, O.P., Pres.; Catherine Rose Quigley, O.P., Prin. Sisters 13; Lay Teachers 41; Students 830.

Convent of the Sacred Heart (Girls) , One E. 91st St., 10128-0654. Tel: 212-722-4745; Fax: 212-996-1784. Email: mblake@cshnyc.org. Web: www.cshnyc.org. Dr. Mary Blake, Headmistress. Religious of the Sacred Heart Sisters 3; Priests 1; Lay Teachers 78; Students 639.

Dominican Academy (Girls) , 44 E. 68th St., 10021. Tel: 212-744-0195; Fax: 212-744-0375. Email: dominica@adnysch.org. Web: www.dominicanacademy.org. Sr. Martha Kunesh, O.P., Prin. Sisters 4; Lay Teachers 24; Students 250.

Fordham Preparatory School (Boys) , E. Fordham Rd., 10458. Tel: 718-367-7500; Fax: 718-367-7598. Email: parkesj@fordhamprep.org. Web: www.fordhamprep.com. Mr. James F. Murray, Bd. Chm.; Rev. Joseph P. Parkes, S.J., Pres.; Mr. Robert J. Gomprecht, Prin.; Mr. Dennis M. Ahern, Asst. Prin.; Mr. Bruce G. Bott, Dean of Students; Revs. Mallick J. Fitzpatrick, S.J., Dir. Guidance; Matthew C. Flood, S.J.; John J. Leonard, S.J.; Stanley J. O'Konsky, S.J.; William J. O'Malley, S.J.; Charles D. Sullivan, S.J.; Raymond M. Sweitzer, S.J.; Thomas G. Benz, S.J. Priests 10; Lay Teachers 65; Students 900.

St. Joseph by the Sea, High School (Coed) , 5150 Hylan Blvd., 10312. Tel: 718-984-6500; Fax: 718-984-6503; 718-227-6816. Email: j.f.bolger@msn.com. Rev. Msgr. Joseph C. Ansaldi, Prin.; Rev. Michael P. Reilly. Priests 2; Sisters 5; Lay Teachers 69; Students 1,400.

La Salle Academy (Boys) , 44 E. Second St., 10003. Tel: 212-475-8940; Fax: 212-529-3598. Web: www.lasalleacademy.org. Bros. James Martino, F.S.C., Pres.; James Furlong, F.S.C.; Brendan Fitzgerald, F.S.C.; Leslie Luker, F.S.C.; John Bassett, F.S.C.; Timothy Jones, F.S.C.; Louis Ruch, F.S.C.; Stephen Caplice, F.S.C.; Charles O'Connell, F.S.C.; Raymond Buck, F.S.C.; Leonard Wojtanowski, C.F.X. Brothers of The Christian Schools Brothers 11; Lay Teachers 35; Students 550.

Loyola School (Coed) , 980 Park Ave., 10028. Tel: 212-288-3522; Fax: 212-861-1021. Email: skatsouros@loyola-nyc.org. Web: www.loyola-nyc.org. Mr. Francis Serbaroli, Bd. Chm.; Revs. Stephen N. Katsouros, S.J., Pres.; James J. Curry, S.J.; Eugene J. Prior, S.J.; Thomas S. Prout, S.J.; Michael E. Sehler, S.J. Society of Jesus Priests 3; Lay Teachers 27; Students 208.

Mother Cabrini High School, (Grades 9-12), 701 Ft. Washington Ave., 10040. Tel: 212-923-3540; Fax: 212-781-2051. Email: info@cabrinihs.com. Web: www.cabrinihs.com. Brian Donahue, Headmaster; Joan Close, Dean of Academics; Susan Fraleigh, Dean of Students; Sr. Sharon Casey, M.S.C., Campus Min.; Kathleen B. Muskopf, Devel. Dir. (Girls) Sisters 6; Lay Teachers 32; Students 456.

Notre Dame Academy High School, 134 Howard Ave., 10301. Tel: 718-447-8878; Fax: 718-447-2926. Email: ndastatenisland@aol.com. Web: www.notredameacademy.org. Dr. Lorraine Pasadino, Pres.; Dr. Gregory Rosscinc, Prin. Congregation of Notre Dame Sisters 1; Lay Teachers 29; Girls 397.

Notre Dame School of Manhattan (Girls) , 327 W. 13th St., 10014. Tel: 212-620-5575; Fax: 212-620-0432. Email: ntdamehs@adnyschools.org. Web: www.cheznous.org. Mr. John Joven, Prin. Sisters 5; Lay Teachers 17; Students 240.

Preston High School (Girls) , 2780 Schurz Ave., 10465. Tel: 718-863-9134; Fax: 718-863-6125. Email: lcoldrick@prestonhs.org. Web: www.prestonhs.org. Sr. Lucille Coldrick, R.D.C., Prin.; Linda Youngren, Asst. Prin.; Sr. Laura Donovan, R.D.C., Asst. Prin. Sisters of the Divine Compassion 7; Lay Teachers 42; Students 550.

Regis High School (Boys) , 55 E. 84th St., 10028. Tel: 212-288-1100; Fax: 212-794-1221. Email: vbiagi@regis-nyc.org. Web: www.regis-nyc.org. Revs. J. Thomas McClain, S.J., Pres.; Vincent L. Biagi, S.J., Prin.; Mr. James F. X. Lyness, Asst. Prin.; Mr. Daniel T. Dougherty, Dean of Students; Revs. Arthur C. Bender, S.J.; Christopher J. Devron, S.J.; Kenneth J. Caufield, S.J. Society of Jesus Priests 5; Lay Teachers 55; Students 517.
Res.: 53 E. 83rd St., 10028.

Rice High School (Boys) , 74 W. 124th St., 10027. Tel: 212-369-4100; Fax: 212-348-4631. Email: adnyricehs@connectinc.com. Web: www.ricehighschool.com. Bro. John M. Walderman, C.F.C., Pres. Congregation of Christian Brothers Diocesan Priest 1; Brothers 4; Lay Teachers 30; Students 376.

Xavier High School (Boys) , 30 W. 16th St., 10011. Tel: 212-924-7900; Fax: 212-924-0303. Web: www.xavierhs.org. Revs. Daniel J. Gatti, S.J., Pres.; David S. Ciancimino, S.J., Headmaster; Mr. Michael LiVigni, Asst. Headmaster; Mr. Joseph Sweeney, Dean of Students; Miss Janet Bonica, Registrar; Revs. John F. Replogle, S.J.; William J. McGowan, S.J.; Robert V. O'Hare, S.J.; James Coughlin, S.J.; Pierce A. Brennan, S.J.; Bros. Christopher Derby, S.J.; Anthony SooHoo, S.J. Society of Jesus, (See listing for Xavier Jesuit Community for additional names of priests and brothers.) Priests 5; Brothers 1; Jesuit Scholastic

1; Lay Teachers 56; Students 913.

BARDONIA. *Albertus Magnus*, 798 Rte. 304, 10954. Tel: 914-623-8842; Fax: 914-623-0009. Email: amadmin@albertusmagnus.org. Web: www.lanline.com/~armadm. Sisters of St. Dominic (Sparkill) 4; Lay Teachers 35; Students 468.

BRONX. *St. Catharine Academy* (Girls) , 2250 Williamsbridge Rd., 10469. Tel: 718-882-2882; Fax: 718-231-9099. Email: stcatharineaca@aol.com. Web: www.scahs.org. Sr. Ann M. Welch, R.S.M., Prin. Sisters 7; Lay Teachers 42; Students 704.

Mount St. Michael Academy (Boys) , 4300 Murdock Ave., 10466. Tel: 718-515-6400; Fax: 718-994-7729. Email: brothermichael@mtstmichael.org. Web: www.mountstmichael.org. Bros. Michael Flanigan, Pres.; Steven E. Murphy, Prin. Deacons 3; Brothers 9; Sisters 2; Lay Teachers 61; Students 968.

Junior High School Tel: 718-515-6400; Fax: 718-994-7729. Mrs. Lillian Dippolito, Prin. Lay Teachers 7; Students 160.

DOBBS FERRY. *Our Lady of Victory Academy High School* (Girls) , 565 N. Broadway, 10522. Tel: 914-693-1633; Fax: 914-693-5250. Email: olvamain@victoryhs.org. Web: www.victoryhs.org. Sr. Joan Agro, O.P., Prin. Sisters of Mercy Sisters 7; Lay Teachers 29; Students 415.

NEW ROCHELLE. *Iona Preparatory School* (Boys) , 255 Wilmot Rd., 10804. Tel: 914-632-0714; Fax: 914-632-9760. Email: jjoc97@ionaprep.org. Web: www.ionaprep.org. Bro. Gerard M. Gaffney, C.F.C., Pres.; Mr. Anthony R. Baxter, Headmaster; Mr. Gregory Quirolo, Asst. Headmaster; Mr. George F. Teasdale, Asst. Headmaster; Mr. Christopher J. Farrell, Vice Pres. for Advancement; Mr. Brian E. Terhune, Vice Pres. Finance; Bros. James J. Adams; Daniel S. Adams; James R. Kelly; Carmine P. Pellegrino; John A. Reynolds. Congregation of Christian Brothers Brothers 4; Sisters 1; Lay Teachers 50; Students 750.

Salesian High School, 148 Main St., 10801. Tel: 914-632-0248; Fax: 914-632-1362. Email: salhsnr@aol.com. Web: www.members.aol.com/salhsnr. Rev. John Nazzaro, S.D.B., Dir. & Pres.; Mr. John P. Flaherty, M.A., Prin.; Sr. Barbara Wright, O.P., Asst. Prin.; Mr. Robert Molinaro, Dean of Students; Rev. Danh Cong Tvan, Coord. of Youth Ministry; Mr. Donald Jordan, Business Mgr.; Mr. Louis Calvelli, Vice Pres. Institutional Advancement; Mr. Jerry Coliaio, Guidance; Revs. James Mulloy, S.D.B.; Richard Putnam, S.D.B.; Bros. Donald Caldway; Tom Sweeney; Michael Leschinsky, S.D.B. Priests 4; Brothers 3; Sisters 1; Lay Teachers 23; Students 430.

Ursuline School, (Grades 6-12) , (Girls) , 1354 North Ave., 10804. Tel: 914-636-3950; Fax: 914-636-3949. Email: admin@ursuline.pvt.k12.ny.us. Web: www.ursuline.pvt.k12.ny.us. Sr. Jean Baptiste Nicholson, O.S.U., Prin. Priests 1; Sisters 9; Lay Teachers 70; Students 795.

RYE. *School of the Holy Child*, (Grades 5-12) , (Girls) , 2225 Westchester Ave., 10580. Tel: 914-967-5622; Fax: 914-967-6476. Email: a.sorrentino@holychildrye.org. Web: www.holychildrye.org. Ann F. Sullivan, Headmistress; Andrea Fletcher, Admisssions Dir. Society of the Holy Child Jesus 1; Lay Teachers 70; Students 310.

STATEN ISLAND. *St. John Villa Academy High School*, 26 Landis Ave., 10305-3729. Tel: 718-442-6240; Fax: 718-447-6729. Email: sjvilla@aol.com. Web: sjva.org. Sr. Antonia Zuffante, C.S.J.B., Prin. Brothers 1; Sisters 15; Lay Teachers 35; Girls 630.

St. Joseph Hill Academy (Girls) , 850 Hylan Blvd., 10305-2095. Tel: 718-447-1374; Fax: 718-447-3041. Email: joshill@adnyschools.org. Web: stjosephhill.org. Sr. Marie Claire, F.D.C., Prin. Daughters of Divine Charity Sisters 4; Lay Teachers 31; Students 399.

WHITE PLAINS. *Academy of Our Lady of Good Counsel* (Girls) , 52 N. Broadway, 10603. Tel: 914-949-0178; Fax: 914-682-3531. Email: olgdcoun@adny.org. Web: www.goodcounsel.pvt.k12.ny.us. Sr. Carol Peterson, R.D.C., Prin. Sisters of the Divine Compassion 6; Lay Teachers 27; Students 325.

[G] SPECIAL SCHOOLS

NEW YORK. *Grace Institute*, 1233 Second Ave., 10021. Tel: 212-832-7605; Fax: 212-486-2869. Email: graceinsti@rcn.com. Web: www.graceinstitute.org. Dr. Mary Mulvihill. Sisters of Charity, Mt. St. Vincent Sisters 4; Lay Teachers 4; Part-time Lay Teachers 6; Students 300.

Lavelle School for the Blind, 221st St. and Paulding Ave., 10469. Tel: 718-882-1212; Fax: 718-882-0005. William F. Simpson, Supt. Sisters of St. Dominic of Blauvelt Capacity 177; Lay Teachers 26; Total Staff 112; Total Enrollment 157.

Mount St. Ursula Speech Center, 2885 Marion Ave., Bronx, 10458. Tel: 718-584-7679; Fax: 718-584-7954. Email: msuspeech@aol.com. Sr. Bernadette Hannaway, O.S.U., Admin. Ursuline Nuns Sisters 1; Lay Clinicians 8; Support Staff 5 Total Enrollment 140.

Seton Foundation for Learning, Inc., 315 Arlene St., Staten Island 10314. Tel: 718-982-5084; Fax: 718-982-5114. Email: seton@adnysch.org. Rev. Msgr. James Dorney, Chm.; Diane Cunningham Exec. Dir.; Mr. John Haugen, Pres. Lay Teachers 11; Assistants 14 Total Enrollment 110.

BRONX. *St. Joseph's School for the Deaf* St. Joseph's School for the Deaf , 1000 Hutchinson River Pkwy., 10465. Tel: 718-828-9000; 718-828-1671 (TDD); Fax: 718-792-6631. Email: PMartin@SJSDNY.org. Ms. Patricia Martin, Exec Dir. Directed by Daughters of the Heart of Mary. Capacity 200 Enrollment 130.

MILLBROOK. *Cardinal Hayes School for Special Children*, St. Joseph Dr., P.O. Box CH, 12545. Tel: 845-677-6363; Fax: 845-677-6691. Email: fapers@cardinalhayeshome.org. Web: www.cardinalhayeshome.org. Fred Apers Exec. Dir. Educational programs for multi-handicapped children. Lay Teachers 5; Capacity 45; Total Enrollment 40.

[H] ELEMENTARY SCHOOLS, PRIVATE

NEW YORK. *Academy of St. Dorothy*, 1305 Hylan Blvd., 10305. Tel: 718-351-0939; Fax: 718-351-0661. Email: dorothy@adnysch.org. Sr. Sharon A. McCarthy, S.S.D., Prin. Sisters of St. Dorothy 4; Lay Teachers 12; Students 320.

Convent of the Sacred Heart (Girls) , 1 E. 91st St., 10128. Tel 212-722-4745; Fax: 212-996-1784. Email: mblake@cshnyc.org. Web: cshnyc.org. Dr. Mary Blake, Headmistress. Sisters 2; Lay Teachers 103; Students 656.

St. John Villa Academy Elementary School Mailing Address: 57 Cleveland Pl., 10305. Sr. Rita Marie Carey, C.S.J.B., Prin. Sisters 9; Lay Teachers 10; Students 418.

St. Joseph Hill Academy Elementary, 850 Hylan Blvd., 10305. Tel: 718-981-1187; Fax: 718-448-7016. Email: joshiles@adnyschools.org. Web: www.stjosephhill.org. Mary Jane Truckenbrodt, Prin. Sisters 1; Lay Teachers 30; Students 525.

Marymount School, (Grades N-12), 1026 Fifth Ave., 10028. Tel: 212-744-4486; Fax: 212-744-0163. Email: kathleen_pagan@marymount.k12.ny.us. Sr. Kathleen Fagan, R.S.H.M., Headmistress. Religious of the Sacred Heart of Mary Sisters 3; Lay Teachers 58; Students 510.

Sacred Heart Private Elementary School, Inc., 1651 Zerega Ave., 10462. Tel: 718-863-5047; Fax: 718-828-1946. Email: shps@adnyschools.org. Web: www.sacredheartprivate.org. Sr. Judith Musco, A.S.C.J., Prin. Apostles of the Sacred Heart of Jesus Sisters 5; Lay Teachers 12; Students 162.

Villa Maria Academy, 3335 Country Club Rd., 10465. Tel: 718-824-3260; Fax: 718-824-7315. Email: villa@adnyschools.org. Web: www.vmafc.org. Sr. Teresa Barton, C.N.D., Prin. Congregation of Notre Dame Sisters 3; Lay Teachers 24; Students 470.

NEW ROCHELLE. *Iona Grammar School*, (Grades PreK-8) , (Boys) , 173 Stratton Rd., 10804. Tel: 914-633-7744; Fax: 914-235-6338 Email: JDDugan1@aol.com. Web: www.ionagrammar.org. Bro. John D. Dugan, C.F.C., Pres. & Headmaster. Brothers 2; Lay Teachers 36; Students 293.

NEWBURGH. *Bishop Dunn Memorial School* 50 Gidney Ave., 12550. Tel: 845-569-3494; Fax: 845-569-3303. Email: bishdunn@nyarchschool.org. Web: www.bdms.org. Mr. James Delviscio, Prin. Sisters of St. Dominic Sisters 2; Lay Teachers 13; Students 260.

PORT JERVIS. *Trinity Catholic School*, 10 Faith Dr., P.O. Box 1001, 12771. Tel: 845-856-6868; Fax: 845-856-6869. Carol Doll, Prin. Lay Teachers 6; Enrollment 65.

STATEN ISLAND. *Notre Dame Academy-Elementary School*, 78 Howard Ave., 10301. Tel: 718-273-9096; Fax: 718-442-6919. Email: ntdames@adnysch.org. Web: www.notredameacademy.org. Sr Rose Mary Galligan, C.N.D., Prin. Congregation of Notre Dame Lay Teachers 14; Students 319.

WHITE PLAINS. *Academy of Our Lady of Good Counsel* (Elementary Dept.), Tel: 914-761-4423; Fax: 914-761-4427. Email: gdounes@adrysch.org. 52 N. Broadway, 10603. Sr. Clare Arenholz, R.D.C., Prin. Sisters 3; Lay Teachers 14; Students 190.

[I] THE CATHOLIC CHARITIES OF THE ARCHDIOCESE OF NEW YORK

NEW YORK. *Catholic Charities Alliance*, 1011 First Ave., 10022. Tel: 212-371-1011, Ext. 2400. Beatriz Diaz-Taveras, Contact Person.

The Catholic Charities of the Archdiocese of New York, 1011 First Ave., 10022. Tel: 212-371-1000; Fax: 212-826-8795. Web: www.catholiccharitiesny.org. Rev. Msgr. Kevin L. Sullivan, Exec. Dir.; Joseph Buttigieg, Chief Prog. Operating Officer; Mr. Kenneth Dempsey, CFO; Rev. Richard F. Gorman, Assoc. Dir., Dept. of Social Research; Ms. Joanne Abruzzese, Dir. Personnel; Rev. Robert Pagliari, C.Ss.R., Assoc. Dir.

Departments: Ann Tommaso, Dir. Behavioral Health Svcs.; Mr. Mario Russell, Dir. Migration & Refugee Svcs.; Ms. Mary Ellen Ros, Dir. Parish & Community Outreach; Mr. George B. Horton, Dir. Social & Community Devel. Tel: 212-371-1000, Ext. 2475; Mr. Joseph Panepinto, Exec. Dir. CYO & Youth Svcs.

The Ladies of Charity of the Catholic Charities of the Archdiocese of New York, 1011 First Ave., 10022. Tel: 212-371-1000, Ext. 2540; Fax: 212-319-8265. Ms. Susan Grady, Exec. Dir.; Rev. Msgrs. William J. Toohy, Spiritual Dir.; Peter G. Finn, M.Div., M.S., M.Ed., Spiritual Dir.

Catholic Charities Community Services, Archdiocese of New York, 1011 First Ave., 10022. Tel: 212-371-1000; Fax: 212-826-8795. Joseph Buttigieg.

Roman Catholic Fund for Children and Other Purposes, 1011 First Ave., 10022. Tel: 212-371-1000; Fax: 212-826-8795. Rev. Msgr. Kevin L. Sullivan.

Holy Name Centre for Homeless Men, Inc., 18 Bleeker St., 10012. Tel: 212-226-5848. Rev. Msgr. John B. Ahern, Dir.

Providence Health Services, 1249 Fifth Ave., 10029. Karl Adler, Pres.

St. Michael's Home, c/o The Catholic Charities of the Archdiocese of New York, 1011 First Ave., 10022. Tel: 212-371-1000. Web: cathwww.org. Bernard E. Reidey, Vice Pres.

[J] HOUSING

NEW YORK. *Catholic Charities Department of Housing, Housing Development Institute, Inc.*, 1011 First Ave., 10022. Tel: 212-371-1000.

BRONX. *Angela House, Inc.*, 3323 Steuben Ave., 10467. Tel: 718-231-7592; Fax: 718-231-9487. Sr. M. Winifred Danwitz, O.S.U., Ph.D., Exec. Dir. A transitional residence for homeless women and their young children.

[K] MENTAL HEALTH SERVICES

NEW YORK. *Catholic Charities Department of Behavioral Health Services*, 1011 First Ave., 10022. Tel: 212-371-1000, Ext. 3608; Fax: 212-421-0021. Email: anne.tommaso@archny.org. Web: www.archny.org. Anne Tommaso, Dir., Behavioral Health Services; Denise Bauer, Dir. of Outpatient Services.

Inwood/Washington Hts:
652 E. 187th St., 10033. Tel: 212-795-6860; Fax: 212-928-4351. Corina Harten, Clinic Supvr.

Bronx:
2380 Belmont Ave., Bronx, 10458. Tel: 718-364-7700; Fax: 718-364-1513. Charles Eisenberg, Clinic Supvr.

Yonkers:
4 St. Mary's St., Yonkers, 10701. Tel: 914-476-2700; Fax: 914-965-4241. Jackie Williams-Walsh, Clinic Supvr.

Peekskill:
1045 Park St., Peekskill, 10566. Tel: 914-737-7338; Fax: 914-737-1050. Mrs. Suzanne DeLasho, Clinic Supvr.

Hudson Valley Counseling Corps:

Rockland County Tel: 845-942-5791; Fax: 845-429-2938.

Orange County Tel: 845-561-3452; Fax: 845-561-2825.

Dutchess County Tel: 845-452-1400; Fax: 845-452-3336.

Sullivan County Tel: 845-791-6023; Fax: 845-791-6104.

Ulster County Tel: 212-371-1011, Ext. 3631; Fax: 212-421-0021. Kathryn Howard, Regional Dir.

SVCMA Health Services Inc.,, 130 W. 12th St., Ste. 2-E, 10011. Tel: 212-604-7536. Email: estclair@svcmcny.org. Elizabeth St. Clair, E.s.q., Contact Person.

[L] IMMIGRATION SERVICES

NEW YORK. *Catholic Charities Department of Immigrant and Refugee Services*, 1011 First Ave. 12th Fl., 10022. Tel: 212-419-3700; Fax: 212-751-3197. Web: www.archny.org. Mr. C. Mario Russell, Dept. Dir.; Ms. Penni Bunyaviroch, Assoc. Dir. for Admin. Svcs.; Mr. Dan R. Smulian, Assoc. Dir. for Legal Svcs.

Refugee Resettlement, 1011 First Ave., 12th Fl., 10022. Tel: 212-419-3700; Fax: 212-751-3197. Ms. Patricia O'Callaghan, Assoc. Dir. for Ref. Res.

Project Irish Outreach, 1011 First Ave., 12th Fl., 10022. Tel: 212-419-3700; Fax: 212-751-3197. Ms. Patricia O'Callaghan, Coord.

New York Immigration Hotline, 1011 First Ave., 12th

Fl., 10022. Tel: 212-419-3737; 800-566-7636. Yolanda Bastidas, Coord.
Asylum Information and Referral Hotline, 1011 First Ave.. Tel: 212-419-3737; Fax: 800-354-0365.

[M] PARISH AND COMMUNITY OUTREACH

NEW YORK. *Catholic Charities Department of Parish and Community Outreach*, 1011 First Ave., 10022. Tel: 212-371-1000, Ext. 2004; Fax: 212-317-8719. Ms. Mary Ellen Ros, Dir.
Catholic Charities Centers:
Central Harlem, 202 W. 141st St., 10030. Tel: 212-694-3939; Fax: 212-694-4242.
Lower Manhattan, 530 Grand St., 10002. Tel: 212-777-3111; Fax: 212-677-9057.
Central Manhattan, 1011 First Ave., 10022. Tel: 212-371-1000, Ext. 2031; Fax: 212-826-8377.
Washington Hts., 652 W. 187 St., 10033. Tel: 212-795-6860; Fax: 212-928-4351.
Bronx, 2380 Belmont Ave., Bronx, 10458. Tel: 718-364-7770; Fax: 718-364-1513.
South Bronx, 402 E. 152nd St., Bronx, 10455. Tel: 718-292-9090; Fax: 718-993-6130.
Staten Island, 120 Anderson Ave., Staten Island, 10302. Tel: 718-447-6330; Fax: 718-447-6060.
Westchester County/Peekskill, 1045 Park Ave., Peekskill, 10566. Tel: 914-737-7338; Fax: 914-737-1050.
Westchester County/Yonkers, 4 St. Mary's St., Yonkers, 10701. Tel: 914-476-2700; Fax: 914-965-4241.
Dutchess County, 218 Church St., Poughkeepsie, 12601. Tel: 845-452-1400; Fax: 845-452-3336.
Orange County, 185 Liberty Ave., P.O. Box 64, Newburgh, 10977. Tel: 845-561-3452; Fax: 845-561-2825.
66 Bennett St., Middletown. Tel: 845-344-4244.
Rockland County, 78 Hudson Ave., Haverstraw, 10927. Tel: 845-942-5791; Fax: 845-429-2938.
Sullivan County, North St. & Liberty St., P.O. Box 395, Monticello, 12701. Tel: 845-791-6023; Fax: 845-791-6104.
Ulster County, 157 Broadway, Kingston, 12401. Tel: 845-340-9170; Fax: 845-340-9596.
Parish Social Ministry, 1011 First Ave., 10022. Tel: 212-371-1000, Ext. 2032; Fax: 212-826-8377. Mrs. Dorothy Meehan.
Ministry to Seniors, 1011 First Ave., 10022. Tel: 212-371-1000, Ext. 2003; Fax: 212-826-8377. Mrs. Eleanor Ramos.
Office for the Homeless and Hungry, 1011 First Ave., 10022. Tel: 212-371-1000, Ext. 2529; Fax: 212-319-0405. Ms. Maureen Sheehan.

[N] SOCIAL AND COMMUNITY DEVELOPMENT

NEW YORK. *Catholic Charities Department of Social and Community Development*, 1011 First Ave., Room 1287, 10022. Tel: 212-371-1000, Ext. 2480; Fax: 212-319-0405. Mr. George B. Horton, Dir. Tel: 212-371-1000, Ext. 2475. Email: george.horton@archny.org..
Offices and Staff:
Criminal Justice Ministry Email: kenneth.hoffarth@archny.org. Mr. Kenneth Hoffarth, Dir. Tel: 212-371-1000, Ext. 3166; Linda Panzella. Tel: 212-371-1000, Ext. 2526. Email: linda.panzella@archny.org.
Justice and Peace Ministry Thomas Dobbins Jr., Outreach Coord. Tel: 212-371-1000, Ext. 2473. Email: thomas.dobbins@archny.org.
Education Outreach Program Alison Hughes-Kelsick, Dir.. Email: alison.hughes-kelsick@archny.orgTel: 212-371-1000, Ext. 2450.
Public Policy Network Wendy Ramadar. Tel: 212-371-1000, Ext. 2490. Email: wendyramadar@worldnet.att.net; Thomas Dobbins Jr. Tel: 212-371-1000, Ext. 2473. Email: thomas.dobbins@archny.org.
Community Development and The Guild for Dorothy Day Ms. Lourdes Ferrer. Tel: 212-371-1000, Ext. 2474. Email: lourdes.ferrer@archny.org.
Office for the Disabled Rev. Robert Pagliari, C.Ss.R. Tel: 212-371-1000, Ext. 2040. Email: robert.pagliari@archny.org.

[O] SPECIAL SERVICES FOR THE ELDERLY/HANDICAPPED

BEACON. *Metropolitan Association of Contemplative Communities, Inc.*, 89 Hiddenbrooke Dr., 12508. Tel: 845-831-5572. Sr. Rita Donahue, O.C.D., Contact Person.

[P] SERVICES TO THE DISABLED

NEW YORK. *Catholic Guild for the Blind*, 1011 First Ave., 6th Floor, 10022. Tel: 212-371-1000, Ext. 2017; Fax: 212-826-8377. Email: tsnyder@archny.org. Ms. A. Therese Snyder, Exec. Dir. Total Staff 12.
New York Catholic Deaf Center, 1011 First Ave., Room 670, 10022. Tel: 212-371-1000 (Voice); 212-758-3045 (TTY); Fax: 212-317-8719. Rev. Msgr. Patrick P. McCahill, Dir.

Mental Health & Community Residences:

NEW YORK. *Beacon of Hope House*, Catholic Charities, 1011 First Ave., 10022. Tel: 212-371-1000; Fax: 212-421-0021. Email: anne.tommaso@archny.org. Web: www.archny.org. Joy Jasper, Assoc. Dir. Personnel.
Supervised Units, 1400 Waters Pl., Bronx, 10461. Tel: 718-892-3494; Fax: 718-892-5507. Bob Franco, Prog. Mgr.
Terence Cardinal Cooke Residence, 2467 Bathgate Ave., Bronx, 10458. Tel: 718-367-6990; 718-367-5405 (TTY); Fax: 718-365-2544. Pearl Johnson, Prog. Mgr.
Supervised Units, 777 Seaview Ave., Bldg. D, 2nd Fl., Staten Island, 10305. Tel: 718-980-1072; Fax: 718-980-1077. Dennis Scimone, Dir. of Housing Services; Sharon Quattrachi, Admin. Sec.
Beacon I: Kimmberli Flury, Prog. Supvr. Tel: 718-980-0041.
Beacon II: Vanessa Harmon, Prog. Supvr. Tel: 718-980-1072.
Staten Island Apartment Programs Tel: 718-979-6241; Fax: 718-979-6941. Sandy Mormile, Prog. Mgr.
90-92 Hancock St., Staten Island, 10305. Tel: 718-979-6241; Fax: 718-979-6941.
Highbridge Neighborhood Supported Housing Program, 1484 Nelson Ave., Suite A, Bronx, 10452. Tel: 718-503-8106; Fax: 718-293-0939. Cindy Aquan, Prog. Supvr.
Kingsborough Intensive Supported Apartment Program, 647 Vanderbilt Ave., Brooklyn, 11238. Tel: 718-398-4556; Fax: 718-398-4807. Gregory Hinds, Prog. Mgr.
Services to the St. Anthony's Residence, 410 E. 156th St., Bronx, 10455. Tel: 718-993-5060; Fax: 718-993-4758. Stanley Hart, Prog. Mgr.
East Bronx Supported Housing, 707 Brady Ave., Bronx, 10462. Tel: 718-829-7177; Fax: 718-829-7376. LaVelle Walton, Program Mgr.; Patricia Iriebi, Assoc. Dir. Supported Housing.
The Clubhouse, 512 Southern Blvd., Bronx, 10455. Tel: 718-993-1078; Fax: 718-993-0216. Yvonne Howe, Prog. Dir.

BARRYVILLE. *New Hope Manor*, 35 Hillside Rd., 12719. Tel: 845-557-8353; Fax: 845-557-6603. Email: newhopemnr@aol.com. Web: www.newhopemanor.org. Nicholas A. Roes, Dir.; Sisters Joanne Maloney, O.P., Bd. of Directors; Rita Moriarity, S.C.C., R.N., Bd. of Directors; Joan Correra, O.F.M., Bd. of Directors; Bro. Charles Kinney, S.A., Bd. of Directors. See listing in the Miscellaneous section for further details.
Staff: Sisters Maureen Conway, O.P., Dir. of Education, Housemother, Counselor & Teacher; Patricia Conway, O.P., Housemother, Counselor & Teacher; Rose Respol, O.P., D.R.E.; Marie Cecelia Landis, S.C.C., Coord. of Infant & Mother Svcs.

SPRING VALLEY. *Good Counsel*, 1157 Fulton Ave., Bronx, 10456. Tel: 718-328-8620; 800-723-8331 (Info. & Referrals); Fax: 718-378-0341. Christopher Bell, Exec. Dir.; Delores Morgan, House Mgr.
Good Counsel, 38 N. Clinton St., Poughkeepsie, 12601. Tel: 845-452-2944; 800-723-8331 (Info. & Referrals); Fax: 845-452-6390. Christopher Bell, Exec. Dir.; Christine Furlano, House Mgr.
Good Counsel, 38 Wiman Pl., Staten Island, 10305. Tel: 718-727-8266; 800-723-8331 (Info. & Referrals); Fax: 718-447-6625. Christopher Bell, Exec. Dir.; Laila Mejia, House Mgr.
Good Counsel/Daystar Program, 275 North St., Harrison, 10528. Tel: 914-925-9834; 800-723-8331 (Info. & Referrals); Fax: 914-925-9101. Christopher Bell, Exec. Dir.; Araceli Nunez, House Mgr. Total Assisted 380; Total Staff 60.

[Q] YOUTH SERVICES

NEW YORK. *Catholic Youth Organization of the Archdiocese of New York Inc.*, Executive Office, 1011 First Ave., 10022-4187. Tel: 212-371-1000; Fax: 212-826-3347. Mr. Henry Humphreys, Pres.; Mr. Joseph E. Panepinto, Exec. Dir.; Mrs. Judith Trancucci, Asst. Dir.; Ms. Lisette Morales, Exec. Asst. & Events Coord.; Mrs. Antoinette Kerins, Dir. Teenage Federation & Blair Lodge; Mr. Jeffrey NS. Rumpf, Coord. East Hudson Region.
Archdiocesan Committee on Scouting Tel: 212-371-1000; Fax: 212-826-3347. Rev. Msgr. Anthony D. Marchitelli, Archdiocesan Boy Scout Chap.; Rev. Lawrence J. Quinn, Sea Cadet Chap.; Eugene Joconetti, Scouting Coord.
CYO Manhattan County and Bronx County Tel: 212-371-1000; Fax: 212-826-3347. Mr. Anthony D'Angelo, Dir.
242 Bathgate Ave., Bronx, 10458. Tel: 718-367-7659; Fax: 718-904-1863.
Grace Youth Ministry Center Tel: 212-666-6598; Fax: 212-665-2271. Mrs. Carmen Castro, Coord.
218 W. 108th St., 10025. Tel: 212-666-6598; Fax: 212-665-2271.
Cardinal Spellman Center Tel: 212-677-6600; Fax: 212-995-8537. Mr. Thomas Rosati, Dir.
137 E. Second St., 10009. Tel: 212-677-6600; Fax: 212-995-8537.
Lt. Joseph P. Kennedy, Jr., Memorial Center Tel: 212-862-6401; Fax: 212-862-6421. Mr. David Dennis, Dir.
34 W. 134th St., 10037. Tel: 212-862-6401; Fax: 212-862-6421.
CYO Staten Island Office Tel: 718-448-4949; Fax: 718-273-8361. Anthony Navarrino, Dir.
120 Anderson Ave., Staten Island, 10302. Tel: 718-448-4950; Fax: 718-448-0576.
Staten Island Center Tel: 718-448-4949; Fax: 718-273-8361. Fran Mitilieri, Dir.; Frank Brucato, Asst. Dir.
120 Anderson Ave., Staten Island, 10302. Tel: 718-448-4949; Fax: 718-273-8361.
CYO Westchester/Putnam Offices Tel: 845-623-2785; Fax: 845-624-0889. Frank Magaletta, Dir.
9 Brookview Blvd., Chestnut Ridge, 10977. Tel: 845-623-2785; Fax: 845-624-0889.
Blair Lodge Youth Ministry Center, Peekskill Rd., Putnam Valley, 10579. Tel: 845-528-5005; Fax: 845-528-6137. Mrs. Antoinette Kerins, Dir.
1011 First Ave., 10022. Tel: 845-783-1254; Fax: 212-826-3347.
CYO Orange Office Tel: 845-783-1254; Fax: 212-826-3347. Ann Lawrence, Teen Federation Coord.
260 Carpenter, Newburgh, 12550. Tel: 845-561-6264; Fax: 212-826-3347. John Smith, Sports Coord.
P.O. Box 234, Highland Mills, 10930. Tel: 845-534-7700; Fax: 212-826-3347.
CYO Rockland Office Tel: 845-620-1662. Thomas F. Collins.
34 Granecy Ct., Pearl River, 10965. Tel: 845-620-1662; Fax: 845-452-3336.
CYO Dutchess Office Tel: 845-452-1400; Fax: 845-452-3336. Andrea Tighe, Youth Min. Coord.
Catholic Center, 240 Church St., Poughkeepsie, 12601. Tel: 845-452-1400; Fax: 845-452-3336.
CYO Ulster Office Tel: 845-340-9170; Fax: 845-340-9596.
157 Broadway, Kingston, 12401. Tel: 845-340-9170; Fax: 845-340-9596.
CYO Sullivan County Tel: 845-292-9100. Sr. Kevin John Shields, O.P.
Box 1011, Liberty, 12750. Tel: 845-292-9100.

BRONX. *St. Francis Youth Center, Inc.*, 420 E. 156th St., 10455. Tel: 718-993-3405. Bro. Thomas McGrinder, C.F.R., Contact Person.

GARRISON. *Capuchin Youth and Family Ministries* A ministry of the Capuchin Franciscan Province of St. Mary , 781 Rt 9D. Tel: 845-424-3609; Fax: 845-424-4403. Email: cyfm@cyfm.org. Web: www.cyfm.org. P.O. Box 192, 10524. Thomas Brinkmann, Dir.

[R] SOCIETY OF ST. VINCENT DE PAUL

NEW YORK. *Society of St. Vincent De Paul, Archdiocesan Central Council of New York* Territory: Archdiocese of New York. , 1011 First Ave., 10022. Tel: 212-755-8615; Fax: 212-755-0151. Email: svdpny@stjohns.edu. Mr. Ramon Vidal, Pres.; Rev. Robert T. Ritchie, Spiritual Advisor.
Legal Title: *The Society of St. Vincent de Paul of the Archdiocese of New York, Inc.*
District Council of Manhattan, 1011 First Ave., Ste. 607, 10022. Tel: 212-755-8615; Fax: 212-755-0151. Mr. Jim Young, Pres.; Rev. Msgr. Wallace A. Harris, Spiritual Advisor; Mr. Vincent D. Reilly, Exec. Sec.
Legal Title: *The Society of St. Vincent de Paul in the City of New York*, Territory: Manhattan.
District Council of the Bronx, 402 E. 152nd St., Bronx, 10455. Tel: 718-824-3157; Fax: 718-824-3157. Frank Cushing, Pres.
District Council of Staten Island, 28 Bryson Ave., Staten Island, 10302. Tel: 718-356-0147. Ray Martin, Pres.

BRONX. *District Council of the Bronx* Territory: Borough of The Bronx & Lower Westchester. , 402 E. 152nd St., 10455. Tel: 718-292-9090; Fax: 718-993-6130. Rev. Tom Dicks; Dominick Galdieri, Pres.
Legal Title: *The Society of St. Vincent de Paul, District Council of the Bronx, Inc.*

STATEN ISLAND. *Particular Council of Staten Island*, Tel: 718-727-3171. Carmen Malandro, Pres.; Deacon Joseph Graf, Spiritual Dir.

[S] INSTITUTIONS FOR DEPENDENT CHILDREN

NEW YORK. *Covenant House Under 21* (Runaway and Homeless Youth.) , 460 W. 41st St., 10036. Tel: 212-613-0300; Fax: 212-629-3756. Sr. Mary Rose McGeady, D.C., Pres.; Bruce J. Henry, Exec. Dir.

Total Assisted 8,593; Total Staff 539.

Vincent J. Fontana Center for Child Protection, 27 Christopher St., 10014. Tel: 212-206-4155; Fax: 212-206-4115. Email: mels@nyfoundling.org. Children & Families 250; Total Staff 12.

BLAUVELT. *St. Dominic Home* 10913. Tel: 845-359-3400; Fax: 845-359-4253. Email: sjm@st.dominicshome.org. Web: www.st.dominichome.org. Sr. Joseph Mary, O.P., Exec. Dir. Capacity: Boys 12; Girls 12; In Foster Homes 558; Group Homes: 43; Boys 17; Girls 50; Sisters 10.

New York Offices, 343 E. 137th St., Bronx, 10454. Tel: 718-993-5765; Fax: 718-402-8202.

Special education program Tel: 845-359-3400; Fax: 845-359-5286. (Emotionally disturbed mentally ill children ages 6-15.) Capacity 72.

Preschool Tel: 718-515-3664; Fax: 718-515-3841. (Ages 3-5) Capacity 48.

Community residences for developmentally disabled Tel: 845-359-3400; Fax: 845-359-3673. Capacity 110.

Community residences for emotionally handicapped Tel: 845-359-3400; Fax: 845-359-7361. Capacity 46.

TORCH (To Reach Children), 2340 Andrews Ave., Bronx, 10463. Tel: 718-365-7238; Fax: 718-584-3057.

Friends of St. Dominic, 500 Western Hwy., 10913. Tel: 914-359-3400; Fax: 914-398-0466. Sr. Joseph Mary Mahoney, O.P.

BRONX. *Saint Dominic's Home - Prevention Program (ASTAAN)* Parent Aide Counseling Advocacy Information and Referral. , 2345 University Ave., 10468. Tel: 718-584-4407; Fax: 718-584-4540. Email: annettet@stdominicshome.org. Web: www.stdominicshome.org. Families 100; Families Served 200.

Pius XII Youth and Family Services, Inc. Central Offices. ; Provides foster care, community and family services, work force development, employee assistance and chemical dependence services. ; Non-Secure Detention and Group Homes. ; Temporary group care provided at 3 homes in Middletown and Poughkeepsie. , 188 W. 230th St., 10463. John G. Kelly, Acting CEO.

The Victor J. Riley Jr. Center for Human Services, 188 W. 230th St., 10463. Tel: 718-561-2073; Fax: 718-562-4538.

11 King Center, Middletown, 10940. Tel: 914-343-7487; Fax: 914-343-1842.

Foster Boarding Homes & Adoption Tel: 718-562-7855; Fax: 718-562-1815. Foster care and adoption services for 500 infants, children and adolescents in the Bronx. Program provides services and medical care to natural families, children and foster parents and recruitment of new foster parents. Adoptive parents are sought for children freed for adoption.

188 W. 230th St., 10463.

Community Services:

North Bronx Family Service Center, 2190 University Ave., 10453. Tel: 718-365-1400; Fax: 718-365-1411. Preventive services center for local community.

Bronx Community Services Tel: 718-931-2611; 718-822-2325.

1967 Turnbull Ave., 10473. Tel: 718-931-2611.

University Heights Day Care, 2167 University Ave., 10453. Tel: 718-584-6400; Fax: 718-584-2724. On-site day care for preschool children and after-school care for school-age children. Office for family day care that provides in-home services for families. Children 101.

Goshen Early Learning Center, 59 St. John St., Goshen, 10924. Tel: 914-294-7502; Fax: 914-294-9619. Montessori-based day care for 60, ages 3-5.

Employment Training and Youth Development Services Training and placement in auto mechanics, word processing and secretarial skills. Special family support and resource program which coordinates job training with family services. After-school education and recreational services.

Snow House, 135 Hall of Fame Terr., 10453. Tel: 718-365-7755; Fax: 718-365-7756.

Student Services - Dropout Prevention Intergenerational program between Jewish Home Hospital and P.S. 79.; Counseling services to identified population of students considered high risk for dropping out of school.

Theodore Roosevelt High School, 500 E. Fordham Rd., 10458. Tel: 718-365-5051.

Morris High School, 166th St. & Boston Rd., 10456. Tel: 718-542-3700, Ext. 1003.

P.S. 79, 125 E. 181st St., 10453. Tel: 718-584-5158.

Adlai Stevenson High School, 1980 Lafayette Ave., 10473. Tel: 718-918-2700, Ext. 560.

Walton High School, West 196 St. & Reservoir Ave., 10468. Tel: 718-365-6215.

After School Programs Supervised Latch-key program of classes, workshops and recreation for 6-18 year olds. Teen Program for adolescents provides recreational program year round.

Family Service Center, 2190 University Ave., 10453.

"Aimin' High Family Service Center One hundred at-risk teens involved in sports and education programs with added community service.; Community Center serving youths, children and adults in educational, recreational and social services after school, evenings, and weekends.; Tutoring for students 6-18 who are one year or more behind grade level. G.E.D. program for high school equivalency. English as a second language classes

Beacon Program, Middle School 45, 2502 Lorillard Pl., 10458. Tel: 718-584-1952.

Chemical Dependency Services:

Administrative Office, 224 Main St., Goshen, 10924. Tel: 845-294-5124; Fax: 845-294-1369.

Chemical Dependency Clinics:, 224 Main St., Goshen, 10924. Tel: 914-294-5888; Fax: 845-294-1402. Medically supervised outpatient clinics for chemically dependent adults and their families.

62 Grand St., Newburgh, 12550. Tel: 845-562-8255; Fax: 845-562-4140.

10 Orchard St., Middletown, 10940. Tel: 845-343-7675; Fax: 845-343-2501.

520 Rte. 17M, Monroe, 10950. Tel: 845-782-0295; Fax: 845-782-5164.

146 Pike St., Port Jervis, 12771. Tel: 845-856-8440.

Alcohol Clinic, 440 Rte. 17M, Monroe, 10950. Tel: 845-782-6600; Fax: 845-782-4408. Specialized clinic for the treatment of alcoholics and their families.

School-based Services:

Alternatives, 14 Scotchtown Ave., Box 87 Goshen, 10924. Tel: 845-294-3501; Fax: 845-294-3501. Chemical dependency awareness and prevention program. Taught to school districts in Orange County. Summer and year-round programs in chemical dependency, AIDS, coping with behavioral problems and others.

Gateway Center, 46 Roe St., Newburgh, 12550. Tel: 845-569-0034; Fax: 845-569-0047. Chemical dependency outpatient clinic for Newburgh high school students, located on school grounds.

Student Assistance Services:

Employee Assistance Services Office Tel: 845-294-2501; Fax: 845-294-9932.

Box 87, Goshen, 10924. Tel: 845-294 3501; Fax: 845-294-9932.

Marie Smith Urban Street Academy, 2900 Exterior St., 10463. Tel: 718-561-7842; Fax: 718-561-5283. Employment Training Program, GED Program, Computer Classes and ESOL Program. Total Assisted 21,848; Total Staff 400.

NANUET. *St. Agatha Home of the New York Foundling Hospital* (Residential.) , 135 Convent Rd., 10954. Tel: 914-623-3461. Kathleen McGlade Ph.D., Dir.; Rev. Michael F. Gannon, Chap. Sisters of Charity of St. Vincent de Paul of New York., Runaway Youth Program.; Refugee Assistance Program.; Ulster County Prevention. Bed Capacity 126; Diagnostic Facilities 26; In Foster Homes 38; Group Homes 81; Non-secure Detention 8; Adult Intermediate Care Facilities 35; Family Support/Respite 10.

WEST PARK. *St. Cabrini Home* 12493. Tel: 845-384-6500; Fax: 845-384-6001. Email: cabrini@ulster.net. Web: cabrinihome.com. James J. Lavelle, Exec. Dir. Served by Redemptionist Fathers Children 80; Agency Operated Boarding Home 1; Group Homes 13; Missionary Sisters of Sacred Heart 5.

Cabrini-on-Hudson Tel: 845-384-6720; Fax: 845-384-6002. An adult community. Residents 71.

WHITE PLAINS. *Cardinal McCloskey Services*, Two Holland Ave., 10603. Tel: 914-997-8000; Fax: 914-997-2166. Email: mmcloughlin@cardinalmccloskey.org. Mrs. Marjorie McLoughlin, Exec. Dir. Sisters 3; In Foster Homes 500; In Group Homes 18; In Family Day Care: Site I: Capacity 541; Site II: Capacity 115; Site III: Capacity 145.

Cardinal McCloskey Emergency Residential School, 155 N. Highland Ave., 10562. Tel: 914-762-5302; Fax 914-762-7844. Capacity 20; Clients in Preventative Services 270; Total Assisted 2,000; Total Staff 415.

[T] SPECIALIZED CHILD CARING HOMES

NEW YORK. *Good Shepherd Services*, 305 7th Ave., 9th Fl., 10001. Tel: 212-243-7070; Fax: 212-929-3412. Email: plomonaco@goodshepherds.org. Web: www.goodshepherds.org. Sr. Paulette LoMonaco, R.G.S., Exec. Dir. Provides foster care and adoption services (formerly McMahon Services for Children) and five residential programs for troubled adolescents, a training program for social service workers and a comprehensive range of neighborhood family services to individuals and youth from the South Brooklyn community. These services include a range of educational support, counseling, crisis intervention, and advocacy services. Total Assisted 10,000; Total Staff 430.

Kennedy Child Study Center, 151 E. 67th St., 10021. Tel: 212-988-9500; Fax: 212-570-6690. Email: k.c.s.c@worldnet.att.net. Web: www.kennedychildstudycenter.org. Ann Williams, Ph.D., Exec. Dir. Preschool Special Education 100; Infant/Parent Services 50.

Case Management Services Tel: 212-988-9500; Fax: 212-327-2601. Family Support Services 40; Clinic Program 400.

Bronx Site, 1028 E. 179th St., Bronx, 10460. Tel: 718-842-0200; Fax: 718-842-1328. Preschool Special Education 160; Infant/Parent Services 100.

Case Management Services Tel: 718-842-0200; Fax: 718-842-1328. Family Support Services 40.

Mission of the Immaculate Virgin Tel: 718-317-2803; Fax: 718-317-2830. Email: mtloretto@msn.com.

Legal Title: *Mission of the Immaculate Virgin for the Protection of Homeless and Destitute Children*

Mount Loretto, Staten Island, 10309. Tel: 718-317-2600; Fax: 718-317-2830. Stephen Rynn, Exec. Dir. In Res. Rev. Msgr. Joseph C. Ansaldi; Rev. Michael P. Reilly.

Intermediate Care Facility Tel: 718-966-6185. Capacity 12.

Community Residence Tel: 718-966-6185. Capacity 4.

Day Care Center Tel: 718-317-2849. Capacity 85.

Individual Residential Alternatives:

St. Matthew Cottage Tel: 718-317-2695. Capacity 8.

108 Bedell St.. Tel: 718-227-2246. Capacity 6.

Residential & Day Care Tel: 718-317-2600; Fax: 718-317-2830. Total Assisted 130; Total Staff 117.

New York Foundling Charitable Corp., 590 Avenue of the Americas, 10011. Tel: 212-633-9300. Sr. Elizabeth Vermaelen, S.C., Pres.

New York Foundling Hospital for Pediatric, Medical and Rehabilitative Care, Inc., 590 Avenue of the Americas, 10011. Tel: 646-459-3600; Fax: 646-459-3636. Email: patriciat@nyfoundling.org. Web: www.nyfoundling.org. Patricia A. Tursi, Exec. Dir. Sponsored by Sisters of Charity of St. Vincent de Paul of New York. Children 136.

New York Foundling Hospital, The (Children from Infancy to 21) , 590 Avenue of the Americas, 10011. Tel: 212-633-9300; Fax: 212-741-7516. Email: ritan@nyfoundling.org. Mr. Michael Garber, Exec. Dir. Children cared for during the year 0; In the institution 236; In foster homes 867; In adoptive homes 286; Mothers cared for in St. Mary's Maternity Residence 93; Group residences 415; Diagnostic reception centers 241; Sisters of Charity of St. Vincent de Paul of New York 15; Family day care 800; Group day care 128; Mother and abusing parent and child program 0; Families 560; Mother and child program 55; Community-based services 0; Families 700; Children 1,400; Programs for handicapped children 204; Foster Boarding Home Program 867; Children with AIDS 21; Total Assisted 7,843; Total Staff 1,700.

Sr. Una McCormack Maternity Services, Inc., 1011 First Ave., 10022. Tel: 212-371-1000; Fax: 212-755-4110. Email: pgeorgini@chbureau.org. Web: www.chbmaternityservices.org. Philip Georgini, Exec. Dir.

MILLBROOK. *Cardinal Hayes Home for Children* Residential care for developmentally disabled children and young adults. , St. Joseph Dr., P.O. Box CH, 12545. Tel: 845-677-6363; Fax: 845-677-6691. Email: fapers@cardinalhayeshome.org. Web: www.cardinalhayeshome.org. Fred Apers, Exec. Dir. Franciscan Missionaries of Mary 5; Capacity of Residential Facilities: Millbrook Intermediate Care Facility 45; Community Intermediate Care Facilities 50.

RHINEBECK. *Astor Home for Children, The* Residential Treatment Facility for severe emotionally disturbed-mentally ill boys and girls, ages 5-12. , 6339 Mill St., P.O. Box 5005, 12572-5005. Tel: 845-871-1000; Fax: 845-876-2020. Email: jmcguirk@astorservices.org. Web: www.astorservices.org. Bed Capacity 20.

Residential Treatment Center (Rhinebeck) Bed Capacity 55; Therapeutic Foster Boarding Homes 24; Family-Based Treatment 10.

Counseling Centers: Red Hook, Poughkeepsie, Beacon and Bronx (Ages birth-18) Capacity: unlimited 0.

Day Treatment Programs (Ages 3-12) Capacity Dutchess Co. 65; Bronx 160; Therapeutic Nursery, Bronx 40; Adolescent Day Treatment 120; School-Based Services: Unlimited 0.

Astor Family Services Program, Bronx (Ages birth-18) Capacity 90.

Head Start-Day Care Centers: Poughkeepsie, Beacon, Salt Point, Millerton, Wingdale, Wappingers Falls Capacity 384.

Day Care Centers: Beacon, Salt Point, Millerton, Poughkeepsie, Wingdale Capacity 35.

Special Class Integrated Services (Ages 3-5) Capacity 58.

Early Head Start Capacity 125; Total Assisted 5,270; Total Staff 575.

Astor Learning Center, The The Astor Learning Center provides individualized special education for children with emotional disturbances in conjuction with the mental health services of the Residential Treatment programs. The ALC serves children between the ages of 5-11 at time of admission. , 6339 Mill St., P.O. Box 5005, 12572-5005. Tel: 845-871-1000; Fax: 845-876-2020. Email: skeegan@astorservices.org. Web: www.astorservices.org. Capacity 75; Total Assisted 105; Total Staff 40.

[U] CHILDREN'S AGENCIES & PROTECTIVE INSTITUTIONS

NEW YORK. *Catholic Guardian Society*, 1011 First Ave., 10022. Tel: 212-371-1000; Fax: 212-935-7820. Email: jfrei@catholicguard.org. Mr. John Frein, Exec. Dir. Intermediate care facilities, individual residential alternatives and family support programs for mentally retarded, developmentally disabled adults. Group home program for boys and girls, ages 13-21 years; agency operated boarding homes and adoption services for boys and girls ages 0-16; provides regular and therapeutic foster homes for boys and girls ages 0-21; and specialized foster homes for children with AIDS; Child abuse and neglect prevention program; Specialized group care programs for mother-child population and children with special needs. Total Assisted 1,074; Total Staff 621.

Catholic Home Bureau, 1011 First Ave., 10022. Tel: 212-371-1000; Fax: 212-755-4110. Email: 6269xx@dfa.state.ny.us pgeorgini@chbureau.org. Web: www.catholichoicebureau.org. Philip Georgini, Exec. Dir. Placement of dependent and neglected boys and girls ages birth-18 in foster and adoptive homes and agency-operated boarding homes. Three shelters serve 45 homeless women with 26 preschool children. Family day care program serves 352 yearly. Maternity Services Program provides free, confidential counseling, medical & shelter care to single and married parents seeking help in planning for their unborn children. Toll-free hotline 1-800-592-HELP. Post Adoption Services and Kinship Caregiver Assistance for lowerincome families. Total Assisted 2,770; Total Staff 165.

Guild of the Infant Savior, 1011 First Ave., Room 1150, 10022. Tel: 212-371-1000, Ext. 2440.

Pelletier School & Services, 147 W. 70th St., 10023. Mary Ellen Murphy, Prog. Dir. Day School-Day Treatment Program for girls and boys 13-17. Bed Capacity 50.

LINCOLNDALE. *Lincoln Hall*, P.O. Box 600, 10540. Tel: 914-248-7474; Fax: 914-248-8391. Email: pt.lincolnhall@worldnet.att.net. John Michael Chiaravalloti, Acting Exec. Dir.

City Office, 220 E. 23rd St., 10010. Capacity Boys 207; Total Staff 351; Total Assisted 421.

[V] CATHOLIC CHARITIES - CHILD CARING AGENCIES

OSSINING. *The Cardinal McCloskey Emergency Residential School*, 155 N. Highland Ave., 10562. Tel: 914-762-5302; Fax: 914-762-7844. Email: eesaunders@aol.com.

STATEN ISLAND. *Sisters of Charity Healthcare System Nursing Home, Inc.* dba Saint Elizabeth Anns Health Care & Rehabilitation Center , 91 Tompkins Ave., 10304. Tel: 718-876-1099. Email: pmcgrann@svcmcny.org. Patricia McGrann, Contact Person.

THORNWOOD. *Catholic World Mission, Inc.*, 582 Columbus Ave., 10594. Tel: 914-749-3900; Fax: 914-749-3939. Web: www.catholicworldmission.org. Rev. Thomas Moylan, Contact Person.

[W] DAY NURSERIES

NEW YORK. *St. Benedict's Day Nursery, Day Care Center*, 21 W. 124th St., 10027. Tel: 212-423-5715; Fax: 212-423-5917. Email: stben124@aol.com. Sr. Rose Mary, Dir. Handmaids of the Most Pure Heart of Mary 4; Children 79.

St. Cecilia's Day Nursery, 118 E. 106th St., 10029. Tel: 212-534-8423. Sr. Frances Arduini, S.A., Dir. Franciscan Sisters of the Atonement 3; Capacity 30; Total Served 30.

Featherbed Lane Day Care Center, 98108 Featherbed Ln., Bronx, 10452. Tel: 212-583-8970. Mrs. Joyce Thompson, Dir. Group Day Care Children 33; Family Day Care Children 76.

Nazareth Nursery Montessori Day Care. , 214-216 W. 15th St., 10011-6501. Tel: 212-243-1881; Fax: 212-929-1466. Web: www.mindspring.com/nazareth.html. Sr. Lucy Sabatini, O.S.F., Dir. & Admin. Sisters of St. Francis of the Mission of the Immaculate Virgin 2; Capacity 55; Total Staff 14.

Providence Rest Child Day Care Center, Inc., 3310 Campbell Dr., 10465. Tel: 718-823-3588; Fax: 718-823-3588. Total Assisted 30; Total Staff 5.

San Jose Day Nursery, 432 W. 20th St., 10011. Tel: 212-929-0839; Fax: 212-924-0891. Sisters Rocio Campana, Supr.; Trinidad Fernandez, Dir. Mothers of the Helpless 6; Children 57.

MILLBROOK. *Hayes Nursery School and Day Care Center*, St. Joseph Dr., P.O. Box CH, 12545. Tel: 845-677-6363; Fax: 845-677-6691. Email: fapers@cardinalhayeshome.org. Web: www.cardinalhayeshome.org. Fred Apers, Exec. Dir. Capacity 75.

YONKERS. *Queen's Daughters Day Care Center, Inc.*, 73 Buena Vista Ave., 10701. Tel: 914-969-4491; Fax: 914-969-4491. Email: qddcc@excite.com. Barbara Berrios, Dir. Children 125; Total Staff 20.

[X] GENERAL HOSPITALS

NEW YORK. *Benefice Advantage*, 155 E. 56th St., 2nd Fl., 10022. Tel: 212-752-7959. Email: mmegalli@chcsnet.org. Maguid R. Megalli, M.D., Pres. & Contact.

Cabrini Medical Center (Cabrini Development Council, Inc.), 227 E. 19th St., 10003. Tel: 212-995-6000; Fax: 212-995-6568. Mr. Robert S. Chaloner, Pres. & CEO; Sr. Arlene Primus, M.S.C., Exec. Dir. for Mission & Ministry. Bed Capacity Acute Hospital 467; Available for Use 329; Skilled nursing facility at Dobbs Ferry 306; New York City, Beds 240; Missionary Sisters of the Sacred Heart 10; Patients assisted annually (includes Homecare visits) 66,832; Cabrini Hospice Program (home care) 900; Total Staff 2,376.

Stuyvesant Polyclinic, Inc. Tel: 212-674-0220; Fax: 212-533-2251. Patients Assisted Annually 62,891.

St. Clare's Hospital and Health Center, 415 W. 51st St., 10019. Tel: 212-459-8000; Fax: 212-459-8127. Email: mbloom@stclaresny.org. Web: www.stclares.org. Len Walsh, Pres. & CEO; Sr. Pascal Conforti, Mission Effectiveness. Bed Capacity 250; Total Services 150,815.

Our Lady of Mercy Medical Center Acute Care General Hospital. Tel: 718-920-9000; Fax: 718-920-9245. Web: www.ourladyofmercy.com.

233rd St. Division, 600 E. 233 St., Bronx, 10466. Tel: 718-920-9000; Fax: 718-920-9245.

Florence D'Urso Pavilion, 1870 Pelham Pkwy. S., Bronx, 10461. Tel: 718-430-6000; Fax: 718-430-6071. Mr. James A. Rutherford, Pres. & CEO; Rev. Msgr. Frederick J. Becker, Vice Pres. Pastoral Svcs.; Rev. John Uko, Catholic Chap. Capacity 612; Patients Assisted Annually 260,358; Total Staff 2,276.

Rosalie Hall Shelter for Unwed Mothers Tel: 718-290-9800; Fax: 718-920-9896. Diane Prusinski, S.M., Dir. Bed Capacity 28; Total Assisted Annually 2,100; Total Staff 25.

Sisters of Charity Health Care System Corp. Tel: 1-8-0-2-7-34. Web: www.schsi.org. 75 Vanderbilt Ave., Staten Island, 10304. Tel: 718-354-5080. Web: http://www.schcs.com. Bed Capacity 866; Total Annually Assisted 29,794; Total Staff 4,000.

Bayley Seton Campus Tel: 718-354-6000; Fax: 718-876-1234.

St. Vincent's Medical Center of Richmond

Saint. Vincent Catholic Medical Centers of New York, Formerly St. Vincents Catholic Medical Centers of New York, 130 W. 12 St., 10011. Tel: 212-604-7554; 212-604-2300; Fax: 212-604-7533. Email: mackermann@svcmcny.org. Web: svcmc.org. David J. Cambell, Pres. & CEO; Mark Ackermann, Contact Person. Bed Capacity 2,083; Total Assisted Annually 600,000; Total Staff 11,393.

St. Vincent's Manhattan, 153 West 11th St., 10011.

St. Vincent's Staten Island, 355 Bard Ave., Staten Island, 10310. Tel: 718-876-2413; Fax: 718-876-2293.

Bayley Seton Campus, 75 Vanderbilt Ave., Staten Island, 10304. Tel: 718-354-6000; Fax: 718-354-6011.

Mary Immaculate, 152-11 89th Ave., Jamaica, 11432. Tel: 718-558-2000; Fax: 718-558-2425.

St. John's Queens, 90-02 Queens Blvd., Elmhurst, 11373. Tel: 718-558-1000; Fax: 718-558-1818.

St. Joseph's, 158-40 79th Ave., Flushing, 11366. Tel: 718-558-6200; Fax: 718-558-6209.

St. Mary's Brooklyn, 170 Buffalo Ave., Brooklyn, 11213. Tel: 718-221-3000; Fax: 718-221-3971.

St. Vincent's Westchester, 275 North St., Harrison, 10528. Tel: 914-967-6500; Fax: 914-925-5157.

BEACON. *St. Francis Hospital*, 11 Hastings Dr., 12508. Tel: 845-838-4500; Fax: 845-831-8131. Email: CDeFreest@SFHHC.org. Web: saintfrancishospital.com. Constance DeFreest, M.S., R.N. This Facility is a 100 bed facility for the treatment of chemical dependency, and is a division of St. Francis Hospital, North Rd., Poughkeepsie, NY. Bed Capacity 100; Total Assisted Annually 2,050; Total Staff 148.

KINGSTON. *Benedictine Hospital*, 105 Mary's Ave., 12401. Tel: 914-338-2500; Fax: 914-334-3149. Web: www.benedictine.org. Sisters Mary Feehan, O.S.B., Senior Vice Pres., Mission Effectiveness; Mary Dorothy Huggard, O.S.B., Dir., Pastoral Care. Sisters of St. Benedict (Federation of St. Scholastica) 4; Capacity 222; Patients Assisted Annually 75,212; Total Staff 940.

PORT JERVIS. *Bon Secours Community Hospital*, 160 E. Main St., 12771. Tel: 845-858-7000; Fax: 845-858-7415. Email: TBrunelle@TSHS.org. Web: www.bonsecourscommunityhosp.org. Thomas R. Brunelle, Exec. Vice Pres. & Admin. Capacity 141; SNF Beds 46; Patients Assisted Annually 77,444; Total Staff 491.

POUGHKEEPSIE. *St. Francis Hospital*, 241 North Rd., 12601. Tel: 845-483-5000; Fax: 845-485-3762. Web: www.saintfrancishospital.com. Robert L. Savage, Pres. & CEO; Revs. Thomas Heffernan, Dir. Pastoral Care; Thomas Heffernan; Emagalir Zeverin, Pastoral Care Assoc. Sisters of St. Francis of Hastings-on-Hudson Capacity 295.

St. Francis Health Care Foundation, 241 North Rd., 12601. Tel: 845-431-8707; Fax: 845-483-5097.

Saint Francis Hospital, Beacon, 11 Hastings Dr., Beacon, 12538. Tel: 845-831-8131; Fax: 845-838-4500. Constance DeFreest, Admin. Capacity (Certified Beds) 100; OP Visits 280,260; Admissions 9,886; Total Staff 1,520.

SUFFERN. *Good Samaritan Hospital of Suffern* 10901. Tel: 845-368-5000; Fax: 845-368-5430. Web: www.GoodSamHosp.org. Dominick Stanzione, CEO, Bon Secours Charity Health System; Sr. Margaret Strauch, S.S.N.D., Dir. Pastoral Care; Revs. George Mattioni, O.A.R., Chap.; Francis A. Cregan, O.A.R., Chap.; Sr. Sheila M. Mullins, O.P., Chap. Sisters of Charity of St. Elizabeth 2; Capacity 370; Patients Assisted Annually 165,000; Total Staff 1,575.

WARWICK. *St. Anthony Community Hospital, Inc.* Franciscan System of Warwick, Inc. , 15-19 Maple Ave., 10990. Tel: 845-986-2276; Fax: 845-986-2687. Leah Cerkvenik, R.N., EVP; Pam Corbett, Dir. Pastoral Care; Rev. Joseph McAndrew, Chap. Capacity 73; Patients Assisted Annually 34,262.

WHITE PLAINS. *St. Agnes Hospital and Children's Rehabilitation Center*, 305 North St., 10605. Tel: 914-681-4500; Fax: 914-681-4974. Email: JSalandra@chcsnet.org. Web: www.saintagneshospital.com. Thomas Dee, Pres. & CEO; Sr. Mary Virginia, R.D.C., Dir. Pastoral Care. Capacity 184; Children's Rehabilitation Center 66,360; Hospital 31,879; Total Staff 765.

YONKERS. *St. Joseph's Medical Center*, 127 S. Broadway, 10701. Tel: 914-378-7000; Fax: 914-965-4838. Email: public.relations@saintjosephs.org. Web: saintjosephs.org. Mr. Michael J. Spicer, Pres.; Rev. Thomas Murphy, O.F.M.Cap.; Sr. Dolores Doyle, Dir. of Pastoral Care. Bed Capacity 394; Nursing Home Beds 200; Sisters of Charity of St. Vincent de Paul 7; Patients Assisted Annually 359,714; Total Staff 1,278.

[Y] SPECIAL HOSPITALS AND SANATORIA FOR INVALIDS

NEW YORK. *Calvary Hospital* For advanced cancer patients. Tel: 718-863-6900; Fax: 718-518-2674. Email: DLattarulo@cavalryhospital.org. Web: www.cavalryhospital.org. 1740 Eastchester Rd., Bronx, 10461. Tel: 718-863-6900; Fax: 718-518-2674. Frank A. Calamari, Exec. Dir.; Rev. Msgr. Michael J. Alessandro, Chap. (Retired); Eileen Pesek, Asst. Admin. & Dir. Pastoral Svcs. Pastoral Staff 16; Accommodations for 225; Patients Assisted Annually 3,300.

St. Rose's Home Free home for incurable cancer patients. , 71 Jackson St., 10002. Tel: 212-677-8132; Fax: 212-982-3485. Email: maureendominican@verizon.net. Sisters Maureen, O.P., Supr.; Mary Joseph, O.P., Admin.; Rev. Francis R. Mullin, O.P., Chap.

Legal Title: *The Servants of Relief for Incurable Cancer* Dominican Sisters of the Congregation of St. Rose of Lima 8; Bed Capacity 35; Patients Assisted Annually 60.

Terence Cardinal Cooke Health Care Center, 1249 Fifth Ave., 10029. Tel: 212-360-1000; Fax: 212-289-2739. Email: tcchcc@chcsnet.org. Web: www.catholichealthcaresystem.org/tcc. Mr. James D. Cameron, Pres. & CEO. Hospital for developmentally disabled. Bed Capacity 50.

Developmental Disabilities Clinic, 1249 Fifth Ave., 10029. Tel: 212-360-3703; Fax: 212-360-3842. Comprehensive Outpatient medical, therapeutic and educational services. On site and off site OMRDD Article 16 services. Patients Assisted Annually 44,000.

Hemodialysis, 1249 Fifth Ave., 10029. Tel: 212-360-3860; Fax: 212-860-3862. 22 End Stage Renal Dialysis Stations; (For information concerning nursing home see Homes for Aged category.) Patients Assisted Annually 22,000.

BRONX. *St. Eleanora's Home for Convalescents*, Sisters of Charity Center, 6301 Riverdale Ave., 10471. Tel: 718-549-9200, Ext. 240; Fax: 718-884-3013. Email: dsmith@scny.org. Web: scny.org. Total Assisted Annually 100; Total Staff 10.

HARRISON. *St. Vincent's Hospital and Medical Center Westchester Branch*, 275 North St., 10528. Tel: 914-967-6500; Fax: 914-925-5157. Web: www.svvmc.org. Brian L. Fitzsimmons, Ph.D. Psychiatric Hospital.; Clergy Consultation Program; Women Religious Program.; Services for pre/postpartum women. Inpatient and outpatient mental health and substance abuse services for adults, adolescents, children and their families. Sites in Harrison, Tuckahoe and Hawthorne. Services available in Spanish. Capacity 133; Patients Assisted Annually 2,891; Sisters of Charity of St. Vincent de Paul 3; All outpatient program admissions 4,452; Partial Hospital 270; Methadone Maintenance Treatment Program 43.

HAWTHORNE. *Rosary Hill Home* Free home for incurable cancer patients. , 10532. Tel: 914-769-0114; Fax: 914-769-3916. Web: www.hawthorne.dominicans.org. Sisters Mary Brigid, O.P, Admin.; Mary Damien, O.P., Supr. Legal Title: *The Servants of Relief for Incurable Cancer* Professed Sisters of St. Dominic 24; Capacity 72; Patients Assisted Annually 183.

[Z] ORDERS OF NURSING SISTERS

NEW YORK. *Little Sisters of the Assumption Family Health Service, Inc.*, 426 E. 119th St., 10035. Tel: 212-987-4422; Fax: 212-987-4430. Email: lsafhs@mindspring.com. Sr. Judith Garson, Exec. Dir.

BRONX. *Convent of the Sisters Servants of Mary S.M.* Mission: Private nursing in the homes. , 3305 Country Club Rd., 10465-1296. Tel: 718-829-0428; Fax: 718-829-2346. Sr. Ema Munoz. Sisters 22.

OSSINING. *Dominican Sisters Family Health Services, Inc. (Central Services/Administration)* Community-based, certified, voluntary Home Health Agency and Long Term Home Health Care and AIDS Programs serving all of Westchester, Suffolk and the South Bronx. , 299 N. Highland Ave., 10562. Tel: 914-941-1710; Fax: 914-941-0518. Email: VHanrahan@dsfhs.org. Web: www.dsfhs.org; www.DominicanSistersFamilyHealthService.org. Sisters Virginia Hanrahan, O.P., B.S.N., M.S., Ph.D., Pres. & CEO; Margaret Flood, O.P., B.S.N., M.A., M.P.A., COO.

Bronx Office, 279 Alexander Ave., Bronx, 10454. Tel: 718-665-6557; Fax: 718-292-9113. Email: PSweeney@dsfhs.org. Margaret Sweeney, B.S.N., M.S.N., Admin.

Westchester Office, 299 N. Highland Ave., 10562. Tel: 914-941-1654; Fax: 914-941-1556. Email: EBobh@dsfhs.org. Evelyn Bobb, B.S.N., M.P.A., Admin.

Suffolk County Offices (3 Offices in Suffolk), 103-6 W. Montauk Hwy., Box 209, Hampton Bays, 11946. Tel: 631-728-0181; Fax: 631-728-2943. Email: pash@dsfhs.org.

Box 866, Amagansett, 11930. Tel: 631-267-1090; Fax: 631-728-2943. Email: pash@dsfhs.org. Pamella Ash, B.S.N., M.A., Admin., Suffolk Offices.

**Family Home Health Care, Inc.*, 65 S. Broadway, Tarrytown, 10591. Diane Ozure, Admin.

STATEN ISLAND. *Pax Christi Hospice* Hospice and Home Care Services for the terminally ill. Sisters of Charity Health Care System. , 355 Bard Ave., 10310. Tel: 718-876-1022; Fax: 718-876-1803.

[AA] NURSING HOMES

NEW YORK. *Cabrini Center for Nursing & Rehabilitation*, 542 E. 5th St., 10009. Tel: 212-358-3000; Fax: 212-358-6269. Email: mdevlin@ccnr.cabrininy.org. Mary Devlin, Admin. Total SNF Beds 240; Total Staff 250.

Kateri Residence Skilled Nursing Care/Residential Health Care Facility for the Elderly. , 150 Riverside Dr., 10024-2201. Tel: 212-769-0744; 646-505-3500; Fax: 212-873-0658. Email: lbond@chcsnet.org. Web: www.catholichealthcaresystem.org/kateri. Lascelles L. Bond, Pres., CEO & Admin.; Robert G. Sussingham, Assoc. Admin.; Patricia E. Schneider, R.N., Ph.D., Asst. Admin.; Bruce L. Adler, CFO; Doris Hung, Controller; Wellington Y. Liu, M.D., Medical Dir.; Janet Levine, R.N., Dir., Nursing Svcs.; Agnes Hsu, R.N., Dir., Resident Assessment; Wanda Taylor, Dir. Admissions; Riva Gottesman, Dir., Medical Records; Lisa Orriola, Dir., Recreation Therapy; Mary B. Fisher, Dir., Volunteers & Devel.; Sisters Patricia Geoghegan, P.B.V.M., Dir. Pastoral Care; Miriam Poveda, R.S.H.M., Pastoral Care Assoc.; Padraic Mary McGuinness, O.P., Pastoral Care Assoc.; Linda Saisselin, Dir. of Social Services. Bed Capacity 520; Total Assisted Annually 1,323; Total Staff 632.

Mary Manning Walsh Home, 1339 York Ave., 10021. Tel: 212-628-2800; Fax: 212-585-3896. Email: mmwhome@msn.com. Sr. Sean William O'Brien, Admin.; Rev. Msgr. James J. Murray, Chap. Carmelite Sisters for the Aged and Infirm Total Staff 530; Total Assisted 362.

Terence Cardinal Cooke Health Care Center Skilled Nursing Facility. ; Skilled Nursing Facility AIDS Program. , 1249 Fifth Ave., 10029. Tel: 212-360-1000; Fax 212-289-2739. Email: tcchcc@chcsnet.org. Web: www.catholichealthcaresystem.org/tcc. Mr. James D. Cameron, Pres. & CEO. (See Special Hospitals Category for additional services offered from this Health Care Center.) Bed Capacity 523; Bed Capacity 153.

BRONX. *Bon Secours New York Health System, Inc.*, 2975 Independence Ave., 10463-4699. Tel: 718-548-1700; Fax: 718-601-3384. Email: nboccia@fhsny.org. Web: scherviercares.org. Jeanne Lee, CEO; Sr. Sheila Moroney, P.B.V.M., Dir. of Pastoral Care.
Legal Title *Schervier Nursing Care Center*
Legal Title: *Frances Schervier Housing Development Fund Corporation*

Bon Secours Health System, Inc., 1505 Marriottsville Rd, Marriottsville, MD 21104. Tel 410-442-5511; Fax 410-442-1082. Total Staff 565.

Jeanne Jugan Residence, 2999 Schurz Ave., P.O. Box 1002, 10465. Tel: 718-464-1800; Fax: 718-464-0254. Email: psbklynlsp@attgolbal.net. Sr. Bernice Marie Wall, L.S.P., Pres.

Medical Missionaries of Mary, 563 Minneford Ave., 10464-1118. Tel: 718-885-0945; Fax: 718-885-0010. Email: mmmci@aol.com. Web: www.mmmusa.org. Sisters Margaret Quinn, M.M.M., Congregational Leader; Siobhan Corkery, M.M.M., Zonal Coord. of the Americas.

St. Patrick's Home for the Aged and Infirm, 66 Van Cortlandt Park S., 10463. Tel: 718-519-2800; Fax: 718-519-2817. Email: www.admissions@stpatrickshome.org. Web: www.stpatrickshome.org/. Sr. M. Patrick Michael, O.Carm., Admin.; Rev. James Larkin, M.S.A. (NOR), Chap. Carmelite Sisters for the Aged and Infirm Sisters 16; Bed Capacity 264; Total Assisted Annually 429; Total Staff 350.

Providence Rest, 3304 Waterbury Ave. 10465. Tel: 718-931-3000; Fax: 718-863-0185. Email: providencerest@aol.com. Web: www.providencerest.org. Sisters Seline Mary Flores, Admin.; Margaret Mary. Sisters of St. John the Baptist 20; Bed Capacity 200; Total Assisted 180; Total Staff 300.

St. Vincent de Paul Residence, 900 Intervale Ave., 10459. Tel: 917-645-9200; Fax: 718-589-7010. Email: fcianciotto@chcsnet.org. Web: www.svdpres.org. Mr. Frank Cianciotto, CEO.

DOBBS FERRY. *St. Cabrini Nursing Home*, 115 Broadway, 10522. Tel: 914-693-6800; Fax: 914-693-1731. Patricia Krasnausky, Pres. & CEO; Rev. Edwin Robinson, O.F.M., Dir. Pastoral Care. Missionary Sisters of the Sacred Heart 5; Bed Capacity 304; Home Health Care 250; Total Staff 450.

Cabrini Home Care, 115 Brodway, 10522. Tel: 914-693-6800, Ext. 500. Email: pkrasnau@ccnr.cabrininy.org. Patricia Krasnausky, Contact Person.

MIDDLETOWN. *St. Teresa's Nursing Home*, 120 Highland Ave., 10940. Tel: 914-342-1033; Fax: 914-344-5631. Email: jwallace@chcsnet.org. Bed Capacity 98; Total Assisted 98; Total Staff 120.

RHINEBECK. *Ferncliff Nursing Home*, 21 Ferncliff Dr., 12572. Tel: 845-876-2011; Fax: 845-876-4810. Sr. M. Bernadette Therese Reilly, Admin.; Rev. Peter J. Smith, Chap. Carmelite Sisters for the Aged and Infirm Bed Capacity 328; Total Assisted 400; Total Staff 450.

STATEN ISLAND. *Carmel Richmond Healthcare and Rehabilitation Center*, Formerly Carmel Richmond Nursing Home, Inc., 88 Old Town Rd., 10304-4299. Tel: 718-979-5000; Fax: 718-979-8027. Sr. Maureen T. Murray, O.Carm., Pres. & CEO; Rev. Eric Kyle, O.F.M., Chap. Carmelite Sisters for the Aged and Infirm Bed Capacity 300.

Friends of Carmel Richmond, Inc. Tel: 718-979-5000; Fax: 718-979-8027. Total Assisted 330; Total Staff 352.

WARWICK. *Villa Frances at the Knolls* Franciscan Health Partner, Inc. , 22 Van Duzer Pl., 10990. Tel: 914-987-5717; Fax: 914-986-1231. Leah Cerkvenik, Exec. Vice Pres., Warwick Campus; Rev. Joseph McAndrew, Chap. Capacity 120.

[BB] ADULT RESIDENCES

NEW YORK. *St. Agnes' Residence* For students and working women. , 237 W. 74th St., 10023. Tel: 212-874-1361. Sr. Mary Pius Friel, R.S.M., Admin. Franciscan Fathers of St. Francis Monastery. Daughters of Mary of the Immaculate Conception 2; Accommodations for 99; Total Assisted 101; Total Staff 6.

Centro Maria, Inc. For young students and working women. , 539 W. 54th St., 10019. Tel: 212-581-5273; Fax: 212-307-5687. Email: cenmariany@mindspring.com. Web: www.religiosasdemariaimmaculada. Sr. Clara Echeverria, R.M.I., Supr. Religious of Mary Immaculate 6; Bed Capacity 54.

Cor Mariae, c/o 1011 First Ave., Rm. 1130, 10022. Tel: 212-371-1000, Ext. 2435. Residence for formerly homeless senior women.

The Dwelling Place For homeless women. , 409 W. 40th St., 10018. Tel: 212-564-7887; Fax: 212-695-3642. Email: thedwellingplace@juno.com. Sr. Nancy Chiarello, O.S.F., Admin. Shelter: 15; Dinner Program: 60; Total Assisted: 22,000; Total Staff: 5.

El Carmelo Residence, 249 W. 14th St., 10011. Tel: 212-242-8224. Sr. Modesta Perez, Supr.

The Jeanne d'Arc Residence Women 18 to 40. , 253 W. 24th St., 10011. Tel: 212-989-5952; Fax: 212-691-0257. Email: sramenke@yahoo.com. Sr. Rose Ann Menke, Admin. Women 18 to 40. Accommodations for 140; Sisters of Divine Providence 8; Lay Staff 11.

St. Joseph's Immigrant Home For students and working women. , 425 W. 44th St., 10036-4402. Tel: 212-246-5363. Sr. Mary Celine, D.M., Admin. Daughters of Mary of the Immaculate Conception 2; Accommodations for 90.

Kolping Society of New York Men's Residence (Catholic Kolping Society New York, Inc.) For young Catholic men. , 165 E. 88th St., 10128. Tel: 212-369-6647; Fax: 212-987-5652. Email: residence@kolpingny.org. Ernst Endrich, Mgr. Total in Residence 88; Total Staff 11.

The Leo House For the Clergy, Sisters & Laity. , 332 W. 23rd St., 10011. Tel: 212-929-1010; Fax: 212-366-6801. Thomas E. Freeburn, Exec. Dir. Senior Citizens in Residence 2; Total Staff 36; Catholic Hotel for Travelers 9,352.

St. Mary's Residence For students and young working women. , 225 E. 72nd St., 10021. Tel: 212-249-6850; Fax: 212-249-4336. Email: St.MarysRes72@aol.com. Sr. M. Perpetua Kodba, F.D.C., Admin.; Mrs. Lisa Rodriguez, Dir. of Admissions. Daughters of Divine Charity 6; Accommodations for 147.

Padre Pio Shelter for Homeless Men, 419 E. 155th St., Bronx, 10455. Tel: 718-292-3713. Email: www.franciscanfriars.com. Bros. Shawn O'Connor, C.F.R., Dir.; Dominic Miriam Bormans, C.F.R., Asst. Dir.; Pier Giorgio Lobiudice, Asst. Dir. Total Assisted 18.

Sacred Heart Residence Working or studying young ladies ages 19-29. , 432 W. 20th St., 10011. Tel: 212-929-5790; Fax: 212-924-0891. Email: sacredheartresidence@hotmail.com. Sr. Rocio Campana, Admin. Congregation of Mothers of the Helpless Capacity 30; Total Staff 3.

Thorpe Family Residence, Inc., 2252 Crotona Ave., 10457. Tel: 718-933-7312; Fax: 718-933-7311. Email: SrBarbTFR@aol.com. Web: www.bronxmall.com/com/thorpe. Sr. Barbara Lenniger, O.P., Exec. Dir. Residents 65; Total Assisted 130; Total Staff 12.

The Crotona-Thorpe Housing Development Fund Corporation Tel: 914-359-6400; Fax: 914-359-6503. Sr. Muriel Cooney, O.P., Pres. (Sub of Thorpe Family Residence, Inc.),

BRONX. *Kolping-on-Concourse*, 2916 Grand Concourse, 10458. Tel: 718-733-6119. Jorge Paris, Mgr. (Catholic Kolping Society New York, Inc.) Total in Residence 96; Total Staff 11.

DOBBS FERRY. *Cabrini Housing Development Fund Corporation*, c/o of St. Cabrini Nursing Home, Inc., 115 Broadway, 10522. Tel: 914-693-6800, Ext. 500. Email: pkrasnau@ccnr.cabrininy.org.

GARRISON. *St. Christopher's Inn* Temporary shelter for homeless men. , P.O. Box 150, 10524-0150. Tel: 914-424-3616; Fax: 914-424-3786. Email: bpalka@atonementfriars.org. Web: atonementfriars.org. Rev. Bernard Palka, S.A., Pres. & CEO. Atonement Friars Total Assisted 1,200; Total Staff 52.

MONTROSE. *Kolping-on-Hudson* (Catholic Kolping Society New York, Inc.) , 95 Montrose Point Rd., 10548. Tel: 914-737-9547. Total Assisted 2,000; Total Staff 10.

MOUNT VERNON. *St. Theresa's Residence*, 30 S. 10th Ave., 10550. Tel: 914-664-5900; Fax: 914-664-6733. John Schroeder, Exec. Dir. Bed Capacity 12.

[CC] CATHOLIC CAMPS

NEW YORK. *The Catholic Camp Association Inc.*, 1011 First Ave., Room 1287, 10022. Tel: 212-371-1000.
John V. Mara CYO Camps, Putnam Valley, 10579.
Hill Camp Capacity 120.
Valley Camp Capacity 120; Total Assisted 147; Total in Residence 271; Total Staff 48.

THORNWOOD. *Challenge NA, Inc.*, 582 Columbus Ave., 10594. Tel: 914-749-3900; Fax: 914-749-3939. Bro. Alexander Kim, L.C., Contact Person.

[DD] COMMUNITY CENTERS

NEW YORK. *Cardinal Spellman Center, Inc.*, 137 E. Second St., 10009. Tel: 212-677-6600; Fax: 212-995-8537. Mr. Thomas Rosati, Dir. All Centers are engaged in full-time recreational and educational activities.; Serves Lower East Side parishes and includes Cardinal Spellman Headstart and Catholic Charities. Lower East Side office for Parish and Community Outreach. Total Staff 35; Total Assisted 1,550.
Casita Maria Inc., 928 Simpson St., Bronx, 10459. Tel: 718-589-2230; Fax: 718-842-4622. Email: casitam@aol.com. Web: www.casitamaria.org. Lue Ann Eldar, Exec. Dir. & CEO; Mrs. Jacqueline Weld, Chm. Serves the Bronx and East Harlem.; Casita Maria serves over 10,000 individuals each year through after-school programs, social services, senior citizen centers, homebound seniors and recreation programs.
Casita Maria-Carver Community Center, 55 E. 102nd St., 10029. Cristina Toosie, Exec. Dir.; Orlando Tomas Martinez, Dir. Serves Carver Houses and adjacent areas of East Harlem.
Drew-Hamilton CYO Center, 220 W. 143rd St., 10030. Serves Central Harlem.
Lieut. Joseph P. Kennedy, Jr. Memorial Community Center, 34 W. 134th St., 10037. Mr. Les Edwards, Exec. Dir. Serves Central Harlem. Serves 200 youth in afternoon and after-school programs and 500 teenagers in evening programs.
Life Experience and Faith Sharing Association, 149 E. 117th St., 10035. Tel: 212-996-7303; Fax: 212-828-5904. Email: lefslitera@aol.com. James Addison, LEFS Team; Timothy Dunnington, LEFS Team; Sr. Dorothy Gallant, S.C., LEFS Team; Vaughn McLamb, LEFS Team; Ann Quintano, LEFS Team; Jimmie Robinson, LEFS Team; Sisters Cecilia Palange, S.C.I.M., LEFS Team; Rosemary O'Donnell, S.C., LEFS Team; Ralph Thomas, LEFS Team; Godfrey Xaba, LEFS Team; Stephany Veluz, LEFS Team. Total Assisted 1,500.
Staten Island CYO Center, Tel: 718-420-1010. Serves residents of Port Richmond and surrounding areas.
120 Anderson Ave., Port Richmond, Staten Island, 10302. Tel: 718-273-8361. Frances M. Mitilieri, Dir.

NYACK. *Catholic Community Services of Rockland, Inc.*, 33 Jefferson St., 10960. Tel: 845-353-7540; 845-353-5562; Fax: 845-353-7360. Email: rockcath@aol.com. Rev. Edward J. Weber, Chm. Provides emergency services to those in need.

YONKERS. *Casa Juan Diego, Inc.*, 97 Yonkers Ave., 10701. Tel: 914-476-7279. Bro. Francis Mary Roaldi, C.F.R. Services to the needy; especially Spanish Speaking immigrants, day laborers.

[EE] MONASTERIES AND RESIDENCES OF PRIESTS AND BROTHERS

NEW YORK. *All Saints Friary* (Order of Friars Minor-The Franciscans-Province of the Most Holy Name of Jesus) , 47 E. 129th St., 10035. Tel: 212-534-3535; Fax: 212-987-1930. Bro. Charles F. Gilmartin, O.F.M.; Revs. Christopher B. Keenan, O.F.M.; Neil O'Connell, O.F.M.; Bro. Daniel P. Sulmasy, O.F.M.
"America;" Residence and publication office of the America Press, 106 W. 56th St., 10019. Tel: 212-581-4640; Fax: 212-399-3596. Email: jesuits@americamagazine.org. Web: www.americamagazine.org. Revs. Robert A. Mitchell, S.J., Supr.; Thomas J. Reese, S.J., Editor-in-Chief; Andrew J. Christiansen, S.J.; Robert C. Collins, S.J.; James J. DiGiacomo, S.J.; John W. Donohue, S.J.; D. James French, S.J.; John J. Gallen, S.J.; Dennis Linehan, S.J.; John F. Long, S.J.; James J. Martin, S.J.; Carlos Novoa, S.J.; Eugene J. O'Brien, S.J.; Frederick J. O'Brien, S.J.; Leo J. O'Donovan, S.J.; Joseph A. O'Hare, S.J.; Vincent T. O'Keefe, S.J.; Robert E. O'Toole, S.J. (STL); Michael E. Sehler, S.J.; Thomas R. Slon, S.J.; Charles M. Whelan, S.J.; Bro. Francis W. Turnbull, S.J. Priests 21; Brothers 1.
Apostolic Society of the Crusade of the Holy Spirit, Blessed Kateri Rectory, 1810 Rte. 82, Lagrangeville, 12540-6095. Tel: 845-227-1457 Crusade; 845-227-1710 (Rectory); Fax: 845-227-1734. Email: CrusadeHSp@aol.com. Web: www.holyspiritcrusade.org. Revs. Ignatius Peries, C.H.S. (Argentina), Dir. Gen., Argentina; Bernard Kelly, C.H.S. (England), Vicar Gen., U.K.; Nimal Mendis, C.H.S., Asst. Gen., Sec. Gen. & Treas. Gen., U.S.A.; Edwin Torres, C.H.S. (Argentina), Sec. Gen., Argentina.
Atonement Friars, 138 Waverly Pl., 10014-3845. Tel: 212-243-4692; Fax: 212-675-6160. Web: www.atonementfriars.org. Rev. Elias D. Mallon, S.A.; Bro. William Martyn, S.A.; Revs. James Loughran, S.A.; Charles Sharon, S.A., Admin.; Henry Marchese, S.A.
Augustinian Recollects Provincial Residence, Province of St. Nicholas of Tolentine, 2800 Schurz Ave., 10465. Tel: 718-823-0460; Fax: 718-239-9554. Email: snezequiel@aol.com. Rev. Francisco Legarra, O.A.R., Delegate.
Legal Title: *The Province of St. Nicholas of Tolentine of the Augustinian Recollect*
Brothers of the Christian Schools of Manhattan College, Inc. Tel: 718-884-0613; Fax: 718-884-3500. 4415 Post Rd., Bronx, 10471. Tel: 718-884-0613; Fax: 718-884-3500. Bros. Kenneth Fitzgerald, F.S.C., Dir.; Luke Salm, F.S.C., Sub Dir.; Anthony Flynn, F.S.C., Sub Dir.; Thomas Scanlan, F.S.C., Pres. Total Staff 9; Total in Residence 30. In Res. Rev. Rinaldo Borzaga, F.S.C.A.
Calasanzian Fathers (Piarists), 88 Convent Ave., 10027. Tel: 212-234-1919; Fax: 212-281-7205. Email: frfelix@mail.con2.com. Revs. Felix Jimenez, Sch.P.; Jose M. Clavero, Sch.P. (Spain); Felix Ganuza, Sch.P.
St. Catherine of Siena Priory, 411 E. 68th St., 10021. Tel: 212-988-8300; Fax: 212-988-6918. Email: stcatsiena@aol.com. Revs. Christopher Johnson, O.P., Prior; Vincent Ferrer McHenry, O.P.; John Jerome Conroy, O.P.; David Aloysius Butler, O.P., Subprior; John Thaddeus Murphy, O.P.; Robert Philip Fitzsimmons, O.P.; George Lawrence Concordia, O.P.; Scott Matthew Erickson, O.P.
St. Clare Friary, 440 W. 36th St., 10018-6326. Tel: 212-594-4108; Fax: 212-563-0787. Email: sground440@aol.com. Web: www.solidgroundministry.com. Rev. James E. Goode, O.F.M., Ph.D., Guardian; Bro. Pius Abooki, B.S.C.L., Instructor, Cardinal Hayes High School; Harold Williams Jr., Affiliate, Solid Ground Prog. Coord.; Carmela Rodriguez, Affiliate, Confraternity of Solid Ground; James P. Newson Jr., Black Catholic Apostolate for Life Coord.
Shrine of Saint Josephine Bakhita Tel: 212-868-1847; Fax: 212-563-0787. In the Holy Mother of God Chapel
Solid Ground Ministry: A Franciscan Ministry with African American Families Tel: 212-868-1847; Fax: 212-563-0787.
National Black Catholic Apostolate for Life Tel: 212-594-4108; Fax: 212-563-0787. Web: www.blackcatholicsforlife.org.
St. Crispin Friary
Franciscan Friars of the Renewal, 420 E. 156th St., Bronx, 10455. Tel: 718-665-2441; Fax: 718-993-4754. Revs. Robert Lombardo, C.F.R., Local Servant; Angelus M. Houle, C.F.R.; Benedict J. Groeschel, C.F.R. Priests 3; Brothers 6.
Saint Francis Monastery, Inc., 135W. 31 St., 10001. Tel: 212-736-8500. Rev. Peter Brophy, O.F.M., Contact Person.
Franciscan Friars, Order of Friars Minor, Holy Name Province, Holy Name Province Provincialate, 158 W. 27th St., 6th Fl., 10001-6206. Tel: 212-924-1451; Fax: 646-201-9620. Email: hnp@hnp.org. Web: www.hnp.org. Revs. John M. Felice, O.F.M., Prov. Min.; Charles J. Miller, O.F.M., Prov. Vicar.
Legal Title: *Franciscan Friars, Order of Friars Minor of the Province of the Most Holy Name*
Priests of the Province in Residences not listed elsewhere:
Seton Hall University, 400 S. Orange Ave., South Orange, NJ 07079-2696. Tel: 973-761-9770. Rev. David M. Bossman, O.F.M.
Bethany Ministries, Box 420, 26C Mill Ln., Middleburgh, 12122-0420. Tel: 518-827-4699. Rev. Peter S. Chepaitis, O.F.M.
Holy Name College, 1650 St. Camillus Dr., Silver Spring, MD 20903. Tel: 301-408-3918; Fax: 301-434-4624. Rev. Russel Murray, O.F.M.
4165 Eaton St., Denver, CO 80212-7306. Tel: 303-936-9738; Fax: 303-936-6250. Rev. Joseph Ganssle, O.F.M.
Catholic Theological Union, 5401 S. Cornell Ave., Chicago, IL 60615-5608. Tel: 773-753-5315; Fax: 773-324-4360. Rev. Depaul A. Genska, O.F.M.
FrancisCare, Elmwood Park Plaza, 475 Market St., Elmwood Park, NJ 07407-3104. Tel: 201-791-1499; Fax: 201-791-3529. Rev. J. Patrick Kelly, O.F.M.
St. Agnes Rectory, 143 E. 43 St., 10017-4065. Tel: 212-682-5722; Fax: 212-370-5791. Rev. Venant Lalonde, O.F.M.
St. Anthony Hermitage, 8817 Brys Drive, Tampa, FL 33635. Tel: 813-888-5616; Fax: 813-886-3624. Rev. Leonard Lencewicz, O.F.M.
850 Thomas Ln., Angola, 14006-9572. Tel: 716-549-7930. Rev. Rene F. Phillips, O.F.M.
Create Inc., 73 Lenox Ave., 10026. Tel: 212-663-1975; Fax: 212-663-1293. Rev. Benedict M. Taylor, O.F.M.
St. Anthony Church: 5 South Main, Helper, UT 84526. Tel: 435-472-5661; Fax: 435-472-3235. Rev. Edward C. Metzger, O.F.M.
Arzobispado de San Juan, P.O. Box 9021967, San Juan, PR 00902-1967. Tel: 787-725-4975; Fax: 787-723-4040. Rev. Alfonso D. Guzman, O.F.M.
Seminario del Espiritu Santo Espada: Casilla 2329, La Paz, Bolivia. Tel: 011-691-2-813-5045; Fax: 011-691-2-813-5045. Rev. Clement Comesky, O.F.M.
Military Chaplains:
Deputy Chief of Chaplains, 2 Naval Annex (Code NO97B), Washington, DC 20370-4000. Tel: 703-614-4043; Fax: 703-614-4725. Rev. Louis V. Iasiello, O.F.M.
3310 First Ave., Apt.7A, San Diego, CA 92103-5659. Tel: 619-260-3640. Rev. Alan Sullivan, O.F.M.
2510 E. 104th Ave., G2-1, Denver, CO 80233-4401. Tel: 303-450-6298; Fax: 303-452-7993. Rev. Conrad W. Loftus, O.F.M.
Preakness Hospital, Box V, Unit 1, Paterson, NJ 07509. Tel: 973-904-5000. Rev. Carmel Lluria, O.F.M.
Priests Abroad:
67 Chen-kund Rd., Sec. 3, Neihu Taipei 11410 Taiwan. Tel: 011-886-2-2-790-0000; Fax: 011-886-2-2-790-9537. Rev. Pius Liu, O.F.M.
34, Rue Roux Alpheran, Aix-En-Provence 13100, France. Tel: 011-33-4-4226-7789; Fax: 011-33-4-4226-7789. Rev. Howard O'Shea.
Vietnamese Franciscan Province, 03 Mai Thi Luu, Dakao, Quani, Tp Ho Chi Minh, Vietnam. Rev. Khoa Nguyen, O.F.M.
Catholic University, Curley Hall, Washington, DC 20064-0001. Tel: 202-319-5867; Fax: 202-238-1657. Rev. Alexander DiLella, O.F.M.
St. Mary's Hospital, 901 45th St., West Palm Beach, FL 33407. Tel: 561-881-2899. Rev. Emmett Mulligan, O.F.M.
All Saints, 47 E. 129 St., 10035. Tel: 212-534-3535. Rev. Neil O'Connell, O.F.M.
Comunidad de San Francisco, 1125 W. 35 St., Hialeah, FL 33012. Tel: 305-822-4367. Rev. John Anglin, O.F.M.
Our Lady Queen of Peace: 1911 Union Valley Rd., Hewitt, NJ 07421. Tel: 973-728-8162; Fax: 973-728-4650. Rev. Richard Mucowski, O.F.M. Solemnly Professed Priests (including 2 Bishops) 320; Brothers 74; Temporary Vows: Brothers 12; Clerics 4; Novices 8; Permanant Deacons 2; Affiliates 7.
Franciscan Province of the Immaculate Conception, 125 Thompson St., 10012. Tel: 212-674-4388; Fax: 212-533-8034. Revs. Robert M. Campagna, O.F.M., Min. Prov.; Patrick Boyle, O.F.M., Vicar Prov.; Armand Padula, O.F.M., Prov. Sec.; Louis D. De Tommaso, O.F.M., Prov. Treas.; Bro. Courtland Campbell, O.F.M., Prov. Promoter of Missions.
Legal Title: *Friars Minor of the Order of St. Francis, Incorporated, New York, 1871* Franciscan Province of the Immaculate Conception of New York City Priests 138; Brothers 27; Permanent Deacons 3; Bishops 4. In Res. Rev. Antonio Nardoianni, O.F.M.
Franciscan Mission Associates, 274-280 W. Lincoln Ave., Mt. Vernon, 10550. Tel: 914-664-5604; Fax: 914-664-3017. Ms. Madeline Bonnici, Exec. Dir.; Bro. Mark Brown, O.F.M., Dir. of Secular Franciscans.
St. Christopher Friary, 18 North Bennet, Street, Boston, MA 02113.
Pious League of Saint Anthony, 151 Thompson St., P.O. Box 489, 10013-0489. Tel: 212-674-4388; Fax: 212-533-8034.
Priests of the Province Abroad: Revs. Richard Martignetti, O.F.M.; Antonio Nardoianni, O.F.M.; Michael Della Penna, O.F.M.; Romano Almagno, O.F.M.
Pontificio Ateneo Antonianum, Via Merulana, 125, Rome 00185 Italy. Rev. Edwin Paniagua, O.F.M.
St. Saviour Monastery, POB 186, Jerusalem 91001 Israel.
Military Chaplains:
NAS Corpus Christi, 10651 E. Street, Corpus Christi, TX 78419-5000. Tel: 361-961-3751. Rev. Charles Soto, O.F.M.
Hunter Army Airfield, P.O. Box 42098, Savannah, GA 31409. Rev. Michael Travaglione, O.F.M.
Retired Military Chaplains:
1427 Ave. de las Adelsas, Encinatas, CA 92024. Tel: 619-436-5355. Rev. Edwin Bobrek, O.F.M.
Priests of the Province Residing Elsewhere: Rev. Sigmund Brambilla, O.F.M.
97 Franklin St., Northampton, MA 01060. Tel: 413-584-4482. Rev. Thaddeus Palmieri, O.F.M.
Mary Help of the Christians Church: 6281 N.W.

66th Way, Parkland, FL 33067. Tel: 954-752-2717. Rev. Clement Procopio, O.F.M.
306 S.18th St., Cottonwood, AZ 86326. Tel: 520-634-3490. Rev. Ciro Iodice, O.F.M.
1111 Langley St., Fall River, MA 02720. Tel: 508-679-2105. Rev. John Bucchino, O.F.M.
14 Stuyvesant Oval #5D, 10009. Tel: 212-228-8798. Rev. Ralph Di Pasquale, O.F.M.
2008 Crowberry Dr., Port St. Lucie, FL 34983. Tel: 407-871-1588.
On Sick Leave: Rev. Xavier Carnicelli, O.F.M.
St. Cabrini Nursing Home, 115 Broadway, Dobbs Ferry, 10552. Tel: 914-693-0798. Rev. Stephen Caforio, O.F.M.
St. Patrick's Manor Inc., 863 Central St., Framingham, MA 01701. Tel: 508-879-8000, Ext. 668. Bro. Anthony Dugas, O.F.M.
Ferncliff Nursing Home, 29 River Rd., Rhinebeck, 12572. Tel: 845-876-2011.
Residing in Canada:
Immaculate Conception Friary, 2 Richardson Ave., Toronto ON M6M 3R4 Canada. Tel: 416-651-1787; Fax: 416-651-7881. Revs. Blaise Tranchida, O.F.M.; Lawrence Parent, O.F.M.
St. Charles Borromeo Friary, 811 Lawrence Ave., Toronto ON M6A 1C3 Canada. Tel: 416-787-0369; Fax: 416-256-4466. Revs. Gregory E. Imbroll, O.F.M.; Michael D'Cruz, O.F.M.
St. Francis Friary, 72 Mansfield Ave., Toronto ON M6J 2B2 Canada. Tel: 416-536-8195; Fax: 416-531-6883. Revs. Gregory Botte, O.F.M.; Frederick Mazzarella, O.F.M.; Raymond Falzon, O.F.M.
St. Lawrence Friary, 2210 Lawrence Ave. E., Scarborough ON M1P 2P9 Canada. Tel: 416-759-9359; Fax: 416-759-6725. Rev. Ralph Paonessa, O.F.M.
St. Jane Frances de Chantal Friary, 2747 Jane St., Downsview ON M3L 2E8 Canada. Tel: 416-741-1463; Fax: 416-741-1469. Revs. Celestino Canzio, O.F.M.; Amedeo Nardone, O.F.M.
St. Jude Friary, 3265 Weston Rd., Weston ON M9M 2T9 Canada. Tel: 416-742-9072; Fax: 416-742-9081. Revs. Octavio Jose Salinas, O.F.M.; Nery Aguirre, O.F.M.
St. Francis Center for Religious, 208501 Hwy. #9, R.R. #8 (Mono Mills), Orangeville ON L9W 3T5 Canada. Tel: 519-941-1747; Fax: 519-941-6961. Bros. Philip Adamo, O.F.M.; Courtland Campbell, O.F.M.; Rev. James Wells, O.F.M.
St. Peter Friary, 100 Bainbridge Ave., Woodbridge ON L4L-3YL Canada. Tel: 905-851-3600; Fax: 905-856-0171. Revs. Claudio Moser, O.F.M.; Michael Corcione, O.F.M.
The Franciscan Vocation Ministry of Holy Name Province, 135 W. 31st St., 10001-3439. Tel: 212-924-1451; 800-677-7788; Fax: 646-201-9619. Email: vocations@hnp.org. Web: www.hnp.org/vocations. Rev. Francis J. DiSpigno, O.F.M., Dir., HNP Vocation Dir.
St. Ignatius Loyola Residence, 53 E. 83rd St., 10028. Tel: 212-288-6200; Fax: 212-606-3460. Revs. Thomas E. Smith, S.J., Rector; Thomas F. Denny, S.J., Min.; Arthur C. Bender, S.J.; Joseph T. Browne, S.J.; Bro. Paul C. Acer, S.J.; Revs. William J. Bergen, S.J.; Vincent L. Biagi, S.J.; Gerard E. Braun, S.J; Bro. John J. Campbell, S.J.; Revs. James R. Carney, S.J.; Kenneth J. Caufield, S.J.; Arthur A. Clarke, S.J.; James J. Curry, S.J.; Richard R. Galligan, S.J.; Donald G. Devine, S.J. (PAT); Mark C. Hallinan, S.J.; Timothy A. Healey, S.J.; Stephen N. Katsouros, S.J.; Anthony F. LaBau, S.J.; Joseph A. Latella, S.J.; Bro. Jerome P. Menkhaus, S.J.; Revs. Walter F. Modrys, S.J.; Robert E. O'Brien, S.J.; Daniel G. O'Hare, S.J.; Eugene J. Prior, S.J.; Thomas S. Prout, S.J.; Michael J. Sala, S.J.; William J. Scanlon, S.J.; Bro. Gilbert J. Scott, S.J.
Immaculate Conception Friary, 754 E. Gun Hill Rd., 10467. Tel: 212-653-2200. Revs. Robert Grix, O.F.M.Cap.; Pius Caccavalle, O.F.M.Cap.; Robert Yurgel, O.F.M.Cap.; Eric Hall, O.F.M.Cap. Capuchin Friars of the Province of the Stigmata of St. Francis Total Assisted 190; Total Staff 20; Priests 4; Brothers 2.
Jesuit Community at Fordham University, 441 E. Fordham Rd., 10458. Tel: 718-817-5322; Fax: 718-733-4456. Very Rev. Vincent J. Duminuco, S.J., Rector, Jesuit Communities of Loyola Hall and Cardinal Spellman Hall & Kohlmann.
Loyola Hall, Jesuit Community Tel: 718-817-5322; Fax: 718-733-4456. Revs. Edward F. Maloney, S.J., Supr.; David J. Casey, S.J., Min.; Joseph V. Dolan, S.J., Sub Min.; John D. Alexander, S.J.; Bro. Sebastian A. Boccabella, S.J.; Revs. John J. Conley, S.J.; Francis P. Canavan, S.J.; W. Norris Clarke, S.J.; G. Richard Dimler, S.J.; Robert R. Dobbins, S.J.; Edward T. Dowling, S.J.; Rev. Msgr. Charles J. Fahey (SY); Revs. Kizito S. Forbi, S.J.; Daniel J. Fitzpatrick, S.J.; L. Augustine Grady, S.J.; Thomas C. Hennessy, S.J.; Bro. Frank W. Jensen, S.J.; Revs. J. Raymond Johnson, S.J.; Robert G. Kelly, S.J., M.A.T.; John R. Keating, S.J.; Edward F.X. Kennedy, S.J.; George C. McCauley, S.J.; Gerald A. McCool, S.J.; Charles Moutenot, S.J.; Thomas Murphy, S.J.; Donald O'Brien, S.J.; Vincent M. Novak, S.J.; Ladislas Orsy, S.J.; Jung-Woo Park, S.J. (Korea, South); Louis B. Pascoe, S.J.; William L. Reilly, S.J.; Herbert W. Rogers, S.J.; James A. Sadowsky, S.J.; Bro. Gerard W. Schade, S.J. Revs. J. Francis Stroud, S.J.; Daniel J. Sullivan, S.J.
Jesuit Community, Kohlmann Hall Tel: 718-584-1638; Fax: 718-584-0760. Revs. Raymond M. Sweitzer, S.J.; John J. Scully, S.J., Min.; John J. Leonard, S.J., Sub Min.; Thomas G. Benz, S.J.; Michael P. Corcoran, S.J.; Robert G. Cregan, S.J.; Mallick J. Fitzpatrick, S.J.; Matthew C. Flood, S.J.; Joseph P. Parkes, S.J.; Stanley J. O'Konsky, S.J.; William J. O'Malley, S.J.; Charles D. Sullivan, S.J.
Cardinal Spellman Hall, Jesuit Community Tel: 718-817-5330; Fax: 718-817-5717. Revs. Daniel J. O'Brien, S.J., Min.; Gerald R. Blaszczak, S.J.; Dean P. Bechard, S.J.; Robert D. Cloney, S.J.; Martin Chase, S.J.; Joseph A. Currie, S.J. John B. Breslin, S.J.; Godehard Bruntrup, S.J. (Germany); Christopher M. Cullen, S.J.; Terence M. Curry, S.J.; His Eminence Avery Dulles, S.J.; Revs. John T. Dziedzicwicz, S.J.; Garrett J. Fitzgerald, S.J.; Robert R. Grimes, S.J.; Martin A. Hegyi, S.J. (Hungary) George Hunt, S.J.; Joseph W. Koterski, S.J.; Joseph T. Lienhard, S.J.; Nicholas D. Lombardi, S.J.; Mark S. Massa, S.J.; Gerard Reedy, S.J.; Richard J. Regan, S.J.; Jose Luis Salazar, S.J.; Michael E. Suarez, S.J.; Jeffrey P. von Arx, S.J.; William L. Wizeman, S.J. Priests 79; Brothers 3; Scholastics 1; Total in Residence 83.
Jesuit Provincial's Office, 39 E. 83rd St., 10028. Tel: 212-774-5500; Fax: 212-774-5510 Email: nykprov@nysj.org. Web: www.nysj.org. Very Rev. Gerald J Chojnacki, S.J., Prov.; Rev. Richard R. Galligan, S.J., Exec. Asst. to Prov.; Bro. John J. Cambell, S.J., Asst. Treas.; Sr. Nora M. Cronin, P.B.V.M., Asst. for Secondary Education; Revs. D. James French, S.J., Asst. for Formation for the Maryland & New York Provinces; Mark C. Hallinan, S.J., Asst. Social Min.; Bro. Gilbert J. Scott, S.J., Asst. to Prov.; Revs. J. Raymond Johnson, S.J., Prov. Treas., Auditor & American Rep. of the Missions of the Society of Jesus, Vatican City; William J. Scanlon S.J., Dir. Province Devel. Office; Thomas E. Smith, S.J., Asst. to the Prov. for the Intl. Apostolate; Robert E. Reiser, S.J., Vocation Dir. for Maryland & New York Provinces; James J. Yannarell, S.J., Province Health Care Coord.; Jose Ojeda, Office Manager; Mr. John R. Raslowsky; Jose Soyangco, Business Mgr.
Priests of the Province Abroad:
C.P. 6139, 00195 Rome Prati, Italy. Tel: 39-06-689-77447; Fax: 39-06-686-8214. Rev. James J. Bowes, S.J.
Pontificia Universita Gregoriana, Piazza della Pilotta 4, 00187 Rome, Italy. Tel: 39-06-6701-5452; Fax: 39-06-6701-5412. Rev. Michael P. Hilbert, S.J.
Pontifical Bible Institute, via della Pilotta 25, 00187 Rome, Italy. Tel: 39-06-69526-6126; Fax: 39-06-69526-6151. Rev. James L. Dugan, S.J.
Coll Bellarmino, Via del Seminario 120, 00186 Rome, Italy. Tel: 39-06-69527-6638; Fax: 39-06-6701-5413. Rev. Keith F. Pecklers, S.J.
Raimundus-Lullus Institute der Universitat-Freiburg, Frankenweg 20, Freiburg 79117 Germany. Tel: 49-761-203-2082. Rev. Charles H. Lohr, S.J.
Priests of the Province in Residences Not Listed Elsewhere:
10-01 162nd St., Apt. 5-D, Whitestone, 11357. Tel: 718-767-5895. Rev. Gerard H. Ettlinger, S.J.
1S 150 Spring Rd., Apt. 2E, Oakbrook Terrace, IL 60181. Tel: 630-833-0645; Fax: 708-756-6863. Rev. Edward J. Mally, S.J.
850 Hylan Blvd., Staten Island, 10305. Tel: 718-448-3980. Rev. John J. Gerhard, S.J.
2674 Valentine Ave., Apt., 1A, Bronx, 10458. Tel: 718-430-4940; Fax: 718-365-8650. Rev. Joseph P. Kane, S.J.
15107 Interlachen Dr., Apt. 722, Silver Spring, MD 20906. Tel: 301-438-3753. Rev. Gerard P. Bell, S.J.
St Regis P.O. Box 429, Hogansburg, 13655. Tel: 613-575-2066. Rev. George H. Belgarde, S.J.
Regis College, 567 Huron St., Toronto ON M5R 2R6 Canada. Tel: 416-960-0297. Rev Adelmo P. Dunghe, S.J.
P.O. Box 954, Rochester, MN 55903. Rev. Eugene J. Quigley, S.J.
370 First Ave., Apt. 12C, 10010. Tel: 646-215-5347. Rev. Walter J. Smith, S.J.
c/o Provincial's Office, 39 E. 83rd St., 10028. Rev. Michael E. Donahue, S.J.
Development Office of the New York Province, 39 E. 83rd St., 10028-0810. Tel: 212-734-1144; Fax: 212-794-1036. Email: development@nysj.org. Web: www.nysj.org. Revs. William J. Scanlon, S.J., Dir.; Gerard E. Braun, S.J; Anthony F. LaBau, S.J. a.k.a. Jesuit Seminary and Mission Bureau, Inc.
St. Joseph's Friary (Franciscan Friars of the Renewal) ; (Postulancy) , 523 W. 142nd St., 10031. Tel: 212-234-9089; Fax: 212-281-4355. Web: www.franciscanfriars.com. Revs. Richard Roemer, C.F.R., Local Servant & Postulant Dir.; Luke Mary Fletcher, C.F.R., Vocation Dir.; Bro. Peter Westall, C.F.R. Postulants 18.
The Little Brothers of the Gospel, 58 E. Fourth St., #10, 10003. Tel: 212-982-2431.
Maryknoll House Catholic Foreign Mission Society. , 121 E. 39th St., 10016. Tel: 212-697-4470; Fax: 212-697-4472. Email: mklnyc@aol.com. Web: www.maryknoll.org. Bro. Anthony Lopez, Dir.; Rev. Clyde Phillips.
Murray-Weigel Hall, 515 E. Fordham Rd., 10458-5004. Tel: 718-430-4900; Fax: 718-365-8650. Email: stevepug2@aol.com. Revs. Steven J. Pugliese, S.J., Min.; Roy A. Drake, S.J., Sub Min.; John D. Boyd, S.J.; Robert W. Dahlke, S.J.; Charles F.X. Dolan, S.J. (NEW); William B. Cogan, S.J.; Richard P. Grogan, S.J.; Eugene K. Culhane, S.J.; Herbert T. Kane, S.J.; Stephen V. Duffy, S.J.; Aidan C. McMullen (NEW); John L. Farrand, S.J.; Most Rev. Martin J. Neylon, S.J.; Revs. Robert J. Haskins, S.J.; Cornelius P. Hurley, S.J.; Joseph P. Kane, S.J.; Joseph V. Landy, S.J.; John M. McConnell, S.J.; James P. Jurich, S.J.; John J. McDonald, S.J., Supr. Community; Joseph E. Moltesz, S.J.; Louis A. Mounteer, S.J.; Edward J. Murphy, S.J.; John A. Nicholson, S.J.; Richard J. Pendergast, S.J.; Francis V. Rooney, S.J.; Peter J. Roslovich, S.J.; Gustav H. Schmidt, S.J.; Bernard E. Shannon, S.J.; Louis E. Soloman, S.J.; Patrick J. Sullivan, S.J.; Francis J. Tierney, S.J.; Richard F. Timone, S.J.; Francis P. Valentino, S.J.; James J. Wheeler, S.J.; Patrick T. Sullivan, S.J.; Robert H. Vogt, S.J.; Ladislas Cser, S.J.; John M. Doolan, S.J.; Joseph F. Fitzpatrick, S.J.; George J. McMahon, S.J.; Gerald J. McMahon, S.J.; Alfredo S. Quevedo, S.J.; Bro. Joseph J. Griffin, S.J. Priests 60; Brothers 6; Scholastic 1.
Scholastics: Mr. John S. Quigley, S.J.; Bros. Theodore C. Bender, S.J.; Ignatius J. Fitzroy, S.J.; Raymond V. Whalen, S.J.
Our Lady of Consolation Residence Tel: 718-548-0888; Fax: 718-548-7824.
3103 Arlington Ave., Corner of W. 231st St., Bronx, 10463. Tel: 718-548-0889; Fax: 718-548-7824. Mrs. Mary Lynch, R.N., Residence Coord.; Rev. Msgrs. Myles Bourke; Augustine Di Blasi; Joseph A. Dunne (Retired); Francis J. Glynn (Retired); Cyril Potocek; Joseph Quinn; Revs. John Cavanaugh; Aloysius Jenko (Retired); William E. Kelly (Retired); William Kennedy; John J. Maher (Retired); Matthew Mulloy (Retired); Eugene P. O'Hara; George Reinheimer; Thomas Tolentino; John B. Vala (Retired).
Padua Friary, 151 Thompson St., 10012. Tel: 212-254-9553; Fax: 212-254-9644. Revs. John R. Scarangello, O.F.M., Guardian, Instructor (Cathedral High Sch.); John-Marie Cassese, O.F.M., Chronicler; Marion Cascino, O.F.M.; Emmanuel Faraone, O.F.M., Parochial Ministry; Sebastian Buccellato, O.F.M., FMU Prom. & Parochial Ministry; Louis Troiano, O.F.M., Parochial Ministry; Adolph Giorda, O.F.M., Parochial Ministry; Louis D. De Tommaso, O.F.M., Provincial Treasurer; Bros. Giles Kelly, O.F.M., Dir. Spiritual Svcs. & Hazelden Center; Luke Storino, O.F.M., Prov. Bookkeeper; Paschal De Mattia, O.F.M., Provincial Curia Staff; Courtland Campbell, O.F.M., Secretary/Missions; Michael Joseph Recinelli, O.F.M., Provincial Curia Staff.
Pallottine Fathers, Society of the Catholic Apostolate, 448 E. 116th St., 10029. Tel: 212-534-0681; Fax: 212-534-0629. Revs. Peter J. Rofrano, S.A.C.; Severino Dominicis, S.A.C., Mt. Carmel Society & Catholic Apostolate Assoc.; Girolamo D'Ambrosi, S.A.C.; Tony Kelly, S.A.C., Spanish Apostolate. Total Assisted 300; Total Staff 15.
Passionist Spiritual Center, 5801 Palisade Ave., Riverdale, 10471. Tel: 718-549-6500; Fax: 718-884-9732. Email: PassSpiritCtr@cpprov.org. Web: www.passionist.org. Rev. Paul R. Fagan, C.P., Retreat Dir & Local Leader; Bro. James Johnson, C.P., Hosted & Special Events Coord.
Redemptorist Priests and Brothers, C.Ss.R. (Prov. of Baltimore) , Our Lady of Perpetual Help, 323 E. 61st St., 10021-8703. Tel: 212-828-1324; Fax: 212-838-4154. Email: JDOCOC@aol.com. Very Rev. Francis J. O'Rourke, C.Ss.R.; Revs. Raymond McCarthy, C.Ss.R.; Lawrence Murphy, C.Ss.R.; John O'Connor, C.Ss.R.; Russell Abata, C.Ss.R.; William R. Bonner, C.Ss.R.; Robert Pagliari, C.Ss.R.; Bro. Christopher Colarossi, C.Ss.R.
St. Vincent de Paul Residence, 900 Intervale Ave., 10459. Tel: 718-589-6965; Fax: 718-589-7010. Email: svdpres@chcn.org. Web: www.svdpres.org. Total Assisted 3,120; Total Staff 8.

St. Vincent Ferrer Priory Dominican Friars Provincial House (Province of St. Joseph). , 869 Lexington Ave., 10021. Tel: 212-744-2080; Fax: 212-327-3011. Very Revs. David Dominic Izzo, O.P., Prior Prov.; Carleton Parker Jones, O.P., Vicar Prov. & Socius; Kevin Dominic Robb, O.P., Prior & Pastor; Revs. Christopher Johnson, O.P., Subprior; William Robert Gannon, O.P.; Bernard Lawrence Keitz, O.P.; Raymond Ferrer Halligan, O.P.; Kevin Anthony McGrath, O.P.; Scott Matthew Erickson, O.P.; George Philip Schommer, O.P.; George Lawrence Concordia, O.P.; Peter John Cameron, O.P., M.F.A.; James Mary Sullivan, O.P.; Bros. Martin Michael Downey, O.P.; John Damian McCarthy, O.P.

Priests assigned but serving elsewhere: Revs. John Aedan McKeon, O.P.; James Moneta Moyna, O.P.; Robert William Vaughn, O.P.; Ronald Henery, O.P. (NO); Robert Urban Sharkey, O.P.; Joseph Anthony Scordo, O.P.; John Patrick McGuire, O.P.; Edmund Augustine Ditton, O.P.; Jerome Joachim Haladus, O.P.; Kevin Palmer McCaffrey, O.P.

Vincentian Fathers, 1834 Third Ave., 10029. Tel: 212-289-5589; Fax: 212-289-8321. Revs. Victor Elia, C.M., Supr.; Candido Arrizurieta, C.M.; Venancio Goyeneche, C.M.

Legal Title: *Padres Paules Community (Vincentians) Inc.*

West Side Jesuit Community, 220 West 98th St., 10025. Tel: 212-663-4615; Fax: 212-866-3241. Email: robjkeck@aol.com. Revs. Robert J. Keck, S.J., Supr.; Daniel J. Berrigan, S.J.; W. Alan Briceland, S.J.; Robert E. Carter, S.J.; Owen W. Daley, S.J.; G. Simon Harak, S.J.; Gerald T. Huyett, S.J.; Bro. Edward L. McCarthy, S.J.; Revs. John G. McSherry, S.J.; Donald J. Moore, S.J.; Peter Murray, S.J.; Enrico Raulli, S.J.; Bro. Joel Magallan Reyes, S.J.; Revs. Joseph Roccosalvo; Joseph C. Towle; Brian F. Zinnamon, S.J.; Edward G. Zogby, S.J.

Xavier Jesuit Community, 30 West 16th St., 10011. Tel: 212-924-7900; Fax: 212-337-7545. Email: hzen@juno.com. Revs. Francis P. Golden, S.J., Rector; Alfred E. Caruana, S.J.; John J. Cecero, S.J.; Edward J. Coughlin, S.J.; Michael T. Kelly, S.J.; Michael C. Lee, S.J.; William J. McGowan, S.J.; Edward J. McMahon, S.J.; John A. Mullin, S.J.; James F. O'Brien, S.J.; Harold F. O'Donnell, S.J.; James L. Pierce, S.J.; Pedro Ruiz, S.J.; Steven A. Schoenig, S.J.; Wagner R. Suarez, S.J.; Michael V. Tueth, S.J.; Yoshitaka Ura, S.J.; James J. Yannarell, S.J.; Henry J. Zenorini, S.J. (For list of faculty see the high school listing for Xavier High School)

BEACON. *St. Joachim Friary* Serving Capuchin Youth and Family Ministries, Garrison, NY , 61 Leonard St., 12508. Tel: 845-838-0000; Fax: 845-838-0004. Email: cyfm@cyfm.org. Web: www.capuchins.org. Revs. Frederick Nickle, O.F.M.Cap., Guardian; Joseph McCarthy, O.F.M.Cap.; Bro. Carlos Hernandez, O.F.M.Cap.

BRONX. *Idente Missionaries - Santa Maria Residence*, 2352 St. Raymond Ave., 10462. Tel: 718-828-2380; Fax: 718-828-4296. Revs. Fernando Real, M.Id., Prov. Supr.; Cristobal Martin, M.Id., Ph.D.; Bros. Francisco Sanchez, M.Id.; Joseph Tran, M.Id.; Marek Wasilewski, M.Id.

Our Lady of the Angels Friary (Franciscan Friars of the Renewal) ; (Postulant House) , 427 E. 155th St., 10455. Tel: 718-993-3405; Fax: 718-993-9997. Web: www.franciscanfriars.com. Revs. Thomas Francis Cacciola; Stanley Fortuna, C.F.R.; Juniper Mary Sistare, C.F.R.; Shawn Conrad O'Connor, C.F.R., Local Servant; Bros. Martin de Porres Maria Ervin, C.F.R.; Dominic Miriam Bormans, C.F.R.; Thomas Joseph McGrinder, C.F.R.; Pier Giorgio Marie Logiudice, C.F.R.; Louis Marie Leonelli, C.F.R.

Passionist Residence, 5801 Palisade Ave., 10471. Tel: 718-548-1182; Fax: 718-548-2945. Revs. Robert Joerger, C.P.; Edward Beck, C.P.; Columkille Regan; Paul Ruttle, C.P.; Bros. Michael Moran, C.P.; August Parlavechio, C.P. Total in Residence 6.

Yarumal Mission Society, Inc., Office of the Pres., 2317 Washington Ave., 10458. Tel: 718-561-8248; Fax: 718-562-2521. Email: imeyusa@aol.com. Web: www.hometown.aol.com. Revs. Jorge I. Fernandez, M.X.Y.; David Guzman, M.X.Y.; Orlando Corrales, M.X.Y.; Jose Gabriel Piedrahita, M.X.Y.

CORNWALL. *Jogues Retreat*, Mailing Address: P.O. Box 522, 12518-0522. Tel: 914-534-7570; Fax: 914-534-3276. Email: jogues.ret@verizon.net. Revs. Alfred L. Fiorino, S.J., Supr. & Guest Master; J. Peter Conroy, S.J., Asst. to Supr., Sabbatical.

ESOPUS. *Marist Brothers F.M.S. (Province of St. Joseph)*, Mailing Address: P.O. Box 197, 12429. Tel: 845-384-6625; Fax: 845-384-6277. Email: brohen@aol.com. Bros. Henry J. Sawicki, F.M.S., Dir.; Gregory De LaNoy, F.M.S.; Todd Patenaude, F.M.S.; Michael Mullin, F.M.S. Brothers 4.

Redemptorist Priests and Brothers C.Ss.R. (Province of Baltimore), Mount Saint Alphonsus, Rte. 9W, P.O. Box 219, 12429. Tel: 845-384-8000; Fax: 845-384-8088. Email: gkeav@aol.com. Web: www.msaretreat.com. Very Rev. George J. Keaveney, C.Ss.R.; Bros. Robert Skinner, C.Ss.R.; Gerard St. Hilaire, C.Ss.R.; Rev. Thomas Travers, C.Ss.R. Priests 6; Brothers 3. In Res. Revs. Dennis Billy, C.Ss.R.; Eugene J. Grohe, C.Ss.R.; John Kiwus, C.Ss.R.; Raymond Weithman, C.Ss.R.

GARRISON. *St. Christopher's Friary*, Mailing Address: Box 150, 10524-0150. Tel: 845-424-3616; Fax: 845-424-3786. Web: www.atonementfriars.org. Revs. Charles Angell, S.A., Guardian; William Drobach, S.A.; Robert Warren, S.A.; Bros. James Daly, S.A.; Donald Perry, S.A.; Benedict Terasawa, S.A.; Thomas Banacki, S.A.; Charles Kenny, S.A.; Robert Taylor, S.A.

Franciscan Friars of the Atonement, Graymoor, P.O. Box 300, 10524-0300. Tel: 845-424-3671; 845-424-3672; 845-424-3673; Fax: 845-424-2166. Email: glucrezia@atonementfriars.org. Web: www.atonementfriars.org. Revs. Fred Alvarez, S.A.; Norman Boyd, S.A.; Bro. Joseph Buettner, S.A.; Revs. Joseph Dimauro, S.A.; Walter Gagne, S.A.; James Gardiner, S.A.; Bros. Francis Gutman, S.A.; Stephen Hanley, S.A.; Daniel Houde, S.A.; Revs. Robert Langone, S.A.; Thomas Orians, S.A.; Bros. Pius MacIsaac, S.A.; Joseph O'Gara, S.A.; Dominic McDonnell, S.A.; Revs. Kevin McMorrow, S.A.; Charles Murphy, S.A.; Owen Murphy, S.A.; Bro. Theodore Novak, S.A.; Rev. Mark O'Connor, S.A.; Bro. Rocco Pace, S.A.; Revs. Peter Tomaino, S.A.; Peter Taran; Bosco Schmidt, S.A.; Bros. Edmund Sheridan, S.A.; Richard Skolinski, S.A.; Rev. Emmanuel Sullivan, S.A.; Bros. Robert Taylor, S.A.; Liam Young, S.A.

St. Francis of Assisi Novitiate, Graymoor, P.O. Box 300, 10524-0300. Tel: 845-424-4055; Fax: 845-424-4673. Revs. Edward Boes, S.A., Novice Dir.; Emil Tomaskovic, S.A.; Bros. Raymond Saville, S.A.; William Weeks, S.A.; Leo Hall, S.A.; Peter Gannon, S.A.

St. Christopher's Inn, Graymoor, P.O. Box 150, 10524-0150. Tel: 845-424-3616; Fax: 845-424-3786. Rev. Bernard Palka, S.A., Pres. & CEO; Bros. Thomas Banacki, S.A.; James Daly, S.A.; Rev. William Drobach, S.A.; Bros. Charles Kenney, S.A.; Donald Perry, S.A.; Benedict Terasawa, S.A.; Revs. Robert Warren, S.A.; Charles Angell, S.A.

Graymoor Ecumenical and Interreligious Institute, 475 Riverside Dr., Room 1960, 10115-1999. Tel: 212-870-2342; 212-870-2330; Fax: 212-870-2001. Rev. James Loughran, S.A., Dir.

Priests of the Province Serving Elsewhere: Revs. Gerald DiGiralamo, S.A., St. John of God Parish, Central Islip, NY; David Fitzgerald, S.A., St. Andrew the Apostle, Apex, NC; Aquinas Thomas, S.A., New Hope Manor, Barryville, NY; Elias Mallon, S.A., Atonement Friars, 138 Waverly Pl., NYC, 10014; Daniel Sylvain, S.A. Tel: 718-574-5772 O.L. of Victory, 583 Throop Ave., Brooklyn, NY, 11216-2496; Blase Burniston, S.A. (Retired). Tel: 813-249-1507 Rocky Creek Village, 8401 Markle St. Lot 239, Tampa, FL, 33615; Simeon Heine, S.A. (Retired). Tel: 212-628-2800 Mary Manning Walsh Nurseing Home, 1339 York Ave. Room 327, New York, NY, 10021; Alexander Kelliher, S.A. (Retired). Tel: 518-732-7617 Resurrection Nursing Home, 90 N. Main St., Caslleton, NY, 12033; Norman Boyd, S.A., Graymoor.

Franciscan Friars of the Atonement, Minister General Office, Graymoor, P.O. Box 300, 10524-0300. Tel: 845-424-2113; Fax: 845-424-2166. Email: ajohnson@atonementfriars.org. Web: www.atonementfriars.org. Very Rev. Arthur M. Johnson, S.A., Min. Gen.; Rev. Daniel O'Shea, S.A., Vicar Gen.; Bro. Gregory Lucrezia, S.A., Sec. Gen.; Revs. John Keane, S.A., 2nd Gen. Councilor; Charles Sharon, S.A., 3rd Gen. Councilor; Bro. Gregory Lucrezia, S.A., 4th Gen. Councilor; Rev. Daniel O'Shea, S.A., Procurator General to the Holy See.

Friar-Priests serving in Japan, Diocese of Yokohama: Tel.: 011-81-45-581-6374; Fax: 011-81-45-581-9068. Revs. Pacificus Von Essen, S.A.; Fidelis Fujihara, S.A. (Japan); Charles Brozat, S.A.; Joseph Hiramatsu, S.A. (Japan); Gabriel Shiraki, S.A. (Japan), Regl. Min.; Damian Sato, S.A.; Eric Tampe, S.A.; Bro. Ignatius Kobayashi, S.A. (Japan).

Friars on assignments or studies: Tel,: 845-424-3671; Fax: 845-424-2166. Revs. Pius F. Keating, S.A.; Joseph Scerbo, S.A.; Edward Gallagher, S.A.

Friars stationed in England: Tel.: 011-44-171-828-4163; Fax: 011-44-171-798-9090. Revs. Robert Mercer, S.A. (England); Michael Seed, S.A. (England); Bros. Gerard Hand, S.A.; Denis Burgelin, S.A.

Friars stationed in Canada, Archdiocese of Vancouver: Tel.: 604-277-8353; Fax: 604-275-4034. Revs. William Linakis, S.A.; Dennis Polanco, S.A.; Bro. Timothy MacDonald, S.A.

Archdiocese of Toronto, Canada:

St. Joan of Arc Parish: Toronto ON M6P 1B1 Canada. Tel: 416-762-1026; Fax: 416-762-4194. Rev. John Kiesling, S.A.

Corpus Christi Parish: 16 Lockwood Rd., Toronto ON M4L 3M8 Canada. Tel: 416-694-0382; Fax: 416-934-3445. Rev. Damian MacPherson, S.A. (Canada).

Paul Wattson Friary, 15 Laxton Ave., Toronto ON M6K 1K8 Canada. Tel: 416-537-0327; Fax: 416-532-8472. Revs. Paschal Breau, S.A. (Canada); Patrick Cogan, S.A.

St. Andrew's Parish: 2547 Kipling Ave., Toronto ON M9V 3A8 Canada. Tel: 416-749-4396.

St. Joan of Arc Parish: Toronto ON Canada. Tel: 416-769-5382; Fax: 416-762-4194. Rev. Bede MacEachen, S.A. (Canada).

St. Joan of Arc Parish: 1701 Bloor St. W., Toronto ON M6P 1B1 Canada. Tel: 416-762-1026; Fax: 416-762-4194. Rev. Timothy Sullivan, S.A.

Archdiocese of Halifax, N.S. Canada: Rev. David Poirier, S.A. Tel: 902-462-3569; Fax: 902-434-5787.

Friars in Military Service: Tel.: 619-524-8820. Rev. William Dillon, S.A. Tel: 619-524-8820.

Friars residing in Italy: Tel.: 011-39-06-687-9552; Fax: 011-39-06-683-3631. Revs. James Puglisi, S.A.; Brian Terry, S.A.

St. Joseph's Rehabilitation Center, Inc., Saranac Lake. Tel: 518-891-3950; Fax: 518-891-3986. Bro. Alan LeMay, S.A.; Revs. Daniel Callahan, S.A.; Carmen Guiliano, S.A.

Graymoor Ecumenical & Interreligious Institute, 475 Riverside Dr., Room 1960, 10115-1999. Tel: 212-870-2330; Fax: 212-870-2001.

Legal Title: *Friars of the Atonement, Inc.*

Legal Title: *St. Christopher's Inn, Inc.*

Legal Title: *Union That Nothing Be Lost, Inc.*

Legal Title: *St. Joseph's Rehabilitation Center, Inc.*

Legal Title: *Paul Wattson Human Resources Fund, Inc.*, (G.E.I.I.)

HARTSDALE. *Mill Hill Fathers Residence*, 222 W. Hartsdale Ave., 10530-1667. Tel: 914-682-0645; Fax: 914-682-0862. Revs. Matthew Grier, M.H.M., Admin.; Robert J. O'Neil, M.H.M., Regl. Representative; James Brian Coffey, M.H.M.; Cornelius M. Snoeren, M.H.M.; Bro. Theodore Tolboom, M.H.M.; Rev. Lester Lonergan, M.H.M. (CHL) (Retired), 1415 Abbey Pl., Apt. 14, Charlotte, NC 28209.

JAMAICA ESTATES. *Paulist Fathers Generalate*, 86-11 Midland Pkwy., 11432. Tel: 718-291-5995; Fax: 718-291-6646. Web: www.paulist.org. Very Rev. John F. Duffy, C.S.P., Pres.; Revs. Michael J. Kallock, C.S.P.; Stephen J. Connor.

Paulist Priests at Paulist Foundations outside the U.S.: Tel.: 011-3906-488-2748; Fax: 011-3906-474-0236.

Via Venti Settembre 14, Rome 00187 Italy. Tel: 011-3906-488-2748; Fax: 011-3906-474-0236. Revs. Paul G. Robichand, C.S.P.; Gerard P. Tully, C.S.P. (TUC).

659 Markham St., Toronto ON M6G 2M1 Canada. Tel: 416-534-4219; Fax: 416-534-4219. Revs. Michael P. Kerrigan, C.S.P.; Philip W. Hart, C.S.P.; Thomas R. Marshall, C.S.P.; Thomas P. Murphy, C.S.P.; James F. McCabe, C.S.P.; Deacon Richard J. Boudreau, C.S.P.

Military Chaplains: Rev. Thomas P. Hall, C.S.P.

On Special Assignment in the U.S. and Abroad: Tel.: 011-39095-564-295. Revs. Justin J. McCormick, C.S.P.; Thomas A. Kane, C.S.P.; James Kolb, C.S.P.; Michael B. McGarry, C.S.P.; Thomas F. Stransky, C.S.P.

Retired: Revs. Martin J. O'Looney, C.S.P.; George R. Fitzgerald, C.S.P. (DEN); Lawrence V. McDonnell, C.S.P.; James R. O'Gara, C.S.P.; Thomas J. Connellan, C.S.P.; Frank M. Sweeney, C.S.P.; Robert T. Scott, C.S.P.; Walter Anthony, C.S.P.; Robert W. Baer, C.S.P.; Edward R. Donovan, C.S.P.; Wilfred A. Brimley, C.S.P.; William J. Cantwell, C.S.P.; John A. Carr, C.S.P.; Robert P. Curtis, C.S.P.; Wilfred Dewan, C.S.P.; Francis X. Diskin, C.S.P.; Charles A. Donovan, C.S.P. (Retired); Harry J. Dooley, C.S.P.; Thomas J. Dove; Joseph P. Flynn, C.S.P.; Harold J. Foye, C.S.P.; Joseph M. Hanly, C.S.P.; George F. Helmich, C.S.P.; Donald E. Howard, C.S.P.; William J. Kenney, C.S.P.; James B. Lloyd, C.S.P.; Stanley F. MacNevin, C.S.P.; Edward A. Maher, C.S.P.; Thomas J. Marley, C.S.P.; Edward J. McDonald, C.S.P.; Neil J. McEleney, C.S.P.; Kenneth H. McGuire, C.S.P.; Louis F. McKernan, C.S.P.; James D. McNulty, C.S.P.; Robert P. Michele, C.S.P.; Ernest C. Mort, C.S.P.; Thomas P. Murphy, C.S.P.; Robert A. O'Donnell, C.S.P.; Harold J. Powers, C.S.P.; Robert F. Quinn, C.S.P.; John C. Reynolds, C.S.P.; Vincent J. Sampietro, C.S.P.; Warren H. Seedorf, C.S.P.; Rudolph T. Vorisek, C.S.P.; Rev. Msgr. Richard J. Walsh, C.S.P.; Rev. Edward D. Wroblewski, C.S.P.

MARYKNOLL. *M.M.A.F. Charitable Trust*, Treasury Office, P.O. Box 306, 10545-0306. Tel: 914-941-7590; Fax: 914-941-2411. Email: rcallahan@maryknoll.org. Rev. Richard B. Callahan, M.M., Contact Person.

Maryknoll Fathers and Brothers 10545-0305. Tel: 914-941-7590; Fax: 914-944-3605. Email: mklcouncil@maryknoll.org. Web: www.maryknoll.org.

General Council: Revs. John C. Sivalon, M.M., Supr. Gen.; Francis T. McGourn, M.M., Vicar Gen.; John C. Barth, M.M., Asst. Gen.; John J. McAuley, M.M., Sec. Gen.; Richard B. Callahan, M.M., Treas. Gen.; Norbert J. Rans, M.M., Asst. Treas.; Joseph P. LaMar, M.M., Asst. Treas.; Joseph B. Arsenault, M.M.; Richard M. Baker, M.M.; Lionel A. Bouffard, M.M.; J. Ernest Brunelle, M.M. (SEA) (Retired); Dennis W. Cleary, M.M.; William J. Coy, M.M.; Wayman P. Deasy, M.M.; Francis A. Diffley, M.M.; Daniel D. Dolan, M.M.; Michael A. Duggan, M.M.; Thomas P. Golden, M.M.; Robert A. Jalbert, M.M.; Leo R. Kennedy, M.M; William T. Knipe, M.M.; Carl P. Meulemans, M.M.; James M. Travis, M.M.; Lawrence J, Lewis, M.M.; Lawrence W. Flynn, M.M.; William B. Frazier, M.M.; Richard R. Fries, M.M.; Charles F. Girnius, M.M.; Ronald L. Green, M.M.; Clyde Phillips, M.M. (CHI); Joseph A. Heim, M.M.; Carroll B. Houle, M.M.; Charles T. Huegelmeyer, M.M.; William E. McCarthy, M.M.; David J. Jones, M.M.; Thomas H. Keefe, M.M.; Martin P. Keegan, M.M.; Alfonso Kim, M.M.; John R. King, M.M.; Joseph P. LaMar, M.M.; James W. Lehr, M.M.; Peter M. Le Jacq, M.M.; Martin J. Lowery, M.M.; Robert J. Lloyd, M.M.; James D. McAuley, M.M.; John J. McAuley, M.M.; William D. McCarthy, M.M.; Robert J. Reiley, M.M.; Joseph J. McGahren, M.M.; Charles J. McPadden, M.M.; William T. Madden, M.M.; Alphonse A. Schiavone, M.M.; Kenneth J. Moody, M.M.; John J. Moran, M.M.; Most Rev. Gerald J. Nagle, M.M.; Revs. Cuong H. Nguyen, M.M.; John B. Northrop, M.M.; George H. Ratermann, M.M.; J. Daniel Schneider, M.M.; Leo B. Shea, M.M.; Michael A. Simone, M.M.; Raymond F. Sullivan, M.M.; William J. Tokus, M.M.; Thomas E. Pesaresi, M.M.; Joseph R. Veneroso, M.M.; Michael J. Snyder, M.M.; Donald J. Vittengl, M.M.; John J. Walsh, M.M.; Michael P. Walsh, M.M.; Edward M. Wroblewski, M.M.

Maryknoll St. Teresa's Residence, 10545-0321. Tel: 914-941-4240; 914-941-4247; Fax: 914-923-3407.

Staff: Revs. Thomas P. McDonnell, M.M., Dir.; John P. Hudert, M.M., Staff; Thomas A. Ahearn, M.M., Asst. Dir. In Res. Most Rev. Richard J. Ham, M.M.; Revs. Thomas A. Ahearn, M.M.; Frederick J. Allen, M.M.; John M. Breen, M.M. (SJ); Donat W. Chatigny, M.M.; William J. Coleman, M.M.; Gervis J. Coxen, M.M.; Richard E. Downey, M.M.; John J. Drew, M.M.; Joseph R. English, M.M.; Joseph A. Farrell, M.M.; Edward J. Flanigan, M.M.; J. Francis Flynn, M.M.; Thomas F. Foley, M.M.; Thomas Fox, M.M.; Thomas F. Garrity, M.M.; Christopher W. Gibbons, M.M.; Thomas F. Gibbons, M.M.; Robert Golish, M.M.; Fidelis C. Goodman, M.M.; John P. Grady, M.M.; J. Gerard Greene, M.M.; John K. Halbert, M.M.; Leon A. Harter, M.M.; Thomas C. Higgins, M.M.; John P. Hudert, M.M.; James A. Jackson, M.M.; Roman A. Kasprzak, M.M.; Alfred V. Keane, M.M.; Walter T. Kelleher, M.M.; Edward R. Killackey, M.M.; James J. Kuhn, M.M.; John P. Lomasney, M.M.; Robert L. Mackesy, M.M.; Robert L. Mackesy, M.M.; William F. Marley, M.M.; Stephen J. Maskell, M.M.; Thomas P. McDonnell, M.M.; Francis S. Meccia, M.M.; Leo F. Melancon, M.M.; George M. Mikolajczyk, M.M.; William H. Moeschler, M.M.; Henry J. Murphy, M.M.; James B. Nagle, M.M.; James B. Nagle, M.M.; James M. O'Brien, M.M.; John J. O'Brien, M.M.; John J. O'Brien, M.M.; Patrick F. O'Donoghue, M.M.; Alan J. Ryan, M.M.; James M. Scanlon, M.M.; Robert R. Sprinkle, M.M.; Lionel G. Trudel, M.M.; C. Thomas Wilcox, M.M.; Walter W. Winrich, M.M. (SJ); Louis J. Wolken, M.M.

Special Assignments: Revs. Brian V. Albright, M.M.; Stephen R. Booth, M.M.; Roy L. Bourgeois, M.M.; Curtis R. Cadorette, M.M.; Michael G. Callahan, M.M. (LA) (Retired); John P. Casey, M.M.; James P. Colligan, M.M. (LA); Miguel F. d'Escoto, M.M.; Marvin F. Deutsch, M.M.; Donald J. Doherty, M.M.; Bernard R. Garritty, M.M.; John E. Keegan, M.M.; Joseph R. Lang, M.M.; Daniel A. Lanza, M.M.; Robert R. Lefebvre, M.M.; Robert A. Lilly, M.M.; Thomas J. Maney, M.M.; John J. Meaney, M.M.; Laurence T. Murphy, M.M.; James P. Nieckarz, M.M.; James K. Nishimuta, M.M.; Richard E. Paulissen, M.M.; Raymond G. Pierini, M.M.; Joseph S. Pulaski, M.M.; Albert I. Reymann, M.M.; John A. Rich, M.M.; James R. Roy, M.M.; Peter L. Ruggere, M.M.; Patrick J. Ryan, M.M.; Daniel J. Sherman, M.M.; Donald R. Steed, M.M.; Wayne T. Weinlader, M.M.; David J. Schwinghamer, M.M.; John F. Wymes, M.M.

Maryknoll Fathers and Brothers Charitable Trust, P.O. Box 306, 10545-0306. Tel: 914-941-7590 Ext. 2422; Fax: 914-941-2411. Revs. Richard B. Callahan, M.M., Trustee; Wayman P. Deasy, M.M., Trustee; Arthur J. Dwyer, M.M., Trustee; Charles T. Huegelmeyer, M.M., Trustee; Thomas H. Keefe, M.M., Trustee; William T. Madden, M.M., Trustee; Bro. Joseph J. Ziegler, M.M., Trustee.

MIDDLETOWN. *St. Albert's Priory* Tel: 845-342-2220; Fax: 845-342-4412. P.O. Box 908, Carmelite Dr., 10940-0908. Tel: 914-344-2220; Fax: 914-342-4412. Revs. Albert Daly, O.Carm.; Vincent McDonald, O.Carm.; Christopher Byrnes, O.Carm.; Daniel Lynch, O.Carm.; Leo Broniszewski, O.Carm.; Francis Amodio, O.Carm.; Esteban Rodriguez, O.Carm.; Bros. James Andrews; Peter Seitzberg, O.Carm.

The National Shrine of Our Lady of Mount Carmel Tel: 845-343-1879; Fax: 845-343-1912. P.O. Box 2162, Carmelite Dr., 10940-2162. Tel: 914-343-1879; Fax: 914-343-1912. Rev. James Sidoti, O.Carm., Dir.

Brandsma Priory, Carmelite Novitiate, 1 Carmelite Dr., P.O. Box 2127, 10940-0439. Tel: 845-343-2959; Fax: 845-344-1808. Email: gpayea@carmelnet.org. Revs. Gerald Payea, O.Carm., Novice Dir.; Timothy Ennis, O.Carm., Novice Dir. Carmelite Friars (North American Prov. of St. Elias and Most Pure Heart of Mary Province) Novices 3.

Carmelite Friars (North American Province of St. Elias) Tel: 914-344-2223; Fax: 914-344-2210. Email: proelias@frontiernet.net. Web: www.carmelites.com. P.O. Box 3079, 10940-0890. Fax: 914-344-2210. Revs. Michael Kissane, O.Carm., Prior Prov. Tel: 914-344-2223; Patrick Mcguigan, O.Carm., Prov. Procurator. Tel: 914-344-2224; Matthew Faulkner, O.Carm., Vocation Dir. Tel: 914-344-2225.

MOUNT VERNON. *St. Bernardine of Siena Friary*, 25 Laurel Ave., 10552-1018. Tel: 914-699-1221. Franciscan Friars, Province of Immaculate Conception Priests 2. In Res. Revs. Andre Cirino, O.F.M.; Benedict J. D'Alessandro, O.F.M., Guardian; James Villa, O.F.M.

Kolbe Friary, 274-280 W. Lincoln Ave., 10550. Tel: 914-664-7169. Bro. Angelo Monti, O.F.M., Guardian. Franciscan Friars, Province of the Immaculate Conception

NEW PALTZ. *St. Joseph Friary*, 34 S. Chestnut St., 12561. Tel: 914-255-5635; Fax: 914-255-5679. Bro. Timothy Jones, O.F.M.Cap., Guardian, Coord. & Vocation Ministry; Revs. Barnabas Keck, O.F.M.Cap.; Maurice Moreau, O.F.M.Cap.; John Mellitt, O.F.M.Cap. Capuchin Friars, Province of St. Mary

NEW ROCHELLE. *Brothers of Holy Cross of the Eastern Province of the United States of America, Inc.*, 85 Overlook Cir., 10804-4501. Tel: 914-632-4468; 914-632-4469; Fax: 914-632-2490. Email: gcscsc@aol.com. Web: www.holycrossbrothers.org. Bros. George Schmitz, C.S.C., Prov.; William Zaydak, C.S.C. Asst. Prov.; Jerome Donnelly, C.S.C., Councilor; John Paige, C.S.C., Councilor; Mark Knightly, C.S.C., Councilor. Professed Brothers (Total in Province) 124. In Res. Bros. Frederick Cosgrove, C.S.C.; John Nicpon, C.S.C.; Robert Russo, C.S.C.

Holy Cross Brothers, Eastern Province, Charitable Trust 85 Overlook Cir., 10804. Tel: 914-632-4468; Fax: 914-632-2490. Email: gcscsc@aol.com. Web: www.holycrossbrothers.org. Bros. George Schmitz, C.S.C., Pres. & Trustee; Peter Martin, C.S.C., Treas. & Trustee; Renatus Foldenauer, C.S.C., Trustee; Richard Kiniry, C.S.C., Trustee; Stephen LaMendola, C.S.C., Trustee.

Saint Joseph's Residence, Inc., 30 Montgomery Cir., 10804-4413. Tel: 914-633-6851; Fax: 914-633-5579. Email: rroepke@atgnet.com. Bros. Brian M. Walsh, C.F.C.; Robert J. Roepke, C.F.C., Vice Pres. Admin.; Thomas C. Higgins, Sec.; Thomas F. Feerick, Vice Pres. Finance. Congregation of Christian Brothers, A facility of limited care for male religious. Total in Residence 14; Total Staff 4.

St. Patrick's Province Center (Congregation of Christian Brothers), Formerly St. Patrick's Provincial House (Congregation of Christian Brothers), 21 Pryer Terrace, 10804. Tel: 914-636-6194; Fax: 914-636-0021. Email: alb@cbinstitute.org. Bros. Brian M. Walsh, C.F.C., Prov. Leader; Kevin G. Cawley, C.F.C., Dep. Prov. Leader. Brothers Living in Community 6; Limited Care Center Total in Residence 15; Total Staff 10. Councilors: Bros. Timothy D. Bray, C.F.C., Dir. Advancement; John W. Casey, C.F.C., Dir. Educational Svcs.; Kevin Griffith, C.F.C.

Saint Joseph Residence, Formerly St. Joseph Residence 30 Montgomery Circle, 10804. Tel: 914-633-6851; Fax: 914-633-5579.

Salesian Cooperators of St. John Bosco, 148 Main St.. Tel: 914-636-4225. Email: MarianShrine@aol.com. Mrs. Lucille Hahn-Cook, Prov. Coord.; Rev. John Puntino, S.D.B., Prov. Delegate.

Salesian Provincial House, 148 Main St., P.O. Box 639, 10802-0639. Tel: 914-636-4225; Fax: 914-636-0159. Email: sdbsue@aol.com. Web: www.salesians.org. Very Revs. James Heuser, S.D.B., Prov.; Patrick Angelucci, S.D.B.; Revs. Vincent Duffy, S.D.B.; Edward Cappelletti, S.D.B.; James Cerbone, S.D.B.; Sean Rooney, S.D.B.; Joseph Doran, S.D.B.; James Mulloy, S.D.B.; John Nazarro, S.D.B.; Terrence O'Donnell, S.D.B.; Richard Putnam, S.D.B.; Robert Savage, S.D.B., Archives; Waclav Swierzbiolek, S.D.B.; Dominic Dahn Cong Tran, S.D.B.; Thomas Valukaran, S.D.B. (NEW); Vincent Zuliani, S.D.B., Supr.; Bros. Thomas Dion, S.D.B.; Andrew Lacombe, S.D.B.; Emile Dube, S.D.B.; John Zito, S.D.B.; Charles Thenier, S.D.B.; Donald Caldwell, S.D.B.; Michael Leschinsky, S.D.B.; Thomas Sweeney, S.D.B. Priests 16; Brothers 8.

PELHAM. *Marist Provincial Office*, 26 First Ave, 10803. Tel: 914-738-0740; Fax: 914-738-0915. Email: pkpsepo@aol.com.

Our Lady of Grace Residence, 850 E. 226th St., Bronx, 10466. Tel: 718-652-1848; Fax: 718-655-2614. Bros. John Byrd; Michael Mullin; Eugene Birmingham.

Marist Brothers Champagnat Hall Community, 4300 Murdock Ave., Bronx, 10466. Tel: 718-994-4227; Fax: 718-994-0145. Bros. Nicholas Caffrey; Denis Caverley; Valerian Doiron; Luke Driscoll; James Gaffney, F.S.C.; Simeon Gerald; Francis Hughes; Patrick Magee; George L. Mathews; Godfrey Robertson; Thomas Kelly; James Devine, Dir.; Matthew Snowden; Sixtus Victor; Vincent Xavier.

Marist Residence, 272 West 91st St., 10024. Tel: 212-769-4951; Fax: 212-769-0446. Bros. James Adams; James Kearney, Dir.; George Kopper; Joseph Sacino, F.M.S.; Francis Zaglauer.

Marist Residence, 143 W. 87th St., 10024. Tel: 212-362-4039. Bros. Gerald Doherty, Dir.; Emil Denworth; Thomas Schady.

Marist Provincial House, 26 First Ave., 10803. Tel: 914-738-1218; Fax: 914-738-0915. Bros. Donnell Neary; Michael Flanigan, Asst. Prov.; Eugene Birmingham.

Marist Brothers, 40 S. Hamilton St., Poughkeepsie, 12601. Tel: 914-471-4077; Fax: 914-471-0205. Bros. Lawrence Gordon; Robert LeClerc; James Stevens.

Marist Brothers, 2 Eden Ter., Poughkeepsie, 12601-4803. Tel: 914-471-8354; Fax: 914-575-3299. Bros. John Nash; Michael Williams.

Marist Lay Volunteer Residence, 67 Sharpe Blvd. S., Mt. Vernon, 10550. Tel: 914-668-5349. Bros. Armand Lamagna, F.M.S., Dir.; Frederick Sambor. 2567 Tenbroeck Ave., Bronx, 10469. Tel: 718-547-6317. Bro. John Bantz, F.M.S.

PELHAM MANOR. *St. Vincent's Residence*, 190 Mt. Tom Rd., 10803-3309. Tel: 914-738-6138; Fax: 914-738-6138. Email: cpstephen@aol.com. Revs. Stephen Haslach, C.P., Supr.; Paschal Smith, C.P.; Leo J. Gorman, C.P. (ORL); James R. Gillette, C.P. The Passionists

SCARBOROUGH. *Carmelite Fathers, NY Prov. of St. Elias*, Carmelite Priory, 3 Woodlea Ln., 10510. Tel: 914-762-3719. Email: wa2svo@bestweb.net. Revs. Timothy C. Donohue, O.Carm.; Joachim J. Snyder, O.Carm.

STATEN ISLAND. *St. Francis Friary*, 500 Todt Hill Rd., 10304. Tel: 718-981-3131; Fax: 718-981-2742. Email: juniperjas@aol.com. Revs. Juniper Alwell, O.F.M.Conv., Guardian; Blase B. Kardos, O.F.M.Conv., Chap.; Stephen Valenta, O.F.M.Conv., Preaching Min.; Shawn Nolan, O.F.M.Conv., Retreat Dir.; Philip Blaine, O.F.M.Conv., Spiritual Center Dir.; Edward Ondrako, O.F.M.Conv.; Bro. Edward Handy, O.F.M.Conv., Social Svc.

Friars Minor Conventual Immaculate Conception Province Charitable Trust Tel: 718-981-3131; Fax: 718-981-2742. Priests 6; Brothers 1.

Scalabrinian Missionaries Scalabrinian Mission Office, The Center for Migration Studies; St. Charles Residence. , 209 Flagg Pl., 10304. Tel: 718-351-0232; Fax: 718-979-1241. Email: cms@cmsny.org. Web: WWW.SCALABRINI.ORG. Revs. Joseph Fugolo, C.S., Dir., Center for Migration Studies & St. Charles Devel. Office; Rene Manenti, C.S., Asst. Dir., Center for Migration Studies; Bro. Louis Calisto, C.S.

TAPPAN. *St. Eliseus Priory*, P.O. Box 27, 10983-0027. Tel: 845-359-5299; Fax: 845-359-0856. Email: ocarmvoc@frontiernet.net. Web: www.frontiernet.net/~ocarmvoc. Rev. Matthew Faulkner, O.Carm., Dir. Students 3.

Carmelite House of Formation

Office of Lay Carmelites Tel: 845-359-0535; Fax: 845-359-0856. Rev. Brocard Connors, O.Carm., Dir. (Carmelite Third Order)

THORNWOOD. *Legionaries of Christ*, 582 Columbus Ave., 10594. Tel: 914-749-3900; Fax: 914-749-3939.

Email: twlc@legionaries.org. Web: www.legionofchrist.org.

WEST PARK. *Congregation of Christian Brothers*, Santa Maria-on-Hudson, 12493. Tel: 845-384-6750; Fax: 845-384-6456. Bros. D. D. Crimmins, Contact Person; W. S. Barry; R.J. Lasik; T.C. Ford. Total in Residence 4.

WHITE PLAINS. *St. Conrad Friary* Provincial Headquarters of the Province of St. Mary of the Capuchin Order. , 30 Gedney Park Dr., 10605-3599. Tel: 914-761-3008; Fax: 914-948-6429. Email: stmaryprov@juno.com. Web: www.capuchin.org.
Legal Title: *The Province of St. Mary of the Capuchin Order*
Legal Title: *Capuchin Friars International, Inc.*, (Nature of Apostolate: Provincial Administration, Hospital, Prison, Preaching, Recruitment); Subject to the Provincial. Total in Residence 54; Total Staff 11.

Development Office:, 210 W. 31st St., 10001. Tel: 212-564-0759; Fax: 212-563-5120. Very Rev. Michael Banks, O.F.M.Cap., Min. Prov.; Revs. David Couturier, O.F.M.Cap., Vicar Prov.; Jerome McHugh, O.F.M.Cap., Sec. & Treas.; Bros. Joseph Yakimovich, O.F.M.Cap., Asst. Sec. & Treas.; Richard Therrien, O.F.M.Cap., Admin. Asst.; Sr. Anna Daly, S.H.C.J., Archivist; Revs. Joel Daniels, O.F.M.Cap., White Plains, NY; Gregory Reisert, O.F.M.Cap., Washington, DC; Paul Engel, O.F.M.Cap., New York, NY; Joseph Flynn, O.F.M.Cap., New Rochelle, NY; Michael Marigliano, O.F.M.Cap., New Rochelle, NY; George J. Dash, O.F.M.Cap., Carmel, NY; Julian Phelan, O.F.M.Cap., Hawthorne, NY. Priests 3; Brothers 2.
Serving in the Military: Rev. James W. Jones, O.F.M.Cap., Chap., U.S.A.

Capuchin Friars International, Inc., St. Conrad Friary, 30 Gedney Park Dr., 10605-3599. Tel: 914-761-3008, Ext. 21; Fax: 914-948-6429. Revs. Giampiero Gambaro, O.F.M.Cap., Treas.; Joseph Albert Wild, O.F.M.Cap, Sec.; Jerome McHugh, O.F.M.Cap., Asst. Sec. Treas.

St. Francis of Assisi Foundation, c/o Capuchin Franciscans, St. Conrad Friary, 30 Gedney Park Dr., 10605-3599. Tel: 914-761-3008, Ext. 21; Fax: 914-948-6429. Dr. Livio Camozzi, Pres.; Revs. Paul Hinder, O.F.M.Cap., Vice Pres.; Giampiero Gambaro, O.F.M.Cap., Treas.; Jerome McHugh, O.F.M.Cap., Asst. Sec. Treas.

YONKERS. *Cathedral Preparatory Seminary Residence*, 201 Seminary Ave., 10704-1896. Revs. Arthur Mastriola; Mark G. Vaillancourt. Priests 2; Students 20.

St. Clare Friary Residence for Senior Friars. , 110 Shonnard Pl., 10703. Tel: 914-423-2392. Revs. Darius Devito, O.F.M.Cap.; Senan Taylor, O.F.M.Cap., Guardian; Sylvan J. Conover, O.F.M.Cap.; Donatus Goetz, O.F.M.Cap.; Raymond Hand, O.F.M.Cap.; James McIntyre, O.F.M.Cap.; John Proppe, O.F.M.Cap.; Charles Repole, O.F.M.Cap.; Owen Shelley, O.F.M.Cap.; Oliver O'Connor; Michael Connolly, Vicar. Capuchin Franciscan Friars, Province of St. Mary Total in Residence 11; Total Staff 3.

St. Felix Friary (Franciscan Friars of the Renewal) ; (House of Studies) , 15 Trinity Plaza, 10701. Tel: 914-476-7279; Fax: 914-476-5033. Revs. Slyvester Mary Mann, C.F.R.; Glenn Sudano, C.F.R., Gen. Community Servant; Bros. Leopold Mariae, C.F.R.; Isaac Mary, C.F.R.; Simon Marie, C.F.R.; Gerard Matthias Kanapes, C.F.R.; Francis Mary Roaldi, C.F.R.; Philip Maria, C.F.R.

St. Leopold's Friary (Franciscan Friars of the Renewal) ; (House of Studies) , 259 Nepperhan Ave., 10701-3461. Tel: 914-965-8143. Web: www.ewtn.com/renewal. Revs. Conrad Osterhout, Servant; Andrew Apostoli; Bros. Lawrence Joseph Schroedel, C.F.R.; Augustine Conner; Gabriel Mary Bakker; Albert Maria Osewski; Leo Fisher, C.F.R.; John Anthony Boughton, C.F.R., Vicar; Sylvester Mary Mann, C.F.R.A; Joseph Mary Deane, C.F.R.; Anthony Marie Baetzold, C.F.R.; Revs. Luke Mary Fletcher, C.F.R.; Juniper Mary Sistare, C.F.R.; Bros. Juan Diego Sutherland; Paulus Marie Tautz; Michael Kmlotek; Ephraim Marie Ali; Christopher Paul Metzger; Solanhs Maria Benfatti; Robert Stanion.

[FF] CONVENTS AND RESIDENCES OF SISTERS

NEW YORK. *Academy of St. Dorothy*, 1305 Hylan Blvd., Staten Island, 10305. Tel: 718-987-0677; 718-351-0939; Fax: 718-351-0661. Email: dorothy@adnyschools.org. Sr. Mary Ann Keegan, S.S.D., Coord. Sisters of St. Dorothy Sisters 8.

Blessed Trinity Missionary Cenacle Missionary Social Work and Parish Ministry. Parish & Community Services, and Catholic Charities of New York , 414 E. 14th St., 10009. Tel: 212-475-1450; Fax: 212-254-8565. Missionary Servants of the Most Blessed Trinity 6; Total Assisted 4,240; Total Staff 6.

Catholic Charities Family and Children's Services, 137 E. 2nd St., 10003. Tel: 212-777-3111; Fax: 212-677-9057.

Carmelite Sisters Teresas of St. Joseph, Inc., 249 W. 14th St., 10011. Tel: 212-242-8224; Fax: 212-242-7233. Email: hnascarmelitaj@aol.com. Sr. Angela Perez, Supr.

Convent of Our Lady of the Presentation, 419 Woodrow Rd., 10312. Tel: 718-356-2121; Fax: 718-948-4115. Email: cquinnpbvm@si.rr.com. Motherhouse and Novitiate of the Sisters of the Presentation. Sisters 22.

Convent of Sisters of the Congregation de Notre Dame, 76 Howard Ave., 10301. Tel: 718-447-0291; Fax: 718-273-0462. Sisters 7.

Corpus Christi Monastery, 1230 Lafayette Ave., 10474. Tel: 718-328-6996; Fax: 718-328-1974. Sr. Maria Pia, Prioress. Solemnly Professed 14; Temporarily Professed 3; Perpetually Professed 2; Novices 1; Postulants 1.

Dalton Center for Mission and Peace Sisters of the Holy Child Jesus , 325 E. 33rd St., 10016-9401. Tel: 212-689-3548; 212-889-3886; Fax: 212-545-7804. Email: shcjapdo@aol.com. Web: shcj.org. Total in Residence 6; Total Staff 3.

The Dwelling Place of New York, Inc., 409 W. 40th St., 10018. Tel: 212-564-7887; Fax: 212-695-3642. Email: nancydpny@aol.com. Sr. Nancy Chiarello, Admin. Sisters 5.

Franciscan Handmaids of Mary Convent Generalate of the Franciscan Handmaids of Mary. , 15 W. 124th St., 10027. Tel: 212-289-5655; Fax: 212-987-5447. Email: mannix4@aol.com. Web: www.fhm.members.aol.com/fhm.nyc. Sr. Maria Goretti Mannix, Congregation Min. Sisters 22; Total Assisted 20.
Other Convents:

Camp St. Edward, 445 Woodvale Ave., Staten Island, 10309. Tel: 718-984-1625; Fax: 718-996-0814.

Handmaids of Mary Novitiate, 444 Woodvale Ave., Staten Island, 10309. Tel: 718-984-1625; Fax: 718-966-0814. Sr. Loretta Theresa Richards, Dir., Formation. Novitiate of the Franciscan Handmaids of the Most Pure Heart of Mary. Associates 50.

Franciscan Missionaries of Mary Tel: 718-547-4693; Fax: 718-325-5102. Email: mmotte@aol.com. Web: www.fmmusa.org.

Provincialate, 3305 Wallace Ave., Bronx, 10467-6599. Tel: 718-547-4693; Fax: 718-325-5102. Email: mmotte@aol.com. Web: www.fmm.org or www.fm-musa.org.

Holy Name Convent, 204 W. 97th St., 10025-5620. Tel: 212-678-6901; Fax: 212-678-6865.

Cardinal Hayes Home Convent, Box K, Millbrook, 12545. Tel: 845-677-6739; Fax: 845-677-6530.

Franciscan Sisters of Little Falls, MN., 20 Walden Ave., 10306-1345. Tel: 718-351-1328. Sisters Elizabeth Weier; Judine Cassidy. Sisters 2.

Franciscan Sisters of the Poor Foundation, Inc., 708 Third Ave., Ste. 1858, 10017. Tel: 212-818-1987; Fax: 212-808-0096. Email: lchristian@franciscanfoundation.org. Web: www.franciscanfoundation.org.

International Presentation Association of the Sisters of the Presentation of the Blessed Virgin Mary, 410 W. 40 St., 4th Fl., 10018-1204. Tel: 212-629-4258; Fax: 212-629-4259. Email: PBVMipa@aol.com. Web: www.ipa.ozehosting.com. Sr. Sharon Allendorf, Contact Person.

St. Joseph Provincialate, 205 Major Ave., 10305. Tel: 718-720-4377; Fax: 718-442-9247. Email: josiefdc@aol.com. Web: www.godslovefdc.org. Provincialate of the Daughters of Divine Charity. Sisters 2; In Province 51.

Missionary Sisters of the Immaculate Heart of Mary District House , 238 E. 15th St., Apt. 5, 10003-3901. Tel: 212-677-2959; Fax: 212-475-7455. Email: icmusdist@juno.com. Sr. Annie Claes, I.C.M., Dist. Leader.

St. Joseph Convent, 238 E. 15th St., 10003-3901. Tel: 212-254-0658; Fax: 212-475-7455. Sisters 9.

Parish Visitors of Mary Immaculate Tel: 718-823-0350; Fax: 718-823-0350. 2151 Watson Ave., Bronx, 10472. Tel: 718-823-0350; Fax: 718-823-0350. Sr. Mary Roberta White, P.V.M.I., Supr. Sisters 5.

Parish Visitors of Mary Immaculate, Marycrest, 164 Quaker Hill Rd., P.O. Box 658, Monroe, 10950-0658. Tel: 845-783-2251; Fax: 845-783-2085. Sisters Mary Gemma Spoldi, Gen. Supr.; Ann Marie, Juniorate Dir.; Dolores Marie, Novice Dir. A contemplative-missionary community serving the Church by person-to-person evangelization through visiting parish families on behalf of their priests; religious education for children and adults not connected with the Catholic schools, giving spiritual counsel and serving as a liaison for social service needs of family members. Total in Community 62.

Schoenstatt Sisters of Mary, Secular Institute, 337 Cary Ave., 10310. Tel: 718-727-8005; Fax: 718-727-3155. Email: sistersofmary@aol.com. Sisters 7; Total Staff 4.

Shalom Convent, 714 W. 231st St., 10463. Tel: 718-884-1663; Fax: 718-432-5843. Email: srritapauline@aol.com. Franciscan Sisters of the Poor 3.

Sisters of Charity Center, Mount Saint Vincent, 6301 Riverdale Ave., 10471-1093. Tel: 718-549-9200; Fax: 718-884-3013. Web: www.scny.org. Sr. Dorothy Metz, Pres.
Legal Title: *The Sisters of Charity of Saint Vincent de Paul of New York*
Legal Title: *Sisters of Charity Center*
Legal Title: *Mount Saint Vincent on Hudson*
Legal Title: *The Sisters of Charity of Saint Vincent de Paul of New York Pension Trust* Total in Congregation 470; In Archdiocese 449.

The Elizabeth Seton Federation, Inc., Sisters of Charity Center, 6301 Riverdale Ave., Bronx, 10471. Tel: 718-549-9200; Fax: 718-884-3013.

Sisters of Life, 450 W. 51 St., 10019. Tel: 212-397-1396. Sr. Agnes Mary Donovan, S.V., Supr. Gen.

Sisters of the Good Shepherd, 337 E. 17th St., 10003-3804. Tel: 212-475-4245; Fax: 212-777-9260.

Legal Title: *Sisters of the Good Shepherd-New York City* Sisters 10.

Society of Helpers Tel: 718-884-3100; Fax: 718-884-3101. 385 W. 263rd St., Bronx, 10471. Tel: 718-884-3100; Fax: 718-884-3101. Email: nyhelper@claret.org. Web: www.claret.org/~srmoore/goodc.html. Sr. Geraldine Finan, Supr. Sisters 6.

Society of the Sacred Heart, R.S.C.J., 515 E. 118th St., 10035. Tel: 212-578-2895; Fax: 212-410-0446. Email: mlufkin@rscj.org. Web: RSCJ.org.
Other Residences:
436 W. 49th St., 10019. Tel: 212-581-3894.
222 E. 93rd St., 10128. Tel: 212-876-2276; Fax: 212-996-5277.
406 E. 80th St., 10021. Tel: 212-288-1986; 212-288-5116; Fax: 212-861-8851.
519 E. 118th St., 10035. Tel: 212-410-3465.

Ursuline Bedford Park Convent, 2885 Marion Ave., 10458. Tel: 718-364-1289; 718-220-3387; Fax: 718-561-4896. Email: bedfordpark@aol.com. Sr. Sheila Murphy, O.S.U., Supr. Sisters 26.

Ursuline Provincialate, 323 E. 198th St., Bronx, 10458. Tel: 718-365-7410; Fax: 718-733-4498. Email: ursruepr@aol.com. Sr. Dorothy Ann Kelly, O.S.U., Prov. Provincialate of the Ursulines of the Roman Union, Eastern Province Sisters in Province 168.

Ursuline Sisters of Andrews Avenue, Inc., 323 E. 198th St., Bronx, 10458. Tel: 718-365-7410; Fax: 718-733-4498. Sr. Dorothy Ann Kelly, O.S.U., Pres.

BEACON. *Carmelite Monastery*, 89 Hiddenbrooke Dr., 12508-2230. Tel: 845-831-5572; Fax: 845-831-5579. Email: bcarmel@prodigy.net. Sr. Marjorie Robinson, O.C.D., Prioress. Professed Nuns 25.

BLAUVELT. *Congregation of Sisters of St. Dominic of Blauvelt*, 496 Western Hwy., 10913. Tel: 845-359-5600; Fax: 845-359-5773. Email: mcollins@opblauvelt.org. Web: www.opblauvelt.org. Sisters Mary Ann Collins, O.P., Pres.; Rose Ellen Gorman, O.P., Asst. to the Pres.
Legal Title: *The Sisters of St. Dominic of Blauvelt, New York* Sisters 187.

BRONX. *Convent of San Damiano* (Franciscan Sisters of the Renewal) , 1661 Haight Ave., 10461. Tel: 718-829-9466; Fax: 718-829-1488. Web: www.franciscansisterscfr.com. Sisters Lucille Cutrone, C.F.R., Community Servant; Francis Teresa O'Donnell, C.F.R.; Agnes Mary Holtz, C.F.R.; Cecilia Francis Jesse, C.F.R.; Jacinta Maria Pollard, C.F.R.; Miriam Therese Johnson, C.F.R.; Mary Francis Roufs, C.F.R. (Mother House, Novitiate House) Sisters 7.

Missionaries of Charity, Inc., 335 E. 145th St., 10451. Tel: 718-292-0019; Fax: 718-292-2929. Sisters M. Dominga, M.C., Regl. Supr.; M. Leticia, M.C., Supr.
406 W. 127th St., 10027. Tel: 212-222-7229. Sr. M. Aloka, M.C., Supr.
657 Washington St., 10014. Tel: 212-645-0587. Sr. M. Lisseria, M.C., Supr. Total Assisted 1,200; Total Staff (shared apostolates) 24.

Our Lady of Guadalupe, Formerly Our Lady of Guadalupe Friary, 3537 Bainbridge Ave., 10467. Tel: 718-547-9840. Sisters Regina Marie; Clare Marie. (Franciscans Friars of the Renewal)

Sisters of St. John the Baptist, Provincial Residence, 3308 Campbell Dr., 10465-1358. Tel: 718-518-7820; Fax: 718-518-8930. Email: usajohnag@aol.com. Web: home.att.net/~baptistines. Sr. John Agnes Barone, C.S.J.B., Prov. Supr. In Province 114; In Archdiocese 96.

Mt. St. John Convent, 150 Anderson Hill Rd.,

Purchase, 10577. Tel: 914-761-7965; Fax: 914-761-2315. Sr. Theresa Ann D'Onofrio, C.S.JB., Supr. (Retired Sisters' Residence) Sisters in residence 32.

Ursuline Communities, Inc., 323 E. 198 St., 10458. Tel: 718-365-7410; Fax: 718-733-4498. Email: ursruepr@aol.com. Sr. Dorothy Ann Kelly, O.S.U., Pres.

CORTLANDT MANOR. *Sisters of the Good Shepherd*, 2226 Crompond Rd, 10567. Tel: 914-526-8587; Fax: 914-526-0291. Sisters of the Good Shepherd 3.

ESOPUS. *Mother of Perpetual Help Monastery* 12429. Tel: 845-384-6533; Fax: 845-384-6654. Email: rednuns@juno.com. Web: www.catholic.org/macc/redemptoristine. Sr. Moira Quinn, O.SS.R., Prioress. Redemptoristine Nuns Professed Sisters 9.

GARRISON. *Motherhouse and Novitiate of the Franciscan Sisters of the Atonement*, St. Francis Convent - Graymoor, 41 Old Highland Tpke., 10524. Tel: 845-424-3623; Fax: 845-424-3298. Email: edonahue@graymoor.org. Web: www.graymoor.org. Sisters Ellen Donahue, S.A., Min. Gen.; Mary Kathleen Murray, S.A., Co-Coord.; Paul Marie Gouthro, S.A., Co-Coord.

Legal Title: *Franciscan Sisters of the Atonement, Inc.* Sisters 75.

Our Lady's Guest and Retreat House, St. Francis Convent, 41 Old Highland Tpke., 10524. Tel: 914-424-3300; Fax: 914-424-3971. Email: retreathouse@graymoor.org. Web: www.graymoor.org. Sr. Josephine Dullaghan, S.A., Directress. Franciscan Sisters of the Atonement Sisters 2.

GRAYMOOR. *Mother Lurana House* Adult Social Day Care. , 166 Old W. Point Rd., Garrison, 10524. Sr. Barbara Ohl, S.A., Directress. Franciscan Sisters of the Atonement

HARRIMAN. *St. Patrick's Villa* Provincial Retirement Home and Provincialate of the Sisters of the Catholic Apostolate (Pallottine). , 13 St. Pat's Dr., P.O. Box 1043, 10926. Tel: 845-783-9381; Fax: 845-783-1248. Web: www.apostle-csac.org. Sisters Theresa Martin, Supr.; Michele Ruggiero, Prov.; Rev. Lawrence X. McCaffrey, S.J., Chap. Sisters 31.

HARTSDALE. *Institute of the Sisters of Mercy of the Americas, Regional Community of New York*, 150 Ridge Rd., 10530-2205. Tel: 914-328-3200; Fax: 914-328-3761. Email: selliottrsm@nymercy.org. Web: www.newyorkmercy.org. Sr. Suzanne Elliot, R.S.M., Regl. Pres.

Legal Title: *The Sisters of Mercy, Inc.* Sisters of Mercy Sisters of Mercy of the Americas 169.

HASTINGS-ON-HUDSON. *Sisters of St. Francis* Motherhouse and Novitiate. , 49 Jackson Ave., 10706-3217. Tel: 914-478-3932; Fax: 914-478-5470. Email: hastingsosf@aol.com. Sr. Roberta Stark Smith, O.S.F., Gen. Min.; Rev. Gary W. Schwartzkopf, S.J., Chap. Sisters of St. Francis, Hastings-on-Hudson Sisters 62.

HAVERSTRAW. *Sisters of St. Francis of Peace*, Congregation Center, 20 Ridge St., 10927. Tel: 845-942-2527; Fax: 845-429-8141. Email: rholtz@fspnet.org. Web: www.fspnet.org. Sr. Regina Holtz, F.S.P., Congregation Min.

HAWTHORNE. *Motherhouse & Novitiate of the Sisters of St. Dominic, Congregation of St. Rose of Lima* 10532. Tel: 914-769-0114; Fax: 914-769-3916. Web: www.hawthorne-dominicans.org. Sr. Marie Edward, O.P., Supr. Gen.; Rev. Julian Phalen, O.F.M.Cap.

Legal Title: *Motherhouse and Novitiate of the Sisters of St. Dominic, Congregation of St. Rose of Lima.* Professed Sisters 22; Sisters in Community 70; In Archdiocese 30.

HIGHLAND MILLS. *Religious of Jesus and Mary*, 202 County Rt.105, P.O. Box 1003, 10930-1003. Tel: 845-928-2213; Fax: 845-928-9437. Email: thevenet@frontiernet.net. Web: www.rc.net/newyork/bethany. Sr. Mary John Horan, R.J.M., Supr. Sisters 12. In Res. Rev. Thomas E. Clarke, S.J.

HOPEWELL JUNCTION. *St. Aloysius Novitiate*, Beekman Rd., P.O. Box 98, 12533. Tel: 914-226-5671; Fax: 914-226-5671. Email: jstab35097@aol.com. Web: www.staloysius.ny.org. Sr. Gloria Castro, Supr. Gen. Oblates to the Blessed Trinity Sisters 9; Postulants 2; Total in Residence 37; Total Staff 31.

LIBERTY. *Blessed Kateri Tekakwitha Religious Education Center*, Mailing Address: Box 1011, 12754. Tel: 914-292-9100; Fax: 914-292-9100. Email: BKT@in4web.com. Dominican Sisters

LIVINGSTON MANOR. *Monastic Sisters of Bethlehem and of the Assumption of the Virgin*, Grooville Rd., 12758. Tel: 845-439-4300; Fax: 845-439-3069. Sr. Amena Figeat, M.S.B.A.V., Supr. Total in Residence 13.

MARYKNOLL. *Maryknoll Communities, Inc.*, 77 Ryder Rd., P.O. Box 133, 10545-0133. Tel: 914-941-7590; Fax: 914-941-2411. Email: rcallahan@maryknoll.org

Maryknoll Residential Care Skilled Nursing home for the Maryknoll sisters only. , Maryknoll Sisters Center, 10545-0311. Tel: 914-941-9230; Fax: 914-941-0213. Email: pedmiston@mksisters.org Web: www.maryknoll.org. Sr. Patricia Edmiston, Admin. Bed Capacity 42; Sisters 33.

Maryknoll Sisters Charitable Trust, Treasury Office, P.O. Box 306 10545-0306. Tel: 914-941-7590; Fax: 914-941-2411. Email: rcallahan@maryknoll.org. Rev. Richard B. Callahan, M.M., Trustee.

Maryknoll Sisters Contemplative Community Contemplative Community of the Maryknoll Sisters of St. Dominic. , Mailing Address: P.O. Box 311, 10545-0311. Tel: 914-941-7575; Fax: 914-923-0733. Email: mkcontemplativecom@juno.com. Sr. Grace Myerjack, M.M., Coord. Sisters 8.

Maryknoll Sisters of St. Dominic Inc., P.O. Box 311, 10545-0311 Tel: 914-941-7575; Fax: 914-923-0733. Email: cerisman@mksisters.org. Web: www.maryknoll.org. Sr. Catherine Erisman, M.M., Center Coord. Professed Sisters 216; Total in Residence 207.

MILLBROOK. *Franciscan Missionaries of Mary*, Mailing Address: Box K, 12545. Tel: 845-677-6363; Fax: 845-677-6739. Email: fmmch@aol.com. Web: fmmusa.org. Sr. Beatrice Costagliola, F.M.M., Local Coord. Sisters 6.

MONROE. *St. Joseph's Convent-Preschool*, 121 Harriman Heights Rd., 10950. Tel: 914-783-3006; Fax: 914-782-5645. Email: littlepals@frontiernet.net. Sr. M. Olivia Reginella, Coord. Sisters of the Catholic Apostolate (Pallottine) 3; Total Assisted 50; Total Staff 5.

MONSEY. *St. Zita's Villa* Motherhouse and Novitiate of Sisters of Reparation of the Congregation of Mary. , 10952. Tel: 914-356-2011; Fax: 914-352-5209. Sr. Maureen Francis, Supr. Sisters 10.

MONTICELLO *St. Thomas Villa* 12701. Sr. Agnes White, C.S.J., Admin. .; Summer residence for Sisters of St. Joseph, Brentwood.

NANUET. *St. Patrick Villa*, 2 Duryea Ln., 10954. Tel: 845-623 3371; Fax: 845-623-0496. Email: stpatrickvilla@aol.com. Sr. Maria Regina Bronner, Admin. Sisters of Charity of St. Vincent de Paul Sisters 23.

NEW ROCHELLE. *Monastery of St. Clare - Franciscan Poor Clare Nuns*, 86 Mayflower Ave., 10801-1615. Tel: 914-632-5227; Fax: 914-632-2227. Email: claresnyeme@juno.com. Sr. Mary Bernadette Quinn, O.S.C., Abbess.

Legal Title: *Franciscan Poor Clare Nuns* Sisters 13.

Ursuline Convent of St. Teresa's, 39 Willow Dr., 10805 Tel: 914-632-1199; Fax: 914-633-5281. Sr. Alice Gallin, O.S.U., Supr.

Legal Title: *Ursuline Convent of St. Teresa's, New York* Sisters 43.

Ursuline Residence, Inc., 1338 North Ave., 10804. Tel: 914-636-3456; Fax: 914-576-2620. Email: ursres@aol.com. Sr. Regina Kehue O.S.U., Supr. Sisters 30.

NEW WINDSOR. *Mt. St. Joseph* Motherhouse of the Sisters of the Presentation of the Blessed Virgin Mary of New Windsor. , 880 Jackson Ave., 12553. Tel: 914-564-6620; Fax: 914-567-0219. Email: pbvmadmin@juno.com. Web: sistersofthepresentation.org. Sisters Catherine Cleary, Pres.; Luke Mulraney, Community Archivist. Ministry in the field of academic education in parochial elementary and high schools; pastoral services; health care; social services. Sisters 165.

NEWBURGH. *Center of Hope Sisters Residence*, 320 Powell Ave., 12550. Sr. Maura Schefter, O.P., Admin. Dominican Sisters of Hope

Daughters of Mary Immaculate Italian Apostolate in Sacred Heart Church. , 15 Stori Rd., 12550. Tel: 914-565-5034. Sr. Putorti, Admin. Total Assisted 225; Total Staff 2.

Sisters of St. Dominic Charitable Trust, 320 Powell Ave., 12550. Tel: 845-561-6520; Fax: 845-569-8748. Email: hdowney@ophope.org. Sr. Ellen Carney, Trustee.

NYACK. *Sisters of Our Lady of Christian Doctrine* aka Institute of Christian Doctrine, Visitation House , 629 N. Midland Ave., 10960-1032. Tel: 845-727-1011; Fax: 845-727-1011. Email: AgnesRCDPres@aol.com. Web: www.sistersrcd.org. Sr. Agnes O'Connor, R.C.D., Pres. Sisters 33; Total in Residence 6; Total Staff 1.

Marydell Faith & Life Center, 640 N. Midland Ave., 10960. Tel: 845-358-5399; Fax: 845-358-1671. Email: marydell@netzero.net.

OSSINING. *Dominican Sisters of Hope*, 299 N. Highland Ave., 10562. Tel: 914-941-4420; Fax: 914-941-1125. Email: cmcdonnell@ophope.org. Web: www.ophope.org. Sr. Catherine McDonnell, O.P., Prioress. Total number in community 278.

Dominicare, Inc., Office of the President, 299 N. Highland Ave., 10562. Tel: 914-941-4420; Fax: 914-941-1125.

PEEKSKILL. *Mt. St. Francis, Motherhouse & Infirm of Franciscan Missionary Sisters of Sacred Heart* Canonical Name: Franciscan Missionary Sisters of the Sacred Heart. , 250 South St., 10566. Tel: 914-737-5409; Fax: 914-736-9614. Email: sajfmsc@mail.com. Sisters Anne James Guerin, F.M.S.C., Prov. Supr.; Teresina Thoravasseril, F.M.S.C., Supr.

Legal Title: *Missionary Sisters of the Third Order of St. Francis*

Mt. St. Francis Infirmary, 250 South St., 10566. Tel: 914-737-3373; Fax: 914-736-9614.

Novitiate

PURCHASE. *Society of the Sacred Heart*, Manhattanville College, 10577. Tel: 914-694-2200; Fax: 914-694-3488. Web: sofie.org/rscj/.

RHINEBECK. *Linwood Spiritual Center*, 50 Linwood Rd., 12572-2507. Tel: 914-876-4178; Fax: 914-876-1920. Email: linwood@ulster.net. Web: www.societyofstursula.org. Sisters Catherine Gormley, S.U., Regl. Supr.; Maureen Steeley, S.U., Dir. Spiritual Center. Society of St. Ursula

RYE. *Convent of the Holy Child*, 25 Convent Ln., 10580-1904. Tel: 914-967-5544; Fax: 914-925-2575. Email: holychildd@aol.com. Sisters of the Holy Child Jesus 17; Sisters of Mercy (NY Region) 1.

SCARSDALE. *Blessed Sacrament Monastery*, 86 Dromore Rd., 10583-1706. Tel: 914-722-1657; Fax: 914-722-1665. Email: obsny@aol.com. Web: www.catholic.org/macc. Sr. Mary Francis Blackmore, Prioress. Sacramentine Nuns Sisters 11.

SLOATSBURG. *St. Mary's Villa, Spiritual & Educational Center*, 150 Sisters Servants Ln., P.O. Box 9, 10974-0009. Tel: 845-753-5100; Fax: 845-753-1956. Email: ssminy@aol.com. Sisters Servants of Mary Immaculate

SPARKILL. *Dominican Convent of Our Lady of the Rosary* Motherhouse and General Novitiate of Dominican Sisters of Congregation of Our Lady of the Rosary. , 175 Rte. 340, 10976-1047. Tel: 914-359-6400; Fax: 914-359-6053. Email: catherine.morgan@sparkill.org. Web: www.sparkill.org. Sr. Maryann Summa, O.P., Pres.; Rev. Raymond Daley, O.P., Chap. Sisters 115; Sisters 409.

STATEN ISLAND. *Daughters of St. Paul, Pious Society*, 78 Fort Pl., 10301. Tel: 718-447-5071; Fax: 718-816-1332. Email: fspny@aol.com. Web: pauline.org. Sr. Patricia Mary Maresca, F.S.P., Supr. Missionary Sisters of the Communications Media Sisters 11.

Eastern Franciscan Common Novitiate, Inc., 444 Woodvale Ave., 10309. Tel: 718-966-4851; Fax: 718-966-0814. Email: srkking@yahoo.com. Sisters Annette Lucchese, F.S.R., Pres.; Jacinta Doyle, S.F.P., Sec.

Pious Disciples of the Divine Master, Regional and Formation House, 60 Sunset Ave., 10314. Tel: 718-761-2323; 718-494-8597; Fax: 718-494-2123. Email: srjosephin@aol.com. Web: www.pddm.us. Sr. M. Josephine Fallon, Regl. Supr. Sisters 7; Novices 5.

TARRYTOWN. *Provincial Center, Religious Sacred Heart of Mary*, 50 Wilson Park Dr., 10591. Tel: 914-631-8872; Fax: 914-631-7803. Email: mod@rshmeap.org. Web: www.rshm.org. Sisters Rosamand Blanchet, R.S.H.M., Prov. Supr.; Michaeline O'Dwyer, R.S.H.M., Prov. Counselor; Mary Heyser, R.S.H.M., Prov. Counselor; Catherine Deubel, R.S.H.M., Provincial Sec.; Martina Crowley, R.S.H.M., Treas.; Loretta Ruvo, Dir. Formation; Eymard Gallagher, R.S.H.M., Dir. of Development; Lucia Kenny, R.S.H.M.; Virginia McNally, R.S.H.M., Dir., Ongoing Formation. Total Staff 8.

WALDEN. *Convent of Most Precious Blood*, 100 Ulster Ave., 12586. Tel: 845-778-7616. Sisters 2.

Little Sisters of the Assumption, Provincial House, 100 Gladstone Ave., 12586. Tel: 845-778-0667; Fax: 845-778-0676. Email: lsaprovsec@aol.com. Web: www.littlesisters.org. Sr. Jean McCormack, Prov. Coord. Sisters in Province 40.

Other residences in New York:

475 E. 115th St., 10029. Tel: 212-369-2097.

310 E. 120th St., 10035. Tel: 212-876-4661; Fax: 212-831-1892.

159-A Johnston St., Newburgh, 12550. Tel: 845-562-1757.

Little Sisters of the Assumption, P.O. Box 677, 12586-0677. Tel: 845-778-7252; Fax: 845-778-2457. Sisters Jean McCormack, Prov.; Joseph McCloat, Local Coord. Sisters 6.

WARWICK. *Mt. Alverno Center, Bon Secours Charity Health System*, 20 Grand St., 10990. Tel: 845-986-2267; Fax: 845-986-9269. Email: alombard@

tshs.org. Web: www.stanthonycommunityhosp.org. Leah Cerkvenik, R.N., EVP Warwick Campus; Mrs. Kathleen Deak, Admin., Mt. Alverno Center, Adult Home/Assisted Living Program; Pam Corbett, Pastoral Care; Rev. Joseph McAndrew, Chap. St. Francis Center at the Knolls, Villa Francis at the Knolls

WHITE PLAINS. *Convent of Our Lady of Good Counsel* Motherhouse of the Sisters of the Divine Compassion. , 52 N. Broadway, 10603. Tel: 914-798-1300; Fax: 914-949-5169. Email: alicefeeley@email.msn.com. Web: divinecompassion.org. Sr. Alice Feeley, R.D.C., Pres. To provide counseling services for laity, religious and clergy. Individual and group counseling are offered as well as marital and family therapy. Sisters 27.

RDC Center for Counseling and Human Development, Inc., 52 N. Broadway, 10603. Tel: 914-949-0504; Fax: 914-997-1979.

YONKERS. *Sisters of Life*, St. Paul the Apostle Convent, 586 McLean Ave., 10705. Tel: 914-968-8094; Fax: 914-968-0462. Sr. Agnes Mary Donovan, S.V., Supr. Gen. Professed Sisters 34; Novices 8; Postulants 8.

[GG] RETREAT HOUSES

BRONX. *Cardinal Spellman Retreat House*, The Passionist Spiritual Center, 5801 Palisade Ave., 10471. Tel: 718-549-6500; Fax: 718-884-9732. Email: PassSpiritCtr@cpprov.org. Web: www.passionists.org & www.preacherman.org. Rev. Paul R. Fagan, C.P., Dir. & Local Coord.; Mr. William J. Gilberg, Admin.; Bro. James Johnson, C.P., Coord. of Special Events.

St. Joseph's Center, 275 W. 230th St., 10463. Tel: 718-796-4340. Rev. Jose Luis Martinez, O.A.R. (LA), Dir.; Bro. Mario Alvarez, O.A.R., Admin. (Spanish Cursillo Center) Total in Residence 1; Total Staff 2.

ESOPUS. *Marist Brothers of Ulster County* Mid Hudson Valley Camp - Summer camp for disadvantaged children / Retreat house for youth. , Mailing Address: P.O. Box 197, 12429. Tel: 845-384-6106 (residence); 845-384-6620 (office); Fax: 845-384-6479. Email: esopusdon1@aol.com. Bro. Donald Nugent, F.M.S., Dir. Total Staff 2.

Mount St. Alphonsus Redemptorist Retreat Center, 1001 Broadway, P.O. Box 219, 12429. Tel: 845-384-8000; Fax: 845-384-8088. Web: www.msaretreat.com. Very Rev. John G. Kingsbury, C.Ss.R., Rector; Bros. Robert Skinnner, C.Ss.R.; Gerard St. Hilaire, C.Ss.R.; Rev. John Murray, C.Ss.R. Redemptorist Fathers and Brothers, Groups and individual retreats, conferences, workshops, and days of prayer. Available for Religious Chapters. Capacity 106; Bed Capacity 161.

HIGHLAND MILLS. *Bethany Retreat House*, 202 County Rd. 105, P.O. Box 1003, 10930-1003. Tel: 845-928-2213; Fax: 845-928-9437. Email: thevenet@frontiernet.net. Web: www.rc.net/newyork/bethany. Sr. Catherine McIntyre, R.J.M., Dir. Religious of Jesus and Mary Total in Residence 14. In Res. Rev. Thomas E. Clarke, S.J.

LARCHMONT. *St. Francis Retreat, Inc.*, 1 Pryer Manor Rd., 10538. Tel: 914-235-6839; Fax: 914-576-6540. Rev. Benedict J. Groeschel, C.F.R. Tel: 914-632-3743.

Trinity Retreat, 1 Pryer Manor Rd., 10538. Tel: 914-235-6839; Fax: 914-576-6540. Email: trinityret@aol.com. Revs. Eugene Fulton, Dir.; Benedict J. Groeschel, C.F.R., Assoc. Dir.

MIDDLETOWN. *National Shrine of Our Lady of Mount Carmel*, Carmelite Dr., P.O. Box 2162, 10940-2162. Tel: 914-343-1879; Fax: 914-343-1912. Email: nsolmc@frontiernet.net. Web: www.ourladyofmtcarmelshrine.com; www.carmelitegiftstore.com. Rev. James Sidoti, O.Carm., Dir. Total Staff 5.

NEWBURGH. *Our Lady of Hope Center* Conducted by the Oblates of Mary Immaculate of the U.S. Province. , 532 River Rd., 12550. Tel: 914-568-0780; Fax: 914-561-7956. Revs. Richard Kulwiec, O.M.I., Supr.; Patrick Brady, O.M.I.; Michael O'Hara, O.M.I.; Robert Leising, O.M.I.; George M. White, O.M.I.; John King, O.M.I.

SLOATSBURG. *St. Mary's Villa*, 150 Sisters Servants Ln., P.O. Box 9, 10974-0009. Tel: 845-753-5100; Fax: 845-753-1956. Email: ssminy@aol.com. Sisters Servants of Mary Immaculate, Spiritual and Educational Center. (Retreats) Total in Residence 6; Total Staff 6.

STATEN ISLAND. *Mount Manresa Jesuit Retreat House*, 239 Fingerboard Rd., 10305. Tel: 718-727-3844; Fax: 718-727-4881. Email: mtmanresa@hotmail.com. Web: www.manresasi.org. Revs. Edward J. Quinnan, S.J., Dir. & Supr.; Brian Frain, S.J.; John J. King, S.J.; Thomas J. Quinn, S.J. (Retired); Sr. Maureen Skelly, S.C.; Mrs. Doroty Berman, Youth Min.; Ms. Arlene Volsario, Admin. Society of Jesus Total in Residence 4; Total Staff 7.

STONY POINT. *Don Bosco Retreat Center and Marian Shrine* Founded 1947. , 174 Filors Ln., 10980. Tel: 914-947-2200; Fax: 914-947-2203. Email: marianshrine@aol.com. Web: www.marianshrine.org. Bros. Emmanuel Alicino, S.D.B.; John Andres, S.D.B.; Mario Audero, S.D.B.; Jerome Cincotta, S.D.B.; Alfred Flatoff, S.D.B.; Richard Pasiak, S.D.B.; David Tierney, S.D.B., Vocations; Bernard Zdanowicz, S.D.B.; Revs. George Atok, S.D.B.; Paul Bedard, S.D.B.; William Burke, S.D.B., Retreats Coord.; James Chiosso, S.D.B., Dir.; John Divizia, S.D.B.; August Kita, S.D.B.; Anthony Luzzi, S.D.B.; Paul Chuong Nguyen, S.D.B.; Philip Pascucci, S.D.B.; John Puntino, S.D.B., Dir.; Gennaro J. Sesto, S.D.B. (NEW), Shrine Coord.; Kenneth Shaw, S.D.B.; Chester Szemborski, S.D.B.; Eugene Walter, S.D.B.; Frank Wolfram, S.D.B. Total in Residence 23; Total Staff 37.

Marian Shrine, 174 Filors Ln., 10980. Tel: 914-947-2200; Fax: 914-947-2203. Email: marianshrine@aol.com. Web: www.marianshrine.org. Revs. George Atok, S.D.B.; Paul Bedard, S.D.B.; William Burke, S.D.B., Retreats Coord.; James Chioso, S.D.B.; John Divizia, S.D.B.; August Kita, S.D.B.; Anthony Luzzi, S.D.B.; Paul Choung Nguyen, S.D.B.; Philip Pascucci, S.D.B.; John Puntino, S.D.B., Dir.; Gennaro Sesto, S.D.B., Shrine Coord.; Kenneth Shaw, S.D.B. (SP); Chester Szemborski, S.D.B.; Eugene Walter, S.D.B.; Frank Wolfram, S.D.B.; Bros. Emmanuel Alicino, S.D.B.; John Andres; Mario Audero, S.D.B.; Jerome Cincotta, S.D.B.; Alfred Flatoff, S.D.B.; Richard Pasaik, S.D.B.; David Tierney, S.D.B.; Bernard Zdanowicz, S.D.B. Total in Residence 23; Total Staff 37.

WALDEN. *St. Andrew's Retreat House*, 257 St. Andrew's Rd., 12586. Tel: 914-778-5941; Fax: 330-627-1935. Sr. Martha Hernandez, Supr. North American Union Sisters of Our Lady of Charity

WAPPINGERS FALLS. *Mt. Alvernia Retreat House* 12590. Tel: 845-297-5706; Fax: 845-298-0309. Email: mtalverniarh@optonline.net. Revs. Michael Nappo, O.F.M., Guardian, Retreat Staff; Roch Ciandella, O.F.M., Dir. Retreats; Thomas Garone, O.F.M., Assoc. Dir., Retreats; Regis Gallo, O.F.M., Retreat Staff; Frank Genevive, O.F.M., Retreat Staff.

In Res. Revs. Thomas More Nicastro, O.F.M.; Ernest D'Onofrio, O.F.M.; Deacon Kenneth Ghastin, O.F.M.

WARWICK. *Franciscan Sisters of the Poor Convent*, 24 Grand St., 10990. Tel: 914-986-2267. Miss Jean Wetstine, Exec. Dir.; Sr. Paula Adelman, Local Community Min.; Rev. Edward Sullivan, O.F.M., Chap. Franciscan Sisters of the Poor

YONKERS. *Sisters of Mary Reparatrix*, 287 Hayward St., 10704. Sr. Margaret Hoey, S.M.R., Prov. Supr. Sisters 4.

[HH] UNIVERSITY APOSTOLATES

NEW YORK. *University Apostolate*, 1011 First Ave., 10022. Tel: 212-371-1000, Ext. 2803; Fax: 212-758-3018. Email: vicared@aol.com. Sr. Deanna Sabetta, C.N.D., Dir.

Bard College, MSC-1227, P.O. Box 5000, Annondale-on-Hudson, 12504-5000. Tel: 845-758-7542. Rev. Paul Murray, Ph.D.

Bronx Community College, Loew Hall-Room 422, University Ave. & W. 181st St., Bronx, 10453. Tel: 718-289-5954. Rev. James Sheehan.

City College of New York, Baskerville, 204, 137th St. & Convent Ave., 10031. Tel: 212-650-5866. Mr. Gregory Pope.

Columbia University, 110 Earl Hall, 10027. Tel: 212-854-5110; 212-866-1500 (Notre Dame Rectory). Email: catholics@columbia.edu. Revs. Jacek Buda, O.P.; Andrzej J. Fornal, O.P.

Culinary Institute of America, 157 Broadway, Kingston, 12401-6057. Tel: 914-331-3459; Fax: 914-340-9596. Email: chaplains@ulster.net. Rev. Marc K. Oliver.

Dutchess Community College, 93 Wurts St., Kingston, 12401-4509. Tel: 845-331-0436. Email: chaplains@bestweb.net. Rev. Marc Oliver.

Vassar College, St. Mary's Convent, 157 Broadway, Kingston, 12401-6057. Tel: 914-331-3459; Fax: 914-340-9596. Email: chaplains@ulster.net. Rev. Marc Oliver.

Dominican College, 470 Western Hwy., Orangeburg, 10962. Tel: 845-359-7800, Ext. 255. Sr. Barbara McEneany, O.P.

Fashion Institute of Technology (SUNY), 227 W. 27th St., 10001. Tel: 212-564-9070, Ext. 232. Email: gavreilly@yahoo.com. Rev. Gavin Reilly, O.F.M-.Cap.

210 W. 31st St., 10001-2876. Tel: 212-564-9070, Ext. 232. Email: gavreilly@yahoo.com.

Fordham University at Lincoln Center, 113 W. 60th St. (Lowenstein 217), 10023. Tel: 212-636-6267. Email: jcavanagh@fordham.edu. Rev. Damian O'Connell, S.J., Asst. Tel: 212-636-6318; Ms. Joan Cavanagh, Dir. Tel: 212-636-6268; Ms. Anna Pfeiffer, Global Outreach. Tel: 212-636-6269.

Fordham University at Rosehill, Bronx, 10458. Tel: 718-817-4500; Fax: 718-817-4505. Email: devitto@fordham.edu. Rev. Joseph Currie, S.J.; Sr. Regina DeVitto, C.N.D.; Mr. Denis Kelly; Mr. Robert Minotti; Mr. Michael Kravatz; Rev. Lito Salazar, S.J.

Herbert H. Lehman College, Student Life Bldg., 220 Bedford Park Blvd. W. (222E), Bronx, 10468. Tel: 718-960-4979. Email: neilofm2000@aol.com. Rev. Neil O'Connell, O.F.M., Dir.; Mrs. Kathryn Mastriaco.

Hostos Community College, 500 Grand Concourse (Room C371), Bronx, 10451. Tel: 718-518-4423 (Mon-Tues). Rev. James Sheehan.

Hunter/Baruch College, Newman Catholic Center, 695 Park Ave., Room 1317 E. Bldg., 10021. Tel: 212-772-4752 (Hunter); 646-312-4762 (Baruch); Fax: 914-694-2496. Sr. Barbara Ann Mueller, O.P.

Iona College, 715 North Ave., New Rochelle, 10801. Tel: 914-633-2340; 914-633-2632; Fax: 914-633-2363. Email: cprocario-foley@iona.edu. Mr. Carl Procario-Foley, Dir.; Bro. Jim Carroll, C.F.C.; Ms. Peggy Clarke; Ms. Kate Byrnes; Rev. John F. Replogle, S.J.

John Jay College, 445 W. 59th St., Room 2311, 10019-1128. Tel: 212-237-8281; Fax: 212-237-8465. Sr. Suzanne Wallin, SC.

Manhattan College, Bronx, 10471. Tel: 718-862-7972; Fax: 718-862-8016. Email: lois.harr@manhattan.edu. Lois Harr, Dir.; Rev. James Cerbone, S.D.B. Tel: 718-862-7972; Mr. Kevin McCloskey. Tel: 718-862-7477; Kinah Ventura.

Manhattanville College, 2900 Purchase St., Purchase, 10577. Tel: 914-323-5150, Ext. 447; Fax: 914-694-2496. Ms. Joanne Carrubba.

Marist College, Poughkeepsie, 12601. Tel: 845-575-3130; 845-575-3000, Ext. 2275; Fax: 845-575-3299. Email: francis.kelly@marist.edu. Rev. Richard LaMorte; Bros. Frank Kelly, F.M.S.; Michael Williams, F.M.S.

Marymount College, 100 Marymount Ave., Tarrytown, 10591. Tel: 914-332-8248; Fax: 914-332-8228. Email: sullivak@mmc.marymt.edu. Karen Schroer-Sullivan.

Marymount Manhattan College, 221 E. 71st St., 10021. Tel: 212-517-0597. Sr. Virginia Dorgan.

Mt. St. Mary College, 330 Powell Ave., Newburg, 12550. Tel: 845-569-3517. Rev. Mark Connell.

College of Mt. St. Vincent, Riverdale, 10471. Tel: 718-405-3200; 718-405-3215; 718-405-3216. Sisters Ann Citerella, S.C., Dir.; Theresa Capria, S.C.; Rev. David Gallo.

College of New Rochelle, 29 Castle Pl., New Rochelle, 10805. Tel: 914-654-5339; 914-654-5867; Fax: 914-654-5958. Email: Tmccorry@cnr.ed. Mr. Terence McCorry, Dir. Tel: 914-654-5867; Helen Wolf, Assoc. Dir.; Rev. John Joseph Flynn, O.F.M.Cap., Chap.

New York Maritime College, 6 Pennyfield Ave., Fort Schuyler, Bronx, 10465-4198. Tel: 718-409-7200. Rev. Michael Moynihan.

New York Medical College, Valhalla, 10595. Tel: 914-594-4646. Email: deacon_otoole@nymc.edu. Deacon Lawrence O'Toole.

New York University, Catholic Center at NYU, 58 Washington Sq. S., 10012. Tel: 212-674-7236; 212-998-1065 (voice mail); Fax: 212-473-2971. Email: mcquire@is3.nyu.edu. Rev. John McGuire, O.P.

Pace University, One Pace Plaza, 20 Cardinal Hayes Pl., 10038. Tel: 212-962-3972. Rev. John McGuire, O.P.

Pace University/Westchester SUNY/Purchase, 72 Carman Rd., Scarsdale, 10583. Tel: 914-543-3340. William Mulligan.

Rockland Community College, 145 College Rd., Suffern, 10901. Tel: 845-574-4531; Fax: 845-574-4134. Email: mverschn@suynrockland.edu. Mr. Michael Ver'Schneider.

St. John's University, 300 Howard Ave. - Room B9, Staten Island, 10301. Tel: 718-390-4475. Email: mahoney@stjohns.edu. Sr. Joan Mahoney, C.N.D., Dir. Tel: 718-390-4473; Rev. Thomas Concagh, C.M. Tel: 718-390-4492; Mr. Jason Valaquez. Tel: 718-390-4475; Ms. Angela Seegel. Tel: 718-390-4497; Beatrice Bruna.

St. Thomas Aquinas, 125 Rte. 340, Sparkill, 10976. Tel: 845-398-4197; Fax: 845-398-4061. Sr. Madeleine Murphy, O.P.

SUNY/New Paltz, 5 Van Alst St., New Paltz, 12561. Tel: 845-257-3024. Email: hgrimsland@hvc.rr.com. Mr. Henry Grimsland.

Wagner College & The College of Staten Island, Kairos House, Wagner College, 1 Campus Rd., Staten Island, 10301. Tel: 718-390-3461 (Wagner); 718-982-2652 (College of Staten Island). Email: elaine.schenk@verizon.net. Sr. Elaine R. Schenk, M.ID.

[II] MISCELLANEOUS

NEW YORK. *Aid to the Church in Need, Inc.*, 378 Broome St., 10013. Tel: 212-334-5340; Fax: 212-334-6163. Email: info@acnusa.org. Web: www.churchinneed.org. Sarkis Boghjalian, National Dir.

Alfred E. Smith Memorial Foundation, Inc., The, 1011 First Ave., 10022-4134. Tel: 212-371-1000, Ext. 3315; Fax: 212-753-5980.

America Press, Inc., The Business & Editorial Offices, 106 W. 56th St., 10019. Tel: 212-581-4640; Fax: 212-399-3596. Email: america@americamagazine.org. Web: www.americamagazine.org. Revs. Thomas J. Reese, S.J., Pres.; Charles M. Whelan, S.J., Vice Pres.; Robert C. Collins, S.J., Sec. & Treas.

American Committee on Italian Immigration, Inc., 352 W. 44th St., 10036-5419. Tel: 212-247-7373; Fax: 212-265-5793. Email: ACIMNY@aol.com. Web: www.acimny.com. Rev. Joseph Fugolo, C.S., Natl. Exec. Sec. To insure fair immigration policy favoring reunion of families and cultural integration of Italian Americans. Total Staff 3.

St. Ansgar Scandinavian Catholic League, 3E. 28th St., 8th Fl., 10016. Tel: 212-675-0400; Fax: 212-620-4687. Email: viggor@rambusch.com. Web: www.saintansgars.org. Dr. Astrid M. O'Brien, Pres.; Revs. Thomas A. Nielson, Chap.; John E. Halborg, Dir. Programs, Editor of the Bulletin; Philip Sandstrom, Spiritual Dir.; Mr. Viggo B. Rambusch, Chm.

St. Anthony Welfare Center, c/o Chancery Office, Room #1940, 1011 First Ave., 10022. Tel: 212-371-1000; Fax: 212-813-9538.

Apostolate for Family Consecration, Inc., Canonical Global Center, PMB #26N, 350 5th Ave., Ste. 3304, 10018-0069. Tel: 212-971-1370. Email: jconiker@familyland.org. Web: www.familyland.org. Jerome Coniker, Pres.

Archdiocesan Council of Catholic Nurses (Includes Manhattan) , 1011 First Ave., 10022. Tel: 212-371-1000.

Brooklyn Prep Alumni Association, Loyola Hall, Fordham Univ., 10458. Tel: 718-817-5447; Fax: 718-733-4456. Web: www.brooklynprep.org. Rev. John D. Alexander, S.J., Moderator. Membership 4,427.

Calvary Fund, Inc., 1740 Eastchester Rd., Bronx, 10461. Tel: 718-518-2077; Fax: 718-518-2477. Email: webmaster@calvaryhospital.org. Web: calvaryhospital.org. Frank A. Calamari, Pres.; Dennis E. Berberich, Chm.

Cardinal Cooke Guild, 1011 First Ave., 10022. Tel: 212-371-1000, Ext. 2740; Fax: 212-371-1011. Email: abbeykkmoy@aol.com. Web: www.activo.com/ccg. Official organization for information on the cause of canonization of Cardinal Terence J. Cooke.

Cardinal Cooke Memorial Foundation, 1011 First Ave., Room 1940, 10022. Tel: 212-371-1000; Fax: 212-813-9538.

Cardinal's Fund for Children, 1011 First Ave., Room 1130, 10022.

Carmel Housing Development Fund Co., Inc., 1011 First Ave., 10022. Tel: 212-371-1000; Fax: 212-826-8795. Rev. Msgr. Kevin L. Sullivan, Pres.

Catholic Alumni Club of the Archdiocese of New York, 83 Christopher St., 10014. Tel: 212-243-6513. Email: nycacemail.@aol.com. Web: www.caci.org/cac/newyorkcac.html. Mary Doherty, Pres.

Catholic Big Brothers of New York, Inc., 45 E. 20th St., 10003. Tel: 212-477-2250; Fax: 212-477-2739. Email: cbbnyc@aol.com. Web: www.cbbnyc.org. Total Assisted 350; Total Staff 12.

The Catholic Big Sisters Archdiocese of New York Family Outreach & Education Center , 220A East 4th St., 3rd Floor, 10009. Tel: 212-475-3291; Fax: 212-475-0280. Email: director@catholicbigsisters.org. Web: www.catholicbigsisters.org. Total Families Assisted 180; Total Staff 6.

Catholic Daughters of the Americas and Its Courts, 10 W. 71st St., 10023. Tel: 212-877-3041; Fax: 212-724-5923. Email: cdofanatl@aol.com. Web: www.catholicdaughters.org. Grace DiCairano, Natl. Regent; Mrs. Margaret O'Brien, Contact Person.

Catholic Family and Human Rights Institute, 866 United Nations Plaza, Ste. 427, 10017. Tel: 212-754-5948; Fax: 212-754-9291. Email: c-fam@c-fam.org. Web: www.c-fam.org. Austin Ruse, Pres.

Catholic Foundation for the Dominican Republic, 1011 First Ave., Room 1940, 10022. Tel: 212-371-1000. Rev. Msgr. James P. Cassidy, Ph.D., Pres.

Catholic Health Care Foundation of the Archdiocese of New York, Inc., 155 E. 56th St., 2nd Fl., 10022. Tel: 212-752-7300; Fax: 212-752-7547. Email: mkeegan@chcsnet.org. Web: www.phsf.org. Mary E. Keegan, Contact Person.

Catholic Health Care System, 155 East 56th St., 2nd Floor, 10022. Tel: 212-752-7300; Fax: 212-752-7547. Email: rrogenhaugh@chcsnet.org. Web: www.chcsnet.org. Karl P. Alles, M.D., Archbishop's Delegate for Health Care.

Catholic High School Association of New York 1011 First Ave., Room 1856, 10022. Tel: 212-371-1000; Fax: 212-758-3018. Email: supt@adnyschools.org. Web: www.ny-archdiocese.org.

Catholic High Schools' Athletic Association of the Archdiocese of New York, 650 Grand Concourse, 10451. Tel: 718-585-5556.

4300 Murdock Ave., Bronx, 10466. Tel: 718-325-6423. Mr. Richard Tricario, Pres.

Catholic Interracial Council of N.Y., The, 899 10th Ave., 10019. Tel: 212-237-8600. Gerard W. Lynch, Pres.

**Catholic League for Religious and Civil Rights*, 450 Seventh Ave., 34th Fl., 10123. Tel: 212-371-3191; Fax: 212-371-3394. Email: cl@catholicleague.org. Web: www.catholicleague.org. Dr. William A. Donohue, Pres.; Bernadette Brady, Vice Pres. Total Staff 12.

Catholic Medical Mission Board, Inc., National Headquarters, 10 W. 17th St., 10011-5765. Tel: 212-242-7757; Fax: 212-807-9161; 212-242-0930. Email: info@cmmb.org. Web: www.cmmb.org. Rev. Msgrs. Ferdinando D. Berardi; Robert J. Fuhrman (NEW); Rev. William J. Scanlon, S.J.; Most Rev. William S. Skylstad, D.D.; Sr. Marilyn Fischer, S.F.P.; Thomas Flynn, M.D.; Thomas P. Melady, Ambassador; Patricia Smith, M.D.; Terry Kirch, Pres. & CEO; James A. Cunningham, C.P.A.; Mr. Charles J. Casamento; Sr. Peggy Egan, O.S.F.

Catholic Near East Welfare Association (CNEWA), 1011 First Ave., 10022. Tel: 212-826-1480; Fax: 212-826-8979. Email: cnewa@cnewa.org. Web: www.cnewa.org. His Eminence Edward Cardinal Egan, Pres. & Treas.; William H. Keeler, Vice Pres.; Rev. Msgrs. Robert L. Stern, Sec. Gen.; Denis Madden, Deputy Sec. Gen.; Chorbishops John D. Faris, Under Sec. Gen.

Catholic Social Policy Coalition of the Archdiocese of New York, The, 1011 First Ave., Room 1150, 10022. Agnes Kearns, Pres.

Catholic Women's Union, c/o Eunice Vasile, 2664 Salt Point Tpke., Clinton Corners, 12514. Tel: 845-266-3074; Fax: 845-266-3666. Eunice Vasile, Pres.; Anna K. Weisz, Vice Pres.; Hilda McGlew, Treas.; Mary Sophie Ruedi, Sec.

The Catholic World Wide Web Corporation, 1011 First Ave., 10022. Tel: 212-371-1000. Email: bernard.reidy@archny.org. Web: cathwww.org. Bernard E. Reidy, Vice Pres.

The Center for Spirituality and Justice, Tel: 914-633-8367; Fax: 914-633-5281. Email: miriamcosu@juno.com. 323 E. 198th St., Bronx, 10458. Tel: 914-633-8667; Fax: 914-633-5281. Bro. Charles A. Reutemann, F.S.C., Vice Pres.; Sr. Miriam Cleary, O.S.U., Sec.; Rev. Michael Wastag, O.Carm. (NEW). Total Assisted 15; Total Staff 3.

Centro Carismatico Catolico Hispano De La Arquidiocesis De Nueva York, Tel: 718-378-1734; Fax: 718-378-1819. Email: catholicny@aol.com. Web: centrocarismatico.com. 826 E. 166th St., Bronx, 10459. Tel: 718-378-1734; Fax: 718-378-1819. Most Rev. Josu Iriondo, Dir.

Chinese Catholic Information Center, 86 Riverside Dr. 10024. Tel: 212-787-6969; Fax: 212-787-0260. Email: chanpaulus@juno.com. Rev. Paul Chan (Taiwan), Dir. Total in Residence 3; Total Staff 3.

Christ House, Inc. Shared Residence for Religious and Young Men Lacking Family Support. , 432 E. 142nd St., Bronx, 10454. Tel: 718-665-8740; Fax: 718-665-1665. Email: jhanney@christhouse-nyc.org. Bro. James V. Hanney, C.F.C., Dir.

The Christophers, 12 E. 48th St., 10017. Tel: 212-759-4050; Fax: 212-759-7449. Email: mail@christophers.org. Web: www.christophers.org. Dennis W. Heaney, Pres. A multi-media organization reaching millions with the Gospel message. Total Staff 36.

CNEWA UNITED STATES, 1011 First Ave., 10022. His Eminence William H. Keeler, Pres.; Chorbishop John D. Faris, Contact Person & Sec.

Committee for Mission Responsibility Society, Inc. The Propagation of the Faith , 1011 First Ave., 10022. Tel: 212-371-1000, Ext. 2700; Fax: 212-371-7220. Email: spofny@aol.com. Rev. Michael C. Crimmins, Dir.

Community of St. Egidio, U.S.A., Inc., P.O. Box 250299, 10025-1534. Tel: 212-663-1483; Fax: 212-663-4178. Email: ppiscitell@hotmail.com. Web: www.santegidio.org. Paola Piscitelli, Pres.

Cor Mariae Development Fund Corporation, 1011 First Ave., 10022. Rev. Msgr. Kevin L. Sullivan, Pres. & Contact Person.

Cor Mariae Housing Development Fund, Inc., 1101 First Ave., 10022. Tel: 212-371-1000, Ext. 2400. Rev. Kevin L. Sullivan, Pres.

Cornelia Connelly Center for Education, Holy Child Middle School, 220 E. 4th St., 10009. Tel: 212-982-2287; Fax: 212-982-0547. Email: mcryan@connellycenter.org. Web: www.holychild.com. Mary Claire Ryan, Dir.; Sr. Marcia Sichol, S.H.C.J., Contact Person.

Courage, Church of St. John the Baptist, 210 W. 31st St., 10001. Tel: 212-268-1010; Fax: 212-268-7150. Email: NYcourage@aol.com. Web: couragerc.net. Rev. John F. Harvey, O.S.F.S., Dir. Total Staff 2.

**CUSA - An Apostolate of the Sick or Disabled, Inc.*, 63 Wall St., Ste. 1802, 10005. Tel: 201-437-0412. Email: ams4@juno.com. Web: www.cusan.org. Mrs. Joan Donnelly, Pres.

Descubriendo Siglo XXI, Inc. (Discovering Century, XXI, Inc.), Holy Cross Church, 329 W. 42nd St., 10036. Tel: 212-244-4778; Fax: 212-868-6997. Email: ptomassiglo21@aol.com. Web: www.descubriendoelsiglo21.org. Rev. Thomas Del Valle-Reyes, Contact Person.

Dominican Friars' Guilds, 141 E. 65th St., 10021. Tel: 212-744-2410; Fax: 212-737-3875. Web: www.op-stjoseph.org.

St. Jude Dominican Missions, 141 E. 65th St., 10021. Tel: 212-744-2410; Fax: 212-737-3875. Rev. Raymond Ferrer Halligan, O.P., Dir.

Dominican Rosary Apostolate, 141 E. 65th St., 10021. Tel: 212-744-2410; Fax: 212-737-3875.

Deserving Poor Boys Priesthood Association, 141 E. 65th St., 10021. Tel: 212-744-2410; Fax: 212-737-3875.

St. Martin de Porres Guild, 141 E. 65th St., 10021. Tel: 212-744-2410; Fax: 212-737-3875.

Dominican Shrine of St. Jude, Inc., St. Catherine of Siena Priory, 411 E. 68th St., 10021. Tel: 212-249-6067; 212-988-8300; Fax: 212-988-8920. Email: concog@ prodigy.net. Web: www.ophomily.org. Very Rev. Edmund M. Gorman, O.P.; Rev. George Lawrence Concordia, O.P., Admin. Dir.

**Don Bosco Harlem Association, Inc.*, 147-159 St. Nicholas Ave., 10026. Tel: 212-662-2693. Rev. George Hanna, S.D.B., Contact Person.

**The Elizabeth Seton Housing Development Fund Corporation*, 1991 Lexington Ave., 10035. Tel: 212-348-1655; Fax: 212-348-1822. Sr. Elizabeth Vermaelon, Pres. Total Assisted 87; Total Staff 3.

**St. Elizabeth Seton Women's Center, Inc.*, 133 W. 70th St., 10023. Tel: 212-579-3657; Fax: 212-579-3659. Email: eswc@aol.com. Sisters Dorothy Metz, Pres.; Arleen Ketchum, S.C., Dir.

Felix Varela Foundation, Inc., The, 1011 First Ave., 10022. Tel: 718-229-8001, Ext. 201; Fax: 718-224-0295. Rev. Msgr. Octavio Cisneros, Pres.

Foundation of the Order of Friars Minor of the Province of the Most Holy Name, Formerly Foundation of the Order of Friars Minor Province of the Most Holy Name158 W. 27th St., 6th Fl., 10001-6206. Tel: 212-924-1451; Fax: 646-201-9620. Email: hnp@hnp.org. Web: www.ofm.org. Rev. John M. Felice, O.F.M., Pres.

St. Francis Counseling Center, Inc., 135 W. 31st St., 10001. Tel: 212-736-8500; Fax: 212-736-8545. Julie D. Berwick, C.S.W., Dir.

St. Francis Monastery Breadline for the Poor, Inc., 135 W. 31st St., 10001-3439. Tel: 212-736-8500; Fax: 212-736-8545. Email: stfra135@aol.com. Rev. Peter Brophy, O.F.M., Contact Person.

Franciscan Missionary Charities, Inc., 135 W. 31st St., 10001. Tel: 212-631-0852; Fax: 212-736-8545. Email: cowofm@hanmail.net. Revs. Ronald P. Stark, O.F.M., Pres.; Francis Kim, O.F.M., Exec. Vice Pres.

Franciscan Missionary Union, Province of the Most Holy Name Headquarters , St. Francis Friary, 135 W. 31st St., 10001-3439. Tel: 212-924-1451; Fax: 212-924-1994. Email: nyce1999@msn.com. Rev. Russell C. Becker, O.F.M., Prov. Promoter. Three schools in Brazil.; The Franciscan Missionary Union also maintains 3 Medical Clinics in Lima, Peru and a Social Center for the poor in Mexico City, Mexico. Various social services in Bolivia; local assistance in Vietnam, Taiwan, Japan and East Africa.

Franciscans International, Inc., 211 E. 43rd St., 11th Floor, 10017-4707. Tel: 212-490-4624; Fax: 866-283-0134. Email: franintl@franciscansinternational.org. Web: www.franciscansinternational.org. Sr. Florence Deacon, O.S.F., Contact Person.

Franciscans of Holy Name Province Benevolence Trust, Inc., 158 W. 27th St., 6th Fl., 10001-6206. Tel: 212-924-1451; Fax: 646-201-9620. Email: hnp@hnp.org. Web: hnp.org. Rev. Dennis M. Wilson, O.F.M., Trustee.

Franciscans of Holy Name Province Sick, Aged and Retired Trust, 158 W. 27th St., 6th Fl., 10001-6206. Tel: 212-924-1451; Fax: 646-201-9620. Email: hnp@hnp.org. Web: www.ofm.org.

Franciscans of Holy Name Province Education and Formation Trust, 158 W. 27th St., 6th Fl., 10001. Tel: 212-924-1451; Fax: 646-201-9620.

Email:hnp@hnp.org.

The Fratecelli Corporation, 158 W. 27 St., 6th Fl., 10001-6206. Tel: 212-924-1451; Fax: 646-201-9620. Email: hnp@hnp.org. Web: www.hnp.org.

Friends of American Art in Religion, Inc., 143 E. 43rd St., 10017. Tel: 212-682-5722; Fax: 212-370-5791. His Eminence Edward Cardinal Egan, Pres.; Rev. Msgr. Eugene V. Clark, P.A., Sec. & Treas.

Friends of RADIO MARIA, Inc., 352 W. 44th St., 10036. Tel: 718-417-0550; Fax: 718-417-5188. Email: radiomny@radiomaria.org. Web: www.radiomaria.org. Rev. Joseph Fugolo, C.S., Dir.

The Good Shepherd Volunteers, Inc., 337 E. 17th St., 10003. Tel: 212-475-4245, Ext. 718; Fax: 212-979-8604. Email: gsv@goodshepherds.org. Web: www.goodshepherdvolunteers.org. Sr. Maureen McGowan, R.G.S., Contact Person.

Gregorian University Foundation, The, 106 W. 56th St., 10019. Tel: 212-582-5433; Fax: 212-956-2921. Email: gregorian@mindspring.com. Web: www.the-gregorian.com. Rev. Robert E. O'Toole, S.J. (STL), Pres.

Guild of Catholic Lawyers, The, c/o Kelly, Drye, & Warren, 101 Park Ave., 10178. 1011 First Ave., 10022. Tel: 212-808-7847; Fax: 212-808-7897. Rev. George W. Rutler, Spiritual Dir.

Healing Through God Word Ministries, Inc., 320 Powell Ave., Newburgh, 12550. Tel: 845-561-6520; Fax: 845-569-8139. Sr. Jean Marie Timko, O.P., Pres.
Legal Title: *Healing Through God Word Ministries, Inc./Apostolate of Intercession Healing & Teaching the Word of God*, An evangelistic ministry of teaching the scriptures, intercession, and healing. Involves missions, retreats, days of renewal, healing services, and Bible studies.

Hispanic Catholic Charismatic Center of the Archdiocese of New York, Tel: 718-378-1734; Fax: 718-378-1819. Email: catholicny@aol.com. Web: centrocarismatico.com. 826 E. 166th St., Bronx, 10459. Tel: 718-378-1734; Fax: 718-378-1819. Most Rev. Josu Iriondo.

House of Peace, Inc., Tel: 718-547-3230; Fax: 718-547-1765. Web: members.aol.com/healing.svc. 1291 Allerton Ave., P.O. Box 696, Bronx, 10469-0696. Tel: 718-547-3230; Fax: 718-547-1765. Maryanne Lacy. Healing Prayer Center for the Peace of Christ Prayer Ministry.

The Housing Fund of the Archdiocese of New York, 1011 First Ave., 10022. Tel: 212-371-1000. Rev. Msgrs. Kevin L. Sullivan, Vice. Pres.; Donald Sakano, Sec. & Treas.

Hungarian Catholic League of America, Inc., 414 E. 82 St., 10016. Tel: 212-327-2959; Fax: 212-535-9221. Rev. Dominic L. Csorba, O.F.M., Pres.; Rev. Msgr. William I. Varsanyi, P.A., Bd. Chm.; A. Petrak, Sec.

Incarnation Children's Center Fund, Inc., 42 Audubon Ave., 10032. Tel: 212-928-2590, Ext. 2400; Fax: 212-928-1500. Email: ccastro@incarnationchildrenscenter.org. Web: www.icc-palsaids.org. Carolyn Castro, Exec. Dir. Capacity 21.

Institute of the Helpers, 385 W. 263rd St., Bronx, 10471. Sr. Teresa Cole, Pres.

Intercommunity Center for Justice & Peace, 20 Washington Square N., 10011. Tel: 212-475-6677; Fax: 212-475-6969. Email: icjp@icjp.org. Web: www.icjp.org. Sr. Arlene Flaherty, O.P., Exec. Dir. Peace and Justice Center is a coalition of 40 religious congregations. The ICJP assists its members in implementing actions of peace and justice according to social teachings of the church. Total Staff 3.

International Catholic Child Bureau/North America, Inc., 595 West End Ave., #10C, 10024. Tel: 212-595-9180; Fax: 212-595-3917. Mr. David J. Sauer, Vice Pres., Admin. Svcs., The Catholic Health Association. An international convening agency for child care professionals interested in developing pilot projects, training seminars, research and advocacy for the physical, psychological, social, spiritual and religious well-being of all children worldwide.

International Catholic Organizations Information Center, Inc., 323 E. 47 St., 10017. Tel: 212-355-5557; Fax: 212-355-9865. Email: icony@unmail.org. Ellen Shafer, Pres. of Board; Dorothy Farley, Exec. Dir.

Jesuit Seminary and Mission Bureau, Inc. See Jesuit Provincial's office.

John LaFarge Institute, The, c/o America Press, Inc., 106 W. 56th St., 10019. Tel: 212-581-4640; Fax: 212-399-3596. Rev. Vincent T. O'Keefe, S.J., Dir.

St. Joseph's Union of Staten Island, New York Inc., 108 Bedell St., Staten Island, 10309. Tel: 718-984-9296. Sr. Una McCormack, O.P., Treas.

Korean Christian Life Community, Inc., 372 5th Ave., #4D, 10018. Tel: 203-855-0698; Fax: 203-855-0698. Email: cmkhang@opronline.net. Catherine M. Khang, Vice Pres.

LAMP Ministries, Inc., 2704 Schurz Ave., Bronx, 10465. Tel: 718-409-5062; Fax: 718-904-0048. Email: tscheuring@lampministries.org. Web: www.lampministries.org. Tom Scheuring, Ph.D., Co-Dir.; Lyn Scheuring, Ph.D., Co-Dir.; Marybeth Greene, Assoc. Dir.; Ed Greene, Assoc. Dir.

LaSalle New York City, Inc., 44 E. 2nd St., 10003. Tel: 212-475-8940; Fax: 212-529-3598. Email: jmartino@lasalleny.com. Web: www.lasalleacademy.org. Bros. Franc Byrnes, F.S.C., Chm.; James Martino, F.S.C., Vice Chm. Total Assisted 550; Total Staff 53.

Legion of Mary, Office, 1011 First Ave., 10022. Tel: 212-752-7966. Email: ny.sanatus@worldnet.att.net.

Lower East Side Catholic Area Conference-Pastoral Center, 23 Oliver St., 10038. Tel: 212-962-1850; Fax: 212-571-4126.

Lumen Dei, 340 W. 53rd St., 10019. Tel: 212-586-4447; Fax: 212-586-1640. Email: ld.prodein@att.net. Rev. Wilberto Reyes Garced, Regl. Supr. Priests of Lumen Dei 1; Sisters of Lumen Dei 5.

Manhattan North Community Services, Inc., 91 Arden St., 10040. Niki Montaluo, Pres.

Maria Droste Services, 386 Park Ave. S., Ste. 903, 10016-8804. Tel: 212-889-4042; Fax: 212-889-3936. Betsy Selman-Babinecz, Dir.
Legal Title: *St. Germaine's Services*

**Monsignor Robert Fox Memorial Shelter Housing Development, Inc.*, Fox House, 111 E. 117th St., 10035. Tel: 212-534-6634; Fax: 212-427-8507. Email: foxsheller@aol.com. Sr. Florence Speth, Exec. Dir. Total Assisted: 450; Total Staff 17.

Narnia Catechetical & Cultural Centre, Inc., 20 Sutton Pl. S., 10022. Mrs. Charles Teetor, Pres.; Mr. George Sim Johnston, Sec. & Treas.

National Federation for Life, 1011 First Ave., Room 1417, 10022.

National Office of the Devotees of Padre Pio, Inc., 1154 1st Ave., 10021. Tel: 212-838-6549. Mr. Mario Bruscki, Dir.

Nativity Mission Center, Inc., 204 Forsyth St., 10002. Tel: 212-477-2472; Fax: 212-473-0538. Email: director@nativitymission.org. Web: www.nativitymission.org. Rev. Vincent DeCola, S.J., Pres. Students 60; Total Staff 10.

**Nazareth Housing, Inc.*, 519 E. 11th St., 10009. Tel: 212-777-1010; Fax: 212-777-1867. Email: nazareth@earthlink.net smadaniel@naarethhousing.com. Web: www.nazarethhousing.com; nazarethhousing.com/index.htm.

New York Catholic Forum, c/o St. Thomas More Church, 65 E. 89th St., 10128. Tel: 212-838-0530. Mr. George Sim Johnston, Chm.

New York Society of the John Paul II Foundation, Inc., 101 East 7th St., 10009. Tel: 718-383-8030; Fax: 718-349-2773. Email: polstar.shop@verizon.net. Mr. Michael Pajak, Pres. Tel: 718-383-9587.

Nocturnal Adoration Society of the United States, 184 E. 76th St., 10021. Tel: 212-288-5082; Fax: 212-717-8397. Email: sjbrcc@aol.com. Web: www.sjbrcc.org. Congregation of the Blessed Sacrament

North American College of Rome, Alumni Assoc. of, Tel: 718-828-3403; Fax: 718-829-1304. *St. Benedict Church*, 2969 Otis Ave., Bronx, 10465. Tel: 718-828-3403; Fax: 718-829-1304. Rev. Msgr. Edmund J. Whalen, S.T.D.

Northeast Hispanic Catholic Center, 1011 First Ave., 10022. Tel: 212-751-7045; Fax: 212-753-5321. Email: nhcc1011@aol.com. Rudy Vargas IV, Exec. Dir.

Partnership for Quality Education, Inc., 1011 First Ave., 10022. Tel: 212-371-1011, Ext. 3356; Fax: 212-371-6461. Email: tpotenza@archny.org. Web: projectyess.org. Helen T. Lowe, Dir. Devel. Partnership for quality education, assisting 148 inner-city schools, Operates Project YESS (Young Executives Supporting Schools), an initiative for capital improvements or repairs in inner-city schools.

St. Patrick's International Inc., c/o Cusack and Stiles LLP, 61 Broadway, Ste. 2100, 10006-2894. Tel: 212-480-0400; Fax: 212-943-8534. Email: spsbur@iol.ie. Web: www.spms.org. Rev. Seamus O'Neil, Pres.

Patrons of the Arts in the Vatican Museums, 143 E. 43rd St., 10017. Tel: 212-682-5722; Fax: 212-370-5791. His Eminence Edward Cardinal Egan, Chm. of the Bd.; Rev. Msgr. Eugene V. Clark, P.A., Treas. & Sec. Total Staff 2.

St. Paul's Guild, Inc., 1011 First Ave., Room 1940, 10022. Tel: 212-371-1000; Fax: 212-813-9538.

Pauline Books & Media, 78 Fort Pl., Staten Island, 10301. Tel: 718-447-5071; 718-447-5086; Fax: 718-816-1332. Email: fspny@aol.com. Web: www.pauline.org.
Legal Title: *Pauline Books & Media*
Other location:, 150 E. 52nd St., 10022. Tel: 212-754-1110; Fax: 212-754-2268. Total in Residence 11; Total Staff 18.

Pax Christi Metro New York, 135 W. Fourth St., 10012. Tel: 212-420-0250; Fax: 212-420-1628. Email: nypaxchristi@igc.org. Web: www.serve.com/pcmny. Rosemarie Pace, Coord. We are a regional chapter of Pax Christi USA, the national Catholic movement for peace.

Perpetual Help Center, Tel: 718-585-3678; Fax: 718-993-5870. Web: www.perpetualhelpcenter.org. 294 E. 150th St., Bronx, 10451. Tel: 718-585-3678; Fax: 718-993-5870. Bro. Stephen Lendvay, C.SS.R. Redemptorist Fathers of New York

Pius XII Foundation, Inc., 570 Lexington Ave., 33rd Fl., 10022. Tel: 212-319-0464; Fax: 212-319-5578. Email: foundation@piusxii.org. Bro. Robert Fontaine, C.S.C., Pres.

Regina Coeli Society First Friday Club for the Catholic Women of New York City Police Dept. , Mailing Address: P.O. Box 939, 10272-0604. Tel: 212-374-5060. Jacquelyn Fleming, Pres.

St. Rose's Settlement, 1011 First Ave., Room 1940, 10022. Tel: 212-371-1000; Fax: 212-813-9538.

S.H.A.R.E. - New York, Inc., 1601 Bronxdale Ave., Bronx, 10462. Tel: 718-518-1513. Email: SHARNYFood@aol.com. Ms. Elisa Perry, Exec. Dir.

Scalabrini Pastoral Center, 352 W. 44th St., 10036-5419. Tel: 212-247-7373; Fax: 212-265-5793. Email: jfugolo@aol.com. Web: www.scalabrini.org. Rev. Joseph Fugolo, C.S., Dir. Directed by The Pius Society of the Missionaries of St. Charles Borromeo, Inc. (NY Prov.) Total Staff 2.
American Committee on Italian Migration (A.C.I.M.) Tel: 212-247-7373; Fax: 212-265-5793.
Scalabrini Promotion Office & Press Office for Migration Tel: 212-247-7374; Fax: 212-265-5793.

Shrine of St. Jude, Inc., St. Stephen of Hungary Parish, 414 E. 82nd St., 10028. Tel: 800-688-JUDE; Fax: 212-535-9221. Email: judehope@covad.net. Web: www.saintstephenofhungary.org. Revs. John M. Felice, O.F.M., Pres.; Angelus Gambatese, O.F.M., Spiritual Dir.; Sr. Natalie M. Runfola, R.S.C.J., Exec. Sec.

Sisters of Charity of New York Charitable Trust, Tel: 718-549-9200; Fax: 718-884-3013. Web: www.scny.org.
Sisters of Charity Center, 6301 Riverdale Ave., Bronx, 10471-1093. Tel: 718-549-9200; Fax: 718-884-3013. Sisters Dorothy Metz, Trustee; Audrey Boylan, Trustee; Mary Ellen Butler, Trustee; Margaret Brick, Trustee; Margaret O'Brien, Trustee.

Sisters of the Holy Child Jesus-African Province Office, 325 E. 33rd St., 10016-9401. Tel: 212-696-5503; Fax: 212-545-7804. Email: shcjapdo@aol.com. Web: shcj.org. Sr. Margaret Rogers, S.H.C.J., Dir.
Legal Title: *Sisters of the Holy Child Jesus - African Province Office for the African Apostolates*

Society for the Renewal of Christian Art, The, 217 E. 66th St., 10021. Tel: 212-288-8186. Rt. Rev. Alban W. Boultwood, O.S.B., Chm. of the Bd.; Emily J. Bouchard, Pres. Purpose: To work for the renaissance of Christian Art in our time and to foster a Christian dimension in the New York art world.
Contemporary Christian Art, Inc., 217 E. 66th St., 10021. Tel: 212-288-8186. Emily Bouchard, Dir. (Affiliated with the Society for the Renewal of Christian Art.); Purpose: To work with artists in designing and producing Christian Art, art used in worship, presented in a contemporary manner. To bring the creators of Christian art and their works into contact with those who seek good art.

Society of Helpers, Tel: 718-884-3100; Fax: 718-884-3101. 385 W. 263rd St., Bronx, 10471. Tel: 718-884-3100; Fax: 718-884-3101. Email: nyhelper_nyhelper@claret.org nyhelper@crols.com. Web: www.claret.org/~srmoore/goodc.html. Sr. Geraldine Finan, Supr. Sisters 5.

Saint Vincent's Catholic Medical Centers Foundation, Inc., 153 W. 11th St., 10011. Tel: 212-604-7554. Email: mackermann@saintvincentsnyc.org. Mr. Mark G. Ackermann, Pres.

St. Thomas Aquinas Foundation National Headquarters (Order of Preachers, St. Joseph Prov.) , 141 E. 65th St., 10021-6618. Tel: 212-737-5757; Fax: 212-861-4216. Email: provincial@stjoseph-usa.op.org. Very Rev. David Dominic Izzo, O.P., Pres.
Legal Title: *St. Thomas Aquinas Foundation of the Dominican Fathers of the United States (STAF)*

Thorpe Family Residence, Inc., Tel: 718-933-7311; Fax: 718-933-7311. 2252 Crotona Ave., Bronx, 10457. Tel: 718-933-7312; Fax: 718-933-7311. Total Assisted Families 16; Total Staff 10.

Tri-State Coalition for Responsible Investment, 20 Washington Sq. N., 10011. Tel: 212-475-6677; Fax: 212-475-6969. Email: tricri@mindspring.com. Sr. Patricia Daly, O.P., Exec. Dir.

Trust for the Center for Migration Studies in New York, 27 Carmine St., 10014-4423. Tel: 212-675-3993; Fax: 212-727-3139. Email: jfugolo@aol.com. Web: www.cmsny.org. Rev. Joseph Fugolo, C.S.

United States Catholic Historical Society, The, 1011 First Ave., Ste. 1940, 10022. Tel: 800-225-7999. Dr. Brian Butler, Pres. & Chm. of the Bd.; Mr. Charles J. James, Exec. Dir.

The United States Catholic Widows and Widowers Assoc., Inc., 1011 First Ave., Room 1940, 10022. Tel: 212-371-1000, Ext. 2900; Fax: 212-813-9538.

Xavier Society for the Blind, 154 E. 23rd St., 10010. Tel: 212-473-7800. Revs. Alfred E. Caruana, S.J., Exec. Dir.; James F. O'Brien, S.J.; Joseph A. Latella, S.J.

BARRYVILLE. *New Hope Manor*, 35 Hillside Rd., 12719. Tel: 914-557-8353; Fax: 914-557-6603. Email: newhopemnr@aol.com. Web: www.newhopemanor.org. Nicholas A. Roes, Exec. Dir.; Sr. Patricia Conway, O.P., Counselor & House Mother; Jennifer Redish, C.S.W., Clinical Dir.; Sisters Maureen Conway, O.P., Dir. Education, Counselor & Teacher; Rose Respil, O.P., Dir. Rel. Education; Revs. Aquinas Thomas, S.A.; Arte Johnson, S.A., Bd. Member; Sisters Joan Correia, O.P., Bd. Member; Joanne Malone, O.P., Bd. Member; Rita Moriarity, S.C.C., R.N., Bd. Member; Bro. Charles Kinney, S.A., Bd. Member. Sparkill Dominican Sisters, A live-in therapeutic community for the substance abuse rehabilitation of women, pregnant women, and infants.

BEACON. *Carmelite Communion, Inc.*, 89 Hiddenbrooke Dr., 12508-2230. Tel: 845-831-5572; Fax: 845-831-5579. Email: bcarmel@prodigy.net. Sr. Marjorie Robinson, O.C.D., Contact Person.

Metropolitan Association of Contemplative Communities, Inc., 89 Hiddenbrooke Dr., 12508. Tel: 845-831-5572; Fax: 845-831-5579. Web: www.catholic.org/macc. Sr. Rita Donahue, O.C.D., Contact Person.

BRONX. *Abraham House, Inc.*, 342 Willis Ave., 10452. Tel: 718-292-9321; Fax: 718-292-5925. Email: abrahamhse@aol.com. Rev. Msgr. Howard W. Calkins, Pres. Total Assisted 6,000; Total Staff 18.

American St. Boniface Society, Incorporated, Mailing Address: P.O. Box 1352, 10466-1352. Tel: 718-994-0989; Fax: 718-994-6119. Rev. Joachim Von Kerssenbrock, S.J., Prov.; Germainiae Septentrionalis, Exec. Dir.

St. Benedict the Moor Center, 281/283 St. Ann's Ave., 10454. Tel: 718-665-9693; Fax: 718-402-9536. Email: moorcenter@aol.com. Anthony R. Jordan, Dir. Operations. Total Staff 12.

Calvary Holding Company, Inc., 1740 Eastchester Rd., 10461. Tel: 718-518-2251; Fax: 718-518-2674. Frank A. Calamari, Pres.; Thomas J. Fahey Jr., M.D., Chm.

Foundation of Christ the Redeemer Institute Id Misioneros y Misioneras Identes, , 2352 St. Raymond Ave., 10462. Tel: 718-828-2380; Fax: 718-828-4296.

St. Joseph's Center For the development of Lay Leaders, Cursillo Center, Marriage Encounter. (Spanish) , 275 W. 230th St., 10463. Tel: 718-796-4340; Fax: 718-796-4340. Rev. Jose Luis Martinez, O.A.R. (LA), Dir. Total in Residence 2; Total Staff 4; Capacity 45.

St. Joseph's School for the Deaf Childrens Fund, Inc., 1000 Hutchinson River Pkwy., 10465. Tel: 718-792-8308; Fax: 718-792-2532. Email: dorothydhm@aol.com. The Children's Fund assists St. Joseph's School for the Deaf in meeting the needs of the children and their educational experiences.

Saint Jutta Foundation, Inc., c/o Rev. John Adam, S.J., Fordham University, Loyola Hall, 10458. Tel: 718-817-3671; Fax: 718-817-5717. Email: hegyi@fordham.edu. Rev. John Adam, S.J., Contact Person.

Marian Residence Fund, 323 E. 198th St., 10458. Tel: 718-365-7410; Fax: 718-733-4498. Email: ursruepr@aol.com. Sr. Dorothy Ann Kelly, O.S.U., Prov./Trustee.

**Mercy Center, Inc.*, 377 E. 145th St., 10454. Tel: 718-993-2789; Fax: 718-402-1594. Email: administration@mercycenterbronx.org. Web: www.mercycenterbronx.org. Joseph S. Dirr, Co-Dir.; Sr. Mary Galeone, R.S.M., Co-Dir. Parenting skills courses, business training, support groups, spirituality groups, & ESL.

Metro New York Life Communities, Inc., Loyola Faber Hall, Fordham University, 10458. Tel: 718-817-5454; Fax: 718-733-4456. Email: frfitz@juno.com. Web: www.fordham.edu/clc. Rev. Daniel J. Fitzpatrick, S.J., Moderator & Contact Person.

NACAR, Inc., 1720 Metropolitan Ave., 10462. Tel: 718-918-9420; Fax: 718-918-9421. Email: eocsc@aol.com. Web: www.catholic-church.org/nacar. Sr. Ellen Rose O'Connell, S.C., Pres.

O.S.U. Charitable Trust, 323 E. 198th St., 10458. Tel: 718-365-7410; Fax: 718-733-4498. Email: ursruepr@aol.com. Sr. Dorothy Ann Kelly, O.S.U., Prov./Trustee.

**The Resource Center for Community Development, Inc.*, 1900 Crotona Pkwy., 10460. Tel: 718-893-0778. Most Rev. Francisco Garmedia, Pres. Total Assisted 15,000; Total Staff 6.

**Tolentine-Zeiser Community Life Center, Inc.*, 2345 University Ave., 10468. Tel: 718-933-6935; Fax: 718-733-1653. Total Assisted 172; Total Staff 19.

Youth Ministries for Peace & Justice, Inc., 1384 Stratford Ave., 10472. Tel: 718-328-5622; Fax: 718-328-5630. Email: ympj@yahoo.com. Alexie Torres-Fleming, Exec. Dir.

BRONXVILLE. *Polish Knights of Malta, Inc.*, 1 Stoneleigh Plaza, #5-K, 10708. Tel: 914-793-4596; Fax: 914-771-4034. Email: witoldsulimirski@cs.com. Mr. Witold S. Sulimirski, Pres.

ESOPUS. *Holy Shroud Guild*, Tel: 716-394-2606; Fax: 716-394-9215. Email: fcb@shroud.org. Web: www.shroud.org. P.O. Box 993, Canandaigua, 14424. Tel: 716-394-2606; Fax: 716-394-9215. Email: fcbrink@aol.com. Web: shroud.org.

Material Distribution Center, 294 E. 150th St., Bronx, 10451. Tel: 718-585-3678; Fax: 718-292-4603.

Executive Council: Very Rev. Frederick C. Brinkmann, C.SS.R., Pres.; Rev. John Kennington, C.Ss.R.

GARRISON. *House of Nazareth Life Institute Ltd. (Nazareth Life Center)*, Philipse Brook Rd., Box 242, 10524. Tel: 845-424-3116. Sr. Marita Paul, F.S.P., Dir. Total in Residence 8; Total Staff 2.

HARTSDALE. *Marian Woods, Inc.*, 152 Ridge Rd., 10530. Tel: 914-750-6000; Fax: 914-750-6100. Nancy Clifford, Admin.

HAWTHORNE. *The Rose Hawthorne Guild*, 600 Linda Ave., 10532. Tel: 914-769-0111, Ext. 4. Sr. Marie Edward, C.P., Pres. & Contact Person.

HIGHLAND FALLS. *Ladycliff College Alumnae Association, Inc.*, P.O. Box 104, 10928. Tel: 914-446-2973; 914-446-5921.

HIGHLAND MILLS. *Thevenet Montessori School*, 202 Country Rte. 105, Box 1003, 10930-1003. Tel: 914-928-6981; Fax: 914-928-9437. Email: thevenet@frontiernet.net. Religious of Jesus and Mary PreK-1 Enrollment 120.

HYDE PARK. *Focolare Movement National Center*, 204 Cardinal Rd., 12538. Tel: 914-229-0230, Ext. 133; Fax: 914-229-1770. Email: czf.luminosa@att.net. Web: rc.net/focolare. Miss Marcella Ferrari, Dir. Tel: 914-229-9712; Fax: 914-229-1770 (Women); Founded in Trent, Italy in 1943. International Headquarters are in Rome, Italy. Movement was approved in March 1962 with the aim of working toward the fulfillment of Christ's prayer for unity, that all may be one. More than four million people, in all walks of life, married and single, are committed in or connected with the Movement. Centers in over fifty countries. Call for additional information.

Focolare Women's Centers:

2615 Schurz Ave., Bronx, 10465. Tel: 718-828-1969; Fax: 718-892-0419. Email: nyff@att.net. Hortensia Lopez, Dir.

1017 Calhoun Ave., Bronx, 10465. Tel: 718-904-1898. Lucia Compostella.

99-28 64 Rd., Rego Park, 11374. Tel: 718-275-2824; Fax: 718-275-5085. Donna Kempt.

Focolare Movement National Center (Men) , 196 Cardinal Rd., 12538. Tel: 914-229-0307; Fax: 914-229-0259. Email: czmlumi@aol.com. Web: rc.net/focolare. Mr. William Neu, Dir.

Focolare Men's Centers:

167 Commonwealth Ave., Mount Vernon, 10552. Tel: 914-667-5916; Fax: 914-268-2451. Email: czmny@aol.com. Carlos Bajo, Dir.

257 E. 71st St., 10021. Tel: 212-535-3795; Fax: 212--58--379. Paul Catipon.

JAMAICA. *The Fellowship of the Beloved Disciple*, Tel: 718-739-6502; Fax: 718-739-7770. Email: lallycp@aol.com. Web: www.john17.org. *Immaculate Conception Monastery*, 86-45 Edgerton Blvd., 11432. Rev. Owen Lally, C.P., Chap.; Yvonne Zeller, Dir.

LIVINGSTON MANOR. *The Monastic Family of Bethlehem*, Grooville Rd., 12758. Tel: 845-439-4300; Fax: 845-439-3069.

MARYKNOLL. *The Asian Catholic News Fund*, P.O. Box 306, 10545-0306. Tel: 914-941-7590 Fax: 914-941-2411. Email: rcallahan@maryknoll.org. Rev. Richard Callahan, M.M., Contact Person.

Friends of St. Maria Goretti, U.S.A. Inc., P.O. Box 0043, 10545-0043. Tel: 914-941-6372; Fax: 914-945-0715. Email: gzilli@maryknoll.org. Web: www.mariagoretti.org. Bro. Goretti Zilli, Pres. Tel: 914-941-6372; 914-941-7590; Rev. William T. Madden, M.M., Treas.; Mr. Ronald Finn, Vice Pres.; Mrs. Marie Finn, Sec.; Marie Candide Bouffard Inkel, Dir. Society St. Maria Goretti.

Maryknoll Mission Association of the Faithful, P.O. Box 307, 10545-0307. Tel: 914-762-6364; Fax: 914-762-7031. Email: mmaf@mkl-mmaf.org. Web: www.maryknoll.org. Kevin Mestrich, Association Leadership Team; Alicia Butkiewicz, Association Leadership Team; Gerry G. Lee, Association Leadership Team. Purpose: promoting and further developing a Catholic global mission effort which is open to Catholic lay, clerical, and religious mission vocations. The Association recruits and trains Catholic lay women, lay men , Priests, Brothers, and Sisters to conduct mission work. The Association sponsors Catholic lay men, lay women, Priests, Brothers, and Sisters in the performance of mission work and provides them with financial and other necessary support in the performance of mission work. Active in Bolivia, Brazil, Cambodia, Chile, El Salvador, Kenya, Mexico, Peru, Sudan, Tanzania, Thailand, United States, Venezuela, Vietnam, Zimbabwe, East Timor & Nepal.

Maryknoll Mission Association of the Faithful, Inc., Philadelphia, PA. Tel: 215-724-2747; Fax: 215-724-2747.

Maryknoll Mission Association of the Faithful, Inc., El Paso, TX. Tel: 915-533-7708.

Maryknoll Mission Association of the Faithful, Inc., Castro Valley, CA. Tel: 510-889-1787.

MOUNT VERNON. *St. Dymphna Devotion*, 274-280 W. Lincoln Ave., P.O. Box 598, 10550. Tel: 914-664-5604; Fax: 914-664-3017. Rev. Robert M. Campagna, O.F.M., Prov.; Madeline Bonnici, Exec. Dir. Province of the Immaculate Conception

Franciscan Mission Associates, 274-280 W. Lincoln Ave., P.O. Box 598, 10550. Tel: 914-664-5604; Fax: 914-664-3017. Rev. Robert M. Campagna, O.F.M., Prov.; Madeline Bonnici, Exec. Dir. Province of the Immaculate Conception

MT. KISCO. *Regina Apostolorum, Inc.*, 773 Armonk Rd., 10549. Tel: 914-773-1368; Fax: 914-773-1438. Rev. Juan Sabadell, L.C., Contact Person.

NEW ROCHELLE. *Christian Brothers Foundation, Inc.*, 33 Pryer Ter., 10804. Tel: 914-636-6194; Fax: 914-636-0021. Bro. Brian M. Walsh, C.F.C., Contact Person.

Songcatchers, Inc., 44 Liberty Ave., 10801. Tel: 914-654-1178 (Day); 914-576-6774 (Eve.); Fax: 914-654-1178 (Call First). Email: bdowdmus@aol.com. Sr. Beth Dowd, O.S.U., Dir. Program activities for elementary school children, including Summer Choir Camp, Concert Choir, and an after-school music program, Kindermusik. Young adults: volunteer staff of after-school program and camp; member concert.

Ursuline Social Outreach, Inc., 39 Willow Dr., 10805. Tel: 914-633-7298; Fax: 914-633-7393. Email: usoalc@aol.com. Sr. Eileen Fane, O.S.U., Exec. Dir. Ursuline Outreach sponsors The Adult Learning Center, 572 Marn St., New Rochelle.

NEWBURGH. **Newburgh Ministry*, 9 Johnston St., 12550. Tel: 845-561-0070; Fax: 845-561-5087. Sr. Margaret Anderson, O.P., Chairperson, Bd. of Dir.; James McElhinney, Coord.

Our Lady of Comfort Women's Center, 91 Ann St., 12550. Tel: 914-561-6267; Fax: 914-565-0572. Nina Faulkner, Treas. Shelter for Women & Children.

OSSINING. *Dominican Sisters of Hope Ministry Trust*, 299 N. Highland Ave., 10562. Tel: 914-941-4420; Fax: 914-941-1125. Email: mwatts@ophope.org. Web: www.ophope.org.

PEEKSKILL. *My Father's House, Inc.*, 143 Lafayette Pl., 10566. Tel: 914-737-8704. Email: rdlxmfh@aol.com. Rev. Ronald D. Lemmert, Pres.

PELHAM. *Passionist Communications, Inc.*, Mailing Address: P.O. Box 440, 10803-0440. Tel: 914-738-3344; Fax: 914-738-7652. Email: sundaymass@aol.com. Web: www.thesundaymass.org. Revs. Leo J. Gorman, C.P. (ORL), Exec. Producer; Paschal Smith, C.P., Assoc. Producer; Stephen Haslach, C.P., Assoc. Producer; James R. Gillette, C.P., Business Mgr. & Assoc. Producer.

Passionist Communications Center, 19 Second Ave., 10803-1417. Tel: 914-738-3344; Fax: 914-738-7652. Rev. Michael Salvagna, C.P. (PIT), Exec. Producer.

RHINEBECK. **The Children's Fund of the Astor Home, Inc.*, 6339 Mill St., 12572. Tel: 845-871-1127; Fax: 845-876-2020. Email: elyons@astorservices.org. Web: www.astorservices.org. Edward J. Lyons, Vice Pres.

RIVERDALE. *Holy Innocents Foundation*, 5272 Post Rd., 10471. Fax: 718-593-0248. Kevin T. O'Reilly, Pres.

RYE. *Catholic Women@Work Inc.*, 815 Boston Post Rd., 10580. Tel: 203-795-2800; Fax: 203-281-6051. Rev. Anthony Bannon, L.C.

Center for Spiritual Development, 96 Milton Rd.,

10580. Tel: 914-967-7328; Fax: 914-967-7387. Ann Marie Wallace, Ph.D., Dir.
Legion of Christ North America, Inc., 815 Boston Post Rd., 10580. Tel: 914-773-1368. Rev. Juan Sabadell, L.C., Contact Person.
Pastoral Support Services, Inc, 815 Boston Post Rd., 10580. Tel: 914-773-1368. Bro. Juan Sabadell, Sec.

SCARSDALE. *Catholic Charismatic Renewal Office*, 194 Gaylor Rd., 10583. Tel: 914-725-1773; Fax: 914-725-5227. Email: charismny@juno.com. Web: www.catholiccharismaticny.org. Sr. Pauline Cinquini, S.C., Co-Liaison; Rev. William B. Cosgrove, Co-Liaison.
Tel: 914-227-8382; Fax: 914-227-3951. Email: cosgrove@idsi.net.

SLEEPY HOLLOW. *RSHM Life Center, Inc.*, 32-34 Beekman Ave. N., 10591. Tel: 914-366-9710; Fax: 914-366-9713. Email: susan@rshmlifecenter.org. Web: www.rshmlifecenter.org. Sacred Heart of Mary Total Assisted 500; Adults 240; Children 260; Total Staff 7.

SLOATSBURG. *St. Mary's Villa, Inc.*, 150 Sisters Servants Ln., P.O. Box 9, 10974-0009. Tel: 845-753-5100; Fax: 845-753-1956. Email: ssminy@aol.com. Sisters Michele Yakymovitch, S.S.M.I., Pres.; Kathleen Hutsko, S.S.M.I., Sec.
The Blessed Josaphata Fund, 9 Emmanuel Dr., 10974-0006. Tel: 215-587-0107. Email: rmulcahey@sbcq.com. Richard T. Mulcahey Jr., Esq., Contact Person.

SPARKILL. *Hallel Institute*, 175 Rte. 340, 10976-1047. Tel: 845-365-2277; Fax: 845-365-2279. Email: hallel@worldnet.att.net. Web: hallelvision.org. Rev. George J. Torok, Pres. Total in Residence 37; Total Staff 9.
One to One Learning, Inc., Office of the President, 175 Rte. 340, 10976. Tel: 845-359-3171; Fax: 845-359-6053. Email: clpangel@aol.com. Sr. Cecilia LaPietra, O.P., Contact Person.

STATEN ISLAND. *Emmaus Ministries, Ltd.*, c/o Church of St. Clare, 110 Nelson Ave., 10308. Tel: 718-984-7873; Fax: 718-966-8420. Web: www.stclares.com. Monica Brown, Pres.; Rev. Msgr. Joseph P. Murphy, Vice Pres. & Contact Person.
Indian Knanaya Catholic Community of Greater NY, Inc., 94 Wilcox St., 10303. Tel: 914-494-7571; Fax: 914-494-9183. Email: ikcc@hotmail.com. Jose Chummar, Pres.
Priests for Life, P.O. Box 141172, 11314. Tel: 718-980-4400; Fax: 718-980-6515. Email: mail@priestsforlife.org. Web: www.priestsforlife.org. Rev. Frank A. Pavone, Natl. Dir.; Anthony DeStefano, Exec. Dir.
**Sisters of Charity Housing Development, Corp.*, 150 Brielle Ave., 10314-6400. Tel: 718-477-6803; Fax: 718-477-1356. Email: epfeldmann@worldnet.att.net. Eric Feldmann, Exec. Dir.

SUFFERN. *Covenant Corporation of Suffern, NY*, c/o Good Samaritan Hospital, 255 Lafayette Ave., 10901. Tel: 914-368-5000; Fax: 914-368-5430. Sr. Barbara Conroy, Pres.
Good Samaritan Foundation for Better Health, Inc., 255 Lafayette Ave., 10901-4869. Tel: 845-368-5151; Fax: 845-368-5596. Email: cpalmer@tshs.org. Web: goodsamhosp.org. Sr. M. Angelica Doris, Pres.; Christine Maraia, Exec. Vice Pres. Fundraising arm of Good Samaritan Hospital, Suffern, NY.

TARRYTOWN. *Ladycliff College Alumnae Association*, 88 Wilson Park Dr., 10591.
Religious of the Sacred Heart of Mary Charitable Trust, 50 Wilson Park Dr., 10591. Tel: 914-631-2979; Fax: 914-332-4735. Sr. Bernadette Kenny, Contact Person.

THORNWOOD. *Alpha Omega Family Center, Inc.*, 582 Columbus Ave., 10594. Tel: 914-749-3900; Fax: 914-749-3939. Rev. Daniel Massick, L.C., Contact Person.
Catholic Kid's Net, Inc., 582 Columbus Ave., 10594. Tel: 914-749-3900; Fax: 914-749-3939. Email: cknet@flash.net. Web: catholickidsnet.org. Rev. Juan Sabadell, L.C., Contact Person.
Catholic Net, Inc., 582 Columbus Ave., 10594. Tel: 914-749-3900; Fax: 914-749-3939. Rev. Emilio Diaz-Torre, L.C., Contact Person.
Consolidated Catholic Administrative Services, Inc., 590 Columbus Ave., 10594. Tel: 914-773-1368; Fax: 914-773-1438. Rev. Juan Sabadell, L.C., Contact Person.
Familia USA, Inc., 582 Columbus Ave., 10594. Tel: 914-749-3900; Fax: 914-749-3939. Rev. Juan Sabadell, L.C., Contact Person.
Helping Hands Medical Missions, Inc., 582 Columbus Ave., 10594. Tel: 914-749-3900; Fax: 914-749-3939. Rev. Emilio Diaz Torre, L.C.
Legion of Christ and Consecrated Regnum Christi Members Assistance Foundation, 584-590 Columbus Ave., 10594. Tel: 914-773-1368; Fax: 914-773-1438. Axel Diaz, Contact Person.
Legion of Christ, Incorporated, 582 Columbus Ave., 10594. Tel: 914-749-3900; Fax: 914-749-3939. Rev. Peter Hopkins, L.C., Contact Person.
Montessori Community, Inc., 118 Whittier Dr., 10594. Mary McElroy, Vice Pres.
Nueva Primavera Inc., 590 Columbus Ave., 10594. Tel: 914-773-1368. Rev. Juan Sabadell, L.C., Contact Person.
Youth and Family Encounter, Inc., 590 Columbus Ave., 10594. Tel: 914-773-1368; Fax: 914-773-1438. Bro. Alexander Kim, L.C., Contact Person.

WALDEN. *Contemplative Outreach, Ltd.*, 257 St. Andrews Rd., 12586. Tel: 973-838-3384; Fax: 973-492-5795. Email: office@coutreach.org. Web: www.contemplativeoutreach.org. Rt. Rev. Thomas Keating, O.C.S.O., Chairperson; Gail Fitzpatrick-Hopler, Pres. Total Staff 7.

WEST HEMPSTEAD. *La Casa Sollievo Della Sofferenza Opera Di Padre Pio* (The Home for the Relief of Suffering) ; Official United States Office. , c/o St. Thomas the Apostle Church, 24 Westminster Rd., 11552. Tel: 516-538-7465; Fax: 516-538-6991. Rev. Francis A. Sariego, O.F.M.Cap., Natl. Dir. & Coord.

WHITE PLAINS. *Company of St. Paul*, 52 Davis Ave., 10605. Tel: 914-946-1019. Rev. Stuart Sandberg, Pres.
Religious of Divine Compassion Charitable Trust, 52 N. Broadway, 10603. Tel: 914-949-2950; Fax: 914-949-5169. Email: alicefeeley@msn.com. Web: divinecompassion.org.

YONKERS. *Leviticus 25:23 Alternative Fund, Inc.*, 928 McLean Ave., 10704-4103. Tel: 914-237-3306; Fax: 914-237-3916. Email: info@leviticusfund.org. Web: www.leviticusfund.org. David C. Raynor, Exec. Dir.; Sisters Patricia Russell, O.S.U., Loan Officer; Margaret Murphy, O.P., Finance Officer; Alice Greenwald, Development Officer.
**Peace Through Divine Mercy, Inc.*, 25 Cambridge Ave., 10707. Tel: 914-337-0600. Email: PeaceThruMercy@aol.com. Kathleen Keefe, Contact Person.

[JJ] PERSONAL PRELATURES

NEW YORK. *Prelature of the Holy Cross and Opus Dei*, 139 E. 34th St., 10016. Tel: 646-742-2700; Fax: 646-742-2747. Email: newyork@opusdei.org. Web: www.opusdei.org. Very Rev. Thomas Bohlin, Regl. Vicar for the U.S.; Rev. Msgr. Javier Garcia de Cardenas; Very Rev. Arne A. Panula; Revs. George M. Rossman; Robert A. Brisson; James W. Albrecht.
Other priests residing in New York: Revs. Bradley K. Arturi, J.C.D.; Martin Heneghan.
Overlook Study Center Tel: 914-235-0199; Fax: 914-637-9597.
99 Overlook Cir., New Rochelle, 10804. Tel: 914-235-6128. Rev. Malcolm M. Kennedy.
330 Riverside Dr., 10025. Tel: 212-222-3285; Fax: 212-316-3629.

RELIGIOUS INSTITUTES OF MEN REPRESENTED IN THE ARCHDIOCESE

For further details refer to the corresponding bracketed number in the Religious Institutes of Men or Women section.

[0130]—*Assumptionists*—A.A.
[0140]—*The Augustinians* (Prov. of St. Joseph)—O.S.A.
[0330]—*Brothers of the Christian Schools* (New York Prov.)—F.S.C.
[0600]—*Brothers of the Congregation of Holy Cross*—C.S.C.
[0400]—*Canons Regular of the Order of the Holy Cross* (Prov. of St. Odilia, Minneapolis, MN)—O.S.C.
[0470]—*The Capuchin Friars* (St. Mary Prov.)—O.F.M.Cap.
[0270]—*Carmelite Fathers & Brothers* (St. Elias Prov.)—O.Carm.
[0310]—*Congregation of Christian Brothers* (Eastern U.S.)—C.F.C.
[0220]—*Congregation of the Blessed Sacrament*—S.S.S.
[1330]—*Congregation of the Mission*—C.M.
[1210]—*Congregation of the Missionaries of St. Charles*—C.S.
[1000]—*Congregation of the Passion* (St. Paul Prov.)—C.P.
[0480]—*Conventual Franciscans* (Immaculate Conception Prov.)—O.F.M.Conv
[0520]—*Franciscan Friars* (Provs. of Most Holy Name of Jesus, Immaculate Conception; Commissariats of Holy Cross, Holy Family)—O.F.M.
[0530]—*Franciscan Friars of the Atonement*—S.A.
[0650]—*Holy Ghost Fathers* (Eastern Prov.)—C.S.Sp.
[0690]—*Jesuit Fathers and Brothers* (New York Prov.)—S.J.
[0730]—*Legionaries of Christ*—L.C.
[]—*Little Brothers of the Gospel*
[0770]—*The Marist Brothers*—F.M.S.
[0780]—*Marist Fathers* (Northeastern Prov.)—S.M.
[0800]—*Maryknoll*—M.M.
[0830]—*Mill Hill Missionaries*—M.H.M.
[0720]—*The Missionaries of Our Lady of La Salette*—M.S.
[0910]—*Oblates of Mary Immaculate* (Eastern Prov.)—O.M.I.
[0430]—*Order of Preachers-Dominicans* (St. Joseph Prov.)—O.P.
[0150]—*Order of the Augustinian Recollects*—O.A.R.
[1020]—*Pauline Fathers and Brother*—S.S.P.
[1030]—*Paulist Fathers*—C.S.P.
[1040]—*Piarist Fathers*—Sch.P.
[1070]—*Redemptorist Fathers* (Baltimore Prov.)—C.SS.R.
[1190]—*Salesians of Don Bosco* (St. Philip Prov.)—S.D.B.
[0990]—*Society of the Catholic Apostolate*—S.A.C.
[1280]—*Stigmatine Fathers and Brothers*—C.S.S.
[1300]—*Theatine Fathers*—C.R.
[0560]—*Third Order Regular of Saint Francis*—T.O.R.

RELIGIOUS INSTITUTES OF WOMEN REPRESENTED IN THE ARCHDIOCESE

[0130]—*Apostles of the Sacred Heart of Jesus*—A.S.C.J.
[0230]—*Benedictine Sisters of Pontifical Jurisdiction*—O.S.B.
[0330]—*Carmelite Sisters for the Aged and Infirm*—O.Carm.
[3110]—*Congregation of Our Lady of the Retreat in the Cenacle*—R.C.
[2410]—*Congregation of the Marianites of Holy Cross*—M.S.C.
[3710]—*Congregation of the Sisters of Saint Agnes*—C.S.A.
[1920]—*Congregation of the Sisters of the Holy Cross*—C.S.C.
[1710]—*Congregation of the Third Order of St. Francis of Mary Immaculate*—O.S.F.
[0760]—*Daughters of Charity of St. Vincent de Paul*—D.C.
[0790]—*Daughters of Divine Charity* (St. Joseph Prov.)—F.D.C.
[0850]—*Daughters of Mary Help of Christians*—F.M.A.
[0860]—*Daughters of Mary of the Immaculate Conception*—D.M.
[0950]—*Daughters of St. Paul*—F.S.P.
[0810]—*Daughters of the Heart of Mary*—D.H.M.
[0420]—*Discalced Carmelite Nuns*—O.C.D.
[1050]—*Dominican Contemplative Nuns*—O.P.
[1070-02]—*Dominican Sisters*—O.P.
[1070-06]—*Dominican Sisters*—O.P.
[1070-03]—*Dominican Sisters*—O.P.
[1070-05]—*Dominican Sisters*—O.P.
[1070-11]—*Dominican Sisters*—O.P.
[1070-15]—*Dominican Sisters*—O.P.
[1070-23]—*Dominican Sisters*—O.P.
[1070-16]—*Dominican Sisters*—O.P.
[1070-13]—*Dominican Sisters*—O.P.
[1120]—*Dominican Sisters of the Roman Congregation*—O.P.
[1170]—*Felician Sisters*—C.S.S.F.
[1260]—*Franciscan Handmaids of the Most Pure Heart of Mary*—F.H.M.
[1370]—*Franciscan Missionaries of Mary*—F.M.M.
[1400]—*Franciscan Missionary Sisters of the Sacred Heart* (Peekskill, NY)—F.M.S.C.
[1180]—*Franciscan Sisters of Allegany, New York*—O.S.F.
[1310]—*Franciscan Sisters of Little Falls, Minnesota*—O.S.F.
[1425]—*Franciscan Sisters of Peace*—F.S.P.
[1190]—*Franciscan Sisters of the Atonement*—S.A.
[1440]—*Franciscan Sisters of the Poor*—S.F.P.
[2070]—*Holy Union Sisters*—S.U.S.C.
[]—*Idente Missionaries*—M.Id.
[3790]—*Institute of the Sisters of St. Dorothy*—S.S.D.
[2310]—*Little Sisters of the Assumption*—L.S.A.
[2340]—*Little Sisters of the Poor*—L.S.P.
[2470]—*Maryknoll Sisters of St. Dominic*—M.M.
[2480]—*Medical Missionaries of Mary*—M.M.M.
[2680]—*Misericordia Sisters*—S.M.
[2720]—*Mission Helpers of the Sacred Heart*—M.H.S.H.
[2710]—*Missionaries of Charity*—M.C.
[1360]—*Missionary Franciscan Sisters of the Immaculate Conception*—O.S.F.
[2790]—*Missionary Servants of the Most Blessed Trinity*—M.S.B.T.

[2900]—*Missionary Sisters of St. Charles Borromeo*—M.S.S.C.B.
[2750]—*Missionary Sisters of the Immaculate Heart of Mary*—I.C.M.
[2860]—*Missionary Sisters of the Sacred Heart*—M.S.C.
[2920]—*Mothers of the Helpless*—M.D.
[3030]—*Oblates of the Most Holy Redeemer*—O.SS.R.
[3035]—*Oblates of the Mother of Orphans*—O.M.O.
[3760]—*Order of St. Clare*—O.S.C.
[2010]—*Order of the Most Holy Redeemer*—O.SS.R.
[3160]—*Parish Visitors of Mary Immaculate*—P.V.M.I.
[3450]—*Religious of Jesus-Mary*—R.J.M.
[3460]—*Religious of Mary Immaculate*—R.M.I.
[3465]—*Religious of the Sacred Heart of Mary* (Eastern North American Prov.)—R.S.H.M.
[2519]—*Religious Sisters of Mercy, Alma, MI*—R.S.M.
[3490]—*Sacramentine Nuns*—O.S.S.
[2970]—*School Sisters of Notre Dame*—S.S.N.D.
[1680]—*School Sisters of St. Francis*—O.S.F.
[0980]—*Sister Disciples of the Divine Master*—P.D.D.M.
[1830]—*Sister of the Good Shepherd*—R.G.S.
[3020]—*Sisters Oblates of the Blessed Trinity*—O.B.T.
[0590]—*Sisters of Charity of Saint Elizabeth, Convent Station*—S.C.
[0650]—*Sisters of Charity of St. Vincent de Paul, New York*—S.C.
[0660]—*Sisters of Christian Charity*—S.C.C.
[2360]—*Sisters of Loretto*—S.L.
[2575]—*Sisters of Mercy of the Americas*—R.S.M.
[3000]—*Sisters of Notre Dame de Namur*—S.N.D.deN.
[3080]—*Sisters of Our Lady of Christian Doctrine*—R.C.D.
[3740]—*Sisters of St. Casimir*—S.S.C.
[1510]—*Sisters of St. Francis of the Mission of the Immaculate Virgin*—O.S.F.
[3820]—*Sisters of St. John the Baptist*—C.S.J.B.
[3830-05]—*Sisters of St. Joseph*—C.S.J.
[3890]—*Sisters of St. Joseph of Peace*—C.S.J.P.
[0260]—*Sisters of the Blessed Sacrament for Indians and Colored People*—S.B.S.
[3140]—*Sisters of the Catholic Apostolate (Pallottine)*—C.S.A.C.
[2980]—*Sisters of the Congregation de Notre Dame*—C.N.D.
[0970]—*Sisters of the Divine Compassion*—R.D.C.
[1000]—*Sisters of the Divine Providence of Kentucky*—C.D.P.
[1990]—*Sisters of the Holy Names of Jesus & Mary*—S.N.J.M.
[3320]—*Sisters of the Presentation of the B.V.M.* (Newburgh; Staten Island)—P.B.V.M.
[3320]—*Sisters of the Presentation of the B.V.M.* (Aberdeen, SD)—P.B.V.M.
[3470]—*Sisters of the Reparation of the Congregation of Mary*—S.R.C.M.
[3480]—*Sisters of the Resurrection*—C.R.
[1490]—*Sisters of the Third Franciscan Order (Syracuse)*
[3600]—*Sisters, Servants of Mary*—S.M.
[2160]—*Sisters, Servants of the Immaculate Heart Of Mary*—I.H.M.
[1890]—*Society of Helpers*—H.H.S.
[2460]—*Society of Mary Repartrix*—S.M.R.
[4040]—*Society of St. Ursula*—S.U.
[4060]—*Society of the Holy Child Jesus*—S.H.C.J.
[4070]—*Society of the Sacred Heart*—R.S.C.J.
[4110]—*Ursuline Nuns*—O.S.U.
[4130]—*Ursuline Sisters (Tildonk)*—O.S.U.
[4230]—*Xaverian Missionary Sisters*—X.M.M.

ARCHDIOCESAN CEMETERIES

HAWTHORNE. *Cemetery of the Gate of Heaven*
LONG ISLAND CITY. *Calvary*
MONSEY. *Cemetery of the Ascension*
STATEN ISLAND. *Cemetery of the Resurrection*

NECROLOGY

† Toner, Rev. Msgr. Francis X., Bronx, NY St. Barnabas—Died 2003
† Aneski, Gabriel—Died 2003
† Daniels, Eugene, Milton, NY St. James—Died May, 2001
† Magee, Andrew T., Maybrook, NY Assumption—Died 2003
† O'Toole, Kenneth E., (Retired)—Died 2003

Diocese of Norwich

(Dioecesis Norvicensis)

Most Reverend

MICHAEL R. COTE, D.D.

Bishop of Norwich; ordained June 29, 1975; appointed Titular Bishop of Cebarades and Auxiliary Bishop of Portland May 9, 1995; ordained July 27, 1995; appointed Bishop of Norwich March 11, 2003; installed May 14, 2003. *Res.: 274 Broadway, Norwich, CT 06360.*

Chancery: 201 Broadway, Norwich, CT 06360. Tel: 860-887-9294; Fax: 860-886-1670.

Web: www.norwichdiocese.org

Most Reverend

DANIEL A. HART, D.D.

Bishop Emeritus of Norwich; ordained February 2, 1953; consecrated Auxiliary Bishop of Boston October 18, 1976; appointed September 12, 1995; installed as Bishop of Norwich November 1, 1995; retired March 11, 2003. *Res.: 213 Broadway, Norwich, CT 06360.*

ESTABLISHED AUGUST 6, 1953.

Square Miles 1,978.

Corporate Title: The Norwich Roman Catholic Diocesan Corporation.

Comprises the Counties of Middlesex, New London, Tolland and Windham in the State of Connecticut and Fishers Island, a portion of Suffolk County in the State of New York.

Legal Title: For legal titles of parishes and diocesan institutions, consult the Chancery Office.

STATISTICAL OVERVIEW

Personnel	
Bishop	1
Retired Bishops	1
Priests: Diocesan Active in Diocese	91
Priests: Diocesan Active Outside Diocese	1
Priests: Diocesan in Foreign Missions	1
Priests: Retired, Sick or Absent	37
Number of Diocesan Priests	130
Religious Priests in Diocese	57
Total Priests in Diocese	187
Extern Priests in Diocese	11
Ordinations:	
Diocesan Priests	4
Permanent Deacons in Diocese	59
Total Brothers	21
Total Sisters	244
Parishes	
Parishes	78
With Resident Pastor:	
Resident Diocesan Priests	67
Resident Religious Priests	12
Without Resident Pastor:	
Administered by Priests	1
Missions	10
Pastoral Centers	23
Professional Ministry Personnel:	
Brothers	5
Sisters	13
Lay Ministers	29
Welfare	
Homes for the Aged	3
Total Assisted	244
Special Centers for Social Services	1
Total Assisted	192
Educational	
Diocesan Students in Other Seminaries	6
Total Seminarians	6
High Schools, Diocesan and Parish	4
Total Students	2,061
High Schools, Private	1
Total Students	55
Elementary Schools, Diocesan and Parish	23
Total Students	4,169
Catechesis/Religious Education:	
High School Students	2,259
Elementary Students	17,146
Total Students under Catholic Instruction	25,696
Teachers in the Diocese:	
Priests	3
Brothers	6
Sisters	35
Lay Teachers	419
Vital Statistics	
Receptions into the Church:	
Infant Baptism Totals	2,836
Adult Baptism Totals	148
Received into Full Communion	290
First Communions	3,073
Confirmations	2,016
Marriages:	
Catholic	501
Interfaith	158
Total Marriages	659
Deaths	2,274
Total Catholic Population	228,520
Total Population	674,804

Former Bishops—Most Revs. BERNARD J. FLANAGAN, D.D., J.C.D. (Retired), ord. Dec. 8, 1931; consecrated Nov. 30, 1953; installed Dec. 9, 1953; transferred to See of Worcester, Aug. 12, 1959; retired March 31, 1983; died Jan. 28, 1998; VINCENT J. HINES, D.D., J.C.D. (Retired), ord. May 2, 1937; appt. Nov. 27, 1959; consecrated March 17, 1960; retired June 17, 1975; died April 23, 1990; DANIEL P. REILLY, D.D., ord. May 30, 1953; appt. June 17, 1975; consecrated Aug. 6, 1975; transferred to See of Worcester, Oct. 27, 1994; installed Dec. 8, 1994; DANIEL A. HART, D.D. (Retired), ord. Feb. 2, 1953; consecrated Auxiliary Bishop of Boston Oct. 18, 1976; appt. Sept. 12, 1995; installed Bishop of Norwich Nov. 1, 1995; retired March 11, 2003.

Office of the Bishop—Most Rev. MICHAEL R. COTE, D.D. Tel: 860-887-9294. Email: bpcote@norwichdiocese.org; Mrs. ALICE PUDVAH, Administrative Asst. Tel: 860-887-9294, Ext. 234.

The Chancery

Chancery—201 Broadway, Norwich, 06360. Tel: 860-887-9294; Fax: 860-886-1670.

Vicar General—Rev. Msgr. THOMAS R. BRIDE, K.C.H.S., V.G., P.A. Tel: 860-887-9294, Ext. 231; Mrs. REGINA WIEGERT, Sec. Tel: 860-887-9294, Ext. 246.

Chancellor—Rev. Msgr. ROBERT L. BROWN. Tel: 860-887-9294, Ext. 232. Email: chancellor@norwichdiocese.org; Mrs. SUSAN SULLIVAN, Sec. Tel: 860-887-9294, Ext. 236.

Diocesan Attorney—MICHAEL E. DRISCOLL, Esq., 22 Courthouse Sq., Norwich, 06360. Tel: 860-889-3321.

Diocesan Attorney Emeritus—JAMES J. DUTTON JR., Esq., K.S.G., 22 Courthouse Sq., Norwich, 06360. Tel: 860-889-3321.

Diocesan Computer Center—Mrs. ANITA SINCLAIR, System Admin. Tel: 860-887-9294, Ext. 240.

Diocesan Finance Office—Mr. WILLIAM RUSSELL, C.P.A., Diocesan Finance Officer. Tel: 860-887-9294, Ext. 241; Mr. VICTOR WELTIG, Asst. Controller. Tel: 860-887-9294, Ext. 242; Ms. JANET WEST, Finance Analyst. Tel: 860-887-9294, Ext. 243; Mrs. ANN MARIE OSOWSKI, Accounts Payable/Medical/Lay Pension. Tel: 860-887-9294, Ext. 245; Ms. KAREN HUFFER, Accounts Receivable. Tel: 860-887-9294, Ext. 244; Ms. ROBIN HOLTSCLAW, Risk Mgr. (CMRS). Fax: 860-885-1512.

College of Consultors—Rev. Msgrs. THOMAS R. BRIDE, K.C.H.S., V.G., P.A.; HENRY N. ARCHAMBAULT, P.A., J.C.D.; ROBERT L. BROWN; RICHARD P. LAROCQUE; ANTHONY S. ROSAFORTE; Very Revs. LAURENCE A.M. LAPOINTE; JOHN J. WHITE, P.A.; Revs. MARK D. O'DONNELL; ROBERT WASHABAUGH.

Presbyteral Council—Most Rev. MICHAEL R. COTE, D.D., Pres.; Very Rev. ROLAND CLOUTIER, Chm. Members: Rev. Msgrs. THOMAS R. BRIDE, K.C.H.S., V.G., P.A.; HENRY ARCHAMBAULT, P.A., J.C.D.; ROBERT L. BROWN; RICHARD P. LAROCQUE; ANTHONY S. ROSAFORTE; Very Revs. MICHAEL L. PHILLIPPINO, Vice Chm.; LAURENCE A.M. LAPOINTE; JOHN J. WHITE, P.A.; Revs. ARTHUR ARCHER; JAMES P. CARINI; ROBERT CRONIN; LESZEK T. JANIK, J.C.L.; EDWARD KONOPKA; WILLIAM MCNULTY; MARK D. O'DONNELL, Sec.; WILLIAM OLESIK; DENNIS M. PERKINS; Very Rev. MICHAEL L. PHILLIPPINO; Revs. RICHARD J. RICARD; MICHAEL S. SMITH; ROBERT WASHABAUGH.

Deans—Very Revs. ROLAND C. CLOUTIER, Putnam; LAURENCE A.M. LAPOINTE, Willimantic; JOHN J. WHITE, P.A., Vernon; Rev. Msgr. HENRY N. ARCHAMBAULT, P.A., J.C.D., Norwich; Very Revs. THOMAS J. SMITH, Middletown; MICHAEL L. PHILLIPPINO, Old Saybrook; MICHAEL T. DONOHUE, New London.

Diocesan Pastoral Council—Most Rev. MICHAEL R. COTE, D.D., Chm.; Rev. Msgrs. HENRY ARCHAMBAULT, P.A.; THOMAS BRIDE, P.A., K.C.H.S., V.G.; ROBERT BROWN; Mrs. NOREEN GRAVEL, R.N.; Bro. J. ROBERT HOULIHAN, C.F.X.; Sr. MARY ALICE KLINE, R.S.M.; Ms. HELENE LABELLE; Mr. JAMES LANDHERR; Mr. JAMES MATHIAS; Dr. ROBERT MILLER, Ph.D.; Mrs. ESPERANZA NUGENT; Mr. BERTRAND PELLETIER, D.D.S.; Mr. DAVID ROY; Ms. JOAN SIENKIEWICZ; Rev. Msgr. WILLIS WEST.

The Tribunal

Diocesan Tribunal—

Judicial Vicar—Rev. Msgr. HENRY N. ARCHAMBAULT, P.A., J.C.D.

Adjutant Judicial Vicar—Rev. LESZEK T. JANIK, J.C.L.

Defenders of the Bond—Revs. ROGER J. LAMOUREUX, O.M.I., J.C.L.; JOSEPH CASTALDI, J.C.L.

Coordinator of the Tribunal—Sr. SALLY TOLLES, D.H.S., J.D., J.C.L.

Judges—Revs. WILLIAM J. FLYNN; GEORGE J. RICHARDS JR., J.C.L.; TED F. TUMICKI, S.T.L., J.C.L.; Very Rev. JOHN J. WHITE, P.A.; Sr. SALLY TOLLES, D.H.S., J.D., J.C.L.

Archivist—Rev. GREGOIRE J. FLUET, Ph.D.

Auditor/Assessors—Full Time: Rev. WILLIAM J. FLYNN; Sr. BEATRICE THEROUX, D.H.S. Part Time: Rev. Msgr. RICHARD L. LAROCQUE; Very Rev. JOHN J. WHITE, P.A.; Revs. DENNIS G. CAREY; GREGOIRE J. FLUET, Ph.D.; RUSSELL F. KENNEDY; CHARLES R. LEBLANC; RICHARD J. RICARD; ROBERT J. WASHABAUGH; Deacon MELVIN G. NYGAARD.

Secretary of the Tribunal—Mrs. MARY J. SHEA.

Notaries—Rev. Msgrs. THOMAS R. BRIDE, K.C.H.S., V.G., P.A.; ROBERT L. BROWN; Mrs. MARY J. SHEA.

Vicar for Clergy—Rev. Msgr. RICHARD P. LAROCQUE. Tel: 860-887-9294, Ext. 258. Email: vicarclergy@norwichdiocese.org; Deacon MICHAEL C. BERSTENE, Dir. Deacon Personnel; Mrs. SUSAN GARDINER, Sec. Tel: 860-887-9294, Ext. 261.

Diocesan Offices, Ministries and Societies

Annual Bishop's Appeal (ABA)— See Development, Diocesan Office

Bishop's Liaison with Retired Clergy—Rev. Msgr. RICHARD P. LAROCQUE, The Chancery, 201 Broadway, Norwich, 06360. Tel: 860-887-9294, Ext. 258.

Bishop's Delegate to Hispanic Permanent Deacons—VACANT.

Diocesan Finance Council—Most Rev. MICHAEL R. COTE, D.D., Chm.; Rev. Msgr. THOMAS R. BRIDE, K.C.H.S., V.G., P.A.; Mr. DONALD BRODEUR, C.P.A.; Mr. JAMES CRONIN; Mr. PETER LAMALFA; Mr. BERNARD PHANEUF; Mr. WILLIAM MCGURK; Mr. TERRENCE CAHILL; Mr. VINCENT ROEMMELE; Mr. PETER SIPPLES, Attorney; Mr. FRED PERKINS, C.P.A.

Diocesan Panel of Pastors, Canon 1742—Rev. Msgr. ANTHONY ROSAFORTE; Very Rev. JOHN J. WHITE, P.A.

Diocesan Pastoral Council— See Chancery listing

Board of Education— See School Office

Building Commission—Very Rev. JOHN J. WHITE, P.A., Chm.; Rev. Msgr. WILLIS W. WEST; Very Rev. MICHAEL T. DONOHUE; Rev. ROBERT A. MURPHY, M.S.A.; Mr. ANTHONY JOYCE; Mr. GEORGE SCHILLER.

Campaigns—

Campaign for Human Development—Very Rev. MICHAEL T. DONOHUE, Diocesan Dir., St. Matthias Church, 317 Chesterfield Rd., P.O. Box 25, East Lyme, 06333-0025. Tel: 860-739-5208; Fax: 860-739-0524.

Catholic Relief Services—Rev. Msgr. ROBERT L. BROWN, Dir.; Mrs. SUSAN SULLIVAN, 201 Broadway, Norwich, 06360-4328. Tel: 860-887-9294.

Campus Ministry—Very Rev. LAURENCE A.M. LAPOINTE, Diocesan Dir., Newman Hall, 290 Prospect St., Willimantic, 06226. Tel: 860-423-0856; Fax: 860-456-8083 (See separate category under Institutions for details).

Middletown—Rev. LOUIS A. MANZO, C.S.C., Wesleyan University - The University Chaplains, 171 Church St., Middletown, 06459-3625. Tel: 860-685-2777, Ext. 2706; Fax: 860-685-2821. Email: lmanzo@wesleyan.edu.

New London—Very Rev. LAURENCE A.M. LAPOINTE, Catholic Chap., Connecticut College, P.O. Box 5203, New London, 06320-5203. Tel: 860-439-2452; Fax: 860-439-2463.

Storrs—Chaplains: Revs. JAMES DRESSMAN, S.J.; PAUL D. HOLLAND, S.J.; GERARD R. MCKEON, S.J.; Sr. ALBERTA SUROWIEC, F.S.S.J., University of Connecticut - St. Thomas Aquinas Chapel, 46 N. Eagleville Rd., Storrs, 06268-1710. Tel: 860-429-6436; Fax: 860-429-2809. Email: stthoffice@worldnet.att.net; Very Rev. LAURENCE A.M. LAPOINTE, Campus Minister, Eastern Connecticut State University, Newman Hall, 290 Prospect St., Willimantic, 06226-2304. Tel: 860-423-0856; Fax: 860-456-8083.

Catechetical Ministry— See School Office

Catholic Charities and Family Services, Diocese of Norwich, Inc.—

Diocesan Director—JOHN J. SMEY, L.C.S.W., Exec. Dir., 331 Main St., Norwich, 06360. Tel: 860-889-8346; Fax: 860-889-2658.

Emergency Financial Assistance, Pregnancy Employment Success Program— Intensive Outreach and Monitoring, Mentoring Program Norwich Office: ANN ELIZABETH GRABOWSKI, B.A., Program Mgr. Tel: 860-889-8346; Fax: 860-889-2658. Willimantic Office: VACANT. Tel: 860-423-7065; Fax: 860-456-1096. New London Office: VACANT. Tel: 860-443-5328; Fax: 860-443-6013.

Emergency Financial Assistance—Sr. SUSANNE GEBRIAN, M.H.S.H., M.A., Social Worker, Norwich Office; IRIS ORTIZ, Supvr., New London Office, 32 Huntington St., New London, 06320. Tel: 860-443-5328; Fax: 860-443-6013; JEANNE WEHLING, B.A., Social Worker, New London Office, 32 Huntington St., New London, 06320. Tel: 860-443-5328; Fax: 860-443-6013.

Pregnancy Program, Mentoring Program—VACANT, Social Worker, Norwich Office; KAREN GRAF, L.C.S.W. Program Mgr.; MARY DUNSMORE, R.N., Coord.

Adolescent Subtance Abuse Program—DIANE SVENNING, M.S.W., B.S., A.S., Social Worker, Coord.

Adoption Program—CHRISTINA SALVIO, L.M.F.T., Coord., Norwich Office; PATRICIA SHELBERG, B.A., Office of Family Life, Norwich Office.

Behavioral Health Clinic—BRIDGETTE JACKSON, Supvr., Norwich Office.

Office of Family Life—MICHAEL PETRIDES, M.S.

Willimantic Office—DIANE LAMBERT, M.P.H., Supvr., 115 Ash St., Willimantic, 06226. Tel: 860-423-7065; Fax: 860-456-1096.

ESP Program—New London Office: KATHY BROWN, M.A., B.A.; CHELSEA SALVIDIO, B.A., 32 Huntington St., New London, 06320.

Catholic Mutual Relief Society— Diocesan Property and Liability Insurance, Ms. ROBIN HOLTSCLAW, Claims/Risk Mgr.. Email: rholtsclaw@catholicmutual.org; Office for all claims: Catholic Mutual Group, 467 Bloomfield Ave., Bloomfield, 06002. Tel: 800-331-2561; Fax: 860-726-9412. National Office: Catholic Mutual Relief Society, 10843 Old Mill Rd., Ste. 300, Omaha, NE 68154. Tel: 800-228-6108.

Catholic Youth Organization (CYO)— See Faith Formation Office for

Cemetery Corporation and Subsidiaries, Diocesan Cemeteries—Rev. Msgr. WILLIS W. WEST, Dir., St. Joseph Rectory, 99 Jackson St., Willimantic, 06226-3077. Tel: 860-423-8439; NICHOLAS W. MIGNONE, Cemetery Mgr., Office, 815 Boswell Ave., Norwich, 06360-2536. Tel: 860-887-1019; Fax: 860-889-4804 (For details on individual cemeteries see separate listing); The following cemeteries are subsidiaries of the Norwich Diocesan Cemetery Corp.

New London—St. Mary Cemetery of New London Corp., 300 Jefferson Ave., New London, 06320-2412. Tel: 860-443-3465 (Office).

Norwich—St. Mary & St. Joseph Cemetery Corp., 815 Boswell Ave., Norwich, 06360-2536. Tel: 860-887-1019.

Taftville—Sacred Heart Cemetery Corp. Harland Rd., Taftville, 06380. Cemetery Office, 815 Boswell Ave., Norwich, 06360-2536. Tel: 860-887-1019.

Uncasville—St. Patrick Cemetery, Depot Rd., Uncasville, 06382. Cemetery Office, 815 Boswell Ave., Norwich, 06360-2536. Tel: 860-887-1019.

Westbrook—Resurrection Cemetery Corp., Rte. 145, Westbrook, 06498. Tel: 860-399-6503 (Cemetery Office).

Censor of Books—Revs. WILLIAM O'ROURKE, S.T.D., St. Stephen Rectory, 130 Old Turnpike Rd., Box 222, Quinebaug, 06262-0222. Tel: 860-935-5205; ROBERT W. CRONIN (Retired), 11 Middlefield Dr., West Hartford, 06107. Tel: 860-232-1886; Very Rev. LAURENCE A.M. LAPOINTE, Newman Hall, 290 Prospect St., Willimantic, 06226. Tel: 860-423-0856.

Commission on Women—201 Broadway Norwich, 06360-4328. Tel: 860-887-9294, Ext. 217. Mrs. SUSAN SEDENSKY; Ms. SHERRY BASSI; Mrs. MAUREEN BUTLER; Mrs. ELLEN BURTON; Mrs. MARYELLEN GRACE; Mrs. PATRICIA LABONTE; Ms. ANGELA MESICK; Mrs. FLORENCE PARKER; Ms. JANICE PIKAL; Mrs. CONSTANCE STOLL; Mrs. JOHANNA REILLY.

Communications, Office of and Diocesan Teleconference Center—JACQUELINE M. KELLER, Dir. Tel: 860-848-2237, Ext. 215. Bishop Flanagan Ministry Center, 1595 Norwich-New London Tpke., Uncasville, 06382-1319. Tel: 860-848-2237; Fax: 860-848-2816.

Four County Catholic—Most Rev. MICHAEL R. COTE, D.D., Publisher; MARY ZUROLO, Editor. Tel: 860-848-2237, Ext. 216. Email: fcceditor@norwichdiocese.org; For Calendar Events: Email: fccevents@norwichdiocese.org.

Community Ministries—

Norwich—Sr. MARYANNE GUERTIN, S.S.J., Dir., St. Vincent dePaul Place, 10 Railroad Place, Norwich, 06360. Tel: 860-889-7374; 860-889-7375.

Middletown—Mr. PETER A. HARDING, Dir.; Sr. ANN LOUGHARY, R.S.M., Meals Prog. Mgr.; TERRY CARBONE, Svc. Coord., St. Vincent dePaul Place, 617 Main St., P.O. Box 398, Middletown, 06457-0398. Tel: 860-344-0097; Fax: 860-343-0023.

Connecticut Catholic Conference—Dr. MARIE HILLIARD, Exec. Dir., 134 Farmington Ave., Hartford, 06105-3784. Tel: 860-524-7882; Fax: 860-525-0750. Email: lobby134@aol.com ccclobby@aol.com. Web: www.ctcatholic.org.

Continuing Education and Formation Commission—Rev. MARK D. O'DONNELL, Chm.; Very Rev. ROLAND C. CLOUTIER; Revs. PETER B. LISZEWSKI; WILLIAM OLESIK; DENNIS M. PERKINS; MICHAEL S. SMITH; RICHARD RICARD; LOUIS MANZO, C.S.C.

Council of Catholic Nurses—Very Rev. THOMAS SMITH, Diocesan Moderator, St. Sebastian Church, 155 Washington St., Middletown, 06457. Tel: 860-347-2638; Fax: 860-437-1889.

Council of Catholic Women—Mrs. JANICE L. PIKAL, Pres., 63 Kaya Ln., Mansfield Center, 06250. Tel: 860-455-1262; Rev. EDWARD M. KONOPKA, Diocesan Moderator, St. Peter Rectory, P.O. Box 707, Higganum, 06441. Tel: 860-345-8018. District Moderators: Rev. Msgr. WILLIS W. WEST, Willimantic Deanery; Revs. EUGENE PILATOWSKI, Norwich Deanery; CHARLES R. LEBLANC, Middletown Deanery; JOSEPH DECOSTA, New London Deanery; WILLIAM J. MCNULTY, Putnam Deanery; JAMES CARINI, Rockville Deanery.

The Deaf, Ministry to—31 Perkins Ave., Norwich, 06360. Tel: 860-886-1281; 860-887-3933 (TTY).

Delegate to Consecrated Life—Sr. SALLY J. TOLLES, D.H.S., J.D., J.C.L., The Tribunal, Diocese of Norwich, 17 Otis St., Norwich, 06360-4419. Tel: 860-887-9294, Ext. 255.

Delegate for Safe Environments—Rev. TED F. TUMICKI, S.T.L., J.C.L., The Tribunal, Diocese of Norwich, 17 Otis St., Norwich, 06360-4419. Tel: 860-887-9294, Ext. 251.

Development, Diocesan Office of (DOD)—Mr. RICHARD COSTELLO, Exec. Dir., 197 Broadway, Norwich, 06360-4407. Tel: 860-886-1928, Ext. 13; Fax: 860-886-2651. Email: dodrc@snet.net.

Annual Bishop's Appeal—Mr. RICHARD COSTELLO, Dir., 197 Broadway, Norwich, 06360. Tel: 860-886-1928, Ext. 13; Fax: 860-886-2651. Email: dodrc@snet.net.

Planned Giving Office—Mr. JOHN BUTLER, Dir., 197 Broadway, Norwich, 06360. Tel: 860-886-1928, Ext. 14. Email: dodjb@snet.net.

Stewardship Office—Mr. TIM SMITH, Dir., 197 Broadway, Norwich, 06360. Tel: 860-886-1928, Ext. 17. Email: stewardship@norwichdiocese.org.

Disabilities-People with— See His Able People, Ministry of

Ecumenism—

Diocesan Commission for Ecumenical and Interreligious Affairs—Ms. KATHLEEN BURTON; Mrs. SANDRA CALABRO, Chm.; Mrs. MARY DILLMAN; Mrs. SHEILA ELLIOTT; Sr. BARBARA HOBBS, P.B.V.M.; Rev. LOUIS MANZO, C.S.C.; Deacon MELVIN NYGAARD; Rev. MARK D. O'DONNELL; MICHAEL OLOCK; Revs. FRANCIS C. ROULEAU; TED F. TUMICKI, S.T.L., J.C.L.; Deacon RONALD FREEDMAN; Mrs. CAROL FREEDMAN; Rev. THEODORE J. KLEIN, Ph.D., Emeritus (Retired).

Ecumenical and Interreligious Affairs, Office of—VACANT, Dir., Bishop Flanagan Ministry Center, 1595 Norwich-New London Tpke., Uncasville, 06382-1319. Tel: 860-848-2237, Ext. 204; Fax: 860-848-2816. Email: eandi@norwichdiocese.org.

Evangelization & Catechumenate (RCIA), Office of—Mrs. SUSAN MYSHRALL, Dir. Tel: 860-848-2237, Ext. 317. Diocesan Evangelization Catechumenate Team: Rev. STANLEY J. SZCZAPA; ERNEST GOLNIK; Sr. KATHERINE MCKENNA, P.B.V.M.; GAYLE MADDEN; THOMAS MADDEN; MILDRED STEARNS; Mrs. SUSAN MYSHRALL, The Bishop Flanagan Ministry Center, 1595 Norwich-New London Tpke., Uncasville, 06382-1319. Tel: 860-848-2237.

Faith Formation, Office for—Bishop Flanagan Ministry Center, 1595 Norwich-New London Tpke., Uncasville, 06382-1319. Tel: 860-848-2237, Ext. 312; Fax: 860-848-2816. Email: resourcescenter@norwichdiocese.org. Sr. ELEANOR O'MALLEY, P.B.V.M., Dir.. Email: faithformationdir@norwichdiocese.org; MARJORIE VANNER, Assoc. Dir., Resource Center. Tel: 860-848-2237, Ext. 207. Email: faithformation@norwichdiocese.org; Rev. GREGORY P. GALVIN, Scout Chaplain. Email: scouting@norwichdiocese.org. Diocesan Scouting Committee: ISABEL GREENBAUGH, Co-Chm.; PAMELA PLASSE, Co-Chm. Consultants: Mrs. OLIVE GREEN; Mrs. LORRAINE MORRONE; Mrs. JANET WALSH; Mrs. SANDY RUSSO.

"Four County Catholic"— See Newspaper

Haitian Ministries—EMILY SMACK, Dir., Bishop Flanagan Ministry Center, 1595 Norwich-New London Tpke., Uncasville, 06382-1319. Tel: 860-848-2237, Ext. 206. Email: haiti.ministry@snet.net. Web: www.haitianministries.org. Haitian Ministries Board: Dr. THOMAS GORIN; Mrs. JUDITH SECORD; Mrs. MARIETTE STEVENS MCCOURT; Mr.

GREGORY SECORD; Mr. KYN TOLSON; TERRANCE CAHILL; MICHAEL DELVECCHIO; PETER HARDING; PETER LODEN; ROBERT MCNALLY; BARBARA WYSOCKI; Sr. MARY HEALY, R.S.M.

Local Haitian Apostolate/Apostola Ayisyun—Rev. FRANCIS C. ROULEAU, 31 Perkins Ave., Norwich, 06360. Tel: 860-460-0794. St. Mary Church, 70 Central Ave., Norwich, 06360. Haitian Creole Mass: Sun. 12:15 pm.

Hispanic Ministry—Sr. MARY JUDE LAZARUS, S.C.M.C., Diocesan Dir., Hispanic Apostolate Office, 61 Club Rd., Windham, 06280-1007. Tel: 860-456-3349; Fax: 860-423-4157.

Evangelization—Sisters FRANCISCA VALLE, H.M.S.P.; RUFINA CARRILLO, St. Mary Star of Sea Convent, 22 Huntington St., New London, 06320. Tel: 860-444-9673. Hispanic Ministry Board: Mr. LUIS BATISTE, Clinton; Mr. JAVIER CRUZ, New London; Mr. DANIEL CHONG, Norwich; Miss ZOILA DIAZ, Willimantic; Mrs. IVONNE FIGUEROA, Willimantic.

Clinton—

St. Mary of the Visitation Church - Spanish Apostolate—Rev. MICHAEL SEQUIRA, Pastor; Sr. MAIRENY SOTO ROJAS, R.O.D.A, Pastoral Assoc., 54 Grove St., Clinton, 06413-1999. Tel: 860-669-8512; Fax: 860-669-9052.

Middletown—

St. Francis of Assisi Church - Spanish Apostolate—Rev. MARTIN JONES, Pastor; Sr. MAIRENY SOTO ROJAS, R.O.D.A, Pastoral Assoc., 10 Elm St., Middletown, 06457-4426. Tel: 860-347-4684; Fax: 860-347-7669.

New London—

St. Mary, Star of the Sea Church - Spanish Apostolate—Rev. ROBERT WASHABAUGH, Pastor; Sr. ROSA MARIA CAMPOS, R.O.D.A., Pastoral Assoc.; Deacon JESUS DIEZ-CANSECO, 10 Huntington St., New London, 06320-6198. Tel: 860-447-1431; Fax: 860-437-1889. Email: stmarysnl@aol.com.

Norwich—

St. Mary Church - Spanish Apostolate—Revs. ROBERT LYNCH, Pastor; RUSSELL KENNEDY, Parochial Vicar; Sr. MARIA DE LOS ANGELES BALLESTERO, R.O.D.A., Pastoral Assoc., 70 Central Ave., Norwich, 06360-4794. Tel: 860-887-2565.

Windham—

Iglesia del Sagrado Corazon de Jesus - Spanish Apostolate—Rev. PAUL J. MURDOCK, Pastor, Res.: 310 Elizabeth Lane, Stonegate Manor, North Windham, 06256. Pastoral Associates: Sr. ROSA MARIA CAMPOS, R.O.D.A.; Mrs. VIRGINIA RODRIGUEZ; Deacon FELIPE SILVA, 61 Club Rd., Windham, 06280-1007. Tel: 860-423-8617; Fax: 860-423-4157.

Holy Childhood— See Pontifical Association of the Holy Childhood

Holy Name Societies— Address all mail to: *Holy Name Societies, 201 Broadway, Norwich, 06360-4328*. Tel: 860-887-9294.

Internal Affairs Office of Sexual Misconduct Services and Information—201 Broadway, Norwich, 06360-4328. Tel: 800-624-7407; 860-889-4455. Deacon AL FECTEAU, Delegate for Internal Investigations; Ms. SHEREE ANTOCH, Asst. Coord. Tel: 800-844-5669.

Insurance— See Catholic Mutual Relief Society (C.M.R.S.)

Justice & Peace, Catholic Social Action for—Mr. RAYMOND MASTRONUNZIO, Dir., Bishop Flanagan Ministry Center, 1595 Norwich-New London Tpke., Uncasville, 06382-1319. Tel: 860-848-2237, Ext. 211; Fax: 860-848-2816. Email: socialaction@norwichdiocese.org. Advisory Council: Dr. LORETTA ANDERSON; Mr. MAURICE BOWEN; Sr. M. JOHN BAPTIST DONOVAN, S.C.M.C.; Ms. CATHERINE FOLEY; Rev. RUSSELL F. KENNEDY; Mr. ANTHONY LONARDELLI SR.; Mr. RUSSELL MCDONOUGH; Mr. JAMES VALLARIO.

His Able People, Ministry of— A ministry for persons with Disabilities *1595 Norwich-New London Tpke., Uncasville, 06382-1319*. Tel: 860-848-2237, Ext. 320; Fax: 860-848-2816.

Lawyers, Guild of Catholic—Mailing Address, 201 Broadway, Norwich, 06360-4328. Tel: 860-887-9294, Ext. 246. MICHAEL E. DRISCOLL, Esq., Pres.; Mrs. REGINA WIEGERT, Sec. Tel: 860-887-9294, Ext. 246; Rev. Msgr. HENRY ARCHAMBAULT, P.A., J.C.D., Chap.

Legion of Mary—Rev. ROBERT B. LYNCH, Diocesan Spiritual Dir., St. Mary Rectory, 70 Central Ave., Norwich, 06360-4794. Tel: 860-887-2565.

Worship, Office of—VACANT, Diocesan Dir., Bishop Flanagan Ministry Center, 1595 Norwich-New London Tpke., Uncasville, 06382-1319. Tel: 860-848-2237, Ext. 209; Fax: 860-848-2816. Email: worship@norwichdiocese.org. Liturgical Commission: Mrs. CLARA BURNSIDE; Mrs. CLAIRE KIRITSIS; Sr. ELEANOR O'MALLEY, P.B.V.M.; Mrs. SANDY RUSSO; Mrs. SUSAN MYSHRALL; Revs. DAVID CHOQUETTE; PAUL J. MURDOCK; Mr. THOMAS P. GOUIN; Mr. MARK SCHLEICHER; Sr. ANN MACK, R.S.M.; Rev. R. THOMAS MCCONAGHY; Ms. NANCY MIGNAULT.

Marriage Encounter/Catholic Charities/Family Life Office—VACANT, Dir., 331 Main St., Norwich, 06360. Tel: 860-889-8346; Fax: 860-889-2658.

Mercy Xavier Development Corporation—Mr. JAMES JOYCE, Pres., 181 Randolph Rd., Middletown, 06457. Tel: 860-347-2343; 860-346-7735.

Ministry Formation, Office of—The Bishop Flanagan Ministry Center, 1595 Norwich-New London Tpke., Uncasville, 06382-1319. Tel: 860-848-2237, Ext. 308; Fax: 860-848-2816.

Newspaper— Official monthly newspaper of Diocese of Norwich-- MARY ZUROLO, Editor. Tel: 860-367-0130, Ext. 216. Email: fcceditor@norwichdiocese.org; Office of Communications, Bishop Flanagan Ministry Center, 1595 Norwich-New London Tpke., Uncasville, 06382-1319. Tel: 860-889-0202; 860-848-2237 (Editor); 860-367-0130 (Advertising); Fax: 860-848-2816. Email: 4cc@norwichdiocese.org. "Four County Catholic"

Nurses— See Council of Catholic Nurses

Pastoral Planning, Office of—Sr. MARY ALICE KLINE, R.S.M., Coord., Bishop Flanagan Ministry Center, 1595 Norwich-New London Tpke., Uncasville, 06382-1319. Tel: 860-848-2237, Ext. 203; Fax: 860-848-2816. Email: pastoralplan@norwichdiocese.org.

People with Disabilities— See His Able People, Ministry of

Permanent Deacon, Office of—Deacon MICHAEL C. BERNSTENE, Diocesan Dir., Deacon Personnel. Tel: 860-887-9294, Ext. 258; Mrs. SUSAN GARDINER, Sec. Tel: 860-887-9294, Ext. 261. The Chancery, 201 Broadway, Norwich, 06360. Tel: 860-887-9294; Fax: 860-886-1670.

Planned Giving Office— See Development, Diocesan Office of

Pontifical Association of the Holy Childhood—Rev. WILLIAM J. OLESIK, St. Maurice Church, 32 Hebron Rd., Bolton, 06043-7606. Tel: 860-643-4466.

Pontifical Society for the Propagation of the Faith—Rev. WILLIAM J. OLESIK, Dir., St. Maurice Church, 32 Hebron Rd., Bolton, 06043-7606. Tel: 860-643-4466.

Prison Ministry for Diocese of Norwich—Ms. SHEREE L. ANTOCH, Dir., Bishop Flanagan Ministry Center, 1595 Norwich-New London Tpke., Uncasville, 06382-1319. Tel: 860-848-2237, Ext. 212; Fax: 860-848-2816.

Brooklyn—

Brooklyn Correctional Institution—59 Hartford Rd., Brooklyn, 06234. Tel: 860-779-4568. Rev. JUSTINIAN RWEYEMAMU, Chap., St. Bernard Rectory, 25 St. Bernard Terr., Rockville, 06066-3258. Tel: 860-875-0753.

Niantic—

Gates Correctional Institution—131 N. Bridebrook Rd., Niantic, 06357. Tel: 860-691-4756. Sr. PATRICIA COOK, R.S.M., Chap., Siena House, 100 Rte. 165, Preston, 06365-8417.

York Correctional Institution—201 W. Main St., Niantic, 06357. Tel: 860-691-6544; 860-691-6673. Chaplains: Deacon DENNIS F. DOLAN; Rev. RUSSELL KENNEDY, St. Mary Rectory, 70 Central Ave., Norwich, 06360-4794. Tel: 860-887-2565.

Somers—

Northern Correctional Institution—287 Bilton Rd., Somers, 06071. Tel: 860-763-8686. Deacon ROBERT BERND, Chaplain, 159 Brainard Rd., Apt. 23, Enfield, 06082.

Osborn Correctional Institution—100 Bilton Rd., Somers, 06071. Tel: 860-749-8391, Ext. 5476. Deacon GERALD GERACI, Chaplain.

Willard-Cybulski Correctional Institution—391 Shaker Rd., Enfield, 06082. Tel: 860-763-6106. Chaplains: Deacon ROBERT LAMBERT; Rev. WILLIAM HILLIARD, Holy Family Rectory, 23 Simon Rd., Enfield, 06082-5903. Tel: 860-741-2101.

Uncasville—

Corrigan Correctional Institution—986 Norwich-New London Tpke., Uncasville, 06382. Tel: 860-848-5764. Rev. JUSTINIAN RWEYEMAMU, St. Bernard Rectory, 25 St. Bernard Terr., Rockville, 06066-3258. Tel: 860-875-0753.

Radgowski Correctional Institution—982 Norwich-New London Tpke., Uncasville, 06382. Tel: 860-848-5034. Rev. JUSTINIAN RWEYEMAMU, St. Bernard Rectory, 25 St. Bernard Terr., Rockville, 06066-3258. Tel: 860-875-0753.

Pro-Life Activities—Mr. JOSEPH P. COLLISON, Dir., 201 Broadway, Norwich, 06360-4328. Tel: 860-887-9294, Ext. 247; Fax: 860-886-1670.

Project Northeast— A program of Evangelization for the unchurched poor. Rev. RICHARD L. ARCHAMBAULT, Dir., 81 Church St., Putnam, 06260-1809. Tel: 860-928-4078; Sr. ELEANOR BALDONI, D.H.S., Assoc. Dir., 22 Pearl Ave., Putnam, 06260-1625. Tel: 860-928-5965.

RCIA— See Evangelization & Catechumenate, Office of

Religious— See Vicar for Religious

Priests Retirement Plan Board—Most Rev. MICHAEL R. COTE, D.D.; Revs. DENNIS PERKINS; KENNETH FLINT (Retired); Mr. JAMES LITTLE; Ms. MARY OLIVER; Rev. DENNIS CAREY.

Retirement—

Priests' Retirement Plan Board—Most Rev. MICHAEL R. COTE, D.D.; Revs. KENNETH FLINT (Retired); JOSEPH CASTALDI; DENNIS PERKINS; DENNIS G. CAREY; Mr. JAMES LITTLE; Ms. MARY OLIVER.

School Office, Diocesan—Dr. HOWARD B. BENNETT, Supt.; Sr. JOAN A. O'CONNER, C.S.J., Assoc. Supt.. Email: joanoconnorcsj@snet.net; DEBRA JADOFSKY, Exec. Sec. to Supt., 43 Perkins Ave., Norwich, 06360-3698. Tel: 860-887-4086; 860-887-9371; Fax: 860-887-9371. Email: bennett.supt@snet.net.

Diocesan School Technology Consultant—ANDRE ARCHAMBAULT. Email: aarchambault@att.net.

Board of Education—Mr. ELMO GIANANTONI, Chm.; Most Rev. MICHAEL R. COTE, D.D., Ex Officio; Rev. Msgr. THOMAS R. BRIDE, K.C.H.S., V.G., P.A.; Dr. HOWARD B. BENNETT; Sr. JOAN A. O'CONNOR, C.S.J.; LINDA CORONA; Rev. CHARLES LEBLANC; Mr. JOHN TOSCHES.

Scouting— See Faith Formation, Office for

Sick, Ministry to the—Sr. RITA JOHNSON, S.S.N.D., Dir., W.W. Backus Hospital, 326 Washington St., Norwich, 06360-2742. Tel: 860-889-8331; 860-886-6948. Res.: 7 Otis St., Norwich, 06360. Tel: 860-886-6948.

Soup Kitchen— See Community Ministries, Saint Vincent de Paul Place

Spanish Speaking Apostolate— See Hispanic Ministry

Spiritual Renewal Services—Co-Directors: Rev. RAYMOND D. INTROVIGNE; Mrs. JUDITH HUGHES. Tel: 860-267-8611. Office, 11 Bath St., P.O. Box 6, Norwich, 06360-5836. Tel: 860-887-0702. Email: srs@ctol.net; Res.: St. Mary Rectory, 1600 Main St., P.O. Box 250, Coventry, 06238-0250. Tel: 860-742-0681; 860-887-7767 (Dial-A-Prayer); Fax: 860-859-1366.

Vicar for Clergy, Office of—The Chancery, 201 Broadway, Norwich, 06360-4328. Tel: 860-887-9294; Fax: 860-885-1512; 860-886-1670. Rev. Msgr. RICHARD P. LAROCQUE. Tel: 860-887-9294, Ext. 258.

Director of Deacon Personnel—Deacon MICHAEL C. BERNSTENE.

Secretary—Mrs. SUSAN GARDINER. Email: vicarclergy@norwichdiocese.orgTel: 860-887-9294, Ext. 261.

Vicar for Religious— See Delegate to Consecrated Life.

Victim Assistance Coordinator—Ms. SHEREE ANTOCH. Tel: 800-844-5669.

Vocations—Rev. Msgr. THOMAS R. BRIDE, K.C.H.S., V.G., P.A., Diocesan Dir.; Very Rev. MICHAEL PHILLIPPINO, Asst. Dir., 201 Broadway, Norwich, 06360-4328. Tel: 860-887-9294.

Director for Promotion & Development—Rev. MARK D. O'DONNELL, 201 Broadway, Norwich, 06360-4328. Tel: 860-887-9294, Ext. 248. Res.: St. John Rectory, 22 Maple Ave., P.O. Box 468, Uncasville, 06382-2327. Tel: 860-848-9335. Email: mdod@worldnet.att.net vocation@downcity.net; Mrs. REGINA WIEGERT, Sec. Tel: 860-887-9294, Ext. 246. Email: contedu@norwichdiocese.org.

Diocesan Vocation Review Committee—Rev. Msgrs. THOMAS R. BRIDE, K.C.H.S., V.G., P.A.; RICHARD P. LAROCQUE; WILLIS W. WEST; Revs. R. THOMAS MCCONAGHY; MARK D. O'DONNELL; Very Rev. MICHAEL PHILLIPPINO; Bro. WILLIAM CIGANEK, C.F.X.

Women, Commission on— See Commission on Women

Apostolate—

Jewett City— The World apostolate of Fatima, Inc., Norwich Diocesan Div. *41 John Rd., Jewett City, 06351*. Tel: 860-376-1041; Fax: 860-376-1041. DENISE DUDEK, Pres.. Email: norwichaf@hotmail.com; LIONEL SANTOS, Pilgrim Statue Guardian.

CLERGY, PARISHES, MISSIONS AND PAROCHIAL SCHOOLS

CITY OF NORWICH
(NEW LONDON COUNTY)

1—ST. PATRICK CATHEDRAL (1879), Rev. Msgr. Anthony S. Rosaforte; Revs. David P. Choquette; Joseph B. Whittel; Deacon Al R. Fecteau.
Res.: 213 Broadway, 06360-4307. Tel: 860-889-8441; Fax: 860-889-2978.
School—211 Broadway, 06360. Tel: 860-889-4174; Fax: 860-889-0040. Email: stpatsnorwich@sbcglobal.net. Sr. Mary Bernard Rivest, S.C.M.C., Prin. Sisters of Charity of Our Lady Mother of the Church 1; Lay Teachers 12; Students 201.
Catechesis/Religious Program—Agnes Carvel, D.R.E. Students 307.

2—ST. JOSEPH (1904), (Polish), Rev. Eugene Pilatowski; Deacon Thomas A. Lewis.
Res.: 120 Cliff St., 06360-5134. Tel: 860-887-1565; Fax: 860-889-3560.
School—Tel: 860-887-4565; Fax: 860-886-6468. Sr. M. Martin LeClair, S.C.M.C., Prin.
Catechesis/Religious Program—Tel: 860-887-4565. Students 68.

3—ST. MARY (1845), Revs. Robert B. Lynch; Russell Kennedy; Sr. Marielos Ballestero, R.O.D.A., Hispanic Min. In Res., Rev. Joseph G. Finnerty.
Res.: 70 Central Ave., 06360-4794. Tel: 860-887-2565; Fax: 860-892-1692. Email: st.marys@99main.com.
Catechesis/Religious Program—Students 72.

4—SS. PETER AND PAUL (1938), Revs. Philip A. Pusateri, S.J.; John R.. d' Anjou, S.J.; Deacon Dennis A. Doyle III.
Res.: 181 Elizabeth St., 06360-6199. Tel: 860-887-9857; Fax: 860-886-4728.
Catechesis/Religious Program—Students 154.

5—SACRED HEART (Norwichtown) (1902), Rev. R. Thomas McConaghy; Deacon Robert P. Hayes.
Res.: 52 W. Town St., Norwichtown, 06360-2296. Tel: 860-887-1030; Fax: 860-887-6550.
Catechesis/Religious Program—Tel: 860-887-1715. Paula Wiencek, D.R.E. Students 127.
Mission—St. John 190 Fitchville Rd., Bozrah, New London Co. 06334.

OUTSIDE THE CITY OF NORWICH

ASHFORD, WINDHAM CO., ST. PHILIP (1937), [CEM 2] Rev. Joseph D. Nguyen.
Res.: 64 Pompey Hollow Rd., 06278-1540. Tel: 860-429-2860; Fax: 860-487-5703.
Catechesis/Religious Program—Tel: 860-429-1921; Fax: 860-487-5703. John Doughty, D.R.E. Students 151.

BALLOUVILLE, WINDHAM CO., ST. ANNE (1882), Rev. Sylva P. LeCours.
Res.: 227 Ballouville Rd., Box 125, 06233-0125. Tel: 860-774-6164; Fax: 860-774-6164.
Catechesis/Religious Program—Tel: 860-774-4023. Students 91.

BALTIC, NEW LONDON CO., ST. MARY OF THE IMMACULATE CONCEPTION (1886), [CEM] Rev. Joseph Tito.
Res.: 70 W. Main St., 06330-1348. Tel: 860-822-6378.
School—St. Joseph, 10 School Hill Rd.. Tel: 860-822-6141; Fax: 860-822-6141. Sr. M. Christina Van Beck, S.C.M.C., Prin. Sisters of Charity of Our Lady Mother of the Church 4; Lay Teachers 5; Students 133.
Catechesis/Religious Program—Students 97.

BOLTON, TOLLAND CO., ST. MAURICE (1954), Rev. William J. Olesik.
Res.: 32 Hebron Rd., 06043-7606. Tel: 860-643-4466.
Catechesis/Religious Program—Tel: 860-643-8374. Mrs. Karen Bergin, D.R.E. Students 280.

BROOKLYN, WINDHAM CO., OUR LADY OF LA SALETTE (1968), Rev. John J. O'Neill, M.S.; Bros. Ronald Lafleche, M.S., Pastoral Assoc.; Robert Russell, M.S., Admin.
Res.: 06234-0211. Tel: 860-774-6275; Fax: 860-774-0679.
Catechesis/Religious Program—Students 232.
Mission—Our Lady of Lourdes Cedar Swamp Rd., Hampton, Windham Co. 06247.

CANTERBURY, WINDHAM CO., ST. AUGUSTINE (1978), Rev. Frank W. McKenna.
Res.: 144 Westminster Rd., 06331-1417. Tel: 860-546-6074.
Catechesis/Religious Program—Tel: 860-546-6225. Students 127.

CHESTER, MIDDLESEX CO., ST. JOSEPH (1885), [CEM] Rev. Robert Murphy, M.S.A.; Deacon Lawrence Moneypenny.
Res.: 48 Middlesex Ave., 06412-1309. Tel: 860-526-5495; Fax: 860-526-7880.
Catechesis/Religious Program—Tel: 860-526-2152. Students 219.

CLINTON, MIDDLESEX CO., ST. MARY OF THE VISITATION (1934), [CEM] Rev. Michael Sequeira; Sr. Marieny Soto, R.O.D.A., Pastoral Assoc.; Deacon Paul Weber.
Res.: 54 Grove St., 06413-1999. Tel: 860-669-8512; Fax: 860-669-9052.
Catechesis/Religious Program—Tel: 860-669-7375. Students 526.

COLCHESTER, NEW LONDON CO., ST. ANDREW (1860), [CEM 2] [JC 2] Rev. Michael C. Giannitelli; Deacons Robert Barlow; Dennis Dolan.
Res.: 128 Norwich Ave., 06415-1269. Tel: 860-537-2355; Fax: 860-537-2356.
Catechesis/Religious Program—Tel: 860-537-5415. Students 900.

COLUMBIA, TOLLAND CO., ST. COLUMBA (1960), Rev. Daniel C. Cronin.
Res.: Rte. 66 at Rte. 87, P.O. Box 146, 06237-0146. Tel: 860-228-3735; Fax: 860-228-8777.
Catechesis/Religious Program—Tel: 860-228-3727. Students 195.

COVENTRY, TOLLAND CO., ST. MARY (1877), [CEM] Revs. Raymond D. Introvigne; Victor Chaker.
Res.: 1600 Main St., P.O. Box 250, 06238-0250. Tel: 860-742-0681; Fax: 860-742-1318.
Catechesis/Religious Program—Tel: 860-742-1092. Students 382.
Mission—St. Joseph Eagleville, Tolland Co.

CROMWELL, MIDDLESEX CO., ST. JOHN (1882), Revs. Raymond Borkowski, O.F.M.Conv.; John M. Voytek, O.F.M.Conv. (TR).
Res.: 5 St. John Ct., 06416-2118. Tel: 860-635-5590; Fax: 860-635-5591.
Catechesis/Religious Program—Tel: 860-635-5156. Students 513.

DANIELSON, WINDHAM CO., ST. JAMES (1869), (French), [CEM] Revs. John J. O'Neill, M.S.; John F. Welch, M.S.; Joseph Whalen, M.S.; Cyriac Mattathilanckal, M.S.; Deacon Rene N. Barbeau Jr. In Res., Rev. Hugh J. Murphy (Retired).
Res.: 12 Franklin St., 06239. Tel: 860-774-3900; Fax: 860-774-4205.
School—Tel: 860-774-3281; Fax: 860-779-2137. Ms. Marguerite Ouellette, Prin. Lay Teachers 13; Students 282.
Catechesis/Religious Program—Tel: 860-774-8459. Students 298.
Mission—Our Lady of Peace East Killingly, Windham Co. 06239.

DAYVILLE, WINDHAM CO., ST. JOSEPH (1874), [CEM] Rev. William J. McNulty.
Res.: 350 Hartford Pike, Box 487, 06241-0109. Tel: 860-774-8656; Fax: 860-774-8656.
Catechesis/Religious Program—Tel: 860-774-2451. Alyce Chartier, D.R.E.; Norma Pokoski, D.R.E. Students 104.
Convent—Parish House Daughters of the Holy Spirit, 21 Williamsville Rd., Box 158 Rogers, 06263. Tel: 860-774-8154.

DURHAM, MIDDLESEX CO., NOTRE DAME (1955), Rev. Augustine Naduvilekoot.
Res.: 272 Main St., 06422-1611. Tel: 860-349-3058; Fax: 860-349-8949.
Catechesis/Religious Program—Students 380.

EAST HAMPTON, MIDDLESEX CO., ST. PATRICK (1879), (Irish), [CEM] Rev. Charles R. LeBlanc; Sr. Dominic Joseph Valla, A.S.C.J., Pastoral Assoc.
Res.: 47 W. High St., P.O. Box 177, 06424-0177. Tel: 860-267-6644; Fax: 860-267-7807. Email: stpatrickchurch@earthlink.net.
Catechesis/Religious Program—Students 513.

EAST LYME, NEW LONDON CO., ST. MATTHIAS (Flannders) (1939), Very Rev. Michael T. Donohue; Sr. M. Rita Clare, R.S.M.; Deacon Steven Reed.
Res.: 186 Chesterfield Rd., P.O. Box 25, 06333-0025. Tel: 860-691-2235.
Church: 317 Chesterfield Rd., P.O.Box 25, 06333-0025. Tel: 860-739-5208; Fax: 860-739-0524.
Catechesis/Religious Program—Tel: 860-739-5208; Fax: 860-739-0524. Students 370.

ELLINGTON, TOLLAND CO., ST. LUKE (1961), Rev. Thomas Flathottam, C.S.T.
Rectory—141 Maple St., P.O. Box 246, 06029-0246. Tel: 860-875-8552; Fax: 860-872-6548.
Church: 141 Maple St., 06029.
Catechesis/Religious Program—Tel: 860-875-4951. Students 393.
Convent—St. Luke Convent, 8 Berr Ave., 06029-0246.

ESSEX, MIDDLESEX CO., OUR LADY OF SORROWS (1926), Rev. Paul J. Gaumond.
Res.: 14 Prospect St., 06426-1049. Tel: 860-767-1284; Fax: 860-767-7874.
Catechesis/Religious Program—Tel: 860-767-2938. Students 264.

FISHERS ISLAND, SUFFOLK CO., OUR LADY OF GRACE (1902), (Irish), Rev. Andrew Waszczenko, S.D.S., Admin.
Res.: Alpine Ave., Box 425, NY 06390-0425. Tel: 631-788-7353; Fax: 631-788-7312.

GALES FERRY, NEW LONDON CO., OUR LADY OF LOURDES (1960), Revs. Joseph F. DeCosta; David P. Choquette.
Res.: 1650 Rte. 12, 06335-1534. Tel: 860-464-7251; Fax: 860-464-7252.
Catechesis/Religious Program—Tel: 860-464-6676. Students 385.

GROTON, NEW LONDON CO.

1—ST. MARY (1964), Rev. Grzegorz P. Brozonowicz; Deacons Peter H. Danesi III; Paul Wallen.
Res.: 69 Groton Long Point Rd., 06340. Tel: 860-445-1446; Fax: 860-448-7269.
Catechesis/Religious Program—Tel: 860-448-0529. Mrs. Barbara Simoncini, D.R.E.; Mrs. Theresa Seals, D.R.E. Students 321.

2—SACRED HEART (1905), Rev. Gregory C. Mullaney; Deacon Julius Pereira.
Res.: 56 Sacred Heart Dr., 06340-4431. Tel: 860-445-2905; 860-445-6648; Fax: 860-445-6648.
School—(Grades PreK-8) Tel: 460-445-0611; Fax: 860-448-4999. Linda Corona, Prin. Lay Teachers 24; Aides 12; Students 385.
Catechesis/Religious Program—Tel: 860-446-8343. Students 360.

HEBRON, TOLLAND CO., THE CHURCH OF THE HOLY FAMILY (1987), Rev. Michael S. Smith.
Mailing Address: P.O. Box 146, 06248-0146. Tel: 860-228-0096; Fax: 860-228-1629.
Catechesis/Religious Program—Tel: 860-228-0096, Ext. 3. Barbara Rodegher, D.R.E. Students 625.

HIGGANUM, MIDDLESEX CO., ST. PETER (1958), Rev. Edward M. Konopka.
Res.: 30 St. Peter Ln., P.O. Box 707, 06441-0707. Tel: 860-345-8018; Fax: 860-345-4067.
Catechesis/Religious Program—Tel: 860-345-4726. Students 186.

JEWETT CITY, NEW LONDON CO., ST. MARY (1870), (Polish), [CEM 2] Rev. Peter B. Liszewski; Deacon Paul R. Baillargeon.
Res.: 34 N. Main St., 06351-2012. Tel: 860-376-2044; Fax: 860-376-2044.
School—54 N. Main St., 06351. Tel: 860-376-0446; Fax: 860-376-4200. Barbara Polanski, Prin. Lay Teachers 9; Students 107.
Catechesis/Religious Program—Tel: 860-376-5771. Students 206.

KILLINGWORTH, MIDDLESEX CO., ST. LAWRENCE (1978), Very Rev. Michael L. Phillippino; Deacons Raymond Gosselin; John A. Balchus.
Res.: 7 Hemlock Dr., 06419-2227. Tel: 860-663-2576; Fax: 860-663-4238.
Catechesis/Religious Program—Tel: 860-873-2956. Students 381.

LEBANON, NEW LONDON CO., ST. FRANCIS OF ASSISI (1980), Rev. Brian J. Converse.
Res.: 67 W. Town St., 06249-0172. Tel: 860-642-6711; Fax: 860-642-4032.
Catechesis/Religious Program—Students 205.

MIDDLEFIELD, MIDDLESEX CO., ST. COLMAN (1890), Rev. Lester G. Morris; Deacon Peter L. Gill.
Res.: 145 Hubbard St., P.O. Box 457, 06455-0457. Tel: 860-349-3868; Fax: 860-349-3150.
Catechesis/Religious Program—Tel: 860-347-1725. Barbara-Jean DiMauro, D.R.E. Students 161.

MIDDLETOWN, MIDDLESEX CO.

1—ST. FRANCIS (1903), Rev. Martin Jones.
Res.: 10 Elm St., 06457-4426. Tel: 860-347-4684; Fax: 860-347-7669.
Catechesis/Religious Program—Tel: 860-344-1098. Students 129.

2—ST. JOHN (1843), [CEM] Rev. Dennis G. Carey; Sr. Ann Mack, R.S.M., Pastoral Assoc.
Res.: 19 John's Sq., 06457-2201. Tel: 860-347-5626; Fax: 860-638-3633.
School—Tel: 860-347-3202; Fax: 860-347-3537. Lay Teachers 13; Students 215.
Catechesis/Religious Program—Students 59.

3—ST. MARY OF CZESTOCHOWA (1903), (Polish), [CEM] Revs. Marek Masnicki; Jan Swiderski.
Res.: 79 S. Main St., 06457-3606. Tel: 860-347-2365; Fax: 860-347-2110.
School—87 S. Main St., 06457. Tel: 860-347-2978; Fax: 860-347-7267. Mrs. Kathleen Dutil, Prin. Lay Teachers 10; Students 270.
Catechesis/Religious Program—Students 150.

4—ST. PIUS X (1957), Revs. Robert Abbatiello, O.F.M-.Cap.; James Hammer, O.F.M.Cap.; Bro. Eugene Sheehan, O.F.M.Cap. In Res., Revs. Ephrem Karwowski, O.F.M.Cap. (RVC) (Retired); Cyprian Murray, O.F.M.Cap.; Bruce Quinn, O.F.M.Cap., Hospital Chap.; Walter O'Brien, O.F.M.Cap. (Retired).
Res.: 310 Westfield St., 06457-2047. Tel: 860-347-4441; 860-347-4442; Fax: 203-347-3001.
Catechesis/Religious Program—Tel: 860-346-9100. Mary Ann Fagan, D.R.E. Students 697.

5—ST. SEBASTIAN (1930), (Italian), [CEM] Very Rev. Thomas J. Smith, V.F.; Revs. Christopher J. Zmuda, Th.Psy.D.; Patrick G. McCorry; Ephrem Karwowski, O.F.M.Cap. (RVC) (Retired); Daniel Karempelis, M.S.A.; Deacons John P. Catalano; Nicholas J. Cannata.
Res.: 155 Washington St., 06457-2800. Tel: 860-347-2638; Fax: 860-347-6736 Office; 860-343-1821 Rectory.

Parish Hall (Parish Activity Center)—Tel: 860-685-9764.
School—61 Durant Ter., 06457. Tel: 860-347-3438; Fax: 860-343-0543. Mrs. Joan Bennett, Prin.; Mrs. Rosemary Lundell, Vice Prin. Lay Teachers 12; Students 190.
Catechesis/Religious Program—90 Pearle St., 06457. Tel: 860-347-2638, Ext. 14. Mr. Edward Smythe, D.R.E. Students 900.
Convent—Daughters of Our Lady of the Garden, 67 Round Hill Rd., 06457. Tel: 860-346-5765; Fax: 860-346-6361. Sr. Donna Breauregard, O.L.G., Supr.

MONTVILLE, NEW LONDON CO., ST. JOHN (1881), [CEM] Revs. Stephen Gulino; Brian J. Romanowski; Francis C. Rouleau; Deacon Melvin Nygaard.
Mailing Address: P.O. Box 468, Uncasville, 06382-2327. In Res., Rev. Msgr. Robert L. Brown, Chancellor. Tel: 860-887-9294 (Chancery); 860-848-3771 (Private); Rev. Mark D. O'Donnell, Dir. Vocations. Tel: 860-887-9294.
Res.: 22 Maple Ave., Uncasville, 06382-2327. Tel: 860-848-9335; Fax: 860-848-1258.
Catechesis/Religious Program—Tel: 860-848-1409; Fax: 860-848-1258. Rev. Jonathan Reardon, D.R.E. Students 199.

MOODUS, MIDDLESEX CO., ST. BRIDGET (1914), [CEM] Rev. Gregoire J. Fluet, Ph.D.
Res.: 75 Moodus-Leesville Rd., P.O. Box 422, 06469-0422. Tel: 860-873-8623; Fax: 860-873-9407.
Catechesis/Religious Program—Students 294.

MOOSUP, WINDHAM CO., ALL-HALLOWS (1859), [CEM] Revs. Darius Ziebowicz, S.D.S., Admin.; Tadeusz Pieniazek, S.D.S.
Res.: 130 Prospect St., 06354-1499. Tel: 860-564-2668; Fax: 860-564-3941.
School—Plainfield Catholic, Tel: 860-564-3476; Fax: 860-564-3476. Joint with St. John, Plainfield.
Catechesis/Religious Program—Tel: 860-230-0141. Julian Michelle, D.R.E. Students 308.
Mission—St. Joseph Sterling, Windham Co.

MYSTIC, NEW LONDON CO., ST. PATRICK (1870), [CEM] Rev. Charles A. McGrail.
Res.: 32 E. Main St., P.O. Box 236, 06355-0236. Tel: 860-536-1800; Fax: 860-572-1513.
Catechesis/Religious Program—Tel: 860-536-6808. Susan Waters, D.R.E. Students 202.

NEW LONDON, NEW LONDON CO.

1—ST. JOSEPH (1907), (Italian—Spanish), Revs. Joseph Castaldi; Charles Rodrigo; James Thaikoottathil; Bro. Robert Vozzo, Hospital Chap.; Deacon Gerard Gaynor Jr.
Res.: 17 Squire St., 06320-4891. Tel: 860-443-5393; Fax: 860-443-0113.
School—Tel: 860-442-1720; Fax: 860-443-5247. Lay Teachers 10; Students 226.
Catechesis/Religious Program—Students 240.

2—ST. MARY, STAR OF THE SEA (1870), (Spanish), Rev. Robert Washbaugh; Deacon Jesus A. Diez Canseco, Hispanic Min.; Sr. Rosa Maria Campos, R.O.D.A., Pastoral Assoc., Hispanic Min. Tel: 860-443-5870. The Oblate Sisters of Divine Love.
Res.: 10 Huntington St., 06320-6198. Tel: 860-447-1431; 860-440-2844 (Parish Hall); Fax: 860-437-1889.
School— (1879),Tel: 860-443-7758; Fax: 860-444-2465. Deacon Frank Farina, Prin. Priests 1; Lay Teachers 12; Students 134.
Catechesis/Religious Program—Tel: 860-443-5870; Fax: 860-443-8552. Mrs. Millie Ramos, D.R.E. Students 237.
Convent—Congregation of Oblate Sisters of Divine Love, 28 River Ave., 06360. Tel: 860-886-6092. Sr. Brta Najela, R.O.D.A., Supr.
Hispanic Ministry—60 Jay St., 06320. Tel: 860-437-1285.

NIANTIC, NEW LONDON CO., ST. AGNES (1922), [JC] Rev. Arthur A. Archer; Deacons Roland J. LaCasse; Maurice J. Walsh; James Delaney.
Res.: 22 Haigh Ave., 06357-3129. Tel: 860-739-9722; Fax: 860-691-2187.
Catechesis/Religious Program—Tel: 860-739-9992. Students 199.
Chapel—Crescent Beach, St. Francis Chapel (Summer) [JC]

NORTH GROSVENORDALE, WINDHAM CO., ST. JOSEPH (1872), [CEM] Revs. Richard J. Ricard; Robert E. Buongirno.
Res.: 12 Main St., P.O. Box 897, 06255-0897. Tel: 860-923-2361; Fax: 860-923-3396.
School—Tel: 860-923-2090; Fax: 860-923-3609. Sharon Briere, Prin. Lay Teachers 13; Students 114.
Catechesis/Religious Program—Tel: 860-923-0155. Students 290.
Mission—Sacred Heart 15 Sacred Heart Dr., P.O. Box 897, Mechanicsville, Windham Co. 06255. Tel: 860-923-0166.

NORTH STONINGTON, NEW LONDON CO., ST. THOMAS MORE (1967), Rev. V. Antony Alaharasan.
Res.: 87 Mystic Rd., 06359. Tel: 860-535-1601; Fax: 860-535-2828.
Catechesis/Religious Program—Students 120.

OAKDALE, NEW LONDON CO., OUR LADY OF THE LAKES (1966), Rev. Walter M. Nagle.
Res.: 752 Norwich, Salem Tpke., 06370. Tel: 860-859-1575; Fax: 860-859-3273.
Catechesis/Religious Program—Students 209.

OCCUM, NEW LONDON CO., ST. JOSEPH (1878), Rev. Leszek T. Janik, J.C.L.; Deacon Lawrence E. Hill.
Res.: 11 Baltic Rd., Box 256, Versailles, 06383-0256. Tel: 860-822-8020; Fax: 860-822-8007.
Catechesis/Religious Program—Tel: 860-822-6963. Mrs. Monica Bernier, D.R.E. Students 140.
Saint Society Church— (Corporate Title: St. Joseph Church Society of Occum, CT, Inc.)

OLD LYME, NEW LONDON CO., CHRIST THE KING (1934), Rev. Msgr. Richard P. LaRocque. In Res., Rev. Thomas W. Ahern (Retired).
Office:—30 Lyme St., P.O. Box 443, 06371-0443. Tel: 860-434-1669; 860-434-1660 (Res.); Fax: 860-434-7140.
Catechesis/Religious Program—Tel: 860-434-9873. Louise Young, D.R.E. Students 380.
Chapel—Our Lady of Good Counsel at Sound View Shore Rd., 06371. Tel: 860-434-5560. (Summer Chapel)

OLD SAYBROOK, MIDDLESEX CO., ST. JOHN (1884), [CEM] Revs. Joseph C. Ashe; Kevin M. Reilly; Deacons Joseph Giuliano; John Hancock.
Res.: 161 Main St., 06475-2367. Tel: 860-388-3787; Fax: 860-388-6008.
School—42 Maynard Rd., 06475. Tel: 860-388-0849; Fax: 860-388-6265. Sr. M. Loreto, S.C.M.C., Prin. Sisters 2; Lay Teachers 15; Students 304.
Catechesis/Religious Program—Tel: 860-388-6288. Sr. M. Kathleen, S.C.M.C., D.R.E. Students 248.

PAWCATUCK, NEW LONDON CO., ST. MICHAEL (1860), [CEM 2] Rev. Dennis M. Perkins.
Res.: 60 Liberty St., 06379. Tel: 860-599-5580; Fax: 860-599-8079.
School—Tel: 860-599-1084. Richard B. Woodworth, Prin. Lay Teachers 9; Students 201.
Catechesis/Religious Program—Mrs. Crystal F. Wilcox, D.R.E. Students 311.

PLAINFIELD, WINDHAM CO., ST. JOHN THE APOSTLE (1907), [CEM] Rev. Michael J. Gill; Deacon Leo N. Bernard.
Res.: 10 Railroad Ave., 06374-1215. Tel: 860-564-3313; Fax: 860-564-3314.
School—Plainfield Catholic School, 12 Railroad Ave., 06374-1215. Tel: 860-564-3476. Sr. Marie Arthur, S.C.M.C., Prin. Lay Teachers 10; Students 232.
Catechesis/Religious Program—12 Railroad Ave., 06374. Tel: 860-564-8380. Students 168.

POMFRET, WINDHAM CO., MOST HOLY TRINITY (1886), Rev. Paul L. Hebert.
Res.: 568 Pomfret St., P.O. Box 235, 06258-0235. Tel: 860-928-5830; Fax: 860-928-4035.
Catechesis/Religious Program—Students 243.

PORTLAND, MIDDLESEX CO., ST. MARY (1872), [CEM] Rev. John F. Ashe; Sr. Mary Ida Dolan, R.S.M., Pastoral Assoc. Tel: 860-342-4913.
Res.: 51 Freestone Ave.,, 06480. Tel: 860-342-2328; Fax: 860-342-1433.
Catechesis/Religious Program—Tel: 860-342-2308. Students 440.

PRESTON, NEW LONDON CO., ST. CATHERINE OF SIENA (1975), Rev. George J. Richards Jr., J.C.L.
Res.: 243 Rte. 164, 06365-8726. Tel: 860-887-9966; Fax: 860-889-7640.
Catechesis/Religious Program—Students 163.

PUTNAM, WINDHAM CO., ST. MARY (1866), [CEM] Very Rev. Roland C. Cloutier; Rev. Krystian Kot; Deacons Pierre M. Desilets; Bernard A. Phaneuf.
Res.: 218 Providence St., 06260-1514. Tel: 860-928-6535; Fax: 860-928-7246.
School—23 Marshall St., 06260. Tel: 860-928-7046; 860-928-1104; Fax: 860-928-9379. Miss Phyllis A. Hickey, Prin.
Catechesis/Religious Program—15 Marshall St., 06260. Tel: 860-928-7246; Fax: 860-928-2032. Mrs. Carol Paul, D.R.E. Students 178.

QUAKER HILL, NEW LONDON CO., OUR LADY OF PERPETUAL HELP (1904), (Polish), Rev. Msgr. Thomas R. Bride, K.C.H.S., V.G., P.A.; Deacon Ronald S. Kitlinski.
Res.: 63 Old Norwich Rd., P.O. Box 329, 06375-0329. Tel: 860-443-1875; Fax: 860-437-1125.
Catechesis/Religious Program—Tel: 860-447-3550. Sr. Michelle Sokol, S.S.J.-T.O.S.F., D.R.E. Students 94.
Convent—Sisters of St. Joseph of Third Order of St. Francis, 59 Old Norwich Rd., 06375. Tel: 860-447-3550.

QUINEBAUG, WINDHAM CO., ST. STEPHEN (1955), Rev. William J. O'Rourke.
Res.: 130 Old Turnpike Rd., 06262-0222. Tel: 860-935-5205; Fax: 860-935-5205.
Catechesis/Religious Program—Students 45.

ROCKVILLE, TOLLAND CO.

1—ST. BERNARD (1854), [CEM] Very Rev. John J. White, P.A.; Revs. Justinian B. Rweyemamu; Sebastian A. Perumbilly; Deacons Michael Berstene; Alexander Saunders.
Res.: 25 St. Bernard's Ter., 06066-3258. Tel: 860-875-0753; Fax: 860-871-7460.
School—20 School St., 06066. Tel: 860-875-0475; Fax: 860-872-2444. Sr. Mary Gerald Creeden, R.S.M., Prin. Sisters 1; Lay Teachers 9; Students 120.
Catechesis/Religious Program—22 School St., 06066. Tel: 860-872-3828. Students 456.
Convent—Sisters of Mercy, 32 School St., 06066. Tel: 860-875-4016.
Cemetery Office—Tel: 860-872-6601.

2—ST. JOSEPH (1905), (Polish), Revs. Joseph M. Olczak, O.S.P.P.E.; Thaddeus Olzacki, O.S.P.P.E.
Res.: 33 West St., 06066-6154. Tel: 860-871-1970; Fax: 860-872-0333.
School—41 West St., 06066. Tel: 860-875-4943. Sr. Joan A. O'Connor, C.S.J., Prin. Felician Sisters 3; Lay Teachers 8; Students 125.
Catechesis/Religious Program—Students 180.

ROGERS, WINDHAM CO., ST. IGNATIUS (1939), Rev. William J. McNulty.
Res.: 350 Hartford Pike, Box 487, Dayville, 06241. Tel: 860-774-8656; Fax: 860-774-8656.
Church: 21 Williamsville Rd., Box 158, 06263.
Convent—St. Ignatius Parish House Daughters of the Holy Spirit, 17 Williamsville Rd., Box 158, 06263. Tel: 860-774-8154.
Catechesis/Religious Program— Combined with St. Joseph, Dayville, CT

SOMERSVILLE, TOLLAND CO., ALL SAINTS (1915), Rev. Timothy C. Valliere; Deacons James J. Burgess; Lawrence W. Deraleau; John J. Abdalla.
Res.: 25 School St., P.O. Box M, 06072-0913. Tel: 860-749-8625; Fax: 860-763-1890.
Catechesis/Religious Program—Tel: 860-763-0348. Sandy E. Russo, D.R.E. Students 496.

STAFFORD SPRINGS, TOLLAND CO., ST. EDWARD (1869), [CEM] Revs. Richard-Jacob Forcier, O.F.M.Conv.; Daniel Fink, O.F.M.Conv.; Jude Surowiec, O.F.M-.Conv.; Bro. Hugh Dymski, O.F.M.Conv.
Mailing Address: 6 Benton St., 06076-0433. Tel: 860-684-2705; Fax: 860-684-0757.
Res.: 55 High St., 06076.
School—(Grades PreK-8) Tel: 860-684-2600; Fax: 860-684-4030. Kathleen Walsh, Prin. Lay Teachers 10; Students 166.
Catechesis/Religious Program—Students 341.
Mission—St. Joseph 6 Benton St., Staffordville, Tolland Co. 06076.

STONINGTON, NEW LONDON CO., ST. MARY (1850), [CEM] Rev. Philip J. Geogan; Deacon Henry E. O'Reilly.
Res.: 95 Main St., 06378-1219. Tel: 860-535-1700; Fax: 860-535-3433.
Catechesis/Religious Program—Tel: 860-535-4252. Matthew West, D.R.E. Students 123.

STORRS, TOLLAND CO., ST. THOMAS AQUINAS (1947), Revs. Paul D. Holland, S.J.; Gerard R. McKeon, S.J. (WOR); James J. Dressman, S.J.; Sr. Alberta Surowiec, F.S.S.J.
Res.: 46 N. Eagleville Rd., 06268-1710. Tel: 860-429-6436; Fax: 860-429-2809.
Catechesis/Religious Program—Tel: 860-429-6436. Susan Salesses, D.R.E. Students 294.

TAFTVILLE, NEW LONDON CO., SACRED HEART (1883), (French), Rev. Msgr. Henry N. Archambault, P.A., J.C.D. In Res., Rev. William J. Flynn.
Res.: 156 Providence St., P.O. Box 208, 06380. Tel: 860-887-3072; Fax: 860-204-9338.
School—15 Hunters Ave., 06380-0208. Tel: 860-887-1757; Fax: 860-889-7276. Sr. Mary David, S.C.M.C., Prin. Sisters of Charity of Our Lady Mother of the Church 4; Lay Teachers 7; Students 165.
Catechesis/Religious Program—Tel: 860-887-4363; Fax: 860-889-7276. Students 130.

TOLLAND, TOLLAND CO., ST. MATTHEW (1964), Revs. James P. Carini; Rysard Slininski; Deacon Ronald Freedman.
Mailing Address: P.O. Box 100, 06084-0100. Tel: 860-872-0200; Fax: 860-875-4413.
Catechesis/Religious Program—Tel: 860-875-8663; Fax: 860-875-4572. Mrs. Nancy Rudek, (Grades 7-12); Mrs. Cynthia Yaconiello, D.R.E. (Grades 1-6). Students 878.

VERNON, TOLLAND CO., SACRED HEART (1958), [JC] Rev. Stanley J. Szczapa; Rella Bernabucci, Pastoral Assoc.; Ernest Golnik, Liturgy and Music Dir.
Church: 550 Hartford Tpke., 06066-5000. Tel: 860-875-4563; Fax: 860-872-2535.
Catechesis/Religious Program—Students 113.

VOLUNTOWN, NEW LONDON CO., ST. THOMAS APOSTLE (1892), [CEM] [JC] Rev. James Joseph Sucholet.
Res.: 61 Preston City Rd., P.O. Box 99, 06384-0099. Tel: 860-376-2293; Fax: 860-376-0287.
Catechesis/Religious Program—49 Preston City Rd., 06384. Tel: 860-376-8352. Alanna Malinowski, Asst. Dir. & D.R.E. Tel: 860-376-4880; Ginger

Coleman, D.R.E. Tel: 860-376-3874. Students 157.
Mission—St. Anne (1891), Rte. 201, Glasgo, New London Co.

WATERFORD, NEW LONDON CO., ST. PAUL (1960), Rev. Richard F. Roughan; Deacon Richard K. Walker.
Res.: 170 Rope Ferry Rd., 06385-2609. Tel: 860-443-5587; Fax: 860-442-9308.
Catechesis/Religious Program—Tel: 860-443-3375. Mrs. Roseann Ward, D.R.E. Students 298.

WAUREGAN, WINDHAM CO., SACRED HEART (1889), (French), [CEM] Revs. Darius Ziebowicz, S.D.S.; Tadeusz Pieniazek, S.D.S.
Res.: 620 Wauregan Rd., P.O. Box 468, 06387-0468. Tel: 860-774-6892; Fax: 860-779-9529.
Catechesis/Religious Program—Students 30.

WEST WILLINGTON, TOLLAND CO., ST. JUDE (1981), Rev. Thomas W. Sennik.
Res.: 25 Old Farms Rd., P.O. Box 240, Willington, 06279-0240. Tel: 860-429-9655.
Catechesis/Religious Program—Tel: 860-429-8604. Students 75.

WESTBROOK, MIDDLESEX CO., ST. MARK (1962), Rev. Richard J. Albamonti; Deacon Thomas E. Rymut.
Res.: 222 McVeagh Rd., 06498-1515. Tel: 860-399-9207; Fax: 860-399-7751.
Catechesis/Religious Program—Tel: 860-399-6208. Students 328.

WILLIMANTIC, WINDHAM CO.
1—ST. JOSEPH (1859), [CEM] Rev. Msgr. Willis W. West; Revs. Walter M. Nagle; Mariadas J. Lipton; Deacon Lawrence Godwin. In Res., Rev. Edward F. Frigault (Retired).
Res.: 99 Jackson St., 06226-3077. Tel: 860-423-8439; Fax: 860-423-6825.
School—St. Mary-St. Joseph, 35 Valley St., 06226. Tel: 860-423-8479; Fax: 860-423-8365. Sr Elaine Moorcraft, Prin.
Catechesis/Religious Program—Students 233.
Convent—88 Jackson St., 06226. Tel: 203-423-5122.
Mission—St. Margaret Rte. 14, Scotland, Windham Co. 06264. Tel: 203-423-1791.

2—ST. MARY (1903), (French), Rev. Roger J. Lamoureux, O.M.I., J.C.L. In Res., Rev. Edward Poulin.
Res.: 80 Maple Ave., 06226-2733. Tel: 860-423-5835; Fax: 860-423-9933.
School—St. Mary-St. Joseph, 35 Valley St., 06226. Tel: 860-423-8479; Fax: 860-423-8365. Sr. M. Elaine Moorcraft, S.C.M.C., Prin. Sisters 2; Lay Teachers 14; Students 198.
Catechesis/Religious Program—Tel: 860-423-9700; Fax: 860-455-9407. Students 117.
Convent—Sisters of Charity of Our Lady, 88 Jackson St., 06226. Tel: 860-423-5122.
Faith Formulation—Tel: 860-423-9700. Mrs. Tina Popeleski, Dir.

WINDHAM, WINDHAM CO., SAGRADO CORAZON DE JESUS (1991), (Hispanic), Rev. Paul J. Murdock; Sisters Rosa M. Campos, R.O.D.A., Pastoral Assoc.; Minerva Salgado, M.S.P.; Deacon Felipe Silva; Ms. Virginia Rodriguez, Pastoral Assoc.
Mailing Address: 61 Club Rd., 06280-1007. Tel: 860-423-8617; Fax: 860-423-4157.
Catechesis/Religious Program—Students 124.

Chaplains of Public Institutions

NORWICH. *William W. Backus Hospital* 06360. Tel: 860-889-8331. Sr. Rita Johnson, S.S.N.D., Chaplaincy Svcs.

MIDDLETOWN. *Connecticut Valley Hospital*, Eastern Dr., P.O. Box 351, 06457. Tel: 860-262-5900; Fax: 860-262-5900. Rev. Jose Rizal Dimapilis, O.P., Prin. Chap.
Long Lane School, P.O. Box 882, 06457. Tel: 860-344-2820.
Middlesex Memorial Hospital, 28 Crescent St., 06457-0822. Tel: 860-347-9471, Ext. 6725. Rev. Bruce Quinn, O.F.M.Cap.

NEW LONDON. *Lawrence and Memorial Hospitals*, Montauk Ave., 06320. Tel: 860-442-0711, Ext. 2609. Bro. Robert Vozzo, C.S.C., Chap., Rev. Glenays Ulchack.
U.S. Coast Guard Memorial Chapel, U.S. Coast Guard Academy, 15 Mohegan Ave., 06320-4195. Tel: 860-444-8418; Fax: 960-701-6729. Rev. Thomas E. Murphy, Capt., C.H.C., U.S.N.

STORRS. *Bergin Correctional Center*, 251 Middletown Tpke., Storrs Mansfield, 06268.

On Duty Outside the Diocese:
Revs.—
Angelo, Thomas M.
Boudreau, C. Paul
Caiazzo, Nicholas
Dudzik, Dariusz
Gwudz, John S.
Kirby, Gerald S., Norwich Mission House, c/o Lynx Air, P.O. Box 407139, Fort Lauderdale, FL 33340.
Klimanskis, Adolfo, St. Casimir Rectory, 350 Smith St., Providence, RI 02908.
Maltese, James L., Church of Holy Name of Mary, 55 E. Jamaica Ave., Valley Stream, NY 11580.
Martin, Patrick A., P.O. Box 16, Stafford Springs, 06076.
Randall, Kevin S., 3339 Massachusetts Ave., N.W., Washington, DC 20008-3687.
Tumicki, Ted

Military Chaplains:
Revs.—
Angelo, Thomas M., Ch. Capt., 23 Wg/MC, Pope AFB, NC 28308.
Gwudz, John S., Office of Chap., U.S.S. Independence, CV 62, FPO, AP 96618-2760.

Absent on Leave:
Revs.—
Bolieau, Henry G.
Dempsey, Edward M., 75 Bushnell St., Hartford, 06114.
Gaulin, Roger M.
Gruber, Anthony P.
Lee, Edward
Liszewski, Francis A.
Nash, John C.
O'Keefe, Francis J.
Surprenant, John L., 943 High St., Akron, PA 17501.
Twomey, Thomas

Retired:
Most Rev.—
Hart, Daniel A., 274 Broadway, 06360.
Rev. Msgrs.—
Gadarowski, Bronislaw A., Winter, 357 Pineview Dr., Venice, FL 34293.
Malanowski, Thaddeus F., 908 S. Prospect Ave., Clearwater, FL 34616.
St. Onge, Paul J., 310 Montauk Ave., New London, 06320.
Vytautas, Balciunas, Matulitis Nursing Home, 10 Thurber Rd., Putnam, 66260. Tel: 860-928-7976
Revs.—
Ahern, Thomas W.
Almendra, Leoncio T., Real St. Abuyog, Leyte, Philippines.
Barnes, Robert W.
Bialkowski, Henry A., 162 Eddy Glover Blvd., New Britain, 06053. Tel: 203-223-4242
Cronin, Robert W., 11 Middlefield Dr., West Hartford, 06107.
Davis, Edward J., 179 Train St., Dorchester, MA 02122. Tel: 617-282-0479
Drummond, Elsyn J.
Flint, Kenneth, P.O. Box 399, Mystic, 06355.
Frigault, Edward F., St. Joseph, 99 Jackson St., Willimantic, 06226.
Giaquinto, Albert C., Theological College, 401 Michigan Ave., N.E., Washington, DC 20064.
Klein, Theodore J., Ph.D., 140 Greemanville Ave., Apt. 2, Mystic, 06355.
Kozon, John A., 3780 Isherwood Cove, Memphis, TN 38125.
Kuzdal, Anthony P., 1714 Beach Pkwy. A-2, Cape Coral, FL 33904. Tel: 813-542-9261
LaChance, Marcel, Sun Haven Mobile Home Park, 19500 Dixie Hwy., North Miami Beach, FL 33180.
Marciniak, John, 70 W. 18th Rd., Broad Channel, NY 11693.
McGrath, Daniel F., 2433 Main St., Rocky Hill, 06067.
McNulty Robert E., 65 Beach St., P.O. Box 356, Green Harbor, MA 02041.
Morrissette, Joseph H., 30 School Hill Rd., Baltic, 06330.
Murphy, Hugh J., P.O. Box 261, Pomfret, 06258.
Nichols, Joseph E., 810 Walnut St., Lebanon, PA 17042.
Poulin, Edward C., 13 Blissville Rd., Lisbon, 06351. Tel: 860-887-3689
Pupsys, Adam, P.O. Box 2163, Westerly, RI 02891.
Ramen, Paul F., 350 Pond Hill Rd., Moosup, 06354. Tel: 860-887-2565
Ricard, Joseph M., 233 Spanish Moss Rd., Davenport, FL 33837.
Sutula, Leo S., 19 Maxwell Sr., Rocky Hill, 06067.
Wisneski, Edward, S.T.D., Ph.D., 78 E. Ridge Rd., Middletown, 06457.

Permanent Deacons:
Abdalla, John, All Saints, Somerville
Bachand, Francis J., St. Mary, Jewett City
Baillargeon, Paul R., St. Mary, Jewett City
Balchus, John A., St. Lawrence, Killingworth
Barbeau, Rene N., Jr., St. James, Danielson
Barlow, Robert C., St. Andrew, Colchester
Bernard, Leo N., St. John, Plainfield
Berstene, Michael C., Diocesan Dir. of Deacon Personnel, St. Bernard, Rockville
Burgess, James J., Office of Evangelization & All Saints, Somersville
Burke, John J., Jr., 15 Black Bear Tr., Hendersonville, NC 28739-9348.
Cannata, Nicholas J., St. Sebastian, Middletown
Cartier, L. Roger, Pineallas Park, FL
Catalano, John P., St. Sebastian, Middletown
Cote, Albert J., (Retired), St. Francis, Lebanon
Cyr, Warren, St. Patrick, East Hampton
Danesi, Peter H., III, St. Mary, Groton
Delaney, James, St. Agnes, Niantic
Deraleau, Lawrence W., All Saints, Somersville
Desilets, Pierre M., St. Mary, Putnam
Diez Conseco, Jesus A., St. Mary, Hispanic Apostolate New London & Bishop's Delegate to Hispanic Permanent Deacons
Dogue, Eduardo, (Retired), Staten Island, N.Y.
Dolan, Dennis F., Prison Ministry, Niantic and St. Andrew, Colchester
Donahue, Donald J., St. Thomas More, North Stonington
Doyle, Dennis A., III, Saints Peter & Paul, Norwich
Fecteau, Al R., Cathedral of St. Patrick, Norwich
Freedman, Ronald, St. Matthew, Tolland
Gaynor, Gerard J., Saint Joseph, New London
Gill, Peter L., St. Colman, Middlefield
Giuliano, Joseph, St. John, Old Saybrook
Goodwin, Lawrence M., St. Joseph, Williamantic
Goodwin, Lawrence, St. Margaret Mission, Scotland
Gosselin, Raymond P., St. Lawrence, Killingworth
Grospitch, Harry J., St. Bernard, Rockville
Hayes, Robert P., Sacred Heart, Norwichtown
Hill, Lawrence, St. Joseph, Occum
Jolin, Joseph, 3501 Heritage Lake, North Fort Meyers, Fl 33903
Kitlinski, Ronald S., Our Lady Perpetual Help, Quaker Hill
LaCasse, Roland J., St. Agnes, Niantic
LaPlante, Joseph A., Southwest Harbor, ME
Lewis, Thomas A., St. Joseph, Norwich
McMahon, James R., Sr.
Melendez, Carlos, Port St. Lucie, FL
Midwood, Barry R., Exton, PA
Moneypenny, Lawrence, St. Joseph, Chester
Nygaard, Melvin G., St. John, Uncasville
O'Reilly, Henry E., St. Mary, Stonington
Osuba, Jose, Columbia
Pereira, Julias A., Sacred Heart, Groton
Phaneuf, Bernard A., St. Mary, Putnam
Ramos, Mariano, Hispanic Ministry House, Enders Island, Mystic
Reed, Steven W., St. Matthias, East Lyme
Rymut, Thomas E., St. Mark, Westbrook
Saunders, Alexander, St. Bernard, Rockville
Silva, Felipe, Sagrado Corazon de Jesus, Windham
Walker, Richard K., St. Paul, Waterford
Wallen, Paul A., St. Mary, Groton Long Point
Walsh, Maurice, St. Agnes, Niantic
Weber, F. Paul, St. Mary of the Visitation, Clinton
Whittle, Joseph B.

INSTITUTIONS LOCATED IN THE DIOCESE

[A] SEMINARIES, RELIGIOUS OR SCHOLASTICATES

CROMWELL. *Holy Apostles College and Seminary*, 33 Prospect Hill Rd., 06416-2005. Tel: 860-632-3000; 860-632-3010 (Admissions); Fax: 860-632-3030. Email: rector@holyapostles.edu. Web: www.holyapostles.edu. Revs. Douglas L. Mosey, C.S.B., Ph.D., Pres. & Rector; Maurice Sheehan, O.F.M.Cap., Academic Dean; Michel Legault, M.S.A.; Raymond Halliwell, M.S.A.; Addison Hallock, M.S.A., Spiritual Dir.; Bradley Pierce, M.S.A.; Ronan P. Callahan, C.P.; Gerard Gibeault, M.S.A.; David Q. Liptak; Luis Luna, M.S.A.; David Zercie, M.S.A.; Joseph M. Olczak, O.S.P.P.E.; Jude Surowiec, O.F.M.Conv.; John Hillier; James Turro; Sr. Mary Anne Linder, F.S.E., Dir. Field Education; Dr. Cynthia Toolin, Registrar; William J. Russell, C.P.A., Finance Officer. Priests 18; Brothers 2; Sisters 5; Lay Teachers 13; Seminarians 70; Seminary Division Lay Students 60; Total 150.

ENDERS ISLAND. *St. Edmund's Novitiate*, P.O. Box 399, 06355. Tel: 860-536-0565; Fax: 860-572-7655. Email: endersisle@aol.com. Web: www.endersisland.com. Revs. Thomas F.X. Hoar, S.S.E., Supr.; Paul Pinard, S.S.E.; Bro. Martin Slattery, S.S.E. Society of St. Edmund Priests 2; Brothers 1.

[B] HIGH SCHOOLS, DIOCESAN

MIDDLETOWN. *Mercy High School*, 1740 Randolph Rd.,

06457-5155. Tel: 860-346-6659; Fax: 860-344-9887. Email: info@mercyhigh.com. Web: www.mercyhigh.com. Sisters Mary A. McCarthy, R.S.M., Prin.; Patty Moriarty, R.S.M., Vice Prin. Student Life; Mr. Steven Brickey, Vice Prin. Academics; Sr. Peggy O'Neill, R.S.M., Vice Prin. & Registrar; Miss Ann Derbacher, Campus Min. Sisters of Mercy Sisters 12; Lay Teachers 55; Students 677; Total Staff 82.

Xavier High School, 181 Randolph Rd., 06457-5635. Tel: 860-346-7735; Fax: 860-346-6859. Email: donnajc@xavierhighschool.org. Web: www.xavierhighschool.org. Bro. William Ciganek, C.F.X., Headmaster; Rev. Gregory Galvin, Chap.; Rory Donaldson, Devel. Dir.; Bro. James Boyle, C.F.X., Community Dir.; Mr. William Garrity, Prin.; Mr. David Sizemore, Academic Dean; Bro. Thomas Ryan, C.F.X., Academic Dean; Mr. Kevin Calkins, Dean of Students. Brothers of St. Francis Xavier Brothers 9; Lay Teachers 56; Students 838.

UNCASVILLE. *St. Bernard High School*, 1593 Norwich-New London Tpke., 06382-1399. Tel: 860-848-1271; Fax: 860-848-1274. Email: info@saint-bernard.com. Web: www.saint-bernard.com. Roy F. Dado, Prin.; James Venditto, Asst. Prin. Priests 1; Lay Teachers 25; Students 325.

St. Bernard Academy (Grades 6-8), 1593 Norwich-New London Tpke., 06382-1399. Tel: 860-848-3007; Fax: 860-848-0261. Rev. Santino Casimano, Chap.; Ms. Mary C. Dillman, Prin.; Mrs. Carlene Martin, Admin. Asst. (Middle School) Lay Teachers 7; Students 144.

[C] HIGH SCHOOLS, PRIVATE

BALTIC. *Academy and Boarding-School of the Holy Family*, 54 W. Main St., P.O. Box 691, 06330-0691. Tel: 860-822-9272; Fax: 860-822-1318. Email: academy.holy.family@snet.net. Web: www.academyoftheholyfamily.org. Sr. Mary Patrick Mulready, S.C.M.C., Prin.; Rev. Michael Wood, Chap. Sisters of Charity of Our Lady Mother of the Church Sisters 6; Lay Teachers 8; Students 56.

THOMPSON. *Marianapolis Preparatory School*, P.O. Box 304, 06277-0304. Tel: 860-923-2220; Fax: 860-923-1884. Email: mebbitt@marianapolis.org. Mrs. Marilyn Ebbitt, Headmistress; Revs. Timothy J. Roth, M.I.C., Chap.; Albin Gurkis, M.I.C.; John Petrauskas, M.I.C.; Mr. James Ringer, Chief Financial Operating Officer. Priests 2; Lay Teachers 27; Students 230.

Congregation of Marians of the Immaculate Conception, P.O. Box 368, 06277-0368. Tel: 860-923-2220; Fax: 860-923-1884. Rev. John Petrauskas, M.I.C.

[D] CHILDREN, RESIDENTIAL CARE FOR

DEEP RIVER. *Mount St. John*, 135 Kirtland St., 06417-1816. Tel: 860-526-5391; Fax: 860-526-1636. Email: coridanc@mtstjohn.org. Web: www.mtstjohn.org. Catherine T. Coridan, M.A., Exec. Dir./Dir. of Ministry; Mr. Andrew George, Prin. Lay Staff 130; Boys 90; Total Assisted 192; Total Staff 155.

[E] HOMES FOR AGED

WILLIMANTIC. *Holy Family Home and Shelter, Inc.*, 88 Jackson St., P.O. Box 884, 06226-0884. Tel: 860-423-7719; Fax: 860-423-3770. Email: holyfamily2@mindspring.com. Web: www.holyfamilyshelter.org. Bonnie Reilein, Exec. Dir.; Sr. M. Peter, S.C.M.C., Dir. Public Rels. Residents 23; Total Assisted 165; Total Staff 12. In Res. Rev. Stephen Fronckewicz, O.S.B.

WINDHAM. *St. Joseph Living Center*, 14 Club Rd., 06280-1000. Tel: 860-456-1107; Fax: 860-450-7114. Email: mkolaczendo@wcmh.org. Maureen Kolaczenko, M.B.A., Admin.; Dr. Michael Keenan, Medical Dir.; Patricia Duffy, R.N., Dir. Nursing Svcs.; Valerie Oliver, R.N., Case Mgr.; Paula Haney, R.P.T., Dir. Rehabilitation Svcs.; Rev. Peter Arulrajan, Chap. Sisters 2; Lay Staff 200; Capacity 120; Total Assisted 120; Total Staff 202.

[F] MONASTERIES AND RESIDENCES OF PRIESTS AND BROTHERS

CROMWELL. *Society of the Missionaries of the Holy Apostles*, 22 Prospect Hill Rd., 06416-2005. Tel: 860-632-3039; Fax: 860-635-4823. Revs. Raymond Halliwell, M.S.A., Prov. Animator; Edward C. Doherty, M.S.A.; Stanley Grove, M.S.A.; Addison Hallock, M.S.A.; Daniel Karempelis, M.S.A.; Benedict Klucinec, M.S.A.; William McCarthy, M.S.A.; Robert Murphy, M.S.A.; Bradley Pierce, M.S.A.; George Realmuto, M.S.A.; Robert Sickler, M.S.A.; Richard Skarbek, M.S.A.; Pasquale Taliercio, M.S.A. Society of the Missionaries of the Holy Apostles

Working Outside the Diocese: Revs. Humberto Almazan, M.S.A.; James Anderson, M.S.A.; J. Patrick Boyhan, M.S.A.; James J. Creedon, M.S.A.; James Downs, M.S.A.; Harold Dunn, M.S.A.; Francis Fajella, M.S.A.; Richard Hite, M.S.A.; Joseph Kenney, M.S.A.; Vincent Kilidjian, M.S.A.; James Larkin, M.S.A.; Marius Morin, M.S.A.; Michael Nofi, M.S.A.; Maximo Asencius Pablo, M.S.A.; Gerard Petta, M.S.A.; Laurence Preston, M.S.A.; Edward Przygocki, M.S.A.; Isaac Raney, M.S.A.; Martin Rooney, M.S.A.; Vincent Salamoni, M.S.A.; Jose Salazar, M.S.A.; Thomas Simon, M.S.A.; David Zercie, M.S.A.; Deacons Richard Gray, M.S.A.; Peter Kucer, M.S.A.

GRISWOLD. *Marian Friary of Our Lady of Guadalupe*, 199 Colonel Brown Rd., 06351. Tel: 860-376-6840; Fax: 860-376-6848. Email: ffi1@mindspring.com. Web: www.marymediatrix.com. Revs. Angelo Mary Geiger, Guardian & Novice Master; American Supr.; Maximilian M. Warnisher, F.F.I. (FR), Vicar. Priests 3; Brothers 4.

MIDDLETOWN. *Congregation of the Brothers of St. Francis Xavier*, 181 Randolph Rd., 06457-5635. Tel: 860-346-8585; Fax: 860-346-6859. Bros. William Ciganek, C.F.X., Prin.; James Boyle, C.F.X., Dir.; Eugene Behenna, C.F.X.; Labre Dillon, C.F.X.; Thomas Fahey, C.F.X.; J. Robert Houlihan, C.F.X.; Rev. Gregory Galvin, Chap.; Bros. John J. McDonald, C.F.X.; H. Lawrence Nyhan, C.F.X.; Thomas Ryan, C.F.X. Total in Residence 10.

MYSTIC. *Society of St. Edmund*, P.O. Box 399, 06355-0399. Tel: 860-536-0565; Fax: 860-572-7655. Email: endersisle@aol.com. Web: www.endersislamo. Revs. Richard Myhalyk, S.E.E., Supr. General; Thomas F.X. Hoar, S.S.E., Sec.; Paul Pinard, S.S.E.; Bro. Martin Slattery, S.S.E. Total in Residence 3.

THOMPSON. *Marian Fathers*, Marianapolis Prep School, 06277-0368. Tel: 860-923-9798; Fax: 860-923-3730. Email: timothy.roth@snet.net. Revs. Timothy Roth, M.I.C., First Councillor, & Vice Provincial; Albin Gurkis, M.I.C.; Bros. Donald Schaefer, M.I.C., Prov. Treas. & Second Councillor; Brian Manian, M.I.C., Supr., Fourth Provincial Councilor. Total in Residence 5.

WILLIMANTIC. *Missionary Oblates of Mary Immaculate*, 289 Windham Rd., P.O. Box 55, 06226-0055. Tel: 860-423-8484; Fax: 860-423-5285. Email: oblates@omict.org. Web: www.omict.org. Revs. Roger Couture, O.M.I., Supr.; Olivier Renaud, O.M.I.; Leroy Landry, O.M.I.; Lon Konold, O.M.I.; Bros. Donat Daigle, O.M.I.; Paul Ricard, O.M.I. Total in Residence 6; Total Staff 12.

[G] CONVENTS AND RESIDENCES FOR SISTERS

NORWICH. *School Sisters Notre Dame*, 7 Otis St., 06360. Tel: 860-886-6948. Email: sisterrjohnson@juno.com.

BALTIC. *Holy Family Motherhouse*, 54 W. Main St., 06330-0691. Tel: 860-822-8241; Fax: 860-822-9842. Email: tjtmvocscmc@juno.com. Web: www.sistersofcharity.com. Sr. M. Anthony, Supr. Gen.; Rev. Michael Wood, Chap. Tel: 860-822-1561. Sisters of Charity of Our Lady, Mother of the Church Professed 72; Junior Professed 7; Novices 2.

GALES FERRY. *Society of the Sisters for the Church* 06335. Tel: 860-464-4023. P.O. Box 295, 06335. Tel: 860-423-8484 (Work); 860-464-4023 (Home). Sr. Jeanette Serra, S.S.C.

HIGGANUM. *Apostles of the Sacred Heart of Jesus*, Sacred Heart on the Lake, 529 Brainard Hill Rd., 06441-4010. Tel: 860-345-4653; Fax: 860-345-4469. Email: sdjvl@juno.com. Total in Residence 3.

MIDDLETOWN. *Mill Hill Sisters*, 6 Bluebird Rd., 06457. Total in Residence 3.

Sisters of Mercy, 421 High St., 06457. Tel: 860-346-6619. Email: RTGarneau@aol.com. Other residences located in Lyme, Hebron, Norwich and Rockville

Sisters of Our Lady of the Garden Convent and Nursery School. , 67 Round Hill Rd., 06457-6119. Tel: 806-346-5765. Sr. Donna Beauregard, O.L.G., Supr. Total Assisted 82; Total Staff 9.

Sisters of St. Joseph, T.O.S.F., 46 Camp St., Apt. 2, 06457-2445. Tel: 860-347-8936.

MOODUS. *Sisters of St. Joseph of Chambery*, P.O. Box 22, 06469-0022. Tel: 860-873-1581; Fax: 860-873-2357. Email: myfathershouse@prodigy.net. Web: www.myfathershouse.com. P.O. Box 22, 06469-0022. Tel: 860-873-1581; Fax: 860-873-2357.

PUTNAM. *Holy Spirit Provincial House*, 72 Church St., 06260-1810. Tel: 860-928-0891; Fax: 860-928-6469. Sr. Jacqueline Robillard, D.H.S., Prov.; Rev. Richard L. Archambault, Chap. Daughters of the Holy Spirit Sisters 63.

Other Locations:

Notre Dame Community, 4 Ravine St., 06260. Tel: 860-928-6163; 860-928-9129.

Daughters of the Holy Spirit, 26 Church St., 06260. Tel: 860-928-6869.

St. Ignatius Parish House Community, 17 Williamsville Rd., Rogers, 06263. Tel: 860-774-8154.

185 Farm Hill Rd., Middletown, 06457. Tel: 860-347-4382.

Provincialate Community, 31 Ravine St., 06260. Tel: 860-928-7072; 860-928-3882.

All Hallows Convent, 152 Prospect St., Moosup, 06354. Tel: 860-564-5409.

Immaculate Conception Convent, Spiritual Renewal Center and Novitiate, 600 Liberty Hwy., 06260-2503. Tel: 860-928-7955; Fax: 860-928-1930. Rev. Vytautas Gedvainis, Chap.; Sr. M. Paul Savickas, Prov. Sisters of the Immaculate Conception of the Blessed Virgin Mary 8; Total in Residence 16; Total Staff 6.

Matulaitis Nursing Home Inc., 10 Thurber Rd., 06260-2522. Tel: 860-928-7976; Fax: 860-963-1920. Web: matulaitisnursinghome.org. Jane Logan, Admin.; Rev. Rapolas Krasauskas, Chap. Sisters of the Immaculate Conception of the Blessed Virgin Mary Sisters 7; Residents 119.

Provincialate Community of the Daughters of the Holy Spirit, 31 Ravine St., 06260-1817. Fax: 860-928-6197. Email: jardhs@juno.com. Sisters Jacqueline Robillard, D.H.S., Prov. Tel: 860-928-7072; Anne Marie Berthiaume, D.H.S., Prov. Councillor. Tel: 860-928-3882.

UNCASVILLE. *Emmaus Community*, 24 Maple Ave., 06382. Tel: 860-848-3379; Fax: 860-848-0755. Email: emmausslc@aol.com. Total in Residence 3; Total Staff 3.

WILLIMANTIC. *Sisters of Charity of Our Lady, Mother of the Church*, St. Joseph Convent, 88 Jackson St., 06226. Tel: 860-423-5122. Total in Residence 4; Total Staff 4.

[H] PRIVATE ASSOCIATIONS OF THE FAITHFUL

ASHFORD. *Benedictine Monastery* Community of Our Lady of Mount Caritas Monastery, O.S.B.; Sisters of the Order of St. Benedict. Contemplative. , Seckar Rd., 06278. Tel: 860-429-7457; Fax: 860-429-9196. Web: mountcaritasmonastery.org. Sr. Mary Peter, O.S.B., Supr. Professed 2; Lay Oblates 7.

[I] RETREAT HOUSES

NORWICH. *Ministry of His Able People* Tel: 860-887-9294.

Ave Maria Place

MYSTIC. *St. Edmund's Retreat*, P.O. Box 399, 06355-0399. Tel: 860-536-0565; Fax: 860-572-7655. Email: endersisle@aol.com. Web: www.endersisland.com. Rev. Thomas F.X. Hoar, S.S.E., Exec. Dir.; Deacon Ronald D. Henderson, Dir. of Operations and Programs; Mrs. Claire St. Clair, Office Mgr.; Brian Pearson, Chair of Board of Advisers; John J. Foley II, Chair Finance Committee. Total in Residence 6; Total Staff 20.

WILLIMANTIC. *Immaculata Retreat House*, 289 Windham Rd., P.O. Box 55, 06226-0055. Tel: 860-423-8484; Fax: 860-423-5285. Email: immaculata@omict.org. Web: www.omict.org. 06226. Revs. Roger Couture, O.M.I., Supr.; Olivier Renaud, O.M.I.; Lon Konold, O.M.I.; Leroy Landry, O.M.I.; Bros. Donat Daigle, O.M.I.; Paul Ricard, O.M.I.; Mrs. Paulette Bard, Dir. Missionary Oblates of Mary Immaculate: U.S. Province Total in Residence 6; Total Statff 12.

[J] RENEWAL CENTERS

PORTLAND. *Affirmation Counseling Center*, 553 Portland Cobalt Rd., 06480-1968. Tel: 860-342-0760; Fax: 860-342-4226. John J. Smey, L.C.S.W., Exec. Dir.; Rev. Roland Cloutier, M.S.W., L.C.S.W., Consultant; Adriana Gabarron, L.C.S.W., Psychotherapist; Ann D. Cady, M.A., Psychotherapist; Julie S. Dudek, M.A., Psychotherapist; Judith L. Siena, M.A., Psychotherapist; John J. Thimm, Psychotherapist. Total Assisted 152; Total Staff 6.

UNCASVILLE. *Emmaus-Diocesan Spiritual Life Center*, 24 Maple Ave., 06382. Tel: 860-848-3427; Fax: 860-848-0755. Email: emmausslc@aol.com. Sisters Mary Barbara Hobbs, P.B.V.M., Dir.; Mary Ann De Francesco, R.S.M., Assoc. Dir.; Rev. Joseph G. Finnerty, Assoc. Dir.; Sr. Agnes Therrien, S.S.Ch., Assoc. Dir. Sisters 3; Total in Residence 3; Total Staff 4.

St. Mary Rectory, 70 Central Ave., 06382. Tel: 860-889-6657; Fax: 860-848-0755.

[K] CAMPUS MINISTRY

WILLIMANTIC. *Campus Ministry* , Eastern Connecticut State University, Newman Hall. , 290 Prospect St., 06226. Tel: 860-423-0856; Fax: 860-456-8083. Email: lapointel@easternct.edu. Web: www.norwichdiocese.org. Rev. Laurence A.M. LaPointe, Diocesan Dir. Campus Ministry.

Wesleyan University-The University Ministry, Office

of the University Chaplains, 171 Church St., Middletown, 06459-3625. Tel: 860-685-2277; Fax: 860-685-2821. Rev. Louis Manzo, C.S.C.

Connecticut College, Harkness Chapel, 270 Mohegan Ave., New London, 06320-4196. Tel: 860-439-2452; Fax: 860-439-2463. Email: lalap@conncoll.edu lapointel@easternet.edu. Rev. Laurence A.M. LaPointe, College Chap.

University of Connecticut, St. Thomas Aquinas Chapel, 46 N. Eagleville Rd., Storrs, 06268-1710. Tel: 860-429-6436; Fax: 860-429-2809. Email: stthoffice@worldnet.att.net. Revs. James J. Dressman, S.J., Chap.; Gerard R. McKeon, S.J (WOR), Chap.; Paul D. Holland, S.J., Chap.; Sr. Alberta Surowiec, F.SS.J., Chap.

[L] MISCELLANEOUS

NORWICH. *The Annual Bishop's Appeal of the Diocese of Norwich, Inc.*, 197 Broadway, 06360. Tel: 860-886-1928; Fax: 860-886-2651. Email: dodrc@snet. Web: www.norwichdiocese.org. Mr. Richard Costello, Dir.; Mr. John Butler, Dir. Planned Giving; Mr. Tim Smith, Dir. Stewardship.

The Catholic Foundation of the Diocese of Norwich, Inc., 201 Broadway, 06360. Tel: 860-887-9294; Fax: 860-886-2651. Email: dodrc@snet.com. Web: www.norwichdiocese.org.

Diocese of Norwich Assisted Living Services, Inc., 201 Broadway, 06360-4328. Tel: 860-887-9294; Fax: 860-886-1670.

The Donor Advised Funds of the Diocese of Norwich, Inc., 201 Broadway, 06360. Tel: 860-887-9294.

ASHFORD. *Our Lady of Mount Caritas Monastery* Contemplative Sisters, Spirit of St. Benedict Primitive Observance , 54 Seckar Rd., 06278. Tel: 860-429-7457; Fax: 860-429-9196. Web: mountcaritasmonastery.org. Sr. Mary Peter, Prioress.

CROMWELL. *Basilian Fathers of Connecticut, Inc.*, 33 Prospect Hill Rd., 06416. Tel: 860-632-3010; Fax: 860-632-3030. Email: fr_mosey@juno.com. Rev. Douglas L. Mosey, C.S.B., Ph.D., Pres. & Rector.

Marian Housing Corporation, Tel: 860-632-1688; Fax: 860-632-1542. 201 Broadway, 06360-4328. Tel: 860-887-9294.

JEWETT CITY. *The World Apostolate of Fatima, Inc., Norwich Diocesan Division*, P.O. Box 605, 06351. Tel: 860-377-7802; Fax: 860-374-2187. Email: norwichwaf@hotmail.com. Denise Dudek, Pres.

MIDDLETOWN. *Mercy Development Office*, 1740 Randolph Rd., 06457. Tel: 860-347-8957; Fax: 860-344-9887. Email: jhall@mercyhigh.com. Web: www.mercyhigh.com. Janet Hall, Devel. Dir.

Mercy-Xavier Fund Corporation, 181 Randolph Rd., 06457. Tel: 860-346-7735; Fax: 860-346-6859.

Xavier Development Office, 181 Randolph Rd., 06457. Tel: 860-347-6079; Fax: 860-346-6859. Email: development@xavierhighschool.org. Web: www.xavierhighschool.org. Mr. Rory Donaldson, Dir.; Mr. Joseph E. Lane, Asst. Devel. Office; Mrs. Kit La Rosa, Sec. Total Staff 3.

PUTNAM. *The Daughters of the Holy Spirit Charitable Trust*, 72 Church St., 06260-1810. Tel: 860-928-0891; Fax: 860-928-6496. Sr. Bonnie Morrow, Trustee & Contact Person.

The Holy Spirit Health Care Center, Inc., 72 Church St., 06260. Tel: 860-928-0891; Fax: 860-928-1312. Email: bmorrowdhs@juno.com. Sr. Jacqueline Robillard, D.H.S., Prov. & Contact Person; Mrs. Annemarie Shiroka, Admin.

WILLIMANTIC. *Saint Joseph's Home for the Aged, Inc.*, 88 Jackson St., 06226. Tel: 860-423-8439. Email: ww_westl@yahoo.com.

WINDHAM. *Sagrado Corazon de Jesus, Inc. of Windham*, 61 Club Rd., 06280. Tel: 860-423-8617; Fax: 860-423-4157. Email: aposthisano@juno.com.

RELIGIOUS INSTITUTES OF MEN REPRESENTED IN THE DIOCESE

For further details refer to the corresponding bracketed number in the Religious Institutes of Men or Women section.

[0200]—*Benedictine Monks*—O.S.B.
[1350]—*Brothers of St. Francis Xavier* (St. Joseph Prov.)—C.F.X.
[0610]—*Brothers of the Congregation of Holy Cross*—C.S.C.
[0470]—*The Capuchin Friars* (Prov. of St. Mary)—O.F.M. Cap
[0340]—*Cistercian Fathers*—O.Cist.
[]—*Congregation of Christian Brothers*—C.F.C.
[0480]—*Conventual Franciscans*—O.F.M.Conv
[0533]—*Franciscan Friars of the Immaculate*—F. I.
[0690]—*Jesuit Fathers and Brothers*—S.J.
[]—*Little Flower Congregation*—C.S.T.
[0740]—*Marian Fathers*—M.I.C.
[0720]—*The Missionaries of Our Lady of La Salette* (Prov. of Our Lady of the Americas)—M.S.
[0910]—*Oblates of Mary Immaculate* (Missionary Oblates of Mary Immaculate, U.S. Prov.)—O.M.I.
[0430]—*Order of Preachers (Dominicans)*—O.P.
[1010]—*Order of St. Paul*—O.S.P.
[1190]—*Salesians of Don Bosco*—S.D.B.
[1260]—*Society of Mary*—S.M.
[0440]—*Society of St. Edmund*—S.S.E.
[1200]—*Society of the Divine Savior*—S.D.S.
[0590]—*Society of the Missionaries of the Holy Apostles*—M.S.A.
[1280]—*Stigmatine Fathers and Brothers*—C.S.S.

RELIGIOUS INSTITUTES OF WOMEN REPRESENTED IN THE DIOCESE

[0130]—*Apostoles of the Sacred Heart of Jesus*—A.S.C.J.
[1920]—*Congregation of Sisters of Holy Cross*—C.S.C.
[0820]—*Daughters of the Holy Spirit*—D.H.S.
[1170]—*Felician Sisters*—C.S.S.F.
[]—*Franciscan Apostolic Sisters*—F.A.S.
[1190]—*Franciscan Sisters of Atonement*—S.A.
[1180]—*Franciscian Sisters of Allegany*—O.S.F.
[2575]—*Institute of the Sisters of Mercy of the Americas*—R.S.M.
[1410]—*Mill Hill Sisters*—F.M.S.J.
[2720]—*Mission Helpers of the Sacred Heart*—M.H.S.H.
[]—*Missionary Servants of the Word*—H.M.S.P.
[3465]—*Religious of the Sacred Heart of Mary*—R.S.H.M.
[]—*Religious Teachers Fillippini*—M.P.F.
[]—*Roncalli Sisters*
[2970]—*School Sisters of Notre Dame*—S.S.N.D.
[]—*Servants of Immaculate Heart of Mary*—I.H.M.
[]—*Sisters Oblates to Divine Love*—R.O.D.A.
[0530]—*Sisters of Charity of Our Lady, Mother of the Church*—S.C.M.C.
[3000]—*Sisters of Notre Dame de Namur* (Connecticut Prov.)—S.N.D.deN.
[]—*Sisters of Our Lady of the Garden*—O.L.G.
[3750]—*Sisters of St. Chretienne*—S.S.Ch.
[3830]—*Sisters of St. Joseph*—S.S.J.
[]—*Sisters of St. Joseph*—C.S.J.
[3930]—*Sisters of St. Joseph of the Third Order of St. Francis*—S.S.J.-T.O
[3937]—*Sisters of St. Martha*—C.S.M.
[2140]—*Sisters of the Immaculate Conception of the Blessed Virgin Mary (Lithuanian)*
[3320]—*Sisters of the Presentation of the B.V.M.*—P.B.V.M.

NECROLOGY

† Balciunas, Rev. Msgr. Vytatas—Died March 28, 2003
† Berube, Theodore E., (Retired)—Died May 26, 2003
† Curtin, J. Clifford, Somersville, CT All Saints Church—Died Feb. 6, 2003
† Kisluk, Aloysius J., Middletown, CT St. Mary of Czestochowa—Died March 4, 2003

Diocese of Oakland

(Dioecesis Quercopolitana)

Most Reverend

ALLEN H. VIGNERON, D.D.

Bishop of Oakland; ordained July 27, 1975; appointed Auxiliary Bishop of Detroit and Titular Bishop of Sault Ste. Marie June 12, 1996; consecrated July 9, 1996; appointed Coadjutor Bishop of Oakland January 10, 2003; installed February 26, 2003; succeeded to See October 1, 2003. *Office: 2900 Lakeshore Ave., Oakland, CA 94610-3697.*

Most Reverend

JOHN S. CUMMINS, D.D.

Retired Bishop of Oakland; ordained January 24, 1953; appointed Titular Bishop of Lambesi and Auxiliary Bishop of Sacramento February 26, 1974; consecrated May 16, 1974; appointed Bishop of Oakland May 3, 1977; installed June 30, 1977; retired September 30, 2003. *Res.: 634 21st St., Oakland, CA 94612.*

ESTABLISHED JANUARY 13, 1962.

Square Miles 1,467.

Comprises two Counties in the State of California--viz., Alameda and Contra Costa.

Legal Title: The Roman Catholic Bishop of Oakland, a Corporation Sole.

For legal titles of parishes and diocesan institutions, consult the Chancery Office.

Chancery Office: 2900 Lakeshore Ave., Oakland, CA 94610-3697. Tel: 510-893-4711; Fax: 510-893-0945.

Email: chancellor@oakdiocese.org

STATISTICAL OVERVIEW

Personnel	
Bishop	1
Retired Bishops	1
Priests: Diocesan Active in Diocese	135
Priests: Diocesan Active Outside Diocese	2
Priests: Retired, Sick or Absent	57
Number of Diocesan Priests	194
Religious Priests in Diocese	98
Total Priests in Diocese	292
Ordinations:	
Diocesan Priests	1
Transitional Deacons	20
Permanent Deacons	96
Permanent Deacons in Diocese	92
Total Brothers	56
Total Sisters	360
Parishes	
Parishes	85
With Resident Pastor:	
Resident Diocesan Priests	51
Resident Religious Priests	14
Without Resident Pastor:	
Administered by Priests	17
Administered by Deacons	1
Administered by Lay People	2
Missions	2
Pastoral Centers	16
Professional Ministry Personnel:	
Brothers	3
Sisters	33
Lay Ministers	184
Welfare	
Catholic Hospitals	1
Total Assisted	130,415
Homes for the Aged	2
Total Assisted	3,000
Day Care Centers	5
Total Assisted	1,600
Specialized Homes	6
Total Assisted	30,500
Special Centers for Social Services	3
Total Assisted	31,000
Residential Care of Disabled	1
Total Assisted	1,500
Other Institutions	4
Total Assisted	30,000
Educational	
Students from This Diocese	14
Diocesan Students in Other Seminaries	3
Total Seminarians	17
Colleges and Universities	3
Total Students	5,191
High Schools, Diocesan and Parish	3
Total Students	1,890
High Schools, Private	6
Total Students	4,404
Elementary Schools, Diocesan and Parish	51
Total Students	13,673
Catechesis/Religious Education:	
High School Students	2,235
Elementary Students	25,552
Total Students under Catholic Instruction	52,962
Teachers in the Diocese:	
Priests	14
Brothers	13
Sisters	40
Lay Teachers	2,034
Vital Statistics	
Receptions into the Church:	
Infant Baptism Totals	9,373
Adult Baptism Totals	472
Received into Full Communion	619
First Communions	8,203
Confirmations	3,345
Marriages:	
Catholic	1,062
Interfaith	276
Total Marriages	1,338
Deaths	2,663
Total Catholic Population	450,934
Total Population	2,464,668

Former Bishops—Most Revs. FLOYD L. BEGIN, S.T.D., consecrated May 1, 1947; appt. Bishop of Oakland on Feb. 21, 1962; died April 26, 1977; JOHN S. CUMMINS, D.D. (Retired), ordained January 24, 1953; appointed Titular Bishop of Lambesi and Auxiliary Bishop of Sacramento February 26, 1974; consecrated May 16, 1974; appointed Bishop of Oakland May 3, 1977; installed June 30, 1977; retired Sept. 30, 2003.

Chancery Office—2900 Lakeshore Ave., Oakland, 94610-3697. Tel: 510-893-4711; Fax: 510-893-0945. Office Hours: 8:30-4:45

Moderator of the Curia/Vicar General—Rev. LARRY SILVA.

Chancellor/Director Office of the Bishop—Sr. BARBARA FLANNERY, C.S.J.

Vicar of Temporalities—Rev. PATRICK GOODWIN.

Director of Services and Resources—Deacon THOMAS MCGOWAN.

Judicial Vicar—Rev. RAYMOND BRETON, J.C.L.

Bishop's Representative for Eastern Rite Catholics—Rev. DAVID LINK.

Bishop's Representative for Permanent Deacons—Deacon DAVID REZENDES.

Bishop's Representative for Catholic Charismatics (English)—Mr. CHARLES PEISSNER.

Bishop's Representative for Catholic Charismatics (Spanish)—Mr. JESUS MACIAS.

Bishop's Representative for Italian Speaking Faithful—Rev. DANIEL E. CARDELLI.

The Roman Catholic Welfare Corporation of Oakland—2900 Lakeshore Ave., Oakland, 94610. Tel: 510-893-4711.

Consultors—Revs. DANIEL CARDELLI; FERNANDO CORTEZ; VINCENT COTTER; DANIEL DANIELSON; QUANG DONG; JAYSON LANDEZA; JOHN MAXWELL; GERARD MORAN; FRED RICCIO; LARRY SILVA; PAUL VASSAR.

Presbyteral Council—Revs. DANIEL E. DANIELSON, Pres.; DANIEL CARDELLI; VINCENT COTTER; LAWRENCE D'ANJOU; DECLAN DEANE; QUANG MINH DONG; RAMIRO FLORES; RAMON J. GOMEZ; JAYSON LANDEZA; PAUL D. MINNIHAN; JESUS NIETO; MICHAEL P. NORKETT; RAYMOND SACCA; RONALD SCHMIT; LARRY SILVA.

Diocesan Pastoral Council—Most Rev. ALLEN H. VIGNERON, D.D. Region 1: Ms. ANNA DEL BECCARO; Ms. MARY STARRS. Region 2: AL STAROSCIAK; Mr. RUBEN RODRIGUEZ. Region 3: Dr. MARIANELA CARTER; LUI GONZALES; Mr. GEORGE SHELTON. Region 4: Ms. LINN BAUTISTA; Ms. CONSUELO MARTIN. Region 5: Mr. MARKUS MULLARKY; Ms. ELSA ZAVALA; Sr. ELIZABETH LANG, O.S.U.; Deacon HOCK CHUAN OEY; Revs. GEOFFREY BARAAN; JOSE M. LEON; DANA MICHAELS; SERGIO LOPEZ; LARRY SILVA; Sr. BARBARA FLANNERY, C.S.J.; Mr. CHUCK SIEBENAND.

Deacon Council—Deacons WILLIAM ARCHER; WILLIAM DROBICK; GARY EVANS; DICK FOLGER; Mrs. SYLVIA GALL; Deacons TIMOTHY MOORE; CHARLES PALOMARES; DAVE REZENDES; Mrs. ROSE ANNE RYKEN.

Lay Ecclesial Ministers Council (ELMC)—Region 1: Mr. TONY MILLETTE; Ms. KATE NAUER. Region 2: Mrs. JACKIE HOOKE; GAIL MCGUIRE; Ms. BEATRIZ CARBALLO. Region 3: Ms. NORAH HIPPOLYTE. Region 4: Ms. VIRGINIA MOLLOY; Mr. KEVIN STASZKOW. Region 5: Ms. TINA POSAS. Special Works: KELLY O'LAGUE DULKA; Ms. MARGARET RONCALLI. Priest Representative: Rev. PAUL D. MINNIHAN. Ex Officio: Sr. BARBARA FLANNERY, C.S.J.; Mr. CHUCK SIEBENAND.

Diocesan Finance Committee—Mr. RICHARD CAMPBELL; Mr. MICHAEL CANIZZARO; Rev. PATRICK GOODWIN; Mr. GLEN HENTGES; Mr. PHILIP JENSEN; Mr. MIKE

NIEDERMEYER; Rev. FRED RICCIO; Mr. GREGORY THRONBURY; Mr. BILL UTIC; Mr. KIP WIXSON.

Pastoral Leadership Placement Board (PLPB)—Most Rev. ALLEN H. VIGNERON, D.D.; Rev. RAYMOND G. BRETON, Chm.; Ms. JOANN MASS; Revs. MICHAEL NORKETT; JOHN PROCHASKA; Mrs. BERNIE PURCELL; Rev. WILLIAM J. O'DONNELL; Sr. FELICIA SARATI; Revs. PAUL SCHMIDT; ANTONIO VALDIVIA; LARRY E. YOUNG; RAY ZIELEZIENSKI.

Deans—Revs. DANIEL DANIELSON, Deanery #1; FRED RICCIO, Deanery #2; VINCE SCOTT, Deanery #3; JOHN KASPER, O.S.F.S., Deanery #4; BRIAN JOYCE, Deanery #5; RONALD G. SCHMIT, Deanery #6; HELMUT RICHTER, Deanery #7; RICHARD MANGINI, Deanery #8; VINCE COTTER, Deanery #9; SEAMUS GENOVESE, Deanery #10; MARCO ANTONIO FIGUEROA, O.F.M., Deanery #11; JAMES MATTHEWS, Deanery #12; PETER MCGRATH, S.J., Deanery #13; LARRY SILVA, Deanery #14; RAMON J. GOMEZ, Deanery #15; VACANT, Deanery #16; Revs. SEAMUS J. FARRELL, Deanery #17; KEVIN MULLINS, Deanery #18; JOHN PROCHASKA, Deanery #19; GEORGE MATANIC, O.P., Deanery #20; JOSE DE JESUS NIETO, Deanery #21; JOHN F. MAXWELL, Deanery #22; DANA MICHAELS, Deanery #23.

Diocesan Departments

Apostleship of the Sea—Rev. PAUL DEVINE, Port Chaplain (Retired), Berth 40, Oakland, 94607. Tel: 510-444-7885.

Archivist/Records Management—Ms. MARY C. BATIZA, 3014 Lakeshore Ave., Oakland, 94610. Tel: 510-273-4980; Fax: 510-273-4983.

Campaign for Human Development—Mrs. BARBARA TERRAZAS, Dir., 433 Jefferson St., Oakland, 94607.

Canon Law Department—2900 Lakeshore Ave., Oakland, 94610. Tel: 510-267-8375.

Director & Judicial Vicar—Rev. RAYMOND G. BRETON.

Adjutant Judicial Vicars and Canonical Consultant to the Bishop—Revs. RAYMOND G. BRETTON, J.C.L.; ROBERT MCCANN, J.C.L.; GARY M. LUIZ, C.PP.S., J.C.L.

Defenders of the Bond—Revs. ANTHONY PHAN LAM, J.C.D.; DAVID O'ROURKE, O.P.; FRANCISCO VICENTE, O.P.

Canonical Consultant to the Bishop—Rev. DONALD HUDSON, J.C.L. (Retired).

Judges—Revs. RAYMOND BRETTON; GARY LUIZ, C.PP.S., J.C.L.; ROBERT MCCANN, J.C.L.; Mr. DAVID T. MCCARTHY, J.C.L.

Notaries of the Tribunal—JACQUELINE COMPTON; MARY O'SULLIVAN; NORMA HERNANDEZ.

Promoter of Justice—VACANT.

Auditors of the Tribunal—ADALID GARCIA; THERESA KOBAK; JOANNE MORGRET; GINA RUBIN; SEANA PANGIA; DIANA O. SANTANA; MYRNA GODINEZ.

Court of Second Instance—Rev. GARY M. LUIZ, C.PP.S., J.C.L., Presiding Judge.

Notary—CAROL IZO.

Catholic Charities—Mrs. BARBARA TERRAZAS, Dir., Legal Title: Catholic Charities of the East Bay, Diocese of Oakland.

Catholic Relief Services—Mrs. BARBARA TERRAZAS, Assoc. Dir.

Catholic Schools Office—Mr. MARK DE MARCO, Supt. Assistant Superintendents: Sisters JOHNELLEN TURNER, O.P.; BARBARA BRAY, S.N.J.M., 3000 Lakeshore Ave., Oakland, 94610. Tel: 510-273-4982.

FACE (Family Aid Catholic Education, tuition assistance)—Ms. ANNE RYNDERS, Dir., 3000 Lakeshore Ave., Oakland, 94610. Tel: 510-628-2169.

Cemeteries and Mausoleums—Mr. ROBERT W. SEELIG, Dir., 1965 Reliez Valley Rd., P.O. Box 488, Lafayette, 94549. Oakland, Alameda County, St. Mary's Cemetery; Antioch, Contra Costa County, Holy Cross Cemetery; Hayward, Alameda County, Holy Sepulchre Cemetery and Mausoleum; Lafayette, Contra Costa County, Queen of Heaven Cemetery; Pleasanton, Alameda County, Christ the King Cemetery; San Pablo, Contra Costa County, St. Joseph's Cemetery and Mausoleum; Livermore, Alameda County, St. Michael's Cemetery.

Censor—Rev. ROBERT MCCANN, J.C.L., 2900 Lakeshore Ave., Oakland, 94610. Tel: 510-267-8375.

Christian Initiation—Ms. LINDA KREHMEIER.

Clergy Services—Rev. MICHAEL NORKETT, Dir., 2900 Lakeshore Ave., Oakland, 94610. Tel: 510-267-8366.

Office of Clergy Personnel—Rev. PAUL SCHMIDT, 2900 Lakeshore Ave., Oakland, 94610. Tel: 510-267-8308.

Cursillo Movement—Rev. LEO EDGERLY, Spiritual Dir.

Deaf and Hard of Hearing—ARDITH A. LYNCH, Dir., St. Joseph's Center, 25580 Campus Dr., Hayward, 94542. Tel: 510-489-9784 (Voice); 510-489-9786 (TTY). Email: sjdeafctr@aol.com.

Development/Stewardship—Ms. KATHERINE KING, Dir.

Episcopal Liturgies—Rev. JOHN BLAKER, Dir., 2900 Lakeshore Ave., Oakland, 94610.

Ethnic Pastoral Centers—

Director of Ethnic & Cultural Services Division—Sr. FELICIA SARATI, C.S.J., 3014 Lakeshore Ave., Oakland, 94610. Tel: 510-273-4998.

Facilities, Planning and Services—Mr ALEX HERNANDEZ, Dir.; Mr. JAMES H. MCCANN, Assoc. Dir.

African American Pastoral Center—Dr. TOINETTE EUGENE, 3014 Lakeshore Ave., Oakland, 94610. Tel: 510-273-4988.

Asian/Indian Pastoral Center—Ms. BELLA COMELO, 2048 Juneau St., San Leandro, 94577. Tel: 510-357-0940.

Brazilian Community—JOSE FREITAS, 1528 Elm St., El Cerrito 94530.

Chinese Pastoral Center—Rev. THOMAS NG, Dir., 176 Ridgeway Ave., Oakland, 94611.

Filipino Catholic—Mr. SIMON REBULLIDA, Dir., 3014 Lakeshore Ave., Oakland, 94610. Tel: 510-273-4999.

French Speaking Community—Rev. THIBAUS D'OULTREMONT, 2621 Ridge Rd., Berkeley, 94709. Tel: 510-847-8865.

Ge'ez Community—Rev. GEBRIEL WOLDAI, Bay Area Regl. Dir., 1640 Addison St., Berkeley, 94703. Tel: 510-549-7529.

Haitian Pastoral Center—PIERRE LABOSSIERE, 2822 55th Ave. Oakland, 94605. Tel: 510-534-5149.

Indonesian Community—RUDY WIDJAJA, 3556 Cour De Charles, San Jose, 95148.

Khmmu/Lactian Pastoral Center—Rev. DON MACKINNON, C.SS.R., 2215 Rose St., Berkeley, 94709. Tel: 510-582-8888.

Korean Pastoral Center—Rev. PAUL OH, Dir., Mr. Andrew Kim Catholic Pastoral Center, 6226 Camden St., Oakland, 94605. Tel: 510-562-3843.

Hispanic Pastoral Center—HECTOR MEDINA, Dir., 3014 Lakeshore Ave., Oakland, Ca 94610. Tel: 510-628-2180.

Polish Pastoral Center—Co Directors Deacon WITOLD CHICHON; Rev. ROBERT WAIVER, 11 Fulton Ave., San Leandro, 94577.

Portuguese Pastoral Center—Co Directors: Ms. MARIA ALCORTA; Rev. ANTONIO DOS REIS, 5800 Thornton Ave., Newark, 94560. Tel 510-794-7910.

Tongan Pastoral Center—Co Chm.: Ms. TENISIA FINAU, East Bay Rep., 1515 Dolan Ave., San Mateo, 94401. Tel: 415-342-2470; MELE MAUSIA, 1433 88th St., Oakland, 94601.

Vietnamese Pastoral Center—Sr. ROSALINE NGUYEN, Dir., 3014 Lakeshore Ave., Oakland, 94610. Tel: 510-273-4941.

Faith and Ministerial Formation—Mrs. KELLY DULKA, Dir., 3014 Lakeshore Ave., Oakland, 94610. Tel: 510-273-4964; Mr. TOM RICHARDSON, Assoc. Dir. In-Service Programming; Mr. CARLOS RIVAS, Assoc. Dir. Spanish Programming.

Family Life Office—Mrs. RITA BILLECI, Dir., 2350 Pacheco St., Concord, 94520. Tel: 510-680-8510.

Associate Director—Mr. JUAN AMBRIZ.

Coordinator for Divorced & Separated Catholics—Ms. OLETA PROCTOR FERNANDEZ.

Respect Life, Women's Pregnancy Service and Bioethics Coordinator—Ms. MONIKA RODMAN.

Services to Gays and Lesbians and Their Families—Mrs. RITA BILLECI.

Financial Services—Mr. MICHAEL CANIZZARO, Dir., 2900 Lakeshore Ave., Oakland, 94610.

Holy Childhood—Ms. KATHERINE KING, Dir., 2900 Lakeshore Ave., Oakland, 94610. Tel: 510-267-8357.

Hospital Ministry—Deacon REX EHLING, Interim Dir., 2900 Lakeshore Ave., Oakland, 94610.

Human Resources—Dr. PENNY PENDOLA, Dir., 2900 Lakeshore Ave., Oakland, 94610. Tel: 510-267-8359.

Newspaper: "The Catholic Voice"—Ms. MONICA CLARK, Editor, 3014 Lakeshore Ave., Oakland, 94610. Tel: 510-893-5339.

Parish Resources—Mrs. NORA PETERSEN, Dir., 2900 Lakeshore Ave., Oakland, 94610. Tel: 510-983-4711. Catechetics: VACANT, English; Ms. JESSY LIRA, Spanish.

Small Christian Communities—NORA PETERSEN, English; Ms. YOLANDA GARCIA, Spanish.

Liturgy—Ms. LINDA KREHMEIER.

Pastoral Planning—Mr. CHUCK SIEBENAND, Dir., 2900 Lakeshore Ave., Oakland, 94610. Tel: 510-267-8368.

Propagation of the Faith—Ms. KATHERINE KING, Dir., Legal Title: Oakland Society for the Propagation of the Faith.

St. Peter the Apostle Society—Ms. KATHERINE KING, Dir.

Special Religious Education Department (SPRED)—Sr. AURORA PEREZ, Dir., 3000 Lakeshore Ave., Oakland, 94610. Tel: 510-273-4982.

Vicar for Religious—Sr. BARBARA FLANNERY, C.S.J., 3705 Dorisa Ave., Oakland, 94605. Tel: 510-635-7252.

Victim Assistance Coordinator—Sr. BARBARA FLANNERY, C.S.J. Tel: 510-267-8334. Email: bflannery@oakdiocese.org.

Vocations—

Priestly and Religious & Director for Seminarians—Rev. LARRY D'ANJOU, 2900 Lakeshore Ave., Oakland, 94610. Tel: 510-267-8345.

Youth and Young Adults—Mr. WILLIAM FORD, Dir., 3014 Lakeshore Ave., Oakland, 94610. Tel: 510-893-4711; Mr. WILLIAM FORD, Dir. CYO Athletics & Catholic Scouting; Ms. EVELYN GONZALEZ, Dir. Youth and Young Adults Ministry; Ms. YVETTE ESPINOZA, Dir. Latino Ethnic Youth Ministry; Ms. EUNICE PARK, Coord. Youth and Young Adult.

Organizations—

St. Vincent de Paul Society—Mr. VAUGHN DONAHUE, Pres., Alameda County, 9235 San Leandro St., Oakland, 94603. Tel: 510-636-4246; Mr. RICK RICHARDSON, Pres., Contra Costa, 2210 Gladstone Dr., Pittsburg, 94565. Tel: 925-439-5060, Ext. 19.

Diocesan Council of Catholic Women—Mrs. SHIRLEY BURNELL, Pres., 1393 Via Vista, San Lorenzo, 94580-2249. Tel: 510-278-5494. Email: symburnell@aol.com.

CLERGY, PARISHES, MISSIONS AND PAROCHIAL SCHOOLS

CITY OF OAKLAND
(ALAMEDA COUNTY)

1—CATHEDRAL OF ST. FRANCIS DE SALES (1886), Merged, with St. Mary, Immaculate Conception to form St. Mary, Immaculate Conception-St. Francis de Sales.

2—ST. ANDREW-ST. JOSEPH (1965), (Latino—African American), Rev. John Direen; Deacons Morris Soublet; Leo Edgerly; Eugene Stelly. In Res., Rev. Ernest B. Brainard (Retired).
Res.: 925 Brockhurst St., 94608. Tel: 510-653-7411; Fax: 510-652-5839.
School—St. Martin De Porres School
School—St. Patrick Campus, (Grades 6-8) Tel: 510-832-1757; Fax: 510-832-6481.
School—Sacred Heart Campus, (Grades K-5) Tel: 510-652-2220; Fax: 510-652-2294.
Catechesis/Religious Program—Students 50.

3—ST. ANTHONY'S (1871), Revs. Joseph Duong Phan; Ramiro Flores.
Res.: 1535 16th Ave., 94606. Tel: 510-534-2117; Fax: 510-534-2119.
School—Tel: 510-534-3334; Fax: 510-534-3378. Lay Teachers 9; Students 164.
Catechesis/Religious Program—Tel: 510-534-4420. Students 250.

4—ST. AUGUSTINE'S (1907), Rev. Ray Zielezienski; Deacon Rex Ehling; Rev. Karen Miller.
Res.: 400 Alcatraz Ave., 94609. Tel: 510-653-8631; Fax: 510-653-4256.
School—410 Alcatraz Ave., 94609. Tel: 510-652-6727; Fax: 510-652-4219. Sisters 1; Lay Teachers 6; Students 73.
Catechesis/Religious Program—Tel: 510-653-4418, Ext. 109. Students 26.

5—ST. BENEDICT (1930), (African American), Rev. James Matthews. In Res., Rev. Cuthbert Aronyu (Uganda).
Res.: 2245 82nd Ave., 94605. Tel: 510-632-1847; Fax: 510-633-2092.
Catechesis/Religious Program—Students 42.

6—ST. BERNARD'S (1912), (Hispanic—African American), Revs. Eric P. Vargas, S.V.D.; Damian Kabot, S.V.D.; Jesus Zamarripa, S.V.D.; Deacon Javier Fuentes. In Res., Rev. Stephen Ernest, S.V.D.
Res.: 1620-62nd Ave., 94621. Tel: 510-632-3013; Fax: 510-632-5286. Email: st.bernard.church@sbcglobal.net.
School—1630-62nd Ave., 94621. Tel: 510-632-6323; Fax: 510-632-6110. Lay Teachers 9; Students 143.
Catechesis/Religious Program—Students 151.

7—ST. COLUMBA'S (1898), (African American), Rev. Jayson Landeza; Deacons Gaston Dube; Frank Beville.
Res.: 6401 San Pablo Ave., 94608. Tel: 510-654-7600; Fax: 510-654-7615.
Catechesis/Religious Program—Students 30.

8—ST. CYRIL (1926), (Korean), Revs. John Fernandes, Parochial Admin.; Paul Oh; Deacon Leslie Miyashiro.
Res.: 6226 Camden St., 94605. Tel: 510-553-9434.

Res.: Web: www.oakcc.org.
School—3200 62nd Ave., 94605. Tel: 510-638-9445; Fax: 510-638-0744. Lay Teachers 7; Students 188.
Catechesis/Religious Program—Students 62.

9—ST. ELIZABETH'S (1892), (Hispanic), Revs. Marco Antonio Figueroa, O.F.M.; Peter Krieg, O.F.M.; Deacon Gabriel Hernandez. In Res., Revs. Kenny Scott, O.F.M.; Melvin Stanley, O.F.M.
Res.: 1500 34th Ave., 94601. Tel: 510-536-1266; Fax: 510-536-8560.
School—Tel: 510-532-7392; Fax: 510-532-0321. Sisters 5; Lay Teachers 23; Students 436.
Catechesis/Religious Program—Tel: 510-532-3766. Students 732.
Mission—Mary Help of Christians 2611 E. 9th St., Alameda Co. 94601. Tel: 510-534-3501; Fax: 510-436-5157.

10—ST. JARLATH'S (1910), Rev. Salvador Macias.
Res.: 2620 Pleasant St., 94602. Tel: 510-532-2068; Fax: 510-532-3745.
School—2634 Pleasant St., 94602. Tel: 510-532-4387; Fax: 510-532-1001. Lay Teachers 10; Students 241.
Catechesis/Religious Program—Students 92.

11—ST. LAWRENCE O'TOOLE (1916), Rev. John Fernandes; Deacons Leslie Miyashiro; Cesar Vega; Dat Vu. In Res., Revs. Anthony Phan Lam; Louis Young Han Jeung (Korea, South); Ken Hamilton, S.V.D.
Res.: 3725 High St., 94619. Tel: 510-530-0761; Fax: 510-530-0974. Res.: Email: slotscjp@juno.com.
School—Tel: 510-530-0266; Fax: 510-530-7568. Lay Teachers 14; Students 262.
Catechesis/Religious Program—Tel: 510-530-0764. Students 80.

12—ST. LEO'S (1911), Rev. Timothy K. Johnson. In Res., Revs. Thomas Ng; Joseph Li (China); Gabriel Msoka (Africa).
Res.: 176 Ridgeway Ave., 94611-5122. Tel: 510-654-6177; Fax: 510-654-4203.
School—Tel: 510-654-7828; Fax: 510-654-4057. Lay Teachers 10; Students 264.
Catechesis/Religious Program—Students 22.

13—ST. LOUIS BERTRAND (1908), (Hispanic—African American), Revs. Antonio A. Valdivia; Enrique Ballesteros; Deacon Noe Gonzalez.
Res.: 1410-100th Ave., 94603. Tel: 510-568-1080; Fax: 510-635-8618.
Catechesis/Religious Program—Tel: 510-632-2865. Students 1,700.

14—ST. MARGARET MARY (1922), Rev. Paul J. Schmidt, Admin.; Jennifer Sacramento.
Res.: 1219 Excelsior Ave., 94610. Tel: 510-482-0596; Fax: 510-482-2093.
Catechesis/Religious Program—Students 15.

15—MARY HELP OF CHRISTIANS CHURCH (1915), (Spanish), Rev. Marco Antonio Figueroa, O.F.M.; Reyna Lupian, Admin.
Mailing Address: P.O. Box 7116, 94601.
Res.: 2611 E. Ninth St., 94601. Tel: 510-534-3501.

16—ST. MARY, IMMACULATE CONCEPTION, Merged, with St. Francis de Sales to form St. Mary, Immaculate Conception-St. Francis de Sales.

17—ST. MARY, IMMACULATE CONCEPTION-ST. FRANCIS DE SALES (1993), Rev. Peter R. McGrath, S.J. In Res., Revs. Hoc Thai Kieu, O.C.S.O.; Victor Tran.
Res. & Office St. Francis de Sales Rectory: 634 21st St., 94612. Tel: 510-832-5057; Fax: 510-832-0212.
Catechesis/Religious Program—Students 150.

18—OUR LADY OF LOURDES (1921), [CEM] Rev. Seamus D. Genovese.
Res.: 2808 Lakeshore Ave., 94610. Tel: 510-451-1790; Fax: 510-893-6443.
Catechesis/Religious Program—Students 25.

19—ST. PASCHAL BAYLON (1955), Rev. Michael Norkett.
Res.: 3700 Dorisa Ave., 94605. Tel: 510-636-0335; Fax: 510-636-0287.
School—Tel: 510-635-7922; Fax: 510-635-4219. Lay Teachers 13; Students 133.
Catechesis/Religious Program—Students 3.

20—ST. PATRICK'S (1879), (African American—Hispanic), Revs. Timothy S. Godfrey, S.J.; Sean O. Carroll, S.J.
Res.: 1023 Peralta St., 94607. Tel: 510-444-1081; Fax: 510-444-1113.
School—1630 10th St., 94607. Tel: 510-832-1757; Fax: 510-832-6481. Lay Teachers 9; Students 92.
Catechesis/Religious Program—Students 30.

21—SACRED HEART (1876), Rev. Thomas Hayes, O.M.I. In Res., Revs. Tom J. Edwards; William Hallahan, O.M.I.
Res.: 4025 Martin Luther King Way, 94609-2317. Tel: 510-655-9209; Fax: 510-652-1958.
School—St. Martin De Porres, 675 41st St., 94609. Tel: 510-652-2220; Fax: 510-652-2294. Mrs. Sue Taylor, Prin. Lay Teachers 8; Students 90.
Catechesis/Religious Program—Students 8.

22—ST. THERESA OF THE INFANT JESUS (THE LITTLE FLOWER) (1925), Rev. Patrick Goodwin. In Res., Rev. Msgr. Bernard J. Moran, Pastor Emeritus (Retired).
Res.: 30 Mandalay Rd., 94618. Tel: 510-547-2777; Fax: 510-653-3575.
School—Tel: 510-547-3146; Fax: 510-547-3253. Lay Teachers 29; Students 278.
Catechesis/Religious Program—Students 100.

OUTSIDE THE CITY OF OAKLAND

ALAMEDA, ALAMEDA CO.

1—ST. ALBERT (1976), Rev. Fernando Cortez.
Res.: 1022 Holly St., 94502. Tel: 510-522-2185; Fax: 510-522-1055.
Catechesis/Religious Program—Students 60.

2—ST. BARNABAS (1925), Rev. Joseph Brown, C.PP.S. In Res., Rev. Mbondo Emmanuel, C.I.C.M.
Res.: 1427 Sixth St., 94501. Tel: 510-522-8933; Fax: 510-522-8380.
School—Tel: 510-521-0595; Fax: 510-521-3560. Lay Teachers 9; Students 141.
Catechesis/Religious Program—Tel: 510-337-8962; Fax: 510-521-3560. Students 80.

3—ST. JOSEPH BASILICA (1885), Rev. Richard J. Danyluk, SS.CC. In Res., Revs. Jeremiah Holland, SS.CC.; Patrick J. Crowley, SS.CC.
Res.: 1109 Chestnut St., 94501. Tel: 510-522-0181; Fax: 510-522-2864.
School—St. Joseph Elementary School, Tel: 510-522-4457; Fax: 510-522-2890. Lay Teachers 28; Students 307.
High School—Tel: 510-523-1526; Fax: 510-523-2181. See separate listing under High Schools, Parochial.
Catechesis/Religious Program—Tel: 510-749-7158. Anne Marie Fourre, D.R.E. Students 135.

4—ST. PHILIP NERI (1925), Rev. Vincent Cotter.
Res.: 3108 Van Buren St., 94501. Tel: 510-522-2299; Fax: 510-522-8123.
School—1335 High St., 94501. Tel: 510-521-0787; Fax: 510-521-2418. Lay Teachers 13; Students 278.
Catechesis/Religious Program—Tel: 510-865-2626. Students 98.

ANTIOCH, CONTRA COSTA CO.

1—HOLY ROSARY (1874), (Hispanic), [CEM] [JC] Revs. Francisco Vicente; LaSalle Hallissey, O.P.; Very Rev. Edward Krasevac, O.P.; Revs. Jordan Bradshaw, O.P.; Anselm Ramelow, O.P.; Bro. Vincent Kelber, O.P.; Sisters Lidya Hernandez, O.P.; Monica Terrazas, O.P.; Deacons Charles Silvernale; Jerry Grigg; Mrs. Jackie Hooke, Pastoral Assoc.
Res.: 1313 A St., 94509. Tel: 925-757-4020; Fax: 925-757-6828.
School—Tel: 925-757-1270; Fax: 925-757-9309. Lay Teachers 63; Students 630.
Catechesis/Religious Program—21 E. 15th St., 94059. Tel: 915-757-9515. Students 1,125.

2—ST. IGNATIUS (1979), [CEM] Rev. Geoffrey Baraan; Deacon Al Fleischer; June Kirk, Pastoral Assoc.
Res.: 3351 Contra Loma Blvd., 94509. Tel: 925-778-0768; Fax: 925-778-0845.
Catechesis/Religious Program—3351 Contra Loma Blvd., 94509. Tel: 925-778-1631. Students 670.

BAY POINT, CONTRA COSTA CO., OUR LADY QUEEN OF THE WORLD (1962), Revs. Richard J. Culver, Admin.; Theo Palis, Pastor Emeritus; James J. Thottapally.
Res.: 3155 Winterbrook Dr., 94565. Tel: 925-458-4718; Fax: 925-458-3161.
Catechesis/Religious Program—Tel: 925-458-4574. Students 340.

BERKELEY, ALAMEDA CO.

1—ST. AMBROSE (1909), Revs. George Alengadan, S.D.B.; Joseph Paradayil, S.D.B.
Res.: 1145 Gilman St., 94706. Tel: 510-525-2620; Fax: 510-525-5399.
Catechesis/Religious Program—Students 24.

2—HOLY SPIRIT PARISH/NEWMAN HALL (1967), Revs. Richard Sparks, C.S.P.; Albert Moser, C.S.P.; Peter Abdella, C.S.P.
Res.: 2700 Dwight Way, 94704-3113. Tel: 510-848-7812; Fax: 510-848-0179.
Catechesis/Religious Program—Frances Rojek, D.R.E. Students 150.

3—ST. JOSEPH THE WORKER (1879), Revs. George E. Crespin; William J. O'Donnell. In Res., Revs. Thomas Martin (Australia); Gerard E. Reid (Jamaica) (Montego Bay); Ghebriel Woldai (Eritrea).
Res.: 1640 Addison St., 94703. Tel: 510-843-2244; Fax: 510-843-2730.
School—2125 Jefferson St., 94703. Tel: 510-845-6266; Fax: 510-845-6185. Sisters 1; Lay Teachers 9; Students 122.
Catechesis/Religious Program—Tel: 510-843-1588. Students 246.

4—ST. MARY MAGDALEN (1923), Rev. George M. Matanic, O.P. In Res., Revs. Bruno Gibson, O.P.; Paul C. Raferty, O.P.; Very Rev. Roberto Corral, O.P.; Revs. Jose Pimentel, O.P.; Michael J. Dodds, O.P.
Res.: 2005 Berryman St., 94709. Tel: 510-526-4811; Fax: 510-525-3638.
School—School of the Madeleine, 1225 Milvia St., 94709. Tel: 510-526-4744; Fax: 510-526-5152. Lay Teachers 17; Students 287.
Catechesis/Religious Program—Students 35.

BRENTWOOD, CONTRA COSTA CO., IMMACULATE HEART OF MARY (1949), (English—Spanish), Revs. Joseph Fiedorowicz; Jesus Hernandez Vidal; Jesus Hernandez.
Res.: 813 First St., 94513. Tel: 925-634-4154; Fax: 925-516-9340.
Catechesis/Religious Program—Students 498.

BYRON, CONTRA COSTA CO., ST. ANNE (1916), Rev. Ronald G. Schmit; Sr. Ruth Faisca, S.H.F.; Deacons Ron Horan; Ed Spano; Gail McGuire, Pastoral Assoc.
Mailing Address: P.O. Box 476, 94514. Tel: 925-634-6625; Fax: 925-634-4194.
Catechesis/Religious Program—Tel: 925-634-9637. Students 198.

CASTRO VALLEY, ALAMEDA CO.

1—OUR LADY OF GRACE (1947), Revs. Kevin C. Mullins, O.S.A.; Thomas J. McLaughlin, O.S.A.; Deacons Robert Dowling; Matthew Dulka. In Res., Rev. Paul E. Quante, O.S.A.
Res.: 3433 Somerset Ave., 94546-3398. Tel: 510-537-0806; Fax: 510-537-6281.
School—19920 Anita Ave., 94546-3398. Tel: 510-581-3155; Fax: 510-581-1059. Lay Teachers 14; Students 285.
Catechesis/Religious Program—Tel: 510-538-3464; 510-582-9266; 510-889-7017; Fax: 510-537-6281. Students 445.

2—TRANSFIGURATION (1961), Rev. Mario L. Borges; Deacons Timothy L. Moore; Burt J. Rigley; Garry L. Evans. In Res., Revs. Walter Scott Chavez; Narcis Kabipi (Tanzania).
Res.: 4000 E. Castro Valley Blvd., 94552. Tel: 510-538-7941; Fax: 510-538-7983.
Catechesis/Religious Program—Tel: 510-537-1502. Students 380.

CONCORD, CONTRA COSTA CO.

1—ST. AGNES (1964), Rev. George E. Mockel.
Res.: 3966 Chestnut Ave., 94519. Tel: 925-689-0838; Fax: 925-689-7899.
School—3886 Chestnut Ave., 94519. Tel: 925-689-3990; Fax: 925-689-3455. Sisters 2; Lay Teachers 16; Students 346.
Catechesis/Religious Program—Tel: 925-689-3757. Students 215.

2—ST. BONAVENTURE (1957), Revs. Richard A. Mangini; James J. McGee; David Lawrence, S.J.; Deacons William Gall; Tim Walsh.
Res.: 5562 Clayton Rd., 94521. Tel: 925-672-5800; Fax: 925-672-4606.
Catechesis/Religious Program—Tel: 925-672-5500. Students 570.

3—ST. FRANCIS OF ASSISI (1984),, (Formerly Most Precious Blood, 1955) Revs. Sergio Lopez; Jerry W. Brown; Deacon Charles Palomares; Mrs. Elizabeth Rogers, Pastoral Assoc. In Res., Rev. Reynaldo Hernandez (El Salvador).
Res.: 860 Oak Grove Rd., 94518. Tel: 925-682-5447; Fax: 925-682-5491.
School—866 Oak Grove Rd., 94518. Tel: 925-682-5414; Fax: 925-682-5480. Sisters 1; Lay Teachers 14; Students 322.
Catechesis/Religious Program—Students 186.

4—QUEEN OF ALL SAINTS (1923), [CEM] Revs. Michael Cunningham; Robert Rein; Mathew Vellankal; Reynaldo Hernandez (El Salvador); Ellen L. Midgley, Pastoral Assoc.; Patty Urias, Coord. Hispanic Min.
Res.: 2390 Grant St., 94520. Tel: 925-825-0350; Fax: 925-825-6975.
School—2391 Grant St., 94520. Tel: 925-685-8700; Fax: 925-685-2034. Maryalice Clare, Prin. Lay Teachers 30; Students 250.
Catechesis/Religious Program—Tel: 925-685-8707. Nancy Tomsic, D.R.E. Students 290.

CROCKETT, CONTRA COSTA CO., ST. ROSE OF LIMA (1912), Rev. Ciarian Dillon, O.M.I.
Res.: 555 Third Ave., 94525. Tel: 510-787-2052; Fax: 510-787-2163.
Catechesis/Religious Program—Tel: 510-787-1203. Students 17.
Mission—St. Patrick c/o St. Rose, Port Costa, Contra Costa Co. 94525.

DANVILLE, CONTRA COSTA CO., ST. ISIDORE'S (1910), Revs. Daniel E. Cardelli; Stan Zak; Anthony W. Herrera. In Res., Revs. James E. Driscoll (Retired); Frank L. Colacicco (SAN) (Retired).
Parish Office:—440 LaGonda Way, 94526. Fax: 925-362-1919. Web: www.st-isidore-danville.org.
Res.: 445 LaGonda Way, 94526-2522. Tel: 925-837-2122; Fax: 925-837-3954.
School—Tel: 925-837-2977; Fax: 925-837-2407. Web: www.stisidore.org. Julie Thomas, Prin. Lay Teachers 50; Students 649.
Catechesis/Religious Program—Tel: 925-362-1900; Fax: 925-362-1909. Students 1,170.

DUBLIN, ALAMEDA CO., ST. RAYMOND (1961), Unassigned. Rev. Robert J. McCann.
Res.: 11555 Shannon Ave., 94568. Tel: 925-828-2460; Fax: 925-828-8610.
School—Tel: 925-828-4064; Fax: 925-828-2454.

Lay Teachers 15; Students 296.
Catechesis/Religious Program—Tel: 925-828-4033. Students 625.

El Cerrito, Contra Costa Co.
1—St. Jerome's (1941), Rev. Paul D Minnihan, S.T.D.
Res.: 308 Carmel Ave., 94530. Tel: 510-525-0876; Fax: 510-526-2721.
School—320 San Carlos, 94530. Tel: 510-525-9484; Fax: 510-525-5227. Lay Teachers 15; Students 277.
Catechesis/Religious Program—Students 55.
2—St. John the Baptist (1925), Revs. John Maxwell; John Blaker. In Res., Rev. Raymond Ogbemure.
Res.: 11150 San Pablo Ave., 94530. Tel: 510-232-5659; Fax: 510-236-0960.
School—Tel: 510-234-2244; Fax: 510-234-3726. Lay Teachers 12; Students 299.
Catechesis/Religious Program—Students 65.

El Sobrante, Contra Costa Co., St. Callistus (1952), Rev. Dana Michaels.
Res.: 3580 San Pablo Dam Rd., 94803. Tel: 510-223-1153; Fax: 510-223-1137.
Catechesis/Religious Program—Tel: 510-222-0432. Students 155.

Fremont, Alameda Co.
1—Corpus Christi (1914), Rev. Timothy Stier.
Res.: 37891 Second St., 94536. Tel: 510-790-3207; Fax: 510-790-3227.
Catechesis/Religious Program—Tel: 510-790-3226. Students 245.
2—Holy Spirit (1886), [CEM] [JC] Revs. Gerard K. Moran; Terrence P. Tompkins; David Weise; Deacons Rudolph Brazil; William Drobick; Richard Yee; Steve Taylor.
Res.: 37588 Fremont Blvd., 94536. Tel: 510-797-1660; Fax: 510-797-7080.
School—Tel: 510-793-3553; Fax: 510-793-2694. Lay Teachers 20; Students 298.
Catechesis/Religious Program—Tel: 510-797-5395; Fax: 510-797-4400. Students 718.
3—St. James The Apostle (1972), Rev. Paul E. Cleu.
Res.: P.O. Box 7084, 94537. Tel: 510-792-1962.
Catechesis/Religious Program—Students 40.
4—St. Joseph Mission Church (1797), [CEM] Rev. Msgr. Manuel C. Simas; Rev. Leo Alban Asuncion.
Res.: P.O. Box 3276, Mission San Jose, 94539. Tel: 510-656-2364; Fax: 510-656-2438.
School—43222 Mission Blvd., 94539. Tel: 510-656-6525; Fax: 510-656-3608. Dominican Sisters of San Jose 1; Lay Teachers 15; Students 286.
Catechesis/Religious Program—Tel: 510-657-0905; Fax: 510-657-4165. Students 215.
5—St. Leonard (1959), Merged, with Santa Paula, Fremont to form St. Leonard-Santa Paula, Fremont.
6—Our Lady of Guadalupe, Formerly St. Leonard - Santa Paula Parish (2000), Revs. Larry Silva; Jan Rudzewicz; Scott Chavez; Deacons Ovide P. Guesnon; Steven Budnik Sr.; Jorge Lara; Michael Cantlon.
Office—41933 Blacow Rd., 94538. Tel: 510-657-4043; Fax: 510-657-4055.
Res.: 40382 Fremont Blvd., 94538. Tel: 510-656-4921; Fax: 510-226-0714.
School—40374 Fremont Blvd., 94538. Tel: 510-657-1674; Fax: 510-657-3659. Sisters 2; Lay Teachers 10; Students 243.
Catechesis/Religious Program—Tel: 510-651-4966 (St. Leonard's Campus). Students 716.
7—Santa Paula (1965), Merged, with St. Leonard, Fremont to form St. Leonard-Santa Paula, Fremont.

Hayward, Alameda Co.
1—All Saints (1898), [CEM] Revs. Carl H. Seewald, S.V.D.; Terrence O'Malley, S.C.J.; Deacon Nelson Gonsalves; Stephen P. Mullin, Parish Life Dir. In Res., Rev. Luke Ssemakula (Uganda).
Church: 22824 Second St., 94541. Tel: 510-581-2570; Fax: 510-581-9538.
School—Tel: 510-582-1910; Fax: 510-582-0866. Linda Knox, Prin. Lay Teachers 9; Students 300; Religious 1.
Catechesis/Religious Program—Tel: 510-538-2711; Fax: 510-581-3642. Students 236.
2—St. Bede (1955), Revs. Seamus J. Farrell; Fernando Sampaio (Brazil); Deacon Denis Ryken. In Res., Rev. Rudolph Alumam (Ghana).
Res.: 26950 Patrick Ave., 94544. Tel: 510-782-2171; Fax: 510-782-9712.
School—26910 Patrick Ave., 94544. Tel: 510-782-3444; Fax: 510-782-2243. Lay Teachers 11; Students 265.
Catechesis/Religious Program—Tel: 510-782-4292. Students 730.
3—St. Clement (1951), Revs. Vincent R. Brylka; Francisco J. Figueroa Esquer.
Office—750 Calhoun St., 94544. Tel: 510-582-7282; Fax: 510-582-1875.
Res.: 738 Calhoun St., 94544.
School—790 Calhoun St., 94544. Tel: 510-538-5885; Fax: 510-538-1643. Mrs. Mary Pult, Prin. Lay Teachers 13; Students 303.
Catechesis/Religious Program—Students 496.
4—St. Joachim (1950), Rev. Sergio Mora; Deacons Rigo Cabezas; Ernest Jaramillo; Oscar Macachor.
Res.: 21250 Hesperian Blvd., 94541. Tel: 510-783-2766; Fax: 510-783-2760.
School—Tel: 510-783-3177. Armond Seishas. Lay Teachers 12 Students 301.
Catechesis/Religious Program—Tel: 510-785-1818. Students 975.

Lafayette, Contra Costa Co., St. Perpetua (1952), Rev. John Kasper, O.S.F.S. In Res., Rev. Francis J. Houdek, S.J.
Res.: 3454 Hamlin Rd., 94549. Tel: 925-283-0272; Fax: 925-283-6534.
School—Tel: 925-284-1640; Fax: 925-284-5676. Lay Teachers 20; Students 262.
Catechesis/Religious Program—Tel: 925-283-0272, Ext. 204. Students 337.

Livermore, Alameda Co.
1—St. Charles Borromeo (1964), [JC] Rev. Robert Mendonca, Parish Admin.; Deacon John Durden. In Res., Rev. Richard McCafferty, S.J.
Res.: 1315 Lomitas Ave., 94550. Tel: 925-447-4549; Fax: 925-373-7088.
Catechesis/Religious Program—Tel: 925-449-0133. Students 150.
2—St. Michael (1878), (Spanish), [CEM] Rev. Msgr. Robert Adams, Pastor Emeritus; Revs. Raymond Sacca; David E. Staal; Sisters Yoshio Komiyama, O.P., Dir. Hispanic Min.; Lorena Ramirez, O.P., Dir. Hispanic Min.; Deacons David Rezendez; Bill Archer. In Res., Revs. Augustine Koilparampil (India); Walter W. Mayer (Retired).
Res.: 458 Maple St., 94550. Tel: 925-447-1585; Fax: 925-447-0520.
School—Tel: 925-447-1888; Fax: 925-447-6720. Sr. Emmanuel Cardinale, O.P. Sisters 2; Lay Teachers 15; Students 317.
Catechesis/Religious Program—Tel: 925-447-8814; Fax: 925-447-6720. Sr. Kathleen Kennedy, D.R.E. Students 537.

Martinez, Contra Costa Co., St. Catherine of Siena (1873), [CEM] Revs. Antonio A. Valdivia; Michael Van Dinh; Neal C. Clemens.
Mailing Address: *Parish Activity Center Office:*, 1125 Ferry St., 94553.
Res.: 1100 Estudillo St., 94553. Tel: 925-228-2230; Fax: 925-228-1318.
School—Tel: 925-228-4140; Fax: 925-228-0697. Mrs. Nancy Libby, Prin. Lay Teachers 12; Students 210.
Catechesis/Religious Program—1125 Ferry St., 94553. Tel: 925-228-2230, Ext. 0. Students 211.

Moraga, Contra Costa Co., St. Monica (1965), Rev. Declan Deane; Deacon Jack Jordan; Mrs. Cath McGhee, Pastoral Admin. In Res., Rev. Michael A. Russo.
Res.: 1001 Camino Pablo, P.O. Box 128, 94556. Tel: 925-376-6900; Fax: 925-376-9796.
Catechesis/Religious Program—Tel: 925-376-0500; 925-376-0558. Students 375.

Newark, Alameda Co., St. Edward's (1920), Revs. Jeffrey Finley, C.PP.S.; Johnson C. Abraham; Paulson Mundanmani, S.D.B. (India); Sr. Jeanne Sullivan, S.N.D., Pastoral Assoc.; Deacons Ernest Perez; Rolito C. Roque; Nick Bruckner; Roger Wedl; Antonio Barreto; Alfonso Perez.
Res.: 5788 Thornton Ave., 94560. Tel: 510-797-0241; Fax: 510-797-4557.
School—Tel: 510-793-7242; Fax: 510-793-3189. Sisters 1 Lay Teachers 12; Students 306.
Catechesis/Religious Program—Tel: 510-797-5588. Students 870.

Oakley, Contra Costa Co., St. Anthony (1925), (Spanish—Portuguese), [JC] Rev. Bernardino Andrade; Joann Mass, Admin.; Deacons Joseph Tovar; Alan Layden; John Kortuem.
Res.: 971 O'Hara Ave., 94561. Tel: 925-625-2048; Fax: 925-625-4433.
Catechesis/Religious Program—Tel: 925-625-2077. Students 512.

Orinda, Contra Costa Co., Santa Maria (1947), Rev. Msgr. Theodore W. Kraus, S.J.
Res.: 40 Santa Maria Way, 94563. Tel: 925-254-2426; Fax: 925-254-2468. In Res., Rev. Paul Ojibway S.A.
Catechesis/Religious Program—Dorothy Harrington, D.R.E., (Children); Mary Eaton, D.R.E., (Youth). Students 342.

Piedmont, Alameda Co., Corpus Christi (1929), Rev. Leo J. Edgerly Jr. In Res., Rev. Basil DePinto.
Res.: 322 St. James Dr., 94611. Tel: 510-530-4343; Fax: 510-530-6824.
School—One Estates Dr., 94611. Tel: 510-530-4056; Fax: 510-530-5926. Lay Teachers 15; Students 280.
Catechesis/Religious Program—Tel: 510-531-2576. Students 263.

Pinole, Contra Costa Co., St. Joseph's (1947), Revs. Quang Minh Dong; Cezar deLeon. In Res., Rev. Richard Gagliardi (Retired).
Parish Center, Office & Mailing Address: 2100 Pear St., 94564. Tel: 510-741-4900; Fax: 510-724-9185.
Church: 837 Tennent Ave., 94564.
School—Tel: 510-724-0242; Fax: 510-724-9886. Lay Teachers 12; Students 317.
Catechesis/Religious Program—Students 430.

Pittsburg, Contra Costa Co.
1—Good Shepherd (1965), Revs. Helmut W. Richter; Herman Leong; Deacon Ferris J. Anthony.
Res.: 3200 Harbor St., 94565. Tel: 925-432-6404; Fax: 925-432-6748.
Catechesis/Religious Program—Tel: 925-439-1091. Students 557.
2—St. Peter Martyr of Verona (1914), Rev. Ricardo A. Chavez. In Res., Rev. William Johnson.
Res.: 740 Black Diamond St., 94565. Tel: 925-432-4771; Fax: 925-432-3389.
School—Tel: 925-439-1014; Fax: 925-439-1506. Lay Teachers 12; Students 315.
Catechesis/Religious Program—Tel: 925-432-7200. Students 518.

Pleasant Hill, Contra Costa Co., Christ the King (1951), Revs. Brian T. Joyce; Gerard A. Murphy. In Res., Rev. Brian Timoney.
Res.: 199 Brandon Rd., 94523. Tel: 925-682-2486; Fax: 925-682-5021.
School—Tel: 925-685-1109; Fax: 925-685-1289. Sr. Carmel Garcia, C.S.J., Prin. Sisters of St. Joseph of Carondelet 3; Lay Teachers 19; Students 324.
Catechesis/Religious Program—Tel: 925-686-1017. Students 1,238.

Pleasanton, Alameda Co.
1—St. Augustine (1901), Merged, with St. Elizabeth Seton, Pleasanton to form The Catholic Community of Pleasanton.
2—The Catholic Community of Pleasanton (1905), [CEM] Revs. Daniel E. Danielson; Nicholas Glisson; Joseph Trin Tran; Padraig Greene; Deacons Richard Martin; Ernest Freeman.
Res.: 3999 Bernal, P.O. Box 817, 94566. Tel: 925-846-4489; Fax: 925-426-5061.
Catechesis/Religious Program—Tel: 925-846-3531; Fax: 925-846-3543. Students 1,763.
3—St. Elizabeth Seton (1991), Merged, with St. Augustine, Pleasanton to form The Catholic Community of Pleasanton.

Point Richmond, Contra Costa Co., Our Lady of Mercy (1902), Rev. David K. O'Rourke, O.P.
Res.: 301 W. Richmond Ave., 94801. Tel: 510-653-4274.

Richmond, Contra Costa Co.
1—St. Cornelius (1952), [CEM] Rev. Filiberto Barrera, Admin.; Sr. Margarita Cortez, O.P., D.R.E.
Res.: 225-28th St., 94804. Tel: 510-233-5215; Fax: 510-233-7342.
School—201-28th St., 94805. Tel: 510-232-3326; Fax: 510-232-4071. Lay Teachers 12; Students 225.
Catechesis/Religious Program—Students 286.
2—St. David of Wales (1952), Rev. Ronald E. Atwood.
Res.: 5641 Esmond Ave., 94805. Tel: 510-237-1531; Fax: 510-237-3801.
School—871 Sonoma St., 94805. Tel: 510-232-2283; Fax: 510-231-0484. Mrs. Barbara Kringle-Fabiani, Prin. Sisters 1; Lay Teachers 28; Students 328.
Catechesis/Religious Program—5418 Esmond Ave., 94805. Students 328.
3—St. Mark's (1912), Rev. Jose de Jesus Nieto-Ruiz, Admin.
Res.: 159 Harbour Way, 94801. Tel: 510-234-5886; Fax: 510-236-5711.
Catechesis/Religious Program—Tel: 510-234-7351. Students 288.

Rodeo, Contra Costa Co., St. Patrick's (1923), Rev. Larry E. Young.
Res.: 825 Seventh St., 94572. Tel: 510-799-4406; Fax: 510-799-5681.
School—907 Seventh St., 94572. Tel: 510-799-2506; Fax: 510-799-6781. Lay Teachers 30; Students 288.
Catechesis/Religious Program—Tel: 510-799-4434. Students 126.

San Leandro, Alameda Co.
1—St. Alphonsus Liguori (1955), [CEM] Rev. Paul Vassor; Deacon George Peters. In Res., Revs. Robert LaBarbera; Paul Ngoko (Kenya).
Res.: 2085 Miramar Ave., 94578. Tel: 510-276-3907; Fax: 510-276-3955. Email: stalphonsas@sbcglobal.net.
Catechesis/Religious Program—Students 14.
2—Assumption of the Blessed Virgin Mary (1951), Rev. Msgr. Michael Lucid; Revs. Mark Wiesner; Michael Galvan.
Res.: 1100 Fulton Ave., 94577. Tel: 510-352-1537; Fax: 510-352-9155.
School— 94577. Tel: 510-357-8772; Fax: 510-357-7018. Lay Teachers 16; Students 296.
Catechesis/Religious Program—Tel: 510-351-1235. Students 80.
3—St. Felicitas (1952), Rev. Wayne Campbell; Deacon Jose Prado, (Retired). In Res., Rev. Tran Thuc Dinh (Vietnam) (Retired).
Res.: 1662 Manor Blvd., 94579. Tel: 510-351-5244;

Fax: 510-351-5730.
School—1650 Manor Blvd., 94579. Tel: 510-357-2530; Fax: 510-357-5358. Sisters of St. Joseph of Wichita 2; Lay Teachers 12; Students 260.
Catechesis/Religious Program—Tel: 510-483-4880. Sandi Walton, D.R.E. Students 317.
4—ST. LEANDER (1864), Revs. John Prochaska; Bich N. Nguyen; Deacons Dennis Davis; Victor Silveira; Antonio Baptista. In Res., Revs. Thomas Lester (Retired); Antonio Reis (Brazil).
Office—474 W. Estudillo Ave., 94577. Tel: 510-895-5631; Fax: 510-352-3578.
School—Tel: 510-351-4144; Fax: 510-483-6060. Lay Teachers 10; Students 292.
Catechesis/Religious Program—Students 538.
5—OUR LADY OF GOOD COUNSEL (1966), (Vietnamese), [JC] Rev. Dominic Thuong Nguyen.
Res.: 14112 Azores Pl., 94577. Tel: 510-895-1165; Fax: 510-483-7705.
Catechesis/Religious Program—2500 Bermuda Ave., 94577. Tel: 510-483-2513. Students 74.
SAN LORENZO, ALAMEDA CO., ST. JOHN THE BAPTIST (1925), Revs. Michael Lacey; William Rozario (India); Deacons Leonard J. Bettencourt; Ernest Molloy. In Res., Rev. William J. Dunn (Retired).
Res.: 264 E. Lewelling Blvd., 94580. Tel: 510-351-5050; Fax: 510-276-0397.
School—Tel: 510-276-6632; Fax: 510-276-5645. Arlene Marseille, Prin. Sisters 1; Lay Teachers 14; Students 271.
Catechesis/Religious Program—Tel: 510-278-5080. Students 186.
SAN PABLO, CONTRA COSTA CO., ST. PAUL (1864), Revs. Paul Fazio, O.F.M.Conv.; Masseo Gonzalez, O.F.M.Conv.; Deacons Ysidro Madrigal; Donaciano Perez.
Res.: 1845 Church Ln., 94806. Tel: 510-232-5931; Fax: 510-232-1846.
School—Tel: 510-233-3080; Fax: 510-231-8777. Lay Teachers 12; Students 254.
Catechesis/Religious Program—1825 Church Ln., 94806. Students 336.
SAN RAMON, CONTRA COSTA CO., ST. JOAN OF ARC (1979), Rev. Fred A. Riccio; Deacons Ruben Gomez; Chuan Oey.
Res.: 2601 San Ramon Valley Blvd., 94583-1630. Tel: 925-830-0600; Fax: 925-830-5059.
Catechesis/Religious Program—Tel: 925-830-4710. Students 1,850.
UNION CITY, ALAMEDA CO.
1—ST. ANNE (1973), Revs. Ramon J. Gomez; Dante Tamayo.
Res.: 32223 Cabello St., P.O. Box 292, 94587. Tel: 510-471-7766; Fax: 510-487-6540.
Catechesis/Religious Program—Tel: 510-489-2080. Students 912.
2—OUR LADY OF THE ROSARY (1951), Rev. Jose M. Leon; Deacons Federico Ceja, (Retired); Richard L. Folger; Gustaaf Roemers; Luis Trucios.
Res.: 703 C St., 94587. Tel: 510-471-2609; Fax: 510-471-4601.
School—Tel: 510-471-3765. Lay Teachers 9; Students 174.
Catechesis/Religious Program—Tel: 510-471-7419. Students 405.
WALNUT CREEK, CONTRA COSTA CO.
1—ST. ANNE (1965), Rev. Msgr. John T. McCracken; Revs. Anthony S. Hannick (YAK) (Retired); William M. Kegel, S.J.; Sr. Carole Pesce, S.H.F., Pastoral Assoc.
Res.: 1600 Rossmoor Pkwy., 94595-2507. Tel: 925-932-2324; Fax: 925-932-4628.
2—ST. JOHN VIANNEY (1965), Revs. Vincent J. Scott; Christopher Berbena; Deacons John Jee; John Mazibrook.
Res.: 1650 Ygnacio Valley Rd., 94598. Tel: 925-939-7911; Fax: 925-939-0450.
Catechesis/Religious Program—Tel: 925-939-9544. Students 431.
3—ST. MARY'S (1941), [JC] Revs. E. Donald Osuna; Joseph Parekkatt, S.D.B.; Olman Solis.
Res.: 1201 Alpine Rd., 94596. Tel: 510-891-8900; Fax: 510-934-1358.
School—Tel: 510-935-5054; Fax: 510-935-5063. Mrs. Mary Lou Curtis, Prin. Lay Teachers 17; Students 278.
Catechesis/Religious Program—2039 Mt. Diablo Blvd., 94596. Tel: 925-891-8930; Fax: 925-891-8940. Students 396.
4—ST. STEPHEN (1966), Rev. Denis A. DesRosiers; Deacon William Bothe.
Res.: 525 Madonna Ln., 94597. Tel: 925-939-3826; Fax: 925-988-0417.
Catechesis/Religious Program—Students 68.

Chaplains of Public Institutions
Hospitals

OAKLAND. *Children's Hospital*. Sr. Bernice Gotelli, P.B.V.M. Tel: 510-428-3325; 510-428-3000.
Highland Hospital. Rev. Basil DePinto. Tel: 510-425-2774, Deacon Dennis Lee. Tel: 510-437-4219.
Kaiser-Permanente Medical Center. Sr. Moira MacPherson. Tel: 510-372-1000, Rev. William Johnson. Tel: 510-372-1000, Deacon Rex Ehling. Tel: 510-483-2112.
Summit Medical Center, Pastoral Care, Tel: 510-835-4500; 510-655-9209. Attended by Sacred Heart.
ANTIOCH. *Delta Memorial Hospital*, Tel: 510-757-4020. Attended by Holy Rosary.
BERKELEY. *Alta Bates Hospital*. Sr. Kathleen Corbett, C.S.J. Tel: 510-204-2064, Rev. John O' Leary. Tel: 510-204-6732; Pager: 510-802-1963.
Alta Bates-Herrick Hospital. Attended by St. Joseph the Worker, Berkeley.
CASTRO VALLEY. *Eden Hospital*. Rev. John Ranallo. Tel: 510-538-7941.
CONCORD. *Mount Diablo Hospital, Director of Pastoral Care*, Tel: 510-682-8200. Rev. William Johnson, Chap., Dir. Pastoral Care. Tel: 925-682-8200. Attended by St. Peter Martyr Church.
FREMONT. *Washington Hospital*. Revs. Richard Peiris. Tel: 510-477-9713; 510-797-1111, Jeffrey Finley, C.PP.S. Tel: 510-797-1111 Corpus Christi Parish. Attended by Corpus Christi Parish.
HAYWARD. *Kaiser Permanente Medical Center*, Tel: 510-781-2171. Attended by St. Bede Parish.
LIVERMORE. *Veterans Administration Hospital*. Rev. Augustine Koilparampil. Tel: 510-447-2560; 510-447-1585.
MARTINEZ. *Contra Costa Regional Medical Center and VA Administrative Skilled Nursing Center*, Tel: 925-370-4704. Rev. William Johnson. Tel: 925-432-4771, Sr. Moira McPherson, O.P. Tel: 925-370-4704 St. Catherine of Siena Parish. Attended by St. Catherine of Siena.
PINOLE. *Doctor's Hospital*, Tel: 510-724-3025. Attended by St. Joseph, Pinole.
PITTSBURG. *Delta Memorial Hospital*, Tel: 925-432-6404. Attended by Good Shepherd.
RICHMOND. *East Bay Hospital*, Tel: 510-233-5215. , VA 23260. Tel: 510-234-5886 St. Cornelius Parish. Attended by St. Cornelius & St. Mark.
Kaiser-Permanente, Tel: 510-234-5886. Attended by St. Mark.
SAN LEANDRO. *Fairmont Hospital, Catholic Chaplain*, Tel: 510-667-3251. Deacon George Peters. Tel: 510-667-3251.
Humana Hospital, Tel: 510-895-5631 St. Leander Parish. Attended by St. Leander (510) 895-5631.; Attended by Assumption Parish (510) 352-1537.
Physicians Community Hospital, Tel: 510-352-1537. Attended by San Leandro Hospital and Vencor Hospital, Assumption.
SAN PABLO. *Brookside-Hospital*, Tel: 510-235-7000 Brookside Hospital; 510-233-5931 St. Paul Parish. Attended by St. Paul.
SAN RAMON. *San Ramon Regional Medical Center*, Tel: 510-830-0600 St. Joan of Arc Parish; 510-275-9200 (Hospital). Attended by St. Joan of Arc.
WALNUT CREEK. *John Muir Memorial Hospital, Pastoral Care*, Tel: 925-939-7911 St. John Vianney Parish; 510-939-3000 (Hospital). Attended by St. John Vianney.
Kaiser-Permanente Medical Center, Tel: 925-372-1000.
Walnut Creek Hospital, Tel: 925-933-7990; 925-939-7911. Attended by St. John Vianney.

Prisons and Jails

OAKLAND. *Community Re-entry Center*. Deacon Gus Roemers.
Detention Ministry, Tel: 510-768-3168; Fax: 510-630-7568. Ms. Jacqueline Manibusan, Dir. & Detention Min.
Glen Dyer Jail. Rev. John Ranallo, Deacon Gus Roemers. (formerly North County Jail)
Victim Offender Reconciliation Program. Mr. Rick Mockler, Dir. Tel: 510-834-5656. (VORP)
DUBLIN. *Federal Correctional Institution*, Tel: 925-833-7500, Ext. 385. Kyung Lee, Chap. Tel: 925-833-7500, Ext. 385.
MARTINEZ. *Contra Costa County Jails*.
Contra Costa County Juvenile Hall Facility. Deacon Frank Beville. Tel: 510-834-5656.
PLEASANTON. *Alameda County Jail-Santa Rita Rehabilitation Center*. Rev. John Ranallo.
RICHMOND. *West County Detention Facility*. (formerly Richmond Jail)
SAN LEANDRO. *Alameda County Juvenile Hall Facility*.

On Special Assignment:
Rev.—
Vella, Francis M., Chap. (Retired), V.A. Medical Center, Alexandria, LA

Military Chaplains:
Rev.—
Wydeven, John L., 293 BSB Box 24, APO, AE 09086.

Graduate Studies:
Revs.—
Breton, Ray
Minihan, Paul

On Leave of Absence:
Rev.—
Kappler, Stephan

Administrative Leave:
Rev.—
Link, David

Retired:
Rev. Msgrs.—
Adams, Robert
Moran, Bernard J., Pastor Emeritus
Moran, Bernard J.
Mullen, William J.
Walsh, Martin E.
Revs.—
Brainard, Ernest B.
Cantillon, John Joseph
Charm, Robert
Clift, James C.
Daly, George
DePinto, Basil
Devine, Paul
Dinh, Tran Thuc (Vietnam)
Dollard, John J.
Domingos, Jaques
Driscoll, James E.
Dunn, William J.
Dybdal, Gerald
Eggerling, Milton
Ferraro, Joseph
Ferreira, Joseph A.
Gagliardi, Richard
Gallagher, Thomas B.
Haasl, Edgar
Hayburn, Edmund L.
Hudson, Donald, J.C.L.
Jaques, Domingos
Joyce, Michael
Kenny, John
Kozina, Vladimir
Lagasse, Ronald
Lester, Thomas
Lima, John
Lu, Matthias
Macchi, William
Manning, John
Marshall, William
Mayer, Walter W.
Mifsud, Carmelo
Morgan, John
Palis, Theo
Picket, James B.
Poon, Stanislaus
Ranallo, John
Ruffing, Norman
Russell, Kenneth
Schexnayder, James
Snyder, Alexander
Starbuck, James
Timoney, Brian
Vella, Francis M.
Welch, Joseph

Permanent Deacons:
Agustin, Benjamin, St. Jerome, El Cerrito
Anthony, Ferris J., (Retired), Good Shepherd, Pittsburg
Archer, William, St. Michael, Livermore
Arteaga, Gustavo, St. Michael, Livermore
Baptista, Antonio, St. Leander, San Leandro
Barnes, Frank, On Duty Outside the Diocese
Barnes, James, (Retired)
Barreto, Antonio, Mark Parish, Richmond
Beltran, Juan, St. Cornelius, Richmond
Bettencourt, Leonard, St. John the Baptist Church, San Lorenzo
Beville, Frank, (Retired), St. Columba, Oakland
Bothe, William, St. Stephen, Walnut Creek
Brazil, Rudolph, Holy Spirit, Fremont
Bruckner, Nick, St. Edward, Newark
Budnik, Steve, Our Lady of Guadalupe, Fremont
Bustos, Frank, (Retired), Immaculate Heart of Mary, Brentwood
Cabezas, Rigoberto, St. Joachim, Hayward
Cain, Jerry, Inactive - Out of Diocese
Calub, Benigno, St. Ann, Union City
Cantlon, Michael, Holy Spirit, Fremont
Ceja, Federico, (Retired)
Chichon, Witold, Polis Pastoral Center, Martinez
Custodio, Maurice, Santa Maria, Orinda
Davis, Dennis, St. Leander, San Leandro
Dowling, Robert, Our Lady of Grace, Castro Valley
Drobick, William, Holy Spirit, Fremont
Duhe, Gaston J., (Retired)
Dulka, Matthew, Our Lady of Grace, Castro Valley

Durden, John, St. Charles, Livermore
Edgerly, Leo, Sr., (Retired)
Ehling, Rex, St. Augustine, Oakland
Evans, Garry, Transfiguration, Castro Valley
Fleischer, Alfred, St. Ignatius, Antioch
Flores, Isidore, St. Mark's, Richmond
Folger, Richard, Our Lady of the Rosary, Union City
Freeman, Ernest, St. Augustine, Pleasanton
Frumkin, Paul, St. Clement, Hayward
Fuentes, Javier, St. Bernard, Oakland
Gall, William, St. Bonaventure, Concord
Gomez, Ruben, St. Joan of Arc, San Ramon
Gonsalves, Nelson, All Saints, Hayward
Gonzalez, Noe, St. Louis Bertrand, Oakland
Grigg, Jerry, Most Holy Rosary, Antioch
Guesnon, Ovide, St. Leonard, Fremont
Hernandez, Gabriel, St. Elizabeth, Oakland
Hoblitzell, Ross, (Retired)
Horan, Ronald, St. Anne, Byron
Jaramillo, Ernest, St. Joachim, Hayward
Jee, John, St. John Vianney, Walnut Creek
Jordan, Jack, St. Monica, Moraga
Karp, Robert, (Retired)
Kortuem, John, St. Anthony, Oakley
Kortuem, John, St. Anthony, Oakley
Lara, Jorge, St. Leonard, Stanta Paula, Fremont
Layden, Alan, St. Anthony, Oakley
Lee, Stanley, On Duty Outside the Diocese-Philippines
Lewandowski, Daniel, On Duty Outside the Diocese
Macachor, Oscar, St. Joachim, Hayward
Madrigal, Ysidro, St. Paul, San Pablo
Marchese, Charles, Jr., On Duty Outside the Diocese
Martin, Richard, St. Augustine, Pleasanton
Mazibrook, John, St. John Vianney, Walnut Creek
McGowan, Thomas, St. John, El Cerrito
Miyashiro, Leslie, Korean Pastoral Center, Oakland
Moll, Herbert, On Duty Outside the Diocese
Molloy, Ernest, St. John the Baptist, San Lorenzo
Moore, Timothy, Transfiguration, Castro Valley
Oey, Hock Chuan, St. Joan of Arc, San Ramon
Palomares, Charles, St. Francis of Assisi, Concord
Pearce, James, St. Agnes, Concord
Perez, Alfonso, St. Edward, Newark
Perez, Donaciano, St. Paul, San Pablo
Perez, Ernest, (Retired)
Perry, Thomas, (Inactive)
Peters, George, St. Alphonsus, San Leandro
Prado, Jose, (Retired)
Preza, Mariano, Concord Hispanic Community, Concord
Quigley, Edward, On Duty Outside the Diocese
Rabuy, Carlos, St. Ann, Union City
Rezendes, David, St. Michael, Livermore
Rigley, Burton, Transfiguration, Castro Valley
Rivilla, Luis, On Duty Outside the Diocese
Roemers, Gustaaf, Our Lady of the Rosary, Union City
Ryken, Dennis, St. Bede, Hayward
Silva, Richard, On Duty Outside the Diocese
Silveira, Victor, St. Leander, San Leandro
Silvernale, Charles, Holy Rosary, Antioch
Smith, Leo, (Retired)
Soublet, Morris, (Retired)
Spano, Edward, St. Ann, Byron
Stelly, Eugene, St. Andrew-St. Joseph, Oakland
Taylor, Stephen, Holy Spirit, Fremont
Tovar, Joseph, St. Anthony, Oakley
Turcios, Luis, Our Lady of the Rosary, Union City
Victoria, Hector, Unassigned
Walsh, Jerome, St. Bonaventure, Concord
Warren, William, Jr., On Duty Outside the Diocese
Wedl, Roger, St. Edward, Newark
Yee, Richard, Holy Spirit, Fremont

INSTITUTIONS LOCATED IN THE DIOCESE

[A] SEMINARIES, RELIGIOUS OR SCHOLASTICATES

OAKLAND. *School of Applied Theology Graduate Theological Union-Berkeley* An Affiliate of the Graduate Theological Union, Berkeley , 5890 Birch Ct., 94618. Tel: 510-652-1651; Fax: 510-420-0542. Email: satgtu@aol.com. Web: www.satgtu.org. Bro. Bernard LoCoco, F.S.C., Pres. & Dean; Sr. Therese McGroddy, R.S.H.M., Dir. Admissions. Brothers 1; Sisters 1; Lay Teachers 30; Students 37; Staff 3.
Trustees: Revs. Francis J. Houdek, S.J.; Eugene Ludwig, O.F.M.Cap.; Eugene R. Zimmers, S.J., Emeritus; Sr. Mary T. Grove, I.H.M.; Bros. Mel Anderson, F.S.C.; Bernard LoCoco, F.S.C.; Sylvia Chu; Ron Courtney; James A. Donahue, Ph.D.; Mr. Robert Mallon; John McMahon; Mr. James Penna, J.D.; Mrs. Sarah Seybold; Ms. Sharon-Gay Smith; Claude Welch, Ph.D., Emeritus.

BERKELEY. *Brother Giles Franciscan Formation Community* (Province of St. Barbara) , 1920-7th St., 94710. Email: Sevenstr@hotmail.com. Bro. John Kiesler, O.F.M., Guardian; Rev. Dan Lackie, O.F.M., Formation Dir.; Bros. Rami Fodda; Ed Sarrazin; William Minkel, O.F.M.; John Gutierrez, O.F.M.; Bonaventure Pearsall; Brian Trawick; Hajime Okuhara. Priests 1; Brothers 8.

Dominican School of Philosophy and Theology (Dominican House of Studies at the Graduate Theological Union) , 2401 Ridge Rd., 94709. Tel: 510-849-2030; Fax: 510-849-1372. Email: grocca@dspt.edu. Web: www.dspt.edu. Revs. Gregory Rocca, O.P., Pres. & Faculty (Regular); Eugene M. Ludwig, O.F.M.Cap., Academic Dean & Faculty; Mr. Scott Connolly, Registrar & Dean of Students; Susan McGinnis Hardie, Dir. Admissions & Recruitment; Mrs. Eleanor Westbrooke, Sec. Priests 15; Sisters 2; Lay Teachers 3 Students 121.
Faculty (Regular): Revs. Joseph Boenzi, S.D.B.; Michael Dodds, O.P.; Edward Krasevac, O.P.; Eugene M. Ludwig, O.F.M.Cap.; Michael Monshau, O.P.; Michael T. Morris, O.P.; Gregory Rocca, O.P.; Gregory T. Tatum, O.P.; Sr. Barbara Green, O.P.; Mr. Mark Delp.
Faculty (Adjunct): Revs. Luke D. Buckles, O.P.; Owen Carroll; Stephen Ernest, S.V.D.; Arthur Lenti, S.D.B.; Michael S. Sherwin, O.P.; Sr. Mary Greenan, F.M.A.; Dr. Marilyn Anne Coffy.

Franciscan School of Theology, 1712 Euclid Ave., 94709. Tel: 510-848-5232; Fax: 510-549-9466. Email: info@fst.edu. Web: www.fst.edu. Revs. William M. Cieslak, O.F.M.Cap., Pres.; Joseph P. Chinnici, O.F.M., Academic Dean; Sisters Ramona Miller, O.S.F., Dir. Spiritual Formation; Rita Dougherty, R.D.C., Registrar, Business Officer; Jonathan Diaz, Dir. Recruitment; Michael Sullivan, Dir. Devel.; Patricia Jimenez, Dir. Student Services. Priests 9; Brothers 2; Sisters 4; Lay Teachers 1; Total Enrollment 95.
Faculty: Revs. Rigoberto Caloca-Rivas, O.F.M.; Joseph P. Chinnici, O.F.M.; William M. Cieslak, O.F.M.Cap.; Faustino Cruz, S.M.; Michael D. Guinan, O.F.M.; Richard Gula, S.S.; Xavier J. Harris, O.F.M.; Kenan B. Osborne, O.F.M.; Thomas West, O.F.M.; Sisters Eva Lumas, S.S.S.; Mary McGann, R.S.C.J.; Bros. John Kiesler, O.F.M.; William J. Short, O.F.M.

The Jesuit School of Theology at Berkeley A Pontifical Faculty of Theology. One of two theological centers of the U.S. Jesuit Conference, Society of Jesus. A Member of the Graduate Theological Union (GTU), Berkeley. , 1735 LeRoy Ave., 94709. Tel: 510-549-5000; Fax: 510-841-8536. Email: gbyrd@jstb.edu. Web: jstb.edu. Revs. Joseph P. Daoust, S.J., Pres.; George R. Murphy, S.J., Coord. Formation Programs; Ms. April M. Collier, Vice Pres. Institutional Advancement; Dr. Bruce Lescher, Dir. Sabbatical Programs; Ms. Lorna Wallace McKeown, Asst. Academic Dean & In-House Registrar; Ms. Linda A. Menes, Dir. of Admissions; Garfield Byrd, Bus. Mgr. & Treas.; Ms. Jill K. Marshall, Dean Students. Priests 16; Sisters 4; Lay Teachers 6; Full-time Faculty 20; Students 193.
Faculty (Emeriti): Revs. Donald L. Gelpi, S.J.; John H. Wright, S.J.
Faculty: Revs. Thomas E. Buckley, S.J.; Joseph P. Daoust, S.J.; John C. Endres, S.J.; Eduardo Fernandez, S.J.; George E. Griener, S.J.; Francis X. McAloon, S.J.; William R. O'Neill, S.J.; James Redington, S.J.; T. Howland Sanks, S.J.; Thomas J. Scirghi, S.J.; Peter Siu, S.J.; Jack Treibar, S.J., Academic Dean; Sisters Mary Ann Donovan, S.C.; Sandra M. Schneiders, I.H.M.; Dr. Jerome P. Baggett; Dr. Lisa Fullum; Dr. Alejandro Garcia-Rivera; Dr. Gina Hens-Piazza; Dr. Jean-Francois Racine.

[B] COLLEGES AND UNIVERSITIES

OAKLAND. *Holy Names College* (1868), Chartered 1880. Resident and Non-Resident Students. , 3500 Mountain Blvd., 94619. Tel: 510-436-1000; Fax: 510-436-1199. Web: www.hnc.edu.
Legal Title: *Sisters of the Holy Names of Jesus and Mary, A Corporation*
Legal Title: *Holy Names College, A Corporation*
Sisters of the Holy Names of Jesus and Mary Priests 2; Sisters 18; Lay Professors 37; Students 947.
Administration: Revs. James Conlon; Henry Ormond, O.Carm.; Sisters Elizabeth Adams, S.N.J.M.; Mary Anderson, S.N.J.M. Margaret Campbell, S.N.J.M.; Sharon Casey, O.P., Dir. Campus Ministry; Deborah Church, S.N.J.M.; Marcia Frideger, S.N.J.M.; Maureen Hester, S.N.J.M.; Donna Maynard, S.N.J.M.; Rosemarie Nassif, S.S.N.D., Pres.; Christine Patrinos, S.N.J.M.; JoAnne Quinliven, S.N.J.M.; Delores Rashford, S.N.J.M.; Carol Sellman, S.N.J.M., Vice Pres. Mission Effectiveness; Nancy Teskey, S.N.J.M.; Irene Woodward, C.F.C.; JoAnn Berridge, Dean Undergraduate Admissions & Financial Aid; Bitta Farahmand, Dir. Residence Life; David J. Fike, Vice Pres. Academic Affairs; John McCready, Vice Pres. Finance & Admin.; Joyce McLean, Dir. Library Svcs.; Danita Nelms, Dir. Adult & Graduate Programs; Claire Olivares, Dir. Devel.; Erik Stilling, Dir. Continuing Education; Jeanette Honstein Tobler, Registrar.
Religious Staff: Sisters Sylvia Barthold, S.N.J.M.; Mary Christine Fleitz, S.N.J.M.; June Kearney, S.N.J.M.; Ethel Mary Tinnemann, S.N.J.M.; Francesca Cabrini Weber, S.N.J.M.

FREMONT. *Queen of the Holy Rosary College* Tel: 510-657-2468; Fax: 510-657-1734. Email: marypaul@msjdominicans.org. Web: www.msjdominicans.org/college.html. P.O. Box 3908, Mission San Jose, 94539-0391. Sisters Rose Marie Hennessy, O.P., Pres.; Mary Paul Mehegan, O.P., Dean.
Legal Title: *Queen of the Holy Rosary College*
Dominican Sisters of Mission San Jose Sisters 15; Lay Teachers 2; Total Enrollment 243.

MORAGA. *St. Mary's College* Coed. Resident and Non-Resident Students. , 1928 St. Mary's Rd., 94575. Tel: 925-631-4000; Fax: 925-376-1847. Web: www.stmarys-ca.edu. Bros. Craig J. Franz, F.S.C., Pres.; Jack Curran, F.S.C., Vice Pres. Student Affairs; Michael Meister, F.S.C., Asst. Academic Vice Pres.
Legal Title: *Saint Mary's College of California*
Brothers of the Christian Schools Priests 4; Sisters 2; Brothers 12; Professors 456; Total Enrollment 4,127.
Saint Mary's College Community: Bros. Martin Fallin, F.S.C., Sub Dir.; Donald Mansir, F.S.C., Dir.
Alemany Community: Bro. Michael Meister, F.S.C., Dir.
Campus Ministers: Sr. Ingrid Clemmensen, O.P., Dir. Campus Ministry.
Faculty: Rev. Msgr. Edgar P. McCarren (RVC) (Retired); Revs. Owen Carroll (Canada); John Morris, O.P.; Michael A. Russo; Sisters Carolyn Krohn, R.S.M.; Clare Wagstaffe; Bros. Michael S. Avila, F.S.C.; William Beatie, F.S.C.; Kenneth W. Cardwell, F.S.C.; Camillus Chavez, F.S.C.; Craig J. Franz, F.S.C.; Ronald Gallagher, F.S.C.; James J. Leahy, F.S.C., (On Leave); Brenden Madden, F.S.C.; Michael F. Meister, F.S.C.; John O'Neill, F.S.C.; Raphael Patton, F.S.C.; O. DeSales Perez, F.S.C.; Theophane Nguyen Van Ke, F.S.C., (Retired); T. Jerome West, F.S.C., (Retired); Martin Yribarren.

[C] HIGH SCHOOLS, DIOCESAN

OAKLAND. *Bishop O'Dowd High School*, 9500 Stearns Ave., 94605. Tel: 510-577-9100; Fax: 510-638-3259. Email: admin@bishopodowd.org. Web: www.bishopodowd.org. Revs. John Huber, C.S.B.; Donald J. McLeod, C.S.B., Prin.; John B. Malo, C.S.B.; Robert H. Glass, C.S.B.; Benjamin Owens, C.SS.R.; Les F. Schaefer, C.S.B.; James Murphy, C.S.B., Supr. Basilian Fathers (Congregation of St. Basil) Priests 6; Lay Teachers 73; Students 1,099.

St. Elizabeth High School, 1530-34th Ave., 94601. Tel: 510-532-8947; Fax: 510-532-9754. Email: smliam@msjdominicans.org. Sr. Mary Liam Brock, Prin. Sisters 2; Lay Teachers 19; Students 300.

[D] HIGH SCHOOLS, PAROCHIAL

ALAMEDA. *Saint Joseph Notre Dame High School*, 1011 Chestnut St., 94501. Tel: 510-523-1526; Fax: 510-523-2181. Email: kmontserrat@sjnd.org. Web: www.sjnd.org. Mr. Anthony V. Aiello, Prin. Lay Teachers 58; Total Staff 58; Students 521.

[E] HIGH SCHOOLS, PRIVATE

OAKLAND. *Holy Name High School*, 4660 Harbord Dr., 94618. Tel: 510-450-1110; Fax: 510-547-3111. Sally Slyngstad, SNJM, Prin. Sisters of the Holy Names of Jesus and Mary Sisters 3; Lay Teachers 28; Students 277.

BERKELEY. *Saint Mary's College High School*, Peralta Park, 1294 Albina Ave., 94706. Tel: 510-526-9242; Fax: 510-559-6277. Web: www.saintmaryschs.org. Bro. Edmond Larouche, F.S.C., Pres.; Mrs. Kathleen Ryan McGuire, Prin. Brothers of the Christian Schools Brothers 3; Lay Teachers 35; Students 630.

CONCORD. *Carondelet High School*, 1133 Winton Dr., 94518-3598. Tel: 925-686-5353; Fax: 925-671-9429. Email: chs@carondelet.pvt.k12.ca.us. Web: www.carondelet.pvt.k12.ca.us. Sr. James Marien Dyer, C.S.J., Prin. Sisters of St Joseph of Carondelet Brothers 1; Sisters 1; Lay Teachers 45; Students 850.

De La Salle High School of Concord, Inc. dba De La Salle High School (Boys) , 1130 Winton Dr.,

94518. Tel: 925-686-3310; Fax: 925-686-3474. Email: edlundm@dlshs.org. Web: www.dlshs.org. Mr. Bruce Shoup, Pres.; Bro. Christopher Brady. Brothers of the Christian Schools (De La Salle Christian Brothers) Priests 1; Brothers 3; Lay Teachers 64; Students 1,038.

Co-Assistant Principals: Mr. Jack Dyer, Student Life; Mr. Roger Hassett, Dir. of Campus Min.; Mr. Mary-Ann Lemire Mattos, Academic Life.

HAYWARD. *Moreau Catholic High School*, 27170 Mission Blvd., 94544. Tel: 510-881-4300; Fax: 510-581-5669. Email: tguevara@moreaucatholic.org. Web: www.moreaucatholic.org. Patricia Geister, Prin.; Joseph Connell, Ph.D., Pres.; Margaret J. Walsh, Corp. Treas. Brothers of Holy Cross Priests 1; Lay Teachers 51; Students 1,188.

RICHMOND. *Salesian High School*, 2851 Salesian Ave., 94804. Tel: 510-234-4433; Fax: 510-236-4636. Email: info@salesian.com. Web: www.salesian.com. Rev. Nicholas J. Reina, S.D.B., Dir. & Pres.; Mr. Timothy Chambers, Prin.; Bro. Ernest Martinez, S.D.B., Asst. Prin.; Revs. Laurence Byrne, S.D.B. (Retired); Jesse Montes, S.D.B.; Bros. Joseph R. Lockwood, S.D.B., Business Mgr.; Tho Bui, S.D.B., Faculty; Thomas Mass, S.D.B., Student Activities; Patrick Maloney, S.D.B. Salesians of St. John Bosco Priests 4; Brothers 4; Lay Teachers 47; Students 573. In Res. Rev. Joseph Boenzi, S.D.B.

[F] EARLY CHILDHOOD EDUCATION CENTERS

MISSION SAN JOSE. *Dominican Kindergarten*, 43326 Mission Blvd., P.O. Box 3908, 94539. Tel: 510-651-7978; Fax: 510-657-1734. Email: Kinderkate@aol.com. Web: msjdominicans.org. Sr. Kathleen McAvoy, O.P., Dir. & Teacher. Sisters 2; Students 32.

[G] SUMMER SCHOOLS

OAKLAND. *Holy Names College*, 3500 Mountain Blvd., 94619. Tel: 510-436-1000; Fax: 510-436-1199. Web: www.hnc.edu. Sisters of the Holy Names of Jesus and Mary, Resident and Non-Resident Students. Total Enrollment 888.

MISSION SAN JOSE. *Queen of the Holy Rosary College*, 43326 Mission Blvd., P.O. Box 3908, 94539. Tel: 510-657-2468; Fax: 510-657-1734. Email: marypaul@msjdominicans.org. Web: www.msjdominicans.org/college.html. Sisters of the Third Order of St. Dominic of the Congregation of the Queen of the Holy Rosary Sisters 15; Lay Teachers 2; Students 243.

MORAGA. *St. Mary's College* 94575. Tel: 925-631-4000; Fax: 925-376-1847. Web: www.stmarys-ca.us. Brothers of the Christian Schools, District of San Francisco Priests 3; Brothers 12; Lay Teachers 467; Students 4,127.

[H] CATHOLIC CHARITIES OF THE DIOCESE OF OAKLAND

OAKLAND. *Catholic Charities of the Diocese of Oakland, Inc.*, 433 Jefferson St., 94607. Tel: 510-768-3100; Fax: 510-451-6998. Email: info@cceb.org. Web: www.cceb.org.

Legal Title: *Catholic Charities of the Diocese of Oakland, Inc., A Non-Proft Corporation.*

Oakland Family Service Center, 433 Jefferson St., 94607. Tel: 510-768-3100; Fax: 510-451-6998. Carol Leahy, FSC Dir.

Office and School Counseling Carol Leahy, Dir.; Roy Hammond, Supvr.

Refugee & Immigration Services Raquel Aguirre, Dir.

Southeast Asian Senior Services Bau Ta, Dir.

Employment & Training Services David Lyons, Dir.

Catholic Campaign for Human Dev. Sr. Barbara Dawson, Coord.

Catholic Relief Services Sr. Barbara Dawson, Dir.

Youth Services Stephanie O'Loughlin, Dir.

Detention Ministry Services Ms. Jacqueline Manibusan, Prog. Coord.

Concord Family Service Center, 2350 Pacheco St., Diablo, 94528. Tel: 925-825-3099; Fax: 925-825-5503. Rueben Garza, Dir.

Brentwood Family Service Center, Delta Regional Community Center, 760 1st St., Brentwood, 94513. Tel: 925-516-3880; Fax: 925-516-3889. Solomon Belette, FSC Dir.

Richmond Family Service Center, 2369 Barrett Ave., Richmond, 94804. Tel: 510-234-5110; 510-234-5110, Ext. 356 (ESL Message Line); Fax: 510-237-1522. Lisa Raffel, FSC Dir.

[I] SOCIETY OF ST. VINCENT DE PAUL

OAKLAND. *Society of St. Vincent de Paul of Alameda County*, 9235 San Leandro St., 94603. Tel: 510-638-7600; Fax: 510-638-8354. Email: info@svdp-alameda.org. Web: www.svdp-alameda.org. Vaughn Donahue, Pres.; Philip Arca, Exec. Dir.. Email: parca@svdp-alomeda.org.

PITTSBURG. *Society of St. Vincent de Paul of Contra Costa County*, 2210 Gladstone Dr., 94565. Tel: 925-439-5060; Fax: 925-439-7863. Email: stvincen@stvincen.org. Web: www.stvincen.org. Rick Richardson, Pres.

[J] DAY NURSERIES

OAKLAND. *Saint Vincent's Day Home, Inc.*, 1086 Eighth St., 94607-2697. Tel: 510-832-8324; Fax: 510-832-5021. Email: info@svdh.org. Web: www.svdh.org. Corinne M. Mohrmann, CEO.

Legal Title: *Saint Vincent's Day Home, A Corporation*, Purpose: SVDH strives to set the standard for quality education in the field of early childhood and youth development. Through these services we provide both hope and stability to families throughout the East Bay. Religious 2; Lay Staff 43; Capacity 275; Total Assisted 390; Total Staff 45.

[K] GENERAL HOSPITALS

HAYWARD. *St. Rose Hospital* (1962), Affiliated with Via Christi Health System, Inc. , 27200 Calaroga Ave., 94545-4383. Tel: 510-264-4000; Fax: 510-887-7421. Email: smurray@strosehospital.org. Web: www.strosehospital.org. Mr. Michael Mahoney, Pres. & CEO; Sr. Mary Alice Girrens, C.S.J., Dir. of Mission Svcs.; Rev. Roy V. Eco, Chap.; Ruthanne Vihinen, Chap.; Sally Hussey, Chap.; Joan M. Silva, Chap.; Rev. Edward K. Dondi, Chap. Sisters of St. Joseph of Wichita, KansasSisters of the Sorrowful Mother. Religious 7; Bed Capacity 175; Total Staff 877; Patients Assisted Annually 129,504.

St. Rose Medical Office Bldg., Inc., 27200 Calaroga, 94545. Tel: 510-264-4000; Fax: 510-887-7421.

St. Rose Hospital Foundation Tel: 510-264-4007; Fax: 510-887-7421. Sr. Antoinette Yelek, C.S.J., Exec. Dir.

27200 Calaroga Ave., 94545-4383. Tel: 510-264-4008; Fax: 510-887-7421.

Silva Pediatric Clinic, 680 W. Tennyson Rd., 94544. Tel: 510-782-4470; Fax: 510-782-4756.

Dental Clinic Tel: 510-780-9119; Fax: 510-780-9211.

[L] ORGANIZATIONS FOR DEAF AND HARD OF HEARING

HAYWARD. *St. Joseph's Center for Deaf and Hard of Hearing*, 25580 Campus Drive, 94542. Tel: 510-881-2245 (Voice); 510-881-2247 (TDD); Fax: 510-881-2248. Email: sjcd@sjcd.org. Web: www.sjcd.org. Ardith A. Lynch, Diocesan Dir.

Legal Title: *St. Joseph's Center for the Deaf and Hard of Hearing, A Corporation*

[M] RETIREMENT AND CARE FACILITIES

OAKLAND. *Bishop Begin Villa* (Retired Priests) , 3418 E. 18th St., 94601. Tel: 510-536-0719; Fax: 510-536-3561. Rev. Msgr. Martin E. Walsh (Retired); Revs. Edmund L. Hayburn (Retired); John R. Kenny; Thomas B. Gallagher (Retired); James C. Clift (Retired); Joseph A. Ferreira (Retired). Residents 6; Total Assisted 6.

Mercy Retirement and Care Center (Affiliated with Elder Care Alliance) , 3431 Foothill Blvd., 94601. Tel: 510-534-8540; Fax: 510-261-7551. Sr. Patricia Creedon, Admin. Sponsored by the Sisters of Mercy. Sisters of Mercy 4; Sisters of the Holy Names 2; Employees 160.

Convalescent Hospital - Skilled Nursing Facility Residential Care & Assisted Living. Bed capacity 59.

Retirement Facility for Priests in the Oakland Diocese Extensive community services.

Seton Senior Center, 211 - B Foothill Blvd., 94606. Tel: 510-663-4681; Fax: 510-663-4411. Email: setonsenior@yahoo.com. Web: nicolekim.trirod.com/unsh.html. Sr. Nichole Nguyen, D.C., Exec. Dir. & Contact Person.

[N] MONASTERIES AND RESIDENCES OF PRIESTS AND BROTHERS

OAKLAND. *Dominican Order (Western Province), St. Albert's Priory*, Dominican House of Formation, 5890 Birch Ct., 94618. Tel: 510-596-1800; Fax: 510-596-1860. Web: www.op.org/opwest/sap. Very Rev. Paul Scanlon, O.P., Prior; Revs. Michael Monshau, O.P., Subprior; Christopher J. Renz, O.P., Master of Students; Richard Schenk, O.P., Regent of Studies; Luke D. Buckles, O.P.; Finbarr Hayes, O.P.; Fabian Parmisano, O.P.; Antoninus Wall, O.P.; Janko Zagar, O.P.; Martin Walsh, O.P., Dir. Vocations; Bros. Bernhard Blankenhorn, O.P.; Gary Cappleman, O.P.; Jerome Cudden, O.P.; peter Do, O.P.; Bryan Dolejsi, O.P.; John Evans, O.P.; Zechariah Foreman, O.P.; Louis Garcia, O.P.; Augustine Hilander, O.P.; Harris Ingle, O.P.; Anthony Garcias, O.P.; Michael Hurley, O.P.; Thomas Irish, O.P.; Vincent Kelber, O.P.; Francis-Hung Le, O.P.; Jeremiah Loverich, O.P.; Jesson Mata; John Mellein, O.P.; James Moore, O.P.; Raphael Salzillo, O.P.; Dismas Sayre, O.P.; Thomas Stoffel, O.P.; Alphonsus Von Hazmburg; Paul Woodward, O.P.; Raphael Domingo, O.P.; Peter Rogers, O.P.; James Thompson, O.P.

Dominican Order, Siena House, 5730 Presley Way, 94618. Tel: 510-654-8735; Fax: 510-654-8735. Revs. Anthony Cordeiro, O.P., Supr. Provincial Treas; David K. O'Rourke, O.P.; Leo Tubbs, O.P.; Gregory Rocca, O.P., Pres., Dominican School of Philosophy and Theology; Michael Morris, O.P., Prof., Dominican School of Philosophy and Theology; Terence Reilly, O.P. Priests 6.

Franciscan Friars, St. Elizabeth Friary, 1500 34th Ave., 94601. Tel: 510-536-1287; Fax: 510-536-3578. Email: stefriary@mail.com. Web: www.sbfranciscans.org. Revs. Kenny Scott, O.F.M.; Rigoberto Caloca-Rivas, O.F.M.; Marco Antonio Figueroa, O.F.M., Pastor; Peter Krieg, O.F.M.; Melvin Stanley, O.F.M.; Thomas West, O.F.M.; Bros. Thomas More Ganmy, O.F.M.; Javier Garcia, O.F.M.; lawrence Goodwin, O.F.M.; David Gutierrez, O.F.M.; Tom Herbst, O.F.M.; Marcos Hernandez, O.F.M.; Antonio Herrera, O.F.M.; Tran Nguyen, O.F.M.; Richard O'Lea, O.F.M.; Sungtae Thomas Kim, O.F.M.; Nghia Phan, O.F.M.; Josef Prochnow, O.F.M.; Balbino Rodriguez, O.F.M., Vicar; Cesar Rodriguez, O.F.M.; James Swan, O.F.M.; Ponchie Vasquez, O.F.M., Guardian; Rufino Zaragoza, O.F.M.

Franciscan Friars Provincial Office, Province of St. Barbara, 1500-34th Ave., 94601-3092. Tel: 510-536-3722; Fax: 510-536-3970. Email: ofmcamain@att.net. Web: www.sbfranciscans.org. Very Rev. Melvin A. Jurisich, O.F.M., Prov. Min.; Revs. Thomas West, O.F.M., Prov. Vicar; Charles Talley, O.F.M., Vocation Coord.; Ms. Guadalupe Aceves, Treas.; Bros. Thomas Nichols, O.F.M., Assoc. Treas.; John Summers, O.F.M., Prov. Sec. Priests 3; Total Staff 20.

On Duty Outside the Province: Revs. Kenneth Laverone, O.F.M., Rome, Italy; Christopher Tomatis, O.F.M., Torino, Italy; Michael Weldon, O.F.M. Franklin, WI; Bro. Garrett Galvin, O.F.M., Catholic University of America, Washington DC.

Franciscan Friars, 1508 Arch St., Berkeley, 94708. Tel: 510-845-1124. Revs. John Hardin, O.F.M., Guardian; Joseph P. Chinnici, O.F.M.; Very Rev. Melvin A. Jurisich, O.F.M.; Rev. William M. Cieslak, O.F.M.Cap.; Bros. Raul Alejos, O.F.M.; Lawrence Abraham, C.M.S.F.; Thomas Nichols, O.F.M.; Martin Ibarra, O.F.M.; John Summers, O.F.M.; Rev. Daniel Lackie, O.F.M.; Bros. John Kiesler, O.F.M., Guardian; John Gutierrez, O.F.M.

Murray Residence Community, 171 Santa Rosa Ave., 94610-1316. Tel: 510-655-8334; Fax: 510-655-4816. Revs. John A. Baumann, S.J., Supr.; Thomas C. Weston, S.J.; Michael Proterra, S.J.; Lester E. Love, S.J.; Stephen M. Kelly, S.J.; Hee-Wan Geong.

Oblate Residence (1953), Headquarters of the Oblates of Mary Immaculate, Pacific area Office and Residence , 290 Lenox Ave., 94610. Tel: 510-452-1550; Fax: 510-452-3421. Email: jrarong@juno.com. Web: www.omiusa.org. Rev. Jose Arong, O.M.I., Dir. & Pacific Area Supr.

Legal Title: *Oblate Fathers Western Province Inc.; Western Oblates Support Trust Fund* Total in Residence 6; Total Staff 2. In Res. Revs. Jose Gago, O.M.I.; Michael Holly, O.M.I.; James P. McSorley, O.M.I.; Umberto Nespolo, O.M.I.; Jerry Orsino.

Order of Preachers (Southern Province) De Porres House of Studies. , 2215 Rose St., Berkeley, 94709. Tel: 510-644-8247; Fax: 510-644-8249. Revs. Jude Siciliano, O.P., Supr. & Prof., DSPT. Tel: 510-644-8247; John J. Markey, O.P., Assoc. Dir. Formation.

Redemptorists, 8945 Golf Links Rd., 94605. Tel: 510-562-9740; Fax: 510-562-1406. Email: CSSRRAY@aol.com. Web: www.holyredeemercenter.org. Very Rev. Raymond Maiser, C.SS.R., Supr.; Revs. Sean Murray, C.SS.R.; Gregory Schmitt, C.SS.R.; Richard Ochiltree; Richard Schiblin, C.SS.R.; Anthony Smith, C.SS.R.; Deacon Dennis Lee, C.SS.R.

Legal Title: *Redemptorist Society of California; Redemptorists of Oakland.*

Western Dominican Province, 5877 Birch Ct., 94618-1626. Tel: 510-658-8722; Fax: 510-658-1061. Email: WDOMPROV@aol.com. Web: www.opwest.org. Very Revs. Roberto Corral, O.P., Prior Prov.; Bartholomew Hutcherson, O.P., Vicar Prov. & Socius; Edward Krasevac, O.P., Vicar Prov.; Revs. Martin Walsh, O.P., Dir. Dominican Mission Foundation; Michael Fones, O.P., Promoter Camlpus Min.; Dominic DeDomenico, O.P., Treas.; Paul Duffner, O.P., Promoter Rosary Confraternity; Kenneth R. Gumbert, O.P. (Oakland Prov.), Promoter Media; Thomas Hayes, O.P., Promoter Holy Name Society; Jude Eli, O.P., Dir. Western Dominican Preaching; Patrick LaBelle, O.P., Promoter Permanent Formation;

Francis Goode, O.P., Promoter Social Justice; George M. Matanic, O.P., Promoter Dominican Laity; Christopher J. Renz, O.P., Student Master & Sec. Dominican Family; Anthony Rosevear, O.P., Novice Master; Jordan Bradshaw, O.P., Promoter Parochial Min.; Michael Dodds, O.P., Regent Studies; Michael Sweeney, O.P., Dir. Catherine of Siena Institute; Bro. John Evans, O.P., Dir. Province Web Site; Rev. Mark Padrez, O.P., Dir. Vocations. Province of the Most Holy Name of Jesus Total in the Province 171.

Serving in Latin America: Revs. David Bello, O.P.; Timothy Conlan, O.P.; Thomas Kraft, O.P.

Serving in Kenya: Rev. Kieran J. Healy, O.P.

Serving in Vatican City: Rev. Allen Duston, O.P., Dir., Office of the Patrons of the Arts in the Vatican Museums.

Serving in Rome: Rev. Robert Christian, O.P., Prof. Pontificia Universita San Tommaso.

BERKELEY. *Capuchin Franciscan Order, House of Studies*, 1534 Arch St., 94708. Tel: 510-841-2229; Fax: 510-849-0809. Email: piusofmcap@hotmail.com.

Saint Conrad Friary Tel: 510-841-2229; Fax: 510-849-0809. Revs. Michael O'Shea, O.F.M.Cap.; Alan Wilson, O.F.M.Cap., Vicar; Christopher Kearney; Bros. Mark Mance, O.F.M.Cap., Student Dir.; Pius Higgins, O.F.M.Cap., Guardian & Asst. Student Dir. Friars in Residence 10; Friars in Formation 5; Total Staff 5.

Holy Cross Fathers-Holy Cross Center, 2597 Virginia St., 94709. Tel: 510-548-8515; Fax: 510-548-7903. Revs. Harry Cronin, C.S.C., Dir.; Daniel Issinq, C.S.C.; John Dunne, C.S.C.; Bro. James Newberry, C.S.C.

Jesuit Community at Jesuit School of Theology at Berkeley, 2621 Ridge Rd., 94709. Tel: 510-841-2487; Fax: 510-549-1114. Email: jstbmwistcn@hotmail.com. Web: www.jstbjesuits.org. Revs. David L. Andrus, S.J. (NO); Alvaro Balsas, S.J. (Portugal); Kevin M. Bradt, S.J. (New York); James T. Bretzke, S.J.; Thomas E. Buckley, S.J.; Gregory I. Carlson, S.J. (OM), Rector; Joseph P. Carroll, S.J. (California); Sean O. Carroll, S.J.; Michael T. Castori, S.J. (NY); Mark K. Ciccone, S.J. (California), Asst. Rector & Min.; Stephen J. Corder, S.J.; Donald F. Crosby, S.J. (California); Joseph P. Daoust, S.J. (DET), Pres., JSTB; Virgilio Domingos, S.J. (Mozambique); Sidney O'Souza, S.J. (East Africa); John C. Endres, S.J.; Eduardo C. Fernandez, S.J. (NO); Miguel Garaizabal, S.J. (Thailand); Donald L. Gelpi, S.J.; Timothy S. Godfrey, S.J. (Missouri); George E. Griener, S.J. (New Orleans); Fedelis Jeyabalan, S.J. (Andhra); J. Raymond Johnson, S.J. (NY); Jean-Pierre Karegeye, S.J. (Rowanda); William M. Kegel, S.J.; Michael Tong-uk Ku, S.J. (Korea, South); Peter R. McGrath, S.J. (New England); Jose Lukoli Minaku, S.J. (Central Africa); Perianayagam Moses, S.J.; George R. Murphy, S.J. (New England); William P. O'Brien, S.J. (CHI); Robert J. Ochs, S.J. (Chicago); William R. O'Neill, S.J. (California); Mathew Pampackal, S.J. (Kerala); Joao Carlos Pinto, S.J. (Portugal); Mamy Oden Evariste Rakotondrazanany, S.J. (Madagascar); Thomas Aquino Deshi Ramadhani, S.J. (Indonesia); Emile Ranaivoariso, S.J. (Madagascar); Jean de Dieu Randrianaivo, S.J. (Madagascar); Selva Rathinam, S.J. (India); Rosario Rocha, S.J. (India); James H. Ryan, S.J. (DM); T. Howland Sanks, S.J. (Maryland); Thomas J. Scirghi, S.J.; Peter Kin Chung Siu, S.J. (California); Gaspar Sunhwa, S.J. (Tanzania); Pius Thekemury, S.J. (Patna); John L. Treloar, S.J. (Wisconsin), Dean, JSTB; Michael M. Turnacliff, S.J. (SFR); Joseph F. Wagner, S.J. (CHI); Gregory Waldrop, S.J. (New Orleans); Robert Wawer, S.J. (Poland); Salvador C. Wee, S.J. (Philippines); Bros. David Antonelli; Lawrence J. Huck, S.J.; Dominic T. Shoniwa, S.J. (Zimbabwe). (See also listing for The Jesuit School of Theology at Berkeley) Total in Residence 95; Scholastics 38; Total Staff 2.

Marist Fathers and Brothers, 2335 Warring St., 94704. Tel: 510-486-1232; 510-486-1276; Fax: 510-848-7204. Web: www.maristsociety.org. Revs. Thomas E. Ellerman, S.M., Supr. & Formation Dir.; Bill Rowland, S.M., Dir. for Vocations, Formation Staff.

Legal Title: *Marist Society Inc.*, Seminary Name: St. Peter Chanel Seminary - Marist Pre-novitate Program.

Redemptorists (St. Clemens Maria House), Formerly Maria HouseRedemptorist Asian Pacific Ministry Center, 2215 Rose St., 94709. Tel: 510-981-9005; Fax: 510-981-9004. Email: kunpah@aol.com. Web: www.kmhmu-catholic.org. Revs. James Farrell, C.SS.R.; David Tobin, C.SS.R.; Caryle Blake, C.SS.R.; Donald Mac Kinnon, C.SS.R.; Donald MacKinnon, C.SS.R.

Legal Title: *The Redemptorists of Berkeley*

Salesian Community, Don Bosco Hall, 1831 Arch St., 94709. Tel: 510-204-0800; Fax: 510-843-4335. Email: BoscoHall1@aol.com. Web: www.donboscowest.org. Total in Residence 24; Total Staff 6.

Core Team: Revs. Jerry Bonjean, S.D.B., Vice Dir.; Arthur Lenti, S.D.B., Councilor; Thomas Prendiville, S.D.B., Dir.; Gerald Wertz, S.D.B., Business Mgr.; Sr. Mary Greenan, F.M.A., Prog. Coord.; Bro. John Rasor, S.D.B., Councilor.

Students in Residence: Revs. Hiroki Amemiya, S.D.B. (Japan); Rafael DelaCruz, S.D.B. (Philippines); Max Egli; Stanislaw Jagodzinski, S.D.B. (South Africa); Kei Kato, S.D.B. (Japan); Alexander Kim-Dae-Shik, S.D.B. (Korea, South); Bogdan Kolar, S.D.B.; Luis German Prato-Quintana, S.D.B. (Venezuela); Andrew Lee Seung Koo (Korea South); Jose Vattaparambil, S.D.B. (East Timor); Paul Felix Vernal, S.D.B. (Kenya); Sisters Hyacintha Chang, I.B.V.M.; Celia Aquino Tacujan F.M.A.; Bros. Tho Phuoc Bui, S.D.B.; Chinh Nguyen, S.D.B.; Steve Way, S.D.B.; Steve Way, S.D.B.

Servite Community, Sarpi Priory (United States of America Province) , 2414 Virginia St., 94709-1206. Tel: 510-848-4086; Fax: 510-549-0593. Email: fsteveryan@earthlilnk.net. Total in Residence 4.

Society of the Precious Blood, 2800 Milvia St., 94703-2209. Tel: 510-665-8434; Fax: 510-665-8437. Revs. Gary M. Luiz, C.PP.S., J.C.L., Dir.; James D. Sloan, C.PP.S.

SAN LEANDRO. *Society of the Precious Blood* Province of the Pacific, Provincial Headquarters, Provincial Center. , 2337 W. Ave. 134th, 94577-4132. Tel: 510-357-4982; Fax: 510-357-4036. Email: rpwcpps@juno.com. Web: www.rc.net/oakland/cpps. Very Rev. Ronald P. Wiecek, C.PP.S., Prov. Dir.; Revs. Marvin J. Steffes, C.PP.S.; Gene R. Wilson, C.PP.S. Total in Residence 3; Total Staff 3.

[O] CONVENTS AND RESIDENCES FOR SISTERS

OAKLAND. *Dominican Sisters of Mission San Jose*, St. Elizabeth Convent, 1555-34th Ave., P.O. Box 7465, 94601. Tel: 510-532-8344; Fax: 510-533-2365. Email: johnnie@msjdominicans.org. Web: www.msjdominicans.org. Sisters 17.

Dominican Sisters of Oakford, Bethany House, 919 Aileen St., 94608. Tel: 510-652-0985. Email: bethanyop@earthlink.net. Web: oakford.op.org/. Sisters 2.

Holy Names Sisters, Provincial Administration, P.O. Box 907, Los Gatos, 95031. Tel: 408-395-5150; Fax: 408-354-8305. Email: snjmcaasm@yahoo.com. Web: www.holynames.net. Sisters Reside In Numerous Residences; Holy Names High School, St. Bede, St. Theresa, & San Antonio, and other residences in Oakland, Alameda, Concord, Castro Valley, Livermore, Hayward. Sisters 57.

Holy Names College Sisters' Residence, 3500 Mountain Blvd., 94619. Tel: 510-436-1635. Email: jmhnc@yahoo.com. Sr. Margaret Spiller, S.N.J.M., Prov. Sisters working in the Diocese 58.

St. Lawrence O'Toole Convent, 3693 High St., 94619-2105. Tel: 510-530-2621; Fax: 510-530-4120.

Adrian Dominican Sisters 3; San Rafael Dominican 1.

Presentation Sisters Tel: 415-422-5001; Fax: 415-422-5026. Email: pelower@pbvmsf.org. Web: presentationsistersf.org. *Sisters of the Presentation*, 281 Masonic Ave., San Francisco, 94118.

11 Warren St., No. 7, 94611. Tel: 510-654-6407; Fax: 510-652-7270.

1725 Oxford St., #308, Berkeley, 94709. Tel: 510-548-6217; Fax: 510-644-9619.

1725 Oxford St., #104, Berkeley, 94709. Tel: 510-549-1256; Fax: 510-644-9472.

1055 47th St., #C, Emeryville, 94608. Tel: 510-655-8132; Fax: 510-655-9159.

1515 Lincoln St., Berkeley, 94703. Tel: 510-848-4851; Fax: 510-486-8247.

Sisters of Charity of Cincinnati, 809-42nd St., 94608. Tel: 510-658-7990.

529-41st St., No. 9, 94609. Tel: 510-654-7328.

Sisters of Mercy, Burlingame, Mercy Retirement and Care Center, 3431 Foothill Blvd., 94601. Tel: 510-534-8540. Sisters 4.

Sisters of Sacred Hearts of Jesus and Mary, 2150 Lake Shore Ave., 94606. Tel: 510-832-2935; Fax: 510-839-5256. Email: lornashjm@jps.net. Sisters 6.

Sisters of St. Francis of Penance and Christian Charity, Casa Guadalupe/Novitiate House, 1815-33rd Ave., 94601. Tel: 510-534-4330; Fax: 510-436-5298. Email: Mariamercado@earthlink.net. Sisters Maria Elena Martinez, OS.F., Dir.; Maria Teresa Mercado, O.S.F., Novice Dir. Sisters 3.

House of Hope, 2027 Nina Ct., Hayward, 94541. Tel: 510-537-1026; Fax: 510-655-3520. Novices 1; Professed 2.

Sisters of St. Joseph of Carondelet Tel: 925-674-8884; Fax: 925-682-5491. Email: noreen50@aol.com. Web: www.csjla.org.

Carondelet Community, 1133 Winton Dr., Concord, 94518-3598. Tel: 925-686-9697; Fax: 925-671-9429. Sisters 4.

Bay Area Crisis Nursery, Inc., 1506 Mendocino Dr., Concord, 94521. Tel: 925-685-8052; 925-685-9740; Fax: 925-689-5815.

Concord Residential Club, 2141 California St., Concord, 94520-7800. Tel: 925-689-4939; Fax: 925-825-4423.

Kwanza House Community, 529 Jean St., 94610-1906. Tel: 510-655-2382; Fax: 510-655-0249. Sisters 2.

Christ the King Community, 3095 Diablo View Rd., Pleasant Hill, 94523-4535. Tel: 925-280-1562; Fax: 925-685-1289. Sisters 3.

St. Anthony Community, 1520 E. 15th St., 94606-4422. Tel: 510-532-9455; Fax: 510-451-8920. Sisters 3; Holy Family Sister 1.

Social Service Sisters, 4000 Waterhouse, 94602. Sisters 6.

851 Trestle Glen Rd., 94610.

BERKELEY. *Dominican Sisters of Mission San Jose*, St. Mary Magdalen Community, 2004 Eunice St., 94709-1932. Tel: 510-527-4817; Fax: 510-527-4818. Email: berkeley@msjdominicans.org. Web: www.msjdominicans.org. Sisters 5.

Franciscan Sisters of Little Falls, MN, 1418 A Fifth St., 94710. Tel: 510-526-2321; Fax: 510-526-2321. Email: paulaosf@america.net. Sisters 5.

Sisters of Charity, B.V.M., 1746 Addison St., 94703. Tel: 510-841-8791. Email: helen.thompson@aatbi.com.

Sisters of Notre Dame de Namur, 1717 Oxford St., No. 101, 94709. Tel: 510-845-2113.

1717 Oxford St., No. 202, 94709. Tel: 510-540-6896.

1725 Oxford St., No. 210, 94709. Tel: 510-848-7439.

BRENTWOOD. *Religious Missionary Congregation of the Most Holy Sacrament and Mary Immaculate*, 636 - 3rd St., 94513. Tel: 925-513-8154. Email: cctrap.com.

CONCORD. *Quinhon Missionary Sisters of the Holy Cross*, Provincial House, 1685 Humphrey Dr., 94519-1810. Tel: 925-674-9639; Fax: 925-676-9320. Sr. Rosaline Lieu Nguyen, L.H.C., Prov.

Aspirant House, 50 Santa Maria Way, Orinda, 94563. Tel: 925-253-0831.

Sisters of St. Joseph of the Third Order of St. Francis, 2301 Mt. Diablo St., 94520. Tel: 925-680-7396; 925-825-2091; Fax: 925-825-2439.

EL CERRITO. *Franciscan Sisters of Perpetual Adoration (FSPA)*, 1317 Liberty St., No. 17, 94530. Tel: 510-233-9797.

2629 34th Ave., 94601. Tel: 510-536-1266.

Mercy Sisters, Ireland, St. John the Baptist Convent, 11154 San Pablo Ave., 94530. Tel: 510-233-6769. Sisters 4.

EL SOBRANTE. *Sisters of St. Joseph of the Third Order of St. Francis, S.S.J.-T.O.S.F.*, 5427 Valley View Rd., 94803. Tel: 510-222-0492. Email: phil4389@aol.com. Sisters 5.

FREMONT. *Sisters of the Holy Family Motherhouse*, 159 Washington Blvd., P.O. Box 3248, 94539-0324. Tel: 510-624-4500; Fax: 510-624-4537. Sr. Sharon Flannigan, S.H.F., Congregational Pres.

HAYWARD. *Dominican Sisters of Adrian, MI*, 1128 D St., 94541. Tel: 510-582-2568.

Holy Names Sisters, St. Bede Convent, 26900 Patrick Ave., 94544. Tel: 510-782-6700. Email: jmbede@aol.com. Sisters 5.

Sisters of St. Joseph of Wichita, KS., 1626 Ashbury Ln., 94545. Tel: 510-782-5960. Email: magirrens@strosehospital.org. Web: www.feist.com/~wichitacsj. Sisters 5.

HERCULES. *Congregation of the Mother of Mount Carmel*, 142 Weiss Ct., 94547. Tel: 510-724-4178. Email: weisscarmel@yahoo.com. Sisters 4.

KENSINGTON. *Discalced Carmelite Nuns*, 68 Rincon Rd., 94707. Tel: 510-526-5050. Solemn Professed 5.

LIVERMORE. *Dominican Sisters of San Rafael*, St. Michael Convent, 375 Maple St., 94550. Tel: 925-443-1666; Fax: 925-447-6720. Email: St-Michael@csdo.org. Sisters 3.

MISSION SAN JOSE. *Dominican Sisters of Mission San Jose*, 43326 Mission Blvd., P.O. Box 3908, 94539. Tel: 510-657-2468; Fax: 510-657-1734. Email: evangela@msjdominicans.org. Web: www.msjdominicans.org. Sr. Rose Marie Hennessy, O.P., Prioress Gen. Generalate Motherhouse and Novitiate of the Dominican Sisters of Mission San Jose, Congregation of The Queen of the Holy Rosary. Sisters 111.

Queen of Peace Community Tel: 510-657-2468; Fax: 510-657-1734. Sr. Sylvia Conant, O.P., Supr.

St. Joseph Priory Tel: 510-657-2468; Fax: 510-657-1734. Sr. Mary Jarlath McGrath, O.P., Prioress.

St. Martin Residence, Formerly St. Martin Infirmary Tel: 510-657-2468; Fax: 510-657-1734. Sr. Mary Jarlath McGrath, O.P., Supr.

Siena House Tel: 510-657-2468; Fax: 510-657-1734. Sr. Mary Joseph Lyons, O.P., Supr.

St. Edward Convent, 37088 Arden St., Newark, 94560-3702. Tel: 510-793-9447; Fax: 510-793-3189. Sr. Cecilia Canales, O.P., Supr.

St. Elizabeth Convent, 1555-34th Ave., P.O. Box 7465, 94601-0465. Tel: 510-532-8344; Fax: 510-533-2365. Sr. John Martin Fixa, O.P., Supr.

St. Mary Magdalen Convent, 2004 Eunice St., Berkeley, 94709-1926. Tel: 510-527-4817; Fax: 510-527-4818. Sr. Veronica Lonergan, O.P., Supr.

Our Lady of Guadalupe Convent, 46752 Crawford St., Fremont, 94539-7164. Tel: 510-490-6902. Sr. Kathleen McAvoy, O.P., Supr.

NEWARK. *Dominican Sisters of Mission San Jose*, St. Edward Convent, 37088 Arden St., 94560. Tel: 510-793-9447; Fax: 510-793-3189 (School). Email: cecilia@msjdominicans.org. Sisters 4.

PLEASANT HILL. *Holy Family Sisters*, Holy Family Center, 2059 Pleasant Hill Rd., 94523. Tel: 925-935-6151; Fax: 925-935-1394. Email: holyfamcen@aol.com. Sisters 8; Total in Residence 5.

SAN LEANDRO. *Dominican Sisters of Oakford*, Our Lady of Guadalupe House of Formation, 327 Woodland Park, 94577. Tel: 510-569-9189. Email: sisterdominic@aol.com. Total in Residence 4; Sisters 4.

Marist Missionary Sisters, 1515 Boxwood Ave., 94579. Tel: 510-357-7876; Fax: 510-357-7816. Email: smsmvo@aol.com. Web: www.maristmissionarysmsm.org. Sr. Georgeanne Marie Donovan, S.M.S.M. Sisters 3.

Marist Missionary Sisters-Vocation Ministry Office, 1515 Boxwood Ave., 94579. Tel: 510-357-7876; Fax: 510-357-7876. Email: smsmvoc@aol.com. Web: www.maristmissionarysmsm.org. Sr. Annemarie Woeste, Vocation Ministry.

Sisters of St. Joseph of Wichita, St. Felicitas Convent, 1662 Manor Blvd., 94579. Tel: 510-351-5577; Fax: 510-351-5577. Sisters 2.

SAN LORENZO. *Presentation Sisters, Kildare, Ireland*, St. John the Baptist Convent, 16642 Ashland Ave., 94580. Tel: 510-278-7128; Fax: 510-278-5145. Email: sjcnv@aol.com. Web: www.gnofn.org/~presis. Sisters 7.

[P] PASTORAL CENTERS

OAKLAND. *Holy Redeemer Center*, Formerly Holy Redeemer Center, Redemptorist Retreat Center Spiritual hospitality center. , 8945 Golf Links Rd., P.O. Box 5007, 94605. Tel: 510-635-6341; Fax: 510-562-1406. Email: gregcssr@aol.com. Web: www.holyredeemercenter.org. Rev. Gregory Schmitt, C.SS.R., Dir.

DANVILLE. *San Damiano Retreat* Retreat House for men, women and married couples. , *Franciscan Retreat House*, 710 Highland Dr., P.O. Box 767, 94526. Tel: 925-837-9141; Fax: 925-837-0522. Email: info@sandamiano.org. Web: www.sandamiano.org. Rev. Raymond J. Bucher, O.F.M., Dir. Total in Residence 5; Total Staff 41. In Res. Revs. Barry Brunsman, O.F.M., Retreat Master & Guardian; Sebastian Drake, O.F.M.; Emmanuel Muessiggang, O.F.M.; Bro. Marion Alfonso, O.F.M.

LAFAYETTE. *Diocesan Youth Retreat Center*, 1977 Reliez Valley Rd., 94549. Tel: 925-934-5802; 925-934-5801; Fax: 925-934-0642. Web: www.members.ad.com/~oakdiocythrtr. Total in Residence 2; Total Staff 2.

PLEASANT HILL. *Holy Family Center*, 2059 Pleasant Hill Rd., 94523. Tel: 925-935-6151; Fax: 925-935-1394. Email: holyfamcen@aol.com. Ministries: Personal Growth Programs, Counseling, Spiritual Direction, Adult Faith Formation.

[Q] NEWMAN CENTERS

OAKLAND. *Holy Names College Campus Ministry* 3500 Mountain Blvd., 94619. Tel: 510-436-1081; Fax: 510-436-1199. Email: casey@hnc.edu. Web: www.hnc.edu. Sr. Sharon Casey, O.P., Dir. Campus Min.

MORAGA. *St. Mary's College Campus Ministry* Box 4777, 94575-4777. Tel: 510-631-4366; Fax: 510-631-4332. Web: www.stmarys-ca.edu. Revs. Thomas J. McElligott (SFR); Salvatore Ragusa, S.D.S.; Sr. Ingrid Clemmensen, O.P., Dir. Campus Ministry; Mr. Christopher Fuller; Ms. Pamela Thomas; Ms. Anna Adams.

[R] PERSONAL PRELATURES

BERKELEY. *Opus Dei* Prelature of the Holy Cross and Opus Dei , Garber House, 2710 College Ave., 94705. Tel: 510-548-2819; Fax: 510-644-3898. Email: padlan@mymailstation.com. Rev. Paul A. Donlan.

[S] MISCELLANEOUS LISTINGS

OAKLAND. *Adventus*, 2900 Lakeshore Ave., 94610. Tel: 510-893-4711; Fax: 510-893-0945. Email: pgoodwin@aol.com. Purpose: To support the mission of the Roman Catholic Diocese of Oakland.

The Benilde Religious & Charitable Trust, c/o Plageman, Lund & Miller LLP, 1999 Harrison St., Ste. 2700, 94612. Tel: 510-273-8553; Fax: 510-273-8559. Email: plageman@plmlawfirm.com. Web: www.plmlawfirm.com. Mr. William H. Plageman Jr., Contact Person. Charitable trust fund to benefit the educational activities of the Brothers of the Christian Schools of San Francisco. Lasallian Education Opportunities.

Casa Vincentia Home for single pregnant women, 18-25 yrs. , 3210 62nd Ave., 94605. Tel: 510-729-0316; Fax: 510-729-0319. Barbara Jackson, Exec. Dir. Total in Residence 6; Total Staff 3.

Dominican Community Support Charitable Trust, 5877 Birch Ct., 94618. Fax: 510-658-1061. Anthony J. Cordeiro, O.P., Contact Person. Tel: 510-655-0521; Rev. Dominic DeDomenico, O.P., Contact Person.

Dominican Sisters Vision of Hope, 1555 34th Ave., P.O. Box 7465, 94601. Tel: 510-533-5768; Fax: 510-533-2365. Email: donna@msjdominicans.org. Web: visionofhope.org. Sr. Donna Johnson, O.P., Contact Person.

A Friendly Manor/A Friendly Place, 2298 San Pablo Ave., 94612. Tel: 510-451-8923; Fax: 510-451-8920. Sr. Maureen Lyons, C.S.J. Purpose: Daytime hospitality center for homeless women. Total Assisted 19,500; Total Staff 3.

**The Gamelin-California Association* Apartment building designed for disabled persons and persons with AIDS. , Providence House, 540-23rd St., 94612-1718. Tel: 510-444-0639; Fax: 510-465-5420. Email: phoakland@aol.com. Web: www.providence.org. Timothy Zaricznyj, Dir. Units 40.

Hesed Community, Benedictine Urban Community for Christian Meditation, 3745 Elston Ave., 94602. Tel: 510-482-5573; Fax: 510-482-8769. Email: Hesedone@aol.com. Web: hesedcommunity.org. Sr. Barbara Hazzard, O.S.B., Dir. Total in Residence 1; Total Staff 3.

Italian Catholic Federation, 675 Hegenberger Rd., Ste. 230, 94621. Tel: 510-633-9058; 888-423-1924; Fax: 510-633-9758. Email: info@icf.org. Web: www.icf.org. Rev. Daniel E. Cardelli.

St. Mary's Center, 635 22nd St., 94612. Tel: 510-893-4723; Fax: 510-893-0119. Email: ed@stmaryscenter.org. Web: www.stmaryscenter.org. Sisters Marilyn Medau, P.B.V.M., Dir. Food for all Ages Prog.; Veronica Lonergan, O.P., Co-Dir. Senior Outreach & Advocacy Prog.; Dorothy Green, Co-Dir. Senior Outreach & Advocacy Prog.; Georgia Barnes, Dir. Recovery 55 Prog.; Corinne Lund, Dir. Pre-School Prog.; Sisters Mary Nolan, O.P., Dir. Coaching Elders; Joanna Bramble, C.S.J., Dir. Devel.; Carol Johnson, Exec. Dir. Total Assisted 2,423; Total Staff 35.

Missionaries of the Kingship of Christ A Franciscan Secular Institute for Women, Men, Priests. , 1500-34th Ave., 94601. Tel: 510-536-1266. Rev. Guglielmo Lauriola, O.F.M., Contact Person. Tel: 510-647-2704.

**Oakland Elizabeth House*, 6423 Colby St., 94618. Tel: 510-601-1213; Fax: 510-653-4256. Email: oakehouse@aol.com. Web: oakehouse@oakehouse.org. Courtenay Redis, Dir. Purpose: Transitional housing for low-income women and children.

Pacific Institute for Community Organization, 171 Santa Rosa Ave., 94610. Tel: 510-655-2801; Fax: 510-655-4816. Email: BaumannPICO@aol.com. Web: www.piconetwork.org. Rev. John A. Baumann, S.J., Exec. Dir.; Most Rev. Roy Dixon, Chm.; Ms. Sybil Morial, Vice Chm.

Redemptorist Community Support Charitable Trust, 8945 Golf Links Rd., 94605. Tel: 510-562-9740; Fax: 510-562-1406. Email: pobcssr@aol.com. Web: www.holyredeemercenter.org. Patrick O'Brien, Trustee.

Vietnamese Senior Care Center, 3014 Lakeshore Ave., 94610. Tel: 510-273-4986; Fax: 510-273-4982. Email: nicolekim23@yahoo.com. Web: www.setonsenior.org. Sr. Nicole Nguyen, D.C., Contact Person. Purpose: special outreach to the elder Vietnamese population. Total Staff 4; Total Assisted 200.

BERKELEY. *Academy of American Franciscan History*, 1712 Euclid Ave., 94709. Tel: 510-548-1755; Fax: 510-549-9466. Email: AcadAFH@aol.com. Web: www.aafh.org. Total Staff 1.

Franciscan Charities, Inc., 1712 Euclid Ave., 94709. Tel: 510-849-0234; Fax: 510-849-0234. Email: ofmcafc@aol.com.

Incarnation Monastery, Camaldolese Benedictines, 1369 La Loma Ave., 94708. Tel: 510-845-0601; Fax: 510-548-6439. Email: fr_robert-hale@msn.com. Web: www.contemplation.com. Rev. Andrew Colnaghi, Prior. Total in Residence 3. In Res. Revs. Robert Hale, O.S.B.Cam.; Arthur Poulin, O.S.B.Cam.

Inter-Friendship House Association, Friendship Center, 1646 Addison St., 94703. Tel: 510-843-7675; Fax: 510-843-7675. Email: ifha_ucb@cal.berkeley.edu. Web: www.ifha-usa.org. Rev. Bernard M.C. Chu, S.J. (China), Dir. Total Staff 1.

Multicultural Institute, 1712 Euclid Ave., 94709. Tel: 510-848-4075; Fax: 510-848-4095. Email: rcaloca@pacbell.net. Web: www.multiculturalinstitute.org. Board of Directors: Cass Candell, Pres. Tel: 510-848-2900; Beatriz Leyva-Cutler, Vice Pres. Tel: 510-528-0264; Eugene McCabe, Treas. Tel: 925-254-8373; Revs. James Lockman, O.F.M.; Kenan B. Osborne, O.F.M. Tel: 510-848-5232; Rigoberto Caloca Rivas, O.F.M.; Philip J. Murphy, B.A. Tel: 415-457-7482; Abby M. Rincon, M.P.H. Tel: 510-643-9089; Thomas F. Rogan. Tel: 510-649-8021. Administrative Staff: Revs. Rigoberto Caloca-Rivas, O.F.M., Ph.D., Exec. Dir.; Martin Ibarra, O.F.M., Life Skills Prog. Asst.; Amalia Barrera, M.F.P., Familias Unidas Prog. Dir.; Tony Lacayo, Life Skills Prog. Asst.; Claudia Luna, MAS Prog. Co-ord.; Teresita Mejia, Accountant; Mary Moran, MAS Prog. Coord.; Mary Moran, Summer School Prog. Coord.; Noe B. Moran, Life Skills Prog. Dir.; Tran Nguyen, Summer School Prog. Coord. (Vietnamese Component); Teresa Perez-Martinez, Admin. Asst.; Julie Preza, MAS Prog. Coord.; Julie Preza, Summer School Prog. Coord.

CONCORD. *Carondelet High School Foundation*, 1133 Winton Dr., 94518. Tel: 925-686-5353; Fax: 925-686-4901. Email: SKL@carondelet.pvt.K12.ca.us. Web: www.carondelet.pvt.k12.ca.us. Sr. Kathleen Lang, C.S.J., Pres.

East Bay Services to the Developmentally Disabled, 1485 Enea Cir., Ste. 1470, 94520. Tel: 925-825-2091; Fax: 925-825-2439. Nonresidence Serves 1,800; Residence 65; Total Staff 70.

EL CERRITO. *Catholic Ladies' Aid Society, Grand Chaplain*, 11150 San Pablo Ave., 94530. Tel: 510-232-5659; Fax: 510-236-0960. Elizabeth Oishi.

EMERYVILLE. *LaSallian Educational Opportunities, Inc.*, 3815 Telegraph Ave., 94609. Tel: 510-450-0555; Fax: 510-450-0554. Email: cbassen@stmarys-ca.edu. Bro. Christopher Bassen, F.S.C., Prog. Dir. Total Assisted 210; Total Staff 7.

FREMONT. *Pia Backes Support Trust*, Dominican Sisters of Mission San Jose, 43326 Mission Blvd., P.O. Box 3908, 94539-0391. Tel: 510-657-2468; Fax: 510-683-0712. Email: jarcher@msjdominicans.org. Sr. Ellen Mary Cunningham, Pres.

MISSION SAN JOSE. *Dominican Sisters of Mission San Jose Foundation (A Non-Profit Corp.)*, Mailing Address: P.O. Box 3908, 94539. Tel: 510-657-2468; Fax: 510-657-1734. Email: dsmsjdev@infolane.com. Web: www.msjdominicans.org/. Sisters Charlotte Shea, O.P., Exec. Vice Pres.; Charlotte Shea, O.P., Pres.; Dan Caputo, Sec. & Treas.

SAN LEANDRO. *Venerable Merlini Foundation*, 2337 W. Ave. 134th, 94577-4132. Tel: 510-357-4982. James Franck, Pres.; Joseph L. Brown, Treas.

RELIGIOUS INSTITUTES OF MEN REPRESENTED IN THE DIOCESE

For further details refer to the corresponding bracketed number in the Religious Institutes of Men or Women section.

[0140]—*The Augustinians*—O.S.A.
[0170]—*Basilian Fathers*—C.S.B.
[0330]—*Brothers of the Christian Schools* (Prov. of San Francisco)—F.S.C.
[0600]—*Brothers of the Congregation of Holy Cross* (Southwest Prov.)—C.S.C.
[0200]—*Camaldolese Benedictines*—O.S.B.Cam.
[0470]—*The Capuchin Friars*—O.F.M.Cap.
[0480]—*Conventual Franciscans*—O.F.M.Conv
[0260]—*Discalced Carmelite Friars*—O.C.D.
[1140]—*Fathers of the Sacred Hearts*—SS.CC.
[0520]—*Franciscan Friars* (Santa Barbara Prov.)—O.F.M.
[0530]—*Franciscan Friars of the Atonement*—S.A.
[0690]—*Jesuit Fathers and Brothers*—S.J.
[0770]—*The Marist Brothers*—F.M.S.
[0910]—*Oblates of Mary Immaculate* (Western Prov.)—O.M.I.
[0920]—*Oblates of St. Francis De Sales*—O.S.F.S.
[0430]—*Order of Preachers-Dominicans* (Prov. of Holy Name of Jesus)—O.P.
[1030]—*Paulist Fathers*—C.S.P.
[0610]—*Priests of the Congregation of Holy Cross*—C.S.C.
[1070]—*Redemptorist Fathers* (Oakland Prov.)—C.SS.R.
[1190]—*Salesians of Don Bosco* (Turin, Italy)—S.D.B.
[1240]—*Servites* (Western Prov.)—O.S.M.

[0760]—*Society of Mary*—S.M.
[0420]—*Society of the Divine Word* (Techny, IL)—S.V.D.
[1060]—*Society of the Precious Blood* (Prov. of the Pacific)—C.PP.S.

RELIGIOUS INSTITUTES OF WOMEN REPRESENTED IN THE DIOCESE

[0340]—*Carmelite Sisters of Charity*—C.ach.
[1780]—*Congregation of the Sisters of the Third Order of St. Francis of Perpetual Adoration* (Spokane, WA)—F.S.P.A.
[0420]—*Discalced Carmelite Nuns*—O.C.D.
[1070-03]—*Dominican Sisters*—O.P.
[1070-04]—*Dominican Sisters*—O.P.
[1070-13]—*Dominican Sisters*—O.P.
[1070-30]—*Dominican Sisters*—O.P.
[1070-12]—*Dominican Sisters*—O.P.
[1310]—*Franciscan Sisters of Little Falls, Minnesota*
[2420]—*Marist Missionary Sisters*
[2470]—*Maryknoll Sisters of St. Dominic*—M.M.
[]—*Quinhon Sisters of the Holy Cross*
[]—*Sisters for Christian Community*—S.F.C.C.
[0430]—*Sisters of Charity of the Blessed Virgin Mary* (Mt. Carmel, Dubuque, IA)—B.V.M.
[2360]—*Sisters of Loretto at the Foot of the Cross* (Nerink, KY)—S.L.
[2516]—*Sisters of Mercy*—S.M.
[2570]—*Sisters of Mercy* (Burlingame, CA)—S.M.
[3000]—*Sisters of Notre Dame de Namur* (Prov. of California)—S.N.D.deN.
[3350]—*Sisters of Providence* (Sacred Heart Prov.)—S.P.
[4080]—*Sisters of Social Service of Los Angeles, Inc.*—S.S.S.
[1630]—*Sisters of St. Francis of Penance and Christian Charity*—O.S.F.
[1650]—*Sisters of St. Francis of Philadelphia*—O.S.F.
[3840]—*Sisters of St. Joseph of Carondelet* (Los Angeles Prov.)—C.S.J.
[3830-03]—*Sisters of St. Joseph of Orange*—C.S.J.
[3930]—*Sisters of St. Joseph of the Third Order of St. Francis* (Prov. of Our Lady of Czestochowa)—S.S.J.-T.O
[3830-18]—*Sisters of St. Joseph of Wichita*—C.S.J.
[]—*Sisters of the Congregation of the Mother of Mount Carmel*
[1960]—*Sisters of the Holy Family*—S.H.F.
[1990]—*Sisters of the Holy Names of Jesus and Mary* (Prov. of Calif.)—S.N.J.M.
[3320]—*Sisters of the Presentation of the B.V.M.* (San Francisco, CA)—P.B.V.M.
[3680]—*Sisters of the Sacred Heart of Jesus and Mary*—S.H.J.M.
[2150]—*Sisters, Servants of the Immaculate Heart of Mary*—I.H.M.
[3330]—*Union of the Sisters of the Presentation of the Blessed Virgin Mary*—P.B.V.M.

NECROLOGY

† Charankat, Peter, Walnut Creek, CA St. Mary—Died July 24, 2003
† Cloutier, Edmund, (Retired)—Died April 9, 2003
† Garcia, John, Ripon, CA St. Patrick—Died April 5, 2003
† Mallon, John J., Walnut Creek, CA St. Mary—Died Aug. 6, 2003
† Mathews, Robert, Alameda, CA St. Barnabas—Died May 21, 2003

Diocese of Ogdensburg

(Dioecesis Ogdensburgensis)

Most Reverend

ROBERT JOSEPH CUNNINGHAM

Bishop of Ogdensburg; ordained May 24, 1969; appointed Bishop of Ogdensburg March 9, 2004; installed May 18, 2004. *P.O. Box 369, Ogdensburg, NY 13669.*

Chancery Office: P.O. Box 369, Ogdensburg, NY 13669. Tel: 315-393-2920; Fax: 315-394-7401.

Email: chancery@dioogdensburg.org

Square Miles 12,036.

Erected by His Holiness Pius IX, February 16, 1872.

Incorporated by a special act of the Legislature of the State of New York, April 10, 1945, with the title: The Roman Catholic Diocese of Ogdensburg, New York.

Comprises that part of Herkimer and Hamilton Counties north of the northern line of the townships of Ohio and Russia as existing in 1872 with the entire Counties of Lewis, Jefferson, St. Lawrence, Franklin, Clinton and Essex in the State of New York.

For legal titles of parishes and diocesan institutions, consult the Chancery Office.

STATISTICAL OVERVIEW

Personnel	
Priests: Diocesan Active in Diocese	92
Priests: Diocesan Active Outside Diocese	8
Priests: Retired, Sick or Absent	50
Number of Diocesan Priests	150
Religious Priests in Diocese	8
Total Priests in Diocese	158
Extern Priests in Diocese	3
Ordinations:	
Diocesan Priests	2
Permanent Deacons	12
Permanent Deacons in Diocese	67
Total Brothers	12
Total Sisters	157
Parishes	
Parishes	119
With Resident Pastor:	
Resident Diocesan Priests	71
Resident Religious Priests	4
Without Resident Pastor:	
Administered by Priests	43
Administered by Religious Women	1

Missions	19
Pastoral Centers	20
Closed Parishes	1
Professional Ministry Personnel:	
Brothers	2
Sisters	18
Lay Ministers	554
Welfare	
Homes for the Aged	3
Total Assisted	300
Special Centers for Social Services	6
Total Assisted	10,500
Educational	
Diocesan Students in Other Seminaries	6
Total Seminarians	6
High Schools, Diocesan and Parish	2
Total Students	768
Elementary Schools, Diocesan and Parish	21
Total Students	2,747
Catechesis/Religious Education:	
High School Students	2,453

Elementary Students	8,187
Total Students under Catholic Instruction	14,161
Teachers in the Diocese:	
Priests	1
Sisters	21
Lay Teachers	244
Vital Statistics	
Receptions into the Church:	
Infant Baptism Totals	1,156
Adult Baptism Totals	390
Received into Full Communion	145
First Communions	1,565
Confirmations	1,448
Marriages:	
Catholic	417
Interfaith	186
Total Marriages	603
Deaths	1,839
Total Catholic Population	128,326
Total Population	423,000

Former Bishops—Rt. Revs. EDGAR P. WADHAMS, D.D., consecrated May 5, 1872; died Dec. 5, 1891; HENRY GABRIELS, D.D., consecrated May 5, 1892; died April 23, 1921; Most Revs. JOSEPH H. CONROY, D.D., LL.D., consecrated May 1, 1912; succeeded to the See, Nov. 21, 1921; died March 20, 1939; FRANCIS J. MONAGHAN, S.T.D., LL.D., consecrated June 29, 1936; succeeded to the See, March 20, 1939; died Nov. 13, 1942; BRYAN J. MCENTEGART, D.D., LL.D. (Retired), consecrated Aug. 3, 1943; transferred to Titular See of Aradi, Aug. 19, 1953; appt. June 26, 1953; to Rectorship of Catholic University of America, Washington, D.C.,; appt. Bishop of Brooklyn, April 16, 1957; installed June 13, 1957; appt. Archbishop, April 15, 1966; retired and appt. Titular Archbishop of Gabii, July 17, 1968; died Sept. 30, 1968; WALTER P. KELLENBERG, D.D., consecrated Oct. 5, 1953; appt. to Ogdensburg, Jan. 19, 1954; transferred to See of Rockville Centre, April 16, 1957; installed May 27, 1957; died Jan. 11, 1986; JAMES J. NAVAGH, D.D., consecrated Sept. 24, 1952; appt. to Ogdensburg, May 8, 1957; transferred to Paterson, Feb. 12, 1963; died in Rome, Oct. 2, 1965; LEO R. SMITH, D.D., appt. Auxiliary Bishop of Buffalo, July 9, 1952; consecrated Sept. 24, 1952; appt. Bishop of Ogdensburg, Feb. 12, 1963; died in Rome Oct. 9, 1963; THOMAS A. DONNELLAN, D.D., appt. March 4, 1964; consecrated April 9, 1964; appt. to Atlanta, May 29, 1968; transferred to Archdiocese of Atlanta, July 16, 1968; died in Atlanta, Oct. 15, 1987; STANISLAUS J. BRZANA, S.T.D., LL.D (Retired), ord. June 7, 1941; appt. Titular Bishop of Cufruta and Auxiliary of Buffalo, May 24, 1964; consecrated June 29, 1964; transferred to Ogdensburg, Oct. 22, 1968; retired Nov. 11, 1993; died March 1, 1997; PAUL S. LOVERDE, D.D., S.T.L., J.C.L., ord. Dec. 18, 1965; appt. Titular Bishop of Ottabia and Auxiliary Bishop of Hartford, Feb. 3, 1988; consecrated April 12, 1988; transferred to Ogdensburg, Nov. 11, 1993; installed Jan. 17, 1994; appt. Bishop of Arlington, Jan. 25, 1999; installed March 25, 1999; GERALD M. BARBARITO, D.D., J.C.L., ordained Jan. 31, 1976; appointed Titular Bishop of Gisipa and Auxiliary Bishop of Brooklyn June 28, 1994; consecrated Aug. 22, 1994; transferred to Ogdensburg Oct. 26, 1999; installed Jan. 7, 2000; appointed Bishop of Palm Beach July 1, 2003; installed Aug. 28, 2003.

Diocesan Offices

Unless otherwise noted, all mail for the following offices to go to: *Spratt Memorial Bldg., 604 Washington St., P.O. Box 369, Ogdensburg, 13669.* Office Hours: Mon.-Fri. 8:15-4:30 (Sept.-June); Summer Hours: 8:45-4

Office of the Bishop—VACANT.

Secretary to the Bishop—Rev. DOUGLAS J. LUCIA, J.C.L.

Bishop's Office Secretary—Mrs. KATHY K. TAYLOR. Fax: 315-393-2150.

Fiscal Officer—Mr. MICHAEL J. TOOLEY. Fax: 315-393-5911.

Parish Administrative Services Coordinator—Mr. VINCE THOUIN.

Employee Benefits—Ms. DEBRA L. MOUSAW.

Insurance Claims and Risk Management Department—Mr. HARRY A. GRANGER, Mgr. Tel: 315-393-0441; Fax: 315-393-1490.

Unless otherwise noted, all mail for the following offices to go to: *Bishop Stanislaus J. Brzana Diocesan Pastoral Center, 622 Washington St., P.O. Box 369, Ogdensburg, 13669.* Office Hours: Mon.-Fri. 8:15-4:30 (Sept.-June); Summer Hours: 8:45-4

Diocesan Administrator—Rev. Msgr. ROBERT L. LAWLER, P.A., St. Mary's Rectory, P.O. Box 187, Waddington, 13694. Tel: 315-388-4466; Fax: 315-388-4722.

Moderator of the Curia—Rev. Msgr. JOHN R. MURPHY, S.T.L., M.A.

Chancellor—Rev. TERRY R. LAVALLEY, J.C.L.

Vice Chancellors—Revs. DOUGLAS J. LUCIA, J.C.L.; CHRISTOPHER J. FUSCO, J.C.L.

Diocesan Director of Christian Formation—Rev. Msgr. ROBERT H. AUCOIN, S.T.L., M.Ed., Wadhams Hall Seminary-College, 6866 State Hwy. 37, Ogdensburg, 13669. Tel: 315-393-4231; Fax: 315-393-4249. Email: aucoin@wadhams.edu.

Matrimonial Tribunal and Office of Canonical Affairs—

Judicial Vicar and Vicar for Canonical Affairs—Rev. Msgr. HARRY K. SNOW, M.A., J.C.L., V.F.

Office Manager—Sr. MARY PATRICK MURPHY, S.S.J., M.S.

Adjutant Judicial Vicars—Revs. PHILIP T. ALLEN; TERRY R. LAVALLEY, J.C.L.; DOUGLAS J. LUCIA, J.C.L.

Auditor—Rev. CHRISTOPHER J. FUSCO, J.C.L.

Promoter of Justice—Rev. Msgr. PETER R. RIANI, S.T.D., M.Ed., V.F.

Defenders of the Bond—Revs. LAWRENCE E. COTTER, S.T.L., B.S., M.S. (Retired); RAYMOND J. MOREAU; JOSEPH MORGAN; ALAN D. SHNOB; JOHN R. YONKOVIG.

Judges—Rev. Msgrs. BERNARD E. CHRISTMAN; ANTHONY A. MILIA; FRANCIS A. WHITE (Retired); Revs. ROBERT L. COTTER (Retired); DANIEL T. KEEFE, V.F.; CLYDE A. LEWIS; GILBERT B. MENARD (Retired).

Notary—Mrs. DIANNA L. SHAVER.

Advocates—Sr. MARY PATRICK MURPHY, S.S.J., M.S.; Rev. Msgrs. DENNIS J. DUPREY, V.F.; JOHN R. MURPHY, S.T.L., M.A.; Revs. DOUGLAS A. DECKER; GARVIN J. DEMARAIS; GARRY B. GIROUX, J.C.L.; ALBERT J. HAUSER; ALAN J. LAMICA; WILLIAM G. REAMER.

Bishop's Delegates for Religious—Rev. Msgr. DENNIS J. DUPREY, V.F.; Sr. JOAN MARIE CASEY, R.S.M., Notre Dame Church, P.O. Box 547, Malone, 12953. Tel: 518-483-4074; Fax: 518-483-4185.

Development Office—Mrs. JANICE SHOEN, Dir.,

Bishop's Fund Appeal; Planned Giving; Bishop's Heritage Circle.
Stewardship Office—VACANT.
Evangelization—Sr. MARY ELLEN BRETT, S.S.J., Dir.
Formation for Ministry—Sr. JUDITH BAUMERT, S.S.J., Dir.
Mission Aid Societies—Rev. GEORGE F. MAROUN, Dir.; Sr. MARY ELLEN BRETT, S.S.J., Assoc. Dir. Fax: 315-393-0981 Society for The Propagation of the Faith; Holy Childhood Association; Society of St. Peter the Apostle; Missionary Union of Clergy and Religious; Ogdensburg Peruvian Apostolate.
Office of Planning—Sr. JENNIFER VOTRAW, S.S.J., Dir.
Director of Priest Personnel and Director of Seminaries—Rev. JOSEPH A. MORGAN, Dir. Seminarians.
Department of Worship—Rev. ALBERT J. HAUSER, Dir.
Unless otherwise noted, all mail for the following offices to go to: *Bishop Paul S. Loverde Center for Education and Formation, 100 Elizabeth St., P.O. Box 369, Ogdensburg, 13669*. Fax: 315-393-8977. Office Hours: Mon.-Fri. 8:15-4:30 (Sept.-June); Summer Hours: 8:45-4
Diocesan Director of Christian Formation—Rev. Msgr. ROBERT H. AUCOIN, S.T.L., M.Ed. Tel: 315-393-4231; Fax: 315-393-4249.
Department of Christian Formation—
Ogdensburg Regional Center—Mrs. HEIDI MACKO, Dir.
Plattsburgh Regional Center—Sr. ELIZABETH MENARD, O.P., Dir., 114A Cornelia St., Plattsburgh, 12901. Tel: 518-563-2022; Fax: 518-563-2138.
Watertown Regional Center—Mr. MICHAEL WAGNER, Dir., 866 Arsenal St., Watertown, 13601. Tel: 315-782-3620; Fax: 315-782-2009.
Youth Ministry—Sr. ROSEMARY CASALENO, S.S.J., Pius X Center, 32 River St., Saranac Lake, 12983. Tel: 518-891-7576.
Catholic Scouting—Sr. MARY RITA KEMPNEY, S.S.J., Diocesan Liaison, St. Mary's Convent, P.O. Box 12, Copenhagen, 13626-0012. Tel: 315-688-2683.
Department of Education—Sr. KATHLEEN MURPHY, O.S.F., Supt.; Mrs. DOROTHY HOBBS, Asst. Supt.; Sr. MARY EAMON LYNG, S.S.J., Asst. Supt. of Faith Formation.
Family Life Department and Pre-Cana—Directors: Deacon GARY FRANK; Mrs. GAYLE FRANK.

Consultative Bodies

Deans—Revs. J. MICHAEL GAFFNEY, V.F., Adirondack; DANIEL T. KEEFE, V.F., Clinton; Rev. Msgrs. PETER R. RIANI, S.T.D., M.Ed., V.F., Essex; DENNIS J. DUPREY, V.F., Franklin; Revs. SCOTT D. FOBARE, V.F., Hamilton-Herkimer; ARTHUR J. LABAFF, V.F., Jefferson; TIMOTHY J. SOUCY, V.F., Lewis; Rev. Msgr. HARRY K. SNOW, M.A., J.C.L., V.F., St. Lawrence.
Diocesan Consultors—Rev. Msgrs. ROBERT L. LAWLER, P.A.; WILLIAM J. ARGY (Retired); PAUL WHITMORE; Revs. PIERRE AUBIN, M.S.C.; ARTHUR J. LABAFF, V.F.; DONALD J. MANFRED; STEVEN M. MURRAY; KEVIN J. O'BRIEN; F. JAMES SHURTLEFF; TERRY R. LAVALLEY, J.C.L., Sec.
Council of Religious—Sisters CONSTANCE SYLVER, S.S.J., Pres.; CAROLYN MADDEN, R.S.M., Vice Pres.; BARBARA ST. ANDREWS, Sec.; MARY PATRICK MURPHY, S.S.J., M.S., Treas.
Priest Personnel Board—Rev. Msgrs. ROBERT L. LAWLER, P.A.; JOHN R. MURPHY, S.T.L., M.A.; Revs. TERRY R. LAVALLEY, J.C.L.; JOSEPH A. MORGAN; MARK R. REILLY; KEVIN J. O'BRIEN; DANIEL T. KEEFE, V.F.; F. JAMES SHURTLEFF; TIMOTHY J. SOUCY, V.F.

Other Diocesan Offices and Directors

Diocesan Archivist—Rev. LAWRENCE E. COTTER, S.T.L., B.S., M.S. (Retired), P.O. Box 369, Ogdensburg, 13669.
Apostleship of Prayer—Rev. ALBERT J. HAUSER, Dir., P.O. Box 369, Ogdensburg, 13669.
Building Commission—Rev. TERRY R. LAVALLEY, J.C.L., P.O. Box 369, Ogdensburg, 13669.
Campus Ministry—Revs. J. ROGER MCGUINNESS, Dir., John XXIII College Community, 90 Broad St., Plattsburgh, 12901. Tel: 518-561-7545; Fax: 518-561-1004; TIMOTHY G. CANAAN; THOMAS E. KORNMEYER; ROBERT L. DECKER; GARRY B. GIROUX, J.C.L.; Deacon PHILIP GIARDINO; RITA MAWN; Sisters JULIANA RAYMOND, S.S.J.; CONSTANCE SYLVER, S.S.J.
Catholic Charities—Sr. DONNA FRANKLIN, D.C., Diocesan Dir., Wadhams Hall, 6866 State Hwy. 37, Ogdensburg, 13669. Tel: 315-393-2255; Fax: 315-393-2402. Ogdensburg Office: MARY DALTON, Dir., P.O. Box 56, Ogdensburg, 13669. Tel: 315-393-2660; Fax: 315-393-9362. Watertown Office: KATHLEEN MATTIS, Dir., 812 State St., Watertown, 13601. Tel: 315-788-4330; Fax: 315-786-0539. Plattsburgh Office: KAREN MISCAVAGE, Dir., 4914 S. Catherine St., Plattsburgh, 12901. Tel: 315-561-0470; Fax: 315-561-0472. Malone Office: CLAIRE POIRIER, Dir., 42 Fort Covington St., Malone, 12953. Tel: 518-483-1460; Fax: 518-483-1478. Lowville Office: VACANT, 7514 S. State St., Lowville, 13367. Tel: 315-376-4141; Fax: 315-376-4141. Port Henry Office: PATRICIA MCCAUGHIN, Project Dir., 14 Park Pl., Port Henry, 12974. Tel: 518-546-3565. Tupper Lake Office - Foster Grandparent Program: VIVIAN SMITH, 114 Wawbeck Ave., Tupper Lake, 12986 Tel: 518-359-7688; Fax: 518-359-3927.
RSVP of Clinton County—SANDRA SEXTON, 46 Flynn Ave., Plattsburgh, 12901. Tel: 518-566-0944; Fax: 518-566-0945.
Seaway House—CAROL WHITCOMBE, Dir., 212 Caroline St., Ogdensburg, 13669. Tel: 315-393-3133.
Catholic Relief Services—Sr. DONNA FRANKLIN, D.C., P.O. Box 296, Ogdensburg, 13669. Tel: 315-393-2255. Fax: 315-393-2402.
Cemeteries—Rev. CHRISTOPHER J. FUSCO, J.C.L., P.O. Box 369, Ogdensburg, 13669. Tel: 315-393-2920; Fax: 315-394-7401.
Censor Librorum—Rev. LAWRENCE E. COTTER, S.T.L., B.S., M.S. (Retired), P.O. Box 369, Ogdensburg, 13669.
Charismatic Renewal—Rev. FRANCIS J. CORYER, Liaison, Church of the Assumption, 78 Clinton St., Redford, 13630. Tel: 518-293-6259.
Department of Communications—Sr. JENNIFER VOTRAW, S.S.J., Dir., P.O. Box 369, Ogdensburg, 13669. Tel: 315-393-2920; Fax: 315-394-7401.
Bureau of Information—Rev. TERRY R. LAVALLEY, J.C.L., P.O. Box 369, Ogdensburg, 13669. Tel: 315-393-2920; Fax: 315-394-7401.
Newspaper—Mrs. MARY LOU KILIAN, Editor; Mr. SCOTT A. WILSON, Circulation & Advertising, P.O. Box 326, Ogdensburg, 13669. Tel: 315-393-2540. "The North Country Catholic"
Bureau of Media—Mrs. LINDA J. KELLEY, 1900 State Hwy. 11B, Potsdam, 13617. Tel: 315-265-0261; Fax: 315-268-7104.
Committee for the Continuing Education of Clergy—Rev. J. ROGER MCGUINNESS, Chm., 90 Broad St., Plattsburgh, 12901. Tel: 518-561-7545; Fax: 518-561-1004.
Ecumenical Commission—Mr. THOMAS SCHNEEBERGER, Chm., St. Francis Christian Formation Center, P.O. Box 38, Croghan, 13327-0038. Tel: 315-346-6963; Fax: 315-346-1200.
Legion of Mary—VACANT.
Natural Family Planning Services—Mr. ANGELO PIETROPAOLI; Mrs. SUZANNE PIETROPAOLI, 36 First St., Malone, 12953.
Permanent Diaconate Program—
Director of Deacon Formation and Director of Ordained Deacons—Rev. Msgr. ROBERT H. AUCOIN, S.T.L., M.Ed., Wadhams Hall, 6866 State Hwy. 37, Ogdensburg, 13669.
Priests' Eucharistic League—Rev. ALBERT J. HAUSER, Dir., P.O. Box 369, Ogdensburg, 13669. Tel: 315-393-2920; Fax: 315-394-7401.
Pro-Life Office—Rev. THOMAS E. KORNMEYER, Dir., St. Bernard's Church, 19 St. Bernard St., Saranac Lake, 12983.
Director of Seminarians—Rev. JOSEPH A. MORGAN, P.O. Box 369, Ogdensburg, 13669. Tel: 315-393-2920; Fax: 315-394-7401.
St. Vincent de Paul Society—VACANT.
Vocations—Rev. DOUGLAS J. LUCIA, J.C.L., Dir., P.O. Box 369, Ogdensburg, 13669. Tel: 315-393-2920; Fax: 315-394-7401. Associate Vocations Directors: Rev. CHRISTOPHER CARRARA; Sr. EILEEN SPANIER, G.N.S.H.; Rev. JOSEPH W. GIROUX; Sr. ROSEMARY CASALENO, S.S.J.; Rev. CHRISTOPHER J. LOOBY; Sr. ELIZABETH MENARD, O.P.
Young Adult Ministry—Rev. HARRY E. GIROUX, Dir., St. Joseph's Church, P.O. Box 224, West Chazy, 12992. Tel: 518-493-4521; Fax: 518-493-5880.

CLERGY, PARISHES, MISSIONS AND PAROCHIAL SCHOOLS

CITY OF OGDENSBURG
(ST. LAWRENCE COUNTY)

1—ST. MARY'S CATHEDRAL (1748), [CEM] Rev. Terry R. LaValley, J.C.L., Rector; Rev. Msgr. William J. Argy (Retired); Rev. Scott R. Seymour; Sr. Mary Theresa La Brake, G.N.S.H., Pastoral Assoc.; Deacons Richard E. Winter, Emeritus; Francis F. Bateman.
Res.: 415 Hamilton St., 13669. Tel: 315-393-3930; Fax: 315-393-6680.
Catechesis/Religious Program—Tel: 315-393-1820; Fax: 315-393-1670. Mrs. Martha Valley, D.R.E. Students 222.

2—NOTRE DAME (1859), (French), [CEM] Rev. F. James Shurtleff; Deacons Victor Demers, Deacon Emeritus; Thomas Kilian; Mark A. LaLonde; Elizabeth J. Bernhard, Pastoral Assoc. In Res., Rev. Joseph A. Morgan; Rev. Msgrs. George M. Phillips (Retired); John R. Murphy.
Res.: 125 Ford Ave., P.O. Box 149, 13669. Tel: 315-393-5050; Fax: 315-393-5962.
School—St. Marguerite D'Youville Academy, (Grades PreK-6), 315 Gates St., 13699. Tel: 315-393-0165; Fax: 315-394-0499. Mr. Daniel Hazen, Prin. Lay Teachers 12; Students 123.
Catechesis/Religious Program—Bishop Conroy Christian Formation Program, 214 Morris St., 13669. Tel: 315-393-1820. Students 117.

OUTSIDE CITY OF OGDENSBURG

ADAMS, JEFFERSON CO., ST. CECILIA (1870), [CEM] Rev. Douglas Decker.
Res.: 19 Grove St., 13605. Tel: 315-232-2392.
Catechesis/Religious Program—Students 230.

ALEXANDRIA BAY, JEFFERSON CO., ST. CYRIL OF ALEXANDRIA (1000 Islands) (1885), [CEM] Rev. Msgr. Robert H. Aucoin, S.T.L., M.Ed.; Deacon Bernard E. Slate.
Res.: Box 477, 13607. Tel: 315-482-2670; Fax: 315-482-4970.
Catechesis/Religious Program—Students 159.

ALTONA, CLINTON CO., HOLY ANGELS (1865), (Irish—French Canadian), [CEM] Rev. Gilbert O. Boisvert.
Res.: P.O. Box 113, 12910. Tel: 518-236-5848; Fax: 518-236-4249.
Oratory—Jericho, St. Alexis
Catechesis/Religious Program—Tel: 518-594-3916. Mary Ellen Tomo, D.R.E. Students 171.

AU SABLE FORKS, CLINTON CO., HOLY NAME (1848), [CEM] Rev. Philip T. Allen; Deacon John J. Ryan.
Res.: 10 Church St., P.O. Box 719, 12912. Tel: 518-647-8225; Fax: 518-647-5394.
School—(Grades PreK-6), 5 Pleasant St., 12912. Tel: 518-647-8444. Mrs. Jean Louis, Prin. Sisters 1; Lay Teachers 8; Students 87.
Catechesis/Religious Program—Students 45.

BLACK BROOK, CLINTON CO., ST. MATTHEW (1848), [CEM] Rev. Philip T. Allen; Deacon John J. Ryan.
Res.: 10 Church St., P.O. Box 719, Au Sable Forks, 12912. Tel: 518-647-8225; Fax: 518-647-5394.
Catechesis/Religious Program—Students 7.

BLACK RIVER, JEFFERSON CO., ST. PAUL (1901), Rev. Andrew R. Mulvaney; Deacon William S. Raven.
Res.: 208 LeRay St., 13612. Tel: 315-773-5672.
Church: 210 LeRay St., 13612.
Catechesis/Religious Program—Students 91.

BLOOMINGDALE, ESSEX CO., ST. PAUL (1897), [CEM 2] Revs. Thomas E. Kornmeyer; Kevin D. McEwan.
Res.: 50 Saranac Ave., P.O. Box 356, 12913. Tel: 518-891-0144; Fax: 518-891-5259.
Mission—Assumption of the B.V.M. Rte. 86, Gabriels, Franklin Co. 12939.
Catechesis/Religious Program—Tel: 518-891-3111. Kathy Gonyea, D.R.E., (Grades 1-12). Students 105.

BOMBAY, FRANKLIN CO., ST. JOSEPH (1912), [CEM] Revs. Kris C. Lauzon; Stephen Rocker.
Res.: 393 Church St., P.O. Box 427, Hogansburg, 13655. Tel: 518-358-2557; Fax: 518-358-2500.
Office: P.O. Box 499, Fort Covington, 12937.
Catechesis/Religious Program—Tel: 518-358-2500. Students 36.

BRASHER FALLS, ST. LAWRENCE CO., ST. PATRICK (1830), (Irish—French), [CEM] Rev. Stephen H. Gratto; Deacon Francis Horan.
Res.: P.O. Box 208, 13613. Tel: 315-389-5401; Fax: 315-389-4066.
Parish Center—Tel: 315-389-5191. Email: parish@twcny.rr.com. Web: www.stpatrick-stlawrence.org.
Catechesis/Religious Program—Helen Brown, D.R.E. Students 165.

BROWNVILLE, JEFFERSON CO., IMMACULATE CONCEPTION OF THE B.V.M. (1874), (Irish—Italian), Revs. John P. Kennehan; Kevin J. O'Brien; Deacon David F. Moltz.
Res.: 119 W. Main St., P.O. Box 99, 13615. Tel: 315-782-1143; Fax: 315-782-7616.
Catechesis/Religious Program—Tel: 315-788-7240. Sr. M. Kateri Rose, S.S.J., D.R.E. Students 194.
Mission—St. Elizabeth Seton P.O. Box 99, Dexter, Jefferson Co. 13615. Tel: 315-639-3888.

BRUSHTON, FRANKLIN CO., ST. MARY'S CHURCH (1870), [CEM] Rev. Howard J. Vennette.
Res.: P.O. Box 249, 12916. Tel: 518-529-7433.
Catechesis/Religious Program—Tel: 518-529-6580. Marion Roscoe, D.R.E. Students 245.

BURKE, FRANKLIN CO., ST. GEORGE (1874), [CEM] Rev. John M. Demo.
Res.: 797 Depot St., P.O. Box 105, 12917. Tel: 518-483-5687; Fax: 518-483-5687.

CADYVILLE, CLINTON CO., ST. JAMES CHURCH (1854),

[CEM] Rev. Msgr. Lawrence M. Deno.
Res.: P.O. Box 117, 12918-0117. Tel: 518-293-7026; Fax: 518-293-8246.
Catechesis/Religious Program—Students 75.

CANTON, ST. LAWRENCE CO.
1—ST. MARY (1868), [CEM] Revs. Timothy G. Canaan; Douglas J. Lucia, J.C.L., Admin.
Res.: 66 Court St., P.O. Box 308, 13617. Tel: 315-386-2543; Fax: 315-386-2543.
School—(Grades PreK-6), 2 Powers St., 13617. Tel: 315-386-3572. Ms. Susan Proulx, Prin. Lay Teachers 10; Students 123.
Catechesis/Religious Program—Ms. Jamie Burns, D.R.E. Students 196.
2—ST. THOMAS MORE (1959),, (Campus Parish) Revs. Timothy G. Canaan; Douglas J. Lucia, J.C.L., Admin.
Res.: 39 Court St., P.O. Box 424, 13617. Tel: 315-386-8425; Fax: 315-386-1200.
Catechesis/Religious Program—St. Mary's. Students 19.

CAPE VINCENT, JEFFERSON CO., ST. VINCENT OF PAUL, Formerly St. Vincent De Paul (1832), [CEM 2] Rev. Pierre Aubin, M.S.C.; Deacon Robert V. Ruddy.
Res.: Box 288, 13618. Tel: 315-654-2662; Fax: 315-654-4721.
Catechesis/Religious Program—Students 60.

CARTHAGE, JEFFERSON CO., ST. JAMES MINOR (1818), [CEM 2] [JC] Rev. George F. Maroun; Sr. Mary Rita Kempney, S.S.J., Pastoral Assoc.; Deacons James J. Gillen; Richard J. Staab, Pastoral Assoc.
Res.: 327 West St., 13619. Tel: 315-493-3224; Fax: 315-493-3280.
School—Augustinian Academy, (Grades PreK-8), 317 West St., 13619. Tel: 315-493-1301; Fax: 315-493-0632. Sr. John Mary Brockway, S.S.J., Prin. Sisters of St. Joseph 1; Lay Teachers 11; Students 170.
Catechesis/Religious Program—Students 181.
Convent—Tel: 315-493-1672.

CHAMPLAIN, CLINTON CO., ST. MARY (1861), [CEM 2] Rev. James W. Seymour; Deacon Leonard Patrie.
Res.: 86 Church St., P.O. Box 368, 12919. Tel: 518-298-8244; Fax: 518-298-2879.
School—(Grades PreK-6) Tel: 518-298-3372; Fax: 518-298-3886. Sr. Marie Cordata Kelly, S.S.J., Prin. Sisters of St. Joseph 1; Lay Teachers 8; Students 107.
Catechesis/Religious Program—Students 137.

CHASM FALLS, FRANKLIN CO., ST. HELEN (1881), [CEM] Rev. Msgr. Dennis J. Duprey, V.F.; Revs. Shane M. Lynch; David C. Gearwar; Sr. Sheila Jane Moran, S.S.J., Admin.
Res. & Church Office: 306 W. Main St., Malone, 12953. Tel: 518-483-1300; Fax: 518-483-1307.
Catechesis/Religious Program—Students 62.
Mission—St. Mary Lake Titus, Franklin Co. 12953.
Mission—St. Joseph Owl's Head, Franklin Co. 12953.

CHATEAUGAY, FRANKLIN CO., ST. PATRICK (1848), [CEM] Rev. John M. Demo; Sr. Mary Hallahan, O.S.U., Pastoral Assoc.
Res.: 132 W. Main St., P.O. Box 908, 12920. Tel: 518-497-6673; Fax: 518-497-6165.
Catechesis/Religious Program—Tel: 518-497-6165. Students 180.
Oratory—St. Jude Brainardsville, Franklin Co. 12920.

CHAUMONT, JEFFERSON CO., ALL SAINTS (1922), Rev. Pierre Aubin, M.S.C.; Deacon Robert V. Ruddy.
Res.: P.O. Box 288, Cape Vincent, 13618. Tel: 315-654-2662; Fax: 315-654-4721.
Catechesis/Religious Program—139 N. Kanady St., Cape Vincent, 13618. Students 26.

CHAZY, CLINTON CO., SACRED HEART (1898), [CEM 2] Rev. L. William Gordon; Deacon Robert J. LeClair.
Res.: P.O. Box 459, 12921. Tel: 518-846-7650; Fax: 518-846-7655.
Catechesis/Religious Program—Tel: 518-846-7180. Students 209.

CHURUBUSCO, CLINTON CO., IMMACULATE HEART OF MARY (1880), [CEM 2] Rev. Howard McCasland, Admin.
Res.: Rte. 189, 12923. Tel: 518-497-9956.
Catechesis/Religious Program—*St. Edmund's Center*, Ellenburg. Tel: 518-594-3907. Students 49.

CLAYTON, JEFFERSON CO., ST. MARY OF CLAYTON (1838), [CEM 2] Rev. Christopher Carrara; Deacon Gary A. Frank.
Res.: 521 James St., 13624. Tel: 315-686-3398 (Rectory); 315-686-2638 (Rel. Education Office); Fax: 315-686-2639.
Catechesis/Religious Program—Tel: 315-686-2638. Students 102.

COLTON, ST. LAWRENCE CO., ST. PATRICK (1864), [CEM] [JC] Revs. Raymond J. Moreau; Lawrence E. Cotter, S.T.L., B.S., M.S., Pastor Emeritus (Retired).
Res.: P.O. Box 315, 13625. Tel: 315-262-2871; Fax: 315-262-2188.
Church: 4897A SH56, 13625.
Catechesis/Religious Program—Students 55.
Mission—St. Paul South Colton, St. Lawrence Co. 13687.
Mission—St. Michael Parishville, St. Lawrence Co. 13625. Tel: 315-268-1733.

CONSTABLE, FRANKLIN CO., THE CATHOLIC COMMUNITY OF CONSTABLE, WESTVILLE AND TROUT RIVER (1872), [CEM] Rev. Francis J. Flynn; Deacon Garry N. Burnell.
Res.: 1197 State Rte. 122, P.O. Box 78, 12926. Tel: 518-483-2775 (Rectory); 518-483-0486 (Parish Office); Fax: 518-483-1618.
Catechesis/Religious Program—Students 68.
Mission— 4326 State Rte. 37, Westville, Franklin Co. 12926.

CONSTABLEVILLE, LEWIS CO., ST. MARY (1820), [CEM] [JC 2] Rev. Lawrence E. Marullo.
Res.: 3070 N. Main St., P.O. Box 382, 13325. Tel: 315-397-2556.
Catechesis/Religious Program—Students 60.

COOPERSVILLE, CLINTON CO., ST. JOSEPH (1790), [CEM] Revs. Clyde A. Lewis; Normand C. Cote, Pastor Emeritus.
Res.: P.O. Box 217, Rouses Point, 12979. Tel: 518-297-7361; Fax: 518-297-3181.
Catechesis/Religious Program—Tel: 518-846-7180. Students 25.

COPENHAGEN, LEWIS CO., ST. MARY (1901), (Irish—French), [CEM 2] Rev. George F. Maroun; Sr. Mary Rita Kempney, S.S.J., Pastoral Assoc.; Deacons Richard J. Staab; James Gillen.
Res.: 9790 NYS Rte. 12, P.O. Box 12, 13626-0012. Tel: 315-688-2683.
Catechesis/Religious Program—Students 32.

CROGHAN, LEWIS CO., ST. STEPHEN (1869), [CEM] [JC 3] Rev. Leo A. Wiley.
Res.: 9748 State Rte. 812, P.O. Box 38, 13327-0038. Tel: 315-346-6958; Fax: 315-346-1200.
Catechesis/Religious Program—Tel: 315-346-6963. Mr. Thomas Schneeberger, D.R.E. Students 207.
Oratory—Belfort, St. Vincent de Paul
Oratory—New Bremen, St. Peter [CEM 3]

CROWN POINT, ESSEX CO., SACRED HEART CHURCH (1874), [CEM] Rev. William G. Muench; Sr. Carol Daul, S.A., Pastoral Assoc.; Deacon Elliott A. Shaw.
Mailing Address: c/o 22 Father Jogues Pl., Ticonderoga, 12883.
Church: 12928. Tel: 518-597-3924.
Catechesis/Religious Program—Students 45.

DANNEMORA, CLINTON CO., ST. JOSEPH (1853), [CEM 2] Rev. John J. Looby; Deacon Edward Mazuchowski. In Res., Rev. Guy Edwards.
Res.: 179 Smith St., Box 418, 12929-0418. Tel: 518-492-7118; Fax: 518-492-7742.
Catechesis/Religious Program—Tel: 518-492-2524. Lynn Lynch, D.R.E. Students 146.

DE KALB JUNCTION, ST. LAWRENCE CO., ST. HENRY (1893), [CEM] Rev. John M. Hunt.
Res.: 3 Josephine St., 13630. Tel: 315-347-3540; Fax: 315-347-4925.
Catechesis/Religious Program—Students 20.
Mission—St. Rene Goupil 24 Pestle St., Russell, St. Lawrence Co. 13684.

DEFERIET, JEFFERSON CO., ST. RITA (1900), Rev. Andrew R. Mulvaney.
Mailing Address: 31 Riverside Dr., 13628.
Res.: 208 Leray St., Black River, 13612. Tel: 315-773-5673; Fax: 315-773-5673.
Catechesis/Religious Program—Students 25.

EDWARDS, ST. LAWRENCE CO., SACRED HEART (1894), Rev. John M. Hunt; Deacon Peter J. Lawless.
Res.: 3 Josephine St., De Kalb Junction, 13630. Tel: 315-347-3540; Fax: 315-347-4925.
Catechesis/Religious Program—Students 25.

ELIZABETHTOWN, ESSEX CO., ST. ELIZABETH (1881), [CEM] Rev. Msgr. Peter R. Riani, S.T.D., M.Ed., V.F.
Res.: P.O. Box 368, 12932. Tel: 518-873-6760; Fax: 518-873-6530.
Catechesis/Religious Program—Students 45.

ELLENBURG, CLINTON CO., ST. EDMUND (1869), [JC 2] Rev. Joseph P. Wheelock; Deacon John A. Levison.
Res. & Church: 5526 Rte. 11, P.O. Box 119, 12933. Tel: 518-594-8843 (Rectory); 518-594-3907 (Office); Fax: 518-594-3222.
Catechesis/Religious Program—Tel: 518-594-7645; Fax: 518-594-3222. Mona LaBombard, D.R.E. Students 342.

ESSEX, ESSEX CO., ST. JOSEPH, [CEM] [JC] Rev. James A. Delbel.
Res.: P.O. Box 607, Willsboro, 12996. Tel: 518-963-4524; Fax: 518-963-7719.

EVANS MILLS, JEFFERSON CO., ST. MARY (1847), [CEM] Rev. Bernard Jakubco, M.S.C.
Res.: 8408 S. Main St., 13637. Tel: 315-629-4425.
Catechesis/Religious Program—Students 66.
Oratory—St. Michael (1849), [CEM] Antwerp, Jefferson Co. Tel: 315-659-8372. Rev. Bernard Jakubco, M.S.C. Antwerp, NY
Mission—St. Joseph Philadelphia, Jefferson Co.
Mission—St. Theresa of Avila Theresa, Jefferson Co. Tel: 315-628-4512.

FORT COVINGTON, FRANKLIN CO., ST. MARY (1837), [CEM 2] Revs. Kris C. Lauzon; Stephen Rocker.
Res.: P.O. Box 427, Hogansburg, 13655. Tel: 518-358-2557; Fax: 518-358-2500.
Office: P.O. Box 499, 12937.
Catechesis/Religious Program—Tel: 518-358-2500. Students 76.

GLENFIELD, LEWIS CO., ST. MARY (1919), [CEM] Revs. Timothy J. Soucy, V.F.; Joseph W. Giroux. In Res., Rev. Robert L. Cotter (Retired).
Res.: 5457 Shady Ave., Lowville, 13367. Tel: 315-376-6662; Fax: 315-376-6663.
Catechesis/Religious Program—Tel: 315-376-7570. Students 41.
Mission—St. Thomas (1876), [CEM] Greig, Lewis Co.

GOUVERNEUR, ST. LAWRENCE CO., ST. JAMES (1875), [CEM 2] Rev. Daniel L. Chapin.
Res.: 164 E. Main St., 13642. Tel: 315-287-0114; Fax: 315-287-0606.
School—(Grades PreK-6), S. Gordon St., 13642. Tel: 315-287-0130. Sr. Ronald Marie Hax, S.S.J., Prin. Sisters 1; Lay Teachers 11; Students 100.
Catechesis/Religious Program—Elizabeth Bradford, D.R.E. Students 71.

HAMMOND, ST. LAWRENCE CO., ST. PETER (1905), (French—Irish), Rev. Albert J. Hauser.
Res.: P.O. Box 216, Morristown, 13664. Tel: 315-375-6571; Fax: 315-375-4832.
Catechesis/Religious Program—Students 50.
Mission—St. Patrick [CEM] P.O. Box 218, Rossie, St. Lawrence Co. 13646.

HARRISVILLE, LEWIS CO., ST. FRANCIS SOLANUS (1879), (French—Irish), [CEM] Rev. Robert L. Decker, Admin.; Deacon Ken Seymour.
Res.: P.O. Box 208, 13648. Tel: 315-543-2421; Fax: 315-543-2421.
Catechesis/Religious Program—Students 45.
Oratory—St. Rita Lake Bonaparte.
Oratory—St. Henry Natural Bridge, Jefferson Co. 13665. Tel: 315-543-2431.

HEUVELTON, ST. LAWRENCE CO., ST. RAPHAEL'S (1880), Rev. Christopher J. Fusco, J.C.L.; Deacon Richard L. Van Kirk.
Res.: 5 Clinton St., P.O. Box 377, 13654. Tel: 315-344-2383.
Catechesis/Religious Program—Students 98.

HOGANSBURG, FRANKLIN CO., ST. PATRICK (1834), (Irish), [CEM] [JC] Revs. Kris C. Lauzon; Stephen Rocker.
Res.: 393 Church St., P.O. Box 427, 13655. Tel: 518-358-2557; Fax: 518-358-2500.
Office: P.O.Box 499, Fort Covington, 12937.

HOPKINTON, ST. LAWRENCE CO., CHURCH OF THE HOLY CROSS (1877), [CEM] Rev. Alfred H. Fish.
Res.: P.O. Box 288, St. Regis Falls, 12980. Tel: 518-856-9456.

HOUSEVILLE, LEWIS CO., ST. HEDWIG (1922), (Polish), Revs. Timothy J. Soucy, V.F.; Joseph W. Giroux.
St. Peter's Church: 5457 Shady Ave., Lowville, 13367-1615. Tel: 315-376-6662; Fax: 315-376-6663.
Catechesis/Religious Program—Students 4.

INDIAN LAKE, HAMILTON CO., ST. MARY'S (1958), [CEM] Rev. Rolland A. Hart.
Res.: Rte. No. 28, P.O. Box 332, 12842. Tel: 518-648-5422; Fax: 518-648-0323.
Catechesis/Religious Program—Students 42.
Mission—St. Paul P.O. Box 332, Blue Mountain Lake, Hamilton Co. 12842.

INLET, HAMILTON CO., ST. ANTHONY OF PADUA (1929), Rev. Scott D. Fobare, V.F.; Deacon Ronald Ste.-Marie.
Mailing Address: P.O. Box 236, Old Forge, 13420. Tel: 315-357-2811; Fax: 315-369-2049.
Catechesis/Religious Program—Students 10.

KEENE, ESSEX CO., ST. BRENDAN (1868), Rev. Patrick W. Mundy.
Res.: P.O. Box 130, 12942-0130. Tel: 518-576-4434; Fax: 518-576-9318.
Mission—St. Margaret Wilmington, Essex Co.

KEESEVILLE, CLINTON AND ESSEX COS.
1—CHURCH OF THE IMMACULATE CONCEPTION (1835), (Irish—French), [CEM] Rev. Msgr. Leeward J. Poissant.
Res.: 1804 Main St., 12944-3745. Tel: 518-834-7100; Fax: 518-834-4612.
Catechesis/Religious Program— Twinned with St. John the Baptist, Keeseville.
Oratory—St. Catherine of Sienna Clintonville. (Closed)
2—ST. JOHN THE BAPTIST (1853), (French—Irish), [CEM] Rev. Msgr. Leeward J. Poissant.
Res.: 1804 Main St., 12944-3745. Tel: 518-834-7100; Fax: 518-834-4612.
Catechesis/Religious Program—1806 Main St., 12944-3745. Tel: 518-834-6002. Students 140.

LAFARGEVILLE, JEFFERSON CO., ST. JOHN THE EVANGELIST (1898), [CEM] Rev. Christopher Carrara.
Res.: 521 James St., Clayton, 13624. Tel: 315-686-3398; Fax: 315-686-2700.

Church: 35923 Rte.180, P.O. Box 157, 13656.
Catechesis/Religious Program—25923 Rte. 180. Students 23.

LAKE CLEAR, FRANKLIN CO., ST. JOHN IN THE WILDERNESS (1887), [CEM] [JC] Revs. Kevin McEwan; Thomas E. Kormeyer; Sr. Constance Marie Sylver, S.S.J., Pastoral Assoc.
Mailing Address: P.O. Box 260, 12945. Tel: 518-891-2286.
Res.: 19 St. Bernard's St., Saranac Lake, 12983. Tel: 518-891-4616; Fax: 518-891-4619.
Catechesis/Religious Program—Pius X Inter-Parish Religious Education Center, 32 River St., Saranac Lake, 12983. Tel: 518-891-3111. Students 23.
Mission—St. Gabriel Pickett Hall #105, Paul Smiths, Franklin Co. 12970. Tel: 518-327-6225.
Summer Station—Fish Creek, State Campsite. Tel: 518-891-3239.

LAKE PLACID, ESSEX, CO., ST. AGNES (1896), [CEM] Rev. J. Michael Gaffney, V.F.; Deacon Bruce Carley Wadsworth.
Res.: 6 Hillcrest Ave., 12946. Tel: 518-523-2200; Fax: 518-523-2203.
School—(Grades PreK-6), 4 Hillcrest Ave., 12946. Tel: 518-523-3771. Kathy Miner, Prin. Lay Teachers 8; Students 105.
Catechesis/Religious Program—Tel: 518-523-3202. Mrs. Mary Lawrence, D.R.E. Students 115.

LAKE PLEASANT, HAMILTON CO., ST. JAMES MAJOR (1924), Rev. Paul J. Kelly.
Res.: P.O. Box 214, Speculator, 12164. Tel: 518-548-6275.
Catechesis/Religious Program—Students 12.

LISBON, ST. LAWRENCE CO., SS. PHILIP AND JAMES (1872), Rev. Christopher J. Fusco, J.C.L.; Sr. Joan Marie Casey, R.S.M., Pastoral Delegate; Elaine Craig, Lay Min.; David Sandburg, Lay Min.
Mailing Address: P.O. Box 175, 13658. Tel: 315-393-3796.
Catechesis/Religious Program—Students 13.

LONG LAKE, HAMILTON CO., ST. HENRY (1899), [JC] Rev. Peter M. Berg.
Mailing Address: P.O. Box 455, 12847. Tel: 518-624-2541; Fax: 518-582-5483.
Res.: 18 Adams Ln., Newcomb, 12852. Tel: 518-582-3671; Fax: 518-582-5483.
Catechesis/Religious Program—Students 16.

LOUISVILLE, ST. LAWRENCE CO., ST. LAWRENCE (1930), [CEM] Revs. Donald J. Manfred; Sean Murray.
Res.: 30 Willard Rd., Massena, 13662. Tel: 315-769-3120; Fax: 315-705-0070.
Catechesis/Religious Program—Tel: 315-764-0488. Students 75.

LOWVILLE, LEWIS CO., ST. PETER (1870), Revs. Timothy J. Soucy, V.F.; Joseph W. Giroux; Deacon Ronald J. Pominville.
Res.: 5457 Shady Ave., 13367. Tel: 315-376-6662; Fax: 315-376-6663.
School—(Grades K-6), 5445 Shady Ave., 13367. Tel: 315-376-2424; Fax: 315-376-2568. Lay Teachers 8.
Catechesis/Religious Program—Tel: 315-376-7570. Students 180.

LYON MOUNTAIN, CLINTON CO., ST. BERNARD (1875), [CEM] [JC] Rev. Msgr. Bernard E. Christman; Deacons Francis Siskavich; Reginald Merrill, (Retired).
Res.: 10 Church Pond Rd., P.O. Box 23, 12952. Tel: 518-735-4357.
Catechesis/Religious Program—Students 71.
Mission—St. Michael [CEM 2] Standish, Clinton Co.

MADRID, ST. LAWRENCE CO., ST. JOHN THE BAPTIST (1869), [CEM] Rev. Msgr. Robert L. Lawler, P.A. In Res., Rev. Lawrence E. Cotter, S.T.L., B.S., M.S. (Retired).
Res.: 34 Oak St., Waddington, 13694. Tel: 315-388-4466.
Church: 3715 County Rte. 14, P.O. Box 68, 13660. Tel: 315-322-5661.
Catechesis/Religious Program—Tel: 315-322-5661. Students 50.

MALONE, FRANKLIN CO.

1—ST. JOHN BOSCO (1935), [CEM] Rev. Msgr. Dennis J. Duprey, V.F.; Revs. Thomas A. Moody; Shane M. Lynch; David C. Gearwar.
Res.: 57 Rennie St., 12953. Tel: 518-483-3642; Fax: 518-483-2595.
Office: 306 W. Main St., 12953.
Catechesis/Religious Program—Students 170.

2—ST. JOSEPH'S (1849), (Irish), [CEM 2] Rev. Msgrs. C. John McAvoy; Dennis J. Duprey, V.F.; Revs. David C. Gearwar; Shane M. Lynch.
Office & Res.: 306 W. Main St., P.O. Box 547, 12953. Tel: 518-483-1300; Fax: 518-483-1307.
Catechesis/Religious Program—Mrs. Tamra Murphy, D.R.E. Students 193.

3—NOTRE DAME (1868), (French-Canadian), [CEM] Rev. Msgr. Dennis J. Duprey, V.F.; Revs. Shane M. Lynch; David C. Gearwar; Sr. Maureen Welch, O.S.U., Pastoral Assoc.
Res.: 11 Church Pl., P.O. Box 547, 12953. Tel: 518-483-1300; Fax: 518-483-1307.
Office: 306 W Main St., 12953.
School—Holy Family, (Grades PreK-8) Tel: 518-483-4443; Fax: 518-481-6762. Anne Marie Wiseman, Prin. (Multi-Parish) Sisters 1; Lay Teachers 16; Students 205.
Catechesis/Religious Program—Mrs. Tamra Murphy, D.R.E. (Grades K-10). Students 230.

MASSENA, ST. LAWRENCE CO.

1—ST. JOSEPH (1947), [JC] Rev. John L. Downs.
Res.: 72 Malby Ave., 13662. Tel: 315-769-3972 (Rectory); 315-769-9076 (Office/Religious Ed.); Fax: 315-764-5409.
Catechesis/Religious Program—Students 127.

2—ST. MARY (1913), [JC] Rev. Alan D. Snnob; Sr. Maureen Sweeney, S.S.J., Pastoral Assoc. In Res., Rev. Richard Demers.
Res.: 105 Cornell Ave., P.O. Box 609, 13662. Tel: 315-764-0239; Fax: 315-769-5526.
School—Trinity Catholic School, (Grades PreK-6), 188 Main St., 13662. Tel: 315-769-5911; Fax: 315-769-6973. Sr. Bernadette Marie Collins, S.S.J., Prin. Sisters of Saint Joseph and Servants of Mary 4; Lay Teachers 14; Students 277.
Catechesis/Religious Program—Anne Borsellino, D.R.E., (Grades K-6); Sr. Maureen Sweeney, S.S.J., D.R.E., (Grades 7-12). Students 189.

3—SACRED HEART (1874), [CEM] Revs. Donald J. Manfred; Sean Murray; Sr. Juliana Fitzpatrick, O.S.M., Pastoral Assoc.; Deacon James J. Hotte.
Res.: 212 Main St., P.O. Box 329, 13662. Tel: 315-769-2469; Fax: 315-769-6973.
Catechesis/Religious Program—Students 341.

MINEVILLE, ESSEX CO., THE CHURCH OF ALL SAINTS (1872), [CEM] Rev. Msgr. C. John McAvoy, Admin.
Mailing Address: P.O. Box C, 12956. Tel: 518-942-5953.
Res.: 17 St. Patrick's Pl., Port Henry, 12974. Tel: 518-546-7254; Fax: 518-546-3439.
Catechesis/Religious Program—Tel: 518-942-3326. Students 83.

MOOERS FORKS, CLINTON CO., ST. ANN (1860), (French-Canadian), [CEM] Rev. Gerald A. Cerank; Deacons Tyrone A. Rabideau; Dennis Monty.
Res.: 3062 Rte. 11, P.O. Box 89, 12959. Tel: 518-236-5632; Fax: 518-236-4446.
Catechesis/Religious Program—Tel: 518-236-4436. Students 129.

MOOERS, CLINTON CO., ST. JOSEPH (1910), (French-Canadian), [CEM] Rev. Gerald A. Cerank.
Mailing Address: P.O. Box 89, Mooers Forks, 12959. Tel: 518-236-5632; Fax: 518-236-4446. In Res., Rev. Cyril W. Rapin (Retired). Tel: 518-236-7142.
P.O. Box 226, 12958.
Catechesis/Religious Program—Tel: 518-236-4436. Students 104.

MORRISONVILLE, CLINTON CO., ST. ALEXANDER (1897), [CEM] Rev. Joseph W. Elliott; Mrs. Pamela J. Ballantine, Pastoral Assoc.
Res.: Church St., P.O. Box 159, 12962. Tel: 518-561-5039; Fax: 518-561-5040.
Catechesis/Religious Program—Tel: 518-563-7855. Students 119.

MORRISTOWN, ST. LAWRENCE CO., ST. JOHN THE EVANGELIST (1941), Rev. Albert J. Hauser.
Res.: P.O. Box 216, 13664. Tel: 315-375-6571; Fax: 315-375-4832.
Catechesis/Religious Program—Students 90.
Oratory—Our Lady of Grace Brier Hill, St. Lawrence Co. 13664.

NEWCOMB, ESSEX CO., ST. THERESE (1950), [CEM] Rev. Peter M. Berg.
Res.: 18 Adams Ln., 12852. Tel: 518-582-3671; Fax: 518-582-5483.
Catechesis/Religious Program—Students 8.

NORFOLK, ST. LAWRENCE CO., VISITATION OF THE B.V.M. (1880), [CEM] Rev. Andrew J. Amyot. In Res., Rev. Msgr. Thomas J. Robillard (Retired); Deacon Lawrence A. Connelly.
Res.: 11 Hepburn St., P.O. Box 505, 13667. Tel: 315-384-3847; Fax: 315-384-3575.
Church: 3 Morris St., P.O. Box 639, 13667.
Catechesis/Religious Program—Tel: 315-384-4242. Students 67.

NORTH BANGOR, FRANKLIN CO., ST. AUGUSTINE (1887), [CEM] Rev. Thomas A. Moody, Admin.
Res.: 2472 S.R. 11, P.O. Box 327, 12966. Tel: 518-483-6674; Fax: 518-481-6351.
Catechesis/Religious Program—Mary Cartier, D.R.E. Students 88.
Mission—St. Edward, Franklin Co. 12966.

NORTH LAWRENCE, ST. LAWRENCE CO., ST. LAWRENCE (1875), (Irish—French), [CEM] Rev. Stephen H. Gratto; Deacon Francis Horan.
Res.: P.O. Box 208, Brasher Falls, 13613. Tel: 315-389-5401; Fax: 315-389-4066. Email: parish@twcny.rr.com. Web: www.stpatrick-stlawrence.org.
Catechesis/Religious Program— Clustered with St. Patrick, Brasher Falls. Students 126.

NORWOOD, ST. LAWRENCE CO., ST. ANDREW (1876), [CEM] Rev. Msgr. Harry K. Snow, M.A., J.C.L., V.F., Admin.; Rev. Paul F. Worczak.
Res.: 2 Park Ave., 13668. Tel: 315-353-7303; Fax: 315-353-4650.
Catechesis/Religious Program—Students 130.

OLD FORGE, HERKIMER CO., ST. BARTHOLOMEW (1897), Rev. Scott D. Fobare, V.F.
Res.: P.O. Box 236, 13420. Tel: 315-369-3554; Fax: 315-369-2049.
Catechesis/Religious Program—Students 21.

OLMSTEDVILLE, ESSEX CO., ST. JOSEPH (1871), [CEM 2] Rev. Richard S. Sturtz.
Mailing Address: Box 368, Schroon Lake, 12870. Tel: 518-251-2565; 518-532-7100; Fax: 518-532-7461.
Rectory—639 Church Rd., P.O. Box 1, 12857.
Catechesis/Religious Program—Students 19.

PERU, CLINTON CO., ST. AUGUSTINE (1883), Rev. Vicente F. Jazmines; Deacon George Grady Benson.
Res.: 3035 Main St., P.O. Box 569, 12972. Tel: 518-643-2435; Fax: 518-643-0960.
School—Tel: 518-643-9505. Sr. Mary Helen Herman, S.S.J., Prin. Sisters 2; Lay Teachers 7; Students 180.
Catechesis/Religious Program—Tel: 518-643-0089; Fax: 518-643-2435. Students 370.
Oratory—St. Patrick [CEM 2] West Peru, Clinton Co. 12972.

PLATTSBURGH, CLINTON CO.

1—ST. JOHN THE BAPTIST (1837), (Irish), [CEM 3] Revs. Normand C. Cote; Kris C. Lauzon.
Res.: 7 Margaret St., 12901. Tel: 518-563-0730; Fax: 518-563-0754.
School—(Grades PreK-6), 59 Broad St., 12901. Tel: 518-563-2260; Fax: 518-563-4553. Sr. Brian Marie Latour, R.S.M., Prin.; Kathleen Toner, Vice Prin. Priests 1; Sisters 1; Lay Teachers 17; Students 210.
Catechesis/Religious Program—Tel: 518-561-6694. Students 133.

2—ST. JOSEPH (Treadwells Mill) (1935), Rev. Joseph W. Elliott; Bro. Roland Gaudette, F.I.C., Pastoral Assoc.
Res. & Mailing Address: Church St., P.O. Box 159, Morrisonville, 12962. Tel: 518-563-6301.
Catechesis/Religious Program—1349 Military Tpke. Rd., 12901. Tel: 518-563-6301. Students 146.

3—ST. MARY OF THE LAKE (Cumberland Head) (1965), [CEM] Rev. Danel T. Keefe.
Res.: 1202 Cumberland Head Rd., P.O. Box 704, 12901. Tel: 518-561-2488; Fax: 518-561-3732.
Catechesis/Religious Program—Eunice Trombly, D.R.E. Students 127.

4—NEWMAN PARISH, JOHN XXIII COLLEGE COMMUNITY (1970), Rev. J. Roger McGuinness; Sr. Bernadette Ducharme, S.C.S.L., Pastoral Assoc.; Mrs. Eileen Ward, Admin. Asst.
Res.: 90 Broad St., 12901. Tel: 518-563-6852 (Res.); 518-561-7545 (Office); Fax: 518-561-1004.

5—OUR LADY OF VICTORY (1907), (French), Rev. Floyd J. Bleaux Jr.; Mrs. Carol Pulsifer, Pastoral Assoc.
Res.: 4919 S. Catherine St., 12901. Tel: 518-561-1842; Fax: 518-561-2269.
Catechesis/Religious Program—Students 125.
Convent—4907 S. Catherine St., 12901. Tel: 518-563-7419; Fax: 518-563-0383. Sr. Louise Marceau, S.C.S.L., Supr.

6—ST. PETER (1853), [CEM] Revs. John R. Yonkovig; Christopher J. Looby; Deacons Robert King; Robert Diehl, Spiritual Life Dir. In Res., Rev. Msgrs. Morris L. Dwyer (Retired); Joseph Aubin.
Res.: 114 Cornelia St., 12901. Tel: 518-563-1692; Fax: 518-566-9420.
School—(Grades PreK-6), St. Charles St., 12901. Tel: 518-561-7132; Fax: 518-561-7806. Mrs. Jean Mockry, Prin. Lay Teachers 14; Students 272.
Catechesis/Religious Program—Tel: 518-563-3278. Melissa LaBarre, D.R.E. Students 129.

PORT HENRY, ESSEX CO., ST. PATRICK (1854), (Irish), [CEM] Rev. Msgr. C. John McAvoy, Admin.
Res.: 17 St. Patrick's Pl., 12974. Tel: 518-546-7254; Fax: 518-546-3439.
Catechesis/Religious Program—Tel: 518-546-3374. Students 104.

PORT LEYDEN, LEWIS CO., ST. MARTIN (1879), [CEM] Rev. Msgr. Paul E. Whitmore.
Res.: P.O. Box 431, 13433. Tel: 315-348-6104; Fax: 315-348-6353.
Catechesis/Religious Program—Students 135.
Mission—St. John Lyons Falls, Lewis Co.

POTSDAM, ST. LAWRENCE CO.

1—ST. FRANCIS OF ASSISI CAMPUS PARISH (NEWMAN CENTER) (1969), Rev. Garry B. Giroux, J.C.L.
Office—41 Main St., 13676-2004. Tel: 315-265-9520; Fax: 315-268-1946.
Catechesis/Religious Program—Students 51.

2—ST. MARY (1841), [CEM] Revs. Garry B. Giroux, J.C.L.; Edward E. Papp; Deacon Frederick A. Brousseau.
Res.: 17 Lawrence Ave., 13676. Tel: 315-265-9680; Fax: 315-268-1443.
School—(Grades PreK-6) Tel: 315-265-3511; Fax:

315-265-5693. Lay Teachers 8; Students 110.
Catechesis/Religious Program—Tel: 315-265-6220. Students 70.

RAQUETTE LAKE, HAMILTON CO., ST. WILLIAM (1890), Rev. Scott D. Fobare, V.F.
Mailing Address: c/o P.O. Box 236, Old Forge, 13420. Tel: 315-369-3554; Fax: 315-369-2049.

RAYMONDVILLE, ST. LAWRENCE CO., ST. RAYMOND (1920), [CEM] Rev. J. Everett Denesha.
Res.: P.O. Box 178, 13678-0178. Tel: 315-384-3191.
Catechesis/Religious Program—Students 8.

REDFORD, CLINTON CO., CHURCH OF THE ASSUMPTION (1869), [CEM] Rev. Francis J. Coryer.
Res.: 78 Clinton St., 12978. Tel: 518-293-6259; Fax: 518-293-6435.
School—(Grades K-6) Tel: 518-293-6231; Fax: 518-293-8173. Lay Teachers 6; Students 35.

REDWOOD, JEFFERSON CO., ST. FRANCIS XAVIER (1848), [CEM] Rev. Msgr. Robert H. Aucoin, S.T.L., M.Ed.
Mailing Address: P.O. Box 477, Alexandria Bay, 13607. Tel: 315-482-2670; Fax: 315-482-4970. In Res., Rev. James L. Meehan (Retired).
Res.: P.O. Box 903, 13679. Tel: 315-482-6359.
Catechesis/Religious Program—Students 18.

ROSIERE, JEFFERSON CO., ST. VINCENT DE PAUL (1871), [CEM] Rev. Pierre Aubin, M.S.C. In Res., Rev. E. John Silver, Pastor Emeritus; Deacon Robert V. Ruddy.
Res.: 31385 County Rte. 4, Cape Vincent, 13618. Tel: 315-654-2576; Fax: 315-654-4721.

ROUSES POINT, CLINTON CO., ST. PATRICK (1860), (Irish), [CEM] [JC] Rev. Clyde A. Lewis; Deacon Noel A. Hinerth.
Res.: 138 Lake St., P.O. Box 217, 12979. Tel: 518-297-7361; Fax: 518-297-3181.
Catechesis/Religious Program—Mary Franke, D.R.E. Students 112.

SACKETS HARBOR, JEFFERSON CO., ST. ANDREW (1886), Rev. Douglas G. Comstock; Deacon Norman Hunneyman.
Res.: 112 E. Main St., Box 530, 13685. Tel: 315-646-3341.
Catechesis/Religious Program—Students 118.
Mission—Queen of Heaven 8900 NYS Rte. 3, Henderson, Jefferson Co. 13650.

SAINT REGIS FALLS, FRANKLIN CO., ST. ANN (1883), [CEM] Rev. Alfred H. Fish.
Res.: P.O. Box 288, St. Regis Falls, 12980. Tel: 518-856-9456; Fax: 518-856-9456.
Catechesis/Religious Program—Students 59.
Oratory—St. Peter Santa Clara.

SARANAC LAKE, FRANKLIN CO., ST. BERNARD (1888), [CEM] [JC] Revs. Thomas E. Kornmeyer; Kevin D. McEwan; Sr. Rita Mary Morrissette, O.S.M., Pastoral Assoc.; Deacons Frederick R. Oberst; Joseph Szwed; Jerome A. Cheney.
Res.: 27 St. Bernard St., 12983. Tel: 518-891-4616; Fax: 518-891-4619.
School—Tel: 518-891-2830. Rebecca P. Marlowe, Prin. Lay Teachers 7; Students 150.
Catechesis/Religious Program—Pius X Center, 32 River St., 12983. Tel: 518-891-3111. Kathy Gonyea, D.R.E. Students 195.

SCHROON LAKE, ESSEX CO., OUR LADY OF LOURDES (1883), [CEM] Rev. Richard S. Sturtz.
Res.: P.O. Box 368, 12870. Tel: 518-532-7100; Fax: 518-532-7461.
Rectory—1114 U.S. Rte. 9, 12870.
Catechesis/Religious Program—Students 34.

SCIOTA, CLINTON CO., ST. LOUIS (1899), (French-Canadian), [CEM] Rev. Gilbert O. Boisvert.
Res.: P.O. Box 113, Altona, 12910. Tel: 518-236-5848; Fax: 518-236-4249.
Catechesis/Religious Program—Tel: 518-236-4436. Students 35.

STAR LAKE, ST. LAWRENCE CO., ST. HUBERT (1893), (French—Irish), [JC] Revs. Robert L. Decker, Admin.; Fay W. Ager; Deacon Philip F. Giardino.
Res.: 1046 Oswegatchie Trail Rd., P.O. Box 9, 13690. Tel: 315-848-3612; Fax: 315-848-2510.
Catechesis/Religious Program—Students 46.
Oratory—St. Anthony of Padua P.O. Box 9, Newton Falls, St. Lawrence Co. 13690.
Oratory—St. Michael P.O. Box 9, Fine, St. Lawrence Co. 13690.

TICONDEROGA, ESSEX CO., ST. MARY (1852), [CEM] Rev. William G. Muench; Sr. Carol Daul, S.A., Pastoral Assoc.; Deacon Elliott A. Shaw.
Res.: 22 Father Jogues Pl., 12883. Tel: 518-585-7144; Fax: 518-585-3632.
School—(Grades K-8), 301 Amherst Ave., 12883. Tel: 518-585-7433; Fax: 518-585-3632. Sr. Sharon Anne Dalton, S.S.J., Prin. Sisters 1; Lay Teachers 8; Students 193.
Catechesis/Religious Program—Tel: 518-597-3924. Students 130.

TROUT RIVER, FRANKLIN CO., ST. BRIDGET'S ORATORY (1865), [CEM] Rev. Francis J. Flynn; Deacon Garry Burnell.
Res.: 1197 State Rte. 122, P.O. Box 78, Constable, 12926. Tel: 518-483-2775 (Rectory); 518-483-0486 (Office); Fax: 518-483-1618.

TUPPER LAKE, FRANKLIN CO.

1—ST. ALPHONSUS (1890), [CEM] Rev. Donald F. Kramberg; Sisters Barbara R. McCarthy, O.P., Pastoral Assoc.; Shirley Anne Brown, S.S.J., Pastoral Assoc.; Deacons James T. Ellis; Joseph H. Gilbert; Gerald H. Savage; James R. Keough.
Res.: 48 Wawbeek Ave., P.O. Box 1166, 12986. Tel: 518-359-3405; Fax: 518-359-2364. Email: stalphon@adelphia.net.
Catechesis/Religious Program—Tel: 518-359-2551. Students 377.

2—HOLY NAME OF JESUS (Faust) (1904), [CEM] Rev. Donald F. Kramberg; Sisters Shirley Anne Brown, S.S.J., Pastoral Assoc.; Barbara R. McCarthy, O.P., Pastoral Assoc.; Deacons James T. Ellis; Gerald H. Savage; James R. Keough.
Res.: 48 Wawbeek Ave., 12986. Tel: 518-359-9194; Fax: 518-359-9360.
Catechesis/Religious Program—Tel: 518-359-2551. Students 272.

WADDINGTON, ST. LAWRENCE CO., ST. MARY (1826), [CEM 3] Rev. Msgr. Robert L. Lawler, P.A.
Res.: P.O. Box 187, 13694. Tel: 315-388-4466; Fax: 315-388-4722.
Catechesis/Religious Program—Msgr. Arquett Parish Center, Tel: 315-388-4423. Students 65.

WATERTOWN, JEFFERSON CO.

1—ST. ANTHONY (1913), (Italian), [JC] Rev. Donald A. Robinson; Deacon Richard C. Warner Sr.
Res.: 850 Arsenal St., 13601. Tel: 315-782-1190; Fax: 315-786-3489.
School—(Grades PreK-6) Tel: 315-788-1461; Fax: 315-779-1140. Mrs. Annette M. Connolly, Prin. Lay Teachers 8; Students 94.
Catechesis/Religious Program—Students 45.

2—HOLY FAMILY (1895), Revs. Theodore A. Crosby; Steven M. Murray; Deacons Edward R. Miller; Douglas J. Marlow; Richard Gaebel; Michael J. Allan; Bruce Wayne Daugherty. In Res., Rev. Mark R. Reilly.
Res.: 129 Winthrop St., 13601. Tel: 315-782-2468; Fax: 315-782-4684.
School—(Grades N-6) Tel: 315-788-7011. Sr. Ellen Rose Coughlin, S.S.J., Prin. Sisters of St. Joseph 3; Lay Teachers 13; Students 256.
Catechesis/Religious Program—Holy Family Religious Education Office, Sterling Pl., 13601. Tel: 315-782-6750. Students 219.

3—OUR LADY OF THE SACRED HEART (1876), Rev. Andrew Torma, M.S.C.; Deacons David N. Henningan; William Michael Johnston; Theresa M. Reed-Male, Business Mgr.
Parish Office—664 Thompson St., 13601. Tel: 315-782-1474; Fax: 315-782-0473.
School— (1922),(Grades K-6), 320 W. Lynde St.. Tel: 315-782-3060; Fax: 315-782-4939. Sr. Sheila Jane Moran, S.S.J., Prin. Sisters 2; Lay Teachers 9; Students 84.
School—Preschool and Day Care, Tel: 315-782-3060.

4—ST. PATRICK (1854), [CEM] Rev. Arthur J. LaBaff, V.F.; Sr. Mary William Argy, S.S.J., Pastoral Assoc.; Deacons William G. Schmidt; Kevin Thomas Mastellon.
Res.: 724 Ives St., 13601. Tel: 315-782-6086.
School—(Grades K-6), 733 S. Massey St., 13601. Tel: 315-788-3935; Fax: 315-788-4447. Mrs. Gail Baker Graham, Prin. Lay Teachers 8; Students 122.
Catechesis/Religious Program—Mrs. Elizabeth Bamann, D.R.E. Students 82.

WELLS, HAMILTON CO., ST. ANN'S (1890), [CEM] Rev. Paul J. Kelly.
Mailing Address: P.O. Box 214, Speculator, 12164. Tel: 518-548-6275.
Catechesis/Religious Program—Students 10.

WEST CHAZY, CLINTON CO., ST. JOSEPH (1884), [CEM] Rev. Harry E. Giroux; Deacon Gerald Defayette.
Res.: P.O. Box 224, 12992. Tel: 518-493-4521; Fax: 518-493-5880.
Catechesis/Religious Program—Students 173.

WEST LEYDEN, LEWIS CO., ST. MARY'S NATIVITY (1900), [CEM] Rev. Sony G. Pulickal, C.M.F.
Res.: P.O. Box 305, 13489. Tel: 315-942-2595; Fax: 315-942-2595.
Catechesis/Religious Program—Students 52.
Mission—SS. Peter & Paul [CEM] Fish Creek.

WESTPORT, ESSEX CO., ST. PHILIP NERI (1879), [CEM] Rev. Msgr. Peter R. Riani, S.T.D., M.Ed., V.F.
Res.: P.O. Box 368, Elizabethtown, 12932. Tel: 518-873-6760; Fax: 518-873-6530.
Catechesis/Religious Program—Students 30.

WILLSBORO, ESSEX CO., ST. PHILIP OF JESUS (1909), [CEM] Rev. James A. Delbel.
Res.: P.O. Box 607, 12996. Tel: 518-963-4524; Fax: 518-963-7719.
Catechesis/Religious Program—Students 65.

WITHERBEE, ESSEX CO., ST. MICHAEL (1911), Closed. For inquiries for parish records contact the chancery.

Chaplains of Public Institutions

FORT DRUM. *U.S. Army Headquarters.* Rev. Peter Uhde.

Military and Medical

OGDENSBURG. *St. Lawrence Psychiatric Center*, St. Vincent's Chapel, 13669. Tel: 315-541-2001, Ext. 2414; Fax: 315-541-2049. Sr. Kathryn Healey, G.N.S.H., Chap., Rev. Msgr. John R. Murphy.

FORT DRUM. *U.S. Army Headquarters Fort Drum*, 25 Vincent Ln., 13603. Tel: 315-772-5591; Fax: 315-772-6725. Rev. Peter Uhde.

PLATTSBURGH. *Champlain Valley Physicians Hospital Medical Center*, 75 Beekman St., 12901. Tel: 518-561-2000. Rev. William G. Reamer, Chap.

TUPPER LAKE, (SUNMOUNT).. *Sunmount Developmental Center*, 403 Park St., 12986. Tel: 518-359-3311; Fax: 518-359-4133. Deacon Joseph Szwed, Chap.

WATERTOWN. *Samaritan Medical Center*, 830 Washington St., 13601. Tel: 315-785-4000; Fax: 315-785-4195. Bro. John Paul Paradis, M.S.C., Chap. & Coord., Casey Shortt, Chap. & Coord.

Prisons

OGDENSBURG. *Ogdensburg Correctional Facility*, One Correction Way, 13669. Tel: 315-393-0281. Deacon Thomas F. Kilian, Rev. Scott R. Seymour.
Riverview Correctional Facility, Box 158, 13669. Tel: 315-393-8400. Deacon Mark A. LaLonde, Rev. Joseph A. Morgan.

ALTONA. *Altona Correctional Facility*, P.O. Box 125, 12910. Tel: 518-236-7841; Fax: 518-236-6235. Rev. Garvin J. Demarais, Deacon John A. Levison.

CAPE VINCENT. *Cape Vincent Correctional Facility* 13618. Tel: 315-654-4100, Ext. 548. Deacon Robert V. Ruddy, Rev. Pierre Aubin, M.S.C.

DANNEMORA. *Clinton Correctional Facility*, P.O. Box 798, 12929-0798. Tel: 518-492-2511, Ext. 4800. Deacon Larry R. Debiec, Rev. Guy F. Edwards. Tel: 518-492-7118.

GABRIELS. *Gabriel's Correctional Facility*, P.O. Box 100, 12939. Tel: 518-327-3111, Ext. 258. Rev. Victor E. Lamore, Chap.

GOUVERNEUR. *Gouverneur Correctional Facility*, Scotch Settlement Rd., P.O. Box 370, 13642. Tel: 315-287-7351; Fax: 315-287-2533. Deacon Thomas F. Kilian, Rev. Daniel L. Chapin, Deacon Kenneth A. Seymour.

LYON MOUNTAIN. *Lyon Mountain Correctional Facility*, P.O. Box 23, 12952. Tel: 518-735-4540. Rev. Msgr. Bernard E. Christman.

MALONE. *Barehill Correctional Facility*, Cady Rd., 12953. Tel: 518-483-8411, Ext. 409. Deacon James J. Hotte, Rev. Alan J. Lamica.
Franklin Correctional Facility, P.O. Box 10, 12953-9720. Tel: 518-483-6040, Ext. 2402. Deacon Joseph R. Szwed, Rev. Garvin J. Demarais.
Upstate Correctional Facility, P.O. Box 2000, 12953. Tel: 518-483-6997. Deacon Richard D. Hart, Rev. Garvin J. Demarais. Tel: 518-483-6997.

MORIAH. *Moriah Shock Incarceration Correctional Facility*.
Fisher Hill Rd., P.O. Box 999, Mineville, 12956-0999. Tel: 518-942-7561. Rev. James A. Delbel, Deacon Elliott Shaw.

RAY BROOK. *Adirondack Correctional Facility*, Box 110, 12977-0110. Tel: 518-891-1343. Rev. Victor E. Lamore.
Res.: Star Rte., Box 152, Saranac Lake, 12983. Tel: 518-891-6540.
Federal Correctional Institution, P.O. Box 300, 12977. Tel: 518-891-5400. Rev. Robert O. Lamitie (Retired).

WATERTOWN. *Watertown Correctional Facility* 13601. Tel: 315-782-7490, Ext. 445. Deacon Kenneth A. Seymour, Rev. Kevin J. O'Brien, Chap.

On Duty Outside the Diocese:
Revs.—
Kennehan, John P., St. John's Mercy Hospital, Springfield, MO.
Ledermann, Paul F., Veterans Home, P.O. Box 7, Yountville, CA 94599.
Schudde, Derk M., Diocese of Orlando, Orlando, FL 32801.
Sestito, Joseph N., 114 Stanwood Ln., Manlius, 13104.
Wertman, Raymond, 2292 Costa Rican Dr., Brahmin #56, Clearwater, FL 34623.

Graduate Studies:
Rev.—
Stitt, Bryan D., North American College, Rome, Italy.

Military Chaplains:
Revs.—
Ratigan, Patrick A., Chap., US Army, 904 Ringneck Way, Hinesville, GA 31313.
Sykes, Gregory P., Chap. U.S. Army, 222 BSB, CMR 405, Box 1394, Apo, AE 09034.

Absent on Sick Leave:
Revs.—
Demers, Richard D., Mary's Rectory, P.O. Box 609, Massena, 13662.
Helfrich, Peter G., 10 Knoll Brook Rd., Apt. 3, Rochester, 14610.

Retired:
Rev. Msgrs.—
Argy, William J., St. Mary's Cathedral Rectory, 13669. Tel: 315-393-3930
Aubin, Joseph G., St. Peter's Rectory, 114A Cornelia St, Plattsburgh, 12901.
Dwyer, Morris L., St. Peter's Rectory, 114 Cornelia St., Plattsburgh, 12901.
Gefell, Gerard J., 2332 Humphrey Rd., Cape Vincent, 13618. Tel: 315-654-3504
McCarthy, Robert J., 324 Pratt St., 13601.
Phillips, George M., Notre Dame Rectory, P.O. Box 149, 13669.
Robillard, Thomas J., 11 Hepburn St., Norfolk, 13667.
White, Francis A., St. Francis Neri Church, 66 Pleasant St., Box M, Westport, 12993.
Revs.—
Beaudet, Eugene J., Buena Vista Park, 30 Frisbie Rd., Willsboro, 12996.
Beyette, Paul V., HC Box 218, Loon Lake, 12989.
Chase, Charles E., P.O. Box 2434, Duxbury, MA 02331.
Cosmic, John J., 39 Anderson Ave., P.O. Box 117, Deferiet, 13628.
Cote, Norman J., St. John the Baptist Rectory, 7 Margaret St., Plattsburgh, 12901.
Cotter, Lawrence E., S.T.L., B.S., M.S., P.O. Box 606, 13669.
Cotter, Robert L., St. Mary Rectory, P.O. Box 26, Glenfield, 13343.
Crable, John M., 4 Edgewater Estates, Plattsburgh, 12901.
DeRoche, Wilfred L., South Meadow Village, #26-5, Carver, MA 02330.
Igo, James P., 10 Daniel St., Arlington, MA 02174.
Jarecki, Michael S., R.R. 1, Box 258, Constable, 12926.
LaLonde, Emile G., Cambry Court, 68 W. Main St., Apt. 2A4, Gouverneur, 13642.
Lamitie, James F., 510 Lake Shore Dr., Apt. 27, Lake Park, FL 33403.
Lamitie, Robert O., Box 35 C, Star Rte., Saranac Lake, 12983.
Martin, Roger, 54 W. Main St., P.O. Box 25, Baltic, CT 06330.
McCasland, Howard, Immaculate Heart of Mary, Rt. 189-560, Churubusco, 12923.
Meehan, James L., St. Francis Xavier, P.O. Box 185, Redwood, 13679.
Menard, Francis A., 3860 State Rte. 11, Malone, 12953.
Menard, Gilbert B., 2 Garrett Way, Schuyler Falls, 12985.
Njeim, Elias, Colonial Manor, Apt. A9, 13601.
Patterson, Terrence R., Box 288, Potsdam, 13676. Tel: 315-265-2986
Poupore, Norman E., P.O. Box 824, Pierrepont Manor, 13674.
Rapin, Cyril W., St. Joseph's Church, P.O. Box 226, Mooers, 12958-0288.
Richard, Charles J., St. Joseph's Home, 420 Lafayette St., 13669.
Silver, John E., St. Vincent de Paul Rectory, 31385 County Rt. 4, Cape Vincent, 13618.
Votraw, Thomas G., United Helpers Nursing Home, 8101 State Hwy. 68, 18669.

Permanent Deacons:
Allen, Michael J., Holy Family, Watertown
Bashaw, Bryan J., Malone
Bateman, Francis F., Ogdensburg
Benson, George Grady, Peru
Brousseau, Frederick A., St. Mary, Potsdam
Burnell, Garry N., St. Francis of Assisi, Constable
Cheney, Jerome A., Saranac Lake
Connelly, Lawrence A., Norfolk
Daugherty, Bruce Wayne, Watertown
Debiec, Larry, Clinton Correctional Facility, Dannemora
Defayette, Gerald R., St. Joseph, West Chazy
Demers, Victor, Notre Dame, Ogdensburg
Diehl, Robert, St. Peter, Plattsburgh
Dwyer, John C., 140 Marlborough Rd., Syracuse, 13206
Ellis, James T., St. Alphonsus, Tupper Lake
Frank, Gary A., St. Mary, Clayton
Gaebel, Richard M., Holy Family, Watertown
Giardino, Philip F., St. Hubert, Star Lake
Gilbert, Joseph H., St. Alphonsus, Tupper Lake
Gillen, James J., St. James Minor, Carthage
Gilner, Gerard, St. Mary, Indian Lake
Hart, Richard D., Upstate Correctional Facility, Malone
Hennigan, David N., Our Lady of the Sacred Heart, Watertown
Hinerth, Noel A., St. Patrick, Rouses Point
Hotte, James J., Sacred Heart, Massena; Bare Hill Correctional Facility, Malone
Hunneyman, Norman L., St. Andrew's, Sackets Harbor
Johnston, William Michael, Watertown
Keough, James R., St. Alphonsus, Tupper Lake
Kilian, Thomas F., Gouverneur Correctional Facility, Gouverneur; Notre Dame, Ogdensburg; Ogdensburg Correctional Facility
King, Robert A., St. Peter, Plattsburgh
LaLonde, Mark A., Notre Dame, Ogdensburg; Riverview Correctional Facility, Ogdensburg
Lawless, Peter J., Sacred Heart, Edwards
LeClair, Robert J., Sacred Heart, Chazy
Levison, John A., Altona Correctional Facility, Altona
Looby, Phillip M., St. Francis, Solanus, Harrisville
Mader, Frederick J., St. Paul, Bloomingdale
Marlow, Douglas, Holy Family, Watertown
Mastellon, Kevin Thomas, Watertown
Mazuchowski, Edward, St. Joseph, Dannemora
Merrill, Reginald F., St. Bernard, Lyon Mountain
Miller, Edward R., Holy Family, Watertown
Moltz, David, St. Elizabeth Seton, Dexter
Monty, Dennis, Mooers Forks
Oberst, Frederick R., St. Bernard, Saranac Lake
Patrie, Leonard L., St. Mary, Champlain
Pominville, Ronald J., St. Peter, Lowville
Rabideau, Tyrone, St. Ann, Mooers Forks
Raven, William S., St. Paul, Black River
Ruddy, Robert V., St. Vincent of Paul & Cape Vincent Correctional Facility, Cape Vincent
Ryan, John J., Holy Name, Ausable Forks
Savage, Gerald H., St. Alphonsus, Tupper Lake
Schmidt, William G., St. Patrick, Watertown
Seymour, Kenneth A., Gouverneur Correctional Facility, Gouverneur; Watertown Correctional Facility, Watertown
Shaw, Elliott A., St. Mary's, Ticonderoga; Moriah Shock Incarceration Facility, Mineville
Siskavich, Francis, St. Bernard, Lyon Mountain
Slate, Bernard E., Alexandria Bay
Staab, Richard J., St. James, Carthage
Ste.-Marie, Ronald, St. Anthony, Inlet
Szwed, Joseph, St. Bernard, Saranac Lake; Sunmount Developmental Center, Tupper Lake; Franklin Correctional Facility, Malone
Trombly, John J., 678 Grant St., 13601.
Van Kirk, Richard L., Heuvelton
Wadsworth, Bruce Carley, Lake Placid
Warner, Richard C., Sr., St. Anthony, Watertown
Winter, Richard E., St. Mary's Cathedral, Ogdensburg
Yarchuk, Andrew, All Saints, Chaumont

INSTITUTIONS LOCATED IN THE DIOCESE

[A] SEMINARIES, DIOCESAN

OGDENSBURG. *Wadhams Hall*, 6866 State Hwy. 37, 13669-4420. Tel: 315-393-4231; Fax: 315-393-4249. Email: inquiry@wadhams.edu. Web: www.wadhams.edu. Mr. Jeffrey Ward, A.A.S., Dir. Finance. Total Staff 2.

[B] HIGH SCHOOLS, INTERPAROCHIAL

PLATTSBURGH. *Seton Catholic Central*, 5135 N. Catherine St., 12901. Tel: 518-561-4031; Fax: 518-563-1193. Email: gcote@setonchs.com. Web: www.setonchs.com. Sr. Gwenda Cote, R.S.M., Prin. Sisters 2; Brothers 2; Lay Teachers 26; Students 324.

WATERTOWN. *Immaculate Heart Central High School*, 1316 Ives St., 13601. Tel: 315-788-4670; 315-788-8982 (Guidance); Fax: 315-788-4672. Email: ihc@gisco.net. Web: www.gisco.net/ihc. Mr. Pat A. Fontana, Prin.; Rev. Mark R. Reilly, Spiritual Dir. Priests 1; Sisters 4; Lay Teachers 24; (Grades 7-12) 441.

[C] RELIGIOUS EDUCATION

OGDENSBURG. *Bishop Conroy School of Religion*, 214 Morris St., 13669-1714. Tel: 315-393-1820; Fax: 315-393-1670. Email: bcsr@gisco.net. Sisters 1; Lay Teachers 40; Total Staff 2; Students 290.

SARANAC LAKE. *Pius X Center*, 61 River St., 12983. Tel: 518-891-3111; Fax: 518-891-4619. Email: stpiusx@adelphia.net. Total Staff 42; Students 400.

WATERTOWN. *Watertown Catechetical Office*, Sterling Pl., 13601. Tel: 315-782-0030. Sisters 1; Students 216.

Special Religious Education Tel: 315-782-0030. Sr. Mary Maurice Black, S.S.J., Coord.

[D] SPECIAL HOSPITALS AND HOMES FOR INVALIDS AND AGED

OGDENSBURG. *St. Joseph's Home*, 420 Lafayette St., 13669. Tel: 315-393-3780; Fax: 315-393-3847. Email: administrator@stjh.org. Web: www.stjh.org. Andrew Peterson, Admin. Total Staff 110; Total Assisted 120.

LAKE PLACID. *St. Margaret Convent*, 420 Old Military Rd., 12946. Tel: 518-523-2929; Fax: 518-523-1401. Email: sistercamillus@webtv.net. Sr. M. Camillus O'Keefe, R.S.M., Supr. Sisters of Mercy

Uihlein Mercy Center, 420 Old Military Rd., 12946. Tel: 518-523-2464; Fax: 518-523-1401. Email: mwilliams@muhc.org. Web: muhc.org. Edward W. Bell, Admin.; Rev. Patrick J. O'Reilly, Chap. Institute of the Sisters of Mercy of the Americas, Regional Community of New York., Skilled Nursing Facility. Sisters 3; Total Staff 200; Total Assisted 224.

SARANAC LAKE. *St. Joseph's Rehabilitation Center, Inc.* Alcoholism & Substance Abuse Rehab. , 99 Glenwood Estates, P.O. Box 470, 12983. Tel: 518-891-3950; 518-891-4135 (Admissions); Fax: 518-891-3986. Email: stjoes@sjrcrehab.org. Web: sjrcrehab.org. Rev. Daniel P. Callahan, S.A., Chap.; Bros. Alan Lemay, S.A. Paschal Steen, S.A. Franciscan Friars of the Atonement. Priests 1; Brothers 2; Residents 58.

TUPPER LAKE. *Mercy Healthcare Center, Inc.* Skilled Nursing Facility. , 114 Wawbeek Ave., 12986. Tel: 518-359-3355; Fax: 518-359-9044. Email: boreilly@muhc.org. Web: muhc.org. Sisters of Mercy of the Americas (Hartsdale) 1; Capacity 80.

[E] MONASTERIES AND RESIDENCES OF PRIESTS AND BROTHERS

SARANAC LAKE. *Atonement Friars*, 69 Franklin Ave., 12983. Tel: 518-891-2395. Email: dancallahan@adelphia.net. Web: graymoor.org. Revs. Daniel P. Callahan, S.A.; Carmen Guiliano, S.A. Total in Residence 2.

St Joseph's Friary, P.O. Box 470, 12983. Tel: 518-891-3494. Bros. Alan Lemay, S.A.; Paschal Steen, T.S.A. Total in Residence 2.

WATERTOWN. *Missionaries of the Sacred Heart*, 668 Thompson St., 13601. Tel: 315-782-3480; Fax: 315-782-0473. Email: shfound@gisco.net. Revs. Bernard Jakubco, M.S.C., Supr.; Benoit Dostie, M.S.C.; William Connor, M.S.C.; Richard Huber, M.S.C.; Pierre Aubin, M.S.C.; Andrew Torma, M.S.C.; Bros. Peter Marceau, M.S.C.; Jean-Paul Paradis, M.S.C.; Deacon Michael Tomsics, M.S.C.

[F] CONVENTS AND RESIDENCES FOR SISTERS

OGDENSBURG. *St. Joseph's Convent, Grey Nuns of the Sacred Heart*, 709 Franklin St., 13669. Tel: 315-393-1763. Email: greynuns@qisco.com. Sr. Joan McElwain, G.N.S.H., Facilitator.

Sisters of St. Joseph, 251 Proctor Ave., 13669. Tel: 315-393-6511.

CARTHAGE. *St. James Convent, Sisters of St. Joseph*, 317 West St., 13619. Tel: 315-493-1672. Sr. Marie Angele Ellis, S.S.J., Supr. Total Staff 2; Total in Residence 2.

CHAMPLAIN. *St. Mary's Convent*, 1060 Main St., 12919. Tel: 518-298-3141.

CLAYTON. *Sisters of Holy Cross*, 415 John St, #1, 13624. Tel: 315-686-3640.

ELLENBURG CENTER. *Our Lady of the Adirondack's Inc. House of Prayer*, 7270 Star Rd., Rte. 190, 12934-2501. Tel: 518-594-3253; Fax: 518-594-7143. Email: olahouse@northnet.org. Sr. Jean T. Beyette, S.A., Dir.; Rev. Thomas A. Moody, Spiritual Dir. Franciscan Sisters of the AtonementOur Lady of the Adirondacks Community.

Our Lady of the Adirondacks Community

Our Lady of the Adirondacks Prayer Association Tel: 518-594-3253; Fax: 518-594-7143. Members 151.

GOUVERNEUR. *St. James' Convent, Sisters of St. Joseph*, 28 S. Gordon St., 13642. Tel: 315-287-0658. Total Staff 2; Total in Residence 2.

MALONE. *St. Joseph's Ursuline Convent, Ursuline Nuns*, 49 Morton St., 12953. Tel: 518-483-2880; Fax: 518-483-5356. Email: ursulmal@twcny.rr.com. Sisters 5.

MASSENA. *St. Joseph's Convent, Sisters of St. Joseph*, 36 Alden St., 13662. Tel: 315-764-0379. Total in Residence 3.

Sacred Heart Convent, 188 Main St., P.O. Box 91, 13662. Tel: 315-769-6238. Email: mas-osm@northnet.org. Total in Residence 3.

MORRISONVILLE. *St. Augustine's Convent*, 1736 Rte.

22B, 12962. Tel: 518-563-1723. Email: augustin@westelcom.com. Sisters of St. Joseph (S.S.J.), Dominican Sisters (O.P.) Total in Residence 2.

PLATTSBURGH. *St. John's Convent*, 62-64 Court St., 12901. Tel: 518-561-9689; Fax: 518-563-4553. Email: sisterb@northnet.org. Sisters of Mercy 4.

St. Peter's Convent, 2 Deland Way, 12901. Tel: 518-566-7315. Email: dshope2@juno.com. Sr. Mary Stephanie Frenette, O.P., Contact Person. Total in Residence 2.

Regina Maria Retreat House Daughters of the Heart of Mary, 77 Brinkerhoff St., 12901. Tel: 518-561-3421; Fax: 518-561-3816. Email: reginamh@westelcom.com. Mary Curran, D.H.M.

Sisters of Charity of St. Louis, 4907 S. Catherine St., 12901. Tel: 518-563-7410; Fax: 518-563-0383.

SARANAC LAKE. *Sisters of Mercy of the Americas*, 35 Trudeau Rd., 12983. Tel: 518-891-3234.

TICONDEROGA. *St. Mary's Convent, Sisters of St. Joseph*, 145 Lake George Ave., 12883. Tel: 518-585-6547; Fax: 518-585-7505. Email: sschoo3@nycap.rr.com. Sr. Sharon Anne Dalton, S.S.J. Total Staff 1; Total in Residence 1.

TUPPER LAKE. *Dominican Sisters of Hope, Ossining*, 37 Lake St., Apt. 2, 12986. Tel: 518-359-9632.

Holy Spirit Convent, 48 High St., 12986. Tel: 518-359-3838.

WATERTOWN. *Precious Blood Monastery, Sister Adorers of the Precious Blood*, 400 Pratt St., 13601. Tel: 315-788-1669; Fax: 315-779-9046. Email: swashb2252@aol.com. Web: www.catholic.org/mace/sistersadorers.html; sisterspreciousblood.org. Sisters Mary Grace Ayotte, Supr.; Martha Emery, A.P.B., Asst. Supr. Total Staff 6; Total in Residence 6.

Sisters of St. Joseph Motherhouse, 1425 Washington St., 13601-4533. Tel: 315-782-3460; Fax: 315-788-2794. Email: ogdssjwa@yahoo.com. Web: www.home.gisco.net/users/sisssj. Sisters Diane Marie Ulsamer, S.S.J., Supr.; Annunciata Collins, S.S.J., Major Supr. Total Staff 24; Total in Residence 41.

[G] RETREAT HOUSES

PLATTSBURGH. *Regina Maria Retreat House*, 77 Brinkerhoff St., 12901. Tel: 518-561-3421; Fax: 518-561-3816. Email: reginamh@westelcom.com. Sr. Mary A.E. Curran, D.H.M. Daughters of the Heart of Mary 3.

[H] INCORPORATED CEMETERIES

BRASHER FALLS. *St. Patrick's Cemetery Association of Brasher Falls, N.Y.*, Box 208, 13613. Tel: 315-389-5401; Fax: 315-389-4066. Email: parish@twcny.rr.com. Web: www.stpatrick-stlawrence.org.

CARTHAGE. *St. James Cemetery Corporation*, 327 West St., 13619. Tel: 315-493-3224; Fax: 518-493-3280. Email: sjcarth@northnet.org.

CROGHAN. *St. Stephen's Cemetery Association, Inc.*, Main St., Box 38, 13327. Tel: 315-346-6958; Fax: 315-346-1200. Email: llwiley@northnet.org.

MALONE. *St. Joseph's Cemetery of Malone, N.Y., Inc.*, 306 W. Main St., 12953. Tel: 518-483-1300; Fax: 518-483-1307. Email: mcp@twcny.rr.com.

Notre Dame Cemetery of Malone, N.Y., Inc., Office, 306 W. Main St., 12953. Tel: 518-483-1300; Fax: 518-483-1307. Email: mcp@twcny.RR.com.

PLATTSBURGH. *Mount Carmel Cemetery*, St. John the Baptist Church, 7 Margaret St., 12901. Tel: 518-563-0730; Fax: 518-563-0754. Email: sjplatt@northnet.org.

WATERTOWN. *Calvary Cemetery Association of Watertown, N.Y.*, Sacred Heart Church, 664 Thompson, 13601. Tel: 315-782-1474; Fax: 315-782-0473. Email: sacredhe@twcny.rr.com. Web: www.olshparish.org.

[I] MISCELLANEOUS LISTINGS

OGDENSBURG. *St. Joseph's Foundation, Inc.*, 420 Lafayette St., 13669. Tel: 315-394-0463; Fax: 315-393-3847. Email: info@stjh.org. Web: www.stjh.org.

CAPE VINCENT. *Mission Project Service*, 139 N. Kanady St., P.O. Box 288, 13618. Tel: 315-654-2447; Fax: 315-654-4721. Email: misprojser@aol.com. Web: www.missionprojectservice.org. Beverly Hennigan, Exec. Dir.; Rev. Pierre Aubin, M.S.C., Dir.

HOGANSBURG. *St. Regis Mission* (Akwesasne) ; Reservation and parish on both sides of U.S.-Canadian border. , Box 429, 13655. Tel: 613-575-2066. Rev. George H. Belgarde, S.J. (NY), Pastor. Priests 1; Brothers 1.

Roman Catholic Community Center, Inc. (Kateri Tekakwitha Center) Mrs. Lucille Peters, Rel. Educ. Coord. Tel: 518-358-2931.

LAKE PLACID. *Mercy Uihlein Health Foundation*, 420 Old Military Rd., 12946. Tel: 518-523-2464; Fax: 518-523-1401. Edward W. Bell, Pres. & CEO.

PLATTSBURGH. *Christ Child Day Nursery*, 5115 N. Catherine, 12901. Tel: 518-561-6451. Mrs. Nancy Fournier, Dir. Total Staff 5; Total Assisted 26.

SARANAC LAKE. *Guggenheim Center for Religious Programs*, P.O. Box 664, 12983. Tel: 518-891-0809 (Lodge); 518-891-3323 (Dorm). Mr. Ralph Bennett, Dir.
Res.: 33 Leona St., 12983. Tel: 518-891-2844.

WATERTOWN. *Sacred Heart Foundation*, 668 Thompson St., 13601. Tel: 315-782-3344; Fax: 315-782-0473. Email: shfound@gisco.net. Web: www.sacredheartfoundation.com. Diana L. Logsdon, Exec. Dir.

The Federation of Sisters of the Precious Blood, Inc., 400 Pratt St., 13601. Tel: 315-783-9838. Sr. Marilyn McGillan, A.P.B., Pres.

Watertown Catholic Education Council, 724 Ives St., 13601. Tel: 315-782-6086; Fax: 315-788-4447. Email: labaff@twcny.rr.com. Rev. Arthur LaBaff, V.F.

RELIGIOUS INSTITUTES OF MEN REPRESENTED IN THE DIOCESE

For further details refer to the corresponding bracketed number in the Religious Institutes of Men or Women section.

[0320]—*Brothers of Christian Instruction* (Alfred, ME)—F.I.C.
[0360]—*Claretian Missionaries*—C.M.F.
[0480]—*Conventual Franciscans*—O.F.M.Conv
[0530]—*Franciscan Friars of the Atonement*—S.A.
[0690]—*Jesuit Fathers and Brothers* (French Canadian Prov. of Montreal)—S.J.
[1110]—*Missionaries of the Sacred Heart*—M.S.C.

RELIGIOUS INSTITUTES OF WOMEN REPRESENTED IN THE DIOCESE

[0760]—*Daughters of Charity of St. Vincent de Paul*—D.C.
[0750]—*Daughters of the Charity of the Sacred Heart of Jesus*—F.C.S.C.J.
[0810]—*Daughters of the Heart of Mary*—D.H.M.
[0820]—*Daughters of the Holy Spirit*—D.H.S.
[1070-03]—*Dominican Sisters*—O.P.
[1070-22]—*Dominican Sisters*—O.P.
[1105]—*Dominican Sisters of Hope*—O.P.
[1190]—*Franciscan Sisters of the Atonement*—S.A.
[1840]—*Grey Nuns of the Sacred Heart*—G.N.S.H.
[2575]—*Institute of the Sisters of Mercy of the Americas* (Burlington, VT; Providence, RI; New York, NY)—R.S.M.
[3580]—*Servants of Mary* (Servite Sisters)—O.S.M.
[3360]—*Sister of Providence*—S.P.
[0110]—*Sisters Adorers of the Precious Blood*—A.P.B.
[0620]—*Sisters of Charity of St. Louis*—S.C.S.L.
[1930]—*Sisters of Holy Cross*—C.S.C.
[1800]—*Sisters of St. Francis of the Third Order Regular*—O.S.F.
[3840]—*Sisters of St. Joseph of Carondelet*—C.S.J.
[3830-12]—*Sisters of St. Joseph of Watertown*—S.S.J.
[4110]—*Ursuline Nuns*—O.S.U.

NECROLOGY

† Branche, John S., (Retired)—Died Sept. 3, 2003
† Driscoll, Thomas F., Alexandria Bay, NY St. Cyril's; Redwood, NY St. Francis Xavier—Died Aug. 29, 2003
† Ladden, Timothy M., (Retired)—Died Jan. 31, 2003
† Marier, Euclid A., (Retired)—Died March 29, 2003
† Snow, J. Lee, Diocese of Ogdensburg—Died Nov. 15, 2003

Archdiocese of Oklahoma City

(Archidioecesis Oklahomapolitana)

Most Reverend

EUSEBIUS J. BELTRAN, D.D.

Archbishop of Oklahoma City; ordained May 14, 1960; appointed Bishop of Tulsa February 28, 1978; installed April 20, 1978; appointed Archbishop of Oklahoma City November 24, 1992; installed January 22, 1993 *Res.: P.O. Box 32180, Oklahoma City, OK 73123.*

Catholic Pastoral Center: 7501 Northwest Expwy., P.O. Box 32180, Oklahoma City, OK 73123. Tel: 405-721-5651; Fax: 405-721-5210.

ESTABLISHED FEBRUARY 6, 1973.

Square Miles 42,470.

Erected into a Vicariate Apostolic by Brief of May 29, 1891. Erected into the Diocese of Oklahoma with the See in Oklahoma City by a Brief of Pope Pius X, August 17, 1905. Name changed to Diocese of Oklahoma City and Tulsa by Bull of Pope Pius XI, November 14, 1930. Erected into Archdiocese of Oklahoma City by a Bull of Pope Paul VI, December 13, 1972. The Province includes the Dioceses of Tulsa and Little Rock.

Comprises the following 46 Counties: Alfalfa, Beaver, Beckham, Blaine, Caddo, Canadian, Carter, Cimarron, Cleveland, Comanche, Cotton, Custer, Dewey, Ellis, Garfield, Garvin, Grady, Grant, Greer, Harmon, Harper, Jackson, Jefferson, Johnston, Kay, Kingfisher, Kiowa, Lincoln, Logan, Love, McClain, Major, Marshall, Murray, Noble, Oklahoma, Pontotoc, Pottawatomie, Roger Mills, Seminole, Stephens, Texas, Tillman, Washita, Woods and Woodward.

For legal titles of parishes and archdiocesan institutions, consult the Pastoral Office.

STATISTICAL OVERVIEW

Personnel	
Archbishops	1
Abbots	1
Retired Abbots	3
Priests: Diocesan Active in Diocese	68
Priests: Diocesan Active Outside Diocese	1
Priests: Retired, Sick or Absent	27
Number of Diocesan Priests	96
Religious Priests in Diocese	23
Total Priests in Diocese	119
Extern Priests in Diocese	18
Ordinations:	
Diocesan Priests	1
Permanent Deacons in Diocese	71
Total Brothers	10
Total Sisters	132
Parishes	
Parishes	71
With Resident Pastor:	
Resident Diocesan Priests	64
Resident Religious Priests	7
Missions	46
Professional Ministry Personnel:	
Brothers	2
Sisters	31
Lay Ministers	78
Welfare	
Catholic Hospitals	6
Total Assisted	705,629
Health Care Centers	2
Total Assisted	360
Homes for the Aged	5
Total Assisted	375
Day Care Centers	2
Total Assisted	350
Residential Care of Disabled	1
Total Assisted	30
Educational	
Diocesan Students in Other Seminaries	16
Total Seminarians	16
Colleges and Universities	1
Total Students	813
High Schools, Diocesan and Parish	2
Total Students	896
Elementary Schools, Diocesan and Parish	17
Total Students	3,464
Elementary Schools, Private	3
Total Students	642
Catechesis/Religious Education:	
High School Students	3,261
Elementary Students	8,915
Total Students under Catholic Instruction	18,007
Teachers in the Diocese:	
Priests	10
Scholastics	1
Brothers	4
Sisters	15
Lay Teachers	389
Vital Statistics	
Receptions into the Church:	
Infant Baptism Totals	2,180
Adult Baptism Totals	344
Received into Full Communion	476
First Communions	1,952
Confirmations	1,344
Marriages:	
Catholic	399
Interfaith	315
Total Marriages	714
Deaths	800
Total Catholic Population	112,951
Total Population	2,643,608

Former Bishops—Rt. Rev. THEOPHILE MEERSCHAERT, D.D., ord. Dec. 23, 1871; appt. first Vicar-Apostolic of Indian Territory and Titular Bishop of Sidyma by Bulls of June 2, 1891; consecrated in Natchez, Sept. 8, 1891; appt. first Bishop of Oklahoma, Aug. 23, 1905; made assistant at the pontifical throne, Nov. 30, 1916;; died Feb. 21, 1924; Most Revs. FRANCIS C. KELLEY, D.D., LL.D., Ph.D., Litt.D., Bishop of Oklahoma City & Tulsa; ord. Aug. 24, 1893; appt. Bishop of Oklahoma, June 25, 1924; consecrated Holy Name Cathedral, Chicago, IL, Oct. 2, 1924; died Feb. 1, 1948; EUGENE J. MCGUINNESS, D.D., Bishop of Oklahoma City & Tulsa; ord. May 22, 1915; consecrated Bishop of Raleigh, Dec. 21, 1937; appt. Coadjutor, Oklahoma City and Tulsa "cum jure successionis," Nov. 11, 1944; installed Jan. 10, 1945; succeeded to the See, Feb. 1, 1948; died Dec. 27, 1957; VICTOR J. REED, D.D., Bishop of Oklahoma City & Tulsa; ord. Dec. 21, 1929; consecrated March 5, 1958; died Sept. 8, 1971; JOHN R. QUINN, D.D., ord. July 19, 1953; appt. Auxiliary Bishop of San Diego and Titular Bishop of Thisiduo, Oct. 21, 1967; Episcopal ordination, Dec. 12, 1967;; transferred to Oklahoma City and Tulsa, Nov. 18, 1971; appt. as Archbishop of the Archdiocese of Oklahoma City, Dec. 13, 1972; installed as Archbishop of Oklahoma City, Feb. 6, 1973; transferred to Archbishop of San Francisco, April 26, 1977; CHARLES A. SALATKA, D.D. (Retired), ord. Feb. 24, 1945; appt. Titular Bishop of Cariana and Auxiliary of Grand Rapids Dec. 9, 1961; consecrated March 6, 1962; appt. Bishop of Marquette Jan. 10, 1968; installed March 25, 1968; appt. Archbishop of Oklahoma City Sept. 27, 1977; installed Dec. 15, 1977; retired Nov. 24, 1992; died March 17, 2003.

Vicar General—Rev. EDWARD J. WEISENBURGER, V.G., M.A., J.C.L.

Regional Vicars—Region I: Rev. RICHARD STANSBERRY, M.A., J.C.L., P.O. Box 60569, Oklahoma City, 73146. Region II: Rev. LOWELL STIEFERMAN, 7336 W. Britton Rd., Oklahoma City, 73132. Region III: Rev. RAY ACKERMAN, P.O. Box 1585, Ada, 74821. Region IV: Rev. JAMES D.M. STAFFORD, P.O. Box 2546, Lawton, 73502. Region V: Rev. HOA NGUYEN, P.O. Box 371, Hobart, 73651. Region VI: Rev. JAMES KNIGHT, P.O. Box 708, Woodward, 73802. Region VII: Rev. MARK MASON, 211 N. Cherokee, Hennessey, 73742. Region VIII: Rev. JOHN MICHALICKA, P.O. Box 1330, Ponca City, 74602. Region IX: Rev. STEPHEN J. BIRD, P.O. Box 185, Okarche, 73762.

Catholic Pastoral Center—7501 Northwest Expwy., P.O. Box 32180, Oklahoma City, 73123. Tel: 405-721-5651; Fax: 405-721-5210. Office Hours: Mon.-Fri. 8:30-4:30

Chancellor—Rev. JOHN A. STEICHEN.

Vicar for Ministries—Rev. ANTHONY B. TAYLOR.

Archdiocesan Tribunal—7501 Northwest Expwy., P.O. Box 32180, Oklahoma City, 73123. Tel: 405-721-5651.

Judicial Vicar—Rev. CHARLES H. SCHETTLER, S.T.L., J.C.D.

Adjutant Judicial Vicar—Rev. RICHARD STANSBERRY, M.A., J.C.L.

Pro-Synodal Judge—Rev. EDWARD WEISENBURGER, V.G., M.A., J.C.L.; Mr. GEORGE RIGAZZI, J.C.L.

Defenders of the Bond—Revs. LOWELL STIEFERMAN; ALAN J. LOTH; JOHN W. FEEHILY.

Advocates—Rev. EDWARD MENASCO; Mrs. MONA CROSS; Mrs. WANDA J. LANE; Mrs. SUSAN LINDLEY; Mrs. JUDY REILLY.

Notaries—Mrs. MONA CROSS; Mrs. TONI NICHOLLS.

Interdiocesan Tribunal of Second Instance for the Province of Oklahoma City—P.O. Box 32180, Oklahoma City, 73123. Tel: 405-721-5651.

Judicial Vicar—Rev. ROBERTO QUANT.

Judge—Rev. EDWARD WEISENBURGER, V.G., M.A., J.C.L.

Defenders of the Bond—Revs. PHILIP M. DONOHOE; ELMER C. SCHWARZ.

Consultors Archdiocesan—Revs. THOMAS BOYER; BRUCE NATSUHARA; JOSEPH A. JACOBI; JOHN A. STEICHEN; EDWARD J. WEISENBURGER, V.G., M.A., J.C.L.; JOACHIM SPEXARTH, O.S.B.; RICHARD STANSBERRY, M.A., J.C.L.

Council of Priests Archdiocesan—Revs. TIMOTHY D. LUSCHEN, Chm., 2001 N. Western, Edmond, 73003; JOHN METZINGER; TIMOTHY D. LUSCHEN, Chm.; DONALD WOLF, Vice Chm.; BRUCE NATSUHARA, Sec. & Treas.; JOACHIM SPEXARTH, O.S.B.; JOHN A. STEICHEN; BILL PRUETT; EDWARD J. WEISENBURGER, V.G., M.A., J.C.L.; JOSEPH A. JACOBI; ANTHONY B. TAYLOR.

Health Panel, Archdiocesan—Rev. WILLIAM B. ROSS, Chm. (Retired), P.O. Box 1280, Purcell, 73080. Tel: 405-527-3077.

Personnel Committee—Revs. ANTHONY B. TAYLOR; THOMAS J. BOYER; ALAN J. LOTH.

Archdiocesan Offices and Directors

Office of Stewardship and Development—Mr. JOSEPH H. COMBS, C.S.A., Dir., P.O. Box 32180, Oklahoma City, 73123. Tel: 405-721-5651.

Archdiocesan Development Fund— formerly Diocesan Development Fund; also formerly known as Diocesan Fund, Bishop's Fund for Diocesan Development, Mr. JOSEPH H. COMBS, C.S.A., Dir., 7501 N.W. Expwy., P.O. Box 32180, Oklahoma City, 73123. Tel: 405-721-5651.

Archdiocese of Oklahoma City Educational Trust Fund—Sr. CATHERINE POWERS, C.N.D., Dir., 7501 N.W. Expwy., P.O. Box 32180, Oklahoma City, 73123.

Catholic Charities of the Archdiocese of Oklahoma City, Inc.—Mr. TIMOTHY O'CONNOR, Dir., 1501 N.

Classen Blvd., Oklahoma City, 73106. Tel: 405-523-3000; Fax: 405-523-3030.

Archdiocesan Finance Council—Most Rev. EUSEBIUS J. BELTRAN, D.D.; Revs. JOHN A. STEICHEN; RICHARD D. STANSBERRY JR.; ANTHONY B. TAYLOR; Mr. JOHN TORBETT; Mr. MICHAEL BLUBAUGH; Mr. FLOYD ANDERSON; Mrs. ELLEN FLEMING; Mr. MELVIN MARTIN; Mrs. SUSAN LOOSEN; Mr. MICHAEL MILLIGAN; Mr. HUGH D. RICE; Mr. MICHAEL R. STERKEL; Mr. DAVID JOHNSON, Business Mgr., Business Office, P.O. Box 32180, Oklahoma City, 73123. Tel: 405-721-5651.

Building Committee—Mr. DAVID JOHNSON, P.O. Box 32180, Oklahoma City, 73123. Tel: 405-721-5651.

Catholic Foundation of Oklahoma, Inc.—Mr. DAVID JOHNSON, Sec. & Treas.; Mr. JOSEPH H. COMBS, C.S.A., 7501 Northwest Expwy., P.O. Box 32180, Oklahoma City, 73123. Tel: 405-721-5651.

Catholic Lawyers Guild—Rev. RAYMOND K. ACKERMAN, Spiritual Moderator, P.O. Box 1585, Ada, 74821. Tel: 580-332-4811.

Catholic Physicians Guild—Rev. DANIEL MCCAFFREY, Chap., P.O. Box 32180, Oklahoma City, 73123. Tel: 405-942-4084.

Catholic Social Services—Mr. TIM O'CONNOR, 1501 N. Classen Blvd., Oklahoma City, 73106. Tel: 405-523-3000; Fax: 405-523-3030.

Charismatic Renewal—Rev. MARVIN F. LEVEN, Episcopal Moderator, P.O. Box 404, Okarche, 73762. Tel: 405-263-7798.

Communications, Archdiocesan Department of—P.O. Box 32180, Oklahoma City, 73123. Tel: 405-721-1810; 405-721-5651.

Correction Related Ministry—VACANT.

Council of Catholic Women, Archdiocesan—Rev. JOSEPH C. KOLB (Retired).

Ecumenical and Interreligious Affairs, Office for Archdiocesan Dir.—VACANT, P.O. Box 510, Edmond, 73083. Tel: 405-340-0691.

Education—Sr. CATHERINE POWERS, C.N.D., Archdiocesan Dir., P.O. Box 32180, Oklahoma City, 73123. Tel: 405-721-4202; 405-721-5651.

Catholic Schools, Office of—Sr. CATHERINE POWERS, C.N.D., Supt.; Mrs. CRIS CARTER, Assoc. Supt., P.O. Box 32180, Oklahoma City, 73123. Tel: 405-721-4202; 405-721-5651.

Religious Education, Office of—Ms. PATRICIA KOENIG, Dir., P.O. Box 32180, Oklahoma City, 73123. Tel: 405-721-1415; 405-721-5651.

Pastoral Ministry Office—Sr. M. DIANE KOORIE, R.S.M., Dir., P.O. Box 32180, Oklahoma City, 73123. Tel: 405-721-1415; 405-721-5651 Affiliated with Kansas Newman College, Wichita, KS and Aquinas Institute, St. Louis, MO.

Campus Ministry, Department of—Rev. BILL PRUETT, 100 E. Stinson, Norman, 73072. Tel: 405-321-0990.

Clergy Education, Department of—P.O. Box 32180, Oklahoma City, 73123. Tel: 405-721-5651.

Victim Assistance Coordinator—Mrs. CAROLINE LINEHAN, P.O. Box 32180, Oklahoma City, 73123. Tel: 405-721-5651, Ext. 150. Email: clinehan@catharchdioceseokc.org.

Family Life Department—Mr. GEORGE RIGAZZI, P.O. Box 32180, Oklahoma City, 73123. Tel: 405-721-8943; 405-721-5651.

Indian Ministries, Inc.— (Oklahoma), Rev. MARIO PULUGUJJU, Liaison, P.O. Box 628, Anadarko, 73005. Tel: 405-247-5255.

Justice and Human Development, Commission for—Mrs. SHIRLEY COX, 1501 N. Classen Blvd., Oklahoma City, 73106. Tel: 405-532-3000.

Legal Counsel—Mr. JACK R. LAWRENCE, 4900 Richmond Sq., Oklahoma City, 73118. Tel: 405-841-6000.

Master of Ceremonies—Revs. ROBERT WOOD; TIMOTHY FULLER, Asst.

Ministry to Priests Program—Rev. ANTHONY B. TAYLOR, Dir., P.O. Box 32180, Oklahoma City, 73123. Tel: 405-721-5651.

Mission "Micatokla"--Archdiocesan Mission of Santiago Atitlan, Guatemala—Rev. JOHN A. STEICHEN, Archdiocesan Coord., P.O. Box 32180, Oklahoma City, 73123. Tel: 405-721-5651; Fax: 405-721-5210.

Newspaper—Ms. RAY DYER, Editor, P.O. Box 32180, Oklahoma City, 73123. Tel: 405-721-1810; 405-721-5651. "The Sooner Catholic"

Pastoral Planning—Mr. JAMES WEINMANN, Dir., 7501 Northwest Expwy., P.O. Box 32180, Oklahoma City, 73123. Tel: 405-721-5651.

Permanent Diaconate—Rev. EDWARD T. MENASCO, Dir., P.O. Box 32180, Oklahoma City, 73123. Tel: 405-721-5651.

Priests' Medical Fund— formerly known as Infirm Priest Fund Rev. JOHN A. STEICHEN, P.O. Box 32180, Oklahoma City, 73123. Tel: 405-721-5651.

Priests' Retirement Board—Most Rev. EUSEBIUS J. BELTRAN, D.D.; Revs. JOHN A. STEICHEN; ANTHONY B. TAYLOR, Chm., Catholic Pastoral Center, P.O. Box 32180, Oklahoma City, 73123. Tel: 405-721-5651.

Propagation of the Faith, Holy Childhood Assoc., Missionary Cooperation Plan—Rev. JOHN A. STEICHEN, P.O. Box 32180, Oklahoma City, 73123. Tel: 405-721-5651.

Rural Life—Rev. JAMES GREINER, Dir., 1100 N. Sara Rd., P.O. Box 246, Mustang, 73064. Tel: 405-376-9435.

Scouting—Rev. MICHAEL WHEELAHAN, P.O. Box 360, Medford, 73759. Tel: 580-395-2148.

St. Ann's Retirement Village—Mr. ROBERT O'CONNOR, Dir. Admin., 9400 St. Ann Dr., Oklahoma City, 73162. Tel: 405-728-7888.

St. Francis de Sales Seminary (Legal Title)—Most Rev. EUSEBIUS J. BELTRAN, D.D., Pres.; Revs. JOHN A. STEICHEN, Sec., Trustees:; DAVID F. MONAHAN (Retired); Mr. DAVID JOHNSON, Treas., P.O. Box 32180, Oklahoma City, 73123.

St. Vincent dePaul, Society of Oklahoma City District Council—Rev. BRUCE K. NATSUHARA, Spiritual Moderator, P.O. Box 408, Oklahoma City, 73101. Tel: 405-235-4565.

Vocations and Seminarians—Rev. LOWELL STIEFERMAN, Dir. Associate Directors: Revs. TIMOTHY LUSCHEN; RICHARD STANSBERRY, M.A., J.C.L., Catholic Pastoral Center, P.O. Box 32180, Oklahoma City, 73123. Tel: 405-721-9351; 405-721-5651.

Worship and Spiritual Life, Office of—Rev. STEPHEN BIRD, Dir.; Sr. JOANNE YANKAUSKIS, O.S.B., Co-Dir., P.O. Box 32180, Oklahoma City, 73123. Tel: 405-721-5651.

Youth and Young Adult Ministry, Office of—Mrs. NANCY HOUSH, Dir.; Mrs. BECKY JAIME, Assoc. Dir., P.O. Box 32180, Oklahoma City, 73123. Tel: 405-721-9220; 405-721-5651.

CLERGY, PARISHES, MISSIONS AND PAROCHIAL SCHOOLS

OKLAHOMA CITY
(OKLAHOMA COUNTY)

1—CATHEDRAL OF OUR LADY OF PERPETUAL HELP (1919), (Vietnamese), [JC] Revs. Edward J. Weisenburger, V.G., M.A., J.C.L.; Thanh Van Nguyen; Deacons William Enos; Paul Lewis; Anthony Le; Sang Ninh. In Res., Rev. Paul Mollan.
Res.: 3214 N. Lake Ave., 73118. Tel: 405-525-2349; Fax: 405-525-3628.
School—Bishop John Carroll, 1100 N.W. 32, 73118. Tel: 405-525-0956; Fax: 405-523-3053. Lay Teachers 16; Students 217.
Catechesis/Religious Program—Tel: 405-525-2349, Ext. 140. Students 85.

2—ST. ANDREW DUNG-LAC (1994), (Vietnamese), [JC] Rev. Dominic Hung Hoang.
Mailing Address: P.O. Box 891584, 73189.
Church: 3000 S.W. 55th St., 73119. Tel: 405-681-2665; 405-681-6918; Fax: 405-681-7951.
Catechesis/Religious Program—Students 236.

3—ST. CHARLES BORROMEO (1954), [JC] Revs. Paul H. Gallatin; Oby J. Zunmas; James A. Goin; Deacons John Pitt, (Retired); Marc LeWand.
Res.: 5024 N. Grove St., 73122. Tel: 405-789-2595; Fax: 405-789-4394.
School—5000 N. Grove St., 73122. Tel: 405-789-0224; Fax: 405-789-3583. Lay Teachers 21; Students 264.
Catechesis/Religious Program—Students 259.

4—CHRIST THE KING (1949), [JC] Revs. Joseph R. Ross; Balasamy Nagineni; Deacon David Best.
Mailing Address: P.O. Box 20508, 73156. Tel: 405-842-1481; Fax: 405-842-0539.
Rectory—1900 Elmhurst Ave., 73120. Tel: 405-841-6680.
Church: 8005 Dorset Dr., 73120.
School—Tel: 405-843-3909; Fax: 504-843-6519. Sally Howard, Prin. Lay Teachers 23; Students 322.
Catechesis/Religious Program—Tel: 405-843-4766. Students 128.

5—CHURCH OF THE EPIPHANY OF THE LORD (1976), Rev. Lowell L. Stieferman; Alveria Kopp, Pastoral Assoc.
Res.: 7336 W. Britton Rd., 73132. Tel: 405-722-2110; Fax: 405-722-6719.
Catechesis/Religious Program—Tel: 405-722-0051. Roxann Lackner, D.R.E. Students 650.

6—CORPUS CHRISTI (1924), (African American), [JC] Rev. David M. Lafferty; Deacons James Barton; Dunn Cumby.
Res.: 1005 N.E. 15th St., 73117. Tel: 405-236-4301; Fax: 405-235-0032.
Catechesis/Religious Program—Students 55.
Mission—St. Robert Bellarmine 115 N. 3rd, Jones, Oklahoma Co. 73049.

7—ST. EUGENE'S (1958), [JC] Rev. Joseph A. Jacobi; Deacons Patrick Reynolds; Duane Descher.
Res.: 2400 W. Hefner Rd., P.O. Box 20930, 73156. Tel: 405-751-7115; Fax: 405-751-8722.
School—Tel: 405-751-0067. Lay Teachers 28; Students 365.
Catechesis/Religious Program—Students 285.

8—ST. FRANCIS OF ASSISI (1925), [JC] Rev. Richard D. Stansberry Jr. In Res., Rev. Charles H. Schettler, S.T.L., J.C.D.
Res.: 1901 N.W. 18th St., P.O. Box 60569, 73146. Tel: 405-528-0485; Fax: 405-524-1260.
School—Rosary, 1910 N.W. 19th St., 73106. Tel: 405-525-9272; Fax: 405-525-5643. Mrs. Karen Carter, Prin. Sisters 1; Lay Teachers 15; Students 209.
Catechesis/Religious Program—Students 98.

9—HOLY ANGELS (1924), (Hispanic), [JC] Rev. Roberto Quant; Deacon Lucio Nieto.
Res.: 317 N. Blackwelder St., 73106. Tel: 405-232-6572; Fax: 405-235-8334.
Convent—Carmelite Missionaries of St. Teresa, 1522 N.W. Third St., 73106. Tel: 405-231-1935.
Catechesis/Religious Program—Students 360.

10—IMMACULATE CONCEPTION (1892), [CEM] Rev. George Pupius; Deacon James Keene.
Res.: 3901 S.W. 29th St., 73119. Tel: 405-685-4224; Fax: 405-685-4483.
Catechesis/Religious Program—Tel: 405-685-4806. Students 49.

11—ST. JAMES (1954), Rev. Robert T. Wood; Deacon Marti Gulikers.
Res.: 4308 S. Blackwelder St., 73119. Tel: 405-636-6800; Fax: 405-636-6848.
School—1224 S.W. 41st St., 73109. Tel: 405-636-6810; Fax: 405-636-6818. Sisters 2; Lay Teachers 15; Students 207.
Convent—Sisters of Charity of Leavenworth, 4212 S. Blackwelder, 73119. Tel: 405-636-6830.
Catechesis/Religious Program—Tel: 405-636-6840. Students 194.

12—ST. JOSEPH (1889), [JC], (Old Cathedral) Rev. Bruce K. Natsuhara.
Mailing Address: P.O.Box 408, 73101. In Res., Rev. George Parackal.
Res.: 307 N.W. 4th St., 73102. Tel: 405-235-4565; Fax: 405-815-6644.
Church: 307 N.W. 4th St., 73102.
Catechesis/Religious Program—Students 18.

13—KOREAN MARTYRS (1996), (Korean), Rev. Hyogeum M. Park.
Church: 2600 S.W. 74th St., 73159. Tel: 405-681-6464; Fax: 405-688-5586.
Res.: 7517 S. Lynn, 73159. Tel: 405-688-5585; Fax: 405-688-5586.
Catechesis/Religious Program—Students 20.

14—OUR LADY OF MOUNT CARMEL AND ST. THERESE LITTLE FLOWER (1921), [JC] Revs. Jenaro De La Cruz, O.C.D.; Henry Bordeaux, O.C.D.
Mailing Address: P.O.Box 1196, 73101-1196. Tel: 405-235-2037; Fax: 405-235-7023.
Mission—Our Lady of Guadalupe 2123 S.W. 11th St., Packing Town, Oklahoma Co. 73108.
Catechesis/Religious Program—Tel: 405-235-5259. Students 570.

15—ST. PATRICK (1950), Rev. Thomas McSherry; Deacon Dennis Frazier.
Res.: 2121 N. Portland, P.O. Box 75835, 73147. Tel: 405-947-2275; 405-946-4441; Fax: 405-946-4894.
Catechesis/Religious Program—Students 120.

16—ST. PAUL, APOSTLE (1956), [JC] Rev. Kenneth E. Kulinski; Deacon Raymond LaChance.
Res.: 3901 S. Sunnylane Rd., Del City, 73115. Tel: 405-677-4873; Fax: 405-619-0596.
Mission— Del City, Mission Co.
Catechesis/Religious Program—Students 130.

17—ST. PHILIP NERI (Midwest City) (1946), [JC] Rev. Charles R. Murphy; Deacon James G. Young, Pastoral Assoc.
Church & Mailing Address: 1107 Felix Pl., Midwest City, 73110. Tel: 405-737-4476; Fax: 405-741-0531.
Rectory—301 Wilson Dr., Midwest City, 73110.
School—1121 Felix Pl., Midwest City, 73110. Tel: 405-737-4496; Fax: 405-732-7823. Lay Teachers 20; Students 267.
Catechesis/Religious Program—Tel: 405-737-4476, Ext. 108. Students 169.

18—SACRED HEART (1911), [JC] Revs. Anthony B. Taylor; Scott A. Boeckman; Jose Acosta; Deacons George Leal; Mariano Martinez.
Res.: 2706 S. Shartel Ave., 73109. Tel: 405-634-2458; Fax: 405-634-2459.
School—2700 S. Shartel Ave., 73109. Tel: 405-634-5673; Fax: 405-634-7011. Ms. Joana Camacho, Prin. Lay Teachers 12; Students 173.
Catechesis/Religious Program—Tel: 405-634-6448. Students 665.

OUTSIDE OKLAHOMA CITY

ADA, PONTOTOC CO., ST. JOSEPH (1902), Rev. Raymond K. Ackerman; Deacon Michael Radosevich.
Res.: 1300 E. Beverly St., P.O. Box 1585, 74821. Tel: 580-332-4811; Fax: 580-436-1226.
Catechesis/Religious Program—Students 80.
Mission—St. Francis Xavier 1313 E. 7th St., Sulphur, Murray Co. 73086. Tel: 580-622-3070.

ALTUS, JACKSON CO., PRINCE OF PEACE (1964), Rev. Joseph H. Arledge.
Res.: 1500 Falcon Rd., 73521. Tel: 580-482-3363; Fax: 580-482-6657.
Mission—Our Lady of Guadalupe P.O. Box 107, Hollis, Harmon Co. 73550. Tel: 580-688-2233; Fax: 580-688-9234.
Catechesis/Religious Program—Students 303.

ALVA, WOODS CO., SACRED HEART (1897), [CEM] Rev. Shane I. Tharp.
Res.: 627 12th St., 73717. Tel: 580-327-0339; Fax: 580-327-0710.
Mission—Our Mother of Mercy 210 S. Main St., Waynoka, Woods Co. 73860.
Mission—St. Cornelius (1895), 404 S. Massachusetts, Cherokee, Alfalfa Co. 73728. Tel: 580-596-3328.
Catechesis/Religious Program—Tel: 580-327-3006. Students 56.

ANADARKO, CADDO CO., ST. PATRICK'S (1892), (Native American), [JC 5] Rev. Mariyanandam Pulugujju (India), Co-Admin.; Deacon John Butler, Co-Admin.
Res.: 1115 W. Petree Rd., Box 628, 73005. Tel: 405-247-5255; Fax: 405-247-5249.
Mission—Our Lady of the Most Holy Rosary Binger. Hwy. 152, Binger, Caddo Co. 73009.
Mission—St. Richard Hwy. 9, Carnegie, Caddo Co. 73015. Tel: 580-654-2177.
Catechesis/Religious Program—Students 57.

ARDMORE, CARTER CO., ST. MARY (1898), [CEM] Revs. Thomas O'Toole; Juan Manuel Guerrero.
Res.: 125 E St. S.W., 73401. Tel: 580-223-0231; Fax: 580-226-2129.
Mission—St. Cecilia 300 E. Lincoln Ave., Healdton, Carter Co. 73438.
Mission—Good Shepherd Broadway & N. 7th, Marietta, Love Co. 73448.
Mission—Holy Cross 14 W. Francis St., Madill, Marshall Co. 73446-3234. Tel: 580-795-7107; Fax: 580-795-7206. P.O. Box 791, Madill, 73446.
Mission—St. Anthony 305 E. Wilson St., Tishomingo, Johnston Co. 73460-3124.
Catechesis/Religious Program—Students 358.

BETHANY, OKLAHOMA CO., LATIN MASS COMMUNITY (2000), Rev. Joseph Poisson, F.S.S.P. (Canada).
Mailing Address: 4701 N. McMillion Ave., 73008. Tel: 405-440-9168; Fax: 405-782-0767.
Church & Chapel: 4703 N. McMillian Ave., 73008.

BISON, GARFIELD CO., ST. JOSEPH'S (1911), (Czech), [CEM] Rev. Larry B. Gatlin.
Res.: Box 117, 73720. Tel: 580-758-3558; Fax: 580-758-1219.
Mission—St. Ann 6th & Locust, Fairview, Major Co. 73737. Tel: 580-227-2270.
Catechesis/Religious Program—Students 28.

BLACKWELL, KAY CO., ST. JOSEPH'S (1901), Rev. Martin Larok Obwona, F.C.
Res.: 315 W. Blackwell Ave., P.O. Box 578, 74631. Tel: 580-363-2096; Fax: 580-363-2096.
Catechesis/Religious Program—Tel: 580-363-0441. Students 87.

CALUMET, CANADIAN CO., IMMACULATE HEART OF MARY (1940), (German—Irish), Rev. Omar Tabing.
Mailing Address: P.O. Box 99, 73014. Tel: 405-893-2336; Fax: 405-893-2715.
Church: 107 S. Freehome, 73014. Tel: 405-893-2336; Fax: 405-893-2715.
Catechesis/Religious Program—Students 6.

CHANDLER, LINCOLN CO., OUR LADY OF SORROWS (1894), [CEM] Rev. James J. Mickus (Retired).
Res.: 409 Price Ave., P.O. Box 543, 74834. Tel: 405-258-1239; Fax: 405-258-0010.
Mission—St. Louis Hwy. 99 & Eighth Ave., Stroud, Lincoln Co. 74079.
Catechesis/Religious Program—Students 90.

CHEROKEE, ALFALFA CO., ST. CORNELIUS (1958),, A mission of Sacred Heart, Alva.

CHICKASHA, GRADY CO., HOLY NAME (1895), [CEM] Rev. Elmer C. Schwarz.
Res.: 210 S. Seventh St., Box 748, 73023. Tel: 405-224-7513; Fax: 405-224-4434.
Catechesis/Religious Program—Tel: 405-224-6068. Students 122.

CLINTON, CUSTER CO., ST. MARY'S (1944), Rev. Carl William Janocha; Deacon Pedro Maldonado.
Res.: 714 S. 12th St., 73601. Tel: 580-323-0309; Fax: 580-323-0345.
Mission—St. Anne 522 E. 3rd, Cordell, Washita Co. 73632.
Catechesis/Religious Program—1218 Knox Ave., P.O. Box 1295, 73601. Tel: 580-323-0345. Students 160.

DUNCAN, STEPHENS CO., ASSUMPTION (1902), [CEM] Revs. Donald J. Wolf; Victor Kurapati; Deacons Bernard T. O'Loughlin; James Conway.
Res.: 711 Hickory Ave., 73533. Tel: 580-255-0590; Fax: 580-252-3866.
Mission—Immaculate Conception Fourth & Comanche, Marlow, Stephens Co. 73055. Tel: 580-658-2365.
Mission—St. Francis of Assisi Fifth & Choctaw, Rush Springs, Grady Co. 73082.
Mission—San Jose 1117 Lincoln Ave., Ryan, Jefferson Co. 73565. Tel: 580-757-2830.
Catechesis/Religious Program—Mrs. Melissa Garcia, D.R.E.; Mr. Marco Ocana, D.R.E. Students 174.

EDMOND, OKLAHOMA CO.

1—ST. JOHN THE BAPTIST (1889), Revs. John R. Metzinger; Louis Vanderley, O.S.B.; Francis T. Nguyen; Deacons Bill Bawden; Bill Coyle; John Morris.
Res.: 900 S. Littler St., P.O. Box 510, 73083. Tel: 405-340-0691; Fax: 405-340-5715.
School—St. Elizabeth Ann Seton School, 925 South Blvd., 73033. Tel: 405-348-5364; Fax: 405-340-9627. Lay Teachers 26; Students 486.
Catechesis/Religious Program—Tel: 405-340-9871. Students 830.

2—ST. MONICA (1993), [CEM] Rev. Timothy D. Luschen.
Mailing Address: 2001 N. Western, 73003. Tel: 405-359-2700; Fax: 405-341-0023.
Res.: 1121 N.W. 199th St., 73003. Tel 405-330-2699; Fax 405-330-2699.
Catechesis/Religious Program—Students 491.

EL RENO, CANADIAN CO., SACRED HEART (1890), [CEM] Rev. Philip M. Donohoe.
Res.: 208 S. Evans St., 73036. Tel: 405-262-1405; Fax: 405-262-2251.
School—Sacred Heart School, 210 S. Evans, 73036. Tel: 405-262-2284; Fax: 405-262-3818. Adawnya Wiewel, Prin. Teachers 11; Students 121.
Catechesis/Religious Program—Tel: 405-262-2273. Students 93.

ELGIN, COMANCHE CO., ST. ANN (1914), (German), [CEM] [JC 2] Rev. Irudayayaraj Yeddanapalli.
Res.: 8432 St. Hwy. 17, P.O. Box 10, 73538. Tel: 580-492-5914; Fax: 580-492-5908.
Mission—Our Lady of Perpetual Help 220 N. A St., Sterling, Comanche Co. 73567.
Mission—Mother of Sorrows 521 E. Wallace, Apache, Caddo Co. 73006.
Catechesis/Religious Program—Students 76.

ELK CITY, BECKHAM CO., ST. MATTHEW'S (1970), (German), [CEM] [JC 3] Rev. Timothy Fuller.
Mailing Address: 3001 E. Hwy. 66, 73648. Tel: 580-225-0066; Fax: 580-225-3522.
Res.: 2900 E. Highway 66, 73648. Tel: 580-225-3980.
Mission—Queen of All Saints 914 N. 5th St., Sayre, Beckham Co. 73662. Tel: 580-928-5124.
Catechesis/Religious Program—Students 175.

ENID, GARFIELD CO.

1—ST. FRANCIS XAVIER (1893), [CEM] [JC] Rev. Kevin J. Ratterman, Admin.; Deacon Anthony Crispo. In Res., Rev. Ernest A. Flusche (Retired).
Res.: 110 N. Madison, P.O. Box 3527, 73702. Tel: 580-237-0812; Fax: 580-237-0909.
School—St. Joseph Catholic School, (Grades PreK-4) Tel: 580-242-4449; Fax: 580-242-3541. Lay Teachers 7; Students 83.
Catechesis/Religious Program—Tel 580-234-0152. Students 253.

2—ST. GREGORY THE GREAT (1971), Rev. Lawrence T. Kowalski.
Church: 1924 W. Willow, 73703. Tel: 580-233-4589; Fax: 580-233-4590.
Res.: 2045 Lantern Ln., 73703. Tel: 580-233-1845.
Mission—St. Michael [CEM] Main St., Goltry, Alfalfa Co. 73739.
Catechesis/Religious Program—Fax: 580-233-4589. Students 232.

FREDERICK, TILLMAN CO., ST. HELEN (1927), Rev. Louis Sellam (India); Ray Wallace, Co-Admin.
Res.: 507 E. Highview Ave., 73542. Tel: 580-335-3298; Fax: 580-335-3953.
Catechesis/Religious Program—Students 58.
Mission—Our Lady of Perpetual Help S. Main & 8th St., Grandfield, Tillman Co. 73546.
Mission—St. Patrick 209 E. Iowa, Walters, Cotton Co. 73572. Tel: 580-875-3855.

GUTHRIE, LOGAN CO., ST. MARY'S (1889), [CEM] Rev. Denis G. Hanrahan; Deacons Roy Ellison; Richard Washko.
Mailing Address: P.O. Box 1556, 7304.
Res.: 411 N. Elm St., 73044. Tel: 405-282-4239; Fax: 405-282-5610.
School—Tel: 405-282-2071; Fax: 405-282-2924. Lay Teachers 8; Students 125.
Mission—St. Margaret Mary P.O. Box 632, Crescent, Logan Co. 73028. Tel: 405-969-2351.
Catechesis/Religious Program—Students 71.

GUYMON, TEXAS CO., ST. PETER'S (1906), (Hispanic), [CEM] Revs. Stephen V. Hamilton; Scott Adams; Deacons Joe Cruz; Simon Guerra.
Res.: 1220 N. Quinn St., P.O. Box 731, 73942. Tel: 580-338-7212; Fax: 580-338-5584; 580-338-8746.
Mission—Sacred Heart 106 N. Albright, P.O. Box 468, Hooker, Texas Co. 73945. Tel: 580-652-2320.
Mission—Good Shepherd S. Ellis at Second, P.O.Box 966, Boise City, Cimarron Co. 73933. Tel: 580-544-3443.
Catechesis/Religious Program—Tel: 405-454-9940. Students 250.

HARRAH, OKLAHOMA CO., ST. TERESA OF AVILA (1907), (Polish), [CEM] Rev. Alan J. Loth.
Res.: 1576 Tim Holt Dr., Box 418, 73045. Tel: 405-454-2819; Fax: 405-454-0981.
Catechesis/Religious Program—Tel: 405-454-9940. Students 201.

HENNESSEY, KINGFISHER CO., ST. JOSEPH'S (1890), [CEM] Rev. Mark E. Mason.
Res.: 211 N. Cherokee St., 73742. Tel: 405-853-4425; Fax: 405-853-2166.
Mission—St. Camillus Main St., Marshall, Logan Co. 73056.
Catechesis/Religious Program—Tel: 405-853-2158; Fax: 405-853-2158. Students 138.

HITCHCOCK, BLAINE CO., SACRED HEART MISSION, Closed., For inquiries for parish records contact St. Anthony of Padua Church, Okeene.

HOBART, KIOWA CO., STS. PETER AND PAUL (1902), Rev. Hoa Van Nguyen.
Mailing Address: 328 S. Randlett, 73651. Tel: 580-726-3925; Fax: 580-726-3925. 409 N. Byers, P.O. Box 310, Mangum, 73554. Tel: 580-782-2657; Fax: 580-782-2457.
Res.: 324 S. Randlett, 73651. Tel: 580-726-3925; Fax: 580-726-3925.
Mission—Sacred Heart Mangum, Greer Co.
Catechesis/Religious Program—Students 78.

JONES, OKLAHOMA CO., ST. ROBERT BELLARMINE (1948),, A mission of Corpus Christi, Oklahoma City.
Mission—St. Theresa of the Infant Jesus Luther, Oklahoma Co. 73054. Closed. See Corpus Christi Church, Oklahoma City for records.

KINGFISHER, KINGFISHER CO., SS. PETER AND PAUL (1896), [CEM] Rev. M. Price Oswalt.
Res.: 309 S. Main St., 73750. Tel: 405-375-4581; Fax: 405-375-3858.
School—Tel: 405-375-4616; Fax: 405-375-5296. Lay Teachers 10; Students 110.
Catechesis/Religious Program—Students 85.

KONAWA, POTTAWATOMIE CO., SACRED HEART (1876), [CEM] Rev. Matthew J. Brown, O.S.B.
Res.: Rte. 1, Box 101, 74849. Tel: 580-925-2145; Fax: 580-925-2145.
Mission—St. Mary Wanette, Pottawatomie Co.
Mission—St. Joseph Wewoka, Seminole Co.
Catechesis/Religious Program—Tel: 580-925-2058. Students 38.

LAWTON, COMANCHE CO.

1—BLESSED SACRAMENT (1902), Rev. James D.M. Stafford; Deacon Bill Adamson.
Res.: 12 S.W. Seventh St., Box 2546, 73502. Tel: 580-355-2054; Fax: 580-355-2055.
School—St. Mary's, 611 A Ave., 73501. Tel: 580-355-5288; Fax: 580-355-4336. Lay Teachers 12; Students 120.
Catechesis/Religious Program—Tel: 580-353-8182. Students 65.

2—HOLY FAMILY (1959),, (Formerly St. Barbara) Rev. Philip Seeton. Fax: 580-536-2607; Deacons Herman Lawrence; Leo Martinez Jr.; Peter Dulcamara; Celine Benoit, Pastoral Assoc.
Res.: 1010 N.W. 82nd St., P.O. Box 7948, 73506. Tel: 580-536-6351; Fax: 580-536-6352.
Catechesis/Religious Program—Tel: 580-536-6355; Fax: 580-536-6352. Students 300.

LEXINGTON, CLEVELAND CO., ST. JOHN THE BAPTIST, Closed., For parish records contact Our Lady of Victory, Purcell.

LOYAL, KINGFISHER CO., ST. JOSEPH MISSION, Closed., For inquiries for parish records contact Sts. Peter & Paul Church, Kingfisher.

MANGUM, GREER CO., SACRED HEART, , Became a mission of Sts. Peter and Paul, Hobart

MCLOUD, POTTOWATOMIE CO., ST. VINCENT DE PAUL (1903), Rev. Eugene C. Marshall, O.S.B.
Res.: 122 S. 10th St., P.O. Box 585, 74851. Tel: 405-964-5606 (Res.); 405-878-5452; Fax: 405-878-5189.
Catechesis/Religious Program—Students 39.

MEDFORD, GRANT CO., ST. MARY'S (1940), [CEM 3] Rev. Michael Wheelahan.
Res.: 214 W. Cherokee, Box 360, 73759. Tel: 580-395-2148; Fax: 580-395-2960.
Mission—St. Mary's Assumption Main & Birch, Wakita, Grant Co. 73771. Tel: 580-594-2541.
Mission—St. Joseph's S. Hwy. 81, Pond Creek, Grant Co. 73766.
Catechesis/Religious Program—Tel: 580-395-2290. Students 78.

MOORE, CLEVELAND CO., ST. ANDREW'S (1962), [CEM] Rev. John W. Feehily; Deacons Jerome Caplinger;

Angus Watford; Margaret Hochla, Pastoral Assoc. Res.: 800 N.W. Fifth, 73153. Tel: 405-799-3334; Fax: 405-799-4880.
Catechesis/Religious Program—Tel: 405-799-3334, Ext. 16. Students 330.

MUSTANG, CANADIAN CO., CHURCH OF THE HOLY SPIRIT (1983), Rev. James A. Greiner.
Church: 1100 N. Sara Rd., P.O. Box 246, 73064. Tel: 405-376-9435; 405-376-5218; Fax: 405-376-4929.
Catechesis/Religious Program—Tel: 405-376-9162. Students 116.

NEWKIRK, KAY CO., ST. FRANCIS OF ASSISI (1894), Rev. Richard J. Beckman.
Res.: 610 W. Ninth St., P.O. Box 11, 74647. Tel: 580-362-3320.
Catechesis/Religious Program—Students 58.

NICOMA PARK, OKLAHOMA CO., OUR LADY OF FATIMA (1949), Rev. Wilbur E. Moore.
Res.: 2255 W. Meyer Cir., Box 368, 73066. Tel: 405-769-2490; Fax: 405-769-9113.
Catechesis/Religious Program—Tel: 405-769-2655. Students 93.

NORMAN, CLEVELAND CO.

1—CHURCH OF ST. MARK THE EVANGELIST (1991), Rev. Thomas J. Boyer; Deacon Byron Jacobson.
Mailing Address: 3939 W. Tecumseh Rd., 73072-1708. Tel: 405-366-7676; Fax: 405-366-7842.
Res.: 3701 Castlerock Rd., 73072. Tel: 405-447-3085; Fax: 405-447-0480.
Catechesis/Religious Program—Students 348.

2—ST. JOSEPH'S (1896), [CEM] Rev. Edward J. Menasco; Deacons Larry Sousa; Patrick Gabrish; Jeff Willard.
Res.: 425 E. Tonhawa, P.O. Box 1227, 73070. Tel: 405-321-8080; Fax: 405-321-4360.
Catechesis/Religious Program—Tel: 405-321-8084. Students 318.

3—ST. THOMAS MORE UNIVERSITY PARISH (1979), [JC] Rev. Bill H. Pruett; Deacons Larry Rossow; Lawrence F. Rossow, Pastoral Assoc.; John D. Piggott.
Church: 100 E. Stinson, 73072. Tel: 405-321-0990; Fax: 405-321-0964.
Res.: 1501 Lincoln, 73072. Tel: 405-329-5319.
Catechesis/Religious Program—Tel: 405-321-0990, Ext. 223. Sr. Ursula Schones, A.S.C., D.R.E. Students 118.

OKARCHE, KINGFISHER CO., HOLY TRINITY (1893), [CEM] Rev. Stephen J. Bird; Deacon Max Schwarz.
Res.: 211 W. Missouri, Box 185, 73762. Tel: 405-263-7930; Fax: 405-263-4518.
School—Box 485, 73762. Tel: 405-263-4422; Fax: 405-263-7475. Diane Floyd, Prin. Lay Teachers 10; Students 95.
Catechesis/Religious Program—Tel: 405-263-4640. Students 98.

OKEENE, BLAINE CO., ST. ANTHONY'S (1901), [CEM] Rev. David A. Cowden.
Res.: 211 S. Fifth St., Box 767, 73763. Tel: 580-822-3511; 580-822-3544; Fax: 580-822-3542.
Mission—St. Thomas 105 W. McAlister, Seiling, Dewey Co. 73663. Tel: 580-922-4376.
Mission—St. Rose of Lima 900 N. Clarence Nash Blvd., P.O. Box 58, Watonga, Blaine Co. 73772. Tel: 580-623-7740.
Catechesis/Religious Program—Tel: 580-822-4799. Students 59.

PAULS VALLEY, GARVIN CO., ST. CATHERINE OF SIENA (1949), [JC] Rev. Mike Vaught.
Res.: 205 W. Bert St., 73075. Tel: 405-238-3741; Fax: 405-238-5325.
Mission—St. Peter's E. Second & Quapah, Lindsay, Garvin Co. 73052. Fax: 405-238-3542.
Catechesis/Religious Program—Students 60.

PERRY, NOBLE CO., ST. ROSE OF LIMA (1893), [CEM] Rev. Thomas Dowdell; Sandy Soulek, Pastoral Assoc.
Mailing Address: P.O. Box 603, 73077-0603.
Res.: 421 Ninth St., 73077. Tel: 580-336-9300; Fax: 580-336-9795.
Mission—Sacred Heart Broadway & Lowe, Billings, Noble Co. 74630.
Catechesis/Religious Program—Students 54.

PONCA CITY, KAY CO., CHURCH OF ST. MARY (1893), [CEM] [JC] Revs. John J. Michalicka; Maria J. Kumar Ugdagandla; Deacon Richard Robinson.
Res.: 707 E. Ponca St., Box 1330, 74602. Tel: 580-765-6031; Fax: 580-765-1327.
School—St. Mary, 415 S. 7th, 74601. Tel: 580-765-4387; Fax: 580-765-1352.
School—Sisters of St. Joseph of Wichita, 3616 Wellington, 74604. Tel: 580-765-0482; Fax: 580-765-0562. Shirley Zink, Prin. Lay Teachers 18; Students 135.
Catechesis/Religious Program—Tel: 580-765-7794. Students 111.

PRAGUE, LINCOLN CO., ST. WENCESLAUS, NATIONAL SHRINE OF THE INFANT JESUS OF PRAGUE (1899), (Czech), [CEM] Rev. Adrian Vorderlandwehr, O.S.B.
Res.: 304 Jim Thorpe Blvd., Box 488, 74864. Tel: 405-567-3404; Fax: 405-567-0365.
Mission—St. Michael 217 S. Koonce, P.O. Box 684, Meeker, Lincoln Co. 74855.
Catechesis/Religious Program—Students 52.

PURCELL, MCCLAIN CO., OUR LADY OF VICTORY (1886), (Hispanic), [CEM] Rev. William B. Ross (Retired).
Res.: 316 W. Jefferson St., Box 1280, 73080. Tel: 405-527-3077; Fax: 405-527-7842; 405-527-6817 (Office).
Catechesis/Religious Program—Students 250.

SEMINOLE, SEMINOLE CO., IMMACULATE CONCEPTION (1928), Rev. Basil Keenan, O.S.B.; Deacon E. Charles Collier, (Retired).
Mailing Address: P.O. Box 164, 74818-0164.
Res.: 815 W. Wrangler Blvd., 74868. Tel: 405-382-3602; Fax: 405-382-3602.
Mission—St. Cecelia Main St., Maud, Seminole Co. 74854.
Catechesis/Religious Program—Students 73.

SHAWNEE, POTTAWATOMIE CO., ST. BENEDICT (1895), [CEM] Rev. Maurus P. Jaeb, O.S.B.; Deacon David Schrupp.
Res.: 632 N. Kickapoo, 74801. Tel: 405-275-0001; Fax: 405-214-9181.
Catechesis/Religious Program—Tel: 405-275-5399. Students 219.

SULPHUR, MURRAY CO., ST. FRANCIS XAVIER (1974),, Became a mission of St. Joseph, Ada.

TONKAWA, KAY CO., ST. JOSEPH'S (1909), [JC] Rev. Martin Larok Obwona, F.C.
Res.: 320 W. North St., P.O. Box 525, 74653. Tel: 580-628-2416; Fax: 580-363-2096.
Catechesis/Religious Program—Students 51.

UNION CITY, CANADIAN CO., ST. JOSEPH'S (1893), [CEM] Rev. John A. Steichen.
Res.: 404 N. Kate Boevers Ave., Box 100, 73090. Tel: 405-483-5329; Fax: 405-483-5329.
Catechesis/Religious Program—Tel: 405-381-2569. Students 74.

WEATHERFORD, CUSTER CO., ST. EUGENE'S (1960), [CEM 3] Rev. Michael L. Chapman; Deacon Joseph Dubey.
Res.: 704 N. Bryan, Box 407, 73096. Tel: 580-772-3209; Fax: 580-772-3541.
Mission—Blessed Sacrament 520 N. Oklahoma, Thomas, Custer Co. 73669.
Mission—Sacred Heart 204 N. Clark Ave., Hinton, Caddo Co. 73047.
Catechesis/Religious Program—Students 85.

WOODWARD, WOODWARD CO., ST. PETER'S (1905), (German), Revs. James D. Knight; Russell L. Hewes.
Res.: 2020 Oklahoma Ave., Box 708, 73801. Tel: 580-256-5305; Fax: 580-256-5840.
Mission—Sacred Heart 301 N. Main, Mooreland, Woodward Co. 73852.
Mission—Holy Name 600 S. Main, Shattuck, Ellis Co. 73858.
Mission—St. Frances Cabrini 101 Ave. C, Beaver, Beaver Co. 73932.
Mission—St. Joseph 325 S.W. 2nd, Buffalo, Harper Co. 73834.
Catechesis/Religious Program—Tel: 580-256-2966. Students 180.

YUKON, CANADIAN CO., ST. JOHN NEPOMUK (1889), Rev. William L. Novak; Deacons Jeffrey Kelly; John Teague.
Mailing Address: P.O. Box 850249, 73085. Tel: 405-354-2743; Fax: 405-354-2770.
Church: 600 S. Garth Brooks Blvd., 73099. Tel: 405-354-2743; Fax: 405-354-2770.
School—(Grades K-8) Tel: 405-354-2509. Sr. Laurentia Koehler, A.S.C., Prin. Sisters 2; Lay Teachers 20; Students 165.
Catechesis/Religious Program—Students 280.

Special Assignment:
Revs.—
Bash, Cletus, Chap. Mercy Health Center (Retired), 4300 W. Memorial Rd., 73120.
Bird, Stephen J., Dir., Office of Worship & Spiritual Life, P.O. Box 32180, 73123. Tel: 405-721-5651
Boeckman, Scott A., Chap., Mt. St. Mary High School, 2801 S. Shartel, 73109.
Leven, Marvin, Chap., Mercy Health Center, 4300 W. Memorial, 73120.
McCaffrey, Daniel, Natural Family Planning Outreach, 3366 N.W. Expressway, Bldg. D, #630, 73112.
Menasco, Edward J., Diaconate Program, P.O. Box 32180, 73123.
Mollan, Paul F., Chap., Deaconess and Baptist Hospitals, 3214 N. Lake, 73118.
Moore, Donald C., St. Ann's Home, 9400 St. Ann's Dr., 73162.
Nguyen, Francis T., Chap., Bishop McGuinness High School, 901 N.W. 50th, 73118.
Paracka1, George, Chap. St. Anthony Hospital, 1000 N. Lee St., P.O. Box 205, 73101. Tel: 405-272-6263
Roberson, Henry, Chap., 2829 Williamsburg, Enid, 73702.
Taylor, Anthony B., Vicar for Ministries, P.O. Box 32180, 73123. Tel: 405-721-5651
Zunmas, Oby J., Chap., Bishop McGuinness High School, 901 N.W. 50th, 73118.

Military Chaplains:
Rev.—
Creider, Philip B., Command Chap., U.S.S. Tarawa (LHA-1), FPD AP.

Absent on Leave:
Rev.—
Ashurst, Peter

Absent on Sick Leave:
Revs.—
Grimes, Price D., Jr., P.O. Box 32180, 73123. Tel: 405-720-9871
Parker, Rick, 26245 Ocean View Ave., Carmel, CA 93923.
True, David

Retired:
Revs.—
Bash, Cletus, P.O. Box 32180, 73123.
Darnall, Thomas W., P.O. Box 32180, 73123. Tel: 405-720-9875
Devlin, Kevin, 1044 W. 80th Ave., Conway Spring, KS 67031.
Flusche, Ernest A.
Imming, David B., 416 W. Mission, St. Mary's, KS 66536.
Kastner, James A., 9400 St. Ann's Dr., 73162.
Kolb, Joseph C., Box 183, Edmond, 73083.
Lamb, Louis J., 7501 W. Britton Rd., 73132.
MacAulay, Gerard, 2000 E. Bay Dr., #161, Largo, FL 33771.
Monahan, David F., P.O. Box 32180, 73212.
Ross, James H., P.O. Box 32180, 73123. Tel: 405-720-9874
Ross, William B., 1506 W. Walnut, El Reno, 73036.
Scheller, John, P.O. Box 32180, 73123. Tel: 405-722-1902
VandeWalle, Victor, P.O. Box 32180, 73123. Tel: 405-720-9873
Vas, Joseph S.
Vrana, John P.
Wrigley, Franklin, 10804 Greystone, 73120. Tel: 405-751-3185
Zoeller, Benedict, P.O. Box 32180, 73123.

Permanent Deacons:
Adamson, Bill, Blessed Sacrament, Lawton
Albert, Paul, St. Matthew, Elk City
Amend, Carl, On Duty Outside the Archdiocese
Avila, Tomas, On Duty Outside the Archdiocese
Barton, James D., Corpus Christi, Oklahoma City
Bautista, Teofilo, Jr., St. Francis of Assisi, Tinker AFB
Bawden, William, St. John the Baptist Church, Edmond
Best, David, Church of Christ the King, Oklahoma City
Brashers, Bart, St. Joseph, Blackwell
Browne, Matthew, (Retired)
Butler, John, St. Patrick Church, Anadarko
Caplinger, Jerome, St. Andrew, Moore
Christophe, Norman, (Retired)
Collier, E. Charles, (Retired)
Conway, James, Immaculate Conception, Marlow
Coyle, William St. John the Baptist, Edmond
Crispo, Anthony, St. Francis Xavier, Enid
Cruz, Joseph M., St. Peter, Guymon
Cumby, Dunn, Corpus Christi Church, Oklahoma City
Descher, Duane, (Retired)
Dollins, Belvin G., (Retired)
Dubey, Joseph, St. Eugene, Weatherford
Dulcamara, Peter, Holy Family Church, Lawton
Ellison, Roy, St. Mary's, Guthrie
Enos, William, Cathedral of Our Lady of Perpetual Help, Oklahoma City
Fahy, Richard, Epiphany of the Lord, Oklahoma City
Forgue, Joseph, Chap., Federal Penitentiary, El Reno
Frazier, Dennis, St. Patrick Church, Oklahoma City
Gabrish, Patrick, St. Joseph Church, Norman
Gorden, William, St. Charles, Oklahoma City
Guerra, Simon, St. Peter, Guymon
Gulikers, Marti, St. James, Oklahoma City
Heskamp, Robert, Epiphany of the Lord, Oklahoma City
Hunt, Lee, St. John the Baptist, Edmond
Jacobsen, Byron, St. Mark Church, Norman
Keene, James, Immaculate Conception Church, Oklahoma City

Kelly, Jeffrey, St. John Nepomuk Church, Yukon
LaChance, Raymond, St. Joseph Church, Norman
Lawrence, Herman, Holy Family, Lawton
Le, Anthony, Cathedral, Oklahoma City
Leal, George, Sacred Heart Church, Oklahoma City
LeWand, Mark, St. Charles Borromeo, Oklahoma City
Lewis, Paul, Cathedral, Oklahoma City
Maldonado, Pedro, St. Peter and Paul, Hobart
Martinez, Leopoldo, Holy Family Church, Lawton
Martinez, Mariano, Sacred Heart, Oklahoma City
McKaskle, Sherman, Queen of All Saints, Sayre
McLauchlin, Robert, (Retired)
Means, Gary, St. Cornelius, Cherokee
Mejstrik, Robert, St. Philip Neri, Midwest City
Morris, John St. John the Baptist, Edmond
Nguyen, Manh San, St. Andrew Dung-Lac Church, Oklahoma City
Nieto, Lucio, Holy Angels, Oklahoma City
Ninh, Sang, Cathedral, Oklahoma City
O'Loughlin, Bernard, Church of the Assumption, Duncan
Pigott, John, (Retired)
Pitt, John, (Retired)
Radosevich, Michael, St. Joseph, Ada
Reisinger, Conrad C. (Retired)
Reynold, Patrick, St. Eugene, Oklahoma City
Robinson, Richard, (Retired), Church of St. Mary, Ponca City
Rossow, Lawrence F., St. Thomas More University Parish, Norman
Rutherford, Gerard, Church of St. Mary, Ponca City
Schrupp, David, St. Benedict, Shawnee
Schwarz, Max, Holy Trinity, Okarche
Sousa, Lawrence, St. Joseph, Norman
Teague, John
Vance, Herbert, Oklahoma Medical Complex, Oklahoma City
Wade, James Lee, St. Francis Xavier, Sulphur
Wallace, Wenum Ray, St. Helen, Frederick
Warnke, Jim E., St. Matthew, Elk City
Warren, John, Our Lady of Victory Church, Purcell
Washko, Richard, St. Mary Church, Guthrie
Watford, Angus, St. Andrew, Moore
Willard, Jeff, St. Joseph, Norman
Young, James G., St. Philip Neri, Midwest City

INSTITUTIONS LOCATED IN THE ARCHDIOCESE

[A] COLLEGES AND UNIVERSITIES

SHAWNEE. *St. Gregory's University* (Coed) ; Liberal Arts and Sciences. , 1900 W. MacArthur Dr., 74804. Tel: 405-878-5100; Fax: 405-878-5198. Email: frlawrence@stgregorys.edu. Web: www.stgregorys.edu. Rev. Lawrence Stasyszen, O.S.B., S.T.D., Pres. Benedictine Monks Priests 4; Brothers 2; Lay Teachers 35; Students 813; Total Staff 190.

[B] HIGH SCHOOLS, ARCHDIOCESAN

OKLAHOMA CITY. *Bishop McGuinness Catholic High School* (Coed) , 801 N.W. 50th St., 73118. Tel: 405-842-6638; Fax: 405-848-9363; 405-858-9550 (Prin. Office). Email: pgiorgio@ionet.net. Web: bmchs.org. Mr. David Morton, Pres. & Prin.; Revs. Oby Zunmas; Francis Nguyen. Priests 2; Sisters 1; Lay Teachers 58; Students 662.

[C] HIGH SCHOOLS, PRIVATE

OKLAHOMA CITY. *Mount St. Mary High School* (Coed) , 2801 S. Shartel Ave., 73109. Tel: 405-631-8865; Fax: 405-631-9209. Email: themount@mountstmary.org. Web: mountstmary.org. Rev. Scott A. Boeckman, Chap.; Mr. Doug Kretchmar, Prin.; Mr. Brian Boeckman, Chm., Rel. Studies Dept. Sisters of Mercy of the Americas, Archdiocese of Oklahoma City Priests 1; Lay Teachers 22; Students 234.

[D] ELEMENTARY SCHOOLS, PRIVATE

OKLAHOMA CITY. *Villa Teresa*, (Grades PreK-4), 1216 Classen Dr., 73103. Tel: 405-232-4286; Fax: 405-552-2658. Email: principal@villateresa.com. Web: villateresa.com. Joana Camacho, Prin. Carmelite Sisters of St. Therese of the Infant Jesus Sisters 4; Lay Teachers 13; Total Staff 25; Students 146.

Villa Teresa Moore, (Grades N-K), 13501 S. Western Ave., 73170. Tel: 405-691-7737; Fax: 405-691-7981. Email: villateresamoore@hotmail.com. Sisters Veronica Higgins, Prin.; Patricia Ann Miller, Dir. Carmelite Sisters of St. Therese of the Infant Jesus Lay Teachers 7; Students 96.

NORMAN. *All Saints Catholic School*, 4001 36th Ave., N.W., 73072. Tel: 405-447-4600; Fax: 405-447-7227. Email: lemigh@ascsn.org. Web: www.ascsn.org. Leslie Emigh, Prin. Lay Teachers 23; Pre-K Students 40; Students 400; Total Staff 42.

[E] GENERAL HOSPITALS

OKLAHOMA CITY. *St. Anthony Hospital*, 1000 N. Lee St., P.O. Box 205, 73101. Tel: 405-272-7000; Fax: 405-272-7075. Email: steven_hunter@ssmhc.com. Web: www.saintsok.com. Mr. Steven L. Hunter, Pres.; Rev. George Parackal, Chap. A member of SSM Health Care. Sisters 3; Bed Capacity 800; Total Staff 2,365; Patients Assisted Annually 173,195.

Mercy Health Center Owned and operated by Sisters of Mercy Health System, St. Louis. , 4300 W. Memorial Rd., 73120. Tel: 405-755-1515; Fax: 405-752-3811. Email: 1ryan@okla.smhs.com. Web: www.mhso.okla.smhs.com. Michael J. Packnett, Pres. & CEO; Rev. Cletus Bash. Chaplains 7; Sisters 2; Sister Volunteers 2; Bed Capacity 368; Total Staff 2,657; Patients Assisted Annually 283,236.

Saint Michael Hospital, 2129 S.W. 59th St., 73119. Tel: 405-685-6671; Fax: 405-680-2817. Email: valinda_rutledge@ssmhc.com. Valinda Rutledge, Pres. A member of SSM Health Care. Total Staff 400; Bed Capacity 193; Patients assisted annually 60,000.

ARDMORE. *Mercy Memorial Health Center, Inc. (MMHC)*, 1011 14th Ave., N.W., 73401. Tel: 580-221-6611; Fax: 580-220-6580. Email: bthompson@ok.mercy.net. Web: www.mercyok.net. Mr. Bobby Thompson, Pres. & CEO. Total Staff 911; Bed Capacity 195; Patients Assisted Annually 106,320.

PONCA CITY. *Via Christi Oklahoma Regional Medical Center-Ponca City*, 1900 N. 14th St., 74602. Tel: 580-765-3321; Fax: 580-765-0341. Email: susan_nolan@via-christi.org. Web: viachristick.org. W. Charles Waters, Pres. & CEO; Sisters Charita Waner, C.S.J., Dir. Pastoral Care; Nora Phelan, Vice Pres. Mission Svcs. Sisters of St. Joseph of Wichita/Sisters of the Sorrowful Mother of Broken Arrow, OK Sisters 2; Total Staff 461; Bed Capacity 150; Patients Assisted Annually 76,000.

(Sub. of Via Christi Health System, Inc.) , 1900 N. 14th, P.O. Box 1270, 74602-1270. Tel: 580-765-0500; Fax: 580-765-0341.

[F] SPECIAL CARE FACILITIES

OKLAHOMA CITY. *St. Ann's Home Inc.*, 9400 St. Ann's Dr., 73162. Tel: 405-728-7888; Fax: 405-728-1302. Email: stann@swbell.net. Mr. Robert O'Connor, Admin.; Rev. Donald C. Moore, Chap. Sisters 2; Total Staff 95; Bed Capacity 120; Total Assisted 108.

Bone and Joint Hospital, 1111 North Dewey Ave., 73103. Tel: 405-272-9671; Fax: 405-552-9197. Email: cathy_mckinney@ssmhc.com. Web: www.boneandjoint.com. Mr. James A Hyde, Pres.; Revs. Joseph S. Vas, Chap. (Retired) Evon Siegel, Chap. A member of SSM Health Care Bed Capacity 102; Patients Assisted Annually 5,315.

[G] ECUMENICAL CENTERS

OKLAHOMA CITY. *Catholic Pastoral Center*, 7501 Northwest Expwy., 73123. Tel: 405-721-5651; Fax: 405-721-5210. Email: jweinmann@catharchdioceseokc.org. Web: catharchdioceseokc.org. P.O. Box 32180, 73123. Mr. James Weinmann, Dir. Mrs. Jeanine McFall, Events Coord. Used for Archdiocesan Chancery; ecumenical activities; retreat-meeting center for ecumenical and nonprofit organizations; and retired priests' residence.

[H] HOMES FOR THE AGED

OKLAHOMA CITY. *St. Ann's Retirement Village, Inc.*, P.O. Box 32180, 73123. Tel: 405-721-5651; Fax: 405-721-5210. Email: djohnson@catharchdioceseokc.org. Mr. David J. Johnson, Business Mgr. Total Assisted 50; Total Staff 45.

Trinity Gardens Apartments, 1501 N. Classen Blvd., 73106. Tel: 405-523-3000; Fax: 405-523-3030. Email: toconnor@catholiccharitiesok.org. Mr. Timothy O'Connor, Contact Person. 58 low income apartments for senior citizens.

Catholic Charities, 3825 N.W. 19th St., 73107. Tel: 405-523-3000; Fax: 405-523-3030. Residents 67.

Villa Isenbart, Inc., c/o Catholic Charities, 1501 Classen Blvd., 73106. Tel: 405-523-3000; Fax: 405-523-3030. Email: toconnor@catholiccharitiesok.org. 40 Apartment Residences for Low-Income Elderly.

3801 N.W. 19th St., 73107. Tel: 405-947-4143; Fax: 405-947-4199. Mr. Timothy O'Connor, Dir. Residents 41.

PONCA CITY. *St. Mary's Housing Foundation*, P.O. Box 1330, 74602. Tel: 580-765-7794; Fax: 580-765-1327. Email: stmarys@poncacity.net. 408 S. 8th St., 74601. Rev. John J. Michalicka, Pres. Senior Citizens Residences 6.

Westminster Village, Inc. Via Christi Health System. 1601 Academy Rd., 74604. Tel: 580-762-0927; Fax: 580-762-0933. Norma Vanman, CEO. Continuum of Care for the Aged Residents 58; Total Staff 92; Total Assisted 87.

[I] MONASTERIES AND RESIDENCES OF PRIESTS AND BROTHERS

OKLAHOMA CITY. *Monastery of Our Lady of Mount Carmel and Little Flower*, 1125 S. Walker Ave., P.O. Box 1196, 73101-1196. Tel: 405-235-2037; Fax: 405-235-7035. Email: florecita1@msn.com. Web: www.florecita1.com. Order of Discalced Carmelites (Oklahoma Province), Little Flower Clinic: Free medical service for the poor. Assisted annually 1,500.

SHAWNEE. *St. Gregory's Abbey* Order of St. Benedict, including University, Novitiate, and Mabee-Gerrer Museum of Art. , 1900 W. MacArthur Dr., 74804. Tel: 405-878-5491; Fax: 405-878-5189. Email: abbotmartin@sgc.edu. Web: www.sgc.edu. Rt. Rev. Martin Lugo, O.S.B., Abbot; Revs. Patrick McCool, O.S.B., Prior; Joachim Spexarth, O.S.B., Subprior.

Legal Title: *Benedictine Fathers of Sacred Heart Mission, Inc.* Priests 21; Brothers 11; Deacons 1. Retired Abbots: Rt. Revs. Philip A. Berning, O.S.B.; Charles Massoth, O.S.B.; Adrian R. Vorderlandwehr, O.S.B.; Revs. Nicholas K. Ast, O.S.B.; Matthew J. Brown, O.S.B.; Charles Buckley, O.S.B., Dir.; Brendan Helbing, O.S.B.; Augustine S. Horn, O.S.B.; Maurus P. Jaeb, O.S.B.; Basil Keenan, O.S.B.; Manuel Magallanes, O.S.B.; Timothy Maloney, O.S.B.; Eugene C. Marshall, O.S.B.; Theodore T. Seneschal, O.S.B.; Lawrence R. Stasyszen, O.S.B.; Daniel M. Suellentrop, O.S.B.; Louis Vanderley, O.S.B.; Paul J. Zahler, O.S.B.

[J] CONVENTS AND RESIDENCES FOR SISTERS

OKLAHOMA CITY. *Carmelite Sisters of St. Therese of the Infant Jesus Motherhouse, Villa Teresa*, 1300 Classen Dr., 73103. Tel: 405-232-7926; Fax: 405-236-3170. Email: library@villateresa.com. Web: www.oksister.com. Sr. Maria Francesca Forst, C.S.T., Supr. Sisters in Community 23; Resident Sisters 20.

Sisters of Mercy of the Americas Retirement Center for Sisters of Mercy of Oklahoma. , Mercy Health Center Convent, 4300 W. Memorial Rd., 73120. Tel: 405-755-1515; Fax: 405-936-5498. Email: rpower@okla.smhs.com. Web: www.mercyok.com. Sr. M. Rose Elizabeth Power, R.S.M., Coord. Sisters 15.

PIEDMONT. *Carmel of St. Joseph*, 20,000 N. County Line Rd., 73078. Tel: 405-348-3947; Fax: 405-348-4916. Email: dcn@qns.com. Sr. Monica Lotter, O.C.D., Prioress. Discalced Carmelite Nuns (Cloistered) Professed Sisters 11; Novices 1.

Sisters of Benedict Red Plains Monastery, 728 Richland Rd., S.W., 73078-9324. Tel: 405-373-4565; 405-373-4569; Fax: 405-373-3392. Email: osbokc@ionet.net. Web: www.redplainsmonastery.org. Sr. Jan Futrell, O.S.B., Prioress. Professed Sisters 11.

[K] CAMPUS MINISTRY & NEWMAN CENTERS

NORMAN. *Campus Ministry for the Archdiocese of Oklahoma City* 100 East Stinson, 73072. Tel: 405-321-0990; Fax: 405-321-0964. Email: bpruett@stm-ou.org. Web: stm-ou.org. Rev. Bill H. Pruett, Dir.

University of Oklahoma, 100 E. Stinson, 73072. Tel: 405-321-0990; Fax: 405-321-0964. Web: stm-ou.org. Rev. C. Joseph Meinhart.

East Central State University, P.O. Box 1585, Ada, 74820. Tel: 580-332-4811; Fax: 580-436-1226. Rev. Ray Ackerman.

Northwestern Oklahoma State College, 627 12th St., Alva, 73717. Tel: 580-327-0339; Fax: 580-327-0710. Rev. Shane I. Tharp.

University of Science & Arts of Oklahoma, P.O. Box 748, Chickasha, 73023. Tel: 405-224-7513; Fax: 405-224-4434. Rev. Elmer C. Schwarz.

University of Central Oklahoma, 321 E. Clegern, Edmond, 73034. Tel: 405-340-6300; Fax: 405-340-5715. Rev. Louis Vanderley, O.S.B.

Oklahoma Panhandle State University, P.O. Box 277, Goodwell, 73942. Tel: 580-338-7212; Fax: 580-338-5584. Rev. Scott Adams.

Cameron University, P.O. Box 7948, Lawton, 73506. Tel: 580-536-6351. Rev. Philip Seeton.

Northern Oklahoma College, P.O. Box 525, Tonkawa, 74653. Tel: 580-628-2416; Fax: 580-531-2607. Rev. Larok Martin.

Southwestern Oklahoma State University, P.O. Box

407, Weatherford, 73096. Tel: 580-772-3209; Fax: 580-772-3541. Rev. Michael L. Chapman; Deacon Joe Dubey.

[L] MISCELLANEOUS

OKLAHOMA CITY. *St. Anthony Hospital Foundation, Inc., Oklahoma City, Oklahoma* Member of SSM Health Care , P.O. Box 205, 73101. 826 N.W. 11, 73106. Tel: 405-272-7070; Fax: 405-270-7607. Email: saintsfoundation@ssmhc.com. Web: www.saintsfoundation.com. Sherry Rhodes, Exec. Dir.

Bishop McGuinness Catholic High School Building Trust, 4900 Richmond Sq. (200), 73118. Tel: 405-841-6000; Fax: 405-841-6006. Email: dgeason@telepath.com. Douglas G. Eason, Contact Person.

SSM Health Care of Oklahoma, Inc. (For staff listings please see St. Anthony Hospital located under General Hospitals) , 1000 N. Lee, P.O. Box 205, 73101. Tel: 405-272-7000.

CANTON. *Las Casas: Dominicans in Ministry with Native Americans*, 524 W. Pine, 73724-9703. Tel: 580-886-3413. Email: whiteearth@pldi.net. Web: www.lascasasproject.org. Self-governing board of trustees.

The White Earth Center Tel: 580-886-3413. Senior Citizens Nutrition Center

Children of the Plains Recreation Center Tel: 580-886-3413. Youth Activities

LAWTON. *Columbia Square, Inc.*, Catholic Charities, 1501 N. Classen, 73109. Tel: 405-523-3000; 580-248-2550; Fax: 580-248-2550. Email: toconnor@catholicharities.org.

304 W. 4th, 73505. Tel: 405-523-3000; Fax: 405-523-3030. Tim O'Connor, Exec. Dir.

OKARCHE. *New Leaven Ministries Foundation*, 507 Memorial Dr., 73762. Tel: 405-263-7798. Email: frsamxi@aol.com. Rev. Marvin Leven.

PIEDMONT. *Benedictine Spirituality Center* Location at Red Plains Monastery , 728 Richland Rd., SW, 73078-9324. Tel: 405-373-4565; Fax: 405-373-3392. Email: ministry@gbronline.com. Web: www.redplainsmonastery.org.

PONCA CITY. *Via Christi Charitable Foundation Oklahoma Regional Medical Center* (A subsidiary of Via Christi Health System, Inc.) , 1900 N. 14th, P.O. Box 1270, 74602-1270. Tel: 580-765-3321; Fax: 580-765-0536. Email: kshiflet@via-christi.org. Web: www.viachristiok.org.

PRAGUE. *National Shrine of the Infant Jesus of Prague*, Tel: 405-567-3080; Fax: 405-567-3404. Email: shrine@brightok.net. *St. Wenceslaus Church*, P.O. Box 488, 74864. 304 Jim Thorpe Blvd., 74864. Tel: 405-567-3404; Fax: 405-567-0365. Novena to the Infant Jesus of Prague takes place the 17th through 25th of each month. Pilgrimages take place on Sunday prior to the 25th of the month.

SHAWNEE. *National Institute on Development Delays, Inc.*, 1900 W. MacArthur, 74804. Tel: 405-878-5288; Fax: 405-878-5114. Email: pop@nidd.org. Web: www.nidd.org. Rev. Paul J. Zahler, O.S.B., Dir.

Early Developmental Integration Center Tel: 405-878-5289; Fax: 405-878-5114.

C. Harold and Connie Brand Early Child Development Center Tel: 405-878-5289; Fax: 405-878-5114.

Home Start Program Tel: 405-878-5289; Fax: 405-878-5114.

Lyle H. Boren Child Development Center Tel: 405-878-5289; Fax: 405-878-5114.

Home Integration, Inc. Tel: 405-878-5289; Fax: 405-878-5114.

Community Integration Program Tel: 405-878-5289; Fax: 405-878-5114.

Employment Integration Program Tel: 405-878-5289; Fax: 405-878-5114.

St. Michael Foundation, Inc. Tel: 405-878-5289; Fax: 405-878-5114.

International Institute on Mental Retardation Tel: 405-878-5289; Fax: 405-878-5114.

RELIGIOUS INSTITUTES OF MEN REPRESENTED IN THE ARCHDIOCESE

For further details refer to the corresponding bracketed number in the Religious Institutes of Men or Women section.

[0200]—*Benedictine Monks*—O.S.B.

[0260]—*Discalced Carmelite Friars* (Oklahoma Prov.)—O.C.D.

[0690]—*Jesuit Fathers* (Missouri Prov.)—S.J.

[0920]—*Oblates of St. Francis De Sales*—O.S.F.S.

RELIGIOUS INSTITUTES OF WOMEN REPRESENTED IN THE ARCHDIOCESE

[0100]—*Adorers of the Blood of Christ*—A.S.C.

[0230]—*Benedictine Sisters of Pontifical Jurisdiction*—O.S.B.

[0380]—*Carmelite Sisters of St. Therese of the Infant Jesus*—C.S.T.

[0390]—*Congregation of Missionary Carmelites of St. Therese* (Houston, TX)—C.M.S.T.

[0420]—*Discalced Carmelite Nuns*—O.C.D.

[1070-13]—*Dominican Sisters* (Adrian, MI)—O.P.

[1070-06]—*Dominican Sisters* (Newburgh, NY)—O.P.

[1070-03]—*Dominican Sisters* (Sinsinawa, WI)—O.P.

[1900]—*Eucharistic Missionaries of St. Theresa* (Mexico)—M.E.S.T.

[1415]—*Franciscan Sisters of Mary*—F.S.M.

[]—*Hermanas Catequistas Guadalupanas*—H.C.G.

[1680]—*School Sisters of St. Francis*—S.S.S.F.

[0480]—*Sisters of Charity of Leavenworth*—S.C.L.

[2980]—*Sisters of Congregation de Notre Dame*—C.N.D.

[1010]—*Sisters of Divine Providence of San Antonio, Texas*—C.D.P.

[2575]—*Sisters of Mercy of the Americas*—R.S.M.

[3360]—*Sisters of Providence of St. Mary-of-the-Woods*—S.P.

[3840]—*Sisters of St. Joseph of Carondelet*—C.S.J.

[2150]—*Sisters, Servants of the Immaculate Heart of Mary*—I.H.M.

CEMETERIES

OKLAHOMA CITY. *Resurrection Memorial*, P.O. Box 32865, 73123. Tel: 405-721-4191.

NECROLOGY

✠ Salatka, Most Rev. Charles A., Retired Archbishop of Oklahoma City—Died March 17, 2003

† Petuskey, John A., (Retired)—Died Nov. 8, 2003

† Schwarz, Bernard F., (Retired)—Died June 12, 2003

† Walch, John L., (Retired)—Died June 29, 2003

† Zagar, John T., (Retired)—Died Oct. 8, 2003

Archdiocese of Omaha

(Archidioecesis Omahensis)

Most Reverend

ELDEN FRANCIS CURTISS

Archbishop of Omaha; ordained May 24, 1958; appointed Bishop of Helena March 4, 1976; consecrated April 28, 1976; appointed Archbishop of Omaha May 4, 1993; installed June 25, 1993 *Chancery Office: 100 N. 62nd St., Omaha, NE 68132-2795.*

Chancery Office: 100 N. 62 St., Omaha, NE 68132-2795. Tel: 402-558-3100; Fax: 402-558-3026.

Web: www.archomaha.com

Email: archbishop@archomaha.org

ESTABLISHED AS A VICARIATE-APOSTOLIC JANUARY 6, 1857.

Square Miles 14,051.

Erected a Diocese October 2, 1885; Archdiocese August 7, 1945.

Comprises the Counties of Boyd, Holt, Merrick, Nance, Boone, Antelope, Knox, Pierce, Madison, Platte, Colfax, Stanton, Wayne, Cedar, Dixon, Dakota, Thurston, Cuming, Dodge, Burt, Washington, Douglas and Sarpy in the State of Nebraska.

Legal Title: For legal titles of parishes and archdiocesan institutions, consult the Chancery Office.

STATISTICAL OVERVIEW

Personnel	
Archbishops	1
Abbots	1
Retired Abbots	1
Priests: Diocesan Active in Diocese	137
Priests: Diocesan Active Outside Diocese	9
Priests: Retired, Sick or Absent	69
Number of Diocesan Priests	215
Religious Priests in Diocese	100
Total Priests in Diocese	315
Extern Priests in Diocese	21
Ordinations:	
Diocesan Priests	4
Transitional Deacons	2
Permanent Deacons	9
Permanent Deacons in Diocese	176
Total Brothers	23
Total Sisters	337
Parishes	
Parishes	138
With Resident Pastor:	
Resident Diocesan Priests	91
Resident Religious Priests	3
Without Resident Pastor:	
Administered by Priests	43
Administered by Deacons	1
Missions	15
Pastoral Centers	3
Professional Ministry Personnel:	
Brothers	1
Sisters	19
Lay Ministers	100
Welfare	
Catholic Hospitals	6
Total Assisted	409,872
Health Care Centers	2
Total Assisted	106,500
Homes for the Aged	3
Total Assisted	323
Day Care Centers	5
Total Assisted	895
Specialized Homes	2
Total Assisted	645
Special Centers for Social Services	14
Total Assisted	131,200
Other Institutions	1
Total Assisted	36,405
Educational	
Diocesan Students in Other Seminaries	33
Total Seminarians	33
Colleges and Universities	2
Total Students	8,400
High Schools, Diocesan and Parish	12
Total Students	3,210
High Schools, Private	5
Total Students	2,477
Elementary Schools, Diocesan and Parish	59
Total Students	14,182
Elementary Schools, Private	2
Total Students	199
Non-residential Schools for the Disabled	1
Total Students	41
Catechesis/Religious Education:	
High School Students	4,259
Elementary Students	14,934
Total Students under Catholic Instruction	47,735
Teachers in the Diocese:	
Priests	39
Scholastics	3
Brothers	4
Sisters	24
Lay Teachers	1,552
Vital Statistics	
Receptions into the Church:	
Infant Baptism Totals	4,323
Adult Baptism Totals	582
Received into Full Communion	628
First Communions	4,031
Confirmations	3,868
Marriages:	
Catholic	791
Interfaith	546
Total Marriages	1,337
Deaths	1,867
Total Catholic Population	229,952
Total Population	867,531

Former Bishops—Rt. Revs. JAMES O'GORMAN, O.C.S.O., D.D., Vicar-Apostolic and Titular Bishop of Raphanea; consecrated May 8, 1859; died July 4, 1874; JAMES O'CONNOR, D.D., Vicar-Apostolic and Titular Bishop of Dibona; consecrated Aug. 20, 1876; appt. first Bishop of Omaha, Oct. 2, 1885; died May 27, 1890; RICHARD SCANNELL, D.D., consecrated Bishop of Concordia, Nov. 30, 1887; transferred to Omaha, Jan. 30, 1891; died Jan. 8, 1916; Most Revs. JEREMIAH J. HARTY, D.D., ord. April 28, 1878; consecrated Archbishop of Manila, P.I., Aug. 15, 1903; transferred to Omaha, May 16, 1916; died Oct. 29, 1927 June 1, 1926 to July 4, 1928; FRANCIS J. BECKMAN, D.D. Bishop of Lincoln and Apostolic Administrator of Omaha from June 1, 1926 to July 4, 1928; JOSEPH FRANCIS RUMMEL, D.D., Bishop of Omaha; appt. March 30, 1928; consecrated May 29, 1928; installed July 4, 1928; transferred to the Archdiocese of New Orleans, March 9, 1935; JAMES H. RYAN, D.D., appt. Titular Bishop of Modra, Aug. 15, 1933; consecrated Oct. 25, 1933; transferred to See of Omaha, Aug. 3, 1935; installed Nov. 21, 1935; elected to Archepiscopal dignity, Aug. 7, 1945;; died Nov. 23, 1947; GERALD T. BERGAN, D.D. (Retired), ord. Oct. 28, 1915; appt. Bishop of Des Moines, March 24, 1934; consecrated June 13, 1934; promoted to Omaha, Feb. 7, 1948; retired June 18, 1969; made Titular Archbishop of Tacarata;; died July 12, 1972; DANIEL E. SHEEHAN, D.D., J.C.D. (Retired), ord. May 23, 1942; appt. Titular Bishop of Capsu and Auxiliary, Jan. 4, 1964; consecrated March 19, 1964; succeeded to See, June 11, 1969; retired May 14, 1992; died Oct. 24, 2000.

Vicar General—Very Rev. MICHAEL W. GREWE, V.G.

Chancery Office—100 N. 62nd St., Omaha, 68132-2795. Tel: 402-558-3100 Fax: 402-558-3026. Email: archbishop@archomaha.org. Office Hours: Mon.-Fri. 9-5

Chancellor—Rev. GREGORY P. BAXTER, S.T.L.

Vice Chancellor—Rev. JOSEPH C. TAPHORN, J.C.L.

Moderator of the Curia—Rev. MICHAEL F. GUTGSELL, J.C.L.

Finance Director (canonical)—Mr. HERBERT L. KARRER.

Consultor to Finance Office—Rev. GREGORY P. BAXTER, S.T.L.

Archdiocesan Tribunal—100 N. 62nd St., Omaha, 68132.

Judicial Vicar—Rev. PATRICK C. HARRISON, J.C.L.

Associate Judicial Vicar—Rev. MICHAEL F. GUTGSELL, J.C.L.

Judges—Deacon JERRY OVERKAMP, J.C.L.; Rev. JOSEPH C. TAPHORN, J.C.L.

Promoter of Justice—Rev. R. MICHAEL FITZPATRICK, S.T.L., J.C.L.

Defenders of the Bond—Revs. R. MICHAEL FITZPATRICK, S.T.L., J.C.L.; VALENTINE J. PETER, S.T.D., J.C.D.

Advocates—Deacon JERRY OVERKAMP.

Attorneys— Appointed for each matrimonial case

Appeal Court— The Tribunal of the Diocese of Lincoln, NE is the Appeal Court for Omaha The Tribunal of the Diocese of Lincoln, NE is the Appeal Court for Omaha.

Metropolitan Tribunal—

Judge—Rev. JOSEPH C. TAPHORN, J.C.L.

Consultors—Very Rev. MICHAEL W. GREWE, V.G.; Revs. RONALD A. BATTIATO; ROSS C. BURKHALTER; Rev. Msgr. WILLIAM J. DENDINGER; Revs. R. MICHAEL FITZPATRICK, S.T.L., J.C.L.; NORMAN F. HUNKE.

Deans—Revs. FRANK LORDEMANN, U.S.; CHARLES F. SWANSON, U.S.C.; JAMES E. GILG, U.S.E.; KENNETH VAVRINA, U.N.E.; DANIEL KAMPSCHNEIDER, U.N.W.; STEVEN J. STILLMUNKS, U.W.; GERALD A. LEISE, R.S.W.; ROSS C. BURKHALTER, R.N.C.; DENNIS U. DEGUZMAN, R.S.E.; THOMAS E. BAUWENS, R.C.; JAY L. KRUSE, R.N.W.; STEVEN E. BOES, R.N.E.

Finance Council—Most Rev. ELDEN FRANCIS CURTISS; Rev. R. MICHAEL FITZPATRICK, S.T.L., J.C.L.; Very Rev. MICHAEL W. GREWE, V.G.; Revs. MICHAEL F. GUTGSELL, J.C.L.; ROBERT H. NIENABER; RONALD S. WASIKOWSKI; GREGORY P. BAXTER, S.T.L.; Mr. HERBERT L. KARRER; Mr. MIKE KIRK; Ms. MARCIA KOORY; Mr. ROMAN UHING; Mr. HERMAN D. WEIST.

Archdiocesan Offices and Directors

Boy Scouts—Rev. TIMOTHY PODRAZA, Chap.

Building Commission—Rev. GREGORY P. BAXTER, S.T.L.; Mr. LEE KARRER; Mr. JOHN ANDREWS; Rev. CHARLES F. SWANSON; Ms. ANNA BESPOYASNY; R. J. DESROSIERS; Mr. TERRY FICENEC; Mr. RAYMOND ALVINE; Mr. PAUL C. JEFFREY; Bro. WILLIAM WOEGER, F.S.C.

Catholic University, Friends of—Rev. GREGORY P. BAXTER, S.T.L.

Cemeteries—Rev. R. MICHAEL FITZPATRICK, S.T.L., J.C.L., Dir.

Censor Librorum—Rev. MICHAEL F. GUTGSELL, J.C.L.

Catholic Charities—SCOT L. ADAMS, Dir., 3300 N. 60th St., Omaha, 68104.

Omaha Priests Retirement Plan and Trust, The—Rev. Msgr. JAMES R. CAIN (Retired); Rev. JAMES R. TIEGS; Mr. JAMES KINEEN; Mr. JOSEPH BEVERIDGE; Mr. DAVID DUREN; Mr. HERBERT L. KARRER.

Commission for Ecumenical Affairs—Rev. JOSEPH C. TAPHORN, J.C.L., Interim.

Commission on Divine Worship—Bro. WILLIAM WOEGER, F.S.C., Coord.

Council of Catholic Women, Archdiocesan—Rev. EDGAR J. WORTMANN, Archdiocesan Moderator, 3020 Curtis, Omaha, 68111.

Diaconate Program—Revs. RODNEY T. ADAMS, Urban Dir. Tel: 402-733-9327; KEITH D. REZAC, Rural Dir. Tel: 402-358-3596.

Catholic School Office—Sr. MICHELLE FALTUS, S.F.C.C., Supt. Schools, 3212 N. 60th St., Omaha, 68104. Tel: 402-554-8493.

Religious Formation, Office of—3212 N. 60th St., P.O. Box 4130, Omaha, 68104. Mr. JAMES CORR, Dir.; Sr. LEE AGNES HODAPP, Asst. Dir. Rural Rel. Education; MARTY KALKOWSKI, Asst. Dir. Young Adult Ministry; Ms. CAROLYN MEEKS, Asst. Dir. Adult Formation; Ms. RITA RAMOS, Asst. Dir., Youth; Ms. CATHI SNYDER, Asst. Dir. Elementary Catechesis; TERESA MONAGHEN, Campus Ministry. Tel: 402-554-8493; Fax: 402-554-8402.

Computer Support Manager—Mr. DARREL GIESBRECHT, Chancery, 100 N. 62nd St., Omaha, 68132. Tel: 402-558-3100; Fax: 402-558-3026.

Family Life—Sr. BARBARA MARKEY, N.D., Dir., 3214 N. 60th St., Omaha, 68104. Tel: 402-551-9003.

Office for Formation and Education in Sexuality—DEBBIE SHEEHAN, Coord., 3218 N. 60th St., Omaha, 68104. Tel: 402-556-8219.

Hispanic Ministry—Sr. ANGELA EREVIA, M.C.D.P., 3218 N. 60th St., Omaha, 68104. Tel: 402-551-2255.

Holy Name Society—Rev. JOHN S. MICHALAK, Dir.

Hospitals—Rev. DAVID W. LAPLANTE.

Management Information Services Manager—Mr. RICHARD STIBOR, Chancery, 100 N. 62nd St., Omaha, 68132. Tel: 402-558-3100; Fax: 402-558-3026.

Legion of Mary—Rev. Msgr. PETER F. DUNNE, Dir. (Retired).

Natural Family Planning—Sr. BARBARA MARKEY, N.D., Dir., 3214 N. 60th St., Omaha, 68104. Tel: 402-551-9003.

Newspaper—Mr. CHARLIE WIESER, Editor, 6060 N.W. Radial Hwy., Omaha, 68104. Tel: 402-558-6611; Fax: 402-558-6614. "The Catholic Voice"

Nocturnal Adoration Society—VACANT.

Office For Consecrated Life—Sr. JACQUELINE THORN, O.S.M., 100 N. 62nd St., Omaha, 68132. Tel: 402-558-3100; Fax: 402-558-3026.

Pastoral Planning Office—MARY JO HUSTEN, Dir. Tel: 402-551-2255.

Priests' Eucharistic League—VACANT.

Propagation of the Faith, Pontifical Assoc. of Holy Childhood and Catholic Students Mission Crusade—Rev. GREGORY P. BAXTER, S.T.L., Dir., 100 N. 62nd St., Omaha, 68132.

Retreats, Laymen—Rev. ALBAN SUEPER, S.S.C., Dir.

Rural Life Conference—Rev. FRANK J. BAUMERT.

St. Vincent de Paul Society—Rev. HAROLD J. BUSE, Spiritual Dir.; Mr. PATRICK MCCARTHY, Pres., 2101 Leavenworth St., Omaha, 68102.

St. Vincent de Paul Store, Inc.—2101 Leavenworth St., Omaha, 68102.

Priests' Council—

Officers—Revs. DAMIAN J. ZUERLEIN, Pres.; NORMAN F. HUNKE, Vice Pres.; JAMES E. GILG, Sec.; THOMAS E. BAUWENS, Treas.

Age Groups—Revs. WILLIAM DENDINGER; EMMETT F. MEYER; OWEN W. KORTE; DAMIAN J. ZUERLEIN; DAVID M. KORTH; MICHAEL P. ECKLEY; DERMOT J. DUNNE; DAMIEN J. COOK.

Religious Orders—Revs. JAMES KEENA, C.SS.R.; THOMAS AQUINAS LEITNER, O.S.B.; RICHARD MCCASLIN, S.J.

Deans—Revs. CHARLES F. SWANSON, (USC); JAMES E. GILG, (USE); FRANK LORDEMANN, (US); KENNETH VAVRINA, (UNE); HAROLD J. BUSE, (UNW); STEVEN J. STILLMUNKS, (UW); GERALD A. LEISE, (RSW); ROSS C. BURKHALTER, (RNC); JAY L. KRUSE, (RNW); GERALD E. GONDERINGER, (RSE); STEVEN E. BOES, (RNE); THOMAS E. BAUWENS, (RC).

Archbishop's Appointees—Revs. GREGORY P. BAXTER, S.T.L.; MICHAEL F. GUTGSELL, J.C.L.; PATRICK C. HARRISON, J.C.L.; JOSEPH C. TAPHORN, J.C.L.

Ex Officio—Very Rev. MICHAEL W. GREWE, V.G., Vicar Gen.; Revs. RONALD A. BATTIATO, Consultor; ROSS C. BURKHALTER; Rev. Msgr. WILLIAM J. DENDINGER; Revs. NORMAN F. HUNKE; R. MICHAEL FITZPATRICK, S.T.L., J.C.L.

Social Ministry Commission—KELLY KELLER, 3300 N. 60th St., Omaha, 68104. Tel: 402-554-0520; Fax: 402-554-0365.

Sodalities—VACANT.

Office for Lay Ministry Formation—Rev. THOMAS A. GREISEN, Dir., 3218 N. 60th St., Omaha, 68104-3494. Tel: 402-561-9274; Fax: 402-551-3050.

Catholic Charities, Inc.—SCOT L. ADAMS, Exec. Dir., 3300 N. 60th St., Omaha, 68104. Tel: 402-554-0520.

Catholic Charities, Inc. Satellite Offices and Services—

The Shelter— Care for battered women, children, therapy for spouse abusers. CHRIS CARLSON, Contact Person, P.O. Box 4346, Omaha, 68104. Tel: 402-558-5700.

St. Martin de Porres Center— Social Justice education, counseling, food pantry, refugee program. A'JAMAL BYNDON, Emergency Svcs.; VIOLA JACKSON, Vision of H.O.P.E., 2417 Burdette St., Omaha, 68111. Tel: 402-341-4004.

Omaha. Archdiocesan Deposit and Loan Fund, Inc.— A pool of funds from archdiocesan parishes providing low interest loans for capital improvements and new construction by archdiocesan parishes. This nonprofit religious, charitable and educational corporation, whose president is the Archdiocese of Omaha, is duly constituted under the laws of the State of Nebraska. Mr. LEE KARRER, Finance Dir., 100 N. 62nd St., Omaha, 68132. Tel: 402-558-3100; Fax: 402-558-3026.

Omaha. Archdiocesan Retreat and Conference Centers— Located in renovated Sheehan Center and Cathedral Center space, overnight, day and weekend accommodations for teens, young adults and adult groups, large and small meeting space, chapel and food service area. *3330 N. 60th St., Omaha, 68104.* Tel: 402-558-1442; Fax: 402-551-1482. CHRISTINE FINOCCHIARO, Dir.

Omaha Campus for Hope— Detoxification, inpatient treatment and extended care for low-income and indigent alcoholics. VICKI MACA, Contact Person, 1490 N. 16th St., Omaha, 68102. Tel: 402-827-0570.

UCSS Counseling Services—JACK WRIGHT, Sheehan Center, 3300 N. 60th St., Omaha, 68104. Tel: 402-554-0520; RAY WILSON, Substance Abuse, 3300 N. 60th St., Omaha, 68104. Tel: 402-554-0520.

Catholic Family Services—CARROLL BARNES, Contact Person, 1761 26th Ave., P.O. Box 573, Columbus, 68602-0573. Tel: 402-563-3833.

Catholic Family Services—1255 4th St., Ste. 220, Norfolk, 68701. Tel: 402-371-3555.

Victim Assistance Coordinator—Tel: 402-558-3100.

Vocations—Rev. RALPH B. O'DONNELL.

Youth-Young Adult Ministry—Ms. RITA RAMOS, 3216 N. 60th St., Omaha, 68104. Tel: 402-551-5070.

CLERGY, PARISHES, MISSIONS AND PAROCHIAL SCHOOLS

CITY OF OMAHA
(DOUGLAS COUNTY)

1—ST. CECILIA'S CATHEDRAL, Revs. Norman F. Hunke; Mark T. Beran; Ukachukwu Sebastian Onyeabor.
Res.: 701 N. 40 St., 68131. Tel: 402-551-2313; Fax: 402-551-2306.
School—Tel: 402-556-6655. Congregation of the Most Holy Rosary, (Sinsinawa, WI) 1; Lay Teachers 23; Students 504.
Catechesis/Religious Program—Bonnie Pryor, D.R.E. Students 40.

2—ST. ADALBERT (1919), Rev. William D. L'Heureux. In Res., Rev. Gregory Baxter.
Res.: 2617 S. 31st St., 68105. Tel: 402-345-1621.
Catechesis/Religious Program—2124 S. 32nd Ave., 68105. Tel: 402-341-5604.

3—ST. AGNES, (Irish—Spanish), Revs. Carl J. Zoucha; Jose Manuel Equihua Gonzalez (Mexico). In Res., Rev. Joseph C. Taphorn, J.C.L.
Res.: 2215 Q St., 68107. Tel: 402-731-0100; Fax: 402-731-2196.
Catechesis/Religious Program—Tel: 402-738-8240. Students 300.

4—ST. ANN, (Hispanic), Revs. Damian Zuerlein; Francisco Hernandez. In Res., Rev. Nguyen Loi.
Res.: 2247 Poppleton Ave., 68108. Tel: 402-341-6613; Fax: 402-341-1753.
School—All Saints Catholic School See Elementary Schools, Interparochial Under Institutions Located in the Archdiocese.
Catechesis/Religious Program—Students 134.

5—ST. ANTHONY (1907), (Lithuanian), Revs. Peter M.J. Stravinskas, Admin.; Nicholas Gregoris, S.T.D. (SCR). In Res., Bro. Joshua Kibler.
Res.: 5401 S. 33rd St., 68107. Tel: 402-733-2423; Fax: 402-733-9033.
Catechesis/Religious Program—Students 16.

6—ASSUMPTION, B.V.M. (1894), (Czech), Rev. J. Brian Beilman.
Res.: 5434 S. 22nd St., 68107. Tel: 402-734-4500; Fax: 402-734-4501.
School—Tel: 402-734-4504; Fax: 402-734-4504. Lay Teachers 12; Students 163.
Catechesis/Religious Program—Fax: 402-734-4505. Students 16.

7—ST. BENEDICT THE MOOR (1918), Rev. Robert W. Dundon, S.J.; Deacons Frank Barbour; Ernie Spicer.
Res.: 2423 Grant St., 68111. Tel: 402-348-0631; Fax: 402-348-0631.
Catechesis/Religious Program—Students 29.

8—ST. BERNADETTE (1963), Revs. Robert F. Preisinger; Paschal Jong-A-Kiem, Asst.; Deacons Ron Casart; Gary Chladek; Pete Digilio; Sebastian Enzolera; Jean Plourde. In Res., Rev. Msgr. Albert L. Krejci (Retired).
Res.: 7600 S. 42nd St., 68147. Tel: 402-731-4694; Fax: 402-733-4890.
School—Tel: 402-731-3033; Fax: 402-731-8735. Mrs. Jean Ernesti, Prin. Lay Teachers 20; Students 313.
Catechesis/Religious Program—Tel: 402-731-9421; Fax: 402-733-4890. Students 143.

9—ST. BERNARD (1905), Revs. Jerome I. Spenner; Paul C. Hoesing, Asst.; Deacons Donald Kemp; Skip Baughman; Edward Osterhaus; Paul Dreismeier.
Res.: 3601 N. 65 St., 68104. Tel: 402-551-0269; Fax: 402-551-2311.
School—Tel: 402-553-4993; Fax: 402-551-4939. Ellie Seward, Prin. Lay Teachers 15; Students 245.
Catechesis/Religious Program—Tel: 402-556-1679. JoAnne Raleigh, D.R.E. Students 54.

10—BLESSED SACRAMENT (1919), [CEM] Rev. Edgar J. Wortmann.
Res.: 3020 Curtis Ave., 68111. Tel: 402-455-5200; Fax: 402-455-6699.
School—Tel: 402-455-4030; Fax: 402-455-6699. Lay Teachers 10; Students 84.
Catechesis/Religious Program—Students 10.

11—ST. BRIDGET (1887), (Irish), Rev. Rodney T. Adams. In Res., Revs. Paul Begley; Ralph B. O'Donnell.
Res.: 4112 S. 26th St., 68107. Tel: 402-733-8811; Fax: 402-733-1272.
Catechesis/Religious Program—Tel: 402-734-5227; Fax: 402-734-1272. Students 17.

12—CHRIST THE KING (1953), Revs. Steven J. Stillmunks; Daniel R. Andrews; Wayne W. Schlautman; Deacon Glenn Tylutki.
Res.: 654 S. 86th St., 68114. Tel: 402-391-3606; Fax: 402-391-1498.
School—Tel: 402-391-0977; Fax: 402-391-2418. Lay Teachers 26; Students 334.
Catechesis/Religious Program—Tel: 402-391-3624. Colleen Leise, D.R.E. Students 107.

13—ST. ELIZABETH ANN (1981), Revs. Joseph G. Hanefeldt; Walter L. Nolte, Asst. In Res., Rev. David La Plante; Deacons Jack Finney; Richard Nelson; Ernie Gencarelli; Martin Crowley; Dennis Connor; John Dagerman; Thomas Wade.
Res.: 5425 North 114th St., 68164. Tel: 402-498-9103; Fax: 402-493-0630.
School—St. James-Seton School, Tel: 402-572-0339; Fax: 402-572-0347. See Elementary Schools, Interparochial Under Institutions Located in the Archdiocese.
Catechesis/Religious Program—Tel: 402-572-0369; Fax: 402-572-0368. Ms. Jo Kusek, D.R.E. Students 228.

14—ST. FRANCES CABRINI, Rev. Roger Kalscheuer; Deacons Anthony Filipcic; Yano DiGiacomo.
Res.: 1334 S. Ninth St., 68108. Tel: 402-342-2464; Fax: 402-342-2470.
Catechesis/Religious Program—Students 20.
School—All Saints Catholic School, Tel: 402-346-5757; Fax: 402-346-3794. See Elementary Schools, Interparochial Under Institutions Located in the Archdiocese.

15—ST. FRANCIS ASSISI, (Polish—Spanish), Rev. Carl J. Zoucha.
Res.: 4513 S. 32nd St., 68107-1403.
Catechesis/Religious Program—Students 165.

16—HOLY CROSS (1922), Revs. Charles F. Swanson; Timothy W. Forget; John Mark Nolte. In Res., Rev. Ralph Librea; Deacon George Elster.
Res.: 4803 William St., 68106. Tel: 402-553-7500; Fax: 402-553-7735.
School—Tel: 402-551-3773; Fax: 402-556-1896. Lay Teachers 24; Students 331.
Catechesis/Religious Program—Students 83.

17—HOLY FAMILY (1876), Deacon Ralph L. Hueser, Admin.
Res.: 1715 Izard St., 68102. Tel: 402-345-1062; Fax: 402-344-8136.

18—HOLY GHOST, Rev. Gregory Benkowski; Deacons Tom Schulte; Paul Eubanks; Andy Sommer.
Res.: 5219 S. 53rd St., 68117. Tel: 402-731-3176; Fax: 402-738-1409.
School—Tel: 402-731-5161; Fax: 402-738-1409. Pam Shiffbauer, Prin. Lay Teachers 12; Students 196.
Catechesis/Religious Program—Tel: 402-731-4574. Diane Hernandez, D.R.E. Students 60.

19—HOLY NAME (1917), Revs. James R. Keena, C.SS.R.; Edward Morgan, C.SS.R.; Bro. John Kuehner, C.SS.R.; Rev. John Morton, C.SS.R.; Bro. William Cloughley, C.SS.R.
Res.: 3014 N. 45th St., 68104. Tel: 402-451-6622; Fax: 402-457-6901.
School—(Grades K-8) Tel: 402-451-5403; Fax: 402-453-7950. Sofia Kock, Prin. Lay Teachers 17; Students 195.
Catechesis/Religious Program—Tel: 402-453-0873. J. Diane Van Ornam, D.R.E. Students 43.

20—IMMACULATE CONCEPTION, B.V.M. (1897), (Polish), Rev. Anthony Espinosa; Deacons Paul Matukewicz; Tim Koziel.
Res.: 2708 S. 24th St., 68108. Tel: 402-342-1074; Fax: 402-342-1074.
School—All Saints Catholic School, Tel: 402-346-5757; Fax: 402-346-8794. See Elementary Schools, Interparochial Under Institutions Located in the Archdiocese.
Catechesis/Religious Program—Students 2.

21—ST. JAMES (1963), Very Rev. Michael W. Grewe, V.G.; Rev. Alexander Okoro; Deacons Jerry Gau; Larry Heck; Stan Kurtz; Pat Lenz; Wayne Young. In Res., Rev. James V. Brown, O.A.R.
Res.: 9025 Larimore Ave., 68134. Tel: 402-572-0499; Fax: 402-573-9345.
School—St. James-Seton School, Tel: 402-572-0339; Fax: 402-572-0347. See Elementary Schools, Interparochial Under Institutions Located in the Archdiocese.
Catechesis/Religious Program—Tel: 402-572-0369; Fax: 402-572-0368. Ms. Jo Kusek, D.R.E. Students 175.

22—ST. JOAN OF ARC (1955), Rev. Carl F. Sodoro. In Res., Rev. Patrick C. Harrison, J.C.L.
Res.: 3122 S. 74th St., 68124. Tel: 402-393-2005; Fax: 402-398-9438.
School—Tel: 402-393-2314; Fax: 402-393-4405. Sisters of Mercy 1; Lay Teachers 18; Students 234.
Catechesis/Religious Program—Tel: 402-391-1906; 402-393-2315. Marilyn Opitz, D.R.E. Students 148.

23—ST. JOHN (1897), Revs. Bert Thelen, S.J.; Philip R. Amidon, S.J.; Thomas N. Schloemer, S.J.; Deacon Ken Kalkowski.
Office—2500 California Pl., 68178. Tel: 402-280-3030; Fax: 402-280-2465.
Catechesis/Religious Program—Tel: 402-280-1128. Students 12.

24—ST. JOHN VIANNEY (1974), Revs. R. Patrick McCaslin; Thomas R. Ward; Deacons Pete DesRosiers; Frank Telich; John Kronschnabel. In Res., Rev. James M. Sullivan (HEL).
Res.: 5801 Oak Hills Dr., 68137. Tel: 402-895-0808; Fax: 402-895-0808.
Catechesis/Religious Program—Tel: 402-895-0896; Fax: 402-895-1336. Sr. Marietta Kerkvliet, O.S.B. Students 356.

25—ST. JOSEPH (1887), (German—Hispanic), Rev. Anthony Espinosa.
Church: 1723 S. 17th St., 68108.
School—All Saints Catholic School, Tel: 402-346-5757. See Elementary Schools, Interparochial Under Institutions Located in the Archdiocese.
Catechesis/Religious Program—Students 213.

26—ST. LEO (1978), Revs. Harold J. Buse; David L. Fulton; Deacons George Knockenhauer; Jerry Steenson; Ira Miller.
Res.: 1920 N. 102nd St., 68114. Tel: 402-397-0407; Fax: 402-397-2887.
School—St. Pius X-St. Leo School, Tel: 402-551-6667; Fax: 402-551-8123. See Elementary Schools, Interparochial Under Institutions Located in the Archdiocese.
Catechesis/Religious Program—Students 342.

27—ST. MARGARET MARY (1919), Revs. Melvin Merwald; Jeffrey Loseke.
Res.: 6116 Dodge St., 68132. Tel: 402-558-2255; Fax: 402-551-6644.
School—Tel: 402-551-6663; Fax: 402-551-5631. Lay Teachers 22; Students 566.
Catechesis/Religious Program—Tel: 402-558-9119; Fax: 402-551-5631. Students 124.

28—ST. MARY (1902), Rt. Rev. William E. Sanderson.
Res.: 3529 Q St., 68107. Tel: 402-731-0204; Fax: 402-731-0793.
School—Tel: 402-738-9533; Fax: 402-738-1425. Lay Teachers 5; Students 84.
Catechesis/Religious Program—Students 6.

29—ST. MARY MAGDALENE (1868), Rev. James E. Gilg.
Res.: 109 S. 19th St., 68102. Tel: 402-342-4807; Fax: 402-344-6941.
School—All Saints Catholic School, Tel: 402-346-5757. See Elementary Schools, Interparochial Under Institutions Located in the Archdiocese.

30—MARY OUR QUEEN, Revs. Richard L. Swoboda, Sr. Assoc. Pastor; Carl A. Salanitro; John P. Broheimer; Deacons Paul Rooney; Ron Hesson; Robert Hamilton.
Res.: 3535 S. 119th St., 68144. Tel: 402-333-8662; Fax: 402-333-4504.
School—3405 S. 119th St., 68144. Tel: 402-333-8663; Fax: 402-334-3948. Lay Teachers 30; Students 579.
Catechesis/Religious Program—Tel: 402-333-8231. Barb Eastridge, D.R.E. Students 375.

31—MOTHER OF PERPETUAL HELP (1975),, (Church of the Deaf) Marlene Rowe, Lay Coord. Tel: 402-493-7220.
Res.: 5215 Seward St., 68104. Tel: 402-558-4214.
Catechesis/Religious Program—Students 5.

32—OUR LADY OF GUADALUPE, (Spanish), Revs. Carl J. Zoucha; Jose Manuel Equihua Gonzalez (Mexico); Deacons Joe Ramirez; Duane Bronk; Luis Valadez; Jesus Herrera; Martin Franco.
Res.: 2310 O St., 68107. Tel: 402-731-2196; Fax: 402-827-6764.
School—Tel: 402-731-1601. Susan Aguilera Robles, Prin. Students 100.
Catechesis/Religious Program—Tel: 402-738-8240. Sr. Marcianne Trujillo, D.R.E. Students 165.

33—OUR LADY OF LOURDES (1917), Rev. William D. L'Heureux; Deacon Frank Hilt. In Res., Rev. Richard J. Reiser.
Res.: 2110 S. 32nd Ave., 68105. Tel: 402-346-0900; Fax: 402-344-3315.
School—2124 S. 32nd Ave., 68105. Tel: 402-341-5604. Mary Lottinville, Prin. Sisters 1; Lay Teachers 22; Students 369.
Catechesis/Religious Program—Students 397.

34—ST. PATRICK (1883), Revs. Stephen J. Gutgsell; Howard Remski, F.S.S.P. (SCR).
Res.: 1404 Castelar St., 68108. Tel: 402-341-1305; Fax: 402-342-5510.
School—All Saints Catholic School, Tel: 402-346-5757; Fax: 402-346-8794. See Elementary Schools, Interparochial Under Institutions Located in the Archdiocese.
Catechesis/Religious Program—Students 9.

35—ST PETER, Revs. Damian Zuerlein; Jose Herrera; Deacon John Zak.
Res.: 709 S. 28th St., 68105. Tel 402-341-4560; Fax: 402-341-6483.
Our Lady of Fatima Vietnamese Community—Tel: 402-341-5722. Rev. Nygen Loi.
Catechesis/Religious Program—Students 80.

36—SS. PETER AND PAUL (1917), (Croatian), Revs. Frank A. Partusch; Charles Okorougo (Nigeria).
Res.: 5912 S. 36th St., 68107. Tel: 402-731-4578; Fax: 402-738-8808.
School—Tel: 402-731-4713; Fax: 402-731-2633. Richard Leimbach, Prin. Lay Teachers 10; Students 187.
Catechesis/Religious Program—Tel: 402-733-3344; Fax: 402-731-2633. Wilma Smith, D.R.E. Students 160.

37—ST. PHILIP NERI (1904), Revs. Daniel J. Kampschneider; John Paul Joyce; Sr. Susan Ivis, Pastoral Min. Tel: 402-451-6921; Deacon Fred Hendrick.
Res.: 8200 N. 30th St., 68112. Tel: 402-455-1289; Fax: 402-455-8398.
School—Tel: 402-455-8666; Fax 402-453-3620. Barbara Marchese, Prin. Lay Teachers 14; Students 224.
Catechesis/Religious Program—Tel: 402-455-2190. Marsha Moon, D.R.E. Students 91.

38—ST. PIUS X (1954), Revs. Lloyd A. Gnirk; Vitalis E. Anyanike.
Res.: 6905 Blondo St., 68104. Tel: 402-558-8446; Fax: 402-558-4986.
School—St. Pius X-St. Leo School, Tel: 402-551-6667; Fax: 402-551-8123. See Elementary Schools, Interparochial Under Institutions Located in the Archdiocese.
Catechesis/Religious Program—Tel: 402-558-1898. Elizabeth Field, D.R.E. Students 96.

39—ST. RICHARD (1963), Rev. Kenneth P. Vavrina.
Res.: 4320 Fort St., 68111. Tel: 402-455-2865; Fax: 402-455-0679.
School—Tel: 402-451-0692. Ms. Sue McCaslin, Prin. Sisters 1; Lay Teachers 10; Students 170.
Catechesis/Religious Program—Students 21.

40—ST. ROBERT BELLARMINE (1966), Revs. Donald W. Shane; Mario D. Rapose; Deacons Larry Sampier; Thomas Murphy; Michael Fletcher.
Res.: 11802 Pacific St., 68154. Tel: 402-333-8989; Fax: 402-333-5489.
School—(Grades PreK-8) Tel: 402-334-1929; Fax: 402-333-7188. Sandra Suiter, Prin. Lay Teachers 29; Students 577.
Catechesis/Religious Program—Tel: 402-333-1959. Deb Poledna, D.R.E. Students 217.

41—ST. ROSE (1919), Rev. Rodney T. Adams.
Res.: 4102 S. 13th St., 68107. Tel: 402-733-9327; Fax: 402-731-9937.
Catechesis/Religious Program—Students 6.

42—SACRED HEART (1890), Rev. Thomas M. Fangman; Deacons Charles Weskirchen; James Chambers.
Res.: 2218 Binney St., 68110. Tel: 402-451-5755; Fax: 402-451-1731.
School—Tel: 402-451-5858; Fax: 402-451-7480. Lay Teachers 11; Students 140.
Catechesis/Religious Program—Students 62.

43—ST. STANISLAUS (1919), Rev. R. Michael Fitzpatrick, S.T.L., J.C.L.; Deacons Daniel Saniuk; James Staroski.
Res.: 4002 J St., 68107. Tel: 402-731-4152; Fax: 402-731-4389.
School—Tel: 402-731-0484; Fax: 402-733-4898. Lay Teachers 9; Students 141.
Catechesis/Religious Program—Students 15.

44—ST. STEPHEN THE MARTYR (1989), Rev. Msgr. William J. Dendinger; Rev. John S. Andrews.
Res.: 17053 M St., 68135. Tel: 402-896-9682; Fax: 402-896-1990.
Church: 16701 S St., 68135. Tel: 402-896-9675; Fax: 402-896-1990.
School—Tel: 402-896-0754. Mr. David Peters, Prin. Students 862.
Catechesis/Religious Program—Tel: 402-896-9683. Students 1,467.

45—ST. THERESE OF THE CHILD JESUS (1918), Rev. Kenneth P. Vavrina.
Res.: 4320 Fort St., 68111. Tel: 402-455-2865; Fax: 402-455-0679.

46—ST. THOMAS MORE (1958), Rev. Msgr. Frank E. Chiodo; Rev. Thomas J. Magnuson.
Res.: 4804 Grover St., 68106. Tel: 402-556-1456; Fax: 402-556-1395.
School—Tel: 402-551-9504; Fax: 402-551-9507. Lay Teachers 25; Students 279.
Catechesis/Religious Program—Tel: 402-551-9816; Fax: 402-551-9507. Students 81.

47—ST. VINCENT DE PAUL (1991), Revs. Dennis A. Hanneman; Patrick A. McLaughlin, Asst.; Deacons Donald K. Clausen; William J. Barnes; Gary J. Hennessey. In Res., Rev. Thomas F. O'Brien.
Res.: 14330 Eagle Run Dr., 68164. Tel: 402-496-7988 (Pastoral Center); 402-498-8425 (Rectory); Fax: 402-496-9933.
School—Tel: 402-492-2111. Patricia Buttell, Prin. Students 787.
Catechesis/Religious Program—Tel: 402-493-1642; Fax: 402-496-9933. Students 526.

48—ST. WENCESLAUS (1877), (Czech), Revs. Franklin A. Dvorak; Dermot J. Dunne; Thomas J. Adams; Michael P. Keating; Deacons John Cerveny; Elvon Anderson; Donald Cowles; Joseph Friend; Michael J. DeSelm.
Res.: 15353 Pacific St., 68154. Tel: 402-330-0304; Fax: 402-330-1476.
School—(Grades K-8) Tel: 402-330-4356. Mary McGuire, Prin. Students 841.
Catechesis/Religious Program—Tel: 402-330-1889. Joan Fleming, D.R.E. Students 543.

OUTSIDE THE CITY OF OMAHA

ALBION, BOONE CO., ST. MICHAEL (1877), [CEM] Rev. Frank J. Baumert.
Res.: 524 W. Church St., 68620. Tel: 402-395-2393; Fax: 402-395-2393.
School—Tel: 402-395-2926; Fax: 402-395-2926. Priests 1; Lay Teachers 11; Students 117.
Catechesis/Religious Program—Students 162.

ALOYS, CUMING CO., ST. ALOYSIUS (1891), (German), [CEM] Rev. Mark J. McKercher.
700 Hwy. 32, West Point, 68788.
Res.: 1318 Ave. G., P.O. Box 623, Wisner, 68791. Tel: 402-529-3242; Fax: 402-529-6239.
Catechesis/Religious Program—Students 10.

ATKINSON, HOLT CO., ST. JOSEPH (1886), [CEM] Rev. LuVerne W. Steffes; Deacons Gerald Gonderinger, (Retired); Art Villemure.
Res.: 317 W. State St., P.O. Box 220, 68713. Tel: 402-925-2122.
School—Tel: 402-925-2104; Fax: 402-925-2104. Lay Teachers 8; Students 73.
Catechesis/Religious Program—Tel: 402-925-5854. Students 100.

BANCROFT, CUMING CO., HOLY CROSS (1884), (German), [CEM] Rev. Leo Rigatuso.
Res.: P.O. Box 524, Lyons, 68038. Tel: 402-687-2102; Fax: 402-687-2102.
Catechesis/Religious Program—Students 37.

BATTLE CREEK, MADISON CO., ST. PATRICK'S (1875), [CEM] Rev. Joseph M. Wray.
Res.: 107 N. Third St., P.O. Box 40, 68715. Tel: 402-675-2485.
Catechesis/Religious Program—Tel: 402-675-6345. Danni Arduser, D.R.E. Students 113.

Mission—St. Francis de Sales Schoolcraft, Madison Co.

BEEMER, CUMING CO., HOLY CROSS (1913), [CEM] Rev. Mark K Merkel.
Res.: 517 Fraisier St. N., P.O. Box 212, 68716. Tel: 402-528-3475; Fax: 402-528-3374.
Catechesis / Religious Program—Students 59.

BELLEVUE, SARPY CO.

1—ST. MARY (1921), Revs. Francis W. Lordemann; Timothy Podraza; Deacons Ralph Hueser; Duane Iwanski; Chuck L'Archevesque; Andy Foray; John Huck; John Wacha.
Res.: 811 W. 23rd Ave., 68005. Tel: 402-291-1350; Fax: 402-291-1375.
School—(Grades PreK-8) Tel: 402-291-1666; Fax: 402-291-9667. Jean Seibel, Prin. Lay Teachers 20; Students 251.
Catechesis / Religious Program—Tel: 402-291-7222; Fax: 402-291-3964. Leslie Trantow, D.R.E. Students 267.

2—ST. MATTHEW THE EVANGELIST CHURCH OF BELLEVUE (1996), Rev. Dennis R. Stolinski.
Res.: 3605 Looking Glass Dr., 68123. Tel: 402-292-7418; Fax: 402-292-7451.
School—(Grades K-8), 12210 S. 36th St., 68123. Tel: 402-291-2030; Fax: 402-291-2047. Donna Blazek, Prin. Lay Teachers 14; Students 214.
Catechesis / Religious Program—Students 177.

BLAIR, WASHINGTON CO., ST. FRANCIS BORGIA (1865), [CEM] Rev. Alfred J. Salanitro.
Res.: 2005 Davis Dr., 68008. Tel: 402-426-3823; Fax: 402-426-5131.
Catechesis / Religious Program—Tel: 402-426-5145. Deb Kaslon, D.R.E.; Paul M. Cerio, D.R.E. Students 455.

BLOOMFIELD, KNOX CO., ST. ANDREW (1892), [CEM] Rev. Stanley J. Schmit.
Res.: 304 S. McNamara St., P.O. Box 419, 68718. Tel: 402-373-2233; Fax: 402-373-2233.
Catechesis / Religious Program—Tel: 402-373-2696. Barb Jackson, D.R.E. Students 92.

BOW VALLEY, CEDAR CO., SS. PETER AND PAUL, Merged, with Sacred Heart, Wynot; Ss. Philip and James, St. James and Immaculate Conception, St. Helena to form Holy Family Church of Cedar County, Hartington.

BOYS TOWN, DOUGLAS CO., IMMACULATE CONCEPTION B.V.M. (1936), Rev. Valentine J. Peter, S.T.D., J.C.D. In Res., Rev. Msgr. Peter F. Dunne (Retired); Rev. Eugene McReynolds, O.S.B.
Res.: 68010. Tel: 402-498-1000; Fax: 402-498-1010.
Catechesis / Religious Program—Tel: 402-498-1885. Students 622.

BUTTE, BOYD CO, SS. PETER AND PAUL (1906), [CEM 2] Rev. Thomas S. Gall.
Res.: 721 1st St., P.O. Box 8, 68722. Tel: 402-775-2452; Fax: 402-775-2452.
Office: 304 E. South St., P.O. Box 149, Spencer, 68777. Tel: 402-589-0067; Fax: 402-589-1013.
Catechesis / Religious Program—Tel: 402-775-2622; Fax: 402-775-2244. Students 65.
Mission—Sacred Heart [CEM] Naper, Boyd Co. (Closed)

CEDAR RAPIDS, BOONE CO., ST. ANTHONY (1884), [CEM] Rev. Ralph J. Steffensmeier.
Res.: P.O. Box 56, 68627. Tel: 308-358-0773; Fax: 308-358-0773.
Catechesis / Religious Program—Students 85.
Mission—St. Mary [CEM] Primrose, Boone Co. 68627.

CENTRAL CITY, MERRICK CO., ST. MICHAEL (1910), Rev. Nelson A. Newman; Deacon Robert Flesch.
Res.: 2402 20th Ave., 68826. Tel: 308-946-2855; Fax: 308-946-2214.
Catechesis / Religious Program—Kendra Jefferson, D.R.E.; Dave Varley, D.R.E. Students 100.

CLARKS, MERRICK CO., ST. PETER (1918), [CEM] Rev. Donald M. Cleary.
Res.: 315 N. Esther, Fullerton, 68638. Tel: 308-536-2574; Fax: 308-536-9604.
Catechesis / Religious Program—Tel: 308-548-2573. Linda Yrkoski, D.R.E. Students 56.

CLARKSON, COLFAX CO., SS. CYRIL AND METHODIUS (1901), (Czech), Rev. Floyd A. Wessling.
Res.: 120 Cherry St., P.O. Box 457, 68629. Tel: 402-892-3464; Fax: 402-892-9879.
School—St. John Neumann, Tel: 402-892-3407; Fax: 402-892-3090. Lay Teachers 4; Students 42.
Catechesis / Religious Program—Students 126.

COLERIDGE, CEDAR CO., ST. MICHAEL (1886), (German—Irish), [CEM] Revs. John L. Pietramale; Garry A. Welsh.
Mailing Address: P.O. Box 278, Hartington, 68739.
Res.: 315 S. Madison, 68727. Tel: 402-254-6559; Fax: 402-254-6553.
Catechesis / Religious Program—Students 45.

COLUMBUS, PLATTE CO.

1—ST. ANTHONY (1913), Rev. Lydell T. Lape; Deacons Michael Placzek; Michael McGuire; Kelly McGowan.
Res.: 562 17th Ave., 68601. Tel: 402-564-3313; Fax: 402-563-1005.
School—Tel: 402-564-4767; Fax: 402-563-1005. Norma Cremers, Prin. Lay Teachers 7; Students 138.
Catechesis / Religious Program—Lori Olson, D.R.E. Students 135.

2—ST. BONAVENTURE (1877), [CEM] Revs. Thomas Weisbecker; Mark D. Bridgman. In Res., Deacons Arthur Spenner; Lawrence Mielak.
Res.: 1565 18th Ave., 68601. Tel: 402-564-7151; Fax: 402-562-6025.
School—Tel: 402-564-7153; Fax: 402-564-2587. Mr. Chris Vos, Prin. Sisters 2; Lay Teachers 12; Students 207.
Catechesis / Religious Program—Gail Benesch, D.R.E.; Belinda Keiter, D.R.E. Students 393.

3—ST. ISIDORE (1963), [JC] Revs. Joseph A. Miksch; William Bord.
Res.: 3921 20th St., 68601. Tel: 402-564-8993; Fax: 402-564-8955.
School—Tel: 402-564-2604; Fax: 402-564-5349. Lay Teachers 20; Students 215.
Catechesis / Religious Program—Tel: 402-246-5455. Students 158.

CONSTANCE, KNOX CO., ST. JOSEPH, [CEM], (Mission of Crofton) Rev. Robert K. English.
Mailing Address: Box 335, Crofton, 68730. Tel: 402-388-4814.
School—West Catholic Elementary See Elementary Schools, Interparochial Under Institutions Located in the Archdiocese.
Catechesis / Religious Program—Students 22.

CREIGHTON, KNOX CO., ST. LUDGER (1885), (German—Czech), [JC] Rev. Keith D. Rezac.
Res.: 908 Lake St., 68729-2917. Tel: 402-358-3596; Fax: 402-358-3596.
School—410 Bryant Ave., 68729. Tel: 402-358-3501; Fax: 402-358-3501. Sisters 1; Lay Teachers 4; Students 40.
Catechesis / Religious Program—Tel: 402-358-3501. Karen Boyle, D.R.E.; Ellen Jundt, D.R.E.; Darla Frisch, D.R.E. Students 123.
Mission—St. Ignatius Brunswick, Antelope Co.

CROFTON, KNOX CO., ST. ROSE OF LIMA, [CEM] Rev. Robert K. English.
Res.: 1316 W. Fifth St., P.O. Box 335, 68730. Tel: 402-388-4814; Fax: 402-388-2680.
School—Tel: 402-388-4393; Fax: 402-388-4393. Lay Teachers 8; Students 112.
Catechesis / Religious Program—Cindy Stucky, D.R.E., (Grades 1-8); Deacon Don Seamann, D.R.E., (Grades 9-12). Students 127.

DELOIT TOWNSHIP, HOLT CO., ST. JOHN THE BAPTIST (1910), [CEM] Rev. William J. Safranek.
Res.: P.O Box 37, Ewing, 68735. Tel: 402-626-7605; Fax: 402-626-7668.
Catechesis / Religious Program—Students 27.

DODGE, DODGE CO., ST. WENCESLAUS (1883), (Czech), [CEM 2] [JC] Rev. Dennis U. DeGuzman.
Res.: 743 Second St., 68633. Tel: 402-693-2235; Fax: 402-693-2255.
School—Tel: 402-693-2819; Fax: 402-693-2347. Elizabeth Gibney, Prin. Lay Teachers 5; Students 67.
Catechesis / Religious Program—Tel: 402-693-2347. Joan Ruskamp, D.R.E. Students 67.
Mission—Sacred Heart Olean, Colfax Co.
Mission—St. Mary Tabor, Colfax Co.

DUNCAN, PLATTE CO., ST. STANISLAUS, [CEM] Revs. David M. Korth; Frank E. Jindra.
Res.: P.O. Box 192, 68634. Tel: 402-897-2625; Fax: 402-897-2626.
Catechesis / Religious Program—Students 91.

ELGIN, ANTELOPE CO., ST. BONIFACE (1902), (German), [CEM] Rev. Thomas E. Bauwens; Deacons Dennis Wiehn; Bill Camp.
Res.: P.O. Box B, 68636-0433. Tel: 402-843-2345; Fax: 402-843-2253.
School—Tel: 402-843-5460; Fax: 402-843-5842. Lay Teachers 8; Students 115.
Catechesis / Religious Program—Students 37.

ELKHORN, DOUGLAS CO., ST. PATRICK, [CEM] Rev. Ronald S. Wasikowski. In Res., Rev. Thomas A. Greisen.
Res.: 20500 W. Maple Rd., P.O. Box 10, 68022. Tel: 402-289-4289; Fax: 402-763-9530.
School—(Grades PreK-6) Tel: 402-289-5407. Donald Ridder, Prin. Students 390.
Catechesis / Religious Program—Tel: 402-289-4947. Students 363.

EMERSON, DAKOTA CO., SACRED HEART (1886), [CEM] Rev. Michael B. Malloy.
Res.: Sixth St. & Main St., P.O. Box 250, 68733. Tel: 402-695-2342; Fax: 402-695-2513.
School—Tel: 402-695-2513. Lay Teachers 4; Students 13.
Catechesis / Religious Program—Students 84.

EWING, HOLT CO., ST. PETER DE ALCANTARA, [CEM] Rev. William J. Safranek.
Res.: P.O. Box 37, 68735. Tel: 402-626-7605; Fax: 402-626-7668.
Catechesis / Religious Program—Tel: 402-626-7905. Students 130.

FORDYCE, CEDAR CO., ST. JOHN THE BAPTIST (1909), (German), [CEM] Rev. Michael Schmitz; Deacon Marcus Potts.
Res.: P.O. Box 170, 68736. Tel: 402-357-3506; Fax: 402-357-3795.
School—West Catholic Elementary, Tel: 402-357-3507. See Elementary Schools, Interparochial Under Institutions Located in the Archdiocese.
Catechesis / Religious Program—Tel: 402-357-2548. Kathy Magorian, D.R.E. Students 5.

FORT CALHOUN, WASHINGTON CO., ST. JOHN THE BAPTIST (1883), Rev. Michael F. Gutgsell, J.C.L.
Res.: 215 N. 13th St., P.O. Box 148, 68023. Tel: 402-468-5348; Fax: 402-468-4619.
Catechesis / Religious Program—Tel: 402-468-5659. Students 150.

FREMONT, DODGE CO., ST. PATRICK (1858), [CEM] Revs. Owen W. Korte; Roland A. Peschel; Damien J. Cook; Deacons Robert Chapman; Edward Gentrup; Hugh Robinson; LeRoy Spieker; Vic Henry; Duane Kosmicki; Dan Mueller; Joe Uhlik.
Res.: 422 E. Fourth St., 68025. Tel: 402-721-6611; Fax: 402-727-8167.
High School—Archbishop Bergan, (Grades 9-12) Tel: 402-721-9683; Fax: 402-721-5366. Don Cunningham, Prin. Lay Teachers 18; Students 112.
School—Bergan Middle School, (Grades 6-8) Tel: 402-721-9766; Fax: 402-721-5366. Lay Teachers 14; Students 91.
Catechesis / Religious Program—Tel: 402-721-9710. Margaret Iossi, D.R.E. Students 595.

FULLERTON, NANCE CO., ST. PETER (1917), (Polish), [CEM] Rev. Donald M. Cleary.
Res.: 315 N. Esther, P.O. Box 368, 68638. Tel: 308-536-2574; Fax: 308-536-2574.
Catechesis / Religious Program—Tel: 308-536-2481. Students 135.

GENOA, NANCE CO., ST. ROSE OF LIMA (1900), [JC] Rev. Robert H. Nienaber.
Res.: 116 N. Elm St., P.O. Box 490, 68640-0490. Tel: 402-993-2323; Fax: 402-993-2323.
Catechesis / Religious Program—Students 110.

GRETNA, SARPY CO., ST. PATRICK (1858), (Irish), [CEM] Rev. Daniel F. Soltys; Deacon Joseph Krajicek.
Res.: 214 No. Cherokee Dr., 68028. Tel: 402-332-5505; Fax: 402-332-5107.
Church: 508 Angus St., 68028.
Catechesis / Religious Program—Tel: 402-332-4444. Students 551.

HARTINGTON, CEDAR CO.

1—HOLY FAMILY CHURCH OF CEDAR COUNTY (2000), (German), [CEM] Rev. Ross C. Burkhalter.
Parish Office—106 W. 889th Rd., 68739-6079. Tel: 402-254-3311; Fax: 402-254-3311.
Catechesis / Religious Program—Tel: 402-357-2178. Students 139.

2—HOLY TRINITY (1886), (German—Irish), [CEM] Revs. John L. Pietramale; John S. Andrews.
Res.: 404 S. Broadway Ave., P.O. Box 278, 68739. Tel: 402-254-6559; Fax: 402-254-6553.
School—Tel: 402-254-6496. Lay Teachers 10; Students 168.
Catechesis / Religious Program—Students 123.

HEUN, COLFAX CO., HOLY TRINITY (1878), (Czech), [CEM] Rev. Paul R. Ortmeier.
Res.: 1733 Road 12,, Clarkson, 68629. Tel: 402-986-1627; Fax: 402-986-1627.
School— See Elementary Schools, Interparochial Under Institutions Located in the Archdiocese.
Catechesis / Religious Program—Fax: 402-986-1627 ext. 51. Students 13.

HOOPER, DODGE CO., ST. ROSE OF LIMA, [CEM] Rev. Michael P. Eckley.
Res.: 405 Elk St., P.O. Box 443, 68031. Tel: 402-654-3449.
Catechesis / Religious Program—Students 52.
Mission—St. Lawrence [CEM] 405 Elk St. Box 443,, Scribner, Dodge Co. 68031. Tel: 402-654-3449.
Catechesis / Religious Program—Students 52.

HOWELLS, COLFAX CO.

1—ST. JOHN NEPOMUCENE (1893), [CEM] Rev. Paul Ortmeier.
Res.: 614 Center St., 68641. Tel: 402-986-1653; Fax: 402-986-1653.
School—Howells Community Catholic School See Elementary Schools, Interparochial Under Institutions Located in the Archdiocese.
Catechesis / Religious Program—Students 6.

2—SS. PETER AND PAUL (1890), (German), [CEM] Rev. Paul Ortmeier.
Res.: 614 Center St., 68641. Tel: 402-986-1653; Fax: 402-986-1653.
School—Howells Community Catholic School See Elementary Schools, Interparochial Under Institutions Located in the Archdiocese.
Catechesis / Religious Program—Students 66.

HUMPHREY, PLATTE CO., ST. FRANCIS (1883), [CEM] [JC 2] Rev. James M. Buckley. In Res., Rev. Wayne S. Pavela.
Res.: P.O. Box 116, 68642. Tel: 402-923-0913; Fax:

402-923-1931.
School—(Grades K-6) Tel: 402-923-0611; Fax: 402-923-1590. Lay Teachers 7; Students 129.
High School—Tel: 402-923-0818. Lay Teachers 16; Students 151.
Catechesis/Religious Program—Students 59.

JACKSON, DAKOTA CO., ST. PATRICK (1856), Rev. Richard Whiteing.
Res.: 203 E. Elk St., P.O. Box 87, 68743. Tel: 402-632-4292.
Catechesis/Religious Program—Tel: 402-632-4258; Fax: 402-632-4312. Claudette Albenesius, D.R.E. Students 84.
Mission—St. Mary [CEM 2] P.O. Box 126, Hubbard, Dakota Co. 68741. Tel: 402-632-4283.

KRAKOW, NANCE CO., SS. PETER AND PAUL (1893), (Polish), [CEM] Rev. Robert H. Nienaber.
Res.: P.O. Genoa, R.R. 2, P.O. Box 18, 68640. Tel: 402-993-6600.
Catechesis/Religious Program—Students 18.

LAUREL, CEDAR CO., ST. MARY (1894), [CEM] Rev. James F. McCluskey; Deacon LeRoy Creamer, (Retired).
Res.: 406 Elm St., P.O. Box 828, 68745. Tel: 402-256-3303; Fax: 402-256-3019.
Catechesis/Religious Program—Susan Mohr, D.R.E. Students 85.
Mission—St. Anne Dixon, Dixon Co.

LEIGH, COLFAX CO., ST. MARY (1900), [CEM] Rev. Melvern A.. Wiese.
Res.: 220 W. Third St., P.O. Box 385, 68643. Tel: 402-487-2666; Fax: 402-487-2666.
Catechesis/Religious Program—Laurie Urban, D.R.E. Students 67.

LINDSAY, PLATTE CO., HOLY FAMILY (1895), [CEM] Rev. James F. Novotny.
Res.: P.O. Box 68, 68644. Tel: 402-428-2455; Fax: 402-428-5205.
School—(Grades 1-6) Tel: 402-428-3455; Fax: 402-428-3231. Lay Teachers 7; Students 107.
High School—(Grades 7-12) Tel: 402-428-3215; Fax: 402-428-3231. Lay Teachers 10; Students 101.
Catechesis/Religious Program—Students 75.

LYNCH, BOYD CO., ASSUMPTION B.V.M. (1892), [CEM] Rev. Thomas S. Gall.
Office: P.O. Box 167, 68746. Tel: 402-569-2421; Fax: 402-569-2421.
Res.: 721 1st. St., P.O. Box 8, Butte, 68722. Tel: 402-775-2452; Fax: 402-775-2452.
Catechesis/Religious Program—Students 31.

LYONS, BURT CO., ST. JOSEPH (1884), Rev. Leo Rigatuso.
Res.: 430 Lincoln St., P.O. Box 524, 68038. Tel: 402-687-2102; Fax: 402-687-2102.
Catechesis/Religious Program—Students 62.

MADISON, MADISON CO., ST. LEONARD, [CEM] Revs. Stanley L. Kasun; Frank Parrinello; Deacons Frederick Ridder; Robert Chadwick.
Res.: 504 S. Nebraska St., P.O. Box 368, 68748. Tel: 402-454-3529; Fax: 402-454-3529.
School—Tel: 402-454-3525; Fax: 402-454-6653. Lay Teachers 5; Students 64.
Catechesis/Religious Program—Students 64.

MENOMINEE, CEDAR CO., ST. BONIFACE (1872), (German), [CEM] Rev. Michael D. Schmitz; Deacon Clarence Jansen.
Res.: P.O. Box 170, Fordyce, 68736. Tel: 402-357-3506; Fax: 402-357-3507.
School—West Catholic Elementary, Fax: 402-357-3795. See Elementary Schools, Interparochial Under Institutions Located in the Archdiocese.
Catechesis/Religious Program—Tel: 402-357-2548. Kathy Magorian, D.R.E. Students 55.

MONTEREY, CUMING CO., ST. BONIFACE (1905), (German), [CEM] Rev. Mark K. Merkel.
Res.: 450 12th Rd., West Point, 68788. Tel: 402-372-3681; Fax: 402-372-3681.

NELIGH, ANTELOPE CO., ST. FRANCIS, Rev. Steven Emanuel; Deacon Bernard Burbach.
Res.: 702 W. 11th St., P.O. Box 259, 68756. Tel: 402-887-4521; Fax: 402-843-2297.
Catechesis/Religious Program—Students 131.

NEWCASTLE, DIXON CO., ST. PETER (1873), [CEM] Rev. David F. Liewer.
Mailing Address: P.O. Box 898, Ponca, 68770-0898. Tel: 402-755-2773; Fax: 402-755-2525.
Res.: P.O. Box 127, 405 Annie St., 68757. Tel: 402-355-2620 (Rectory).
Catechesis/Religious Program—Tel: 402-355-2280. Angie Bennett, D.R.E. Students 61.

NORFOLK, MADISON CO., SACRED HEART (1881), (German), Revs. David D. Belt; James E. Keiter; Dermot J. Dunne; Deacons Jim Doolittle; Irving St. Arnold; Roger D. Pribnow.
Res.: 202 S. Fifth St., 68701. Tel: 402-371-2621; Fax: 402-371-0403. Web: www.shpo.org.
School—(Grades PreSchool-12) Tel: 402-371-4584 (Pre-School-6); 402-371-2784 (7-12); Fax: 402-379-8129 (Pre-School-6); 402-379-2929 (7-12). Vicki Hodge, Co. Prin. (Pre-School-6); Anne Miller, Co. Prin. (Pre-School-6); Jeff Bellar, Prin. (Grades 7-12). Priests 4; Lay Teachers 54; Students 754.
Catechesis/Religious Program—Tel: 402-371-8658. Marilyn Kathol, D.R.E. (Pre-School-12). Students 542.

NORTH BEND, DODGE CO., ST. CHARLES BORROMEO (1892), [JC] Rev. Gerald P. Melchior.
Res.: P.O. Box 457, 68649. Tel: 402-652-8484; Fax: 402-652-3418.
Catechesis/Religious Program—Tel: 402-652-8437. Betty Marxsen, D.R.E. (Grades K-6). Students 157.

O'NEILL, HOLT CO., ST. PATRICK (1877), [CEM] Revs. Mark D. Filips; Eric S. Olsen.
Res.: 301 E Adams, 68763. Tel: 402-336-1602; Fax: 402-336-1613.
School—Tel: 402-336-2664; Fax: 402-336-2055. Lay Teachers 10; Students 130.
High School—Tel: 402-336-4455; Fax: 402-336-1533. Sisters 1; Lay Teachers 9; Students 111.
Catechesis/Religious Program—Tel: 402-336-1602; Fax: 402-336-1533. Mary Novak, D.R.E Students 183.
Mission—St. Joseph Amelia, Holt Co. Tel: 402-482-5283.

OLEAN, COLFAX CO., SACRED HEART, [CEM], (Mission of St. Wenceslaus, Dodge) Rev. Dennis U. DeGuzman.
Res.: 743 Second St., Dodge, 68633. Tel: 402-693-2356.
School—Howells Community Catholic School See Elementary Schools, Interparochial Under Institutions Located in the Archdiocese.

OSMOND, PIERCE CO., ST. MARY OF THE SEVEN DOLORS (1904), [CEM] Rev. Stanley J. Schmit.
Res.: 509 Hill St., P.O. Box 397, 68765. Tel: 402-748-3340; Fax: 402-748-3433.
School—Tel: 402-748-3433. Lay Teachers 4; Students 36.
Catechesis/Religious Program—Students 59.

PAPILLION, SARPY CO., ST. COLUMBKILLE (1897), Revs. Francis A. Nigli; Charles L. Jurgensmeier, S.J.; Deacons Frank Mascarello; Jerry Overkamp; William Hill; Eldon Lauber; Mike Leick; Roland Kaiser; Joseph Morley; Duane Thome; Steve Jordan; Paul Powers; Bob Stier; John J. Zurek.
Res.: 200 E. Sixth St., 68046. Tel: 402-339-3285; Fax: 402-592-4753.
School—Tel: 402-339-8706; Fax: 402-592-4147. Lay Teachers 23; Students 662.
Catechesis/Religious Program—Tel: 402-339-0990; Fax: 402-339-3977. Students 817.

PENDER, THURSTON CO., ST. JOHN (1889), [JC] Rev. Michael B. Malloy.
Res.: 601 N. Main St., P.O. Box 250, Emerson, 68733-0250. Tel: 402-385-3258; Fax: 402-385-3400.
Catechesis/Religious Program—Students 75.

PETERSBURG, BOONE CO., ST. JOHN THE BAPTIST (1896), [CEM] Rev. Frank J. Baumert.
Res.: P.O. Box 608, 68652. Tel: 402-395-2393; Fax: 402-395-2393.
School—Tel: 402-386-5472. Lay Teachers 2; Students 20.
Catechesis/Religious Program—Students 82.

PIERCE, PIERCE CO., ST. JOSEPH (1905), (German), [CEM] Rev. Gerald A. Connealy.
Res.: 118 W. Willow St., 68767. Tel: 402-329-4200; Fax: 402-329-4579.
Catechesis/Religious Program—Tel: 402-329-6655. Students 178.

PLAINVIEW, PIERCE CO., ST. PAUL (1912), [CEM] Rev. Stanley J. Schmit.
Res.: P.O. Box 397, Osmond, 68765. Tel: 402-748-3340; Fax: 402-748-3340.
Catechesis/Religious Program—Students 49.

PLATTE CENTER, PLATTE CO., ST. JOSEPH (1884), (German—Irish), [CEM] [JC] Rev. Rodney V. Kneifl.
Res.: P.O. Box 155, 68653-0155. Tel: 402-246-2255; Fax: 402-246-2045.
Catechesis/Religious Program—Tel: 402-246-5700. Angela Dolezal, D.R.E. Students 107.

PONCA, DIXON CO., ST. JOSEPH (1890), [CEM] Rev. David F. Liewer.
Res.: P.O. Box 898, 68757 Tel: 402-355-2620; 402-755-2773 (Office); Fax: 402-755-2525.
Catechesis/Religious Program—Tel: 402-755-4273. Kari Richards, D.R.E. Students 81.

RAEVILLE, BOONE CO., ST. BONAVENTURE (1882), (German), [CEM] Rev. Thomas E. Bauwens.
Res.: 301 S. 2nd St., Box B, Elgin, 68636. Tel: 402-843-2345; Fax: 402-843-2253.
Catechesis/Religious Program—Students 11.

RALSTON, DOUGLAS CO., ST GERALD (1957), Revs. Gary L. Ostrander; Ralph A. Lammers (Retired); Perry Robinson, S.J.
Res.: 7859 Lakeview St., 68127. Tel: 402-331-1955; Fax: 402-339-8733.
School—Tel: 402-331-4223; Fax: 402-331-4523. David Garland, Prin. Lay Teachers 20; Students 294.
Catechesis/Religious Program—Tel: 402-331-4223. Students 490.

RANDOLPH, CEDAR CO., ST. FRANCES DE CHANTAL (1892), (German), [CEM] Rev. Ronald A. Battiato; Deacons Vincent Schmit; Doug Tunink.
Res.: 402 N. Bridge St., 68771. Tel: 402-337-0644.
Catechesis/Religious Program—Tel: 402-337-0341. Sandy Thies, D.R.E. Students 199.

ST. CHARLES, CUMING CO., ST. ANTHONY (1862), (German), [CEM] Rev. Mark K. Merkel.
Res.: 445 15th Rd., West Point, 68788. Tel: 402-372-3681.

ST. EDWARD, BOONE CO., ST. EDWARD (1888), [CEM] Rev. James F. Novotny.
Res.: 805 Washington St., P.O. Box A, 68660-0136. Tel: 402-678-2642; Fax: 402-678-2341.
Catechesis/Religious Program—Sheryl Rosno, D.R.E. Students 71.

ST. HELENA, CEDAR CO., IMMACULATE CONCEPTION, Merged, with Ss. Philip and James, St. James; Ss. Peter and Paul, Bow Valley and Sacred Heart, Wynot to form Holy Family Church of Cedar County.

ST. JAMES, CEDAR CO., SS. PHILIP AND JAMES, Merged, with Immaculate Conception, St. Helena; Ss. Peter and Paul, Bow Valley and Sacred Heart, Wynot to form Holy Family Church of Cedar County.

SCHUYLER, COLFAX CO.
1—ST. AUGUSTINE (1878), (Irish—German), [CEM] Revs. Gerald A. Leise Jr.; Gustavo Barrientos; Deacons Marvin Capoun; James DeBlauw.
Res.: 619 Banner St., 68661. Tel: 402-352-3521; Fax: 402-352-3521.
Catechesis/Religious Program—320 W. 10 St., 68661. Tel: 402-352-2149. Students 188.
2—ST. MARY (1914), (Czech), Revs. Gerald A. Leise; Gustavo Barrientos; Deacons Evan Drozda, (Retired); Jim Conrad; Carl Perrin.
Res.: 308 W. 10 St., 68661. Tel: 402-352-3540; Fax: 402-352-5971.
Catechesis/Religious Program—Tel: 402-352-2149. Kathy Mares, D.R.E. Students 116.

SILVER CREEK, MERRICK CO., ST. LAWRENCE (1902), (Polish), [CEM] Revs. David M. Korth; Frank E. Jindra.
Res.: P.O. Box 332, 68663. Tel: 308-773-2282; Fax: 308-773-8281.
Catechesis/Religious Program—Tel: 308-773-2430; Fax: 308-773-8281. Joan Sock, D.R.E. Students 51.

SNYDER, DODGE CO., ST. LEO, [CEM] Rev. Gerald P. Melchior.
Res.: P.O. Box 188, 68664. Tel: 402-652-8484.
Catechesis/Religious Program—Tel: 402-568-2586. Betty Marxsen, D.R.E. Students 38.

SOUTH SIOUX CITY, DAKOTA CO., ST. MICHAEL (1898), [CEM] Revs. Daniel L. Wittrock; Paul Albenesius; Jose Mendoza.
Office:—P.O. Box 128, 68776.
Res.: 1405 First Ave., 68776. Tel: 402-494-5423; Fax: 402-494-6342.
School—Tel: 402-494-1526; Fax: 402-494-4283. Lay Teachers 14; Students 130.
Catechesis/Religious Program—1414 Third Ave., 68776. Tel: 402-494-2827. Students 250.
Mission—St. Cornelius Homer, Dakota Co. Rev. Daniel L. Wittrock.

SPENCER, BOYD CO., ST. MARY (1892), [CEM 2] Rev. Thomas S. Gall.
Office: 304 E. South St., P.O. Box 149, 68777. Tel: 402-589-0067; Fax: 402-589-1013.
Res.: 721 1st St., P.O. Box 8, Butte, 68722. Tel: 402-775-2452; Fax: 402-775-2452.
Catechesis/Religious Program—Mary Kirpatrick, D.R.E. Tel: 402-589-1266. Students 44.

SPRINGFIELD, SARPY CO., ST. JOSEPH (1980), [JC] Rev. Joseph Broudou, Temp. Admin.
Res.: 102 S. Ninth St., P.O. Box 345, 68059. Tel: 402-253-2889; Fax: 402-253-2949.
Catechesis/Religious Program—Tel: 402-253-2949. Sherry Huntwork, D.R.E. Students 118.

STANTON, STANTON CO., ST. PETER (1893), Rev. Timothy J. Lange.
Res.: P.O. Box 557, 68779. Tel: 402-439-2147; Fax: 402-439-2149.
Catechesis/Religious Program—Tel: 402-379-1234; 402-439-2331. Valerie Morfeld, D.R.E.; Karen Petersen, D.R.E. Students 93.

STUART, HOLT CO., ST. BONIFACE (1899), [CEM] Rev. Douglas P. Scheinost.
Res.: 106 E. Fourth, P.O. Box 190, 68780. Tel: 402-924-3262; Fax: 402-924-3494.
School—Tel: 402-924-3803; Fax: 402-924-3803. Lay Teachers 4; Students 33.
Catechesis/Religious Program—Students 95.

TARNOV, PLATTE CO., ST. MICHAEL (1884), (Polish), [CEM] Rev. Rodney Kneifl.
Res.: P.O. Box 155, Platte Center, 68653. Tel: 402-246-2255; Fax: 402-246-2045.
Catechesis/Religious Program—Tel: 402-923-1308. Students 40.

TEKAMAH, BURT CO., ST. PATRICK, [JC] Rev. James V. Kramper.
Res.: 1323 R St., 68061-1542. Tel: 402-374-1692; Fax: 402-374-1692.

Catechesis/Religious Program—Tel: 402-374-1696. Romaine Boerma, D.R.E. Students 84.
Mission—Holy Family 2801 Co. Rd. U, Decatur, Burt Co. 68020. Rev. James V. Kramper.

TILDEN, MADISON CO., OUR LADY OF MT. CARMEL (1887), [CEM] Rev. Steven Emanuel.
Res.: P.O. Box 458, 68781. Tel: 402-368-7710; Fax: 402-368-7710.
Catechesis/Religious Program—Tel: 402-368-5919. Corine Frey, D.R.E. Students 95.

VALLEY, DOUGLAS CO., ST. JOHN (1917), Rev. Emmett F. Meyer.
Res.: 209 E. Sunset, 68064. Tel: 402-359-5783; Fax: 402-359-5217.
Catechesis/Religious Program—Tel: 402-779-2814. Connie Schnoes, D.R.E. Students 128.

VERDIGRE, KNOX CO., ST. WENCESLAUS (1884), [CEM] Rev. Jay L. Kruse.
Res.: 409 S. Third St., P.O. Box 9, 68783-0009. Tel: 402-668-2331; Fax: 402-668-2375.
Catechesis/Religious Program—Students 110.
Mission—St. William P.O. Box 9, Niobrara, Knox Co. 68783-0009. Tel: 402-857-3438. Rev. Jay L. Kruse.

WALTHILL, THURSTON CO., ST. JOSEPH, (Native American), Revs. David M. Korth; Steven Boes.
Res.: 501 Main St., 68067. Tel: 402-846-5550; Fax: 402-878-2760.
Mission—Our Lady of Fatima Box 404, Macy, Thurston Co. 68067. Revs. David M. Korth; Steven Boes.

WAYNE, WAYNE CO., ST. MARY (1881), [CEM] Rev. Mark A. Tomasiewicz.
Res.: 412 E. 8th St., 68787. Tel: 402-375-2000; Fax: 402-375-5782.
School—Tel: 402-375-2337. Lay Teachers 6; Students 31.
Catechesis/Religious Program—Students 180.

WEST POINT, CUMING CO., ASSUMPTION B.V.M. (1875), [CEM] Revs. Gerald E. Gonderinger; Mark J. McKercher; Deacons Vincent Maly; Kenneth Batenhorst.
Res.: 343 N. Monitor St., 68788. Tel: 402-372-2188; Fax: 402-372-3563.
School—Guardian Angel, Tel: 402-372-5328. Sr. Mary Ann Tupy, Prin. Priests 2; Sisters 2; Lay Teachers 18; Students 269.
Catechesis/Religious Program—Sr. Judanne Stratman, O.S.F., D.R.E. Students 134.

WINNEBAGO, THURSTON CO.
1—ST. AUGUSTINE'S, (Native American),, (Indian Mission), Revs. Steven Boes, Mission Dir.; David M. Korth, Asst. Dir.
Res.: P.O. Box GG, 68071. Tel: 402-878-2577; Fax: 402-878-2760.
School— 68071. Tel: 402-878-2291; Fax: 402-878-2760. Missionary Benedictine Sisters 4; Lay Teachers 8; Students 88.
2—OUR LADY OF FATIMA OF MACY, Closed., This is a mission of St. Joseph, Walthill.

WISNER, CUMING CO., ST. JOSEPH (1879), (Irish—German), [CEM] [JC] Rev. Mark J. McKercher.
Res.: 1318 G Ave. W., P.O. Box 623, 68791. Tel: 402-529-3242; Fax: 402-529-6239.
Catechesis/Religious Program—Tel: 402-529-3891. Anne McManigal, D.R.E. Students 129.

WYNOT, CEDAR CO., SACRED HEART, Merged, with Ss. Philip and James, St. James; Immaculate Conception, St. Helena and Ss. Peter and Paul, Bow Valley to form Holy Family Church of Cedar County.

Special Assignment:
Revs.—
Fitzpatrick, R. Michael, Dir. Catholic Cemeteries, 7710 W. Center Rd., 68124. Tel: 402-391-3711
Gonderinger, Gerald E., Language Studies
Keller, Daniel E., St. Robert Bellarmine, 11802 Pacific St., 68154.
Richling, Theodore L., 7323 Shirley St., 68124.

On Duty Outside the Archdiocese:
Rev.—
McKamy, Eldon J., Providence St. Vincent Medical Center, Portland, OR

Graduate Studies:
Rev.—
Lewis, Ryan, The Catholic University of America, Washington, D.C.

Military Chaplains:
Revs.—
Dillon, Jerome V., Chap., U.S.N.R.
Hall, Douglas C., U.S.A.F.
Reeson, David G., U.S.A.F.

Absent on Leave:
Revs.—
Allgaier, Robert A.
Grimmond, Christopher J.
Kasun, Stanley L., St. Pius X Priory, Schuyler
Loecker, Craig J., Archdiocese of Anchorage, Alaska
Noecker, Ronald J.
Whalen, John J., Diocese of Burlington (VT)
Zaccone, Paul C., Congregation of the Sacred Hearts, Honolulu (HI)

Retired:
Rev. Msgrs.—
Ariano, Joseph W.
Brodersen, Charles F., 9230 Burt St., #223, 68114.
Cain, James R.
Dunne, Peter F., Boys Town Center, Boys Town, 68010.
Furlong, Thomas D., 3605 Looking Glass Dr., Bellevue, 68123.
Gass, Robert J., 14948 G St., 68137.
Kelligar, William L., 7232 Shirley Ct., 68124.
Kerwin, Eugene H., 7232 Shirley Ct., 68124.
Krejci, Albert L., 7600 S. 42nd St., 68147.
Meister, Andrew H., P.O. Box 25D, Cedar Bluffs, 68015.
Michalak, John S., 7232 Shirley St. #301, 68124.
Mickells, Anthony B., 2405 S. 48th Ave., 68106.
O'Donnell, Edward C., 1870 S. 75th St., 68124.
Werner, Cyril J., P.O. Box 562, Hartington, 68739.
Wolbach, Richard A., 4001 S. 36th St., 68107.
Revs.—
Astuto, Lucian S., 15676 Webster St., 68118.
Bartek, William C., 7323 Shirley Ct., 68124.
Beacom, John F., 757 E. Decatur, West Point, 68788.
Begley, Paul, 4112 S. 26th St., 68107.
Benliro, Fernando C.
Bonham, Ray O., 7323 Shirley St., 68124.
Carroll, Patrick A., 4752 N. 14th Ave., 68110.
Ciurej, Richard S., 4107 S. 38th St., 68107.
Conley, Martin P., 7323 Shirley St., 68124.
Dickes, Jerome H., 500 E. 8th St., Yankton, SD 57078.
Fangman, Paul J., Rte. 1, Box 139, Humphrey, 68642.
Ficenec, Leonard C., R.R. 1, Box 202, Tarnov, 68642.
Finch, Joseph E., Germantown, NY.
Fitzgerald, William F., 7655 East Main, Scottsdale, AZ 85251.
Galas, Daniel D., 7323 Shirley St., 68124.
Gill, Edward B., 736 W. Fairview St., Albion, 68620.
Golik, Stanislaus, 7323 Shirley St., 68124.
Hunkeler, Edward J., 5605 105th Plaza-3, 68134.
Kenny, James E., 7232 Shirley St., 68124.
Krajicek, Robert P., 5204 E. Mavi Ln., Glendale, AZ 85306.
Kreikemeier, Leo A., Rte. 1, P.O. Box 25E, Cedar Bluffs, 68015.
Kros, Donald M., HC 76, Box 51, Lynch, 68748.
Lammers, Ralph A., 7323 Shirley St., 68124.
LaRocque, Benedict J., O.S.B., Saint Benedict Abbey, Atchison, KS 66002.
Librea, Raphael B., 4803 William St., 68106.
McCaslin, John O., 7323 Shirley St., #305, 68124.
McMahon, Aloysius J., 7323 Shirley St., 68124.
Meiergerd, Godfrey A., 320 E. Decatur St., West Point, 68788.
Micek, Joseph S., 1655 E. Sahara, Apt. 1056, Las Vegas, NV 89104.
Musteikis, Leonard, Lithuania.
O'Brien, Thomas, 2422 150th St., 68116.
Parr, Norman B., 7323 Shirley St., 68124.
Petrasic, Martin J., 2603 S. 50th St., 68106.
Petrusic, Anthony A., 322 Virginia St., Hollywood, FL 33019.
Schmitz, Robert A., 7323 Shirley St., 68124.
Schwartz, Hugh F., 7323 Shirley St., #205, 68124.
Schwertley, James F., 109 S. 19th St., 68102.
Smith, Robert J., 2724 N. 98th St., 68114.
Stevens, Clifford J., 709 S. 28th St., 68105.
Tuma, Anthony F., 7323 Shirley St., 68124.
Vernon, John E., Tulsa, OK.
Whelan, William S., Conception College Seminary, Hwy. 136 and W., Conception, MO 64433.
Wilwerding, Anthony P., #8 Madonna Dr., Hardy, AR 72542.

Permanent Deacons:
Abbott, Ernest, Jr.
Anderson, Andy
Archbold, Steve
Archibald, Joseph
Barbour, Frank
Barnes, William J.
Batenhorst, Kenneth F.
Baughman, Charles
Brich, James
Brisson, Ralph
Bronk, Duane
Burbach, Bernie
Camp, William J.
Cantrell, Charles D.
Capoun, Marvin
Casart, Ronald
Cerveny, John
Chadwick, Robert H.
Chambers, James
Chapman, Robert, (Retired)
Chladek, Gary F.
Choi, Joseph
Clausen, Donald
Connor, Dennis
Conrad, James J., Jr.
Cowles, Donald
Creamer, LeRoy
Crowley, Martin
Dahlseid, John
Davis, Dennis, (Retired)
DeBlauw, James L.
DeGilio, John J.
DeSelm, Michael J.
DesRosiers, Peter
Dethlefs, Dennis
DiGiacomo, Yano, (Retired)
Digilio, Peter
Dineen, Lonnie
Doolittle, James
Dreifuerst, Lester, (Retired)
Dreismeier, Paul
Drozda, Evan
Dunn, Donald
Edgerton, Richard
Elster, George
Enzolera, Sebastian
Eubanks, Paul
Filipcic, Anthony, (Retired)
Finney, Jack
Fitzgerald, Thomas
Flesch, Robert
Fletcher, Michael
Foray, Andrew
Franco, Martin
Frankenfield, Thomas H.
French, Gary
Friend, Joseph, (Retired)
Gau, Jerome
Gencarelli, Ernest
Gentrup, Edward
Goldsmith, Edwin G.
Gonderinger, Gerald, (Retired)
Gurney, David
Guzman, Luis
Hamilton, Robert
Heck, Lawrence
Hendricks, Fred
Hennessey, Gary
Henry, Victor R.
Herrara, Jesus
Hesson, Ronald W.
Hill, William H., Jr.
Hilt, Frank
Horner, Ron
Huck, John
Hueser, Ralph
Hughes, Thomas J.
Iwanski, Duane
Jansen, Clarence
Johnson, Donald
Jordan, Steve
Kaiser, Roland G.
Kalkowski, Kenneth
Kemp, Donald, (Retired)
Knockenhauer, George F.
Knudsen, Dennis
Kosmicki, Duane E.
Koziel, Timothy J.
Krajicek, Joseph
Krieski, Timothy
Kronschnabel, John
Kube, Norman
Kurtz, Stanley
L'Archevesque, Charles
Lauber, Eldon
Leick, Mike
Lenz, Patrick
Livingston, Tom
Lukowski, Ray
Maly, Vince
Mascarello, Frank
Mascarello, John, (Retired)
Matukewicz, Paul
Mayhan II, Leo
McGowan, Kelly
McGuire, Michael
Mendick, Daniel, (Retired)
Menke, Maurice
Mielak, Lawrence
Miles, Patrick
Miller, Carl
Miller, Ira
Morley, Joseph Edward

Mueller, Daniel D.
Mueting, Richard
Murphy, Thomas
Nelson, Richard
Newell, James M.
O'Donnell, William L.
Osterhaus, Edwin
Overkamp, Jerry
Perchal, Daniel E.
Perrin, Carl A.
Perry, Russ
Placzek, Michael
Plourde, Jean
Potts, Marcus
Poulosky, Paul
Powers, Paul
Preister, Tim
Pribnow, Otto
Pribnow, Roger D.
Purnell, Thomas, (Retired)
Ramirez, Joseph, (Retired)
Ridder, Frederick
Robinson, Hugh
Rooney, Paul
Ryan, Ronald R.
Sampier, Larry D.
Sanders, Thomas, (Retired)
Saniuk, Daniel
Sawtelle, Harold
Schimonitz, Eugene
Schlautman
Schmit, Vincent
Schulte, Thomas
Schumacher, Allan
Seamann, Donald M.
Sommer, Andrew
Sommer, Fred, (Retired)
Spenner, Arthur
Spicer, Ernest
Spieker, LeRoy
St. Arnold, Skip
Staroski, Jim
Steenson, Gerald
Steffen, Andrew
Steffen, Paul
Stier, Robert A.
Telich, Frank
Tharp, Bud
Thoene, Sylvan
Thome, Duane, (Retired)
Tomaso, Paul
Tunink, Douglas G.
Tylutki, Glenn
Uhlik, Joseph R.
Valadez, Luis
Valasek, Thomas W.
Villemure, Arthur
Wade, Thomas W.
Weskirchen, Charles
Wiehn, Dennis
Wocha, John
Zak, John J., Jr.
Zurek, John J.

INSTITUTIONS LOCATED IN THE ARCHDIOCESE

[A] COLLEGES AND UNIVERSITIES

OMAHA. *College of St. Mary*, 1901 S. 72nd St., 68124. Tel: 402-399-2400; Fax: 402-399-2342. Email: enroll@csm.edu. Web: www.csm.edu. Sr. Maryanne Stevens, R.S.M., Pres.; Dr. Martin Larrey, Vice Pres. for Academic Affairs; Robert Gass, Chap.; Martin Larrey, Publications Coord. Sisters 9; Lay Teachers 51; Students 910.

**Creighton University*, 2500 California Plaza, 68178. Tel: 402-280-2700; Fax: 402-280-2727. Email: jpschlegel@creighton.edu. Web: www.creighton.edu. Rev. John P. Schlegel, S.J., Pres. & Contact. Priests 8; Sisters 2; Lay Teachers 660; Total Enrollment 7,490; Total Staff 2,326.

The University is comprised of the following schools:

College of Arts and Sciences Tel: 402-280-2431; Fax: 402-280-4729. Dr. Timothy R. Austin, Dean.

College of Business Administration Tel: 402-280-2390; Fax: 402-280-2172. Dr. Robert E. Pitts, Dean.

Graduate School and University College/ Summer Sessions Tel: 402-280-1253; Fax: 402-280-2423. Dr. Barbara J. Braden, Dean.

School of Law Tel: 402-280-2874; Fax: 402-280-3161. Patrick Borchers, J.D., Dean.

School of Dentistry Tel: 402-280-5061; Fax: 402-280-5094. Dr. Wayne W. Barkmeier, Dean.

School of Medicine Tel: 402-280-2300; Fax: 402-280-4027.

School of Nursing Tel: 402-280-2004; Fax: 402-280-2045. Dr. Eleanor Howell, Dean.

School of Pharmacy and Health Professions Tel: 402-280-1828; Fax: 402-280-5738. Dr. J. Chris Bradberry, Dean. Priests 24; Sisters 2; Lay Teachers 662; Students 6,513; Total Staff 1,656.

[B] HIGH SCHOOLS, ARCHDIOCESAN

OMAHA. *Daniel J. Gross Catholic High School of Omaha*, 7700 S. 43rd St., 68147. Tel: 402-734-2000; Fax: 402-734-4270. Email: cleve@gross.creighton.edu. Web: www.gross.creighton.edu. Rev. Thomas Kocik, Chap.; Rebecca Cleveland, Pres. & Contact; Dorothy Ostrowski, Prin.; Joe Blazevich, Asst. Prin.; Tom Kerkman, Asst. Prin.; Marie Angele, Campus Ministry. Priests 1; Lay Teachers 44; Students 570; Total Staff 56.

Roncalli Catholic High School of Omaha, 6401 Sorensen Pkwy., 68152. Tel: 402-571-7670; Fax: 402-571-3216. Email: DGross@roncallicatholic.org. Web: www.roncallicatholic.org. Dr. Duane Gross, Pres. & Contact; Mr. Curt Feilmeier, Prin.; Mr. Chad Holtz, Dean; Rev. Paul C. Hoesing, Chap.; Mr. Clayton Freeman, Campus Min.; Sr. Rosalee Burke, N. D. Devel.; Mr. David Miller, Activities Dir. Lay Teachers 20; Students 318; Total Staff 51.

V.J. & Angela Skutt Catholic High School of Omaha, 3131 S. 156th St., 68130. Tel: 402-333-0818; Fax: 402-333-1790. Email: vjskutt@creighton.edu. Web: www.skuttcatholic.com. Rev. James E. Gilg, Pres. & Prin.; Rob Meyers, Asst. Prin.; Sr. Clarice Faltus, O.S.F., Acedemic Affairs; Michael McMahon, Activities Dir. Priests 1; Sisters 2; Lay Teachers 49; Students 662; Total Staff 50.

COLUMBUS. *Scotus Central Catholic High School*, (Grades 7-12), 1554 18th Ave., 68601. Tel: 402-564-7165; Fax: 402-564-6004. Email: wgannon@esu7.org. Web: www.scotuscc.org. Mr. William Gannon, Supt./Prin.; Mr. Wayne Morfield, Prin. & Contact; Rev. William D. Bond. Priests 1; Lay Teachers 26; Students 389.

ELGIN. *Pope John XXIII Central Catholic High School at Elgin*, P.O. Box 179, 68636. Tel: 402-843-5325; Fax: 402-843-2297. Email: dcannon@esu8.esu8.K12.ne.us. Dennis Cannon, Prin.; Rev. Steven D. Emanuel, Teacher & Campus Min. Priests 2; School Sisters of St. Francis 1; Lay Teachers 11; Students 140.

HARTINGTON. *Cedar Catholic High School*, 401 S. Broadway, P.O. Box 15, 68739. Tel: 402-254-3906; Fax: 402-254-3976. Email: mmccabe@esu1.org. Web: cchs.cedar.esu1.K12.ne.us. Mike McCabe, Admin. & Contact; Rev. Garry A. Welsh, Spiritual Dir. Lay Teachers 18; Students 234; Total Staff 30.

NORFOLK. *Norfolk Catholic High School*, 2300 Madison Ave., 68701. Tel: 402-371-2784 Fax: 402-379-2929. Email: jeffbellar@ncknights.org. Web: www.ncknights.org. Mr. Jeff Beller, Prin. & Contact. Priests 3; Lay Teachers 30; Students 375.

WEST POINT. *Central Catholic High School*, 419 E. Decateur 68788. Tel: 402-372-5326; Fax: 402-372-5327. Email: central@cathschls.creighton.edu. Web: myweb.cableone.net/cencat/. Mrs. Peggy Thayer, Prin. & Contact. Priests 3; Franciscan Sisters of Christian Charity 1; Lay Teachers 13; Students 158.

[C] HIGH SCHOOLS, PRIVATE

OMAHA. *Creighton Preparatory School*, 7400 Western Ave., 68114. Tel: 402-393-1190; Fax: 402-393-0260. Email: dmcca@prep.creighton.edu. Web: www.creightonprep.creighton.edu. Revs. Robert V. Hotz, S.J., Pres.; Richard F. McCaslin, S.J., Supr. & Contact; Mr. John Naatz, Prin.; Revs. William J. Doran, S.J.; Willard J. Dressel, S.J.; Michael J. Marco, S.J. (CLV); Mark E. Niemann, S.J.; William F. O'Leary, S.J.; Kevin C. Schneider, S.J.; James A. Sinnerud, S.J.; Charles J. Tilley, S.J. (MRY); Bros. James E. Garvey, S.J.; Paul J. Kemper, S.J. Priests 11; Brothers 2; Scholastics 3; Lay Teachers 48; Students 989.

Duchesne Academy of the Sacred Heart, 36th & Burt Sts., 68131. Tel: 402-558-3800; Fax: 402-558-0051. Email: shaggas@duchesne.creighton.edu. Web: duchesne.creighton.edu. Mrs. Sheila K. Haggas, Head of School & Contact. Society of the Sacred Heart 4; Lay Teachers 31; Girls 271.

Marian High School, 74th and Military Ave., 68134. Tel: 402-571-2618; Fax: 402-571-2978. Email: ekmarian@marian.creighton.edu. Web: marian.creighton.edu. Elizabeth Kish, Head of School, Prin. & Contact. Servants of Mary Sisters 1; Lay Teachers 51; Girls 702.

Mercy High School, 1501 S. 48th St., 68106. Tel: 402-553-9424; Fax: 402-553-0394. Email: burnellj@mercyhigh.org. Web: www.mercyhigh.org. Sr. Johanna Burnell, R.S.M., Pres. & Contact; Carolyn Jaworski, Prin. Sisters of Mercy of the Americas 3; Lay Teachers 26; Girls 350.

BOYS TOWN. *Father Flanagan's Boys' Home* 68010. Tel: 402-498-1000; Fax: 402-498-1010. Email: peterv@boystown.org. Rev. Valentine J. Peter, S.T.D., J.C.D., Contact. See Protective Institutions. Priests 1; Lay Teachers 43; Total Enrollment 636; Total Staff 44.

ELKHORN. *Mount Michael High School*, 22520 Mt. Michael Rd., 68022-3400. Tel: 402-289-2544; Fax: 442-289-4539. Email: bosborne@knightnet.creighton.edu. Web: www.mountmichaelhs.com. Rt. Rev. Theodore Wolff, O.S.B., Abbot; Brian Osborne, Prin. & Contact; Revs. Richard Thell, O.S.B.; John Hagemann, O.S.B.; Michael Liebl, O.S.B.; Daniel Lenz, O.S.B.; Louis L. Sojka, C.S.B.; Stephen J. Plank, O.S.B. Priests 7; Sisters 1; Professed Brothers 2; Lay Teachers 13; Students 144.

[D] ELEMENTARY SCHOOLS, INTER-PAROCHIAL

OMAHA. *All Saints Catholic School*, 1335 S. 10th St., 68108. Tel: 402-346-5757; Fax: 402-346-8794. Email: allsts@cathschls.creighton.edu. Gretchen Olsen, Prin. & Contact. Serving parishes of St. Ann, St. Frances Cabrini, St. Joseph, St. Mary Magdalene Immaculate Conception, St. Patrick Lay Teachers 15; Students 210.

Catholic Academy, 2326 S. 14th St., 68108. Tel: 402-345-3500; Fax: 402-342-8005. Email: bev_luna@yahoo.com. Beverly Luna, Head Teacher. Lay Teachers 8; Students 90.

St. James-Seton School, 9212 Tomahawk Blvd., 68134. Tel: 402-572-0339; Fax: 402-572-0347. Email: tcrum@marian.creighton.edu. Web: sjs.creighton.edu. Terry Crum, Prin. & Contact. Lay Teachers 35; Students 780; Total Staff 60.

St. Pius X-St. Leo School, 6905 Blondo St., 68104. Tel: 402-551-6667; Fax: 402-551-8123. Email: jgubbels@creighton.edu. Web: www.SPSL.creighton.edu. Mrs. Joyce Gubbels, Prin. & Contact. Sisters 2; Lay Teachers 47; Students 847.

FORDYCE. *West Catholic Elementary* Serving parishes in Constance, Fordyce & Menominee , 303 Omaha St., P.O. Box 167, 68736-0167. Tel: 402-357-3507; Fax: 402-357-3795. Joseph Schroeder, Prin. & Contact. Lay Teachers 3; Students 53.

HARTINGTON. *East Catholic Elementary* Serving parishes in Bow Valley, St. Helena & Wynot , 108 W. 889th Rd., 68739-6079. Tel: 402-357-2146; Fax: 402-357-3758. Email: jschroeder@esul.org. Joseph Schroeder, Prin. Lay Teachers 5; Students 50.

HOWELLS. *Howells Community Catholic School* Serving parishes in Howells, Olean, Heun, Aloys & Tabor , 114 N. 6th St., 68641. Tel: 402-986-1689; Fax: 402-986-1653. Mrs. Mary Ann Spicka, Head Teacher (Grades 1-6). Lay Teachers 6; Students 75.

[E] ELEMENTARY SCHOOLS, PRIVATE

BOYS TOWN. *Father Flanagan's Boys' Home*Rev. Valentine J. Peter, S.T.D., J.C.D., Contact. See Protective Institutions below.

[F] SPECIAL EDUCATION

OMAHA. *Christian Urban Education Service Foundation*, 2207 Wirt St., 68110. Tel: 402-451-5755; Fax: 402-451-1731. Web: www.sacredheart-cues.org. Rev. Thomas M. Fangman, Exec. Dir. of CUES. Lay Teachers 10; Students 142.

The Jesuit Middle School of Omaha, 2311 N. 22nd St., 68110. Tel: 402-346-4464; Fax: 402-341-1817. Email: ski@jesuit.coxatwork.com. Rev. James L. Michalski, S.J., Pres. & Contact. Lay Teachers 8; Students 68; Total Staff 11.

Madonna School for Exceptional Children, 2537 N. 62nd, 68104. Tel: 402-556-1883; Fax: 402-556-7332. Email: madonnaschool@cov.net. Web: www.madonnaschool.org. Dr. Deirdre Milobar, Prin. Lay Teachers 8; Students 41.

Madonna Shop, 2014 N. 66th, 68104. Tel: 402-551-5441; Fax: 402-551-6910. Email: rdm7911@aol.com. Robin Moses, Mgr. Total Staff 6; Total Enrollment 31.

[G] GENERAL HOSPITALS

OMAHA. *Alegent Health - Bergen Mercy Health System*, 1010 N. 96th St., Ste. 200, 68114. Tel: 402-343-4430; Fax: 402-343-4337. Email: ncooney@alegent.org. Web: www.alegent.com. Sr. Norita Cooney, R.S.M., Board Chair. Affiliate of Catholic Health Initiatives. General Hospitals 3; Bed Capacity 675; Inpatient 21,269; Outpatient 195,497; Total Assisted Annually 216,766; Total Staff 2,762.

**Archbishop Bergan Mercy Medical Center*, 7500 Mercy Rd., 68124. Tel: 402-398-6060; Fax: 402-398-6920. Web: alegent.com. Michael Tiesi, Admin.; Sisters Elaine Abels, R.S.C.J., Chap.; Duchesne Maxwell, O.P., Chap.; Mary Mason, Chap.; Thomas Backer, Chap. and CPE Supvr.-in-Training; Rev. David W. LaPlante, Chap.; Deacon

Tom Murphy, Chap.; Loretta Siegale, Dir. Pastoral Care; Marian Standeven, Operations Leader Mission Svcs./Community Affairs. Affiliate of Catholic Health Initiatives. Sisters 2; Bed Capacity 400; Patients Assisted Annually 147,728.

Bergan Mercy Foundation, Inc. Tel: 402-343-4438; Fax: 402-343-4316. Tilman Adair, Chief Dev. Officer; Marian Standeven, Contact.

Boys Town National Research Hospital, 555 N. 30 St., 68131. Tel: 402-498-6511; Fax: 402-498-6357. Web: www.boystownhospital.org. Dr. Patrick Brookhouser, Dir. Bed Capacity 42; Total Assisted Annually 35,000; Total Staff 630.

NORFOLK. *Faith Regional Health Services*, 1500 Koenigstein Ave., 68701. Tel: 402-644-7205; Fax: 402-644-7468. Email: proche@frhs.org. Web: www.frhs.org. Sisters Mary Paula Lieck, O.S.B., Pres.; Mary Kevin Hermsen, Prioress; Patrick Roche, Contact & Vice Pres. for Mission Svcs.; Revs. Gerald A. Connealy, Chap.; Timothy J. Lange, Chap. The Missionary Benedictine Sisters Bed Capacity 166; Patients Assisted Annually 63,005; Newborn 1,847.

O'NEILL. *Avera St. Anthony's Hospital*, 2nd and Adams St., 68763. Tel: 402-336-2611; Fax: 402-336-5135. Email: Ron.Cork@avera-sta.org. Web: www.avera-sta.org. Ronald J. Cork, Admin.; John T. Porter, Pres. & CEO. Attended by St. Patrick Church. Bed Capacity 25; Bassinets 10; Patients Assisted Annually 17,451; Total Staff 186.

WAYNE. *Providence Medical Center*, 1200 Providence Rd., 68787. Tel: 402-375-3800; Fax: 402-375-7989. Email: mthomas@providencemedical.com. Marcile Thomas, Admin., Contact; Sisters Monica Backes, Supr.; Hilda Choi, Pastoral Care. Missionary Benedictine Sisters Bed Capacity 25; Patients Assisted Annually 11,500; Staff 132.

WEST POINT. *Franciscan Care Services, Inc.* dba St. Francis Memorial Hospital , 430 N. Monitor St., 68788-1595. Tel: 402-372-2404; Fax: 402-372-2360. Email: rbriggs@fcswp.org. Web: www.fesup.org. Ronald O. Briggs, CEO & Contact; Deacon Vince Maly, Chap. Franciscan Sisters of Christian Charity Sisters 6; Bed Capacity 25; Patients Assisted Annually 66,150; Total Staff 230.

[H] NURSING AND CONVALESCENT HOMES

OMAHA. *Mercy Villa* Retirement Home for the Sisters of Mercy of the Americas for the Omaha Region , 1845 S. 72nd St., 68124. Tel: 402-391-6224; Fax: 402-391-1872. Email: jeannew@mercyoma.org. Sr. Jeanne Ward, R.S.M., Coord. Resident Sisters 46; Total Assisted 30; Total Staff 55.

New Cassel Retirement Center, 900 N. 90th St., 68114. Tel: 402-393-2277; Fax: 402-393-3784. Web: www.newcassel.org. Mr. Joseph H. Schulte, Dir.; Rev. James R. Tiegs; Mary Kerres, Dir. Pastoral Care; Mr. Joseph H. Schulte, Contact. School Sisters of St. Francis Sisters 1; Aged Residents 165; Total Staff 70.

NORFOLK. *St. Joseph's Rehabilitation and Care Center*, 401 N. 18th St., 68701. Tel: 402-644-7375; Fax: 402-379-4867. Email: bdisch@frhs.org. Bill Disch, Admin. & Contact. Missionary Benedictine Sisters 1; Aged Residents 83.

WEST POINT. *Franciscan Care Services, Inc.* dba St. Joseph Retirement Community , 320 E. Decatur, 68788. Tel: 402-372-3477; Fax: 402-372-6600. Web: www.fcswp.org. Sr. Emy Beth Furrer. Franciscan Sisters of Christian Charity, Manitowoc, WI 6; Residents 75; Total Assisted Annually 70; Total Staff 37.

[I] PROTECTIVE INSTITUTIONS

BOYS TOWN. **Father Flanagan's Boys' Home* 68010. Tel: 402-498-1000; Fax: 402-498-1010. Email: peterv@boystown.org. Web: www.boystown.org. Rev. Valentine J. Peter, S.T.D., J.C.D., Exec. Dir.; Dr. Dan Daly, Dir. Education; Rev. Eugene McReynolds, O.S.B.; Robert Gehringer, High School Prin.; Cathy DeSalvo, Grade School Prin. High School: Teachers 29; Students 494; Grade School: Teachers 15; Students 142.

Boys Town USA Tel: 402-498-1928; Fax: 402-498-1010. Dr. Jerry Davis, Assoc. Exec. Dir., U.S.A.; Robert Pick, Assoc. Exec. Dir. (Prog. & Staff Devel.); Dr. Dan Daly, Assoc. Exec. Dir., Home Campus.

Boys Town National Research & Training Center Tel: 402-498-1560; Fax: 402-498-1500. Dr. Ruby Asugha, Natl. Resource & Training Center Assoc. Exec. Dir.; Jeff Peterson, Dir. of Operations.

Boys Town National Research Hospital for Children Tel: 402-498-6501; Fax: 402-498-6357. Dr. Patrick Brookhouser, Dir.

Boys Town Crisis Hotline Tel: 800-448-3000; Fax: 402-498-6357. Dee Kohler, Coord.

Boys Town Religious Education Program Tel: 402-498-1885; Fax: 402-498-1010. Laura Budenberg, Dir.; Kathy McGee, Assoc. Dir. Total Assisted 36,405; Total Staff 2,481.

[J] FAMILY SERVICE CENTERS

OMAHA. *Catholic Charities*, Daniel E. Sheehan Center, 3300 N. 60th St., 68104. Tel: 402-554-0520; Fax: 402-829-9268. Email: catholiccharities@ccomaha.org. Web: www.ccomaha.org. Scot L. Adams, Contact.

COLUMBUS. *Catholic Charities*, 3020 18th St., Suite 17, 68601. Tel: 402-563-3833; Fax: 402-562-8714. Email: shellic@ccomaha.org. Shelli Cornwell, Dir. & Contact.

NORFOLK. *Catholic Charities Counselling Services*, 109 S. 15th St., Ste. 14A, 68701. Tel: 402-371-3555; Fax: 402-379-4662. Email: shellic@ccomaha.org. Shelli Cornwell, Prog. Supr.

[K] MONASTERIES AND RESIDENCES OF PRIESTS AND BROTHERS

OMAHA. *Jesuit Community at Creighton University*, 2500 California St., 68178. Tel: 402-280-2700; Fax: 402-280-5590. Email: jesuits@creighton.edu. Web: www.creighton.edu. Revs. Richard J. Hauser, S.J., Rector; William F. Gerut, S.J., Min.; Philip R. Amidon, S.J.; Andrew Alexander, S.J.; Thomas E. Bannantine, S.J.; Bro. James F. Becwar, S.J.; Revs. Burnell B. Bisbee, S.J.; Gail G. Bohr, S.J.; Robert E. Brodzeller, S.J.; Raymond A. Bucko, S.J. (NY); Robert O. Burns, S.J.; James F. Clifton; Donald A. Doll, S.J.; Donald D. Driscoll, S.J.; Robert W. Dundon, S.J.; Harry S. Eglsaer, S.J.; Robert H. Fitzgerald, S.J.; Lawrence W. Flanagan, S.J.; Michael J. Flecky, S.J.; Lawrence D. Gillick, S.J.; John M. Ginsterblum, S.J.; M. Dennis Hamm, S.J.; Thomas J. Hansen, S.J.; William J. Harmless, S.J.; Bro. James F. Heidrick, S.J.; Revs. Thomas A. Hoffman, S.J.; John P. Horn, S.J.; Eugene J. Jakubek, S.J.; Charles L. Jurgensmeier, S.J.; Howard E. Kalb, S.J.; Charles T. Kestermeier, S.J.; William T. Kolarec, S.J.; Edward A. Larkin, S.J.; Leland E. Lubbers, S.J.; Paul A. Mahowald, S.J.; Richard D. McGloin, S.J.; Robert F. McEniry, S.J.; Dennis P. McNeilly, S.J.; Bro. Tesfa Michael Haile Mehari, S.J.; Revs. James L. Michalski, S.J.; John F. Montag; Robert F. O'Connor, S.J.; Richard W. Ott, S.J.; Joseph N. Pershe, S.J.; Francis A. Prokes, S.J.; James J. Quinn, S.J.; Perry L. Robinson, S.J.; Luis Rodriguez, S.J.; James H. Ryan, S.J.; Gregory A. Schissel, S.J.; John P. Schlegel, S.J.; Thomas N. Schloemer, S.J.; Thomas J. Shanahan; David L. Smith, S.J.; Bros. Robert E. Smith, S.J.; Edmund W. Stetzen, S.J.; Revs. Paul J. Strittmatter, S.J. (DM); Albert R. Thelen, S.J.; John S. Thiede, S.J.; Charles J. Tilley, S.J. (MRY); Ernesto Travieso, S.J.; Martin O. Vaske, S.J.; Bro. Michael R. Wilmot, S.J.; Revs. M. John Wymelenberg, S.J.; John D. Zuercher, S.J.

Legal Title: *Jesuit Community at Creighton University* Priests 60; Brothers 5.

The Redemptorists of Nebraska, 3014 N. 45th St., 68104. Tel: 402-451-6622; Fax: 402-457-6901. Revs. James R. Keena, C.SS.R., Supr.; Charles A. Wehrley Jr., C.SS.R. (LA); John Morton, C.SS.R.; Bro. William Cloughley, C.SS.R.

ELKHORN. *Mount Michael Abbey*, 22520 Mount Michael Rd., 68022-3400. Tel: 402-289-2541; Fax: 402-289-4539. Email: twolff@mountmichaelabbey.org. Web: www.mountmichaelabbey.org. Rt. Rev. Theodore J. Wolff, O.S.B., Abbot & Contact; Bro. Jerome Kmiecik, O.S.B., Prior; Rev. Michael Liebl, O.S.B., Subprior; Rt. Rev. Raphael Walsh, O.S.B.; Revs. Benedict Dohle, O.S.B.; Adrian Liable, O.S.B.; Nathanael Foshage, O.S.B.; Eugene McReynolds, O.S.B.; Richard Thell, O.S.B.; John Hagemann, O.S.B.; Daniel Lenz, O.S.B.; Louis L. Sojka, O.S.B.; Stephen J. Plank, O.S.B. Benedictine Fathers Priests 12; Professed Brothers 10.

ST. COLUMBANS. *St. Columban's Foreign Mission Society* (Corporate Title: St. Columban's Foreign Mission Society) ; Regional Headquarters and Administration Offices of the Columban Fathers in the United States. , 68056. Tel: 402-291-1920; Fax: 402-291-8693. Email: director@columban.org. Web: www.columban.org. Revs. Richard Steinhilber, S.S.C.; Denis Bartley, S.S.C., Local Supr.; John Burger, S.S.C., Regl. Dir.; Salvatore Caputo; Paul E. Casey, S.S.C. (Retired); J. Donald Devine, S.S.C.; Edward Dolan, S.S.C., Pannned Giving; Oliver Kennedy, S.S.C.; Donal O'Farrell, S.S.C., Archivist; Robert O'Rourke, S.S.C., Bursar-Local; Colm Stanley, S.S.C.; Alban Sueper, S.S.C.; William Sweeney, S.S.C., Bursar-Regl. Priests 13. Other Assignments: Revs. Thomas Normanly, S.S.C., Buffalo, NY; Clarence Beckley, S.S.C., Chicago, IL; Robert Clark, S.S.C., Fontana, CA; John A. Buckley, S.S.C. (Brazil); George Da Roza, S.S.C., Studies; Michael Donnelly, S.S.C., Bristol, RI; Thomas Vaughan, S.S.C. (Retired), St. Paul, MN; Robert Burke, S.S.C. (Retired); Vincent McCarthy, S.S.C., El Paso, TX; William Morton, S.S.C., El Paso, TX; Victor Gaboury, S.S.C. (Retired), Bristol, RI; Cathal Gallagher (SFS); Donald Kelley, S.S.C., Mission, TX; James Needham, S.S.C., St. Paul, MN; Paul O'Malley, S.S.C. (Retired), Worcester; John Wanaurny, El Paso, TX; Brendan Murray, S.S.C. (BO); Gerald Wilmsen, S.S.C., Supr. (Retired); Victor Babin, S.S.C. (MIA); Paul Bradley, S.S.C. (ORG); John Clifford, S.S.C. (SD); Michael Cody, S.S.C. (CHI); Thomas Cusack, S.S.C. (LA); Leo Distor, S.S.C. (CHI); Michael Dodd, S.S.C. (WDC); P. Gerard Dunne, S.S.C. (LA); Howard Eisel, S.S.C. (DUL); Sean John McGrath, S.S.C. (LA); Anthony Mortell, S.S.C. (LA); Kevin Mullins, S.S.C. (ELP); Timothy Mulroy, S.S.C. (CHI); Tien Nguyen, S.S.C. (LA); James O'Brien, S.S.C. (BO); Dennis O'Mara, S.S.C. (CHI); Albert Utzig, S.S.C. (CHI); Paul White, S.C.C. (LA).

SCHUYLER. *Benedictine Mission House*, Christ the King Priory, 68661. Tel: 402-352-2177; Fax: 402-352-2176. Email: bmh.schuyler@dtnspeed.net. Web: www.megavision.net/benedict. Very Rev. Germar Neubert, O.S.B., Prior & Contact; Revs. Volker Futter, O.S.B., Subprior; Thomas Aquinas Leitner, O.S.B.; Stanley L. Kasun. Brothers 4.

[L] CONVENTS AND RESIDENCES FOR SISTERS

OMAHA. *Monastery of St. Clare*, 3626 N. 65th Ave., 68104. Tel: 402-558-4916; Fax: 402-558-5046. Web: www.omahapoorclare.org. Sr. Mary Clare Brown, Contact. Poor Clares (Second Order of St. Francis), Attended by Jesuit Fathers. Sisters 8.

Motherhouse of the Servants of Mary, Convent of Our Lady of Sorrows, 7400 Military Ave., 68134. Tel: 402-571-2547; Fax: 402-573-6055. Web: www.osms.org. Sisters Jean Morrow, O.S.M., Prov. & Contact; Doris Durant, O.S.M., Asst. Prov. Professed 101; Novice 1; Sisters in Motherhouse 34.

Provincial Motherhouse and Novitiate of the Notre Dame Sisters, 3501 State St., 68112. Tel: 402-455-2994; Fax: 402-455-3974. Email: notredamesisters@juno.com. Web: www.notredamesisters.org. Sr. Margaret Hickey, N.D., Prov. Pres. & Contact. Professed 61; Sisters living at Motherhouse 31; Novices 1.

Sisters of Mercy of the Americas, Regional Community of Omaha, 7262 Mercy Rd., 68124-2389. Tel: 402-393-8225; Fax: 402-393-8145. Email: patriciaf@mercyoma.org. Web: www.mercyoma.org. Sr. Patricia Forret, R.S.M., Pres. & Contact. Perpetually Professed 198.

Sisters of the Annunciation of the Archdiocese of Omaha, 14849 "G" St., 68137. Tel: 402-891-0001; Fax: 402-891-0333. Email: revrobertj@msn.com. Rev. Msgr. Robert J. Gass (Retired).

Sisters of the Good Shepherd (R.G.S.), 1106 N. 36th St., 68131. Tel: 402-551-2966; Fax: 402-551-2495. Email: ssreileen@aol.com. Web: www.goodshepherdsisters.org. Sisters 2.

NORFOLK. *Immaculata Convent*, 300 N. 18th St., 68701-3687. Tel: 402-371-3438; Fax: 402-379-2877. Email: skhermsen@conpoint.com. Web: www.norfolkosb.org. Sr. Kevin Hermsen, O.S.B., Prioress & Contact.

Legal Title: *Immaculata Convent, Priory Motherhouse and Novitiate of the Missionary Benedictine Sisters* Sisters 47; Postulants 1.

[M] SECULAR INSTITUTES

OMAHA. *Institute of the Apostolic Oblates*, 6762 Western Ave., 68132. Tel: 402-553-4418; Fax: 402-553-1388. Email: ao-omaha@mitec.net. Web: www.prosanctitate.org. Teresa J. Monaghen, Natl. Moderator; Rev. Carl J. Zoucha; Franca Salvo, Contact. A secular institute for women with the aim of promoting the universal call to holiness, through working apostolate of the Pro Sanctity Movement.

Apostolic Sodales - Secular Institute for Priests

ELKHORN. *Pro Sanctity Movement*, 11002 N. 204th St., 68022. Tel: 402-289-2670; Fax: 402-289-1938. Email: psm@prosanctity.org. Web: www.prosanctitate.org. Teresa Monaghen, Natl. Dir. Tel: 402-289-2670; Teresa Monaghen, Contact. Ecclesial organization: Promotes apostolates of holiness; teaches, supports and guides people seeking to deepen their spiritual life.

[N] EDUCATIONAL FOUNDATIONS AND TRUST FUNDS

OMAHA. *The Omaha Archdiocesan Educational Foundation, Inc.*

The Office of Stewardship and Development, 3212 North 60th St., P.O. Box 4130, 68104-0130. Tel: 402-554-8493; Fax: 402-551-3426. Email: jtamisie@creighton.edu.

Archbishop Sheehan Adult Education Endowment Trust

All Saints Catholic School Educational Endowment Trust Tel: 402-346-5757.

Black Students Catholic Educational Endowment Trust

Music in Catholic Schools Endowment Trust
Roncalli Catholic High School Educational Endowment Trust Tel: 402-571-7670.
Roncalli Catholic High School Scholarship Endowment Trust Tel: 402-571-7670.
Religious Education Evangelization Commission Endowment Trust
The Catholic Voice Educational Endowment Trust Tel: 402-558-6611.
Marian High School Scholarship Endowment Trust Tel: 402-571-2618.
Marian High School Endowment Trust Tel: 402-571-2618.
The Omaha Archdiocesan Parish Foundation, Inc.
St. Michael Church of Albion, NE, Educational Endowment Trust, Albion. Tel: 402-395-2393.
St. Michael Church of Albion, NE, Parish Endowment Trust, Albion. Tel: 402-395-2393.
St. Aloysius Parish Endowment Trust, Aloys. Tel: 402-372-3681.
St. Aloysius Parish Educational Endowment Trust Tel: 402-372-3681.
St. Joseph Parish Endowment Trust, Amelia. Tel: 402-336-1602.
St. Joseph Parish Educational Endowment Trust, Amelia. Tel: 402-336-1602.
St. Joseph Church Educational Endowment Trust, Atkinson. Tel: 402-925-2122.
St. Joseph Parish Endowment Trust, Atkinson. Tel: 402-925-2122.
Holy Cross Parish Endowment Trust, Bancroft. Tel: 402-687-2102.
Holy Cross Parish Educational Endowment Trust, Bancroft. Tel: 402-687-2102.
St. Patrick Parish Endowment Trust, Battle Creek. Tel: 402-675-2495.
St. Patrick Parish Educational Endowment Trust, Battle Creek. Tel: 402-675-2485.
Cedar Catholic High School Educational Endowment Trust, Hartington. Tel: 402-254-6559.
Holy Cross Parish Endowment Trust, Beemer, Beemer, 68716. Fax: 402-528-3475.
Holy Cross Parish Educational Endowment Trust, Beemer. Tel: 402-528-3475.
St. Mary Church Educational Endowment Trust, Bellevue. Tel: 402-291-1350.
St. Mary Church Endowment Trust, Bellevue. Tel: 402-291-1350.
St. Matthew the Evangelist Parish Endowment Trust, Bellevue. Tel: 402-292-7418.
St. Francis Borgia Parish Endowment Trust, Blair. Tel: 402-426-3823.
St. Francis Borgia Parish Educational Endowment Trust, Blair. Tel: 402-426-3823.
St. Andrew Parish Endowment Trust, Bloomfield. Tel: 402-373-2233.
St. Andrew Parish Educational Endowment Trust, Bloomfield. Tel: 402-373-2233.
SS. Peter and Paul Parish Endowment Trust, Bow Valley. Tel: 402-254-3311.
SS. Peter and Paul Parish Educational Endowment Trust, Bow Valley. Tel: 402-254-3311.
East Catholic Elementary School Educational Endowment Trust, Bow Valley. Tel: 402-357-2146.
St. Ignatius Parish Endowment Trust, Brunswick. Tel: 402-582-4288.
St. Ignatius Parish Educational Endowment Trust, Brunswick. Tel: 402-582-4288.
SS. Peter and Paul Parish Endowment Trust, Butte. Tel: 402-775-2452.
SS. Peter and Paul Parish Educational Endowment Trust, Butte. Tel: 402-775-2452.
St. Anthony Parish Endowment Trust, Cedar Rapids. Tel: 308-358-0773.
St. Anthony Parish Educational Endowment Trust, Cedar Rapids. Tel: 308-358-0773.
St. Michael Catholic Church Parish Endowment Trust, Central City. Tel: 308-946-2855.
St. Michael Parish Educational Endowment Trust, Central City. Tel: 308-946-2855.
St. Peter Parish Endowment Trust, Clarks. Tel: 308-536-2574.
St. Peter Parish Educational Endowment Trust, Clarks. Tel: 308-536-2574.
SS. Cyril and Methodius Parish Endowment Trust, Clarkson. Tel: 402-892-3464.
SS. Cyril and Methodius Parish Educational Endowment Trust, Clarkson. Tel: 402-892-3464.
Church of St. Theresa of Avila Parish Educational Endowment Trust, Clearwater. Tel: 402-887-4521.
St. Theresa of Avila Parish Endowment Trust, Clearwater. Tel: 402-887-4521.
St. Michael Parish Endowment Trust, Coleridge. Tel: 402-283-4614.
St. Michael Parish Educational Endowment Trust, Coleridge. Tel: 402-283-4614.
St. Anthony Parish Endowment Trust, Columbus. Tel: 402-564-3313.
St. Anthony Parish Educational Endowment Trust, Columbus. Tel: 402-564-3313.
St. Anthony Elementary School Endowment Trust, Columbus. Tel: 402-564-3313.
St. Bonaventure Church Endowment Trust, Columbus. Tel: 402-564-7151.
St. Isidore Church Endowment Trust, Columbus. Tel: 402-564-8993.
St. Isidore Parish Educational Endowment Trust, Columbus. Tel: 402-564-8993.
St. Isidore Elementary School Endowment Trust, Columbus. Tel: 402-564-8993.
Scotus Central Catholic High School Endowment Trust, Columbus. Tel: 402-564-7165.
St. Joseph Parish Endowment Trust, Constance. Tel: 402-388-4814.
St. Joseph Parish Educational Endowment Trust, Constance. Tel: 402-388-4814.
St. Ludger Parish Endowment Trust, Creighton. Tel: 402-358-3596.
St. Ludger Parish Educational Endowment Trust, Creighton. Tel: 402-358-3596.
St. Ludger Elementary School Endowment Trust, Creighton. Tel: 402-358-3596.
St. Rose of Lima Parish Endowment, Crofton. Tel: 402-388-4814.
St. Rose of Lima Parish Educational Endowment Trust, Crofton. Tel: 402-388-4814.
Holy Family Parish Endowment Trust, Decatur. Tel: 402-374-1692.
Holy Family Parish Educational Endowment Trust, Decatur. Tel: 402-374-1692.
St. Anne Parish Endowment Trust, Dixon. Tel: 402-256-3303.
St. Anne Parish Educational Endowment Trust, Dixon. Tel 402-256-3303.
St. Wenceslaus Parish Endowment Trust, Dodge. Tel: 402-693-2235.
St. Wenceslaus Church Educational Endowment Trust, Dodge. Tel: 402-693-2235.
St. Stanislaus Parish Endowment Trust Duncan. Tel: 402-897-2625.
St. Stanislaus Parish Educational Endowment Trust, Duncan. Tel: 402-897-2625.
St. Boniface School Endowment Trust, Elgin. Tel: 402-843-2345.
St. Boniface Parish Endowment Trust, Elgin. Tel: 402-843-2345.
St. Boniface Parish Educational Endowment Trust, Elgin. Tel: 402-843-2345.
Pope John XXIII Central Catholic High School Endowment Trust, Elgin. Tel: 402-843-2345.
Mt. Michael Foundation, Inc., Elkhorn. Tel: 402-289-2541.
St. Patrick School Tuition Assistance Endowment Trust, Elkhorn. Tel: 402-289-4289.
St. Patrick School Endowment Trust, Elkhorn. Tel: 402-289-4289.
St. Patrick Parish Endowment Trust, Elkhorn. Tel: 402-289-4289.
Sacred Heart Parish Endowment Trust, Emerson. Tel: 402-695-2342.
Sacred Heart Parish Educational Endowment Trust, Emerson. Tel: 402-695-2342.
St. Peter de Alcantara Parish Endowment Trust, Ewing. Tel: 402-626-7605.
St. Peter de Alcantara Parish Educational Endowment Trust, Ewing. Tel: 402-626-7605.
St. John the Baptist Parish Endowment Trust, Fordyce. Tel: 402-357-3506.
Archbishop Bergan Jr./Sr. Catholic High School Educational Endowment Trust, Fremont. Tel: 402-721-6611.
St. John the Baptist Parish Educational Endowment Trust, Fordyce. Tel: 402-357-3506.
West Catholic Educational Endowment Trust, Fordyce. Tel: 402-357-3506.
St. John the Baptist Parish Endowment Trust, Fort Calhoun. Tel: 402-468-5348.
St. John the Baptist Church Educational Endowment Trust, Fort Calhoun. Tel: 402-468-5348.
St. Patrick Catholic Church Endowment Trust, Fremont. Tel: 402-721-6611.
St. Patrick Parish Educational Endowment Trust, Fremont. Tel: 402-721-6611.
St. Peter Catholic Church Endowment Trust, Fullerton. Tel: 308-536-2574.
St. Peter Parish Educational Endowment Trust, Fullerton. Tel: 308-536-2574.
St. Rose of Lima Parish Endowment Trust, Genoa. Tel: 402-993-2323.
St. Rose of Lima Parish Educational Endowment Trust, Genoa. Tel: 402-993-2323.
St. Patrick Parish Endowment Trust, Gretna. Tel: 402-332-4444.
St. Patrick Parish Educational Endowment Trust, Gretna. Tel: 402-332-4444.
Holy Trinity Parish Endowment Trust, Hartington. Tel: 402-254-6559.
Holy Trinity Parish Educational Endowment Trust, Hartington. Tel: 402-254-6559.
Holy Trinity Grade School Endowment Trust, Hartington. Tel: 402-254-6559.
Holy Trinity Parish Endowment Trust, Heun. Tel: 402-986-1627.
Holy Trinity Parish Educational Endowment Trust, Heun. Tel: 402-986-1627.
St. Cornelius Parish Endowment Trust, Homer. Tel: 402-494-5423.
St. Cornelius Parish Educational Endowment Trust, Homer. Tel: 402-494-5423.
St. Rose of Lima Parish Endowment Trust, Hooper. Tel: 402-654-3449.
St. Rose of Lima Parish Educational Endowment Trust, Hooper. Tel: 402-654-3449.
St. John Nepomucene Parish Endowment Trust, Howells. Tel: 402-986-1653.
St. John Nepomucene Parish Educational Endowment Trust, Howells. Tel: 402-986-1653.
SS. Peter and Paul Parish Endowment Trust, Howells. Tel: 402-986-1653.
SS. Peter and Paul Parish Educational Endowment Trust, Howells. Tel: 402-986-1653.
SS. Peter and Paul Catholic Church Endowment for Howells Community Catholic School, Howells. Tel: 402-986-1653.
St. Mary Parish Endowment Trust, Hubbard. Tel: 402-256-3303.
St. Mary Parish Educational Endowment Trust, Hubbard. Tel: 402-256-3303.
St. Francis Parish Endowment Trust, Humphrey. Tel: 402-923-0913.
St. Francis Parish Educational Endowment Trust, Humphrey.
St. Patrick Parish Endowment Trust, Jackson. Tel: 402-632-4292.
St. Patrick Parish Educational Endowment Trust, Jackson. Tel: 402-632-4292.
SS. Peter and Paul Parish Endowment Trust, Krakow. Tel: 402-993-6600.
SS. Peter and Paul Parish Educational Endowment Trust, Krakow. Tel: 402-993-6600.
St. Mary Parish Endowment Trust, Laurel. Tel: 402-256-3303.
St. Mary Parish Educational Endowment Trust, Laurel. Tel: 402-256-3303.
St. Mary Parish Endowment Trust, Leigh. Tel: 402-487-2666.
St. Mary Parish Cemetery Endowment Trust, Leigh.
Holy Family Parish Endowment Trust, Lindsay. Tel: 402-428-2455.
Holy Family Parish Educational Endowment Trust, Lindsay. Tel: 402-428-2455.
Assumption Parish Endowment Trust, Lynch. Tel: 402-569-2421.
Assumption Parish Educational Endowment Trust, Lynch. Tel: 402-569-2421.
Assumption Parish Cemetery Endowment Trust, Lynch.
St. Joseph Parish Endowment Trust, Lyons. Tel: 402-569-2421.
St. Joseph Parish Educational Endowment Trust, Lyons. Tel: 402-569-2421.
Our Lady of Fatima Parish Endowment Trust, Macy. Tel: 402-878-2402.
Our Lady of Fatima Parish Educational Endowment Trust, Macy. Tel: 402-878-2402.
St. Leonard Parish Endowment Trust, Madison. Tel: 402-454-3529.
St. Leonard Parish Educational Endowment Trust, Madison. Tel: 402-454-3529.
St. Boniface Parish Educational Endowment Trust, Menominee. Tel: 402-357-3506.
St. Boniface Parish Endowment, Menominee. Tel: 402-357-3506.
St. Boniface Parish Endowment Trust, Monterey. Tel: 402-372-3681.
St. Boniface Parish Educational Endowment Trust, Monterey. Tel: 402-372-3681.
Sacred Heart Parish Endowment Trust, Naper. Tel: 402-775-2452.
Sacred Heart Parish Educational Endowment Trust, Naper. Tel: 402-775-2452.
St. Francis of Assisi Parish Educational Endowment Trust, Neligh. Tel: 402-887-4521.
St. Francis of Assisi Parish Endowment Trust, Neligh. Tel: 402-887-4521.
St. Peter Parish Endowment Trust, Newcastle. Tel: 402-755-2773.
St. Peter Parish Educational Endowment Trust, Newcastle. Tel: 402-755-2773.
St. William Parish Endowment Trust, Niobrara. Tel: 402-668-2331.
St. William Parish Educational Endowment Trust, Niobrara. Tel: 402-668-2331.
Sacred Heart Parish Endowment Trust, Norfolk. Tel: 402-371-2621.
Sacred Heart Parish Religious Education Endowment Trust, Norfolk.
Sacred Heart Elementary School Educational Endowment Trust, Norfolk.
Norfolk Catholic High School Educational Endowment Trust, Norfolk.
St. Charles Borromeo Parish Endowment Trust, North Bend. Tel: 402-652-8484.

St. Charles Borromeo Parish Educational Endowment Trust, North Bend. Tel: 402-652-8484.
Sacred Heart Parish Endowment Trust, Olean. Tel: 402-693-2235.
Sacred Parish Educational Endowment Trust, Olean. Tel: 402-693-2235.
Blessed Sacrament Parish Endowment Trust Tel: 402-455-5200.
Blessed Sacrament Parish Educational Endowment Trust Tel: 402-455-5200.
Blessed Sacrament School Educational Endowment Trust Tel: 402-455-5200.
Christ the King Parish Endowment Trust Tel: 402-391-3606.
Christ the King Educational Endowment Trust Tel: 402-391-3606.
Church of the Assumption Educational Endowment Trust Tel: 402-734-4500.
Church of the Assumption Endowment Trust Tel: 402-734-4500.
Church of the Assumption Scholarship Educational Endowment Trust Tel: 402-734-4500.
Holy Cross Parish Endowment Trust Tel: 402-553-7500.
Holy Family Parish Endowment Trust Tel: 402-345-1062.
Holy Family Parish Educational Trust Tel: 402-345-1062.
Holy Ghost Parish Endowment Trust Tel: 402-731-3176.
Holy Ghost Educational Endowment Trust Tel: 402-731-3176.
Holy Name Parish Endowment Trust Tel: 402-451-6622.
Holy Name Parish Educational Endowment Trust Tel: 402-451-6622.
Holy Name Elementary School Endowment Trust Tel: 402-451-6622.
Immaculate Conception Parish Endowment Trust Tel: 402-342-1074.
Immaculate Conception Parish Educational Endowment Trust Tel: 402-342-1074.
Mary Our Queen Educational Endowment Trust Tel: 402-333-8662.
Mother of Perpetual Help Parish Endowment Trust Tel: 402-333-8662.
Mother of Perpetual Help Parish Educational Endowment Trust Tel: 402-558-4214.
Our Lady of Fatima Parish Endowment Trust Tel: 402-341-5772.
Our Lady of Fatima Parish Educational Endowment Trust Tel: 402-341-5772.
Our Lady of Guadalupe Parish Endowment Trust Tel: 402-734-2196.
Our Lady of Guadalupe Educational Endowment Trust, 68131. Tel: 402-734-2196.
Our Lady of Lourdes Parish Endowment Trust Tel: 402-346-0900.
Our Lady of Lourdes of Parish Educational Endowment Trust Tel: 402-346-0900.
Our Lady of Lourdes School Educational Endowment Trust Tel: 402-346-0900.
Sacred Heart Parish Endowment Trust Tel: 402-451-5755.
Sacred Heart Parish Educational Endowment Trust Tel: 402-451-5755.
St. Adalbert Parish Endowment Trust Tel: 402-345-1621.
St. Adalbert Parish Educational Endowment Trust Tel: 402-345-1621.
St. Agnes Parish Endowment Trust Tel: 402-731-2196.
St. Agnes Parish Educational Endowment Trust Tel: 402-731-2196.
St. Ann Parish Endowment Trust Tel: 402-341-6613.
St. Ann Parish Educational Endowment Trust Tel: 402-341-6613.
St. Anthony Parish Endowment Trust Tel: 402-733-2433.
St. Anthony Parish Educational Endowment Trust Tel: 402-733-2433.
St. Benedict Parish Endowment Trust Tel: 402-348-0631.
St. Benedict Parish Educational Endowment Trust Tel: 402-348-0631.
St. Bernadette Parish Endowment Trust Tel: 402-731-4694.
St. Bernadette Parish Educaitonal Endowment Trust Tel: 402-731-4694.
St. Bernard Parish Memorial Endowment Trust Tel: 402-551-0269.
St. Bernard Parish Religious Educational Endowment Trust Tel: 402-551-0269.
St. Bridget Parish Endowment Trust Tel: 402-733-8811.
St. Bridget Parish Educational Endowment Trust Tel: 402-733-8811.
St. Cecilia Cathedral Endowment Trust Tel: 402-551-2313.
St. Elizabeth Ann Parish Endowment Trust Tel: 402-493-2186.
St. Elizabeth Ann Parish Educational Endowment Trust Tel: 402-493-2186.
St. Francis of Assisi Church of South Omaha Endowment Trust Tel: 402-731-2699.
St. Francis of Assisi Church of South Omaha Educational Endowment Fund Tel: 402-731-2699.
St. Frances Cabrini Parish Endowment Trust Tel: 402-342-2464.
St. Frances Cabrini Parish Educational Endowment Trust Tel: 402-342-2464.
St. James Parish Endowment Trust Tel: 402-572-0499.
St. James Parish Educational Endowment Trust Tel: 402-572-0499.
St. James/Seton School Educational Endowment Fund Tel: 402-572-0499.
St. Joan of Arc Parish Educational Endowment Fund Tel: 402-393-2005.
St. Joan of Arc Parish Endowment Trust Tel: 402-393-2005.
St. Joan of Arc Grade School Educational Endowment Trust Tel: 402-393-2005.
St. John Vianney Church of Millard Parish Endowment Trust Tel: 402-895-0808.
St. John Vianney Parish Educational Endowment Trust Tel: 402-895-0808.
St. Joseph Parish Endowment Trust Tel: 402-342-2836.
St. Joseph Parish Educational Endowment Trust Tel: 402-342-2836.
St. Leo Parish Endowment Trust Tel: 402-397-0407.
St. Leo Parish Educational Endowment Trust Tel: 402-397-0407.
St. Margaret Mary Parish Endowment Trust Tel: 402-558-2255.
St. Margaret Mary Parish Educational Endowment Trust Tel: 402-558-2255.
St. Margaret Mary School Educational Endowment Trust Tel: 402-558-2255.
St. Mary Parish Endowment Trust Tel: 402-731-0204.
St. Mary Parish Educational Endowment Trust Tel: 402-731-0204.
St. Mary Elementary School Endowment Trust Tel: 402-731-0204.
St. Patrick Church Educational Endowment Trust Tel: 402-341-1305.
St. Patrick Parish Endowment Trust
St. Peter Parish Endowment Trust Tel: 402-341-4560.
St. Peter Parish Educational Endowment Trust Tel: 402-341-4560.
SS. Peter and Paul Church Endowment Trust Tel: 402-731-4578.
SS. Peter and Paul Parish Educational Endowment Trust Tel: 402-731-4578.
SS. Peter and Paul Elementary School Educational Endowment Trust Tel: 402-731-4578.
St. Philip Neri Church Endowment Trust Tel: 402-455-1289.
St. Philip Neri Parish Educational Endowment Trust Tel: 402-455-1289.
St. Pius X Parish Endowment Trust Tel: 402-558-8446.
St. Pius X Parish Educational Endowment Trust Tel: 402-558-8446.
St. Pius X/St. Leo School Educational Endowment Trust Tel: 402-558-8446.
St. Richard Parish Endowment Trust Tel: 402-455-2865.
St. Richard Parish Educational Endowment Trust Tel: 402-455-2865.
St. Richard Grade School Educational Endowment Trust Tel: 402-455-2865.
St. Robert Bellarmine Parish Endowment Trust Tel: 402-333-8989.
St. Rose Parish Endowment Trust Tel: 402-733-9327.
St. Rose Parish Educational Endowment Trust Tel: 402-733-9327.
St. Stanislaus Parish Endowment Trust Tel: 402-731-4152.
St. Stanislaus Parish Educational Endowment Trust Tel: 402-731-4152.
St. Stephen the Martyr Parish Endowment Trust Tel: 402-896-9675.
St. Stephen the Martyr Parish Educational Endowment Trust Tel: 402-896-9675.
St. Stephen the Martyr Elementary School Educational Endowment Trust Tel: 402-896-9675.
St. Therese of the Child Jesus Parish Endowment Trust Tel: 402-455-4966.
St. Therese of the Child Jesus Parish Educational Endowment Trust Tel: 402-455-4966.
St. Thomas More Parish Endowment Trust Tel: 402-556-1456.
St. Thomas More Parish Educational Endowment Trust Tel: 402-556-1456.
St. Thomas More School Educational Endowment Trust Tel: 402-556-1456.
St. Vincent de Paul Parish Endowment Trust Tel: 402-496-7988.
St. Vincent de Paul Parish Educational Endowment Trust Tel: 402-496-7988.
St. Wenceslaus Parish Endowment Trust Tel: 402-330-0304.
St. Wenceslaus Parish Educational Endowment Trust Tel: 402-330-0304.
St. Patrick Educational Endowment Trust, Oneill, 68763. Tel: 402-336-1602.
St. Patrick Foundation, Inc., O'Neill. Tel: 402-336-1602.
St. Mary School Foundation, Inc., O'Neill. Tel: 402-336-1602.
St. Mary of the Seven Dolors Parish Endowment Trust, Osmond. Tel: 402-748-3340.
St. Columbkille Parish Endowment Trust, Papillion. Tel: 402-339-3285.
St. Columbkille Educational Endowment Trust, Papillion. Tel: 402-339-3285.
St. John the Baptist Parish Endowment Trust, Pender. Tel: 402-385-3285.
St. John the Baptist Parish Educational Endowment Trust, Pender. Tel: 402-385-3285.
St. John the Baptist Center Maintenance Endowment Trust, Petersburg. Tel: 402-386-5580.
St. John the Baptist Parish Endowment Trust, Petersburg. Tel: 402-386-5580.
St. John the Baptist Endowment Trust Tel: 402-386-5580.
St. Joseph Parish Endowment Trust, Pierce. Tel: 402-329-4200.
St. Joseph Parish Educational Endowment Trust, Pierce. Tel: 402-329-4200.
St. Paul Parish Endowment Trust, Plainview. Tel: 402-582-4413.
St. Paul Parish Educational Endowment Trust, Plainview. Tel: 402-582-4413.
St. Joseph Parish Endowment Trust, Platte Center. Tel: 402-246-2255.
St. Joseph Parish Educational Endowment Trust, Platte Center. Tel: 402-246-2255.
St. Joseph Parish Endowment Trust, Ponca. Tel: 402-755-2773.
St. Joseph Parish Educational Endowment Trust, Ponca. Tel: 402-755-2773.
St. Mary Parish Endowment Trust, Primrose. Tel: 308-358-0773.
St. Mary Parish Educational Endowment Trust, Primrose. Tel: 308-358-0773.
St. Bonaventure Parish Endowment Trust, Raeville. Tel: 402-386-5254.
St. Bonvaventure Parish/Pope John XXIII High School Educational Endowment Trust, Raeville. Tel: 402-386-5254.
St. Gerald Parish Endowment Trust, Ralston. Tel: 402-331-1955.
St. Gerald Parish Educational Endowment Trust, Ralston.
St. Gerald School Educational Endowment Trust, Ralston.
St. Frances de Chantal Parish Endowment Trust, Randolph. Tel: 402-337-0644.
St. Frances de Chantal Parish Educational Endowment Trust, Randolph. Tel: 402-337-0644.
St. Anthony Parish Endowment Trust, St. Charles. Tel: 402-572-3681.
St. Anthony Parish Educational Endowment Trust, St. Charles. Tel: 402-572-3681.
St. Edward Parish Endowment Trust, St. Edward. Tel: 402-395-2926.
St. Edward Parish Educational Endowment Trust, St. Edward. Tel: 402-395-2926.
Immaculate Conception Parish Endowment Trust, St. Helena. Tel: 402-245-3311.
Immaculate Conception Parish Educational Endowment Trust, St. Helena. Tel: 402-245-3311.
SS. Philip and James Parish Endowment Trust, St. James. Tel: 402-357-2400.
SS. Philip and James Parish Educational Endowment, St. James. Tel: 402-357-2400.
St. John Parish Endowment Trust, St. John.
St. John Parish Educational Endowment Trust, St. John.
St. Francis de Sales Parish Endowment Trust, Schoolcraft. Tel: 402-675-2485.
St. Augustine Parish Endowment Trust, Schuyler. Tel: 402-352-3521.
St. Augustine Parish Educational Endowment Trust, Schuyler. Tel: 402-352-3521.
St. Mary Parish Endowment Trust, Schuyler. Tel: 402-352-3540.
St. Mary Parish Educational Endowment Trust, Schuyler. Tel: 402-352-3540.
St. Lawrence Parish Endowment Trust, Scribner. Tel: 402-654-3449.
St. Lawrence Parish Educational Endowment Trust, Scribner. Tel: 402-654-3449.
St. Lawrence Parish Endowment Trust, Silver Creek. Tel: 402-897-2625.
St. Lawrence Parish Educational Endowment Trust, Silver Creek. Tel: 402-897-2625.
St. Leo Parish Endowment Trust, Snyder. Tel:

402-897-2625.
St. Leo Parish Educational Endowment Trust, Snyder. Tel: 402-568-2520.
St. Michael Educational Endowment Trust, South Sioux City. Tel: 402-494-5423.
St. Michael Parish Endowment Trust, South Sioux City.
St. Mary Catholic Church Endowment Trust, Spencer. Tel: 402-589-0067.
St. Mary Parish Educational Endowment Trust, Spencer. Tel: 402-589-0067.
St. Mary Cemetery Endowment Trust, Spencer.
St. Joseph Parish Endowment Trust, Springfield. Tel: 402-253-2899.
St. Joseph Parish Educational Endowment Trust, Springfield. Tel: 402-253-2899.
St. Peter Parish Endowment Trust, Stanton. Tel: 402-439-2147.
St. Peter Parish Educational Endowment Trust, Stanton. Tel: 402-439-2147.
St. Boniface Parish Endowment Trust, Stuart. Tel: 402-924-3262.
St. Boniface Parish Educational Endowment Trust, Stuart. Tel: 402-924-3262.
St. Boniface Elementary School Endowment Trust, Stuart. Tel: 402-924-3263.
St. Mary Parish Endowment Trust, Tabor. Tel: 402-986-1627.
St. Mary Parish Educational Endowment Trust, Tabor. Tel: 402-986-1627.
St. Michael Parish Endowment Trust, Tarnov. Tel: 402-246-4821.
St. Michael Parish Educational Endowment Trust, Tarnov. Tel: 402-246-4821.
St. Patrick Parish Endowment Trust, Tekamah. Tel: 402-374-1692.
St. Patrick Parish Educational Endowment Trust, Tekamah. Tel: 402-374-1692.
Our Lady of Mt. Carmel Parish Endowment Trust, Tilden. Tel: 402-368-7710.
Our Lady of Mt. Carmel Parish Educational Endowment Trust, Tilden. Tel: 402-368-7710.
St. John the Evangelist Parish Endowment Trust, Valley. Tel: 402-359-5783.
St. John the Evangelist Parish Educational Endowment Trust, Valley. Tel: 402-359-5783.
St. Wenceslaus Church Parish Endowment Trust, Verdigre. Tel: 402-668-2331.
St. Wenceslaus Parish Educational Endowment Trust, Verdigre. Tel: 402-668-2331.
St. Joseph Parish Endowment Trust, Walthill. Tel: 402-878-2402.
St. Joseph Parish Educational Endowment Trust, Walthill. Tel: 402-878-2402.
St. Mary Parish Endowment Trust, Wayne. Tel: 402-375-2000.
St. Mary Educational Endowment Trust, Wayne. Tel: 402-375-2000.
Church of the Assumption of the B.V.M. Parish Endowment Trust, West Point. Tel: 402-372-2188.
Church of the Assumption of the B.V.M. Parish Educational Endowment Trust, West Point. Tel: 402-372-2188.
Guardian Angels Grade School Educational Endowment Trust, West Point. Tel: 402-372-2188.
West Point Central Catholic High School Activity Center Endowment Trust Tel: 402-372-5326.
West Point Central Catholic High School Educational Endowment Trust, West Point. Tel: 402-372-5326.
St. Augustine Indian Mission Endowment Trust, Winnebago. Tel: 402-878-2402.
St. Augustine Indian Mission Educational Endowment Trust, Winnebago. Tel: 402-878-2402.
St. Augustine Indian Mission Tuition Relief Educational Endowment Trust, Winnebago. Tel: 402-878-2402.
St. Joseph Parish Endowment Trust, Wisner. Tel: 402-529-3242.
St. Joseph Parish Educational Endowment Trust, Wisner. Tel: 402-529-3242.
Sacred Heart Parish Endowment Trust, Wynot. Tel: 402-357-2400.
Sacred Heart Parish Educational Endowment Trust, Wynot. Tel: 402-357-2400.

ST. COLUMBANS. *Columban Fathers Regional Administration*, P.O. Box 10, 68056-0010. Tel: 402-291-1920; Fax: 402-291-8693. Email: stcolneus@aol.com. Web: www.st.columban.org. Rev. William Sweeney, S.S.C., Contact.
St. Columban's Central Administration
St. Columban's Medical and Retirement Tel: 402-291-1920; Fax: 402-291-4984.
St. Columban's Gift Annuity Trust Tel: 402-291-1920; Fax: 402-291-4984.
St. Columban's Education Trust Tel: 402-291-1920; Fax: 402-291-4984.
St. Columban's Priests Health Program Trust Tel: 402-291-1920; Fax: 402-291-4984.
St. Columban's Retirement Fund Trust Tel: 402-291-1920; Fax: 402-291-4984.
St. Columban's Masses in Trust Tel: 402-291-1920; Fax: 402-291-4984.
St. Columban's Donors/Personal Trust Tel: 402-291-1920; Fax: 402-291-4984.
St. Columban's Regional Trust Tel: 402-291-1920; Fax: 402-291-4984.
St. Columban's Burse Estate Trust Tel: 402-291-1920; Fax: 402-291-4984.
St. Columban's Gift Annuity Trust California Tel: 402-291-1920; Fax: 402-291-4984.

[O] MISCELLANEOUS

OMAHA. *Archdiocesan Consultation Service*, 3300 N. 60th St., 68104. Tel: 402-551-1135; Fax: 402-554-0365. Email: mmicheletto@archomaha.org. Sr. Marie Micheletto, R.S.M., Dir. & Contact.
Archdiocesan Hispanic Ministry Office, 3216 N. 60th St., 68104-3421. Tel: 402-558-3134; Fax: 402-551-3050. Email: amerevia@archomaha.org. Sr. Angela Erevia, M.C.D.P., Dir.
Beginning Experience, 3214 N. 60th St., 68104. Tel: 402-551-9003; Fax: 402-551-3050. Email: jgould@omahaflo.creighton.edu. Sr. Barbara Markey, N.D., Contact.
**Bergan Mercy Foundation, Inc.* (Provides support to the mission of Bergen Mercy Health System dba Alegent Health), 7500 Mercy Rd., 68124. Tel: 402-343-4430; Fax: 402-343-4337. Email: ncooney@alegent.org. Web: www.alegent.com. Sr. Norita Cooney, R.S.M., Contact.
Black Student Catholic Scholarship Trust Fund A trust for the purpose of providing eligible black Catholic students scholarships and assistance for Catholic high school education. The board of 10 trustees for a nonprofit religious and educational corporation, whose president is the Archbishop of Omaha oversees the affairs of this trust. , c/o Office of Stewardship and Development, P.O. Box 4130, 68104-0130. Tel: 402-554-8493. Tessie Edwards, Contact.
C.M.G. Agency, Inc. An insurance agency supporting the religious and business activities of the Catholic Mutual Relief Society of America and The Catholic Relief Insurance Company of America. , 10843 Old Mill Rd., Ste. 300, 68154-2600. Tel: 800-228-6108, Ext. 2405; Fax: 402-551-2943. Email: dnovak@catholicmutual.org. Richard A. Novak, Contact.
Cathedral Arts Project, Inc., 100 N. 62nd St., 68132. Tel: 402-558-3100, Ext. 243; Fax: 402-558-3026. Email: WJWOEGER@archomaha.org DATUMA@archomaha.org. Web: www.cathedralartsproject.org. Bro. William J. Woeger, F.S.C., Exec. Dir. & Contact; Sr. Dorothy Tuma Assoc. Dir.
**Catholic Charities Foundation*, 3300 N. 60th St., 68104. Tel: 402-554-0520; Fax: 402-829-9268. Email: catholiccharities@ccomaha.org. Web: www.ccomaha.org. Scot L. Adams, Pres. & Contact.
Catholic Jail and Prison Ministry, 701 S. 28th St., 68105-1511. Tel: 402-342-7142; Fax: 402-330-5842. Email: RPVON@prodigy.net. Richard P. Vondenkamp, Dir.
Catholic Mutual of Canada, 10843 Old Mill Rd., Ste. 300, 68154-2600. Tel: 800-228-6108; Fax: 402-551-2943. Email: dnovak@catholicmutual.org. Richard A. Novak, Sec. & Contact. To support the religious and business activities of the Catholic Mutual Relief Society of America and its subsidiary Catholic Relief Insurance Company of America
Catholic Umbrella Pool, 10843 Old Mill Rd., Ste. 300, 68154-2600. Tel: 402-551-8765; Fax: 402-551-2943. Email: dennis@catholic-doc.org. Mr. Dennis F. Atwood, K.S.G., Contact.
St. Cecilia Schola Cantorum, Inc. A nonprofit religious, charitable, educational center, duly constituted under the laws of the State of Nebraska, provides education and resources in church music and promoting the performance of church music in the Archdiocese of Omaha. , 3843 Webster St., 68131. Tel: 402-558-3100; 402-553-5524; Fax: 402-551-4212; 402-551-2306. Email: scholacantorum@stceciliacathedral.org. Kevin Vogt, Contact & Dir.
Christ Child Society of Omaha, 1248 S. 10th St., 68108. Tel: 402-342-4566; Fax: 402-342-4541. C. Timothy Connor, Exec. Dir. & Contact. Day Care Centers 2; Total Assisted Annually 100; Special Care Centers 3; Total Assisted Annually 5,000.
Christian Family Movement (CFM), 3514 N. 63rd St., 68104. Tel: 402-558-1710. Edwin Osterhaus, Contact; Sheila Osterhaus, Contact.
Christian Urban Education Service, 2207 Wirt St., 68110. Tel: 402-451-5755; Fax: 402-451-1731. Rev. Thomas M. Fangman.
Christians Encounter Christ, 1938 S. 149th Cir., 68144. Tel: 402-334-2497. Rick Ekstrom, Contact. Purpose: To promote the transferring of environments through Christian leaders who are willing to live and share their principles of being Christian. Through the ongoing development of their Christian Personality, strengthened by their 4th Day, these leaders strive to instill the spirit and sense of gospel to all environments in which they are actively involved.
Daughters of the Eternal Father, 2216 Poppleton Ave., 68108-3436. Tel: 402-342-1032; Fax: 402-342-9094. Email: srmlucy.cox.net. Web: www.heartofmaryministry.com. Sr. Mary Lucy Astuto, Contact.
FOCCUS, Inc An agency creating, marketing and training in the use of marriage preparation and marriage enrichment programs and services, as well as supporting research and program development relating to healthy family life. , 3214 N. 60th St., 68104. Tel: 402-551-9003; Fax: 402-551-3050. Email: foccus@foccusinc.com. Web: www.foccusinc.com. Sr. Barbara Markey, N.D., Contact.
Francis House (Men's Sheltering.) , 1702 Nicholas St., 68102. Tel: 402-341-1821; Fax: 402-341-5270. Email: siena1702@sienafrancis.omhcoxmail.com. Web: www.sienafrancis.org. Mike Saklar, Dir. & Contact.
Health and Retirement Trust of Sisters of Mercy of the Americas, Regional Community of Omaha, 7262 Mercy Rd., 68124-2389. Tel: 402-393-8225; Fax: 402-393-8145. Email: patriciaf@mercyoma.com. Web: www.mercyoma.org. Sr. Patricia Forret, R.S.M., Contact.
Heart of Mary Publishing Company, Incorporated dba Heart of Mary Ministry, 2216 Poppleton Ave., 68108-3436. Tel: 402-342-9265; Fax: 402-342-9094. Email: srmarylucy@cox.net. Web: www.heartofmaryministry.com. Sr. Mary Lucy Astuto, Contact.
Holy Name Housing Corp., 3014 N. 45th St., 68104. Tel: 402-453-6100; Fax: 402-451-7187. Sr. Marilyn Ross, R.S.M., Exec. Dir. & Contact.
Holy Trinity Church of Colfax, County Parish and Cemetery Endowment Trust Fund, 100 North 62nd St., 68132. Tel: 402-986-1627; Fax: 402-986-1627.
Institute for Priestly Formation, Creighton University, 2500 California Plaza, 68178. Tel: 402-546-6384; Fax: 402-280-2423. Email: ipf@creighton.edu. Web: www.creighton.edu/ipf. Rev. Richard J. Gabuzda, Contact. Purpose: To offer programs and support for the integration of theological study, spiritual growth and direction, and retreat experiences for diocesan seminarians and priests.
Intecessors of the Lamb, 4014 N. Post Rd., 68112. Tel: 402-455-5262; Fax: 402-455-1323. Email: bellwether@novia.net. Web: www.bellwetheromaha.org. Sr. Nadine, Contact.
St. James Manor, Inc., 3102 No. 60th St., 68104. Tel: 402-551-4243; Fax: 402-558-8023. Email: JoeR@ccomaha.org. Joseph V. Rysavy, Pres. & Contact.
Latino Catholic Scholarship Fund Receives and distributes funds as financial aid to Latino students attending Catholic schools. , P.O. Box 4130, 68104-0130. Tel: 402-554-8493. Email: jtamisie@archomaha.org. Web: www.archomaha.com. Judy Tamisiea, Contact Person.
St. Mary's Church of Tabor Parish and Cemetery Endowment Trust Fund, 100 North 62nd St., 68132. Tel: 402-986-1627; Fax: 402-986-1627.
McAuley Bergan Center, 3552 Farnam St., 68131. Tel: 402-342-1688; Fax: 402-342-7043. Paul Maginn, Dir. & Contact. Adult Day Care Centers.
McAuley Ministry Fund (Provides support to the mission of the Sisters of Mercy of the Americas, Regional Community of Omaha) , 7262 Mercy Rd., 68124-2389. Tel: 402-393-8225; Fax: 402-393-8145. Email: patriciaf@mercyoma.com. Web: www.mercyoma.org. Sr. Patricia Forret, R.S.M., Contact.
Mercy Holdings, 7262 Mercy Rd., 68124-2389. Tel: 402-393-8225; Fax: 402-393-8145. Email: patriciaf@mercyoma.com. Web: www.mercyoma.org. Sr. Patricia Forret, R.S.M., Contact.
Mercy Housing Midwest, 7262 Mercy Rd., 68124. Tel: 402-398-6614; Fax: 402-393-2144. Email: cwehrwein@mercyhousing.org.
Mercy Housing, 7262 Mercy Rd., 68124. Tel: 402-398-6614; Fax: 402-393-2144.
Mercy Northglen, 7262 Mercy Rd., 68124. Tel: 402-398-6614; Fax: 402-393-2144.
Mercy Western Manor, 7262 Mercy Rd., 68124. Tel: 402-398-6614; Fax: 402-393-2144.
Mercy Crestview Village, 7262 Mercy Rd., 68124. Tel: 402-398-6614; Fax: 402-393-2144.
Mercy Oakwood Gardens, 7262 Mercy Rd., 68124. Tel: 402-398-6614; Fax: 402-393-2144. To provide affordable housing to the economically poor.
The Most AMYable Roman Catholic Lending

Library, Inc., 5404 William St., 68106-2355. Tel: 402-553-1837. Email: athanasius.rwe@catholicexchange.com. Roger Elliott, Contact; Judy Elliott, Contact. Purpose: a nonprofit corporation religious, charitable and educational corporation is duly constituted under the laws of the State of Nebraska and operated by a Board of Directors for the purpose of collecting and lending orthodox Catholic books and magazines, Videos and audiotapes, Prayers and Petitions.

New Cassel Foundation A nonprofit religious, charitable and educational corporation, duly constituted under the laws of the State of Nebraska, to provide support and benefit for the New Cassel Retirement Center and the Franciscan Adult Day Center. , 900 N. 90th St., 68114-2769. Tel: 402-393-2277; Fax: 402-393-3784. Rev. James R. Tiegs, Pres. & Contact.

New Covenant Center: Education for Justice and Peace, 703 S. 28th St., 68105-1528. Tel: 402-345-5111. Email: mcosssf@juno.com. Sr. Maureen Connolly, S.S.S.F., Prog. Coord.

Notre Dame Housing, Inc., 3501 State St., 68112-1709. Tel: 402-455-2994; Fax: 402-455-3974. Email: maz@creighton.edu. Web: www.notredamesisters.org. Sr. Mary Ann Zimmer, N.D., Contact. Purpose: To provide housing for elderly and persons of low-income or otherwise unable to afford market rate housing.

Notre Dame Living Center, Inc., 3501 State St., 68112-1709. Tel: 402-455-2994; Fax: 402-455-3974. Email: maz@creighton.edu. Web: www.notredamesisters.org. Sr. Mary Ann Zimmer, N.D., Contact. Purpose: Provides affordable housing to the elderly, particularly those of low-income status.

Pope Paul VI Institute for the Study of Human Reproduction, 6901 Mercy Rd., 68106. Tel: 402-390-6600; Fax: 402-390-9851. Email: popepaul@mitec.net. Web: www.popepaulvi.com. Thomas W. Hilgers, M.D., Dir.

Siena - Francis House, Inc., P.O. Box 217, D.T.S., 68101. Tel: 402-341-1821; Fax: 402-341-5270. Email: siena1702@aol.com. Web: www.sienafrancis.org. Mike Saklar, Dir. & Contact.

Siena House (Women's Sheltering) , 1702 Nicholas St., 68102. Tel: 402-341-1821; Fax: 402-341-5270. Web: www.sienafrancis.org. Mike Saklar, Dir. & Contact.

Teachers' Salary Endowment Trust Fund of St. Stephen Church of Omaha, St. Stephen Church of Omaha, 16704 "S" St., 68135. Tel: 402-896-9675; Fax: 402-896-1990. Email: jstover@stephen.org. Purpose: providing endowment support for teachers employed by St. Stephen Church of Omaha.

TEC, Box 4130, 68104. Tel: 402-554-8493; Fax: 402-554-8402. Email: rmramos@archomaha.org. Web: www.oarch.org/orf/orfpages/tec.html. Rita Ramos, Asst. Dir. Youth Ministry.

Widowed and Divorced Catholics of Omaha, 3214 N. 60th St., 68104. Tel: 402-551-9003; Fax: 402-551-3050. Web: jgould@omahaflo.creighton.edu. Jean Gould, Contact.

Womens' Care Center of the Heartland (Holy Family House) Provides housing, spiritual and pastoral support to women facing crisis pregnancy and post-birth or post abortion circumstances of need. , 1404 Castelar St., 68108. Tel: 402-341-1305; Fax: 402-352-5510. Email: stpatricko@cox.net. Web: www.womenscch.org. Rev. Stephen F. Gutgsell, Contact.

The Young Adult Beginning Experience, 3214 N. 60th St., 68104. Tel: 402-551-9003; Fax: 402-551-3050. Sr. Barbara Markey, N.D., Contact.

EWING. *St. Theresa Church of Clearwater Cemetery Endowment Trust Fund*, P.O. Box 37, 68735. Tel: 402-626-7605; Fax: 402-626-7668. Rev. William Safranek, Contact.

GRETNA. *Holy Family Shrine* A place of pilgrimage, prayer and resource for the public and private prayer. This nonprofit religious, charitable and educational corporation is duly constituted under the laws of the State of Nebraska and operated by a Board of Trustees. , 23132 Pflug Rd., 68028. Tel: 401-332-4565. Web: www.holyfamilyshrine.org. Sr. Renee Mirkes, O.S.F., Contact.

HUMPHREY. *St. Francis Church of Humphrey Cemetery Endowment Trust Fund*, P.O. Box 116, 68642. Tel: 402-923-0913; Fax: 402-923-1931. Email: rectory@megavision.com. Rev. James M. Buckley, Contact.

LAVISTA. *Marriage Encounter*, 9930 Idora St., 68128. Tel: 402-331-3107. Email: ja-k@cox.net. Web: www.geocities.com/capecanaveral/6748/mesect9/. John & Jackie Riesberg, Contact.

LAUREL. *St. Ann Church of Dixon Cemetery Endowment Trust Fund*, P.O. Box 828, 68745. Tel: 402-256-3303; Fax: 402-256-3019. Email: maryann68745@yahoo.com.

LYNCH. *Niobrara Valley House of Renewal*, P.O. Box 167, 68746. Tel: 402-569-2421. Email: marypmin@threeriver.net. Web: www.threeriver.net/retreat. Mary Hildman, Contact.

OAKDALE. *Tintern Retreat and Resource Center*, 52619 843 Rd., 68761. Tel: 402-776-2188. Email: tintern@gpcom.net. Web: www.tinternrrc.org. Phyllis A. Camp, Contact.

PETERSBURG. *St. John the Baptists' Church of Petersburg Cemetery Endowment Trust Fund*, c/o St. John the Baptist Church, P.O. Box 608, 68652. Tel: 402-386-5580. A trust for the purpose of providing for the support and benefit of the cemeteries maintained by St. John the Baptist Church of Petersburg. The nonprofit, charitable and educational corporation is duly constituted under the laws of the State of Nebraska and is operated by a 3 member Board of Trustees.

Rural Central Deanery Faith and Ministry Formation Center, P.O. Box 9, 68652-0009. Tel: 402-386-5395. Email: rcdeanery@yahoo.com. Sr. Patricia Throener, O.S.F., Contact.

ST. EDWARD. *St. Edward's Church (of St. Edward) Cemetery Endowment Trust Fund*, 805 Washington St., 68660. Tel: 402-678-2642; Fax: 402-678-2341. A trust for the purpose of providing for the support and benefit of the cemeteries maintained by St. Edward Church, St Edward, NE. The nonprofit, charitable and educational corporation is duly constituted under the laws of the State of Nebraska and is operated by a 3 member Board of Trustees.

SCHUYLER. *St. Benedict Center Endowment Fund* An endowment for the purpose of providing for the support and benefit of development, maintenance and supplemental funding of programs and services of St. Benedict Center and the receipt and management of gifts and bequests to the same center. The nonprofit, charitable and educational corporation is duly constituted under the laws of the State of Nebraska , 1126 Rd. "I", P.O. Box 528, 68661-0528. Tel: 402-352-8819; Fax: 402-352-8884. Email: benedict.center@alltel.net. Web: www.megavision.net/benedict. Very Rev. Germar Neubert, O.S.B., Contact at Benedictine Mission House/Christ the King Priory.

SILVER CREEK. *St. Lawrence Church of Silver Creek Cemetery Endowment Trust Fund*, P.O. Box 332, 68663. Tel: 308-773-2282; Fax: 308-773-8281. Email: dkorth@megavision.

WINNEBAGO. *St. Augustine's Indian Mission*, P.O. Box GG, 68071. Tel: 402-878-2402; Fax: 402-878-2760. Email: sboes@mother.esul.org. Web: www.staugustinemission.com. Revs. Steven Boes, Contact & Dir.; Dave Kurth, Asst. Dir.

FEATHERS An endowment, duly constituted under the laws of the State of Nebraska as a nonprofit religious, charitable and educational corporation, to provide scholarships to Native American children of the Winnebago nation to attend high school, grade school, college. , c/o St. Augustine Indian Mission, P.O. Box GG, 68071. Tel: 402-878-2402; Fax: 402-878-2760. Rev. Steven Boes, Contact & Dir.

[P] PUBLIC ASSOCIATIONS OF THE CHRISTIAN FAITHFUL

OMAHA. *Christian Life Community-North Central Region (CLC)* A public association of the Christian faithful of Pontificial Right providing spiritual support and guidance in the Jesuit tradition of the Spiritual Exercises. , 2500 California Plaza, 68178. Tel: 402-280-2692; Fax: 402-280-5590. Email: jzsj@creighton.edu. Rev. Jack Zuercher, S.J., Contact & Regional Ecclesial Asst.

Intercessors of the Lamb A community of the consecrated hermits and a center of formation with the charism of intercessory prayer; provides retreats, conferences and resources for charismatic, marian and spiritual warfare spirituality. , 4014 North Post Rd., 68112. Tel: 402-455-1514; Fax: 402-455-1323. Email: bellwether@novia.net. Web: www.bellwetheromaha.org. Sr. Nadine Brown, Contact.

RELIGIOUS INSTITUTES OF MEN REPRESENTED IN THE ARCHDIOCESE

For further details refer to the corresponding bracketed number in the Religious Institutes of Men or Women section.

[0200]—*Benedictine Monks*—O.S.B.
[0330]—*Brothers of the Christian Schools* (St. Louis, MO)—F.S.C.
[0690]—*Jesuit Fathers and Brother* (Wisconsin Prov.)—S.J.
[0150]—*Order of the Augustinian Recollects* (St. Augustine Prov.)—O.A.R.
[1070]—*Redemptorist Fathers* (St. Louis Prov.)—C.SS.R.
[0370]—*Society of St. Columban*—S.S.C.

RELIGIOUS INSTITUTES OF WOMEN REPRESENTED IN THE ARCHDIOCESE

[0230]—*Benedictine Sisters of Pontifical Jurisdiction*—O.S.B.
[1070-03]—*Dominican Sisters*—O.P.
[1230]—*Franciscan Sisters of Christian Charity*—O.S.F.
[1430]—*Franciscan Sisters of Our Lady of Perpetual Help*—O.S.F.
[2575]—*Institute of the Sisters of Mercy of the Americas*—R.S.M.
[0210]—*Missionary Benedictine Sisters*—O.S.B.
[2960]—*Notre Dame Sisters*—N.D.
[3760]—*Order of St. Clare*—O.S.C.
[1680]—*School Sisters of St. Francis* (Our Lady of Angels Prov.)—O.S.F.
[3580]—*Servants of Mary*—O.S.M.
[1630]—*Sisters of St. Francis of Peace and Christian Charity* (Denver Prov.)—O.S.F.
[1640]—*Sisters of St. Francis of Perpetual Adoration* (Colorado Springs, CO)—O.S.F.
[1830]—*Sisters of the Good Shepherd*—R.G.S.
[3270]—*Sisters of the Most Precious Blood* (O'Fallon, MO)—C.PP.S.
[3320]—*Sisters of the Presentation of the B.V.M.*—P.B.V.M.
[4070]—*Society of the Sacred Heart*—R.S.C.J.

ARCHDIOCESAN CEMETERIES

OMAHA. *Calvary*
Holy Sepulchre
St. Mary
St. Mary Magdalene
Resurrection

NECROLOGY

† DeBacker, Rev. Msgr. Thomas, (Retired)—Died March 10, 2003
† Hupp, Rev. Msgr. Robert P., (Retired)—Died Aug. 29, 2003
† Kelly, Michael J., (Retired)—Died Dec. 6, 2003
† Massmann, Albert, Elkhorn, NE Mount Michael Abbey—Died July 13, 2003
† Moreci, Francis A., (Retired)—Died Sept. 21, 2003
† Sheehan, Bernard, Elkhorn, NE Mount Michael Abbey—Died Jan. 27, 2003
† Weeke, James L., (Retired)—Died Dec. 10, 2003

Diocese of Orange in California

(Arausicanae in California)

Most Reverend

TOD DAVID BROWN, D.D.

Bishop of Orange; ordained May 1, 1963; appointed Bishop of Boise December 27, 1988; Episcopal Ordination April 3, 1989; appointed Bishop of Orange June 29, 1998; installed September 3, 1998. *Office: Marywood Center,* 2811 E. Villa Real Dr., Orange, CA 92867.

Chancellors Office: 2811 E. Villa Real Dr., P.O. Box 14195, Orange, CA 92863-1595. Tel: 714-282-3000; Fax: 714-282-3029.

Web: www.rcbo.org

Email: sgiacomi@rcbo.org

Most Reverend

NORMAN F. MCFARLAND, D.D., J.C.D.

Retired Bishop of Orange; ordained June 15, 1946; appointed Titular Bishop of Bida and Auxiliary of San Francisco June 5, 1970; consecrated September 8, 1970; appointed Apostolic Administrator December 6, 1974; appointed Bishop of Reno-Las Vegas February 10, 1976; installed March 31, 1976; appointed Bishop of Orange December 29, 1986; installed February 24, 1987; retired June 30, 1998. *Res.: 200 W. La Veta Ave., Orange, CA 92866. Office: Marywood Center,* 2811 E. Villa Real Dr., Orange, CA 92867.

Most Reverend

JAIME SOTO, D.D., M.S.W.

Auxiliary Bishop of Orange; ordained June 12, 1982; appointed Auxiliary Bishop of Orange March 23, 2000; installed May 31, 2000.

Most Reverend

DOMINIC MAI LUONG

Auxiliary Bishop of Orange; ordained May 21, 1966; appointed Auxiliary Bishop of Orange April 25, 2003; installed June 11, 2003.

ESTABLISHED JUNE 18, 1976.

Square Miles 782.

Comprises the County of Orange in the State of California.

Diocesan Patron: Our Lady of Guadalupe.

Legal Titles:
(Prot. No. CD 528-76)
The Roman Catholic Bishop of Orange, a Corporation Sole.
Diocese of Orange Education and Welfare Corporation.
Catholic Charities of Orange.

For legal titles of parishes and diocesan institutions, consult the Diocesan Pastoral Service Office

STATISTICAL OVERVIEW

Personnel	
Bishop	1
Auxiliary Bishops	2
Retired Bishops	1
Abbots	1
Priests: Diocesan Active in Diocese	107
Priests: Diocesan Active Outside Diocese	11
Priests: Retired, Sick or Absent	63
Number of Diocesan Priests	181
Religious Priests in Diocese	116
Total Priests in Diocese	297
Extern Priests in Diocese	22
Ordinations:	
Diocesan Priests	6
Religious Priests	1
Permanent Deacons	14
Permanent Deacons in Diocese	70
Total Brothers	9
Total Sisters	320
Parishes	
Parishes	56
With Resident Pastor:	
Resident Diocesan Priests	49
Resident Religious Priests	7
Missions	4
Pastoral Centers	4
Professional Ministry Personnel:	
Brothers	4
Sisters	36
Lay Ministers	209
Welfare	
Catholic Hospitals	3
Total Assisted	402,021
Health Care Centers	3
Total Assisted	13,502
Homes for the Aged	1
Total Assisted	60
Day Care Centers	2
Total Assisted	200
Specialized Homes	6
Total Assisted	286
Special Centers for Social Services	9
Total Assisted	840,633
Other Institutions	1
Total Assisted	98
Educational	
Diocesan Students in Other Seminaries	29
Total Seminarians	29
High Schools, Diocesan and Parish	3
Total Students	4,608
High Schools, Private	3
Total Students	1,029
Elementary Schools, Diocesan and Parish	36
Total Students	13,735
Elementary Schools, Private	2
Total Students	671
Catechesis/Religious Education:	
High School Students	7,985
Elementary Students	37,370
Total Students under Catholic Instruction	65,427
Teachers in the Diocese:	
Priests	17
Brothers	4
Sisters	40
Lay Teachers	1,143
Vital Statistics	
Receptions into the Church:	
Infant Baptism Totals	16,462
Adult Baptism Totals	669
Received into Full Communion	591
First Communions	13,954
Confirmations	5,564
Marriages:	
Catholic	2,184
Interfaith	636
Total Marriages	2,820
Deaths	2,718
Total Catholic Population	1,170,480
Total Population	3,000,000

Former Bishops—Most Revs. WILLIAM R. JOHNSON, appt. Titular Bishop of Biera and Auxiliary Bishop of Los Angeles, Feb. 9, 1971; consecrated March 25, 1971; installed as first Bishop of Orange, June 18, 1976; died July 28, 1986; NORMAN F. MCFARLAND, D.D., J.C.D. (Retired), ord. June 15, 1946; appt. Titular Bishop of Bida and Auxiliary of San Francisco, June 5, 1970; consecrated Sept. 8, 1970; appt. Apostolic Administrator, Dec. 6, 1974; appt. Bishop of Reno-Las Vegas, Feb. 10, 1976; installed March 31, 1976; appt. Bishop of Orange, Dec. 29, 1986; installed Feb. 24, 1987; retired June 30, 1998.

Vicar General—Rev. Msgr. JOHN URELL, Office: Marywood Center.

Chancellor—SHIRL GIACOMI, Office: Marywood Center.

Moderator of the Curia—Rev. Msgr. JOHN URELL, Office: Marywood Center.

Director of Clergy Personnel—Rev. J. MICHAEL MCKIERNAN, Office: Marywood Center.

Secretary to the Bishop—Rev. J. MICHAEL MCKIERNAN, Office: Marywood Center.

Vicar for Religious Communities—Sr. EYMARD FLOOD, O.S.C., Office: Marywood Center.

Vicar for Priests—Rev. KERRY BEAULIEU, Office: Marywood Center.

Vicar for Religious Education—Rev. CHRISTOPHER SMITH, Office: Marywood Center.

Vicar for Pastoral and Community Affairs—Rev. Msgr. JOHN F. SAMMON, P.A., Res.: 200 W. La Veta Ave., Orange, 92866. Office: Marywood Center.

Diocesan Pastoral Service Office—2811 E. Villa Real Dr., P.O. Box 14195, Orange, 92863-1595. Tel: 714-282-3000; Fax: 714-282-3029. Office Hours: Mon.-Fri. 9-5

Office of Canonical Services—2811 E. Villa Real Dr., P.O. Box 14195, Orange, 92863-1595. Tel: 714-282-3080; Fax: 714-282-3087.

Judicial Vicar—Rev. DOUGLAS COOK, J.C.L.

Adjutant Judicial Vicars—Rev. Msgr. DANIEL J. MURRAY, J.C.L.

Promoters of Justice—Rev. Msgr. HUGH O'CONNOR (Retired); Rev. TUAN PHAM, J.C.L.

Judges—Rev. Msgrs. JOHN G. CAMPBELL, J.C.L.; PAUL MARTIN; DANIEL J. MURRAY, J.C.L.; Very Rev. ARTHUR A. HOLQUIN, S.T.L.; Revs. JAMES HARTNETT; THOMAS HA; DANIEL R. HOPCUS; DOUGLAS COOK, J.C.L.; JOHN R. KELLER (Retired); JOSEPH NETTEKOVEN; TED OLSON; TUAN PHAM, J.C.L.; JOHN CARONAN O.Praem., J.C.L.; MARGARET ANN RAMSDEN, S.F.C.C., J.C.L.; Ms. PEGGY JEAN PAOLI, J.C.L.; PAULA MODAFF, S.P., J.C.L.

Defenders of the Bond—Revs. JOHN A. BRADLEY; TUAN JOSEPH PHAM, J.C.L.; THOMAS KELLER, M.S.C.

Ecclesiastical Notaries—LUCY DOMINQUES; LINDA BRAUN; PAULA LYNN; SANDRA DALTON; LILLIAN ESQUIVEL; SUSAN STANKIS.

National Organization for Decent Literature—Rev. Msgr. JOHN F. SAMMON, P.A., Dir., Office: Marywood Center.

Newman Apostolate—Rev. PATRICK PHILBIN, S.M., Dir., P.O. Box 6030, Irvine, 92616. Tel: 714-856-0211.

Parish Councils and Parish Development—SHIRL GIACOMI, Chancellor, Office: Marywood Center.

Diaconate—Mr. FRANK CHAVEZ, Office: Marywood Center.

Clergy Personnel Board—Rev. Msgr. JOHN URELL, V.G.; Revs. FRED BAILEY; CIRILO FLORES; MICHAEL HEHER; TIMOTHY MACCARTHY; TUYEN NGUYEN; EAMON O'GORMAN; J. MICHAEL MCKIERNAN, Auditor, Office: Marywood Center.

Media Relations—Rev. Msgr. LAWRENCE J. BAIRD, Dir., Office: Marywood Center.

Conciliation & Arbitration Office—Ms. DOLORES CHURCHILL, L.C.S.W., Office: Marywood Center.

Orange Diocesan Council of Catholic Women—Sr. EYMARD FLOOD, O.S.C., Moderator; MARY HAYES, Pres., Office: Marywood Center.

Priests' Relief—Rev. KERRY BEAULIEU, Office: Marywood Center.

Council of Priests—Most Revs. TOD DAVID BROWN, D.D.; JAIME SOTO, D.D., M.S.W.; Rev. Msgrs. JOHN SAMMON; PAUL MARTIN; Rev. DOUGLAS COOK; Rev. Msgr. JOHN URELL; Rev. MICHAEL HOAN; Rev. Msgrs. WILBUR DAVIS; DANIEL MURRAY; Very Rev. ARTHUR HOLQUIN; Revs. JEROME KARCHER; ED POETTGEN; RUDOLPH PRECIADO; STEVE SALLOT; COLM CONLON; STEPHEN DUFFIN; ENRIQUE SERA; GILBERTO ESCOBEDO; JUSTIN M. PISCIOTTA, O.S.M.; TED OLSON; MICHAEL HEHER; KERRY BEAULIEU; MARITO REBAMONTAN; GERALD M. HORAN, O.S.M.; JOSEPH SCERBO, S.A.; JOHN CARONAN, O.Praem., Office: Marywood Center.

Consultors—Rev. DOUGLAS COOK; Rev. Msgr. JOHN SAMMON; Most Rev. JAIME SOTO, D.D., M.S.W.; Rev. MICHAEL HOAN; Rev. Msgrs. JOHN URELL; WILBUR DAVIS; Revs. KERRY BEAULIEU; MICHAEL HEHER; STEVE SALLOT; Very Rev. ARTHUR HOLQUIN; Revs. GERALD HORAN, O.S.M.; MARITO REBAMONTAN.

Propagation of the Faith—Rev. Msgr. JOHN F. SAMMON, P.A., Dir., Office: Marywood Center.

Council for Religious—Sisters EYMARD FLOOD, O.S.C., Dir.; FRANCINE GUNTHER, S.H.C.J.; YOLANDA MAGALLANES, S.D.S.H.; Bros. AUGUSTINE PACKARD, O.H.; JOEL A. LECHNER, O.S.M.

Society of St. Vincent de Paul of Orange County—ED HARTMANN, Pres.; Rev. PATRICK AILBE BRENNAN, O.S.A., Spiritual Dir., 180 S. Cypress, Orange, 92866. Tel: 714-633-9194.

Schools Office—Bro. WILLIAM CARRIERE, F.S.C., Supt.; Mrs. SALLY TODD, Assoc. Supt., Office: Marywood Center.

Schools Advisory Board of Education— Office: Marywood Center

Vocations Office—Rev. Msgr. WILBUR DAVIS, Dir., Office: Marywood Center.

Catholic Campaign for Human Development—Local Board: DOLORES CHURCHILL; Deacon FRANK CHAVEZ; WALTER DALY; DIETER MYERS GONZALES; VIRGINIA FAULKNER, Office: Marywood Center.

Diocesan Offices and Directors

Apostleship of Prayer—Rev. Msgr. HUGH O'CONNOR (Retired), 2050 W. Ball Rd., Anaheim, 92804. Tel: 714-774-2595.

Archivist—Rev. WILLIAM KREKELBERG, Office: Mission Basilica San Juan Capistrano, 31522 Camino Capistrano, San Juan Capistrano, 92675-0691.

Boy Scouts—Rev. Msgr. JOHN F. SAMMON, P.A., Office: Marywood Center.

Liturgical Commission—Very Rev. ARTHUR HOLQUIN, Chm.; Revs. KERRY BEAULIEU; JOHN P. MCANDREW; J. MICHAEL MCKIERNAN; TUAN JOSEPH PHAM, J.C.L.; Ms. JO ANN DAVIS; Mr. FRANK CHAVEZ; Ms. CHARLENE DUMITRU; Mr. FERMIN GOMEZ; Dr. KATHLEEN DEJARDIN; Ms. KATHY LEWIS; Ms. LESA TRUXAW; Mr. MICHAEL SHAFFER, Office: Marywood Center.

Building and Renovation Committee of the Liturgical Commission—Revs. JOHN P. MCANDREW; KERRY BEAULIEU; J. MICHAEL MCKIERNAN; Very Rev. ARTHUR HOLQUIN; Dr. KATHLEEN DEJARDIN; Mr. MICHAEL SHAFFER; Mrs. LESA TRUXAW, Chm., Office: Marywood Center.

Land Advisory Board—Most Rev. TOD DAVID BROWN, D.D.; Rev. ED POETTGEN; Mr. ARTHUR BIRTCHER; Mr. TERENCE K. BARRY, Chm.; Ms. SHARON HENNESSEY; Mr. DANIEL HOLDEN; Mr. R. RAND SPERRY; Rev. Msgr. JOHN URELL; KENNETH TAIT. Staff: Mr. PHIL REIS; LILY FUNK; Rev. J. MICHAEL MCKIERNAN; JOE NOVOA; SHIRL GIACOMI.

Diocesan Construction Board—Most Rev. TOD DAVID BROWN, D.D.; Rev. Msgr. JOHN URELL; Rev. THEODORE OLSON; Mr. TERRANCE BARRY; Mr. RON GAGNON; Mr. ARTHUR BIRTCHER, Chm.; Mr. MARKO E. BOTICH; Mr. EDWARD REYNOLDS; Mr. HARRY G. KREIDER. Staff: Mr. PHIL RIES; Mr. JOE NOVOA, Construction Mgr.; Rev. J. MICHAEL MCKIERNAN; SHIRL GIACOMI.

Diocesan Finance Council—Most Revs. TOD DAVID BROWN, D.D.; JAIME SOTO, D.D., M.S.W.; Rev. Msgr. WILLIAM MCLAUGHLIN; Mr. TOM KLEINBAUER; Rev. Msgrs. JOHN URELL; LAWRENCE BAIRD; THERESA CAGNEY MORRISON; Mr. WILLIAM CRAWFORD; Mr. GUY WILSON; Mr. ROGER KIRWAN; Mr. PAUL SCHLOEMER. Staff: Rev. J. MICHAEL MCKIERNAN; Mr. PHIL RIES, Dir.; Mr. CARLOS VASQUEZ; Mr. JEAN FRANCOIS TROUNG; Mr. KEVIN LARSON; SHIRL GIACOMI.

Director of Finance—Mr. PHIL RIES, Dir.; Mr. CARLOS VASQUEZ, Controller, Office: Marywood Center.

Catholic Charities of Orange—CATHERINE SPEAR, Exec. Dir., Office, 1800 E. McFadden, Santa Ana, 92705. Tel: 714-347-9600.

Cemeteries—Mr. MICHAEL WESNER, Dir., Office: Marywood Center.

Ministry to Priests—Revs. KERRY BEAULIEU, Vicar, Priests; MICHAEL HOAN; RUDOLPH PRECIADO; TIM FREYER; ROY KIM; RICHARD DELAHUNTY; ROD KELLER; KEN SCHMIT; JOHN P. MCANDREW; JOHN MONESTERO; GORDON MORELAND, S.J.; TUAN NGUYEN; AL BACA; STEVE SALLOT, Office: Marywood Center.

Cursillo Movement—Revs. RAYMOND SKONEZNY, Exec. Spiritual Dir.; DAVID VUELVAS-ARIAS, Spiritual Dir., Hispanic Cursillo; RAPHAEL NGUYEN, Spiritual Dir., Vietnamese Cursillo, Office: Marywood Center.

Office for Deaf Ministry—CONNIE WILD, Dir.; Deacon FRANK LUNA, 2050 W. Chapman Ave., Ste. 217, Orange, 92868. Tel: 714-940-0884; 714-940-0880 (TDD); Fax: 714-639-8670; 714-939-9905.

Office for Religious Education—Rev. CHRISTOPHER H. SMITH, Vicar; RUTH BRADLEY, Dir.; OLIVIA CORNEJOS, Elementary/Junior High. Youth & Young Adult Ministries: NANCY HORMUTH, Dir.; JAVIER CASTILLO, Assoc. Dir.

Library/Media Center—DIANE MURRAY, Dir.

Institute of Pastoral Ministry—JOAN KULIK, Dir.; NURIA CHEKOURAS, Assoc. Dir., Office: Marywood Center.

Ecumenical and Interreligious Affairs—Revs. RAFAEL LUEVANO, Officer; JOHN MONESTERO; Mrs. SUE MONTANO FENWICK; Dr. GEORGE E. SAINT-LAURENT; Judge MARY FINGAL ERICKSON, Chm.; Very Rev. HUGH C. BARBOUR, O.Praem., Ph.D.; Rev. MINH C. BUI; Mrs. NURIA CHEKOURAS; Mrs. OLIVIA CORNEJO; Ms. SUSAN DEAN; Rev. ALLAN DECK, S.J.; Mrs. ORALIE ENOS; Rev. GILBERTO ESCOBEDO; Sr. JEANNE FALLON, C.S.J.; Mr. JOHN FITZSIMONS; Sr. MARIE JEANNE GAILLAC, C.S.F.; Ms. RENATE GOUTIER; Mr. GREG KELLEY; Rev. ROY KIM; Mr. COREY J. TIMPSON; Judge DAVID MCEACHEN; Rev. CHRISTIAN MONDOR, O.F.M.; Mrs. LISA RAMIREZ; Mrs. ANN NGUYEN; Dr. JOSE SANCHEZ-NUNEZ, Office: Marywood Center.

Family Life—CARMELA TREANOR, Dir., Office: Marywood Center.

Marriage Preparation - Spanish—PATRICIA LEHMAN, Coord.

Marriage Preparation - English—Coords.: Deacon JERRY PYNE; JOANN PYNE.

Natural Family Planning—MARY DAUSCH, Coord.

RAINBOWS—DOLORES CERVANTES, Coord.

Engaged Encounter—VINNIE DEFALCO; MARY KAY DEFALCO.

Marriage Encounter - English—CATHY MAURER; STEVE MAURER.

Marriage Encounter - Spanish—SALVADOR GONZALES; DOLORES GONZALES.

Vietnamese Community Couples Retreat—Mr. PETER NHUE NGUYEN; Mrs. PETER NHUE NGUYEN, Vietnamese Catholic Center, 1538 Century Blvd., Santa Ana, 92703-1301. Tel: 714-554-4211.

Retrouvaille - English—BRIAN CHU; DINAH CHU; LARRY HERICH; ELLEN HERICH.

Retrouvaille - Spanish—ANGELES JUAREZ; ARNULFO JUAREZ; FRANCISCO LEYVA; ESPERANZA LEYVA.

Office of Hispanic Ministry—Sr. LETICIA SALAZAR, O.D.N., Dir., Office: Marywood Center.

Holy Childhood—Rev. Msgr. JOHN F. SAMMON, P.A., Dir., Office: Marywood Center.

Holy Name Society—Rev. Msgr. JOHN F. SAMMON, P.A., Dir., Office: Marywood Center.

Risk Management and Insurance Services—Mr. MICHAEL SHAFFER, Dir., Office: Marywood Center.

Legion of Mary—Rev. Msgr. HUGH O'CONNOR (Retired), Res.: 2050 W. Ball Rd., Anaheim, 92804. Tel: 714-774-2595.

Worship—Mrs. LESA TRUXAW, Dir., Office: Marywood Center.

Evangelization—MARIA BARRIENTOS, Dir., Office: Marywood Center.

Respect Life Program NCCB—Rev. Msgr. JOHN F. SAMMON, P.A., Dir., Office: Marywood Center.

Catecumenate—Mrs. LESA TRUXAW, Dir., Office: Marywood Center.

Stewardship Office—BARBARA NELSON, Dir., Office: Marywood Center.

Development Office—Rev. Msgr. LAWRENCE BAIRD, Office: Marywood Center.

Perpetual Adoration Programs—Rev. Msgr. JOHN SAMMON, Dir., Office: Marywood Center.

Victim Assistance Coordinator—DIANE GOMEZ-VALENZUELA. Tel: 714-293-9050. Email: dgomezval@cs.com.

CLERGY, PARISHES, MISSIONS AND PAROCHIAL SCHOOLS

CITY OF ORANGE

1—CATHEDRAL OF THE HOLY FAMILY (1921), Very Rev. Donald Romito, Rector; Rev. Robert Capone; Deacon Joseph Esparza.
Res.: 566 S. Glassell St., 92866. Tel: 714-639-2900; Fax: 714-639-8022.
School—530 S. Glassell St., 92866. Tel: 714-538-6012; Fax: 714-633-5892. Lay Teachers 25; Students 600.
Catechesis/Religious Program—Tel: 714-538-2800; Fax: 714-633-6769. Students 1,137.

2—LA PURISIMA (1964), Revs. Christopher Heath; Ismael Silva; Ahn Nguyen; Deacons Anthony Bube; Juan Espinoza; Richard Lovett.
Res.: 11712 N. Hewes, 92869. Tel: 714-633-5800; Fax: 714-633-8364.
School—Tel: 714-633-5411; Fax: 714-633-1588. Kathleen Manulkin, Prin. Lay Teachers 19; Students 306.
Catechesis/Religious Program—Tel: 714-633-5344; Fax: 714-633-1588. Students 971.

3—ST. NORBERT (1963), Rev. Msgr. John Urell; Rev. John Monestero. In Res., Most Rev. Peter Esterka; Deacon Timothy Carver.
Res.: 300 E. Taft Ave., 92865. Tel: 714-637-4360; Fax: 714-637-0201.
School—Tel: 714-637-6822. Lay Teachers 11; Students 291.
Catechesis/Religious Program—Tel: 714-998-1070. Carmen Estrada, D.R.E.; Edith Marik, D.R.E. Students 775.

ORANGE COUNTY OUTSIDE THE CITY

ALISO VIEJO, CORPUS CHRISTI, Rev. Fred Bailey.
6 "A" Liberty, Ste. 100, 92656. Tel: 949-389-9008; Fax: 949-831-6540.
Catechesis/Religious Program—Students 292.

ANAHEIM

1—ST. ANTHONY CLARET (1955), Rev. Rudolph J. Preciado; Rev. Msgr. James F. Nash, Pastor Emeritus (Retired); Revs. John Paul Hopping; Josephat Ddungu.
Res.: 1450 E. La Palma Ave., 92805. Tel: 714-776-0270; Fax: 714-776-6022.
School—Tel: 714-535-3284; Fax: 714-535-8558. Lay Teachers 12; Students 185.
Catechesis/Religious Program—Tel: 714-778-0580; 714-778-1399 Spanish; Fax: 714-956-2701. Margarita Navarro; Leonard Beckman, D.R.E. Students 1,124.

2—ST. BONIFACE (1987), Revs. Timothy Freyer; Armando Virrey; Thomas DeNguyen.
Res.: 120 N. Janss St., 92805. Tel: 714-956-3110; Fax: 714-956-3034.
School—500 W. Chartres St., 92805. Tel: 714-772-3060; Fax: 714-956-5170. Dominican Sisters (Mission San Jose) O.P. 1; Lay Teachers 14; Students 256.
Catechesis/Religious Program—Tel: 714-956-3461; Fax: 714-956-3060. Students 1,587.

3—ST. JUSTIN MARTYR (1958), Rev. Joseph Nettekoven; Rev. Msgr. Hugh O'Connor, Pastor Emeritus (Retired); Revs. Joseph Droessler; Efrain Flores; Deacon Raymond Duthoy. In Res., Rev. John Monestero.
Res.: 2050 W. Ball Rd., 92804. Tel: 714-774-2595; Fax: 714-774-9849.
Church: Ball Rd. and Empire, 92804.
School—2030 W. Ball Rd., 92804. Tel: 714-772-4902; Fax: 714-772-2092. Lay Teachers 15; Students 210.
Catechesis/Religious Program—Students 349.
Mission—Sacred Heart 10852 Harcourt, Orange Co. 92804. Tel: 714-821-3133.

4—SAN ANTONIO (1977), Revs. Seamus A. Glynn; Sy Uy Nguyen. In Res., Deacon Doug Cook.
Res.: 5800 E. Santa Ana Canyon Rd., 92807. Tel: 714-974-1416; Fax: 714-974-9630.
School—Tel: 714-695-3700; Fax: 714-695-3704. Please see St. Francis of Assisi School located under Multi-Parish Schools in the Institution Section.
Catechesis/Religious Program—Tel: 714-974-2053. Carolyn Buehler, D.R.E. Students 1,452.

BREA, ST. ANGELA MERICI (1962), Rev. Theodore Olson; Rev. Msgr. Emmett McCarthy, Pastor Emeritus; Rev. Bill T. Cao; Deacons Tom McGuine; Carlos Navarro.
Res.: 585 Walnut St., 92821. Tel: 714-529-1821; Fax: 714-529-0569.
Church: Walnut and Fir, 92821.
School—575 S. Walnut Ave., 92821. Tel: 714-529-6372; Fax: 714-529-7755. Religious 1; Lay Teachers 16; Students 283.

Catechesis/Religious Program—Tel: 714-529-2311. Students 815.

Buena Park, St. Pius V (1948), Revs. Thomas McManus, O.S.A.; Thomas Tevington, O.S.A.; John Grace, O.S.A.; Patrick A. Brennan, O.S.A.; Ray Elam, O.S.A. (SD).
Res.: 7691 Orangethorpe Ave., 90621. Tel: 714-522-2193; Fax: 714-522-1730.
School—Tel: 714-522-5313; Fax: 714-522-1767. Lay Teachers 21; Students 615.
Catechesis/Religious Program—Tel: 714-522-3971. Students 650.

Capistrano Beach, San Felipe de Jesus (1950), (Hispanic), Rev. John A. Bradley; Rev. Msgr. John V. Coffield, Pastor Emeritus (Retired); Deacon Victor Samano.
Res.: 27526 Paseo Verano, San Juan Capistrano, 92675-5314. Tel: 949-661-7500; Fax: 949-661-7500.
Church: Domingo St. & Sepulveda, 92624.
Catechesis/Religious Program—Students 214.

Costa Mesa

1—St. Joachim (1947), Revs. Joseph R. Robillard; George Blais; Augustin Escobar.
Res.: 1964 Orange Ave., 92627. Tel: 949-574-7400; Fax: 949-574-7407.
School—Tel: 949-574-7411, Ext. 316; Fax: 949-646-8948. Lay Teachers 12; Students 272; Teacher's Aides 5; Day Care Personnel 4.
Catechesis/Religious Program—Tel: 949-574-7400; Fax: 949-575-7407. Students 685.

2—St. John the Baptist (1960), Revs. Martin Benzoni, O.Praem; Philip Smith, O.Praem; Vincent Gilmore, O.Praem; Pascal Bao Nguyen, O.Praem. In Res., Rev. Luke S. Laslavich, O.Praem.
Res.: 1015 Baker St., 92626. Tel: 714-540-2214; Fax: 714-540-5902.
School—Tel: 714-557-5060; Fax: 714-557-9263. Sr. M. Vianney Ennis, S.M., Prin. Sisters of Mercy 1; Lay Teachers 22; Students 600.
Catechesis/Religious Program—Tel: 714-546-4102. Sisters Sharon Richards, S.D.S.H., D.R.E.; Tam Thoy Huang, L.H.C., D.R.E.; Elvira Diaz, D.R.E. Students 680.

Cypress, St. Irenaeus (1961), Revs. Patrick Rudolph; Joseph D. Fenton, S.M.; Deacon Jose Campos.
Res.: 5201 Evergreen Ave., 90630. Tel: 714-826-0760; Fax: 714-826-1608.
School—9201 Grindlay St., 90630. Tel: 714-827-4500; Fax: 714-827-2930. Sisters 2; Lay Teachers 23; Students 558.
Catechesis/Religious Program—9211 Grindlay St., 90630. Tel: 714-826-1140; Fax: 714-826-1608. Students 809.

Dana Point, St. Edward (1969), Revs. Steve Sallot; Steven Correz; Deacon Jesse Michel.
Res.: 33926 Calle La Primavera, 92629. Tel: 949-496-1307; Fax: 949-496-1557.
School—33866 Calle La Primavera, 92629. Tel: 949-496-1241; Fax: 949-496-1819. Lay Teachers 19; Students 520.
Catechesis/Religious Program—Tel: 949-496-6011. Students 900.

El Toro, Santiago de Compostela (1979), Revs. David Gruver; Gilberto Escobedo.
Res.: 21682 Lake Forest Dr., Lake Forest, 92630. Tel: 949-951-8599; Fax: 949-951-2687.
School—Tel: 949-888-1990; Fax: 949-888-1994. Please see Serra Catholic School located under Multi-Parish schools, in the Institution Section.
Catechesis/Religious Program—Tel: 949-951-0792; Fax: 949-951-2687. Students 868.

Fountain Valley, Holy Spirit (1972), Revs. Mario F. Rebamontan; Joseph Tuan Pham; Sean Condon; Deacons Jerry Dao; William Cobbett.
Res.: 17270 Ward St., 92708. Tel: 714-963-1811; Fax: 714-968-1775.
Catechesis/Religious Program—Tel: 714-963-7871; Fax: 714-968-1775. Sisters Anna Tom, D.R.E.; Agnes Thuah Hoang, D.R.E. Students 741.

Fullerton

1—St. Juliana Falconieri (1965), Revs. Jude M. Herlihy, O.S.M.; Luke Stano, O.S.M.; Patrick J. Donovan, O.S.M., Chap. (California State Univ. - Newman Club); Deacons William Schlater; Jay L. Milam; Gerhard P. Stadel.
Office—1319 N. Acacia Ave., 92831. Tel: 714-879-1965; Fax: 714-526-6673.
Res.: 1316 N. Acacia Ave., 92831. Tel: 714-879-1965.
School—1320 N. Acacia Ave., 92831. Tel: 714-871-2829; Fax: 714-871-8465. Lay Teachers 9; Students 320; Part-Time Teachers 8.
Catechesis/Religious Program—Students 257.

2—St. Mary's (1912), Revs. James C. Ries; Salvador Landa; Deacons Carlos Gonzalez; Manuel Chavira.
Res.: 400 W. Commonwealth Ave., 92832. Tel: 714-525-2500; Fax: 714-525-3837.
School— Please see St. Philip Benizi, Fullerton for details.
Catechesis/Religious Program—Tel: 714-992-5070. Students 570.

3—St. Philip Benizi (1958), Revs. Ignatius M. Kissel, O.S.M. (CHI); Manuel Maya, O.S.M.; Justin M. Pisciotta, O.S.M.; Deacons Jack Brennan; Richard Glaudini; Fidel Rodriguez.
Res.: 235 S. Pine Dr., 92833-3294. Tel: 714-871-3610; Fax: 714-871-5827.
School—215 S. Pine Dr., 92833-3293. Tel: 714-871-6121; Fax: 714-992-4167. Roman Fernando, Admin.; Mrs. Dolan, Prin. Religious 1; Lay Teachers 16; Students 269.
Catechesis/Religious Program—Tel: 714-870-0561. Ms. Carmelita Yanez, D.R.E. Students 514.

Garden Grove

1—St. Callistus (1961), Revs. Tuyen Nguyen; Ramon Cisneros; Jude Lucier O. Praem; Viet-Peter Ho.
Res.: 12921 Lewis St., 92840. Tel: 714-971-2141; Fax: 714-971-9112.
Church: Garden Grove Blvd. and Lewis St., 92840.
School—St. Callistus Preschool, 12132 Faster St., 92840. Tel 714-750-6777.
School—12901 Lewis St., 92840. Tel: 714-971-2023; Fax: 714-971-2031. Lay Teachers 21; Students 323.
Catechesis/Religious Program—Tel: 714-971-2091. Maureen Ross, D.R.E. Students 1,683.

2—St. Columban (1953), Revs. Juan Caboboy; Miguel A. Hernandez; Quang Chu; Joseph Luan Nguyen; Deacons Robert Kelleher; Anthony Carrasco. In Res., Rev Michael Heher.
Res.: 10801 Stanford Ave., 92840. Tel: 714-534-1174; Fax: 714-534-1937.
School—10855 Stanford Ave., 92840. Tel: 714-534-3947; Fax: 714-590-9153. Religious Sisters of Charity 1; Lay Teachers 13; Students 263.
Catechesis/Religious Program—Tel: 714-537-2015. Students 1,500.

Huntington Beach

1—St. Bonaventure (1965), Revs. Bruce Patterson; Douglas Dale; Raphael Xuan Nguyen; John R. Keller (Retired); Deacons Matt Calabrese; Vincent Tran.
Res.: 16400 Springdale St., 92649. Tel: 714-846-3350; 714-846-3359; Fax: 714-840-0430.
School—Tel: 714-846-2472; Fax: 714-840-0498. Union of the Sisters of the Presentation of the Blessed Virgin Mary 6; Lay Teachers 24; Students 638.
Catechesis/Religious Program—16377 Bradbury Ln., 92647. Tel: 714-846-2472. Virginia Curley, D.R.E. Students 1,160.

2—St. Mary's by the Sea (1977), Revs. Daniel Johnson; Eamon Mackin, C.H.S.
Res.: 321 10th St., 92648. Tel: 714-536-6913; Fax: 714-536-2464.
Catechesis/Religious Program—Students 102.

3—SS. Simon and Jude (1912), Revs. Christian Mondor, O.F.M.; Michael L. Harvey, O.F.M. In Res., Revs. Emery Tang, O.F.M.; Alex Manville, O.F.M. (LA) Sr. Maureen Sheehan, B.V.M. Pastoral Assoc.
Res. 20444 Magnolia St., 92646. Tel: 714-962-3333; Fax: 714-965-6456.
School—Tel: 714-962-4451; Fax: 714-968-1329. Lay Teachers 36; Students 687.
Catechesis/Religious Program—Tel: 714-963-0014. Ernesto Zamora Gallardo, D.R.E. Students 696.

4—St. Vincent de Paul (1977), Revs. Antonio Lopez; Jerome T. Karcher; Deacons Scotty Bourne; Fred Canlas.
Res.: 8345 Talbert Ave., 92646. Tel: 714-842-3000; Fax: 714-842-6780.
Catechesis/Religious Program—Tel: 714-842-3000; Fax: 714-842-6780. Students 315.

Irvine

1—St. Elizabeth Ann Seton (1976), Rev. Thomas Pado.
Res.: 9 Hillgate, 92612-3265. Tel: 949-854-1000; Fax: 949-854-0079.
Catechesis/Religious Program—Students 392.

2—St. John Neumann (1978), Revs. Colm Conlon; John E. Shetler; Ray Skonezny.
Res.: 5101 Alton Pkwy., 92604-8605. Tel: 949-559-4006; Fax: 949-857-4788.
Catechesis/Religious Program—Tel: 949-786-6105; Fax: 949-786-6102. Sr. Maria Lai, D.R.E. Students 700.

3—St. Thomas More (1996), Rev. John E. Janze. In Res., Rev. William Krekelberg.
Res.: 14010 Remington, 92620-3212. Tel: 949-551-8601; Fax: 949-551-5879.
Catechesis/Religious Program—Tel: 949-551-8029; Fax: 949-551-5879. Students 590.

La Habra, Our Lady of Guadalupe (1947), Revs. Justin H. MacCarthy; Matthew M. Munoz.
Res.: 900 W. La Habra Blvd. 90631. Tel: 562-691-0533; Fax: 562-694-8328.
School—Tel: 562-697-9726; Fax: 562-905-0095. Sisters of St. Joseph of Orange 1; Lay Teachers 20; Students 453.
Catechesis/Religious Program—Tel: 562-691-2104; Fax: 562-697-6391. Students 670.

Laguna Beach, St. Catherine of Siena (1923), Rev. Eamon T. O'Gorman. In Res., Rev. Thomas J. McIntyre, C.M.
Res.: 990 Temple Ter., 92651. Tel: 949-494-9701; Fax: 949-497-2610.
School—3090 S. Coast Hwy., 92651. Tel: 949-494-7339; Fax: 949-376-5752. Lay Teachers 13; Students 277.
Catechesis/Religious Program—Tel: 949-499-5876. Students 276.

Laguna Hills, St. Nicholas (1965), Revs. Richard A. Delahunty; Tuan John Nguyen; Deacons Ray Havert; Michael Fletcher.
Res.: 24252 El Toro Rd., Laguna Woods, 92653. Tel: 949-837-1090; Fax: 949-837-9510.
Catechesis/Religious Program—Tel: 949-837-7676. Students 460.

Laguna Niguel, St. Timothy (1980), Revs. Bruce Lavery; Donald Kolda, S.J.; Deacon Ed Salgado.
Res.: 29102 Crown Valley Pkwy., 92677. Tel: 949-249-4091; Fax: 949-249-4094.
Catechesis/Religious Program—Tel: 949-495-4126. Students 768.

Los Alamitos, St. Hedwig (1960), Revs. Kenneth A. Schmit; Roy Kim.
Res.: 11482 Los Alamitos Blvd., 90720. Tel: 562-430-0509; Fax: 562-431-9989.
School—Tel: 562-431-5001; Fax: 562-799-1791. Lay Teachers 26; Students 514.
Catechesis/Religious Program—Tel: 562-493-2521. Students 608.

Mission Viejo, St. Kilian (1970), Rev. James P. Dunning; Deacon Dick Naumann.
Res.: 26872 Estanciero Dr., 92691. Tel: 949-586-4440; Fax: 949-454-1043.
School—Tel: 949-888-1990; Fax: 949-888-1994. Please see Serra Catholic School located under Multi-Parish Schools, in the Institution Section.
Catechesis/Religious Program—Tel: 949-586-4550; Fax: 949-454-1043. Marcia Burns, D.R.E. Students 1,150.

Newport Beach

1—Our Lady of Mount Carmel (1923), Rev. Msgr. Daniel J. Murray, J.C.L.; Rev. Patrick A. Doherty.
Res.: 1441 W. Balboa Blvd., 92661-1010. Tel: 949-673-3775; Fax: 949-673-3137.
Catechesis/Religious Program—Tel: 949-673-2719; Fax: 949-673-3137. Students 250.

2—Our Lady Queen of Angels (1953), Rev. Msgr. William McLaughlin; Revs. Joseph Phien Nguyen; Paul F. Bradley, S.S.C.; Deacon Charlie Boyer.
Res.: 2046 Mar Vista Dr., 92660. Tel: 949-644-0200; Fax: 949-644-1349.
School—750 Domingo Dr., 92660. Tel: 949-644-1166; Fax: 949-644-6213. Lay Teachers 20; Students 350.
Catechesis/Religious Program—Tel: 949-219-1497; Fax: 949-644-1349. Students 643.
Chapel—St. John Vianney, Tel: 714-675-2221. Rev. Msgr. Lawrence J. Baird.

Placentia, St. Joseph (1953), Revs. Timothy Ramaekers; Benjamin Benedicto; Deacon Ed Faulk; Rev. Thomas Keller, M.S.C.; Deacon Jorge Ramirez.
Res.: 717 N. Bradford Ave., 92870-4515. Tel: 714-528-1487; Fax: 714-579-3791.
School—801 N. Bradford Ave., 92870-4515. Tel: 714-528-1794; Fax: 714-528-0668. Lay Teachers 21; Students 300.
Catechesis/Religious Program—Tel: 714-528-1487; Fax: 714-579-3791. Teri Kleckner, D.R.E.; Eloisa Ramirez, D.R.E. (Spanish). Students 826.
Mission—St. Theresa Chapel 636 Van Buren Ave., Atwood, Orange Co. 92811.

Rancho Santa Margarita, San Francisco Solano Church (1989), Revs. Craig M. Butters; Bao Q. Thai; Sr. Barbara Reder, S.P., Pastoral Assoc.
Res.: 22082 Antonio Pkwy., 92688-1993. Tel: 949-589-7767; Fax: 949-589-7768.
School—Serra Catholic School, 23652 Antonio Pkwy., 92688-1993. Tel: 949-888-1990; Fax: 949-888-1994. Angeline Trudell, Prin. Lay Teachers 51; Students 910; Total Staff 128.
Catechesis/Religious Program—Tel: 949-589-1709; Fax: 949-589-2840. Students 1,300.

San Clemente, Our Lady of Fatima (1947), Revs. Jack Sewell; Reynold Furrell; Rev. Msgr. Anthony McGowan, Pastor Emeritus.
Res.: 105 La Esperanza, 92672. Tel: 949-492-4101; Fax: 949-492-4856.
School—Tel: 949-492-7320; Fax: 949-492-3793. Lay Teachers 13; Students 313.
Catechesis/Religious Program—Tel: 949-492-4101; Fax: 949-492-4856. Students 454.

San Juan Capistrano, Mission Basilica (1776), [CEM] Very Rev. Arthur Holquin; Rev. Gregory Marquez; Deacons Joseph Halka; David Sire; Charles Stanton. In Res., Rev. Joseph Scerbo, S.A.
Res.: 31520 Camino Capistrano, 92675. Tel: 949-234-1360; Fax: 949-248-2008 (Parish Office).
School—Tel: 949-234-1385; Fax: 949-248-2178. Lay Teachers 17; Students 371.
Catechesis/Religious Program—Tel: 949-234-1370; Fax: 949-248-2056. Linda Berkshire, D.R.E.

Students 1,090.

SANTA ANA

1—ST. ANNE'S (1923), (Hispanic), Most Rev. Cirilo B. Flores; Revs. Michael Galinada, S.M.; Timothy Peters; Deacons Carlos Euyoque; Francisco Martinez.
Res.: 109 Borchard Ave., P.O. Box 2425, 92707. Tel: 714-835-7434; Fax: 714-835-4506.
School—Tel: 714-542-9328; Fax: 714-542-3431. Sisters 3; Lay Teachers 14; Students 293.
Catechesis/Religious Program—Tel: 714-542-1213; Fax: 714-542-6608. Students 823.

2—ST. BARBARA'S (1962), Revs. Richard C. Kennedy; Antonio Zapata; Vincent Hung Pham; Joseph Truc Dinh, S.D.B.
Res.: 730 S. Euclid St., 92704. Tel: 714-775-7733; Fax: 714-775-9467.
School—Tel: 714-775-9477; Fax: 714-775-9468. Lay Teachers 21; Students 480.
Catechesis/Religious Program—Tel: 714-775-9475. Students 1,725.

3—IMMACULATE HEART OF MARY (1960), Revs. Enrique J. Sera; Alfonso Garcia-Espino; Rafael Echevarria; Deacon Gerardo de Santos. In Res., Rev. Ignatius Lau (Retired).
Res.: 1100 S. Center St., 92704. Tel: 714-751-5335.
School—Tel: 714-545-8185; Fax: 714-545-2362. Lay Teachers 4; Students 100.
Catechesis/Religious Program—Tel: 714-546-5186. Students 1,338.

4—ST. JOSEPH'S (1887), Revs. Christopher H. Smith; Cesar Salazar.
Res.: 727 Minter St., 92701. Tel: 714-542-4411; Fax: 714-542-9770.
School—Tel: 714-542-2704; Fax: 714-542-2132. Lay Teachers 12; Students 261.
Catechesis/Religious Program—Tel: 714-550-8096; Fax: 714-245-2319. Students 973.

5—OUR LADY OF GUADALUPE (1927), (Hispanic), Rev. Alonso Caceres.
Res.: 541 E. Central Ave., 92707. Tel: 714-540-0902; Fax: 714-540-3053.
Catechesis/Religious Program—Tel: 714-540-9231. Rosa Castro, D.R.E. Students 1,160.

6—OUR LADY OF GUADALUPE (1938), (Hispanic), Revs. Ramon Gaitan, O.A.R.; Paul Goni, O.A.R.; Deacon Miguel Gonzalez.
Res.: 1322 E. Third St., 92701. Tel: 714-836-4142; Fax: 714-836-7417.
Catechesis/Religious Program—Tel: 714-835-8933. Margarita Garza, D.R.E. Students 1,486.

7—OUR LADY OF LA VANG (1985), (Hispanic), Rev. William Barman.
Res.: 5021 W. 16th St., 92703. Tel: 714-636-3260; Fax: 714-539-0783.
Catechesis/Religious Program—Students 343.

8—OUR LADY OF THE PILLAR (1965), (Hispanic), Revs. Alfredo de Dios, O.A.R.; Gabino Perez; Jose Luis Jimenez; Deacon Ulises Feliciano, O.A.R. In Res., Revs. Joachim Goni, O.A.R.; Luis Eduardo Ramirez, O.A.R.
Res.: 1622 W. 6th St., 92703. Tel: 714-543-1700; Fax: 714-543-9640.
School—601 N. Western Ave., 92703. Tel: 714-542-5177; Fax: 714-541-5748.
Catechesis/Religious Program—Tel: 714-542-4684. Students 1,600.

SEAL BEACH

1—ST. ANNE'S (1921), Rev. Robert S. Vidal; Rev. Msgr. Michael Collins, Pastor Emeritus.
Res.: 340 Tenth St., 90740. Tel: 562-431-0721; Fax: 562-431-3050.
Catechesis/Religious Program—Tel: 562-431-8524; Fax: 562-431-3050. Students 95.

2—HOLY FAMILY (1969), Rev. Msgrs. Brian Coghlan; James J. Pierse, Pastor Emeritus (Retired).
Res.: 13900 Church Pl., 90740. Tel: 562-430-8170; Fax: 562-493-4643.

STANTON, ST. POLYCARP (1961), Revs. Edward Poettgen; Gabriel Ramirez; Binh Nguyen; Deacons Javier Antunez; Ramiro Lopez. In Res., Rev. Matthias Ho (Retired).
Res.: 8100 Chapman Ave., 90680. Tel: 714-893-2766; Fax: 714-898-6675.
School—8182 Chapman Ave., 90680. Tel: 714-893-8882; Fax: 714-897-3357. Lay Teachers 9; Students 185.
Catechesis/Religious Program—Tel: 714-892-3158. Students 559.

TUSTIN, ST. CECILIA (1957), (Spanish—Vietnamese), Revs. Timothy MacCarthy; John P. McAndrew; Kiem Van Tran; Deacons Domingo Garza; Jon Schlemmer.
Res.: 1301 Sycamore, 92780. Tel: 714-544-3250; Fax: 714-838-1996.
School—Tel: 714-544-1533; Fax: 714-544-0643. Lay Teachers 20; Students 344.
Catechesis/Religious Program—Tel: 714-838-4466. Students 950.

WESTMINSTER, BLESSED SACRAMENT (1947), Revs. James Hartnett; Scott C. Nguyen (WCH); Robert Wiley; David Vuelvas-Arias; Deacons Arturo Gimenez; Joseph Stripling.
Res.: 14072 S. Olive St., 92683. Tel: 714-892-4489; Fax: 714-892-5560.
School—14146 S. Olive St., 92683. Tel: 714-893-7701; Fax: 714-891-7186. Roisin McAree, Prin. Lay Teachers 16; Students 298.
Catechesis/Religious Program—14144 S. Olive St., 92683. Tel: 714-897-2142; Fax: 714-892-5560. Ana Marie Gimenez, D.R.E. Students 1,195.

YORBA LINDA

1—ST. MARTIN (1970), Revs. Joseph Knerr; John T. Hiltz (Retired); James Overend; Deacon Frank Chavez.
Res.: 19767 Yorba Linda Blvd., 92886. Tel: 714-970-2771; Fax: 714-970-5654.
School—*St. Francis of Assisi*, 5330 Eastside Cir., 92887. Tel: 714-695-3700; Fax: 714-695-3704. Debra Declues, Prin. Lay Teachers 30; Students 585; Total Staff 50.
Catechesis/Religious Program—Tel: 714-970-2521; Fax: 714-970-5654. Pam Bender, D.R.E.; Cindy Piszyk, D.R.E. (Adult); David Glaudini, D.R.E. (Youth). Students 862.

2—SANTA CLARA DE ASIS, Rev. Michael Hanifin.
Mailing Address: 22605 E. La Palma Ave., Ste. 509, 92887-6713. Tel: 714-692-5030; Fax: 714-692-5380.
Catechesis/Religious Program—Tel: 714-692-5030; Fax: 714-692-5380. Students 175.

Chaplains Of Public Institutions

ORANGE. *Orange County Medical Center*, 101 The City Dr. S., 92868. Tel: 714-634-5678. (Served by St. Callistus Parish.)
12921 Lewis St., Garden Grove, 92840. Tel: 714-971-2141.

COSTA MESA. *Fairview Developmental Center*, 2501 Harbor, 92626. Tel: 714-545-9331. Mary Brosseau.

SANTA ANA. *All Adult and Juvenile Jail Facilities*, 2112 N. Main St., Ste. 290, 92706. Tel: 714-547-7082. Revs. Clif Marquis, S.T., Nicholas Barille, S.T.

Special Assignment:
Rev. Msgr.—
Sammon, John F., P.A., Vicar for Pastoral & Community Affairs
Revs.—
Cook, Douglas, Dir., Polish Center, Yorba Linda
Hoan, Michael, Dir., Vietnamese Center, 1538 N. Century Blvd., 92703. Tel: 714-554-4211
Hogan, John, S.S.C., Dir., Korean Center, 7655 Trask Ave., Westminster, 92683.
Kim, Alex, St. Thomas Korean Catholic Center, Anaheim, 92801-6710.
McKiernan, J. Michael, Sec. to the Bishop & Dir. of Clergy Personnel Marywood Center
Moreland, J. Gordon, S.J., Dir., House of Prayer for Priests, 7734 Santiago Canyon Rd., 92869.

On Duty Outside the Diocese:
Revs.—
Hopcus, Daniel, St. Mary of the Woods, IN 47876-1089.
Puhlman, Robert, Our Lady of Las Vegas, 3104 Alta Dr., Las Vegas, NV 89107.
Rudolph, Patrick, P.O. Box 31356, Las Vegas, NV 89173-1356.

Military Chaplains:
Revs.—
Fry, James Q.
Shimotsu, John M.
Sweeney, Kevin

Absent on Sick Leave:
Revs.—
DiStefano, Joseph
Ha, Thomas Do Thanh (Retired)
Karp, Joseph A.
Kinzer, Gary
Kolberg, Lawrence R.
Monestero, John

Inactive Leave:
Revs.—
Duffin, Stephen
Sun Kim, Simon Chung

Education Leave:
Revs.—
Moses, Patrick
Nguyen, Michael

Administrative Leave:
Rev. Msgrs.—
Murray, Daniel J., J.C.L.
Tanilong, Gerardo J.
Revs.—
Henson, Jerome
Nguyen, Dominic
Salazar, Cesar

Sabbatical:
Rev.—
Luevano, Rafael

Retired:
Most Rev.—
McFarland, Norman F.
Rev. Msgrs.—
Campbell, John
Coffield, John V.
Collins, Michael
Falvey, Sinon
Keenan, John C.
Martin, Paul M.
McCarthy, Emmett
McGowan, Anthony
Nash, James F.
O'Connor, Hugh
Pierse, James J.
Scannell, Peter
Tien, Peter
Revs.—
Chinh, Peter
Croal, Thomas
Fee, Pat
Ho, Matthias
Joyce, John M.
Keller, J. Rod
Lau, Ignatius
Luongo, John
Lyons, Denis
Sheahan, John A.
Vu, Joachim

Permanent Deacons:
Antunez, Jay, St. Polycarp, Stanton
Barth, John, On Duty Outside the Diocese
Bourne, Scotty, St. Vincent de Paul
Boyer, Charles, Our Lady Queen of Angels
Brenes-Rios, Anthony, Our Lady of Guadalupe, La Habra
Brennan, John, St. Philip Benizi, Fullerton
Bube, Anthony, La Purisima, Orange
Calabrese, Matt, St. Bonaventure, Huntington Beach
Campos, Jose, St. Ireaneus, Cypress
Canlas, Fred, St. Vincent de Paul, Huntington Beach
Carrasco, Anthony, St. Columban, Garden Grove
Carver, Timothy, St. Norbert, Orange
Chavez, Frank, St. Martin de Porres, Yorba Linda
Chavira, Manuel, St. Mary, Fullerton
Cobbett, William, Holy Spirit, Fountain Valley
Cook, Douglas, San Antonio de Padua, Anaheim Hills
Coughlin, Charles, St. Thomas More, Irvine
Dao, Jerry, Holy Spirit, Fountain Valley
Davis, Clyde, St. Boniface, Anaheim
Dennis, Irving, On Duty Outside the Diocese
DeSantos, Gerardo, Immaculate Heart of Mary, Santa Ana
Devore, Robert, Corpus Christi, Aliso Viejo
Duthoy, Raymond, St. Justin Martyr, Anaheim
Erwin, Glenn, Our Lady of Mt. Carmel, Newport Beach
Esparza, Joseph, Holy Family Cathedral
Espinoza, Juan, La Purisima, Orange
Esposito, Robert, (On Duty Outside the Diocese)
Euyoque, Carlos, St. Anne, Santa Ana
Faulk, Edward, St. Joseph, Placentia
Fletcher, Michael, St. Nicholas, Laguna Woods
Garza, Domingo, St. Cecilia, Tustin
Gimenez, Arturo, Blessed Sacrament, Westminster
Glaudini, Richard, St. Philip Benizi, Fullerton
Gonzales, Carlos, St. Mary, Fullerton
Gonzalez, Miguel, St. Bonaventure and Our Lady of Guadalupe
Halka, Joseph, Mission Basilica San Juan Capistrano (Tuscon)
Havert, Raymond, St. Nicholas, Laguna Hills
Hurst, Larry, St. Hedwig, Los Alamitos
Jensen, Don, St. Thomas More, Irvine
Jones, Wesley, St. Boniface, Anaheim
Kelleher, Robert, St. Columban, Garden Grove
Lee, Moon Chul, Korean Martyrs
Leon, Ramon, St. Justin Martyr, Anaheim
Lopez, Ramiro, St. Polycarp, Stanton
Lovett, Richard, La Purisima, Orange
Luna, Frank, Catholic Deaf Center, Orange
Mackey, Robert, San Antonio de Padua, Anaheim
Martinez, Francisco, St. Anne, Santa Ana
McGuine, Thomas, St. Angela Merici, Brea (Milwaukee)
Melton, Harold, On Duty Outside the Diocese
Meyer, Leon, St. Cecilia, Tustin
Michel, Jesse, St. Edwards, Dana Point
Milam, Jay, St. Juliana Falconieri, Fullerton

Miller, Gerald, On Duty Outside the Diocese
Mutz, Steve, Our Lady of Mt. Carmel, Newport Beach
Myers, Paul, On Duty Outside the Diocese
Naumann, Richard, St. Kilian (Santa Rosa)
Navarro, Carlos, St. Angela Merici, Brea
Porcella, Roger, On Duty Outside the Diocese
Pyne, Gerald, Our Lady of Guadalupe, La Habra
Ramirez, Jorge, St. Joseph, Placentia
Reynoso, Jose Luis, St. Boniface, Anaheim
Richeson, James, (On Duty Outside the Diocese)
Rivera, Manuel, Anchorage; (On Leave of Absence)
Rodriguez, Fidel, St. Philip Benizi, Fullerton
Romero, Rafael, St. Callistus, Garden Grove
Salgado, Fernando, St. Timothy, Laguna Niguel
Samano, Victor, San Felipe de Jesus, Capistrano Beach
Schlater, William, St. Juliana Falconieri, Fullerton
Schlemmer, Jon, St. Cecilia, Tustin
Seagraves, Veral M. N., St. John Vianney Chapel, Balboa
Sire, David, Mission San Juan Capistrano, San Juan Capistrano
Song, Thomas, St. Thomas Korean Center. Anaheim
Stadel, Gerhard P., St. Juliana Falconieri, Fullerton
Stanton, Charles, Mission Basilica San Juan Capistrano (Santa Rosa)
Stripling, Joseph, Blessed Sacrament, Westminster
Sullivan, Neill, Our Lady Queen of Angels, Newport Beach
Swift, Bernard, (Retired)
Tran, Vincent, St. Bonaventure
vonVoigt, Fred, (On Duty Outside the Diocese)
Yang, William, Hmong Community
Zambrano, Jose, On Duty Outside the Diocese

INSTITUTIONS LOCATED IN THE DIOCESE

[A] SEMINARIES AND SCHOLASTICATES FOR RELIGIOUS

MIDWAY CITY. *St. Patrick's Novitiate and Scholasticate*, 7820 Bolsa Ave., 92655. Tel: 714-897-8181; Fax: 714-898-9020. Email: BrosStPatrick@aol.com. Conducted by the Brothers of St. Patrick Brothers 4.

SILVERADO. *St. Michael's Norbertine Postulancy, Novitiate and Juniorate*, 19292 El Toro Rd., 92676. Tel: 949-858-0222; Fax: 949-858-4583. Rt. Rev. Eugene J. Hayes, O.Praem., Abbot; Revs. Thomas W. Nelson, O.Praem., Dir. Formation; Augustine R. Puchner, O.Praem., Asst. Dir. Formation; Very Rev. Hugh C. Barbour, O.Praem., Ph.D., Prof. Philosophy; Revs. John E. Caronan, O.Praem., Prof. Latin; Gregory M. Dick, O.Praem., Prof. Scripture. Conducted by the Norbertine Fathers, For listing of other Norbertine priests working in the Diocese, refer to St. Michael College Prep High School. Priests 6; Total Enrollment 18.

[B] COLLEGES AND UNIVERSITIES

ORANGE. *St. Joseph College, Orange* Branch Campus of University of San Francisco; St. Joseph Library. , 480 S. Batavia St., 92868. Tel: 714-633-8121; Fax: 714-744-3166. Sr. Anne Hennessy, C.S.J.

[C] HIGH SCHOOLS, DIOCESAN

FULLERTON. *Rosary High School* (Girls) , 1340 N. Acacia Ave., 92831. Tel: 714-879-6302; Fax: 714-879-0853. Email: rosary@rosaryhs.org. Web: www.rosaryhs.org. Mrs. Trudy Mazzarella, Pres., Prin.; Terry Gonzales, Prin. Lay Teachers 48; Students 652; Total Staff 76.

RANCHO SANTA MARGARITA. *Santa Margarita Catholic High School*, 22062 Antonio Pkwy., 92688. Tel: 949-766-6000; Fax: 949-766-6005. Email: information@smhs.org. Web: www.smhs.org. Bro. Lawrence Monroe, F.S.C., Prin. Priests 1; Brothers 1; Sisters 1; Lay Teachers 93; Students 1,650.

SANTA ANA. *Mater Dei High School* (Coed) , 1202 W. Edinger, 92707-2191. Tel: 714-754-7711; Fax: 714-754-1880. Email: admissions@materdei.org. Web: www.materdei.org. Ms. Frances Clare, Prin. & Contact; Mr. Patrick Murphy, Pres.; Revs. Tuan Pham; Eugene David Burnett, O.F.M.; Luke S. Laslavich, O.Praem. Priests 3; Brothers 1; Sisters 3; Lay Teachers 148; Students 2,200; Total Staff 155.

[D] HIGH SCHOOLS, PRIVATE

ANAHEIM. *Cornelia Connelly School of the Holy Child* (Girls) , 2323 W. Broadway, 92804. Tel: 714-776-1717; Fax: 714-776-2534. Email: cornelia@connellyhs.org. Web: www.connellyhs.org. Sr. Francine Gunther, S.H.C.J., Head of School. Sisters of the Holy Child Jesus

Cornelia Connelly School Development Fund
Cornelia Connelly School Scholarship Fund Lay Teachers 29; Students 215; Total Staff 44.

Servite High School, A California Corporation, 1952 W. La Palma, 92801. Tel: 714-774-7575; Fax: 714-774-1404. Email: mail@servitehs.org. Web: servitehs.org. Rev. Gerald M. Horan, O.S.M., Pres.; Mr. Raymond Dunne, Prin.; Revs. Richard M. Boyle, O.S.M.; Edward M. Penonzek, O.S.M.; Michael M. Pontarelli, O.S.M.; Eugene M. Smith, O.S.M.; Bros. Joel A. Lechner, O.S.M.; Arnaldo M. Sanchez, O.S.M. Servite Friars Priests 5; Brothers 2; Sisters 1; Lay Teachers 52; Students 772; Total Staff 75.

SILVERADO. *St. Michael's Preparatory School*, (Grades 9-12) , (Boarding school for boys) , 19292 El Toro Rd., 92676-9710. Tel: 949-858-0222; Fax: 949-858-7365. Email: stmichaelsprep@juno.com. Web: www.stmichaelsprep.org. Revs. Gabriel D. Stack, O.Praem., Headmaster; James G. Garceau, C.R.I.C. (LA); Godfrey E. Bushmaker, O.Praem.; Alphonsus B. Hermes, O.Praem.; Jerome M. Molokie, O.Praem.; Adrian J. O'Connor, O.Praem.; Justin S. Ramos, O.Praem.; James G. Smith, O.Praem., Treas.; Hubert S. Szanto, O.Praem.; Victor S. Szczurek, O.Praem.; Charles W. Willingham, O.Praem. Priests 11; Seminarians 3; Lay Teachers 4; Students 63; Total Staff 18.

[E] ELEMENTARY SCHOOLS AND DAY NURSERIES, PRIVATE

ANAHEIM. *St. Catherine's Military School*, 215 N. Harbor Blvd., 92805. Tel: 714-772-1363; Fax: 714-772-3004. Email: scms@msjdominicans.org. Web: stcatherinesmilitary.com. Sr. Mary Menegatti, Admin. & Prin.

Legal Title: *St. Catherine's Military School, a Corp.* Dominican Sisters of Mission San Jose 13; Sisters 11; Lay Teachers 14; Students 160; Total Staff 25.

SANTA ANA. *Santa Clara Day Nursery and Kindergarten*, 1021 N. Newhope, 92703. Tel: 714-554-8850 Fax: 714-554-5886. Email: clarisas@netzero.net. Sr. Susana Guzman, M.C., Contact. Poor Clare Missionary Sisters (M.C.) Sisters 14; Children 100; Total Staff 11.

TUSTIN. *Saint Jeanne de Lestonnac School*, 16791 E. Main, 92780. Tel: 714-542-4271; Fax: 714-542-0644. Email: jeanne@stjeanne.com. Web: www.stjeanne.com. Sisters Doris Louise, O.D.N., Head of School; Sharon Lamprecht, O.D.N., Prin. Sisters of the Company of Mary 5; Adrian Dominican 1; Lay Teachers 34; Students 501; Total Staff 49.

[F] MULTI-PARISH SCHOOLS

RANCHO SANTA MARGARITA. *Serra Catholic School*, 23652 Antonio Pkwy., 92688-1993. Tel: 949-888-1990; Fax: 949-635-1921. Email: serra@serraschool.org. Web: www.serraschool.org. Mrs. Angeline Trudell, Prin.; Mrs. Mary Alvarado, Assoc. Prin. Lay Teachers 51; Students 910; Total Staff 113.

YORBA LINDA. *St. Francis of Assisi School*, 5330 Eastside Circle, 92887. Tel: 714-695-3700; Fax: 714-695-3704. Email: info@stfrancis-yorbalinda.com. Web: www.stfrancis-yorbalinda.com. Ms. Debra Decluies, Prin. Lay Teachers 30; Students 574; Total Staff 50.

[G] GENERAL HOSPITALS

ORANGE. *St. Joseph Hospital of Orange*, 1100 W. Stewart Dr., 92868. Tel: 714-771-8000, Ext. 8020; Fax: 714-744-8600. Larry Ainsworth, Pres. & CEO; Rev. Elly S. Tavarro; Robert Minkin, Contact Person. Patients Assisted Annually 89,627; Beds 448; Other Employees 1,902; Nurses 1,161.

FULLERTON. *St. Jude Medical Center*, 101 E. Valencia Mesa Dr., 92835-3875. Tel: 714-871-3280; Fax: 714-446-5067. Web: www.stjudemedicalcenter.org. Sr. Claudette Des Foyes, C.S.J., Dir. Spiritual Care; Revs. William Caffrey, S.V.D., Chap.; William Patrick, Chap.; Raymundus Bhia Wea, S.V.D., Chap.; Mary Jane Steed, B.C.C., Chap.; Rosa Perez Williams, Chap.; Lucy Davies, Chap.; Rev. Ray Hommes, Chap. Bed Capacity 309; Nurses 765; Total Staff 2,163; Total Assisted Inpatient & Outpatient 133,000

MISSION VIEJO. *Mission Hospital Regional Medical Center*, 27700 Medical Center Rd., 92691. Tel: 949-364-1400; Fax: 949-364-2056. Email: srma@mhr.stjoe.org. Web: www.mission4health.com. Peter Bastone, Pres. & CEO. Sponsored by Sisters of St. Joseph of Orange Staff 1,903; Patients assisted: Inpatient days 70,411; Outpatients 103,911; Bed Capacity 338.

[H] SPECIAL SERVICES

ORANGE. *Loyola Institute for Spirituality*, 480 S. Batavia St., 92868. Tel: 714-997-9587; Fax: 714-997-9588. Email: loyinst@pacbell.net. Web: www.loyolainstitute.org. Rev. Allan F. Deck, S.J., Exec. Dir.; Lupe Amezquita Admin.; Revs. Chi Ngo, S.J., Assoc. Dir.; Anastacio S. Rivera, S.J., Assoc. Dir.; David C. Schwartz, S.J., Assoc. Dir.

Search of Orange County, Inc., P.O. Box 4191, 92867. Tel: 949-753-3533. Web: www.rc.net/orange/search. David Wilmes, Contact. Tel: 949-636-7343.

St. Vincent de Paul Society, 130 S. Cypress, 92866. Tel: 714-547-5566; Fax: 714-771-2739. Web: svdpoc.org. Mr. Edward C. Hartmann, Pres.; Denis F. Zaun, Exec. Dir.; Rev. Roy Kim; Joyce Foley, Contact. Total Staff 139; Total Assisted 346,206.

Special Works of the St. Vincent de Paul Society:

Second Harvest Food Bank of Orange County, 426-A W. Almond, 92866. Tel: 714-771-1343; Fax: 714-771-2748. Mr. Thomas M. Seeberg.

St. Vincent de Paul Center for Community Reconciliation, 2525-N. North Grand Ave., Santa Ana, 92705. Tel: 714-288-5600; Fax: 714-288-5619. Scott Mather, Dir. Programs include: Friends Outside and Institute for Conflict Management

Stores and Workshops, 180 Cypress, 92866. Tel: 714-633-9194; Fax: 714-997-1703. Charles A. Reich, Dir.

ANAHEIM. *St. Thomas Korean Catholic Center*, 412 N. Crescent Way, 92801. Tel: 714-772-3995; Fax: 714-772-3636. Email: st_thomas@stkcc.org. Rev. Alex K. Kim, Contact; John Lee, Admin.

SANTA ANA. *St. Francis Home*, 1718 W. 6th St., 92703. Tel: 714-542-0381; Fax: 714-542-4654. Email: stfrancis@yahoo.com. Sr. Elia Caro, O.S.F., Admin. & Contact Person. Franciscan Sisters of the Immaculate Conception, Inc. Sisters 20.

Holy Family Services, Adoption and Foster Care, 1403 S. Main St., 92707. Tel: 714-835-5551; Fax: 714-973-4971. Email: hfsadopt@aol.com. Web: hfs.org. Debra Richardson, Exec. Dir.

Vietnamese Catholic Center, 1538 N. Century Blvd., 92703. Tel: 714-554-4211; 714-554-5565; Fax: 714-265-1161. Email: info@vnco.org vanphong@vnco.org. Web: www.vnco.org. Rev. Michael Hoan, Dir. & Contact Person. Total in Residence 2; Total Staff 6.

SILVERADO. *St. Michael's Summer Camp* Boys aged 7-12 years. , St. Michael's Abbey, 19292 El Toro Rd., 92676-9701. Tel: 949-858-0222, Ext. 226; Fax: 949-858-4583. Rev. Anthony Kopp, O.Praem., Contact. Capacity 120; Total in Residence 95; Total Staff 25.

WESTMINSTER. *Korean Catholic Ministry*, 7655 Trask Ave., 92683. Tel: 714-897-6510; Fax: 714-897-0832. Email: church@kmccoc.org. Web: www.kmccoc.org. Rev. John Hogan, S.S.C., Dir. Korean Martyrs Center & Contact Person.

YORBA LINDA. *Polish Center*, 3999 Rose Dr., 92886. Tel: 714-996-8161; Fax: 714-996-8161. Web: www.polishcenter.org. Revs. Douglas Cook, Dir.; Henry K. Noga, S.V.D., Asst. Dir.

[I] MONASTERIES AND RESIDENCES OF PRIESTS AND BROTHERS

ORANGE. *Trinity Missionaries/Missionary Servants of the Most Holy Trinity, St. Joseph Church*, 727 Minter St., Santa Ana, 92701-4132. Tel: 714-542-4411; Fax: 714-542-9770. Rev. Nicholas Barille, S.T., Contact.

ANAHEIM. *Servite Fathers and Brothers* Servite Friars , Servite Priory, 1922 W. La Palma Ave., 92801-3544. Tel: 714-774-8869; Fax: 714-774-6792. Revs. Eugene M. Smith, O.S.M.; Peregrine M. Graffius, O.S.M. (CHI); Michael M. Pontarelli, O.S.M.; Thomas M. Crotty, O.S.M. (CHI); Paul M. Gins, O.S.M.; Bros. Arnaldo Sanchez, O.S.M.; Joel A. Lechner, O.S.M., Contact.

Servite High School, 1952 W. La Palma Ave., 92801-3595. Tel: 714-774-7575; Fax: 714-774-1404.

BUENA PARK. *Augustinian Fathers*, St. Pius V, 7691 Orangethorpe Ave., 90621. Tel: 714-522-2193; Fax: 714-522-1730. Email: cherbers@pacbell.net. Web: stpiusv.org. Total in Residence 5; Total Staff 12.

Order of Friar Servants of Mary (Servites) U.S.A. Province, Servite Residence, 5210 Somerset St., 90621-1498. Tel: 714-739-0553. Email: gmh@adelphia.net. Rev. Gerald M. Horan, O.S.M. (CHI); Bro. Michael M. Callary, O.S.M., Contact Person.

St. Juliana Falconieri Priory, 1316 N. Acacia Ave., Fullerton, 92831. Tel: 714-879-1971; Fax: 714-526-6673. Revs. Patrick M. Donovan, O.S.M. (CHI). Tel: 714-879-1971; George M. Luznicky, O.S.M. (CHI); Jude M. Herlihy, O.S.M.; Luke Stano, O.S.M.; Bro. Philip M. Eikmeyer, O.S.M.

St. Philip Benizi Priory, 235 S. Pine Dr., Fullerton,

92833-3294. Tel: 714-871-3613; Fax: 714-871-5827. Revs. Ignatius M. Kissel, O.S.M. (CHI); Justin M. Pisciotta, O.S.M.; Manuel Maya Chavez, O.S.M.

Seven Holy Founders Priory, 1922 W. LaPalma Ave., Anaheim, 92801-3595. Tel: 714-774-8869; Fax: 714-774-6792. Revs. Thomas M. Crotty, O.S.M. (CHI); Paul M. Gins, O.S.M.; Peregrine M. Graffius, O.S.M. (CHI); Michael M. Pontarelli, O.S.M.; Eugene M. Smith, O.S.M.; Bros. Arnaldo M. Sanchez, O.S.M.; Joel Lechner, O.S.M.

Sisters of St. Joseph - Chaplain, Regina Residence, 430 S. Batavia, 92868. Tel: 714-744-3109. Rev. George M. Luznicky, O.S.M. (CHI), Chap.

FULLERTON. *Servite Fathers and Brothers*, St. Juliana Falconieri, 1316 N. Acacia, 92831. Tel: 714-879-1971; Fax: 714-526-6673. Email: info@stjulianachurch.org. Web: www.stjulianachurch.org. Rev. Jude Herlihy, O.S.M., Contact Person. Total in Residence 3; Total Staff 3.

St. Philip Benizi, 235 S. Pine Dr., 92833-3294. Tel: 714-871-3613.

GARDEN GROVE. *Manresa Jesuit Residence*, 12712 Fletcher Dr., 92840-4853. Tel: 714-530-8650; 714-997-9587; Fax: 714-530-8813. Email: loyinst@pacbell.net. Web: loyolainstitute.org. Revs. Allan Deck, S.J., Supr.; Chi Ngo, S.J.; Anastacio S. Rivera, S.J.; David C. Schwartz, S.J.

HUNTINGTON BEACH. *Franciscan Friars*, SS. Simon and Jude, 20444 Magnolia St., 92646. Tel: 714-962-3333; Fax: 714-965-6456. Email: mharvey@ssj.org. Rev. Michael L. Harvey, O.F.M., Contact Person.

MIDWAY CITY. *Brothers of St. Patrick, St. Patrick's Novitiate and Scholasticate*, 7820 Bolsa Ave., 92655. Tel: 714-897-8181; Fax: 714-898-9020. Email: brossrpatrick@aol.com. Bros. Livinus Bellew, F.S.P.; Aquinas Cassin, F.S.P.; Edwin Guidera, F.S.P., Contact; Matthew Regan, F.S.P.

SANTA ANA. *Augustinian Recollects*, Our Lady of Guadalupe, 1322 E. 3rd St., 92701-5104. Tel: 714-836-4142; Fax: 714-836-7417. Rev. Ramon Gaitan, O.A.R., Contact Person.

Our Lady of the Pillar, 1622 6th St., 92703. Tel: 714-543-1700; Fax: 714-543-9640. Rev. Luis Ramirez.

SILVERADO. *Norbertine Fathers of Orange Inc.* For detailed information regarding the high school and seminary, please refer to High Schools, Private and Seminaries and Scholastics for Religious in the Institution section. , St. Michael's Abbey (O.Praem.), 19292 El Toro Rd., 92676-9710. Tel: 949-858-0222; Fax: 949-858-4583. Rt. Revs. Eugene J. Hayes, O.Praem., Abbot; Ladislas K. Parker, O.Praem., Abbot Emeritus; Very Rev. Hugh C. Barbour, O.Praem., Ph.D., Prior; Revs. James G. Smith, O.Praem., Subprior; Jordan S. Anderson, O.Praem.; Martin R. Benzoni, O.Praem.; Stephen M. Boyle, O.Praem.; Godfrey E. Bushmaker, O.Praem.; John E. Caronan, O.Praem.; Leo J. Celano, O.Praem.; Adrian J. Connor, O.Praem.; Raphael J. Davis, O.Praem.; Gregory M. Dick, O.Praem.; Patrick D. Foutts, O.Praem.; Paul L. Gelencser, O.Praem.; Vincent M. Gilmore, O.Praem.; Francis M. Gloudeman, O.Praem.; Alphonsus B. Hermes, O.Praem.; Robert S. Hodges, O.Praem.; Joseph K. Horn, O.Praem.; Gerlac A. Horvath, O.Praem.; Bernard M. Johnson, O.Praem.; Lawrence C. Johnson, O.Praem.; Anthony Mary J. Kopp, O.Praem.; Luke S. Laslavich, O.Praem.; Jerome M. Molokie, O.Praem.; Peter D. Muller, O.Praem.; Thomas W. Nelson, O.Praem.; Pascal B. Nguyen, O.Praem.; Michael U. Perea, O.Praem.; Augustine R. Puchner, O.Praem.; Justin S. Ramos, O.Praem.; Hermann-Joseph K. Rettig, O.Praem.; Clement A. Rudnay, O.Praem.; Philip T. Smith, O.Praem., S.T.M.; Theodore R. Smith, O.Praem.; Gabriel D. Stack, O.Praem.; Hubert S. Szanto, O.Praem.; Victor S. Szcurek, O.Praem.; Nicholas M. Tacito, O.Praem.; Charles W. Willingham, O.Praem.; Norbert J. Wood, O.Praem. For detailed information concerning St. Michael's Abbey and St. Michael's College Preparatory High School please refer to the Seminary and High School categories in this Diocese. Priests 42; Clerics 16; Novices 3; Postulants 5.

WESTMINSTER. *Columban Fathers*, Korean Martyrs Catholic Center, 7655 Trask Ave., 92683. Tel: 714-897-6510; Fax: 714-897-0832. Email: church@kmccoc.org. Web: www.kmccoc.org. Rev. John Hogan, S.S.C. Tel: 714-897-2825.

[J] CONVENTS AND RESIDENCES FOR SISTERS

ORANGE. *Sisters of Providence*, Marywood Center, 2811 E. Villa Real Dr., 92867. Tel: 714-282-3099; Fax: 714-282-3029. Email: srconcetta@rcbo.org.

Sisters of St. Joseph of Orange Motherhouse Community, 480 S. Batavia, 92868. Tel: 714-633-8121, Ext. 7735; Fax: 714-744-3165. Email: ahennessy@osjorane.org. Sr. Anne Hennessy, C.S.J., Gen. Sec. & Contact Person. Sisters 33.

Regina Residence Community, 430 S. Batavia St., 92868. Tel: 714-744-3109; Fax: 714-744-3163. Email: rreginares@earthlink.net. Sisters 48.

Formation Community, 940 W. Palmyra, 92868. Tel: 714-771-4706. Email: formcomcsj@aol.com formcom@aol.com. Sisters 5.

Casa Magnolia Community, 954 W. Palmyra, 92868. Tel: 714-639-1030. Email: casamag@aol.com. Sisters 2.

St. Joseph Hospital Community, P.O. Box 5600, 92863-5600. Tel: 714-633-9111; 714-771-8040. Email: cnvntsjo@corp.stjoe.org. Sisters 8.

Greengrove Community, 2075 Greengrove St., 92665. Tel: 714-974-9079. Email: csjgr@earthlink.net. Sisters 3.

Valencia Community, 5742 E. Valencia Dr., 92869. Tel: 714-639-2665. Email: csjval@yahoo.com. Sisters 3.

Palmyra Community, 1000 W. Palmyra St., 92868-3812. Tel: 714-997-0590. Email: sisters@sbcglobal.net. Sisters 2.

Sisters of the Presentation of the Blessed Virgin Mary, St. Norbert Convent, 343 E. Chestnut, 92867. Tel: 714-637-7390; Fax: 714-637-7473. Email: orangePBVM@aol.com. Sr. Marilyn Omieczynski, Contact Person. Sisters 3.

ANAHEIM. *Dominicans, Mission San Jose*, St. Catherine Military School, 215 N. Harbor Blvd., 92805-2596. Tel: 714-772-1363; Fax: 714-772-3004. Email: scms@msjdominicans.org. Web: www.stcatherinesmilitary.com. Sr. Mary Menegatti, Admin., Prin. & Contact Person. Sisters 12.

BREA. *Sisters of St. Clare*, 446 S. Poplar Ave., 92821-6649. Tel: 714-256-1278. Sr. Anne Otter, Contact Person. Sisters 3.

St. Clare's Garden, 449 S. Pine Ave., 92821-6649. Tel: 714-257-1113; Fax: 714-257-1068. Sr. Briegeen Moore, O.S.C., Contact Person.

BUENA PARK. *Sisters of Our Lady of Perpetual Help*, 6751 Western Ave., 90621. Tel: 714-521-1345; Fax: 714-521-7611. Email: solphca@hanmail.net. Sr. M. Lucia, Contact Person. Sisters 6.

COSTA MESA. *Sisters of Mercy of Ireland*, St. John the Baptist Convent, 2960 Mendoza Dr., 92626. Tel: 714-545-2116; Fax: 714-557-9263. Email: mvianney@sjbschool.net. Sr. Mary Vianney, Contact Person. Sisters 2.

CYPRESS. *Union of the Presentation of the Blessed Virgin Mary*, 5151 Evergreen Ave., 90630. Tel: 323-563-1051. Email: gemmapires@aol.com. Sr. Mary Dunlea, P.B.V.M., Contact Person.

DANA POINT. *Sisters of St. Joseph of Orange*, Dana Point Community, 33392 Via Lenita, 92629. Tel: 949-488-0433. Email: srma@mhr.stjoe.org. Sr. Martha Ann Fitzpatrick, Contact Person. Sisters 2.

FOUNTAIN VALLEY. *Sisters of Social Service*, 9076 La Colonia, 92708-2719. Tel: 714-847-8981; Fax: 213-747-4499. Email: srsusankam@aol.com. Sr. Susan Kam, Contact Person.

FULLERTON. *Sisters of St. Joseph of Orange*, East Alto Community, 1601 E. Alto Ln., 92831. Tel: 714-526-3141. Email: csjoalto@earthlink.net. Sr. Adele Marie Korhummel, Contact Person. Sisters 5.

St. Jude Hospital Community, 3642 Coronado Dr., 92835. Tel: 714-879-7159. Sisters 2.

GARDEN GROVE. *Eucharistic Missionaries of the Most Holy Trinity*, 11892 E. Lampson Ave., 92840. Tel: 714-530-5727; Fax: 714-636-5192. Email: orangemest@aol.com. Rt. Rev. Yolanda Barroso, M.E.S.S.T., Contact Person. Sisters 5.

Religious Sisters of Charity, St. Columban Convent, 12555 Westlake St., 92840. Tel: 714-534-1003. Email: rscgg@aol.com. Sr. Bernadette Moran, Contact Person. Sisters 5.

Sisters of St. Joseph of Orange, Garden Grove Community, 9731 Acacia Ave., 1- C, 92841. Tel: 714-530-4695. Email: srrcsj@earthlink.net. Sr. Rebecca Rodriguez, Contact Person.

HUNTINGTON BEACH. *Sisters of Charity of the Blessed Virgin Mary*, SS. Simon & Jude Convent, 20512 Tobermory Cir., 92646-5837. Tel: 714-968-2237; Fax: 714-965-6456. Email: msheehan@ssj.org. Web: www.brmcong.org. Sr. Maureen Sheehan, B.V.M., Contact Person.

Sisters of the Presentation of the Blessed Virgin Mary, St. Bonaventure Convent, 16441 Bradbury Ln., 92647. Tel: 714-846-6212; Fax: 714-840-0480. Email: presentation@linkline.com. Web: www.gnofn.org/~presis/. Sr. Annunciata Murtagh, P.B.V.M., Contact. Sisters 6.

LA HABRA. *Sisters of St. Joseph of Orange*, Our Lady of Guadalupe Community, 920 W. La Habra Blvd., 90631. Tel: 562-697-9726; Fax: 562-905-0095. Email: olglh@hotmail.com. Sr. Kathleen Marie, Contact Person.

LAGUNA HILLS. *Sisters of Little Company of Mary*, St. Nicholas Convent, 24652 La Cienega, 92653. Tel: 949-643-8688; Fax: 949-831-5022. Sisters 3.

LAKE FOREST. *School Sisters of St. Francis*, 24001 Muirlands Blvd. #146, 92630. Tel: 949-951-8681; Fax: 949-951-8681. Email: generalate@sssf.org. Web: www.sssf.org.

RANCHO PALOS VERDES. *Daughters of Mary and Joseph Provincialate*, 5300 Crest Rd., 90275-5004. Tel: 310-377-9968; Fax: 310-541-5967. Email: dmjca@dmjca.org. Web: www.dmjca.org.

Daughters of Mary and Joseph, 215 N. Harbor Blvd., Anaheim, 92805-2596. Tel: 714-772-1363; Fax: 714-772-3004.

RANCHO SANTA MARGARITA. *Sisters of Providence*, 252 Montana Del Lago, 92688. Tel: 949-589-3322; Fax: 949-589-7768. Email: sbr@sfsolano.org. Web: www.sfsolano.org. Sr. Barbara Reder, S.P.

SANTA ANA. *Dominicans, Mission San Jose*, St. Callistus Convent, 2541 N. Forest Ave., 92706. Tel: 714-953-4322. Email: callistus@msjdominicans.org. Web: www.msjdominicans.org. Sisters 4.

Franciscan Missionary Sisters of the Immaculate Conception, St. Francis Home for the Aged, 1718 W. 6th St., 92703. Tel: 714-542-0381; Fax: 714-542-4654. Email: stfrancishome@yahoo.com. Sisters 20.

Poor Clare Missionary Sisters of the Blessed Sacrament, 1019 N. Newhope St., 92703-1534. Tel: 714-554-8850; Fax: 714-554-5886. Email: clarisas@netzero.net. Sr. Susana Guzman, M.C., Contact Person. Sisters 15.

Sisters of St. Joseph of Carondelet, Hogar de San Jose, 507 N. Linwood Ave., 92701. Tel: 714-541-6480. Email: adcsj@sbcglobal.net. Sr. Maureen O'Connor, C.S.J., Contact Person.

St. Joseph, 727 Minter St., 92701. Tel: 714-550-8096; Fax: 714-542-9770.

Sisters of St. Joseph of Orange, Casa Guadalupe Community, 414 S. Broadway, 92701. Tel: 714-834-9381. Email: csj414@yahoo.com. Sisters 4.

Olive Street Community, 2109 N. Olive St., 92706. Tel: 714-542-3380. Email: 2109csj@sbcglobal.net. Sisters 4.

Sisters of the Company of Mary, St. Anne's Convent, 1339 S. Broadway, 92707. Tel: 714-558-1340; Fax: 707-221-2207. Sisters 6.

Sisters of the Lovers of the Holy Cross, 1401 S. Sycamore St., 92707. Tel: 714-973-1951; Fax: 714-667-0711. Web: www.lhcla.org. Sisters 7.

920 N. Bewley St., 92703. Tel: 714-554-9376; Fax: 714-554-5925. Email: monicaphi@usa.com. Sr. Monica Phi Tran, L.H.C., Contact Person. Sisters 17.

Society Devoted to the Sacred Heart, Heart of Jesus Retreat Center, 2927 S. Greenville St., 92704. Tel: 714-557-4538; Fax: 714-668-9780. Email: sdshrc@juno.com. Sisters 6.

Sacred Heart Convent, 2911 S. Greenville St., 92704. Tel: 714-751-6335; Fax: 714-546-0873. Sisters 5.

SEAL BEACH. *Franciscans, Syracuse*, St. Anne Convent, 328 1/2 10th St., 90740. Tel: 562-493-4630. Email: sealbeachsam@yahoo.com.

SILVERADO. *Rosarian Dominicans*, St. Michael's Convent, 19292 El Toro Rd., 92676. Tel: 949-858-0487. Sisters 7.

TUSTIN. *Adrian Dominicans*, St. Jeanne de Lestonnac Convent, 16791 E. Main St., 92780. Tel: 714-541-3125; Fax: 714-835-0648. Email: srterry@stjeanne.com. Web: www.lestonnac.org. Sr. Doris Louise, O.D.N., Contact Person.

Sisters de L'Union-Chretienne de Saint Chaumond, 14391 Clarissa Ln., 92780. Tel: 714-730-1475; Fax: 714-731-7315. Sr. Marie-Agnes Clisson, Contact Person. Sisters 4.

Sisters of Providence, 14692 Charloma Dr., 92780. Tel: 714-544-9021. Email: jsmithsp@juno.com. Web: www.sistersofprovidence.org. Sisters 1.

Sisters of the Company of Mary, Provincial House, 16791 E. Main St., 92780-4034. Tel: 714-541-3125; Fax: 714-835-0648. Email: srdorisodn@sbcglobal.net. Web: www.lestonnac.org. Sr. Doris Louise, O.D.N., Contact Person. Sisters 17.

Lestonnac Retreat Center: Tel: 714-542-2496; Fax: 714-835-0648.

Lestonnac Residence: Tel: 714-558-9872; Fax: 714-835-0648.

St. Jeanne de Lestonnac School: Tel: 714-542-4271; Fax: 714-542-0644. Email: jeanne@stjeanne.com. Web: www.stjeanne.com.

WESTMINSTER. *Korean Sisters of Our Lady of Perpetual Help*, 7655 Trask Ave., 92683. Tel: 714-373-2556; Fax: 714-897-0832. Sisters 2.

[K] CATHOLIC CHARITIES

SANTA ANA. *Catholic Charities of Orange County, Inc.*, 1800 E. McFadden Ave., 92705. Tel: 714-347-9600; Fax: 714-542-3020. Email: ccocinfo@ccoc.org. Web: www.ccoc.org. Catherine Spear, M.S., C.F.R.E., Exec. Dir.; Most Rev. Jaime Soto, M.S.W., Vicar of Charities. Total Staff 60; Total Assisted 92,971.

Counseling Services Tel: 714-347-9601; Fax: 714-542-3020. Regina Lindner, Prog. Dir.
Employment Services, Anaheim. Tel: 714-635-5230; Fax: 714-635-9896. Xang Yang, Prog. Dir.
Family Service Center Tel: 714-668-1130; Fax: 714-957-2523. Lupe Savastano, Prog. Dir.
Resettlement, Immigration & Citizenship Services Tel: 714-347-9613; Fax: 714-542-3541. Thu Tran, Prog. Dir.
Legal Services and Advocacy, Formerly Community Social Action 92705. Tel: 714-347-9656; Fax: 714-542-3541. Lisa Ramirez, Esq.

[L] RETREAT HOUSES

ORANGE. *Center for Spiritual Development*, 434 S. Batavia St., 92868-3907. Tel: 714-744-3175, Ext. 4421; Fax: 714-744-3176. Email: csdinfo@csjorange.org. Web: www.thecsd.com. Sr. Anne Mary Huepper, C.S.J., Exec. Dir. Total Staff 14.
House of Prayer for Priests, 7734 Santiago Canyon Rd., 92869. Tel: 714-639-9740; Fax: 714-639-9313. Email: jgmhop@aol.com. Rev. J. Gordon Moreland, S.J., Dir. & Contact Person. Total in Residence 2; Total Staff 1. In Res. Rev. Patrick B. Philbin, S.M.
Marywood Retreat Center, 2811 E. Villa Real Dr., 92867. Tel: 714-282-3098 (Days Mon-Fri); 714-282-3099 (Evenings & Weekends); Fax: 714-282-3029. Email: sr.cbanez@rcbo.org. Web: www.rcbo.org. Elizabeth Sandoval, Reservations & Facilities Coord.; Sr. M. Concetta Banez, S.P., Retreat Hostess. Tel: 714-282-3099 (evenings & weekends). The facilities of Marywood are available for retreats, days of prayer, and other religious activities. Capacity 109.

LA HABRA. *Villa Maria House of Prayer*, 1252 N. Citrus Dr., 90631-2652. Tel: 562-691-5838; Fax: 562-691-2572. Sr. Grace Ann Loperena, C.S.J., Contact Person. Sisters of St. Joseph of Carondelet Sisters 4.

SANTA ANA. *Heart of Jesus Retreat Center*, 2927 S. Greenville St., 92704. Tel: 714-557-4538; Fax: 714-668-9780. Email: sdshrc@juno.com. 2911 S. Greenville St., 92704. Society Devoted to the Sacred Heart Sisters 6; Total Staff 6.

[M] NEWMAN CENTERS

FULLERTON. *California State University Fullerton, Newman Center* St. Juliana Falconieri, 1316 N. Acacia Ave., 9283--202. Tel: 714-879-1965; Fax: 714-526-6673. Web: www.newman-csuf.com. Rev. Patrick J. Donovan, O.S.M., Chap. & Adviser, Newman Catholic Club. Tel: 714-871-1086.

IRVINE. *U.C.I. Interfaith Center* P.O. Box 6030, 92616-6030. Tel: 949-856-0211; 949-753-3373; Fax: 714-639-9313. Email: pphilbin@netzero.net. Web: spirit.dos.uci.edu/ucc. Rev. Patrick B. Philbin, S.M., Chap. & Diocesan Dir. Campus Ministry.

[N] SECULAR INSTITUTES

FULLERTON. *Pro Sanctity Spirituality Center, Retreat House*, 205 S. Pine Dr., 92833. Tel: 714-956-1020; Fax: 714-525-8948. Email: psmcal@aol.com. Web: prosanctitate.org. Agnes Rus, Dir. Capacity: 26 overnight, 32 day use
Pro Sanctity Movement Tel: 714-956-1020; Fax: 714-525-8948. Cathy McDonnell, Dir.

[O] MISCELLANEOUS LISTINGS

ORANGE. *St. Joseph Health System*, 500 S. Main St., Ste. 400, 92868. Tel: 714-347-7579; Fax: 714-347-7590. Web: www.stjhs.org. Sr. Katherine Gray, C.S.J., Bd. Chm.; Mr. Richard Statuto, Pres. & CEO.
St. Joseph Health System Foundation, 500 S. Main St., Ste. 400, 92868. Tel: 714-347-7579; Fax: 714-347-7590. Maya Dunn, Contact Person.
St. Jude Hospital Yorba Linda, St. Joseph Health System, 500 S. Main St., 92868-4515. Tel: 714-347-7579; Fax: 714-347-7590. Robert J. Frashetti.
Orange Catholic Foundation, 2811 E. Villa Real Dr., 92867-1999. Tel: 714-282-3020; Fax: 714-282-3136. Email: msgr.LBaird@rcbo.org. Web: www.rcbo.org/offices/development/ocf.htm. Rev. Msgr. Lawrence J. Baird.
Orange County Catholic Alumni Club, P.O. Box 6054, 92863-6054. Tel: 714-502-8086 Email: orangecountyCAC@juno.com. Web: www.caci.org/cac/occac.html.
Sisters of St. Joseph Healthcare Foundation, 480 S. Batavia St., 92868. Tel: 714-633-8121; Fax: 714-744-3165. Email: sbecker@corp.stjoe.org. Sr. Sharon Becker, C.S.J., Exec. Dir.

EL TORO. *Aid to the Church in Need, Inc.*, P.O. Box 1000, 92630. Joseph Cornelius, Pres.

FULLERTON. *Apostolic Oblates* House of Formation for Professed Apostolic Oblates. Secular Institute of the Apostolic Oblates, Inc. , 2125 W. Walnut Ave., 92833. Tel: 714-871-5768; Fax: 714-525-8948. Email: ApostolicO@aol.com. Agnes Rus, Local Moderator.
St. Jude Memorial Foundation, P.O. Box 4138, 92834. Tel: 714-992-3033; Fax: 714-446-5430.

SILVERADO. *Norbertine Association of St. Joseph, Inc.*, St. Michael's Abbey, 19292 El Toro Rd., 92676-9710. Tel: 949-858-0222, Ext. 213; Fax: 949-858-4583.
Officers: Revs. Eugene J. Hayes, O.Praem., Pres.; John E. Caronan, O.Praem., Sec.; Sr. Mary Augustine, O.Praem, Moderator.

RELIGIOUS INSTITUTES OF MEN REPRESENTED IN THE DIOCESE

For further details refer to the corresponding bracketed number in the Religious Institutes of Men or Women section.

[0530]—*Atonement Friars*—S.A.
[0140]—*Augustinian Fathers*—O.S.A.
[0150]—*Augustinian Recollects*—O.A.R.
[1160]—*Brothers of St. Patrick*—F.S.P.
[0330]—*Brothers of the Christian Schools*—F.S.C.
[0360]—*Claretian Missionaries*—C.M.F.
[0370]—*Columban Fathers*—S.S.C.
[0380]—*Comboni Missionaries of the Heart of Jesus* (Verona)—M.C.C.J.
[]—*Crusade of the Holy Spirit*—C.H.S.
[]—*Divine Word*—S.V.D.
[0520]—*Franciscan Fathers*—O.F.M.
[0670]—*Hospitaller Brothers of St. John of God*—O.H.
[0690]—*Jesuit Fathers and Brothers*—S.J.
[0780]—*Marist Fathers*—S.M.
[0660]—*Missionaries of the Holy Spirit*—M.Sp.S.
[1110]—*Missionaries of the Sacred Heart*—MSC
[0900]—*Norbertine Fathers*—O.Praem.
[0610]—*Priests of the Holy Cross*—C.S.C.
[1190]—*Salesians of Don Bosco*—S.D.B.
[1240]—*Servite Fathers and Brothers*—O.S.M.
[0840]—*Trinity Missionaries*—S.T.

RELIGIOUS INSTITUTES OF WOMEN REPRESENTED IN THE DIOCESE

[]—*Congregation of Divine Providence*
[1920]—*Congregation of Sisters of the Holy Cross*—C.S.C.
[0880]—*Daughters of Mary and Joseph*—D.M.J.
[1070-13]—*Dominican Sisters* (Adrian, MI)—O.P.
[]—*Dominican Sisters* (Mission San Jose)—O.P.
[]—*Dominican Sisters* (Western Australia)—O.P.
[]—*Dominican Sisters* (Caldwell, NJ)—O.P.
[1070-03]—*Dominican Sisters* (Sinsinawa)—O.P.
[]—*Eucharistic Missionaries of the Most Holy Trinity*—M.E.S.S.T.
[1350]—*Franciscan Missionary Sisters of the Immaculate Conception*—O.S.F.
[1540]—*Franciscan Sisters* (Clinton, IA)—O.S.F.
[]—*Franciscan Sisters* (Syracuse, NY)—O.S.F.
[2390]—*Lovers of the Holy Cross Sisters*—L.H.C.
[2490]—*Medical Missionary Sisters*—M.M.S.
[2840]—*Poor Clare Missionaries of Blessed Sacrament*—M.C.
[3280]—*Presentation Sisters of Blessed Virgin Mary*—P.B.V.M.
[3400]—*Religious Sisters of Charity*—R.S.C.
[2575]—*Religious Sisters of Mercy of the Americas*—R.S.M.
[]—*Religious Sisters of the Sacred Heart of Mary*—R.S.H.M.
[]—*Rosarian Dominican Sisters*—O.P.
[]—*School Sisters of Notre Dame*—S.S.N.D.
[1680]—*School Sisters of St. Francis*—S.S.S.F.
[]—*Sisters de L'Union-Chretienne de Saint Chaumond*—U.C.S.C.
[]—*Sisters for Christian Community*—S.F.C.C.
[0430]—*Sisters of Charity of the Blessed Virgin Mary*—B.V.M.
[0990]—*Sisters of Devine Providence*—C.D.P.
[]—*Sisters of Mercy of Ireland*—R.S.M.
[2575]—*Sisters of Mercy of the Americas*—R.S.M.
[]—*Sisters of Our Lady of Perpetual Help*—S.O.L.P.H.
[]—*Sisters of Providence* (Montreal)—S.P.
[]—*Sisters of Providence* (Seattle)—S.P.
[3340]—*Sisters of Providence* IN—S.P.
[4090]—*Sisters of Social Service*—S.S.S.
[3770]—*Sisters of St. Clare*—O.S.C.
[3830-03]—*Sisters of St. Joseph* (Orange)—C.S.J.
[3840]—*Sisters of St. Joseph of Carondelet*—C.S.J.
[3840]—*Sisters of St. Joseph of Carondelet* (Albany Prov.)—C.S.J.
[3930]—*Sisters of St. Joseph of the Third Order of St. Francis*—S.S.J.-T.O.
[3935]—*Sisters of St. Louis*—S.S.L.
[0700]—*Sisters of the Company of Mary*—O.D.N.
[1990]—*Sisters of the Holy Names of Jesus and Mary*—S.N.J.M.
[2270]—*Sisters of the Little Company of Mary*—L.C.M.
[4050]—*Sisters of the Society Devoted to the Sacred Heart*—S.D.S.H.
[4060]—*Society of the Holy Child Jesus*—S.H.C.J.

DIOCESAN CEMETERIES

ORANGE. *Holy Sepulcher*, 7845 Santiago Canyon Rd., 92869. Kevin Haynes, Supt.

ANAHEIM. *Holy Cross*, 619 S. Euclid, 92802.

HUNTINGTON BEACH. *Good Shepherd Cemetery and Mausoleum*, 8301 Talbert Ave., 92646. Guadalupe Ramirez, Supt.

LAKE FOREST. *Ascension*, 24754 Trabuco Rd., 92630. John D. Callaghan Jr., Supt.

NECROLOGY

† Brennan, Rev. Msgr. Daniel H., Costa Mesa, CA St. John the Baptist—Died Oct. 30, 2003
† Trac, Peter Vu Dinh, (Retired)—Died Sept. 30, 2003

Diocese of Orlando

(Dioecesis Orlandensis)

Most Reverend

NORBERT L. DORSEY, C.P., D.D., S.T.D.

Bishop of Orlando; ordained April 28, 1956; appointed Auxiliary Bishop of Miami January 10, 1986; ordained Titular Bishop of Mactaris and Auxiliary Bishop of the Archdiocese of Miami March 19, 1986; appointed Bishop of Orlando March 20, 1990; installed as Third Bishop of Orlando May 25, 1990 *Office: 50 E. Robinson St., Orlando, FL 32801. P.O. Box 1800, Orlando, FL 32802.*

Most Reverend

THOMAS G. WENSKI, V.G.

Coadjutor Bishop of Orlando; ordained May 15, 1976; appointed Auxiliary Bishop of Miami June 24, 1997; installed September 3, 1997; appointed Coadjutor Bishop Of Orlando July 1, 2003; installed August 20, 2003 *Office: 50 E. Robinson St., Orlando, FL 32801.*

Chancery: 50 E. Robinson St., Orlando, FL 32801P.O. Box 1800, Orlando, FL 32802. Tel: 407-246-4800; Fax: 407-246-4942.

Web: www.orlandodiocese.org

Email: cbrinati@orlandodiocese.org

ESTABLISHED JUNE 18, 1968.

Square Miles 11,256.

Comprises the Counties of Brevard, Lake, Marion, Orange, Osceola, Polk, Seminole, Sumter and Volusia in the State of Florida.

Legal Title: For legal titles of parishes and diocesan institutions, consult the Chancery.

STATISTICAL OVERVIEW

Personnel	
Bishop	2
Priests: Diocesan Active in Diocese	93
Priests: Diocesan Active Outside Diocese	6
Priests: Retired, Sick or Absent	22
Number of Diocesan Priests	121
Religious Priests in Diocese	44
Total Priests in Diocese	165
Extern Priests in Diocese	28
Ordinations:	
Diocesan Priests	1
Transitional Deacons	6
Permanent Deacons in Diocese	137
Total Brothers	16
Total Sisters	103
Parishes	
Parishes	72
With Resident Pastor:	
Resident Diocesan Priests	64
Resident Religious Priests	8
Missions	10
Professional Ministry Personnel:	
Brothers	4
Sisters	29
Lay Ministers	181
Welfare	
Day Care Centers	11
Total Assisted	975
Special Centers for Social Services	7
Total Assisted	19,286
Residential Care of Disabled	1
Educational	
Diocesan Students in Other Seminaries	20
Total Seminarians	20
High Schools, Diocesan and Parish	5
Total Students	2,627
Elementary Schools, Diocesan and Parish	31
Total Students	12,457
Non-residential Schools for the Disabled	1
Total Students	60
Catechesis/Religious Education:	
High School Students	4,360
Elementary Students	22,329
Total Students under Catholic Instruction	41,853
Teachers in the Diocese:	
Priests	1
Brothers	4
Sisters	26
Lay Teachers	1,049
Vital Statistics	
Receptions into the Church:	
Infant Baptism Totals	6,108
Adult Baptism Totals	540
Received into Full Communion	689
First Communions	5,884
Confirmations	4,357
Marriages:	
Catholic	928
Interfaith	488
Total Marriages	1,416
Deaths	3,864
Total Catholic Population	361,085
Total Population	3,535,994

Former Bishops—Most Revs. WILLIAM D. BORDERS, D.D., ord. May 18, 1940; appt. Bishop of Orlando, May 2, 1968; consecrated June 14, 1968; transferred to Baltimore, March 25, 1974 as Archbishop; THOMAS J. GRADY, D.D. (Retired), ord. April 23, 1938; appt. Second Bishop of Orlando, Nov. 9, 1974; installed Dec. 16, 1974; retired May 25, 1990; died April 21, 2002.

Chancery—50 E. Robinson St., Orlando, 32801. Tel: 407-246-4800; Fax: 407-246-4942. Email: cbrinati@orlandodiocese.org. Web: www.orlandodiocese.org. *P.O. Box 1800, Orlando, 32802.*

Vicars General—Most Rev. THOMAS G. WENSKI; Very Rev. PATRICK J. CAVERLY, V.G., P.O. Box 1800, Orlando, 32802. Tel: 407-246-4800.

Archivist and Librarian—STEVEN GATALETTO.

Chancellor—Sr. LUCY VAZQUEZ, O.P., J.C.D., P.O. Box 1800, Orlando, 32802. Tel: 407-246-4825.

Marriage Tribunal—50 E. Robinson St., Orlando, 32801. Tel: 407-246-4850.

Judicial Vicar—Rev. MATTHEW J. CONNOLLY.

Adjutant Judicial Vicar—Rev. PAIGE BLAKELY, J.C.L.

Director of Tribunal—Sr. LUCY VAZQUEZ, O.P., J.C.D.

Promoter of Justice—Sr. LUCY VAZQUEZ, O.P., J.C.D.

Defenders of the Bond—Revs. FERNANDO GIL, J.D., J.C.D.; GREGORY PARKES; Sr. LUCY VAZQUEZ, O.P., J.C.D.

Judges—Revs. PAIGE BLAKELY, J.C.L.; RONALD KRISMAN, J.C.L.; MATTHEW CONNOLLY; JOHN GIEL, J.C.L.; JOSE BAUTISTA, J.C.L.

Regional Advocate—Sr. ANN ENGLERT, O.P. Tel: 386-668-1426.

Chief Financial Officer—GERALD F. HILBRICH.

Comptroller—ROGER BARNES.

Deans—Revs. MANUEL FERNANDEZ, Northern Deanery; PAUL J. HENRY, Central Deanery South; RICHARD WALSH, Central Deanery North; RAYMOND O'LEARY, Eastern Deanery; ANTHONY BLUETT, Western Deanery; ROBERT J. HOEFFNER, Southern Deanery.

Priests' Council—Executive Committee: Most Rev. NORBERT L. DORSEY, C.P., D.D., S.T.D., Pres.; Revs. NICHOLAS KING, Chm.; VAL SHEEDY, Vice Chm. (Retired); MIGUEL GONZALEZ, Sec.; Very Rev. PATRICK J. CAVERLY, V.G., Ex Officio; Rev. EMILE GENTILE, T.O.R., Ex Officio. Members: Revs. PHIL EGITTO; ANTHONY BLUETT; MANUEL FERNANDEZ; MIGUEL GONZALEZ; ROBERT HOEFFNER; NICHOLAS KING; NICHOLAS O'BRIEN; PAUL J. HENRY; RAYMOND O'LEARY; VAL SHEEDY (Retired); RICHARD WALSH; RICHARD TROUT.

Consultors—Most Rev. THOMAS G. WENSKI; Very Rev. PATRICK J. CAVERLY, V.G.; Revs. ROBERT HOEFFNER; ANTHONY BLUETT; MANUEL FERNANDEZ; ROBERT MARKUNAS; RAYMOND O'LEARY; RICHARD WALSH.

Bishop's Executive Staff—Most Revs. NORBERT L. DORSEY, C.P., D.D., S.T.D.; THOMAS G. WENSKI; Very Rev. PATRICK J. CAVERLY, V.G.; Revs. PAUL HENRY; EMILE GENTILE, T.O.R.; ROBERT WEBSTER; Sr. LUCY VAZQUEZ, O.P., J.C.D.; CAROL BRINATI; STEPHEN G. RICHARDVILLE; GERALD F. HILBRICH.

Vicar for Religious—Sr. LUCY VAZQUEZ, O.P., J.C.D., P.O. Box 1800, Orlando, 32802.

Vicar for Clergy—Rev. EMILE GENTILE, T.O.R.

Diocesan Offices and Organizations

Office of Stewardship & Development—MARILYN L. BLANCHETTE, Dir., P.O. Box 1800, Orlando, 32802. Tel: 407-246-4841.

Office of Communications—CAROL BRINATI, Dir., P.O. Box 1800, Orlando, 32802. Tel: 407-246-4814.

Ethnic Ministries—Rev. JOHN MCCORMICK, Dir. Tel: 407-422-2005.

Advisory Board—

Black Community—Rev. LEO HODGES.

Portuguese/Brazilian—Rev. VOLMAR SCARRABELLI, C.S.

Filipino—Rev. PETER PUNTAL.

Haitian—Rev. LEMIER GUILLAME.

Hispanic—Rev. JOSE BAUTISTA.

Korean—Rev. LEE "LUKE" JUNG-NAM.

Vietnamese—Revs. CHAU NGUYEN; JOSEPH DUNG BUI.
Building Commission—WILLIAM G. KRAMER, A.I.A., Coord., P.O. Box 1800, Orlando, 32802. Tel: 407-246-4870.
Campus Ministry—Rev. PAUL HENRY, Dir., c/o St. John Vianney Parish, 6200 S. Orange Blossom Trail, Orlando, 32809. Tel: 407-855-5391.
Catholic Charities—STEPHEN G. RICHARDVILLE, Dir., 1771 N. Semoran Blvd., Orlando, 32807-3598. Tel: 407-658-1818; Fax: 407-282-2891.
Cemeteries—Rev. THOMAS BARRETT, Dir., P.O. Box 1800, Orlando, 32802. Tel: 407-246-4870.
Censor of Books—Rev. STEVEN OLDS, St. Vincent de Paul Seminary, 10701 S. Military Trail, Boynton Beach, 33436.
Cursillos de Cristiandad—Rev. CARL VACEK, T.O.R., Dir., San Pedro Center, 2400 Dike Rd., Winter Park, 32792. Tel: 407-671-6322.
Criminal Justice Office—THOMAS GILLAN, 1771 N. Semoran Blvd., Orlando, 32807-3544. Tel: 407-658-1818.
Office of Ecumenism—Rev. LARRY LOSSING, P.O. Box 1800, Orlando, 32802. Tel: 407-246-4922.
Education, Board of—JERRY ALLENDER, Chm.
Education, Department of—HARRY V. PURPUR, Ed.D., Supt., P.O. Box 1800, Orlando, 32802. Tel: 407-246-4900; Fax: 407-246-4940.
Family Life—HEIDI PECKHAM, Dir., P.O. Box 1800, Orlando, 32802. Tel: 407-246-4866.
Farmworker Ministry, Office for—VACANT, Dir., P.O. Box 1800, Orlando, 32802. Tel: 407-246-4930; Fax: 407-246-4932.
Finance Committee—WILLIAM OROSZ, Chm.
Fiscal Management—GERALD F. HILBRICH.
Immigration Services—RICHARD LOGUE, Dir., 1771 N. Semoran Blvd., Orlando, 32807-3598. Tel: 407-658-0110; Fax: 407-249-5699.
Insurance Committee—Dr. MARGARET CURRAN, Chm.
Lay Ministry Development—MARTHA GRAVOIS, M.A., M.R.E., Dir., P.O. Box 1800, Orlando, 32802. Tel: 407-246-4880; Fax: 407-246-4942.
Office of Worship—Rev. ROBERT WEBSTER, Dir., P.O. Box 1800, Orlando, 32802. Tel: 407-246-4860.
Office of Liturgical Music—WILLIAM BRISLIN, Dir., P.O. Box 1800, Orlando, 32802. Tel: 407-246-4830.
Newspaper—Mr. CHRISTOPHER GUNTY, Assoc. Publisher, P.O. Box 609512, Orlando, 32860-9512. Tel: 407-660-9141; Fax: 407-660-2977; JULIE GREENE, Orlando Editor, P.O. Box 1800, Orlando, 32802. Tel: 407-246-4924. "The Florida Catholic"
Permanent Diaconate—Rev. EMILE GENTILE, T.O.R., Dir. Co-Directors: Deacons BOB KINSEY; JERRY KELLY, P.O. Box 1800, Orlando, 32802. Tel: 407-246-4875; Fax: 407-246-4942.
Priests' Continuing Education—Rev. RICHARD WALSH, St. Margaret Mary, 526 Park Ave., Winter Park, 32789. Tel. 407-647-3392.
Priests' Personnel—Rev. EMILE GENTILE, T.O.R., P.O. Box 1800, Orlando, 32802. Tel: 407-246-4875.
Propagation of the Faith—Rev. JOHN McCORMICK, Dir., St. James Cathedral, 215 N. Orange Ave., Orlando, 32801. Tel: 407-422-2005.
Real Estate Committee—Rev. NICHOLAS KING, Chm., St. Mary, 75 Barton Ave., Rockledge, 32955-2939. Tel: 407-636-6834.
Refugee Resettlement—RICHARD LOGUE, Dir., 1771 N. Semoran Blvd., Orlando, 32807-3598. Tel: 407-658-0110; Fax: 407-249-5699.
Religious Education—Sr. LINDA L. GAUPIN, C.D.P., Ph.D., Dir., P.O. Box 1800, Orlando, 32802. Tel: 407-246-4910; Fax: 407-246-4940.
Media Center—ROZAN JORDAN, Dir., 50 E. Robinson St., Orlando, 32801. Tel: 407-246-4895; Fax: 407-246-4935.
Respect Life Office—DEBORAH SHEARER, Dir., P.O. Box 1800, Orlando, 32802. Tel: 407-246-4820; Fax: 407-246-4942.
Girl Scouting—BOB BIRMINGHAM, P.O. Box 1800, Orlando, 32802. Tel: 407-246-4910.
Sister Diocese-Mission Office—Sr. BERNADETTE MACKAY, O.S.U., Dir., P.O. Box 1800, Orlando, 32802. Tel: 407-246-4890; Fax: 407-246-4892.
Sister's Council—Sr. LORETTA MORGAN, S.F.C.C., Pres., P.O. Box 1800, Orlando, 32802.
Society of St. Vincent de Paul—THOMAS MCNAUGHTON, Pres., P.O. Box 1800, Orlando, 32802.
Spiritual Development—Rev. CARL VACEK, T.O.R., 2400 Dike Rd., Winter Park, 32792. Tel: 407-671-6322.
Vocations—Rev. THOMAS BARRETT, Dir., P.O. Box 1800, Orlando, 32802. Tel: 407-246-4875; Fax: 407-246-4942.
Youth Ministry—TONY MAIONE, P.O. Box 1800, Orlando, 32802. Tel: 407-246-4911; Fax: 407-246-4940.
Apostleship of the Sea Chaplain— Port Canaveral: Deacon WILLIAM WANCA SR., Our Lady of Grace Parish, 300 Malabar Rd., S.E., Palm Bay, 32907. Tel: 321-725-3066.
Victim Assistance Coordinator—Sr. LUCY VAZQUEZ, O.P. Tel: 407-246-4826. Email: slvafj@aol.com.

CLERGY, PARISHES, MISSIONS AND PAROCHIAL SCHOOLS

CITY OF ORLANDO
(ORANGE COUNTY)

1—ST. JAMES CATHEDRAL (1881), Revs. John M. McCormick; Frank J. Mutsko; Philip Nunez; Deacon Sam Ryan.
Church: 215 N. Orange Ave., 32801. Tel: 407-422-2005; Fax: 407-422-2009.
School—Tel: 407-841-4432; Fax: 407-648-4603. Lay Teachers 23; Students 474.
Catechesis/Religious Program—Students 392.
Mission—St. Ignatius Kim Korean Mission 1504 Muriel St., Orange Co. 32806. Tel: 407-897-6587; Fax: 407-897-6587. Rev. Luke Jung-Nam.

2—ST. ANDREW (1957), Revs. Andrew O'Reilly, C.PP.S.; Humberto Jana, C.P.P.S.; Deacons Jose Cruz; Rafael Hernandez.
Res.: 801 Hastings, 32808. Tel: 407-293-0730; Fax: 407-293-0739.
School—Tel: 407-295-4230; Fax: 407-290-0959. Lay Teachers 19; Students 376.
Catechesis/Religious Program—Students 280.

3—BLESSED TRINITY (1965), Revs. Joe Aquino, M.S., Co-Pastor; Ron Gagne, M.S., Co-Pastor; Michael J. Flanagan, M.S.; Deacon Edwin De Jesus.
Res.: 4545 E. Anderson Rd., 32812. Tel: 407-277-1702; Fax: 407-277-1973.
Catechesis/Religious Program—Tel: 407-277-1702; Fax: 407-277-1973. Students 616.

4—ST. CHARLES BORROMEO (1954), (English-Vietnamese), Revs. Thomas Barrett; Chau Nguyen; Deacons Richard Rupp; James Smith.
Res.: 4001 Edgewater Dr., 32804. Tel: 407-293-9556; Fax: 407-293-9213.
School—Tel: 407-293-7691; Fax: 407-295-9839. Lay Teachers 24; Students 598.
School—Preschool, Tel: 407-295-7041. Lay Teachers 2; Students 33.
Catechesis/Religious Program—Tel: 407-293-9556, Ext. 121. Students 90.

5—GOOD SHEPHERD (1956), Revs. Brian R. Sheridan, M.S.; Stephen J. Krisanda, M.S.; Deacons Jose "Manny" Garcia; John T. Crotty; Confesor De Jesus; Dr. Steven B. Colon, D.Min.
Mailing Address: 5900 Oleander Dr., 32807. Tel: 407-277-3939; Fax: 407-273-5148.
Res.: 567 Hewett Dr., 32807. Tel: 407-275-5486.
School—Tel: 407-277-3973; Fax: 407-277-2605. Sisters 2; Lay Teachers 33; Students 631.
School—Preschool, Tel: 407-277-3939, Ext. 220. Sisters 1; Lay Teachers 11; Students 93.
Catechesis/Religious Program—Tel: 407-277-3939, Ext. 211. Maria Virgen Jimenez, D.R.E. Students 735.

6—HOLY CROSS (1992), Rev. Esau Garcia.
Res.: 12600 Marsfield Ave., 32837. Tel: 407-438-0990; Fax: 407-438-4090.
Catechesis/Religious Program—Students 1,105.

7—HOLY FAMILY (1975), [JC] Revs. William Ennis; Gregory Parkes; Felicito Baybay; Deacons Charles Mallon; Robert Pleus.
Res.: 5125 S. Apopka-Vineland Rd., 32819. Tel: 407-876-2211; Fax: 407-876-1167.
School—5129 S. Apopka-Vineland Rd., 32819. Tel: 407-876-9344; Fax: 407-876-8775. Sr. Dorothy Sayers, M.P.F., Prin. Sisters 2; Lay Teachers 30; Students 645.
Catechesis/Religious Program—Tel: 407-876-6331; Fax: 407-876-8775. Students 1,040.

8—ST. ISAAC JOGUES (1987), Revs. Fernando Gil, J.D., J.C.D.; Ybain F. Ramirez; Deacons Robert Kloznick; Orlando Lendoiro; Angel Pacheco; Rafael Mena.
Mailing Address: 4301 S. Chickasaw Tr., 32829. Tel: 407-249-0906; Fax: 407-273-3236.
Catechesis/Religious Program—(Grades PreK-12) Lay Teachers 120; Students 800.

9—ST. JOHN THE EVANGELIST (2001), Revs. Laurence Olszewski, C.S.C.; Robert Wiseman, C.S.C.
Mailing Address: 7380 Murrell Rd., Ste. 104, Viera, 32940. Tel: 321-751-3400; Fax: 321-751-3413.
Catechesis/Religious Program—Students 250.

10—ST JOHN VIANNEY (1959), Revs. Paul J. Henry; Vidal Arboleda (Retired); Miguel Gonzalez; Deacons Miguel Beltran; Rene Morales; Tom Tagye, Dir. Ministry to the Sick.
Res.: 6200 S. Orange Blossom Tr., 32809. Tel: 407-855-5391; Fax: 407-859-3631.
School—Tel: 407-855-4660; Fax: 407-857-7932. Sr. Elizabeth Murphy, Prin. Sisters of St. Francis of Philadelphia 2; Lay Teachers 31; Students 704.
Catechesis/Religious Program—Tel: 407-855-5391, Ext. 235. Terri Tagye, D.R.E. Students 600.

11—ST. JOSEPH (1962), (Polish—Filipino), Revs. Robert W. Brown; Larry Lossing.
Res.: 1501 N. Alafaya Tr., 32828. Tel: 407-275-0841; Fax: 407-275-0841.
Catechesis/Religious Program—Tel: 407-282-7784; Fax: 407-282-7348. Students 600.

OUTSIDE THE CITY OF ORLANDO

ALTAMONTE SPRINGS, SEMINOLE CO.

1—ANNUNCIATION (1982), Very Rev. Patrick J. Caverly, V.G.; Revs. Stephen D. Parkes; Charles J. Deeney, O.M.I.; Stephen A. Baumann.
Mailing Address: P.O. Box 915887, Longwood, 32791-5887. Tel: 407-869-9472; Fax: 407-869-4661.
Res.: 1020 Montgomery Rd., 32714.
School—Annunciation Catholic Academy, (Grades K-8) Tel: 407-774-2801; Fax: 407-774-2826. Lay Teachers 30; Students 496.
Catechesis/Religious Program—Tel: 407-869-0934. Students 1,135.

2—ST. MARY MAGDALEN (1959), Revs. Charles I. Mitchell; Edward J. Thompson; Tito Rojas; Thomas Smith; Deacons Henry Libersat; Norm Kazyk; Jerry Kelly; Marshall Gibbs.
Res.: 861 Maitland Ave., 32701. Tel: 407-831-1212; Fax: 407-831-1560.
School—Tel: 407-339-7301; Fax: 407-339-9556. Sisters 2; Lay Teachers 40; Students 478.
Catechesis/Religious Program—Tel: 407-834-2211. Students 664.

APOPKA, ORANGE CO., ST. FRANCIS OF ASSISI (1966), Revs. Timothy P. Labo; Humberto Jana, C.P.P.S.; Deacon Frank Diaz; Rev. Jose Bautista (Haiti); Deacon Laurence Herbert.
Res.: 834 S. Orange Blossom Trail, 32703-6560. Tel: 407-886-4602; Fax: 407-886-9758.
Catechesis/Religious Program—Students 381.

BAREFOOT BAY, BREVARD CO., ST. LUKE (1986), [JC] Rev. Patrick J. O'Carroll; Deacon Roland Benoit.
Res.: 5055 Micco Rd., 32976. Tel: 561-664-9310; Fax: 561-664-3374.
Catechesis/Religious Program—Students 34.

BARTOW, POLK CO., ST. THOMAS AQUINAS (1956), Rev. Peter Mitchell.
Res.: 1305 E. Mann Rd., 33830. Tel: 863-533-8578; Fax: 863-533-5090.
Catechesis/Religious Program—Tel: 863-533-4514. Students 118.
Mission—St. Elizabeth Ann Seton 101 Edgewood, Fort Meade, Polk Co. 33841. Tel: 863-285-7390.
Mission—Our Lady of Guadalupe 2150 State Rd. 559, Wahneta, Polk Co. 33880. Tel: 863-299-3854; Fax: 863-299-8247. Rev. Norman Farland.

BELLEVIEW, MARION CO., ST. THERESA (1951), Rev. James MacLoughlin.
Res.: 11526 S.E. U.S. Hwy. 301, 34420-4430. Tel: 352-245-2458; Fax: 352-245-1521.
Catechesis/Religious Program—Tel: 352-245-5300; Fax: 352-245-1521. Students 119.

BUSHNELL, SUMTER CO., ST. LAWRENCE (1995), Rev. Peter A. Sagorski.
Office and Mailing Address: 320 E. Dade Ave., 33513. Tel: 352-793-7788; Fax: 352-793-4787.
Res.: 223 E. Vermont Ave., 33513. Tel: 352-793-4636.
Catechesis/Religious Program—Students 57.
Mission—St. Vincent de Paul Mission Wildwood, Sumter Co.

CANDLER, MARION CO., IMMACULATE HEART OF MARY (1983), Rev. Stephen Phillips.
Mailing Address: P.O. Box 310, 32111. Tel: 352-687-4031; Fax: 352-687-1811.
Catechesis/Religious Program—Tel: 352-687-8818. Students 63.
Mission—Christ the King 14045 N. Hwy. 301, Citra, Marion Co. 32113. Tel: 352-595-5605.

CASSELBERRY, SEMINOLE CO., ST. AUGUSTINE (1969), Rev. Michael J. Hughes, O.S.A.
Res.: 375 N. Sunset Dr., 32707. Tel: 407-695-3262; Fax: 407-699-8998.
Catechesis/Religious Program—Students 337.

CLERMONT, LAKE CO., BLESSED SACRAMENT (1961), Rev. Christopher Hoffmann; Deacons Paul Schneider; Rafael Gonzalez; Michael Shortell; Ismael Pineiro.
Res.: 720 12th St., 34711. Tel: 352-394-3562; Fax: 352-241-0062.
Catechesis/Religious Program—Tel: 352-394-3562, Ext. 19. Students 600.

COCOA BEACH, BREVARD CO., CHURCH OF OUR SAVIOUR (1956), Rev. Sean Heslin.
Res.: 5301 N. Atlantic Ave., 32931. Tel: 321-783-4554; Fax: 321-868-6743.
School—Tel: 321-783-2330; Fax: 321-784-6330. Lay Teachers 16; Students 229.
Catechesis/Religious Program—Students 250.

COCOA, BREVARD CO., BLESSED SACRAMENT (1967),

Rev. Anthony F. Quinlivan, C.Ss.R.; Deacon Richard J. Basso.
Office: 5135 N. U.S. Hwy. 1, 32927. Tel: 321-632-6333; Fax: 321-631-2560.
Catechesis/Religious Program—Students 193.

DAYTONA BEACH, VOLUSIA CO.

1—OUR LADY OF LOURDES (1953), Rev. Philip J. Egitto.
Res.: 201 University Blvd., 32118. Tel: 386-255-0433; Fax: 386-238-1175.
School—Tel: 386-252-0391; Fax: 386-238-1175. Lay Teachers 16; Students 234.
Catechesis/Religious Program—Students 46.

2—ST. PAUL'S (1881), Revs. Robert E. Webster; Jose Munoz; Deacons Robert Landers; Jim Flynn.
Res.: 317 Mullally St., P.O. Box 646, 32115. Tel: 386-252-5422; Fax: 386-252-1936.
School—Tel: 386-252-7915; Fax: 386-238-7903. Lay Teachers 17; Students 268.
Catechesis/Religious Program—Students 40.

DE LAND, VOLUSIA CO., ST. PETER'S (1883), Revs. Thomas Connery; Joseph Bui (OAK); R. Alfredo Ortiz; Deacons Chester DeMarsh; Michael Alverez; Robert LaPlante; Gerard Smith; Robert Kinsey; Wilfred Steinmetz; Ronald Keehner.
Mailing Address: P.O. Box 3700, 32721. Tel: 386-822-6000; Fax: 386-822-6034.
Res.: 359 W. New York Ave., 32720.
School—Tel: 386-822-6010; Fax: 386-822-6013. Mrs. Joan Kinsey, Prin. Lay Teachers 30; Students 283.
Catechesis/Religious Program—Students 352.
Mission—San Jose Mission 165 Emporia Rd., Barberville, Volusia Co. 32005. Tel: 386-749-9372.

DEBARY, VOLUSIA CO., ST. ANN'S (1961), Rev. Paige A. Blakely; Deacon Jim Lathan.
Office:—26 Dogwood Tr., P.O. Box 530218, 32753-0218. Tel: 386-668-8270; Fax: 386-668-8471.
Res.: 10 Larkspur Ln., 32713.
Catechesis/Religious Program—Students 259.

DELTONA, VOLUSIA CO.

1—ST. CLARE (1989), (Anglo—Hispanic), Rev. Charles Viviano; Deacons Joseph Robert; Gilberto Torres.
Res.: 2961 Day Rd., 32738. Tel: 386-789-9990; Fax: 386-789-2430.
Catechesis/Religious Program—Students 300.

2—OUR LADY OF THE LAKES (1970), Revs. Edward J. McCarthy; Ralph I. DuWell; Deacons Hervey Mondor; Ray Doyle; Dan Feinbaum; Gilberto Perez; Ricardo Gonzalez.
Res.: 1310 Maximilian St., 32725. Tel: 407-574-2131; Fax: 407-860-0074.
Catechesis/Religious Program—Tel: 407-574-4620. Students 511.

DUNNELLON, MARION CO., ST. JOHN THE BAPTIST (1976), Rev. Joseph Pinchock; Deacons Fred Crawford Jr.; Joseph Interlandi.
Res.: 7525 S. Hwy. 41, 34432. Tel: 352-489-3166; Fax: 352-489-3156.
Catechesis/Religious Program—Students 94.

EUSTIS, LAKE CO., ST. MARY OF THE LAKES (1912), Rev. Manuel A. Fernandez; Deacons Louis Klein; Francis McDonald.
Res.: 218 Ocklawaha Ave., 32726-4840. Tel: 352-483-3500; Fax: 352-483-1370.
Catechesis/Religious Program—Tel: 352-483-3500, Ext. 109. Students 290.

HAINES CITY, POLK CO., ST. ANN (1969), (Anglo—Hispanic), [JC], (Formerly Transfiguration) Revs. Carlos Bedoya; Mark Wegg.
Res.: 1311 E. Robinson Dr., P.O. Box 1285, 33845. Tel: 863-422-4370; Fax: 863-421-2522.

INDIALANTIC, BREVARD CO., HOLY NAME OF JESUS (1959), Rev. David Page; Deacons Charles Foy; Joseph Richiuso; James Seidel.
Res.: 3050 Hwy. A1A, 32903. Tel: 321-773-2783; Fax: 321-777-0929.
School—(Grades K-8) Tel: 321-773-1630; Fax: 321-773-7148. Lay Teachers 28; Students 468.
Catechesis/Religious Program—Tel: 321-773-3905. Students 686.

KISSIMMEE, OSCEOLA CO.

1—ST. CATHERINE OF SIENA (1994), (Latino), Revs. Jose Bautista (Haiti); Yvon Hache; Deacons Roberto Ocasio; Eliezer Maldonado.
Office: 2750 E. Osceola Pkwy., 34745. Tel: 407-344-9607; Fax: 407-344-9160.
Res. & Mailing Address: P.O. Box 450698, 34745-0698. Tel: 407-344-1735.
Catechesis/Religious Program—Students 286.

2—HOLY REDEEMER (1917), (Hispanic), Revs. Robert W. Mitchell; Pedro (Peter) Puntal; Franklin Salazar.
Res.: 1603 N. Thacker Ave., 34741. Tel: 407-847-2500; 407-846-3700; Fax: 407-847-9687.
School— (1993),(Grades PreK-8), 1800 W. Columbia Ave., 34741. Tel: 407-870-9055; Fax: 407-870-2214. Mary Kay Spencer, Prin. Sisters of St. Joseph 1; Lay Teachers 24; Students 435.
Catechesis/Religious Program—Tel: 407-870-8196. Mrs. Rose Dzejak, D.R.E. Students 1,285.

LADY LAKE, LAKE CO., ST. TIMOTHY (1985), Revs. Robert Fucheck; Gerald Shovelton (Retired); Deacons John Sullivan; Frederick Giel; Nicholas Deutsch; Ronald L'Huillier; George Mattison.
1351 Paige Pl., 32159. Tel: 352-753-0989; Fax: 352-753-9602.
Catechesis/Religious Program—Students 60.

LAKE WALES, POLK CO., HOLY SPIRIT (1927), Revs. Anthony Bluett; Leon Dobosiewiez; Leo Dobo (Retired); Deacons Donald E. Raymond; John Avery.
Res.: 644 S. 9th St., P.O. Box 232, 33853. Tel: 863-676-1556; Fax: 863-676-2962.
Catechesis/Religious Program—Tel: 863-678-1083. Students 209.
Mission—St. Leo the Great Nalcrest, Polk Co. 33856. Tel: 863-679-1919. 10721 E. Leisure, 33898.

LAKELAND, POLK CO.

1—ST. ANTHONY'S (1982), Revs. Michael E. Giglio; Joseph M. Hayden (Retired); Deacon Jean Hughes Desir; Sr. Patricia Sipan, S.N.D., Pastoral Assoc.
Res.: 820 Marcum Rd., P.O. Box 90164, 33804-0164. Tel: 863-858-8047; Fax: 863-859-1036.
School—(Grades PreK-8), 820 Marcum Rd., 33809. Tel: 863-858-0671. Mrs. Colleen Ehlenbeck, Prin. Lay Teachers 11; Students 150.
Catechesis/Religious Program—Sr. Patricia Sipan, S.N.D., D.R.E. Students 195.

2—CHURCH OF THE RESURRECTION (1963), Rev. Matthew Mello; Deacon Joseph Wortman.
Res.: 3855 S. Florida Ave., 33813-1109. Tel: 863-646-3556; Fax: 863-644-8697.
School— (1990),(Grades PreK-8), 3720 Old Hwy. 37, 33813. Tel: 863-644-3931; Fax: 863-648-0625. Lay Teachers 35; Students 578.
Catechesis/Religious Program—Tel: 863-644-0585. Students 396.

3—ST. JOHN NEUMANN (1988), Rev. Frank Buck.
Res.: P.O. Box 7155, 33807. Fax: 863-647-0888.
Church: 501 E. Carter Rd., 33813. Tel: 863-647-3400.
Catechesis/Religious Program—Tel: 863-607-9458; Fax: 863-647-9845. Students 169.

4—ST. JOSEPH'S (1898), Revs. John Caulfield; Ramon Bolantete; Reynord Araya-Morales; Deacon Antonio Martinez. In Res., Rev. Felix Banos (Retired).
Res.: 210 W. Lemon St., P.O. Box 30, 33802. Tel: 863-682-0555; Fax: 863-686-9546.
School—Tel: 863-686-6415; Fax: 863-687-8074. Lay Teachers 19; Students 267.
Catechesis/Religious Program—Tel: 863-687-8873. Students 290.

LEESBURG, LAKE CO., ST. PAUL'S (1954), Revs. John C. Giel; Nicholas J. O'Brien; Deacon Lawrence Holder.
Res.: 1330 Sunshine Ave., 34748. Tel: 352-787-6354; Fax: 352-787-5971.
School—Tel: 352-787-4657; Fax: 352-787-0324. Lay Teachers 15; Students 164.
Catechesis/Religious Program—Tel: 352-787-6354; Fax: 352-787-5971. Students 206.

LONGWOOD, SEMINOLE CO., CHURCH OF THE NATIVITY (1960), Revs. Benjamin A. Berinti, C.Pp.S.; Henry L. Frantz, C.Pp.S.; Deacon Constantino Ferriola. In Res., Rev. Norbert Adelman, C.Pp.S.
Res.: 3255 N. Ronald Reagan Blvd., 32750. Tel: 407-322-3961; Fax: 407-322-3981.
Catechesis/Religious Program—Students 934.

MELBOURNE BEACH, BREVARD CO., IMMACULATE CONCEPTION (1978), Rev. Joseph A. Nolan; Deacons Howard Pettengill Jr.; Michael J. Biennas.
Res.: 3780 S. Hwy. A1A, 32951. Tel: 321-725-0552; Fax: 321-727-8218.
Catechesis/Religious Program—Tel: 321-726-8111. Students 94.

MELBOURNE, BREVARD CO.

1—ASCENSION (1959), Rev. Eamon Tobin; Deacons Michael McElwee; Sergio Colon.
Mailing Address: 2950 N. Harbor City Blvd., 32935-6259. Tel: 321-254-1595; Fax: 321-255-3490.
School—Tel: 321-254-5495; Fax: 321-259-0993. Sisters of Mercy (Ardee, Ireland) 1; Lay Teachers 30; Students 636.
Catechesis/Religious Program—Tel: 321-254-1595, Ext. 3080; Fax: 321-254-1595. Students 437.

2—OUR LADY OF LOURDES (1931), (Hispanic), Revs. William Hanley; Carlos Puerto; Deacons Michael J. Biennas; Ed Stives.
Res.: 1626 Oak St., 32901-4517. Tel: 321-723-3636; Fax: 321-951-8029.
School—420 E. Fee Ave., 32901. Tel: 321-723-3631; Fax: 321-723-7408. Lay Teachers 17; Students 206.
Catechesis/Religious Program—Students 171.

MERRITT ISLAND, BREVARD CO., DIVINE MERCY (1964), Rev. Michael A. Farrell.
Res.: 1940 N. Courtenay Pkwy., 32953. Tel: 321-452-5955; Fax: 321-455-2268.
School—Tel: 321-452-0263; Fax: 321-453-7573. Lay Teachers 19; Students 233.
Catechesis/Religious Program—Students 341.
Convent—1930 N. Courtenay Pkwy., 32953. Tel: 321-452-1279. Sisters 2.

MIMS, BREVARD CO., HOLY SPIRIT (1967), Rev. Bill Zamborsky.
Office & Res.: 2399 Holder Rd., 32754-2103. Tel: 321-269-2282; Fax: 321-269-2252.
Catechesis/Religious Program—Tel: 321-269-7785. Students 208.

MOUNT DORA, ORANGE CO., ST. PATRICK'S (1973), (Hispanic), [CEM] Revs. Emile A. Gentile, T.O.R.; Roderick Soha, T.O.R.; Luis Barrera; Deacon William Fisher Jr.
Res.: 6803 Old Hwy. 441 S., 32757. Tel: 352-383-8556; Fax: 352-383-8443.
Catechesis/Religious Program—Tel: 352-383-8556, Ext. 34. Students 205.

NEW SMYRNA BEACH, VOLUSIA CO.

1—OUR LADY STAR OF THE SEA (1973), Rev. Thomas J. Bergin; Deacon Paul Rock.
Res.: 3837 Sandstone Ct., 32169. Tel: 386-427-4530; Fax: 386-423-6245.
Catechesis/Religious Program—Tel: 386-423-6245. Students 62.

2—SACRED HEART (1926), Revs. Francis Browne, C.Ss.R.; John G. Barry, C.Ss.R.; Donald J. Winter, C.Ss.R.; John Cavanaugh, C.Ss.R.; Eugene Daigle, C.Ss.R.; Deacon Thomas Murray.
Res.: 998 Father Donlan Dr., P.O. Box 729, 32170. Tel: 386-428-6426; Fax: 904-423-4088.
School—Tel: 386-428-4732; Fax: 386-428-4087. Sisters of Notre Dame (Toledo) 3; Lay Teachers 18; Students 218.
Catechesis/Religious Program—Tel: 386-427-8372; Fax: 386-428-4087. Blake Buruazos, D.R.E. Students 225.
Mission—St. Gerard 3171 S. Ridgewood Ave., Edgewater, Volusia Co. 32141. Tel: 386-428-6930.

OCALA, MARION CO.

1—BLESSED TRINITY (1922), Revs. Patrick J. Sheedy; Pedro Zapata; Gabriel Ipasu; Deacons James Schwartz; James Boerstler; Heriberto Berrios. In Res., Rev. Michael O'Keeffe.
Res.: 5 S.E. 17th St., 34471. Tel: 352-629-8092; Fax: 352-351-8872.
School—Tel: 352-622-5808; Fax: 352-622-1660. Lay Teachers 38; Students 687.
Catechesis/Religious Program—Students 515.

2—ST. JUDE'S CATHOLIC COMMUNITY (1983), Rev. Anthony Palmese; Deacon Santos Santiago.
Church: 443 Marion Oaks Dr., 34473-3203. Tel: 352-347-0154; Fax: 352-347-5211.
Catechesis/Religious Program—Students 72.

3—OUR LADY OF THE SPRINGS (1982), Revs. Andrew Mallick; Ronald E. Oser.
Office—4047 N.E. 21st St., 34470. Tel: 352-236-2230; Fax: 352-236-1475.
Catechesis/Religious Program—Fran Lopez, D.R.E. (Grades K-8). Students 105.
Mission—St. Joseph of the Forest Silver Springs. 17301 E. Hwy. 40, Ocala National Forest, Marion Co. 34488. Tel: 352-625-4222; Fax: 352-625-4922.
Mission—St. Hubert of the Forest P.O. Box 715, Astor, Lake Co. 32102. Tel: 352-759-3983.

4—QUEEN OF PEACE (1987), Rev. Patrick J. O'Doherty.
Res.: 6455 S.W. State Rd. 200, 34476. Tel: 352-854-2181; Fax: 352-854-7840.
Catechesis/Religious Program—Students 110.

ORMOND BEACH, VOLUSIA CO.

1—ST. BRENDAN (1960), Rev. John J. Ryan.
Res.: 1000 Ocean Shore Blvd., 32176. Tel: 386-441-1505; Fax: 386-441-0774.
School—Tel: 386-441-1331. Lay Teachers 23; Students 237.
Catechesis/Religious Program—Tel: 386-441-1505, Ext. 307. Students 120.

2—PRINCE OF PEACE (1966), Revs. Thomas P. McMackin; Timothy P. Daly; Deacons John J. Mann; Harold Timmis.
Res.: 600 S. Nova Rd., 32174. Tel: 386-672-5272; Fax: 386-677-3224.
Catechesis/Religious Program—Students 406.

PALM BAY, BREVARD CO.

1—ST. JOSEPH (1914), [CEM] Rev. Robert J. Hoeffner; Deacon Alfred P. Somma.
Res.: 5330 Babcock St. N.E., P.O. Box 060507, 32906. Tel: 321-727-1565; Fax: 321-676-2579.
School—Tel: 321-723-8866; Fax: 321-727-1181. Lay Teachers 22; Students 380.
Catechesis/Religious Program—Students 216.

2—OUR LADY OF GRACE (1989), Rev. Leo Hodges; Deacons Richard C. Shaw; Francis Falotico; William T. Wanca Sr.; Jack Rhine.
Church & Mailing Address: 300 Malabar Rd. S.E., 32907-3005. Tel: 321-725-3066; Fax: 321-725-9534.
Res.: 949 Haas St., 32907. Tel: 321-726-8742.
Catechesis/Religious Program—Students 268.

POINCIANA, KISSIMMEE CO., ST. ROSE OF LIMA (1994), Unassigned.
Res.: 140 Pompei Dr., 34758. Tel: 407-932-5004; Fax: 407-932-0407.
Catechesis/Religious Program—Students 370.

PORT ORANGE, VOLUSIA CO.

1—EPIPHANY (1962), Rev. Paul T. Kamide.
Res.: 201 Lafayette St., 32127. Tel: 386-767-6111; Fax: 386-767-0017.
Catechesis/Religious Program—Students 223.

2—OUR LADY OF HOPE (1981), [CEM] Rev. Raymond

J. O'Leary.
Res.: P.O. Box 290216, 32129. Tel: 386-788-6144; Fax: 386-761-8840.
Catechesis/Religious Program—Tel: 386-788-6747. Betsy Glasenapp, D.R.E. Students 418.

ROCKLEDGE, BREVARD CO., ST. MARY'S (1917), [JC] Rev. Nicholas King; Rev. Msgr. Terence J. Farrelly, Pastor Emeritus (Retired); Rev. David Vivero.
Mailing Address: *Mailing Address*, 75 Barton Ave., 32955. Tel: 321-636-6834; Fax: 321-632-4301.
School—Tel: 321-636-4208; Fax: 321-636-0591. Sisters of Mercy (Limerick) 4; Lay Teachers 23; Students 394.
Catechesis/Religious Program—Tel: 321-633-9985. Students 204.

ST. CLOUD, OSCEOLA CO., ST. THOMAS AQUINAS (1968), Revs. Fabian G. Gimeno; Kent Walker.
Mailing Address: P.O. Box 700368, 34770-0368.
Res.: 721 Brown Chapel Rd., 34769. Tel: 407-957-4495; Fax: 407-957-1771.
Church: 700 Brown Chapel Rd., 34769.
School—800 Brown Chapel Rd., 34769. Tel: 407-957-1772; Fax: 407-957-8700. Lay Teachers 18; Students 297.
Catechesis/Religious Program—Tel: 407-957-4057. Students 499.

SANFORD, SEMINOLE CO., ALL SOULS (1911), [CEM] Revs. Richard W. Trout; Mark Christopher; Luis Barrera.
Res.: 301 W. 8th St., 32771. Tel: 407-322-3795; Fax: 407-322-1131.
School—Tel: 407-322-7090; Fax: 407-321-7255. Lay Teachers 17; Students 290.
Catechesis/Religious Program—Students 245.

TITUSVILLE, BREVARD CO., ST. TERESA (1958), Revs. John S. Murray; Joseph L. Roberts III; Deacons Donald Boland; Charles I. Robichaud.
Res.: 203 Ojibway Ave., P.O. Box 1598, 32781-1598. Tel: 321-268-3441; Fax: 321-268-3270.
School—Tel: 321-267-1643; Fax: 321-268-5124. Sisters of Mercy (Gort, Ireland) 3; Lay Teachers 19; Students 360.
Catechesis/Religious Program—Tel: 321-268-0440; Fax: 321-268-3720. Students 270.
Convent—3380 Muirfield Dr., 32780. Tel: 321-267-1610; Fax: 321-267-1610. Sisters 2.

WINTER GARDEN, ORANGE CO., RESURRECTION (1967), Rev. Alex Dalpiaz, C.S.
Church & Mailing Address: 1211 S. Vineland Rd., 34787. Tel: 407-656-3113; Fax: 407-654-4935.
Res.: 1211 S. Vineland Rd., 34787.
Catechesis/Religious Program—Students 520.

WINTER HAVEN, POLK CO.
1—ST. JOSEPH'S (1923), Revs. William J. Neumann; Mark Wegg; Deacons Nuoc Van Dang; John Landry.
Res.: 532 Ave. M N.W., 33881. Tel: 863-294-3144; Fax: 863-299-9709.
School—Tel: 863-293-3311; Fax: 863-299-7894. Sisters of Notre Dame, Chardon, Ohio Province 1; Lay Teachers 26; Students 496.
Catechesis/Religious Program—Tel: 863-299-9709. Students 266.
2—ST. MATTHEW (1973), Rev. Fred R. Ruse; Deacon Donald W. Worland.
Church & Mailing Address: 1991 Overlook Dr., 33884. Tel: 863-324-3040; Fax: 863-324-9198.
Res.: 365 Pasco Ct., 33884. Tel: 863-324-0357; Fax: 863-324-9181.
Catechesis/Religious Program—Tel: 863-324-3559. Students 292.

WINTER PARK, ORANGE CO., ST. MARGARET MARY (1947), Revs. Richard Walsh; Derk Schudde; Francis Smith; Deacons Robert Kreps; Nemsy Gubatan; Ralph Eckoff.
Res.: 526 N. Park Ave., 32789. Tel: 407-647-3392; Fax: 407-647-4492.
School—Tel: 407-644-7537; Fax: 407-644-7357. Lay Teachers 31; Students 559.
Catechesis/Religious Program—Tel: 407-647-5171; Fax: 407-647-4492. Students 499.

WINTER PARK, SEMINOLE CO., SAINTS PETER AND PAUL (1967), Revs. Sean K. Cooney; David Scotchie; Deacons Al Castellana; James Campbell; Donald Warner; Jerry Vaughan; Nick Nichols; Jose Gonzalez; Nick Nichols.
Res.: 5300 Old Howell Branch Rd., 32792. Tel: 407-657-6114; Fax: 407-657-9375.
Catechesis/Religious Program—Tel: 407-657-9530; Fax: 407-657-9530. Students 900.

WINTER SPRINGS, SEMINOLE CO., ST. STEPHEN (1985), Revs. John J. Bluett; George W. Dunne, S.S.S. (Ireland).
Res.: 575 Tuskawilla Rd., 32708. Tel: 407-699-5683; Fax: 407-699-8408.
Catechesis/Religious Program—Students 1,763.

SHRINES

MARY QUEEN OF THE UNIVERSE SHRINE (1986), Revs. F. Joseph Harte; Barry Dowd; John McMullan; Daniel Greene (Retired); Leo J. Gorman, C.P.
Res.: 8300 Vineland Ave., 32821. Tel: 407-239-6600; Fax: 407-239-1362.

Special Assignment:
Revs.—
Barrett, Thomas, Office of Cemeteries & Office of Vocations
Connolly, Matthew J., Judicial Vicar
Gentile, Emile A., T.O.R., Vicar for Clergy
Lossing, Larry, Office of Ecumenism
Walsh, Richard, Priests' Continuing Education
Webster, Robert E., Office of Worship

On Duty Outside the Diocese:
Revs.—
Bastos, Luiz C., Palm Beach
Henry, Peter, Switzerland
Kandel, Timothy, Miami
Mueller, Michael, U.S. Military
Olds, Steven, St. Vincent de Paul Seminary, Boynton Beach, FL
Stahl, Allen M., U.S. Military
Traupman, Robert, Maryland

Retired:
Rev. Msgrs.—
Bartok, Charles, 900 Broom St., Unit 4, Wilmington, DE 19806.
Farrelly, Terence J., 56 Barton Ave., Rockledge, 32955. Tel: 407-636-9099
Farris, Semaan, 604 Tupelo Dr., Melbourne, 32935. Tel: 407-255-2505
Revs.—
Angles, Sebastian, 2601 Muscatello St., 32837. Tel: 407-851-1934
Arboleda, Vidal, St. John Vianney, 6200 S. Orange Blossom Tr., 32809. Tel: 407-855-5391
Banos, Felix, P.O. Box 30, Lakeland, 33802-0030.
Benitez, Eduardo, P.O. Box 1524, Davenport, 33837.
Cosgrove, J. Kelly, 4182 Mount Vernon Ave., Titusville, 32780. Tel: 407-267-8601
Dobo, Leo, 1070 Tequesta Tr., Lake Wales, 33853. Tel: 863-769-1919
Donnelly, Brendan, Ireland
Donohue, Peter, C.S.C., Christopher Lodge, 323 Arthur Ave., Cocoa Beach, 32931. Tel: 407-799-8383
Edwards, James F., P.O. Box 2188, Ormond Beach, 32175. Tel: 904-258-5293
Foley, William A., S.M., 31 Fillmore Ct., Satellite Beach, 32937. Tel: 407-773-7631
Freitas, Daniel, 4905 Buttonwood Dr., Melbourne, 32940. Tel: 407-242-7365
Garcia, Emilio, P.O. Box 1757, Dunnellon, 34430.
Garvy, John, Blue Ridge Apartments, 108 N. Blue Ridge Rd., Black Mountain, NC 28711.
Grasso, Richard E., 415 N. Halifax Dr., Ormond Beach, 32176. Tel: 904-677-0188
Hamilton, Edward A., 1600 Hagys Ford Rd. Apt. 4M, Penn Valley, 19072. Tel: 610-949-0443
Harmon, Michael, P.O. Box 217, Palm Harbor, 34685. Tel: 727-781-7619
Hayden, Joseph Mark, 4927 Lakeland Harbor Blvd., Lakeland, 33805. Tel: 941-686-8046
Holland, Cajetan, C.S.C., 325 Arthur Ave., Cocoa Beach, 32931-4065.
Jennings, Francis, C.SS.R., St. Alphonsus Villa, P.O. Box 548, New Smyrna Beach, 32170.
Lambour, Stephen, C.S.C., 325 Arthur Ave., Cocoa Beach, 32931-4065.
Lochner, Robert J., C.S.C. (FTW), Christopher Lodge, 323 Arthur Ave., Cocoa Beach, 32931. Tel: 407-799-8383
McNicholas, Stephen, (Ireland)
Mena, Jose, 501 N. Ocean St., Apt. 1703, Jacksonville, 32202.
Nebus, Vincent, P.O. Box 060507, Palm Bay, 32906-0507.
Molin, Joseph A., 219 Essex Dr., Ormond Beach, 32176. Tel: 904-441-2055
Pawlak, Edwin F., 1315G Cheney Hwy., Titusville, 32780. Tel: 407-269-6089
Quinn, Peter, P.O. Box 7022, Daytona Beach, 32116.
Redmond, Lawrence, P.O. Box 4159, St. Augustine, 32085.
Rimshaw, Joseph J., S.S.J., 411 E. Lincoln Ave., Melbourne, 32901-4536. Tel: 407-723-1708
Ross, Kenneth, 62 Archer St., Yonkers, NY 10701-1540. Tel: 914-969-4560
Serraino, Frederick, C.S.C., Christopher Lodge, 325 Arthur Ave., Cocoa Beach, 32931. Tel: 407-783-6312
Sheedy, Val, Oceans 3, 3043 S. Atlantic Ave., Apt. 202, Daytona Beach, 32118.
Shine, Sean, P.O. Box 495 Candler, 32111. Tel: 352-687-4282
Slafkosky, Andrew L., 610 Pine Rd., Silver Springs Shores, 34472. Tel: 352-687-8677
Smith, Frank, 678 Scarlet Oak Cir. #114, Altamonte Springs, 32701.
Smith, Thomas, 621 Swallow Dr., Casselberry, 32707. Tel: 407-695-1720
VanNufflen, Albert, C.I.C.M., Aliki Condominium, 2828 N. Atlantic Ave., #202, Daytona Beach, 32118. Tel: 904-672-9098
Wallace, Harry, 4031 Saxson Dr., New Smyrna Beach, 32169. Tel: 904-426-7808
Zammit, Francis X., P.O. Box 291242, Port Orange, 32129. Tel: 904-761-1388

Permanent Deacons:
Agers, Allen, (Retired), Holy Spirit, Mims
Almodovar, Ismael, Resurrection, Winter Garden
Alvarez, Jose M., St. Peter, DeLand
Avery, John, Holy Spirit, Lake Wales
Barbieri, Robert, Inactive
Basso, Richard, Blessed Sacrament, Sharpes
Beltran, Miguel, St. John Vianney, Orlando
Benoit, Roland, St. Luke, Barefoot Bay
Berrios, Heriberto, Blessed Trinity, Ocala
Biennas, Michael, Our Lady of Lourdes, Melbourne
Boerstler, James, Blessed Trinity, Ocala
Boland, Donald, St. Teresa, Titusville
Bonneau, Louis, Immaculate Heart of Mary, Candler
Campbell, James, Sts. Peter & Paul, Winter Park
Castellana, Al, Sts. Peter & Paul, Winter Park
Cavins, William, (Inactive)
Collier, John, (Inactive)
Colon, Hector, St. Ann, Haines City
Colon, Sergio, Ascension, Melbourne
Crawford, Fred J., Jr., St. John the Baptist, Dunnellon
Crotty, John, Good Shepherd, Orlando
Cruz, Jose F., St. Andrew, Orlando
Dang, Nuoc Van, St. Joseph, Winter Haven
de la Fuente, Richard
DeJesus, Confesor, Good Shepherd, Orlando
DeJesus, Edwin
DeMarsh, Chester, St. Peter, DeLand
Desjardins, Roland, On Duty Outside the Diocese
Deutsch, Nicholas, (Retired)
Diaz, Celso, Holy Cross, Orlando
Diaz, Frank, Resurrection, Winter Garden
Dignan, Paul, Sr., St. Joseph, Lakeland
Doyle, Raymond, (Retired), Our Lady of the Lakes, Deltona
Dwyer, Bruce, Holy Spirit, Mims
Eckoff, Ralph R., St. Margaret Mary, Winter Park
Falotico, Francis E., Our Lady of Grace, Palm Bay
Feinbaum, Daniel, Our Lady of the Lakes, Deltona
Ferriola, Constantino, Nativity, Longwood
Fisher, William, Jr., St. Patrick, Mount Dora
Flynn, James, Sacred Heart, New Smyrna Beach
Foy, Les, Holy Name of Jesus, Indialantic
Garcia, Jose M., Good Shepherd, Orlando
Gibbs, Marshall, St. Mary Magdalen, Altamonte Springs
Giel, Frederick, St. Timothy, Lady Lake
Giron, Jose, St. Lawrence, Bushnell
Glennon, John, St. Paul, Leesburg
Gonzalez, Jose, Sts. Peter & Paul, Winter Park
Gonzalez, Julio, Resurrection, Winter Garden
Gonzalez, Rafael, Blessed Sacrament, Clermont
Gonzalez, Ricardo, Our Lady of the Lakes, Deltona
Gubatan, Nemsy, St. Margaret Mary, Winter Park
Hamilton, James, Our Lady of the Springs, Ocala
Henry, Vernon, Our Saviour, Cocoa Beach
Herbert, Larry, St. Francis of Assisi, Apopka
Hernandez, Rafael, St. Andrew, Orlando
Hindes, John T., St. Joseph of the Forest Mission, Silver Springs
Holder, Lawrence, St. Paul, Leesburg
Interlandi, Joseph, St. John the Baptist, Dunnellon
Iskra, Joseph J., Holy Spirit, Lake Wales
Kazyk, Norm, St. Mary Magdalen, Altamonte Springs
Keehner, Ron, St. Peter, DeLand
Kelly, Gerard, St. Mary Magdalen, Altamonte Springs
Kinsey, Robert, St. Peter, DeLand
Klein, Louis, St. Mary of the Lakes, Eustis
Kloznick, Robert, St. Isaac Jogues, Orlando
Kreps, Bob, St. Margaret Mary, Winter Park
L'Huillier, Ron
Lammers, Jack, St. Joseph of the Forest Mission, Silver Springs
Landers, Robert, St. Paul, Daytona Beach
Landry, John, St. Joseph, Winter Haven
LaPlante, Robert, St. Peter, DeLand
Lathan, Jim, St. Ann, DeBary
Lendoiro, Orlando, St. Issac Jogues, Orlando
Libersat, Henry, St. Mary Magdalen, Altamonte Springs
Lysaght, Evan, Our Lady of Lourdes, Daytona
Maldonado, Eliezer, St. Catherine of Siena, Kissimmee
Mallon, Charles A., Holy Family, Orlando
Mann, John J., Prince of Peace, Ormond Beach
Martin, Jack, Holy Cross, Orlando
Martinez, Antonio, St. Joseph, Lakeland
Mattison, George, St. Timothy, Lady Lake

McDonald, Francis L., St. Mary of the Lakes, Eustis
McElwee, Michael, Ascension, Melbourne
McMahon, George, On Duty Outside the Diocese
Messinger, George, Epiphany, Port Orange
Monat, Noe, St. Ann, Haines City
Mondor, Hervey, Our Lady of the Lakes, Deltona
Morales, Ramon, Holy Cross, Orlando
Morales, Rene, St. Catherine of Siena Church, Kissimmee
Murello, Andrew, St. Mary, Rockledge
Murphy, Mike, St. Mary, Rickledge
Murray, Thomas, Sacred Heart, New Smyrna Beach
Neris, Susano, Blessed Trinity, Orlando
Nichols, Nick, Sts. Peter & Paul, Winter Park
O'Heru, Eugene, Blessed Sacrament, Cocoa
Ocasio, Roberto, St. Catherine of Siena, Kissimmee
Oettinger, Frank, St. Anthony, Lakeland
Orbon, Carl, Holy Family, Orlando
Otradovec, Byron, St. Lawrence, Bushnell
Pacheco, Angel, St. Isaac Jogues, Orlando
Parn, Harold, Queen of Peace, Ocala
Pellosie, John C., (Retired)
Perez, Gilberto, Our Lady of the Lakes, Deltona
Perez, Primitivo, Blessed Trinity, Ocala
Pettengill, Howard, Jr., Immaculate Conception, Melbourne Beach
Phelps, Wayne, Good Shepherd, Orlando
Pineiro, Ismael, Blessed Sacrament, Clermont
Pleus, Robert, Holy Family, Orlando
Ramos, Jose Vidal, St. Rose of Lima, Poinciana
Ramos, Jose A.
Raymond, Donald, Holy Spirit, Lake Wales
Reid, Joseph, St. Ann, Haines City; St. Ann, Haines City
Reilly, Eugene, Our Savior, Cocoa
Rhine, Jack, Our Lady of Grace, Palm Bay
Richiuso, Joseph, Holy Name of Jesus, Indialantic
Rinderle, Edward, (Inactive)
Robert, Joseph, St. Clare, Deltona
Robichaud, Charles, St. Teresa, Titusville
Rock, Paul J., Our Lady Star of the Sea, New Smyrna Beach
Rupp, Richard T., St. Charles Borromeo, Orlando
Ryan, Sam, St. James, Orlando
Santana, Heriberto, St. Francis of Assisi, Apopka
Santiago, Santos, St. Jude, Ocala
Schneider, Paul A., Blessed Sacrament, Clermont
Schwartz, James, Blessed Trinity, Ocala
Seidel, James, St. John the Evangelist, Viero
Shaw, Richard, Our Lady of Grace, Palm Bay
Shortell, Mike, Blessed Sacrament, Clermont
Simpson, Bruce, Ss. Peter & Paul, Winter Park
Smith, Gerard F., St. Peter, DeLand
Smith, James, St. Charles Borromeo, Orlando
Somma, Alfred P., St. Joseph, Palm Bay
Steinmetz, Wilfred, St. Peter, DeLand
Stives, Edward, Our Lady of Lourdes, Melbourne
Sullivan, John, St. Timothy, Lady Lake
Tagye, Thomas, St. John Vianney, Orlando
Timmis, Harold, St. Brendan, Ormond Beach
Torres, Gilberto, St. Clare, Deltona
Vaughn, Jerry, Sts. Peter & Paul, Winter Park
Wanca, William T., Sr., Our Lady of Grace, Palm Bay
Warner, Donald, Sts. Peter & Paul, Winter Park
Wendel, David, St. John Neumann, Lakeland
Whale, William, Epiphany, Port Orange
Wiencek, Bruno, St. Lawrence, Bushnell
Worland, Donald, St. Matthew, Winter Haven
Wortman, Joseph, Resurrection, Lakeland

INSTITUTIONS LOCATED IN THE DIOCESE

[A] HIGH SCHOOLS, DIOCESAN AND PAROCHIAL

ORLANDO. *Bishop Moore High School*, 3901 Edgewater Dr., 32804. Tel: 407-293-7561; Fax: 407-296-8135. Email: kanem@bishopmoore.org. Web: www.bishopmoore.org. Rev. Thomas Barrett. Lay Teachers 63; Students 1,097; Total Staff 41.

DAYTONA BEACH. *Father Lopez Catholic High School*, 960 Madison Ave., 32114. Tel: 904-253-5213; Fax: 904-252-6101. Email: ldowdy@fatherlopez.org. Web: www.fatherlopez.org. Sr. M. Jane Veldof, R.S.M., Prin.; Mrs. Linda Dowdy, Prin. Lay Teachers 22; Students 288; Total Staff 22.

LAKELAND. *Santa Fe Catholic High School*, (Grades 9-12), 3110 Highway 92 E., 33801. Tel: 863-665-4188; Fax: 863-665-4151. Email: mboyd-sfhs@doschool.org. Web: www.santafecatholic.org. Mike Boyd, Prin. Priests 1; Sisters 1; Lay Teachers 16; Students 190.

MELBOURNE. *Central Catholic High School*, 100 E. Florida Ave., 32901. Tel: 407-727-0793; Fax: 407-727-1134. Email: mancinij@melbournecc.org. Web: melbournecc.org. Mr. Joe Mancini, Prin.; Rev. Doug Bailey, School Pastor. Lay Teachers 39; Students 600.

OCALA. *Trinity Catholic High School*, 2600 S.W. 42nd St., 34474. Tel: 352-622-9025; Fax: 352-861-8164. Email: aprendergast@tchs.us. Web: www.trinitycatholichs.org. Bro. Thomas Andrew Prendergrast, C.F.C., Prin.; Rev. Patrick J. Sheedy, School Pastor. Brothers 4; Lay Teachers 27; Students 452.

[B] SPECIAL SCHOOLS

ORLANDO. *Morning Star School*, 954 Leigh Ave., 32804-2299. Tel: 407-295-3077; Fax: 407-522-1700. Email: mss954@aol.com. Kathryn Harding, Ph.D., Prin. School for Exceptional Children. Sisters of St. Joseph of St. Augustine 1; Lay Teachers 7; Students 60.

[C] HOUSING ACCOMMODATIONS FOR THE ELDERLY

ORLANDO. *Monsignor Bishop Manor Apts., Inc.*, 824 Borders Cir., 32808. Tel: 407-293-3339; Fax: 407-293-0085. Email: crobertson@cartereturgent.com. Total Staff 5; Total in Residence 176.

DAYTONA BEACH. *Casa San Pablo*, 401 N. Ridgewood Ave., 32114. Tel: 386-253-2828; Fax: 386-253-0842. Email: marlene0110@aol.com. Marlene H. Palmer, Admin. Total in Residence 64; Total Staff 9.

MELBOURNE. *Ascension Manor*, 2960 Pineapple Ave., 32935. Tel: 321-757-9828; Fax: 321-752-9437. Email: ascensionmanor@carteretmgmt.com. Donna Rafanello, Mgr. Total in Residence 80; Total Staff 9.

OCALA. *Trinity Villas I, Inc.*, 3728 N.E. 8th Pl., 34470-1093. Tel: 352-694-5507; Fax: 352-694-1434. Email: dcraw51898@aol.com. Debra Crawford, Mgr. Total in Residence 98; Total Staff 5.

Trinity Villas II, Inc., 3728 N.E. 8th Pl., 34470-1093. Tel: 352-694-5507; Fax: 352-694-7434. Email: dcraw51898@aol.com. Debra Crawford, Mgr. Total in Residence 64; Total Staff 3.

ORMOND BEACH. *Prince of Peace Housing, Inc.* dba Prince of Peace Villas , 664 S. Nova Rd., 32174. Tel: 904-673-5080; Fax: 904-673-2008. Email: styson@carteretmgmt.com. Sue Tyson, Mgr. Total in Residence 70; Total Staff 4.

PORT ORANGE. *Epiphany Manor*, 4792 S. Ridgewood Ave., 32127. Tel: 904-767-2556; Fax: 904-761-0490. Total in Residence 73; Total Staff 5.

WINTER HAVEN. *Episcopal Catholic Apartments*, 500 Ave. L, N.W., 33881. Tel: 863-299-4481; Fax: 863-299-5719. Email: kathyl@episcopal-catholic.com. Web: www.episcopal-catholic.com. Kathy Lang, Admin. Total in Residence 199; Total Staff 13.

[D] RETREAT CENTERS

WINTER PARK. *San Pedro Spiritual Development Center*, 2400 Dike Rd., 32792. Tel: 407-671-6322; Fax: 407-671-3992. Email: info@sanpedrocenter.org. Web: www.sanpedrocenter.org. Rev. Carl Vacek, T.O.R., Dir. Tel: 407-671-6322, Ext. 223. Total in Residence 5; Total Staff 3.
Friars on Staff: Revs. John Vianney Cunningham, T.O.R. Tel: 407-671-6322, Ext. 229; Robert D'Aversa, T.O.R.
Friars in Residence: Revs. Columba James Enright, T.O.R.; Patrick Seelman, T.O.R.

[E] MONASTERIES AND RESIDENCES OF PRIESTS AND BROTHERS

ORLANDO. *Bethany House of Beutel*, 1600 Lakeside Dr., 32803-1508. Tel: 407-894-8175; Fax: 407-897-1133. Revs. Jordan K. Grimes, C.P., Supr.; Emmet Linden, C.P. Prayer Center for Passionist Priests and Brothers.

COCOA BEACH. *Congregation of Holy Cross, Eastern Province*, 325 Arthur Ave., 32931-4065. Tel: 321-799-8383; Fax: 321-783-6312. Revs. Fred Serraino, C.S.C., Asst. Supr.; William Donahue, C.S.C.; Peter Donohue, C.S.C.; Cajetan Holland, C.S.C. (Retired); Stephen Lambour, C.S.C.; Robert McDonnell, C.S.C.; James Murphy, C.S.C.; Bros. Dennis Fleming, C.S.C., Superior; Jerome Healey, C.S.C.; Herman Zaccarelli, C.S.C. Total in Residence 10; Total Staff 5.

KISSIMMEE. *Presentation Brothers*, 1602 Pettis Blvd., 34741-3117. Tel: 407-846-2033; Fax: 407-846-7473. Email: fpm1802@Juno.com. Web: www.presentationbrothers.org. Bros. Francis Schafer, F.P.M., Region Leader; James Needham, F.P.M.; Bernard Murphy, F.P.M.

NEW SMYRNA BEACH. *St. Alphonsus Villa-Redemptorist Fathers and Brothers*, 318 N. Riverside Dr., P.O. Box 548, 32170-0548. Tel: 386-428-6481; Fax: 386-428-6481. Revs. George Dorn, C.SS.R., Supr.; Joseph Gribbon, C.SS.R.; Francis Jennings, C.SS.R. (Retired); Leo Lanigan, C.SS.R.; James McGonagle, C.SS.R.; Jerome Murphy, C.SS.R.; Francis Sands, C.SS.R.; Alfred Sieradski, C.SS.R.; Joseph Gorney, C.SS.R.; Bro. Thomas Rochacewicz, C.SS.R. Total in Residence 10; Total Staff 8.

Redemptorist Fathers of the Vice Province of Richmond, 313 Hillman St., P.O. Box 1529, 32170. Tel: 386-427-3094; Fax: 386-423-1270. Email: vprichmond@aol.com. Very Rev. Jerome Chavarria, C.Ss.R.; Revs. Vincent Douglass, C.Ss.R., Vice Prov. Procurator; George Kelly, C.SS.R.; Robert M. Pagliari, C.SS.R.; Michael Varady, C.SS.R. Total in Residence 46; Total Staff 5.

Villa Madonna, 4385 Saxon Dr., 32169. Tel: 386-427-4660. Email: seraphintor@aol.com. Very Rev. Seraphin Conley, T.O.R., Contact Person In Res. Rev. Seamus Corcoran, T.O.R.

OCALA. *Congregation of Christian Brothers* (Eastern U.S. American Province) , 1384 S.E. 54th Pl., 34480-5760. Tel: 352-622-1374. Email: brtap@aol.com. Bro. Thomas A. Prendergast, C.F.C., Contact Person.

WINTER PARK. *Franciscan Friars, T.O.R., Provincial Residence, San Pedro Friary*, 2400 Dike Rd., 32792. Tel: 407-671-6322; Fax: 407-671-3992. Email: info@sanpedrocenter.org. Web: www.sanpedrocenter.org. For detailed information of staff and residences in this diocese, please see Retreat Centers in the Institution section. Total in Residence 5; Total Staff 3.

[F] NEWMAN CENTERS OF CENTRAL FLORIDA

ORLANDO. *Embry-Riddle Aeronautical University Office of the Chaplain*, 600 S. Clyde Morris Blvd., Daytona Beach, 32114-3900. Tel: 386-226-6580; Fax: 386-226-6007. Email: csu_erau@yahoo.com. Web: www.db.erau.edu/campus/student/clubs/csunion.

Office of the Chaplain, 600 S. Clyde Morris Blvd., Daytona Beach, 32114-3900. Tel: 386-226-6581; Fax: 386-226-6007. Email: dalyt@cts.db.erau.edu. Rev. Timothy P. Daly, Univ. Chap. & Dir. Catholic Campus Ministry.

DE LAND. *Stetson University Catholic Campus Ministry* Newman House, 523 N. Amelia Ave., 32724. Tel: 386-822-8156; Fax: 386-822-6034. Email: tcon497830@aol.com. Rev. Thomas Connery. Total Staff 1.

LAKELAND. *Florida Southern College Newman Center* c/o St. Joseph, 210 W. Lemon St., 33815. Tel: 862-682-0555; Fax: 863-686-9546. Email: fr.ramon@stjosephlakeland.org. Web: www.stjosephlakeland.org. Rev. Robert Moses, Chap. Total in Residence 1; Total Staff 1.

MELBOURNE. *Florida Institute of Technology Campus Ministry* 150 W. University Blvd., 32901-6988. Tel: 321-674-8045; Fax: 321-674-8938. Email: dbailey@fit.edu. Web: www.fit.edu. Rev. Douglas S. Bailey, S.D.S. Total Staff 2.

WINTER PARK. *Rollins College Campus Ministry* c/o St. Margaret Mary, 526 Park Ave. N., 32789. Tel: 407-647-3392; Fax: 407-647-4492. Web: stmargaretmary.org.

University of Central Florida Catholic Campus Ministry Sts. Peter & Paul Parish, 5300 Old Howell Branch Rd., 32792. Tel: 407-657-6114, Ext. 226; Fax: 407-657-9375. Email: davsco@catholicweb.com. Web: pegasus.cc.ucf.edu/~ccm. Rev. David Scotchie.

[G] MISCELLANEOUS

ORLANDO. *Bishop Grady Villas*, 401 Bishop Grady Ct., St. Cloud, 34770. Tel: 407-892-6078; Fax: 407-892-3081. Christina Montauiti, Dir.

**Catholic Volunteers in Florida, Inc.* National recruitment for statewide (FL) placement of full-time volunteers in one-year service assignments. Co-sponsored by Florida's bishops, Sisters of St. Joseph of St. Augustine, FL, and New Hope Charities. The Episcopal Advisor is Most Reverend John H. Ricard, S.S.J. of the Diocese of Pensacola-Tallahassee. , P.O. Box 536476, 32853-6476. Tel: 407-660-8800; Fax: 407-660-8833. Email: volunteer@cvif.org. Web: www.cvif.org. Timmy Rupeiks, Prog. Coord.; Mr. Richard Galentino, Exec. Dir., Owned and operated by the Sisters of St. Joseph of St. Augustine, FL. Lay Volunteers 19; Staff 4.

Good Shepherd Corporation of Orlando, Inc., 599 Bablonica Dr., 32807. Tel: 407-658-2909; Fax: 407-658-0005. Email: flowrsmtl@jumo.com. Web: www.geocities.com/goodshepherdservices. Mr. John Custis, Pres. Total Assisted 170; Total Staff 4.

RELIGIOUS INSTITUTES OF MEN REPRESENTED IN THE DIOCESE

For further details refer to the corresponding bracketed number in the Religious Institutes of

Men or Women section.
[0140]—*Augustinians*—O.S.A.
[]—*Congregation of Christian Brothers* (Eastern U.S. American Province)—C.F.C.
[0220]—*Congregation of the Blessed Sacrament*—S.S.S.
[0610]—*Congregation of the Holy Cross (Southern Province)*—C.S.C.
[1000]—*Congregation of the Passion*—C.P.
[0520]—*Franciscan Fathers*—O.F.M.
[]—*Legionaries of Christ*—L.C.
[0760]—*Marist Fathers Society of Mary*—S.M.
[0720]—*Missionaries of Our Lady of LaSalette*—M.S.
[]—*Missionaries of St. Charles*—C.S.
[]—*Missionhurst Congregation of the Immaculate Heart of Mary*—C.I.C.M.
[0910]—*Oblates of Mary Immaculate*—O.M.I.
[]—*Presentation Brothers*—F.P.M.
[1070]—*Redemptorist Fathers (Baltimore Province)*—C.SS.R.
[1200]—*Society of the Divine Savior*—S.D.S.
[1060]—*Society of the Precious Blood (Cincinnati Province)*—C.PP.S.
[]—*St. Joseph Society of the Sacred Heart*—S.S.J.
[0560]—*Third Order Regular of Saint Francis (Province of the Immaculate Conception)*—T.O.R.

RELIGIOUS INSTITUTES OF WOMEN REPRESENTED IN THE DIOCESE

[]—*Alianza in Jesus through Mary (Secular Institution)*—A.J.M.
[0230]—*Benedictine Sisters of Pontifical Jurisdiction* (St. Petersburg)—O.S.B.
[]—*Congregation of the Sisters of St. Joseph*—C.S.J.
[]—*Congregation of the Sisters of the Holy Family*—S.S.F.
[1070]—*Dominican Sisters*—O.P.
[1180]—*Franciscan Sisters of Allegany, New York*—O.S.F.
[]—*Immaculate Heart of Mary Reparatrix, Gqogonya*—I.H.M.R.
[]—*Incarnatio-Consecratio-Missio*—I.C.M.
[2720]—*Mission Helpers of the Sacred Heart*—M.H.S.H.
[3770]—*Order of St. Clare*—O.S.C.
[3130]—*Our Lady of Victory Missionary Sisters*—O.L.V.M.
[3320]—*Presentation Sisters of the Blessed Virgin Mary*—P.B.V.M.
[2070]—*Religious of the Holy Union of the Sacred Hearts*—S.U.S.C.
[3430]—*Religious Teachers Filippini*—M.P.F.
[3590]—*Servants of Mary (Servite Sisters)*—O.S.M.
[]—*Sisters for Christian Community*—S.F.C.C.
[0440]—*Sisters of Charity of Cincinnati, Ohio*—S.C.
[0430]—*Sisters of Charity of the Blessed Virgin Mary*—B.V.M.
[0990]—*Sisters of Divine Providence*—C.D.P.
[2360]—*Sisters of Loretto at the Foot of the Cross*—S.L.
[2640]—*Sisters of Mercy from Ireland* (Meath Community)—R.S.M.
[2523]—*Sisters of Mercy from Ireland* (Longford)—R.S.M.
[2530]—*Sisters of Mercy from Ireland* (Ardee-Dundalk)—R.S.M.
[2550]—*Sisters of Mercy from Ireland* (Limerick)—R.S.M.
[2560]—*Sisters of Mercy from Ireland* (Ennis)—R.S.M.
[2535]—*Sisters of Mercy from Ireland* (Galway)—R.S.M.
[2575]—*Sisters of Mercy of the Americas*—R.S.M.
[2990]—*Sisters of Notre Dame* (Chardon, OH)—S.N.D.
[3000]—*Sisters of Notre Dame de Namur*—S.N.D.deN.
[1630]—*Sisters of St. Francis of Penance & Christian Charity*—O.S.F.
[1650]—*Sisters of St. Francis of Philadelphia*—O.S.F.
[]—*Sisters of St. Francis of Syracuse*—O.S.F.
[1570]—*Sisters of St. Francis of the Holy Family*—O.S.F.
[3840]—*Sisters of St. Joseph of Carondelet* (St. Louis, MO)—C.S.J.
[3850]—*Sisters of St. Joseph of Chambery*—C.S.J.
[3900]—*Sisters of St. Joseph of St. Augustine, Florida*—S.S.J.
[1830]—*Sisters of the Good Shepherd*—R.G.S.
[1990]—*Sisters of the Holy Names of Jesus and Mary*—S.N.J.M.
[4110]—*Ursuline Nuns*—O.S.U.

NECROLOGY

† Campagnone, Rev. Msgr. Francis, (Retired)—Died March 20, 2003
† Denehy, Rev. Msgr. John, (Retired)—Died Aug. 22, 2003
† Bueche, Walter, St. Alphonsus Villa-Redemptorist Fathers and Brothers New Smyrna Beach, FL—Died 2003
† Collins, John, St. Alphonsus Villa-Redemptorist Fathers and Brothers New Smyrna Beach, FL—Died 2003
† O'Toole, Henry, St. Alphonsus Villa-Redemptorist Fathers and Brothers New Smyrna Beach, FL—Died 2003

Diocese of Owensboro

(Dioecesis Owensburgensis)

Most Reverend

JOHN J. McRAITH, D.D.

Bishop of Owensboro; ordained February 21, 1960; appointed October 23, 1982; consecrated December 15, 1982. *Res.: 501 W. Fifth St., Owensboro, KY 42301. 600 Locust St., Owensboro, KY 42301-2130.* Fax: 270-683-6883.

Catholic Pastoral Center: 600 Locust St., Owensboro, KY 42301. Tel: 270-683-1545; Fax: 270-683-6883.

Web: www.owensborodio.org

Email: ja@pastoral.org

CREATED DECEMBER 9, 1937.

Square Miles 12,502.

Erected February 23, 1938.

Comprises the following thirty-two Counties in the western part of the State of Kentucky: Allen, Ballard, Breckinridge, Butler, Caldwell, Calloway, Carlisle, Christian, Crittenden, Daviess, Edmonson, Fulton, Graves, Grayson, Hancock, Henderson, Hickman, Hopkins, Livingston, Logan, Lyon, McCracken, McLean, Marshall, Muhlenberg, Ohio, Simpson, Todd, Trigg, Union, Warren and Webster.

For legal titles of parishes and diocesan institutions, consult the Catholic Pastoral Center.

STATISTICAL OVERVIEW

Personnel	
Bishop	1
Priests: Diocesan Active in Diocese	59
Priests: Diocesan Active Outside Diocese	1
Priests: Diocesan in Foreign Missions	3
Priests: Retired, Sick or Absent	14
Number of Diocesan Priests	77
Religious Priests in Diocese	18
Total Priests in Diocese	95
Extern Priests in Diocese	2
Ordinations:	
Diocesan Priests	2
Transitional Deacons	1
Total Brothers	5
Total Sisters	198
Parishes	
Parishes	79
With Resident Pastor:	
Resident Diocesan Priests	47
Resident Religious Priests	5
Without Resident Pastor:	
Administered by Priests	20
Administered by Professed Religious Men	1
Administered by Religious Women	4
Administered by Lay People	2
Pastoral Centers	1
Professional Ministry Personnel:	
Brothers	3
Sisters	17
Lay Ministers	47
Welfare	
Catholic Hospitals	1
Total Assisted	399,685
Homes for the Aged	2
Total Assisted	219
Day Care Centers	3
Total Assisted	1,780
Special Centers for Social Services	3
Total Assisted	52,000
Educational	
Diocesan Students in Other Seminaries	4
Total Seminarians	4
Colleges and Universities	1
Total Students	713
High Schools, Diocesan and Parish	3
Total Students	934
Elementary Schools, Diocesan and Parish	18
Total Students	3,716
Catechesis/Religious Education:	
High School Students	1,526
Elementary Students	3,497
Total Students under Catholic Instruction	10,390
Teachers in the Diocese:	
Priests	3
Sisters	11
Lay Teachers	332
Vital Statistics	
Receptions into the Church:	
Infant Baptism Totals	949
Adult Baptism Totals	147
Received into Full Communion	190
First Communions	879
Confirmations	924
Marriages:	
Catholic	186
Interfaith	175
Total Marriages	361
Deaths	536
Total Catholic Population	51,847
Total Population	836,162

Former Bishops—Most Revs. FRANCIS R. COTTON, D.D., First Bishop of Owensboro; ord. June 17, 1920; appt. Dec. 16, 1937; consecrated Feb. 24, 1938; died Sept. 25, 1960; HENRY J. SOENNEKER, D.D. (Retired), Second Bishop of Owensboro; ord. May 26, 1934; appt. March 10, 1961; consecrated April 26, 1961; installed May 9, 1961; retired June 17, 1982; died Sept. 24, 1987.

Catholic Pastoral Center—600 Locust St., Owensboro, 42301. Tel: 270-683-1545; Fax: 270-683-6883. Refer all official business to this address.

Vicar General—Rev. GERALD CALHOUN, Res.: Christ the King Parish, 1600 Kingsway Dr., Madisonville, 42431. Tel: 270-821-5494.

Vicar of Clergy—Rev. DARRELL VENTERS, St. Thomas Aquinas, 1403 College St., P.O. Box 10170, Bowling Green, 42101. Tel: 270-843-3638; Fax: 270-843-3638.

Chancellor—Sr. JOSEPH ANGELA BOONE, O.S.U.

Archivist—Sr. EMMA CECILIA BUSAM, O.S.U.

Diocesan Tribunal—

Judicial Vicar—Rev. GREGORY G. TRAWICK; Ms. SANDY MORRIS, Admin. Asst.

Adjutant Judicial Vicar—VACANT.

Defender of the Bond—Rev. JOSEPH M. MILLS, J.C.L.

Judges—Revs. LEONARD ALVEY, Ed.S.; J. PATRICK REYNOLDS, J.C.L.; JOHN VAUGHAN, J.C.D.; RICHARD MEREDITH; J. MICHAEL CLARK, J.C.L.

Advocates— Priests and pastoral ministers of the diocese.

Case Promoters—Sr. VIVIAN MARIE BOWLES, O.S.U., Ed.D.; Mrs. DONNA MURPHY; Ms. LOUANNE GELARDEN.

Notaries—Mrs. MARY ANN KURZ; Ms. LOUANNE GELARDEN.

Clinical Psychologists—PATRICIA G. CAMPBELL; WILLIAM G. BACH, M.D.

Diocesan Boards and Councils

Diocesan Pastoral Council—Rev. GERALD CALHOUN; Ms. JANET THOMASON; Ms. DOROTHY LEE; Mr. JEFF LAMB; Sr. AUDREY RECKTENWALD, M.S.B.T.; Bro. KEN GRONDIN, C.F.C.; Rev. JOHN VAUGHAN, J.C.D.; Mr. TOM HAYDEN; Mr. PERRY ELDER; SUZANNE WILSON; Ms. SHARON EBELHAR; BARB CARPER; Ms. BETTY ELDER; Mr. PAUL BACHI; SUZANNE RUSH; Ms. MARILYN CHANDLER; Mr. JOE HANCOCK; Mr. STEVE SHOULTA; Mr. BILL CLARK; DELPHINE OPERLE.

Consultors—Revs. LARRY HOSTETTER; RANDY HOWARD; RICHARD POWERS; J. PATRICK REYNOLDS, J.C.L.; JOHN THOMAS.

Deans—Revs. FRANK RUFF, G.H.M., Bowling Green; J. EDWARD BRADLEY, Central; KEN MIKULCIK, Eastern; MIKE WILLIAMS, Fancy Farm; BEN LUTHER, Hopkinsville; RAY GOETZ, The Lakes; JOHN VAUGHAN, J.C.D., Owensboro; BRUCE McCARTY, Paducah; GERALD CALHOUN, Ex Officio.

Age Group Six Representative—Rev. PHIL RINEY.

Priests' Council—Revs. LARRY HOSTETTER; RICHARD POWERS; RANDY HOWARD; J. PATRICK REYNOLDS, J.C.L.; DELMA CLEMONS; JOHN THOMAS; GERALD CALHOUN; JOHN VAUGHAN, J.C.D.; J. EDWARD BRADLEY; KEN MIKULCIK; DARRELL VENTERS; FRANK RUFF, G.H.M.; BEN LUTHER; RAY GOETZ; BRUCE McCARTY; PHIL RINEY.

Council of Religious—Sisters MARY COLETTE GEERY, O.S.F.; PAT RHOTEN, O.S.U.; Rev. TIMOTHY SWEENEY, O.S.B.; Sisters MARTHA SCHULER, G.H.M.S.; EULA JOHNSON, S.C.N.; RITA LECHNER S.P.; CHERYL UEBELHOR, O.S.B.; AUDREY RECKTENWALD, M.S.B.T.; Bro. KEN GRONDIN, C.F.C.

Pastoral Office for Administration—Sr. JOSEPH ANGELA BOONE, O.S.U., Dir.; KAY HARDIN, Assoc. Dir.

Pastoral Office for Stewardship—Mr. KEVIN KAUFFELD, Dir.

Committee for Administration—Mr. HOMER BARTON; Ms. JANET BERRY; Ms. DONNA SAUER; Sr. BARBARA JEAN HEAD, A.S.C.; Mr. CHARLES KAMUF; Mr. JOSEPH HANCOCK; Mr. BOB OGLE; Revs. BRAD WHISTLE; GERALD CALHOUN; MARTY HAYES; Mr. MIKE THOMPSON.

Pastoral Office for Education—

Superintendent of Schools—Mr. JOSEPH O'BRYAN.

Director of Office for Religious Education—Ms. PATTY BLAIR.

Committee for Education—Revs. LEONARD ALVEY; BRIAN JOHNSON; Bro. KEN WOODS; Sr. PAT RHOTEN, O.S.U.; Mr. STEVE SHOULTA; Ms. ANNE O'BRYAN; ED CALHOUN; Ms. DONNA LAZZARO; Ms. JANICE CALHOUN; Ms. ROSE WHEELER; Ms. BONNIE MARKS; Mr. WAYNE HAGAN; Ms. LORRAINE LUKEN; Ms. CAROL HIGDON; Ms. BONNIE GIBSON; Ms. BARBARA HERTEL.

Director of Ecumenism—VACANT.

Youth Ministry—Ms. MELINDA PRUNTY, Dir.

Director of Communications and Editor of the Diocesan Newspaper—MEL HOWARD. "Western Kentucky Catholic"

Director of Television and Radio Broadcast Communications—Mr. CLIFF RUSSELL.

Pastoral Office for Worship—Rev. LARRY McBRIDE, Dir.; Ms. MARTHA HAGAN, Assoc. Dir.; Mr. MIKE BOGDAN, Dir. Office for Music.

Diocesan Liturgical Committee—Revs. CARL McCARTHY; LARRY McBRIDE; TONY BICKETT; Sr. LARRAINE LAUTER, O.S.U.; Ms. MARTHA HAGAN; Ms. PATTY BROWN; Mr. MICHAEL BOGDAN; Sr. ANNALITA LANCASTER, O.S.U.; Rev. JOHN THOMAS;

Ms. CLEO HIGDON; Sr. ALICIA COOMES, O.S.U.
Pastoral Office for Spiritual Life—Sr. AMELIA STENGER, O.S.U., Dir., Mount St. Joseph, 8001 Cummings Rd., Maple Mount, 42356. Tel: 270-229-0200; Fax: 270-229-0279.
Cursillo—Sr. ELAINE BURKE, O.S.U., Mount St. Joseph, 8001 Cummings Rd., Maple Mount, 42356. Tel: 270-229-0200.
Pastoral Office for Outreach—Sr. PATRICIA FRONING, O.S.F., Dir.
Catholic Charities—RITA HEINZ, Dir. Programs, 600 Locust St., Owensboro, 42301. Tel: 270-683-1545. Board Members: JAN BASILE; MARK PFIEFER; Revs. ED BRADLEY; PHIL RINEY; Sisters LUCY BONIFAS; JOSEPH ANGELA BOONE, O.S.U.; BETH CARRICO; RANDALL HARDESTY; PEGGY HOWARD; EDIE KEENEY; JUDY MCCLELLAN; CHIP PRIDE; GENE ROBERTS; KAYE CASTLEN; BETH CARRICO; STEVE TEASLEY; BOB HOWARD; MIKE BOONE; Bro. KEN WOODS.
Catholic Campaign for Human Development—RICHARD MURPHY, Dir.
Catholic Relief Service—RICHARD MURPHY, Dir.
Pastoral Office for Social Concerns—RICHARD MURPHY, Dir.
Social Concerns Committee—LIZ FRANCIS; Sr. MARTHA SCHULER, G.H.M.S.; GLORIA ADAMS; MARILYN CHANDLER; MIKE MORROW; MARTHA CRABTREE; BERNADETTE HOWARD; MARY DANHAUER; SUZANNE ROSE.
Office for Safe Environment for the Protection of Children and Young People—Ms. MARTHA HAGAN, Coord.
Respect Life Office—RICHARD MURPHY.
African-American Office—VERONICA WILHITE.
Hispanic Office—Rev. STAN PURYEAR, Dir., St. Joseph Parish, 434 Church St., Bowling Green, 42101-1810. Tel: 270-842-2525.
Pastoral Office of Family Life—BETTY MEDLEY, Dir.
Family Life Committee—Mr. TOM HAYDEN; Ms. JOYCE HAYDEN; JUDY KAPELSOHN; Ms. GAIL CRITCHELOW; Mr. DON WEAVER; Ms. MARY WEAVER; Mr. JERRY CRITCHELOW; Mr. DENNY MANN; BETTY MEDLEY; EDWINA HYLAND.
Natural Family Planning—DEANNA PAYNE; ANGIE SIMS; MICHELLE ROBERTS.
Society for the Propagation of the Faith—Rev. JOSEPH M. MILLS, J.C.L.
Pastoral Office for Personnel—Rev. DARRELL VENTERS.
Priest Personnel Committee—Revs. DAN KREUTZER; FREDDIE BYRD; PAT REYNOLDS; JOHN VAUGHAN, J.C.D.; RICHARD POWERS; BRAD WHISTLE; DARRELL VENTERS, Vicar of Clergy.
Vocations Office—Rev. BRAD WHISTLE, Precious Blood Parish, 3306 Fenmore St., Owensboro, 42301. Tel: 270-684-6888; Fax: 270-684-1304.
Continuing Education for Priests—Rev. RICHARD MEREDITH, St. Pius Tenth Parish, 3512 E. 6th St., Owensboro, 42303. Tel: 270-684-4745; Fax: 270-684-2709.
**Roman Catholic Diocese of Owensboro Charitable Trust Fund, Inc.*—Most Rev. JOHN J. MCRAITH; Revs. JOE MILLS; JOE RHODES; PAUL POWELL; BOB OSBORNE.

Organizations

St. Vincent de Paul Society—Rev. DARRELL VENTERS, Chap., P.O. Box 10170, Bowling Green, 42102-4770.
Scouting Activities—Rev. KENNETH MIKULCIK, Chap., 600 Locust St., Owensboro, 42301. Tel: 270-683-1545.
Holy Childhood Association—Rev. JOSEPH M. MILLS, J.C.L.
Teens Encounter Christ—Rev. FREDDIE BYRD, 600 Locust St., Owensboro, 42301. Tel: 270-683-1545.
Legion of Mary—VACANT.
Serra Club—Rev. JOE MILLS, Chap.; JOY BACH, Pres.
Lourdes Hospital—1530 Lone Oak Rd., P.O. Box 7100, Paducah, 42002-7100. Tel: 270-444-2444; Fax: 270-444-2980. WILLIAM G. WHEELER, M.D., Pres. & CEO.
Victim Assistance Coordinator—RITA HEINZ. Tel: 270-683-1545. Email: heinzr@pastoral.org.

CLERGY, PARISHES, MISSIONS AND PAROCHIAL SCHOOLS

CITY OF OWENSBORO
(DAVIESS COUNTY)

1—ST. STEPHEN CATHEDRAL, Revs. John R. Vaughan; Tony Shonis; Sr. Martha Keller, Pastoral Assoc.; Mr. Michael Conley, Pastoral Assoc.; Mr. Ron Greenwell, Pastoral Assoc.; Mr. Larry Lyon, Pastoral Assoc.
Res.: 614 Locust St., 42301. Tel: 270-683-6525; Fax: 270-683-3621. Web: www.ststephencathedral@pastoral.org.
Chapel—Blessed Sacrament [CEM] 602 Sycamore St., 42301. Tel: 270-926-4741. Veronica White, Admin.

2—BLESSED MOTHER, Revs. Freddie Byrd; Mark Buckner; Jan Storm, Admin. Asst.; Dr. Margaret Ayers, Pastoral Assoc.; Sr. Alicia Coomes, O.S.U., Pastoral Assoc.
Office: 601 E. 23rd St., 42303.
Res.: 515 E. 22nd St., 42303. Tel: 270-683-8444; Fax: 270-683-6423.

3—THE IMMACULATE, Rev. Timothy Sweeney, O.S.B.; Sr. Julia Head, O.S.U., Pastoral Assoc.
Parish Office—2516 Christie Pl., 42301. Tel: 270-683-0689; Fax: 270-926-9016.
Res.: 2601 Christie Pl., 42301.

4—SS. JOSEPH AND PAUL, Rev. Brian J. Roby; Martha McCarty, Pastoral Assoc.
Res.: 609 E. 4th St., 42303. Tel: 270-683-5641; Fax: 270-685-4766.

5—OUR LADY OF LOURDES, Rev. John R. Meredith.
Res.: 4029 Frederica St., 42301. Tel: 270-684-5369; Fax: 270-683-8008.

6—ST. PIUS TENTH, Rev. Richard Meredith.
Res.: 3512 E. Sixth St., 42303. Tel: 270-684-5517; 270-684-4745 (Office); Fax: 270-684-2709.

7—PRECIOUS BLOOD, Revs. Brad Whistle; Pete Hughes; Sr. Rosanne Spalding, O.S.U., Pastoral Assoc.
Res.: 3306 Fenmore St., 42301. Tel: 270-684-6888; Fax: 270-684-1304.

OUTSIDE THE CITY OF OWENSBORO

AURORA, MARSHALL CO., ST. HENRY, [CEM] Rev. Robert Drury.
Res.: 16097 U.S. Hwy. 68 E., Hardin, 42048. Tel: 270-474-8058; Fax: 270-474-9867.

AXTEL, BRECKINRIDGE CO., ST. ANTHONY, [CEM] Rev. Kenneth Mikulcik.
Res.: R.R. 3, Hardinsburg, 40143. Tel: 270-257-2132; Fax: 270-257-2132.

BARDWELL, CARLISLE CO., ST. CHARLES, [CEM] Most Rev. Thomas J. Buckman.
Res.: 6922 State Rte. 408, 42023. Tel: 270-642-2586; Fax: 270-642-2222.

BEAVER DAM, OHIO CO., HOLY REDEEMER, Rev. Fideles Levri, G.H.M.; Sr. Luisa Bickett, O.S.U., Pastoral Assoc.
768 Horse Branch Loop, Horse Branch, 42349. Tel: 270-274-4285.
Office—P.O. Box 106, 42320. Tel: 270-274-3414; Fax: 270-274-4245.

BIG CLIFTY, GRAYSON CO., ST. MARY, Closed., Records kept at St. Paul's Church, 1821 St. Paul Rd., Leitchfield, KY 42754. Tel: 270-242-7436.

BOWLING GREEN, WARREN CO.

1—HOLY SPIRIT, Revs. W. Jerry Riney; Mark Buckner; Ms. Anita Willoughby, Pastoral Assoc.
Res.: 2232 Smallhouse Rd., 42104-4141. Tel: 270-842-7777; Fax: 270-842-6174.

2—ST. JOSEPH'S, Revs. Stan Puryear; Manuel D. Rivas (El Salvador), Hispanic Min.; Dan Fortier, Pastoral Assoc.
Res.: 434 Church Ave., 42101. Tel: 270-842-2525; Fax: 270-843-9624.

BROWN'S VALLEY, DAVIESS CO., ST. ANTHONY, [CEM] Rev. J. Michael Clark, J.C.L.; Kathi Lat_a, Pastoral Assoc.
Church: 261 St. Anthony Rd., Utica, 42376. Tel: 270-733-4341.

CADIZ, TRIGG CO., ST. STEPHEN, Revs. Carl McCarthy, Co-Pastor; John Thomas, Co-Pastor.
Res.: 1698 Canton Rd., 42211. Tel: 270-522-3801; Fax: 270-522-3901.

CALHOUN, MCLEAN CO., ST. SEBASTIAN, [CEM] Rev. Peter Hughes.
Res.: 130 State Rte. 136 W., 42327-9521. Tel: 270-273-3185; Fax: 270-273-3185.

CALVERT CITY, MARSHALL CO., ST. PIUS TENTH, Rev. Robert Drury.
Res.: P.O. Box 495, 42029. Tel: 270-395-4727; Fax: 270-395-5747.
Catechesis/Religious Program—911 Fifth Ave., P.O. Box 798, 42029. Tel: 270-395-4431.

CENTRAL CITY, MULENBERG CO., ST. JOSEPH, Rev. Benjamin F. Luther; Sisters Rose Karen Johnson, O.S.U., Pastoral Assoc.; Rose Theresa Johnson, O.S.U., Pastoral Assoc.
Res.: 113 S. Third St., 42330. Tel: 270-754-1164.

CLARKSON, GRAYSON CO., ST. ELIZABETH OF HUNGARY, [CEM] Rev. Martin E. Hayes.
Res.: 1821 St. Paul Rd., Leitchfield, 42754. Tel: 270-242-7436.
Catechesis/Religious Program—306 Clifty Ave., 42726. Tel: 270-242-4414.

CLINTON, HICKMAN CO., ST. JUDE, Rev. Michael E. Williams; Steve Ross, Pastoral Assoc.
Res.: 42031. Tel: 270-653-6869.

CLOVERPORT, BRECKINRIDGE CO., ST. ROSE, [CEM] Rev. Gary Hayes.
Res.: 118 Chestnut St., 40111. Tel: 270-788-6422; Fax: 270-788-6422.

CURDSVILLE, DAVIESS CO., ST. ELIZABETH, Rev. Pike Powell, Admin.
Mailing Address: 6143 First St., P.O. Box 9-A, 42334. Tel: 270-229-4134.

DAWSON SPRINGS, HOPKINS CO., RESURRECTION, Rev. Bruce Fogle.
Church: 530 Industrial Park Rd., 42408. Tel: 270-383-4743; 270-797-8665; Fax: 270-383-4744.

EARLINGTON, HOPKINS CO., IMMACULATE CONCEPTION, Rev. Bruce Fogle.
Res.: 125 S. Day St., 42410. Tel: 270-383-4743; Fax: 270-383-4744.

EDDYVILLE, LYON CO., ST. MARK CHURCH, Rev. Maurice J. Tiell, Admin.
Res.: 302 Peachtree Ln., 42038. Tel: 270-388-2133.

ELKTON, TODD CO., ST. SUSAN, Rev. Frank Ruff, G.H.M.; Bro. Ken Woods, G.H.M., Pastoral Assoc.; Mr. Paul Witte, Pastoral Assoc.
Res.: P.O. Box 788, 42220. Tel: 270-265-5263; Fax: 270-265-5288.

FANCY FARM, GRAVES CO., ST. JEROME, [CEM] Rev. Dave Johnson.
Res.: P.O. Box 38, 42039. Tel: 270-623-8181; Fax: 270-623-6341.
Catechesis/Religious Program—Lisa Marie Cipolla, D.R.E.

FANCY FARM, HICKMAN CO., ST. DENIS, [CEM] Rev. Thomas J. Buckman.
St. Charles Church: 6922 State Rte. 408, Bardwell, 42023. Tel: 270-642-2586; Fax: 270-642-2222.

FORDSVILLE, OHIO CO., ST. JOHN THE BAPTIST, Revs. Patrick M. Bittel; Ralph Earl Patterson; Sr. Marie Michael Hayden, O.S.U., Pastoral Assoc.
Mailing Address: P.O. Box 127, 42343. Tel: 270-276-3619.

FRANKLIN, SIMPSON CO., ST. MARY OF THE WOODS, [CEM] Rev. Eric Riley.
Res.: Box 388, 42135. Tel: 270-586-4515.

FULTON, FULTON CO., ST. EDWARD, Rev. Michael E. Williams.
Res.: 504 Eddings St., 42041. Tel: 270-472-2742.

GRAND RIVERS, LIVINGSTON CO., ST. ANTHONY OF PADUA, , (Grand Rivers Catholic Church) Rev. Msgr. George H. Hancock; Sisters Rosemary Esterkamp, G.H.M.S.; Martha Schuler, G.H.M.S.; Carol York, Pastoral Assoc.
Res.: 1518 J.H. O'Bryan Ave., P.O. Box 447, 42045. Tel: 270-362-0408.
Church: Tel: 270-362-7121; Fax: 270-362-7121.

GRAYSON SPRINGS, GRAYSON CO., ST. AUGUSTINE, [CEM] Rev. Brian A. Johnson.
Res. & Mailing Address: c/o St. Anthony Church, 1256 St. Anthony Church Rd., Clarkson, 42726. Tel: 270-242-4791; Fax: 270-242-2601.

GUTHRIE, TODD CO., STS. MARY & JAMES, Rev. Frank Ruff, G.H.M.; Sisters Bernadette Hengstebeck, G.H.M.S., Pastoral Min.; Catherine Schoenborn, G.H.M.S., Pastoral Min.
Res.: P.O. Box 325, 42234. Tel: 270-483-2571.

HARDINSBURG, BRECKINRIDGE CO., ST. ROMUALD, [CEM] Rev. Tony Bickett.
Res.: 40143. Tel: 270-756-2356; Fax: 270-756-2099.

HAWESVILLE, HANCOCK CO., IMMACULATE CONCEPTION, [CEM] Rev. David Kennedy; Sr. Rita Lechner, S.P., Pastoral Assoc.
Res.: 430 Main Cross, P.O. Box 219, 42348. Tel: 270-927-8419; Fax: 270-927-6783.

HENDERSON, HENDERSON CO., HOLY NAME OF JESUS, [CEM] Revs. J. Edward Bradley; Jason Wayne McClure; Sr. Margaret Ann Aull, O.S.U., Pastoral Assoc.
Res.: 511 Second St., 42420. Tel: 270-826-2096; Fax: 270-827-1494.
School—618 Second St., 42420. Tel: 270-827-3425; Fax: 270-827-3432. Ursuline Sisters 1; Lay Teachers 34; Students 631.

HENSHAW, UNION CO., ST. AMBROSE, [CEM] Rev. Richard Cash.
Res.: *c/o St. Francis Borgia*, 1317 N. Main St., Sturgis, 42459. Tel: 270-333-4645; Fax: 270-333-4342.
Catechesis/Religious Program—Tel: 270-333-2806.

HICKMAN, FULTON CO., SACRED HEART, Rev. Michael E. Williams; Sr. Mary Agnes VonderHaar, O.S.U., Pastoral Assoc.
Res.: 411 Moulton St., 42050-1327. Tel: 270-236-2071.

HOPKINSVILLE, CHRISTIAN CO., SS. PETER AND PAUL, Revs. Carl McCarthy, Co-Pastor; John Thomas, Co-Pastor.
Res.: 902 E. Ninth St., 42240. Tel: 270-885-8522; Fax: 270-885-5296.
School—Tel: 270-886-0172; Fax: 270-887-9924. Lay Teachers 10; Students 210.

IRVINGTON, BRECKINRIDGE CO., HOLY GUARDIAN ANGELS, Rev. Gary Hayes.
Mailing Address: 118 Chestnut St., Cloverport, 40111. Tel: 270-788-6422; Fax: 270-788-6422. 301 W. High St., 40146.

KNOTTSVILLE, DAVIESS CO., ST. WILLIAM, [CEM] Rev.

Anthony R. Stevenson.
Res.: 9515 Kentucky 144, Philpot, 42366. Tel: 270-281-4802; Fax: 270-281-9556.
School—Mary Carrico Memorial School, Tel: 270-281-5526; Fax: 270-281-9556. Lay Teachers 6; Students 84.

LACENTER, BALLARD CO., ST. MARY, [CEM] Rev. Dan Kreutzer; Sr. Teresa Riley, O.S.U., Pastoral Assoc.
Church: P.O. Box 570, 42056. Tel: 270-665-5551 (Office); 270-665-5654 (Res.).

LEITCHFIELD, GRAYSON CO., ST. JOSEPH'S, [CEM] Rev. Randy Howard; Sr. Ruth Mattingly, O.S.U., Pastoral Min.
Res.: 109 W. Walnut St., 42754. Tel: 270-259-3028; Fax: 270-259-9860.

LEWISPORT, HANCOCK CO., ST. COLUMBA, [CEM] Rev. David Kennedy; Sr. Rita Lechner, S.P., Pastoral Assoc.
Res.: 815 Pell St., P.O. Box 358, 42351. Tel: 270-927-8419; Fax: 270-295-3682.

LIVERMORE, MCLEAN CO., ST. CHARLES, Rev. Benjamin F. Luther.
Mailing Address: 113 S. 3rd St., Central City, 42330. Tel: 270-754-1164.
Church: 506 Hill Ave., 42352. Tel: 270-754-1164; 270-273-3185 (Res.); Fax: 270-754-1164.

MADISONVILLE, HOPKINS CO., CHRIST THE KING, Rev. Gerald Calhoun.
Res.: 1600 Kingsway Dr., 42431. Tel: 270-821-5494; Fax: 270-825-8612.
School—Tel: 270-821-8271. Lay Teachers 10; Students 119.
School—Preschool, Tel: 270-821-3954. Students 56.

MARION, CRITTENDEN CO., ST. WILLIAM, [CEM] Rev. Richard Cash.
Res.: 860 S. Main St., 42064. Tel: 270-965-2477; Fax: 270-965-0918.

MAYFIELD, GRAVES CO., ST. JOSEPH, [CEM] Rev. Tony Jones.
Res.: 702 W. Broadway St., 42066. Tel: 270-247-2843; Fax: 270-247-6835.
School—Tel: 270-247-4420; Fax: 270-247-6835. Lay Teachers 9; Students 118.

MCQUADY, BRECKINRIDGE CO., ST. MARY-OF-THE-WOODS, [CEM 2] Rev. Ken Mikulcik.
Res.: R.R. 3, Hardinsburg, 40143. Tel: 270-756-2093.

MORGANFIELD, UNION CO., ST. ANN'S, [CEM] Rev. Gerald H. Baker.
Res.: 304 Church St., 42437. Tel: 270-389-2287; Fax: 270-389-0219.
Catechesis/Religious Program—Melissa Alvey-Polites, D.R.E.

MORGANTOWN, BUTLER CO., HOLY TRINITY, Rev. Fideles Levri, G.H.M.; Sr. Marie Colette Gerry, O.S.F., Pastoral Assoc.
Res.: 766 Logansport Rd., P.O. Box 222, 42261. Tel: 270-526-3723; Fax: 270-274-4245.

MURRAY, CALLOWAY CO., ST. LEO, Rev. Ray Goetz; William Duffield, M.Div., Admin./Pastoral Assoc.
Res.: 401 N. 12th St., 42071. Tel: 270-753-3876; Fax: 270-759-2074.

OAK GROVE, CHRISTIAN CO., ST. MICHAEL THE ARCHANGEL, Revs. David William Kennedy; Carl McCarthy, Co-Pastor; John Thomas, Co-Pastor.
Res.: 448 State Line Rd., P.O. Box 505, 42262. Tel: 270-640-9850; Fax: 931-552-5518.

PADUCAH, MCCRACKEN CO.

1—ST. FRANCIS DE SALES, Revs. Larry McBride; Al Bremer.
Res.: 116 S. Sixth St., 42001. Tel: 270-442-1923; Fax: 270-443-4616.

2—ST. JOHN THE EVANGELIST, Rev. Bruce McCarty.
Parish Office—7430 St. John Church Rd., 42003.
Res.: 6705 Old U.S. Hwy. 45, 42003. Tel: 270-554-3810; Fax: 270-534-9163.
School—7450 St. John Church Rd., 42003. Tel: 270-554-8826; Fax: 270-554-8826. Lay Teachers 8; Students 51.

3—ROSARY CHAPEL, Revs. Larry McBride; Al Bremer.
Mailing Address: P.O. Box 1481, 42002-1481.
Res.: 711 Ohio St., 42001. Tel: 270-444-6383; Fax: 270-444-0553.

4—ST. THOMAS MORE, Rev. J. Patrick Reynolds, J.C.L.
Church: 5645 Blandville Rd., 42001. Tel: 270-534-9000; Fax: 270-534-4339.
Catechesis/Religious Program—Faith Formation, 1241 Elmdale Rd., 42003. Tel: 270-443-0295.

PEONIA, GRAYSON CO., ST. ANTHONY'S, [CEM] Rev. Brian A. Johnson.
Res.: 1256 St. Anthony Church Rd., Clarkson, 42726. Tel: 270-242-4791.

PHILPOT, DAVIESS CO., ST. LAWRENCE, [CEM] Rev. Anthony R. Stevenson.
Res.: 9515 Kentucky 144, Knottsville, 42366. Tel: 270-281-4802; Fax: 270-281-9556.

PRINCETON, CALDWELL CO., ST. PAUL, [CEM] Rev. Richard T. Danhauer.
Res.: 813 S. Jefferson, 42445. Tel: 270-365-6786.

PROVIDENCE, WEBSTER CO., HOLY CROSS, Rev. Bruce Fogle.
Church: 730 North Highway 41A, 42450. Tel: 270-383-4743; Fax: 270-383-4744.

REED, HENDERSON CO., ST. AUGUSTINE, [CEM] Rev. Maury D. Riney.
Res.: 16777 Hwy. 60 E., 42451. Tel: 270-764-5599.

ROME, DAVIESS CO., ST. MARTIN, Rev. Leonard Arcilesi.
Res.: 5856 Kentucky 81, 42301. Tel: 270-685-0339; Fax: 270-684-5444.

RUSSELLVILLE, LOGAN CO., SACRED HEART, Rev. Peter Stryker, C.P.M.
Res.: 296 W. 6th St., 42276. Tel: 270-726-6963; Fax: 270-726-2232.

ST. JOSEPH, DAVIESS CO., ST. ALPHONSUS, [CEM] Rev. Gregory G. Trawick.
Mailing Address: 7925 KY 500, 42301. Tel: 270-229-4164.
Res.: 7950 Cummings Rd., 42301. Tel: 270-229-4566; Fax: 270-229-4164.

ST. PAUL, GRAYSON CO., ST. PAUL, [CEM] Rev. Martin E. Hayes.
Res.: 1821 St. Paul Rd., Leitchfield, 42754. Tel: 270-242-7483.
School—Tel: 270-242-7483. Lay Teachers 4; Students 29.

SCOTTSVILLE, ALLEN CO., CHRIST THE KING, Rev. Dennis Holly, G.H.M.; Sr. Davida Loosbrock, O.S.F., Pastoral Assoc.
Res.: P.O. Box 463, 42164. Tel: 270-237-4404.

SEBREE, WEBSTER CO., ST. MICHAEL, Rev. Ray Clark; Bros. Ken Grondin, C.F.C., Pastoral Assoc.; Tim Smyth, C.F.C., Pastoral Assoc.
Res.: P.O. Box 705, 42455. Tel: 270-835-2584; Fax: 270-835-9919.

SORGHO, DAVIESS CO., ST. MARY MAGDALENE, [JC] Rev. Richard Powers.
Res.: 7232 Kentucky 56, 42301. Tel: 270-771-4436; Fax: 270-771-4478.

STANLEY, DAVIESS CO., ST. PETER OF ALCANTARA, [CEM 2] Rev. Ray Clark.
Res.: 81 Church St., 42301. Tel: 270-764-1983; Fax: 270-764-0931.

STURGIS, UNION CO., ST. FRANCIS BORGIA, Rev. Richard Cash.
Res.: 1308 N. Adams St., 42459. Tel: 270-333-5915; Fax: 270-333-4342.
Catechesis/Religious Program—1317 N. Main St., 42459. Tel: 270-333-2806; Fax: 270-333-4342.

SUNFISH, EDMONSON CO., ST. JOHN THE EVANGELIST, [CEM] Rev. Randy Howard.
Church: 430 St. John Church Rd., 42284. Tel: 270-259-3028; Fax: 270-259-9860.

UNIONTOWN, UNION CO., ST. AGNES, [CEM] Rev. Terry Devine; Libby Downs, Pastoral Assoc.
Res.: P.O. Box 607, 42461. Tel: 270-822-4416; Fax: 270-822-5316.

WAVERLY, UNION CO.

1—ST. PETER, [CEM] Rev. Terry Devine.
Res.: 201 E. Market St., 42462. Tel: 270-389-4224; Fax: 270-389-4224.

2—SACRED HEART, [CEM] Rev. Terry Devine.
Res.: 201 E. Market St., 42462. Tel: 270-389-4224; Fax: 270-389-4224.

WAX, GRAYSON CO., ST. BENEDICT, [CEM] Rev. Brian A. Johnson.
St. Anthony Church: 1256 St. Anthony Church Rd., Clarkson, 42726. Tel: 270-242-4791.

WHITESVILLE, DAVIESS CO., ST. MARY OF THE WOODS, [CEM] Revs. Patrick M. Bittel; Ralph Earl Patterson.
Res.: 10534 Main Cross, P.O. Box 1, 42378. Tel: 270-233-4196; Fax: 270-233-5557.
School—St. Mary's Grade School, Tel: 270-233-5253; Fax: 270-233-9360. Lay Teachers 14; Students 183.

Non-Parochial Assignments:
Revs.—
Alvey, Leonard J., Brescia University, 717 Frederica St., 42301.
Garner, Andy, Chap., Owensboro Catholic High School, 42301.
Hostetter, Larry, Brescia University, 717 Frederica St., 42301.
Mills, Joseph M., J.C.L., Chap., Mount St. Joseph, Maple Mount, 42356.
Reisz, Leonard, 617 E. 23rd St., 42301.

On Duty Outside the Diocese:
Rev.—
Roof, Frank, Chap., U.S. Penitentiary, 4200 Bureau Rd. N., Terre Haute, IN 47808.

Absent on Leave:
Revs.—
Ausenbaugh, J. Andrew
Karl, Kevin
Little, John
Payne, Gary
Ulrich, Steve
Weider, Henry

Military Chaplains:
Revs.—
Arflack, Gregory A., 4033 Custer Dr., Fort Knox, 40121.
Wheatley, Carroll, 900 Talon Cir., Apt. #1-A, Jacksonville, NC 28540.
Willett, William D., 5955 Wainwright Dr., Fort Hood, TX 76544.

Retired:
Rev. Msgr.—
Powers, Bernard, Bishop Cotton Apartments, 2501 Old Hartford Rd., 42303.
Revs.—
DeNardi, Charles A., Ambassador Shores, 1705 St. Paul Rd., Leitchfield, 42754.
Glahn, Carl, Bishop Cotton Apts., 2501 Old Hartford Rd., 42303.
Hagman, William J., Bishop Cotton Apts., 2501 Old Hartford Rd., 42303.
Miller, Joseph C., Box 319, Nevis, MN 56467.
Powers, Aloysius, 2501 1/2 Old Hartford Rd., Apt 6, 42303.
Reisz, Leonard, 617 E. 23rd St., 42303.
Rhodes, Joseph, Bishop Cotton Apts., 2501 Old Hartford Rd., 42303.
Riney, Philip C., P.O. Box 95, McDaniels, 40152-0095.

INSTITUTIONS LOCATED IN THE DIOCESE

[A] COLLEGES AND UNIVERSITIES

OWENSBORO. *Brescia University*, 717 Frederica St., 42301. Tel: 270-685-3131; 877-273-7242; Fax: 270-686-6422. Web: www.brescia.edu. Sr. Vivian Marie Bowles, O.S.U., Ed.D., Pres.. Email: vivianb@brescia.edu; Kathleen H. McKee, Ph.D., Dean; Sr. Helena Fischer, O.S.U., Registrar; Revs. Larry Hostetter; Leonard J. Alvey; Joseph T. Merkt. Priests 3; Sisters 12; Administrators 9; Lay Teachers 41; Students 750.

[B] HIGH SCHOOLS, INTER-PAROCHIAL

OWENSBORO. *Owensboro Catholic High School*, 1524 W. Parrish Ave., 42301. Tel: 270-684-3215; Fax: 270-684-7050. Email: harold.staples@owensborocatholic.org. Web: www.owensborodio.org/schools/ocs/index.htm. Mr. Harold Staples, Prin.; Rev. Andy Garner, Chm. Religion Dept.; Mr. Steve Garvin, Dean of Students; Ms. Karen Dueker, Devel. Dir. Priests 1; Lay Teachers 43; Students 570.

PADUCAH. *St. Mary High School*, 1243 Elmdale Rd., 42003. Tel: 270-442-1681; Fax: 270-442-7920. Email: rwhiting@smss.org. Web: www.smss.org. Mrs. Rosann Whiting, Prin. Sisters 1; Lay Teachers 16; Students 200.

WHITESVILLE. *Trinity High School* 42378. Tel: 270-233-5533; Fax: 270-233-9293. Web: www.trinityhs.com. Dr. Leonard D. Ralph, Prin.. Email: donralph@trinityhs.com. Lay Teachers 10; Students 164.

[C] ELEMENTARY SCHOOLS, INTER-PAROCHIAL

OWENSBORO. *St. Angela Merici School*, (Grades K-6), 525 E. 23rd St., 42303. Tel: 270-683-6989; Fax: 270-684-5956. Email: tracy.conkright@owensborocatholic.org. Ms. Tracy Conkright, Prin. Ursuline Sisters 1; Lay Teachers 17; Students 290.

Catherine Spalding School, (Grades K-6), 4017 Frederica St., 42301. Tel: 270-684-7583; Fax: 270-684-4938. Email: pj.hayden@owensborocatholic.org. Web: www.owensborocatholic.org. Mr. P. J. Hayden, Prin. Lay Teachers 8; Students 170.

Francis R. Cotton School, (Grades K-6), 3418 E. 4th St., 42303. Tel: 270-683-2268; Fax: 270-684-8309. Email: mike.clark@owensborocatholic.org. Web: www.bishopcotton.org. Mr. Mike Clark, Prin. Lay Teachers 11; Students 133.

Holy Angels Elementary, 5712 Kentucky Hwy. 56, 42301. Tel: 270-771-4773; Fax: 270-771-4310. Email: bill.hagan@owensborocatholic.org. Bill Hagan, Prin. Lay Teachers 8; Students 130.

Holy Family (Middle) School, (Grades 7-8) , (Owensboro Catholic Middle School) , 2540 Christie Pl., 42301. Tel: 270-683-0480; Fax: 270-683-0495. Email: jim.duffy@owensborocatholic.org. Web: www.owensborocatholic.org. Mr. James T.

Duffy, Prin. Lay Teachers 19; Students 247.

BOWLING GREEN. *St. Joseph School*, 416 Church Ave., 42101-1887. Tel: 270-842-1235; Fax: 270-842-9072. Email: stjosephbgky@hotmail.com. Web: home.catholicweb.com/stjoebg. Janice Lange, Prin. Lay Teachers 19; Students 318.

HARDINSBURG. *St. Romuald School*, 295 N. Main St., 40143. Tel: 270-756-5504; Fax: 270-756-5167. Email: srisprincipal@hotmail.com. Mr. Louis Mattingly, Prin. Lay Teachers 10; Students 206.

MORGANFIELD. *St. Ann Interparochial School*, 320 S. Church St., 42437-1600. Tel: 270-389-1898; Fax: 270-389-1834. Email: sais@pennyrile.net. Web: www.st-ann.com. Mrs. Janet Gill, Prin. Lay Teachers 13; Students 231.

PADUCAH. *St. Mary Elementary*, 377 Highland Blvd., 42003. Tel: 270-442-1681, Ext. 252; Fax: 270-442-7920. Email: glasoski@smss.org. Web: www.smss.org. Mrs. Genie Lasoski, Prin. Lay Teachers 22; Students 350.

St. Mary Middle School, (Grades 6-8), 1243 Elmdale Rd., 42003. Tel: 270-442-1681, Ext. 231; Fax: 270-442-7920. Email: rwhiting@smss.org. Web: www.smss.org. Ms. Rosann M. Whiting, Prin. Religious 1; Lay Teachers 9; Students 149.

[D] GENERAL HOSPITALS

PADUCAH. *Lourdes Hospital*, 1530 Lone Oak Rd., P.O. Box 7100, 42002-7100. Tel: 270-444-2444; Fax: 270-444-2980. Email: wwheeler@lourdes-pad.org. Web: www.lourdes-pad.org. William G. Wheeler, M.D., Pres. & CEO; Sr. Marie Moore, Vice. Pres. of Mission Svcs. Sisters of Mercy of the Americas, Region of Cincinnati. Bed Capacity 389; Patients assisted annually 442,399.

McAuley Manor, Inc. Tel: 270-575-0050; Fax: 270-444-7144. Housing for Elderly.

Mercy Manor, Inc. Tel: 270-415-9166. Apartments for Elderly.

Dublin Manor, Inc. Apartments for the Elderly

Lourdes Foundation, Inc., 1530 Lone Oak Rd., 42002-7100. Tel: 270-444-2205; 270-444-2101; Fax: 270-444-2732. Missie Hendley, Dir.

Mercy Regional Emergency Medical Services, Inc. Tel: 270-443-6529.

Legal Title: *Mercy Health Partners - Lourdes, Inc.*, Ambulance Service.

[E] HOMES FOR AGED

OWENSBORO. *Carmel Home*, 2501 Old Hartford Rd., 42303. Tel: 270-683-0227; Fax: 270-688-0630. Sisters M. Angela Therese Kim, Carmel. D.C.J., Supr.; M. Frances Teresa Scully, Carmel, D.C.J., Admin.; Rev. Joseph Rhodes, Chap. (Retired). Carmelite Sisters of the Divine Heart of Jesus Sisters 3; Residents 115.

KNOTTSVILLE. *Bishop Soenneker Home* Residential Care of the Handicapped. , 9545 Kentucky 144, 42366. Tel: 270-281-4881; Fax: 270-281-5804. Residents 55; Total Staff 27; Total Assisted Annually 14.

[F] MONASTERIES AND RESIDENCES OF PRIESTS AND BROTHERS

AUBURN. *Fathers of Mercy*, 806 Shaker Museum Rd., 42206. Tel: 270-542-4146; Fax: 270-542-4147. Email: fathers@fathersofmercy.com. Web: www.fathersofmercy.com. Very Rev. William P. Casey, C.P.M., Supr. Gen. In Res. Revs. Denis Blais, C.P.M.; Ben Cameron, C.P.M.; Louis Caporiccio, C.P.M.; Shannon Collins, C.P.M.; James P. Costigan, C.P.M.; Christopher Crotly, C.P.M.; Francis Fusare, C.P.M., C.P.M.; Robert M. Gregor, C.P.M.; Louis Guardiola, C.P.M.; Christopher Henderson, C.P.M.; Sean Kopczynski, C.P.M.; Wade Menezes, C.P.M.; John Molloy, C.P.M.; Dan Sheehan, C.P.M.; James Walling, C.P.M.; David M. Wilton, C.P.M., Vicar Gen., Mission Dir.

HARTFORD. *Glenmary House*, 300 Peach Alley, 42347. Tel: 270-298-9886; Fax: 270-298-9398. Email: ljohnson@glenmary.org. Rev. Thomas S. Charters, G.H.M., Novice Dir.; Bro. Larry Johnson, Dir. The Home Missioners of America In Res. Rev. Tom Kirkendoll, G.H.M.

[G] CONVENTS AND RESIDENCES FOR SISTERS

OWENSBORO. *The Glenmary Center*, P.O. Box 22264, 42304-2264. Tel: 270-686-8401; Fax: 270-686-8759. Email: info@glenmarysisters.org. Web: www.glenmarysisters.org. Sr. Patricia Leighton, Pres. Home Mission Sisters of America, Inc. aka Glenmary Sisters Professed Sisters in Community 9.

Service to the Home Missions Total Assisted Annually 10,000; Total Staff 6.

MAPLE MOUNT *Mount St. Joseph* Motherhouse and Convent of the Ursuline Nuns of the Congregation of Paris. , 8001 Cummings Rd., 42356. Tel: 270-229-4103; Fax: 270-229-4127. Email: robryan@maplemount.org. Web: www.ursulinesmsj.org. Sr. Rose Marita O'Bryan, O.S.U., Congregational Leader; Rev. Joseph Mills, Chap.; Sr. Vickie Cravens, O.S.U., Archivist. Professed Sisters in Community 176.

WHITESVILLE. *St. Joseph's Monastery*, 8564 Crisp Rd., 42378. Tel: 270-233-4571; Fax: 270-233-4356. Email: nunsp@bellsouth.net. Web: www.passionistnuns.org. Sr. Catherine Marie Schuhmann, C.P., Supr. Religious of the Passion of Jesus Christ, (Passionist Nuns, Cloistered Contemplative) Postulants 4; Novices 1; Final Vows 15

[H] RETREAT CENTERS

MAPLE MOUNT. *Mount St. Joseph Conference and Retreat Center, Inc.*, 8001 Cummings Rd., 42356. Tel: 270-229-0200; Fax: 270-229-0279. Email: msjcenter@maplemount.org. Web: www.msjcenter.org. Sisters Amelia Stenger, O.S.U. Dir.; Elaine Burke, O.S.U., Assoc. Dir.

[I] NEWMAN CENTERS

BOWLING GREEN. *Western Kentucky University Newman Center* St. Thomas Aquinas Chapel, 1403 College St., P.O. Box 10170, 42102-4770. Tel: 270-843-3638; Fax: 270-843-3638. Email: ventersd@insightbb.com. Web: www.wkucatholiccenter.com. Rev. Darrell Venters, Dir.; Sr. Elaine Byrne, O.S.U., Pastoral Min. Students 1,651.

MURRAY. *Murray State University Newman House* 220 N. 13th St., 42071. Tel: 270-753-1391; Fax: 270-759-2074. Email: newman.house@murraystate.edu. Web: www.newmanhouse.org. William Duffield, M.Div.; Rev. J. Raymond Goetz. Students 800.

[J] MISCELLANEOUS LISTINGS

OWENSBORO. *Cathedral Preschool*, 500 Locust St., 42301. Tel: 270-926-1652; Fax: 270-683-3621. Email: nancy.neal@pastoral.org. Nancy Neal, Dir. Students 206.

The Catholic Foundation of Western Kentucky, 600 Locust St., 42301. Tel: 270-683-1545; Fax: 270-683-6883. Email: ja@pastoral.org. Web: www.owensborodio.org.

Centro Latino, 524 Locust St., 42301. Tel: 270-683-2541; Fax: 270-683-2541. Email: ocentrolatino@aol.com. Total Staff 4; Total Assisted Annually 12,000.

**Daniel Pitino Shelter, Inc.* Provides soup kitchen seven days a week, shelter for 65 homeless, education facilities, legal aid and medical services for those unable to pay. , 501 Walnut St., 42301. Tel: 270-688-9000; Fax: 270-688-0093. Email: dpsjim@hotmail.com. Total Assisted Annually 30,000; Employees 14; Volunteers 210.

Gideon Productions, Inc., 4029 Frederica St., 42301. Tel: 270-688-9040; Fax: 270-688-9040. Email: frjohn@gideonproductions.com. Web: www.gideonproductions.com. Rev. John R. Meredith, Contact Person.

**Glenmary Sisters Charitable Trust*, P.O. Box 22264, 42301. Tel: 270-686-8401; Fax: 270-686-8759.

Interparish Deposit Loan Fund Corp., 600 Locust St., 42301-2130. Tel: 270-683-1545; Fax: 270-683-6883. Email: ja@pastoral.org. Web: www.owensborodio.org. Sr. Joseph Angela Boone, O.S.U., Contact Person.

Mercy Health Partners. Kentucky Indiana, Inc., The Corporate Center, Bldg. A, Ste. 202, 401 Frederica St., 42301. Tel: 270-683-7590; Fax: 270-683-5055. Email: dborders@health-partners.org. Doug Borders, Pres. & CEO.

Owensboro Catholic Consolidated School System, 1524 W. Parrish Ave., 42301. Tel: 270-686-8896; Fax: 270-686-8997. Email: al.thompson@owensborocatholic.org. Web: www.owensborodio.org/schools/ocs/index.htm. Al Thompson, Dir.

**The Roman Catholic Diocese of Owensboro Kentucky Charitable Trust Fund, Inc.*, 600 Locust St., 42301. Tel: 270-683-1545; Fax: 270-683-6883. Email: ja@pastoral.org. Web: www.owensborodio.org. Sr. Joseph Angela Boone, O.S.U.

BOWLING GREEN. *Diocesan Shrine of Mary Mother of the Church and Model of all Christians*, St. Joseph, 434 Church St., 42101. Tel: 270-842-2525; Fax: 270-554-3810. Email: stjoseph@muhlon.com.

PADUCAH. *St. Mary School System*, 1243 Elmdale Rd., 42003. Tel: 270-442-1681, Ext. 225; Fax: 270-442-7920. Email: learn@smss.org. Web: www.smss.org.

St. Mary School System Benefit Fund, 1243 Elmdale Rd., 42003. Tel: 270-442-1681; Fax: 270-442-7920. Email: learn@smss.org. Web: www.smss.org.

RELIGIOUS INSTITUTES OF MEN REPRESENTED IN THE DIOCESE

For further details refer to the corresponding bracketed number in the Religious Institutes of Men or Women section.

[0200]—*Benedictine Monks*—O.S.B.

[0820]—*Congregation of the Fathers of Mercy*—C.P.M.

[]—

[0570]—*Glenmary Home Missioners* (Glendale OH)—Glmy.

RELIGIOUS INSTITUTES OF WOMEN REPRESENTED IN THE DIOCESE

[0360]—*Carmelite Sisters of the Divine Heart of Jesus*—Carmel D.C

[]—*Congregation of Divine Providence*—C.D.P.

[2080]—*Home Mission Sisters of America*—G.H.M.S.

[2575]—*Institute of the Sisters of Mercy of the Americas* (Cincinnati, OH; Detroit, MI)—R.S.M.

[2790]—*Missionary Servants of the Most Blessed Trinity*—M.S.B.T.

[]—*Missioneras del Sagrado Corazon de Jesus Ad Gentes*—M.A.G.

[3170]—*Religious of the Passion of Jesus Christ*—C.P.

[1070-03]—*Sinsinawa Domincan Sisters*—O.P.

[0500]—*Sisters of Charity of Nazareth*—S.C.N.

[3360]—*Sisters of Providence of Saint Mary-of-the-Woods, Indiana*—S.P.

[]—*Sisters of St. Benedict*—O.S.B.

[1650]—*Sisters of St. Francis of Philadelphia* (PA)—O.S.F.

[2260]—*Sisters of the Lamb of God*—A.D.

[1760]—*Sisters of the Third Order of St. Francis of Penance and Charity* (Tiffin, OH)—O.S.F.

[1720]—*Sisters of the Third Order Regular of St. Francis of the Congregation of Our Lady of Lourdes* (Rochester, MN)—O.S.F.

[4120]—*Ursuline Nuns, of the Congregation of Paris*—O.S.U.

[1570]—*Sisters of St. Francis of the Holy Family* (Dubuque, IA)—O.S.F.

INTERPAROCHIAL CEMETERIES

OWENSBORO. *Mater Dolorosa*, 1860 W. 9th St., 42301.

Resurrection, 5404 Leitchfield Rd., 42303. Mr. Art Hodde, Dir.

BOWLING GREEN. *St. Joseph Interparochial Cemetery*, St. Joseph Cemetary Foundation, P.O. Box 10334, 42102. Tel: 270-842-2525. Mr. Ray Grudzielaner, Pres.

NECROLOGY

† Fischer, Charles G., (Retired)—Died July 2, 2003

† Mattingly, Martin Dawson Springs, KY Resurrection; Earlington, KY Immaculate Conception—Died Sept. 9, 2003

Diocese of Palm Beach

(Dioecesis Littoris Palmensis)

Most Reverend

GERALD M. BARBARITO

Bishop of Palm Beach; ordained January 31, 1976; appointed Auxiliary Bishop of Brooklyn June 28, 1994; installed August 22, 1994; appointed Bishop of Ogdensburg October 26, 1999; appointed Bishop of Palm Beach July 1, 2003; installed August 28, 2003. *Office: 9995 N. Military Tr., Palm Beach Gardens, FL 33410.*

The Pastoral Center Office: 9995 N. Military Tr., Palm Beach Gardens, FL 33410. Tel: 561-775-9500; Fax: 561-775-9556. *Mailing Address: P.O. Box 109650, Palm Beach Gardens, FL 33410-9650*

Web: diocesepb.org

Email: info@diocesepb.org

ESTABLISHED OCTOBER 24, 1984.

Square Miles 5,115.

Comprises the Counties of Palm Beach, Martin, Indian River, Okeechobee and St. Lucie in the State of Florida.

Legal Corporate Title: The Diocese of Palm Beach.

For legal titles of parishes and diocesan institutions, consult the Chancery.

STATISTICAL OVERVIEW

Personnel	
Bishop	1
Retired Bishops	2
Priests: Diocesan Active in Diocese	75
Priests: Diocesan Active Outside Diocese	3
Priests: Retired, Sick or Absent	33
Number of Diocesan Priests	111
Religious Priests in Diocese	32
Total Priests in Diocese	143
Extern Priests in Diocese	12
Ordinations:	
Diocesan Priests	4
Transitional Deacons	4
Permanent Deacons in Diocese	44
Total Brothers	5
Total Sisters	145
Parishes	
Parishes	49
With Resident Pastor:	
Resident Diocesan Priests	44
Resident Religious Priests	5
Missions	4
Professional Ministry Personnel:	
Sisters	25
Lay Ministers	98
Welfare	
Special Centers for Social Services	23
Total Assisted	9,600
Residential Care of Disabled	3
Total Assisted	18
Other Institutions	4
Total Assisted	400
Educational	
Seminaries, Diocesan	1
Students from This Diocese	5
Students from Other Diocese	74
Diocesan Students in Other Seminaries	11
Total Seminarians	16
High Schools, Diocesan and Parish	3
Total Students	2,245
Elementary Schools, Diocesan and Parish	15
Total Students	5,659
Elementary Schools, Private	2
Total Students	622
Catechesis/Religious Education:	
High School Students	3,176
Elementary Students	16,434
Total Students under Catholic Instruction	28,152
Teachers in the Diocese:	
Priests	7
Brothers	2
Sisters	21
Lay Teachers	570
Vital Statistics	
Receptions into the Church:	
Infant Baptism Totals	4,319
Adult Baptism Totals	342
Received into Full Communion	337
First Communions	3,820
Confirmations	2,332
Marriages:	
Catholic	628
Interfaith	246
Total Marriages	874
Deaths	2,348
Total Catholic Population	259,729
Total Population	1,806,524

Former Bishop—Most Revs. THOMAS V. DAILY, D.D., ord. Jan. 10, 1952; appt. Titular Bishop of Bladia and Auxiliary Bishop of Boston, Dec. 31, 1974; consecrated Feb. 11, 1975; appt. first Bishop of Palm Beach, July 17, 1984; installed Oct. 24, 1984; transferred to Bishop of Brooklyn, Feb. 20, 1990; J. KEITH SYMONS, D.D., ord. May 18, 1958; appt. Auxiliary Bishop of St. Petersburg, Jan. 16, 1981; consecrated March 19, 1981; appt. second Bishop of Pensacola-Tallahassee, Sept. 29, 1983; installed Nov. 8, 1983; appt. second Bishop of Palm Beach, June 2, 1990; installed July 31, 1990; resigned June 2, 1998; ANTHONY J. O'CONNELL, D.D., ord. March 30, 1963; appt. Bishop of Knoxville, May 27, 1988; ord. and installed Sept. 8, 1988; appt. Bishop of Palm Beach Nov. 6, 1998; resigned March 8, 2002; SEAN P. O'MALLEY, O.F.M.Cap., Ph.D., ordained Aug. 29, 1970; appointed Coadjutor May 30, 1984; appointed Bishop of St. Thomas, Virgin Islands; ordained Aug. 2, 1984; installed Oct. 16, 1985; appointed Bishop of Fall River June 16, 1992; installed Aug. 11, 1992; appointed Bishop of Palm Beach Sept. 3, 2002; installed Oct. 19, 2002; appointed Archbishop of Boston July 1, 2003; installed July 30, 2003.

The Pastoral Center—Mailing Address, P.O. Box 109650, Palm Beach Gardens, 33410-9650. Tel: 561-775-9500; Fax: 561-775-9556. *9995 N. Military Trail, Palm Beach Gardens, 33410.*

Vicar General—Rev. CHARLES NOTABARTOLO.

Moderator of Curia—Rev. CHARLES NOTABARTOLO.

Episcopal Secretary—Rev. BRIAN KING.

Executive Secretary to Bishop—Mrs. ANNETTE RUSSELL.

Chancellor—Mrs. LORRAINE SABATELLA.

Assistant Archivist—Mrs. MERKE BARONI.

Matrimonial Tribunal—

Judicial Vicar—Rev. Msgr. THOMAS J. KLINZING, J.C.L.

Adjutant Judicial Vicar—Rev. GLEN J. POTHIER, J.C.L.

Judges—Rev. Msgrs. RAYMOND BLAIR, S.T.L., J.C.D.; THOMAS J. KLINZING, J.C.L.; Revs. GLEN J. POTHIER, J.C.L.; DAMIAN TOWEY, C.P., J.C.D.

Defenders of the Bond—Rev. Msgr. RONALD BESHARA, S.T.L., J.C.L.; Rev. DAMIAN TOWEY, C.P., J.C.D.

Assessors—Rev. Msgr. JAMES BURKE; Rev. MICHAEL W. EDWARDS, B.S.; Mrs. LORRAINE SABATELLA, B.A.

Promoter of Justice—Rev. DAMIAN TOWEY, C.P., J.C.D.

Notaries—Rev. CHARLES NOTABARTOLO; Mrs. LORRAINE SABATELLA, B.A.

Director of the Tribunal—Mr. SANDI MARTINEZ, M.A.

Case Directors & Secretaries—Mrs. HELEN COUGHTER, B.A.; Mrs. DEBORAH DUXBURY, B.A.; Ms. ALICE RIVERA.

Advocates—Rev. Msgr. JAMES BURKE; Mr. BERNARD CONKO, B.M.M., J.D.; Ms. KATHLEEN CONTE; Ms. SYLVIA RAFTERY.

Secretariat for Ministerial Personnel

Secretary—Rev. Msgr. JAMES M. BURKE (Retired).

Office of Vocations—Rev. GAVIN BADWAY, Dir.; Sr. HELEN KILIJANSKI, A.S.C.J., Assoc. Dir.

Vicar for Religious—Rev. MARK A. SZANYI, O.F.M.Conv.; Sr. MARIA CONSILIA MANTELLO, A.S.C.J., Assoc. Vicar for Religious.

Religious Vocations—Sr. MARIA CONSILIA MANTELLO, A.S.C.J., Assoc. Vicar.

Vicar for Permanent Deacons—Deacon JACK PIERCE.

Office for Permanent Diaconate Formation—Deacon DENNIS DEMES, Dir.

Secretariat for Personnel

Secretary—Rev. EDWARD SZPIEG.

Office of Human Resources—Mrs. LIZ DOUGHERTY, Dir.

Serving Children Office—Ms. DIANE CARTIER, Coord.

Secretariat for Family Life

Secretary—Rev. THOMAS E. BARRETT.

Office of Family Life, Engaged Encounter—Mrs. JANICE PETERSEN MINSHEW, Dir.

Marriage Encounter—Very Rev. JAMES MURTAGH, Spiritual Moderator.

Office for Respect Life—Mr. DONALD KAZIMIR, Dir.

Spiritual Moderator—Rev. JOSEPH PAPES.

Office of Prison Ministry—Sr. BETTY FRASCINO, O.S.F., Dir. Tel: 561-775-9500.

Office of Substance Abuse Ministry—Mr. ERIK A. VAGENIUS, Dir. Tel: 561-775-9527.

Victim Assistance Coordinator—Ms. THERESA FRETTERD. Tel: 561-801-0999. Email: tfretterd@cardinalnewman.com.

Secretariat for Communications

Secretary—Rev. LEO F. ARMBRUST.

Office of Communications—Mr. JAMES BROSEMER, Dir.

Office of "The Florida Catholic"—Mrs. IRENE HEY, Editor.

Secretariat for Spiritual Development

Secretary—Rev. THOMAS J. SKINDELESKI.

Office for Liturgy—Rev. MICHAEL DRISCOLL, O.Carm., Dir.

Cursillo Movement for Hispanics—Revs. CHARLES NOTABARTOLO, Spiritual Dir. Tel: 561-684-4152; TIMOTHY O'TOOLE, V.F., Spiritual Dir.; JAIME DORADO, Assoc. Dir.

Charismatic Renewal for Hispanics—Revs. RICK GEORGE, Spiritual Dir.; MARIO CASTANEDA, Dir. Tel: 561-775-9500.

Legion of Mary—Rev. KEVIN MACGABHANN, Spiritual Moderator.

Secretariat for Diverse Apostolates

Secretary—Rev. NESTOR RODRIGUEZ.

Office for Black Catholic—Mrs. LORRAINE LYLES, Dir.

Office for Hispanic Ministry—Sr. VIVIAN GONZALEZ, R.M.I., Dir.

Office for Mayan Ministry—Sr. RACHEL SENA, O.P., Dir.

Office for Haitian Ministry—Rev. YVES GEFFRARD, Dir.

Office for Rural Life/Migrant Ministry—P.O. Box 1203, Stuart, 34995. Mrs. MARIA CHRISTINA MARQUEZ, Dir., P.O. Box 1203, Stuart, 34995.

Secretariat for Youth & Young Adults

Secretary—Rev. JAMES HESS, O.Carm.

Office of Youth and Young Adults—Sr. JUDE RUGGERI, A.S.C.J., Dir.

Office for Campus Ministry—Sr. NANCY STRILLACCI, A.S.C.J., Dir. Tel: 561-775-9500.

Office of Scouting—Deacon ROBERT JAMES DANIELS, Chap.

Secretariat for Education

Secretary—Rev. ALFREDO HERNANDEZ, V.F.

Superintendent of Schools—Sr. JOAN DAWSON, O.S.F. Assistant Superintendents: Mrs. PATRICIA CANTIERI; Mrs. MARIE PRIVUZNAK.

Office of Special Education - C.O.M.E.—Mrs. PATRICIA CANTIERI.

Office of Catechesis and Leadership Development—Vacant Deacon JAMES CAMPBELL, Dir.

School of Christian Formation-English & Spanish—Sr. VIVIAN GONZALEZ, R.M.I.

R.C.I.A.—Deacon JAMES CAMPBELL, Dir.

Secretariat for Evangelization

Secretary—Rev. JULIAN P. HARRIS.

Propagation of the Faith/Mission Support—Rev. JOHN A. BARROW, Dir.

Holy Childhood Association—Rev. JOHN A. BARROW, Dir., P.O. Box 109650, Palm Beach Gardens, 33410-9650.

Office of Ecumenical and Interfaith Activities—Rev. BRIAN FLANAGAN, Dir.

Office of Stewardship—Mr. EDWARD LAUGHLIN, Dir.

Office for Diocesan Services Appeal—Mr. EDWARD LAUGHLIN, Dir.

Secretariat for Catholic Charities

Secretary—Rev. Msgr. JOHN MCMAHON.

Executive Director—VACANT.

Catholic Charities—Administrative Offices, 9995 N. Military Trail, Palm Beach Gardens, 33410-9650. Tel: 561-775-9567; Fax: 561-625-5906. *Mailing Address, P.O. Box 109650, Palm Beach Gardens, 33410-9650.* Rev. Msgr. JOHN R. MCMAHON, Sec.; VACANT, Exec. Dir.

Aim for the Best—900 54th St., West Palm Beach, 33407. Tel: 561-842-2406; Fax: 561-863-5379. *Mailing Address, P.O. Box 8246, West Palm Beach, 33407.* ELENA M. GARCIA.

Elder Affairs—900 54th St., West Palm Beach, 33407. Tel: 561-842-2406; Fax: 561-863-5379. *Mailing Address, P.O. Box 8246, West Palm Beach, 33407.* Sr. MARYROSE CROWLEY, S.S.N.D.

Counseling, Adoption Services and Foster Care—900 54th St., West Palm Beach, 33407. Tel: 561-842-2406; Fax: 561-863-5379. *Mailing Address, P.O. Box 8246, West Palm Beach, 33407.* GLORIA STEVENSON.

Lifeline—900 54th St., West Palm Beach, 33407. Tel: 561-842-5301. *P.O. Box 8246, West Palm Beach, 33407.* MAFY RODRIGUEZ.

In-Home Family Therapy (Bridge to Success)—900 54th St., West Palm Beach, 33408. Tel: 561-842-2406; Fax: 561-863-5379. *P.O. Box 8246, West Palm Beach, 33407.* KELLI KUZNIAR.

Residences for Adults with Developmental Challenges—

Alhambra House—399 N.E. 25th Terr., Boca Raton, 33431. Tel: 561-392-9474.

Bethlehem House—2280 N.E. 5th Ave., Boca Raton, 33431. Tel: 561-368-1570.

Columbia House—424 N.E. 8th St., Boca Raton, 33432. Tel: 561-862-5990; Fax: 561-862-5989. MICHAEL PERRY.

Counseling Services—1040 S. Federal Hwy., Ste. 101, Delray Beach, 33483. Tel: 561-274-0801; Fax: 561-274-7056. DIANN JASINSKI.

Birthline—1040 S. Federal Hwy., Ste. 101, Delray Beach, 33483. Tel: 561-278-0894; Fax: 561-274-7056. MARY RODRIGUEZ.

Belle Glade Office—425 S.W. 4th St., Belle Glade, 33430. Tel: 561-996-0485; Fax: 561-996-4467. *P.O. Box 1000, Belle Glade, 33430.* EURANDA CLARKE.

GladesKids Out of School Program—Belle Glade. Tel: 561-993-0066; Fax: 561-993-0061. *Mailing Address, 900 S.W. Avenue J, Belle Glade, 33430.* Sr. LAURA CAVANAUGH, S.B.S.

Family Empowerment—425 S.W. 4th St., Belle Glade, 33430. Tel: 561-996-4402; Fax: 561-996-4467. *Mailing Address, P.O. Box 1000, Belle Glade, 33430.* JANNIE SUTHERLAND.

Maurawood Community Outreach—900 54th St., West Palm Beach, 33407. Tel: 561-842-2406; Fax: 561-863-5379. *Mailing Address, P.O. Box 8246, West Palm Beach, 33407.* SUSAN ZACCHEO.

Office of Housing Development & Management—9995 N. Military Trail, Palm Beach Gardens, 33410. Tel: 561-775-9571; Fax: 561-625-5906. *Mailing Address, P.O. Box 109650, Palm Beach Gardens, 33410.* ROBIN LUNN.

Office of Social Concerns—9995 N. Military Trail, Palm Beach Gardens, 33410. Tel: 561-775-9579; Fax: 561-625-5906. *Mailing Address, P.O. Box 109650, Palm Beach Gardens, 33410.* AL MINUTOLI.

Pahokee Pals Out of School Program—1200 E. Main St., Pahokee, 33476. Tel: 561-924-5677; Fax: 561-924-3595. KAREN ROMANI.

Refugee and Immigration Services—900 54th St., West Palm Beach, 33407. Tel: 561-863-9255; Fax: 561-863-1680. *Mailing Address, P.O. Box 8246, West Palm Beach, 33407.* ANNE MARIE ALEXANDRE.

Immigration Legal Services-Site 1—900 54th St., West Palm Beach, 33407. Tel: 561-434-0928; Fax: 561-202-2310. *P.O. Box 8246, West Palm Beach, 33407.* MARISOL ZEQUERIA BURKE, Attorney.

Immigration Legal Services-Site 2—1111 S. Federal Hwy. Ste. 218, Stuart, 34995. P.O. Box 2687, Stuart, 34995. MARISOL ZEQUERIA BURKE, Attorney.

Residences for Seniors—

Villa Franciscan—2101 Avenue F, Riviera Beach, 33404. Tel: 561-840-0444; Fax: 561-840-9444. BILL KERR.

Villa Madonna—4809 Lake Worth Rd., Lake Worth, 33463. Tel: 561-963-1900; Fax: 561-963-1476. ROSEMARY MCMAHON.

Villa Assumpta—2539 N.E. Mission Dr., 9-8, Jensen Beach, 34957. Tel: 772-334-0009; Fax: 772-334-2168. Ms. LINDA MATZ.

Villa Seton—3300 S.W. Chartwell St., Port St. Lucie, 34953.

Counseling, Adoption and Foster Care—1111 S.E. Federal Hwy., Ste. 218, Stuart, 34995. Tel: 772-283-0541; Fax: 772-220-9894. *Mailing Address, P.O. Box 2687, Stuart, 33995.* HELEN KELLY.

Indiantown Outreach Center—15305 S.W. Adams Ave., Indiantown, 34956. Tel: 772-597-2812. *Mailing Address, P.O. Box 67, Indiantown, 34956.* MARIA CRISTINA MARQUEZ.

St. Lucie County Outreach Office—217 N. U.S. Hwy. #1, Fort Pierce, 34948. Tel: 772-460-1419; Fax: 772-460-9664. *Mailing Address, P.O. Box 3936, Fort Pierce, 34948.* CARMEN SIBRUN.

Counseling Office—St. Lucie Church, 280 S.W. Prima Vista Blvd., Port St. Lucie, 34983. Tel: 772-562-5957; Fax: 772-562-2209. MARIA DUBOY.

Okeechobee County Youth Outreach—P.O. Box 2891, Okeechobee, 34974. Tel: 772-979-0857; Fax: 772-336-4827. MAGALI ARMAND.

Samaritan Center—3650 41st St., Vero Beach, 32960. Tel: 772-770-3039; Fax: 772-567-0812. JOYCE WILD.

Indian River Counseling Office—St. Helen Church, 2025 20th Ave., Vero Beach, 32961. Tel: 772-562-5957; Fax: 772-562-2209. MARY LAMARR.

Secretariat for Temporalities

Secretary—Rev. CHARLES NOTABARTOLO.

Financial Administrator—Mr. BASIL ZALOOM.

Financial Council—VACANT.

Property and Liability—Rev. RICHARD MURPHY.

Office for Building and Renovations—Mr. JIM BANNON, Dir.

Real Estate—Rev. RICHARD MURPHY.

Parish Formation and Planning—Rev. CHARLES NOTABARTOLO.

Office for Benefits and Pension—Mrs. ANA JAROSZ, Dir.

Office of Data Processing—Mr. BASIL ZALOOM.

Office for Facilities—Ms. MARIAN LOYND, Dir.

Office of Cemeteries—Rev. THOMAS VENGAYIL, V.F., Dir.; Mr. CHARLES FREEBOLD, Admin.

Legal Affairs—Mr. J. PATRICK FITZGERALD, Esq., 110 Merrick Way, Ste. 3-B, Coral Gables, 33134. Tel: 561-659-6438.

Secretariat for Canonical Services

Secretary—Rev. Msgr. THOMAS J. KLINZING, J.C.L.

Consultative Bodies

College of Consultors—Rev. Msgrs. JAMES BURKE; THOMAS J. KLINZING, J.C.L.; JOHN MCMAHON; Very Rev. JAMES MURTAGH; Revs. CHRISTOPHER ALLEN; MICHAEL W. EDWARDS, B.S.; GERALD GRACE; FRANCIS LECHIARA; RICHARD MURPHY; CHARLES NOTABARTOLO; ARTHUR VENEZIA.

Presbyteral Council—Rev. CHARLES NOTABARTOLO; Rev. Msgrs. JAMES BURKE; THOMAS J. KLINZING, J.C.L.; Revs. GERALD GRACE; ALFREDO HERNANDEZ, V.F.; THOMAS VENGAYIL, V.F.; TIMOTHY O'TOOLE, V.F.; MARIO CASTANEDA; RAYMOND HUBERT; TIMOTHY JOHNSON, O.Carm.; JOHN KASPAREK; FRANCIS LECHIARA; NOEL MCGRATH; SEAMUS MURTAGH; KEVIN NELSON; IRVINE NUGENT; FRANCIS REARDON; NESTOR RODRIGUEZ.

CLERGY, PARISHES, MISSIONS AND PAROCHIAL SCHOOLS

CITY OF PALM BEACH GARDENS
(PALM BEACH COUNTY)

CATHEDRAL OF ST. IGNATIUS LOYOLA (1984), Revs. John A. Kasparek, Pastor & Rector; John Gallagher.
Res.: 9999 N. Military Tr., 33410. Tel: 561-622-2565; Fax: 561-624-9489.
School—All Saints Interparochial School For a complete listing, please see Interparochial Schools in the Institution section.
Catechesis/Religious Program—Students 370.

OUTSIDE THE CITY OF PALM BEACH GARDENS

BELLE GLADE, PALM BEACH CO., ST. PHILIP BENIZI (1961), Revs. Luis Aineto, S.D.B.; Jeremiah Reen, S.D.B.; Jonn DiFiore; Bro. Vilaire Philius, S.D.B.
Res.: 710 S. Main St., 33430-4202. Tel: 561-996-3870; Fax: 561-996-1281.
Catechesis/Religious Program—Tel: 561-996-5928; Fax: 561-996-1281. Students 533.

BOCA RATON, PALM BEACH CO.

1—ASCENSION (1968), Revs. Charles Hawkins; Brian Lehnert; Deacon Dennis Demes. In Res., Rev. Joseph R. Lang, M.M.
Res.: 7250 N. Federal Hwy., 33487-1606. Tel: 561-997-5486; Fax: 561-997-5862.
Catechesis/Religious Program—Students 207.

2—ST. JOAN OF ARC (1956), Rev. Msgr. John McMahon; Revs. Roger F. McDonough (BGP); Semanhyia Boateng-Mensah.
Res.: 370 S.W. 3rd St., 33432. Tel: 561-392-0007; Fax: 561-392-0074.
School—Sisters of Mercy, Skibbereen, Tel: 561-392-7974; Fax: 561-368-6671. Sr. Ellen Murphy, R.S.M., Prin. Sisters 3; Lay Teachers 28; Students 689.
Catechesis/Religious Program—Tel: 561-391-4345; Fax: 561-368-6671. Students 784.

3—ST. JOHN THE EVANGELIST (1992), Rev. Michael O'Flaherty.
Res.: 10300 Yamato Rd., 33498. Tel: 561-488-1373; Fax: 561-488-5562.
Catechesis/Religious Program—Students 490.

4—ST. JUDE (1979), Very Rev. Michael Driscoll, O.Carm., Pastor & Carmelite Prov.; Revs. Timothy Johnson, O.Carm.; Aquinas Stack, O.Carm.
Res.: 2235 S.W. 16th Pl., 33486-8560. Tel: 561-392-8172.
Church: 21689 Toledo Rd., 33433. Tel: 561-392-8172; Fax: 561-362-2184.
School—Preschool, Tel: 561-392-9579; Fax: 561-362-0845. Ms. Ruth A. Doran, Dir. Staff 18; Students 84.
School—Tel: 561-392-9160; Fax: 561-392-5815. Miss Debbie Armstrong, Prin. Lay Teachers 34; Students 470.
Catechesis/Religious Program—Tel: 561-362-8597; Fax: 561-362-0845. Students 557.

5—OUR LADY OF LOURDES (1977), Revs. Francis Reardon; Yves Geffrard.
Res.: 22094 Lyons Rd., 33428. Tel: 561-483-2440; Fax: 561-482-0626.
Catechesis/Religious Program—Tel: 561-483-2440, Ext. 1429; Fax: 561-558-1434. Students 898.

BOYNTON BEACH, PALM BEACH CO.

1—ST. MARK (1952), Revs. Mark Szanyi, O.F.M.-Conv.; Samuel Zebron, O.F.M.Conv.; Ignatius Piatek, O.F.M.Conv.
Res.: 643 N.E. 4th Ave., 33435. Tel: 561-734-9330; Fax: 561-735-3463.
School—730 N.E. 6th Ave., 33435. Tel: 561-732-9934; Fax: 561-732-0501. Mrs. Marcia Seamans, Prin. Lay Teachers 22; Students 270.
Catechesis/Religious Program—Students 117.

2—ST. THOMAS MORE (1972), Revs. Julian P. Harris; Richard Schaefer; Peter Troug.
Res.: 10935 S. Military Tr., 33436. Tel: 561-737-3095; Fax: 561-737-8697.
Catechesis/Religious Program—Tel: 561-737-3521; Fax: 561-737-3596. Students 840.

DELRAY BEACH, PALM BEACH CO.
1—EMMANUEL (1983), Revs. James Fiore; Raymond P. Hubert, Pastor Emeritus (Retired).
Res.: 15700 S. Military Tr., 33484. Tel: 561-496-2480; Fax: 561-496-5755.
Catechesis / Religious Program—Students 109.
2—OUR LADY OF PERPETUAL HELP MISSION (1987), Rev. Roland Desormeaux, C.S.
Church & Res.: 510 S.W. Eighth Ave., 33444. Tel: 561-276-4880; Fax: 561-276-7036.
Catechesis / Religious Program—Students 267.
3—OUR LADY QUEEN OF PEACE (1963), Rev. Matthew Didone, C.S., Admin.
Res.: 9600 W. Atlantic Ave., 33446. Tel: 561-499-6234; Fax: 561-499-5513.
Catechesis / Religious Program—Students 350.
4—ST. VINCENT FERRER (1941), Revs. Frank Guinan; John A. Skehan, Pastor Emeritus (Retired); Timothy Sockol.
Res.: 840 George Bush Blvd., 33483. Tel: 561-276-6892; Fax: 561-276-8068.
School—715 N.E. 8th Ave., 33483. Tel: 561-276-3882; Fax: 561-279-9505. Sisters of Mercy (Kinsale, Ireland) 2; Lay Teachers 25; Students 228.
Catechesis / Religious Program—Tel: 561-279-8041; Fax: 561-276-6274. Students 313.
FELLSMERE, INDIAN RIVER CO., OUR LADY OF GUADALUPE MISSION (1991), Rev. Noel McGrath (Ireland).
Catechesis / Religious Program—Students 225.
Mission— Rte. 512, P.O. Box 9, Indian River Co. 32948. Tel: 772-571-9875; Fax: 772-571-8321.
FORT PIERCE, ST. LUCIE CO.
1—ST. ANASTASIA (1911), Revs. Timothy O'Toole, V.F.; Mark Christopher, Pastor Emeritus; Ducasse Francois, I.V. Dei. (Haiti).
Res.: 407 S. 33rd St., P.O. Box 430, 34954-0430. Tel: 772-461-2233; Fax: 772-461-2242.
School—Tel: 772-461-2232; Fax: 772-468-2037. Mrs. Vickie Guettler, Prin. Sisters 1; Lay Teachers 39; Students 692.
Catechesis / Religious Program—Students 92.
2—ST. MARK (1972), Revs. Thomas E. Barrett; Sean de Leis, C.S.Sp.
Res.: 1924 Zephyr Ave., 34982. Tel: 772-461-8150; Fax: 772-464-2367.
Catechesis / Religious Program—Tel: 772-464-8955. Students 130.
3—NOTRE DAME MISSION (1995), Revs. Timothy O'Toole, V.F.; Ducasse Francois, I.V. Dei. (Haiti).
Res.: 217 N. U.S. Hwy. #1, 34950. Tel: 561-466-9617; Fax: 561-466-4075.
Catechesis / Religious Program—Tel: 772-335-9540. Students 32.
HIGHLAND BEACH, PALM BEACH CO., ST. LUCY (1968), Revs. Gerald Grace; Anthony J. Chepanis, Pastor Emeritus (Retired).
Res.: 3510 S. Ocean Blvd., 33487. Tel: 561-278-1280; Fax: 561-278-8509.
HOBE SOUND, MARTIN CO., ST. CHRISTOPHER (1960), Revs. Aidan Hynes; Kevin Nelson.
Res.: 12001 S.E. Federal Hwy., 77233-55. Tel: 772-546-5150; Fax: 772-546-8820.
School—All Saints Interparochial School, Tel: 561-748-8994. For a complete listing, please see Interparochial Schools in the Institution section.
Catechesis / Religious Program—Students 284.
INDIANTOWN, MARTIN CO., HOLY CROSS (1960), Revs. Nestor Rodriguez; Juan de la Calle, Pastor Emeritus.
Mailing Address: P.O. Box 999, 34956.
Res.: 15927 S.W. 150 St., 34956. Tel: 772-597-2798; Fax: 772-597-2741.
Catechesis / Religious Program—Students 100.
JENSEN BEACH, MARTIN CO., ST. MARTIN DE PORRES (1973), Revs. Robert L. Magee; Thomas J. Rynne, Pastor Emeritus (Retired).
Mailing Address: P.O. Box 1087, 34958.
Res.: 2555 N.E. Savanna Rd., 34958. Tel: 772-334-4214; Fax: 772-334-8627.
Catechesis / Religious Program—Tel: 772-334-4492. Students 360.
JUNO BEACH, PALM BEACH CO., ST. PATRICK (1987), Revs. Brian Flanagan; Lucas Chacha. In Res., Rev. Bernard Dooley, S.J.
Res.: 2549 Hope Ln., W., 33410. Tel: 561-626-8626; Fax: 561-622-6471.
School—All Saints Interparochial School, Tel: 561-748-8994; Fax: 561-748-8779. For a complete listing, please see Interparochial Schools in the Institution section.
Catechesis / Religious Program—Students 170.
JUPITER, PALM BEACH CO., ST. PETER (1987), Revs. Donald T. Finney, M.I.C.; David C. Downey; Deacons John Kucera; Stephen McMahon; Donald Battison.
Res.: 1701 Indian Creek Pkwy., 33458. Tel: 561-575-0837; Fax: 561-575-6784.
School—All Saints Interparochial School For a complete listing, please see Interparochial Schools in the Institution section.
Catechesis / Religious Program—Students 625.
LAKE WORTH, PALM BEACH CO.
1—ST. MATTHEW (1992), Rev. Clemens Hammerschmitt.
Res. & Mailing: 6090 Hypoluxo Rd., 33463-7312. Tel: 561-966-8878; Fax: 561-968-1238.
Catechesis / Religious Program—Tel: 561-966-1538. Students 483.
2—SACRED HEART (1917), Revs. Peter Van Nguyen; Francis X. Fenech, Pastor Emeritus (Retired); Dumarsais Pierre-Louis; Edgar Mazariegos.
Res.: 425 N. M St., 33460. Tel: 561-582-4736; Fax: 561-588-5238.
School—410 N. M St., 33460. Tel: 561-582-2242; Fax: 561-547-9699. Stephen Smith, Prin. Sisters 1; Lay Teachers 22; Students 215.
Catechesis / Religious Program—Tel: 561-588-0837. Students 311.
LANTANA, PALM BEACH CO., HOLY SPIRIT (1964), Revs. Kevin MacGabhann; Ronald Schulz.
Res. and Mailing: 1000 Lantana Rd., P.O. Box 3978, 33465. Tel: 561-585-5970; Fax: 561-575-8482.
Catechesis / Religious Program—Tel: 561-585-3930. Students 140.
NORTH PALM BEACH, PALM BEACH CO.
1—ST. CLARE (1960), Revs. William D. O'Shea; Giuseppe Savaia (Italy).
Res.: 821 Prosperity Farms Rd., 33408. Tel: 561-622-7477; Fax: 561-624-0022.
School—Tel: 561-622-7171; Fax: 561-627-4426. Mr. Andrew J. Houvouras, Prin. Lay Teachers 30; Students 529.
Catechesis / Religious Program—Students 158.
2—ST. PAUL OF THE CROSS (1970), Revs. Arthur Venezia; James Molgano.
Res.: 10970 State Rd. AIA, 33408. Tel: 561-626-1873; Fax: 561-622-7307.
School—All Saints Interparochial School, Tel: 561-748-8994; Fax: 561-748-8979. For a complete listing, please see Interparochial Schools in the Institution section.
Catechesis / Religious Program—Students 181.
OKEECHOBEE, OKEECHOBEE CO., SACRED HEART (1964), Rev. Hugh Duffy.
Mailing Address: P.O. Box 716, 34973.
Res.: 901 S.W. 6th St., 34974. Tel: 863-763-3727; Fax: 863-763-9334.
Catechesis / Religious Program—Tel: 863-763-2745. Students 513.
PAHOKEE, PALM BEACH CO., ST. MARY (1932), Rev. John J. Mericantante.
Res.: 1200 E. Main St., 33476. Tel: 561-924-7305; Fax: 561-924-9394.
Catechesis / Religious Program—Tel: 561-924-5888. Students 60.
PALM BEACH, PALM BEACH CO., ST. EDWARD (1926), Rev. Francis J. Lechiara.
Res.: 144 N. County Rd., 33480. Tel: 561-832-0400; Fax: 561-833-3359.
Catechesis / Religious Program—Students 80.
PALM CITY, MARTIN CO., HOLY REDEEMER (1983), Revs. Martin B. Mulqueen; Anthony Basso, S.D.V.
Mailing Address: P.O. Box 916, 34991.
Res.: 1964 Capri St., 34990. Tel: 561-286-4590; Fax: 561-286-8792.
Catechesis / Religious Program—Tel: 772-463-1579. Students 464.
PALM SPRINGS, PALM BEACH CO., ST. LUKE (1961), Revs. David W. Carr (WOR); Daniel V. Cronin, Pastor Emeritus (Retired); Larkin Connolly, Pastor Emeritus; Juan Raul Cardenas; Claude D'Souza (RVC).
Res.: 2892 S. Congress Ave., 33461. Tel: 561-965-8980; Fax: 561-965-1384.
School—Tel: 561-965-8190; Fax: 561-965-2404. Sr. Janet Finley, O.S.F., Prin. Lay Teachers 11; Students 255.
Catechesis / Religious Program—Tel: 561-969-1242. Students 439.
PORT ST. LUCIE, ST. LUCIE CO.
1—ST. BERNADETTE (2001), Rev. Victor Ulto.
Church: 350 N.W. California Blvd., 34986. Tel: 772-336-9956; Fax: 772-336-5266.
Catechesis / Religious Program—Students 65.
2—ST. ELIZABETH ANN SETON (1993), Rev. Edmund L. Szpieg.
Church: 930 S.W. Tunis Ave., 34953. Tel: 772-336-0282; Fax: 772-336-1494.
Catechesis / Religious Program—Tel: 772-336-0363; Fax: 772-336-1494. Students 405.
3—HOLY FAMILY (1987), Revs. Thomas F. Cauley; Rodney Q. Titus.
Mailing Address: 2330 Mariposa Ave., 34952. Tel: 772-335-2385; Fax: 772-335-2517.
Catechesis / Religious Program—Tel: 772-337-4313. Students 365.
4—ST. LUCIE (1961), Revs. D. Brian Horgan; Paul Chung Nguyen; Marco Tulio DeLeon.
Res.: 425 S.W. Irving St., 34983. Tel: 772-878-1215; Fax: 772-878-1299.
Catechesis / Religious Program—Students 550.
RIVIERA BEACH, PALM BEACH CO., ST. FRANCIS OF ASSISI (1948), Revs. Arthur Obin, O.M.I.; Martin McMahon, O.M.I. In Res., Revs. Rolland Bennett, O.M.I.; Robert Colfer, O.M.I.
Res.: 200 W. 20th St., 33404. Tel: 561-842-2482; Fax: 561-863-2985.
School—Tel: 561-844-5971; Fax: 561-844-5784. Mrs. Marcia Mariani, Prin. Lay Teachers 15; Students 141.
ROYAL PALM BEACH, PALM BEACH CO., OUR LADY QUEEN OF THE APOSTLES (1988), Revs. Thomas J. Skindeleski; Mark Mlay, A.L.C.P. (Tanzania).
Res.: 100 Crestwood Blvd. S., 33411. Tel: 561-798-5661; Fax: 561-798-5663.
Catechesis / Religious Program—Students 618.
SEBASTIAN, INDIAN RIVER CO., ST. SEBASTIAN (1981), Revs. John Morrissey; Noel McGrath (Ireland); Deacon Henk Toussaint.
Mailing Address: P.O. Box 78-1212, 32978-1212.
Res.: 13075 U.S. Hwy. 1, 32958. Tel: 772-589-5790; Fax: 772-388-0084.
Catechesis / Religious Program—Tel: 772-589-4147. Students 315.
STUART, MARTIN CO.
1—ST. ANDREW (1999), Rev. John A. Barrow.
Church & Mailing: 2100 S.E. Cove Rd., 34997. Tel: 772-781-4415; Fax: 772-781-2906.
Catechesis / Religious Program—Students 168.
2—ST. JOSEPH (1916), Revs. A. Christopher Allen; Benedict Ndeyekiyo Mosha, A.L.C.P. (Africa); Son Linh Hoang.
Res.: 1200 E. 10th St., 34996. Tel: 772-287-2727; Fax: 772-287-4998.
School—Tel: 772-287-6975; Fax: 772-287-4733. Mrs. Judith H. Edelman, Prin. Lay Teachers 32; Students 484.
TEQUESTA, PALM BEACH CO., ST. JUDE (1962), Revs. Thomas Vengayil; Joseph Papes.
Mailing Address: P.O. Box 3726, 33469.
Res.: 204 U.S. Hwy. 1, 33469. Tel: 561-746-7974; Fax: 561-743-6127.
School—All Saints Interparochial School, Tel: 561-748-8994; Fax: 561-748-8979. For a complete listing, please see Interparochial Schools in the Institution section.
Catechesis / Religious Program—Tel: 561-746-1890. Students 444.
VERO BEACH, INDIAN RIVER CO.
1—ST. HELEN (1919), Rev. Michael W. Edwards, B.S.; Rev. Msgr. Irvine Nugent, Pastor Emeritus; Rev. Adrian Torres.
Res.: 2085 Tallahassee Ave., P.O. Box 2927, 32961. Tel: 772-567-5129; Fax: 772-567-1061.
School—2050 Vero Beach Ave., 32960. Tel: 772-567-5457; Fax: 772-567-4823. Lay Teachers 14; Students 299.
Catechesis / Religious Program—2025 20th Ave., 32960. Tel: 772-562-5954; Fax: 772-562-2209. Students 360.
2—HOLY CROSS (1981), Revs. Richard M. Murphy (ROC) (Retired); Michael Massaro, C.S.C.; John B. O'Hare, Pastor Emeritus (Retired).
Res.: 500 Iris Ln., 32964. Tel: 772-231-0671; Fax: 772-234-5653.
Catechesis / Religious Program—Tel: 772-234-1102. Students 215.
3—ST. JOHN OF THE CROSS (1989), Rev. John A. Crowley.
Res.: 950 82nd Ave., 32966. Tel: 772-563-0057; Fax: 772-563-9176.
Catechesis / Religious Program—Tel: 772-563-6457. Students 56.
WELLINGTON, PALM BEACH CO.
1—ST. RITA (1980), Revs. Donald Munro; Mario Castaneda.
Res.: 13645 Paddock Dr., 33414. Tel: 561-793-8544; Fax: 561-793-4082.
Catechesis / Religious Program—Students 3,096.
2—ST.THERESE DE LISIEUX (2000), Rev. Louis Guerin.
Res.: 11800 Lake Worth Rd., 33467. Tel: 561-784-0689; Fax: 561-784-8346.
Catechesis / Religious Program—Tel: 561-784-8262. Students 404.
WEST PALM BEACH, PALM BEACH CO.
1—ST. ANN (1895), Very Rev. James Murtagh; Rev. Msgr. Yves LaPierre.
Res.: 310 N. Olive Ave., 33401. Tel: 561-832-3757; Fax: 561-659-1465.
School—Tel: 561-832-3676; Fax: 561-832-1791. Karen DeMar, Prin. Lay Teachers 30; Students 320.
Catechesis / Religious Program—Students 120.
2—HOLY NAME OF JESUS (1954), Revs. Aidan Lacy; Irvine Nugent; Alex J. Vargas; John C. D'Mello (India).
Res.: 345 S. Military Tr., 33415. Tel: 561-683-3555; Fax: 561-683-1051.
School—Tel: 561-683-2990; Fax: 561-683-0803. Sr. Kathleen Cumins, R.S.H.M., Prin. Sisters 3; Lay Teachers 16; Students 317.
Catechesis / Religious Program—Tel: 561-683-4603. Students 215.
3—ST. JOHN FISHER (1963), Revs. Terence J. Figel,

O.M.I., Pastor; John Vereb, Pastor Emeritus.
Res.: 4001 North Shore Dr., 33407. Tel: 561-842-1224; Fax: 561-842-8750.
Catechesis/Religious Program—Students 50.

4—St. Juliana (1949), Revs. Alfredo Hernandez, V.F.; John J. Pasquini; Raciel Trevino. In Res., Rev. Jose Crucet.
Res.: 4500 S. Dixie Hwy., 33405. Tel: 561-833-9745; Fax: 561-833-4992.
School—Tel: 561-655-1922; Fax: 561-655-8552. Mrs. Mary Schmitz, Prin. Sisters of St. Joseph 1; Lay Teachers 33; Students 502.
Catechesis/Religious Program—Students 577.

5—Mary Immaculate (1974), Revs. Tomasz Makowski; Glen Pothier; Jimmy Habablag (Philippines).
Res.: 390 Sequoia Dr., 33409. Tel: 561-686-8128; Fax: 561-686-8406.
Catechesis/Religious Program—Students 104.

Special Assignment:
Revs.—
Armbrust, Leo F., 11380 Prosperity Farms Rd., 33410.
O'Loughlin, Frank
Redden, Don, Hispanic Ministry, 2410 Florida Ave., Fort Pierce, 34950.

On Duty Outside the Diocese:
Revs.—
Euteneuer, Thomas J., Human Life International, 4 Family Life, Front Royal, VA 22630.
McNally, Michael J., M.Div., M.Th., M.A., Ph.D., St. Charles Borromeo Seminary - Overbrook, 100 E. Wynnewood Rd., Wynnewood, PA 19096.
O'Flanagan, Thomas
Ryan, Patrick

Retired:
Rev. Msgrs.—
Burke, James M.
Nugent, Irvine
Revs.—
Block, John G.
Calle, Juan de la
Chepanis, Anthony J.
Christopher, Mark
Connolly, Larkin
Cronin, Daniel V.
Devereaux, Martin C.
Dockerill, Walter
Dolan, Peter C.
Fenech, Francis X.
Fitzgerald, Matthew
Flynn, Francis
Hubert, Raymond P.
Maloney, Francis E.
Malvey, James
McAtavey, John J.
Murphy, Richard
O'Hare, John B.
Otto, Thomas
Powell, Bernard F.
Profeta, Salvatore
Rynne, Thomas J.
Skehan, John A.
Stack, Christopher
Vereb, John

Permanent Deacons:
Ambroise, Emile
Barbaro, Sam
Battison, Donald
Beres, Ronald
Blake, Richard
Brooks, James
Collins, George
Crary, Lawrence
Daniels, Robert
Demes, Dennis
DiMauro, Joseph
Dingee, Richard
Draughon, Woodworth R., Jr.
Fathauer, Ronald
Gallagher, Daniel
Garamella, Robert
Gardyna, Henry
Gluhosky, Frank
Hamilton, Jack
Hayes, Stephen
Kucera, John
Leone, Charles
Lopez, Jesus
Lucente, Salvatore
Mancuso, Terry
McMahon, Stephen
Melendez, Carlos
Mostler, John
Murray, Paul
Ortiz, Jose
Pagliara, Daniel
Pierce, Jack
Powell, David R.
Raisch, Jack
Ramos, Mariano
Santana, Richard
Sawney, Ira (Grenada)
Seppanen, Henry
Toussaint, Henk
Wesley, Albert
Whalen, Charles
Zatarga, Michael
Ziemianski, Lawrence L.

INSTITUTIONS LOCATED IN THE DIOCESE

[A] SEMINARIES, RELIGIOUS OR SCHOLASTICATES

Boynton Beach. *St. Vincent de Paul Regional Seminary*, 10701 S. Military Tr., 33436. Tel: 561-732-4424; Fax: 561-737-2205. Web: svdp.edu. Rev. Msgr. Stephen C. Bosso (PT), Rector & Pres.; Revs. Steven Olds (ORL), Dean of Human Formation; Guillermo Arias, S.J., M.Ed.; Sr. Maureen Grady, C.S.C., D.Min., Dean of Pastoral Formation; Dr. Sixto Garcia, Ph.D.; Dr. Antonio Lopez, Ph.D.; Mr. Art Quinn, M.L.S., L.S., Librarian; Most Rev. Raymond Lessard, D.D., S.T.L., J.C.L., J.C.L.; Revs. Felipe Estevez, S.T.D. (MIA), Dean of Spiritual Formation; Piotr Paciorek, S.T.D. (Poland); Robert Bauer, S.D.B., S.S.L.; Michael Muhr, M.Div., S.P.; Steven O'Hala, S.T.D. (MIA), Vice Rector, Dean of Academic Formation; Jose Juan Quijano, S.T.L. (MIA), S.T.D. Candidate; Sr. Margarita Gomez, RMI, STL, D. Min., R.M.I., S.T.L.; Dr. Emilio Chavez, S.T.D., Ph.D.; Sr. Joyce Lavoy, O.P., M.A.

[B] HIGH SCHOOLS, DIOCESAN AND PAROCHIAL

Boca Raton. *Pope John Paul II High School*, 4001 N. Military Tr., 33431. Tel: 561-314-2100; Fax: 561-989-8582. Email: pjphs@pjpii.org. Web: www.pjpii.org. Revs. Guy Fiano, O.Carm., Pres.; Thomas Zalewski, O.Carm., Dir.of Facilities; James Hess, O.Carm.; Bros. Robert Chiulli, O.Carm.; Robert Bathe, O.Carm.; Dr. Jerrold Robinson, Prin.; Mrs. Susan Hanley, Asst. Prin. Priests 3; Brothers 2; Lay Teachers 71; Students 902.

Fort Pierce. *John Carroll High School*, 3402 Delaware Ave., 34947-6116. Tel: 772-464-5200; Fax: 772-464-5233. Email: jchs@johncarrollhigh.com. Web: www.johncarrollhigh.com. Rev. Thomas E. Barrett, Pres.; Mr. Clyde L. Russell, Prin. Priests 2; Lay Teachers 31; Students 515.

West Palm Beach. *Cardinal Newman High School*, 512 Spencer Dr., 33409. Tel: 561-683-6266; Fax: 561-683-7307. Email: cnhs@cardinalnewman.com. Web: www.cardinalnewman.com. Rev. David W. Carr (WOR), Pres.; John F. Clarke, Prin.; James E. Carver, Asst. Prin.; Rev. Richard George, Chap. Lay Teachers 60; Students 840.

[C] INTERPAROCHIAL SCHOOLS

Jupiter. *All Saints Catholic School*, 1759 Indian Creek Pkwy., 33458. Tel: 561-748-8994; Fax: 561-748-8979. Email: ascs@allsaintsjupiter.org. Web: www.allsaintsjupiter.org. Mrs. Mary Beth Quick, Prin. Lay Teachers 14; Total Enrollment 234.

[D] SCHOOLS, PRIVATE

Indiantown. *Hope Rural School*, (Grades K-5), 15929 S.W. 150th St., 34956. Tel: 772-597-2203; Fax: 772-597-2259. Email: hopesch@onearrow.net. Web: www.gate.net/~hopesch. Sisters Marie Celeste Gatti, O.P., Dir.; Marion Hangsterfer, O.P., Prin. Sisters 2; Lay Teachers 11; Students 190.

West Palm Beach. *Holy Cross Catholic Preschool & Center*, 930 Southern Blvd., 33405. Tel: 561-366-8026; Fax: 561-366-8577. Sr. Maureen Minihane, C.S.C. Admin.

**Rosarian Academy*, (Grades PreK-8), 807 N. Flagler Dr., 33401. Tel: 561-832-5131; Fax: 561-820-8750. Email: info@rosarian.org. Web: www.rosarian.org. Sr. Corienne Sanders, O.P., Prin. Sisters of St. Dominic (Adrian, MI) Sisters 6; Lay Teachers 41; Students 525.

[E] GENERAL HOSPITALS

West Palm Beach. *St. Mary's Hospital, Inc.*, 901 45th St., 33407-2495. Affiliated Support Organizations:
St. Mary's Ancillary Services, Inc.
St. Mary's Care Services, Inc.
Women's Health Servies, Inc.
Allegany Franciscan Foundation, Palm Beach County, Inc.

[F] HOMES FOR AGED

West Palm Beach. *Noreen McKeen Residence for Geriatric Care*, 315 Flagler Dr. S., 33401. Tel: 561-655-8544; Fax: 561-650-8952. Sr. Mary Anne Dennehy, O.Carm., Admin.; Rev. Edward Campbell, O.S.B., Chap.

[G] NAZARETH HOMES

Boca Raton. *Alhambra House*, 399 NE 25th Ter., 33431. Tel: 561-862-5990; Fax: 561-862-5989. Email: nazhomes@aol.com. Michael Perry, Contact Person.

Bethlehem House, 2280 N.E. 5th Ave., 33431. Tel: 561-862-5990; Fax: 561-862-5989. Email: nazhomes@aol.com. Michael Perry, Contact Person.

Columbia House, 424 N.E. 8th St., 33432. Tel: 561-862-5990; Fax: 561-862-5989. Email: nazhomes@aol.com. Michael Perry, Contact Person.

[H] SOCIETY OF ST. VINCENT DE PAUL

West Palm Beach. *Palm Beach District Council*, 4863 Elmhurst Rd., 33417. Tel: 561-683-6570. Rev. Clemens Hammerschmitt, Spiritual Advisor. Tel: 772-344-1341.

Archbishop Feehan Council, 5480 85th St., Vero Beach, 32967-5544. Tel: 561-539-3338.

Martin County Council, 1200 E. 10th St., Stuart, 34996. Tel: 772-220-2759.

Palm Beach Council, 2647 Old Dixie Hwy., 33404. Tel: 561-845-0562.

Treasure Coast District Council, 1063 S.W. McCoy Ave., Port St. Lucie, 34953. Tel: 561-336-9054.

[I] PERSONAL PRELATURES

Delray Beach. *Prelature of the Holy Cross and Opus Dei*, 4409 Frances Dr., 33445. Tel: 561-498-1249; Fax: 561-498-0054. Rev. Christopher Schmitt. Legal Title: *The Work of God, Inc.*

[J] MONASTERIES AND RESIDENCES OF PRIESTS AND BROTHERS

Boca Raton. *St. Elias Priory-Order of Carmelites, NY*, 4944 Rabbit Hollow, 33487. Tel: 561-995-6762; Fax: 561-995-0769. Revs. Thomas Zalewski, O.Carm.; Guy Fiano, O.Carm., Prior; James Hess, O.Carm.; Bros. Robert Chiulli, O.Carm.; Robert Bathe, O.Carm.

North Palm Beach. *Our Lady of Florida Spiritual Center*, 1300 U.S. Hwy. No. 1, 33408. Tel: 561-626-1300; Fax: 561-627-3956. Email: rsullivan@cpprov.org. Web: www.ourladyofflorida.org. Revs. Francis Finnigan, C.P., Dir. Retreats; Damian Towey, C.P.; Emmanuel Gardon, C.P.; Raphael Amrhein, C.P.; Bro. Matthew Krawchyk, C.P. Priests 4.

Tequesta. *P.I.M.E. Missionaries*, 1550 Beach Rd., 33469. Tel: 561-746-7767; Fax: 561-747-9549. Email: nichom@aol.com. Web: www.pime.org. Revs. Nicholas Maestrini, P.I.M.E., Rector; Pasquale Persico, P.I.M.E.

Vero Beach. *Paulist Fathers Residence*, 1225 20th Ave., 32960. Tel: 772-562-0500; Fax: 772-794-9810. Revs. Thomas J. Marley, C.S.P.; William J. Cantwell, C.S.P.; George F. Helmich, C.S.P.; Thomas J. Connellan, C.S.P.

[K] CONVENTS AND RESIDENCES FOR SISTERS

Delray Beach. *Christ the King Monastery of St. Clare* (Solemn Vows, Papal Enclosure) , 3900 Sherwood Blvd., 33445-5699. Tel: 561-498-3294; Fax: 561-498-2281. Email: ctkm.delray@juno.com. Sr. Mary Veronica Butler, O.S.C., Abbess. Cloistered Sisters 9; Extern Sisters 2.

Lake Charles Shores. *Claretian Missionary, Sisters of Florida, Inc.*, 7700 Westlake Dr., 33406. Tel: 561-433-4731; Fax: 561-963-0789. Email: claretian.sr.delray@worldnet.att.net. Web: www.claretiansisters.org.

Stuart. *Congregation of the Sisters of the Most Holy Soul of Christ*, 1042 E. 9th St., 34996. Tel: 772-286-5720. Sr. Anita Gabarczyk, S.S.C.H., Supr.

West Palm Beach. *Adrian Dominican Sisters, Florida Mission Chapter*, 810 N. Olive Ave., 33401-3710. Tel: 561-832-6521; Fax: 561-832-0365. Email: flmich@aol.com. Web: www.adriansisters.org. Sr. Mary Ann Caulfield, O.P., Chapter Prioress.

[L] RETREAT HOUSES

Lantana. *The Cenacle Spiritual Life Center*, 1400 S. Dixie Hwy., 33462-5492. Tel: 561-582-2534; Fax: 561-582-8070. Email: cenaclefl@aol.com. Web: www.cenaclesisters.org. Spiritual Life Center for laity and religious. Sisters 5.

NORTH PALM BEACH. *Our Lady of Florida Spiritual Center,* 1300 U.S. Hwy. No. 1, 33408. Tel: 561-626-1300; Fax: 561-627-3956. Email: rsullivan@cpprov.org. Web: www.ourladyofflorida.org.

[M] MISCELLANEOUS LISTINGS

PALM BEACH GARDENS. *Catholic Charities of the Diocese of Palm Beach, Inc.,* P.O. Box 109650, 34410-9650. 9995 N. Military Tr., 34410.
GladesKids Out of School Program, St. Philip Benizi, 1102 N.W. Ave. A, Belle Glade, 33430. Tel: 561-996-3970; Fax: 561-993-0061. 900 S.W. Ave. J, Belle Glade, 33430. Sr. Laura Cavanaugh, S.B.S.
Con El, Inc., P.O. Box 109650, 33410-9650.
Diocesan Council of Catholic Women Rev. Clemens Hammerschmitt, Diocesan Moderator; Mrs. Judy Powers, Pres. Tel: 561-820-1349.
Diocese of Palm Beach, Inc., P.O. Box 109650, 33410-9650.
Diocese of Palm Beach Burse Fund Trust
Diocese of Palm Beach Endowment Trust
Diocese of Palm Beach Health Plan Trust Revs. Charles E. Notabartolo, Chm.; Louis T. Guerin, Chm.
Diocesan Pension Plan Trust Rev. Charles E. Notabartolo, Chm.
Diocesan Property & Liability Insurance Committee Rev. Richard Murphy, Chm.
The Florida Catholic of Palm Beach, Inc., P.O. Box 109650, 33410-9650. Mrs. Irene Hey, Editor.
Helping Hands Scholarship Fund, Diocese of Palm Beach, Tel: 561-775-9547. P.O. Box 109650, 33410-9650.

BOCA RATON. *Christ Child Society of Boca Raton,* P.O. Box 811025, 33481-1025. Tel: 561-368-3932; Fax: 561-368-2318. Email: agnesgreg@aol.com.
Cross International Catholic Outreach, Inc., 370 W. Camino Gardens Blvd., 33432. Tel: 561-392-9212, Ext. 408; Fax: 561-367-0564. Email: info@crossinternational.org. Web: www.crosscatholic.org. Mr. James J. Cavnar, Pres.

BOYNTON BEACH. *St. Vincent de Paul Regional Seminary Endowment Trust,* 10701 S. Military Tr., 33436.

CORAL SPRINGS. *South Florida Lay Cistercians, Inc.,* 6311 N.W. 47th Ct., 33067. Tel: 954-340-5705; Fax: 954-344-9231. Email: deserttraveler@aol.com. Natalie Smith, Pres.
Vocations Placement Service, Inc., 6311 N.W. 47th Ct., 33067. Tel: 954-340-5705; Fax: 954-344-9231. Email: deserttraveler@aol.com. Web: vocationsplacement.org.

GREENACRES. *Villa Madonna,* 4809 Lake Worth Rd., 33463-3455. Tel: 561-963-1900; Fax: 561-963-1476. Email: thirdvilla@aol.com. Rosemary McMahon, Resident Mgr.

JENSEN BEACH. *Villa Assumpta, Inc.,* 2539 N.E. Mission Dr., 9-8, 34957. Tel: 561-334-0009; Fax: 561-334-2168. Email: villaassumpta1994@hotmail.com. Ms. Linda Matz, Resident Mgr.

JUPITER. *Pan-American Catholic Health Care Network, Inc.,* 200 Beach Rd., Apt. 302, 33469. Tel: 718-356-8006; Fax: 718-356-8006. Email: mhealysedutto@netscape.net. Mary Healy-Sedutto, Ph.D., Contact Person.

NORTH PALM BEACH. *Christ Child Society of Palm Beach,* P.O. Box 14441, 33408. Tel: 561-795-0134; Fax: 561-793-6505. Email: mbishop110@aol.com.

PALM CITY. *St. Raphael Family Life Center,* 9440 S.W. 48th Ave., 34991. Tel: 561-781-0350.

PORT ST. LUCIE. *Villa Seton, Inc.,* 3300 S.W. Chartwell St., 34953. Tel: 561-775-9571; Fax: 561-775-5906. Email: cc_housing@hotmail.com. Robin Lunn, Dir. Housing Devel.

RIVIERA BEACH. *Villa Franciscan, Inc.,* 2101 Avenue F, 33404. Tel: 561-840-0444; Fax: 561-840-9444. Email: vfan@bellsouth.net. Web: villafranciscan.catholicweb.com. Mr. William Kerr, Mgr.

STUART. *Christ Child Society of Stuart,* 6189 Baltusroi Ter., 34997. Tel: 772-220-9943. Gloria McGuirk, Pres.

WELLINGTON. *Magnificat Palm Beach Center, Inc.,* 1500 Corporate Center Way, Ste. 202, West Palm Beach, 33414. Tel: 561-793-2218. Britta Neinast, Treas.

RELIGIOUS INSTITUTES OF MEN REPRESENTED IN THE DIOCESE

For further details refer to the corresponding bracketed number in the Religious Institutes of Men or Women section.

[]—*Apostolic Life Community of Priests in the Opus Spiritus Sancti* (Tanzania)—A.L.C.P.
[0200]—*Benedictine Monks*—O.S.B.
[0030]—*Congregation of St. Paul*—C.S.P.
[0610]—*Congregation of the Holy Cross*—CSC
[0650]—*Congregation of the Holy Ghost*—C.S.Sp.
[1000]—*Congregation of the Passion*—C.P.
[0520]—*Franciscan Friars* (Holy Name Prov.)—O.F.M.
[0520]—*Franciscan Friars* (Immaculate Conception Prov.)—O.F.M.
[]—*Franciscan Friars Minor of Puglia* (Italy)—O.F.M.
[0470]—*Franciscan Friars, Capucin*—O.F.M.Cap.
[0480]—*Franciscans Friars, Conventual*—O.F.M.Conv
[0670]—*Hospitaller Brothers of St. John of God*—O.H.
[]—*Institute Voluntas Dei* (Canada - Province of Haiti)—I.V.Dei.
[0800]—*Maryknoll Missionary Fathers*—M.M.
[1210]—*Missionaries of St. Charles Borromeo*—C.S.
[0910]—*Oblates of Mary Immaculate*—O.M.I.
[0270]—*Order of Carmelites*—O.Carm.
[1050]—*Pontifical Institute for Foreign Missions*—P.I.M.E.
[1190]—*Salesians of Don Bosco*—S.D.B.
[0690]—*Society of Jesus*—S.J.
[]—*Society of the Divine Vocations* PMB—S.D.V.

RELIGIOUS INSTITUTES OF WOMEN REPRESENTED IN THE DIOCESE

[0130]—*Apostles of the Sacred Heart of Jesus*—A.S.C.J.
[0330]—*Carmelite Sisters for the Aged and Infirm*—O.Carm.
[0685]—*Claretian Missionary Sisters*—R.M.I.
[1930]—*Congregation of the Sisters of the Holy Cross*—C.S.C.
[1710]—*Congregation of the Third Order of St. Francis of Mary Immaculate*—O.S.F.
[1070-03]—*Dominican Sisters* (Sinsinawa, WI)—O.P.
[1070-13]—*Dominican Sisters* (Adrian, MI)—O.P.
[1070-16]—*Dominican Sisters of Hope*—O.P.
[1070-17]—*Dominican Sisters of St. Catherine de Ricci*—O.P.
[1140]—*Eucharistic Missionaries of St. Dominic*—O.P.
[1180]—*Franciscan Sisters of Allegany, NY*—O.S.F.
[1845]—*Guadalupana Missionaries of the Holy Spirit*—M.G.Sp.S
[]—*Hermitage of the Diocese of Palm Beach*
[2470]—*Maryknoll Sisters of St. Dominic*—M.M.
[2490]—*Medical Mission Sisters*—M.M.S.
[3760]—*Order of St. Clare*—O.S.C.
[3110]—*Religious of Our Lady of the Cenacle*—R.C.
[3465]—*Religious of the Sacred Heart of Mary*—R.S.H.M.
[]—*Sisters for Christian Community*—S.F.C.C.
[0590]—*Sisters of Charity of St. Elizabeth* (Convent Station, NJ)—S.C.
[2110]—*Sisters of Humility of Mary*—H.M.
[2560]—*Sisters of Mary Reparatrix*—S.M.R.
[2520]—*Sisters of Mercy* (Dublin, Ireland)—R.S.M.
[2575]—*Sisters of Mercy of the Americas*—R.S.M.
[3000]—*Sisters of Notre Dame de Namur*—S.N.D.deN.
[1630]—*Sisters of St. Francis of Penance and Christian Charity*—O.S.F.
[1530]—*Sisters of St. Francis of the Congregation of Our Lady of Lourdes* (Sylvania, OH)—O.S.F.
[3840]—*Sisters of St. Joseph of Carondelet*—C.S.J.
[3900]—*Sisters of St. Joseph of St. Augustine*—S.S.J.
[0260]—*Sisters of the Blessed Sacrament*—S.B.S.
[1830]—*Sisters of the Good Shepherd*—R.G.S.
[1990]—*Sisters of the Holy Names of Jesus and Mary*—S.N.J.M.
[]—*Sisters of the Most Holy Soul of Jesus*—S.S.C.H.
[2150]—*Sisters, Servants of the Immaculate Heart of Mary*—I.H.M.

DIOCESAN CEMETERIES

WEST PALM BEACH. *Our Lady Queen of Peace Catholic Cemetery, Inc.,* 10941 Southern Blvd., 33406. Tel: 561-793-0711; Fax: 561-793-0182. Email: email@ourqueen.org. Web: www.ourqueen.org. Rev. Thomas Vengayil, Dir.; Mr. Charles Freebold, Admin.

NECROLOGY

† O'Shea, Rev. Msgr. Joseph H., (Retired)—Died Feb. 9, 2003
† Aymanamkuzhy, Jacob, (Retired)—Died July 19, 2003
† Morgan, Matthew, (Retired)—Died July 7, 2003

Diocese of Paterson

(Dioecesis Patersonensis)

Most Reverend

FRANK J. RODIMER, D.D., J.C.D.

Bishop of Paterson; ordained May 19, 1951; appointed Bishop of Paterson December 13, 1977; ordained and installed February 28, 1978 *Res.: 178 Derrom Ave., Paterson, NJ 07504.*

ESTABLISHED DECEMBER 9, 1937.

Square Miles 1,214.

Comprises the Counties of Passaic, Morris and Sussex in the State of New Jersey.

Legal Title: For legal titles of parishes and diocesan institutions, consult the Chancery Office.

Diocesan Center: 777 Valley Rd., Clifton, NJ 07013. Tel: 973-777-8818; Fax: 973-777-8976.

Web: www.patersondiocese.org

STATISTICAL OVERVIEW

Personnel	
Bishop	1
Abbots	2
Retired Abbots	5
Priests: Diocesan Active in Diocese	152
Priests: Diocesan Active Outside Diocese	17
Priests: Retired, Sick or Absent	75
Number of Diocesan Priests	244
Religious Priests in Diocese	161
Total Priests in Diocese	405
Extern Priests in Diocese	12
Ordinations:	
Diocesan Priests	3
Religious Priests	1
Transitional Deacons	2
Permanent Deacons	22
Permanent Deacons in Diocese	192
Total Brothers	33
Parishes	
Parishes	111
With Resident Pastor:	
Resident Diocesan Priests	96
Resident Religious Priests	10
Without Resident Pastor:	
Administered by Priests	5
Pastoral Centers	5
Professional Ministry Personnel:	
Brothers	2
Sisters	60
Lay Ministers	161
Welfare	
Catholic Hospitals	3
Total Assisted	770,000
Homes for the Aged	8
Total Assisted	490
Residential Care of Children	3
Total Assisted	98
Day Care Centers	5
Total Assisted	1,600
Specialized Homes	2
Total Assisted	1,600
Special Centers for Social Services	13
Total Assisted	65,000
Residential Care of Disabled	11
Total Assisted	80
Educational	
Diocesan Students in Other Seminaries	6
Seminaries, Religious	2
Students Religious	5
Total Seminarians	11
Colleges and Universities	2
Total Students	1,801
High Schools, Diocesan and Parish	5
Total Students	2,475
High Schools, Private	4
Total Students	1,250
Elementary Schools, Diocesan and Parish	57
Total Students	15,693
Elementary Schools, Private	3
Total Students	545
Catechesis/Religious Education:	
High School Students	11,784
Elementary Students	35,352
Total Students under Catholic Instruction	68,911
Teachers in the Diocese:	
Priests	15
Scholastics	7
Brothers	13
Sisters	136
Lay Teachers	1,522
Vital Statistics	
Receptions into the Church:	
Infant Baptism Totals	8,274
Adult Baptism Totals	196
Received into Full Communion	291
First Communions	8,032
Confirmations	4,634
Marriages:	
Catholic	1,266
Interfaith	345
Total Marriages	1,611
Deaths	3,581
Total Catholic Population	420,172
Total Population	1,124,058

Former Bishops—Most Revs. THOMAS H. MCLAUGHLIN, S.T.D., LL.D., consecrated July 25, 1935; transferred to Paterson, Dec. 16, 1937; died March 17, 1947; THOMAS A. BOLAND, S.T.D., consecrated July 25, 1940; transferred to Paterson, June 21, 1947; transferred to Newark as Archbishop, Nov. 15, 1952; died March 16, 1979; JAMES A. MCNULTY, D.D., appt. Auxiliary Bishop of Newark, Aug. 2, 1947; consecrated Oct. 7, 1947; appt. Bishop of Paterson, April 9, 1953; transferred to Diocese of Buffalo, Feb. 12, 1963; died Sept. 4, 1972; JAMES J. NAVAGH, D.D., consecrated Sept. 24, 1952; appt. Bishop of Ogdensburg, May 8, 1957; transferred to Bishop of Paterson, Feb. 12, 1963; died Oct. 2, 1965; LAWRENCE B. CASEY, D.D., appt. Auxiliary Bishop of Rochester, Feb. 10, 1953; consecrated May 5, 1953; appt. Bishop of Paterson, March 9, 1966; died June 15, 1977.

Vicar General, Moderator of the Curia—Rev. Msgr. HERBERT K. TILLYER, M.Ch.A.

Vicar for Planning and Priorities—Rev. Msgr. JAMES T. MAHONEY.

Vicar for Retired Priests—Rev. Msgr. RAYMOND LOPATESKY.

Coordinator for Religious—Sr. ELLEN JOYCE, S.C.

Vicar for Deacons—Rev. Msgr. ROBERT DIACHEK.

Deans—Rev. Msgr. THOMAS J. COLETTA, Paterson; Revs. VICTOR J. MAZZA, Clifton; HERNAN ARIAS, Passaic; Rev. Msgrs. EUGENE BOLAND, Mid Passaic County; REMIGIO G. ROCCO, Northern Passaic County; Rev. DAVID MCDONNELL, Southwestern Morris County; Rev. Msgr. PATRICK E. BROWN, Southeastern Morris County; Revs. PATRICK RICE Eastern Morris County; DENNIS J. HOGAN, Northeastern Morris County; Rev. Msgr. JOSEPH T. ANGINOLI, J.C.L., Northern Morris County; Revs. P. CHRISTOPHER MULDOON, Western Morris County; STANLEY BARRON, Sussex County.

Diocesan Center—777 Valley Rd., Clifton, 07013. Tel: 973-777-8818; Fax: 973-777-8976. Office Hours: Mon.-Fri. 9-4:30; All mail should be addressed to this office.

Chancellor—Rev. Msgr. JOHN E HART, J.C.L.

Vice Chancellor—Rev. Msgr. T. MARK CONDON, J.C.L.

Archivist—Rev. Msgr. RAYMOND J. KUPKE.

Secretary to the Bishop—Rev. Msgr. T. MARK CONDON, J.C.L.

Administrative Assistant to the Bishop—Mrs. BARBARA FIERRO.

Administrative Assistant to the Chancellor—Mrs. ARLINE PERRO.

Secretary to the Vice Chancellor—Ms. KERRY DOLAN.

Diocesan Counsel— Dwyer, Connell & Lisbona.

Diocesan Tribunal—

Judicial Vicar—Rev. Msgr. EDWARD J. KURTYKA, J.C.D.

Adjutant Judicial Vicar—Rev. Msgr. JOSEPH T. ANGINOLI, J.C.L.

Advocates—Revs. JOHN T. CONNOLLY, M.Div.; MICHAEL BURKE, S.T.M., J.D.; JOHN J. FOLEY, C.S.P., J.C.D.

Auditors—Revs. PAUL IOVINO; JOHN P. HANLEY; Deacon ANTHONY SALERNO.

Defenders of the Bond—Rev. Msgrs. KENNETH E. LASCH, J.C.D.; T. MARK CONDON, J.C.L.; Rev. EDWARD J. HINDS, J.C.L.; Rev. Msgr. GEORGE F. HUNDT, J.C.L.

Pro-Synodal Judges—Rev. Msgr. JOHN J. CARROLL, Ed.D.; Revs. JOHN T. CATOIR, J.C.D. (Retired); MARK A. MANCINI, M.Div.; Rev. Msgrs. JOHN E. HART, J.C.L.; JOHN J. DEMKOVICH; HERBERT K. TILLYER, M.Ch.A; THOMAS J. TRAPASSO, S.T.L. (Retired); Rev. REGIS P. WALLACE, O.S.B.

Administrative Assistants and Notaries—Mrs. SHAWN VACCA; Mrs. ROSE LUCIGNANI.

Consulting Psychologist—EDMUND J. RUBIN, Ph.D.; JAMES A. SAVAGE, Psy.D.

Presbyteral Council—Rev. Msgrs. JOHN J. CARROLL, Ed.D.; HERBERT K. TILLYER, M.Ch.A; ELIAS TAMAYO; PETER J. DOODY; Rev. ROBERT J. GORDON; Rev. Msgr. JOHN E. HART, J.C.L.; Revs. WAYNE M. VARGA; PATRICK RICE; MARC MANCINI; RICHARD RENTO; ROBERT SANDOZ, O.F.M.; ANTONIO RODRIGUEZ; A. RICHARD CARTON; STANLEY BARRON.

College of Consultors—Rev. Msgrs. HERBERT K. TILLYER, M.Ch.A; ELIAS TAMAYO; PETER J. DOODY; JOHN E. HART, J.C.L.; Revs. WAYNE M. VARGA; ROBERT J. GORDON; PATRICK RICE; MARC MANCINI; RICHARD RENTO; ANTONIO RODRIGUEZ; RICHARD CARTON; STANLEY BARRON.

Finance Council—Most Rev. FRANK J. RODIMER; Rev. Msgrs. HERBERT K. TILLYER, M.Ch.A; JAMES T. MAHONEY; JOHN E. HART, J.C.L.; Sr. MARY ANN TIERNEY, S.C.; Mr. EDWARD HENNESSY; Mr. WILLIAM HINKES; Mr. JOSEPH LIPARI; Mr. THOMAS P. LOFTUS; Mr. WAYNE LONG; Ms. THERESE PICK; Mr. EUGENE SYLVA.

Diocesan Secretariats

Communications Secretariat—Mr. RICHARD A. SOKERKA, 597 Valley Rd., P.O. Box 1887, Clifton, 07015. Tel: 973-278-3202; Fax: 973-279-2265.

Diocesan Newspaper, "The Beacon"—Mr. RICHARD A. SOKERKA, Editor & Gen. Mgr.; Ms. TERRI MAURO, Mng. Editor, 597 Valley Rd., P.O. Box 1887, Clifton, 07015. Tel: 973-279-8845.
Communications Office—MARIANNA THOMPSON, Dir., 597 Valley Rd., P.O. Box 1887, Clifton, 07015. Tel: 973-278-3202; Fax: 973-279-2265.
Secretariat For Parish Life—Mr. PHILIP A. RUSSO, Exec. Sec., 777 Valley Rd., Clifton, 07013. Tel: 973-777-8818.
Office of Family Life—Mrs. MARIE RYAN, Consultant.
Engaged Encounter—Rev. ROBERT J. MITCHELL, Spiritual Dir. Tel: 973-691-1561. Coordinators: TODD SCHMIDT; DEBBIE SCHMIDT. Tel: 973-726-7016. Registration Couple: DAVID DE MARTINO; LINDA DE MARTINO. Tel: 973-764-5711.
Respect Life—Mrs. MARIE RYAN, Consultant.
Office of Parish Catechetics—Mr. THOMAS BROWN, Consultant.
Catechetical Leaders Association—Ms. BARBARA BUCK. Tel: 973-334-5257.
Office of Ministry Among Hispanics—Rev. TERENCE MORAN, C.SS.R., Consultant; Ms. IVANNIA VEGA-MC TIGHE, Consultant for Hispanic Youth & Family Ministry.
Commission for Hispanic Catholic Ministry—Mr. RAUL E. PAMPLONA, Chm. Tel: 973-790-8132.
Office of Worship and Spirituality—Dr. PATRICIA BARTLE, Consultant.
Liturgical Commission—Rev. EDWARD J. HINDS, J.C.L., Chm. Tel: 973-538-3231.
Environment & Architecture Commission—Rev. ROBERT J. GORDON. Tel: 973-779-6201.
RCIA Commission—Rev. EDWARD A. COLLINS. Tel: 973-696-1234.
Office of Youth Ministry—Consultants: Mr. PHILIP RUSSO; Ms. IVANNIA VEGA-MC TIGHE.
Young Prophets Catholic Youth Program in Paterson—Rev. GENO SYLVA, Dir. Tel: 973-694-3702, Ext. 13. Email: gsylva@depaulcatholic.org.
Catholic Scouting—Rev. WAYNE VARGA. Tel: 973-334-2090.
Office for Campus Ministry—Rev. LOUIS J. SCURTI, Coord., Catholic Campus Ministers. Tel: 973-595-6184.
Ecumenical Officer—Rev. CHARLES J. PARR, 737 Valley Rd., Clifton, 07013. Tel: 973-777-5651.
Related Organizations—
Catholic Deaf Society—Rev. Msgrs. JOSEPH J. GOODE, Moderator, 2 Miller Rd., Kinnelon, 07405. Tel: 973-838-6838; THOMAS J. TRAPASSO, S.T.L., Asst. Moderator (Retired).
Charismatic Renewal—Rev. NICHOLAS BOZZA, Liaison. Tel: 973-347-0032.
English Cursillos—Ms. JEAN TAHAN, Lay Dir. Tel: 973-772-1759. Spiritual Advisors: Rev. PHILIP A. LEBEAU; Deacon DON O'LEARY; Sr. MARIANNE JOYCE, S.C.
Spanish Cursillos—WILLIAM TORRES, Lay Dir. Tel: 973-361-9073; Rev. BRANDO IBARRA. Tel: 973-742-2142.
World Wide Marriage Encounter—Executive Couple: DAN WOLFE; MARCIA WOLFE. Tel: 973-347-1499. Registration Couple: EILEEN PEREZ; RALPH PEREZ. Tel: 800-499-6552.

Pastoral Administration

Division of Clergy and Personnel—
Clergy Personnel Office—Rev. Msgr. GEORGE F. HUNDT, J.C.L., Dir.; Mrs. ROSEMARY J. DONNELLY, Admin. Asst., 737 Valley Rd., Clifton, 07013. Tel: 973-777-2955.
Deacon Internship Program—Rev. Msgr. FRANCIS J. DUFFY, Dir., 6 Sussex Ave., Morristown, 07960. Tel: 973-538-4851.
Ministry for Priestly Formation and Education—Rev. CHARLES J. PARR, Dir., 737 Valley Rd., Clifton, 07013. Tel: 973-777-5651.
Mission Office—Rev. Msgr. JOHN J. DEMKOVICH, Dir.; Rev. STANLEY C. BARRON, Assoc. Dir.; Mrs. ELEANOR MATAS, Office Mgr., 24 DeGrasse St., Paterson, 07505. Tel: 973-278-3491.
Office of Health Care Ministry—Rev. Msgr. ROBERT M. DIACHEK, Dir., 205 Madison Ave., Madison, 07940-1003. Tel: 973-443-9300.
Office of the Permanent Diaconate—Rev. Msgr. ROBERT M. DIACHEK, Vicar, 205 Madison Ave., Madison, 07940-1003. Tel: 973-443-9300; Fax: 973-443-4140.
Consultant for Religious Communities—Sr. ELLEN JOYCE, S.C., Consultant. Tel: 973-777-8818.
Victim Assistance Coordinator—Ms. PEGGY ZANELLO. Tel: 973-879-1489.
Vocations Office—Revs. PAUL S. MANNING, Dir.; HERNAN ARIAS, Assoc. Dir., 737 Valley Rd., Clifton, 07013. Tel: 973-472-2812.
Division of Finance and Budget—
Business Office—Mr. WAYNE G. LONG, Finance Officer; Mr. JOSEPH LIPARI, Controller; Ms. CAROL TUMINELLO, Bookkeeper; Mrs. BETTY ANN GREENE, Sec.; Mr. TIMOTHY POTTER, Dir. Devel., 777 Valley Rd., Clifton, 07013.
Diocesan Facilities Manager—Mr. JAMES FIERRO.
Insurance Office—Mrs. EILEEN FOGARTY, Employee Benefits; Ms. DENISE SCHMIDT, Risk Mgr., 777 Valley Rd., Clifton, 07013. Tel: 973-777-8818.
Diocesan Cemetery Office—Rev. Msgr. HERBERT K. TILLYER, M.Ch.A, Dir.; Mr. JOHN M. CAVANAUGH, Asst. Dir., 58 McLean Blvd., Paterson, 07513. Tel: 973-279-2900.
School Division—Mr. FRANK PETRUCELLI, Supt.; Sr. DOROTHY BANASHAK, S.S.C., Asst. Supt. Secondary Educ. and Governmental Programs. Assistant Superintendents Elementary Educ.: Sisters JOSEPH SPRING, S.C.C.; IRENE LAURENCE, M.F.I.C.; Mrs. LINDA KOSTENKO, Asst. Supt.; Mr. JOHN FANELLI, Dir. Technology; Mr. PATRICK PEACE, Dir. Finances and Admin. Svcs.; Mr. RAYMOND CERCHIONE, Educ. Council Pres.; Sr. RITA MARIE FRITZEN, O.S.F., Elementary Principals' Assoc. Pres., 777 Valley Rd., Clifton, 07013. Tel: 201-777-8818.
Secretariat for Catholic Charities—JOHN F. DUFFY, Exec. Sec.; Rev. EDWARD LAMBRO, Dir. Devel. & Public Rels., 24 De Grasse St., Paterson, 07505. Tel: 973-279-7100; Fax: 973-523-1150.
Hispanic Information Center—Mr. LORENZO HERNANDEZ, Dir., 270 Passaic St., Passaic, 07055. Tel: 973-779-7022.
Catholic Family and Community Services—JOHN F. DUFFY, Exec. Dir.; Mr. ROBERT JACOB, Assoc. Dir. & CFO; Ms. CATHERINE SPINA, Admin. Asst.; Rev. MICHAEL BURKE, Staff Attorney, 24 De Grasse St., Paterson, 07501. Tel: 973-279-7100.
Aging Services—Ms. PATRICIA REIDY, Dir. Tel: 973-279-4300.
Adoption and Counseling Services—Rev. THOMAS MCGRATH, Dir., 476 17th Ave., Paterson, 07504. Tel: 973-523-9595.
Friendship Corner—Ms. WANDA ALICEA, Dir., 279 Carroll St., Paterson, 07509. Tel: 973-569-0001.
Parish Social Ministries—Mr. THOMAS MCCANN, Dir., 476 17th Ave., Paterson, 07504. Tel: 973-523-7361.
Immigration and Refugee Services—Ms. MAI LIEU, Dir., 24 DeGrasse St., Paterson, 07501. Tel: 973-279-7100.
Italian Catholic Center—Miss PHILOMENA DESOPO, Dir., 24 DeGrasse St., Paterson, 07501. Tel: 973-278-4955.
Mt. St. Joseph's Children Center—Sr. DOROTHY SHEAHAN, S.C., 124 Shepherd Ln., Totowa, 07512. Tel: 973-595-5720.
Multi-Lingual Center—Ms. ROSE KARDASHIAN, Dir., 24 DeGrasse St., Paterson, 07501. Tel: 973-279-7100.
The Palloti Center—Ms. ANITA MORAWSKI, Dir., 476 17th Ave., Paterson, 07054. Tel: 973-523-1544.
Partnership for Social Services—Sr. THOMASINA GEBHARD, S.S.M., Dir., 48 Wyker Rd., Franklin, 07416. Tel: 973-827-4702.
Sancta Maria House of Mercy—Sr. MARIA ELIZABETH WHILIFER, Dir., 360 E. 37th St., Paterson, 07504. Tel: 973-523-1338.
Father English Multi-Purpose Community Center—Deacon ROBERT VESOTA, Exec. Dir., 435 Main St., Paterson, 07501. Tel: 973-881-0280.
Preschool Day Care Center Programs— A Child's World-El Mundo del Nino; EUNICE RAMIREZ, Dir., A Child's Time-El Tiempo del Nino;; AIDA ZARATE, Dir., 433 Main St., Paterson, 07501. Tel: 973-278-3110 El Mundo de Colores;; LAURA ZARIFE, Dir., 44 Ward St., Paterson, 07505. Tel: 973-523-0919.
After School Program—PABLO RIVERA, Dir.
Teenage After School Program—JUAN GONZALEZ, Dir.
Work Assistance Program—JUAN GONZALEZ, Dir.
Senior and Disabled Transportation—MICHAEL DRAKE FORD, Dir.
Emergency Food and Clothing Programs—CARLOS ROLDAN, Dir.
Passaic Teen Center—Ms. DENISE MEZA, 228 Hope Ave., Passaic, 07055. Tel: 973-473-5755.
Youth Haven—Ms. DENISE MEZA, Dir., 212 Slater St., Paterson, 07501. Tel: 973-881-1611. Shelter-Crisis Intervention.
Catholic Social Services of Morris County, Inc. (Hope House)—Mrs. PHILOMENA D'SA, Exec. Dir.; Ms. LISA KELLY, Dir. Devel. & Publicity; Mrs. BARBARA LONGO, Coord. Fix-It Prog.; Ms. AMANDA VILLALBA RICKERT, Coord. Alcoholism Programs; Ms. CAROLINE JACOBUS, Dir. AIDS Center. Coord. Home Sharing Program: Ms. CAROLE KELLY; Mr. PAUL CHIESA; Ms. LYNNE PASTOR, Dir. Behavioral Health Svcs.; Mr. RAM MUPPIRALA, Dir. Finance & Admin.; Ms. ANGELA VANCE, Dir. Operations; Ms. CECILIA HALL, Clinical Supvr., 19-21 Belmont Ave., Dover, 07801. Tel: 973-361-5555.
Department for Persons with Disabilities—Mr. THOMAS A. BARRETT, Exec. Dir.; Ms. JULIE TATTI, Assoc. Dir.; Sr. JOAN KATHLEEN GERCKE, S.S.J., Dir., Human Resources; Mr. ROCCO ZAPPILE, Comptroller; Mr. ROY DE FRANCO, Dir. Devel., 1049 Weldon Rd., Oak Ridge, 07438. Tel: 973-697-4394.
Group Homes—
Murray House—Ms. WANDA PEREZ, Dir., 86 Allwood Pl., Clifton, 07015. Tel: 973-470-5694.
Wayne Marathon House—Mrs. MARIA ARCE, Dir., 648 Black Oak Ridge Rd., Wayne, 07470. Tel: 973-628-9074.
Finnegan House—Ms. LYNNE OLIVARI, Dir., 1049 Weldon Rd., Oak Ridge, 07438. Tel: 973-697-1246.
Alexander House—Ms. ARLENE GROSENBECK, Dir., 1049 Weldon Rd., Oak Ridge, 07438. Tel: 973-697-1812.
Columbus House—Ms. CHERYL SLATE, Dir., 1049 Weldon Rd., Oak Ridge, 07438. Tel: 973-697-1644.
Fitzpatrick House—Ms. PAMELA VAN ECK, Dir., 215 Mountain Ave., Pompton Lakes, 07442. Tel: 973-248-1569.
Wehrlen House—Ms. MARGARET DOYLE, Dir., 18 Bisset Dr., West Milford, 07480. Tel: 973-208-1883.
Gruenert Employment Center—Mrs. KATHY DE YOUNG, Dir., 725 Rte. 15 S., Lake Hopatcong, 07849. Tel: 973-663-9102.
Basile Apartment—Mrs. JANET WASHINGTON, Dir., Brittany Chase, Wayne, 07470. Tel: 973-694-9591.
Calabrese House—Sr. CHRISTINE STEVENSON, Dir., 829 Littleton Rd., Parsippany, 07054. Tel: 973-299-8360.
Wallace House—KIM WALTER, Dir., 447 Glen Rd., Sparta, 07871. Tel: 973-726-3470.
Keleher Apartments—Ms. ISABEL ALMONTE, Dir., 124 Barrister Dr., Butler, 07405. Tel: 973-283-8475.
Straight and Narrow, Inc.—NORMA TANGARA, M.P.H., Exec. Dir.; Dr. JUDITH HERSCHLAG, Ph.D., Dir. Adult Residential Treatment; Mrs. ARLENE PELLER, Dir. Alpha-II Prog.; Ms. PHYLLIS ANDERSON, R.N., Dir. Mt. Carmel Hospital; Ms. KAREN ROCCISANO, Dir., Alpha I & III Programs; NANCY DIMITROVSKI, Dir. Cedar Out-Patient Clinic; REINA RIVAS, Dir. Juvenile Treatment Unit; Rev. GREG DROGON, Dir. Pastoral Care Unit; Dr. RUDOLFO MOISES, Medical Dir., 296 Straight St., Paterson, 07501. Tel: 973-345-6000.
McNulty Half-Way House—Mr. RAYMOND MC CUTCHEN, Dir., 101 Cedar St., Paterson, 07501. Tel: 973-279-7003.
Medical Day Care Center—HENRIETTA LEMON, R.N., Dir., 180 E. 19th St., Paterson, 07524-1537.
Methadone Maintenance Centers—Rev. Msgr. LOUIS J. BIHR, Dir., Bergen Pines Hospital, E. Ridgewood Ave., Paramus, 07652. Bergen Pines Hospital, 75 E. Broadway, Hackensack, 07601.
Affiliated Organizations—
Apostleship of Prayer—Rev. Msgr. CHRISTOPHER DILELLA, Dir., 26 Green Village Rd., Madison, 07040. Tel: 973-377-4000.
Diocesan Council of Catholic Women—Rev. Msgr. JOSEPH A. CIAMPAGLIO, Dir., 152 Mt. Pleasant Ave., Dover, 07801. Tel: 973-366-7095; Mrs. MAUREEN JOYCE, 8 Glenwood Mountain Rd., Sussex, 07461.
Justice and Peace Commission—Rev. PATRICK RICE.
Diocesan Holy Name Federation—Mr. FRANK STEINER, Pres.
Legion of Mary—Rev. Msgr. JOHN J. DEMKOVICH, Spiritual Dir.; Mrs. LUCY LEONE, Pres., 63 Monroe St., Passaic, 07055. Tel: 973-779-0427.
Priests Eucharistic League—Rev. Msgr. CHRISTOPHER DILELLA, Dir., 26 Green Village Rd., Madison, 07040. Tel: 973-377-4000.
Commission for Black Catholic Ministries—Mrs. RUTH LAWSON, Pres. Tel: 973-898-9260.
Commission for Hispanic Catholic Ministries—Mr. RAUL E. PAMPLONA, Chm. Tel: 973-790-8132.

CLERGY, PARISHES, MISSIONS AND PAROCHIAL SCHOOLS

CITY OF PATERSON
(PASSAIC COUNTY)

1—CATHEDRAL OF ST. JOHN THE BAPTIST (1820), [CEM] Rev. Msgr. Mark J. Giordani; Revs. Ruben Dario Cortez, S.X.; Luis A. Rendon (Colombia); Luis Espinoza; Deacons Manuel Santiago; Jose Pomales; Guido Pedraza; Luis Gil.
Res.: 381 Grand St., Paterson, 07505. Tel: 973-345-4070; Fax: 973-345-7831.
School—Pope John Paul II School See Elementary Schools, Diocesan under Institutions Located in the Diocese for details.

Catechesis/Religious Program—Students 350.

2—ST. AGNES (1883), Rev. Msgr. Mark J. Giordani, Admin.; Deacons Gilberto Vazquez; Pedro Cruz.
Res.: 681 Main St., Paterson, 07503. Tel: 973-279-0250; Fax: 973-357-1218.
Catechesis/Religious Program—Students 184.

3—ST. ANTHONY'S (1909), (Italian), Revs. Armand R. Quinto, S.D.B.; Jacob Champanil, S.D.B.; Vincent Duffy, S.D.B. (NY); Miroslaw Panczyk, S.D.B.; Thomas Provenzano, S.D.B. (CHI); Adelard Labonee, S.D.B.; Bro. Sal Sammarco, S.D.B. In Res., Revs. Paul Avallone, S.D.B.; Adelard Labonte, S.D.B.
Res.: 138 Beech St., Paterson, 07501. Tel: 973-742-9695; Fax: 973-881-0522.
School— (1921), 144 Beech St., Paterson, 07501. Tel: 973-279-3510; Fax: 973-523-1757. Salesian Sisters, Daughters of Mary Help of Christians 3; Lay Teachers 9; Students 228.
Catechesis/Religious Program—Students 75.

4—BLESSED SACRAMENT (1911), (Italian), Rev. Patrick Ryan.
Res.: 224 E. 18th St., Paterson, 07524. Tel: 973-523-5002; Fax: 973-523-3766.
School— (1953), 289-Sixth Ave., Paterson, 07524. Tel: 973-278-8787; Fax: 973-278-6436. Maestre Pie Filippini (Religious Teachers Filippini) 5; Lay Teachers 10; Students 300.
Catechesis/Religious Program—Students 76.

5—ST. BONAVENTURE (1877), Revs. John T. Piccione, O.F.M.; Christian F. Camadella, O.F.M.; Deacon Joseph Balough.
Res.: 174 Ramsey St., Paterson, 07501. Tel: 973-279-1016; Fax: 973-279-2507.
Catechesis/Religious Program—Students 137.

6—ST. CASIMIR'S (1911), (Lithuanian), Rev. John P. Hanley, Admin.
Res.: 147 Montgomery St., Paterson, 07501. Tel: 973-279-1922.

7—ST. GEORGE (1897), Revs. John J. Klein; Nelson Betancur; Deacon William Hussey.
Res.: 408 Getty Ave., Paterson, 07503. Tel: 973-742-0350; Fax: 973-754-0657.
School—(1897), 30 Michigan Ave., Paterson, 07503. Tel: 973-684-6754; Fax: 973-684-1988. Lay Teachers 12; Students 300.
Catechesis/Religious Program—Students 80.

8—ST. GERARD MAJELLA (1962), Revs. Charles J. Waller; John P. Hanley; Deacons Joseph Sisco; George Forshay.
Res.: 501 W. Broadway, Paterson, 07522. Tel: 973-595-8446; Fax: 973-790-0778.
School— (1965),Tel: 973-595-5640; Fax: 973-595-5475. Sisters 2; Lay Teachers 8; Students 265.
Catechesis/Religious Program—Students 130.

9—ST. JOSEPH'S (1867), Rev. Robert W. Wisniefski; Deacons Ronald Romano; Hector Casillas. In Res., Rev. Gregory Colucci.
Res.: 399 Market St., Paterson, 07501. Tel: 973-278-0030.
School—Pope John Paul II School See Elementary Schools, Diocesan under Institutions Located in the Diocese for details.

10—ST. MARY'S (1873),, (Auxilium Christianorum) Rev. Joseph G. Buffardi; Deacons Antonio Salierno; Juan Carlos Carnero. In Res., Rev. Andrew Velez.
Res.: 410 Union Ave., Paterson, 07502. Tel: 973-790-8651; Fax: 973-790-8534.
School— (1874), 95 Sherman Ave., Paterson, 07502. Tel: 973-956-1542; Fax: 973-956-1759. Salesian Sisters of St. John Bosco 3; Lay Teachers 12; Students 260.
Catechesis/Religious Program—Students 211.

11—ST. MICHAEL THE ARCHANGEL (1903), (Italian), Rev. Joseph J. Orlandi.
Res.: 70 Cianci St., Paterson, 07501. Tel: 973-523-8413; Fax: 973-253-4279.

12—OUR LADY OF LOURDES (1882), Rev. Donald Sella.
Res.: 440 River St., Paterson, 07524. Tel: 973-742-2142; Fax: 973-345-9136.
School— (1883),Tel: 973-278-0164; Fax: 973-278-3030. Lay Teachers 9; Students 240.
Catechesis/Religious Program—Students 56.

13—OUR LADY OF POMPEI (1916), (Italian), Rev. Sal J. Panagia; Deacon Henry Gallo.
Res.: 70 Murray Ave., Paterson, 07501. Tel: 973-742-1969; Fax: 973-742-1335.
Catechesis/Religious Program—Students 160.

14—OUR LADY OF VICTORIES (1882), Rev. Msgr. Thomas J. Coletta; Deacons Leo Gardner; Mario Munoz; Jesus Davila; Maximo Paulino.
Res.: 100 Fair St., Paterson, 07501. Tel: 973-279-0487; Fax: 973-977-8506.
Catechesis/Religious Program—Students 75.

15—ST. STEPHEN'S (1903), (Polish), Rev. John T. Connolly, M.Div. In Res., Rev. Francis Maliszewski; Deacon Candelario Espinal.
Res.: 86 Martin St., Paterson, 07501. Tel: 973-742-2822; Fax: 973-742-1679.
Catechesis/Religious Program—Students 50.

16—ST. THERESE (1926), Rev. Luciano Cruz; Deacons Nicholas Varsalona; Raul Pamplona; Luis Ramirez.
Res.: 80 13th Ave., Paterson, 07504. Tel: 973-881-0400; Fax: 973-881-7638.
School— (1953), 765-14th Ave., Paterson, 07504. Tel: 973-278-4135; Fax: 973-278-3228. Deacon Nicholas Varsalona, Prin. Lay Teachers 10; Students 320.
Catechesis/Religious Program—Students 50.

OUTSIDE THE CITY OF PATERSON

ANDOVER, SUSSEX CO., GOOD SHEPHERD (1979), [CEM] Rev. Msgr. Richard A. Steiger; Deacons Thomas Sullivan; Edmund Galinski; Keith Harris; Mrs. Sharon Mazuza, Pastoral Assoc.
Office—Rte. 517 (48 Tranquility Rd.), P.O. Box 464, 07821. Tel. 973-786-6631; 973-786-552[illegible] (Res.); 973-786-5811 (CEM); Fax: 973-786-5233.
Catechesis/Religious Program—Tel: 973-786-6632. Students 600.

BOONTON, MORRIS CO.

1—SS. CYRIL AND METHODIUS (1907), (Slovak), [CEM] Rev. Zbigniew Tyburski.
Res.: 215 Hill St., 07005. Tel: 973-334-0139; Fax: 973-402-9512.
Catechesis/Religious Program—Students 20.

2—OUR LADY OF MOUNT CARMEL (1847), [CEM] Rev. Michael A. Walsh; Deacon Joseph Richardson.
Res.: 910 Birch St., 07005. Tel: 973-334-1017; Fax: 973-335-1833.
School— (1868), 205 Oak St., 07005. Tel: 973-334-2777; Fax: 973-334-0975. Lay Teachers 12; Students 163.
Catechesis/Religious Program—Tel: 973-334-0429. Students 280.

BRANCHVILLE, SUSSEX CO., OUR LADY QUEEN OF PEACE (1951), Rev. Msgr. William P. Stober.
Res.: 209 Rte. 206, 07826. Tel: 973-948-3185; Fax: 973-948-4799.
Catechesis/Religious Program—Tel: 973-948-2741. Students 328.

BUDD LAKE, MORRIS CO., ST. JUDE (1943), Rev. Robert J. Mitchell; Deacon Anthony C. Siino; Donna M. Cole, Pastoral Assoc.
Res.: 17 Mt. Olive Rd., 07828. Tel: 973-691-1561; Fax: 973-691-9060.
Catechesis/Religious Program—Students 730.

BUTLER, MORRIS CO., ST. ANTHONY (1878), [CEM] Revs. Thomas R. Hartle, O.F.M.; Emmet Murphy, O.F.M.; Sr. Joanne Beirne, O.P., Pastoral Assoc. In Res., Rev. Jude Murphy, O.F.M.
Res.: 65 Bartholdi Ave., 07405. Tel: 973-838-0031; Fax: 973-838-0649.
School— (1882),Tel: 973-838-085[illegible]; Fax: 973-838-1460. Sisters 1; Lay Teachers 10; Students 169.
Catechesis/Religious Program—Students 380.
Parish House—71 Bartholdi Ave. 07405. Tel: 973-838-8585.

CEDAR KNOLLS, MORRIS CO., NOTRE DAME OF MT. CARMEL (1917), Revs. Jude S. Salus, O.S.B.; Justin Capato, O.S.B.; Deacons Joseph Harris; Victor Lupi; Bro. James Konchalski, O.S.B.
Res.: 75 Ridgedale Ave., 07927. Tel: 973-538-1358; Fax: 973-538-7403.
Catechesis/Religious Program—Students 598.

CHATHAM TOWNSHIP, MORRIS CO., CORPUS CHRISTI (1966), Rev. Msgr. James Mahoney.
Res.: 234 Southern Blvd., 07928. Tel: 973-635-0070; Fax: 973-635-5518.
Catechesis/Religious Program—Students 1,000.

CHATHAM, MORRIS CO., ST. PATRICK'S (1874), Revs. Edward J. Hinds, J.C.L.; Sigmund Peplowski; Deacons Joseph A. Wisneski; Mark Nixon.
Res.: 85 Washington Ave., 07928. Tel: 973-635-0625; Fax: 973-635-0119.
School— (1872), 45 Chatham St., 07928. Tel: 973-635-4623; Fax: 973-635-2311. Lay Teachers 30; Students 446.
Catechesis/Religious Program—Students 790.

CHESTER, MORRIS CO., ST. LAWRENCE THE MARTYR (1950), Rev. Msgr. P. Kevin Flanagan; Rev. Lancelot Reis; Deacon Frank Owens.
Res.: Main St., P.O. Box 730, 07930. Tel: 908-879-5371; Fax: 908-879-7701.
Catechesis/Religious Program—Main St., P.O. Box 31. Tel: 908-879-6714; Fax: 908-879-7701. Students 700.

CLIFTON, PASSAIC CO.

1—ST. ANDREW THE APOSTLE (Allwood) (1938), Rev. Msgr. Peter J. McHugh; Rev. Boguslaw Kobus; Deacon Robert J. Ayers.
Res.: 400 Mt. Prospect Ave., 07012. Tel: 973-779-6873; Fax: 973-779-0573.
School— (1953), 418 Mt. Prospect Ave., 07012. Tel: 973-473-3711; Fax: 973-473-6611. Sisters of the Presentation 2; Lay Teachers 10; Students 215.
Catechesis/Religious Program—Tel: 973-473-2863. Students 164.

2—ST. BRENDAN (1945), Rev. Frank W. Weber. In Res., Rev. Msgr. Francis Matarazzo; Rev. Alan F. Savitt.
Res.: 154 E. First St., 07011. Tel: 973-772-1115; Fax: 973-772-0497.
School— (1946), 154 E. First St., 07011. Tel: 973-772-1149; Fax: 973-773-1163. Sisters 1; Lay Teachers 15; Students 368.
Catechesis/Religious Program—Tel: 973-772-6775; Fax: 973-772-6213. Students 207.

3—ST. CLARE'S (1913), Rev. Msgr. Brendan P. Madden; Rev. Thomas J. Fitzgerald.
Res.: 69 Allwood Rd., 07014. Tel: 973-777-7588.
School— (1959),Tel: 973-777-7582; Fax: 973-473-0127. Lay Teachers 12; Students 245.
Catechesis/Religious Program—Students 260.

4—SS. CYRIL AND METHODIUS (1913), (Slovak), Rev. Paul O'Donnell Duggan, Admin. In Res., Rev. Hector Melendez.
Res.: 218 Ackerman Ave., 07011. Tel: 973-546-4390; Fax: 973-546-3269.

5—ST. JOHN KANTY (1930), (Polish), Revs. Raphael Zwolenkiewicz, O.F.M.Conv.; Andrzes Urbaniak, O.F.M.Conv.; Roger Haas, O.F.M.Conv.; Deacon Robert Altilio.
Res.: 49 Speer Ave., 07013. Tel: 973-779-4102; Fax: 973-773-0857.
School— (1958), 37 Speer Ave., 07013. Tel: 973-773-8090; Fax: 973-773-0421. Felician Sisters 3; Lay Teachers 10; Students 152.
Catechesis/Religious Program—Tel: 973-779-6214. Students 300.

6—ST. PAUL (1914), Revs. Victor J. Mazza; Brian Flanagan; Deacons Joseph Puskas; Peter Casamento. In Res., Rev. Robert K. Hooper.
Res.: 124 Union Ave., 07011. Tel: 973-546-2746; Fax: 973-340-2083.
School— (1916),Tel: 973-546-2161; Fax: 973-546-0057. Lay Teachers 11; Students 200.
Catechesis/Religious Program—Students 340.

7—ST. PHILIP THE APOSTLE (1943), Rev. Msgr. Peter J. Doody; Revs. David P. Long; Thomas G. Rainforth; Deacons Gregory DeLorenzo; Arthur Bandel.
Res.: 797 Valley Rd., 07013. Tel: 973-779-6200; Fax: 973-779-2959.
School— (1954),Tel: 973-779-4700. Lay Teachers 27; Students 420.
Catechesis/Religious Program—Tel: 973-779-1439. Students 645.

8—SACRED HEART (1897), (Italian), Rev. Msgr. Julian B. Varettoni; Rev. Andrew T. Perretta. In Res., Rev. Michael D. Joly.
Res.: 145 Randolph Ave., 07011. Tel: 973-546-6012; Fax: 973-546-1814.
School— (1953), 43 Clifton Ave., 07011. Tel: 973-546-4695; Fax: 973-546-8774. Lay Teachers 14; Students 245.
Catechesis/Religious Program—Students 28.

CONVENT STATION, MORRIS CO., ST. THOMAS MORE (1966), Rev. Arthur S. Colaicovo; Deacon Kenneth Rado. In Res., Rev. Zbigniew Kluba.
Res.: Madison Ave., Box 286-C, 07961. Tel: 973-267-5330.
Catechesis/Religious Program—Students 220.

DENVILLE, MORRIS CO., ST. MARY'S (1926), Rev. Msgr. James H. Murray; Rev. Richard V. Tartaglia; Deacons Al Klose; Charles Burrows.
Res.: 15 Myers Ave., 07834. Tel: 973-627-0269; Fax: 973-627-6355.
School— (1954),Tel: 973-627-2606; Fax: 973-627-9316. Lay Teachers 16; Students 168.
Catechesis/Religious Program—Tel: 973-627-8276. Students 690.

DOVER, MORRIS CO.

1—ST. MARY'S (1845), [CEM] Rev. Msgr. Richard A. Rusconi; Deacons Thomas P. Beirne; Richard Goglia; Stuart Hartnett.
Res.: 425 W. Blackwell St., 07801. Tel: 973-366-0184; Fax: 973-366-5377.
School— (1878), S. Main St., 07801. Tel: 973-366-0309; Fax: 973-366-6252. Sisters of Christian Charity 1; Lay Teachers 17; Students 207.
Catechesis/Religious Program—Tel: 973-366-0236. Students 375.

2—OUR LADY QUEEN OF THE MOST HOLY ROSARY (1959), (Hispanic), Rev. Jorge I. Rodriguez (DEN); Deacon Percy Silva.
Res.: 77 Richards Ave., 07801. Tel: 973-361-2725; Fax: 973-361-4058.
Catechesis/Religious Program—. Students 260.

3—SACRED HEART (1904), Rev. Msgr. Ronald J. Tully; Deacons Brian Drury; Gary Gordon; Ralph Weichand; Henry Hyle. In Res., Rev. Msgr. Charles F. Powers (Retired).
Res.: 4 Richards Ave., 07801. Tel: 973-366-0060; Fax: 973-366-8636.
School— (1923), 30 N. Essex St., 07801. Tel: 973-366-2068; Fax: 973-366-9428. Sisters of Sorrowful Mother 1; Lay Teachers 15; Students 196.
Catechesis/Religious Program—Students 271.

EAST HANOVER, MORRIS CO., ST. ROSE OF LIMA (1957), Rev. Msgr. William McCarthy (Retired); Rev. Owen Moran; Deacon Robert A. Lang; Sisters Dolores Alfone, F.S.R., Pastoral Assoc.; Concepta D'Amato, F.S.R., Pastoral Assoc.
Res.: 312 Ridgedale Ave., 07936. Tel: 973-887-5572; Fax: 973-884-0476.

School— (1961),Tel: 973-887-6990; Fax: 973-887-8655. Lay Teachers 28; Students 464.
Catechesis/Religious Program—Tel: 973-887-0357. Students 649.

FLANDERS, MORRIS CO., ST. ELIZABETH ANN SETON (1985), Rev. Msgr. John B. Wehrlen; Rev. Gerard P. Lair, O.S.B.; Deacons James McGrory; Frank Puglia.
Res.: 61 Main St., 07836. Tel: 973-927-1629; Fax: 973-927-0327.
Catechesis/Religious Program—Tel: 973-927-7077. Students 990.

FLORHAM PARK, MORRIS CO., HOLY FAMILY (1951), Rev. Msgr. Raymond J. Kupke; Rev. William J. Mooney; Deacons William F. Ward, Pastoral Assoc.; Mark McCabe, Pastoral Assoc.; Mrs. Barbara Froetscher, Pastoral Assoc.; Mrs. Patricia Danishek, Pastoral Assoc.; Mrs. Virginia Akhoury, Pastoral Assoc.; Mrs. Mary Jane McGuire.
Res.: 1 Lloyd Ave., 07932. Tel: 973-377-1817; Fax: 973-377-6350.
School— (1954),Tel: 973-377-4181; Fax: 973-377-0273. Sisters of Christian Charity 2; Lay Teachers 19; Students 246.
Catechesis/Religious Program—Tel: 973-377-3101. Students 620.

FRANKLIN, SUSSEX CO., IMMACULATE CONCEPTION (1867), [CEM] Rev. Martin G. Glynn; Deacon Jerome Schenker.
Res.: 75 Church St., 07416. Tel: 973-827-9575; Fax: 973-827-7375.
Catechesis/Religious Program—Tel: 973-827-9501. Students 332.

GREEN POND, MORRIS CO., ST. SIMON THE APOSTLE (Rockaway Twp.) (1942), Rev. Msgr. Joseph T. Anginoli, J.C.L.
Res.: 1010 Green Pond Rd., 07435. Tel: 973-697-4699; Fax: 973-697-1784.
Catechesis/Religious Program—Students 130.

HAINESVILLE, SUSSEX CO., ST. THOMAS THE APOSTLE (1941), Rev. A. Richard Carton; Deacon Wayne Von Doehren.
Mailing Address: P.O. Box 187, Layton, 07851. Tel: 973-948-2296; Fax: 973-293-8933.
Catechesis/Religious Program—Tel: 973-293-3536. Students 75.

HAMBURG, SUSSEX CO., ST. JUDE THE APOSTLE (1966), Rev. William B. Collins.
Res.: Beaver Run Rd., P.O. Box 1, 07419. Tel: 973-827-8030; Fax: 973-827-8382.
Catechesis/Religious Program—Tel: 973-827-2280. Students 365.

HASKELL, PASSAIC CO., ST. FRANCIS OF ASSISI (1905), Rev. Msgr. Remigio G. Rocco; Deacon Jose Rivera.
Res.: 868 Ringwood Ave., 07420. Tel: 973-835-0480; Fax: 973-835-3277.
School— (1912),Tel: 973-835-3268; Fax: 973-616-7644. Lay Teachers 10; Students 206.
Catechesis/Religious Program—Tel: 973-835-1946. Students 274.

HAWTHORNE, PASSAIC CO., ST. ANTHONY'S (1908), Rev. Msgr. George F. Hundt, J.C.L.; Rev. T. Kevin Corcoran; Deacons Richard J. Brudzynski; Anthony E. Bernardine; Anthony Fadlalla.
Res.: 276 Diamond Bridge Ave., 07506. Tel: 973-427-1478; Fax: 973-427-4826.
School— (1912), 270 Diamond Bridge Ave., 07506. Tel: 973-423-1818; Fax: 973-423-6065. Sisters 2; Lay Teachers 14; Students 253.
Catechesis/Religious Program—Tel: 973-427-7873. Students 752.

HEWITT, PASSAIC CO., OUR LADY QUEEN OF PEACE (1921), Rev. William Scully, O.F.M.; Deacons Charles Roche; Joseph Verboys; Philip Thiuri. In Res., Rev. Richard Mucowski, O.F.M.; Bro. Paul Santoro, O.F.M.
Friary: 1911 Union Valley Rd., 07421. Tel: 973-728-8162; Fax: 973-728-4650.
School— (1960),Tel: 973-728-9339; Fax: 973-728-6850. Franciscan Sisters 1; Lay Teachers 12; Students 220.
Catechesis/Religious Program—Tel: 973-728-8264. Students 700.

HIGHLAND LAKES, SUSSEX CO., OUR LADY OF FATIMA (1954), Rev. Msgr. Robert B. Carroll.
Mailing Address: P.O. Box 242, 07422. Tel: 973-764-4457; Fax: 973-764-4504.
Catechesis/Religious Program—Tel: 973-764-7277. Students 410.

HOPATCONG, SUSSEX CO., ST. JUDE'S (1931), Revs. George J. Gothie; John J. McGuigan; Deacon Thomas Friel.
Res.: 40 Maxim Dr., 07843. Tel: 973-398-6377; Fax: 973-398-0121.
Catechesis/Religious Program—Students 535.

KINNELON, MORRIS CO., OUR LADY OF THE MAGNIFICAT (1961), [CEM] Rev. Msgrs. John J. Carroll, Ed.D.; Joseph J. Goode.
Res.: 2 Miller Rd., 07405. Tel: 973-838-6838; Fax: 973-838-0710.
School— (1964),Tel: 973-838-6222; Fax: 973-838-0409. Ms. Judith Clayton, Prin. Lay Teachers 18; Students 221.
Catechesis/Religious Program—Tel: 973-838-0567. Sr. Ellen Denise O'Connor, F.S.P. Students 710.

LAKE HOPATCONG, MORRIS CO., OUR LADY STAR OF THE SEA (Jefferson Twp.) (1910), Rev. P. Christopher Muldoon; Deacon Vincent Pisano.
Res.: Espanong Rd., P.O. Box 337, 07849. Tel: 973-663-0211; Fax: 973-663-4302.
Catechesis/Religious Program—Tel: 973-663-0124. Students 460.

LINCOLN PARK, MORRIS CO., ST. JOSEPH'S (1922), Rev. Dennis J. Hogan; Deacons Stephen Marabeti; Joseph Parlapiano.
Res.: 216 Comly Rd., 07035. Tel: 973-696-4411; Fax: 973-305-8466.
Catechesis/Religious Program—Students 583.

LITTLE FALLS, PASSAIC CO., OUR LADY OF THE HOLY ANGELS (1883), Revs. Robert Sandoz, O.F.M.; Gregory Gebbia, O.F.M.; Robert J. Norton, O.F.M.; Sisters Nancy Grassia, O.S.F., Pastoral Assoc.; Mary Judith Lynch, O.P., Pastoral Assoc.
Res.: 465 Main St., 07424. Tel: 973-256-5200; Fax: 973-256-0185.
School— (1903), 471 Main St., 07424. Tel: 973-256-1132; Fax: 973-890-0904. Ms. Karen Sturz, Prin. Sisters 1; Lay Teachers 9; Students 145.
Catechesis/Religious Program—Students 780.

LONG VALLEY, MORRIS CO.

1—ST. LUKE (1982), Rev. Michael J. Drury.
Res.: 3 Carl Ln., P.O. Box 416, 07853. Tel: 908-876-3515; Fax: 908-876-5277.
Church: 265 W. Mill Rd., 07853.
Catechesis/Religious Program—Students 888.

2—ST. MARK THE EVANGELIST (1986), Revs. Allen F. Stepien; Robert J. Gordon, Admin.
Res.: 59 Spring Ln., 07853. Tel: 908-850-0652; Fax: 908-850-0648.
Catechesis/Religious Program—Students 500.

MADISON, MORRIS CO., ST. VINCENT MARTYR (1805), [CEM] Rev. Msgr. Christopher C. DiLella; Rev. Peter B. Wells.
Res.: 26 Green Village Rd., 07940. Tel: 973-377-4000; Fax: 973-377-8242.
School— (1848),Tel: 973-377-1104; Fax: 973-377-2632. Lay Teachers 29; Students 408.
Catechesis/Religious Program—Tel: 973-966-1771. Students 764.

MCAFEE, SUSSEX CO., ST. FRANCIS DE SALES (1963), Rev. Msgr. John V. Boland; Rev. Frederick Walters.
Mailing Address: P.O. Box 785, 07428. Tel: 973-827-3248; Fax: 973-827-7534.
Catechesis/Religious Program—Tel: 973-827-8300. Students 1,000.

MENDHAM, MORRIS CO., ST. JOSEPH'S (1853), [CEM] Rev. Msgr. Kenneth E. Lasch, J.C.D.; Deacons Robert F. Santos; William P. Long.
6 New St., 07945. Tel: 973-543-5950; Fax: 973-543-6025.
School— (1963),Tel: 973-543-7474; Fax: 973-543-7817. Lay Teachers 9; Students 244.
Catechesis/Religious Program—Students 860.

MONTAGUE, SUSSEX CO., ST. JAMES THE GREATER (1943), Rev. A. Richard Carton; Deacon Wayne Von Doehren.
Res.: 75 River Rd., 07827. Tel: 973-293-3379; Fax: 973-293-8933.
Catechesis/Religious Program—Tel: 973-293-3536. Students 90.

MONTVILLE, MORRIS CO., ST. PIUS X (1959), Revs. Joseph J. Garbarino; John F. Tarantino; Deacons Andrew L. Cavaliere; Jack Callahan.
Parish Ministry Office—Tel: 973-335-2894; Fax: 973-394-0069.
Res.: 18 Changebridge Rd., 07045. Tel: 973-331-1706.
School— (1963),Tel: 973-335-1253; Fax: 973-335-2392. Sr. June Morrissey, S.C., Prin. Religious 2; Lay Teachers 12; Students 280.
Catechesis/Religious Program—24 Changebridge Rd., 07045. Students 900.

MORRIS PLAINS, MORRIS CO., ST. VIRGILIUS (1881), Rev. William L. Winston; Sr. Mary Zaino, Pastoral Assoc.; Deacons Sylvester Mazzoccoli; Daniel Scrone; Peter McNally; Merle Sisler. In Res., Rev. Msgr. James L. Fallon, Pastor Emeritus (Retired).
Res.: 250 Speedwell Ave., 07950. Tel: 973-538-1418; Fax: 973-538-2992.
School— (1910),Tel: 973-539-7267; Fax: 973-292-5157. Mrs. Joyce Middleton. Lay Teachers 11; Students 200.
Catechesis/Religious Program—Tel: 973-267-1366. Students 615.

MORRISTOWN, MORRIS CO.

1—ASSUMPTION OF THE BLESSED VIRGIN MARY (1848), [CEM] Rev. Msgr. Martin F. Rauscher; Rev. Dennis J. Crowley; Deacons P. Michael Hanly; William Harty; Tony DiLorenzo; Frank Para; Tom Spruiell; Richard Pinto. In Res., Deacon Donatus Nnagha; Rev. Joseph M. Casey.
Res.: 91 Maple Ave., 07960. Tel: 973-539-2141; Fax: 973-984-0632.
School— (1850), 63 MacCulloch Ave., 07960. Tel: 973-538-0590; Fax: 973-984-3632. Sisters of Charity 3; Lay Teachers 38; Students 567.
Catechesis/Religious Program—Tel: 973-267-5638. Students 636.

2—ST. MARGARET'S (1930), Rev. Msgr. Francis J. Duffy; Rev. J. Brando Ibarra. In Res., Rev. Msgr. Thomas J. Trapasso, S.T.L. (Retired).
Res.: 6 Sussex Ave., 07960. Tel: 973-538-0874; Fax: 973-538-4581.
Catechesis/Religious Program—Tel: 973-267-8354. Students 245.

MOUNT ARLINGTON, MORRIS CO., OUR LADY OF THE LAKE (1888), Revs. Joseph Ryan; Desmond O'Connor, S.P.S.
Res.: One Park Ave., 07856. Tel: 973-398-0240; Fax: 973-398-3667.
Catechesis/Religious Program—Tel: 973-770-0291. Students 380.

MOUNT HOPE, MORRIS CO., ST. BERNARD'S (1855), Rev. Msgr. Richard A. Rusconi.
Res.: 446 Mt. Hope Rd., Wharton, 07885-2814. Tel: 973-627-0066; Fax: 973-627-3631.
Catechesis/Religious Program—Students 28.

MOUNTAIN LAKES, MORRIS CO., ST. CATHERINE OF SIENA (1956), Revs. Patrick Rice; Regis P. Wallace, O.S.B.
Res.: 10 N. Pocono Rd., 07046. Tel: 973-334-7131; Fax: 973-334-3202.
Catechesis/Religious Program—Tel: 973-334-5257. Students 850.

NETCONG, MORRIS CO., ST. MICHAEL'S (1873), [CEM] Revs. Nicholas G. Bozza; Arthur S. Colaicovo; Deacons Joseph Keenan; Stuart Murphy.
Res.: 4 Church St., 07857. Tel: 973-347-0032; Fax: 973-347-1560.
School— (1922),Tel: 973-347-0039; Fax: 973-347-0054. Lay Teachers 29; Students 450.
Catechesis/Religious Program—Tel: 973-347-1465. Students 560.

NEW VERNON, MORRIS CO., CHRIST THE KING (1956), Rev. Patrick G. O'Donovan.
Res.: Blue Mill Rd., P.O. Box 368, 07976. Tel: 973-539-4955; Fax: 973-267-7070.
Catechesis/Religious Program—Tel: 973-539-5729. Students 340.

NEWTON, SUSSEX CO., ST. JOSEPH'S (1854), [CEM] Rev. Peter Filipkowski; Deacons Gerald Hanifan; Alfred Kucinski; Arthur Van Vleet; Larry D'Amico.
Res.: 17 Elm St., 07860. Tel: 973-383-1985; Fax: 973-383-8164.
Catechesis/Religious Program—Tel: 973-383-8413. Students 418.

OAK RIDGE, MORRIS CO., ST. THOMAS, THE APOSTLE (1949), [CEM] Rev. Msgr. John E. Fitzpatrick.
Res.: 5635 Berkshire Valley Rd., 07438. Tel: 973-208-0090; Fax: 973-208-0092.
Catechesis/Religious Program—Tel: 973-208-0096. Students 294.

OGDENSBURG, SUSSEX CO., ST. THOMAS OF AQUIN (1881), [CEM] Rev. Stanley C. Barron; Deacons Edward Reading; Dominic Zampella.
Res.: 53 Kennedy Ave., 07439. Tel: 973-827-3190; Fax: 973-827-9738.
Catechesis/Religious Program—Students 200.

PARSIPPANY, MORRIS CO.

1—ST. ANN (1982), Rev. Msgr. Martin McDonnell; Sr. Frances Sanzo, S.S.C., Pastoral Assoc.; Deacons Donald O'Leary; Alfred Frank.
Res.: 781 Smith Rd., 07054. Tel: 973-884-1986; Fax: 973-884-0940.
Catechesis/Religious Program—Students 246.

2—ST. CHRISTOPHER (1944), Rev. Msgr. Frank B. Ferraioli; Rev. Sean McDonnell (Ireland); Deacons John J. Kelly; John Bernero; Henry Rohrman.
Res.: 1050 Littleton Rd., 07054. Tel: 973-539-7050; Fax: 973-539-3601.
School— (1962),Tel: 973-539-7053; Fax: 973-539-0207. Sisters of St. Dominic 4; Lay Teachers 16; Students 332.
Catechesis/Religious Program—Tel: 973-539-6208. Students 700.

3—ST. PETER THE APOSTLE (1938), Rev. Msgr. Herbert K. Tillyer, M.Ch.A; Revs. Wayne M. Varga; Frank P. Agresti; Frank P. Agresti; Sr. Sylvia Berzinski, S.S.C., Pastoral Assoc.; Deacons Louis Chiocco; Daniel Ferry; Joseph Marsicoveti.
Res.: 179 Baldwin Rd., 07054. Tel: 973-334-2090; Fax: 973-334-5397.
School— (1958),Tel: 973-334-4704; Fax: 973-334-0622. Lay Teachers 18; Students 231.
Catechesis/Religious Program—189 Baldwin Rd., 07054. Tel: 973-335-9713. Students 854.

PASSAIC, PASSAIC CO.

1—ST. ANTHONY OF PADUA (1917), (Italian), Revs. Hernan Arias; Ramilo Esplana.
Res.: 95 Myrtle Ave., 07055. Tel: 973-777-4793; Fax: 973-779-6864.
School— (1960), 40 Tulip St., 07055. Tel: 973-773-0970; Fax: 973-473-4681. Sisters 4; Lay Teachers 8; Students 199.
Catechesis/Religious Program—Students 403.

2—Assumption of the Blessed Virgin Mary (1891), (Slovak), Rev. Msgr. John J. Demkovich. In Res., Rev. John T. Catoir, J.C.D. (Retired).
Res.: 63 Monroe St., 07055. Tel: 973-779-0427; Fax: 973-472-5033.
3—Holy Rosary (1918), (Polish), Revs. Stefan Las; Stanley Lesniowski.
Res.: 6 Wall St., 07055. Tel: 973-473-1578; Fax: 973-473-1773.
Catechesis/Religious Program—Students 350.
4—Holy Trinity (1900), (German), Rev. Antonio Rodriguez.
Res.: 226 Harrison St., 07055. Tel: 973-778-9763; Fax: 973-778-7582.
Catechesis/Religious Program—Students 285.
5—St. Joseph's (1892), (Polish), Rev. Msgr. Joseph Czerkies; Rev. Dariusz Kaminski.
Res.: 7 Parker Ave., 07055. Tel: 973-473-0921; Fax: 973-473-4085.
Catechesis/Religious Program—Students 235.
6—St. Nicholas (1868), Rev. Msgr. Felipe N. Carvajal.
Res.: 153 Washington Pl., 07055. Tel: 973-779-7867; Fax: 973-815-1893.
School— (1874), 123 Jefferson St., 07055. Tel: 973-779-1987; Fax: 973-779-1931. Sisters of Charity 1; Lay Teachers 10; Students 250.
Catechesis/Religious Program—Tel: 973-779-7867; Fax: 973-815-1893. Students 60.
7—Our Lady of Fatima (1954), (Hispanic), Revs. Gilberto Gutierrez; Hector Melendez.
Res.: 32 Exchange Pl., 07055. Tel: 973-472-0815; Fax: 973-472-0250.
Catechesis/Religious Program—Students 215.
8—Our Lady Of Mt. Carmel (1902), (Italian), Rev. Sam Frapaul, O.F.M.Cap.
Res.: 10 St. Francis Way, 07055. Tel: 973-473-0246; Fax: 973-473-3404.
School— (1954),Tel: 973-473-8183; Fax: 973-473-0937. Franciscan Sisters 4; Lay Teachers 12; Students 310.
9—St. Stephen's (1902), (Magyar), Rev. Stephen N. Mustos, Sch.P.
Res.: 223 Third St., 07055. Tel: 973-779-0332; Fax: 973-778-4263.
Catechesis/Religious Program—Students 5.

Pequannock, Morris Co.
1—Holy Spirit (1949), Revs. Alfred J. Lampron; Edward A. Collins; Deacon Michael Scruggs.
Res.: 318 Tpke., 07440. Tel: 973-696-1234; Fax: 973-305-9390.
School— (1956),Tel: 973-835-5680; Fax: 973-835-1757. Maestre Pie Filippini (Religious Teachers Filippini) 4; Lay Teachers 17; Students 319.
Catechesis/Religious Program—330 Newark-Pompton Tpke., 07440. Tel: 973-835-5696. Students 230.
Convent—Tel: 973-694-2111.
2—Our Lady of Fatima Chapel (Tridentine) (1994), Revs. Mark Fischer, F.S.S.P. (ATL), Arnaud Mortemard De Boisse, F.S.S.P. In Res., Rev. Kenneth Baker, S.J.
Res.: 32 West Franklin Ave., 07440. Tel: 973-694-6727; Fax: 973-694-7629.
School—St. Maximilian Kolbe School, 18 First St., 07440. Tel: 973-694-1034; Fax: 973-694-1304. Mrs. Mary Lou Bednar, Prin. Lay Teachers 6; Students 48.

Pompton Lakes, Passaic Co., Our Lady of the Assumption (1906), Revs. John Carnevale, O.F.M.; Jude Murphy, O.F.M.; Kevin Downey, O.F.M.; Sr. Arlene Kollar, S.S.C., Pastoral Assoc.; Deacons Thomas Kimak; Hal Clark.
Parish Office—17 Pompton Ave., 07442. Tel: 973-835-0374; Fax: 973-835-8173.
St. Mary's Friary: 64 Lenox Ave., 07442. Tel: 973-839-1975.
School— (1951),Tel: 973-835-2010; Fax: 973-835-7529. Bro. Vincent Casamento, O.F.M., Prin. Lay Teachers 15; Students 249.
Catechesis/Religious Program—Tel: 973-835-7750; Fax: 973-616-6307. Students 1,891.

Pompton Plains, Morris Co., Our Lady of Good Counsel (1962), Rev. Msgr. Patrick J. Scott; Deacons Don X. Bancroft; Edward Jaroszewski; Charles Mallory; Ron Ochner. In Res., Rev. Richard H. Oliveri (Retired).
Res.: 155 W. Pkwy., P.O. Box 218, 07444. Tel: 973-839-2447; Fax: 973-839-9492.
Catechesis/Religious Program—Tel: 973-839-3311. Students 855.

Prospect Park, Passaic Co., St. Paul's (1924), Rev. Msgr. Edward J. Kurtyka, J.C.D. In Res., Revs. Marc Mancini; Michael A. Burke.
Res.: 286 Haledon Ave., Paterson, 07508. Tel: 973-790-8169.
Catechesis/Religious Program—Tel: 973-790-8135. Students 131.

Randolph, Morris Co.
1—St. Matthew the Apostle (1988), Rev. David McDonnell; Deacons Edward Keegan; Patrick Sheehan.
Res.: 267 Dover-Chester Rd., 07869. Tel: 973-584-1101; Fax: 973-584-0499.
Catechesis/Religious Program—Students 628.
2—Resurrection (1978), Rev. John Andrew Connell; Deacons Roger Lacouture; Kenneth Weaver; Raymond Latour. In Res., Rev. Msgr. George Dudak.
Res.: 651 Millbrook Ave., 07869. Tel: 973-895-4224; Fax: 973-895-3224.
Catechesis/Religious Program—Tel: 973-895-4226; Fax: 973-895-3224. Students 1,047.

Ringwood, Passaic Co., St. Catherine of Bologna (1917), Rev. Msgr. Patrick G. Panos; Deacons James Elliott; Richard Michalski.
Res.: 112 Erskine Rd., 07456. Tel: 973-962-7032; Fax: 973-962-1776.
School— (1948),Tel: 973-962-7131; Fax: 973-962-0585. Franciscan Sisters of Ringwood 3; Lay Teachers 17; Students 320.
Catechesis/Religious Program—Tel: 973-962-4966. Students 503.

Rockaway, Morris Co.
1—St. Cecilia's (1869), [CEM] Revs. John E. Hart; Brendan J. Murray; Brian Sullivan; Brian Sullivan; Deacons John F. Taylor; Paul D. Willson. In Res., Rev. Paul S. Manning.
Res.: 70 Church St., 07866. Tel: 973-627-0313; 973-627-0816; Fax: 973-627-4811.
School— (1958), Halsey Ave., 07866. Tel: 973-627-6003; Fax: 973-627-5217. Sisters of Christian Charity 1; Lay Teachers 12; Students 289.
Catechesis/Religious Program—Tel: 973-252-0760. Students 900.
2—St. Clement, Pope and Martyr (1964), Rev. James J Termyna; Deacons Harry Dachisen; Robert Morton.
Res.: 154 Mt. Pleasant Ave., Dover, 07801. Tel: 973-366-7095; Fax: 973-366-6083.
Catechesis/Religious Program—Tel: 973-366-7547; Fax: 973-366-6084. Students 324.
3—Sacred Heart (1923), (Slovak), Revs. John E. Hart, Admin.; Brendan J. Murray; Brian Sullivan. In Res. Rev. Volodymyr Baran.
Res.: 63 E. Main St., 07866. Tel: 973-627-0422; Fax: 973-627-6249.
School— (1965),Tel: 973-627-7689. Sisters of the Sorrowful Mother 1; Lay Teachers 10; Students 310.

Schooley's Mountain, Morris Co., Our Lady of the Mountain (1954), [CEM] Revs. Ralph H. Sodano; Mark Olenowski, Admin.
Res.: Rte. 24, 07870. Tel: 908-876-4395; Fax: 908-876-3744.
Catechesis/Religious Program—Tel: 908-876-4003. Students 723.

Sparta, Sussex Co.
1—Blessed Kateri Tekakwitha (1983), Revs. Albert Nix; Thomas H. Fallone; Sr. Barbara Moore, O.P., Pastoral Assoc.; Deacons Andrew Calandriello; Paul Puleo; Charles Mathias; William Pearson; James Cammarano; Joseph Cote.
Res. 427 Stanhope Rd., 07871. Tel: 973-729-1682; Fax: 973-729-0702.
Catechesis/Religious Program—Tel: 973-729-0489. Students 1,400.
2—Our Lady of the Lake (1935), Rev. Msgr. Paul F. Knauer; Rev. Thomas Mangieri; Deacon Edward Maron.
Res.: 294 Sparta Ave., 07871. Tel: 973-729-6107; Fax: 973-729-7203.
School— (1954),Tel: 973-729-9174; Fax: 973-729-0318. Ms. Barbara Campione, Prin. Lay Teachers 28; Students 502.
Catechesis/Religious Program—Tel: 973-729-2918. Students 780.

Stirling, Morris Co., St. Vincent de Paul (1886), [CEM] Rev. Msgr. Patrick E. Brown; Rev. James P. Bono; Deacon Peter O'Neill. In Res., Rev. Hugh Murphy.
Res.: Bebout Ave., 07980. Tel: 908-647-0118; Fax: 908-647-5992.
School— (1955),Tel: 908-647-0421; Fax: 908-647-3878. Lay Teachers 23; Students 286.
Catechesis/Religious Program—Tel: 908-647-6772. Students 918.

Stockholm, Sussex Co., St. John Vianney (1958), Rev. Matthew J. Twiggs; Deacon Stanley Sisson.
Res.: 2823 Rte. 23, P.O. Box 505, 07460. Tel: 973-697-6550; Fax: 973-697-6882.
Catechesis/Religious Program—Tel: 973-764-7071. Students 350.

Succasunna, Morris Co., St. Therese (1957), Revs. Joseph P. Davis; James A.D. Smith; Timothy Dowling; Deacons Anthony Signorelli; Bruce Olsen.
Res.: 7 Hunter St., 07876. Tel: 973-584-8271; Fax: 973-584-0684.
School— (1963),Tel: 973-584-0812; Fax: 973-584-2029. Sisters 1; Lay Teachers 9; Students 288.
Catechesis/Religious Program—Tel: 973-584-9442; Fax: 973-584-9492. Students 819.

Sussex, Sussex Co., St. Monica (1881), Rev. Charles A. Perricone; Carol Bezak, Pastoral Assoc.
Res.: 33 Unionville Ave., 07461. Tel: 973-875-4521; Fax: 973-875-7538.
Catechesis/Religious Program—Tel: 973-875-2252; Fax: 973-875-5531. Students 600.

Swartswood, Sussex Co., Our Lady of Mt. Carmel (1951), Rev. John J. Quinlan; Deacons Ellis F. Schweitzer; Anthony P. Barile Jr.; Robert T. Davis; Edward J. Muller; Debra M. Tripi, Pastoral Assoc.
Mailing Address: P.O. Box 124, 07877. Tel: 973-383-3566; Fax: 973-383-3831.
Catechesis/Religious Program—Tel: 973-579-2355. Students 268.

Totowa Borough, Passaic Co., St. James of the Marches (1926), Rev. Msgr. Eugene M. Boland; Rev. Paul Iovino.
Res.: 32 St. James Pl., 07512. Tel: 973-790-0288; Fax: 973-790-7064.
School— (1956),Tel: 973-956-8824; Fax: 973-956-8824. Sr. Mary Ann Grimes, Prin. Sisters 1; Lay Teachers 11; Students 170.
Catechesis/Religious Program—31 St. James Pl.. Tel: 973-790-4860; Fax: 973-790-4644. Students 355.

Wayne, Passaic Co.
1—Annunciation (1963), Rev. Msgr. Stanislaus E. Schinski; Deacons Charles Tenga; Andrew Kostic.
Res.: 45 Urban Club Rd., 07470. Tel: 973-694-5700; Fax: 973-694-5706.
Catechesis/Religious Program—Tel: 973-694-0787. Students 225.
2—Holy Cross (1925), Rev. Charles J. Parr.
Res.: 17 Van Duyne Ave., 07470. Tel: 973-696-1065; Fax: 973-696-3641.
Catechesis/Religious Program—Tel: 973-696-3500. Students 100.
3—Immaculate Heart of Mary (1956), Rev. Daniel A. Kelly; Sr. Maureen Corcoran, S.C.
Res.: 580 Ratzer Rd., 07470. Tel: 973-694-3400; Fax: 973-694-3459.
School— (1958),Tel: 973-694-1225; Fax: 973-872-9043. Lay Teachers 16; Students 223.
Catechesis/Religious Program—Tel: 973-694-4891. Students 632.
4—Our Lady of Consolation (1963), Rev. Michael Lombardo; Deacons Robert Pringle; Joseph Crowley. In Res., Rev. Eugene R. Sylva.
Res.: 1799 Hamburg Tpke., 07470. Tel: 973-839-3444; Fax: 973-839-9695.
School— (1967),Tel: 973-839-2323; Fax: 973-839-2428. Lay Teachers 13; Students 145.
Catechesis/Religious Program—Students 428.
5—Our Lady of the Valley (1960), Rev. Daniel W. Murphy; Deacons Michael Wallace; Vincent Cocilovo.
Res.: 630 Valley Rd., 07470. Tel: 973-694-4585; Fax: 973-696-5451.
School— (1962),Tel: 973-696-2212; Fax: 973-696-0238. Sisters of St. Joseph 1; Lay Teachers 22; Students 319.
Catechesis/Religious Program—630 Valley Rd.. Tel: 973-696-8307. Students 900.

West Milford Township, Passaic Co., St. Joseph (1765), Revs. Ronald Sordillo; Philip Le Beau; Deacons Milton Smilek; Anthony Curcio; Harry White.
Res.: 454 Germantown Rd., 07480. Tel: 973-697-6100; Fax: 973-697-3716.
School— (1956),Tel: 973-697-6896; Fax: 973-208-7111. Lay Teachers 12; Students 179.
Catechesis/Religious Program—Tel: 973-208-0636. Students 650.

Whippany, Morris Co., Our Lady of Mercy (1854), [CEM] Revs. John DeMattia; John P. Pilipie; Sr. Ann McKeon, G.N.S.H., Youth Min.
Res.: 9 Parsippany Rd., 07981. Tel: 973-887-0050; Fax: 973-887-0991.
School—Tel: 973-887-2611; Fax: 973-887-6629. Sr. Catherine Duignan, C.S.J.P., Prin. Lay Teachers 8; Students 175.
Catechesis/Religious Program—94-96 Whippany Rd.. Tel: 973-887-0767. Students 361.

Chaplains of Public Institutions
Hospitals

Paterson. *St. Joseph Hospital*, 703 Main St., 07503. Tel: 973-754-2000; 973-754-2060 (Office). Sr. Jane Frances Brady, Pres. & CEO, Revs. Martin Rooney, Janusz Rzadca.
Preakness Hospital, P.O. Box V, 07509. Tel: 973-278-6800. Revs. Andrew Velez, James Moss.

Denville. *St. Clare Hospital*, Pocono Rd., 07834. Tel: 973-627-3000. (Vacant)

Dover. *Dover General Hospital*, Jardine St., 07801. Tel: 973-939-3000. Rev. Wolodomyr Baran.

Morris Plains. *Greystone Park Psychiatric Hospital* 07950. Tel: 973-538-1800. Rev. Joseph M. Casey.

Morristown. *Morristown Memorial Hospital*, 100 Madison Ave., 07960. Tel: 973-540-5307. Revs. Zbigniew Kluba, Michael A. Walsh, Sr. Jo Mascera, S.S.C.

Newton. *Newton Memorial Hospital*, 175 High St.,

07860. Tel: 973-383-2121. (Vacant)

PASSAIC. *St. Mary Hospital*, 211 Pennington Ave., 07055. Tel: 973-473-1000. Revs. Luke Guastella, O.F.M.Cap., Vincent Liuzzo, O.F.M.Cap.

Passiac General Hospital, 350 Blvd., 07055. Tel: 973-345-4300. Revs. Robert K. Hooper, Andrew Velez, Deacon Enio Simeone.

POMPTON PLAINS. *Chilton Memorial Hospital* 07444. Tel: 973-831-5000. Deacon Edward Jaroszewski.

TOTOWA. *North Jersey Developmental Center*. Rev. Louis J. Scurti.

WAYNE. *St. Joseph's Wayne Hospital*, Hamburg Tpke., 07470. Tel: 973-942-6900. (Vacant)

Correctional Facilities

PATERSON. *Passaic County Jail*. Rev. Msgr. Mark J. Giordani, Rev. Luis Rendon.

MORRIS PLAINS. *Morris County Youth Center*. (Vacant)

MORRISTOWN. *Morris County Jail*. Rev. Msgr. Patrick E. Brown.

NEWTON. *Sussex County Jail*. (Vacant)

Special Assignment:
Rev. Msgrs.—
Bihr, Louis J., 296 Straight St., Paterson, 07501.
Condon, T. Mark, J.C.L., 178 Derrom Ave., Paterson, 07504.
Diachek, Robert M., 205 Madison Ave., Madison, 07940-1053. Tel: 973-236-1333
Revs.—
Lambro, Edward, 476 17th Ave., Paterson, 07504. Tel: 973-523-4456
McGrath, Thomas M., 476 17th Ave., Paterson, 07504. Tel: 201-523-9595

On Duty Outside the Diocese:
Revs.—
Erwin, Patrick O., Mayaguez, PR.
Grasso, Richard, Daytona Beach, FL
Holterhoff, Edward G., Monterey, CA
Mastroeni, Anthony J., Christendom College, Front Royal, VA
McLeod, David H., Manahawkin, NJ
McLoughlin, Brendan, Denville, NJ
Pavlick, Raymond A., Walden, NY
Reading, Edward, Ortley Beach, NJ
Stephenson, Alphonse J., Point Pleasant, NJ
Vitillo, Robert J., Washington, DC
Weis, John H., Bad Axe, MI

Military Chaplains:
Rev. Msgr.—
Cusack, John J., USAF
Revs.—
Briganti, Philip J., USA
O'Grady, Frank, USA
Parisi, Michael, USN

Sabbatical:
Rev. Msgr.—
Tamayo, Elias

Absent on Leave:
Revs.—
Coutinho, Absalom
Drogon, Greg
Kanzic, Gerald B.
Nieves, Jose Javier

Unassigned:
Rev. Msgr.—
Naughton, William M.
Revs.—
Cramer, William N.
Dillon, Edward J.
Mabango, Ashiono Anthony
O'Connor, John H.
Scolamiero, Dominic A.
Scott, James C.
Treglio, Vincent

Retired:
Rev. Msgrs.—
Bertasius, Anthony, 600 Liberty Hwy., Putnam, CT 06260.
Biesiada, Louis W., 2001 N.E. 38th St., Lighthouse Point, FL 33064.
Bischoff, Francis J., 140 Shepherd Ln., Totowa, 07512.
Busch, Aloysius J., Nazareth Village, Main St., Chester, 07930.
Carey, Leo P., Nazareth Village, Main St., Box 635, Chester, 07930.
Cassidy, Charles C., 516 Oak Hill Ct., Lanoka Harbor, 08734.
Ciampaglio, Joseph M.
Conway, Michael, 3900 S. University Dr., Davie, FL 33328.
Corr, John F., 83 Primose Tr., Morristown, 07960.
Dericks, John H., 288 Lackawanna Dr., Andover, 07821.
Dudak, George A., P.O. Box 257, Hibernia, 07842.
Fallon, James L., 10 W. Hanover Ave., Morris Plains, 07950.
Feenan, J. Francis, Ireland.
Ferrito, Joseph L., 15 Sea Girt Ln., Waretown, 08758.
Flek, Ladislaus J., 140 Shepherd Ln., Totowa, 07512.
Hayes, Denis A., 140 Shepherd Ln., Totowa, 07512.
Introini, Elso C.
Lee, Thaddeus, P.O. Box 2044, Beach Haven, 08008.
Longua, Paul A., Nazareth Village, P.O. Box 745, Chester, 07930.
Matarazzo, Frank, 154 E. 1st St., 07011.
McBride, Peter A., Nazareth Village, Main St., Chester, 07930.
McCarthy, William
McQuaid, Eugene, 21 Pocono Rd., Room 628, Denville, 07834.
Morris, John E., 140 Shepard Ln., Totowa, 07512.
O'Rorke, James H., 58 Portsmouth Ct., Hamburg, 07419.
Podgorny, John, (Poland)
Powers, Charles F., 4 Richards St., Dover, 07801.
Puma, Vincent E., 970 Black Oak Ridge Rd., Wayne, 07470.
Rugel, James J., 12 Grove Rd., Oak Ridge, 07438.
Russo, Charles J., 27 Livingston Rd., Morristown, 07960.
Ryan, Leo P., Nazareth Village, Main St. Box 635, Chester, 07930.
Trapasso, Thomas J., S.T.L., 6 Sussex Ave., Morristown, 07960.
Zazella, Thomas J., 4270 E. Agaze Rd., Phoenix, AZ 85044.
Revs.—
Catoir, John T., J.C.D., 63 Monroe St., Passaic, 07055.
Colucci, Gregory, 399 Market St., Paterson, 07501.
Costigan, George, Puentenans, Spain.
Davey, Edward M., Nazareth Village, Main St., Chester, 07930.
Fanning, Leo M., Nazareth Village, Main St., Chester, 07930.
Heekin, John M., 3912 S. Ocean Blvd., Apt. 505, Highland Beach, FL 33487.
Hertel, James R., 2 Ann St., Unit F112, 07013.
Heusser, John F., 509 Goffle Hill Rd., Hawthorne, 07506.
Hewitt, Kenneth R., 490 Windemere Ave., Mount Arlington, 07856.
Jacobs, Richard A., 157 Bridge St., Catskill, NY 12414.
Klim, Vincent, 2510 Hemlock Farms, Hawley, PA 18428.
Krajewski, Paul A., 10 Prime Rose Ln., Mount Arlington, 07856.
Kuzhippallil, George, P.O. Box 871, Camillus, NY 13031.
Lewis, Gerald F., 2 Heritage Dr., Sparta, 07871.
LoGatto, Joseph J., Cosenza, Italy.
Lugo, Joseph W., 78 Chestnut St., Bridgewater, 08807.
Maliszewski, Francis, 86 Martin St., Paterson, 07501.
McHugh, Dennis, Our Lady's Shrine, Knock, County Mayo, Ireland.
Mullan, Patrick, Nazareth Village, Main St., Box 635, Chester, 07930.
Murphy, Joseph E., Narareth Village, Main St., Box 635, Chester, 07930.
Mushinsky, John E., 22 Boston Rd., Neptune, 07753.
O'Kielty, James P., Nazareth Village, Main St., Box 635, Chester, 07930.
O'Riordan, Jeremiah, 1202 157th St., Beachurst, NY 11357-1959.
Oliveri, Richard H.
Pisarcik, John G., 1415 Farmview Dr., Dover, DE 19904-3392.
Pruschowitz, Walter M., Beverwyck Nursing Home, 420 Beverwyck Rd., Parsippany, 07054.
Rento, Richard G., 33 Murray Ln., Lavalette, 08735.
Shema, George T., Nazareth Village, Main St., Box 635, Chester, 07930.
Sullivan, John A., 905-B S.W. Central Ave., Seaside Park, 08752.

Permanent Deacons:
Kostic, Andrew, Annunciation, Wayne
Altilio, Robert M., St. John Kanty, Clifton
Ayers, Robert, St. Andrew the Apostle, Clifton
Balough, Joseph, St. Bonaventure, Paterson
Bancroft, Don X., Our Lady of Good Counsel, Pompton Plains
Bandel, Arthur, St. Philip, Clifton
Barile, Anthony P., Jr., Our Lady of Mount Carmel, Swartswood
Beirne, Thomas P., St. Mary, Dover
Bernardine, Anthony E., St. Anthony, Hawthorne
Bernero, John, St. Christopher, Parsippany
Bianchi, Roland, Archdiocese of Newark
Biersbach, Raymond, (Unassigned)
Brudzynski, Richard, St. Anthony, Hawthorne
Buckholtz, Alexander E., (Retired)
Calandriello, Andrew, Blessed Kateri Tekakwitha, Sparta
Callahan, Jack, St. Pius X, Montville
Cammarano, James, Blessed Kateri Tekakwitha, Sparta
Carnero, Juan Carlos, St. Mary, Paterson
Casamento, Peter, St. Paul, Clifton
Casillas, Hector, St. Joseph, Paterson
Cassidy, Joseph, (Retired)
Cavaliere, Andrew L., St. Pius X, Montville
Chiocco, Louis, St. Peter the Apostle, Parsippany
Ciampa, Alfred, Unassigned
Clark, Hal G., St. Mary, Pompton Lakes
Cleary, Kevin, St. Luke, Long Valley
Cocilovo, Vincent, Our Lady of the Valley, Wayne
Collins, David, (Unassigned)
Cortes, Jesus, Our Lady of Fatima, Passaic
Costello, Barry, (Retired)
Cote, Joseph, Blessed Kateri Tekakwitha, Sparta
Crowley, Joseph C., Jr., Our Lady of Consolation, Wayne
Cruz, Pedro, St. Agnes, Paterson
Curcio, Anthony, Jr., St. Joseph, West Milford
D'Amico, Larry, St. Joseph, Newton
Dachisen, Harry, St. Clement Pope and Martyr, Rockaway Township
DaSilva, Joao, Morristown Memorial Hospital
Davilas, Jesus, Our Lady of Victories, Paterson
Davis, Robert T., Our Lady of Mount Carmel, Swartswood
de Mena, Henry, Notre Dame of Mt. Carmel, Cedar Knolls
DeLorenzo, Gregory, St. Philip Church, Clifton
DiLorenzo, Anthony, Assumption, Morristown
Dolan, Eugene P., Sacred Heart, Dover
Drury, Brian, Sacred Heart, Dover
Elliott, James, St. Catherine of Bologna, Ringwood
Espinal, Candelario, St. Stephen, Paterson
Fadalla, Gerald J., St. Anthony, Hawthorne
Fanelli, Alfredo, Notre Dame of Mt. Carmel, Cedar Knolls
Ferry, Daniel F., St. Peter the Apostle, Parsippany
Forshay, George W., St. Gerard Majella, Paterson
Frank, Alfred E., St. Ann, Parsippany
Friel, Thomas, St. Jude, Hopatcong
Galinski, Edmund V., Good Shepherd, Andover
Gallo, Henry, Our Lady of Pompei, Paterson
Gardner, Leo, Our Lady of Victories, Paterson
Gibbons, Thomas P., Our Lady of the Mountain, Schooley's Mountain
Gil, Luis, St. John's Cathedral, Paterson
Giron, Jose D., (Unassigned)
Goglia, Richard, St. Mary, Dover
Gordon, Gary, Sacred Heart, Dover
Grish, Kevin, (Unassigned)
Gutierrez, Carlos, (Unassigned)
Hanifen, Gerald B., St. Joseph, Newton
Hanly, P. Michael, Assumption, Morristown
Harris, Joseph, Notre Dame, Cedar Knolls
Harris, Keith, Good Shepherd, Andover
Hartnett, Stuart, St. Mary, Dover
Harty, William, Assumption, Morristown
Head, Robert C., Our Lady of the Mountain, Schooley's Mountain
Healy, Philip, Immaculate Heart of Mary, Wayne
Healy, Thomas F., Jr., St. Luke, Long Valley
Higgins, Edward J., St. Mary, Pompton Lakes
Hilber, Joseph, (Unassigned)
Hussey, William E., St. George Church, Paterson
Hyle, Henry, Sacred Heart, Dover
Jaroszewski, Edward, Our Lady of Good Counsel Church, Pompton Plains
Jones, Frederick B., Jr., Military Archdiocese.
Keegan, Edward, St. Matthew, Randolph
Keenan, Joseph, St. Michael, Netcong
Kelly, John, St. Christopher, Parsippany
Kimak, Thomas J., St. Mary, Pompton Lakes
Klose, Albert P., St. Mary, Denville
Kronyak, Thomas, St. Jude, Hamburg
Kucinski, Al, St. Joseph, Newton.
Lacouture, Roger, Resurrection, Randolph
Lally, Edward J., (Unassigned)
Lang, Robert A., St. Rose of Lima, East Hanover
Larkin, John S., Diocese of Charleston
Latour, Raymond, Resurrection, Randolph
Lebron, Florencio G., (Unassigned)
Leo, Vincent, Jr., St. Rose of Lima, East Hanover
Liotard, Paul A., (Unassigned)
Llanso, Jamie, (Retired)
Llibre, John, Unassigned
Long, William P., St. Joseph, Mendham
Lupi, Victor, Notre Dame, Cedar Knolls

Madreperla, Steven A., (Unassigned)
Mallory, Charles, Our Lady of Good Counsel Church, Pompton Plains
Marabeti, Stephen J., St. Joseph Church, Lincoln Park
Maron, Edward, Our Lady of the Lake, Sparta
Marsicoveti, Joseph, St. Peter the Apostle, Parsippany
Mathias, Charles T., Bl. Kateri Tekakwitha, Sparta
Mazzaccoli, Sylvester A., St. Virgil Church, Morris Plains
McCabe, Mark, Holy Family, Florham Park
McCaffrey, David, (Unassigned)
McGrory, James G., St. Elizabeth Ann Seton, Flanders
McMullin, Robert, St. Gerard Majella, Paterson
McNally, Peter J., St. Virgil, Morris Plains
McQuaid, Francis P., (Unassigned)
Meyer, John, (Unassigned)
Michalski, Richard, St. Catherine of Bologna, Ringwood
Morris, James, (Unassigned)
Morton, Robert, St. Clement, Rockaway Twp.
Muller, Edward J., Our Lady of Mount Carmel, Swartswood
Munoz, Mario, Blessed Sacrament, Paterson
Murphy, Stuart, St. Michael, Netcong
Natafalusy, Stephen P., St. Elizabeth Ann Seton, Flanders
Nixon, Mark G., St. Patrick, Chatham
O'Leary, Donald, St. Ann, Parsippany
O'Neill, Peter, St. Vincent de Paul, Stirling
Ochner, Ronald, Diocese of Venice, FL,
Olsen, Bruce, St. Therese, Succasunna
Owens, Frank, St. Lawrence the Martyr, Chester
Pamplona, Raul, St. Therese, Paterson
Para, Frank, Assumption, Morristown
Parlapiano, Joseph J., St. Joseph, Lincoln Park
Paulino, Maximo, Our Lady of Victories, Paterson
Pearson, William J., (Unassigned)
Pedraza, Guido, St. John the Baptist, Paterson
Peters, William L., Raleigh, NC
Pilek, John E., St. Luke, Long Valley
Pinto, Richard, Assumption, Morristown
Pirylis, Michael, (Unassigned)
Pisano, Vincent F., Our Lady Star of the Sea, Hopatcong
Pluciniak, Edward, Our Lady of the Mountain, Schooley's Mountain
Pomales, Jose, St. John Cathedral, Paterson
Pringle, Robert H., Our Lady of Good Counsel, Pompton Plains
Puglia, Frank, St. Elizabeth Ann Seton, Flanders
Puleo, Paul A., Blessed Kateri Tekakwitha, Sparta
Puskas, Joseph, St. Paul, Clifton
Quinn, Joseph, Notre Dame of Mt. Carmel, Cedar Knolls
Rado, Kenneth, St. Thomas More, Convent Station
Ramirez, Edward, St. Nicholas, Passaic
Ramirez, Luis, St. Therese, Paterson
Reading, Edward J., St. Thomas of Aquin, Ogdensburg
Reed, Daniel, Unassigned
Richardson, Joseph, Our Lady of Mount Carmel, Boonton
Rivera, Jose M., St. Francis of Assisi, Haskell
Roche, Charles, St. Francis of Assisi, Haskell
Rohrman, Harry, (Unassigned)
Romano, Ron, St. Joseph, Paterson
Salierno, Anthony, St. Mary, Paterson
Sanchez, Armando, Blessed Sacrament, Paterson
Santiago, Manuel, St. John the Baptist Cathedral, Paterson
Santos, Robert F., St. Joseph, Mendham
Schenker, Jerome, Immaculate Conception, Franklin
Schwietzer, Ellis F., Our Lady of Mount Carmel, Swartswood
Scrone, Daniel, St. Virgil, Morris Plains
Scruggs, Michael K., Holy Spirit, Pequannock
Sheehan, Patrick, St. Matthew, Randolph
Signorelli, Anthony, St. Therese, Succasunna
Siino, Anthony C., St. Jude, Budd Lake
Silva, Percy, (Unassigned)
Simeone, Enio, Passaic General Hospital
Sisco, Joseph, St. Gerard Majella, Paterson
Sisler, Merle F., St. Virgil, Morris Plains
Sisson, Stanley, St. John Vianney, Stockholm
Smilek, Milton, St. Joseph, West Milford
Spruiell, Thomas, Assumption, Morristown
Sullivan, Thomas, Good Shepherd, Andover
Taylor, John F., St. Cecilia, Rockaway
Tenga, Charles, Annunciation, Wayne
Teresinski, John S., (Unassigned)
Thiuri, Phillipe, Our Lady Queen of Peace, Hewitt
Turner, John, Leave of Absence
Van Orman, Patrick, Our Lady of the Mountain, Schooleys Mountain
Van Vleet, Arthur H., St. Joseph, Newton
Varsalona, Nicholas, St. Therese Church, Paterson
Vazquez, Gilberto, St. Agnes, Paterson
Verboys, Joseph R., Our Lady Queen of Peace, Hewitt
Vesota, Robert, Father English Center, Paterson
Von Doehren, Wayne, St. James, Montague; St. Thomas, Hainesville
Walker, John, (Unassigned)
Wallace, Michael J., Our Lady of the Valley, Wayne
Ward, William, Holy Family, Florham Park
Weaver, Kenneth, Resurrection, Randolph
Whelan, Edward, (Unassigned)
White, Harry, St. Joseph, West Milford
Wiekand, Ralph, (Unassigned)
Willson, Paul D., St. Cecilia, Rockaway
Wisneski, Joseph A., St. Patrick, Chatham
Zampella, Dominic, St. Thomas of Aquin, Ogdensburg

INSTITUTIONS LOCATED IN THE DIOCESE

[A] SEMINARIES, RELIGIOUS OR SCHOLASTICATES

OAK RIDGE. *Paulist Novitiate*, 243 Mount Paul Rd., 07438-9512. Tel: 973-697-6341; Fax: 973-697-7814. Email: mountpaulnj@c.s.com. Rev. John J. Foley, C.S.P., J.C.D., Dir. Ministries. Missionary Society of St. Paul the Apostle (Paulist Fathers)

[B] COLLEGES AND UNIVERSITIES

MENDHAM. *Assumption College for Sisters*, 350 Bernardville Rd., 07945. Tel: 973-543-6528; Fax: 973-543-1738. Email: acs@scceast.org. Web: www.acscollegeforsisters.org. Sisters Mary Joseph Schultz, S.C.C., Pres.; Mary Theresa Wojnicki, S.C.C., Academic Dean & Registrar; Mary Lawrence Cassidy, S.C.C., Treas. Conducted by Sisters of Christian Charity. Religious 12; Students 24.

MORRISTOWN. *College of Saint Elizabeth*, 2 Convent Rd., 07960-6989. Tel: 973-290-4000; 973-290-4354; Fax: 973-290-4488. Web: www.st-elizabeth.edu. Sr. Francis Raftery, S.C., Pres.; Dr. Johanna Glazewski, Vice Pres. for Academic Affairs & Dean of Studies; Maria Cammarata, Vice Pres. for Finance & Admin. and Treas.; Mrs. John A. Kruglinski, Comptroller; Dr. Carol Strobeck, Registrar; Mrs. Donna Tatarka, Dean of Admissions & Financial Aid; Rev. Anthony J. Ciorra, Chap. Sisters of Charity, Full-time Admin. and Faculty: Priests 3; Religious 22; Lay Teachers 141; Students 1,766.

[C] HIGH SCHOOLS, DIOCESAN

PATERSON. *Paterson Catholic Regional High School*, 764 11th Ave., 07514. Tel: 973-278-1024; Fax: 973-684-7244. Email: patersoncatholic-hs@hotmail.com. Rev. Hugh Murphy, Pres.; Florence Pisano, Prin.; Teresa Kerr, Asst. Prin.; Michele R. Neves, Asst. Prin. Priests 1; Sisters 1; Lay Teachers 33; Students 420.

DENVILLE. *Morris Catholic High School* 07834. Tel: 973-627-6674; Fax: 973-627-4351. Email: mchs@morriscatholic.org. Web: www.morriscatholic.org. Rev. Paul S. Manning, Pres.; Sr. Marie Pauline Demek, S.C.C., Prin. Priests 1; Sisters 7; Lay Teachers 25; Students 375.

MADISON. *Bayley-Ellard High School* 07940. Tel: 973-377-2486; Fax: 973-377-6639. Email: info@bayley.org. Web: www.bayley.org. Deacon Daniel Scrone, Acting Dir.; Rev. Msgrs. John F. Corr (Retired); James L. Fallon (Retired). Priests 3; Lay Teachers 30; Students 250.

SPARTA. *Pope John XXIII High School* 07871. Tel: 973-729-6125; Fax: 973-729-4313. Email: dipathspj@impresso.com. Rev. Kieran A. McHugh, Pres. Lay Teachers 65; Students 870.

WAYNE. *De Paul High School*, 1512 Alps Rd., 07470. Tel: 973-694-3702; Fax: 973-633-5381. Email: tsmithling@depaulcatholic.org. Web: depaulcatholic.org. Rev. Eugene R. Sylva, Pres.; Thomas Smithling, Prin. Sisters 5; Brothers 1; Lay Teachers 48; Students 610.

[D] HIGH SCHOOLS, PRIVATE

CONVENT STATION. *Academy of St. Elizabeth* 07961. Tel: 973-290-5200; Fax: 973-290-5232. Sr. Patricia Mary McMullen, S.C., Prin. Sisters of Charity Sisters 3; Lay Teachers 25; Students 225.

MORRISTOWN. *Delbarton School*, 230 Mendham Rd., 07960. Tel: 973-538-3231; Fax: 973-538-8836. Email: homepage@delbarton.org. Web: www.delbarton.org. Rev. Luke L. Travers, O.S.B., Headmaster; Mr. Edward Kim, Asst. Headmaster; Mr. Charles Ruebling, Dean of Faculty; Mr. David Donovan, Dir. of Admissions; Mr. David Hajduk, Dir. Campus Min.; Rev. Anthony Sargent, O.S.B. Day School for Boys. (Grades 7-12) Monks 18; Laymen 70; Students 540.

Villa Walsh Academy 07960. Tel: 973-538-3680; Fax: 973-538-6733. Email: villawalsh@aol.com. Web: www.villawalsh.org. Sr. Patricia Pompa, M.P.F., Prin. College Preparatory for girls (Grades 7-12) Conducted by Religious Teachers Filippini Sisters 9; Lay Teachers 25; Students 235.

NORTH HALEDON. *Mary Help of Christians Academy*, 659-723 Belmont Ave., 07508. Tel: 973-790-6200; Fax: 973-790-6125. Email principal@maryhelp.org. Web: www.maryhelp.org. Sisters Theresa Kelly, F.M.A., Supr.; Margaret Wilhelm, F.M.A., Prin. Daughters of Mary Help of Christians (Salesian Sisters) Sisters 22; Lay Teachers 27; Students 250.

[E] ELEMENTARY SCHOOLS, DIOCESAN

CLIFTON. *Pope John Paul II School* Serving St. John the Baptist Cathedral and St. Joseph, Paterson , 775 Valley Rd., 07013. Tel: 973-458-9282; Fax: 973-458-9820. Email: principal@pjpii.com. Sr. Theresa Samson, F.M.A., Prin.; Ms. Kathleen Fields, Vice Prin. Sisters 4; Lay Teachers 27; Students 650.

[F] REGIONAL ELEMENTARY SCHOOLS

FRANKLIN. *Immaculate Conception Regional School*, 65 Church St., 07416. Tel: 973-827-3777; Fax: 973-827-8728. Email: oleary@icrschool.com. Ms. Diane Di Spaena, Prin. Serves Immaculate Conception, Franklin; Our Lady of Fatima, Highland Lakes; St. John Vianney, Stockholm; St. Monica, Sussex; St. Thomas of Aquin, Ogdensburg; St. Francis De Sales, McAfee; St. Jude, Hamburg Lay Teachers 18; Students 294.

NEWTON. *St. Joseph Regional School*, Jefferson St., 07860. Tel: 973-383-2909; Fax: 973-383-6353. Email: sjrs@nac.net. Web: www.sjccs.com. Sr. Betty Ann Martinez, F.M.A., Prin. Serves St. Joseph, Newton; Our Lady Queen of Peace, Branchville; Our Lady of Mount Carmel, Swartswood Lay Teachers 12; Students 235.

PASSAIC. *Passaic Catholic Regional School*, 212 Market St., 07055. Tel: 973-773-4644; Fax: 973-773-2735. Email: pcrs212market@aol.com. Sr. Joselle Ratka, C.S.S.F., Prin. Serves Holy Rosary, St. Joseph, St. Stephen, St. Mary, Our Lady of Fatima, in Passaic Sisters 2; Lay Teachers 10; Students 210.

[G] PRIVATE PRESCHOOL

FLORHAM PARK. *Magic Kingdom Day Nursery*, 88 Brooklake Rd., 07932. Tel: 973-966-9762; Fax: 973-377-3994. Email: gelsym@yahoo.com. Sr. Gelsey Mosca, S.D.V., Prin. Vocationist Sisters Sisters 13; Lay Teachers 1; Students 90.

NEWTON. *Camp Auxilium Learning Center*, 14 Old Swartswood Rd., 07860. Tel: 973-383-2621; Fax: 973-383-3214. Email: campauxilium@nac.net. Web: www.campauxilium.org. Sr. Lou Ann Fantauzza, F.M.A., Prin. Salesian Sisters Sisters 3; Lay Teachers 14; Students 275.

PARSIPPANY. *St. Elizabeth's Nursery and Montessori School, Inc.*, 499 Park Rd., 07054. Tel: 973-540-0721; Fax: 973-540-9186. Sr. Gina Maria Amico, F.S.S.E., Contact Person. Students 180.

[H] CHILDREN'S CENTERS

DENVILLE. *St. Peter's Village*, 170 Diamond Spring Rd., 07834. Tel: 973-627-0212; Fax: 973-627-3338. Email: srkatherine@nac.net. Sr. Katherine M. Kinnally, S.S.N.D., Dir. Staffed by School Sisters of Notre Dame Sisters 1; Residents 16.

TOTOWA. *Mt. St. Joseph Children's Center*, 124 Shepherd Ln., 07512. Tel: 973-595-5720; Fax: 973-595-1930. Sr. Dorothy Sheahan, S.C., Dir. Residential school for classified emotionally disturbed boys, 6-14, referred from public school districts. Under the direction of Catholic Family and Community Services. Residents 37.

[I] RETREAT HOUSES & HOUSES OF PRAYER

BRANCHVILLE. *Sanctuary of Mary-Our Lady of the Holy Spirit*, 252 Wantage Ave., 07826. Tel: 973-875-7625. Rev. Silvester J. Livolsi (NEW).

CHESTER. *Hermits of Bethlehem in the Heart of Jesus*, 82 Pleasant Hill Rd., 07930. Tel: 908-879-7059; Fax: 908-879-7059. Rev. Eugene C. Romano, Desert Father. Priests 1; Sisters 5.

CONVENT STATION. *Xavier Center* A retreat & conference center. , 07961. Tel: 973-290-5100; Fax: 973-290-5121. Email: cahxavier@aol.com. Web: www.xaviercenter.org. Sr. Carol Heller, S.C., Admin.

FLORHAM PARK. *Vocationist Fathers Retreat Center*, 90 Brooklake Rd., 07932. Tel: 973-966-6262; Fax: 973-593-8381. Email: vocationist@aol.com. Web: www.vocationist.org. Rev. Armando M. Palmieri, S.D.V. (Italy) (NEW), Dir.

MENDHAM. *Villa Pauline* 07945. Retreat House for Men & Women Sisters of Christian Charity 7.

MORRISTOWN. *Loyola House of Retreats*, 161 James St., 07960. Tel: 973-539-0740; Fax: 973-898-9839. Email: retreathouse@loyola.org. Web: www.loyola.org. Revs. Patrick J. Sullivan, Supr. & Dir.; Donald G. Devine, S.J.; Edmund W. Nagle, S.J.; Emmet J. Norton, S.J.; William R. O'Leary, S.J., Admin.; Louis P. Sogliuzzo, S.J.; Thomas F. Walsh, S.J.; Richard J. Anable, S.J.; William P. Poorten, S.J.; Kirk R. Reynolds, S.J.; Sisters Barbara Connell, S.C.; Mary Ann Pfund, S.S.J. Society of Jesus Priests 9; Sisters 2.

St. Mary's Abbey Retreat Center, 230 Mendham Rd., 07960. Tel: 973-538-5231, Ext. 2100; Fax: 973-538-7109. Email: abbeyretreat@juno.com. Web: delbarton.org. Very Rev. Patrick M. Hurley, O.S.B., Dir. & Guestmaster.

MOUNT ARLINGTON. *Claremount Retreat Center*, 35 Windemere Ave., 07856. Tel: 973-601-1475; Fax: 973-601-1495. Sr. Mary Jean Ryder, C.S.S.F., Dir.

NEWTON. *Sacred Heart Retreat Center*, 20 Old Swartswood Rd., 07860. Tel: 973-383-2620; Fax: 973-383-3083. Email: shcenter@juno.com. Sr. Catherine Hurley, F.M.A., Supr. Daughters of Mary Help of Christians (Salesian Sisters of St. John Bosco) Sisters 4.

OAK RIDGE. *Mount Paul Retreat Center*, 243 Mount Paul Rd., 07438-9512. Tel: 973-697-6341; Fax: 973-697-7814. Email: mountpaulnj@cs.com. Rev. John J. Foley, C.S.P., J.C.D., Dir. Ministries.

RINGWOOD. *Franciscan Spiritual Center-Ringwood*, 474 Sloatsburg Rd., 07456. Tel: 973-962-9778; Fax: 973-962-0445. Email: fsrretreat@aol.com. Sr. Rosemary Napolitano, O.S.F., Dir. Sisters of St. Francis of Philadelphia

[J] GENERAL HOSPITALS

PATERSON. *St. Joseph's Hospital and Medical Center*, 703 Main St., 07503. Tel: 973-754-2000; Fax: 973-754-3273. Mr. Patrick R. Wardell, Pres. & CEO; Kathleen Silard, Vice Pres. & COO; Sr. Ann Stango, S.C., Vice Pres., Mission; Revs. William N. Cramer, Dir. Pastoral Care; Janusz Rzadca; Martin Rooney. Sisters of Charity of St. Elizabeth, NJ 35; Bed Capacity 792; Patients assisted annually 315,607.

DENVILLE. *Saint Clare's Community Care, Inc.* dba Saint Clare's Health Services , c/o 25 Pocono Rd., 07834. Tel: 973-989-3124; Fax: 973-989-3195. Email: jmccaffrey@stclares.org. Web: www.stclares.org. Sr. M. Johnice Thone, S.S.M., Chm.; Mr. Garu J. Bain, Pres. & CEO.

Affiliates:

St. Clare's Hospital, Inc.
St. Clare's Foundation, Inc.
St. Francis Life Care Corporation
St. Francis Assisted Living Corporation
St. Clare's Management Services, Inc.
St. Francis Health Resort, Inc.
St. Clare's Home Care, Inc.
Wallkill Valley Health Care Foundation, Inc.
Visiting Nurse Association of Sussex County
Sisters of the Sorrowful Mother Housing Corporation I, Inc.
Sisters of the Sorrowful Mother Housing Corporation II, Inc.

Saint Clare's Hospital, Inc., 25 Pocono Rd., 07834. Tel: 973-625-6194; Fax: 973-625-6184. Email: jmccaffrey@saintclares.org. Web: www.saintclares.org. Sr. M. Johnice Thone, S.S.M., Chm.; Mr. Gary J. Bain, Pres. & CEO. (Parent Corp.: Saint Clare's Health Services) Patients Assisted Annually 340,000; Bed Capacity 690.

Campuses:

Saint Clare's Hospital-Denville Tel: 973-625-6194; Fax: 973-625-6184.

Saint Clare's Hospital-Boonton Township Tel: 973-316-1802; Fax: 973-316-1815.

Saint Clare's Hospital-Sussex Tel: 973-702-2770; Fax: 973-702-2893.

Saint Clare's Hospital-Dover Tel: 973-989-3000; Fax: 973-989-3290.

Pastoral Care Department: Revs. Ignatius Arokiam; Wolodymyr Baran; William Freeswick; Victor Razumov; Sisters Katherin M. Belongia; Diane Duprey, S.S.M.; Mary Joan Phillips, S.S.M.; Deacon Edward Lally.

PASSAIC. *St. Mary's Hospital*, 211 Pennington Ave., 07055. Tel: 973-470-3000; Fax: 973-470-0184. Email: petersonp@smh-passaic.org. Web: www.smh-passaic.org. Patricia Peterson, Pres. & CEO; Rev. Vincent Liuzzo, O.F.M.Cap., Dir. Pastoral Care. Sisters of Charity of St. Elizabeth, NJ 10; Bed Capacity 200; Patients Assisted Annually 116,472.

St. Mary's Health Corporation

[K] HOMES FOR AGED

PATERSON. *St. Joseph Rest Home for Aged Women* Conducted by Daughters of Charity of the Most Precious Blood , 46 Preakness Ave., 07522. Tel: 973-956-1921; Fax: 973-956-1582. Email: dcpbchalouxi@aol.com. Sr. Josephine Alderuccio, D.C.P.B., Supr. Residents 35.

DENVILLE. *St. Francis Residential Community* 07834. Tel: 973-627-5000; Fax: 973-625-9245. Email: abrown@saintclares.org. Web: www.saintfrancisres.com. Alice Brown, Exec. Dir.; Rev. William J. Freeswick, Chap. Rest and Residential Home Sisters of the Sorrowful Mother 6; Bed Capacity 100; Apartments 62; Guests 150.

Franciscan Oaks Independent Living Units & Health Center, 21 Pocono Rd., 07834. Tel: 973-586-5000; Fax: 973-586-5039. Sponsored by Sisters of the Sorrowful Mother.

TOTOWA. *St. Joseph's Home for the Elderly*, 140 Shepherd Ln., 07512. Tel: 973-942-0300; Fax: 973-942-7201. Sr. Mary Vincent, L.S.P.; Rev. Raymond Beach, O.F.M., Chap. Conducted by Little Sisters of the Poor Sisters 16; Residents 134.

[L] RESIDENCES FOR WOMEN

PATERSON. *St. Frances Residence*, 25 Jackson St., 07501. Tel: 973-278-7074; Fax: 973-278-7544. Sr. Marian Farrell, Admin. Sisters of Charity of St. Elizabeth, NJ 3; Residents 25.

WAYNE. *Bethany Residence*, 738 Rte. 23, 07470. Tel: 973-628-8109. Sr. Joseph Loretto, M.S.B.T., Admin. Residents 12.

Kilroy Residence, 584 Ratzer Rd., 07470. Tel: 973-694-3594. Sr. Maria Francis Shebellock, F.S.P., Dir. Residents 12.

[M] MONASTERIES AND RESIDENCES OF PRIESTS AND BROTHERS

PATERSON. *St. Benedict the Moor Friary*, 146 Danforth Ave., 07501. Tel: 973-523-0808; Fax: 973-523-5904. Bros. Vincent Casamento, O.F.M.; Paul Santoro, O.F.M., Guardian.

BUTLER. *St. Anthony Friary*, 63 Bartholdi Ave., 07405. Tel: 973-838-4080; Fax: 973-492-5483. Revs. Frederick McKeever, O.F.M., Guardian; John S. Ahearn, O.F.M.; Alvin A. Black, O.F.M.; Patrick M. Brown, O.F.M.; Bernard R. Creighton, O.F.M., Vicar; Emmanuel Duffy, O.F.M.; Matthew L. Gaskin, O.F.M.; Charles V. Hayes, O.F.M.; John J. Kull, O.F.M.; Gerard R. McDonald, O.F.M.; Anthony McGuire, O.F.M.; Theodore A. McNally, O.F.M.; Quintin A. Neyland, O.F.M. (NY); Samuel D. O'Connor, O.F.M.; LaSalle O'Friel, O.F.M.; Neil Padden, O.F.M.; John J. Pierce, O.F.M.; Leon C. Ristuccia, O.F.M.; Edwin F.D. Robinson, O.F.M.; Edward J. Sullivan, O.F.M.; Lambert F. Valentine, O.F.M. (NY); Bernardine Ward, O.F.M.; Bros. Fintan Duffy, O.F.M.; Thomas Sullivan, O.F.M.; Rosario Vieira, O.F.M. Order of Friars Minor Priests 22; Brothers 3.

CLIFTON. *Holy Face of Jesus Monastery*, 1697 State Hwy. 3, P.O. Box 691, 07012. Tel: 973-778-1177; Fax: 973-778-3809. Email: holyface@worldnet.att.net. Revs. Bernard Schinn, O.S.B.; Paul Kariekatt, O.S.B.; Bernard Ramanaden, O.S.B. Sylvestrine Benedictine Monks Priests 3.

FLORHAM PARK. *Father Justin Vocationary*, 90 Brooklake Rd., 07932. Tel: 973-966-6262; Fax: 973-593-8381. Web: www.vocationist.org. Revs. Michael Reardon, S.D.V. (LA), Supr.; Mario Muccitelli, S.D.V.; Ezio Antunes, S.D.V.; Vernon Kohlmann, S.D.V. (NEW).

LAFAYETTE. *St. Francis Center* 07848. Tel: 973-383-6465. Bro. Julius Tkaczyk, O.F.M.Cap., Vicar; Rev. Brian Tomlinson, O.F.M.Cap., Local Min. Capuchin Friars Priests 1; Brothers 1.

MORRISTOWN. *St. Mary's Abbey*, Delbarton, 230 Mendham Rd., 07960. Tel: 973-538-3231; Fax: 973-538-7109. Email: osbmonks@delbarton.org. Web: www.osbmonks.org. Rev. Thomas J. Confroy, O.S.B., Abbot; Rt. Revs. Brian H. Clark, O.S.B., Abbot Emeritus; Leonard G. Cassell, O.S.B., Abbot Emeritus; Rev. Gerard P. Lair, O.S.B., Abbot Emeritus; Very Rev. Patrick M. Hurley, O.S.B., Prior; Revs. Jerome Borski, O.S.B.; Benet W. Caffrey, O.S.B.; Gabriel M. Coless, O.S.B.; Michael J. Collins, O.S.B.; Richard J. Cronin, O.S.B.; Edward Seton Fittin, O.S.B.; Germain L. Fritz, O.S.B.; Simon P. Gallagher, O.S.B.; Giles P. Hayes, O.S.B.; John E. Hesketh, O.S.B.; Elias R. Lorenzo, O.S.B.; Joel J. Leikhim, O.S.B.; Beatus T. Lucey, O.S.B.; Kenneth H. Mayer, O.S.B.; Peter J. Meaney, O.S.B.; James O'Donnell, O.S.B., Treas.; Hilary O'Leary, O.S.B.; Rembert F. Reilly, O.S.B., Subprior; Anthony G. Sargent, O.S.B.; Wilfred G. Schulz, O.S.B.; Joachim B. Schweitzer, O.S.B.; Andrew T. Smith, O.S.B.; Luke L. Travers, O.S.B.; Bros. John Babicz, O.S.B.; Paul J. Diveny, O.S.B., Novicemaster; Eamon H. Drew, O.S.B.; Jeremiah R. Grosse, O.S.B.; Tarcisius Hoang-Hoa, O.S.B.; Jonathan M. Hunt, O.S.B.; Christopher K. Rosa, O.S.B.; Kieran M. Shiek, O.S.B.; Brendan A. Tumulty, O.S.B. Priests 39; Serving Outside the Diocese 8; Brothers 10.

Resident Outside the Abbey: Revs. Damian B. Breen, O.S.B.; Timothy J. Brennan, O.S.B.; Justin Capato, O.S.B.; Conall R. Coughlin, O.S.B.; Donal R. Fox, O.S.B. (NEW); Simon P. Gallagher, O.S.B.; Karl J. Roesch, O.S.B.; Jude S. Salus, O.S.B.; Bruno A. Ugliano, O.S.B.; Regis P. Wallace, O.S.B.; Benedict M. Worry, O.S.B.; Bro. James Konchalski, O.S.B.

NEWTON. *St. Paul's Abbey*, P.O. Box 7, 07860. Tel: 973-383-2470; Fax: 973-383-5782. Email: osbnewton@catholic.or.kr. Rt. Revs. Joel P. Macul, O.S.B., Abbot; Justin E. Dzikowicz, O.S.B., (Resigned); Augustine J. Hinches, O.S.B., (Resigned); Revs. Bosco Kuin Kim, O.S.B., Prior; Patrick J. Bonner, O.S.B.; Basil J. Wallace, O.S.B.; Odilo Yi, O.S.B.; Samuel Kim, O.S.B.; Peter Ahn, O.S.B. Order of St. Benedict, Congregation of St. Ottilien, (Formerly the Little Flower Monastery) Priests 11; Lay Monks 7.

Priests Residing Outside the Monastery: Rev. Damian J. Milliken, O.S.B., P.O. Box 213, Lushoto. Tel: 255-2726-40210; Fax: 255-2726-40212.

Inkamana Abbey, P/Bag X9333, Vryheid, 3100, South Africa. Tel: 27-34-982-2577. Rev. Peter W. Blue, O.S.B.

OAK RIDGE-MILTON. *St. Stanislaus B. M. Friary*, Manor Dr., 07438. Tel: 973-697-7757. Revs. Francis Majewski, O.F.M.Cap., Supr.; Eugene Mixtacki, O.F.M.Cap.; Sigmund M. Klimowicz, O.F.M.Cap.; Norbert Karava, O.F.M.Cap.; Joseph Kubiak, O.F.M.Cap. Capuchin Fathers Priests 9.

RINGWOOD. *Holy Name Friary, Inc.*, 2 Morris Rd., 07456. Tel: 973-962-7200; Fax: 973-962-9766. Email: hnfringwood@netscape.net. Revs. A. Francis Soucy, O.F.M., Supr. & Contact Person; Declan Bailey, O.F.M.; Giles Bello, O.F.M.; Maurice Brick, O.F.M.; Amadeus Burke, O.F.M.; Edward Burke, O.F.M.; Michael Feeny, O.F.M.; Clement Healy, O.F.M.; Joseph Keernan, O.F.M.; Cornelius Kelly, O.F.M.; Hugh King, O.F.M.; Gerard Lewis, O.F.M.; Edward McGuire, O.F.M.; Zachary O'Friel, O.F.M.; Lawrence F. Pafchik, O.F.M.; Bros. Gordan Clark, O.F.M.; Gilbert McEvoy, O.F.M.; Marion Ressel, O.F.M.; Paul Slaby, O.F.M.; Joseph P. Trunk, O.F.M.

STIRLING. *Holy Spirit Missionary Cenacle*, 1050 Long Hill Rd., 07980. Tel: 908-647-0208; Fax: 908-647-5770. Email: religious@stshrine.org. Web: stshrine.org. Revs. Peter Krebs, S.T., Dir.; Stephen Ernest, S.T.; Vincent Fitzpatrick, S.T.; Joseph Keenan, S.T.; Cajetan McDyre, S.T.; Odel Medina, S.T.; Campion Murphy, S.T.; Stephen Quinn, S.T.; Marco Antonio Sanchez, S.T. (LA); Kent M. Weidie, S.T.; Bro. Martin Pacholek, S.T. Missionary Servants of the Most Holy Trinity Priests 10; Brothers 1.

Shrine of St. Joseph, 1050 Long Hill Rd., 07980. Tel: 908-647-0208; Fax: 908-647-5770. Email: religious@stshrine.org. Web: stshrine.org. Rev. Peter Krebs, S.T., Custodian. Priests 10; Brothers 1; Sisters 7.

WAYNE. *P.I.M.E. Missionaries Residence*, 34 Grandview Dr., 07470. Tel: 973-694-1790; Fax: 973-694-0444. Email: pimenj@optonline.net. Web: www.beamissionary.org. Revs. Luigi Acerbi, P.I.M.E.; Giancarlo Ghezzi, P.I.M.E.

Xaverian Missionary Fathers, Provincial House, 12 Helene Court, 07470. Tel: 973-942-2975; Fax: 973-942-5012. Email: xavwayne@optonline.net. Web: www.xaviermissionaries.org. Revs. Ivan Marchesin, S.X., Prov.; Herondi Fernandes De Araujo; Frank B. Grappoli, S.X.; Dario Maso, S.X.

Mission Assignments: Makeni, Sierra Leone: Most Rev. George Biguzzi, S.X.; Revs. Luigi Brioni, S.X.; Jesus Evan, S.X.; Eugene Montesi, S.X. (BO); Luciano Peterlini, S.X.; Graziano Rossato, S.X.

Belem, Brazil: Revs. Francis Gugliotta, S.X.; Danilo Lago, S.X.; Vasco Miloni, S.X.; Mario Pezzotti, S.X.

Cameroon: Revs. Rene Lovat, S.X.; Pierino Zoni, S.X.

Sao Paulo, Brazil: Rev. Gino Nasini, S.X.

Jakarta, Indonesia: Revs. Bruno Orru, S.X.; Franco Qualizza, S.X.

Buenaventura, Colombia: Revs. Mauro Loda, S.X.; Mark Marangone, S.X.

Torreon, Mexico: Revs. Dan Boschetto, S.X.; Ramon Cerratos, S.X.; Pablo Nieves, S.X.

Taiwan: Revs. Edi Foschiatto, S.X.; Joseph Matteucig, S.X.; Martino Roia, S.X.; Joe Vignato, S.X.

Japan: Revs. Renato Filippini, S.X.; Frank Sottocornula, S.X.; Bro. Alberto Bertozzi, S.X.

Philippines: Rev. Carl Chudy, S.X.

Mozambique Rev. Horacio Perez, S.X.

[N] CONVENTS AND RESIDENCES FOR SISTERS

PATERSON. *Daughters of Charity of the Most Precious Blood*, 46 Preakness Ave., 07522. Tel: 973-956-1921; Fax: 973-956-1582. Sr. Josephine Alderuccio, D.C.P.B., Supr. Sisters 11.

Missionary Sisters of the Immaculate Conception of the Mother of God, 779 Broadway, 07509. Tel: 973-279-3790; Fax: 973-742-8231. Email: smicdev@aol.com. P.O. Box 3026, 07509-3026. Sr. Eleanor Goekler, S.M.I.C., Prov. Coord.

Missionary Sisters of the Immaculate Conception of the Mother of God, 396 E. 38th St., 07504. Tel: 973-279-2885; Fax: 973-742-8281. Email: smicdev@aol.com. Sisters 3.

Missionary Sisters of the Immaculate Conception of the Mother of God, 374-18th Ave., 07504-1333. Tel: 973-523-4988. Sisters 6.

BOONTON. *Society of the Sisters of the Church*, 24 Deer Hill Ct., 07005. Tel: 973-299-8365; Fax: 973-884-0940. Email: SRBW@ssoc.org. Web: www.ssoc.org. Sr. Frances Sanzo, S.S.C., Coord. Sisters 11.

CHESTER. *Carmel of the Immaculate Heart of Mary*, 80 Pleasant Hill Rd., 07930-2135. Tel: 908-879-4990; Fax: 908-879-0884. Email: hercarmnj@earthlink.net. Sr. Mary of Jesus and St. Joseph, O.Carm., Desert Mother. Hermits of Our Lady of Mt. Carmel Sisters 4.

CONVENT STATION. *Motherhouse of the Sisters of Charity*, P.O. Box 476, 07961. Tel: 973-290-5424; Fax: 973-290-5335. Email: escharity@aol.com. Web: www.scnj.org. Sr. Barbara Conroy, S.C., Gen. Supr. Professed Sisters 83.

DENVILLE. *Our Lady of Sorrows Convent, Sisters of Sorrowful Mother*, 9 Pocono Rd., 07834. Tel: 973-627-9008; Fax: 973-625-9245. Email: olsconventnj@aol.com. Web: www.ssmfranciscans.org.
Residences:
4 Pocono Rd., 07834. Tel: 973-983-8456.
45 N. Shore Dr., 07834. Tel: 973-625-8433.
40 E. Main St., Rockaway, 07866. Tel: 973-627-4643.
32 Wits End Dr., Hamburg, 07419. Tel: 973-827-0191. Sisters 16.

FLORHAM PARK. *St. Anne Villa*, P.O. Box 476, Convent Station, 07961. Tel: 973-867-1502. Email: rcaiazzo@saintannevilla.org. Sr. Rosanne Caiazzo, S.C., Admin.; Rev. Wilfred Schulz, O.S.B., Chap. Sisters of Charity of St. Elizabeth, Home for retired and infirm Sisters Bed Capacity 101.

Sister Joanna House of Formation, 88 Brooklake Rd., 07932. Tel: 973-966-9762; Fax: 973-377-3994. Email: gelsym@yahoo.com. Sisters Perpetuva Da Conceicao, S.D.V., Supr.; Louisa Garcione, S.D.V., Delegate; Gelsey Mosca, S.D.V., Prin. Sisters 15.

GLADSTONE. *Mt. St. John Convent*, 22 St. John's Dr., 07934. Tel: 908-234-0640; Fax: 908-781-7814. Email: baptistines@worldnet.att.net. Web: www.baptistines.home.att.net. Sr. Angelita Vazzano, C.S.J.B., Admin. Sisters of St. John the Baptist Sisters 9.

HALEDON. *Institute of the Daughters of Mary Help of Christians*, 655 Belmont Ave., 07508. Tel: 973-790-7963; Fax: 973-790-6485. Email: secretarysya@aol.com. Web: www.salesiansisters.org. Sisters Judith Suprys, F.M.A., Prov.; Helene Godin, F.M.A., Supr.; Rev. Paul P. Avallone, S.D.B., Chap. Provincialate of Daughters of Mary Help of Christians Daughters of Mary Help of Christians (Salesian Sisters) 43.

MENDHAM. *Mallinckrodt Convent-Motherhouse and Novitiate of the Sisters of Christian Charity* 07945. Tel: 973-543-6528; Fax: 973-543-9459. Web: scceast.org. Sr. Mary Edward Spohrer, S.C.C., Prov. Supr. Daughters of the Blessed Virgin Mary of the Immaculate Conception Sisters 48; Novices 3; Postulants 1.

MORRISTOWN. *St. Lucy Provincialate of the Religious Teachers Filippini, Novitiate, Villa Walsh Academy*, 455 Western Ave., 07960-4928. Tel: 973-538-2886; Fax: 973-538-6107. Email: atizzano@hotmail.com. Web: www.filippiniusa.org. Sisters Ascenza Tizzano, M.P.F., Prov.; Rita Tassinari, M.P.F., Supr.; Lillian Ernest, M.P.F., Dir. Formation.
Legal Title: *Pontifical Institute of the Religious Teachers Filippini* Sisters 88; Junior Professed 1; Novices 1; Postulants 1.

Monastery Discalced Carmelite Nuns of the Most Blessed Virgin Mary of Mt. Carmel, 189 Madison Ave., 07960. Tel: 973-539-0773; Fax: 973-984-0509. Sr. Therese Katulski, O.C.D., Prioress. Professed Nuns 7; Extern Sisters 1; Novices 1.

MOUNT ARLINGTON. *Felician Sisters of St. Francis of Assisi Convent*, 37 Windemere Ave., 07856. Sr. Mary Josita, C.S.S.F., Local Supr. Professed Sisters 7.

PARSIPPANY. *St. Francis of Assisi Novitiate-Franciscan Sisters of St. Elizabeth*, 499 Park Rd., 07054. Tel: 973-539-3797; 973-605-8729; Fax: 973-539-3347. Email: ludovico@franciscansisters.com. Web: www.franciscansisters.com. Sr. Gina Marie Amico, F.S.S.E., Delegate Gen.; Rev. Philip W. Nielsen, O.F.M., Chap. Perpetually Professed Sisters 17; Temporarily Professed Sisters 4.

PASSAIC. *St. Joseph Convent*, 9 Quincy St., 07055. Sr. Krystyna Kwasniak, D.P.H.M., Supr.

Our Lady of Mt. Carmel Convent, Sisters of Saint Francis of Philadelphia, 47 Reid Ave., 07055. Tel: 973-471-6352. Sr. M. Berard, O.S.F., Supr. Sisters 5.

RINGWOOD. *Sisters of St. Francis of Philadelphia, Mt. St. Francis Convent*, 474 Sloatsburg Rd., 07456. Tel: 973-962-7411; Fax: 973-962-0445. Email: caz973@juno.com. Sr. Carol Ann Zurlo, Admin. Sisters of St. Francis 2.

Sisters of St. Francis of Philadelphia, St. Clare Convent, 474 Sloatsburg Rd., 07456. Tel: 973-962-4705. Sisters of St. Francis 2.

Sisters of St. Francis of Philadelphia, 474 Sloatsburg Rd., 07456. Tel: 973-962-6416. Sr. Francis Paul Torre, O.S.F., Admin. Total in Residence: Sisters of St. Francis of Philadelphia 6; Missionary Sisters of the Immaculate Conception 7.

STIRLING. *Blessed Trinity Missionary Cenacle*, 1190 Long Hill Rd., 07980. Tel: 908-647-1165. Missionary Servants of the Most Blessed Trinity 1.

Holy Trinity Convent, 1026 Long Hill Rd., 07980. Tel: 908-647-6584. Sr. Sophia Kozikowska, Supr. Servants of Jesus 6.

WEST PATERSON. *Missionary Sisters of the Immaculate Conception of the Mother of God*, Generalate, 48 Garden Ave., 07424. Tel: 973-279-1484; Fax: 973-279-2991. Email: smicgen@worldnet.att.net. Sr. Corona Chung, S.M.I.C., Coord. Gen. Sisters 5.

The Society of Sisters for the Church, 396 Rifle Camp Rd., 07424. Tel: 973-345-1816. Email: eustach@aol.com. Sr. Anne Marie McNicholl, Pres. Sisters 22.

[O] NEWMAN CENTERS

HALEDON. *William Paterson University of New Jersey*, Jesus Christ, Prince of Peace Chapel & Bishop Frank J. Rodimer Catholic Campus Ministry Center, 219 Pompton Rd., 07508. Tel: 973-720-3524; Fax: 973-595-5312. Email: scurti@wpunj.edu. Web: www.princeofpeacechapel.com. Rev. Louis J. Scurti.

MADISON. *Drew University Catholic Campus Ministry Chaplain's Office, President's House Annex*, 07940. Tel: 973-408-3027; Fax: 973-627-3631. Email: jfarias@drew.edu. Revs. Joseph G. Farias. Tel: 973-443-8496; Kieran Fergeus, O.P. Tel: 908-227-6472.
Res.: P.O. Box 387, Convent Station, 07961-0387. Fax: 973-443-8651.

Fairleigh Dickinson University
Catholic Campus Ministry, Fairleigh Dickinson University, 285 Madison Ave., 07940. Tel: 973-443-8651; Fax: 973-627-3631. Email: madisonccm@aol.com. Revs. Joseph G. Farias; Kieran Fergeus, O.P. Tel: 908-227-6472.
Res.: P.O. Box 387, Convent Station, 07961-0387. Tel: 973-443-8496; Fax: 973-443-8651.

[P] MISCELLANEOUS LISTINGS

PATERSON. *St. Anthony's Guild* 07509. Tel: 973-777-3737; Fax: 212-594-2769. Email: anthonian@aol.com. Web: anthonian.org. Revs. Joseph M. Hertel, O.F.M., Dir.; Cassian A. Miles, O.F.M.; Allan G. Von Kobs, O.F.M.; Rayner F. Williams, O.F.M. Membership organization supports the work of The Franciscan Friars of Holy Name Province.

The Association of the Marian Apostolate of Mercy, Inc., 360 E. 37th St., 07504. Tel: 973-523-1338; Fax: 973-523-7241. Email: marianassociates@aol.com. Sr. Maria Elizabeth Whilifer, Pres.; Rev. John Gordon, Sec.; Judith A. Bonnesen, Treas.; Rev. Msgr. Mark J. Giordani, Spiritual Dir.

Martin de Porres Village Corporation, Green St., 07501. Tel: 973-881-8022; Fax: 973-881-0149. Rev. Msgr. Herbert K. Tillyer, M.Ch.A, Pres. Sponsoring Martin De Porres, Vill.

Reese Corporation, c/o R.P. Marzulli Co., 264 Belleville Ave., Bloomfield, 07003. Tel: 973-279-2262; Fax: 973-279-8625. Rev. Msgr. Herbert K. Tillyer, M.Ch.A, Pres. Sponsoring Governor Paterson Towers, Maurice Brick Residence, Brestel Residence, William F. Hinchcliffe Pavilion, Ralph J. Diverio Residence, Murray M. Bisgaier Residence, William Levine Residence.

CHESTER. *Nazareth Village* Retirement residence for diocesan priests. , 6 Meadow Ln., Box 635, 07930. Tel: 908-879-6991; Fax: 908-879-7461. Email: nazarethvillage@hotmail.com. Web: www.nazarethvillage.com. Rev. Msgr. Raymond M. Lopatesky, Dir. In Res. Rev. Msgrs. Aloysius J. Busch (Retired); Leo P. Carey (Retired); Paul A. Longua (Retired); Peter A. McBride (Retired); Leo P. Ryan (Retired); Revs. John T. Catoir, J.C.D. (Retired); Edward M. Davey (Retired); Patrick Mullan (Retired); Joseph E. Murphy (Retired); James P. O'Kielty (Retired); Jeremiah O'Riordan; Walter Pruschowitz; George T. Shema (Retired).

CONVENT STATION. *Seton Health Care, Inc.*, Convent of Saint Elizabeth, P.O. Box 476, 07961. Tel: 973-290-5450; Fax: 973-290-5335. Email: mshaughnessy@scnj.org. Web: www.scnj.org. Sr. Maureen Shaughnessy, S.C., Pres.

MADISON. *Priests Residence*, 205 Madison Ave., 07940-1003. Tel: 973-443-9300; Fax: 973-443-4140. Email: user567964@aol.com. Rev. Msgr. Robert M. Diachek.

MORRISTOWN. *Abbey Woods at Delbarton Inc.*, 230 Mendham Rd., 07960. Tel: 973-538-3231, Ext. 3035; Fax: 973-538-7109. Mr. Adolf E. Schimpf, Vice Pres., Business Affairs. Order of Saint Benedict

College of St. Elizabeth, Center for Theological and Spiritual Development, 2 Convent Rd., 07960. Tel: 973-290-4300; Fax: 973-290-4312. Email: aciorra@lcsu.edu. Web: csespirit.org. Rev. Anthony J. Ciorra.

PASSAIC. *St. Jude Media Ministries*, 63 Monroe St., 07055. Tel: 973-777-0303; Fax: 973-472-5033. Email: jtcatoir@aol.com. Web: www.fatherjohncatoir.com. Rev. John T. Catoir, J.C.D., Dir. (Retired).

POMPTON LAKES. *Pathways Counseling Center, Inc.*, 31 Pompton Ave., 07442. Tel: 973-835-6337; Fax: 973-616-4688. Email: paulaf@pathwayscounseling.org. Web: www.pathwayscounseling.org. Ms. Paula Fitzsimmons, Clinic Dir.; Ms. Peg Buczek, Advertising Mgr.

STIRLING. *Father Judge Apostolic Center*, 1292 Long Hill Rd., 07980. Tel: 908-647-7112; 908-647-2422 (Res.); Fax: 908-632-0350. Email: fjac3@psac.com. Web: www.fjac.org. Sr. Gail Lambert, M.S.B.T., Dir.; Rev. Kent M. Weidie, S.T., Assoc. Dir.; Kathleen Warren, Prog. Liasion; Kristen Wisniewski, Admin. Asst.; Sr. Thomas Mary Gore, M.S.B.T., Young Adult Ed.

WAYNE. *Siena Village*, 1000 Siena Village, 07470. Tel: 973-696-2811; Fax: 973-696-2721. Email: aldors@aol.com. Sr. Alice Matthew, O.P., Dir.

RELIGIOUS INSTITUTES OF MEN REPRESENTED IN THE DIOCESE

For further details refer to the corresponding bracketed number in the Religious Institutes of Men or Women section.

[0200]—*Benedictine Monks* (St. Mary, St. Paul Abbeys; Holy Face of Jesus Monastery)—O.S.B.
[0470]—*The Capuchin Friars*—O.F.M.Cap
[0480]—*Conventual Franciscans*—O.F.M.Conv
[0520]—*Franciscan Friars* (Holy Name Prov.)—O.F.M.
[0690]—*Jesuit Fathers and Brothers* (New York Prov.)—S.J.
[0840]—*Missionary Servants of the Most Holy Trinity* (Silver Spring, MD)—S.T.
[1030]—*Paulist Fathers* (New York)—C.S.P.
[1050]—*Pontifical Institute for Foreign Missions*—P.I.M.E.
[1190]—*Salesians of Don Bosco* (Turin, Italy)—S.D.B.
[1340]—*Vocationist Fathers*—S.D.V.
[1360]—*Xaverian Missionary Fathers* (Wayne)—S.X.

RELIGIOUS INSTITUTES OF WOMEN REPRESENTED IN THE DIOCESE

[0230]—*Benedictine Sisters of Pontifical Jurisdiction*—O.S.B.
[0740]—*Daughters of Charity of the Most Precious Blood*—D.C.P.B.
[0850]—*Daughters of Mary Help of Christians*—F.M.A.
[]—*Daughters of the Most Pure Heart of the Most Holy Virgin Mary* (Passaic)
[0420]—*Discalced Carmelite Nuns*—O.C.D.
[1070-06]—*Dominican Sisters*—O.P.
[1070-18]—*Dominican Sisters*—O.P.
[1170]—*Felician Sisters*—C.S.S.F.
[1400]—*Franciscan Missionary Sisters of the Sacred Heart* (Peekskill)—F.M.S.C.
[]—*Hermits of Our Lady of Mt. Carmel*—H.O.Carm.
[2340]—*Little Sisters of the Poor*—L.S.P.
[2790]—*Missionary Servants of the Most Blessed Trinity*—M.S.B.T.
[2760]—*Missionary Sisters of the Immaculate Conception of the Mother of God*—S.M.I.C.
[3430]—*Religious Teachers Filippini*—M.P.F.
[2970]—*School Sisters of Notre Dame*—S.S.N.D.
[1700]—*School Sisters of the Third Order of St. Francis*—O.S.F.

[3560]—*Servants of Jesus* (Starling)—S.J.
[3580]—*Servants of Mary*—O.S.M.
[0590]—*Sisters of Charity of Saint Elizabeth, Convent Station*—S.C.
[0660]—*Sisters of Christian Charity*—S.C.C.
[3820]—*Sisters of St. John the Baptist*—C.S.J.B.
[3830]—*Sisters of St. Joseph* (Chestnut Hill, PA)—C.S.J.
[3890]—*Sisters of St. Joseph of Peace*—C.S.J.P.
[1830]—*Sisters of the Good Shepherd*—R.G.S.
[3320]—*Sisters of the Presentation of the B.V.M.*—P.B.V.M.
[4100]—*Sisters of the Sorrowful Mother (Third Order of St. Francis)*—S.S.M.
[]—*The Society of the Sisters of the Church* (Passaic)
[4210]—*Vocationist Sisters*—S.D.V.

NECROLOGY

† Alonso, Rev. Msgr. Jose A., (Retired)—Died Sept. 29, 2003
† Gallo, Rev. Msgr. Louis J., Paterson, NJ St. Mary's—Died Dec. 21, 2003
† Glennon, Rev. Msgr. William, (Retired)—Died Nov. 23, 2003
† Daly, M. Paul—Died Dec. 23, 2003
† Lovato, Charles, (Retired)—Died April 27, 2003
† Ruddy, Edward J., (Retired)—Died Jan. 20, 2003

Diocese of Pensacola-Tallahassee

(Dioecesis Pensacolensis-Tallaseiensis

Most Reverend

JOHN H. RICARD, S.S.J., D.D., PH.D.

Bishop of Pensacola-Tallahassee; ordained May 25, 1968; ordained Auxiliary Bishop of Baltimore July 2, 1984; appointed Bishop of Pensacola-Tallahassee January 21, 1997

Monsignor James Amos Pastoral Center P.O. Drawer 17329, Pensacola, FL 32522. Tel: 850-432-1515; Fax: 850-436-6424.

Web: www.ptdiocese.org

Email: chancellor@ptdiocese.org

ESTABLISHED NOVEMBER 6, 1975.

Square Miles 14,044.

Comprises the following Counties: Bay, Calhoun, Escambia, Franklin, Gadsden, Gulf, Holmes, Jackson, Jefferson, Leon, Liberty, Madison, Okaloosa, Santa Rosa, Taylor, Wakulla, Walton and Washington Counties.

Legal Title: For legal titles of parishes and diocesan institutions, consult the Pastoral Center.

STATISTICAL OVERVIEW

Personnel	
Bishop	1
Priests: Diocesan Active in Diocese	49
Priests: Diocesan Active Outside Diocese	7
Priests: Retired, Sick or Absent	19
Number of Diocesan Priests	75
Religious Priests in Diocese	9
Total Priests in Diocese	84
Extern Priests in Diocese	31
Ordinations:	
Diocesan Priests	1
Permanent Deacons in Diocese	57
Total Brothers	4
Total Sisters	50
Parishes	
Parishes	49
With Resident Pastor:	
Resident Diocesan Priests	47
Resident Religious Priests	7
Without Resident Pastor:	
Administered by Priests	10
Administered by Deacons	1
Missions	9
Welfare	
Catholic Hospitals	1
Total Assisted	276,936
Homes for the Aged	3
Total Assisted	250
Special Centers for Social Services	4
Total Assisted	39,850
Other Institutions	1
Total Assisted	1,833
Educational	
Diocesan Students in Other Seminaries	14
Total Seminarians	14
High Schools, Diocesan and Parish	2
Total Students	676
Elementary Schools, Diocesan and Parish	9
Total Students	2,159
Non-residential Schools for the Disabled	1
Total Students	16
Catechesis/Religious Education:	
High School Students	1,703
Elementary Students	4,663
Total Students under Catholic Instruction	9,231
Teachers in the Diocese:	
Priests	1
Sisters	9
Lay Teachers	182
Vital Statistics	
Receptions into the Church:	
Infant Baptism Totals	1,010
Adult Baptism Totals	190
Received into Full Communion	292
First Communions	1,055
Confirmations	924
Marriages:	
Catholic	212
Interfaith	131
Total Marriages	343
Deaths	610
Total Catholic Population	62,289
Total Population	1,267,077

Former Bishops—Most Revs. RENE H. GRACIDA, D.D., ord. May 23, 1959; appt. Titular Bishop of Masuccaba and Auxiliary of Miami, Dec. 6, 1971; consecrated Jan. 25, 1972; appt. first Bishop of Pensacola-Tallahassee, Oct. 1, 1975; installed Nov. 6, 1975; transferred to Bishop of Corpus Christi, May 19, 1983; J. KEITH SYMONS, D.D., Bishop of Pensacola-Tallahassee; ord. May 18, 1958; Titular Bishop of Siguritanus and Auxiliary of St. Petersburg; appt. Jan. 16, 1981; consecrated March 19, 1981; Bishop of Pensacola-Tallahassee; appt. Sept. 29, 1983; installed Nov. 8, 1983; transferred to Bishop of Palm Beach, June 2, 1990; JOHN M. SMITH, J.C.D., D.D., Bishop of Pensacola-Tallahassee; ord. May 27, 1961; Titular Bishop of Tre Taverne and Auxiliary of Newark; appt. Dec. 1, 1987; consecrated Jan. 25, 1988; Bishop of Pensacola-Tallahassee; appt. June 25, 1991; installed July 31, 1991; transferred to Coadjutor Bishop of Trenton, Nov. 21, 1995; appt. Bishop of Trenton July 1, 1997.

Monsignor James Amos Pastoral Center—11 N. B St., Pensacola, 32501. Tel: 850-435-3500; Fax: 850-436-6424. *Mailing Address, P.O. Drawer 17329, Pensacola, 32522.*

Chancellor—Rev. Msgr. MICHAEL V. REED, J.C.L.

Vicar for Priests—Rev. Msgr. JOHN CASSIDY.

Vicar for Permanent Deacons—Deacon GERARD WILLIAMSON.

Vicar for Religious—Rev. Msgr. MICHAEL REED, J.C.L.

Vice Chancellor & Notary—Rev. JOSEPH FOWLER.

Vicars Forane—Rev. STEVEN J. O'CONNOR, Northwest Vicariate Forane; Very Rev. PATRICK FOLEY, Southwest Vicariate Forane; VACANT, West Central Vicariate Forane; Very Revs. MARTIN BRATEK, C.R., East Central Vicariate Forane; DENNIS O'BRIEN, Eastern Vicariate Forane.

Vicar General—Rev. Msgr. LUKE HUNT.

Diocesan Tribunal—11 N. B St., Pensacola, 32501. Mailing Address, P.O. Drawer 17329, Pensacola, 32522. Tel: 850-436-6454; Fax: 850-436-6457.

Judicial Vicar—Rev. Msgr. JAMES J. FLAHERTY, J.C.L., J.V.

Associate Judicial Vicar—VACANT.

Advocate—Deacon WILLIAM SCHAAL.

Judges—Rev. Msgr. JAMES J. FLAHERTY, J.C.L., J.V.; Rev. WILLIAM P. BROWN, J.C.L.; Deacon DANIEL MCAULIFFE, J.C.L.

Promoter of Justice—Rev. Msgr. MICHAEL REED, J.C.L.

Auditors—Rev. JOSEPH CALLIPARE; Deacon DANIEL MCAULIFFE, J.C.L.

Assessor—Deacon WILLIAM SCHAAL.

Defender of the Bond—Rev. EUGENE CASSERLY, M.Ch.A.

Notaries—Rev. JOSEPH CALLIPARE; Deacons DANIEL MCAULIFFE, J.C.L.; RAMON BONANNO; WILLIAM SCHAAL; Mrs. RUBY RIVIAS.

College of Consultors—Rev. Msgrs. MICHAEL CHERUP; MICHAEL MOONEY, V.F.; Rev. ROY MARIEN; Rev. Msgr. JOHN O'SULLIVAN.

Administrative Council—Rev. Msgrs. MICHAEL CHERUP; JAMES J. FLAHERTY, J.C.L., J.V.; MICHAEL MOONEY, V.F.; MICHAEL REED, J.C.L., Chancellor; Sisters BETTY ANNE MEADE, M.S.B.T., M.S.W.; MARY CAPLICE, C.N.D.; Deacon JEFFERY TRUMPS.

Council of Permanent Deacons—Most Rev. JOHN H. RICARD, S.S.J., D.D., Ph.D.; Deacons GERARD WILLIAMSON, Chm., Vicar for Deacons; THOMAS KENNELL; REYMOND CASTELLANO; JOHN HOWELL; LOUIS MARINI; SAL CIRABISI; RUDY RAYMAKER.

Council of Sisters—Sisters MAUREEN JOSEPH KIRWAN, S.C., Pres.; MARGUERITE GIBBS, I.H.M., Vice-Pres.; PATRICIA ANN PEPITONE, R.S.M., Sec.; MARY GILLESPIE, C.N.D., Treas.

Diocesan Commissions, Departments, and Offices

Apostleship of the Sea, Office of the—VACANT, Chap., P.O. Drawer 17329, Pensacola, 32522. Tel: 850-435-3500.

Archivist—CARLISLE SEMMES, Ed.D., P.O. Drawer 17329, Pensacola, 32522. Tel: 850-435-3520.

Black Catholics, Office of—VACANT, P.O. Drawer 17329, Pensacola, 32522. Tel: 850-435-3500.

Building & Renovation, Diocesan Commission for—Rev. Msgrs. LUKE HUNT; MICHAEL REED, J.C.L.; Deacons JEFFERY TRUMPS; JOHN MORGAN; Mr. JOHN KENNEDY; Mr. THEODORE J. RUCKSTUHL; Mr. J. PATRICK REMICH; JAN L. VIAU, P.O. Drawer 17329, Pensacola, 32522. Tel: 850-435-3500.

Building & Renovation, Office of—Deacon JOHN MORGAN, P.O. Drawer 17329, Pensacola, 32522. Tel: 850-435-3500.

Campaign for Human Development, Office of—Rev. Msgr. MICHAEL REED, J.C.L., Dir., P.O. Drawer 17329, Pensacola, 32522. Tel: 850-435-3500.

Campus Ministry—P.O. Drawer 17329, Pensacola, 32522. Tel: 850-435-3500. *Pensacola-University of West Florida: Nativity of Our Lord Parish, 9945 Hillview Dr., Pensacola, 32514.* Tel: 850-477-3221. Tallahassee-Florida Agricultural & Mechanical University, St. Eugene Chapel: Rev. FELIX I. OSASONA, M.S.P., Dir., 701 Gamble St., Tallahassee, 32310. Tel: 850-222-6482. Florida State University: Rev. MICHAEL SHAW, Dir., P.O. Box 2395, Tallahassee, 32316. Tel: 850-222-9630.

Catholic Daughters of the Americas—Rev. ROBERT F. MORRIS, Court Chap.; Mrs. JOYCE PFEIFFER, Regent, 304 N. Sunset Blvd., Gulf Breeze, 32507.

Catholic Women, Diocesan Council of—SHEILA HOPKINS, Pres., P.O. Drawer 17329, Pensacola, 32522. Tel: 850-435-3500.

Catholic Charities of Northwest Florida—Sr. BETTY

ANNE MEADE, M.S.B.T., M.S.W., Exec. Dir.. Email: meadb@ptdiocese.org; A. LARRY MALTBY, Assoc. Dir., Offices--Pensacola: 11 North B St., Pensacola, 32501. Tel: 850-435-3518; Fax: 850-436-6424. Email: maltbyl@ptdiocese.org. Fort Walton Beach: ADAIR PICKARD, Regl. Dir., 11 First St., S.E., Fort Walton Beach, 32548. Tel: 850-244-2825; Fax: 850-244-2963. Email: cathcharfwb@gnt.net.

Pensacola—VACANT, Regl. Dir., 222 E. Government St., Pensacola, 32502. Tel: 850-436-6410; Fax: 850-436-6419. Panama City: CONSTANCE MARTINEC, Regl. Dir., 3218 E. 11th St., Panama City, 32401. Tel: 850-763-0475; Fax: 850-763-2969. Email: cathcharpc@aol.com. Tallahassee: WENDY J. BLAIR, Regl. Dir., P.O. Box 20165, Tallahassee, 32316. Tel: 850-222-2180; Fax: 850-681-6963. Email: ccoftall@tfn.net. Quincy: VACANT, 27 N. Shadow St., Quincy, 32351. Tel: 850-875-1353; Fax: 850-627-6755.

Cemetery Office—Mr. GARY BENNETT, Dir., P.O. Drawer 17329, Pensacola, 32522. Tel: 850-435-3500. Holy Cross Cemetery, 1300 E. Hayes St., Pensacola, 32503. Tel: 850-432-0878; Fax: 850-434-9031; Mr. FRED MCEVOY, Dir., Calvary Cemetery, 4298 Country Club Blvd., Sunny Hills, 32428. Tel: 850-773-2165.

Charismatic Renewal, Diocesan Commission for—Rev. EUGENE PATHE, Moderator; JOE BROWN, Chm., P.O. Drawer 17329, Pensacola, 32522. Tel: 850-435-3500.

Christian Formation, Office of—Sr. MARGARET KUNTZ, A.S.C.J., Dir.; Deacon STEPHEN WULF, Assoc. Dir.; JENNIFER HARRINGTON, Project Middle School Coord.; Mrs. RITA TOLBERT, Resource Center Coord., P.O. Drawer 17329, Pensacola, 32522. Tel: 850-435-3524; Fax: 850-436-6424. Email: christianformation@ptdiocese.org.

Office of RENEW—Sr. MARGARET KUNTZ, A.S.C.J., Dir., P.O. Drawer 17329, Pensacola, 32522. Tel: 850-435-3523; Fax: 850-436-6424.

Communications, Office of—Rev. Msgr. MICHAEL MOONEY, V.F., Dir., P.O. Drawer 17329, Pensacola, 32522. Tel: 850-435-3527; Fax: 850-435-7756.

"The Florida Catholic"—VACANT, Reporter, P.O. Drawer 17329, Pensacola, 32522. Tel: 850-435-3528; Fax: 850-435-7756.

Cursillo Movement—Rev. MICHAEL SHAW, Spiritual Dir.; Mrs. YVONNE BEYERS, Diocesan Lay Dir., P.O. Drawer 17329, Pensacola, 32522. Tel: 850-435-3500.

Ecumenical & Interreligious Affairs, Office of—Rev. JOHN GRAY, Dir., 5200 Saufley Field Rd., Pensacola, 32526. Tel: 850-456-5966; Fax: 850-453-3138.

Education, Department of—P.O. Drawer 17329, Pensacola, 32522. Tel: 850-432-3540.

Catholic Youth Sports League—JEFF SCHMITT, Dir., P.O. Drawer 17329, Pensacola, 32522. Email: jschmitt@uwf.edu.

Schools, Diocesan Commission for—Sr. MARY CAPLICE, C.N.D., Admin. Officer; STEPHANY ALFT; Very Rev. MARTIN BRATEK, C.R.; ELEANOR GASI; THERESA HARRELL; BRENDA LONG; DONNA MARIE HENDRICKSON; DONNA BLOOMER; HENRY ZMUDA, P.O. Drawer 17329, Pensacola, 32522. Tel: 850-435-3500.

Superintendent of Schools, Office of the—Sisters MARY CAPLICE, C.N.D., Supt.; MARGUERITE RENUART, O.P., Assoc. Supt., P.O. Drawer 17329, Pensacola, 32522. Tel: 850-435-3540; Fax: 850-436-6424.

Marriage & Family Life Ministries, Department of—Mrs. LOUISE RITZ, Dir., P.O. Drawer 17329, Pensacola, 32522. Tel: 850-435-3532 Ministries: Engaged Encounter, Marriage Encounter, Natural Family Planning, Foccus, Bereavement, Marriage Enrichment, The Third Option, Refoccus, Evenings for the Engaged, Pre Cana, To Trust Again, Parenting Programs, New Beginnings, Divorce & Beyond.

Respect Life Committee—Deacon JEFFREY TRUMPS, Chm.; Rev. Msgr. MICHAEL MOONEY, V.F.; Rev. KEVIN JOHNSON; Deacon SANTIAGO MOLINA; Mr. BOB BRADY; Mr. MARK FARMER; Mrs. JANICE FARMER; Mrs. MONIQUE HUTCHINSON; Mr. JIM KANE; Mrs. INGRID KANE; Dr. MICHAEL MANGAN; Mrs. MICHAEL MANGAN; Dr. ROBERT SAXER; Mrs. MARTHA SEEP; Mrs. VALERIE SCHUMM; Dr. DAVID HARRIS.

Finance, Diocesan Commission for—Mr. ROBERT EMMANUEL, Chm.; Rev. Msgrs. LUKE HUNT, Sec.; MICHAEL REED, J.C.L.; JOHN CASSIDY; Mr. ROBERT HAMEL; Mr. ERIC NICKELSEN; Mr. VINCE WHIBBS JR.; Mr. ALBERT WILLIAMS JR.; Mr. J. PATRICK REMICH; Deacon JEFFERY TRUMPS, P.O. Drawer 17329, Pensacola, 32522. Tel: 850-435-3500.

Finance, Department of—Deacon JEFFERY TRUMPS, Dir., P.O. Drawer 17329, Pensacola, 32522. Tel: 850-435-3500.

Hispanic Ministry, Office of—Very Rev. DENNIS O'BRIEN, Dir., P.O. Drawer 17329, Pensacola, 32522. Tel: 850-435-3500.

Holy Childhood Association—Sr. MARY CAPLICE, C.N.D., Dir., P.O. Drawer 17329, Pensacola, 32522. Tel: 850-435-3500. Email: ptschools@aol.com.

Holy Name Society—Rev. Msgr. MICHAEL REED, J.C.L., P.O. Drawer 17329, Pensacola, 32522. Tel: 850-432-1515.

Justice and Peace, Office of—Catholic Charities, P.O. Drawer 17329, Pensacola, 32522. Tel: 850-435-3500.

Independent Review Board—P.O. Drawer 17329, Pensacola, 32522. Tel: 850-432-1515; Fax: 850-436-6424. Rev. DOUG HALSEMA; The Honorable WILLIAM HENDERSON; Mr. BARRY KELLY; Mrs. STEPHANIE ALFT; Mrs. ANGELA GUILLAUME; Mr. MARVIN KAIMAN; Dr. ANITA NUSBAUM; Mr. ROBERT EMMANUEL, Esq.

Information Systems, Department of—TIM VIAU, P.O. Drawer 17329, Pensacola, 32522. Tel: 850-435-3537; Fax: 850-436-6424. Email: viaut@ptdiocese.org.

Orders & Ministries, Commission for—P.O. Drawer 17329, Pensacola, 32522. Tel: 850-435-3500; Fax: 850-436-6424. Rev. DANIEL BUTLER; Rev. Msgr. SLADE CRAWFORD; Rev. THOMAS GUIDO; Very Rev. DENNIS O'BRIEN; Rev. Msgrs. JOHN O'SULLIVAN; MICHAEL REED, J.C.L.

Knights of Columbus—Rev. Msgr. LUKE HUNT, Diocesan Chap., P.O. Box 1057, Gulf Breeze, 32562. Tel: 850-934-0222; Fax: 850-934-2804.

Legion of Mary—Rev. HECTOR R.G. PEREZ, S.T.D., Diocesan Spiritual Dir., P.O. Drawer 12001, Pensacola, 32589. Tel: 850-432-9362.

Liturgy, Office of—VACANT, Dir., P.O. Drawer 17329, Pensacola, 32522. Tel: 850-435-3500.

Moderator of the Curia—Rev. Msgr. MICHAEL REED, J.C.L.

Permanent Diaconate Formation Board—Rev. Msgr. JAMES J. FLAHERTY, J.C.L., J.V.; Rev. PAUL T. WHITE; Rev. Msgr. LUKE HUNT; Deacons GERARD WILLIAMSON; JOHN MORGAN; TOM KENNELL; JAMES MURRAY; JOHN HOWELL; PATRICK REMICH; MINNIE SEABROOK; Sr. CHRISTINE KELLY, S.S.J., P.O. Drawer 17329, Pensacola, 32522. Tel: 850-435-3500.

Permanent Diaconate, Office of—Deacon GERARD WILLIAMSON, Vicar for Deacons, P.O. Drawer 17329, Pensacola, 32522. Tel: 850-435-3531.

Priestly Life and Ministry, Office of—Very Rev. ROBERT MORRIS, Dir., P.O. Drawer 17329, Pensacola, 32522. Tel: 850-435-3500.

Priests' Pension Plan, Board for—Most Rev. JOHN H. RICARD, S.S.J., D.D., Ph.D.; Rev. Msgrs. LUKE HUNT; MICHAEL REED, J.C.L.; MICHAEL MOONEY, V.F.; MICHAEL TUGWELL; Rev. JACK GRAY; Rev. Msgrs. JOHN T. CASSIDY; JOHN O'SULLIVAN. Consultants:: Deacon JEFFERY TRUMPS; Mr. ROBERT EMMANUEL.

Clergy Concerns—Rev. Msgrs. MICHAEL CHERUP, Chm.; JOHN CASSIDY; Very Revs. ROBERT MORRIS; DENNIS O'BRIEN, P.O. Drawer 17329, Pensacola, 32522. Tel: 850-435-3500.

Propagation of the Faith, Office of—Rev. Msgr. FRANCIS SZCZYKUTOWICZ, Dir., P.O. Drawer 17329, Pensacola, 32522. Tel: 850-435-3500.

Real Estate, Diocesan Commission for—Rev. Msgrs. LUKE HUNT, Chm.; JOHN V. O'SULLIVAN, V.F.; FRANCIS SZCZYKUTOWICZ; Mr. ROBERT EMMANUEL; Mr. J. PATRICK REMICH; Mr. JOHN DONOVAN; Deacon JOHN MORGAN, Sec., P.O. Drawer 17329, Pensacola, 32522. Tel: 850-435-3500.

Real Estate, Office of—Deacon JOHN MORGAN, Dir., P.O. Drawer 17329, Pensacola, 32522. Tel: 850-435-3538.

St. Vincent de Paul Society— Pensacola Particular Council, BRENDA CROSBY, Pres., 2200 W. Desoto St., Pensacola, 32505. Tel: 850-434-6615. Tallahassee Chapter: BILL RYAN, Pres.; HERMI HADI, Vice Pres., 4409 Blountstown Hwy., Tallahassee, 32304. Tel: 850-576-6099.

Seminarian Candidate Review Board—Rev. ROY MARIEN; Rev. Msgr. C. SLADE CRAWFORD; Very Rev. DENNIS O'BRIEN; Mr. WILLIAM NADICKSBERND; Deacon JOHN MORGAN; Sr. MARY CAPLICE, C.N.D.; Mrs. ROSEMARY MASON, P.O. Drawer 17329, Pensacola, 32522. Tel: 850-435-3500.

Seminarians, Office of—Rev. Msgr. C. SLADE CRAWFORD, Dir.; Mrs. LINDA BARRETT, Sec., P.O. Drawer 17329, Pensacola, 32522. Tel: 850-435-3552. Email: barrettl@ptdiocese.org.

Vocations, Office of—Rev. Msgr. C. SLADE CRAWFORD, Dir.; Mrs. LINDA BARRETT, Sec., Drawer 17329, Pensacola, 32522. Tel: 850-435-3552.

Serra Club—Pensacola: Rev. DOUG HALSEMA, Chap.; Mr. ESMOND DROTT, Pres. Tallahassee: Rev. PHILIP FORTIN, Chap.; Mr. PAUL KACZOROWSKI, Pres.

Victim Assistance Coordinators—Ms. DANIELLE MALONE, L.M.H.L. Tel: 850-438-3131, Ext. 17. Email: maloned@ptdiocese.org; Dr. JAMES GAGNON, M.S.W., L.C.S.W. Tel: 850-877-0205.

Youth Ministry, Office of—Rev. Msgr. MICHAEL A. CHERUP, Dir.; LISA KURNIK, Assoc. Dir.; LUCRETIA JONES, Sec., P.O. Drawer 17329, Pensacola, 32522. Tel: 850-435-3553.

CLERGY, PARISHES, MISSIONS AND PAROCHIAL SCHOOLS

GREATER PENSACOLA
(ESCAMBIA COUNTY)

1—CATHEDRAL OF THE SACRED HEART (1905), Rev. Msgr. Michael V. Reed, J.C.L., Rector; Rev. Joseph Fowler; Deacon Jean White. Apostles of the Sacred Heart In Res., Rev. Msgr. George Sindik.
Res.: 1101 E. Mallory St., P.O. Box 2248, 32503. Tel: 850-438-3131; Fax: 850-436-6428.
School—Sacred Heart Cathedral School, 1603 N. 12th Ave., 32503. Tel: 850-436-6440; 850-438-0560; Fax: 850-436-6444. Sr. Elizabeth Knight, A.S.C.J., Prin.
Catechesis/Religious Program—Tel: 850-438-3131; Fax: 850-436-6428. Students 145.
Convent—1700 Conway Dr., 32503. Tel: 904-438-0560.

2—ST. ANNE (Brownsville) (1953), Closed., For inqueries for Sacramental records, please see the Cathedral of the Sacred Heart, Pensacola.

3—ST. ANNE'S (Bellview) (1964), Rev. John F. Gray; Deacon Thomas Donnelly. In Res., Rev. Thomas O'Flaherty.
Res.: 5200 Saufley Field Rd., 32526-1626. Tel: 850-456-5966; Fax: 850-453-3138.
Catechesis/Religious Program—Students 181.

4—ST. ANTHONY OF PADUA (1941), (African American), Very Rev. Patrick Foley.
Res.: 1804 N. Davis St., 32503. Tel: 850-436-6422.
Catechesis/Religious Program—Students 10.

5—HOLY SPIRIT (Warrington) (1968), Rev. Msgr. James J. Flaherty, J.C.L., J.V.; Deacons Eugene Geri; Jeffrey Trumps.
Res.: 10650 Gulf Beach Hwy., 32507. Tel: 850-492-0837 (Office); Fax: 850-492-4968.
Catechesis/Religious Program—Tel: 852-492-0837, Ext. 210. Students 156.

6—ST. JOHN THE EVANGELIST (1851), [CEM] Rev. Richard L. Altenbaugh; Deacon Gerard Williamson.
Res.: 303 S. Navy Blvd., 32507. Tel: 850-455-0356; Fax: 850-453-5109.
School—Sisters of Mercy, Tel: 850-456-5218; Fax: 850-456-5956. Sr. Patricia Ann Pepitone, R.S.M., Prin. Sisters 1; Lay Teachers 16; Students 201.
Catechesis/Religious Program—Students 69.
Convent—325 S. Navy Blvd., 32507. Tel: 850-456-3046; Fax: 850-456-3046.

7—ST. JOSEPH (1891), [CEM] Very Rev. Patrick Foley; Sr. Maureen Joseph Kirwan, S.C., Pastoral Assoc.
Mailing Address: P.O. Box 13566, 32591. Tel: 850-436-6461; Fax: 850-436-6462.
Res.: 141 W. Intendencia St., 32501. Tel: 850-436-6461; Fax: 850-436-6462.
Catechesis/Religious Program—Tel: 850-436-6461; Fax: 850-436-6462. Students 83.

8—LITTLE FLOWER (1945), Rev. Martin D. Holley; Deacons Reymond Castellano; Stephen Wulf.
Res.: 6495 Lillian Hwy., P.O. Box 3009, 32516. Tel: 850-455-5641; Fax: 850-455-4508.
School—Tel: 850-455-4851; Fax: 850-457-8982. Barbara McDermott, Prin. Lay Teachers 18; Students 199.
Catechesis/Religious Program—Tel: 850-455-8434. Students 90.

9—ST. MARY (1941), Revs. Eugene D. Casserly; Dominic Phan Sa; Deacon Crisostomo Buenavista.
Mailing Address: P.O. Box 6117, 32503. Tel: 850-478-2797; Fax: 850-478-2739.
Res.: 401 Van Pelt Ln., 32505. Tel: 850-478-2797; Fax: 850-478-2739. Email: stmaryca@bellsouth.net.
Catechesis/Religious Program—Tel: 850-478-1635; Fax: 850-478-2739. Students 80.

10—ST. MICHAEL (1559), Unassigned.
Res.: 19 N. Palafox St., P.O. Box 12423, 32582. Tel: 850-438-4985; Fax: 850-433-9758.

11—NATIVITY OF OUR LORD (1969), Rev. Msgr. Michael P. Mooney; Deacons Randall Comeau; Dennis Dobransky. In Res., Rev. Msgr. Raymond Mullins.
Res.: 9945 Hillview Dr., 32514-5702. Tel: 850-477-3221; Fax: 850-494-1503.
Catechesis/Religious Program—Tel: 850-478-5584, Ext. 5; Fax: 850-478-5584. Students 294.

12—Our Lady Queen of Martyrs, Mission (1977), (Vietnamese), Rev. Augustine Nguyen Thanh Hue (Vietnam).
Res.: 3295 S. Barrancas Ave., 32507. Tel: 850-455-2712; Fax: 850-455-0264.
Catechesis/Religious Program—Tel: 850-455-2712; Fax: 850-455-0264.

13—St. Paul (1963), Revs. Douglas Halsema; Dominic Dat Tran; Deacons John P. Morgan; Robert Leblanc.
Res.: 3131 Hyde Park Rd., 32503. Tel: 850-434-2551; Fax: 850-436-6449.
School—Apostles of the Sacred Heart (Hamden, CT), Tel: 850-436-6435; Fax: 850-436-6437. Sr. Maureen Fitzgerald, A.S.C.J., Prin. Sisters 1; Lay Teachers 16; Students 295.
Catechesis/Religious Program—Tel: 850-436-6446; Fax: 850-436-6449. Students 229.
Convent—1700 Conway Dr., 32503. Tel: 850-438-0560.
Mission—Church of Our Savior 6700 Old Spanish Tr., Escambia Co. 32504. Tel: 850-434-2551; Fax: 850-436-6449.

14—St. Stephen (1922), Rev. Hector R.G. Perez, S.T.D.
Res.: 900 W. Garden St., 32501. Tel: 850-432-9362; Fax: 850-435-9946.
Catechesis/Religious Program—Tel: 850-432-9362; Fax: 850-435-9946. Students 37.

15—St. Thomas More (1954), Rev. Msgr. John T. Cassidy; Rev. Paul Honer.
Mailing Address: 510 Bayshore Dr., 32507. Tel: 850-456-2543; Fax: 850-455-5203.
Catechesis/Religious Program—Tel: 850-456-0001; Fax: 850-455-5203. Students 113.

CITY OF TALLAHASSEE
(Leon County)

1—Blessed Sacrament (1845), Very Rev. John V. O'Sullivan, V.F.; Rev. Edward T. Jones.
Res.: 624 Miccosukee Rd., 32308. Tel: 850-222-1321; Fax: 850-222-9772.
School—Trinity Catholic, Tel: 850-222-0444; Fax: 850-224-5067. Mrs. Janet Gendusa, Prin. Lay Teachers 27; Students 476.
School—John Paul II Catholic High School, Tel: 850-201-5744; Fax: 850-205-3299. For a complete listing, please see High Schools, Diocesan in the Institution section.
Catechesis/Religious Program—Students 231.

2—Co-Cathedral of St. Thomas More (1968), Rev. Msgr. Michael Tugwell, Rector; Revs. Michael Shaw; Siluvai R. Selvappan; Deacon Santiago Molina.
Res.: 900 W. Tennessee St., P.O. Box 2395, 32316. Tel: 850-222-7371; 850-222-9630 (Office); Fax: 850-222-6430.
School—John Paul II Catholic High School, Tel: 850-201-5744; Fax: 850-205-3299. For a complete listing, please see High Schools, Diocesan in the Institution section.
Catechesis/Religious Program—Students 147.
Chapel—St. Eugene, Florida A&M University [JC] 701 W. Gamble St., 32310. Tel: 850-222-6482; Fax: 850-222-6482. Rev. Felix I. Osasona, M.S.P. (GAL).

3—Good Shepherd (1973), Revs. Michael Foley; Philip Fortin; Deacons Andrew Radigan; Gary Brinkworth; Marcus Hepburn.
Office—4665 Thomasville Rd., 32309. Tel: 850-893-1837; 850-893-2381; Fax: 850-894-6912.
School—John Paul II Catholic High School For a complete listing, please see High Schools, Diocesan in the Institution section.
Catechesis/Religious Program—Bette Scaringe, D.R.E. Students 826.

4—St. Louis (1979), Rev. Kevin Johnson; Deacons Nelson Madera, Ph.D.; Mack Shook.
School— For a complete listing, please see High Schools, Diocesan in the Institution Section.
Res.: 4151 Miraflores Ln., 32303. Tel: 850-562-5140; Fax: 850-562-7356. Email: stlouischurch@earthlink.net.
Catechesis/Religious Program—Tel: 850-562-5140. Students 107.

OUTSIDE THE CITIES OF PENSACOLA AND TALLAHASSEE

Apalachicola, Franklin Co., St. Patrick (1851), [JC] Rev. Roger Latosynski.
Res.: 27 Sixth St., P.O. Box 550, 32320. Tel: 904-653-9453; Fax: 850-653-4528.

Bayou George, Bay Co., Our Lady of the Rosary, Rev. W. P. Brown.
Res.: 5622 Julie Dr., Panama City, 32404. Tel: 850-769-5067; Fax: 850-769-1229.
Catechesis/Religious Program—Tel: 850-764-5067; Fax: 850-769-1227. Students 30.
Mission—Our Lady Queen of Peace P.O. Box 213, Fountain, Bay Co. 32438.

Blountstown, Calhoun Co., St. Francis of Assisi (1972), Rev. Msgr. Francis Szczykutowicz.
Res.: 16498 S.W. Gaskin St., 32424. Tel: 850-674-4482; Fax: 850-237-2045.
Catechesis/Religious Program—Students 11.

Bonifay, Holmes Co., Blessed Trinity (1979), Rev. Richard Dawson.
Res.: 2331 Hwy. 177A, 32425. Tel: 850-547-3735; Fax: 850-547-7477.

Cantonment, Escambia Co., St. Jude Thaddeus (1966), [CEM] [JC] Revs. Thomas Keyickal; George Thekkummattatil; John Bartoszewicz, Admin.
Res.: 303 Rocky Ave., 32533. Tel: 850-968-6189; Fax: 850-968-1578.
Mission—St. Elizabeth of Hungary 303 Rocky Ave., Barrineau Park, Escambia Co. 32533. Tel: 850-587-2550.
Catechesis/Religious Program—Students 47.

Chattahoochee, Gadsden Co., Holy Cross Parish (1972), Rev. Jacob M. Pallivathukkal (India), Admin.
Res.: 4034 Memorial Blue Star Hwy., 32324. Tel: 850-663-4610; Fax: 850-663-9555.

Chipley, Washington Co., St. Joseph the Worker (1968), Rev. Paul T. White.
Res.: P.O. Box 266, 32428. Tel: 850-482-3734; Fax: 850-482-7241.
Catechesis/Religious Program—Tel: 850-482-3734; Fax: 850-482-7241. Students 25.

Crestview, Okaloosa Co., Our Lady of Victory (1954), Deacon Kenneth Mayfield.
Office: 550 Adams Dr., 32536.
Res.: 143 Jeff Dr., 32536. Tel: 850-682-4622; Fax: 850-689-0335.
Catechesis/Religious Program—Tel: 850-682-4622; Fax: 850-689-0335. Students 216.

De Funiak Springs, Walton Co., St. Margaret (1931), Rev. Richard Dawson.
Mailing Address: P.O. Box 590, 32435-0590. Tel: 850-892-9247; Fax: 850-892-2065.
Res.: 247 U.S. Hwy. 331 N., 32435. Tel: 850-892-9247; Fax: 850-892-2065.
Catechesis/Religious Program—Tel: 850-892-9247; Fax: 850-892-2065. Students 57.

Destin, Okaloosa Co., Corpus Christi (1977), Rev. Robert F. Morris; Deacon Joseph Rose.
Res.: 307 Beach Dr., 32541. Tel: 850-654-5422; Fax: 850-837-3807.
Catechesis/Religious Program—Tel: 850-654-5423; Fax: 850-837-3807. Students 75.

Destin, Walton Co., Church of the Resurrection (1981), Rev. Michael J. Flynn; Deacon Matthew Rezmer.
Res.: 259 Miramar Beach Dr., 32550. Tel: 850-837-0357; Fax: 850-837-2062.
Catechesis/Religious Program—Tel: 850-837-0357; Fax: 850-837-2062. Students 123.

Fort Walton Beach, Okaloosa Co., St. Mary (1914), Very Rev. Michael Cherup; Rev. John J. Licari; Sr. Evelyn Rogers, S.U.S.C., Pastoral Assoc.; Deacons Robert J. Saxer; Charles Wolf; John Howell; William Bodisch; Ramon Bonnano; Walter Richardson; Daniel McAuliffe, J.C.L.; Anthony Restivo.
Res.: 110 St. Mary Ave., S.W., 32548-6645. Tel: 850-243-3742; Fax: 850-243-1271.
School—Tel: 850-243-8913; Fax: 850-243-7895. Mrs. Regina Nadicksbernd, Prin. Lay Teachers 21; Students 348.
Catechesis/Religious Program—Tel: 850-244-1833; Fax: 850-243-1271. Students 224

Fountain, Bay Co., Our Lady Queen of Peace Mission, Rev. William P. Brown, J.C.L.
Mailing Address: 5622 Julie Dr., Panama City, 32404. Tel: 850-769-5067; Fax: 850-796-1227.
Church: 18005 Lazy Ln., 32438.
Catechesis/Religious Program—Students 18.

Freeport, Walton Co., Christ the King Mission (1984), Rev. Thomas S. Collins; Deacon Dave Casey.
Mailing Address: c/o St. Rita, P.O. Box 1223, Santa Rosa Beach, 32459.
Church: 15542 U.S. Hwy. 3315, 32439. Tel: 850-267-2558; Fax: 850-267-3711.
Catechesis/Religious Program—Students 2.

Gulf Breeze, Santa Rosa Co., St. Ann (1948), Rev. Msgr. Luke Hunt; Rev. Sean Vincent Knox.
Res.: 100 Daniel Dr., P.O. Drawer 1057, 32562. Tel: 850-932-2859; Fax: 850-934-2804.
School—St. Ann Discovery School, Tel: 850-932-9330; Fax: 850-934-2804. Carol Lyvers. (Learning Center & Afterschool) (Ages 1-11) Teachers 43; Students 169.
Catechesis/Religious Program—Tel: 850-932-2859, Ext. 234; Fax: 850-934-2804. Students 301.
Mission—Our Lady of the Assumption Pensacola Beach. 920 Via de Luna, P.O. Box 1057, Santa Rosa Co. 32561. Tel: 850-934-0222; Fax: 850-934-6020.

Lanark Village, Franklin Co., Sacred Heart of Jesus (1960), Rev. James F. Gregan.
Res.: 109 Newman Dr., P.O. Box 729, 32323. Tel: 850-697-3445.

Madison, Madison Co., St. Vincent de Paul (1907), Rev. Ernest Sylvestre, O.M.I. In Res., Rev. Joseph C. Schwab, O.M.I.
Res.: 402 N.W. Sumter St., 32340-2048. Tel: 850-973-2428; Fax: 850-973-9311.
Catechesis/Religious Program—Students 27.

Marianna, Jackson Co., St. Anne (1947), [JC] Rev. Paul T. White.
Res.: 3009 Fifth St., P.O. Box 1547, 32447. Tel: 850-482-3734; Fax: 850-482-7241.
Catechesis/Religious Program—Tel: 850-482-3734; Fax: 850-482-7241. Students 66.

Mary Esther, Okaloosa Co., St. Peter (1975), Rev. Joseph P. Callipare; Deacon David P. Robinson.
Res.: 100 Francis St., 32569. Tel: 850-581-2556; Fax: 850-581-2640.
Catechesis/Religious Program—Tel: 850-581-7263. Students 200.

Medart, Wakulla Co., St. Elizabeth Ann Seton (1975), [CEM] Rev. James B. MacGee, O.M.I.
Mailing Address: 3609 Coastal Hwy., Crawfordville, 32327. Tel: 850-926-1797; Fax: 850-926-1737.
Catechesis/Religious Program—Students 42.
Mission—St. Stephen the Protomartyr Natural Bridge Rd., P.O. Box 1142, Woodville, Leon Co. 32362. Tel: 850-421-9094.

Mexico Beach, Bay Co., Our Lady of Guadalupe Mission, , See St. Dominic, Panama City.

Milton, Santa Rosa Co., St. Rose of Lima (1957), [JC] Revs. Steven J. O'Connor; Kurian Manikuttiyil; Deacon Thomas Kennell.
Church: 5965 Sleepy Hollow, 32570.
Res.: 6451 Park Ave., 32570. Tel: 850-623-3600; Fax: 850-983-3043.
Catechesis/Religious Program—Students 250.

Monticello, Jefferson Co., St. Margaret (1917), Rev. Ernest Sylvestre, O.M.I.
Res.: 402 Sumter St., Madison, 32340. Tel: 850-973-2428; Fax: 850-973-9311.
Church: U.S. Hwy. 90 E., 32344. Tel: 850-997-3622.
Catechesis/Religious Program—Students 19.

Niceville, Okaloosa Co.

1—Christ Our Redeemer (1989), Rev. Roy C. Marien; Deacons Michael Carucci; Joaquin Trevino; James Murray; William Schaal.
Res.: 1028 White Point Rd., 32578. Tel: 850-897-7797; Fax: 850-897-2422.
Catechesis/Religious Program—Tel: 850-897-2974; Fax: 850-897-2422. Students 228.

2—Holy Name of Jesus (1964), Rev. Daniel J. Butler; Deacons Thomas Fraites; Louis Marini; Willie O'Neal; James Cox; Gary McBride.
Res.: 1200 Valparaiso Blvd., P.O. Box 1475, 32588-1475. Tel: 850-678-7813; Fax: 850-678-5775.
Catechesis/Religious Program—Tel: 850-678-6790; Fax: 850-678-5775. Students 430.

Panama City Beach, Bay Co., St. Bernadette (1956), Rev. David T. O'Shea.
Res.: 1214 Moylan Rd., 32407. Tel: 850-234-3490; Fax: 850-234-3266.
Catechesis/Religious Program—Tel: 850-234-3266. Students 153.
School—Child Development Center & School, Tel: 850-230-0009; Fax: 850-230-6989. Rosie Hendrickson, Prin.; Kate Mullen, Dir.; Laura Condron, Dir. Lay Teachers 3; Students 39.
St. Bernadette John Lee Outreach Center—1329 Moylan Rd., 32407. Tel: 850-236-5252. Email: stbernadette@knology.net. Web: www.stbernadette.com. Juli Roock, Office Mgr.

Panama City, Bay Co.

1—St. Dominic (1917), Rev. Peter L. Zaleswki; Deacons Salvatore Cirabisi; Estal Daron. In Res., Revs. Viet Huynh; John Selleck.
Res.: 3308 E. 15th St., 32405-7414. Tel: 850-785-4574; Fax: 850-872-0800.
Catechesis/Religious Program—Tel: 850-763-7393; Fax: 850-872-0800. Students 345.
Mission—Our Lady of Guadalupe [CEM] 1500 N. 15th St., Mexico Beach, Bay Co. 32410. Tel: 850-648-3006. Rev. James J. Lambert.

2—St. John the Evangelist (1945), Very Rev. Martin Bratek, C.R.; Rev. Glen Baptiste, C.R.; Deacons Dale Johnson; Earl C. Mirus; John Renick, M.D.
Res.: 1008 Fortune Ave., 32401. Tel: 850-763-1821; Fax: 850-784-1739.
School—Tel: 850-763-1775; Fax: 850-784-4461. Thomas Collins, Ph.D., Prin. Lay Teachers 24; Students 254.
Catechesis/Religious Program—Tel: 850-763-1821. Students 370.

3—SS. Peter & Paul Mission (1981), (Vietnamese), [JC] Rev. Viet Tan Huynh, Admin.
Mailing Address: P.O. Box 3627, 32401. Tel: 850-914-0390.
Res.: 1003 E. Ave., 32401. Tel: 850-785-4574.
School—Students 14.
Catechesis/Religious Program—Students 50.

Pensacola Beach, Escambia Co., Our Lady of the Assumption Mission (1979),, Mailing Address: P.O. Box 1057, Gulf Breeze, 32561. Tel: 850-934-0222; Fax: 850-934-6020. See St. Ann, Gulf Breeze.
920 Via de Luna, 32561. Tel: 850-934-0222; Fax:

850-934-6020.
Catechesis/Religious Program—Tel: 850-934-0222; Fax: 850-934-6020. Students 50.

PERRY, TAYLOR CO., IMMACULATE CONCEPTION (1914), Rev. Msgr. C. Slade Crawford. In Res., Rev. Francis Bagan, O.M.I.
Res.: 2750 S. Byron Butler Pkwy., 32348. Tel: 850-584-3169; Fax: 850-584-5736. Email: immac@perry.gulfnet.com.
Catechesis/Religious Program—Tel: 850-584-8853. Students 90.
Center—Tel: 850-584-8853.

PORT ST. JOE, GULF CO., ST. JOSEPH (1925), Rev. Thomas J. Guido.
Res.: 2006 Monument Ave., P.O. Box 820, 32457-0820. Fax: 850-229-1922.
Church: 20th & Monument Sts., 32457-0820. Fax: 850-229-1922.
Catechesis/Religious Program—Tel: 850-227-1417. Students 41.
Mission—San Blas Catholic Mission C30E, Gulf Co. 32456.
Mission—St. Lawrence Mission Wewahitchka, Gulf Co.

QUINCY, GADSDEN CO., ST. THOMAS THE APOSTLE (1957), Very Rev. Dennis O'Brien.
Res. & Mailing Address: 27 N. Shadow St., P.O. Box 549, 32353. Tel: 850-627-2350; Fax: 850-627-6755.
Catechesis/Religious Program—Tel: 850-627-8807; Fax: 850-627-6755. Students 175.
Hispanic Ministry Office of St. Thomas—Religious Education Office. Tel: 850-627-8807; Fax: 850-627-6755.

SANTA ROSA BEACH, WALTON CO., ST. RITA (1982), Rev. Thomas S. Collins; Deacon David Casey.
Mailing Address: P.O. Box 1223, 32459. Tel: 850-267-2558; 850-622-2751 (Rectory); Fax: 850-267-3711.
Res.: Tel: 850-267-2558; Fax: 850-267-3711. Email: saintritacatholic.church@mchsi.com.
Catechesis/Religious Program—Students 105.
Mission—Christ the King Catholic Mission Freeport, Walton Co.

SUNNY HILLS, WASHINGTON CO., ST. THERESA (1972), Rev. Msgr. Francis S. Szczykutowicz.
Res.: 2056 Sunny Hills Blvd., 32428. Tel: 850-773-3406; Fax: 850-773-7008.
Catechesis/Religious Program—Tel: 850-773-3406; Fax: 850-773-7008.

TIGER POINT, SANTA ROSA CO., ST. SYLVESTER (1979), Rev. John F. Kelly.
Res.: 3551 Gulf Breeze Pkwy., Gulf Breeze, 32563. Tel: 850-932-6807; Fax: 850-932-6338. Email: saintsylv@mchsi.com. See St. Joseph, Port St. Joe
Catechesis/Religious Program—Tel: 850-932-6807; Fax: 850-932-6338. Students 286.

WEWAHITCHKA, GULF CO., ST. LAWRENCE MISSION, , Mailing Address: c/o P.O. Box 820, Port St. Joe, 32457.
Catechesis/Religious Program—Students 6.

WOODVILLE, LEON CO., ST. STEPHEN THE PROTOMARTYR (1979), Rev. James B. MacGee, O.M.I.
Mailing Address: P.O. Box 1142, 32363. Tel: 850-421-9094. See St. Elizabeth Ann Seton, Medart.
Res.: 3609 Coastal Hwy., Crawfordville, 32327. Tel: 850-926-1797; Fax: 850-926-1737. Email: seascp@aol.com.
Catechesis/Religious Program—Students 9.

Chaplains of Public Institutions

PENSACOLA. *Escambia County Jail*. Deacon Dennis Dobransky.
Saufley Field Federal Prison Camp. Rev. J. Deffenbaugh.
TALLAHASSEE. *Federal Correctional Institution*. Deacon Ted Horbowy.
CHATTAHOOCHEE. *Florida State Hospital*. Vacant.
CHIPLEY. *Washington Correctional Institution*. Rev. John Selleck.
CRAWFORDVILLE. *Wakulla Correctional Institution*. Joan Sharman, Dir., Deacon Marcus Hepburn.
CRESTVIEW. *Okloosa Correctional Facility*. Deacon James Cox.
EGLIN. *Eglin Federal Prison Camp Eglin Air Force Base*. Deacon Gary McBride.
MARIANNA. *Florida Correctional Institutions*.
SNEADS. *Apalachee Correctional Institution*.
WEWAHITCHKA. *Gulf Coast Institution*. Rev. John Selleck.

On Duty Outside the Diocese:
Rev. Msgrs.—
Bosso, Stephen C., St. Vincent de Paul Regional Seminary, 10701 E. Military Tr., Boynton Beach, 33436.
Kerr, William A., Ph.D. (PIT), La Roche College, 9000 Babcock Blvd., Pittsburgh, PA 15237.
Revs.—
Roland, Charles, 1706 S. Hendrickson, Adel, GA 31620.
Sarmiento, Oscar, St. Joseph Parish, 8670 Byron Ave., Miami Beach, 33141.

Military Chaplains:
Revs.—
Bluett, James K., Fort Richardson, Fort Richardson, AK 99505-5999.
Krzywicki, Lance P., Chap., ILVA,1, 07024 La Maddalena, Italy.
McClanahan, Robert P., Jr., Chap., Cmdr.
Voyt, Stephen A., Lt. Col., McChord AFB, WA 98438.

On Leave of Absence:
Revs.—
Caffrey, Joseph
Castillo, Richard
Cayer, John
Crandall, Thomas
Hevia, Todd O.
Stewart, Paul
Wood, Peter N.

Retired:
Rev. Msgrs.—
Bowles, Richard (COS)
Mullins, Raymond
Sindik, George
Revs.—
Condren, William
Dolan, Hugh
Hogarty, Paul
Jorden, James A.
Joseph, William
Kiem, Anthony
Kirby, Edward A.
White, Philip

Permanent Deacons:
Barrows, Stanley, (On Duty Outside Diocese)
Bartoszewicz, John M., St. Jude Thaddeus, Cantonment
Benevides, Luis, (On Duty Outside Diocese)
Bodish, William, St. Mary, Fort Walton Beach
Bonanno, Frederick R., St. Mary, Fort Walton Beach
Brinkworth, Gary, Good Shepherd, Tallahassee
Buenavista, Crisostomo, St. Mary, Pensacola
Carucci, Michael J., Christ Our Redeemer, Niceville
Casey, David R., St. Rita, Santa Rosa Beach
Castellano, Reymond, Little Flower, Pensacola
Cirabisi, Sal, St. Dominic, Panama City
Comeau, Randall O., Nativity of Our Lord, Pensacola
Cox, James, Holy Name of Jesus, Niceville
Daron, Estal, St. Dominic, Panama City
Davey, David, (Retired)
Dobransky, Dennis, Nativity, Pensacola
Donnelly, Thomas, St. Anne, Pensacola
Fraites, Thomas J., Holy Name of Jesus, Niceville
Gardner, James L., (Retired)
Geri, Eugene A., Holy Spirit, Pensacola
Hepburn, Marcus, Good Shepard, Tallahassee
Horbowy, Thadeous, Blessed Sacrament, Tallahassee
Horner, Paul, St. Thomas More, Pensacola
Howell, John, St. Mary, Fort Walton Beach
Johnson, Dale R., St. John the Evangelist, Panama City
Kennell, Thomas H., St. Rose of Lima, Milton
Kreppein, Joan, (On Duty Outside Diocese)
L'Huillier, Ron, (On Duty Outside Diocese)
Landry, Alduce, (Retired)
Leblanc, Robert
Madera, Nelson I., St. Louis, Tallahassee
Marini, Louis, Holy Name of Jesus, Niceville
Martinez, Desiderio, St. John the Evangelist, Panama City
Mayfield, Kenneth, Our Lady of Victory, Crestview
Mc Auliffe, Daniel, St.Mary, Ft. Walton Beach
McBride, Gary, Holy Name of Jesus, Niceville
Mirus, Earl C., St. John the Evangelist, Panama City
Molina, Santiago, St. Thomas More, Tallahassee
Morgan, John P., St. Paul, Pensacola
Murphy, Michael, (On Duty Outside Diocese)
Murray, James, Christ Our Redeemer, Blue Water Bay
O'Neal, Willie, Holy Name of Jesus, Niceville
Packard, Russell C., (On Duty Outside Diocese)
Pallone, Eugene, St. Anthony/St. Joseph, Pensacola
Provencher, Conrad, St. Bernadette, Panama City Beach
Radigan, Terence A., Good Shepherd, Tallahassee
Raymaker, Terence, Blessed Sacrament, Tallahassee
Renick, John, St. John the Evangelist, Panama City
Restivo, Anthony, St. Mary, Fort Walton Beach
Rezmer, Matthew, Resurrection, Miramar Beach
Richardson, Walter H., St. Mary, Fort Walton
Robinson, David P., St. Peter, Mary Esther
Rose, Joseph, (Retired)
Saxer, Robert J., St. Mary, Fort Walton Beach
Schaal, William, Christ Our Redeemer, Blue Water Bay
Seabrook, Bradley M., (Retired)
Shook, Mack D., St. Louis, Tallahassee
Simard, Thomas, St. Jude, Cantonment
Trevino, Joaquin D., Christ Our Redeemer, Niceville
Trumps, Jeffery, Holy Spirit, Pensacola
White, Jean, (Retired)
Williamson, Gerard, St. John the Evangelist, Warrington
Wolf, Charles R., St. Mary, Fort Walton Beach
Wulf, Stephen

INSTITUTIONS LOCATED IN THE DIOCESE

[A] HIGH SCHOOLS, DIOCESAN

PENSACOLA. *Pensacola Catholic High School*, 3043 W. Scott St., 32505. Tel: 850-436-6400; Fax: 850-436-6405. Email: martinK5@juno.com. Web: pensacolachs.org. Sr. Kierstin Martin, A.S.C.J., Prin. Sisters 2; Lay Teachers 38; Students 595; Total Staff 55.

TALLAHASSEE. *John Paul II Catholic High School*, 5100 Terrebone Dr., 32311-7848. Tel: 850-201-5744; Fax: 850-205-3299. Email: rfelton@jpiichs.org. Web: www.jpiichs.org. Randall G. Felton, Ph.D., Prin. Sisters 3; Lay Teachers 14; Students 81; Total Staff 6.

[B] ELEMENTARY SCHOOLS, DIOCESAN

PENSACOLA. *St. Michael*, 601 N. Palafox St., 32501. Tel: 850-436-6464; Fax: 850-436-6458. Email: srassj@pensacolastmichael.org. Web: pensacolastmichael.org. Sr. S. Robert Anne, S.S.J., Prin. Sisters of St. Joseph (Buffalo) Sisters 1; Lay Teachers 16; Students 212.

[C] GENERAL HOSPITALS

PENSACOLA. *The Mother Seton Guild of Sacred Heart Hospital, Inc.* 32504. Mr. Jim Wharton, Pres.
Sacred Heart Foundation, Inc., 5151 N. 9th Ave., 32504. Tel: 850-416-4660; Fax: 850-416-4664. Email: shf@shhpens.org. Web: sacred-heart.org. P.O. Box 2700, 32513-2700. Rosilan Leahy, Pres. Bed Capacity 431; Total Assisted Annually 800; Total Staff 8.
Sacred Heart Health Ventures, Inc., 5151 N. Ninth Ave., 32504. Tel: 850-416-6500. Email: kemmanue@shhpens.org. Karen Emmanuel, Gen. Council.
Sacred Heart Hospital of Pensacola, 5151 N. Ninth Ave., 32504. Tel: 850-416-7000; Fax: 850-416-6119. Email: pmadden@shhpens.org. Web: sacred-heart.org. Patrick J. Madden, Pres. & CEO. Annual Admissions 20,269; Total Staff 3,147; Total Assisted 276,936; Bed Capacity 431.

[D] HOMES FOR AGED

PENSACOLA. *Haven of Our Lady of Peace, Inc.*, 1900 Sumit Blvd., 32503. Tel: 850-436-5900; Fax: 850-436-5959. Email: mperez@shhpens.org. Martha Perez, Admin. Guests 120; Total Staff 185.

[E] APARTMENTS FOR THE ELDERLY AND HANDICAPPED

TALLAHASSEE. *Casa Calderon, Inc.*, 800 W. Virginia St., 32304. Tel: 850-222-4026; Fax: 850-561-6868. Email: karkoel@aol.com. Rev. Msgr. C. Slade Crawford, Pres.; Ms. Barbara Bolden. Total Assisted 111; Total Staff 5.

[F] MONASTERIES AND RESIDENCES FOR PRIESTS AND BROTHERS

TALLAHASSEE. Brotherhood of Hope: 2302 Mission Rd., 32304-2629. Tel: 850-580-3122; Fax: 850-580-3122. Web: www.brotherhoodofhope.org. Bros. Stephen Quense; Gary Davis; Samuel Gunn; Allen Marquez.
Missionary Servants of the Most Holy Trinity: 7997 Mahan Dr., P.O. Box 10429, 32301-2429. Tel: 850-224-4955. Email: fvrst@mail.instal.com. Revs. Francisco Valdovinos, S.T.; Alexis Zunga, S.T.

[G] CONVENT AND RESIDENCES FOR SISTERS

PENSACOLA. *Blessed Trinity Missionary Cenacle*, 412 Bayshore Dr., 32507. Tel: 850-456-4141. Sisters 4.
St. Michael Convent, 18 W. Jackson St., 32501-3956. Tel: 850-436-6460. Email: srassj@pensacolastmichael.org. Web: pensacolastmichael.org. Sisters of Mercy of the Americas; Sisters of St. Joseph (Buffalo) Sisters 2.

Notre Dame Convent, Sisters of the Congregation of Notre Dame, 1001 Deason St., 32505. Tel: 850-438-5906. Email: cndpens@juno.com. Sisters 3.

Sacred Heart Hospital Convent, 1657 Trinity Dr., 32504. Tel: 850-416-7920; Fax: 850-416-6119. Email: dc@sacred-heart.org. Web: www.shhint.net.

APALACHICOLA. *Martin House*, 149 10th St., 32320. Tel: 850-653-8774; 850-653-3478. Email: apalachop@gtcom.net. Sinsinawa Dominican Congregation of the most Holy Rosary 3.

MARIANNA. *Sisters of St. Francis of Philadelphia*, 3007 Fifth St., 32446. Tel: 850-526-3291. Sisters 1.

SUNNY HILLS. *Vestiarki Sisters of Jesus (Poland)*, 3919 Vistula Dr., 32428. Tel: 850-773-3302. Sisters 4; Total Assisted 3.

[H] HOMELESS SHELTERS

PANAMA CITY. *St. Barnabas House*, 2943 E. 11th St., 32401. Tel: 850-763-0475; Fax: 850-763-2969. Email: catholicchari@comcast.net. c/o Catholic Charities, 3128 E. 11th St., 32401. Sheila Harmon, Coord. Total in Residence 20; Total Staff 4.

Naomi House, 2941 E. 11th St., 32401. Tel: 850-763-0475; Fax: 850-763-2969. Email: catholicchari@comcast.net. c/o Catholic Charities, 3128 E. 11th St., 32401.

[I] RETREAT HOUSES

TALLAHASSEE. *The Saint John Neumann Spiritual Renewal Center*, 685 Miccosukee Rd., 32308. Tel: 850-224-2971; Fax: 850-224-2941. Sr. Christine Kelly, S.S.J., Dir. Sisters 3.

NAVARRE. *Casa Stella Maris*, 7650 Clark St., 32566. Tel: 850-623-3600. Rev. Steven J. O'Connor, Dir. Total Staff 1.

[J] MISCELLANEOUS

PENSACOLA. *Diocese of Pensacola-Tallahassee Education Foundation, Inc.*, P.O. Drawer 17329, 32522. Tel: 850-432-1515; Fax: 850-436-6424. Email: ptschools@ptdiocese.org.

St. Michael Cemetery Foundation, Inc., P.O. Box 13602, 32561. Tel: 850-436-4643. Web: www.stmichaelcemetery.org.

TALLAHASSEE. *Florida Catholic Conference*, 313 S. Calhoun St., 32301-1807. Tel: 850-222-3303; Fax: 850-681-9548. Email: flacathconf@flacathconf.org. Web: www.flacatlconf.org. D. Michael McCarron, Ph.D., Exec. Dir.

RELIGIOUS INSTITUTES OF MEN REPRESENTED IN THE DIOCESE

For further details refer to the corresponding bracketed number in the Religious Institutes of Men or Women section.

[1080]—*Congregation of the Resurrection* (Chicago Prov.)—C.R.

[0840]—*Missionary Servants of the Most HolyTrinity*—S.T.

[]—*Missionary Society of St. Paul* (Gwagwalda-Abuja)

[0910]—*Oblates of Mary Immaculate* (Eastern American Prov.)—O.M.I.

[1260]—*Society of Christ*—S.Ch.

[0975]—*Society of our Lady of the Most Holy Trinity*—S.O.L.T.

RELIGIOUS INSTITUTES OF WOMEN REPRESENTED IN THE DIOCESE

[0130]—*Apostles of the Sacred Heart of Jesus*—A.S.C.J.

[0760]—*Daughters of Charity of St. Vincent de Paul* (Eastern Prov.)—D.C.

[]—*Daughters of the Blessed Trinity*—F.S.T.

[1070-03]—*Dominican Sisters*—O.P.

[1070-13]—*Dominican Sisters*—O.P.

[1070-14]—*Dominican Sisters*—O.P.

[2790]—*Missionary Servants of the Most Blessed Trinity*—M.S.B.T.

[0430]—*Sisters of Charity of Blessed Virgin Mary*—B.V.M.

[0590]—*Sisters of Charity of Saint Elizabeth, Convent Station*—S.C.

[0660]—*Sisters of Christian Charity*—S.C.C.

[2575]—*Sisters of Mercy of the Americas* (Baltimore, MD)—R.S.M.

[1660]—*Sisters of Saint Francis of the Providence of God*—O.S.F.

[3840]—*Sisters of St. Joseph of Carondelet*—C.S.J.

[3900]—*Sisters of St. Joseph of St. Augustine, Florida*—S.S.J.

[2980]—*Sisters of the Congregation de Notre Dame* (Blessed Sacrament Prov.)—C.N.D.

[2070]—*Sisters of the Holy Union*—S.U.S.C.

[2150]—*Sisters, Servants of the Immaculate Heart of Mary*—I.H.M.

[]—*Society of Our Lady of the Most Holy Trinity*—S.O.L.T.

[]—*Vestiarski Sisters of Jesus* (Poland)—V.S.S.

NECROLOGY

(No Deaths)

Diocese of Peoria

(Dioecesis Peoriensis)

Most Reverend

DANIEL R. JENKY, C.S.C.

Bishop of Peoria; ordained April 6, 1974; appointed Auxiliary Bishop of Fort Wayne-South Bend and Titular Bishop of Amantia October 21, 1997; consecrated December 16, 1997; appointed Bishop of Peoria February 12, 2002; installed April 10, 2002 *Office: 607 N.E. Madison Ave., Peoria, IL 61603.*

Chancery: 607 N.E. Madison Ave., Peoria, IL 61603. Tel: 309-671-1561; Fax: 309-671-5079.

ESTABLISHED 1877.

Square Miles 16,933.

A cross-section of Illinois, bounded on the north by the Counties of Whiteside, Lee, De Kalb, Grundy and Iroquois, and on the east by Kendall, Grundy, Kankakee and Ford, and on the south by Adams, Brown, Cass, Menard, Sangamon, Macon, Moultrie, Douglas and Edgar; comprising the Counties of Bureau, Champaign, Dewitt, Fulton, Hancock, Henderson, Henry, Knox, La Salle, Livingston, Logan, Marshall, Mason, McDonough, McLean, Mercer,Peoria, Piatt, Putnam, Rock Island, Schuyler, Stark, Tazewell, Vermilion, Warren and Woodford.

Legal Title: For legal titles of parishes and diocesan institutions, consult the Chancery.

STATISTICAL OVERVIEW

Personnel	
Auxiliary Bishops	1
Abbots	1
Retired Abbots	2
Priests: Diocesan Active in Diocese	149
Priests: Diocesan Active Outside Diocese	10
Priests: Retired, Sick or Absent	72
Number of Diocesan Priests	231
Religious Priests in Diocese	45
Total Priests in Diocese	276
Extern Priests in Diocese	10
Ordinations:	
Diocesan Priests	7
Religious Priests	1
Transitional Deacons	2
Permanent Deacons in Diocese	111
Total Brothers	6
Total Sisters	240
Parishes	
Parishes	165
With Resident Pastor:	
Resident Diocesan Priests	134
Resident Religious Priests	16
Without Resident Pastor:	
Administered by Priests	15
Missions	26
Pastoral Centers	6
Closed Parishes	2
Professional Ministry Personnel:	
Brothers	6
Sisters	32
Lay Ministers	55
Welfare	
Catholic Hospitals	8
Total Assisted	2,945,453
Homes for the Aged	6
Total Assisted	583
Day Care Centers	2
Total Assisted	250
Special Centers for Social Services	1
Total Assisted	18,500
Educational	
Diocesan Students in Other Seminaries	35
Total Seminarians	35
Colleges and Universities	1
Total Students	148
High Schools, Diocesan and Parish	7
Total Students	155
High Schools, Private	7
Total Students	2,624
Elementary Schools, Diocesan and Parish	45
Total Students	12,115
Catechesis/Religious Education:	
High School Students	2,835
Elementary Students	11,834
Total Students under Catholic Instruction	29,746
Teachers in the Diocese:	
Priests	16
Brothers	3
Sisters	36
Lay Teachers	975
Vital Statistics	
Receptions into the Church:	
Infant Baptism Totals	3,998
Adult Baptism Totals	425
Received into Full Communion	500
First Communions	2,936
Confirmations	3,523
Marriages:	
Catholic	623
Interfaith	359
Total Marriages	982
Deaths	2,315
Total Catholic Population	195,553
Total Population	1,562,868

Former Bishops—Most Revs. JOHN LANCASTER SPALDING, D.D., consecrated May 1, 1877; resigned Sept. 11, 1908; Titular Archbishop of Scitopolis; appt. Oct. 14, 1908; died Aug. 25, 1916; EDMUND M. DUNNE, D.D., ord. June 24, 1887; consecrated Sept. 1, 1909; died Oct. 17, 1929; JOSEPH H. SCHLARMAN, Ph.D., J.C.D., ord. June 29, 1904; consecrated June 17, 1930; named Assistant at Papal Throne, Nov. 16, 1950; Archbishop ad personam; appt. June 27, 1951; died Nov. 10, 1951; WILLIAM E. COUSINS, D.D., ord. April 23, 1927; Titular Bishop of Forma and Auxiliary Bishop of Chicago; appt. Dec. 17, 1948; consecrated March 7, 1949; Bishop of Peoria; appt. May 19, 1952; Archbishop of Milwaukee; appt. Dec. 17, 1958; died Sept. 14, 1988; JOHN B. FRANZ, D.D. (Retired), ord. June 13, 1920; Bishop of Dodge City; appt. May 29, 1951; consecrated Aug. 29, 1951; transferred to Peoria, Aug. 8, 1959; retired June 1, 1971; died July 3, 1992; EDWARD W. O'ROURKE, D.D. (Retired), ord. May 28, 1944; Bishop of Peoria; appt. May 24, 1971; consecrated July 15, 1971; retired Jan. 23, 1990; died Sept. 29, 1999; JOHN J. MYERS, J.C.D., ord. Dec. 17, 1966; appt. Coadjutor Bishop of Peoria July 7, 1987; ord. Sept. 3, 1987; succeeded to Bishop of Peoria, Jan. 23, 1990; appt. Archbishop of Newark July 24, 2001; installed Oct. 9, 2001.

Bishop's Office—607 N.E. Madison Ave., Peoria, 61603. Tel: 309-671-1561; Fax: 309-671-5079. Please direct all calls for the Bishop's Office to this number; Office Hours: Mon.-Fri. 8:30-4:30

Vicar General—Rev. Msgr. STEVEN P. ROHLFS, S.T.D., V.G., Sheen Pastoral Center, 412 N.E. Madison Ave., Peoria, 61603. Tel: 309-671-1550; Fax: 309-671-1558.

Chancellor—Rev. Msgr. STEVEN P. ROHLFS, S.T.D., V.G., Sheen Pastoral Center, 412 N.E. Madison Ave., Peoria, 61603. Tel: 309-671-1550; Fax: 309-671-1558.

Moderator of the Curia—Rev. Msgr. STEVEN P. ROHLFS, S.T.D., V.G., Sheen Pastoral Center, 412 N.E. Madison Ave., Peoria, 61603. Tel: 309-671-1550; Fax: 309-671-1558.

Vice Chancellors—Rev. Msgr. JOSEPH A. ZUBE, J.C.L.; Rev. JASON GRAY, S.T.L., 607 N.E. Madison Ave., Peoria, 61603. Tel: 309-671-1561; Fax: 309-671-5079; Ms. PATRICIA GIBSON, J.D., J.C.L., 412 N.E. Madison Ave., Peoria, 61603-3720. Tel: 309-671-1550; Fax: 309-671-1576.

Director of Development—Mr. JOHN HOWARD, Sheen Pastoral Center, 412 N.E. Madison Ave., Peoria, 61603. Tel: 309-671-1550; Fax: 309-671-1595.

Director of Finance—Mr. TOBY GUALANDRI, Sheen Pastoral Center, 412 N.E. Madison Ave., Peoria, 61603. Tel: 309-671-1550; Fax: 309-671-1595.

Legal Department—Ms. PATRICIA GIBSON, J.D., J.C.L., Sheen Pastoral Center, 412 N.E. Madison Ave., Peoria, 61603-3720. Tel: 309-671-1550; Fax: 309-671-1576.

Diocesan Tribunal—Rev. EDWARD J. ROBERTS, J.C.L., Sheen Pastoral Center, 412 N.E. Madison Ave., Peoria, 61603. Tel: 309-671-1550; Fax: 309-677-6798.

Judicial Vicar—Rev. Msgr. RICHARD SOSEMAN, M.A., J.C.L.

Defender of the Bond—Rev. Msgr. J. BRIAN REJSEK, J.C.L.

Promoter of Justice—Rev. Msgr. J. BRIAN RESJEK, J.C.L.

Adjutant Judicial Vicars—Rev. Msgrs. JOSEPH A. ZUBE, J.C.L.; RICK OBERCH, J.C.L.

Auditor—Sr. MARIANNE BURKHARD, O.S.B., J.C.L.

Judges—Sr. MARIANNE BURKHARD, O.S.B., J.C.L.; Rev. EDWARD ROBERTS, J.C.L.

Advocates—Mrs. CHERYL CRISS; Deacon DAVID REISING.

Notaries—Mrs. DEBRA WILLIAMS; Mrs. JANICE VICARY; Mrs. NANCY PAUL.

Diocesan College of Consultors—Rev. Msgrs. STEVEN P. ROHLFS, S.T.D., V.G.; STUART SWETLAND, S.T.D.; RICHARD SOSEMAN, M.A., J.C.L.; JEROME HAM; DALE WELLMAN; THOMAS E. MACK; Revs. PHILIP HALFACRE; JEFFREY LAWRENCE; WILLIAM MILLER, I.C.; KENNETH MARCHULONES, Sheen Pastoral Center, 412 N.E. Madison Ave., Peoria, 61603. Tel: 309-671-1550; Fax: 309-671-1558.

Vicariates and Vicars—Rev. Msgrs. J. MARK WILLIAMS, S.T.L., Bloomington; ALBERT W. HALLIN, Champaign; Revs. THADDEUS PRACZ, Danville; STANLEY L. DEPTULA, Henry; Rev. Msgr. DONNELLY J. FITZPATRICK, Kewanee; Rev. JAMES E. KRUSE, La Salle; Rev. Msgrs. E. E. HIGGINS, Lincoln; RICHARD PRICCO, Macomb; Rev. ERNEST PIZZAMIGLIO, Monmouth; Rev. Msgr. RAYMOND BOYLE, Ottawa; Revs. TIMOTHY NOLAN, Pekin; STEVE MCKINLEY, O.F.M.Conv., V.F., Peoria, N.W.; MICHAEL C. BLISS, Peoria, S.E.; Rev. Msgrs. THOMAS E. MACK, Pontiac; PAUL E. SHOWALTER, Rock Island.

Diocesan Offices and Directors

Finance Council (Canon 492)—Rev. Msgr. STEVEN P. ROHLFS, S.T.D., V.G.; Sr. DIANE MARIE MCGREW, O.S.F.; Rev. Msgr. THOMAS MILLER; Deacon MATTHEW LEVY; Mr. GERALD T. WOMBACHER; Ms. JEAN SOMERS; Mr. DANIEL REYNOLDS; Mr. TOBY GUALANDRI; Mr. JOHN HOWARD; Ms. PATRICIA GIBSON, J.D., J.C.L.; Mr. ROBERT MANNING; Mr. ROBERT BRADY, Sheen Pastoral Center, 412 N.E. Madison Ave., Peoria, 61603. Tel: 309-671-1550; Fax: 309-671-1595.

Art and Architecture Commission—Rev. Msgr. STEVEN ROHLFS, S.T.D., V.G., 412 N.E. Madison Ave., Peoria, 61603. Tel: 309-671-1550; Fax: 309-671-1558.

Catholic Cemeteries—Rev. Msgr. STEVEN P. ROHLFS, S.T.D., V.G., Sheen Pastoral Center, 412 N.E. Madison Ave., Peoria, 61603. Tel: 309-671-1550; Fax: 309-671-1558.

Catholic Education Office—Mrs. PATRICIA

KAWCZYNSKI, Supt., Catholic Schools. Associate Superintendents: Mr. VERNON CARR; Mr. KENNETH J. SANDERSON; Mr. RONALD BOLSTER, Dir., Office of Catechetics; Mr. MICHAEL FILAMORE; Mr. JEREMY PITT-PAYNE, Assoc. Dir. Chastity Formation, Sheen Pastoral Center, 412 N.E. Madison Ave., Peoria, 61603. Tel: 309-671-1550; Fax: 309-671-1595.

Catholic Relief Services—Rev. Msgr. STEVEN P. ROHLFS, S.T.D., V.G., 412 N.E. Madison Ave., Peoria, 61603. Tel: 309-671-1550; Fax: 309-671-1558.

Catholic Women, Council of—Rev. Msgr. DALE WELLMAN, Moderator, 1608 13th St., Moline, 61265. Tel: 309-762-2362.

Censor Librorum—Rev. Msgr. STEVEN P. ROHLFS, S.T.D., V.G.

Clergymen's Aid, Inc.—Most Rev. DANIEL JENKY, C.S.C., Trustee & Ex Officio; Rev. Msgr. STEVEN P. ROHLFS, S.T.D., V.G., Trustee & Ex Officio; Revs. JEFF LAWRENCE, Pres.; MARK MERDIAN, Sec.; Rev. Msgr. DOUGLAS HENNESSY; Revs. ROBERT SPILMAN; MARK DESUTTER; KENNETH MARCHULONES; Rev. Msgrs. THOMAS MILLER, Trustee; ALBERT W. HALLIN, 412 N.E. Madison Ave., Peoria, 61603. Tel: 309-671-1550; Fax: 309-671-1558.

Commission for Ecumenism—Rev. Msgr. ALBERT W. HALLIN, 405 W. Clark St., Champaign, 61820. Tel: 217-352-8748.

Communications, Office of—Mrs. KATE KENNY, Dir., Bishop Franz Center, 613 N.E. Jefferson, Peoria, 61603. Tel: 309-671-1568; Fax: 309-671-1578.

Conciliation and Arbitration Process—Rev. Msgr. STEVEN P. ROHLFS, S.T.D., V.G., Chm., Sheen Pastoral Center, 412 N.E. Madison Ave., Peoria, 61603-2720. Tel: 309-671-1550; Fax: 309-671-1558.

Cursillo Program—Rev. BRIAN BROWNSEY, Spiritual Dir.; Deacon WILLIAM READ, Asst. Diocesan Dir., Spalding Renewal Center, 401 N.E. Madison Ave., Peoria, 61603. Tel: 309-676-4001.

Diocesan Office of Development—Mr. JOHN HOWARD, Dir.; Mr. SHAWN RIEDELL, Assoc. Dir., Sheen Pastoral Center, 412 N.E. Madison Ave., Peoria, 61603. Tel: 309-671-1550; Fax: 309-671-1595.

Diocesan Education Commission—Rev. PHILIP D. HALFACRE, Chm., Sheen Pastoral Center, 412 N.E. Madison Ave., Peoria, 61603. Tel: 309-671-1550; Fax: 309-671-1595.

Diocesan Evangelization Office—Deacon GREG SERANGELI, Dir., Bishop Franz Center, 613 N.E. Jefferson Ave., Peoria, 61603. Tel: 309-671-1568; Fax: 309-671-1578.

Diocesan Office of Finance—Mr. TOBY GUALANDRI, Dir., Finance Office: Sheen Pastoral Center, 412 N.E. Madison Ave., Peoria, 61603. Tel: 309-671-1550; Fax: 309-671-1595.

Diocesan Hispanic Ministry Office—Rev. Msgr. BRIAN REJSEK, Dir., Bishop Franz Center, 613 N.E. Jefferson Ave., Peoria, 61603. Tel: 309-671-1568; Fax: 309-671-1578.

Diocesan Office of Insurance—Sheen Pastoral Center, 412 N.E. Madison Ave., Peoria, 61603. Tel: 309-671-1550; Fax: 309-671-1576.

Diocesan Pastoral Council—Rev. Msgr. STEVEN P. ROHLFS, S.T.D., V.G., Sheen Pastoral Center, 412 N.E Madison Ave., Peoria, 61603. Tel: 309-671-1550; Fax: 309-671-1558.

Diocesan Personnel Board—Rev. Msgr. STEVEN P. ROHLFS, S.T.D., V.G., Dir., Sheen Pastoral Center, 412 N.E Madison Ave., Peoria, 61603. Tel: 309-671-1550; Fax: 309-671-1558.

Diocesan Director of Music—Mr. PETER KURDZIEL, 613 N.E. Jefferson, Peoria, 61603. Tel: 309-671-1568; Fax: 309-671-1578.

Divine Worship, Office of—Rev. JASON A. GRAY, S.T.L., Diocesan Chancery, 607 N.E. Madison Ave., Peoria, 61603. Tel: 309-671-1561; Fax: 309-671-5079.

Office of Marriage and Family—Mr. TIM RODER, Dir., Sheen Pastoral Center, 412 N.E. Madison Ave., Peoria 61603. Tel: 309-671-1550; Fax: 309-671-1595.

Office of Pastoral Services—Ms. JEANNE WHALEN, Dir., Sheen Pastoral Center, 412 N.E. Madison Ave., Peoria, 61603. Tel: 309-671-1550; Fax: 309-671-1595.

Holy Childhood Association—Rev. Msgr. STEVEN P. ROHLFS, S.T.D., V.G., Dir., 412 N.E Madison Ave., Peoria, 61603. Tel: 309-671-1550; Fax: 309-671-1558.

Office of Victims Assistance—412 N.E Madison Ave., Peoria, 61603. Tel: 309-671-1550 Fax: 309-671-1576.

Newspaper--"The Catholic Post"—Mr. THOMAS DERMODY, Editor-in-Chief, 409 N.E. Monroe Ave., Peoria, 61603. Tel: 309-673-3601; Fax: 309-673-0384.

Nurses Council of—VACANT.

Permanent Diaconate, Office of—Rev. Msgr. CHARLES J. BEEBE, 503 Bryan St., Peoria, 61603. Tel: 309-671-1582.

Priests' Eucharistic League—Rev. Msgr. JOSEPH A. ZUBE, J.C.L., Sheen Pastoral Center, 412 N.E. Madison Ave., Peoria, 61603. Tel: 309-671-1550; Fax: 309-677-6798.

Propagation of the Faith—Rev. Msgr. STEVEN P. ROHLFS, S.T.D., V.G., Dir., 412 N.E. Madison Ave., Peoria, 61603. Tel: 309-671-1550; Fax: 309-671-1558.

Priests' Purgatorial Society—Rev. Msgr. STEVEN P. ROHLFS, S.T.D., V.G., Dir., Sheen Pastoral Center, 412 N.E. Madison Ave., Peoria, 61603. Tel: 309-671-1550; Fax: 309-671-1558.

Rural Life Conference—Deacon WILLIAM GRAY, Dir., 1225 N. County Rd. 1000, Hamilton, 62341. Tel: 217-847-3818. Email: gfpltd@adams.net.

Presbyteral Council—Rev. Msgr. STUART W. SWETLAND, S.T.D., Pres.; Rev. PHILIP D. HALFACRE, Vice Pres.; Rev. Msgr. THOMAS MACK, Sec./Treas., Sheen Pastoral Center, 412 N.E. Madison, Peoria, 61603. Tel: 309-671-1550; Fax: 309-671-1558.

Catholic Charities—Miss PEGGY A. ARIZZI, Diocesan Dir.; TRICIA FOX, Assoc. Dir., 2900 W. Heading Ave., Peoria, 61604. Tel: 309-636-8000; Fax: 309-671-0253. Bloomington Offices, 603 N. Center St., Bloomington, 61701. Tel: 309-829-6307; Fax: 309-829-3254. 2714 W. McGraw Dr., Bloomington, 61704. Tel: 309-662-3840; Fax: 309-663-2883. Canton Office, 162 E. Chestnut St., Canton, 61520. Tel: 309-647-5014; Fax: 309-647-8287. Champaign Office, 610 1-2 E. Park St., Champaign, 61820. Tel: 217-352-5179. Danville Office, 102 N. Robinson, Danville, 61832. Tel: 217-443-1772; Fax: 217-443-1701. Galesburg Office, 292 N. Chambers, Galesburg, 61401. Tel: 309-342-1136; Fax: 309-342-1891. LaSalle Office, 542 Crosat, LaSalle, 61301. Tel: 815-223-4007; Fax: 815-223-4550. Lincoln Office, 310 S. Logan, Lincoln, 62656. Tel: 217-732-3771; Fax: 217-735-1738. Macomb Office, 527 Grant St., Macomb, 61455. Tel: 309-833-1791; Fax: 309-836-1462. Pekin Office, 15 S. Capitol, Pekin, 61554. Tel: 309-353-9500; Fax: 309-353-3528. Rock Island Office, 816 20th St., Rock Island, 61201. Tel: 309-788-9581.

TEC—Rev. BRIAN BROWNSEY, Dir., Spalding Renewal Center, 401 N.E. Madison Ave., Peoria, 61603. Tel: 309-676-4001.

Vocations Office—Rev. BRIAN K. BROWNSEY, Dir., 613 N.E. Jefferson Ave., Peoria, 61655. Tel: 309-671-1569; Fax: 309-671-1577. Associate Directors: Revs. STANLEY L. DEPTULA; JAMES E. KRUSE.

CLERGY, PARISHES, MISSIONS AND PAROCHIAL SCHOOLS

CITY OF PEORIA

(PEORIA COUNTY)

1—ST. MARY'S CATHEDRAL (1846), Most Rev. Daniel R. Jenky, C.S.C.; Rev. Msgr. J. Brian Rejsek, J.C.L. Office: 613 N.E. Jefferson, 61603.
Res.: 607 N.E. Madison Ave., 61603. Tel: 309-671-1568; Fax: 309-671-1578.

2—ST. ANN (1994), Rev. Terry A Cassidy; Deacon Joseph Koeppel; Sr. Judith Croegaert, Pastoral Assoc.
Mailing Address: 1010 S. Louisa St., 61605. Tel: 309-674-5072; Fax: 309-655-1566.
St. Ann's Youth Center,—1009 S. Louisa St., 61605. Tel: 309-674-0225.

3—ST. BERNARD'S, Rev. James G. Pallardy.
Res.: 509 E. Kansas Ave., 61603. Tel: 309-682-1221; Fax: 309-682-3462.
School—Tel: 309-682-5823. Leroy Pesch, Prin. Lay Teachers 7; Students 76.

4—ST. BONIFACE'S (1881), (German), Closed., For inquiries for parish records contact St. Ann, Peoria.

5—ST. CECILIA'S, Closed., For Sacramental records write St. Philomena, 3300 N. Twelve Oaks Dr., Peoria, IL 61604.

6—HOLY FAMILY (1956), Revs. Steve McKinley, O.F.M.Conv., V.F.; Patrick Stoffer, O.F.M.Conv.; Alejandro Lopez, O.F.M.Conv.; Deacons James Maubach; Joseph Lahood.
Res.: 3720 N. Sterling, 61615. Tel: 309-688-3427; Fax: 309-688-2174.
School—2329 W. Reservoir, 61615. Tel: 309-688-2931; Fax: 309-681-5687. Pat Kellogg, Prin. Lay Teachers 23; Students 347.

7—ST. JOHN'S (1890), (Irish), Closed., For inquiries for parish records contact St. Ann, Peoria.

8—ST. JUDE'S (1975), [CEM] Rev. Bruce Lopez; Deacons Thomas Rapach; Roger Hunter.
Res.: 10811 Knoxville Ave., 61615. Tel: 309-243-7811; Fax: 309-243-7810.
Catechesis / Religious Program—Tel: 309-243-7811, Ext. 212; 309-243-7811, Ext. 213; Fax: 309-243-7810. Students 197.

9—ST. MARK'S (1891), Revs. Benjamin B. Reese; Anthony Maanzo; Deacon John Skender.
Res.: 1113 W. Bradley Ave., 61606. Tel: 309-673-1263; Fax: 309-637-1484.
School—Tel: 309-676-7131; Fax: 309-677-8060. John Crumrine, Prin. Lay Teachers 17; Students 300.
Catechesis / Religious Program—Tel: 309-497-2838. Students 35.

10—ST. MARTIN DE PORRES (1976) Rev. Terry Cassidy; Sr. Judith Croegaert, O.S.B., Pastoral Assoc.
Res.: 103 Richard Pryor Pl., 61605. Tel: 309-676-0726; Fax: 309-676-4090.
Southside Catholic Child Care Center—1010 W. Johnson, 61605. Tel: 309-674-7340.

11—ST. PETER'S (1897), Rev. Jason A. Gray, S.T.L.; Deacon Richard Zimmerman. In Res., Revs. Brian K. Brownsey; Charles Klamut.
Res.: 2719 N.E. Madison Ave., 61603. Tel: 309-685-3861; Fax: 309-685-4523.

12—ST. PHILOMENA'S (1945), [JC] Revs. Gregory K. Ketcham; Attilio Morelli (NEW); Deacons Robert England, (Retired); Harry Ohl; David Reising.
Res.: 3300 N. Twelve Oaks Dr., 61604-1464. Tel: 309-682-8642; Fax: 309-682-8955.
School—Sisters of St. Francis, Tel: 309-685-1208; Fax: 309-681-5676. Sisters Mary Joseph Bickett, O.S.F., Prin.; Kathleen Maurisse, O.S.F., Prin. Sisters 4; Lay Teachers 23; Students 425.
St. Philomena Endowment Trust—

13—SACRED HEART (1879), (German), Revs. Sergius Scherpenberg, O.F.M.; Marne Breckensiek, O.F.M.
Res.: 504 Fulton St., 61602. Tel: 309-673-6316; 309-673-6317.

14—ST. THOMAS (1937), Rev. Msgr. William A. Watson; Rev. Scott Engelbrecht; Sr. Rachel Bergschneider, O.S.B., Pastoral Assoc. & D.R.E.; Deacons Donald Efinger; Robert Waldschmidt; Francis S. Eaton; Earl Hietter; William Kelley Sr.
Res.: 904 E. Lake Ave., Peoria Heights, 61616. Tel: 309-688-3446; Fax: 309-688-3467.
School—4229 N. Monroe, Peoria Heights, 61614. Tel: 309-685-2533. Mrs Ann Ribando, Prin. Lay Teachers 26; Students 485.
Catechesis / Religious Program—Students 169.

15—ST. VINCENT DE PAUL (1962), Rev. Msgr. Thomas R. Miller; Rev. Dennis E. Spohrer; Deacon Robert W. Myers Sr. In Res., Deacon Thomas DeBernardis.
Res.: 6001 N. University St., 61614. Tel: 309-691-3602; Fax: 309-691-3637.
School—6003 N. University St., 61614. Tel: 309-691-5012; Fax: 309-683-1036. Mr. Michael Birdaes, Prin. Lay Teachers 29; Students 613.
Catechesis / Religious Program—Tel: 309-691-6513. Students 156.

OUTSIDE THE CITY OF PEORIA

ABINGDON, KNOX CO., SACRED HEART (1924), Revs. William T. Miller, I.C., Admin.; Joseph Presley, I.C.
Res. & Mailing: 506 N. Main St., 61410. Tel: 309-462-3421.

ALEDO, MERCER CO., ST. CATHERINE'S CHURCH (1914), [CEM] Revs. John Thieryoung; John Cyr. In Res., Rev. Robert O'Conner.
Res.: 106 N.E. Fourth, 61231. Tel: 309-582-7500; Fax: 309-582-5155.
Catechesis / Religious Program—Students 130.
Mission—St. Mary's 602 S. 10th St., Keithsburg, Mercer Co. 61442. Tel: 309-374-2420.
Mission—St. Theresa of the Little Flower New Boston, Mercer Co. Closed. For inquiries for mission records contact St. Mary's Mission, Keithsburg.

ALEXIS, WARREN CO., ST. THERESA'S (1877), (Swedish), [CEM] Rev. Ronald Enderlin, Admin.
Res.: 131 Main St., P.O. Box 26, 61412. Tel: 309-482-3935.
Mission—St. Aloysius N. Depot St., Wataga, Knoxville Co. 61488. Tel: 309-375-6835. Rev. Ernest E. Pizzamiglio, Admin.

ANDALUSIA, ROCK ISLAND CO., ST. PATRICK'S (1974), Rev. Richard L. Barclift.
Mailing Address: Box 249, 61232.
Res.: 9616 140th St. W., Taylor Ridge, 61284. Tel: 309-798-2098; Fax: 309-798-2840.
Catechesis / Religious Program—Tel: 309-798-2630. Students 145.

ANNAWAN, HENRY CO., SACRED HEART (1893), [CEM] Rev. Timothy J. Sauppe.
Res.: 305 W. South Ave., 61234. Tel: 309-935-6911.

ARLINGTON, BUREAU CO., ST. PATRICK'S (1864), [CEM] Rev. Kevin D. Gorman, O.S.B.
Res.: 106 Church St., P.O.Box 78, 61312. Tel: 815-638-2323.
Catechesis / Religious Program—Students 68.

ATKINSON, HENRY CO., ST. ANTHONY'S (1870), (Belgian), [CEM] Rev. Msgr. Donnelly J. Fitzpatrick.

Res.: 204 W. Main St., P.O. Box 210, 61235-0210. Tel: 309-936-7900; Fax: 309-936-7900.

BARTONVILLE, PEORIA CO., ST. ANTHONY (1969), Rev. David C. Heinz; Deacons Richard Hammond; Louis Tomlianovich.
Res.: 2525 Skyway Rd., 61607. Tel: 309-697-0645; Fax: 309-697-2188.
Catechesis/Religious Program—Students 169.

BEMENT, PIATT CO., ST. MICHAEL, Rev. Greg Nelson.
Res.: 1301 N. Market St., Monticello, 61856. Tel: 217-762-2566.

BENSON, WOODFORD CO., ST. JOHN (1873), [CEM] Rev. Msgr. Charles J. Beebe.
Res.: c/o 506 W. Randolph, Roanoke, 61561. Tel: 309-394-2615; Fax: 309-923-3031.

BLACKSTONE, LIVINGSTON CO., ST. BERNARD, Closed., For inquiries for sacramental records contact Immaculate Conception, Streater.

BLOOMINGTON, MCLEAN CO.

1—HOLY TRINITY (1853), [CEM] Rev. Msgr. J. Mark Williams, S.T.L.; Rev. Vincent C. Peters; Deacons Brendan Carolan; Lewis Roesch; James Gore.
1909 E. Lincoln St., 61701. Tel: 309-662-3712; Fax: 309-663-9115.
Res.: 704 N. Main St., 61701. Tel: 309-829-2197; Fax: 309-829-2243.
School—705 N. Roosevelt, 61701. Tel: 309-828-7151; Fax: 309-827-8131. Mrs. Kay O'Brien, Prin. Sisters 4; Lay Teachers 30; Students 569.
Catechesis/Religious Program—Tel: 309-828-8242. Mrs. Sharon Priester, D.R.E. Students 260.

2—ST. MARY'S (1867), (German), [CEM] Revs. Ric Schneider, O.F.M.; Dacian Batt, O.F.M.; Bros. Kevin Duckson, O.F.M.; Tim Lamb, O.F.M.; Deacons Darrel Petri; Jerry Hozie.
Res.: 527 W. Jackson St., 61701. Tel: 309-827-8526; Fax: 309-829-3061.
School—603 W. Jackson St., 61701. Tel: 309-828-5954. Lay Teachers 12; Students 159.
Catechesis/Religious Program—Students 158.

3—ST. PATRICK CHURCH OF MERNA (1890), [CEM] Rev. Gerald T. Ward.
Church: 1001 N. Towanda Barnes Rd., 61704. Tel: 309-662-7361; Fax: 309-664-6167.
Catechesis/Religious Program—Sr. Rita Ann Bregenhorn, O.S.U., Pastoral Assoc. Students 550.

4—ST. PATRICK'S (1892), [JC] Revs. Patrick K. O'Neal; Vincent E. Dietzen, Pastor Emeritus (Retired).
Res.: 1209 W. Locust St., 61701. Tel: 309-829-1355; Fax: 309-828-0577.

BRADFORD, STARK CO., ST. JOHN THE BAPTIST (1876), [CEM] Rev. Robert Rayson.
Res.: 218 First St., Box 310, 61421. Tel: 309-897-4081; Fax: 309-897-8007.
Catechesis/Religious Program—Students 41.

BRIMFIELD, PEORIA CO., ST. JOSEPH'S (1852), (Irish), [CEM] Rev. Lawrence P. Morrissey.
Res.: 314 W. Clay St., 61517. Tel: 309-446-3275; Fax: 309-446-3275.
Mission—St. James Williamsfield, Knox Co. 61489. Tel: 309-446-3275.

BUDD, LIVINGSTON CO., ST. BERNARD'S, Closed., For parish records contact Church of the Immaculate Conception, Streator.

BUSHNELL, MCDONOUGH CO., ST. BERNARD (1877), Rev. David L. Kurt.
Res.: 376 W. Hail St., 61422. Tel: 309-772-2333.
Catechesis/Religious Program—Students 62.

CAMP GROVE, MARSHALL CO., ST. PATRICK (1866), (Irish), [CEM] Rev. Robert Rayson.
Res.: 115 W. Camp St., 61424. Tel: 309-493-5261.

CAMPUS, LIVINGSTON CO., SACRED HEART (1882), (Irish), [CEM] Rev. William M. Gardner.
Res.: 313 W. Hamilton, Odell, 60460. Tel: 815-998-2197.

CANTON, FULTON CO., ST. MARY'S (1862), [CEM 2] Rev. Arthur D. Meyer.
Mailing Address: 159 E. Chestnut St., 61520. Fax: 309-647-1580.
Res.: 140 N. 2nd Ave., 61520. Tel: 309-647-1473; Fax: 309-647-1476.
Catechesis/Religious Program—Tel: 309-647-0261. Students 142.

CARTHAGE, HANCOCK CO., IMMACULATE CONCEPTION (1860), [CEM] Revs. Anthony J. Trosley; Luke A Spannagel.
Res.: 125 N. Fayette, 62321. Tel: 217-357-3087.
Mission—St. Mary West Point, Hancock Co.

CHAMPAIGN, CHAMPAIGN CO.

1—HOLY CROSS (1912), Rev. Msgr. Albert W. Hallin; Rev. Donald Henderson; Deacons Henry Hart; Edward Mohrbacher.
Res.: 405 W. Clark St., 61820. Tel: 217-352-8748; Fax: 217-366-2929.
School—410 W. White St., 61820. Tel: 217-356-9521; Fax: 217-356-1745. Mrs. Rose Costello, Prin. Lay Teachers 25; Students 405.
Catechesis/Religious Program—Tel: 217-352-8748; Fax: 217-366-2929. Marc Cardaronella, D.R.E. Students 154.

2—ST. JOHN'S CATHOLIC CHAPEL (1918),, (For Catholic Students at the University of Illinois), Rev. Msgr. Stuart W. Swetland, S.T.D., Chap.; Revs. Thomas Holloway, Asst. Chap.; Brian L. Herlocker. In Res., Revs. Fortunatus Bijura (Rulenge, Tanzania); Johndamascene Zilimu (Rulenge, Tanzania).
Newman Hall: 604 E. Armory Ave., 61820. Tel: 217-344-1184; Fax: 217-344-4957.

3—ST. MARY'S (1854), [CEM] Rev. Thomas J. Royer.
Res.: 612 E. Park Ave., 61820. Tel: 217-352-8364; Fax: 217-352-6859.

4—ST. MATTHEW (1965), Revs. Mark J. Merdian; David P. Richardson.
Res.: 1303 Lincolnshire Dr., 61821. Tel: 217-359-4224; Fax: 217-359-9846.
School—1307 Linconshire Dr., 61821. Tel: 217-359-4114; Fax: 217-359-7507. Mrs. Kathleen Scherek, Prin. Lay Teachers 25; Students 464.
Catechesis/Religious Program—Tel: 217-359-8761. Students 251.

CHATSWORTH, LIVINGSTON CO., SS. PETER AND PAUL (1877), (German—Irish), [CEM] Rev. Richard W. Brunskill.
Res.: 406 N. Fifth St., P.O. Box 546, 60921. Tel: 815-635-3127; Fax: 815-635-3756.
Mission—St. James Forrest, Livingston Co.

CHENOA, MCLEAN CO., ST. JOSEPH'S (1859), [CEM] Rev. Carl LoPresti.
Res.: 225 W. Owsley, 61726. Tel: 815-945-2561; Fax: 815-945-7634.
Catechesis/Religious Program—Students 39.
Mission—St. Mary Lexington, McLean Co.

CHERRY, BUREAU CO., HOLY TRINITY (1904), [CEM] Rev. Kevin D. Gorman, O.S.B.
Res.: P.O. Box 159, 212 S. Main, 61317. Tel: 815-894-2006; Fax: 815-894-2090.

CHILLICOTHE, PEORIA CO., ST. EDWARD'S (1900), [CEM] Rev. Glenn H. Harris; Deacons Gregory Serangeli; Bob Pomazal.
Res.: 1216 N. 6th St., 61523. Tel: 309-274-3809.
School—Tel: 309-274-2994; Fax: 309-274-4141. Ms. Jeannine McAllister, Prin. Lay Teachers 11; Students 129.

CLINTON, DE WITT CO., ST. JOHN THE BAPTIST'S (1879), Rev. Gordon Pillon. In Res., Rev. Ben M. Rodriguez.
Res.: 502 N. Monroe St., 61727. Tel: 217-935-3727.
Catechesis/Religious Program—Tel: 217-935-3727. Students 103.

COAL VALLEY, ROCK ISLAND CO., ST. MARIA GORETTI (1972), Rev. R. Michael Schaab, Admin.; Sr. Sandra Brunenn, O.S.B., Pastoral Assoc.; Deacons Charles Breeden; Robert Zimmerman.
Res.: P.O. Box 159, 210 E. 22nd Ave., 61240. Tel: 309-799-3414; Fax: 309-799-3436.
Catechesis/Religious Program—Tel: 309-799-7283. Students 145.

COLFAX, MCLEAN CO., ST. JOSEPH'S (1850), Rev. Carl LoPresti.
Res.: P.O. Box 169, 107 W. North, 61728. Tel: 309-723-6229; Fax: 309-723-6229.

COLONA, HENRY CO., ST. PATRICK'S (1941), [JC] Rev. Duane C. Jack.
Res.: 201 First St., 61241. Tel: 309-792-3854; Fax: 309-278-0015.
Catechesis/Religious Program—Tel: 309-949-3176. Marc Possin, D.R.E. Students 222.

CREVE COEUR, TAZEWELL CO., SACRE COEUR (1954), Rev. Joseph W. Anderson.
Res.: 301 Roosevelt St., 61610. Tel: 309-699-8223; Fax: 309-698-3692.
Church: 601 Rusche Ln., 61610. Tel: 309-699-8511.

CULLOM, LIVINGSTON CO., ST. JOHN'S (1881), Rev. Msgr. Thomas E. Mack; Rev. Steven P. Loftus.
Res.: 119 E. Howard, Pontiac, 61764. Tel: 815-689-2367.

DALZELL, BUREAU CO., ST. THOMAS MORE (1934), (Italian), Rev. Bernard A. Horzen, O.S.B.
Res.: 302 Chestnut, 61320. Tel: 815-663-6201.

DANVILLE, VERMILION CO.

1—HOLY FAMILY (1978), [CEM] Rev. Ted Pracz; Deacons Herman Bott; Richard Smith.
Church: 444 E. Main St., 61832. Tel: 217-431-5100; Fax: 217-431-5103.
School—Tel: 217-431-5108. Mrs. Peggy Cray, Prin. Lay Teachers 14; Students 255.

2—ST. PAUL'S (1915), Rev. Msgr. Douglas J. Hennessy; Sr. Charles Allen, Pastoral Assoc.
Res.: 1303 N. Walnut St., 61832. Tel: 217-442-5313; Fax: 217-442-5356.
School—1307 N. Walnut St., 61832. Tel: 217-442-3880; Fax: 217-442-5852. Mrs. Mary Shepherd, Prin. Lay Teachers 25; Students 355.
Catechesis/Religious Program—Students 86.

DELAVAN, TAZEWELL CO., ST. MARY'S (1859), [CEM] Rev. Gerald J. Verdun.
Res.: Box 769, 61734. Tel: 309-244-8516.
Mission—St. Joseph's Hopedale, Tazewell Co.

DEPUE, BUREAU CO., ST. MARY'S (1908), [CEM] Rev. Bailey T. Clemens.
Res.: 312 Park St., Box 19, 61322. Tel: 815-447-2552.

DOWNS, MCLEAN CO., ST. MARY'S (1910), Rev. Patrick Henehan.
Church: 108 E. Washington St., P.O. Box 66, 61736. Tel: 309-378-4679; Fax: 309-378-4679.
Catechesis/Religious Program—Students 168.

DUNLAP, PEORIA CO., ST. CLEMENT'S, Closed., For inquiries for parish records contact St. Jude, 10811 N. Knoxville, Peoria, IL 61615.

DWIGHT, LIVINGSTON CO., ST. PATRICK'S (1862), (Irish), [CEM] Rev. James E. Rickey.
Res.: 126 W. Mazon Ave., P.O. Box 70, 60420. Tel: 815-584-3522; Fax: 815-584-3518.
Catechesis/Religious Program—Tel: 815-584-3110; Fax: 815-584-3518. Ginger Connor, D.R.E. Students 356.

EAGLE TOWNSHIP, LA SALLE CO., ANNUNCIATION OF BLESSED VIRGIN MARY (1869), (Irish), [CEM] Rev. Charles A. McCarthy, C.S.Sp.
Church: Rte. 3, Eagle Township, Streator, 61364. Tel: 815-672-6500.
Res.: Rte 1, 957 N. 17th Rd., Tonica, 61370. Tel: 815-856-2502.

EARLVILLE, LA SALLE CO., ST. THERESA'S (1904), [CEM 2] Rev. Robert D. Spilman.
Res.: 221 Union St., Box 190, 60518. Tel: 815-246-4321; Fax: 815-246-9581.

EAST MOLINE, ROCK ISLAND CO.

1—ST. ANNE (1919), Rev. James K. Ramer; Sr. Mary O'Connor, B.V.M, Pastoral Assoc.
Res.: 555 18th Ave., 61244. Tel: 309-755-5071; Fax: 309-755-5343.
School—Tel: 309-755-9771; Fax: 309-755-7407. Mr. Todd Morris, Prin. Lay Teachers 14; Students 201.

2—ST. MARY'S (1907), (Belgian—Spanish), [JC] Rev. John Burns; Deacon Jerry Buyck.
Res.: 1908 13th St., 61244. Tel: 309-755-4111; Fax: 309-755-2384.
School—Tel: 309-755-4352. Mrs. Jeanne La Gatta, Prin. Lay Teachers 16; Students 140.
Catechesis/Religious Program—1925 13th St., 61244. Students 167.

EAST PEORIA, TAZEWELL CO., ST. MONICA'S (1898), Rev. Kenneth L. Marchulones; Sr. Marjorie Meismer, O.S.F., Pastoral Assoc.; Deacon Charles Robbins.
Res.: 303 Campanile Dr., 61611. Tel: 309-694-2061.
Catechesis/Religious Program—Tel: 309-699-8458. Sr. Marjorie Miesmer, O.S.F., D.R.E. Students 110.

EL PASO, WOODFORD CO., ST. MARY'S (1863), [CEM 2] Rt. Rev. Roger F. Corpus, O.S.B., Admin.
Res.: 79 W. Third, P.O. Box 197, 61738. Tel: 309-527-4555; Fax: 309-527-7750.
Catechesis/Religious Program—Tel: 309-744-2490. Mrs. Judy Hinshaw, D.R.E. Students 131.

ELKHART, LOGAN CO., ST. PATRICK (1856), Rev. Msgr. E. Edward Higgins; Rev. Thomas Shaw.
Res.: 213 S. Bogardus, P.O. Box 19, 62634. Tel: 217-947-2714; Fax: 217-947-2524.
Mission—St. Thomas Aquinas Mount Pulaski, Logan Co.
Mission—St. John the Baptist Middletown, Logan Co. Closed.
Mission—St. Columba Mason City, Mason Co. Closed.

ELMWOOD, PEORIA CO., ST. PATRICK'S (1870), (Irish), [CEM] Rev. Bruce King, I.C.
Res.: P.O. Box 440, 61529. Tel: 309-742-4921; Fax: 309-742-8243.
Catechesis/Religious Program—Students 72.

EUREKA, WOODFORD CO., ST. LUKE'S (1982), [JC] Rev. Edward J. Roberts, J.C.L.
Mailing Address: 705 E. Jefferson, Washington, 61571. Tel: 309-467-4855; Fax: 309-444-7070.
Church: 904 E. Regan Dr., P.O. Box 226, 61530.

FAIRBURY, LIVINGSTON CO., ST. JOHN THE BAPTIST (1857), [CEM] Rev. Scott Archer.
Res.: 110 E. Ash, 61739. Tel: 815-692-2555.
Catechesis/Religious Program—Students 61.
Mission—St. Rose Strawn, Livingston Co.

FARMER CITY, DE WITT CO., SACRED HEART (1899), [CEM] Rev. Donald F. Roszkowski.
Res.: 612 N. Plum St., 61842. Tel: 309-928-3855; Fax: 309-928-3855.
Mission—St. John Bellflower, McLean Co.

FARMINGTON, FULTON CO., ST. MATTHEW'S (1904), (Italian), Rev. Bruce King, I.C.; Deacon John Burton.
Res.: 156 E. Vernon St., 61531. Tel: 309-245-4001; Fax: 309-245-4351.

GALESBURG, KNOX CO.

1—CORPUS CHRISTI (1885), [CEM] Revs. William T. Miller, I.C., Admin.; Joseph Presley, I.C.
Res.: 273 S. Prairie St., 61401. Tel: 309-343-8256; Fax: 309-343-4793.
School—Costa Catholic School, 2726 Costa Dr., 61401. Tel: 309-344-3151; Fax: 309-344-1594. Mrs. Sandra Holm, Prin. Operates with Immaculate Heart and St. Patrick. Lay Teachers 25; Students 278.
Catechesis/Religious Program—Students 155.

2—IMMACULATE HEART OF MARY (1956), Rev. Ernest E. Pizzamiglio.

Mailing Address: P.O. Box 550, 61402. Tel: 309-344-3108; Fax: 309-344-1205.
Res.: 2401 N. Broad St., 61401.
School— See Corpus Christi Parish.
Catechesis/Religious Program—Students 123.
Mission—St. Aloysius Wataga, 61488.

3—ST. PATRICK'S (1863), [JC] Revs. William T. Miller, I.C.; Joseph Presley, I.C.; Deacon James D. Haneghan.
Mailing Address: P.O. Box 589, 61402-0589. Tel: 309-343-9874; Fax: 309-343-9944.
Res.: 858 S. Academy St., 61401.
School— See Corpus Christi Parish.

GALVA, HENRY CO., ST. JOHN'S (1882), (Swedish), [CEM] Rev. Eugene Radosevich.
Res.: 212 N.E. 1st St., 61434. Tel: 309-932-2409; Fax: 309-932-8238.

GENESEO, HENRY CO., ST. MALACHY'S (1866), Rev. Michael G. Pakula; Deacons Harley Chaffee; Harley Harris; Thomas Wachtel; Larry Honzel; Walter Verbeck, (Retired).
Res.: 595 E. Ogden Ave., 61254. Tel: 309-944-5393; Fax: 309-944-5319.
School—Tel: 309-944-3230. Mrs. Donna Osbourne, Prin. Lay Teachers 7; Students 136.
Catechesis/Religious Program—Tel: 309-944-3518. M. Elizabeth Fristensky, D.R.E. Students 330.

GEORGETOWN, VERMILION CO., ST. ISAAC JOGUES (1942), Rev. John Paninski, M.S.
Res.: 109 W. Seventh St., 61846. Tel: 217-662-6708.

GRANVILLE, PUTNAM CO., SACRED HEART OF JESUS (1908), (Italian), [CEM] Rev. Duane Leclercq.
Res.: P.O. Box 217, 61326. Tel: 815-339-2138; Fax: 815-339-2138.
Catechesis/Religious Program—Students 120.
Mission—St. Francis Xavier P.O. Box 217, Bureau, Bureau Co. 61323.

HAVANA, MASON CO., ST. PATRICK'S (1865), [CEM] Rev. Michael Monclova; Deacons Stanley Buczko; Jon Dosher.
Res.: 437 S. Orange, P.O. Box 545, 62644. Tel: 309-543-6373; Fax: 309-543-3241.
Mission—Immaculate Conception 505 S. Adams, P.O. Box 242, Manito, Mason Co. 61546. Tel: 309-968-6826. Deacon William Meyer.

HENNEPIN, PUTNAM CO., ST. PATRICK'S (1865), [CEM] Rev. Duane Leclercq.
Mailing Address: P.O. Box 217, Granville, 61326.
Res.: 10 St., P.O. Box 200, 61327. Tel: 815-925-7500; Fax: 815-339-6133.

HENRY, MARSHALL CO.

1—ST. JOSEPH'S (1878), (Irish), [CEM 2] Rev. Harry A Pierjok.
Res.: 418 N. Center, Lacon, 61540-1104. Tel: 309-246-5145; Fax: 309-246-5417.

2—ST. MARY'S (1851), (German), [CEM 2] Rev. Harry A Pierjok.
Res.: 418 Center, Lacon, 61540-1104. Tel: 309-246-5145.
Catechesis/Religious Program—Tel: 309-364-2011. Sr. Anita, D.R.E. Students 137.

HOOPESTON, VERMILION CO., ST. ANTHONY'S (1877), Rev. R. Anthony Lee.
Church: 423 S. Third St., P.O. Box 414, 60942. Tel: 217-283-6211; Fax: 217-283-6252.
Mission—Holy Trinity Rankin, Vermilion County 60960.

HOOPPOLE, HENRY CO., ST. MARY'S, Attended by, Annawan.

IVESDALE, CHAMPAIGN CO., ST. JOSEPH'S (1863), (Irish), [CEM] Rev. Joseph Dondanville.
Res.: 612 E. Park, Champaign, 61820. Tel: 217-352-8364; Fax: 217-352-6859.

KEWANEE, HENRY CO.

1—ST. FRANCIS OF ASSISI (1906), (Polish), Revs. Chris G. Haake; Fredi Gomez-Torres.
Res.: 406 Central Blvd., 61443. Tel: 309-852-2761; Fax: 309-852-0222.
Mission—St. John Vianney 313 S. West St., Cambridge, Henry Co. 61238. Tel: 309-937-3304.

2—ST. MARY'S CATHOLIC CHURCH (1855), [CEM 2] Revs. Chris G. Haake; Fredi Gomez-Torres; Deacons Martin Van Meltebeck; John T. Mock; Raymond Van Wassenhove.
Res.: 406 W. Central Blvd., 61443-2010. Tel: 309-852-4549; Fax: 309-853-4106.
School—Visitation, 107 S. Lexington, 61443. Tel: 309-856-7451; Fax: 309-852-4259. Ms. Penny Rowan, Prin. Lay Teachers 13; Students 114.
Catechesis/Religious Program—Tel: 309-856-5451. Mrs. Phyllis Elliott, D.R.E. Students 80.

KICKAPOO, (EDWARDS) PEORIA CO., ST. MARY OF KICKAPOO (1837), [CEM] Rev. Patrick M. Riordan.
Res.: 9910 W. Knox St., Kickapoo (Edwards), 61528. Tel: 309-691-2030 (Church); Fax: 309-691-2898.
School—Tel: 309-691-3015. Mr. Ron Dwyer, Prin. Lay Teachers 8; Students 132.

LA SALLE, LA SALLE CO.

1—ST. HYACINTH'S (1875), [CEM] Revs. Gordon Pillon; Ben M. Rodriguez; Deacon Charles Burgess.
Res.: 927 10th St., 61301. Tel: 815-223-0934; Fax: 815-223-9939.
School—LaSalle Catholic, Tel: 815-223-5088; Fax: 815-223-5366. Sr. Alice Ann Harcharik, O.S.F., Prin. Sisters 1; Lay Teachers 16; Students 169.

2—ST. PATRICK'S (1838), (Irish), [CEM] Revs. Gordon Pillon; Ben M. Rodriguez.
Res.: 725-Fourth St., 61301. Tel: 815-223-0641; Fax: 815-223-0523.
School—Tel: 815-223-1166; Fax: 815-223-7650. Mr. Steve Siska, Prin. Lay Teachers 14; Students 177.

3—QUEEN OF THE HOLY ROSARY (1925), (Italian), [JC] Revs. Gordon Pillon; Ben M. Rodriguez. In Res., Rev. DeoGratias Rweyongeza.
Res.: 529 Fourth St., 61301. Tel: 815-223-7129.

4—RESURRECTION (1979), Rev. John M. Onderko; Deacon Ronald Rager.
Res.: 913 Fifth St., 61301. Tel: 815-223-1459; Fax: 815-223-1585.
School—LaSalle Catholic School, Tel: 815-223-5088; Fax: 815-223-5366. Lay Teachers 16; Students 158.
Mission—Sacred Heart Dimmick Township. Tel: 815-223-1459.

LACON, MARSHALL CO., IMMACULATE CONCEPTION (1853), [CEM 2] Rev. Harry A Pierjok; Deacon J. Robert Murphy.
Res.: 418 N. Center St., 61540. Tel: 309-246-5145; Fax: 309-246-5417.

LADD, BUREAU CO., ST. BENEDICT'S (1893), Rev. Harold L. Datzman, O.S.B.
Res.: 314 Bureau St., 61329. Tel: 815-894-2319; Fax: 815-894-2265.
Mission—St. Gertrude 711 Railroad Ave., Seatonville, Bureau Co. 61359.

LEONORE, LA SALLE CO., SS. PETER AND PAUL'S (1860), (German), [CEM] Rev. Charles A. McCarthy, C.S.Sp.
Res.: Rte. 1,, Tonica, 61370. Tel: 815-856-2502; Fax: 815-856-2502.

LEWISTOWN, FULTON CO., ST. MARY'S (1865), [CEM] Rev. Msgr. Robert W. O'Connor.
Res.: 705 N. Broadway St., P.O. Box 106, 61542. Tel: 309-547-3226; Fax: 309-547-3226.
Mission—St. Michael St. David, Fulton Co.

LINCOLN, LOGAN CO., HOLY FAMILY (1857), [CEM 2] Rev. Msgr. E. Edward Higgins; Rev. Thomas Taylor.
Res.: 316 S. Logan St., 62656. Tel: 217-732-4019; Fax: 217-735-2650.
School—Carroll Catholic School, Tel: 217-732-7518; Fax: 217-732-7518. Mrs. Linda Mahler, Prin. Lay Teachers 10; Students 147.
Catechesis/Religious Program—Holy Family Religious Education Center, 109 Fifth St., 62656. Tel: 217-735-3520. Students 94.
Mission—St. Mary Atlanta, Logan Co. 61723.

LORETTO, LIVINGSTON CO., ST. MARY'S (1873), (German), Closed., For inquiries contact St. Patrick, Dwight.

LOSTANT, LA SALLE CO., ST. JOHN THE BAPTIST'S (1862), [CEM] Rev. Stanley Deptula.
Res.: P.O. Box 486, Wenona, 61377. Tel: 815-853-4558; Fax: 815-853-0111.
Church: 301 S. Sheridan, 61334. Tel: 815-368-3339.

MACOMB, MCDONOUGH CO., ST. PAUL'S (1854), [CEM] Rev. Msgr. Richard A. Pricco; Deacon Lawrence Adams.
Res.: 309 W. Jackson, 61455. Tel: 309-833-2496.
School—Tel: 309-833-2470. Mrs. Barbara Shrode, Prin. Lay Teachers 8; Students 109.
Catechesis/Religious Program—Tel: 309-837-1024. Students 140.
Mission—Sacred Heart Tennessee, McDonough Co.

MAHOMET, CHAMPAIGN CO., OUR LADY OF THE LAKE (1981), Rev. John C. Horton; Deacon Edward Mueller.
Res.: 501 W. State St., P.O. Box 109, 61853. Tel: 217-586-5153; Fax: 217-586-5924.
Catechesis/Religious Program—Tel: 217-586-6283. Mr. Roger L. Phelps, D.R.E. Students 400.

MARSEILLES, LA SALLE CO., ST. JOSEPH'S (1902), Rev. Bowen Schmitt.
Res.: 200 Broadway St., P.O. Box 26, 61341. Tel: 815-795-2240; Fax: 815-795-2240.
Catechesis/Religious Program—Tel: 815-795-2251. Students 73.
Mission—St. Patrick Ransom, La Salle Co.

MATHERVILLE, MERCER CO., ST. ANTHONY'S CHURCH (1916), [CEM 2] Revs. John Thieryoung; John Cyr.
Office—P.O. Box 208, 61263. Tel: 309-754-8711.
Mission—St. John Viola, Mercer Co. 61486. Tel: 309-596-2950.

MENDOTA, LA SALLE CO., HOLY CROSS (1863), [CEM] Revs. James E. Kruse; Steven Bird; Deacon Vincent Slomian.
Res.: 1010 Jefferson St., 61342. Tel: 815-538-6151; Fax: 815-539-5014.
School—1008 Jefferson St., 61342. Tel: 815-539-7003; Fax: 815-539-9082. Mrs. Anita Kobilsek, Prin. Lay Teachers 11; Students 176.
Catechesis/Religious Program—Tel: 815-539-6050. Karen Zolper, D.R.E. Students 250.

METAMORA, WOODFORD CO.

1—ST. MARY OF LOURDES (1831), Rev. Neri Greskoviak, O.F.M.; Bro. Xavier Gedeon, O.F.M., Pastoral Assoc.; Deacons Jack Gaetz; Robert Heiple; William Reed.
Res.: 424 Lourdes Rd., 61548. Tel: 309-383-4460; Fax: 309-383-4467.

2—ST. MARY'S (1864), (German), [CEM] Rev. John M. Verrier; Deacons Marvin Smith; Joseph Lowry.
Res.: 415 W. Chatham St., P.O.Box 319, 61548. Tel: 309-367-4407; Fax: 309-367-9456.
School—Tel: 309-367-2528; Fax: 309-367-2169. Mrs. Dareen Shipman, Prin. Sisters of St. Francis of the Immaculate Conception 1; Lay Teachers 13; Students 171.
Catechesis/Religious Program—Brenda Gualandri, D.R.E. Students 106.
Mission—St. Elizabeth Washburn, Woodford Co.

MILAN, ROCK ISLAND CO., ST. AMBROSE (1924), Rev. Anthony M. Ego; Sr. Charlotte Sonneville, O.S.B., Pastoral Assoc.
Res.: 312 W. First St., 61264. Tel: 309-787-4593; Fax: 309-787-6403.
Catechesis/Religious Program—Tel: 309-787-6240. Diane Hansen, D.R.E. Students 120.

MINONK, WOODFORD CO., ST. PATRICK'S (1878), [CEM] Rev. Stanley Deptula, Admin.
Res.: 420 E. Sixth St., Box 107, 61760-0107. Tel: 309-432-2700; Fax: 309-432-3399.
Catechesis/Religious Program—Students 115.

MOLINE, ROCK ISLAND CO.

1—CHRIST THE KING (1967), Rev. Donald L. Levitt.
Parish Center—3205 60th St., 61265. Tel: 309-762-4634; Fax: 309-762-7848.
Catechesis/Religious Program—Tel: 309-797-5202. Janet Myers, D.R.E. (PreK-6 & Junior High); Matt Sivertsen, (High School Youth Ministry). Students 200.

2—ST. MARY'S (1875), (Hispanic), [CEM] Rev. Jerome R. Pilon; Deacon Russell W. Swim.
Res.: 412 10th St., 61265. Tel: 309-764-1562; Fax: 309-764-0317.
Catechesis/Religious Program—Tel: 309-762-6575. Mrs. Claire Sally Van Oteghem, D.R.E. Students 223.

3—SACRED HEART (1906), (Belgian), Rev. Msgr. Dale L. Wellman; Rev. Vien Van Do; Sr. Kathleen Mullin, Pastoral Assoc.; Deacons Dennis De Vooght; Patrick Murphy; Bob Vogelbaugh. In Res., Rev. Michael J. Andrejek.
Lee Parish Center—1608 13th St., 61265. Tel: 309-762-2362; Fax: 309-757-5502.
School—Seton Catholic School, (Grades PreK-8) Tel: 309-757-5500. Mrs. Jane Barrett, Prin. Sisters 1; Lay Teachers 33; Students 601.
Catechesis/Religious Program—Sara Tucker, D.R.E. Students 409.

MONMOUTH, WARREN CO., IMMACULATE CONCEPTION (1864), [CEM] Revs. R. E. Enderlin; Kevin Creegan; Deacon William Clark.
Church: 210 W. Broadway, 61462. Tel: 309-734-7533; Fax: 309-734-6082.
School—Tel: 309-734-6037. Mrs. Mary Wurtzberger, Prin. Lay Teachers 11; Students 140.
Mission—St. Andrew Oquawka, Henderson Co.

MONTICELLO, PIATT CO., ST. PHILOMENA, Rev. Greg Nelson.
Res.: 1301 N. Market St., 61856. Tel: 217-762-2566.

MORTON, TAZEWELL CO., BLESSED SACRAMENT (1957), Rev. Mark A. DeSutter; Deacons Thomas Moran; Dan Murphy.
Res.: 217 E. Greenwood St., 61550. Tel: 309-266-9721; Fax: 309-266-9201.
School—Tel: 309-263-8442; Fax: 309-263-8443. Mr. James Eckhart, Prin. Lay Teachers 14; Students 202.
Catechesis/Religious Program—Tel: 309-266-6791. Students 344.

NAUVOO, HANCOCK CO., SS. PETER AND PAUL'S (1848), (German), [CEM 2] Rev. Gregory K. Ketcham.
Res.: 150 N. Wells St., 62354. Tel: 217-453-2428; Fax: 217-453-2015.
School—Tel: 217-453-2511. Mr. Alan Thompson, Prin. Lay Teachers 7; Students 101.
Catechesis/Religious Program—Students 25.
Mission—Sacred Heart Dallas City, Hancock Co. 62330.

NORMAL, MCLEAN CO., EPIPHANY (1966), Rev. Msgr. Eric S. Powell; Deacon Richard Grimler.
Res.: 1006 E. College Ave., 61761. Tel: 309-452-2585; 309-452-3223; Fax: 309-452-4851.
School—Tel: 309-452-3268. Mr. Richard Marehouse, Prin. Lay Teachers 23; Students 441.
Catechesis/Religious Program—Mary Jean Kraft, D.R.E. Students 350.

ODELL, LIVINGSTON CO., ST. PAUL'S (1873), (Irish), [CEM 2] Rev. William M. Gardner.
Res.: 313 W. Hamilton, 60460. Tel: 815-998-2197; Fax: 815-998-2197.
School—Tel: 815-998-2194; Fax: 815-998-1514. Sr.

Maria Semonski, Prin. Lay Teachers 5; Students 62; Religious 1.
OGLESBY, LA SALLE CO., HOLY FAMILY (1953), Rev. Gregory Jozefiak.
Res.: 311 N. Woodland Ave., 61348. Tel: 815-883-8233; Fax: 815-883-8771.
School—Tel: 815-883-8916; Fax: 815-883-8943. Mr. James Narczewski, Prin. Lay Teachers 15; Students 178.
Catechesis/Religious Program—Students 100.
OHIO, BUREAU CO., IMMACULATE CONCEPTION CHURCH (1875), (Irish), [CEM] Rev. Binh K. Tran.
Res.: *c/o St. John's*, 204 N. Main St., Walnut, 61376-0370. Tel: 815-379-2602; Fax: 815-379-2626.
ORION, HENRY CO., MARY, OUR LADY OF PEACE (1962), Rev. R. Michael Schaab.
Res.: 1402 10th St., P.O.Box 175, 61273-0175. Tel: 309-526-8106.
Catechesis/Religious Program—Students 177.
OTTAWA, LA SALLE CO.
1—ST. COLUMBA (1844), (Irish), [CEM] Revs. David Kipfer; Keith A. Walder.
Res.: 122 W. Washington St., 61350. Tel: 815-433-0700; Fax: 815-433-0305.
School—1110 LaSalle St., 61350. Tel: 815-433-1199; Fax: 815-433-1219. Mr. Joseph Benning, Prin. Lay Teachers 17; Students 280.
Catechesis/Religious Program—Students 125.
Mission—St. Mary's RR 1, Grand Ridge, La Salle Co. 61235. Tel: 815-249-6871.
2—ST. FRANCIS OF ASSISI (1858), [CEM] Rev. Gerald J. Meyer.
Res.: 820 Sanger St., 61350. Tel: 815-434-0969; Fax: 815-434-1073.
3—ST. MARY'S (1927), Revs. Philip Halfacre, Admin.; Peter Pilon.
Res.: 2005 Center St., Ottawa (Naplate), 61350. Tel: 815-433-2404; Fax: 815-433-9458.
4—ST. PATRICK'S (1893), (Irish), Rev. Philip Halfacre.
Res.: 726 W. Jefferson St., 61350. Tel: 815-434-0768; Fax: 815-434-0793.
School—801 W. Jefferson St., 61350. Tel: 815-433-2889; Fax: 815-431-9419. Mr. Steven Brockman, Prin. Lay Teachers 10; Students 145.
Catechesis/Religious Program—Mrs. Mary Jean Weihman, D.R.E. Students 130.
Convent—727 W. Jefferson, 61350. Tel: 815-433-2637.
PEKIN, TAZEWELL CO., ST. JOSEPH'S (1863), [CEM 2] Revs. Timothy Nolan; David Whiteside; Glenn J. Fontana; Deacons Charles Murray; Martin Pogioli; Mark Wilder; Ernie Whited.
Res.: 303 S. Seventh St., 61554. Tel: 309-347-6108; Fax: 309-347-6959.
School—Tel: 309-347-7194. Joan Moore, Prin. Lay Teachers 17; Students 342.
Catechesis/Religious Program—Tina Sondag, D.R.E. Students 214.
PENFIELD, CHAMPAIGN CO., ST. LAWRENCE'S (1898), [CEM] Rev. William C. Keebler Jr.
Res.: P.O. Box 49, 61862. Tel: 217-595-5560; Fax: 217-595-5439.
PERU, LA SALLE CO.
1—ST. JOSEPH'S (1854), [CEM] Revs. Henry H. Fritz, O.S.B.; Joseph J. Heyd, O.S.B.
Res.: 1925 5th St., P.O. Box 608, 61354. Tel: 815-223-0718; Fax: 815-223-5690.
School—Peru Catholic School System, (Grades PreK-8), 2003 Fifth St., 61354. Tel: 815-224-1914. Mrs. Janice Corrigan, Prin. Operated jointly by the Peru parishes. Lay Teachers 12; Students 226.
Catechesis/Religious Program—Sandra Weger, D.R.E. Students 150.
2—ST. MARY'S (1867), (Irish), Rev. Henry H. Fritz, O.S.B., Admin.
Res.: 1319 Sixth St., 61354. Tel: 815-223-2672; Fax: 815-223-1230.
School—Peru Catholic School System, Tel: 815-224-1914. See St. Joseph's for details.
3—ST. VALENTINE'S (1891), (Polish), [CEM] Rev. Thomas Badovsky.
Res.: 1109 Pulaski St., 61354. Tel: 815-223-0315.
School—Peru Catholic School System, Tel: 815-224-1914. See St. Joseph's for details.
Catechesis/Religious Program—Tel: 815-223-8471. Lynda Martin, D.R.E. Students 106.
PESOTUM, CHAMPAIGN CO.
1—ST. JOSEPH (1904), (German), [CEM] Rev. Joseph M. Mai Chi Thanh.
Res.: P.O. Box 169, 61863. Tel: 217-867-2434.
2—ST. MARY (1875), (German), [CEM] Rev. Joseph M. Mai Chi Thanh.
Res.: P.O. Box 169, 61863. Tel: 217-867-2434.
PETERSTOWN, LA SALLE CO., SS. PETER AND PAUL (1872), [CEM] Revs. James E. Kruse; Steven Bird.
Res.: 1010 Jefferson St., Mendota, 61342. Tel: 815-538-6151; Fax: 815-539-5014.
PHILO, CHAMPAIGN CO., ST. THOMAS (1869), [CEM] Rev. Stephen A. Willard.
Res.: 310 E. Madison, P.O. Box 266, 61864. Tel: 217-684-2571; Fax: 217-684-2571.
School—Tel: 217-684-2309; Fax: 217-684-2309. Mr. Michael Hough, Prin. Sisters 0; Lay Teachers 10; Students 104.
Mission—Immaculate Conception [CEM] Bongard, Champaign Co. 61864.
PONTIAC, LIVINGSTON CO., ST. MARY'S (1877), [CEM] Rev. Msgr. Thomas E. Mack; Rev. Steven P. Loftus.
Res.: 119 E. Howard St., P.O. Box 374, 61764. Tel: 815-844-7683; Fax: 815-842-4345.
School—414 N. Main St., 61764. Tel: 815-844-6585; Fax: 815-844-6987. Mrs. Sharon Warfield, Prin. Lay Teachers 14; Students 247.
Catechesis/Religious Program—Students 80.
PRINCETON, BUREAU CO., ST. LOUIS (1865), Rev. Jeffrey D. Stirniman.
Res.: 616 S. Gosse Blvd., 61356. Tel: 815-879-0181; Fax: 815-879-5042.
School—Tel: 815-872-8521; Fax: 815-879-8010. Mrs. Mary Paula Schmitt, Prin. Sisters 2; Lay Teachers 12; Students 123.
Catechesis/Religious Program—Tel: 815-872-1033; Fax: 815-879-5042. Students 217.
PRINCEVILLE, PEORIA CO., ST. MARY OF THE WOODS (1867), [CEM] Rev. Msgr. Richard Soseman.
Res.: 407 S. Walnut, 61559. Tel: 309-385-4370; Fax: 309-385-1754.
Catechesis/Religious Program—Students 60.
RANSOM, LA SALLE CO., ST. PATRICK'S (1883), [CEM] Rev. Bowan M. Schmitt.
Res.: 110 Wallace, P.O. Box 127, 60470. Tel: 815-586-4266.
RANTOUL, CHAMPAIGN CO., ST. MALACHY'S (1888), [CEM] Revs. Jeffrey G. Laible; Stanley J. Malinowski, Pastor Emeritus (Retired); Deacon William Shipp. Tel: 217-893-0741.
Office:—Tel: 217-892-2023; Fax: 217-892-2378.
Res.: 311 E. Grove Ave., 61866. Tel: 217-892-2044.
School—340 E. Belle Ave., 61866. Tel: 217-892-2011. Sr. Sara Koch, Prin. Sisters 3; Lay Teachers 12; Students 191.
Convent—Sisters of the Third Order of St. Dominic (Springfield), 304 E. Belle Ave., 61866. Tel: 217-892-2870.
RAPIDS CITY, ROCK ISLAND CO., ST. JOHN THE BAPTIST (1857), [CEM] Rev. James P. DeBisschop.
Res.: 1416 Third Ave., P.O. Box 258, 61278. Tel: 309-496-2414; Fax: 309-755-1650.
Catechesis/Religious Program—Fax: 309-496-3414. Students 139.
Mission—St. Mary 708 State Ave., Rte. 84, Hampton, Rock Island Co. 61256. Tel: 309-496-2414.
RARITAN, HENDERSON CO., CHURCH OF ST. PATRICK (1876), (Irish), Revs. R. E. Enderlin; Kevin Creegan; Deacon William Clark.
Res.: P.O. Box 24, 61471. Tel: 309-734-7533.
ROANOKE, WOODFORD CO., ST. JOSEPH (1874), Rev. Msgr. Charles J. Beebe.
Res.: 508 W. Randolph, 61561. Tel: 309-923-3031; Fax: 309-926-3031.
ROCK ISLAND, ROCK ISLAND CO.
1—ST. JOSEPH'S (1876), Rev. Patrick DeMeulemeester; Sr. Germaine Cupp, O.S.B., Pastoral Assoc.
Res.: 1316 Second Ave., 61201. Tel: 309-794-9793; Fax: 309-794-9950.
School— Operates as part of Jordan Catholic School of Rock Island.
2—ST. MARY (1851), (German),, (Formerly Immaculate Conception) Revs. Patrick DeMeulemeester; George J. Schroeder, Pastor Emeritus (Retired). 2208 Fourth Ave., 61201. Tel: 309-793-1897.
Rectory: 2208 Fourth Ave., 61201-8904. Tel: 309-788-3322.
3—ST. PIUS X (1955), Rev. Msgr. Paul E. Showalter; Rev. Thomas Mizeur; Deacons Timothy Granet; Paul Martin; Philip Sailer; Philip Dockery-Jackson. In Res., Rev. Msgr. Ambrose Nwohw.
Res.: 2502 29th Ave., 61201. Tel: 309-793-7373; Fax: 309-793-7376.
School—Tel: 309-793-7350; Fax: 309-793-7361. Daniel Lievens, Prin. Operates as part of Jordan Catholic School of Rock Island. Lay Teachers 32; Students 249.
Catechesis/Religious Program—Students 150.
4—SACRED HEART (1900), Rev. Msgr. Ambrose Cunningham.
Res.: 2810 Fifth Ave., 61201. Tel: 309-794-0660.
School—Jordan Catholic School of Rock Island, Tel: 309-793-7350. Lay Teachers 30; Students 537.
RUSHVILLE, SCHUYLER CO., ST. ROSE (1870), [JC] Rev. David Kurt.
Res.: 319 N. Franklin St., P.O. Box 194, 62681-0292. Tel: 217-322-3424.
RUTLAND, LA SALLE CO., SACRED HEART (1895), (Irish), [CEM] Rev. James C. Kretz.
Res.: c/o 311 W. Santa Fe Ave., P.O. Box 165, Toluca, 61369. Tel: 815-452-2043.
ST. AUGUSTINE, KNOX CO., ST. AUGUSTINE (1863), [CEM] Rev. David L. Kurt.
Mailing Address: 376 W. Hail, Bushnell, 61422. Tel: 301-462-3421; 309-772-2333.
SENECA, LA SALLE CO., ST. PATRICK'S (1856), [CEM] Rev. Msgr. Raymond J. Boyle.
Parish Center—183 W. Union, 61360. Tel: 815-357-8509.
Res.: 176 W. Union St., 61360. Tel: 815-357-6239; Fax: 815-357-6476.
Catechesis/Religious Program—Tel: 815-357-8509; Fax: 815-357-8509. Students 196.
SEYMOUR, CHAMPAIGN CO., ST. BONIFACE (1878), [CEM] Rev. Thomas J. Royer.
Res.: 416 County Rd., 1100 N., 61875. Tel: 217-863-2190; Fax: 217-352-6859.
SHEFFIELD, BUREAU CO., ST. PATRICK'S (1854), [CEM] Rev. Msgr. Donnelly J. Fitzpatrick, Admin.
Res.: 231 W. Atkinson St., P.O. Box 338, 61361. Tel: 815-454-2251; Fax: 815-454-2541.
Mission—St. Margaret Mary Wyanet, Bureau Co.
SILVIS, ROCK ISLAND CO., OUR LADY OF GUADALUPE (1927), (Hispanic), Rev. J. M. Logan.
Res.: 800 17th St., 61282. Tel: 309-792-3867.
Catechesis/Religious Program—Students 56.
SPRING VALLEY, BUREAU CO.
1—ST. ANNE'S, Closed., For sacramental records contact SS. Peter and Paul's, Spring Valley.
2—ST. ANTHONY'S (1904), (Italian), Rev. Joseph T. Hogan.
Res.: P.O. Box 150, 510 Richard A. Mautino Dr., 61362-0150. Tel: 815-663-3731; Fax: 815-663-0012.
Catechesis/Religious Program—Tel: 815-663-3731. Angela M. Hermes, D.R.E. Students 137.
3—IMMACULATE CONCEPTION (1884), [CEM] Rev. Paul J. Meismer.
Res.: 202 N. Greenwood St., 61362. Tel: 815-663-5351.
Catechesis/Religious Program—
4—SS. PETER AND PAUL'S (1891), (Polish), [CEM] Rev. Edward S. Kopec.
Res.: 220 N. Terry St., P.O. Box 209, 61362. Tel: 815-663-3041.
STREATOR, LA SALLE CO.
1—ST. ANTHONY OF PADUA (1881), [CEM] Rev. Msgr. Jerome Ham.
Res.: 407 S. Park St., 61364. Tel: 815-672-4523; Fax: 815-672-0378.
School—410 S. Park St., 61364. Tel: 815-672-3847; Fax: 815-673-3590. Sr. Carol Royston, Prin. Sisters 1; Lay Teachers 14; Students 258.
Catechesis/Religious Program—Students 120.
2—ST. CASIMIR (1916), (Polish), [CEM] Rev. Msgr. Jerome Ham.
Res.: 405 Illinois St., 61364. Tel: 815-672-2206.
Catechesis/Religious Program—Students 4.
3—IMMACULATE CONCEPTION (1868), (Irish), [CEM] Rev. Msgr. John J. Prendergast.
Res.: 404 N. Park St., 61364. Tel: 815-672-2034; Fax: 815-673-3796.
4—ST. STEPHEN'S (1884), (Slovak), [CEM 2] Rev. Jeffrey C. Lawrence. In Res., Rev. Msgr. Peter E. Bolerasky, Pastor Emeritus (Retired).
Res.: 711 Lundy St., 61364. Tel: 815-672-2474; Fax: 815-672-2040.
School—807 E. Lundy St., 61364. Tel: 815-672-3265; Fax: 815-672-9402. Mrs. Deborah Jayed. Sisters 3; Lay Teachers 15; Students 159.
Catechesis/Religious Program—Students 181.
THOMASBORO, CHAMPAIGN CO., ST. ELIZABETH'S (1893), [CEM] Revs. Jeffrey G. Laible; Stanley J. Malinowski (Retired).
Res.: 100 Church St., Box 307, 61878. Tel: 217-643-3395; Fax: 217-643-2217.
TISKILWA, BUREAU CO., ST. MARY'S (1881), [CEM] Rev. Jeffrey D. Stirniman; Deacon John Murphy.
Res.: P.O. Box 179, 61368. Tel: 815-646-4451; Fax: 815-646-4376.
TOLONO, CHAMPAIGN CO., ST. PATRICK'S (1859), [CEM] Rev. Joseph Dondanville.
Res.: 212 E. Washington St., P.O. Box K, 61880. Tel: 217-485-5194.
Mission—St. Charles Borromeo 110 S. East, Homer, Champaign Co. 61849.
TOLUCA, MARSHALL CO., ST. ANN'S (1895), (Italian), [CEM] Rev. James C. Kretz.
Res.: 311 W. Santa Fe Ave., Box 165, 61369. Tel: 815-452-2043.
URBANA, CHAMPAIGN CO., ST. PATRICK'S (1901), Rev. George F. Remm; Sr. Charlene Cesario, S.S.C.M., Pastoral Assoc.; Deacon Dan Murphy.
Res.: 708 W. Main St., 61801. Tel: 217-367-2665; Fax: 217-383-1002.
Catechesis/Religious Program—Carolyn McElrath, D.R.E. Students 396.
UTICA, LA SALLE CO., ST. MARY (1858), [CEM] Rev. Msgr. James J. Swaner.
Res.: 303 Division St., 61373. Tel: 815-667-4677; Fax: 815-667-4097.
WALNUT, BUREAU CO., ST. JOHN'S (1912), Rev. Binh K. Tran.
Res.: P.O. Box 370, 204 N. Main St., 61376-0370. Tel: 815-379-2602; Fax: 815-379-2626.
WAPELLA, DE WITT CO., ST. PATRICK'S (1858), [CEM] Rev. Donald F. Roszkowski.

Res.: 308 S. Locust St., 61777. Tel: 217-935-9242.

WARSAW, HANCOCK CO., SACRED HEART (1874), (German), [CEM] Rev. Michael Menner.
Res.: 245 S. 9th St., 62379. Tel: 217-256-3657.
Catechesis/Religious Program—Students 69.
Mission—St. Mary 560 Lakeview Ave., Hamilton, Hancock Co. 62341. Deacons William Gray; Eugene Heintz.

WASHBURN, WOODFORD CO., ST. ELIZABETH, [CEM] Rev. John M. Verrier.
Mailing Address: P.O. Box 219, Metamora, 61548. Tel: 309-367-4407 (St. Mary's Metamora); Fax: 309-367-9456.

WASHINGTON, TAZEWELL CO., ST. PATRICK'S (1941), Rev. Joseph P. Donton; Deacons Paul Neakrase; Joseph Venzon.
Res.: 705 E. Jefferson, 61571. Tel: 309-444-3524; Fax: 309-444-7070.
School—Tel: 309-444-4345; Fax: 309-444-7100. Mrs. Sharon Weiss, Prin. Lay Teachers 15; Students 229.
Catechesis/Religious Program—Tel: 309-444-4139. Sr. Rose Therese Sevigny, D.R.E. Students 166.

WEDRON, LA SALLE CO., ST. JOSEPH'S (1947), Rev. John G. Waugh.
Res.: Box 60, 60557. Tel: 815-433-2962.

WENONA, MARSHALL CO., ST. MARY'S (1867), [CEM] Rev. Stanley L. Deptula.
Res.: P.O. Box 486, 61377. Tel: 815-853-4558.
Mission—Immaculate Conception Mt. Falatine, La Salle Co.

WESTVILLE, VERMILION CO.
1—ST. MARY'S (1903), [CEM] Rev. David Erickson.
Res.: 231 N. State St., 61883. Tel: 217-267-3334; Fax: 217-267-3335.
School—225 N. State St., 61883. Tel: 217-267-7730; Fax: 217-267-3327. Mr. David Boyd, Prin. Lay Teachers 13; Students 138.
2—SS. PETER AND PAUL, Closed., For inquiries for parish records contact St. Mary's, Westville.

WOODHULL, HENRY CO., ST. JOHN'S (1889), (Swedish), [CEM 2] Rev. Eugene A. Radosevich.
Res.: 390 E. Highway Ave., P.O. Box 249, 61490. Tel: 309-334-2180; Fax: 309-334-3317.

WYOMING, STARK CO., ST. DOMINIC'S (1881), [CEM] Rev. Robert Rayson.
Res.: 303 Galena Ave., 61491. Tel: 309-695-4031.

Chaplains of Public Institutions

DANVILLE. *Veterans' Administration Hospital*, Tel: 217-442-8000. Rev. John Schultz, Military Chap.

DWIGHT. *Dwight Correctional Center*, Tel: 815-584-3522. Rev. James E. Rickey. Attended from St. Patrick's, Dwight.

LINCOLN. *Logan Correctional Center*, Tel: 217-947-2714; 309-244-8516. Vacant.

PONTIAC. *Illinois State Penitentiary*. Rev. William Gardner, Chap. Attended from St. Paul, Odell
Res.: 811 Hill St., 61704. Tel: 815-842-1150.

SHERIDAN. *Illinois Industrial School for Boys*. Rev. John G. Waugh, Chap.

Special Residence:
Rev. Msgr.—
Rohlfs, Steven, S.T.D., V.G.
Rev.—
Zube, Joseph

On Duty Outside the Diocese:
Revs.—
Amar, Mubarak, F.S.S.P. (LIN)
Collins, Patrick W., Archdiocese of Chicago
Guthrie, Raymond, Diocese of Rockford
Henseler, J. Thomas, Diocese of Springfield, IL
Hochstatter, Theodore
Myers, James E., 32 Middlefield Rd., Menlo Park, CA 94025.
Ohm, Edward U., (Military)
Smith, Jerome, Military
Virtue, William D., Diocese of Rockford
Vitaliano, Dominic J., (Military)

Graduate Studies:
Rev.—
Szydlik, Thomas, North American College Vatican City State.

On Leave:
Rev.—
Shea, Thomas, Rte. 1, Secor, 61771.

Retired:
Rev. Msgrs.—
Bolerasky, Peter E., P.O. Box 904, Streator, 61364.
Campbell, James F.
Duncan, Edward J.
Maloney, Thomas, Rt. 2, Box 85A, Lexington, 61753.
Morrissey, James L., 3509 W. Willow Knolls Rd., #F, 61615.
Motsett, C. Bourke, 1806 Washington, Danville, 61832.
Revs.—
Anderson, John Flattery, 2822 W. Heading Ave., 61604.
Bawiec, Edward J., 424 W. First St., Oglesby, 61348.
Brajkovich, Thomas R., 114 N. 2nd St., Chillicothe, 61523.
Bresnahan, Richard F., 2435 - 29th St., Moline, 61265.
Breuning, Walter, 514 Front St., Henry, 61537.
Bush, Edward, 920 S. Chicago St., Geneseo, 61254.
Carney, Edward, 1295 Millpoint Rd., East Peoria, 61611.
Colgan, Marvin, St. Joseph's, 401 9th St., Lacon, 61540.
Crawford, Richard E., 1414 S. Monroe, Streator, 61364.
Creager, Robert, 726 W. Jefferson, Ottawa, 61350.
Culleton, James P., 101 Park Ave., Morris, 60450.
Dietzen, John J., 2705 W.. Willow Lake Dr., #82, 61614.
Dietzen, Vincent E., 436 South St., Danville, 61832.
Divan, Anthony L., 4187 SE 23rd Court, Okeechobee, FL 34974.
Engels, Francis, P.O. Box 272, Kewanee, 61443.
Finnell, Eugene, 3785 Tyrrell Rd., Mackinaw, 61755
Fitzsimmons, Ricahrd, 830 Garfield Ave., Batavia, 60510.
Gaughran, John, Illinois Veterans Home, 1707 N. 12th St., Quincy, 62301.
Gildner, Leo H., 1523 Ottawa Ave.,, Ottawa, 61350.
Goodman, Norman, P.O. Box 1087, Pekin, 61554.
Hiland, George, 374 Benchop, Sebastian, FL 32958.
Hoffman, Robert, 343 Hickory Ct., Oakwood, 61858.
Hughes, Robert, 1103 Peppertree Ln., Eureka, 61530.
Jesiolowski, Sylvester E., 315 E. Second Ave., Box 21, Oglesby, 61348.
Kane, Eugene, 1831 County Rd. 2500 N., Thomasboro, 61878.
Karl, Charles E., 10904 N.Rhonda Way, Dunlap, 61525.
Kelly, Thomas F., W6881 W. Lake Shore Dr., Elkhorn, WI 53121.
King, John, P.O. Box 79, Starrucla, PA 18462.
Kolczaski, Richard, 1001 Monks Ave., Peru, 61354.
Krewer, Edward M., 1177 N. Gooding St., La Salle, 61301-1581.
Lee, Robert E., 1011 - 11th Ave., Moline, 61265.
Lukoskie, Raymond M., 2102 LeClaire St., Warsaw, 62379.
Malinowski, Stanley J., P.O. Box 307, Thomasboro, 61878.
Malcy, Dale, 1709 Char-Lu, Mendota, 61342.
Mann, Robert G., 19614 N. Star Ridge Dr., Sun City West, AZ 85375.
Morrissey, Jerome V., 207 S. Third, Wenona, 61377.
Mullen, Richard, 2414 Heritage Dr., Champaign, 61822.
Niemeyer, John, 132 Mobile-Land Ct., Bloomington, 61701.
O'Connor, John F., 407 N. Franklin, River Forest, 60305.
O'Connor, Robert D., 106 NE 4th St., Aledo, 61231.
O'Riley, Dennis H., 618 Greenbriar, North Vernon, IN 47765.
Prendergast, Robert E., P.O. Box 548, Kewanee, 61443.
Purcell, James, 19 Pinewood Park, Chillcothe, 61523.
Raney, Richard E., 685 Mantanzas Ct., Fort Myers Beach, FL 33931.
Reynolds, Robert E., Culbertson Gardens, 400 Logan, Apt.B-1, Rushville, 62681.
Roche, David, 728 E. Water St., Pontiac, 61764.
Russo, Nicodemus A., 613 Fenwick, San Antonio, TX 78239.
Ryan, Francis, 2223 W. Heading Ave., West Peoria, 61604.
Ryan, William A., 610 E. First St., Spring Valley, 61362.
Schladen, Robert, P.O. Box 6105, 61601.
Schroeder, George J., 16 Waverly Dr., Rock Island, 61201.
Sors, Vladimir, 308 S. Monroe St., Streator, 61364.
Thompson, George M., 3026 55th St., Moline, 61265.
Verhoye, Gerard A., 202 N. State, Box 603, Atkinson, 61235.
Wuellner, George E., St. Boniface Church, 416 County Rd. 1110 N., Seymour, 61875.

Permanent Deacons:
Mendoza, Elias A., St. Malachy, Rantoul
Adams, John L., St. Paul's, Macomb
Barr, Earl, Diocese of Phoenix
Beltramini, Robert, (On Leave of Absence)
Bott, Herman J., Holy Family, Danville
Breeden, Charles, St. Maria Goretti, Coal Valley
Briggs, James W., St. Anne's, E. Moline
Buczko, Stanley, St. Patrick, Havana
Burgess, Charles E., St. Hyacinth's, LaSalle
Burton, John, St. Matthew, Farmington
Carolan, Brendan, Holy Trinity, Bloomington
Cenek, Stephen, St. Ann, Peoria
Chaffee, Harley, St. Malachy, Genesco
Clark, William H., Immaculate Conception, Monmouth
Crutcher, Steven, St. Patrick of Merna
DeBernardis, Thomas, St. Vincent de Paul, Peoria
DeVooght, Dennis, Sacred Heart, Moline
Dockery-Jackson, Joseph, St. Pius X, Rock Island
Dosher, Jon, St. Patrick, Havana
Eaton, Francis, St. Thomas, Peoria Heights
Efinger, Donald, St. Thomas, Peoria Heights
England, Robert, (Retired)
Filzen, Bernard R., (Retired), St. Mark's Church, Peoria
Gaetz, Dale, Co. Admin. of Permanent Deacons, St. Mary, Lourdes
Gore, James, Holy Trinity, Bloomington
Granet, Timothy, St. Pius X, Rock Island
Gray, William, St. Mary Mission, Hamilton
Grimler, Richard, (Retired)
Hammel, Richard F., (Retired)
Hammond, Richard G., St. Anthony's Church, Bartonville
Haneghan, James, St. Patrick, Galesburg
Harris, Harley, St. Malachy, Geneseo
Hart, Henry, Holy Cross, Champaign
Heintz, Eugene, St. Mary Mission, Hamilton
Heipel, Robert, St. Mary of Lourdes, Metamora
Hietter, Earl E., St. Thomas, Peoria Heights
Honzel, Larry, St. Malachy, Genesco
Hozie, Jerome, St. Mary, Bloomington
Hunter, Roger, St. Jude, Dunlap
Jones, Robert, St. Patrick, Seneca
Kauth, Richard, (On Leave of Absence)
Kelley, William, (Retired), St. Thomas, Peoria Heights
Kettering, Jack M.
Koeppel, Joseph, St. Ann's, Peoria
Kovachevich, Victor, St. Mary, Canton
La Hood, Joseph, Holy Family, Peoria; Prison Ministry
Lalande, John, Oswego, NY
Landry, John, (Retired)
Leonard, John, St. John's, Bellflower
Levy, Matthew, St. John's. Rapids City
Lowry, Joseph, St. Mary of Lourdes, Metamora
Maduzia, Elias, St. Patrick, Urbans
Martin, Paul, St. Pius X, Rock Island
Maubach, James, Holy Family, Peoria
McClellan, William, (Retired)
Meyer, William, Immaculate Conception, Manito
Mock, John, St. Mary, Kewanee
Mohrbacher, Edward, Holy Cross, Champaign
Moran, Thomas, Blessed Sacrament, Morton
Mueller, Edward, Our Lady of the Lake, Mahomet
Murphy, John R., Immaculate Conception, Lacon
Murphy, John P., St. Louis, Princeton
Murphy, Patrick, Sacred Heart, Moline
Murphy, R. Daniel, Blessed Sacrament, Morton
Murray, Charles, St. Joseph, Pekin
Myers, Robert, St. Vincent de Paul, Peoria
Neakrase, Paul, St. Patrick, Washington
Oenning, Frank W., (On Leave of Absence)
Ohl, Harry, St. Philomena, Peoria
Petri, Darrel, St. Mary, Bloomington
Pinheiro, Edwin, Holy Cross, Champaign
Pogioli, Martin, St. Joseph, Pekin
Pomazal, Robert, St. Edward, Chillicothe
Rager, Ronald L., Valley Community Hospital, LaSalle
Randazzo, Frank G., St. Joseph, Rock Island
Rapach, Thomas, St. Jude's, Dunlap
Read, William, St. Monica, East Peoria, Asst. dio director Cursillo-Tec, Local Director Cursillo-Tec
Reid, Michael, (On Leave of Absence)
Reising, David, St. Philomena, Peoria
Robbins, Charles, St. Monica, E. Peoria
Roesch, Lewis, Holy Trinity, Bloomington
Sailer, Philip, St. Pius X, Rock Island
Sandoval, Henry, (On Leave of Absence)
Scanlan, Richard, St. Matthew, Champaign
Serangeli, Gregory, St. Edward's, Chillicothe, Co-Admin. of Permanent Deacons, Director of Evangelization, Diocese oc Peoria
Shipp, William, St. Malachy's, Rantoul
Simon, Nicholas, St. Anthony, Atkinson
Sims, Fred, St. Patrick, LaSalle
Skender, John, St. Mark, Peoria
Sloman, William, St. Francis Medical Center, Peoria
Slomian, Vincent, Holy Cross, Mendota
Smith, Frank, (Retired)
Smith, Marvin, St. Mary, Metamora

Smith, Richard, Holy Family, Danville
Swim, Russ, St. Mary, Moline
Tomlianovich, Louis A., St. Anthony's, Bartonville
Tyler, Raymond Toby, Holy Family, Peoria
Van Meltebeck, Martin, St. Mary, Kewanee
Van Wassenhove, Raymond, St. Mary, Kewanee
Vargas, Ausencio, Hispanic Ministry, St. Mary's Cathedral
Venzon, Joseph, St. Patrick, Washington
Verbeck, Walter, (Retired)
Vogelbaugh, Bob, Sacred Heart, Moline
Wachtel, Thomas, St. Malachy, Geneseo
Wagner, George, St. Mary's, Pontiac
Waldschmidt, Robert, St. Thomas, Peoria Heights
Wallace, Ray, St. Mary's, Pontiac
Whited, Ernie, St. Joseph, Pekin
Wilder, Mark, St. Joseph, Perkins
Zimmerman, Richard, St. Peter, Peoria
Zimmerman, Robert, St. Maria Goretti, Coal Valley
Zulz, Charles, St. Mary, Wenona

INSTITUTIONS LOCATED IN THE DIOCESE

[A] SEMINARIES, RELIGIOUS OR SCHOLASTICATES

PEORIA. *Rosminian Novitiate*, 2327 W. Heading Ave., 61604. Tel: 309-676-6341; Fax: 309-676-1087. Email: wtmic@juno.com. Revs. Paul Stiene, Novice Master; William T. Miller, I.C., Provincial Supr. Priests 2; Laymen 3; Total Staff 5.

PERU. *St. Bede Abbey and Academy* 61354. Tel: 815-223-3140; Fax: 815-223-8580. Email: stbede@ivnet.com. Web: www.st-bede.com. Benedictine Fathers and Brothers Priests 25; Brothers 6; Permanent Staff: Priests 11; Brothers 3; Sisters 1; Lay Staff 60.

Staff: Rev. Claude J. Peifer, O.S.B., Abbot; Very Rev. Sebastian Lewis, O.S.B., Prior, Jr. Master; Rev. Michael Calhoun, Sub-Prior; Rt. Revs. Marion E. Balsavich, O.S.B., (Resigned); Roger F. Corpus, O.S.B., (Resigned); Revs. Gabriel G. Bullock, O.S.B.; Harold L. Datzman, O.S.B.; Philip D. Davey, O.S.B.; Patrick A. Fennell, O.S.B.; Henry H. Fritz, O.S.B.; Dominic M. Garramone, O.S.B.; Kevin D. Gorman, O.S.B.; Placid W. Hatfield, O.S.B.; Ambrose B. Hessling, O.S.B.; Joseph J. Heyd, O.S.B.; William J. Kirk, O.S.B.; Sebastian C. Lewis, O.S.B.; Ronald L. Margherio, O.S.B.; Matthew C. Mazzuchelli, O.S.B.; Benedict B. McKean, O.S.B.; Dunstan R. Morrissey, O.S.B.; James M. Murray, O.S.B.; Arthur G. Schmit, O.S.B.; Stephen J. Souse, O.S.B.; Bros. Nathaniel Grossman, O.S.B.; George J. Matsouka, O.S.B.; Luke E. McLachlan, O.S.B.; Bede D. Schuda, O.S.B.; Anthony Shaughnessy, O.S.B.; Mark F. Strassburger, O.S.B.

[B] HIGH SCHOOLS, DIOCESAN AND INTER-PAROCHIAL

PEORIA. *Notre Dame High School* 5105 N. Sheridan, 61614. Tel: 309-691-8741; Fax: 309-691-0875. Web: peorianotredame.com. Patricia O'Connell, Prin.; Rev. Charles Klamut, Chap. Priests 1; Sisters 3; Lay Teachers 63; Students 889.

Peoria Notre Dame Scholarship Trust, 5105 N. Sheridan Rd., 61614. Rev. Msgr. William A. Watson, Pres.; Amy Vonachen, Vice Pres.; Carl Anderson, Sec.; Scott Cicciarelli, Treas.

BLOOMINGTON. *Central Catholic High School*, 712 N. Center St., 61701. Tel: 309-827-5373; Fax: 309-827-0173. Email: srutledge71@hotmail.com. Web: www.blmcchs.org. Mrs. Joy Allen, Prin.; Rev. Patrick Henehan. Priests 1; Lay Teachers 29; Students 326.

CHAMPAIGN. *High School of St. Thomas More*, 3901 N. Mattis, 61822. Tel: 217-352-7210; Fax: 217-352-7213. Email: admin@hs-stm.org. Web: www.hs-stm.org. Tim Millage, Prin.; Rev. Joseph Dondanville, Chap. Priests 1; Lay Teachers 25; Students 222.

DANVILLE. *Schlarman High School* 61832. Tel: 217-442-2725; Fax: 217-442-0293. Email: pstitt@schlarman.com broderic@schlarman.com. Web: www.schlarman.com. Dr. Raymond Broderick, Admin.; Rev. Anthony Lee. Lay Teachers 18; Students 214.

OTTAWA. *Marquette High School*, 1000 Paul St., 61350. Tel: 815-433-0125; Fax: 815-433-2632. Email: xavmhs@roe35.k12.il.us. Web: marquettehs.com. Ronald Spandet, Prin.; Rev. Peter Pilon, Chap. Priests 3; Lay Teachers 19; Students 246.

ROCK ISLAND. *Alleman High School*, 1103 40th St., 61201. Tel: 309-786-7793; Fax: 309-786-7834. Email: allemanhs@mchsi.com. Web: www.allemanhighschool.org. Colin Letendre, Prin.; Revs. Daniel J. Mirabelli, C.S.V., Dir. of Devel.; Michael J. Andrejek, Chap. Priests 2; Sisters 5; Deacons 2; Lay Teachers 24; Students 490.

[C] HIGH SCHOOLS, PRIVATE

PERU. *St. Bede Academy* 61354. Tel: 815-223-3140; Fax: 815-223-8580. Web: www.st-bede.com. Benedictine Fathers and Brothers Benedictine Priests 5; Brothers 2; Lay Teachers 19; Students 302; Full-time Teachers: Priests 1; Sisters 1; Lay Teachers 17.

Teachers: Rev. Philip Davey, O.S.B., Supt.; Mrs. Michelle Mershon, Prin.; Revs. Stephen J. Souse, O.S.B., Registrar; Michael M. Calhoun, O.S.B., Chap.; Bro. Bede Schuda, O.S.B., CFO; Mr. Bernie Moore, Asst. Prin.; Mr. Robert Leclercq, Dir. Guidance; Mr. Thomas McGunnigal, Business Mgr.

[D] ELEMENTARY SCHOOLS INTER-PAROCHIAL

LA SALLE. *La Salle Catholic School*, 1055 Sixth St., 61301. Tel: 815-223-5088; Fax: 815-223-5366. Email: laser2@insight.com. Web: www.asd.com. Sr. Alice Ann Harcharik, O.S.F., Prin. Sisters 1; Lay Teachers 16; Students 159.

MOLINE. *Seton Catholic School*, 1320-16th Ave., 61265. Tel: 309-764-5418; Fax: 309-762-0545. Email: jbarrett@setonschool.com. Mrs. Jane Barrett, Prin. Sisters 1; Lay Teachers 35; Students 602.

ROCK ISLAND. *Jordan Catholic School of Rock Island, Inc.* Facilities at St. Ambrose, St. Pius, and Sacred Heart. , 2901-24th St., P.O. Box 3490, 61204-3490. Tel: 309-793-7350; Fax: 309-793-7361. Web: www.jordanschool.com; home.revealed.netJCSoffice/index.html. Daniel Lievens, Admin. Directs the Elementary School System for the Rock Island-Milan area, operating facilities at Sacred Heart, St. Pius X. Parishes in Rock Island and St. Ambrose in Milan. Lay Teachers 27; Students 460.

Commission on Education for Jordan Catholic School, P.O. Box 3490, 61204-3490. Tel: 309-793-7350; Fax: 309-793-7361.

WEST PEORIA. *Immaculate Conception Pre-Kindergarten*, 2408 W. Heading Ave., 61604-5096. Tel: 309-674-6168; Fax: 309-674-2006. Email: infosf@yahoo.com. Web: osfsisterswpeoria.org. Sr. M. Elaine Haertjens, O.S.F., Dir. Sponsored by the Sisters of St. Francis of the Immaculate Conception Students 10.

[E] RELIGIOUS EDUCATION CENTERS, PRIVATE

PERU. *Sisters of St. Benedict*, 26 W. U.S. Hwy. 6, 61354. Tel: 815-223-6741. Sisters Margaret Suerth, O.S.B., (Retired); Mary Core, O.S.B., St. Bede Academy.

[F] CATHOLIC SOCIAL SERVICE OF PEORIA

WEST PEORIA. *Catholic Social Service of Peoria*, 2900 W. Heading Ave., 61604. Tel: 309-671-5700; Fax: 309-674-1664. Email: jknapp@ccdop.org. Ms. Peggy A. Arizzi, Exec Dir.; Ms. Tricia C. Fox, Assoc. Dir. Total Institutional Staff 33; Other Staff 625; Total Assisted 33,658.

Catholic Charities West, Formerly Catholic Social Services West 2900 W. Heading Ave., 61604. Tel: 309-636-8000; Fax: 309-674-1664.

Foster Home Programs Tel: 309-636-8000; Fax: 309-671-1046.

Catholic Charities Institutions, Formerly Catholic Social Services Institutions 2900 W. Heading Ave., 61604.

Guardian Angel Home Tel: 309-671-5700; Fax: 309-673-3405.

Jesu Children's Enrichment Center Tel: 309-686-7550; Fax: 309-671-8905.

Peoria Community Area Project/LaCasa Center, 1406 W. Antoinette St., 61605. Tel: 309-637-2600; Fax: 309-637-6327. Family Counseling, Adoption Services, Senior Citizens In-Home Counseling, Women's Counseling & Support Services, Cabrini Maternity Services.

Catholic Charities Counseling, Formerly Catholic Social Service Counseling 413 N.E. Monroe, 61603. Tel: 309-671-5720; Fax: 309-671-0257.

Catholic Charities Branch Offices:
603 N. Center St., Bloomington, 61701. Tel: 309-829-6307; Fax: 309-829-3254.
502 S. Morris Ave., Bloomington, 61701. Tel: 309-820-7617; Fax: 309-820-7617.
1315A Curt Dr., Champaign, 61820. Tel: 217-352-5179; Fax: 217-352-0318.
102 N. Robinson, Danville, 61832. Tel: 217-443-1772; Fax: 217-443-1701.
292 N. Chambers, Galesburg, 61401. Tel: 309-342-1136; Fax: 309-342-1891.
542 Crosat, LaSalle, 61301. Tel: 815-223-4007; Fax: 815-224-4550.
310 S. Logan, Lincoln, 62656. Tel: 217-732-3771; Fax: 217-735-1738.
310 E. Washington, Macomb, 61455-0355. Tel: 309-833-1791; Fax: 309-836-1462.
303 S. 7th St., Pekin, 61554. Tel: 309-347-6108, Ext. 220.
823 20th St., Rock Island, 61201. Tel: 309-786-0770; Fax: 309-786-3856.

Fort Armstrong, 1900 3rd Ave., Rock Island, 61201. Tel: 309-788-9581; Fax: 309-788-9608.

Catholic Charities Outreach Offices:
Watseka Outreach Office, 1120 Walnut St., Watseka, 60970. Tel: 815-432-6120.
Geneseo Outreach Office, 217 N. Russell, Geneseo, 61254. Tel: 309-944-3165.
Kewanee Outreach Office, 406 W. Central Blvd., Kewanee, 61443. Tel: 309-852-4549.
Pontiac Outreach Office, 501 N. Chicago, Pontiac, 61764. Tel: 815-844-3629.
Canton Outreach Office, 162 N. Chestnut, Canton, 61520. Tel: 309-647-5014; Fax: 309-647-8287.

[G] CHILDREN'S HOMES

WEST PEORIA. *Catholic Charities Foster Care Program*, Formerly Catholic Social Service Foster Care Program, 2900 W. Heading Ave., 61604. Tel: 309-636-8000; Fax: 309-671-1046. Web: cssdop.org. Ms. Peggy A. Arizzi, Exec. Dir.; Ms. Trish Fox, Asst. Exec. Dir. Clients placed in Foster Care during year 1,338; Total Staff 215.

Guardian Angel Home, 2900 W. Heading Ave., 61604. Tel: 309-636-7500; Fax: 309-673-3405. Web: ccdop.org. Peggy Arizzi, Exec. Dir. Treatment for Abused and Neglected Youth. Staff 27; Capacity 16; Served 26.

[H] DAY CARE CENTERS

PEORIA. *South Side Catholic Child Care Center*, 1010 W. Johnson St., 61605. Tel: 309-674-7340; Fax: 309-682-2065. Ollie Bracket, Dir. Children 103; Total Staff 15.

MOLINE. *Pedals Preschool-Daycare Inc.*, 1602 13th St., 61265-3901. Tel: 309-797-8279; Fax: 309-757-5502. Email: pedals@qconline.com. Karyn Fritzsche, Dir. & Contact Person.

WEST PEORIA. *Jesu Children's Enrichment Centers*, 2900 W. Heading Ave., 61604. Tel: 309-671-5660. Web: ccdop.org. Staff 24; Capacity 158; Served 165.

[I] GENERAL HOSPITALS

PEORIA. *Saint Francis' Medical Center*, 530 N.E. Glen Oak Ave., 61637. Tel: 309-655-2000; Fax: 309-655-2347. Email: keith.e.steffen@osfhealthcare.org. Mr. Keith Steffen, Admin.; Sr. M. Ildefonsa, O.S.F., Supr.; Rev. Michael Bliss, Dir. Bed Capacity 550; Patients Assisted Annually 740,448; Staff 3,703.

OSF Healthcare System, 800 N.E. Glen Oak Ave., 61603-3200. Tel: 309-699-2852; Fax: 309-655-6869. Web: www.osfhealthcare.org. Total Annually Assisted 1,576,400; Total Staff 10,568; Bed Capacity 1,556.

OSF Healthcare Foundation, 800 N.E. Glen Oak Ave., 61603-3200. Tel: 309-655-4817. Mr. Kevin Schoeplein, Pres.

BLOOMINGTON. *OSF St. Joseph Medical Center*, 2200 E. Washington, 61701. Tel: 309-662-3311; Fax: 309-662-7143. Web: www.osfstjoseph.org. Mr. Kenneth J. Natzke, Admin. Bed Capacity 182; Annually Assisted 133,729; Total Staff 978.

DANVILLE. *Provena United Samaritans Medical Center*, 812 N. Logan, 61832. Tel: 217-443-5000; Fax: 217-443-1965. Web: provenausmc.com. William A. McDonald, Admin.

Legal Title: *Provena Hospitals.* Sisters 2; Capacity 308; Patients Assisted Annually 231,053; Staff 1,103.

Provena Samaritan Health Partners

GALESBURG. *St. Mary Medical Center*, 3333 N. Seminary St., 61401-1299. Tel: 309-344-3161; Fax: 309-344-9494. Web: osfhealthcare.org. Sr. M. Joan, O.S.F., Supr.; Deacon Robert Myers, Pastoral Care Dir. Sisters of the Third Order of St. Francis 1; Patients assisted annually 45,000; Total Staff 576.

The Galesburg St. Mary Medical Center Foundation, 3333 N. Seminary St., 61401.

PONTIAC. *OSF St. James-John W. Albrecht Medical Center*, 2500 W. Reynolds, 61764. Tel: 815-842-2828; Fax: 815-842-4912. Web: www.osfsaintjames.org. David T. Ochs, Admin.; Deacon George Wagner, Chap. Sisters of the Third Order of St. Francis 5; Capacity 47; Patients Assisted Annually 73,544; Total Staff 390.

SPRING VALLEY. *St. Margaret's Hospital*, 600 E. First St., 61362. Tel: 815-664-5311; Fax: 815-664-1335. Email: admin@aboutsmh.org. Web:

www.aboutsmh.org. Timothy Muntz, Pres.; Sr. Mary Jo Zacher, Pastoral Care Dir. Sisters of Mary of the Presentation 3; Bed Capacity 123; Patients Assisted Annually 220,321; Total Staff 625.

STREATOR. *St. Mary's Hospital*, 111 E. Spring St., 61364. Tel: 815-673-2311; Fax: 815-673-4541. Web: www.stmaryshospital.org. Sr. Laura Northcraft, Pastoral Care Dir.; Mark S. O'Halla, Exec. Vice Pres. Hospital Sisters of St. Francis. Sisters 1; Patients Assisted Annually 44,308; Bed Capacity 251; Bassinets 28; Total Staff 511.

URBANA. *Provena Covenant Medical Center*, 1400 W. Park St., 61801. Tel: 217-337-2000; Fax: 217-337-4541. Email: dianehfriedman@provenahealth.com. Web: www.provenacovenant.org. Sr. Agnes Cunningham, S.S.C.M., Supr.; Mark S. Wiener, Pres. & CEO; Sr. Mary Robert Morton, S.S.C.M., Dir. & Pastoral Min.; Vera Duncanson, Pastoral Min.; Ginny Conron, Pastoral Min.; Revs. Peter Dyck, Pastoral Min.; Jerry Nichols, Pastoral Min.; Jeff McPike, Pastoral Min.

Legal Title: *Provena Covenant Medical Center.* Sisters 8; Capacity 280; Patients Assisted Annually 93,201; Total Staff 906.

[J] SPECIAL HOSPITALS AND SANATORIA

LACON. *St. Joseph's Nursing Home*, 401 Ninth St., 61540. Tel: 309-246-2175; Fax: 309-246-3609. Email: stjosephs@stjosephs-lacon.om. Web: stjoseph-lacon.com. Mr. Thomas Becher, Admin.; Rev. Harold F. Schmitt, Chap. Daughters of St. Francis of Assisi Sisters 10; Bed Capacity 93; Total Staff 105.

PEORIA HEIGHTS. *Saint Clare Home*, 5533 N. Galena Rd., 61614. Tel: 309-682-5428. Sr. Mary Dries, O.S.F., Pastoral Care Dir.; Ms. Lisa J. Denning, Admin. Sponsored and owned by the Sisters of the Third Order of St. Francis., Skilled nursing facility. Total Staff 94; Bed capacity 98.

ROCK ISLAND. *St. Anthony's Continuing Care Center*, 767 30th St., 61201. Tel: 309-788-7631; Fax: 309-788-9823. Bed Capacity 119; Total Staff 120.

[K] HOMES FOR AGED

PEORIA. *St. Augustine Manor*, 1301 N.E. Glendale Ave., 61603. Tel: 309-674-7069; Fax: 309-494-6547. Jeri Myers, Admin. Residents 81; Total Staff 34; Total Assisted 115.

St. Joseph's Home of Peoria, 2223 W. Heading Ave., West Peoria, 61604. Tel: 309-673-7425; Fax: 309-673-7430. Email: sjhp@mtco.com. Web: www.stjjome.org. Rev. Frank Ryan, Chap.; Sr. Mary Barbara Buckley, O.S.F., Interim Admin. Sisters of St. Francis of the Immaculate Conception Sisters 8; Residents 144; Retired Sisters 6; Total Assisted 151; Total Staff 110. In Res. Rev. Francis J. Ryan.

[L] RETREAT HOUSES

HENRY. *Christ the King Retreat Center - Diocese of Peoria*, Box 165, 61537. Tel: 309-364-3084. Rev. John M. Verrier, Admin.; Deacon Frederick J. Kruse, Dir. Priests 1; Total in Residence 2; Total Staff 3.

[M] MONASTERIES AND RESIDENCES FOR PRIESTS AND BROTHERS

PEORIA. *Congregation of St. John*, 1116 W. College, 61606-1728. Tel: 309-674-0208; Fax: 309-497-3759. Email: stjohn@bobcat.bradley.edu. Web: www.stjean.com. Revs. Antoine Thomas, Prior; John Therese Creus, Prior; Bros. John Mary Ignatius Crawley; Nathan Cromly; Michael Guadalupe Mozqueda.

GEORGETOWN. *La Salette Missionaries, c/o St. Isaac Jogues Parish*, 109 W. Seventh St., 61846. Tel: 217-662-6708. Revs. John Paninski, M.S., c/o St. Issac Joques Parish, Georgetown; Thaddeus Plawny, M.S.

Legal Title: *La Salette Fathers, Inc.* Priests 2; Total Staff 2.

PRINCEVILLE. *St. Joseph Priory and Novitiate*, 11223 W. Legion Hall Rd., 61559. Tel: 309-385-1193; Fax: 309-385-1830. Email: stjohn@ocslink.com. Web: www.st.jean.com. Revs. Joseph Mary Brown, F.J.; Didier-Marie, F.J., Novice Master. Priests 2; Professed Brothers 5; Novices 4; Postulants 1.

[N] CONVENTS AND RESIDENCES FOR SISTERS

PEORIA. *St. Francis Medical Center Hospital - Convent*, 740 N. Glen Oak Ave., 61603. Tel: 309-655-4014; 309-655-2083; 309-655-2044; Fax: 309-655-2347. Email: sisterildefonsa@osfhealthcare.org. Sr. M. Ildefonsa Richter, O.S.F., Supr. The Sisters of the Third Order of St. Francis 6.

Immaculate Conception Convent Tel: 309-674-6168; Fax: 309-674-2006. Email: imfosf@yahoo.com. Web: osfsisterswpeoria.org. 2408 W. Heading Ave., West Peoria, 61604-5096. Tel: 309-674-6168; Fax: 309-674-2006. Sr. Irene Marie Fritch, O.S.F., Pres.; Rev. Msgr. James F. Campbell, Chap. (Retired). Motherhouse of the Sisters of St. Francis of the Immaculate Conception. Sisters 46; Professed Sisters 50.

Missionaries of Charity Convent, 506 Hancock St., 61603. Tel 309-674-7160. Sr. M. Sumati, Supr. Sisters 4; Total Assisted 17,000; Total Volunteer Staff 2.

The Poor Clares Tel: 309-682-3182; Fax: 309-682-3182. Email: paxbonum@aol.com. Web: www.poorclare.org/rockford. Sisters 4.

Our Lady of the Angels Convent, 3432 W. Baskin Ridge, 61604. Tel: 309-682-3182; Fax: 309-682-3182.

EAST PEORIA. *Motherhouse, The Sisters of the Third Order of St. Francis*, 1175 Saint Francis Ln., 61611-1299. Tel: 309-699-7215. Sr. Mary Ellen Flannery, O.S.F., Major Supr. Sisters in Residence 32; Total Sisters in Community 52.

Mt. Alverno Novitiate, 1175 Saint Francis Ln., 61611-1299. Tel: 309-699-9313. Email: vocation.info@osfhealthcare.org. Web: www.osfhealthcare.org. Rev. Msgr. Rick J. Oberch, Chap. Novitiate of The Sisters of the Third Order of St. Francis Sisters 2; Novices 2.

LACON. *St. Joseph Motherhouse and Novitiate* 61540. Tel: 309-246-2175; Fax: 309-246-2708. Email: spirit@joysta.com. Sr. M. Vaclava Ballon, Prov. Supr. Congregation of the Daughters of St. Francis of Assisi - American Province. Sisters 13; Sisters in Community (Professed) 28.

OTTAWA. *Sisters of Mercy of the Americas*, 306 Canal St., Apt. 516, 61350. Tel: 815-433-1357. Sisters 1; Total Staff 1.

PONTIAC. *Handmaids of Nazareth*, St. Mary Convent, 111 E. Howard St., 61764-1917. Tel: 815-842-1890; Fax: 815-842-1582. Email: srdonnamarie@hotmail.com. P.O. Box 507, Pittsford, NY 14534. Sisters in Residence 5.

PRINCEVILLE. *Sisters of St. John*, 11227 W. Legion Hall Rd., 61559. Fax: 309-385-2550. Sr. Miriam, Supr. Sisters 13.

ROCK ISLAND. *St. Mary Monastery, Motherhouse and Novitiate*, 2100-88th Ave., W., 61201-7649. Tel: 309-283-2100; Fax: 309-283-2200 Email: benedictines@stmarymonastery.org. Web: www.stmarymonastery.org. Sr. Ruth Ksycki, O.S.B., Prioress. Benedictine Sisters of Pontifical Jurisdiction Sisters in Community 64.

STREATOR. *Franciscan Sisters*, 905 S. Park St., 61364. Tel: 815-673-1259; Fax: 815-673-1259. Web: www.springfieldfranciscans.org. *St. Francis Convent*, LaVerna Rd., P.O. Box 19431, Springfield, 62794-9431.

WEST PEORIA. *Mother of Peace Home*, 2223 W. Heading Ave., 61604. Tel: 309-673-4657. Total Residents 7; Total Staff 15.

[O] NEWMAN CENTERS

PEORIA. *Newman Foundation at Bradley University & Illinois Central College* 1116 W. College Ave., 61606-1728. Tel: 309-674-0208 (Office); Fax: 309-497-3759. Email: bradleynewmancenter@hotmail.com. Web: www.geocities.com/bradleynewmancenter/. Gina McKenna, Office Mgr.; Revs. Antoine Thomas; John Therese Creus; Bro. Nathan Cromly. Congregation of St. John Total Residence 4.

CHAMPAIGN. *St. John's Catholic Student Chapel and Newman Foundation, University of Illinois* 604 E. Armory Ave., 61820. Tel: 217-344-1266; Fax: 217-344-6606. Email: webmaster@newmanfoundation.org. Web: newmanfoundation.org. Rev. Msgrs. Edward J. Duncan, Emeritus (Retired); Stuart W. Swetland, S.T.D., Dir.; Revs. Thomas Holloway; Brian L. Herlocker; Fortunatus Bijura; Johndamascene Zilimu. Total in Residence 6; Total Staff 6; Newman Center Residence 339; Newman Center Staff 95.

MACOMB. *St. Francis of Assisi Newman Center* 1401 W. University Dr., 61455. Tel: 309-837-3988; Fax: 309-837-4179. Email: fatherKH@aol.com or newman@macomb.com. Web: www.wiunewmancenter.com. Rev. Kenneth J. Hummel.

NORMAL. *St. Robert Bellarmine Newman Center, Illinois State Univ., Wesleyan Univ., Heartland Community & Eu* 501 S. Main St., 61761-2996. Tel: 309-452-5046; Fax: 309-452-3845. Email: gccaste@ilstu.edu. Rev. Gary C. Caster, Chap. Total Staff 4.

ROCK ISLAND. *Augustana College Catholic Campus Ministry* 61201. Tel: 309-794-7272. Email: AMNMR@Augustana.edu. Sr. Marilyn Ring, O.S.B. Staff 1.

[P] PERSONAL PRELATURES

URBANA. *Opus Dei* Prelature of the Holy Cross and Opus Dei , Lincoln Green Foundation, 715 W. Michigan Ave., 61801. Tel: 217-367-6650; Fax: 217-344-2987. Email: mseelinger@yodersoftware.com. Web: www.opusdei.org. In Res. Rev. Barry Cole.

[Q] MISCELLANEOUS

PEORIA. *Archbishop Fulton J. Sheen Foundation*, P.O. Box 728, 61652-0728. Tel: 309-671-1550; Fax: 309-677-6798. Rev. Msgr. Richard Soseman.

Franciscan Spirituality and Resource Center, 2408 W. Heading Ave., 61604. Tel: 309-674-8432; Fax: 309-674-2006. Sisters Betty Jean Haverback, O.S.F., Contact Person; Diane VandeVoorde, O.S.F., Contact Person.

Northside Office of Christian Response 1825 N.E. Adams St., 61603. Tel: 309-637-0322; 800-637-5508; Fax: 309-637-0307. Mr. John Truitt, Dir. Total Assisted 139; Total Staff 1.

Notre Dame High School of Peoria, Inc. 61656.

SHARE Food Program of Central Illinois, Inc., 1825 N.E. Adams St., 61603. Tel: 309-637-0282; 800-637-5508; Fax: 309-637-0307. Total Staff 5; Assisted: 156,000.

St. Vincent De Paul Society, 3612 N.E. Monroe St., 61603. Tel: 800-637-5508; Fax: 309-637-0307. John and Mary Truitt, Co-Pres. Diocesan Council and Particular Council of Peoria.

ALEDO. *Family of Mary Coredemptrix*, 1331 230th St., 61231. Tel: 309-372-4654; Fax: 309-372-4462. Email: triumph@winco.net.

BLOOMINGTON. *Central Catholic High School of Bloomington, Inc.* 61799.

Homes of Hope, Inc.

Homes of Hope, 1570 Hunt Dr., Normal, 61761.

CHAMPAIGN. *The High School of St. Thomas More of Champaign, Inc.* 61826.

DANVILLE. *Schlarman High School of Danville, Inc.* 61834.

LASALLE. *Starved Rock-LaSalle Manor, Inc.*, 1135 S. 10th St., 61301. Tel: 815-223-0557; Fax: 815-223-0559. Ms. Susan Dillberg, Contact Person.

LACON. *St. Francis of Assisi Fund, NFP*, 507 N. Prairie St., 61540-1152. Tel: 309-246-2175. Sr. M. Vaclava Ballon, Contact Person.

Religious Sisters Aid, NFP, 507 N. Prairie St., 61540-1152. Tel: 309-246-2175. Email: spirit@joysta.com. Sr. M. Vaclava Ballon, Contact Person.

MOLINE. *The Order of the Legion of Little Souls of the Merciful Heart of Jesus*, 428 39th St., 61265-1641. Tel: 309-797-8491; Fax: 309-736-5570. Email: littlesoul@littlesouls.org. Web: www.littlesouls.org. Teresa I. Huyten, Dir.; Rev. Michael L. Menner, Diocesan Chap.

OTTAWA. *Marquette High School of Ottawa, Inc.* 61350.

ROCK ISLAND. *Alleman High School of Rock Island, Inc.* 61299.

St. Anthony's Continuing Care Center, 767 30th St., 61201. Tel: 309-788-7631; Fax: 309-488-9823. Email: Eileen.moseley@bhshealthcare.org. Web: www.bhshealth.org. Dale M. Thompson, Pres. & CEO. Sponsored by: The Sisters of St. Scholastica Monastery, Sponsor: Benedictine Health System

RELIGIOUS INSTITUTES OF MEN REPRESENTED IN THE DIOCESE

For further details refer to the corresponding bracketed number in the Religious Institutes of Men or Women section.

[]—*Apostles of Jesus - Peoria Community*

[0200]—*Benedictine Monks* (St. Bede Abbey)—O.S.B.

[]—*Congregation of St. John*—F.J.

[1320]—*Clerics of St. Viator*—C.S.V.

[0480]—*Conventual Franciscans*—O.F.M.Conv

[0520]—*Franciscan Friars* (Prov. of St. John the Baptist)—O.F.M.

[0300]—*Institute of Charity* (Rome, Italy)—I.C.

[0720]—*The Missionaries of Our Lady of La Salette*—M.S.

RELIGIOUS INSTITUTES OF WOMEN REPRESENTED IN THE DIOCESE

[0230]—*Benedictine Sisters of Pontifical Jurisdiction*—O.S.B.

[0920]—*Congregation of the Daughters of St. Francis of Assisi, (American Prov.)*—D.S.F.

[2100]—*Congregation of the Humility of Mary*—C.H.M.

[1920]—*Congregation of the Sisters of the Holy Cross*—C.S.C.

[1730]—*Congregation of the Sisters of the Third Order of St. Francis, Oldenburg, IN*—O.S.F.

[1710]—*Congregation of the Third Order of St. Francis of Mary Immaculate, Joliet, IL*—O.S.F.

[0760]—*Daughters of Charity of St. Vincent de Paul*—D.C.

[1070-03]—*Dominican Sisters*—O.P.

[1070-10]—*Dominican Sisters*—O.P.
[1450]—*Franciscan Sisters of the Sacred Heart*—O.S.F.
[1770]—*Hospital Sisters of the Third Order of St. Francis*—O.S.F.
[2575]—*Institute of the Sisters of Mercy of the Americas*—R.S.M.
[2710]—*Missionaries of Charity*—M.C.
[3230]—*Poor Handmaids of Jesus Christ*—P.H.J.C.
[2970]—*School Sisters of Notre Dame*—S.S.N.D.
[1680]—*School Sisters of St. Francis*—O.S.F.
[3520]—*Servants of the Holy Heart of Mary*—S.S.C.M.
[0430]—*Sisters of Charity of the Blessed Virgin Mary*—B.V.M.
[0660]—*Sisters of Christian Charity*—S.C.C.
[2450]—*Sisters of Mary of the Presentation*—S.M.P.
[3360]—*Sisters of Providence of Saint Mary-of-the-Woods, Indiana*—S.P.
[1540]—*Sisters of Saint Francis, Clinton, Iowa*—O.S.F.
[1705]—*The Sisters of St. Francis of Assisi*—O.S.F.
[1580]—*Sisters of St. Francis of the Immaculate Conception*—O.S.F.
[3840]—*Sisters of St. Joseph of Corondelet*—C.S.J.
[]—*Sisters of the Community of St. John*
[1820]—*Sisters of the Third Order of St. Francis (East Peoria, Illinois)*—O.S.F.

CEMETERIES/CEMETARY ASSOCIATIONS

PEORIA. *Catholic Cemetery Association of Peoria, IL*, 412 N.E. Madison Ave., 61603. Tel: 309-674-2760. Rev. Msgr. Steven P. Rohlfs, S.T.D., V.G. Operates St. Mary's Cemetery, St. Joseph's Cemetery and Resurrection Cemetery in Peoria.

BLOOMINGTON. *Holy Cross Cemetery Association of Bloomington, IL*, Tel: 309-829-2197.

DANVILLE. *Resurrection Catholic Cemetery Association of Danville, IL*, Tel: 217-431-5100.

FARMER CITY. *St. Joseph Cemetery Association of Farmer City, IL*, Tel: 309-928-3855.

GALESBURG. *St. Joseph's Cemetery Association of Galesburg, IL*, Tel: 309-342-1913.

PEKIN. *Catholic Cemetery Association of Pekin, IL*, Tel: 309-347-6109.

ROCK ISLAND. *Calvary Cemetery Association of Rock Island, IL*, Tel: 309-788-6197; 309-764-1928.

NECROLOGY

† Hettinger, Rev. Msgr. Clarence J.—Died Nov. 19, 2003
† O'Dea, Rev. Msgr. Joseph J.—Died July 13, 2003
† Blough, E. C.—Died Jan. 12, 2003
† Graves, Joseph A.—Died Dec. 29, 2002
† Harbert, William—Died April 25, 2003
† Hettinger, Paul W.—Died April 5, 2003
† Mahoney, John A.—Died Nov. 23, 2003

Archdiocese of Philadelphia

(Archidioecesis Philadelphiensis)

His Eminence

ANTHONY CARDINAL BEVILACQUA, D.D., M.A., J.C.D., J.D.

Archbishop Emeritus of Philadelphia; ordained June 11, 1949; appointed Titular Bishop of Aquaealba and Auxiliary Bishop of Brooklyn October 7, 1980; consecrated November 24, 1980; appointed Bishop of Pittsburgh October 7, 1983; installed December 12, 1983; installed Archbishop of Philadelphia February 11, 1988; Created Cardinal Priest June 28, 1991; retired July 15, 2003. *Office: 100 E. Wynnewood Rd., Wynnewood, PA 19096.*

Most Reverend

MARTIN N. LOHMULLER, D.D.

Retired Auxiliary Bishop of Philadelphia; ordained June 3, 1944; appointed Auxiliary Bishop of Philadelphia and Titular Bishop of Ramsbury February 11, 1970; consecrated April 2, 1970; retired October 11, 1994. *Res.: Villa Maria House of Studies,* 1140 King Rd., Immaculata, PA 19345.

Most Reverend

LOUIS A. DESIMONE, D.D.

Retired Auxiliary Bishop of Philadelphia; ordained May 10, 1952; appointed Auxiliary Bishop of Philadelphia and Titular Bishop of Cillio June 27, 1981; consecrated August 12, 1981; retired April 2, 1997. *Res.: St. Justin Martyr Rectory,* 1222 Hagysford Rd., Narberth, PA 19072.

His Eminence

JUSTIN CARDINAL RIGALI, J.C.D.

Archbishop of Philadelphia; ordained April 25, 1961; appointed Archbishop of Roman Curia June 8, 1985; installed September 14, 1985; appointed Archbishop of St. Louis January 25, 1994; installed March 16, 1994; appointed Archbishop of Philadelphia July 15, 2003; installed October 7, 2003; Created Cardinal Priest October 21, 2003. *Office: 222 North 17th St., Philadelphia, PA 19103.*

The Chancery: 222 N. 17th St., Philadelphia, PA 19103-1299. Tel: 215-587-4538; Fax: 215-587-3907.

Web: www.archdiocese-phl.org

Email: chancery@adphila.org

Most Reverend

ROBERT P. MAGINNIS, D.D., V.G.

Auxiliary Bishop of Philadelphia; ordained May 13, 1961; appointed Auxiliary Bishop of Philadelphia and Titular Bishop of Siminina January 24, 1996; consecrated March 11, 1996. *Res.: St. Colman Rectory,* 11 Simpson Rd., Ardmore, PA 19003-2812. Tel: 610-642-0545.

Most Reverend

MICHAEL F. BURBIDGE, D.D., ED.D., V.G.

Auxiliary Bishop of Philadelphia; ordained May 19, 1984; appointed Auxiliary Bishop of Philadelphia and Titular Bishop of Cluain Iraird June 21, 2002; consecrated September 5, 2002. *Res.: St. Charles Borromeo Seminary, Overbrook,* 100 E. Wynnewood Rd., Wynnewood, PA 19096. Tel: 610-785-6200.

DIOCESE ESTABLISHED APRIL 8, 1808.

Square Miles 2,183.

Erected an Archdiocese February 12, 1875.

Comprises all the City and County of Philadelphia, and the Counties of Bucks, Chester, Delaware and Montgomery in the State of Pennsylvania.

Patrons of the Diocese: I. Immaculate Conception B.V.M., December 8; II. Saints Peter and Paul, Apostles, June 29. This Archdiocese was solemnly consecrated to the Sacred Heart of Jesus on the Feast of Saint Teresa of Avila, October 15, 1873. On May 23, 1952, the Archdiocese of Philadelphia was solemnly consecrated to the Immaculate Heart of Mary at the Shrine of Our Lady of Fatima, Portugal.

For legal titles of parishes and archdiocesan institutions, consult The Chancery.

STATISTICAL OVERVIEW

Personnel	
Cardinals	1
Retired Cardinals	1
Auxiliary Bishops	2
Retired Bishops	2
Abbots	1
Retired Abbots	1
Priests: Diocesan Active in Diocese	521
Priests: Diocesan Active Outside Diocese	34
Priests: Diocesan in Foreign Missions	1
Priests: Retired, Sick or Absent	168
Number of Diocesan Priests	724
Religious Priests in Diocese	372
Total Priests in Diocese	1,096
Extern Priests in Diocese	35
Ordinations:	
Diocesan Priests	9
Religious Priests	2
Transitional Deacons	5
Permanent Deacons	1
Permanent Deacons in Diocese	210
Total Brothers	122
Total Sisters	3,366
Parishes	
Parishes	279
With Resident Pastor:	
Resident Diocesan Priests	258
Resident Religious Priests	21
Missions	7
Pastoral Centers	22
Closed Parishes	3
Professional Ministry Personnel:	
Brothers	1
Sisters	140
Lay Ministers	375
Welfare	
Catholic Hospitals	7
Total Assisted	722,296
Health Care Centers	1
Total Assisted	228
Homes for the Aged	37
Total Assisted	8,118
Residential Care of Children	4
Total Assisted	852
Day Care Centers	3
Total Assisted	201
Specialized Homes	5
Total Assisted	1,479
Special Centers for Social Services	15
Total Assisted	76,937
Residential Care of Disabled	7
Total Assisted	445
Other Institutions	8
Total Assisted	15,295
Educational	
Seminaries, Diocesan	1
Students from This Diocese	52
Students from Other Diocese	102
Seminaries, Religious	1
Students Religious	8
Total Seminarians	60
Colleges and Universities	11
Total Students	35,820
High Schools, Diocesan and Parish	22
Total Students	22,726
High Schools, Private	15
Total Students	7,525
Elementary Schools, Diocesan and Parish	212
Total Students	73,132
Elementary Schools, Private	13
Total Students	4,490
Non-residential Schools for the Disabled	5
Total Students	340
Catechesis/Religious Education:	
High School Students	7,264
Elementary Students	50,499
Total Students under Catholic Instruction	201,856
Teachers in the Diocese:	
Priests	109
Brothers	49
Sisters	609
Lay Teachers	8,609
Vital Statistics	
Receptions into the Church:	
Infant Baptism Totals	16,153
Adult Baptism Totals	1,245
Received into Full Communion	620
First Communions	17,502
Confirmations	16,243
Marriages:	
Catholic	3,946
Interfaith	1,749
Total Marriages	5,695
Deaths	12,733
Total Catholic Population	1,486,058
Total Population	3,872,783

Former Bishops—Most Revs. MICHAEL FRANCIS EGAN, O.F.M., D.D., consecrated Oct. 28, 1810; died July 22, 1814; HENRY CONWELL, D.D., consecrated Sept. 24, 1820; died April 22, 1842; FRANCIS PATRICK KENRICK, D.D., consecrated June 6, 1830; transferred to Baltimore in 1851; died July 8, 1863; JOHN NEPOMUCENE NEUMANN, C.SS.R., D.D., consecrated March 28, 1852; died Jan. 5, 1860; Canonized June 19, 1977.; JAMES FREDERIC WOOD, D.D., consecrated coadjutor, cum iure successionis, April 26, 1857; Bishop of Philadelphia, Jan. 5, 1860; appt. Archbishop Feb. 12, 1875; Sacred Pallium, June 17, 1875; died June 20, 1883; PATRICK JOHN RYAN, D.D., consecrated April 14, 1872; Bishop of Tricomia and Coadjutor with right of succession to the Archbishop of St. Louis;; appt. Titular Archbishop of Salamis, Jan. 6, 1884; Archbishop of Philadelphia, June 8, 1884; died Feb. 11, 1911; EDMOND FRANCIS PRENDERGAST, D.D., consecrated Feb. 24, 1897, Titular Bishop of Scillio; Auxiliary Bishop of Philadelphia; Archbishop of Philadelphia, May 27, 1911; died Feb. 26, 1918; His Eminence DENNIS CARDINAL DOUGHERTY, appt. Bishop of Nueva Segovia, P.I., April 7, 1903; consecrated June 14, 1903; transferred to Jaro, P.I., April 19, 1908; transferred to Buffalo Nov. 30, 1915; transferred to Philadelphia April 30, 1918; installed as Archbishop of Philadelphia July 10, 1918; Pallium conferred May 6, 1919; created Cardinal Priest, March 7, 1921; died May 31, 1951; JOHN CARDINAL O'HARA, C.S.C., appt. Military Delegate of Armed Forces and Titular Bishop of Mylasa Dec. 11, 1939; consecrated Jan. 15, 1940; transferred to Buffalo March 10, 1945; transferred to Philadelphia Nov. 28, 1951; installed as Archbishop of Philadelphia Jan. 9, 1952; Pallium conferred Jan. 12, 1953;; created Cardinal Priest Dec. 15, 1958; died Aug. 28, 1960; JOHN CARDINAL KROL, D.D., J.C.D. (Retired), ord. Feb. 20, 1937; appt. Titular Bishop of Cadi and Auxiliary Bishop of Cleveland July 11, 1953; consecrated Sept. 2, 1953; appt. Archbishop of Philadelphia Feb. 11, 1961; created Cardinal Priest June 26, 1967; retired Feb. 11, 1988; died

March 3, 1996.

Vicars General—Most Revs. MICHAEL F. BURBIDGE, D.D., M.A., Ed.D., V.G. Tel: 610-785-6200; ROBERT P. MAGINNIS, D.D., V.G. Tel: 610-642-0545; Rev. Msgr. JOSEPH R. CISTONE, V.G. Tel: 215-587-4507.

Office of the Cardinal—His Eminence JUSTIN CARDINAL RIGALI, J.C.D., Archbishop of Philadelphia; Rev. Msgr. JOHN J. MCINTYRE, Sec. to the Cardinal Archbishop, 222 N. 17th St., Philadelphia, 19103-1299. Tel: 215-587-3800.

Office of the Vicar for Administration—Rev. Msgrs. JOSEPH R. CISTONE, V.G., Vicar General. Tel: 215-587-4507; Fax: 215-587-4545; MICHAEL T. MCCULKEN, Asst. Vicar Admin. Tel: 215-587-4511. Assocs. to the Vicar Admin.: Rev. Msgr. JOSEPH P. DUNCAN; Bro. JOSEPH WILLARD, F.S.C.; Mr. JAMES J. BOCK JR.; Sr. LINDA M. SARIEGO, O.S.F., 222 N. 17th St., Philadelphia, 19103-1299.

Regional Vicars—Rev. Msgrs. JAMES D. BEISEL, Vicar for Bucks County, 685 York Rd., Warminster, 18974. Tel: 215-957-1525; JAMES T. MCDONOUGH, M.S.W., Vicar for Chester County, 2 Forrest Lane, Strafford, 19087-2504. Tel: 610-995-9450; JOHN E. BRESLIN, Vicar for Delaware County, 1797 S. Sproul Rd., Springfield, 19064-1195. Tel: 610-543-6759; JOHN C. MARINE, Vicar for Montgomery County, 354 Conshohocken State Rd., Gladwyne, 19035. Tel: 610-896-0567; FRANCIS W. BEACH, Vicar for Philadelphia-North, 240 Hermitage St., Philadelphia, 19127. Tel: 215-508-4250; JOHN T. CONWAY, Vicar for Philadelphia-South, 525 Cobbs Creek Pkwy., Philadelphia, 19143. Tel: 215-476-7484. 502 S. 12th St., Philadelphia, 19147. Tel: 215-735-3164, Ext. 1052. 4404 N. 5th St., Philadelphia, 19140. Tel: 215-324-8291 The Vicar for Philadelphia-South Supervises The St. Peter Claver Evangelization Center.; The Vicar for Philadelphia-North Supervises The Catholic Institute for Evangelization.

Office of the Vicar for Religious—

Vicar for Religious—Rev. Msgr. ALEXANDER J. PALMIERI, M.A., J.C.L.

Coordinator for Vocations to Religious Life—Sr. KATHLEEN LEARY, S.S.J., Office, 222 N. 17th St., Philadelphia, 19103-1299. Tel: 215-587-3795; Fax: 215-587-3790.

The Chancery—Rev. Msgr. ALEXANDER J. PALMIERI, M.A., J.C.L., Chancellor; Rev. JAMES M. OLIVER, J.C.D., Vice Chancellor, 222 North 17th St., Philadelphia, 19103-1299. Tel: 215-587-4538; Fax: 215-587-3907.

Archivist—JOSEPH J. CASINO, M.A., M.S.L.S., Office, 100 E. Wynnewood Rd., Wynnewood, 19096-3001. Tel: 610-667-2125.

Metropolitan Tribunal—222 N. 17th St., Philadelphia, 19103-1299. Tel: 215-587-3750; Fax: 215-587-0508. Communications should be sent to the above address.

Judicial Vicar—Rev. Msgr. JAMES J. GRAHAM.

Assistant Judicial Vicars—Revs. JOSEPH C. DIECKHAUS, J.C.L.; PAUL A. DIGIROLAMO, J.C.D.; EDUARDO G. MONTERO.

Archdiocesan Judges—Rev. Msgr. MICHAEL J. FITZGERALD, J.C.D., J.D.; Rev. STEVEN J. HARRIS, J.C.D.; Rev. Msgr. ALEXANDER J. PALMIERI, M.A., J.C.L.; Mrs. MELISSA L. SCHOOLS, J.C.L.; Rev. Msgrs. SAMUEL E. SHOEMAKER, J.C.D.; VINCENT M. WALSH, J.C.D.; Sr. CARLOTTA BARTONE, S.H.C.J., J.C.L.

Promoters of Justice—Rev. Msgr. MICHAEL J. FITZGERALD, J.C.D., J.D.; Revs. GERARD C. MESURE, J.C.D., J.D.; JAMES M. OLIVER, J.C.D.; Rev. Msgr. VINCENT M. WALSH, J.C.D.

Defenders of the Bond—Rev. Msgr. JOHN P. BOLAND, M.A.; Revs. GERARD C. MESURE, J.C.D., J.D.; JAMES M. OLIVER, J.C.D.; ROBERT J. POWELL, D.M.A, M.A., M.Div.; JOHN D. REARDON, M.Div.; VINCENT F. WELSH, J.C.L., M.A.

Approved Advocates—Revs. EDWARD H. BELL, M.Div.; JOSEPH W. BONGARD, M.A.; JOSEPH E. HOWARTH, M.A.L.S.; KENNETH P. MCATEER, M.Div.; JOSEPH J. NICOLO, M.Div.; KARL A. ZEUNER, S.T.L.; Sr. CAROL MOCKUS, C.S.F.N.; Deacons EDWARD A. KONARSKI; JOHN C. HYNES.

Secretary—Rev. JOHN D. REARDON, M.Div.

Notaries—JOAN MCDOWELL; WINIFRED CANNON; MARY KAY DEVLIN.

Office for Ecumenical and Interreligious Affairs—VACANT, Dir., 222 N. 17th St., Philadelphia, 19103-1299. Tel: 215-587-3624; Fax: 215-587-3628.

Information Technology Services—Mr. MARK D'ERAMO, Dir. Tel: 215-587-2426; Fax: 215-587-3808.

Office for Audit Services—Mr. PHILIP H. GALLAGHER JR., C.P.A., Dir. Tel: 215-587-2474; Fax: 215-587-0512.

Office for General Services—Tel: 215-587-3633; Fax: 215-587-2481.

Office for Special Projects—Tel: 215-587-3992; Fax: 215-587-2481.

Ecclesiastical Exchange Program—Rev. Msgr. LOUIS A. D'ADDEZIO, Dir.; Mr. GEORGE G. SHARRETTS, Asst. Dir. Tel: 215-587-3996; Fax: 215-587-2481.

Office for Research and Planning—ROBERT J. MILLER, Ed.D., Dir. Tel: 215-587-3545; Fax: 215-587-3817.

Secretariat for Catholic Education

All addresses are: 222 N. 17th St., Philadelphia, PA 19103-1299 unless otherwise indicated

Secretary for Catholic Education—Dr. RICHARD MCCARRON. Tel: 215-587-3700; Fax: 215-587-5644; 215-587-5638.

Office of Catholic Education—Dr. RICHARD MCCARRON, Sec. for Catholic Education; Mr. THOMAS J. SMITH, Deputy Sec. Catholic Education; Deacon THOMAS F. O'BRIEN, Ph.D., Ed.D., Supt. of Schools. Assistant Superintendents: Mr. STEPHEN PAWLOWSKI, Asst. Supt. Secondary Staff Rels.; Ms. MARY ROCHFORD, Asst. Supt. for Elementary Schools; Mrs. SHARON R. QUAY, Asst. Supt. Special Education.

Office for Catechetical Formation—Rev. MARTIN T. CIOPPI, Ed.D., Deputy Sec. Catechetical Formation.

Office for Youth and Young Adults—PATRICIA MANION, Dir.; Mr. MICHAEL MULLEN, Asst. Dir., 105 Argyle Rd., Ardmore, 19003. Tel: 610-649-9476; Fax: 610-649-9520.

Parish Youth Ministry—Mr. MICHAEL MULLEN, Dir. Tel: 610-649-9410.

Archdiocesan Boy Scout—Rev. Msgr. JOHN B. WENDRYCHOWICZ, Chap. Tel: 610-649-9476.

Camp Neumann Conference Center—STEPHEN TAYLOR, Dir. Tel: 215-343-6552.

Community Service Corps—KATHLEEN PFEFFER, Dir. Tel: 215-567-4280.

Secretariat for Catholic Human Services

All addresses are: 222 N. 17th St., Philadelphia, PA 19103. Tel: 215-587-3900, unless otherwise indicated

Secretary for Catholic Human Services—Rev. Msgr. TIMOTHY C. SENIOR, M.B.A., M.S.W. Tel: 215-587-3903; Rev. JOSEPH A. TRACY, S.T.D., M.S.W., Deputy Sec. Tel: 215-587-3908; EDWARD T. CAHILL, CFO. Tel: 215-587-3889; EDWARD J. LIS, M.A., M.Div., M.S., Dir. of Catholic Mission Integration. Tel: 215-965-1710.

Catholic Social Services (300)—

Catholic Charities of the Archdiocese of Philadelphia—Rev. Msgr. TIMOTHY C. SENIOR, M.B.A., M.S.W., Sec. Catholic Human Svcs. Tel: 215-587-3903; JAMES AMATO, L.S.W., Deputy Sec. Catholic Social Svcs. Tel: 215-587-3754; EDWARD T. CAHILL, CFO. Tel: 215-587-3889; TERESA THOMPSON, L.S.W., Dir. Children Svcs. Tel: 215-587-0529; KAREN K. BECKER, L.S.W., Dir. Family Svcs. Tel: 215-587-3590; LORRAINE KNIGHT, M.Ed., Dir. Administrative & Support Svcs. Tel: 215-587-3906; JOHN M. WAGNER, Dir. Housing & Homeless Svcs. Tel: 215-587-3589; Bro. DENNIS MALLOY, F.S.C., A.C.S.W, M.A., Dir. Juvenile Justice Svcs., St. Gabriel's System, 117 S. 17th St., Philadelphia, 19103. Tel: 215-665-8777; MARK E. FITZGERALD, M.S.W., N.H.A., Dir. Mental Retardation Svcs., Don Guanella School, Administrative Office, 1797 S. Sproul Rd., Springfield, 19064. Tel: 610-543-6602.

Family Service Centers—

Cardinal Bevilacqua Community Center—2646 Kensington Ave., Philadelphia, 19125. Tel: 215-426-9422; Fax: 215-426-9426. ESTELA REYES-BUGG, Prog. Coord.

Casa del Carmen Family Services—W. GIOVANNI MORANTE, M.A., Admin., Reese & Blavis Sts., Philadelphia, 19140. Tel: 215-329-5660.

Holy Family Center—Intake and Information & Referral, 227 N. 18th St., Philadelphia, 19103. Tel: 215-854-7090. MICHAEL MONTIE, L.C.S.W., Supvr.

Northeast Philadelphia Service Center—AMY STONER, L.S.W., Admin., 7340 Jackson St., Philadelphia, 19136. Tel: 215-624-5920.

South Philadelphia Family Service Center—1941 Christian St., Philadelphia, 19146. Tel: 215-790-9530; Fax: 215-790-9765. AMY STONER, L.S.W., Admin.

Southwest Family Service Center—6214 Grays St., P.O. Box 16986, Philadelphia, 19142. Tel: 215-724-8550. AMY STONER, L.S.W., Admin.

Bucks County Family Service Centers—MARGUERITE POWERS, L.S.W., Asst. Dir., 100 Levittown Pkwy., Levittown, 19054. Tel: 215-945-2550.

Middle Bucks County—607 W. Street Rd., Warminster, 18974. Tel: 215-957-6699.

Upper Bucks County—427 N. Main St., Sellersville, 18960. Tel: 215-453-7098.

Chester County Family Services Centers—JAMES MCMASTER, M.B.A., Admin., 141 E. Lancaster Ave., Downingtown, 19335. Tel: 610-269-4060. 105 Prospect Ave., West Grove, 19390. Tel: 610-869-6500.

Delaware County Family Services Center—JAMES MCMASTER, M.B.A., Admin., 240 N. Bishop Ave., Springfield, 19064. Tel: 610-626-6550. 130 E. 7th St., Chester, 19013. Tel: 610-876-7101.

Montgomery County Family Service Center—MARGUERITE POWERS, L.S.W., Asst. Dir., 353 E. Johnson Hwy., Norristown, 19401. Tel: 610-279-7372.

Specialized Services— are all located at the Holy Family Center unless otherwise noted: *227 N. 18th St., Philadelphia, 19103.*

Adoption Services—MARY LARK MERMAN, L.S.W., Admin. Tel: 215-854-7050.

Child Care Services—PHYLLIS ADORNO, L.S.W., Admin., 222 N. 17th St., Philadelphia, 19103. Tel: 215-587-3575.

Counseling Services—MICHAEL MONTIE, L.C.S.W., Supvr. Tel: 215-854-7090.

Immigration and Refugee Services—PHYLLIS FORMAN ESQ., Admin. Tel: 215-854-7019.

Housing/Homeless Services—DEBORAH WAGNER, L.S.W., Admin. Tel: 215-854-7080.

Senior Adult Services—GEORGE SALLOOM, L.S.W. Tel: 215-854-7029.

Volunteer & Community Relations Services—WILLIAM TANGRADI, M.S.W., Mgr. Tel: 215-854-7058.

Catholic Campaign for Human Development—227 N. 18th St., Philadelphia, 19103. Tel: 215-587-5656.

Catholic Health Care Services—Rev. Msgr. TIMOTHY C. SENIOR, M.B.A., M.S.W., Sec. Catholic Human Svcs. Tel: 215-587-3903; JUDITH A. PASSERINI, C.N.H.A., M.Mgmt., Deputy Sec. Catholic Health Care Svcs. Tel: 215-587-2436; JOSEPH J. SWEENEY JR., M.B.A., N.H.A., CFO. Tel: 215-242-2062; LOUISE M. SULLIVAN, N.H.A., Dir. Facility Based Svcs. Tel: 215-587-2496; KENNETH P. LEWIS, M.S.W., B.C.D., N.H.A., Dir. Planning & Program Devel. Tel: 215-587-2487; BEVERLEE JOHANNSEN, B.S.N., N.H.A., Dir. Quality Assurance. Tel: 215-587-3663; Rev. Msgr. TIMOTHY C. SENIOR, M.B.A., M.S.W., Diocesan Coord. for Health Care Affairs. Tel: 215-587-3903.

Information Technology Services (ITS) Division—ANNE H. AYELLA, Archdiocesan Dir., Catholic Relief Services, 111 S. 38th St., Philadelphia, 19104. Tel: 215-895-3470; ARIK HILL, Consultant. Tel: 215-965-1737.

Information Systems—LEILA C. COOPER, Dir. Tel: 215-854-7023.

Information Technology—M. LEE MYERS, Dir. Tel: 215-368-0900.

Nutritional Development Services—PATRICK F.E. TEMPLE-WEST, Dir., 111 S. 38th St., Philadelphia, 19104. Tel: 215-895-3470.

Office for Community Development—JOHN M. WAGNER, Dir. Tel: 215-587-3589.

Secretariat For Evangelization

All addresses are: 222 N. 17th St., Philadelphia, PA 19103-1299. Fax: 215-587-3561, unless otherwise indicated.

Secretary for Evangelization—BERNADETTE A. O'CONNELL, M.S., M.S.W. Tel: 215-587-5629.

Deputy Secretary for Evangelization—THOMAS WAVRO, A.M. Tel: 215-587-5666.

Office for Black Catholics—PATRICIA SHELTON, Dir. Tel: 215-587-3634.

Director for Evangelization—DOMINIC LOMBARDI, S.T.L. Tel: 215-587-0500.

Adult Faith Formation—MARYANNE HARRINGTON, Asst. Dir. Tel: 215-587-3514.

Evangelization—VACANT, Asst. Dir. Tel: 215-587-0500; CONSTANCE SCHARFF, Prog. Coord. Tel: 215-587-0504; Fax: 215-587-0502; Mr. WILLIAM C. DONAGHY, Prog. Coord. Tel: 215-587-0547; Fax: 215-587-0502.

Family Life Office—MARY BERGAN, Asst. Dir., 100 E. Wynnewood Rd., Wynnewood, 19096-3069. Tel: 610-660-9002.

Parish Pastoral Councils—ROBERT CHOINIERE, Coord. Tel: 215-587-3694.

Prison Ministry Program—LAURA FORD RUCINSKI, Coord. Tel: 215-331-3640.

Church Ministry Institute—MARYANNE HARRINGTON, Admin. Tel: 215-587-3514.

Office for Hispanic Catholics—ANNA C. VEGA, M.A., Dir. Tel: 215-587-3786.

Office for Pastoral Care of Migrants and Refugees—Rev. WILLIAM G. AYRES, Dir. Tel: 215-587-3540.

African Outreach— Contact the Office for Pastoral Care for Migrants and Refugees. Tel: 215-587-3540.

Apostleship of the Sea—Rev. KURIAKOSE CHEERAN, C.M.I., Coord., Seamen's Church Institute, 475 N. Fifth St., Philadelphia, 19123. Tel: 215-922-2562.

Cambodian Apostolate—Sr. MARY THERESA NGUYEN, A.C.J., Contact, St. Thomas Aquinas Rectory, 1719

Morris St., Philadelphia, 19145. Tel: 215-334-2312.

Chinese Apostolate—Rev. THOMAS BETZ, O.F.M.Cap., Coord. Tel: 215-592-7552.

Filipino Apostolate—Sr. LORETTO MAPA, R.A., Coord., St. Thomas Aquinas Rectory, 1719 Morris St., Philadelphia, 19145. Tel: 215-334-2312.

Haitian Apostolate—Rev. JEAN-CLAUDE MOMPOINT, Coord., Incarnation of Our Lord, 5105 N. 5th St., Philadelphia, 19120. Tel: 215-329-2320.

Indian Apostolate, Syro Malabar Rite—Rev. JACOB CHRISTY, Immaculate Conception, 602 West Ave., Jenkintown, 19046-2708. Tel: 215-884-4022.

Indian Apostolate, Syro Malankara Rite—Rev. VAIDHIAN KOTTARAMALLASERIL, Coord., Incarnation of Our Lord, 5105 N. Fifth St., Philadelphia, 19120. Tel: 215-329-2320.

Indian Apostolate-Knanayan Comm.—Rev. THOMAS VATTOTHUPARAMBIL, Coord., St. Anthony Padua, 259 Forest Ave., Ambler, 19002. Tel: 215-646-4742.

Indian Apostolate, Latin Rite—Rev. RAJU B. SELVARAJ, St. Mary Medical Center, Langhorne-Newtown Rd., Langhorne, 19047. Tel: 215-750-2000.

Indonesian Apostolate—Rev. YULIANUS ASTANTO, C.M., St. Thomas Aquinas, 17th & Morris Streets, Philadelphia, 19145. Tel: 215-334-2312.

Irish Apostolate—Rev. COLM CAMPBELL, Coord., St. Cyril of Alexandria, 153 Penn Blvd., East Lansdowne, 19050. Tel: 610-623-1929.

Korean Apostolate—Revs. SUNG-KOOK LEE, Coord., Holy Angels, 7000 Old York Rd., Philadelphia, 19126. Tel: 215-548-5535; PAUL BON YOUNG KOO, Holy Cross, Bishop & Springfield Roads, Springfield, 19064. Tel: 610-626-3321.

Laotian Apostolate— Contact the Office for Pastoral Care for Migrants and Refugees Tel: 215-587-3540.

Pakistani Outreach—Rev. DOMINIC ISAAC, St. William, Rising Sun Ave. & Devereaux St., Philadelphia, 19111. Tel: 215-745-1389.

Polish Apostolate—Rev. Msgr. FRANCIS S. FERET, St. Adalbert, Allegheny Ave. & Thompson St., Philadelphia, 19134. Tel: 215-739-3500.

Portuguese and Brazilian Apostolates—Rev. LUIZ DE GONZAGA FURTADO, Coord., St. Martin of Tours, 5450 Roosevelt Blvd., Philadelphia, 19124. Tel: 215-535-2962.

Vietnamese Apostolate—Rev. JOSEPH TRAN, Coord., Office, 150 Hampden Rd., Upper Darby, 19082. Tel: 610-352-1431.

Respect Life Office—Deacon DAVID B. SCHAFFER, Dir. Tel: 215-587-5661. Email: www.archdiocese-phl.org/respectlife.

Department for AIDS Ministry—Deacon DAVID B. SCHAFFER, Admin. Tel: 215-587-5661.

Department for Pastoral Care for Persons with Disabilities—Sr. KATHLEEN SCHIPANI, I.H.M., Admin. Tel: 215-587-3530 (Voice); 215-587-5010 (TTY).

Deaf Apostolate—Sr. KATHLEEN SCHIPANI, I.H.M., Admin. Tel: 215-587-3913 (Voice); 215-587-5010 (TTY); Rev. ANTHONY T. RUSSO, C.SS.R., Coord., St. Boniface Rectory. Tel: 215-423-9547. Web: www.archdiocese-phl.org/respectlife. For information on Mass schedule call office or visit our web site.

Department for Pro-Life Activities—VACANT, Admin. Tel: 215-587-3703.

Pontifical Society for the Propagation of the Faith—Rev. Msgr. JAMES J. FITZPATRICK, Dir. Tel: 215-587-3944.

Pontifical Society of St. Peter Apostle—Rev. Msgr. JAMES FITZPATRICK, Dir. Tel: 215-587-3944.

Pontifical Missionary Society of the Holy Childhood (Holy Childhood Assoc.)—Rev. JAMES FITZPATRICK, Dir. Tel: 215-587-3944.

Pontifical Missionary Union—Rev. Msgr. JAMES FITZPATRICK, Dir. Tel: 215-587-3944.

Office for Worship—Rev. DANIEL E. MACKLE, Dir. Tel: 215-587-3537.

Secretariat For Clergy

All addresses are: 222 N. 17th St., Philadelphia, PA 19103-1299 unless otherwise indicated.

Secretary for Clergy—Rev. Msgr. WILLIAM J. LYNN. Tel: 215-587-4532.

Office for Clergy—Rev. Msgr. WILLIAM J. LYNN, Dir.; Rev. VINCENT F. WELSH, J.C.L., M.A., Asst. Dir. Tel: 215-587-4532.

Priests' Personnel Board—Most Revs. MICHAEL F. BURBIDGE, D.D., M.A., Ed.D., V.G.; ROBERT P. MAGINNIS, D.D., V.G.; Rev. Msgrs. FRANCIS W. BEACH; JAMES D. BEISEL; JOHN E. BRESLIN; JOSEPH R. CISTONE, V.G.; JOHN T. CONWAY; Rev. HENRY B. DEGNAN (Retired); Rev. Msgrs. WILLIAM J. LYNN; JOHN C. MARINE; JAMES T. MCDONOUGH, M.S.W.; Revs. JOHN F. BABOWITCH; JOHN B. FLANAGAN; PATRICK G. MCCORMICK; JOSEPH P. MCGEOWN; MICHAEL S. OLIVERE; Rev. Msgr. CHARLES P. VANCE.

Department of Continuing Formation for Diocesan Priests—Rev. JOSEPH P. GENTILI, M.Div., S.T.L., S.T.D., Dir.

Department Retired Clergy—Rev. Msgr. FRANCIS A. MENNA, Admin.

Permanent Diaconate Department—Rev. DENNIS J. CARBONARO, M.Div., M.A., Admin.; Sr. VERONICA GROSS, R.S.M., Asst. Admin.; Deacon JAMES T. OWENS, Assoc. to Admin., St. Charles Borromeo Seminary, 100 E. Wynnewood Rd., Wynnewood, 19096. Tel: 610-664-2213.

St. Charles Borromeo Seminary—Most Rev. MICHAEL F. BURBIDGE, D.D., M.A., Ed.D., V.G., Rector, 100 E. Wynnewood Rd., Wynnewood, 19096. Tel: 610-667-3394.

Vocation Office for Diocesan Priesthood—Rev. JOHN F. BABOWITCH, Dir., St. Charles Borromeo Seminary, 100 E. Wynnewood Rd., Wynnewood, 19096. Tel: 610-667-5778.

Secretariat For Temporal Services

All addresses are: 222 N. 17th St., Philadelphia, PA 19102 unless otherwise indicated.

Temporal Services—Mr. GLENN J. MASAKOWSKI, M.MGT., Sec. & CFO. Tel: 215-587-3959; Fax: 215-965-1711; Ms. MAUREEN VAN THUYNE, Deputy Sec. Tel: 215-587-3958; Fax: 215-965-1711; Ms. ANITA GUZZARD, M.B.A., Deputy Sec. Tel: 215-587-3943; Fax 215-587-3939.

Investment Services—Mr. ROBERT J. GUNN Dir. Tel: 215-587-3969; Fax: 215-965-1711.

Office for Property Services—Mr. ARTHUR FRIEDMAN, M.S., Dir. Tel: 215-587-3560; Fax: 215-587-0599.

Catholic Cemeteries Office—Mr. ROBERT WHOMSLEY, Dir., 111 S. 38th St., Philadelphia, 19104. Tel: 215-895-3450; Fax: 215-895-3458.

Human Resources Office—Mrs. MARLENE M. LOGLISCI, M.B.A., SPHR., Dir. Tel: 215-587-3910 Fax: 215-587-3572.

Office for Insurance Services—CHARLES J. DEBEVEC, C.P.C.U., Dir. Tel: 215-587-3644; Fax: 215-587-2498.

Office for Legal Services—Rev. Msgr. MICHAEL J. FITZGERALD, J.C.D., J.D., Dir. Tel: 215-587-0511; Fax: 215-587-0512.

Office for Accounting Services—ANITA GUZZARDI, M.B.A., Controller. Tel: 215-587-3943; Fax: 215-587-3939.

Parish Financial Services—PETER DAVIS, M.A., Dir. Tel: 215-587-2477; Fax: 215-587-3939.

Educational Financial Services—DAVID J. MAGEE, M.B.A., Ed.D., Dir. Tel: 215-587-3755; Fax: 215-587-3525.

Secretariat for External Affairs

All addresses are: 222 N. 17th St., Philadelphia, PA 19103-1299 unless otherwise indicated.

Secretary for External Affairs—STAN H. RETIF. Tel: 215-587-3507; Fax: 215-587-3649.

Office for Public Affairs—GUY L. CIARROCCHI, Esq., Dir. Tel: 215-587-3509; Fax: 215-587-0515.

Office for Communications—CATHERINE L. ROSSI, Dir. Tel: 215-587-3747; Fax: 215-587-3871.

Newspaper - "Catholic Standard and Times"—MICHELLE L. JOHNSON, Editor. Tel: 215-587-3668; Fax: 215-587-3979.

Office for Development—STAN H. RETIF, Dir. Tel: 215-587-5650; Fax: 215-587-3647; ANTONIA BUTTO, Asst. Dir. Tel: 215-587-5650; Fax: 215-587-3647; REGINA DIGUILIO, Assoc. Dir. Tel: 215-587-0590; Fax: 215-587-2442.

Archdiocesan Offices, Boards, Commissions and Committees

All addresses are: 222 N. 17th St., Philadelphia, PA 19103-1299 unless otherwise indicated.

Blind, Guild for all the—Rev. EDMUND J. MAHER (Retired). Tel: 215-854-7042.

Board of Trustees of Lay Employees Retirement Plan—His Eminence JUSTIN CARDINAL RIGALI, J.C.D., Chm.; Mr. GLENN J. MASAKOWSKI, M.MGT., Vice Chm.

Diocesan Priests' Compensation and Benefits Committee—Rev. Msgrs. WILLIAM J. LYNN, Chm.; FRANCIS A. MENNA; DANIEL J. SULLIVAN; Revs. ROBERT B. MCDERMOTT; FRANCIS P. GROARKE; Mr. GLENN MASAKOWSKI; Mr. ROBERT SIMS; Revs. RALPH J. CHIEFFO; MATTHEW W. GUCKIN; Rev. Msgrs. RICHARD T. LAHART (Retired); JOSEPH P. MCFADDEN.

Building Committee—Rev. Msgr. RICHARD J. SKELLY, Chm. (Retired), (Drawings of building plans are reviewed by this committee).

Cardinal's Committee for Christian Home and Family—MARY BERGAN, Asst. Dir., Family Life Office, 100 E. Wynnewood Rd., Wynnewood, 19096. Tel: 610-660-9002.

Censores Librorum—Rev. Msgrs. JOSEPH J. ANDERLONIS, S.T.D.; FRANCIS A. BARSZCZEWSKI, S.T.L., M.S.L.S.; Rev. JOSEPH G. PRIOR, S.T.D., S.S.L., M.A.

Archbishop's Delegate to Charismatic Prayer Groups—Rev. JOHN J. KELLY, St. Bridget Rectory, 3667 Midvale Ave., Philadelphia, 19129-1712. Tel: 215-844-4126.

College of Consultors—Rev. Msgr. HERBERT A. BEVARD; Most Rev. MICHAEL F. BURBIDGE, D.D., M.A., Ed.D., V.G.; Rev. Msgrs. JOSEPH R. CISTONE, V.G.; CHARLES V. DEVLIN (Retired); WILLIAM J. LYNN; Most Revs. ROBERT P. MAGINNIS, D.D., V.G.; JOSEPH F. MARTINO, D.D., H.E.D., V.G.; Rev. JOSEPH C. MCLOONE, M.A.; Rev. Msgrs. ROBERT T. MCMANUS (Retired); THOMAS M. MULLIN; ALBERT V. NORRELL (Retired); ALEXANDER J. PALMIERI, M.A., J.C.L.

Council of Managers for Development—Rev. Msgr. JOSEPH R. CISTONE, V.G., Chm.; Most Rev. ROBERT P. MAGINNIS, D.D., V.G., Vice Chm. Tel: 215-587-4507.

Council of Priests—His Eminence ANTHONY CARDINAL BEVILACQUA, D.D., M.A., J.C.D., J.D., Presider (Retired); Most Revs. MICHAEL F. BURBIDGE, D.D., M.A., Ed.D., V.G.; ROBERT P. MAGINNIS, D.D., V.G.; Rev. Msgrs. JOSEPH R. CISTONE, V.G.; GREGORY J. PARLANTE; NELSON J. PEREZ; Revs. JOSEPH L. LOGRIP; HANS A.L. BROUWERS; SIDNEY C. BURGOYNE (Retired); ROBERT B. MCDERMOTT; MICHAEL P. MCCORMAC; Rev. Msgrs. ALEXANDER J. PALMIERI, M.A., J.C.L.; WILLIAM J. LYNN; CHARLES V. DEVLIN (Retired); ROBERT T. MCMANUS (Retired); Revs. GASPER A. GENUARDI; JOSEPH C. DIECKHAUS, J.C.L.; MICHAEL J. FITZPATRICK; NICHOLAS F. MARTORANO, O.S.A.; JAMES A. LYONS; JOSEPH C. MCLOONE, M.A.; STEPHEN D. THORNE; NICHOLAS R. WASELINE, O.S.F.S.; Rev. Msgrs. HERBERT A. BEVARD; THOMAS M. MULLIN.

Educational Fund—Tel: 215-587-3774. Office for Financial Services.

Philadelphia Archdiocesan Holy Name Union—Rev. MICHAEL J. FITZPATRICK, Spiritual Dir., St. Peter Rectory, 1080 North Manor Rd., Honey Brook, 19344-9610. Tel: 610-942-9112; Fax: 610-942-3385. Email: stpeterchesco@comcast.net.

Information Line, Archdiocesan—Tel: 215-587-3600.

Interparochial Cooperation, Commission for—Rev. Msgr. DANIEL J. SULLIVAN, Holy Innocents Rectory, 1337 E. Hunting Park Ave., Philadelphia, 19124-4938. Tel: 215-743-2600.

Legion of Mary—Rev. FRANCIS G. LENDACKY, St. Agnes-St. John Nepomucane Rectory, 319 Brown St., Philadelphia, 19123-2228. Tel: 215-627-0340.

Moderator of Priests Conferences—Rev. JOSEPH P. GENTILI, M.Div., S.T.L., S.T.D., Dir. Dept. Continuing Formation for Diocesan Priests. Tel: 215-587-4532.

Parish Sites and Boundaries, Commission for—Rev. Msgr. JAMES P. MCCOY, Chm.

Pastors Review Board—Rev. Msgr. HERBERT A. BEVARD; Rev. GASPER A. GENUARDI; Rev. Msgrs. THOMAS M. MULLIN; GREGORY J. PARLANTE.

Pennsylvania Catholic Conference— (Harrisburg) Board of Governors: His Eminence JUSTIN CARDINAL RIGALI, J.C.D. Administrative Board: Rev. Msgr. JOSEPH R. CISTONE, V.G.; GUY L. CIARROCCHI, Esq. Education Department: Dr. RICHARD MCCARRON; Dr. THOMAS F. O'BRIEN. Social Concerns: Rev. Msgr. TIMOTHY C. SENIOR, M.B.A., M.S.W.; Deacon DAVID B. SCHAFFER.

Victim Assistance Coordinators—MARTIN R. FRICK, L.S.W., M.P.A.; KAREN BECKER. Tel: 215-587-2485; 215-587-3590.

CLERGY, PARISHES, MISSIONS AND PAROCHIAL SCHOOLS

CITY OF PHILADELPHIA
(PHILADELPHIA COUNTY)

1—CATHEDRAL BASILICA OF SS. PETER AND PAUL (1846), Rev. Msgr. John A. Close; Rev. Gerald P. Carey. In Res., Rev. Msgrs. John J. Caulfield (Retired); Louis A. D'Addezio; Revs. Frederick Clement, M.SS.CC. (CAM); Daniel E. Mackle; Deacon Epifanio DeJesus.

Res.: 1723 Race St., 19103. Tel: 215-561-1313; 215-561-1314; Fax: 215-561-1580.

Catechesis/Religious Program—Students 20.

Chapel—*Our Lady of the Miraculous Medal*, Tel: 215-972-8116.

2—ST. ADALBERT (1904), (Polish), Rev. Msgr. Francis S. Feret; Rev. Thaddeus Gorka, Pastoral Assoc.

Res.: 2645 E. Allegheny Ave., 19134. Tel: 215-739-3500; Fax: 215-739-5706.
School—3236 Edgemont St., 19134. Tel: 215-739-1920; Fax: 215-739-0519. Sisters of the Holy Family of Nazareth 3; Lay Teachers 10; Students 250.

3—ST. AGATHA-ST. JAMES (1976), Consolidated Revs. Steven J. Marinucci; William E. Grogan; George Strausser; Charles J. Pfeffer.
Res.: 3728 Chestnut St., 19104. Tel: 215-386-9732; Fax: 215-386-9734.
Catechesis/Religious Program—Students 4.

4—ST. AGNES-ST. JOHN NEPOMUCENE (1907), (Slovak), Consolidated, January 1, 1980. Rev. Francis G. Lendacky.
Res.: 319 Brown St., 19123. Tel: 215-627-0340.

5—ALL SAINTS (Bridesburg) (1860), [CEM] Rev. Edward P. Burke.
Res.: 2651 Buckius St., 19137. Tel: 215-535-4411; Fax: 215-744-6533.
School—4623 E. Thompson St., 19137. Tel: 215-743-0715; Fax: 215-744-0563. Sisters of St. Francis of Philadelphia 1; Lay Teachers 8; Students 177.
Catechesis/Religious Program—Tel: 215-289-8810. Students 60.

6—ALL SAINTS CHAPEL, Closed., (1877-1977) Formerly located at Philadelphia General Hospital, 700 Civic Center Blvd. Spiritual records are kept at St. Agatha-St. James Church. Tel.: 215-386-9732; 386-9733.

7—ST. ALOYSIUS (1894-2003), (German), Closed., Formerly located at 26th & Tasker Sts. Spiritual records are kept at St. Gabriel Church. Tel.: 215-463-4060

8—ST. ALPHONSUS, Closed., (1852-1972) Formerly located at 1400 S. Fourth St. Spiritual records are kept at Sacred Heart of Jesus Church. Tel.: 215-465-4050; 465-4051.

9—ST. AMBROSE (1923), Revs. James N. Catagnus; John M. Harkins; Deacons Jose M. Mendez; Luis Ruiz.
Res.: 363 E. Roosevelt Blvd., 19120. Tel: 215-329-7900; 215-329-7901; Fax: 215-329-9206.
Church: C St. & Roosevelt Blvd., 19120.
School—405 E. Roosevelt Blvd., 19120. Tel: 215-457-3083; Fax: 215-457-9261. Lay Teachers 11; Students 271.
Catechesis/Religious Program—Tel: 215-455-8160. Students 81.

10—ST. ANDREW (1924), (Lithuanian), Rev. Peter M. Burkauskas.
Res.: 1913 Wallace St., 19130. Tel: 215-765-2322; Fax: 215-765-0124.

11—ST. ANNE (1845), [CEM] Rev. Joseph D. Brandt. In Res., Rev. Kuriakose Cheeran, C.M.I.
Res.: 2328 E. Lehigh Ave., 19125. Tel: 215-739-4590; Fax: 215-739-0983.
School—2343 E. Tucker St., 19125. Tel: 215-634-4231; Fax: 215-427-0608. Sr. Margaret Duffy, S.S.J., Prin. Sisters of St. Joseph 1; Lay Teachers 16; Students 318.
Catechesis/Religious Program—Cedar & Tucker Sts.. Students 52.

12—ANNUNCIATION B.V.M. (1860), Rev. Gary Pacitti. In Res., Rev. Msgr. Michael J. Fitzgerald, J.C.D., J.D.; Rev. Eduardo G. Montero.
Res.: 1511 S. 10th St., 19147. Tel: 215-334-0159; Fax: 215-462-5065.
School—12th & Wharton Sts., 19147. Tel: 215-465-1416; Fax: 215-465-0308. Sisters, Servants of the Immaculate Heart of Mary 2; Lay Teachers 13; Students 317.
Catechesis/Religious Program—Students 245.

13—ST. ANSELM (1962), Revs. Thomas J. Dunleavy; David A. Fernandes. In Res., Deacon Gerald J. Whartenby.
Res.: 12669 Dunks Ferry Rd., 19154. Tel: 215-637-3525; Fax: 215-637-4915.
School—12670 Dunks Ferry Rd., 19154. Tel: 215-632-1133; Fax: 215-632-3264. Mrs. Geraldine Murphy, Prin. Lay Teachers 30; Students 702.
Catechesis/Religious Program— Miss Jane Rowles, D.R.E. Students 181.

14—ST. ANTHONY OF PADUA (1886), Closed., Formerly Located at 2321 Fitzwater St. Spiritual records are kept at St. Charles Borromeo Church. Tel. 215-735-0600.

15—ASCENSION OF OUR LORD (1899), Rev. Michael A. Chapman; Deacon Leo Gladnick; Sr. Joan Reithmiller, S.S.J., Dir. Parish Svcs.
Res.: 725 E. Westmoreland St., 19134. Tel: 215-739-1670; Fax: 215-739-1455.
School—735 E. Westmoreland St., 19134. Tel: 215-739-6226; Fax: 215-739-7317. Teresa Richardson, M.A., Prin. Sisters 2; Lay Teachers 11; Students 202.
Catechesis/Religious Program— Sr. Catherine Langle, S.S.J., D.R.E. Students 48.

16—ASSUMPTION B.V.M. (1848), Closed., (1848-1995) Formerly located at 1131 Spring Garden St. Spiritual records are kept at St. John the Evangelist Church. Tel.: 215-563-4145.

17—ST. ATHANASIUS (1928), Rev. Msgr. Herbert A. Bevard; Deacon Fred Poellnitz. In Res., Rev. John J. Shellem (Retired).
Res.: 2050 Walnut Ln., 19138. Tel: 215-548-2700; Fax: 215-548-7453.
School—St. Athanasius-Immaculate Conception School See Consolidated Parish Schools under Institutions Located in the Archdiocese. Tel: 215-424-5045; Fax: 215-927-6615. Sisters 3; Lay Teachers 10; Students 284.
Catechesis/Religious Program—Students 396.

18—ST. AUGUSTINE (1796), Revs. John F. O'Rourke, O.S.A.; Pascal A. DeCicco, O.S.A., Pastoral Assoc. First foundation of Augustinian Order in U.S.A. In Res., Rev. W. Howard McGraw, O.S.A.
Res.: 243 N. Lawrence S., 19106-1195. Tel: 215-627-1838; Fax: 215-627-3911.
School—St. Mary Interparochial School See Consolidated Parish Schools under Institutions Located in the Archdiocese.

19—ST. BARBARA (1921), Rev. Msgr. Wilfred J. Pashley.
Res.: 5359 Lebanon Ave., 19131. Tel: 215-473-1044; Fax: 215-473-5252.
Catechesis/Religious Program—Students 5.
Convent—5336 Diamond St., 19131. Tel: 215-477-3839.

20—ST. BARNABAS (1919), Revs. Joseph P. Devlin; Peter N. Quinn; Deacons Leonard J. Wolkowicz; John J. Ellis; John J. Kreczkevich.
Res.: 6300 Buist Ave., 19142-3098. Tel: 215-726-1119; 215-726-1120; Fax: 215-726-1180.
School—64th St. & Buist Ave., 19142-3097. Tel: 215-729-3603; Fax: 215-724-8728. Sisters of Immaculate Heart of Mary 4; Lay Teachers 19; Students 442.
Catechesis/Religious Program—Tel: 215-724-8728. Students 100.
Convent—6328 Buist Ave., 19142-3097. Tel: 215-729-1572.

21—ST. BARTHOLOMEW (1919), Revs. Joseph P. Denny; Edward E. Brady. In Res., Revs. Ildebrando E. Schifalacqua; Joseph C. McCaffrey, M.B.A., M.Div.; Deacon John J. Bean.
Res.: 5600 Jackson St., 19124. Tel: 215-831-1224; 215-831-1225; Fax: 215-831-0467.
School—Jackson & Sanger St., 19124. Tel: 215-744-6393; Fax: 215-744-9377. Lay Teachers 12; Students 270.
Catechesis/Religious Program—Students 82.

22—ST. BENEDICT (1922), Rev. George B. Moore; Deacons Stephen Hopkins; James T. Walker; Calvin C. Smith.
1942 E. Chelten Ave., 19138. Tel: 215-924-2876.
Res.: 1940 E. Chelten Ave., 19138. Tel: 215-924-4401; Fax: 215-924-4390.
School—1935 Medary Ave., 19138. Tel: 215-424-8073. Lisa McLish, Prin. Lay Teachers 9; Students 175.
Catechesis/Religious Program—Students 20.

23—ST. BERNARD (1927), Revs. Charles J. Sullivan; George J. Szparagowski; W. Frederick Kindon; David Machain (Retired); John G. Fala (Retired); Deacon Richard F. Hunter.
Res.: 7341 Cottage St., 19136. Tel: 215-333-0446; Fax: 215-333-3215.
School—7340 Jackson St., 19136. Tel: 215-624-5204; Fax: 215-624-8806. Lay Teachers 19; Students 398.
Catechesis/Religious Program—Students 175.

24—ST. BONAVENTURE (1889-1993), Closed., Formerly located at 9th & Cambria Sts. Spiritual records are kept at St. Veronica Church. Tel: 215-228-4878.

25—ST. BONIFACE (1865), Revs. Charles McDonald, C.SS.R.; James Cascione, C.SS.R.; Bro. Manuel Martinez, C.SS.R. In Res., Revs. Anthony T. Russo, C.SS.R., Deaf Apostolate; Gerard J. Brinkmann, C.SS.R.; Alexander F. Ortiz, C.SS.R.; Kevin R. Murray, C.SS.R.
Res.: 174 W. Diamond St., 19122. Tel: 215-739-6376.
School—142 W. Diamond St., 19122. Tel: 215-634-6588. Lay Teachers 10.
Catechesis/Religious Program—Students 166.

26—ST. BRENDAN (1925-1934), Closed., Formerly located at 507 Manheim St. Spiritual records are kept at St. Francis of Assisi Church. Tel.: 215-842-1287.

27—ST. BRIDGET (1853), Rev. John J. Kelly. In Res., Rev. Michael J. Reilly.
Res.: 3667 Midvale Ave., 19129. Tel: 215-844-4126; Fax: 215-842-2536.
School—3636 Stanton St., 19129. Tel: 215-843-2828. Sisters of St. Joseph 1; Lay Teachers 13; Students 170.
Catechesis/Religious Program—Students 217.
Convent—3665 Midvale Ave., 19129. Tel: 215-844-5663.
St. Francis Friary—3685 Midvale Ave.. Tel: 215-844-1125.

28—ST. CALLISTUS (1921), Rev. Eugene M. Tully; Deacon Francis J. Connors.
Res.: 700 N. 67th St., 19151-3614. Tel: 215-473-4417; Fax: 215-473-6728.

29—ST. CARTHAGE (1915-2000), Closed., Formerly located at 525 Cobbs Creek Pkwy. Spiritual records are kept at St. Cyprian Church. Tel.: 215-747-3250.

30—ST. CASIMIR (1893), (Lithuanian), Rev. Peter M. Burkauskas.
Res.: 324 Wharton St., 19147. Tel: 215-468-2052; Fax: 215-468-0354.
School—Tel: 215-334-8407; Fax: 215-334-0521. Mrs. Angelina Clair, Prin. Lay Teachers 9; Students 127.
Catechesis/Religious Program—Students 161.

31—ST. CATHERINE OF SIENA (1910-1972), Closed., Formerly located at 436 W. Penn St. Spiritual records are kept at St. Vincent de Paul Church. Tel.: 215-438-2925.

32—ST. CECILIA (1911), Revs. Charles E. Bonner; Thomas M. Sodano; Dennis Z. Fedak; Deacon Louis Malfara.
Res.: 535 Rhawn St., 19111. Tel: 215-725-1240; Fax: 215-725-2130.
School—525 Rhawn St., 19111. Tel: 215-725-8588; Fax: 215-725-0247. Sisters of the Immaculate Heart of Mary 8; Lay Teachers 35; Students 903.
Catechesis/Religious Program—Tel: 215-725-2580. Students 96.

33—CHAPEL OF OUR LADY OF THE MIRACULOUS MEDAL (LA MILAGROSA) (1912), (Spanish), Attended by, Cathedral Basilica of SS. Peter and Paul, 1723 Race St., Philadelphia, PA 19103. Tel: 215-561-1313; 1314. Rev. Msgr. John A. Close.
Church: 1903 Spring Garden St., 19130. Tel: 215-972-8116.
Catechesis/Religious Program—Students 16.

34—ST. CHARLES BORROMEO (1868), Rev. Joseph Watson; Deacon William C. Mayes.
Res.: 902 S. 20th St., 19146. Tel: 215-735-0600; Fax: 215-735-6630.
Church: 20th & Christian Sts., 19146.
Catechesis/Religious Program—Tel: 215-735-6898; Fax: 215-732-6253. Students 25.

35—CHRIST THE KING (1963), Revs. James A. Callahan; John C. O'Driscoll, M.Div., S.L.L.
Res.: 3252 Chesterfield Rd., 19114. Tel: 215-632-1144; Fax: 215-632-4933.
School—3205 Chesterfield Rd., 19114. Tel: 215-632-1375; 215-637-3838. Sisters of St. Joseph 3; Lay Teachers 22; Students 449.
Catechesis/Religious Program—Tel: 215-632-2144. Students 106.

36—ST. CHRISTOPHER (1950), Rev. Msgr. Joseph P. Garvin; Revs. Thomas J. Rooney; John P. Gutekunst.
Res.: 13301 Proctor Rd., 19116. Tel: 215-673-5177; Fax: 215-698-0585.
School—13307 Proctor Rd., 19116. Tel: 215-673-5787; Fax: 215-673-8511. Lay Teachers 37; Students 839.
Catechesis/Religious Program— Sr. Michele Fisher, C.S.F.N., D.R.E. Students 203.

37—ST. CLEMENT (1865), Rev. Robert T. Feeney.
Res.: 2240 S. 71st St., 19142-1108. Tel: 215-729-0500; Fax: 215-729-3003.
School—SS. Clement-Irenaeus Consolidated School See Consolidated Parish Schools under Institutions Located in the Archdiocese. Tel: 215-729-8368; Fax: 215-729-1274. Sisters, Servants of the Immaculate Heart of Mary 4; Lay Teachers 9; Students 205.
Catechesis/Religious Program—Fax: 215-279-3003. Students 16.

38—ST. COLUMBA (1895-1993), Closed., Formerly located at 2340 W. Lehigh Ave. Spiritual records are kept at St. Martin de Porres Church. Tel.: 215-228-8330; 228-8331.

39—CORPUS CHRISTI (1921-1987), Closed., (1912-1987) Formerly located at 29th & Allegheny Ave. Spiritual records are kept at St. Martin de Porres Church. Tel.: 215-228-8330; 228-8331.

40—SAINT CYPRIAN (2000), (African American), Rev. Msgr. Federico A. Britto. In Res., Rev. Stephen D. Thorne; Rev. Msgr. John T. Conway.
Res.: 525 Cobbs Creek Pkwy., 19143. Tel: 215-747-3250; Fax: 215-747-2372.
School—6225 Cedar Ave., 19143. Tel: 215-748-4450; Fax: 215-747-7794. Camille Brown, Ph.D., Prin. Lay Teachers 27; Students 420.
Catechesis/Religious Program—Students 16.
Convent—5501 Cedar Ave., 19143. Tel: 215-472-2936.

41—ST. DOMINIC (1849), [CEM] Revs. John D. Gabin; Bernard J. Benischeck (Retired); Michael J. Heim.
Res.: 8504 Frankford Ave., 19136. Tel: 215-624-5502; 215-624-5503; Fax: 215-333-1750.
School—8512 Frankford Ave., 19136. Tel: 215-333-6703; Fax: 215-333-9930. Sisters, Servants of the Immaculate Heart of Mary 9; Lay Teachers 16; Students 482.
Catechesis/Religious Program—Tel: 215-624-5301. Students 90.
Convent—8510 Frankford Ave., 19136. Tel: 215-333-0144.

42—ST. DONATO (1910), (Italian), Rev. Ferdinand Buccafurni.
Res.: 403 N. 65th St., 19151. Tel: 215-747-4131; Fax: 215-747-7884.
School—405 N. 65th St., 19151. Tel: 215-748-2994; Fax: 215-748-0288. Sr. Christine Marie Baltas, H.S.C., Prin. Sisters 2; Lay Teachers 13; Students 256.
Catechesis/Religious Program—Students 8.
43—ST. EDMOND (1912), Rev. Francis P. Groarke; Deacon James J. Stewart. In Res., Rev. Michael S. Olivere.
Res.: 2130 S. 21st St., 19145. Tel: 215-334-3755; Fax: 215-334-2081.
Catechesis/Religious Program—Students 20.
44—ST. EDWARD THE CONFESSOR (1865-1993), Closed., Formerly located at 8th & York Sts. Spiritual records are kept at Visitation B.V.M. Church. Tel.: 215-228-8330; 228-8331.
45—ST. ELIZABETH (1872-1993), Closed., Spiritual records are kept at St. Martin De Porres Church.
46—EPIPHANY OF OUR LORD (1889), (Italian—Irish), Revs. Dominic M. Chiaravalle; John E. Calabro; Quan N. Tran, M.Div.; Dennis J. Witalec.
Res.: 1121 Jackson St., 19148. Tel: 215-334-1035; Fax: 215-334-7885.
School—13th & Jackson Sts., 19148. Tel: 215-467-5385; Fax: 215-336-5103. Lay Teachers 19; Students 295.
Catechesis/Religious Program—Tel: 215-467-5621. Students 90.
47—ST. FRANCIS DE SALES (1890), Revs. Roland D. Slobogin; Silvester Kuris; Sr. Alice Daly, I.H.M., Pastoral Assoc.; Deacon Trac Mai Huynh. In Res., Rev. John Pidgeon.
Res.: 4625 Springfield Ave., 19143. Tel: 215-222-5819; Fax: 215-222-5821.
School—917 S. 47th St., 19143. Tel: 215-387-1749; 215-727-3929; Fax: 215-387-6605. Sisters, Servants of the Immaculate Heart of Mary 7; Lay Teachers 17; Students 543.
Catechesis/Religious Program—Students 32.
48—ST. FRANCIS OF ASSISI (1899), Rev. Richard J. Rock, C.M. In Res., Revs. James Kiernan, C.M.; John P. Timlin, C.M.
Res.: 4821 Greene St., 19144. Tel: 215-842-1287; Fax: 215-842-3338.
School—St. Martin De Porres School (Germantown) See Consolidated Parish Schools under Institutions Located in the Archdiocese. Tel: 215-842-1266; Fax: 215-842-1400. Sr. Nancy Cassidy, D.C., Prin. Lay Teachers 11; Students 210.
49—ST. FRANCIS XAVIER (1839), Revs. Paul C. Convery, C.O.; Alberto Mejia; Deacon Vincent J. Thompson. In Res., Rev. Georges G. Thiers, C.O.; Bro. Brian Gaffney, C.O.
Res.: 2319 Green St., 19130. Tel: 215-765-4568; Fax: 215-765-4049.
Oratory— 2321 Green St., 19130.
School—24th & Wallace Sts., 19130. Tel: 215-763-6564; Fax: 215-236-2818. Lay Teachers 11; Students 249.
50—ST. GABRIEL (1895), Rev. Michael J. Lee, O.Praem.; Mr. Chris Marano, Youth Minister; Sisters Marie Claire, I.H.M., Pastoral Min.; Felice Marie, I.H.M., Pastoral Min.; Rev. James C. Rodia, O.Praem.
Res.: 2917 Dickinson St., 19146. Tel: 215-463-4060; Fax: 215-755-2680.
School—Our Lady of Angels See Consolidated Parish Schools under Institutions Located in the Archdiocese. Tel: 215-468-7230; Fax: 215-468-2554. Lay Teachers 22; Students 300.
Catechesis/Religious Program—Tel: 215-334-0374; Fax: 215-334-0374. Students 290.
Convent—2916 Dickinson St.. Tel: 215-334-2620.
51—ST. GEORGE (1902), (Lithuanian), Rev. Msgr. Joseph J. Anderlonis, S.T.D.
Res.: 3580 Salmon St., 19134. Tel: 215-739-3102; Fax: 215-739-7217.
School—2700 E. Venango St., 19134. Tel: 215-634-8803. Lay Teachers 10; Students 214.
Convent—3570 Salmon St., 19134. Tel: 215-739-0472.
52—GESU (1868-1993), Closed., Formerly located at 18th & Thompson Sts. Spiritual records are kept at St. Malachy Church. Tel.: 215-763-1305.
53—GOOD SHEPHERD (1925), Rev. Gerard C. Mesure, J.C.D., J.D.; Louise Bailey, Business Mgr.
Res.: 6667 Chester Ave., 19142. Tel: 215-727-8300; Fax: 215-727-5932.
Catechesis/Religious Program—Students 3.
54—ST. GREGORY, Closed., (1895-1981) Formerly located at 52nd and Warren Sts. Spiritual records are kept at St. Rose of Lima Church. Tel: 215-877-2991, 2992.
55—ST. HEDWIG (1907-2000), (Polish),, Formerly located at 802 N. 24th St. Spiritual records are kept at St. Francis Xavier Church. Tel.: 215-765-4568.
56—ST. HELENA (1924), Rev. Albert C. DiGiacobbe; Rev. Msgr. Joseph T. Trinh; Deacons Victor Seda; Francis Urmson. In Res., Rev. Francis M. Gallagher (PEO).
Res.: 6161 N. Fifth St., 19120-1497. Tel: 215-424-1300; Fax: 215-424-9152.
School—6101 N. Fifth St., 19120. Tel: 215-549-2947; Fax: 215-549-5947. Sisters of St. Joseph 3; Lay Teachers 16; Students 336.
Catechesis/Religious Program—Students 47.
57—ST. HENRY (1916-1993), (German), Closed., Formerly located at 4400 N. 5th St. Spiritual records are kept at Incarnation Church. Tel.: 215-329-2320; 329-2321.
58—HOLY ANGELS (1906), Rev. Paul S. Lee In Res., Rev. In-Cheng Yu.
Res.: 7000 Old York Rd., 19126. Tel: 215-548-5535; 215-548-5536; Fax: 215-224-6615.
Catechesis/Religious Program—Students 200.
59—HOLY CHILD (1909-1993), Closed., Formerly located at 5200 N. Broad St. Spiritual records are kept at Our Lady of Hope Church. Tel.: 215-329-8100; 329-3164.
60—HOLY CROSS (1890), Rev. Leo P. Oswald; Deacon Richard Coyne. In Res., Rev. Ronald M. Jakows.
Res.: 154 E. Mt. Airy Ave., 19119. Tel: 215-247-0661; Fax: 215-247-1849.
School—144 E. Mt. Airy Ave., 19119. Tel: 215-242-0414; Fax: 215-242-0414. Sisters of St. Joseph 3; Lay Teachers 10; Students 194.
Convent—148 E. Mt. Airy Ave., 19119. Tel: 215-247-0262.
Catechesis/Religious Program—Tel: 215-247-3405. Mr. James Nelson, D.R.E. Students 41.
61—HOLY FAMILY (1885), Revs. Francis X. McKee; James J. Martin. In Res., Deacon Eugene R. Leahy.
Res.: 234 Hermitage St., 19127. Tel: 215-482-0450; 215-482-8608; Fax: 215-482-7531.
School—242 Hermitage St., 19127. Tel: 215-487-2796; 215-483-0903; Fax: 215-487-8134. Lay Teachers 13; Students 215.
Catechesis/Religious Program—Interparochial C.C.D. Program - St. Josaphat's, Tel: 215-483-4470; Fax: 215-483-4471. Students 20.
62—HOLY INNOCENTS (1927), Rev. Msgr. Daniel J. Sullivan, Revs. Wilfred F. Maloney; Quan M. Trinh.
Res.: 1337 E. Hunting Park Ave., 19124. Tel: 215-743-2600; Fax: 215-743-8041.
School—1312 E. Bristol St., 19124. Tel: 215-743-5909. Sisters, Servants of the Immaculate Heart of Mary 16; Lay Teachers 26; Students 640.
Catechesis/Religious Program—Tel: 215-288-5911. Students 20.
63—HOLY NAME OF JESUS (Fishtown) (1904), Rev. Msgr. Gregory J. Parlante.
Res.: 701 E. Gaul St., 19125-2896. Tel: 215-739-3960; Fax: 215-739-7597.
School—E. Berks & Gaul Sts., 19125. Tel: 215-423-3334; Fax: 215-425-9353. Sisters, Servants of the Immaculate Heart of Mary 4; Lay Teachers 8; Students 271.
School—Preschool, Kensington. Tel: 215-423-3041. Sr. Janet Walters, I.H.M., Prin.
64—HOLY REDEEMER (1941), (Chinese) Unassigned., (Mission Chapel of the Church of St. John the Evangelist)
School—915 Vine St., 19107. Tel: 215-922-0999; Fax: 215-922-6674. Lay Teachers 9; Students 249.
Parish House—916 Wood St., 19107 Tel: 215-627-5293; Fax: 215-563-9980.
65—HOLY SPIRIT (1964), Rev. David C. Sicoli; Deacon Albert George.
Res.: 1900 Geary St., 19145. Tel: 215-334-4242; Fax: 215-334-8787.
School—1845 Hartranft St., 19145. Tel: 215-389-0715; Fax: 215-336-7719. Lay Teachers 11; Students 243.
Catechesis/Religious Program—Students 67.
66—HOLY TRINITY (1789), (German), [CEM] Attended by, Old St. Mary's Church, Sixth and Spruce Sts. , 252 South Fourth St., 19106. Tel: 215-923-7930.
School—St. Mary Interparochial School See Consolidated Parish Schools under Institutions Located in the Archdiocese. Tel: 215-923-7522.
67—ST. HUBERT (1924), Closed., Formally located at Torresdale and Cottman Aves. from 1924-1940. Spiritual records transferred to St. Bernard Church. Tel: 215-333-0446.
68—ST. HUGH OF CLUNY (1922), Rev Scott Brockson; Deacon Jose L. Lozada-Figueroa.
Res.: 145 W. Tioga St., 19140. Tel: 215-634-1800; Fax: 215-427-0303.
School—3533 N. Mascher St., 19140. Tel: 215-634-3060; 215-634-3183; Fax: 215-634-2690. Sisters of St. Joseph 5; Lay Teachers 8; Students 250.
Catechesis/Religious Program—Students 250.
69—ST. IGNATIUS OF LOYOLA (1893 , (African American), Rev. Joseph F. Okonski.
Res.: 636 N. 43rd St., 19104. Tel: 215-386-5065; 215-386-1058; Fax: 215-386-2832
School—617 N. 43rd St., 19104. Tel: 215-222-3626. Mrs. Patricia Jerome, Prin. Sisters of the Blessed Sacrament 1; Sisters of St. Joseph 1; Lay Teachers 9; Students 190.
Catechesis/Religious Program—Ms. Cora Murphy, D.R.E.
Convent—644 N. 43rd St., 19104. Tel: 215-386-0302.
Chaplaincy—St. Ignatius Nursing Home. Tel: 215-349-8800; Fax: 215-222-3078.
70—IMMACULATE CONCEPTION (1869), Rev. Herbert J. Sperger. In Res., Revs. Edmund C. Wesolowski (Retired); Michael F. Hennelly, M.Div.
Res.: 1020 N. Front St., 19123. Tel: 215-627-2702; Fax: 215-627-7344.
St. Michael Rectory—1445 N. 2nd St., 19122. Tel: 215-739-2358; Fax: 215-739-5766.
Catechesis/Religious Program—Students 3.
Mission—Central Shrine of the Miraculous Medal
71—IMMACULATE CONCEPTION (1902), (African American), Rev. Timothy V. Lyons, C.M. In Res., Rev. Gregory P. Cozzubbo, C.M.; Deacon Brouycie P. Isley.
Res.: 1020 E. Price St., 19138. Tel: 215-843-9468; Fax: 215-843-6570.
School—St. Athanasius-Immaculate Conception School See Consolidated Parish Schools under Institutions located in the Archdiocese. Tel: 215-424-5045; Fax: 215-927-6615.
Catechesis/Religious Program—Tel: 215-843-9468; Fax: 215-843-6570. Students 51.
72—IMMACULATE HEART OF MARY (1952), Rev. Msgr. Bartholomew J. O'Brien; Revs. Stephen C. White; John B. Flanagan; Deacon Salvatore R. Bianco.
Res.: 819 Cathedral Rd., 19128. Tel: 215-483-1000; Fax: 215-483-1732.
School—815 Cathedral Rd., 19128. Tel: 215-482-2029; Fax: 215-482-1075. Lay Teachers 31; Students 511.
Catechesis/Religious Program—Tel: 215-483-4266. Students 75.
73—INCARNATION OF OUR LORD (1900), Revs. John M. Halloran; Vaidhian Babu (India); Rayford E. Emmons; Jean-Claude Mompoint, (Haitian Apostolate); Deacons Felipe Cruz; Jose A. Fontanez; Jose Hernandez.
Res.: 5105 N. Fifth St., 19120. Tel: 215-329-2320; Fax: 215-329-6149.
School—Tel: 215-457-2779; Fax: 215-457-1328. Sr. Janet Regina, I.H.M., Prin. Sisters, Servants of the Immaculate Heart of Mary 7; Lay Teachers 15; Students 397.
Catechesis/Religious Program—Students 130.
Convent—401 W. Lindley Ave., 19120. Tel: 215-329-0672.
74—SAINT IRENAEUS (1966), Rev. Thomas A. Nasta; Deacon Michael R. Arno.
Res.: 2728 South 73rd St., 19153. Tel: 215-727-2888; Fax: 215-365-4751.
School—SS. Clement-Irenaeus Consolidated School See Consolidated Parish Schools under Institutions Located in the Archdiocese. Tel: 215-729-8368; Fax: 215-729-1274.
75—ST. JAMES (1850-1976), Consolidated, with St. Agatha to form St. Agatha-St. James. See separate listing for details.
76—ST. JEROME (1955), Revs. Joseph B. Graham; Eugene J. McBride, O.S.F.S.; William T. Small; Deacon Charles Pavonarius. In Res., Rev. Edward V. Avery.
Res.: 8100 Colfax St., 19136. Tel: 215-333-4461; Fax: 215-333-6791.
School—3031 Stamford St., 19136. Tel: 215-624-0637; Fax: 215-624-5711. Sharon Nendza, Prin. Sisters of St. Joseph 1; Lay Teachers 33; Students 690.
Catechesis/Religious Program—Students 63.
77—ST. JOACHIM (1845), [CEM] Rev. Robert Bazzoli, O.S.F.S. In Res., Revs. Mark Plaushin, O.S.F.S.; Vincent Smith, O.S.F.S.
Res.: 1527 Church St., 19124. Tel: 215-535-0580; Fax: 215-831-1788.
School— Closed. Please see Holy Innocents Area Catholic School.
Catechesis/Religious Program—Tel: 215-288-5911. Students 90.
Convent—1509 Church St.. Tel: 215-535-6177. Servants of the Immaculate Heart of Mary 7.
78—ST. JOAN OF ARC (1919), Rev. Edward H. Bell, M.Div. In Res., Rev. Paul A. DiGirolamo, J.C.D.; Rev. Msgr. Charles V. Devlin (Retired).
Res.: 2025 E. Atlantic St., 19134. Tel: 215-535-4641; 215-535-5138; Fax: 215-535-7477.
School— Closed. Please see Holy Innocents Area Catholic School.
Catechesis/Religious Program—Students 40.
Convent—3550 Frankford Ave., 19134. Tel: 215-533-0959.
79—ST. JOHN CANTIUS (1892), (Polish), Revs. Joseph J. Zingaro; Marcel Kolakowski, O.F.M.; Jan Palkowski.
Res.: 4415 Almond St., 19137. Tel: 215-535-6667; Fax: 215-535-7107.
School—4435 Almond St., 19137. Tel: 215-535-3446; Fax: 215-535-3858. Lay Teachers 13; Students 185; Kindergarten 9.

Catechesis/Religious Program—Students 22.

80—ST. JOHN NEPOMUCENE, (Slovak), Consolidated, with St. John Nepomucene and St. Agnes January 1, 1980. Spiritual records transferred to St. Agnes Church, 319 Brown St., Philadelphia, PA 19123. Tel.: 215-627-0340.

81—ST. JOHN THE BAPTIST (1831), [CEM] Revs. Louis C. Bier; Stephen C. McDermott; Deacon Gaspero P. Baratta. In Res., Rev. Gregory J. Fairbanks.
Res.: 146 Rector St., 19127. Tel: 215-482-4600; Fax: 215-482-2976.
School—119 Rector St., 19127. Tel: 215-482-0449; Fax: 215-482-2451. Sisters, Servants of the Immaculate Heart of Mary 3; Lay Teachers 13; Students 342.
Catechesis/Religious Program—Students 60.

82—ST. JOHN THE EVANGELIST (1830), [CEM] Revs. Francis X. Russo, O.F.M.Cap.; Senan Glass, O.F.M-.Cap.; Benjamin Regotti, O.F.M.Cap.; Joseph Tuscan, O.F.M.Cap.; John McCloskey, O.F.M.Cap. (HBG); Bernard Ukwuegbu; Bro. James Gavin, O.F.M.Cap. In Res., Rev. Anselm Martin, O.F.M.Cap.
Res.: 21 S. 13th St., 19107. Tel: 215-563-4145; Fax: 215-563-1770.
School—St. Mary Interparochial School See Consolidated Parish Schools under Institutions Located in the Archdiocese. Tel: 215-923-7522.
Mission—Holy Redeemer Chinese Church 915 Vine St., Philadelphia Co. 19107. Tel: 215-922-0999; Fax: 215-922-6674.

83—ST. JOSAPHAT (1898), (Polish), Rev. Msgr. John B. Wendrychowicz. In Res., Revs. Edward A. Pelczar; Brian P. Hennessy.
Res.: 124 Cotton St., 19127. Tel: 215-483-4470; Fax: 215-483-4037.
School—137 Grape St., 19127. Tel: 215-482-0285; Fax: 215-483-4053. Bernardine Sisters of St. Francis 1; Lay Teachers 9; Students 217.
Catechesis/Religious Program—Students 15.

84—ST. KATHERINE OF SIENA (1922), Rev. Msgr. James P. McBride; Revs. Paul J. Stenson; James T. McCabe; Dennis G. Wilde, O.S.A.; Andrews Athapilly, C.M.I.; Anne Rhodes, Business Mgr.; Deacons James J. Duffy; David Brink.
Res.: 9700 Frankford Ave., 19114. Tel: 215-637-7548; Fax: 215-637-0146.
School—9720 Frankford Ave., 19114. Tel: 215-637-2181; Fax: 215-637-4867. Sr. M. John, C.S.F.N., Prin. Sisters of the Holy Family of Nazareth 3; Lay Teachers 29; Students 650.
Catechesis/Religious Program—Tel: 215-637-1464. Cynthia Kay, D.R.E. Students 86.

85—KING OF PEACE (1926), (Italian), Rev. Thomas J. Rossi, O.Praem.
Res.: 2530 Wharton St., 19146. Tel: 215-468-4107; Fax: 215-468-2882.
School—Our Lady of Angels, Tel: 215-468-7230; Fax: 215-468-2554.
Catechesis/Religious Program—Our Lady of Angels School, 30th & Dickinson Sts.. Tel: 215-334-0374. Students 28.
Convent—1315 S. 26th St., 19146. Tel: 215-468-7009.

86—ST. LADISLAUS (1906-2003), (Polish), Closed., Formerly located at 1650 W. Hunting Park Ave. Spiritual records are kept at St. Josaphat Church. Tel.: 215-483-4470

87—ST. LAURENTIUS (1882), (Polish), Rev. Francis A. Gwiazda. In Res., Rev. Joseph C. Stec, M.A. (Retired).
Res.: 1608 E. Berks St., 19125. Tel: 215-739-1776; 215-739-9387; Fax: 215-739-9663.
School—1612 E. Berks St., 19125. Tel: 215-423-8834; Fax: 215-426-4675. Felician Sisters of St. Francis 1; Lay Teachers 10; Students 224.
Catechesis/Religious Program—Students 270.
Convent—1648 E. Berks St., 19125. Tel: 215-739-4447.

88—ST. LEO (1884), Revs. John J. Farry; John J. Sibel; Joseph E. O'Brien (Retired).
Res.: 6658 Keystone St., 19135. Tel: 215-333-0340; Fax: 215-333-7590.
School—6649 Tulip St., 19135. Tel: 215-624-8669. Sisters of St. Joseph 3; Lay Teachers 11; Students 247.
Catechesis/Religious Program—Tel: 215-331-3399. Students 80.
Convent—4900 Unruh St., 19135. Tel: 215-624-1253.

89—ST. LUCY (1905), (Italian), Rev. Francis J. Sabatini. In Res., Rev. John F. Babowitch.
Res.: 4503 Smick St., 19127. Tel: 215-483-0554; Fax: 215-483-2450.
School—146 Green Ln., 19127. Tel: 215-482-6578; Fax: 215-482-7702. Elizabeth Veneziale, Prin. Lay Teachers 14; Students 197.

90—ST. LUDWIG (1891-1975), (German), Closed., Formerly located at 28th & Master Sts. Spiritual records are kept at St. Francis Xavier Church. Tel.: 215-765-4568.

91—ST. MADELEINE SOPHIE (1925), Rev. Leo P. Oswald. In Res., Rev. Msgr. Thomas J. Hilferty (Retired).
Res.: 6440 Greene St., 19119. Tel: 215-438-9464; Fax: 215-848-7953.
School—St. Martin De Porres School (Germantown) See Consolidated Parish Schools under Institutions Located in the Archdiocese. Tel: 215-842-1266; Fax: 215-842-1400.
Catechesis/Religious Program—Students 15.

92—ST. MALACHY (1850), (African American), Rev. John P. McNamee.
Res.: 1429 N. 11th St., 19122. Tel: 215-763-1305; Fax: 215-763-2023.
School—1419 N. 11th St., 19122. Tel: 215-232-0696; Fax: 215-236-1434. Lay Teachers 12; Students 211.
Catechesis/Religious Program—Students 35.

93—SAINT MARTHA (1966), Revs. Alexander Masluk; Paul Obrimski; Deacon Raymond F. Gwynn. In Res., Rev. Christopher D. Lucas.
Res.: 11301 Academy Rd., 19154-3304. Tel: 215-632-3720; Fax: 215-632-7737.
School—11321 Academy Rd., 19154-3304. Tel: 215-632-0320; Fax: 215-632-5546. Lay Teachers 29; Students 625.
Catechesis/Religious Program—Students 90.

94—ST. MARTIN DE PORRES (1993), Rev. Edward J. Hallinan; Deacons Edward J. Andrews; Thomas A. Shields.
Res.: 2340 W. Lehigh Ave., 19132. Tel: 215-228-8330; Fax: 215-221-6516.
School—23rd St. & Lehigh Ave., 19132. Tel: 215-223-6872; Fax: 215-223-4126. Sisters of St. Joseph 4; Lay Teachers 20; Students 440.
Catechesis/Religious Program—Students 70.

95—ST. MARTIN OF TOURS (1923), Revs. Anthony W. Janton; Marshall J. Kloda; Paul J. Castellani; Charles D. Smith; Deacon Jack Gravlin; Sr. Anastasia Watson, I.H.M., Pastoral Assoc. In Res., Rev. Luis Furtado (Brazil).
Res.: 5450 Roosevelt Blvd., 19124. Tel: 215-535-2962; Fax: 215-535-3091.
School—Loretto Ave. & Sanger St., 19124. Tel: 215-533-3050. Sisters of the Immaculate Heart of Mary 18; Lay Teachers 47; Students 1,100.
Catechesis/Religious Program—Tel: 215-535-3090; Fax: 215-535-3091. Stephen Guckin, D.R.E. Students 145.

96—ST. MARY MAGDALEN DE PAZZI, (Italian), Closed., (1852-2000). Formerly located at 712 Montrose St. Spiritual records are kept at Saint Paul Church. Tel.: 215-923-0355.

97—ST. MARY OF CZESTOCHOWA, (Polish), Closed., (1927-2000) Formerly located at 59th St. and Elmwood Ave. Spiritual records are kept at St. Barnabas Church. Tel.: 215-726-1119; 1120.

98—ST. MARY OF THE ASSUMPTION (1849), (German), [CEM] Rev. James McGuinn; Deacon Joseph Sexton.
Res.: 176 Conarroe St., 19127. Tel: 215-482-4264; Fax: 215-508-1731.
School—167 Conarroe St., 19127. Tel: 215-482-1611; Fax: 215-508-1536. Sisters 2; Lay Teachers 11; Students 217.
Catechesis/Religious Program—Students 284.

99—ST. MARY OF THE ETERNAL, (Italian), Closed., (1911-1976) Formerly located at 2222 W. Clearfield St. Spiritual records are kept at St. Martin de Porres. Tel.: 215-228-8330; 228-8331.

100—MATER DOLOROSA (1911), (Italian), Rev. Charles F. Engelhardt, O.S.F.S. In Res., Rev. Cornelius F. Kilty, O.S.F.S.
Res.: 1676 Ruan St., 19124. Tel: 215-535-4036; 215-743-4718; Fax: 215-535-1267.
Catechesis/Religious Program—Students 25.

101—MATERNITY B.V.M. (1870), Rev. George A. Majoros; Rev. Msgr. Bernard E. Witkowski; Revs. John F. McCole; Francis E. Fox; Joseph V. Accardi; Deacons Phillip Heaney; John C. Hynes.
Res.: 9220 Bustleton Ave., 19115. Tel: 215-673-8127; 215-676-5144; Fax: 215-673-6597.
School—9322 Bustleton Ave., 19115. Tel: 215-673-0235; Fax: 215-671-1347. Miss Kathleen Veasy, Prin. Sisters of Mercy 1; Lay Teachers 28; Students 693.
Catechesis/Religious Program—Students 118.
Convent—Tel: 215-673-8118.

102—ST. MATTHEW (1927), Rev. Msgr. Charles E. McGroarty; Revs. James E. Goerner; Edward C. Kelly; Daniel M. Dooley; Deacon Robert Burns. In Res., Rev. Msgr. Thomas J. Kelley (Retired).
Res.: 3000 Cottman Ave., 19149. Tel: 215-333-0585; Fax: 215-333-0757.
School—3040 Cottman Ave., 19149. Tel: 215-333-3142. Sisters, Servants of the Immaculate Heart of Mary 9; Lay Teachers 46; Students 1,188.
Catechesis/Religious Program—Students 75.

103—ST. MICHAEL (1831), [CEM] Rev. Herbert J. Sperger; Sr. Louise Goeller, I.H.M., Coord. Parish Svcs.; Deacon Zoilo Martes.
Res.: 1445 N. Second St., 19122. Tel: 215-739-2358; Fax: 215-739-5766.
Catechesis/Religious Program—Students 71.

104—ST. MICHAEL MISSION, , (1923-1958) Formerly located at Red Lion & Knights Rd. in Torresdale. Spiritual records are kept at Our Lady of Calvary Church. Tel.: 215-637-7515.

105—ST. MICHAEL OF THE SAINTS, Closed., (1924-1982) Formerly located at 4811 Germantown Ave. Spiritual records kept at St. Francis of Assisi Church. Tel.: 215-842-1287.

106—ST. MONICA (1895), Revs. Joseph Kelley; Anthony J. Cossavella; Clement Kurowski, O.F.M.; Ignatius Marneni; Charles Zlock; Deacons John C. Orlando; Leonard D. DeMasi.
Res.: 2422 S. 17th St., 19145. Tel: 215-334-4170; 215-334-4171; Fax: 215-389-6045.
School—Junior School, 1714 Ritner Ave., 19145. Tel: 215-467-5338; Fax: 215-467-4599. Sisters, Servants of the Immaculate Heart of Mary 9; Lay Teachers 33; Students 610.
School—Senior School, 2500 S. 16th St., 19145. Tel: 215-334-3777.
Catechesis/Religious Program—Tel: 215-334-1659; Fax: 215-389-0355. Students 182.

107—MOST BLESSED SACRAMENT (1901), (African American), Rev. Roland D. Slobogin.
Res.: 5628 Chester Ave., 19143. Tel: 215-729-0694; Fax: 215-729-0712.
Catechesis/Religious Program—Students 15.

108—MOST PRECIOUS BLOOD OF OUR LORD (1907-1993), Closed., (1907-1993) Formerly located at 28th & Diamond Sts. Spiritual records are kept at St. Martin De Porres Church. Tel.: 215-228-8330.

109—MOTHER OF DIVINE GRACE (1926), (Italian), Rev. John J. LaRosa; Deacon Joseph A. Micucci.
Res.: 2918 E. Thompson St., 19134. Tel: 215-739-0353; Fax: 215-739-9910.
School—2612 E. Monmouth St., 19134. Tel: 215-426-7325; Fax: 215-426-0753. Lay Teachers 10; Students 225.
Catechesis/Religious Program—Students 20.

110—NATIVITY OF THE BLESSED VIRGIN MARY (1882), Revs. Anthony F. Orth; Kevin B. McGoldrick. In Res., Rev. Daniel J. Moriarity.
Res.: 2535 E. Allegheny Ave., 19134. Tel: 215-739-2735; Fax: 215-739-2748.
School—2541 E. Madison St., 19134. Tel: 215-739-8761; Fax: 215-739-8781. School Sisters of Notre Dame 1; Lay Teachers 17; Students 320.
Catechesis/Religious Program—Tel: 215-739-1173. Sr. Marie Notwick, S.S.J., D.R.E. Students 84.
Convent—Capuchin Friars, 3224 Belgrade St., 19134. Tel: 215-739-0291. Revs. Thomas Betz, O.F.M.Cap.; James Menkhus, O.F.M.Cap.; Paul Dressler, O.F.M.Cap. Padre Pio Friary.

111—ST. NICHOLAS OF TOLENTINE (1912), (Italian), Revs. Nicholas Martorano, O.S.A.; John Brynes, O.S.A.; James R. Keating, O.S.A. (ORL). In Res., Bro. John Holt, O.S.A.
Res.: 910 Watkins St., 19148. Tel: 215-463-1326; Fax: 215-463-0888.
Church: Ninth St. below Morris St., 19148.
School—913 Pierce St., 19148. Tel: 215-468-0353; Fax: 215-334-9661. Religious Sisters Filippini 3; Religious 1; Lay Teachers 22; Students 470.
Catechesis/Religious Program—Students 75.

112—OLD ST. JOSEPH'S (1733), Revs. Mark F. Horak, S.J. (CHL); Leo A. Murray, S.J.; Joseph M. Alminde, S.J.; Michael A. Hricko (BAL); William F. Gavin, S.J. In Res., Revs. Joseph P. Logan, S.J.; James A.P. Bryne, S.J.
Res.: 321 Willings Alley, 19106. Tel: 215-923-1733; 215-923-1734; Fax: 215-574-8529.
School—St. Mary Interparochial School See Consolidated Parish Schools under Institutions Located in the Archdiocese.

113—OLD ST. MARY'S (1763), [CEM] Rev. Msgr. John A. Sharkey.
Res.: 252 S. Fourth St., 19106. Tel: 215-923-7930.
School—St. Mary Interparochial School See Consolidated Parish Schools under Institutions Located in the Archdiocese. Tel: 215-923-7522. Lay Teachers 9; Students 242.

114—OUR LADY HELP OF CHRISTIANS (1885), (German), Rev. Edward J. Kelly.
Res.: 3160 Gaul St., 19134. Tel: 215-739-2211; Fax: 215-739-9273.
School—2424 E. Allegheny Ave., 19134. Tel: 215-427-3499; Fax: 215-427-2296. Sisters of Christian Charity 3; Lay Teachers 9; Students 227.
Catechesis/Religious Program—Students 342.
Convent—Tel: 215-739-7890.

115—OUR LADY OF ANGELS (1907), (Italian), Rev. Ferdinand Buccafurni, Admin.
Res.: *St. Donato Church*, 403 N. 65th St., 19151. Tel: 215-747-4131; Fax: 215-747-7884.
Church: 4970 Master St., 19131.

116—OUR LADY OF CALVARY (1958), Revs. John P. Paul; John S. Hutter; Santo Garzarelli (Retired); Peter Talocci.
Res.: 11024 Knights Rd., 19154. Tel: 215-637-7515; Fax: 215-637-7517.

School—11027 Kipling Ln., 19154. Tel: 215-637-1648; Fax: 215-632-3810. Sisters of the Holy Family of Nazareth 5; Lay Teachers 33; Students 921.
Catechesis/Religious Program—Fax: 215-632-3816. Students 110.

117—OUR LADY OF CONSOLATION (1917), (Italian), Revs. Michael C. DiIorio; Christopher D. Lucas. In Res., Rev. John P. Betoni, O.S.A.
Res.: 7056 Tulip St., 19135. Tel: 215-333-0442; 215-333-5774; Fax: 215-333-2884. Web: www.olctacony.org.
School—Princeton & Edmund Sts., 19135. Tel: 215-624-0505. Web: www.olcschool.catholicweb.com. Ms. Margaret A. Clinton, Prin. Lay Teachers 11; Students 236.
Catechesis/Religious Program—Students 46.
Convent—7052 Tulip St., 19135. Tel: 215-332-4426.

118—OUR LADY OF GOOD COUNSEL (1898-1932), Closed., Formerly located at 816 Christian St. Spiritual records are kept at St. Paul Church. Tel.: 215-923-0355.

119—OUR LADY OF HOPE (1993), Revs. James J. McGinnis; Anthony M. Bozeman; Deacons William Champagne; Israel Rosario. In Res., Rev. Renato T. Oliveros, S.J.
Res.: 5200 N. Broad St., 19141-1628. Tel: 215-329-8100; 215-329-8164; Fax: 215-324-4660.
School—5218 N. Broad St., 19141-1626. Tel: 215-329-8100; Fax: 215-324-4660. Teresa Diamond, Prin. Lay Teachers 12; Students 240.
Catechesis/Religious Program—Students 110.

120—OUR LADY OF LORETO (1932-2000), (Italian), Closed., Formerly located at 6214 Grays Ave. Spiritual records are kept at St. Barnabas Church. Tel.: 215-726-1119; 1120.

121—OUR LADY OF LOURDES (1894), Rev. James C. Sherlock. In Res., Rev. Martin T. Cioppi, Ed.D.
Res.: 6315 Lancaster Ave., 19151. Tel: 215-473-1669; 215-473-1670; Fax: 215-473-1670.
School—1940 N. 63rd St., 19151. Tel: 215-877-2727; Fax: 215-877-6042. Sisters of Mercy 2; Lay Teachers 12; Students 235.
Catechesis/Religious Program—Students 14.

122—OUR LADY OF MERCY (1889-1984), Closed., Formerly located at Broad St. & Susquehanna Ave. Spiritual records are kept at St. Malachy Church. Tel.: 215-763-1305.

123—OUR LADY OF MT. CARMEL (1896), Revs. Kenneth W. Sharp; James A. Lyons; Sebi Antony Palamattath, C.M.I. (India).
Res.: 2319 S. Third St., 19148. Tel: 215-334-7766; Fax: 215-334-3269.
School—2329 S. Third St., 19148. Tel: 215-334-0584; Fax: 215-336-4519. Sisters of Mercy 4; Lay Teachers 16; Students 400.
Catechesis/Religious Program—Students 70.
Convent—251 Ritner St., 19148. Tel: 215-334-6800.

124—OUR LADY OF POMPEII (1914-1993), (Italian), Closed., Formerly located at 6th St. & Erie Ave. Spiritual records are kept at St. Veronica Church. Tel.: 215-228-4878.

125—OUR LADY OF RANSOM (1955), Revs. William F. McGeown; Christopher M. Walsh; Deacons Dominic A. Garritano; Joseph M. Cella.
Res.: 6701 Calvert St., 19149. Tel: 215-332-6166; Fax: 215-332-6811.
School—6740 Roosevelt Blvd., 19149. Tel: 215-332-4352. Lay Teachers 15; Students 315.
Catechesis/Religious Program—Tel: 215-708-2495. Students 65.
Convent—Tel: 215-624-1954.

126—OUR LADY OF THE BLESSED SACRAMENT (1910-1972), Closed., Formerly located at 712 N. Broad St. Spiritual records are kept at the Cathedral Basilica of SS. Peter and Paul. Tel.: 215-561-1313; 561-1314.

127—OUR LADY OF THE HOLY SOULS (1909-1993), Closed., Formerly located at 19th & Tioga Sts. Spiritual records are kept at Our Lady of Hope Church. Tel.: 215-329-8100.

128—OUR LADY OF THE ROSARY (1886), Rev. Thomas P. Kletzel; Sr. Patricia Tirrell, S.H.C.J., Dir. Parish Svcs.
Res.: 345 N. 63rd St., 19139. Tel: 215-476-6511; 215-476-2050; Fax: 215-476-3230.
School—344 N. Felton St., 19139. Tel: 215-474-4011; Fax: 215-474-7807. Mrs. Marguerite Henry, Prin. Lay Teachers 10; Students 215.
Catechesis/Religious Program—Students 16.

129—OUR LADY OF THE ROSARY (Germantown) (1928-1977), (Italian), Closed., Formerly located at 528 E. Haines St. Spiritual records are kept at Immaculate Conception Church. Tel.: 215-843-9468.

130—OUR LADY OF VICTORY (1899), Rev. Thomas P. Kletzel; Deacon Richard G. Nightingale.
Res.: 5412 Vine St., 19139. Tel: 215-747-7567; 215-747-6731; Fax: 215-748-6269.
School—54th & Summer Sts., 19139. Tel: 215-747-8004. Sr. Barbara Farrell, S.S.J., Prin. Sisters of St. Joseph 6; Lay Teachers 9; Students 210
Catechesis/Religious Program—Students 10.
Convent—5330 Vine St., 19139. Tel: 215-747-7040.

131—OUR MOTHER OF CONSOLATION (1855), Revs. James T. Dever, O.S.F.S.; Steven P. Wetzel, O.S.F.S.; Michael J. McCue, O.S.F.S.; Deacon Clifford W. Brown. In Res., Rev. Nicholas R. Waseline, O.S.F.S.
Res.: 9 E. Chestnut Hill Ave., 19118. Tel: 215-247-0430; Fax: 215-247-2506.
School—17 E. Chestnut Hill Ave., 19118. Tel: 215-247-1060; Fax: 215-247-0590. Michael C.. Kimble, Prin. Lay Teachers 11; Students 222.
Catechesis/Religious Program—Students 60.
Convent—23 E. Chestnut Hill Ave., 19118. Tel: 215-247-0552.

132—OUR MOTHER OF SORROWS (1852), Rev. Joseph F. Okonski.
Res.: 1030 N. 48th St., 19131. Tel: 215-878-0875; Fax: 215-878-7420.
School—1020 N. 48th St., 19131. Tel: 215-473-5828; Fax: 215-477-3096. Sisters of St. Joseph 2; Lay Teachers 10; Students 240.
Catechesis Religious Program— Joan Munkanta, D.R.E. Students 30.

133—ST. PATRICK (1839), Rev. Msgr. Philip J. Dowling.
Res.: 242 S. 20th St., 19103. Tel: 215-735-9900; Fax: 215-732-0998.
School—*St. Mary Interparochial School*, Tel: 215-923-7522.
Catechesis/Religious Program—Students 17.

134—ST. PAUL (1843), Rev. Louis P. Bellopede.
Res.: 808 S. Hutchinson St., 19147. Tel: 215-923-0355; Fax: 215-923-1803.
Worship Site:— Saint Mary Magdalen dePazzi Church, 712 Montrose St.
Catechesis/Religious Program—Students 140.

135—ST. PETER CLAVER (1889-1985), Closed., Formerly located at 12th & Lombard Sts. Spiritual records are kept at St. John the Evangelist Church. Tel.: 215-563-4145.

136—ST. PETER THE APOSTLE (1842), [CEM] Revs. Thomas J. Gavigan, C.SS.R.; Michael Hopkins, C.SS.R.; William J. Harbison, C.SS.R.; Dennis Demko, C.SS.R.; Deacons Jose Miguel Betancourt; Juan Ramos; Mr. Eugene McGarvey. In Res., Revs. Herman Brinkmann, C.SS.R.; Seamus M. Quinn, C.SS.R.; Rev. Msgr. George Tomichek D.C., P.A.; Revs. William C. Maggs, C.SS.R.; Donald Miniscalco, C.SS.R.
Church, Rectory and Mailing Address: 1019 N. Fifth St., 19123. Tel: 215-627-2386; Fax: 215-627-2366.
School—1009 N. Fifth St., 19123. Tel: 215-922-5958. Sr. Rosalia Federici, S.S.N.D. School Sisters of Notre Dame 1; Lay Teachers 11; Students 308.
Catechesis/Religious Program— Sr. Clare Marsico, I.H.M., D.R.E. Students 45.
Convent—1005 N. 5th St., 19123. Tel: 215-627-3954.
Shrine—*St. John Neuman*, Tel: 215-627-3080; Fax: 215-627-3296. Mary Arghenbright, Office Mgr.

137—ST. PHILIP NERI (1840), Revs. Vincent F. Welsh, J.C.L., M.A.; Francis Piro; Luke L. Chow (Retired).
Res.: 218 Queen St., 19147. Tel: 215-468-1922; Fax: 215-465-3147.
Catechesis/Religious Program— Twinned with Sacred Heart, Philadelphia. Tel: 215-462-4129; Fax: 215-462-9429. Students 46.

138—ST. RAPHAEL (1904-1989), Closed., Formerly located at 86th St. & Tinicum Ave. Spiritual records are kept at St. Irenaeus Church. Tel.: 215-727-2888.

139—ST. RAYMOND OF PENAFORT (1941), Rev. Msgr. John F. O'Brien. In Res., Rev. Daniel J. Kearns.
Res.: 1350 Vernon Rd., 19150. Tel: 215-549-3760; Fax: 215-549-1271.
School—7940 Williams Ave., 19150. Tel: 215-548-1919 Sisters of Mercy 1; Lay Teachers 10; Students 290.
Catechesis/Religious Program—Students 42.

140—RESURRECTION OF OUR LORD (1928), Revs. William C. Kaufman; Robert L. Brennan; Philip G. Bochanski; John E. Fitzgerald. In Res., Rev. Msgr. William A. Dombrow.
Res.: 2000 Shelmire Ave., 19152. Tel: 215-745-3211; Fax: 215-745-0587.
School—2020 Shelmire Ave., 19152. Tel: 215-742-1127; Fax: 215-742-0947. Stephen J. Hewitt, Prin.; Lucille Hillerman, Vice Prin. Lay Teachers 31; Students 807.
Catechesis/Religious Program—Tel: 215-742-1127. Students 140.

141—ST. RICHARD (1924), (Irish—Italian), Rev. Joseph J. Gallagher.
Res.: 3010 S. 18th St., 19145. Tel: 215-468-4777; Fax: 215-468-3161.
School—19th & Pollock Sts., 19145. Tel: 215-467-5430. Lay Teachers 10; Students 258.
Convent—1827 Pollock St., 19145. Tel: 215-465-5209. Sisters of Mercy 5.

142—ST. RITA OF CASCIA (1907), Revs. Michael F. Di Gregorio, O.S.A., Pastor & Shrine Dir.; James L. Galligan, O.S.A., Shrine Ministry; Edward E. Doran, O.S.A., Pastoral Assoc.; Deacon Leroy F. O'Kedas. In Res., Revs. Edward V. Griffin, O.S.A.; James R. Flynn, O.S.A.; Michael P. Sullivan, O.S.A.
Res.: 1166 S. Broad St., 19146. Tel: 215-546-8333; Fax: 215-732-3510.

143—ST. ROSE OF LIMA (1921), Rev. Msgr. Wilfred J. Pashley.
Res.: 1535 N. 59th St., 19151. Tel: 215-877-2991; Fax: 215-877-8255.
School—1522 N. Wanamaker St., 19131. Tel: 215-473-6030; Fax: 215-473-2338. Sisters, Servants of the Immaculate Heart of Mary 1; Lay Teachers 9; Students 240.
Catechesis/Religious Program—Students 14.

144—SACRED HEART (1913-1977), (Hungarian), Closed., Formerly located at Mascher & Master Sts. Spiritual records are kept at St. Michael Church. Tel: 215-739-2358

145—SACRED HEART OF JESUS (1871), Revs. Michael J. Sheehan; William E. Dean. In Res., Rev. John J. Bradley (Retired).
Res.: 1404 S. Third St., 19147-6099. Tel: 215-465-4050; 215-465-4051; Fax: 215-465-0400.
School—1329 Moyamensing Ave., 19147. Tel: 215-462-4129; Fax: 215-462-9429. Web: www.sacredheartsp.com. Sr. Regina Mullen, I.H.M., Prin. Sisters of the Immaculate Heart of Mary 4; Lay Teachers 9; Students 238.
Catechesis/Religious Program—Students 9.
Convent—1420 S. Third St., 19147. Tel: 215-463-8719. Sr. Mary Ann Bolger, I.H.M., Supr.

146—ST. STANISLAUS (1891), (Polish), Rev. Msgr. Joseph P. Duncan.
Res.: 242 Fitzwater St., 19147. Tel: 215-925-2631; Fax: 215-925-3585.
School—*St. Mary Interparochial School* See Consolidated Parish Schools under Institutions Located in the Archdiocese. Tel: 215-923-7522; Fax: 215-923-8502.

147—STELLA MARIS (1954), Rev. Msgr. James F. Connelly, S.T.L., H.E.D.; Revs. George B. Cadwallader, M.A.; George W. Crowe; Deacon James Thompson.
Res.: 2901 S. 10th St., 19148. Tel: 215-465-2336; 215-465-2337; Fax: 215-465-1061.
School—814 Bigler St., 19148. Tel: 215-467-6262; Fax: 215-389-6040. Sisters of St. Joseph 3; Lay Teachers 15; Students 285.
Catechesis/Religious Program—Students 105.
Convent—2929 S. 10th St., 19148. Tel: 215-462-1111.

148—ST. STEPHEN (1843-1993), Closed., Formerly located at Broad & Butler Sts. Spiritual records are kept at Our Lady of Hope Church. Tel: 215-329-8100.

149—ST. TERESA OF AVILA (1853-1972), Closed., Formerly located at Broad & Catherine Sts. Spiritual records are kept at St. Rita Church. Tel: 215-546-8333.

150—ST. THERESE OF THE CHILD JESUS (1925), Rev. Joseph C. McLoone, M.A.; Deacon Edward M. Purnell.
Res.: 6611 Ardleigh St., 19119. Tel: 215-438-5279; Fax: 215-438-8031.
School—Anderson & Upsal Sts., 19119. Tel: 215-844-5654; Fax: 215-844-8461. Mrs. Donna-Maria Meyers, Prin. Lay Teachers 12; Students 170.
Catechesis/Religious Program—Tel: 215-438-5746. Students 10.

151—ST. THOMAS AQUINAS (1885), Revs. Arthur I. Taraborelli; Joseph Dinh C. Huynh (Vietnam). In Res., Revs. Astanto Adi, C.M. (Indonesia); Joseph W. McCloskey.
Res.: 1719 Morris St., 19145. Tel: 215-334-2312; Fax: 215-755-9369.
School—18th & Morris Sts., 19145. Tel: 215-334-0878; Fax: 215-334-2357. Lay Teachers 23; Students 565.
School—*Day Care*, 1700 Fernon St.; 1800 Morris St.. Tel: 215-334-6480; Fax: 215-334-8221. Staff 12; Children 62.
Catechesis/Religious Program—Tel: 215-334-5998. Students 35.

152—ST. TIMOTHY (1928), Revs. Kevin C. Lawrence; Mark S. Kunigonis; Joseph E. Howarth, M.A.L.S.; Rev. Msgr. James J. Flood.
Res.: 3001 Levick St., 19149. Tel: 215-624-6188; Fax: 215-624-1316.
School—Hawthorne & Levick Sts., 19149. Tel: 215-338-9797; Fax: 215-331-6457. Stephen DiCicco, Prin.; Margaret Presutti, Vice Prin. Sisters of St. Joseph 3; Lay Teachers 33; Students 891.
Catechesis/Religious Program—Students 140.
Convent—3033 Levick St., 19149. Tel: 215-624-8333.

153—TRANSFIGURATION OF OUR LORD (1905-2000),, Formerly located at 5533 Cedar Ave. Spiritual records are kept at St. Cyprian Church. Tel.: 215-747-3250.

154—ST. VERONICA (1872), Revs. Eduardo Coll, I.V.E.;

Leonardo Lopez, I.V.E.; Deacon Rafael Maldonado; Mrs. Maureen Maher, Business Mgr. In Res., Rev. Manuel Jesus Taco Montalgo, I.V.E.
Res.: 533 W. Tioga St., 19140. Tel: 215-228-4878; 215-225-5677; Fax: 215-228-0381.
School—Sixth & Tioga St., 19140. Fax: 215-225-2595. Sr. Elizabeth Monica Acri, I.H.M., Prin. Sisters, Servants of the Immaculate Heart of Mary 3; Lay Teachers 8; Students 242.
Catechesis/Religious Program—Tel: 215-228-4878. Sr. Alba M. Bonilla, O.P., D.R.E. Students 175.
Convent—Sisters, Servants of the Immaculate Heart of Mary, 3521 N. Sixth St., 19140. Tel: 215-223-9107. Sr. Katherine Ward, I.H.M., Supr.
Convent—Dominican Sisters of Our Lady of the Rosary of Fatima, 632 W. Erie Ave., 19140. Tel: 215-226-3507.

155—ST. VINCENT DE PAUL (1851), Revs. John Kettelberger, C.M.; Stephen M. Grozio, C.M.; Juan F. Polanco, C.M.; Bro. Alfred J. Smith, C.M.
Res.: 109 E. Price St., 19144. Tel: 215-438-2925; Fax: 215-438-4856.
School—St. Martin De Porres School (Germantown) See Consolidated Parish Schools under Institutions Located in the Archdiocese. Tel: 215-842-1266.

156—VISITATION B.V.M. (1874), Revs. Hugh Joseph Shields; Thomas M. Higgins; Deacons Edwin Manzano; Apolonio Collazo.
Res.: 2625 B St., 19125. Tel: 215-634-1133; Fax: 215-634-6662.
School—300 E. Lehigh Ave., 19125. Tel: 215-634-7280; Fax: 215-634-4062. Sisters of St. Joseph 5; Lay Teachers 19; Students 467.
Catechesis/Religious Program—Sr. Margaret Doherty, S.H.C.J., D.R.E. Students 147.

157—ST. WILLIAM (1920), Rev. Msgr. Nelson J. Perez; Revs. Antony Thanickal, C.M.I.; Angelo Hernandez. In Res., Revs. Edmund J. Maher (Retired); Dominic Issac, J.C.D.
Res.: 6200 Rising Sun Ave., 19111. Tel: 215-745-1389; Fax: 215-745-2650.
School—Primary School, 6200 Palmetto St., 19111. Tel: 215-342-3369; Fax: 215-342-3115.
School—Intermediate School, Rising Sun and Robbins Aves., 19111. Tel: 215-342-4488.
School—Middle School, Rising Sun and Devereaux Aves., 19111. Tel: 215-725-2574. Sisters, Servants of the Immaculate Heart of Mary 9; Lay Teachers 26; Students 570.
Catechesis/Religious Program—Tel: 215-745-0921. Students 65.
Little Learners Center—514 McKinley St., 19111. Tel: 215-745-7708.
Convent—6226 Rising Sun Ave., 19111. Tel: 215-745-3513.
Pastoral Care Ministry—Tel: 215-742-9992.

OUTSIDE THE CITY OF PHILADELPHIA

ABINGTON, MONTGOMERY CO., OUR LADY HELP OF CHRISTIANS (1953), Rev. Joseph D. Bowen; Deacon Joseph T. Rooney. In Res., Revs. Albert J. Santorsola; Francis Farsaci, O.S.A.
Res.: 1500 Marian Rd., 19001. Tel: 215-886-3456; Fax: 215-886-7312.
School—Preschool, Tel: 215-887-8503. Lay Teachers 8; Students 46.
School—Elkins & Crater Rds., 19001. Tel: 215-887-3067; Fax: 215-887-3250. Lay Teachers 16; Students 261.
Catechesis/Religious Program—Tel: 215-672-7074. Noreen McDonnell. Students 302.

AMBLER, MONTGOMERY CO.

1—ST. ANTHONY OF PADUA (1886), [CEM] Revs. Stephen P. McHenry; Thomas Vattothuparambil (India); Deacons David E. Jones; Kevin Gentilcore.
Res.: 259 Forest Ave., 19002-5999. Tel: 215-646-4742; Fax: 215-646-4864.
School—Ambler Catholic Elementary School See Consolidated Parish Schools under Institutions Located in the Archdiocese. Tel: 215-646-6150; Fax: 215-654-5254. Sisters of St. Joseph 1; Lay Teachers 11; Students 213.
Catechesis/Religious Program—Tel: 215-646-0586. Students 280.

2—ST. JOSEPH (1920), Rev. Daniel J. Cavanaugh; Deacon Francis Clark. In Res., Rev. William Benonis.
Res.: 16 S. Spring Garden St., 19002-4797. Tel: 215-646-0494; Fax: 215-643-6389.
School—Ambler Catholic Elementary School See Consolidated Parish Schools under Institutions Located in the Archdiocese. Tel: 215-646-2007.
Catechesis/Religious Program—Students 328.

ARDMORE, MONTGOMERY CO., ST. COLMAN (1907), Most Rev. Robert P. Maginnis; Rev. Joseph M. Arnholt; Deacon David B. Schaffer. In Res., Rev. Richard J. Wright (Retired).
Res.: 11 Simpson Rd., 19003. Tel: 610-642-0545; Fax: 610-642-6853.
School—SS. Colman-John Neumann School See Consolidated Parish Schools under Institutions Located in the Archdiocese. Tel: 610-642-0545.

ARDSLEY, MONTGOMERY CO., QUEEN OF PEACE (1954), Rev. Msgr. James P. Matteo; Rev. James F. Sullivan. In Res., Rev. Msgr. William J. Lynn; Deacon Raymond Jacobucci.
Res.: 820 North Hills Ave., 19038. Tel: 215-887-1838; Fax: 215-887-8328.
School—835 North Hills Ave.. Tel: 215-886-4782. Sisters, Servants of the Immaculate Heart of Mary 3; Lay Teachers 14; Students 205.
Catechesis/Religious Program—Tel: 215-886-3014. Sr. Joyce Bell, I.H.M., D.R.E. Students 267.
Convent—825 North Hills Ave.. Tel: 215-887-4785.

ASTON, DELAWARE CO., ST. JOSEPH (1947), Revs. Robert C. Vogan; Geraldo J. Pinero; Rev. Msgr. Richard J. Skelly (Retired).
Res.: 3255 Concord Rd., 19014. Tel: 610-497-3340; Fax: 610-497-3383.
School—Tel: 610-494-0147. Ms. Anne Cook, Prin. Lay Teachers 19; Students 307.
Catechesis/Religious Program—Tel: 610-494-4358. Mrs. Linda Rowe, D.R.E. Students 415.

BALA CYNWYD, MONTGOMERY CO., ST. MATTHIAS (1906), Rev. Arthur E. Rodgers; Mr. John Yura, Dir. Parish Svcs.; Deacon Gerald Kelly. In Res., Revs. Charles E. Gormley (Retired); Philip J. Lowe, Ed.D.
Res.: 128 Bryn Mawr Ave., 19004-3099. Tel: 610-664-0207; Fax: 610-664-3559.
Catechesis/Religious Program—120 Bryn Mawr Ave., 19004-3098. Tel: 610-664-1942. Marie Faiss, D.R.E. Students 83.
Convent—108 Highland Ave., 19004. Tel: 610-667-1399.

BENSALEM, BUCKS CO.

1—ST. CHARLES BORROMEO (1903), Rev. Msgr. Francis A. Carbine; Rev. Patrick G. McCormick. In Res., Rev. John F. Meyers, Coord., Hispanic Min.
Res.: 1731 Hulmeville Rd., 19020. Tel: 215-638-3625; Fax: 215-245-8578.
School—(Grades PreK-8), 1704 Bristol Pike. Tel: 215-639-3456; Fax: 215-639-0496. Sisters, Servants of the Immaculate Heart of Mary 4; Lay Teachers 18; Students 409.
Catechesis/Religious Program—Tel: 215-638-3650. Students 185.
Convent—1080 Kings Ave.. Tel: 215-639-0113. Sisters Servants of the Immaculate Heart of Mary 9.

2—ST. ELIZABETH ANN SETON (1976), Rev. Michael J. Lonergan; Deacons Francis C. Klauder; Joseph W. Niland; Lawrence J. Gibson.
1200 Park Ave., 19020-4652. Tel: 215-245-6122; Fax: 215-245-4211.
Catechesis/Religious Program—Tel: 215-638-1498. Students 154.

3—SAINT EPHREM (1966), [CEM] Rev. Msgr. Kenneth P. McAteer; Revs. Timothy F. O'Sullivan; Stephen F. Katziner; Deacons Edward J. Dymek; James Debow.
Res.: 5400 Hulmeville Rd., 19020. Tel: 215-245-1698; Fax: 215-245-4787.
School—5340 Hulmeville Rd., 19020. Tel: 215-639-9488; Fax: 215-639-0206. Sisters, Servants of the Immaculate Heart of Mary 4; Lay Teachers 25; Students 632.
Catechesis/Religious Program—Tel: 215-639-4895. Students 246.
Convent—5300 Hulmeville Rd., 19020. Tel: 215-638-1024.

4—OUR LADY OF FATIMA (1954), Revs. Thomas D. Homa; Victor Warkulwiz, M.S.S.
Res.: Fatima Acres, 2933 Street Rd., 19020. Tel: 215-639-4254; Fax: 215-639-4589.
Early Childhood Center—Fatima Acres, 2915 Street Rd., 19020. Tel: 215-639-1916.
School—Tel: 215-638-3256; Fax: 215-639-6424. Sisters, Servants of the Immaculate Heart of Mary 3; Lay Teachers 9; Students 230.
Catechesis/Religious Program—2915 Street Rd.. Tel: 215-639-8814. Students 110.

BERWYN, CHESTER CO., ST. MONICA (1897), [CEM] Rev. William A. Trader. In Res., Rev. Vincent R. Morabito.
Res.: 635 First Ave., 19312. Tel: 610-644-0110; Fax: 610-695-0850.
School—First and Woodside Aves.. Tel: 610-644-8848; Fax: 610-695-8515. Mrs. Diana Thompson, Prin. Lay Teachers 16; Students 204.
Catechesis/Religious Program—Tel: 610-647-4757. Mrs. Mary Francisco, D.R.E. Students 270.

BOOTHWYN, DELAWARE CO., ST. JOHN FISHER (1971), Rev. John T. Lyons. In Res., Rev. Hans Kwakman, M.S.C. (Netherlands Antilles).
Res.: 4225 Chichester Ave., 19061. Tel: 610-485-0441; Fax: 610-859-2109.
School—Holy Saviour-St. John Fisher School See Consolidated Parish Schools under Institutions Located in the Archdiocese. Tel: 610-485-0363; Fax: 610-485-7809.
Catechesis/Religious Program—Tel: 610-485-0581. Students 335.

BRIDGEPORT, MONTGOMERY CO.

1—ST. AUGUSTINE (1892), [CEM] Rev. Msgr. Francis X. Schmidt. In Res., Rev. Robert J. Murray, O.S.A.
Res.: 464 Ford St., 19405. Tel: 610-272-4088; Fax: 610-272-6396.
School—Holy Trinity Catholic School See Consolidated Parish Schools under Institutions Located in the Archdiocese. Tel: 610-279-4630 (Upper); 610-277-4133 (Lower); Fax: 610-279-5579 (Upper); 610-277-4725 (Lower). Sisters, Servants of the Immaculate Heart of Mary 6; Lay Teachers 10; Students 170.
Catechesis/Religious Program—Students 90.
Station—Our Mother of Sorrows Worship Site:

2—OUR LADY OF MT. CARMEL (1924), (Italian), Rev. Salvatore J. Pronesti.
Res.: 502 Ford St., 19405. Tel: 610-272-3479; Fax: 610-272-5449.
School—Holy Trinity Catholic School See Consolidated Parish Schools under Institutions Located in the Archdiocese. Tel: 610-279-4630; Fax: 610-279-5579.
Catechesis/Religious Program—Tel: 610-272-3479; Fax: 610-272-5449. Students 236.

3—OUR MOTHER OF SORROWS (1926), (Slovak), Closed. For inquiries for parish records contact the chancery.

BRISTOL, BUCKS CO.

1—ST. ANN (1906), (Italian), Revs. James R. Day, O.SS.T.; John DiMatteo, O.SS.T., Pastor Emeritus; Claude J. Gravel, O.SS.T.; Thomas A. Morris, O.SS.T. (BAL).
Res.: 357 Dorrance St., P.O. Box 1175, 19007. Tel: 215-788-2128; Fax: 215-781-9782.
School—418 Jefferson Ave., 19007. Tel: 215-788-2030; Fax: 215-788-2979. Sisters of the Most Holy Trinity 3; Lay Teachers 10; Students 200.
Catechesis/Religious Program—Students 90.
Convent—430 Jefferson Ave., 19907. Tel: 215-788-2531.
Mission—Sacred Heart of Jesus Main St., Tullytown, Bucks Co. 19007.

2—ST. MARK (1845), [CEM] Rev. Dennis M. Mooney. In Res., Rev. Vincent Tung The Pham.
Res.: 1025 Radcliffe St., 19007. Tel: 215-826-0597; 215-788-2493; Fax: 215-785-4121.
School—1024 Radcliffe St., 19007. Tel: 215-785-0973; Fax: 215-781-0268. Karen Pezza, Prin. Lay Teachers 13; Students 197.
Catechesis/Religious Program—Tel: 215-788-2319. Students 155.
Convent—921 Radcliffe St., 19007.

BROOKHAVEN, DELAWARE CO., OUR LADY OF CHARITY (1952), Rev. Msgr. Andrew J. Hanlon; Rev. Joseph J. Martin.
Res.: 231 Upland Rd., 19015. Tel: 610-872-6192; Fax: 610-872-1120.
Parish Center—245 Upland Rd., 19015. Tel: 610-876-4198.
School—249 Upland Rd., 19015. Tel: 610-874-0410; Fax: 610-874-5879. Lay Teachers 20; Students 380.
Catechesis/Religious Program—Students 150.

BROOKLINE, DELAWARE CO., ANNUNCIATION B.V.M. (1927), Rev. Msgr. Ignatius L. Murray; Rev. George J. Boyle, Pastor Emeritus (Retired). In Res., Rev. Msgr. Michael T. McCulken.
Res.: 410 Sagamore Rd., Havertown, 19083. Tel: 610-449-1613; Fax: 610-449-7041.
School—411 Brookline Blvd., Havertown, 19083. Tel: 610-446-8430; Fax: 610-446-0627. Sisters of Mercy 1; Lay Teachers 21; Students 360.
Catechesis/Religious Program—Tel: 610-449-9858. Students 309.
Convent—421 Brookline Blvd., Havertown, 19083. Tel: 610-449-4065.

BROOMALL, DELAWARE CO., ST. PIUS X (1955), Revs. James Hutchins; Joseph M. Derrig; Mark J. Haynes; Deacon Joseph E. Iannucci.
Res.: 220 Lawrence Rd., 19008. Tel: 610-353-4880; Fax: 610-356-1084.
School—204 Lawrence Rd., 19008. Tel: 610-356-7222; Fax: 610-356-5380. Sisters, Servants of the Immaculate Heart of Mary 6; Lay Teachers 27; Students 608.
Catechesis/Religious Program—Tel: 610-353-6950. Students 488.

BRYN MAWR, DELAWARE CO., ST. JOHN NEUMANN (1964), Rev. James J. McKeaney; Sr. Carol Kelly, S.S.J., Dir. Parish Ministries. In Res., Rev. Msgr. Michael J. Matz.
Res.: 380 Highland Ln., 19010. Tel: 610-525-3100; Fax: 610-525-6363.
School—SS. Colman-St. John Neumann School See Consolidated Parish Schools under Institutions Located in the Archdiocese. Tel: 610-525-3266; Fax: 610-525-6103. Mrs. Mary Ann DeAngelo, Prin. Lay Teachers 19; Students 238.
Catechesis/Religious Program—Students 125.
Convent—340 Highland Ln., 19010. Tel: 610-527-1220; 610-527-3115.

BRYN MAWR, MONTGOMERY CO., OUR MOTHER OF GOOD COUNSEL (1885), Revs. James E. Martinez, O.S.A.; Adrian Gilligan, O.S.A. In Res., Revs.

Anthony P. Burrascano, O.S.A.; Harry A. Cassel, O.S.A. (Retired); Joseph A. Duffey (Retired); James D. McBurney, O.S.A.
Res.: 31 Pennswood Rd., 19010. Tel: 610-525-0147; Fax: 610-525-0157.
School—St. Thomas-Good Counsel School See Consolidated Parish Schools under Institutions Located in the Archdiocese. Tel: 610-525-1407; Fax: 610-525-4701. Lay Teachers 16; Students 160.
Catechesis/Religious Program—Fax: 610-525-0157. Students 140.

BUCKINGHAM, BUCKS CO., OUR LADY OF GUADALUPE (2000), Revs. Joseph J. Quindlen; Robert B. McDermott; Deacon Joseph N. Gousie.
Mailing Address: P.O. Box 406, 18912-0406.
Parish Office—5667 York Rd., Lahaska, 18931. Tel: 215-794-2004; Fax: 215-794-5004.
Res.: 3686 W. Long Ln., Doylestown, 18901-1292. Tel: 215-230-4625.
Catechesis/Religious Program—Tel: 215-794-4105; Fax: 215-794-4106. Students 817.

CENTER SQUARE, MONTGOMERY CO., ST. HELENA (1919), Revs. Joseph J. Nicolo, M.Div.; Thomas J. Duffy; Deacon A. Kenneth Belanger. In Res., Rev. Christopher Redcay.
Res.: 1489 DeKalb Pike, Blue Bell, 19422. Tel: 610-275-7711; Fax: 610-275-7610.
School—Tel: 610-279-3345. Sisters of Mercy 1; Lay Teachers 23; Students 384.
Catechesis/Religious Program—Tel: 215-277-3573. Students 250.
Convent—Tel: 610-272-1383.

CHADDS FORD, DELAWARE CO., ST. CORNELIUS (1963), Rev. James E. Locke; Deacons Clement J. McGovern; Richard G. Wirth.
Res.: 160 Ridge Rd., 19317. Tel: 610-459-2502; Fax: 610-459-3942.
School—St. Cornelius School, Tel: 610-459-8663; Fax: 610-459-7728.
Catechesis/Religious Program—Tel: 610-459-2130; Fax: 610-459-3942. Students 197.

CHALFONT, BUCKS CO., ST. JUDE (1962), Rev. Msgr. James P. McCoy; Rev. Sean P. Bransfield; Mr. Robert T. O'Sullivan, Business Mgr.; Deacons John T. Riordan; Claude B. Granese. In Res., Rev. Robert P. Lepleiter (Retired).
Res.: 321 W. Butler Ave., 18914-2329. Tel: 215-822-0179; Fax: 215-822-0638.
School—323 W. Butler Ave., 18914. Tel: 215-822-9225; Fax: 215-822-0722. Sr. Marie Melanie, R.S.M., Prin. Sisters 1; Lay Teachers 32; Students 477.
Catechesis/Religious Program—Tel: 215-822-7553. Sr. Ruth J. Mulligann, R.S.M., D.R.E. Students 715.

CHELTENHAM, MONTGOMERY CO.

1—ST. JOSEPH (1953), Rev. William S. Harrison.
Res.: 120 Hilldale Rd., 19012. Tel: 215-635-5533; Fax: 215-635-4578.
School—Boncouer & Water Rds.. Tel: 215-635-0102; Fax: 215-635-4881. Daughters of Our Lady of the Sacred Heart 2; Lay Teachers 8; Students 190.
Catechesis/Religious Program—Students 46.
Convent—7633 Waters Rd.. Tel: 215-224-2159.

2—PRESENTATION OF BLESSED VIRGIN MARY (1890), Revs. William S. Harrison; John R. McFadden; Sr. Joan B. Melley, S.S.J., Parish Svcs. Dir.
Res.: 100 Old Soldiers Rd., 19012. Tel: 215-379-1364; 215-379-1599; Fax: 215-379-1456.
School—Hasbrook Ave. & Old Soldiers Rd., 19012. Tel: 215-379-3798; Fax: 215-379-4430. Lay Teachers 20; Students 403.
Catechesis/Religious Program—Tel: 215-379-2054. Students 162.
Convent—107 Old Soldiers Rd., 19012. Tel: 215-379-8343.

CHESTER HEIGHTS, DELAWARE CO., ST. THOMAS THE APOSTLE (1729), [CEM] Revs. Richard C. Williams; Francis J. Cauterucci; Deacons Anthony DiIenno; Charles Devine.
Res.: 430 Valley Brook Rd., Glen Mills, 19342. Tel: 610-459-2224; Fax: 610-459-2677.
School—Tel: 610-459-8134; Fax: 610-459-8120. Lay Teachers 17; Students 410.
Catechesis/Religious Program—Tel: 610-459-3477. Joseph Doyle, D.R.E. Students 550.
Chaplaincies— Glen Mills Schools; Delaware County Prison; Brinton Manor; Rosehill; Riddle Hospital; 4 Seasons Assisted Living.

CHESTER, DELAWARE CO.

1—ST. ANTHONY OF PADUA (1908-1993), (Italian), Closed., Formerly located at 308 W. 3rd St. Spiritual records are kept at Saint Katharine Drexel Church, Chester. Tel: 610-872-3731.

2—ST. HEDWIG (1902-1993), (Polish), Closed., Formerly located at 4th & Hayes Sts. Spiritual records are kept at Sacred Heart Church, Clifton Heights. Tel: 610-623-0409.

3—IMMACULATE HEART OF MARY (1873-1993), Closed., Formerly located at 2nd & Norris Sts. Spiritual records are kept at Saint Katharine Drexel Church, Chester. Tel: 610-872-3731.

4—SAINT KATHARINE DREXEL (1993), Revs. Kevin P. Murray; William G. Ayers; Peter J. Welsh.
1920 Providence Ave., 19013. Tel: 610-872-3731; Fax: 610-872-0545. In Res., Deacon Michael J. Finn.
School—Tel: 610-872-7358; Fax: 610-872-7833.
Catechesis/Religious Program—Tel: 610-872-0192. Students 39.
Convent—1902 Providence Ave., 19013. Tel: 610-876-4913.
Saint Katharine Drexel Center—2nd & Norris St., 19013. Tel: 610-872-3731; Fax: 610-872-0545.

5—ST. MICHAEL (1842-1993), Closed., Formerly located at 7th St. & Avenue of the States. Spiritual records are kept at Saint Katharine Drexel Church, Chester. Tel: 610-872-3731.

6—OUR LADY OF VILNA (1924-1972), (Lithuanian), Closed., Formerly located at 4th & Madison Sts. Sacramental records are kept at Saint Katharine Drexel Church, Chester. Tel: 215-872-3731.

7—RESURRECTION OF OUR LORD (1911-1993), Closed., Formerly located at 9th St. & Highland Ave. Spiritual records are kept at Saint Katharine Drexel Church, Chester. Tel: 610-872-3731.

8—ST. ROBERT (1922-1993), Closed., Formerly located at 20th St. & Providence Ave. Spiritual records are kept at Saint Katharine Drexel Church, Chester. Tel: 610-872-3731.

CLIFTON HEIGHTS, DELAWARE CO., SACRED HEART (1910), (Polish), Rev. Msgr. Francis A. Barszczewski, S.T.L., M.S.L.S.; Deacon Boleslaw S. Wojewodka.
Res.: 316 E. Broadway, 19018. Tel: 610-623-0409; Fax: 610-623-2926.
School—Kindergarten & Preschool, 301 E. Berkley Ave., 19018. Tel: 610-623-4861.
Catechesis/Religious Program—Students 61.
Convent—300 E. Berkley Ave., 19018. Tel: 610-623-8804.
Mission—St. Hedwig Chapel 4th & Hayes Sts., Chester, Delaware Co. 19013.

COATESVILLE, CHESTER CO.

1—ST. CECILIA (1870), [CEM] Revs. Francis J. Schlett; Donald P. McNamara; Vacant (GB); Deacon Frederick H. Kerr.
Res.: 99 N. 6th Ave., 19320. Tel: 610-384-0422; Fax: 610-384-4415.
School—Coatesville Area Catholic Elementary School See Consolidated Parish Schools under Institutions Located in the Archdiocese. Tel: 610-384-5961. Sisters, Servants of the Immaculate Heart of Mary 3; Lay Teachers 23; Students 505.
Catechesis/Religious Program—Students 168.
Convent—603 E. Lincoln Hwy.. Tel: 610-384-0733; Fax: 610-384-5730.

2—ST. JOSEPH (1924), (Slovak), Rev. John V. Oulds.
Res.: 404 Charles St., 19320. Tel: 610-384-0360; Fax: 610-384-8545.
School—Coatesville Area Catholic Elementary School See Consolidated Parish Schools under Institutions Located in the Archdiocese. Tel: 610-384-5961; Fax: 610-383-6592.
Catechesis/Religious Program—Students 40.

3—OUR LADY OF THE ROSARY (1917), (Italian), Rev. Hans A.L. Brouwers; Deacon Richard Stoughton.
Res.: 80 S. 17th Ave., 19320. Tel: 610-384-1415; Fax: 610-383-6592.
School—Coatesville Area Catholic Elementary School See Consolidated Parish Schools under Institutions Located in the Archdiocese. Tel: 610-384-5961; Fax: 610-384-5730.
Catechesis/Religious Program—Tel: 610-384-1415. Students 207.

4—ST. STANISLAUS KOSTKA (1907), (Polish), [CEM] Rev. John V. Oulds.
Res.: 209 W. Lincoln Hwy., 19320. Tel: 610-384-1172; Fax: 610-384-8545.
School—Coatesville Area Catholic Elementary School See Consolidated Parish Schools under the Institutions Located in the Archdiocese. Tel: 610-384-5961; Fax: 610-383-6592.
Catechesis/Religious Program—Students 8.

COLLEGEVILLE, MONTGOMERY CO., ST. ELEANOR (1911), Revs. Patrick E. Sweeney; Andrew C. Brownholtz; Deacons James Burns; Joseph R. DeRosa. In Res., Rev. Msgr. John M. Galyo (Retired); Rev. Joseph Bongard.
Res.: 647 Locust St., 19426. Tel: 610-489-1647; Fax: 610-489-7469.
School—Tel: 610-489-9434; Fax: 610-489-6137. Lay Teachers 22; Students 495.
Catechesis/Religious Program—Tel: 610-489-4677. Students 986.

COLLINGDALE, DELAWARE CO., ST. JOSEPH (1916), Rev. James E. McVeigh; Deacon Paul McBlain; Revs. Mark S. Gaspar; Michael J. Davis.
Res.: 500 Woodlawn Ave., 19023. Tel: 610-583-4530; Fax: 610-583-7730.
School—Bartram & Woodlawn Aves.. Tel: 610-586-0356; Fax: 610-586-7710. Sr. Susan Immaculate, I.H.M., Prin. Sisters, Servants of the Immaculate Heart of Mary 5; Lay Teachers 25; Students 528.
Catechesis/Religious Program—Tel: 610-586-1520. Students 180.

CONSHOHOCKEN, MONTGOMERY CO.

1—SS. COSMAS AND DAMIAN (1912), (Italian), Rev. Gasper A. Genuardi. In Res., Rev. Msgr. Alexander J. Palmieri, M.A., J.C.L.; Rev. John J. McKenzie, O.S.A.; Deacon Armand J. Maresca.
Res.: 209 W. Fifth Ave., 19428. Tel: 610-828-0101; Fax: 610-828-5294.
School— See Consolidated Parish Schools under Institutions Located in the Archdiocese. , Conshohocken Catholic School. Tel: 610-828-2007; Fax: 610-825-8796.
Catechesis/Religious Program—Students 145.

2—ST. MARY (1905), (Polish), [CEM] Rev. Msgr. Robert J. Grudowski. In Res., Rev. Msgr. Edward S. Musial (Retired); Rev. James G. Mercer (ARL).
Res.: 140 W. Hector St., 19428. Tel: 610-828-0260; Fax: 610-828-9665.
Catechesis/Religious Program—Students 23.

3—ST. MATTHEW (1851), (Irish), [CEM] [JC 2] Rev. James W. Donlon. In Res., Rev. John J. Ames.
Res.: 219 Fayette St., 19428. Tel: 610-828-0424; Fax: 610-825-5168.
School—Conshohocken Catholic School See Consolidated Parish Schools under Institutions Located in the Archdiocese. Tel: 610-828-2007; Fax: 610-825-8796.
Catechesis/Religious Program—Students 183.
Convent—Third Ave. & Harry St.. Tel: 610-828-0174.

CROYDON, BUCKS CO., ST. THOMAS AQUINAS (1922), Rev. Lawrence F. Crehan.
Res.: 601 Bristol Pike, 19021-5496. Tel: 215-788-2989; 215-788-5813; Fax: 215-788-7626.
School—Walnut Ave. & Bristol Pike. Tel: 215-785-1130; Fax: 215-785-2564. Barbara A. Rutecki, Prin. Lay Teachers 12; Students 267.
Catechesis/Religious Program—Students 150.

DARBY, DELAWARE CO., BLESSED VIRGIN MARY (1913), Rev. Joseph Corley. In Res., Rev. Edward Kennedy.
Res.: 1101 Main St., 19023. Tel: 610-583-2128; Fax: 610-583-9829.
School—47 MacDade Blvd., 19023. Tel: 610-586-0638; Fax: 610-586-1582. Sisters, Servants of the Immaculate Heart of Mary 5; Lay Teachers 10; Students 213.
Catechesis/Religious Program—Tel: 610-586-2490. Students 84.

DELPHI, MONTGOMERY CO., ST. MARY (1926), Revs. Charles J. McElroy; Joseph L. Farrell.
Res.: 40 Spring Mount Rd., Schwenksville, 19473. Tel: 610-287-8156; Fax: 610-287-4226.
School—Tel: 610-287-7757. Lay Teachers 19; Students 357.
Catechesis/Religious Program—Tel: 610-287-4517. Students 415.

DOWNINGTOWN, CHESTER CO., ST. JOSEPH (1851), [CEM] Rev. Msgr. Joseph P. McFadden; Revs. Gregory J. Hamill; George J. Monahan; Stephen C.A. Kazanjian; Deacons Edward R. Schiappa; Paul Ruffo. In Res., Rev. Edward J. Jablonski.
Res.: 338 Manor Ave., 19335. Tel: 610-269-8294; Fax: 610-269-2487.
School—340 Manor Ave., 19335. Tel: 610-269-8999; Fax: 610-269-2252. Sisters, Servants of the Immaculate Heart of Mary 4; Lay Teachers 29; Students 794.
Catechesis/Religious Program—Tel: 610-873-8798. Mrs. Kathy Aaronson, D.R.E. Students 968.
Convent—336 Manor Ave., 19335. Tel: 610-269-8314.

DOYLESTOWN, BUCKS CO., OUR LADY OF MOUNT CARMEL (1850), [CEM] Rev. Charles H. Hagan; Rev. Msgr. James J. Mulligan, S.T.L., M.A.; Rev. Gerald J. Hoffman, M.Div.; Deacons George Corwell; Walter Kelly. In Res., Rev. Benet Hill, O.S.B. (WDC).
Res.: 235 E. State St., 18901. Tel: 215-348-4190; Fax: 215-348-3104.
School—E. Ashland St., 18901. Tel: 215-348-5907; Fax: 215-348-5671. Sisters of St. Francis of Philadelphia 2; Lay Teachers 25; Students 445.
Catechesis/Religious Program—Tel: 215-345-7089; Fax: 215-345-4216. Sr. Christa DeBacher, D.R.E. Students 1,068.
Convent—209 E. State St., 18901. Tel: 215-348-4663.

DREXEL HILL, DELAWARE CO.

1—ST. ANDREW (1916), Rev. Msgr. John E. Breslin; Revs. Joseph M. Glatts; Girard J. Cusatis; Deacon Daniel N. DeLucca.
Res.: 3500 School Ln., 19026. Tel: 610-259-1169; Fax: 610-259-0556.
School—529 Mason Ave., 19026. Tel: 610-259-5145; Fax: 610-284-6956. Ronald F. Duska Jr., Prin. Sisters of St. Joseph 2; Lay Teachers 24; Students 468.
Catechesis/Religious Program—Students 330.
Convent—535 Mason Ave., 19026. Tel: 610-259-6130.

2—ST. BERNADETTE (1947), Revs. William A. Wright; John H. Roebuck; Deacon Frank B. Burke, Business Mgr.
Res.: 1035 Turner Ave., 19026. Tel: 610-789-7676; Fax: 610-789-9539.
School—1015 Turner Ave., 19026. Tel: 610-449-6126; Fax: 610-789-0890. Oblate Sisters of St. Francis de Sales 3; Lay Teachers 23; Students 408.
Catechesis/Religious Program—Tel: 610-853-1740. John Blisard, D.R.E. Students 330.
Convent—Tel: 610-789-2325.

3—ST. CHARLES BORROMEO (1849), [CEM] Rev. Msgr. Daniel A. Murray, S.T.L., S.S.L.; Rev. Stephen A. Moerman; Deacons Francis Fabrizio; Peter Calabrese.
Res.: 3422 Dennison Ave., 19026. Tel: 610-623-3800; Fax: 610-284-9583.
School—3400 Dennison Ave., 19026. Tel: 610-626-4687; Fax: 610-626-1935. Sisters, Servants of the Immaculate Heart of Mary 4; Lay Teachers 17; Students 280.
Catechesis/Religious Program—Tel: 610-259-4389. Students 210.
Convent—3407 Dennison Ave., 19026. Tel: 610-623-0965.

4—ST. DOROTHY (1947), Rev. Michael D. Murphy; Deacon John J. Davaro. In Res., Rev. Daniel J. Dougherty.
Res.: 4910 Township Line, 19026. Tel: 610-789-7788; 610-789-7338; Fax: 610-789-6936.
School—Tel: 610-789-4100. Lay Teachers 23; Students 441.
Catechesis/Religious Program—Tel: 610-853-1499. Students 360.
Convent—1201 Burmont Rd., 19026. Tel: 610-789-4112.

EAST GOSHEN, CHESTER CO., SS. PETER AND PAUL (1967), Revs. James J. Foley; Joseph W. Dragon; Deacons Arthur G. Harrison; Thomas J. Horan; Robert F. Pierce.
Res.: 1325 Boot Rd., West Chester, 19380. Tel: 610-692-2216; Fax: 610-692-7103.
School—(Grades PreK-5), 1327 Boot Rd., West Chester, 19380-5901. Tel: 610-696-1000. Mrs. Margaret Egan, Prin. Lay Teachers 16; Students 308.
Catechesis/Religious Program—Tel: 610-692-5886. Patricia B. Ehrhart, D.R.E. Students 653.

EAST LANSDOWNE, DELAWARE CO., ST. CYRIL OF ALEXANDRIA (1928), Revs. Edward T. Kearns; Colm Campbell (Ireland); Deacon James E. Dalton.
Res.: 153 Penn Blvd., 19050-2698. Tel: 610-623-5160; Fax: 610-622-2479.
School—716 Emerson Ave., 19050. Tel: 610-623-1113; Fax: 610-623-2427. Sisters, Servants of the Immaculate Heart of Mary 4; Lay Teachers 13; Students 288.
Catechesis/Religious Program— 19050. Tel: 610-623-1406; Fax: 610-622-2479. Students 150.
Convent—171 Penn Blvd., 19050. Tel: 610-623-6590.

EDDYSTONE, DELAWARE CO., ST. ROSE OF LIMA (1890), Rev. Gerald D. Canavan; Deacon Lawrence P. Schnepp.
Res.: 1901 Chester Pike, 19013. Tel: 610-876-6170; Fax: 610-876-6128.
School—*St. Madeline-St. Rose School* See Consolidated Parish Schools under Institutions Located in the Archdiocese. Tel: 610-583-3662; Fax: 610-583-3683.
Catechesis/Religious Program—Students 175.

ELKINS PARK, MONTGOMERY CO., ST. JAMES (1923), Rev. Raymond J. Himsworth.
Res.: 8320 Brookside Rd., 19027. Tel: 215-635-6210; Fax: 215-635-3346.
School—8304 Brookside Rd., 19027. Tel: 215-635-4673; Fax: 215-635-3521. Lay Teachers 11; Students 225.
Catechesis/Religious Program—Students 106.

ESSINGTON, DELAWARE CO., ST. MARGARET MARY ALACOQUE (1921), Rev. John J. Nevins.
Res.: 500 Wanamaker Ave., 19029. Tel: 610-521-9177; Fax: 610-595-0230.
Catechesis/Religious Program—Students 55.

EXTON, CHESTER CO., SS. PHILIP AND JAMES (1959), Rev. Msgr. Michael J. Burke; Rev. Christopher B. Rogers; Deacons Frank M. Bizal; Charles W. Polley Jr.; William C. Fahy. In Res., Revs. James C. Otto; Samuel A. Verruni, Chap.
Res.: 107 N. Ship Rd., 19341. Tel: 610-363-6536; Fax: 610-524-7359.
School—721 N. Ship Rd., 19341. Tel: 610-363-6530; Fax: 610-363-6495. Sr. Mary Anne Winterberg, I.H.M., Prin. Sisters, Servants of the Immaculate Heart of Mary 6; Lay Teachers 32; Students 750.
Catechesis/Religious Program—Tel: 610-363-1307. Sr. Eunice Marie, I.H.M., D.R.E. Students 577.
Convent—105 N. Ship Rd., 19341. Tel: 610-363-7068.

FAIRLESS HILLS, BUCKS CO., ST. FRANCES CABRINI (1953), Rev. Msgr. John J. Miller; Rev. Timothy J. Buckley; Deacons Louis F. Hoelzle; Mace M. Mazzoni.
Res.: 325 S. Oxford Valley Rd., 19030. Tel: 215-946-4040; 215-943-1116.
School—10 Goble Ct., 19030. Tel: 215-946-6334. Lay Teachers 23; Students 416.
Catechesis/Religious Program—Tel: 215-946-1115. Students 295.

FALLSINGTON, BUCKS CO., ST. JOSEPH THE WORKER (1956), Rev. Donald G. Birch. In Res., Rev. Mark J. Hunt.
Res.: 9172 New Falls Rd., 19054. Tel: 215-945-4486; Fax: 215-945-3292.
School—9160 New Falls Rd., 19054. Tel: 215-945-4312; Fax: 215-945-8733. Lay Teachers 14; Students 239.
Catechesis/Religious Program—Tel: 215-945-4680. Students 169.

FEASTERVILLE, BUCKS CO., ASSUMPTION B.V.M. (1950), Revs. Daniel P. Devine; James J. Brennan; Sr. Diane Wolf, S.S.J., Pastoral Assoc. In Res., Rev. Robert H. Roedel.
Res.: 1900 Meadowbrook Rd., 19053. Tel: 215-357-1221; Fax: 215-357-2283.
School—Tel: 215-357-5499. Sisters, Servants of the Immaculate Heart of Mary 5; Lay Teachers 18; Students 395.
Catechesis/Religious Program—Tel: 215-357-3445. Mrs. Joyce Boag. Students 339.
Convent—55 Bristol Rd., 19053. Tel: 215-355-3898.

FLOURTOWN, MONTGOMERY CO., ST. GENEVIEVE (1953), Rev. Msgr. Robert J. Carroll. In Res., Revs. John D. Reardon, M.Div.; Carl F. Janicki; Deacons Joseph Manson; Joseph Nines.
Res.: 1225 Bethlehem Pike, 19031. Tel: 215-836-2828; Fax: 215-836-7218.
School—1237 Bethlehem Pike, 19031. Tel: 215-836-5644; Fax: 215-836-0159. Sisters of St. Joseph 4; Lay Teachers 16; Students 238.
Catechesis/Religious Program—Tel: 215-836-1994. Students 169.
Station—*Seven Dolors Church* Worship Site: 1301 Bethlehem Pike, 19031. Tel: 215-233-4392; Fax: 215-233-4392.

GLADWYNE, MONTGOMERY CO., ST. JOHN BAPTIST VIANNEY (1927), Rev. Donald E. Leighton; Deacon Paul Kern. In Res., Rev. Msgr. Joseph A. Shields (Retired).
Res.: 1110 Vaughans Ln., 19035. Tel: 610-642-0938; Fax: 610-642-1432.
Catechesis/Religious Program—1222 Hagysford Rd., Penn Valley, 19072. Tel: 610-664-0165; Fax: 610-664-5612. Sr. Mary Sarah, R.S.M., D.R.E. Students 115.

GLENOLDEN, DELAWARE CO., ST. GEORGE (1923), Rev. Michael P. McCormac.
Res.: 22 E. Cooke Ave., 19036-1497. Tel: 610-237-1633; Fax: 610-237-9626.
School—15 Lamont Ave., 19036-1497. Tel: 610-583-0419. Lay Teachers 9; Students 212.
Catechesis/Religious Program—Students 135.
Convent—11 E. Lamont Ave., 19036-1497. Tel: 610-583-5160.

GLENSIDE, MONTGOMERY CO., ST. LUKE THE EVANGELIST (1905), Rev. Msgr. J. Michael Flood; Rev. Anthony J. DiGuglielmo; Deacon Thomas Croke.
Res.: 2316 Fairhill Ave., 19038. Tel: 215-572-0128; Fax: 215-572-0482.
School—2330 Fairhill Ave., 19038. Tel: 215-884-0843; Fax: 215-884-4607. Sr. William Adele, S.S.J., Prin. Sisters of St. Joseph 5; Lay Teachers 22; Students 352.
Catechesis/Religious Program—2324 Fairhill Ave., 19038. Tel: 215-884-2080. Sharon D'Amore, D.R.E. Students 354.
Convent—2324 Fairhill Ave., 19038. Tel: 215-884-0225.

HATBORO, MONTGOMERY CO., ST. JOHN BOSCO (1953), Revs. Kenneth Putz; Zachary W. Nauit; Deacons Daniel J. Rouse; William F. Kruckenberger.
Res.: 235 E. County Line Rd., 19040. Tel: 215-672-7280; Fax: 215-672-1105.
School—215 E. County Line Rd., 19040-1298. Tel: 215-675-1484. Sisters, Servants of the Immaculate Heart of Mary 4; Lay Teachers 16; Students 224.
Catechesis/Religious Program—Tel: 267-803-0774. Students 348.
Convent—189 E. County Line Rd., 19040. Tel: 215-675-2301.

HATFIELD, MONTGOMERY CO., ST. MARIA GORETTI (1953), Revs. Leonard N. Peterson; Jeffrey M. Stecz.
Res.: 1601 Derstine Rd., 19440. Tel: 215-721-0199; Fax: 215-721-4320.
School—2980 Cowpath Rd., 19440. Tel: 215-721-9098; Fax: 215-721-3394. Lay Teachers 10; Students 225.
Catechesis/Religious Program—Tel: 215-721-6559. Students 697.

HAVERTOWN, DELAWARE CO., ST. DENIS (1825), [CEM] Rev. Msgr. Joseph T. Marino; Rev. Kevin J. Gallagher; Deacon John F. Schlegel. In Res., Rev. Msgr. Bernard J. Trinity (Retired).
Res.: 2401 St. Denis Ln., 19083. Tel: 610-446-0200; Fax: 610-446-4638.
School—300 E. Eagle Rd., 19083. Tel: 610-446-4608; Fax: 610-446-5705. Sisters of Mercy 1; Lay Teachers 31; Students 505.
Catechesis/Religious Program—Tel: 610-449-7892; Fax: 610-446-5705. Students 270.
Convent—Tel: 610-446-1263.

HIGHLAND PARK, DELAWARE CO., ST. LAURENCE (1917), Rev. Msgr. Thomas J. Herron; Revs. Francis J. Mulranen; John D. Silcox Jr.; Deacon Mark Wallace.
Res.: 30 St. Laurence Rd., Upper Darby, 19082. Tel: 610-449-0600; 610-449-0601; Fax: 610-449-4299.
School—8245 W. Chester Pike, 19082. Tel: 610-789-2670; Fax: 610-789-1128. Sisters, Servants of the Immaculate Heart of Mary 10; Lay Teachers 21; Students 416.
Catechesis/Religious Program—Tel: 610-789-4854. Students 200.
Convent—Tel: 610-449-7042.
H.O.P.E. Program—Tel: 610-449-0600; Fax: 610-449-4299.

HILLTOWN, BUCKS CO., OUR LADY OF THE SACRED HEART (1919), [CEM] Rev. Michael J. Kelly; Deacon Vincent G. Ceneviva. In Res., Rev. Joseph F. Rymdeika.
Res.: Rte. 152 & Broad St., 18927. Tel: 215-822-9224; Fax: 215-712-0278.
School—*St. Agnes-Sacred Heart School* See Consolidated Parish Schools under Institutions Located in the Archdiocese. Tel: 215-822-9174; Fax: 215-822-7942.
Catechesis/Religious Program—Tel: 215-822-9020. Students 397.

HOLLAND, BUCKS CO., ST. BEDE THE VENERABLE (1966), Revs. Eugene G. Cusick; Michael J. McCleane; Andrew McCormick; Deacon Joseph Orlando.
Res.: 1071 Holland Rd., 18966. Tel: 215-357-5720; Fax: 215-396-0704.
School—1053 Holland Rd., 18966. Tel: 215-357-4720; Fax: 215-355-9526. Sisters of St. Casimir 2; Lay Teachers 22; Students 511.
Catechesis/Religious Program—Tel: 215-357-2130; Fax: 215-357-0232. Students 812.
Convent—35 Vanderveer Dr., 18966. Tel: 215-355-2132.

HONEY BROOK, CHESTER CO., ST. PETER (1963), Rev. Michael J. Fitzpatrick; Virginia L. Giles, Business Mgr.; Deacon John J. D'Amico.
Res.: 1080 N. Manor Rd., 19344-9610. Tel: 610-942-2112; Fax: 610-942-3385.
Catechesis/Religious Program—Tel: 610-942-4518; Fax: 610-942-4518. Patrice A. Peterson, D.R.E. Students 310.

HORSHAM, MONTGOMERY CO., ST. CATHERINE OF SIENA (1963), Revs. J. Jerome Wild; Laurence Gleason; Deacons Timothy Urbanski; Richard Haddon. In Res., Rev. John J. Nordeman.
Res.: 321 Witmer Rd., 19044. Tel: 215-672-2881; Fax: 215-674-1025.
School—317 Witmer Rd., 19044. Tel: 215-674-1904; Fax: 215-674-1466. Sisters of Mercy 1; Lay Teachers 25; Students 342.
Catechesis/Religious Program—Tel: 215-674-8549. Students 550.
Convent—319 Witmer Rd., 19044. Tel: 215-672-7221.

HUNTINGDON VALLEY, MONTGOMERY CO., ST. ALBERT THE GREAT (1962), Rev. Msgr. Paul F. Curran; Revs. Kevin J. Parker; John P. Gallagher (Retired); Sr. Marie Rachfalski, O.S.F., Parish Svcs. Dir.
Res.: 212 Welsh Rd., 19006. Tel: 215-947-3500; Fax: 215-938-9071.
School—216 Welsh Rd., 19006. Tel: 215-947-2332; Fax: 215-938-9360. Mary Randles, Prin. Lay Teachers 23; Students 483.
Catechesis/Religious Program—Tel: 215-947-3641. Students 290.

JAMISON, BUCKS CO., ST. CYRIL OF JERUSALEM (1965), Rev. Robert J. Powell, D.M.A, M.A., M.Div.; Deacons Joseph F. Windish; Joseph Owen. In Res., Rev. Patrick S. McManus, M.A.
Res.: 1410 Almshouse Rd., 18929. Tel: 215-343-1288; Fax: 215-343-3924.
Catechesis/Religious Program—Tel: 215-343-3139. Students 771.

JENKINTOWN, MONTGOMERY CO., IMMACULATE CONCEPTION (1866), Rev. Msgr. John J. Conahan; Rev. Jacob Christy (SYM); Deacons Paul Hagerty; Alvin Clay. In Res., Rev. William J. Chiriaco.
Res.: 604 West Ave., 19046-2708. Tel: 215-884-4022; 215-887-0181; Fax: 215-887-4163.
School—606 West Ave., 19046. Tel: 215-887-1312; Fax: 215-887-5517. Diane Greco, Prin. Lay Teachers 20; Students 235.
Catechesis/Religious Program—Tel: 215-885-5586. Students 275.

KENNETT SQUARE, CHESTER CO., ST. PATRICK (1869), [CEM] Rev. Victor F. Sharrett; Deacon James K. Madonna.

Res.: 218 S. Meredith St., 19348. Tel: 610-444-2128; Fax: 610-444-4941.
Parish Office:—212 Meredith St., 19348. Tel: 610-444-4364; Fax: 610-444-2129.
School—210 Meredith St., 19348. Tel: 610-444-3104; Fax: 610-444-3166. Lay Teachers 10; Students 204.
Catechesis/Religious Program—Tel: 610-444-2214. Marianne Kane, D.R.E. Students 305.

KIMBERTON, CHESTER CO., ST. BASIL THE GREAT (1965), Rev. Robert A. McLaughlin; Deacon Barry R. Midwood.
Res.: 2300 Kimberton Rd., Box 637, 19442-0637. Tel: 610-933-2110; 610-933-4730; Fax: 610-933-0627.
School—Tel: 610-933-2453; Fax: 610-933-7590. Lay Teachers 12; Students 250.
Catechesis/Religious Program—Tel: 610-935-1261. Students 218.
Convent—Sisters of St. Francis Residence, Tel: 610-933-2345.

KING OF PRUSSIA, MONTGOMERY CO., MOTHER OF DIVINE PROVIDENCE (1954), Rev. Thomas J. Furey. In Res., Revs. Frank A. Giuffre; James Cox.
Res.: 333 Allendale Rd., 19406-1640. Tel: 610-265-4178; Fax: 610-265-1653.
School—405 Allendale Rd., 19406. Tel: 610-265-2323; Fax: 610-265-1816. Grey Nuns of the Sacred Heart 2; Lay Teachers 20; Students 346.
Catechesis/Religious Program—Tel: 610-337-2173. Students 215.
Convent—Tel: 610-278-9439.

LAFAYETTE HILL, MONTGOMERY CO., ST. PHILIP NERI (1945), Rev. Msgr. Charle P. Vance. In Res., Rev. Paul C. Brandt.
Res.: 437 Ridge Pike, 19444. Tel: 610-828-5717; 610-834-1975; Fax: 610-834-0392.
School—3015 Chestnut St., 19444. Tel: 610-828-3082; Fax: 610-828-2943. Sisters of St. Joseph 5; Lay Teachers 22; Students 502.
Catechesis/Religious Program—Tel: 610-834-9868. Students 209.
Convent—Tel: 610-828-2866.

LANSDALE, MONTGOMERY CO., ST. STANISLAUS (1876), [CEM] Rev. Msgr. Joseph W. Murray; Revs. David A. Doyne; John C. Nguyen; Robert A. Roncase; Deacons Mathieu Tielemans; C. Stephens Vondercrone.
Res.: 51 Lansdale Ave., 19446. Tel: 215-855-3133; Fax: 215-855-5478.
School—493 E. Main St., 19446. Tel: 215-368-0995; Fax: 215-393-4869. Diane McCaughan, Prin.; Miss Maureen Drumm, Asst. Prin. Lay Teachers 23; Students 545.
Catechesis/Religious Program—Tel: 215-855-9893. Students 320.

LANSDOWNE, DELAWARE CO., ST. PHILOMENA (1898), Rev. David H. Benz; Deacon Charles Tobin. In Res., Rev. A. Jason Kulczynski.
Res.: 41 E. Baltimore Ave., 19050. Tel: 610-622-2420; Fax: 610-622-1215.
School—21 N. Highland Ave., 19050. Tel: 610-259-6817; Fax: 610-259-5656. Email: stphilomenaoffice@juno.com. Dr. Joan Ciccone, Prin. Lay Teachers 13; Students 218.
Catechesis/Religious Program—Students 50.

LENNI, DELAWARE CO., ST. FRANCIS DE SALES (1894), [CEM] Revs. Michael A. Colagreco; Joseph E. Walsh, Pastor Emeritus (Retired).
Res.: 35 New Rd., P.O. Box 97, 19052. Tel: 610-459-2203; Fax: 610-459-5029.
School—Tel: 610-459-0799; Fax: 610-558-3058. Sisters of St. Francis of Philadelphia 2; Lay Teachers 9; Students 189.
Catechesis/Religious Program—Tel: 610-459-0554. Students 257.
Convent—28 New Rd., Aston, 19014. Tel: 610-459-2501.
Station—Delco Juvenile Detention Center Old Chester.
Station—Fair Acres Geriatric Center Lima. Tel: 610-891-5600.
Station—Sleighton Farms Darling. Tel: 610-558-6500.
Station—Granite Farms Est. Media. Tel: 610-358-3440.
Station—Riddle Village Media. Tel: 610-891-3777.
Station—The Residence at Glen Riddle Media. Tel: 610-358-9933.
Station—Riddle Hospital Media. Tel: 610-566-9400.
Station—Penn State Lima Campus Media. Tel: 610-892-1350.
Station—Williamson School Media. Tel: 610-566-1776.

LEVITTOWN, BUCKS CO.

1—IMMACULATE CONCEPTION B.V.M. (1954), Rev. Joseph L. Logrip. In Res., Rev. Alan Okon.
Res.: 5201 Emilie Rd., 19057-2505. Tel: 215-946-1638; 215-946-1639; Fax: 215-946-2149.
School—3810 Oxford Valley Rd., 19057. Tel: 215-949-2848. Sisters, Servants of the Immaculate Heart of Mary 2; Lay Teachers 14; Students 256.
Catechesis/Religious Program—Tel: 215-945-0826. Students 135.
Convent—Tel: 215-945-4664.

2—ST. MICHAEL THE ARCHANGEL (1953), Rev. Msgr. Richard T. Powers; Revs. Francis X. Trauger; Michael J. Saban; Deacon Harry J. Simpson.
Res.: 66 Levittown Pkwy., 19054. Tel: 215-945-1166; Fax: 215-945-6988.
School—130 Levittown Pkwy., 19054. Tel: 215-943-0222; Fax: 215-943-9068. Lay Teachers 32; Students 678.
Catechesis/Religious Program—Tel: 215-547-2518. Students 458.
Convent—85 Levittown Pkwy., 19054. Tel: 215-943-8232.

3—QUEEN OF THE UNIVERSE (1955), Revs. Paul A. Wiedmann; John C. Moloney; Deacon Joseph Upcavage.
Res.: 2443 Trenton Rd., 19056. Tel: 215-945-8750; Fax: 215-945-0413.
School—Tel: 215-945-1866. Sisters of St. Joseph 1; Lay Teachers 12; Students 260.
Catechesis/Religious Program—Tel: 215-945-2704. Students 498.
Convent—Tel: 215-945-6116.

LINFIELD, MONTGOMERY CO., ST. CLARE (1963), Rev. Joseph P. McGeown.
Res.: 1223 Main St., 19468-1020. Tel: 610-495-7263; Fax: 610-495-9928.
Catechesis/Religious Program—Tel: 610-495-0464. Students 394.

LINWOOD, DELAWARE CO., HOLY SAVIOUR (1915), Rev. Michael J. Gerlach. In Res., Rev. Peter J. Foley.
Res.: 108 E. Ridge Rd., 19061. Tel: 610-485-2520; 610-485-2521; Fax: 610-485-7727.
School—Holy Saviour-St. John Fisher School See Consolidated Parish Schools under Institutions Located in the Archdiocese. Tel: 610-485-0363; Fax: 610-485-7809. Barbara Virga, B.A., M.A., Prin.
Catechesis/Religious Program—Tel: 610-485-2520; Fax: 610-485-7727. Students 110.
Convent—122 E. Ridge Rd., 19061. Tel: 610-485-7320.

LOWER MAKEFIELD, BUCKS CO., ST. JOHN THE EVANGELIST (1964), Rev. Msgr. James J. Fitzpatrick; Rev. Vito J. Carbone; Deacons James E. Hartman; Robert P. Gellentien. In Res., Rev. Robert J. Conner (Retired).
Res.: 752 Big Oak Rd., Morrisville, 19067. Tel: 215-295-4102; Fax: 215-295-3128.
School—728 Big Oak Rd., Morrisville, 19067. Tel: 215-295-0629; Fax: 215-295-6258. Bernardine Sisters of St. Francis 1; Lay Teachers 17; Students 240.
Catechesis/Religious Program—Tel: 215-295-9239. Students 437.
Convent—Tel: 215-295-8201.

MALVERN, CHESTER CO., ST. PATRICK (1915), Revs. James J. Ambrogi; Nicholas J. Dirinni; Deacons Lawrence P. Froio; Paul Cox. In Res. Rev. Matthew W. Guckin.
Res.: 126 Woodland Ave., 19355. Tel: 610-647-2345; Fax: 610-647-4997.
School—115 Channing Ave., 19355. Tel: 610-644-5797; Fax: 610-647-0535.
Catechesis/Religious Program—Tel: 610-296-8899; Fax: 610-296-8384. Students 675.

MANOA, DELAWARE CO., SACRED HEART (1927), Revs. Henry J. McKee; Michael Murtha; Deacons John J. Suplee; Thomas J. Woods; Mike Small.
Res.: 105 Wilson Ave., Havertown, 19083. Tel: 610-449-3000; Fax: 610-449-2364.
School—Tel: 610-446-9198; Fax: 610-446-4861. Sisters, Servants of the Immaculate Heart of Mary 2; Lay Teachers 12; Students 231.
Catechesis/Religious Program—Tel: 610-446-7597; Fax: 610-446-3176. Sr. Kathleen McCafferty, S.S.J., D.R.E. Students 310.
Convent—108 Shelbourne Rd., 19083. Tel: 610-446-3694.

MAPLE GLEN, MONTGOMERY CO., ST. ALPHONSUS (1963), Rev. Msgr. Thomas J. Owens; Rev. John C. Crowley; Deacon Peter H. Burghart.
Res.: 33 Conwell Dr., 19002. Tel: 215-646-4600; Fax: 215-646-0180.
School—29 Conwell Dr., 19002. Tel: 215-646-0150; Fax: 215-646-7150. Lay Teachers 23; Students 343.
Catechesis/Religious Program—Tel: 215-643-7938. Students 351.
Convent—1563 Temple Dr., 19002. Tel: 215-646-6644.

MARCUS HOOK, DELAWARE CO., IMMACULATE CONCEPTION (1917), (Italian) Rev. Joseph A. Amalfitano.
Res.: 21 W. Eighth St., P.O. Box 355, 19061. Tel: 610-485-1026; Fax: 610-485-7829.
Catechesis/Religious Program—Students 45.

MEDIA, DELAWARE CO.

1—ST. MARY MAGDALEN (1963), Revs. Ralph J. Chieffo; John E. Mulgrew, M.A.; Deacon E. Peter Zurbach.
Res.: 2400 N. Providence Rd., 19063. Tel: 610-566-8821; Fax: 610-566-1005.
School—2430 N. Providence Rd., 19063. Tel: 610-565-1822; Fax: 610-627-9670. Lay Teachers 29; Students 424.
Catechesis/Religious Program—Tel: 610-565-5782. Students 200.

2—NATIVITY OF THE BLESSED VIRGIN MARY (1868), [CEM] Rev. Msgr. Francis A. Giliberti; Rev. Patrick J. Welsh. In Res., Rev. Joseph J. Kennedy, Pastor Emeritus (Retired).
Res.: 30 E. Franklin St., 19063. Tel: 610-566-0185; Fax: 610-566-2873.
School—Gayley St., 19063. Tel: 610-566-6881; Fax: 610-566-2010. Servants of the Most Sacred Heart of Jesus 2; Lay Teachers 13; Students 200.
Catechesis/Religious Program—Tel: 610-566-3910. Students 267.
Convent—Tel: 610-565-8399.

MILMONT PARK, DELAWARE CO., OUR LADY OF PEACE (1922), Revs. John P. Collins; Matthew C. Chadwick, O.F.M.Conv.
Res.: 501 Belmont Ave., 19033-3308. Tel: 610-532-8081; 610-532-8082; Fax: 610-532-7402.
School—Milmont and Rees Aves., 19033-3395. Tel: 610-534-0689; Fax: 610-534-4856. Sr. Denise Clifford, S.S.J., Prin. Sisters of St. Joseph 2; Lay Teachers 10; Students 205.
Catechesis/Religious Program—Students 175.
Convent—Tel: 610-532-4699.

MORRISVILLE, BUCKS CO., HOLY TRINITY (1900), [CEM] Rev. John C. Eckert; Deacon Warren C. Leonard.
Res.: 201 N. Pennsylvania Ave., 19067. Tel: 215-295-3045; Fax: 215-295-8317.
School—Osborne Ave. & Stockham Ave., 19067. Tel: 215-295-6900; Fax: 215-337-9079. Mrs. Barbara Nuzzolo, Prin. Lay Teachers 11; Students 263.
Catechesis/Religious Program—Tel: 215-295-3079. Students 120.

MORTON, DELAWARE CO., OUR LADY OF PERPETUAL HELP (1907), Rev. Msgr. John M. Savinski, M.Div., M.A.; Rev. John R. DiOrio; Deacon Joseph M. Oliver. In Res., Rev. Michael P. O'Malley, Ed.D.
Res.: O.L.P.H. Ct., 2130 Franklin Ave., 19070. Tel: 610-543-1046; Fax: 610-543-6150.
School—#5 O.L.P.H. Ct., 2130 Franklin Ave., 19070. Tel: 610-543-8350; Fax: 610-544-3203. Sisters of St. Francis of Philadelphia 2; Lay Teachers 20; Students 338.
Catechesis/Religious Program—Tel: 610-543-5448. Students 304.
Convent—#3 O.L.P.H. Ct., 2130 Franklin Ave., 19070. Tel: 610-543-0186.

NARBERTH, MONTGOMERY CO., ST. MARGARET (1900), Rev. Robert J. Chapman; Sr. Mary Alice Feenane, R.S.M., Parish Svcs. Dir. In Res., Revs. Stephen J. Dougherty; Thomas J. McManus.
Res.: 208 N. Narberth Ave., 19072. Tel: 610-664-3770; Fax: 610-664-5001.
School—227 N. Narberth Ave., 19072. Tel: 610-664-2640; Fax: 610-664-4677. Sisters of Mercy 1; Lay Teachers 14; Students 207.
Catechesis/Religious Program—Tel: 610-664-5715. Ms. Mary Katherine Roach, D.R.E. Students 143.
Convent—506 Haverford Ave., 19072. Tel: 610-664-2748.

NEW GARDEN TOWNSHIP, CHESTER CO., ST. GABRIEL OF THE SORROWFUL MOTHER (1988), Rev. Richard J. Maisano.
Mailing Address: P.O. Box 709, Avondale, 19311. Tel: 610-268-0296; Fax: 610-268-5022.
Catechesis/Religious Program—Students 241.

NEW HOPE, BUCKS CO., ST. MARTIN OF TOURS (1885), [CEM] Rev. John P. Schmeer.
W. Bridge St. & Riverstone Cir., 18938.
Res.: 1 Riverstone Cir., P.O. Box 88, 18938. Tel: 215-862-5472; Fax: 215-862-1829.
School—Elementary School Mrs. Deborah Jaster, Prin.
Catechesis/Religious Program—Students 336.

NEWTOWN SQUARE, DELAWARE CO., ST. ANASTASIA (1912), Rev. Msgr. Philip J. Cribben; Revs. James P. McKelvey; Paul J. O'Donnell; Paul Bon Young Koo. In Res., Rev. Robert E. Steinman, O.S.A.; Deacon Frank Colgan.
Res.: 3301 W. Chester Pike, 19073. Tel: 610-356-1613; Fax: 610-356-8332.
School—Tel: 610-356-6225; Fax: 610-356-5748. Sisters of St. Joseph 4; Lay Teachers 37; Students 710.
Catechesis/Religious Program—Tel: 610-356-5069. Students 430.
Convent—3305 W. Chester Pike, 19073. Tel: 610-356-0273.

NEWTOWN, BUCKS CO., ST. ANDREW (1880), [CEM] Revs. Michael C. Picard; William S. Lange; John A. Freeman; Deacon Albert T. Derivan.
Res.: 81 Swamp Rd., 18940. Tel: 215-968-2262; Fax: 215-579-9344.
School—51 Wrights Rd., 18940. Tel: 215-968-2685; Fax: 215-968-4795.

School—Preschool, 138 S. Sycamore St., 18940. Tel: 215-968-3464; Fax: 215-968-8606. Lay Teachers 49; Students 1,056.
Catechesis/Religious Program—Tel: 215-968-6929. Students 1,081.

NORRISTOWN, MONTGOMERY CO.

1—ST. FRANCIS OF ASSISI (1923), Revs. Kevin C. Trautner; Robert Marczewski. In Res., Rev. Dominick F. Finn, O.S.F.S.
Res.: 600 Hamilton St., 19401. Tel: 610-272-0402; Fax: 610-272-1794.
School—Oak & Buttonwood Sts., 19401. Tel: 610-272-0501; Fax: 610-272-8011. Sisters of St. Joseph 1; Lay Teachers 15; Students 221.
Catechesis/Religious Program—Students 125.
Convent—Tel: 610-272-3686.

2—HOLY SAVIOUR (1903), (Italian), Revs. Charles L. Sangermano; Brian A. Izzo; Rev. Msgr. J. John Busco; Deacons John Parker; Donald Kretsch. In Res., Rev. Harry A. Romano (Retired).
Res.: 407 E. Main St., 19401. Tel: 610-275-0958; Fax: 610-275-8464.
School—Airy & Walnut Sts., 19401. Tel: 610-272-8864; Fax: 610-272-0311. Lay Teachers 12; Students 203.
Catechesis/Religious Program—Students 148.
Mission—Our Lady of Mount Carmel 460 Fairfield Rd., Black Horse, Montgomery Co. 19401. Tel: 610-277-7739.

3—ST. PATRICK (1835), [CEM] Revs. William S. Murphy; Charles J. Kennedy, Coord., Hispanic Min., Montgomery Co.; Bernard Kranicka, Business Mgr.
Res.: 714 DeKalb St., 19401. Tel: 610-272-1408; Fax: 610-275-0238.
Catechesis/Religious Program—Religious Educ. Bldg., Chestnut & Green Sts., 19401. Tel: 610-272-4500. Mary Ann Mitchell, D.R.E. Students 103.
Convent—Missionaries of Charity, 630 DeKalb St., 19401. Tel: 610-277-5962.

4—ST. PAUL (1963), Rev. Harry E. McCreedy; Sr. Rosellen Bracken, R.S.M., Parish Svcs. Dir.; Mary Rose Edmonds, Business Mgr.; Deacon Michael Dayoc. In Res., Rev. Henry B. Degnan (Retired).
Res.: 2007 New Hope St., 19401. Tel: 610-279-6725; Fax: 610-275-6771.
School—351 E. Johnson Hwy., 19401. Tel: 610-275-2990; Fax: 610-275-0470. Lay Teachers 11; Students 180.
Catechesis/Religious Program—Tel: 610-279-5330. Mrs. Meg Farrell, D.R.E. Students 85.

5—ST. TITUS (1962), Rev. Edward A. Windhaus; Rev. Msgr. Thomas J. Scanlon; Deacon Joel Ziff; John Hotz, Business Mgr.
Res.: 3006 Keenwood Rd., East Norriton, 19403. Tel: 610-279-4990; Fax: 610-279-8640.
School—Keenwood Rd. & Norriton Dr., East Norriton, 19403. Tel: 610-279-6043; Fax: 610-279-8090. Lay Teachers 18; Students 340.
Catechesis/Religious Program—3000 Keenwood Rd., Norriton, 19401. Tel: 610-279-5662. Mrs. Claire Boyle, D.R.E. Students 73.

NORTH WALES, MONTGOMERY CO.

1—MARY, MOTHER OF THE REDEEMER (1987), Rev. Msgrs. Philip C. Ricci; James J. Shields; Rev. William J. Teverzczuk; Deacons Francis M. Cavaliere; George H. Klinger; Paul John, Business Mgr.
Res.: 1325 Upper State Rd., 19454. Tel: 215-362-7400; 215-362-8966; Fax: 215-362-4127.
School—1321 Upper State Rd., 19454. Mrs. Joanne Zinn, Prin.
Catechesis/Religious Program—Tel: 215-412-2251. Nancy Franks, D.R.E. Students 800.

2—ST. ROSE OF LIMA (1919), Rev. Msgr. John P. Boland, M.A. In Res., Rev. Msgr. James J. Graham; Rev. Gerald S. Smith; Deacons Edward A. Konarski; John J. Campbell.
Res.: 428 S. Main St., 19454-3224. Tel: 215-699-4617; Fax: 215-699-4452.
School—425 W. Pennsylvania Ave., 19454-3498. Tel: 215-699-8831; Fax: 215-661-1691. Lay Teachers 14; Students 248.
Catechesis/Religious Program—Tel: 215-699-4434. Students 283.

NORWOOD, DELAWARE CO., ST. GABRIEL (1891), Revs. J. Thomas Heron; John F. McBride; John J. Large.
Res.: 233 Mohawk Ave., 19074. Tel: 610-586-1225; Fax: 610-586-6068.
School—Cleveland Ave.. Tel: 610-532-3234; Fax: 610-532-5523. Lay Teachers 20; Students 340.
Catechesis/Religious Program—Tel: 610-532-5057. Students 475.

ORELAND, MONTGOMERY CO., HOLY MARTYRS (1949), Rev. Michael J. Ryan. In Res., Revs. Charles J. Noone (Retired); Raymond F. Tribuiani.
Res.: 120 Allison Rd., 19075. Tel: 215-884-8575; Fax: 215-884-5924.
School—(Grades PreK-8), 121 Allison Rd., 19075. Tel: 215-887-2044; Fax: 215-887-0024. David Hayden, Prin. Lay Teachers 12; Students 155.
School—Preschool, 207 Ulmer Ave., 19075. Tel: 215-572-8605.
Catechesis/Religious Program—Tel: 215-887-0360. Students 210.

OTTSVILLE, BUCKS CO., ST. JOHN THE BAPTIST (1743), [CEM] Rev. Joseph Tobias, M.S.C.; Deacon Ernest D'Angelo.
Res.: 4050 Durham Rd., 18942. Tel: 610-847-5521.
School—Tel: 610-847-5523; Fax: 610-847-8549. Lay Teachers 15; Students 235.
Catechesis/Religious Program—Tel: 610-847-5522; Fax: 610-847-5522. Students 270.

OXFORD, CHESTER CO., SACRED HEART (1914), Rev. John F. Hummell, Ed.D.; Deacon Francis Murphy.
Res.: 203 Church Rd., 19363. Tel: 610-932-5040; Fax: 610-932-5041.
School—Tel: 610-932-3633; Fax: 610-932-6051. Miss Kathleen McCabe, Prin.
Catechesis/Religious Program—Tel: 610-932-5863. Students 366.

PAOLI, CHESTER CO., ST. NORBERT (1956), Revs. Domenic A. Rossi, O.Praem.; Maurice C. Avicolli, O.Praem.; Deacon William Masapollo.
Res.: 50 Leopard Rd., 19301. Tel: 610-644-1655; Fax: 610-644-1928.
School—Greenlawn & Leopard Rds., 19301. Tel: 610-644-1670; Fax: 610-644-0201. Lay Teachers 18; Students 227.
Catechesis/Religious Program—Tel: 610-664-1342. Students 436.

PARKESBURG, CHESTER CO., OUR LADY OF CONSOLATION (1853), [CEM] Rev. Victor J. Eschbach. In Res., Rev. John Van De Paer, C.I.C.M.; Deacon Eugene Favinger.
Res.: 603 Second Ave., 19365. Tel: 610-857-3510; Fax: 610-857-2353.
School—Coatesville Area Catholic Elementary School See Consolidated Parish Schools under Institutions Located in the Archdiocese. Tel: 610-384-5961; Fax: 610-384-5730.
Catechesis/Religious Program—10 Cemetery Rd., 19365. Tel: 610-857-1003. Delores Cain, D.R.E. Students 350.
Mission—St. Malachy (1838), [CEM] 76 St. Malachi Rd., Doe Run, Chester Co. 19330.

PENN VALLEY, MONTGOMERY CO., ST. JUSTIN MARTYR (1964), Rev. Donald E. Leighton; Sr. Mary Sarah, R.S.M., Parish Svcs. Dir.; Mary Rose Edmonds, Business Mgr. In Res., Most Rev. Louis A. DeSimone.
Res.: 1222 Hagysford Rd., Narberth, 19072. Tel: 610-664-0165; Fax: 610-664-5612.
Catechesis/Religious Program—Students 42.

PENNDEL, BUCKS CO., OUR LADY OF GRACE (1908), [CEM] Revs. William B. Dooner; James R. Casey; Sean F. O'Neill.
Res.: 225 Bellevue Ave., 19047. Tel: 215-757-7700; 215-757-7786; Fax: 215-757-5377.
School—300 Hulmeville Ave., 19047. Tel: 215-757-5287; Fax: 215-757-6199. Mrs. Margaret M. Secoda, Prin. Lay Teachers 25; Students 550.
Catechesis/Religious Program—Tel: 215-757-5530. Students 366.
Parish Service Center—338 Hulmeville Ave., 19047. Tel: 215-757-5052; Fax: 215-757-5530.

PENNSBURG, MONTGOMERY CO., ST. PHILIP NERI (1919), [CEM] Rev. John J. Scarcia; Deacon Michael J. Franks Sr. In Res., Rev. Raymond W. Smart (Retired).
Res.: 1325 Klinerd Rd., 18073. Tel: 215-679-9275; 215-679-9330; Fax: 215-679-0386.
School—Sixth & Washington Sts., East Greenville, 18041. Tel: 215-679-7481; Fax: 215-679-8370. Students 115.
Catechesis/Religious Program—Tel: 215-541-3120. Students 245.

PHOENIXVILLE, CHESTER CO.

1—ST. ANN (1905), [CEM] Rev. John J. Newns.
Res.: 502 Main St., 19460. Tel: 610-933-3732; Fax: 610-935-7958.
School—Holy Family School See Consolidated Parish Schools under Institutions Located in the Archdiocese. Tel: 610-933-7562; Fax: 610-933-8823. Lay Teachers 30; Students 480.
Catechesis/Religious Program—Tel: 610-933-2354; Fax: 610-935-7958. Students 386.
Parish Center—602 S. Main St., 19460. Tel: 610-983-3751.

2—HOLY TRINITY (1903), (Polish), [CEM] Rev. Michael W. Rzonca.
Res.: 219 Dayton St., 19460. Tel: 610-933-3023; Fax: 610-935-9261.
School—Holy Family School See Consolidated Parish Schools under Institutions Located in the Archdiocese. Tel: 610-933-7562; Fax: 610-933-8823.
Catechesis/Religious Program—Students 12.
Convent—Bernardine Sisters of the Third Order of St. Francis, 221 Dayton St., 19460. Tel: 610-983-9446.

3—ST. MARY OF THE ASSUMPTION (1840), [CEM 2] Rev. Thomas J. Brennan.
Res.: 212 Dayton St., 19460. Tel: 610-933-2526; Fax: 610-935-1706.
School—Holy Family School See Consolidated Parish Schools under Institutions Located in the Archdiocese. Tel: 610-933-7562; Fax: 610-933-8823.
Catechesis/Religious Program—Students 97.

4—SACRED HEART (1900), (Slovak), [CEM] Rev. Michael W. Rzonca. In Res., Rev. James V. Leary (Retired).
Res.: 148 Church St., 19460. Tel: 610-933-3830; Fax: 610-935-9261.
School—Holy Family School See Consolidated Parish Schools under Institutions Located in the Archdiocese. Tel: 610-933-7562; Fax: 610-933-8823.
Catechesis/Religious Program—Students 70.

PLYMOUTH MEETING, MONTGOMERY CO., EPIPHANY OF OUR LORD (1957), Revs. Richard J. McAndrews; Dominic L. Rossi; Deacons William R. Radetzky; Kenneth P. Clancy; Emil J. Wernert. In Res., Rev. James J. Kelly (Retired).
Res.: 3050 Walton Rd., 19462-2361. Tel: 610-828-8634; Fax: 610-828-1802.
School—3040 Walton Rd., 19462-2361. Tel: 610-825-0160; Fax: 610-825-0460. Miss Miriam A. Havey, Prin. Lay Teachers 14; Students 218.
Catechesis/Religious Program—Tel: 610-825-6790. Donna Heeney, D.R.E. Students 325.

POTTSTOWN, MONTGOMERY CO.

1—ST. ALOYSIUS (1856), [CEM 2] Revs. Walter J. Benn; Dominic Tran Minh Duc; Robert W. Povish; Deacons James Anderson; Ismael Fuentes.
Res.: 214 N. Hanover St., 19464. Tel: 610-326-5877; Fax: 610-326-0901.
School—Third & Hanover Sts., 19464. Tel: 610-326-6167; Fax: 610-970-9960. Sisters of St. Francis of Philadelphia 1; Lay Teachers 22; Students 463.
Catechesis/Religious Program—Tel: 610-326-4407. Students 262.
Convent—370 South St., 19464. Tel: 610-326-1498; Fax: 610-326-0901.

2—HOLY TRINITY (1899), (Slovak), [CEM] Rev. Walter J. Benn.
Res.: 370 South St., 19464. Tel: 610-326-2432; Fax: 610-326-4106.
Catechesis/Religious Program—St. Aloysius School, Tel: 610-326-6167. Students 7.

3—ST. PETER (1924), (Polish), Rev. Edward P. Kuczynski; Deacon David M. Kubczak.
Res.: 1128 South St., 19464. Tel: 610-326-5023; Fax: 610-323-4297.
School—1126 South St., 19464. Tel: 215-323-6730; Fax: 610-326-0478. Lay Teachers 9; Students 200.
Catechesis/Religious Program—Students 95.

PRIMOS, DELAWARE CO., ST. EUGENE (1955), Rev. Joseph J. Meehan; Deacon James V. Walsh. In Res., Rev. Joseph C. Bordonaro, D.Min.
Res.: 200 S. Oak Ave., 19018. Tel: 610-626-2866; Fax: 610-626-1904.
School—110 S. Oak Ave., 19018. Tel: 610-622-2909; Fax: 610-622-6358. Lay Teachers 9; Students 255.
Catechesis/Religious Program—Students 180.

QUAKERTOWN, BUCKS CO., ST. ISIDORE (1886), [CEM] Revs. Frederick J. Riegler; John F. Wackerman.
Res.: 531 W. Broad St., 18951. Tel: 215-536-4389; Fax: 215-536-4137.
School—603 W. Broad St.. Tel: 215-536-6052; Fax: 215-536-8647. Lay Teachers 13; Students 265.
Catechesis/Religious Program—Tel: 215-536-6498. Students 375.

RICHBORO, BUCKS CO., ST. VINCENT DE PAUL (1968), Revs. Joseph J. McLaughlin; Richard E. Rudy; Deacon John M. Golaszewski.
Res.: 654 Hatboro Rd., 18954-1039. Tel: 215-357-5905; Fax: 215-953-8190.
Catechesis/Religious Program—Tel: 215-322-1932. Students 601.

RIDLEY PARK, DELAWARE CO., ST. MADELINE (1908), Rev. Msgr. George J. Mazzotta; Revs. John D. Hand; Thomas P. McKelvey; Deacon Gregory R. O'Brien. In Res., Rev. Sidney C. Burgoyne (Retired).
Res.: 110 Park St., 19078. Tel: 610-532-6880; Fax: 610-532-6653.
Church: Penn St. & Morton Ave., 19078.
School—St. Madeline-St. Rose School See Consolidated Parish Schools under Institutions Located in the Archdiocese. Tel: 610-583-3662; Fax: 610-583-3683. Lay Teachers 17; Students 363.
Catechesis/Religious Program—Tel: 610-583-6120. Students 320.

RIEGELSVILLE, BUCKS CO., ST. LAWRENCE (1974), [JC] Rev. Gavin W. Muir.
Res.: 345 Elmwood Ln., P.O. Box 126, 18077. Tel: 610-749-2684; Fax: 610-749-2695.
Catechesis/Religious Program—Students 41.

ROSLYN, MONTGOMERY CO., ST. JOHN OF THE CROSS (1953), Rev. Msgr. Thomas J. Duane; Rev. John J. Kilgallon. In Res., Rev. Donald J. Mills; Deacon Edward R. Luczkowski.
Res.: 2741 Woodland Rd., 19001. Tel: 215-659-4460; Fax: 215-659-2551.
School—2805 Woodland Rd.. Tel: 215-659-1365; Fax: 215-659-7996. Mrs. Christine Weiseman, Prin. Lay Teachers 13; Students 273.
Catechesis/Religious Program—Tel: 215-659-1451.

Students 190.
Convent—Grey Nuns of the Sacred Heart, 2803 Woodland Rd.. Tel: 215-659-4483.

ROYERSFORD, MONTGOMERY CO., SACRED HEART (1973), Rev. Thomas F. Doyle; Deacon Joseph Houser.
Res.: 838 Walnut St., P.O. Box 64, 19468. Tel: 610-948-5915; 610-948-4087; Fax: 610-948-9177.
School—Area Catholic Elementary School of the Sacred Heart, Lewis Rd. & Washington St., 19468. Tel: 610-948-7206; Fax: 610-948-6508. Lay Teachers 14; Students 240.
Catechesis/Religious Program—Tel: 610-792-2997. Mary Anne Stephens, D.R.E. Students 433.

RYDAL, MONTGOMERY CO., ST. HILARY OF POITIERS (1962), Rev. Msgr. Michael J. Carroll; Deacon John K. Hunter. In Res., Rev. Paul M. Kennedy, M.A.
Res.: 820 Susquehanna Rd., 19046. Tel: 215-884-3252.
School—920 Susquehanna Rd., 19046. Tel: 215-887-4520; Fax: 215-887-6337. Students 238.
Catechesis/Religious Program—Students 125.

SECANE, DELAWARE CO., OUR LADY OF FATIMA (1952), Revs. Engelbert G. Michel; William S. Kirk. In Res., Rev. Thomas R. Urian, M.A., D.Min.
Res.: 1 Fatima Dr., 19018. Tel: 610-532-5800.
School—10 Fatima Dr., 19018. Tel: 610-586-7539; Fax: 610-586-0117. Sisters, Servants of the Immaculate Heart of Mary 4; Lay Teachers 15; Students 452.
Catechesis/Religious Program—Tel: 610-586-3633. Students 230.
Convent—5 Fatima Dr., 19018. Tel: 610-532-1190.

SELLERSVILLE, BUCKS CO., ST. AGNES (1919), [CEM] Rev. Msgr. James E. Molloy; Rev. John F. Bowe; Deacon Harry Tucker.
Res.: 445 N. Main St., 18960. Tel: 215-257-2128; Fax: 215-257-4561.
School—St. Agnes-Sacred Heart School See Consolidated Parish Schools under Institutions Located in the Archdiocese. Tel: 215-257-3571; Fax: 215-257-8036. Lay Teachers 25; Students 440.
Catechesis/Religious Program—Tel: 215-257-1811; Fax: 215-257-0525. Students 461.

SHARON HILL, DELAWARE CO., HOLY SPIRIT (1892), Revs. Martin E. Woodeshick; Daniel J. Kehoe, Pastor Emeritus (Retired); Deacons Albert Rayner; Thomas Butcavage.
Res.: 1028 School St., 19079. Tel: 610-583-2220; Fax: 610-583-5130.
Catechesis/Religious Program—Tel: 610-532-1154. Sr. Teresa Conner, S.M.G. Students 60.

SOUTH COVENTRY, CHESTER CO., ST. THOMAS MORE (1968), Rev. Hugh J. Dougherty; Deacon George W. Leonhardt Jr.
Res.: 2101 Pottstown Pike, Pottstown, 19465. Tel: 610-469-9304; Fax: 610-469-9315.
Catechesis/Religious Program—Tel: 610-469-9302. Students 221.

SOUTHAMPTON, BUCKS CO., OUR LADY OF GOOD COUNSEL (1923), Revs. Anthony J. D'Angelico; James T. Henry; Clemens J. Gerdelmann.
Res.: 611 Knowles Ave., 18966-4198. Tel: 215-357-1300, Ext. 100; Fax: 215-357-4452.
School—Second St. Pike, 18966. Tel: 215-357-1300, Ext. 101. Mr. Frank Mokriski, Prin. Lay Teachers 25; Students 521.
Catechesis/Religious Program—Tel: 215-357-1300, Ext. 126. Students 535.

SPRING CITY, CHESTER CO., ST. JOSEPH (1919), Rev. John J. Dinda. In Res., Revs. Robert H. Mulligan; Donato P. Silveri.
Res.: 3640 Schuylkill Rd., 19475. Tel: 610-948-7760; Fax: 610-948-8509.
Catechesis/Religious Program—Tel: 610-792-0375. Students 105.

SPRINGFIELD, DELAWARE CO.

1—ST. FRANCIS OF ASSISI (1923), Revs. Salvatore M. Riccio; Michael A. Filippello; Deacons James D. Kane Sr.; Arthur M. McGuire. In Res., Rev. Thomas J. Smith.
Res.: 136 Saxer Ave., 19064. Tel: 610-543-0848; Fax: 610-604-0283.
School—112 Saxer Ave.. Tel: 610-543-0546; Fax: 610-544-9431. Lay Teachers 18; Students 368.
Catechesis/Religious Program—Students 331.

2—HOLY CROSS (1948), Revs. Edward B. Cahill; Joachim Ha Young-Re; Mardean E. Miller; Sr. Mary Carmela SanDusky, R.S.M., Pastoral Min. In Res., Rev. Msgr. Arthur J. Centrella (Retired); Deacon Robert Frankenberger.
Res.: 651 E. Springfield Rd., 19064. Tel: 610-626-3321; Fax: 610-622-2920.
School—Bishop & Springfield Rds., 19064. Tel: 610-626-1709; Fax: 610-626-1859. Sisters of Mercy 1; Lay Teachers 19; Students 439.
Catechesis/Religious Program—Tel: 610-626-1057; Fax: 610-626-8057. Students 212.
Convent—Tel: 610-626-2492.

3—ST. KEVIN (1955), Rev. James J. Whelan; Sr. Eleanor McFadden, S.S.J., Pastoral Assoc.; Deacons Thomas Eichman; Leonard Diana. In Res., Rev. Raymond J. Overstreet.
St. Kevin Rectory: 200 W. Sproul Rd., 19064-2016. Tel: 610-544-3777; 610-544-8778; Fax: 610-544-7832.
School—Tel: 610-544-4455; Fax: 610-544-7092. Sisters of St. Joseph 2; Lay Teachers 16; Students 221.
Catechesis/Religious Program—Tel: 610-544-3236; Fax: 610-544-7382. Students 257.
Convent—Tel: 610-544-4535.

STOWE, MONTGOMERY CO., ST. GABRIEL OF THE SORROWFUL MOTHER (1929), Rev. James W. Gormley.
Parish Center—127 E. Howard St., 19464. Tel: 610-326-5127; Fax: 610-326-5749.
Res.: 421 Jefferson St., 19464. Tel: 610-327-2248.
Catechesis/Religious Program—Tel: 610-327-5376. Students 95.

STRAFFORD, CHESTER CO., OUR LADY OF THE ASSUMPTION (1908), (Italian), [CEM] Rev. Joseph A. Vadino; Deacons John P. Rose; George Bolter. In Res., Rev. Msgr. James T. McDonough, M.S.W.; Rev. Daniel J. Hoy (Retired).
Res.: 35 Old Eagle School Rd., 19087-2577. Tel: 610-688-1178; 610-688-6147; Fax: 610-293-9680.
School—Preschool, 135 Fairfield Ln., 19087. Tel: 610-688-5277.
Catechesis/Religious Program—Tel: 610 688-6590. Students 160.

SWARTHMORE, DELAWARE CO., NOTRE DAME DE LOURDES (1959), Rev. Karl A. Zeuner, S.T.L.; Deacons James Basilio; Michael McAndrews.
Res.: 950 Michigan Ave., 19081. Tel: 610-544-1270; Fax: 610 544-4310.
School—990 Fairview Rd., 19081. Tel: 610-328-9330; Fax: 610-328-3955. Lay Teachers 14; Students 247.
Catechesis/Religious Program—Tel: 610-544-9739; Fax: 610-543-3412. Students 180.

SWEDESBURG, MONTGOMERY CO., SACRED HEART (1907), (Polish), Rev. Leonard A. Lewandowski; Rev. Msgr. Anthony E. Jaworowski (Retired).
Res.: 120 Jefferson St., 19405. Tel: 610-275-1750; Fax: 610-275-0480.
School—Holy Trinity Catholic School See Consolidated Parish Schools under the Institutions Located in the Archdiocese. Tel: 610-277-4133; Fax: 610-277-4725. Lay Teachers 11; Students 186.
Catechesis/Religious Program—Students 40.
Convent—635 E. Fourth St., 19405. Tel: 610-275-3348; Fax: 610-272-6166.

TROOPER, MONTGOMERY CO., VISITATION B.V.M. (1954), Rev. Msgr. Thomas A. Murray; Revs. Eugene C. Wilson; Khoa M. Nguyen.
Res.: 196 N. Trooper Rd., Norristown, 19403. Tel: 610-539-5572; Fax: 610-539-3240.
School—N. Trooper Rd., R.D. 1, Norristown, 19403. Tel: 610-539-6080; Fax: 610-630-7956. Sisters of the Holy Family of Nazareth 2; Lay Teachers 32; Students 695.
Catechesis/Religious Program—Tel: 610-539-6211. Roseanne Terranova, D.R.E. Students 585.
Convent—Tel: 610-539-5558.

UPPER DARBY, DELAWARE CO., ST. ALICE (1922), Revs. William P. Donnelly; Joseph Tran Kim Thien, Pastoral Assoc. In Res., Deacon Joseph F. Coyle.
Res.: 150 Hampden Rd., 19082. Tel 610-352-1431.
School—(Grades K-8), 135 Copley Rd., 19082. Tel: 610-352-0725; Fax: 610-352-7288. Sisters, Servants of the Immaculate Heart of Mary 3; Lay Teachers 10; Students 196.
Catechesis/Religious Program—Students 65.

UPPER GWYNEDD, MONTGOMERY CO., CORPUS CHRISTI (1964), Rev. Msgr. Thomas P. Flanigan, Ed.D.; Revs. James J. McLaughlin; Kevin J. Kelly; Sr. Mary Corbett, S.S.J., Dir. Human Svcs.
Res.: 900 Sumneytown Pike, Lansdale, 19446. Tel: 215-855-1311; Fax: 215-855-3631.
School—920 Sumneytown Pike, Lansdale, 19466. Tel 215-368-0582; Fax: 215-361-5927. Sisters of St. Joseph 3; Lay Teachers 21; Students 476.
Catechesis/Religious Program—Tel: 215-362-2292. Trish Keen, D.R.E. Students 753.
Convent—1622 Supplee Rd., Lansdale, 19446. Tel: 215-368-0737.

UPPER UWCHLAN, CHESTER CO., SAINT ELIZABETH (2000), Rev. Msgr. Thomas M. Mullin; Deacon Richard L. Fremont.
Res.: 2 Fox Ridge Rd., Glenmoore, 19343-9546. Tel: 610-321-9616; Fax: 610-321-1275.
Parish Office—941 Pottstown Pike, P.O. Box 695, Uwchlan, 19480-0695. Tel: 610-321-0283; Fax: 610-321-0257.
Catechesis/Religious Program—Tel: 610-321-1191. Students 875.

VALLEY FORGE, MONTGOMERY CO., ST. TERESA OF AVILA (1918), Rev. Msgr. Andrew J. Golias, S.T.D., S.T.L.; Deacon Robert P. Gohde. In Res., Rev. Edward J. Casey, M.Div.
Res. & Mailing Address: 1260 S. Trooper Rd., Norristown, 19403-3659. Tel: 610-666-5820; Fax: 610-666-7511.
School—2550 S. Parkview Dr. Norristown, 19403. Tel: 610-666-6069; Fax: 610-666-0195. Janet Lazorcheck, Prin. Lay Teachers 10; Students 218.
Catechesis/Religious Program—Tel: 610-666-0644. Nance Morrisroe, D.R.E. Students 293.

VILLANOVA, DELAWARE CO., ST. THOMAS OF VILLANOVA PARISH (1848), Revs. Richard O'Leary, O.S.A.; Keith Hollis, O.S.A. In Res., Rev. Anthony M. Genovese, O.S.A.
Res.: 1229 W. Lancaster Ave., Rosemont, 19010. Tel: 610-525-4801; Fax: 610-525-6041.
School—St. Thomas-Good Counsel School See Consolidated Parish Schools under Institutions Located in the Archdiocese. Tel: 610-525-1407; Fax: 610-525-0157.
St. Thomas of Villanova Preschool—1236 Montrose Ave., Rosemont, 19010. Tel: 610-525-7554.
Catechesis/Religious Program—Students 205.

WALLINGFORD, DELAWARE CO., ST. JOHN CHRYSOSTOM (1952), Revs. James R. Bajorek; Robert F. Lucas; Deacons Raymond Vadino; Walter Lance. In Res., Rev. Thomas J. Donaghy (BAL) (Retired).
Res.: 617 S. Providence Rd., 19086. Tel: 610-874-3418; Fax: 610-872-1741.
School—607 Providence Rd., 19086. Tel: 610-876-7110; Fax: 610-876-5923. Sisters of St. Joseph 1; Lay Teachers 25; Students 297.
Catechesis/Religious Program—605 S. Providence Rd., 19086. Tel: 610-872-4673. Students 425.
Convent—Tel: 610-872-7194.

WARMINSTER, BUCKS CO., NATIVITY OF OUR LORD (1956), Revs. Angelo R. Cilino; Thomas J. Cavanaugh; Gary J. Kramer. In Res., Rev. James F. Endres.
Res.: 625 W. Street Rd., 18974. Tel: 215-675-1925; Fax: 215-674-3787.
School—585 W. Street Rd., 18974. Tel: 215-675-2820; Fax: 215-675-9413. Sisters of St. Joseph 1; Lay Teachers 31; Students 592.
Catechesis/Religious Program—Tel: 215-672-5316. Students 400.
Convent—605 W. Street Rd., 18974. Tel: 215-672-0147.

WARRINGTON, BUCKS CO.

1—ST. JOSEPH (1922), Revs. James A. Grant; Robert G. Suskey; Deacon Karl Hartmann. In Res., Rev. Ronald M. Vierling, M.F.C.
Res.: 1795 Columbia Ave., 18976. Tel: 215-672-3020; Fax: 215-672-3114.
School—St. Joseph/St. Robert Bellarmine School See Consolidated Parish Schools under Institutions Located in the Archdiocese. Tel: 215-672-0724. Lay Teachers 23; Students 458.
Catechesis/Religious Program—Tel: 215-672-9990. Mrs. Cathy Cain, D.R.E. Students 265.
Station—Willow Grove Naval Air Station Willow Grove. Tel: 215-443-6002.

2—ST. ROBERT BELLARMINE (1968), Rev. Msgr. Joseph T. Kane; Rev. Joseph M. McDermott; Deacon George E. Morris.
Res.: 856 Euclid Ave., 18976. Tel: 215-343-0315; Fax: 215-343-8592.
School—St. Joseph & St. Robert Bellarmine School See Consolidated Parish Schools under Institutions Located in the Archdiocese. Tel: 215-343-5100; Fax: 215-491-4148.
Catechesis/Religious Program—850 Euclid Ave., 18976. Tel: 215-343-9433. Students 577.

WAYNE, CHESTER CO., ST. ISAAC JOGUES (1970), Rev. Msgr. Joseph C. Cunningham; Rev. Paschal U. Onunwa (Nigeria); Filee Parry, Business Mgr.; Mary D. Schachinger, Parish Svcs. Dir.; Joan M. Carey, Parish Svcs. Dir.
Res.: 50 W. Walker Rd., 19087. Tel: 610-687-3366; Fax: 610-293-9529.
School—Preschool, Tel: 610-687-2481; Fax: 610-293-9529.
Catechesis/Religious Program—Tel: 610-687-2481. Louis M. Valenti, D.R.E. Students 174.

WAYNE, DELAWARE CO., ST. KATHARINE OF SIENA (1893), Rev. Msgr. John J. Jagodzinski; Sisters Kathleen Callaghan, S.S.J., Dir. Parish Life & Ministry; Elizabeth O'Hara, S.S.J., Parish Svcs. Dir.; Deacons Dennis Bingham; Charles Ginn. In Res., Rev. Joseph T. Shenosky, M.A., D.Min.
Res.: 104 S. Aberdeen Ave., 19087. Tel: 610-688-4584; Fax: 610-688-7951.
School—229 Windermere Ave., 19087. Tel: 610-688-5451; Fax: 610-688-6796. Maria Brown, Prin. Lay Teachers 25; Students 387.
Catechesis/Religious Program—Tel: 610-688-7890. Sr. Patricia Feeley, S.S.J., D.R.E. Students 349.
Convent—235 Windermere Ave., 19087. Tel: 610-688-0655.

WEST CHESTER, CHESTER CO.

1—ST. AGNES (1793), [CEM] Rev. Msgr. Edward M. Deliman; Revs. John A. Franey; Philip M. Forlano; Christopher J. Papa; Deacon Victor Gonzalez.
Res.: 233 W. Gay St., 19380. Tel: 610-692-2990; Fax: 610-692-9623.
School—211 W. Gay St., 19380. Tel: 610-696-1260;

Fax: 610-436-9631. Sisters, Servants of the Immaculate Heart of Mary 3; Lay Teachers 24; Students 539.
Catechesis/Religious Program—207 W. Gay St., 19380. Tel: 610-436-4640; Fax: 610-719-1961. Students 485.
Convent—205 W. Gay St., 19380. Tel: 610-692-9430.

2—SS. SIMON AND JUDE (1961), Rev. Msgr. Francis X. Meehan; Rev. Kevin P. McCabe; Mr. Ronald B. Avellino, Business Mgr.; Deacons James Lyon; James Owens; Ben Stam. In Res., Rev. Msgr. Richard LaHart; Rev. Dennis O'Donnell.
Res.: 8 Cavanaugh Ct., 19382. Tel: 610-696-3624; Fax: 610-696-3971.
School—6 Cavanaugh Ct.. Tel: 610-696-5249; Fax: 610-696-4682. Sisters, Servants of the Immaculate Heart of Mary 6; Lay Teachers 21; Students 509.
Catechesis/Religious Program—Tel: 610-692-3118. Sr. Rose Caritas, I.H.M., D.R.E. Students 566.
Convent—Tel: 610-692-4394.

WEST CONSHOHOCKEN, MONTGOMERY CO., ST. GERTRUDE (1888), Rev. Msgr. Robert J. Grudowski. 209 Merion Ave., 19428. Tel: 610-828-0268; Fax: 610-828-7024.
Catechesis/Religious Program—Students 21.

WEST GROVE, CHESTER CO., ASSUMPTION B.V.M. (1873), [CEM] Rev. Msgr. John W. Graf; Most Rev. James J. Melle; Joyce Malchione, Business Mgr.; Deacons Thomas Hannan; Michael DeGrasse. In Res., Rev. Msgr. Francis J. Depman.
Res.: 107 W. Evergreen St., 19390. Tel: 610-869-2722; Fax: 610-869-3252.
School—290 State Rd., 19390. Tel: 610-869-9576; Fax: 610-869-4049. Sr. Michele Smith, I.H.M., Prin. Sisters, Servants of the Immaculate Heart 3; Lay Teachers 15; Students 290.
Catechesis/Religious Program—Tel: 610-869-8575. Jacqueline Smith, D.R.E. Students 650.
Convent—105 W. Evergreen St., 19390. Tel: 610-869-9832.
Mission—Santa Maria, Madra de Dios P.O. Box 1019, Avondale, Chester Co. 19311. Tel: 610-268-3365; Fax: 610-869-9395.

WESTTOWN, CHESTER CO., ST. MAXIMILIAN KOLBE (1986), Rev. Msgr. Hugh P. Campbell; Rev. John D. Schiele; Deacons Lawrence Brandon; Alfred Mauriello; William Hickey.
Res.: 15 E. Pleasant Grove Rd., West Chester, 19382. Tel: 610-399-6936; Fax: 610-399-4828.
School—(Grades PreK-8) Tel: 610-399-8400; Fax: 610-399-4684. Students 470.
Catechesis/Religious Program—Tel: 610-399-9642. Students 470.

WILLOW GROVE, MONTGOMERY CO., ST. DAVID (1919), Rev. Msgr. Richard T. Bolger; Rev. John J. Shelley; Deacon William F. Eliason. In Res., Rev. Richard P. Connors.
Res.: 316 N. Easton Rd., 19090. Tel: 215-657-0252; Fax: 215-659-6516.
School—401 N. Easton Rd., 19090. Tel: 215-659-6393; Fax: 215-659-6377. Sisters, Servants of the Immaculate Heart of Mary 5; Lay Teachers 21; Students 380.
Catechesis/Religious Program—Tel: 215-659-4059. Students 430.
Convent—400 N. Easton Rd., 19090. Tel: 215-659-0445.

WYNDMOOR, MONTGOMERY CO., SEVEN DOLORS (1916-2003), Closed., Formerly located at 1200 E. Willow Grove Ave. spiritual records are kept at St. Genevieve Church. Tel.: 215-836-2828

WYNNEWOOD, MONTGOMERY CO., PRESENTATION B.V.M. (1954), Rev. Msgr. Vincent M. Walsh, J.C.D.
Res.: 204 Haverford Rd., 19096. Tel: 610-642-8341; Fax: 610-896-1970.
School—230 Haverford Rd., 19096. Tel: 610-642-0208. Kay Kelly, Prin. Lay Teachers 11; Students 148.
Catechesis/Religious Program—Students 80.
Convent—240 Haverford Rd., 19096. Tel: 610-642-3803. Sisters 4.

YARDLEY, BUCKS CO., ST. IGNATIUS OF ANTIOCH (1920), [CEM] [JC] Rev. Msgr. Samuel E. Shoemaker, J.C.D.; Revs. Joseph R. Hess, M.Div.; Louis J. Kolenkiewicz, M.Div.; Deacons Robert J. Skawinski; Robert J. Stewart.
Res.: 999 Reading Ave., 19067. Tel: 215-493-3377; Fax: 215-493-0450.
School—Tel: 215-493-3867; Fax: 267-573-3550. Lay Staff 21; Students 237.
Catechesis/Religious Program—Tel: 215-493-5204; Fax: 215-493-0956. Students 611.

YEADON, DELAWARE CO., ST. LOUIS (1928), Rev. Steven J. Harris, J.C.D.
Res.: 821 W. Cobbs Creek Pkwy., 19050. Tel: 610-623-0553; Fax: 610-623-8191.
Catechesis/Religious Program—Students 17.

Chaplains of Public Institutions

PHILADELPHIA. *Philadelphia Prison System*, 8001 State Rd., 19136. Tel: 215-276-2288. Rev. Gregory P. Cozzubbo, C.M.
Veterans Administration Medical Center, University & Woodland Aves., 19104. Tel: 215-823-5800, Ext. 2776. Revs. James E. King, Michael A. Lipareli.

COATESVILLE. *Veterans Administration Medical Center* 19320. Tel: 215-384-7711, Ext. 190. Rev. Joseph S. Hasiebar.

GRATERFORD. *Graterford State Correctional Institution* 19426. Tel: 215-489-4151. Rev. Robert W. Povish.

NORRISTOWN. *Norristown State Hospital* 19401. Tel: 215-270-1104. Rev. Dominick F. Finn, O.S.F.S., Chap.

SPRING CITY. *Southeastern Pennsylvania Veterans Center* 19475. Tel: 215-948-2400. Rev. Donato P. Silveri.

On Special or Other Archdiocesan Assignment:
Rev. Msgrs.—
Beach, Francis W., Regl. Vicar, Philadelphia-North, 240 Hermitage St., 19127.
Cistone, Joseph R., V.G., Vicar for Admin. Ridley Park, Spiritual Life Center, 405 Tome St., Ridley Park, 19078.
Marine, John C., Vicar for Montgomery Co., 354 Conshohocken State Rd., Gladwyn, 19035.
Palmieri, Alexander J., M.A., J.C.L., Chancellor, Office of the Chancellor, Sisters of Mercy Convent, 515 Montgomery Ave., Merion Station, 19066.
Senior, Timothy C., M.B.A., M.S.W., Secretary, Secretary for Catholic Human Services, Divine Providence Village, 686 Old Maple Rd., Springfield, 19064.
Revs.—
DiMaria, Peter, Faculty, Bishop Shanahan High School, St. Mary of Providence Center, 227 Isabella Rd., Elverson, 19520.
McGee, Leo J., Chaplain, Little Flower Manor, 1201 Springfiield Rd., Darby, 19023.
McIntyre, John J., Admin. Sec., Office of the Archbishop, Cardinal's Residence, 5700 City Ave., 19131.
Tracy, Joseph A., S.T.D., M.S.W., Deputy Secretary, Cardinal's Residence, 5700 City Ave., 19131.
Wilz, John C., Chaplain, Motherhouse, Grey Nuns of the Sacred Heart, 1750 Quarry Rd., Morrisville, 19067.

On Duty Outside the Archdiocese:
Rev. Msgrs.—
Bransfield, Michael J., National Shrine of the Immaculate Conception, Fourth St. & Michigan Ave., N.E., Washington, DC 20017.
Green, James P., Secretariat of State, Vatican Apostolic Palace, Vatican City State 00120.
Kutys, Daniel J., N.C.C.B. Office for the Catechism, 3211 4th St., N.E., Washington, DC 20017.
Malone, Richard, Saint John Vianney Theological Seminary Joatican City State, 1300 S. Steele St., Denver, CO 80210.
Thomas, Daniel E., Official, Congregation for Bishops, Pontifical North American College, Vatican City State 00120 Vatican City State. Tel: 011-39-6849-3846
Revs.—
Benonis, Richard R., Veteran's Administration Hospital, San Antonio, TX.
Bonavitacola, John M., Our Lady of Mount Carmel Parish, 2121 S. Rural Rd., Tempe, AZ 85282.
Concha, Augusto, Our Lady of Mount Carmel, Box 2062, Barceloneta, PR 00617.
Funk, Peter C., Diocese of Beaumont, 703 Archie St., P.O. Box 3948, Beaumont, TX 77704.
Gill, Dennis G., Pontifical North American College 00120 Vatican City State.
Grous, Albin J., Congregation for Catholic Education, Piazza Pio XII 3, 00193, Rome, Italy.
Jugenheimer, James R., 1910 S. Webster, P.O. Box 23066, Green Bay, WI 54305.
Magee, Michael K. Focolare Sacerdotale Congregation for Divine Worship, Via Tor de' Conti, 17/1, Rome 00184 Italy.
McGann, Thomas A., Our Lady of the Angels Church, 75A Molynes Rd., Kingston 10, Jamaica.
Mendez, Rafael, Diocese of Arecibo, Puerto Rico, 206 Dr. Salas St., P.O. Box 616, Arecibo, PR 00613.
Menei, Francis T., Saint Richard Parish, 201 Adele Ave., Manheim, 17545.
Perzan, Stephen B., Our Lady of Mount Carmel, Box 2062, Barcelona, PR 00617.
Quinter, Paul S., L'Osservatore Romano, 00120 Vatican City State.
Shields, Hugh Joseph, Society of St. James the Apostle, 24 Clark St., Boston, MA 02109.
York, Richard R., Holy Cross Catholic Church, 506 26th St. W., Palmetto, FL 34221.

Military Chaplains:
Rev. Msgr.—
Burns, Vincent P.
Revs.—
Boyle, Dennis P.
Coffey, Joseph L.
Concha, Alfonso J.
DiGregorio, Joseph L.
Foley, Francis P.
McManus, Gerald D.

Graduate Studies:
Revs.—
Brady, Patrick J., Casa Santa Maria, Via dell'Umilta 30, Rome 00187 Italy.
Bransfield, Brian J., Catholic University, Curley Hall #116, Washington, DC 20064.
Donovan, William G., Casa Santa Maria, Via dell'Umilta 30, Rome 00187 Italy.
Fairbanks, Gregory J., Casa Santa Maria, Via dell'Umilta 30, Rome, Italy.
Giuffre, Frank A., Casa Santa Maria, Via dell'Umilta 30, Rome 00187 Italy.
Gorman, James P., The oblate School of Theology, 109 Oblate Ct., San Antonio, TX 78216.
Hennelly, Michael F., M.Div., Immaculate Conception Rectory, 1020 N. Front St., 19123-1717.
Hennessy, Brian P., Casa Santa Maria, Via dell'Umilta 30, Rome, Italy.
Spitzer, Michael H., Casa Santa Maria, Via dell'Umilta 30, Rome, Italy.

Absent on Sick Leave:
Revs.—
Anziano, James J.
Crowe, George W.
Fitzgibbons, John A.
Toth, Joseph A.
Van Thuyne, Dennis G.

Absent on Leave:
Rev. Msgrs.—
Gillespie, John E.
Walls, David E.
Revs.—
Blaine, Michael J.
Brinkman, Charles J.
Brugger, Craig F.
Delli Carpini, John J.
DePaoli, Edward M.
Donofrio, Michael J.
Dougherty, William J.
Gallagher, Francis J.
Gallagher, Joseph P.
Gana, Stanley M.
Givey, David W.
Grumm, Thomas J.
Kohler, Thomas M.
Kornacki, Matthew J., M.Div.
Martino, Nicholas J.
McCarthy, Michael J.
McGuire, James E.
McLoughlin, Richard J.
Morrison, Robert A.
Taraborelli, Carmen F.
Wisniewski, Thomas J.

Retired:
Rev. Msgrs.—
Bennington, J. Clement, Villa St. Joseph, 1436 Lansdowne Ave., Darby, 19023-1298.
Busco, John J., Holy Savior Rectory, 407 E. Main St., Norristown, 19041-5119.
Carbo, Eugene J., Villa Saint Joseph, 1436 Lansdowne Ave., Darby, 19023-1298.
Caulfield, John J., Cathedral Basilica SS. Peter and Paul, 1723 Race St., 19103.
Centrella, Arthur J., Holy Cross Rectory, 651 E. Springfield Rd., Springfield, 19064.
Craven, Thomas P., Villa Saint Joseph, 1436 Lansdowne Ave., Darby, 19023-1298.
Daly, James P., Villa Saint Joseph, 1436 Lansdowne Ave., Darby, 19023-1298.
Devlin, Charles V., 180 Ocean Ave., Island Heights, NJ 08732.
Dreger, Francis X., 2700 W. Brigantine Ave., Brigantine, NJ 08203.
Falls, Thomas B., Villa Saint Joseph, 1436 Lansdowne Ave., Darby, 19023-1298.
Fitzmaurice, Francis J., Villa Saint Joseph, 1436 Lansdowne Ave., Darby, 19023.
Gallen, Charles V., Saint Francis Country House, 1412 Lansdowne Ave., Darby, 19023-1218.
Galyo, John M., Saint Eleanor Rectory, 647 Locust St., Collegeville, 19426-2541.
Hilferty, Thomas J., Saint Madeleine Sophie Rectory, 6440 Greene St., 19119-3298.
Howard, James J., 9224 Grace Ln., 19115.
Jaworowski, Anthony E., Sacred Heart Rectory, 120 Jefferson St., Swedesburg, 19405.
LaHart, Richard T., SS. Simon and Jude Rectory, 8 Cavanaugh Ct., West Chester, 19382.

McGrath, James, Villa Saint Joseph, 1436 Lansdowne Ave., Darby, 19023-1298.
McGuire, Anthony W., 400 E. Allens Lane, 19119-1103.
McManus, Robert T., 72 Parkridge Dr., Bryn Mawr, 19010.
Meehan, James H., Villa Saint Joseph, 1436 Lansdowne Ave., Darby, 19023-1298.
Monaghan, Charles J., Villa Saint Joseph, 1436 Lansdowne Ave., Darby, 19023-1298.
Mortimer, James E., 406 Solly Ave., 19111.
Musial, Edward S., Villa Saint Joseph, 1436 Lansdowne Ave., Darby, 19023-1298.
Mynaugh, Charles B., Villa Saint Joseph, 1436 Lansdowne Ave., Darby, 19023-1298.
Nace, Arthur J., 104 Sycamore Rd., Havertown, 19083.
Norrell, Albert V., Villa Saint Joseph, 1436 Lansdowne Ave., Darby, 19023-1298.
Nugent, Arthur W., 1341 Osbourne Ave., Roslyn, 19001.
Peck, Leon J., Regina Coeli Residence for Priests, 685 York Rd., Warminster, 18974.
Pryor, Thomas P., Villa Saint Joseph, 1436 Lansdowne Ave., Darby, 19023.
Schaeflein, Charles J., Mount Nazareth, 2755 Holme Ave., 19152.
Shields, Joseph A., Saint John the Baptist, Vianney Rectory, 1110 Vaughan Ln., Gladwyne, 19035.
Skelly, Richard J., Saint Joseph Rectory, 256 Concord Rd., Aston, 19014-1905.
Statkus, Francis J., 208 E. Trenton Ave., Wildwood Crest, NJ 08260.
Trinity, Bernard J., Saint Denis Rectory, 2401 Saint Denis Ln., Havertown, 19083.

Revs.—
Barnes, Gerard J., Villa Saint Joseph, 1436 Lansdowne Ave., Darby, 19023-1298.
Barr, Philip R., 1511 Grant Rd., West Chester, 19382.
Bartos, Francis J., Villa Saint Joseph, 1436 Lansdowne Ave., Darby, 19023-1298.
Benischeck, Bernard J., Saint Dominic Rectory, 8504 Frankford Ave., 19136.
Benonis, William J., Saint Joseph Rectory, 16 S. Spring Garden St., Ambler, 19002-4797.
Birkhead, Henry G., Villa Saint Joseph, 1436 Lansdowne Ave., Darby, 19023-1298.
Boyle, George J., Annunciation B.V.M. Rectory, 410 Sagamore Rd., Havertown, 19083-3998.
Brackenridge, David F., Saint Francis Country House, 1412 Lansdowne Ave., Darby, 19023-1218.
Bradley, James F., Saint Francis Country House, 1412 Lansdowne Ave., Darby, 19023-1218.
Bradley, John J., Sacred Heart of Jesus Rectory, 1404 S. Third St., 19147-6099.
Breen, Robert H., Villa Saint Joseph, 1436 Lansdowne Ave., Darby, 19023-1298.
Burgoyne, Sidney C., Saint Madeline Rectory, 110 Park St., Ridley Park, 19078.
Callahan, Joseph W., Villa Saint Joseph, 1436 Lansdowne Ave., Darby, 19023-1298.
Carey, Paul J., Regina Coeli Residence for Priests, 685 York Rd., Warminster, 18974.
Catullo, Pasquale R., Villa Saint Joseph, 1436 Lansdowne Ave., Darby, 19023-1298.
Cellucci, Carl D., 902 Surf Ave., North Wildwood, NJ 08260.
Chow, Luke L., Saint Philip Neri Rectory, 218 Queen St., 19147.
Chwieroth, Edward J., Salem Harbour Apartments, 106 Moorsgate, Andalusia, 19020.
Coates, John T., Saint Mary's Manor, 701 Lansdale Ave., Lansdale, 19446-2900.
Conner, Robert J., Saint John the Evangelist Rectory, 752 Big Oak Rd., Morrisville, 19067.
Coonan, James J.
Cornely, Francis J., Regina Coeli Residence for Priests, 685 York Rd., Warminster, 18974.
Cox, William J., Regina Coeli Residence for Priests, 685 York Rd., Warminster, 18974.
Cudemo, Nicholas V.
Cullen, John F., Regina Coeli Residence for Priests, 685 York Rd., Warminster, 18974.
Daly, John J., Villa Saint Joseph, 1436 Lansdowne Ave., Darby, 19023-1298.
Degnan, Henry B., St. Paul Rectory, 2007 New Hope St., East Norriton, 19401.
DeMayo, John B., P.O. Box 380, Blakeslee, 18610.
Dougherty, Henry E., Villa Saint Joseph, 1436 Lansdowne Ave., Darby, 19023-1298.
Duddy, Patrick A., Villa Saint Joseph, 1436 Lansdowne Ave., Darby, 19023-1298.
Dunne, Peter J.
Durney, Charles W., P.O. Box 138, Tuscarora, 17982.
Dux, James M.
Dziadosz, Edward T., P.O. Box 95, Mahanoy City, 17948-0095.
Fala, John G., Saint Bernard Rectory, 7341 Cottage St., 19136.
Feeney, Thomas M., 1341 Osbourne Ave., Roslyn, 19001.
Foster, John J., Regina Coeli Residence for Priests, 685 York Rd., Warminster, 18974.
Gallagher, Daniel J., Villa Saint Joseph, 1436 Lansdowne Ave., Darby, 19023-1298.
Gallagher, John P., Saint Albert the Great Rectory, 212 Welsh Rd, Huntingdon Valley, 19006-6598.
Gallen, Francis H., Hershey Mill, 118 Chandler Dr., West Chester, 19380.
Garzarelli, Santo R., Our Lady of Calvary Rectory, 11024 Knights Rd., 19154-4295.
Gormley, Charles E., Saint Matthias Rectory, 128 Bryn Mawr Ave., Bala Cynwyd, 19004.
Graf, Henry C., Regina Coeli Residence for Priests, 685 York Rd., Warminster, 18974.
Graham, Thomas D., Villa Saint Joseph, 1436 Lansdowne Ave., Darby, 19023-1298.
Hagenbach, George G., Villa Saint Joseph, 1436 Lansdowne Ave., Darby, 19023-1298.
Hartnett, Walter J., Villa Saint Joseph, 1436 Lansdowne Ave., Darby, 19023-1298.
Heim, John S., 4527 Salmon St., 19137.
Herron, Bernard J., Villa Saint Joseph, 1436 Lansdowne Ave., Darby, 19023-1298.
Herron, Francis X., 9 N. Pelham Ave., Longport, NJ 08403.
Hoy, Daniel J., Our Lady of the Assumption Rectory, 35 Old Eagle School Rd., Strafford, 19087.
Hughes, James F., 1060 Lenape Dr., East Stroudsburg, 18301.
Jaworowski, Leon E., Villa Saint Joseph, 1436 Lansdowne Ave., Darby, 19023-1298.
Joseph, William T.
Jung, Joseph B., Villa Saint Joseph, 1436 Lansdowne Ave., Darby, 19023-1298.
Kane, Aloysius T., Villa Saint Joseph, 1436 Lansdowne Ave., Darby, 19023-1298.
Kehoe, Daniel J., Holy Spirit Rectory, 1028 School St., Sharon Hill, 19079.
Kelly, Francis E., 4972 Skippack Pike, P.O. Box 259, Creamery, 19430-0259.
Kelly, James J., Villa Saint Joseph, 1436 Lansdowne Ave., Darby, 19023-1298.
Kelly, James Joseph, Epiphany of Our Lord Rectory, 3050 Walton Rd., Norristown, 19462.
Kennedy, Joseph J., Nativity B.V.M. Rectory, 30 E. Franklin St., Media, 19063.
Koob, Edward H., 6612 Pleasure Ave., Sea Isle City, NJ 08243-1450.
Kostelnick, Albert T., Villa Saint Joseph, 1436 Lansdowne Ave., Darby, 10923-1298.
Krick, Howard K., Regina Coeli Residence for Priests, 685 York Rd., Warminster, 18974.
Leary, James V., Sacred Heart Rectory, 148 Church St., Phoenixville, 19460.
Lepleiter, Robert P., St. Jude Rectory, 321 W. Butler Ave., Chalfont, 18914-2329.
Loughran, Francis J., St. Mary's Manor, 701 Lansdale Ave., Lansdale, 19446-2900.
Machain, David B., Saint Bernard Rectory, 7341 Cottage St., 19136.
Maguire, Connell J., 2800 N. Ocean Dr., Apt. B15a, Riviera Beach, FL 33404.
Maher, Edmund J., St. William Rectory, 6200 Rising Sun Ave., 19111.
Murphy, James A., St. Gabriel Rectory, 421 Jefferson St., Stowe, 19464.
Murphy, James J., 237 W. Montgomery Ave., Apt. 2Q, Haverford, 19041.
Murphy, Joseph T., 812 Rowland Ave., Cheltenham, 19012.
Murray, John J.
Noone, Charles J., Holy Martyrs Rectory, 120 Allison Rd., Oreland, 19075-1896
O'Brien, Joseph E., Saint Leo Rectory, 6658 Keystone St., 19135.
O'Connor, John P., Villa Saint Joseph, 1436 Lansdowne Ave., Darby, 19023-1298.
O'Donnell, William J. (ALN), Regina Coeli Residence for Priests, 685 York Rd., Warminster, 18974.
Pohl, Jerome H., 2982 Richmond St., 19134.
Rogers, Francis P.
Romano, Harry A., Holy Saviour Rectory, 407 E. Main St., Norristown, 19401-5119.
Ryan, Robert F., Villa Saint Joseph, 1436 Lansdowne Ave., Darby, 19023-1298.
Schifalacqua, Ildebrando E., St. Bartholomew Rectory, 5600 Jackson St., Philadelphia, 19124.
Schneider, George P., Villa Saint Joseph, 1436 Lansdowne Ave., Darby, 19023-1219.
Senske, Joseph A., Gillet Convent, Immaculata College, P.O. Box 731, Immaculata, 19345.
Shea, Thomas F.
Shellem, John J., St. Athanasius Rectory, 2050 Walnut Ln., 19138.
Smart, Raymond W., Saint Philip Neri Rectory, 1325 Klinerd Rd., Pennsburg, 18073.
Smith, William J., Villa Saint Joseph Church Rd., 1436 Lansdowne Ave., Darby, 19023-1298.
Smyth, Henry J., Regina Coeli Residence for Priests, 685 York Rd., Warminster, 18974.
Speitel, Edmond J., 805 3rd St., Ocean City, NJ 08226.
Stanton, William J., Regina Coeli Residence for Priests, 685 York Rd., Warminster, 18974.
Stec, Joseph C., M.A., Saint Laurentius Rectory, 1608 East Berks St., 19125-2499.
Sweeney, Joseph J., 504 15th St., Ocean City, NJ 08226.
Szal, Ignatius J., 460 Sunbury St., Minersville, 17954.
Van Stone, John J., Villa Saint Joseph, 1436 Lansdowne Ave., Darby, 19023-1298.
Walsh, John M., Villa Saint Joseph, 1436 Lansdowne Ave., Darby, 19023-1298.
Walsh, Joseph E., Villa Saint Joseph, 1436 Lansdowne, Darby, 19023-1298.
Walsh, Michael L., Camilla Hall, Immaculata, 19345.
Walsh, Thomas F., Villa Saint Joseph, 1436 Lansdowne Ave., Darby, 19023-1298.
Wassel, Eugene A., Saint Francis Country House, 1412 Lansdowne Ave., Darby, 19023-1298.
Wesolowski, Edmund C., Immaculate Conception Rectory, 1020 N. Front St., 19123-1717.
Wright, Richard J., Saint Colman Rectory, 11 Simpson Rd., Ardmore, 19003.

Permanent Deacons:
All locations are Philadelphia unless otherwise indicated.
Anderson, James
Andrews, Edward J., St. Martin De Porres Church
Arno, Michael R., St. Irenaeus Church
Baratta, Gaspero P.
Basilio, James A., Notre Dame De Lourdes Church, Swarthmore
Bean, John J., St. Bartholomew Church
Belanger, A. Kenneth, St. Helena Church, Blue Bell
Bentacourt, Jose M., St. Peter the Apostle Church
Bianco, Salvatore R., Immaculate Heart of Mary Church
Bingham, Dennis J., St. Katharine of Siena Church, Wayne
Bizal, Francis M., SS. Philip and James Church, Exton
Bolter, George A., Our Lady of the Assumption Church, Strafford
Bonilla, Victor M., Hispanic Ministry for Bucks County
Brandon, Lawrence G., St. Maximilian Kolbe Church, West Chester
Brink, David C., St. Katherine of Siena Church
Brown, Clifford W., Our Mother of Consolation Church
Burghart, Peter H., St. Alphonsus Church, Maple Glen
Burke, Francis B., St. Bernadette, Drexel Hill
Burns, James H., St. Eleanor Church, Collegeville
Burns, Robert C., St. Matthew Church
Butcavage, Thomas E., Holy Spirit Church, Sharon Hill
Calabrese, Peter J., St. Charles Borromeo Church, Drexel Hill
Campbell, John J., St. Rose of Lima, North Wales
Cavaliere, Francis M., On loan to the Diocese of Saint Petersburg, Florida
Cella, Joseph M., Our Lady of Ransom Church
Ceneviva, Vincent G., Our Lady of Sacred Heart Church, Hilltown
Champagne, William E., Our Lady of Hope Church
Clancy, Kenneth P., Epiphany of Our Lord Church, Plymouth Meeting
Clark, Francis T., St. Joseph Church, Ambler
Clay, Alvin A., Immaculate Conception Church, Jenkintown
Colgan, Francis M., St. Anastasia Church, Newtown Square
Collazo, Apolonio, Visitation B.V.M. Church
Connors, Francis J., St. Callistus
Corwell, George V., Our Lady of Mt. Carmel Church, Doylestown
Cox, Paul R., St. Patrick, Malvern
Coyle, Joseph P., St. Alice Church, Upper Darby
Coyne, Richard C., Holy Cross Church
Croke, Thomas M., St. Luke the Evangelist Church, Glenside
Cruz, Felipe, Incarnation of Our Lord Church
D'Amico, John J., St. Peter Church, Honey Brook
D'Angelo, Ernest, St. John the Baptist Church, Ottsville
Dalton, James E., St. Cyril of Alexandria Church, East Lansdowne
Davaro, John J., St. Dorothy Church, Drexel Hill
Dayoc, Michael J., St. Paul Church, East Norriton
DeBow, James P., St. Ephrem Church, Bensalem
DeGrasse, Michael J., Assumption B.V.M. Church, West Grove

DeJesus, Epifanio, Cathedral Basilica of SS. Peter & Paul
DeLucca, Daniel N., St. Andrew Church, Drexel Hill
DeMasi, Leonard D., St. Monica Church
Derivan, Albert T., St. Andrew Church, Newtown
DeRosa, Joseph R., St. Eleanor, Collegeville
Devine, Charles F., St. Thomas the Apostle Church, Glen Mills
Diana, Leonard J., St. Kevin Church, Springfield
DiIenno, Anthony J., St. Thomas the Apostle, Glen Mills
Duffy, James J., St. Katherine of Siena
Dymek, Edward J., St. Ephrem Church, Bensalem
Eichman, Thomas E., St. Kevin Church, Springfield
Eliason, William F., St. David Church, Willow Grove
Ellis, John J., St. Barnabas Church
Fabrizio, Francis S., St. Charles Borromeo Church, Drexel Hill
Fahy, William C., SS. Philip and James Church, Exton
Favinger, M. Eugene, Our Lady of Consolation Church, Parkesburg
Finn, Michael J., Saint Katharine Drexel Church, Chester
Fontanez, Jose, Incarnation of Our Lord Church
Frankenberger, Robert, Holy Cross Church, Springfield
Franks, Michael J., Sr., St. Philip Neri Church, Pennsburg
Fremont, Richard L., St. Elizabeth Church, Uwchlan
Froio, Lawrence P., St. Patrick Church, Malvern
Fuentes, Ismael, St. Aloysius Church, Pottstown
Fulmer, Walter C., Christ the King Church
Garritano, Dominic A., Our Lady of Ransom Church
Gellentien, Robert P., St. John the Evangelist Church, Morrisville
Gentilcore, Kevin F., St. Anthony of Padua Church, Ambler
George, Albert J., Holy Spirit Church
Gibson, Lawrence J., St. Elizabeth Ann Seton Church, Bensalem
Ginn, Charles, St. Katharine of Siena Church, Wayne
Gladnick, Leo T., Ascension of Our Lord Church
Gohde, Robert P., St. Teresa of Avila Church, Norristown
Golaszewski, John M., St. Vincent De Paul Church, Richboro
Gonzalez, Victor, St. Agnes Church, West Chester
Gousie, Joseph N., Our Lady of Guadalupe Church, Buckingham
Granese, Claude B., St. Jude Church, Chalfont
Grant, John D., Saint Mary Medical Center
Gravlin, John J., St. Martin of Tours Church
Gwynn, Raymond F., St. Jerome Church
Haddon, Richard S., St. Catherine of Siena Church, Horsham
Hagerty, Paul B., Immaculate Conception Church, Jenkintown
Hannan, Thomas J., Assumption B.V.M. Church, West Grove
Harrison, A. Gerald, SS. Peter and Paul Church, West Chester
Hartmann, James F., St. John the Evangelist Church, Morrisville
Hartmann, Karl J., St. Joseph Church, Warrington
Heaney, Philip E., Maternity B.V.M. Church
Hernandez, Jose, Incarnation of Our Lord Church
Hickey, William L., St. Maximilian Kolbe, West Chester
Hoelzle, Louis F., St. Frances Cabrini Church, Fairless Hills
Hopkins, Stephen, St. Benedict Church
Horan, Thomas J., SS. Peter & Paul Church, West Chester
Houser, Joseph F., Sacred Heart Church, Royersford
Hunter, John K., St. Hilary of Poitiers Church, Rydal
Hunter, Richard F., St. Bernard Church
Huynh, Trac Mai, St. Francis De Sales Church
Hynes, John, Maternity B.V.M. Church
Iannucci, Joseph E., St. Pius X Church, Broomall
Isley, Brouycie P., Immaculate Conception Church
Jacobucci, Raymond, Queen of Peace Church, Ardsley
Jones, David E., St. Anthony of Padua Church, Ambler
Kane, James D., St. Francis of Assisi Church, Springfield
Kelly, Gerald F., St. Matthias Church, Bala Cynwyd
Kelly, Walter F., Our Lady of Mount Carmel Church, Doylestown
Kern, Paul R., St. John Baptist Vianney Church, Gladwyne
Kerr, Frederick H., St. Cecilia Church, Coatesville
Klauder, Francis C., St. Elizabeth Ann Seton Church, Bensalem
Klinger, George H., Mary, Mother of the Redeemer Church, North Wales
Konarski, Edward A., St. Rose of Lima Church, North Wales
Kreczkevich, John J., St. Barnabus Church
Kretsch, Donald J., Holy Savior Church, Norristown
Kruckenberger, William F., St. John Bosco Church, Hatboro
Kubczak, David M., St. Peter Church, Pottstown
Lance, Walter C., St. John Chrysostom Church, Wallingford
Leahy, Eugene R., Holy Family Church
Leonard, Warren C., Holy Trinity, Morrisville
Leonhardt, George W., Jr., St. Thomas More Church, Pottstown
Lozada, Jose Luis, St. Hugh of Cluny Church
Luczkowski, Edward R., St. John of the Cross Church, Roslyn
Lyon, James E., SS. Simon & Jude Church, West Chester
Madonna, James K., St. Patrick Church, Kennett Square
Maldonado, Rafael, St. Veronica Church
Malfara, Louis S., St. Cecilia Church
Manson, Joseph J., St. Genevieve Church, Flourtown
Manzano, Edwin R., Visitation B.V.M. Church
Maresca, Armand J., SS. Cosmas & Damian Church, Conshohocken
Martes, Zoilo, St. Michael Church
Masapollo, William M., St. Norbert Church, Paoli
Mauriello, Alfred J., St. Maximilian Kolbe, West Chester
Mayes, William C., St. Charles Borromeo Church
Mazzoni, Mace M., St. Frances Cabrini Church, Fairless Hills
McAndrews, Michael J., Notre Dame DeLourdes Church, Swarthmore
McBlain, Paul J., St. Joseph Church, Collingdale
McGovern, Clement J., St. Cornelius Church, Chadds Ford
McGuire, Arthur M., St. Francis of Assisi Church, Springfield
Mendez, Jose M., St. Ambrose Church
Micucci, Joseph A., Mother of Divine Grace Church
Midwood, Barry R., St. Basil the Great Church, Kimberton
Morris, George E., St. Robert Bellarmine Church, Warrington
Murphy, Francis X., Sacred Heart Church, Oxford
Nightingale, Richard G., Our Lady of Victory Church
Niland, Joseph W., St. Elizabeth Ann Seton Church, Bensalem
Nines, Joseph L., St. Genevieve Church, Flourtown
O'Brien, Gregory R., St. Madeline Church, Ridley Park
O'Kedas, Leroy F., (On Leave of Absence)
Oliver, Joseph M., Our Lady of Perpetual Help, Morton
Orlando, John C., St. Monica Church
Orlando, Joseph P., St. Bede the Venerable Church, Holland
Owen, Joseph T.
Owens, James T., Associate to the Administrator, Permanent Diaconate Department
Parker, John, Holy Saviour Church, Norristown
Pavonarius, Charles A., St. Jerome Church
Pierce, Robert F., SS. Peter & Paul Church, West Chester
Poellnitz, Fredrick E., St. Athanasius Church
Polley, Charles W., Jr., Ss. Philip and James Church, Exton
Purnell, Edward M., St. Theresa of the Child Jesus Church
Radetsky, William R., Epiphany of Our Lord Church, Plymouth Meeting
Ramos, Juan F., St. Peter the Apostle
Rayner, Albert E., Holy Spirit Church, Sharon Hill
Riordan, John T., St. Jude Church, Chalfont
Rooney, Joseph T., Our Lady Help of Christians Church, Abington
Rosario, Israel, Our Lady of Hope Church
Rose, John P., Our Lady of the Assumption Church, Strafford
Rouse, Daniel J., St. John Bosco Church, Hatboro
Ruffo, Paul E., St. Joseph Rectory, Downingtown
Ruiz, Luis, St. Ambrose Church
Schaffer, David B., Saint Colman Church, Ardmore
Schiappa, Edward R., St. Joseph Church, Downingtown
Schlegel, John F., St. Denis Rectory, Havertown
Schnepp, Lawrence P., St. Rose of Lima Church, Eddystone
Seda, Victor I., St. Helena Church
Sexton, Joseph F., St. Mary of the Assumption Church
Shields, Thomas A., St. Martin De Porres Church
Simpson, Harry J., St. Michael the Archangel, Levittown
Skawinski, Robert J., St. Ignatius Church, Yardley
Small, Michael C., Sacred Heart Church, Havertown
Smith, Calvin C., St. Benedict Church
Stam, Bernardus C., SS. Simon & Jude Church, West Chester
Stewart, James J., St. Edmond Church
Stewart, Robert J., St. Ignatius Church, Yardley
Stoughton, Richard L., Our Lady of the Rosary Church, Coatesville
Suplee, John J., Sacred Heart Church, Havertown
Thompson, James A., Stella Maris
Thompson, Vincent J., St. Francis Xavier Church
Tielemans, Mathieu M., St. Stanislaus Church, Lansdale
Tobin, Charles A., St. Philomena Church, Lansdowne
Tormey, James M., Sr., Our Mother of Consolation Church
Tucker, Henry E., St. Agnes Church, Sellersville
Upcavage, Joseph R., Queen of the Universe Church, Levittown
Urbanski, Timothy E., St. Catherine of Siena Church, Horsham
Urmson, Francis B., St. Helena
Vadino, Raymond M., St. John Chrysostom Church, Wallingford
Vondercrone, C. Stephens, St. Stanislaus Church, Lansdale
Walker, James, St. Benedict Church
Wallace, Mark M., St. Laurence Church, Upper Darby
Walsh, James V., St. Eugene Church, Primos
Wernert, Emil J., Epiphany of Our Lord, Plymouth Meeting
Whartenby, Gerald J., St. Anselm Church
Windish, Joseph F., St. Cyril of Jerusalem Church, Jamison
Wirth, Richard D., St. Cornelius Church, Chadds Ford
Wojewodka, Boleslaw S., Sacred Heart Church, Clifton Heights
Wolkowicz, Leonard J., St. Barnabas Church
Woods, Thomas J., Sacred Heart Church, Havertown
Ziff, Joel M., St. Titus Church, Norristown
Zurbach, E. Peter, St. Mary Magdalen Church, Media

INSTITUTIONS LOCATED IN THE ARCHDIOCESE

[A] SEMINARIES, ARCHDIOCESAN

WYNNEWOOD. *Theological Seminary of St. Charles Borromeo, Overbrook*, Administration: 100 E. Wynnewood Rd., 19096. Tel: 610-667-3394; Fax: 610-667-7635. Email: seminary@adphila.org. Web: www.scs.edu. Most Rev. Michael F. Burbidge, D.D., M.A., Ed.D., V.G., Rector; Rev. Christopher J. Schreck, S.T.B., S.S.L., Ph.D., S.T.D. (SAV) Vice Rector; Elaine K. Rice, M.B.A., Vice Pres., Finance & Operations; Revs. Joseph Prior, M.Div., M.A., S.S.L., S.T., Chief Academic Officer; Robert A. Pesarchick, M.Div., M.A., S.T.L., S.T., Academic Dean, Theology Division; David E. Diamond, M.Div., M.A., Ph.D., Academic Dean, College Division; Anthony J. Costa, M.Div., M.A., S.T.L., S.T., Academic Dean, Rel. Studies Div.; Joseph T. Szolack, M.Div. (CAM), Dean of Men, Theology Division; Joseph L. Maloney, M.Div., Dean of Men, College Division; Sandra R. Lovascio, B.A., Dir. Devel.; Rev. Joseph F. Gleason, M.Div., M.S., Dir. Spiritual Formation, Theology Division; Rev. Msgr. Paul V. Dougherty, M.Div., M.A., Dir. Spiritual Formation, College Division; Revs. Efren V. Esmilla, D.Min., Asst. Dir. of Pastoral and Apostolic Formation; Joseph P. Gentili, M.Div., S.T.L., S.T.D., Dir. Pastoral and Apostolic Formation; Cait Kokolus, M.S.L.S., M.A., Dir. Library Svcs.; Lawrence A. Heyman, Ed.M., M.S., Registrar; Bruce Grear, Dir. Facilities; James P. Gibbons, Dir. Dining & Guest Svcs.; Rev. James P. Olson, M.Div., M.A., Dir., Spirituality Year Prog. Priests 25; Sisters 2; Lay Staff 21; College and Theology Division Students 159; Religious Studies Division Students 266; Seminarians from Archdiocese 52; Seminarians from other Dioceses 102; Religious Communities 5.

Full Time Instructional Faculty: Candida Antonelli, M.Ed.; Janet Haggerty, M.A., Ph.D.; Alfred Hanley, M.A., Ph.D.; Rev. Jay Harrington, O.P., Ph.D., S.T.D., S.T.L., M.Div., M.A.; Atherton C. Lowry, M.A., Ph.D.; Theodore E. Kiefer, M.A., D.M.A.; Revs. Matthew J. Kornacki, M.Div.; Shaun L. Mahoney, M.Div., S.T.L., S.T.D.; Kevin T. McMahon, S.T.B., S.T.L., S.T.D. (WIL), John Cardinal Krol

Chair Prof. of Moral Theology; Gerald H. Malsbary, M.A., Ph.D.; Rev. Michael J. McNally, M.Div., M.Th., M.A., Ph.D. (PMB); Mr. William G. Murphy, S.T.L., S.T.D.; Elizabeth M. Nagel, M.A., S.S.L., S.S.D.; Rev. Msgr. William J. J. O'Donnell, M.A., Spiritual Dir. of Spirituality Year Prog.; Rev. James M. Oliver, J.C.D., M.Div., M.A., J.C.L., J.C.D.; John H. Sceski, M.A., Ph.D.; Christian Washburn, M.A. Adjunct Faculty: J. Brian Benestad, M.A., S.T.L., Ph.D.; Rev. Dennis J. Carbonaro, M.Div., M.A.; Carmina M. Magnusen Chapp, M.A., Ph.D.; Revs. Daniel N. DeLucca, M.A., Ph.D.; Stephen J. Dougherty; Augustine M. Esposito, O.S.A., M.Div., M.A., Ph.D.; Jennifer Fetter, M.S.; Sr. Mary Elizabeth Kratzinger, S.S.J., M.A.; Revs. Thomas J. McManus, M.Div., M.A., S.T.L.; John C. O'Driscoll, M.Div., S.L.L.; Rev. Msgr. Alexander J. Palmieri, M.A., J.C.L.; Sr. Rita Small, R.S.M., M.A.; Rabbi David A. Wortman, M.A., M.Phil. In Res. Rev. Dennis J. Carbonaro, M.Div., M.A.

[B] SEMINARIES, RELIGIOUS OR SCHOLASTICATES

PHILADELPHIA. *Brothers of the Christian Schools*, Jeremy House, 6633 Ardleigh St., 19119-3824. Tel: 215-843-1884; Fax: 215-843-1617. Email: jeremyhouse@juno.com. Bro. Richard Buccina, F.S.C., F.S.C., Dir. Professed Brothers 4; Scholastics 2.

DePaul Novitiate, 5710 Magnolia St., 19144. Tel: 215-843-1581; Fax: 215-844-9634. Email: joeccm@ix.netcom.com. Rev. Joseph V. Cummins, C.M., Dir. National Novitiate for the Congregation of the Mission (Vincentians). Priests 2. In Res. Very Rev. Thomas F. McKenna, C.M.; Revs. Charles M. Shanley, C.M.; Charles P. Strollo, C.M.; Bro. Peter A. Campbell, C.M.

St. Vincent's Seminary, 500 E. Chelten Ave., 19144-1296. Tel: 215-848-1985; Fax: 215-844-2085. Email: cmphila88@aol.com. Web: www.cmeast.org. Very Rev. Thomas F. McKenna, C.M., Prov.; Revs. Charles P. Strollo, C.M., Asst. Prov.; William W. Sheldon, C.M., Supr.; Stephen M. Grozio, C.M., Prov. Treas. & Second Councillor; Jerry J. McGovern, Corp. Treas.; Revs. James O. Kiernan, C.M., Dir. Miraculous Medal Association; John W. Carven, C.M., Prov. Archivist; Jerry J. McGovern, Corp. Treas. Central House of the Eastern Province of the Congregation of the Mission, (Vincentians). Residence for retired priests & brothers.

PAOLI. *Daylesford Abbey*, 220 S. Valley Rd., 19301-1900. Tel: 610-647-2530; Fax: 610-651-0219. Email: nobertines@daylesford.org. Web: www.daylesford.org. Rt. Rev. Ronald J. Rossi, O.Praem., Abbot; Very Rev. John J. Novielli, O.Praem., Prior; Rt. Rev. John E. Neitzel, O.Praem., Abbot Emeritus; Revs. Steven J. Albero, O.Praem., Vocation Dir.; Joseph A. Serano, O.Praem., Treas.
Legal Title: *Norbertine Fathers, Inc.* Priests 28; Brothers 4.

SPRINGFIELD. *Don Guanella House of Formation*, 1795 S. Sproul Rd., 19064. Tel: 610-328-3406; Fax: 610-328-1019. Email: servantsofcharity@msn.com. Web: www.servantsofcharity.org. Rev. Silvio De Nard, S.C. Congregation of the Servants of Charity Priests 1.

VILLANOVA. *St. Augustine Friary*, 214 Ashwood Rd., 19085. Tel: 610-527-0325; Fax: 610-527-0640. Revs. Joseph F. Girone, O.S.A.; Daniel E. Doyle, O.S.A.; Francis Gallogly, O.S.A.; Stanley C. Smith, O.S.A. Priests 4.

[C] COLLEGES AND UNIVERSITIES

PHILADELPHIA. *Chestnut Hill College*, 9601 Germantown Ave., 19118-2693. Tel: 215-248-7000; Fax: 215-248-7155. Email: chcapply@chc.edu. Web: www.chc.edu. Sr. Carol Jean Vale, S.S.J., Ph.D., Pres. Sisters 19; Lay Teachers 42; Students 1,600.

Holy Family University, Formerly Holy Family College (1954), Grant and Frankford Aves., 19114. Tel: 215-637-7700; Fax: 215-637-3787. Email: fonley@holyfamily.edu. Web: www.holyfamily.edu. Sr. Francesca Onley, C.S.F.N., Pres.; Rev. Albert J. Smith, O.S.F.S., Chap. & Campus Min. Congregation of the Sisters of the Holy Family of Nazareth Priests 5; Sisters 15; Lay Faculty 253; Undergraduate Students 1,781; Graduate 888. In Res. Rev. James J. Collins, S.O.E.D., Dept. of Religious Studies.

St. Joseph's University Regis Hall , 5600 City Ave., 19131. Tel: 610-660-1000; Fax: 610-660-1201. Web: www.sju.edu. Under the direction of the Jesuit Fathers. Incorporated January 29, 1851. Priests 21; Sisters 4; Lay Teachers 250; Students 7,180.

Jesuit Fathers Tel: 610-660-1400; Fax: 610-664-6464. Revs. Timothy R. Lannon, S.J., Pres.; George W. Bur, S.J., Spec. Asst. to Pres.; Nicholas J. Rashford, S.J.; James W. Moore, S.J., Assoc. Dean College of Arts and Sciences; Anthony J. Berret, S.J.; H. Cornell Bradley, S.J.; Thomas Brennan, S.J.; Francis F. Burch, S.J.; Very Rev. Joseph F. Chorpenning, O.S.F.S., S.T.L., Ph.D.; Revs. Peter A. Clark, S.J.; Donald G. Clifford, S.J.; Jerome B. Coll, S.J.; Joseph J. Feeney, S.J.; Gerald F. Finnegan, S.J. (BO); Vincent J. Genovesi, S.J.; Joseph J. Godfrey, S.J.; Albert H. Jenemann, S.J.; Joseph L. Lombardi, S.J.; Richard G. Malloy, S.J.; Dennis E. McNally, S.J.; Patrick Samway, S.J.; Sisters Ann Bernadette, G.N.S.H.; Frances Hart, S.S.J.; Frances Joseph, R.A.; Elizabeth Ann Linehan, R.S.M.

LaSalle University, 1900 W. Olney Ave., 19141. Tel: 215-951-1000; Fax: 215-951-1488. Bro. Michael J. McGinnis, F.S.C., Ph.D., Pres.; Richard A. Nigro, Ph.D., Provost; David C. Fleming, M.B.A., Vice Pres. Business Affairs; R. Brian Elderton M.Ed., Vice Pres. Advancement; Raymond A. Ricci, Ed.M., Vice Pres. Enrollment Svcs.; Thomas A. Keagy, Ph.D., Dean, School of Arts and Sciences; Gregory C. Bruce, M.B.A., Dean, School of Business Admin.; Zane Robinson Wolf, Ph.D., Dean, School of Nursing; Robert G. Voss, A.B., Dean of Admissions & Financial Aid; Joseph J. Cicala, Ph.D., Dean of Students; Bro. Charles F. Echelmeier, F.S.C., Dir. University Ministry & Svc. (Incorporated under the auspices of the Brothers of the Christian Schools) Brothers 22; Priests 3; Sisters 4; Lay Teachers 465; Students 5,937.

ASTON. *Neumann College*, One Neumann Dr., 19014-1298. Tel: 610-459-0905; Fax: 610 459-1370. Email: neumann@neumann.edu. Web: www.neumann.edu. Dr. Rosalie M. Mirenda, D.N.S., Pres.; Rev. Jude Michael Krill, O.F.M.Conv., Chap. Sponsored by the Sisters of St. Francis of Philadelphia, Opened September 1965. Priests 1; Sisters 19; Administrators 99; Faculty and Staff 127; Adjuncts 144; Lay Teachers 52; Students 2,589.

GWYNEDD VALLEY. *Gwynedd-Mercy College* 19437. Tel: 215-646-7300; Fax: 215-641-5573. Email: dobbs.a@gmc.edu. Web: www.gmc.edu. Rev. John Collins, C.S.S.R., Chap. Sisters of Mercy 10; Sisters 2; Lay Teachers 77; Students 2,558.

IMMACULATA. *Immaculata University* (1920), 19345. Tel: 610-647-4400; Fax: 610-251-1668. Web: www.immaculata.edu. Sisters R. Patricia Fadden, I.H.M., Pres.; M. Carroll Isselmann, I.H.M., Vice Pres. for Academic Affairs; Stephen Pugliese, M.A., Vice Pres. for Student Affairs; Dr. Thomas Ford, Vice Pres. for Financial Affairs; Dr. Linda Hopkins, Vice Pres. for Institutional Advancement; Janice Bates, Registrar; Dr. Elke Franke, Dean College of Lifelong Learning; Sr. Ann Heath, I.H.M., Dean College of Graduate Studies; Dr. Janet Kane, Dean Women's College; Marie Moughan, Exec. Dir. Public Rels. & Mktg.; Peter Lysionek, Dir. Financial Aid; Rev. Gregory J. Hickey, M.A., M.Div. Conducted by Sisters, Servants of the Immaculate Heart of Mary Priests 1; Sisters 22; Total Staff 251; Enrollment 3,062.

RADNOR. *Cabrini College* (1957), 610 King of Prussia Rd., 19087-3698. Tel: 610-902-8100; Fax: 610-902-8309. Email: cmay@cabrini.edu. Web: www.cabrini.edu. Dr. Antoinette Iadarola, Pres.; Frederick Pratt, Campus Min.; Rev. Michael Bialecki, O.S.A., Campus Min. Missionary Sisters of the Sacred Heart Priests 2; Sisters 1; Lay Teachers 211; Students 2,458.

ROSEMONT. *Rosemont College of the Holy Child Jesus* 19010-1699. Tel: 610-527-0200; Fax: 610-527-0341. Email: ann.amore@rosemont.edu. Web: www.rosemont.edu. Ann M. Amore, Ph.D., Pres.; Sr. Tobie Tondi, S.H.C.J., Vice Pres., Mission; Joshua Snyder, Campus Min. Sisters of the Holy Child Jesus 6; Full Time Lay Teachers 46; Part Time Lay Teachers 70; Students 1,210.

VILLANOVA. *Villanova University* 19085. Tel: 610-519-7499; Fax: 610-519-5333. Email: Stephen.Merritt@Villanova.edu. Web: www.villanova.edu. Revs. Edmund J. Dobbin, O.S.A., Pres. & Bd. Trustee; Francis J. Caponi, O.S.A., Bd. Trustee; James R. Flynn, O.S.A., Bd. Trustee; John E. Deegan, O.S.A., Bd. Trustee; Raymond F. Dlugos, O.S.A., Bd. Trustee; Kevin F. Dwyer, O.S.A. (BO), Bd. Trustee; William T. Garland, O.S.A., Bd. Trustee; Gary N. McCloskey, O.S.A., Bd. Trustee; Donald F. Reilly, O.S.A., Bd. Trustee; James A. Anderson, Ph.D., Bd. Trustee; Herbert F. Aspbury Esq., Bd. Trustee; James R. Birle, Bd. Trustee; Kimble A. Byrd Esq., Bd. Trustee; Gerald S.J. Cassidy Esq., Bd. Trustee; Tara S. Cortes, Ph.D., Bd. Trustee; James C. Curvey, Bd. Trustee; James D. Danella, Bd Trustee; John G. Drosdick, Bd. Trustee; William B. Finnerman, Bd. Trustee; John G. Gilfillan III, Esq., Bd. Trustee; Harry R. Halloran Jr., Bd. Trustee; Patricia H. Imbesi, Bd. Trustee; Maureen H. McCullough Esq., Bd. Trustee; James F. Orr III, Bd. Trustee; Terence M. O'Toole, Bd. Trustee; Michael B. Picotte, Bd. Trustee. Founded 1842 by the Augustinians, Province of St. Thomas of Villanova. Colleges of Liberal Arts and Sciences, Engineering, Commerce and Finance, Nursing, Part-time and Continuing Education, Graduate Studies and the School of Law and Continuing Education. Priests 19; Brothers 1; Lay Teachers 503; Students 10,300; Clerical Faculty: Total Staff 525; Full-time Enrollment 6,300; Part-time Enrollment 350; Total Enrollment 10,300.
Administration: Dr. John R. Johannes, Vice Pres. Academic Affairs; Dr. Helen K. Lafferty, Univ. Vice Pres.; Revs. William A. McGuire, O.S.A., Senior Vice Pres. Admin.; John P. Stack, O.S.A., Vice Pres. Student Life; Mr. John M. Elizandro, Vice Pres. Institutional Advancement; Dr. Mark A. Sargent, Dean School of Law; Mr. Vincent Nicastro, Dir. Athletics; Ms. Dorothy A. Malloy, Vice Pres. Univ. Counsel; Rev. George F. Riley, O.S.A., Special Asst. to Pres. External Affairs; Mr. Kenneth G. Valosky, CFO; Stephen A. Stumpf, Int. Dean College of Commerce & Finance; Dr. Barry Johnson, Dean of Engineering; Rev. Kail C. Ellis, O.S.A., Dean of Liberal Arts & Sciences; Mr. Paul Pugh, Dean of Students; Dr. M. Louise Fitzpatrick, Dean College of Nursing; Mr. Stephen R. Merritt, Dean Office of Enrollment Mgmt.; Mr. Stephen Fugale, CIO - UNIT; Revs. Joseph Calderone, O.S.A., Campus Ministry; T. Shawn Tracy, O.S.A., Campus Ministry; Gordon E. Marcellus, O.S.A., Dir. Devel.; John P. Betoni, O.S.A., Student Employment Asst.; John F. McAtee, O.S.A., Campus Ministry; Revs. Thomas Murnane, O.S.A., Office of Univ. Admission; Dennis J. Gallagher, O.S.A., Archivist; Thomas J. Mahony, O.S.A., Facilities Mgmt.
Clerical Faculty: Revs. Richard G. Cannuli, O.S.A., Dir. Art Gallery; Frank E. Chambers, O.S.A., Office of Univ. Admission; John T. Denny, O.S.A.; Peter M. Donohue, O.S.A.; Daniel E. Doyle, O.S.A.; Francis A. Eigo, O.S.A.; Edward J. Enright, O.S.A.; John J. Farrell, O.S.A.; John J. Hagen, O.S.A.; Robert Hagan, O.S.A., Asst. Athletic Dir.; Richard Jacobs, O.S.A.; Charles P. Laferty, O.S.A.; Martin Laird, O.S.A.; Bernard A. Lazor, O.S.A.; Joseph Loya, O.S.A.; Lee J. Makowski, O.S.A.; Thomas F. Martin, O.S.A.; James J. McCartney, O.S.A.; Neil J. McGettigan, O.S.A.; John J. McKenzie, O.S.A.; Robert J. Murray, O.S.A.; Joseph Ryan, O.S.A.; Michael J. Scanlon, O.S.A.; Bro. John Stagliano, O.S.A.

[D] HIGH SCHOOLS, ARCHDIOCESAN

PHILADELPHIA. *Archbishop Ryan High School*, 11201 Academy Rd., 19154-3397. Tel: 215-637-1800; Fax: 215-637-8833. Email: ryanlibrary@onebox.com. Web: www.archbishopryan.org. Revs. Charles Newman, O.F.M., Pres.; Rene Barczak, O.F.M.; Carl Graczyk, O.F.M.; Francis Kelly, O.F.M.; Gabriel A. Rosetti, O.F.M.; William Stout, O.F.M. Franciscan Friars, Order of Friars Minor, Opened September 7, 1966. Priests 2; Sisters 5; Lay Teachers 122; Total Staff 129; Students 2,579.

Cardinal Dougherty High School, 6301 N. 2nd St., 19120-1599. Tel: 215-276-2300; Fax: 215-276-2306. Email: cdhs@libertynet.org. Web: www.cardinaldougherty.org. Rev. Paul M. Kennedy, M.A., Pres.; Mrs. Mary Harkins, M.A., Prin.; Rev. Carl F. Janicki, School Min. (Coed) Opened September 1956. Priests 4; Sisters 14; Lay Teachers 48; Students 1,173.

Father Judge High School for Boys, 3301 Solly Ave., 19136-2396. Tel: 215-338-9494; Fax: 215-338-0250. Email: principal@fjquest.com. Web: fjquest.com. Revs. Thomas P. Gallagher, O.S.F.S.; Eugene L. Kelly, O.S.F.S.; Dennis W. Killion, O.S.F.S.; Gerard J. Mahoney, O.S.F.S.; David M. Merchant, O.S.F.S.; Gerald M. Dunne, O.S.F.S. (SUP); Bros. Thomas Brophy, O.S.F.S.; James Williams, O.S.F.S.; Dr. Joseph DeAngelis, Prin.; Rev. Joseph G. Campellone, O.S.F.S., Pres. Oblates of St. Francis de Sales, Opened September 1954. Priests 7; Brothers 2; Lay Teachers 61; Students 1,304.

St. Hubert's Catholic High School for Girls, 7320 Torresdale Ave., 19136. Tel: 215-624-6840; Fax: 215-624-5940. Email: contactus@huberts.org. Web: huberts.org. Sr. Alma Rose Schlosser, S.S.J., Pres.; Rev. Christopher D. Lucas, Dir. School Ministry; Sr. Marie Esther Hart, I.H.M., Prin. Opened September 1941. Priests 1; Sisters 22; Lay Teachers 56; Students 1,164.

St. John Neumann High School (Formerly Southeast Catholic High School) , 2600 Moore St., 19145-1798. Tel: 215-389-4900; Fax: 215-462-3577. Email: neumann@netaxs.com. Web: www.netaxs.com~neumann. Revs. Michael S. Olivere, Pres.; Quan H. Tran, School Ministry; Stephen D. Thorne. Canons Regular of Premontre Diocesan Priests forming Faculty, (Boys) Opened September 1, 1934. Priests 3; Sisters 1; Lay Teachers 31; Students 597.

John W. Hallahan Catholic Girls High School, 311 N. 19th St., 19103-1198. Tel: 215-563-8930; Fax: 215-563-3809. Email: jhpres@adphila.org. Web: www.jhallahan.org. Mrs. Margaret A. Gallagher, Pres.; Sr. Susan Marie Kuk, I.H.M., Prin.; Rev. Michael J. Reilly, School Min. Opened September 18, 1901. Priests 1; Sisters 5; Lay Teachers 27; Students 679.

Little Flower Catholic High School for Girls, 1000 W. Lycoming St., 19140. Tel: 215-455-6900; Fax: 215-329-0478. Web: littleflowerhighschool.org. Sisters Kathleen Klarich, R.S.M., Prin.; Donna Shallo, I.H.M., Pres.; Rev. Joseph C. McCaffrey, M.B.A., M.Div., School Min. Opened September 1, 1939. Sisters 5; Lay Teachers 32; Students 793.

St. Maria Goretti High School, 1736 S. 10th St., 19148. Tel: 215-465-8437; Fax: 215-462-2410. Email: mgpres@adphila.org. Web: www.goretti.com. Ms. Rita Frey, R.N., Pres.; Mrs. Patricia Sticco, Acting Prin.; Rev. Charles Zlock, School Min. (Girls) Opened September 1955. Sisters 12; Lay Teachers 34; Students 685.

Northeast Catholic High School for Boys, 1842 E. Torresdale Ave., 19124-4418. Tel: 215-831-1234; Fax: 215-743-0926. Email: preznechs@aol.com. Web: www.northcatholic.com. Revs. Vincent E. Smith, C.S.F.S.; Nicholas R. Waseline, O.S.F.S., Prin.; Mr. Michael Cunningham. Oblates of St. Francis de Sales, Opened September 7, 1926. Priests 6; Brothers 1; Sisters 1; Lay Faculty 35; Students 786.

Roman Catholic High School for Boys, 301 N. Broad St., 19107. Tel: 215-627-1270; 215-627-1570; Fax: 215-627-4979. Email: mail@cahillite.com. Web: www.cahillite.com. Revs. Paul C. Brandt, Pres. & Rector; Ronald M. Jakows, School Min. Opened September 8, 1890. Priests 2; Sisters 2; Lay Teachers 45; Students 899.

West Philadelphia Catholic High School, 4501 Chestnut St., 19139. Tel: 215-386-2244; Fax: 215-222-1651. Email: westcatholic@hotmail.org. Web: www.westcatholic.org. Bro. Richard Kestler, F.S.C.; Rev. John Pidgeon, Dir. School Ministry. Opened September 6, 1989. Priests 1; Religious 15; Lay Teachers 36; Students 730.

DOWNINGTOWN. *Bishop Shanahan High School*, 220 Woodbine Rd., 19335. Tel: 610-518-1300; Fax: 610-343-6220. Email: rplunkett@shanahan.org. Web: www.shanahan.org. Sisters Regina Plunkett, I.H.M., Pres.; Maureen L. McDermott, I.H.M., Prin.; Revs. James Otto; Matthew W. Guckin; Peter DiMaria. (Coed) Formerly St. Agnes High School opened in 1909; became diocesan high school September 1957, moved from West Chester to Downingtown in 1998. Sisters, Servants of the Immaculate Heart of Mary 9; Priests 3; Lay Teachers 63; Students 1,420.

DREXEL HILL. *Archbishop Prendergast High School*, 401 N. Lansdowne Ave., 19026. Tel: 610-259-0265; Fax: 610-259-3676. Email: prendie@nni.com. Web: www.prendie.com. Sr. Catherine Robinson, S.S.J., Pres.; Mrs. Mary Berner, Prin.; Rev. Jason Kulczynski, Dir. School Ministry. Opened September 1956. Priests 1; Sisters 6; Lay Teachers 45; Girls 936.

Monsignor Bonner High School, 403 N. Lansdowne Ave., 19026-1196. Tel: 610-259-0280; Fax: 610-259-1630. Web: www.bonnerhigh.com. Revs. Augustine M. Esposito, O.S.A., M.Div., M.A., Ph.D., Pres.; William E. Atkinson, O.S.A.; Francis X. Devlin, O.S.A.; Daniel McLaughlin, O.S.A.; Stephen Baker, O.S.A., Prior. (Boys) Opened September 1953 as Archbishop Prendergast High School for Boys. New name adopted September 1956. Priests 5; Sisters 4; Lay Teachers 48; Students 963.

FAIRLESS HILLS. *Conwell-Egan Catholic High School*, 611 Wistar Rd., 19030. Tel: 215-945-6200; Fax: 215-945-6206. Email: cecinfo@conwell-egan.org. Web: conwell-egan.org. Dr. Lorraine Rice, Pres.; MaryJane McHugh, Prin.; Revs. Fidelis F. Weber, T.O.R., Guidance Dir.; Alan Okon, Campus Min. Formerly Bishop Egan High School, Fairless Hills, and Bishop Conwell High School, Levittown. Priests 2; Sisters 8; Brothers 1; Lay Teachers 48; Students 1,033.

NORRISTOWN. *0.Kennedy-Kenrick Catholic High School*, 250 E. Johnson Hwy., 19401. Tel: 610-275-2846; Fax: 610-277-6699. Web: www.kkchs.org. Rev. T. Christopher Redcay, Pres.; Rosemary Naab, Prin.; Rev. James Cox; Crista Anders, Dir. of Campus Min. Formerly Bishop Kenrick High School, Norristown, and Archbishop Kennedy High School, Conshohocken. Priests 2; Sisters 12; Lay Teachers 27; Students 574; Administrators 4.

POTTSTOWN. *St. Pius X High School*, 844 N. Keim St., 19464. Tel: 610-326-8990; Fax: 610-323-8594. Email: president@stpiusxhs.org. Web: www.stpiusxhs.org. Dr. David W. Brennan, Prin.; Rev. Joseph W. Bongard, M.A., Pres. Opened 1954. Priests 2; Sisters 1; Lay Teachers 32; Students 590.

RADNOR. *Archbishop John Carroll High School*, 211 Matson Ford Rd., 19087. Tel: 610-688-7610; Fax: 610-688-8326 (Prin.); 610-971-0827 (Pres.). Email: carroll@jcarroll.org. Web: www.jcarroll.org. Rev. Vincent R. Morabito. Opened September 1967. Priests 3; Sisters 6; Lay Teachers 59; Students 1,124.

SPRINGFIELD. *Cardinal O'Hara High School*, 1701 S. Sproul Rd., 19064. Tel: 610-544-3800; Fax: 610-544-1189. Email: cohs.com. William J. McCusker, Ed.D., Pres.; Revs. Michael P. O'Malley, Ed.D., Prin.; Joseph C. Bordonaro, D.Min.; Raymond J. Overstreet; Thomas R. Urian, M.A., D.Min.; Joseph T. Shenosky, M.A., D.Min. (Coed) Opened September, 1963. Priests 5; Sisters 4; Lay Teachers 101; Students 2,010.

WARMINSTER. *Archbishop Wood Catholic High School*, 655 York Rd., 18974. Tel: 215-672-5050; Fax: 215-672-9572. Email: fciao@archwood.org. Web: www.archwood.org. Dr. Frederick J. Ciao, Ph.D., Pres.; Mrs. Catherine Murray, Prin.; Revs. James F. Endres; Patrick S. McManus, M.A. Opened September 1964. Priests 2; Sisters 2; Lay Teachers 62; Students 1,170.

WYNCOTE. *Bishop McDevitt High School*, 125 Royal Ave., 19095-1198. Tel: 215-887-5575; Fax: 215-887-1371. Email: bmcdhs1@nni.com. Web: www.mcdevitths.org. Salvatore DiNenna, Ph.D., Pres.; Revs. William J. Chiriaco; John J. Nordeman; Albert J. Santorsola. Opened September 1958. Priests 3; Sisters 4; Lay Teachers 40; Students 816.

[E] VOCATIONAL HIGH SCHOOLS

PHILADELPHIA. *Mercy Vocational High School*, 2900 W. Hunting Park Ave., 19129-1803. Tel: 215-226-1225; Fax: 215-228-6337. Email: admin@mercyvhs.org. Web: www.mercyvocational.org. Sisters Rosemary Herron, R.S.M., Prin.; Susan Walsh, R.S.M., Vice Prin. Sisters of Mercy 12; Lay Teachers 40; Students 404.

[F] HIGH SCHOOLS, PAROCHIAL

LANSDALE. *Lansdale Catholic High School*, 700 Lansdale Ave., 19446-2995. Tel: 215-362-6160; 215-242-6160 (Philadelphia); Fax: 215-362-5746. Email: jrymdeika@lansdalecatholic.com. Web: www.lansdalecatholic.com. Mrs. Linda Robinson, Prin.; Rev. Joseph F. Rymdeika, Pres. Opened 1949. 1983 joined the System of Secondary Schools in Philadelphia. Priests 2; Lay Teachers 48; Students 850.

[G] HIGH SCHOOLS, PRIVATE

PHILADELPHIA. *St. Joseph's Preparatory School*, Office of the President, 1733 W. Girard Ave., 19130. Tel: 215-978-1950; Fax: 215-765-1710. Web: www.sjprep.org. Rev. Bruce M. Bidinger, S.J., Pres.; Dr. Michael J. Coury, Prin.; Mr. Daniel A. Brennan, Vice Pres. for Devel.; Mr. Charles J. Johnson, Vice Pres. Finance; Mrs. Rose Marie Kettinger, Registrar; Mr. Christopher Cosentino, Dean of Students; Revs. Thomas F. Clifford, S.J.; Francis E. Skechus, S.J. Priests 3; Sisters 1; Lay Teachers 69; Students 993.

Nazareth Academy High School, 4001 Grant Ave., 19114-2999. Tel: 215-637-7676; Fax: 215-637-8523. Email: jacobs@nazarethacademyhs.org. Web: www.nazarethacademyhs.org. Sr. Mary Joan Jacobs, C.S.F.N., Ed.D., Prin. Sisters 9; Lay Teachers 59; Girls 449.

BENSALEM. *Holy Ghost Preparatory School*, 2429 Bristol Pike, 19020. Tel: 215-639-2102; Fax: 215-639-4225. Email: jduaim01@holyghostprep.org. Web: www.holyghostprep.org. Rev. Jeffrey T. Duaime, C.S.Sp., Pres. Tel: 215-639-2102. Spiritan Fathers 2; Lay Teachers 45; Boys 509.

BRYN MAWR. *Country Day School of the Sacred Heart*, 480 Bryn Mawr Ave., 19010. Tel: 610-527-3915; Fax: 610-527-0942. Email: smacdonald@cdssh.org. Web: www.cdssh.org. Sr. Matthew Anita MacDonald, S.S.J., Head of School; Rev. Thomas P. Gillin. Sisters 42; Lay Teachers 42; Students 371; Total Staff 62.

DEVON. *Devon Preparatory School* 19333. Tel: 610-688-7337; Fax: 610-688-2409. Email: info@devonprep.com. Revs. James P. Shea, Sch.P., Headmaster; Richard S. Wyzykiewicz, Sch.P., Chap. & Rector; Ferdinand Negrillos, Sch.P.; Louis G. Mesko, Sch.P.; Geza Pazmany, Sch.P. Piarist Fathers Priests 3; Lay Teachers 30; Students 280.

FLOURTOWN. *Mt. St. Joseph Academy*, 120 W. Wissahickon Ave., 19031. Tel: 215-233-3177; Fax: 215-233-4734. Email: mdacey@msjacad.org. Web: www.msjacad.org. Sisters Mary Dacey, S.S.J., Pres.; Karen Dietrich, S.S.J., Prin. Sisters of St. Joseph 16; Lay Teachers 43; Students 562.

GWYNEDD VALLEY. *Gwynedd-Mercy Academy*, 1345 Sumneytown Pike, 19437-0902. Tel: 215-646-8815; Fax: 215-646-4361. Email: skathleen@gmahs.com. Web: www.gmahs.com. Sr. Kathleen Boyce, R.S.M., Prin. Sisters 11; Lay Teachers 39; Girls 397.

HOLLAND. *Villa Joseph Marie High School for Girls* 18966. Tel: 215-357-8810; Fax: 215-357-2477. Email: dkoop@vjmhs.com. Sr. M. Elaine, S.S.C., Prin.; Diana Koopman, Int. Prin.; Rev. John A. Cannon, Chap. (Retired). Priests 1; Sisters of St. Casimir 3; Lay Teachers 26; Students 338.

MALVERN. *Malvern Preparatory School for Boys*, 418 S. Warren Ave., 19355-2707. Tel: 484-595-1100; Fax: 484-595-1118. Web: www.malvernprep.com. Revs. David J. Duffy, O.S.A., Pres.; Stephen M. Curry, O.S.A., Faculty, Campus Min.; James R. Flynn, O.S.A., Dean of Middle School; Patrick B. McStravog, O.S.A., Prior, Chair of Theology. Priests 4; Lay Teachers 75; Students 597.

Villa Maria Academy High School, 370 Old Lincoln Hwy., 19355. Tel: 610-644-2551; Fax: 610-644-2866. Email: info@vmahs.org. Web: www.vmahs.org. Sr. Marita Carmel, I.H.M., Prin. Sisters, Servants of the Immaculate Heart of Mary 14; Lay Teachers 45; Total Staff 59; Girls 440.

MERION. *Merion Mercy Academy*, Merion Station, 19066. Tel: 610-664-6655; Fax: 610-664-6322. Email: mma@merion-mercy.com. Web: www.merion-mercy.com. Sr. Regina Ward, Prin. Day School for Girls. Sisters of Mercy 10; Lay Teachers 45; Students 449.

VILLANOVA. *Academy of Notre Dame de Namur*, 560 Sproul Rd., 19085. Tel: 610-687-0650; Fax: 610-687-1912. Email: broughton_ma@ndapa.org. Web: www.ndapa.org. Sr. Mary Anne Broughton, Pres.; Ms. Jean Phalan, Junior School Prin.; Mrs. Maria Marino, High School Prin. Sisters 9; Lay Teachers 68; Girls 493.

WYNDMOOR. *LaSalle College High School*, 8605 Cheltenham Ave., 19038. Tel: 215-233-2911; Fax: 215-233-1418. Email: admissions@lschs.org. Web: www.lschs.org. Bro. Rene Sterner, F.S.C., Pres.; Mr. Fred Assaf, Prin.; Bro. Brendan Garwood, F.S.C., Religious Supr. Priests 1; Brothers of the Christian Schools 12; Lay Teachers 86; Students 1,040.

[H] CONSOLIDATED PARISH SCHOOLS

PHILADELPHIA. *St. Athanasius-Immaculate Conception School*, 7105 Limekiln Pike, 19138. Tel: 215-424-5045; Fax: 215-927-6615. Email: apathanic05@nni.com. Web: www.sa-ic.org. Consolidated school for St. Athanasius Parish and Immaculate Conception Parish. Sisters 3; Lay Teachers 11; Students 284.

SS. Clement-Irenaeus School, 72nd St. & Paschall Ave., 19142-1108. Tel: 215-729-8368; Fax: 215-729-1274. Consolidated school for St. Clement Parish and St. Irenaeus Parish. Servants of the Immaculate Heart of Mary 5; Lay Teachers 10; Students 204.

St. Martin de Porres School (Germantown), 44 W. Logan St., 19144. Tel: 215-842-1266. Consolidated school for St. Francis of Assisi Parish, St. Madeleine Sophie Parish and Saint Vincent de Paul Parish. Sisters 2; Lay Teachers 10; Priests 2; Students 210.

St. Mary Interparochial School, 5th & Locusts Sts., 19106. Tel: 215-923-7522; Fax: 215-923-8502. Email: st.mary@verizon.net. Consolidated school for St. Stanislaus Parish, Old St. Joseph Parish, Old St. Mary Parish, St. John the Evangelist Parish, St. Augustine Parish, Holy Trinity Parish, St. Mary Magdalen dePazzi and St. Patrick. Lay Teachers 10; Students 241.

Our Lady of Angels School, 2917 Dickinson Streets, 19146. Tel: 215-468-7230; Fax: 215-468-2554. Email: apgabe03@nni.com. Web: www.olangels.org. Sr. Noreen James Friel, I.H.M., Prin. Consolidated school for St. Gabriel Parish, St. Aloysius Parish, King of Peace Parish, Philadelphia, PA. Sisters 3; Lay Teachers 9; Students 250.

AMBLER. *Ambler Catholic Elementary School*, 260 Forest Ave., 19002. Tel: 215-646-6150; Fax: 215-646-7435. Email: kaleslie@amblercatholic.org. Web: www.amblercatholic.org. Consolidated school for St. Anthony of Padua Parish and St. Joseph Parish. Sisters of St. Joseph 1; Lay Teachers 12; Students 245.

BRIDGEPORT. *Holy Trinity Catholic School* Tel: 610-277-4133; Fax: 610-277-4725. Web: HOLY-TRINITY-CATHOLIC.org.

Holy Trinity Lower School (Grades PreK-4), 631 E. Fourth St., Swedesburg, 19405. Tel: 610-277-4133; Fax: 610-277-4725.

Holy Trinity Upper School (Grades 5-8), 504 Ford St., 19405. Tel: 610-279-4630; Fax: 610-279-5579. Sr. Patricia Mengel, I.H.M., Prin. Consolidated schools for St. Augustine, Bridgeport; Our Lady of

Mount Carmel, Bridgeport; Sacred Heart, Swedesburg. Servants of the Immaculate Heart of Mary 4; Lay Teachers 13; Students (PreK-4) 105; Students (5-8) 66.

Holy Trinity School, 504 Ford St., 19405. Tel: 610-279-4630; Fax: 610-279-5579. Email: pmnostop@juno.com. Web: HOLY-TRINITY-CATHOLIC.org. Sr. Patricia Mengel, I.H.M., Prin. Consolidated school for St. Augustine, Bridgeport; Our Lady of Mount Carmel, Bridgeport; Sacred Heart, Swedesburg. Sisters 4; Lay Teachers 13; Students 66.

BRYN MAWR. *SS. Colman-John Neumann School*, 372 Highland Ln., 19010. Tel: 610-525-3266; Fax: 610-525-6103. Email: scjnschool.org. Web: www.scjnschool.org. Mrs. Mary Ann DeAngelo, Prin. Consolidated school for St. Colman Parish and St. John Neumann Parish. Lay Teachers 20; Students 238.

St. Thomas-Good Counsel School, 575 Lancaster Ave., 19010. Tel: 610-525-1407; Fax: 610-525-4701. Email: stgc@stgcschool.org. Web: www.stg@school.org. Consolidated school for St. Thomas of Villanova Parish and Our Mother of Good Counsel Parish. Lay Teachers 15; Students 160.

COATESVILLE. *Coatesville Area Catholic Elementary School*, 605 E. Lincoln Hwy., 19320. Tel: 610-384-5961; Fax: 610-384-5730. Email: apcaces09@aol.com. Web: www.coatesvillecatholicsch.org. Consolidated for St. Cecilia, St. Joseph, St. Stanislaus and Our Lady of the Rosary, Coatesville, and St. Peter Parish, Honeybrook. Servants of the Immaculate Heart of Mary 4; Lay Teachers 16; Students 505.

CONSHOHOCKEN. *Conshohocken Catholic School* Tel: 610-828-2007; Fax: 610-825-8796. Email: conshohockencatholic@yahoo.com. Mrs. Jacqueline Kerrigan, Prin. Consolidated school for SS. Cosmas & Damian Parish and St. Matthew Parish.

St. Matthew Elementary Campus (Grades 1-8), 205 Fayette St., 19428. Tel: 610-828-2007; Fax: 610-825-8796.

SS. Cosmas & Damian Primary Campus (Grades PreK-K), 5th Ave. & Maple St., 19428. Tel: 610-828-0755; Fax: 610-828-5191. Sisters 3; Lay Teachers 15; Students 243.

HILLTOWN. *St. Agnes-Sacred Heart School*, Rte. 152 & Broad St., P.O. Box 31, 18927. Tel: 215-822-9174; Fax: 215-822-7942. Margaret Graham, Prin.

LINWOOD. *Holy Saviour-St. John Fisher School*, 122 E. Ridge Rd., 19061. Tel: 610-485-0363; Fax: 610-485-7809. Email: apsavior10@nni.com. Ms. Barbara Virga, M.A. Consolidated school for Holy Saviour Parish and St. John Fisher Parish. Lay Teachers 14; Students 260.

PHOENIXVILLE. *Holy Family School*, 221 Third Ave., 19460. Tel: 610-933-7562. Consolidated school for St. Ann Parish, Holy Trinity Parish, St. Mary of the Assumption Parish and Sacred Heart Parish. Lay Teachers 14; Students 350.

RIDLEY PARK. *St. Madeline-St. Rose School*, 500 Tome St., 19078. Tel: 610-583-3662; Fax: 610-583-3683. Email: smsboss@comcast.net. Web: www.smsrcentral.com. Consolidated School for St. Madeline Parish and St. Rose of Lima Parish. Lay Teachers 18; Students 363.

SELLERSVILLE. *St. Agnes-Our Lady of the Sacred Heart*, 393 N. Main St., 18960. Tel: 215-257-3571; Fax: 215-257-8036. Margaret Graham, Prin. Consolidated school for St. Agnes Parish and Our Lady of the Sacred Heart, Hilltown. Lay Teachers 19; Students 435.

WARRINGTON. *SS. Joseph-St. Robert School*, 850 Euclid Ave., 18976. Tel: 215-343-5100; Fax: 215-343-7434. Web: stjstr.org. Consolidated school for St. Joseph Parish and St. Robert Bellarmine Parish. Lay Teachers 20; Students 458.

[I] ELEMENTARY SCHOOLS, PRIVATE

PHILADELPHIA. *The Gesu School*, 1700 W. Thompson Sts., 19121. Tel: 215-763-3660; 215-763-9077 (Development); Fax: 215-763-9844. Email: neil@gesuschool.org. Web: www.gesuschool.org. Christine Beck, Pres.; Sr. Ellen Convey, I.H.M., Prin.; Rev. Neil L. Ver-Schneider, S.J.; Sr. Patricia McGrenra, I.H.M. Priests, Society of Jesus 1; Sisters, Servants of the Immaculate Heart of Mary 2; Lay Teachers 31; Students 433.

**La Salle Academy*, (Grades 3-8), 1434 N. 2nd St., 19122. Tel: 215-739-5804. Email: jeannemcgowan2002@yahoo.com. Sr. Jeanne McGowan, S.S.J., Pres.

Nazareth Academy Grade School, 4701 Grant Ave., 19114. Tel: 215-637-7777; Fax: 215-637-5696. Email: duffy@nni.com. Web: www.nazarethacademy.net. Sr. M. Martin, C.S.F.N., Prin. Sisters of the Holy Family of Nazareth 4; Lay Teachers 12; Students 233.

Norwood-Fontbonne Academy, Formerly Norwood-Frontbonne Academy for Boys and Girls, 8891 Germantown Ave., 19118. Tel: 215-247-3811; 215-242-1611; Fax: 215-247-8405; 215-248-9721. Email: jlaurich@norfon.org. Web: www.norfon.org. Sr. Jean Laurich, S.S.J., Prin.; Mr. George Aspen, Asst. Prin.; Mrs. Deborah Wood, Asst. Prin.; Sr. Joannie Cassidy, S.S.S., Campus Min.; Mrs. Joanne Baillie, Admissions Dir.; Mrs. Robbie Hain, Devel. Dir. Sisters of St. Joseph 10; Lay Teachers 44. Students 540.

BRYN MAWR. *St. Aloysius Academy*, (Grades PreK-8), 401 S. Bryn Mawr Ave., 19010. Tel: 610-527-0506; 610-525-1670; Fax: 610-525-5140. Email: soar@staloysiusacademy.org. Web: www.staloysiusacademy.org. Sr. Carolyn M. Dimick, I.H.M., Prin. Sisters, Servants of the Immaculate Heart of Mary 11; Lay Teachers 28; Students 312.

DREXEL HILL. *Holy Child Academy*, (Grades PreK-8), 475 Shadeland Ave., 19026. Tel: 610-259-2712; Fax: 610-259-1862. Email: shcadm@hotmail.com. Web: holychildacademy.com. Mrs. Anita P. Coll, Head. Lay Teachers 29; Students 235.

IMMACULATA. *Villa Maria Academy*, 1140 King Rd., P.O. Box 600, 19345. Tel: 610-644-4864; Fax: 610-647-6403. Email: rwalsh@villamaria.org. Web: www.villamaria.org. Sr. Mary Ellen Tennity, I.H.M., Prin. Sisters, Servants of the Immaculate Heart of Mary 4; Lay Teachers 26; Girls 358.

MERION. *Waldron Mercy Academy* 23158123, 513 Montgomery Ave., Merion Station, 19066. Tel: 610-664-9847; Fax: 610-664-6364 Email: waldronmercy.org. Web: www.waldronmercy.org. Sr. Patricia Smith, R.S.M., Prin.; Mr. Stephen Stritch, Vice Prin. for Inst. Advancement; Mrs. Susan Smith, Admissions Dir. Private, coeducational elementary school with child care, preschool & Montessori programs. Sisters of Mercy 5 Lay Teachers 45; Students 512.

RADNOR. *Armenian Sisters Academy*, 440 Upper Gulph Rd., 19087. Tel: 610-687-4100; Fax: 610-687-2430. Email: asaphila@aol.com. Web: www.armeniansrsacademy.org. Sr. Louisa Kassarjian, Prin. Montessori for ages 3-6. Ungraded Elementary for ages 7-14. Sisters 3; Lay Teachers 21; Students 195.

ROSEMONT. *Rosemont School of the Holy Child*, 1344 Montgomery Ave., 19010. Tel: 610-922-1000; Fax: 610-525-7128. Email: mbroderi@rosemontschool.org. Web: www.rosemontschool.org. Sr. Mary Broderick, S.H.C.J., Prin. Sisters of the Holy Child Jesus 2; Lay Teachers 35; Students 292.

SPRING HOUSE. *Gwynedd-Mercy Academy*, (Grades K-8), Elementary Division, 816 Norristown Rd., P.O. Box 241, 19477. Tel: 215-646-4916; 215-646-2406 (Business Office); Fax: 215-628-8441. Email: mkenney@gmaelem.org. Web: www.gmaelem.org. Sr. Anne Crampsie, R.S.M., Prin. Sisters of Mercy 1; Lay Teachers 42; Students 445; Total Staff 50.

WYNCOTE. *Ancillae-Assumpta Academy*, (Grades PreK-8), (Coed), 2025 Church Rd., 19095. Tel: 215-885-1636; Fax: 215-885-2740. Email: emccoy@ancillae.org mgillespie@ancillae.org. Sisters Elizabeth McCoy, A.C.J., Dir.; Maureen Gillespie, A.C.J., Prin. Handmaids of the Sacred Heart of Jesus 5; Lay Teachers 56; Students 579.

YARDLEY. *Grey Nun Academy*, 1750 Quarry Rd., 19067. Tel: 215-968-4151; Fax: 215-860-7418. Email: jmc@gnaedu.org. Web: www.gnaedu.org. Joanne M. Cornell, Prin. (Coed Day School) Grey Nuns of the Sacred Heart 1; Lay Teachers 28; Students 235.

[J] SPECIAL EDUCATION

PHILADELPHIA. *Our Lady of Confidence Day School* Tel 215-276-2300; Fax: 215-657-9312. Email: APConf01@nni.com. Web: www.ourladyofconfidence.com/. Mentally Handicapped. Sisters of St. Joseph 1; Lay Teachers 10; Students 130.

Main School and Office, 314 N. Easton Rd., Willow Grove, 19090-2506. Tel: 215-657-5311; Fax: 215-657-9312. Email: APConf01@nni.com.

High School Site, 6301 N. Second St., 19020-1599. Tel: 215-276-2300, Ext. 262;; Fax: 215-657-9312. Sr. Francis Christi, S.S.J., Prin.

LEVITTOWN. *Queen of the Universe Day Center*, 2477 Trenton Rd., 19056. Tel: 215-945-6090; Fax: 215-945-7320. Email: qudc1@nni.com. Web: www.qudaycenter.org. Mrs. Clara Chirchirillo, Prin. Mentally Retarded and Developmental Delay Students. Lay Teachers 3; Students 31.

NORWOOD. *Archbishop Ryan School for Deaf and Hard of Hearing Children*, 233 Mohawk Ave., 19074. Tel: 610-586-7044; Fax: 610-586-7053. Email: APRyanGab01@nni.com. Web www.ces-msa.org. Sr. Margaret Langer, I.H.M., Prin. Sisters 4; Lay Teachers 10; Students 35.

UPPER DARBY. *St. Lucy Day School for Children with Visual Impairments*, 130 Hampden Rd., 19082. Tel: 610-352-4550; 610-352-4555; Fax: 610-352-4582. Email: APLucy01@nni.com. Web: www.stlucydayschool.org. Sr. M. Margaret Fleming, I.H.M., Prin. Day school for children who are blind or visually impaired. Sisters, Servants of the Immaculate Heart of Mary 6; Lay Teachers 3; Students 25.

WYNNEWOOD. *St. Katherine Day School*, 930 Bowman Ave., 19096. Tel: 610-667-3958; Fax: 610-667-3625. Email: APKath01@nni.com. Margaret Devaney, Prin. Children with Developmental Delay/Mental Retardation. Lay Teachers 12; Students 138.

[K] THE CATHOLIC SOCIAL SERVICES OF THE ARCHDIOCESE OF PHILADELPHIA

PHILADELPHIA. *The Catholic Social Services of the Archdiocese of Philadelphia*, 222 N. 17th St., 19103. Tel: 215-587-3900; Fax: 215-587-2479. Email: Chumsrv@chs-adphila.org. Web: www.archdiocese-phl.org. Rev. Msgr. Timothy C. Senior, M.B.A., M.S.W., Sec., Catholic Human Svcs.; Edward T. Cahill, CFO; James Amato, L.S.W., Deputy Sec.; Teresa Thompson, L.S.W., Dir. Children's Svcs.; Karen K. Becker, L.S.W., Dir. Family Svcs.; Lorraine Knight, M.Ed., Dir. Admin. & Support Svcs.; John M. Wagner, Dir. Housing & Homeless Svcs.; Bro. Dennis Malloy, F.S.C., A.C.S.W, M.A., Dir. Juvenile Justice Svcs. All addresses unless otherwise indicated.

St. Gabriel's System, 117 S. 17th St., 19103. Tel: 215-665-8777; Fax: 215-665-8821. Mark E. Fitzgerald, M.S.W., N.H.A., Dir. Mental Retardation Svcs.

Administrative Office, 1797 S. Sproul Rd., Springfield, 19064. Tel: 610-543-5410; Fax: 610-543-5397. Phyllis Adorno, L.S.W., Admin. Child Care Svcs.

Catholic Campaign for Human Development, 227 N. 18th St., 19103. Tel: 215-587-5656; Fax: 215-587-5626.

Northeast Philadelphia, 7340 Jackson St., 19136. Tel: 215-624-5920; Fax: 215-624-9197. Amy Stoner, L.S.W., Admin.

North Philadelphia, Casa del Carmen, 4400 N. Reese St., 19140. Tel: 215-329-5660; Fax: 215-329-6722. W. Giovanni Morante, M.A., Admin.

Bucks County:

Levittown, 100 Levittown Pkwy., Levittown, 19054. Tel: 215-945-2550; Fax: 215-945-3595. Marguerite Powers, L.S.W., Asst. Dir.

Middle Bucks County:

Sellersville, 427 N. Main St., Sellersville, 18960. Tel: 215-453-7098; Fax: 215-453-6572. Marguerite Powers, L.S.W., Asst. Dir.

Warminster, 607 W. Street Rd., Warminster, 18974. Tel: 215-957-6699; Fax: 215-957-9189. Marguerite Powers, L.S.W., Asst. Dir.

Chester County:

West Grove, 105 Prospect Ave., West Grove, 19390. Tel: 610-869-6500; Fax: 610-869-6258. James McMaster, M.B.A., Admin.

Downingtown, 141 E. Lancaster Ave., Downingtown, 19335. Tel: 610-269-4060; Fax: 610-269-4065. James McMaster, M.B.A., Admin.

Delaware County:

Chester City, 130 E. 7th St., Chester, 19013. Tel: 610-876-9183; Fax: 610-876-9243. James McMaster, M.B.A., Admin.

Springfield, 240 N. Bishop Ave., Springfield, 19064. Tel: 610-626-6550; Fax: 610-626-2069. James McMaster, M.B.A., Admin.

Montgomery County:

Norristown, 353 E. Johnson Hwy., Norristown, 19401. Tel: 610-279-7372; Fax: 610-270-0626. Marguerite Powers, L.S.W., Asst. Dir. & Admin.

Holy Family Center, 227 N. 18th St., 19103. Tel: 215-587-3900; Fax: 215-854-7100. Michael Montie, L.C.S.W., Supvr. (Intake and Information & Referral); All addresses unless otherwise indicated.

South Philadelphia Family Service Center, 1941 Christian St., 19146. Tel: 215-790-9530; Fax: 215-790-9765. Amy Stoner, L.S.W., Admin.

Southwest Family Service Center, 6214 Grays St., P.O. Box 16986, 19142. Tel: 215-724-8550; Fax: 215-724-8521. Amy Stoner, L.S.W., Admin.

Volunteer & Community Relations Services Tel: 215-854-7058; Fax: 215-854-7100. William Tangradi, M.S.W., Mgr. Tel: 215-854-7058.

Immigration and Refugee Services, 19103. Tel: 215-854-7010; Fax: 215-854-7100. Phyllis Forman Esq., Admin.

Counseling Services, 227 N. 18th St., 19103. Tel: 215-854-7030; Fax: 215-854-7100. Michael Montie, L.C.S.W., Supvr.

Adoption Services Tel: 215-854-7050; Fax: 215-854-7100. Mary Lark Merman, L.S.W., Admin.

Housing/Homeless Services Tel: 215-854-7080; Fax: 215-854-7100. Deborah Wagner, Admin.

Senior Adult Services Tel: 215-854-7029. George Sallom, L.S.W., Admin. Total Assisted Annually

76,937; Total Staff 3,000.

[L] INSTITUTIONS FOR DEPENDENT CHILDREN

PHILADELPHIA. *St. Joseph Catholic Home for Children*, 5238 N. Broad St., 19141. Tel: 215-324-2610; Fax: 215-457-8240. Email: srlouise@adphila.org knorris@chs-adphia.org. Karen Norris, M.S., Dir. Operations; Sr. Louise Kane, S.S.J., L.S.W., Exec. Dir. Provides Therapeutic Group Home Care; Maternity Home Care; Mother/Baby Residential Care. Mental Health services available on site for all residents. Sisters of St. Joseph 3; Capacity 87.

St. Vincent's Home, 7201 Milnor St., 19135. Tel: 215-624-5600; Fax: 215-624-8355. Email: jlavoritano@chs-adphila.org. Provides Family Oriented residential care for children 6 mos.-16 years of age.; Residential program with 72 beds that provides comprehensive emergency shelter to over 300 boys and girls annually.; Mother/baby/ for girls 12 to 21 years of age. Capacity - 12 mothers - 12 children. Capacity 72; Total Staff 132.

AMBLER. *St. Mary's Villa for Children and Families*, 701 Bethlehem Pike, P.O. Box 388, 19002-0388. Tel: 215-643-7676; Fax: 215-542-9219. Email: fanning.rita@hfi-pgh.org. Web: www.hfi.org. Sr. M. Rita Fanning, C.S.F.N., M.S., Exec. Dir. Provides services for dependent-neglected children with emotional problems 4-18 and their families. Sisters of the Holy Family of Nazareth 5; Capacity 87; Total Staff 103; Total Assisted Annually 120.

BENSALEM. *St. Francis - St. Joseph Homes for Children*, 3400 Bristol Pike, 19020. Tel: 215-638-9310; Fax: 215-638-2498. Web: sfsj.org. Email: francisjoe2001@yahoo.com. Francis E. Swiacki Jr., L.S.W., Admin. Provides residential treatment at 15 sites for boys, ages 9 to 21; also Supervised Living for boys 17 and older. Total Assisted 240; Capacity 155; Total Staff 200.

[M] RESIDENTIAL SCHOOLS FOR MENTALLY HANDICAPPED CHILDREN AND ADULTS

SPRINGFIELD. *Cardinal Krol Center*, 1799 S. Sproul Rd., 19064. Tel: 610-543-3380; Fax: 610-544-1207. Email: fr.dweber@chs-adphila.org. Web: www.cssmrserv.org. Rev. Dennis M. Weber, S.C., Admin. A residential facility for 131 mentally retarded male adults which provides an environment, both day and residential, that contributes to the individuals own growth and development by fulfilling their potential in the physical, mental, emotional, social, psychological, and spiritual areas of their lives. Priests 4; Residential Capacity 131; Day Program 45; Total Assisted Annually 176; Total Staff 150.

Divine Providence Village, 686 Old Marple Rd., 19064. Tel: 610-328-7730; Fax: 610-544-1710. Sr. Esther Leroux, D.S.M.P., Admin.; Rev. Msgr. Timothy C. Senior, M.B.A., M.S.W., Chap. Care & specialized training for developmentally disabled females. Sisters 5; Capacity 96.

Don Guanella School, 1797 S. Sproul Rd., 19064-1195. Tel: 610-543-1418; Fax: 610-328-2136. Email: fr.dweber@chs-adphila.org. Web: www.cssmrserv.org. Rev. Dennis M. Weber, S.C., Admin. Provides specialized care and residential treatment program for mentally retarded boys ages 6-21. Capacity: Residents 40; Day Students 100.

[N] RESIDENTIAL HOMES FOR PHYSICALLY HANDICAPPED CHILDREN

ROSEMONT. *St. Edmond's Home for Children*, 320 S. Roberts Rd., 19010. Tel: 610-525-8800; Fax: 610-525-2693. Web: cssmrserv.org. Denise Clofine, Admin.; Rev. Romano DiRuscio, S.C., Chap. Licensed I.C.F./M.R. care for severely/profoundly impaired, physically handicapped boys and girls ages 2-21. Capacity 40; Total Staff 100.

[O] PROTECTIVE INSTITUTIONS

PHILADELPHIA. *St. Gabriel's System*, Administrative Offices, 117 S. 17th St., Ste. 1701, 19103. Tel: 215-665-8777; Fax: 215-665-8821. Email: br.dmalloy@chs-adphila.org. Bro. Dennis Malloy, F.S.C., A.C.S.W, M.A., Exec. Dir. Administrative and Intake services for residential treatment; Group Home care and Day Treatment for Court-committed delinquent boys, ages 12-17. (See St. Gabriel's Hall, De LaSalle in Towne, De LaSalle Vocational and De LaSalle Aftercare and Brother Rousseau Academy). Total Staff 417; Total Assisted 2,000.

AUDUBON. *St. Gabriel's Hall*, Box 7280, 19407-7280. Tel: 215-247-2776 (Philadelphia); 610-666-7970 (Audubon); Fax: 610-666-1479. Email: bromalloy@chs_adphila.org. Bros. Dennis Malloy, F.S.C., A.C.S.W, M.A., Exec. Dir.; Brian Henderson, F.S.C., Dir. Offers residential treatment for court-committed delinquent boys, ages 12-18. Capacity 201; Total Staff 261; Total Assisted 200.

[P] DAY TREATMENT CENTERS

PHILADELPHIA. *De La Salle-In-Towne Day Treatment Center*, 25 S. Van Pelt St., 19103. Tel: 215-567-5500; Fax: 215-567-6922. Email: cguas@chs-adphila.org. Bro. Dennis Malloy, F.S.C., A.C.S.W, M.A., Exec. Dir.; Charles E. Gaus, Dir. A community based day treatment program for court-committed delinquent boys, ages 14-17. Capacity 110; Total Staff 35; Total Assisted 260.

BENSALEM. *De La Salle Vocational Day Treatment Center*, Box 344, 19020. Tel: 215-464-0344; Fax: 215-638-3767. Bro. Dennis Malloy, F.S.C., A.C.S.W, M.A., Exec. Dir.; Mr. James Logan, M.S.S., Dir. A community based day treatment program for court-committed delinquent boys, ages 15-18. Capacity 125; Total Staff 40.

[Q] RESIDENCES FOR UNMARRIED MOTHERS

HAVERTOWN. *St. Vincent's Maternity Residence*, 104 E. Township Line Rd., 19083. Tel: 610-446-0105; Fax: 610-446-0105. Sr. Louise Kane, S.S.J., L.S.W., Admin. Total Assisted 100; Total Staff 12; Capacity 11.

Information and Referrals Tel: 215-324-2610; Fax: 215-457-8240.

[R] SENIOR COMMUNITY CENTERS

PHILADELPHIA. *St. Anne's Senior Community Center*, 2607 E. Cumberland St., 19125. Tel: 215-423-2772; Fax: 215-423-2423. Barbara Jo Hartzell, Center Coord. Total Staff 6; Total Assisted 11,288.

St. Bernard's Senior Adult Program, Formerly St. Bernard's Senior Community Center, 7340 Jackson St., 19136. Tel: 215-624-5920; Fax: 215-624-9197. Email: kpagni@chs-adphila.org.

St. Charles Senior Community Center, 1941 Christian St., 19146. Tel: 215-790-9530; Fax: 215-790-9765. Daryl Kezell, Coord.

Norris Square Senior Community Center, 2121 N. Howard St., 19133. Tel: 215-423-7241; Fax: 215-634-7751. Email: mfraziere@adphila.org. Web: cconstable/po/web/aoc. Maria P. Frazier, Coord. Total Assisted 120; Total Staff 9.

Star Harbor Senior Community Center, 4700 Springfield Ave., 19143. Tel: 215-726-7468; Fax: 215-726-7496. Email: bjhartze@chs-adphila.org. Ernestine Patterson, Coord.

[S] OUTREACH CENTERS

PHILADELPHIA. *Casa del Carmen*, 4400 N. Reese St., 19140. Tel: 215-329-5660; Fax: 215-329-6722. W. Giovanni Morante, M.A., Admin. Offers emergency crisis social services to the Spanish speaking community in Philadelphia and surrounding areas.

Drueding Center/Project Rainbow, 413 W. Master St., 19122. Tel: 215-769-1830; 215-769-1931; Fax: 215-787-0999. Email: emarvel@holyredeemer.com. Web: www.holyredeemer.com. Sr. Ellen M. Marvel, C.S.R., Pres. Sponsor: Sisters of the Holy Redeemer, C.S.R., Subsidiary of Holy Redeemer Health System.; Provides transitional housing and support services for homeless women with children; daycare is provided for the children.

Marketing/Public Affairs Department, c/o 1602 Huntingdon Pike, Meadowbrook, 19046. Tel: 215-938-3226; Fax: 215-938-3232.

St. Francis Inn, 2441 Kensington Ave., 19125. Tel: 215-423-5845; Fax: 215-423-2289. Rev. Michael A. Duffy, O.F.M., Contact Person. Hot meals for the poor. Priests 2; Brothers 2.

St. Benedict Thrift Shop, 437 W. Girard Ave., 19122. Tel: 215-235-1848. Karen Pushaw, Contact Person. A clothing and furniture thrift store operated by Franciscans.

St. Benedict's Thrift Store A clothing and furniture store operated by Franciscans. , 437 W. Girard Ave., 19122. Tel: 215-235-1848.

Thea Bowman's Women's Center, 2858 Kensington Ave., 19134. Sr. Xavier Kozubal, C.S.F.N., Contact Person. Women's day activity center.

St. John's Hospice for Men 231352063, 1221 Race St., 19107. Tel: 215-563-7763; Fax: 215-563-0108. Web: www.saintjohnshospice.org. Joseph Pinhak, Prog. Dir. Staffed by Catholic Social Services Archdiocese of Philadelphia. Total Assisted 50,000; Total Staff 33.

Mercy Hospice, 334 S. 13th St., 19107. Tel: 215-545-5153; Fax: 215-545-1872. Marilyn Mock, Dir. Provides temporary and extended shelter care, hot meals, clothing, casework and referral services to homeless and transient women and women with children. Total Staff 33; Total Assisted 2,700.

Visitation Homes, 2638 Kensington Ave., 19125. Tel: 215-425-2080; Fax: 215-425-1412. Patrick Mehaffey, Prog. Dir. Residential service program for families making the transition from homelessness to permanent housing. The program offers 18 furnished one to three bedroom apartments and on site case managemet and life skill services. Referrals come through the City's Office of Emergency Shelter and Services. For a period of up to 2 years, residents are helped to achieve economic self sufficiency and address the other issues which led to their homelessness.

Women of Hope, 1210 Lombard St., 19147. Tel: 215-732-1341; Fax: 215-732-0659. Mary Darden, Prog. Dir. Residential Facility for chronically mentally ill homeless women. Capacity 24.

Women of Hope, 251 N. Lawrence St., 19106. Tel: 215-592-9116; Fax: 215-592-0650. Sr. Maureen Crissy, R.S.M., Prog. Dir. Residential facility for chronically mentally ill homeless women. Capacity 22; Total Staff 22; Total Assisted 22.

CHESTER. *Bernardine Center*, 2625 Ninth St., 19013. Tel: 610-497-3225; Fax: 610-497-3659. Email: bernardinecenter@hotmail.com. Web: www.bernardinecenter.org. Sr. Rose MacDermott, O.S.F., Dir. Svcs. West Side Brunch, Emergency Food Cupboard, Supercupboard Program, Advocacy, Social Justice and Spirituality Education. Sisters 4.

[T] DAY CARE CENTERS

PHILADELPHIA. *Bambino Gesu Child Development Center*, 5210 N. Broad St., 19141. Tel: 215-457-4330; Fax: 215-457-4216. Sr. Louise Kane, S.S.J., L.S.W., Exec. Dir. Total Staff 15.

Casa del Carmen Day Care Center, 4400 N. 5th St., 19140. Tel: 215-457-4325; Fax: 215-457-4339. W. Giovanni Morante, M.A., Admin.

St. Monica Day Care Center, 1441 Porter St., 19145. Tel: 215-334-6001; Fax: 215-467-4599. Email: DOCIHM@aol.com. Web: stmonica.org. Sr. Colleen Dougherty, I.H.M., Admin. Sister, Servants of the Immaculate Heart of Mary Total Staff 12; Total Assisted 120.

St. Vincent's Day Care Center, 7201 Milnor St., 19135. Tel: 215-624-5600; Fax: 215-624-8355. Agnes Healey, Dir. Day Care.

[U] GENERAL HOSPITALS

PHILADELPHIA. *St. Agnes Medical Center*, 1900 S. Broad St., 19145. Tel: 215-339-4100. Web: www.stagnesmedicalcenter-pa.org. Sr. Margaret T. Sullivan, O.S.F., Pres.; Revs. Dennis J. Witalec, Chap.; Joseph McCloskey, Chap. Opened May 15, 1888.; Affiliate of Catholic Health East/Mercy Health System. Bed Capacity 153; Total Staff 765; Annually Assisted 133,825.

Mercy Hospital of Philadelphia, 501 S. 54th St., 19143. Tel: 215-748-9000; Fax: 215-748-9709. Web: www.mercyhealth.org. Sr. Christine McCann, R.S.M., Bd. Chm.; Gavin Kerr, Pres. & CEO, Mercy Health System; Bernadette M. Mangan, Senior Vice Pres. & CEO Mercy Hospital of Philadelphia; Sr. Megan Brown, R.S.M., Vice Pres., Mission Svcs. Opened July 2, 1918. Incorporated May 1, 1969. Sisters of Mercy 10; Bed Capacity 286; Patients Assisted Annually 96,090; Total Staff 1,075.

Nazareth Hospital, 2601 Holme Ave., 19152. Tel: 215-335-6000; Fax: 215-335-6598. Patricia B. DeAngelis, Pres. & CEO; Revs. Edward V. Avery; Leonard A. Furmanski. Affiliate of Catholic Health East & Mercy Health System. Bed Capacity 241; Total Staff 1,100; Patients Assisted Annually 162,000.

DARBY. *Mercy Catholic Medical Center* 19023.

Mercy Fitzgerald Hospital, 1500 Lansdowne Ave., 19023-1291. Tel: 610-237-4000; Fax: 610-237-4202. Sr. Christine McCann, R.S.M., Bd. Chm.; Mary C. Morrison, Senior Vice Pres. & CEO; Revs. Lawrence H. Hansen, Chap.; Selvan Albert, O.Praem., Chap.; Joseph C. Laenen, O.Praem., Chap. Opened July 1, 1933. Incorporated May 1, 1969. Sisters of Mercy 7; Bed Capacity 391; Admissions 15,512; Total Outpatient and ED Visits 176,313.

HAVERTOWN. *Mercy Haverford Hospital* dba Mercy Community Hospital , 2000 Old W. Chester Pike, 19083. Tel: 610-853-7000; Fax: 610-449-0415. George F. McLaughlin, CEO. Sisters of Mercy, Opened Haverford Hospital in 1958; Haverford Community Hospital in 1977; Mercy Community Hospital June 28, 1991.; Attended by Local Parishes. Bed Capacity 107; Patients Assisted Annually 27,208.

HUNTINGDON VALLEY. *Holy Redeemer Health Care Corporation and Foundation*, 521 Moredon Rd., 19006. Tel: 215-938-4650; Fax: 215-914-4020. Web: www.holyredeemer.com. Subsidiary of Holy Redeemer Health System; Sponsor: Sisters of the Holy Redeemer, C.S.R.; Foundation solicits and manages funds for future growth and development. Total Staff 3,487; Total Assisted 212,000.

Marketing & Public Affairs Department, c/o 1602 Huntingdon Pike, Meadowbrook, 19046. Tel: 215-938-3226; Fax: 215-938-3232.

HRH Management Corporation, 667 Welsh Rd., 19006. Tel: 215-938-4650; Fax: 215-938-4671. Web: www.holyredeemer.com. Subsidiary of Holy Redeemer Health System. Sponsor: Sisters of the Holy Redeemer, C.S.R.

Marketing & Public Affairs Department, c/o 1602 Huntingdon Pike, Meadowbrook, 19046. Tel: 215-938-3226; Fax: 215-938-3232.

LANGHORNE. *St. Mary Medical Center*, Langhorne-Newton Rd., 19047. Tel: 215-710-2520; Fax: 215-710-2298. Email: aoshea@che-east.org. Web: www.stmaryhealthcare.org. Gregory T. Wozniak, Pres. & CEO; Revs. Raju Pilla, Chap.; George Wallace, S.M., Chap.; Lawrence H. Hansen, Dir. of Spiritual Care. Opened February 21,1973.; Affiliate of Catholic Health East. Bed Capacity 227; Patients Assisted Annually 118,000; Total Staff 2,030.

Langhorne MRI, Inc., Langhorne-Newton Rd., 19047. Tel: 215-710-5280; Fax: 215-710-5287.

MEADOWBROOK. *Holy Redeemer Hospital and Medical Center*, 1648 Huntingdon Pike, 19046. Tel: 215-947-3000; Fax: 215-938-3945. Email: tjudge@holyredeemer.com. Web: www.holyredeemer.com. Gail Latimer, COO; Revs. Michael C. Bolesta, Chap.; Timothy M. Judge, Dir., Spiritual Svcs. Sponsor: Sisters of the Holy Redeemer, C.S.R., Subsidiary of Holy Redeemer Health System, Inc.; Acute care community hospital, providing broad spectrum of services, including preventive, rehabilitative, emergency and obstetrical care plus pastoral counseling. Bed Capacity 283; Total Assisted 11,800; Total Staff 1,200.

NORRISTOWN. *Mercy Suburban Hospital*, 2701 DeKalb Pike, 19401. Tel: 610-278-2001; Fax: 610-272-4642. Web: www.mercyhealth.org. Bed Capacity 131; Assisted Annually 108,577; Total Staff 364.

[V] SPECIAL HOSPITALS AND SANATORIA

PHILADELPHIA. *Mount Nazareth*, 2755 Holme Ave., 19152. Tel: 215-338-8992; Fax: 215-338-8752. Sr. M. Rita Partyka, Supr.; Rev. Msgr. Charles J. Schaeflein, Chap. (Retired). Sisters of the Holy Family of Nazareth, Home for retired and infirm sisters. Resident Sisters 50; Total Assisted Annually 40; Total Staff 18.

ASTON. *Assisi House*, 600 Red Hill Rd., 19014. Tel: 215-459-8990; Fax: 610-558-5344. Email: JLAMANNA@osfPHILA.org. Sr. Jane La Manna, O.S.F., Admin.; Rev. George Maslar, O.F.M.Conv. (BRK). Home for retired Sisters of St. Francis of Philadelphia. Total Assisted Annually 118; Total Staff 160.

DARBY. *Villa Saint Joseph*, 1436 Lansdowne Ave., 19023-1298. Tel: 610-586-8535; Fax: 610-586-2810. Rev. Msgr. Francis A. Menna, Rector. Home for aged, infirm and convalescent priests of the Archdiocese of Philadelphia. Sisters 1; Total Staff 43; Residents 62.

DOWNINGTOWN. *St. John Vianney Center*, 151 Woodbine Rd., 19335. Tel: 610-269-2600; Fax: 610-873-8028. Web: sjvcenter.org. Revs. Charles R. O'Hara, Chap.; Thomas F. Dugan, Admin. Center for Healing for Priests, Brothers, and Sisters. Bed Capacity 50; Total Assisted Annually 238; Total Staff 54.

IMMACULATA. *Camilla Hall Nursing Home*, P.O. Box 100, 19345-0100. Tel: 610-644-1152; Fax: 610-695-0691. Email: ihmcamilla@worldnet.att.net. Sisters Margaret Gradl, I.H.M., Admin.; M Patrizia O'Connor, Supr.; Revs. Michael L. Walsh, Chap. (Retired); Patrick O.Neill, Chap. Sisters, Servants of the Immaculate Heart of Mary Bed Capacity 240; Skilled Care 92; Residents 176; Total Staff 175.

MERION STATION. *McAuley Convent*, 517 Montgomery Ave., 19066. Tel: 610-667-2775; Fax: 610-667-9650. Sisters Mary Anne Basile, Supr. & Admin.; Mary Bonaventure, R.S.M., Dir. of Nursing. Infirmary for Religious Sisters of Mercy. Total Staff 50; Total Assisted 36.

VENTNOR. *Villa St. Joseph by the Sea*, 114 S. Princeton Ave., 08406. Tel: 609-822-7184. Rev. Msgr. Francis A. Menna, Rector; Mrs. HelenMarie Kolicius, Admin. Summer residence for aged, infirm, and convalescent priests of the Archdiocese of Philadelphia.

WARMINSTER. *Regina Coeli Residence for Priests*, 685 York Rd., 18974. Tel: 215-441-4642. Rev. Msgr. James D. Beisel, Admin. Home for retired priests of the Archdiocese of Philadelphia. Total Staff 5; Total in Residence 12.

[W] AFFILIATED SERVICES

PHILADELPHIA. **Holy Redeemer Home Health & Hospice Services* Holy Redeemer Support Services , 12265 Townsend Rd., Ste. 400, 19154. Tel: 215-671-9200; Fax: 215-671-1950. Web: www.holyredeemer.com. Denise Collins, COO. Subsidiary of Holy Redeemer Health System, Inc. Sponsor: Sisters of the Holy Redeemer.; Medicare certified home health agency serving patients in their own homes; Medicare certified hospice program serving terminally ill patients and their families.

Marketing/Public Affairs Department, c/o 1602 Huntingdon Pike, Meadowbrook, 19046. Tel: 215-938-3226; Fax: 215-938-3232.

PHOENIXVILLE. *St. Mary's Franciscan Shelter*, 209 Emmett St., 19460. Tel: 610-933-3097; Fax: 610-917-9845. Email: stmarysfs@verizon.net. Total Staff 5; Families Assisted 30.

Staff: Sr. Emma Mary Steckel, O.S.F.; Kate Garges; Sr. Christine Kranichfeld, Dir.; Sherri Zahorchak, Case Mgr.; Betty Mastrangelo.

[X] NURSING AND CONVALESCENT HOMES

PHILADELPHIA. *St. Ignatius Nursing Home*, 4401 Haverford Ave., 19104. Tel: 215-349-8800; Fax: 215-222-3078. Email: smagatha@stignatiusnursinghome.org. Sr. Mary Agatha Cebula, C.S.S.F., N.H.A., Admin. Attended from St. Ignatius Church. Felician Sisters 8; Bed Capacity 176; Total Assisted 295; Total Staff 230; Total in Residence 176.

St. John Neumann Nursing Home, 10400 Roosevelt Blvd., 19116. Tel: 215-698-5600; Fax: 215-698-5755. Email: adminsec.sjnh@erols.com. Web: SJN-PHL.org. Michelle Bieszczad, C.N.H.A., Admin.; Rev. Bernard C. Farley, Chap. Sisters of the Holy Family of Nazareth Bed Capacity 226; Total Assisted Annually 415; Total Staff 212.

Sacred Heart Free Home for Incurable Cancer, 1315 W. Hunting Park Ave., 19140. Tel: 215-329-3222; Fax: 215-329-4197. Email: sacredheartm@verizon.net. Sisters Carol Marie, O.P., Supr.; M. Florence, O.P., Admin.

Legal Title: *The Servants of Relief for Incurable Cancer* Dominican Sisters of Hawthorne, Opened April 27, 1930.; Attended by Oblates of St. Francis de Sales. Bed Capacity 37; Total Assisted 57; Total Staff 32.

DARBY. *St. Francis Country House*, 1412 Lansdowne Ave., 19023-1218. Tel: 610-461-6510; Fax: 610-461-3558. Mrs. Cynthia O'Brien, C.N.H.A., Admin.; Rev. Edward J. Kennedy, Chap. Opened June 30, 1913. Total Assisted Annually 448; Total Staff 347.

DOWNINGTOWN. *St. Martha Manor*, 470 Manor Ave., 19335. Tel: 610-873-8490; Fax: 610-873-5927. Web: SMARTHAM-PHL.org. Maureen Reisinger, N.H.A., Admin.; Rev. Edward J. Jablonski, Chap. Capacity 128; Total Assisted Annually 201; Total Staff 179.

FLOURTOWN. *St. Joseph Villa*, 110 W. Wissahickon Ave., 19031-1898. Tel: 215-836-4179; Fax: 215-248-7889. Email: apprichd@stjosephvilla.opg. Web: www.stjosephvilla.org. Sr. Dorothy Apprich, S.S.J., Admin. Bed Capacity 324; Licensed beds 108; Convent beds 216; Total Staff 313.

[Y] BOARDING HOMES FOR THE AGED

PHILADELPHIA. *Holy Family Home*, 5300 Chester Ave., 19143-4993. Tel: 215-729-5153; Fax: 215-727-5332. Sr. Catherine, L.S.P., Supr.; Rev. Douglas M. McKay, Chap. Little Sisters of the Poor Total Staff 100; Residents 102.

Immaculate Mary Home, 2990 Holme Ave., 19136-1829. Tel: 215-335-2100; Fax: 215-331-1016. Email: admin.imn@erols.com. Web: IMH-PHL.org. Stuart K. Skinner, N.H.A., Admin.; Rev. John H. Mulholland, Chap. Opened March 1976. Capacity 296; Total Assisted Annually 471; Total Staff 383.

St. Joseph Housing Corporation Tel: 215-248-7200; Fax: 215-248-7277. Email: msjc@ssjphila.org. Web: www.ssjphila.org.

Mount St. Joseph Convent, 19118-2694. Tel: 215-248-7200; Fax: 215-248-7277. Email: msjc@ssjphila.net. Web: www.ssjphila.org. Staffed by the Sisters of St. Joseph. Total Staff 4; Total in Residence 107.

Sacred Heart Manor, 6445 Germantown Ave., 19119. Tel: 215-438-5268; Fax: 215-951-0798. Email: michaelshm@aol.com. Web: www.sacredheartmanor.com. Sr. M. Patricia Michael, O.Carm., Admin.; Rev. Eduardo G. Montero, Chap. Carmelite Sisters for the Aged and Infirm Nursing Care Residents 171; Personal Care Boarding Home 96; Total Staff 250.

DARBY. *Little Flower Manor*, 1201 Springfield Rd., 19023. Tel: 610-534-6000; Fax: 610-534-6039. Rev. Leo J. McGee, Chap. Staffed by Sisters of the Divine Redeemer, All Skilled Nursing Care. Total Staff 185; Patients Assisted Annually 180.

Villa St. Teresa, 1215 Springfield Rd., 19023. Tel: 610-583-0700; Fax: 610-583-5011. Sr. M. Anne Angelcyk, S.D.R., Admin. Staffed by Sisters of the Divine Redeemer, Residential. Total Assisted Annually 89; Residents 45; Total Staff 30.

DOWNINGTOWN. *Catholic Health Care Services-Villa Saint Martha*, 490 Manor Ave., 19335. Tel: 610-873-5300; Fax: 610-873-2855. Email: admissions.vsm@chs-adphila.org. Web: www.vsm-phl.org. Judith P. Horvath, N.H.A., Admin.; Rev. Edward J. Jablonski, Chap. Independent Living, Assisted Living, Memory Support Assisted Living. Units 120; Staff 70.

ELVERSON. *St. Mary of Providence Center*, 227 Isabella Rd., 19520. Tel: 610-942-4166; Fax: 610-942-4259. Email: stmaryofprov@msn.com. Web: stmaryofprov-pa.org. Sr. Anna Bilotta, D.S.M.P., Supr.; Rev. Peter DiMaria, Chap. Residence for Senior Citizens. Center of Spirituality, Retreats and Days of Recollection. Sisters 3; Capacity 39; Overnight and day retreats 110; Total Staff 15; Total in Residence 52.

FLOURTOWN. *Bethlehem Retirement Village*, 100 W. Wissahickon Ave., 19031. Tel: 215-233-0998; Fax: 215-233-9052. Email: JoanGrelis@aol.com. Sr. Joan Grelis, S.S.J., Mgr. Staffed by the Sisters of St. Joseph Apartments 100; Total Staff 4; Total in Residence 104.

HOLLAND. *St. Joseph Home for the Aged*, 1182 Holland Rd., 18966. Tel: 215-357-5511; Fax: 215-357-1707. Cecile F. Shocket, M.S.N., R.N., N.H.A., Admin.; Rev. John A. Cannon, Chap. (Retired). Sisters of St. Casimir, Personal Care and Licensed Nursing facility. Senior Residents 58; Total Staff 124; Nursing Care Total Assisted 38.

HUNTINGDON VALLEY. *Redeemer Village - Redeemer Village II*, 1551 Huntingdon Pike, 19006. Tel: 215-947-8168. Web: www.holyredeemer.com. *Marketing/Public Affairs Department*, Holy Redeemer Health System, c/o 1602 Huntingdon Pike, Meadowbrook, 19046. Joseph Munizza, Mgr., Redeemer Village. Sisters of the Holy Redeemer, C.S.R., Subsidiary of Holy Redeemer Health System. Low income housing for the elderly or handicapped, subsidized by HUD. Apartments 151.

Redeemer Village II, 1551 Huntingdon Pike, 19006. Tel: 215-947-8168. Sisters of the Holy Redeemer, C.S.R., Subsidiary of Holy Redeemer Health System, Inc. Low income housing for the elderly or handicapped, subsidized by HUD. Apartments 49.

LANSDALE. *St. Mary Manor*, 701 Lansdale Ave., 19446. Tel: 215-368-0900; Fax: 215-362-2891. Web: SMM_PHL.org. John T. Chapman, N.H.A., Admin.; Rev. Joseph F. McCafferty, Chap. Immaculate Heart of Mary Sisters Total Assisted Annually 295; Total Staff 229.

YARDLEY. *D'Youville Manor*, 1750 Quarry Rd., 19067. Tel: 215-579-1750; Fax: 215-579-3054. Email: dyouvillemanor@greynun.org. Web: www.dyouvillemanor.org. Cecile F. Shocket, M.S.N., R.N., N.H.A., Admin. Operated by Grey Nuns of the Sacred Heart. Assisted living retirement residence for the elderly. Capacity 51; Total Staff 30; Total in Residence 45.

[Z] RESIDENCES FOR WOMEN

PHILADELPHIA. *Saint Katharine Drexel Residence*, 7919 Forrest Ave., 19150. Tel: 215-549-5765; Fax: 215-549-2375. Carolyn Harrington, Dir.

St. Mary's Residence, 5th and Locust Sts., 19106. Tel: 215-922-4228; Fax: 215-922-5131. Susan M. Steir, Prog. Dir. Religious Sisters of Mercy Catholic Social Services Residents 33; Total Staff 7.

[AA] MONASTERIES AND RESIDENCES OF PRIESTS AND BROTHERS

PHILADELPHIA. *Augustinian Community (O.S.A.)*, 910 Watkins St., 19148. Tel: 215-463-1326; Fax: 215-463-0888. Rev. Nicholas Martorano, O.S.A., Prior.

Brothers of Charity (F.C.), 6522 Belmar St., 19142. Tel: 215-729-4417; Fax: 215-887-6372. Bro. William Riley, F.C.

The Brothers of the Christian Schools, Roncalli Community, 6519 N. 12th St., 19126. Tel: 215-424-4032. Bros. Thomas McPhillips, F.S.C., Dir.; Martin Fahey, F.S.C., Dist. Sec.

Brothers of the Christian Schools, St. Mary's Community, 7018 Boyer St., 19119-1801. Tel: 215-248-2434; Fax: 215-248-4327. Bro. Edward Davis, F.S.C., Dir. Total in Residence 5.

Congregation of the Mission, St. Vincent's Seminary, 500 E. Chelten Ave., 19144-1203. Tel: 215-848-1985; Fax: 215-844-2085. Email: cmphila88@aol.com. Web: cmeast.org. Central House of the Congregation of the Mission (Vincentian Community), Eastern Province. Novitiate, Central Shrine of the Miraculous Medal in the United States, The Central Association of the Miraculous Medal and St. Catherine's Infirmary, Assisted Living Facility, The Brother Bertrand Ducournau Archives of the Eastern Province of the Congregation of the Mission. Total in Residence 35.

Provincial Administration: Very Rev. Thomas F. McKenna, C.M., Prov.; Revs. Charles P. Strollo, C.M., Asst. Prov.; Stephen M. Grozio, C.M., Prov. Treas.; Jerry J. McGovern, Corp. Treas.
House Administration: Revs. William W. Sheldon, C.M., Supr.; William J. Bamber, C.M., Asst. Supr.; Gerald E. Deitzer, C.M., Treas. In Res. Revs. William J. Bamber, C.M.; Robert J. Brandenberger, C.M.; John J. Buckley, C.M.; John W. Carven, C.M., Prov. Archivist; John J. Cusack, C.M.; Gerald E. Deitzer, C.M.; Lester T. DeMott, C.M.; Daniel E. Donovan, C.M.; Thomas M. Finley, C.M.; William P. Finn, C.M.; Frederick J. Gaulin, C.M.; John J. Hodnett, C.M.; John V. Kennedy, C.M.; Thomas R. Kennedy, C.M.; Daniel J. Kramer, C.M.; Paul M. Murphy, C.M.; William W. Sheldon, C.M.; Joseph R. Wright, C.M.

St. Catherine Infirmary Tel: 215-848-1985, Ext. 142; Fax: 215-848-6078. Revs. Joseph L. Boegel, C.M.; Gearoge E. Krock, C.M.; Terence J. Mooney, C.M.; John S. Pearce, C.M.; Walter F. Dirig, C.M.; Donald L. Doyle, C.M.; John A. Doyle, C.M.; William P. Finn, C.M.; Aloysius P. Grass, C.M.; John F. King, C.M.; Edward C. Mannion, C.M.; William E. McKeon, C.M.; Charles J. O'Connor, C.M.; Joseph M. O'Donnell, C.M.; Joseph J. Symes, C.M.; Robert R. Virgnola (C.M.); Louis B. Storms, C.M.; Vincent E. Trunk, C.M.
Vincentian Fathers of the Eastern Province of the Congregation of the Mission serving on special assignments other than the Motherhouse:
Rome, Italy: Very Rev. Robert P. Maloney, C.M.; Rev. Elmer Bauer III, C.M.
California: Rev. Peter J. Albano, C.M.
District of Columbia: Revs. Harry Arnone, C.M.; David M. O'Connell, C.M.
Florida: Revs. Edward F. McQuillan, C.M.; Jose Sanchez, C.M.
Maine: Rev. John W. Gouldrick, C.M.
Michigan: Revs. Vincent J. O'Malley, C.M.; Robert Prior, C.M.; Michael M. Shea, C.M.
New Hampshire: Rev. Francis X. Maguire, C.M.
New York: Rev. William J. Gormley, C.M.
South Carolina: Rev. John J. Lawlor, C.M.
Texas: Rev. Carl L. Pieber, C.M.

Father Louis Brisson Residence, 3301 Solly Ave., 19136-2340. Tel: 215-624-1604; Fax: 215-332-3478. Revs. Robert D. Ashenbrenner, O.S.F.S.; Leon V. Bonikowski, O.S.F.S.; Joseph G. Campellone, O.S.F.S.; William W. Davis, O.S.F.S.; John J. Dennis, O.S.F.S.; John V. DiFilippo, O.S.F.S.; Gerald M. Dunne, O.S.F.S. (SUP); Thomas P. Gallagher, O.S.F.S.; Joseph J. Griffin, O.S.F.S.; Eugene L. Kelly, O.S.F.S.; Dennis W. Killion, O.S.F.S.; Gerard J. Mahoney, O.S.F.S.; Eugene J. McBride, O.S.F.S.; David M. Merchant, O.S.F.S.; Edward L. Rauch, O.S.F.S.; Peter J. Harvey, O.S.F.S.; James P. Kelly, O.S.F.S.; R. Douglas Smith, O.S.F.S.; John J. Sullivan, O.S.F.S.; Bros. Thomas P. Brophy, O.S.F.S.; James F. Williams, O.S.F.S. Total Staff 11; Total in Residence 10.

Gesu School Jesuit Community and Outreach Center (S.J.), 1700 W. Thompson St., 19121. Tel: 215-763-3660; Fax: 215-763-9844. Email: neil@gesuschool.org. Rev. Neil L. Ver-Schneider, S.J., Contact Person. Total Assisted 500; Total Staff 2.

Holy Spirit Missonary Cenacle, 1301 Oak Ln., 19126. Tel: 215-924-2257; Fax: 215-224-6808. Bro. Paul Michalenko, S.T. Missionary Servants of the Most Holy Trinity

Inner City House, 1904 N. 22nd St., 19121. Tel: 215-765-1904. Email: frdave1904@hotmail.com. Rev. David I. Hagan, O.S.F.S., Dir. Total in Residence 1; Total Assisted 750.

Jesuit Community at St. Joseph's University, 5600 City Ave., 19131. Tel: 610-660-1400; Fax: 610-664-6640. Email: jesuits@sju.edu. Web: www.sju.edu/jesuits.

Loyola Center and Manresa Hall Revs. George W. Bur, S.J., Rector; Thomas F. Gleeson, S.J., Asst. Rector; H. Cornell Bradley, S.J., Asst. to the Rector; Harry F. Geib, S.J., Dir. of Manresa Hall; Joseph A. Arroyo, S.J. (Spain); Robert S. Curry, S.J., Supr. of Manresa Hall; Francis F. Burch, S.J.; Bro. Thomas S. Kretz, S.J., Min.; Revs. Peter A. Clark, S.J.; Donald G. Clifford, S.J.; Richard J. Colgan, S.J.; Jerome B. Coll, S.J.; Timothy R. Lannon, S.J., Pres.; Gerald F. Finnegan, S.J. (BO); Stephen A. Garber, S.J.; Vincent J. Genovesi, S.J.; Thomas F. Gleeson, S.J.; James J. Gormley, S.J.; Howard J. Heim, S.J.; Frederick A. Homann, S.J.; Albert H. Jenemann, S.J.; Joseph F. Curran, S.J.; Joseph L. Lombardi, S.J.; John J. Mawhinney, S.J.; Alfred D. Cutajar, S.J.; John W. McDaniel, S.J.; John P. McGinty, S.J.; Dennis E. McNally, S.J.; Donald J. Freeze, S.J.; James W. Moore, S.J.; Richard G. Malloy, S.J.; Robert J. Paquet, S.J.; Anthony P. Roberts, S.J.; William A. Ryan, S.J.; Francis E. Skechus, S.J.; Herbert F. Smith, S.J.; Robert A. Thoman; Bro. Walter F. Quistgaard, S.J.; Rev. Martin R. Tripole, S.J.; Bro. Robert J. Fitzgerald, S.J. Priests 39; Brothers 2.

St. Alphonsus House, 5800 Overbrook Ave., 19131. Tel: 215-477-9220; Fax: 215-477-1519. Revs. Anthony J. Berret, S.J.; Thomas J. Brennan, S.J.; Joseph J. Feeney, S.J.; Patrick H. Samway, S.J.; Mark P. Scalese, S.J.; Bro. John J. McLane, S.J. Priests 5; Brothers 1.
Residing Elsewhere:
Thomas Jefferson Univ., Orlowitz Hall, 1000 Walnut St., Apt. 1513, 19107. Tel: 215-928-1614. Rev. Edward C. Bradley, S.J., Counselor for Students and Faculty.
The St. John Neuman Nursing Home, 10400 Roosevelt Blvd., 19116. Rev. Ralph C. Campbell, S.J., 183 Planters Run Ct., Dover, DE 19901. Tel: 302-698-3381.
Business: 183 Planters Run Ct., Dover, DE 19901. Tel: 302-698-3381. Rev. Patrick R. Shaules, S.J., Dir. Operation HELP, Inc.
McAuley Convent, 517 Montgomery Ave., Merion Station, 19066-1296. Tel: 610-660-7841; Fax: 610-667-9680. Rev. Thomas Wheeler, S.J., Infirmary Chap.
Stella Maris Parish Rev. Patrick T. Brannan, S.J.Business: 2901 S. 10th St., 19148.

Jesuit Community, Arrupe House, 1226 N. 18th St., 19121. Tel: 215-765-1875; Fax: 215-765-1710. Email: tclifford@sjprep.org. Revs. Bruce M. Bidinger, S.J., Pres.; Thomas F. Clifford, S.J., Supr.; Neil L. Ver-Schneider, S.J.; Ramon Prudencio Toledo, S.J. Residence of Jesuit Fathers and Brother.

Monastery of Our Lady of Mercy, 6398 Drexel Rd., 19151-2596. Tel: 215-879-0594; Fax: 215-877-7625. Email: vocations@orderofmercy.org. Web: www.orderofmercy.org. Revs. James W. Mayer, O.de.M., Local Supvr.; Matthew H. Phelan, O.de.M, Master of Students; Gene A. Costa, O.de.M., Spiritual Dir. Order of the B.V.M. of Mercy (Mercedarian Friars), Post Novitiate House of Studies for the Order. Total in Residence 7.

Order of Friars Minor of the Province of the Most Holy Name aka Holy Name Province, The Franciscans, 1802 E. Hagert St., 19125. Tel: 215-423-2859. Revs. William DeBiase, O.F.M.; Michael A. Duffy, O.F.M.; Charles Finnegan, O.F.M.; Francis Pompei, O.F.M.; Bros. Xavier de la Huerta, O.F.M.; Thomas Ennis, O.F.M.; John Gill, O.F.M.

The Philadelphia Congregation of The Oratory of St. Philip Neri, 2321 Green St., 19130-3196. Tel: 215-765-4568; Fax: 215-765-4049. Revs. Georges G. Thiers, C.O., Provost; Paul C. Convery, C.O., Vicar; Alberto Royo-Mejia, C.O., J.C.D.; Bro. Brian Gaffney, C.O.

St. Pius X Friary, 11051 Academy Rd., 19154. Tel: 215-632-1300; Fax: 215-632-2550. Revs. Rene Barczak, O.F.M.; Roderick Drag, O.F.M.; Carl Graczyk, O.F.M.; Francis X. Kelly, O.F.M.; William Stout, O.F.M.; Charles Newman, O.F.M.; Warren Rector, O.F.M.; Gabriel A. Rosetti, O.F.M.; Joel F. Szydlowski, O.F.M.; Rudolph Wieszczek, O.F.M.; Francis Berna, O.F.M. Order of Friars Minor, Assumption B.V.M. Province, Faculty Residence for Archbishop Ryan High School.

The Brothers of the Christian Schools Jeremy House, 6633 Ardleigh St., 19119-3824. Tel: 215-843-1884; Fax: 215-843-1617. Email: jeremyhouse@juno.com. Bro. Richard Buccina, F.S.C., F.S.C., Dir. Professed Brothers 4; Scholastics 2.

AUDUBON. *Christian Brothers (F.S.C.)*, St. Gabriel Hall Community, Pawlings Rd., P.O. Box 7280, 19407-7280. Tel: 215-247-2776; 610-666-7970.

BENSALEM. *Congregation of the Holy Ghost*, Spiritan Hall, 2401 Bristol Pike, 19020. Tel: 215-638-0980; Fax: 215-639-5439. Email: jtduaime@verizon.net. Revs. Jeffrey T. Duaime, C.S.Sp., Supr.; Christopher H. McDermott, C.S.Sp., Bursar; Norman E. Bevan, C.S.Sp. Faculty Residence for Priests Teaching at Holy Ghost Preparatory School.

BRYN MAWR. *Augustinians Friars (O.S.A.)*, Our Mother of Good Counsel Community, 31 Pennswood Rd., 19010-3475. Tel: 610-525-0327; Fax: 610-525-0157. Email: austinfriarsomgc@yahoo.com. Rev. James E. Martinez, O.S.A., Prior & Contact Person.

DEVON. *Piarist Fathers (Order of the Pious Schools)*, 363 Valley Forge Rd., 19333. Tel: 610-688-6807; Fax: 610-688-2409. Email: sjcalasanctius@juno.com. Web: azeg@juno.com. Total Staff 6; Total in Residence 5.
Priests who teach at Devon Preparatory School: Revs. James J. Shea, Sch.P., Headmaster; Richard S. Wyzykiewicz, Sch.P., Rector & Prov. Asst.; Louis G. Mesko, Sch.P.; Ferdinand Negrillos, Sch.P.; Geza Pazmany, Sch.P.; Stephen Mustos, Sch.P.
Piarist Fathers Latin Mission Tel: 305-279-2333; Fax: 305-279-0925. Revs. David Powers, Sch.P.; Mario B. Vizcaino, Sch.P.

DOYLESTOWN. *Pauline Fathers Monastery, Shrine of Our Lady of Czestochowa*, 654 Ferry Rd., P.O. Box 2049, 18901. Tel: 215-345-0607; Fax: 215-348-2148. Email: cshrine@aol.com. Web: www.polishshrine.com.
Office Tel: 215-345-0600; 215-345-0601; Fax: 215-348-2148. Revs. Krzyysztof Wieliczko, O.S.P.P.E., Prov. & Prior; Anzelm Chalupka, O.S.P.P.E., Sub Prior; Jan Michalak, O.S.P.P.E.; Jan Kolmaga, O.S.P.P.E., Prior; Stephen Z. Wozniczka, O.S.P.P.E., Shrine Dir.; Bartlomiej Marciniak, O.S.P.P.E.; Tadeusz Olzacki, O.S.P.P.E.; Simon Shaner, O.S-.P.P.E.; Mikolaj Socha, O.S.P.P.E.; Marian Zalecki, O.S.P.P.E.; Faustyn Muir, O.S.P.P.E.; Sebastian Hanes, O.S.P.P.E.; Bros. Casimir Pasnik; Didak Turi; Luke Mitura; Peter Lisiecki; Tomasz Fabiszewski, O.S.P.P.E.; Krzysztof Oleksik, O.S-.P.P.E.

ELKINS PARK. *Society of the Brother Servants of the Holy Spirit (B.H.S.)*, 7605-A Washington Ln., 19027-1036. Tel: 215-886-9787. Bro. Darryl-Joseph Branch, B.H.S., Contact Person. Total in Residence 3.

FAIRLESS HILLS. *St. Anthony Friary*, 607 Wistar Rd., 19030. Tel: 215-943-4810; Fax: 215-943-7410. Revs. Fidelis F. Weber, T.O.R., Guidance Dir. & Local Min.; Neil Saller, T.O.R.; Donald F. Vuketich, T.O.R.; Bro. Lawrence Hilferty, T.O.R. Franciscan Friars T.O.R., Faculty residence for priests and brothers who teach at Conwell-Egan Catholic High School. Total in Residence 4.

LANGHORNE. *Society of Mary, Marist Fathers*, St. Mary's Hospital, 19047. Tel: 215-750-2558. Rev. George Wallace, S.M., Contact.

LAVEROCK. *Brothers of Charity (F.C.)*, Triest Hall, 7720 Doe Ln., 19038. Tel: 215-887-6361; Fax: 215-877-6372. Email: mlonswayfc@aol.com. Web: www.fracarita.com. Total Staff 4; Total in Residence 5.

MALVERN. *Augustinian Friars (O.S.A.)*, Malvern Prep School Community, St. Augustine Friary, 418 S. Warren Ave., 19355-2707. Tel: 610-647-8281; Fax: 610-647-8281. Web: www.malvernprep.org. Revs. David J. Duffy, O.S.A., Pres.; Stephen M. Curry, O.S.A., Faculty, Campus Min.; James R. Flynn, O.S.A., Dean of Middle School; Patrick B. McStravog, O.S.A., Prior, Chair of Theology; James D. Paradis, O.S.A., Prov. Admin. Total in Residence 5; Students 597.

PAOLI. *Daylesford Abbey*, 220 S. Valley Rd., 19301-1900. Tel: 610-647-2530; Fax: 610-651-0219. Email: norbertines@daylesford.org. Web: www.daylesford.org. Rt. Rev. Ronald J. Rossi, O.Praem., Abbot; Very Rev. John J. Novielli, O.Praem., Prior; Revs. Steven J. Albero, O.Praem., Vocation Dir.; Joseph A. Serano, O.Praem., Treas.; Andrew D. Ciferni, O.Praem.; Joseph P. McLaughlin, O.Praem.; Richard J. Antonucci, O.Praem.; Theodore J. Antry, O.Praem.; Maurice C. Avicolli, O.Praem.; John M. Cagney, O.Praem.; Very Rev. Michael T. Collins, O.Praem. (WIL); Revs. Francis X. Cortese, O.Praem.; Willliam R. Craig, O.Praem.; Paul J. DeAntoniis, O.Praem.; William J. Fischer, O.Praem.; Edward J. Kimpel, O.Praem.; Blaise R. Krautsack, O.Praem.; Joseph C. Laenen, O.Praem.; David T. Lawlor, O.Praem.; Michael J. Lee, O.Praem.; Thomas O. Meulemans, O.Praem.; Rt. Rev. John E. Neitzel, O.Praem., Abbot Emeritus; Revs. James C. Rodia, O.Praem.; Domenic A. Rossi, O.Praem.; Thomas J. Rossi, O.Praem.; Nicholas R. Terico, O.Praem.; Charles T. Urban, O.Praem.; John C. Zagarella, O.Praem.; Bros. Blase G. Corso, O.Praem.; John B. Ginder, O.Praem.; William J. Kelly, O.Praem.; Joseph P. Mulholland, O.Praem.
Legal Title: *Norbertine Fathers, Inc.* Priests 28; Brothers 4.

SPRINGFIELD. *Servants of Charity (S.C.)* Don Guanella Village , Cardinal Krol Center, 1799 S. Sproul Rd., 19064. Tel: 610-543-3380; Fax: 610-544-1207. Email: frdweber@chs-adphila.org. Rev. Dennis M. Weber, S.C., Contact Person. Total in Residence 4.

VILLANOVA. *Fray de Leon Community*, Burns Hall - West Campus, Villanova University, 19085. Tel: 610-519-5020; Fax: 610-519-7479. Revs. Peter M. Donohue, O.S.A.; John T. Denny, O.S.A.; Robert Hagan, O.S.A.; Joseph S. Mostardi, O.S.A., Prior. Augustinians Total in Residence 5.
P.O. Box 340, 19085. Tel: 610-527-3330, Ext. 279; Fax: 610-527-0618. Rev. Thomas Martin, O.S.A.
St. John Stone Friary, 37 Aldwyn Ln., 19085. Tel: 610-527-7925; Fax: 610-527-2307. Revs. John E. Deegan, O.S.A.; William J. Donnelly, O.S.A.; Kail C. Ellis, O.S.A.; Michael J. Scanlan, O.S.A.; T. Shawn Tracy, O.S.A., Prior.
Provincial Offices of the Order of St. Augustine, Province of St. Thomas of Villanova, P.O. Box 340, 19085-0340. Tel: 610-527-3330; Fax: 610-520-0618. Email: secretary@augustinian.org. Web: www.augustinian.org. Revs. Donald F. Reilly,

O.S.A., Prior Prov. Tel: 610-527-3330, Ext. 225; Anthony P. Burrascano, O.S.A., Treas. & Mission Procurator. Tel: 610-527-3330, Ext. 226; John J. Sheridan, O.S.A., Prov. Archivist. Tel: 610-527-3330, Ext. 247; James R. Flynn, O.S.A., Contact Person, Prov. Sec. Tel: 610-527-3330, Ext. 223; Richard D. Appicci, O.S.A., Mission Office. Tel: 610-527-3330, Ext. 238; James D. McBurney, O.S.A., Dir. Vocations. Tel: 610-527-3330, Ext. 284; James D. Paradis, O.S.A., Dir. Ongoing Formation & Personnel. Tel: 610-527-3330, Ext. 233; Joseph S. Mostardi, O.S.A., Dir. Office of the Augustinian Volunteers. Tel: 610-527-3330, Ext. 279.

St. Augustine Friary, 214 Ashwood Rd., P.O. Box 340, 19085. Tel: 610-527-0325; Fax: 610-527-0640. Joseph F. Girone, O.S.A. Total in Residence 4.

St. Thomas Monastery 19085. Tel: 610-519-7500; Fax: 610-519-5040. Revs. Richard D. Appicci, O.S.A.; John P. Betoni, O.S.A.; John E. Bresnahan, O.S.A.; Donald X. Burt, O.S.A.; George J. Callaghan, O.S.A.; Angus N. Carney, O.S.A.; John V. Casey; Francis E. Chambers; James P. Conway; James T. Deery, O.S.A.; Russell J. DeSimone, O.S.A.; Edmund J. Dobbin, O.S.A., Pres., Villanova Univ.; John M. Driscoll, O.S.A.; Gerard M. Duff, O.S.A.; Francis A. Eigo, O.S.A.; John J. Farrell, O.S.A.; John J. Fitzgerald, O.S.A.; Dennis J. Gallagher, O.S.A.; John J. Gallagher, O.S.A.; Raymond E. Geisser; Karl A. Gersbach, O.S.A.; Dante L. Girolami, O.S.A.; Edwin T. Grimes, O.S.A.; John J. Hagen, O.S.A.; Joseph A. Jordan, O.S.A., Treas.; Charles P. Laferty, O.S.A.; Martin S. Laird, O.S.A.; Joseph F. Laverty, O.S.A.; Bernard A. Lazor, O.S.A.; John F. Lipp, O.S.A.; John F. McAtee, Prior; Neil J. McGettigan, O.S.A.; Robert F. Andrews, O.S.A.; John J. McKenzie, O.S.A.; Robert M. Burke, O.S.A.; Thomas J. Mahony, O.S.A.; Lee J. Makowski, O.S.A.; Thomas M. Murnane, O.S.A.; Alfred E. Murphy, O.S.A.; Robert J. Murray, O.S.A.; John J. Murray (Retired); James L. Nolan, O.S.A.; Bernard J. O'Dowd, O.S.A.; Francis A. Farsaci, O.S.A.; John M. Quinn, O.S.A.; Patrick J. Rice, O.S.A.; George F. Riley, O.S.A.; Joseph C. Schnaubelt, O.S.A.; Joseph L. Shannon, O.S.A.; Thomas J. Shea, O.S.A.; John J. Sheridan, O.S.A.; Ralph V. Shuhler, O.S.A.; Ralph C. Shurer, O.S.A.; Arthur F. Smith, O.S.A.; John P. Stack, O.S.A.; Robert E. Steinman, O.S.A.; Michael P. Sullivan, O.S.A.; Dennis G. Wilde, O.S.A. Total Staff 17; Total in Residence 58.

St. Thomas of Villanova Friary, 109 Willowburn Rd., 19085-1313. Tel: 610-527-0856; Fax: 610-527-8812. Revs. Donald F. Reilly, O.S.A.; Richard G. Cannuli, O.S.A.; Joseph D. Calderone, O.S.A.

WYNDMOOR. *Christian Brothers (F.S.C.)*, LaSalle High School Community, 8605 Cheltenham Ave., 19038. Tel: 215-233-3030; Fax: 215-233-0297. Email: Brotherbrendan@juno.com. Web: www.lschs.org. Bro. Brendan Garwood, F.S.C., Contact Person. Total in Residence 16.

Oblates of St. Francis de Sales (O.S.F.S.) Villa de Sales Oblate Residence, 8501 Flourtown Ave., 19038. Tel: 215-836-1472; Fax: 215-836-7213. Very Rev. Joseph F. Chorpenning, O.S.F.S., S.T.L., Ph.D., Religious Supr. & Contact Person. Total in Residence 8.

Villa de Sales Oblate Residence, 8501 Flourtown Ave., 19038. Tel: 215-836-1472; Fax: 215-836-7213. Very Rev. Joseph F. Chorpenning, O.S.F.S., S.T.L., Ph.D.; Rev. Raymond J. Christ, O.S.F.S.; Bro. Robert J. Drelich, O.S.F.S.; Revs. William A. Guerin, O.S.F.S.; Richard T. Reece, O.S.F.S.; Bro. Harry G. Schneider, O.S.F.S.; Revs. Albert J. Smith, O.S.F.S.; Richard Wojnicki. Total in Residence 8.

[BB] CONVENTS AND RESIDENCES OF SISTERS

PHILADELPHIA. *Assumption Convent*, 1001 S. 47th St., 19143. Tel: 215-386-5016; Fax: 215-386-1780. Email: rabowman227@juno.com. Sr. Clare Teresa, R.A., Prov. Supr.

Assumption Hall, Sisters of St. Joseph, 8900 Norwood Ave., 19118-2711. Tel: 215-247-3665; 215-248-2564. Sr. Marjorie Lawless, S.S.J., Contact. Residence for Norwood-Fontbonne Academy Faculty. Total Staff 15.

Blessed Trinity Mother Missionary Cenacle, 3501 Solly Ave., 19136. Tel: 215-335-7550; Fax: 215-335-7559. Email: msbtphl@aol.com. Sisters Barbara DeMoranville, M.S.B.T., Gen. Custodian; Mary E. Butler, M.S.B.T., Gen. Sec. Generalate, Novitiate and Candidacy of the Missionary Servants of the Most Blessed Trinity. Mother Boniface Center. Total Staff 25; Total in Residence 95.

Carmelite Monastery, 66th Ave. and Old York Rd., 19126. Tel: 215-424-6143; Fax: 215-424-6143 (*5). Sr. Barbara of the Holy Ghost, Prioress.

Carmelite Sisters for the Aged and Infirm (O.Carm.), Sacred Heart Manor, 6445 Germantown Ave., 19119-2345. Tel: 215-438-5268; Fax: 215-951-0798. Web: www.sacredheartmanor.com.

Congregation of the Sisters of St. Felix, St. Ignatius Convent, 4401 Haverford Ave., 19104. Tel: 215-222-2296; Fax: 215-222-3078. Email: smagatha@stignatiusnursinghome.org. Sr. Mary Agatha Cebula, C.S.S.F., N.H.A., Local Min.

Daughters of Charity, Formerly Convent of the Daughters of Charity, 449 E. Locust Ave., 19144-1323. Tel: 215-438-3536; Fax: 215-438-5232. Email: philadtrs@aol.com. Web: dc-northeast.org. Sr. Patricia Bouza, D.C., Supr. Total in Residence 7.

Daughters of St. Paul, 9171 A Roosevelt Blvd., 19114. Tel: 215-676-9494; Fax: 215-676-9928. Email: philadelphia@pauline.org. Web: www.pauline.com. Sr. Catherine Bennett, F.S.P., Supr.

Daughters of St. Paul Convent, 9610 Evans St., 19115. Tel: 215-969-5068. Email: philadelphia@pauline.org. Web: www.pauline.org. Sr. Catherine Bennett, F.S.P., Supr. Sisters 5.

Dominican Sisters of Our Lady of the Rosary of Fatima, Convent of Mother M. Dominga, 606 W. Erie Ave., 19140-4431. Tel: 215-226-5507; Fax: 215-226-3507. Email: fatimapa@juno.com. Web: www.macredominga.org/. Sr. M. Alba Bonilla, O.P., Local Supr. Dominican Sisters of Our Lady of the Rosary of Fatima Total in Residence 4.

Emmaus Convent, 5358 Cedar Ave., 19143. Tel: 215-471-7260. Email: rsmemmaus@aol.com Sisters of Mercy (R.S.M.) Total in Residence 3.

St. Francis Convent, 1727 S. 11th St., 19148. Tel: 215-463-7343. Email: gpfrancis@alt.net. Residence of Sisters of St. Francis of Philadelphia employed at St. Maria Goretti and Hallahan High Schools, St. Agnes Hospital, Sacred Heart School, (Child/Family Treatment), and Archdiocesan Office, Grant Writing in Aston and Southern Homes.

Franciscan Sisters of Allegany (O.S.F.), 2622 Potter St., 19125. Tel: 215-739-6441; Fax: 215-739-5607.

Grey Nuns of the Sacred Heart Tel: 215-269-9783; Fax: 215-269-9789. Web: www.greynun.org.

St. Joseph the Worker Convent, 9168 New Falls Rd., Fallsington, 19054-1805. Tel: 215-269-9783; Fax: 215-269-9789. Total in Residence 7.

Handmaids of the Sacred Heart of Jesus, 1242 S. Broad St., 19146-3119. Tel: 215-468-6368; Fax: 215-271-1488. Email: gjpetrone@msn.com. Web: acjusa.org. Sr. Gloria Petrone, A.C.J., Supr. Total in Residence 6.

Hannah House, Sisters of St. Joseph, 2458 N. 16th St., 19132. Tel: 215-221-0211; Fax: 215-228-4410. Email: virginiajenkins@comcast.net. Sr. Virginia Jenkins, S.S.J., Contact Person. Sisters 2.

Immaculate Heart Convent, 7310 Torresdale Ave., 19136. Tel: 215-332-8299; Fax: 215-332-6077. Email: rmlenihan@yahoo.com. Sr. Rita Lenihan, I.H.M., Contact Person. Faculty Residence for Sisters, Servants of the Immaculate Heart of Mary, teaching at St. Hubert High School. Total in Residence 13.

Immaculate Heart Convent, 4904 Chestnut St., 19139. Tel: 215-474-8971. Sr. Regina Havens, I.H.M., Supr. Faculty Residence for Sisters, Servants of the Immaculate Heart of Mary, who teach at West Philadelphia Catholic High School and Archbishop Prendergast High School. Total Staff 5; Total in Residence 5.

St. Isaac House, Society of the Daughters of the Heart of Mary Tel: 610-664-9546; Fax: 610-617-0504. 226 N. Essex Ave., #106, Narberth, 19072. Tel: 610-664-9546; Fax: 610-617-0504. Sr. Kathleen F. Devine, D.H.M., Supr.

St. Joseph Convent, 7300 Torresdale Ave., 19136. Tel: 215-338-4884. Email: ssjtorr@netcarrier.com. Faculty Residence for Sisters of St. Joseph, who teach at St. Hubert and Father Judge High School, St. Vincent's Orphanage and Nazareth Academy.

St. Joseph the Worker Convent, 2846 W. Allegheny Ave., 19132. Tel: 215-228-4030. Sr. Mary Urban, R.S.M., Coord. Sisters of Mercy (R.S.M.)

Little Servants of the Holy Family of Seoul, 70th & Old York Rd., 19126. Tel: 215-548-5535. Sr. Andrew Kim, L.S.H.F., Local Supr.

Little Sisters of the Assumption, 1211 S. 15th St., 19146-3116. Tel: 215-218-9157; Fax: 215-218-9159. Email: srmarielsa@aol.com. Web: www.littlesisters.org. Sr. Marie Gervasi, L.S.A., Contact. Total in Residence 3.

Little Sisters of the Poor, Holy Family Home, 5300 Chester Ave., 19143. Tel: 215-729-5153; Fax: 215-729-5158.

Little Workers of the Sacred Hearts, Sacred Hearts Convent, 160 Carpenter Ln., 19119-2563. Tel: 215-843-2266.

Mary Immaculate Convent, 1731 S. 11th St., 19148. Tel: 215-468-9133; Fax: 215-336-7463. Email: MARYIM1731@aol.com. Sr. Helen Rapine, I.H.M., Supr. Faculty Residence for Sisters, Servants of the Immaculate Heart of Mary, who teach at St. Maria Goretti High School and John W. Hallahan High School. Total in Residence 16; Total Staff 16.

Medical Mission Sisters (M.M.S.), 136 E. Price St., 19144. Tel: 215-844-3672. Email: veramms@hotmail.com. Sisters Vera Sheenan, M.M.S., Contact Person; Teresa Arae; Yumiko Nobue. Total in Residence 3.

Medical Mission Sisters, North American Sector, 8400 Pine Rd., 19111. Tel: 215-742-6100; Fax: 215-342-3948. Email: mmsorg@medicalmissionsisters.org. Web: www.medicalmissionsisters.org. Sisters Joan Foley, M.M.S., Sector Coord.; Denise Elliott, M.M.S., Dist. Coord. Sisters in Sector 134; Total in Residence 51.

St. Michael Hall, 9001 Germantown Ave., 19118. Tel: 215-247-3698. Email: SSJsmhall@aol.com. Faculty Residence for Sisters of St. Joseph who staff Chestnut Hill College. Total in Residence 9.

Missionary Sisters of the Sacred Heart (Cabrini Sisters), 6701 Callowhill St., 19151. Tel: 215-472-7911; Fax: 215-472-4289. Sr. Mary Ann Hawes, M.S.C., Supr.

Monastery of the Visitation Nuns, 5820 City Ave., 19131-1295. Tel: 215-473-5888; Fax: 215-473-7512. Sr. Frances de Sales Paganelli, V.H.M., Supr.; Rev. Howard J. Heim, S.J., Chap. Total Staff 9; Total in Residence 8.

Mother of Peace House, 2622 Potter St., 19125. Tel: 215-739-6441; Fax: 215-739-5607. Franciscan Sisters of Allegany

Mt. St. Joseph Convent, 9701 Germantown Ave., 19118-2694. Tel: 215-248-7200; Fax: 215-248-7277. Email: msjc@ssjphila.org. Web: ssjphila.org. Sr. Patricia Kelly, S.S.J., Supr. Gen. Motherhouse of the Sisters of St. Joseph of Chestnut Hill, Philadelphia.

Nazareth Convent, Religious Sisters of Mercy, 6369 Woodbine Ave., 19151. Tel: 215-477-3022. Sr. Kathleen Lyons, R.S.M., Contact Person.

Peace Hermitage, 8400 Pine Rd., 19111. Tel: 215-742-6100; 215-342-2039; Fax: 215-342-3948. Email: ednavmms@juno.com. Sr. Edna C. Villafuerte, M.M.S., Contact Person. Society of Catholic Medical Missionaries (Medical Mission Sisters) Total in Residence 5.

Provincial House of the Sisters of the Holy Family of Nazareth Immaculate Conception Province , 4001 Grant Ave., 19114. Tel: 215-268-1050; Fax: 215-268-1075. Email: sisters-csfn@att.net. Web: www.phila-csfn.org. Sr. M. Celine Warnilo, Prov. Supr.; Rev. Ronald J. Ferrier, Chap. Total in Residence 148.

School Sisters of Notre Dame, St. Vincent Community, 7201 Milnor St., 19135. Tel: 215-624-5635. Email: SSNDvincent@aol.com. Total in Residence 3.

School Sisters of Notre Dame, 2141 N. Howard St., 19122. Tel: 215-634-2227; Fax: 215-634-4990. Email: nsnp.org.

School Sisters of Notre Dame, Visitation Community, 3978 Constance Rd., 19114. Tel: 215-824-0754. Email: sisterbernie@yahoo.com. Web: www.ssnd.org. Sr. Bernadette Marie Ravenstahl, S.S.N.D., Contact.

Sister Servants of the Holy Spirit of Perpetual Adoration (S.Sp.S.A.P.), Convent of Divine Love, 2212 Green St., 19130. Tel: 215-567-0123; Fax: 215-569-8314. Email: cdl.phl@verizon.net. Web: www.holyspiritadorationsisters. Sr. Mary Catherine, S.Sp.S.A.P., Supr.; Rev. Joseph C. Dieckhaus, J.C.L., Chap.

Sisters of St. Francis of Philadelphia, Santa Chiara, 2238 S. 12th St., 19148. Tel: 215-465-2227. Email: RRBARBAOSF@aol.com. Sisters Residence for those who work at Our Lady of Angels Convent, Aston and Epiphany Church.

Sisters of St. Francis of Philadelphia, St. Agnes Convent, 1900 S. Broad St., 19145. Tel: 215-465-1597. Email: smcspell@aol.com. Total in Residence 7.

Sisters of St. Francis of Philadelphia (Assumption Convent), Assumption Convent, 609 S. Convent Rd., Aston, 19014. Tel: 610-558-7672. Sr. Eileen Valerie Kulacz, O.S.F., Congregational Sec. Total in Residence 6.

Sisters of St. Francis of Philadelphia (Franciscan Formation House), 609 S. Convent Rd., Aston, 19014. Tel: 610-558-7731. Sr. Eileen Valerie Kulacz, O.S.F., Congregational Sec. Total in Residence 4.

Sisters of St. Francis of Philadelphia (O.S.F.), 214 Gerritt St., 19147. Tel: 215-755-2352. Email: msullivan@che-east.org.

Sisters of St. Francis of Philadelphia, Canticle

House, 1626 Mifflin St., 19145. Tel: 215-551-2586. Email: mlucey@osfphila.org. Web: www.osfphila.org.

Sisters of St. Joseph, Neumann Hall, 58 E. Northwestern Ave., 19118. Tel: 215-248-7277. Email: msjc@ssjpila.org. Web: ssjhila.org. Total in Residence 4.

Sisters of St. Joseph of Philadelphia, Immaculate Heart of Mary Convent, 823 Cathedral Rd., 19128. Tel: 215-482-8540. Sisters in Residence 6.

Sisters of St. Joseph of Philadelphia Elizabeth House, 138 Carpenter Ln., 19119-2563. Tel: 215-849-3362. Sr. Charlene Diorka, S.S.J., Contact Person.

Sisters of St. Joseph of Philadelphia, Cecilian Academy, 6818 Cresheim Rd., 19119. Tel: 215-438-7515. Total in Residence 10.

Sisters of St. Joseph of Philadelphia, Fournier Community, Administration, 9701 Germantown Ave., 19118-2694. Tel: 215-248-7200; Fax: 215-248-7277. Email: msjc@ssjphila.org. Web: ssjphila.org. Sr. Patricia Kelly, S.S.J., Supr. Gen. Sisters 3.

Sisters of St. Joseph of Philadelphia, Nazareth House Tel: 215-836-2613. Email: nazareth@peoplepc.com. 931 Bethlehem Pike, Erdenheim, 19038. Tel: 215-836-2613. Total in Residence 5.

Sisters of the Blessed Sacrament, Acacia Community, 3533 N. 19th St., 19140. Tel: 215-223-9132. Email: ELENAMH@aol.com. Total in Residence 3.

Sisters of the Good Shepherd, 5356 Chew Ave., 19138. Tel: 215-843-9411; Fax: 215-843-3141. Email: marynorad@juno.com. Neighborhood ministry, mediation program. Total in Residence 2.

Sisters of the Good Shepherd (RGS), 9736 Walley Ave., 19115-3014. Tel: 215-677-7583; Fax: 215-677-0075. Web: goodshepherdsistersna.com. Sr. M. Holy Spirit Doherty, Contact Person. Total in Residence 3.

Sisters of the Good Shepherd (Contemplative), 715 Susquehanna Rd., 19111. Tel: 215-722-3970; Fax: 215-722-0786. Sr. Mary Euphrasia Gibson, Supr. Total in Residence 8.

Sisters of the Good Shepherd (R.G.S.), P.O. Box 44258, 19144. Tel: 215-849-2070; Fax: 215-849-4385. Sr. M. Loretta Clancy, R.G.S., Contact Person. Total in Residence 1.

Sisters of the Holy Child, 2362 E. York St., 19125-3029. Tel: 215-423-9514. Email: york@shcj.org.

Response-Ability Residence, 4724 Cedar Ave., 19143-2098. Tel: 215-726-3947. Email: ra@shcj.org. Residence for volunteers for Teacher Service Project sponsored by the Society of Holy Child.

Sisters of the Holy Family of Nazareth, St. Joseph Convent, Grant and Frankford Aves., 19114. Tel: 215-637-6262; Fax: 215-637-5689.

Sisters of the Holy Family of Nazareth, Jesus of Nazareth Convent (aka Mount Nazareth), 2755 Holme Ave., 19152. Tel: 215-338-8992; Fax: 215-338-8752. Total in Residence 60.

Sisters of the Holy Family of Nazareth, Infant Jesus Convent, 2723 Holme Ave., 19152-2015. Tel: 215-335-6380; Fax: 215-335-3764. Email: nazcon@aol.com. Web: www.csfn.org. Total in Residence 25.

Sisters of the Holy Redeemer, Angelus Community, 705 Medary Ave., 19126. Tel: 215-276-0262; Fax: 215-914-4111. Email: emarvel@holyredeemer.com. Web: www.sistersholyredeemer.org. Total in Residence 4.

AMBLER. *Sisters of the Holy Family of Nazareth (C.S.F.N.)*, 701 Bethlehem Pike, Box 388, 19002. Tel: 215-643-7676; Fax: 215-542-9219. Email: sisterritasmv@cs.com. Residential Treatment Center for Children.; St. Mary's Villa for Children and Families.

ARDMORE. *Missionary Sisters of the Holy Rosary (M.S.H.R.)*, 205 Cricket Ave., 19003. Tel: 610-896-1786; Fax: 610-896-9063. Email: ts741@hotmail.com. Web: mshr.org. Total in Residence 5.

ASTON. *Anna Bachmann House*, 606 S. Convent Rd., 19014. Tel: 610-558-3240. Web: www.osfphila.org. Sr. Julie McCole, O.S.F., Contact Person.

Convent of Our Lady of Angels (Formerly Glen Riddle) , 609 S. Convent Rd., 19014. Tel: 215-459-4125; Fax: 610-459-0195. Email: ekulacz@osfphila.org. Web: www.osfphila.org. Sr. Lynn Patrice Lavin, O.S.F., Congregational Min. Motherhouse of the Sisters of St. Francis of Philadelphia.

Mt. Alvernia Convent, 602A S. Convent Rd., 19014. Tel: 610-459-5989. Email: hherberi@comcast.net. Sr. Helen St. Paul, O.S.F., Contact Person. Sisters of St. Francis of Philadelphia. Total in Residence 3.

Sisters of St. Francis, 607 S. Convent Rd., 19014. Tel: 610-358-5417. Email: cwright@osfphila.org. Web: www.osfphila.org. Sr. Eileen Valerie Kulacz, O.S.F., Congregational Sec.

Sisters of St. Francis of Philadelphia, Our Lady of the Valley Convent, 10 Red Hill Rd., 19014-1119. Tel: 610-358-4008. Web: www.osfphila.org. Sr. Mary Beth Antonelli, O.S.F., Contact. Total in Residence 4.

Sisters of St. Francis of Philadelphia, Assisi House, 600 Red Hill Rd., 19014. Tel: 610-459-8990; Fax: 610-558-5344. Email: jlamanna@osfphila.org. Total in Residence 118; Total Staff 160.

Sisters of St. Francis of Philadelphia, Portiuncula Convent, 610 Red Hill Rd., 19014. Tel: 610-558-5350; Fax: 610-558-5344. Email: portiuncula@hotmail.com. Sisters 10.

Sisters of St. Francis of Philadelphia, TAU Convent, 4000 Concord Rd., 19014. Tel: 610-494-7322. Sr. Helen Budzik, O.S.F., Contact. Total in Residence 4.

BENSALEM. *St. Elizabeth Convent*, 1663 Bristol Pike, 19020-8502. Tel: 215-244-9900; Fax: 215-244-8174. Email: kathdrexel@aol.com. Web: www.katharinedrexel.org. Sisters Monica Loughlin, S.B.S., Pres.; Jane Norton, S.B.S., Local Dir.

Legal Title: *Sisters of the Blessed Sacrament*, Motherhouse of the Sisters of the Blessed Sacrament for Indians and Colored People. Total in Residence 40; Total Staff 17.

St. Michael Hall, 1663 Bristol Pike, 19020. Tel: 215-244-9900; 215-638-0865; Fax: 215-244-6222. Email: stmichhall@aol.com.

Legal Title: *Sisters of the Blessed Sacrament* The Infirmary of the Sisters of the Blessed Sacrament.

Sisters of the Blessed Sacrament, Formerly Sisters of the Blessed Sacrament Novitiate, 1663 Bristol Pike, 19020. Tel: 215-244-1859. Email: maxwellam@aol.com. P.O. Box 8502, 19020. Sr. Amedee Maxwell, S.B.S.

Legal Title: *Sisters of the Blessed Sacrament, Bensalem, PA* Professed Sisters 3; Candidate 1; Total in Residence 4.

BROOKHAVEN. *Sisters of St. Francis of Philadelphia*, Claddagh House, 160 Meadowbrook Ln., 19015. Tel: 610-490-5367. Email: mirmurray@comcast.net. Web: www.osfphila.org. Total in Residence 3.

BRYN MAWR. *Missionary Sisters of the Holy Rosary*, 741 Polo Rd., 19010. Tel: 610-520-1974; Fax: 610-520-2002. Email: ts741@hotmail.com. Web: www.mshr.org. Total in Residence 8.

Society of the Holy Child Jesus, 700 Old Lancaster Rd., 19010. Tel: 610-527-5076; Fax: 610-527-4671. Email: apenrose@juno.com. Retirement Residence for Sisters of the Holy Child Jesus. Total in Residence 4.

CHELTENHAM. *Daughters of Our Lady of the Sacred Heart*, St. Joseph Convent, 7633 Waters Rd., 19012. Tel: 215-224-2159. Email: fdnsc@aol.com. Total in Residence 2.

CHESTER. *Bernardine Sisters of St. Francis*, Sacred Heart Convent, 2601 W. Tenth St., 19013. Tel: 610-497-9788; Fax: 610-497-3434. Email: conlab1@juno.com. Total in Residence 14.

Bernardine Sisters of St. Francis, Bernardine Center, 2625 W. Ninth St., 19013. Tel: 610-497-3225.

Bernardine Sisters of St. Francis, Sacred Heart Convent, 2061 W. 10th St., 19013. Tel: 610-497-9788.

Missionaries of Charity, Gift of Mary, 2714 W. 9th St., 19013. Tel: 610-494-7424. Sr. M. Vineeth, M.C., Supr. Total Assisted 300; Total Staff 5.

COATESVILLE. *Comboni Missionary Sisters*, 58 S. 6th Ave., 19320. Tel: 610-380-9229. Sr. Angela Sesana, C.M.S., Supr.

DARBY. *Religious Sisters of Mercy*, Bethlehem Convent, 3 Golf Rd., 19023. Tel: 610-461-7634; Fax: 610-567-6333. Web: sistersofmercyoi@rcn.com. Sr. Donna M. Watto, Coord. Sisters 3.

Sisters of the Divine Redeemer, Divine Redeemer Convent, 1215 Springfield Rd., 19023. Tel: 610-534-1688.

DREXEL HILL. *St. Joseph Convent*, 435 N. Lansdowne Ave., 19026-1190. Tel: 610-622-0440. Email: srsj@erols.com. Faculty Residence for Sisters of St. Joseph who teach at Archbishop Prendergast High School, Msgr. Bonner High School, and Bishop Neuman.

Society of the Holy Child Jesus, Provincial Office, 460 Shadeland Ave., 19026. Tel: 610-626-1400; Fax: 610-626-1454. Email: msichol@shcj.org. Web: www.shcj.org. Sr. Marcia Sichol, S.H.C.J., Prov. Leader.

Legal Title: *Society of the Holy Child Jesus American Province, Inc.*

Xavier House Provincial Offices, 460 Shadeland Ave., 19026. Tel: 610-626-1400; Fax: 610-626-0451. Email: phope@shcj.org. Web: www.shcj.org. Society of the Holy Child Jesus

ERDENHEIM. *Sisters of St. Joseph of Philadelphia*, Divine Shepherd Convent, 927 Bethlehem Pike, 19038. Total in Residence 6.

Divine Shepherd Convent, 927 Bethlehem Pike, 19038. Tel: 215-836-2082.

ELKINS PARK. *St. Catherine Hall*, 750 Ashbourne Rd., 19027-2596. Tel: 215-635-4540; Fax: 215-635-2372. Email: stcathall@aol.com. Retirement Residence for Dominican Sisters of St. Catherine de Ricci. Total Staff 5; Total in Residence 30.

Dominican Retreat House, Convent of Our Lady of Prouille, 750 Ashbourne Rd., 19027-2596. Tel: 215-782-8520; 215-224-0945; Fax: 215-782-1744. Email: mariadrh@yahoo.com. Web: www.elkinsparkop.org. Total Staff 35; Total in Residence 15.

Dominican Sisters Administrative Offices, Dominican Congregation of St. Catherine de Ricci, 750 Ashbourne Rd., 19027-2596. Tel: 215-635-6027; Fax: 215-635-2071. Email: cgaekeop@verizon.net. Web: www.elkinsparkop.org. Sr. Carolyn Krebs, O.P., Pres.

ELVERSON. *Daughters of St. Mary of Providence (D.S.M.P.)*, St. Mary of Providence Center, 227 Isabella Rd., 19520. Tel: 610-942-4166; Fax: 610-942-4259. Email: stmaryofprov@msn.com. Web: stmaryofprov-pa.org. Sr. Anna Maria Bilotta, D.S.M.P., Contact Person. Total in Residence 3; Total Staff 15.

ESSINGTON. *Bernardine Sisters of St. Francis*, St. Margaret Mary Convent, 546 Wanamaker Ave., 19029. Tel: 610-521-3286; Fax: 610-521-3280. Email: jperose@aol.com.

FEASTERVILLE. *Grey Nuns of the Sacred Heart*, 1825 Bridgetown Pike, 19053.

FLOURTOWN. *St. Rita Convent*, 1410 Bethlehem Pike, 19031. Tel: 215-836-1615. Sr. Maureen B. McCann, R.S.M. Sisters of Mercy of the Americas Total in Residence 2.

Sisters of St. Joseph of Philadelphia, Mt. St. Joseph Academy, 120 W. Wissahickon Ave., 19031-1922. Tel: 215-233-4368; Fax: 215-233-4734. Email: scmcwill@msjacad.org. Total in Residence 16.

Sisters of St. Joseph of Philadelphia, St. Joseph Villa Staff Visitation Community, 110 W. Wissahickon Ave., 19031-1898. Tel: 215-836-4179; Fax: 215-248-7802. Email: visitationcommunity@msn.com. Sr. Lillian Devlin, S.S.J., Contact Person. Total 13.

FOX CHASE MANOR. *Sisters of St. Basil (O.S.B.M.)* Motherhouse of the Sisters of St. Basil. , 710 Fox Chase Rd., 19046-4198. Tel: 215-663-9153; Fax: 215-728-6129. Email: basilians@aol.com. Web: www.basiliansfoxchase.org. Sr. Dorothy Ann Busowski, O.S.B.M., Prov.

Basilian Spirituality Center, 710 Fox Chase Rd., 19046. Tel: 215-780-1227; Fax: 215-728-6129.

GLENSIDE. *Medical Mission Sisters* (Society of Catholic Medical Missionaries, Inc.) , 15 E. Glenside Ave., 19038. Tel: 215-886-4036. Email: eunice@medicalmissionsisters.org. Web: medicalmissionsisters.org. Total in Residence 3.

Sisters of St. Francis of Assisi (Milwaukee), 229 Edge Hill Rd., 19038. Tel: 215-886-7388. Web: www.lakeosfs.org.

GWYNEDD VALLEY. *Religious Sisters of Mercy - St. Joseph Convent*, 1349 Sumneytown Pike, P.O. Box 902, 19437-0902. Tel: 215-646-5259.

Religious Sisters of Mercy - Transfiguration Convent, 1325 Sumneytown Pike, P.O. Box 901, 19437-0901. Tel: 215-641-5512.

Religious Sisters of Mercy - Visitation Convent, 1325 Sumneytown Pike, P.O. Box 901, 19437. Tel: 215-641-5537.

HOLLAND. *Villa Joseph Marie*, 1180 Holland Rd., 18966. Tel: 215-357-4259; Fax: 215-357-9366. Email: library1@vjmhs.org. Sr. Ann Therese, S.S.C., Supr.; Rev. John A. Cannon, Chap. (Retired).

HUNTINGDON VALLEY. *Sisters of the Holy Redeemer Provincialate*, 521 Moredon Rd., 19006. Tel: 215-914-4100; Fax: 215-914-4111; 215-914-4171. Email: rheilman@holyredeemer.com. Web: www.sistersholyredeemer.org. Sisters M. Regina Heilman, C.S.R., Prov. Supr.; Anne Marie Haas, C.S.R., Formation Dir.; Revs. Michael C. Bolesta, Chap.; Timothy M. Judge, Chap. Annunciation Formation Community Total in Residence 14.

IMMACULATA. *Sisters, Servants of the Immaculate Heart of Mary (I.H.M.)*, Pacis Hall, 19345-0700. Tel: 610-889-1668; Fax: 610-695-0691 (Camilla Hall). Email: pacishall@netzero.net. Sr. Mary Richard, I.H.M., Contact. Total in Residence 37.

Sisters, Servants of the Immaculate Heart of Mary (I.H.M.), Gillet Hall, Box 400, 19345-0400. Tel: 610-647-4400, Ext. 3650. Email: gillet@immaculata.edu. Total in Residence 53.

Sisters, Servants of the Immaculate Heart of Mary, (I.H.M.), Camilla Hall, Box 100, 19345. Tel: 610-644-1152; Fax: 610-695-0691.

Villa Maria House of Studies, 1140 King Rd., 19345-0200. Tel: 610-647-2160; Fax: 610-889-4874. Email: betmc97@aol.com.

Legal Title: *Villa Maria House of Studies, Motherhouse of the Sisters, Servants of the Immaculate Heart of Mary*, Ministry in the field of Academic Education at all levels, Early Childhood Center, Congregation Retirement and Health Care Center, Pastoral Ministry, Diocesan and Parish Administration, Literacy Center, Spirituality Center, Directors of Religious Education, Drug and Alcohol Counseling, Ministry to Hispanics. Total in Residence 1,107.

JENKINTOWN. *Grey Nuns of the Sacred Heart*, Immaculate Conception Convent, 600 West Ave., 19046. Tel: 215-884-9145. Sr. Maureen Quigley, G.N.S.H., Coord.

Sisters of the Holy Redeemer, St. Elizabeth Convent, 615 Fox Chase Rd., 19046. Tel: 215-379-0112; Fax: 215-914-4111. Email: sranita@holyredeemer.com. Web: www.sistersholyredeemer.org. Total in Residence 4.

KING OF PRUSSIA. *The Bernardine Sisters of the Third Order of St. Francis* (also known as Bernardine Franciscan Sisters) , 403 Allendale Rd., 19406. Tel: 610-337-3864; Fax: 610-337-4359. Email: bfgeneralate@aol.com. Web: www.bfranciscan.org. Sisters Madonna Marie Harvath, O.S.F., Gen. Min.; Amalia Vivian, O.S.F., Gen. Councilor; Charlene Dalrymple, O.S.F., Gen. Councilor; Marilisa Helena da Silva, O.S.F., Gen. Councilor.

Legal Title: *The Bernardine Sisters of the Third Order of St. Francis, Generalate*

LANGHORNE. *Monastery of St. Clare, Poor Clares* Prayer and Altar Bread Ministry. , 1271 Langhorne-Newton Rd., 19047-1297. Tel: 215-968-5775; Fax: 215-968-6254. Email: stclare@voicenet.com. Web: www.voicenet.com/~stclare. Cloistered Contemplative Nuns

San Damiano Convent, 104 Alberts Way, 19047. Tel: 215-860-7185.

Legal Title: *Sisters of St. Francis of Philadelphia* Total in Residence 2.

Sisters of St. Francis of Philadelphia, St. Mary Convent, 19047. Tel: 215-757-9494. Total in Residence 10.

Sisters of St. Francis of Philadelphia, Franciscan Residence, 113 Alberts Way, 19047. Tel: 215-860-1059. Sisters serving at St. Mary Medical Center.

LANSDALE. *Religious of the Assumption, Assumption Convent*, 506 Crestview Rd., 19446. Tel: 215-368-4427; Fax: 215-368-4427. Email: ralansdale@verizon.net.

MALVERN. *Villa Maria Convent*, 370 Old Lincoln Hwy., 19355. Tel: 610-647-4878; Fax: 610-644-2866. Email: info@vmahs.org. Web: www.vmahs.org. Sisters, Servants of the Immaculate Heart of Mary (I.H.M.) Total in Residence 15.

MEADOWBROOK. *Sisters of the Holy Redeemer*, Emmanuel Convent, 1600 Huntingdon Pike, 19046. Tel: 215-938-5650; Fax: 215-914-4111. Email: snicklaus@holyredeemer.com. Web: www.sistersholyredeemer.org. Total in Residence 6.

MERION. *Sisters of Mercy*, Formerly Religious Sisters of Mercy, St. Anne Convent, 276 Meeting House Ln., Merion Station, 19066. Tel: 610-667-4531.

Sisters of Mercy, Bethany House of Prayer, Formerly Religious Sisters of Mercy, Bethany House of Prayer 272 Meeting House Ln., Merion Station, 19066. Tel: 610-667-3066.

Sisters of Mercy, McAuley Convent (Infirmary), Formerly Religious Sisters of Mercy, McAuley Convent (Infirmary) 517 Montgomery Ave., Merion Station, 19066. Tel: 610-667-2775; Fax: 610-667-9680. Rev. Thomas F.X. Wheeler, S.J., Chap.

Agape Convent, 515 Montgomery Ave., Merion Station, 19066. Tel: 610-664-2861.

Sisters of Mercy of the Americas, Merion Regional Community, Convent, Merion Station, 19066. Tel: 610-664-6650; Fax: 610-664-3429. Email: mfk@sistersofmercymerion.org. Sisters Christine McCann, R.S.M., Regl. Pres.; Marian Francis Kelly, R.S.M., Local Coord.; Rev. Msgr. Alexander J. Palmieri, M.A., J.C.L., Chap. Motherhouse of the Sisters of Mercy of Merion, PA. Sisters 83.

Sisters of Mercy of the Americas, Regional Community of Merion, Formerly Sisters of Mercy of the Americas, Merion Regional Community, Agape, 515 Montgomery Ave., Merion Station, 19066. Tel: 610-664-6650. Email: www.sistersofmercymerion.org. Sisters 394.

MORTON. *Sisters of St. Francis of Philadelphia (O.S.F.)*, 2130 Franklin Ave., Ct. No. 3, 19070-1217. Tel: 610-543-0186. Total in Residence 5; Total Staff 5.

NEWTOWN. *Grey Nuns of the Sacred Heart*, 4 Stockton Ct., 18940. Tel: 215-968-0735. Sisters Jean Liston, G.N.S.H.; Patricia Geary, G.N.S.H. Total in Residence 2.

NORRISTOWN. *Immaculate Heart Convent*, 1834 Arch St., 19401. Tel: 610-279-2616. Email: cnews1834@aol.com. Sr. Rose Patrice, I.H.M., Supr. Faculty Residence for Sisters, Servants of the Immaculate Heart of Mary, who teach at Kennedy-Kenrick Catholic High School.

Missionaries of Charity, 630 DeKalb St., 19401-3944. Tel: 610-277-5962. Sr. Regi Paul, M.C., Supr. Services include Food Distribution and Emergency Night Shelter. Sisters 4.

RADNOR. *Armenian Sisters of the Immaculate Conception*, 440 Upper Gulph Rd., 19087. Tel: 610-688-9360; Fax: 610-687-2430. Email: ASAARMENIANSRS@aol.com. Web: www.armeniansrsacademy.org. Sr. Louisa Kassarjian, Supr. Total in Residence 3.

Missionary Sisters of the Sacred Heart of Jesus (Cabrini Sisters), Cabrini College Convent, 610 King of Prussia Rd., 19807-3698. Tel: 610-995-1210; Fax: 610-995-1210. Email: vandusen49@aol.com. Web: www.mothercabrini.com. Total in Residence 2.

ROSEMONT. *American Province Archives, Sisters of the Holy Child Jesus*, 1308 Wendover Rd., 19010. Tel: 610-525-8951; Fax: 610-525-8952. Sr. Helena Mayer, S.H.C.J., Archivist.

Holy Child Infirmary, 1341 Montgomery Ave., 19010. Tel: 610-525-1329; Fax: 610-527-2428. Email: cmmshcj@cs. Web: www.shcj.org. Total in Residence 23; Total Staff 29.

Sisters of the Holy Child Jesus (S.H.C.J.), New Sharon Community, 1341 Montgomery Ave., 19010. Tel: 610-525-9900; Fax: 610-527-2428. Email: cmmshcj@cs. Web: www.shcj.org. Sr. Catherine M. Murray, S.H.C.J., Coord. Total in Residence 13.

Infirmary - Community Tel: 610-525 1329; Fax: 610-527-2428. Total in Residence 23.

Sisters of the Holy Child Jesus (S.H.C.J.), Gracemere Convent, 1316 Wendover Rd., 19010. Tel: 610-525-5601. Email: gracemere@juno.com. Total in Residence 6.

Sisters of the Holy Child Jesus (S.H.C.J.), Midhill Convent, 1355 Montgomery Ave., 19010. Tel: 610-527-3483; Fax: 610-527-2428. Email: cmmshc@cs. Web: www.shcj.org. Total in Residence 10.

SHARON HILL. *Poor Servants of the Mother of God S.M.G. Novitiate*, 209 Felton Ave., 19079. Tel: 610-532-6769; Fax: 610-532-6765. Email: poorservents@rcn.com. Web: www.poorservants.com. Sr. Teresa Conner, S.M.G., Contact.

SPRINGFIELD. *St. Anthony Convent*, 1715 S. Sproul Rd., 19064. Tel: 610-544-4066. Email: sasisters@rcn.com. Residence for Sisters of St. Francis of Philadelphia who teach in Cardinal O'Hara High School and other Ministries. Total Staff 8; Total in Residence 8.

Daughters of St. Mary of Providence, Divine Providence Village, 686 Old Marple Rd., 19064. Tel: 610-328-7730; Fax: 610-544 1710. Email: DPVDSMP@aol.com.

Immaculate Heart of Mary Convent, 1725 S. Sproul Rd., 19064. Tel: 610-544-0275. Email: ihmconvent@comcast.net. Sr. Marie Jerome, I.H.M., Supr. Faculty Residence for Sisters, Servants of the Immaculate Heart of Mary, who teach in Cardinal O'Hara High School and Archbishop Prendergast High School.

St. Joseph Convent, 1705 S. Sproul Rd., 19064. Tel: 610-544-4230. Email: ssjoh@nni.com. Sr. Helen Cantwell, S.S.J. Sisters of St. Joseph Faculty House, Cardinal O'Hara High School. Total in Residence 11.

Our Lady of Mercy Convent, 1735 S. Sproul Rd., 19064. Tel: 610-544-0238. Faculty Residence for Sisters of Mercy who teach in Cardinal O'Hara and Mercy Vocational High Schools.

STRAFFORD. *Our Lady of the Assumption Convent*, 139 Fairfield Ln., 19087. Tel: 610-688-7889. Sr. Rose Marie Adams, I.H.M., Supr. Sisters, Servants of the Immaculate Heart of Mary Total in Residence 8.

VILLANOVA. *Sisters of Notre Dame de Namur*, Notre Dame Convent, 560 Sproul Rd., 19085. Tel: 610-688-8810; Fax: 610-687-1912. Web: ndapa.org. Residence for Sisters of Notre Dame de Namur who teach at Academy of Notre Dame.

WARMINSTER. *Sisters of St. Joseph of Philadelphia*, Nativity of Our Lord Convent, 605 W. Street Rd., 18974. Tel: 215-672-0147; Fax: 215-675-9413. Residence of Sisters St. Joseph.

WYNCOTE. *Handmaids of the Sacred Heart of Jesus*, 2025 Church Rd., 19095. Tel: 215-576-6250; Fax: 215-576-8052. Email: emccoy@ancillae.org. Web: www.ancillae.org. Sr. Elizabeth McCoy, A.C.J., Supr. Total in Residence 8.

WYNNEWOOD. *Sisters of the Holy Child Jesus (S.H.C.J.)*, Connell House, 105 Old Forest Rd., 19096. Tel: 610-649-8462. Web: www.shcj.org. Total in Residence 4.

YARDLEY. *Motherhouse of the Grey Nuns of the Sacred Heart*, 1750 Quarry Rd., 19067-3998. Tel: 215-968-4236; Fax: 215-968-6656. Email: mfinnick@greynun.org. Web: www.greynun.org. Sisters Marlene G. Butler, GNSH, Pres.; Mary Finnick, GNSH, Coord., Motherhouse Community. Total in Residence 41.

YEADON. *St. Michael Convent*, 14 Baily Rd., 19050. Tel: 610-623-3631. Sr. Nancy Donovan, R.S.M., Supr. Residence of Religious Sisters of Mercy who staff Mercy Health Corporation of Southeastern PA.

[CC] RETREAT HOUSES

PHILADELPHIA. *Center for Marianist Spirituality & Communities (CMSC)*, 1341 N. Delaware Ave., Ste. 302A, 19125-4300. Tel: 215-634-4116; Fax: 215-634-4955. Email: CMARSCOM@aol.com. Web: www.marianist-cmsc.org. CMSC is committed to the misssion and spirit of Mary. This spirit fosters spiritual growth and formation, the building of lay faith/action communities and social justice according to the unique gifts of the Marianist tradition. Programs offered in Spirituality, Mary & Community Building for groups, staff, faculty, and parishes. Total Staff 2; Total Assisted 600.

Mother Boniface Center, 3501 Solly Ave., 19136. Tel: 215-335-7541; Fax: 215-335-7511. Sr. Virginia Morris, M.S.B.T. Sponsored by Missionary Servants of the Most Blessed Trinity. Mid-week and weekend programs; retreats, days of recollection, scripture study, meetings, workshops and hosting programs. Capacity 67; Total Staff 6; Total in Residence 4.

Urban House of Prayer, 1919 Cambridge St., 19130. Tel: 215-236-8328. Sr. Marie Bodell, S.N.D.deN., Dir.; Rev. George W. Bur, S.J. Sisters of Notre Dame de Namur Total in Residence 1.

ASTON. *Clare House*, 608 B. Legion Rd., 19014. Tel: 610-459-4077; Fax: 610-558-6122. Email: fsc@osfphila.org. Web: www.fscaston.org. Sr. Christa Thompson, O.S.F. Directed and Private Retreats. Staffed by Sisters of St. Francis of Philadelphia. Capacity 6; Total Staff 2; Total Guests 400.

DOYLESTOWN. *Shrine of Our Lady of Czestochowa*, 654 Ferry Rd., P.O. Box 2049, 18901. Tel: 215-345-9146; Fax: 215-348-2148.

ELKINS PARK. *Dominican Retreat House* Convent of Our Lady of Prouille , 750 Ashbourne Rd., 19027-2596. Tel: 215-782-8520; Fax: 215-782-1744. Email: info@elkinsparkretreats.org. Web: www.elkinsparkretreats.org. Retreat house for laity and religious Total Staff 35; Total in Residence 11.

HAVERFORD. *Saint Raphaela Center*, 616 Coopertown Rd., 19041. Tel: 610-642-5715; Fax: 610-642-6788. Email: acihaverford@juno.com. Sr. Dorothy Beck, A.C.J., Dir.

MALVERN. *St. Joseph's-in-the-Hills* (The Malvern Retreat House) , 313 Warren Ave., P.O. Box 315, 19355-0315. Tel: 610-644-0400; Fax: 610-644-4363. Email: mail@malvernretreat.com. Web: malvernretreat.com. Rev. Dennis J.W. O'Donnell, Ph.D., Rector. Tel: 610-644-0400, Ext. 28; Stephen Tulli, Chm. Owned and Operated by the Laymen's Retreat League.; Offers weekend and weekday, overnight, twilight programs for men, women, students, seniors and clergy. Daily Capacity 350; Annual Retreatants over 20,000.

YARDLEY. *Providence Center*, 1750 Quarry Rd., 19067-3998. Tel: 215-968-4236; Fax: 215-968-6656. Email: tmckittrick@greynun.org. Tom McKittrick, Dir. Providence Center shares space at the Grey Nuns Motherhouse. Individually directed retreats available on a limited basis. Able to provide space for Days of Prayer for groups up to 25 persons.

[DD] CAMPS

JAMISON. *Camp Neumann Conference Center*, Tel: 215-343-6552; Fax: 215-343-8849. Email: office@campneumann.com. Web: www.campneumann.com. P.O. Box 297, 18929. Tel: 215-343-6552. Summer resident camp for boys and girls.

[EE] NEWMAN APOSTOLATE

PHILADELPHIA. *Newman Apostolate for Archdiocese of Philadelphia* 222 N. 17th St., 19103. Tel: 215-587-4544; Fax: 215-964-1749. Email: frcioppm@adphila.org. Web: www.archdiocese-phl.org/offices/na.htm. Rev. Martin T. Cioppi, Ed.D., Archdiocesan Dir.

Full Time Chaplaincies:

University of Pennsylvania, Newman Hall, 3720 Chestnut St., 19104-6189. Tel: 215-898-7575; Fax: 215-386-5899. Email: cpfeffer@adphila.org. Web: www.newman.upenn.edu. Rev. Charles J. Pfeffer, Newman Chap.; Ms. Susan Harte, Asst. to the Chap.

Drexel University, Newman Center, 30 S. 33rd St., 19104-2509. Tel: 215-590-8760; Fax: 215-590-8634. Email: wegrogan@drexel.edu. Web: www.drexel.edu/

newmancenter. Rev. William E. Grogan, Chap.
Temple University, Newman Center, 2129 N. Broad St., 19122-1193. Tel: 215-232-3779; Fax: 215-235-7302. Email: plowe@astro.temple.edu. Web: www-.templenewmancenter.org. Rev. Philip J. Lowe, Ed.D., Chap.; Sr. Helen Victor, S.S.J., Asst. to Chap.
West Chester University, Newman Center, 409 Trinity Dr., West Chester, 19382-5362. Tel: 610-436-0891; Fax: 610-436-6247. Email: 103624.2035@compuserve.com. Web: iws.wcupa.edu/stu/newman. Rev. Samuel A. Verruni, Chap.; Ms. Christine M. Silsby, M.A., Assoc. to Chap.
Tri-College Newman Cluster-Bryn Mawr, Haverford and Swarthmore Colleges, 219 Fayette St., Conshohocken, 19042. Tel: 610-828-0424; Fax: 610-825-5168. Email: james1@swarthmore.edu. Rev. John J. Ames, Chap.
Part-time Chaplaincies:
Tenet Hahnemann (Center City Campus), Formerly MCP-Hahnemann University (Center City Campus) Chaplaincy Vacant.
MCP Medical College of Pennsylvania (East Falls Campus), St. Bridget Church, 3667 Midvale Ave., 19129-1712. Tel: 215-844-4126.
Warminster Hospital, Formerly Allegheny University Hospitals, Bucks County St. John Bosco Church, 235 East County Line Rd., Hatboro, 19040-1298. Tel: 215-672-7280.
Moss Rehab Einstein at Elkins Park, Formerly Allegheny University Hospitals, Elkins Park St. James Church, 8320 Brookside Dr., Elkins Park, 19027. Tel: 215-635-6210. Rev. Raymond J. Himsworth, Chap.
Arcadia University, St. Luke the Evangelist Church, 2316 Fairhill Ave., Glenside, 19038-4107. Tel: 215-572-0128. Rev. Msgr. J. Michael Flood, Chap.
Bucks County Community College, St. Andrew Church, 81 Swamp Rd., Newtown, 18940. Tel: 215-968-2262.
Cheney University Tel: 610-399-2353. Dr. O'dell Edward Jack, Dean, School of Education. Tel: 610-399-2353.
Community College of Philadelphia Chaplaincy Vacant.
Delaware County Community College, St. Anastasia Church, 3301 W. Chester Pk., Newtown Square, 19073. Tel: 610-356-3303; 610-359-5206. Frank Mulvaney, D.C.C.C., Contact, Math/Science Dept.
Delaware County Community College, Math Science Dept., Media, 19063. Tel: 610-359-5206.
St. Anastasia Church, 3301 West Chester Pike, Newtown Square, 19073. Tel: 610-356-1613; 610-356-3303; Fax: 610-356-8332.
Delaware Valley College of Science and Agriculture, St. Jude Church, 321 W. Butler Ave., Chalfont, 18914-2329. Tel: 215-822-0179; Fax: 215-822-0638. Rev. James B. McCoy.
Harcum Junior College, Our Mother of Good Counsel, 31 Pennswood Rd., Bryn Mawr, 19010. Tel: 610-525-0147.
Harcum College Chaplaincy Vacant.
Haverford College Chaplaincy Vacant
Thomas Jefferson University Chaplaincy Vacant.
Lincoln University, Sacred Heart Church, 101 Church Rd., Oxford, 19363. Tel: 610-932-5040. Rev. John F. Hummell, Ed.D., Chap.
Montgomery County Community College, St. Helena Church, P.O. Box 5085, Center Square, 19422. Tel: 610-275-7711. Chaplaincy Vacant.
Pennsylvania State University-Abington , Chaplaincy Vacant.
Pennsylvania State University - Ogontz Campus, Our Lady Help of Christians, 1500 Marian Rd., Abington, 19001. Tel: 215-886-3456.
Pennsylvania State University - Delaware County Campus, St. Francis de Sales Church, New Rd., Box 97, Lenni, 19062. Tel: 610-459-2203.
Pennsylvania State University-Great Valley Campus, 19104. Chaplaincy Vacant
Philadelphia College of Pharmacy and Science, St. Francis de Sales Church, 4625 Springfield Ave., 19143. Tel: 215-222-5819.
Philadelphia College of Textiles and Science, St. Bridget Church, 3667 Midvale Ave., 19129-1712. Tel: 215-844-4126.
Philadelphia University, St. Bridget Church, 3667 Midvale Ave., 19129-1712. Tel: 215-844-4126.
Roxborough Memorial School of Nursing, St. John the Baptist, 146 Rector St., 19107. Tel: 215-482-4600.
Temple University, Ambler Campus, St. Alphonsus Church, 33 Conwell Dr., Maple Glen, 19002. Tel: 215-646-4600; Fax: 215-646-0180. Web: www.libertynet.org/~tunewman.
University of the Arts, Assoc. Dean's Office, Broad and Pine Sts., 19102. Tel: 215-875-2236.
St. John the Evangelist Church, 21 S. 13th St., 19107. Tel: 215-563-4145. Dr. Annelte DiMedio, Ph.D., Contact.
University of the Sciences in Philadelphia, Newman Center, 30 S. 33rd St., 19104-2509. Tel: 215-590-8760.
Ursinus College, St. Eleanor Church, 647 Locust St., Collegeville, 19426-2541. Tel: 610-489-1647; Fax: 610-489-7469. Rev. Patrick E. Sweeney, Chap.
Widener University, Blessed Katherine Drexel Church, 20th and Providence Ave., Chester, 19013-5695. Tel: 610-872-0545.

[FF] MISCELLANEOUS LISTINGS

PHILADELPHIA. *St. Agnes Foundation*, 1900 S. Broad St., 19145. Tel: 215-339-4323; Fax: 215-339-5570. Email: thearen@che-east.org. Web: www.stagnesmedicalcenter-pa.org. Sr. Marge Sullivan, Pres. & CEO.
Apostleship of Prayer, St. Joseph's University, 5600 City Ave., 19131. Tel: 610-660-1400; Fax: 610-664-6640. Rev. Timothy Brown, S.J., Contact.
Br. Rousseau Academy, 5900 A Elmwood Ave., 19143. Tel: 215-724-4572; Fax: 215-724-4572. Larry Patrick, M.P.A., Dir.
Catholic Health Care Services, 222 N. 17th St., 19103. Tel: 215-587-3663; Fax: 215-587-3773. Web: chcs-phl.org.
Catholic Heritage Center, c/o Archdiocese of Philadelphia, 222 N. 17th St., 19103-1299. Email: heritage@adphila.org. Web: www.catholicheritage-phl.org. Bro. Joseph J. Willard, F.S.C., Chm., Exec. Committee. Scheduled to open in the future, the Catholic Heritage Center is a state-of-the-art, multi-purpose facility, owned and operated by the Archdiocese of Philadelphia. It will include a museum featuring both permanent and temporary exhibits on Catholic history, heritage, art and culture, a research library and archives, an education resource center, and a gift shop. Located in Philadelphia's historic district near Independence National Historical Park, the center will offer school groups, families and other visitors an opportunity to encounter their Catholic heritage with an experience which is both educational and entertaining.
Catholic Kolping Society, 1285 Southampton Rd., 19116. Tel: 215-676-8977. Email: phlkolping@aol.com. Rev. Engelbert G. Michel, Praeses; Mr. Charles Morris, Pres.; Mr. Anne Suttmann, Vice Pres.; Mr. Earl Asimos, Treas.
Catholic League For Persons With Disabilities, 4110 Glenview St., 19135. Tel: 215-331-2617. Board of Directors 15; Total Membership 85.
Catholics United for the Faith (St. John Neumann Philadelphia Area Chapter) , 183 Hillcrest Ave., 19118. Tel: 215-247-2585; Fax: 215-247-6335. Email: annemwilson@yahoo.com. Mrs. Anne M. Wilson, Chm.
Center for Human Integration, 8400 Pine Rd., 19111. Tel: 215-742-3505; Fax: 215-742-3507. Email: chi4wellness@aol.com. Web: www.ctrforhumanintegration.org. Sr. Mary Em McGlone, MMS Dir. School of Integrative Body Mind Therapies, classes and client services.
The Central Association of the Miraculous Medal, 475 E. Chelten Ave., 19144-5785. Tel: 215-848-1010; Fax: 215-848-1014; 800-523-3674. Email: kiernan@cammonline.org. Web: www.cammonline.org. Rev. James O. Kiernan, C.M., Dir.; Mr. Charles P. Kelly, Gen. Mgr. & Contact Person Miraculous Medal Magazine.
CORA Services, 733 Susquehanna Rd., 19111. Tel: 215-342-7660; 215-535-2957 (Neumann Center); Fax: 215-745-9857. Email: afchunn@coraservices.org. Web: www.coraservices.org. Anthony F. Chunn, Ph.D., CEO; Sr. Mary Charity Kohl, Founding Admin.
Legal Title: *CORA Services, Inc., Philadelphia, Pennsylvania*, Services provided for children, families and teen pregnancy. Programs available: counseling, speech and language, remediation and GED, Early Childhood, Drug & Alcohol and Summer Recreational. Total Assisted 30,000; Total Staff 264.
Euphrasia House, Inc., P.O. Box 44258, 19144-3016. Tel: 215-849-3371 (Intake); 215-844-7686 (Bus.); Fax: 215-849-4385. Sr. Mary Loretta Clancy, Dir. & Contact Person. Women and Children-in-Transition. Sponsored by the Sisters of the Good Shepherd.; Residential and Outreach Services Total Staff 11; Total in Residence 15 Adults; 20 Children 0.
Fournier Retirement Fund Corporation, Mount St. Joseph Convent, 9701 Germantown Ave., 19118-2694. Tel: 215-248-7205; Fax: 215-248-7277. Email: msjc@ssjphila.org. Web: www.ssjphila.org. Sr. Joanne Fehrenbach, S.S.J., Gen. Sec. & Contact Person.
Franciscan Volunteer Ministry, Inc., P.O. Box 29276, 19125. Tel: 215-427-3070; Fax: 215-427-3059. Email: fvmpd@aol.com. Web: www.fvm89.org. Katie Sullivan, Prog. Dir. Purpose: To create and run a Franciscan lay volunteer program in the United States.
Good Shepherd Mediation Program, 5356 Chew Ave., 19138. Tel: 215-843-5413; Fax: 215-843-2080. Email: gsmediation@phillymediators.org. Web: www.phillymediators.org. Cheryl Cutrona, Exec. Dir.
Legal Title: *Good Shepherd Corporation, Philadelphia, Pennsylvania*
IHM Center for Literacy and GED Programs, 425 W. Lindley Ave., 19120. Tel: 215-457-2232; Fax: 215-457-5209. Email: ihmcenter@dca.net. Sisters M. Anne Smith, I.H.M., M.A., Dir.; Ann M. Harrison, I.H.M., Site Coord. Full-time program with courses in Adult Basic Education (ABE); English for Speakers of Other Languages (ESOL) and General Educational Development (GED).
929 S. Farragut St., 19143. Tel: 215-382-0292; Fax: 215-726-4811.
Katherine Kiernan Chateau, Inc., c/o Catholic Social Services, 222 N. 17th St., Ste. 300, 19103. Tel: 215-587-3903; Fax: 215-587-2479. Email: chumsrv@chs-adphila.org. Web: www.archdiocese-phl.org.
Ladies of Charity, 227 N. 18th St., 19103. Tel: 215-854-7025. His Eminence Anthony J. Bevilacqua, D.D., M.A., J.C.D., J.D.; Rev. Msgrs. Timothy C. Senior, M.B.A., M.S.W.; James T. McDonough, M.S.W., Moderator; Mrs. Dominick Lazanski, Pres. Emeritus; Miss Marie E. Bergmaier, Pres. Purpose is to provide volunteer services for hospitals, nursing homes and home-bound individuals.
Marianist Lay Network of North America, 1341 N. Delaware Ave., 302A, 19125-4300. Tel: 215-634-4116; Fax: 215-634-4955. Email: mlnna@aol.com. Web: www.mlnna.com.
Missionary Cenacle Apostolate, 3501 Solly Ave, 19136. Tel: 310-632-0641; Fax: 310-258-4096. Email: josiemorales@juno.com. Web: www.mcenacle.org/mca/mca.htm. Mrs. Josie Morales, Gen. Custodian. The MCA is a branch of the Missionary Cenacle Family. Lay people called to be missionaries in the Church in the providence of everyday life. MCA members live and work in the United States, Mexico, Puerto Rico, Colombia, and Costa Rica.
1602 E. Helmick St., Carson, CA 90746. Tel: 310-632-0641; Fax: 310-258-4096.
The Papal Foundation, 222 N. 17th St., 19103-1299. Tel: 215-587-4501; 215-587-2491; Fax: 215-965-1712. Email: pf1988@aol.com. Mr. James V. Coffey, S.T.M., M.Div., Contact Person.
Sisters of Saint Joseph Welcome Center, 728 E. Allegheny Ave., 19134-2428. Tel: 215-634-1696; Fax: 215-634-0760. Email: emarnien@earthlink.net. Web: ssjwelcomecenter.org. Sisters Eileen Marnien, Dir.; Marian Behrle, Dir. Literacy Project. Sisters 4.
Society of Catholic Medical Missionaries Generalate, Inc. (Effective 1991) , 8400 Pine Rd., 19111. Tel: 215-742-6100; Fax: 215-342-3948. Email: medmisisters@gn.apc.org. Web: www.medicalmissionsisters.org. Sisters Clarita Hackman, M.M.S., Contact Person; Elizabeth Koothanam, M.M.S., Pres. Corporation collects funds for charitable and missionary work, for Medical Mission Sisters; Assists in operation of hospitals, clinics and primary health care programs; Assists in care of poor, sick and infirm, in U.S. and overseas; Assists in training and educating men and women in medicine and nursing, and other health professions; Trains candidates for the Community; Provides assisted living care to sick and elder Medical Mission Sisters.
Society of St. Vincent de Paul of Philadelphia, 901 E. Luzerne St., 19124. Tel: 215-288-9540; Fax: 215-288-9540. Email: carreygroberts@cs.com. Most Rev. Robert P. Maginnis, Spiritual Advisor; Salvatore Talamo, Pres.; Carey G. Roberts, Exec. Dir.; Robert Lanzilotta, Gen Mgr. Catholic Lay Organization serving those in need with spiritual, moral, material and financial support regardless of race, creed, etc.
The Saint Thomas More Society of Philadelphia, 2600 One Commerce Sq., 19103-7098. Tel: 215-564-8126; Fax: 215-564-8120. Email: jmcrowley@msn.com. Web: www.stmsphl.org. Mr. James M. Crowley, Pres. Purpose: The Society is an association of catholic lawyers organized to strengthen the religious and charitable commitment of its members and to promote high ethical standards in the legal profession, as exemplified by the life of Saint Thomas More.
St. Vincent's Orphan Asylum-St. Vincent's Comprehensive Emergency Shelter Program, 7201 Milnor St., 19135. Tel: 215-624-5600; Fax: 215-624-8355. Bed Capacity 72; Total Assisted Annually 300; Total Staff 140.
The Warner Perpetual Trust for the Benefit of Catholic Charities, Provident National Bank, P.O.

Box 7648, 19101. Tel: 610-585-5698; Fax: 610-358-4275.

Legal Title: *The Warner Perpetual Trust for the Benefit of Catholic Charities of the Archdiocese of Philadelphia,* (The "Perpetual" Trust)

ARDMORE. **Catholic Leadership Institute*, P.O. Box 373, Malvern, 19355. Tel: 610-251-3750; Fax: 610-251-3751. Email: info@CatholicLeaders.org. Web: www.CatholicLeaders.org. Most Rev. Robert P. Maginnis, D.D., Honorary Chair; Timothy C. Flanagan, Founder; Matthew F. Manion, Pres.; Rev. Charles J. Pfeffer, Spiritual Dir. Lay organization providing leadership training and personal development programs to help people reach their God given potential as Catholic leaders and Christian witnesses in their family, workplace, community and Church.

ASTON. *Franciscan Ministries Foundation, Inc.*, 609 S. Convent Rd., 19014. Tel: 610-558-7713; Fax: 610-558-5357. Email: mvdgeest@osfphila.org. Web: www.osfphila.org. Sr. Mary Vandergeest, O.S.F., Exec. Dir. Purpose: Raises funds to fulfill the needs of the Ministries and Retired Sisters of the Sisters of St. Francis of Philadelphia.

Sisters of St. Francis of Philadelphia, Charitable Trust I and Charitable Trust II, Our Lady of Angels Convent, 19014. Tel: 610-558-6794; Fax: 610-459-0195. Email: ekulacz@osfphila.org. Web: www.osfphila.org. Sr. Lynn Patrice Lavin, O.S.F., Congregational Min.

CONSHOHOCKEN. *Mercy Health System of Southeastern PA*, One West Elm St., 19428. Tel: 610-567-6106; Fax: 610-567-6150. Email: mwhitty@mercyhealth.org. Web: www.mercyhealth.org. Sr. Mary Christine McCann, R.S.M., Bd. Chm.; Gavin R. Kerr, Pres. & CEO. Mercy Health System is a regional health corporation of Catholic Health East, sponsored by the Sisters of Mercy and Hope Ministries. The health care services operated by Mercy Health System include:

Mercy Hospital of Philadelphia Tel: 215-748-9300; Fax: 215-748-9709.

Mercy Fitzgerald Hospital Tel: 610-237-4000; Fax: 610-237-4202.

Mercy Suburban Hospital Tel: 610-278-2002; Fax: 610-272-4642.

St. Agnes Medical Center Tel: 215-339-4220; Fax: 215-339-0482.

Nazareth Hospital Tel: 215-335-6039; Fax: 215-335-6598.

Keystone Mercy Health Plan Tel: 215-937-8201; Fax: 215-937-8202.

Mercy Management Services Tel: 610-567-6106; Fax: 610-567-6150.

Mercy Health Foundation Tel: 610-567-6105; Fax: 610-567-6150.

Mercy Home Health Services Tel: 610-690-2526; Fax: 610-690-4644.

Mercy Court Tel: 610-623-3083; Fax: 610-259-1414.

DREXEL HILL. *National Communicators Network for Women Religious*, 435 N. Lansdowne Ave., 19026-1113. Tel: 610-626-7360; Fax: 610-626-7360. Email: coordinator@ncnwr.org. Web: www.ncnwr.org. Sr. Arlene Ronollo, S.S.J., Natl. Coord. Sponsor: Communication personnel of congregations of Women Religious who are members.; NCNWR is organized to promote and assist in the understanding of women religious and specifically to enhance their image and advance their mission. The organization is also provides a network of professional support and education for its members.

ELKINS PARK. *Dominican Pastoral Counseling*, 750 Ashbourne Rd., 19027. Tel: 215-635-6027; Fax: 215-635-2017. Email: CGAEKEOP@verizon.net. Web: www.elkinsparkop.org. Richard T. Mulcahey Jr., Esq., Contact Person.

Lucy Eaton Smith Fund, 750 Ashbourne Rd., 19027. Tel: 215-635-6027; Fax: 215-635-2017. Email: CGAEKEOP@verizon.net. Web: www.elkinsparkop.org. Richard T. Mulcahey Jr., Esq., Contact Person.

FLOURTOWN. *Saint Joseph Guild*, 110 W. Wissahickon Ave., P.O. Box 36, 19031-0036. Tel: 215-248-7838; Fax: 215-248-7802. Email: sjguild19@aol.com. Web: www.ssjphila.org. Sr. Frances DeLisle, S.S.J., Coord.

FORT WASHINGTON. *John Paul II Foundation for Peace, Justice & Human Rights*, The Copernicus House, P.O. Box 267, 19034. Tel: 215-646-4101; Fax: 215-628-8944. Email: KEENCORNER@aol.com.

HUNTINGDON VALLEY. **Holy Redeemer Health System*, 667 Welsh Rd., 19006. Tel: 215-938-4650; Fax: 215-938-4671. Web: www.holyredeemer.com. *Marketing/Public Affairs Department*, c/o 1602 Huntingdon Pike, Meadowbrook, 19046. Michael B. Laign, Pres. & CEO. Sponsor: Sisters of the Holy Redeemer, C.S.R., Parent organization which maintains, manages, and operates the health care system composed of the various corporations sponsored and established by the Sisters of the Holy Redeemer, C.S.R. as follows: Drueding Center; Holy Redeemer Home Health and Hospice Services; Holy Redeemer Health Care Corporation and Foundation; HRH Management Corp.; Holy Redeemer Visiting Nurse Agency (NJ); Holy Redeemer Managed Care Org.; HR Physician Services; Holy Redeemer Hosp. & Med. Ctr.; Redeemer Med. Supply Co.

Holy Redeemer Hospital and Medical Center Tel: 215-947-3000.

Redeemer Center Tel: 215-938-4100.

St. Joseph's Manor Tel: 215-938-4000.

The Lafayette - Redeemer Tel: 215-214-2877. Benjamin Pieczynski, Vice Pres.

Holy Redeemer Health Care Corporation and Foundation Tel: 215-938-4650.

Holy Redeemer Home Health and Hospice Services Tel: 215-671-9200.

Holy Redeemer Transitional Care Unit Tel: 215-947-3000.

Holy Redeemer Multicare Tel: 609-465-2082.

Holy Redeemer Visiting Nurse Agency Tel: 609-465-2082.

Holy Redeemer Hospice Tel: 215-671-9200.

Redeemer Village - Redeemer Village II Tel: 215-947-8168.

Drueding Center/Project Rainbow Tel: 215-769-1830.

HRH Management Corporation Tel: 215-938-4650.

**HR Physician Services (aka Holy Redeemer Physician and Ambulatory Services)* Tel: 215-938-4600.

**Holy Redeemer Managed Care Organization* Tel: 215-938-4600.

IMMACULATA. *Enserv Inc.*, King Rd., 19345. Tel: 610-647-4400, Ext. 3147; Fax: 610-251-1668.

KING OF PRUSSIA. *Bernardine Franciscan Sisters Mission and Ministries Charitable Trust*, 403 Allendale Rd., 19406. Tel: 610-337-3864; Fax: 610-337-4359. Email: bfgeneralate@aol.com. Web: www.bfranciscan.org. Sr. Madonna Marie Harvath, O.S.F., Contact Person.

Bernardine Franciscans, Delaware County, 403 Allendale Rd., 19406. Tel: 610-337-3864; Fax: 610-337-4359. Email: bfgeneralate@aol.com. Web: www.bfranciscan.org. Total Assisted Annually 10,401; Total Staff 7.

Bernadine Center, 2625 W. Ninth St., Chester, 19013. Tel: 610-497-3225; Fax: 610-497-3659. Sr. Madonna Marie Harvath, O.S.F., Contact Person.

MEADOWBROOK. **Holy Redeemer Physician and Ambulatory Services*, 1602 Huntingdon Pike, 2nd Floor, 19046. Tel: 215-938-4600; Fax: 215-938-4610. Web: www.holyredeemer.com. Michele Urofsky, Senior Vice Pres. Sponsor: Sisters of the Holy Redeemer C.S.R., Subsidiary of Holy Redeemer Health System.; Nonprofit corporation formed to establish, operate and maintain family health clinics and practices, laboratories, dispensaries, buildings, and facilities relating to these purposes, and provide the services of physicians and other health care professionals in connection with the provision of health care services at Holy Redeemer Hospital and Medical Center, and other hospitals, clinics and health care facilities.

MERION. *Greaton Properties, Inc.*, 701 City Line Ave., Merion Station, 19066. Tel: 610-660-1321; Fax: 610-660-1319. Email: jpease@sju.edu. Mr. Joseph R. Pease, Treas.

NEWTOWN SQUARE. *Catholic Health East*, 14 Campus Blvd., Ste. 300, 19073-3277. Tel: 610-355-2004; Fax: 610-355-2050. Email: sfoti@che.org. Web: che.org. Mr. Robert V. Stanek, Pres. & CEO. Catholic Health East is a multi-institutional, Catholic health system co-sponsored by 14 congregations: Franciscan Sisters of Allegany in St. Bonaventure, NY; Sisters of Providence in Holyoke, MA; nine Regional Communities of the Sisters of Mercy of the Americas The Franciscan Sisters of St. Joseph in Hamburg, NY; the Sisters of St. Joseph of St. Augustine, FL; Sisters of Charity of Seton Hill Greensburg, PA; and Hope Ministries, a Public Juridic Person of Pontifical Right within Catholic Health East, Newtown Square, PA. Founded in 1997, Catholic Health Care East facilities serve communities through 18 regional systems in 11 eastern states.

Global Health Ministry, 14 Campus Blvd., Ste. 300, 19073-3277. Tel: 610-355-2003; Fax: 610-355-2050. Email: lmanley@globalhealthministry.org. Web: www.globalhealthministry.org. Sr. Elizabeth Scanlon, R.S.M., Pres. & CEO; Lynn E. Manley, Dir., Prog. Opers.

YEADON. *Mercy Court*, 550 S. Lansdowne Ave., 19050. Tel: 610-623-3083; Fax: 640-259-1414. Email: mercycourt@rcm.com. Sr. Juliana Kozman, R.S.M., Prog. Mgr. Sisters of Mercy, Low income apartments for independent living for older adults. Total Apartments 100; Total Staff 5.

RELIGIOUS INSTITUTES OF MEN REPRESENTED IN THE ARCHDIOCESE

For further details refer to the corresponding bracketed number in the Religious Institutes of Men or Women section.

[0140]—*The Augustinians* (Provs. of St. Thomas Villanova & Our Mother of Good Counsel)—O.S.A.

[0290]—*Brothers of Charity*—F.C.

[0330]—*Brothers of the Christian Schools* (Baltimore Prov.)—F.S.C.

[]—*Brothers of the Holy Spirit*—B.H.S.

[0900]—*Canons Regular of Premontre*—O.Praem.

[0470]—*Capuchin Friars*—O.F.M.Cap.

[0275]—*Carmelites of Mary Immaculate*—C.M.I.

[0650]—*Congregation of the Holy Spirit* (Eastern Prov.)—C.S.Sp.

[0860]—*Congregation of the Immaculate Heart of Mary (Missionhurst)*—C.I.C.M.

[1330]—*Congregation of the Mission* (Eastern Prov.)—C.M.

[]—*Institute of the Incarnate Word*—I.V.E.

[0800]—*Maryknoll Fathers and Brothers*—M.M.

[0850]—*Missionaries of Africa*—M.Afr.

[0825]—*Missionaries of the Blessed Sacrament*—M.S.S.

[1110]—*Missionaries of the Sacred Heart* (American Prov.)—M.S.C.

[0840]—*Missionary Servants of the Most Holy Trinity*—S.T.

[0920]—*Oblates of St. Francis de Sales*—O.S.F.S.

[0520]—*Order of Friars Minor* (Assumption B.V.M. & Most Holy Name Provs.)—O.F.M.

[0480]—*Order of Friars Minor, Conventual*—O.F.M.Conv

[0970]—*Order of Our Lady of Mercy*—O.deM.

[]—*Order of Preachers*—O.P.

[1310]—*Order of the Holy Trinity*—O.SS.T.

[1010]—*Pauline Fathers*—O.S.P.P.E.

[0950]—*The Philadelphia Congregation of the Oratory of Saint Philip Neri*—C.O.

[1040]—*Piarist Fathers*—Sch.P.

[1070]—*Redemptorist Fathers* (Baltimore Prov.)—C.SS.R.

[1220]—*Servants of Charity*—S.C.

[0690]—*Society of Jesus (Jesuits)* (Maryland Prov.)—S.J.

[0780]—*Society of Mary (Marists)*—S.M.

[0560]—*Third Order Regular of Saint Francis* (Prov. of the Most Sacred Heart)—T.O.R.

RELIGIOUS INSTITUTES OF WOMEN REPRESENTED IN THE ARCHDIOCESE

[1070-13]—*Adrian Dominican Sisters*—O.P.

[]—*Armenian Sisters of the Immaculate Conception*—C.I.C.

[1810]—*Bernardine Sisters of the Third Order of St. Francis*—O.S.F.

[0330]—*Carmelite Sisters for the Aged and Infirm*—O.Carm.

[0690]—*Comboni Missionary Sisters*—C.M.S.

[0270]—*Congregation of Bon Secours*—C.B.S.

[]—*Contemplative Sister of the Good Shepherd*—C.G.S.

[0760]—*Daughters of Charity of St. Vincent de Paul*—D.C.

[0900]—*Daughters of Our Lady of the Sacred Heart*—F.D.N.S.C.

[0940]—*Daughters of St. Mary of Providence*—D.S.M.P.

[0810]—*Daughters of the Heart of Mary*—D.H.M.

[0420]—*Discalced Carmelite Nuns*—O.C.D.

[1070-23]—*Dominican Sisters of Hawthorne*—O.P.

[1105]—*Dominican Sisters of Hope*—O.P.

[]—*Dominican Sisters of Our Lady of the Rosary*—O.P.

[]—*Dominican Sisters of St. Catherine de Ricci* (Elkins Park, PA)—O.P.

[1170]—*Felician Sisters*—C.S.S.F.

[1180]—*Franciscan Sisters of Allegany, New York*—O.S.F.

[1840]—*Grey Nuns of the Sacred Heart*—G.N.S.H.

[1870]—*Handmaids of the Sacred Heart of Jesus*—A.C.J.

[]—*Little Servants of the Holy Family of Seoul*—L.S.H.F.

[2300]—*Little Servants Sisters of the Immaculate Conception*—L.S.I.C.

[2310]—*Little Sisters of the Assumption*—L.S.A.

[2340]—*Little Sisters of the Poor*—L.S.P.

[2345]—*Little Workers of the Sacred Hearts*—P.O.S.C.

[2490]—*Medical Mission Sisters*—M.M.S.

[2710]—*Missionaries of Charity*—M.C.

[2790]—*Missionary Servants of the Most Blessed Trinity*—M.S.B.T.

[2730]—*Missionary Sisters of the Holy Rosary*—M.S.H.R.
[2800]—*Missionary Sisters of the Most Sacred Heart of Jesus of Hiltrup*—M.S.C.
[2860]—*Missionary Sisters of the Sacred Heart* (Eastern Prov.)—M.S.C.
[3060]—*Oblates Sisters of St. Francis de Sales*—O.S.F.S.
[3730]—*Order of St. Basil the Great*—O.S.B.M.
[3760]—*Order of St. Clare*—O.S.C.
[1705]—*Order of St. Francis of Assisi*—O.S.F.
[0950]—*Pious Society Daughters of St. Paul*—F.S.P.
[3640]—*Poor Servants of the Mother of God*—S.M.G.
[3390]—*Religious of the Assumption*—R.A.
[3430]—*Religious Teachers Filippini*—M.P.F.
[2970]—*School Sisters of Notre Dame*—S.S.N.D.
[1700]—*School Sisters of St. Francis*—O.S.F.
[]—*Servants of the Lord and of the Virgin of Matara*—S.S.V.M.
[3540]—*Sister Servants of the Holy Spirit of Perpetual Adoration*—S.Sp.S.deA
[3630]—*Sister Servants of the Most Sacred Heart of Jesus*—S.S.C.J.
[0500]—*Sisters of Charity of Nazareth*—S.C.N.
[0660]—*Sisters of Christian Charity*—S.C.C.
[2575]—*Sisters of Mercy of the Americas, Merion, PA*—R.S.M.
[3000]—*Sisters of Notre Dame de Namur*—S.N.D.deN.
[3893]—*Sisters of Saint Joseph of Chestnut Hill, Philadelphia*—S.S.J.
[3740]—*Sisters of St. Casimir*—S.S.C.
[1650]—*Sisters of St. Francis of Philadelphia*—O.S.F.
[0260]—*Sisters of the Blessed Sacrament for Indians and Colored People*—S.B.S.
[0970]—*Sisters of the Divine Compassion*—R.D.C.
[1020]—*Sisters of the Divine Redeemer*—S.D.R.
[1830]—*Sisters of the Good Shepherd*—R.G.S.
[1970]—*Sisters of the Holy Family of Nazareth*—C.S.F.N.
[2000]—*Sisters of the Holy Redeemer*—C.S.R.
[2060]—*Sisters of the Most Holy Trinity*—O.SS.T.
[3270]—*Sisters of the Most Precious Blood*—C.PP.S.
[2160]—*Sisters Servants of the Immaculate Heart of Mary* (Scranton)—I.H.M.
[2170]—*Sisters, Servants of the Immaculate Heart of Mary (Immaculata)*—I.H.M.
[4060]—*Society of the Holy Child Jesus*—S.H.C.J.
[4120]—*Ursuline Sisters of the Immaculate Conception*—O.S.U.
[4190]—*Visitation Nuns*—V.H.M.

ARCHDIOCESAN CEMETERIES

PHILADELPHIA. *Cathedral*, 48th St. and Lancaster Ave., 19131. Tel: 215-477-8918.
Holy Sepulchre, Cheltenham Ave. & Ivy Hill Rd., 19150. Tel: 215-247-0691.
New Cathedral, 2nd & Butler Sts., 19140. Tel: 215-634-3212.

BENSALEM. *Resurrection*, 5201 Hulmeville Rd., 19020. Tel: 215-639-0965.

CHALFONT. *St. John Neumann*, 3797 County Line Rd., 18914. Tel: 215-822-0680.

NEWTOWN. *All Saints*, R.R. 413, Twining Bridge Rd., 18940.

SPRINGFIELD. *SS. Peter and Paul*, 1600 S. Sproul Rd., 19064. Tel: 610-544-4933.

WEST BRANDYWINE TWP.. *All Souls*, R.R. 322, 19343.

WEST CONSHOHOCKEN. *Calvary*, Gulph & Matsonford Rd., 19428. Tel: 610-525-2214.

WEST GROVE. *Holy Saviour* Penn Township

YEADON. *Holy Cross*, 626 Bailey Rd., 19050. Tel: 610-626-2206; 215-476-3656.

NECROLOGY

† Doolin, Rev. Msgr. William A.—Died Oct. 22, 2003
† Helduser, Rev. Msgr. Frederick J., Drexel Hill, PA St. Dorothy—Died July 2, 2003
† Kane, Rev. Msgr. Thomas A., (Retired)—Died July 10, 2003
† Marley, Rev. Msgr. Michael F., (Retired)—Died May 7, 2003
† Paul, Rev. Msgr. William J., Morrisville, PA St. John the Evangelist—Died June 15, 2003
† Donohie, John M., Philadelphia, PA Immaculate Heart of Mary—Died Jan. 16, 2003
† Dougherty, John C.—Died Oct. 5, 2003
† Dougherty, Joseph D., (Retired)—Died Feb. 23, 2003
† Duffy, John J., (Retired)—Died June 21, 2003
† Hagan, Thomas C., Philadelphia, PA St. Cecilia—Died Jan. 31, 2003
† Lewis, Francis C., Bristol, PA St. Mark—Died March 20, 2003
† Loughrey, Thomas F., (Retired)—Died Nov. 22, 2003
† Monteleone, Rev. Pascal A.—Died March 19, 2003
† Morley, John J., (Retired)—Died Sept. 6, 2003
† Morrison, Francis X., (Retired)—Died April 13, 2003
† O'Rourke, Charles M., (Retired)—Died Nov. 11, 2002
† Oestreich, Emil C., (Retired)—Died Nov. 29, 2002
† Ostaszewski, George, (Retired)—Died Sept. 3, 2003
† Schuyler, Henry C.—Died June 8, 2003

Diocese of Phoenix

(Dioecesis Phoenicensis)

Most Reverend

THOMAS J. OLMSTED

Bishop of Phoenix; ordained July 2, 1973; appointed Coadjutor Bishop of Wichita February 16, 1999; Episcopal ordination April 20, 1999; appointed Bishop of Wichita October 4, 2001; appointed Bishop of Phoenix November 25, 2003; installed December 20, 2003. *Office: 400 E. Monroe St., Phoenix, AZ 85004-2336.*

Diocesan Pastoral Center: 400 E. Monroe St., Phoenix, AZ 85004-2336. Tel: 602-257-0030; Fax: 602-354-2427.

Web: www.diocesephoenix.org

Email: communications@diocesephoenix.org

ESTABLISHED DECEMBER 2, 1969.

Square Miles 43,967.

Comprises the Counties of Maricopa; Mohave; Yavapai & Coconino not to include the territorial boundaries of the Navajo Indian Reservation; Pinal--that portion of land known as the Gila River Indian Reservation in the State of Arizona.

Patroness of Diocese: Our Lady of Guadalupe.

For legal titles of parishes and diocesan institutions, consult the Chancery Office.

STATISTICAL OVERVIEW

Personnel	
Retired Archbishops	1
Bishop	1
Retired Bishops	2
Priests: Diocesan Active in Diocese	94
Priests: Retired, Sick or Absent	38
Number of Diocesan Priests	132
Religious Priests in Diocese	98
Total Priests in Diocese	230
Extern Priests in Diocese	70
Ordinations:	
Diocesan Priests	3
Transitional Deacons	2
Permanent Deacons in Diocese	211
Total Brothers	12
Total Sisters	213
Parishes	
Parishes	89
With Resident Pastor:	
Resident Diocesan Priests	64
Resident Religious Priests	18
Without Resident Pastor:	
Administered by Deacons	5
Administered by Lay People	1
Missions	27
Professional Ministry Personnel:	
Brothers	6
Sisters	44
Lay Ministers	420
Welfare	
Catholic Hospitals	1
Total Assisted	262,596
Health Care Centers	1
Total Assisted	98,899
Homes for the Aged	11
Total Assisted	972
Day Care Centers	27
Total Assisted	1,456
Specialized Homes	9
Total Assisted	29,680
Special Centers for Social Services	13
Total Assisted	1,710,862
Residential Care of Disabled	1
Total Assisted	3,250
Educational	
Diocesan Students in Other Seminaries	21
Total Seminarians	21
High Schools, Diocesan and Parish	6
Total Students	3,443
High Schools, Private	1
Total Students	1,210
Elementary Schools, Diocesan and Parish	28
Total Students	9,271
Catechesis/Religious Education:	
High School Students	6,734
Elementary Students	33,106
Total Students under Catholic Instruction	53,785
Teachers in the Diocese:	
Priests	9
Scholastics	2
Brothers	9
Sisters	40
Lay Teachers	808
Vital Statistics	
Receptions into the Church:	
Infant Baptism Totals	12,465
Adult Baptism Totals	1,286
Received into Full Communion	1,068
First Communions	9,414
Confirmations	5,060
Marriages:	
Catholic	1,269
Interfaith	422
Total Marriages	1,691
Deaths	3,404
Total Catholic Population	556,692
Total Population	3,650,019

Former Bishops—Most Revs. EDWARD A. MCCARTHY, D.D., installed Bishop of the Diocese of Phoenix, Dec. 2, 1969; transferred to Coadjutor Archbishop of Miami, July 7, 1976; installed Sept. 17, 1976; JAMES S. RAUSCH, D.D., Ph.D., installed March 22, 1977; died May 18, 1981; THOMAS J. O'BRIEN, D.D. (Retired), ord. May 7, 1961; consecrated Jan. 6, 1982; installed Bishop of the Diocese of Phoenix Jan. 18, 1982; retired June 18, 2003.

Moderator of the Curia—Rev. Msgr. RICHARD MOYER, Diocesan Pastoral Center, 400 E. Monroe, Phoenix, 85004. Tel: 602-257-0030.

Vicar General—Rev. Msgrs. RICHARD MOYER, Diocesan Center. Tel: 602-257-0030. St. Timothy Catholic Community, 1730 W. Guadalupe Rd., Mesa, 85202-7424. Tel: 480-775-5200; DALE FUSHEK, V.G., St. Timothy Catholic Community, 1730 W. Guadalupe Rd., Mesa, 85202-7424. Tel: 480-775-5200.

Diocesan Office—400 E. Monroe St., Phoenix, 85004-2336. Tel: 602-257-0030; Fax: 602-354-2427.

Chancellor—Sr. MARY ANN WINTERS, S.C., 400 E. Monroe St., Phoenix, 85004-2336. Tel: 602-257-0030; Fax: 602-354-2427.

Assistant Chancellor—Rev. MICHAEL L. DISKIN, 400 E. Monroe St., Phoenix, 85004-2336. Tel: 602-257-0030; Fax: 602-354-2427.

College of Consultors—Rev. Msgr. RICHARD W. MOYER, V.G. (Retired); Rev. TIMOTHY DAVERN, J.V.; Rev. Msgr. DALE FUSHEK, V.G.; Revs. ROBERT SKAGEN; CHARLES KIEFFER; NATHAN CASTLE, O.P.; MICHAEL STRALEY; MICHAEL L. DISKIN; KIERAN KLECZEWSKI; GREG MENEGAY; PATRICK MOWRER; THOMAS ZURCHER, C.S.C.

Finance and Administration—Rev. Msgr. RICHARD MOYER, Vicar; Mr. JOSEPH ANDERSON, Dir., 400 E. Monroe St., Phoenix, 85004-2336. Tel: 602-354-2185; Fax: 602-354-2448.

Diocesan Tribunal—Office, 400 E. Monroe St., Phoenix, 85004-2336. Tel: 602-354-2275; Fax: 602-354-2424.

Judicial Vicar—Rev. TIMOTHY R. DAVERN, J.C.L.. Email: frdavern@diocesephoenix.org.

Adjutant Judicial Vicars—Revs. PHILIP ACQUARO, C.S.B., J.C.L.. Email: frphil@diocesephoenix.org; PAUL OREL. Email: frpaul@diocesephoenix.org.

Diocesan Judges—Rev. Msgr. ALAN MALONE (Retired); Deacons DOUGLAS LECLAIR, J.C.L.; WILLIAM FINNEGAN.

Defenders of the Bond—Revs. ROBERT J. CARUSO; PETER DOBROWSKI; CHARLES G. KIEFFER; VALENTINE BOYLE, O.Carm.; Sr. FRANCES WETZEL, O.P.

Advocates—Revs. MICHAEL L. DISKIN; CHARLES C. PARKER; JOHN D. EHRICH; NICHOLAS FLORIDI; FAUSTO PENAFIEL; GARY REGULA; Deacon PAUL HURSH; Sisters BRIDGET CHAPMAN, M.M.; RUTH KARNITZ, S.S.N.D.; ELLEN SINCLAIR, S.D.S.; Mrs. SANDRA J. CONSIGLIO, M.A.; BOBBIE FRIEDRICH; DEBORAH MALATIN; MARY ESTHER STEWART.

Auditors—Rev. CHARLES C. PARKER; Sisters RUTH KARNITZ, S.S.N.D.; ELLEN SINCLAIR, S.D.S.

Promoter of Justice—Deacon DOUGLAS LECLAIR, J.C.L.. Email: dcndoug@diocesephoenix.org.

Censor Librorum—Rev. TIMOTHY R. DAVERN, J.C.L.

Notaries—Rev. DONALD J. KLINE; Sr. M. ANTHONY POERIO, I.B.V.M.; Mrs. JUSTINA SANCHEZ; Mrs. MARY LYN PYEATTE; Mrs. WALDA SWEENEY.

Appellate Court Administrator-Diocese of Phoenix—Sr. RUTH KARNITZ, S.S.N.D.

Youth Protection Advocate—JENNIFER O'CONNOR, 400 E. Monroe, Phoenix, 85004. Tel: 602-354-2396; Fax: 602-354-2496.

Archives—JOHN PAUL, Archivist, 400 E. Monroe St., Phoenix, 85004-2336. Tel: 602-354-2457.

Arizona Catholic Conference—Mr. RONALD JOHNSON, Exec. Dir., 400 E. Monroe St., Phoenix, 85004-2336. Tel: 602-354-2390; Fax: 602-354-2466; 602-354-2394.

Buildings & Property—JOHN MINIERI, Dir., Real Property & Facilities; TOM CHERMACK, Asst. Dir. Construction, Diocesan Center, 400 E. Monroe St., Phoenix, 85004-2336. Tel: 602-257-0030; Fax: 602-354-2440.

Catholic Community Foundation - Diocese of Phoenix—JOHN SCOLA, CFRE, Exec. Dir., 400 E. Monroe St., Phoenix, 85004-2336. Tel: 602-354-2400; Fax: 602-354-2423.

Catholic Cemeteries— St. Francis, Holy Redeemer, Holy Cross, Queen of Heaven, Calvary, All Souls (under development) Rev. MICHAEL L. DISKIN, Spiritual Advisor; GARY L. BROWN, Exec. Dir., Administrative Offices, 2033 N.48th St., Phoenix, 85008. Tel: 602-267-1329; Fax: 602-685-1516. Calvary Cemetery, 201 W. University, Flagstaff, 86001. Tel: 928-774-1105; Fax: 928-774-1105 (call first). St. Francis Cemetery, 2033 N. 48th St., Phoenix, 85008. Tel: 602-267-1329; Fax: 602-267-7942. Holy Redeemer Cemetery, 23015 N. Cave Creek Rd., Phoenix, 85040. Tel: 480-573-3243; Fax: 480-513-3293. Holy Cross Cemetery, 10045 W. Thomas Rd., Avondale, 85323. Tel: 623-936-1710; Fax: 623-936-6605. Queen of Heaven Cemetery, 1500 E. Baseline Rd., Mesa, 85204. Tel: 480-892-3729; Fax: 480-892-2891. All Souls Cemetery (under development), 700 N. Bill Gray

Rd., Cottonwood, 86326. Tel: 928-649-1998; Fax: 602-685-1516.

"The Catholic Sun"— (Diocesan Newspaper) *400 E. Monroe St., Phoenix, 85004-2336.* Tel: 602-257-0030; 602-257-5565; Fax: 602-258-6404. Email: info@catholicsun.org. Web: www.catholicsun.org.

Public Information Officer—MARY JO WEST, 400 E. Monroe, Phoenix, 85004-2336. Tel: 602-354-2121; Fax: 602-354-2273.

Stewardship Office— (Charity & Development Appeal) BILL SCHWANEKAMP, Dir., 400 E. Monroe St., Phoenix, 85004. Tel: 602-354-2215; Fax: 602-354-2432; JIM CRUTHOFF, Assoc. Dir. Tel: 602-354-2216 (Endowments/Planned Giving); JOHN SCOLA, Exec Dir., 400 E. Monroe St., Phoenix, 85004. Tel: 602-354-2400.

Ecumenical and Interreligious Affairs—Rev. MICHAEL L. DISKIN, Dir., 400 E. Monroe, Phoenix, 85004. Tel: 602-257-0030; Fax: 602-354-2427.

Vicariate of Christian Formation and Education—Sr. DOLORETTE FARIAS, S.S.N.D., Exec. Dir., 400 E. Monroe, Phoenix, 85004. Tel: 602-257-0030; Fax: 602-354-2444.

Diaconate Ministry—Deacons DANIEL PETERSON, Dir., 400 E. Monroe, Phoenix, 85004. Tel: 602-354-2011; Fax: 602-354-2437; KEITH DAVIS, Dir. Formation. Tel: 602-354-2012.

Vocations—Rev. DONALD KLINE, Dir., 400 E. Monroe, Phoenix, 85004. Tel: 602-257-0030; Fax: 602-354-2442. Email: frkline@diocesephoenix.org.

Worship and Liturgy, Office of—Sr. MARY ANTHONY POERIO, I.B.V.M., Dir., 400 E. Monroe, Phoenix, 85004. Tel: 602-257-0030; Fax: 602-354-2432.

Schools—MARYBETH MUELLER, Supt. Schools; Sr. MELITA M. PENCHALK, O.S.B.M., Asst. Supt. School; JOANNE JOHNSON, Coord. Instructional Svcs., 400 E. Monroe, Phoenix, 85004. Tel: 602-257-0030; Fax: 602-354-2432.

Catechetical Ministry—Deacon JOHN MEYER, Dir.; CAROL GASTELUM, Assoc. Dir.; STACY FILEWICZ-ROSS, Assoc. Dir., 400 E. Monroe, Phoenix, 85004. Tel: 602-257-0030; Fax: 602-354-2431.

Youth-Young Adult Campus Ministry—LARRY FRAHER, Dir., 400 E. Monroe, Phoenix, 85004. Tel: 602-354-2380; Fax: 602-354-2431.

The Catholic Scouting Program—Rev. DENNIS O'ROURKE, Liaison, St. Benedict Parish, 6400 W. Del Rio St., Chandler, 85226. Tel: 480-961-1610; Fax: 480-961-1794.

Office of Family Life and Life Issues—RICHARD BERGKESSEL, Dir., 400 E. Monroe, Phoenix, 85004. Tel: 602-257-0030; Fax: 602-354-2431.

Mount Claret Center—Directors: Rev. Msgr. JOHN J. MCMAHON; Rev. EUGENE MAGUIRE; Ms. JO SWIGER, Asst. Dir.; Sr. REGINA MARIE BOSLET, S.C., Asst. Dir.

Office of Disability Ministry—ISABELLA RICE, Dir., 400 E. Monroe, Phoenix, 85004. Tel: 602-354-2370; 602-354-2369 (TTY); Fax: 602-354-2432.

Native American Ministry Office—Sisters ANNE FISCHER, S.S.N.D., Dir.; ROSE MARIE DEIBEL, S.N.D.deN., Assoc. Dir., 400 E. Monroe, Phoenix, 85004. Tel: 602-354-2050; Fax: 602-354-2432.

Native American Ministry - Field Office—Sr. ANNE FISCHER, S.S.N.D., Dir., 120 Church St., Sacaton, 85247. P.O. Box 545, Sacaton, 85247. Tel: 520-562-3716.

Social Ministry Office—Mr. GUY MIKKELSEN, 1201 E. Thomas Rd., Phoenix, 85014. Tel: 602-285-1800; Fax: 602-285-1838.

Diocesan Attorney—GREGORY J. LEISSE, 400 E. Monroe, Phoenix, 85004. Tel: 602-257-0030; Fax: 602-354-2427.

Priests' Assurance Association—Rev. MICHAEL L. DISKIN, Sec., 400 E. Monroe, Phoenix, 85004. Tel: 602-257-0030.

Priest Personnel—Rev. THOMAS ZURCHER, C.S.C., Vicar, 400 E. Monroe, Phoenix, 85004. Tel: 602-257-0030; Fax: 602-354-2427.

Advisory Board for the Continuing Formation of Priests—Rev. THOMAS ZURCHER, C.S.C., 400 E. Monroe, Phoenix, 85004. Tel: 602-257-0030.

Priestly Life and Ministry Board—Rev. THOMAS ZURCHER, C.S.C., 400 E. Monroe, Phoenix, 85004. Tel: 602-257-0030.

Priests' Placement Board—Rev. THOMAS ZURCHER, C.S.C., 400 E. Monroe, Phoenix, 85004. Tel: 602-257-0030.

Prisons, Catholic Ministries To—Deacon PETER MURPHY, Dir., 400 N. 30th St., Phoenix, 85008. Tel: 602-354-2485. Email: dcnmurphy@diocesephoenix.org.

Youth at Risk—KEVIN STARRS, Coord., 320 N. 20th Dr., Phoenix, 85009-3881. Tel: 602-267-1531.

State Adult Facilities— Phoenix Prison Complex, Perryville Prison (female), Lewis Prison, ACW Prison.

State Juvenile Facilities— Adobe Mountain, Black Canyon, Encanto, Eagle Point, Sunrise

County Jails (Adult & Juvenile)— Madison Jail, Durango Jail, Estrella Jail (female), Towers Jail

Federal Prison (Adult)— Federal Correction Institute (male & female)

Private Prison (Adult)— Phoenix West

Diocesan Prison Ministry Staff—Black Canyon Hwy., 2800 W. Pinnacle Peak Rd., Phoenix, 85027. Tel: 602-869-9050, Ext. 270.

County Juvenile Detention Center—3125 W. Durango, Phoenix, 85009. Diocesan Prison Ministry Staff.

Propagation of the Faith—Sr. JEAN STEFFES, C.S.A., 400 E. Monroe, Phoenix, 85004. Tel: 602-257-0030; Fax: 602-354-2442.

Holy Childhood Association—Sr. JEAN STEFFES, C.S.A., 400 E. Monroe, Phoenix, 85004. Tel: 602-257-0300; Fax: 602-354-2442.

Hispanic Ministry—

Office of Hispanic Ministry—Rev. TIMOTHY CONLON, O.S.C., Vicar; JOSE ROBLES, Dir.; IGNACIO RODRIGUEZ, Office Mgr., 400 E. Monroe, Phoenix, 85004. Tel: 602-257-0030; Fax: 602-354-2432.

Human Resources (Personnel and Benefits)—JOHN UNGVARY, Chief Human Resources Officer, 400 E. Monroe, Phoenix, 85004. Tel: 602-257-0030; Fax: 602-354-2428.

Information Technology—JOHN UNGVARY, Dir.; SILVIA RADVAK, Supvr., 400 E. Monroe St., Phoenix, 85004. Tel: 602-257-0030; Fax: 602-354-2458.

Religious, Office of—Sr. JEAN STEFFES, C.S.A., Dir., 400 E. Monroe, Phoenix, 85004. Tel: 602-257-0030; Fax: 602-354-2442.

Catholic Tuition Organization of the Diocese of Phoenix (CTODP)—Rev. Msgr. RICHARD W. MOYER, V.G., Pres. (Retired); KAREN L. SHEPARD, Prog. Coord., Diocesan Center, 400 E. Monroe St., Phoenix, 85004. Tel: 602-354-2416; Fax: 602-354-2432.

Office of Black Catholic Ministry—Mrs. JACQUELIN RIDEAU, Coord.; CHERRIE HOLLAND, Chm., Diocesan Center, 400 E. Monroe St., Phoenix, 85004. Tel: 602-354-2025.

Research and Planning Office—CARYN MERON, Dir., 400 E. Monroe St., Phoenix, 85004. Tel: 602-257-0030; Fax: 602-354-2431.

Victim Assistance Coordinator—JENNIFER O'CONNOR. Tel: 602-354-2396. Email: joconnor@diocesephoenix.org.

CLERGY, PARISHES, MISSIONS AND PAROCHIAL SCHOOLS

CITY OF PHOENIX
(MARICOPA COUNTY)

1—SS. SIMON AND JUDE CATHEDRAL (1953), Rev. Msgr. Michael O'Grady, Rector; Rev. Chauncey Winkler; Deacons Matias Valle; William West; Rick Curran. In Res., Revs. Francis A. Peacock; Donald Kline.
Res.: 6351 N. 27th Ave., 85017. Tel: 602-242-1300; Fax: 602-249-3768.
School—Tel: 602-242-1299. Sr. Raphael Quinn, I.B.V.M., Prin. Sisters 1; Lay Teachers 28; Students 560.
Convent—Tel: 602-242-2544.
Mission—Santa Rosa Chapel 1901 W. Ocotillo, Maricopa Co. 85017.

2—ST. AGNES (1940), Revs. Michael Sgarioto, O.Carm., Admin.; John Long, O.Carm.; Peter J. Liuzzi, O.Carm. (LA); Deacons Angel Guzman; Eduardo Lopez; Robert England. In Res., Revs. Ernest Larkin, O.Carm.; Michael Kwiecien, O.Carm.
Res.: 1954 N. 24th St., 85008. Tel: 602-244-0349; Fax: 602-244-0054.
School—2311 E. Palm Ln., 85006. Tel: 602-244-1451. Connie Emminger, Prin. Lay Teachers 15; Students 208.
Convent—1818 N. 23rd St., 85006. Tel: 602-244-1174.

3—SS. ANTHONY AND PIUS X (1943), Revs. Patrick Mowrer; Mario Garcia Restrepo; Juvenal Perez-Monterrosa; Deacon Lowell O'Grady.
Church & Res.: 909 S. First Ave., 85003. Tel: 602-252-1771; Fax: 602-258-4714.
Mission—St. Pius X 809 S. Seventh Ave., Maricopa Co. 85007.
Mission—Our Lady of Fatima 1418 S. 17th Ave., Maricopa Co. 85007. Tel: 602-254-4944. Rev. Francis A. Peacock, Admin.

4—ST. AUGUSTINE (1970), Rev. Alonso Saenz.
Res.: 3630 N. 71st Ave., 85033. Tel: 623-849-3131; Fax: 623-849-5689.

5—ST. CATHERINE OF SIENA (1947), Revs. David Sanfilippo; Michael D. Reinhardt; Francisco Saenz, O.P.; Deacons Carlos Terrazas; Albert Gonzalez.
Res.: 6401 S. Central Ave., 85040. Tel: 602-276-5581; Fax: 602-276-2119.
School—6413 S. Central Ave., 85040. Tel: 602-276-2241, Ext. 251; Fax: 602-268-7886. Ms. Pat DeVito, Prin. Lay Teachers 14; Students 240.

6—CORPUS CHRISTI (1985), Revs. Albert F.H. Hoorman; Bruce Downs; Sr. Frances Ellsperman, O.P., Pastoral Assoc.; Deacons Alexander Gaudio; Patrick Flynn; Philip Simeone.
Res.: 3550 E. Knox, 85044. Tel: 480-893-8770; Fax: 480-893-3291.

7—ST. EDWARD CONFESSOR (1976), Rev. Jorge Canez; Deacon Peter Fejes.
Res.: 4410 E. Southern Ave., 85040. Tel: 602-438-0043; Fax: 602-438-9305.

8—ST. FRANCIS XAVIER (1928), Revs. Russell J. Roide, S.J., Admin.; Joseph Dube, S.J.; Daniel J. Sullivan (SJ); Deacons Charles VanDyke; William Clower; Clark Rutledge.
Res.: 4715 N. Central Ave., 85012-1796. Tel: 602-279-9547; Fax: 602-248-8968.
School—Tel: 602-266-5364. Lisa Westfall-Elliot, Prin. Lay Teachers 28; Students 520.

9—ST. GREGORY (1947), Revs. John J. Dougherty, C.S.C., Admin.; Michael Floreth, C.S.C.; Deacon Lee Kloft.
Res.: 3424 N. 18th Ave., 85015. Tel: 602-264-4488; Fax: 602-266-5210.
School—3440 N. 18th Ave., 85015. Tel: 602-266-9527. Ms. Maureen Fyan, Prin. Sisters 2; Lay Teachers 14; Students 263.
Convent—Sisters of the Institute of B.V.M., 3437 N. 18th Ave., 85015. Tel: 602-265-2396.

10—HOLY FAMILY (1968), Rev. Jorge Canez.
Res.: 6802 S. 24th St., 85040. Tel: 602-268-2632; Fax: 602-268-8909.

11—IMMACULATE HEART OF MARY (1924), Rev. Patrick Mowrer; Deacon Richard Yanez.
Res.: 909 E. Washington St., 85034. Tel: 602-253-6129; Fax: 602-253-4210.

12—ST. JEROME (1962), Revs. L. Pierre Hissey; Steven A. Kunkel; Deacons Michael Phelan; James Mickens; Joseph Stickney; Bill Bidleman. In Res., Rev. Charles Parker.
Church: 10815 N. 35th Ave., 85029. Tel: 602-942-5555; Fax: 602-504-9115.
School—Tel: 602-942-5644. Carl Hodus, Prin. Sisters 1; Lay Teachers 21; Students 299.

13—ST. JOAN OF ARC (1979), Revs. Larry W. Weidner; John F. Cullinan (Retired); Deacons James Springer; Donald Fischer; Phil LoCascio; Guy Goubeaux; Juan Guzman.
Parish Center—3801 E. Greenway Rd., 85032-4698. Tel: 602-867-9171; Fax: 602-482-7930.

14—ST. JOSEPH (1969), Rev. Frank Fernandez; Deacons Harry Schwan; Charles Kelly.
Res.: 11001 N. 40th St., 85028. Tel: 602-996-5120; Fax: 602-996-4011.

15—ST. LUKE (1985), Rev. Richard A. Milligan.
Res.: 19644 N. Seventh Ave., 85027. Tel: 623-582-0561.
Mission—Good Shepherd Mission 45033 N. 12th St., New River, Maricopa Co. 85087. Tel: 623-465-9740; Fax: 623-742-7031. Deacons James Fogle, Admin.; Daniel L. Peterson.

16—ST. MARK (1946), Rev. David Cooney, S.D.S., Admin. In Res., Rev. Fred Peters, S.D.S.; Bro. Roger Pelky, S.D.S.
Res.: 400 N. 30th St., 85008. Tel: 602-267-0503.
Mission—St. Philip the Deacon Catholic Center 615 N. 20th St., Maricopa Co. 85006. Tel: 602-253-1076. Deacons Pedro Mesa; Richard Rein.

17—ST. MARTIN DE PORRES (1973), Deacon Jose Olivarez.
Res.: 3851 W. Wier Ave., 85041. Tel: 602-276-2466 (Church); Fax: 602-232-2147.

18—ST. MARY'S BASILICA (1881), Revs. Vincent Mesi, O.F.M. (LA); Michael Weldon, O.F.M. In Res., Revs. Luis Baldonado, O.F.M.; Alonso De Blas, O.F.M.; Bro. Kevin Dunne, O.F.M.
Res.: 231 N. Third St., 85004. Tel: 602-354-2100; Fax: 602-354-2060.

19—ST. MATTHEW (1939), Rev. Raymond Ritari; Bros. Charles Fitzsimmons, C.F.C.; Charles Avendano, C.F.C.; Douglas Zlatis, C.F.C.; Deacon Tony Beltran.
Res.: 320 N. 20th Dr., 85009. Tel: 602-258-1789; Fax: 602-258-6507.
School—2038 W. Van Buren, 85009. Tel: 602-254-0611. Mary Pat Waldmann. Lay Teachers 13; Students 168.
Convent—2106 W. Van Buren, 85009. Tel: 602-253-9124.

20—MOST HOLY TRINITY (1951), Revs. Joshua R. Alvero, D.S. (GAL), Admin.; Leonardo J. Vargas, D.S.; Mariano E. Talay, D.S.; Joseph Thuan Nguyen, O.P.; Bro. Pasquale Manalio, O.P.; Deacon Lorenzo Salazar.
Res.: 8620 N. Seventh St., 85020. Tel: 602-944-3375; Fax: 602-943-2323.
School—535 E. Alice Ave., 85020. Tel: 602-943-9058. Ms. Jane Segovia, Prin. Lay Teachers 23;

Students 283.
McHugh Hall/Small Hall—8820 N. Seventh St., 85020. Tel: 602-997-6726.

21—OUR LADY OF CZESTOCHOWA (POLISH PASTORAL MISSION), Rev. Eugeniusz Bolda, S.C.
Church: 6530 N. 7th Ave., 85014. Tel: 602-212-1172; Fax: 602-212-1173.

22—OUR LADY OF THE VALLEY (1973), Rev. David M. Ostler, Admin.
Church: 3220 W. Greenway Rd., 85053. Tel: 602-993-1213; Fax: 602-993-1223.

23—ST. PAUL (1976), Rev. Eugene O'Carroll; Deacon Bill Vivio.
Res.: 330 W. Coral Gables Dr., 85023. Tel: 602-942-2608; Fax: 602-548-0708.

24—SACRED HEART (1954), Ms. Ann Conway, Parish Life Coord.
Church: 1421 S. 12th St., 85034. Tel: 602-258-2089.

25—ST. THERESA (1955), Revs. Charles G. Kieffer; Nicholas Floridi; Deacons Colin Campbell; Sione Hola.
Res.: 5045 E. Thomas Rd., 85018. Tel: 602-840-0850; Fax: 602-840-0871.
School—5001 E. Thomas Rd., 85018. Tel: 602-840-0010. Peter Morkert, Prin. Sisters 1; Lay Teachers 27; Students 497.

26—ST. THOMAS THE APOSTLE (1950), Revs. James Wall; John D. Ehrich; Deacons Donald Kuban; Thomas Bills.
Res.: 2312 E. Campbell Ave., 85016-5597. Tel: 602-954-9089; Fax: 602-956-3454.
School—4510 N. 24th St., 85016. Tel: 602-954-9088. Sr. Patricia Gehling, S.S.N.D., Prin. Sisters 3; Lay Teachers 37; Students 593.

27—ST. VINCENT DE PAUL (1957), Revs. Jeffrey H. Harvey, C.M. (STO), Admin.; Michael J. Boyle, C.M.; Ruben Dario Restrepo, C.M.; Victor Pacheco, C.M. (LA); Deacon Bill Jenkins.
Res.: 3140 N. 51st Ave., 85031. Tel: 623-247-6871; Fax: 623-247-4457.
School—3130 N. 51st Ave., 85031. Tel: 623-247-8595. Sr. Louise Camous, D.C., Prin. Sisters 1; Lay Teachers 18; Students 281.
Convent—*Daughters of Charity*, 3130 N. 51st Ave., 85031. Tel: 623-247-8916.

OUTSIDE THE CITY OF PHOENIX

AVONDALE, MARICOPA CO., ST. THOMAS AQUINAS, Revs. Kieran Kleczewski; Thaddeus McGuire; Deacon Chuck Shaw.
Res.: 13720 W. Thomas Rd., 85323. Tel: 623-935-2151; 623-935-3625; Fax: 623-935-5044.
School—Tel: 623-935-0945. Dagoberto Batista, Prin. Sisters 1; Lay Teachers 14; Students 175.

BAGDAD, YAVAPAI CO., ST. FRANCIS OF ASSISI (1949), George Rojas, Parish Life Coord.; Maria Rojas, Parish Life Coord.
Mailing Address: P.O. Box 768, 86321.
Church & Rectory: 220 Cook St., 86321. Tel: 928-633-2389.

BAPCHULE, PINAL CO., ST. PETER'S (1949), Deacon Sidney Martin.
Mailing Address: P.O. Box 545, Sacaton, 85247. Tel: 520-562-3716; 602-319-0742 (Mobile); Fax: 520-315-3963.
School—P.O. Box 10840, 85221. Tel: 520-315-3835; Fax: 520-315-3963. Sr. Martha Mary Carpenter, O.S.F., Prin. Franciscan Sisters of Christian Charity (Manitowoc, WI) 7; Lay Teachers 8; Students 209.
Missions of Gila River Catholic Community Team—
Mission—*Holy Family* Blackwater, Pinal Co.
Mission—*Our Lady of Victory* Sacaton Flats, Pinal Co.
Mission—*St. Anne* Santan, Pinal Co.
Mission—*St. Anthony* Sacaton, Pinal Co.

BUCKEYE, MARICOPA CO., SAINT HENRY (1956), Rev. Charles Goraieb; Deacons George Cameron; Jesus Ruiz.
Res.: 128 S. Third St., 85326. Tel: 623-386-6407; Fax: 623-386-4328.
Mission—*San Isidoro Labrador* Harquahala Valley, Maricopa Co.

BULLHEAD CITY, MOHAVE CO., ST. MARGARET MARY (1947), Rev. Peter P. Dobrowski; Deacons Richard Eckert; Philip Wisely.
Res.: 1691 N. Oatman Rd., 86442. Tel: 928-758-7117; Fax: 928-758-2345.

CAMP VERDE, YAVAPAI CO., ST. FRANCES CABRINI (1962), Rev. James Kelly; Deacon David Kaminsky.
Res.: P.O. Box 1677, 86322. Tel: 928-567-3543.
Church: 608 W. General Crook Trail, 86322. Tel: 928-567-3543; Fax: 928-567-7058.
Mission—*St. Philip Benizi* P.O. Box 138, Black Canyon City, Yavapai Co. 85324. Tel: 623-374-5392; Fax: 623-374-9768. Deacons Jim Sejba, Parish Life Coord.; Leslie Stokes. Though this mission is canonically part of St. Frances Cabrini Parish, pastoral responsibility is currently being handled by St. Germaine Parish, Prescott Valley.

CAREFREE, MARICOPA CO., OUR LADY OF JOY (1972), Revs. Greg Menegay; Mathew Plathottam.
Res.: P.O. Box 1359, 85377. Tel: 480-488-2229 (Church); 480-488-0469 (Rectory); Fax: 480-488-1085.

CASHION, MARICOPA CO., ST. WILLIAM (1973), Rev. Loren Gonzales, Admin.; Deacon Albert Scheller.
Mailing Address: P.O. Box 329, 85329.
Res.: 11003 W. Third St., 85329. Tel: 623-936-6115; Fax: 623-936-8308.
Mission—*Our Lady of Guadalupe* 6807 Lower Buckeye Rd., Santa Maria, Maricopa Co. 85043.

CAVE CREEK, MARICOPA CO., ST. GABRIEL (2002), Rev. John D. Spaulding.
32648 N. Cave Creek Rd., 85331. Tel: 480-595-0883; Fax: 480-595-0886. In Res., Rev. Oliver Mohan, O.M.I.

CHANDLER, MARICOPA CO.

1—ST. ANDREW THE APOSTLE (1985), Revs. Joseph I. Hennessy; Christopher J. Fraser; Deacons Buddy Clapham; Ernest Garcia; Michael Carr Thomas Monday; John Benware.
Res.: 3450 W. Ray Rd., 85226. Tel: 480-899-1990; Fax: 480-917-8475.

2—ST. BENEDICT (1985), Rev. Dennis J. O'Rourke; Deacon Richard Cuprak.
Church: 6400 W. Del Rio St., 85226. Tel: 480-961-1610; Fax: 480-961-1794.

3—ST. MARY'S (1937), Revs. Robert Clements; Tomasz Wesolowski; George Highberger; Alvin Cayetano S.O.L.T.; Deacons Craig Hirtze; Bruce Bennett, Ed.D.
Res.: 230 W. Galveston, 85224. Tel: 480-963-3207; Fax: 480-814-9417.
School—*St. Mary-Basha Catholic Elementary*, 200 W. Galveston, 85224. Tel: 480-963-4951. Sr. Mary Norbert Long, S.C., Prin. Sisters of Charity, Seton Hill 3; Lay Teachers 24; Students 509.

COTTONWOOD, YAVAPAI CO., IMMACULATE CONCEPTION (1966), Rev. Emile "Bud" Pelletier; Deacon Onofre Duran.
Church: 700 N. Bill Gray Rd., 86326. Tel: 928-634-2933; Fax: 928-634-3326.
Mission—*St. Cecilia* Clarkdale, Yavapai Co. Closed 2002, for sacramental records contact Immaculate Conception, 928-634-2142.

EL MIRAGE, MARICOPA CO., SANTA TERESITA (1968), Rev. David Kelash; Deacon Jose Garza.
Church: 14016 N. Verbena St., 85335.
Res.: P.O. Box 67, 85335. Tel: 623-583-8183; Fax: 623-583-2963.

FLAGSTAFF, COCONINO CO., SAN FRANCISCO DE ASIS (1997), Revs. Michael Straley; Gary Regula; Deacons James Arnold; Lawrence Whelan.
Mailing Address: 2257 E. Cedar Ave., 86004-1918. Tel: 928-779-1341; Fax: 928-779-2903.
Rectory—520 W. Riordan Rd., 86002
School—*St. Mary's Catholic School*, 320 N. Humphrey, 86001. Tel: 928-779-1337. Ms. Marilyn Johnson, Prin. Lay Teachers 19; Students 249.
Convent—*Institute of the Blessed Virgin Mary Loretto Sisters*, 202 S. Kendrick, 86001. Tel: 520-744-3680.
Chapel—*Nativity of B.V.M.* 16 W Cherry Ave., 86001.
Chapel—*Our Lady of Guadalupe* 225 S. Kendrick, 86001.
Chapel—*St. Pius X* 2257 E. Cedar Ave., 86004.

FOUNTAIN HILLS, MARICOPA CO., ASCENSION (1976), Rev. John T. McDonough.
Church: 12615 Fountain Hills Blvd., 85268. Tel: 480-837-1066; Fax: 480-837-9093.
Mission—*St. Dominic* 25603 N. Danny Ln., Ste. 2, Rio Verde, Maricopa Co. 85263. Tel: 480-471-1516.

GILA BEND, MARICOPA CO., ST. MICHAEL (1963), Unassigned.
Res.: 515 W. Norma St., P.O. Drawer F, 85337. Tel: 928-683-2336.
Church: 314 Dodson St., 85337.
Mission—*St. Lucy, Paloma Ranch* Tohono O'Odham, Maricopa Co. Deacon Tom Swisher, Admin. Tel: 520-550-2034. (Native American Village)

GILBERT, MARICOPA CO., ST. ANNE (1943), Revs. Douglas E. Lorig; William Kosco Stephen Schack; Deacons Ken Kulinowski; Gerald O'Toole; David Barraza; Keith Boswell; Thomas Pintar; John Berger; Bob Carey.
Mailing Address: P.O. Box 228 85299-0228. Tel: 480-892-0905; Fax: 480-505-6034.
Church: 440 E. Elliot Rd., 85299-0228.
School—*Little Flower Montessori* Dee Dee Tamminen, Dir. Lay Teachers 10; Students 221.
Mission—*Our Lady of Guadalupe* P.O. Box 856, Queen Creek, Maricopa Co. 85242. Tel: 480-963-3207. Rev. George Highberger.

GLENDALE, MARICOPA CO.

1—ST. HELEN (1974), Revs. Robert Skagen; Louis Mraz, O.S.C.; Deacons Joseph Shinske; Rudolph Campas; Paul Csuy.
Res.: 5510 W. Cholla, 85304. Tel: 623-979-4202; Fax: 623-412-1226.

2—ST. JAMES (1982), Rev. Kenneth A. Van De Ven; Deacons Richard Kijewski; Alan Bowslaugh; Frank Devine.
Church: 19640 N. 35th Ave., 85308. Tel: 623-581-0707; Fax: 623-581-0110.
Res.: 18225 N. 35th Dr., 85308. Tel: 623-843-0421.

3—ST. LOUIS THE KING (1962), Rev. John Slobig.
Mailing Address: 4331 W. Maryland Ave., 85301. Tel: 623-930-1127; Fax: 623-930-1129.
School—Tel: 623-939-4260. Gregory Pizzolato, Prin. Lay Teachers 10; Students 220.

4—OUR LADY OF PERPETUAL HELP (1948), Revs. Fausto Penafiel; John Ebbesmier; Deacons Tony Lopez; Robert Myers; Eddie Molina; Vincent Torres; Charles Heeter.
Res.: 5614 W. Orangewood Ave., 85301. Tel: 623-939-9785; Fax: 623-934-8854.
School—7521 N. 57th Ave., 85301. Tel: 623-931-7288. Cecilia Frakes, Prin. Sisters 1; Lay Teachers 23; Students 367.
Chapel—*Our Lady of Guadalupe* 55th Ave. & Lamar, 85301.

5—ST. RAPHAEL (1974), Rev. Cyprian Hibner, O.Carm., Admin.; Deacons Richard Meidl; Robert Manthie.
Res.: 5504 W. Acoma, 85306.
Church: 5525 W. Acoma, 85306. Tel: 602-938-4227; Fax: 602-978-0305.

6—ST. THOMAS MORE (1997), Rev. James Turner; Deacons Roy Drapeau; Keith Davis.
6180 W. Utopia Rd., 85308-7111. Tel: 623-566-8222; Fax: 623-825-1468.

GOODYEAR, MARICOPA CO., SAINT JOHN VIANNEY (1956), Revs. John A. Herman, C.S.C., Admin.; John DeRiso, C.S.C.; Deacons James Cascio; Charles A. Witschorik, C.S.C.
Office—539 La Pasada Blvd., 85338. Tel: 602-932-3313; Fax: 602-932-1896.
Res.: 11 Loma Linda Blvd., Avondale, 85323. Tel: 602-925-0418.
School—Tel: 623-932-2434. Catherine Lucero, Prin. Sisters 2; Lay Teachers 22; Students 366.
Convent—15 W. Loma Linda Blvd., Avondale, 85323. Tel: 623-932-2652; Fax: 623-932-1243.

GRAND CANYON, COCONINO CO., EL CRISTO REY (1960), Rev. Francis D. Zagorc, C.S.C. (FTW).
Mailing Address: P.O. Box 505, 86023. Tel: 928-638-2390.

GUADALUPE, MARICOPA CO., OUR LADY OF GUADALUPE (1970), Rev. Joseph A. Baur, O.F.M., Admin.; Deacon Santo Bernasconi.
Office—5445 San Angelo, St. Guadalupe, 85283. Tel: 480-839-2860.
Res.: 9004 Calle Maravilla, 85283. Tel: 480-839-2376.

HIGLEY, MARICOPA CO., ST. MARY MAGDALENE, Revs. John Cunningham; Mathew Mampara.
Res.: P.O. Box 849, 85263-6786. Tel: 480-279-6737; Fax: 480-279-6786.

JEROME, YAVAPAI CO., HOLY FAMILY (1908), Unassigned.
Immaculate Conception—P.O. Box 995, Cottonwood, 86326-0995. Tel: 928-634-2933. (Sacramental Records)

KINGMAN, MOHAVE CO., ST. MARY'S (1906), Rev. James Alling; Deacons Bill Del Monaco; Jose Rodriguez; Brian Lewis.
Res.: 302 E. Spring St., 86401. Tel: 928-753-3359; Fax: 928-753-2581.
Mission—*Our Lady of the Desert* P.O. Box 491, Dolan Springs, Mohave Co. 86441. Tel: 928-767-3154.

LAKE HAVASU CITY, MOHAVE CO., OUR LADY OF THE LAKE (1969), Most Rev. Michael Deptula; Revs. Charles C. Murphy, S.J. (SJ); Fidelis Igwinwanne; Deacons Thomas C. Coe; Thomas DeFilippis.
Res.: 1975 Daytona Dr., 86403. Tel: 928-855-2685; Fax: 928-855-7172.

LAVEEN, MARICOPA CO., ST. JOHN THE BAPTIST (1910), Deacon Joseph "Tom" Swisher, Parish Life Coord.
Res.: P.O. Box 693, 85339-0693. Tel: 520-550-2034.
Mission—*St. Catherine* Santa Cruz, Pinal Co.
Mission—*St. Francis* Ak-Chin, Pinal Co.
Mission—*San Lucy* Gila Bend, Maricopa Co.
Mission—*Indian Care Center* Gila River, Yuma Co.
Station—*St. Francis Xavier* Lone Butte.

MESA, MARICOPA CO.

1—ALL SAINTS (1972), Rev. Robert Caruso; Deacons Gene Messer; Ronald Wilson; William Finnegan; Walter Reiman.
Church: 1534 N. Recker Rd., 85205. Tel: 480-985-7655; Fax: 480-396-0837.

2—ST. BRIDGET (1985), Rev. W. Scott Brubaker; Deacons Joe Scaccia; Gordon Aird.
Res.: 2850 E. Lockwood St., 85213. Tel: 480-924-9138.
Church: 2213 N. Lindsay Rd., 85213. Tel: 480-924-9111; Fax: 480-924-3103.

3—CHRIST THE KING (1959), Revs. Christopher Carpenter; Daniel Vollmer; Jose David Lopez-Silvestre; Deacons Joseph Cady; Joseph Spadafino; Ronald Ruiz.
Res.: 1505 E. Dana Ave., 85204.

Church: 1551 E. Dana Ave., 85204. Tel: 480-964-1719; Fax: 480-844-4498.
School—Tel: 480-844-4480. Casimir (Casey) Kozlik, Prin. Lay Teachers 12; Students 253.
4—HOLY CROSS (1978), Revs. Dennis Riccitelli; James Vasil (GBG); Deacon James Gersitz.
Res.: 1244 S. Power Rd., 85206. Tel: 480-981-2021; Fax: 480-981-6844.
5—QUEEN OF PEACE (1934), Revs. Leonard Walker, Admin.; Lloyd P. Kramlich, S.D.S.; Deacons John Reidel; Richard Areyzaga; Santiago Rodriguez.
Res.: 141 N. Macdonald St., 85201. Tel: 480-969-9166; Fax: 480-969-8102.
School—109 N. Macdonald St., 85201. Tel: 602-969-0226. Mr. Michaels Evans, Prin. Lay Teachers 15; Students 211.
6—ST. TIMOTHY (1978), Rev. Msgr. Dale J. Fushek, V.G.; Rev. Carlos Gomez; Deacons Thomas Bolduc; Barry Smith; Richard Petersen; Kevin Bassett; Paul Hursh; Donald Crawford. In Res., Rev. Msgr. Richard W. Moyer, V.G. (Retired); Rev. Paul Orel.
Res.: 1730 W. Guadalupe, 85202. Tel: 480-775-5200; Fax: 480-820-7984.
School—2045 S. Pennington, 85202. Tel: 480-775-2650. Pamela Gomez, Prin. Lay Teachers 11; Students 157.
Convent—2754 S. Pennington, 85202. Sisters 4.
Catholic Life Productions, Inc. dba LIFE TEEN Program—Tel: 480-820-7001. Phil Baniewicz, Exec. Dir.
PEORIA, MARICOPA CO., ST. CHARLES BORROMEO (1968), Rev. Hugo Gonzalez; Deacon Ernesto Ramirez.
Mailing & Church: 8615 W. Peoria Ave., 85345-0819.
Res.: 8617 W. Peoria Ave., 85345. Tel: 623-979-3418.
PRESCOTT VALLEY, YAVAPAI CO., ST. GERMAINE (1984), Revs. John Shetler; Benjamin Maatuokuu.
Res.: 7997 E. Dana Dr., 86314. Tel: 928-772-6350; Fax: 928-772-4413.
Mission—St. Joseph S. Hwy. 69, P.O. Box 446, Mayer, Yavapai Co. 86333. Tel: 928-632-4018. Rev. Kevin Hunt Diaz, Admin.
PRESCOTT, YAVAPAI CO., SACRED HEART (1877), Revs. Richard H. DeTore, C.M.F., Admin.; Daryl Olds, C.M.F.; Albert M. Vazquez, C.M.F.; Gerald Caffrey, C.M.F.; Deacons Thomas Kayser; John Lamon; Tony Humphrey.
Res.: 150 Fleury Ave., 86301. Tel: 928-445-3141; Fax: 928-717-1074.
School—131 N. Summit Ave., 86301. Tel: 520-445-2621. Ms. Donna Walsh, Prin. Institute of the Blessed Virgin Mary Sisters 1; Lay Teachers 9; Students 123.
Convent—229 N. Summit St., 86301. Tel: 520-445-7861.
Mission—Good Shepherd of the Desert Congress Junction, Yavapai Co. Rev. Brian Bell, Admin.
Mission—St. Mary's P.O. Box 706, Yarnell, Yavapai Co. 85362. Tel: 928-427-0276. George Rojas, Parish Life Coord.; Maria Rojas, Parish Life Coord.
Mission—St. Catherine Laboure P.O. Box 152, Chino Valley, Yavapai Co. 86323. Tel: 928-636-4071. Rev. H. Fred LeClaire, C.M.F. (SAT), Admin.
SCOTTSDALE, MARICOPA CO.
1—ST. BERNADETTE (1995), Rev. Richard Felt; Deacons John Meyer; Roy Rooker. In Res., Rev. Thomas A. Walsh (Retired).
Office—16245 N. 60th St., 85254. Tel: 480-905-0221; Fax: 480-905-0249.
2—ST. BERNARD OF CLAIRVAUX (1994), Rev. Robert Voss; Deacons Anthony Dudzic; Louis Cornille; Michael Carlomagno; Willard Capistrant.
Res.: 10755 N. 124th St., 85259. Tel: 480-661-9843; Fax: 480-614-8092.
3—BLESSED SACRAMENT (1974), Revs. Patrick Robinson; Gerald Thaar, O.S.C.; Deacons Bernard Rekiere; Harry Hude; Clemens Czapinski; Jack Ehrlich.
Res.: 11300 N. 64th St., 85254. Tel: 480-948-8370; Fax: 480-951-3844.
4—ST. DANIEL THE PROPHET (1961), Revs. Joseph McGaffin; Cyprian Okoronkwo; Raul Lopez Marzetti; Deacons Martin Dippre; Jesse Sanchez. In Res., Rev. Patrick Smith.
Res.: 1030 N. Hayden Rd., 85257. Tel: 480-945-8437; Fax: 480-945-4335.
School—Tel: 480-949-8034. Deacon Bruce Bennett, Ed.D., Prin. Clergy 1; Lay Teachers 10; Students 187.
Convent—7830 E. Roosevelt, 85257. Tel: 480-423-5240.
Korean Catholic Community— 85257. Rev. Columbano Chin-SuSin.
5—ST. MARIA GORETTI (1967), Rev. Gregory J. Schlarb; Deacons Herve Lemire; Jose Orozco.
Res.: 8344 E. Edward Ave., 85250.
Church: 6261 N. Granite Reef Rd., 85250. Tel: 480-948-8380; Fax: 480-948-8815.
6—OUR LADY OF PERPETUAL HELP (1949), Revs. Thomas Hever; John Bernbrock, S.J.; Peter Rossa; Deacons Irving Fleming; James Hoyt; Thomas Phelan.
Res.: 7655 E. Main St., 85251. Tel: 480-947-4331; Fax: 480-874-3798.
School—3801 N. Miller Rd., 85251. Tel: 480-874-3720. Sr. Marian Grace Brandt, S.C., Prin. Sisters of Charity 2; Lay Teachers 24; Students 565.
Convent—7634 E. Second St., 85251. Tel: 480-945-3867.
7—ST. PATRICK (1980), Rev. Eric Tellez; Deacon Fred Giesner. In Res., Rev. Vernon Meyer.
Office—10815 N. 84th St., 85260. Tel: 480-998-3843; Fax: 480-998-5218.
SEDONA, YAVAPAI CO., ST. JOHN VIANNEY (1965), Rev. J.C. Ortiz; Deacon Ronald Martinez.
Res.: 180 Soldiers Pass Rd., P.O. Box 3909, W. Sedona, 86340. Tel: 928-282-7545; Fax: 928-282-1798. Dr. Charles E. Reaume, Dir. Admin.
Chapel—Holy Cross 780 Chapel Rd., P.O. Box 1043, 86339. Tel: 928-282-4069; Fax: 928-282-3701.
SELIGMAN, YAVAPAI CO., ST. FRANCIS (1940), Unassigned.
Res.: P.O. Box 308, 86337. Tel: 928-422-3354.
Church: 104 Schoney, 86337.
Mission—St. Anne 47047 7th St., Ashfork, Yavapai Co. 86320.
SUN CITY WEST, MARICOPA CO., OUR LADY OF LOURDES (1979), Revs. Michael Minogue; Richard Ryan; Deacons Thomas Henn; George Koch; Eugene Phillips; Jerome Reicks.
Res.: 19002 N. 128th Ave., 85375. Tel: 623-546-2767; Fax: 623-214-1246.
SUN CITY, MARICOPA CO.
1—CHURCH OF ST. JOACHIM & ST. ANNE (1961), Rev. Mark Harrington, Admin.; Deacon William Phares.
Mailing Address: P.O. Box 748, 85372.
Res.: 11625 111th Ave., 85351-3746. Tel: 623-972-1179; Fax: 623-972-1170.
2—ST. CLEMENT OF ROME (1970), Revs. Earl D'Eon; Blase Meyer; Matthias Feit (Retired); Deacon Stanley Giza.
Res.: 15800 Del Webb Blvd., 85351. Tel: 623-974-5867; Fax: 623-974-0562.
3—ST. ELIZABETH SETON (1976), Revs. Franklin Bartel; Raymond Greco; William Harnischfeger; Deacon Forrest Briesch.
Res.: 9728 Palmeras Ln., 85373. Tel: 623-972-2129; Fax: 623-974-0654.
SUN LAKES, MARICOPA CO., ST. STEVEN (1988), Rev. Emmett J. FitzPatrick.
Mailing Address: 24827 S. Dobson Rd., 85248. Tel: 480-895-9266.
Res.: 10324 E. Michigan Ave., 85248. Tel: 480-895-9304.
SURPRISE, MARICOPA CO., ST. CLARE OF ASSISI, Rev. Hans Ruygt, Admin.; Deacons Stephen Martin; James Martin.
Mailing Address: 17111 W. Bell Rd., 85374. Tel: 623-546-3444.
TEMPE, MARICOPA CO.
1—HOLY SPIRIT (1973), Revs. John Hanley; Edward J. Kaminski, C.S.C.; Deacons Stephen Beard; Gary Johnson.
Office—1800 E. Libra Dr., 85283. Tel: 480-838-7474; Fax: 480-838-6720.
Rectory—1871 E. Libra Dr., 85283.
Church: 1800 E. Libra Dr., 85283.
2—ST. MARGARET (1972), Deacons Frank G. Galarza, Parish Life Coord.; Manuel Olivas.
Res.: 2435 E. McArthur Dr., 85281. Tel: 480-967-0379; Fax: 480-967-3825.
Mission—St. Francis Scottsdale. P. O. Box 3334, Salt River Indian, Maricopa Co. 85271. Tel: 520-562-3716. Deacon Sidney Martin.
Mission—St. Paschal Baylon Sacaton. P.O. Box 545, Lehi, Maricopa Co. 85247.
3—OUR LADY OF MT. CARMEL (1932), Revs. John Bonavitacola, Admin.; John R. Coleman; Deacons James Salamone; Charles Voss; James Brett.
Res.: 2121 S. Rural Rd., 85282. Tel: 480-967-8791; Fax: 480-967-4919.
School—2117 S. Rural Rd., 85282. Tel: 480-967-5567. Dr. Vincent Sheridan, Prin. Lay Teachers 24; Students 492.
Tongan Catholic Community— 85282. Rev. Timothy R. Davern, J.C.L., Liaison.
4—RESURRECTION (1970), Revs. Fred Adamson; Timothy R. Davern, J.C.L.; Deacons Dwight Morton; Wayne Morten. In Res., Rev. Joseph G. Krijnen (Retired).
Res.: 3201 S. Evergreen Rd., 85282. Tel: 480-838-0207; Fax: 480-756-1501.
TOLLESON, MARICOPA CO., BLESSED SACRAMENT (1953), Rev. Daniel McBride; Deacon Antonio M. Chavez Sr.
Res.: 512 N. 93rd Ave., 85353. Tel: 623-936-7107; Fax: 623-936-9536.
WICKENBURG, MARICOPA CO., ST. ANTHONY OF PADUA (1941), Rev. Brian Bell.
Res.: 232 N. Tegner St., 85390. Tel: 928-684-2096; Fax: 928-684-3539.
Mission—Our Lady of Guadalupe 50627 Eagle Eye Rd., P.O. Box 294, Aguila, Maricopa Co. 85320.
WILLIAMS, COCONINO CO., ST. JOSEPH'S (1928), Deacon James Buchanan, Parish Life Coord.
Res.: 900 W. Grant, 86046. Tel: 928-635-2430; Fax: 928-635-0177.

Chaplains of Public Institutions

PHOENIX. *Arizona State Hospital*, 2500 E. Van Buren St., 85008. Tel: 602-220-6190. Sr. Patricia Pieper, S.N.D.deN., Chap., Charles R. Johnson, Chap.
Good Samaritan Medical Center, 1111 E. McDowell Rd., 85006. Tel: 602-239-4324. Vacant.
St. Joseph's Hospital, P.O. Box 2071, 85001. Tel: 602-406-3690. Rev. Milton N. Adamson, C.S.C., Chap., Sr. Margaret McBride, Dir. Chap. Svcs., Michaelle Hennessey, Dir. Chap. Svcs.
St. Luke's Medical Center, 1800 E. Van Buren St., 85006. Tel: 602-251-8480. Don Mitchum, Chap. Coord.
Maricopa Medical Center, 2601 E. Roosevelt St., 85008. Tel: 602-267-5011. Rev. Fred Peters, S.D.S., Chap.
Phoenix Indian Medical Center, 4212 N. 16th St., 850. Tel: 602-263-1017. Vacant (For Sacramental Records Contact St. Francis Xavier at 602-279-9547)
United States Veterans Affairs Medical Center, 650 E. Indian School Rd., 85012. Tel: 602-222-6422.
CHANDLER. *Chandler Regional Hospital*, 475 S. Dobson Rd., 85224. Tel: 480-821-7639. Sr. Joan Pfeiffer, S.N.D.deN., Chap.
LUKE AIR FORCE BASE. *Luke Catholic Community*, 58 FW/HC, 13968 Shooting Star St., 85309-1932. Tel: 623-856-6211; Fax: 623-856-6968. Rev. John Regan, Auxiliary Chap., Deacon James Pfleger.
PRESCOTT. *United States Veterans Hospital (Prescott)*, Veterans Administration Medical Center, 86313. Tel: 520-776-6029. Rev. Gerald Caffrey, C.M.F., Chap.
SCOTTSDALE. *Scottsdale Memorial Hospital*, 7400 E. Osborn Rd., 85251. Tel: 480-481-4000; 602-945-8437. Rev. Patrick Smith, Chap.

Special Assignment:
Rev. Msgrs.—
Fushek, Dale J., V.G., 1730 W. Guadalupe Rd., Mesa, 85202. Tel: 480-775-5200
McMahon, John J., Dir. Mount Claret Center, 4633 N. 54th St., 85018. Tel: 602-840-5066
Moyer, Richard W., V.G., Vicar Admin. Svcs. & Moderator of the Curia (Retired), 400 E. Monroe, 85004. Tel: 602-257-0030
Revs.—
Acquaro, Philip A., C.S.B., Diocesan Ctr., Tribunal Office, 400 E. Monroe, 85004. Tel: 602-257-0030
Conlon, Timothy, O.S.C., Vicar, Hispanic Ministry, Diocesan Center, 400 E. Monroe, 85004. Tel: 602-257-0030
Davern, Timothy R., J.C.L., Judicial Vicar, Tribunal Office, 400 E. Monroe, 85004. Tel: 602-257-0030
Diskin, Michael L., Asst. Chancellor & Ecumenical Officer, Diocesan Center, 400 E. Monroe. Tel: 602-257-0030
Goulet, Wayne F., 8540 N. Central Ave., #13, 85020.
Kline, Donald, Vocation Dir., 400 E. Monroe St., 85004. Tel: 602-257-0030
Makacinas, Stanley, O.Carm., Exec. Dir. Kino Institute, 1224 E. Northern Ave., 85020. Tel: 602-997-7397
Orel, Paul, Diocesan Center Tribunal Office, 400 E. Monroe.
Parker, Charles, Tribunal Office, 400 E. Monroe St., 85004. Tel: 602-257-0030
Ryle, Edward J., Exec. Dir., Arizona Catholic Conference, 400 E. Monroe St., 85004. Tel: 602-257-0030
Sharp, David L., C.S.B., Campus Min., 6000 W. Olive Ave., Glendale, 85302. Tel: 623-435-3525 Glendale Community College

On Leave:
Revs.—
Draves-Arpaia, Cornelius
Hall, John
Healy, William P.
Meyer, Vernon
Young, Eugene

Retired:
Rev. Msgrs.—
Maguire, Eugene, 4701 N. 68th St., #147, 85251.
Malone, Alan, Eyrecourt, Ballinasloe, Galway, Co. Ireland.
McKay, William E., 6457 E. Dodge St., Mesa, 85205.
Moyer, Richard W., V.G., St. Timothy Catholic Community, 1730 W. Guadalupe Rd., Mesa, 85202-7424.
Revs.—

Bain, J.F. Michael, 380 Celestial Dr., Clarkdale, 86234-3368.
Baumann, Lawrence L., 5516 Boulder Hwy., #2F, P.O. Box 373, Las Vegas, NV 89122.
Bormann, Charles P., 5029 E. Smokehouse Tr., Cave Creek, 85331.
Boulanger, Andre, 2239 E. Cheery Lynn, 85016.
Boyle, Thomas, 325 W. Holly St., 85003.
Brogan, Leo, 5895 Friars Rd. Unit 5316, San Diego, CA 92110.
Colton, Bernard, 122A Clanabogan Rd., Omagh, Co. Tyrone BT 7815 N Northern Ireland.
Cullinan, John F., St. Joan of Arc, 3801 E. Greenway Rd., 85032-4698.
Faustina, John M., P.O. Box 135, Island Pond, VT 05846-0135.
Feit, Matthias, 15800 Del Webb Blvd., Sun City, 85351-1698.
Gauthier, John C., Diocese of Phoenix, 400 E. Monroe St., 85004.
Gillespie, Joseph, 13605 N. Del Webb Blvd., Sun City, 85351.
Glass, Gerald J., 8141 N. 16th St., #7, 85020.
Groves, Edmund, St. Paul's Convent, Bushmount, Clonakilty, Co. Cork Ireland.
Hurley, Michael F., P.O. Box 366, Clarkdale, 86324-0366.
Kelly, Martin C., Riverview Killonan, Ballysimon, Co, Limerick Ireland.
Kotnis, Gregory M., 15735 W. Arrowhead Dr., Suprise, 85374.
Krijnen, Joseph G., Resurrection Parish, 3201 S. Evergreen Rd., Tempe, 85282.
Mitchell, William J., 1675 Leisure World, Mesa, 85206.
Morales, Raul, P.O. Box 6412, Mesa, 85216-6412.
O'Dea, Thomas, 1822 S. 39th St., Unit 116, Mesa, 85206.
O'Reilly, Francis J., 2345 W. Orangewood Ave., 85021.
Pirrung, George, P.O. Box 1144, Cottonwood, 86326.
Portmann, Frederick, 1825 W. Emelita Ave., Mesa, 85202.
Sigman, Louis A., 1272 E. La Costa Pl., Chandler, 85226.
Simlik, Frank P., 10713 W. El Dorado Dr., Sun City, 85351.
Sotelo, Antonio, 1027 N. 27th Ln., 85009.
Vogt, John, 9450 N. 95th St., Unit 109, 85258.
Wajda, Edward J., 214 S. Laveen Ave., Chandler, 85226.
Waldron, William, 10417 Saratoga Cir., Sun City, 85351-2210.
Walsh, Thomas A., St. Bernadette Parish, 16245 N. 60th St., 85254. Tel: 602-905-0221
Wasielewski, Henry R., P.O. Box 939, Tempe, 85280-0939.
Zappitelli, Francis, P.O. Box 17906, Fountain Hills, 85269.

Permanent Deacons:
Aird, Gordon, St. Bridget, Mesa
Anderson, Roy, (Retired)
Anselmo, Clement, Native American Ministry
Anselmo, Thomas A., (Retired)
Areyzaga, Richard, Queen of Peace, Mesa
Arnold, James, San Francisco de Asis, Flagstaff
Arnold, Maurice, (Retired)
August, Joe, (Retired)
Babbits, Oliver, (Retired)
Barelli, John, Sky Harbor Chaplaincy, Phoenix
Barraza, David, St. Anne, Gilbert
Bassett, Kevin, St. Timothy, Mesa
Battista, James, (Retired)
Beard, Stephen, Holy Spirit, Tempe
Beltran, Anthony N., St. Matthew's, Phoenix
Bennett, Bruce, St. Mary, Chandler
Benware, John, St. Thomas the Apostle, Chandler
Berger, John, St. Anne, Gilbert
Bernasconi, Santino R., Our Lady of Guadalupe, Guadalupe
Bidleman, William, St. Jerome, Phoenix
Bills, Tom, St.Thomas the Apostle, Phoenix
Bolduc, Thomas, St. Timothy, Mesa
Bolton, Edward L., (Retired)
Boswell, Keith, St. Anne, Gilbert
Bowslaugh, Alan P.
Brett, James, Our Lady of Mt. Carmel, Tempe
Briesch, Forrest, St. Elizabeth Seton, Sun City
Buchanan, James, St. Joseph, Williams
Burgin, Edward, (Unassigned)
Burke, Edward, (Unassigned)
Cady, Joseph, Christ the King, Mesa
Cameron, George, St. Henry, Buckeye
Campas, Rudolph, St. Helen, Glendale
Campbell, Colin, St. Theresa, Phoenix
Capistrant, Willard, St. Bernard of Clairvaux, Scottsdale
Carey, Robert, St. Anne, Gilbert
Carlomagno, Micheal, St. Bernard of Clairvaux, Scottsdale
Carr, Michael, St. Andrew the Apostle, Chandler
Cascio, James, St. John Vianney, Avondale
Chavez, Antonio, Blessed Sacrament, Tolleson
Clapham, Buddy, St. Andrew the Apostle, Chandler
Clower, William, St. Francis Xavier, Phoenix
Coe, Tom, Our Lady of the Lake, Lake Havasu City
Cornille, Louis, St. Bernard of Clairvaux, Scottsdale
Crawford, Don, St. Timothy, Mesa
Csuy, Paul E., St. Elizabeth Seton, Sun City
Cummings Jack, (Retired)
Cuprak, Richard, St. Benedict, Chandler
Curran, Richard, Ss. Simon & Jude Cathedral, Phoenix
Czapinski, Clemens, Blessed Sacrament, Scottsdale
Davey, Bob, (Retired)
Davis, Keith, St. Thomas More, Glendale
Davis, William, Sacred Heart, Prescott
DeFelippis, Thomas, Our Lady of the Lake, Lake Havasu City
Del Monaco, William, St. Mary, Kingman
Dennis, Irving, (Retired)
Devine, Frank, St. James, Glendale
Dippre, Martin, St. Daniel the Prophet, Scottsdale
Drapeau, Roy, St. Thomas More, Glendale
Dudzic, Anthony, St. Bernard of Clairvaux, Scottsdale
Duran, Onofre, Immaculate Conception, Cottonwood
Eckert, Dick, St. Margaret Mary, Bullhead City
Ehrlich, Jacob, Blessed Sacrament, Scottsdale
England Robert, St. Agnes, Phoenix
Fejes, Peter, St. Edward, Phoenix
Ferski, Andy, (Retired)
Finnegan, William, All Saints, Mesa
Fischer, Donald, St. Joan of Arc, Phoenix
Fleming, Irving, Our Lady of Perpetual Help Church, Scottsdale
Flynn, Patrick F., Corpus Christi, Phoenix
Fogle, James, Good Shepherd Mission, New River
Galarza, Frank, St. Margaret, Tempe
Garcia, Ernie, St. Andrew the Apostle, Chandler
Garza, Jose, Santa Teresita, El Mirage
Gaudio, Alexander L., Corpus Christi Phoenix
Gergosian, Edward, (Retired)
Gersitz, James, Holy Cross, Mesa
Giesner, Fred, St.Patrick, Scottsdale
Giza, Stanley, St. Clement of Rome, Sun City
Gonzales, Albert, St. Catherine of Siena, Phoenix
Gonzalez, Ronald, FCI Chapel
Goubeaux, Guy, St. Joan of Arc, Phoenix
Gouveia, Americo, (Retired)
Gregory, Tom, (Retired)
Guldan, Ranald, (Retired)
Guzman, Angel, St. Agnes, Phoenix
Guzman, Juan, St. Joan of Arc, Phoenix
Heeter, Charles, Our Lady of Perpetual Help, Glendale
Henn, Thomas, Our Lady of Lourdes, Sun City West
Hernandez, Jose, (Retired)
Hickcox, Edward M., San Francisco de Asis, Flagstaff
Hintze, Craig, St. Mary, Chandler
Hola, Sione, St. Theresa, Phoenix
Hoyt, James, Our Lady of Perpetual Help, Scottsdale
Hude, Harry, Blessed Sacrament, Scottsdale
Humphrey, Charles A., Sacred Heart, Prescott
Hurley, Dan A., (Retired)
Hurrish, Dutch, (Retired)
Hursh, Paul, St. Timothy, Mesa
Jenkins, William, St. Vincent de Paul, Phoenix
Jimenez, Ramon H., (Retired)
Johnson, Gary, Holy Spirit, Tempe
Kaminsky, David, St. Francis Cabrini, Camp Verde
Kayser, Thomas E., Sacred Heart, Prescott
Kelly, Charles, St. Joseph, Phoenix
Kijewski, Richard, St. James, Glendale
Kloft, Lee, St. Gregory Parish, Phoenix
Koch, George, Our Lady of Lourdes, Sun City West
Kuban, Donald, St. Thomas the Apostle, Phoenix
Kulinowski, Kenneth, St. Anne, Gilbert
Lamon, John, Sacred Heart Parish, Prescott
Lazok, George, (Retired)
LeClair, Douglas, St. Thomas Byzantine, Gilbert
Lemire, Herve, St. Maria Goretti, Scottsdale
Leone, Robert, (Retired)
Lessard, Joseph M., (Retired)
Lewis, Brian, St. Mary, Kingman
LoCascio, Phil, St. Joan of Arc, Phoenix
Lopez, Ed, St. Agnes, Phoenix
Lopez, Tony, Our Lady of Perpetual Help, Glendale
Lukaszewski, Don, (Unassigned)
Manalio, Pasquale, Most Holy Trinity, Phoenix
Manthie, Robert, St. Raphael, Glendale
Marth, Jim, St. Clare of Assisi Surprise
Martin, Sidney, St. Peter Indian Mission, Bapchule
Martin, Stephen J., St. Clare of Assisi, Surprise
Martinez, Ronald, St. John Vianney, Sedona
Meidl, Richard, St. Raphael, Glendale
Meli, John, (Retired)
Mesa, Pedro, St. Philip the Deacon, Phoenix
Messer, Gene, All Saints, Mesa
Meyer, John A., Diocesan Dir. of Catechetical Ministry, St. Bernadette, Scottsdale
Micek, Theodore, (Unassigned)
Mickens, James, St. Jerome, Phoenix
Miller, John, (Retired)
Molina, Eddie, Our Lady of Perpetual Help, Glendale
Monday, Thomas, St. Andrew the Apostle, Chandler
Morton, Dwight, Resurrection, Tempe
Murphy, Peter, Dir., Prison Ministry
Myers, Robert P., Our Lady of Perpetual Help, Glendale
Neely, Theodore, (Retired)
O'Grady, Lowell, St. Anthony, Phoenix
O'Toole, Gerald, St. Anne Parish, Gilbert
Olivarez, Jose D., St. Martin de Porres, Phoenix
Olivas, Manuel, St. Margaret Tempe
Orozco, Jose, St. Maria Goretti, Scottsdale
Pardini, Louis, Ph.D., (Retired)
Pelton, Ron, (Retired)
Petersen, Richard, St. Timothy, Mesa
Peterson, Daniel L., Dir., Diaconate; Good Shepherd Mission, New River
Pfleger, James, Luke Air Force Base, Litchfield
Phelan, Mike, St. Jerome, Phoenix
Phelan, Thomas J., Our Lady of Perpetual Help, Scottsdale
Phillips, Eugene, Our Lady of Lourdes, Sun City West
Pintar, Thomas, St. Anne, Gilbert
Rade, Douglas, (Retired)
Ramirez, Ernesto, St. Charles Borromeo, Peoria
Raymond, Charles J., (Retired)
Raymond, Robert, (Retired)
Regan, W. Richard, (Retired)
Reicks, Jerome, Our Lady of Lourdes, Sun City West
Reiman, Walter, All Saints, Mesa
Rein, Richard, St. Phillip the Deacon Mission, Phoenix
Rekiere, Bernard, Blessed Sacrament, Scottsdale
Riedel, John, Queen of Peace, Mesa
Rodriguez, Jose, St. Mary, Kingman
Rodriguez, Santiago, Queen of Peace, Mesa
Roger, Ray, (Unassigned)
Rooker, Roy, St. Bernadette, Scottsdale
Root, Joseph, (Retired)
Roy, Alex, Native American Ministry
Ruiz, Jesus, St. Henry, Buckeye
Ruiz, Ron, Christ the King, Mesa
Rutledge, Clark, St. Francis Xavier, Phoenix
Salamone, James, Our Lady of Mount Carmel, Tempe
Salazar, Lorenzo, Most Holy Trinity, Phoenix
Sanchez, Jesse, St. Daniel the Prophet, Scottsdale
Santa, Reed, (Retired)
Scaccia, Joseph, St. Bridget, Mesa
Scheller, Albert, St. William, Cashion
Schwan, Harry, St. Joseph, Phoenix
Sejba, Jim, St. Philip Benizi Mission, Black Canyon City
Shaw, Chuck, St. Thomas Aquinas, Litchfield Park
Shea, William, All Saints Newman Center, Tempe
Shinske, Joseph, St. Helen's, Glendale
Simeone, Philip, Corpus Christi, Phoenix
Smith, Barry, St. Timothy, Mesa
Spadafino, Joseph, Christ the King, Mesa
Springer, James, St. Joan of Arc, Phoenix
Starrs, William, (Retired)
Stickney, Joseph, St. Jerome, Phoenix
Stokes, Leslie, St. Philip Benizi, Black Canyon City
Swisher, Thomas, St. John the Baptist, Laveen; Prison Ministry
Terrazas, Carlos, St. Catherine of Siena, Phoenix
Torres, Vincent, Our Lady of Perpetual Help, Glendale
Treichel, Robert, (Retired)
Valle, Matias, Ss. Simon & Jude, Phoenix
Valverde, W. George, (Retired)
Van Dyke, Charles, St. Francis Xavier, Phoenix
Vasquez, Manuel, St. Catherine of Siena, Phoenix
Vera, Emidio B., (Retired)
Vivio, William, St. Paul, Phoenix
Voss, Charles, Our Lady of Mount Carmel, Tempe
West, Tony, SS. Simon & Jude Cathedral, Phoenix
Whelan, Laurence, San Francisco de Asis, Flagstaff
White, Jim, (Retired)
Wilson, Ronald, All Saints, Mesa
Wisely, Phil, St. Margaret Mary, Bullhead City
Wood, Stewart, (Retired)
Yanez, Richard, Immaculate Heart of Mary, Phoenix

INSTITUTIONS LOCATED IN THE DIOCESE

[A] HIGH SCHOOLS, DIOCESAN

PHOENIX. *Bourgade Catholic High School*, 4602 N. 31st Ave., 85017. Tel: 602-973-4000; Fax: 602-973-5854. Email: srmary@diocesephoenix.org. Web: www.bourgade.org. Sisters Mary McGreevy, S.S.N.D., Prin.; Kathleen Janiak, R.S.M., Dir. Students; Lori Pieper, Dir. Studies. Sisters 3; Brothers 1; Lay Teachers 30; Students 403.

St. Mary's High School, 2525 N. Third St., 85004. Tel: 602-254-6371; Fax: 602-253-0337. Email: st_mary_hs_p@diocesephoenix.org. Web: www.smks.org. Dr. Monica Jones, Prin.; Mrs. Suzanne Fessler, Asst. Prin.; Sr. Linda Campbell, O.S.B., Academic Advisors. Brothers 2; Sisters 1; Lay Teachers 66; Students 783.

Xavier College Preparatory, 4710 N. Fifth St., 85012. Tel: 602-277-3772; Fax: 602-279-1346. Email: sjfphx@xcp.org. Web: www.xcp.org. Sisters M. Joan Fitzgerald, B.V.M., Prin.; Lynn Winsor, B.V.M., Vice Prin. Sisters 9; Lay Teachers 78; Students 1,197.

CHANDLER. *Seton Catholic High School*, 1150 N. Dobson Rd., 85224. Tel: 480-963-1900; Fax: 480-963-1974. Email: setoncatholic@diocesephoenix.org. Web: www.setoncatholic.org. Dr. Richard Riley, Prin.; Mrs. Regina Wainwright, Asst. Prin.; Mrs. Shelley Connor, Devel. Dir. Sisters of Charity of Seton Hill 1; Lay Teachers 42; Students 607.

SCOTTSDALE. *Notre Dame Preparatory High School*, 9701 E. Bell Rd., 85260. Tel: 480-634-8200; Fax: 480-634-8299. David Gonsalves, Prin.; Preston Colao, Asst. Prin.; Dr. David Harris, Asst. Prin. Sisters 1; Brothers 1; Lay Teachers 37; Students 453.

[B] HIGH SCHOOLS, PRIVATE

PHOENIX. *Brophy College Preparatory*, 4701 N. Central Ave., 85012. Tel: 602-264-5291; Fax: 602-266-3642. Web: www.brophyprep.org. Rev. Edward Reese, S.J., Pres.; Mr. Edwin J. Hearn, Prin.; Mr. William Kopas, Asst. Prin.; Mrs. Dorothy Dunnion, Asst. Prin.; Mr. A. Joseph Helm Jr., Treas.; James Gmelich, Dean of Students; Revs. E. Louis Bishop, S.J.; Kevin Dilworth, S.J.; James E. Flynn, S.J.; Anton J. Renna, S.J.; John R. Becker, S.J.; Michael Gilson, S.J.; Jesus Palomino, Scholastics; Minh Dang, Scholastics. Jesuit Fathers, Boys day school. Priests 6; Scholastics 2; Lay Teachers 79; Students 1,210.

[C] ELEMENTARY SCHOOLS, PAROCHIAL

PHOENIX. *St. John Bosco Interparish School Community*, Formerly St. John Bosco Catholic School Community, 16035 S. 48th St., 85048. Tel: 480-219-4848; Fax: 480-219-5767. Email: selliott@sjbosco.org. Web: www.sjbosco.org. Mr. Sherman Elliott, Prin. Intraparish school for Corpus Christi, Phoenix; Holy Spirit, Tempe; St. Andrew, Chandler and St. Benedict, Chandler. Lay Teachers 22; Students 465.

SCOTTSDALE. *Pope John XXIII Catholic School Community*, 16235 N. 60th St., 85254. Tel: 480-905-0939; Fax: 480-905-0955. Email: popejohnXXIII@diocesephoenix.org. Rev. Patrick Robinson, Liaison Pastor; Mr. William C. Langley, Prin. Intraparish School for St. Bernadette, Scottsdale; Blessed Sacrament, Scottsdale; St. Joan of Arc, Phoenix and Our Lady of Joy, Carefree. Sisters 1; Lay Teachers 25; Students 590.

[D] GENERAL HOSPITALS

PHOENIX. *St. Joseph's Hospital and Medical Center*, 350 W. Thomas Rd., 85001. Tel: 602-285-3000; Fax: 602-406-6149. Web: www.ichosestjoes.com. Linda Hunt, Pres. dba of Catholic Healthcare West; Sponsored by Burlingame Regional Community of the Sisters of Mercy Sisters 4; Bed Capacity 519; Patients Assisted Annually 262,596; Total Staff 3,721.

[E] HOMES FOR THE AGED & HANDICAPPED

PHOENIX. *Avondale Senior Village*, 2702 N. 44th St., Ste. 102-A, 85008. Tel: 602-952-9525; Fax: 602-952-9539. Web: www.mercyhousing.org.

Camelot Casitas, 2702 N. 44th St., Ste. 102-A, 85008. Tel: 602-952-9525; Fax: 602-952-9539. Web: www.mercyhousing.org.

Casa De Merced, 2702 N. 44th St., Ste. 102-A, 85008. Tel: 602-952-9525; Fax: 602-952-9539. Web: www.mercyhousing.org.

El Mirage Senior Village, c/o Wishing Well II, Clubhouse Office, 5530 N. 17th Ave., 85015. Tel: 602-242-1020; Fax: 602-249-7550. Web: www.mercyhousing.org. Sherry Wheelock, Contact Person.

Guadalupe Senior Village, 2702 N. 44th St., Ste. 102-A, 85008. Tel: 602-952-9525; Fax: 602-952-9539. Web: www.mercyhousing.org.

Mesa Senior Meadows, 2702 N. 44th St., Ste.102-A, 85008. Tel: 602-952-9525; Fax: 602-952-9539. Web: www.mercyhousing.org.

Peoria Place, 2702 N. 44th St., Ste. 102-A, 85008. Tel: 602-952-9525; Fax: 602-952-9539. Web: www.mercyhousing.org.

Plazas de Merced, 2702 N. 44th St., Ste. 102-A, 85008. Tel: 602-952-9525; Fax: 602-952-9539. Web: www.mercyhousing.org.

Senior Village, 3541 W. Vogel, 85051. Tel: 602-843-3008.

Sweetwater Gardens Apartments (Handicapped) , 2035 E. Sweetwater, 85022. Tel: 602-867-4549.

Vista Alegre, 2702 N. 44th St., Ste. 102-A, 85008. Tel: 602-952-9525; Fax: 602-952-9539. Web: www.mercyhousing.org.

AVONDALE. *Vianney Villas Apartments* (Retirement)-HUD Rent Subsidized , 750 S. Fourth St., 85323. Tel: 623-932-2036.

KINGMAN. *Kingman Heights Apartments* (Retirement)-HUD Rent Subsidized , 1020 Detroit Ave., 86401. Tel: 928-753-2425; Fax: 928-753-2425.

LAKE HAVASU CITY. *Becket House Apartments* (Retirement) , 865 Cashmere Dr., 86403. Tel: 928-855-7178.

WICKENBURG. *Padua Hills Apartments* (Retirement)-HUD Rent Subsidized , 460 S. West Rd., 85390. Tel: 928-684-7034.

WILLIAMS. *St. Agnes Apartments* (Retirement) , 200 S. Ninth, 86046. Tel: 928-635-2913.

[F] CONVENTS AND RESIDENCES OF SISTERS

PHOENIX. *Institute of Blessed Virgin Mary (I.B.V.M.)* (Regional House) , 2521 W. Maryland Ave., 85017. Tel: 602-433-0658; Fax: 602-864-8620. Email: srraphael@simonjude.org. Sr. Raphael Quinn, Regl. Supr. Sisters 4.

Missionaries of Charity, 1414 S. 17th Ave., 85007. Tel: 602-258-5504. Sr. M. Christena, M.C., Regl. Supr. Sisters 4.

Our Lady of Guadalupe Monastery Sisters of St. Benedict , 8502 W. Pinchot, 85037. Tel: 623-848-9608; Fax: 623-846-4029. Email: bensrs@aol.com. Sr. Linda Campbell, O.S.B., Prioress. Sisters 2; Affiliate 1.

Retreat/Conference Center Overnight Capacity 25; Daylong Capacity 70.

Sisters of Charity of the Blessed Virgin Mary (Xavier Convent) , 4712 N. Third St., 85012. Tel: 602-264-0445. Sr. Joan Nuckols, B.V.M., Community Representative. Sisters 7.

Sisters of Divine Savior, 323 E. Elm St., 85012-1703. Tel: 602-274-0228. Email: sdselmst@fastq.com. Web: www.sds.sisters.org. Sr. Georgene Faust, S.D.S., Cluster Coord. for Region. Sisters 8.

Union of Sisters of the Presentation of the Blessed Virgin Mary (Provincial House) , 729 W. Wilshire Dr., 85007. Tel: 602-271-9687; 602-258-9476; Fax: 602-253-9166. Email: unionpressprov@aol.com. Sr. Joan O'Sullivan, P.B.V.M., Prov. Sisters 2.

MESA. *Sisters of Notre Dame de Namur* (Casa Guadalupe) , 548 W. Third St., 85201. Tel: 480-964-3685; Fax: 480-655-9975. Email: mesasnd@aol.com. Sisters 2.

TEMPE. *Sisters of Charity* (Seton House) , 1014 S. George Dr., 85281. Tel: 480-967-5538. Email: setonwest@msn.com. Sisters 3.

[G] MONASTERIES AND RESIDENCES OF PRIESTS AND BROTHERS

PHOENIX. *Carmelite Community*, 1717 W. Flower, 85015. Tel: 602-274-0442; Fax: 602-274-0442 (Call First). Email: sboyle@juno.com. Revs. Tiernan O'Callaghan, O.Carm. (Retired); Silvan Boyle, O.Carm. (Retired); John R. Larkin, O.Carm., Prior, (Retired). Priests 3.

Crosier Community of Phoenix (Canons Regular of the Order of the Holy Cross), 2617 E. Campbell Ave., 85016. Tel: 602-224-0434; Fax: 602-224-0722. Email: yimyansil@qwest.net. Revs. Joseph P. Cain, O.S.C.; Joseph J. Bruemmer, O.S.C.; Richard N. Ohlemacher, O.S.C.; Louis R. Mraz, O.S.C.; Robert J. Bliven, O.S.C.; Joseph A. Fichtner, O.S.C.; Neil Emon, O.S.C., Prior; Robert V. Zylla, O.S.C.; John Vincent, O.S.C.; Timothy Conlon, O.S.C.; Gerald Thoar, O.S.C.; Bros. James Scher, O.S.C., Admin.; Gabriel Guerrero, O.S.C. Priests 11; Brothers 2.

Holy Cross Congregation/Casa Santa Cruz, 7126 N. Seventh Ave., 85021. Tel: 602-944-6000; Fax: 602-944-1221. Revs. Milton N. Adamson, C.S.C.; Joseph F. O'Donnell, C.S.C.; John P. Keefe, C.S.C., Supr.; James T. Burtchaell, C.S.C.; Howard Kuhns, C.S.C.; John P. Schuneman, C.S.C.; Ambrose J. Wheeler, C.S.C.; Robert L. Kramer, C.S.C.; James W. Thornton, C.S.C.; Thomas K. Zurcher, C.S.C.; Bro. Lewis T. Brazil, C.S.C. Priests 10; Brothers 1.

TEMPE. *Dominicans (Dominican Community-Jordan House)*, 1042 E. Campus, 85282. Tel: 480-829-1804. Revs. Nathan G. Castle, O.P., Supr.; Frederick Lucci, O.P.; Miguel Rolland, O.P. Priests 3.

[H] RETREAT HOUSES

PHOENIX. *Mt. Claret Center*, 4633 N. 54th St., 85018. Tel: 602-840-5066; Fax: 602-840-5732. Rev. Msgr. John J. McMahon, Dir.; Rev. Eugene Maguire, Dir.; Sr. Regina Marie Boslet, S.C., Assoc. Dir.; Josephine Swiger, Assoc. Dir. Priests 2.

Cursillo Movement: Rev. Msgr. John J. McMahon, Spiritual Dir.; Sr. Janice Bohn, S.N.D.deN., Assoc. Spiritual Dir.

BLACK CANYON CITY. *Contemplative House of Prayer* (Our Lady of Solitude) , P.O. Box 1140, 85324. Tel: 623-374-9204; Fax: 623-374-9204 (Call First). Sr. Mary Therese Sedlock, O.S.F., Dir.

SCOTTSDALE. *Franciscan Renewal Center, Inc. (Casa de Paz Y Bien)*, 5802 E. Lincoln Dr., 85253. Tel: 480-948-7460; Fax: 480-948-2325. Email: casa@thecasa.org. Web: www.thecasa.org. Bro. Joseph Schwab, O.F.M., Dir.; Revs. Laurence P. Dolan, O.F.M.; Michael Weldon, O.F.M.; William Shaughnessy, O.F.M.; Bro. Mario Vasquez, O.F.M. Priests 3; Brothers 1.

[I] NEWMAN CENTERS

PHOENIX. *Office of Youth and Young Adult Ministries* 400 E. Monroe, 85004. Tel: 602-257-5559; Fax: 602-288-2918. Email: lfraher@diocesephoenix.org. Web: www.diocesephoenix.org. Larry Fraher, Dir. Mesa Community College, Chandler; Gilbert Community College; Glendale Community College; Scottsdale Community College; Paradise Valley Community College; ASU West.

American Graduate School of International Management, Thunderbird Campus, 15249 N. 59th Ave., Glendale, 85306. Tel: 602-978-7011. Joaquin Duarte. Tel: 602-978-7184. (Glendale)

Glendale Community College, 35949 S. Ricon Rd., Wickenburg, 85390. Tel: 520-684-7779. Rev. David L. Sharp, C.S.B.

Yavapai College, Emery Riddle Aeronautical University, Sacred Heart Parish, 150 Fleury Ave., Prescott, 86301. Tel: 520-445-3141. Mr. Vincent Gallegos. (Prescott)

Arizona State University, All Saints Catholic Newman Center, 230 E. University Dr., P.O. Box 1987, Tempe, 85281. Tel: 480-967-7823. Revs. Nathan Castle, O.P., Dir.; Frederick Lucci, O.P. (Tempe)

Catholic Committee on Scouting Tel: 480-961-1610. Rev. Dennis J. O'Rourke, Chap.

[J] ACADEMIES OF RELIGIOUS TEACHING

PHOENIX. *Kino Institute of Theology*, Formerly Kino Institute, 400 E. Monroe, 85004. Tel: 602-354-2300; 602-254-7977 (Library); Fax: 602-354-2251. Email: kino@diocesephoenix.org. Web: www.kinoinstitute.org. Revs. Stanley Makacinas, O.Carm., Exec. Dir.; Ernest Larkin, O.Carm., Emeritus Faculty; Barry Sargent, Ph.D., Academic Dean; Tricia Hoyt, Faculty, Student Advisor; Rev. Michael Kwiecien, O.Carm., Faculty, Student Advisor; Sisters Maria Celia Molina, S.S.N.de N., Coord. Programa de Formacion and Agua Viva; Darcy Peletich, O.F.M., Librarian; Diana Stickney, Dir. University San Francisco Graduate Prog.; Gina Milligan, Operations Mgr. Tel: 602-906-9798; Dyanna Pedroza, Registrar.

[K] MISCELLANEOUS LISTINGS

PHOENIX. *Andre House of Arizona*, 213 S. 11th Ave., 85007-3132. Tel: 602-255-0580; Fax: 602-254-3834. Email: director@andrehouseaz.org. Web: www.andrehouseaz.org. P.O. Box 2014, 85001-2014. Tel: 602-255-0580; Fax: 602-254-3834. Revs. William Wack, C.S.C., Dir.; Duane Balcarski, C.S.C.; Chela Sullivan; Tom Parks; Nancy Bartholomew; Mike Lueken; Joseph Ushinski; Bro. Richard Armstrong, C.S.C. Hospitality House, Indiana Province of the Congregation of Holy Cross.

Catholic Social Services of Central and Northern Arizona, Inc., 1610 W. Camelback Rd., 85015. Tel: 602-285-1999; Fax: 602-285-0311. Email: css_communications@diocesephoenix.org. Web: www.catholicsocialserviceaz.org. Linda Nadolski, Pres.; Paul Martodam, M.P.A., CEO; Kristen Schmidt, M.S.W., Ph.D., COO.

Regional Service Centers:

Catholic Social Service, Phoenix, Formerly Catholic Social Service of Phoenix 1825 W. Northern Ave., 85021. Tel: 602-997-6105; Fax: 602-870-3891. Maureen Webster, A.C.S.W, C.I.S.W., Regl. Dir.

Catholic Social Service, West Valley, Formerly Catholic Social Service of the West Valley 14010 N. El Mirage Rd., El Mirage, 85323. Tel: 623-972-1576; Fax: 623-875-0519. Cathy Tompkins, M.S., C.P.C., Regl. Dir.

Catholic Social Service, East Valley, Formerly Catholic Social Service of the East Valley 430 N. Dobson Rd., Ste. 110, Mesa, 85201. Tel: 480-964-8771; Fax: 480-964-8865. Tara vanden Bosch, Regl. Dir. 24 hour Domestic Violence Hotline Tel: 480-821-1024

Catholic Social Service, Coconino, Formerly Catholic Social Service 43 S. San Francisco, Flagstaff, 86001. Tel: 928-774-9125; Fax: 928-774-0697. J.R. Brown, Ed.D., Regl. Dir.

Catholic Social Service, Mohave, Formerly Catholic Social Service of Mohave 1370 Ramar Rd., Ste. D, Bullhead City, 86442. Tel: 928-758-4176; Fax: 928-758-5141. J.R. Brown, Ed.D., Regional Dir. 2438 Kingman Ave., Kingman, 86401. Tel: 928-718-1117; Fax: 928-718-1124.

Catholic Social Service, Yavapai, Formerly Catholic Social Service of Yavapai 434 W. Gurley, Prescott, 86301. Tel: 928-778-2531; Fax: 928-771-9531.

Verde Valley Office, 736 North Main St., Cottonwood, 86326. Tel: 928-634-4254; Fax: 928-639-4368. John Allen, M.C.C.P.C., Regl. Dir.

Westside Head Start, 7400 W. Olive Ave., Ste. 10, Peoria, 85345. Tel: 623-486-9868; Fax: 623-486-9988. Cathy Tompkins, M.S., C.P.C., Regional Dir. 51 Head Start Classrooms

Office of Peace & Justice, 1610 W. Camelback Rd., 85015. Tel: 602-285-1999; Fax: 602-285-0311. Kathy Saile, M.S.W., Dir.

Residential Facilities:

Casa Linda Lodge Tel: 602-943-6461; Fax: 602-943-4173. Diane Ellis, C.I.S.W., Resident Prog. Supvr. Pregnant and parenting teens

Dignity House Tel: 602-274-3680. Carrie Mascaro, Prog. Supvr. Group living for homeless women leaving prostitution.

My Sister's Place Tel: 480-821-1024; Fax: 480-963-9532. Domestic Violence Shelter

Spring Haven Group Home Tel: 602-997-6105; Fax: 602-870-3891. Diane Ellis, C.I.S.W., Resident Prog. Supvr. Abused and neglected adolescent girls

Aspen House, 304 S. O'Leary, Flagstaff, 86001. Tel: 928-226-8600; Fax: 928-226-8603. J.R. Brown, Ed.D., Regl. Dir.

The Catholic Tuition Organization of the Diocese of Phoenix, 400 E. Monroe, 85004-2336. Tel: 602-744-6345; Fax: 602-288-2908. Email: ctodp@diocesephoenix.org. Web: www.ctodp.org. Karen L. Shepard, Prog. Coordinator; Rev. Msgr. Richard Moyer, Pres.

Christ Child Society, 4633 N. 54th St., 85018-1904. Tel: 602-667-3355; Fax: 602-667-0380. Sheila Hill, Pres.; Rosemary Dolmage, Treas.

Foundation for Senior Living, 1201 E. Thomas Rd., 85014. Tel: 602-285-1800. Email: gmikkelsen@diocesephoenix.org.

Affordable Services for Seniors, Inc. 1201 E. Thomas Rd., 85014. Tel: 602-285-1800. Email: gmikkelsen@diocesephoenix.org. Mr. Guy Mikkelsen, Pres.

Foundation for Senior Adult Living, Inc. Tel: 602-285-1800; Fax: 602-285-1838. Email: chollinger@diocesephoenix.org. Charles Hollinger, Contact Person. Sweetwater Gardens (Apartments for the Handicapped), Phoenix; Kingman Heights Apartments, Kingman.

FSAL Development Corporation, 1201 E. Thomas Rd., 85014. Tel: 602-285-1800.

FSAL Management Tel: 602-285-1800; Fax: 602-285-1838. Email: switt@diocesephoenix.org. Selina Witt, Contact Person.

FSAL Nursing Care Centers, 1201 E. Thomas Rd., 85014. Tel: 602-285-1800.

FSAL Programs Tel: 602-285-1800; Fax: 602-285-1838. Email: lmartin@diocesephoenix.org. Ms. Linda Martin, Dir. Adult Day Health Care Centers; In-Home Care Services; Home Safety & Repair Program; Community Action Programs/Senior Centers; Adult Foster Care; Oasis (Older Adult Service & Information System); Pathways Program (Resources and Referral-Care Management).

FSAL Real Estate Services Tel: 602-285-1800; Fax: 602-285-1838. Email: gmikkelsen@diocesephoenix.org. Mr. Guy Mikkelsen, Contact Person.

FSAL Rural Development Tel: 602-285-1800; Fax: 602-285-1838. Email: chollinger@diocesephoenix.org. Charles Hollinger. Becket House Apartments, Lake Havasu City; Vianney Villas Apartments, Avondale; Padua Hills Apartments, Wickenburg; St. Agnes Apartments, Williams, Amy Neal Retirement Center, Kingman.

FSAL Services, Inc., 1201 E. Thomas Rd., 85014. Tel: 602-285-1800.

FSL Home Improvements, 1201 E. Thomas Rd., 85014-5734. Tel: 602-285-1800; Fax: 602-285-1838. Email: gmikkelsen@diocesephoenix.org. Mr. Guy Mikkelsen, Pres. & Contact Person. Foundation for Senior Living

FSL Pathways Tel: 602-285-1800; Fax: 602-285-1838. Email: chill@diocesephoenix.org. Carolyn hill, Contact Person. Assisted Group Living Program (11 Houses). Phoenix.

Payson Senior Living, Inc. Tel: 602-285-1800; Fax: 602-285-1838. Email: chollinger@diocesephoenix.org. Charles Hollinger, Contact Person. (Pineview Manor Apartments, Payson)

St. Clair Senior Living, 1201 E. Thomas Rd., 85014. Tel: 602-285-1800. Email: gmikkelsen@diocesephoenix.org. Mr. Guy Mikkelsen, Pres.

Guadalupe Senior Village, 2702 N. 44th St., Ste. 102-A, 85008. Tel: 602-952-9525; Fax: 602-952-9539. Web: www.mercyhousing.org.

St. Joseph the Worker (Job Service), 213 S. 11th Ave., 85007-3503. Tel: 602-257-4390; Fax: 602-254-3834. Email: jobs@stjoetheworker.org. Web: stjoetheworker.org. P.O. Box 13503, 85002-3503. Thomas Ryan, Chm. Bd. of Directors; Janet M. Gray, Exec. Dir.; Tom Gryp, Vice Pres.; Peter Ziebron, Treas. To assist homeless people and those on the verge of homelessness in their efforts to secure and keep full-time, meaningful employment.

St. Mary's Scholarship & Benefit Fund, 2525 N. Third St., 85004. Tel: 602-254-6371; Fax: 602-253-0337. Email: pfarrell@smks.org. Web: www.smks.org. Barney McShane, Pres.

Mercy Properties Arizona, 2702 N. 44th St., Ste. 102-A, 85008. Tel: 602-952-9525; Fax: 602-952-9539. Web: www.mercyhousing.org.

Mesa Senior Meadows, 2702 N. 44th St., Ste. 102-A, 85008. Tel: 602-952-9525; Fax: 602-952-9539. Web: www.mercyhousing.org.

National Catholic Council for Hispanic Ministry, Inc., 3131 E. Camelback Rd., Ste. 200, 85016. Tel: 602-266-8623; Fax: 602-606-5705. Email: ncchm1@aol.com. Web: www.ncchm.org. Mr. Armando Contreras, Exec. Dir.

**Natural Family Planning*, 400 N. 30th St., 85008. Tel: 602-225-0636; Fax: 602-225-0175. Email: phxnfp@aol.com. Web: www.phxnfp.org. Peggy Frei, Dir. & Diocesan Coord. for N.F.P. Svcs. Center provides Natural Family Planning Services, Instructional Series, Introductions to Natural Family Planning for Marriage Preparation. Program is endorsed by the Diocesan Development Plan for N.F.P., U.S. Conference of Catholic Bishops (USCCB).

**Southwest Catholic Health Network Corp.*, 2800 N. Central Ave., Ste. 400, 85004. Tel: 602-263-3066; Fax: 602-263-2098. Email: saronovitch@schalleranderson.com. Stanley Aronovitch, Pres. & CEO.

St. Vincent De Paul Society, P.O. Box 13600, 85002. Tel: 602-254-3338; Fax: 602-261-6829. Web: www.stvincentdepaul.net. Stephen J. Zabilski, Exec. Dir.; Nancy B. Spencer, Pres.; Rev. Msgr. John J. McMahon, Spiritual Advisor.

GOODYEAR. *St. John Vianney School Development Fund*, 539 La Pasada Blvd., 85338. Tel: 623-932-3313; Fax: 623-932-1896. Email: frherman@diocesephoenix.org. Web: www.stjohnvianneyparish.com. Rev. John A. Herman, C.S.C. (FTW), Pres.

MESA. **Life Teen, Inc.*, 1730 W. Guadalupe Rd., 85202. Tel: 480-820-7001; Fax: 480-820-8653. Email: philb@lifeteen.com. Web: www.lifeteen.org. Mr. Phil Baniewicz, Exec. Dir.

PEORIA. *The Catholic Retreat for Young Singles, Inc.*, 8219 W. Salter Dr., 85382. Tel: 623-825-3889. Email: davidjgannon@cox.net. David Gannon, Liaison.

SCOTTSDALE. *Mercy Housing Southwest*, 6501 E. Greenway Pkwy., Ste. 102-506, 85254. Tel: 602-923-7395; Fax: 602-795-0497. Email: lrossi@mercyhousing.org. Web: www.mercyhousing.org. Cherie Kirschbaum, Pres.

TEMPE. **City of the Lord*, 711 W. University Dr., 85281-3411. Tel: 480-968-5895; 480-968-5990; Fax: 480-921-9175. Email: ewcotl@aol.com. Web: www.cityofthelord.org. Edward Wilmowski, Pres.; James R. Jones, Vice Pres.; Robert Carmody, Vice Pres.

**Friends of the Orphans*, 424 E. Southern Ave, Ste. 102, 85282. Tel: 480-967-9449; Fax: 480-967-9288. Email: fotoaz@fotoaz.org. P.O. Box 25507, 85285-5507Web: www.helptheorphans.org. Suzanne M. McCarthy, Exec. Dir.

RELIGIOUS INSTITUTES OF MEN REPRESENTED IN THE DIOCESE

For further details refer to the corresponding bracketed number in the Religious Institutes of Men or Women section.

[0170]—*Basilian Fathers* (Western Prov.)—C.S.B.

[0200]—*Benedictine Monks* (St. Meinrad Archabbey)—O.S.B.

[0600]—*Brothers of the Congregation of Holy Cross*—C.S.C.

[0400]—*Canons Regular of the Order of the Holy Cross*—O.S.C.

[0270]—*Carmelite Fathers and Brothers* (Prov. of St. Elias)—O.Carm.

[0350]—*Cistercian Order of the Strict Observance (Trappists)*—O.C.S.O.

[0360]—*Claretian Missionaries* (Western Prov.)—C.M.F.

[0310]—*Congregation of Christian Brothers*—C.F.C.

[1330]—*Congregation of the Mission* (Prov. of the West)—C.M.

[]—*Disciples of Hope*—D.S.

[0520]—*Franciscan Friars* (Prov. of Santa Barbara)—O.F.M.

[0650]—*Holy Ghost Fathers* (Western Prov.)—C.S.Sp.

[0690]—*Jesuit Fathers and Brothers* (California, Oregon & Chicago Provs.)—S.J.

[0910]—*Oblates of Mary Immaculate* (Our Lady of Hope)—O.M.I.

[0430]—*Order of Preachers (Dominicans)* (Western Prov.)—O.P.

[0610]—*Priests of the Congregation of Holy Cross*—C.S.C.

[1220]—*Servants of Charity*—S.C.

[1240]—*Servites* (Western Prov.)—O.S.M.

[0975]—*Society of Our Lady of the Most Holy Trinity*—S.O.L.T.

[1200]—*Society of the Divine Savior* (North American Prov.)—S.D.S.

RELIGIOUS INSTITUTES OF WOMEN REPRESENTED IN THE DIOCESE

[0230]—*Benedictine Sisters of Pontifical Jurisdiction* (Duluth, St. Paul, MN)—O.S.B.

[0990]—*Congregation of Divine Providence* (Pittsburgh, PA)—C.D.P.

[2715]—*The Congregation of Missionary Sisters of Christ the King for Polish Immigrants* (Poznan, Poland; Chicago, IL)—M.Chr.

[1780]—*Congregation of Sisters of the Third Order of St. Francis of Perpetual Adoration* (La Crosse, WI)—F.S.P.A.

[3710]—*Congregation of the Sisters of St. Agnes* (Fond du Lac, WI)—C.S.A.

[1920]—*Congregation of the Sisters of the Holy Cross* (Notre Dame, IN)—C.S.C.

[1710]—*Congregation of the Third Order of St. Francis of Mary Immaculate* (Joliet, IL)—O.S.F.

[0760]—*Daughters of Charity* (Los Altos Hills, CA)—D.C.

[0850]—*Daughters of Mary Help of Christians* (San Antonio, TX)—F.M.A.

[0810]—*Daughters of the Heart of Mary* (Holyoke, MA)—D.H.M.

[1070-03]—*Dominican Sisters* (Sinsinawa, WI)—O.P.

[1070-13]—*Dominican Sisters* (Adrian, MI)—O.P.

[1070-28]—*Dominican Sisters* (Akron, OH)—O.P.

[1070-30]—*Dominican Sisters* (Mountain View, CA)—O.P.

[1070-24]—*Dominican Sisters* (Great Bend, KS)—O.P.

[1120]—*Dominican Sisters of Roman Congregation* (Iowa City, IA)—O.P.

[1170]—*Felician Sisters* (Livonia, MI)—C.S.S.F.

[1230]—*Franciscan Sisters of Christian Charity* (Manitowoc, WI)—O.S.F.

[1310]—*Franciscan Sisters of Little Falls, Minnesota* (Little Falls, MN)—O.S.F.

[1430]—*Franciscan Sisters of Our Lady of Perpetual Help* (St. Louis, MO)—O.S.F.

[1440]—*Franciscan Sisters of the Poor* (Brooklyn, NY)—F.S.P.

[2370]—*Institute of the Blessed Virgin Mary (Loretto Sisters)* (Toronto, Ont., Canada)—I.B.V.M.

[2380]—*Institute of the Blessed Virgin Mary (Loretto Sisters)* (Rathfarnham, Dublin, Ireland)—I.B.V.M.

[2740]—*Maryknoll Sisters of St. Dominic* (Maryknoll, NY)—M.M.

[]—*Missionarias Carmelitas de Santa Teresa del Nino Jesus* (Pueblo, Mexico)—M.C.S.T.N.

[2710]—*Missionaries of Charity* (Calcutta, India)—M.C.

[]—*Missionaries of the Kingship of Christ, a Secular Institute* (Bethesda, MD)—S.I.M.

[2860]—*Missionary Sisters of the Sacred Heart of Jesus* (New York, NY)—M.S.C.

[3130]—*Our Lady of Victory Missionary Sisters* (Huntington, IN)—O.L.V.M.

[2970]—*School Sisters of Notre Dame* (Milwaukee, WI; Irving, TX; Mankato, MN; Wilton, CT)—S.S.N.D.

[1680]—*School Sisters of St. Francis* (Milwaukee, WI)—S.S.S.F.

[1690]—*School Sisters of the Third Order of St Francis* (Pittsburgh, PA)—O.S.F.

[3590]—*Servants of Mary Servite Sisters* (Lady Smith, WI)—O.S.M.

[0440]—*Sisters of Charity of Cincinnati, Ohio*—S.C.

[0570]—*Sisters of Charity of Seton Hill, Greensburg, Pennsylvania*—S.C.

[0430]—*Sisters of Charity of the B.V.M.* (Dubuque, IA)—B.V.M.

[2575]—*Sisters of Mercy of the Americas* (Pittsburgh, PA; Burlingame, CA; Chicago, IL; Omaha, NE)—R.S.M.

[3000]—*Sisters of Notre Dame de Namur* (Cincinnati, OH)—S.N.D.deN.

[1540]—*Sisters of St. Francis* (Clinton, IA)—O.S.F.

[1705]—*The Sisters of St. Francis of Assisi* (Milwaukee, WI)—O.S.F.

[1570]—*Sisters of St. Francis of the Holy Family* (Dubuque, IA)—O.S.F.

[3830-15]—*Sisters of St. Joseph* (Concordia, KS)—C.S.J.

[3840]—*Sisters of St. Joseph of Carondelet*—C.S.J.

[3930]—*Sisters of St. Joseph of the Third Order of St. Francis* (South Bend, IN)—S.S.J.-T.O

[1030]—*Sisters of the Divine Savior* (Milwaukee, WI)—S.D.S.

[3730]—*Sisters of the Order of St. Basil the Great* (Uniontown, PA)—O.S.B.M.

[3260]—*Sisters of the Precious Blood* (Dayton, OH)—C.PP.S.

[2150]—*Sisters, Servants of the Immaculate Heart of Mary*—I.H.M.

[3330]—*Union of the Sisters of the Presentation of the B.V.M.* (Phoenix, AZ)—P.B.V.M.

NECROLOGY

† Long, Francis C., (Retired)—Died Sept. 5, 2003

Diocese of Pittsburgh

(Dioecesis Pittsburgensis)

Most Reverend

DONALD W. WUERL, S.T.D.

Bishop of Pittsburgh; ordained December 17, 1966; appointed Titular Bishop of Rosemarkie and Auxiliary Bishop of Seattle December 3, 1985; consecrated January 6, 1986; appointed and canonically installed Bishop of Pittsburgh February 12, 1988; liturgically installed March 25, 1988 *Office: 111 Blvd. of the Allies, Pittsburgh, PA 15222-1618.*

Pastoral Center: 111 Blvd. of the Allies, Pittsburgh, PA 15222-1618. Tel: 412-456-3000.

Web: www.diopitt.org

Email: communications@diopitt.org

Most Reverend

JOHN B. MCDOWELL, PH.D.

Retired Auxiliary Bishop of Pittsburgh; ordained November 4, 1945; appointed Auxiliary Bishop of Pittsburgh and Titular Bishop of Tamazuca July 18, 1966; consecrated September 8, 1966; resigned September 30, 1996 *c/o Diocese of Pittsburgh,* 111 Blvd. of the Allies, Pittsburgh, PA 15222-1618.

Most Reverend

WILLIAM J. WINTER, V.G., S.T.D.

Auxiliary Bishop of Pittsburgh; ordained December 17, 1955; appointed Auxiliary Bishop of Pittsburgh and Titular Bishop of Uthina December 27, 1988; consecrated February 13, 1989 *Res.: Sacred Heart Church,* 310 Shady Ave., Pittsburgh, PA 15206-4389.

ESTABLISHED AUGUST 8, 1843.

Square Miles 3,754.

Comprises the Counties of Allegheny, Beaver, Lawrence, Washington, Greene, and Butler in the State of Pennsylvania.

Legal Title: For legal titles of parishes and diocesan institutions, consult the Legal Office.

STATISTICAL OVERVIEW

Personnel	
Bishop	1
Auxiliary Bishops	2
Retired Bishops	1
Priests: Diocesan Active in Diocese	314
Priests: Diocesan Active Outside Diocese	21
Priests: Diocesan in Foreign Missions	2
Priests: Retired, Sick or Absent	121
Number of Diocesan Priests	458
Religious Priests in Diocese	123
Total Priests in Diocese	581
Extern Priests in Diocese	45
Ordinations:	
Diocesan Priests	1
Religious Priests	1
Permanent Deacons in Diocese	50
Total Brothers	35
Total Sisters	1,443
Parishes	
Parishes	215
With Resident Pastor:	
Resident Diocesan Priests	197
Resident Religious Priests	11
Without Resident Pastor:	
Administered by Priests	7
Pastoral Centers	1
Professional Ministry Personnel:	
Brothers	4
Sisters	69
Lay Ministers	258
Welfare	
Catholic Hospitals	2
Total Assisted	489,213
Homes for the Aged	9
Total Assisted	1,379
Day Care Centers	11
Total Assisted	1,845
Specialized Homes	8
Total Assisted	6,023
Special Centers for Social Services	7
Total Assisted	73,221
Residential Care of Disabled	1
Total Assisted	176
Educational	
Seminaries, Diocesan	1
Students from This Diocese	12
Diocesan Students in Other Seminaries	16
Total Seminarians	28
Colleges and Universities	3
Total Students	13,530
High Schools, Diocesan and Parish	8
Total Students	3,347
High Schools, Private	3
Total Students	648
Elementary Schools, Diocesan and Parish	104
Total Students	23,133
Elementary Schools, Private	4
Total Students	960
Non-residential Schools for the Disabled	2
Total Students	176
Catechesis/Religious Education:	
High School Students	6,444
Elementary Students	48,458
Total Students under Catholic Instruction	96,724
Teachers in the Diocese:	
Priests	3
Brothers	14
Sisters	79
Lay Teachers	1,897
Vital Statistics	
Receptions into the Church:	
Infant Baptism Totals	7,240
Adult Baptism Totals	361
Received into Full Communion	904
First Communions	8,096
Confirmations	8,596
Marriages:	
Catholic	1,840
Interfaith	831
Total Marriages	2,671
Deaths	9,402
Total Catholic Population	815,719
Total Population	1,966,067

Former Bishops—Rt. Revs. MICHAEL J. O'CONNOR, D.D., ord. June 1, 1833; consecrated Aug. 15, 1843; transferred to Erie and then to Pittsburgh Dec. 20, 1853; resigned May 23, 1860; entered the Society of Jesus Dec. 22, 1860; died at Woodstock College, MD, Oct. 18, 1872; MICHAEL DOMENEC, C.M., D.D., ord. June 30, 1839; consecrated Dec. 9, 1860; transferred to Allegheny, Jan. 11, 1876; resigned July 29, 1877; died at Tarragona, Spain, Jan. 5, 1878; JOHN TUIGG, D.D., ord. May 14, 1850; consecrated March 19, 1876; transferred to as Apostolic Administrator of Allegheny 1877; died at Altoona Dec. 7, 1889; RICHARD PHELAN, D.D., ord. May 4, 1854; consecrated Aug. 2, 1885; Titular Bishop of Cibyra and Coadjutor to the Rt. Rev. John Tuigg; succeeded to Bishop Tuigg, Dec. 7, 1889; died at Idlewood Dec. 20, 1904; Most Revs. J. F. CANEVIN, D.D., ord. June 4, 1879; consecrated Titular Bishop of Sabrata and Coadjutor, Feb. 24, 1903; succeeded to the See of Pittsburgh, Dec. 20, 1904; resigned Nov. 26, 1920; Titular Archbishop of Pelusium; appt. Jan. 9, 1921; died at Pittsburgh March 22, 1927; HUGH C. BOYLE, D.D., ord. July 2, 1898; succeeded to the See of Pittsburgh, June 16, 1921; consecrated June 29, 1921; died at Pittsburgh Dec. 22, 1950; His Eminence JOHN CARDINAL DEARDEN, S.T.D., ord. Dec. 8, 1932; Titular Bishop of Sarepta and Coadjutor Bishop of Pittsburgh; appt. March 13, 1948; consecrated May 18 1948; succeeded to the See, Dec. 22, 1950; assistant at the Pontifical Throne, Oct. 15, 1957; installed at the Archdiocese of Detroit, Dec. 18, 1958 created Cardinal, April 28, 1969; died at Southfield, MI Aug. 2, 1988; JOHN CARDINAL WRIGHT, S.T.D., ord. Dec. 8, 1935; appt. May 10, 1947; consecrated June 30, 1947; transferred to Bishop of Worcester, Jan. 28, 1950; transferred to Pittsburgh, Jan. 23, 1959; to the Roman Curia as Prefect of the Sacred Congregation for the Clergy; appt. April 23, 1969; created Cardinal, April 28, 1969; died at Cambridge, MA, Aug. 10, 1979; Most Rev. VINCENT M. LEONARD, D.D., ord. June 16, 1935; appt. Titular Bishop of Arsacal and Auxiliary, Feb. 28, 1964; consecrated April 21, 1964; succeeded to the See, June 1, 1969; resigned June 30, 1983; died at Pittsburgh Aug. 28, 1994; His Eminence ANTHONY CARDINAL BEVILACQUA, D.D., J.C.D., J.D., ord. June 11, 1949; appt. Oct. 4, 1980; consecrated Nov. 24, 1980; Bishop of Pittsburgh; appt. Oct. 10, 1983; installed Dec. 12, 1983; appt. Archbishop of Philadelphia, Feb. 11, 1988; created Cardinal, June 29, 1991; resigned Oct. 7, 2003.

Pastoral Center—111 Blvd. of the Allies, Pittsburgh, 15222-1618. Tel: 412-456-3000. All official correspondence should be directed to this office.

Chancellor—VACANT. Tel: 412-456-3129.

Vicars General—Most Rev. WILLIAM J. WINTER, V.G., S.T.D.; Very Rev. PAUL J. BRADLEY, V.G., M.S.W.

Bishop's Office—Most Rev. DONALD W. WUERL, S.T.D.; Revs. ROBERT J. GRECCO, M.Div., Admin. Sec.; DENNIS P. YUROCHKO, Master of Ceremonies Direct all official correspondence to the Bishop at this address 111 Blvd. of the Allies, Pittsburgh, 15222-1618. Tel: 412-456-3010.

General Secretary—Very Rev. PAUL J. BRADLEY, V.G., M.S.W. Tel: 412-456-3131; Fax: 412-456-3197.

Associate General Secretary—Mr. JOHN P. FLAHERTY, M.A. Tel: 412-456-3146.

Vicar for Canonical Services—

Director, Department of Canon and Civil Law

Services—Very Rev. LAWRENCE A. DINARDO, M.Ch.A., J.C.L., V.E. Address all correspondence to 111 Blvd. of the Allies, Pittsburgh, 15222-1698. Tel: 412-456-1618; Fax: 412-456-3183.

Assistant Director, Department of Canon and Civil Law Services—Rev. BRIAN J. WELDING, S.T.L., J.C.D. Tel: 412-456-3135.

Matrimonial Concerns, Office for—Revs. RICHARD M. LELONIS, J.C.L., Dir.; JAMES P. MCDONOUGH, S.T.L., J.C.L., Canonical Consultant, Address all correspondence to: 2900 Noblestown Rd., Pittsburgh, 15205-4227. Tel: 412-928-5530.

Tribunal Office— Address all correspondence to: *2900 Noblestown Rd., Pittsburgh, 15205-4227*. Tel: 412-928-5530; Fax: 412-928-5990.

Judicial Vicar—Very Rev. ROBERT J. AHLIN, J.C.L.

Director of Cases—Ms. ELAINE M. BUZZINOTTI, J.D., M.A.

Judges—Revs. JAMES L. AARON, M.Ed. (Retired); MARTIN F. BARKIN, M.Div.; CHARLES S. BOBER, S.T.D.; Very Revs. PAUL J. BRADLEY, V.G., M.S.W.; ROBERT J. CEDOLIA, V.F., M.Div., M.A.; Rev. DAVID D. DEWITT; Very Rev. LAWRENCE A. DINARDO, M.Ch.A., J.C.L., V.E.; Revs. KEVIN J. DOMINIK, M.Div.; WILLIAM P. FEENEY, M.Div.; Very Rev. ROBERT F. GUAY, V.F., M.Div.; Mrs. RITA F. JOYCE, J.D., J.C.L.; Revs. JAMES E. KUNKEL, S.T.M.; RICHARD M. LELONIS, J.C.L.; JOSEPH R. LEMP, S.T.L.; THOMAS M. O'DONNELL, M.Div.; JOHN R. RUSHOFSKY, M.Ed.; THEODORE A. RUTKOWSKI, S.T.L.; JOSEPH C. SCHEIB, M.A., J.C.L., M.Div.; CHARLES W. SPEICHER, Ph.D., S.T.M.; BENEDETTO P. VAGHETTO, J.C.L.; LEO V. VANYO, J.C.D. (Retired).

Promoters of Justice—Revs. BRIAN J. WELDING, S.T.L., J.C.D.; JAMES P. MCDONOUGH, S.T.L., J.C.L.

Advocate—Deacon DAVID E. LAMM, J.D.

Defenders of the Bond—Revs. J. LAWRENCE BRUNEY, M.Div.; DENNIS J. COLAMARINO, M.Div.; LOUIS L. DENINNO, M.Div., J.C.L.; Very Rev. ROBERT M. FRANCO, V.F., M.Ch.A.; Rev. JAMES P. MCDONOUGH, S.T.L., J.C.L.

Notaries—Mrs. THERESE M. BINKNEY; Ms. MARTHA J. BRAUN; Ms. ANNETTE W. SEMAN; Mrs. DARLENE WILCE.

Secretary for Education—Rev. KRIS D. STUBNA, S.T.D.; Sr. IGNATIUS ROONEY, R.S.M., M.Ed., Special Asst. to Sec., 111 Blvd. of the Allies, Pittsburgh, 15222-1618. Tel: 412-456-3100; Fax: 412-456-3101.

Secretary for Ministerial Leadership—Very Rev. JAMES G. YOUNG, V.E., M.Div.; Mrs. RITA E. FLAHERTY, M.S.W., Assistance Coord., 111 Blvd. of the Allies, Pittsburgh, 15222-1618. Tel: 412-456-3060; Fax: 412-456-3188.

Secretary for Pastoral and Social Concerns—Ms. SUSAN L. RAUSCHER, 111 Blvd. of the Allies, Pittsburgh, 15222-1618. Tel: 412-456-3157; Fax: 412-456-3180.

Deans and Deaneries—Most Rev. WILLIAM J. WINTER, V.G., S.T.D., Chm., College of Deans; Very Revs. EDWARD M. BRYCE, V.F., S.T.L., Central (Allegheny County); THOMAS B. FERRIS, V.F., North Side (Allegheny County); ANDREW C. FISCHER, V.F., M.Div., Allegheny Valley (Allegheny County); KENNETH E. OLDENSKI, V.F., Northwest (Allegheny County); ROBERT J. CEDOLIA, V.F., M.Div., M.A., East Suburban (Allegheny County); ROBERT M. FRANCO, V.F., M.Ch.A., South Pittsburgh (Allegheny County); DANIEL A. VALENTINE, V.F., D.Min., Steel Valley (Allegheny County); WALTER A. SOBON, V.F., M.Ed., Southwest (Allegheny County); DONALD P. BREIER, V.F., M.Div., South Hills (Allegheny County); STEPHEN M. CHERVENAK, V.F., S.T.L., Mon Yough (Allegheny County); ROBERT F. GUAY, V.F., M.Div., Beaver County; HARRY R. BIELEWICZ, V.F., M.Div., Butler County; MAURO J. CAUTELA, V.F., M.Div., Lawrence County; VACANT, Greene County; Very Revs. ROBERT J. BOYLE, V.F., Washington County East; JOHN A. HARVEY, V.F., M.Div., Washington County West.

Department for Consecrated Life—Sr. PATRICIA ROGAN, O.S.F., Delegate for Religious, 2900 Noblestown Rd., Pittsburgh, 15205-4227. Tel: 412-921-5800, Ext. 13.

Priest Council—Most Revs. DONALD W. WUERL, S.T.D., Pres.; WILLIAM J. WINTER, V.G., S.T.D.; Very Rev. PAUL J. BRADLEY, V.G., M.S.W.; Rev. NORMAN E. BEVAN, C.S.Sp.; Very Rev. EDWARD M. BRYCE, V.F., S.T.L.; Rev. CARMEN A. D'AMICO, M.Div.; Very Rev. LAWRENCE A. DINARDO, M.Ch.A., J.C.L., V.E.; Revs. JOHN P. GALLAGHER, S.T.L.; JOHN R. HANEY, M.Div.; JOSEPH J. KLEPPNER, S.T.L., Ph.D.; JOSEPH R. LEMP, S.T.L.; THOMAS R. MILLER; DAM D. NGUYEN, M.Div.; Rev. Msgr. WILLIAM M. OGRODOWSKI, S.T.L.; Very Rev. KENNETH E. OLDENSKI, V.F.; Revs. THOMAS D. O'NEIL, M.Div.; GEORGE E. SALADNA, S.T.L., S.S.L.; DANIEL SULLIVAN, C.P.; DAVID H. TAYLOR, M.Div.; LOUIS F. VALLONE, M.Div.; Very Rev. JAMES G. YOUNG, V.E., M.Div.

College of Consultors—Most Revs. DONALD W. WUERL, S.T.D.; WILLIAM J. WINTER, V.G., S.T.D.; Very Revs. PAUL J. BRADLEY, V.G., M.S.W.; EDWARD M. BRYCE, V.F., S.T.L.; Revs. JOHN R. HANEY, M.Div.; JOSEPH J. KLEPPNER, S.T.L., Ph.D.; JOSEPH R. LEMP, S.T.L.; THOMAS R. MILLER; Rev. Msgr. WILLIAM M. OGRODOWSKI, S.T.L.; Very Rev. KENNETH E. OLDENSKI, V.F.; Rev. DAVID H. TAYLOR, M.Div.

Diocesan Development Board—Mr. FREDERICK P. O'BRIEN, C.F.O. & Chm.; Sr. PATRICIA CAIRNS, C.S.J.; Mr. JOSEPH F. DIMARIO; Mr. JOSEPH G. LUTTRINGER; Mr. AMBROSE MURRAY; Rev. JOHN M. O'TOOLE; Mr. MATTHEW J. STOESSEL; Rev. KRIS D. STUBNA, S.T.D.

Diocesan Finance Council—Most Rev. DONALD W. WUERL, S.T.D., Pres.; Very Rev. PAUL J. BRADLEY, V.G., M.S.W.; Ms. KATHLEEN GEIS; Mr. MICHAEL J. HANNON; Mr. JAMES MCLAUGHLIN; Mr. HARRY F. MURRAY; Mr. LEO W. YOCHUM.

Diocesan Pastoral Council—Most Revs. DONALD W. WUERL, S.T.D., Chm.; WILLIAM J. WINTER, V.G., S.T.D.; Very Rev. PAUL J. BRADLEY, V.G., M.S.W.; Mrs. HELEN J. BEDNARCZYK; Mr. JAMES C. CAVANAUGH; Deacon RICHARD R. CESSAR; Rev. MARK A. ECKMAN, M.Div.; Mrs. NICOLA ESTES; Mrs. CHERYL J. FINN; Mrs. JOANNE M. FRONCZEK; Bro. RICHARD GRZESKIEWICZ, F.S.C.; Mr. DONALD G. HENDERSON; Sr. ELAINE HROMULAK, O.S.F.; Mr. ROBERT A. KORCHECK, Ph.D.; Mr. KEVIN L. LANDER; Sr. EILEEN MAGILL, O.S.F.; Rev. DANIEL J. MAURER, S.T.L.; Sr. ANNE CELINE MUTSCHELLER, C.S.J.; Mrs. NANCY R. NETCHI; Ms. SHIRLEY NOVAK; Mr. KENNETH G. OGILVIE; Mrs. NIDIA OLIVER; Ms. LINDA L. RENDULIC; Mr. GUY J. RUBINO; Mr. JOHN SEARLES; Mr. GERALD R. SHRUM; Mr. TIMOTHY TASSONE.

Clergy Personnel Board—Most Revs. DONALD W. WUERL, S.T.D.; WILLIAM J. WINTER, V.G., S.T.D.; Very Revs. PAUL J. BRADLEY, V.G., M.S.W.; JAMES G. YOUNG, V.E., M.Div., Chm.; Revs. JOHN R. RUSHOFSKY, M.Ed., Exec. Sec.; DAVID J. BONNAR, S.T.B.; Very Rev. ROBERT J. CEDOLIA, V.F., M.Div., M.A.; Revs. WILLIAM P. FEENEY, M.Div.; JOHN R. HANEY, M.Div.; RONALD P. LENGWIN, M.Div.; ROBERT M. MILLER; ALBERT J. SEMLER; DANIEL W. WHALEN, S.T.L., J.D.; PAUL J. ZYWAN, M.Div.

Diocesan Administration

Administrative Procedures, Office for—Mrs. RITA F. JOYCE, J.D., J.C.L., Admin. Tel: 412-456-3135.

Adult Faith Formation, Office for—VACANT, Dir.; Deacon STEPHEN J. BYERS, Asst. Tel: 412-456-3117.

Archives and Record Center—Mr. KENNETH A. WHITE, Dir.; Mr. BURRIS E. ESPLEN, Archivist, 4721 Fifth Ave., Pittsburgh, 15213. Tel: 412-621-6217.

Assistance Coordinator, Office of the—Mrs. RITA E. FLAHERTY, M.S.W. Tel: 412-456-3060.

Auditors/Analysts, Office for the—Mr. JAMES E. STIERHEIM, Supvr. Tel: 412-456-3028.

Bishop, Office of the Diocesan—Revs. ROBERT J. GRECCO, M.Div., Admin. Sec.; DENNIS P. YUROCHKO, Master of Ceremonies. Tel: 412-456-3010.

Black Catholic Ministries, Office for—Mrs. MARGRETTA STOKES TUCKER, M.Ed., Dir. Tel: 412-456-3170.

Black Catholics, Ethnic and Cultural Communities, Dept. for—Mrs. MARGRETTA STOKES TUCKER, M.Ed., Dir. Tel: 412-456-3170.

Blind Persons— Refer to Disabilities, Dept. for Persons with

Budget and Planning - Secretariat for Education, Office for—Mr. ROY CARTIER, M.B.A., M.R.P., Dir. Tel: 412-456-3108.

Building Commission—Very Rev. PAUL J. BRADLEY, V.G., M.S.W., Chm.; Mr. JAMES J. ZIELINSKI, Exec. Sec. Tel: 412-456-3034.

Building Services, Office for—Mrs. DARLENE M. HOLZER, Dir. Tel: 412-456-3000.

Business Services, Dept. for—Mr. FREDERICK P. O'BRIEN, C.F.O. & Dir. Tel: 412-456-3137.

Campus Ministry, Office for—Rev. W. PETER HORTON, M.A., M.Div., Dir., 1010 McNeilly Rd., Pittsburgh, 15226. Tel: 412-563-6373.

Canon and Civil Law Services, Dept. for—Very Rev. LAWRENCE A. DINARDO, M.Ch.A., J.C.L., V.E., Dir.; Rev. BRIAN J. WELDING, S.T.L., J.C.D., Asst. Dir. Tel: 412-456-3135.

Canonical Services, Office for—Very Rev. LAWRENCE A. DINARDO, M.Ch.A., J.C.L., V.E., Vicar; Rev. BRIAN J. WELDING, S.T.L., J.C.D., Asst. Dir. Tel: 412-456-3135.

Catechesis, Office for—Mr. KENNETH M. OGOREK, M.A., Dir. Tel: 412-456-3115.

Catechetical Ministries, Office for—Ms. SHARON T. TYBOROWSKI, Dir. Tel: 412-456-3110.

Catholic Charities—Sr. PATRICIA CAIRNS, C.S.J., Exec. Dir., 212 9th St., Pittsburgh, 15222. Tel: 412-456-6999. Allegheny County, 212 9th St., Pittsburgh, 15222. Tel: 412-456-6999. Beaver County, 3582 Brodhead Rd., Ste. 108, Monaca, 15601. Tel: 724-775-0758. Butler County, 407 A W. Jefferson St., Butler, 16001. Tel: 724-287-4011. Greene County, 95 E. High St., Rm. 107, Waynesburg, 15370. Tel: 724-627-6410. Lawrence County, 413 Highland Ave., New Castle, 16101. Tel: 724-658-5526. Washington County, 331 S. Main St., Washington, 15301. Tel: 724-228-7722. Roselia Center, 624 Clyde St., Pittsburgh, 15213. Tel: 412-682-4410; 412-682-4411. St. Joseph's House of Hospitality, Inc., 1635 Bedford Ave., Pittsburgh, 15219. Tel: 412-471-0666.

Challenges: Options in Aging—*Shenley Square, 2706 Mercer Rd., New Castle, 16105-1422*. Tel: 724-658-3729.

Catholic Cemeteries Assoc., The—Ms. ANNABELLE MCGANNON, Exec. Dir., 718 Hazelwood Ave., Pittsburgh, 15217-2807. Tel: 412-521-9133.

Catholic Schools, Dept. for—Mr. ROBERT L. PASERBA, Ed.D., Supt. Catholic Schools; Sr. MARY JO MUTSCHLER, S.C., Asst. Supt. Catholic Elementary Schools; Mrs. ANNA MARIE CATANZARO, M.Ed., Asst. Supt. Catholic Secondary Schools; Mr. RONALD T. BOWES, D.A., Asst. Supt. Public Policy & Devel. Tel: 412-456-3090.

Educational Consultants—Sr. BRIGID MARIE GRANDEY, S.C.; Ms. MADONNA J. HELBLING, Ph.D.; Sisters URSULA KELLY, S.S.N.D., M.A.; CATHERINE ANN KOLLER, C.D.P., M.A.; LORETTA KRALL, C.S.J., M.A.; M. DENISE MAHER, C.S.J., M.A.; Mr. KENNETH M. OGOREK, M.A.; Sr. IRENE MARY WILBURN, S.C., M.A., 135 First Ave., Pittsburgh, 15222. Tel: 412-456-3070.

Chaplain Services, Office for—Very Rev. JAMES G. YOUNG, V.E., M.Div., Dir. Tel: 412-456-3057.

Charismatic Prayer Groups—Rev. JOHN P. SWEENEY, Moderator, St. Titus Parish, 952 Franklin Ave., Aliquippa, 15001-3359. Tel: 724-378-8561.

Chief Financial Officer—Mr. FREDERICK P. O'BRIEN. Tel: 412-456-3137.

Civil Legal Services, Office for—Mrs. RITA F. JOYCE, J.D., J.C.L., Dir.; Mr. WILLIAM A. STEIDLE JR., J.D., Counsel for Parishes & Schools; Mr. CHRISTOPHER G. PONTICELLO, J.D., Counsel for Real Estate; Ms. ELAINE M. BUZZINOTTI, J.D., M.A., Counsel to the Office. Tel: 412-456-3126.

Clergy Personnel, Dept. for—Rev. JOHN R. RUSHOFSKY, M.Ed., Dir. Tel: 412-456-3060.

Communications Commission—Mr. ROBERT P. LOCKWOOD, Chm. Tel: 412-456-3020.

Communications, Dept. for—Mr. ROBERT P. LOCKWOOD, Dir.; Mr. WILLIAM W. HILL, Sr. Staff Communicator; Ms. JOYCE M. DURIGA, Staff Communicator. Tel: 412-456-3020.

Community Service Liaison, Office of the—Mr. W. JOHN HANNIGAN, M.S.W. Tel: 412-456-3162.

Cultural Diversity, Commission—Mrs. MARGRETTA STOKES TUCKER, M.Ed., Chm. Tel: 412-456-3170.

Deaf Persons— Refer to Disabilities, Dept. for Persons with

Diaconate, Office for the—Rev. JAMES A. WEHNER, S.T.D., Dir., St. Paul Seminary, 2900 Noblestown Rd., Pittsburgh, 15205-4227. Tel: 412-921-5800, Ext. 22.

Diocesan National Black Catholic Congress Leadership Team—Ms. SHELLEY SIMS, Team Leader, 912 Finland St., Pittsburgh, 15219. Tel: 412-687-3271.

Diocesan Purchasing Commission—Mr. JAMES W. PEARCE, Exec. Dir., 2900 Noblestown Rd., Pittsburgh, 15205. Tel: 412-922-6400.

Disabilities, Dept. for Persons with—Ms. GRACE T. HARDING, M.A., Dir.; Sr. MICHELLE GRGURICH, V.S.C., Assoc. Dir.; Revs. PATRICK F. RAGER, Chap. to Persons with Physical Disabilities; WALTER G. RYDZON, Chap. to Deaf Persons, 135 First Ave., Pittsburgh, 15222. Tel: 412-456-3119 (Voice); 412-456-3122 (TTY).

Ecumenical and Interfaith Commission—Rev. RONALD P. LENGWIN, M.Div., Chm. Tel: 412-456-3021.

Educational Media, Dept. for—Mr. JEFFREY A. HIRST, Dir., St. Paul Seminary, 2900 Noblestown Rd., Pittsburgh, 15205-4227. Tel: 412-921-5800, Ext. 24.

Electronic Media, Office for—Mrs. NANCY K. LIPPERT, Dir., St. Paul Seminary, 2900 Noblestown Rd., Pittsburgh, 15205-4227. Tel: 412-921-5800, Ext. 16.

Ethnic Ministries, Office for—Chaplains to Korean Catholic Community: Revs. ALEXIS ANANIA, O.F.M.; MATTHEW BYEONG-HYEON WOO. Chaplains to Latino Catholic Community: Revs. ALVIN P. GUTIERREZ; DANIELE VALLECORSA; DAM D. NGUYEN, M.Div., Chap to Vietnamese Catholic Community. Tel: 412-456-3170.

Evangelization, Dept. for—Rev. JAMES A. WEHNER,

S.T.D., Dir., St. Paul Seminary, 2900 Noblestown Rd., Pittsburgh, 15205-4227. Tel: 412-921-5800, Ext. 22.

Family Life and Catechesis, Office for—Mrs. MAUREEN H. WOOD, M.R.E., Dir.; Deacon PAUL M. HOOVER, M.D., Asst. Tel: 412-456-3160.

Financial Services, Office for—Mr. JOSEPH G. LUTTRINGER, Dir. Tel: 412-456-3025.

Central Accounting Services—Tel: 412-456-3032.

Parish Accounting Services—Tel: 412-456-3027.

Foundation, Catholic Diocese of Pittsburgh—Mr. JOSEPH F. DIMARIO, Dir. Tel: 412-456-3085.

Gilmary Diocesan Center—Mr. RONALD W. RAGAN, M.P.A., Dir., 601 Flaugherty Run Rd., Coraopolis, 15108-3899. Tel: 412-264-8400.

Health Care Liaison, Office of the—Very Rev. LAWRENCE A. DINARDO, M.Ch.A., J.C.L., V.E. Tel: 412-456-3135.

Information Technology, Office for—Mr. JOHN F. ZDILLA, M.S., Dir. Tel: 412-456-3152.

Insurance/Benefits, Office for—Mr. DAVID S. STEWART, Dir. Tel: 412-456-3045.

Justice and Peace Commission—Mrs. VERONICA C. MORGAN-LEE, Ph.D., Chm. Tel: 412-456-3162.

Lay Personnel, Office for—Mrs. DARLENE M. HOLZER, Dir. Tel: 412-456-3016.

Learning Media Center—Mr. JEFFREY A. HIRST, Dir., St. Paul Seminary, 2900 Noblestown Rd., Pittsburgh, 15205-4227. Tel: 412-921-5800, Ext. 24.

Matrimonial Concerns, Office for—Revs. RICHARD M. LELONIS, J.C.L., Dir.; JAMES P. MCDONOUGH, S.T.L., J.C.L., Canonical Consultant, 2900 Noblestown Rd., Pittsburgh, 15205-4227. Tel: 412-928-5530.

Ministerial Assessment, Office for—Very Rev. LAWRENCE A. DINARDO, M.Ch.A., J.C.L., V.E., Exec. Sec. Tel: 412-456-3135.

Ministries, Institute for—Sr. PATRICIA ROGAN, O.S.F., Dir., St. Paul Seminary, 2900 Noblestown Rd., Pittsburgh, 15205-4227. Tel: 412-921-5800, Ext. 15.

Mission Office—Rev. RONALD P. LENGWIN, M.Div., Dir. Tel: 412-456-3065.

Music, Office for—Rev. JAMES J. CHEPPONIS, M.Div., M.A., Dir., St. Paul Seminary, 2900 Noblestown Rd., Pittsburgh, 15205-4227. Tel: 412-921-5800, Ext. 36.

Natural Family Planning Advisory Committee—Deacon PAUL M. HOOVER, M.D., Chm. Tel: 412-456-3160.

Newspaper—Most Rev. DONALD W. WUERL S.T.D., Pres.; Mr. ROBERT P. LOCKWOOD, Gen. Mgr., 135 First Ave., #200, Pittsburgh, 15222-1506. Tel: 412-471-1252. "Pittsburgh Catholic"

Payroll, Office for—JOHN G. CVETIC, Dir. Tel: 412-456-3006.

Pilgrimage Office—Rev. RONALD P. LENGWIN, M.Div., Dir. Tel: 412-456-3065.

Pornography, Commission to Counter—Mrs. NORMA NORRIS, Chm. Tel: 412-456-3157.

Post-Ordination Formation, Office for—Rev. JAMES A. WEHNER, S.T.D., Dir., St. Paul Seminary, 2900 Noblestown Rd., Pittsburgh, 15205-4227. Tel: 412-921-5800, Ext. 22.

Pre-Ordination Formation, Dept. for—Rev JAMES A. WEHNER, S.T.D., Dir., St. Paul Seminary, 2900 Noblestown Rd., Pittsburgh, 15205-4227. Tel: 412-921-5800, Ext. 22.

Property Planning and Development, Office for—Mr. JAMES J. ZIELINSKI, Dir. Tel: 412-456-3034.

Public and Community Affairs, Office for—Rev. RONALD P. LENGWIN, M.Div., Dir. Tel: 412-456-3021.

Religious Education, Dept. for—Mrs. JUDITH A. KIRK, Dir. Tel. 412-456-3112.

Respect Life, Office for—Ms. SUSAN L. RAUSCHER, Dir. Tel: 412-456-3161.

Retired Priests, Office for—Very Rev. JEROME A. DIXON, V.E., Vicar; Deacon JAMES R. GRAB, Asst. Tel: 412-761-2187.

Retired Priests, Residences for—Rev. H. MICHAEL KERNAN, Dir., Cardinal Dearden Center, 4721 Fifth Ave., Pittsburgh, 15213. Tel: 412-687-8022; Mr. PAUL MERLO, Admin., St. John Vianney Manor, 2600 Morange Rd., Pittsburgh, 15205. Tel: 412-928-0825.

St. Paul Cathedral—Very Rev. DONALD P. BREIER, V.F., M.Div., Rector and Pastor, 108 N. Dithridge St., Pittsburgh, 15213-2694. Tel: 412-621-4951.

St. Paul Seminary—Revs. JAMES A. WEHNER, S.T.D., Rector; EDWARD L. YUHAS, Vice Rector & Dean of Studies; BRIAN J. WELDING, S.T.L., J.C.D., Spiritual Dir. & Dir. Spiritual Formation; Sr. JUDITH WORDEN, R.S.M., Coord. of Apostolic Works; Mrs. MARY ALICE BUCK, Admin. Asst. to Rector, 2900 Noblestown Rd., Pittsburgh, 15205-4227. Tel: 412-921-5800, Ext. 10.

Social Advocacy and Convening, Dept. for—Ms. SUSAN L. RAUSCHER, Dir. Tel: 412-456-3157.

Society for the Propagation of the Faith—Rev. RONALD P. LENGWIN, M.Div., Dir. Tel: 412-456-3065.

Stewardship and Development, Office for—Mr. JOSEPH F. DIMARIO, Dir.; Mr. JAMES M. GALLAGHER, Assoc. Dir.; Mr. PAUL F. STABILE, Dir. of Planned Giving; Mr. MATTHEW J. STOESSEL, Asst. Dir., Parishes & Schools. Tel: 412-456-3085.

Television and Radio Production— Refer to Electronic Media, Office for

Theological Commission—Rev. JOSEPH J. KLEPPNER, S.T.L., Ph.D., Chm. Tel: 724-775-6363.

Victim Assistance Coordinator—Mrs. RITA E. FLAHERTY, M.S.W. Tel: 412-456-3060. Email: rflaherty@diopitt.org.

Vision Impairments, Persons with— Refer to Disabilities, Dept. for Persons with

Vocations, Office for—Co Directors: Revs. THOMAS J. BURKE; THOMAS A. SPARACINO, St. Paul Seminary, 2900 Noblestown Rd., Pittsburgh, 15205-4227. Tel: 412-921-5800, Ext. 23.

Worship Commission—Rev. EDWARD L. YUHAS, Chm. Tel: 412-921-5800, Ext. 32.

Worship, Dept. for—Revs. EDWARD L. YUHAS, Dir.; DENNIS P. YUROCHKO, Asst. Dir., St. Paul Seminary, 2900 Noblestown Rd., Pittsburgh, 15205-4227. Tel: 412-921-5800, Ext. 32.

Youth and Young Adult Ministry, Dept. for—Mrs. JOYCE A. GILLOOLY, M.Ed., Dir.; Mr. ROBERT A. SHERWIN, Assoc. Dir.; Mr. GARY M. SLIFKEY, M.A., Assoc. Dir., 1010 McNeilly Rd., Pittsburgh, 15226. Tel: 412-563-6373.

CLERGY, PARISHES, MISSIONS AND PAROCHIAL SCHOOLS

CITY OF PITTSBURGH, PROPER
(ALLEGHENY COUNTY)

1—ST. PAUL CATHEDRAL (1834), Very Rev. Paul J. Bradley, V.G., M.S.W., Rector; Rev. Daniel J. Maurer, S.T.L. In Res., Rev. Robert J. Grecco, M.Div.; Deacon George W. Gaines.
Res.: 108 N. Dithridge St., 15213. Tel: 412-621-4951; Fax: 412-621-1079.
School—St. Agnes Diocesan School, 120 Robinson St., 15213. Tel: 412-682-1129; Fax: 412-687-8091. Mrs. Michelle Peduto, Prin. Lay Teachers 11; Students 160.
Catechesis/Religious Program—Students 40.

2—ST. AGNES, Closed., For sacramental records contact St. Paul Cathedral.

3—ST. ANN, (Hungarian), Closed., See St. Stephen.

4—ST. AUGUSTINE, (German), Closed., See Our Lady of the Angels.

5—ST. BEDE (1922), Very Rev. Edward M. Bryce, V.F., S.T.L. In Res., Revs. Felix Owino, A.J.; Frederick Leo Nkasibwe, A.J.; Sr. Mary Elizabeth Schrei, S.C., Pastoral Assoc.
Res.: 509 S. Dallas Ave., 15208. Tel: 412-661-7222; Fax: 412-661-9337.
School—6920 Edgerton Ave., 15208. Tel: 412-661-9425; Fax: 412-661-0447. Lay Teachers 24; Students 350.
Catechesis/Religious Program—Students 83.

6—ST. BENEDICT THE MOOR (1889), (African American), Rev. Carmen A. D'Amico, M.Div.; Deacon Reynold Wilmer. In Res., Rev. Michael L. Komakec (Uganda).
Res.: 91 Crawford St., 15219. Tel: 412-281-3141; Fax: 412-391-7151.
School—2900 Webster Ave., 15219. Tel: 412-682-3755; Fax: 412-682-4058. Sisters of St. Joseph 6; Lay Teachers 7; Students 196.
Catechesis/Religious Program—Students 90.
Convent—Tel: 412-621-0519.

7—ST. CATHERINE OF SIENA (Beechview) (1902), Very Rev. Robert M. Franco, V.F., M.Ch.A.; Deacon Thomas O'Neill.
Res.: 1810 Belasco Ave., 15216. Tel: 412-531-2135; Fax: 412-531-8543.
Catechesis/Religious Program—Tel: 412-561-0399. Students 130.

8—ST. CHARLES LWANGA PARISH (1992), Consolidated Revs. David H. Taylor, M.Div.; Jeffrey T. Molnar. from the following churches: Corpus Christi, Holy Rosary, Mother of Good Counsel, Our Lady Help of Christians, Our Lady of the Most Blessed Sacrament and SS. Peter & Paul. In Res., Rev. Edward Hoffmann.
Res. 7114 Kelly St., 15208. Tel: 412-731-3020; Fax: 412-731-1615.
School—Holy Rosary, 7120 Kelly St., 15208. Tel: 412-731-2567; Fax: 412-731-3476. Lay Teachers 9; Students 181.
Catechesis/Religious Program—Students 45.

9—CORPUS CHRISTI, Closed., See St. Charles Lwanga.

10—ST. ELIZABETH OF HUNGARY, (Slovak), Closed., See St. Patrick-St. Stanislaus Kostka.

11—EPIPHANY (1902), (Irish), Rev. James W. Garvey. In Res., Revs. John F. Walsh, Hospital Chap.; James McDonough; Patrick George (West Africa).
Res.: 1018 Centre Ave., 15219-3502. Tel: 412-471-0557; Fax: 412-471-1345. Email: epiphany@access-4-free.com.

12—HOLY FAMILY, (Polish), Closed., See Our Lady of the Angels.

13—HOLY ROSARY, Closed., See St. Charles Lwanga.

14—ST. HYACINTH, (Polish), Closed., See St. Regis.

15—IMMACULATE CONCEPTION (1905), (Italian), Merged, with St. Joseph, Pittsburgh to form Immaculate Conception-St. Joseph Parish, Pittsburgh

16—IMMACULATE CONCEPTION-ST. JOSEPH (2001), (Italian—German), Revs. Dale E. DeNinno; Edward J. Kunco.
Res.: 4712 Liberty Ave., 15224. Tel: 412-682-5353; Fax: 412-682-6766.
School—Tel: 412-621-5199; Fax: 412-621-5601.
Catechesis/Religious Program—Tel: 412-682-2354. Students 261.

17—IMMACULATE HEART OF MARY (1897), (Polish), Rev. Joseph E. Swierczynski.
Res.: 3058 Brereton Ave., 15219. Tel: 412-621-5170; Fax: 412-621-7445.
Catechesis/Religious Program—Tel: 412-682-2886; Fax: 412-682-6889. Twinned with Our Lady of Angels. Students 35.

18—ST. JOACHIM, Closed., See St. Rosalia.

19—ST. JOHN THE BAPTIST, Closed., See Our Lady of the Angels.

20—ST. JOSEPH (1872), (German), Merged, with Immaculate Conception, Pittsburgh to form Immaculate Conception-St. Joseph Parish, Pittsburgh

21—ST. KIERAN, Closed., See St. Matthew.

22—ST. LAWRENCE O'TOOLE (East End) (1897), Rev. James G. Graham.
Res.: 5323 Penn Ave., 15224. Tel: 412-363-1771; Fax: 412-363-7552.
Catechesis/Religious Program—4235 Stanton Ave., 15201. Students 47.

23—ST. MARTIN (West End), Closed., See Guardian Angels.

24—ST. MARY ASSUMPTION (Lawrenceville), Closed., See St. Matthew.

25—ST. MARY OF MERCY (1870), Rev. John M. O'Toole. In Res., Revs. Ronald P. Lengwin, M.Div.; Andre Quenum (West Africa) (Cotonou).
Res.: 202 Stanwix St., 15222. Tel: 412-261-0110; Fax: 412-261-0113.

26—ST. MARY'S (Lawrenceville), Closed., See Our Lady of the Angels.

27—ST. MATTHEW (1993), Consolidated, from St. Kieran and St. Mary Assumption. Rev. Joseph J. Janiszeski, T.O.R.
Res.: 5322 Carnegie St., 15201. Tel: 412-781-6701; Fax: 412-781-1331.
Catechesis/Religious Program—Tel: 412-781-5192. Students 71.

28—MOTHER OF GOOD COUNSEL, (Italian), Closed., See St. Charles Lwanga.

29—OUR LADY HELP OF CHRISTIANS, (Italian), Closed., See St. Charles Lwanga.

30—OUR LADY OF THE ANGELS (1993), [CEM] Consolidated, from St. Augustine, Holy Family, St. John the Baptist and St. Mary. Revs. John Daya, O.F.M.Cap.; Leon Leitem, O.F.M.Cap.; Deacon Francis J. Dadowski. In Res., Revs. Ralph Zehe, O.F.M.Cap.; Reginald Russo, O.F.M.Cap.
Res.: 225 37th St., 15201. Tel: 412-682-0929; Fax: 412-682-6889.
School—St. John Neumann Regional Catholic Elementary School, Tel: 412-682-5096; Fax: 412-682-0811. See Consolidated Schools under Institutions Located in the Diocese.
Catechesis/Religious Program—Tel: 412-682-2886. Students 112.

31—OUR LADY OF THE MOST BLESSED SACRAMENT, Closed., See St. Charles Lwanga.

32—ST. PATRICK (Strip District), Closed., See St. Patrick-St. Stanislaus Kostka.

33—ST. PATRICK-ST. STANISLAUS KOSTKA (1993), (Polish), Consolidated Rev. Thomas J. McKenna, Admin. of St. Stanislaus, St. Patrick and St. Elizabeth of Hungary.
Res. & Parish Office: 57 21st St., 15222. Tel: 412-471-4767; Fax: 412-471-1209.
Catechesis/Religious Program—Students 8.

34—SS. PETER AND PAUL (East Liberty), Closed., See St. Charles Lwanga.

35—ST. PHILOMENA (Squirrel Hill), Closed., See St. Bede.

36—ST. RAPHAEL (1911), Revs. Joseph V. Kurutz;

Daniele Vallecorsa.
Res.: 1118 Chislett St. E., 15206. Tel: 412-661-3100; Fax: 412-661-4105.
School—1154 Chislett St., 15206. Tel: 412-661-0288; Fax: 412-661-0428. Sisters of St. Joseph 1; Lay Teachers 11; Students 156.
Catechesis/Religious Program—Tel: 412-661-0290. Students 65.

37—ST. REGIS (1993), Merged, with St. Hyacinth. Rev. Donald C. Fisher, M.A.
Res.: 3235 Parkview Ave., 15213. Tel: 412-681-9365; Fax: 412-681-1175.
Catechesis/Religious Program—Students 12.

38—ST. ROSALIA (1993), Merged, with St. Joachim. Rev. Joseph W. Reschick. In Res., Rev. Joseph C. Beck.
Res.: 411 Greenfield Ave., 15207. Tel: 412-421-5766; Fax: 412-421-4529.
School—Tel: 412-521-3005; Fax: 412-521-2763. Sisters of the Immaculate Heart of Mary 2; Lay Teachers 11; Students 159.
Catechesis/Religious Program—Tel: 412-521-7836. Students 105.

39—SACRED HEART (1872), Most Rev. William J. Winter, V.G., S.T.D.; Revs. Edward S. Litavec; C. William Hausen. In Res., Rev. John A. Reifsnyder.
Res.: 310 Shady Ave., 15206. Tel: 412-661-0187; Fax: 412-661-7932.
School—325 Emerson St., 15206. Tel: 412-441-1582; Fax: 412-441-2798. Sisters of Charity 1; Lay Teachers 23; Students 439.
Catechesis/Religious Program—Students 50.

40—ST. STANISLAUS (Strip District), (Polish), Closed., See St. Patrick-St. Stanislaus Kostka.

41—ST. STEPHEN (1993), Merged, Wtih St. Ann. Rev. Cornelius W. McCaulley, S.T.L.
Mailing Address: 5115 Second Ave., 15207. Tel: 412-421-9210; Fax: 412-421-6421.
Res.: 131 E. Elizabeth St., 15207. Tel: 412-421-9210.
School—134 E. Elizabeth St., 15207. Tel: 412-421-9447; Fax: 412-421-4748. Sisters of Charity 1; Lay Teachers 8; Students 89.
Catechesis/Religious Program—Students 45.

SOUTH SIDE

1—ST. ADALBERT, (Polish), Closed., See Prince of Peace.

2—ST. BASIL (1907), (German), Rev. Robert J. Meyer. In Res., Rev. Joseph C. Scheib, M.A., J.C.L., M.Div.
Res.: 1735 Brownsville Rd., 15210. Tel: 412-882-9763; Fax: 412-882-2476.
Catechesis/Religious Program—Tel: 412-881-4440. Students 295.
Convent—30 W. Willock Rd., 15227. Tel: 412-881-0638.

3—ST. CANICE (Knoxville), Closed., See St. John Vianney.

4—ST. CASIMIR, (Lithuanian), Closed., See Prince of Peace.

5—ST. GEORGE (Allentown), Closed., See St. John Vianney.

6—GUARDIAN ANGELS (West End) (1994), [CEM] Merged, with St. James and St. Martin. Rev. John E. Hissrich. In Res., Rev. Joseph Marie Obama (Cameroon).
Res.: 1030 Logue St., 15220. Tel: 412-921-4077; Fax: 412-922-4945.
School—Elizabeth Seton Elementary, Tel: 412-331-4529; Fax: 412-331-8734. See Consolidated Schools under Institutions Located in the Diocese.
Catechesis/Religious Program—Tel: 412-921-3223. Students 103.

7—ST. HENRY, Closed., See St. John Vianney.

8—HOLY ANGELS (1903), Very Rev. Robert J. Ahlin, J.C.L., Admin.
Res.: 408 Baldwin Rd., 15207. Tel: 412-461-6906; Fax: 412-461-0961.
Catechesis/Religious Program—Tel: 412-461-8500. Students 536.

9—HOLY INNOCENTS (1900), Rev. Donald N. Buchleitner.
Res.: 3011 Landis St., 15204. Tel: 412-331-0268; Fax: 412-331-1219.
School—Elizabeth Seton Elementary, Tel: 412-331-4529; Fax: 412-331-8734. See Consolidated Schools under Institutions Located in the Diocese.
Catechesis/Religious Program—Tel: 412-771-4893. Students 58.

10—ST. JAMES (West End), Closed., See Guardian Angels.

11—ST. JOHN THE EVANGELIST, Closed., See Prince of Peace.

12—ST. JOHN VIANNEY (Hilltop) (1994), [CEM] [JC], Consolidation of the following churches: St. Canice, St. George, St. Henry, and St Joseph. Revs. Frank D. Almade; Daniel W. Whalen, S.T.L., J.D.
823 Climax St., 15210. Tel: 412-381-8300; Fax: 412-431-3790. In Res., Revs. William R. Terza; Thomas M. O'Donnell, M.Div.; Tae Woo Jung (Korea, South).
School—Bishop Leonard Catholic School, 434 Ormsby Ave., 15210. Tel: 412-381-3557; Fax: 412-381-8611. Students 283.
Catechesis/Religious Program—Tel: 412-381-5581. Students 195.

13—ST. JOSAPHAT, (Polish), Closed., See Prince of Peace.

14—ST. JUSTIN (Mt. Washington) (1917), Rev. Walter C. Rydzon.
Res.: 539 Boggs Ave., 15211. Tel: 412-381-9878; 412-381-9825 (TTY); Fax: 412-431-8017. Catholic Deaf Community.
Catechesis/Religious Program—Tel: 412-381-3774; Fax: 412-381-0371. Students 102.

15—ST. MARY OF THE MOUNT (Mt. Washington) (1873), Rev. Louis F. Vallone, M.Div.; Deacon Robert Barth. In Res., Rev. Clement Okoye (Nigeria).
Res.: 403 Grandview Ave., 15211. Tel: 412-381-0212; Fax: 412-381-9921.
School—Bigham St. & Grandview Ave., 15211. Tel: 412-431-4645; Fax: 412-381-0770. Sisters of the Immaculate Heart of Mary 2; Lay Teachers 10; Students 166.
Catechesis/Religious Program—Tel: 412-381-3310. Students 120.

16—ST. MATTHEW, (Slovak), Closed., See Prince of Peace.

17—ST. MICHAEL, (German), Closed., See Prince of Peace.

18—OUR LADY OF LORETO (1959), Rev. George F. Chortos.
Res.: 1905 Pioneer Ave., 15226. Tel: 412-341-6161; Fax: 412-341-3399.
Catechesis/Religious Program—Tel: 412-341-2360. Students 119.

19—ST. PAMPHILUS (1960), Rev. Alexis Anania, O.F.M. In Res., Rev. Byeong-Hyeon (Korea, South); Bro. John-Michael Pinto, O.F.M.; Deacon Leon F. Miles.
Res.: 948 Tropical Ave., 15216. Tel: 412-341-1000; 412-531-8449; Fax: 412-341-6956.
Church: 1000 Tropical Ave., 15216.
Catechesis/Religious Program—Tel: 412-561-0330. Students 63.

20—ST. PETER, Closed., See Prince of Peace.

21—ST. PIUS X (1954), Rev. Robert J. Miller.
Res.: 3040 Pioneer Ave., 15226. Tel: 412-563-5423; Fax: 412-561-3868.
School—Brookline Regional Catholic School, Tel: 412-563-0858. See Consolidated Schools under Institutions Located in the Diocese.
Catechesis/Religious Program—Tel: 412-563-1588. Students 127.

22—PRINCE OF PEACE (1992), [CEM 6] Consolidated, from the following churches: St. Adalbert, St. Casimir, St. John the Evangelist, St. Josaphat, St. Matthew, St. Michael and St. Peter. Revs. Bernard M. Harcarik; Richard J. Thompson.
Res.: 81 S. 13th St., 15203-1897. Tel: 412-481-8380; Fax: 412-431-0209.
Catechesis/Religious Program—Tel: 412-381-5458. Students 70.

23—RESURRECTION (Brookline) (1909), Revs. Frank Mitolo; James E. Seeger; Deacon Richard Very. In Res., Rev. Victor J. Rocha (Retired).
Res.: 1100 Creedmoor Ave., 15226. Tel: 412-563-4400; Fax: 412-563-4403.
Catechesis/Religious Program—Tel: 412-343-9551. Students 256.

24—ST. VINCENT (Esplen), Closed., See St. John of God, McKees Rocks.

25—ST. WENDELIN (Carrick) (1873), [CEM] Rev. Gary W. Oehmler.
Res.: 2728 Custer Ave., 15227. Tel: 412-882-1480; Fax: 412-884-2334.
School—Bishop John B. McDowell Regional School, Tel: 412-884-5676; Fax: 412-884-8610. See Consolidated Schools under Institutions Located in the Diocese.
Catechesis/Religious Program—Tel: 412-882-3414. Students 101.

NORTH SIDE

1—ST. AMBROSE, Merged, with St. Boniface to form Holy Wisdom.

2—ANNUNCIATION, Closed., See Incarnation of the Lord.

3—ST. BONIFACE, Merged, with St. Ambrose to form Holy Wisdom.

4—ST. CYRIL OF ALEXANDRIA (1924), Very Rev. Thomas B. Ferris, V.F.
Res.: 3854 Brighton Rd., 15212. Tel: 412-761-1552; Fax: 412-761-3318.
School—Tel: 412-761-5043; Fax: 412-761-0840. Lay Teachers 14; Students 198.
Catechesis/Religious Program—Tel: 412-734-0505. Students 140.

5—ST. FRANCIS XAVIER, Closed., See Risen Lord.

6—ST. GABRIEL ARCHANGEL, (Slovak), Closed., See Risen Lord.

7—HOLY WISDOM (1994), [CEM] Very Rev. Lawrence A. DiNardo, M.Ch.A., J.C.L., V.E. In Res., Revs. Louis L. DeNinno, M.Div., J.C.L.; Vincent F. Kolo.
Res.: 1025 Haslage Ave., 15212-3429. Tel: 412-231-1116; Fax: 412-231-1072.
Catechesis/Religious Program—Tel: 412-321-3186; Fax: 412-321-7807. Twinned with St. Peter, North Side. Students 10.

8—INCARNATION OF THE LORD (1993), Consolidated, from Annunciation and Nativity of Our Lord. Rev. John M. Bachkay.
Res.: 4071 Franklin Rd., 15214. Tel: 412-931-2911; Fax: 412-931-2832.
School—4072 Franklin Rd., 15214. Tel: 412-931-2330; Fax: 412-931-2406. Sr. Roberta Kardell, S.F.C.C. Sisters 1; Lay Teachers 9; Students 122.
Catechesis/Religious Program—Students 75.

9—ST. JOSEPH, Closed., See St. Peter.

10—ST. LEO, Closed., See Risen Lord.

11—MOST HOLY NAME OF JESUS (Troy Hill) (1868), (German), [CEM] Rev. W. David Schorr; Deacon G. Gregory Jelinek. In Res., Revs. James L. Aaron, M.Ed. (Retired); Joseph Henry, S.J.
Res.: 1700 Harpster St., 15212-4393. Tel: 412-231-2994; Fax: 412-231-7180.
School—Cardinal Wright Regional School, Tel: 412-231-8248. See Consolidated Schools under Institutions Located in the Diocese.
Catechesis/Religious Program—Tel: 412-231-3002. Students 140.
Chapel—St. Anthony's (1880),Tel: 412-323-9504. Sr. Margaret Liam Glenane, S.A., Asst. Dir.

12—NATIVITY OF OUR LORD, Closed., See Incarnation of the Lord.

13—OUR LADY QUEEN OF PEACE, Closed., See St. Peter.

14—ST. PETER (1993), (Polish), [CEM] Consolidated, from St. Cyprian, St. Mary's, Mary Immaculate & Our Lady, Queen of Peace, St. Joseph, St. Peter and St. Wenceslaus. Revs. Benjamin R. Walker, O.S.B.; Ralph Tajak, O.S.B.
Res.: 720 Arch St., 15212. Tel: 412-321-0711; Fax: 412-321-7807.
School—Cardinal Wright Regional School, Tel: 412-231-8248; Fax: 412-231-0835. See Consolidated Schools under Institutions Located in the Diocese.
Catechesis/Religious Program—Tel: 412-321-3186. Students 41.

15—REGINA COELI, (Italian), Closed., For sacramental records contact St. Cyril of Alexandria.

16—RISEN LORD (1993), Consolidated, from the following churches: St. Francis Xavier, St. Gabriel Archangel, St. Leo and Our Lady of Perpetual Help. Rev. Thomas J. Galvin; Deacon David Gruseck.
Res.: 3250 California Ave., 15212. Tel: 412-761-1507; Fax: 412-761-6454.
Catechesis/Religious Program—Tel: 412-766-1726. Students 107.

17—ST. WENCESLAUS, Closed., See St. Peter.

OUTSIDE THE CITY OF PITTSBURGH

ALEPPO TOWNSHIP, ALLEGHENY CO., ST. MARY (1852), [CEM] Rev. J. Lawrence Bruney, M.Div., Admin. In Res., Rev. Sylvester Moijueh.
Res.: 444 Glenfield Rd., Sewickley, 15143. Tel: 412-741-6460; Fax: 412-749-9271.
Catechesis/Religious Program—Tel: 412-741-3959. Students 151.

ALIQUIPPA, BEAVER CO., ST. TITUS (1994), [CEM 2] [JC 2] Merged, with St. Joseph, West Aliquippa. Revs. John P. Sweeney; James M. Bachner.
Res.: 952 Franklin Ave., 15001. Tel: 724-378-8561; Fax: 724-378-4851.
School—107 Sycamore St., 15001. Tel: 724-378-7940; Fax: 724-375-8893. Lay Teachers 10; Students 145.
Catechesis/Religious Program—Tel: 724-378-8665. Students 309.

ALLISON PARK, ALLEGHENY CO., ST. URSULA (1908), Revs. Garrett D. Dorsey; Ernest Strelinski, P.A.
Res.: 3937 Kirk Ave., 15101. Tel: 412-486-6700; Fax: 412-486-2562.
School—Tel: 412-486-5511; Fax: 412-492-7295. Sisters 1; Lay Teachers 14; Students 198.
Catechesis/Religious Program—Tel: 412-486-3374; Fax: 412-486-3374. Students 450.

AMBRIDGE, BEAVER CO.

1—CHURCH OF CHRIST THE KING, Closed., See Good Samaritan.

2—DIVINE REDEEMER, Closed., See Good Samaritan.

3—GOOD SAMARITAN (1994), [CEM] Consolidated, from the following churches: St. Veronica, Divine Redeemer, St. Stanislaus, Christ the King and Holy Trinity. Revs. Samuel J. Esposito; Charles J. Baptiste.
Res.: 725 Glenwood Ave., 15003. Tel: 724-266-6565; Fax: 724-266-5570.
School—Glenwood Ave. & 8th St., 15003. Tel: 724-266-1670; Fax: 724-266-5570. Mary Frances Panian, Prin. Lay Teachers 6; Students 130.
Catechesis/Religious Program—Students 336.

4—HOLY TRINITY, (Croatian), Closed., See Good Samaritan.

5—ST. STANISLAUS, Closed., See Good Samaritan.

6—ST. VERONICA, Closed., See Good Samaritan.

ASPINWALL, ALLEGHENY CO., ST. SCHOLASTICA (1903), Rev. Robert G. Duch, Ph.D.
Res.: 309 Brilliant Ave., 15215. Tel: 412-781-0186; Fax: 412-781-4316.
School—Christ the Divine Teacher Academy, Tel: 412-781-7927. See Consolidated Schools under Institutions Located in the Diocese.
Catechesis/Religious Program—Tel: 412-781-0608. Students 423.

AVELLA, WASHINGTON CO., ST. MICHAEL (1917), [CEM] Rev. Pierre G. Sodini, S.T.L.
Res.: 95 Highland Ave., 15312. Tel: 724-587-3570; Fax: 724-587-5203.
Catechesis/Religious Program—Students 133.

BADEN, BEAVER CO., ST. JOHN THE BAPTIST (1866), [CEM] Rev. Joseph J. Dascenzo.
Res.: 375 Linmore Ave., P.O. Box 171, 15005. Tel: 724-869-2280; Fax: 724-869-0305.
Catechesis/Religious Program—Students 32.

BAIRDFORD, ALLEGHENY CO., ST. VICTOR (1919), Rev. Robert R. Coyne; Deacon Silverio Rubio.
Res.: P.O. Box 149, 15006. Tel: 724-265-2070; Fax: 724-265-6316.
Catechesis/Religious Program—Tel: 724-265-4040. Students 478.

BALDWIN BORO, ALLEGHENY CO., ST. ALBERT THE GREAT (1956), Rev. Edward M. Czemerda.
Res.: 3171 Churchview Ave., 15227. Tel: 412-884-7744; Fax: 412-884-2300.
School—Bishop John B. McDowell Regional School, Tel: 412-884-5676; Fax: 412-884-8610. See Consolidated Schools under Institutions Located in the Diocese.
Catechesis/Religious Program—Tel: 412-884-8282. Students 260.

BEAVER FALLS, BEAVER CO.

1—DIVINE MERCY (1994), (Polish), [CEM] Consolidated, from St. Mary and Holy Trinity. Rev. Donald R. Bischof. In Res., Rev. Paul J. Savage, S.T.L.
Res.: 605 Tenth St., 15010. Tel: 724-846-4585; Fax: 724-846-6868.
School—609 Tenth St., 15010. Tel: 724-846-5955; Fax: 724-846-1894. Lay Teachers 10; Students 118.
Catechesis/Religious Program—Tel: 724-846-8133. Students 115.

2—HOLY TRINITY, (Polish), Closed., See Divine Mercy.

3—ST. PHILOMENA (1948), Rev. David E.F. Scharf.
Res.: 3908 Sixth Ave., 15010. Tel: 724-843-7375; Fax: 724-843-7575.
School—Tel: 724-846-2272; Fax: 724-846-7110. Lay Teachers 8; Students 77.
Catechesis/Religious Program—Students 82.

BEAVER, BEAVER CO., SS. PETER AND PAUL (1830), [CEM] Rev. Msgr. William M. Ogrodowski (STL). In Res., Rev. Kenneth E. Myers, M.S.Ed.
Res.: 200 Third St., 15009. Tel: 724-775-4111; Fax: 724-775-1117.
School—370 E. End Ave., 15009. Tel: 724-774-4450; Fax: 724-774-5192. Lay Teachers 14; Students 151.
Catechesis/Religious Program—Students 305.

BELLEVUE, ALLEGHENY CO., ASSUMPTION OF THE BLESSED VIRGIN MARY ON THE BEAUTIFUL RIVER (1903), Revs. Dennis M. Buranosky; Michael J. Stumpf.
Res.: 45 N. Sprague Ave., 15202. Tel: 412-766-6660; Fax: 412-766-4836.
School—35 N. Jackson Ave., 15202. Tel: 412-761-7887; Fax: 412-761-7620. Lay Teachers 15; Students 200.
Catechesis/Religious Program—Tel: 412-766-4046. Students 67.

BENTLEYVILLE, WASHINGTON CO.

1—AVE MARIA (1994), [CEM 2] Consolidated, from St. Luke, St. Clement, and St. Joseph. Rev. John B. Lendvai.
Res.: 126 Church St., 15314-1406. Tel: 724-239-3591; Fax: 724-239-4667.
School—Box 590, Ellsworth, 15331. Tel: 724-239-2226; Fax: 724-239-2272. Lay Teachers 5; Students 120; Preschool Students 32.
Catechesis/Religious Program—Students 124.

2—ST. LUKE, Closed., See Ave Maria, Ellsworth.

BESSEMER, LAWRENCE CO., ST. ANTHONY (1909), Merged, with St. Lawrence, Hillsville to form Christ the King, Hillsville.

BETHEL PARK, ALLEGHENY CO.

1—ST. GERMAINE (1957), Rev. Nicholas A. Pesanka; Mary Beth Green, Pastoral Assoc.
Res.: 7003 Baptist Rd., 15102. Tel: 412-833-0661; Fax: 412-833-4036.
School—7001 Baptist Rd., 15102. Tel: 412-833-0223. Lay Teachers 17; Students 172.
Catechesis/Religious Program—Tel: 412-833-0662. Students 300.

2—ST. THOMAS MORE (1953), Revs. Kenneth R. White; Joseph B. Cordori.
Res.: 126 Fort Couch Rd., 15241. Tel: 412-833-0031; Fax: 412-833-5995.
School—134 Fort Couch Rd., 15241. Tel: 412-833-1412; Fax: 412-833-5597. Lay Teachers 22; Students 265.
Catechesis/Religious Program—Tel: 412-835-6996. Students 620.

3—ST. VALENTINE (1931), Revs. J. Francis Frazer; Thomas A. Sparacino.
Res.: 2710 Ohio St., 15102. Tel: 412-835-4415; Fax: 412-835-4417.
School—(Grades PreK-8), 2709 Mesta St., 15102. Tel: 412-835-3780. Lay Teachers 12; Students 255.
Catechesis/Religious Program—Tel: 412-831-6466. Students 710.

BLAWNOX, ALLEGHENY CO., ST. EDWARD (1938), Rev. Russell J. Maurer.
Res.: 450 Walnut St., 15238. Tel: 412-828-4066; Fax: 412-828-3084.
Catechesis/Religious Program—Tel: 412-828-7310. Students 130.

BOBTOWN, GREENE CO., ST. IGNATIUS OF ANTIOCH (1924), Rev. Lawrence V. Holpp.
Res.: Box 63, 15315. Tel: 724-839-7122; Fax: 724-839-7315.
Catechesis/Religious Program—Students 45.

BOYERS, BUTLER CO., ST. ALPHONSUS (1841), [CEM] [JC 3] Merged, with Epiphany, St. Paschal and St. Louis, W. Sunbury. Rev. Albert C. Koser.
Mailing Address: P.O. Box 46, 16020. Tel: 724-791-2393; Fax: 724-791-9971.
Res.: 2709 W. Sunbury Rd., 16020. Tel: 724-791-2393.
Catechesis/Religious Program—Students 135.

BRADDOCK HILLS, ALLEGHENY CO., SACRED HEART (1897), (Polish), Rev. Thomas A. Wagner, Admin.
Administration Office:—416 Verona St., 15104.
Res.: 1600 Brinton Rd., 15221-4902. Tel: 412-271-4222; Fax: 412-271-1222.
Catechesis/Religious Program— Twinned with Good Shepherd, Braddock. Students 1.

BRADDOCK, ALLEGHENY CO., GOOD SHEPHERD (1985), Rev. Thomas A. Wagner. In Res., Rev. Douglas A. Boyd.
Res.: 416 Verona St., 15104. Tel: 412-271-1515; Fax: 412-271-1222.
School—1025 Braddock Ave., 15104 Tel: 412-271-2492; Fax: 412-271-3248. Sr. Marie Diane Novachek, V.S.C., Prin. Sisters 3; Lay Teachers 10; Students 144.
Catechesis/Religious Program—Tel: 412-271-2630. Students 85.
Convent—Tel: 412-271-1736.

BRENTWOOD, ALLEGHENY CO., ST. SYLVESTER (1924), Revs. Mark A. Eckman, M.Div.; Leroy A. DiPietro. In Res., Deacon Joseph R. Mueller.
Res. 3754 Brownsville Rd., 15227. Tel: 412-882-8598; Fax: 412-882-0153.
School—30 W. Willock Rd., 15227. Tel: 412-882-9900. Sisters of Divine Providence 1; Lay Teachers 8; Students 160.
Catechesis/Religious Program—Tel: 412-881-4142. Students 510.

BRIDGEVILLE, ALLEGHENY CO.

1—ST. AGATHA (1894), Closed., See Holy Child.

2—ST. ANTHONY (1915), (Lithuanian), Closed., See Holy Child.

3—ST. BARBARA (1894), [CEM] Rev Donald Chortos.
Res.: 45 Prestley Rd., 15017-1971. Tel: 412-221-5152; Fax: 412-221-7935.
Catechesis/Religious Program—Students 195.

4—HOLY CHILD (1994), [CEM] Consolidated, from St. Agatha and St. Anthony. Revs. Frederick L. Cain; Thaddeus S. Maida; Paul W. Merkovsky.
Res.: 212 Station St., 15017. Tel: 412-221-5213; Fax: 412-257-2461.
School—Tel: 412-221-4720; Fax: 412-257-9742. Sisters 1; Lay Teachers 10; Students 166.
Catechesis/Religious Program—Tel: 412-221-6514. Students 476.
Convent—509 Coulter St., 15017. Tel: 412-221-3930.

BULGER, WASHINGTON CO., ST. ANN (1917), Unassigned.
Res.: 967 Grant St., Box 488, 15019-0488. Tel: 724-796-3791; 724-796-9151 (Social Hall); Fax: 724-796-5173.
Catechesis/Religious Program—Students 58.

BURGETTSTOWN, WASHINGTON CO., OUR LADY OF LOURDES (1916), [CEM] Rev. Richard J. Tusky.
Res.: 1109 Main St., 15021. Tel: 724-947-3363; Fax: 724-947-9348.
School—1111 Main St., 15021. Tel: 724-947-3363 Rectory; Fax: 724-947-9348. Lay Teachers 10; Students 123.
Catechesis/Religious Program—Tel: 724-587-3775. Students 148.

BUTLER, BUTLER CO.

1—ST. FIDELIS OF SIGMARINGEN (1995), Revs. James F. Murphy; George Palick.
Res.: 125 Buttercup Rd., 16001. Tel: 724-482-2690; Fax: 724-482-2315.
Catechesis/Religious Program—Tel: 724-482-2362. Students 325.

2—ST. MICHAEL THE ARCHANGEL (1909), (Italian—French), [CEM] Rev. James W. Dolan.
Res.: 432 Center Ave., 16001. Tel: 724-282-4107; Fax: 724-282-3156.
School—Butler Catholic School, Tel: 724-285-4276; Fax: 724-285-4896. See Consolidated Schools under Institutions Located in the Diocese.
Catechesis/Religious Program—Tel: 724-282-9365. Students 160.

3—ST. PAUL (1867), (Territorial), Very Rev. Harry R. Bielewicz, V.F., M.Div.; Rev. F. Raymond Trance; Deacons Mitchell M. Natali; Gerald C. Stein, (Retired). In Res., Rev. Henry S. Preneta (GBG), Hospital Chap., (Retired).
Res.: 128 N. McKean St., 16001. Tel: 724-287-1759; Fax: 724-287-2081.
School—Butler Catholic School, Tel: 724-285-4276; Fax: 724-285-4896. See Consolidated Schools under Institutions Located in the Diocese.
Catechesis/Religious Program—Students 375.

4—ST. PETER (1821), (German), [CEM] Rev. Jack Nanz.
Res.: 127 Franklin St., 16001. Tel: 724-287-2743; Fax: 724-287-8447.
School—Butler Catholic School, Tel: 724-285-4276. See Consolidated Schools under Institutions Located in the Diocese.
Catechesis/Religious Program—Students 545.

5—ST. WENDELIN (1863), [CEM] Rev. Michael J. Maranowski.
Res.: 210 St. Wendelin Rd., 16002. Tel: 724-287-0820; Fax: 724-287-6253.
School—*Preschool*, Tel: 724-285-4986. Students 42.
School—(Grades K-8), 211 St. Wendelin Rd., 16002. Tel: 724-285-4986. Lay Teachers 8; Students 73.
Catechesis/Religious Program—Students 183.

CABOT, BUTLER CO., ST. JOSEPH (1904), Rev. John Getsy, O.F.M.Cap.
Res.: 315 Stoney Hollow Rd., 16023. Tel: 724-352-2149; Fax: 724-352-7174.
Catechesis/Religious Program—Tel: 724-352-3030; Fax: 724-352-3443. Students 362.

CALIFORNIA, WASHINGTON CO., ST. THOMAS AQUINAS (1888), [CEM] Rev. Mark J. Skertich.
Res.: 213 Fourth St., 15419. Tel: 724-938-3204; Fax: 724-938-0434.
Catechesis/Religious Program—Tel: 724-938-7775. Students 95.

CANONSBURG, WASHINGTON CO.

1—ST. GENEVIEVE, (Polish), Closed., See St. Patrick.

2—ST. PATRICK (1993), [CEM] Merged, with St. Genevieve. Revs. Philip J. Przybyla; Alfred C. Cicola; John B. Gizler (Retired).
Res.: 317 W. Pike St., 15317. Tel: 724-745-6560; Fax: 724-746-1112.
School—Hutchinson & Murdock Sts., 15317. Tel: 724-745-7977; Fax: 724-746-1112. Priests 3; Lay Teachers 11; Students 183.
Catechesis/Religious Program—Tel: 724-745-3787. Students 551.

CARMICHAELS, GREENE CO., ST. HUGH (1951), (Polish), Rev. John M. Bauer.
Res.: 408 Rte. 88, 15320. Tel: 724-966-7270; Fax: 724-966-9118.
Catechesis/Religious Program—Students 22.

CARNEGIE, ALLEGHENY CO.

1—ST. ELIZABETH ANN SETON (1992), (Italian—German), [CEM] [JC 4] Consolidated, from the following churches: Holy Souls, St. Ignatius de Loyola, Immaculate Conception, St. Joseph, St. Luke and St. Vincent de Paul, Walkers Mill. Revs. Joseph G. Luisi; Steven M. Palsa. In Res., Rev. James G. Young.
Res.: 206 Mary St., 15106-2489. Tel: 412-276-1011; Fax: 412-276-0816.
Catechesis/Religious Program—127 Finley Ave., 15106. Tel: 412-279-8118; Fax: 412-279-2757. Students 350.

2—HOLY SOULS, Closed., See St. Elizabeth Ann Seton.

3—ST. IGNATIUS DE LOYOLA, (Polish), Closed., See St. Elizabeth Ann Seton.

4—IMMACULATE CONCEPTION, (Polish), Closed., See St. Elizabeth Ann Seton.

5—ST. JOSEPH, (German), Closed., See St. Elizabeth Ann Seton.

6—ST. LUKE, Closed., See St. Elizabeth Ann Seton.

CASTLE SHANNON, ALLEGHENY CO., ST. ANNE (1889), [CEM] Very Rev. Donald P. Breier, V.F., M.Div.; Rev. James R. Gretz. In Res., Rev. Msgr. Charles O. Rice, Pastor Emeritus (Retired).
Res.: 400 Hoodridge Dr., 15234. Tel: 412-531-5964; Fax: 412-531-6901.
School—4040 Willow Ave., 15234. Tel: 412-561-7720; Fax: 412-561-7927. Lay Teachers 15; Students 230.
Catechesis/Religious Program—Tel: 412-561-0101. Students 753.

CECIL, WASHINGTON CO., ST. MARY (1909), [CEM] Rev. Robert P. Connolly.
Res.: 10 St. Mary's Ln., 15321. Tel: 412-221-1560; Fax: 412-221-9544.
Catechesis/Religious Program—Tel: 412-221-0595. Students 240.

CENTER TOWNSHIP, BEAVER CO., ST. FRANCES CABRINI (1961), Revs. Joseph J. Kleppner, S.T.L., Ph.D.; Michael John Lynam. In Res., Rev. Msgr. Jeremiah J. McCarthy.
Res.: 115 Trinity Dr. Center Twp., Aliquippa, 15001. Tel: 724-775-6363; Fax: 724-775-3848.
Catechesis/Religious Program—Tel: 724-774-4888; Fax: 724-775-3848. Students 500.

CENTER TOWNSHIP, BUTLER CO., ST. ANDREW (1964), Rev. James G. Salberg.
Res.: 1660 N. Main St. Ext., Butler, 16001. Tel: 724-287-7781; Fax: 724-287-7346.
Catechesis/Religious Program—Students 171.

CHARLEROI, WASHINGTON CO.
1—SS. CYRIL AND METHODIUS, (Slovak), Closed., See Mary Mother of the Church.
2—ST. JEROME, Closed., See Mary Mother of the Church.
3—MARY MOTHER OF THE CHURCH (1992), [CEM] Consolidated, from SS. Cyril & Methodius, St. Jerome and Mother of Sorrows. Revs. David F. Dzermejko; Bernard B. Costello.
Res.: 624 Washington Ave., 15022-1989. Tel: 724-483-4572; 724-483-5533; Fax: 724-483-0122.
Catechesis/Religious Program—Students 218.
4—MOTHER OF SORROWS, (Italian), Closed., See Mary Mother of the Church.

CHICORA, BUTLER CO., MATER DOLOROSA (1910), Rev. David D. DeWitt. In Res., Rev. William Komakech.
Res.: P.O. Box 243, 16025. Tel: 724-445-2275; Fax: 724-445-7507.
Catechesis/Religious Program—Students 120.

CHIPPEWA TOWNSHIP, BEAVER CO., CHRIST THE DIVINE TEACHER (1969), Rev. Harry R. Sangl.
Res.: 116 Thorndale Dr., Beaver Falls, 15010. Tel: 724-846-7540.
Catechesis/Religious Program—Tel: 724-847-4750. Students 251.

CHURCHILL BOROUGH, ALLEGHENY CO., ST. JOHN FISHER (1960), Very Rev. Carl J. Gentile, V.F.
Res.: 33 Lewin Ln., 15235. Tel: 412-241-4722; Fax: 412-241-4653.
Catechesis/Religious Program—Tel: 412-241-4653. Students 140.

CLAIRTON, ALLEGHENY CO.
1—ST. CLARE OF ASSISI (1994), [CEM] Consolidated, from the following churches: St. Joseph, St. Paulinus and St. Clare. Revs. Richard J. Zelik, O.F.M.Cap.; Michael P. Masich, O.F.M.Cap.; Bros. Charles O'Connor, O.F.M.Cap., Pastoral Asst.; Gregory Brown, O.F.M.Cap.
314 Wilson Ave., 15025. Tel: 412-233-7870; Fax: 412-233-0742. In Res., Rev. John Carey, O.F.M.Cap.
School—336 Wilson Ave., 15025. Tel: 412-233-7598.
Catechesis/Religious Program—Tel: 412-233-4416. Students 59.
2—ST. JOSEPH, Closed., See St. Clare of Assisi.
3—ST. PAULINUS, Closed., See St. Clare of Assisi.

CLARKSVILLE, WASHINGTON CO., ST. THOMAS (1992), (Polish—Italian), Rev. Thomas R. Miller.
Res.: 30 Main St., 15322. Tel: 724-377-2588; Fax: 724-377-0707.
Catechesis/Religious Program—Students 80.

CONWAY, BEAVER CO., OUR LADY OF PEACE (1941), Revs. Robert Guay; Patrick Barkey. In Res., Rev. David C. Menegay.
Res.: 1000 Third Ave., 15027. Tel: 724-869-3024; Fax: 724-869-3025.
Catechesis/Religious Program—Tel: 724-869-4723. Students 329.

CORAOPOLIS, ALLEGHENY CO., ST. JOSEPH (1891), [CEM] Rev. G. Malcolm McDonald.
Res.: 1304 Fourth Ave., 15108. Tel: 412-264-6162; Fax: 412-264-5370.
School—Tel: 412-264-6141; Fax: 412-264-1518. Felician Sisters 3; Lay Teachers 12; Students 167; Pre-School 20.
Catechesis/Religious Program—Tel: 412-262-2828. Students 160.

COYLESVILLE, BUTLER CO., ST. JOHN (1853), [CEM] Rev. Louis F. Pascazi, Admin.
Res.: 668 Clearfield Rd., Fenelton, 16034-9743. Tel: 724-287-7590; Fax: 724-287-3550.
Catechesis/Religious Program—Tel: 724-287-0426. Students 121.

CRAFTON, ALLEGHENY CO., ST. PHILIP (1839), (Irish), [CEM] Rev. Walter W. Dworak.
Res.: 50 W. Crafton Ave., 15205. Tel: 412-922-6300; Fax: 412-920-7310.
School—52 W. Crafton Ave., 15205. Tel: 412-928-2742. Sisters of Charity 4; Lay Teachers 25; Students 368.
Catechesis/Religious Program—Tel: 412-928-2744. Students 224.

CRANBERRY TOWNSHIP, BUTLER CO., ST. FERDINAND (1961), Revs. John P. Gallagher, S.T.L.; Gary W. Krummert; Joseph P. Newell; Barbara McCarthy, Pastoral Assoc.
Res.: 2535 Rochester Rd., 16066-6496. Tel: 724-776-2888; Fax: 724-776-2378.
Catechesis/Religious Program—Tel: 724-776-9177; Fax: 724-776-6640. Students 1,243.

CREIGHTON, ALLEGHENY CO., HOLY FAMILY (East Deer Twp.) (1949), (Territorial), Rev. Miroslaw Stelmaszczyk.
Res.: 787 Freeport Rd., 15030. Tel: 724-224-1626; Fax: 724-224-0609.
Catechesis/Religious Program—Students 38.

DARLINGTON, BEAVER CO., ST. ROSE OF LIMA (1854), [CEM] Rev. James B. Krah.
Res.: 3357 Constitution Blvd., 16115. Tel: 412-843-0152; Fax: 724-843-7810.
Catechesis/Religious Program—Students 196.

DONORA, WASHINGTON CO.
1—ST. CHARLES, Closed., See Our Lady of the Valley.
2—ST. DOMINIC, (Slovak), Closed., See Our Lady of the Valley.
3—HOLY NAME OF THE BLESSED VIRGIN MARY, Closed., See Our Lady of the Valley.
4—OUR LADY OF THE VALLEY (1992), [CEM] Consolidated, from the following churches: St. Charles Borromeo, St. Dominic, Holy Name of the Blessed Virgin Mary and St. Philip Neri. Rev. David J. Kriss. In Res., Rev. Joseph Oppong (Ghana).
Res.: 571 Thompson Ave., 15033. Tel: 724-379-4777; 724-379-7777; Fax: 724-379-6242.
Catechesis/Religious Program—Students 125.
5—ST. PHILIP NERI, (Italian), Closed., See Our Lady of the Valley.

DUQUESNE, ALLEGHENY CO.
1—CHRIST THE LIGHT OF THE WORLD (1994), [CEM 2] Consolidated, from St. Hedwig and Holy Name. Rev. Dennis Colamarino.
Res.: 32 S. First St., 15110. Tel: 412-469-0196; Fax: 412-466-6845.
Catechesis/Religious Program—Students 109.
2—HOLY NAME, Closed., See Christ the Light of the World.
3—ST. JOSEPH (1897), (German), [CEM] Rev. Dennis Colamarino. In Res., Rev. Emmanuel C. Agbakwuru (Nigeria).
Res.: 817 W. Grant Ave., 15110. Tel: 412-466-1304; Fax: 412-466-3130.
Catechesis/Religious Program— Twinned with Christ the Light of the World.

EAST MCKEESPORT, ALLEGHENY CO., ST. ROBERT BELLARMINE (1951), Rev. John G. Oesterle.
Res.: 1313 Fifth Ave., 15035. Tel: 412-824-2644; 412-824-2635; Fax: 412-824-4786.
Catechesis/Religious Program—Tel: 412-824-3688; Fax: 412-829-1266. Students 233.

EAST PITTSBURGH, ALLEGHENY CO.
1—ST. HELEN, (Slovak), Closed., See Holy Cross.
2—HOLY CROSS (1994), Consolidated, from St. William and St. Helen. Rev. Miroslaus A. Wojcicki.
Res.: 905 Main St., 15112. Tel: 412-829-1146; Fax: 412-816-2059.
Catechesis/Religious Program—Students 50.
Convent—Sisters of Divine Providence, 515 Howard St., 15112. Tel: 412-829-0815. (Allison Park) Sisters 3.
3—ST. WILLIAM, Closed., See Holy Cross.

ELIZABETH, ALLEGHENY CO., ST. MICHAEL (1849), [CEM] Rev. Rudolph F. Smoley.
Res.: 101 McLay Dr., 15037. Tel: 412-751-0663; Fax: 412-751-2161.
School—Sixth & Bayard St., 15037. Tel: 412-384-9400; Fax: 412-384-3727. Lay Teachers 6; Students 59.
Catechesis/Religious Program—Students 371.

ELLWOOD CITY, LAWRENCE CO.
1—ST. AGATHA (1895), (Territorial), Merged, with Purification of the Blessed Virgin Mary, Ellwood City to form Holy Redeemer, Ellwood City.
2—HOLY REDEEMER PARISH (2000), Very Rev. Mauro J. Cautela, V.F., M.Div.; Rev. Michael L. Yaksick.
300 Crescent Ave., Ste. 1, 16117. Tel: 724-758-4411; Fax: 724-752-1466.
Catechesis/Religious Program—610 Bridge St., 16117. Tel: 724-758-1271; Fax: 724-758-5562. Students 723.
3—PURIFICATION OF THE BLESSED VIRGIN MARY (1914), Merged, with St. Agatha, Ellwood City to form Holy Redeemer, Ellwood City.

ELRAMA, ALLEGHENY CO., ST. ISAAC JOGUES (1950), Rev. Robert Andrew Kohuch.
Church: 1216 Collins Ave., Clairton, 15025.
P.O. Box 600, 15038. Tel: 412-384-4406; Fax: 412-384-5740.
Catechesis/Religious Program—Students 77.

EMSWORTH, ALLEGHENY CO., SACRED HEART (1891), Revs. John P. Skaj, C.S.Sp.; Francis P. Meenan, C.S.Sp.
Res.: 154 Orchard Ave., 15202. Tel: 412-761-6651; Fax: 412-766-8298.
Catechesis/Religious Program—Tel: 412-761-3806. Students 170.

ETNA, ALLEGHENY CO., ALL SAINTS (1902), Rev. John Vojtek; Bess Biamonte, Pastoral Assoc. In Res., Rev. Ameh Ambrose Ejeh (Nigeria).
Res.: 19 Wilson St., 15223-1798. Tel: 412-781-0530; Fax: 412-784-8769.
School—Preschool, 20 Wilson St., 15223. Tel: 412-781-4692.
School—19 Dewey St., 15223. Tel: 412-782-0939; Fax: 412-782-6214. Lay Teachers 9; Students 101.
Catechesis/Religious Program—Tel: 412-782-3307. Students 100.
Social Service—Tel: 412-781-0530.

EVANS CITY, BUTLER CO., ST. MATTHIAS (1939), Rev. William J. Ritzert.
Res.: 417 E. Main St., 16033. Tel: 724-538-5331.
Catechesis/Religious Program—Students 197.

FINLEYVILLE, WASHINGTON CO., ST. FRANCIS OF ASSISI (1893), [CEM] Very Rev. Robert J. Boyle, V.F.; Deacon Victor P. Satter.
Res.: 3609 Washington Ave., 15332. Tel: 724-348-7145; Fax: 724-348-7522.
Catechesis/Religious Program—Tel: 724-348-6190. Students 256.

FOREST HILLS, ALLEGHENY CO., ST. MAURICE (1949), Rev. John W. Skirtich. In Res., Rev. Pachomius Okogie, O.S.B.
Res.: 2001 Ardmore Blvd., 15221. Tel: 412-271-0809; Fax: 412-271-2415.
School—Tel: 412-351-5403. Sisters 3; Lay Teachers 29; Students 325.
Catechesis/Religious Program—Tel: 412-271-6606. Students 242.

FRANKLIN PARK BOROUGH, ALLEGHENY CO.
1—ST. JOHN NEUMANN (1979), Rev. William R. Bovard. In Res., Rev. Ambrose Mootheril.
Res.: 1543 Old Orchard Rd., 15237. Tel: 412-366-2020; Fax: 412-366-2866.
Catechesis/Religious Program—2230 Rochester Rd., 15237. Tel: 412-366-5885. Students 797.
2—SAINTS JOHN AND PAUL (1994), Rev. Joseph R. McCaffrey.
Res.: 2586 Wexford-Bayne Rd., Sewickley, 15143. Tel: 724-935-2104; Fax: 724-935-8320.
Catechesis/Religious Program—Students 1,125.

FREDERICKTOWN, WASHINGTON CO.
1—ST. MICHAEL THE ARCHANGEL, Closed., See St. Oliver Plunkett, Marianna.
2—ST. OLIVER PLUNKETT (1994), [CEM] Consolidated, from Saints Mary & Ann, Marianna, and St. Michael Archangel, Fredericktown. In Res., Rev. Francis A. Nazimek (Retired).
Res.: Box 638, 15333. Tel: 724-377-0128; Fax: 724-377-0129.
Catechesis/Religious Program—Students 150.

FREEDOM, BEAVER CO., ST. FELIX (1906), (Italian), [CEM] Rev. Raymond M. Utz.
Res.: 450 13th St., 15042. Tel: 724-775-1476; Fax: 724-775-5684.
Catechesis/Religious Program—Tel: 724-728-4421. Students 70.

GLADE MILLS, BUTLER CO., HOLY SEPULCHER (1955), Rev. John P. Maloney.
Res.: 1304 E. Cruikshank Rd., Butler, 16002. Tel: 724-586-7610; Fax: 724-586-7247.
School—Tel: 724-586-5022; Fax: 724-586-5073. Lay Teachers 13; Students 193.
Catechesis/Religious Program—Tel: 724-586-7276. Students 479.

GLASSPORT, ALLEGHENY CO.
1—ST. CECILIA, Closed., See Queen of the Rosary.
2—QUEEN OF THE ROSARY (1994), Consolidated, from Holy Cross and St. Cecilia. Rev. Casimir Kedzierski.
Res.: 530 Michigan Ave., 15045. Tel: 412-672-7209; Fax: 412-672-6390.
School—St. Joseph Regional School 15045. Tel: 412-678-0659. See Consolidated Schools under Institutions Located in the Diocese.
Catechesis/Religious Program—Students 163.

GLENSHAW, ALLEGHENY CO.
1—ST. BONAVENTURE (1957), Revs. Pierre M. Falkenhan, V.F.; Mark A. Thomas.
Res.: 2001 Mount Royal Blvd., 15116. Tel: 412-486-2606; Fax: 412-492-9329.
School—Tel: 412-486-2608; Fax: 412-487-8657. Sisters of Divine Providence 1; Lay Teachers 27; Students 460.
Catechesis/Religious Program—Tel: 412-486-0800. Students 471.
2—ST. MARY OF THE ASSUMPTION (1834), [CEM] Revs. John A. Marcucci; Edward Schleicher.
Res.: 2510 Middle Rd., 15116. Tel: 412-486-4100; Fax: 412-486-4150.
School—Tel: 412-486-7611; Fax: 412-487-9509. Sisters of Divine Providence 1; Lay Teachers 26; Students 447.
Catechesis/Religious Program—Tel: 412-486-5521; Fax: 412-486-5177. Students 670.

GREEN TREE, ALLEGHENY CO., ST. MARGARET (1938), Revs. Harry E. Nichols; Shawn O. Malarkey.
Res.: 310 Mansfield Ave., 15220. Tel: 412-921-0745; Fax: 412-921-0707.
School—915 Alice St., 15220. Tel: 412-922-4765; Fax: 412-922-4647. Lay Teachers 22; Students 260.
Catechesis/Religious Program—912 Alice St., 15220.

Tel: 412-921-7999; Fax: 412-921-7999. Students 260.
HARMARVILLE, ALLEGHENY CO., ST. FRANCIS OF ASSISI (1940), Rev. Hugh J. McCormley.
Res.: 2599 Freeport Rd., 15238. Tel: 412-828-3123; Fax: 412-828-0527.
Catechesis/Religious Program—Rte. 910, Indianola, 15051. Tel: 412-767-9971. Students 51.
HARWICK, ALLEGHENY CO., OUR LADY OF VICTORY (1944), Rev. Albert L. Zapf.
Res.: 1319 Low Grade Rd., Box 198, 15049. Tel: 724-274-8575; Fax: 724-274-0529.
Catechesis/Religious Program—Tel: 724-274-6445. Students 200.
HERMAN, BUTLER CO., ST. MARY OF THE ASSUMPTION (1842), [CEM] Rev. Lester Knoll, O.F.M.Cap.
Res.: 821 Herman Rd., P.O. Box 26, 16039. Tel: 724-285-3285; Fax: 724-285-4715.
School—Tel: 724-283-2129. Lay Teachers 8; Students 108; PreK 24.
Catechesis/Religious Program—Students 100.
HILLSVILLE, LAWRENCE CO.
1—CHRIST THE KING (2000), Rev. James A. Downs.
Mailing Address: P.O. Box 23, 16132. Tel: 724-667-7721; Fax: 724-667-0827.
Catechesis/Religious Program—Students 209.
2—ST. LAWRENCE (1904), (Italian), Merged, with St. Anthony, Bessemer to form Christ the King, Hillsville.
HOLIDAY PARK, ALLEGHENY CO., OUR LADY OF JOY (1968), Very Rev. Robert J. Cedolia, V.F., M.Div., M.A.
Res.: 2000 O'Block Rd., 15239. Tel: 412-795-3388; Fax: 412-793-5308.
Catechesis/Religious Program—Tel: 412-795-4389. Students 725.
HOMESTEAD, ALLEGHENY CO.
1—ST. ANNE, Closed., See St. Maximilian Kolbe, Homestead.
2—ST. ANTHONY, Closed., See St. Maximilian Kolbe, Homestead.
3—ST. MARY MAGDALENE, Closed., See St. Maximilian Kolbe, Homestead.
4—ST. MAXIMILIAN KOLBE (1992), [CEM 3] Consolidated, from the following churches: St. Anne, Homestead; St. Anthony, Homestead; St. Margaret, Homestead; St. Mary Magdalene, Homestead; St. Michael, Homestead; SS. Peter & Paul, Homestead. Rev. Mark L. Thomas. In Res., Rev. Mark W. Glasgow. Tel: 412-462-1807.
Parish Center: 363 W. 11th Ave. Extension, 15120. Tel: 412-461-1054; Fax: 412-462-1744.
Catechesis/Religious Program—Students 48.
5—SS. PETER AND PAUL, (Lithuanian), Closed., See St. Maximilian Kolbe, Homestead.
HOPEWELL TOWNSHIP, BEAVER CO., OUR LADY OF FATIMA (1954), Revs. Howard W. Campbell; Terrence P. O'Connor.
Res.: 2270 Brodhead Rd., Aliquippa, 15001. Tel: 724-375-7626; Fax: 724-375-0219.
School—Tel: 724-375-7565. Lay Teachers 18; Students 199.
Catechesis/Religious Program—Tel: 724-378-8020. Students 553.
IMPERIAL, ALLEGHENY CO., ST. COLUMBKILLE (1908), [CEM] Rev. Domenic Mancini.
Res.: 103 Church Rd., 15126. Tel: 724-695-7325; Fax: 724-695-9202.
Catechesis/Religious Program—101 Church Rd., 15126. Tel: 724-695-2146. Students 477.
INDUSTRY, BEAVER CO., ST. CHRISTINE, Closed., See St. Blaise, Midland.
INGRAM, ALLEGHENY CO., ASCENSION (1967), Very Rev. Walter A. Sobon, V.F., M.Ed.
Res.: 114 Berry St., 15205. Tel: 412-921-1230; Fax: 412-922-1279.
Catechesis/Religious Program—Tel: 412-922-6808. Students 130.
JEFFERSON HILLS, ALLEGHENY CO., ST. THOMAS A'BECKET (1957), Rev. Robert L. Seeman.
Res.: 509 Gill Hall Rd., 15025. Tel: 412-655-2885; Fax: 412-655-0615.
Catechesis/Religious Program—Tel: 412-653-4322; Fax: 412-653-9979. Students 460.
KENNEDY TOWNSHIP, ALLEGHENY CO., ST. MALACHY (1953), Rev. Richard S. Jones; Deacon David Lamm.
Res.: 343 Forest Grove Rd., Coraopolis, 15108. Tel: 412-771-5483; Fax: 412-331-7312.
School—Tel: 412-771-4545; Fax: 412-771-0922. Lay Teachers 12; Students 257.
Catechesis/Religious Program—Tel: 412-771-7480. Students 553.
KOPPEL, BEAVER CO.
1—QUEEN OF HEAVEN (1992), [CEM] Consolidated, from St. Monica, Wampum and St. Teresa, Koppel. Rev. Joseph R. Lemp, S.T.L.
Res.: 6421 Sixth Ave., P.O. Box A, 16136-0601. Tel: 724-846-5702; 724-846-9559 (Office); Fax: 724-846-2219.
Catechesis/Religious Program—Students 101.
2—ST. TERESA, Closed., See Queen of Heaven.
LAWRENCE, WASHINGTON CO., ST. ELIZABETH, Closed., See St. Mary, Cecil.
LIBERTY BORO, ALLEGHENY CO., ST. EUGENE, Closed., See St. Mark, Port Vue.
LYNDORA, BUTLER CO.
1—ST. JOHN (1904), (Slovak), Closed., See St. Fidelis of Sigmaringen, Butler.
2—ST. STANISLAUS KOSTKA (1919), (Polish), Merged, with St. Conrad, Meridian, and St. John, Lyndora, to form St. Fidelis, Butler.
MARS, BUTLER CO., ST. KILIAN (1920), Rev. Charles S. Bober, S.T.D.; Deacon Ralph W. Bachner Jr.
Res.: Clarke & Cherry Sts., P.O. Box 394, 16046. Tel: 724-625-1665; Fax: 724-625-1922.
Catechesis/Religious Program—212 Hook St., Box 394, 16046. Tel: 724-625-1288. Students 900.
MCDONALD, WASHINGTON CO., ST. ALPHONSUS (1892), Rev. John A. Harvey.
Res.: 219 W. Lincoln Ave., 15057. Tel: 724-926-2984; Fax: 724-926-5120.
Catechesis/Religious Program—Students 140.
MCKEES ROCKS, ALLEGHENY CO.
1—SS. CYRIL AND METHODIUS, (Polish), Closed., See St. John of God.
2—ST. FRANCIS DE SALES, Closed., See St. John of God.
3—ST. JOHN OF GOD (1993), [CEM 2] Consolidated, from the following churches: St. Francis de Sales, SS. Cyril & Methodius, St. Maria Goretti Chapel, St. Mark, St. Mary Help of Christians, Mother of Sorrows and St. Vincent, Pittsburgh. Revs. Paul C. Householder; Lawrence R. Smith; Deacon Joseph Compomizzi. In Res., Revs. Harold Baily; Regis J. Ryan; Christopher Mbogu (Nigeria).
Parish Office—1 Desiderio Way, 15136. Tel: 412-771-5646; Fax: 412-331-0678.
School—3 Desiderio Way, 15136. Tel: 412-331-8501; Fax: 412-331-0678. Lay Teachers 9; Students 139.
Catechesis/Religious Program—Tel: 412-331-8573. Students 181.
4—ST. MARIA GORETTI CHAPEL, Closed., See St. John of God.
5—ST. MARK, (Slovak), Closed., See St. John of God.
6—ST. MARY HELP OF CHRISTIANS, (German), Closed., See St. John of God.
7—MOTHER OF SORROWS, (Italian), Closed., See St. John of God.
MCKEESPORT, ALLEGHENY CO.
1—HOLY TRINITY, Closed., See St. Martin de Porres.
2—ST. MARTIN DE PORRES (1993), [CEM 3] Consolidated, from St. Mary, Holy Trinity, Sacred Heart and St. Peter. Revs. John L. Gudewicz; Richard J. Wesoloski; Deacon Steve Pikula. In Res., Revs. John A. Palko (Retired); Ignatius Kayita (Uganda).
Res.: 704 Market St., 15132. Tel: 412-672-9763; Fax: 412-672-2817.
School—St. Joseph Regional School, Mc Keesport, 15133. See Consolidated Schools under Institutions Located in the Diocese.
Catechesis/Religious Program—Tel: 412-672-7440. Students 70.
3—ST. MARY, (German), Closed., See St. Martin de Porres.
4—ST. MARY CZESTOCHOWA (1893), (Polish), [CEM] Rev. Francis B. Lachowicz.
Res.: 2515 Versailles Ave., 15132. Tel: 412-672-0765; Fax: 412-672-2220.
Catechesis/Religious Program—2412 Versailles Ave., 15132. Tel: 412-751-2873. Students 96.
5—ST. PATRICK (1993), [CEM] Merged, with St. Denis, Versailles and St. Perpetua, McKeesport. Rev. Vincent P. Velas.
Res.: 310 32nd St., 15132. Tel: 412-673-4110; Fax: 412-678-7259.
Catechesis/Religious Program—305 32nd St., 15132. Tel: 412-664-7417. Students 120.
6—ST. PERPETUA, Closed., See St. Patrick, Versailles.
7—ST. PETER, Closed., See St. Martin de Porres.
8—ST. PIUS V (1903), [CEM] Merged, with St. Stephen. Rev. John J. Keane (HRT), Admin.
Res.: 2911 Versailles Ave., 15132. Tel: 412-673-8878; Fax: 412-673-8704.
Catechesis/Religious Program—Students 65.
9—SACRED HEART, (Croatian), Closed., See St. Martin de Porres.
10—ST. STEPHEN (1899), (Hungarian), Closed., See St. Pius V.
MEADOWLANDS, WASHINGTON CO., OUR LADY OF THE MIRACULOUS MEDAL (1949), [JC] Rev. John L. O'Shea.
Res.: Box 366, 15347. Tel: 724-222-1911; Fax: 724-222-5688.
Catechesis/Religious Program—Tel: 724-228-9088; 724-228-8575 CCD Activities Center; Fax: 724-228-1488. Students 166.
MERIDIAN, BUTLER CO., ST. CONRAD, Merged, with St. John and St. Stanislaus Kostka, Lyndora to form St. Fidelis, Butler.
MIDLAND, BEAVER CO., ST. BLAISE (1994), Rev. John M. Jordan.
Res.: 772 Ohio Ave., 15059. Tel: 724-643-4050; Fax: 724-643-6533.
Catechesis/Religious Program—Tel: 724-643-4663. Students 170.
MILLVALE, ALLEGHENY CO.
1—ST. ANN, Closed., See Holy Spirit.
2—ST. ANTHONY, (German), Closed., See Holy Spirit.
3—HOLY SPIRIT (1994), Consolidated, from St. Anthony and St. Ann. Revs. George J. Spangenberg, C.S.Sp.; Ekpaa Mallo, C.S.Sp. from St. Anthony and St. Ann. In Res., Rev. John Marandu, C.S.Sp.
Res.: 608 Farragut St., 15209. Tel: 412-821-4424; Fax: 412-821-8258.
School—100 Howard St., 15209. Tel: 412-821-4805; Fax: 412-821-4714. Lay Teachers 12; Students 195.
Catechesis/Religious Program—Tel: 412-821-2099. Students 234.
4—ST. NICHOLAS, (Croatian), Closed., See the new St. Nicholas.
5—ST. NICHOLAS (1894), (Croatian), [JC 2] Very Rev. Gabriel Badurina, T.O.R.
Administrative Center—24 Maryland Ave., 15209. Tel: 412-821-3438; Fax: 412-821-8726.
Catechesis/Religious Program—414 Kinkura Dr., 15212. Tel: 412-322-3732. Students 131.
MONACA, BEAVER CO., ST. JOHN THE BAPTIST (1888), [CEM] Rev. Frank M. Kurimsky.
Res.: 1409 Pennsylvania Ave., 15061. Tel: 724-775-3940; Fax: 724-775-6886.
School—Virginia Ave. & 15th St., 15061. Tel: 724-775-5774; Fax: 724-775-2997. Lay Teachers 12; Students 340.
Catechesis/Religious Program—Students 305.
MONONGAHELA, WASHINGTON CO.
1—ST. ANTHONY (1904), (Italian—Slovak), Rev. Joseph E. Feltz, Admin.
Res.: 225 Park Ave., 15063. Tel: 724-258-9710; Fax: 724-258-3362.
Catechesis/Religious Program—Tel: 724-258-9233. Students 175.
2—TRANSFIGURATION (1865), [CEM 2] Rev. John J. Baver.
Res.: 722 W. Main St., 15063. Tel: 724-258-7742; Fax: 724-258-8733.
School—Madonna Regional Catholic School, Tel: 724-379-5977; Fax: 724-379-7633. See Consolidated Schools under Institutions Located in the Diocese.
Catechesis/Religious Program—Students 125.
MONROEVILLE, ALLEGHENY CO.
1—ST. BERNADETTE (1955), Revs. Michael W. Decewicz; Joseph F. Keenan; Deacon Michael W. Kelly.
Res.: 245 Azalea Dr., 15146. Tel: 412-373-0050; Fax: 412-374-8113.
School—(Grades PreK-8) Tel: 412-372-7255; Fax: 412-372-7649. Sisters 2; Lay Teachers 20; Students 378.
Catechesis/Religious Program—Tel: 412-373-1797. Students 780.
2—NORTH AMERICAN MARTYRS (1960), Rev. Francis J. Murhammer. In Res., Rev. Thomas V. Manning.
Res.: 2526 Haymaker Rd., 15146. Tel: 412-373-0330; Fax: 412-380-1306.
School—(Grades K-6) Tel: 412-373-0889. Lay Teachers 10; Students 106.
Catechesis/Religious Program—Tel: 412-372-8149. Students 386.
MOON TOWNSHIP, ALLEGHENY CO., ST. MARGARET MARY (1956), Revs. John Ayoob; Robin Evanish.
Res.: One Parish Pl., 15108-2697. Tel: 412-264-2573; Fax: 412-264-4327.
Catechesis/Religious Program—Tel: 412-264-9368. Students 680.
MT. LEBANON, ALLEGHENY CO.
1—ST. BERNARD (1919), (Irish—German), Revs. David A. Driesch; George R. Dalton; James R. Torquato. In Res., Rev. Leo V. Vanyo, J.C.D. (Retired).
Res.: 311 Washington Rd., 15216. Tel: 412-561-3301; Fax: 412-563-0211.
School—(Grades PreK-8), 315 Washington Rd., 15216. Tel: 412-341-5444; Fax: 412-341-2044. Lay Teachers 30; Students 524.
Catechesis/Religious Program—401 Washington Rd., 15216. Tel: 412-561-0199. Students 981.
2—ST. WINIFRED (Pittsburgh) (1960), Rev. Jeremiah T. O'Shea; Deacon Joseph Kosko.
Res.: 550 Sleepy Hollow Rd., 15228. Tel: 412-344-5010; Fax: 412-563-7279.
Catechesis/Religious Program—Tel: 412-563-1414. Students 358.
MUNHALL, ALLEGHENY CO.
1—ST. MARGARET, Closed., See St. Maximilian Kolbe, Homestead.
2—ST. MICHAEL, (Slovak), Closed., See St. Maximilian Kolbe, Homestead.
3—ST. RITA (1936), (Slovak), Rev. Alvin J. Adams.
Res.: 219 W. Schwab Ave., 15120. Tel: 412-461-4204; Fax: 412-462-5484.
Catechesis/Religious Program—Tel: 412-462-4646. Students 84.

4—St. Therese of Lisieux (1925), Very Rev. Hugh J. Lang; Rev. Nicholas Mastrangelo.
Res.: One St. Therese Ct., 15120. Tel: 412-462-8161; Fax: 412-462-4817.
School—Three St. Therese Ct., 15120. Tel: 412-462-8163. Sisters of Charity 2; Lay Teachers 19; Students 269.
Catechesis/Religious Program—Students 294.
Muse, Washington Co., Holy Rosary (1963), Rev. George T. DeVille.
Res.: Orchard St., P.O. Box 447, 15350-0447. Tel: 724-745-3531; Fax: 724-745-0669.
Catechesis/Religious Program—Students 189.
Natrona Heights, Allegheny Co.
1—Blessed Sacrament, Closed., See Our Lady of the Most Blessed Sacrament.
2—Our Lady of Perpetual Help, Closed., See Our Lady of the Most Blessed Sacrament.
3—Our Lady of the Most Blessed Sacrament (1992), (Polish—Slovak), Consolidated, from Most Blessed Sacrament and Our Lady of Perpetual Help. Revs. Stan M. Gregorek; Anthony Gargotta; Deacon Patrick Wood.
Res.: 1526 Union Ave., 15065-2008. Tel: 724-226-4900; Fax: 724-224-3559.
Catechesis/Religious Program—800 Montana Ave., Natrona Hts., 15065. Tel: 724-224-3339. Students 315.
Natrona, Allegheny Co.
1—St. Joseph (1992), [CEM] [JC] Merged, with St. Ladislaus and St. Mathias. Rev. Donald J. Sotak.
Res.: 96 Pond St., 15065-2671. Tel: 724-224-1336; Fax: 724-224-6926.
High School—800 Montana Ave., Natrona Heights, 15065. Tel: 724-224-5552; Fax: 724-224-0235.
Catechesis/Religious Program—Students 75.
2—St. Ladislaus, (Polish), Closed., See St. Joseph.
3—St. Mathias, Closed., See St. Joseph.
Nemacolin, Greene Co., Our Lady of Consolation (1923), (Polish), [CEM] Rev. John M. Bauer.
Mailing Address: c/o St. Hugh, 408 Rte. 88, Carmichael, 15320. Tel: 724-966-7270; Fax: 724-966-9118.
Res.: 837 Wood Ext., 15351. Tel: 724-966-7909.
Catechesis/Religious Program—Students 18.
Mission—Sacred Heart Rices Landing, Greene Co.
Mission—St. Mary Crucible, Greene Co.
Neshannock, Lawrence Co., St. Camillus (1959), Rev. Philip N. Farrell, M.A., M.Div.; Sr. Barbara Ann Johnston, Pastoral Assoc. In Res., Rev. Francis C. Graff.
Res.: 314 W. Englewood Ave., New Castle, 16105. Tel: 724-652-9471; Fax: 724-654-1430.
Catechesis/Religious Program—Tel: 724-652-9497. Students 500.
New Bedford, Lawrence Co., St. James (1844), [CEM] Rev. John W. Rebel.
Res.: P.O. Box 207, 16140. Tel: 724-964-8276; Fax: 724-964-1108.
Catechesis/Religious Program—Students 180.
New Brighton, Beaver Co.
1—SS. Cyril and Methodius, (Slovak), Closed., See Holy Family.
2—Holy Family (1994), [CEM] Consolidated, from St. Joseph and SS. Cyril and Methodius. Rev. James R. Orr, M.Div., M.A.
Rectory & Office—1851 3rd Ave., 15066. Tel: 724-847-3538; 724-847-3548; Fax: 724-847-3585.
Church: 521 7th Ave., 15066.
Catechesis/Religious Program—Tel: 724-846-9622. Students 200.
New Castle, Lawrence Co.
1—St. Joseph the Worker (1888), [JC] Rev. Robert J. Schweitzer.
Res.: 1111 S. Cascade St., 16101. Tel: 724-658-1683; Fax: 724-658-1684.
Catechesis/Religious Program—Tel: 724-654-9739; Fax: 724-654-7076. Students 325.
2—St. Lucy, (Italian), Closed., See St. Vincent de Paul.
3—Madonna of Czestochowa, Closed., See Mary, Mother of Hope.
4—St. Margaret, Closed., See St. Vincent de Paul.
5—St. Mary, Closed., See Mary, Mother of Hope.
6—Mary, Mother of Hope (1993), (Irish—Polish), [CEM] [JC] Consolidated, from St. Mary and Madonna of Czestochowa. Rev. Victor J. Molka Jr.
Res.: 124 N. Beaver St., 16101. Tel: 724-658-2564; Fax: 724-658-9024.
Catechesis/Religious Program—119 N. Beaver St., 16101. Tel: 724-658-2564, Ext. 21. Students 255.
7—St. Michael, (Slovak), Closed., See St. Vincent de Paul.
8—SS. Philip and James, (Polish), Closed., See St. Vincent de Paul.
9—St. Vincent de Paul (1993), [CEM 2] Consolidated, from the following churches in New Castle: St. Lucy, St. Michael, SS. Philip & James, St. Margaret; and Holy Cross, West Pittsburg. Revs. Benedetto P. Vaghetto, J.C.L.; Kenneth R. Keene, M.Div.; Frank G. Erdeljac, M.Div.; Deacon S. Daniel Kielar.
Res.: One Lucymont Dr., 16102. Tel: 724-652-5829; Fax: 724-656-0413.
Catechesis/Religious Program—Tel: 724-654-2822. Students 276.
10—St. Vitus (1901), (Italian), [JC] Rev. John D. Petrarulo.
Res.: 910 S. Mercer St., 16101. Tel: 724-652-3422; Fax: 724-652-2322.
School—915 S. Jefferson St., 16101. Tel: 724-654-9297; Fax: 724-654-9364. Lay Teachers 10; Students 154.
Catechesis/Religious Program—Tel: 724-654-9371. Students 501.
North Oakland, Butler Co., St. Joseph (1872), [CEM] Rev. David D. DeWitt, Admin.
Res.: 409 N. Main St., P.O. Box 243, Chicora, 16025. Tel: 724-445-2275; Fax: 724-445-7507.
Catechesis/Religious Program—864 Chicora Rd., Chicora, 16025. Tel: 724-445-3713. Students 67.
North Rochester, Beaver Co., St. Pudentiana, Closed., See St. Cecilia, Rochester.
O'Hara Township, Allegheny County, St. Joseph (1845), [CEM] Rev. Thomas R. Miller.
Res.: 330 Dorseyville Rd., 15215. Tel: 412-963-8885; Fax: 412-963-1945.
Catechesis/Religious Program—342 Dorseyville Rd., 15215. Tel: 412-963-9252. Students 410.
Oakdale, Allegheny Co., St. Patrick (1866), [CEM] Rev. William J. Schwartz.
Res.: 7322 Noblestown Rd., 15071. Tel: 724-693-9260; Fax: 724-693-9247.
Catechesis/Religious Program—Tel: 724-693-8447. Students 85.
Oakmont, Allegheny Co., St. Irenaeus (1908), Rev. Paul D. Cwynar.
Res.: 387 Maryland Ave., 15139. Tel: 412-828-3065; Fax: 412-828-1587.
School—Tel: 412-828-8444; Fax: 412-828-8749. Sr. Carol Ann Papp, O.S.F., Prin. Lay Teachers 13; Students 110.
Catechesis/Religious Program—Tel: 412-828-9450. Students 281.
Overbrook, Allegheny Co., St. Norbert (1914), (German), Revs. Michael C. MacVeigh; Joseph P. Pudichery.
Res.: 2413 Off Saw Mill Run Blvd., 15234. Tel: 412-881-1316; 412-881-2474; Fax: 412-881-6728.
Catechesis/Religious Program—Tel: 412-881-2040. Students 52.
Penn Hills, Allegheny Co.
1—St. Bartholomew (1950), Rev. David J. Bonnar, S.T.B.
Res.: 111 Erhardt Dr., 15235. Tel: 412-242-3374; Fax: 412-242-1488.
School—Tel: 412-242-2511; Fax: 412-242-8317. Sisters 1; Lay Teachers 20; Students 263.
Catechesis/Religious Program—Tel: 412-242-7207. Students 150.
2—St. Gerard Majella (1964), Rev. John D. Brennan.
Res.: 121 Dawn Dr., Verona, 15147. Tel: 412-793-3333; Fax: 412-793-4726.
Catechesis/Religious Program—Tel: 412-793-3959. Students 175.
3—St. Susanna (1960), Rev. Martin F. Barkin, M.Div.
Res.: 200 Stotler Rd., 15235-3554. Tel: 412-731-7465; Fax: 412-798-0479.
Catechesis/Religious Program—Tel: 412-793-9448. Students 80.
Perrysville, Allegheny Co., St. Teresa of Avila (1867), [CEM] Very Rev. James S. Ruggiero; Revs. William P. Siple; Robert J. Vular.
Res.: 1000 Avila Ct., 15237. Tel: 412-367-9001; Fax: 412-366-8415.
School—800 Avila Ct., 15237. Tel: 412-367-9001, Ext. 530; Fax: 412-364-1172. Religious 2; Lay Teachers 26; Students 350.
Catechesis/Religious Program—Students 513.
Peters Township, Washington Co., St. Benedict the Abbot (1962), Revs. Philip J. Donatelli; John J. Arnott; Deacon John Layton; Dennis Gehlrlein, Pastoral Assoc.
Res.: 120 Abington Dr., McMurray, 15317. Tel: 724-941-9406; Fax: 724-941-9517.
Catechesis/Religious Program—Tel: 724-941-9587. Students 1,666.
Pitcairn, Allegheny Co., St. Michael (1895), Rev. John E. Dinello.
Church: 750 Wall Ave., 15140. Tel: 412-373-3400; Fax: 412-373-5652.
Res.: 740 Wall Ave., 15140. Tel: 412-373-2610. Email: saintmichael@stargate.net.
Catechesis/Religious Program—Students 69.
Pleasant Hills, Allegheny Co., St. Elizabeth (1942), Revs. Roy H. Conley; Michael S. Suslowicz; Paul R. Staud.
Res.: Grove Pl., 15236. Tel: 412-882-8744; Fax: 412-882-8320.
School—Tel: 412-881-2958; Fax: 412-882-0111. Lay Teachers 32; Students 630.
Catechesis/Religious Program—Tel: 412-882-5023; Fax: 412-207-1647. Students 605.
Chapel of Convenience—St. David, Baldwin Boro, 15236. Tel: 412-882-8744.
Plum, Allegheny Co., St. Januarius (1946), Rev. Peter R. Pilarski.
Res.: 1450 Renton Rd., 15239. Tel: 412-793-4439; Fax: 412-793-7135.
Catechesis/Religious Program—Students 80.
Port Vue, Allegheny Co.
1—St. Joseph, Closed., See St. Mark.
2—St. Mark (1993), Revs. Gerald S. Mikonis; Deo Gratias Mugisha (Uganda).
Administration Center—1101 Romine Ave., 15133. Tel: 412-678-6275; Fax: 412-673-1393.
St. Joseph Worship Site—1125 Romine Ave., 15133.
Res. & St. Eugene Worship Site—3210 Liberty Way, Liberty Borough, 15133. Tel: 412-678-6275.
School—St. Joseph Regional School, Tel: 412-678-0659; Fax: 412-678-1301. See Consolidated Schools under Institutions Located in the Diocese.
Catechesis/Religious Program—Students 454.
Prospect, Butler Co., St. Christopher at the Lake (1974), Rev. Matthew Tosello.
Res.: 229-232 N. Franklin St., 16052. Tel: 724-865-2430; Fax: 724-865-1120.
Catechesis/Religious Program—Tel: 724-865-9840. Students 109.
Rankin, Allegheny Co., Visitation of the Blessed Virgin Mary, (Croatian), Closed., See Word of God, Swissvale.
Reserve Township, Allegheny Co., St. Aloysius (1892), Rev. Dennis J. Bradley.
Res.: 3616 Mt. Troy Rd., 15212. Tel: 412-821-2351; Fax: 412-821-6480.
Catechesis/Religious Program—Tel: 412-821-2792. Students 135.
Richeyville, Washington Co., St. Agnes (1994), Rev. Francis Z. Jurewicz.
Res.: Box 406, 15358. Tel: 724-632-5858; Fax: 724-632-5858.
Catechesis/Religious Program—Pike Run Dr., Daisytown, 15427. Tel: 724-938-2007. Students 65.
Richland Township, Allegheny Co., Saint Richard (1992), Very Rev. Kenneth E. Oldenski, V.F.
Res.: 3841 Dickey Rd., Gibsonia, 15044. Tel: 724-444-1971; Fax: 724-444-6001.
Catechesis/Religious Program—Fax: 724-444-1977. Students 850.
Robinson Township, Allegheny Co., Holy Trinity (Moon Run) (1944), Revs. Robert W. Herrmann; William J. Scholz; Deacon Tim Killmeyer. In Res., Rev. John Fitzgerald.
Res.: 5718 Steubenville Pike, McKees Rocks, 15136-1311. Tel: 412-787-2140; 412-787-2143; Fax: 412-787-3799.
School—(Grades PreK-8) Tel: 412-787-2656; Fax: 412-787-9487. Lay Teachers 23; Students 409.
Catechesis/Religious Program—Tel: 412-859-3467. Students 480.
Rochester, Beaver Co., St. Cecilia (1856), (German—Italian), [CEM] Merged, with St. Pudentiana. Revs. Ward G. Stakem, O.F.M.Cap.; William Gillum, O.F.M.Cap.; Philip Fink, O.F.M-.Cap.; Philip J. Bernier, O.F.M.Cap.
Res.: 303 Jackson St., 15074. Tel: 724-775-0801; Fax: 724-774-3056.
Catechesis/Religious Program—Tel: 724-775-2761. Students 227.
Roscoe, Washington Co., St. Joseph (1904), In Res., Rev. George J. Moneck, Admin.
Res.: Box 486, 15477. Tel: 724-938-2324; Fax: 724-938-2983.
Catechesis/Religious Program—Students 75.
Ross Township, Allegheny Co., St. Sebastian (North Hills) (1952), Revs. Joseph M. Mele; Clinton P. Zadroga; James M. Stover; Deacon Richard R. Cessar.
Res.: 311 Siebert Rd., 15237. Tel: 412-364-8999; Fax: 412-364-6330.
School—307 Siebert Rd., 15237. Tel: 412-364-7171; Fax: 412-364-5891. Sisters 6; Lay Teachers 30; Students 401.
Catechesis/Religious Program—Tel: 412-366-4000. Students 576.
Russellton, Allegheny Co., Transfiguration (1916), [CEM] Rev. Robert W. Habe.
Res.: 15 Poma St., 15076. Tel: 724-265-1030; Fax: 724-265-1030.
School—(Grades K-8), McKrell Rd., 15076. Tel: 724-265-3350. Lay Teachers 10; Students 125.
Catechesis/Religious Program—Tel: 265-724-4860. Students 100.
Scott Township, Allegheny Co.
1—Our Lady of Grace (1947), Revs. Theodore A. Rutkowski, S.T.L.; Kenneth A. Sparks. In Res., Rev. John Obasi.
Res.: 310 Kane Blvd., 15243. Tel: 412-279-7070; Fax: 412-276-0278.
School—1734 Bower Hill Rd., 15243. Tel: 412-279-6611; Fax: 412-279-6755. Lay Teachers 16; Students 274.

Catechesis/Religious Program—1730 Bower Hill Rd., 15243. Tel: 412-276-0277; Fax: 412-276-0277. Students 540.
2—SS. SIMON AND JUDE (1955), Rev. Richard E. Ward. In Res., Rev. Kris D. Stubna, S.T.D.
Res.: 1607 Greentree Rd., 15220. Tel: 412-563-3189; Fax: 412-563-8524.
School—1625 Greentree Rd., 15220. Tel: 412-563-1353; Fax: 412-563-8617. Lay Teachers 14; Students 206.
Catechesis/Religious Program—Tel: 412-563-1199. Students 279.
SEWICKLEY, ALLEGHENY CO., ST. JAMES (1863), [CEM] Revs. Albert Semler; David Poecking; Deacon Robert Sabatelle.
Res.: 200 Walnut St., 15143. Tel: 412-741-6650; Fax: 412-741-4782.
School—201 Broad St., 15143. Tel: 412-741-5540; Fax: 412-741-9038. Sisters of St. Joseph 2; Lay Teachers 11; Students 230.
Catechesis/Religious Program—Tel: 412-741-6766. Students 493.
SHARPSBURG, ALLEGHENY CO.
1—ST. JOHN CANTIUS (1906), (Polish), Very Rev. Andrew C. Fischer, V.F., M.Div., Admin.
Res.: 201 9th St., 15215. Tel: 412-784-8700; Fax: 412-781-1101.
Catechesis/Religious Program—Tel: 412-781-5150. Students 155.
2—MADONNA OF JERUSALEM (1904), (Italian), Very Rev. Andrew C. Fischer, V.F., M.Div., Admin.
Res.: 201 Ninth St., 15215. Tel: 412-784-8700; Fax: 412-781-1101.
Catechesis/Religious Program—Tel: 412-781-5150. Students 152.
3—ST. MARY (1904), (Italian), Very Rev. Andrew C. Fischer, V.F., M.Div., Admin.
Res.: 201 Ninth St., 15215. Tel: 412-784-8700; Fax: 412-781-1101.
Catechesis/Religious Program—Tel: 412-781-5150; Fax: 412-781-5150. Students 155.
SLIPPERY ROCK, BUTLER CO., ST. PETER (1938), [CEM] Rev. James L. Armstrong, D.Min.
Res.: 670 S. Main St., 16057. Tel: 724-794-2880; Fax: 724-794-1255.
Catechesis/Religious Program—Tel: 724-794-5101. Students 200.
SOUTH PARK, ALLEGHENY CO.
1—ST. JOAN OF ARC (1923), Rev. Phillip Pribonic.
Res.: 6414 Montour St., 15129. Tel: 412-833-2400; Fax: 412-835-1764.
School—6470 Library Rd., 15129. Tel: 412-833-2433. Lay Teachers 13; Students 129.
Catechesis/Religious Program—Tel: 412-835-3724. Students 530.
2—NATIVITY (1905), Rev. Richard A. Infante.
Res.: 5802 Curry Rd., 15236. Tel: 412-655-3000; Fax: 412-650-4658.
School—(Grades PreK-8), 5811 Curry Rd., 15236. Tel: 412-653-1500; Fax: 412-653-2619. Lay Teachers 13; Students 123.
Catechesis/Religious Program—5807 Curry Rd., 15236. Tel: 412-655-1565. Students 635.
SPRINGDALE, ALLEGHENY CO., ST. ALPHONSUS (1901), Rev. George E. Saladna, S.T.L., S.S.L.
Res.: 750 Pittsburgh St., 15144-1699. Tel: 724-274-5084; Fax: 724-274-7035.
Catechesis/Religious Program—Tel: 724-274-2547. Students 145.
SWISSVALE, ALLEGHENY CO.
1—ST. ANSELM, Closed., See Word of God.
2—SAINT BARNABAS, (Slovak), Closed., See Word of God.
3—MADONNA DEL CASTELLO (1920), (Italian), Rev. John J. Cassella, M.Div.
Res.: 2021 S. Braddock Ave., 15218. Tel: 412-271-5666; Fax: 412-271-2335.
Catechesis/Religious Program—Tel: 412-271-4711; Fax: 412-271-2335. Students 43.
4—WORD OF GOD (1994), (Irish—Croatian), Consolidated, from the following churches: St. Anselm, St. Barnabus and Visitation of the Blessed Virgin Mary, Rankin. Revs. Frank J. Drabiska; Alvin Gutierrez; Kevin McKnight. In Res., Rev. Peter Debo (Uganda).
Res.: 7446 McClure Ave., 15218. Tel: 412-241-1372; Fax: 412-241-0168.
School—7438 McClure Ave., 15218. Tel: 412-371-8587. Sisters of Charity 2; Lay Teachers 19; Students 400.
Catechesis/Religious Program—Tel: 412-351-0670. Students 326.
TARENTUM, ALLEGHENY CO.
1—ST. CLEMENT, Closed., See Holy Martyrs.
2—HOLY MARTYRS (1992), (Slovak), [CEM] [JC 2] Consolidated, from St. Clement and Sacred Heart, St. Peter.
Res.: 353 W. Ninth Ave., 15084. Tel: 724-224-0770; Fax: 724-224-7070.
Catechesis/Religious Program—216 W. 9th Ave., 15084. Tel: 724-224-1234. Students 224.
3—SACRED HEART - ST. PETER, Closed., See Holy Martyrs.
TURTLE CREEK, ALLEGHENY CO., ST. COLMAN (1882), Rev. James E. Kunkel, S.T.M.
Res.: 100 Tri-Boro Ave., 15145. Tel: 412-823-2564; Fax: 412-823-6436.
School—(Grades PreK-8), 547 Hunter St. 15145. Tel: 412-823-4871; Fax: 412-823-6326. Sisters of Mercy of the Americas 1; Lay Teachers 11; Students 166.
Catechesis/Religious Program—Tel: 412-823-9114. Students 175.
UNITY, ALLEGHENY CO., ST. JOHN THE BAPTIST (1915), [CEM] Revs. Charles W. Speicher, Ph.D., S.T.M.; Aaron Kriss.
Res.: 444 St. John St., 15239. Tel: 412-793-4511; 412-793-4580; Fax: 412-793-4311.
School—418 Unity Center Rd., 15239. Tel: 412-793-0555; Fax 412-793-4001. Lay Teachers 22; Students 333.
Catechesis/Religious Program—Tel: 412-795-6536. Students 815.
UPPER ST. CLAIR, ALLEGHENY CO.
1—ST. JOHN CAPISTRAN (1968), Rev. James J. Chepponis, M.Div., M.A.; Deacon William F. Strathmann Jr.
Res.: 1610 McMillan Rd., 15241. Tel: 412-221-6275; Fax: 412-257-3789.
Catechesis/Religious Program—Tel: 412-221-5445. Students 387.
2—ST. LOUISE DE MARILLAC (1961), Rev. Thomas E. Kredel; Sr. M. Justice Przybocki, C.S.S.F., Pastoral Assoc.
Res.: 320 McMurray Rd., 15241. Tel: 412-833-1010; Fax: 412-833-6624.
School—310 McMurray Rd., 15241 Tel: 412-833-0600; Fax: 412-835-2898. Felician Sisters 2; Lay Teachers 25; Students 504.
Catechesis/Religious Program—Tel: 412-835-1155; Fax: 412-833-3952. Students 1,450.
VERONA, ALLEGHENY CO., ST. JOSEPH (1866), [CEM] Rev. Edwin J. Wichman.
Res.: 825 Second Ave., 15147-1498. Tel: 412-795-5114.
School—Tel: 412-828-7213. Lay Teachers 15; Students 173.
Catechesis/Religious Program—Tel: 412-828-7715. Students 156.
VERSAILLES, ALLEGHENY CO., ST. DENIS, Closed., See St Patrick, McKeesport.
WAMPUM, LAWRENCE CO., ST. MONICA, Closed., See Queen of Heaven, Koppel.
WASHINGTON, WASHINGTON CO.
1—ST. HILARY (1919), Rev. Thomas D. O'Neil, M.Div.
Res.: 320 Henderson Ave., 15301. Tel: 724-222-4087; Fax: 724-222-2130.
Catechesis/Religious Program—340 Henderson Ave., 15301. Tel: 724-222-1381. Students 128.
2—IMMACULATE CONCEPTION (1854), [CEM 3] Rev. William P. Feeney, M.Div.; Sr. Margaretta Nussbaumer, C.D.P., Pastoral Assoc.; Rev. Nicholas A. Spirko; Deacons Leon Abraham, (Retired); Joseph Cerenzia; John Manion; Rev. Thomas J. Lewandowski.
Res.: 119 W. Chestnut St., 15301. Tel: 724-225-1425; Fax: 724-229-7946.
School—111 W. Spruce St., 15301. Tel: 724-225-1680; Fax: 724-225-4651. Lay Teachers 24; Students 473.
Catechesis/Religious Program—135 W. Chestnut St., 15301. Tel: 724-225-0382. Students 645.
WAYNESBURG, GREENE CO., ST. ANN (1839), [CEM] Rev. John J. Batykefer.
Res.: 232 E. High St., 15370. Tel: 724-627-7568; Fax: 724-627-7568.
Catechesis/Religious Program—Students 234.
WEST ALIQUIPPA, BEAVER CO., ST. JOSEPH, Closed., See St. Titus, Aliquippa.
WEST MIFFLIN, ALLEGHENY CO.
1—ST. AGNES (1867), [CEM] Rev. Joseph R. Grosko, M.Div., Admin. In Res., Rev. Benedict Faneye, O.P. (Nigeria).
Res.: 622 St. Agnes Ln., 15122. Tel: 412-466-2655.
School—(Grades PreSchool-8), 653 St. Agnes Ln., 15122. Tel: 412-466-6238; Fax: 412-466-2013. Sisters of the Holy Spirit 2; Lay Teachers 10; Students 134.
Catechesis/Religious Program—Students 90.
Convent—635 St. Agnes Ln., 15122. Tel: 412-466-3554.
2—HOLY SPIRIT (1963), Very Rev. Daniel A. Valentine, V.F., D.Min.
Res.: 2603 Old Elizabeth Rd., 15122-2598. Tel: 412-466-5048; Fax: 412-466-4983.
Catechesis/Religious Program—Tel: 412-466-1264. Students 282.
3—HOLY TRINITY (1901), (Slovak), [CEM] Rev. Joseph R. Grosko, M.Div.
Res.: 529 Grant Ave. Ext., 15122. Tel: 412-466-6545; Fax: 412-466-6968.
Catechesis/Religious Program—1439 Sylvan Ave., 15122. Tel: 412-466-4490. Students 110.
4—RESURRECTION (1936), Rev. Robert G. Turner.
Res.: 3909 Donna Ave., 15122. Tel: 412-461-8087; Fax: 412-461-0142.
School—*James LaVelle*, (Grades PreSchool-8), One Majka Dr., 15122. Tel: 412-462-4344; Fax: 412-461-1230. Lay Teachers 11; Students 151.
Catechesis/Religious Program—Tel: 412-461-7944. Students 190.
WEST PITTSBURG, LAWRENCE CO., HOLY CROSS, Closed., See St. Vincent de Paul, New Castle.
WEST SUNBURY, BUTLER CO., ST. LOUIS, Closed., See St. Alphonsus, Boyers.
WEST VIEW, ALLEGHENY CO., ST. ATHANASIUS (1905), Revs. Robert A. Norton; John E. Forbidussi.
Res.: 7 Chalfonte Ave., 15229. Tel: 412-931-4624; Fax: 412-939-3516.
School—2 Wentworth Ave., 15229. Tel: 412-931-6633; Fax: 412-459-0104. Ms. Gabrielle Yingling, Prin. Lay Teachers 13; Students 151.
Catechesis/Religious Program—Tel: 412-931-3670. Students 432.
WEXFORD, ALLEGHENY CO.
1—ST. ALEXIS (1961), Revs. Paul J. Zywan, M.Div.; Matthew R. McClain. In Res., Rev. Harry F. Petrie (Retired).
Res.: 10090 Old Perry Hwy., 15090. Tel: 724-935-4343; Fax: 724-935-1270.
School—(Grades PreK-8) Tel: 724-935-3940; Fax: 724-935-6070. Lay Teachers 25; Students 378.
Catechesis/Religious Program—Tel: 724-935-0877. Students 448.
2—ST. ALPHONSUS (1840), [CEM] [JC] Revs. Peter P. Murphy; Thomas J. Burke.
Res.: 201 Church Rd., 15090. Tel: 724-935-1151; Fax: 724-934-3877.
School—Tel: 724-935-1152; Fax: 724-935-1110. Sisters 1; Lay Teachers 22; Students 530.
Catechesis/Religious Program—Tel: 724-935-1160; Fax: 724-934-3788. Students 305.
WHITE OAK BORO, ALLEGHENY CO., ST. ANGELA (1958), Very Rev. Stephen M. Chervenak, V.F., S.T.L.
Res.: 1732 Fawcett Ave., 15131. Tel: 412-672-9641; Fax: 412-672-1576.
School—1640R Fawcett Ave., 15131. Tel: 412-672-2360; Fax: 412-672-0880. Lay Teachers 12; Students 242.
Catechesis/Religious Program—Tel: 412-672-0913. Students 170.
WHITEHALL, ALLEGHENY CO., ST. GABRIEL OF THE SORROWFUL VIRGIN (1944), Revs. John R. Haney, M.Div.; Dam D. Nguyen, M.Div.; Deacon James F. Leonard. In Res., Rev. John E. Suhoza.
Res.: 5200 Greenridge Dr., 15236. Tel: 412-881-8115; 412-881-8117; Fax: 412-440-0160.
School—Tel: 412-882-3353; Fax: 412-882-2125. Lay Teachers 22; Students 475.
Catechesis/Religious Program—5302 Greenridge Dr., 15236. Tel: 412-881-7950. Students 400.
WILDWOOD, ALLEGHENY CO., ST. CATHERINE OF SWEDEN (1953), Revs. Regis M. Farmer; David J. Jastrab.
Res.: 2308 W. Hardies Rd., 15091. Tel: 412-961-0399; 724-443-2087; Fax: 724-443-3633.
Catechesis/Religious Program—Students 674.
WILKINSBURG, ALLEGHENY CO., ST. JAMES (1869), Rev. Warren W. Metzler.
Res.: 718 Franklin Ave., 15221. Tel: 412-241-1392; 412-241-1318 Bus. Mgr.; Fax: 412-241-6625.
School—721 Rebecca Ave., 15221. Tel: 412-242-3515; Fax: 412-241-3199. Lay Teachers 17; Students 221.
Catechesis/Religious Program—Tel: 412-242-2246. Students 26.
WILMERDING, ALLEGHENY CO.
1—ST. JUDE THE APOSTLE (1994), [CEM] Consolidated, from St. Aloysius and St. Leocadia. Rev. Norbert J. Campbell.
Res.: 405 Westinghouse Ave., 15148. Tel: 412-823-8390; Fax: 412-823-8399.
Catechesis/Religious Program—Tel: 412-823-1066. Students 86.
2—ST. LEOCADIA, (Polish), Closed., See St. Jude the Apostle.
WIRETON, ALLEGHENY CO., ST. CATHERINE OF SIENA (1959), Rev. Thomas R. Wilson.
Res.: 199 McGovern Blvd., Crescent, 15046. Tel: 724-457-7026; 724-457-0106 (Church Hall); Fax: 724-457-3292.
Catechesis/Religious Program—Tel: 724-457-1679. Students 295.
ZELIENOPLE, BUTLER CO., ST. GREGORY (1906), [CEM] Rev. Robert M. Miller.
Res.: 2 W. Beaver St., 16063. Tel: 724-452-7245; Fax: 724-452-4064.
School—115 Pine St., 16063. Tel: 724-452-9731; Fax: 724-452-4064. Lay Teachers 11; Students 210.
Catechesis/Religious Program—Students 195.

Chaplains of Public Institutions

ALLEGHENY COUNTY. *Depaul Institution*, Tel: 412-924-1012. Rev. Walter G. Rydzon. Tel: 412-381-9878.
St. Joseph House of Hospitality, Tel: 412-471-0666.

Rev. John E. Suhoza. Tel: 412-881-8115.
Pittsburgh International Airport. Rev. John P. Fitzgerald. Tel: 412-472-0155.

BEAVER COUNTY. *McGuire Memorial Home*, Tel: 724-843-3400. Rev. William Gillium, O.F.M.Cap., Director of Pastoral Care. Tel: 724-775-0801. (Vacant)

Hospitals

ALLEGHENY COUNTY. *Children's Hospital*, Tel: 412-647-5326. UPMC Chaplains, Tel: 412-647-7615
St. Clair Memorial Hospital, Tel: 412-561-4900. Attended by Our Lady of Grace, Pittsburgh. Tel:412-279-7070
Jefferson Hospital, Tel: 412-469-5000. Rev. Robert Andrew Kohuch. Tel: 412-384-4406, Sr. Nancy Kline, Pastoral Care. Tel: 412-469-5855.
Magee-Women's Hospital, Tel: 412-647-1000. Sr. Nora Egan, C.S.J. Tel: 412-372-6758.
McKeesport UPMC, Tel: 412-664-2000. Rev. John M. Elanjileth (ROM). Tel: 412-673-5552.
Mercy Health System of Pittsburgh-Mercy Providence Hospital, Tel: 412-323-5600. Attended by St. Peter. Tel: 412-321-0711
Mercy Health System of Pittsburgh-Pittsburgh Mercy Hospital, Tel: 412-232-8198 (PC Office). Revs. Joseph Monahan, T.O.R., John L. McKenna.
Ohio Valley General Hospital, Tel: 412-777-6161. Attended by St. Malachy. Tel: 412-741-6656 and St. John of God. Tel: 412-771-5646
Sewickley Valley Hospital, Tel: 412-741-6600. Attended by St. James. Tel: 412-741-6656 and St. Catherine of Siena. Tel: 724-457-7026
UPMC Braddock, Tel: 412-636-5000. Rev. Douglas A. Boyd. Tel: 412-271-1515.
UPMC Passavant Hospital, Tel: 412-367-6700. Sr. Caritas Marshall, C.S.J. Tel: 412-364-5938. Sacramental Coordination by St. Catherine of Sweden Parish.
UPMC Shadyside Hospital, Tel: 412-623-2121. Revs. Gilbert Puznakoski. Tel: 412-623-1692, Michael A. McDermott.
UPMC Southside Hospital, Tel: 412-488-5550. Rev. John F. Walsh. Tel: 412-471-0654.
UPMC St. Margaret Hospital, Tel: 412-767-4672. St. Scholastica Parish, Tel: 412-781-0186; Pastoral Care, Tel: 412-784-4749
UPMC University of Pittsburgh Medical Center, Tel: 412-647-7560. Revs. Michael A. McDermott, Richard Terdine, Sr. Mary Kay Hamond, C.S.J. Patient and Family Support, Tel: 412-647-7615
West Penn Allegheny Health System-Allegheny General, Tel: 412-359-3131. Rev. Thomas J. McKenna. Tel: 412-359-4269.
West Penn Allegheny Health System-Alley-Kiski Medical Center, Tel: 724-224-5100. Attended by Our Lady of the Most Blessed Sacrament, Natrona Heights. Tel: 724-226-4900
West Penn Allegheny Health System-Forbes Regional. Rev. John E. Dinello. Tel: 412-373-2610. Sacramental coordination by St. John Fisher. Tel: 412-241-4722
West Penn Allegheny Health System-Life Care Hospital of Pittsburgh, Tel: 412-247-2424. Attended by St. James, Wilkinsburg. Tel:412-241-1392
West Penn Allegheny Health System-Suburban General Hospital. Attended by Assumption of the Blessed Virgin Mary on the Beautiful River, Bellevue. Tel:412-766-6660; 412-734-6000
West Penn Allegheny Health System-West Penn Hospital, Tel: 412-578-5000. Revs. James P. Holland. Tel: 412-621-5679, Edward L. Hoffman. Tel: 412-242-2002.

BEAVER COUNTY. *The Medical Center Beaver*, Tel: 724-728-7000. Rev. Kenneth E. Myers, M.S.Ed. Tel: 724-775-4111.
UPMC Beaver, Tel: 724-875-1212. Attended by St. Titus, Aliquippa. Tel:724-378-8561

BUTLER COUNTY. *Butler Memorial Hospital*, Tel: 724-283-6666. Attended by St. Fidelis Parish. Tel. 724-482-2690

GREENE COUNTY. *Greene County Memorial*, Tel: 724-627-3101. Attended by St. Ann, Waynesburg. Tel:724-627-7568

LAWRENCE COUNTY. *Ellwood City Hospital*, Tel: 724-752-0081. Attended by Holy Redeemer Parish, Ellwood City. Tel:724-758-4441.
Jameson Memorial Hospital, Tel: 724-658-9001. Rev. Frank G. Erdeljac, M.Div. Tel: 724-535-4786.

WASHINGTON COUNTY. *Mon Valley Hospital*, Tel: 724-258-2000. Attended by Transfiguration, Monongahela. Tel:724-258-7742
Washington County East Deanery, Tel: 724-377-0128. Deacon Thomas W. Raymond.
Washington Hospital, Tel: 724-225-7000. Attended by Immaculate Conception, Washington. Tel:724-225-1425
West Penn Allegheny Health System-Canonsburg Hospital, Tel: 724-745-6100. Rev. Kenneth E. Kezmarsky. Being handled by St. Patrick until assignment is made. Tel:724-745-6560

Veterans Administration Hospitals

ALLEGHENY COUNTY. *VA Pittsburgh Health Care System-H.J. Heinz and University Drive Divisions*, Tel: 412-688-6000, Ext. 6729. Revs. Emett Schuler, O.F.M.Cap. Tel: 412-531-4545, Mark W. Glasgow. Tel: 412-461-1054, Robert Craig, O.F.M.Cap. Tel: 412-682-6430. Tel: 412-688-6000

BUTLER COUNTY. *Department of Veterans Affairs-Deshon Hospital*, Tel: 724-287-4781. Rev. William J. Ritzert. Tel: 724-538-5331.
Va Medical Center Butler. Rev. Marvin Justi, Tel: 724-352-2149.

Rehabilitation, Nursing and Geriatric Care Facilities

ALLEGHENY COUNTY. *Arden Courts.* Attended by Rev. Ladis Cizik '87 Tel: 412-795-3388
Asbury Heights, Tel: 412-341-1030. Attended by St. Bernard, Mt. Lebanon. Tel: 412-561-3300.
Baldwin Health Care, Tel: 412-885-8400. Attended by St. Elizabeth of Hungary, Pittsburgh. Tel: 412-882-8744.
Beatty Pointe Village. Attended by Rev. Ladis Cizik '87 Tel: 412-795-3388 or Tel: 412-374-9000
Beverly Manor of Monroeville, Tel: 412-856-7570. Rev. Thomas V. Manning.
Canterbury Place, Tel: 412-622-9000. Attended by Our Lady of the Angels, Pittsburgh. Tel: 412-682-0929.
Cedars of Monroeville, Tel: 412-373-3900. Attended by Rev. Ladis Cizik '87 Tel: 412-795-3388
Children's Institute, St. Bede, Tel: 412-661-7222; Fax: 412-420-2400. (Vacant)
Collins Nursing Center, Tel: 412-661-1740. Rev. Edward L. Hoffman. Tel: 412-242-2002.
DT Watson Rehab Hospital, Tel: 412-741-9000. Attended by St. James, Sewickley. Tel: 412-741-6650.
Forbes Nursing Center, Tel: 412-665-3232. Rev. Joseph C. Beck. Tel: 412-421-5766.
Greater Pittsburgh Rehab Hospital, Tel: 412-856-2400. Rev. Joseph C. Beck. Tel: 412-421-5766.
Hamilton Hills Personal Care. Rev. Ladis Cizik. Tel: 412-795-3388.
Healthsouth Harmarville Rehabilitation Hospital, Tel: 412-826-4929. Attended by Saint Francis of Assisi, Tel: 412-828-3123
Heartland Health Care Center, Tel: 412-665-2400. Rev. Edward L. Hoffman. Tel: 412-242-2002.
Heritage Shadyside, Tel: 412-422-5100. Attended by St. Rosalia, Pittsburgh. Tel: 412-421-5766.
Independence Court of Mt. Lebanon, Tel: 412-341-4400. Attended by St. Ann, Castle Shannon. Tel: 412-531-5964; St. Thomas More, Bethel Park. Tel: 724-883-0031
Independent Court of Monroeville, Tel: 412-373-3030. Rev. Joseph C. Beck. Tel: 412-421-5766.
Kane Regional Center - Glen Hazel, Tel: 412-422-6800. Rev. Joseph C. Beck. Tel: 412-422-6839.
Kane Regional Center - McKeesport, Tel: 412-675-8600. Sr. Thomas Joseph Gaines, S.C. Tel: 412-675-8640.
Kane Regional Center - Ross, Tel: 412-369-2000. Attended by St. Sebastian.
Kane Regional Center - Scott, Tel: 412-429-3000. Rev. Richard L. Conboy, S.T.L. Tel: 412-429-3040.
Ladies of the Grand Army Republic (LGAR), Tel: 412-825-9000. Rev. Ladis Cizik. Tel: 412-795-3388.
Little Sisters of the Poor (James P. Wall Home for the Aged), Tel: 412-761-5373. Rev. Jerome A. Dixon (Retired). Tel: 412-761-2187.
Longwood at Oakmont, Tel: 412-826-5917. St. Irenaeus. Tel: 412-828-3065
Manorcare Health Services, Highland Dr.. Tel: 412-831-6050. Attended by St. Thomas More. Tel: 412-833-0031.
Manorcare Health Services Green Tree, Greentree Rd.. Tel: 412-344-7744. Attended by SS. Simon & Jude, Tel: 412-563-3189.
Manorcare Health Services McMurray, McMurray Rd.. Tel: 412-941-3080. Sr. Ruth Ann Walsh, O.S.F.
Manorcare Health Services Monroeville, Tel: 412-856-7071. Rev. Ladis Cizik. Tel: 412-795-3388. Tel: 412-856-7071
Manorcare Health Services North Hills, Tel: 412-369-9955. Rev. Joseph C. Beck. Tel: 412-421-5766.
St. Margaret Seneca Place, Tel: 412-798-8000. Rev. Thomas V. Manning. Attended by St. Bartholomew, Penn Hills. Tel: 412-242-3374.
Marian Manor, Inc., Tel: 412-563-4222, Ext. 304. Rev. Regis R. Alberth. Tel: 412-561-1320.
Mt. Lebanon Manor Convalescent Center, Tel: 412-257-4444. Attended by St. Thomas More. Tel: 412-833-0031.
Oakmont Nursing Center, Tel: 412-828-7300. Attended by St. Irenaeus, Oakmont. Tel: 412-828-3065
Presbyterian Seniorcare Westminister Place, Tel: 412-826-6136. Rev. Ladis Cizik. Tel: 412-795-3388. Attended by St. Irenaeus, Oakmont.
Ridgepoint, Tel: 412-653-6870. Attended by Nativity, South Park Twp. Tel: 412-655-3000.
Riverview Center for Jewish Seniors, Tel: 412-521-5900. Attended by St. Rosalia, Pittsburgh. Tel: 412-421-5766.
Seneca Hills Retirement Village. Rev. Ladis Cizik. Tel: 412-795-3388. Tel: 412-793-1700
Seneca Manor Assisted Living. Rev. Ladis Cizik. Tel: 412-795-3388. Tel: 412-798-6000
Shadyside Nursing and Rehabilitation Center, Tel: 412-362-3500. Rev. Edward L. Hoffman. Tel: 412-242-2002.
Southwestern Nursing and Rehabilitation Center, Tel: 412-466-0600, Ext. 5989. Attended by Holy Spirit, West Mifflin. Tel: 412-466-5048
St. Margaret Seneca Place. Rev. Ladis Cizik. Tel: 412-795-3388. Tel: 412-798-8000
Sunrise Assisted Living. Rev. Ladis Cizik. Tel: 412-795-3388. Tel: 412-380-2589
UPMC Cranberry Place. Attended by St. Killian Parish, Tel: 724-625-1665 or Tel: 724-772-5350
UPMC Rehabilitation Hospital, Tel: 412-420-2400. Attended by St. Bede, Pittsburgh. Tel: 412-661-7222.
Vicentian de Marillac Home. Attended by St. Raphael, Tel: 412-661-3100 or Tel: 412-361-2833
Vincentian Home, Tel: 412-366-5600. Rev. Reginald Russo, O.F.M.Cap.
Vincentian Regency Home, Tel: 412-366-8540. Revs. Ambrose Mootheril, David C. Dixon, Asst. (Retired). Tel: 412-928-0825. Tel: 412-366-8540
Woodhaven Convalescent Center, Tel: 412-856-4770. Rev. Joseph C. Beck. Tel: 412-421-5766.
Woven Hearts of Penn Hills, Tel: 412-798-3400. St. John the Baptist. Tel: 412-793-4511

BEAVER COUNTY. *Friendship Ridge Skilled Nursing*, Tel: 724-775-7100. Revs. Paul J. Savage, S.T.L. Tel: 724-846-4585, Kenneth E. Myers, M.S.Ed. Tel: 724-775-4111.
Villa St. Joseph, Tel: 724-869-6300. Rev. Philip Fink, O.F.M.Cap. Tel: 724-775-0801.

BUTLER COUNTY. *Sunnyview Home*, Tel: 724-282-1800. Attended by St. Fidelis. Tel: 724-482-2690.

GREENE COUNTY. *Curry Memorial Home*, Tel: 724-627-3153. Attended by St. Ann, Waynesburg. Tel: 724-627-7568.
Franklin Care Center, Tel: 724-852-2020. Attended by St. Ann, Waynesburg. Tel: 724-627-7568.

LAWRENCE COUNTY. *Almira Home*, Tel: 724-652-4131. Rev. Francis C. Graff. Tel: 724-652-9471.
Belvedere Residence, Inc., Tel: 724-924-2191. Rev. Francis C. Graff. Tel: 724-652-9471.
Castle Manor, Tel: 724-654-4377. Rev. Francis C. Graff. Tel: 724-652-9471.
Cedar Manor, Tel: 724-654-8050. Rev. Francis C. Graff. Tel: 724-652-9471.
Golden Hill Nursing, Inc., Tel: 724-654-7791. Rev. Francis C. Graff. Tel: 724-652-9471.
Haven Convalescent Home, Tel: 724-654-8833. Rev. Francis C. Graff. Tel: 724-652-9471.
Highland Hall Care Center, Tel: 724-658-4781. Rev. Francis C. Graff. Tel: 724-652-9471.
Hillview Manor, Tel: 724-658-1521. Rev. Francis C. Graff. Tel: 724-652-9471.
Indian Creek Nursing Home, Tel: 724-652-6340. Rev. Francis C. Graff. Tel: 724-652-9471.
Jack Rees Nursing and Rehabilitation Center, Tel: 724-652-3863. Rev. Francis C. Graff. Tel: 724-652-9472.
Majors Manor, Tel: 724-924-9568. Rev. Francis C. Graff. Tel: 724-652-9471.
Overlook Nursing Home, Tel: 724-946-3511. Rev. Francis C. Graff. Tel: 724-652-9471.
Shenango United Presbyterian Home, Tel: 724-946-3516. Rev. Francis C. Graff. Tel: 724-652-9471.
Silver Oak Nursing, Tel: 724-652-3863. Rev. Francis C. Graff. Tel: 724-652-9471.

WASHINGTON COUNTY. *Beverly South Hills*, Tel: 724-746-1300. Rev. Kenneth E. Kezmarsky. Tel: 724-745-6560, Tel: 724-746-1300
Canon House, Tel: 724-745-7771. Rev. Kenneth E. Kezmarsky. Tel: 724-745-6560, Tel: 724-745-7771
Charles House Home for the Aged, Tel: 724-745-6355. Rev. Kenneth E. Kezmarsky. Tel: 724-745-0950, Tel: 724-745-6355
Greenery Nursing Home, Tel: 724-745-8000. Rev. Kenneth E. Kezmarsky. Tel: 724-745-6560, Tel: 724-745-8000
Horizon Senior Care, Tel: 724-746-5040. Rev. Kenneth E. Kezmarsky. Tel: 724-745-6560, Tel: 724-746-5040
Humbert Lane Health Care, Tel: 724-228-4740. Rev. Richard R. Ragni. Tel: 412-343-9558 Tel: 412-276-1383 Residence.
Kade's Nursing Home, Tel: 724-222-2148. Rev. Richard R. Ragni. Tel: 412-222-2148 Tel: 412-276-1383 Residence.
Pine Lawn Home, Tel: 724-746-1460. Rev. Kenneth E. Kezmarsky. Tel: 724-745-6560. Tel: 724-746-1460
Presbyterian Senior Care, Tel: 724-222-4300. Rev. Richard R. Ragni. Tel: 412-276-1383 Residence.
Rest Haven Personal Care Home I, Tel: 724-745-3333. Rev. Kenneth E. Kezmarsky. Tel: 724-745-6560.

Rest Haven Personal Care Home II, Tel: 724-746-3233. Rev. Kenneth E. Kezmarsky. Tel: 724-745-6560.
Rest Haven Personal Care Home V, Tel: 724-746-4666. Rev. Kenneth E. Kezmarsky. Tel: 724-745-6560. Tel: 724-746-4666
Washington City Health Center, Tel: 724-228-5010. Rev. Richard Ragni. Tel: 412-276-1383 Residence.

Mental Health Facilities

ALLEGHENY COUNTY. *Mayview State Hospital*, Tel: 412-257-6500. Rev. Harold Bailey. Tel: 412-771-5646. Holy Rosary Parish (724-745-3531)
Western Psychiatric Institute & Clinic, Tel: 412-647-3060. Attended by UPMC Chaplains. Tel: 412-647-7615.

WASHINGTON COUNTY. *Bradley Center South*, Tel: 724-746-1212; 724-746-2400. Rev. Kenneth E. Kezmarsky. Tel: 724-745-6560. Tel: 724-746-1212

Correctional Institutions

ALLEGHENY COUNTY. *Allegheny County Jail*, Tel: 412-350-2000. Rev. George F. Chortos. Tel: 412-350-2057, Deacons James A. Kenny, Thomas J. O'Neill.
Shuman Center, Tel: 412-661-6806. Rev. James A. Wehner, S.T.D. Tel: 724-921-5800, Ext. 22. Social Services. Tel: 412-665-4135.
State Correctional Institute at Pittsburgh, Tel: 412-381-8300. Rev. William R. Terza. Tel: 412-761-1955.

BEAVER COUNTY. *Beaver County Jail*. Saints Peter and Paul. Tel: 724-775-4111

BUTLER COUNTY. *Butler County Jail*. St. Paul

GREEN COUNTY. *State Correctional Institute at Greene*, Tel: 724-852-2902. Rev. George J. Moneck. Tel: 724-938-2324.
State Correctional Institution at Waynesburg (Women's Facility), Tel: 724-627-6185. St. Ann Parish (724-627-7568).
Waynesburg County Jail, Tel: 724-627-7780. St. Ann Parish (724-627-7780)

LAWRENCE COUNTY. *Lawrence County Jail*, Tel: 724-654-5384. Rev. James A. Downs. Tel: 724-667-7721.
Youth Development Center, Tel: 412-656-7300. Rev. John W. Rebel. Tel: 724-964-8276, Sr. Noreen Stearns, H.M. Tel: 330-395-8401.

WASHINGTON COUNTY. *Washington County Jail*, Tel: 412-561-7557. Attended by Immaculate Conception, Washington. Tel: 724-225-1425.

On Duty Outside the Diocese:
Revs.—
Bleichner, Howard P., Sulpicians, 2-1151 E. Cliff Dr., Santa Cruz, CA 95062.
Burns, Edward J., U.S.C.C.B., 3211 4th St. N.E., DC 20017-1194.
Cellini, Ronald R., St. Peter Parish, 70 Lady's Island Dr., Beauford, SC 29901.
Cizik, Ladis, Exec. Dir., Blue Army of Our Lady of Fatima, Lanteri House, 668 Mountain View Rd., E., Asbury, NJ 08802-1400.
Connolly, Brian W., 2444 Madison Rd., Apt. 911, Cincinnati, OH 45208.
Dominik, Kevin J., M.Div., St. Vincent Seminary, 300 Frasier Purchase Rd., Latrobe, 15650.
Fay, William J., St. Vincent Seminary, 300 Frasier Purchase Rd., Latrobe, 15650.
Friday, Robert M., S.T.D., Catholic University, 620 Michigan Ave., N.E., DC 20064-0001.
Hebda, Bernard A., Palazzo Delle Congregazioni, Piazza pio XII, 00120 Citta' del Vaticano, Italy.
Kozar, John E., Ponifical Mission Societies in the U.S.A., 366 Fifth Ave., New York, NY 10001.
Lauer, Eugene F., Catholic Theological Union, 5401 S. Cornell Ave., Chicago, IL 60615.
Mazurek, James K., M.Div., SS. Cyril & Methodius Seminary, 3535 Indian Tr., Orchard Lake, MI 48324.
Mueller, Richard J., St. John the Evangelist, 625 111th Ave., N., Naples, FL 34108.
Roos, H. Jules, Centro de Obras Sociales, Apartado 473, Chimbote, Peru.
Taylor, Augustus R., Jr., 1812 W. 48th St., Los Angeles, CA 90062.
Whalen, Timothy F., M.Div., Chancellor, Orchard Lake School, 3535 Indian Tr., Orchard Lake, MI 48324.

Graduate Studies:
Revs.—
Farnan, James B., Casa Santa Maria, Via dell'Umilta 30, 00187, Rome, Italy.
Gizler, John B. (Retired), St. Paul Seminary, 2900 Noblestown Rd., 15205.
Yurochko, Dennis P., Diocese of Pittsburgh Pastoral Center, 111 Blvd. of the Allies, 15222.

Military Chaplains:
Revs.—
Brzek, Jon J., Office of the Chaplain, 3012 Mink Point Blvd., Beaufort, SC 29902-5813.
Dansak, Thomas E., PSC 824, Box 2640, Fpo, AE 09627-1000.
Fix, Donald P., PSC 561, Box 1064, Fpo, AP 96310-0021.
Geinzer, John A., Chap., USN, USS Essex, (LHD-2), FPO, AP 96643-1661.
Glasgow, Mark W., Chap. VA Medical Center, c/o St. Maximilian Kolbe, 303 E. 10th Ave., Homestead, 15120.
Lamonde, Joseph R., P.O. Box 429, Ridge, MD 20680.
Yagesh, Richard C., PSC 557, Box 424, Fpo, AP 96379-0424.

Absent on Sick Leave:
Revs.—
Bunchek, Edward P.
Cirilli, Matthew R.
Manning, Thomas V.
Patriquin, Garry D.
Rager, Patrick F.

Retired:
Rev. Msgrs.—
Darkowski, Leon S., 235 The Boulevard, 15210.
Findlan, Joseph G., St. John Vianney Manor, 2600 Morange Rd., 15205.
Garland, Robert P., 96 S.W. 15th Ct., Boynton Beach, FL 33426.
Kraus, Donald W., Little Sisters of the Poor, 1028 Benton Ave., 15212-1694.
Kraus, Donald W., St. John Vianney Manor, 2600 Morange Rd., 15205.
Lackner, Paul M., Vincentian Home, 111 Perrymont Rd., 15237-5239.
Rice, Charles O., St. Anne Church, 400 Hoodridge Dr., 15234-1794.
Seli, John J., Cape Hacienda #202, 6655 Ridgewood Ave., Cocoa Beach, FL 32931.
Revs.—
Aaron, James L., M.Ed., Most Holy Name of Jesus, 1700 Harpster St., 15212.
Blough, William G., 421 Washington Ave., Oakmont, 15139.
Boccardi, Raymond C., 616 Fourth St., Apt. A, Ellwood City, 16117-2051.
Charnoki, John J., St. John Vianney Manor, 2600 Morange Rd., 15205.
Cheetham, William J., Cardinal Dearden Center, 4721 Fifth Ave., 15213.
Conner, Glenn T., St. John Vianney Manor, 2600 Morange Rd., 15205.
Czepinski, Richard J., 4510 Stilley Rd., 15227-1326.
DeBlasio, Dominck A., 605 Market St., Freeport, 16229.
DeCarlo, Philip J., 801 Somerville Dr., 15243.
DeLuca, Anthony, 409 Shady Ridge Dr., Monroeville, 15146.
Dixon, David C., St. John Vianney Manor, 2600 Morange Rd., 15205.
Dixon, Jerome A., Little Sisters of the Poor, 1028 Benton Ave., 15212-1694.
Dougherty, Eugene J., St. John Vianney Manor, 2600 Morange Rd., 15205.
Fording, John D., St. John Vianney Manor, 2600 Morange Rd., 15205.
Gelati, Dario, Parrocchia de Birbesi, 46040 Guidizzolo (MN), Italy.
Getty, Roy G., Cardinal Dearden Center, 4721 Fifth Ave., 15213-2915.
Gibson, John W., Vincentian Home, 111 Perrymont Rd., 15237-5239.
Gloninger, Hugh M., St. John Vianney Manor, 2600 Morange Rd., 15205.
Gualtieri, Raymond A., 4940 Brightwood Rd., Apt. A102, Bethel Park, 15102.
Henne, Paul G., Felician Sisters Motherhouse, 1500 Woodcrest Ave., Coraopolis, 15108-3099.
Henry, Leo G., St. John Vianney Manor, 2600 Morange Rd., 15205.
Jackovic, George V., 124 Bennington Dr., Canonsburg, 15317.
Jones, Donald R., 202 Williamsburg Dr., Elizabeth, 15037-2442.
Kelly, Gerard D., St. John Vianney Manor, 2600 Morenge Rd., 15205.
Kernan, Michael H., Cardinal Dearden Center, 4721 Fifth Ave., 15213-2915.
Kirby, Thomas M., Sisters of the Divine Redeemer, 999 Rock Run Rd., Elizabeth, 15037.
Kohler, William F., 2611 Ventana Dr., Coraopolis, 15108.
Kopecky, Joseph A., 1503 Sylvan Ave., Natrona Heights, 15065-1642.
Kram, Thomas J., 103 Chesna Dr., 15234-2348.
Kuenzig, Aloysius A., 2715 Custer Ave., 15227.
Kuenzig, Peter A., 2715 Custer Ave., 15227.
Laboon, Joseph D., 912 Eagle Pointe Dr., Canonsburg, 15317.
Lackner, Francis J. X., St. John Vianney Manor, 2600 Morange Rd., 15205.
Le, Trieu Ngoc, St. John Vianney Manor, 2600 Morange Rd., 15205.
Lech, Ferdinand F., Vincentian Home, 111 Perrymont Rd., 15237.
Leech, George T., 28 Emerson Ave., 15205.
Luteri, Evaristo, Vincentian Assisted Living, 111 Perrymont Rd., 15237.
Lutz, Gerald J., St. Peter Parish, 70 Lady's Island Dr., Beaufort, SC 29901.
Majda, Francis A., Vincentian Home, 111 Perrmont Rd., 15237.
Maliszewski, Edward C., Fox Hills Towers, Apt. 216, 1120 Fox Hill Dr., Monroeville, 15146-1075.
Manion, Thomas F., Cardinal Dearden Center, 4721 Fifth Ave., 15213-2915.
Markell, John W., 938 Broadway, East Mc Keesport, 15035.
Massung, Francis G., St. John Vianney Manor, 2600 Morange Rd., 15205.
Mastrangelo, Joseph A., 1111 S. Mercer St., New Castle, 16101.
McColligan, Raymond A., St. John Vianney Manor, 2600 Morange Rd., 15205.
McIlvane, Donald W., 265 46th St., Apt. 1207, 15201.
McSweeney, Edward F., 3619 Parkview Ave., 15213.
Michaels, John L., Vincentian Home, 111 Perrymonth Rd., 15237.
Miller, William J., St. John Vianney Manor, 2600 Morange Rd., 15205.
Murphy, Thomas R., Vincentian Home, 111 Perrymont Rd., 15237.
Nazimek, Francis A., St. Oliver Plunkett, P.O. Box 638, Fredericktown, 15333-0638.
Nee, Thomas M., St. John Vianney Manor, 2600 Morange Rd., 15205.
O'Brien, John, Cardinal Dearden Center, 4721 Fifth Ave., 15213-2915.
Palko, John A., St. Martin de Porres, c/o 705 Shaw Ave., McKeesport, 15132-2334.
Paluse, Richard V., 37 Forsythe Rd., 15220.
Parsons, Harry E., St. John Vianney Manor, 2600 Morange Rd., 15205.
Petrie, Harry F., St. Alexis, 10090 Old Perry Hwy., Wexford, 15090-9320.
Plantes, Francis P., Marian Manor, 2695 Winchester Dr., 15220-4099.
Polak, Michael J., St. John Vianney Manor, 2600 Morange Rd., 15205.
Rishel, Robert F., Vincentian Home, 111 Perrymont Rd., 15237.
Rocha, Victor J., Resurrection, 1100 Creedmoor Ave., 15213-2299.
Rutledge, William G., 1150 Calmwood Rd., Glenshaw, 15116.
Sedlak, Valentine G., Cardinal Dearden Center, 4721 Fifth Ave., 15213-2915.
Smith, Thomas E., 658 Lake Villas Dr., Altamonte Springs, FL 32701-4909.
Szarnicki, Henry A., St. John Vianney Manor, 2600 Morange Rd., 15205.
Szarnicki, Zygmunt V., St. John Vianney Manor, 2600 Morange Rd., 15205.
Trzeciakowski, Edward J., St. John Vianney Manor, 2600 Morange Rd., 15205.
Unger, John M., St. John Vianney Manor, 2600 Morange Rd., 15205.
Vanyo, Leo V., J.C.D., St. Bernard Parish, 311 Washington Rd., 15216.
Vecchio, Michael J., 5775 Fernley Dr. W., Apt. 76, West Palm Beach, FL 33415.
Vollmer, Raymond A., Villa Maria Center, 1050 N.W. 125th St., Rm. 344, North Miami, FL 33161.
Weirauch, William P., Vincentian Home, 111 Perrymont Rd., 15237.
Wichmanowski, Walter F., St. John Vianney Manor, 2600 Morange Rd., 15205.
Wilt, George A., St. John Vianney Manor, 2600 Morange Rd., 15205.

Permanent Deacons:
Abraham, Leon B., (Retired)
Bachner, Ralph W., Jr., St. Kilian, Mars
Bane, John J., (Retired)
Barth, Robert V., Catholic Office for the Deaf
Brueckner, Joseph P., (Retired)
Byers, Stephen J., Dept. for Religious Education/CCD
Cerenzia, Joseph A., Immaculate Conception, Washington
Cessar, Richard R., Northwest Deanery
Compomizzi, Joseph, St. John of God, McKees Rocks
Cunningham, Regis C., (Retired)
Dadowski, Francis J., Our Lady of the Angels, Lawrenceville
Deskevich, Stephen M., Holy Family Institute
DiSanto, Dale J., Mon Yough Deanery
Gaines, George W., St. Paul Cathedral
Gleason, Kenneth V., (Retired)
Gruseck, David J., Risen Lord, North Side

Hoover, Paul M., M.D., Office for Adult & Family Catechesis
Jelinek, G. Gregory, Most Holy Name of Jesus, Troy Hill
Kelly, Michael W., East Suburban Deanery
Kenny, James A., Allegheny County Jail
Kielar, S. Daniel, St. Vincent de Paul, New Castle
Killmeyer, Tim M., St. John of God, St. Malachy, Holy Trinity
Kosko, Joseph J., St. Winifred, Mt. Lebanon
Kriston, Louis H., Allegheny Valley Deanery
Kuhns, Elbert A., Greene County Deanery
Lamm, David E., J.D., Office for the Tribunal
Layton, John, St. Benedict the Abbot, Peters Twp.
Leonard, James F., St. Gabriel of the Sorrowful Virgin, Whitehall
Manion, John F., Immaculate Conception Parish
McKelvey, Albert T., (Retired)
Meyer, Joseph C., Jr., St. Patrick, Canonsburg
Miles, Leon F., St. Pamphilus, Beechview
Mueller, Joseph R., St. Sylvester, Brentwood
Natali, Mitchell M., St. Paul, Butler
O'Keefe, Charles L., (Retired)
O'Neill, Thomas J., Allegheny County Jail
Pikula, Stephen C., Saint Martin de Porres, McKeesport
Raymond, Thomas W., Washington East Deanery
Rubio, Silverio, St. Victor, Bairdford
Sabatelle, Robert C., Northwest Deanery
Satter, Victor P., St. Francis of Assisi, Finleyville
Sheil, James M., Greene County Deanery
Stein, Gerald C., (Retired)
Strathmann, William F., Jr., St. John Capistran, Upper Saint Clair
Sutton, Lawrence R., Our Lady of Grace, Scott Township
Very, Richard, Resurrection, Brookline
Wilmer, Reynold, St. Benedict the Moor, Hill District
Witter, David R., St. Alexis, Wexford
Wood, Patrick G., Our Lady of the Most Blessed Sacrament

INSTITUTIONS LOCATED IN THE DIOCESE

[A] SEMINARIES, RELIGIOUS OR SCHOLASTICATES

PITTSBURGH. *Saint Paul Seminary*, College & Pre-Theology, 2900 Noblestown Rd., 15205. Tel: 412-921-5800; Fax: 412-928-5842. Email: seminaryprog@diopitt.org. Web: www.diopitt.org. Revs. James A. Wehner, S.T.D., Rector. Tel: 724-921-5800, Ext. 22; Edward L. Yuhas, Vice Rector & Dean of Studies; Brian J. Welding, S.T.L., J.C.D., Dir. of Spirtual Formation; Sr. Judith Worden, R.S.M., Coord. Apostolic Works. Priests 3; Sisters 1; Students (attending Duquesne University) 12.

[B] COLLEGES AND UNIVERSITIES

PITTSBURGH. *Carlow College*, 3333 5th Ave., 15213. Tel: 412-578-6059; Fax: 412-578-6668. Email: admission@carlow.edu. Web: www.carlow.edu. Sr. Grace Ann Geibel, R.S.M., Ph.D., Pres.; Gary Smith, Ph.D., Vice Pres. for Academic Affairs. Sisters of Mercy Sisters 3; Lay Teachers 76; Total Staff 79; Total Enrollment 2,135.

Duquesne University of the Holy Spirit, 600 Forbes Ave., 15282. Tel: 412-396-6000; Fax: 412-396-4334. Web: www.duq.edu. Dr. Charles J. Dougherty, Pres.; Revs. William F. Crowley, C.S.Sp.; Francis Hanley, C.S.Sp.; Sean M. Hogan, C.S.Sp., Exec. Vice Pres. Student Life; Matthias Idyu, C.S.Sp.; Sean Kealy, C.S.Sp.; Raymond D. French, C.S.Sp.; Luke Mbefo, C.S.Sp.; Naos McCool, C.S.Sp.; David L. Smith, C.S.Sp., Supr.; John A. Sawicki, C.S.Sp.; Edmund R. Supple, C.S.Sp.; Jocelyn Gregorie, C.S.Sp.; Very Rev. James P. McCloskey, C.S.Sp. Holy Ghost Fathers Priests 16; Lay Teachers 409; Students 9,595; Total Staff 1,447.

The University is coeducational and comprises the following Colleges and Schools and Institutes:

College of Liberal Arts Tel: 412-396-5097; Fax: 412-396-4859. Dr. Constance Ramirez, Dean College & Graduate School of Liberal Arts.

School of Business Administration Tel: 412-396-6238; Fax: 412-396-4764. James C. Stalder, Dean.

School of Music Tel: 412-396-6080; Fax: 412-396-5479. Dr. Edward Kocher, Dean.

School of Law Tel: 412-396-6300; Fax: 412-396-5219. Nicholas Cafardi, Dean.

School of Leadership and Professional Advancement Tel: 412-396-5600; Fax: 412-396-5072. Dr. Benjamin Hodes, Dean.

School of Education Tel: 412-396-6093; Fax: 412-396-5585. Dr. Rick McCown, Interim Dean.

School of Nursing Tel: 412-396-6550; Fax: 412-396-6346. Dr. Eileen Zungolo, Dean.

School of Pharmacy Tel: 412-396-6380; Fax: 412-396-1810. Dr. R. Pete Vanderveen, Dean.

School of Health Sciences Tel: 412-396-6652; Fax: 412-396-5554. Dr. Gregory Frazer, Dean; Dr. David W. Seybert, Dean School of Natural & Environmental Sciences. Tel: 412-396-4900; Dr. Ralph L. Pearson, Provost & Academic Vice Pres.; Mr. Stephen Schillo, Vice Pres., Mgmt. & Business; Rev. Sean M. Hogan, C.S.Sp., Exec. Vice Pres. Student Life; Linda S. Drago, Esq., Gen. Counsel & Univ. Sec.

La Roche College, 9000 Babcock Blvd., 15237. Tel: 412-367-9300; Fax: 412-536-1038. Email: admsas@laroche.edu. Web: www.laroche.edu. Rev. Msgr. William A. Kerr, Ph.D., Pres.; Sr. Carolyn Winschel, C.D.P., Ph.D., Senior Vice Pres., Mission & Planning; Dan Soller, Exec. Vice Pres., Admin.; Rev. W. Peter Horton, M.A., M.Div., Campus Min.; Dr. Howard Ishiyama, Vice Pres. for Academic Affairs; Kenneth Service, Vice Pres. Inst. Resources; Fred Vey, CFO; Rev. Patrick O'Brien, S.T.D., M.S.Ed., Dept. Chair Religious Studies. Sisters of Divine Providence Priests 5; Sisters 9; Lay Teachers 212; Total Staff 187; Students 1,800.

[C] HIGH SCHOOLS, DIOCESAN

PITTSBURGH. *Bishop Canevin High School*, Formerly Canevin Catholic High School, 2700 Morange Rd., 15205. Tel: 412-922-7400; Fax: 412-922-7403. Email: mainoffice@canevin.com. Web: www.bishopcanevin.org. Mr. Kenneth Sinagra, Prin.; Rev. Alvin J. Adams, Chap. Priests 1; Sisters 1; Lay Teachers 29; Students 349.

Central District Catholic High School, 4720 Fifth Ave., 15213. Tel: 412-621-8189; Fax: 412-208-0555. Email: principal@pittcentralcatholic.org. Web: www.pittcentralcatholic.org. Bro. Richard Grzeskiewicz, F.S.C., Prin. The school is a Diocesan institution under the care of the Christian Brothers. Priests 1; Brothers 10; Lay Teachers 55; Students 869; Total Staff 166.

North Catholic High School, 1400 Troy Hill Rd., 15212. Tel: 412-321-4823; Fax: 412-321-0599. Email: nchs@north-catholic.org. Web: www.north-catholic.org. Sisters 2; Lay Teachers 28; Total Staff 29; Students 381.

Oakland Catholic High School, 144 N. Craig St., 15213. Tel: 412-682-6633; Fax: 412-682-2496. Email: webmaster@oaklandcath.org. Web: www.oaklandcath.org. Dr. Maureen Marsteller, Prin.; Katherine D. Freyvogel, Pres. Priests 1; Lay Teachers 36; Total Staff 40; Students 462.

BADEN. *Quigley Catholic High School*, 200 Quigley Dr., 15005. Tel: 724-869-2188; Fax: 724-869-3091. Email: diopghquighs@impresso.com. Web: www.qchs.org. Rev. David C. Menegay, Prin. Sisters 1; Lay Teachers 16; Students 196; Total Staff 19.

MCKEESPORT. *Serra Catholic High School*, 200 Hershey Dr., 15132. Tel: 412-751-2020; Fax: 412-751-3488. Email: diopghserra@impresso.com. Web: www.serrahs.com. Brothers 1; Sisters 1; Lay Teachers 18; Students 306; Total Staff 24.

Under the direction of the Franciscan Friars (Province of the Most Sacred Heart). Bro. Sean Mary Fitzwater, T.O.R., Pres.; Rev. Edward Stafford, T.O.R.; Bros. Jonathan St. Andre, T.O.R.; Martin O'Malley, T.O.R.

MT. LEBANON. *Seton-LaSalle Catholic High School*, 1000 McNeilly Rd., 15226. Tel: 412-561-3583; Fax: 412-561-9097. Email: slshs1@nauticom.net. Web: www.slshs.org. Priests 1; Sisters 6; Lay Teachers 31; Students 505; Total Staff 38.

Under care of Sisters of Charity. Rev. Robert J. Miller, Chap.

[D] HIGH SCHOOLS, PRIVATE

PITTSBURGH. *Mt. Alvernia High School*, 146 Hawthorne Rd., 15209. Tel: 412-821-3858; Fax: 412-821-2910. Email: office@mtalvernia.com. Web: mtalvernia.com. Kimberly Minick, Prin. Sisters of St. Francis Lay Teachers 10; Students 85.

Vincentian Academy - Duquesne University, Peebles & McKnight Rds., 15237. Tel: 412-364-1616; Fax: 412-367-5722. Email: panich@duq.edu. Web: www.vaduq.org. Vincentian Sisters of Charity 4; Lay Teachers 22; Students 270; Total Staff 32.

CORAOPOLIS. *Our Lady of the Sacred Heart High School*, 1504 Woodcrest Ave., 15108. Tel: 412-264-5140; Fax: 412-264-4143. Email: olshdevelopment@hotmail.com. Web: www.olsh.org. Sr. Mary Francine Horos, C.S.S.F., Prin. Felician Sisters, C.S.S.F., State approved day high school. Priests 1; Sisters 3; Lay Teachers 25; Students 318; Total Staff 40.

[E] CONSOLIDATED SCHOOLS

PITTSBURGH. *Bishop McDowell Regional School*, (Grades PreK-8) , (Baldwin) , 3198 Schieck St., 15227. Tel: 412-884-5676; Fax: 412-884-8610. Email: bishopmcdowell@yahoo.com. Web: www.regionalcatholicschool.com. Berenice Maroney-Turkaly, Prin. Serving the parishes of St. Albert the Great and St. Wendelin. Lay Teachers 12; Students 137; Total Staff 13.

Brookline Regional Catholic School, (Grades PreK-8) , (Brookline) , 2690 Waddington Ave., 15226. Tel: 412-563-0858; Fax: 412-341-5610. Email: brcschool@quest.net. Web: www.nauticom.net/www/pius/BRChome.htm. Janet Salley, Prin. Serving the parishes of Our Lady of Loreto, St. Pius X, and Resurrection. Religious 1; Lay Teachers 16; Students 256; Total Staff 17.

Cardinal Wright Regional School, (Grades PreK-8) , (North Side) , 711 West Commons, 15212. Tel: 412-231-8248; Fax: 412-231-0835. Email: macek@stargate.net. Web: www.cardinalwrightregionalschool.org. Mr. Kenneth E. Macek, Prin. Serving the parishes of St. Aloysius, Most Holy Name of Jesus and St. Peter. Lay Teachers 10; Students 201.

Christ the Divine Teacher Catholic Academy, (Grades K-8) , (Aspinwall) , 205 Brilliant Ave., 15215. Tel: 412-781-7927; Fax: 412-781-0891. Email: cdtca@nauticom.net. Sr. Marilyn Hoeing, O.S.F., Acting Prin. Serving the parishes of St. Edward, St. John Cantius, St. Joseph, Madonna of Jerusalem, St. Mary, and St. Scholastica. Religious 1; Lay Teachers 11; Students 164; Total Staff 13.

Elizabeth Seton Regional Elementary School, (Grades PreK-8), 3021 Landis St., 15204. Tel: 412-331-4529; Fax: 412-331-8734. Email: elizabethseton@stargate.net. Sarah E. Tonski, Prin. Serving the parishes of Guardian Angels and Holy Innocents. Lay Teachers 8; Students 136; Total Staff 11.

St. John Neumann Regional, Catholic Elementary, (Grades K-8), 250 44th St., 15201. Tel: 412-682-5096; Fax: 412-682-0811. Email: sjn15201@yahoo.com. Web: www.geocities.com/sjnpgh. Sr. Coletta Adelsberg, C.S.J., Prin. Serving the parishes of Our Lady of Angels, St. Matthew and St. Lawrence O'Toole. Sisters 1; Lay Teachers 9; Students 149.

BUTLER. *Butler Catholic School* Tel: 724-285-4276; Fax: 724-285-4896. Email: bcsspboffozbzoom.net. Web: www.butlercatholic.org. *St. Paul*, 515 E. Locust St., 16001. Tel: 724-285-4276; Fax: 724-285-4896. Serving the parishes of St. Paul, St. Michael, St. Fidelis, St. Andrew, and St. Peter's, Butler. Lay Teachers 24; Students 319.

DONORA. *Madonna Catholic Regional School*, (Grades K-8), 1 Park Manor Rd., 15033. Tel: 724-379-5977; Fax: 724-379-7633. Email: madon@stargate.net. M. A. Knoll, Prin. Serving the parishes of St. Anthony, Mary, Mother of the Church, Our Lady of the Valley, and Transfiguration. Lay Teachers 15; Students 270; Total Staff 15.

PORT VUE. *St. Joseph Regional School*, (Grades PreK-8), 1125 Romine Ave., 15133. Tel: 412-678-0659; Fax: 412-678-1301. Email: kinolem@stjoesregional.com. Web: www.stjoesregional.com. Mr. Frank J. Napoli, Prin. Serving the parishes of Queen of Rosary, St. Martin de Porres, St. Mark, St. Patrick. Lay Teachers 14; Students 252; Total Staff 16.

[F] ELEMENTARY SCHOOLS, PRIVATE

PITTSBURGH. *Carlow College Campus School*, (Grades PreK-8), 3333 5th Ave., 15213. Tel: 412-578-6157; Fax: 412-578-8850. Email: bgirard@carlow.edu. Web: www.carlow.edu/~ccs. Sisters of Mercy Sisters 2; Lay Teachers 28; Students 270; Total Staff 30.

ALLISON PARK. *Providence Heights Alpha School*, 9000 Babcock Blvd., 15101. Tel: 412-366-4455; Fax: 412-635-6317. Web: www.alphaschool.org. Dr. Brian White, Prin. Sisters of Divine Providence Sisters 6; Lay Teachers 21; Students 194; Total Staff 32.

BADEN. *Mount Gallitzin Academy*, (Grades PreK-8), 1016 State St., 15005-1399. Tel: 724-869-2505; 724-869-2151; Fax: 724-869-4932. Email: mtgallitzin@stargate.net. Web: www.stjoseph-baden.org. Sr. Norma Zanieski, C.S.J., Prin. Sisters of St. Joseph Sisters 6; Lay Teachers 14; Students 272; Preschool Students 14; Total Staff 20.

Mount Gallitzin Academy Corp., 1016 State St., 15005-1399. Tel: 724-869-2505; Fax: 724-869-4932. Email: mtgallitzin@stargate.net. Sr. Norma Zanieski, C.S.J. Purpose: to engage in educational activities and the operation of educational program of the Sisters of St. Joseph. Funds, distributions, gifts, bequests, endowments, grants, and contributions from other charitable organizations and student tuitions will be used to support applicant organization's programs and ministry outreach.

[G] DEPARTMENT OF SPECIAL EDUCATION

PITTSBURGH. *St. Anthony School Programs*, 2718 Custer Ave., 15227. Tel: 412-882-1333; Fax: 412-882-1668. Email: anthcoo@nauticom.net. Thomas O'Toole, Exec. Dir. Resource rooms for students with special needs in 7 elementary schools and 2 high schools. Lay Teachers 10; Students 109; Total Staff 10.

The De Paul Institute, 6202 Alder St., 15206. Tel: 412-924-1012; Fax: 412-924-1036. Email: vp@depaulinst.com. Web: www.depaulinst.com. Dennis Barrett, Ph.D., Supt.; Sr. Virginia Pascaretta, S.C., Educational Dir. Auditory day school for children with hearing, speech and language impairments. Sisters 3; Lay Teachers 14; Students 73.

NEW BRIGHTON. *McGuire Memorial*, 2119 Mercer Rd., 15066-3437. Tel: 724-843-3400; Fax: 724-847-2004. Email: mcgm@mcguirememorial.org. Web: www.mcguirememorial.org. Residential Facility-Intermediate Care for Developmentally Challenged. Priests 1; Sisters 6; Lay Teachers 15; Lay Staff 422; Residents 89; Additional Services: Adult Training 90; Community Living Residents 39; Private Academic Program 48.

[H] CHILD CARE INSTITUTIONS

PITTSBURGH. *Franciscan Child Day Care Center*, 1401 Hamilton Rd., 15234-2399. Tel: 412-882-5085; Fax: 412-885-7210. Email: franchildctr@aol.com. Sisters Linda Kaman, R.S.M., Dir.; Barbara Zilch, O.S.F., Pres. Total Assisted 79; Total Staff 35.

Mt. Alvernia Day Care & Learning Center, 146 Hawthorne Rd., 15209. Tel: 412-821-4302; Fax: 412-821-3318. Web: www.millvaleFranciscans.org. Provides infant, toddler, and preschool care as well as before- and after-school care for school age children. Total Assisted 175; Total Staff 35.

Providence Connections, Inc., Corporate Office, 3113 Brighton Rd., 15212-2456. Tel: 412-766-3860; Fax: 412-766-6775. Email: caconway2@juno.com. Sr. Maria Fest, Exec. Dir.

Providence Child Care Center, South, 400 Hoodridge Ave., 15234-1793. Tel: 412-531-3360; Fax: 412-531-3360. Total Assisted 44; Total Staff 18.

Providence Family Support Center, 3113 Brighton Rd., 15212-2456. Tel: 412-766-6730; Fax: 412-766-6775. Total Assisted 196; Total Staff 36.

Amelia House, Clarion. Tel: 814-226-6682. Purpose: To engage in educational activities and operation of day care centers and other related services to women and children in need. Total Assisted 13; Total Staff 1.

Vincentian Child Care, Inc., 8200 McKnight Rd., 15237. Tel: 412-366-8588; Fax: 412-366-7315. Email: sgeorgine@vincentiansrspgh.org. Web: vincentiansrspgh.org/childcare/index.html. Sr. Georgine Bires, V.S.C., Contact Person. Purpose: to engage in educational activities; operating a day care program; to perform any lawful acts to effectuate purposes of this corporation and in this pursuit to apply funds or incomes exclusively for charitable, religious, scientific, literary, and educational purposes. Total Assisted 100; Total Staff 35.

EMSWORTH. *Holy Family Institute*, 8235 Ohio River Blvd., 15202. Tel: 412-766-4030; Fax: 412-766-5434. Email: schott.sandra@hfi-pgh.org. Web: www.hfi-pgh.org. Sr. Linda Yankoski, Exec. Dir. Sisters of the Holy Family of Nazareth, Holy Family Institute is committed to helping children, preserving families and strengthening communities by providing a network of services including in-home counseling, residential treatment, summer day camp, and out-patient mental health services. Holy Family provides special education and alternative education for grades K through 12. The Bellefonds Method serves K through 12 as well as the adult population. This method uses a technique of assessment and re-education for learning difficulties due to developmental disabilities, stroke, brain trauma or infection. Volunteer opportunities are also available at Holy Family Institute. Sisters 1; Total Assisted: Children 3,506; Families 6,323; Total Staff 465.

[I] GENERAL HOSPITALS

PITTSBURGH. *Mercy Hospital of Pittsburgh* (Affiliate of Pittsburgh Mercy Health System), 1400 Locust St., 15219. Tel: 412-232-7505; Fax: 412-232-7380. Web: www.mercylink.org. J. Penn Krause, Exec. Vice Pres. & COO. Bed Capacity 460; Patients Assisted Annually 252,085; Total Staff 2,612.

Mercy Providence Hospital, 1004 Arch St., 15212. Tel: 412-323-5600; Fax: 412-323-5685. Web: www.mercylink.org. Sr. Patricia Mary Hespelein, Vice Pres. Mission Council. (Affiliate of Pittsburgh Mercy Health System) Sisters 3; Bed Capacity 133; Patients Assisted Annually 229,977; Total Staff 302.

Pittsburgh Mercy Foundation, 1709 Blvd. of the Allies, Ste. 100, 15219-5947. Tel: 412-232-7504; Fax: 412-232-7810. Email: dtrehar@mercy.pmhs.org. Web: www.mercylink.org. Total Staff 7.

Pittsburgh Mercy Health System, Inc., 1400 Locust St., 15219 Tel: 412-232-8111; Fax: 412-232-7380. Web: www.mercylink.org. Mr. Gregg G. Zoller, Pres. & CEO. Bed Capacity 619; Patients Assisted Annually 489,213; Staff 3,974.

Parent company of the following subsidiaries:

Coolock Enterprises, Inc. Tel: 412-232-8111; Fax: 412-232-7380.

Mercy Primary Care, Inc. Tel: 412-232-8111; Fax: 412-232-7380.

The Mercy Hospital of Pittsburgh Tel: 412-232-8111; Fax: 412-232-7380.

Pittsburgh Mercy Foundation Tel: 412-232-5583; Fax: 412-232-7810.

Mercy Life Center Corporation Tel: 412-232-8111; Fax: 412-232-7380.

St. Pius X Residence, Inc. Tel: 412-232-8111; Fax: 412-232-7380.

Mercy Providence Hospital Tel: 412-323-5600; Fax: 412-323-5685. (Formerly Divine Providence Hospital of Pittsburgh)

[J] SPECIAL HOSPITALS AND SANATORIA FOR INVALIDS

PITTSBURGH. *Vincentian de Marillac*, 5300 Stanton Ave., 15206. Tel: 412-361-2833; Fax: 412-361-2833. Email atrzeciak@vcsdemarillac.org. Anne Trzeciak, N.H.A., Contact. Non-sectarian, skilled nursing home. Vincentian Sisters of Charity 1; Total Staff 75; Bed Capacity 52; Total Assisted 92.

Vincentian Home Inc., 111 Perrymont Rd., 15237. Tel: 412-366-5600; Fax: 412-366-1408. Web: www.vcs.org. Sr. Anne Kull, V.S.C., Admin. Vincentian Sisters of Charity Sisters 12; Total Staff 257; Bed Capacity 217; Patients Assisted Annually 217; Assisted Living: Total Assisted 54; Total Staff 27.

[K] HOMES FOR THE AGED

PITTSBURGH. *Little Sisters of the Poor Home for the Aged*, 1028 Benton Ave., 15212. Tel: 412-761-5373; Fax: 412-734-1030. Email: littlesisters1@mindspring.com. Web: www.littlesistersofthepoor-pittsburgh.org. Sr. Mary Vincent Mannin, Supr. & Admin.; Rev. Jerome Dixon. Sisters 10; Total Staff 100; Residents 21; Total Assisted 28; Apartments 12

Marian Manor Corp., 2695 Winchester Dr., 15220-4099. Tel: 412-563-6866 (Admin.); 412-563-1244 (Nursing Service); Fax: 412-563-1250. Email: echlebowski@choiceonemail.com. Web: www.marianmanor.com. Sr. Eileen Chlebowski, N.H.A., Admin.; Rev. Regis Alberth. Sisters of the Holy Spirit 12; Total Staff 280; Residents 194; Total Assisted 271; Child Day Care: Total Assisted 52; Total Staff 13.

St. Pius X Residence, Inc. (Affiliate of Pittsburgh Mercy Health System), 2681 Waddington Ave., 15226. Tel: 412-563-5040; Fax: 412-563-3776. Mary Jo Hummel, Admin. Total in Residence 26; Total Staff 20.

ALLISON PARK. *Vincentian Regency*, 9399 Babcock Blvd., 15101. Tel: 412-366-8540; Fax: 412-369-9789. Email: ddolak@vcsregency.org. Web: www.vcs.org. Sr. Dorothy Dolak, V.S.C., Admin.; Rev. David C. Dixon (Retired). Vincentian Sisters of Charity Bed Capacity 143; Total Staff 200; Adult Day Services: Total Assisted 290; Total Staff 200.

BADEN. **Villa St. Joseph of Baden, Inc.*, 1030 State St., 15005. Tel: 724-869-6300; Fax: 724-869-6399. Sr. Judith Maroni, C.S.J., Pres.; Ms. Mary M. Murray, N.H.A., Admin. Purpose: to operate a 120 bed skilled/intermediate care licensed nursing home, striving to address not only medical needs, but to also maximize opportunities for physical activity, social interaction and spiritual development - holistic care. Beds for Patients with Dementia or Alzheimers 30; Total Assisted 120; Total Staff 160.

[L] REHABILITATION, NURSING AND GERIATRIC CARE FACILITIES

PITTSBURGH. *Marian Hall Home, Inc.*, 934 Forest Ave., 15202-1118. Tel: 412-761-1999; Fax: 412-761-2556. Email: marian@sgi.net. Sr. Marian Sgriccia, O.S.F. Purpose: to provide programs, facilities, and services, including, but not limited to, residential personal care, and long-term care homes for the elderly, ill, or disabled, including supportive services. Total in Residence 57; Total Assisted Annually 75; Total Staff 41.

[M] PERSONAL PRELATURES

PITTSBURGH. *Prelature of the Holy Cross and Opus Dei*, Warwick House, 5090 Warwick Terr., 15213. Tel: 412-683-8448; Fax: 412-687-3806. Email: info@warwickhouse.org. Web: www.opusdei.org. Revs. Rene J. Schatteman (LA); Martin J. Miller.

[N] MONASTERIES AND RESIDENCES OF PRIESTS AND BROTHERS

PITTSBURGH. *St. Augustine Friary*, 221 36th St., 15201. Tel: 412-682-6430; Fax: 412-682-6148. Email: capuchin.friars@att.net. Web: www.capuchin.com. Revs. Robert Craig, O.F.M.Cap., Chap., Oakland VA Medical Center; Gervase Degenhardt Hardt, O.F.M.Cap., Chap., Sisters of St. Francis, Millvale; Francis Fugini, O.F.M.Cap., Dir. for Missions; Paul Kuppe, O.F.M.Cap., Prov. Min.; John Pavlik, O.F.M.Cap., Vicar Prov.; John J. Petrikovic, O.F.M.Cap., Prov. Sec.; Bertin Roll, O.F.M.Cap., Dir. Archconfraternity of Christian Mothers; Scott Seethaler, O.F.M.Cap., Preaching Ministry; DeSales Young, O.F.M.Cap., Confessor, St. Mary of the Point, Pittsburgh; Armand Yeaglin, O.F.M.Cap, Pastoral Supply; John Bednarik, O.F.M.Cap., Definitor Gen.; William Henn, O.F.M.Cap., Prof. Pontifical Gregorian Univ.; Otmar Gallagher, O.F.M.Cap. (VEN), Pastoral Supply; Bonaventure Stefun, O.F.M.Cap., Pastoral Supply; Edward Laurent, O.F.M.Cap.; Thomas A. Dutkiewicz, O.F.M.Cap., Confessor; Maurice Sheehan, O.F.M.Cap. (NOR), Academic Dean, Holy Apostles Seminary; Bro. Richard Lubomski, O.F.M.Cap., Guardian Fraternity Service.

In Res. Rev. Benedict Pope, O.F.M.Cap.

Congregation of the Oratory of St. Philip Neri, The Pittsburgh Oratory, 4450 Bayard St., 15213. Tel: 412-681-3181; Fax: 412-681-2922. Email: dsaepittsburghoratory.org. Web: www.andrew.cmu.edu/USER/oratory. Very Rev. Bryan F. Summers, C.O., Provost; Rev. Drew P. Morgan, C.O.; Very Rev. David S. Abernethy, C.O., Provost; Revs. Joseph E. Sioli, C.O.; Michael J. Darcy, C.O. Total Staff 5.

St. Conrad Friary, 9448 Babcock Blvd., Allison Park, 15101. Tel: 412-364-8240; Fax: 412-366-8331. Web: www.capuchin.com. Rev. W. David Nestler, O.F.M.Cap., Guardian & Dir. Novices; Bro. David Cira, O.F.M.Cap., Chap., Mercy Health System; Revs. Blaise J. Fusco, O.F.M.Cap., Jubilarian; Gabriel Giles, O.F.M.Cap, Jubilarian; Joel Ostrowski, O.F.M.Cap., Jubilarian; Roland Raible, O.F.M.Cap., Jubilarian; Pascal Schaller, O.F.M.Cap., Jubilarian; Brendan Malloy, O.F.M. Cap., Pastoral Supply for St. Mary of Mercy Church, Downtown; Jeff Ernst, O.F.M.Cap. (STL), Asst. Dir. of Novices. Novices 5; Total in Residence 14; Total Staff 1.

Croatian Commissariate, T.O.R., 24 Maryland Ave., 15209. Tel: 412-821-3438; Fax: 412-821-8276. Very Rev. Gabriel Badurina, T.O.R., Commissary Prov.

St. Francis Friary, 2905 Castlegate Ave., 15226. Tel: 412-531-4545; Fax: 412-531-0998. Email: bjstefun@worldnet.att.net. Web: www.capuchin.com. Revs. Thomas A. Dutkiewicz, O.F.M.Cap., Confessor, St. Mary of Mercy Church, Pittsburgh; Emitt Schuler, O.F.M.Cap., VA Chap.; Maurice Sheehan, O.F.M.Cap., Dean, Holy Apostles Seminary, Cromwell, CT; Bonaventure Stefun, O.F.M.Cap., Guardian; Edward Laurent, O.F.M.Cap., Dir. St. Fidelis Devel. Office & Vicar. Residents 6.

Franciscan Friars, T.O.R., Queen of Peace Friary, 5324 Carnegie St., 15201. Tel: 412-782-4755; Fax: 412-782-2377. Bro. Albert Gentile, T.O.R., Local Min.; Rev. Bernard Tickerhoof, T.O.R., Retreat Ministry In Res. Bro. Michael Tripka, T.O.R., Retreat Ministry.

St. John Vianney Manor, 2600 Morange Rd., 15205. Tel: 412-928-0825; 412-928-0908; Fax: 412-928-1947. Retired priests' residence. Total in Residence 29; Total Staff 8. In Res. Rev. Msgr. Joseph G. Findlan (Retired); Revs. Charles B. Bergman; Leo R. Burchianti (Retired); John J. Charnoki (Retired); Glenn T. Conner (Retired); John B. Corbett; David C. Dixon (Retired), St. John Vianney Manor, 2600 Morange Rd., 15205; Eugene J. Dougherty (Retired); John D. Fording (Retired); Hugh M. Gloninger (Retired); Leo G. Henry (Retired); Gerard D. Kelly (Retired); Edward L. Kryston; Francis J. X. Lackner (Retired); Trieu Ngoc Le (Retired); Francis G. Massung (Retired); Raymond McColligan; William M. Miller; Thomas M. Nee (Retired); William P. O'Malley; Harry E. Parsons (Retired); Robert J. Reardon; Bernard P. Shulik; Henry A. Szarnicki (Retired); Zygmunt V. Szarnicki (Retired); Edward J. Trzeciakowski (Retired); John M. Unger (Retired); Walter F. Wichmanowski (Retired); George A. Wilt (Retired).

St. Paul of the Cross Monastery Retreat Center, Passionist Overseas Missions. , 148 Monastery Ave., S.S., 15203. Tel: 412-381-1188; Fax: 412-481-5049. Web: www.catholic-church/

stpaulsmonastery/. Very Rev. Richard A. Nalepa, C.P.; Revs. Donald Ware, C.P., Asst. Local Supr.; William Davin, C.P.; Timothy Fitzgerald, C.P.; John F. McMillan, C.P.; Edwin Moran, C.P.; Daniel Sullivan, C.P.; Bros. Leo Di Fiore, C.P., Passionist Overseas Missions Dir.; Matthew Krawchyk, C.P.

Mission Band: Revs. Timothy Fitzgerald, C.P.; Edwin Moran, C.P.; Daniel Sullivan, C.P.; Michael Salvagna, C.P., Dir. of Passionist Communications. Retreat Center: Revs. Thomas P. Bonacci, C.P., Dir. Tel: 412-381-7676; Joseph Sedley, C.P.

Passionist Overseas Missions: Bro. Leo Di Fiore, C.P., Rel. Admin. Coord. Tel: 412-381-1189, Ext. 21.

Society of The Divine Word, 207 Lytton, 15213. Tel: 412-683-4030. Rev. Walter Ostrowski, S.V.D., Mission Dir. Tel: 412-683-0640. Total in Residence 4. In Res. Revs. Ray Hober, S.V.D.; James Huang, S.V.D.; Bro. John DeBold, S.V.D.

Third Order Regular of Saint Francis - Province of the Most Sacred Heart of Jesus, 128 Woodshire Dr., 15215-1714. Tel: 412-781-8333; Fax: 412-781-1219. Email: MinProvSHP@aol.com. Web: www.franciscantor.org. Very Rev. Edmund F. Carroll, T.O.R., Prov. Min.; Rev. Joseph Monahan, T.O.R., Chap. Mercy Hospital. Residents 1; Total Staff 2.

Queen of Peace Friary, 5324 Carnegie St., 15201. Tel: 412-782-4755; Fax: 412-782-2377. Bros. Albert Gentile, T.O.R., Local Min.; Bernard Tickerhoof, T.O.R., Retreat Min.; Michael Tripka, T.O.R.

Serra Friary, 200 Hershey Dr., McKeesport, 15132. Tel: 412-751-1250; Fax: 412-751-3488. Bros. Sean Mary Fitzwater, T.O.R.; Dominic Foster, T.O.R.; Jonathan St. Andre, T.O.R.; Martin O'Malley, T.O.R.; Rev. Edward Stafford, T.O.R.

AVALON. *Holy Family Friary* (Friars Minor), The Franciscans. , 232 S. Home Ave., 15202-2899. Tel: 412-761-2550; 412-761-8470; Fax: 412-761-2959. Email: holyfamilyfriary@comcast.net. Bros. Allan Schmitz, O.F.M.; David Kohut, O.F.M.; Lawrence Pollak, O.F.M.; Jerome Pavlik, O.F.M.; Revs. David Moczulski, O.F.M. (CIN); Michael Lenz, O.F.M. (CIN). Friars 6.

Franciscan House of Evangelization, 2428 Arlington Ave., 15210. Tel: 412-431-4476; Fax: 412-431-4478. Email: ofmpgh@prodigy.net. Bros. Daniel Barrett, O.F.M.; Thomas Gerchak, O.F.M.; Bill Spond, O.F.M. Friars 3.

BETHEL PARK. *Holy Spirit Fathers and Brothers Provincialate*, 6230 Brush Run Rd., 15102. Tel: 412-831-0302; Fax: 412-831-0970. Email: csspeast@sgi.net. Web: www.spiritans.org. Very Rev. James P. McCloskey, C.S.Sp., Prov. Supr.; Rev. Girard J. Kohler, C.S.Sp., Mission Procurator. Residents 2; Total Staff 7.

HERMAN. *St. Mary's Friary*, P.O. Box 26, 16039. Tel: 724-282-1485; Fax: 724-285-4715. Email: stmarys@stargate.net. Bros. Lester Knoll, O.F.M.Cap., Vicar; Eric Gauchat, O.F.M.Cap., Guardian; DePaul Ripko, O.F.M.Cap.; Gary Stakem, O.F.M.Cap.; James Townsend, O.F.M.Cap. Capuchin Friars

MCKEESPORT. *Franciscan Friars, T.O.R., Serra Friary*, 200 Hershey Dr., Mc Keesport, 15132-7400. Tel: 412-751-1250; Fax: 412-751-3488. Web: www.serrahs.org. Rev. Edward Stafford, T.O.R.; Bros. Martin O'Malley, T.O.R.; Jonathan St. Andre, T.O.R.

ROCHESTER. *St. Cecilia Friary*, 303 Jackson St., 15074. Tel: 724-775-0801; 724-774-6046; Fax: 724-774-3056. Email: stcecilia@access995.com. Web: www.stceciliaroch.org. Revs. Philip J. Bernier, O.F.M.Cap.; Ward Stakem, O.F.M.Cap. Capuchin Friars In Res. Revs. Philip Fink, O.F.M.Cap.; William Gillum, O.F.M.Cap.

[O] CONVENTS AND RESIDENCES FOR SISTERS

PITTSBURGH. *St. Benedict Monastery*, Benedictine Sisters of Pontifical Jurisdiction, 4530 Perrysville Ave., 15229-2296. Tel: 412-931-2844; Fax: 412-931-8970. Email: osbpgh@osbpgh.org. Web: www.osbpgh.org. Sr. Michelle Farabaugh, O.S.B., Prioress. Motherhouse and Novitiate of the Benedictine Sisters in the Diocese. Sisters 76.

Benedictine Center, Inc. Tel: 412-931-6051; Fax: 412-931-6003. Sr. Michelle Farabaugh, O.S.B., Pres.

Convent of Mercy, 3333 Fifth Ave., 15213. Tel: 412-578-6225; Fax: 412-578-6180. Email: gscarpino@carlow.edu. Sr. Georgine Scarpino, R.S.M., Pres.; Rev. Robert J. George, Chap. Motherhouse of Sisters of Mercy of the County of Allegheny. Established in 1843. Total Professed Sisters 172.

Holy Family Manor, 301 Bellevue Rd., 15229-2194. Tel: 412-931-6996; Fax: 412-931-2399. Email: celeste_33_66@yahoo.com. Sr. Celeste Hupert, C.S.F.N, Supr. Residence for Retired Sisters. Sisters 43.

Ladies of Bethany, 1004 Oglethorpe Ave., 15201-2151. Tel: 412-781-4022; Fax: 412-858-2532.

Other Convents:

276 Bruin Rd., Petrolia, 16050-2102. Tel: 724-753-0174.

1509 Trinity Ave., 15206-1362. Tel: 412-441-2287.

Motherhouse and Novitiate of the Vincentian Sisters of Charity, 8200 McKnight Rd., 15237. Tel: 412-364-3000; Fax: 412-364-9055. Email: creebel@vincentiansrspgh.org. Web: www.vincentiansrspgh.org. Sr. Charlene Reebel, V.S.C., Gen. Supr.; Rev. Reginald Russo, O.F.M.Cap., Chap.

Motherhouse, Sisters of the Holy Spirit (S.H.S.) (Ross Township) , 5246 Clarwin Ave., 15229-2208. Tel: 412-931-1917; Fax: 412-931-3711. Email: SRSHS@aol.com. Sr. M. Bridget Miller, S.H.S., Gen. Supr.; Most Rev. David A. Zubik, Chap. Professed Sisters 48; Total in Community 50.

Our Lady of Sorrows Convent of the Passionist Nuns, 2715 Churchview Ave., 15227. Tel: 412-881-1155. Sr. Joyce Foga, C.P., Supr. Motherhouse and Novitiate of the Religious of the Passion. (Passionist Nuns). Professed Sisters 8; Novices 1.

Sisters of Our Lady of Charity, N.A.U., 4100 Vinceton St., 15214. Tel: 412-931-2299; Fax: 412-931-6044. Sr. Sheila Rooney, Supr. North American Union of the Sisters of Our Lady of Charity, Inc. Sisters 10.

Sisters of St. Francis of the Providence of God, St. Francis Convent Motherhouse, 3603 McRoberts Rd., 15234-2398. Tel: 412-882-9911; Fax: 412-885-7210. Email: srsosfprov@aol.com. Sisters Joanne Brazinski, O.S.F., Gen. Min.; J. Lora Dambroski, O.S.F., Prov. Min.; Rev. John E. Suhoza, Chap. Sisters 95.

Sisters of the Holy Family of Nazareth of Western Pennsylvania, 285 Bellevue Rd., 15229-2195. Tel: 412-931-4778; Fax: 412-931-9746. Email: csfnstjoseph@yahoo.com. Web: www.csfn.org.

Legal Title: *Sisters of the Holy Family of Nazareth of Western Pennsylvania, Inc.* Professed Sisters in Provincialate 16; Total Professed Sisters 96.

ALLISON PARK. *Congregation of The Sisters of Divine Providence of Allegheny County*, Providence Heights Motherhouse, 9000 Babcock Blvd., 15101-2793. Tel: 412-931-5241; Fax: 412-635-5416. Email: mjcoultas@yahoo.com. Web: www.sistersofdivineprovidence.org/. Sr. Mary Joan Coultas, C.D.P., Prov. Dir. & Pres. Motherhouse and Novitiate (Kingstons, MA) of the Sisters of Divine Providence in the Diocese (Pittsburgh Province). In Motherhouse 99; In Province (including Puerto Rico) 310.

BADEN. *Sisters of St. Joseph-St. Joseph Convent*, Formerly St. Joseph Convent, 1020 State St., 15005. Tel: 724-869-2151; 412-761-3700; Fax: 724-869-3336. Email: secofcsj@usaor.net. Web: www.stjoseph-baden.org. Sr. Sharon Costello, Congregational Moderator; Rev. Philip Fink, O.F.M.Cap., Chap. Motherhouse of Sisters of St. Joseph. In Community 265; Temporary 3; Novices 2; Residents 82.

BELLEVUE. *Mount Assisi Convent, Motherhouse of the School Sisters of the Third Order of St. Francis*, 934 Forest Ave., 15202. Tel: 412-761-6004; Fax: 412-761-0290. Email: mtassisi@sgi.net. Web: www.franciscansisters-pa.org. Sisters 69; Residents 42; Total Staff 5. In Res. Rev. Richard Lelonis, Chap.

CORAOPOLIS. *Our Lady of the Sacred Heart Convent*, 1500 Woodcrest Ave., 15108. Tel: 412-264-2890; Fax: 412-264-7047. Email: cssfpa@nauticom.net. Web: www.felicianspa.org. Sr. Mary Cabrini Procopio, C.S.S.F., Prov. Min.; Revs. Paul Henne, Chap.; Richard Conboy, Chap. Provincial House and Novitiate of the Felician Sisters of Pennsylvania C.S.S.F. Professed 113; Total in Residence 73; Total Staff 40.

ELIZABETH. *Divine Redeemer Motherhouse*, 999 Rock Run Rd., 15037. Tel: 412-751-8600; Fax: 412-751-0355. Email: SrMonicaSDR@aol.com. Sr. M. Monica Kosztolnyik, S.D.R., Prov.; Rev. Thomas M. Kirby. Motherhouse and Novitiate of the Sisters of the Divine Redeemer. In the Community 43.

MILLVALE. *St. Francis Convent, Mt. Alvernia*, 146 Hawthorne Rd., 15209. Tel: 412-821-2200; Fax: 412-821-3318. Email: acarville@millvalefranciscans.org. Web: www.millvalefranciscans.com. Rev. Gervase Degenhardt, O.F.M.Cap., Chap. Sisters of St. Francis of Millvale, PA, Motherhouse and Novitiate of the Order in the Diocese.; Attended by Capuchin Fathers from St. Augustine, Pittsburgh. In the Community: Professed Sisters 183; Juniors 1; Associates 37; In the Motherhouse: Professed Sisters 101.

VILLA MARIA. *Sisters of the Humility of Mary*, Villa Maria Community Center, P.O. Box 914, 16155. Tel: 724-964-8861; Fax: 724-964-8082. Email: info@humilityofmary.org. Web: www.humilityofmary.org. Sr. Ruthmary Powers, H.M., Major Supr.; Rev. Frank G. Erdeljac, M.Div. Tel: 724-535-4786. Professed Sisters in Congregation 211; Sisters in Residence 60; Novices 1; Residents 41.

[P] RETREAT HOUSES

PITTSBURGH. **The Burning Bush: Franciscan House of Prayer*, 32-40 Pius St., 15203-1617. Tel: 412-381-3819; 866-517-7612 (Toll Free); Fax: 412-381-1585. Email: burnbush@nb.net. Purposes: A Franciscan-oriented House of Prayer and retreat facility for contemplation, rest, prayer and spiritual nourishment; motherhouse for formation and prayer of Lay Franciscans of Adoration. Total in Residence 3.

Contact Persons: Fred Koerner, L.F.A., Moderator; Sr. Damian Tosi, O.L.C., L.F.A,, Asst. Moderator.

Franciscan Spirit and Life Center, 3605 McRoberts Rd., 15234-2340. Tel: 412-881-9207; Fax: 412-885-7247. Email: FSLCCOM@aol.com. Rev. Bernard Tickerhoof, T.O.R., Dir. Sisters of St. Francis of the Providence of God., Purpose: To provide a facility to individuals for retreats and spiritual programs.; Overnight accommodations for 23. Conference room and dining facility. Three hermitages available on daily, overnight or weekly basis. Total Staff 4.

Martina Spiritual Renewal Center, Inc., To provide a facility to individuals and groups for retreats and spiritual programs. 5244 Clarwin Ave., 15229-2208. Tel: 412-931-9766; Fax: 412-931-1823. Email: martina5244@worldnet.att.net. Sisters Bridget Miller, S.H.S., Pres.; Cindy Ann Kibler, S.H.S. Ministry of the Sisters of the Holy Spirit.

St. Paul of the Cross Retreat Center, 148 Monastery Ave., 15203. Tel: 412-381-7676; 412-381-7677; Fax: 412-431-3044. Email: stpaulrcpa@cpprov.org. Web: trfn.clpgh.org/stpaulrc/. Revs. Tom Bonacci, C.P., Dir.; Joe Sedley, C.P.; Dr. Susan Stangl, Assoc.; Dr. Salvatore Mascari, Assoc. Total in Residence 2; Total Staff 25.

ALLISON PARK. *Kearns Spirituality Center*, 9000 Babcock Blvd., 15101-2713. Tel: 412-366-1124; Fax: 412-635-6318. Email: kearnsscl@aol.com. Web: www.divineprovidenceweb.org. Sisters Agnes Raible, C.D.P., Dir.; Loretta Jean Schorr, C.D.P., Prog. Coord. Sisters of Divine Providence, Conference room for 250; overnight accommodations for 60; dining facilities for 200. Call for more information on programs offered. Total Staff 6.

BETHEL PARK. *Holy Spirit Animation Center*, 6230 Bush Run Rd., 15102. Tel: 412-835-3510; Fax: 412-835-3541. Email: bethel41@juno.com. Revs. Constantine J. Conan, C.S.Sp.; Louis F. Dolan, C.S.Sp.; Jeremiah A. Falvey, C.S.Sp.; William J. Jackson, C.S.Sp.; John R. Kanda, C.S.Sp.; Girard J. Kohler, C.S.Sp.; Heinrich J. Lemmens, C.S.Sp.; Francis X. Malinowski, C.S.Sp.; John P. McAndrew, C.S.Sp.; John S. Rondeau, C.S.Sp.; Albert M. Seichpine, C.S.Sp.; J. Gerald Walsh, C.S.Sp.; Francis P. Kanda, C.S.Sp. (PRO); Richard F. Wersing, C.S.Sp.; Timothy T. McDonough, C.S.Sp. (VEN); Joseph L. Kelly, S.S.Sp.; John R. Weber, C.S.Sp. Total in Residence 17; Total Staff 30.

CORAOPOLIS. *Gilmary Diocesan Center*, 601 Flaugherty Run Rd., 15108-3899. Tel: 412-264-8400; Fax: 412-264-8415. Email: gilmary@diopitt.org. Web: www.gilmarycenter.org. Mr. Ronald W. Ragan, M.P.A., Dir. Overnight facilities for 219; meeting rooms for one-day programs; separate adult and youth facilities; 150-seat dining room, 200-seat chapel, indoor heated swimming pool, gymnasium, outdoor volleyball and basketball courts and ballfield. Total Staff 10.

[Q] OFFICES FOR CAMPUS MINISTRY

PITTSBURGH. *Chaplain Services*, Formerly Office of Chaplaincies 111 Blvd. of the Allies, 15222. Tel: 412-456-3057; Fax: 412-456-3188. Email: kwinwood@diopitt.org.

Office for Campus Ministry 1010 McNeilly Rd., 15226. Tel: 412-536-1050, Ext. 141; Fax: 412-536-1048. Email: hortonp1@laroche.edu. Rev. W. Peter Horton, M.A., M.Div., Dir.

Art Institute of Pittsburgh St. Peter Church, 720 Arch St., 15212-5296. Tel: 412-321-0711. Rev. Benjamin R. Walker, O.S.B.

La Roche College 9000 Babcock Blvd., 15237. Tel: 412-536-1050.

Carlow College, 3333 5th Ave., 15213. Tel: 412-578-6069. Sr. Eleanore Loftos, R.S.M.

Carnegie-Mellon University, Ryan Catholic Newman Center, 4450 Bayard St., 15213. Tel: 412-681-3181; Fax: 412-681-2922. Rev. David Abernathy, C.O.; Sr. Bernadette Young, C.D.P.; Revs. Michael Darcy, C.O.; Joseph E. Sioli, C.O.

Chatham College, Ryan Catholic Newman Center, 4450 Bayard St., 15213. Tel: 412-681-3181; Fax:

412-681-2922. Rev. David Abernathy, C.O.; Sr. Bernadette Young, C.D.P.; Rev. Joseph E. Sioli, C.O.

Community College of Allegheny County - Boyce Campus, St. Bernadette Church, 5245 Azalea Dr., Monroeville, 15146. Tel: 412-373-0050; Fax: 412-374-8113. Rev. Michael W. Decewicz.

Community College of Allegheny County - Northside Campus, St. Peter Church, 720 Arch St., 15212-5296. Tel: 412-321-0711; Fax: 412-321-7807.

Community College of Allegheny County- South Campus, Holy Spirit Church, 2603 Old Elizabeth Rd., West Mifflin, 15122. Tel: 412-466-5048; Fax: 412-466-4983. Very Rev. Daniel A. Valentine, V.F., D.Min.

Community College of Allegheny County - North Hills Campus, St. Teresa of Avila, 1000 Avila Ct., 15237-2176. Tel: 412-367-9001; Fax: 412-366-8415.

Duquesne University, Campus Ministry, 15282. Tel: 412-396-6020. Revs. Raymond D. French, C.S.Sp., Dir.; Timothy Hickey, C.S.Sp.; Matthias Idyu, C.S.Sp.

Geneva College, Campus Ministry, 289 Ridge Rd., New Brighton, 15066. Tel: 724-846-5978. Patrick Corcoran, Dir.; Rev. David E. Scharf.

Pennsylvania State University, Beaver Campus, Campus Ministry, 289 Ridge Rd., New Brighton, 15066. Tel: 724-846-5978. Mr. Patrick W. Corcoran, Dir.

Point Park College, St. Mary of Mercy Church, 202 Stanwix St., 15222. Tel: 412-261-0110; Fax: 412-261-0113.

Robert Morris College, Moon Township Campus Rev. Harold E. Baily.

St. Benedict the Moor, 1500 Centre Ave., 15219. Tel: 412-281-3141.

Epiphany, 1018 Centre Ave., 15219. Tel: 412-471-0654.

12 Maple Ave., Carnegie, 15106.

Robert Morris College, Downtown Pittsburgh Campus, St. Benedict the Moor Church, 1500 Centre Ave., 15219. Tel: 412-281-3141; Fax: 412-391-7151. Rev. Carmen A. D'Amico, M.Div.

University of Pittsburgh, Ryan Catholic Newman Center, 4450 Bayard St., 15213. Tel: 412-681-3181; Fax: 412-681-2922. Rev. David Abernathy, C.O., Dir.; Sr. Bernadette Young, C.D.P.; Revs. Michael Darcy, C.O.; Joseph E. Sioli, C.O.

California University (California), St. Thomas Aquinas Church, 4th & Union Streets, California, 15419. Tel: 724-938-3204; Fax: 724-938-0434. Rev. Mark J. Skertich, Dir.

Westminster College, St. Camillus Church, 313 W. Englewood Ave., New Castle, 16105. Tel: 724-652-9471; Fax: 724-654-1430. Rev. Philip Farrell.

Slippery Rock University, Newman Center (Slippery Rock), 342 Normal Ave., Slippery Rock, 16057. Tel: 724-794-8459; Fax: 724-794-1150. Rev. James L. Armstrong, D.Min., Dir.; Ms. Diane Magliocca, Campus Min.

Washington and Jefferson College (Washington), Newman Center, 1 S. College St., Washington, 15301. Tel: 724-228-5004. Rev. Tom Lewandowski.

Waynesburg College (Waynesburg), St. Ann Church, 232 E. High St., Waynesburg, 15370. Tel: 724-627-7568. Rev. John J. Batykefer.

[R] MISCELLANEOUS LISTINGS

PITTSBURGH. *The Capuchin Franciscan Volunteer Corps, Inc.*, 220 37th St., 15201. Tel: 412-682-6011; Fax: 412-682-0506. Email: volunteers@capuchin.com. Web: www.capuchin.com. Bro. Robert Toomey, O.F.M.Cap., Dir. Province of St. Augustine of the Capuchin Order, Purpose: To promote, train, supervise and support Catholic lay missions and missionaries throughout the world, especially in conjunction with the ministries and fraternities of the Capuchin Order.

Catholic Diocese of Pittsburgh Foundation, 111 Blvd. of the Allies, 15222. Tel: 412-456-3085; Fax: 412-456-3169. Email: development@diopitt.org. Web: www.diopitt.org.

The Catholic Historical Society of Western Pennsylvania, Synod Hall, 125 N. Craig St., 15213. Tel: 412-531-5725. Email: ajosephll@aol.com. Anthony P. Joseph Jr., Pres. Purpose: To promote the teaching of the Catholic Church in the United States, especially the Church in Western Pennsylvania; to recognize the growth, development and contribution of the Catholic Church by the preservation of artifacts, records and documents related to that history; to make available the results of research and study.

The Catholic Institute of Pittsburgh, PA, 111 Blvd. of the Allies, 15222. Tel: 412-456-3137; Fax: 412-456-3139. Email: fobrien@diopitt.org. Mr. Frederick P. O'Brien, CFO.

Catholic Long Term Care Network of Western Pennsylvania, Inc., 1028 Benton Ave., 15212. Tel: 412-761-5373; Fax: 412-307-0074. Email: littlesisters1@mindspring.com. Web: www.c1tcn.org. Sr. Elizabeth Judith Garrett, Contact. A collaborative effort of seven religious communities and the Diocese of Pittsburgh. The sponsors operate nine skilled nursing facilities and five assisted living-personal care homes, low income apartments. Sponsors: Diocese of Pittsburgh, Felician Sisters, Little Sisters of the Poor, School Sisters of St. Francis, Sisters of St. Joseph, Sisters of the Holy Spirit, Sisters of Mercy, Sisters of St. Basil the Great, Sisters of St. Francis of Millvale, Vincentian Sisters of Charity.

Chimbote Foundation, 111 Blvd. of the Allies, 15222-1618. Tel: 412-456-3065; Fax: 412-456-3069. Email: rlengwin@diopitt.org. Web: www.diopitt.org.

Christ Child Society of Pittsburgh, P.O. Box 11324, 15238-1824. Tel: 412-682-4102; Fax: 412-682-4102. Patricia DiGiovine, Contact; Rev. Frank D. Almade, Chap. Purpose: To foster a personal love of Christ expressed in service for needy children and youths. Total Assisted 912; Volunteers 72.

The City of God Foundation, 285 Bellevue Rd., 15229. Tel: 412-931-3510, Ext. 1300; Fax: 412-931-7255. Sr. Patricia Phillips, C.S.J., Contact Person.

Cursillo Movement-Diocese of Pittsburgh, P.O. Box 213, Wildwood, 15091. Tel: 888-386-3631. Email: mkfleck@hotmail.com. Web: www.cursillo.org/pittsburgh. Rev. Stan M. Gregorek; Mary K. Fleckenstein, Lay Dir.

Elizabeth Seton Center Inc., 1900 Pioneer Ave., 15226. Tel: 412-561-8400; Fax: 412-561-8488. Email: SrBarb@setoncenter.com. Web: www.setoncenter@setoncenter.com. Sr. Barbara Ann Boss, S.C., Pres. Day Care Programs for Children and Adults; Senior Citizens Center; School of Music; Seton Pioneer Theater Group. Sisters of Charity 15; Total Assisted 3,225; Total Staff 90.

Epiphany Association, 820 Crane Ave., 15216-3050. Tel: 412-341-7494; Fax: 412-341-7495. Email: smuto@epiphanyassociation.org. Web: www.epiphanyassociation.org. Purpose: Under the auspices of its Epiphany Academy of Formative Spirituality, the Association strives with God's help to meet the needs of parents, pastors, teachers, counselors, chaplains, and directors in pursuit of a deeper understanding of the spiritual life in accordance with the wisdom of their faith and formation traditions. Total Staff 6; Total in Residence 1.

St. Francis Academy Corporation, 1401 Hamilton Rd., 15234. Tel: 412-882-9911; Fax: 412-885-7210. Email: usaprovosf@aol.com. Sr. Mary Ann Lostoski, O.S.F., Pres.

Holy Family Foundation, 8325 Ohio River Blvd., Ste. 200, 15202-1594. Tel: 412-766-4030; Fax: 412-766-5434. Email: fryer.diane@hfi-pgh.org. Web: hfi-pgh.org. The Holy Family Foundation was formed in 1992 to promote & support the public charitable works & educational purposes of Holy Family Institute and any other exempt activities affiliated with Holy Family Institute.

Holy Family Social Services, To promote the inherent worth of children youth and families without regard to race, nationality, or religious beliefs and to provide comprehensive services for children, youth and families, including residential and treatment services social, emotional, educational, physical and spiritual support.8235 Ohio River Blvd., 15202. Tel: 412-766-4030; Fax: 412-766-5434. Email: jenkins.kevin@hfl-pgh.org. Web: www.hfl-pgh.org. Kevin Jenkins, Exec. Dir. Sisters 1; Total Staff 209; Children 2,596; Families 6,474.

Mercy Outreach Ministries, Inc., 3333 Fifth Ave., 15213. Tel: 412-578-6191; Fax: 412-578-6180. Sr. Susan Welsh, Contact Person.

Millvale Franciscans, Inc, 146 Hawthorne Rd., 15209. Tel: 412-821-2200; Fax: 412-821-3318. Email: acarville@millvalefranciscans.org. Betsy Miksic, Contact Person.

Mount Assisi Academy Preschool, 934 Forest Ave., 15202. Tel: 412-761-0381; Fax: 412-761-0290. Sr. Elaine Hromulak, O.S.F. Sisters 2; Lay Teachers 4; Students 111.

Mount Nazareth Center, Inc., 285 Bellevue Rd., 15229-2195. Tel: 412-931-9761; Fax: 412-931-7255. Email: info@mtnazarethcenter.org. Web: www.mtnazarethcenter.org. Total Staff 445.

Mt. Nazareth Learning Center Tel: 412-931-9761, Ext. 5200; 412-931-9241, Ext. 5200; Fax: 412-931-7255. Child Care: Infants; Toddlers; Pre-School; Kindergarten. Total Assisted 436; Total Staff 40.

Nazareth Housing Services Tel: 412-931-3510, Ext. 1320; Fax: 412-931-7255. Housing Counseling; Low Income Home Ownership. Total Assisted 592; Total Staff 35.

Nazareth Family Services Tel: 412-931-1026, Ext. 2090; Fax: 412-931-7255. Family Counseling; Family Life Education. Total Assisted 1,500; Total Staff 1.

Nazareth Family Foundation, 285 Bellevue Rd., 15229. Tel: 412-931-4778; Fax: 412-931-9746. Email: srmariak@yahoo.com. Sr. Maria Kruszewski, Pres. Purpose: To promote family life through financial support of facilities, programs, and services which enhance individual and family well-being. Total Assisted 16,376; Total Staff 3.

North Catholic Endowment Fund, 111 Blvd. of the Allies, 15222. Tel: 412-456-3100; Fax: 412-456-3101. Email: education@diopitt.org. Web: www.diopitt.org.

Pension Plan for the Diocese of Pittsburgh (Lay Pension Plan) , 111 Blvd. of the Allies, 15222. Tel: 412-456-3137; Fax: 412-456-3139. Email: benefits@diopitt.org. Mr. Frederick P. O'Brien, Dir.

Pittsburgh Catholic Publishing Associates Purpose: To promote for Catholics and other readers an understanding of the mission and teachings of the Church and its role in the community , 135 First Ave., Ste. 200, 15222-1506. Tel: 412-471-1252; Fax: 412-471-4228. Email: info@pittsburghcatholic.org. Web: www.pittsburghcatholic.org. Mr. Robert P. Lockwood, Gen. Mgr.; Ms. Carmella A. Weismantle, Comptroller. Purpose: To promote for Catholics and other readers an understanding of the mission and teachings of the Church and its role in the community.

Pittsburgh Diocese Knights of Columbus Bishop Wright Project, (Incorporated), 2718 Custer Ave., 15227. Tel: 412-882-1333; Fax: 412-882-1668. Email: anthexdi@nauticom.net. Web: www.diopitt.org/education/sas2.htm. Project for benefit of St. Anthony School for Programs and McGuire Memorial.

The Portiuncula Foundation of the Sisters of St. Francis of Millvale, 146 Hawthorne Rd., 15209. Tel: 412-821-2200. Sr. Ann Carville, O.S.F., Contact Person.

Priests' Benefit Plan of the Diocese of Pittsburgh, 111 Blvd. of the Allies, 15222. Tel: 412-456-3060; Fax: 412-456-3139. Email: centralaccounting@diopitt.org. Rev. Charles S. Bober, S.T.D., Chm. Purpose: To provide certain retirement and health-related benefits to eligible priests.

Scholastic Opportunity Scholarships of the Diocese of Pittsburgh, 111 Boulevard of the Allies, 15222. Tel: 412-456-3100; Fax: 412-456-3101. Email: kstubna@diopitt.org. Web: wwwdiopitt.org. Rev. Kris D. Stubna, S.T.D., Contact Person.

Sisters of Mercy Continuing Support Trust Fund, 3333 Fifth Ave., 15213. Tel: 412-578-6224; Fax: 412-578-6180. Email: gscarpino@carlow.edu. Sr. Georgine Scarpino, Pres.

Sisters of St. Francis of the Providence of God Ministries Corporation, 3603 McRoberts Rd., 15234-2398. Tel: 412-882-9911; Fax: 412-885-7210. Email: usaprovosf@aol.com. Sr. J. Lora Dambroski, O.S.F., Pres. Program: Franciscan Spirit and Life Center.

Society of Saint Vincent de Paul, Council of Pittsburgh, 1243 N. Franklin St., 15233. Tel: 412-321-1071; Fax: 412-321-9131. Email: council@svdppitt.org. Web: www.svdppitt.org. Patricia Janoski, Pres. Total Assisted 85,000; Total Staff 60.

Saint Thomas More Society, 1015 Irwin Dr., 15236. Tel: 412-884-1597; Fax: 412-884-5847. Email: damienschorr@comcast.net. Mr. John W. Giltinan, Pres.

Tri-Diocesan Sisters Leadership Conference, c/o 3603 McRoberts Rd., 15234-2398. Fax: 412-885-7210. Email: jdlosf@aol.com. Sr. J. Lora Dambroski, O.S.F., Contact Person.

ALLISON PARK. *Congregations of Religious Women Charitable Trust*, 9000 Babcock Blvd., 15101. Tel: 412-931-5241; Fax: 412-635-5406. Email: dmacpa@juno.com. Dorothy M. Antonucci, Chm.

Divine Providence Foundation, 9000 Babcock Blvd., 15101. Tel: 412-931-5241; Fax: 412-635-5416. Email: dpfoundation@juno.com. Sr. Mary Joan Coultas, C.D.P., Pres. Purpose: To perform public charitable works in the area of health care and education..

Sisters of Divine Providence Charitable Trust, 9000 Babcock Blvd., 15101-2793. Tel: 412-931-5241; Fax: 412-635-5416. Email: bbastin@juno.com. Web: www.sistersofdivprovidence.org. Sr. Carolyn Winschel, C.D.P., Chm.

Vincentian Collaborative Services, 9399 Babcock Blvd., 15101-2092. Tel: 412-630-9980; Fax: 412-630-9441. Email: tnovak@vcsregency.org. Web: www.vcs.org. Sr. Theresa Novak, V.S.C., Exec. Dir. Purpose: To provide coordination and supervision of facilities and services operating under the auspices of the Vincentian Sisters of Charity.

Vincentian Collaborative Services Rehabilitation Services, 9399 Babcock Blvd., 15101. Tel: 412-562-3745. Rosemary L. Corsetti, Contact Person.

BADEN. **Girls Hope of Pittsburgh, Inc.*, 1020 State St., 15005. Tel: 412-869-2868; Fax: 724-869-6576. Email: girlshope@bhgh.org. Sr. Donna Marie

Tahaney, Contact Person. Purpose: To provide a supportive home environment and a quality education through college for girls who have potential for leadership but who because of poverty, abuse, neglect or abandonment cannot remain in their own homes. Total Assisted 23; Total Staff 11.

BETHEL PARK. *Spiritan Support Trust*, 6320 Brush Run Rd., 15102. Tel: 412-831-0302; Fax: 412-831-0970. Email: csspeast@sgi.net. Web: www.spiritans.org. Very Rev. James P. McCloskey, C.S.Sp., Prov. Supr.

CLAIRTON. *Sisters Place, Inc.*, 460 Reed St., 15025. Tel: 412-233-3903; Fax: 412-233-3904. Email: sistersplace@comcast.net. Web: www.sistersplace.org. Sherry Wilson, Pres. Purpose: To provide hospitality, housing and advocacy to women and children who are homeless or of low income. Total Staff 12; Total Assisted 73.

ELIZABETH. *Divine Redeemer Health Care Ministeries Corp.*, 999 Rock Run Rd., 15037. Tel: 412-751-8600; Fax: 412-751-0355. Email: SrMonicaSDR@aol.com.

Sisters of Divine Redeemer Charitable Trust, 999 Rock Run Rd., 15037. Tel: 412-751-8600; Fax: 412-751-0355. Email: SrMonicaSDR@aol.com.

MCKEESPORT. *Auberle*, 1101 Hartman St., 15132-1500. Tel: 412-673-5800; Fax: 412-673-5805. Email: geraldm@auberle.org. Web: www.auberle.org. Gerald M. Meyer, Exec. Dir. Purpose: To provide services to at risk children and their families. Total in Residence 140; Total Staff 291.

Intersection, 115 Seventh Ave., P.O. Box 827, Mc Keesport, 15134. Tel: 412-678-6948. Sr. Peg O'Neill, R.S.M., Contact Person.

Pauline Auberle Foundation, 1101 Hartman St., 15132. Tel: 412-673-5800; Fax: 412-673-5805. Email: raymondn@auberle.org. Web: trfn.clpgh.org/auberle. Everett Tademy, Chm. Bd. Continues mission of Pauline Auberle Foundation while providing support to Auberle through facilities and funds. Total Staff 1.

VILLA MARIA. *The Center for Learning*, Administrative/Customer Svc. Office, Evergreen Rd., Box 910, 16155. Tel: 800-767-9090; 724-964-8083; Fax: 888-767-8080. Email: rschaffer@centerforlearning.org. Web: www.centerforlearning.org. Sr. Rose Schaffer, H.M., Pres. & CEO. Educational Publisher of values-based curriculum: Religion for Catholic schools and parishes; English/Language Arts, Social Studies and Novel/Drama Curriculum Units for all schools.; Owned and operated by the Sisters of the Humility of Mary. Directed by an Ecumenical Lay Board. Shipping-business office in Villa Maria.

Editorial/Prepress Office, 24600 Detroit Rd., Ste. 201, Westlake, OH 44145. Tel: 440-250-9341; Fax: 440-250-9715.

Sisters of the Humility of Mary Charitable Trust, Villa Maria Community Center, P.O. Box 313, 16155. Tel: 724-964-8861; Fax: 724-964-8082. Email: JBurkhart@humilityofmary.org. Web: www.humilityofmary.org. Sr. Janet Burkhart, H.M., Contact Person.

Villa Maria Apartments, Formerly Villa Maria Residential ServicesP.O. Box 230, 16155. Tel: 724-964-8099; Fax: 724-964-8082. Email: fflanigan@humilityofmary.com. Web: www.humilityofmary.org. Sr. Frances Flanigan, H.M., Exec. Dir. (Villa Maria Apartments); Housing for low & moderate income for senior citizens 58 & over. Apartments 37.

Villa Maria Education Center 16155. Tel: 724-964-8886; Fax: 724-964-8815. Email: RKramer@humilityofmary.com. Web: www.humilityofmary.org. Sr. Rose Marie Kramer, H.M., Dir. A center for adolescents and pre-adolescents which provides programs to foster the development of strong spiritual and personal values, self-worth, respect for others, and social awareness. Total Assisted 2,500; Total Staff 16.

RELIGIOUS INSTITUTES OF MEN REPRESENTED IN THE DIOCESE

For further details refer to the corresponding bracketed number in the Religious Institutes of Men or Women section.

[0200]—*Benedictine Monks* (St. Vincent Archabbey)—O.S.B.
[0330]—*Brothers of the Christian Schools* (Prov. of Baltimore)—F.S.C.
[0470]—*The Capuchin Friars* (Prov. of St. Augustine)—O.F.M.Cap.
[0650]—*Congregation of the Holy Spirit* (Eastern Prov.)—C.S.Sp.
[1000]—*Congregation of the Passion* (Eastern Prov.)—C.P.
[]—*Croatian Franciscans* Croatian Commissariate—T.O.R.
[0520]—*Franciscan Friars* (Provs. of Assumption B.V.M. & Immaculate Conception; St. John the Baptist)—O.F.M.
[0950]—*Oratorians*—C.O.
[]—*Society of the Brother-Servants of the Holy Spirit*—B.H.S.
[0420]—*Society of the Divine Word*—S.V.D.
[0560]—*Third Order Regular of Saint Francis* (Prov. of Sacred Heart of Jesus)—T.O.R.

RELIGIOUS INSTITUTES OF WOMEN REPRESENTED IN THE DIOCESE

[0230]—*Benedictine Sisters of Pontifical Jurisdiction*—O.S.B.
[]—*Dominican Sisters, Congregation of the Most Holy Rosary*
[]—*Dominican Sisters, St. Mary of the Springs* (Columbus, OH)—O.P.
[1170]—*Felician Sisters*—C.S.S.F.
[1190]—*Franciscan Sisters of Atonement*—S.A.
[]—*Ladies of Bethany*—L.B.
[2340]—*Little Sisters of the Poor*—L.S.P.
[2720]—*Mission Helpers of the Sacred Heart*—M.H.S.H.
[3071]—*North American Union Sisters of Our Lady of Charity*—O.L.C.
[3170]—*Religious of the Passion of Jesus Christ*—C.P.
[3430]—*Religious Teachers Filippini* (St. Lucy Filippini Prov.)—M.P.F.
[2970]—*School Sisters of Notre Dame*—S.S.N.D.
[1690]—*School Sisters of St. Francis*—O.S.F.
[0570]—*Sisters of Charity of Seton Hill, Greensburg, Pennsylvania*—S.C.
[0990]—*Sisters of Divine Providence*—C.D.P.
[1660]—*Sisters of Saint Francis of the Providence of God*—O.S.F.
[3830-13]—*Sisters of Saint Joseph*—C.S.J.
[1620]—*Sisters of St. Francis of Millvale, Pennsylvania*—O.S.F.
[]—*Sisters of St. Francis of the Third Order of Buffalo*—O.S.F.
[3840]—*Sisters of St. Joseph of Carondelet* (Albany, NY Prov.)—C.S.J.
[1020]—*Sisters of the Divine Redeemer*—S.D.R.
[1970]—*Sisters of the Holy Family of Nazareth*—C.S.F.N.
[2040]—*Sisters of the Holy Spirit*—S.H.S.
[2110]—*Sisters of the Humility of Mary*—H.M.
[2160]—*Sisters, Servants of the Immaculate Heart of Mary*—I.H.M.
[]—*Ursuline Sisters of the Immaculate Conception* (Cleveland)—O.S.U.
[4160]—*Vincentian Sisters of Charity*—V.S.C.
[]—*Institute of the Sisters of Mercy of the Americas* (Pittsburgh, PA)—R.S.M.

DIOCESAN CEMETERIES

PITTSBURGH. *The Catholic Cemeteries Association of the Diocese of Pittsburgh, Inc.*, Central Office, 718 Hazelwood Ave., 15217-2807. Tel: 412-521-9133; Fax: 412-521-7019.

All Saints Catholic Cemetery & Mausoleum (Braddock Catholic), 1560 Brinton Rd., 15221-4899. Tel: 412-271-5950; Fax: 412-271-8219.

Calvary Catholic Cemetery & Mausoleum, 718 Hazelwood Ave., 15217-2807. Tel: 412-421-9959; Fax: 412-421-3670.

Christ Our Redeemer Catholic Cemetery & Mausoleum (North Side Catholic), 204 Cemetery Ln., 15237-2722. Tel: 412-931-2206; Fax: 412-931-2229.

St. Mary Catholic Cemetery, c/o Calvary Cemetery, 718 Hazelwood Ave., 15217-2807. Tel: 412-421-9959; Fax: 412-621-6439.

St. Stanislaus Catholic Cemetery & Mausoleum & St. Anthony Catholic Cemetery, 700 Soose Rd., 15209-1544. Tel: 412-821-4324; Fax: 412-821-4718.

Queen of Heaven Catholic Cemetery & Mausoleum, 2900 Washington Rd., McMurray, 15317-3278. Tel: 412-831-3360; 724-941-7601; Fax: 724-942-2550.

Resurrection Catholic Cemetery & Mausoleum, 100 Resurrection Rd., Moon Township, 15108. Tel: 724-695-2999; Fax: 724-695-3032.

Sacred Heart Catholic Cemetery and Mausoleum, 97 Sacred Heart Rd., Monongahela, 15063-9605. Tel: 724-258-2885; Fax: 724-258-2275.

Good Shepherd Catholic Cemetery & Mausoleum, 733 Patton St., Monroeville, 15146-4530. Tel: 412-824-0355; Fax: 412-823-9083.

Saint Joseph Catholic Cemetery & Mausoleum, 1443 Lincoln Hwy., North Versailles, 15137-2448. Tel: 412-823-9111; Fax: 412-823-6655.

Holy Souls Catholic Cemetery, c/o Resurrection Catholic Cemetery , 100 Resurrection Rd., Moon Township, 15108. Tel: 724-695-3063; Fax: 724-695-3032.

Our Lady of Hope Catholic Cemetery & Mausoleum, 1898 Bakerstown Rd., Tarentum, 15084. Tel: 724-224-2785; Fax: 724-224-0211.

Holy Savior Catholic Cemetery, 4629 Bakerstown Rd., Gibsonia, 15044. Tel: 724-625-3822; Fax: 724-625-3880.

Mount Carmel Catholic Cemetery & Mausoleum, 7601 Mt. Carmel Rd., Verona, 15147. Tel: 412-241-1260; Fax: 412-241-5041.

NECROLOGY

† Conley, Martin R., Canonsburg, PA St. Patrick—Died Feb. 12, 2003
† Girdis, Joseph C., (Retired)—Died Jan. 29, 2003
† Hutnik, William J., (Retired)—Died Aug. 17, 2002
† Kilarecki, George W., (Retired)—Died Nov. 5, 2002
† Leonard, Albert J.—Died Oct. 1, 2002
† Marpes, Thomas M., Pittsburgh, PA Saint Pius X Parish—Died Aug. 16, 2002
† Miller, Joseph W., (Retired)—Died July 27, 2002
† Newmeyer, George C., Glenshaw, PA St. Bonaventure—Died Nov. 17, 2002
† O'Connell, Thomas C., (Retired)—Died Nov. 1, 2002
† Rodgers, Francis M., (Retired)—Died Feb. 13, 2003
† Schirra, Peter M., (Retired)—Died May 30, 2003
† Somma, James, (Retired)—Died Nov. 26, 2002
† Turlik, Andrew J., (Retired)—Died May 18, 2003

Diocese of Portland (In Maine)

(Dioecesis Portlandensis)

Most Reverend

RICHARD J. MALONE

Bishop of Portland; ordained priest May 20, 1972; appointed Auxiliary Bishop of Boston and Titular Bishop of Aptuca January 27, 2000; ordained March 1, 2000; appointed Bishop of Portland February 10, 2004; installed March 31, 2004. *P.O. Box 11559, 510 Ocean Ave., Portland, ME 04104-7559.*

Most Reverend

JOSEPH JOHN GERRY, O.S.B.

Retired Bishop of Portland; ordained June 12, 1954; ordained Titular Bishop of Praecausa and Auxiliary Bishop of Manchester April 21, 1986; appointed Bishop of Portland December 21, 1988; installed February 21, 1989; retired February 10, 2004. *P.O. Box 11559, Portland, ME 04104-7559.*

Chancery: 510 Ocean Ave., P.O. Box 11559, Portland, ME 04104-7559. Tel: 207-773-6471; Fax: 207-773-0182.

ESTABLISHED JULY 29, 1853.

Square Miles 33,040.

Comprises the State of Maine.

Corporate Title: Roman Catholic Bishop of Portland, a Corporation Sole.

For the legal titles of other diocesan-related institutions, please consult Chancery.

STATISTICAL OVERVIEW

Personnel	
Bishop	1
Priests: Diocesan Active in Diocese	93
Priests: Diocesan Active Outside Diocese	4
Priests: Retired, Sick or Absent	71
Number of Diocesan Priests	168
Religious Priests in Diocese	45
Total Priests in Diocese	213
Extern Priests in Diocese	7
Ordinations:	
Diocesan Priests	3
Transitional Deacons	1
Permanent Deacons in Diocese	27
Total Brothers	26
Total Sisters	371
Parishes	
Parishes	135
With Resident Pastor:	
Resident Diocesan Priests	83
Resident Religious Priests	14
Without Resident Pastor:	
Administered by Priests	35
Administered by Deacons	1
Administered by Religious Women	1
Administered by Lay People	1
Missions	45
Professional Ministry Personnel:	
Sisters	10
Lay Ministers	66
Welfare	
Catholic Hospitals	3
Total Assisted	379,998
Health Care Centers	5
Total Assisted	1,258
Homes for the Aged	6
Total Assisted	604
Day Care Centers	2
Total Assisted	205
Special Centers for Social Services	5
Total Assisted	3,987
Educational	
Diocesan Students in Other Seminaries	9
Total Seminarians	9
Colleges and Universities	1
Total Students	4,943
High Schools, Diocesan and Parish	1
Total Students	360
High Schools, Private	2
Total Students	793
Elementary Schools, Diocesan and Parish	17
Total Students	3,755
Elementary Schools, Private	1
Total Students	164
Catechesis/Religious Education:	
High School Students	2,034
Elementary Students	12,280
Total Students under Catholic Instruction	24,338
Teachers in the Diocese:	
Priests	1
Sisters	23
Lay Teachers	340
Vital Statistics	
Receptions into the Church:	
Infant Baptism Totals	2,340
Adult Baptism Totals	282
Received into Full Communion	298
First Communions	2,914
Confirmations	3,459
Marriages:	
Catholic	676
Interfaith	342
Total Marriages	1,018
Deaths	2,921
Total Catholic Population	217,676
Total Population	1,274,923

Former Bishops—Very Rev. J. COSKERY, V.G., of Baltimore, The first Bishop-Elect, declined the nomination.; Rt. Revs. DAVID W. BACON, D.D., consecrated April 22, 1855; died Nov. 5, 1874; JAMES AUGUSTINE HEALY, D.D., consecrated June 2, 1875; died Aug. 5, 1900; His Eminence WILLIAM CARDINAL O'CONNELL, consecrated Bishop of Portland, May 19, 1901; named Coadjutor Archbishop of Boston, Feb. 8, 1906; succeeded to the See of Boston, Aug. 30, 1907; created Cardinal, Nov. 27, 1911; died April 22, 1944; Rt. Revs. LOUIS S. WALSH, D.D., consecrated Oct. 18, 1906; died May 12, 1924; JOHN GREGORY MURRAY, D.D., ord. April 14, 1900; consecrated April 28, 1920; transferred to the Archdiocese of St. Paul, Oct. 29, 1931; died Oct. 11, 1956; Most Revs. JOSEPH EDWARD MCCARTHY, D.D., ord. July 4, 1903; consecrated Aug. 24, 1932; died Sept. 8, 1955; DANIEL JOSEPH FEENEY, D.D., LL.D., Bishop of Portland; ord. May 21, 1921; appt. Titular Bishop of Sita and Auxiliary of Portland, June 22, 1946; consecrated Sept. 12, 1946; Apostolic Administrator of the Diocese; appt. July 27, 1948; Coadjutor "cum jure successionis"; appt. March 4, 1952; succeeded to See, Sept. 8, 1955; died Sept. 15, 1969; PETER LEO GERETY, D.D., ord. June 29, 1939; appt. March 4, 1966; consecrated June 1, 1966; appt. Apostolic Administrator, Feb. 18, 1967; succeeded to See, Sept. 15, 1969; transferred to Archdiocese of Newark, April 2, 1974; EDWARD C. O'LEARY, D.D., ord. June 15, 1946; Titular Bishop of Moglaena and Auxiliary Bishop of Portland; appt. Nov. 17, 1970; consecrated Jan. 25, 1971; Apostolic Administrator; appt. June 29, 1974; ninth Bishop of Portland, Dec. 4, 1974;; installed Dec. 18, 1974; resigned Sept. 27, 1988; died April 2, 2002.

Vicar General—Rev. Msgr. MICHAEL J. HENCHAL, J.C.L.

Chancery—510 Ocean Ave., P.O. Box 11559, Portland, 04104-7559. Tel: 207-773-3471; Fax: 207-773-0182. Office Hours: Mon.-Fri. 9-4:30 Labor Day to Memorial Day; 8:30-4:30 Memorial Day to Labor Day. Closed Holidays.

Co-Chancellors—Rev. Msgr. MARC B. CARON, S.T.L.; Sr. RITA-MAE BISSONNETTE, R.S.R., J.C.L.

Bishop's Delegate for Clergy—Rev. Msgr. PAUL F. STEFANKO, J.C.L.

Vicars for Priests—Revs. JOHN W. GOULDRICK, C.M.; ANTHONY F. KUZIA, C.M

Director of Communications—Ms. SUSAN BERNARD.

Diocesan Tribunal—510 Ocean Ave., P.O. Box 11559, Portland, 04104-7559. Tel: 207-773-6471.

Officialis—Rev. Msgr. PAUL F. STEFANKO, J.C.L.

Promoter of Justice—Rev. Msgr. MICHAEL J. HENCHAL, J.C.L.

Defenders of the Bond—Sisters RITA-MAE BISSONNETTE, R.S.R., J.C.L.; CLAUDIA BARBRE, R.S.M., J.C.L.; ANN KEEVAN, C.S.J., J.C.D.; Mr. GEORGE G. PAVLOFF, J.C.D.

Advocates—Sisters CLAUDIA BARBRE, R.S.M., J.C.L.; ANN KEEVAN, C.S.J., J.C.D.; Very Rev. MARK P. NOLETTE, V.F.; Mr. GEORGE G. PAVLOFF, J.C.D.; Sr. RITA-MAE BISSONNETTE, R.S.R., J.C.L.

Office Coordinator—Rev. Msgr. PAUL F. STEFANKO, J.C.L.

Notaries—Mrs. NAJLIA KERRIGAN; Mrs. MARY DELANEY.

Associate Judges—Rev. Msgr. RAYMOND F. BEGIN, S.T.L., J.C.D. (Retired); Rev. JOSEPH J. KOURY, J.C.D.; Sr. RITA-MAE BISSONNETTE, R.S.R., J.C.L.; Very Rev. MARK P. NOLETTE, V.F.; Mr. GEORGE G. PAVLOFF, J.C.D.; Rev. Msgr. MICHAEL J. HENCHAL, J.C.L.

Guardian—Rev. Msgr. MARC B. CARON, S.T.L.

Deans—Revs. PHILIP A. TRACY; RICHARD P. RICE; RICHARD C. MALO, V.F.; Very Rev. Msgr. CHARLES M. MURPHY, S.T.D., V.F.; Rev. Msgr. RENE T. MATHIEU, V.F.; Very Rev. Msgr. J. JOSEPH FORD JR., V.F.; Rev. RICHARD R. OULLETTE, V.F.; Very Rev. MARK P. NOLETTE, V.F.; Revs. ALFRED JACQUES; RICHARD C. MCLAUGHLIN, V.F.

Diocesan Consultors—Rev. Msgr. VINCENT A. TATARCZUK (Retired); Very Rev. Msgr. CHARLES M. MURPHY, S.T.D., V.F.; Rev. GEORGES J. PLANTE; Rev. Msgrs. RENE T. MATHIEU, V.F.; MARC B. CARON, S.T.L.; Rev. JAMES J. MORRISON; Rev. Msgr. PAUL F. STEFANKO, J.C.L.; Rev. JOHN R. SKEHAN; Rev. Msgr. MICHAEL J. HENCHAL, J.C.L.

Diocesan Review Board—Judge DANIEL WATHEN,

Chm.; Mrs. KATHLEEN ROSSI; Mr. MICHAEL TARPINIAN; Mr. PAUL FALCONER; Dr. JAMES MORAN; Rev. Msgr. RENE T. MATHIEU, V.F.; Sr. CLAIRE LABBEE, C.S.J.; Mr. JAMES WALSH; Mrs. EDNA CHACE; Dr. ANNE PULSIFIER; Mrs. KAREN MORAN. Staff: Rev. Msgr. MARC B. CARON, S.T.L.; Sr. RITA-MAE BISSONNETTE, R.S.R.

Diocesan Offices and Directors

Office of Support and Assistance Ministry— (Sexual Abuse Victims) Sr. RITA-MAE BISSONNETTE, R.S.R., Dir. Tel: 207-773-6471; Ms. SUSANNE STURM, Asst. Minister. Tel: 866-829-4437.

Office of Professional Responsibility—Deacon JOHN BRENNAN, Dir., P.O. Box 11559, Portland, 04104-7559. Tel: 207-773-6471; 207-799-5528, Ext. 102.

Campaign for Human Development—Mr. LEO PAQUIN, P.O. Box 10660, Portland, 04104-6060. Tel: 207-781-8550; Fax: 207-781-8560.

Catholic Stewardship Appeal—Mr. WILLIAM S. RICHARD, C.P.A., Dir., 510 Ocean Ave., P.O. Box 11559, Portland, 04104-7559. Tel: 207-773-6471.

Catholic Relief Services—Mrs. CARLEEN E. COOK, 510 Ocean Ave., P.O. Box 11559, Portland, 04104-7559. Tel: 207-773-6471.

Catholic Schools Office—Sr. ROSEMARY T. DONOHUE, S.N.D., Supt., Schools, 510 Ocean Ave., P.O. Box 11559, Portland, 04104-7559. Tel: 207-773-6471.

Catholic Scouting—Deacon KEVIN JACQUES, Dir., Catholic Committee on Scouting, St. Dominic High School, 121 Gracelawn Rd., Auburn, 04210-6452; SUSAN VOGEL, Co-Chm., 39 Pillsbury St., South Portland, 04106.

Catholic Charismatic Renewal Diocesan Liaison—Rev. RICHARD P. RICE, 144 Lincoln St., Bath, 04530-2198.

Catholic Charities Maine— Central Services: Mr. JOHN M. KERRY, Exec. Dir., P.O. Box 10660, Portland, 04104-6060. Tel: 207-781-8550; Fax: 207-781-8560; Ms. CONNIE JONES, Human Resources Dir., P.O. Box 10660, Portland, 04104-6060. Tel: 207-781-8550; Fax: 207-781-8560.

Clergy Benefit Plan-Clergy Pension Plan— Prudential Committee: Most Rev. JOSEPH JOHN GERRY, O.S.B., Pres. (Retired); Very Rev. Msgr. J. JOSEPH FORD JR., V.F., Chm. Bd.; Revs. CLAUDE J. ALBERT, Treas.; NORMAND E. CARPENTIER, Sec., Members:; Rev. Msgr. VINCENT A. TATARCZUK (Retired); Revs. LIONEL G. CHOUINARD; GEORGES J. PLANTE; BRIAN D. BLANCHETTE; CLAUDE R. GENDREAU; JAMES KNOX; ROBERT LARIVIERE; TIMOTHY NADEAU; MARK REINHARDT; Rev. Msgr. MARC B. CARON, S.T.L., Ex Officio; Mr. TIMOTHY R. COTNOIR, Plan Accountant.

Diocesan Archivist—Sr. RITA-MAE BISSONNETTE, R.S.R. Contact Chancellor's Office:

Diocesan Board of Education—ROBERT SMITH, Chm.; Sr. ROSEMARY T. DONOHUE, S.N.D., Exec. Sec.; KELLIE M. PIZZO, Recording Sec., Members:; Rev. RENALD D. LABARRE; Mr. MATTHEW FLAHERTY; Mr. WILLIAM RIDGE; PATRICIA ADAMS; PATRICIA BERTHIAUME; JOSEPH DONAHUE, Esq.; MARK RIOUX; Deacon DEAN LACHANCE; DEBORAH SANFORD; SUSAN GAJEWSKI; KAREN HUBER; ROBERT CONNORS; ANNA LYONS; JONATHAN SHAPIRO; Mr. G. MICHAEL WELCH; Rev. TIMOTHY NADEAU.

Diocesan Bureau of Housing—Most Rev. JOSEPH JOHN GERRY, O.S.B., Bishop of Portland Pres. (Retired); Mr. DAVID P. TWOMEY, C.P.A., Treas.; THOMAS KELLY ESQ., Clerk, P.O. Box 11559, Portland, 04104-7559.

Diocesan Council of Priests—Rev. Msgrs. VINCENT A. TATARCZUK (Retired); ROBERT LAVOIE; Very Rev. Msgr. J. JOSEPH FORD JR., V.F.; Revs. PHILIP A. TRACY; SCOTT MOWER; GEORGES J. PLANTE; JAMES ROBICHAUD; Rev. Msgr. RENE T. MATHIEU, V.F., Chm.; Revs. JOSEPH J. KOURY, J.C.D.; FRANCIS P. MORIN; WALTER GAUDREAU, S.M.; RAYMOND PICARD; ROBERT D. LARIVIERE; TIMOTHY NADEAU; JAMES J. MORRISON. Ex Officio: Rev. MICHAEL J. HENCHAL; Very Rev. Msgr. CHARLES M. MURPHY, S.T.D., V.F.; Rev. Msgr. MARC B. CARON, S.T.L.; Rev. JOHN R. SKEHAN; Rev. Msgr. PAUL F. STEFANKO, J.C.L.; Revs. JOHN W. GOULDRICK, C.M.; ANTHONY F. KUZIA, C.M.

College of Consultors—Rev. Msgr. VINCENT A. TATARCZUK (Retired); Rev. GEORGES J. PLANTE; Rev. Msgr. RENE T. MATHIEU, V.F.; Revs. JAMES J. MORRISON; MICHAEL J. HENCHAL; Very Rev. Msgr. CHARLES M. MURPHY, S.T.D., V.F.; Rev. Msgr. MARC B. CARON, S.T.L.; Rev. JOHN R. SKEHAN; Rev. Msgr. PAUL F. STEFANKO, J.C.L.

Diocesan Director of Pastoral and Educational Services—Rev. JOHN R. SKEHAN, Chancery Office, 510 Ocean Ave., P.O. Box 11559, Portland, 04104-7559.

Diocesan Finance Council—Most Revs. JOSEPH JOHN GERRY, O.S.B. (Retired); MICHAEL J. HENCHAL; Rev. CLAUDE ALBERT; Mr. WILLIAM STOLOSKI; Mr. ARTHUR BORDUAS; MARY ARNOLD; DAVID WARREN; JOHN DECKRO, Chm.; Rev. JAMES J. MORRISON; CHARLES PRINN; GREGG H. GINN; JOHN SCHIAVI; RICHARD RODERICK; GREGORY ST. ANGELO, Vice Chm.; Sr. JUDE MURRAY, R.S.M.; Mr. DAN ROUX; Mr. EDWARD SNOOK. Ex Officio Members: Rev. Msgr. MARC B. CARON, S.T.L.; Sr. RITA-MAE BISSONNETTE, R.S.R.; Mr. DAVID P. TWOMEY, C.P.A., Finance Officer. Staff: Mrs. LAURIE J. DOWNEY, C.P.A.; Mr. TIMOTHY R. COTNOIR; WILLIAM S. RICHARDS.

Diocesan Office of Catechetics and Initiation—Ms. BARBARA A. SMITH, Diocesan Dir.; Mrs. KATHY DYER, Region I Resource Person, 25 Coolidge Ave., Caribou, 04736. Tel: 207-496-0520; Sisters CATHERINE GREEN, R.S.M., Region II Resource Person, 44 Bennoch Rd., P.O. Box 333, Stillwater, 04489-0333. Tel: 207-827-5257; CAROL MARTIN, P.F.M., Region III Resource Person, 38 Green St., Augusta, 04330-7437. Tel: 207-622-6859; Ms. BARBARA A. SMITH, Region IV Resource Person, Chancery Office, 510 Ocean Ave., P.O. Box 11559, Portland, 04104-7559. Tel: 207-773-6471, Ext. 107; Fax: 207-773-0182.

Diocesan Office of Communications—Ms. SUSAN BERNARD, Dir., 510 Ocean Ave., P.O. Box 11559, Portland, 04104-7559. Tel: 207-773-6471, Ext. 112.

Diocesan Office of Public Affairs—Mr. MARC R. MUTTY, Dir., 510 Ocean Ave., P.O. Box 11559, Portland, 04104-7559.

Diocesan Office of Ministry to Persons with Disabilities—Ms. CLAIRE P. BLAIS, P.O. Box 11559, Portland, 04104-7559.

Bishop's Delegate for Priests—Rev. Msgr. PAUL F. STEFANKO, J.C.L., Dir., 510 Ocean Ave., P.O. Box 11559, Portland, 04104-7559. Tel: 207-773-6471.

Vicars for Priests—Revs. ANTHONY F. KUZIA, C.M. Tel: 207-576-2703. Email: rakuzia@aol.com; JOHN W. GOULDRICK, C.M. Tel: 207-576-2944. Email: gouldrje@aol.com; 607 Sabattus St., Lewiston, 04240-4193. Tel: 207-784-4613.

Diocesan Office of Small Christian Communities—Ms. BARBARA A. SMITH, Coord., P.O. Box 11559, Portland, 04104-7559. Tel: 207-773-6471.

Diocesan Office for Worship—Rev. Msgr. MARC B. CARON, S.T.L., Dir., 510 Ocean Ave., P.O. Box 11559, Portland, 04104-7559. Tel: 207-773-6471.

Diocesan Office of Youth Ministry—Mrs. JEANNE S. BIGELOW, Dir. Youth Ministry Regional Coordinators: KAREN OUELLETTE, 436 Frenchville Rd., Fort Kent, 04743. Tel: 207-834-8355; Fax: 207-834-6835 Region II,; WILLIAM ROMANO, P.O. Box 623, Waterville, 04901. Tel: 207-862-6149; Fax: 207-862-4041 Region III,; SANDRA THOMPSON, P.O. Box 112, Buckfield, 04220. Tel: 207-388-2875.

Financial Management—Mr. DAVID P. TWOMEY, C.P.A., Finance Officer; Mrs. LAURIE J. DOWNEY, C.P.A., Controller; Mr. TIMOTHY R. COTNOIR, Asst. Controller, 510 Ocean Ave., P.O. Box 11559, Portland, 04104-7559. Tel: 207-773-6471.

General Counsel—Mr. THOMAS KELLY, Robinson Kriger & McCallum, 12 Portland Pier, P.O. Box 568, Portland, 04112-0568. Tel: 207-772-6565.

Maine Diocesan Council of Catholic Women—Most Rev. JOSEPH JOHN GERRY, O.S.B., Episcopal Chm. (Retired); Rev. LAWRENCE CONLEY, V.F., Diocesan Moderator, St. Catherine Parish, 29 Paris St., Norway, 04268-1132; Mrs. SANDY BRETON, Diocesan Pres.

Newman Apostolate—Rev. JOSEPH J. KOURY, J.C.D., Coord. Pastoral Assocs.: Revs. PHILIP A. TRACY; LAWRENCE CONLEY; ROGER P. CHABOT; MICHAEL SHERIDAN; STEPHEN CONCANNON; RICHARD LEMBO; JOHN J. TOPAZ, O.F.M.Cap.; FRANK MURRAY, .; CLAUDE GENDREAU; Sr. SYLVIA COMER; Bro. RICHARD CRAWLEY, O.F.M.Cap; Ms. KAREN OUELLETTE.

Personnel Board—Rev. JOHN R. SKEHAN; Rev. Msgr. MICHAEL J. HENCHAL, J.C.L.; Revs. ANDREW DUBOIS; RICHARD C. MALO, V.F.; Very Rev. MARK P. NOLETTE, V.F.; Revs. PAUL PLANTE; MARK S. REINHARDT; Rev. Msgrs. PAUL F. STEFANKO, J.C.L.; MARC B. CARON, S.T.L.; Revs. JEAN-PAUL LABRIE; ROGER P. CHABOT; Rev. Msgr. RENE T. MATHIEU, V.F. Officio Members: Most Rev. JOSEPH JOHN GERRY, O.S.B., Pres. (Retired); Rev. Msgr. MICHAEL J. HENCHAL, J.C.L., Vicar Gen.; Very Rev. Msgr. CHARLES M. MURPHY, S.T.D., V.F., Dir., Seminarians.

Pontifical Association of Holy Childhood—Mrs. CARLEEN E. COOK, Dir., 510 Ocean Ave., P.O. Box 11559, Portland, 04104-7559. Tel: 207-773-6471.

Pontifical Society for the Propagation of the Faith—Mrs. CARLEEN E. COOK.

Seminarians, Director of—Very Rev. Msgr. CHARLES M. MURPHY, S.T.D., V.F., 510 Ocean Ave., P.O. Box 11559, Portland, 04104-7559. Tel: 207-773-6471.

Victim Assistance Coordinator—Sr. RITA-MAE BISSONNETTE, R.S.R., J.C.L. Tel: 207-773-6471. Email: rbissonnette@portlanddiocese.net.

Vocations—Rev. FRANK J. MURRAY, Diocesan Dir., St. Dominic Regional High School, 179 Blake St., Lewiston, 04240. Tel: 207-782-6911; Fax: 207-795-6439. Res.: Sacred Heart Rectory, 24 Sacred Heart Pl., Auburn, 04210.

Director of Chaplaincy Services—Rev. RICHARD C. McLAUGHLIN, V.F., St. John Parish, 207 York St., Bangor, 04401-5442. Tel: 207-942-6941; Fax: 207-947-5984.

Apostolate of the Sea—VACANT, Ship Visitor.

CLERGY, PARISHES, MISSIONS AND PAROCHIAL SCHOOLS

CITY OF PORTLAND
(CUMBERLAND COUNTY)

1—CATHEDRAL OF THE IMMACULATE CONCEPTION (1853), Rev. James L. Nadeau, Rector. In Res., Rev. Roland P. Nadeau; Rev. Msgr. Marc B. Caron, S.T.L.; Revs. Donald L. McAllister; Albin A. Andrus; John D. Civiello (Retired); Harold D. Moreshead (Retired); Joseph E. Whitlock (Retired); Vincent McCann, M.H.H.
Res.: 307 Congress St., 04101-3695. Tel: 207-773-7746 (Rectory); 207-774-5101 (Res.); Fax: 207-879-5547.
School—14 Locust St., 04101. Tel: 207-775-1491; Fax: 207-828-3989. Sr. Theresa Rand, R.S.M., Prin. Sisters of Mercy 2; Sisters of the Holy Rosary 1; Lay Teachers 16; Students 203.
Catechesis/Religious Program—Tel: 207-772-6597; Fax: 207-879-5547. Donna Lebel, D.R.E. Students 152.

2—ST. CHRISTOPHER'S (Peaks Island) (1923), Rev. Frederick H. Morse.
Mailing Address: 15 Central St., P.O. Box 37, Peaks Island, 04108-0037. Tel: 207-766-2585.
Catechesis/Religious Program—Students 7.
Mission— Long Island, Cumberland Co.

3—ST. DOMINIC'S, Merged, with Sacred Heart, Portland to form Sacred Heart/St. Dominic's, Portland.

4—ST. JOSEPH'S (1909), Revs. Patrick Glavin, O.F.M-.Cap.; Don Bosco Duquette, O.F.M.Cap.; Peter Kaseta, O.F.M.Cap.; John Tokaz, O.F.M.Cap.; Anthony Egan, O.F.M.Cap.; Bro. Richard Crawley, O.F.M.Cap.
Res.: 673 Stevens Ave., 04103. Tel: 207-797-7026; Fax: 207-797-2679.
School—697 Stevens Ave., 04103. Tel: 207-797-7073; Fax: 207-797-7078. Ms. Lori Ann Lee, Prin. Lay Teachers 17; Students 240.
Catechesis/Religious Program—Tel: 207-797-9509. Martha Turner, D.R.E.; Sylvia Harlow, D.R.E. Students 165.

5—ST. LOUIS (1915), (Polish), Rev. Ireneusz Chodakowski, M.I.C. In Res., Rev. Bernard Backiel, M.I.C. (SPR).
Res.: 279 Danforth St., 04102. Tel: 207-773-4176.

6—ST. PATRICK'S (1922), Rev. Thomas M. Murphy.
Res.: 1342 Congress St., 04102. Tel: 207-772-6325.
School—1251 Congress St., 04102. Tel: 207-772-2521; Fax: 207-828-8917. Mrs. Barbara Ann Arnoldo, Prin. Sisters of Mercy 2; Lay Teachers 14; Students 218.
Catechesis/Religious Program—Tel: 207-772-3521. Cynthia McGarry, D.R.E. Students 219.

7—ST. PETER'S (1911), (Italian), Rev. Kieran Monahan, O.F.M.
Res.: 72 Federal St., 04101. Tel: 207-773-0748; Fax: 207-879-0557.
Catechesis/Religious Program—Mrs. Terri St. Angelo, D.R.E. Students 85.

8—ST. PIUS X (1962), Revs. Arthur H. Pare, S.J., Pastor; Robert F. Regan, S.J.
Res.: 492 Ocean Ave., 04103. Tel: 207-775-3032; Fax: 207-874-7514.
Catechesis/Religious Program—Tel: 207-775-2185. Sandra Litcher, D.R.E. Students 202.

9—SACRED HEART/ST. DOMINIC (1997), Merged, with Sacred Heart, Portland and St. Dominic, Portland to form Sacred Heart/St. Dominic, Portland. Rev. Richard D. Bertrand, S.J.
Res.: 80 Sherman St., 04101-2216. Tel: 207-772-6182; Fax: 207-772-9615.
Catechesis/Religious Program—Students 28.

OUTSIDE THE CITY OF PORTLAND

ASHLAND, AROOSTOOK CO., ST. MARK'S, [CEM 3] Rev. Scott Mower.
Res.: 68 School St., P.O. Box 190, 04732-0190. Tel: 207-435-3591.
Catechesis/Religious Program—Tel: 207-435-6440.

Students 31.
Mission—Our Lady of the Lakes Portage, Aroostook Co.
Mission—St. Catherine Washburn, Aroostook Co.
AUBURN, ANDROSCOGGIN CO.
1—ST. LOUIS (1902), Revs. Frank J. Murray; Kevin Martin; Sr. Elizabeth A. Platt, C.O.C., Pastoral Assoc.; Deacon Denis Mailhot.
Mailing Address: *Auburn Catholic Community*, P.O. Box 828, 04212-0828.
Res.: 267 Minot Ave., 04210. Tel: 207-782-8096; Fax: 207-782-9032.
Church: 24 Dunn St., 04210.
Catechesis/Religious Program— Twinned with Sacred Heart, Auburn & St. Philip, Auburn.
Parish Center—36 Sacred Heart Pl., 04210.
2—ST. PHILIP'S (1968), Revs. Frank J. Murray; Kevin Martin; Sr. Elizabeth A. Platt, C.O.C., Pastoral Assoc.; Deacon Denis Mailhot.
Mailing Address: *Auburn Catholic Community*, P.O. Box 828, 04212-0828.
Parish Offices—36 Sacred Heart Pl., 04210.
Res. & Church: 365 Turner Rd., 04210-8410. Tel: 207-782-8096; Fax: 207-782-9032.
Catechesis/Religious Program— Twinned with St. Louis, Auburn & Sacred Heart, Auburn.
3—SACRED HEART (1923), Revs. Frank J. Murray; Kevin Martin; Sr. Elizabeth A. Platt, C.O.C., Pastoral Assoc.; Deacon Denis Mailhot.
Mailing Address: *Auburn Catholic Community*, P.O. Box 828, 04212-0828.
Res.: 267 Minot Ave., 04210. Tel: 207-782-8096; Fax: 207-782-9032.
Church: 8 Sacred Heart Pl., 04210.
Catechesis/Religious Program— Twinned with St. Louis, Auburn & St. Philip, Auburn. Sandra Tardiff, D.R.E. Tel: 207-786-9045. Students 194.
Parish Center—36 Sacred Heart Pl., 04210.
AUGUSTA, KENNEBEC CO.
1—ST. ANDREW'S (1968), Rev. Michael P. Gendreau; Deacon Dean Lachance.
Res.: 20 St. Andrew St., 04330-9752. Tel: 207-623-8543; Fax: 207-623-7574.
Catechesis/Religious Program—Tel: 207-623-3159. Gail Gould, D.R.E. Students 73.
2—ST. AUGUSTINE'S (1888), [CEM 2] Rev. Richard E. St. Cyr.
Res.: One Kendall St., 04330. Tel: 207-622-2184; Fax: 207-621-4064.
School—24 Washington St., 04330. Tel: 207-622-1771. Sr. Rachel Boucher, Prin. Sisters of the Presentation of Mary 2; Lay Teachers 13; Students 165.
Catechesis/Religious Program—Tel: 207-621-4075. Lyn Grothe, D.R.E. Students 30.
3—ST. MARY'S (1834), [CEM 2] Rev. Michael P. Gendreau.
Res.: 41 Western Ave., P.O. Box 555, 04332-0555. Tel: 207-623-8823; Fax: 207-623-7574.
School—56 Sewall St., 04332. Tel: 207-623-3491; Fax: 207-626-5818. Sr. Barbara Brennan, R.S.M., Prin. Sisters of Mercy 1; Lay Teachers 18; Students 258.
Catechesis/Religious Program—Mary-Ellen Mahon, D.R.E. Tel: 207-626-5940; Gail Gould, D.R.E., (Grades K-5); Mary Jane Silva, D.R.E., (Grades 6-12). Students 117.
BAILEYVILLE, WASHINGTON CO., ST. JAMES THE GREATER (1905), Rev. Francis P. Morin.
Res.: 56 Summit St., P.O. Box 369, 04694-0369. Tel: 207-427-6908; Fax: 207-427-6066.
Catechesis/Religious Program—Tel: 207-427-3481. Ms. Mary White, D.R.E. Students 45.
BANGOR, PENOBSCOT CO.
1—ST. JOHN'S (1856), Rev. Richard G. McLaughlin; Sr. Celestine Theriault, R.S.M., Pastoral Assoc.; Mr. Andre Vigneault, Pastoral Assoc. In Res., Rev. John J. Austin.
Res.: 207 York St., 04401. Tel: 207-942-6941; 207-942-0955; Fax: 207-947-5984.
School—All Saints Catholic School, P.O. Box 1749, 04401. Tel: 207-947-7063; Fax: 207-942-2398. Marcia Diamond, Prin. Lay Teachers 26; Students 283.
Catechesis/Religious Program—Tel: 207-945-0023. Joan Winstead, D.R.E. Students 295.
2—ST. MARY'S (1872), Rev. Thomas Lequin.
Res.: 768 Ohio St., 04401-3106. Tel: 207-945-5018; Fax: 207-942-9781.
School—All Saints Catholic School
St. Mary's Campus—Tel: 207-947-7063; Fax: 207-942-7356. (Grades K-3)
St. John's Campus—Tel: 207-947-0955; Fax: 207-942-2398. (Grades 4-8)
Catechesis/Religious Program—Tel: 207-942-1643. Students 474.
BAR HARBOR, HANCOCK CO., HOLY REDEEMER (1907), [CEM] Rev. John O'Hara.
Res.: 21 Ledgelawn Ave., 04609-1303. Tel: 207-288-3535; Fax: 207-288-3324.
Catechesis/Religious Program—Tel: 207-288-3421. Students 20.
BATH, SAGADAHOC CO., ST. MARY (1849), Rev. Richard P. Rice.
Res.: 144 Lincoln St., 04530-2198. Tel: 207-443-3423; Fax: 207-443-5692.
Catechesis/Religious Program—Tel: 207-443-4987. Nancy Lewis, D.R.E. Students 130.
BELFAST, WALDO CO., ST. FRANCIS OF ASSISI (1891), Rev. Costanzo J. Piselli.
Res. & Mailing Address: 81 Court St., 04915-6134. Tel: 207-338-4433; Fax: 207-338-9846.
Catechesis/Religious Program—Tel: 207-930-9884. Students 83.
Mission—St. Mary of the Isles Isleboro, Waldo Co.
BENEDICTA, AROOSTOOK CO., ST. BENEDICT'S (1834), [CEM] Rev. Richard C. Malo, V.F.; Deacon Danny Watson.
Mailing Address: P.O. Box 27, 04733-0024. Tel: 207-365-4294; Fax: 207-365-7378.
Catechesis/Religious Program—Tel: 207-365-4269. Anna Robinson, D.R.E. Students 38.
Mission—St. Joseph's Church 324 Station St., Sherman Station, Penobscot Co. 04777.
BERWICK, YORK CO., OUR LADY OF PEACE (1927), Rev. Hilary J. Cameron; Roger Normand, Pastoral Assoc.
Res.: 25 Saw Mill Hill, 03901-2109. Tel: 207-698-1072; Fax: 207-698-5217.
Catechesis/Religious Program—Students 78.
BIDDEFORD, YORK CO.
1—ST. ANDRE'S (1899), [JC] Rev. Reginald R. Brissette.
Mailing Address: 41 Sullivan St., 04005.
Res.: 73 Bacon St., 04005. Tel: 207-282-3333; Fax: 207-286-8679.
School—St. James School See St. Joseph's for details.
Catechesis/Religious Program— Twinned with St. Joseph Biddeford.
2—ST. JOSEPH'S (1870), Rev. Renald D Labarre; Sr. June Rita Fortier, S.C.I.M.; Nancy P. Labbe, Pastoral Assoc.
Office—41 Sullivan St., P.O. Box 408, 04005. Tel: 207-282-9352; Fax: 207-286-8679.
Res.: 43 Center St., 04005. Tel: 207-282-4817.
School—New Consolidated School - St. James, (Grades K-8), 25 Graham St., 04007. Tel: 207-282-4084. Ms. Patricia Berthiaume, Prin. Lay Teachers 27; Students 490.
Catechesis/Religious Program—Tri-Parish Program Tel: 207-282-4812. Julia Bertolo, D.R.E.; Laurel Grossin-Drake, D.R.E. Students 150.
3—ST. MARY'S (1855), [CEM] Rev. Brendan G. Harnett, Admin.
Office—41 Sullivan St., 04005.
Res.: P.O. Box 515, 04005. Tel: 207-282-9352; Fax: 207-286-8679.
School—St. James School, Tel: 207-282-4084. See St. Joseph's for details.
Catechesis/Religious Program— Twinned with St. Joseph, Biddeford.
Mission—St. Brendan Biddeford Pool, York Co.
BINGHAM, SOMERSET CO., ST. PETER'S (1920), Rev. Georges J. Plante.
Res.: Owens St., Box No. 667, 04920. Tel: 207-672-3912.
Catechesis/Religious Program—Students 13.
BOOTHBAY HARBOR, LINCOLN CO., OUR LADY, QUEEN OF PEACE (1928), Rev. Raymond Picard.
Res.: 82 Atlantic Ave., 04538. Tel: 207-633-2680; Fax: 207-633-4198.
Catechesis/Religious Program—Students 40.
BRADLEY, PENOBSCOT CO., ST. ANN (1934), [JC] Rev. Paul R. Kerns.
Mailing Address: P.O. Box 450, 04411.
Res.: 84 Main St., 04411. Tel: 207-827-2087.
Catechesis/Religious Program—Tel: 207-827-7643. Mary Shorette, D.R.E. Students 45.
BREWER, PENOBSCOT CO.
1—ST. JOSEPH'S (1926), [JC] Rev. Joel R. Cyr.
Res.: 531 N. Main St., 04412. Tel: 207-989-5388; Fax: 207-989-5343.
Catechesis/Religious Program—Tel: 207-989-5343. Students 125.
2—ST. TERESA'S (1894), Rev. Joel R. Cyr.
Res.: 440 S. Main St., 04412. Tel: 207-989-7049; Fax: 207-989-4992.
Catechesis/Religious Program—Tel: 207-989-6129. Students 113.
BRIDGTON, CUMBERLAND CO., ST. JOSEPH (1971), Rev. Joseph E. Daniels.
Mailing Address: P.O. Box 310, 04009-0310. Tel: 207-647-2334.
Catechesis/Religious Program—Tel: 207-647-8651. Students 170.
Mission—St. Elizabeth Ann Seton P.O. Box 332, Fryeburg, Oxford Co. 04037. Tel: 207-935-4245.
BRUNSWICK, CUMBERLAND CO.
1—ST. CHARLES (1930), Rev. Stephen F. Concannon.
Office—132 McKeen St., 04011. Tel: 207-725-2624; Fax: 207-725-4436.
Catechesis/Religious Program—Tel: 207-725-4436. Students 199.
Mission—St. Katharine Drexel Harpswell, Cumberland Co.
2—ST. JOHN THE BAPTIST (1877), [CEM] Revs. Walter Gaudreau, S.M.; Edward Sheehan, S.M.; Kenneth Ridgeway, S.M. In Res., Rev. Robert P. Bouchard.
Res.: 39 Pleasant St., 04011. Tel: 207-725-8756; Fax: 207-798-4792.
School—St. John's School, 39 Pleasant St., 04011. Tel: 207-725-5507. Mr. Edward P. Buckley, Prin. Lay Teachers 26; Students 227.
Catechesis/Religious Program—Tel: 207-729-5966. Carolyn Ruggles, D.R.E. Students 67.
Mission—St. Andrew Rte. 196, Pejepscot, Topsham Co. 04086.
BUCKSPORT, HANCOCK CO., ST. VINCENT DE PAUL (1892), [CEM] Rev. Richard A. Lembo, Admin.
Res.: 60 Franklin St., P.O. Box S, 04416. Tel: 207-469-3322.
Catechesis/Religious Program—Suzanne Castonguay, D.R.E. Students 42.
CALAIS, WASHINGTON CO., IMMACULATE CONCEPTION (1859), Very Rev. Mark P. Nolette, V.F.
Res.: 17 Calais Ave., 04619. Tel: 207-454-3413; Fax: 207-454-0649.
Catechesis/Religious Program—Lisa Howard, D.R.E. Students 56.
CAMDEN, KNOX CO., OUR LADY OF GOOD HOPE (1967), Rev. Arthur C. Pechillo.
Res.: 7 Union St., 04843. Tel: 207-236-4785; Fax: 207-236-9422.
Catechesis/Religious Program—Tel: 207-236-4889. Students 164.
Mission—Our Lady of Peace North Haven, Knox Co.
CAPE ELIZABETH, CUMBERLAND CO., ST. BARTHOLOMEW, Rev. Msgr. Michael J. Henchal, J.C.L.; Deacon John S. Brennan.
Res.: 8 Two Lights Rd., 04107. Tel: 207-799-5528; Fax: 207-799-1532.
Catechesis/Religious Program—Students 282.
CARIBOU, AROOSTOOK CO.
1—HOLY ROSARY (1896), Revs. Jean Paul Labrie; David A. Raymond.
Res.: 31 Thomas Ave., P.O. Box 625, 04736. Tel: 207-498-2536; Fax: 207-498-2537.
Catechesis/Religious Program—Tel: 207-498-8844. Gail Langley, D.R.E. Students 202.
2—SACRED HEART (1881), Rev. Thanh Nguyen.
Res.: 1143 Van Buren Rd., 04736. Tel: 207-498-2763; Fax: 207-498-2763.
Catechesis/Religious Program—Betty Thompson, D.R.E. Tel: 207-498-8741. Students 25.
DAIGLE, AROOSTOOK CO., HOLY FAMILY, Closed., For inquiries for parish records please contact St. Louis, Fort Kent.
DEXTER, PENOBSCOT CO., ST. ANNE'S (1893), Rev. Raymond P. Morency.
Res.: 59 Free St., 04930. Tel: 207-924-7104.
Catechesis/Religious Program—Tel: 207-924-7993. Students 37.
DOVER-FOXCROFT, PISCATAQUIS CO.
1—ST. FRANCIS XAVIER (1929), Rev. James P. Robichaud.
Res.: 45 High St., Dover Foxcroft, 04426. Tel: 207-564-2842; Fax: 207-564-7370.
Catechesis/Religious Program—Tel: 207-943-5160. Deborah Moulton, D.R.E. Students 17.
Mission—St. Paul Milo, Piscataquis Co.
2—ST. THOMAS (1898), Rev. James P. Robichaud.
Res.: 45 High St., 04426. Tel: 207-564-2842.
Catechesis/Religious Program—Tel: 207-564-0867. Louise DuLac, D.R.E. Students 67.
Mission—Holy Family Sangerville, Piscataquis Co.
EAGLE LAKE, AROOSTOOK CO., ST. MARY'S (1892), [CEM] Rev. Wilfred P. Labbe.
Res.: Church St., 04739. Tel: 207-444-5119.
Catechesis/Religious Program—Tel: 207-444-6083. Mildred Pelletier, D.R.E. Students 55.
EAST MILLINOCKET, PENOBSCOT CO., ST. PETER'S (1907), Rev. Richard C. Malo, V.F.; Deacon Daniel Watson.
Res.: 56 Cedar St., P.O. Box 400, 04430. Tel: 207-746-3333; Fax: 207-746-8188.
Catechesis/Religious Program—Julie Fiske, D.R.E. Students 80.
EASTPORT, WASHINGTON CO., ST. JOSEPH (1828), [JC] Rev. Eugene F. Gaffey.
Res.: 51 Washington St., 04631. Tel: 207-853-2825.
Catechesis/Religious Program—Students 40.
Mission—St. John the Evangelist Pembroke, Washington Co.
ELLSWORTH, HANCOCK CO., ST. JOSEPH'S (1862), [CEM] Rev. Louis J. Phillips, Admin.
Res.: 231 Main St., 04605. Tel: 207-667-2342; Fax: 207-667-2043.
Catechesis/Religious Program—Students 125.
Mission—Our Lady of the Lake Green Lake, Hancock Co.
Mission—St. Margaret Winter Harbor, Hancock Co.
FAIRFIELD, SOMERSET CO., IMMACULATE HEART OF

MARY (1871), Rev. Marcel L. Dumoulin; Kimberly Suttie, Pastoral Assoc.
Res.: 21 High St., 04937. Tel: 207-453-6131; Fax: 207-453-8334.
Catechesis/Religious Program—Tel: 207-453-7940. Students 95.

FALMOUTH, CUMBERLAND CO., HOLY MARTYRS (1968), Very Rev. Msgr. Charles M. Murphy, S.T.D., V.F.; Deacon Dennis J. Popadak.
Catechesis/Religious Program—266 Foreside Rd., 04105. Tel: 207-781-4573; Fax: 207-781-3961. Students 533.

FARMINGTON, FRANKLIN CO., ST. JOSEPH'S (1885), Rev. Roger P. Chabot.
Mailing Address: 133 Middle St., 04938-1598. Tel: 207-778-2778.
Catechesis/Religious Program—David Levensalor, D.R.E. Students 99.

FORT FAIRFIELD, AROOSTOOK CO., ST. DENIS (1894), [CEM 2] Revs. Jean Paul Labrie; David A. Raymond.
Res.: 143 Main St., 04742-1223. Tel: 207-473-7329; Fax: 207-473-4189.
Catechesis/Religious Program—Students 42.

FORT KENT, AROOSTOOK CO., ST. LOUIS (1870), [CEM 3] Rev. Claude R. Gendreau.
Res.: 26 E. Main St., 04743. Tel: 207-834-5656; Fax: 207-834-7461.
Catechesis/Religious Program—Tel: 207-834-3970. Phyllis Pettetier, D.R.E. (Grades K-8); Robin Berlanger, D.R.E. (Grades 9-12); Robin Pinette, D.R.E. Students 350.

FRENCHVILLE, AROOSTOOK CO., ST. LUCE'S (Upper) (1843), [CEM] Rev. L. Philip Cyr.
Mailing Address: P.O. Box 10, St. Agatha, 04772-0010. Tel: 207-543-7447; Fax: 207-543-6019.
Catechesis/Religious Program—Tel: 207-543-7313; Fax: 207-543-9332. Judy Michaud, D.R.E. Students 97.

GARDINER, KENNEBEC CO., ST. JOSEPH'S (1863), [CEM] Rev. Paul M. Sullivan, S.J. (BO); Ms. Patricia A. Phillips, Parish Coord.
Res.: One Lincoln Ave., 04345-2188. Tel: 207-582-2385; Fax: 207-588-0650.
Catechesis/Religious Program—Tel: 207-582-1149. Students 99.

GORHAM, CUMBERLAND CO., ST. ANNE (1967), Rev. Lawrence J. Conley.
Res.: 299 Main St., 04038. Tel: 207-839-4857; Fax: 207-839-3082.
Catechesis/Religious Program—Tel: 207-839-3082. Sr. Jackie Moreau, R.S.M., D.R.E. Students 366.
Mission—Our Lady of Sebago East Sebago, Cumberland Co.

GRAND ISLE, AROOSTOOK CO., ST. GERARD-MT. CARMEL (1930), [CEM] Very Rev. Richard R. Ouellette.
Res.: 04746. Tel: 207-895-3436.
Catechesis/Religious Program—Verna Beaulieu, D.R.E. Students 65.

GRAY, CUMBERLAND CO., ST. GREGORY (1967), Rev. Msgr. Robert G. Lavoie.
Res.: 24 N. Raymond Rd., P.O. Box 345, 04039-0345. Tel: 207-657-4241.
Catechesis/Religious Program—Tel: 207-657-5659. Students 140.

GREENVILLE, PISCATAQUIS CO., HOLY FAMILY (1916), Rev. William F. Modlin.
Res.: 145 Pritham Rd., P.O. Box 457, 04441-0457. Tel: 207-695-2262.
Catechesis/Religious Program—Tel: 207-695-2009. Lucy Fay, D.R.E. Students 20.
Mission—St. Joseph's [CEM] Rockwood, Somerset Co.

HALLOWELL, KENNEBEC CO., SACRED HEART (1878), Rev. George W. Hickey.
Res.: 12 Summer St., 04347. Tel: 207-623-3424; Fax: 207-623-3424.
Catechesis/Religious Program—Tel: 207-623-3807. Ann Byron, D.R.E.; Terri Trott, D.R.E. Students 75.

HAMLIN, AROOSTOOK CO., ST. JOSEPH (1920), [CEM] Revs. Joseph Chasse, S.M.; Andre Gosselin, S.M.; Robert McDonald, S.M.
Res.: 336 Main St., Van Buren, 04785. Tel: 207-868-2718; Fax: 207-868-9713.
Catechesis/Religious Program— Twinned with St. Bruno and St. Remi, Van Buren.

HAMPDEN, PENOBSCOT CO., ST. MATTHEW (1968), Rev. Robert C. Vaillancourt.
Res.: 70 Western Ave., P.O. Box 280, 04444. Tel: 207-862-3517; Fax: 207-862-4576.
Catechesis/Religious Program—Tel: 207-862-2683. Melanie Van Aken, D.R.E. Students 147.

HOULTON, AROOSTOOK CO., ST. MARY'S (1839), Rev. Eddy Morin.
Res.: 112 Military St., 04730. Tel: 207-532-2871; Fax: 207-532-4401.
Catechesis/Religious Program—Tel: 207-532-0953. Students 150.

HOWLAND, PENOBSCOT CO., ST. LEO (1945), [CEM] Rev. Andre L. Houle, O.M.I.
Mailing Address: P.O. Box 329, 04448. Tel: 207-732-3495; Fax: 207-732-5112.
Catechesis/Religious Program—Tel: 207-732-5602; Fax: 207-732-4805. Students 40.

INDIAN TOWNSHIP, WASHINGTON CO., ST. ANN (1929), (Native American), Rev. Francis P. Morin; Deacon George Stevens Jr.
Church: P.O. Box 358, 04668-0358. Tel: 207-796-5013.
Catechesis/Religious Program—Students 8.

ISLAND FALLS, AROOSTOOK CO., ST. AGNES (1920), [CEM] Rev. Eddy Morin.
Mailing Address: 112 Military St., Houlton, 04730. Tel: 207-532-2871; Fax: 207-532-4401.
Catechesis/Religious Program—Tel: 207-528-2737. Students 24.
Mission—St. Paul Patten, Aroostook Co.

JACKMAN, SOMERSET CO., ST. ANTHONY (1892), [CEM] Rev. William F. Modlin.
Mailing Address: P.O. Box 338, 04945-0338.
Res.: 04945. Tel: 207-668-2881.
Catechesis/Religious Program—Students 18.
Mission—SS. Philip & James West Forks, Somerset Co.

JAY, FRANKLIN CO., ST. ROSE OF LIMA (1894), Rev. Richard E. Senghas.
Res.: One Church St., 04239. Tel: 207-897-2173; Fax: 207-897-2478.
Catechesis/Religious Program—Tel: 207-897-3940. Students 113.

KENNEBUNK, YORK CO., ST. MARTHA'S (1909), Rev. Laurent R. Laplante; Deacon Darrell Blackwell.
Res.: 34 Portland Rd., P.O. Box 510, 04043. Tel: 207-985-6252; Fax: 207-985-7740.
Catechesis/Religious Program—Mrs. Rosanne Smith, D.R.E. Students 304.

KITTERY, YORK CO., ST. RAPHAEL'S (1916), Rev. Real J. Nadeau.
Res.: 6 Whipple Rd., 03904-1739. Tel: 207-439-0442; Fax: 207-439-0442.
Catechesis/Religious Program—Faith Formation Center, 6 Whipple Rd., 03904-1739. Students 116.

LEWISTON, ANDROSCOGGIN CO.
1—HOLY CROSS (1923), [JC] Rev. Msgr. Rene T. Mathieu, V.F.; Rev. Paul LaBrec.
Res.: 16 St. Croix St., P.O. Box 1540, 04241-1540. Tel: 207-782-9463; Fax: 207-782-5968.
School—17 Baird Ave., 04240. Tel: 207-783-9323; Fax: 207-783-9491. Mr. Shawn Chabot, Prin. Sisters 2; Lay Teachers 25; Students 412.
Catechesis/Religious Program—Tel: 207-783-7241. Ms. Ruth Oakley, D.R.E. Students 142.
2—HOLY FAMILY, Rev. Andrew Dubois; Doreen Gagne, Pastoral Assoc. Tel: 207-783-7333. In Res., Revs. John W. Gouldrick, C.M.; Anthony F. Kuzia, C.M.; Michael J. Seavey.
Res.: 607 Sabattus St., 04240. Tel: 207-782-8928; Fax: 207-782-3179.
Catechesis/Religious Program—Tel: 207-783-7330. Marie Beaulieu, D.R.E. Students 294.
3—ST. JOSEPH'S (1857), [JC] Rev. Michael J. Seavey.
Res.: 253 Main St., 04240. Tel: 207-784-5328; Fax: 207-795-5078.
School—393 Main St., 04240. Tel: 207-784-8811; Fax: 207-783-9522. Mrs. Andree Tostevin, Prin. Lay Teachers 15; Students 186.
Catechesis/Religious Program—Tel: 207-782-2286. Connie Ayotte, D.R.E. Students 90.
4—ST. MARY'S, Closed. For inquiries for parish records contact the chancery.
5—ST. PATRICK'S (1887), [CEM] Rev. Thomas F. Farley.
Rectory/Office: 1 Walnut St., 04240. Tel: 207-782-1997; Fax: 207-782-6722.
Church: 220 Bates St., 04240.
Catechesis/Religious Program—Fax: 207-786-9223. Rita Desjarding, D.R.E. Students 25.
6—SS. PETER AND PAUL (1870), Rev. Robert D. Lariviere.
Mailing Address: 27 Bartlett St., 04240. Tel: 207-777-1200; Fax: 207-786-9223.
School—15 Sacred Heart Pl., Auburn, 04210. Tel: 207-782-0721; Fax: 207-782-0110. Sr. Margaret Walsh, R.S.M., Prin. Lay Teachers 8; Students 137.
Catechesis/Religious Program—Rita Desjarding, D.R.E. Students 50.

LIMERICK, YORK CO., ST. MATTHEW (1921), Rev. Richard A. Nadeau; Deacon Paul Lissandrello.
Res.: 19 Dora Ln., 04048. Tel: 207-793-2244; Fax: 207-793-2191.
Catechesis/Religious Program—Students 195.

LIMESTONE, AROOSTOOK CO., ST. LOUIS, Revs. Jean Paul Labrie; David A. Raymond. In Res., Rev. L. Chanel Cyr (Retired).
Res.: 100 Main St., 04750-1116. Tel: 207-325-4843.
Catechesis/Religious Program—Tel: 207-325-4843. Students 45.

LINCOLN, PENOBSCOT CO., ST. MARY (1902), Revs. Myles Cyr, O.M.I.; Roger Cyr; Deacon Thomas Krapf.
Res.: 164 Main St., P.O. Box 310, 04457. Tel: 207-794-6333; Fax: 207-794-8044.
Catechesis/Religious Program—Carl Cooper, D.R.E. Students 86.
Mission—St. James Kingman, Penobscot Co.
Mission—Sacred Heart Winn, Penobscot Co.
Mission—St. Ann Danforth, Washington Co.
Mission—Guardian Angel Vanceboro, Washington Co.

LISBON FALLS, ANDROSCOGGIN CO.
1—SS. CYRIL AND METHODIUS, (Slovak), Merged, with St. Anne's and Holy Family to form Holy Trinity, Lisbon Falls.
2—HOLY TRINITY (1995), [CEM 3] Rev. Lionel G. Chouinard.
Res.: 67 Frost Hill Ave., 04252. Tel: 207-353-2792 (Office); Fax: 207-353-6192.
Catechesis/Religious Program—Tel: 207-353-6306. Students 66.

LISBON, ANDROSCOGGIN CO., ST. ANNE'S, Merged, with Holy Family and SS. Cyril and Methodius to form Holy Trinity, Lisbon Falls.

LUBEC, WASHINGTON CO., SACRED HEART (1913), Rev. Michael J. Sheridan; Ms. Patricia A. Phillips, Parish Coord.
Mailing Address: P.O. Box 63, 04652-0063.
Res.: 19 Church St., 04652. Tel: 207-733-2214.
Catechesis/Religious Program—Tel: 207-853-2494. Students 6.

LYMAN, YORK CO., ST. PHILIP (1981), [JC] Rev. James Knox, Admin. (Retired).
Res.: 404 Goodwins Mills Rd., 04002. Tel: 207-499-2940.
Catechesis/Religious Program—Tel: 207-282-3037. Lucille Prescott, D.R.E. Students 109.

MACHIAS, WASHINGTON CO., HOLY NAME OF JESUS (1828), Rev. Michael J. Sheridan, Admin.
Res.: 11 Free St., P.O. Box 248, 04654. Tel: 207-255-3731; Fax: 207-255-3337.
Catechesis/Religious Program—Dan Hogan, D.R.E. Students 62.
Mission—St. Michael's Cherryfield, Washington Co.

MADAWASKA, AROOSTOOK CO.
1—ST. DAVID'S (1872), [CEM] Very Rev. Richard R. Ouellette.
Res.: 774 Main St., 04756. Tel: 207-728-3366; Fax: 207-728-3366.
Catechesis/Religious Program—Tel: 207-728-4012. Sharon M. Oullettte, D.R.E. Students 104.
2—ST. THOMAS AQUINAS (1929), [CEM] Rev. James R. Albert.
Mailing Address: P.O. Box 128, 04756. Tel: 207-728-7531; Fax: 207-728-4217.
Catechesis/Religious Program—Tel: 207-728-7135; Fax: 207-728-7173. Ann Marie Clavette, D.R.E. Students 307.

MADISON, SOMERSET CO., ST. SEBASTIAN (1907), [CEM] Rev. Georges J. Plante; Elisabeth Crowley, Pastoral Assoc.
Res.: 161 Main St., 04950-1599. Tel: 207-696-3203; Fax: 207-696-3203.
Catechesis/Religious Program—Tel: 207-696-8153; Fax: 207-696-5560. Students 60.

MARS HILL, AROOSTOOK CO., ST. JOSEPH (1927), Rev. Alfred E. Irving.
Mailing Address: *c/o St. Mary's Rectory*, P.O. Box 813, Presque Isle, 04769. Tel: 207-768-3671; 207-429-9805 (Church); Fax: 207-764-8644.
Catechesis/Religious Program—Tel: 207-764-0161; Fax: 207-764-8092. Students 12.

MECHANIC FALLS, ANDROSCOGGIN CO., OUR LADY OF RANSOM (1931), Rev. Antonio Amato.
Res.: 117 Elm St., P.O. Box 206, 04256. Tel: 207-345-2691.
Catechesis/Religious Program—Sandy Ferland, D.R.E.; Judy Emch, D.R.E.; Ellen Theriault, D.R.E. Students 70.
Mission—St. Mary P.O. Box 206, Oxford Co. 04256.

MEXICO, OXFORD CO., ST. THERESA (1926), [JC] Rev. Alfred Jacques; Deacon Rod Berger.
Res.: 7 Brown St., 04257. Fax: 207-364-2593.
Catechesis/Religious Program—Tel: 207-364-4555. Students 28.
Mission—St. Joseph Dixfield, Oxford Co.

MILLINOCKET, PENOBSCOT CO., ST. MARTIN OF TOURS (1899), Rev. Richard C. Malo, V.F.; Deacon Daniel Watson.
Mailing Address: 112 Maine Ave., 04462.
Res.: 18 Colby St., 04462. Tel: 207-723-5902 (Office); 207-723-9533 (Rectory); Fax: 207-723-9904.
Catechesis/Religious Program—Tel: 207-723-9904. Students 107.

NEWCASTLE, LINCOLN CO., ST. PATRICK (1796), [CEM] Rev. Raymond Picard.
Mailing Address: P.O. Box 598, 04553. Tel: 207-563-3240; Fax: 207-563-7145.
Catechesis/Religious Program—St. Patrick's Parish Ctr., Academy Hill Rd., 04553. Tel: 207-563-6038. Students 84.

NORTH VASSALBORO, KENNEBEC CO., ST. BRIDGET'S (1911), Rev. Joseph W. Cahill.
Mailing Address: P.O. Box 159, 04962. Tel: 207-873-3204.

Catechesis/Religious Program—Tel: 207-465-9751; Fax: 207-465-9158. Mrs. Anna M. Anderson, D.R.E.
Mission—St. Peter China Lake, Kennebec Co.

NORTHEAST HARBOR, HANCOCK CO., ST. IGNATIUS (1929), Rev. John O'Hara; Deacon Joseph LaPlante.
Res.: 21 Ledgelawn Ave., Bar Harbor, 04609-1303. Tel: 207-288-3535; Fax: 207-288-3324.
Catechesis/Religious Program—436 Seawall Rd, 04679. Tel: 207-244-0445.
Mission—Our Lady Star of the Sea Islesford, Hancock Co.
Mission—St. Peter's Manset, Hancock Co.

NORWAY, OXFORD CO., ST. CATHERINE OF SIENNA (1914), Rev. Gerald A. Levesque.
Res.: 32 Paris St., 04268-5633. Tel: 207-743-2606; Fax: 207-743-6601.
Catechesis/Religious Program—Students 118.
Mission—Our Lady of the Snows Rte. 26, Bethel, Oxford Co. 04217. Tel: 207-824-2933.

OAKLAND, KENNEBEC CO., ST. THERESA (1963), Rev. Joseph W. Cahill.
Res.: 35 Church St., 04963. Tel: 207-465-3856; Fax: 207-465-9158.
Catechesis/Religious Program—Tel: 207-465-7951. Anna H. Anderson, D.R.E. Tel: 207-397-2041. Students 85.
Mission—St. Helena Belgrade Lakes, Kennebec Co.

OLD ORCHARD BEACH, YORK CO., ST. MARGARET'S (1926), Rev. Coleman P. O'Toole; Deacon Daniel J. Delargy.
Res.: 6 Saco Ave., P.O. Box 289, 04064-0289. Tel: 207-934-2322; Fax: 207-934-8322.
Catechesis/Religious Program—Tel: 207-934-4232. Students 136.
Chapel—Old Orchard, St. Luke's

OLD TOWN, PENOBSCOT CO.
1—ST. ANN CHURCH, INDIAN ISLAND (1688), (Native American), Rev. Paul R. Kerns.
Mailing Address: P.O. Box 560, 04468-0560. Tel: 207-827-2172.
Catechesis/Religious Program—Mrs. Liz Bard, D.R.E. Students 10.
2—HOLY FAMILY (1992), [JC] Rev. Normand P. Richard.
Res.: 429 Main St., 04468. Tel: 207-827-4000; Fax: 207-827-2113.
Catechesis/Religious Program—Tel: 207-827-2377. Students 87.
3—ST. JOSEPH'S, Closed., See Holy Family.
4—ST. MARY'S, Closed., See Holy Family.

OQUOSSOC, FRANKLIN CO., OUR LADY OF THE LAKES (1927), Unassigned.
Res.: Box 333, 04964. Tel: 207-864-3795.
Catechesis/Religious Program—Students 10.
Mission—St. Luke Rangeley, Franklin Co. Tel: 207-864-2622.
Mission—St. John Stratton, Franklin Co. Tel: 207-246-4892.
Mission—Richard H. Bell Memorial Chapel Sugarloaf U.S.A., Franklin Co.

ORONO, PENOBSCOT CO.
1—ST. MARY'S (1888), [JC] Rev. Joseph J. Koury, J.C.D., Pastor.
Res.: Tel: 207-866-3372; Fax: 207-866-4543.
Church: 89 Main St., 04473.
Catechesis/Religious Program— Twinned with Our Lady of Wisdon, Orono.
2—OUR LADY OF WISDOM PERSONAL CAMPUS PARISH (1946), Rev. Joseph J. Koury, J.C.D.
Res.: *University of Maine*, Newman Center, 83 College Ave., 04473. Tel: 207-866-2155; Fax: 207-866-4543.
Catechesis/Religious Program—JoAnn Hall, D.R.E. Students 100.
Newman Campus Ministry Center—

PERRY, WASHINGTON CO., ST. ANN (Pleasant Point) (1907), (Native American), Very Rev. Mark P. Nolette, V.F.; Sr. Janice Murphy, R.S.M., Parish Coord.; Deacon Francis Nicholas.
Res.: 04667. Tel: 207-853-4718.
Catechesis/Religious Program—Students 35.

PITTSFIELD, SOMERSET CO., ST. AGNES (1909), Rev. Emmanuel Iheaka (BIR).
Res.: 50 Detroit Ave., 04967. Tel: 207-487-2777.
School—6 Pine St., 04967. Tel: 207-487-3899. Sr. Elizabeth Cobb, R.S.M., Prin. Diocesan Sisters of Mercy 2; Lay Teachers 6; Students 66.
Catechesis/Religious Program—Students 30.

PRESQUE ISLE, AROOSTOOK CO., NATIVITY OF B.V.M. (1895), [CEM 2] Rev. Alfred E. Irving.
Res.: 6 Roberts St., P.O. Box 813, 04769-0813. Tel: 207-768-3671; Fax: 207-764-8644.
Catechesis/Religious Program—Tel: 207-764-0161; Fax: 207-764-8092. Ann Albert, D.R.E. Students 105.

RICHMOND, SAGADAHOC CO., ST. AMBROSE (1866), Rev. Angelo B. LeVasseur.
Res.: 27 Kimball St., P.O. Box 38, 04357. Tel: 207-737-4713; Fax: 207-737-4713.
Catechesis/Religious Program—Students 29.

ROCKLAND, KNOX CO., ST. BERNARD'S (1857), [CEM 2] Rev. Mark S. Reinhardt.
Res.: 150 Broadway, 04841. Tel: 207-594-4322; Fax: 207-594-0234.
Catechesis Religious Program—Margaret Cuccinello, D.R.E. Students 100.
Mission—St. James Thomaston, Knox Co.

RUMFORD, OXFORD CO., ST. ATHANASIUS-ST. JOHN (1906), [JC] Rev. Alfred Jacques.
Res.: 126 Maine Ave., 04276. Tel: 207-364-4555; Fax: 207-364-4555.
School—115 Maine Ave., 04276. Tel: 207-364-2528. Donald Fournier, Prin. Lay Teachers 12; Students 108.
Catechesis Religious Program—Mary Therrault, D.R.E. Students 102.
Mission—St. Mary's Chapel Roxbury Pond, Oxford Co.

ST. AGATHA, AROOSTOOK CO., ST. AGATHA'S (1889), Rev. L. Philip Cyr.
Res.: 04772. Tel: 207-543-7447; Fax: 207 543-6019.
Catechesis/Religious Program—Tel: 207 543-7313; Fax: 207-543-9332. Judy Michaud, D.R.E. Students 82.
Mission—St. Michael's Chapel [CEM 2] Birch Point Rd., Madawaska, Aroostook Co. 04756.

ST. FRANCIS, AROOSTOOK CO., ST. CHARLES (1894), [CEM 4] Rev. Claude R. Gendreau.
Res.: P.O Box 100, 04774. Tel: 207-398-3530.
Catechesis/Religious Program—Tel: 207-398-4475.

ST. JOHN, AROOSTOOK CO., ST. JOHN, Merged, with St. Charles and St. Francis, Maine on Jan 1, 2002.

SABATTUS, ANDROSCOGGIN CO., OUR LADY OF THE ROSARY (1975), Rev. Angelo B. LeVasseur.
Res.: 131 High St., 04280. Tel: 207-375-6951; Fax: 207-375-4135.
Catechesis/Religious Program—Tel: 207-375-6581. Students 62.
Mission—St. Francis Greene, Androscoggin Co. Tel: 207-946-5758.

SACO, YORK CO.
1—MOST HOLY TRINITY (1916), Revs. James J. Doherty, C.S.C.; Patrick Walsh, C.S.C.
Res.: 271 Main St., Box 310, 04072. Tel: 207-282-3321; Fax: 207-284-2274.
Catechesis/Religious Program—Tel: 207-282-6392. Students 231.
2—NOTRE DAME DE LOURDES (1929), [JC] Rev. Paul E. Cote.
Res.: 15 Cutts Ave., 04072. Tel: 207-282-1392; Fax: 207-282-0353.
School—50 Beach St., 04072. Tel: 207-283-3111; Fax: 207-286-2750. Sr. Linda Mae Plourde, P.M., Prin. Sisters of the Presentation of Mary 1; Lay Teachers 12; Students 108.
Catechesis/Religious Program—Tel: 207-282-0911. Donna Rivard, D.R.E. Students 40.

SANFORD, YORK CO.
1—HOLY FAMILY (1923), [JC] Revs. Claude J. Albert; Timothy J. Nadeau; Gerald Coutu, Pastoral Assoc.
Res.: 66 North Ave., 04073. Tel: 207 324-2420; Fax: 207-324-5318.
School—St. Thomas Consolidated School, Tel: 207-324-2549; Fax: 207-324-2549. Norman Provost, Prin. For Holy Family, St. Ignatius and Notre Dame, Springvale. Lay Teachers 16; Students 266.
Catechesis/Religious Program— Twinned with St. Ignatius, Sanford and Notre Dame, Springvale. Tel: 207-324-5832. Joyce M. St. Pierre, D.R.E. Students 240
2—ST. IGNATIUS MARTYR (1892), [CEM] Revs. Claude J. Albert; Timothy J. Nadeau; Gerald Coutu, Pastoral Assoc. & D.R.E. In Res., Rev. Rene G. Lavoie (Retired).
Res.: 10 St. Ignatius St., 04073. Tel: 207-324-6040; Fax: 207-324-5318.
Catechesis/Religious Program— Twinned with Holy Family, Sanford and Notre Dame, Springvale. Tel: 207-651-4610; Fax: 207-324-5318.

SCARBOROUGH, CUMBERLAND CO., ST. MAXIMILIAN KOLBE (1988), Rev. James J. Morrison.
Mailing Address: P.O. Box 57, 04070-0057. Tel: 207-883-2597 (Res.); 207-883-0334 (Parish Office); Fax: 207-883-4246.
Catechesis/Religious Program—Tel: 207-883-1742. Kathy Sparda, D.R.E. Students 373.
Mission—St. Jude Rte. 9, Pine Point, Scarborough Co. 04074.

SINCLAIR, AROOSTOOK CO., ST. JOSEPH (1936), [CEM] Rev. L. Philip Cyr.
Mailing Address: P.O. Box 10, St. Agatha, 04772.
Res.: St. Agatha, 04772. Tel: 207-543-7447; Fax: 207-543-6019.
Catechesis/Religious Program—Tel: 207-543-7313; Fax: 207-543-9332. Students 13.

SKOWHEGAN, SOMERSET CO., NOTRE DAME DE LOURDES (1881), [CEM] Rev. Maurice N. Morin; Sr. Claudette Darisse, A.S.V., Pastoral Assoc.
Res.: 273 Water St., P.O. Box 369, 04976. Tel: 207-474-2039; Fax: 207-474-2039.
Catechesis/Religious Program—Tel: 207-474-9844. Students 92.

SOUTH BERWICK, YORK CO., ST. MICHAEL (1886), [CEM] Rev. Hilary J. Cameron.
Res.: 25 Saw Mill Hill, Berwick, 03901. Tel: 207-384-4241; Fax: 207-384-4289.
Catechesis/Religious Program—Students 137.

SOUTH PORTLAND, CUMBERLAND CO.
1—CHURCH OF THE HOLY CROSS (1913), Rev. Paul E. Coughlin.
Mailing Address: P.O. Box 2708, 04116-2708. Tel: 207-772-7489; Fax: 207-772-7480.
Parish Office—29 Aspen Ave., 04106.
Res.: 11 Aspen Ave., 04106. Tel: 207-472-7489; Fax: 207-871-0235.
School—436 Broadway, 04106. Tel: 207-799-6661; Fax: 207-799-8345. Deacon Steven G. Harnois, Prin. Sisters 1; Lay Teachers 20; Students 254.
Catechesis/Religious Program—Tel: 207-773-8710; Fax: 207-772-7480. Joseph Draper, D.R.E. Merged with St. John the Evangelist.
2—ST. JOHN THE EVANGELIST (1940), Rev. Paul E. Coughlin.
Res.: 11 Aspen Ave., 04106. Tel: 207-772-7489; Fax: 207-871-0235.
Catechesis/Religious Program—Tel: 207-773-8710; Fax: 207-772-7480. Joseph Draper, D.R.E. Twinned with Holy Cross, South Portland. Students 201.

SPRINGVALE, YORK CO., NOTRE DAME (1887), [CEM] Revs. Claude A. Albert; Timothy J. Albert.
Res.: 10 Payne St., Box 278, 04083. Tel: 207-324-6630.
Catechesis/Religious Program— Twinned with Holy Family, Sanford and St. Ignatius, Sanford. Rebecca Carlson, D.R.E. Students 240.

STOCKHOLM, AROOSTOOK CO., ST. THERESE (1926), Rev. Joachim Thanh Nguyen.
Mailing Address: 1143 Van Buren Rd., Caribou, 04736.
Church: 04783. Tel: 207-498-2763.
Catechesis/Religious Program—Students 8.

STONINGTON, HANCOCK CO., ST. MARY STAR OF THE SEA (1931), Rev. Richard Lembo, Admin.
Mailing Address: P.O. Box 25, 04681. Tel: 207-367-2343.
Mission—Our Lady of Holy Hope Pleasant St., Box 413, Castine, Hancock Co 04421. Tel: 207-326-8228.

VAN BUREN, AROOSTOOK CO.
1—ST. BRUNO - ST. REMI (1991), [CEM] Revs. Joseph Chasse, S.M.; Robert McDonald, S.M.; Andre Gosselin, S.M.
Res.: 336 Main St., 04785. Tel: 207-868-2718; Fax: 207-868-9713.
Catechesis/Religious Program—Tel: 207-868-2835. Elaine Levesque, D.R.E. Students 139.
Mission—St. Rose Chapel, Aroostook Co.
2—ST. REMI (1923), Merged, with St. Bruno. For further details see separate listing under St. Bruno.

WALLAGRASS, AROOSTOOK CO., ST. JOSEPH'S (1890), [CEM 3] Rev. Wilfred P. Labbe.
Church: 1961 Aroostook Rd., 04781. Tel: 207-444-5135; Fax: 207-444-5135.
Res.: Church St., P.O. Box 249, Eagle Lake, 04739. Tel: 207-444-5119; Fax: 207-444-5119.
Catechesis/Religious Program—Tel: 207-834-6753. Students 50.

WATERVILLE, KENNEBEC CO.
1—NOTRE DAME, Merged, with Sacred Heart and St. Francis de Sales to form Parish of the Holy Spirit, Waterville.
2—PARISH OF THE HOLY SPIRIT (1996), [JC], Merging St. Francis de Sales, Sacred Heart and Notre Dame Parishes. Revs. Philip A. Tracy; Ralph Boisvert; Sr. Line Rioux, C.S.J., Pastoral Assoc.
Res.: 70 Pleasant St., 04901-5405. Tel: 207-872-2281; Fax: 207-877-0675.
Catechesis/Religious Program—Tel: 207-872-2264; Fax: 207-872-2264. Marla Duperry, D.R.E. Students 178.
3—SACRED HEART, Merged, with Notre Dame and St. Francis de Sales to form Parish of the Holy Spirit, Waterville.

WELLS, YORK CO., ST. MARY (1970), Very Rev. Msgr. J. Joseph Ford Jr., V.F.
Res.: Eldredge Rd., P.O. Box 368, 04090-0368. Tel: 207-646-5605; Fax: 207-646-9437.
Catechesis/Religious Program—Students 170.
Mission—All Saints Ogunquit, York Co.

WESTBROOK, CUMBERLAND CO.
1—ST. EDMUND (Prides Corner) (1975), Rev. D. Joseph Manship.
Res.: 355 Bridgton Rd., 04092. Tel: 207-797-8233; Fax: 207-797-8356.
Catechesis/Religious Program—Tel: 207-797-4539. Mrs. Sandra Bois, D.R.E. Students 75.
2—ST. HYACINTH (1892), [CEM] Rev. James P. Brewer; Rosalie Aube, D.R.E. In Res., Rev. Paul R. Marquis.
Res.: 295 Brown St., 04092. Tel: 207-854-2003; Fax: 207-854-4899.
Catechesis/Religious Program—Tel: 207-854-4925. Students 133.
3—ST. MARY'S (1920), [JC] Rev. D. Joseph Manship.

Res.: 625 Main St., 04092. Tel: 207-854-2753; Fax: 207-856-7318.
Catechesis/Religious Program—Tel: 207-854-8669. Larry Guertin, D.R.E. Students 97.

WHITEFIELD, LINCOLN CO., ST. DENIS (1818), [CEM] Rev. Donald R. J. Daigle; Deacon Joseph Reid.
Res.: 298 Grand Army Rd, 04353-3419. Tel: 207-549-7425.
Catechesis/Religious Program—Students 50.

WILTON, FRANKLIN CO., ST. MARY, Closed., For further details see separate listing for St. Joseph, Farmington.

WINDHAM, CUMBERLAND CO., OUR LADY OF PERPETUAL HELP (1974), Rev. Normand E. Carpentier.
Res.: 919 Roosevelt Tr., 04062-5641. Tel: 207-892-8288; Fax: 207-893-1072.
Catechesis/Religious Program—Tel: 207-892-8922. Students 303.
Mission—St. Raymond Chapel Rte. 85 at Crescent Lake, East Raymond, Cumberland Co. 04071.

WINSLOW, KENNEBEC CO., ST. JOHN THE BAPTIST (1926), [JC] Rev. Paul A. Plante; Mrs. Elaine Gordon, Pastoral Assoc.
Res.: 47 Monument St., 04901. Tel: 207-872-2373; 207-877-0953; Fax: 207-873-7301.
School—36 1/2 Garand St., 04901. Tel: 207-872-7115; Fax: 207-872-2500. Mr. Kevin Scully, Prin. Lay Teachers 7; Students 124.
Catechesis/Religious Program—Students 120.

WINTERPORT, WALDO CO., ST. GABRIEL (1850), Rev. Robert C. Vaillancourt.
St. Matthew's: 70 Western Ave., P.O. Box 280, Hampden, 04444. Tel: 207-862-3517; Fax: 207-862-4576.
Catechesis/Religious Program—Tel: 207-223-4088. Beth Thieme, D.R.E. Students 47.

WINTHROP, KENNEBEC CO., ST. FRANCIS XAVIER (1910), [JC] Rev. Brian D. Blanchette.
Res.: 130 Rte. 133, 04364. Tel: 207-377-2922; Fax: 207-377-7087.
Catechesis/Religious Program—Tel: 207-377-6844. Nancy Lynn Yocono, D.R.E. Students 123.
Mission—St. Stanislaus Monmouth, Kennebec Co.
Mission—St. Leo Litchfield, Kennebec Co. 04350. Tel: 207-268-4727.

YARMOUTH, CUMBERLAND CO., SACRED HEART (1876), [CEM] Rev. Msgr. Paul F. Stefanko, J.C.L.; Ann Peacock, Pastoral Assoc.; Cherie Piper, Pastoral Assoc.
Res.: 326 Main St., 04096. Tel: 207-846-5584; Fax: 207-846-6003.
Catechesis/Religious Program—Tel: 207-865-4264. Ann Peacock, D.R.E.; Debra Gagnon, D.R.E. Students 289.
Mission—St. Jude's Freeport, Cumberland Co.

YORK HARBOR, YORK CO., ST. CHRISTOPHER-BY-THE-SEA (1947), Rev. Albert B. Colpitts; Deacon Claude Spencer.
Res.: One Lilac Ln., 03909-1020. Tel: 207-363-2111; Fax: 207-363-1586.
Catechesis/Religious Program—Tel: 207-363-4177; Fax: 207-363-8934. Rose Cronin, D.R.E. Students 330.
Mission—St. Mary, Star of the Sea York Beach, York Co.

Chaplains of Public Institutions

PORTLAND. *St. Joseph's Manor*, Tel: 207-797-0600. (Vacant)
Maine Medical Center, Tel: 207-871-0111. Revs. Patrick Glavin, O.F.M.Cap., Chap., Frederick H. Morse, Chap., Paul R. Marquis, Chap.
Mercy Hospital, Tel: 207-879-3358. Rev. Roland P. Nadeau, Mrs. Agnes LaStoria, Sr. M. Michael Connelly, R.S.M.

AUGUSTA. *Augusta Mental Health Institute*, Tel: 207-289-7334. Rev. Donald R.J. Daigle.
Maine General Medical Center, Tel: 207-626-1000. Sr. Paulette Ducharme, O.S.U., Pastoral Assoc.

BANGOR. *Eastern Maine Medical Center*, Tel: 207-942-6941. Rev. Joseph W. Aprs Jr. Taylor Hospital, Bangor Convalescent Center,
St. Joseph's Hospital, Tel: 207-262-1798. Rev. John J. Austin, Sr. Mary Edmund, C.S.S.F., Pastoral Assoc.

BIDDEFORD. *Southern Maine Medical Center*, Tel: 207-283-3663. Lewella Daigle Landry.

LEWISTON. *Central Maine Medical Center*, Tel: 207-795-0111. Mrs. Kathleen O'Wril, Rev. Donald Gagne, S.M.
St. Mary's Regional Medical Center. Rev. Donald Gagnon, S.M., Sally Brochu.
Campus Ave., P.O. Box 291, 04243. Tel: 207-777-8520. Sisters Madeline Normand, P.M., Huguette Allard, S.G.M., Mr. Kenneth Rancort.

SOUTH PORTLAND. *Maine Youth Center*. Deacon John J. McAuliffe Jr.
Men's Correctional Center, Tel: 207-828-4921. Rev. Robert P. Bouchard.

THOMASTON. *Maine State Prison*, Tel: 207-828-4921. Rev. Robert P. Bouchard.

TOGUS. *Dept. of Veteran Affairs*, Tel: 207-622-1134, Ext. 5176. Rev. Raymond R. Lagace, O.F.M.

WARREN. *Super Maximum Facility & Minimum Facility*, Tel: 207-828-4921. Rev. Robert P. Bouchard.

WATERVILLE. *Mid-Maine Medical Center*, Tel: 207-872-1000. Margaret Crowell.

Special or Other Diocesan Assignment:
Rev. Msgr.—
Caron, Marc B., S.T.L., P.O. Box 11559, 04104-7559. Tel: 207-773-6471; 207-772-5104
Revs.—
Clogan, Paul M. (AUS)
Gosselin, G. Gerard
Greenleaf, Daniel P.
Lee, Thomas M.
Michaud, James L.
Poussard, Bertrand R., Mt. St. Joseph, 7 Highwood St., 04901-5797.
Roux, G. Albert, P.O. Box 127, St. Francis, 04774-0127.
Skehan, John R., P.O. Box 11559, 04104-7559.
Thomson, Edward A.

Military Chaplains:
Rev. Msgr.—
Goudreau, Joseph L., 3704 2nd St. S., Arlington, VA 22204-1604. Tel: 703-696-3532; Fax: 703-696-5996
Revs.—
Cote, David P., USAF Academy, 412 33rd Ave., N.E., Great Falls, MT 59404-4203.
Welch, Bernard J., Brunswick Naval Station, 901 Fitch Ave., Brunswick, 04011. Tel: 207-921-2223; 207-921-2231

Retired:
Rev. Msgrs.—
Begin, Raymond F., S.T.L., J.C.D., Winter, 4951 Summertree Rd., Venice, FL 34293-4254. Tel: 941-493-6869. Summer, 19 Northwood Dr., Windham, 04062-5306. Tel: 207-892-0771
Gleason, Paul D., 1 Nudd Ave., Hampton, NH 03842-2939. Tel: 613-926-5442
Nicknair, Leopold G., St. Mary Rectory, Church St., Eagle Lake, 04739.
Tatarczuk, Vincent A., P.O. Box 218, Raymond, 04071. Tel: 207-655-3672
Tracy, George E., 11 Bangor Mall Blvd., Ste. 400, Bangor, 04401-2596. Tel: 207-866-3100; Fax: 207-866-3105
Revs.—
Auger, Gaston E., Box 476, West Kennebunk, 04094. Tel: 207-985-7059
Auger, Raymond D., 4675 Appletree Cir., P.O. Box 3268, Boynton Beach, FL 33436. Tel: 561-752-0417
Bill, J. Armand, 402A Sandpiper Dr., Fort Pierce, FL 34982-5122. Tel: 772-467-1011
Bureau, Germain H., P.O. Box 748, Sabattus, 04280-0748.
Burns, T. Lee, 22357 Peachland Blvd., Port Charlotte, FL 33952. Tel: 941-236-2521
Caron, Antonin R., 79 Fairlawn Ave., Lewiston, 04240.
Chouinard, Marcel G., Mt. St. Joseph, 7 Highwood St., 04901-5797. Tel: 207-873-0705
Civiello, John D., 75 State St., Apt. 231-Box 181, 04101-0181. Tel: 207-773-9582
Cyr, L. Chanel, 302 Main St., Limestone, 04750-1116. Tel: 207-325-4843
Davis, John P., 68 Webster Ave., Lewiston, 04240. Tel: 207-784-6235
Feeney, John J., 175 A Pine St., 04102. Tel: 207-780-1494
Gilbert, Valmont R., 80 Silver St., #5, 04901. Tel: 207-861-8977
Girouard, Robert J., 10801 Bethel St., Port Richey, FL 34668. Tel: 727-868-7313
Gower, James M., 23 High Brook Rd., Bar Harbor, 04609. Tel: 207-288-9780
Harvey, Richard R., 12 Bayberry Rd., Brewer, 04412-1202. Tel: 207-989-8007
Huot, Leopold J., St. Andre Healthcare Facility, 409 Pool Rd., Biddeford, 04005.
Jacques, Donald W., 17 Lorisa Ln., Milford, NH 03055. Tel: 603-672-1981
Knox, James, 31 Clearview Dr., Scarborough, 04074-8319. Tel: 207-883-9652
L'Heureux, Ernest L., 64 Lebonan St., Sanford, 04073. Tel: 207-459-7090
Lavoie, Rene G., 4808 N.W. 48th Ave., Tamarac, FL 33319-3635. Tel: 954-735-4580
Lebel, Maurice T., 64 Flintlock Village #64, Wells, 04090. Tel: 207-641-8790
Lee, Robert E., St. Joseph Manor, 1133 Washington Ave., 04103. Tel: 207-797-0600
Leveille, Rudolph J., 69 Juniper St., Bangor, 04401. Tel: 207-942-9715
Levesque, Sylvio J., 25 Second St., Apt. 215, Hallowell, 04347. Tel: 207-263-7231
Martel, C. James, 29 Rio De Palmas, Fort Pierce, FL 34951. Tel: 772-489-9538
McAllister, Donald, Cathedral Residence, 307 Congress St., 04101-3695. Tel: 207-775-5129
McCarthy, Richard C., St. Joseph Manor, 1133 Washington Ave., 04103. Tel: 207-797-0600
McGarrigle, Michael, 76 Ward Cir., Brunswick, 04011-9343. Tel: 207-725-5764
McInnis, Richard W., 16 Lochness Rd., Rumford, 04276. Tel: 207-364-8717
McKenna, Joseph R., 100 State St., #321, 04101. Tel: 207-775-1084
Moreshead, Harold D., Cathedral Residence, 307 Congress St., 04101-3695. Tel: 207-828-8638
Mulkern, Stephen M., 1258 Washington Ave., 04103. Tel: 207-677-2881
Neault, Armand R., 54 Blacksmith Rd., #11, Wells, 04090. Tel: 207-646-6417
Nicknair, Harold, (Winter), 5725 80th St. N., Unit #411, St. Petersburg, FL 33709. Tel: 727-545-7876. (Summer), 75 Main St., #22, South Portland, 04106-5925. Tel: 207-828-8835
O'Donnell, Richard A., 61 Cleveland Cir., South Portland, 04106.
Ouellette, Roger J., Mt. St. Joseph Home, Highwood St., 04901-5797. Tel: 207-873-0432
Paquet, Hubert J., 46 Wentworth St., Biddeford, 04405. Tel: 207-286-9674
Pare, Paul M., 860 Main St., P.O. Box 4, North Vassalboro, 04926. Tel: 207-872-5287
Parent, Royal J., Golden Gate Mobile Home Community (Winter), 82010 A. St., Pinellas Park, FL 33781-1718. Tel: 727-568-9163. (Summer), 12 Southern Ave., Augusta, 04330. Tel: 207-724-3358
Patenaude, Gilbert A., 57 Oxford St., Augusta, 04330. Tel: 207-622-3832
Rokos, Richard V., Gull Harbor 4533, 17117 Gull Blvd., North Redington Beach, FL 33708. Tel: 727-394-2675
Rotunno, Anthony R., P.O. Box 297, Rockwood, 04478-0297. Tel: 207-534-8831
St. Pierre, Romeo A., 15 Garden Cir. N., Caribou, 04736.
Thibodeau, Clement D., 1800 Van Buren Rd., Connor, 04736. Tel: 207-498-8542
Tracy, Philip Michael, 148 Breakwater Dr., #404, South Portland, 04106. Tel: 207-767-2334
Whitlock, Joseph E., Cathedral Residence, 307 Congress St., 04101-3695.

INSTITUTIONS LOCATED IN THE DIOCESE

[A] COLLEGES AND UNIVERSITIES

STANDISH. *Association of Mercy Colleges and Universities*, 278 Whites Bridge Rd., 04084-5263. Tel: 207-893-7711; Fax: 207-893-7867. Dr. David B. House, Treas. Sponsor: Colleges and Universities run by the Sisters of Mercy throughout the U.S.A.
Saint Joseph's College, 278 Whites Bridge Rd., 04084-5263. Tel: 207-893-7711; Fax: 207-893-7867. Email: dhouse@sjcme.edu. Web: www.sjcme.edu. Dr. David B. House, Pres.; Dr. Daniel P. Sheridan, Vice Pres. for Academic Affairs & Dean of the College; Dr. Michael P. Connolly, Vice Pres. for Student Affairs; Sisters Mary George O'Toole, R.S.M., Vice Pres. for Sponsorship & Mission Integration; Mary Kneeland, R.S.M., Treas.; Rev. John Tokaz, O.F.M.Cap., Chap.; Sr. Sylvia Comer, R.S.M., Campus Min.; Deacon John McAuliffe Jr.; Philip Yauch, Vice Pres. Fin. & Admin.; Robert Sullivan, Vice Pres. Institutional Advancement; Alexander Popovics, Vice Pres. Enrollment Mgmt. Priests 1; Sisters 8; Deacons 1; Lay Professors 110; Undergraduate Students in Distance Education 2,230; Graduate Students 1,755; Total Students 3,985.
Residential College Program Tel: 207-893-6641; Fax: 207-893-7861. Full Time Enrollment 983; Part Time Enrollment 3,960.

[B] HIGH SCHOOLS, REGIONAL

AUBURN. *St. Dominic Regional High School*, 121 Gracelawn Rd., 04210. Tel: 207-782-6911; Fax: 207-795-6439. Email: gmwelch@st-dominic.net. Web: www.st-dominic.net. Mr. G. Michael Welch, Prin. Sisters 2; Lay Teachers 28; Students 360.

[C] HIGH SCHOOLS, PRIVATE

PORTLAND. *Catherine McAuley High School*, 631 Stevens Ave., 04103. Tel: 207-797-3802; Fax: 207-797-3804. Email: sredwardmary@mcaulleyhs.org.

Sr. Edward Mary Kelleher, R.S.M., Prin. Sisters of Mercy 3; Lay Teachers 27; Girls 290.

Cheverus High School, 267 Ocean Ave., 04103. Tel: 207-774-6238; Fax: 207-828-0207. Email: info@cheverus.org. Web: www.cheverus.org. Rev. John W. Keegan, S.J. (BO), Pres.; Mr. John H.R. Mullen, Prin.; Rev. John W. Keegan, S.J. (BO). Faculty resides at St. Ignatius Residence. See separate listing for details. Priests 1; Lay Teachers 36; Students 503.

[D] ELEMENTARY SCHOOLS, PRIVATE

WATERVILLE. *Mount Merici Elementary School*, 152 Western Ave., 04901. Tel: 207-873-3773; Fax: 207-873-6377. Email: mmpvt-mm@mount-merici.pvt.k12.me.us. Web: www.mount-merici.pvt.k12.me.us. Susan H. Cote, Prin. Lay Teachers 8; Students 164.

[E] CATHOLIC CHARITIES MAINE, INC.

FALMOUTH. *Catholic Charities Maine* Web: www.ccmaine.org. P.O. Box 10660, 04104-6060. 358 U.S. Rte. 1, 04105. Tel: 207-781-8550; Fax: 207-781-8560. Most Rev. Joseph John Gerry, O.S.B., Pres. (Retired); Ms. Patricia Collins, Chm.; Mr. John M. Kerry, CEO; Ms. Connie Jones, Human Resources Dir. Tel: 207-781-8550.

St. Elizabeth's Child Development Center, 87 High St., 04101. Tel: 207-871-7444. Lori Freid Moses, Dir.

St. Michael's Center Emergency Foster Care, 1066 Kenduskeag Ave., Bangor, 04401. Tel: 207-941-2855. Email: pvestal@ccmaine.org. Web: www.cc-maine.org. Mr. Paul K. Vestal Jr., Dir.

Legal Title: *St. Michael's Center Emergency Foster Care, Juvenile Jail Diversion Program and Home Based Family Services and Tracker Services.*

[F] SPECIAL RESIDENTIAL SERVICES

PORTLAND. *McAuley Residence, Inc.*, 91 State St., 04101. Tel: 207-773-5289; Fax: 207-773-2672. Email: mcauleyr@maine.rr.com. Sr. Miriam T. Callnan, R.S.M., Dir. Transitional Housing and support services for women with or without children Number served annually 12.

BIDDEFORD. *St. Andre Home, Inc.*, Admin. Office, 283 Elm St., 04005-3093. Tel: 207-282-3351. Email: SaintAndre@aol.com. Web: www.SaintAndreHome.com. Dr. Gregory C. Foltz, Exec. Dir. Pregnant and Parenting Young Women, Adoption Services, Infant Foster Care Homes, Emergency Placement; Public Information-Education; Community Outreach Services; Residences in Biddeford, Lewiston, Bangor. Number served annually 925.

FALMOUTH. *St. Joseph Child Development Center*, c/o Catholic Charities Maine, 358 U.S. Rte. 1, 04105. Tel: 207-782-2711; Fax: 207-782-8741. Web: stjosephinfo@ccmaine.org. Ms. Constance R. Ouellette, Dir.

LEWISTON. *Neighborhood Housing Intiative, Inc.*, c/o Sisters of Charity Health System, Inc., P.O. Box 7291, 04243-7291. Tel: 207-777-8802; Fax: 207-777-8800. James E. Cassidy, Pres.

[G] HOMES FOR THE AGED

PORTLAND. *Deering Pavilion Apartment House for Senior Citizens*, 880 Forest Ave., 04103. Tel: 207-797-8777; Fax: 207-797-8963. Email: deerpan@maine.rr.com. Web: www.deeringpavilion.com. Helen McGuinness, Exec. Dir. Residents 247; Apartments 200.

St. Joseph's Manor, 1133 Washington Ave., 04103. Tel: 207-797-0600; Fax: 207-797-4168. Email: rtardif@saintjosephsmanor.org. Web: www.saintjosephsmanor.org. Most Rev. Joseph John Gerry, O.S.B., Pres. (Retired); Mr. Ronald G. Tardif, Dir.; Faith Stilphen, R.N., Dir. Nurses. Bed Capacity 165; Served 396.

BANGOR. *St. Xavier's Home*, 119 Somerset St., 04401. Tel: 207-942-4815. *St. John Parish*, 207 York St., 04401-5442. Rev. Richard McLaughlin, Contact Person. Units 18.

BIDDEFORD. *St. Andre Health Care & Rehab Center*, 407 Pool St., 04005-9716. Tel: 207-282-5171; Fax: 207-282-5372. Email: andre@gwi.net. Sr. Madeleine D'Anjou, Admin., 04005. Sponsored by Covenant Health Systems, Inc., Lexington, MA Bed Capacity 96.

LEWISTON. *Maison Marcotte* (Formerly: Marcotte Congregate Housing) , 100 Campus Ave., 04240. Tel: 207-786-0062; Fax: 207-777-8570. Email: cmathieu@sochs.com. Cecile Y. Mathieu, Dir. Total In Residence 130; Total Staff 2.

**St. Marguerite d'Youville Pavilion* (Formerly: Marcotte Nursing Home) , 102 Campus Ave., 04240. Tel: 207-777-4200; Fax: 207-777-4255. Email: dfournier@sochs.com. Web: www.stmarysme.com. Debra Fournier, Admin.; Rev. Raymond Corriveau, O.P., Chap. Bed Capacity 280.

WATERVILLE. *Mt. St. Joseph Holistic Care Community*, Highwood St., 04901. Tel: 207-873-0705; Fax: 207-873-6626. Email: msj@mtsj.org. Web: www.mtsj.org. Revs. Bertrand Poussard; Roger J. Ouellette (Retired); Marcel Chouinard; Sr. Marcelle Roy, C.S.J., Coord.; Gail Hillstrom, Admin., 04901. Sisters of St. Joseph of Lyons, C.S.J. Nursing Facility 137; Assisted Living 26.

Seton Village Inc., 1 Carver St., 04901. Tel: 207-873-0178; Fax: 207-873-1233. Most Rev. Joseph John Gerry, O.S.B., Bishop of Portland, Pres. (Retired); Mr. David P. Twomey, C.P.A., Treas.; Daniel Bard, Chm.; Mr. Harlan Cooper, Admin. Units 140; Guests 148.

[H] GENERAL HOSPITALS

PORTLAND. **Mercy Hospital*, 144 State St., 04101. Tel: 207-879-3000; Fax: 207-897-3429. Web: www.mercyhospital.org. Ms. Eileen Skinner, Pres.; Rev. Roland P. Nadeau, Chap. Lay Nurses (RN's and LPN's) 250; Bed Capacity 230; Patients Assisted Annually 165,000; School of Radiology Students 17.

BANGOR. *St. Joseph Hospital*, 360 Broadway, 04401. Tel: 207-262-1000; Fax: 207-262-1922. Email: sm.norberta@sjhhealth.com. Web: www.stjoeshealing.com. Sisters Barbara Theresa, C.S.S.F., Supr.; Mary Norberta, C.S.S.F., Pres. & CEO. Felician Sisters 6; Nursing Sisters 1; Lay Nurses 162; Bed Capacity 112; Patients Assisted Annually 70,748.

Pastoral Care Dept., 360 Broadway, 04401. Tel: 207-262-1798; Fax: 207-262-1922. Rev. John Austin; Sr. Mary Edmund, C.S.S.F.

BUCKSPORT. *Bridgewell, Inc.*, Box 836, 04416. Tel: 207-469-7616; Fax: 207-469-7616. Sr. Miriam Devlin, Contact Person. Health Care Facility. Number served 225.

LEWISTON. *Community Clinical Services, Inc.* (Formerly: Metropolitan Rehabilitation Institute) , 100 Campus Ave, Ste. #1, 04240. Tel: 207-777-8841; Fax: 207-777-8847. Susan Keiler, Dir.

**St. Mary's Regional Medical Center*, Campus Ave., P.O. Box 291, 04243-0291. Tel: 207-777-8100; Fax: 207-777-8800. Web: www.stmarysmaine.com. Sisters Huguette Allard, S.G.M., Chap.; Madeleine Normand, P.M., Chap.; Sharon Leavitt, S.C.I.M., Chap.; Sally A. Brochu, Dir. & Chap.; Kenn Rancourt, Chap.; Rev. Donald Gagne, S.M., Chap. Sisters 3; Nurses 273; LPN 12; CNA 55; Bed Capacity 160; Patients Assisted Annually 144,250.

Sisters of Charity Health System, Inc., P.O. Box 7291, 04243-0291. Tel: 207-777-8802; Fax: 207-777-8800. James E. Cassidy, Pres. & CEO.

Lifeline Tel: 207-777-8708. Serving 600.

Covenant 50 Tel: 207-777-8823; Fax: 207-777-8570. Subscribers 700.

Genesis Residential Treatment Facility Tel: 207-753-5437; Fax: 207-777-8944. Facility for Adolescent Boys.

Renaissance House Tel: 207-753-5437; Fax: 207-753-5480. Residential Program for Children 3 months to 12 years old.

WorkMed Tel: 207-753-3085; Fax: 207-753-3088. Occupational Health Program.

Health & Wellness Program Tel: 207-777-8898; Fax: 207-753-0873.

[I] MONASTERIES AND RESIDENCES OF PRIESTS AND BROTHERS

PORTLAND. *St. Ignatius Residence*, 77 Read St., 04103-3433. Tel: 207-777-0473; Fax: 207-775-1229. Rev. John Keegan, S.J. Jesuit Fathers (New England Prov.) Priests 1.

ALFRED. *Notre Dame Institute*, Shaker Hill Rd., P.O. Box 159, 04002. Tel: 207-324-6312; Fax: 207-490-2370. Email: alfredfic@gwi.net. Bros. Daniel Caron, F.I.C., Prov. Tel: 207-324-0067; James Lacasse, F.I.C., Supr. Tel: 207-324-6612; Rev. Theodore Letendre, F.I.C., Dir. Provincial House of Brothers of Christian Instruction

Notre Dame Spiritual Center Tel: 207-324-6160; Fax: 207-324-5044. Rev. Theodore Letendre, F.I.C. Tel: 207-324-1017. Brothers 22.

KENNEBUNKPORT. *St. Anthony's Friary*, 28 Beach Ave., P.O. Box 980, 04046. Tel: 207 967-2011; Fax: 207-967-5721. Email: johnbac@adelphia.net. Web: www.framon.net. Revs. Placid Barius, O.F.M., Delegate of Provincial; Gabriel Baltrusaitis, O.F.M., Vicar of the Friary & Procurator; John J. Bacevicius, O.F.M., Guardian, Pastoral Min.; Andrew R. Bisson, Pastoral Ministry; Antana Grabnickas, Pastoral Ministry. Priests 6; Seminarians 1. In Res. Rev. Raphael J. Sakalys, O.F.M.

LEWISTON. *SS. Peter and Paul House*, 10 Richmond Ave, 04240-5346. Tel: 207-784-7309; Fax: 207-777-0056. Revs. James Donovan, O.P. (Canada); Raymond Corriveau, O.P., Supr.; Pierre E. Lachance, O.P. (FR); Bro. Irenee Richard, O.P., Treas. Residence for Dominican Fathers or Friar Preachers Priests 3; Brothers 1.

American Dominican Friars Serving in Canada: Revs. Thomas Demers, O.P.; Thomas R. Potvin, O.P.; Bernard M. Remillard, O.P.; Claude Richard, O.P.; Bro. Robert Beaulieu, O.P.

PEAKS ISLAND. *Mother of the Good Shepherd Monastery by the Sea*, 235 Pleasant Ave., 04108. Tel: 207-766-2717; Fax: 207-766-2707. Email: monks@gwi.net. Web: www.augustinianmonks.org. Rev. A.M. Seamus of Jesus, O.S.A., Prior; Bro. Nicholas of the Immaculate Heart, O.S.A., Subprior. The Servants of God of St. Augustine.

[J] CONVENTS AND RESIDENCES OF SISTERS

PORTLAND. *Frances Warde Convent*, 37 Capisic St., 04102-2203. Tel: 207-772-1140; Fax: 207-772-1873. Email: pmoon@maine.rr.com.

Mercy Convent, 144 State St., 04101. Tel: 207-879-3566. Sr. Mary Michael Connelly, R.S.M., Coord. Sisters of Mercy of the Americas 3.

Monastery of the Precious Blood, 166 State St., 04101-3794. Tel: 207-774-0861; Fax: 207-774-3253. Sr. Mary Jo Divney, A.P.B., Supr. Adorers of the Precious Blood 3; Novices 1.

Motherhouse of the Sisters of Mercy of the Americas, 605 Stevens Ave., 04103-2691. Tel: 207-797-7861; Fax: 207-797-0416. Email: jlittle@maine.rr.com. Sisters Jean Little, R.S.M., Regl. Pres.; Maura Murphy, O.S.U., Local Coord. Motherhouse; Rev. Peter Kaseta, O.F.M.Cap.

St. Joseph Rectory, Stevens Ave.. Tel: 207-797-7026; Fax: 207-797-2679. Sisters in Residence at Motherhouse 27.

St. Patrick, 17 Frances St., 04102. Tel: 207-772-0723. Sr. Rachel Cushman, R.S.M., Coord. Sisters of Mercy of the Americas 3.

Sisters of Charity, 1137 Washington Ave., 04103. Tel: 207-797-8607; Fax: 207-797-6086. Email: jacquiep@juno.com. Sisters 2.

Sisters of Mercy of the Americas, 186 Lane Ave., 04103. Tel: 207-878-6630. Email: strand@maine.rr.com. Sr. Theresa Rand, R.S.M., Contact Person. Sisters of Mercy of the Americas 4.

Sisters of Mercy of the Americas, 84 Plymouth St., 04103-2005. Tel: 207-797-6957; Fax: 207-797-0146. Sr. Mary M. Morey, R.S.M., Contact Person. Sisters of Mercy of the Americas 4.

Sisters of Our Lady of the Holy Rosary, 20 Thomas St., 04102. Tel: 207-774-3756; Fax: 207-772-3130. Email: rsr@maine.rr.com. Sr. Carole Jean Lappa, R.S.R., Regl. Supr. Tel: 207-772-3130. Sisters of Our Lady of the Holy Rosary 4.

AUBURN. *Companions of Christ*, 503 Park Ave., 04210. Tel: 207-784-5960. Email: lizbethcc@midmaine.com. Sr. Elizabeth Platt, C.O.C., Contact Person. Sisters 2.

AUGUSTA. *St. Augustine*, 5 Kendall St., 04330. Tel: 207-622-2494; Fax: 207-261-4074. Email: srrachel@staugustine.pvt.k12.me.us. Sr. Rachel Boucher, P.M., Supr. Sisters of the Presentation of Mary Sisters 2.

St. Mary, 51 Sewall St., 04330. Tel: 207-623-9714. Sr. Theresa Conlogue, R.S.M., Contact Person. Sisters of Mercy of the Americas 1.

BANGOR. *St. Joseph Convent*, 360 Broadway, 04401-3979. Tel: 207-262-1124; Fax: 207-262-1925. Email: srbarbara@sjhhealth.com. Sr. Barbara Theresa Martis, C.S.S.F., Contact Person. Felician Sisters 9.

BIDDEFORD. *St. Joseph's Convent*, 409 Pool St., 04005. Tel: 207-284-8381; Fax: 207-286-9418. Email: scimjoro@gwi.net. Sr. Theresa Bouthot, S.C.I.M., Supr. Sections A, B & C. Sisters of the Immaculate Heart of Mary (Good Shepherd) 45.

Marie Fitzbach Convent, 290 Elm St., 04005. Tel: 207-282-2714. Email: fitzbach@gwi.net. Sr. Theresa Therrien, S.C.I.M., Coord. Servants of the Immaculate Heart of Mary (Good Shepherd) 7.

Marie Joseph Spiritual Center, 10 Evans Rd., 04005. Tel: 207-284-5671; Fax: 207-286-1371. Email: mariejosephcenter@yahoo.com. Web: www.presmarymethuen.org. Sr. Gertrude Robitaille, Supr. Sisters of the Presentation of Mary 13.

BRUNSWICK. *St. John the Baptist Convent*, 37 Pleasant St., 04011. Tel: 207-725-5484. Email: lauri@gwi.net. Sr. Marcella Savoie, O.S.U., Supr. Ursuline Sisters 7.

CASCO. *Community of the Resurrection*, P.O. Box 284, 04015-0284. Tel: 207-627-7184; Fax: 207-627-4840. Email: comrest@juno.com. Sr. Renata Camenzind, Supr. Total in Residence 4.

HOULTON. *Little Franciscans of Mary*, 38 Green St., Augusta, 04330. Tel: 207-622-6859. Email: reg3carol@aol.com. Sr. Juanita Robichaud, P.F.M., Contact Person. Little Franciscans of Mary 2.

INDIAN ISLAND. *St. Ann's Convent* Email: edesjardins@iisbia.edu. *Penobscot Reservation*, P.O. Box 3039, Old Town, 04468. Tel: 207-827-4862. Email: ejar@gwi.net. Sisters of Mercy of the Americas

LEWISTON. *Dominican Sisters of the Roman Congregation*, Provincial Residence, 123 Dumont Ave., Apt. 1, 04240-6107. Tel: 207-782-3535; Fax: 207-782-0435. Email: moniqueb@megalink.net. Web: www.op.org/roman. Sr. Monique Belanger, O.P., Prov. Prioress. Sisters 1.

Holy Cross, 15 Baird Ave., 04240. Tel: 207-782-0263. Sr. Cecile Mondor, Supr. Sisters of the Presentation of Mary 2.

Sisters of Charity, Sisters' Residence, 98 Campus Ave., P.O. Box 701, 04243-0701. Tel: 207-782-0798. Sr. Estelle Lamothe, Supr. Sisters 2.

OLD ORCHARD BEACH. *Sisters of Our Lady of the Holy Rosary, Regional House*, 25 Portland Ave., 04064-2211. Tel: 207-934-0592. Sr. Olla Laplante, Supr. Sisters 3.

PITTSFIELD. *St. Agnes*, 9 High St., 04967-1213. Tel: 207-487-4790; Fax: 207-487-3895. Email: srcobb@mint.net. Sr. Elizabeth Cobb, Contact Person. Diocesan Sisters of Mercy 2.

PLEASANT POINT. *St. Ann's Convent*, P.O. Box 126, Perry, 04667. Tel: 207-853-4718. Email: janicemurphy@mainline.net. Sr. Janice Murphy, R.S.M., Coord.

ST. AGATHA. *Our Lady of Wisdom Convent*, 380 Main St., P.O. Box 172, 04772-0172. Tel: 207-543-7523; Fax: 207-543-7575. Sr. Candide Corriveau, D.W., Coord. Daughters of Wisdom 2.

SABATTUS. *Dominican Sisters*, 61 Lisbon Rd., 04280-4209. Tel: 207-375-6583; Fax: 207-375-2694. Email: srmargg@megalink.net. Sr. Marguerite Gregoire, O.P., Prioress. Dominican Sisters of the Roman Congregation 8.

SACO. *Bay View Community*, 187 Bay View Rd., 04072. Tel: 207-283-3636; 207-284-8863; Fax: 207-282-7376. Email: scimbv@gwi.net. Sr. Dorina Chasse, S.C.I.M., Supr.; Rev. James E. Connor, Chap. Servants of the Immaculate Heart of Mary (Good Shepherd Sisters) 31.

Notre Dame de Lourdes, 27 Thornton Ave., 04072. Tel: 207-284-8943. Sr. Michelle Doyon, Dir. Sisters of the Presentation of Mary 2.

Provincial Residence, 313 Seaside Ave., 04072-3410. Tel: 207-284-6429; Fax: 207-282-7376. Email: scimpro@gwi.net. Sr. Lucille Gamache, S.C.I.M., Prov. Supr. Servants of the Immaculate Heart of Mary Sisters 3.

SOUTH PORTLAND. *Our Lady of Mercy Convent*, 265 Cottage Rd., 04106. Tel: 207-767-5804. Email: eboyd@maine.rr.com. Sr. Carol A. LeTourneau, R.S.M., Supr. Gen. Diocesan Sisters of Mercy of Portland 8.

WATERVILLE. *Blessed Sacrament Convent*, 101 Silver St., 04901. Tel: 207-872-7072; Fax: 207-873-2317. Email: servantsinfo@blesacrament.org. Web: www.blesacrament.org. Sr. Mary Catherine Perko, S.S.S., Supr. Servants of the Blessed Sacrament Sisters 9.

Mt. Merici Convent, 172 Western Ave., 04901-4617. Tel: 207-873-3515; Fax: 207-873-4926. Email: laurim@gwi.net. Sr. Laurianne Michaud, O.S.U., Prioress. Ursuline Sisters 22.

Mt. St. Joseph Sisters' Residence, 7 Highwood St., 04901. Tel: 207-873-4804. Sr. Yvette Poulin, C.S.J., Coord. Sisters of St. Joseph 2.

WINSLOW. *Provincialate of the Sisters of St. Joseph*, 93 Halifax St., 04901. Tel: 207-873-4512; Fax: 207-873-1976. Email: csjwinme@adelphia.net. Web: www.esjwinslowmain.org. Sisters Laurette Levasseur, C.S.J., Prov. Supr.; Gilla Dube, Asst. Sisters 3.

[K] HERMITAGES

ELLSWORTH. *John of the Cross Monastery*, 19 Trinity Way, 04605-2800. Tel: 207-664-0026. Email: gaudeamus@panax.com. Sr. Margaret Dorgan, D.C.M. Carmelite Sisters 2.

ST. ALBANS. *Divine Mercy Hermitage*, 57 Bryant Rd., 04971. Tel: 207-938-3730; Fax: 207-938-3730. Email: dmh@tdstelme.com. Sr. Margaret Mary Cuddeback.

Sky-Arch Hermitage, 47 Bryant Rd., 04971. Tel: 207-938-3458. Email: sky-arch@sky-archhermitage.com. Web: www.sky-archhermitage.com. Sr. B. Emmanuel Bryant.

THORNDIKE. *Transfiguration Hermitage*, 548 Files Hill Rd., 04986-9709. Tel: 207-568-3731. Email: srewagner@uninets.net. Sr. Elizabeth Wagner, Contact Person.

[L] RETREAT HOUSES

ALFRED. *Notre Dame Retreat & Spiritual Center*, P.O. Box 159, 04002-0159. Tel: 207-324-6160; Fax: 207-324-5044. Email: spiritualcenter2002@yahoo.com. Bro. Theodore Letendre, F.I.C., Dir.

BIDDEFORD. *Marie Joseph Spiritual Center*, 10 Evans Rd., 04005. Tel: 207-284-5671; Fax: 207-286-1296. Email: mariejosephcenter@yahoo.com. Web: www.presmarymethuen.org. Sr. Claire Vanasse, P.M., Dir. Sisters of the Presentation of Mary

FRENCHVILLE. *Christian Life Center*, P.O. Box 530, 04745-0530. Tel: 207-543-6193; Fax: 207-543-6193. Email: clc@ainop.com. Mr. Donald Clavette, Dir.

SACO. *Bay View Villa, Guest and Retreat House*, 187 Bay View Rd., 04072. Tel: 207-286-8762. Email: bvv@gwi.net. Sr. Claire Lambert, S.C.I.M., Dir. Servants of the Immaculate Heart of Mary

[M] NEWMAN CENTERS

PORTLAND. *University of New England-Westbrook College*

Res.: *St. Joseph Church*, 673 Stevens Ave., 04103. Tel: 207-797-7026; Fax: 207-797-2679. Revs. Peter Kaseta, O.F.M.Cap.; Don Bosco Duquette, O.F.M-.Cap.

University of Southern Maine Portland Campus, c/o Sacred Heart/St. Dominic Rectory, 80 Sherman St., 04101-2216. Tel: 207-772-6182; Fax: 207-772-9615. Email: shsdp@ime.net. Bro. Richard Crawley, O.F.M.Cap., Campus Min. Tel: 207-749-0256.

Gorham Campus Rev. Lawrence Conley. Tel: 207-839-4857.

BIDDEFORD. *University of New England*

St. Andre: 04005. Tel: 207-282-5893. Email: ashinkel@cheverus.org. Dr. Al Shinkel, Campus Min.

BRUNSWICK. *Bowdoin College* St. Charles Parish, 132 McKeen St., 04011. Email: frchris@aol.com.

Newman Center 04011. Tel: 207-576-3135. Rev. Stephen F. Concannon, Chap. Tel: 207-725-2624; Bro. Richard Crawley, O.F.M.Cap., Campus Min. Tel: 207-749-0256.

CASTINE. *Maine Maritime Academy* 158 Franklin St., P.O. Box S, 04416. Tel: 207-469-3322. Rev. Richard Lembo, Chap.

FARMINGTON. *University of Maine at Farmington* Newman Campus Ministry. 133 Middle St., 04938. Tel: 207-778-2778; Fax: 207-778-0268. Email: stjoefarm@midmaine.com. Rev. Roger P. Chabot, Chap.

FORT KENT. *University of Maine at Fort Kent* 436 Frenchville Rd., 04743. Tel: 207-834-3855; Fax: 207-834-6835. Email: karenouellette@hotmail.com. Karen Ouellette, Chap.

LEWISTON. *Bates College* 163 Wood St., 04240. Tel: 207-786-8272; Fax: 207-786-8282. Email: rvwpl1@juno.com. Web: www.bates.edu/admin/offices/chaplain. Rev. Frank J. Murray.

MACHIAS. *University of Maine at Machias* c/o Holy Name, P.O. Box 248, 04654. Tel: 207-255-3731. Rev. Michael Sheridan.

ORONO. *University of Maine Our Lady of Wisdom Parish/Newman Center*, 83 College Ave., 04473-1596. Tel: 207-866-2155; Fax: 207-866-4543. Email: newmancenter@maine.edu. Web: www.ume.maine.edu/newman. Rev. Joseph J. Koury, J.C.D.; Casey Murphy, Campus Min.

PRESQUE ISLE. *University of Maine at Presque Isle*

St. Mary's Rectory, 6 Roberts St., P.O. Box 813, 04769. Tel: 207-768-3671; Fax: 207-764-8644.

SOUTH PORTLAND. *Southern Maine Technical College Holy Cross Rectory*, 11 Aspen St., 04106. Tel: 207-772-7489. Rev. Paul E. Coughlin.

STANDISH. *Saint Joseph's College* , Campus Ministry Office. , 04084-5263. Tel: 207-893-7792; Fax: 207-893-6605. Email: scomer@sjcme.edu. Rev. John Tokaz, O.F.M.Cap.; Sr. Sylvia Comer, R.S.M., Dir. of Campus Ministry.

WATERVILLE. *Colby College* Mid Maine Campus Ministry, 04901. Tel: 207-872-3559. Email: patracy@colby.edu. Rev. Philip A. Tracy, Chap. Dean of Students Office, Colby College.

Thomas College Mid Maine Campus Ministry, 04901. Tel: 207-872-3559. Email: patracy@colby.edu. Rev. Philip A. Tracy, Chap. Dean of Students Office, Colby College.

[N] MISCELLANEOUS LISTINGS

PORTLAND. *St. Elizabeth's Child Development Center*, 87 High St., 04101. Tel: 207-871-7444; Fax: 207-871-1178. Email: lfreidmoses@ccmaine.org. Lori Freid Moses. Number served annually 100.

BANGOR. *St. Michael's Center*, 1066 Kenduskeag Ave., 04401. Tel: 207-941-2855; Fax: 207-941-2835. Email: pvestal@main.org. Web: www.ccmaine.org. Paul Vestal Jr., Dir. Functional Family Therapy, Juvenile Intensive Supervision Services, Home Based Family Services and Case Management Services. Number served annually 800.

BIDDEFORD. *St. Andre Housing, Inc.*, 39 Sullivan St., 04005. Tel: 207-773-6471. David Twomey, Contact Person. Sponsored by: Roman Catholic Diocese of Portland., Purpose: to provide low income housing for the elderly in a deprived area of the state. Served annually 35.

P.O. Box 11559, 04104-7559.

LEWISTON. *Wisdom's Center*, 97 Blake St., P.O. Box 1016, 04243-1016. Tel: 207-784-0155; Fax: 207-784-0156. Email: wisdomscenter@prodigy.net. Sr. Irene Arsenault, D.W., Admin.

RELIGIOUS INSTITUTES OF MEN REPRESENTED IN THE DIOCESE

For further details refer to the corresponding bracketed number in the Religious Institutes of Men or Women section.

[0320]—*Brothers of Christian Instruction*—F.I.C.
[0470]—*The Capuchin Friars* (Prov. of St. Mary)—O.F.M.Cap.
[0740]—*Congregation of Marians of the Immaculate Conception (St. Stanilaus Kostka Prov.)*—M.I.C.
[0480]—*Conventual Franciscans*—O.F.M.Conv
[0520]—*Franciscan Friars* (Custody of St. Casimer)—O.F.M.
[0690]—*Jesuit Fathers and Brothers* (New England Prov.)—S.J.
[0780]—*Marist Fathers* (Boston Prov.)—S.M.
[0910]—*Oblates of Mary Immaculate* (Prov. of St. John the Baptist)—O.M.I.
[0430]—*Order of Preachers (Dominicans)* (Canadian Prov.)—O.P.
[]—*Order of St. Augustine*—O.S.F.
[0610]—*Priests of the Congregation of the Holy Cross* (Eastern Prov.)—C.S.C.
[0975]—*Society of Our Lady of the Most Holy Trinity*—S.O.L.T.

RELIGIOUS INSTITUTES OF WOMEN REPRESENTED IN THE DIOCESE

[]—*Community of the Resurrection*
[]—*Companions of Christ*—C.O.C.
[3100]—*Congregation of Our Lady of the Holy Rosary*—R.S.R.
[1920]—*Congregation of Sisters of Holy Cross*—C.S.C.
[2230]—*Congregation of the Infant Jesus*—C.I.J.
[0750]—*Daughters of the Charity of the Sacred Heart of Jesus*—F.C.S.C.J.
[0960]—*Daughters of Wisdom*—D.W.
[]—*Diocesan Carmelites of Maine*—D.C.M.
[2655]—*Diocesan Sisters of Mercy*—R.S.M.
[1120]—*Dominican Sisters of the Roman Congregation*—O.P.
[1170]—*Felician Sisters*—C.S.S.F.
[1430]—*Franciscan Sisters of Our Lady of Perpetual Help*—O.S.F.
[2575]—*Institute of the Sisters of Mercy of the Americas*—R.S.M.
[2280]—*Little Franciscan of Mary*—P.F.M.
[2760]—*Missionary Sisters of the Immaculate Conception of the Mother of God*—S.M.I.C.
[3500]—*Servants of the Blessed Sacrament*—S.S.S.
[3550]—*Servants of the Immaculate Heart of Mary*—S.C.I.M.
[0490]—*Sisters of Charity of Montreal (Grey Nuns)*—S.G.M.
[0610]—*Sisters of Charity of St. Hyacinthe (Grey Nuns)*—S.C.S.H.
[3000]—*Sisters of Notre Dame de Namur*—S.N.D.deN.
[3750]—*Sisters of St. Chretienne*—S.S.Ch.
[3870]—*Sisters of St. Joseph (Lyons, France)*—C.S.J.
[0150]—*Sisters of the Assumptions*—S.A.S.V.
[0110]—*The Sisters of the Precious Blood*—A.P.B.
[3310]—*Sisters of the Presentation of Mary*—P.M.
[4110]—*Ursuline Nuns (Roman Union)* (Northeastern Prov.)—O.S.U.

DIOCESAN CEMETERIES

BANGOR. *Mount Pleasant*, 449 Ohio St., 04401. Tel: 207-947-4322. Mr. William Foley.

BIDDEFORD. *St. Joseph*, West St., P.O. Box 391, 04005. Tel: 207-282-0747.

LEWISTON. *St. Peter*, Switzerland Rd., 04240. Tel: 207-782-8721. Gerry Raymond.

SOUTH PORTLAND. *Calvary*, 1461 Broadway, 04106. Tel: 207-773-5796. Mr. Richard Nee.

WATERVILLE. *St. Francis*, 78 Grove St., 04901. Tel: 207-872-2770. P.O. Box 575, 04903-0575. Mr. Clarence Hebert.

NECROLOGY

† Lange, L. Joseph, (Retired)—Died Oct. 17, 2003
† Lonsdale, Richard G., Chap., Waterville, ME Blessed Sacrament Convent—Died June 4, 2003
† Marquis, J. Alphee, (Retired)—Died Sept. 23, 2003
† Martel, Robert T., (Retired)—Died Sept. 13, 2003

Archdiocese of Portland in Oregon

(Archidioecesis Portlandensis in Oregon)

Most Reverend

JOHN G. VLAZNY, D.D.

Archbishop of Portland in Oregon; ordained December 20, 1961; appointed Auxiliary Bishop of Chicago and Titular Bishop of Stagno October 31, 1983; consecrated December 13, 1983; appointed Bishop of Winona May 19, 1987; installed July 29, 1987; appointed Archbishop of Portland in Oregon October 28, 1997; installed December 19, 1997

Most Reverend

KENNETH D. STEINER, D.D.

Auxiliary Bishop of Portland in Oregon; ordained May 19, 1962; appointed Titular Bishop of Avensa and Auxiliary Bishop of Portland in Oregon December 6, 1977; ordained March 2, 1978 *Office: 2838 E. Burnside St., Portland, OR 97214.*

Archdiocesan Pastoral Center: 2838 E. Burnside St., Portland, OR 97214-1895. Tel: 503-234-5334; Fax: 503-234-2545.

Web: www.archdpdx.org

Email: @archdpdx.org

Square Miles 29,717.

Erected as a Vicariate-Apostolic December 1, 1843.

Created Archdiocese of Oregon City, July 24, 1846; Name changed by Papal Decree to "Archdiocese of Portland in Oregon," September 26, 1928.

Comprises that part of the State of Oregon lying between the summit of the Cascades and the Pacific Ocean.

Legal Title: For legal titles of parishes and archdiocesan institutions, consult the Archdiocesan Pastoral Center

STATISTICAL OVERVIEW

Personnel	
Archbishops	1
Auxiliary Bishops	1
Abbots	2
Retired Abbots	1
Priests: Diocesan Active in Diocese	95
Priests: Diocesan Active Outside Diocese	4
Priests: Retired, Sick or Absent	50
Number of Diocesan Priests	149
Religious Priests in Diocese	169
Total Priests in Diocese	318
Extern Priests in Diocese	20
Ordinations:	
Religious Priests	2
Transitional Deacons	3
Permanent Deacons	7
Permanent Deacons in Diocese	38
Total Brothers	82
Total Sisters	487
Parishes	
Parishes	124
With Resident Pastor:	
Resident Diocesan Priests	75
Resident Religious Priests	35
Without Resident Pastor:	
Administered by Priests	9
Administered by Deacons	1
Administered by Lay People	3
Completely Vacant	1
Missions	24
Pastoral Centers	1
Professional Ministry Personnel:	
Brothers	1
Sisters	15
Lay Ministers	182
Welfare	
Catholic Hospitals	9
Total Assisted	1,943,612
Health Care Centers	7
Total Assisted	86,687
Homes for the Aged	8
Total Assisted	1,619
Day Care Centers	4
Total Assisted	1,229
Specialized Homes	6
Total Assisted	869
Special Centers for Social Services	17
Total Assisted	1,327,475
Residential Care of Disabled	3
Total Assisted	86
Educational	
Seminaries, Diocesan	1
Students from This Diocese	19
Students from Other Diocese	123
Diocesan Students in Other Seminaries	5
Students Religious	40
Total Seminarians	64
Colleges and Universities	2
Total Students	4,856
High Schools, Diocesan and Parish	3
Total Students	1,495
High Schools, Private	7
Total Students	3,593
Elementary Schools, Diocesan and Parish	41
Total Students	8,639
Elementary Schools, Private	2
Total Students	451
Catechesis/Religious Education:	
High School Students	3,654
Elementary Students	11,847
Total Students under Catholic Instruction	34,599
Teachers in the Diocese:	
Priests	59
Brothers	17
Sisters	50
Lay Teachers	1,471
Vital Statistics	
Receptions into the Church:	
Infant Baptism Totals	5,558
Adult Baptism Totals	705
Received into Full Communion	624
First Communions	4,864
Confirmations	2,615
Marriages:	
Catholic	750
Interfaith	468
Total Marriages	1,218
Deaths	1,911
Total Catholic Population	389,345
Total Population	3,038,600

Former Bishops—Most Revs. FRANCIS NORBERT BLANCHET, D.D., First Vicar Apostolic of Oregon Territory; consecrated July 25, 1845, Titular Bishop of Drasa; appt. Archbishop of Oregon City, July 24, 1846 when the Vicariate was erected into an ecclesiastical province; resigned 1880; died June 18, 1883; CHARLES JOHN SEGHERS, D.D., consecrated June 29, 1873; Bishop of Vancouver Island, British Columbia; coadjutor to the Archbishop of Oregon City, Dec. 10, 1880; Archbishop, Dec. 20, 1880; resigned 1884; and transferred to Vancouver Island, British Columbia; died Nov. 28, 1886; WILLIAM H. GROSS, C.SS.R., D.D., Archbishop of Oregon City; consecrated Bishop of Savannah, GA April 27, 1873; promoted by His Holiness Leo XIII Feb. 1, 1885 from Savannah to the Archiepiscopal See of Oregon City;; died Nov. 14, 1898; ALEXANDER CHRISTIE, D.D., Archbishop of Oregon City; consecrated June 29, 1898, Bishop of Vancouver Island, B.C.; promoted by His Holiness Leo XIII February 12, 1899 from Vancouver Island to the Archiepiscopal See of Oregon City;; died April 6, 1925; EDWARD D. HOWARD, D.D., LL.D., Titular Archbishop of Albule; ord. June 12, 1906; consecrated Titular Bishop of Isauria and Auxiliary Bishop of Davenport, April 6, 1924; appt. to the See of Oregon City, April 30, 1926; asst. at the Pontifical Throne, May 2, 1939;; transferred to the Titular See of Albule and as Archbishop of Portland in Oregon, Dec. 9, 1966; died Jan. 2, 1983; ROBERT JOSEPH DWYER, D.D., Ph.D., ord. June 11, 1932; consecrated Bishop of Reno, August 5, 1952; appt. Archbishop of Portland in Oregon Dec. 9, 1966; resigned Jan. 22, 1974; died March 24, 1976; CORNELIUS MICHAEL POWER, D.D., J.C.D. (Retired), ord. June 3, 1939; appt. Bishop of Yakima, Feb. 5, 1969; consecrated May 1, 1969; appt. Archbishop of Portland in Oregon, Jan. 22, 1974; retired July 3, 1986; died May 22, 1997; WILLIAM J. LEVADA, S.T.D., ord. Dec. 20, 1961; appt. Titular Bishop of Capri and Auxiliary Bishop of Los Angeles, March 29, 1983; appt. Archbishop of Portland in Oregon, July 1, 1986; installed Sept. 21, 1986; appt. Coadjutor Archbishop of San Francisco, Aug. 17, 1995; transferred to Oct. 24, 1995; FRANCIS E. GEORGE, O.M.I., Ph.D., S.T.D., ord. Dec. 21, 1963; appt. Bishop of Yakima July 10, 1990; installed Sept. 21, 1990; appt. Archbishop of Portland in Oregon, April 29, 1996; installed May 27, 1996; appt. Archbishop of Chicago April 8, 1997; installed May 7, 1997.

Office of the Archbishop

Archdiocesan Pastoral Center—2838 E. Burnside St., Portland, 97214-1895. Tel: 503-234-5334; Fax: 503-234-2545.

Vicars and Directors

Vicar General and Moderator of the Curia—Rev. DENNIS O'DONOVAN, Pastoral Center, 2838 E. Burnside St., Portland, 97214. Tel: 503-233-8331; Fax: 503-234-2545.

Vicar for Clergy—Rev. PATRICK BRENNAN.

Finance Officer—LEONARD VUYLSTEKE.

Department Directors—

Business Affairs—PAULETTE FURNESS.

Clergy—Rev. PATRICK BRENNAN.

Education—ROBERT MIZIA.

Chancellor/Public Services—MARY JO TULLY.

Pastoral Services—Rev. MICHAEL MASLOWSKY.

Evangelization—Deacon THOMAS GORNICK.

Chancellor—MARY JO TULLY.

College of Consultors—Most Revs. JOHN G. VLAZNY, D.D.; KENNETH D. STEINER, D.D.; Rev. Msgr. FRANK CAMPBELL; Revs. JOSEPH BROWNE, C.S.C.; DONALD BUXMAN; JOSEPH JACOBBERGER; CHARLES LIENERT; GREGORY MOYS; DENNIS O'DONOVAN; PAUL PERI; GEORGE WOLF.

Area Vicars—Revs. JOSEPH JACOBBERGER, Downtown Portland; ROBERT KRUEGER, Northeast Portland; ROBERT BARRICKS, Southeast Portland; RICHARD SIRIANNI, East Portland Suburban; CARL FLACH, J.C.L., South Portland Suburban; RICHARD ROSSMAN, West Portland Suburban; WAYNE FORBES, Beaverton Suburban; TERRY O'CONNELL, Yamhill County; LOUIS URBANSKI, Tualatin Valley; JOSEPH BROWNE, C.S.C., Columbia County; NICHOLAS NILEMA, A.L.C.P., North Coast; DAVID ZEGER, Marion County; GEORGE WOLF, Metropolitan Salem; PANNEER SELVAM, Santiam; JOHN HENDERSON, O.F.M.Conv., Albany-Corvallis; STEPHEN CLOVIS, Metropolitan Eugene; VACANT, Middle Coast; Revs. HEIKO JUNGE, South Coast; JUNIPER SCHNEIDER, O.F.M.Conv., Southern Oregon.

Personnel Board—Revs. WAYNE FORBES; DON BUXMAN; PAUL PERI; MARK BACHMEIER; MICHAEL JOHNSTON; PATRICK BRENNAN, Ex Officio; DENNIS O'DONOVAN; SLIDER STEVERNOL.

Tribunal

Judicial Vicar—Rev. PATRICK BRENNAN, J.C.L.; LINDA WEIGEL, J.C.L., Dir. Tel: 503-233-8380.

Adjutant Judicial Vicar—Revs. CARL FLACH, J.C.L.; KELLY VANDEHEY, J.C.L.

Judges—Revs. PATRICK BRENNAN, J.C.L.; CARL J. FLACH; CARL GIMPL; THOMAS BROCKHAUS, O.S.B., J.C.D.; JOSEPH JACOBBERGER; MICHAEL JOHNSTON; JAMES MAYO; MICHAEL PATRICK, J.C.L.; KELLY VANDEHEY, J.C.L.

Defenders of the Bond—Rev. GREGORY MOYS; Sr. MAUREEN ABBOTT, S.P.; LINDA WEIGEL, J.C.L.

Auditor—ALEXANDRIA GUERRA-SUNDBERG.

Case Instructor—Sr. MAUREEN ABBOTT, S.P.

Notaries—MARGARET PALMER; SUSAN OUFFOUE; LYNN HOFFMANN.

Advocates— Priests and pastoral ministers by appointment

Archdiocesan Offices and Agencies

Archives—DAN HASKINS. Tel: 503-233-8334. 2838 E. Burnside St., Portland, 97214-1895.

Building Commission—Most Rev. JOHN G. VLAZNY, D.D.; Revs. THEODORE WEBER, Chm. (Retired); DENNIS O'DONOVAN; JOSEPH HEUBERGER; LESLIE SIEG; JOHN BROCKAMP; FRED SHIPMAN; ROBERT BOILEAU; JOSEPH GEHLEN; MICHAEL KINNE; DAVID HODGIN; PAULETTE FURNESS, Ex Officio; KEN SCOTT, Sec. Tel: 503-234-5334.

Business Affairs—PAULETTE FURNESS, Dir., 2838 E. Burnside St., Portland, 97214-1895. Tel: 503-234-5334.

Campus Ministry—Rev. MICHAEL MASLOWSKY, Dir., 2838 E. Burnside St., Portland, 97214-1895. Tel: 503-233-8385.

Catholic Charities, Inc.—DENNIS KEENAN, Exec. Dir., 231 S.E. 12th Ave., Portland, 97214-1342. Tel: 503-231-4866.

Catholic Deaf Ministry—Sr. LINDA ROBY, B.V.M., Dir., 2838 E. Burnside St., Portland, 97214. Tel: 503-233-8398 (V/TTY).

"Catholic Sentinel"— (Official Newspaper of the Archdiocese), Most Rev. JOHN G. VLAZNY, D.D., Publisher-in-Chief; JOHN J. LIMB, Publisher; ROBERT PFOHMAN, Editor, 5536 N.E. Hassalo, Portland, 97213-3638. Tel: 503-281-1191.

Catholic Youth Organization—Sr. KRISTA VON BORSTELL, S.S.M.O., Exec. Dir., Oregon Plaza, 825 N.E. 20th Ave., Ste. 320, Portland, 97232. Tel: 503-231-9484.

Cemeteries—TIM CORBETT, Supt., Mt. Calvary Cemetery, 333 S.W. Skyline Blvd., Portland, 97221. Tel: 503-292-6621.

Clergy Personnel—Rev. PATRICK BRENNAN, Vicar for Clergy, 2838 E. Burnside St., Portland, 97214-1895. Tel: 503-233-8366.

Communications—BUD BUNCE, Dir., 2838 E. Burnside St., Portland, 97214-1895. Tel: 503-233-8373.

Continuing Education for Clergy—Rev. SLIDER STEURNOL, Dir. Board Members: Revs. ELWIN SCHWAB; MICHAEL SPRAUER; TODD MOLINARI; DICK ROSSMAN; PATRICK BRENNAN; PAT DONOGHUE, 2838 E. Burnside St., Portland, 97214-1895. Tel: 503-234-5334.

Diaconate Office—Rev. RICHARD HUNEGER, Dir.; Deacon VERN KORCHINSKI, Assoc. Dir., 2838 E. Burnside St., Portland, 97214-1895. Tel: 503-233-8344.

Ecumenical and Interreligious Affairs—Rev. RICHARD SIRIANNI, Dir.; MARY JO TULLY, Assoc. Dir., 2838 E. Burnside St., Portland, 97214. Tel: 503-233-8323.

Evangelization—Deacon THOMAS GORNICK, Dir., 2838 E. Burnside St., Portland, 97214-1895. Tel: 503-233-8335.

Finance Council—Most Rev. JOHN G. VLAZNY, D.D.; Revs. PAUL PERI; PATRICK WALSH; DENNIS O'DONOVAN; DOUG WHITE; DONNA RAGAN; PAULETTE FURNESS; DOUG TOLLEFSON; ARTHUR SCHULTE JR., Ph.D.; BOBBIE DORE FOSTER; MIKE PAUL; ROBERT BELDING; REX WARDLAW; CAMERON WILLIAMS; CAROLYN WINTERS; MYRON FLECK; LEONARD VUYLSTEKE, Chm.; GARRETT MORGAN; EDWARD HERINCKX, 2838 E. Burnside St., Portland, 97214-1895. Tel: 503-233-8350.

Financial Services—LEONARD VUYLSTEKE, Dir., 2838 E. Burnside St., Portland, 97214-1895. Tel: 503-233-8359.

Hispanic Ministries—RAUL VELAZQUEZ, Dir., 2838 E. Burnside St., Portland, 97214. Tel: 503-233-8324.

Historical Commission—MARY-CATHERINE CUTHILL, Pres., 2838 E. Burnside St., Portland, 97214-1895.

Holy Childhood, Pontifical Association of—MARY JO TULLY, Dir., 2838 E. Burnside St., Portland, 97214-1895. Tel: 503-233-8323.

Housing—Rev. MICHAEL MASLOWSKY, Dir., 3825 S.E. 80th Ave., Ste. 104, Portland, 97206. Tel: 503-245-7970.

Human Resources—BARBARA BALTZ, Dir., 2838 E. Burnside St., Portland, 97214-1895. Tel: 503-234-5334.

Justice and Peace—ANTHONY GRANADOS, Coord., 2838 E. Burnside St., Portland, 97214-1895. Tel: 503-233-8361.

Liturgical Commission—Revs. PAUL PERI, Chm.; JOHN DOMIN; Sr. JEREMY GALLET, S.P., Ex Officio; Revs. JAMES MAYO; JOSEPH S. MCMAHON; RICHARD RUTHERFORD, C.S.C.; Sr. LORETTA SCHAFF, O.S.F.; MARY JO TULLY; AGNES ZUEGER; SUE HALLET, 2838 E. Burnside St., Portland, 97214-1895.

Marriage and Family Life Office—JAY WONACOTT, Dir., 2838 E. Burnside St., Portland, 97214-1895. Tel: 503-233-8393.

Ministry Formation—Rev. PAUL PERI, Dir., Griffith Center, 11957 S.E. Fuller Rd., Milwaukie, 97222. Tel: 503-652-3765.

Mission Office—MARY JO TULLY, Dir., 2838 E. Burnside St., Portland, 97214-1895. Tel: 503-233-8323.

Oregon Catholic Conference—Most Revs. JOHN G. VLAZNY, D.D., Pres.; ROBERT F. VASA, Vice Pres.; ROBERT CASTAGNA, Gen. Counsel & Exec. Dir., 2838 E. Burnside St., Portland, 97214-1895. Tel: 503-233-8387.

Oregon Catholic Press—Most Rev. JOHN G. VLAZNY, D.D., Publisher-in-Chief; JOHN J. LIMB, Publisher, 5536 N.E. Hassalo, Portland, 97213-3638. Tel: 503-281-1191.

Pastoral Services—Rev. MICHAEL MASLOWSKY, Dir., 2838 E. Burnside St., Portland, 97214-1895. Tel: 503-233-8385.

People with Disabilities—DOROTHY DESMARTEAU-COUGHLIN, Dir., 2838 E. Burnside St., Portland, 97214-1895. Tel: 503-233-8399 (V/TTY).

Pro-Life Activities—Rev. MICHAEL MASLOWSKY, Dir., 2838 E. Burnside St., Portland, 97214-1895. Tel: 503-233-8385.

Project Rachel—447 N.E. 47th Ave., Ste. 100, Portland, 97213. Tel: 800-249-8074.

Propagation of the Faith, Pontifical Society for the—MARY JO TULLY, Dir., 2838 E. Burnside St., Portland, 97214-1895. Tel: 503-233-8323.

Religious Education—CATHY SHANNON, Dir., 2838 E. Burnside St., Portland, 97214-1895. Tel: 503-233-8304.

Refugee Resettlement—CECILIA BARICEVIC, 231 S.E. 12th Ave., Portland, 97214-9813. Tel: 503-231-4866.

Resource Development—DOUG TOLLEFSON, Dir., 2838 E. Burnside St., Portland, 97214-1895. Tel: 503-233-8336.

St. Mary's Home for Boys—EMMA DENNIS, Exec. Dir., 16535 S.W. Tualatin Valley Hwy., Beaverton, 97006. Tel: 503-649-5651.

School Office—ROBERT MIZIA, Supt. Tel: 503-233-8300; VACANT, Asst. Supt., School Personnel & Technology; Sr. RITA RAE SCHNEIDER, R.S.M., Asst. Supt., Faith Formation & Curriculum, 2838 E. Burnside St., Portland, 97214-1895.

Special Projects—TODD COOPER, Dir., 2838 E. Burnside St., Portland, 97214-1895. Tel: 503-233-8386.

Stewardship Office—DOUG TOLLEFSON, Dir., 2838 E. Burnside St., Portland, 97214-1895. Tel: 503-233-8333.

Victim Assistance Coordinator—CATHY SHANNON. Tel: 503-416-8810. Email: cshannon@archdpdx.org.

Vocations—Rev. KELLY VANDEHEY, J.C.L., Dir., 2838 E. Burnside St., Portland, 97214-1895. Tel: 503-233-8368.

Worship—Sr. JEREMY GALLET, S.P., Dir., 2838 E. Burnside St., Portland, 97214-1895. Tel: 503-233-8342.

Youth and Young Adult Ministry—RANDY KOLLARS, Dir., 2838 E. Burnside St., Portland, 97214-1895. Tel: 503-233-8395.

CLERGY, PARISHES, MISSIONS AND PAROCHIAL SCHOOLS

CITY OF PORTLAND
(MULTNOMAH COUNTY)

PORTLAND

1—CATHEDRAL OF THE IMMACULATE CONCEPTION (1851), Rev. Joseph Jacobberger; Kelly Vandehey, J.C.L.; Deacons John Ries; Thomas Gornick.
Res.: 1716 N.W. Davis St., 97209. Tel: 503-228-4397; Fax: 503-242-2568.
School—110 N.W. 17th Ave., 97209. Tel: 503-227-4297; Fax: 503-243-3819. Order of Servants of Mary 2; Lay Teachers 10; Students 225.
Catechesis/Religious Program—Students 50.

2—ST. AGATHA (1911), Revs. Slider Steuernol; Timothy Mockaitis.
Office—1430 S.E. Nehalem St., 97202. Tel: 503-236-4747; Fax: 503-236-6407.
School—(Grades PreK-8) Tel: 503-234-5500; Fax: 503-234-7240. Lay Teachers 10; Students 178.
Catechesis/Religious Program—Students 18.

3—ALL SAINTS (1917), Rev. Richard Thompson.
Res.: 3847 N.E. Glisan, 97232. Tel: 503-232-4305; Fax: 503-238-8847.
School—601 N.E. 39th Ave., 97232. Tel: 503-236-6205; Fax: 503-236-0781. Lay Teachers 32; Students 426.
Catechesis/Religious Program—Students 59.

4—ST. ANDREW (1907), Rev. Robert W. Krueger.
Res.: 806 N.E. Alberta St., 97211. Tel: 503-281-4429; Fax: 503-281-4411.
Catechesis/Religious Program—Students 30.

5—ST. ANTHONY (1917), Rev. James Aidan Mayo.
Res.: 3600 S.E. 79th Ave., 97206. Tel: 503-771-6039; Fax: 503-772-0107.
Catechesis/Religious Program—Students 27.

6—ASCENSION (1892), Revs. Paul Botenhagen, O.F.M.; Armando Lopez, O.F.M. In Res., Rev. Loren Kerkof, O.F.M.
Church: 7507 S.E. Yamhill, 97215. Tel: 503-256-3897; Fax: 503-257-4681.
Res.: 404 S.E. 68th, 97215. Tel: 503-253-8305.
Catechesis/Religious Program—Tel: 503-256-3897; Fax: 503-257-4681. Students 110.

7—ASSUMPTION (1909), Closed. For inquiries for parish records contact the chancery., (North Portland Catholic Community)

8—ST. BIRGITTA (1954), Rev. Joseph P. Browne, C.S.C.
Res.: 11820 N.W. St. Helens Rd., 97231-2319. Tel: 503-286-3929.
Chapel—Portland, Chapel of Our Lady of Sinj
Catechesis/Religious Program—Students 51.

9—BLESSED SACRAMENT (1913), Closed., For inquiries for parish records please contact Holy Cross, Portland (North Portland Catholic Community).

10—ST. CHARLES (1914), Rev. Agnelo Gomes, S.F.X.; Kathy Truman, Pastoral Assoc.
Parish Center—5310 N.E. 42nd, 97218. Tel: 503-281-6461; Fax: 503-281-6828.
Catechesis/Religious Program—Students 71.

11—CHURCH OF ST. JOSEPH THE WORKER (1885), Rev. John Amsberry.
Res.: 2310 S.E. 148th, 97233. Tel: 503-761-8710; Fax: 503-761-8545.
Catechesis/Religious Program—Tel: 503-762-2704. Students 145.

12—CHURCH OF ST. MICHAEL THE ARCHANGEL (1894),

(Italian), Rev. Paul Peri; Patricia Bellamah, Pastoral Assoc.
Res.: 424 S.W. Mill St., 97201. Tel: 503-228-8629; Fax: 503-827-7689.

13—ST. CLARE (1913), Rev. Thomas B. Farley.
Res.: 8535 S.W. 19th Ave., 97219. Tel: 503-244-1037; Fax: 503-246-2665.
School—Tel: 503-244-7600; Fax: 503-293-2076. Lay Teachers 13; Students 227.
Catechesis/Religious Program—Students 163.

14—ST. ELIZABETH OF HUNGARY (1953), Rev. James Kolb.
Res.: 4112 S.W. Sixth Ave. Dr., 97239. Tel: 503-222-2168; Fax: 503-274-2438.

15—ST. FRANCIS OF ASSISI (1876), Rev. Charles J. Lienert, Moderator; Valerie Chapman, Pastoral Admin.; Sr. Denise Anderson, Pastoral Assoc.
Res.: 330 S.E. 11th Ave., 97214. Tel: 503-232-5880; Fax: 503-232-6449.
Catechesis/Religious Program—Students 9.

16—HOLY CROSS (1901), Rev. David Gutmann. (North Portland Catholic Community.)
Office:—5227 N. Bowdoin St., 97203. Tel: 503-289-2834; Fax: 503-283-7056.
School—Tel: 503-289-3010; Fax: 503-286-5006. Sisters 3; Lay Teachers 11; Students 199.
Chapel—Christ The Teacher, University of Portland 5000 N. Willamette Blvd., 97203. Tel: 503-283-7311; Fax: 503-283-7399.
Catechesis/Religious Program—Students 62.

17—HOLY FAMILY (1931), Rev. Robert Barricks.
3732 S.E. Knapp, 97202. Tel: 503-774-1428; 503-788-2051; Fax: 503-774-1854.
Res.: Tel: 503-788-2051.
School—Tel: 503-774-8871; Fax: 503-774-8872. Kathleen Lockie, Prin. Lay Teachers 16; Students 224.
Catechesis/Religious Program—Tel: 503-774-7804 (Youth). Students 100.

18—HOLY REDEEMER (1906), Revs. Joseph V. Corpora, C.S.C.; Bradley Metz, C.S.C.; Bro. Ronald Whelan; Deacon Lou Del Fra.
Res.: 25 N. Portland Blvd., 97217. Tel: 503-285-4539; Fax: 503-285-0666.
School—Tel: 503-283-5197; Fax: 503-283-9479. Sisters of the Holy Names of Jesus and Mary 6; Franciscan Sisters 1; Lay Teachers 16; Students 348.
Catechesis/Religious Program—Students 70.

19—HOLY ROSARY PARISH & DOMINICAN PRIORY (1894), Very Rev. Anthony M. Patalano, O.P. (LA), Pastor & Prior; Revs. Paul Raftery, O.P.; Aquinas Costello, O.P.; Louis O'Halloran, O.P.; James Glavin, Parish Admin.
1333 N.E. MLK Jr. Blvd., 97232. In Res., Revs. Paul A. Duffner, O.P.; Gregory M. Anderson, O.P.; LaSalle Hallissey, O.P. (OAK).
Res.: 375 N.E. Clackamas St., 97232. Tel: 503-235-3163; Fax: 503-235-3164.
Confraternity of the Most Holy Rosary—P.O. Box 3617, 97208. Tel: 503-236-8393; Fax: 503-236-8394.
Catechesis/Religious Program—Students 190.

20—ST. IGNATIUS (1907), [JC] Revs. Peter Byrne, S.J.; Dan Mai, S.J.
Res.: 3400 S.E. 43rd Ave., 97206. Tel: 503-777-1491; Fax: 503-777-3142.
School—3330 S.E. 43rd St., 97206. Tel: 503-774-5533; Fax: 503-788-1134. Sisters of the Holy Names of Jesus and Mary 2; Lay Teachers 13; Students 227.
Convent—Sisters of the Holy Names of Jesus and Mary, 4130 S.E. Brooklyn, 97206. Tel: 503-231-6538. Sisters 4.
Catechesis/Religious Program—Students 67.

21—IMMACULATE HEART OF MARY (1885), Rev. Nicolaus Marandu.
Res.: 2926 N. Williams Ave., 97227-1628. Tel: 503-287-3724; Fax: 503-287-5011.
Catechesis/Religious Program—Students 27.

22—ST. JOHN FISHER (1959), Rev. Wayne A. Forbes; Scott Kolbet, Pastoral Assoc. Tel: 503-244-5784.
Res.: 7007 S.W. 46th Ave., 97219. Tel: 503-246-4686; Fax: 503-452-8570.
School—Tel: 503-246-3234; Fax: 503-246-4117. Lay Teachers 13; Aides 6; Students 257.
Catechesis/Religious Program—Tel: 503-244-5784; Fax: 503-452-8570. Students 88.

23—ST. JUAN DIEGO (2002), Rev. John Kerns; Kathy Yee, Pastoral Assoc.
Church: 1280 N.W. Saltzman Rd., 97229. Tel: 503-644-1617; Fax: 503-626-6540.

24—KOREAN MARTYRS CATHOLIC CHURCH (1990), (Korean), [JC] Rev. Chrysostom Sung-Joo Kim.
Res.: 10840 S.E. Powell Blvd., 97266. Tel: 503-762-6880; Fax: 503-760-6601.
Catechesis/Religious Program—Tel: 503-661-8468. Students 99.

25—ST. MARY MAGDALENE (1911),, (The Madeleine) Rev. E. B. Painter, S.J.
Res.: 3123 N.E. 24th Ave., 97212. Tel: 503-281-5777; Fax: 503-281-0673.
School—3240 N.E. 23rd Ave., 97212. Tel: 503-288-9197; Fax: 503-280-1196. Bernadette Kunnen, Prin.; Marietta Debruhl, Vice Prin. Sisters of the Holy Name 2; Lay Teachers 16; Students 243.
Catechesis/Religious Program—Students 60.

26—OUR LADY OF LAVANG (1999), (Vietnamese), Revs. James Pham-Van-Ninh, S.E.; Joseph Nguyen Duc Hau, S.E.; Peter Hoang Thai Binh.
5404 N.E. Alameda Dr., 97213. Tel: 503-249-5892; Fax: 503-249-1776.
Catechesis/Religious Program—Students 819.

27—OUR LADY OF SORROWS (1917), Rev. Amancio Rodrigues.
Res.: 5221 S.E. Knight St., 97206. Tel: 503-775-6731; Fax: 503-775-6732.
School—Tel: 503-771-3592; Fax: 503-774-5390. Sisters 2; Lay Teachers 10; Students 203.
Catechesis/Religious Program—Students 15.

28—ST. PATRICK (1885), Revs. James Aidan Mayo, Admin.; Ronald P. Raab, C.S.C.
Res.: 1623 N.W. 19th Ave., 97209. Tel: 503-222-4086; Fax: 503-222-6642.

29—ST. PETER (1911), Rev. Dale T. Waddell; Brendan Mallon, Pastoral Assoc.; Teresa Ramirez Sanchez, Hispanic Min.
Mailing Address: 8648 S.E. Foster Rd., 97266. Tel: 503-777-3321; Fax: 503-777-3321.
Res.: 5736 S.E. 86th St., 97266. Tel: 503-777-1026.
Catechesis/Religious Program—Tel: 503-777-3322. Students 155.

30—ST. PHILIP NERI (1912), Revs. Stephen E. Bossi, C.S.P.; Richard Colgan, C.S.P. (BO). In Res., Revs. Vincent J. Sampietro, C.S.P.; Broderick Walsh, C.S.P.
Res.: 2408 S.E. 16th Ave., 97214. Tel: 503-231-4955; Fax: 503-736-1383.
Catechesis/Religious Program—Students 30.

31—ST. PIUS X (Cedar Mill) (1953), Revs. Ronald C. Millican; Joseph Hoang; Deacon Robert Little.
Office—1280 N.W. Saltzman Rd., 97229. Tel: 503-644-5264; Fax: 503-626-6540.
School—1260 N.W. Saltzman Rd., 97229. Tel: 503-644-3244; Fax: 503-646-6568. Lay Teachers 13; Students 268.
Catechesis/Religious Program—Tel: 503-626-3154. Students 716.

32—QUEEN OF PEACE, Closed. For inquiries for parish records contact the chancery., (North Portland Catholic Community.)

33—ST. RITA (1924), Rev. Patrick Brennan; Chris Kresek, Admin.
Mailing Address: 10029 N.E. Prescott St., 97220. Tel: 503-252-3403; Fax: 503-256-9682.
Catechesis/Religious Program—Students 12.

34—ST. ROSE OF LIMA (1911), Rev. Richard J. Hunteger; Deacon Donald Ciffone.
Res.: 2727 N.E. 54th Ave., 97213. Tel: 503-281-5318; Fax: 503-284-8350.
School—Archbishop Howard School, Tel: 503-281-1912; Fax: 503-281-0554. Lay Teachers 12; Students 283.
Catechesis/Religious Program—Students 79.

35—SACRED HEART (1893), Rev. Bruce Brown, Admin.
Res.: 3910 S.E. 11th Ave., 97202. Tel: 503-231-9636; Fax: 503-231-1766.
Catechesis/Religious Program—Students 11.

36—ST. STANISLAUS (1907), (Polish), Rev. Henry Kociolek, S.Ch.
Res.: 3916 N. Interstate Ave., 97227-1063. Tel: 503-281-7532; Fax: 503-281-7532.
Catechesis/Religious Program—Christ Our Life Students 95.

37—ST. STEPHEN (1907), Rev. Stephen Stobie.
Res.: 1112 S.E. 41st Ave., 97214. Tel: 503-234-5019; Fax: 503-239-5985.

38—ST. THERESE OF THE CHILD JESUS (1955), Rev. Jacob A. Mosbrucker; Deacon Vernard Korchinski, Pastoral Assoc.
Res.: 1260 N.E. 132nd Ave., 97230. Tel: 503-256-5850; Fax: 503-253-3560.
School—Tel: 503-253-9400; Fax: 503-253-9571. Dominican Sisters of Mission San Jose 2; Lay Teachers 12; Students 260.
Catechesis/Religious Program—Students 65.

39—ST. THOMAS MORE (1935), Rev. Michael P. Johnston.
Church: 3525 S.W. Patton Rd., 97221. Tel: 503-222-2055; Fax: 503-242-1831.
School—Tel: 503-222-6105; Fax: 503-227-5661. Lay Teachers 16; Students 225.
Catechesis/Religious Program—Students 112.

40—ST. VINCENT DE PAUL (1919),, (Downtown Chapel), Rev. Robert J. Loughery C.S.C. In Res., Rev. Ronald P. Raab, C.S.C.
Res.: 601 W. Burnside St., 97209. Tel: 503-228-0746; Fax: 503-972-1063.

OUTSIDE THE CITY OF PORTLAND

ALBANY, LINN CO., OUR LADY OF PERPETUAL HELP (1885), Rev. John C. Betts Kathleen Reilly, Pastoral Assoc.
Res.: 728 Ellsworth St., 97321. Tel: 541-926-1449; Fax: 541-926-2191.
School—815 S. Broadalbin. Tel: 541-928-7474; Fax: 541-926-9342. Chris Meadows, Prin. Lay Teachers 6; Students 113.
Catechesis/Religious Program—Tel: 541-926-9327. Ellen Ketsdever, D.R.E. Students 250.

ALOHA, WASHINGTON CO., ST. ELIZABETH ANN SETON (1982), Rev. Louis Urbanski.
Res.: 3145 S.W. 192nd Ave., 97006. Tel: 503-649-9044; 503-649-6211; Fax: 503-848-2915.
Catechesis/Religious Program—Tel: 503-848-3766. Students 300.

ASHLAND, JACKSON CO., OUR LADY OF THE MOUNTAIN (1887), Rev. Joseph Betschart.
Res.: 987 Hillview Dr., 97520. Tel: 541-482-1146; Fax: 541-488-5174.
Catechesis/Religious Program—Students 165.

ASTORIA, CLATSOP CO., ST. MARY, STAR OF THE SEA (1874), [JC] Rev. William C. Moisant.
Res.: 1388 Franklin, 97103. Tel: 503-325-3671 Office; Fax: 503-325-7983.
School—(Grades PreSchool-8) Tel: 503-325-3771. Lay Teachers 11; Students 139.
Mission—St. Francis de Sales 867 5th Ave., Hammond, Clatsop Co. 97121.
Catechesis/Religious Program—Students 57.

BANDON, COOS CO., HOLY TRINITY (1883), [CEM] Rev. Heiko Junge.
Res.: 355 Oregon Ave., 97411. Tel: 541-347-2309; Fax: 541-347-9256.
Mission—St. John the Baptist P.O. Box 884, Port Orford, Curry Co. 97465.
Catechesis/Religious Program—Students 34.

BEAVERTON, WASHINGTON CO.

1—ST. CECILIA (1876), Revs. Scott Vandehey; Peter Fernandes, S.F.X.
Res.: 5105 S.W. Franklin Ave., 97005. Tel: 503-644-2619; Fax: 503-626-7204.
School—Tel: 503-644-2619, Ext. 1; Fax: 503-646-4217. Lay Teachers 17; Students 266.
Catechesis/Religious Program—Students 453.

2—HOLY TRINITY (1962), [CEM] Rev. John Waldron.
Res.: 13715 S.W. Walker Rd., 97005. Tel: 503-643-9528; Fax: 503-644-8486.
School—Tel: 503-644-5748; Fax: 503-643-4475. Lay Teachers 14; Students 268.
Catechesis/Religious Program—Tel: 503-646-0331; Fax: 503-626-2030. Students 211.

BROOKINGS, CURRY CO., STAR OF THE SEA (1923), Rev. Joseph J. Bosch.
Mailing Address: Box 1066, 97415. 820 Old County Rd., 97415. Tel: 541-469-2313; Fax: 541-469-9644.
Mission—St. Charles Borromeo 94323 Gauntlet, P.O. Box 33, Gold Beach, Curry Co. 97444. Tel: 541-247-2453. Rev. Thomas F. Mannion (Retired).
Catechesis/Religious Program—Students 40.

CANBY, CLACKAMAS CO., ST. PATRICK (1882), [CEM] Rev. Thomas D. Yurchak.
Res.: 498 N.W. Ninth, P.O. Box 730, 97013. Tel: 503-266-9411; Fax: 503-263-2293.
Catechesis/Religious Program—488 N.W. 9th, 97013. Tel: 503-266-2401. Students 215.

CENTRAL POINT, JACKSON CO., SHEPHERD OF THE VALLEY (1978), Rev. James Clifford, O.S.A.
Office—600 Beebe Rd., 97502. Tel: 541-664-1050; Fax: 541-664-9312.
Catechesis/Religious Program—Students 99.

COOS BAY, COOS CO., ST. MONICA (1888), Rev. Mike Walker.
Mailing Address: 357 S. 6th St., 97420.
Church: 97420. Tel: 541-267-7421; Fax: 541-267-8491.
Catechesis/Religious Program—Students 83.

COQUILLE, COOS CO., HOLY NAME (1915), Rev. John F. McGuire.
Res.: 12 N. Dean St., 97423. Tel: 541-396-3849.
Catechesis/Religious Program—Students 31.
Mission—Sts. Ann and Michael 209 Second St., Myrtle Point, Coos Co. 97458. Tel: 541-396-3849.
Mission—St. Bridget 580 Third & Spruce, Powers, Coos Co. 97466.

CORNELIUS, WASHINGTON CO., ST. ALEXANDER (1881), (Hispanic), Revs. David J. Schiferl, Admin.; Celso Rodriguez (Mexico).
Mailing Address: P.O. Box 644, 97113. Tel: 503-359-0304; Fax: 503-992-8634.
Res.: 268 N. 17th Ave., 97113. Tel: 503-992-0133.
Catechesis/Religious Program—Tel: 503-357-8240. Students 220.

CORVALLIS, BENTON CO., ST. MARY (1861), [CEM] Most Rev. John Henderson, O.F.M.Conv., O.F.M. Conv. (CHI); Rev. Angel Perez; Deacons Francis Potts; Chris Anderson; Sharon Sever, Contact Person.
Res.: 501 N.W. 25th St., 97330. Tel: 541-757-1988; Fax: 541-757-2788.
Catechesis/Religious Program—Tel: 541-757-1675. Students 534.

COTTAGE GROVE, LANE CO., OUR LADY OF PERPETUAL HELP (1897), Rev. Richard Boyle, O.S.M. (CHI).
Res.: 1025 N. 19th St., 97424. Tel: 541-942-3420; Fax: 541-942-4712.

Mission—St. Philip Benizi 406 Holbrook, Creswell, Lane Co.
Catechesis/Religious Program—406 Holbrook, Creswell, 97426. Betty Krumlauf, D.R.E. Students 76.

DALLAS, POLK CO., ST. PHILIP (1920), [JC] Rev. Gerald Quintal.
Office—825 S.W. Mill St., 97338. Tel: 503-623-2440.
Catechesis/Religious Program—Students 90.

ESTACADA, CLACKAMAS CO., ST. ALOYSIUS (1924), [JC] Rev. Robert J. Palladino.
Res.: P.O. Box 1199, 97023. Tel: 503-630-2416.
Catechesis/Religious Program—Students 57.

EUGENE, LANE CO.

1—ST. JUDE (1969), Rev. John E. McGrann.
Office—4330 Willamette, 97405. Tel: 541-344-1191; Fax: 541-345-6001.
Catechesis/Religious Program—Students 97.

2—ST. MARK (1961), Rev. Daniel Reynolds.
Res.: 1760 Echo Hollow Rd., 97402. Tel: 541-689-0725; Fax: 541-689-0569.
Catechesis/Religious Program—Tel: 541-689-1119. Students 125.

3—ST. MARY (1887), [CEM] Revs. Mark V. Bachmeier; Victor Perez; Deacon Thomas Altenhofen.
Res.: 1062 Charnelton St., 97401. Tel: 541-342-1139; Fax: 541-334-6996.
Catechesis/Religious Program—Students 224.

4—ST. PAUL (1955), Rev. Stephen M. Clovis.
Res.: 1201 Satre St., 97401. Tel: 541-686-2345; Fax: 541-686-0037.
School—Tel: 541-344-1401; Fax: 541-344-2572. Sisters 1; Lay Teachers 18; Students 255.
Catechesis/Religious Program—Students 94.

5—ST. PETER (1955), [JC] Rev. David Ronald Cullings.
Res.: 1150 Maxwell Rd., 97404. Tel: 541-688-1051; Fax: 541-689-0782 (call first).
Catechesis/Religious Program—Tel: 541-689-0782. Students 90.

6—ST. THOMAS MORE (1915),, (Catholic Campus Ministry) Revs. David Orique, O.P.; Reginald Martin, O.P. (SEA), Pastoral Assoc.; Kathleen Horton, Ph.D., Dir. In Res., Rev. Thomas More McGreevy, O.P.
Res.: 1850 Emerald St., 97403. Tel: 541-343-7021; 541-346-4468; Fax: 541-686-8028.
Catechesis/Religious Program—Students 32.

FLORENCE, LANE CO., ST. MARY, OUR LADY OF THE DUNES (1951), Rev. Donald K. Gutmann.
Res.: 85060 U.S. Hwy. 101 S., Box 2640, 97439. Tel: 541-997-2312; Fax: 541-902-0417.
Catechesis/Religious Program—Students 84.

FOREST GROVE, WASHINGTON CO., ST. ANTHONY (1908), [JC] Rev. William Holtzinger; Lani Vandehey, Pastoral Assoc. Tel: 503-357-8147.
Res.: 1660 Elm St., 97116. Tel: 503-357-2989; Fax: 503-357-2217.
Catechesis/Religious Program—Students 128.

GERVAIS, MARION CO., SACRED HEART-ST. LOUIS (1847), [CEM] Rev. Vincent Trujillo, O.S.B.
Res.: 680 Elm Ave., P.O. Box 236, 97026. Tel: 503-792-4231; Fax: 503-792-3749.
School—Tel: 503-792-4541; Fax: 503-792-3826. Nicki Medeiros, Prin. Lay Teachers 5; Students 93.
Catechesis/Religious Program—Tel: 503-463-8525. Students 106.

GRAND RONDE, YAMHILL CO., ST. MICHAEL (1860), Rev. Terry O'Connell.
Res.: 48520 S.W. Hebo Rd., 97347. Tel: 503-843-2206; Fax: 503-843-2206.

GRANTS PASS, JOSEPHINE CO., ST. ANNE (1896), Revs. Gregory Moys; Casmir Onyegwara; Deacons James McVeigh; Robert Chapin; Robert Chapin, Rogue River Catholic Community: P.O. Box 1596, Rogue River, Jackson Co. 97537. Tel: 541-582-1373.
Res.: 1131 N.E. 10th St., 97526. Tel: 541-476-2240; Fax: 541-476-2194.
Parish Center—1133 N.E. 10th St., 97526. Tel: 541-479-4848.
School—(Grades PreK-8) Tel: 541-479-1582; Fax: 541-479-1582. Mr. David Stone, Prin. Lay Teachers 7; Students 115.
Kelly Youth Center—1129 N.E. 10th St., 97526. Tel: 541-476-5802; Fax: 541-476-2240.
Catechesis/Religious Program—Tel: 541-479-4848. Students 217.
Mission—St. Patrick 407 W. River St., Cave Junction, Josephine Co. 97523. Tel: 541-592-3658; Fax: 541-592-3580. Rev. Harry Holwell.

GRESHAM, MULTNOMAH CO.

1—ST. ANNE (1957), Revs. J. Michael Morrissey; Michael I. Kueber.
Res.: 1015 S.E. 182nd Ave., 97233-5099. Tel: 503-665-4935; Fax: 503-661-2116.
Catechesis/Religious Program—Students 185.

2—ST. HENRY (1913), Revs. Richard D. Sirianni; Peter Makalla. In Res., Rev. Charles J. Lienert; Deacon Donald Philip.
Office—346 N.W. First St., 97030. Tel: 503-665-9129; Fax: 503-665-8238.
Catechesis/Religious Program—Students 437.

HILLSBORO, WASHINGTON CO., ST. MATTHEW (1902), [CEM] Revs. Juan Jose Gonzalez, M.Sp.S.; Gerardo Alberto, M.Sp.S.; Celso Marquez, M.Sp.S.
Res.: 475 S.E. 3rd Ave., 97123-4499. Tel: 503-648-1998; Fax: 503-648-4489.
School—Tel: 503-648-2512; Fax: 503-648-4518. Lay Teachers 11; Students 246.
Catechesis/Religious Program—Students 300.

INDEPENDENCE, POLK CO., ST. PATRICK (1908), Rev. Carl Ginpl.
Office—1275 E St., 97351. Tel: 503-838-1242; Fax: 503-838-3856.
Res.: 1258 E St., 97351. Tel: 503-838-5137.
Catechesis/Religious Program—Students 215.

JORDAN, LINN CO., OUR LADY OF LOURDES (1885), [CEM] [JC 2] Rev. Kevin O'Conor, O.M.I., Moderator.
Res.: 39043 Jordan Rd., 97374. Tel: 503-394-2437; Fax: 541-327-2343.
Catechesis/Religious Program—Tel: 503-394-3853; Fax: 503-394-7045. Linda Duman, D.R.E. Students 36.
Mission—St. Patrick 7th St., Lyons, Linn Co. 97358. Fax: 503-394-2603.

JUNCTION CITY, LANE CO., ST. HELEN (1916), [CEM] Rev. Charles E. Zach.
Res.: 1350 W. Sixth Ave., 97448. Tel: 541-998-8053; Fax: 541-998-9474.
Catechesis/Religious Program—Students 80.

KEIZER, MARION CO., ST. EDWARD (1967), Rev. Philip G. Sopke, C.S.C. (FTW).
Office—5303 River Rd. N., 97303. Tel: 503-393-5323; Fax: 503-393-5323.
Catechesis/Religious Program—Fax: 503-463-5439. Students 162.

LAKE OSWEGO, CLACKAMAS CO., OUR LADY OF THE LAKE (1890), [CEM] Revs. Joseph S. McMahon; Peter Smith; Deacon Richard Heames.
Mailing Address: 650 A Ave., 97034-2943. Tel: 503-636-7687; Fax: 503-636-9415.
School—716 A Ave., 97034-2943. Tel: 503-636-2121; Fax: 503-635-7760. Joan M. Codd, Prin. Lay Teachers 15; Students 239.
Catechesis/Religious Program—Tel: 503-636-7687; Fax: 503-636-9415. Students 449.

LEBANON, LINN CO., ST. EDWARD (1903), Rev. Paul P. Maher, O.M.I.; Deacon Richard E. Triska.
Mailing Address: *Office*, 100 Main St., 97355. Tel: 541-258-5333; Fax: 541-258-2511.
Res.: 251 Second St., 97355.
Catechesis/Religious Program—Tel: 541-258-2224. Students 96.

LINCOLN CITY, LINCOLN CO., ST. AUGUSTINE (1925), [CEM] Rev. Mell Stead.
Res.: 1139 N.W. Hwy. 101, 97367. Tel: 541-994-2216 (Call First); Fax: 541-994-2216.
Catechesis/Religious Program—Students 80.

MCMINNVILLE, YAMHILL CO., ST. JAMES (1876), [CEM] Rev. Terry J. O'Connell.
Res.: 1145 E. First St., 97128. Tel: 503-472-5232; Fax: 503-472-4414.
School—Tel: 503-472-2661; Fax: 503-472-5201. Lay Teachers 11; Students 132.
Catechesis/Religious Program—Students 260.
Mission—St. Martin de Porres 407 Ferry St., Dayton, Yamhill Co. 97114. Tel: 503-864-2378; Fax: 503-864-3211.

MEDFORD, JACKSON CO., SACRED HEART OF JESUS (1928), [JC] Revs. Liam Cary; Henry Rufo.
Res.: 449 S. Ivy St., 97501. Tel: 541-779-4661; Fax: 541-774-9474.
School—Tel: 541-772-4105; Fax: 541-732-0633. Perry Martin, Prin. Lay Teachers 19; Students 286.
Mission—St. Joseph 280 N. 4th, Jacksonville, Jackson Co. 97530.
Catechesis/Religious Program—Students 458.

MILWAUKIE, CLACKAMAS CO.

1—CHRIST THE KING (1960), Rev. Donald R. Buxman.
Res.: 7414 S.E. Michael Dr., 97222. Tel: 503-659-1475, Ext. 301; Fax: 503-659-6138.
School—Tel: 503-785-2411; Fax: 503-794-9607. Patty Blackburn, Prin. Lay Teachers 14; Students 243.
Catechesis/Religious Program—Tel: 503-785-2413. Students 170.

2—ST. JOHN THE BAPTIST (1912), Rev. Todd Molinari; Sr. Rae Skinner, S.N.J.M., R.C.I.A. Dir. In Res., Rev. Timothy Murphy.
Res.: 10955 S.E. 25th, 97222. Tel: 503-654-5449; Fax: 503-653-9567.
School—10956 S.E. 25th, 97222. Tel: 503-654-0200; Fax: 503-654-8419. Sisters 1; Lay Teachers 11; Students 195.
Catechesis/Religious Program—Tel: 503-659-2760; Fax: 503-653-9567. Students 137.

MOLALLA, CLACKAMAS CO., ST. JAMES (1962), Rev. R. Ed Coleman.
Res.: 301 Frances St., 97038. Tel: 503-829-2080; Fax: 503-829-2806.
Catechesis/Religious Program—Tel: 503-829-2880. Students 128.

MONROE, BENTON CO., ST. ROSE (1883), [CEM] Rev. Charles E. Zach.
Mailing Address: P.O. Box 516, 97456. Tel: 541-847-5454.
Res.: 00470 S. Fifth, 97456. Tel: 541-847-5454.
Catechesis/Religious Program—Students 33.

MT. ANGEL, MARION CO., ST. MARY (1880), (German), [CEM 2] Rev. Philip Waibel, O.S.B.
Res.: 575 East College St., 97362. Tel: 503-845-2296; Fax: 503-845-2297.
Catechesis/Religious Program—Tel: 503-845-4282; Fax: 503-845-2247. Students 275.
Mission—Holy Rosary [CEM] Scotts Mills, Marion Co.

MYRTLE CREEK, DOUGLAS CO., ALL SOULS (1952), [JC] Rev. William A. Ryan, O.S.A.
Res.: 1242 N.E. Spruce St., P.O. Box 810, 97457. Tel: 541-863-3271; Fax: 541-863-6759.
Catechesis/Religious Program—Students 20.
Mission—Holy Family 243 Marshall Ave., Glendale, Douglas Co. 97442.

NEWBERG, YAMHILL CO., ST. PETER (1909), Rev. James Nibler, O.M.V. (SFD); Matthew Floyd, Pastoral Assoc.
Res.: 2315 N. Main, 97132-6081. Tel: 503-538-4312; Fax: 503-538-5693.
Catechesis/Religious Program—Students 130.

NEWPORT, LINCOLN CO., SACRED HEART PARISH (1889), [JC] Rev. Brian V. Allbright.
Res.: 927 N. Coast Hwy., P.O. Box 843, 97365. Tel: 541-265-5101.
Mission—St. Mary 231 E. Logsden Rd., Siletz, Lincoln Co. 97380. Tel: 541-444-1164.
Catechesis/Religious Program—Tel: 541-265-5101. Students 85.

NORTH BEND, COOS CO., HOLY REDEEMER (1906), [JC] Rev. Karl Schray.
Res.: 2250 16th St., 97459. Tel: 541-756-6901; Fax: 541-756-3234.
Catechesis/Religious Program—Tel: 541-756-0161; 541-756-8904 (Youth Min.). Students 190.

NORTH PLAINS, WASHINGTON CO., ST. EDWARD (1913), [CEM] Most Rev. Kenneth Steiner.
Res.: P.O. Box 507, 97133. Tel: 503-647-2131 (Parish).
Catechesis/Religious Program—Tel: 503-647-2131. Students 65.

OAKRIDGE, LANE CO., ST. MICHAEL (1941), Unassigned.
Res.: 76387 Crestview St., P.O. Box 422, 97463. Tel: 541-782-3262.
Mission—St. Henry [JC] 38925 Dexter Rd., P.O. Box 65, Dexter, Lane Co. 97431. Tel: 541-937-3033.
Catechesis/Religious Program—Students 16.

OREGON CITY, CLACKAMAS CO., ST. JOHN THE APOSTLE (1842), [CEM] Rev. Timothy Mockaitis.
Res.: 417 Washington St., 97045. Tel: 503-742-8200; Fax: 503-742-8219.
School—Tel: 503-742-8230; Fax: 503-742-8239. Macelle Nagel, Prin. Lay Teachers 12; Students 204.
Catechesis/Religious Program—Tel: 503-742-8220; Fax: 503-742-8229. Students 370.

RAINIER, COLUMBIA CO., NATIVITY B.V.M. (1909), Rev. Robert Beltrami, O.F.M.
Res.: 204 E. C St., P.O. Box 340, 97048. Tel: 503-556-5641.
Catechesis/Religious Program—Students 63.
Mission—St. John the Baptist High St., Clatskanie, Columbia Co. 97016.

REDLAND, CLACKAMAS CO., ST. PHILIP BENIZI (1969), Rev. Carl J. Flach.
Res.: 18211 S. Henrici Rd., Oregon City, 97045. Tel: 503-631-2882; Fax: 503-631-7443.
Catechesis/Religious Program—Tel: 503-631-7124. Students 125.

REEDSPORT, DOUGLAS CO., ST. JOHN THE APOSTLE (1924), Rev. Don Gutmann; Charlotte Fogarty, Pastoral Assoc.
Res.: 12 St. Johns Way, 97467. Tel: 541-271-5621.
Catechesis/Religious Program—Students 17.

ROCKAWAY, TILLAMOOK CO., ST. MARY BY THE SEA (1927), [JC] Rev. Jack Morris, S.J.
Mailing Address: P.O. Box 390, 97136.
Church: 275 S. Pacific St.. Tel: 503-355-2661 (Office); Fax: 503-355-9611.
Catechesis/Religious Program—Students 4.

ROSEBURG, DOUGLAS CO., ST. JOSEPH (1867), [CEM] Revs. Juniper Schneider, O.F.M.Conv.; Elwin Schwab; Deacon John H. Stenbeck.
Res.: 800 W. Stanton St., 97470. Tel: 541-673-5157; Fax: 541-672-5022.
School—Tel: 541-672-1751; Fax: 541-673-5229. Lay Teachers 6; Students 71.
Catechesis/Religious Program—Tel: 541-672-7239. Students 115.

ROY, WASHINGTON CO., ST. FRANCIS OF ASSISI (1908), [CEM] Rev. Philip M. Hemming.
Res.: 39135 N.W. Harrington Rd., Banks, 97106. Tel: 503-324-2231.
School—39085 N.W. Harrington Rd., Banks, 97106. Tel: 503-324-2182; Fax: 503-324-7032. Lay Teachers 5; Students 89.
Catechesis/Religious Program—Students 94.

ST. HELENS, COLUMBIA CO., ST. FREDERIC (1910), Rev.

Luan Quach Tran.
Res.: 175 S. 13th St., 97051. Tel: 503-397-0148; Fax: 503-366-3870.
Catechesis/Religious Program—Tel: 503-397-0366. Students 60.

ST. LOUIS, MARION CO., ST. LOUIS, Closed., For sacramental records contact Sacred Heart-St. Louis, Gervias.

ST. PAUL, MARION CO., ST. PAUL (1839), [CEM] Rev. Charles D. Borho.
Res.: 20217 Christie St., N.E., P.O. Box 454, 97137. Tel: 503-633-4611.
School—20327 Christie St., N.E., P.O. Box 188, 97137. Tel: 503-633-4622; Fax: 503-633-4624. Mr. Charles F. Geis, M.A.Ed., Prin. Lay Teachers 7; Students 119.
Catechesis/Religious Program—Students 12.

SALEM, MARION CO.
1—ST. JOSEPH (1864), [JC] Revs. James Coleman; Wayne Dawson; John Luat Nguyen, O.F.M. (SFR).
Res.: 721 Chemeketa St., N.E., 97301. Tel: 503-581-1623; Fax: 503-581-7271.
School—Tel: 503-581-2147; Fax: 503-399-7045. Sisters of the Holy Names of Jesus and Mary 2; Lay Teachers 13; Students 196.
Catechesis/Religious Program—Tel: 503-585-5095. Students 210.
Mission—San Jose, Marion Co. Tel: 503-399-6288.
2—QUEEN OF PEACE (1963), Rev. George Wolf; Darlene Joynt, Pastoral Assoc.; Bryce Herrman, Pastoral Assoc.
Office—P.O. Box 3016, 97302. Tel: 503-364-7202; Fax: 503-364-5882.
School—4227 Lone Oak Rd., S.E.. Tel: 503-362-3443; Fax: 503-589-9411. Debilyn Janota, Prin. Lay Teachers 10; Students 150.
Catechesis/Religious Program—Tel: 503-364-7202; Fax: 503-364-5882. Tricia Boyle, D.R.E. (PreK-Elementary); Martin Gay, D.R.E. & Youth Min., Young Adult (Grades 7-12); Cheri Posedel, D.R.E. & Youth Min., Young Adult (Grades 7-12). Students 335.
3—ST. VINCENT DE PAUL (1925), [JC] Rev. Joseph Heuberger; Sr. Joyce Barsotti, S.S.M.O., Pastoral Assoc.
Res.: 1010 Columbia St., N.E., 97303-5198. Tel: 503-363-4589; Fax: 503-363-9493.
School—Tel: 503-363-8457; Fax: 503-363-1516. Lay Teachers 7; Students 88.
Catechesis/Religious Program—1015 Columbia St. N.E., 97303. Tel: 503-363-2166; Fax: 503-363-2339. Students 149.

SANDY, CLACKAMAS CO., ST. MICHAEL THE ARCHANGEL (1898), Rev. Patrick Walsh.
Res.: 18090 S.E. Langensand Rd., 97055-9427. Tel: 503-668-4446; Fax: 503-668-4446.
Mission—St. John the Evangelist Box 1278, Welches, Clackamas Co. 97067. Tel: 503-622-6338.
Catechesis/Religious Program—Students 93.

SCAPPOOSE, COLUMBIA CO., ST. WENCESLAUS (1911), [CEM] Rev. James R. Stange.
Parish Office—Tel: 503-543-2110; Fax: 503-543-5159.
Res.: 51555 Old Portland Rd., 97056.
Catechesis/Religious Program—Tel: 503-534-7425. Students 126.

SCIO, LINN CO., ST. BERNARD (1912), Rev. Kevin O'Conor, O.M.I.
Res.: P.O. Box 45, 97374. Tel: 503-394-2625.
Catechesis/Religious Program—Students 24.
Mission—St. Thomas 647 Third St., Jefferson, Marion Co. 97352. Tel: 541-327-2343.

SEASIDE, CLATSOP CO., OUR LADY OF VICTORY (1913), Rev. Nicholas Nilema, A.L.C.P.; Deacon Alton Stromberg.
Res.: P.O. Box 29, 97138. Tel: 503-738-6161; Fax: 503-738-6182.
Mission—St. Peter the Fisherman P.O. Box 29, Archcape, Clatsop Co. 97138. Tel: 503-436-2876.
Catechesis/Religious Program—Students 131.

SHADY COVE, JACKSON CO., OUR LADY OF FATIMA (1955), Rev. William McHugh, O.M.I.
Res.: 37 Church Ln., P.O. Box 116, 97539. Tel: 541-878-2479.
Catechesis/Religious Program—Students 41.

SHAW, MARION CO., ST. MARY (1906), [CEM] Rev. G. James Brady, C.S.C.
Mailing Address: P.O. Box 338, Aumsville, 97325-0338. Tel: 503-362-6159; Fax: 503-371-6435.
Res.: 9168 Silver Falls Hwy., S.E., Aumsville, 97325.
Catechesis/Religious Program—Students 35.

SHERIDAN, YAMHILL CO., GOOD SHEPHERD (1908), Revs. Terry O'Connell; Joseph J. Bosch.
Res.: 127 N.E. Hill St., 97378. Tel: 503-843-2206; Fax: 503-843-3048.

SHERWOOD, WASHINGTON CO., ST. FRANCIS (1921), Rev. Thomas McCarthy, S.J.
Mailing Address: P.O. Box 279, 97140. Tel: 503-625-6185; Fax: 503-625-6187.
Res.: 400 S. Pine St., 97140. Tel: 503-625-6186; Fax: 503-625-5914.
Church: 400 N.E. Oregon St., 97140. Tel: 503-625-5914.
Catechesis/Religious Program—Tel: 503-625-6185; Fax: 503-625-6187. Students 296.

SILVERTON, MARION CO., ST. PAUL (1914), [CEM] Rev. William Hammelman, O.S.B.; Deacon Loris A. Buccola.
Res.: 1410 Pine St., 97381. Tel: 503-873-2044; Fax: 503-873-0304.
Catechesis/Religious Program—Students 161.

SPRINGFIELD, LANE CO., ST. ALICE (1947), Rev. Roy L. Antunez, S.J.
Res.: 1520 F St., 97477. Tel: 541-747-7041; Fax: 541-746-5213.
Catechesis/Religious Program—Students 115.

STAYTON, MARION CO., IMMACULATE CONCEPTION (1903), [CEM] Rev. Panneer Selvam.
Res.: 1077 N. Sixth Ave., 97383. Tel: 503-769-2656; Fax: 503-769-5621.
School—Tel: 503-769-2718; Fax: 503-769-0560. Lay Teachers 14; Students 217.
Catechesis/Religious Program—Students 56.

SUBLIMITY, MARION CO., ST. BONIFACE (1879), [CEM] Rev. Patrick Donoghue.
Res.: 375 S.E. Church St., 97385. Tel: 503-769-5664; Fax: 503-769-4292.
Catechesis/Religious Program—Students 83.
Mission—St. Catherine of Siena First & Ivy, Mill City, Marion Co. 97360.
Mission—St. Christopher Santiam Ave., Detroit, Marion Co. 97342.

SUTHERLIN, DOUGLAS CO., ST. FRANCIS XAVIER (1957), Rev. Juniper Schneider, O.F.M.Conv.; Deacon John H. Stenbeck.
Mailing Address: 800 Stanton St., Roseburg, 97470. Tel: 541-673-5157 (Office); Fax: 541-672-5022.

SWEET HOME, LINN CO., ST. HELEN (1953), Rev. Andrew Harris, O.M.I.; Deacon Richard Malone.
Res.: 815 Fifth Ave., 97386. Tel: 541-367-2530.
Catechesis/Religious Program—Tel: 541-367-4700. Students 90.
Mission—Holy Trinity 104 Blakely Ave., P.O. Box 145, Brownsville, Linn Co. 97327.

TIGARD, WASHINGTON CO., ST. ANTHONY (1910), [CEM] Revs. Leslie M. Sieg; Jack Murphy.
Res.: 9905 S.W. McKenzie St., 97223 Tel: 503-639-4179; Fax: 503-624-2364.
School—Fax: 503-620-5117. Jeananne Bloudek, Prin. Tel: 503-639-4179. Lay Teachers 27; Students 400.
Catechesis/Religious Program—Students 557.

TILLAMOOK, TILLAMOOK CO., SACRED HEART (1890), [CEM] Rev. Gary Zerr.
2411 Fifth St., 97141. Tel: 503-842-6647; Fax: 503-842-3897.
Catechesis/Religious Program—Tel: 503-842-8984. Students 141.
Mission—St. Joseph P.O. Box 9, Cloverdale, Tillamook Co. 97112. Tel: 503-392-3685. Rev. Menino George A. Nazareth.

TUALATIN, CLACKAMAS CO., CHURCH OF THE RESURRECTION (1981), Rev. Richard Rossman.
Mailing Address: 21060 S.W. Stafford Rd., 97062. Tel: 503-638-1579; Fax: 503-638-8754.
Catechesis/Religious Program—Students 292.

VENETA, LANE CO., ST. CATHERINE OF SIENA (1954), Rev. Thomas More McGreevy, O.P.; Sue Hallett, Parish Admin.
Res.: 25181 E. Broadway, P.O. Box 277, 97487. Tel: 541-935-3933.
Catechesis/Religious Program—Tel: 541-935-1806. Students 33.

VERBOORT, WASHINGTON CO., VISITATION B.V.M. (1875), (Dutch), [CEM] Rev. Scott Vandehey.
Res.: 4285 N.W. Visitation Rd., Forest Grove, 97116. Tel: 503-357-3860; Fax: 503-359-0819.
School—Tel: 503-357-6990; Fax: 503-359-0819. Lay Teachers 9; Students 118.
Catechesis/Religious Program—Tel: 503-357-4190. Students 118.

VERNONIA, COLUMBIA CO., ST. MARY (1923), Rev. Luan Tran, Moderator; Juanita Dennis, Pastoral Assoc.
Church: 960 Missouri Ave., P.O. Box 312, 97064. Tel: 503-429-8841; Fax: 503-429-8841 (call first).
Catechesis/Religious Program—Tel: 503-429-0311. Students 21.
Mission—Our Lady of the Woods [JC]

WALDPORT, LINCOLN CO., ST. ANTHONY (1949), Rev. Gerard Steckler, S.J., Admin.
Mailing Address: P.O. Box 770, 97394. Tel: 541-563-3246; Fax: 541-563-3734. 685 N. Broadway, 97394.
Catechesis/Religious Program—Students 30.

WILSONVILLE, CLACKAMAS CO., ST. CYRIL (1926), Rev. Daniel Adams.
Res.: 9210 S.W. Fifth St., 97070. Tel: 503-682-2332; Fax: 503-685-9294.
Catechesis/Religious Program—Students 155.

WOODBURN, MARION CO., ST. LUKE (1899), [CEM] Revs. David Zegar; Jaime Rojas (Mexico).
Office and Res.: 417 Harrison St., 97071. Tel: 503-981-1531; 503-981-5011 (office); Fax: 503-981-5012 (office).
School—529 Harrison St., 97071. Tel: 503-981-7441; Fax: 503-982-4697. Lay Teachers 11; Students 172.
Catechesis/Religious Program—Students 210.
Mission—St. Agnes 3052 D St., Hubbard, Marion Co. 97032.

YAMHILL, YAMHILL CO., ST. JOHN (1910), Rev. David Janes, Admin.
Mailing Address: P.O. Box 580, 97148. Tel: 503-662-4291.
Catechesis/Religious Program—Students 69.

SOUTHEAST ASIAN VICARIATE

PORTLAND, MULTNOMAH CO., SOUTHEAST ASIAN VICARIATE (1982),, Please refer to Our Lady of Lavang Church, Portland, OR.

Chaplains of Public Institutions

PORTLAND. *Department of Veterans' Affairs Medical Center*, 3710 S.W. U.S. Veterans' Hospital Rd., Box 1034, 97207. Tel: 503-220-8262; 503-220-8262; Fax: 503-721-1049. Rev. William E. Wickham, C.S.C.
Oregon Health Sciences University, St. Elizabeth, 4112 Sixth Ave., 97201. Tel: 503-222-2168. Rev. Jim Kolb, C.S.P.

ROSEBURG. *U.S. Veterans' Administration Hospital*, 913 N.W. Garden Valley Blvd., 97470-6513. Tel: 541-673-5157. Deacon John Stenbeck.

SALEM. *Hillcrest Youth Correctional Facility*, 2450 Strong Rd., 97302. Tel: 503-986-0421; Fax: 503-986-0473. Rev. Ted Frison.
Mill Creek Correctional Facility, 5465 Turner Rd., 97310-9400. Tel: 503-378-2333. Rev. James Jacobson, S.J.
Oregon State Correctional Institution, 3405 Deer Park Dr., S.E., 97310. Tel: 503-373-0146. Doug Farris, Chap., Christian Church.
Oregon State Penitentiary, 2605 State St., 97310. Tel: 503-378-2333; Fax: 503-378-3897. Rev. James Jacobson, S.J.
Oregon Women's Correction Center, 2809 State St., 97310. Tel: 503-570-6604. Sr. Arnadine Bean, S.N.J.M., Chap.
Santiam Correctional Institution, 4005 Aumsville Hwy., S.E., 97310-9112. Tel: 503-378-2144, Ext. 423; Fax: 503-378-3261. Rev. James Jacobson, S.J., Chap.

SHERIDAN. *Federal Correctional Institution*, 27072 Ballston Rd., 97378-9601. Tel: 503-843-4442, Ext. 256. David Holston, Chap.

WHITE CITY. *U.S. Veternan's Affairs Domiciliary* 97503. Tel: 541-826-2111, Ext. 3321. Revs. Joseph E. Shirey, S.J., Paschal Donald Salisbury, O.P.

WOODBURN. *MacLaren Youth Correctional Facility*, 2630 N. Pacific Hwy., 97071. Tel: 503-986-0421. Rev. Ted Frison.

Special Assignment:
Rev.—
Carey, Raymond, P.O. Box 3019, Salem, 97302. P.O. Box 3019, Salem, 97302.

On Duty Outside the Archdiocese:
Revs.—
Clark, David, St. Jospeh College, Lawrence St., Mill Hill, London NW74JX England.
Dillard, William, St. Rose of Lima Parish, 293 H St., Chula Vista, CA 91910.
King, Martin, 6 ARW/HC, 2204 Administration Ave., MacDill AFB, FL 33621.
Wood, Charles, Brotherhood of the People of Praise, 1353 Cleveland Ave. S., St. Paul, MN 55116.

Absent on Leave:
Revs.—
Cach, Mark, 4310 S.E. King Rd., #246, Milwaukie, 97222.
Galluzzo, James
Knusel, Frank, 34799 N. Honeyman Rd., Scappoose, 97056.

Retired:
Rev. Msgrs.—
Campbell, Francis, St. John Vianney Residence, 4525-A S.W. St. John Vianney Way, Beaverton, 97007.
Thielen, Martin, St. John Vianney Residence, 4655-C S.W. St. John Vianney Way, Beaverton, 97007.
Van Der Zanden, Edmund, St. John Vianney Residence, 4525-C S.W. St. John Vianney Way, Beaverton, 97007.
Revs.—
Altstock, Edward, St. John Vianney Residence, 4630-C S.W. St. John Vianney Way, Beaverton, 97007.
Alvares, Augustine, 12075 Mount Hamilton Rd., San Jose, CA 95140.

Baccellieri, Joseph, 13055 S.E. Stark St., #41, 97233.
Beno, Joseph, 484 S. 17th St., P.O. Box 1012, St. Helens, 97051.
Bliven, Edmond, 3311 S.W. First Ave., 97201.
Brennan, Cathal, 14544 S.E. Brightwood Ave., Milwaukie, 97267.
Brouillard, John, 17704 N.W. Shadyfir Loop, Space 39, Beaverton, 97006.
Brown, Bruce, 6005 Skyline Dr., West Linn, 97068.
Chun, Francis, 4635 S.W. 148th Ave., Beaverton, 97007.
Cieslinski, Robert, St. John Vianney Residence, 4630-D S.W. St. John Vianney Way, Beavertown, 97007.
Crunican, James, Mount St. Joseph Residence, 3060 S.E. Stark St., #383, 97214.
Cunniff, Vincent, St. John Vianney Residence, 4655-D S.W. St. John Vianney Way, Beaverton, 97007.
Denman, Donald, St. John Vianney Residence, 4630-B S.W. St. John Vianney Way, Beaverton, 97007.
DePra, Italo, 1148 Third Ave. #62, Chula Vista, CA 91911.
Dernbach, Arthur, St. John Vianney Residence, 4630-A S.W. St. John Vianney Way, Beaverton, 97007.
Dieringer, James J., P.O. Box 683, Pacific City, 97135.
Domin, John M., 14645 S.W. Farmington, Beaverton, 97007.
Dowd, James, P.O. Box 727, Cottage Grove, 97424.
Durand, Donald, 62 N.W. Ava, Gresham, 97030.
Fleming, Brendan, St. John Vianney Residence, 4525-D. S.W. St. John Vianney Way, Beaverton, 97007.
Fritz, Norbert, McAuley Terrace, 3120 S.E. Stark #3007, 97214.
Gage, Gregory A., 2500 N. Main St., Newberg, 97132.
Gothe, Marcus, St. John Vianney Residence, 4655-B S.W. St. John Vianney Way, Beaverton, 97007.
Hume, Kenneth, 19453 Stillmeadow Dr., Oregon City, 97045.
Hwang, Bernard, O.S.B., 19526 Lazy Creek Ln., Oregon City, 97045.
Jacobson, Gary, St. John Vianney Residence, 4595 S.W. St. John Vianney Way, Beaverton, 97007.
Kennedy, Alan, Maryville Nursing Home, 14645 S.W. Farmington Rd., Beaverton, 97007.
Kies, Emil, Evergreen Court, No. 101, 451 O'Connell St., North Bend, 97459.
Krall, Jack, 1167 N.W. Wallula, Gresham, 97030.
Lau, Michael, 19885 S.W. Oak Ct., Aloha, 97007.
Linehan, Cornelius, 7111 N.E. Broadway, 97213.
Linehan, Jeremiah, 6908 N.E. Tillamook St., 97210.
McHugh, Donald, 1623 S.E. Miller St., 97202.
McKean, Louis, St. John Vianney Residence, 4655-A S.W. St. John Vianney Way, Beaverton, 97007.
McMahon, Joseph M., St. John Vianney Residence, 4525-B St. John Vianney Way, Beaverton, 97007.
Moore, Neil, 1619 N.W. Bridgeway Ln., Beaverton, 97006.
Neuville, Joseph, P.O. Box 586, Aurora, 97002.
Norbort, Fritz, Assumption Village, 9121 N. Burr, 97203.
Park, Morton, Assumption Village, 7411 N. Hudson St., #101, 97203.
Reedy, John J., Maryville Nursing Home, 14645 S.W. Farmington Rd., Beaverton, 97007.
Rodakowski, Louis, P.O. Box 177, Vida, 97488.
Saalfeld, Lawrence, 14506 S.E. Carol Ave., Milwaukie, 97267.
Sassano, Rock, 71403 Fishhawk Rd., Birkenfeld, 97016.
Senko, Martin, 20964 S.W. Rock Rd., Aloha, 97606.
Taaffe, Charles, 1085 Columbia St., N.E., Salem, 97303.
Weber, Theodore, 14460 S.E. Sieben Creek Dr., Clackamas, 97015.
Wraszczak, Chester, Summerplace #204, 15727 N.E. Russell, 97230.

Permanent Deacons:

Allor, Ray, St. Edward, Keizer
Altenhofen, Thomas, St. Mary, Eugene
Anderson, Chris, St. Mary, Corvallis
Bentz, Ron, Our Lady of Lourdes, Scio
Buccola, Loris, St. Paul, Silverton
Burke-Sivers, Harold, Immaculate Heart, Portland
Chapin, Robert L., Jr., St. Anne, Grants Pass
Ciffone, Donald, St. Rose, Portland
Cummings, Owen, (Unassigned)
Diehm, Brian, St. Thomas More, Portland
Filardi, Ronald, Sacred Heart, Medford
Gornick, Thomas, (Unassigned)
Heames, Richard, Our Lady of the Lake, Lake Oswego
Jacob, Ramon, St. Andrew, Portland
Korchinski, Vernard, St. Therese, Portland
Little, Robert, St. Pius X, Portland
Lukosh, Robert, Assumption Chapel, Portland
Luz, John, St. Paul, Eugene
Malone, Richard, St. Helen, Sweet Home
McVeigh, James G., St. Anne, Grants Pass
Mendez, Jose R., St. Joseph, Salem
Morin, Edward, St. Cecilia, Beaverton
Myers, James, Church of Resurrection, Tualatin
Partlow, David, Our Lady of the Lake, Lake Oswego
Philip, Donald, St. Henry, Gresham
Potts, Francis, St. Mary, Corvallis
Richardson, Bill, St. Anthony, Tigard; St. Cecilia, Beaverton
Ries, John D., The Cathedral, Portland
Riherd, John, St. Juan Diego, Portland
Rodriguez, Raul, St. James, McMinnville
Seifer, Leo, St. Mary, Mount Angel
Soper, Leonard, St. Benedict Lodge, McKenzie Bridge
Sorensen, David, St. Mary, Florence
Stenbeck, John H., St. Joseph, Roseburg
Stromberg, Alton, Our Lady of Victory, Seaside
Triska, Richard, St. Edward, Lebanon
Vandercoevering, Allen, St. Joseph, Salem
Vu, an, Our Lady of Sorrows, Portland
Wagner, Daniel, St. Ignatius, Portland

INSTITUTIONS LOCATED IN THE ARCHDIOCESE

[A] SEMINARIES, RELIGIOUS, ARCHDIOCESAN OR SCHOLASTICATES

PORTLAND. *Franciscan Formation Community*, 827 N.E. Alberta, 97211. Tel: 503-287-9223; Fax: 503-282-0644. Email: Postulancy@sbfranciscans.org. Web: www.sbfranciscans.org. Rev. Javier Reyes, O.F.M., Dir. & Contact Person. Priests 2; Postulants 4.

Jesuit Novitiate of St. Francis Xavier, 3301 S.E. 45th Ave., 97206. Tel: 503-774-5699; Fax: 503-788-2596. Email: orenev@teleport.com. Revs. Patrick J. Lee, S.J., Dir. Novices; Thomas J. Lamanna, S.J., Asst. Dir. Novices; James R. Laudwein, S.J., Min. Priests 4; Novices 7. In Res. Rev. John J. Kindall, S.J.

MOUNT ANGEL. *Felix Rougier House of Studies*, 585 E. College St., 97362. Tel: 503-845-1181; Fax: 503-845-1189. P.O. Box 499, St. Benedict, 97373. Revs. Antonio Armendariz, M.Sp.S., Rector & Supr. House of Studies; Juan Jose Gonzalez, M.Sp.S., Assoc. Rector. Brothers 11.

ST. BENEDICT. *Mount Angel Seminary* 97373. Tel: 503-845-3951; Fax: 503-845-3126. Email: registrar@mtangel.edu. Rt. Rev. Nathan Zodrow, O.S.B., Abbot & Chancellor; Very Rev. Richard Paperini, O.S.B., Pres. & Rector; Dr. Elaine Park, S.S.L., S.T.D., Academic Dean; Revs. Jerome Young, O.S.B., Vice Rector & Dir. Spiritual Life; Richard Wallace, Dir. of Pastoral Formation; John Cihak, Dir. of Human Formation; Marina Keys, Operations Mgr.; Rev. Odo Recker, O.S.B., Dir. of Admissions; Sisters Virginia Schroeder, S.N.J.M., Asst. Dir. Pastoral Formation; Teresa Gould, F.M., Coord. of Music; Mrs. Dorene Preis, Registrar; Bro. Austin Tallman, O.S.B., Admin. Asst. & Contact Person. Priests 23; Deacons 3; Sisters 4; Brothers 6; Lay Teachers 14.

Formation Directors Revs. John Cihak; William Miller, S.J.; Liem Nguyen, O.S.B.; Rt. Rev. Peter Eberle, O.S.B. (Retired); Revs. Edgar Sanchez, M.Sp.S.; Joseph Nguyen, O.S.B. (MRY); Bro. Samuel Berning, O.S.B.

[B] COLLEGES AND UNIVERSITIES

PORTLAND. **University of Portland*, 5000 N. Willamette Blvd., 97203. Tel: 503-943-7911; Fax: 503-943-7401. Email: webmaster@up.edu. Web: www.up.edu. Endowed by the Congregation of Holy Cross; established 1901. Priests 25; Brothers 3; Sisters 6; Lay Teachers 160; Adjunct Faculty 93; Students 3,113.

Executive Officers of the University: Bro. Donald J. Stabrowski, C.S.C., Provost; Rev. William Beauchamp, C.S.C., Senior Vice Pres.; Dr. John Goldrick, Vice Pres. Student Svcs.; Dr. Roy Heynderickx, Financial Vice Pres.; Madeline Doll, Contact Person.

Faculty Staff: Revs. Robert Antonelli, C.S.C.; William Beauchamp, C.S.C.; James Connelly, C.S.C.; John Donato, C.S.C.; Thomas Hosinski, C.S.C.; William Hund, C.S.C.; John Kurtzke, C.S.C.; Edwin Obermiller, C.S.C.; Peter Pacini, C.S.C.; Claude Pomerleau, C.S.C. (A.), Religious Supr.; Richard Rutherford, C.S.C.; Charles D. Sherrer, C.S.C.; Ronald Wasowski, C.S.C.; Arthur F. Wheeler, C.S.C. In Res. Revs. Frederick Barr, C.S.C.; Richard Berg, C.S.C.; George C. Bernard, C.S.C.; Thomas Bill, C.S.C.; Adrien Ste. Marie, C.S.C.; Chester Prusynski, C.S.C.; Arthur Schoenfeldt, C.S.C.; William E. Wickham, C.S.C.; John Wironen, C.S.C.; Bros. Ken Allen, C.S.C.; Fulgence Dougherty, C.S.C.

Following is the Academic Structure of the University:

College of Arts and Sciences Tel: 503-943-7760; Fax: 503-943-7804. Dr. Marlene Moore, Dean.

School of Nursing Tel: 503-943-7509; Fax: 503-943-7729. Dr. Terry Misener, Dean.

School of Business Administration Tel: 503-943-7224; Fax: 503-943-8041. Dr. Larry Lewis, Dean.

School of Engineering Tel: 503-943-7314; Fax: 503-943-7316. Dr. Zia J. Yamayee, Dean.

School of Education Tel: 503-943-7315; Fax: 503-943-8042. Sr. Maria Ciriello, O.P., Dean.

Graduate School Tel: 503-943-7107. Dr. Patricia Chadwick.

MARYLHURST. *Marylhurst University* 97036. Tel: 503-636-8141; Fax: 503-636-9526. Email: president@marylhurst.edu. Web: www.marylhurst.edu. Dr. Nancy Wilgenbusch, Pres.; Dr. David Plotkin, Vice Pres. Academic Affairs & Contact Person; Pat Wittenberg, Contact Person. Sisters 10; Lay Teachers 406; Students 1,743.

[C] HIGH SCHOOLS, ARCHDIOCESAN

PORTLAND. *Central Catholic High School* (Coed) , 2401 S.E. Stark St., 97214. Tel: 503-235-3138; Fax: 503-233-0073. Email: cpeddicord@centralcatholichigh.org. Web: www.centralcatholichigh.org. Rev. Timothy Murphy, Pres.; Ron Edwards, Prin. & Contact Person. Priests 1; Sisters 2; Lay Teachers 52; Students 784.

MEDFORD. *St. Mary's School* (Coed) , 816 Black Oak Dr., 97504. Tel: 541-773-7877; Fax: 541-772-8973. Email: cstrand@stmarysschool.us. Web: www.stmarysschool.us. Karl Hanf, Prin.; Carroe Strand, Contact Person. Sisters 1; Lay Teachers 33; Lay Staff 13; Students 301.

SALEM. **Archbishop Francis Norbert Blanchet School*, 4373 Market St., N.E., 97301. Tel: 503-391-2639; Fax: 503-399-1259. Email: blanchet@open.org. Web: www.blanchetcatholicschool.com. Lay Teachers 20; Students 293.

STAYTON. *Regis High School* (Coed) , 550 W. Regis St., 97383. Tel: 503-769-2159; Fax: 503-769-1706. Email: principal@regishighschool.net. Web: www.regishighschool.net. Mr. Anthony Guevara, Prin. Lay Teachers 15; Students 169.

Regis High School Foundation, 550 W. Regis St., 97383. Tel: 503-769-2159; Fax: 503-769-1706.

[D] HIGH SCHOOLS, PRIVATE

PORTLAND. *De La Salle North Catholic High School (Coed)*, 7654 N. Delaware Ave., 97217. Tel: 503-285-9385; Fax: 503-285-9546. Email: delasallenorth.org. Web: www.delasallenorth.org. Matthew D. Powell, Pres. Lay Teachers 14; Brothers 3; Sisters 1; Students 192.

Jesuit High School (Coed) , 9000 S.W. Beaverton-Hillsdale Hwy., 97225-2491. Tel: 503-292-2663; Fax: 503-292-0134. Email: dgedrose@jesuitportland.com. Web: www.jesuitportland.com. Mr. Richard Gedrose, Pres. & Contact Person; Rev. Lawrence F. Robinson, S.J., Acting Supr.; Mrs. Sandra Satterberg, Prin.; Mr. Paul Hogan, Academic Vice Prin.; Mrs. Sue Walcutt, Vice Pres. Advancement; Mr. James Naggi, Vice Prin. Admin. Svcs.; Mrs. Shirley Poppe, Admissions Dir.; Mr. Donald Clarke, Campus Min. The Society of Jesus School:Priests 3; Lay Staff 117; Students 1,124; Community:Priests 6.

Faculty: Revs. William E. Hayes, S.J., Chancellor; David S. Olivier, S.J.; Lawrence F. Robinson, S.J. In Res. Revs. Joseph R. DeJardin, S.J.; Edward P. McTighe, S.J.

St. Mary's Academy (Girls) , 1615 S.W. Fifth Ave., 97201. Tel: 503-228-8306; Fax: 503-223-0995. Web: www.stmaryspdx.org. Patricia Barr, Prin. Sisters 2; Lay Teachers 44; Students 572.

BEAVERTON. *Valley Catholic Middle & High Schools* (Coed) , 4275 S.W. 148th Ave., 97007. Tel: 503-644-3745; Fax: 503-646-4054. Web: www.ssmo.org. Mr. Ross Thomas, Prin. Sisters of St. Mary of Oregon Sisters 1; Lay Teachers 37; Students 462.

EUGENE. *Marist High School* (Coed) , 1900 Kingsley Rd., 97401. Tel: 541-686-2234; Fax: 541-342-6451. Email: dorton@marists.org. Web: www.marists.org. Rev. John Legerski; Doug Orton, Prin. Priests 1; Lay Teachers 36; Students 524.

MILWAUKIE. *LaSalle High School* (Coed) , 11999 S.E. Fuller Rd., 97222. Tel: 503-659-4155; Fax: 503-659-2535. Email: lasalle@lasalle.pvt.k12.or.us. Web: www.lasalle.pvt.k12.or.us. William S. George, Prin.; Gregory R. VanderZanden, Pres. Sisters 1; Lay Teachers 37; Students 632.

SALEM. *Archbishop Francis Norbert Blancet School dba Blanchet Catholic School*, 4373 Market St., N.E., 97301. Tel: 503-391-2639; Fax: 503-399-1259. Email: blanchet@open.org. Web: www.blanchetcatholicschools.com. Robert Weber, Prin.

Salem Catholic Schools Foundation, P.O. Box 13207, 97309. Tel: 503-371-9068; Fax: 503-362-0513. Email: kevin@mannixlawfirm.com.

[E] ELEMENTARY SCHOOLS, AREA

EUGENE. *O'Hara Area Elementary Catholic School*, 715 W. 18th, 97402. Tel: 541-485-5291; Fax: 541-484-9138. Mrs. Dianne Bert, Prin. Comprised of students from the following parishes in Eugene: St. Jude, St. Mark, St. Mary, St. Paul, St. Peter, St. Alice and the Newman Center. Lay Teachers 23; Students 404.

[F] ELEMENTARY SCHOOLS, PRIVATE

PORTLAND. *St. Andrew Nativity School*, 4925 N.E. 9th Ave., 97211. Tel: 503-335-9600; Fax: 503-335-9494. Email: kconnellsj@yahoo.com. Web: www.nativityportland.com. Rev. Kevin Connell, S.J., Pres. Priests 2; Lay Teachers 11; Scholastics 2; Students 65.

Franciscan Montessori Earth School, 14750 S.E. Clinton St., 97236. Tel: 503-760-8220; Fax: 503-760-8333. Email: fmessfa@hotmail.com. Web: www.fmessfa.com. Sr. Francine Cardew, F.S.E., Contact Person. Staffed by Franciscan Sisters of the Eucharist. Franciscan Sisters of the Eucharist 4; Lay Teachers 27; Students 335.

BEAVERTON. *St. Mary of the Valley Grade School*, (Grades K-6), 4440 S.W. 148th Ave., 97007. Tel: 503-626-7781; Fax: 503-626-5731. Email: smvgsprincipal@ssmo.org. Web: www.ssmo.org. Susan Friesen, Prin. & Contact Person; Sr. Rita Watkins, Coord. Ministries. Sisters of St. Mary of Oregon Sisters 2; Lay Teachers 21; Students 382.

Valley Catholic School (Grades 7-12), 4275 S.W. 148th Ave., 97007. Tel: 503-644-3745; Fax: 503-646-4054. Web: www.valleycatholic.org. Ross Thomas, Prin. & Contact Person; Sr. Rita Watkins, Coord. Ministries. Sisters 1; Lay Teachers 44; Students 487.

[G] SOCIAL AND MINISTERIAL SERVICES

PORTLAND. *Catholic Charities of the Archdiocese of Portland in Oregon*, 231 S.E. 12th Ave., 97214. Tel: 503-231-4866; Fax: 503-231-4327. Email: dkeenancatholiccharities.oregon.org. Web: www.dkeenancatholiccharitiesoregon.org. Dennis B. Keenan, M.S.W., Exec. Dir.; Richard Deml, C.P.A., Controller; Chance Daniels, Public Rels. Mgr. CSS Group Homes 222; Resettlement Services 157; CCS Foundation Homes 78; Total persons annually served by CSS 119,413.

Catholic Charities Social Service Division of Portland, 231 S.E. 12th Ave., 97214. Tel: 503-231-4866; Fax: 503-231-4327. Douglas Alles, Social Svc. Dir.; Rev. Bruce Cwiekowski, AIDS Ministry Coord. Programs include: maternity and aftercare home, crisis pregnancy counseling adoption, mental health, case management, domestic violence intervention, refugee resettlement, Hispanic health outreach, AIDS ministry, ministry to the elderly, Asian social services, Project Rachel, Immigration Legal Services, Rose Haven day shelter for homeless women, and low income housing.

Catholic Youth Organization/Camp Howard, 825 N.E. 20th, Ste. 320, 97232-2295. Tel: 503-231-9484; Fax: 503-231-9531. Sr. Krista Von Borstel, S.S.M.O., Exec. Dir. Programs include: Youth recreation & camping.

Catholic Community Services of Lane County, 945 W. Seventh Ave., Eugene, 97402. Tel: 541-345-3642; Fax: 541-345-2891. Edward Monks, Exec. Dir. Programs include: Emergency shelter, utilities, and food, single mothers shelter, drug dependent mothers shelter, family shelter, young parents program, family self-sufficiency program.

Catholic Community Services of Mid-Willamette Valley and the Central Coast, 142 Glenbrook N., Keizer, 97307. Tel: 503-390-2600; Fax: 503-304-1343. Jim Seymour, Exec. Dir. Programs include: Center for delinquent youth, developmentally & physically disabled group homes, shelter for displaced youth, counseling center, Hispanic mental health outreach, child abuse, parent/newborn program.

Catholic Community Services of Southern Oregon, 440 S. Ivy St., Medford, 97501. Tel: 541-779-0803; Fax: 541-779-0803. Maria Aranda, Dir. Programs include: Emergency services, health clinics, community education, immigration legal services.

[H] CHILD DEVELOPMENT CENTERS

PORTLAND. *Providence Child Center*, 830 N.E. 45th Ave., 97213. Tel: 503-215-2400; Fax: 503-215-0660. Patricia Budo, Operations Admin.

Legal Title: *Sisters of Providence in Oregon*. Sisters 1; Total Staff 219.

Children's Nursing Center Tel: 503-215-2400; Fax: 503-215-2424. Provides skilled nursing care and habilitation/rehabilitation services for children who have physical and mental disabilities and multiple care needs. Long-term chronic care, short-term care for respite, transition, or pediatric end of life care provided.

Providence Montessori School Tel: 503-215-2409; Fax: 503-215-2442. Preschool and elementary education for children ages 3 to 6 with a broad array of developmental needs and abilities.

Providence Wee Care Tel: 503-215-6832; Fax: 503-215-0333. Child development program for children of Providence Medical Center employees and the community, ages 6 weeks to 6 years. Developmental and age-appropriate activities support child's growth and developement.

Providence Neurodevelopmental Center for Children Tel: 503 215-2233; Fax: 503-215-2478. PNCC provides evaluation and treatment for children with special needs from infancy to 18 years of age. Services include neurodevelopmental assessment, psychological/cognitive assessment, feeding disorders clinic, medical nutrition services, physical therapy, occupational therapy, speech/language pathology, and social services.

[I] RESIDENTIAL SCHOOLS FOR YOUTHS WITH EMOTIONAL-SOCIAL PROBLEMS

BEAVERTON. *St. Mary's Home for Boys, Inc.*, 16535 S.W. Tualatin Valley Hwy., 97006. Tel: 503-649-5651; Fax: 503-649-7405. Emma Dennis, Exec. Dir. & Contact Person. Residential & day treatment center for behaviorally & emotionally disturbed children. Students 500.

[J] GENERAL HOSPITALS

PORTLAND. *Providence Portland Medical Center*, 4805 N.E. Glisan St., 97213. Tel: 503-215-1111; 503-215-6833; Fax: 503-215-6192. Email: kathleen.kirch@providence.org. Web: www.providence.org. Revs. Herbert Wheatley, O.F.M.; Jon Buffington (EST); John Wironen, C.S.C.; Rev. John Hubbard, Presbyterian Chap.; Grethe Barber, Episcopal Chap.; Sandra J. Walker, E.L.C.A., Clinical Pastoral Educ. Supvr.; Sr. Elizabeth Kitanura, Presbyterian Chap.; Rebecca Gurney, Baptist Chap., Oncology; Stacey Morgan, Baptist Chap.; Sisters Kathleen Kircher, S.N.J.M., Dir. Pastoral Care & Contact Person; Rosalie Orr, S.N.J.M., Hospice Home Health; Maureen Niedermeyer, O.S.B., Cardiology; Mary Coakley, O.S.F., Chap.; Brigid Carey, P.B.V.M., Staff Chap.; Joseph Joyce, Lay Chap. Addiction Treatment (Catholic); Martha Leven, Lay Chap. (Catholic); Kathryn Anne, Lay Chap. Child Center & Neurology (Catholic).

Legal Title: *Providence Health Systems, Oregon Region* Sisters 6; Bed Capacity 483; Total Staff 2,551; Patients Assisted Annually 442,009.

Providence Medical Foundation, 4805 N.E. Glisan, 97213. Tel: 503-215-6187; Fax: 503-215-0530. Bryce Streng, Exec. Dir.; Kelly Buechler Exec. Dir.

Providence St. Vincent Medical Center, 9205 S.W. Barnes Rd., 97225. Tel: 503-297-4411; Fax: 503-291-2468. Email: donelson@providence.org. Web: www.providence.org. Russ Danielson, Admin. Health Care Oper., Providence Health System; Donald S. Elsom, Admin., Providence St. Vincent Medical Center & Contact Person; Monica M. Anderson, Dir. Pastoral Svcs.; Revs. Edward P. McTighe, S.J., Chap.; Eldon J. McKamy; Joseph R. Reeves; Bro. Larry Eschweiler, O.H.; Liam Devitt, Catholic Chap.; Ms. Shiela Schaeffer, Catholic Chap.; Charlene K. Epp, Protestant Chap.; Michele Sakuri, Catholic Chap.; Ms. Theresa Edmondson, Catholic Chap.; Jean Keith, Protestant Chap.; Ms. Judith A. McGowan, Catholic Chap.; Sr. Patricia Valentine, S.N.J.M., Catholic Chap.; Ms. Christine Wallace, Protestant Chap.; Simon S. Ho, Protestant Chap.; Laura A. Moya, Music Thanatologist.

Legal Title: *Providence Health System.*, Providence Health System. Sisters 1; Brothers 1; Bed Capacity 451; Patients Assisted Annually 665,000.

**St. Vincent Medical Foundation, Portland* Tel: 503-216-2227; Fax: 503-216-4140.

EUGENE. **Sacred Heart Medical Center*, 1255 Hilyard St., P.O. Box 10905, 97440. Tel: 541-686-7300; Fax: 541-686-7391. Jill Hoggard Green, Admin.; Alan Yordy, CEO, Peace Health OR; Robert V. Scheri, Dir. Pastoral Care & Chap.; Revs. J. Noel Hickie (BAK), Chap.; Ken Olsen, Chap.; Sisters Carol Lee, S.N.J.M., Chap.; Vivian Ripp, S.N.J.M., Chap.; Gerald Jensen, Chap.; Joel Peterson, Chap.; Carol A. Willie, Chap.; David Waggoner, Chap.; Ed McIndoo, Chap. Sisters of St. Joseph of Peace, Div. of Peace Health. Sisters 5; Bed Capacity 432; Total Staff 3,541; Patients Assisted Annually 132,233.

FLORENCE. *Peace Harbor Hospital*, 400 Ninth St., 97439. Tel: 541-997-8412; Fax: 541-997-1478. Email: pbyers@peachhealth.org. Web: www.peacehealth.org. James Barnhart, Regl. CEO; Sr. Noreen Terrault, C.S.J.P., Pastoral Care; Peggy Byers, Contact Person. Acute care hospital owned and operated by Peace Health, Bellevue, WA. Bed Capacity 21; Total Staff 380; Patients Assisted Annually 10,000.

MEDFORD. *Providence Medford Medical Center*, 1111 Crater Lake Ave., 97504-6225. Tel: 541-732-5000; Fax: 541-732-5872. Mr. Charles T. Wright, Chief Exec., Southern Oregon Service Area; Mr. Bartholomew C. Rodrigues, Dir. Mission Integration, Ethics & Spiritual Care; Rev. Joseph E. Shirey, S.J., (Part-time); Sisters Therese Kohles, S.P., Senior Representative to Foundation Bd. (On Call); Mary Grondin, S.P., Representative to Community Bd.; Patricia Marie Landin, S.S.M.O., Chap.

Legal Title: *Providence Health System* Sisters 2; Bed Capacity 168; Total Staff 1,023; Patients Assisted Annually 114,873.

**Providence Community Health Foundation, Medford* Tel: 541-732-5193; Fax: 541-772-2861.

MILWAUKIE. **Providence Milwaukie Hospital*, 10150 S.E. 32nd Ave., 97222. Tel: 503-513-8300; Fax: 503-513-8463. Web: www.providence.org. Camelia Hanemann, Dir. Pastoral Care & Contact Person.

Legal Title: *Providence Health System in Oregon.* Bed Capacity 77; Total Staff 430; Patients Assisted Annually 80,000.

**Providence Milwaukie Foundation, Milwaukie* Tel: 503-513-8625; Fax: 503-513-8319.

NEWBERG. *Providence Newberg Hospital*, 501 Villa Rd., 97132. Tel: 503-537-1701; Fax: 503-537-1811. Mark Meinert, CEO; Jack R. Sumner, Dir. Finance & Contact Person. Bed Capacity 35; Total Staff 335; Patients Assisted Annually 110,000.

ROSEBURG. *Mercy Medical Center, Inc.*, 2700 Stewart Pkwy., 97470. Tel: 541-673-0611; Fax: 541-677-4830. Web: www.mercyrose.org. Victor J. Fresolone, Pres. & CEO; Janet L. Baker, Vice Pres. & CFO & Contact. Tel: 541-677-2458; Janet Buchanan, Vice Pres., Mission Services. Bed Capacity 153; Total Staff 1,196; Patients Assisted Annually 235,220.

Mercy Healthcare, Inc., 2700 Stewart Pkwy., 97470. Tel: 541-673-0611; Fax: 541-677-4830. Sandra R. Pearson, Exec. Asst. Tel: 541-677-2467.

Mercy Foundation, Inc., 2700 Stewart Pkwy., 97470. Tel: 541-677-4818; Fax: 541-677-4891.

Linus Oakes, Inc., 2700 Stewart Pkwy., 97470. Tel: 541-677-4800; Fax: 541-677-2106.

SEASIDE. *Providence Seaside Hospital*, 725 S. Wahanna Rd., 97138-7735. Tel: 503-717-7000; Fax: 503-717-7505. Email: srjeri.renner@providence.org. Web: www.providence.org/northcoast. William Sexton, Admin.; Sr. Jeri Renner, O.P., Contact Person, Spiritual Care.

Legal Title: *Sisters of Providence in Oregon.* Bed Capacity 47; Extended Care 22; Total Staff 270; Patients Assisted Annually 150,000.

**Providence Seaside Hospital Foundation, Inc.* Tel: 503-717-7600; Fax: 503-717-7505.

[K] RETIREMENT AND ASSISTED LIVING

PORTLAND. **St. Anthony Village (activity of St. Anthony Village Enterprise)*, 3560 S.E. 79th Ave., 97206. Tel: 503-775-4414; Fax: 503-771-9189. Email: mkellenbeck@villagesage.com. Web: www.villagesage.com. Rev. Michael Maslowsky, Pres.; Melodie Kellenbeck, Admin. & Contact Person; Deanna Morley, Leasing Coord. Retirement village centered around Catholic parish. Independent and assisted living, Alzheimer's unit, activities director, gardens, interaction with neighbors. Total Assisted Annually 130.

**Assumption Village (activity of St. Anthony Village Enterprise)*, 9121 N. Burr, 97203. Tel: 503-283-5644; Fax: 503-283-5692. Rev. Michael Maslowsky, Pres.; Deanna Morley, Leasing Coord. Retirement Village, Senior independent and assisted living, chapel with daily Mass multiple activities, gardens, intergenerational interaction with neighborhood and local social service agencies. Total Assisted Annually 79.

Mt. St. Joseph, Inc., 3060 S.E. Stark St., 97214-3099. Tel: 503-535-4700; Fax: 503-797-6702. Web: www.mtstjoseph.org. Bill Sherer, Pres. & CEO; Alexis Greshom, Dir. Pastoral Care. Catholic Health Initiatives - Owner/Operator. Sisters 3; Bed Capacity 276; Residents 236.

BEAVERTON. *Maryville Nursing Home*, 14645 S.W. Farmington Rd., 97007. Tel: 503-643-8626; Fax: 503-520-1435. Sr. Geraldine Bernards, Admin.; Rita Williams, R.N., Dir. Nurses; Rev. John M. Domin, Chap. (Retired). Sisters 8; Lay Workers 223; Guests 281; Hospice Care: Total Assisted 281;

Total Staff 301.

Little Flower Development Center, 4415 S.W. 148th Ave., 97007. Tel: 503-520-0214; Fax: 503-626-6220. Lay Staff 70; Children 231.

MOUNT ANGEL. *Providence Benedictine Nursing Center*, 540 S. Main St., 97362-9523. Tel: 503-845-6841; Fax: 503-845-9229. Web: www.providence.org/marion. Emily Dazey, Exec. Dir.; Sr. Joseph Fennimore, Chap.; Rev. Aelred Yockey, O.S.B., Chap.; Rev. Dana McBrien, Interfaith Chap. Sisters of Providence Health System. Sisters 1; Patients Assisted Annually 580.

Providence Benedictine Orchard House Tel: 503-845-2544; Fax: 503-845-2560. Personalized Living Center (ALF). Assisted 67.

Providence Benedictine Garden Homes Tel: 503-845-2544; Fax: 503-845-2560. Adult Foster Care. Assisted 9.

Providence Benedictine Home Health Tel: 503-845-9226; Fax: 503-845-9880. Staff 32; Patients Assisted Annually 1,100.

[L] MONASTERIES AND RESIDENCES OF PRIESTS

PORTLAND. *Colombiere Community*, 3220 S.E. 43rd Ave., 97206. Tel: 503-595-1930; Fax: 503-228-6741. Email: pford@nwjesuits.org. Web: www.nwjesuits.org. Revs. Patrick J. Ford, S.J., Supr.; Peter D. Byrne, S.J.; Kevin T. Clarke, S.J.; Kevin G. Connell, S.J.; James R. Conyard, S.J.; James E. Jacobsen, S.J.; John McBride, S.J.; William T. Miller, S.J.; John J. Morris, S.J.; John V. Murphy, S.J.; Armand M. Nigro, S.J.; Brad R. Reynolds, S.J.; J. Patrick Stewart, S.J.; John D. Whitney, S.J.; Dan Mai, S.J.; Jeffrey N. McDougall, S.J., Min.

The Grotto, The National Sanctuary of Our Sorrowful Mother, 85th and N.E. Sandy Blvd., P.O. Box 20008, 97294-0008. Tel: 503-254-7371; 503-254-7372 (Monastery); Fax: 503-254-7948. Revs. John M. Topper, O.S.M., Prior & Exec. Dir.; Patrick M. McNamara, O.S.M. Brothers 1; Sisters 4. In Res. Revs. Robert S. Anderson, O.S.M.; Louis M. Breton, O.S.M.; Damian M. Kobus, O.S.M.

Holy Cross Fathers & Brothers, C.S.C. - University of Portland, 5000 N. Willamette Blvd., 97203. Tel: 503-286-3457; Fax: 503-286-3457. Email: csc@up.edu. Revs. Claude Pomerleau, C.S.C., Supr.; Robert Antonelli, C.S.C.; William Beauchamp, C.S.C.; Richard Berg, C.S.C.; George C. Bernard, C.S.C.; Frederick Barr, C.S.C.; Thomas Bill, C.S.C.; Joseph P. Browne, C.S.C.; James Connelly, C.S.C.; John Donato, C.S.C; Terry Ehreman, C.S.C.; Thomas Hosinski, C.S.C.; William Hund, C.S.C.; John Kurtzke, C.S.C.; Edwin Obermiller, C.S.C.; Peter Pacini, C.S.C.; Chester Prusynski, C.S.C.; Richard Rutherford, C.S.C.; Charles D. Sherrer, C.S.C.; Arthur Schoenfeldt, C.S.C.; Adrien Ste. Marie, C.S.C.; Ronald Wasowski, C.S.C.; Arthur F. Wheeler, C.S.C.; William E. Wickham, C.S.C.; John Wironen, C.S.C.; Bros. Ken Allen, C.S.C.; Flugence Dougherty, C.S.C.; Donald Stabrowski, C.S.C.

Holy Rosary Priory, 375 N.E. Clackamas St., 97232. Tel: 503-235-3163; Fax: 503-235-3164.

Jesuit Provincial Office (Society of Jesus, Oregon Prov.), P.O. Box 86010, 97286-0010. Revs. John D. Whitney, S.J., Prov.; Patrick J. Ford, S.J., Socius, Chief of Staff; Ignatius F. Ohno, S.J., Treas.; Stephen C. Lantry, S.J., Dir. of Vocations; Joel K. Adams, S.J., Asst. for Secondary Schools, Asst. for Formation; Charles J. Peterson, S.J., Dir. Rocky Mountain Mission / NW, Asst. for Native Ministries; Mr. Matthew Senecal, Dir. of Devel.; Mr. William Lockyear, CFO; Mrs. Joyceann Hagen, Asst. for Pastoral Ministries. Sisters 4.
Oregon Province priests not listed elsewhere:
5441 San Angelo St., Guadalupe, AZ 85283. Tel: 602-838-3143. Rev. David A. Myers, S.J.
Oregon Province Priests serving outside the U.S.: Revs. Francis E. Case, S.J.; Joseph B. Danel, S.J.; Bartholomew J. Murphy, S.J.; John J. Navone, S.J.; Michael J. Schultheis, S.J.; Gary N. Smith, S.J.; Anthony P. Via, S.J.; Thomas E. Zeyen, S.J.; Robert B. Grimm, S.J.; Anthony Anh, S.J. (SPK); Bro. James P. Selinsky, S.J.

AMITY. *Brigittine Priory of Our Lady of Consolation - The Order of the Most Holy Savior*, 23300 Walker Ln., 97101. Tel: 503-835-8080; Fax: 503-835-9662. Email: monks@brigittine.org. Web: www.brigittine.org. Bro. Steven Vargo, O.Ss.S., Prior. Professed 9; Novices 3.

LAFAYETTE. *The Cistercian (Trappist) Abbey of Our Lady of Guadalupe* 97127. Tel: 503-852-7174; Fax: 503-852-7748. Email: community@trappistabbey.org. Rt. Rev. Peter McCarthy, O.C.S.O.; Revs. Dismas Gannon, O.C.S.O., Prior; Casey Bailey, O.C.S.O.; Martin Cawley, O.C.S.O.; Timothy Clark, O.C.S.O.; Howard Curtis, O.C.S.O.; Joseph-Benedict Donnelly, O.C.S.O.; Jerome Ebacher, O.C.S.O.; Francis King, O.C.S.O.; Richard Layton, O.C.S.O.; Timothy Michell, O.C.S.O.; Philip Negele, O.C.S.O. (DEN); Peter Plakut, O.C.S.O.; Mark Weidner, O.C.S.O. Order of Cistercians of the Strict Observance Solemnly Professed 33; Priests 14; Simply Professed 2; Total in Community 35.

MOUNT ANGEL. *Discalced Carmelite Friars (OCD)*, 915 S. Main St., 97362. Tel: 503-845-2240 Carmelite House of Studies. *Carmelite House of Studies*, P.O. Box 260, 97362. Tel: 503-845-2240 Carmelite House of Studies; Fax: 503-845-2243. Rev. Donald Kinney, O.C.D., Rector.

Missionaries of the Holy Spirit, M.Sp.S., 585 E. College St., 97362. Tel: 503-845-1182; Fax: 503-845-1182. P.O. Box 499, St. Benedict, 97373. Tel: 503-845-1181; Fax: 503-845-1189. Email: msps@mspsoregon.org. Web: www.teleport.com/~msps/. Revs. Edgar Sanchez, M.Sp.S., Rector; Celso Marquez, M.S.p.S., Vice-Rector; Jose Ortega, M.Sp.S., Supr. of the Vicariate. Serving the Felix Rougier House of Studies and St. Matthew Parish, Hillsboro:

MYRTLE CREEK. *Augustinian Community*, P.O. Box 810, 97457. Tel: 541-863-3271; Fax: 541-863-6759. Email: warosa@quixnet.net. Web: www.churchbulletin.com. Revs. James Clifford, O.S.A.; William Ryan, O.S.A., Regl. Supr.

ST. BENEDICT. *Mt. Angel Abbey* 97373. Tel: 503-845-3030; Fax: 503-845-3594. Web: www.mtangel.edu. Rt. Revs. Nathan Zodrow, O.S.B.; Joseph Wood, O.S.B. (Retired); Peter Eberle, O.S.B. (Retired); Very Revs. Paul Thomas, O.S.B., Prior & Contact Person; Paschal Cheline, O.S.B., Subprior; Revs. Thomas Brockhaus, O.S.B.; Timothy Sander, O.S.B.; Stephen Hofmann, O.S.B.; Bernard Sander, O.S.B.; Louis Charvet, O.S.B.; David Nicholson, O.S.B.; Athanasius Buchholz, O.S.B.; Benedict Suing, O.S.B.; Leo Rimmele, O.S.B.; Augustine DeNoble, O.S.B.; Placidus Zach, O.S.B.; Bede Partridge, O.S.B.; Bruno Becker, O.S.B.; Cosmas White, O.S.B.; Alexander Plasker, O.S.B.; Gregory Duerr, O.S.B.; Edmund Smith, O.S.B.; Marian Del Monaco, O.S.B.; Vincent Trujillo, O.S.B.; Kenneth Jacques, O.S.B.; William Hammelman, O.S.B.; Jeremy Driscoll, O.S.B.; Philip Waibel, O.S.B.; Jerome Young, O.S.B.; Marius Walter, O.S.B.; Joachim McCann, O.S.B.; Aelred Yockey, O.S.B.; Pius X Harding, O.S.B.; Thomas Thien Dang, O.S.B.; Vincent Liem Nguyen, O.S.B.; Michael Mee, O.S.B.; Odo Recker, O.S.B.; Ezekiel Lotz, O.S.B.; Karl Nielson, O.S.B.; Joseph Nguyen, O.S.B. (MRY). Monks in perpetual vows 60; Divided as follows: Priests 42; Brothers 18.

[M] CONVENTS AND RESIDENCES FOR SISTERS

PORTLAND. *Convent of Sisters of Reparation of the Sacred Wounds of Jesus, Novitiate*, 2120 S.E. 24th Ave., 97214-5504. Tel: 503-236-4207; Fax: 503-236-3400. Email: repsrs@juno.com repsrs@msn.com. Sr. Mary of the Angels, S.R., Supr. Gen. Sisters 3; Donne Members 90.

Convent of the Good Shepherd, 562 N. Portland Blvd., 97217. Tel: 503-283-4931; Fax: 503-283-4894. Email: joanspiering@comcast.net. Sr. Joan Spiering, Contact Person. Sisters 4.

Convent of the Society of the Holy Child Jesus, 5937 N. Denver Ave., 97217. Tel: 503-289-9975.

Holy Cross Convent (1670), 7408 S.E. Alder, 97215. Tel: 503-254-3284; Fax: 503-255-3097. Email: mtgdlhn@yahoo.com. Sr. Agatha Tran Thi Hang, Supr. & Contact Person.
Legal Title: *Adorers of the Holy Cross Sisters*, First foundation in the United States in 1976, founded by Bishop Pierre Lambert de la Motte. Represented in the Archdiocese of Portland in Oregon and the Diocese of Arlington, VA. Sisters 24; Candidates 6.

Holy Spirit Sisters Convent, 1904 S.E. Division, 97202. Tel: 503-239-0328. Email: alcssisters@aol.com. Sr. Catherine P. Msaky, A.L.C.S., Contact Person. Sisters 7.

"Rose Hall" Reparation and Prayer Center, 2120 S.E. 24th Ave., 97214-5504. Tel: 503-236-4207; Fax: 503-236-3400. Email: repsrs@juno.com repsrs@msn.com. Sr. Mary of the Angels, S.R., Dir.

Sisters of Mercy Convent, 3080 S.E. Stark St., 97214. Tel: 503-236-1972; Fax: 503-797-6702. Sisters 16.

Sisters of Social Service, 14405 S.W. Sexton Mt. Dr., Apt. A, 97005-7493. Tel: 503-641-6509. Sisters 3; Capacity: Residents 36; Day Students 100.
Other Addresses:
1554 Madras St., S.E., Salem, 97306. Tel: 503-391-7498.
8046 S.E. Taggart, 97206. Tel: 503-777-2526.

BEAVERTON. *Convent, Franciscan Missionary Sisters of Our Lady of Sorrows*, 3600 S.W. 170th Ave., 97006-5099. Tel: 503-649-1634; Fax: 503-649-8382. Email: franmisisters@juno.com. Web: www.olpretreat.org. Sr. Anne Marie, O.S.F., Supr. Gen., Contact Person. Sisters 15; Novitiate 2.

St. Mary of the Valley Convent, 4440 S.W. 148th Ave., 97007. Tel: 503-644-9181; Fax: 503-464-1102. Email: srbarbarajeanl@ssmo.org. Web: www.ssmo.org. Sisters Barbara Jean Laughlin, S.S.M.O., Supr. Gen.; Adele Marie Altenhofen, Local Supr.; Rev. Francis Chun, Chap. (Retired). Motherhouse of the Sisters of St. Mary of Oregon. Professed Sisters 87.

The Vietnamese Holy Cross Sisters, 7361 S.E. 175th Terr., 97007. Tel: 503-259-8767. Email: ngoan55@hotmail.com. Sr. Maria Ngoan Nguyen, Supr.

BRIDAL VEIL. *Convent, Franciscan Sisters of the Eucharist, Administrative Center*, 48100 E. Crown Point Hwy., 97010. Tel: 503-695-2375; Fax: 503-695-2368. Email: fsebridalveil@fsecommunity.org. Web: www.fsecommunity.org. Sr. Mary Michael Costello, F.S.E., Supr. & Contact Person. Sisters 7.

EUGENE. *Carmel of Maria Regina* (Contemplative Order) , 87609 Green Hill Rd., 97402. Tel: 541-345-8649; Fax: 541-345-4857. Sr. Maria Teresa, O.C.D., Prioress. Professed Sisters 8.

MARYLHURST. *Convent of the Holy Names*, P.O. Box 25, 97036. Tel: 503-675-2467; Fax: 503-675-2453. Email: bstewart@snjmor.org. Sisters Mary Breiling, Leadership Council; Jane Hibbard, S.N.J.M., Leadership Council; Lynda Thompson, Leadership Council; Barbara Stewart, Admin. Asst. & Contact Person. Provincial House of the Sisters of the Holy Names of Jesus & Mary, S.N.J.M. Professed Sisters 191; Temporarily professed 3.

MT. ANGEL. *Queen of Angels Monastery*, 840 S. Main St., 97362-9527. Tel: 503-845-6141; Fax: 503-845-6585. Email: qam@open.org. Web: www.benedictine-srs.org. Sr. Dorothy Jean Beyer, O.S.B., Prioress & Contact Person. Monastery of the Benedictine Sisters of Mt. Angel.; See separate listing for Shalom Prayer Center (retreat center) and St. Joseph Shelter (special center for social services and assistance). Sisters 47; Novices 2; Postulants 1.

[N] RETREAT HOUSES

PORTLAND. *The Jesuit Spirituality Center*, P.O. Box 86040, 97286. Tel: 503-595-1919. Marilyn Kirvin-Quamme, Dir. & Contact Person; Diane Glenn, Admin. Asst.
Legal Title: *Loyola Retreat Association, S.J., Inc. dba The Jesuit Spirituality Center.*

BEAVERTON. *Our Lady of Peace Retreat*, 3600 S.W. 170th Ave., 97006-5099. Tel: 503-649-7127; Fax: 503-649-8382. Email: olpretreat@juno.com. Web: www.olpretreat.org. Sr. Anne Marie Warren, O.S.F., Supr. & Contact Person. Franciscan Missionary Sisters of Our Lady of Sorrows 17.

GOLD HILL. *St. Rita's Retreat Center*, P.O. Box 310, 97525. Tel: 541-855-1333. Email: strita@looped.com. Rev. Stephen J. Fister, Dir. & Contact Person.

MCKENZIE BRIDGE. *St. Benedict Lodge Dominican Retreat & Conference Center*, 56630 North Bank Rd., 97413-9614. Tel: 541-822-3572 (Office & Dominican Res.); Fax: 541-822-3631. Email: bdtop@efn.org tfdeman@msn.com. Web: www.sblodge.org. 91683 Alma Dr., 97413. Tel: 541-822-3937. Email: sjohnbac@efn.org. Bro. Daniel Thomas, O.P., Dir. & Contact; Rev. Thomas DeMan, O.P., Chap. & Assoc. Dir.; Deacon Leonard Soper. Dominican Retreat & Conference Center. Retreat guests: 541-822-6151.
46052 McKenzie Hwy., Vida, 97488. Tel: 541-896-0284. Email: dcnlgjms@earthlink.net. Sr. John Maureen Backenstos, S.N.J.M., Spiritual & Temporal Ministry.

MILWAUKIE. *Franciscan Spiritual Center-West*, Spiritual direction; retreats; educational workshops and body-work in conjunction with retreats and workshops3300 S.E. Dwyer Dr., Ste. 306, 97222-6548. Tel: 503-794-8542; Fax: 503-794-8556. Email: francisspctr@aol.com. Sr. Carol Ann Warnke, O.S.F., Dir. Sisters of St. Francis of Philadelphia

MT. ANGEL. *Benedictine Sisters Shalom Prayer Center*, 840 S. Main St., 97362-9527. Tel: 503-845-6773; Fax: 503-845-6585. Email: shalom@open.org. Web: www.open.org/shalom. Sr. Joan Pokorny, O.S.B., Dir. & Contact Person. Sisters 7.

PACIFIC CITY. *Nestucca Sanctuary*, P.O. Box 670, 97135-0670. Rev. Andrew J. Dufner, S.J., Retreat Dir. & Contact Person.

ST. BENEDICT. *Mount Angel Abbey Guest House* 97373. Tel: 503-845-3025; Fax: 503-845-3027. Email: retreat@mtangel.edu. Web: www.mtangel.edu. Rev. Michael Mee, O.S.B., Dir. & Contact Person.

[O] SOCIETY OF ST. VINCENT DE PAUL

PORTLAND. *Macdonald Center and Residence*, 605 N.W. Couch St., 97209. Tel: 503-222-5720; Fax: 503-241-7375. Email: berg@up.edu. Web: www.macdcenter.org. Rev. Richard F. Berg, C.S.C., Exec. Dir.; Mary Sue Richen, Prog. Dir. Total People Served 750.

Society of St. Vincent de Paul Portland Council , 3601 S.E. 27th Ave., 97202. Tel: 503-235-7837; Fax: 503-233-5581. Email: billconyard@svdppdx.org. Web: www.svdppdx.org. Shari Crawford, Contact Person. Total Assisted Annually 230,000.

EUGENE. *Society of St. Vincent de Paul* Archdiocesan Council. , 705 S. Seneca St., 97402. Tel: 541-687-5820; Fax: 541-683-9423. Email: svdp@svdplanecounty.org. Web: www.svdplanecounty.org. David Santos, Pres.

Society of St. Vincent de Paul Eugene Council. , 705 S. Seneca St., 97402. Tel: 541-687-5820; Fax: 541-683-9423. Email: svdp@svdplanecounty.org. Web: www.svdplanecounty.org. Jacqueline Cole, Pres.; Terrence R. McDonald, Exec. Dir.; Susan Sammons, Contact Person.

MEDFORD. *Society of St. Vincent de Paul* Rogue Valley Council , P.O. Box 1663, 97501. Tel: 541-772-3828; Fax: 541-772-6886. Email: vincent@mind.net. Web: www.sovicariate.org/svdp. Bill Schueller, Pres. Total Assisted Annually 117,794.

SALEM. **Society of St. Vincent de Paul* Council of Mid-Willamette Valley , 3745 Portland Rd., N.E., P.O. Box 7864, 97303. Tel: 503-364-1062; Fax: 503-364-2708. Email: svdp@open.org. Barbara Latham, Pres.; Kimberly Allain, Exec. Dir. & Contact Person. Total Assisted Annually 85,024.

[P] NEWMAN CENTERS

PORTLAND. *University of Portland* Campus Ministry, 5000 N. Willamette Blvd., 97203. Tel: 503-943-7131; Fax: 503-943-7093. Email: ministry@up.edu. Web: www.up.edu. Revs. Edwin Obermiller, C.S.C., Dir.; John Donato, C.S.C., Assoc.; Diane Zbasnik, Assoc.; Maureen Briare, Choir Dir.; Anna Minore, Prog. Asst.

Southern Oregon University (Ashland), 987 Hillview Dr., Ashland, 97520. Tel: 541-482-0825; Fax: 541-488-5174. Email: frjoseph@mind.net. Web: www.sou.edu/su/newman/newman.htm. Rev. Joseph Betschart, Dir. & Chap.; Brian Teipen, Assoc. Dir.

Oregon State University (Corvallis), Newman Center, 2127 N.W. Monroe St., Corvallis, 97330. Tel: 541-752-6818. Email: giffords@peak.org. Sue Gifford, Pastoral Dir.

Trinity Court (Student Housing), 2121 N.W. Monroe, Corvallis, 97330. Tel: 541-245-7970; Fax: 503-245-7977. Rev. John Henderson, O.F.M.Conv., Chap.

University of Oregon (Eugene), Newman Center, 1850 Emerald St., Eugene, 97403. Tel: 541-343-7021; Fax: 541-686-8028. Email: newman@newmanctr-uoregon.org. Web: www.newmanctr-uoregon.org. Revs. Michael Fones, O.P.; David Orique, O.P., Assoc.; Stefani Catoni, Pastoral Assoc.

Lane Community College, 1850 Emerald St., Eugene, 97403. Tel: 541-343-7071; Fax: 541-686-8028. Stefani Catoni, Campus Min.

Pacific University (Forest Grove) Email: parierad@pacificu.edu. Debbie Pariera, Campus Min.; Rev. William Holtzinger, Chap.

St. Anthony Church: 3009 Vista Dr., Forest Grove, 97116. Tel: 503-357-9023; Fax: 503-352-2933.

Lewis & Clark College Rev. Joseph S. McMahon, Chap.; Sr. Loretta Schaff, O.S.F., Campus Min. 0615 S.W. Palatine Hill Rd., PO. Box 171, 97219. Tel: 503-768-7080; Fax: 503-768-7084. Email: schaff@clark.edu.

Linfield College (McMinnville) Email: mdouglass@onlinemac.com. Michael Douglas, Campus Min.

St. James Church: 1145 N.E. First St., McMinnville, 97128. Tel: 503-472-5232.

Western Oregon State College (Monmouth) Tel: 503-838-1242. Rev. Carl Gimpl, Chap.; Teresa Schneiderman, Campus Min.

1275 E St., Monmouth, 97361.

Willamette University (Salem) Heather Pariera, Campus Min.

St. Joseph Church: 721 Chemeketa St., N.E., Salem, 97301. Tel: 503-581-1623; Fax: 503-581-7271.

[Q] MISCELLANEOUS

PORTLAND. **Albina Community Development Corporation*, 3987 N. Mississippi Ave., 97227. Tel: 503-335-0947; Fax: 503-281-0933. Email: albinacdc.org. Sheila Simons, Contact Person; Joice Taylor, Dir. of Community Svcs. & Contact Person. Low income rental properties - 355 units; Served 1,400 individuals

St. Andrew Legal Clinic, 807 N.E. Alberta, 97211. Tel: 503-281-1500; Fax: 503-282-5642. Email: joverlund@salcgroup.org. Joel K. Overlund, Dir. & Contact Person.

Blanchet House of Hospitality, 340 N.W. Glisan St., 97209. Tel 503-226-3911; Fax: 503-222-4071. Email: blanchetcntr@aol.com. Web: www.BlanchetHouse.org. Bill Muir, Dir. Tel: 503-807-4330.

Catholic Broadcasting Northwest, Inc., 88.5 KBVM-FM, P.O. Box 5888, 97228-5888. Tel: 503-285-5200; Fax: 503-285-3322. Email: info@kbvm.com. Web: www.kbvm.com. Steven J. Moffitt, Gen. Mgr.

Catholic Engaged Encounter of Oregon, Inc., 2200 S.W. 75th Ave., 97225. Tel: 503-292-0001; Fax: 503-699-7500. Email: ramsdenfam@msn.com. Web: www.visionww.com/ceeore. Jerry Ramsden; Denise Ramsden. Marriage Preparation Program providing weekend retreats to engaged couples. Couples served 371; Volunteers 55.

Cordero Corporation (dba De LaSalle North Catholic High School), 7654 N. Delaware, 97217. Tel: 503-285-9385; Fax: 503-285-9546. Email: mpowell@delasallenorth.org. Web: www.delasallenorth.org. Matthew Powell, Contact Person.

**Franciscan Ministry Network*, 4725 N.E 9th Ave., 97211. Tel: 503-280-0600. Email: tumultynatt@aol.com. Rev. Matt Tumulty, O.F.M., Exec. Dir. & Contact Person.

**The Gamelin-Oregon Association-Emilie House*, 5520 N.E. Glisan, 97213-3169. Tel: 503-236-9779; Fax: 503-239-1867. Web: www.providence.org/long-term-care/housing/e60emiller.htm. Shannon Stickler, Dir. & Contact. Sisters of Providence, 41 apartments for the elderly and mobility impaired subsidized by the Department of Housing and Urban Development.

Jesuit Development & Communications Office, P.O. Box 86010, 97286-0010. Tel: 503-227-1174; Fax: 503-228-5741. Email: msenecal@nwjesuits.org. Web: www.nwjesuits.org. Mr. P. Matthew Senecal, Dir. Devel.; Ms. Donna Wiench, Communications Dir.; Revs. J. Patrick Stewart, S.J., Assoc. Dir. Devel.; Dan Mai, S.J., Liaison for Jesuit Intl. Min.

**Jesuit Volunteer Corps: Northwest*, P.O. Box 3928, 97208-3928. Tel: 503-335-8202; Fax: 503-249-1118. Email: jvcnw@jesuitvolunteers.org. Web: www.jesuitvolunteers.org. John Matcovich, Exec. Dir.

St. Joseph the Worker Corporate Internship Program, Inc., 7654 N. Delaware, 97217. Tel: 503-285-9385, Ext. 104; Fax: 503-285-9546. Email: mjacobson@delasallenorth.org. Web: www.delasallenorth.org. Michael Jacobson, Dir.

**St. Joseph the Worker Job Fund*, 605 N.W. Couch St., 97209. Tel: 503-222-5720; Fax: 503-241-7375. Email: berg@up.edu. Rev. Richard F. Berg, C.S.C., Exec. Dir. Contact Person.

Northeast Catholic Counseling Center, 8383 N.E. Sandy Blvd., Ste. 205, 97220. Tel: 503-253-0964; Fax: 503-253-7659. Email: northeastcatholic@quest.net. Sr. Barbara Kennedy, O.S.M., Dir. & Contact Person. Sisters 4; Lay Counselors 4.

Oregon Catholic Conference, 2838 E. Burnside St., 97214. Tel: 503-233-8387; Fax: 503-235-2630. Most Revs. John G. Vlazny, D.D., Pres.; Robert F. Vasa, Vice Pres.; Kenneth D. Steiner, D.D., Dir.; Rev. Dennis O'Donovan, Sec. & Treas.; Mr. Robert Castagna, Gen. Counsel & Exec. Dir.

Paulist Fathers Catholic Center for Evangelization, 2408 S.E. 16th Ave., 97214. Tel: 503-231-4955; Fax: 503-736-1383. Email: info@stphilipneripdx.org. Web: www.stphilipneripdx.org. Revs. Stephen E. Bossi, C.S.P.; Richard Colgan, C.S.P. (BO); Ann Jacobson, Contact Person.

**Women's Intercommunity AIDS Resource*, 1608 S.E. Ankeny, 97214. Tel: 503-238-4420; 888-303-4420; Fax: 503-238-4610. Email: dblair@wiar-nw.org. Denise Blair, Contact Person.

BEAVERTON. *Our Lady of Peace Institute in Catholic Teaching*, 3600 S.W. 170th Ave., 97006. Tel: 503-649-7127; Fax: 503-649-8382. Email: olpretreat@juno.com. Web: www.olpretreat.org. Rev. Leo Slatterie, Dir.; Sr. Mary Regina, Coord. & Contact Person. Staff 7; Students 40.

LAKE OSWEGO. **Cornelia Connelly Counseling Center*, 3975 S.W. Mercantile Dr., Ste. #154, 97035. Tel: 503-636-1157; Fax: 503-675 9691. Email: spearing@teleport.com. Web: www.home.teleport.com/~spearing. Sr. Joan Spearing, S.H.C.J., Dir. & Contact Person. Total people assisted annually 590.

**Mary's Woods at Marylhurst, Inc., c/o Provincial Administration Office*, P.O. Box 25, Marylhurst, 97036. Tel: 503-675-2400; Fax: 503-675-2015. Email: rfrawley@maryswoods.com. Web: www.maryswoods.com. Sisters Mary Breiling, S.N.J.M., Pres.; Roswitha Frawley, S.N.J.M., Mission Dir.; Jim Hopke, Exec. Dir.; Kimberly Kern, Dir. Marie Rose Health Center; Barbara Stewart, Contact Person. Current Residency 419.

MARYLHURST. *Holy Names Sisters Foundation, c/o Provincial Admin. Office*, P.O. Box 25, 97036. Tel: 503-675-2445; Fax: 503-636-4253. Email: acarr@snjmor.org. Diane Hood, CFO; Sisters Jane Hibbard, S.N.J.M., Pres.; Mary Breiling, S.N.J.M., Sec.; Adrienna Carr, Devel. Dir.

MILWAUKIE. *La Salle High School Educational Foundation*, 11999 S.E. Fuller Rd., 97222. Tel: 503-353-1417; Fax: 503-659-2535. Email: lasalle@lasalle.pvt.k12.or.us. Web: www.lasalle.pvt.k12.or.us. Mr. Bruce Michieli, Contact Person & Dir. Finance.

MT. ANGEL. *Benedictine Foundation of Oregon*, Box 912, 97362. Tel: 503-845-2556; Fax: 503-845-2815. Email: benfoundation@mtangel.net. Web: www.benedictine-srs.org. Steven Ritchie, Exec. Dir. & Contact Person.

Carmelite House of Studies, 915 S. Main St., P.O. Box 260, 97362. Tel: 503-845-2240; Fax: 503-845-2243. Email: maocd@open.org. Revs. Donald Kinney, O.C.D., Rector, Student Master & Contact Person; James Geoghegan, O.C.D.

St. Joseph's Shelter, 925 S. Main, 97362-9527. Tel: 503-845-6147; Fax: 503-845-2815. Email: fmele@mtangel.net. Web: www.fmele@mtangel.net. Frank Mele, Admin. & Contact Person. Special center for social services and assistance. Total Staff 7; Total People Served 352; Total Shelter Nights 23,559; Total Meals Served 19,539.

MYRTLE CREEK. *Council of Douglas County of the Society of St. Vincent dePaul*, 116 N. Main, P.O. Box 1258, 97457. Tel: 541-863-5489; Fax: 541-863-5489. Email: svdp@pioneer-net.com. Mr. Edward L. Rodrigues, Contact Person & Council Pres. Total Assisted Annually 12,633.

ST. BENEDICT. *The Abbey Foundation of Oregon*, One Abbey Dr., 97373. Tel: 503-845-3257; Fax: 503-845-3257. Email: fredmund@mtangel.edu. Web: www.mangel.edu. Rev. Edmund Smith, O.S.B., Treas. & Contact Person.

RELIGIOUS INSTITUTES OF MEN REPRESENTED IN THE ARCHDIOCESE

For further details refer to the corresponding bracketed number in the Religious Institutes of Men or Women section.

[]—*Apostolic Life Community Of Priests (Holy Spirit Fathers)*—A.L.C.P.
[0140]—*The Augustinians*—O.S.A.
[0200]—*Benedictine Monks* (Mt. Angel, OR)—O.S.B.
[0895]—*Brigittine Monastery of Our Lady of Consolidation*—O.Ss.S.
[0330]—*Brothers of the Christian Schools*—F.S.C.
[0350]—*Cistercians Order of the Strict Observance (Trappists)*—O.C.S.O.
[]—*Conventual Franciscans*—O.F.M.Conv
[]—*Discalced Carmelite Friars*—O.C.D.
[0520]—*Franciscan Friars* (Prov. of Santa Barbara)—O.F.M.
[0690]—*Jesuit Fathers and Brothers* (Oregon Prov.)—S.J.
[0780]—*Marist Fathers*—S.M.
[0660]—*Missionaries Of The Holy Spirit*—M.Sp.S.
[0910]—*Oblates of Mary Immaculate*—O.M.I.
[0430]—*Order of Preachers (Dominicans)* (Western Prov.)—O.P.
[1030]—*Paulist Fathers*—C.S.P.
[0610]—*Priests of the Congregation of Holy Cross*—C.S.C.
[1240]—*Servites* (Western Prov.)—O.S.M.
[1260]—*Society of Christ*—S.Ch.
[]—*Society of the Missionaries of St. Francis Xavier*—S.F.X.-

RELIGIOUS INSTITUTES OF WOMEN REPRESENTED IN THE ARCHDIOCESE

[0230]—*Benedictine Sisters of Pontifical Jurisdiction* (Mount Angel, OR)—O.S.B.
[0420]—*Discalced Carmelite Nuns*—O.C.D.
[1070-12]—*Dominican Sisters*—O.P.
[]—*Dominican Sisters Congregation of the Holy Cross*—O.P.
[]—*Dominican Sisters Of Caldwell, NJ*—O.P.
[1390]—*Franciscan Missionary Sisters of Our Lady of Sorrows*—O.S.F.
[]—*Franciscan Sisters of Our Lady of Perpetual Help*—O.S.F.
[]—*Holy Spirit Sisters*
[1250]—*The Institute of the Franciscan Sisters of the Eucharist*—F.S.E.
[2575]—*Institute of the Sisters of Mercy of the Americas* (Omaha, NE)—R.S.M.
[]—*Maryknoll Missionary Sisters*—M.M.
[]—*Missionaries of the Rosary of Fatima*—M.R.F.
[]—*Oblates of Saint Martha*—O.S.M.

[]—*Presentation Sisters of the Blessed Virgin Mary*—p.b.v.m.
[]—*Religious Sisters of Mercy of Alma, Mich.*—R.S.M.
[3590]—*Servants of Mary (Servite Sisters)*—O.S.M.
[]—*Sisters For Christian Community*—S.F.C.C.
[0430]—*Sisters of Charity of the Blessed Virgin Mary*—B.V.M.
[3350]—*Sisters of Providence* (Mother Joseph Province)—S.P.
[3360]—*Sisters of Providence of St.-Mary-of-the-Woods, IN*—S.P.
[3475]—*Sisters of Reparation of the Sacred Wounds of Jesus*—S.R.
[4080]—*Sisters of Social Service of Los Angeles, Inc.*—S.S.S.
[]—*Sisters of St. Dominic* (Akron, Ohio)—O.P.
[]—*Sisters of St. Dominic* (Blauvelt, NY)—O.P.
[1630]—*Sisters of St. Francis of Penance and Christian Charity*—O.S.F.
[1650]—*The Sisters of St. Francis of Philadelphia*—O.S.F.
[1530]—*Sisters of St. Francis of the Congregation of Our Lady of Lourdes, Sylvania, Ohio*—O.S.F.
[1570]—*Sisters of St. Francis of the Holy Family* (Dubuque, IA)—O.S.F.
[3890]—*Sisters of St. Joseph of Peace* (Western Prov.)—C.S.J.P.
[3960]—*Sisters of St. Mary of Oregon*—S.S.M.O.
[1830]—*The Sisters of the Good Shepherd*—R.G.S.
[1990]—*Sisters of the Holy Names of Jesus and Mary*—S.N.J.M.
[]—*Sisters of the Roman Congregation*—O.P.
[4060]—*Society of the Holy Child Jesus* (American Prov.)—S.H.C.J.
[4155]—*Vietnamese Adorers of the Holy Cross*—M.T.G.
[]—*Vietnamese Holy Cross Sisters*

ARCHDIOCESAN CEMETERIES

PORTLAND. *Gethsemani*
Mount Calvary
EUGENE. *Mount Calvary*
SALEM. *St. Barbara*

NECROLOGY

† Engel, John—Died 2003
† Karath, William, Bandon, OR Holy Trinity—Died Jan. 11, 2003
† Williams, Alfred, (Retired)—Died June 15, 2003

Diocese of Providence

(Dioecesis Providentiensis)

Most Rev.

ROBERT E. MULVEE

Bishop of Providence; ordained June 30, 1957; appointed Auxiliary Bishop of Manchester and Titular Bishop of Summa February 15, 1977; consecrated April 14, 1977; appointed Bishop of Wilmington February 19, 1985; installed April 11, 1985; appointed Coadjutor Bishop of Providence February 9, 1995; succeeded to See June 11, 1997 *Res.: 30 Fenner St., Providence, RI 02903-3603. One Cathedral Sq., Providence, RI 02903-3695.* Tel: 401-278-4545; Fax: 401-278-4548.

Most Reverend

LOUIS E. GELINEAU

Bishop Emeritus of Providence; ordained June 5, 1954; appointed Bishop of Providence December 6, 1971; consecrated January 26, 1972; retired June 11, 1997 *Res.: 30 Fenner St., Providence, RI 02903-3603. One Cathedral Sq., Providence, RI 02903-3695.* Tel: 401-278-4508; Fax: 401-278-4548.

ESTABLISHED APRIL 16, 1872.

Square Miles 1,085.

Corporate Title: Roman Catholic Bishop of Providence, a corporation sole.

Comprises the State of Rhode Island.

Bishop's Office & Chancery Office: One Cathedral Square, Providence, RI 02903-3695. Tel: 401-278-4500; Fax: 401-278-4621.

Web: www.dioceseofprovidence.org

Email: chancellor@dioceseofprovidence.org

STATISTICAL OVERVIEW

Personnel	
Bishop	1
Auxiliary Bishops	1
Retired Bishops	3
Abbots	1
Retired Abbots	1
Priests: Diocesan Active in Diocese	187
Priests: Diocesan Active Outside Diocese	17
Priests: Diocesan in Foreign Missions	1
Priests: Retired, Sick or Absent	94
Number of Diocesan Priests	299
Religious Priests in Diocese	121
Total Priests in Diocese	420
Extern Priests in Diocese	20
Ordinations:	
Diocesan Priests	4
Transitional Deacons	8
Permanent Deacons in Diocese	108
Total Brothers	74
Total Sisters	605
Parishes	
Parishes	152
With Resident Pastor:	
Resident Diocesan Priests	138
Resident Religious Priests	6
Without Resident Pastor:	
Administered by Priests	8
Missions	6
Pastoral Centers	22
Closed Parishes	1
Professional Ministry Personnel:	
Brothers	5
Sisters	14
Lay Ministers	300
Welfare	
Catholic Hospitals	1
Total Assisted	249,454
Health Care Centers	1
Total Assisted	490
Homes for the Aged	9
Total Assisted	836
Day Care Centers	5
Total Assisted	437
Specialized Homes	2
Total Assisted	176
Special Centers for Social Services	7
Total Assisted	27,500
Residential Care of Disabled	1
Total Assisted	3
Other Institutions	10
Total Assisted	142,000
Educational	
Seminaries, Diocesan	1
Students from This Diocese	11
Students from Other Diocese	2
Diocesan Students in Other Seminaries	20
Total Seminarians	31
Colleges and Universities	2
Total Students	8,266
High Schools, Diocesan and Parish	4
Total Students	2,209
High Schools, Private	8
Total Students	4,040
Elementary Schools, Diocesan and Parish	45
Total Students	11,425
Elementary Schools, Private	4
Total Students	1,295
Catechesis/Religious Education:	
High School Students	9,968
Elementary Students	30,408
Total Students under Catholic Instruction	67,642
Teachers in the Diocese:	
Priests	45
Brothers	33
Sisters	99
Lay Teachers	1,786
Vital Statistics	
Receptions into the Church:	
Infant Baptism Totals	5,405
Adult Baptism Totals	209
Received into Full Communion	385
First Communions	6,162
Confirmations	4,772
Marriages:	
Catholic	1,455
Interfaith	343
Total Marriages	1,798
Deaths	5,632
Total Catholic Population	679,275
Total Population	1,069,725

Former Bishops—Rt. Revs. THOMAS F. HENDRICKEN, D.D., consecrated first Bishop of Providence, April 28, 1872; died June 11, 1886; MATTHEW HARKINS, D.D., consecrated second Bishop of Providence, April 14, 1887; died May 25, 1921; Most Revs. WILLIAM A. HICKEY, D.D., ord. Dec. 22, 1893; appt. Coadjutor Bishop of Providence, Cum jure successionis, March 10, 1919; consecrated Titular Bishop of Claudiopolis, April 10, 1919; succeeded to the See of Providence, May 25, 1921; died Oct. 4, 1933; FRANCIS P. KEOUGH, D.D., consecrated fourth Bishop of Providence, May 22, 1934; appt. Archbishop of Baltimore, Nov. 29, 1947; died Dec. 8, 1961; RUSSELL J. MCVINNEY, D.D., appt. May 29, 1948; consecrated July 14, 1948 fifth Bishop of Providence; died Aug. 10, 1971; LOUIS E. GELINEAU, D.D., S.T.L., J.C.L. (Retired), appt. Dec. 6, 1971; consecrated sixth Bishop of Providence, Jan. 26, 1972; retired June 11, 1997.

Vicars General—Most Rev. ROBERT J. MCMANUS, D.D., S.T.D.; Rev. Msgr. WILLIAM I. VARSANYI, P.A.

Episcopal Vicars and Secretaries—

Vicar for Canonical Affairs—Rev. Msgr. WILLIAM I. VARSANYI, P.A.

Vicar for Judicial Matters—Very Rev. JOEL A. LECUIVRE, J.C.L.

Secretary for Diocesan Administration—Rev. Msgr. PAUL D. THEROUX.

Secretary for Catholic Education and Spiritual Formation and Evangelization—Mr. DAVID M. BEAUDOIN, D.Min.

Secretary for Ministerial Services—Most Rev. ROBERT J. MCMANUS, D.D., S.T.D.

Secretary for Planning & Financial Services—Rev. Msgr. WILLIAM J. MCCAFFREY.

Secretary for Social Ministry—Mr. JOHN J. BARRY III.

Deans—Very Revs. JOHN A. KILEY, Deanery No. I; JOHN E. UNSWORTH, Deanery No. II; Rev. EUGENE J. MCKENNA, Deanery No. III; Very Revs. RAYMOND C. THEROUX, Deanery No. IV; CHARLES E. DOWNING, Deanery No. V; RAYMOND B. BASTIA, Deanery No. VI; RANDOLPH G. CHEW, Deanery No. VII; Rev. JOHN C. HALLORAN, Deanery No. VIII; Very Revs. JOHN W. LOLIO, Deanery No. IX; GERALD E. BEIRNE, Deanery No. X; DANIEL M. TRAINOR, Deanery No. XI; ROBERT P. PERRON, Deanery No. XII.

Bishop's Office & Chancery Office—One Cathedral Sq., Providence, 02903-3695. Tel: 401-278-4500; Fax: 401-278-4548. Office Hours: Mon.-Fri. 8:30-4:30

Vicars General—Most Rev. ROBERT J. MCMANUS, D.D., S.T.D. Tel: 401-278-4587; Rev. Msgr. WILLIAM I.

VARSANYI, P.A. Tel: 401-278-4520.
Vicar for Canonical Affairs—Rev. Msgr. WILLIAM I. VARSANYI, P.A. Tel: 401-278-4520.
Moderator of the Curia—Rev. Msgr. PAUL D. THEROUX. Tel: 401-278-4535.
Chancellor—Rev. JOHN J. DARCY, M.A., J.C.L. Tel: 401-278-4663; 401-278-4518; Fax: 401-278-4621.
Diocesan Tribunal—
Judicial Vicar—Very Rev. JOEL A. LECUIVRE, J.C.L. Tel: 401-278-4666; Fax: 401-278-4672.
Judges—Rev. Msgr. PAUL D. THEROUX; Revs. FRANCIS P. KAYATTA; JUDE O. ONUCHUKWU, J.C.D.; RONALD P. SIMEONE; JOHN J. DARCY, M.A., J.C.L.
Assessor and Auditor—Rev. EDWARD J. MCGOVERN (Retired).
Promoter of Justice—Rev. Msgr. WILLIAM I. VARSANYI, P.A.
Defender of the Bond—Most Rev. LOUIS E. GELINEAU, D.D., S.T.L., J.C.L. (Retired).
Advocate—Rev. JOHN J. RAINONE.
Assessor and Counselor—Mrs. DIANE DIFIORE, B.S.
Notary—Mrs. LINDA L. NASTARI.
Secretary—Very Rev. JOEL A. LECUIVRE, J.C.L.
Council of Priests—One Cathedral Sq., Providence, 02903-3695. Tel: 401-278-4517.
Officers—Most Rev. ROBERT E. MULVEE, Pres.; Revs. ROBERT F. HAWKINS, Moderator; JOHN J. DARCY, M.A., J.C.L., Sec. & Treas.
Council Members—Most Rev. ROBERT J. MCMANUS, D.D., S.T.D.; Rev. Msgrs. WILLIAM J. MCCAFFREY; PAUL D. THEROUX; WILLIAM I. VARSANYI, P.A.; Very Revs. JOEL A. LECUIVRE, J.C.L.; DANIEL M. TRAINOR; Revs. STEPHEN P. AMARAL; MICHAEL A. CICCONE, O.P.; JOHN J. DARCY, M.A., J.C.L.; RICHARD P. DESAULNIERS; JOSEPH A. ESCOBAR; WILFRID G. GREGOIRE; ROBERT F. HAWKINS; ANTHONY D. IWUC; ROBERT J. MAYNARD (Retired); JOSEPH A. PESCATELLO; MARK A. SAURIOL.
College of Consultors—Most Rev. ROBERT J. MCMANUS, D.D., S.T.D.; Rev. Msgrs. WILLIAM J. MCCAFFREY; ROBERT C. NEWBOLD (Retired); PAUL D. THEROUX; WILLIAM I. VARSANYI, P.A.; Very Rev. RANDOLPH G. CHEW; Revs. JOHN C. HALLORAN; ROBERT F. HAWKINS; ANTHONY D. IWUC; JAMES T. RUGGIERI.
Finance Council—Most Revs. ROBERT E. MULVEE, Pres.; ROBERT J. MCMANUS, D.D., S.T.D.; Rev. Msgrs. WILLIAM I. VARSANYI, P.A.; WILLIAM J. MCCAFFREY, Sec.; PAUL D. THEROUX; Revs. EDWARD S. CARDENTE; JOHN J. DARCY, M.A., J.C.L.; BERTRAND L. THEROUX; Sr. M. THERESE ANTONE, R.S.M.; Mr. JOSE ALEX ARIZA; Mr. JOHN W. FLYNN; Mr. ANTHONY T. GWIAZDOWSKI; Ms. MARIE J. LANGLOIS; Mr. THOMAS J. SKALA; Hon. PAUL J. TAVARES.
Finance Officer—Mr. MICHAEL F. SABATINO, C.P.A.

Diocesan Offices and Directors

Diocesan Administration—
Secretariat for Diocesan Administration—One Cathedral Sq., Providence, 02903-3695. Tel: 401-278-4535.
Archives—Ms. VERONICA LIMA, Archive Clerk, One Cathedral Sq., Providence, 02903-3695. Tel: 401-278-4522.
Censors of Books—Rev. Msgrs. JOHN F. COX (Retired); ROBERT C. NEWBOLD (Retired).
Communications— (Legal Title: Diocesan Catholic Telecommunications Network of Rhode Island);(News Media, Radio, TV, Public Relations) Mr. WILLIAM G. HALPIN, Dir.; Ms. KAREN DAVIS, Communications Coord.; Mrs. LAURA H. TESTA, Web Page Coord., One Cathedral Sq., Providence, 02903-3695. Tel: 401-278-4600; Fax: 401-278-4649.
Media Services— (Media Production, Audio-Visual, Photography, Creative Media Programming and Consultation) Mrs. ANN FORTE. Tel: 401-278-4678.
Telecommunications— (Produces "Called to Serve" and other Catholic Programming, Liaison with State Interconnect and CATV Companies, ETWN Liaison) Miss SUSAN MCCARTHY. Tel: 401-278-4609.
Education and Compliance—Lt. ROBERT N. MCCARTHY, Dir., 80 St. Mary's Dr., Cranston, 02920. Tel: 401-941-0760.
Government Liaison—Rev. Msgr. ROBERT C. NEWBOLD, Diocesan Dir. (Retired), 493 Mt. Pleasant Ave., Providence, 02908. Tel: 401-331-9870; Rev. BERNARD A. HEALEY, Assoc. Govt. Liaison, 191 School St., P.O. Box 67, Providence, 02908. Tel: 401-333-1568; Fax: 401-333-8941.
Human Resources Office—Mr. WILLIAM G. MEYER III, Dir., One Cathedral Square, Providence, 02903-3695. Tel: 401-278-4584; Fax: 401-751-0049.
Newspaper—Revs. STANLEY T. NAKOWICZ, Exec. Editor; BERNARD A. HEALEY, Theological Consultant & Editorial Writer, 184 Broad St., Providence, 02903-4080. Tel: 401-272-1010; Fax: 401-421-8418 "The Providence Visitor", Diocesan weekly.
Propagation of the Faith— (Legal Title: Society for the Propagation of the Faith, Diocese of Providence) Rev. Msgr. WILLIAM I. VARSANYI, P.A., Dir.; Sr. M. CAROLANNE THEROUX, R.S.M., Sec., One Cathedral Sq., Providence, 02903-3695. Tel: 401-278-4519.
Catholic Relief Services—Rev. Msgr. WILLIAM I. VARSANYI, P.A. Tel: 401-278-4520.
Holy Childhood Association—Rev. Msgr. WILLIAM I. VARSANYI, P.A. Tel: 401-278-4519.
Ministerial Services—
Secretariat for Ministerial Services—Most Rev. ROBERT J. MCMANUS, D.D., S.T.D., Sec., One Cathedral Sq., Providence, 02903-3695. Tel: 401-278-4527.
Clergy Formation— (Priests, Permanent Deacons) Rev. MARCEL L. TAILLON, Dir., One Cathedral Square, Providence, 02903-3695. Tel: 401-278-4516.
Clergy Personnel—Most Rev. ROBERT J. MCMANUS, D.D., S.T.D., Dir., One Cathedral Sq., Providence, 02903-3695. Tel: 401-278-4527.
Ecumenical Commission—Rev. LIONEL A. BLAIN, Chm., 1200 Mendon Rd., Woonsocket, 02895. Tel: 401-766-0626.
Catholic-Jewish Relations—Rev. DAVID L. STOKES, Dir., 67 Cole Ave., Providence, 02906. Tel: 401-751-0196.
Grievance Committee—c/o Clergy Personnel, One Cathedral Sq., Providence, 02903-3695. Tel: 401-278-4527.
Health Care Ministries—Rev. JOHN E. WATTERSON, Dir., St. Mary Star of the Sea, P.O. Box 3329, Narragansett, 02882. Tel: 401-783-0043; Fax: 401-783-0986.
Minister for Priests—Rev. NORMAND J. GODIN, 1045 Douglas Pike, Harrisville, 02830. Tel: 401-568-7101; 401-861-7265.
Minister for Senior Priests—Rev. Msgr. GEORGE L. FRAPPIER (Retired), 341 Ballou St., Woonsocket, 02895. Tel: 401-766-7529.
Clergy Benefit Fund— (Legal Title: Our Lady, Queen of the Clergy) Rev. NORMAND J. GODIN, Sec.
Permanent Diaconate—Deacon BENJAMIN BARBOZA, One Cathedral Sq., Providence, 02903-3695. Tel: 401-278-4650.
Religious—Sr. JACQUELINE DICKEY, S.S.Ch., One Cathedral Sq., Providence, 02903-3695. Tel: 401-278-4633.
Council of Religious—Sr. JACQUELINE DICKEY, S.S.Ch., Coord.
Seminary of Our Lady of Providence— House of Formation for college students and pre-theologians) Most Rev. ROBERT J. MCMANUS, D.D., S.T.D., Rector; Rev. ALBERT A. KENNEY, Dir. Spiritual Formation, 485 Mt. Pleasant Ave., Providence, 02908. Tel: 401-331-1316; Fax: 401-521-4192.
Vocations—Revs. ALBERT A. KENNEY, Dir.; MARCEL L. TAILLON, Vocations Recruiter, 485 Mt. Pleasant Ave., Providence, 02908. Tel: 401-831-8011; Sr. JACQUELINE DICKEY, S.S.Ch., Assoc. Dir., Rel. Vocations, One Cathedral Sq., Providence, 02903-3695. Tel: 401-278-4633.
Secretariat for Catholic Education, Spiritual Formation and Evangelization—
Secretariat for Catholic Education and Spiritual Formation—Mr. DAVID M. BEAUDOIN, D.Min., Dir., One Cathedral Sq., Providence, 02903-3695. Tel: 401-278-4625.
Black Catholic Ministry—Mrs. LOIS TABELA, Coord., One Cathedral Sq., Providence, 02903-3695. Tel: 401-278-4552.
Catholic Campus Ministry—Rev. JOHN P. SOARES, Dir., URI Catholic Student Center, 90 Chapel Way, Kingston, 02881-1228. Tel: 401-847-2324.
Catholic Schools—Bro. WILLIAM DYGERT, C.S.C., Ph.D., Supt.; Ms. SHEILA DURANTE, Asst. Supt., One Cathedral Sq., Providence, 02903-3695. Tel: 401-278-4550.
Diocesan Apostolate for Persons with Handicaps—Rev. GERARD O. SABOURIN, Dir., One Cathedral Sq., Providence, 02903-3695. Tel: 401-278-4630.
Apostolate for Deaf and Hearing Impaired—Mr. JIMMY KELLY, Dir. Tel: 401-278-4630; 401-278-4583 (Voice & TTD).
SPRED (Special Religious Education)—Ms. COLLEEN TOUCHETTE, One Cathedral Sq., Providence, 02903-3695. Tel: 401-658-1174.
Religious Education—Mr. JOSEPH P. SINWELL, D.Min., Dir., 34 Fenner St., Providence, 02903. Tel: 401-278-4646.
Our Lady of Peace Spiritual Life Center—Sr. JEAN MARIE MCGEE, R.S.M., Dir., 333 Ocean Rd., P.O. Box 507, Narragansett, 02882. Tel: 401-884-7676; 401-783-2871.
Worship—Rev. PETER J. ANDREWS, Dir., St. Theresa Parish, 265 Stafford Rd., Tiverton, 02878-2498. Tel: 401-625-5722; Fax: 401-625-5384.
Youth Ministry and Young Adult Ministry—Miss LOUISE DUSSAULT, Dir., One Cathedral Sq., Providence, 02903-3695. Tel: 401-278-4626.
Catholic Scouting-Boy Scouts, Girl Scouts, Camp Fire—Rev. ANGELO N. CARUSI, Chap. Tel: 401-278-4626; Sr. DIANE RUSSO, R.S.M., Pastoral Assoc.
Catholic Youth Organization—Tel: 401-278-4626.
Youth Summer Camps—Mater Spei Day Camp, Box W, Chepachet, 02814. Tel: 401-568-3580. *Tower Hill Camp, 60 St. Dominic Rd., Peacedale, 02883.* Tel: 401-783-9123.
Social Ministry—
Secretariat for Social Ministry—Mr. JOHN J. BARRY III, Sec., 83 Stewart St., Providence, 02903-4006. Tel: 401-421-7833, Ext. 105; Fax: 401-274-5450.
Child Care—Mrs. ALEXANDRA FREED, B.A., Exec. Dir., 485 Mt. Pleasant Ave., Providence, 02908. Tel: 401-274-3094.
Community Services and Advocacy— (Legal Title: Diocesan Bureau of Social Services) Mrs. MARY BRAY, Program Monitor & Supvr., 184 Broad St., Providence, 02903-4029. Tel: 401-421-7833, Ext. 106; Fax: 401-453-6135.
AIDS Ministry—Rev. ROGER L. FORTIN, Coord. Tel: 401-421-7833, Ext. 126; 401-767-3500.
Alzheimer's Respite Care—GLORIA ISABEL HINCAPIE. Tel: 401-421-7833, Ext. 134.
Catholic Campaign for Human Development and Catholic Charities Advocacy Fund—Mr. JOHN J. BARRY III.
Chaplains of Public Institutions— Catholic Chaplaincy Team (All Correctional and Detention Institutions) Ms. PATRICIA JAEHNIG, Coord. Tel: 401-421-7833, Ext. 101. *Youth Correctional Training School*, ROLAND COMEAU. Tel: 401-421-7833, Ext. 125.
Clearinghouse Program—Mrs. MARY BRAY. Tel: 401-421-7833, Ext. 106.
Community Advocacy—VACANT.
Hispanic Ministry—Ms. AIDA HIDALGO, Dir., 184 Broad St., Providence, 02903. Tel: 401-421-7833, Ext. 133.
Immigration and Refugee Services—STELLA CARRERA, Coord. Tel: 401-421-7833, Ext. 129; Fax: 401-277-9027. Email: oirs6@aol.com.
Information Specialist—Sr. PATRICIA ONYEJE, D.M.M.M. Tel: 401-421-7833, Ext. 110.
Interfaith Community Dire Emergency Fund/ Emergency Assistance Network—RICHARD ANDRADE, Coord.; CAROL OWENS, Intake. Tel: 401-421-7833, Ext. 107.
Neighborhood Friendly Visitor Program—GLORIA ISABEL HINCAPIE, Coord. Tel: 401-421-7833, Ext. 134.
Peace and Justice—Ms. PATRICIA JAEHNIG, Coord. Tel: 401-421-7833, Ext. 101.
Respite Care Services/Subsidized Homemaker Program—GLORIA ISABEL HINCAPIE, Coord. Tel: 401-421-7833.
Community Services and Advocacy - Newport Satellite—5 Mann Ave., Newport, 02840. Tel: 401-849-7942.
Community Services and Advocacy - Peacedale Satellite—1231 Kingstown Rd., Peace Dale, 02883.
Community Services and Advocacy - West Warwick Satellite—1289 Main St., West Warwick, 02893. Tel: 401-823-6211; Fax: 401-828-0310.
Community Services and Advocacy - Woonsocket Satellite—204 N. Main St., Woonsocket, 02895. Tel: 401-762-0634.
Life and Family Ministry— (Legal Title: Retreat House of the Immaculate Heart of Mary) Ms. DOROTHY J. LEVESQUE, On-Site Supvr., 184 Broad St., Providence, 02903. Tel: 401-421-7833, Ext. 112; Fax: 401-331-4484.
Divorce and All Other Losses (S.D.R.W.)—Ms. DOROTHY J. LEVESQUE, Coord. Tel: 401-421-7833, Ext. 112.
Adoption Searches—LYNDA NOTTE. Tel: 401-421-7833, Ext. 117.
Evaluations for Maturity for Marriage—LYNDA NOTTE, Marriage Evaluation Consultant.
Hispanic Parish Outreach—Mr. SILVIO CUELLAR, Coord. Tel: 401-421-7833, Ext. 120.
Marriage Enrichment/Natural Family Planning—Deacon STEPHEN R. COTE, Coord. Tel: 401-331-4463, Ext. 114.
Marriage Preparation—Deacon STEPHEN R. COTE, Coord. Tel: 401-331-4463, Ext. 115.
Parenting Education—VICKY EGAN, Coord. Tel: 401-331-4463, Ext. 116.
Peace and Justice—Ms. CATHERINE FOCHLER MCELROY, Coord. Tel: 401-331-4463, Ext. 113.
Project Rachel/Project Gabriel/Elizabeth Ministry—LYNDA NOTTE. Tel: 401-331-4463, Ext. 117.
Rachel's Vineyard's Retreats—DONNA WARNER, Liaison.

Respect Life Program—Ms. KRIS CAPRONI. Tel: 401-331-4463, Ext. 119; Mr. SILVIO CUELLAR. Tel: 401-331-4463, Ext. 120; CAROL OWENS. Tel: 401-331-4463, Ext. 108.

Project Hope/Projecto Esperanza— (Legal Title: Project Hope/Projecto Esperanza) Mrs. MARY BRAY, Prog. Supvr., 400 Dexter St., Center Falls, 02863. Tel: 401-728-0515; Fax: 401-722-2330.

Projecto Hispano de Asistencia—400 Dexter St., Center Falls, 02863. Tel: 401-729-4727.

Senior Care Office—Miss MARY ANN ALTRUI, Exec. Dir., 10 Rhodes Ave., North Smithfield, 02896-6999. Tel: 401-767-3500.

St. Martin de Porres Multi-Service Center— (Legal Title: St. Martin de Porres Center) Mr. WAYNE HOULE, Dir., 160 Cranston St., Providence, 02907-2396. Tel: 401-274-6783; Fax: 401-274-5930.

Planning and Financial Services—

Secretariat for Planning and Financial Services—Rev. Msgr. WILLIAM J. MCCAFFREY, Sec.; Mr. MICHAEL F. SABATINO, C.P.A., Finance Officer, One Cathedral Sq., Providence, 02903-3695. Tel: 401-278-4540; Fax: 401-831-1786.

Building Commission—Mr. GEORGE STAPLES, Dir., Facilities; Ms. CAROL ANN NELSON, Facilities Mgr.; Mr. MICHAEL D. FALCONE, Facilities Engineer; Mr. MAXIME E. GIROUARD JR., Environmental Engineer, One Cathedral Sq., Providence, 02903-3695. Tel: 401-278-4636.

Cemeteries—Rev. ANTHONY W. VERDELOTTI, Dir.; Mr. ARTHUR F. LURGIO, Assoc. Dir., One Cathedral Sq., Providence, 02903-3695. Tel: 401-273-4575.

Fiscal Office—J. TIMOTHY KOCAB, Diocesan Controller, One Cathedral Sq., Providence, 02903-3695. Tel: 401-278-4616; Fax: 401-751-6808.

Insurance Commission—Rev. Msgr. WILLIAM J. MCCAFFREY, Chm., One Cathedral Sq., Providence, 02903-3695. Tel: 401-278-4616.

Catholic Mutual Group—Mr. GREG CARLSON, Claims & Risk Mgr., 80 St. Mary's Dr., Cranston, 02920-5200. Tel: 401-944-5375; 401-944-5379; Fax: 401-944-5380. Email: Mmurphy@catholicmutual.com.

Management Information Services—Ms. MARGARET RYAN, Dir., One Cathedral Sq., Providence, 02903-3695. Tel: 401-278-4598.

Parish Financial Assistant—Ms. CATHERINE MESSIER; Mr. FRANCOIS CAYO; Ms. KATHERINE HARRINGTON, One Cathedral Sq., Providence, 02903-3695. Tel: 401-278-4544.

Pastoral Planning—Ms. CONSTANCE V. THORNTON, Dir., One Cathedral Sq., Providence, 02903-3695. Tel: 401-278-4610.

Stewardship and Development— (Annual Appeal, Stewardship, Planned Giving) Mr. ANTHONY T. GWIAZDOWSKI, Dir.; Rev. Msgr. WILLIAM J. MCCAFFREY, Moderator, 80 St. Mary's Dr., Cranston, 02920. Tel: 401-943-6550.

Bishop's Partnership in Charity—Tel: 401-943-6550.

Catholic Charity Fund Appeal—Tel: 401-943-6550.

Catholic Foundation of R.I.—Ms. KAREN R. COOPER, Asst. Dir. Tel: 401-943-6550.

Victim Assistance Coordinator—Mr. MICHAEL HANSEN. Tel: 401-946-0728; Fax: 401-946-1587. Email: mhansen@dioceseofprovidence.org.

CLERGY, PARISHES, MISSIONS AND PAROCHIAL SCHOOLS

CITY OF PROVIDENCE
(PROVIDENCE COUNTY)

1—CATHEDRAL OF SS. PETER AND PAUL (1837), Rev. Francis J. Giudice, Rector; Most Rev. George H. Pearce, S.M., D.D.
Legal Title: *SS. Peter and Paul's Church, Providence, RI* In Res., Revs. Normand W. Valois (Retired); John J. Darcy, M.A., J.C.L.
Res.: 30 Fenner St., 02903. Tel: 401-331-2434 (Office); 401-278-4510 (Cathedral Residence); Fax: 401-331-2435.
Convent—Tel: 401-272-4502. Sisters of St. Joseph 6.
Catechesis/Religious Program—Students 10.

2—ST. ADALBERT (1902), (Polish), Rev. Frederick V. Slota.
Legal Title: *Saint Adalbert's Church*
Res.: 866 Atwells Ave., 02909-2596. Tel: 401-351-9306; Fax: 401-351-9306.
Convent—Tel: 401-831-3336. Sr. Theresa Mary Gondek, Supr. Felician Sisters of St. Francis 2.
Catechesis/Religious Program—864 Atwells Ave., 02909-2596. Students 73.

3—ST. AGNES (1904), Rev. Normand J. Godin.
Legal Title: *St. Agnes Church*
Res.: 351 Branch Ave., 02904. Tel: 401-861-7265; Fax: 401-454-6839.
Catechesis/Religious Program—Tel: 401-331-2547. Students 80.

4—ST. ANN (1895), (Italian), Very Rev. Raymond B. Bastia; Rev. Dean Patrick Perri.
Legal Title: *Saint Ann's Catholic Church of Providence, Rhode Island*
Res.: 2 Russo St., 02904. Tel: 401-861-5111; Fax: 401-751-5453.
School—525 Branch Ave., 02904. Tel: 401-331-0891; Fax: 401-854-0870. Lay Teachers 13; Students 159.
Catechesis/Religious Program—Tel: 401-521-5220. Students 80.

5—ST. ANTHONY (Olneyville) (1900), Rev. Joseph Protano Jr.
Legal Title: *Saint Anthony's Church Corporation, Rhode Island*
Res.: 549 Plainfield St., 02909. Tel: 401-943-2300; Fax: 401-943-2301.
Catechesis/Religious Program—Students 10.

6—ASSUMPTION OF THE BLESSED VIRGIN MARY (1871), Very Rev. Daniel M. Trainor; Rev. Gildardo Suarez (Colombia).
Legal Title: *The Church of the Assumption, Providence, Rhode Island*
Res.: 791 Potters Ave., 02907. Tel: 401-941-1248; Fax: 401-781-4887.
Catechesis/Religious Program—Tel: 401-941-3768. Students 272.

7—ST. AUGUSTINE (1929), Revs. Barry R.L. Connerton; Edward J. Wilson Jr.; Alfred C. Lonardo. (Legal title: Saint Augustine's Church, Providence, Rhode Island) In Res., Rev. Msgr. Salvatore R. Matano.
Res.: 20 Old Rd., 02908. Tel: 401-831-3503; Fax: 401-421-9060.
School—635 Mt. Pleasant Ave., 02908. Tel: 401-831-1213; Fax: 401-831-4256. Mrs. Paul F. Morry, Prin. Sisters 2; Lay Teachers 26; Students 340.
Catechesis/Religious Program—Students 436.

8—ST. BARTHOLOMEW (1907), (Italian), Revs. Alfred P. Almonte, C.S.; Mario Titotto, C.S.; Sr. Rita Petrarca, A.S.C.J., Pastoral Assoc.; Deacon Robert L. Gallo.
Legal Title: *Saint Bartholomew's Church Corporation*
Res.: 297 Laurel Hill Ave., 02909-3897. Tel: 401-944-4466; Fax: 401-946-5866.
School—315 Laurel Hill Ave., 02909-3898. Tel: 401-944-5662; Fax: 401-946-6422. Mr. Frank D. Spaziano, Prin. Lay Teachers 15; Students 199.
Catechesis/Religious Program—Tel: 401-944-4466, Ext. 114; Fax: 401-946-5866. Students 165.

9—BLESSED SACRAMENT (1888), Rev. Anthony W. Verdelotti.
Legal Title: *The Church of the Blessed Sacrament in Providence, Rhode Island*
Res.: 239 Regent Ave., 02908. Tel: 401-751-7575; Fax: 401-621-9605.
School—240 Regent Ave., 02908. Tel: 401-831-3993. June Spencer, Prin. Lay Teachers 22; Students 341.
Catechesis/Religious Program—Students 99.
Convent—350 Mount Pleasant Ave., 02908. Tel: 401-274-6578. Sisters Faithful Companions of Jesus 4.

10—ST. CASIMIR (1919), (Lithuanian), [JC Rev. Adolph Klimanskis (NOR), Admin.
Legal Title: *Saint Casimir's Church, Providence, Rhode Island*
Res.: 350 Smith St., 02908. Tel: 401-331-1051.

11—ST. CHARLES BORROMEO (1874), (French), Rev. Robert J. Giardina; Deacons Jose Rico, Pastoral Assoc.; Rony Lopez; Joseph Braga.
Legal Title: *Saint Charles Borromeo Roman Catholic Church, Providence, Rhode Island*
Res.: 178 Dexter St., 02907. Tel: 401-421-6441; Fax: 401-454-4986.
Catechesis/Religious Program—Students 228.

12—ST. EDWARD (1874), Revs. Edward S. Cardente; Kris M. Von Maluski; Nolasco Tamayo Alvarez (Colombia).
Legal Title: *The Church of St. Joseph Geneva Rhode Island*
Res.: 10 Caxton St., 02904. Tel: 401-353-3120; Fax: 401-353-5126.
Church: 997 Branch Ave., 02904. Tel: 401-331-4035.
Catechesis/Religious Program—Tel: 401-353-5215. Students 6.

13—GENESIS COMMUNITY, Closed., For inquiries for parish records contact Cathedral of SS. Peter & Paul, Providence.

14—ST. HEDWIG, Closed., For inquiries for sacramental records contact St. Adalbert Parish, Providence.

15—HOLY CROSS (1949), (Italian), Rev. Anthony Mancini, Admin.; Deacon John J. Natalizia.
Legal Title: *Corporation of the Church of the Holy Cross*
Res.: 18 King Philip St., 02909. Tel: 401-274-5225; Fax: 401-274-6635.
Catechesis/Religious Program—Tel: 401-751-1144. Mrs. June Carnevale, D.R.E. Students 133.

16—HOLY GHOST (1889), (Italian), Rev. Tarcisio Bagatin, C.S.
Legal Title: *Corporation of the Church of the Holy Ghost, Rhode Island* In Res., Rev. Michael Tarro, C.S.
Res.: 472 Atwells Ave., 02909. Tel: 401-421-3551; Fax: 401-421-3557.
School—35 Swiss St., 02909. Tel: 401-421-4455; Fax: 401-421-5444. Mrs. Carol Wood-Soltys, Prin. Sisters of Mercy of the Americas 1; Lay Teachers 9; Students 186.
School—Day Care Center, Tel: 401-521-9510. Lay Teachers 3; Children 40.
Catechesis/Religious Program—Mr. Alfred Casinelli, D.R.E. Students 45.

17—HOLY NAME OF JESUS (1882), (Cape Verdean), Rev. Kevin R. Fisette; Deacons Frederick A. Young; Charles L. Hanrahan.
Legal Title: *Church of the Holy Name of Jesus at Providence, Rhode Island*
Res.: 99 Camp St., 02906-1799. Tel: 401-272-4515; Fax: 401-272-4616.
School—Tel: 401-351-0533; Fax: 401-351-0371. Lay Teachers 12; Students 156.
Catechesis/Religious Program—Students 77.

18—IMMACULATE CONCEPTION, Closed., For inquiries for sacramental records contact St. Patrick Parish, Providence.

19—ST. JOHN, Closed., (Legal title: St. John Church of Providence Rhode Island). Sacramental records are located at St. Mary Church, Providence.

20—ST. JOSEPH (Foxpoint) (1851), Rev. Msgr. William J. McCaffrey; Sr. Mary Ellen Maytum, R.S.M., Pastoral Min.
Legal Title: *St. Joseph's Church Providence Rhode Island* In Res., Rev. Henry J. Bodah.
Res.: 92 Hope St., 02906. Tel: 401-421-9137; Fax: 401-621-5349.
Catechesis/Religious Program—Students 47.

21—ST. MARON, Rev. John J. Darcy, M.A., J.C.L.
Legal Title: *Church of St. Maron in Providence*
Res.: One Cathedral Square, 02903-3695. Tel: 401-278-4663; Fax: 401-278-4621.

22—ST. MARY (Broadway) (1853), Rev. Frank S. Salmani; Deacon Robert Nicholson.
Legal Title: *St. Mary's Church Providence Rhode Island*
Res.: 538 Broadway, 02909-3329. Tel: 401-274-3434.
School—30 Barton St., 02909. Tel: 401-274-5250. Dr. Frank Pallotta, Prin. Sisters 2; Lay Teachers 11; Students 150.
Catechesis/Religious Program—Students 30.

23—ST. MICHAEL THE ARCHANGEL (South Providence) (1859), Revs. Raymond B. Malm (Haiti); Jacques E. Chavannes (Haiti); Deacon Juan Andres Perez.
Legal Title: *St. Michael's Providence, Rhode Island*
Res.: 239 Oxford St., 02905. Tel: 401-781-7210; Fax: 401-461-6164.
Catechesis/Religious Program—Students 320.

24—OUR LADY OF CHARITY, Rev. Msgr. William I. Varsanyi, P.A.
Legal Title: *Church of Our Lady of Charity of Providence*
Res.: One Cathedral Sq., 02903-3695.

25—OUR LADY OF LOURDES (1904), (French), Rev. Msgr. Paul D. Theroux; Deacon Anthony Wendolowski.
Legal Title: *Church of Our Lady of Lourdes*
Res.: 901 Atwells Ave., 02909. Tel: 401-272-8127; Fax: 401-861-0226.

26—OUR LADY OF MT. CARMEL (1921), (Italian), Revs. Raymond P. Luft; Hugo Carmona (Colombia); Fredy Jimenez (Colombia).
Legal Title: *Church of Our Lady of Mount Carmel, Providence*
Res.: 12 Spruce St., 02903. Tel: 401-274-2113; Fax: 401-453-1221.
Catechesis/Religious Program—Students 66.

27—OUR LADY OF THE ROSARY (1886), (Portuguese), Revs. Joseph A. Escobar; Antonio M. Paiva, Pastor Emeritus (Retired).
Legal Title: *Church of Our Lady of the Rosary*
Res.: 463 Benefit St., 02903. Tel: 401-421-5621; Fax: 401-421-0783.
Catechesis/Religious Program—Tel: 401-273-1685. Elisa Guerra Thibeault, D.R.E. Students 220.

28—ST. PATRICK (1841), Rev. James T. Ruggieri; Sr. Carol Mary Morrison, R.S.M., Pastoral Assoc.; Eduardo Birbuet, Pastoral Assoc.
Legal Title: *St. Patrick's Church, Providence, Rhode Island*
Res.: 152 Holden St., 02908. Tel: 401-421-7070; Fax: 401-751-7085.
Church: 244 Smith St., 02908.
School—Tel: 401-421-9300; Fax: 401-421-9300. Mr. Stephen M. Raymond, Prin. Lay Teachers 13; Students 159.

Catechesis/Religious Program—Tel: 401-272-7296. Students 80.

29—St. Pius V (1918), Revs. Michael A. Ciccone, O.P.; Aaron J. Cote, O.P; Bernard Mulcahy, O.P.
Legal Title: *Saint Pius Church, Providence, Rhode Island* In Res., Rev. John L. Sullivan, O.P.; Very Rev. John P. Burchill, O.P., Prior; Rev. Joseph McGroarty, O.P.
Res.: 55 Elmhurst Ave., 02908. Tel: 401-751-4871; Fax: 401-273-1089.
School—49 Elmhurst Ave., 02908. Tel: 401-421-9750; Fax: 401-455-3928. Lay Teachers 17; Students 263.
Catechesis/Religious Program—Tel: 401-751-4871, Ext. 117. Students 192.
Convent—30 Elmhurst Ave., 02908. Tel: 401-751-5878.

30—St. Raymond (1911), Rev. Edward L. Pieroni.
Legal Title: *Saint Raymond's Church Corporation*
Res.: 2 Matilda St., 02904-1812. Tel: 401-351-4224; Fax: 401-274-3350.
Church: 1240 N. Main St., 02906. Tel: 401-351-4224; Fax: 401-274-3350.
Catechesis/Religious Program—Tel: 401-274-3350. Students 26.

31—St. Sebastian (1915), Revs. Robert W. Hayman, M.A., Ph.D.; David L. Stokes.
Legal Title: *Church of Saint Sebastian*
Res.: 67 Cole Ave., 02906. Tel: 401-751-0196; Fax: 401-273-7406.
Catechesis/Religious Program—Tel: 401-272-6062. Students 117.

32—St. Teresa of Avila (Olneyville) (1883), Rev. Raymond L. Tetrault.
Legal Title: *Saint Teresa's Church Providence Rhode Island*
Res.: 18 Pope St., 02909. Tel: 401-831-7714; Fax: 401-831-7727.
Catechesis/Religious Program—Students 89.

33—St. Thomas (Fruit Hill) (1886), Rev. Francis P. Kayatta; Deacon Albert DePetrillo.
Legal Title: *St. Thomas' Church of Manton Rhode Island*
Res.: 65 Fruit Hill Ave., 02909. Tel: 401-272-7118; Fax: 401-272-8431.
School—Tel: 401-351-0403. See St. Thomas Regional School
Catechesis/Religious Program—Tel: 401-272-1443. Students 225.
Convent—41 Edendale Ave., 02911. Tel: 401-272-1722.

OUTSIDE THE CITY OF PROVIDENCE

Barrington, Bristol Co.

1—Holy Angels (1913), (Italian), Rev. Raymond J. Ferrick.
Legal Title: *Holy Angel's Church Corporation*
Res.: 341 Maple Ave., 02806. Tel: 401-245-7743; Fax: 401-245-9698.
Catechesis/Religious Program—341 Maple Ave., 02806. Tel: 401-247-1764. Students 100.

2—St. Luke (West Barrington) (1942), Revs. William R. Jenkinson; David F. Gaffney.
Legal Title: *Saint Luke's Church Corporation, Barrington*
Res.: 108 Washington Rd., 02806-1133. Tel: 401-246-1212; Fax: 401-246-1301.
School—Waldron Ave., 02806. Tel: 401-246-0990; Fax: 401-246-2120. Marycarol Gentile, Prin. Lay Teachers 17; Students 296.
Catechesis/Religious Program—Tel: 401-246-1363. Patricia Grattan, D.R.E. (Grades 1-5); Diane Comerford, D.R.E. (Grades 6-10). Students 732.

Bristol, Bristol Co.

1—St. Elizabeth (1913), (Portuguese), Revs. Thomas J. Ferland; Fernando Cabral (Portugal).
Legal Title: *Saint Elizabeth's Church of Bristol* In Res, Rev. Joseph D. Santos Jr. (Portugal).
Res.: 577 Wood St., 02809-2395. Tel: 401-253-8366.
School—10 Monroe Ave., 02809. Tel: 401-253-7622; Fax: 401-253-5910. Mrs. Magdalen Chianese, Prin. Lay Teachers 14; Students 158.
Catechesis/Religious Program—Tel: 401-253-3501; Fax: 401-253-7630. Ms. Loretta Francis, D.R.E.; Mrs. Maureen Jernigan, D.R.E. Students 501.

2—St. Mary (1869), [CEM] Rev. Barry J. Gamache.
Legal Title: *Saint Mary's Church, Bristol, Rhode Island*
Res.: 330 Wood St., 02809. Tel: 401-253-3300; Fax: 401-253-3300.
Catechesis/Religious Program—Tel: 401-253-2270. Students 405.
Mission—Our Lady of Prudence Prudence Island, Newport Co. 02872.

3—Our Lady of Mount Carmel (1917), (Italian), [JC] Rev. Henry P. Zinno Jr.; Deacon Paul Bisbano.
Legal Title: *Church of Our Lady of Mount Carmel, Bristol*
Res.: 141 State St., 02809. Tel: 401-253-9449; Fax: 401-253-5687. Email: hpz612@yahoo.com.
School—Maestre Pie Filippini, 117 State St., 02809. Tel: 401-253-8455; Fax: 401-254-8234. Email: hpz612@yahoo.com. Sr. Ellamae McDonald, M.P.F., Prin. (Religious Teachers Filippini) Sisters 2; Lay Teachers 12; Students 206.
Catechesis/Religious Program—131 State St., 02809. Tel: 401-624-3664. Students 260.

Burrillville, Providence Co.

1—St. Joseph (Pascoag) (1884), Rev. Clifford J. Cabral; Deacon Anthony E. Muscatelli.
Legal Title: *Saint Joseph's Roman Catholic Church of Pascoag*
Res.: 183 Sayles Ave., P.O. Box 188, Pascoag, 02859. Tel: 401-568-2411; Fax: 401-568-2586.
Catechesis/Religious Program—Students 281.

2—Our Lady of Good Help (Mapleville) (1905), Rev. Timothy J. Lemlin; Deacon Richard J. Lapierre.
Legal Title: *Eglise de Notre Dame de Bonsecours*
Res.: 1063 Victory Hwy., Box 158, Mapleville, 02839. Tel: 401-568-5272; Fax: 401-568-5351.
Catechesis/Religious Program— Mrs. Patricia Ducharme, D.R.E. Students 205.

3—St. Patrick (Harrisville) (1854), [CEM] [JC 2] Rev. Bernard M. O'Reilly, M.A., Ph.D., D.Min.
Legal Title: *St. Patrick's Church, Burrillville, Rhode Island*
Res.: 45 Main St., Harrisville, 02830. Tel: 401-568-5600; Fax: 401-568-7132.
Catechesis/Religious Program—Students 244.
Mission—St. Louis Chapel Old Victory Hwy., Glendale, Providence Co. 02826.

4—St. Theresa of the Child Jesus (Nasonville) (1923), [CEM] Rev. Roland L. Simoneau.
Legal Title: *Church of Saint Teresa of the Child Jesus, Nasonville*
Res.: 35 Dion Dr., Harrisville, 02830. Tel: 401-568-8280; Fax: 401-567-9238.
Catechesis/Religious Program—Tel: 401-568-3057. Students 108.

Central Falls, Providence Co.

1—The Holy Spirit Catholic Community (1997), [CEM], Consolidation of the following three parishes: Holy Trinity, (Legal Title: Church of the Holy Trinity, Central Falls); Notre Dame, (Legal Title: Notre Dame Church); and St. Matthew, (Legal Title: Saint Matthew's Church of Central Falls). Revs. Eugene R. Lessard; Otoniel J. Gomez-Serna (Colombia); Gerard J. Caron.
Res.: 1030 Dexter St., 02863-1717. Tel: 401-726-2600; 401-725-1748; 401-723-5326; Fax: 401-722-0224.
Catechesis/Religious Program—Tel: 401-722-3717. Students 405.

2—Holy Trinity (1989), Merged, with Notre Dame, Central Falls and St. Matthew, Central Falls to form The Holy Spirit Catholic Communtity, Central Falls. (Legal title: Church of the Holy Trinity, Central Falls)

3—St. Joseph (1906), (Polish), Rev. Anthony D. Iwuc.
Legal Title: *St. Joseph's Church of Central Falls*
Res.: 391 High St., 02863-3109. Tel: 401-723-5427; Fax: 401-726-5971.
Catechesis/Religious Program—Students 56.

4—St. Matthew's (1906), (French), Merged, with Holy Trinity, Central Falls and Notre Dame, Central Falls to form The Holy Spirit Catholic Community, Central Falls. (Legal title: Saint Matthew's Church of Central Falls).

5—Notre Dame (1873), (French), Merged, with Holy Trinity, Central Falls and St. Matthew, Central Falls to form The Holy Spirit Catholic Community, Central Falls. (Legal title: Notre Dame Church).

Charlestown, Washington Co., St. Mary (Carolina) (1946), Rev. David E. Green; Deacons Paul Theroux; John S. Shea.
Legal Title: *Saint Mary's Church Corporation, Carolina*
Res.: P.O. Box 475, Carolina, 02812. Tel: 401-364-7214; Fax: 401-364-0182.
Catechesis/Religious Program—Tel: 401-864-7935. Students 278.
Mission—St. James 2079 Mat. School House Rd., Washington Co. 02813. Tel: 401-364-7214.

Coventry, Kent Co.

1—SS. John and Paul (1955), Very Rev. Paul R. Grenon; Revs. Michael J. Menna; David C. Procaccini; Deacon Robert A. Turbitt II.
Legal Title: *SS. John and Paul Parish Corporation, Coventry*
Res.: 341 S. Main St., 02816. Tel: 401-821-5764; Fax: 401-828-5351.
343 S. Main St., 02816.
Father John V. Doyle School—343 South Main St., 02816. Tel: 401-821-3756; Fax: 401-828-5351. Email: hpz612@yahoo.com. Mr. J. Robert McDermott, Prin.; Mrs. Vivian Ryan, Vice Prin. Lay Teachers 23; Students 465.
Catechesis/Religious Program—Tel: 401-821-4780. Students 1,296.

2—Our Lady of Czenstochowa (Quidnick) (1905), (Polish), Rev. Stephen P. Amaral.
Legal Title: *Church of Our Lady of Czenstochowa*
Res.: 445 Washington St., 02816. Tel: 401-821-7991; Fax: 401-821-8714.
Catechesis/Religious Program—Students 70.

3—St. Vincent de Paul (Anthony) (1937), (French), Rev. Paul J. Laporte. (Legal title: Church of Saint Vincent de Paul, Anthony, Rhode Island).
Res.: 6 St. Vincent de Paul St., 02816. Tel: 401-821-8719; Fax: 401-827-5071.
Convent—8 St. Vincent de Paul St., 02816. Tel: 401-828-6506. Sr. Lorette Soucy, P.M., Supr. Sisters of the Presentation of Mary 2.
Catechesis/Religious Program—2 St. Vincent de Paul St., 02816. Tel: 401-828-3090. Students 151.

Cranston, Providence Co.

1—St. Ann (1858), Revs. Farrell E. McLaughlin; John J. Rainone. (Legal title: St. Anne's Church, Cranston, Rhode Island).
Res.: 1493 Cranston St., 02920. Tel: 401-942-2767; Fax: 401-942-2773.
Catechesis/Religious Program—Tel: 401-942-0655. Students 310.

2—Holy Apostles (1991), Rev. Richard D. Sheahan.
Legal Title: *Holy Apostles Church, Cranston, Rhode Island*
Res.: 800 Pippin Orchard Rd., 02921. Tel: 401-946-5586; Fax: 401-946-5066.
Catechesis/Religious Program—Students 1,525.

3—Immaculate Conception (Oaklawn) (1958), Rev. Ronald E. Brassard; Deacons Carmine Forlingieri; Thomas R. Raspallo; Vera Candelmo, Pastoral Assoc.
Legal Title: *Immaculate Conception Church Corporation, Cranston*
Res.: 237 Garden Hills Dr., 02920. Tel: 401-942-1854; Fax: 401-942-2897.
Catechesis/Religious Program— Barbara Prata, D.R.E.; Keith Dorsey, D.R.E. Students 552.

4—St. Mark (Garden City) (1950), Revs. Richard A. Donnelly; Giacomo Capoverdi; Deacon Robert C. Persson.
Legal Title: *Saint Mark's Church Corporation of Cranston*
Res.: 9 Garden Ct., 02920. Tel: 401-942-1616.
Catechesis/Religious Program—Tel: 401-942-3231. Students 412.

5—St. Mary (Knightsville) (1925), (Italian),, (Santa Maria della Civita) Revs. James J. Verdelotti; Angelo N. Carusi; Deacon Peter A. Ceprano.
Legal Title: *Saint Mary's Church, Cranston*
Res.: 1525 Cranston St., 02920-5297. Tel: 401-942-1492; Fax: 401-946-2531.
School—Tel: 401-944-4107; Fax: 401-944-2395. Email: hpz612@yahoo.com. Mrs. Elizabeth Mizzoni, Prin. Lay Teachers 16; Students 269.
Catechesis/Religious Program—Tel: 401-944-1323; Fax: 401-944-2461. Phyllis Ann Persson, D.R.E. Students 388.

6—St. Matthew (Auburn) (1909), Revs. James R. Collins; Peter J. D'Ambrosia, S.M.; Charles R. Grondin.
Legal Title: *St. Matthew's Church Corporation*
Res.: 15 Frances Ave., 02910. Tel: 401-461-7172; Fax: 401-461-7339.
Church: Elmwood & Park Ave., 02910.
School—1301 Elmwood Ave., 02910. Tel: 401-941-8954; Fax: 401-781-7722. Email: hpz612@yahoo.com. Ms. Elaine P. Dykstra, Prin. Lay Teachers 16; Students 190.
Catechesis/Religious Program—Tel: 401-781-4568. Sr. Mercian Hassett, R.S.M., D.R.E. Students 396.

7—St. Paul (Edgewood) (1907), Very Rev. Randolph G. Chew; Rev. Robert H. Forcier; Sr. Mary Ann Rossi, C.N.D., Pastoral Assoc.
Legal Title: *Saint Paul's Church of Edgewood* In Res., Rev. Robert J. Maynard (Retired).
Res.: One St. Paul Pl., 02905. Tel: 401-461-5734; Fax: 401-785-3613.
School—1789 Broad St., 02905. Tel: 401-941-2030; Fax: 401-941-2084. Email: hpz612@yahoo.com. Mrs. Jean Patterson, Prin. Lay Teachers 13; Students 183.
Catechesis/Religious Program—Tel: 401-941-5576. Elizabeth Neubauer, D.R.E. Students 367.

Cumberland, Providence Co.

1—St. Aidan (1962), Rev. Donald L. Depatie.
Legal Title: *St. Aidan Church Corporation, Cumberland*
Res.: 1460 Diamond Hill Rd., 02864. Tel: 401-333-5897; Fax: 401-333-5078.
Catechesis/Religious Program—Tel: 401-333-9030. Students 223.

2—St. Joan of Arc (Cumberland Hill) (1929), Rev. Norman W. Bourdon.
Legal Title: *Saint Joan's Church, Cumberland, Rhode Island*
Res.: 3357 Mendon Rd., 02864-2195. Tel: 401-658-2084; Fax: 401-658-2086.
Catechesis/Religious Program—Tel: 401-658-0734. Students 590.

3—St. John Baptist Mary Vianney (Diamond Hill)

(1953), Rev. J. Raymond Theroux; Deacon Paul H. Lambert.
Legal Title: *Saint John Baptist Mary Vianney Church Corporation, Diamond Hill*
Res.: 3609 Diamond Hill Rd., 02864. Tel: 401-333-6060; Fax: 401-333-0766.
Catechesis/Religious Program—3587 Diamond Hill Rd., 02864. Tel: 401-333-2347. Students 931.

4—ST. JOSEPH (Ashton) (1872), [CEM] Rev. John W. Hunt.
Legal Title: *St. Joseph's Church, Ashton, Rhode Island*
Res.: Mendon Rd., P.O Box 7005, 02864. Tel: 401-333-4013; Fax: 401-333-4013.
Catechesis/Religious Program—Tel: 401-333-4014. Students 390.

5—OUR LADY OF FATIMA (Valley Falls) (1953), (Portuguese), Revs. Dennis J. Kieton; Domingos M. da Cunha.
Legal Title: *Church of Our Lady of Fatima, Valley Falls*
Res.: Fatima Dr., 02864. Tel: 401-723-6719; Fax: 401-723-1698.
Catechesis/Religious Program—Tel: 401-724-3454; Fax: 401-724-3454. Students 350.

6—ST. PATRICK (Valley Falls) (1861), [CEM 2] Rev. Lawrence E. Toole.
Legal Title: *St. Patrick's Church Corporation, Valley Falls, Rhode Island*
Res.: 301 Broad St., 02864. Tel: 401-725-0344.
Catechesis/Religious Program—Tel: 401-725-0344. Students 280.

EAST GREENWICH, KENT CO., OUR LADY OF MERCY (1853), [CEM] Very Rev. John W. Lolio; Rev. Michael A. Colello.
Legal Title: *Our Lady of Mercy, Greenwich, Rhode Island*
Res.: 65 Third St., 02818. Tel: 401-884-4968; Fax: 401-884-1415.
Catechesis/Religious Program—Tel: 401-884-1061. Students 698.
Convent—36 Fourth Ave., 02818. Tel: 401-884-9292.
Convent—66 Fifth Ave., 02818. Tel: 401-886-4753.

EAST PROVIDENCE, PROVIDENCE CO.

1—ST. BRENDAN (Riverside) (1909), Very Rev. John E. Unsworth; Rev. Jared J. Costanza.
Legal Title: *St. Brendan's Church*
Res.: 60 Turner Ave., Riverside, 02915. Tel: 401-433-2600; Fax: 401-433-3336.
School—55 Turner Ave., Riverside, 02915. Tel: 401-433-1290; Fax: 401-433-4600. Email: hpz612@yahoo.com. Lay Teachers 12; Students 198.
Catechesis/Religious Program—Tel: 401-433-2680. Robert J. Ferri, D.R.E. Students 830.

2—ST. FRANCIS XAVIER (1915), (Portuguese), Revs. Victor M. Vieira; Edward A. Sousa Jr.; Timothy D. Reilly.
Legal Title: *Saint Francis Xavier's Church* In Res., Rev. Louis M. Diogo (Retired).
Res.: 81 N. Carpenter St., 02914. Tel: 401-434-1878; Fax: 401-438-1950.
Catechesis/Religious Program—Tel: 401-434-3153; 401-434-9421. Students 825.

3—ST. MARGARET (Rumford) (1888), Rev. Thomas L. Keenan; Deacon John F. Needham.
Legal Title: *Saint Margaret's Church Corporation, East Providence Rhode Island*
Res.: 1098 Pawtucket Ave., Rumford, 02916. Tel: 401-438-3230; Fax: 401-438-4221.
School—42 Bishop Ave., Rumford, 02916. Tel: 401-434-2338; Fax: 401-431-0266. Email: hpz612@yahoo.com. Mr. John Rezendes, Prin. Lay Teachers 17; Students 270.
Catechesis/Religious Program—Tel: 401-435-4755. Students 245.

4—ST. MARTHA (1956), Rev. Jude P. McGeough.
Legal Title: *St. Martha's Church Corporation, East Providence*
Res.: 2595 Pawtucket Ave., 02914. Tel: 401-434-4060; Fax: 401-434-4849.
Catechesis/Religious Program—Tel: 401-434-7030. Students 197.

5—OUR LADY OF LORETO (1920), (Italian—Brazilian), Rev. Stanley T. Nakowicz.
Legal Title: *Church of Our Lady of Loreto, East Providence*
Res.: 346 Waterman Ave., 02914. Tel: 401-434-3535; Fax: 401-434-8204.
Catechesis/Religious Program—Students 92.

6—SACRED HEART (1876), Rev. Peter S. DiTullio, S.C.
Legal Title: *Church of the Sacred Heart*
Res.: 118 Taunton Ave., 02914. Tel: 401-434-0326; Fax: 401-434-0326. Email: hpz612@yahoo.com.
School—56 Purchase St., 02914. Tel: 401-434-1080; Fax: 401-434-4638. Email: hpz612@yahoo.com. Lay Teachers 14; Students 179.
School—Nursery-Day Care, 101 Taunton Ave., 02914. Tel: 401-434-2462. Staff 7; Children 80.
Catechesis/Religious Program—Students 62.

EXETER, WASHINGTON CO., BLESSED KATERI TEKAKWITHA MISSION (1981),, (An operation of Saint Hedwig's Church Corporation) Rev. Gerard O. Sabourin, Admin.
84 Exeter Rd., 02822. Tel: 401-295-0234.
Catechesis/Religious Program—Students [illegible]0.

FOSTER, PROVIDENCE CO., ST. PAUL THE APOSTLE (1972), Rev. Paul A. Charland.
Legal Title: *St. Paul's Church Corporation, Foster*
Res.: 116A Danielson Pike, 02825-1468. Tel: 401-647-3664; Fax: 401-647-3680.
Catechesis/Religious Program—Students 306.

GLOCESTER, PROVIDENCE CO., ST. EUGENE (Chepachet) (1956), Rev. Charles P. Quinn; Deacon Norman Bacon.
Legal Title: *St. Eugene's Church Corporation, Chepachet*
Res.: 1251 Putnam Pike, P.O. Box A, Chepachet, 02814. Tel: 401-568-5102; Fax: 401-567-7347.
Catechesis/Religious Program—Students 320.

HOPKINTON, WASHINGTON CO.

1—ST. JOSEPH (Hope Valley) (1939), Rev. Michael J. Leckie.
Legal Title: *Saint Joseph's Church, Hope Valley*
Res.: P.O. Box 388, 1105 Main St., Hope Valley, 02832. Tel 401-539-8311.
Catechesis/Religious Program—Tel: 401-539-8312. Students [illegible]08.

2—OUR LADY OF VICTORY (Ashaway) (1946), Rev. James V. Farley.
Legal Title: *Church of Our Lady of Victory, Ashaway*
Res.: 169[illegible] Main St., P.O. Box 276, Ashaway, 02804. Tel: 401-377-8830; Fax: 401-377-8830.
Catechesis/Religious Program—Tel: 401-377-8435; Fax: 401-377-8830. Students 190.

JAMESTOWN NEWPORT CO., ST. MARK (Jamestown) (1909), [CEM] Rev. William J. O'Neill.
Legal Title: *Saint Mark Church of Jamestown*
Res.: 60 Narragansett Ave., 02835. Tel: 401-423-1421; Fax: 401-423-2067.
Catechesis/Religious Program—Tel: 401-423-1518. Students 328.

JOHNSTON, PROVIDENCE CO.

1—ST. BRIGID (Thornton) (1915), Rev. Robert A. Rochon.
Legal Title: *Saint Brigid's Church of Johnston*
Res.: 1231 Plainfield, 02919. Tel: 401-944-2232; Fax: 401 944-0306.
Catechesis/Religious Program—Tel: 401-949-0330. Students 105.

2—OUR LADY OF GRACE (1913), (Italian), Rev. Douglas J. Spina; Deacons Robert P. Troia; Armand Ragosta.
Legal Title: *Church of Our Lady of Grace*
Res.: 4 Lafayette St., 02919. Tel: 401-231-2220; Fax: 401-231-3905.
Catechesis/Religious Program—Tel: 401-231-8959. Students 190.

3—ST. ROBERT BELLARMINE (1963), Rev. John G. LaPointe.
Legal Title: *St. Robert Bellarmine Church Corporation, Johnston*
Res.: 18[illegible]4 Atwood Ave., 02919-3215. Tel: 401-232-5600; Fax: 401-231-5793.
Catechesis/Religious Program—Tel: 401-232-9321; Fax: 401-232-5793. Students 131.

4—ST. ROCCO (1903), (Italian), Revs. Ralph Bove, C.S.; Mardeo C. Reyes; Sr. Shawn Lyons, A.S.C.J., Pastoral Assoc.; Deacon Robert P. Troia.
Legal Title: *Saint Rocco Church of Johnston*
Res.: 927 Atwood Ave., 02919. Tel: 401-942-5203; Fax: 401-464-6422.
School—931 Atwood Ave., 02919. Tel: 401-944-2993; Fax: 401-944-3019. Sr. Mary Grace Walsh, A.S.C.J., Prin. Apostles of the Sacred Heart of Jesus 2; Lay Teachers 25; Students 500.
Catechesis/Religious Program—Tel: 401-944-6040. Sr. Rose Alfieri, C.P., D.R.E. Students 325.

LINCOLN, PROVIDENCE CO.

1—ST. AMBROSE (Albion) (1905), [CEM] Rev. Bernard A. Healey.
Legal Title: *St. Ambrose Church, Albion, Rhode Island*
Res.: [illegible]91 School St., Albion, 02802. Tel: 401-333-1568; Fax: 401-333-8941.
Catechesis/Religious Program—Tel: 401-334-3735. Students 200.

2—ST. JAMES (Manville) (1874), [CEM] Rev. Richard P. Desaulniers; Deacon Gregory Horton.
Legal Title: *Saint James Church of Manville, Rhode Island*
Res.: 33 Division St., Box 60, Manville, 02838. Tel: 401-766-1558; Fax: 401-766-1561.
Catechesis/Religious Program—57 Division St., Manville, 02838. Tel: 401-769-2676. Students 200.

3—ST. JUDE (Lincoln) (1946), Rev. Bernard C. Lavin; Deacon Lionel J. Remilliard Jr.
Legal Title: *St. Jude's Church, Lincoln*
Res.: 301 Front St., 02865. Tel: 401-725-8140; Fax: 401-726-4946.
Catechesis/Religious Program—Tel 401-725-8120. Sr. Mary Higgins, R.S.M., D.R.E. (Grades 1-6); Natalie Plouff, D.R.E. (Grades 7-10). Students 716.

LITTLE COMPTON, NEWPORT CO., ST. CATHERINE OF SIENA (1930), [CEM] Rev. Gerald W. Hussey.
Legal Title: *St. Catherine's Church Corporation, Little Compton*
Res.: 74 Simmons Rd., P.O. Box 208, 02837-0208. Tel: 401-635-4420; Fax: 401-635-2214.
Catechesis/Religious Program—Students 150.

MIDDLETOWN, NEWPORT CO., ST. LUCY (Middletown) (1952), Rev. Eugene J. McKenna; Deacon John E. Croy.
Legal Title: *Saint Lucy's Church Corp.*
Res.: 909 W. Main Rd., 02842-6351. Tel: 401-847-6153; Fax: 401-846-1545.
Catechesis/Religious Program—Tel: 401-847-6154. Sisters Mary T. Burns, C.P., D.R.E.; Rosemary Burnham, R.S.M., D.R.E.; Assunta Riley, R.S.M., D.R.E. Students 365.

NARRAGANSETT, WASHINGTON CO.

1—ST. MARY, STAR OF THE SEA (Point Judith) (1960), Rev. John E. Watterson.
Legal Title: *St. Mary, Star of the Sea Church Corporation, Point Judith*
Res.: P.O. Box 3329, 02882. Tel: 401-783-4449; Fax: 401-783-0986.
Catechesis/Religious Program—Tel: 401-789-7308; Fax: 401-783-0986. Students 280.

2—ST. THOMAS MORE (1917), Rev. John C. Halloran; Deacon Paul J. Sullivan.
Legal Title: *St. Thomas More Church, Narragansett Pier, Rhode Island*
Res.: 53 Rockland St., 02882. Tel: 401-789-7682; Fax: 401-783-8646.
Catechesis/Religious Program—Tel: 401-783-2113. Students 266.
Chapel—Bonnet Shores, St. Veronica Chapel, Formerly Bonnet Shores, St. Veronica Summer ChapelTel: 401-783-1051.

NEW SHOREHAM, WASHINGTON CO., ST. ANDREW (Block Island) (1917), [JC] Rev. Donal R. Kehew, Admin.
Legal Title: *Saint Andrew's Church Corporation, Block Island*
Res.: Spring St., Block Island, 02807. Tel: 401-466-5519.
Catechesis/Religious Program—Students 22.

NEWPORT, NEWPORT CO.

1—ST. AUGUSTIN (1911), Rev. John McNulty; Sr. Josephine St. Leger, S.J.C., Pastoral Assoc.; Deacon Bernard G. Theroux.
Legal Title: *Saint Augustin's Church of Newport*
Res.: 2 Eastnor Rd., 02840. Tel: 401-847-0518; Fax: 401-848-2411.
Catechesis/Religious Program—Students 110.

2—JESUS SAVIOUR (1926), (Portuguese), Rev. Francis A. O'Loughlin; Deacons James N. Dunbar; James R. Rudnik.
Legal Title: *Church of Jesus-Saviour, Newport*
Res.: One Vernon Ave., 02840. Tel: 401-847-1267; Fax: 401-846-3375.
Catechesis/Religious Program—Tel: 401-846-4095. Students 120.

3—ST. JOSEPH (1885), Rev. John J. Lavin.
Legal Title: *Saint Joseph's Church of Newport, Rhode Island*
Res.: 5 Mann Ave., 02840. Tel: 401-847-0065; Fax: 401-849-2195.
Catechesis/Religious Program—Tel: 401-847-9248; Fax: 401-849-2195. Students 281.

4—ST. MARY (1826), [CEM] Rev. George B. McCarthy.
Legal Title: *St. Mary's, Newport, Rhode Island*
Res.: 12 William St., P.O. Box 547, 02840. Tel: 401-847-0475; Fax: 401-845-9497.
Catechesis/Religious Program—Tel: 401-846-6057. Students 235.

NORTH KINGSTOWN, WASHINGTON CO.

1—ST. BERNARD (Wickford) (1874), Rev. Dennis A. Reardon; Deacons Ronald DePietro; Joseph Turcotte.
Legal Title: *St. Bernard's Roman Catholic Church of Wickford, Rhode Island*
Office—415 Tower Hill Rd., Wickford, 02852. Tel: 401-295-0387; Fax: 401-295-1713.
Catechesis/Religious Program—Tel: 401-295-5235. Michelle Sandham, D.R.E. Students 538.

2—ST. FRANCIS DE SALES (Davisville) (1960), Revs. Bertrand Theroux; Marek S. Kupka.
Legal Title: *St. Francis de Sales Church Corporation, North Kingstown*
Res.: 381 School St., 02852. Tel: 401-884-2105; Fax: 401-885-4315.
Catechesis/Religious Program—Tel: 401-885-3639. Kathleen Kane, D.R.E. Students 780.

NORTH PROVIDENCE, PROVIDENCE CO.

1—ST. ANTHONY (1944), (Italian), Revs. Edward S. Cardente; Kris M. Von Maluski; C. Brian Lagasse.
Legal Title: *Saint Anthony's Church Corporation, North Providence*
Res.: 5 Gibbs St., 02904. Tel: 401-353-3120; Fax: 401-353-5126.

Catechesis/Religious Program—Tel: 401-353-5125. Maryann Pallotta, D.R.E. Students 485.

2—ST. LAWRENCE (Centredale) (1907), Rev. David Piacentini.
Legal Title: *Saint Lawrence Church of Centredale* In Res., Rev. Peter G. Young (Retired).
Res.: 624 Woonasquatucket Ave., 02911-1652. Tel: 401-231-9126; Fax: 401-231-7425.
Catechesis/Religious Program—Tel: 401-231-5255. Students 195.

3—MARY, MOTHER OF MANKIND (1967), Rev. W. Douglas Grant.
Legal Title: *Mary, Mother of Mankind Church Corporation, North Providence*
Res.: 25 Fourth St., 02911. Tel: 401-231-3542; Fax: 401-232-0965.
Catechesis/Religious Program—Tel: 401-231-3544. Students 241.

4—PRESENTATION OF THE BLESSED VIRGIN MARY (Marieville) (1912), (French), Rev. Louis T. Natalizia; Deacon Louis A. Vani.
Legal Title: *Church of the Presentation of the Blessed Virgin Mary*
Res.: 1081 Mineral Spring Ave., 02904. Tel: 401-722-7140; Fax: 401-722-6617.
Catechesis/Religious Program—Tel: 401-722-8824; 401-722-7007 (Rel. Ed. Center). Maryann Dempsey, D.R.E. Students 232.

NORTH SMITHFIELD, PROVIDENCE CO., ST. JOHN THE EVANGELIST (Slatersville) (1872), [CEM] Rev. Raymond A. Tetreault.
Legal Title: *St. John's Church Society, Rhode Island*
Res.: 63 Church St., Slatersville, 02876. Tel: 401-762-0946; Fax: 401-762-0944.
Catechesis/Religious Program—Tel: 401-762-0966. Mrs. Sara D. Hickey, D.R.E. Students 555.

PAWTUCKET, PROVIDENCE CO.

1—ST. ANTHONY (1926), (Portuguese), Rev. John W. O'Brien; Deacon Louis P. Serra.
Legal Title: *Saint Anthony's Church Corporation, Pawtucket*
Res.: 32 Lawn Ave., 02860. Tel: 401-723-9138; Fax: 401-725-5616.
Catechesis/Religious Program—Students 260.

2—ST. CECILIA (1910), (French), Rev. Francis C. Santilli.
Legal Title: *Saint Cecilia's Church Corporation*
Res.: 1253 Newport Ave., 02861. Tel: 401-722-1101; Fax: 401-727-3844.
School—755 Central Ave., 02861. Tel: 401-723-9463; Fax: 401-722-1444. Sisters 2; Lay Teachers 33; Students 466.
Catechesis/Religious Program—Students 420.

3—ST. EDWARD (1904), Rev. Charles H. Galligan; Deacon Raymond E. Batalon.
Legal Title: *St. Edward's Church of Pawtucket*
Office—58 Hancock St., 02860. Tel: 401-725-7036.
Church: 396 Weeden St., 02860.
Catechesis/Religious Program—58 Hancock St., 02860. Students 100.

4—IMMACULATE HEART OF MARY (1979), (Cape Verdean),, (An operation of Church of St. Maron in Providence) Rev. Arlindo A. Amaro, C.S.Sp., Admin.
Res.: 35 Clay St., Central Falls, 02863. Tel: 401-725-1126; Fax: 401-726-4119.
Church: 291 High St., 02860. Tel: 401-725-5456.
Catechesis/Religious Program—Students 130.

5—ST. JOHN THE BAPTIST (1884), (French), Very Rev. Joel A. Lecuivre, J.C.L.; Rev. Jose Omar Zuluaga (Colombia); Deacon Raymond M. Lagesse.
Legal Title: *The Church of St. John the Baptist of Pawtucket Rhode Island*
Res.: 69 Quincy Ave., 02860. Tel: 401-722-9054; Fax: 401-724-3514.
Catechesis/Religious Program—Students 225.

6—ST. JOSEPH (1873), Rev. Charles B. McDermott.
Legal Title: *St. Joseph's Church* In Res., Revs. Richard C. Maynard (Retired); John J. McElroy, Pastor Emeritus (Retired).
Res.: 193 Walcott St., 02860. Tel: 401-724-9190; Fax: 401-724-9314.
Catechesis/Religious Program—Students 71.

7—ST. LEO THE GREAT (1916), (Irish), Very Rev. John A. Kiley; Rev. John A. Sistare.
Legal Title: *Church of Saint Leo the Great in Pawtucket* In Res., Rev. Philip E. Bonvouloir, A.A.
Res.: 697 Central Ave., 02861. Tel: 401-722-1220; Fax: 401-726-3392.
School—723 Central Ave., 02861. Tel: 401-725-3620; Fax: 401-725-1696. Lisa LePore, Prin. Sisters 1; Lay Teachers 22; Students 342.
Catechesis/Religious Program—Students 200.

8—ST. MARIA GORETTI (1953), Rev. Kenneth J. Suibielski; Deacon Thomas Boutier.
Legal Title: *St. Maria Goretti Church Corporation, Pawtucket*
Res.: 165 Power Rd., 02860. Tel: 401-725-4355; Fax: 401-729-5711.
Catechesis/Religious Program—Tel: 401-729-5713. Students 177.

9—ST. MARY OF THE IMMACULATE CONCEPTION (1829), [CEM] Rev. William J. Ledoux; Deacon C. Patrick Sheehy.
Legal Title: *The Church of the Immaculate Conception of Pawtucket, Rhode Island*
Res.: 103 Pine St., P.O. Box 518, 02862. Tel: 401-722-5425; Fax: 401-729-0341.
School—(Grades PreK-8), 167 George St., 02862. Tel: 401-723-6695; Fax: 401-723-6763. Mrs. Patricia Baumgartel, Prin. Lay Teachers 14; Students 219.
Catechesis/Religious Program—Tel: 401-722-5426. Ms. Michelle Laliberte. Students 150.

10—OUR LADY OF CONSOLATION (1895), (French), Rev. Normand L. Courtemanche.
Legal Title: *Church of Our Lady of Consolation Rhode Island*
Res.: 10 Webster St., 02860. Tel: 401-722-2804; Fax: 401-725-2409.
Catechesis/Religious Program—Students 98.

11—SACRED HEART OF JESUS (1872), (Irish—Portuguese), Rev. Paul E. Desmarais.
Legal Title: *The Church of the Sacred Heart of Jesus of Pawtucket, Rhode Island* In Res., Rev. John D. Dreher (Retired).
Res.: 38 Park St., 02860. Tel: 401-722-3226.
Catechesis/Religious Program—Tel: 401-722-9861. Students 225.

12—ST. TERESA OF THE CHILD JESUS (1929), Revs. Joseph Paquette; Mark A. Sauriol; Deacon Roland R. Geoffroy.
Legal Title: *Church of Saint Teresa of the Child Jesus, Pawtucket, Rhode Island*
Res.: 358 Newport Ave., 02861. Tel: 401-722-4470; Fax: 401-722-2958.
School—150 Wood Haven Rd., 02861. Tel: 401-726-1414; Fax: 401-722-6998. Mary Carney, Prin. Sisters of Mercy of the Americas 1; Lay Teachers 15; Students 197.
Catechesis/Religious Program—Tel: 401-723-2266. Michael Lavigne, D.R.E. Students 295.

PORTSMOUTH, NEWPORT CO.

1—ST. ANTHONY (1901), Rev. Daniel J. Gray.
Legal Title: *Saint Anthony's Church of Portsmouth*
Res.: 2836 E. Main Rd., P.O. Box 570, 02871. Tel: 401-683-0089; Fax: 401-683-9680.
Catechesis/Religious Program—Tel: 401-683-3636. Students 231.

2—ST. BARNABAS (1963), Rev. Kevin J. Brassil.
Legal Title: *St. Barnabas Church Corporation, Portsmouth*
Res.: 1697 E. Main Rd., 02871. Tel: 401-683-1343; Fax: 401-683-5065.
Catechesis/Religious Program—Tel: 401-683-3147. Students 625.

SCITUATE, PROVIDENCE CO., ST. JOSEPH (North Scituate) (1940), Rev. Roger A. Houle; Deacon Paul A. Ullucci.
Legal Title: *Saint Joseph's Church Corporation, North Scituate*
Res.: Danielson Pk., P.O. Box 236, North Scituate, 02857. Tel: 401-647-2255; Fax: 401-647-2968.
Catechesis/Religious Program—Tel: 401-647-2650. Students 598.

SMITHFIELD, PROVIDENCE CO.

1—ST. MICHAEL (Georgiaville) (1875), Rev. Richard A. Valentine; Deacon William Small, Ph.D.
Legal Title: *St. Michael's Church, Georgiaville, Rhode Island*
Res.: 80 Farnum Pike, Georgiaville, 02917. Tel: 401-231-5119; Fax: 401-231-0523.
Catechesis/Religious Program—Tel: 401-231-1340. Students 489.

2—ST. PHILIP (Greenville) (1852), Very Rev. Gerald E. Beirne; Revs. Robert L. Bailey; Michael J. Najim; Deacons Harris J. Gederman; Carlo J. Sabetti.
Legal Title: *St. Philip's Church Greenville Rhode Island*
Res.: 622 Putnam Ave., Greenville, 02828-1403. Tel: 401-949-1500; Fax: 401-949-3504.
School—618 Putnam Ave., Greenville, 02828. Tel: 401-949-1130; Fax: 401-949-1141. Sisters of Mercy of the Americas 1; Lay Teachers 17; Students 254.
Catechesis/Religious Program—Tel: 401-949-0330; Fax: 401-949-5630. Jean Cedor, D.R.E. Students 1,110.

SOUTH KINGSTOWN, WASHINGTON CO.

1—CHRIST THE KING (Kingston) (1950), Rev. Joseph D. Creedon.
Legal Title: *Christ the King Church Corporation, Kingston*
Res.: 180 Old North Rd., Kingston, 02881. Tel: 401-783-7459; Fax: 401-789-3671.
Catechesis/Religious Program—Tel: 401-789-0417. Students 875.

2—ST. FRANCIS OF ASSISI (Wakefield) (1879), [CEM] Revs. Nicholas P. Smith; Robert F. Caul; Deacon Paul O. Iacono.
Mailing Address: 114 High St., Wakefield, 02879-3141. Tel: 401-783-4411; Fax: 401-783-9667.
Legal Title: *Saint Francis's Church*
Catechesis/Religious Program—Tel: 401-792-8684. Students 629.
Mission—*St. Romuald* Wakefield. 61 Atlantic Ave., Matunuck, Washington Co. 02879.

TIVERTON, NEWPORT CO.

1—ST. CHRISTOPHER (1910), Rev. Peter J. Andrews.
Legal Title: *Saint Christopher's Church of Tiverton*
Res.: 1660 Main Rd., 02878. Tel: 401-624-6644; Fax: 401-624-9889.
Catechesis/Religious Program—Students 81.

2—HOLY GHOST (North Tiverton) (1913), Rev. Jay A. Finelli; Deacon Raymond E. Levesque.
Legal Title: *Church of the Holy Ghost, North Tiverton*
Res.: 311 Hooper St., 02878. Tel: 401-624-8131; Fax: 401-625-5156.
Catechesis/Religious Program—Tel: 401-624-3664. Students 260.

3—ST. MADELEINE SOPHIE (1948), (Portuguese), Rev. Gerald W. Hussey.
Legal Title: *Saint Madeleine's Church Corporation of Tiverton*
Res.: 35 Lake Rd., 02878. Tel: 401-624-4226; Fax: 401-624-3848.
Catechesis/Religious Program—Students 80.

4—ST. THERESA (1960), Rev. Peter J. Andrews; Deacon Jesse L. Martins.
Legal Title: *St. Theresa's Parish Corporation, Tiverton*
Res.: 265 Stafford Rd., 02878. Tel: 401-624-8746; Fax: 401-625-5384.
Catechesis/Religious Program—Students 216.

WARREN, BRISTOL CO.

1—ST. ALEXANDER (1915), (Italian), [CEM] Rev. David W. Masello, Admin.
Legal Title: *Saint Alexander's Church Corporation, Warren*
Res.: 221 Main St., 02885. Tel: 401-245-6369; Fax: 401-247-5455.
Catechesis/Religious Program—Tel: 401-247-1764. Students 28.

2—ST. CASIMIR (1908), (Polish), [JC] Rev. Matthew J. Strumski.
Legal Title: *Saint Casimir's Church of Warren*
Res.: 228 Child St., 02885-9998. Tel: 401-245-4422.
Catechesis/Religious Program—21 Liberty St., 02885. Tel: 401-245-3925. Mrs. Barbara Karcz, D.R.E. Students 11.

3—ST. JEAN BAPTISTE (1877), (French), [CEM] Rev. Peter J. Gower.
Legal Title: *The Church of Saint Jean Baptiste of Warren Rhode Island*
Res.: 328 Main St., 02885. Tel: 401-245-8392; Fax: 401-245-6582.
Catechesis/Religious Program—Tel: 401-245-7000, Ext. 17. Students 207.

4—ST. MARY OF THE BAY (1851), [CEM] [JC] Rev. Peter J. Gower.
Legal Title: *Church of Saint Mary of the Bay*
Res. and Parish House: 645 Main St., 02885. Tel: 401-245-7000, Ext. 21; Fax: 401-245-7093.
Parish House—430R Water St., 02885. Tel: 401-245-7000, Ext. 21; 2.
Catechesis/Religious Program—Tel: 401-245-7000, Ext. 17; Fax: 401-245-6582. Students 480.

5—ST. THOMAS THE APOSTLE (1952), (Portuguese), Rev. John E. Abreu; Deacon Benjamin Barboza.
Legal Title: *Saint Thomas the Apostle Church Corporation*
Res.: 500 Metacom Ave., 02885. Tel: 401-245-4469; Fax: 401-245-4527.
Catechesis/Religious Program—Tel: 401-245-4488. Anne Furtado, D.R.E. Students 102.

WARWICK, KENT CO.

1—ST. BENEDICT (Conimicut) (1914), Rev. Pierre J. Plante.
Legal Title: *St. Benedict's Church, Conimicut*
Res.: 135 Beach Ave., P.O. Box 9485, 02889. Tel: 401-737-9492; Fax: 401-739-0974.
Catechesis/Religious Program—70 Transit St., 02889. Tel: 401-738-2545. Students 281.

2—ST. CATHERINE (Apponaug) (1916), Rev. Roger G. Champigny; Deacon John F. Baker.
Legal Title: *Saint Catherine's Roman Catholic Church of Warwick, Rhode Island*
Res.: 3252 Post Rd., 02886. Tel: 401-737-4455; Fax: 401-732-7739.
Catechesis/Religious Program—Tel: 401-737-6234; Fax: 401-736-0960. Brenda Newbury, D.R.E.; Kelly Francoeur, D.R.E. Students 144.

3—ST. CLEMENT'S (1961), Merged, with St. Rose of Lima to form St. Rose of Lima/St. Clement, Warwick. (Legal title: St. Clement Church Corporation, Warwick).

4—ST. FRANCIS OF ASSISI (Hillsgrove) (1943), Rev. Timothy J. Gorton; Sr. Arlene Kalin, S.S.J., Pastoral Assoc.; Deacon Kevin P. Masse.
Legal Title: *Saint Francis Church Corporation, Hillsgrove*

Res.: 596 Jefferson Blvd., 02886. Tel: 401-737-5191; Fax: 401-737-1159.
School—610 Jefferson Blvd., 02886. Tel: 401-737-2721; Fax: 401-737-2721. Mrs. Carol Bowen, Prin. Sisters of St. Joseph 2; Lay Teachers 16; Students 131.
Catechesis/Religious Program—Students 81.
Convent—249 Chestnut St., 02888. Tel: 401-781-2464.

5—St. Gregory the Great (Cowesett) (1961), Revs. Alfred V. Ricci; David F. Ricard; Deacon Paul F. Kirk.
Legal Title: *St. Gregory the Great Church Corporation, Warwick*
Res.: 360 Cowesett Rd., 02886. Tel: 401-884-1666; Fax: 401-884-2448.
Catechesis/Religious Program—Tel: 401-884-0797. Students 703.

6—St. Kevin (1956), Revs. Robert F. Hawkins; Francis W. O'Hara; Deacon Paul C. Konold.
Legal Title: *St. Kevin's Church Corporation Warwick*
Res.: 333 Sandy Ln., 02889. Tel: 401-737-2638; Fax: 401-732-2832.
School—39 Cathedral Rd., 02889. Tel: 401-737-7172; Fax: 401-738-2832. Lay Teachers 24; Students 379.
Catechesis/Religious Program—Tel: 401-739-6309. Harriet Duffy, D.R.E. Students 492.

7—St. Peter (Pawtuxet) (1933), Rev. Roger C. Gagne; Rev. Msgr. John F. Cox, Pastor Emeritus (Retired); Deacon Robert Morisseau.
Legal Title: *St. Peter's Church, Warwick, Rhode Island* In Res., Rev. Nicholas J. Iacovacci (Retired).
Res.: 350 Fair St., 02888. Tel: 401-467-4895; Fax: 401-785-9282.
School—Tel: 401-781-9242; Fax: 401-467-5673. Mrs. Maureen Jannetta, Prin. Lay Teachers 24; Students 262.
Catechesis/Religious Program—120 Mayfair Rd., 02888. Tel: 401-461-5691. Margaret Andreozzi, D.R.E.; Elaine Morisseau, D.R.E. Students 340.

8—St. Rita (Oakland Beach) (1935), Rev. Bertil J. Anderson.
Legal Title: *Saint Rita's Church Corporation, Oakland Beach*
Res.: 722 Oakland Beach Ave., 02889. Tel: 401-738-1800; Fax: 401-738-1806.
Catechesis/Religious Program—Students 336.

9—Ss. Rose & Clement (1998),, Consolidation of St. Rose of Lima and St. Clement. (Legal Title: St. Clement's Church Corporation, Warwick) (Legal Title: St. Rose's Church Corporation, Warwick). Rev. Robert L. Marciano; Deacon Noel Edsall.
Res.: 171 Inman Ave., 02886-1700. Tel: 401-739-0213; Fax: 401-732-4144.
School—St. Rose of Lima, 200 Brentwood Ave., 02886. Tel: 401-739-6937; Fax: 401-737-4632. Mrs. Linda E. LeBeau, Prin. Lay Teachers 15; Students 245.
Catechesis/Religious Program—111 Long St., 02886. Tel: 401-737-1330. Mrs. Sue Jarbeau, D.R.E. Students 650.

10—St. Rose of Lima (Greenwood) (1950), Merged, with St. Clement to form St. Rose of Lima/St. Clement, Warwick. (Legal title: Saint Rose's Church Corporation, Warwick).

11—St. Timothy (Hoxie) (1950), Revs. Barry M. Meehan; Robert E. Lacombe.
Legal Title: *Saint Timothy's Church Corporation, Warwick*
Res.: 1799 Warwick Ave., 02889. Tel: 401-739-9552; Fax: 401-738-2466.
Catechesis/Religious Program—101 Lake Shore Dr., 02889. Tel: 401-738-9079. Students 300.

12—St. William (Norwood) (1933), [CEM] Rev. George P. Behan; Deacon Thomas P. O'Hara. (Legal title: Saint William Church Corporation, Norwood).
Res.: 200 Pettaconsett Ave., 02888. Tel: 401-781-7226; Fax: 401-781-4177.
Catechesis/Religious Program—Tel: 401-781-0343. Students 143.

West Warwick, Kent Co.

1—St. Anthony (Riverpoint) (1925), (Portuguese), Rev. Reinaldo M. Cardoso.
Legal Title: *Saint Anthony's Church Corporation, River Point*
Res.: 10 Sunset Ave., 02893. Tel: 401-821-8342.
Catechesis/Religious Program—Students 103.

2—Christ the King (Centreville) (1931), (French), Rev. George L. Allard.
Legal Title: *Church of Christ the King, West Warwick*
Res.: 120 Legris Ave., 02893. Tel: 401-821-9228; Fax: 401-821-0866.
Catechesis/Religious Program—130 Legris Ave., 02893. Tel: 401-823-3443. Mrs. Janice Rousselle, D.R.E.; Mrs. Jeanne Carrier, D.R.E. Students 197.

3—St. James (1908), Merged, with St. John the Baptist, West Warwick to form SS. John and James Parish, West Warwick

4—SS. John and James Parish, Rev. Msgr. Jacques L. Plante; Rev. Dariusz G. Jonczyk; Deacon Paul Shea.
Res.: 20 Washington St., 02893-4919. Tel: 401-821-7323; 401-821-7661.
School—St. John the Baptist School, 17 St. John St., 02893. Tel: 401-821-5285. Dr. Rickard Gannon, Prin. Lay Teachers 16; Students 110.

5—St. John the Baptist (Arctic) (1874), (French), [CEM] Merged, with St. James, West Warwick to form SS. John and James Parish, West Warwick

6—St. Joseph (Natick) (1873), Revs. Charles H. Downing; Fredy Jimenez-Londono, Hispanic Ministry; Deacon Laurence O. Gagnon.
Legal Title: *St. Joseph's Church, Natick RI*
Res.: 854 Providence St., 02893-1140. Tel: 401-821-4072; Fax: 401-821-2408.
School—(Grades PreK-8), Wakefield St., 02893. Tel: 401-821-3450. Deacons 1; Lay Teachers 21; Students 290.
Catechesis/Religious Program—Students 215.

7—St. Mary (Crompton) (1844), [CEM] [JC] Rev. Paul F. Reynolds.
Legal Title: *St. Mary's Church, Crompton Rhode Island*
Res.: 70 Church St., 02893. Tel: 401-821-5555; 401-822-1006; Fax: 401-828-8756.
Catechesis/Religious Program—Tel: 401-828-8756; Fax: 401-828-8756. Students 154.

8—Our Lady of Good Counsel (Phenix) (1897), (French), [CEM] Rev. Paul R. Lemoi; Deacon Raymond LaFrance.
Legal Title: *Church of Our Lady of Good Counsel, Warwick RI*
Res.: 60 Pleasant St., 02893. Tel: 401-821-6428.
Catechesis/Religious Program—Tel: 401-822-1869. Students 100.

9—SS. Peter and Paul (Phenix) (1853), [CEM] Rev. Christopher M. Davenport.
Legal Title: *SS. Peter and Paul's Church, Phoenixville, Rhode Isla*
Res.: 48 Highland St., 02893-5699. Tel: 401-821-2198.
Catechesis/Religious Program—Students 92.

10—Sacred Heart Church (Natick) (1929), (Italian), Rev. Richard A. Bucci.
Legal Title: *Church of the Sacred Heart, Natick RI*
Res.: 820 Providence St., 02893. Tel: 401-821-4184; Fax: 401-828-8883.
Catechesis/Religious Program—Students 79.

Westerly, Washington Co.

1—St. Clare (Misquamicut) (1946), Revs. Peter M. Cavanaugh; Bernard M. Dore (India).
Legal Title: *Saint Clare's Church Corporation, Misquamicut*
Res.: 4 Saint Clare Way, Misquamicut, 02891. Tel: 401-348-8765.
Catechesis/Religious Program—Students 225.

2—Immaculate Conception (1885), (Italian), [CEM] Revs. Wilfrid G. Gregoire; Michael A. Kelley; Deacons Robert G. Alessio; John D. McGregor.
Mailing Address: P.O. Box 556, 02891-0556. Tel: 401-596-2130; Fax: 401-348-2153.
Legal Title: *Church of the Immaculate Conception of Westerly, Rhode Island*
Res.: 111 High St., 02891. Tel: 401-596-2130; Fax: 401-348-2351.
Catechesis/Religious Program—Tel: 401-596-0900; Fax: 401-348-2153. Mrs. Rosemary Buonocore, D.R.E. (Grades 1-6); Mrs. Catherine Kimmel, D.R.E. (Grades 7-10). Students 361.

3—St. Pius X (1955), Rev. Raymond N. Suriani; Deacon Francis J. Valliere.
Legal Title: *St. Pius X Parish Corporation, Westerly*
Res.: 44 Elm St., 02891. Tel: 401-596-2535; Fax: 401-596-9930.
School—32 Elm St., 02891. Tel: 401-596-5735; Fax: 401-596-5791. Lay Teachers 16; Students 157.
Catechesis/Religious Program—Tel: 401-596-8530. Students 149.

4—St. Vincent de Paul (Bradford) (1946), Rev. James V. Farley.
Legal Title: *Saint Vincent's Church Corporation, Bradford*
Res.: P.O. Box 277, 7 Church St., Bradford, 02808. Tel: 401-377-2289; Fax: 401-377-8850.
Catechesis/Religious Program—Tel: 401-377-8435. Students 215.

Woonsocket, Providence Co.

1—St. Agatha (1953), Rev. Msgr. John C. Allard; Rev. Michael A. Sisco; Deacon Eugene Garceau.
Legal Title: *Saint Agatha's Church Corporation, Woonsocket* In Res., Rev. Joseph P. Heaney (Retired).
Res. 34 Joffre Ave., 02895. Tel: 401-767-2950; Fax: 401-767-2951.
Catechesis/Religious Program—Students 160.

2—All Saints Catholic Community (1998), [JC], An alliance of the following three parishes: Our Lady of Victories, (French), est. 1909, (Legal title: Church of Notre Dame des Victoires); St. Aloysius, (French) est. 1902, (Legal title: Saint Aloysius Church of Woonsocket); and St. Ann, (French) est. 1890 (Legal title: St. Ann's Church Corporation of Woonsocket RI). Very Rev. Robert P. Perron; Rev. Daniel J. Sweet; Deacons Roman Manchester; N. David Bouley. In Res., Rev. J.A. Roger Lacasse.
Res.: 323 Rathbun St., 02895. Tel: 401-762-1100; 401-766-0370; Fax: 401-765-6321.
Catechesis/Religious Program—Tel: 401-766-5771. Students 292.
Convent—St. Ann Convent, 120 Gaulin Ave., 02895. Tel: 401-766-2485. Sr. Celia Laliberte, P.M., Supr. Sisters of the Presentation of Mary 5.

3—St. Aloysius, Merged, with Our Lady of Victories, Woonsocket and St. Ann, Woonsocket, to form All Saints Catholic Community, Woonsocket.

4—St. Ann, Merged, with Our Lady of Victory, Woonsocket and St. Aloysius, Woonsocket to form All Saints Catholic Community, Woonsocket.

5—St. Anthony (1924), (Italian), [JC] Rev. Ronald P. Simeone; Deacon Bernard Archambault.
Legal Title: *Saint Anthony's Church, Woonsocket, RI*
Res.: 128 Greene St., 02895. Tel: 401-766-2640; Fax: 401-766-2640.
Catechesis/Religious Program—Students 22.

6—St. Charles (1846), (Irish), [CEM] Rev. D. Bryan Finerty.
Legal Title: *St. Charles Borromeo's Church, Woonsocket, RI*
Res.: 190 N. Main St., 02895-3140. Tel: 401-766-0176; Fax: 401-766-0185.
Catechesis/Religious Program—Tel: 401-766-3088. Students 53.

7—Holy Family (1902), (French), [JC] Rev. Edward G. St-Godard; Deacon James Walsh.
Legal Title: *Church of the Holy Family*
Res.: 414 S. Main St., 02895. Tel: 401-762-0830; Fax: 401-762-3441.
Catechesis/Religious Program—Students 95.

8—St. Joseph (East Woonsocket) (1929), (French-Canadian), Revs. Lionel A. Blain; Michael J. Woolley.
Legal Title: *Saint Joseph's Church, Woonsocket*
Res.: 1200 Mendon Rd., 02895-3999. Tel: 401-766-0626; Fax: 401-766-1632.
Catechesis/Religious Program—1210 Mendon Rd., 02895. Tel: 401-766-8233. Michelle T. Barrette, D.R.E. Students 325.
Station—Woonsocket Health Center, Tel: 401-765-2100; Fax: 401-232-7275.
Station—Wyndemere Woods, Tel: 401-762-4226; Fax: 401-766-5548.

9—Our Lady of Victories, Merged, with St. Alyosius, Woonsocket and St. Ann, Woonsocket to form All Saints Catholic Community, Woonsocket.

10—Our Lady, Queen of Martyrs (1953), Rev. Maurice L. Brindamour; Deacon Robert A. Blais.
Legal Title: *Our Lady, Queen of Martyrs Church Corporation, Woonsocket* In Res., Rev. Joseph A. Pescatello.
Res.: 1409 Park Ave., 02895-6597. Tel: 401-762-5117; Fax: 401-765-8875.
Catechesis/Religious Program—Tel: 401-767-2576. Students 311.

11—Precious Blood (1843), (French), [CEM] Rev. Msgr. John C. Allard, Admin.; Rev. Michael A. Sisco.
Legal Title: *Our Lady, Queen of Martyrs Church Corporation, Woonsocket* In Res., Revs. John M. Fahey (TUC) (Retired); Albert H. Brindamour (Retired).
Res.: 94 Carrington Ave., 02895. Tel: 401-762-0326; 401-883-6600; Fax: 401-767-2951.
Catechesis/Religious Program—34 Joffre Ave., 02895. Tel: 401-767-2950. Students 35.

12—Sacred Heart (1895), Rev. Ronald J. Bengford, Temporary Admin., Woonsocket, RI Sacret Heart.
Legal Title: *Church of the Sacred Heart Woonsocket, RI*
Res.: 415 Olo St., 02895. Tel: 401-766-3150; Fax: 401-766-6864.
Catechesis/Religious Program—Tel: 401-766-3151. Students 105.

13—St. Stanislaus (1905), (Polish), [JC] Rev. Boguslaw T. Gibowski, Admin.
Legal Title: *Saint Stanislaus Kostka Church of Woonsocket*
Res.: 174 Harris Ave., 02895. Tel: 401-762-0021.
Catechesis/Religious Program—Students 38.

Chaplains of Public Institutions

Providence. *Miriam Hospital*, 164 Summit Ave., 02906. Tel: 401-274-3700. Rev. Edward L. Pieroni.
Res.: 2 Matilda St., 02904-1812.
Rhode Island Hospital, 593 Eddy St., 02902. Tel: 401-277-4000. Revs. Gerald G. Harbour, Dir. Pastoral Care, Peter J. D'Ambrosia, S.M.
Res.: 15 Frances Ave., Cranston, 02910. Rev. Jose Q. Dos Reis, Ms. Janice Hart, Coord., Team Member, Sr. Barbara Harrington, O.P., Team Member, Elsa Menegozzo, Team Member.
Roger Williams Hospital, 825 Chalkstone Ave., 02908.

Tel: 401-456-2000. Pastoral care provided by local parishes.
Veterans Administration Hospital, Davis Park, 02908. Tel: 401-273-7100. Rev. Francis J. Crowley (BO).

BURRILLVILLE. *Rhode Island-Zambarano State Hospital*. (Vacant)
Wallum Lake, 02859. Pastoral care provided by Office of Health Ministries.

CRANSTON. *Department of Corrections*.
c/o 83 Steward St., 02903. (Vacant)
9 Alma Ave., East Providence, 02916. Deacon George Yany.
111 Cross St., Central Falls, 02863. Sr. Agnes Bonville, R.S.M.
Eleanor Slater Hospital. Rev. Robert E. Lacombe.
Res.: 1799 Warwick Ave., Warwick, 02889.

NEWPORT. *Newport Hospital*. Rev. Francis A. O'Loughlin.
Res.: 5 Mann Ave., 02840. Tel: 401-847-0065.
Salve Regina University. Rev. John C. Codega.

NORTH SMITHFIELD. *St. Antonie Residence*. Rev. Roger M. Fortin.
Landmark Medical Center, Fogarty Unit. Pastoral care provided by local parishes.

PAWTUCKET. *Memorial Hospital of Rhode Island*. Pastoral care provided by local parishes.
St. Raphael Academy. Rev. Mark A. Sauriol, Part-time.
Res.: 358 Newport Ave., 02861.

SOUTH KINGSTOWN. *South County Hospital*. Rev. Nicholas P. Smith.
Res.: 114 High St., Wakefield, 02879-3141. Tel: 401-782-8000.

WARWICK. *Kent County Memorial Hospital*. Rev. David F. Ricard.
Res.: 41 Sandro Dr., 02886.

WESTERLY. *The Westerly Hospital*, 25 Wells St., 02891. Tel: 401-596-6000. Pastoral care provided by local parishes.

WOONSOCKET. *Landmark Medical Center, Woonsocket Unit*. Pastoral care provided by local parishes.

On Duty Outside the Diocese:
Rev. Msgrs.—
Evans, Robert C., North American College, Rome, Italy.
Haberek, Jerome A., Chap., 7023 Ashleigh Manor Ct., Alexandria, VA 22315-4756. U.S. Army
Matano, Salvatore R., Apostolic Nunciature, Washington, DC 20001.
Montecalvo, Carlo F., Chap., U.S. Air Force
Revs.—
Baker, John C., St. Anthony's Church, 901 N.E. Second St., Fort Lauderdale, FL 53301.
Beirne, Robert M., 1730 Bank St., Baltimore, MD 21231-2401.
Berthelette, Ernest H., Chap., U.S. Air Force
Blais, Robert L., c/o Priests' Personnel Office, One Cathedral Sq., 02903.
Bolton, Paul J., Chap., U.S. Army
Brodeur, Dennis A., 477 N. Lindbergh Blvd., St. Louis, MO 63141.
Collins, Raymond F., Catholic University of America, Washington, DC.
Kelley, Edward J., Chap., U.S. Army
LaMontagne, Bernard L., St. Mary of Woods, IN 47876.
O'Neill, Thomas D., Diocese of Victoria
Pincince, Gerald P., 191 Hadley Rd., Sugar Hill, NH 03585.
Prendiville, Edmond P., St. Helen Church, 3033 NW 33rd Ave., Fort Lauderdale, FL 33310-1123.
Reilly, Timothy D., North American College, Rome, Italy.

Absent on Leave:
Revs.—
Azzarone, Daniel M.
Demers, Normand J.
Petrocelli, John N.
Silipigni, Stephan A.

Retired:
Rev. Msgrs.—
Carey, William J., P.O. Box 16, Jamestown, 02835.
Cavallaro, Galliano J., 493 Mt. Pleasant Ave., 02908.
Cerrito, Albert J., 402 Elm Ave., Port Charlotte, FL 33952.
Cox, John F., 350 Fair St., Warwick, 02888.
Dziob, Michael W., St. John Vianney Residence, 493 Mt. Pleasant Ave., 02908.
Egan, Edward F., St. John Vianney Residence, 493 Mt. Pleasant Ave., 02908.
Frappier, George L., 341 Ballou St., 02895.
Geoghegan, Arthur T. (MIA), 1900 S. Ocean Ave., Fort Lauderdale, FL 33316.
Lloyd, Paul A., Jeanne Jugen Residence, 964 Main St., Pawtucket, 02860.
Metsy, Norman G., 6467 Oak Shore Dr., Panama City, FL 32404.
Murray, William F., P.O. Box 1366, Mashpee, MA 02649.
Newbold, Robert C., St. John Vianney Residence, 493 Mt. Pleasant Ave., 02908-3329.
Revs.—
Barrette, Donat A., 97 Sailfish Dr., East Falmouth, MA 02536-6150.
Beaulieu, Raymond, P.O. Box 433, Jamestown, 02835.
Belhumeur, Roger E., St. John Vianney Residence, 493 Mt. Pleasant Ave., 02908.
Besse, Joseph A., 70 Landmark Ave., Warwick, 02886.
Boland, Edward F., St. John Vianney Residence, 493 Mt. Pleasant Ave., 02908.
Bouressa, Donald J., P.O. Box 592, Narragansett, 02882.
Brindamour, Albert H., 94 Carrington Ave., 02895-4594.
Bushee, Richard J., 650 E. Greenwich Ave., Bldg. 7, Unit 310, West Warwick, 02893.
Carmone, Anthony F., P.O. Box 496264, Port Charlotte, FL 33949-9177.
Carty, John T., 43 Phillips Rd., East Greenwich, 02818-0472.
de Serpa, Roberto, Rua Recreio dos Artistas 46-10.D, 9700 Angra do Heroismo, Terceira, Azores, Portugal.
Dean, Frederic D., St. John Vianney Residence, 493 Mt. Pleasant Ave., 02908-3329.
DeLellis, Francis V., 190 S. Weeden Rd., P.O. Box 28, Wakefield, 02880.
Deneault, Normand J., St. John Vianney Residence, 493 Mt. Pleasant Ave., 02908.
Diogo, Louis M., 81 N. Carpenter St., East Providence, 02914.
Dreher, John D., Sacred Heart Rectory, 38 Park St., Pawtucket, 02860.
Duhaime, James H., 152 Elmdale Rd., North Scituate, 02857.
Dyer, Raymond E., St. John Vianney Residence, 493 Mt. Pleasant Ave., 02908.
Ethier, Robert D., 49 Farm St., Blackstone, MA 01504.
Farrell, John F., 12 Airport Rd., Coventry, 02816.
Fitzgerald, Edmund H., 125 Bucklin St., Apt. 4, Pawtucket, 02861.
Freitas, Fernando P., 29 Bullocks Pt. Ave., Apt. 3A, Riverside, 02915-5341.
Gagne, Rene E., St. John Vianney Residence, 493 Mt. Pleasant Ave., 02908.
Gallagher, Joseph T., P.O. Box 80066, South Dartmouth, MA 02748.
Gallagher, William M., P.O. Box 80066, South Dartmouth, MA 02748.
Gorman, George F., Villa @ St. Antoine, 400 Mendon Rd., North Smithfield, 02896.
Gray, John W., 505 Church Ave., Warwick, 02889.
Greaves, John G., 3 Sea Breeze Ln., Bristol, 02809.
Hamilton, James J., 63 Doris Ave., Warwick, 02889.
Hart, Thomas B., P.O. Box 921, Portsmouth, 02871.
Hazebrouck, Maurice L., c/o One Cathedral Sq., 02903.
Heaney, John F., P.O. Box 84, Carolina, 02812.
Heaney, Joseph P., St. Agatha Rectory, 34 Joffre Ave., Woonsucket, 02895.
Henry, Joseph P., 225 Capstan St., Jamestown, 02835.
Hogan, Ralph R., 30 Kingstown Rd., Narragansett, 02882.
Horgan, Joseph E., 25 Leading St., Johnston, 02919.
Hunt, Patrick J., 23 Willis Dr., Cumberland, 02964.
Hynes, James P., 12 Lane F Ramblewood Estates, Coventry, 02816.
Hynes, Joseph P., 12 Lane F Ramblewood Estates, Coventry, 02816.
Iacovacci, Nicholas J., 350 Fair St., Warwick, 02888.
Johnson, Edward A., P.O. Box 1218, Fitzgerald, GA 31750.
Keefe, Francis J., St. John Vianney Reisdence, 493 Mt. Pleasant Ave., 02908.
Kelly, Raymond M.
King, Donald J., c/o Helen Galogly, 355 Fair St., Warwick, 02888.
Lacasse, Roger, 323 Rathbun St., 02895.
LeThiez, Alphonse D., 2062 Oakridge Cir., Venice, FL 34293.
Lynch, Cornelius B., 125 Bucklin St., Apt. 15, Pawtucket, 02861.
Maher, Charles E., 188 Col. John Gardner Rd., Narragansett, 02882.
Marot, Roger L., Father Marot CYO Center, 53-77 Federal St., 02895.
Maynard, Leon C., 964 Main St., Pawtucket, 02860.
Maynard, Richard C., St. Joseph Rectory, 193 Walcott St., Pawtucket, 02860-3266.
Maynard, Robert J., 1 St. Paul Pl., Cranston, 02905.
McElroy, John J., 193 Walcott St., Pawtucket, 02860.
McGovern, Edward J., St. John Vianney Residence, 493 Mt. Pleasant Ave., 02908.
Murphy, William F., St. John Vianney Residence, 493 Mount Pleasant Ave., 02908.
Narewski, Peter J., St. John Vianney Residence, 493 Mt. Pleasant Ave., 02908.
Paiva, Antonio M., 463 Benefit St., 02903.
Rafferty, Raymond J., St. James Well, Greenore, County Louth, Ireland.
Randall, John F., P.O. Box 114006, North Providence, 02911.
Randall, Robert J., P.O. Box 5617, Wakefield, 02880.
Schenick, Joseph D., St. John Vianney Residence, 495 Mt. Pleasant Ave., 02908.
Sears, William F., 92 Hope St., 02906.
Shanley, Joseph D., 167 Blackstone St., 02895.
Thadeu, Joseph S., 62 Griffith Dr., East Providence, 02915.
Turillo, B. Samuel, 196 Lansdowne Rd., Warwick, 02888.
Valois, Normand W., 30 Fenner St., 02903.
Walsh, Clyde J., St. John Vianney Residence, 493 Mt. Pleasant Ave., 02908.
Young, Peter G., 624 Woonasquatucket Ave., North Providence, 02911.

Permanent Deacons:
Alessio, Robert G., Immaculate Conception, Westerly
Andrade, Charles, St. Patrick, Providence
Archambault, Bernard L., St. Anthony, Woonsocket
Bacon, Normand J., St. Eugene, Chepachet
Baker, John F., St. Catherine, Warwick
Barboza, Benjamin, St. Thomas the Apostle, Warren
Batalon, Raymond E., (Retired)
Bisbano, Paul, (On Leave of Absence)
Blais, Michael, (On Leave of Absence)
Blais, Robert, Our Lady, Queen of Martyrs, Woonsocket
Bouchard, Thomas, St. Joseph, Woonsocket
Bouley, N. David, All Saints Catholic Community, Woonsocket
Boutier, Thomas F., St. Maria Goretti, Pawtucket
Braga, Joseph F., St. Charles, Providence
Caban, Vicente, (On Leave of Absence)
Ceprano, Peter A., St. Mary, Cranston
Conley, James E., St. Mary of the Bay, Warren
Corey, John A., St. Rita, Warwick
Cote, Stephen R., St. Clare, Misquamicut
Dadlez, Mark A., (Retired)
DePetrillo, Albert, St. Thomas, Providence
DePietro, Ronald H., St. Bernard, North Kingstown
DiOrio, Dominic P., Our Lady of Loreto, East Providence
Dufour, John, (On Leave of Absence)
Dunbar, James N., Jesus Saviour, Newport
Edsall, Noel, SS. Rose & Clement, Warwick
Forlingieri, Carmine, Immaculate Conception, Cranston
Gagnon, Laurence O., St. Joseph, West Warwick
Gallo, Robert L., St. Bartholomew, Providence
Garceau, Eugene, St. Agatha, Woonsocket
Garcia, Luis, Assumption, Providence
Gauthier, Clovis, (Retired)
Gederman, Harris J., St. Philip, Greenville
Geoffroy, Roland R., St. Teresa, Pawtucket
Gomez, Oscar, (On Leave of Absence)
Hanrahan, Charles L., Holy Name of Jesus, Providence
Horton, Gregory R., St. James, Manville
Iacono, Paul O., St. Francis of Assisi, South Kingstown
Johnson, Loring F., (Retired)
Keogh, Richard B., Christ the King, Kingston
Kirk, Paul, D.D.S., St. Gregory the Great, Warwick
Konold, Paul C., St. Kevin, Warwick
LaFleur, Norman R., (On Leave of Absence)
LaFleur, W. Carl, St. Clare, Westerly
LaFrance, Raymond, Our Lady of Good Counsel, West Warwick
Lagesse, Raymond M., St. John the Baptist, Pawtucket
Lambert, Paul H., St. John Vianney, Cumberland
Lamont, Edward, (On Leave of Absence)
Lapierre, Richard J., Our Lady of Good Help, Mapleville
Lennon, Thomas J., (Retired)
Levesque, Raymond E., Holy Ghost, Tiverton
Lopez, Pedro, Our Lady of Mt. Carmel, Providence
Lopez, Rony, St. Charles, Providence
Lucian, Robert C., (Retired)
MacLure, Robert, (On Sick Leave)
Martins, Jesse L., St. Theresa, Tiverton
Masse, Kevin P., St. Francis of Assisi, Warwick

Masse, Paul, (On Leave of Absence)
Maynard, Jacques, (Retired)
McAdam, Robert, St. Ambrose, Lincoln
McCarthy, Charles F., St. Timothy, Warwick
McGregor, John D., Immaculate Conception, Westerly
Millard, Charles E., M.D., (Retired)
Morisseau, Robert M., St. Peter, Warwick
Muscatelli, Anthony E., St. Joseph, Burrillville
Napolitano, Michael D., Chaplain, Rhode Island College, Providence
Natalizia, John J., Holy Cross, Providence
Needham, John F., St. Margaret, East Providence
Nicholson, Robert E., St. Mary, Providence
Nova, Leocadio, (Retired)
O'Hara, Thomas P., St. William, Warwick
Ouellette, Lucien, (Retired)
Owen, Jimmie, Blessed Sacrament, Providence
Perez, Juan Andres, St. Michael, Providence
Persson, Robert C., St. Mark, Cranston
Ragosta, Armand R., Our Lady of Grace, Johnston
Raspallo, Thomas R., Immaculate Conception, Cranston
Remillard, Lionel J., St. Jude, Lincoln
Riccio, Raymond L., Chaplain, State Hospitals
Rico, Jose, St. Charles Borromeo, Providence
Risi, Stephen M., St. Anthony, North Providence; St. Edward, Providence
Rose, Joseph, St. Kevin, Warwick
Rudnick, James R., Jesus Saviour, Newport
Sabetti, Carlo J., St. Philip, Greenville
Sardinha, John, (Retired)
Schofield, William J., St. Benedict, Warwick
Scholz, Franz, SS. John & Paul, Coventry
Serra, Louis P., St. Anthony, Pawtucket
Shea, John S., St. Mary, Charlestown
Shea, Paul M., SS. John & James, West Warwick
Sheehy, C. Patrick, St. Mary, Pawtucket
Sinesi, Rugiero A., (Retired)
Small, William A., (Retired)
Stone, Francis J., (Retired)
Stone, Robert V., (On Leave of Absence)
Sullivan, Paul J., St. Thomas More, Narragansett
Tanguay, Paul A., Our Lady of Consolation, Pawtucket
Theroux, Bernard G., Chaplain, RI Vets Home
Theroux, Paul A., St. Mary, Carolina
Troia, Robert, St. Rocco's, Thornton
Tumminelli, Joseph P., St. Robert Bellamine, Johnston
Turbitt, Robert A., II, SS. John and Paul, Coventry
Turcios, Jose, Holy Ghost, Providence
Turcotte, Joseph G., St. Bernard, North Kingstown
Ullucci, Paul A., St. Joseph, Scituate
Urrico, Francis X., (On Leave of Absence)
Valliere, Francis J., St. Pius X, Westerly
Vani, Louis A., Presentation of the Blessed Virgin Mary, North Providence
Walsh, James T., Holy Family, Woonsocket
Wendoloski, Anthony, Our Lady of Lourdes, Providence
West, Harry A., Jr., St. Teresa, Providence
Yany, George, St. Basil Melkite, Lincoln
Young, Frederick A., Holy Name, Providence

INSTITUTIONS LOCATED IN THE DIOCESE

[A] SEMINARIES, DIOCESAN

PROVIDENCE. *Seminary of Our Lady of Providence*, 485 Mt. Pleasant Ave., 02908. Tel: 401-331-1316; Fax: 401-521-4192. Web: www.catholicpriest.com. Most Rev. Robert J. McManus, D.D., S.T.D., Rector; Revs. Albert A. Kenney, Vocation Dir. & Dir. Spiritual Formation; Marcel L. Taillon, Vocations Recruiter.

Legal Title: *Seminary of Our Lady of Providence*, House of Formation for College Students and Pre-Theologians. Staff 6; Students 14.

[B] COLLEGES AND UNIVERSITIES

PROVIDENCE. *Providence College*, River Ave. & Eaton St., 02918. Tel: 401-865-1000; Fax: 401-865-2057. Email: pcadmiss@providence.edu. Web: www.providence.edu. Revs. Philip A. Smith, O.P., Pres.; Terence Keegan, O.P., Exec. Vice Pres.; Thomas L. Canavan, O.P., Vice Pres. Academic Admin.; Mr. Michael V. Frazier, Vice Pres. Finance & Business; Rev. J. Stuart McPhail, O.P., Vice Pres. Student Svcs.; Mr. Joseph P. Brum, Vice Pres. Alumni & Devel.; Mr. Edward J. Caron, Vice Pres. College Rels.; Rev. Mark S. Nowel, O.P., Dean Undergraduate Studies; Joseph G. Marina, Dean School of Continuing Education; Revs. James A. Driscoll, O.P., Dir. Academics for Graduate Rel. Studies Prog. & Dir. Promotions & Publicity of Grad. School of Rel. & Biblical Studies; Brendan Murphy, O.P., Chaplain; Harvey Varnet, Dir. Library.

Legal Title: *Providence College*, Conducted by the Dominican Friars. Dominican Priests Teaching 27; Diocesan Priests Teaching 2; Sisters Teaching 3; Lay Professors 305; Day School Enrollment: Men 1,580; Women 2,170; Graduate School: Men 458; Women 843; Evening Division: Men 354; Women 526.

NEWPORT. *Salve Regina University* 02840-4192. Tel: 401-847-6650; Fax: 401-847-0372. Email: sruadmis@salve.edu. Web: www.salve.edu. Dr. M. Therese Antone, R.S.M., Pres.; Dr. Theresa Madonna, Vice Pres. Academic Affairs; Dr. Leona Misto, R.S.M., Vice Pres. Mission Integration & Planning; William B. Hall, Vice Pres. Business & Financial Affairs; John J. Rok, Vice Pres. Student Life; Laura E. McPhie-Oliveira, Vice Pres. Enrollment Svcs.; Frederick C. Promades, Dir. Institute Research; Aida Mirante, Dir. Financial Aid; Michael Semenza, Vice Pres. Institutional Advancement; Kathleen Boyd, Dir. Library Svcs.; John Quinn, Dean of Students; Thomas H. Brennan, Dir. Information Systems; Stephen Trainor, Undergraduate Dean; Revs. John C. Codega; Michael T. Malone, C.S.Sp.; John Lavin.

Legal Title: *Salve Regina University* Sisters of Mercy of the Americas Priests 3; Brothers 2; Sisters 18; Lay Teachers 97; Students-Men 731; Women 1,542.

[C] HIGH SCHOOLS, DIOCESAN

PAWTUCKET. *St. Raphael Academy*, 123 Walcott St., 02860. Tel: 401-723-8100; Fax: 401-723-8740. Web: www.saintraphaelacademy.org. Rev. Mark A. Sauriol; Bro. Daniel Aubin, F.S.C., Pres.

Legal Title: *Saint Raphael Academy*, Conducted by the Brothers of the Christian Schools with Sisters of Mercy of the Americas. Priests 1; Brothers 3; Sisters 1; Lay Teachers 36; Students-Boys 266; Girls 242.

SOUTH KINGSTOWN. *The Prout School*, 4640 Tower Hill Rd., Wakefield, 02879. Tel: 401-789-9262; Fax: 401-782-2262. Email: info@theproutschool.org. Web: www.theproutschool.org. Bro. Edmond Precourt, F.S.C., Prin.

Legal Title: *The Prout School* Brothers 1; Sisters 2; Lay Teachers 49; Students-Boys 187; Girls 352.

WARWICK. *Bishop Hendricken High School*, 2615 Warwick Ave., 02889. Tel: 401-739-3450 Fax: 401-732-8261. Email: hawks@hendricken.com. Web: www.hendricken.com. Revs. Marcel L. Taillon, Chap.; Jose Q. dos Reis, Chap. of the Brothers; Bro. Thomas R. Leto, Pres.

Legal Title: *Bishop Hendricken High School* Congregation of Christian Brothers Priests 1; Brothers 4; Sisters 2; Lay Teachers 85; Boys 1,050.

[D] HIGH SCHOOLS, REGIONAL

PAWTUCKET. *Bishop Francis P. Keough Regional High School*, 145 Power Rd., 02860. Tel: 401-726-0335; Fax: 401-726-0336. Email: biskeo@netscape.net. Web: www.bishopkeough.org. Jeanne H. Leclerc, Prin. Sisters 1; Lay Teachers 12; Girls 108.

[E] HIGH SCHOOLS, PRIVATE

PROVIDENCE. *La Salle Academy*, (Grades 7-12), 612 Academy Ave., 02908. Tel: 401-351-7750; Fax: 401-444-1782. Email: dlaroche@loa.com. Web: www.loa.com/lasalle. Bro. Michael McKenery, F.S.C., Pres.; Mr. Donald Kavanagh, Prin.; Rev. Albert A. Kenney, Chap.

Legal Title: *St. John Baptist de LaSalle Institute*, Conducted by the Brothers of the Christian Schools. Priests 1; Brothers 7; Lay Teachers 92; Students 1,334; Total Staff 137.

EAST PROVIDENCE. *St. Mary Academy*, (Grades 6-12) Tel: 401-434-0113; Fax: 401-438-5936. Email: conteja@rinet36.org. Web: www.stmaryacademy.bayview.org. *Bayview*, 3070 Pawtucket Ave., Riverside, 02915. Tel: 401-434-0113; Fax: 401-483-5936. Sr. Elizabeth McAuliffe, R.S.M., Ed.D., Pres.; Ms. Colleen Gribbin, Prin. Sisters of Mercy of the Americas and Sisters of St. Joseph, Presentation of Mary Sisters 10; Lay Teachers 63; Girls 884.

PORTSMOUTH. *Portsmouth Abbey School*, Cory's Ln., 02871. Tel: 401-683-2000; Fax: 401-683-5888. Email: abbotmark@portsmouthabbey.org. Web: www.portsmouthabbey.org. Rev. F. Mark Serna, O.S.B., Abbot.

Legal Title: *Order of St. Benedict in Portsmouth, Rhode Island* Priests 8; Brothers 2; Lay Teachers 50; Students 339.

SOUTH KINGSTOWN. *Immaculate Conception Academy* Tel: 401-782-6200; Fax: 401-782-6208. Email: cwilders@inteducators.org. 4780 Tower Hill Rd., Wakefield, 02879. Tel: 401-782-6200; Fax: 401-782-6205. Ms. Caroline Wilders, Dir.; Rev. Javier Fayos, L.C., Chap.

Legal Title: *Overbrook, Inc.* Teachers 11; Boarding School Students 80.

WARREN. *Our Lady of Fatima High School*, (Grades 7-12), 360 Market St., Rte. 136, 02885. Tel: 401-245-4449; Fax: 401-245-1380. Web: www.fatimahs.org. Sr. Mary Margaret Souza, S.S.D., Prin. Sisters of St. Dorothy Sisters 5; Lay Teachers 14; Students 185.

WOONSOCKET. *Mt. St. Charles Academy*, (Grades 7-12) 02895-5599. Tel: 401-769-0310; Fax: 401-762-2327. Email: mscpres@hotmail.com. Web: mountsaintcharles.org. Bros. Robert R. Croteau, S.C., Pres.; Herve Richer, Prin.

Legal Title: *Mount Saint Charles Academy, Inc.* Brothers of the Sacred Heart Brothers 12; Sisters 1; Lay Teachers 58; Students 989.

[F] ELEMENTARY SCHOOLS, PRIVATE

PROVIDENCE. *San Miguel School*, 12 Carter St., 02907. Tel: 401-467-9777; Fax: 401-785-4976. Email: sanmiguel@ride.ri.net. Web: www.sanmiguelprov.org. Michael Vebelherr. Brothers 1; Lay Teachers 11; Students 64.

CUMBERLAND. *Mercymount Country Day School*, Wrentham Rd., 02864. Tel: 401-333-5919; Fax: 401-333-5150. Email: ride5179@ride.ri.net. Web: www.mercymount.org. Sr. Martha Mulligan, R.S.M., Prin. Sisters of Mercy of the Americas Sisters 5; Brothers 1; Lay Teachers 21; Students 367.

EAST PROVIDENCE. *St. Mary Academy*, (Grades PreK-12) *Bay View*, 3070 Pawtucket Ave., Riverside, 02915. Tel: 401-434-0113; Fax: 401-434-0335. Email: emcauliffe@stmaryacademy-bayview.org. Web: www.stmaryacademy-bayview.org. Sr. Norma Fleming, R.S.M., Prin., Elementary School; Ms. Colleen Gribbin, Prin., High School; Sr. Elizabeth McAuliffe, R.S.M., Ed.D., Pres. Sisters of Mercy of the Americas, Day Pupils Sisters 20; Lay Teachers 80; Students 1,164.

NEWPORT. *Cluny School*, (Grades PreK-8) , (Day School) , 75 Brenton Rd., 02840. Tel: 401-847-6043; Fax: 401-848-5678. Email: ride9678@ride.ri.net. Web: www.ri-net/RInet/Cluny. Sisters Joan Vander Zyom, S.J.L., Pres.; Regina Brunelle, Vice Pres.; Mr. Jack Regan, Prin.; Sisters Josephine St. Leger, S.J.C., Sec. & Treas.; Genevieve Marie Vigil, S.J.L.

Legal Title: *St. Joseph of Cluny Sisters' School, Inc.* Sisters 2; Lay Teachers 15; Students 210.

PORTSMOUTH. *St. Philomena School*, 324 Cory's Lane, 02871. Tel: 401-683-0268; Fax: 401-683-6554. Sr. Ann Marie Walsh, F.C.J., Prin. Sisters Faithful Companions of Jesus Teaching Sisters 1; Lay Teachers 28; Students 443.

[G] REGIONAL ELEMENTARY SCHOOLS

PROVIDENCE. *Bishop McVinney Regional School*, (Grades PreK-8), 155 Gordon Ave., 02905. Tel: 401-781-2370; Fax: 401-785-2618. Email: bmv155@aol.com. Mr. Louis Hebert, Prin.

Legal Title: *Catholic Association for Regional Education* Sisters 1; Lay Teachers 17; Students 335.

St. Thomas Regional School, 15 Edendale Ave., 02911. Tel: 401-351-0403; Fax: 401-351-0403 (call first). Email: strspw@rinet36.org. Lisa A. Cardarelli, Prin. Lay Teachers 10; Students 245.

CENTRAL FALLS. *St. Elizabeth Ann Seton Academy*, 909 Lonsdale Ave., 02863. Tel: 401-728-6230; Fax: 401-723-9532. Email: ANNM@rinet36.org. Web: www.myschoolonline.com/ri/seasa. Sr. Ann McKenna, R.S.M., Prin. Sisters 3; Lay Teachers 10; Students 290.

COVENTRY. *Notre Dame Regional School*, (Grades K-8), 2 St. Vincent de Paul St., 02816. Tel: 401-821-6334; Fax: 401-821-0436. Email: rid04177@ride.ni.net. Manuel Perry, Prin. Lay Teachers 9; Students 120.

CRANSTON. *Cranston-Johnston Catholic Regional School*, 43 Poplar Dr., 02920. Tel: 401-942-7245; Fax: 401-943-5738. Email: rid05464@ride.ri.net. Paul A. Zona Jr., Prin. Sisters 1; Lay Teachers 26; Students 430.

EAST GREENWICH. *Our Lady of Mercy Regional School*, (Grades PreK-8), 55 Fourth Ave., 02818. Tel: 401-884-1618; Fax: 401-885-3138. Email: sjbarry@olmschool.org. Sr. Jeanne Barry, Prin. Sisters 1; Lay Teachers 27; Students 415.

MIDDLETOWN. *All Saints Academy*, (Grades K-8), 915 W. Main Rd., 02842. Tel: 401-848-4300; Fax: 401-848-5587. Email: rid40001@ride.ri.net. Web: allsaintsacademy.org. Kevin J. Dillon, Prin. Sisters 2; Lay Teachers 15; Students 175.

PAWTUCKET. *Woodlawn Catholic Regional School*, (Grades K-8), 61 Hope St., 02860. Tel: 401-723-3759; Fax: 401-722-4090. Email: rid26468@ride.ri.net. Web: members.cox.net/regionals. Sr. Martha M. Serbst, R.S.M., Prin. Sisters 3; Lay Teachers 7; Students 227.

SOUTH KINGSTOWN. *Monsignor Matthew F. Clarke Regional School*, (Grades PreK-7), Tower Hill Rd., 02879. Tel: 401-789-0860; Fax: 401-789-3164. Email: PrincipalHFiore@aol.com. Henry Fiore Jr., Prin. Lay Teachers 27; Students 450.

WARWICK. *Overbrook Academy at Our Lady of Providence Center* (Boarding School) , 836 Warwick Neck Ave., 02889. Tel: 401-737-2850; Fax: 401-737-2884. Email: information@overbrookacademy.org. Web: www.overbrookacademy.org. Miss Kristina Pinero, Dir.; Rev. Andrew McNair, L.C., Chap. Lay Teachers 15; Students 165.

[H] THE GREATER WOONSOCKET CATHOLIC REGIONAL SCHOOL SYSTEM
Member Schools

BURRILLVILLE

Father Holland Catholic Regional Elementary School (Grades PreK-8) Tel: 401-568-4589; Fax: 401-567-9069. Email: frholland@cox.net. 180 Sayles Ave., Pascoag, 02859. Tel: 401-568-4589; Fax: 401-567-9069. *Regional Administration*, P.O. Box 487, Woonsocket, 02895. Tel: 401-762-1095. Shawn A. Capron, Prin. Lay Teachers 10; Students 219.

WOONSOCKET

Good Shepherd Catholic Regional Middle School (Grades 4-8), 1210 Mendon Rd., 02895. Tel: 401-767-5906. Email: goodshepherdschool@cox.net. Mrs. Paula Hurteau, Admin.; Mr. Larry Poitras, Prin. Lay Teachers 21; Students 315.

Monsignor Gadoury Regional Primary School (Grades PreK-3) , and a three year old pilot program , 1371 Park Ave., 02895. Tel: 401-767-5902; Fax: 401-767-5902. Email: m.gadoury@cox.net. Mary Chabot, Prin. Lay Teachers 7; Students 161.

Our Lady of Victories Regional Primary School, 148 Spring St., 02895. Tel: 401-767-5904. Anne M. Flood, Prin. Lay Teachers 8; Students 165.

[I] CHILD CARING FACILITIES

PROVIDENCE. *Group Home for Adolescent Boys* (Whitmarsh House) , 1055 N. Main St., 02904. Tel: 401-351-7230; Fax: 401-421-0198. Bro. John McHale, O.L.P., Dir. Boys 70.

NARRAGANSETT. *Ocean Tides*, 635 Ocean Rd., 02882-1314. Tel: 401-789-1016; Fax: 401-788-0924. Email: brob@oceantides.org. Web: http://www.oceantides.org. Bros. Brendan Gerrity, F.S.C., Pres.; John McGann, F.S.C., Social Svcs.; John Norton, F.S.C., Court Liaison; Joseph Schafer, F.S.C., Dir. Social Svcs.; Peter Clifford, F.S.C., Admin. Asst.
Legal Title: *Ocean Tides, Inc.* Brothers 5; Lay Teachers 25; Lay Staff 39; Students 106.

[J] DAY NURSERIES

PROVIDENCE. *Carter Day Nursery*, 239 Public St., 02905. Tel: 401-751-9752; Fax: 401-351-6110. Email: ncurran@dioceseofprovidence.org. Nicole F. Curran, B.S., Dir.; Mrs. Alexandra Moser, B.A., Exec. Dir.
Legal Title: *The Nazareth Home*, Day care provided for 126 children. Total Asisted 100; Total Staff 17.

St. Vincent Day Care Center, 485 Mt. Pleasant Ave., 02908. Tel: 401-274-3094; Fax: 401-274-3092. Email: alexandraf@dioceseofprovidence.org. Mrs. Alexandra Freed, B.A., Exec. Dir.
Legal Title: *Saint Vincent de Paul Infant Asylum*, Day care provided for 71 children. Total Assisted 71; Total Staff 21.

LINCOLN. *Mount St. Francis Day Care Center*, .. Tel: 401-767-2829; Fax: 401-767-3748. Email: mariez@intap.net. 57 Division St., Manville, 02838. Mrs. Alexandra Freed, B.A., Exec. Dir. & Prog. Dir.
Legal Title: *Mount St. Francois of Woonsocket, RI*, Day care provided for 121 children 6 weeks old through Kindergarten full day. Total Assisted 121; Total Staff 15.

NEWPORT. *Garrettson Memorial Day Care Nursery*, 299 Spring St., 02840. Tel: 401-846-6470; Fax: 401-847-7588. Email: karend@intap.net. Mary Ann Altrui, M.S.W., Dir.; Karen Davis, Dir. of Garrettson.
Legal Title: *The Saint Clare Home*, Day care & licensed kindergarten provided for 73 children between the ages of 18 months-6 years old. Lay Teachers 12.

[K] GENERAL HOSPITALS

PROVIDENCE. *St. Joseph Health Services of Rhode Island - St. Joseph Hospital for Specialty Care*, 21 Peace St., 02907. Tel: 401-456-4080; Fax: 401-456-4089. Web: www.saintjosephri.com. Mr. H. John Keimig, Pres.; Rev. C. Leon Kachel, Chap. Bed Capacity 104.
Includes:

Southern New England Rehabilitation Center Tel: 401-456-4500; Fax: 401-456-4501. Jon A. Mukand, M.D., Ph.D., Medical Dir. A joint venture of St. Joseph Hospital and Rhode Island Hospital.

Corporate Care Occupational Health and Safety Services Tel: 401-456-4020; Fax: 401-456-4203. Jay Burstein, M.D., Medical Dir.

St. Joseph Center for Health & Human Services Tel: 401-456-4321; Fax: 401-456-4089. Abdel Hammo, M.D., Medical Dir.

St. Joseph Center for Psychiatric Services Tel: 401-456-4437; Fax: 401-456-4078. Ronald Gobeil, D.O., Medical Dir.

NORTH PROVIDENCE. *St. Joseph Health Services of Rhode Island - Our Lady of Fatima Hospital*, 200 High Service Ave., 02904. Tel: 401-456-3000; Fax: 401-456-3028. Web: www.fatimahospital.com. Mr. H. John Keimig, Pres.; Revs. John N. Petrocelli, Dir. Pastoral Care; Varghese Thekkattayil (India), Dir. Pastoral Care; Marilyn Horan, R.N., Asst. Dir. School of Nursing. Student Nurses 100; Bed Capacity 386; Patients Assisted Annually 249,454; Total Staff 1,850.

[L] VISITING AND NURSING OF THE SICK

PROVIDENCE. *Holy Spirit Convent*, 43 Westerly Ave., 02909. Tel: 401-946-5639. Sisters Louis Ernest Brodeur, D.H.S., Contact Person; Caroline Devinez, D.H.S. Daughters of the Holy Spirit Sisters 2; Visits 480; Number of Patients 10.

[M] HOMES FOR AGED

PROVIDENCE. *St. Joseph Living Center*, 153 Dean St., 02903. Tel: 401-272-3335; Fax: 401-621-8604. Diane E. Evans, R.N., B.S.N., Exec. Dir. Assisted and independent living and respite care facility, a division of St. Joseph Health Services of Rhode Island. Residents 66.

CUMBERLAND. *Mount St. Rita Health Centre*, 15 Sumner Brown Rd., 02864. Tel: 401-333-6352; Fax: 401-333-1012. Email: mail@mountstrita.org. Web: www.mountstrita.org. Julie Richard, Admin.
Legal Title: *Mount St. Rita Health Centre Inc.*, Licensed Nursing Home. Residents 98; Total Staff 163.

NEWPORT. *St. Clare Home*, 309 Spring St., 02840. Tel: 401-849-3204; Fax: 401-849-5780. Email: mbdaigneault@stclarehome.com. Web: stclarehome.com. Mary Beth Daigneault, Admin.; Rev. Richard A. Walsh, Chap.
Legal Title: *The Saint Clare Home*, Nursing Facility. Daughters of the Holy Spirit 5; Lay Nurses 11; Lay Employees 73; Residents 47.

NORTH KINGSTOWN. *Scalabrini Villa*, 860 N. Quidnessett Rd., 02852. Tel: 401-884-1802; Fax: 401-884-4727. Email: admin@scalabrinivilla.com. Web: www.scalabrinivilla.com. Rev. Edward J. Marino, C.S., Admin. Tel: 401-884-1802; Sr. Teresita Tauyan, F.A.S., Supr. Tel: 401-884-4594.
Legal Title: *Scalabrini Villa Inc.*, Full Skilled Nursing Facility. Franciscan Apostolic Sisters 4; Residents 120; Total Staff 126; Total Assisted 42,800.

NORTH SMITHFIELD. *St. Antoine Residence*, 10 Rhodes Ave., 02896. Tel: 401-767-3500; Fax: 401-769-5249. Email: maltrui@stantoine.net. Web: www.stantoine.net. Mary Ann Altrui, M.S.W., Exec. Dir.
Legal Title: *Saint Antoine Residence* Residents 260; Total Staff 415.

The Villa at Saint Antoine, 400 Mendon Rd., 02896-6999. Tel: 401-767-2574; Fax: 401-767-2581. Email: maltrui@stantoine.net. Web: www.stantoine.net. Mary Ann Altrui, M.S.W., Exec. Dir.; Mr. John Hedderson, Dir.
Legal Title: *The Frassati Residence* Total Staff 62; Total Assisted 90.

PAWTUCKET. *Jeanne Jugan Apartments*, 310 Sayles Ave., 02860. Tel: 401-723-4314; Fax: 401-727-2885. 964 Main St., 02860. Apartments for elderly 27; Residents 30; Total Staff 1.

Jeanne Jugan Residence, 964 Main St., 02860. Tel: 401-723-4314; Fax: 401-727-2885. Rev. Msgr. William I. Varsanyi, P.A., Chap.
Legal Title: *Jeanne Jugan Residence of the Little Sisters of the Poor* Little Sisters of the Poor 14; Residents 66; Total Staff 86; Total Assisted 78. In Res. Rev. Msgr. Paul A. Lloyd (Retired); Rev. Leo C. Maynard.

WOONSOCKET. *Saint Francis House*, 167 Blackstone St., 02895. Tel: 401-762-5255; Fax: 401-767-2911. Email: st.francishouse@att.net. Helen Stradone, Dir.; Rev. Joseph D. Shanley, Chap. (Retired).
Legal Title: *Saint Francis House, Woonsocket RI* Residents 59; Total Staff 27.

[N] CAMPS AND COMMUNITY CENTERS

PROVIDENCE. *St. Francis Chapel & City Ministry Center*, 58 Weybosset St., 02903. Tel: 401-331-6510; Fax: 401-453-0034. Email: fsevola@stfrancischapel.com. Web: stfrancischapel.com. Revs. Frank Sevola, O.F.M., Guardian & Exec. Dir.; Michael S. Joyce, O.F.M.; Charles J. O'Connor, O.F.M.; Eric T. Carpine, O.F.M.; Ambrose A. Donehue, O.F.M.; John P. Hogan, O.F.M.; Hugh Eller, O.F.M.; Stephen Lynch, O.F.M.; Bro. Nathnael Necaster, O.F.M.; Rev. Brice Leavins, O.F.M. (BO); Bros. Albert Aldrich, O.F.M.; Kevin McGoff, O.F.M.

St. Martin de Porres Multi-Purpose Center, 160 Cranston St., 02907. Tel: 401-274-6783; Fax: 401-274-5930. Email: stmartinwh@aol.com. Wayne B. Houle, Dir.
Legal Title: *St. Martin de Porres Center* Total under care 2,100; Total Assisted 2,500; Total Staff 13.

McAuley House, 163 Niagara St., 02907. Tel: 401-941-9013; Fax: 401-941-6862. Email: mcauleyhouse@surtglobal.net. Web: www.mcauleyri.org. Sr. Suzanne Lachapelle, R.S.M., Admin.
Legal Title: *The McAuley Corporation* Total under care annually 10,000.

McAuley Village, 325 Niagara St., 02907-2000. Tel: 401-467-3630; Fax: 401-467-2760. Email: info@mcauleyri.org. Web: www.mcauleyri.org. Sr. Dolores Crowley, R.S.M., Exec. Dir.
Legal Title: *The McAuley Corporation* Families assisted 22; Children in day care center 46; Total Staff in village and day care center 20.

BURRILLVILLE. *Mater Spei Day Camp*, Tel: 401-568-3580. Box W, Chepachet, 02814. Maria Piccirilli, Dir.

CRANSTON. *Rejoice in Hope Youth Center*, 804 Dyer Ave., 02920. Tel: 401-942-6571; Fax: 401-943-8686. Email: rejoiceinhope@juno.com. Patricia Kane, Dir.

EAST PROVIDENCE. *Emmaus Youth Center - Region 4*, Tel: 401-433-4327; Fax: 401-433-1320. Email: emmauscyo@juno.com. Web: www.oso.com./community/groups/emmaus. 25 Metropolitan Park Dr., Riverside, 02915. Maria Piccirilli, Dir.

PAWTUCKET. *Father Barry CYO Center*, 38 Denver St., 02860. Tel: 401-723-5111; 401-723-5119; Fax: 401-723-1757. Email: frbarrycyo@juno.com. Web: www.frbarrycyo.com. Ms. Colette M. Savaria, Dir.
Legal Title: *Father Barry CYO Center*

SOUTH KINGSTOWN. *St. Dominic Savio Youth Center*, Tel: 401-783-4055; Fax: 401-789-4630. Email: stdomsavio@juno.com. 60 St. Dominic Rd., Peace Dale, 02883. Tel: 401-783-4055; 401-783-9123; Fax: 401-789-4630. Ms. Marie L. Lachapelle, Dir.
Legal Title: *St. Dominic Savio Boys' Center*

Tower Hill Camp, Tel: 401-783-9123; Fax: 401-789-4630. Email: stdomsavio@juno.com. 60 St. Dominic Rd., Peace Dale, 02883. Tel: 401-783-9123; Fax: 401-789-4630. Ms. Marie L. Lachapelle, Dir.
Legal Title: *Rhode Island Home for Working Boys*

WARWICK. *OLP Center, Inc.*, 836 Warwick Neck Ave., 02889. Tel: 401-739-6850; Fax: 401-738-8058. Email: Aldrichman@ids.net. Web: Aldrichmansion.com. Mrs. Paulette M. Turcotte, Dir.
Legal Title: *OLP Center, Inc.*

WOONSOCKET. *Fr. Marot CYO Center*, 53 Federal St., 02895. Tel: 401-762-3252; Fax: 401-762-3255. Email: cyoregion2@aol.com. Miss Fern Dery, Co-Dir.; Mr. Roland Berard, Admin.; Rev. Roger L. Marot, Spiritual Dir. (Retired).
Legal Title: *CYO of Northern Rhode Island, Inc.*

[O] PERSONAL PRELATURES

PROVIDENCE. *Prelature of the Holy Cross and Opus Dei*, Mathewson House, 224 Bowen St., 02906. Tel: 401-272-7834; Fax: 401-272-7854. Email: info@opusdei.org. Web: www.opusdei.org. Rev. George Crafts.

[P] MONASTERIES AND RESIDENCES OF PRIESTS AND BROTHERS

PROVIDENCE. *Brothers of Our Lady of Providence*, 1055 N. Main St., 02904. Tel: 401-351-7230; Fax: 401-421-0198. Brothers 2.

Office, 1055 N. Main, 02904. Tel: 401-351-7230. Bro. John McHale, O.L.P., Supr.

St. Francis Friary, 58 Weybosset St., 02903. Tel: 401-331-6510; Fax: 401-453-0034. Email: fsevola@stfrancischapel.com. Web: stfrancischapel.com. Revs. Frank Sevola, O.F.M., Guardian & Exec. Dir.; Stephen Lynch, O.F.M., Vicar; Charles J. O'Connor, O.F.M.; Hugh Eller, O.F.M.; Michael S. Joyce, O.F.M.; Ambrose Donehue, O.F.M.; John P. Hogan, O.F.M.; Eric T. Carpine, O.F.M.; Brice Leavins, O.F.M. (BO); Bros. Nathnael Necaster, O.F.M.; Albert Aldrich, O.F.M.; Kevin McGoff, O.F.M.
Legal Title: *St. Francis Weybosset Street Chapel, Inc.* Franciscan Friars Priests 12.

St. John Vianney Residence, 493 Mt. Pleasant Ave., 02908. Tel: 401-331-9870. Rev. Edward J. McGovern, Coord. (Retired). Residence for Senior Priests. Priests 16.
Residents: Rev. Msgrs. Galliano J. Cavallaro (Retired); Michael W. Dziob (Retired); Edward F. Egan (Retired); Robert Newbold; Revs. Roger E. Belhumer; Edward F. Boland (Retired); Frederic D. Dean (Retired); Normand J. Deneault (Retired); Raymond E. Dyer (Retired); Rene E. Gagne (Retired); Francis J. Keefe (Retired); Peter J. Narewski (Retired); Joseph D. Schenick (Retired); Clyde J. Walsh (Retired).

St. Pius Priory, 55 Elmhurst Ave., 02908. Tel: 401-751-4871; Fax: 401-273-1089. Very Rev. John P. Burchill, O.P.; Revs. John L. Sullivan, O.P.; Michael A. Ciccone, O.P.; Joseph McGroarty, O.P.; Bernard Mulcahy, O.P.; Aaron J. Cote, O.P.
Legal Title: *Dominican Fathers* Priests 5

St. Thomas Aquinas Priory at Providence College, 333 Eaton St., 02918-0001. Tel: 401-865-2101 (office); Fax: 401-865-2959.
Legal Title: *Priory of St. Thomas Aquinas* Dominican Friars Bishops in Residence 1; Priests in Residence 46; Brothers in Residence 2; Priests residing outside Priory 3.
Assigned & Residing in the Priory: Very Rev. Edward T. Myers, O.P., Prior; Most Rev. Ernest B. Boland, O.P., Retired Bishop of Multan (Retired); Revs. Jon Alexander, O.P. (Chicago Prov.); John E. Allard, O.P.; J. Iriarte Andujar, O.P.; Albino F. Barrera, O.P.; Robert E. Bond, O.P.; Daniel J. Cassidy, O.P.; Edward L. Cleary, O.P. (Chicago Prov.); George L. Cochran, O.P.; Paul M. Conner, O.P. (Oakland Prov.); Thomas M. Coskren, O.P.; John F. Cunningham, O.P.; G. Adrian Dabash, O.P.; James J. Davis, O.P.; Vincent G. DeLucia, O.P.; James A. Driscoll, O.P.; Francis C. Duffy, O.P.; Thomas J. Ertle, O.P.; Joseph Peter Fegan, O.P. (WDC); William David Folsey, O.P.; Joseph J. Guido, O.P.; Kenneth R. Gumbert, O.P. (Oakland Prov.); Ralph T. Hall, O.P.; Curtis E. Henritzy, O.P.; G. Nicholas Ingham, O.P.; Terence Keegan, O.P.; John A. Langlois, O.P.; Bernard F. Langton, O.P.; Joseph L. Lennon, O.P.; Richard A. McAlister, O.P.; Thomas D. McGonigle, O.P. (Chicago Prov.); J. Stuart McPhail, O.P.; William P. Marquis, O.P.; Robert A. Morris, O.P.; Matthew F. Morry, O.P.; David Brendan Murphy, O.P.; Robert D. Myett, O.P.; Mark D. Nowel, O.P.; John S. Peterson, O.P.; Matthew D. Powell, O.P. (Chicago Prov.); James Ferrer Quigley, O.P., (St. Vincent Ferrer, New York, NY); Paul E. Seaver, O.P.; Kenneth Sicard, O.P.; A. Philip Smith, O.P.; John Vidmar, O.P.; Walter Urban Voll, O.P.; Michael John Paul Walker, O.P.; Bros. M. Francis Liebold, O.P.; F. Kevin O'Connell, O.P.
Assigned but Living Outside the Priory: Rev. Timothy F. Bellamah, O.P., (St. Jacques, Paris, France).

BRISTOL. *St. Columban's Retirement House*, Box 65, Ferry Rd., 02809. Tel: 401-253-6909; Fax: 401-253-7099. Revs. James Dwyer, S.S.C., Supr.; William F. Sullivan, S.S.C.; Thomas L. Convery, S.S.C.; Joseph Crehan, S.S.C.; Michael Donnelly, S.S.C., Vicar & Bursar; Norbert F. Feld, S.S.C.; Brian Gallagher, S.S.C.; Michael Harrison, S.S.C.; Francis Keaney, S.S.C.; Fintan Keegan, S.S.C.; Daniel McGinn, S.S.C.; Joseph McSweeney, S.S.C.; John O'Doherty, S.S.C.; Hugh O'Rourke, S.S.C.; Paul J. O'Rourke, S.S.C.; Matthew Quinn, S.S.C.; Victor Gaboury, S.S.C. (OM) (Retired).
Legal Title: *St. Columban's Foreign Mission Society* Priests 17.

BURRILLVILLE. *Brothers of the Sacred Heart Provincial House* Tel: 401-568-8686; Fax: 401-568-1450. Email: loulaperle@aol.com NEprovincial@bshne.org. 685 Steere Farm Rd., Pascoag, 02859-4601. Tel: 401-568-8686; 401-568-3361; Fax: 401-568-1450. Revs. Ronald S. Dupuis, S.C., Chap.; Nelson Dionne, S.C., Asst. Chap.; Bros. Raymond Reinsant, S.C., Prov. Supr. of New England Prov.; Robert Gagne, S.C., Accounts Mgr.; Louis Laperle, Prov. Sec.; Rev. Ronald S. Dupuis, S.C., Local Supr.; Bros. Paul J. Hebert, S.C., Exec. Asst. for Missions; Roland Ouellette, S.C., Vocation Dir.
Legal Title: *The Order of the Brothers of the Sacred Heart of New England, Inc.* Brothers 30.

NARRAGANSETT. *Christian Brothers' Center*, 635 Ocean Rd., 02882. Tel: 401-789-0244; Fax: 401-783-5303. Email: jdl@cbc.necoxmail.com. Web: www.cbline.org. Rev. Owen F. Goodwin, SS.CC., Chap.; Bros. Daniel Casey, F.S.C., Prov.; Peter Iorlano, F.S.C., Asst. Prov. & Dir. Formation; Frederick Mueller, F.S.C., Dir. Education; Mr. Lee Grossi, Dir. Finance; Mrs. Mary Yakey, Health Care Coord.
Legal Title: *Brothers of the Christian Schools, Long Island-New England Province* Brothers of the Christian Schools Brothers 40; Brothers in the Province 88.

PORTSMOUTH. *Abbey of St. Gregory the Great*, 285 Cory's Lane, 02871. Tel: 401-683-2000; Fax: 401-683-5888. Email: abbotmark@portsmouthabbey.org. Web: www.portsmouthabbey.org. Rt. Revs. F. Mark Serna, O.S.B., Abbot; Matthew Stark, O.S.B., Retired Abbot and Prior (Retired); Revs. Julian Stead, O.S.B.; B. Benedict Lang, O.S.B.; F. Philip Wilson, O.S.B.; A. Damian Kearney, O.S.B.; Michael Stafford, O.S.B.; P. Geoffrey Chase, O.S.B.; Christopher Davis, O.S.B.; Very Rev. R. Ambrose Wolverton, O.S.B.; Revs. T. Edmund Adams, O.S.B.; Caedmon Holmes; P. Paschal Scotti, O.S.B.
Legal Title: *Order of St. Benedict in Portsmouth, Rhode Island* Benedictines of the English Congregation Abbots 2; Priests 11; Brothers 2.

WOONSOCKET. *Brothers of the Sacred Heart*, 800 Logee St., 02895. Tel: 401-769-0313; Fax: 401-769-0065. Email: ride7859@ride.ri.net. Bro. Willie A. Morin, S.C., Local Supr. Brothers 11.

Brothers of the Sacred Heart, St. Ann's Residence, 82 Cumberland St., 02895. Tel: 401-762-4215. Bro. Clifford King, S.C., Dir.

St. John's Residence, 159 Earle St., 02895. Tel: 401-766-9677. Email: Brorol@aol.com. Web: www.Brothersofthesacredheart.org. Bros. Robert R. Croteau, S.C., Supr. & Dir.; Raymond Reinsant, S.C., Prov.; Alan Aubin; Robert Croteau, S.C.; Robert Gagne, S.C.; Tom Greer; Louis Laperle; Marcel Leclerc; Roland Ouellette. Brothers 8.

[Q] CONVENTS AND RESIDENCES FOR SISTERS

BARRINGTON. *Monastery of Discalced Carmelites*, 25 Watson Ave., 02806-4009. Tel: 401-245-3421; Fax: 401-245-5872. Email: myascolt@juno.com. Web: home.att.net/~barringtoncarmel. Sr. Mary Margaret Yascolt, O.C.D., Prioress.
Legal Title: *Monastery of Discalced Carmelites at Nayatt, Barrington, RI* Professed Sisters 14.

BRISTOL. *Mt. St. Joseph Provincialate*, 13 Monkeywrench Ln., 02809-2916. Tel: 401-253-7835; Fax: 401-253-7835. Email: srdot@att.net. Sr. Dorothy Schwarz, S.S.D., Prov. and Local Coord. Sisters of St. Dorothy Sisters 5.

CUMBERLAND. *Sisters of Mercy of the Americas, Regional Community of Providence*, 15 Highland View Rd., 02864-1124. Tel: 401-333-6333; Fax: 401-333-6450. Email: administration@mercyri.org. Web: www.mercyri.org. Sisters Patricia Combies, R.S.M., Pres.; Maureen McElroy, R.S.M., Councilor; Joan Bailey, R.S.M., Councilor; Marlene Laliberte, R.S.M., Councilor; Christina Costigan, R.S.M., Councilor.
Legal Title: *Sisters of Mercy of Providence, Inc.* Sisters 350.

Sisters of Mercy, 15 Highland View Rd., 02864-1124. Tel: 401-333-2439.

Mercycrest Convent, 255 Wrentham Rd., 02864. Tel: 401-333-5283.

Mercyknoll Convent, Highland View Rd., 02864. Tel: 401-333-6804.

Mercymount Convent, Wrentham Rd., 02864. Tel: 401-333-0158. Sisters of Mercy 5.

NEWPORT. *St. Clare Convent, Cutting Memorial*, 301 Spring St., 02840. Tel: 401-846-1025
Legal Title: *The Saint Clare Home* Daughters of the Holy Spirit 5.

Cluny Provincial House, 90 Brenton Rd., 02840-4392. Tel: 401-846-4757; 401-846-4826 (Prov.); Fax: 401-846-2276; 401-845-4826 (Office). Email: clunyusa@hotmail.com. Sisters of St. Joseph of Cluny Sisters 11; Sisters in Diocese 18; Sisters in Cluny Provincial of U.S.A. & Canada 37.

Provincial House Tel: 401-846-4826; Fax: 401-846-4826. Sisters Marie Cooper, S.J.C., Prov. Supr.; Josephine St. Leger, S.J.C., Prov. Councilor.

St. Joseph of Cluny Convent Tel: 401-847-3637; Fax: 401-847-4072. Sr. Marie Cooper, Local Supr.

Corpus Christi Carmel, 516 Broadway, 02840. Tel: 401-847-6165. Sisters Teresa Winefride, O.Carm., Supr.; Delphine, O.Carm., Regl. Supr., U.S.A. Corpus Christi Carmelite Sisters Sisters 2.

Javouhey House, 78 Carroll Ave., 02840. Sisters of St. Joseph of Cluny 4.

NORTH KINGSTOWN. *Holy Family Convent*, 1 Wright Ln., 02852. Tel: 401-294-3554; Fax: 401-295-2077. Email: srmtraynor@aol.com. Web: http://www.passionistsisters.org. Sr. Rosemary Traynor, C.P., Prov.
Legal Title: *Sisters of the Holy Cross and Passion*, Provincial Office of the Sisters of the Cross and Passion. Sisters 2.

NORTH PROVIDENCE. *Daughters of Mary Mother of Mercy*, 2 Pope St., 02904. Tel: 401-353-8654; Fax: 401-353-5126. Sisters 2.

Franciscan Missionaries of Mary 399 Fruit Hill Ave., 02911. Tel: 401-353-5800; Fax: 401-353-2674. Email: fmmalc@aol.com. Web: www.fmmusa.org.
Legal Title: *Franciscan Missionaries of Mary*

Holy Family Community, 399 Fruit Hill Ave., 02911. Tel: 401-353-5800. Sr. Margaret Gargan, F.M.M., Supr. Sisters 13.

Our Lady, Queen of Peace, Assisted Living Community, 399 Fruit Hill Ave., 02911. Tel: 401-353-5800; Fax: 401-354-8296. Sisters Helen Holowinski, F.M.M., Supr.; Lois Ann Pereira, F.M.M., Admin. Sisters 17.

Trinity Community, Assisted Living Community, 399 Fruit Hill Ave., 02911. Tel: 401-353-5800. Sr. Anne Richards, F.M.M., Supr. Sisters 17.

Our Lady of the Lourdes Convent, 385 Fruit Hill Ave., 02911. Tel: 401-353-6381. Sr. Rosemarie Higgins, F.M.M., Supr. Sisters 2.

Bethany, (House of On-Going Formation), 397 Fruit Hill Ave., 02911. Tel: 401-353-5860. Email: fmmbethany@aol.com. Sr. Yvette Hubert, F.M.M., Dir.

De Chappotin Community, 399 Fruit Hill Ave., 02911. Tel: 401-353-9412; Fax: 401-353-2674. Sr. Rosalie McNaughton, F.M.M., Supr. Sisters 6.

NORTH SMITHFIELD. *Franciscan Missionaries of Mary*, Ein Karim Community, 318 Mendon Rd., 02896. Tel: 401-766-8242; Fax: 401-766-6492. Email: karimfmm@aol.com. Sr. Elaine Nazareth, F.M.M., Coord. Sisters 4.

PAWTUCKET. *St. John the Baptist Convent*, 85 Slater St., 02860-2863. Tel: 401-722-1850; Fax: 401-728-6851. Email: fmmpawt@aol.com. Sr. Bernice Moreau, F.M.M., Coord. Franciscan Missionaries of Mary 6.

SOUTH KINGSTOWN. *Congregation of the Sisters of Divine Providence Generalate* Tel: 401-782-1785; Fax: 401-782-6967. Email: cdpgen@hotmail.com. Web: www.divineprovidence-cdp.org.

Mother of Providence Convent, 12 Christopher St., Wakefield, 02879. Tel: 401-782-1785; Fax: 401-782-6967. Sr. Myra Rodgers, C.D.P., Gen. Supr.

WEST GREENWICH. *Mary of Nazareth Novitiate*, 28 Victoria Hwy., 02817. Tel: 401-392-1007; Fax: 401-392-1009. Franciscan Missionaries of Mary 2; Novices 2.

WOONSOCKET. *Emmanuel House*, 67 Highland St., 02895. Tel: 401-766-0525.

Franciscan Apostolic Sisters, 94 Carrington Ave., 02895. Tel: 401-762-0326, Ext. 28; Fax: 401-884-3573. Email: fas@scalabrinivilla.com. Web: www.geocities.com/franapsisters. Sr. Magdalena Obisppo, F.A.S., Acting Regl. Animator. Sisters 7.
860 N. Quidnessett Rd., North Kingstown, 02852. Tel: 401-884-4594; Fax: 401-884-3573. Email: fas@scalabrinivilla.com. Web: www.geocities.com/franapsisters. Sr. Magdalena Obisppo, F.A.S., Acting Regl. Animator. Sisters in USA 19.

[R] RETREAT HOUSES

CUMBERLAND. *Mercy Lodge*, 6 Summer Brown Rd., 02864. Tel: 401-333-2801. 15 Highland View Rd., 02864-1124.

NARRAGANSETT. *Our Lady of Peace Spiritual Life Center*, 338 Ocean Rd., Box 507, 02882. Tel: 401-884-7676; 401-783-2871; Fax: 401-792-8682. Email: OLP@Intap.net. Sisters Jean Marie McGee, R.S.M., Dir.; Elizabeth McLaughlin, S.N.D., Asst. to Dir. & Team Member; Revs. Robert F. Caul, Team Member; Richard M. Friedrichs, Team Member; Ms. Veneta Lorraine, Team Member.
Legal Title: *Our Lady of Peace Retreat House*

NORTH PROVIDENCE. *Bethany Renewal Center*, 397 Fruit Hill Ave., 02911. Tel: 401-353-5860. Email: fmmbethaney@aol.com. Web: www.fmmusa.org. Sisters Joyce C. Gardella, F.M.M.; Yvette Hubert, F.M.M. Conducted by the Franciscan Missionaries of Mary.

[S] NEWMAN CENTERS

PROVIDENCE. *Brown University* Office of Chaplains & Rel. Life, Box 1931, 02912. Tel: 401-863-2344; Fax: 401-863-9359. Email: catholic@brown.edu. Web: www.brown.edu/students/Brown_Catholic. Rev. Henry J. Bodah, Chap.; Mary Beth Reynolds, Catholic Campus Min.

Johnson & Wales University Catholic Campus Ministry-CBCSI Bldg., 8 Abbott Park Place, 02903. Tel: 401-598-1830; Fax: 401-598-1171. Email: sgaumont@jwu.edu. Web: www.jwu.edu/prov/stuac/sp_cath.htm. Sandra Gaumont, Campus Min.

Rhode Island College Catholic Campus Ministry, Donovan Lower Level, 600 Mt. Pleasant Ave., 02908. Tel: 401-456-8168; Fax: 401-456-2849 (Call first). Email: campusministry@ric.edu. Web: www.ric.edu/chaplain. Deacon Michael Napolitano.

BRISTOL. *Roger Williams University* Catholic Chaplain's Office, 1 Old Ferry Rd., 02809. Tel: 401-254-3433. Email: frbj6@aol.com. Rev. Barry J. Gamache.

SMITHFIELD. *Bryant College* Chaplain's Office, 1150 Douglas Pike, Box 33, 02917-1284. Tel: 401-232-6045; Fax: 401-232-6362. Email: revjp@bryant.edu. Rev. Joseph A. Pescatello, Chap.

SOUTH KINGSTOWN. *University of Rhode Island Catholic Center* Tel: 401-874-2324; Fax: 401-874-9099. Email: jso9365u@postoffice.uri.edu. Web: www.uricatholiccenter.org.
Kingston, 02881. Tel: 401-874-2324; Fax: 401-874-9099. Email: jso9365u@postoffice.uri.edu. Revs. John P. Soares, Chap.; Joseph D. Creedon, Chap.; Mrs. Carol Maddock, Chap. & Campus Min.

[T] SECULAR INSTITUTES

GREENVILLE. *Regnum Christi*, 60 Austin Ave., 02828. Tel: 401-949-2820; Fax: 401-949-2310; 401-949-0291. Email: matere@ids.net. Web: www.regnumchristi.org. Ms. Gabriela Garza, Dir.

MANVILLE. *Oblate Missionaries of Mary Immaculate*, P.O. Box 303, 02838. Tel: 207-798-0324. Email: demartori@aol.com. Web: www.inst.secular-ommi.com. Miss Ruth A. Valois.

[U] MISCELLANEOUS LISTINGS

PROVIDENCE. *College Compass Inc.*, P.O. Box 6811, 02940. Tel: 401-739-7779; Fax: 401-739-7760. Email: michelle.burns@collegecompass.org. Web: www.collegecompass.org. Michelle Burns, Dir. Operations.

Miscellaneous Listings for the Diocese of Providence Mailing address for all Providence listings , Chancery Office: 1 Cathedral Sq., 02903. Tel: 401-278-4517; Fax: 401-278-4621. Email: jdarcy@dioceseofprovidence.org. Web: www.dioceseofprovidence.org. Rev. John J. Darcy, M.A., J.C.L., Chancellor. For further information contact:
Catholic Charity Fund
Catholic Information Center of Newport
Catholic Inner City Apostolate, Inc.
Catholic Investment Trust, Inc.
Catholic Teachers' College of Providence
Charismatic Renewal, 32 Lawn Ave., Pawtucket, 02860-3522. Tel: 401-723-9138. Rev. John W. O'Brien.
CharisNewal RI, 244 Smith St., 02908. Tel: 401-253-9457. Bob LaFazia, Co-Dir.; Ted Carlson, Co-Dir.
Cursillo Movement
538 Broadway, 02909-1895. Tel: 401-274-3434. Rev. Frank S. Salmani, Spiritual Dir.
100 Empress Dr., East Greenwich, 02818. Tel: 401-884-2424. Kathryn Robbio, Lay Coord.
The Church of the Immaculate Conception, North Providence
De LaSalle Academy Corporation
Diocesan Administration Corporation Tel: 401-278-4616; Fax: 401-751-6808. J. Timothy Kocab, Diocesan Controller.
Diocesan Service Corporation Tel: 401-278-4616; Fax: 401-751-6808.
Holy Name Society, 391 High St., Central Falls, 02863. Tel: 401-723-5427.
House of the Good Shepherd of Providence
Homes for Hope Foundation
Inter-Parish Loan Fund, Inc.
LaSalle Academy
Little Sisters of the Assumption of Woonsocket
Marian Association of Northern Rhode Island
Mary, Mother of Youth Center
The Mercy Home and School
Mother of Hope Novitiate
New England Conference of Diocesan Directors of Religious Education
Occult Awareness Ministry
Our Lady of Providence Preparatory Seminary
Our Lady, Queen of the Clergy
Pius X Salvage Bureau
Providence Catholic Schools Collaborative
The Rhode Island Catholic Orphan Asylum (St. Aloysius Home)
Roman Catholic Bishop of Providence A Corporation Sole.
St. Benedict's Hearth Corporation, East Providence.
Saint Hedwig's Church Corporation, Providence
St. John's Church of Providence
Saint Margaret's Home
Saint Maria Society
St. Mary Academy of the Visitation
Saint Raphael's Industrial Home and School
St. Vincent de Paul Home, Woonsocket
Stella Maris Home for Convalescents
Vision of Hope, Inc.

BURRILLVILLE. *Father Andre Coindre Charitable Trust*, Tel: 401-568-2379. Email: loulaperle@aol.com. 685 Steere Farm Rd., Pascoag, 02859-4601. Fax: 401-568-1450. Bro. Louis Laperle, Corp. Sec.

CUMBERLAND. *Conference of Regional Treasurers*, 15 Highland View Rd., 02864-1124. Tel: 401-333-9145; Fax: 401-333-6450. Email: mpmurphy@mercyri.org. Sr. Marypatricia Murphy, R.S.M.

GREENVILLE. *Mater Ecclesiae, Inc.*, 60 Austin Ave., 02828. Tel: 401-949-2820; Fax: 401-949-2310; 401-949-0291. Email: matere@ids.net. Web: www.regnumchristi.org. Luly Fernandez, Contact Person.
Pro Values, Inc., 60 Austin Ave., 02828. Tel: 914-773-1368; Fax: 914-773-1438. Rev. Juan Sabadell, L.C., Sec. & Contact Person.

NARRAGANSETT. *Saint Benilde Community Support Charitable Trust*, 635 Ocean Rd., 02882-1314. Tel: 401-789-0244; Fax: 401-783-5303. Email: lee@cbc.necoxmail.com.

NORTH PROVIDENCE. *Franciscan Missionaries of Mary*, 399 Fruit Hill Ave., 02911. Tel: 401-353-5800; Fax: 401-354-8296. Email: mmotte@aol.com. Web: www.fmmusa.org.
Mission Resource Center Tel: 401-353-4470; Fax: 401-353-8779. Sr. Alma Dufault, F.M.M., Dir.

PASCOAG. *The Charles Lwanga Charitable Trust*, 658 Steere Farm Rd., 02859-4601. Tel: 401-568-2379; Fax: 401-568-9810. Email: loulaperle@aol.com. Bro. Robert Croteau, S.C., Treasurer.

SMITHFIELD. *LC Pastoral Services, Inc.*, 60 Austin Ave., Greenville, 02828. Tel: 401-949-2820; Fax: 401-949-2310. Rev. Juan Sabadell, L.C., Contact Person.
Mater Ecclesiae, Inc., 60 Austin Dr., Greenville, 02828. Tel: 401-949-2820; Fax: 401-949-2310. Rev. Juan Sabadell, L.C., Contact Person.

SOUTH KINGSTOWN. *The Legion of Christ (RI) Incorporated*, 4780 Tower Hill Rd., Wakefield, 02879. Tel: 203-281-4798. Rev. Juan Sabadell, L.C., Contact Person.
Overbrook, Incorporated, 4780 Tower Hill Rd., Wakefield, 02879. Tel: 203-281-4798. Rev. Juan Sabadell, L.C., Contact Person.

WARWICK. *Hombre Nuevo (RI), Inc.*, 109 Hardig Rd., 02886. Tel: 401-886-0603.

WEST WARWICK. *Tides Family Services*, Family Counseling, 215 Washington St., 02893. Tel: 401-822-1360; Fax: 401-823-4694. Email: mail@tidesfs.org. Web: www.tidesfs.org. Bro. Michael Reis, F.S.C., Pres. & Treas. Staff 70; Assisted 1,500.
Branch Offices:
Youth New Futures, 790 Broad St., 02907. Tel: 401-467-8888; Fax: 401-467-8899.
Youth New Futures, 242 Dexter St., Pawtucket, 02860. Tel: 401-724-8100; Fax: 401-724-8899.
Tides' Hispanic Outreach Project, 242 Dexter St., Pawtucket, 02860. Tel: 401-724-8201; Fax: 401-724-8899.
Outreach and Tracking Program, 242 Dexter St., Pawtucket, 02860. Tel: 401-724-8380; Fax: 401-724-8899.
Woonsocket Outreach Project, 1 Social St., Woonsocket, 02895. Tel: 401-766-9320; Fax: 401-766-9324.
Learning Centers:
242 Dexter St., Pawtucket, 02860. Tel: 401-724-8060; Fax: 401-724-8899.
790 Broad St., 02907. Tel: 401-467-8228; Fax: 401-467-8899.
222 Washington St., 02893. Tel: 401-823-0157; Fax: 401-823-4694.
Youth Diversion Projects:
215 Washington St., 02893. Tel: 401-822-1360; Fax: 401-823-4694.
242 Dexter St., Pawtucket, 02860. Tel: 401-724-8380; Fax: 401-724-8899.

RELIGIOUS INSTITUTES OF MEN REPRESENTED IN THE DIOCESE

For further details refer to the corresponding bracketed number in the Religious Institutes of Men or Women section.

[]—*Apostolic Life Community of Priests in the Opus Spiritus Sancti*—O.S.S.
[0130]—*Assumptionists*—A.A.
[0200]—*Benedictine Monks*—O.S.B.
[]—*Brothers of Our Lady of Providence*—O.L.P.
[0330]—*Brothers of the Christian Schools* (New England-Long Island Prov.)—F.S.C.
[1100]—*Brothers of the Sacred Heart*—S.C.
[0310]—*Congregation of Christian Brothers*—C.F.C.
[0520]—*Franciscan Friars* (Prov. of the Most Holy Name)—O.F.M.
[0600]—*Holy Cross Brothers*—C.S.C.
[0650]—*Holy Ghost Fathers* (Eastern Prov.)—C.S.Sp.
[0730]—*Legionaires of Christ*—L.C.
[0780]—*Marist Fathers*—S.M.
[1210]—*Missionaries of St. Charles (Scalabrinians)*—C.S.
[1110]—*Missionaries of the Sacred Heart*—M.S.C.
[0430]—*Order of Preachers (Dominicans)* (Prov. of St. Joseph)—O.P.
[1220]—*Servants of Charity*—S.C.
[0370]—*Society of St. Columban*—S.S.C.

RELIGIOUS INSTITUTES OF WOMEN REPRESENTED IN THE DIOCESE

[0130]—*Apostles of the Sacred Heart of Jesus*—A.S.C.J.
[1810]—*Bernadine Franciscan Sisters*—O.S.F.
[0350]—*Carmelite Sisters (Corpus Christi)*—O.Carm.
[0990]—*Congregation of Divine Providence*—C.D.P.
[]—*Congregation of the Immaculate Conception*—C.I.C.
[]—*Daughters of Mary Mother of Mercy*—D.M.M.M.
[0820]—*Daughters of the Holy Spirit*—D.H.S.
[0420]—*Discalced Carmelite Nuns*—O.C.D.
[1070-15]—*Dominican Sisters*—O.P.
[1105]—*Dominican Sisters of Hope*
[1100]—*Dominican Sisters of the Presentation*
[1070]—*Dominicans*—O.P.
[1070-13]—*Dominicans* (Adrian)—O.P.
[1070-15]—*Dominicans* (Blauvelt)—O.P.
[1070-17]—*Dominicans* (de'Ricci)—O.P.
[1070-14]—*Dominicans* (Grand Rapids)—O.P.
[1070-05]—*Dominicans* (Amityville)—O.P.
[1170]—*Felician Sisters*—C.S.S.F.
[]—*Franciscan Apostolic Sisters*—F.A.S.
[1370]—*The Franciscan Missionaries of Mary*—F.M.M.
[]—*Franciscan Sisters*—O.S.F.
[1180]—*Franciscan Sisters of Allegheny*—O.S.F.
[3790]—*Institute of the Sisters of St. Dorothy*—S.S.D.
[2340]—*Little Sisters of the Poor*—L.S.P.
[2470]—*Maryknoll Missionaries*—M.M.
[1360]—*Missionary Franciscan Sisters of the Immaculate Conception*—M.F.I.C.
[3450]—*Religious of Jesus and Mary*—R.J.M.
[2070]—*Religious of the Holy Union of the Sacred Hearts*—S.U.S.C.
[4070]—*Religious of the Sacred Heart*—R.S.C.J.
[3430]—*Religious Teachers Filippini*—M.P.F.
[2970]—*School Sisters of Notre Dame*—S.S.N.D.
[2575]—*Sisters of Mercy of the Americas*—R.S.M.
[3000]—*Sisters of Notre Dame de Namur*—S.N.D.deN.
[3720]—*Sisters of Saint Anne*—S.S.A.
[3750]—*Sisters of St. Chretienne*—S.S.CH.
[0590]—*Sisters of St. Elizabeth, Convent Station*—S.C.
[1570]—*Sisters of St. Francis of the Holy Family* (Dubuque, IA)—O.S.F.
[3860]—*Sisters of St. Joseph of Cluny*—S.J.C.
[3830]—*Sisters of St. Joseph of Springfield*—S.S.J.
[2980]—*Sisters of the Congregation of Notre Dame*—C.N.D.
[3180]—*Sisters of the Cross and Passion*—C.P.
[3310]—*Sisters of the Presentation of Mary*—P.M.
[3320]—*Sisters of the Presentation of the B.V.M.*—P.B.V.M.
[4040]—*Society of St. Ursula*—S.U.
[4048]—*Society of the Sisters, Faithful Companions of Jesus*—F.C.J.

DIOCESAN CEMETERIES

PROVIDENCE. *St. Patrick's*
BARRINGTON. *Maria Del Campo*
CRANSTON. *St. Ann's*
CUMBERLAND. *Resurrection*
EAST PROVIDENCE. *Gate of Heaven*
MIDDLETOWN. *St. Columba*
PAWTUCKET. *St. Francis*
Mount St. Mary's
WEST GREENWICH. *St. Joseph*

NECROLOGY

† Davis, Joseph E., Woonsocket, RI Sacred Heart—Died June 12, 2003
† Doucet, Ovila T., Jeanne Jugan Residence, 964 Main St., Pawtucket, 02860—Died Oct. 19, 2003
† Kelleher, James L., Johnston, RI St. Brigid—Died May 15, 2003
† Mendonsa, August F., (Retired)—Died May 14, 2003
† Morin, Henri D., (Retired)—Died April 23, 2003
† Murphy, Joseph F., St. John Vianney Residence, 495 Mt. Pleasant Ave., 02908. (Retired)—Died Jan. 31, 2003

Diocese of Pueblo

(Dioecesis Pueblensis)

Most Reverend

ARTHUR N. TAFOYA, D.D.

Bishop of Pueblo; ordained May 12, 1962; appointed Bishop of Pueblo July 1, 1980; consecrated and installed September 10, 1980 *1001 Grand Ave., Pueblo, CO 81003.* Tel: 719-544-9861, Ext. 151; Fax: 719-544-1220.

Catholic Pastoral Center: 1001 N. Grand Ave., Pueblo, CO 81003. Tel: 719-544-9861; Fax: 719-544-5202.

Web: www.pueblo-diocese.com

Email: diocesepueblo@usa.net

Most Reverend

CHARLES A. BUSWELL

Retired Bishop of Pueblo; ordained July 9, 1939; appointed Bishop of Pueblo August 8, 1959; consecrated September 30, 1959; installed October 6, 1959; retired September 18, 1979 *Res.: Villa Pueblo Towers,* 855 Hunter Dr., #810, Pueblo, CO 81001-1837.

Square Miles 48,155.

Diocesan Patron: St. Therese of the Child Jesus. Secondary Patroness: Our Lady of Guadalupe.

Erected a Diocese November 15, 1941.

Comprises the 29 Counties of Alamosa, Archuleta, Baca, Bent, Conejos, Costilla, Crowley, Custer, Delta, Dolores, Fremont, Gunnison, Hinsdale, Huerfano, Kiowa, La Plata, Las Animas, Mesa, Mineral, Montezuma, Montrose, Otero, Ouray, Prowers, Pueblo, Rio Grande, Saguache, San Juan and San Miguel in the southern and western part of the State of Colorado.

Legal Title: For legal titles of parishes and diocesan institutions, consult the Business Office.

STATISTICAL OVERVIEW

Statistical report was not submitted for 2004.

Personnel	
Bishop	1
Retired Bishops	1
Abbots	1
Retired Abbots	1
Priests: Diocesan Active in Diocese	34
Priests: Diocesan Active Outside Diocese	1
Priests: Diocesan in Foreign Missions	1
Priests: Retired, Sick or Absent	36
Number of Diocesan Priests	72
Religious Priests in Diocese	32
Total Priests in Diocese	104
Extern Priests in Diocese	3
Ordinations:	
Diocesan Priests	1
Transitional Deacons	2
Permanent Deacons in Diocese	29
Total Brothers	5
Total Sisters	96
Parishes	
Parishes	52
With Resident Pastor:	
Resident Diocesan Priests	33
Resident Religious Priests	14
Without Resident Pastor:	
Administered by Priests	4
Administered by Deacons	2
Missions	56
Professional Ministry Personnel:	
Sisters	9
Lay Ministers	56
Welfare	
Catholic Hospitals	5
Total Assisted	890,800
Homes for the Aged	2
Total Assisted	1,555
Special Centers for Social Services	3
Total Assisted	4,950
Educational	
Diocesan Students in Other Seminaries	6
Total Seminarians	6
High Schools, Diocesan and Parish	1
Total Students	94
Elementary Schools, Diocesan and Parish	4
Total Students	702
Elementary Schools, Private	1
Total Students	176
Catechesis/Religious Education:	
High School Students	2,443
Elementary Students	4,902
Total Students under Catholic Instruction	8,323
Teachers in the Diocese:	
Brothers	1
Sisters	6
Lay Teachers	83
Vital Statistics	
Receptions into the Church:	
Infant Baptism Totals	2,020
Adult Baptism Totals	171
Received into Full Communion	321
First Communions	1,554
Confirmations	890
Marriages:	
Catholic	249
Interfaith	120
Total Marriages	369
Deaths	1,564
Total Catholic Population	110,200
Total Population	601,000

Former Bishops—Most Rev. JOSEPH CLEMENT WILLGING, D.D., First Bishop of Pueblo; ord. June 20, 1908; appt. Dec. 6, 1941; consecrated Feb. 24, 1942; Assistant at Pontifical Throne, Feb. 20, 1958; died March 3, 1959.

Catholic Pastoral Center—1001 N. Grand Ave., Pueblo, 81003. Tel: 719-544-9861; Fax: 719-544-5202. Office Hours: Mon.-Fri. 8-12 & 1-5

Vicar General—Rev. THOMAS M. ADRIANS, V.G.

Chancellor—Rev. Msgr. MARK A. PLEWKA, J.C.L. Tel: 719-544-9861, Ext. 162.

Vice Chancellor—Mrs. LORRAINE GUERIN. Tel: 719-544-9861, Ext. 151.

Diocesan Tribunal—

Judicial Vicar—Rev. Msgr. MARK A. PLEWKA, J.C.L.

Promotor Justitiae—VACANT.

Defensores Vinculi—Rev. GEORGE V. FAGAN, J.C.L.; Ms. DONI R. NEEDHAM. Tel: 719-544-9861, Ext. 161.

Judicial Experts—Rev. Msgr. MARVIN J. KAPUSHION, M.S.W., J.C.L., L.C.S.W.; Dr. MICHAEL MILLARD, Ph.D.

Secretarial to the Tribunal—Ms. DONI NEEDHAM. Tel: 719-544-9861, Ext. 161.

Judge—Rev. Msgr. MARK A. PLEWKA, J.C.L.

Ecclesiastical Notaries—Mrs. LORRAINE GUERIN; Ms. DONI NEEDHAM; Rev. MARK T. BETTINGER.

Presbyteral Council-College of Consultors— Ex Officio: Most Rev. ARTHUR N. TAFOYA, D.D., Ex Officio; Rev. Msgr. MARK A. PLEWKA, J.C.L., Ex Officio. Tel 719-544-9861, Ext. 162; Revs. THOMAS M. ADRIANS, V.G., Chm.; CARLOS ALVAREZ; JOHN J. COSTANZO (Retired); Very Rev. ROGER DORCY, Vice Chm. & Treas.; Rev. Msgr. MARVIN KAPUSHION (Retired); Rev. NATHANAEL FOSHAGE, O.S.B.

Deans—Revs. THOMAS R. HINNI, C.M., V.F., Pueblo Deanery; WILLIAM T. GLEESON, V.F., Alamosa Deanery; JAMES F. KOENIGSFELD, V.F., Durango Deanery; MICHAEL N. SMITH, S.J., V.F., Grand Junction Deanery; CHARLES A. SENA, V.F., La Junta Deanery; RICHARD L. WEHRMEYER, C.M., V.F., Trinidad Deanery.

Archivist—Mrs. LORRAINE GUERIN. Tel: 719-544-9861, Ext. 151.

Diocesan Offices

Administrative Services—

The Bishop of Pueblo, a Corporation Sole—1001 N. Grand Ave., Pueblo, 81003. Tel: 719-544-9861, Ext. 141.

Business and Finance—Tel: 719-544-9861, Ext. 141. Mrs. BARBARA J. DUFF, Dir. Tel: 719-544-9861, Ext. 141.

Finance Advisory Council—Rev. JAMES E. KING, Chm., 611 N. 11th St., Canon City, 81212. Tel: 719-275-7549; Deacon EDWARD RICCILLO, Vice Chm., 24744 Birdsong Dr., Pueblo, 81006. Tel: 719-543-2944, Ext. 123.

Stewardship—Mrs. BARBARA J. DUFF. Tel: 719-544-9861, Ext. 141.

Development—Mrs. BARBARA J. DUFF. Tel: 719-544-9861, Ext. 141.

Human Resources—Mrs. THERESA FARLEY, Dir. Tel: 719-544-9861, Ext. 171.

Liaison for Organizations—Mrs. LORRAINE GUERIN, Contact. Tel: 719-544-9861, Ext. 151.

Department of Pastoral Life—Sr. BETTY WERNER, O.P., Dir. Tel: 719-544-9861, Ext. 114.

Ministry Formation—Sr. BETTY WERNER, O.P. Tel: 719-544-9861, Ext. 114.

Superintendent of Catholic Schools—Sr. BETTY WERNER, O.P. Tel: 719-544-9861, Ext. 114.

Office of Multicultural & Detention Ministry—Mr. RON ROYBAL, Coord. Tel: 719-544-9861, Ext. 110.

Migrant and Hispanic Ministry—Mr. RON ROYBAL, Contact. Tel: 719-544-9861, Ext. 110.

Office of Catechesis—Sr. LAETITIA SLUSSER, S.C., Coord. Tel: 719-544-9861, Ext. 115.

Office of Worship and Spiritual Life—Ms. KATHLEEN CAREY, Ph.D., Coord. Tel: 719-544-9861, Ext. 117.

O.C.I.A. (R.C.I.A.)—Ms. KATHLEEN CAREY, Ph.D., Contact. Tel: 719-544-9861, Ext. 117.

Diocesan Liturgical Council—Most Rev. ARTHUR N. TAFOYA, D.D., Contact.

Office of Social Justice—Mr. LARRY HOWE-KERR, Coord. Tel: 719-544-9861, Ext. 112.

Evangelization—Mr. LARRY HOWE-KERR, Contact. Tel: 719-544-9861, Ext. 112.

Vocation Office—Deacon JACOB SHAFER, Coord. Tel: 719-544-9861, Ext. 116.

Family Life & Youth—VACANT.
Web Master and Secretary—EMILY UNDEM. Tel: 719-544-9861, Ext. 118.
Department of Pastoral Outreach—Sr. ANDREA VASQUEZ, O.S.B., Dir. Tel: 719-544-9861, Ext. 123.
Campus Ministry—Sr. ANDREA VASQUEZ, O.S.B. Tel: 719-544-9861, Ext. 123.
Deanery Coordinator—Sr. ANDREA VASQUEZ, O.S.B., Contact. Tel: 719-544-9861, Ext. 123.
Mission Office—Sr. ANDREA VASQUEZ, O.S.B. Tel: 719-544-9861, Ext. 123.
Propagation of the Faith—Sr. ANDREA VASQUEZ, O.S.B., Contact, 1001 N. Grand Ave., Pueblo, 81003. Tel: 719-544-9861, Ext. 123.
Diocesan Newspaper—Most Rev. ARTHUR N. TAFOYA, D.D., Publisher, 1001 Grand Ave., Pueblo, 81003. Tel: 719-544-9861, Ext. 151; Mr. JOHN PEARRING, Mng. Editor, 109 Pawnee Ave., Manitou Springs, 80829. Tel: 719-685-5202, Ext. 121. "The Chronicle of Catholic Life"
Resource Library—Ms. JOYCE RIVERA, Clerk. Tel: 719-544-9861, Ext. 121.
Catholic Charities of the Diocese of Pueblo, Inc.—Mrs. JANE MAZUR, M.S., M.S.W., Dir., 429 W. 10th St., Ste. 101, Pueblo, 81003. Tel: 719-544-4233; Fax: 719-544-4215.
Victim Assistance Coordinator—Mrs. JANE MAZUR, M.S., M.S.W. Tel: 719-544-4233. Email: jmazur@pueblocharities.org.
Division—Family Counseling Center, 429 W. 10th St., Ste. 101, Pueblo, 81003. Tel: 719-544-4233.
The Bishop Charles A. Buswell Trust—Most Rev. ARTHUR N. TAFOYA, D.D., Contact, 1001 N. Grand Ave., Pueblo, 81003. Tel: 719-544-9861, Ext. 151.
Boy Scouts of America—Deacon MIKE ROVELLA, Chap., 1660 Sneffles, Montrose, 81401. Tel: 970-249-3319; RIK BERGETHON, Committee Chm., 159 McNeil Rd., Pueblo, Co 81001. Tel: 719-544-1255.
Catholic Charismatic Renewal Center—Rev. CARLOS A. ALVAREZ, Contact, Holy Name of Mary Parish, P.O. Box 97, Del Norte, 81132. Tel: 719-657-3147.
Clergy Benefit Society of the Diocese of Pueblo, Inc.—Rev. LEONARD E. RACKI, Pres. (Retired), 31 Terrace Dr., Pueblo, 81001-1135. Tel: 719-583-1988.
Diocesan Catechetical Council—Most Rev. ARTHUR N. TAFOYA, D.D., Contact Person, 1001 N. Grand Ave., Pueblo, 81003. Tel: 719-544-9861, Ext. 151.
Diocesan Council of Catholic Women—Rev. RICHARD F. BECKER, Moderator, 1145 S. Aspen Rd., Pueblo, 81006. Tel: 719-544-1886.
Diocesan Pastoral Council—Mr. DARREN GARCIA, Chm., 405 N. 5th St., Rocky Ford, 81067. Tel: 719-254-3094; Mr. AL PEARSON, Vice Chm., 2837 A Lexington, Grand Junction, 81503. Tel: 970-243-0957.
Father John Powers Memorial Basketball League, Inc.—Mr. ROBERT J. DOUGLASS, Contact Person, 144 Harvard Ave., Pueblo, 81004. Tel: 719-544-7192.
Girl Scouts of America—Mrs. LINDA ROOF, 24 Bellflower Ct., Pueblo, 81001. Tel: 719-544-6725.
St. John Neumann Catholic School Foundation—330 Lake Ave., Pueblo, 81004. Tel: 719-543-8407; Fax: 719-543-8864.
Human Development Commission of the Diocese of Pueblo—Mr. LARRY HOWE-KERR, Contact, 1001 N. Grand Ave., Pueblo, 81003. Tel: 719-544-9861, Ext. 112.
Catholic Campaign for Human Development—Mr. LARRY HOWE-KERR, Chm.
Nocturnal Adoration Society—Sr. JOSEPHINE RONEY, S.S.S., 311 E. Mesa Ave., Pueblo, 81006. Tel: 719-545-PRAY.
Presbyteral Council—Most Rev. ARTHUR N. TAFOYA, D.D., Pres.; Revs. THOMAS M. ADRIANS, V.G., Chm.; CARLOS ALVAREZ; Very Rev. ROGER P. DORCY, Vice Chm. & Treas.; Rev. Msgrs. MARVIN J. KAPUSHION, M.S.W., J.C.L., L.C.S.W.; MARK A. PLEWKA, J.C.L., Sec., Ex Officio; Revs. JOHN J. COSTANZO (Retired); NATHANAEL FOSHAGE, O.S.B.
Standing Committees—
Clergy Assemblies—Revs. THOMAS M. ADRIANS, V.G., Chm., 1708 Horseshoe Dr., Pueblo, 81001. Tel: 719-542-9248; DERREK D. SCOTT, Sec.; LEONARD RACKI, Treas.
Continuing Education and Formation—Revs. TONY WOJCINSKI, Chm.; KEVIN NOVAK; Mrs. BARBARA J. DUFF, Ex Officio; Rev. CHARLIE SENA; Deacon HENRY WERTIN.
Personnel—Revs. TOM ADRIANS, Chm.; BEN BACINO; JOHN FARLEY; JAMES KOENIGSFELD; NATHANAEL FOSHAGE, O.S.B.
**Posada Shelter*—Ms. ANNE STATTELMAN, Dir., 1008 N. Grand Ave., Pueblo, 81003. Tel: 719-545-8776.
Clergy Conference of the Diocese of Pueblo—Rev. THOMAS M. ADRIANS, V.G., 1708 Horseshoe Dr., Pueblo, 81001. Tel: 719-542-9248.
Las Hermanas de Pueblo—Mrs. ROSEANNA PADILLA, Pres., P.O. Box 4116, Pueblo, 81001. Tel: 719-544-2014.
SEARCH—Ms. SANDY HANSEN, 917 E. Evans, Pueblo, 81004. Tel: 719-546-1015; 719-544-8246. Email: info@searchretreatprogram.org. Web: searchretreatprogram.org.
Sisters' Council—Sr. ANDREA VASQUEZ, O.S.B., 1001 N. Grand Ave., Pueblo, 81003-2948. Tel: 719-544-9861, Ext. 123.
Legion of Mary—Ms. MARINA ZAMORA, Pres., 2944 Aster St., Pueblo, 81005. Tel: 719-564-7248.
Catechetical Ministry—Sr. LAETITIA SLUSSER, S.C., Coord. Formation. Tel: 719-544-9861, Ext. 115.
Tribunal—Rev. Msgr. MARK A. PLEWKA, J.C.L. Tel: 719-544-9861, Ext. 162.
Holy Childhood, Association—Sr. ANDREA VASQUEZ, O.S.B., Contact, 1001 N. Grand Ave., Pueblo, 81003. Tel: 719-544-9861, Ext. 123.

CLERGY, PARISHES, MISSIONS AND PAROCHIAL SCHOOLS

CITY OF PUEBLO
(PUEBLO COUNTY)

1—SACRED HEART CATHEDRAL (1872), Very Rev. Roger P. Dorcy, Rector; Sr. Arlene Sanders, Pastoral Min.
Parish Office:—414 W. 11th St., 81003. Tel: 719-544-5175; Fax: 719-586-9922.

2—ST. ANNE (1956), Rev. James E. Friel.
Res.: 2701 E. 12th St., 81001. Tel: 719-545-2644; Fax: 719-542-8089.

3—ST. ANTHONY OF PADUA, Closed. For inquiries for parish records contact the chancery., Contact Chancery for sacremental records.

4—CHRIST THE KING (1957), Rev. Thomas M. Adrians, V.G.; Deacon Mike LaConte.
1708 Horseshoe Dr., 81001. Tel: 719-542-9248; Fax: 719-545-9826.
Convent—11 MacNaughton Rd., 81001. Tel: 719-543-2466; Fax: 719-545-9826.

5—ST. FRANCIS XAVIER (1903), Rev. Thomas R. Hinni, C.M., V.F.; Jack Blanc, Business Mgr.
611 Logan Ave., 81004. Tel: 719-564-1125; Fax: 719-564-1141.
Mission—Our Lady of Lourdes Beulah, Pueblo Co.

6—HISTORIC SOUTHSIDE CATHOLIC COMMUNITY (2000), Rev. John B. Farley; Deacon Philip J. Reynolds; Sr. Marie Vigil, Business Mgr.
Mailing Address: 919 E. Evans Ave., 81004-2567. Tel: 719-296-8778; Fax: 719-562-1195.
Our Lady of the Assumption: 900 E. Routt Ave., 81004. Tel: 719-543-2168.
St. Mary Help of Christians: 307 E. Mesa Ave., 81006. Tel: 719-543-3601.
St. Patrick: 226 Michigan Ave., 81004. Tel: 719-542-4702.
Catechesis/Religious Program—Tel: 719-543-1783. August Cordova, D.R.E. Students 124.

7—HOLY FAMILY (1954), Rev. Jesse L. Perez; Deacon Steve Lumbert.
Mailing Address: 2827 Lakeview Ave., 81005. Tel: 719-564-2696; Fax: 719-564-4396.
Catechesis/Religious Program—Pam Evanoff, D.R.E. Students 350.
Mission—St. Aloysius (1936), Rye, Pueblo Co. Rev. Msgr. Marvin J. Kapushion, M.S.W., J.C.L., L.C.S.W.

8—HOLY ROSARY (1954), Rev. Msgr. Mark A. Plewka, J.C.L.
Office—2400 W. 22nd St., 81003. Tel: 719-545-7219; Fax: 719-545-7259.
Res.: 201 Lamkin St., #403, 81003. Tel: 719-545-3670.

9—ST. JOSEPH (1960), Revs. Richard F. Becker; James F. Koenigsfeld, V.F.; Marco Antonio Salinas.
Res. and Office: 1145 S. Aspen Rd., 81006. Tel: 719-544-1886; 719-543-0835; Fax: 719-544-5137.

10—ST. LEANDER (1902), Rev. Ben Bacino; Deacon Edward Riccillo.
Office—1402 E. Seventh St., 81001. Tel: 719-544-8411; Fax: 719-544-8202.

11—ST. MARY (1895), Consolidated, with Our Lady of the Assumption, Pueblo and St. Patrick, Pueblo to form Historic Southside Catholic Community, Pueblo.

12—OUR LADY OF GUADALUPE CHAPEL (1968),, c/o St. Leander. , Mailing Address: 1402 E. 7th St., 81001. 914 E. Second St., 81001. Tel: 719-544-8411; Fax: 719-544-8202.

13—OUR LADY OF MT. CARMEL (1901), Revs. Richard F. Becker; James F. Koenigsfeld, V.F.; Marco Antonio Salinas.
421 Clark St., 81003. Tel: 719-542-5952; Fax: 719-542-2310.

14—OUR LADY OF THE ASSUMPTION (1949), Consolidated, with St. Mary, Pueblo and St. Patrick, Pueblo to form Historic Southside Catholic Community, Pueblo.

15—OUR LADY OF THE MEADOWS (1979), Rev. Kevin Novack; Deacons Rick Oreskey; John Wertz.
23 Starling Dr., 81005. Tel: 719-561-3580; Fax: 719-561-1271.

16—ST. PATRICK (1882), Consolidated, with Our Lady of the Assumption, Pueblo and St. Mary, Pueblo to form Historic Southside Catholic Community, Pueblo.

17—ST. PIUS X (1955), Rev. J. William Huber, Ph.D.
Parish Center—3130 Morris Ave., 81008. Tel: 719-542-4264; Fax: 719-583-8103.
Catechesis/Religious Program—142 Stardust Dr., Pueblo West, 81007. Students 224.
Mission—St. Paul the Apostle 3130 Morris Ave., Pueblo West, Pueblo Co. 81008. Tel: 719-547-3725 Business Office.

18—SHRINE OF ST. THERESE (1948), Rev. William Courtney; Paula Giordano, Pastoral Assoc.
300 Goodnight Ave., 81004. Tel: 719-542-1788; Fax: 719-542-2130.

OUTSIDE THE CITY OF PUEBLO

AGUILAR, LAS ANIMAS CO., ST. ANTHONY (1875), (Spanish—Italian), [CEM] [JC 2] Rev. Philip Coury, C.M.
Mailing Address: P.O. Box 577, 81020. Tel: 719-941-4124; Fax: 719-941-4124.
Mission—Mount Carmel Trujillo Creek, Las Animas Co.
Mission—San Jose Gulnare, Las Animas Co.

ALAMOSA, ALAMOSA CO., SACRED HEART (1887), Rev. William T. Gleeson, V.F.; Mrs. Marianne Dunne, Pastoral Assoc.
Mailing Address: P.O. Box 547, 81101. Tel: 719-589-3211; 719-589-5829 (Parish Center); Fax: 719-589-5820.
Station—Adams State College (Alamosa), Mosca. Tel: 719-587-7011.

AVONDALE, PUEBLO CO., SACRED HEART (1960), (Spanish), Rev. Kevin J. Bachman, O.S.B.; Mr. John L. Sullivan, Parish Dir.
Mailing Address: P.O. Box 279, 81022. Tel: 719-947-3092; Fax: 719-947-3082.
Mission—St. William Mailing Address: P.O. Box 276, Boone, Pueblo Co. 81025. Tel: 719-947-3432.

CANON CITY, FREMONT CO., ST. MICHAEL (1880), Rev. James E. King; Deacon Merle E. Runck.
611 N. 11th St., 81212. Tel: 719-275-7549; Fax: 719-275-7540.
Catechesis/Religious Program—1016 Mystic, 81212. Tel: 719-275-3368. Students 209.

CAPULIN, CONEJOS CO., ST. JOSEPH (1912), (Hispanic), [CEM] Rev. Edmundo Valera, Ph.D.
Mailing Address: P.O. Box 40, 81124. Tel: 719-274-5304; Fax: 719-274-4454.
Mission—Our Lady of the Valley 19617 S. Hwy. 285, La Jara, Conejos Co. 81140. Tel: 719-274-5647.
Mission—St. Therese of the Child Jesus 115 Main St., Manassa, Conejos Co. 81141.
Mission—St. Anthony 18900 County Rd. 28, Los Sauces, Conejos Co. 81151.
Mission—Our Lady of the Immaculate Conception 211 Blanca St., Romeo, Conejos Co. 81148.

CENTER, SAGUACHE CO., ST. FRANCIS JEROME (1951), Revs. Carlos A. Alvarez, Admin.; Martin Frias.
781 Warden St., 81125. Tel: 719-754-3969; Fax: 719-754-3964.
Mission—St. Agnes P.O. Box 22, Saguache, Saguache Co. 81149.
Station—Sanctuary House Retreat Center Crestone. Tel: 719-256-4778; Fax: 719-256-4719.

CONEJOS, CONEJOS CO., OUR LADY OF GUADALUPE (1857), [CEM] Rev. Pat Valdez, C.R., Admin.
Mailing Address: P.O. Box 305, Antonito, 81120. Tel: 719-376-5985; Fax: 719-376-2530. 6633 Co. Rd. 13, 81129.
Mission—St. Augustine
Mission—Sagrada Familia Antonito. 17344 Co. Rd. G, Lobatos, Conejos Co. 81120.
Mission—San Juan Nepomuceno y San Cayetano Antonito. 684 Co. Rd. B, Ortiz, Conejos Co. 81120.
Mission—San Antonio de Padua Antonito. 13148 Co. Rd. C, San Antonio, Conejos Co. 81120.
Mission—San Pedro y San Rafael Antonito. 5308 Co. Rd. 10.75, San Rafael, Conejos Co. 81120.

CORTEZ, MONTEZUMA CO., ST. MARGARET MARY (1945), Rev. Derrek D. Scott; Deacon Andres Hernandez.
Mailing Address: 28 E. Montezuma, 81321. Tel: 970-565-7308 (Office); Fax: 970-565-0822.
Mission—St. Jude 313 N. Pine, Dove Creek, Dolores Co. 81324.

CRESTED BUTTE, GUNNISON CO., QUEEN OF ALL SAINTS (1883), Attended by, St. Peter Parish, Gunnison. Rev. Steven J. Murray.
Church: P.O. Box 271, 81224. Tel: 970-641-0808; Fax: 970-641-4592.
Catechesis/Religious Program—405 Sopris.

DEL NORTE, RIO GRANDE CO., HOLY NAME OF MARY (1879), [CEM] Revs. Carlos A. Alvarez, Admin.; Martin Frias.
645 Pine Ave., P.O. Box 97, 81132. Tel: 719-657-3147; Fax: 719-657-2855.

Mission—St. Francis of Assisi Los Valdeses, Rio Grande Co.
Mission—Holy Family South Fork, Rio Grande Co.
Mission—Immaculate Conception Creede, Mineral Co.

DELTA, DELTA CO., ST. MICHAEL (1911), Rev. Mark T. Bettinger.
Parish Office—628 Meeker St., 81416. Tel: 970-874-3300; Fax: 970-874-4015.
Res.: 628 Meeker St., 81416. Tel: 970-874-5116; Fax: 970-874-4015.
Mission—St. Philip Benizi P.O. Box 713, Cedaredge, Delta Co. 81413. Tel: 970-856-6495.

DURANGO, LA PLATA CO.

1—ST. COLUMBA (1881), Rev. James F. Koenigsfeld, V.F., Admin.; Mary Therese Ralph, Pastoral Assoc.
1830 E. Second Ave., 81301. Tel: 970-247-0044; Fax: 970-385-5737.
School—Tel: 970-247-5527; Fax: 970-382-9355. Sisters of St. Dominic 2; Lay Teachers 20; Students 254.

2—SACRED HEART (1906), (Hispanic), Rev. Joseph Gallegos, C.R.
254 E. Fifth Ave., 81301. Tel: 970-247-3997; Fax: 970-375-2385.

FLORENCE, FREMONT CO., ST. BENEDICT (1895), Rev. Baaju Izuchi, C.S.Sp., Ph.D., Admin.
622 W. Second St., P.O. Box 189, 81226. Tel: 719-784-4879; Fax: 719-784-2070.
Mission—St. Patrick Rockvale, Fremont Co.

FRUITA, MESA CO., SACRED HEART (1890), Rev. Michael N. Smith, S.J., V.F.; Deacon John Luginbill.
Mailing Address: 513 E. Aspen Ave., 81521. Tel: 970-858-9605; Fax: 970-858-9605.

GARDNER, HUERFANO CO., SACRED HEART (1912), Rev. Richard Wehrmeyer, C.M., V.F.; Deacon John Luginbill.
Mailing Address: P.O. Box 86, Walsenburg, 81089. Tel: 719-738-1204; Fax: 719-738-1206.

GRAND JUNCTION, MESA CO.

1—IMMACULATE HEART OF MARY (1955), Rev. Vincente Paz en la Casa; Deacon Douglas VanHouten.
790 26 1/2 Rd., 81506. Tel: 970-242-6121; Fax: 970-256-0276.
Mission—St. Ann 535 W. 1st St., Palisade, Mesa Co. 81526. Tel: 970-464-5157. Sr. Celine Regan, O.P., Pastoral Assoc.
Station— Debeque.
Station— Collbran.

2—ST. JOSEPH (1884), Rev. Msgr. Edward H. Nunez; Rev. Donald Malin; Deacons William Pewters, Pastoral Assoc.; Stanley G. Neumann, Pastoral Assoc.
Mailing Address: 230 N. Third, 81501. Tel: 970-243-0209; Fax: 970-243-7493.
School—Holy Family School, 786 26 1/2 Rd., 81506. Tel: 970-242-6168; 970-241-1489; Fax: 970-242-4244. Ms. Ann Ashwood, Prin. Sisters 3; Lay Teachers 21; Students 365.

GUNNISON, GUNNISON CO., ST. PETER (1881), Rev. Steven J. Murray.
303 N. Wisconsin St., 81230. Tel: 970-641-0808; Fax: 970-641-4592.
Catechesis/Religious Program—400 W. Georgia Ave.. Tel: 970-641-0268.
Mission—St. Rose of Lima 302 Silver St., Lake City, Hinsdale Co. 81235. Tel: 970-944-0228.

HOLLY, PROWERS CO., ST. FRANCES OF ROME (1920), Rev. Msgr. William P. Doll.
Church: 130 S. Fifth St., 81047. Tel: 719-537-6688.
Mission—St. Mary Bristol, Prowers CoP.O. Box 592, 81047.

IGNACIO, LA PLATA CO., ST. IGNATIUS PARISH (1898), Rev. Edward J. Andary.
Mailing Address: P.O. Box 1350, 81137. Tel: 970-563-4241; Fax: 970-563-1032.
Mission—St. Bartholemew
Mission—SS. Peter & Rose R.R. 2, Arboles, Archuleta Co. 81137.
Station— Tiffany.

LA JUNTA, OTERO CO., OUR LADY OF GUADALUPE/ST. PATRICK (1889), Revs. Charles A. Sena, V.F.; Paul Montez, O.S.B.
222 Lincoln St., Box 1181, 81050. Tel: 719-384-4342; 719-384-4372; Fax: 719-384-7894.

LAMAR, PROWERS CO., ST. FRANCIS DE SALES-OUR LADY OF GUADALUPE (1907), Rev. Anthony A. Wojcinski; Deacon Henry J. Wertin.
600 E. Parmenter St., 81052. Tel: 719-336-7759; Fax: 719-336-0291.
Catechesis/Religious Program—Tel: 719-336-7750.

LAS ANIMAS, BENT CO., ST. MARY (1910), Rev. Raymond P. Grimes.
714 Elm St., 81054. Tel: 719-456-0357; Fax: 719-456-1104.

MANCOS, MONTEZUMA CO., ST. RITA (1914), Rev. Derrek D. Scott; Deacon Andres Hernandez.
28 E. Montezuma Ave., Cortez, 81321. Tel: 970-565-7308; Fax: 970-565-0822.
Mission—Our Lady of Victory Church 101 N. 7th, Dolores, Montezuma Co. 81323. Tel: 970-565-7308.
Mission—Immaculate Heart of Mary Chapel Rico, Dolores Co. Tel: 970-565-7307.
Station—National Park Mesa Verde.

MONTE VISTA, RIO GRANDE CO., ST. JOSEPH (1920), Revs. Carlos A. Alvarez, Admin. Tel: 719-852-4590; Martin Frias; Deacon Don Lamb. Tel: 719-852-3773.
425 Batterson, P.O. Box 587, 81144. Tel: 719-852-2523 (Rectory); 719-852-2673 (Parish); Fax: 719-852-0623.
Station— Lariate.
Station— Morada.
Station—Mountain Meadows Nursing Center, Tel: 719-852-5138.
Station—Colorado State Veterans Center Homelake. Tel: 719-852-5118.
Station—High Valley Manor, Tel: 719-852-5711.

MONTROSE, MONTROSE CO., ST. MARY (1906), Rev. Msgr. Daniel R. Huber; Deacons Dennis Putnam, Parish Assoc.; Michael Rovella.
Parish Center:—1855 St. Mary's Dr., 81401. Tel: 970-249-3319; Fax: 970-249-9088.
Mission—Our Lady of Fatima, Tel: 970-323-5146.

OURAY, OURAY CO., ST. DANIEL THE PROPHET (1883), Rev. Nathanael Foshage, O.S.B.
Mailing Address: P.O. Box 565, 81427. Tel: 970-325-4373.
Mission—St. Patrick 1005 Reece, Silverton, San Juan Co. 81433.

PAGOSA SPRINGS, ARCHULETA CO., IMMACULATE HEART OF MARY (1923), (Hispanic), [CEM] Rev. John C. Bowe, C.R.; Deacons Tom Bomkamp. Tel: 970-731-3115; Roger Behr. Tel: 970-731-0409.
Mailing Address: P.O. Box 451, 81147. Tel: 970-264-5702; Fax: 970-264-3166.
Catechesis/Religious Program—Students 147.
Mission—St. Francis Frances, Archuleta Co. Fax: 970-264-3166.
Mission—St. John Baptist Pagosa Junction, Archuleta Co.
Mission—St. James Trujillo, Archuleta Co.
Station— Chromo.

PAONIA, DELTA CO., SACRED HEART (1923), Rev. William R. Nelson.
235 N. Fork Ave., P.O. Box 988, 81428. Tel: 970-527-3214; Fax: 970-527-5468.
Mission—St. Margaret Mary 331 Bridge St., Hotchkiss, Delta Co. 81419.

ROCKY FORD, OTERO CO., ST. PETER (1910), Revs. Charles A. Sena, V.F.; Paul Montez, O.S.B.
1209 Swink Ave., 81067. Tel: 719-254-3565; Fax: 719-254-3921.
Mission—St. Joseph the Worker 1209 Swink, Manzanola, Otero Co. 81067.
Mission—St. Peter Chapel P.O. Box 218, Ordway, Crowley Co. 81063. Tel: 719-267-4645.
Mission—Mary Queen of Heaven P.O. Box 214, Fowler, Otero Co. 81039. Tel: 719-263-4455.

SAN LUIS, COSTILLA CO., SANGRE DE CRISTO (1881), (Hispanic), [CEM] Rev. Patrick M. Valdez, C.R.
Res.: P.O. Box 326, 81152. Tel: 719-672-3685; Fax: 719-672-0300.
Catechesis/Religious Program—Students 59.
Mission—St. James Blanca, Costilla Co.
Mission—Holy Family Fort Garland, Costilla Co.
Mission—Immaculate Conception Chama, Costilla Co.
Mission—San Acacio San Acacio, Costilla Co.
Mission—SS. Peter and Paul San Pedro, Costilla Co.
Mission—St. Isidro San Isidro, Costilla Co.
Mission—St. Francis of Assisi San Francisco, Costilla Co.
Mission—Sacred Heart of Jesus Garcia, Costilla Co.

SILVERTON, SAN JUAN CO., ST. PATRICK (1883), Rev. Nathanael Foshage, O.S.B.
Mailing Address: P.O. Box 565, Ouray, 81427. Tel: 970-325-4373.

SPRINGFIELD, BACA CO., ANNUNCIATION (1932), Rev. J. Patrick Walsh, S.J.
140 Kansas St., 81073. Tel: 719-523-6645.
Station— Walsh.

TELLURIDE, SAN MIGUEL CO., ST. PATRICK (1896), Rev. Nathanael Foshage, O.S.B., Supvr.; Deacon Michael Doehrman, Parish Dir.
Mailing Address: P.O. Box 398, 81435. Tel: 970-728-3337; Fax: 970-728-8029.
Mission—Our Lady of Sorrows P.O. Box 451, Nucla, Montrose Co. 81424.

TRINIDAD, HUMBOLDT CO., OUR LADY OF MT. CARMEL, TRINIDAD AREA CATHOLIC COMMUNITY (TRINIDAD CLUSTER), Closed., For inquiries for parish records contact Most Holy Trinity, 719-846-3369

TRINIDAD, LAS ANIMAS CO.

1—ST. JOSEPH, TRINIDAD AREA CATHOLIC COMMUNITY (TRINIDAD CLUSTER), Closed., For inquiries for parish records contact Most Holy Trinity, 719-846-3369.

2—MOST HOLY TRINITY, TRINIDAD AREA CATHOLIC COMMUNITY (TRINIDAD CLUSTER) (1885), [CEM] Revs. Robert A. Hagan, S.J.; Eugene C. Renard, S.J.; Thomas J. Melancon, S.J.
235 N. Convent St., 81082. Tel: 719-846-3369; Fax: 719-846-4856.
School—237 Church St., 81082. Tel: 719-846-7541. Sisters 1; Lay Teachers 18; Students 131.
Mission—St. Isidore Vigil, Las Animas Co.
Mission—St. Ignatius Segundo, Las Animas Co.

VINELAND, PUEBLO CO., ST. THERESE (1928), Revs. Richard F. Becker; Marco Antonio Salinas.
Mailing Address: 1145 S. Aspen Rd., 81006. Tel: 719-948-2410; 719-544-1886; Fax: 719-544-5137.
In Res., Rev. Robert F. Carden (Retired).

WALSENBURG, HUERFANO CO., ST. MARY (1896), [CEM] Rev. Richard Wehrmeyer, C.M., V.F.; Deacon John Luginbill; Sr. Carol Tlach, S.N.D., Senior Outreach Dir.
Mailing Address: P.O. Box 86, 81089. Tel: 719-738-1204; Fax: 719-738-1206.
Mission—Christ the King P.O. Box 752, La Veta, Huerfano Co. 81055.
Mission—Sacred Heart P.O. Box 228, Gardner, Huerfano Co. 8104.
Mission—Our Lady of Guadalupe Chama, Huerfano Co.

WESTCLIFFE, CUSTER CO., OUR LADY OF THE ASSUMPTION (1870), Rev. Louis M. Kirby, O.S.B.
Mailing Address: P.O. Box 359, 81252. Tel: 719-783-2340.

Chaplains of Public Institutions

PUEBLO. *Colorado State Hospital*, Tel: 719-546-4434. (Vacant)
St. Mary Corwin Medical Center. Rev. Gary L. Kennedy.
1008 Minnequa Ave., 81004. Tel: 719-560-4000.
1024 Oxford St., #9, 81005. Rev. Ervin Schmitt. Tel: 719-564-0885.
Parkview Hospital. Michael C. DeSciose.
Res.: 1070 Moccasin Dr., 81007.

CANON CITY. *Fremont Correctional Facility*, St. Dismas Chapel. (Vacant)

CROWLEY. *Arkansas Valley Correctional Facility*. (Vacant)

TRINIDAD. *State Home for the Aged*. Administered by priests from Trinity Area Catholic Community

---

On Duty Outside the Diocese:
Revs.—
Haberman, C. Robert, San Rafael, CA
Norman, Clifford A., Mexico

Absent on Leave:
Revs.—
Bonfadini, Leo
Bouchard, Norman
McCleary, Michael L.
Thill, Richard
Trujillo, Carlos B.
Vandenberg, James

Retired:
Rev. Msgrs.—
Delaney, Howard L., 7-C Bonnymede, 81001.
Holland, George T., 2204 Wyoming Ave., 81004.
Kapushion, Marvin, 620 E. Routt, 81004. Tel: 719-545-4599
Revs.—
Bertrand, Aloysius J., 3260 N. 12th, #221, Grand Junction, 81506. Tel: 970-256-9579
Carden, Robert F., 1133 36th Lane, Vineland, 81006.
Cavanagh, Michael J., 543 Bridge St., Lowell, MA 01850.
Cerwonka, Clarence J. (SY), 37 Fayette St., Binghamton, NY 13905. Tel: 607-723-5383
Corbett, Michael E., 2110 "B" Chatalet Lane, 81005. Tel: 719-566-9836
Costanzo, John J., 4947 King St., Denver, 80221. Tel: 303-477-4853
Danowski, Alexander J., 653 Country Court, Grand Junction, 81504-5907.
Gallagher, Maurice O., 116 N. Highland Ave., Boone, 81025. Tel: 719-947-9812
Kiernan, John G., 2185 Linda Ln., Grand Junction, 81501.
Kukucka, Joseph G., P.O. Box 123, Sugar City, 81076.
Marcantonio, Clement, LRMC 799 CMR 402, Apo, AE 09180.
McDevitt, James J., St. Vincent's Church, 840 George Bush Blvd., Delray Beach, FL 33483.
Munson, Thomas N., Res.: 16098 County Rd. 28.3, Dolores, 81323.
O'Flynn, John, 23 Churchill Pl., 81001.
O'Sullivan, John C., Providence Mount St. Vincent, 4831 35th Ave., S.W., Seattle, WA 98126.
Pettit, Edward G., 324 E. Evans, 81004. Tel: 719-595-0217
Powers, William V., 1414 E. 8th St., 81001.

Quinn, Thomas J., S.J. (NY), P.O. Box 607, South Fork, 81154. Tel: 719-657-3147
Racki, Leonard E., 31 Terrace Dr., 81001.
Roche, Ron, 1912 Vinewood Ln., 81005. Tel: 719-565-0813
Rykowski, Jerome A., 587 Eastwood St., Grand Junction, 81504-4814. Tel: 970-243-6234
Schmitt, Ervin J., 1024 Oxford St., #9, 81005. Tel: 719-564-0885
Schoening, Sylvester H., Hermitage, 1250 Mountain View Ln., P.O. Box 553, Norwood, 81423.
Smigiel, Walter J., 3517 Atlantic Dr., Colorado Springs, 80910.
Sutton, John H., 310 3rd Ave., Cando, ND 58324.
Wichmann, Edward W., 1225 Central Blvd., Apt. 903, Brownsville, TX 78520.

Permanent Deacons:
Behr, Roger, Immaculate Heart of Mary, Pagosa Springs
Boies, James A., Sr., V.A. Hospital Chap.
Bomkamp, Thomas, Immaculate Heart of Mary, Pagosa Springs
Doehrman, Michael J., Parish Dir., Telluride/Nucla
Dunn, Joseph, Sacred Heart, Durango
Hawes, Lloyd, St. Peter, Gunnison
Hernandez, Andres, St. Margaret Mary, Cortez
LaConte, Michael, Christ the King, Pueblo
Lamb, Donald, St. Joseph, Monte Vista
Luginbill, John, St. Mary, Walsenburg
Lumbert, Steven, Holy Family, Pueblo
Neumann, Stan, St. Joseph, Grand Junction
Newport, Gary, St. Columba, Durango
Oreskey, Richard, Our Lady of the Meadows, Pueblo
Pewters, William, St. Joseph, Grand Junction
Putnam, Dennis, St. Mary, Montrose
Reynolds, Philip, Historic Southside Catholic Communtity, Pueblo
Riccillo, Edward, St. Leander, Pueblo
Romero, Toby, Sacred Heart, Durango
Rovella, Mike, St. Mary, Montrose
Runck, Merle, St. Michael, Canon City
Shafer, Jacob, Vocation Director and Director of Deacons/Deacon Formation, Catholic Pastoral Center
Stroop, John, Queen of All Saints, Crested Butte
VanHouten, Douglas, Immaculate Heart of Mary, Grand Junction
Wertin, Henry, St. Francis de Sales, Lamar
Wertz, John, Our Lady of the Meadows, Pueblo

INSTITUTIONS LOCATED IN THE DIOCESE

[A] HIGH SCHOOLS, DIOCESAN

TRINIDAD. *Trinidad Catholic Schools*, 201 Church St., 81082. Tel: 719-846-7541; Fax: 719-846-6974. Email: tcadmin@amigo.net. Mrs. Kim Bettger, Prin. Sisters 1; Lay Teachers 7; Students 44.

[B] ELEMENTARY SCHOOLS, DIOCESAN

PUEBLO. *The Shrine of St. Therese Catholic School*, 320 Goodnight Ave., 81004. Tel: 719-561-1121; Fax: 719-561-2252. Web: www.sttherese-school.org. Joseph M. Tanner, Prin. Lay Teachers 9; Total Enrollment 158.

DURANGO. *St. Columba*, (Grades PreK-8), 1801 E. 3rd Ave., 81301-5072. Tel: 970-247-5527; Fax: 970-382-9355. Email: saintc@frontier.net. Sr. Edith Marie Hauser, O.P., Prin. Sisters 2; Lay Teachers 18; Students 254.

GRAND JUNCTION. *Holy Family*, (Grades PreK-8), 786 26 1/2 Rd., 81501. Tel: 970-242-6168; Fax: 970-242-4244. Web: holyfamily-gj.org. Ms. Ann Ashwood, Prin. Sisters 3; Lay Teachers 22; Students 367.

TRINIDAD. *Trinidad Catholic Elementary*, (Grades K-8), 201 Church St., 81082-2606. Tel: 719-846-7218; Fax: 719-846-6974. Email: tcadmin@amigo.net. Mrs. Kim Bettger, Prin. Lay Teachers 11; Students 71.

[C] ELEMENTARY SCHOOLS, PRIVATE

PUEBLO. *John Neumann Catholic Schools*, 330 Lake Ave., 81004. Tel: 719-543-8407; Fax: 719-543-8864. Email: pecoraroj@yahoo.com. Mr. Jack Pecoraro, Admin.; Mr. John Moruzzi, Dir.
Stauter Campus (Grades K-3), 2415 E. Orman Ave., 81004. Tel: 719-561-9419; 719-566-9636; Fax: 719-561-4718. Mr. John Moruzzi, Dir. Lay Teachers 7; Students 66.
Seton Campus (Grades 4-8), 330 Lake Ave., 81004. Tel: 719-543-8864; 719-543-8407; Fax: 719-543-8864. Mr. Jack Pecoraro, Admin. Lay Teachers 8; Students 88.
Preschool, 2415 E. Orman Ave., 81004. Tel: 719-561-9419; Fax: 719-561-4718. Connie Lauer, Dir. Lay Teachers 3; Students 60.

[D] GENERAL HOSPITALS

PUEBLO. *Centura Health-St. Mary-Corwin Medical Center* An operating unit of Catholic Health Initiatives Mountain Region (an affiliate of Catholic Health Initiatives). , 1008 Minnequa Ave., 81004. Tel: 719-560-4000; Fax: 719-560-5950. Email: chaplainsmc@centura.org. Web: www.stmarycorwin.org. Mr. Thomas E. Anderson, CEO; Susan Ortega, Contact Person; Revs. Gary Kennedy, Chap.; Ervin J. Schmitt, Chap. (Retired); Mrs. Irene Behling, Dir. Spiritual Care; Sr. Darleen Mahoney, O.S.F. Bed Capacity 408; Total Staff 1,200; Patients Assisted Annually 217,300.

CANON CITY. *Centura Health-St. Thomas More Hospital*, 1338 Phay Ave., 81212. Tel: 719-269-2000; Fax: 719-269-2016. Web: www.stthomasmorehosp.org. C. Ray Honaker, CEO; Rev. Baaju Izuchi, C.S.Sp., Ph.D., Chap. An operating unit of Catholic Health Initiatives Mountain Region (an affiliate of Catholic Health Initiatives). Bed Capacity 245; Patients Assisted Annually 72,252.

DURANGO. *Centura Health-Mercy Medical Center* An affiliate of Catholic Health Initiatives. , 375 E. Park Ave., 81301. Tel: 970-247-4311. Email: kirkdignum@mercydurango.org. Web: www.mercydurango.org. Kirk Dignum, Ph.D., Pres. & CEO. Beds 83; Patients Assisted Annually 239,925; Total Staff 724.
Chaplains: John Boyd, Dir., Mission & Medical Affairs; Diana McKenna, Contact & Dir., Mission & Spiritual Care.

GRAND JUNCTION. *Marillac Clinic, Inc.*, 2333 N. 6th St., 81501. Tel: 970-255-1782; Fax: 970-255-1711. Email: jcameron@stmarygj.com. Ms. Janet K. Cameron, Exec. Dir.
Legal Title: *Sisters of Charity of Leavenworth Health System* Total Staff 60; Total Assisted 24,931.
St. Mary Hospital and Medical Center, P.O. Box 1628, 81502-1628. Tel: 970-244-2273; Fax: 970-244-2891. Web: www.stmarygj.com. Email: pmontgomery@stmarygj.com. Mr. Robert W. Ladenburger, Pres. & CEO; Pat Montgomery, Exec. Asst. Sisters of Charity of Leavenworth, Kansas 10; Bed Capacity 346; Patients Assisted Annually 350,440; Total Staff 2,015.

[E] SPECIAL CARE FACILITIES

PUEBLO. *Villa Pueblo* An operating unit of Catholic Health Initiatives Mountain Region (an affiliate of Catholic Health Initiatives). , 1111 Bonforte Blvd., 81001. Tel: 719-545-5911; Fax: 719-544-1354. Rev. Ron Kruis, Chap.

CANON CITY. *Centura Health-Progressive Care Center* An operating unit of Catholic Health Initiatives Mountain Region (an affiliate of Catholic Health Initiatives). , 1338 Phay Ave., 81212. Tel: 719-269-2000; Fax: 719-269-2016. Email: barbaracarochi@centura.org. Barbara Carochi, Admin. Bed Capacity 116.

[F] MONASTERIES AND RESIDENCES OF PRIESTS AND BROTHERS

CANON CITY. *Holy Cross Abbey*, P.O. Box 1510, 81215-1510. Tel: 719-275-8631; Fax: 719-275-7125. Email: hcabbey@juno.com. Rt. Rev. Kenneth C. Hein, O.S.B., Retired Abbot (Retired); Revs. Ignatius J. Smith, O.S.B., Supr.; William L. Thompson, O.S.B.; Bernard P. Gervais, O.S.B.; Louis M. Kirby, O.S.B.; Paul J. Montez, O.S.B.; Michael D. Murray, O.S.B.; Martin de Porres J. Muheim, O.S.B.; Kevin J. Bachman, O.S.B.; Bros. Bernard A.F. Best, O.S.B.; Matthew Bach, O.S.B.; David J. Downey, O.S.B. Priests of Monastery 12; Professed Brothers 3.

TRINIDAD. *Trinidad Area Catholic Community*, Rectory, 615 E. Goddard Ave., 81082. Tel: 719-846-3360.
Business Address:, 235 N. Convent St., 81082. Tel: 719-846-3369; Fax: 719-846-4856. Revs. Robert A. Hagan, S.J., Supr.; Eugene C. Renard, S.J.; Thomas J. Melancon, S.J.

[G] CONVENTS AND RESIDENCES FOR SISTERS

PUEBLO. *Servants of the Blessed Sacrament*, 311 E. Mesa Ave., 81006. Tel: 719-545-7729; Fax: 719-542-3094. Email: ssspueblo@juno.com. Sr. Josephine Roney, S.S.S., Supr. Sisters 3.

[H] NEWMAN CENTERS

GUNNISON. *Campus Ministry - Diocese of Pueblo* 1001 N. Grand Ave., 81003. Tel: 970-641-0325. Sr. Andrea Vasquez, O.S.B.
Adams State College (Alamosa), United Campus Ministry College Center, Rm. 329, P.O. Box 1164, Alamosa, 81102-9986. Tel: 719-589-7516; 719-274-5304. Shirley Atencio.
Fort Lewis College (Durango) Tom Eckenrode.
Fort Lewis College Center for Campus Ministry 1830 E. 2nd Ave., Durango, 81301. Tel: 970-247-0044.
Mesa State College (Grand Junction), Newman Center, 1135 College Pl., Grand Junction, 81501. Tel: 970-241-3670. Ms. Janet Johnson, Campus Min.
Western State College (Gunnison), Campus Ministry Center, 600 E. Georgia, 81230. Tel: 970-641-0325. Ms. Susan Searle, Campus Min.
University of Southern Colorado (Pueblo), 1708 Horseshoe Dr., 81001. Tel: 719-542-9248. Christ the King
Colorado State University - Pueblo, Formerly University of Southern Colorado (Pueblo) 419 Petroleum Ave., Florence, 81226. Tel: 719-542-2089; 719-542-9248. Joyce Archuleta, Campus Min.

[I] RETREAT WORK

CANON CITY. *Trinity Ranch Conference & Renewal Center, Inc.*, Mailing Address: 2951 E. Hwy. 50, 81212. Tel: 719-275-8631; Fax: 719-275-7125. Email: hcabbey@juno.com. Rev. Ignatius Smith, O.S.B., Prior.

CRESTONE. *Spiritual Life Institute of America, Inc.*, P.O. Box 219, 81131. Tel: 719-256-4778; Fax: 719-256-4719. Email: nada@fone.net. Web: www.spirituallifeinstitute.org. Revs. David Denny, Prior; John Meoska; Sr. Connie Bielecki, Contact. Priests 2; Brothers 1; Sisters 5.

MONTROSE. *Spes in Deo Franciscan Family Retreat Center, Inc.*, 21661 Hwy. 550, 81401. Tel: 970-249-3526. Email: joyce@spesindeoretreat.com. Web: www.spesindeoretreat.com. M. Joyce Martin, Pres., Bd. of Directors.

WHITEWATER. *Whitewater Community, Inc.*, 8250 Kannah Creek Rd., 81527. Tel: 970-241-3847. Sr. Mary M. Glenn, Contact. Sisters 2.

[J] MISCELLANEOUS

PUEBLO. **Catholic Diocese of Pueblo Foundation*, 1001 N. Grand Ave., 81003. Tel: 719-544-9861, Ext. 131; Fax: 719-544-5202. Email: bfbrandt@usa.net. Web: www.dioceseofpueblo.com. Mr. Bruce F. Brandt, Dir.
St. Charles Community, 18 Dartmouth, 81005. Tel: 719-566-1620. Mr. Ed Sajbel, Contact Person.
Deacon Candidate Formation Council, 1001 N. Grand Ave., 81003. Tel: 719-544-9861, Ext. 116. Deacon Vernon Dobelmann.
Historic Southside Catholic Community, 919 East Evans Ave., 81004. Tel: 719-296-8778; Fax: 719-562-1195. Rev. John B. Farley, Pastor; Deacon Philip Reynolds; Sr. Marie Vigil, Business Mgr. The Historic Southside Catholic Community is an organization which clusters the pastoral and administrative functions for 3 parishes: St. Mary Help of Christians, and St. Patrick Catholic Churches/Parishes, Pueblo
John Neumann Catholic School (Administration & Middle School), 330 Lake Ave., 81004. Tel: 719-543-8407; Fax: 719-543-8864. Email: admissions@johnneumann.org. Web: www.johnneumann.org. Mr. Jack Pecoraro, Admin. (John Neumann Catholic Schools housed at Seton Education Center)
Pueblo Community Soup Kitchen, Inc., 422 W. Seventh, 81003. Tel: 719-545-6540. Myrtle Huff, Coord.
S.E.T. of Pueblo, Inc. A division of Catholic Health Initiatives Colorado. , 1902 E. Orman Ave., 81004. Tel: 719-560-5886; Fax: 719-564-4709. Email: noreenellisonsc@centura.org. Sisters Noreen Ellison, S.C., Exec. Dir.; Jacqueline Riggio, S.C., Asst. Dir. Purpose: A ministry to low-income, disadvantaged, and underserved persons, providing educational and health support services for empowerment and transformation.
SEARCH of Pueblo, 917 E. Evans, 81004. Tel: 719-544-8246. Email: searchofpueblo@aol.com. Ms. Sandy Hansen, Coord.
Serra Club of Pueblo, 5426 Stonemoor Dr., 81005. Tel: 719-566-0511. Mrs. Sally Stricca, Sec.
Sisters for Christian Community, 1081 S. Lynx Dr., 81007. Tel: 719-547-2416; Fax: 719-547-4401. Email: salliewatkins@juno.com. Sr. Sallie Watkins, S.F.C.C., Ph.D., Sec. & Contact.

CENTER. *Artes Del Valle (Hispanic Craft Cooperative)*, P.O. Box 627, 81125. Tel: 719-589-4769; 719-754-3191. Miss Shirley Ortega, Mgr. Artes del Valle is under the auspices of St. Francis Jerome Church, Center.

DURANGO. *Mercy Health Foundation*, 375 E. Park Ave., 81301. Tel: 970-382-2091; Fax: 970-385-5392.

Email: karenmidkiff@mercydurango.org. Ms. Karen Midkiff, Exec. Dir. & Contact. Affiliate of Catholic Health Initiatives.

GRAND JUNCTION. *Grand Valley Catholic Outreach*, 240 White Ave., 81501. Tel: 970-241-3658; Fax: 970-242-3908. Email: gvco@juno.com. Web: www.catholicoutreach.org. Sr. Karen Bland, O.S.B., Exec. Dir.

P.O. Box 246, 81502. Tel: 970-241-3658; Fax: 970-242-3908.

Grand Valley Peace and Justice, c/o St. Joseph Church, 230 N. 3rd St., 81501. Tel: 970-243-4378; Fax: 970-243-7493. Email: bevg3@prodigy.net. Ms. Karen Sjoberg, Dir.

St. Mary's Hospital Foundation, 2635 N. 7th St., P.O. Box 1628, 81502-1628. Tel: 970-244-2015; Fax: 970-244-6108. Email: mmccarthy@stmarygj.com. Mary Frances McCarthy, Exec. Dir.

St. Mary's Rehabilitation Center, Inc., P.O. Box 1628, 81502.

PAGOSA SPRINGS. *Archuleta Housing Corporation*, 713 San Juan Ave. P.O. Box 355, 81147-0355. Tel: 970-264-2195.

RELIGIOUS INSTITUTES OF MEN REPRESENTED IN THE DIOCESE

For further details refer to the corresponding bracketed number in the Religious Institutes of Men or Women section.

[0200]—*Benedictine Monks*—O.S.B.

[1330]—*Congregation of the Mission* (Missouri Prov.)—C.M.

[0260]—*Discalced Carmelite Monks*—O.C.D.

[0690]—*Jesuit Fathers and Brothers* (Missouri Prov.)—S.J.

[1300]—*Theatine Fathers* (Rome, Italy)—C.R.

RELIGIOUS INSTITUTES OF WOMEN REPRESENTED IN THE DIOCESE

[0230]—*Benedictine Sisters of Pontifical Jurisdiction* (Chicago, IL; Covington, KY; Colorado Springs, CO; Yankton, SD)—O.S.B.

[3765]—*Capuchin Poor Clares*—O.S.C.Cap.

[1710]—*Congregation of the Third Order of St. Francis of Mary Immaculate, Joliet, IL*—O.S.F.

[0420]—*Discalced Carmelite Nuns*—O.C.D.

[1070-13]—*Dominican Sisters*—O.P.

[1070-24]—*Dominican Sisters*—O.P.

[1845]—*Guadalupanas Missionaries of the Holy Spirit*—M.G.Sp.S.

[1910]—*Hermanas Josefinas*—H.J.

[2575]—*Institute of the Sisters of Mercy of the Americas*—R.S.M.

[2960]—*Notre Dame Sisters*—N.D.

[3130]—*Our Lady of Victory*—O.L.V.M.

[3580]—*Servants of Mary*—O.S.M.

[3500]—*Servants of the Blessed Sacrament*—S.S.S.

[]—*Sisters for Christian Community*—S.F.C.C.

[0440]—*Sisters of Charity of Cincinnati, Ohio*—S.C.

[0480]—*Sisters of Charity of Leavenworth, Kansas*—S.C.L.

[2360]—*Sisters of Loretto At the Foot of the Cross*—S.L.

[1570]—*Sisters of St. Francis of the Holy Family*—O.S.F.

[3830-15]—*Sisters of St. Joseph*—C.S.J.

[3830-18]—*Sisters of St. Joseph*—C.S.J.

[1720]—*Sisters of the Third Order Regular of St. Francis of the Congregation of Our Lady of Lourdes*—O.S.F.

[]—*Sisters of Whitewater Community*

[4060]—*Society of the Holy Child Jesus*—S.H.C.J.

CEMETERIES, DIOCESAN AND PAROCHIAL

PUEBLO. *Gate of Heaven*

Legal Title: *Gate of Heaven Section, Roselawn Cemetery Assoc.*

AGUILAR. *St. Anthony* (St. Anthony Parish)

CAPULIN. *St. Anthony; St. Francis; St. Joseph; and Capulin* (St. Joseph Parish)

CONEJOS. *Conejos; Las Mesitas; San Antonio; Ortiz; and Labatos* (Our Lady of Guadalupe Parish)

DEL NORTE. *St. Francis of Assisi* (Holy Name of Mary Parish)

FRUITA. *Fruita Catholic* (Sacred Heart Parish)

PAGOSA SPRINGS. *St. John the Baptist; St. Andrew Avelino; St. Francis; and St. James* (Immaculate Heart of Mary Parish)

RYE. *Mount Olivet*

Legal Title: *The Rye Mount Olivet Cemetery.*, (St. Daniel Mission Parish)

SAN LUIS. *San Luis; San Pedro; San Acacio; San Francisco; and Chama* (Sangre de Cristo Parish)

TRINIDAD. *Trinidad Catholic* Legal Title: Trinidad Catholic Cemetery Assoc. (Holy Trinity Parish)

WALSENBURG. *St. Mary* Legal Title: St. Mary Cemetery Association, Inc. (St. Mary Parish)

WESTCLIFFE. *Silver Cliff Assumption Catholic* (Our Lady of the Assumption Parish)

NECROLOGY

† Blanpied, Rev. Msgr. Robert D., (Retired)—Died Oct. 6, 2003

Diocese of Raleigh

(Dioecesis Raleighiensis)

Most Reverend

F. JOSEPH GOSSMAN, D.D., J.C.D.

Bishop of Raleigh; ordained December 17, 1955; appointed Titular Bishop of Aguntum and Auxiliary Bishop of Baltimore July 15, 1968; ordained September 11, 1968; appointed Fourth Bishop of Raleigh April 8, 1975; installed May 19, 1975 *Res.: 1601 Westbridge Ct., Raleigh, NC 27606. Office: 715 Nazareth St., Raleigh, NC 27606.* Tel: 919-821-9702.

Catholic Center: 715 Nazareth St., Raleigh, NC 27606. Tel: 919-821-9700; Fax: 919-821-9705.

Web: www.dioceseofraleigh.org

Square Miles 31,875.

Established as Vicariate-Apostolic of North Carolina by Pope Pius IX, March 3, 1868.

Established as Diocese of Raleigh by Pope Pius XI, December 12, 1924.

Comprises the following Counties in the State of North Carolina: Alamance, Beaufort, Bertie, Bladen, Brunswick, Camden, Carteret, Caswell, Chatham, Chowan, Columbus, Craven, Cumberland, Currituck, Dare, Duplin, Durham, Edgecombe, Franklin, Gates, Granville, Greene, Halifax, Harnett, Hertford, Hoke, Hyde, Johnston, Jones, Lee, Lenoir, Martin, Moore, Nash, New Hanover, Northampton, Onslow, Orange, Pamlico, Pasquotank, Pender, Perquimans, Person, Pitt, Robeson, Sampson, Scotland, Tyrrell, Vance, Wake, Warren, Washington, Wayne and Wilson.

Legal Title: For legal titles of parishes and diocesan institutions, consult the Chancery.

STATISTICAL OVERVIEW

Personnel	
Bishop	1
Priests: Diocesan Active in Diocese	59
Priests: Diocesan Active Outside Diocese	4
Priests: Retired, Sick or Absent	28
Number of Diocesan Priests	91
Religious Priests in Diocese	51
Total Priests in Diocese	142
Extern Priests in Diocese	2
Ordinations:	
Diocesan Priests	3
Permanent Deacons in Diocese	29
Total Brothers	6
Total Sisters	63
Parishes	
Parishes	78
With Resident Pastor:	
Resident Diocesan Priests	44
Resident Religious Priests	21
Without Resident Pastor:	
Administered by Religious Women	8
Administered by Lay People	1
Missions	10
Pastoral Centers	7
Professional Ministry Personnel:	
Brothers	6
Sisters	14
Lay Ministers	100
Welfare	
Special Centers for Social Services	12
Total Assisted	59,943
Educational	
Seminaries, Diocesan	1
Diocesan Students in Other Seminaries	14
Total Seminarians	14
High Schools, Diocesan and Parish	1
Total Students	945
Elementary Schools, Diocesan and Parish	35
Total Students	7,496
Catechesis/Religious Education:	
High School Students	3,420
Elementary Students	14,274
Total Students under Catholic Instruction	26,149
Teachers in the Diocese:	
Priests	2
Brothers	7
Sisters	10
Lay Teachers	680
Vital Statistics	
Receptions into the Church:	
Infant Baptism Totals	4,684
Adult Baptism Totals	267
Received into Full Communion	391
First Communions	3,443
Confirmations	1,854
Marriages:	
Catholic	445
Interfaith	392
Total Marriages	837
Deaths	895
Total Catholic Population	180,909
Total Population	4,024,253

Former Bishops of Diocese—Most Revs. WILLIAM J. HAFEY, D.D., consecrated June 24, 1925; transferred to the See of Scranton, PA, Oct. 2, 1937; installed Nov. 15, 1937; died May 12, 1954; EUGENE J. MCGUINNESS, D.D., consecrated Dec. 21, 1937; transferred to the See of Oklahoma City and Tulsa, OK, Dec. 8, 1944; installed Jan. 10, 1945; died Dec. 27, 1957; VINCENT S. WATERS, D.D., consecrated May 15, 1945; installed June 6, 1945; died Dec. 3, 1974.

Former Bishops of Vicariate-Apostolic—His Eminence JAMES CARDINAL GIBBONS, consecrated Aug. 16, 1868, Titular Bishop of Adramyttum, first Vicar-Apostolic; transferred to Richmond, VA, July 30, 1872; promoted to the See of Baltimore, Oct. 3, 1877; created Cardinal-Priest of S. Maria in Trastevere, June 7, 1886; died March 24, 1921; Most Rev. JOHN J. KEANE, consecrated Bishop of Richmond and Vicar-Apostolic of North Carolina, Aug. 25, 1878; transferred to the Titular See of Jasso, Aug. 12, 1888; elevated to the Archepiscopal Dignity with the title of Archbishop of Damascus, Jan. 9, 1897; transferred to the See of Dubuque, July 24, 1900; resigned April 3, 1911; appt. Titular Archbishop of Cios, April 28, 1911; died June 23, 1918; Rt. Revs. H. P. NORTHROP, consecrated Titular Bishop of Rosalia and Vicar-Apostolic of North Carolina, Jan. 8, 1882; transferred to Charleston, Jan. 27, 1883; died June 7, 1916; LEO HAID, O.S.B. Vicar Apostolic of North Carolina and Abbot-Ordinary of Belmont Abbey consecrated Titular Bishop of Messene, July 1, 1888; died July 24, 1924.

Office of the Bishop—715 Nazareth St., Raleigh, 27606. Tel: 919-821-9702; Fax: 919-821-9779.

Vicar General & Moderator of the Curia—Rev. Msgr. MICHAEL P. SHUGRUE, V.G., 715 Nazareth St., Raleigh, 27606. Tel: 919-821-9708.

Chancellor—RUSSELL C. ELMAYAN, 715 Nazareth St., Raleigh, 27606. Tel: 919-821-9704.

Vice Chancellor for Canonical Affairs—Very Rev. GIRARD M. SHERBA, J.C.D., 219 W. Edenton St., Raleigh, 27603. Tel: 919-832-6030.

Chancery—715 Nazareth St., Raleigh, 27606. Tel: 919-821-9703; Fax: 919-821-9779.

Deans—Very Revs. ROCH T. DROZDZIK, V.F., Albermarle; TERRENCE COLLINS, V.F., Cape Fear; JEFFREY A. INGHAM, V.F., Fayetteville; ERNEST J. RUEDE, V.F., New Bern; JOHN MCGEE, O.S.F.S, V.F., Piedmont; Rev. Msgr. JOHN F. O'CONNOR, V.F., Raleigh; Very Rev. JUSTIN KERBER, C.P., V.F., Tar River.

Diocesan Attorney—CHARLES F. POWERS III, P.O. Box 10096, Raleigh, 27605-0096. Tel: 919-783-1008.

Diocesan Consultors—Rev. PHILLIP M. LEACH; Rev. Msgrs. GERALD L. LEWIS, S.T.L.; JOHN F. O'CONNOR, V.F.; MICHAEL P. SHUGRUE, V.G.; Revs. DONALD F. STAIB; JOSEPH G. VETTER.

Diocesan Tribunal—715 Nazareth St., Raleigh, 27606. Tel: 919-821-9700. All rogatorial commissions should be directed to the Tribunal.

Defenders of the Bond—Revs. JOSEPH G. MULRONEY, J.C.L.; ALBAN HARMON, C.P., J.C.L.

Diocesan Judges—Rev. Msgrs. GERALD L. LEWIS, S.T.L.; THOMAS P. HADDEN (Retired).

Director of the Tribunal—PATRICK MORRIS, J.C.D., Ph.D.

Notaries—VIKKI NEWELL; ANNE SPEICHER.

Officialis—Very Rev. GIRARD M. SHERBA, J.C.D.

Promoter of Justice—VACANT.

Priests' Council—Rev. MARK J. BETTI; Very Revs. TERRENCE COLLINS, V.F.; ROCH T. DROZDZIK, V.F.; JEFFREY A. INGHAM, V.F.; Rev. JOHN R. KELLY; Very Rev. JUSTIN KERBER, C.P., V.F.; Rev. PHILLIP M. LEACH; Very Rev. JOHN MCGEE, O.S.F.S, V.F.; Rev. Msgr. JOHN O'CONNOR, V.F.; Rev. DANIEL D. OSCHWALD; Very Rev. ERNEST RUEDE, V.F.; Revs. WILLIAM J. RUHL, O.S.F.S.; BERNARD E. SHLESINGER; Rev. Msgr. MICHAEL SHUGRUE, V.G.; Revs. DONALD STAIB; BARRY R. STRONG, O.S.F.S.; JOSEPH G. VETTER; Very Rev. STEPHEN WORSLEY. Ex Officio: Rev. Msgr. GERALD LEWIS; Very Rev. FERNANDO TORRES; Rev. Msgr. THOMAS P. HADDEN (Retired).

Sisters' Council—Sisters BARBARA MARIE CADY, S.U.; MARY ANN CZAJA, C.S.A.

Vicar for Priests—Very Rev. STEPHEN WORSLEY, 118 E. St. James St., Tarboro, 27886. Tel: 252-539-4511.

Vicars for Religious—Sisters DAMIAN MARIE JACKSON, O.S.F., 711 Mason Rd., Durham, 27712; MARGARET GALLAGHER, I.H.M., 124 Marshall St., Warrenton, 27589.

Diocesan Divisions and Departments

Business Services Division—KIM MCBRIDE, Dir., Catholic Center, 715 Nazareth St., Raleigh, 27606. Tel: 919-821-9727.

Computer Services—JOHN ALLAN TALLANT. Tel: 919-821-9719.

Development Office—DEBORAH ROSSI. Tel: 919-821-9721.

Property/Construction—ARTHUR WESCHE. Tel: 919-821-9726.

Communications Division—FRANK MOROCK, Dir., Catholic Center, 715 Nazareth St., Raleigh, 27606. Tel: 919-821-9732.

Ecumenical Commission—Rev. DAVID MCBRIAR, O.F.M. Tel: 919-682-3449.

Evangelization Office—TERRENCE JACKSON, Dir. Tel: 919-821-9746.

Freeman Media Resource Center—TERRI RING. Tel: 919-821-9743.

Human Resources—LEO TAPLER, Dir. Tel: 919-821-9711.

NC Catholic Newspaper—JOHN STRANGE, Editor. Tel: 919-821-9736.

Campus Ministry—Rev. PHILLIP LEACH, Dir., Newman Catholic Student Center, 218 Pittsboro St., Chapel Hill, 27516-2738. Tel: 919-929-3730.

Catholic Schools—MICHAEL J. FEDEWA, Supt. Tel: 919-821-9748.

Faith Development—TERRY JACKSON, Interim Dir. Tel: 919-821-9771.

Catechesis & Catechist Formation—JAN VALLERO. Tel: 919-821-8145.

Marriage Preparation—Mrs. LINDA BEDO. Tel: 919-821-9753.
Youth Ministry—MICHAEL HAGARTY. Tel: 919-821-9770.
Young Adult Ministry—MICHELE A. CASTLE. Tel: 919-821-9772.
Adult Faith Development—ROBERT JONES. Tel: 919-821-9740.
African-American Ancestry Ministry—Rev. Msgr. THOMAS P. HADDEN (Retired), Catholic Center, 715 Nazareth St., Raleigh, 27606. Tel: 919-821-9762.
Hispanic Ministry—VERONICA ALVARADO, Dir., Catholic Center, 715 Nazareth St., Raleigh, 27606. Tel: 919-821-9764.
Vicar for Hispanics—Very Rev. FERNANDO TORRES, c/o Diocese of Raleigh, Hispanic Ministry, 715 Nazareth St., Raleigh, 27606. Tel: 919-821-9738.
Office of Liturgy—Rev. Msgr. JOHN F. O'CONNOR, V.F., Our Lady of Lourdes, 2718 Overbrook Dr., Raleigh, 27608. Tel: 919-782-1973.
Vicar for African American Ancestry Ministry—Ms. MARTHA BAILEY, Catholic Center, 715 Nazareth St., Raleigh, 27606. Tel: 919-821-9762.
Vocations—Revs. MICHAEL G. CLAY, Dir. of Formation, 740 Gimghoul Rd., Chapel Hill, 27514-3811. Tel: 919-967-2203; DANIEL OSCHWALD, Dir. of Recruitment, 715 Nazareth St., Raleigh, 27606. Tel: 919-233-9744.
Program for Child & Youth Protection—JOHN PENDERGRASS, Program Dir., Catholic Center, 715 Nazareth Center, Raleigh, 27606. Tel: 919-821-8157.
Catholic Social Ministries—KATHLEEN WALSH, A.C.S.W., Dir., Catholic Center, 715 Nazareth St., Raleigh, 27606. Tel: 919-821-9752.
Peace and Justice—Sr. JOAN JURSKI, O.S.F., Catholic Center, 715 Nazareth St., Raleigh, 27606. Tel: 919-821-9751.
Senior Housing—KATHLEEN WALSH, Catholic Center, 715 Nazareth St., Raleigh, 27606. Tel: 919-821-9752.
Miscellaneous Offices—
Apostleship of the Sea—Very Rev. FRANCIS R. MOESLEIN (Retired), 2106 Joslyn Dr., Morehead City, 28557-9200. Tel: 919-726-3579.
Censor Librorum—VACANT.
Engaged Encounter— Marriage Preparation and Enrichment Office *Catholic Center, 715 Nazareth St., Raleigh, 27606*. Tel: 919-821-9753.
Holy Childhood Pontifical Association—Rev. WILLIAM L. PITTS, Sacred Heart, P.O. Box 1768, Pinehurst, 28374-1768. Tel: 910-295-6550.
Marriage Encounter—MICHAEL WALLACE; REGINA WALLACE. Tel: 252-454-0430.
Human Resources—LEO TAPLER, Catholic Center, 715 Nazareth St., Raleigh, 27606. Tel: 919-821-9711.
Propagation of the Faith—Rev. WILLIAM L. PITTS, Sacred Heart, P.O. Box 1768, Pinehurst, 28374-1768. Tel: 910-295-6550.
Victim Assistance Coordinator—JOHN PENDERGRASS, Dir. Program for Child & Youth Protection. Tel: 866-535-7233; 919-821-8157. Email: safe@raldioc.org; KATHLEEN WALSH, A.C.S.W. Tel: 919-821-9752. Email: walsh@raldioc.org.

CLERGY, PARISHES, MISSIONS AND PAROCHIAL SCHOOLS

CITY OF RALEIGH
(WAKE COUNTY)

RALEIGH

1—CATHEDRAL OF THE SACRED HEART (1924), Very Rev. Girard M. Sherba, J.C.D., Rector; Rev. Jonathan A. Woodhall. In Res., Rev. Edgar Fernando Torres (Colombia).
Office—219 W. Edenton St., 27603-1724. Tel: 919-832-6030; Fax: 919-833-4667.
Res.: 219 W. Edenton St., 27603. Tel: 919-836-1790; Fax: 919-833-4667.
School—Tel: 919-832-4711; Fax: 919-832-8329. Mrs. Donna Moss, Prin. Lay Teachers 18; Students 240.
Catechesis/Religious Program—Bianche Ellison, D.R.E., (Pastoral Svcs.). Students 234.

2—CATHOLIC STUDENT CENTER, NORTH CAROLINA STATE UNIVERSITY (1974),, Mailing Address: 600 Bilyeu St., 27606. Tel: 919-833-9668; Fax: 919-833-1194.
Res.: 2601-203 Bogey Way, 27603. Tel: 919-772-8218.
Doggett Center at Aquinas House—600 Bilyeu St., 27606. Tel: 919-833-9668; Fax: 919-833-1194. Rev. J. William Long, Campus Min.

3—ST. FRANCIS OF ASSISI (1982), [CEM] Revs. Daniel T. Kenna, O.F.M.; Mark G. Reamer, O.F.M.; William E. McConville, O.F.M.
Res.: 11401 Leesville Rd., 27613. Tel: 919-847-8205; Fax: 919-870-1790.
School—The Franciscan School, 10000 St. Francis Dr.. Fax: 919-847-9558. Thomas McLaughlin, Prin. Lay Teachers 32; Students 563.
School—Early Childhood Learning Center Nancy Bourke, Prin. Lay Teachers 20; Students 126.
Catechesis/Religious Program—Tel: 919-847-8205. Maureen Leahy, D.R.E. (Grades PreK-5); Ann Danyluk, D.R.E. (Grades 6-8); Leo Moreda, D.R.E. (Grades 9-12 & Young Adults); Chris Kitts, D.R.E. (Dir. of Evangelization). Students 1,113.

4—ST. JOSEPH (1968), Rev. Msgr. John J. Williams.
Res.: 630 Peartree Ln., 27610. Tel: 919-231-6364; Fax: 919-231-9884.
Catechesis/Religious Program—Deborah Pergerson, D.R.E. Students 90.

5—ST. LUKE THE EVANGELIST (1985), Rev. Joseph G. Mulroney, J.C.L.
Church & Res. Address: 12333 Bayleaf Church Rd., 27614-9165. Tel: 919-848-1533; Fax: 919-848-0662.
Catechesis/Religious Program—Tel: 919-848-3197. Students 375.

6—OUR LADY OF LOURDES (1954), Rev. Msgr. John F. O'Connor, V.F.; Deacon Myles J. Charlesworth.
Office—2718 Overbrook Dr., 27608. Tel: 919-782-1973; Fax: 919-571-9957.
Res.: 2912 Anderson Dr., 27608. Tel: 919-781-9784.
School—2710 Overbrook Dr., 27608. Tel: 919-782-1670. Jane Bourbina, Prin. Sisters of Notre Dame 2; Lay Teachers 23; Students 480.
Catechesis/Religious Program—Tel: 919-782-1973, Ext. 114; Fax: 919-420-2188. Joan Samuels Rose, D.R.E. (Min. Faith Formation); Tracy Kessler, D.R.E. (Youth Min.). Students 240.

7—ST. RAPHAEL (1966), [CEM] Revs. Francis P. Gillespie, S.J.; Shay W. Auerbach, S.J.; Paul J. McCarren, S.J.; Patrick D. Rogers, S.J.; Deacon Robert T. Madey, Pastoral Assoc.; William A. Abel, Pastoral Assoc.; Hector Velazco, Pastoral Assoc.
Res.: 5801 Falls of Neuse Rd., 27609. Tel: 919-865-5700; Fax: 919-865-5701.
School—St. Raphael, Tel: 919-865-5750, Ext. 713; Fax: 919-865-5751. Students 314.
St. Raphael Catholic Early Childhood Center—Carrie Griffith, Dir. Students 314.
Catechesis/Religious Program—Sue Hoying, D.R.E.; Mary Lynn Whittaker, D.R.E.; Pat Foran, D.R.E. Students 796.

OUTSIDE THE CITY OF RALEIGH

AHOSKIE, HERTFORD CO., ST. CHARLES BORROMEO (1944), Rev. Thomas J. McGee, O.S.F.S.
Res.: P.O. Box 605, 27910. Tel: 252-332-2939.
Catechesis/Religious Program—Students 16.
Mission—St. Anne Scotland Neck, Halifax Co.

APEX, WAKE CO.

1—ST. ANDREW THE APOSTLE (1983), Revs. David E. Fitzgerald, S.A.; Alban Carroll, S.A.; George Ribeiro, S.A. (NY).
Res.: 3008 Old Ralegh Rd., 27502. Tel: 919-362-0414; Fax: 919-362-5778.
Catechesis/Religious Program—Tel: 919-362-1673. Students 921.

2—ST. MARY MAGDALENE (1997), Rev. Donald F. Staib.
625 Magdala Pl., 27502. Tel: 919-657-4800; Fax: 919-657-4805.
Catechesis/Religious Program—Students 359.

BURGAW, PENDER CO., ST. JOSEPH (1908), [CEM] Revs. Douglas Smiley; Trent L. Watts. Admin.
Church & Res.: 1303 Hwy. 117 S., 28425. Tel: 910-259-2601; Fax: 910-259-7695.
Catechesis/Religious Program—Brian Wright, D.R.E., (St. Joseph); Marcia Hatcher, D.R.E., (Transfiguration). Students 44.
Mission—Transfiguration (1953), 506 E. Main St., P.O. Box 1601, Wallace, Duplin Co. 28466. Tel: 910-285-1876.

BURLINGTON, ALAMANCE CO., BLESSED SACRAMENT (1928) Revs. Denis Hackett, O.F.M.Conv.; Robert Benko, O.F.M.Conv.
Mailing Address: P.O. Box 619, 27216. Tel: 336-226-8796; Fax: 336-227-2896. In Res., Revs. Terence Pescatore, O.F.M.Conv.; John Ruffo, O.F.M.Conv.
Res.: 1236 Westbrook Ave., Elon, 27244. Tel: 336-446-6753.
School—Tel: 336-570-0019; Fax: 336-570-9623. Mrs. Natalie Tackitt, Prin. Lay Teachers 20; Students 275.
Catechesis/Religious Program—Tel: 336-570-0013. Students 352.

BUTNER, GRANVILLE CO., ST. BERNADETTE (1957), Sr. Carol Loughney, I.H.M., Pastoral Admin.
Mailing Address: 313 Tenth St., 27509. Tel: 919-575-4744; Fax: 919-575-4744.
Catechesis/Religious Program—Students 57.

BUXTON, DARE CO., OUR LADY OF THE SEAS (1935), Rev. Andre C. Izac.
Mailing Address: P.O. Box 399, 27920. Tel: 252-995-6370; Fax: 252-995-6398.
Catechesis/Religious Program—Students 42.

CARY, WAKE CO., ST. MICHAEL THE ARCHANGEL (1962), Rev. Msgr. John A. Wall; Revs. Bill John Acosta-Escobar; Walter Ospina-Briceno.
Res.: 804 High House Rd., 27513. Tel: 919-468-6100; Fax: 919-468-6130.
School—810 High House Rd., 27513. Carolyn Wheelock, Prin.
Catechesis/Religious Program—Tel: 919-468-6120. Mollie Berry, D.R.E. Students 1,600.

CASTLE HAYNE, NEW HANOVER CO., ST. STANISLAUS KOSTKA (1914), (Polish), [CEM] Rev. Ryszard Kolodziej.
Church & Res.: 4849 Castle Hayne Rd., 28429-4849. Tel: 910-675-2336 (Office); Fax: 910-675-3116.
Catechesis/Religious Program—Students 59.

CHAPEL HILL, ORANGE CO.

1—NEWMAN CATHOLIC STUDENT CENTER, UNIVERSITY OF NORTH CAROLINA (1968), Revs. Phillip M. Leach; Edward P. Mahoney.
Res.: 218 Pittsboro St., 27516-2738. Tel: 919-929-3730; Fax: 919-929-3778.
Catechesis/Religious Program—Students 120.

2—ST. THOMAS MORE (1940), Revs. John G. Durbin; John Alex Gonzalez; Ms. Theresa Keller, Pastoral Assoc.
Parish Offices—940 Carmichael St., 27514-4203. Tel: 919-942-1040; Fax: 919-942-6193.
Res.: 301 Rossburn Way, 27516. Tel: 919-967-8485.
School—(Grades K-8), 920 Carmichael St., 27514. Tel: 919-929-1546; Fax: 919-929-1783. Sr. Catherine Michael Fee, S.S.J., Prin. Sisters 1; Lay Teachers 36; Students 445.
Catechesis/Religious Program—Tel: 919-933-1041. Jim Hynes, D.R.E.; Elizabeth Tempia, D.R.E. Students 482.

CLAYTON, JOHNSTON CO., ST. ANN (1935), Rev. Scott E. McCue.
Church: 4057 Hwy. 70 Business W., 27520. Tel: 919-934-2084; Fax: 919-934-4639.
Catechesis/Religious Program—Students 237.

CLINTON, SAMPSON CO., IMMACULATE CONCEPTION (1910), Revs. Philip M. Tighe, Admin.; Gabriel Jaimes Rebollar.
Mailing Address: P.O. Box 859, 28329. Tel: 910-592-1384; Fax: 910-592-8725.
Mission—San Juan San Juan. Old Hwy. 701, Ingold, Sampson Co. Tel: 910-592-1384.
Station—Santa Clara (2000), Hidden Valley.

DUNN, HARNETT CO., SACRED HEART (1916), Rev. Paul M. Parkerson.
Mailing Address: P.O. Box 535, 28335. Tel: 910-891-1972; Fax: 910-891-5767.
Res.: 209 S. Ellis Ave., 28334. Tel: 910-892-3414.
Catechesis/Religious Program—Mrs. Jan Rebman, D.R.E. Students 70.

DURHAM, DURHAM CO.

1—HOLY CROSS (1938), (African American), Rev. Stephen M. Garrity, S.J.
Church: 1400 S. Alston Ave., 27707. Tel: 919-682-4852; Fax: 919-688-6160.
Res.: 1313 Exchange Pl., 27713. Tel: 919-484-1311.
Catechesis/Religious Program—Tel: 919-688-6160. Etheldreda Guion, D.R.E. Students 100.

2—HOLY INFANT (1970), [CEM] Rev. John E. McGee, O.S.F.S.
Res.: 5000 Southpark Dr., 27713-9470. Tel: 919-544-7135; Fax: 919-544-1799.
Catechesis/Religious Program—Tel: 919-544-7135, Ext. 18. Students 251.

3—IMMACULATE CONCEPTION (1906), Revs. David J. McBriar, O.F.M.; Jacek Orzechowski; Steve Patti, O.F.M.; Deacon Laurence DeCarolis.
Res.: 725 Burch Ave., 27701. Tel: 919-682-3449; Fax: 919-682-7999.
School—Immaculata, 721 Burch Ave., 27701. Tel: 919-682-5847; Fax: 919-956-7073. Mary Kay Delaney, Prin.; Rita Fritzgerald, Asst. Prin. Lay Teachers 30; Students 385.
Catechesis/Religious Program—Barbara Pegg, D.R.E. Students 1,082.

4—ST. MATTHEW (1990), [CEM] Rev. John G. Parish (LA).
Res.: 1001 Mason Rd., 27712. Tel: 919-479-1001; Fax: 919-479-4848.
Catechesis/Religious Program—Betsy Strauss, D.R.E. Students 149.

EDENTON, CHOWAN CO., ST. ANNE (1858), [CEM] Very Revs. Roch T. Drozdzik, V.F. (Poland); Roch T. Drozdzik, V.F. (Poland).
Mailing Address: P.O. Box 422, 27932. Tel: 252-482-2716.
Church: 207 N. Broad St., 27932. Tel: 919-482-2617; Fax: 252-482-8702.
Catechesis/Religious Program—Fax: 252-482-2716. Students 74.
Mission—All Souls Creswell. Helen Randlett, 462 Old Cherry Rd., Columbia, Tyrrell 27928. Tel: 252-797-4068.

ELIZABETH CITY, PASQUOTANK CO., HOLY FAMILY (1915), Rev. Samuel James Buchholz.
Mailing Address: 1453 N. Road St., 27906-1525. Tel: 252-338-2521; Fax: 252-338-4183.
Res.: 1453 N. Road St., 27909. Tel: 252-335-4419.
Catechesis/Religious Program—Rev. Alan Meister, D.R.E.; Debora Short, D.R.E. Students 123.
Mission—St. Katherine Drexel Maple, Currituck Co.

FARMVILLE, PITT CO., ST. ELIZABETH (1931), (Lebanese), Sr. Grace Campbell, I.H.M., Pastoral Admin.
Mailing Address: P.O. Box 189, 27828. Tel: 252-753-4367; Fax: 252-753-4367.
Catechesis/Religious Program—Students 10.

FAYETTEVILLE, CUMBERLAND CO.
1—ST. ANDREW KIM CHAPEL, Rev. Andrew Se-Myung Chang.
1380 Pamalee Dr., 28303. Tel: 910-630-2316; Fax: 910-487-8737.
2—ST. ANN (1940), (African American), Rev. Thomas Malloy, O.S.F.S.
Office—357 N. Cool Spring St., 28301. Tel: 910-483-3216; Fax: 910-483-4185.
Res.: 228 Temple Ave., 28301. Tel: 910-483-5871.
School—Tel: 910-483-3902; Fax: 910-483-3195. Sr. Margaret Mary Scally, D.C., Prin. Daughters of Charity 3; Lay Teachers 14; Students 143.
Catechesis/Religious Program—Tel: 910-488-7137; Fax: 910-483-4185. Michael Patterson, D.R.E. Students 94.
Convent—1933 Martindale Dr., 28304. Tel: 910-484-1675.
3—ST. ELIZABETH ANN SETON (1981), Rev. Willard Rucinski, O.S.F.S.
Res.: 700 Carnegie St., 28311. Tel: 910-488-1797; Fax: 910-488-7116.
Catechesis/Religious Program—John Bunting, D.R.E. Students 254.
4—ST. PATRICK (1824), Revs. John R. Kelly; Patrick Keane.
Mailing Address: 2840 Village Dr., 28304-3813. Tel: 910-323-2410; Fax: 910-323-3006.
Res.: 433 Holly Ln., 28305. Tel: 910-484-8253.
School—1620 Marlborough Rd., 28304. Tel: 910-323-1865. Mr. Tom Manion, Prin. Lay Teachers 12; Students 262.
Catechesis/Religious Program—Tel: 910-323-2410, Ext. 107; Fax: 910-323-3006. Margaret Blanc, D.R.E. Students 392.

FUQUAY-VARINA, WAKE CO., ST. BERNADETTE (1987), Rev. Douglas Smiley; Deacons Anthony Meier; Richard Lacina.
Mailing Address: 1005 Wilbon Rd., 27526-9702. Tel: 919-552-8758; Fax: 919-552-1846.
Catechesis/Religious Program—Tel: 919-552-8758. Mrs. Michele Dexter, D.R.E. Students 320.
Hispanic Office—Tel: 919-552-2922.

GARNER, WAKE CO., ST. MARY, MOTHER OF THE CHURCH (1966), Revs. Robert T. Schriber; Joseph J. Yaeger; Deacon Leo Tapler.
Res.: 1008 Vandora Springs Rd., 27529. Tel: 919-772-5777; 919-772-5524 (Office); Fax: 919-772-5534.
Catechesis/Religious Program—Tel: 919-772-5199. Students 398.

GOLDSBORO, WAYNE CO., ST. MARY (1889), Revs. William J. Ruhl, O.S.F.S.; Thomas P. Norris, O.S.F.S.
Res.: 1000 N. Jefferson Ave., 27530-3141. Tel: 919-734-5033; Fax: 919-580-0730.
School—Tel: 919-735-1931; Fax: 919-735-1917. Lynn P. Magoon, Prin. Sisters, Servants of the Immaculate Heart of Mary 2; Lay Teachers 15; Students 226.
Catechesis/Religious Program—Tel: 919-734-5033, Ext. 34. Mrs. Carole M. Sears, D.R.E. Students 142.

GREENVILLE, PITT CO.
1—ST. GABRIEL (1936), Rev. Thomas McCann, C.P.; Lucille Gorham, Pastoral Assoc.
Res.: 1120 Martin Luther King Jr. Dr., 27834. Tel: 252-758-1504; Fax: 252-758-1479.
Catechesis/Religious Program—Students 35.
2—ST. PETER'S (1884), Very Rev. Justin Kerber, C.P., V.F.; Rev. Patrick Daugherty, C.P.
Res.: 2700 E. Fourth St., 27858. Tel: 252-757-3259; Fax: 252-752-1499.
School—Tel: 252-752-3529; Fax: 252-752-7604. Ramon Espinosa, Prin. Lay Teachers 35; Students 523.
Catechesis/Religious Program—Tel: 252-757-3259, Ext. 203. Sarah McPherson, D.R.E. Students 335.

HAMPSTEAD, PENDER CO., ST. JUDE THE APOSTLE (1992), Rev. Terrence Collins.
Mailing Address: 18737 Hwy. 17 N., 28443. Tel: 910-270-1477; Fax: 910-270-1424.
Res.: 557 Osprey Dr., 28443. Tel: 910-273-1689.
Catechesis/Religious Program—Students 75.
Mission—St. Mary, Gate of Heaven P.O. Box 2667, Surf City, Pender Co. 28445. Fax: 910-270-1477.

HAVELOCK, CRAVEN CO., ANNUNCIATION (1953), [CEM] Rev. Roberto Keenan.
Mailing Address: P.O. Box 720, 28532-0177. Tel: 252-447-2112; Fax: 252-447-2595.
School—Tel: 252-447-3137; Fax: 252-447-3138. Mrs. June Pietras, Prin. Lay Teachers 16; Students 200.
Catechesis/Religious Program—246 E. Main St., Stedman, 28391. Tel: 252-447-2436. Mrs. Maureen McInerney, D.R.E. Students 200.

HENDERSON, VANCE CO., ST. JAMES THE GREATER (1995), [CEM] [JC] Consolidated Rev. William J. Upah. St. Paul and St. Catherine of Siena, Oxford merged to form St. James the Greater.
Res.: 3275 Hwy. 158 Bypass, 27536. Tel: 252-438-3124; Fax: 252-438-3214.
Catechesis/Religious Program—Students 160.
Mission—St. Joseph Norlina Rd., Warrenton, Warren Co. 27589. Tel: 252-438-3124.

HILLSBOROUGH, ORANGE CO., HOLY FAMILY (1989), Sr. Marie Therese Bugge, O.S.U., Pastoral Admin.
Mailing Address: 216 Governer Burke Rd., 27278. Tel: 919-732-1030; Fax: 919-732-7852.
Catechesis/Religious Program—Students 145.

HOPE MILLS, CUMBERLAND CO., GOOD SHEPHERD (1981), Rev. Thanh N. Nguyen; Very Rev. Thomas J. Gaul, V.F., Pastor Emeritus.
Res.: 5050 Oak St., 28348. Tel: 910-425-1590; Fax: 910-423-9973.
Catechesis/Religious Program—Tel: 910-425-5617. Janice Carnahan, D.R.E. Students 341.
Mission—St. Isidore 8569 Clinton Rd., Stedman, Cumberland Co. 28391.

JACKSONVILLE, ONSLOW CO., SHRINE OF THE INFANT OF PRAGUE, CHURCH OF THE HOLY SPIRIT (1941), Revs. Thomas R. Davis; William Hernando Rodriguez.
Mailing Address: 205 Chaney Ave., 28540. Tel: 910-347-4196; Fax: 910-347-9338.
Res.: 330 Mildred Ave., 28540. Tel: 910-347-8881.
School—Tel: 910-353-1300; 910-455-0838. Sr. Claudia Bronsing, O.S.F., Prin. Lay Teachers 20; Students 200.
Catechesis/Religious Program—Tel: 910-455-1296. Sr. Cecilia McClain, S.C., D.R.E. Students 509.

KINSTON, LENOIR CO., HOLY SPIRIT CATHOLIC CHURCH (1921), (African American—Hispanic),, (Formerly Holy Trinity-Our Lady of the Atonement) Rev. Douglas Reed.
Mailing Address: P.O. Box 1455, 28503-1455. Tel: 252-523-8898; Fax: 252-527-9495.
Res.: 137 Rae Rd., 28504. Tel: 252-523-4377.
Church: 400 Academy Heights Rd., 28504.
Catechesis/Religious Program—Pat Kaspryzk, D.R.E. Students 83.

KITTY HAWK, DARE CO., HOLY REDEEMER (1935), Rev. William F. Walsh, O.S.F.S.; Thomas Herrity, Business Mgr.
Mailing Address: P.O. Box 510, 27949. Tel: 252-261-4700; Fax: 252-261-1405.
Office—301 W. Kitty Hawk Rd., 27949.
Res.: 109 Sunrise View, 27949. Tel: 252-261-2728.
Catechesis/Religious Program—Tel: 252-261-4700; Fax: 252-261-1405. Students 231.
Mission—Holy Trinity 73315 Virginia Dare Tr., Nags Head, Dare Co. 27959. Tel: 252-261-1168.
Station—Corolla Chapel Corolla.

LAURINBURG, SCOTLAND CO., ST. MARY (1946), [JC] Rev. Robert W. Diegelman.
Mailing Address: P.O. Box 1148, 28353-1148. Tel: 910-276-1478; 910-276-4468 (Office); Fax: 910-276-9519.
Catechesis/Religious Program—Students 105.

LOUISBURG, FRANKLIN CO., OUR LADY OF THE ROSARY (1999), Sr. Elizabeth Bullen, I.H.M., Admin.
Church: 937 N. Main St., 27549. Tel: 919-340-0556; Fax: 919-497-3124 124.
Catechesis/Religious Program—Students 43.

LUMBERTON, ROBESON CO., ST. FRANCIS DE SALES (1938), Revs. Robert J. Yankevitch, S.J.; Carlos Arce, O.F.M.
Mailing Address: P.O. Box 2249, 28359-2249. Tel: 910-739-4723; Fax: 910-739-5443.
Res.: 2000 Elizabethtown Rd., 28358.
Catechesis/Religious Program—Tel: 910-739-4713. Students 139.
Mission—St. Andrew 301 Mercer Ave., Red Springs, Robeson Co. 28377. Tel: 910-843-3440.
Mission—San Pablo 406 W. Broad St., St. Pauls, Robeson Co. 28384.

MOREHEAD CITY, CARTERET CO., ST. EGBERT (1929), Very Revs. Gregory D. Spencer; Francis R. Moeslein, Pastor Emeritus (Retired); Deacon Albert Feneis.
Parish Hall—1706 Evans St., 28557. Tel: 252-726-3559; Fax: 252-726-2232.
Res.: 1612 Evans St., 28557. Tel: 252-726-2535.
School—Tel: 252-726-3418; Fax: 252-727-0150. Mrs. Lesley Ferguson, Prin. Lay Teachers 7; Students 135.
Catechesis/Religious Program—Tel: 919-726-9696. Jolanta Gardas, D.R.E. Students 182.

MOUNT OLIVE, WAYNE CO., ST. MARY (1916), Rev. Frank M. Raffo.
Mailing Address: P.O. Box 1145, 28365. Tel: 919-658-4023; Fax: 919-658-3128.
Mission—Posada Guadalupana Mt. Olive, Duplin Co.

NEW BERN, CRAVEN CO., ST. PAUL (1821), [CEM] Very Rev. Ernest J. Ruede, V.F.; Rev. Msgr. James R. Jones, Pastor Emeritus; Sr. Monique Dissen, H.M., Pastoral Assoc.; Deacon William Hunt, Pastoral Assoc.
Rectory—3108 Farrior Cir., 28562. Tel: 252-638-4436.
Church: 3005 Country Club Rd., 28562. Tel: 252-638-1984; Fax: 252-638-2144.
School—3007 Country Club Rd., 28562. Tel: 252-633-0100; Fax: 252-633-4457. Sr. Susan Therese Armbruster, I.H.M., Prin. Sisters, Servants of the Immaculate Heart of Mary 4; Lay Teachers 16; Students 300.
Catechesis/Religious Program—Tel: 252-633-3030. Joy Harsen, D.R.E. Students 211.

NEWTON GROVE, SAMPSON CO., OUR LADY OF GUADALUPE (1871), [CEM] Rev. Bernard (Ned) Shlesinger III.
Office:—P.O. Box 100, 28366. Tel: 910-594-0287; Fax: 910-594-1749.
Res.: 211 Irwin Dr., 28366. Tel: 910-594-0152.
Catechesis/Religious Program—Students 200.

ORIENTAL, PAMLICO CO., SAINT PETER THE FISHERMAN (2000), Rev. Msgr. Gerald Lewis, Admin.; Deacon Robert J. Whitfield, Pastoral Assoc.
Res.: 504 Broad St., 28571. Tel: 252-249-3687; Fax: 252-249-6576.
Catechesis/Religious Program—Students 6.

PINEHURST, MOORE CO., SACRED HEART (1919), Revs. William L. Pitts; Jose Antonio Galvez-Orellano, O.F.M.Conv.
Mailing Address: P.O. Box 1768, 28370. Tel: 910-295-6550; Fax: 910-255-0299.
Catechesis/Religious Program—Tel: 910-295-3072; Fax: 910-255-0299. Mrs. Barbara Kemple, D.R.E. Students 375.

PLYMOUTH, WASHINGTON CO., ST. JOAN OF ARC (1959), Sr. Dolores Glick, M.H.S.H., Pastoral Admin.; Rebeca Boudreaux, Spanish Min.
Mailing Address: P.O. Box 822, 27962. Tel: 252-793-4052; Fax: 252-793-4052.
Catechesis/Religious Program—Students 24.

RAEFORD, HOKE CO., ST. ELIZABETH OF HUNGARY (1959), Sr. Jeanne Morgan, S.S.J., Pastoral Admin.
Res.: 124 Palmer St., 28376-9322. Tel: 910-875-8803; Fax: 910-875-8803.
Catechesis/Religious Program—Students 50.

RIEGELWOOD, COLUMBUS CO., CHRIST THE KING (1964), (Hispanic), Revs. Matthew D. Hendrick; Edward Burch.
Mailing Address: 1011 Eastwood Rd., Wilmington, 28403. Tel: 910-392-0720; Fax: 910-392-6777.

ROANOKE RAPIDS, HALIFAX CO., ST. JOHN THE BAPTIST (1931), Rev. Mark J. Betti. In Res., Rev. Michael A. Butler, V.F. (Vietnam).
Res.: 115 E. Ninth St., 27870. Tel: 252-537-4667; Fax: 252-535-2076.
Catechesis/Religious Program—Teri Bales, D.R.E. Students 82.

ROCKY MOUNT, NASH & EDGECOMBE COS., OUR LADY OF PERPETUAL HELP (1892), Rev. JaVan J. Saxon.
Mailing Address: 328 Hammond St., 27804. Tel: 252-972-0452; Fax: 252-972-4780.
Res.: 501 Hammond St., 27804. Tel: 252-972-1949; Fax: 252-972-4780.
School—Tel: 252-972-1971; Fax: 252-972-7831. Mrs. Elizabeth Watson, Prin. Lay Teachers 8; Students 81.
Catechesis/Religious Program—Tel: 252-972-0498. Dianne Young, D.R.E. Students 182.
Mission—Immaculate Conception 723 Virginia Ave., Nash & Edgecombe Cos. 27804.

ROXBORO, PERSON CO., SS. MARY AND EDWARD (1935), Rev. Harold V. McGovern, O.S.F.S.
Res.: 611 N. Main St., 27573-5040. Tel: 336-599-4122; Fax: 336-598-0412.
Mission—St. Bernadette Butner. Now a parish under the city of Butner.

SANFORD, LEE CO., ST. STEPHEN THE FIRST MARTYR (1932), Rev. John J. Forbes.
Res.: 2402 Wicker St., 27330-7681. Tel: 919-776-1532; Fax: 919-775-1399.
Catechesis/Religious Program—Tel: 919-776-3843. Students 351.

SHALLOTTE, BRUNSWICK CO., ST. BRENDAN THE NAVIGATOR (1983), [JC] Rev. Patrick O'Connor, O.S.F.S.
Mailing Address: Box 2984, 28459-9999. Tel: 910-754-8544; Fax: 910-755-6046.
Church & Office: 5101 Ocean Hwy. W., 28459.
Catechesis/Religious Program—Tel: 910-754-8544. Students 85.

SILER CITY, CHATHAM CO., ST. JULIA (1961), (Hispanic), Revs. Michael . Lorentsen, O.F.M.Conv.; Joseph Madden, O.F.M.Conv.
Mailing Address: 210 Harold Hart Rd., 27344. Tel: 919-742-5584; Fax: 919-742-4917.
Catechesis/Religious Program—Students 187.

SMITHFIELD, JOHNSTON CO., ST. ANN (1935),, See new

location under Clayton, NC.
SOUTHERN PINES, MOORE CO., ST. ANTHONY OF PADUA (1895), Very Rev. Jeffrey A. Ingham, V.F.
Mailing Address: P.O. Box 29, 28388-0029. Tel: 910-692-6613; Fax: 910-692-4964.
Res.: 23 Village in the Woods, 28387. Tel: 910-692-9847; Fax: 910-692-4964.
School—320 N. Ashe St., 28387-0029. Tel: 910-692-6241. Mr. Patrick J. Scannell, Prin.
Catechesis/Religious Program—Students 168.
SOUTHPORT, BRUNSWICK CO., SACRED HEART (1941), Rev. J. Douglas Lawson; Deacon Eugene J. Gillis; Patricia Ciemnicki, Dir. Pastoral Svcs.
Mailing Address: 5269 Dosher Cutoff, S.E., 28461. Tel: 910-457-6173; Fax: 910-457-6421.
Res.: 213 Yaupon Dr., 28461. Tel: 910-457-0223.
Catechesis/Religious Program—Tel: 910-457-6173. Patricia Novotny, D.R.E. Students 117.
SWANSBORO, ONSLOW CO., ST. MILDRED (1947), [CEM] Rev. Donald G. Baribeau, M.S.
Res.: 616 Sabiston Dr., 28584-9674. Tel: 910-326-4370; Fax: 910-326-7825.
Catechesis/Religious Program—Tel: 910-326-5589. Laura Leblanc, D.R.E. Students 225.
TARBORO, EDGECOMBE CO., ST. CATHERINE (1934), Rev. Edward Deviny, C.P.
Res.: 1004 St. David St., 27886. Tel: 919-823-3866; Fax: 919-824-0412.
Catechesis/Religious Program—Students 16.
WAKE FOREST, WAKE CO., ST. CATHERINE OF SIENA (1940), Rev. Robert J. Kus.
Church: 520 W. Holding Ave., 27587. Tel: 919-570-0070; Fax: 919-570-0071.
Catechesis/Religious Program—Tel: 919-570-0070, Ext. 73. Susan Gammon, D.R.E. Students 855.
WASHINGTON, BEAUFORT CO., MOTHER OF MERCY (1963), Rev. Artura Cabra, M.S.
Res.: 112 W. Ninth St., 27889. Tel: 252-946-2941; Fax: 252-946-1399.
Church: 111 W. Ninth St., 27889.
Catechesis/Religious Program—Tel: 919-946-0769. Dana Lawson, D.R.E. Students 46.
WENDELL, WAKE CO., ST. EUGENE (1948), Revs. Charles Phukuta Khonde, C.I.C.M.; Ramel Portula, C.I.C.M.; Deacon Willie Foggie; Bro. Giovanni Ada, C.I.C.M., Pastoral Assoc.
Mailing Address: P.O. Box 188, 27591. Tel: 919-365-7114; Fax: 919-365-9431.
Catechesis/Religious Program—Tel: 919-365-9431. Gail Hernandez, D.R.E. Students 233.
WHITEVILLE, COLUMBUS CO., SACRED HEART (1938), (Spanish), Rev. James P. Byrne, O.S.F.S.
Res.: 302 N. Lee St., 28472. Tel: 910-642-3895; Fax: 910-640-1948.
Catechesis/Religious Program—Students 73.
Mission—Our Lady of the Snows 701 Broad St., P.O. Box 1766, Elizabethtown, Bladen Co. 28337. Tel: 910-862-4998; Fax: 910-862-7298.
WILLIAMSTON, MARTIN CO., HOLY TRINITY (1951), Sr. Kieran Williams, I.H.M., Pastoral Admin.
Mailing Address: P.O. Box 894, 27892-0894. Tel: 252-792-4091; Fax: 252-792-4091.
Church: 830 East Blvd., 27892. Tel: 252-792-4306; Fax: 252-792-9064.
Catechesis/Religious Program—Students 100.
WILMINGTON, NEW HANOVER CO.
1—IMMACULATE CONCEPTION (1925), Rev. Barry R. Strong, O.S.F.S.
Church: 6650 Carolina Beach Rd., 28412. Tel: 910-791-1003; Fax: 910-791-0081.
Catechesis/Religious Program—Carol Cholette, D.R.E. Students 236.
2—ST. MARK (1978), Revs. Matthew D. Hendrick; Edward Burch.
Church: 1011 Eastwood Rd., 28403. Tel: 910-392-0720; Fax: 910-392-6777.
School—1013 Eastwood Rd., 28403-1905. Tel: 910-392-0720, Ext. 239. Eve MacCurry, Prin.
Catechesis/Religious Program—Tel: 910-793-5974. Ms. Anne Doyle, D.R.E. Students 567.
Mission—Christ the King 100 Burns Rd., Riegelwood, Columbus Co. 28456-0155.
3—ST. MARY (1821), Revs. John L. Gillespie; Marcos Leon-Angulo.
Res.: 405 Ann St., 28401-4592. Tel: 910-762-5491; Fax: 910-762-9664.
School—Michele Lezon, Prin. Lay Teachers 10; Students 160.
Catechesis/Religious Program—Students 160.
WILSON, WILSON CO.
1—ST. ALPHONSUS DE LIGUORI, Closed., For sacramental records contact St. Therese, Wilson.
2—CHURCH OF ST. THERESE (1923), Revs. Walter Ospina; Gregory Lowchy, Admin.
Church & Office: 700 Nash St., N.E., 27893-3047. Tel: 252-237-3019; Fax: 252-237-2042.
Res.: 200 Gray St., N.E., 27893-3710. Tel: 252-237-0143.
School—(Grades PreK-5) Tel: 252-237-3019, Ext. 17; Fax: 252-237-2042. Lay Teachers 11; Students 82.
Catechesis/Religious Program—Tel: 252-237-3019. Students 262.
WRIGHTSVILLE BEACH, NEW HANOVER CO., ST. THERESE (1939), Rev. Eugene Grabowski; Deacon James F. Welch.
Res.: 209 S. Lumina Ave.,, 28480. Tel: 910-256-2471; Fax: 910-256-2459.
Catechesis/Religious Program—Students 115.

Special Assignment:
Revs.—
Clay, Michael G., 744 Gimghoul St., Chapel Hill.
Mahoney, Edward P., Duke University, Durham, 27706
Oschwald, Daniel D., 715 Nazareth St., 27606.
Shugrue, Michael, 715 Nazareth St., 27606.
Tulley, Thomas, P.O. Box 3400, Chapel Hill.

On Duty Outside the Diocese:
Revs.—
Brockman, David D., Rome, Italy.
Carlson, Steven V., Operation Enduring Freedom, 2-82 Avn. Bn., Apo, AE 09355.
Fitzgerald, R. Martin, 2348 Sijan Dr., # 100, USAF Academy, CO 80840.
Garneau, James F., Ph.D., Pontifical College Josephinum, 7625 North High St., Columbus, OH 43235.

Absent on Leave:
Revs.—
Butler, Michael A., V.F. (Vietnam)
Flanagan, Christopher
Labossy, James
Watts, Trent L.

Retired:
Rev. Msgrs.—
Hadden, Thomas P., 801-202 Moratock Dr., 27604.
Jones, James, 2228 Fox Horn Rd., New Bern, 28562. Tel: 252-635-5318
Revs.—
Bryon, Paul J., 211 McCauley St., Chapel Hill, 27516. Tel: 919-968-1657
Butler, James, 5758 Three Oaks Dr., 27612.
Creel, Jesse, St. Albans, 120-32 193rd St., Jamaica, NY 11412-3637. Tel: 708-525-0880
Dash, Alan J., 6702 Rushwood Ct., Wilmington, 28405. Tel: 910-452-0547
Dorsel, John F., P.O. Box 1881, Pinehurst, 28374. Tel: 910-295-2085
Ghisalberti, Giacomo G., P.O. Box 70338, Myrtle Beach, SC 29572.
Giacomini, Antonio, O.F.M.Cap., Stratford Arms, Apt. 9-B, Greenville, 27858.
Harper, John, St. Joseph of the Pines, 103 Gossman St., Room 860, Southern Pines, 28387. Tel: 910-692-5814
Keaney, James P., 1316 E. Ninth St., Roanoke Rapids, 27870. Tel: 252-535-4093
Keenan, Desmond R., 7901 Hinton Rd., Wake Forest, 27587.
Klaus, Joseph J., 197 Ocean Blvd., Kitty Hawk, 27949. Tel: 252-255-0279
Kowal, William D., St. John Vianney Center, 151 Woodbine Rd., Downingtown, PA 19335.
Lawson, Robert T., 590 Central Ave., Villa E-3, Southern Pines, 28389. Tel: 910-695-4340
Lewis, Gerald, P.O. Box 4280, Emerald Isle, 28594.
Maloney, Francis G., 592 Central Ave., Villa F.3, Southern Pines, 28387.
Very Rev.—
Moeslein, Francis R., 2106 Joslyn Dr., Morehead City, 26557-9200. Tel: 252-726-3579
Revs.—
Parker, Kenneth, 704 McIntosh Rd., Carthage, 28327. Tel: 910-245-4640
Richardson, John L., 592 Central Dr., Villa F., Southern Pines, 28387.
Shea, Robert F., 592 Central Ave., Villa F.4, Southern Pines, 28387.
Turner, Richard W., P.O. Box 1039, Spring Hope, 27882. Tel: 252-475-3360

Permanent Deacons:
Barnes, Frank, St. Rafael, Raleigh
Bogdan, James, St. Brendan, Shallotte
Charlesworth, Myles, Our Lady of Lourdes, Raleigh
Colon, Vicente, St. Patrick, Fayetteville
Cortright, William, St. Elizabeth of Hungary, Raeford
DeCarolis, Lawrence, Immaculate Conception, Durham
Evans, Forest, Holy Family, Hillsborough
Feneis, Al, St. Egbert, Morehead City
Foggie, Willie, St. Eugene, Wendell
Gillespie, Patrick, Holy Family, Elizabeth City
Gillis, Eugene, Sacred Heart, Southport
Goodrow, Joseph, Infant of Prague, Jacksonville
Hanemann, Louis, St. Michael, Cary
Henrich, Robert, Our Lady of Lourdes, Raleigh
Hubisz, John, N.C.S.U. Aquinas House, Raleigh
Hunt, William, St. Paul, New Bern
Junginger, George, St. Michael, Cary
Lewandowski, Stephen, St. Joseph, Raleigh
Lucina, Dick, St. Bernadette, Fuquay-Varina
Mack, Tom, Holy Infant, Durham
Madey, Robert, St. Raphael, Raleigh
McGahran, Robert, St. Brendan, Shallotte
Meier, Anthony, St. Bernadette, Fuquay-Varina
Mirande, Mike, Sacred Heart, Pinehurst
Rodriguez, Jorge, Unassigned
Schoebel, James, Ft. Bragg, Fayetteville
Tapler, Leopold, St. Mary, Garner
Welch, James, St. Therese, Wrightsville Beach
Wobser, Don, Holy Redeemer, Kitty Hawk

INSTITUTIONS LOCATED IN THE DIOCESE

[A] HIGH SCHOOLS

RALEIGH. *Cardinal Gibbons High School*, 1401 Edwards Mill Rd., 27607. Tel: 919-834-1625; Fax: 919-834-9771. Email: aj1401@hotmail.com jay@caatholic.org. Web: www.cghs.pvt.k12.nc.us. Bro. Michel Bettigole, O.S.F., Prin. Priests 2; Brothers 2; Sisters 3; Lay Teachers 85; Students 984.
HILLSBOROUGH. *St. Mary School*, 7500 Schley Rd., 27278. Tel: 919-732-7200; Fax: 919-732-1907. Web: www.stmarycs.org. Margaret Rauschenberg, Prin. Sisters 1; Teachers 15; Total Enrollment 150.

[B] CHILD CARE CENTERS

RALEIGH. *St. Joseph Pre-School*, 624 Peartree Ln., 27610. Tel: 919-231-4545; Fax: 919-231-9884. Email: mshaughn@nc.rr.com. Mrs. Marjorie Shaughnessy, Dir. Students 12.
St. Raphael Catholic School and Early Childhood Center, 5815 Falls of the Neuse Rd., 27609. Tel: 919-865-5717; Fax: 919-865-5701. Email: pendergrassj@raldioc.org. Web: srcs.hypermart.net. Marilyn Kasper, Prin.; Carrie Griffith, Dir. Lay Teachers 47; Students 466.
APEX. *Saint Andrew Early Childhood Center*, 3008 Old Raleigh Rd., 27502. Tel: 919-387-8656; Fax: 919-362-5778. Email: anngraf@nc.rr.com. Web: www.saintandrew.org. Ann Graf, Dir. Total Staff 25; Students 146.
CARY. *St. Michael's Early Childhood Center*, 804 High House Rd., 27513. Tel: 919-468-6110; Fax: 919-468-6130. Email: eoconnell@stmichaelcary.org. Web: www.stmichaelcary.org. Ms. Elana O'Connell, Dir. Total Staff 21; Students 188.
GARNER. *St. Mary Child Development Center*, 1008 Vandora Springs Rd., 27529. Tel: 919-772-0009; Fax: 919-772-5534. Email: smgprek@bellsouth.net. Ms. Karen Williams, Dir. Lay Teachers 6; Total Staff 15; Students 115.

[C] GENERAL HOSPITALS

SOUTHERN PINES. *St. Joseph of the Pines*, 590 Central Dr., 28387-2899. Tel: 910-246-3000. Web: www.sjp.org. Mr. John Capasso, Pres. & CEO. Legal Title: *St. Joseph of the Pines, Inc.* Bed Capacity 176; Staff 225.

[D] CATHOLIC SOCIAL SERVICES

RALEIGH. *Catholic Social Ministries of the Diocese of Raleigh, Inc.*, 715 Nazareth St., 27606-2187. Tel: 919-821-9750; Fax: 919-821-9712. Kathleen Walsh, A.C.S.W, Diocesan Dir. Total Staff 50; Total Assisted 34,991.
Regional Office, 226 Hillsborough St., 27605. Tel: 919-832-0225; Fax: 919-832-0736. Rick Miller-Haraway, L.C.S.W.
Regional Office, 4006 Princess Pl. Dr., Wilmington, 28405. Tel: 910-251-8130; Fax: 910-251-8491. Linda K. Pierce, L.C.S.W.
Regional Office, 902 Broad St., P.O. Box 647, Durham, 27702. Tel: 919-286-1964; Fax: 919-286-4001. Susan Gilbertson, L.C.S.W.
Regional Office, 2712 Ft. Bragg Rd., Fayetteville, 28303-4721. Tel: 910-424-2020; Fax: 910-424-8435. Stephen Dow, L.C.S.W.
Regional Office, 502 Middle St., P.O. Box 826, New Bern, 28563. Tel: 252-638-2188; Fax: 252-638-2417. Linda McAlister, L.C.S.W.
Regional Office, 2717 S. Memorial Dr., Greenville, 27835-8241. Tel: 252-355-5111; Fax: 252-355-1088. Betty Byrnes, L.C.S.W.
Regional Office, 123 Market St., Hertford, 27944. Tel: 252-426-7717; Fax: 252-426-9940. Julian Miller, L.C.S.W.
Peace and Justice Office, 715 Nazareth St., 27606-2198. Tel: 919-821-9751; Fax: 919-821-9712.

Sr. Joan Jurski, O.S.F.

[E] MONASTERIES AND RESIDENCE OF PRIESTS AND BROTHERS

RALEIGH. *Dominican Priory*, Dominican Priory of St. Martin de Porres, 304 E. Park Dr., P.O. Box 12927, 27605-2927. Tel: 919-833-1893; Fax: 919-833-1449. Revs. Michael M. Burke, O.P.; James D. Campbell, O.P.; Martin J. Iott, O.P.; Jude Siciliano, O.P.; Steve Smith, O.P.; Brian J. Pierce, O.P.

Jesuit Community, 5801 Falls of the Neuse Rd., 27609. Tel: 919-876-1581; Fax: 919-872-3723. Email: abelb@raldioc.org. Web: www.saintraphael.org. Sisters 3; Bed Capacity 391; Patients Assisted Annually 234,782.

Jesuits in Eastern North Carolina: Revs. Shay W. Auerbach, S.J.; Paul W. Brant, S.J.; Stephen M. Garritty, S.J.; Francis P. Gillespie, S.J.; Paul J. Mc Carren, S.J.; John J. McLain, S.J.; Patrick O. Rogers, S.J.; Robert J. Yankevitch, S.J.

BURLINGTON. *Conventual Franciscans*, Blessed Sacrament Church, 408 W. Davis St., P.O. Box 619, 27216. Tel: 336-226-8796; Fax: 336-227-2896. Email: catholic@netpath.net. Web: www.blessedsacramentnc.org. Revs. Denis Hackett, O.F.M.Conv.; Terence Pescatore, O.F.M.Conv.; Robert Benko, O.F.M.Conv.; John Ruffo, O.F.M.Conv. Total in Residence 4.

CARY. *Franciscan Brothers of Brooklyn*, 304 Gentlewoods Dr., 27511. Tel: 919-303-7732. Email: brmichel@catholic.org. Bro. Michel Bettigole, O.S.F.

NORTH TOPSAIL BEACH. *Marianist Community*, 221 Oyster Ln., 28460. Tel: 910-328-6030; Fax: 910-328-3481. Email: topsailmarianists@juno.com. Rev. Richard Kuhn, S.M.; Bros. Raymond McQuade, S.M., Dir.; Frank Smith, S.M.

PITTSBORO. *Our Lady of Guadalupe Friary*, P.O. Box 1638, 27312. Tel: 919-545-5600; Fax: 919-545-5650. Email: ncfriars@aol.com. Web: www.franciscanseast.org. Revs. Michael Lorentsen, O.F.M.Conv.; Joseph Madden, O.F.M.Conv.; Bro. Raymond Sobocinski, O.F.M.Conv., Contact Person & Guardian.

[F] CONVENTS AND RESIDENCES FOR SISTERS

RALEIGH. *Sisters of Notre Dame*, 3905 Yew Circle, 27612. Tel: 919-781-3739; Fax: 919-420-2188 (School,Work). Email: sndoll@mindspring.com. Web: www.olls.org. Sisters 2.

Sisters of the Holy Cross, 8005 Bark Pl., 27615. Tel: 919-518-1829. Sisters 2.

AHOSKIE. *Sisters of St. Louis--California Region*, 409 W. Church St., 27910. Tel: 919-332-2220. Email: tmssl@yahoo.com. Web: www.St-louis-sisters.org.

CARY. *Sisters of St. Francis of Sylvania, Ohio*, 1204-C Village Greenway, 27511. Tel: 919-460-6218; Fax: 919-821-9705. Email: jurski@raldioc.org.

CHAPEL HILL. *Sisters, Servants of the Immaculate Heart of Mary*, 6 St. James Pl., 27514-3426. Tel: 919-933-8240. Email: cgellings@aol.com. Web: ihmsisters.org.

St. Thomas More Sisters' Residence, 301 Colony Woods Dr., 27514. Tel: 919-929-1547.

DURHAM. *Dominican Congregation of St. Catherine DeRicci*, 711 Mason Rd., 27712-9229. Tel: 919-477-1285; Fax: 919-477-9485. Email: camay711@nc.rr.com. Web: www.raldio.org/auila.htm/.

Sisters of St. Francis of Philadelphia, 711 Mason Rd., 27712-9229. Tel: 919-477-1285; Fax: 919-477-9485. Email: damian711@nc.rr.com. Web: www.raldioc.org/avila.html.

FARMVILLE. *Sisters, Servants of the Immaculate Heart of Mary*, P.O. Box 189, 27828-0189. Tel: 252-753-4367; Fax: 252-753-4367. Email: elizabet@geeksnet.com.

FAYETTEVILLE. *Daughters of Charity*, Marguerite Naseau House, 1933 Martindale Dr., 28304. Tel: 910-484-1675; Fax: 910-484-1675 (Call First). Email: margueritenaseau@hotmail.com. Web: stanncatholicschool.org. Daughters of Charity of St. Vincent de Paul Sisters 3.

GARNER. *Adrian Dominican Sisters*, 606 Windbluff Ct., 27529. Tel: 919-773-1219. Email: maennisop@aol.com.

GOLDSBORO. *St. Mary's Convent*, 1603 Edgerton St., 27530. Tel: 919-735-0838. Sisters, Servants of the Immaculate Heart of Mary Sisters 2.

JACKSONVILLE. *Sisters of Saint Francis*, 2038 W. Wingate Ct., 28546. Tel: 910-347-6783.

Sisters of St. Ursula, 600 Windsor Cir., Apt. 206, 28546. Tel: 910-347-4196; Fax: 910-347-9338. Email: bmcady@aol.com.

NEW BERN. *St. Paul Convent*, 3003 Country Club Rd., 28562. Tel: 252-637-3726. Total in Residence 4.

RAEFORD. *St. Elizabeth of Hungary Parish House*, 124 Palmer St., 28376. Tel: 910-875-8803; Fax: 910-875-8803. Email: srjmorgan@juno.com. Web: www.members.tripod.com/jubilee/st.eliz/index.html.

SANFORD. *St. Mark's Convent*, 807 Valley Rd., 27330. Tel: 919-776-5350. Sisters of St. Joseph of St. Mark 2.

SOUTHERN PINES. *St. Joseph of the Pines*, 125 Longleaf Rd., 28387. Tel: 910-692-6848. Email: srzeno@earthlink.net. Sisters of Providence 2.

TARBORO. *Congregation of St. Agnes*, 701 Cedar Ln., 27886. Tel: 919-823-8801; Fax: 282-823-0989. Email: tcoutreach@tarboronc.com. Web: csasisters.org.

WARRENTON. *Sisters, Servants of the Immaculate Heart of Mary*, 113 Joshua Way, 27589. Tel: 252-257-5605; Fax: 252-257-5605. Email: stjoseph@3rddoor.com.

WILLIAMSTON. *Sisters, Servants of the Immaculate Heart of Mary*, P.O. Box 894, 27892. Tel: 252-792-4091; Fax: 252-792-4091. Email: holytrinity@clis.com.

[G] RETREAT HOUSES

RALEIGH. *Madonna House*, 424 Rose Ln., 27610. Tel: 919-231-4049. Email: madonnah@mv.igs.net. Web: www.mv.igs.net/~madonnah. Echo Lewis; Sue Perreca; Carol Gordon; Miss Theresa Davis, Dir.

DURHAM. *Avila Retreat Center*, 711 Mason Rd., 27712-9229. Tel: 919-477-1285; Fax: 919-477-9485. Email: damian711@nc.rr.org. Web: www.raldioc.org/avila.html. Sr. Damian Marie Jackson, O.S.F., Dir. Total Staff 8; Total in Residence 2.

[H] COLLEGE CAMPUS MINISTRY CENTERS

RALEIGH. *Doggett Center for Catholic Campus Ministry at Aquinas House* North Carolina State University, 600 Bilyeu St., 27606-2152. Tel: 919-833-9668; Fax: 919-833-1194. Email: blong@unity.ncsu.edu. Web: www2.ncsu.edu/ncsu/stud_orgs/aquinas_house/. Rev. J. William Long, Campus Min.

CHAPEL HILL. *Newman Catholic Student Center* University of North Carolina, 218 Pittsboro St., 27516. Tel: 919-929-3730; Fax: 919-929-3778. Web: www.newman-chapelhill.org. Revs. Phillip M. Leach; Edward P. Mahoney.

DURHAM. *Newman Catholic Student Center Duke University* Box 90974, 27708-0974. Tel: 919-684-8959; Fax: 919-681-8660. Email: catholic@duke.edu. Web: www.duke.edu/web/catholic/. Rev. Joseph G. Vetter, Dir.

North Carolina Central University 1400 S. Alston Ave., 27707. Tel: 919-682-4852; Fax: 919-688-6160. Email: sgarrity@nc.rr.com. Web: www.holycrossdurham.org. Rev. Stephen M. Garrity, S.J.

ELON. *Elon University* Tel: 336-278-7355; Fax: 336-278-7299. Email: jruffo@elon.edu. Web: www.elon.edu/ccm. *Catholic Campus Ministry*, Campus Box 2960, 27244-2010. Tel: 336-278-7355. Rev. John Ruffo, O.F.M.Conv., Campus Min.

GREENVILLE. *Newman Catholic Student Center of East Carolina University*, Formerly Catholic Newman Center at East Carolina University 953 E. 10th St., 27858. Tel: 252-757-1991; Fax: 252-757-1991. Email: ecunewman@hotmail.com. Web: www.newman-ecu.org. Emily Preslar, Int. Campus Min.

WILMINGTON. *Newman Catholic Student Center* University of North Carolina at Wilmington, P.O. Box 20044, UNC-W Station, 28407. Tel: 910-792-0507; Fax: 910-792-0507. Email: ccmuncw@aol.com. Web: www.newman-uncw.org. Catherine R. Rusin.

[I] MISCELLANEOUS

RALEIGH. *AngelPlace, Inc.*, 5117 Wickham Rd., 27606. Tel: 919-845-4368. Web: angelplace.org. Rosemary C. Battista, Contact. Childcare and parenting classes for single parents

Catholic Housing Corporation, 715 Nazareth St., 27606. Tel: 919-821-9704; Fax: 919-821-9705. Email: elmayan@raldioc.org.

Catholic Parish Outreach, 2539-C Noblin Rd., 27604. Tel: 919-873-0245; Fax: 919-873-0260. Total Staff 1; Total Assisted 31,309.

The Clergy Retirement Plan of Diocese of Raleigh, 715 Nazareth St., 27606. Tel: 919-821-9711; Fax: 919-821-9712. Email: tapler@raldioc.org.

CHAPEL HILL. *Vocations Office*, 740 Gimghoul Rd., 27514-3811. Tel: 919-967-2205; Fax: 919-967-3048. Email: clay@raldioc.org. Rev. Michael G. Clay, Dir.

DURHAM. *The Emily Krzyzewski Family Life Center (formerly The Burch Avenue Center)*, c/o Immaculate Conception Church, 725 Burch Ave., 27701-2811. Tel: 919-682-3449; Fax: 919-682-7999. Web: www.emilykflc.com.

NORTH TOPSAIL BEACH. *Marianist Family Ministry, Inc.* Christian Family Living Center , 2006 Wicker St., 28460. Tel: 910-328-1584; Fax: 910-328-3481. Email: cflcentertopsail@aol.com. Web: www.christianfamilyliving.org. Joseph Dicostanzo. Total Staff 130; Total in Residence 2.

SMITHFIELD. *Short Journey Retreat Center*, 2323 Cleveland Rd., 27577. Tel: 919-934-7463; Fax: 919-934-7464. Email: yangj@raldioc.org.

SOUTHERN PINES. *St. Joseph of the Pines Retirement Villa*, 592 Central Dr., 28387. Tel: 910-246-3001. Email: newtonp@sjp.org. Pat Newton, Dir. Total Staff 4; Total in Residence 69.

St. Joseph of the Pines, Inc., 590 Central Dr., 28387. Tel: 910-246-3000; Fax: 910-246-3187. Email: capassoj@sjp.org. Web: www.sjp.org.

Legal Title: *St. Joseph of the Pines, Inc.*, Retirement Villas, Low-income Housing for elderly, Belle Meade Retirement Resort Long Term Care Facilities 1.

RELIGIOUS INSTITUTES OF MEN REPRESENTED IN THE DIOCESE

For further details refer to the corresponding bracketed number in the Religious Institutes of Men or Women section.

[1000]—*Congregation of the Passion*—C.P.

[0480]—*Conventual Franciscans*—O.F.M.Conv

[0520]—*Franciscan Friars*—O.F.M.

[0530]—*Franciscan Friars of the Atonement*—S.A.

[0690]—*Jesuit Fathers and Brothers* (Maryland & New York Provs.)—S.J.

[0720]—*The Missionaries of Our Lady of La Salette*—M.S.

[0920]—*Oblates of St. Francis De Sales* (American Prov.)—O.S.F.S.

[0430]—*Order of Preachers (Dominicans)*—O.P.

RELIGIOUS INSTITUTES OF WOMEN REPRESENTED IN THE DIOCESE

[]—*Adrian Dominican Sisters of the Most Holy Rosary* (Adrian, MI)—O.P.

[3710]—*Congregation of the Sisters of Saint Agnes*—C.S.A.

[3935]—*Congregation of the Sisters of St. Louis*—S.S.L.

[1920]—*Congregation of the Sisters of the Holy Cross*—C.S.C.

[0760]—*Daughters of Charity of St. Vincent de Paul*—D.C.

[0960]—*Daughters of Wisdom*—D.W.

[1070-13]—*Dominican Sisters*—O.P.

[1070-17]—*Dominican Sisters*—O.P.

[1190]—*Franciscan Sisters of the Atonement*—S.A.

[]—*Mission Helpers of the Sacred Heart*—M.H.S.H.

[0570]—*Sisters of Charity of Seton Hill, Greensburg, Pennsylvania*—S.C.

[2990]—*Sisters of Notre Dame* (Chardon, OH)—S.N.D.

[3340]—*Sisters of Providence*—S.P.

[1650]—*Sisters of St. Francis of Philadelphia*—O.S.F.

[3830]—*Sisters of St. Joseph*—S.S.J.

[3910]—*Sisters of St. Joseph of St. Mark*—S.J.S.M.

[1830]—*Sisters of the Good Shepherd* (Silver Spring, MD)—R.G.S.

[1990]—*Sisters of the Holy Names of Jesus and Mary*—S.N.J.M.

[2150]—*Sisters, Servants of the Immaculate Heart of Mary*—I.H.M.

[2160]—*Sisters, Servants of the Immaculate Heart of Mary*—I.H.M.

[2170]—*Sisters, Servants of the Immaculate Heart of Mary*—I.H.M.

[4048]—*Society of Sisters Faithful Companions of Jesus*—F.C.J.

[4040]—*Society of St. Ursula*—S.U.

[]—*Ursuline Sisters*—O.S.U.

NECROLOGY

✠ Lynch, Most Rev. George E., Retired Auxiliary Bishop of Raleigh—Died May 25, 2003

† Ketchersid, Corbin W., (Retired)—Died April 5, 2003

Diocese of Rapid City

(Dioecesis Rapidopolitana)

Most Reverend

BLASE J. CUPICH

Bishop of Rapid City; ordained August 16, 1975; appointed Bishop of Rapid City July 7, 1998; ordained and installed September 21, 1998

Square Miles 43,000.

Formerly the Diocese of Lead.

Erected August 4, 1902; See transferred to Rapid City, August 1, 1930.

Comprises the Counties of Bennett, Butte, Corson, Custer, Dewey, Fall River, Gregory, Haakon, Harding, Jackson, Jones, Lawrence, Lyman, Meade, Mellette, Pennington, Perkins, Stanley, Shannon, Todd, Tripp and Ziebach in the State of South Dakota.

Legal Title: For legal titles of parishes and diocesan institutions, consult the Chancery Office.

Chancery Office: 606 Cathedral Dr., Rapid City, SD 57701. Tel: 605-343-3541; Fax: 605-348-7985.

Email: chancery@diorc.org

STATISTICAL OVERVIEW

Personnel	
Bishop	1
Priests: Diocesan Active in Diocese	28
Priests: Diocesan Active Outside Diocese	3
Priests: Retired, Sick or Absent	12
Number of Diocesan Priests	43
Religious Priests in Diocese	21
Total Priests in Diocese	64
Ordinations:	
Diocesan Priests	1
Transitional Deacons	1
Permanent Deacons	5
Permanent Deacons in Diocese	30
Total Brothers	5
Total Sisters	58
Parishes	
Parishes	97
With Resident Pastor:	
Resident Diocesan Priests	22
Without Resident Pastor:	
Administered by Priests	73
Administered by Religious Women	2
Missions	32
Pastoral Centers	4
Professional Ministry Personnel:	
Brothers	2
Sisters	7
Lay Ministers	18
Welfare	
Residential Care of Children	1
Total Assisted	7
Day Care Centers	1
Total Assisted	21
Specialized Homes	2
Total Assisted	2,150
Special Centers for Social Services	11
Total Assisted	10,059
Other Institutions	2
Educational	
Diocesan Students in Other Seminaries	8
Total Seminarians	8
High Schools, Diocesan and Parish	1
Total Students	196
High Schools, Private	1
Total Students	220
Elementary Schools, Diocesan and Parish	1
Total Students	469
Elementary Schools, Private	1
Total Students	367
Catechesis/Religious Education:	
High School Students	1,320
Elementary Students	2,787
Total Students under Catholic Instruction	5,367
Teachers in the Diocese:	
Priests	7
Scholastics	3
Brothers	3
Sisters	6
Lay Teachers	91
Vital Statistics	
Receptions into the Church:	
Infant Baptism Totals	551
Adult Baptism Totals	72
Received into Full Communion	78
First Communions	509
Confirmations	492
Marriages:	
Catholic	82
Interfaith	80
Total Marriages	162
Deaths	490
Total Catholic Population	29,440
Total Population	227,211

Former Bishops—Most Revs. JOHN STARIHA, D.D. (Retired), consecrated Oct. 28, 1902; retired March 29, 1909 and named Titular Bishop of Antipatride; died in Laibach, Austria, Nov. 28, 1915; JOSEPH F. BUSCH, D.D., consecrated May 19, 1910; transferred to Saint Cloud, MN, Feb. 21, 1915; died May 31, 1953; JOHN J. LAWLER, S.T.D., consecrated Titular Bishop of Greater Hermopolis and Auxiliary Bishop of St. Paul, Minnesota, May 19, 1910; transferred to the See of Lead, Jan. 29, 1916; died March 11, 1948; LEO F. DWORSCHAK, D.D. (Retired), consecrated Titular Bishop of Tium and Coadjutor Bishop of Rapid City "cum jure successionis," Aug. 22, 1946; transferred to Fargo, ND, April 10, 1947; WILLIAM T. MCCARTY, C.SS.R., D.D. (Retired), appt. Titular Bishop of Anaea and Delegate to the Military Vicar, Jan. 2, 1943; appt. Coadjutor Bishop of Rapid City "cum jure successionis," April 10, 1947; succeeded to March 11, 1948; retired Sept. 17, 1969; appt. Titular Bishop of Rotdon; died Sept. 14, 1972; HAROLD J. DIMMERLING, D.D., appt. Bishop of Rapid City, Sept. 17, 1969; ord. May 2, 1940; consecrated Oct. 30, 1969; died Dec. 13, 1987; CHARLES J. CHAPUT, D.D., appt. Bishop of Rapid City, April 11, 1988; appt. Archbishop of Denver, Feb. 18, 1997.

Vicar General—Rev. DANIEL JUELFS, J.C.L.

Chancery Office—606 Cathedral Dr., P.O. Box 678, Rapid City, 57709. Tel: 605-343-3541; Fax: 605-348-7985. Email: chancery@diorc.org. Office Hours: Mon.-Fri. 8-5; Address all official business to this office.

Chancellor—MARGARET SIMONSON.

Diocesan Tribunal—606 Cathedral Dr., P.O. Box 678, Rapid City, 57709-0678. Tel: 605-343-3541; Fax: 605-348-7985.

Officialis—Rev. DANIEL JUELFS.

Diocesan Consultors—Revs. WILLIAM PAULY, S.J.; MICHEL MULLOY; DANIEL JUELFS; LEO HAUSMANN; BRIAN LANE; MARK MCCORMICK.

Deaneries—Rev. Msgr. MICHAEL WOSTER, Rapid City; Revs. WILLIAM ZANDRI, Lead; PETER KOVARIK, Hot Springs; ED VANORNY, Presho BRIAN FAWCETT, Lemmon; RAYMOND DEISCH, Gregory.

Presbyteral Council—Rev. ED VANORNY, Pres.

Vicar for Retired Priests—Rev. D. CRAIG COWER (Retired).

Permanent Diaconate Program, Sioux Spiritual Center—Rev. GEORGE WINZENBURG, S.J., Dir., HCR 77, Box 271, 20100 Center Rd., Howes, 57748. Tel: 605-985-5906.

Development and Stewardship Program—ROBERT BICKETT, Dir.

Continuing Education of Clergy—Rev. BRIAN LANE.

Vocation Program—Rev. BRIAN CHRISTENSEN, Dir., P.O. Box 678, Rapid City, 57709-0678. Tel: 605-343-3541.

Diocesan Finance Manager—SUZANNE LAMBERT.

Diocesan Finance Council—Ms. IONA LANGER; CHRIS SCHMID; SHIRLEY STEC; DAN DUFFY; MONTE PALACEK; RAY HILLENBRAND PETE LIEN JR.; Rev. BRIAN LANE; FRANK SHORT; DON STUKEL; PAT BURCHILL; TERESA BIGGS; CHRIS SCHMID.

Holy Childhood Pontifical Association—Rev. PAUL DAHMS.

Propagation of the Faith—Rev. PAUL DAHMS.

Catholic Relief Service—Rev. PAUL DAHMS, Dir., 606 Cathedral Dr., Rapid City, 57701-5498.

Native Concerns Office—VERONICA VALANDRA, Dir., 606 Cathedral Dr., Rapid City, 57701. Tel: 605-343-3541.

Director of Ongoing Formation—Rev. BRIAN LANE, 532 Adams St., Rapid City, 57701. Tel: 605-342-1556.

Secretary Education—Rev. JOHN WADE.

Director of Rural Life—VACANT.

Office of Family Life—KATHLEEN KOVARIK, Dir., 606 Cathedral Dr., P.O. Box 678, Rapid City, 57709-0678. Tel: 605-343-3541; Fax: 605-348-7985.

Family Life Sponsored Ministries—

Pro-Life Commission—SUE JIMMERSON, Chm., 606 Cathedral Dr., Rapid City, 57701.

Retreat Ministry—606 Cathedral Dr., P.O. Box 678, Rapid City, 57709-0678. Tel: 605-343-3541.

Separated, Divorced and Widowed Support Group—606 Cathedral Dr., P.O. Box 678, Rapid City, 57709-0678. Tel: 605-343-3541.

Bereavement Ministry—606 Cathedral Dr., P.O. Box 678, Rapid City, 57709-0678. Tel: 605-343-3541.

Natural Family Planning Ministry—606 Cathedral Dr., P.O. Box 678, Rapid City, 57709-0678. Tel: 605-343-3541.

Independent Ministries—

Rachel's Vineyard—606 Cathedral Dr., P.O. Box 678, Rapid City, 57709-0678. Tel: 605-343-3541.

Retrouvaille—606 Cathedral Dr., P.O. Box 678, Rapid City, 57709-0678. Tel: 605-343-3541.

Right to Life—Tel: 605-342-9101 (local contact).

Birthright—Tel: 605-343-1732.

Catholic Engaged Encounter—606 Cathedral Dr., P.O. Box 678, Rapid City, 57709-0678. Tel: 605-343-3541.

Worldwide Marriage Encounter—606 Cathedral Dr., P.O. Box 678, Rapid City, 57709-0678. Tel: 605-343-3541.

Diocesan Office of Religious Education—ETTA FINN, Ph.D., Dir., 300 Fairmont Blvd., Rapid City, 57701. Tel: 605-341-2508.

Campaign for Human Development—Rev. PAUL DAHMS, Dir., 606 Cathedral Dr., Rapid City, 57701-5498. Tel: 605-343-3541.

Victim Assistance Coordinator—MARYANN TULLY. Tel: 605-209-3418. Email: fredoldford@cs.com.

West River Catholic Newspaper—EILEEN SULLIVAN

ROTERT, Editor, 606 Cathedral Dr., Rapid City, 57701.

West River Catholic Youth Commission—606 Cathedral Dr., Rapid City, 57701.

Archives—SR. CELINE ERK, O.S.B.

CLERGY, PARISHES, MISSIONS AND PAROCHIAL SCHOOLS

CITY OF RAPID CITY
(PENNINGTON COUNTY)

1—CATHEDRAL OF OUR LADY OF PERPETUAL HELP (1890), Rev. Msgr. Michael Woster, J.C.L., Rector; Revs. Valentine Young, O.F.M.; Timothy William Castor; Deacons Tom Lane, (Retired); George Gladfelter.
Church: 520 Cathedral Dr., 57701-5499. Tel: 605-342-0507; Fax: 605-721-5986.
School—St. Elizabeth Seton Central School, Tel: 605-348-1477. See separate listing under Institutions Located in the Diocese.
Catechesis/Religious Program—Students 190.
Chapel—Immaculate Conception, Tel: 605-341-1578.
Mission—St. Michael's Hermosa, Custer Co.

2—BLESSED SACRAMENT (1947), Revs. Michel Mulloy; Kevin Lee Achbach; Deacons Greg Palmer; Patrick Fagan.
Res.: 4500 Jackson Blvd., 57702-4999. Tel: 605-342-3336; Fax: 605-341-5668.
Catechesis/Religious Program—Students 686.
Mission—Our Lady of Mt. Carmel Keystone, Pennington Co.
Mission—St. Rose of Lima 100 Park Ave., Hill City, Pennington Co. 57745.

3—ST. ISAAC JOGUES (1949), (Native American), Rev. David G. Matzko, S.J. (CHY); Deacons James Garnett; Leroy Decory; Luis Usera. In Res., Rev. John Hatcher, S.J.
Res.: 221 Knollwood Dr., P.O. Box 1304, 57709-1304. Tel: 605-343-2165; Fax: 605-343-3257.
Catechesis/Religious Program—Students 124.
Mother Butler Center—Tel: 605-343-2165; Fax: 605-343-3257. Catechetical and Social Center for Indians.
Mission—Indian Health Service, Sioux San Hospital and Pennington County Jail, Pennington Co.

4—ST. THERESE THE LITTLE FLOWER (1941), [JC], Formerly known as The Church of St. John the Evangelist. Revs. Brian Lane; Bryan Sorensen; Deacons Claude Sauer; Michael Curtin. In Res., Rev. Brian Patrick Christensen.
Res.: 532 Adams St., 57701. Tel: 605-342-1556; Fax: 605-348-6272.
Catechesis/Religious Program—Students 239.

OUTSIDE THE CITY OF RAPID CITY

BELLE FOURCHE, BUTTE CO., ST. PAUL (1905), [JC] Revs. Timothy Hoag; Matthew Fallgren; Deacon Ray Klein.
Res.: 855 Fifth St., 57717-1701. Tel: 605-723-3226; Fax: 605-723-3771.
Catechesis/Religious Program—Students 82.

BISON, PERKINS CO., BLESSED SACRAMENT (1918), [JC], Served from Lemmon. Rev. Brian Fawcett. In Res., Rev. Andrew Morvey (Retired).
Res.: P.O. Box 210, Lemmon, 57638. Tel: 605-244-5546.
Catechesis/Religious Program—Students 28.
Mission—St. James Drew, Perkins Co. Tel: 605-374-3767.

BONESTEEL, GREGORY CO., IMMACULATE CONCEPTION (1906), [CEM] Attended by, Church of St. Anthony, Fairfax and St. Francis Xavier, Ponca Creek. Rev. Janusz Korban.
Res.: P.O. Box 376, 57317-0376. Tel: 605-654-2204; Fax: 605-654-2658.
Catechesis/Religious Program—Students 34.

BUFFALO, HARDING CO., ST. ANTHONY (1917), [CEM 2] [JC] Rev. Gary Oreshoski.
Res.: P.O. Box 85, 57720-0085. Tel: 605-375-3438.
Catechesis/Religious Program—Students 35.
Mission—St. Agnes Cox, Harding Co.
Mission—St. Isidore Ralph, Harding Co.
Mission—Our Lady of the Prairie Reva, Harding Co.

BURKE, GREGORY CO., SACRED HEART (1905), [CEM 2] [JC] Attended by, St. Joseph, Gregory.
Res.: P.O. Box 354, 57523-0354. Tel: 605-775-2532.
Catechesis/Religious Program—Students 50.

CLEARFIELD, TRIPP CO., ST. BONIFACE, Closed., For sacramental records contact Immaculate Conception, Winner.

COLOME, TRIPP CO., ST. ISIDORE (1909), [JC] Attended by, Immaculate Conception, Winner. Rev. Leo Hausmann.
Res.: P.O. Box 405, 57528-0405. Tel: 605-842-1437.
Catechesis/Religious Program—Tel: 605-842-2464. Students 44.

CUSTER, CUSTER CO., ST. JOHN THE BAPTIST (1911), [JC] Attended by, St. Anthony's, Hot Springs and St. Rose of Lima, Hill City. Rev. Peter Kovarik.
Res.: P.O. Box 632, 57730-0632. Tel: 605-673-4426; Fax: 605-673-4426.
Catechesis/Religious Program—Tel: 605-673-4426. Students 81.

DEADWOOD, LAWRENCE CO., ST. AMBROSE (1877), [CEM] Rev. Paul G. Dahms.
Res.: 760 W. Main St., 57732-1003. Tel: 605-578-1519.
Catechesis/Religious Program—732 Main St., 57732-0320. Tel: 605-578-1921. Students 40.

EAGLE BUTTE, DEWEY CO., ALL SAINTS (1911), (Native American), [JC] Revs. Thomas Westhoven, S.C.J.; J. Anthony Kluckman, S.C.J.
Res.: P.O. Box 110, 57625-0110. Tel: 605-964-3391; Fax: 605-964-3300.
Catechesis/Religious Program—Students 68.
Mission—Immaculate Conception Bridger, Ziebach Co.
Mission—St. Joseph Cherry Creek, Ziebach Co.
Mission—Sacred Heart Dupree, Ziebach Co.
Mission—St. Catherine Promise, Dewey Co.
Mission—Sacred Heart Red Scaffold, Ziebach Co.
Mission—St. Joseph Ridgeview, Dewey Co.
Mission—St. Luke Thunder Butte, Ziebach Co.
Mission—St. Therese White Horse, Dewey Co.

FAIRFAX, GREGORY CO., ST. ANTHONY'S (1904), [CEM] Attended by, Immaculate Conception, Bonesteel. Rev. Janusz Korban.
Mailing Address: c/o P.O. Box 186, 57335-0186. Tel: 605-654-2204; Fax: 605-654-2658.
Catechesis/Religious Program—Students 21.

FAITH, MEADE CO., ST. JOSEPH (1917), [CEM] Rev. John Heying.
Res.: P.O. Box 307, 57626-0307. Tel: 605-967-2201; Fax: 605-967-2207.
Catechesis/Religious Program—Students 38.
Mission—St. Anthony Red Owl, Meade Co.
Mission—Our Lady of Victory Plainview, Meade Co.
Mission— Mud Butte, Meade Co.

FORT PIERRE, STANLEY CO., ST. JOHN (1905), [JC] Rev. Dale Kutil.
Res.: 206 W. Main, P.O. Box 670, 57532-0670. Tel: 605-223-2176; Fax: 605-223-2482.
Catechesis/Religious Program—Students 94.

GREGORY, GREGORY CO., ST. JOSEPH (1905), [CEM 3] Rev. Raymond J. Deisch.
Res.: 414 Church St., 57533. Tel: 605-835-9290.
Catechesis/Religious Program—Mary Vale Hall, 411 Church St.. Tel: 605-835-9396. Students 70.

HERMOSA, CUSTER CO., ST. MICHAEL'S, Attended by, Our Lady of Perpetual Help Cathedral, Rapid City.

HILL CITY, PENNINGTON CO., ST. ROSE OF LIMA (1898), [JC] Attended by, Blessed Sacrament, Rapid City. Rev. Michel Mulloy.
Res.: 4500 Jackson Blvd., 57702. Tel: 605-342-3336; Fax: 605-341-5668.
Catechesis/Religious Program—Tel: 605-574-2479. Students 65.

HOT SPRINGS, FALL RIVER CO., ST. ANTHONY'S (1890), [JC] Rev. Peter Kovarik; Deacon Pat Coy.
Res.: P.O. Box 969, 57747-0969. Tel: 605-745-3393; Fax: 605-745-3393.
Catechesis/Religious Program—Deacon Earl F. Witte. Students 71.
Mission—St. James 310 3rd St., Edgemont, Fall River Co. 57735.

KADOKA, JACKSON CO., OUR LADY OF VICTORY (1908), [JC] Attended by, St. Patrick's, Wall. Rev. Robert D. Baden; Deacon Eugene A. Heckathorne.
Res.: P.O. Box 159, 57790-0159. Tel: 605-837-2219.
Catechesis/Religious Program—Students 24.

KENEL, CORSON CO., ASSUMPTION OF THE BLESSED VIRGIN MARY (1879), (Native American), Attended by, St. Bernard, McLaughlin.
Res.: P.O. Box 539, McLaughlin, 57642-0539. Tel: 605-823-4401; Fax: 605-823-2325.
Catechesis/Religious Program—Students 30.

KENNEBEC, LYMAN CO., ST. MICHAEL'S (1906), [CEM] Attended by, St. Mary, Reliance. , Mailing Address: P.O. Box 185, Lower Brule, 57548-0185. Tel: 605-473-5335; Fax: 605-473-5453.
Catechesis/Religious Program—Students 18.

KYLE, SHANNON CO., OUR LADY OF SORROWS (1910), (Native American), [CEM 2] Deacon Lawrence Whiting, (Retired).
Res.: P.O. Box 398, 57752-0398. Tel: 605-455-2888.
Catechesis/Religious Program—Students 10.
Mission—St. John of the Cross Allen, Bennett Co.
Mission—St. Stephens Medicine Root, Shannon Co.

LEAD, LAWRENCE CO., ST. PATRICK'S (1878), [CEM] [JC] Rev. William A. Zandri.
Res.: 141 S. Siever St., 57754. Tel: 605-584-2002; Fax: 605-584-3114.
Catechesis/Religious Program—Students 63.

LEMMON, PERKINS CO., ST. MARY'S (1909), [JC] Rev. Brian Fawcett; Deacons Carl Orthman; Bill Dustman.
Res.: P.O. Box 210, 57638. Tel: 605-374-3767; Fax: 605-374-3768.
Catechesis/Religious Program—Dorene Bierwagon, D.R.E. Students 91.
Mission—Sacred Heart Morristown, Corson Co.
Mission—Blessed Sacrament Bison, Perkins Co.

LOWER BRULE, LYMAN CO., ST. MARY'S (1923), (Native American), [CEM] Revs. Stephen Huffstetter, S.C.J.; Charles Wonch, S.C.J.
Office—P.O. Box 185, 57548. Tel: 605-473-5335; Fax: 605-473-5453.
Catechesis/Religious Program—Students 20.

MANDERSON, SHANNON CO., ST. AGNES (1901), (Native American), [CEM] Rev. William Pauly, S.J.
Mailing Address: P.O. Box 88, 57756.
Res.: 100 Mission Dr., Pine Ridge, 57770-2100. Tel: 605-867-5491; Fax: 605-867-5874.
Catechesis/Religious Program—Students 10.
Mission—Sacred Heart P.O. Box 88, Wounded Knee, Shannon Co. 57756. Tel: 605-867-2267.

MARTIN, BENNETT CO., OUR LADY OF THE SACRED HEART (1918), [CEM] [JC] Rev. John J. Hennessy, S.J.; Deacons Calvin Clifford; Lawrence Kocer.
Mailing Address: P.O. Box 567, 57551. Tel: 605-685-6232.
Catechesis/Religious Program—Tel: 605-685-6274. Students 101.

MCINTOSH, CORSON CO., ST. BONAVENTURE'S (1913), [CEM] Revs. Kerry Prendiville; Tony Grossenburg.
Res.: P.O. Box 539, McLaughlin, 57642. Tel: 605-823-4401; Fax: 605-823-2325.
Catechesis/Religious Program—Students 35.

MCLAUGHLIN, CORSON CO., ST. BERNARD (1918), [CEM] Revs. Kerry Prendiville; Tony Grossenburg; Deacon Paul Keller.
Res.: P.O. Box 539, 57642. Tel: 605-823-4401; Fax: 605-823-2325.
Catechesis/Religious Program—Tel: 605-823-4210; Fax: 605-823-4757. Sisters of St. Francis of the Immaculate Conception 2; Lay Teachers 19; Students 95.
Mission—St. Aloysius Bullhead, Corson Co.
Mission—St. Bede Wakpala, Corson Co.
Mission—Our Lady of the Assumption Parish Kenel, Corson Co.
Mission—St. Bonaventure P.O. Box 320, McIntosh, Corson Co. 57641. Tel: 605-273-4334.

MIDLAND, HAAKON CO., ST. WILLIAM (1911), Attended by, Sacred Heart, Philip. , Mailing Address: P.O. Box 309, Philip, 57567. Tel: 605-859-2664; Fax: 605-859-2812.

MISSION, TODD CO., ST. THOMAS THE APOSTLE (1933), (Native American), [CEM] Attended by, St. Francis, Mission. Rev. Ed Witt, S.J.; Deacon Marlon J. Leneaugh.
Church: P.O. Box 151, 57555. Tel: 605-856-4618.
Catechesis/Religious Program—Tel: 605-856-2273. Gladys Bordeaux, D.R.E. Students 35.
Mission—St. Peter's St. Francis. P.O. Box 499, Okreek, Todd Co. 57572. Tel: 605-747-2362.
Mission—St. Rose Soldier Creek, Todd Co.

MORRISTOWN, CORSON CO., SACRED HEART (1912), [JC] Attended by, St. Mary's, Lemmon. , Mailing Address: P.O. Box 210, Lemmon, 57638. Tel: 605-374-3767; Fax: 605-374-3768.
Catechesis/Religious Program—Students 12.

MURDO, JONES CO., ST. MARTIN (1906), [CEM] Attended by, Christ the King, Presho. Rev. Ed Vanorny.
Mailing Address: P.O. Box 399, Presho, 57568. Tel: 605-669-2436; Fax: 605-895-2534.
Catechesis/Religious Program—Tel: 605-895-2534. Students 16.

NEW UNDERWOOD, PENNINGTON CO., ST. JOHN THE EVANGELIST (1921), [JC] Rev. Daniel Juelfs.
Res.: P.O. Box 305, 57761. Tel: 605-754-6446.
Catechesis/Religious Program—Students 34.
Mission—St. Margaret Lakeside, Meade Co.

NEWELL, BUTTE CO., ST. MARY STAR OF THE SEA (1910), Attended by, St. Francis of Assisi, Sturgis , Mailing Address: 1049 Howard St., Sturgis, 57785-1999. Tel: 605-720-3579.
Catechesis/Religious Program—Students 39.

NORRIS, MELETTE CO., SACRED HEART (1955), [JC] Attended by, St. Francis Mission, St. Francis, S.D. Rev. Ronald S. Seminara, S.J.
Res.: HC75, Box 923, 57560. Tel: 605-747-2118.

OGLALA, SHANNON CO., OUR LADY OF THE SIOUX (1916), (Native American), [CEM] Attended by, Holy Rosary Mission, Pine Ridge. Sr. Connie Schmidt, S.S.N.D., Pastoral Coord.
Res.: P.O. Box 140, 57764. Tel: 605-867-5673; Fax: 605-867-1518.
Catechesis/Religious Program—Students 5.

PARMELEE, TODD CO., ST. AGNES (1927), Rev. Christopher J. Manahan, S.J.
Res.: P.O. Box 115, 57566. Tel: 605-747-2118; Fax: 605-747-5057.
Mission—Sacred Heart Upper Cutmeat, Todd Co.

Mission—St. Joseph Hall Black Pipe-Corn Creek, Melette Co.

PHILIP, HAAKON CO., SACRED HEART (1907), [JC] Rev. Ron Garry.
Res.: 307 W. Elm, P.O. Box 309, 57567. Tel: 605-859-2664; Fax: 605-859-2812.
Catechesis/Religious Program—Students 85.
Mission—St. Mary Milesville, Haakon Co.
Mission—St. William Midland, Haakon Co. Tel: 605-843-2544.

PIEDMONT-BLACK HAWK, MEADE CO., OUR LADY OF THE BLACK HILLS (1916), [JC] Rev. Mark McCormick; Deacons Walt Wilson; John Osnes.
Res.: 12365 N. Hwy. 79, 57769-2007. Tel: 605-787-5168.
Catechesis/Religious Program—Students 177.

PINE RIDGE, SHANNON CO., SACRED HEART (1890), (Lakota), [JC], Attended from Holy Rosary Mission. Rev. Stephen J. Sanford, S.J.
Res.: P.O. Box 359, 57770. Tel: 605-867-5551; Fax: 605-867-1969.
Catechesis/Religious Program—Students 60.

PORCUPINE, SHANNON CO., CHURCH OF CHRIST THE KING (1901), (Native American), [CEM] Rev. William Pauly, S.J.
Res.: 100 Mission Dr., Pine Ridge, 57770-2100. Tel: 605-867-1614; Fax: 605-867-2428.
School—Our Lady of Lourdes Mission School, Tel: 605-867-5568. Cynthia Hillman, Prin. Sisters 1; Lay Teachers 9; Students 137.
Catechesis/Religious Program—Students 15.
Mission—St. Paul [CEM] P.O. Box 7, Shannon Co. 57772. Tel: 605-867-1614.

PRESHO, LYMAN CO., CHRIST THE KING (1906), [CEM] Rev. Ed Vanorny.
Res.: P.O. Box 399, 57568-0399. Tel: 605-895-2534; Fax: 605-895-2534.
Catechesis/Religious Program—Students 33.
Mission—St. Martin of Tours P.O. Box 357, Murdo, Jones Co. 57559.
Mission—St. Anthony of Padua P.O. Box 159, Draper, Jones Co. 57531.

RELIANCE, LYMAN CO., ST. MARY'S (1911), [CEM] Attended by, St. Mary's, Reliance. , Mailing Address: P.O. Box 185, Lower Brule, 57548-0185. Tel: 605-473-5335; Fax: 605-473-5453.
Catechesis/Religious Program—Students 18.

ROSEBUD, TODD CO., ST. BRIDGET, (Native American), Rev. Christopher J. Manahan, S.J.
Res.: P.O. Box 340, 57570-0340. Tel: 605-747-2496.

ST. FRANCIS, TODD CO., ST. CHARLES (1886), (Native American), [CEM] Rev. Christopher J. Manahan, S.J.; Deacon Ben Black Bear Jr.
Res.: Box 499, 57572. Tel: 605-747-2533; Fax: 605-747-5057.
Catechesis/Religious Program—Tel: 605-747-4610. Students 132.
Mission—, See listing under Indian Missions for Rosebud Reservation, St. Francis regarding details on personnel and missions.
Mission—St. Patrick Spring Creek, Todd Co.

SPEARFISH, LAWRENCE CO., ST. JOSEPH (1907), [JC] Revs. Timothy Hoag; Matthew Fallgren.
Res.: 844 5th St., 57783-2005. Tel: 605-642-2306; Fax: 605-642-1024.
Catechesis/Religious Program—Students 314.

STURGIS, MEADE CO., ST. FRANCIS OF ASSISI (1840), [CEM] Rev. Arnold Kari.
Res.: 1049 Howard St., 57785-1999. Tel: 605-720-3579; Fax: 605-720-3579.
Catechesis/Religious Program—Tel: 605-720-3996. Carol Rost, D.R.E. Students 149.

TIMBER LAKE, DEWEY CO., HOLY CROSS (1910), Rev. Andrzej Wyrostek.
Res.: P.O. Box 70, 57656-0070. Tel: 605-865-3653.
Catechesis/Religious Program—Students 145.
Mission—St. Mary Isabel, Dewey Co.
Mission—Holy Rosary Trail City, Corson Co.

WALL, PENNINGTON CO., ST. PATRICK'S (1917), [JC] Rev. Robert D. Baden.
Res.: P.O. Box 405, 57790-0405. Tel: 605-279-2542.
Catechesis/Religious Program—Students 58.
Mission—Holy Rosary Interior, Jackson Co.

WANBLEE, JACKSON CO., IGNATIUS LOYOLA (1920), (Native American), [CEM 3] [JC 5] Rev. Frank Schmitt, S.J.
Res.: P.O. Box 229, 57577. Tel: 605-462-6170.
Catechesis/Religious Program—Tel: 605-455-2831. Students 18.
Mission—St. Henry Potato Creek, Jackson Co.

WATAUGA, CORSON CO., ST. MICHAEL (1912) [CEM] Attended by St. Bernard, McLaughlin. , Mailing Address: P.O. Box 539, McLaughlin, 57642. Tel: 605-823-4401; Fax: 605-823-2325.
Catechesis/Religious Program—Students 21.

WHITE RIVER, MELLETTE CO.
1—ST. IGNATIUS (1899), (Native American), [CEM] [JC] Rev. Edward Q. Witt, S.J.
Res.: P.O. Box 245, 57579-0245. Tel: 605-259-3381.
Catechesis/Religious Program—Tel: 605-259-3313. Students 15.
Mission—Our Lady of Good Counsel Wood, Mellette Co. 57585.
2—SACRED HEART (1919), [JC] Rev. Edward G. Witt, S.J.
Mailing Address: P.O. Box 185, 57579-0185.
Catechesis/Religious Program—Students 21.

WINNER, TRIPP CO., IMMACULATE CONCEPTION (1910), Rev. Leo Hausmann.
Res.: 302 W. Fourth, P.O. Box 765, 57580. Tel: 605-842-3520; Fax: 605-842-3520.
Catechesis/Religious Program—Students 180.
Mission—St. Ann [JC] Keyapaha, Tripp Co.

INDIAN MISSIONS

EAGLE BUTTE, DEWEY CO., CHEYENNE RIVER RESERVATION (1911), (Native American), [CEM 8] [JC 2] Revs. Thomas Westhoven, S.C.J.; J. Anthony Kluckman, S.C.J.; Deacon Ted Knife Sr.
Mailing Address: *All Saints*, P.O. Box 110, 57625. Tel: 605-964-3391; Fax: 605-964-3300.
Catechesis/Religious Program—Students 119.
Mission—Immaculate Conception Bridger, Ziebach Co.
Mission—Sacred Heart Dupree, Ziebach Co.
Mission—St. Catherine Promise, Dewey Co.
Mission—St. Joseph Ridgeview, Dewey Co.
Mission—St. Joseph Cherry Creek, Ziebach Co.
Mission—St. Luke Thunder Butte, Ziebach Co.
Mission—Sacred Heart Red Scaffold, Ziebach Co.
Mission—St. Therese White Horse, Dewey Co.

LOWER BRULE, LYMAN CO., LOWER BRULE RESERVATION (1895), (Native American), [CEM] Revs. Stephen Huffstetter, S.C.J.; Charles Wonch, S.C.J.
Mailing Address: P.O. Box 185, 57548. Tel: 605-473-5335; 605-473-5215; Fax: 605-473-5453. Sisters 1.
Catechesis/Religious Program—Students 20.

PINE RIDGE, SHANNON CO., HOLY ROSARY (Pine Ridge Reservation) (1888), (Native American), Revs. Peter J. Klink, S.J.; Patrick Burns, S.J , Supr.; Tom Simonds, S.J.; Steve Sanford, S.J.; Frank Schmitt, S.J., (Wanblee); William Pauly, S.J., (Manderson, Wounded Knee, Porcupine).
Mailing Address: 100 Mission Dr., 57770-2100. Tel: 605-867-5491; Fax: 605-967-1291. Priests 6; Lay Teachers 47; Brothers 3; Scholastics 3.
School—Red Cloud Indian School, Tel: 605-867-5491; Fax: 605-867-1291. Sr. Monica, O.S.F., Coord. Sisters 6; Lay Teachers 42; Students: Elementary 184; High School 214.
Catechesis/Religious Program—Students 398.
Mission—St. Joseph Cuny Table, Shannon Co.
Mission—Our Lady of Sioux P.O. Box 140, Oglala, Shannon Co. 57764. Tel: 605-867-5673; Fax: 605-867-1518.
Mission—Our Lady of Good Counsel No Water, Shannon Co.
Mission—St. Bernard Red Shirt Table, Shannon Co.

ST. FRANCIS, TODD CO., ROSEBUD RESERVATION (1886), (Native American), [CEM], St. Francis Mission and Rosebud Educational Society. Revs. John Hatcher, S.J., Supr., Mission.; Christopher J. Manahan, S.J.; Richard T. Jones, S.J.; Edward G. Witt, S.J.; Bro. Henry Lynch, C.F.X.; Deacons Ben Black Bear Jr.; Marlon Leneaugh.
Mailing Address: P.O. Box 499, 57572-0499. Tel: 605-747-2361; Fax: 605-747-5057. Priests 4; Permanent Deacons 2; Brothers 2; Sisters 3.
Catechesis/Religious Program—Tel: 605-747-2142. Students 293.
Mission—St. Charles, Todd Co. Tel: 605-747-2533.
Mission—St. Peter Okreek, Todd Co. Tel: 605-747-2362.
Mission—St. Rose Soldier Creek, Todd Co. Tel: 605-747-2362.
Mission—St. Patrick Spring Creek, Todd Co. Tel: 605-747-5319.
Mission—St. Agnes Box 115, Parmelee, Todd Co. 57566. Tel: 605-747-2118.
Mission—Sacred Heart Parmelee. Box 115, Upper Cutmeat, Todd Co. 57566. Tel: 605-747-2118.
Mission—St. Bridget P.O. Box 340, Rosebud, Todd Co. 57570. Tel: 605-747-2496.
Mission—St. Ignatius Box 245, White River, Mellette Co. 57579. Tel: 605-259-3381.
Mission—Sacred Heart Box 185, White River, Mellette Co. 57579. Tel: 605-747-2362.
Mission—Our Lady of Good Counsel Wood, Mellette Co. Tel: 605-747-2362.
Mission—Sacred Heart HCR 75, Box 923, Norris, Mellette Co. 57560. Tel: 605-462-6353.
Mission—St. Thomas Box 151, Mission, Todd Co. 57555. Tel: 605-856-4618.

STANDING ROCK, CORSON CO., STANDING ROCK RESERVATION (1918), Revs. Kerry Prendiville; Tony Grossenburg.
St. Bernard's Church: P.O. Box 539, McLaughlin, 57642. Tel: 605-823-4401; Fax: 605-823-2325.
Mission—St. Bede Wakpala, Corson Co.
Mission—St. Aloysius Bullhead, Corson Co.
Mission—Assumption of the Blessed Virgin Mary Church Kenel, Corson Co.
Mission—St. Michael Watauga, Corson Co.

Chaplains of Public Institutions

ELLSWORTH. *Ellsworth AFB*. Rev. David A. Voelker, 28th BW/HC, Ellsworth Afb, 57706.

On Special Assignment:
Rev.—
Biegler, Steven (North American College, Rome)

On Duty Outside the Diocese:
Rev.—
Novotny, Richard

Retired:
Rev. Msgr.—
O'Connell, William, Casa Maria, 12541 N. Hwy. 79, Piedmont, 57769.
Revs.—
Birdsall, John M., Casa Maria, 12541 N. Hwy. 79, Piedmont, 57769.
Cower, D. Craig, 255 Texas St., Westhills Village F211, 57701-7356.
Hight, Michael, 416 6th Ave. #3, Wall, 57790.
Jordan, Collins P., c/o Bennett City Healtcare Box 70-D, Martin, 57551.
Morvay, Andrew, P.O. Box 208, Bison, 57638.
Scherer, Gerald N., P.O. Box 268, Hermoso, 57744-0268.
Valades, Reuben, 304 Denver St. Apt. 101, 57701.

Permanent Deacons:
Black Bear, Ben, Jr., St. Francis Mission, St. Francis
Brown, Larry, Faith
Bush, Gerald, Wanblee
Clifford, Calvin, Martin
Condon, Harold, Howes
Coy, Patrick, Hot Springs
Curtin, Michael, Rapid City
DeCory, Leroy, Rapid City
Dustman, Bill, Lemmon
Fagan, Patrick, Rapid City
Garnet, James W., (Retired), Rapid City
Gladfelter, George, Rapid City
Grant, Albert, (Retired), Rapid City
Heckathorne, Eugene A., Kadoka
Hill, Ken, (Retired), Albuquerque, New Mexico
Keller, Paul, McLaughlin
Klein, Ray, Belle Fourche
Knife, Theodore, Eagle Butte
Kocer, Lawrence, Martin
Lane, Thomas, (Retired), Rapid City
Leneaugh, Marlon, Mission
Orthman, Carl, Lemmon
Osnes, John, Piedmont
Palmer, Greg, Rapid City
Rath, Vern, Spearfish
Sauer, Claude, (Retired), St. Therese, Rapid City
Tully, Frederick G., Hill City
Usera, Luis, Rapid City
Wilson, Walt, Piedmont
Witte, Earl Joseph, (Retired), St. James, Edgemont

INSTITUTIONS LOCATED IN THE DIOCESE

[A] DIOCESAN CATHOLIC SCHOOL SYSTEM

RAPID CITY. *St. Thomas More High School*, 300 Fairmont Blvd., 57701. Tel: 605-343-8484; Fax: 605-348-1318. Email: stm@stm.k12.sd.us. Web: stm.k12.sd.us. Lay Teachers 16; Students 196; Total Staff 42.

St. Elizabeth Elementary and Middle School, 431 Oakland, 57701. Tel: 605-348-1477; Fax: 605-342-4367. Lay Teachers 33; Students 469; Staff 67.

[B] MONASTERIES AND RESIDENCES OF PRIESTS & BROTHERS

EAGLE BUTTE. *Sacred Heart Community House*, P.O. Box 110, 57625-0110. Tel: 605-964-3391; Fax: 605-964-3300. Email: scjhouse@eaglebuttescjs.org. Revs. Thomas Westhoven, S.C.J.; J. Anthony Kluckman, S.C.J. Priests 2.

HOWES. *Kino Jesuit Community*, 20100 Center Rd., 57748-9505. Tel: 605-985-5906; Fax: 605-985-5908. Priests 5. In Res. Revs. John Hatcher, S.J., Dir. of Inculturation, Supr.; Thomas Lawler, S.J.; David G. Matzko, S.J. (CHY); Thomas J. Tierney, S.J.; George Winzenburg, S.J.

LOWER BRULE. *SCJ Community House*, P.O. Box 185, 57548-0185. Tel: 605-473-5335; 605-473-5487;

Fax: 605-473-5453. Email: pastteam@gwtc.net. Revs. Stephen Huffstetter, S.C.J.; Charles Wonch, S.C.J.; Bro. Duane Lemke, S.C.J. Priests 2; Total in Residence 3; Total Staff 4.

PIEDMONT. *Casa Maria Residence for Retired Priests*, 12541 N. Hwy. 79, 57769. Tel: 605-835-9290. Email: wocwalk@rap.midco.net. Rev. Msgr. William O'Connell (Retired).

PINE RIDGE. *Jesuit Community of Holy Rosary Mission*, 100 Mission Dr., 57770-2100. Tel: 605-867-5491; Fax: 605-867-1291. Email: pburns@redcloudschool.org. Web: www.redcloudschool.org. Revs. William Pauly, S.J.; Peter J. Klink, S.J., Pastor & Pres.; Stephen Sanford, S.J.; Paul Manhart, S.J.; Patrick Burns, S.J., Supr.; Tom Simonds, S.J.; Frank Schmitt, S.J.; Bros. Bill Foster, S.J.; Claire Simon, S.J.; Michael Zimmerman, S.J. Priests 9; Brothers 3; Total in Residence 12; Scholastics 3.

[C] CONVENTS AND RESIDENCES FOR SISTERS

RAPID CITY. **Benedictine Convent of St. Martin*, 2110 C St. Martin Dr., 57702-9660. Tel: 605-343-8011; Fax: 605-399-2723. Email: fmartin620@aol.com. Web: www.blackhillsbenedictine.com. Sr. Lorane Coffin, O.S.B., Prioress. Motherhouse and Novitiate of the Sisters of St. Benedict Sisters 35.

Kateri Convent, 624 Adams, 57701-0809. Tel: 605-343-6261. Email: oblatesis@juno.com. Home Visitations, particularly Native Americans, Communion to Homebound, Tutoring in elementary schools Oblate Sisters of the Blessed Sacrament 2.

PORCUPINE. *Our Lady of Lourdes School Convent*, P.O. Box 7, 57772-0007. Tel: 605-867-1056; Fax: 605-867-6141. Email: sistersusan@yahoo.com. School Sisters of Notre Dame

[D] MISCELLANEOUS

RAPID CITY. *Benedictine Convent of St. Martin Retirement Trust*, 2110-C. St. Martin Dr., 57702-9660. Tel: 605-343-8011; Fax: 605-399-2723. Email: fmartin620@aol.com. Web: www.blackhillsbenedictine.com. Sr. Mary Wegher, Trustee & Contact Person.

The Catholic Education Fund, Inc., P.O. Box 678, 57709-0678. Tel: 605-343-3541; Fax: 605-348-7985.

Catholic Parish Association Contingency Fund, Inc., P.O. Box 678, 57709-0678. Tel: 605-343-3541; Fax: 605-348-7985.

Catholic Social Service of the Diocese of Rapid City, 918 5th St., 57701. Tel: 605-348-6086; Fax: 605-348-1050. Email: css@rapidnet.com. Web: www.catholic-social-services.net. James Kinyon, Dir.

St. Martin's Community Center, 2110 C St. Martin Dr., 57702-9660. Tel: 605-343-8011; Fax: 605-399-2723. Web: www.blackhillsbenedictine.com. Sr. Edna Marie Stephenson, O.S.B., Dir.

St. Martin's Learning Center, 2110-C St. Martin Dr., 57702-9392. Tel: 605-343-2243. Email: ckovarik@gwtc.net. Sr. Carol Kovarik, O.S.B., Dir. Sisters 1; Students 21.

Priest Retirement and Aid Association/Pension Plan Board, Westhills Village, F211, 255 Texas St., 57701-7364. Tel: 605-721-3456. Most Rev. Blase J. Cupich; Rev. Msgr. Michael Woster, J.C.L., Pres.; Revs. D. Craig Cower, Exec. Sec. (Retired); Dale Kutil; Brian Lane, Vice Pres. & Recorder; Brian Fawcett.

Western South Dakota Catholic Foundation, Inc., P.O. Box 678, 57709-0678. Tel: 605-343-3541; Fax: 605-348-7985. Email: bbickett@diorc.org.

EAGLE BUTTE. *CPT, Inc.*, P.O. Box 110, 57625-0110. Tel: 605-964-3391; Fax: 605-964-3300. Rev. Thomas Westhoven, S.C.J., Dir.

Sacred Heart Center, 121 Landmark St., P.O. Box 2000, 57625-2000. Tel: 605-964-6062; Fax: 605-964-6060. Email: mcdaniel@shconline.org. Web: www.shconline.org. Frank McDaniel, Dir. Total Assisted 2,150; Total Staff 35.

HOWES. *The Diocese of Rapid City Mahpiya na Maka Okogna* Sioux Spiritual Center , 20100 Center Rd., 57748-7703. Tel: 605-985-5906; Fax: 605-985-5908. Email: ssc@gwtc.net. Web: http://puffin.creighton.edu/jesuit/ssc/. Revs. Thomas A. Lawler, S.J.; George Winzenburg, S.J. Total in Residence 2; Total Staff 6.

MANDERSON. *St. Francis Home*, P.O. Box 122, 57756-0122. Tel: 605-455-2077. Email: cmahoney@gwtc.net. Sisters Geraldine Clifford, O.S.F., Min.; Colleen Mahoney, O.S.F. Sisters of St. Francis Marycrest, Home for abandoned and abused children (Licensed) 2-18 years of age.

RELIGIOUS INSTITUTES OF MEN REPRESENTED IN THE DIOCESE

For further details refer to the corresponding bracketed number in the Religious Institutes of Men or Women section.

[1350]—*Brothers of St. Francis Xavier*—C.F.X.

[1130]—*Congregation of the Priests and Brothers of the Sacred Heart*—S.C.J.

[0690]—*Jesuit Fathers and Brothers*—S.J.

RELIGIOUS INSTITUTES OF WOMEN REPRESENTED IN THE DIOCESE

[0230]—*Benedictine Sisters of Pontifical Jurisdiction* (Rapid City, SD)—O.S.B.

[2950]—*Congregation of Notre Dame de Sion*

[1070-13]—*Dominican Sisters* (Adrian, MI)—O.P.

[2960]—*Notre Dame Sisters* (Omaha, NE)—N.D.

[3010]—*Oblate Sisters of the Blessed Sacrament* (Marty, SD)—O.S.B.S.

[2970]—*School Sisters of Notre Dame*—S.S.N.D.

[]—*Sisters of Charity of Cincinnati (Ohio)*—S.C.

[0660]—*Sisters of Christian Charity* (Wilmette, IL)—S.C.C.

[2560]—*Sisters of Mercy*—R.S.M.

[1630]—*Sisters of St. Francis of Penance and Christian Charity* (Denver, CO)—O.S.F.

[]—*Sisters of St. Francis of the Holy Family* (Dubuque)

[1580]—*Sisters of St. Francis of the Immaculate Conception* (Peoria, IL)—O.S.F.

[2980]—*Sisters of the Congregation of Notre Dame* (Ridgefield, CT)—C.N.D.

[2390]—*Siters of the Living Word*

[3320]—*Sisters of the Presentation of the B.V.M.* (Aberdeen, SD; Dubuque, IA; Fargo, ND)—P.B.V.M.

NECROLOGY

† Becht, James, (Retired)—Died Dec. 9, 2002

† Staricek, Andrew—Died Nov. 29, 2003

Diocese of Reno

(Dioecesis Renensis)

Most Reverend

PHILLIP F. STRALING, D.D.

Bishop of Reno; ordained March 19, 1959; appointed Bishop of San Bernardino July 18, 1978; installed November 6, 1978; appointed Bishop of Reno March 21, 1995; installed June 29, 1995. *290 S. Arlington Ave., Ste. 200, Reno, NV 89501.*

GAUDIUM IN CHRISTO

Pastoral Center: 290 S. Arlington Ave., Ste. 200, Reno, NV 89501. Tel: 775-329-9274; Fax: 775-348-8619.

Web: catholicreno.org

Email: dioceseofreno@catholicreno.org

Square Miles 70,852.

Erected as the Diocese of Reno by His Holiness Pope Pius XI March 27, 1931. Canonical Erection of the Diocese August 19, 1931; Redesignated Diocese of Reno-Las Vegas by Pope Paul VI, October 13, 1976; Reformed Diocese of Reno by His Holiness Pope John Paul II March 21, 1995.

Comprises the Counties of: Carson City, Churchill, Douglas, Elko, Eureka, Humboldt, Lander, Lyon, Mineral, Pershing, Storey, and Washoe.

Patrons of the Diocese: Our Lady of the Snows (August 5); The Holy Family (Sunday in the Octave of Christmas); Established through an Apostolic brief dated August 24, 1933.

Legal Title: "The Roman Catholic Bishop of Reno and His Successors, a Corporation Sole".
Legal Title: *For legal titles of parishes and diocesan institutions, consult the Pastoral Center.*

STATISTICAL OVERVIEW

Personnel	
Bishop	1
Priests: Diocesan Active in Diocese	15
Priests: Diocesan Active Outside Diocese	1
Priests: Retired, Sick or Absent	6
Number of Diocesan Priests	22
Religious Priests in Diocese	11
Total Priests in Diocese	33
Extern Priests in Diocese	14
Ordinations:	
Diocesan Priests	1
Transitional Deacons	3
Permanent Deacons	4
Permanent Deacons in Diocese	10
Total Brothers	3
Total Sisters	38
Parishes	
Parishes	28
With Resident Pastor:	
Resident Diocesan Priests	19
Resident Religious Priests	5
Without Resident Pastor:	
Administered by Priests	1
Administered by Deacons	3
Missions	6
Professional Ministry Personnel:	
Sisters	6
Lay Ministers	26
Welfare	
Catholic Hospitals	1
Total Assisted	327,750
Health Care Centers	3
Total Assisted	15,000
Day Care Centers	2
Total Assisted	277
Special Centers for Social Services	7
Total Assisted	46,562
Educational	
Diocesan Students in Other Seminaries	7
Total Seminarians	7
High Schools, Diocesan and Parish	1
Total Students	493
Elementary Schools, Diocesan and Parish	4
Total Students	1,042
Catechesis/Religious Education:	
High School Students	1,213
Elementary Students	4,313
Total Students under Catholic Instruction	7,068
Teachers in the Diocese:	
Brothers	1
Sisters	2
Lay Teachers	111
Vital Statistics	
Receptions into the Church:	
Infant Baptism Totals	1,857
Adult Baptism Totals	163
Received into Full Communion	195
First Communions	1,495
Confirmations	687
Marriages:	
Catholic	243
Interfaith	80
Total Marriages	323
Deaths	296
Total Catholic Population	91,973
Total Population	607,459

Former Bishops—Most Revs. THOMAS K. GORMAN, D.D., D.Sc.Hist., ord. June 23, 1917; appt. Bishop, April 24, 1931; consecrated July 22, 1931; appt. Coadjutor Bishop of Dallas "cum jure successionis," Feb. 8, 1952; succeeded to the See, Aug. 19, 1954; resigned Aug. 27, 1969; died Aug. 16, 1980; ROBERT J. DWYER, D.D., Ph.D., ord. June 11, 1932; appt. May 20, 1952; consecrated Aug. 5, 1952; elevated to Archiepiscopal Dignity and promoted to Portland in Oregon, Dec. 14, 1966; resigned Jan. 22, 1974; died March 24, 1976; JOSEPH GREEN, D.D., ord. July 14, 1946; appt. Titular Bishop of Trisipa and Auxiliary of Lansing, June 22, 1962; consecrated Aug. 28, 1962; appt. Bishop of Reno, March 10, 1967; installed May 25, 1967; resigned Dec. 6, 1974; died Aug. 31, 1982; NORMAN F. MCFARLAND, D.D., J.C.D. (Retired), ord. June 15, 1946; appt. Titular Bishop of Bida and Auxiliary of San Francisco, June 5, 1970; ord. Bishop, Sept. 8, 1970; appt. Apostolic Admin. of Reno, Dec. 6, 1974; appt. Bishop of Reno, Feb. 10, 1976; transferred to Orange, Dec. 29, 1986; appt. Bishop of Orange, Feb. 24, 1987; retired June 30, 1998; DANIEL F. WALSH, D.D., ord. March 30, 1963; appt. Titular Bishop of Tigia and Auxiliary of San Francisco; ord. Bishop, Sept. 24, 1981; appt. Bishop of Reno-Las Vegas, June 9, 1987; installed Aug. 6, 1987; appt. first Bishop of the newly established Diocese of Las Vegas, March 21, 1995; installed June 28, 1995; appt. Bishop of Santa Rosa April 11, 2000; installed May 22, 2000.

Bishop's Office—

Bishop—Most Rev. PHILLIP F. STRALING, D.D.

Secretary—DONNA KENNEDY. Tel: 775-329-9274, Ext. 428.

Vicar-General—Rev. GEORGE WOLF, V.G.

Chancellor—Bro. MATTHEW CUNNINGHAM, F.S.R. Tel: 775-329-9274, Ext. 429.

Secretary—JOAN TOPOIAN. Tel: 775-329-9274, Ext. 410.

Tribunal—

Judicial Vicar/Officialis—Rev. THOMAS FRANSISCUS, C.SS.R., J.C.L.

Secretary/Notary—JENY HILL. Tel: 775-329-9274, Ext. 419.

Promoter of Justice—Rev. GEORGE WOLF, V.G.

Defenders of the Bond—Revs. GEORGE WOLF, V.G.; GARY M. LUIZ, C.PP.S., J.C.L.

Judges—Revs. ALBERT M. FOSSELMAN, J.C.L.; STEPHEN FROST, J.C.L.

Advocates—Bro. MATTHEW CUNNINGHAM, F.S.R.; Revs. DAVID SCHUYLER, S.M., S.T.L., J.C.D.; CHARLES DURANTE.

Department of Education—

Superintendent of Schools—KITTY BERGIN. Tel: 775-329-9274, Ext. 430.

Office of Faith Formation and Parish Pastoral Services—NANCY WHIPPLE, Dir. Tel: 775-329-9274, Ext. 431; MONIQUE JACOBS, Assoc. Dir. Tel: 775-329-9274, Ext. 439. Secretaries: LETTY ANGUIANO. Tel: 775-329-9274, Ext. 413; BREANNA BALMUT. Tel: 775-329-9274, Ext. 434; DENIS MERLINO. Tel: 775-329-9274, Ext. 441.

Office of Faith Formation Resource Center—BREANNA BALMUT. Tel: 775-329-9274, Ext. 434.

Office of Safe Environment—JANE O'CONNOR. Tel: 775-329-9274, Ext. 445.

Office of Ethnic Ministries—MARIPAZ RAMOS, Dir. Tel: 775-329-9274, Ext. 423; MARIA DODSON, Sec. Tel: 775-329-9274, Ext. 415.

Archives—Bro. MATTHEW CUNNINGHAM, F.S.R., Chancellor. Tel: 775-329-9274, Ext. 429.

Curia—Most Rev. PHILLIP F. STRALING, D.D.; Revs. GEORGE WOLF, V.G., Moderator; TOM FRANSISCUS, C.SS.R.; Bro. MATTHEW CUNNINGHAM, F.S.R.; Ms. NANCY WHIPPLE; Mr. KEVIN DAY; Mr. MICHAEL QUILICI; Mr. TIM WANNER; MONIQUE JACOBS; Ms. KITTY BERGIN; Ms. MARIPAZ RAMOS.

Department of Stewardship and Development—MICHAEL QUILICI. Tel: 775-329-9274, Ext. 432; CARMEN GODOY, Sec. Tel: 775-329-9274, Ext. 433.

Diocesan Communications—Bro. MATTHEW CUNNINGHAM, F.S.R. Tel: 775-329-9274, Ext. 429.

Diocesan Board of Consultors—Revs. GEORGE WOLF, V.G.; ARIEL ARIAS; WILLIAM NADEAU, O.M.I.; PAUL MCCOLLUM; LARRY MORRISON; TOM FRANSISCUS, C.SS.R.; MIKE MAHONE; NORMAN KING; Bro. MATTHEW CUNNINGHAM, F.S.R.

Finance Office—

Finance Committee—Most Rev. PHILLIP F. STRALING, D.D.; Rev. GEORGE WOLF, V.G.; Ms. VIRGINIA ZORIO; Mr. ED HOUSTON; Mr. BOB ARMSTRONG; Bro. MATTHEW CUNNINGHAM, F.S.R.; Mr. TIM WANNER; Mr. RICHARD KWAPIL; Mrs. DEBBIE GRIFFIN; Mr. DENNIS PRICE; Mr. MIKE QUILICI.

Business Manager—TIM WANNER. Tel: 775-329-9274, Ext. 420.

Administrative Assistant and Employee Benefits Coordinator—JUDY LUBICH. Tel: 775-329-9274, Ext. 414.

Accountants and Bookkeepers—LINDA OETKEN. Tel: 775-329-9274, Ext. 424; ANNA HILL. Tel: 775-329-9274, Ext. 422; RITA SAN PAOLO. Tel: 775-329-9274, Ext. 435.

Frontier of the Faith—Mailing Address, P.O. Box 10930, Reno, 89510. Tel: 775-348-6628.

Director—BETTIE ENGEBRETSON. Email: fof_reno@gbis.com.

Missionary Co-Op—Bro. MATTHEW CUNNINGHAM, F.S.R. Tel: 775-329-9274, Ext. 429.

"Northern Nevada Catholic" Newspaper—MAUREEN ANGEL, Editor-in-Chief, 290 S. Arlington, Ste. 200, Reno, 89501-1713. Tel: 775-826-1010; Fax: 775-826-1010. Email: nnc@gbis.com.

Our Mother of Sorrows Cemetery—2700 N. Virginia St., Reno, 89503. Tel: 775-323-0133. *P.O. Box 8505, Reno, 89507.* Fax: 775-323-1229. Email: omos@powernet.net. SOPHIA MITCHELL, Oper. Mgr.; Sr. OFELIA ROIBAS, Counselor.

Presbyteral Council—Revs. MIKE MAHONE; GEORGE WOLF, V.G.; ARIEL ARIAS; WILLIAM NADEAU, O.M.I.; TOM FRANSISCUS, C.SS.R.; LARRY MORRISON; PAUL MCCOLLUM; NORMAN KING; Bro. MATTHEW CUNNINGHAM, F.S.R.

Priests' Personnel Board—Most Rev. PHILLIP F. STRALING, D.D.; Revs. CHARLES DURANTE; JOHN BAIN; MIKE MAHONE; GEORGE WOLF, V.G.; Bro. MATTHEW CUNNINGHAM, F.S.R.

Prison Ministry— Carson City Area: Rev. JIM SETELIK, Corpus Christi Church. Tel: 775-882-1967.

Lovelock Prison—Rev. LORENZO TORRENTE. Tel: 775-273-2189.

Elko Area—SHERRY LAGIER, Chap. Tel: 775-738-6432.

Property Management—TIM WANNER.

Respect Life Core Committee—Most Rev. PHILLIP F. STRALING, D.D.; Rev. RICHARD DEMOLEN; Ms. JULIANNA JERVIS; Mrs. MARILEE RAILTON; Ms. KATHLEEN ROSSI; Ms. PAT GLENN; Mr. DOUG PEARSON; Mr. MARK FOXWELL; Ms. CONNIE FOXWELL; Ms. JEAN SOKOL; Ms. LINDA UGALDE.

Seminary Board—Most Rev. PHILLIP F. STRALING, D.D.; Revs. CHARLES DURANTE; ROBERT SIMPSON; PAUL MCCOLLUM; MARGARET GRAHAM; Sr. MARIA AHEARN, O.C.D.

Victim Assistance Coordinator—PATRICIA R. WILLIAMS. Tel: 775-851-4020. Email: wmsfamrno@earthlink.net.

Vocations Awareness Board—Rev. CHARLES DURANTE, Chm.; Sr. MARIE LOUISE BISHOP; Mr. MIKE NEESER; Mr. ROSS BARKER; Mr. TOM HALL; Deacon RON KLONICKE; Ms. DIANE KLONICKE; Ms. LINDA WANNER.

CLERGY, PARISHES, MISSIONS AND PAROCHIAL SCHOOLS

CITY OF RENO
(WASHOE COUNTY)

1—ST. THOMAS AQUINAS CATHEDRAL (1907), Very Rev. Gregory Gilroy, O.F.M.Conv., Rector; Revs. Arthur Gamboa, O.F.M.Conv.; Manuel Galvez, O.F.M.Conv. In Res., Friar Jacob Carazo, O.F.M.Conv.
Res.: 310 W. Second St., 89503-5398. Tel: 775-329-2571; Fax: 775-329-2456.
Catechesis/Religious Program—Mary Cantwell Doblado, D.R.E. Students 238.

2—ST. ALBERT THE GREAT (1948), Rev. Robert A. Simpson.
Mailing Address: 1259 St. Albert Dr., 89503.
Res.: 1250 Wyoming Ave., 89503. Tel: 775-747-0722; Fax: 775-746-3976.
School—1255 St. Albert Dr., 89503. Tel: 775-747-3392; Fax: 775-747-6209. Mr. Patrick Perry, Prin. Lay Teachers 15; Students 282.
St. Albert's Child Development Center—1259 St. Albert Dr., 89503. Tel: 775-747-1617; Fax: 775-746-3976. Kristen Mareno, Dir.
Catechesis/Religious Program—JoElla Barrie, D.R.E. (Grades K-12). Students 298.

3—OUR LADY OF THE SNOWS (1939), Revs. John Corona; Vince Fallon, SS.CC.; Sr. Anita Minihane, R.S.M., Parish Life Admin.; Deacon Dennis Schreiner.
Office—1138 Wright St., 89509. Tel: 775-323-6894; Fax: 775-323-6749.
School—1125 Lander St., 89509. Tel: 775-322-2773; Fax: 775-322-0827. Mary E. Clark, Prin. Lay Teachers 12; Students 292.
Catechesis/Religious Program—Tel: 775-329-6147; Fax: 775-323-6749. Lauri-Ann Reinhart, D.R.E. Students 324.

4—OUR LADY OF WISDOM (1965), Revs. Charles Durante; Frank Murphy, Pastor Emeritus; Linda Wanner, Pastoral Assoc.
Mailing Address: P.O. Box 8879, 89507.
Office—1101 N. Virginia St., 89503. Tel: 775-322-4336; Fax: 775-322-3616.

5—ST. ROSE OF LIMA (1996), Rev. Thomas Donnelly.
Mailing Address: 100 Bishop Manogue Dr., 89511. Tel: 775-851-1874; Fax: 775-851-1727.
Catechesis/Religious Program—Bud Flocchini, D.R.E.; Mary Lou Flocchini, D.R.E. Students 190.
Mission—Holy Spirit 1025 N. U.S. Hwy. 395, Washoe Valley, Washoe Co. 89704. Tel: 775-849-7764.

6—ST. THERESE CHURCH OF THE LITTLE FLOWER (1947),, (St. Jude Shrine) Revs. Honesto Agustin; Antonio Quijano, M.S.; Cyril Apassa; John E. Rodriguez; Deacons Robert Ruggiero; Ron Klonicke.
Office—875 E. Plumb Ln., 89502. Tel: 775-322-2255; Fax: 775-322-0196.
Res.: 339 Urban Rd., 89509. Tel: 775-826-6579.
School—1300 Casazza Dr., 89502. Tel: 775-323-2931; Fax: 775-323-2997. Mr. David Brancamp, Prin. Sisters of Mercy 1; Lay Teachers 16; Students 309.
Catechesis/Religious Program—Tel: 775-322-3415. Sr. Carol Bettencourt, S.H.F., D.R.E. Students 735.

OUTSIDE THE CITY OF RENO

BATTLE MOUNTAIN, LANDER CO., ST. JOHN BOSCO (1940), Rev. William Paiz, C.M.F., Admin.
Mailing Address: P.O. Box 428, 89820.
Office—392 S. Reese St., 89820.
Res.: 384 S. Reese St., 89820. Tel: 775-635-2576; Fax: 775-635-5729.
Catechesis/Religious Program—Tel: 775-635-0109. Patricia Larsgaard, D.R.E. Students 117.
Mission—St. Augustine 113 Virginia St., Austin, Lander Co. 89310. Tel: 775-635-2576.

CARLIN, ELKO CO., SACRED HEART (1910), Rev. Brian Kennedy, C.SS.R.; Deacon Craig LaGier, Parish Life Coord. & Admin.
Mailing Address: P.O. Box 235, 89822.
Office—651-3rd St., 89822. Tel: 775-754-6425; Fax: 775-754-2942.
Res.: 315 Peters, 89822. Tel: 775-754-2011.

CARSON CITY, CARSON CITY CO.

1—CORPUS CHRISTI (1949), Rev. James Setelik.
Res.: 5335 Snyder Ave., 89701. Tel: 775-882-1967; Fax: 775-882-2435.
Catechesis/Religious Program—Mary Scott, D.R.E. Students 237.

2—ST. TERESA OF AVILA (1858), Revs. Gerald T. Hanley; Robert Chorey; Sr. Marie McGloin, S.A., Pastoral Assoc.; Deacon Bob Evans.
Res.: 3000 N. Lompa Ln., 89706. Tel: 775-882-1968; Fax: 775-883-7063.
School—567 S. Richmond Ave., 89703. Tel: 775-882-2079; Fax: 775-882-6135. Mr. Rick Redican, Prin. Lay Teachers 10; Students 158.
Catechesis/Religious Program—Tel: 775-882-2130. Mary Ann Randall, D.R.E. Students 695.

DAYTON, LYON CO., ST. ANN, Rev. Michael Dallmeier, O.F.M.; Deacon Roger Porcella.
Mailing Address: P.O. Box 309, 89403. Tel: 775-246-7578; Fax: 775-246-7560.

ELKO, ELKO CO., ST. JOSEPH'S (1917), Rev. Brian Kennedy, C.SS.R.; Deacon Craig LaGier, Parish Life Coord. & Admin.; Sherry LaGier, Pastoral Assoc. & Detention Min. Chap.
Office—1035 C St., 89801. Tel: 775-738-6432; Fax: 775-738-3356.
Catechesis/Religious Program—Cathy Higginbotham, D.R.E. Students 608.
Mission—St. Thomas Aquinas 619 Sixth St., P.O. Box 369, Wells, Elko Co. 89835. Tel: 775-752-3400; Fax: 775-752-3400. Rev. Julio Navas.
Mission—Our Lady of Guadalupe P.O. Box 462, Jackpot, Elko Co. 89825. Rev. Julio Navas, Admin.

EUREKA, EUREKA CO., ST. BRENDAN'S (1872), Rev. Brian Kennedy, C.SS.R.; Deacon Craig LaGier, Parish Life Coord.
Mailing Address: P.O. Box 305, 89316.
Res.: 70 N. O'Neill Ave., 89316. Tel: 775-237-5278.

FALLON, CHURCHILL CO.

1—FALLON NAVAL AIR STATION BASE CHAPEL (1977), Rev. Thomas Friedl.
Office—Naval Air Station, 4755 Pasture Rd., Bldg. 351, 89496-5000. Tel: 775-426-8563; Fax: 775-426-2742.

2—ST. PATRICK (1920), Rev. Ariel Arias.
Church & Mailing Address: 850 W. Fourth St., 89406. Tel: 775-423-2846; Fax: 775-423-5210.
Res.: 375 Tedford Ln., 89406.
Catechesis/Religious Program— Mike Golding, D.R.E.; Pam Golding, D.R.E. Students 110.

FERNLEY, LYON CO., ST. ROBERT BELLARMINE (1957), Rev. Thomas Cronin, Pastoral Admin.
Mailing Address: P.O. Box 473, 89408.
Office—190 S. West St., 89408. Tel: 775-575-4011; Fax: 775-575-7601.
Catechesis/Religious Program—Sherry Hall, D.R.E. Students 57.
Mission—St. Joseph the Worker Empire, Washoe Co. 89412.

GARDNERVILLE, DOUGLAS CO., ST. GALL (1917), Revs. William Nadeau, O.M.I.; Jorge Herrera.
Office & Mailing Address—1343 Centerville Rd., 89410. Tel: 775-782-2852; Fax: 775-782-2622.
Catechesis/Religious Program—Tel: 775-782-3784; Fax: 775-782-3930. Julie Davis, D.R.E. Students 429.

HAWTHORNE, MINERAL CO., OUR LADY OF PERPETUAL HELP (1938), Rev. Paul McCollum.
Mailing Address: 37 N. West St., Yerington, 89447.
Office—804 A St., 89415. Tel: 775-945-2020; Fax: 775-945-3559.
Res.: 794 A St., 89415.
Catechesis/Religious Program—Students 20.

INCLINE VILLAGE, WASHOE CO., ST. FRANCIS OF ASSISI (1965), Rev. Michael Q. Mahone.
Mailing Address: P.O. Box 4226, 89450. Tel: 775-831-0490; Fax: 775-831-2045.
Church: Mt. Rose Hwy. at Kelly Dr., 89450.
Catechesis/Religious Program—Students 110.

LOVELOCK, PERSHING CO., ST. JOHN THE BAPTIST (1875), Rev. Lorenzo Torrente.
Mailing Address: P.O. Box 177, 89418-0177.
Res.: 1045 Franklin Ave, 89419-0177. Tel: 775-273-2189; Fax: 775-273-1154.
Church: 1085 Franklin Ave., 89419-0177.
Catechesis/Religious Program—Students 108.

SPARKS, WASHOE CO.

1—HOLY CROSS CATHOLIC COMMUNITY (1967), Rev. George C. Wolf; Deacon Ron Schmitt; Jill McAboy, Pastoral Assoc.
Res.: 5650 Vista Blvd., 89436. Tel: 775-358-2544; Fax: 775-358-8239.
Catechesis/Religious Program—Laura Balmut, D.R.E. (Liturgy of the Word & Grades 1-7); Jill McAboy, D.R.E. (Grades 8-10 & Confirmation). Students 271.

2—IMMACULATE CONCEPTION (1904), Rev. Norman King.
Res.: 590 Pyramid Way, 89431. Tel: 775-358-5977; Fax: 775-359-3951.
Catechesis/Religious Program—Marilyn Heywood, D.R.E., (Elementary). Tel: 775-324-0555; Pat Giannotti, D.R.E., (High School). Tel: 775-358-3107. Students 156.

STEAD, WASHOE CO., ST. MICHAEL'S (1967), Rev. Thomas J. Fransiscus, C.SS.R.
Res.: 14075 Mt. Vida St., 89506. Tel: 775-972-7462; Fax: 775-972-9373.
Catechesis/Religious Program—Constance West, D.R.E. Students 83.

SUN VALLEY, WASHOE CO., ST. PETER CANISIUS (1976), Rev. Larry Morrison.
Res.: 225 E. Fifth Ave., 89433. Tel: 775-673-6800; Fax: 775-673-2028.
Catechesis/Religious Program—Tel: 775-673-6023. Christine Luna, D.R.E. Students 70.

VIRGINIA CITY, STOREY CO., ST. MARY IN THE MOUNTAINS (1862), Rev. Joseph Anthony, Admin.
Mailing Address: P.O. Box 510, 89440.
Res.: Taylor St. & E St., 89440. Tel: 775-847-9099; Fax: 775-246-7560.

WINNEMUCCA, HUMBOLDT CO., ST. PAUL (1883), Rev. Jose Issac (India).
Mailing Address: 350 Melarkey St., 89445.
Res.: Fourth St. & Melarkey St., 89445. Tel: 775-623-2928; Fax: 775-623-6816. Eleanor Taylor, Office Mgr.
Catechesis/Religious Program—Geri DeMattei, D.R.E. Students 303.
Mission—St. Alphonsus Paradise Valley, Humboldt Co. 89426.
Mission—Sacred Heart McDermitt, Humboldt Co. 89421.

YERINGTON, LYON CO., HOLY FAMILY (1901), Rev. Paul McCollum.
Res.: 37 N. West St., 89447. Tel: 775-463-2882; Fax: 775-463-2162.
Catechesis/Religious Program—Cindy Hitchcock, D.R.E. Students 119.
Mission—St. John the Baptist Wellington. Hwy. 208, P.O. Box 36, Smith Valley, Lyon Co. 89444. Tel: 775-465-2220; Fax: 775-465-9989.

ZEPHYR COVE, DOUGLAS CO., OUR LADY OF TAHOE (1966), Rev. Richard DeMolen.
Mailing Address: P.O. Box 115, 89448.
Res.: 630 Don Dr., 89448. Tel: 775-588-2080; Fax: 775-588-0211.
Catechesis/Religious Program—Gracie Connell, D.R.E. Students 85.

On Special Assignment:
Rev.—
O'Brien, John J., Chap., Washoe Medical Center, 2300 Dickerson Rd., #42, 89503.

On Duty Outside the Diocese:
Rev.—
Hoffmann, Frank, 917 Torrence St., #20, San Diego, CA 92103.

Graduate Studies:
Rev.—
Abraham, Joseph, Catholic University, Washington, DC 20064.

Leave of Absence:
Rev.—
Vieages, Harold

Absent on Sick Leave:
Rev.—
Bain, John

Retired:
Rev. Msgr.—
McFadden, Leo E., 3363 Spring Creek Cir., 89509.
Revs.—
Avella, William, 64 Jasper Ln., Dayton, 89403.
Corona, John, 1740 Lavender Ct., Minden, 89423.
Fosselman, Albert, Double Diamond/The Meadows, 1162 Tule Dr., 89511.
Herkowski, Arthur M., 1299 Flora Glen Dr., Sparks, 89434.
Wright, Thomas, 575 Vallejo, Apt. 224, Petaluma, CA 94952.

Permanent Deacons:
Evans, Robert, 877 Thompson St, Carson City, 89703. Tel: 775-883-2341
Garcia, Joseph, 1456 Molly Dr., Carson City, 89706. Tel: 775-834-3914
Gerrich, Don, 19 North West St., Yerington, 89447. Tel: 775-463-4073
Gonzales, Emilio, 1185 Sage Ocean Dr., Gardnerville, 89460. Tel: 775-783-8880
Klonicke, Ron, 490 Golden Vista, 89506. Tel: 775-971-5258
LaGier, Craig, 1035 C St., Elko, 89801. Tel: 775-738-6432
Porcella, Roger, 986 Ridgeview Dr., Carson City, 89705. Tel: 775-267-5110
Ruggiero, Robert L., 1280 Davidson Way, 89509. Tel: 775-337-0735
Schmitt, Ron, 1095 E. York Way, Sparks, 89434. Tel: 775-358-1625
Schreiner, Dennis, 525 Nancy Circle, 89503. Tel: 775-624-6864
Schumacher, Wendell, (Retired)

INSTITUTIONS LOCATED IN THE DIOCESE

[A] HIGH SCHOOLS, DIOCESAN

RENO. *Bishop Manogue High School*, 400 Bartlett St., 89512. Tel: 775-329-0011; Fax: 775-329-5961. Email: tim.petersen@bishopmanogue.org. Web: www.bishopmanogue.org. Tim Petersen, Pres. & Prin.; Martin Barrett, Devel. Dir.; Susan Smith, Business Mgr. Brothers 1; Sisters 1; Lay Teachers 36; Students 493.

[B] GENERAL HOSPITALS

RENO. *St. Mary's Central Nevada Health Care Corp.*, 235 W. Sixth St., 89520-0108. Tel: 775-770-2770; Fax: 775-770-7249. Sr. Maureen McInerney, O.P., VP - Sponsorship.

St. Mary's Foundation, 235 W. Sixth St., 89520-0108. Tel: 775-770-3020; Fax: 775-770-3545. Email: stephanie.hauk@saintmarysreno.com. Stephanie Hauk, Vice Pres. Total Staff 7.

St. Mary's Health Care Corp. dba St. Mary's Health Network , 235 W. Sixth St., 89520-0108. Tel: 775-770-3004; Fax: 775-770-3621. Web: www.saintmarysreno.com. Sr. Maureen McInerney, O.P., VP - Sponsorship; Jeff K. Bills, Pres. & CEO; Ernie Martinelli, Chm. Sisters of St. Dominic, Congregation of the Most Holy Name (Dominican Sisters, San Rafael)

St. Mary's Regional Medical Center, 235 W. Sixth St., 89520-0108. Tel: 775-323-2041; Fax: 775-770-3963. Email: linda.herman@saintmarysreno.com. Sr. Maureen McInerney, O.P., VP - Sponsorship. Tel: 775-770-3004; Jeff Bills, Pres. & CEO; Bobbie Flowers, M.A., Mgr. Spiritual Care; Revs. Ives Aniban, Chaplaincy Svcs.; Art Valmonte; Bill Bartlett, Chap.; Sr. Diane Carroll, O.P.; Valerie Willett, Chap. Sisters of the Third Order of St. Dominic, Congregation of the Most Holy Name (San Rafael, CA) Sisters 3; Total Staff 2,005; Bed Capacity 321; Patients Assisted Annually 327,750.

[C] DAY NURSERIES

RENO. *Holy Child Day Home*, 440 Reno Ave., 89509. Tel: 775-329-2979; Fax: 775-329-8537. Mrs. Karen L. Barreras, Dir. Lay Teachers 33; Boys 99; Girls 71.

[D] MONASTERIES AND RESIDENCES FOR PRIESTS AND BROTHERS

RENO. *Brothers of Our Lady of the Holy Rosary Monastery*, 232 Sunnyside Dr., 89503-3510. Tel: 775-747-4441. Email: bros-reno@moondog.net. Bros. Philip Napolitano, F.S.R.; Matthew Cunningham, F.S.R., Supr.; Edward Zuber, F.S.R. Brothers 3.

[E] CONVENTS AND RESIDENCES FOR SISTERS

RENO. *Carmelite Monastery (O.C.D.)*, 1950 La Fond Dr., 89509-3099. Tel: 775-323-3236; Fax: 775-322-1532. Email: jarc@pyramid.net. Sr. Ann Weber, Prioress. Discalced Carmelite Nuns 16.

Little Flower Convent (S.M.), 660 Casazza Dr., 89502. Tel: 775-322-5966; Fax: 775-322-5265. Sr. Elizabeth O'Neill, S.M., Contact Person. Sisters of Mercy Sisters 3.

St. Mary's Convent (O.P.), 411 W. Sixth St., 89503. Tel: 775-323-5196. Sr. Patricia Simpson, O.P., Supr. Dominican Sisters of San Rafael Sisters 9.

Sisters of the Holy Family, S.H.F., 6730 S. McCarran Blvd., 89509. Tel: 775-827-5370. Email: renoshf@juno.com. Holy Family Sisters. Sisters 3.

SPARKS. *Sisters of St. Philip Neri*, 135 Pascus Pl., 89431. Tel: 775-331-0708; Fax: 775-331-7073. Email: sisterr@nsn.k12.nv.us. Sisters 2.

[F] CAMPUS MINISTRY

RENO. *University of Nevada, Newman Community* 1101 N. Virginia St., 89503. Tel: 775-322-4336; Fax: 775-322-3616. P.O. Box 8879, 89507. Email: olwnewmancenter@gbis.com. Rev. Charles Durante, Chap. Served by Our Lady of Wisdom

[G] CATHOLIC COMMUNITY SERVICES OF NORTHERN NEVADA

RENO. *Catholic Community Services of Northern Nevada*, P.O. Box 5099, 89513-5099. 500 E. Fourth St., 89512. Tel: 775-322-7073; Fax: 775-322-8197. Email: ccsnn@gbis.com. Kevin Day, Dir.

Adoption Jaye Hill, Mgr. Tel: 775-322-7073.

Emergency Assistance Ida Yoas, Dir. Tel: 775-322-0553.

St. Vincent's Food Pantry Grace Turner, Dir. Tel: 775-786-5266.

St. Vincent's Thrift Shop James Baker, Dir. Tel: 775-322-9824.

Holy Child Day Home, 440 Reno Ave., 89509. Tel: 775-329-2979; Fax: 775-329-8537. Karen Barreras, Dir.

St. Vincent's Dining Room, P.O. Box 5099, 89513-5099. 505 W. Third St., 89503. Tel: 775-329-5363. Ray Trevino, Dir.

St. Vincent's Haven, P.O. Box 5099, 89513-5099. 1865 Montello Ave., 89506. Tel 775-329-1189. Dennis Rector, Mgr.

St. Vincent's Residence, 395 Gould St., 89502. Richard Burke, Mgr.

[H] MISCELLANEOUS

RENO. **Fertility Care Center of Reno, Inc.*, 505 S. Arlington Ave., #B-2, 89509. Tel: 775-827-5111; Fax: 775-851-2114. Ms. Julianna Jervis, Contact Person.

Nevada Catholic Conference, 290 S. Arlington Ave., Ste. 200, 89501-1713. Tel: 775-322-7412; Fax: 775-322-1838. Email: veets3@aol.com. V. Robert Payant, Exec. Dir.

RELIGIOUS INSTITUTES OF MEN REPRESENTED IN THE DIOCESE

For further details refer to the corresponding bracketed number in the Religious Institutes of Men or Women section.

[0960]—*Brothers of the Congregation of Our Lady of the Holy Rosary*—F.S.R.
[0360]—*Claretian Missionaries*—C.M.F.
[1140]—*Congregation of the Sacred Hearts of Jesus and Mary*—SS.CC.
[0480]—*Conventual Franciscans*—O.F.M.Conv.
[0520]—*Franciscan Friars*—O.F.M.
[0720]—*Missionaries of Our Lady of La Salette* Philippine Province—M.S.
[0910]—*Oblates of Mary Immaculate*—O.M.I.
[1070]—*Redemptorist Father* (San Juan Prov.)—C.SS.R.
[0990]—*Society of the Catholic Apostolate* (Irish Prov.)—S.A.C.

RELIGIOUS INSTITUTES OF WOMEN REPRESENTED IN THE DIOCESE

[0420]—*Discalced Carmelite Nuns*—O.C.D.
[1070-04]—*Dominican Sisters of San Rafael*—O.P.
[1190]—*Franciscan Sisters of the Atonement*—S.A.
[2560]—*Sisters of Mercy of Ireland* (U.S. Prov.)—R.S.M.
[2575]—*Sisters of Mercy of the Americas* (Burlingame)—R.S.M.
[1705]—*Sisters of St. Francis of Assisi*—O.S.F.
[1650]—*Sisters of St. Francis of Philadelphia*—O.S.F.
[]—*Sisters of St. Philip Neri* (Madrid, Spain)—R.F.
[1960]—*Sisters of the Holy Family*—S.H.F.

DIOCESAN CEMETERIES

RENO. *Our Mother of Sorrows Cemetery & Mausoleum*, 2700 N. Virginia St., 89503. P.O. Box 8505, 89507. Tel: 775-323-0133; Fax: 775-323-1229. Sophia Mitchell, Operations Mgr.; Sr. Ofelia Roibas, Counselor.

NECROLOGY

† Bowling, Rev. Msgr. Robert A., Reno, NV St. Therese Church of the Little Flower—Died June 14, 2003

Diocese of Richmond

(Dioecesis Richmondiensis)

Most Reverend

FRANCIS X. DILORENZO

Bishop of Richmond; ordained May 18, 1968; appointed Titular Bishop of Tigia and Auxiliary Bishop of Scranton January 26, 1988; consecrated March 8, 1988; appointed Apostolic Administrator of Honolulu October 12, 1993; succeeded to See November 29, 1994; appointed Bishop of Richmond March 31, 2004; installed May 24, 2004.

Most Reverend

WALTER F. SULLIVAN, D.D.

Bishop Emeritus of Richmond; ordained May 9, 1953; appointed Titular Bishop of Selsey and Auxiliary Bishop of Richmond October 20, 1970; consecrated December 1, 1970; appointed Apostolic Administrator of Richmond April 30, 1973; succeeded to the See, June 6, 1974; resigned September 16, 2003. *811 Cathedral Pl., Richmond, VA 23220.*

ESTABLISHED IN 1820.

Square Miles 36,711.

Comprises the State of Virginia, with the exception of the Counties of Arlington, Clarke, Culpeper, Fairfax, Fauquier, Frederick, King George, Lancaster, Loudoun, Madison, Northumberland, Orange, Page, Prince William, Rappahannock, Richmond, Shenandoah, Spottsylvania, Stafford, Warren and Westmoreland.

For legal titles of parishes and diocesan institutions, consult the Chancery Office.

The Chancery: 811 Cathedral Pl., Richmond, VA 23220-4801. Tel: 804-359-5661; Fax: 804-358-9159.

Web: www.richmonddiocese.org

Email: aedwards@richmonddiocese.org

STATISTICAL OVERVIEW

Personnel	
Retired Bishops	1
Abbots	1
Priests: Diocesan Active in Diocese	111
Priests: Diocesan Active Outside Diocese	7
Priests: Retired, Sick or Absent	45
Number of Diocesan Priests	163
Religious Priests in Diocese	37
Total Priests in Diocese	200
Extern Priests in Diocese	34
Ordinations:	
Diocesan Priests	1
Transitional Deacons	1
Permanent Deacons in Diocese	87
Total Brothers	12
Total Sisters	193
Parishes	
Parishes	146
With Resident Pastor:	
Resident Diocesan Priests	101
Resident Religious Priests	8
Without Resident Pastor:	
Administered by Priests	20
Administered by Deacons	4
Administered by Religious Women	4
Administered by Lay People	9
Missions	6
Pastoral Centers	2
Professional Ministry Personnel:	
Brothers	2
Sisters	90
Lay Ministers	483
Welfare	
Catholic Hospitals	10
Total Assisted	660,500
Homes for the Aged	18
Total Assisted	1,730
Day Care Centers	2
Total Assisted	100
Special Centers for Social Services	8
Total Assisted	11,300
Residential Care of Disabled	5
Total Assisted	300
Other Institutions	7
Total Assisted	30,000
Educational	
Diocesan Students in Other Seminaries	11
Total Seminarians	11
High Schools, Diocesan and Parish	5
Total Students	1,315
High Schools, Private	4
Total Students	831
Elementary Schools, Diocesan and Parish	24
Total Students	8,370
Elementary Schools, Private	2
Total Students	478
Non-residential Schools for the Disabled	4
Total Students	400
Catechesis/Religious Education:	
High School Students	6,029
Elementary Students	18,838
Total Students under Catholic Instruction	36,272
Teachers in the Diocese:	
Priests	8
Scholastics	4
Sisters	22
Lay Teachers	964
Vital Statistics	
Receptions into the Church:	
Infant Baptism Totals	3,523
Adult Baptism Totals	515
Received into Full Communion	610
First Communions	3,628
Confirmations	1,940
Marriages:	
Catholic	587
Interfaith	568
Total Marriages	1,155
Deaths	1,655
Total Catholic Population	212,189
Total Population	4,771,500

Former Bishops—Rt. Revs. PATRICK KELLY, D.D., first Bishop; consecrated Aug. 24, 1820; transferred to Waterford and Lismore in 1822; died Oct. 8, 1829; RICHARD V. WHELAN, D.D., second Bishop; consecrated March 21, 1841; transferred to Wheeling, July 23, 1850; died July 7, 1874; JOHN MCGILL, D.D., consecrated Nov. 10, 1850; died Jan. 14, 1872; His Eminence JAMES CARDINAL GIBBONS, D.D., consecrated August 16, 1868; Bishop of Adramyttum, and Vicar-Apostolic of North Carolina; transferred to the See of Richmond, July 30, 1872; transferred to the See of Baltimore, Oct. 3, 1877; created Cardinal Priest of S. Maria in Trastevere, June 7, 1886; died March 24, 1921; Rt. Revs. JOHN J. KEANE, D.D., consecrated Aug. 25, 1878; resigned August, 1888; rector of the Catholic University, Washington, DC; transferred to Archbishopric of Dubuque, July 24, 1900; died June 27, 1918; AUGUSTINE VAN DE VYVER, D.D., consecrated Oct. 20, 1889; died Oct. 16, 1911; DENIS JOSEPH O'CONNELL, D.D., consecrated May 3, 1908; Titular Bishop of Sebaste and Auxiliary Bishop of San Francisco; appt. Bishop of Richmond, Jan. 19, 1912; resigned Jan. 15, 1926 and appointed Titular Archbishop of Marianne; died Jan. 1, 1927; Most Revs. ANDREW J. BRENNAN, D.D., ord. December 17, 1904; consecrated Titular Bishop of Thapsus and Auxiliary Bishop of Scranton, April 25, 1923; appt. Bishop of Richmond, May 28, 1926; resigned April 14, 1945; appt. Titular Bishop of Telmissus; died May 23, 1956; PETER L. IRETON, D.D., ord. June 20, 1906; appt. Titular Bishop of Cime Coadjutor Bishop and Apostolic Administrator of Richmond, August 3, 1935; consecrated October 23, 1935; named Bishop of Richmond, April 14, 1945; named Assistant at the Pontifical Throne, May 21, 1956; died April 27, 1958; JOHN J. RUSSELL, D.D. (Retired), ord. July 8, 1923; appt. Bishop of Charleston, Jan. 28, 1950; consecrated March 14, 1950; appt. Bishop of Richmond, July 3, 1958; retired April 3, 1973; died March 17, 1993.

Central Administrative Offices

Unless otherwise indicated all Diocesan Offices are located at: *811 Cathedral Pl., Richmond, 23220-4801.* Tel: 804-359-5661; Fax: 804-358-9159.

Apostolic Administrator—His Eminence WILLIAM CARDINAL KEELER.

Vicars General—Former Delegates: Rev. Msgrs. THOMAS F. SHREVE, V.G., J.C.L., 11000 Smoke Tree Dr., Richmond, 23236. Tel: 804-794-0222; ROBERT M. PERKINS, V.G., 823 Park Ave., Richmond, 23220. Tel: 804-359-5651. Regional Delegates: Rev. Msgrs. THOMAS J. CAROLUZZA, Eastern Vicariate. Tel: 757-650-3663; ROBERT M. PERKINS, V.G., Central Vicariate. Tel: 804-359-5651; J. KENNETH RUSH, D.Min., Western Vicariate. Tel: 434-846-5245.

Chancellor—Mrs. ANNE C. EDWARDS.

Diocesan Tribunal Central Offices—3805 Cutshaw Ave., Ste. 307, Richmond, 23230-3938. Tel: 804-355-9155; Fax: 804-359-2810.

Judicial Vicar—Rev. Msgr. WILLIAM V. SULLIVAN, J.C.L., M.Ch.A.

Adjutant Judicial Vicars—Very Rev. J. SCOTT DUARTE, J.C.D.; Rev. Msgr. R. FRANCIS MUENCH, J.C.L.

Judges—Rev. Msgr. J. KENNETH RUSH, D.Min.; Revs.

WAYNE BALL, J.C.L.; MARTIN E. LAVIN, J.C.D.; RUSSELL E. SMITH, S.T.D.; MICHAEL M. DUFFY, J.C.L.; KEVIN J. O'BRIEN, S.T.B., Ph.D.; Ms. H. ROBERTA SMALL, J.C.L.

Defenders of the Bond—Rev. JOSEPH FACURA, J.C.L.; Deacon JOHN H. THOMAS; Ms. SUSAN VANNICE, J.C.L.

Field Office—

Tidewater—145 Dupre Ave., Norfolk, 23503-3423. Tel: 757-588-2941; Fax: 757-588-6247.

Ecclesiastical Notaries—Ms. ANN NIERMEYER; Mrs. DENISE RYAN; Ms. BARBARA WATTS.

Auditors—Ms. VALERIE MCAVOY.

Delegate for the Causes of Saints—Very Rev. SCOTT DUARTE. Tel: 804-355-9155.

Delegate for the Hispanic Apostolate—Rev. Msgr. MICHAEL S. SCHMIED; ELISA MONTALVO, Dir. Tel: 804-359-5661, Ext. 242; BERENICE BISSETT, Assoc. Dir. Tel: 804-359-5661.

Ethnic and Special Liturgies— Filipino, Hispanic, Korean, Vietnamese; Tridentine Latin Mass, Deaf/Hearing Impaired. Please refer to the diocesan website, or contact the Chancery office for locations and schedules.

Delegate for Ecumenism & Ecumenical Affairs—Rev. Msgr. RAYMOND A. BARTON.

Secretary to the Bishop Emeritus—Rev. PASQUALE J. APUZZO.

Special Assistant to the Bishop—Dr. STEPHEN M. COLECCHI.

Delegate for Vocations—Rev. MICHAEL A. RENNINGER; Mr. VINCENT VANDERHEIJDEN, Assoc. Dir.

Vocation Director for Promotion and Recruitment—Rev. Msgr. MICHAEL MCCARRON.

Liturgical Consultant—Rev. MICHAEL RENNINGER.

Department of Communication & Administration—Rev. PASQUALE J. APUZZO, Moderator.

Office of Communication—Rev. PASQUALE J. APUZZO, Dir.

Office of Archives—Mrs. ANNE EDWARDS, Dir.; Mr. VINCENT SANSONE, Asst. Dir.

Office of Human Resources—Rev. PASQUALE APUZZO, Acting Dir.; Mrs. ETTA SHEPPERD, Benefits Admin.

Office of Development—Mrs. KAREN BISHOP, Dir.

Office of Information Technology—Ms. JOAN PARDUE, Dir.; Mr. LEE JONES, Network Admin.; Ms. LYNN MOONEY, Programmer & Analyst.

Office of Printing—Mr. NORMAN HOWARD, Dir.

Pastoral Coordinator Program—Sr. CORA MARIE BILLINGS, R.S.M., Bishop's Liaison.

Department of Financial & Fiscal Services—Mr. JOHN F. BARRETT, Moderator.

Office of Finance—Mr. JOHN F. BARRETT, Dir.; Ms. CRYSTAL LANG, Controller.

Office of Plant Management—Mrs. SUSAN R. TEAL, Dir.

Office of Risk Management—Mr. KURT HICKMAN, Dir.

Department of Pastoral Services—Ms. DIANE BIALKOWSKI, Moderator.

Office of Christian Formation—Mr. DENNIS EEEMAN, Dir. Associate Directors: Mrs. EMILY FILIPPI; Ms. PATRICIA NOVAK.

Office of Catholic Schools—Ms. DIANE BIALKOWSKI, Supt. Assistant Superintendents: Ms. MAUREEN MCCABE; Mr. MICHAEL BECHELLI.

Office of Campus and Young Adult Ministry—Sr. DIANE GUY, S.N.D., Dir.; Bro. COSMAS RUBENCAMP, Assoc. Dir.; Mr. LEROY CRIE JR., Coord. Encounter Retreats.

Department of Social Action—Dr. STEPHEN M. COLECCHI, Moderator.

Office of Justice and Peace—Dr. STEPHEN M. COLECCHI Dir. Associate Directors: Mr. MICHAEL E. STONE; Dr. KATHLEEN KENNEY.

Appalachian Office of Justice & Peace—KATHY SCHMITT, Dir., P.O. Box 660, St. Paul, 24283. Tel: 276-762-5050.

Migrant Ministry Office—Mr. JAMES ALBRIGHT, Dir., P.O. Box 584, Accomac, 23301. Tel: 757-787-7862.

Office of Refugee & Immigration Services—Mrs. MARILYN BRESLOW, Exec. Dir.

Richmond Regional Dir.—KATHLEEN JACKSON.

Hampton Roads Regional Dir.—KAREN KURILKO, 1615 Kecoughtan Rd., Hampton, 23661. Tel: 757-247-3600.

Norfolk (Immigration Services)—1802 Ashland Ave., Norfolk, 23509-1236. Tel: 757-623-9131.

Roanoke Regional Dir.—BARBARA SMITH, 1106 9th St., S.E., Roanoke, 24013. Tel: 540-342-7561.

Ministry with Older Adults—MARY ELLEN COX, Coord. Tel: 804-227-3116.

Office of Black Catholics—Sr. CORA MARIE BILLINGS, R.S.M., Dir.

Diocesan Councils and Organizations

Apostleship of the Sea—STELLA MARRIS; Rev. Msgr. SANTIAGO C. FRIAS, 155 W. Government Ave., Norfolk, 23503. Tel: 757-623-4222.

Catholic Campaign for Human Development—Mr. MICHAEL STONE, Diocesan Dir.

Catholic Relief Services—Dr. KATHLEEN KENNEY.

Catholic Daughters of America—ANNA PATTI, State Regent, 1020 Charity Dr., Virginia Beach, 23455. Tel: 757-363-2460.

Catholic Golden Age—Sr. ROSE O'BRIEN, C.B.S., 5715 Monument Ave., Richmond, 23226.

"Catholic Virginian" (Diocesan Newspaper)—Mr. STEPHEN S. NEILL, Editor, P.O. Box 26843, Richmond, 23261. Tel: 804-359-5654; Fax: 804-359-5689; Ms. ROBIN PRICE, Mng. Editor; Mrs. JUDITH LINDFORS, Business Mgr. & Circulation Dir.

Council of Catholic Women—Mrs. CHARLENE FOUGHNER, 408 Loura Ct., Hampton, 23666.

Catholic Women's Club—MIDGE SCANNELL, Pres., 13 Glenbrooke Circle E., Richmond, 23229. Tel: 804-282-5327.

Cemeteries—Rev. GEORGE E. ZAHN, Dir. Tel: 804-329-0473.

Councilium Board for Education—Ms. MAUREEN MCCABE, 811 Cathedral Pl., Richmond, 23220. Tel: 804-359-5661.

Council of Priests— See Presbyteral Council

Cursillo—Lay Co-Dirs.: ELLIE HENRIETTA; JEFF HENRIETTA, Rte. 3, Box 965, Louisa, 23093. Tel: 804-589-2139.

Catholic Charities—Dr. STEPHEN M. COLECCHI, Diocesan Dir.

Commonwealth Catholic Charities—1512 Willow Lawn Dr., Richmond, 23230-0565. Tel: 804-285-5900. Rev. DAVID J. BERGNER, S.D.S., Exec. Dir.

Catholic Charities of Hampton Roads, Inc.—4855 Princess Anne Rd., Virginia Beach, 23462. Tel: 757-467-7707. Mrs. MARGARET ROBERTSON, Exec. Dir.

Ecumenical Officer—Rev. Msgr. RAYMOND A. BARTON, 712 Little Neck Rd., Virginia Beach, 23452. Tel: 757-498-7834.

Finance Council—JOSEPH PETRO, 505 Helm Dr., Newport News, 23602.

Haitian Ministry Commission—Bro. COSMOS RUBENCAMP, Exec. Sec., 811 Cathedral Pl., Richmond, 23220. Tel: 804-359-5661.

Holy Childhood Association—Rev. Msgr. THOMAS F. SHREVE, V.G., J.C.L.

Justice & Peace Commission—Dr. STEPHEN M. COLECCHI.

Knights of Columbus—RICHARD C. HEAD, State Deputy, 6637 Rock Lawn Dr., Clifton, 20124-2527.

Nocturnal Adoration Society—Rev. JAMES KAUFFMANN, 300 N. Sheppard St., Richmond, 23220.

Diocesan Pastoral Council—VACANT.

Diocesan School Board—Mr. JAMES GREER, Chm., 3202 Woodland Rd., Glen Allen, 23060.

Pax Christi Richmond—Mr. JOHN GALLINI, 2425 Triton Dr., Richmond, 23235.

Pax Christi Virginia—ADELE DELLA-VALLE RAUTH; BOB DELLA-VALLE RAUTH, 110 Lee Dr., Huddleston, 24104.

Presbyteral Council—VACANT.

Propagation of the Faith—Rev. Msgr. THOMAS F. SHREVE, V.G., J.C.L.

Respect Life—Mr. MICHAEL E. STONE, Coord.

Diocesan AIDS Task Force—Dr. KATHLEEN KENNEY, 811 Cathedral Place, Richmond, 23220. Tel: 804-359-5661.

Secular Carmelite Communities—

Community of the Holy Spirit—SUNNI COWLING, O.C.D.S., Pres., 1211 Mt. Erin Dr., Richmond, 23231.

Community of Our Lady of the Annunciation—TIRA KNIPSEL, O.C.D.S., Pres., 1288 Alanton Dr., Virginia Beach, 23454.

Serra Club of Richmond—JOHN STROTMEYER, 1000 Beveridge Rd., Richmond, 23226.

Scouting (Boys & Girls)—Rev. BRIAN RAFFERTY, Chap. Tel: 757-622-1120; PAUL JANKA, Pres. Tel: 757-424-2619; Mr. JIM TALBERT. Tel: 804-272-1374.

Sowers of Justice—Dr. STEPHEN M. COLECCHI.

Victim Assistance Coordinator—Rev. PASQUALE J. APUZZO. Tel: 804-359-5661. Email: papuzzo@richmonddiocese.org.

Youth Ministry Council—Ms. PATRICIA NOVAK, 811 Cathedral Pl., Richmond, 23220.

CLERGY, PARISHES, MISSIONS AND PAROCHIAL SCHOOLS

CITY OF RICHMOND

1—CATHEDRAL OF THE SACRED HEART (1906), [JC] Most Rev. Walter F. Sullivan, D.D., Pastor Emeritus (Retired); Rev. Msgr. Robert M. Perkins, V.G., Rector; Deacons Melvin Dowdy; Marshall Banks.
Bishop's Office—811 Cathedral Pl., 23220-4801. Tel: 804-359-5661; Fax: 804-358-9159.
Cathedral Office—823 Park Ave., 23220. Tel: 804-359-5651; Fax: 804-358-8043.
Church: 18 N. Laurel, 23220.
Catechesis/Religious Program—Students 146.

2—ST. AUGUSTINE (Chesterfield Co.) (1973), Rev. Msgr. Michael S. Schmied; Deacons Eric Broughton; Eugene Corrigan.
Res.: 9608 Verlinda Ct., 23237. Tel: 804-778-4842.
Church: Corner of Hopkins & Beulah Rd., 23237. Tel: 804-275-7962; Fax: 804-271-4604.
Catechesis/Religious Program—Students 465.

3—ST. BENEDICT (1911), [JC] Rev. James Kauffmann.
Mailing Address: 206 N. Belmont Ave., 23221.
Res.: 1129 West Ave., 23220. Tel: 804-358-2427; Fax: 804-355-5112.
Church: 300 N. Sheppard St., 23221-2407. Tel: 804-254-8810; Fax: 804-355-5112.
School—3100 Grove Ave., 23221. Tel: 804-254-8850; Fax: 804-254-9163. Mr. Ed Rossmore, Prin. Lay Teachers 18; Students 242.
Catechesis/Religious Program—Students 95.

4—ST. BRIDGET (Henrico Co.) (1949), Revs. Michael Renninger; Kenneth J. Shuping; John A. Arkestyn; Robert Giovenco.
Church: 6006 Three Chopt Rd., 23226-2797. Tel: 804-282-9511; Fax: 804-285-7227.
School—6011 York Rd., 23226. Tel: 804-288-1994; Fax: 804-288-1994. Ms. Anne T. Carroll, Prin. Lay Teachers 28; Students 459.
Catechesis/Religious Program—Students 490.

5—CHURCH OF THE EPIPHANY (Chesterfield Co.) (1979), Rev. Msgr. Thomas F. Shreve, V.G., J.C.L.
Mailing Address: 11000 Smoketree Dr., 23236-3144. Tel: 804-794-0222; Fax: 804-378-2013.
School— See St. Edward, Richmond.
Catechesis/Religious Program—Students 799.

6—CHURCH OF THE VIETNAMESE MARTYRS (1983), (Vietnamese), Rev. Msgr. Joseph Than Xuan Pham.
Mailing Address: 12500 Patterson Ave., 23233. Tel: 804-784-5450; Fax: 804-784-9822. In Res., Rev. John M. David.
Catechesis/Religious Program—Students 115.

7—ST. EDWARD THE CONFESSOR (1959), Rev. Donald H. Lemay; Deacons Robert Ewan; James Greer; Thomas B. Elliott.
Mailing Address: 2700 Dolfield Rd., 23235-2618. Tel: 804-272-2948; Fax: 804-560-3565.
Res.: 10908 Ashburn Rd., 23235-2618. Tel: 804-330-0772.
Church: Huguenot Rd. & Dolfield Dr., 23235.
School—Regional School St. Edward-Epiphany, 10701 Huguenot Rd., 23235. Tel: 804-272-2881; Fax: 804-272-2904. Ms. Georgette Richards, Prin. Lay Teachers 23; Students 494.
Catechesis/Religious Program—Students 559.

8—ST. ELIZABETH (1923), (African American), [JC] Sr. Cora Marie Billings, R.S.M., Pastoral Coord.
Mailing Address: 1301 Victor St., 23222-3935. Tel: 804-329-4599; Fax: 804-321-0741.
Church: 2712 Second Ave., 23222. Fax: 804-321-0741.
School—All Saints, 3418 Noble Ave., 23222. Tel: 804-329-7524; Fax: 804-321-1538. Mr. Kenneth Soistman, Prin.
Catechesis/Religious Program—Students 23.

9—ST. GABRIEL (Chesterfield Co.) (1997), Rev. Pasquale Apuzzo.
Mailing Address: P.O. Box 129, Moseley, 23120. Tel: 804-639-6712; Fax: 804-639-6591.
Catechesis/Religious Program—Students 705.

10—HOLY ROSARY (1953), (African American), Rev. Msgr. Walter Barrett.
Parish Office & Mailing Address—1218 N. 34th St., 23223-0416. Tel: 804-222-1105; Fax: 804-226-2204.
Res.: 901 Hunters Run Dr., 23223. Tel: 804-343-7111.
Church: N. 33rd & S St., 23223.
Catechesis/Religious Program—Students 50.

11—ST. JOSEPH (1991), Rev. Adrian W. Harmening, O.S.B.
828 Buford Rd., 23235. Tel: 804-342-1319; 804-320-4932; Fax: 804-355-5112; 804-320-4050.
Catechesis/Religious Program—Tel: 804-744-0075. Students 87.

12—ST. KIM TAEGON (1986), (Korean), Rev. Paul P. Cho.
Mailing Address: 3103 Maury St., 23224-3542. Tel: 804-232-0993; Fax: 804-232-0995.
Church: 3100 Logandale Ave., 23224.
Catechesis/Religious Program—Students 49.

13—ST. MARY (1962), Rev. Walter G. Lewis; Sr. Pat McCarthy, S.F.C.C., Pastoral Assoc.; Deacons Frank Baskind; Chuck Kamper.
Mailing Address: 9505 Gayton Rd., 23229-5319. Tel: 804-740-4044; Fax: 804-740-2197.
School—9501 Gayton Rd., 23229. Tel: 804-740-1048; Fax: 804-740-1310. Mrs. Judith Regec, Prin.

Lay Teachers 27; Students 417.
Catechesis/Religious Program—Students 530.
14—ST. MICHAEL (Glen Allen) (1992), Rev. John E. Leonard; Deacons David Nemetz; Andrew Ferguson; Curtis Hornstra.
Mailing Address: 4491 Springfield Rd., Glen Allen, 23060. Tel: 804-527-1037; Fax: 804-527-1039.
Catechesis/Religious Program—Students 958.
15—OUR LADY OF LOURDES (Henrico Co.) (1944), [JC] Revs. Steven R. Rule; Robert Griffen. In Res., Rev. Charles Fisher.
Church: 8200 Woodman Rd., 23228-3237. Tel: 804-262-7315; Fax: 804-262-7337.
School—Tel: 804-262-1770; Fax: 804-262-1437. Lucy R. Reilley, Prin. Lay Teachers 26; Students 403.
Catechesis/Religious Program—Tel: 804-262-7315; Fax: 804-262-7337. Students 282.
16—ST. PATRICK (1859), Rev. Leo G. Gagnon (MAN) (Retired), Richmond, VA St. Patrick's; Ms. Dorothy Mann.
Mailing Address: 213 N. 25th St., 23223-7115. Tel: 804-648-0504; Fax: 804-648-5216.
School—2600 E. Grace St., 23223. Tel: 804-648-3621; Fax: 804-648-3622. Mr. David Urban, Prin. Lay Teachers 16; Students 196.
17—ST. PAUL (1921), [CEM] Revs. George E. Zahn; Patricio Torres-Lisboa.
Mailing Address: 909 Rennie Ave., 23227. Tel: 804-329-0473; 804-329-5512; Fax: 804-321-6454. In Res., Rev. Frederick J. Feusahrens.
School—All Saints, 3418 Noble Ave., 23227. Tel: 804-329-7524; Fax: 804-321-1538. Mr. Kenneth Soistman, Prin. Lay Teachers 18; Students 203.
Catechesis/Religious Program—Students 93.
18—ST. PETER (1834), [JC] Rev. Robert A. Brownell.
Mailing Address: P.O. Box 933, 23218-0933. Tel: 804-643-4315; Fax: 804-783-6120.
Res.: 4030 Forest Hill Ave., Apt. 27, 23225. Tel: 804-231-3941.
Church: 800 E. Grace St., 23219.
Catechesis/Religious Program—Students 9.
19—SACRED HEART (1901), [JC] Rev. David Stokes, S.J.; Deacon Mark Matte.
Mailing Address: 1415 Perry St., 23224-2057. In Res., Rev. G. Harry Hock, S.J.
Res.: 1409 Perry St., 23224. Tel: 804-230-6430; 804-232-8964 (Office); Fax: 804-231-9931.
Church: 1401 Perry St., 23224.

OUTSIDE THE CITY OF RICHMOND

ABINGDON, WASHINGTON CO., CHRIST THE KING (1983), Rev. Paul Maier.
Res. & Mailing Address: P.O. Box 1201, 24212-1201. Tel: 276-628-2941; Fax: 276-783-7282.
Church: 820 E. Main St., 24212.
Catechesis/Religious Program—Students 57.
AMELIA, GOOD SAMARITAN (1980), Deacon George C. Stonikinis Jr., Admin.
Mailing Address: P.O. Box 759, 23002. Tel: 434-392-6639.
Catechesis/Religious Program—Students 10.
AMHERST, AMHERST CO., ST. FRANCIS OF ASSISI (1995), Rev. Daniel Kelly.
Mailing Address: P.O. Box 663, 24521. Tel: 434-263-8509.
Catechesis/Religious Program—Students 5.
APPOMATTOX, APPOMATTOX CO., OUR LADY OF PEACE (1982), Rev. David L. Nott.
Mailing Address: P.O. Box 668, 24522-0668. Tel: 434-352-0104.
Church: Intersection of Rte. 631 & Rte. 627, 24522.
Catechesis/Religious Program—
ASHLAND, HANOVER CO., ST. ANN (1892), Rev. Msgr. William V. Sullivan, J.C.L., M.Ch.A.
Church & Mailing Address: 105 S. Snead St., 23005-1811. Tel: 804-798-5039; Fax: 804-798-5072. Email: mail@st-anns-online.com.
Res.: 202 Thompson St., 23005-1514. Tel: 804-752-5902.
Catechesis/Religious Program—Students 238.
BEDFORD, BEDFORD CO., HOLY NAME OF MARY (1874), Rev. Stephen McNally; Deacon Raymond Roderique.
Mailing Address: 1307 Oakwood St., 24523-1613. Tel: 540-586-8988; Fax: 540-587-9080.
Res.: 1531 Newton Cir., 24523. Tel: 540-586-9271.
Catechesis/Religious Program—Students 92.
BIG STONE GAP, WISE CO., SACRED HEART (1902), Rev. James Fosnot; Deacon Barron Flanary. In Res., Rev. Leslie Schmidt, G.H.M.
Rectory—1821 Holton Ave., 24219-2611. Tel: 276-523-6546; Fax: 276-523-1602.
Catechesis/Religious Program—Tel: 276-523-1588. Students 30.
BLACKSBURG, MONTGOMERY CO., ST. MARY & NEWMAN COMMUNITY (1938), Revs. James M. Arsenault; Richard Mooney, Campus Min.; Deacons Mike Ellerbrock; Jim Keaney; Ms. Kathy St. Marie, Campus Min.
Mailing Address: 706 Harding Ave., N.E., 24060-3618. Tel: 540-552-1091; Fax: 540-953-2962.
Res.: 1211 Old Mill Rd., 24060. Tel: 540-951-2136.
Newman Community— 203 Otey St., 24060. Tel: 540-951-0032.
Catechesis/Religious Program—Students 397.
BLACKSTONE, NOTTOWAY CO., IMMACULATE HEART OF MARY (1947), Rev. Anthony Dinges; Mrs. Therese Mansfield, Pastoral Coord.
Mailing Address: P.O. Box 266, 23824-0266. Tel: 804-292-5535; Fax: 804-292-5535.
Church: 903 S. Main St., 23824.
Catechesis/Religious Program—Students 23.
BRISTOL, BRISTOL CO., ST. ANNE (1903), [CEM] Rev. Timothy E. Keeney; Deacon Harry Hall, Pastoral Assoc.
Mailing Address: 350 Euclid Ave., 24201-4014. Tel: 276-669-8200; Fax: 276-669-7825.
Res.: 922 Chester St., 24201. Tel: 276-466-4776.
School—300 Euclid Ave., 24201. Tel: 276-669-0048; Fax: 276-669-3523. Dr. Jean Green, Prin. Lay Teachers 26; Students 305.
Catechesis/Religious Program—Students 170.
BROOKNEAL, CAMPBELL CO., ST. ELIZABETH OF HUNGARY (1989), Sr. Edna N. Maier, Pastoral Coord.
Mailing Address: 374 Juniper Cliff Rd., P.O. Box 1097, 24528.
Res.: 1306 N. Main St., South Boston, 24592. Tel: 434-517-0349.
Catechesis/Religious Program—Students 3.
BUCKINGHAM, CHURCH OF THE NATIVITY (1981), [CEM] Mr. Robert Lloyd Brown, Admin.
Mailing Address: P.O. Box 241, 23921-0241. Tel: 434-969-3306.
Church: Rte. 60 E., 23921. Fax: 434-969-1508.
BUCKNER, LOUISA CO., IMMACULATE CONCEPTION (1876), Rev. Rodney Rodis; Deacon Joseph Milkevitch.
Mailing Address: P.O. Box 40, Mineral, 23117-0040. Tel: 540-894-4266; Fax: 540-894-4993.
Church: 1107 Frederick Hall Rd., 23024.
Catechesis/Religious Program—Students 28.
CAPE CHARLES, NORTHAMPTON CO., ST. CHARLES (1886), Rev. J. Michael Breslin; Deacon Donald Donovan.
Mailing Address: 545 Randolph Ave., 23310-3305. Tel: 757-331-1724; Fax: 757-331-2040.
Catechesis/Religious Program—Students 12.
CAROLINE COUNTY, CAROLINE CO., ST. MARY OF THE ANNUNCIATION (1914), [CEM 2] Very Rev. J. Scott Duarte, J.C.D.
Mailing Address: P.O. Box 396, Ladysmith, 22501.
Office & Church: 10306 Ladysmith Rd., Ladysmith, 22501. Tel: 804-448-9064; Fax: 804-448-5464.
Catechesis/Religious Program—Students 62.
CHARLOTTESVILLE, ALBEMARLE CO.
1—CHURCH OF THE HOLY COMFORTER (1880), Rev. Dennis Murphy; Deacon Joseph Morlino.
Mailing Address: 208 E. Jefferson St., 22902-5105. Tel: 434-295-7185; Fax: 434-295-7001.
Res.: 660 Evergreen Ave., 22902. Tel: 434-977-5859.
Catechesis/Religious Program—Tel: 434-295-6559. Students 92.
2—CHURCH OF THE INCARNATION (1976), Revs. Gregory Kandt; Bernard Taylor; Deacon Christopher Morash.
Office—1465 Incarnation Dr., 22901-1716. Tel: 434-973-4381; Fax: 434-973-1757.
Res.: 2414 Commonwealth Dr., 22901. Tel: 434-978-7544.
School—Charlottesville Catholic School, 1205 Pen Park Rd., 22901. Tel: 434-964-0400; Fax: 434-964-1373. Dr. Grace Viere, Prin.; Daniel G. Dolan, Pres.
Catechesis/Religious Program—Students 490.
3—ST. THOMAS AQUINAS (1963), [JC] Revs. Brian Mulcahy, O.P.; Thomas J. Blau; Norman Haddad; Deacon Frank Veraart.
Mailing Address: 331 Kent Rd., 22903. In Res., Rev. Augustine Thompson.
Office—Tel: 434-293-8081; 434-293-6472; Fax: 434-296-1941.
Res.: 308 Alderman Rd., 22903. Tel: 434-977-5658.
Church: 401 Alderman Rd., 22903.
Catechesis/Religious Program—Students 445.
CHESAPEAKE, CHESAPEAKE CO.
1—ST. MARY (1915), Rev. Marion Karzeniowski; Sr. Bernice McCourt, S.N.D., Pastoral Coord.
Mailing Address: P.O. Box 174-B, 23321-0174. Tel: 757-488-2663; Fax: 757-488-9237.
Church: 536 Homestead Rd., 23321.
Catechesis/Religious Program—Students 58.
2—PRINCE OF PEACE (1975), Rev. Christian Haydinger; Deacons Nicholas Marino; Michael Moro.
Mailing Address: 621 Cedar Rd., 23322. Tel: 757-547-0356; 757-547-3903; Fax: 757-436-6477.
Res.: 303 Elberon Ct., 23322. Tel: 757-547-2951.
Catechesis/Religious Program—Students 858.
3—ST. STEPHEN, MARTYR (1997), Rev. James E. Gordon.
Mailing Address: 1544 S. Battlefield Blvd., 23322. Tel: 757-421-7416; Fax: 757-421-7488.
Res.: 1117 Vineyard Dr., 23322. Tel: 757-546-9400.
Catechesis/Religious Program—Students 532.
4—ST. THERESE OF LISIEUX (1954), Rev. Robert L. Cummins.
Mailing Address: 4137 Portsmouth Blvd., 23321-2127. Tel: 757-488-2553; Fax: 757-465-4086.
Res.: 3908 Parkway Rd., 23321.
Catechesis/Religious Program—Students 520.
CHINCOTEAGUE, ACCOMACK CO., ST. ANDREW (1977), Rev. Paschal Kneip, O.S.B.
Mailing Address: 6319 Mumford St., 23336-0229. Tel: 757-336-5432; Fax: 757-336-3515.
Church: 6288 Church St., 23336.
Catechesis/Religious Program—Tel: 757-336-1209. Students 27.
CHRISTIANSBURG, MONTGOMERY CO., HOLY SPIRIT CATHOLIC CHURCH (1995), Rev. John Prinelli.
Mailing Address: P.O. Box 98, 24068.
Our Savior Lutheran Church: 1845 Cambria Rd., 24073. Tel: 540-381-0299; 540-921-3547; Fax: 540-921-3547.
Catechesis/Religious Program—Students 48.
CLARKSVILLE, MECKLENBURG CO., ST. CATHERINE OF SIENA (1947), Rev. Silvio Kaberia; Deacon John Sadowski.
Mailing Address: P.O. Box 1537, 23927.
Res.: 810 Market St., 23927. Tel: 434-374-5040.
Church: 805 Virginia Ave., 23927. Tel: 434-374-8408; Fax: 434-374-9442.
Catechesis/Religious Program—Tel: 434-374-5028. Students 13.
CLIFTON FORGE, ALLEGHANY CO., ST. JOSEPH (1889), [CEM] Rev. Louis Benoit.
Mailing Address: 620 Jefferson Ave., 24422-1715. Tel: 540-863-5371.
Catechesis/Religious Program—Students 50.
CLINTWOOD, DICKENSON CO., ST. JOSEPH (1979), Rev. Robert B. Rademacher, G.H.M.; Christine Ramirez, Pastoral Coord.
Mailing Address: P.O. Box 1250, 24228-1250. Tel: 276-926-5451.
Church: Main St., 24228.
Catechesis/Religious Program—Students 4.
COLONIAL HEIGHTS, COLONIAL HEIGHTS CO., ST. ANN (1925), [CEM] Rev. James Cowles.
Mailing Address: 17111 Jefferson Davis Hwy., 23834-5396. Tel: 804-526-2548; Fax: 804-526-1922.
Res.: 12861 Percival St., Chester, 23831. Tel: 804-796-9342.
Catechesis/Religious Program—Tel: 804-526-1860. Students 522.
COLUMBIA, FLUVANNA CO., ST. JOSEPH/SHRINE OF ST. KATHARINE DREXEL (1967), Rev. Gerald A. Przywara.
Mailing Address: P.O. Box 808, 23038-0808. Tel: 804-842-3970; Fax: 804-589-4463.
Res.: 15 Dogleg Rd., Palmyra, 22963. Tel: 804-589-5200.
Catechesis/Religious Program—Students 15.
COVINGTON, ALLEGHANY CO., SACRED HEART (1924), Rev. Louis Benoit.
Office—214 W. Locust St., 24426-1537. Tel: 540-965-5821; Fax: 540-962-2147.
Res.: 222 W. Locust St., 24426-1537. Tel: 540-962-6541.
Catechesis/Religious Program—Students 8.
CREWE, NOTTOWAY CO., ST. JOHN THE BAPTIST (1939), Rev. Anthony Dinges; Mrs. Therese Mansfield, Pastoral Coord.
Mailing Address: 102 Oliver Ave., 23930-1410. Tel: 434-645-7509; Fax: 434-292-5535.
Catechesis/Religious Program—Students 12.
Mission—Sacred Heart (1913), P.O. Box 62, Meherrin, Prince Edward 23954. Tel: 434-736-9390.
DANVILLE, PITTSYLVANIA CO., SACRED HEART (1878), Rev. Charles Briendel.
Mailing Address: 538 Central Blvd., 24541. Tel: 434-792-9456; Fax: 434-792-9463.
Res.: 154 College Ave., 24541. Tel: 434-792-0081.
School—540 Central Blvd., 24541. Tel: 434-793-2656; Fax: 434-793-2658. Kimberly Meadows, Prin. Lay Teachers 36; Students 367.
Catechesis/Religious Program—Students 44.
DINWIDDIE, DINWIDDIE CO., ST. JOHN (1907), [CEM] Rev. John J. Martinez, S.J.; Deacon Matthew MacLaughlin.
Mailing Address: 7215 Squirrel Level Rd., Petersburg, 23805-7035. Tel: 804-861-0123; Fax: 804-861-0123.
Church: Squirrel Level Rd. & Flank Rd., 23805.
Catechesis/Religious Program—Students 33.
ELKTON, ROCKINGHAM CO., HOLY INFANT (1953), Rev. Daniel Bain.
Mailing Address: 101 W. Marshall Ave., 22827-1221. Tel: 540-298-1341.
Church: Rte. 33 & Rte. 340, 22827.
Catechesis/Religious Program—Students 7.
EMPORIA, GREENSVILLE CO., ST. RICHARD (1940), Rev. Dennis McAuliffe (BRK).
Mailing Address: 117 Laurel St., 23847-2506. Tel: 434-636-7782 (Rectory); Fax: 434-636-4549.
Catechesis/Religious Program—
FARMVILLE, PRINCE EDWARD CO., ST. THERESA (1939), Rev. Carl DeSouza; Deacons Emmett R. McLane;

George C. Stonikinis Jr.
Church & Mailing Address: 709 Buffalo St., 23901-1109. Tel: 434-392-3934; Fax: 434-392-1611.
Res.: 400 Putney St., 23901. Tel: 434-315-0311.
Catechesis / Religious Program—Students 80.
Longwood University—
Hampden-Sydney College—

FINCASTLE, BOTETOURT CO., CHURCH OF THE TRANSFIGURATION (1989), Revs. George C. Heise, Admin.; Ben F. Calip (Philippines); Deacon Mark D. Allison.
Mailing Address: P.O. Box 416, 24090-0416. Tel: 540-473-2656; Fax: 540-473-2193.
Church: 7624 Roanoke Rd., 24090.
Catechesis / Religious Program—Students 194.
Mission—St. John the Evangelist

FORT MONROE, HAMPTON CO., ST. MARY STAR OF THE SEA (1860), Rev. Peter Creed.
Mailing Address: 7 Frank Ln., 23651-1010. Tel: 757-722-9855; 757-722-3138; Fax: 757-726-0083.
School—St. Mary Star of the Sea, 14 N. Willard Ave., Hampton, 23663. Tel: 757-723-6358; Fax: 757-723-7580. Sr. Marie Blanchette Cummings, Prin. Sisters 4; Lay Teachers 12; Students 206.
Catechesis / Religious Program—Students 18.

FRANKLIN, SOUTHAMPTON CO., ST. JUDE (1948), Rev. Martin Lavin, J.C.L.
Mailing Address: 1014 Clay St., 23851-1309. Tel: 757-569-9600; Fax: 757-562-6974.
Catechesis / Religious Program—Students 76.
Mission—Infant of Prague Rte. 460, Wakefield, Southampton Co. 23888.

GATE CITY, SCOTT CO., ST. BERNARD (1956), Rev. Roland Hautz, G.H.M.
Mailing Address: 105 Linda St., 24251. Tel: 276-386-9665; Fax: 276-386-3902.
Catechesis / Religious Program—Students 10.
Mission—St. Patrick (1946), Rte. 1, P.O. Box 135, Dungannon, Scott 24245. Tel: 276-995-2305.

GLOUCESTER, GLOUCESTER CO., ST. THERESE, THE LITTLE FLOWER (1939), Rev. Lee Guarnieri.
Mailing Address & Church: 6262 Main St., 23061. Tel: 804-693-5439.
Office—Tel: 804-693-5939; Fax: 804-693-4766.
Res.: 6262 Main St., 23061.
Catechesis / Religious Program—Tel: 804-693-5939. Students 195.

HAMPTON, HAMPTON CO.

1—CATHOLIC COMMUNITY OF THE KOREAN MARTYRS (1989), (Korean), Rev. Antonius Hyo Kang Jang.
Mailing Address: 2018 Bay Ave., 23661. Tel: 757-245-4485; 757-303-3423; Fax: 757-247-8828.
Catechesis / Religious Program—Students 50.

2—IMMACULATE CONCEPTION (1968), Rev. Robert E. French.
Mailing & Res.: P.O. Box 7382, 23666-0382. Tel: 757-826-0050.
Church: 2150 Cunningham Dr., 23666. Tel: 757-826-0393; Fax: 757-825-0855.
Catechesis / Religious Program—Students 152.

3—ST. JOSEPH (1968), Revs. Anthony Morris, C.SS.R.; Donald Winter, C.SS.R.; Gerald Schreiber, C.SS.R.; Deacon Jose M. Gonzalez.
Mailing Address: P.O. Box 4126, 23664-0126.
Res.: 410 Buckroe Ave., 23664-0126. Tel: 757-851-1711.
Church: 414 Buckroe Ave., 23664-0126. Tel: 757-851-8800; Fax: 757-851-1875.
Catechesis / Religious Program—Students 237.

4—OUR LADY OF VIETNAM CHAPEL (1994), (Vietnamese), Rev. Joseph Hai Nguyen, Ph.D.
Mailing Address: 1806 Ashland Ave., Norfolk, 23509. Tel: 757-622-5345; 757-722-2657.
Chapel— 1307 LaSalle Ave., 23669. Fax: 757-622-4248.

5—ST. ROSE OF LIMA (1948), Rev. Donald J. Cavey.
Mailing Address: 2114 Bay Ave., 23661. Tel: 757-245-5513; Fax: 757-245-1277.
Res.: 2108 Bay Ave., 23661. Tel: 757-245-6313.
Catechesis / Religious Program—Students 14.

HARRISONBURG, ROCKINGHAM CO., BLESSED SACRAMENT (1906), Revs. James E. Gallagher; John A. Grace; Deacon Fred La Spina.
Mailing Address & Church: 154 N. Main St., 22802. Tel: 540-434-4341; 540-434-8601; Fax: 540-434-4655.
Res.: 843 Meadowlark Dr., 22802. Tel: 540-433-5666.
Catechesis / Religious Program—Tel: 540-434-5549. Students 525.

HIGHLAND SPRINGS, HENRICO CO., ST. JOHN (1929), Rev. Wayne Ball.
Mailing Address: P.O. Box 190, 23075-0190. Tel: 804-737-8028; 804-737-5732; Fax: 804-328-4683.
Res.: 7973 Bear Grass Ln., Mechanicsville, 23111. Tel: 804-789-0997.
Church: 813 W. Nine Mile Rd., 23075.
Catechesis / Religious Program—Students 110.

HOPEWELL, HAMPTON CO., ST. JAMES CHURCH (1918), Rev. Daniel Bond.
Mailing Address: 510 W. Poythress St., 23860-2508.
Res.: 102 N. Fifth Ave., 23860. Tel: 804-458-9286.
Church: 500 W. Poythress St., 23860. Tel: 804-458-9223; 804-458-9286 (evening); Fax: 804-458-1216.
Catechesis / Religious Program—Tel: 804-458-2286. Students 99.

HOT SPRINGS, BATH CO., THE SHRINE OF THE SACRED HEART (1922), Rev. John McGinnity (Retired).
Mailing Address: Drawer B, 24445-0027. Tel: 540-839-2603.
Catechesis / Religious Program—Students 5.

HURT, PITTSYLVANIA CO., ST. VICTORIA (1964), Rev. David L. Noct.
Mailing Address: P.O. Box 640, 24563-0640. Tel: 434-324-4824; Fax: 434-324-4824.
Res.: 305 Victoria Dr., 24563.
Catechesis / Religious Program—Students 30.

JONESVILLE, LEE CO., CHURCH OF THE HOLY SPIRIT (1956), Rev. James M. Fosnot; Deacon Barron Flanary.
Mailing Address: P.O. Box 923, 24263. In Res., Rev. Leslie Schmidt, G.H.M.
Res.: 1821 Holton Ave., Big Stone Gap, 24219. Tel: 540-523-6546; Fax: 540-523-1602.
Church: State Rt. 58 E. of Jonesville, 24263.
Catechesis / Religious Program—Students 16.

LAKE GASTON, MECKLENBERG CO., ST. PETER THE APOSTLE (1995), Rev. Dennis McAuliffe (BRK).
Mailing Address: P.O. Box 700, Bracey, 23919. Tel: 434-636-7782; Fax: 434-636-4549.
Church: Rte. 903, 631 Ebony Rd., Ebony.

LEBANON, RUSSELL CO., GOOD SHEPHERD (1959), Rev. Robert L. Krenik.
Mailing Address: P.O. Box 730, 24266-0730. Tel: 276-889-1690; 276-889-0127.
Church: 479 N.W. Main St., 24266.
Catechesis / Religious Program—Students 7.

LEXINGTON, ROCKBRIDGE CO., ST. PATRICK (1873), Rev. N. Alan Lipscomb.
Mailing Address: P.O. Box 725, 24450-0725. Tel: 540-463-3533; Fax: 540-462-2935.
Office—221 W. Nelson St., 24450.
Res.: 225 Denny Lane, 24450. Tel: 540-463-6819.
Church: 219 W. Nelson St., 24450.
Catechesis / Religious Program—Students 116.

LOVINGSTON, NELSON CO., ST. MARY (1979), Rev. Daniel Kelly; Deacon Richard J. Nees.
Mailing Address: P.O. Box 375, 22949-0735. Tel: 434-263-8509; Fax: 434-263-6928.
Catechesis / Religious Program—Tel: 434-263-6923. Students 28.

LYNCHBURG, CAMPBELL CO.

1—HOLY CROSS (1859), [CEM] Rev. Msgr. J. Kenneth Rush, D.Min.; Deacon Gordon Cartwright.
Church & Office Address: 710 Clay St., 24504-2530. Tel: 434-846-5245; Fax: 434-846-7022.
Res.: 2000 Burnt Bridge Rd., 24503. Tel: 434-385-0220.
School—Regional School, (Grades PreK-12), 2125 Langhorne Rd., 24501. Tel: 434-847-5436. Mr. John P. Jones, Prin. Lay Teachers 45; Students 317.
Catechesis / Religious Program—Students 256.

2—ST. THOMAS MORE (1978), Rev. James E. Dorson. 3015 Roundelay Rd., 24502-2036. Tel: 434-237-5911; Fax: 434-237-8854.
Catechesis / Religious Program—Tel: 434-237-8852. Students 344.

MARION, SMYTH CO., ST. JOHN THE EVANGELIST CHURCH (1974), Rev. Paul Maier.
124 Park Blvd., 24354. Tel: 276-783-7282; Fax: 276-783-7282.
Church: 124 Park Blvd., 24354.
Catechesis / Religious Program—Students 20.

MARTINSVILLE, HENRY CO., ST. JOSEPH (1949), (Hispanic), Rev. Joseph Torretto.
Mailing Address: 2481 Spruce St., 24112. Tel: 276-638-4779; 276-638-1192; Fax: 540-638-2218.
Res.: 711 Windsor Ln., 24112. Tel: 276-632-5182.
Catechesis / Religious Program—Students 60.

MATHEWS, MATHEWS CO., CHURCH OF FRANCIS DE SALES (1983), Rev. John D. Boddie.
Mailing Address: P.O. Box 158, 23109-0158. Tel: 804-725-2776; Fax: 804-725-5463.
Church: Rte. 647 & Lover's Ln., 23109.
Catechesis / Religious Program—Students 60.

MECHANICSVILLE, HANOVER CO., CHURCH OF THE REDEEMER (1976), Rev. James J. Begley; Deacons Chris Colville; Chris Malone.
Church & Mailing Address: 8275 Meadowbridge Rd., 23116. Tel: 804-746-4911; Fax: 804-746-8657.
Res.: 8222 N. Mayfield Ln., 23111. Tel: 804-730-1844.
Catechesis / Religious Program—Tel: 804-746-4911. Students 550.

MIDDLESEX, MIDDLESEX CO., CHURCH OF THE VISITATION (1983), [CEM] Rev. John D. Boddie; Mary O'Lenick, Pastoral Assoc.
Mailing Address: P.O. Box 38, Topping, 23169-0038. Tel: 804-758-5160; Fax: 804-758-0676.
Res.: Box 34, Cobbs Creek, 23085. Tel: 804-776-0676; Fax: 804-725-5463.
Church: 8462 Puller Hwy., Topping, 23169.
Catechesis / Religious Program—Students 33.

MINERAL, LOUISA CO., ST. JUDE (1974), Rev. Rodney Rodis; Deacon Joseph Milkevitch.
Mailing Address: P.O. Box 40, 23117-0040. Tel: 540-894-4266; Fax: 540-894-4993.
Church: 1937 Davis Hwy., 23117.
Catechesis / Religious Program—Students 70.

MONETA, BEDFORD CO., RESURRECTION (1984), [CEM] Chris Barrett, Pastoral Coord.; Joe Day, Admin.
Mailing Address: 15353 Moneta Rd., 24121-9804. Tel: 540-297-5530; Fax: 540-297-6316.
Catechesis / Religious Program—Students 52.

NEW CASTLE, CRAIG CO., SAINT JOHN THE EVANGELIST MISSION (1997), Rev. George C. Heise, Admin.
Rte. 3, P.O. Box 680, 24127. Tel: 540-977-1485.
Catechesis / Religious Program—Students 13.

NEWPORT NEWS, NEWPORT CO.

1—ST. JEROME (1966), Revs. Joseph B. Majewski; Charles Sagilio; Deacon Joseph Riss.
Mailing Address: 116 Denbigh Blvd., 23608-3333. Tel: 757-877-5021; Fax: 757-898-1437.
Catechesis / Religious Program—Tel: 757-877-3771. Students 504.

2—OUR LADY OF MOUNT CARMEL (1953), Rev. Msgr. Michael D. McCarron; Rev. Peter Tran; Deacon Bernard H. Taylor.
100 Harpersville Rd., 23601-2324. Tel: 757-595-0385; 757-595-0387; Fax: 757-599-9285.
School—Tel: 757-596-2754; Fax: 757-596-1727. Sr. Mary Aquinas, O.P., Prin. Sisters of St. Dominic 3; Lay Teachers 47; Students 535.
Catechesis / Religious Program—Tel: 757-595-0385, Ext. 119. Students 435.

3—ST. VINCENT DE PAUL (1881), Ms. Therese A. Simon, Pastoral Assoc.
Mailing Address: P.O. Box 258, 23607-0258. Tel: 757-245-4234; Fax: 757-245-0039.
Church: 230 33rd St., 23607.
Catechesis / Religious Program—Students 79.

NORFOLK, NORFOLK CITY CO.

1—BASILICA OF ST. MARY OF THE IMMACULATE CONCEPTION (1791), (African American), [JC] Revs. John J. Dorgan, Rector; Ernest Bulinda; Deacon Calvin Bailey.
Office—1000 Holt St., 23504-4241. Tel: 757-622-4487; Fax: 757-625-7969.
Church: 232 Chapel St., 23504.
Catechesis / Religious Program—Students 177.
Convent—1000 Holt St., 23504. Tel: 757-627-5213.

2—BLESSED SACRAMENT (1921), Rev. Joseph H. Metzger III.
Mailing Address: 170 Painter St., 23505-4557. Tel: 757-423-8305; Fax: 757-451-3335.
Res.: 110 W. Severn Rd., 23505. Tel: 757-489-9636.
Church: Newport Ave. & Painter St., 23505.
Catechesis / Religious Program—Students 143.

3—CHRIST THE KING (1949), Rev. Brian Rafferty; Deacon Keith A. Fournier.
Office & Mailing Address—1803 Columbia Ave., 23509-1298. Tel: 757-622-1120; 757-622-9196; Fax: 757-627-8808.
Res.: 1804 Ashland Ave., 23509. Tel: 757-627-1723.
School—3401 Tidewater Dr., 23509. Tel: 757-625-4951; Fax: 757-623-5212. Ms. Miriam Cotton, Prin. Lay Teachers 20; Students 330.
Catechesis / Religious Program—Tel: 757-625-0208. Students 160.

4—HOLY TRINITY (1921), [JC] Rev. David McGuire.
Mailing Address: 155 W. Government Ave., 23503-2905. Tel: 757-480-3433; Fax: 757-480-8749. In Res., Rev. Msgr. Santiago C. Frias. Tel: 757-480-3434.
School—154 W. Government Ave., 23503. Tel: 757-583-1873; Fax: 757-587-3677. Ms. Deneane Nofplot, Prin. Lay Teachers 20; Students 205.
Catechesis / Religious Program—Students 128.

5—OUR LADY OF LAVANG (1991), [JC] Rev. Joseph Hai-Nguyen, Ph.D.
1806 Ashland Ave., 23509-1236.
Church: 409 Compostella Rd., 23518. Tel: 757-622-5345; 757-545-5606; Fax: 757-622-4248.

6—ST. PIUS X (1955), Rev. Msgr. R. Francis Muench, J.C.L.; Rev. Jesus Enciso; Deacon Walker King.
Res.: 1615 Longdale Dr., 23518. Tel: 757-855-3297.
School—7800 Halprin Dr., 23518. Tel: 757-588-6171; Fax: 757-587-6580. Sr. Marie Renee Murphy, I.H.M., Prin. Sisters Servants of the Immaculate Heart of Mary 3; Lay Teachers 26; Students 408.
Catechesis / Religious Program—Students 275.

7—SACRED HEART (1894), [CEM] Rev. Daniel N. Klem; Deacon Louis Maurelli.
Office—520 Graydon Ave., 23507-1711. Tel: 757-625-6763; Fax: 757-627-1965.
Catechesis / Religious Program—Students 220.

NORGE, JAMES CITY CO., ST. OLAF, PATRON OF NORWAY (1992), Rev. John E. Ridgell.
Mailing Address: 104 Norge Ln., 23188-7229. Tel: 757-564-3819; Fax: 757-565-1099.
Catechesis / Religious Program—Students 125.

NORTON, WISE CO., ST. ANTHONY (1938), Rev. Timothy Drake.
Mailing Address & Church: 1009 Virginia Ave., N.W., 24273-1897. Tel: 276-679-2336.
Catechesis / Religious Program—Students 9.

Mission—St. Mary E. Front St. at Beech Ave., Coeburn, Wise Co.
Station—University of Virginia at Wise Wise.

ONLEY, ACCOMAC CO., ST. PETER'S THE APOSTLE (1942), Revs. Frank Wiggins; Francisco Valle; Deacon Jon D. Shearer.
Mailing Address: P.O. Box 860, 23418-0860. Tel: 757-787-4592; Fax: 757-787-2899.
Church: 25236 Coastal Blvd., 23418.
Catechesis/Religious Program—Students 83.

PALMYRA, FLUVANNA CO., SS. PETER & PAUL (1986), Rev. Gerald A. Przywara.
Mailing Address: 4309 Thomas Jefferson Pkwy., 22963-9506. Tel: 804-589-5201; Fax: 804-589-4463.
Catechesis/Religious Program—Students 136.

PEARISBURG, GILES CO., HOLY FAMILY (1965), Rev. John Prinelli.
Mailing Address: 516 Mason Court Dr., 24134-1832. Tel: 540-921-3547.
Catechesis/Religious Program—Students 16.

PETERSBURG, PRINCE GEORGE CO., ST. JOSEPH (1842), [CEM] Rev. Robert M. Spencer.
Mailing Address: P.O. Box 2006, 23804-1306.
Church & Office: 11 N. Market St., PA 23803. Tel: 804-733-3115; Fax: 804-862-9931.
Res.: 19 Centre Hill Ct., 23803. Tel: 804-732-5127.
School—Tel: 804-732-3931; Fax: 804-863-2635. Ms. Ruth Bonner, Prin. Lay Teachers 10; Students 192.
Catechesis/Religious Program—Tel: 804-862-9977. Students 70.

POCAHONTAS, TAZEWELL CO., ST. ELIZABETH (1896), Rev. Daniel O. Brady.
Mailing Address: P.O. Box 608, 24635-0608. Tel: 276-988-4626; Fax: 276-988-4626.
Catechesis/Religious Program—Students 6.

PORTSMOUTH, PORTSMOUTH CO.

1—CHURCH OF THE RESURRECTION (1971), Rev. James V. Carr; Deacon John Glynn.
Mailing Address: 3501 Cedar Ln., 23703. Tel: 757-484-7335; Fax: 757-484-5857.
Res.: 5130 Castleway, 23703. Tel: 757-484-7336.
School—Portsmouth Catholic Elementary School, 2301 Oregon Ave., 23701. Tel: 757-488-6744; Fax: 757-465-8833. Mr. Edward P. Williams, Prin. Lay Teachers 26; Students 243.
Catechesis/Religious Program—Students 324.

2—HOLY ANGELS (1917), [JC] Rev. Romeo Jazmin.
Office—34 Afton Pkwy., 23702-2739. Tel: 757-485-2142; 757-485-2143; Fax: 757-485-3699.
Catechesis/Religious Program—Students 94.

3—ST. PAUL (1804), [CEM] [JC] Rev. Joseph S. Slowik; Deacon Joseph Grillo.
Res.: 518 High St., 23704-3516. Tel: 757-397-7066; Fax: 757-393-4334.
Church: 522 High St., 23704.
Catechesis/Religious Program—Students 115.

POWHATAN, CAMPBELL CO., ST. JOHN NEUMANN (1948), Rev. J. Morton Biber; Deacon Edward Schmidt.
Church: 2480 Batterson Rd., 23139-7513. Tel: 804-598-3754; 804-794-9098; Fax: 804-598-1467.
Catechesis/Religious Program—Students 140.

PRINCE GEORGE COUNTY, PRINCE GEORGE CO., CHURCH OF THE SACRED HEART (1906), [CEM] Rev. Jay Wagner.
Mailing Address: 4415 County Dr., Petersburg, 23805-7567. Tel: 804-732-6385; Fax: 804-732-6385.
Catechesis/Religious Program—Fax: 804-732-6385. Students 140.

QUINQUE, GREENE COUNTY, SHEPHERD OF THE HILLS (1980), Rev. Daniel Bain.
Mailing Address: P.O. Box 83, 22965-0083. Tel: 804-985-3929.
Res.: 101 W. Marshall Ave., Elkton, 22827. Tel: 540-298-1341.
Church: Rte. 633. Tel: 434-985-3929.
Catechesis/Religious Program—Students 30.

QUINTON, NEW KENT CO., ST. ELIZABETH ANN SETON (1986), Rev. Russell E. Smith, S.T.D.
Mailing Address & Church: 2631 Pocahontas Trail, 23141-0245. Tel: 804-932-4125; Fax: 804-932-8126.
Catechesis/Religious Program—Students 23.

RADFORD, BEDFORD CO., ST. JUDE (1967), Rev. Patrick Golden.
Mailing Address: 1740 Tyler Rd., Christiansburg, 24073-6154. Tel: 540-639-5341; Fax: 540-639-4738.
Res.: 900 Berkley St., 24141. Tel: 540-731-9541.
Catechesis/Religious Program—Students 84.

RICHLANDS, TAZEWELL CO., ST. MARY (1962), Rev. Thomas R. Collins.
Mailing Address: 1118 Farmer St., 24641. Tel: 276-963-8545 (Rectory); Fax: 276-963-8545.
Catechesis/Religious Program—Students 15.
Mission—St. Joseph (1966),, Buchanan Co. Tel: 276-935-2815. Rte. 460 Tookland, Grundy, 24614.

ROANOKE, ROANOKE CO.

1—ST. ANDREW (1890), [JC] Rev. Msgr. Thomas G. Miller.
Mailing Address: 631 N. Jefferson St., 24016-1401. Tel: 540-344-9814; 540-345-9714; Fax: 540-344-7879.
Res.: 120 Windward Dr., 24014. Tel: 540-725-1117.
Catechesis/Religious Program—Students 224.

2—ST. GERARD (1946), Rev. Constance L. Silayo. 809 Orange Ave., N.W., 24016-1117. Tel: 540-343-7744; Fax: 540-343-3599.
School—Roanoke Catholic Regional Elementary and High School, 621 N. Jefferson St., 24016. Tel: 540-982-3756; Fax: 540-345-0785. Ray Eric Correia, Pres.; Anthony Durso, Prin. Upper School; Susan Thompson, Prin. Lower School. Lay Teachers 39; Students 594.
Catechesis/Religious Program—Students 98.

3—OUR LADY OF NAZARETH (1914), [JC] Rev. Msgr. Joseph P. Lehman; Deacon Robert Rowland.
Mailing Address: 2505 Electric Rd., S.W., 24018-3599. Tel: 540-774-0066 (Office); 540-774-0857 (Res.); Fax: 540-774-2148.
Catechesis/Religious Program—Tel: 540-774-0773. Students 549.

ROCKY MOUNT, FRANKLIN CO., FRANCIS OF ASSISI (1984), Rev. Rolo B. Castillo.
Mailing Address: 15 Glennwood Dr., 24151-2111. Tel: 540-483-9591; Fax: 540-483-5232.
Catechesis/Religious Program—Students 70.

ST. PAUL, WISE CO., ST. THERESE (1954), Rev. Robert L. Krenik.
Mailing Address: P.O. Box 56, 24283-0056. Tel: 276-762-5932; Fax: 276-762-5932.
Res.: 3107 Sixth Ave., 24283. Tel: 276-889-1690.
Catechesis/Religious Program—Students 6.

SALEM, PAGE CO., OUR LADY OF PERPETUAL HELP (1947), Rev. Jeremiusz H. Sojka; Deacons Michael Ellerbrock; Eric Surat; Stephen O'Connell.
Mailing Address: 314 Turner Rd., 24153-2399. Tel: 540-387-0491; Fax: 540-389-8237.
Res.: 1408 Kathryn Ln., 24153. Tel: 540-387-1020.
Catechesis/Religious Program—Tel: 540-387-0451. Students 200.

SCOTTSVILLE, ALBEMARLE CO., ST. GEORGE (1975), Deacon Albert Carini.
Mailing Address: P.O. Box 9, 24590-0009. Tel: 434-286-3724.
Catechesis/Religious Program—Students 12.

SMITHFIELD, ISLE OF WIGHT CO., GOOD SHEPHERD (1984), Ms. Joanne R. Gordon, Pastoral Coord.
Mailing Address: P.O. Box 840, 23431-0840. Tel: 757-365-0579; Fax: 757-365-4749.
Church: 300 Smithfield Blvd., 23430.
Catechesis/Religious Program—Students 136.

SOUTH BOSTON, HALIFAX CO., ST. PASCHAL BAYLON (1981), [JC] Sr. Edna N. Maier, Pastoral Coord.
Mailing Address: 800 John Randolph Blvd., 24592-2943.
Res.: 3302 N. Main St., 4592. Tel: 434-572-2285 (Office); Fax: 434-572-1725.
Catechesis/Religious Program—Students 85.

SOUTH HILL, MECKLENBURG CO., GOOD SHEPHERD (1922), Rev. Silvio Kaberia.
Mailing Address: P.O. Box 621, 23970-0621. Tel: 434-447-3622; Fax: 434-447-4729.
Church: 1664 N. Mecklenburg Ave., 23970. Fax: 434-447-3622.
Catechesis/Religious Program—Students 32.

STAUNTON, AUGUSTA CO., ST. FRANCIS OF ASSISI (1844), Rev. John Adam Abe; Kimberly Newcomb, Pastoral Assoc. In Res., Rev. Msgr. Andrew Cassin (WDC); Rev. William O'Brien (Retired).
Church & Mailing Address: 121 N. Augusta St., 24401-3636. Tel: 540-886-2262; Fax: 540-885-5743.
Res.: 126 N. New St., 24401. Tel: 540-886-9121.
Catechesis/Religious Program—Students 289.

SUFFOLK, SUFFOLK CO., ST. MARY OF THE PRESENTATION (1927), Rev. Louis W. Ruoff.
Office—202 S. Broad St., 23434-5715. Tel: 757-539-5732; Fax: 757-538-0103.
Church: 200 S. Broad St., 23434.
Catechesis/Religious Program—Students 96.

TABB, YORK CO., BLESSED KATERI TEKAWITHA (1986), Rev. Lawrence J. Mullaney.
Church & Office: 3800 Big Bethel Rd., 23693-3814. Tel: 757-766-3800; 757-766-1384; Fax: 757-766-1125.
Catechesis/Religious Program—Students 289.

TAPPAHANNOCK, ESSEX CO., ST. TIMOTHY (1972), Rev. Michael M. Duffy, J.C.L.
Mailing Address: P.O. Box 129, 22560-0129.
Church: Rte. 17 & Airport Rd., 22560. Tel: 804-443-2760; 804-443-2570; Fax: 804-443-2022.
Catechesis/Religious Program—Students 77.

TAZEWELL, TAZEWELL CO., ST. THERESA (1980), Rev. Daniel O. Brady.
Mailing Address: P.O. Box 345, 24651-0345. Tel: 276-988-4626; Fax: 276-988-0946.
Church: 304 Tazewell Ave., 24651.
Catechesis/Religious Program—Students 18.

VIRGINIA BEACH, VIRGINIA BEACH CO., CHURCH OF THE ASCENSION (1972), [CEM] Revs. James E. Parke; Charles Faul; Deacons Gary Harmeyer; Thomas McFeely.
Office—4853 Princess Anne Rd., 23462-4446. Tel: 757-495-1887; 757-495-1886; Fax: 757-495-1516.
Catechesis/Religious Program—Tel: 757-495-1886, Ext. 11. Students 842.

VIRGINIA BEACH, VIRGINIA CO.

1—CHURCH OF THE HOLY APOSTLES (1977),, (Anglican-Roman Catholic Congregation of Hampton Roads) Rev. Charles Faul.
Church: 1598 Lynnhaven Pkwy., 23453-2008. Tel: 757-427-0963; Fax: 757-427-9434.
Catechesis/Religious Program—Students 20.

2—ST. GREGORY THE GREAT (1957), Revs. Mario Fulgenzi; Luke Policicchio, O.S.B. (GBG); Damian Abbaticchio, O.S.B.; John Mary Tompkins; Cristiano Aparecido Brito, O.S.B. (GBG); Deacon Raymond Check.
Office—5345 Virginia Beach Blvd., 23462. Tel: 757-497-8330; Fax: 757-490-1492.
School—5343 Virginia Beach Blvd., 23462-1896. Tel: 757-497-1811; Fax: 757-497-7005. Sr. Patricia O'Donnell, I.H.M., Prin. Lay Teachers 48; Students 774; Religious 5.
Catechesis/Religious Program—Tel: 757-499-4494; Fax: 757-490-1492. Students 900.
Chapel—Chesapeake, St. Benedict Tridentine Chapel (1992), 521 McCosh St., Chesapeake, 23320. Tel: 757-543-0561.
Catechesis/Religious Program—Students 29.

3—HOLY FAMILY (1977), Rev. Thomas J. Quinlan.
Parish Center—1279 N. Great Neck Rd., 23454-2117. Tel: 757-481-5702; 757-481-0799; Fax: 757-481-3989.
Catechesis/Religious Program—Students 516.

4—HOLY SPIRIT (1975), [CEM] Rev. Kenneth E. Wood; Deacon Robert F. Durel.
Office—1396 Lynnhaven Pkwy., 23453-2798. Tel: 757-468-3600; 757-468-3601; Fax: 757-468-3342.
Res.: 3345 Clubhouse Rd., 23452. Tel: 757-340-3933.
Catechesis/Religious Program—Students 529.

5—ST. JOHN THE APOSTLE CHURCH (1989), Rev. Thomas Mattingly; Deacon Vernon Krajeski. In Res., Rev. Paul Gaughan (Retired). Tel: 757-426-2550.
Church: 800 Los Conaes Way, 23456-6421. Tel: 757-426-2180; Fax: 757-426-6857.
School—1968 Sandbridge Rd., 23456. Tel: 757-821-1100; Fax: 757-821-1047. Charlene Feliton, Prin. (PreK-8).
Catechesis/Religious Program—Tel: 757-426-2180; Fax: 757-426-6857. Students 849.

6—ST. LUKE (1986), Revs. Salvador Anonuevo, Admin.; Gary Harmeyer; Lawrence Illy.
Mailing Address: 2304 Salem Rd., 23456-1215. Tel: 757-427-5776; Fax: 757-427-2260.
Catechesis/Religious Program—Tel: 757-427-5776; Fax: 757-427-2260. Students 148.

7—ST. MARK (1978), Rev. James Griffin; Deacons Michael Johnson; John Kren.
Mailing Address: 1505 Kempsville Rd., 23464-7210. Tel: 757-479-1010; 757-479-0414; Fax: 757-479-9453.
Res.: 4901 Whitewood Ln., 23464. Tel: 757-467-4932.
Catechesis/Religious Program—Tel: 757-479-9897; Fax: 757-479-9453. Students 361.

8—ST. MATTHEW (1924), Rev. Joseph Facura; Deacons Daniel F. McCormick, (Retired); Chris Romero; Bill Blatnik; Darrell Wentworth.
Office—3314 Sandra Ln., 23464-1736. Tel: 757-420-6310; 757-420-6311; Fax: 757-420-7734.
Res.: 806 Bridgeport Place, 23464. Tel: 757-523-1723.
School—3316 Sandra Ln., 23464. Tel: 757-420-2455; Fax: 757-420-4880. Ms. Barbara White, Prin. Lay Teachers 36; Students 628.
Catechesis/Religious Program—Tel: 757-420-6310; Fax: 757-420-7734. Students 200.

9—ST. NICHOLAS (1963), Rev. Msgr. Raymond A. Barton.
Office & Church: 712 Little Neck Rd., 23452. Tel: 757-340-7231; Fax: 757-340-2727.
Res.: 3340 Old Kirkwood Dr., 23452-5807. Tel: 757-498-7834.
Catechesis/Religious Program—Students 395.

10—STAR OF THE SEA (1915), Rev. Kevin J. O'Brien, S.T.B., Ph.D.
Office—1404 Pacific Ave., 23451-3439. Tel: 757-428-8547; Fax: 757-428-0788.
School—309 15th St., 23451. Tel: 757-428-8400; Fax: 757-428-0788. Mrs. Susan Fentress, Prin. Lay Teachers 24; Students 364.
Catechesis/Religious Program—Tel: 757-428-8547; Fax: 757-428-0788. Students 213.

WAYNESBORO, AUGUSTA CO., ST. JOHN THE EVANGELIST (1946), Rev. Stephen J. Hickman.
Mailing Address: 344 Maple Ave., 22980-4706.
Office—Tel: 540-949-6145; 540-949-6146; Fax: 540-932-8512.
Res.: 329 Walnut Ave., 22980. Tel: 540-943-4051.
Church: 300 Maple Ave., 22980.
Catechesis/Religious Program—Students 198.

WEST POINT, KING WILLIAM CO., OUR LADY OF THE BLESSED SACRAMENT (1918), [CEM] Rev. Edward Moran.
Mailing Address: 207 W. Euclid Blvd., 23181. In Res., Rev. John Brieffies.
Church: 3570 King William Ave., 23181. Tel: 804-843-3125; Fax: 804-843-9158.
Catechesis/Religious Program—Students 67.

WILLIAMSBURG, YORK CO., ST. BEDE'S (1932), Rev.

Msgr. William H. Carr; Rev. Antonio R. Malabad (Retired); Deacon Robert R. Thompson.
Res.: 601 College Ter., 23185. Tel: 757-220-4233.
Church & Mailing Address: 3686 Ironbound Rd., P.O. Box 5400, 23188.
Catechesis/Religious Program—Students 746.

WOODLAWN, CARROLL CO., ST. JOSEPH'S (1981), Rev. Charles W. Brickner; Deacon Bruce K. Dwyer.
Mailing Address: 99 Joy Ranch Rd., 24381-1213. Tel: 276-236-7814; Fax: 276-238-8711.
Catechesis/Religious Program—Students 10.
Mission—Church of the Risen Lord U.S. 58 and County 625, Patrick Springs, Patrick 24133.
Catechesis/Religious Program—Students 5.
Mission—Church of All Saints Rt. 615 & Rt. 693, Floyd, Floyd Co. 24091.
Catechesis/Religious Program—Students 10.

WYTHEVILLE, WYTHE CO., ST. MARY'S (1845), [CEM] Rev. Rene Castillo; Deacon Walter "Barney" Jennings.
Mailing Address: P.O. Box 7, 24382-0007. Tel: 276-228-3104; Fax: 276-228-3322.
Church: 370 E. Main St., 24382.
Catechesis/Religious Program—Students 38.
Mission—St. Edward P.O. Box 1670, Pulaski, Davis Co. 24301. Tel: 276-980-6511.
Catechesis/Religious Program—Students 28.

YORKTOWN, YORK CO., ST. JOAN OF ARC (1954), Rev. James Curran; Deacon Daniel Johnson.
Office—315 Harris Grove Ln., 23692-4014. Tel: 757-898-5570; Fax: 757-898-0737.
Catechesis/Religious Program—Tel: 757-898-7190. Mr. Gary Taylor, D.R.E. Students 80.

Chaplains of Public Institutions

RICHMOND. *International Airport*. Rev. Wayne Ball, J.C.L., Chap.
McGuire VA Medical Center. Rev. Msgr. Walter C. Barrett, Chap. Tel: 804-343-7111.

HAMPTON. *VA Medical Center*, Chaplain Service, Bldg. 69, 23667. Tel: 757-722-9961, Ext. 3600. Revs. Lloyd F. Stephenson (Retired), Donald J. Cavey.

NORFOLK. *Apostleship of the Sea*. Rev. Msgr. Santiago C. Frias. Tel: 757-480-3434.

PETERSBURG. *Federal Correctional Institution*. (Vacant)

SALEM. *Salem VA Medical Center*, Tel: 540-982-2463. Rev. Jeremiusz H. Sojka, Chap.

On Special or Other Diocesan Assignment:
Revs.—
Apuzzo, Pasquale, Chancery Office
D'Aurora, Joseph, Hosp. Chap.
Lane, Mark

On Duty Outside the Diocese:
Rev.—
Natale, Samuel, New York

Graduate Studies:
Rev.—
Trinh, Thai Q., Cailifornia Institute of Integral Studies, San Francisco, CA 94103.

Military Chaplains:
Revs.—
Caiazzo, Nickolas (NOR)
Cowan, Steven
Dang, Chin Van
Huan, Joseph Van Tran
Iaucci, Thomas
Kanicki, Philip A.

Unassigned:
Rev.—
Bostwick, John

Retired:
Most Rev.—
Sullivan, Walter F., D.D., Bishop Emeritus of Richmond
Rev. Msgr.—
Michael, Chester P., 2586 Ennis Mountain Rd., Afton, 22920-6626.
Revs.—
Beardsley, Frederick, 5910 Kensington Ave., 23226-2636.
Blankenship, John P., 1818 Grove Ave., #1, 23220. Tel: 804-359-1952
Cervantes, Leo, 664 Burgos St., Cagayan de Oro City 9000, Philippines.
Chmura, Stanislaus, 717 Cooper Ave., Inverness, FL 34450-6507. Tel: 352-344-8035
Clark, Joseph L., 1016 Donation Dr., Virginia Beach, 23455. Tel: 757-464-1816
Condon, William F., 155 W. Brown Rd., #130, Mesa, AZ 85201. Tel: 602-957-2614
Connelly, William P., 5345 Marian Lane, Virginia Beach, 23462. Tel: 757-456-5018
Dinga, William, P.O. Box 226, Bath, ME 04530.
Dinges, Anthony, 102 Oliver Ave., Crewe, 23920-1410.
Ditty, James, 1316 Mill Lake Quarter, Chesapeake, 23320-2748. Tel: 757-436-6032
Fisher, Charles, 8200 Woodman Rd., 23228. Tel: 804-264-4990
Funk, Virgil C., 12960 S.W. Park Way, Portland, OR 97225. Tel: 503-643-3734
Gallagher, Paul V., 159 Franklin Parke Ct., Christiansburg, 24073-4457. Tel: 540-381-0729
Gaughan, Paul, St. John's Rectory, 800 Los Conaes Way, Virginia Beach, 23456-6421. Tel: 757-426-2550
Goodman, Julian, 11800 Paddock Dr., Midlothian, 23113.
Guttendorf, James R., 24 N. Oak St., Highland Springs, 23075.
Hamlet, Ralph, 141 Green Turtle Ln., Apt. 10, Charlottesville, 22901-2373.
Hanna, Don Michael, 7501 River Rd., Newport News, 23607. Tel: 757-247-6314
Henry, Thomas, 751 Hillsdale Dr., #CC03, Charlottesville, 22901-3300.
Higgins, Phillip, 214 Woodridge Dr., Rustburg, 24588.
Ilano, Jovencio, 606 North Naylor St., Alexandria, 22304. Tel: 703-370-6033
Kloepfer, John S., P.O. Box 1742, Clarksville, 23927.
Kruc, James, 326 Wolf St., Philadelphia, PA 19148-3315. Tel: 215-462-1759
La Fratta, William, 19 Shortwood Cir., Palmyra, 22963-2747. Tel: 434-589-0824
Malabad, Antonio R., 601 College Terr., Williamsburg, 23185. Tel: 757-220-4233
McEleney, Robert J., Rt. 5, P.O. Box 432, Appomattox, 24522-9343. Tel: 434-352-2881
McGinnity, John, P.O. Box B, Hot Springs, 24445-0047. Tel: 540-839-2603
Naro, Carl J., 153 Mayo Creek Ln., Wingina, 24599-3080. Tel: 434-263-4323
Nash, Robert, P.O. Box 1093, Deltaville, 23043-1093.
Naylor, Ronald J., 100 E. Ocean View Ave., #904, Norfolk, 23503-1634. Tel: 757-587-4185
Nee, Thomas B., 5345 Marian Lane, Virginia Beach, 23462. Tel: 757-685-8844
Newell, Matthias, 4000 E. Fletcher Ave. #D-207, Tampa, FL 33613. Tel: 434-575-1607
Ngo, Anthony, 12500 Patterson Ave., 23233-6411.
O'Brien, William, P.O. Box 34, Fisherville, 22939. Tel: 540-942-2945
Pereira, Albert F., 4713 Clintwood Dr., Portsmouth, 23703-4201.
Rodrigues, Anthony, P.O. Box 1014, Denton, MT 59430. Tel: 406-567-2288
Rodriguez, D. Andres G., 49540 San Martin de Tabara, Zamora, Spain.
Ruth, Robert F., P.O. Box 258, Newport News, 23607-0258.
Stephenson, Lloyd F., 8226 Mill Pond Dr., North, 23128. Tel: 804-694-4493
Stickle, William, 128 Clipper Ct., Kill Devil Hills, NC 27948-9113.
Teslovic, Eugene, 107 Maryland Ave., Portsmouth, 23707.
Warren, Robert, P.O. Box 6194, Charlottesville, 22906-6194. Tel: 434-823-2024
Welch, Thomas David, 351 Buntontown, Butler, TN 37640-7804.

Permanent Deacons:
Allison, Mark D., Church of the Transfiguration, Fincastle
Arkesteyn, John Aster, Saint Bridget, Richmond
Bailey, Calvin, Basilica of Saint Mary of the Immaculate Conception, Norfolk
Baker, Robert D., Church of the Sacred Heart, Petersburg
Banks, Marshall, Cathedral of The Sacred Heart, Richmond
Baskind, Frank, Saint Mary, Richmond
Bergen, Brian, St. Mary's Hospital of Richmond Inc., MCV Hospital
Birx, Charles R., (Retired)
Birx, Charles R., Radford
Blatnik, Bill, Saint Matthew, Virginia Beach
Broughton, Eric, Saint Augustine, Richmond
Carini, Albert J., St. George, Scottsville
Cartwright, Gordon, Holy Cross Lynchburg
Check, Raymond P., St. Gregory the Great, Virginia Beach
Colville, Chris, Church of the Redeemer, Mechanicsville
Corrigan, Eugene, Saint Augustine, Richmond
Donovan, Donald, St. Charles, Cape Charles
Dowdy, Melvin, Cathedral of the Sacred Heart, Richmond
Durel, Robert F., Church of the Holy Spirit, Virginia Beach
Dwyer, Bruce K., All Saints, Floyd; Risen Lord, Woodlawn; St. Joseph, Woodlawn
Ellerbrock, Michael, Saint Jude Catholic, Christiansburg; Our Lady Of Perpetual Help, Salem; St. Mary, Blacksburg
Elliott, Thomas B., Saint Edward, Richmond
Ewan, Robert, St. Edward, Richmond
Ferguson, Andrew, Saint Michael, Richmond
Flanary, Barron, Sacred Heart, Big Stone Gap; Church of the Holy Spirit, Jonesville
Fournier, Keith, Christ the King Church, Norfolk
Giovenco, Robert, Saint Bridget, Richmond
Glynn, John, Church of the Resurrection, Portsmouth
Gonzalez, Jose, St. Joseph, Hampton
Greer, James, Saint Edward, Richmond
Griffin, Robert H., Our Lady of Lordes, Richmond
Grillo, Joseph, Saint Paul, Portsmouth
Hall, Harry, St. Anne, Bristol
Hanzlik, Edward, Church of the Sacred Heart, Petersburg
Harmeyer, Gary, Church of the Ascension, Virginia Beach; Saint Luke, Virginia Beach
Hayes, William, (Retired)
Heise, George, Saint John the Evangelist Mission, New Castle; Church of the Transfiguration, Fincastle
Hornstra, Curtis, Saint Michael, Richmond
Illy, Lawrence, Saint Luke, Virginia Beach
Jennings, Walter "Barney", Saint Mary the Mother of God, Wytheville
Johnson, Daniel, Saint Joan of Arc, Yorktown
Johnson, Michael, Saint Mark, Virginia Beach
Kamper, Eugene, Saint Mary, Blacksburg
King, Walker P., St. Pius X, Norfolk
Krajeski, Vernon, St. John the Apostle, Virginia Beach
Kren, John, Saint Mark, Virginia Beach
Kwon, Peter H., Ph.D., (Retired)
La Spina, Fred, Blessed Sacrament, Harrisonburg
LaSpina, Fred C., Blessed Sacrament Church, Harrisonburg
Linden, Raymond K., Church of the Sacred Heart, Prince George County
MacLaughlin, Matthew, Saint John, Petersburg
Malone, Christopher M., Church of the Redeemer, Mechanicsville
Mammi, Nicholas, All Saints, Floyd
Marino, Nicholas, Prince Of Peace, Chesapeake
Matte, Mark, Sacred Heart, Richmond
Maurelli, Louis, Sacred Heart, Norfolk
McCormick, Daniel F., St. Matthew, Virginia Beach
McFeely, Thomas, Church of the Ascension, Virginia Beach
McGrann, Thomas, Saint Bede, Williamsburg
McLane, Emmett R., Saint Theresa, Farmville
Menting, Peter J., (Retired)
Milkevitch, Joseph, Saint Jude, Mineral; Immaculate Conception, Buckner
Morash, Christopher, Incarnation, Charlottesville
Morlino, Joseph, Holy Comforter, Charlottesville
Moro, Michael, Prince Of Peace, Chesapeake
Mullen, Thomas Matthew, Saint Michael, Richmond
Nees, Richard J., Saint Mary, Lovingston
Nemetz, David, St. Michael, Richmond
O'Connell, Stephen, Our Lady Of Perpetual Help, Salem
Ports, Francis J., (Retired)
Riss, Joseph, Saint Jerome, Newport News
Roderique, Raymond, Holy Name of Mary, Bedord
Romero, Crisanto, Saint Matthew, Virginia Beach
Rowland, Robert, Our Lady of Nazareth, Roanoke
Rowland, Robert, Our Lady of Nazareth, Roanoke
Sadowski, John, Saint Catherine of Siena, Clarksville
Schmidt, Edward, Saint John Neumann, Powhatan
Shearer, David, St. Peter the Apostle, Onley
Shearer, Jon D., Saint Peter the Apostle, Onley
Stonikinis, George C., Jr., Saint Theresa, Farmville; Good Samaritan, Amelia Court House
Surat, Eric, Our Lady Of Perpetual Help, Salem
Surat, Eric, Our Lady of Perpetual Help, Salem
Taylor, Bernard F., Our Lady of Mt. Carmel, Newport News
Taylor, Bernard H., Incarnation, Charlottesville
Thomas, John H., (Retired)
Thompson, Robert R., Saint Bede, Williamsburg
Lisboa-Torres, Patricio, Bishop's Office
Veraart, Frank, St. Thomas Aquinas, Charlottesville
Weir, Robert, (Retired)
Wentworth, Darrell, Saint Matthew, Virginia Beach

INSTITUTIONS LOCATED IN THE DIOCESE

[A] HIGH SCHOOLS, DIOCESAN

DANVILLE. *Sacred Heart School*, (Grades PreK-9), 540 Central Blvd., 24541. Tel: 434-793-2656; Fax: 434-793-2658. Email: sacredht@earthlink.net. Web: www.sheartschool.com. Lay Teachers 46; Total Staff 51; Total Enrollment 370.

LYNCHBURG. *Holy Cross Regional School*, (Grades PreK-12), 2125 Langhorne Rd., 24501. Tel: 434-847-5436; 434-847-5464; Fax: 434-847-4156. Email: office@hcrs-va.org. Web: www.hcrs-va.org. Mr. John P. Jones, Prin. Lay Teachers 36; Students 337.

NEWPORT NEWS. *Peninsula Catholic High School*, (Grades 8-12), 600 Harpersville Rd., 23601. Tel: 757-596-7247; Fax: 757-591-9718. Web: www.peninsulacatholic.com. William Hammond, Pres.; Mrs. Frankie Conway, Prin. Lay Teachers 25; Staff 13; Students 306.

ROANOKE. *Roanoke Catholic School*, (Grades PreK-12), 621 N. Jefferson St., 24016-1416. Tel: 540-982-3532; Fax: 540-345-0785. Email: info@roanokecatholic.com. Web: www.roanokecatholic.com. Ray Eric Correia, Pres.; Susan R. Thompson, Elementary Prin.; Anthony Durso, Secondary Prin. Lay Teachers 49; Students 591.

VIRGINIA BEACH. *Bishop Sullivan Catholic High School*, (Grades 9-12), 4552 Princess Anne Rd., 23462. Tel: 757-467-2881; Fax: 757-467-0284. Email: mailbox@chsvb.org. Web: www.chsvb.org. Rev. Msgr. William L. Pitt, Prin. Priests 2; Lay Teachers 46; Students 497.

[B] HIGH SCHOOLS, PRIVATE

RICHMOND. *Benedictine High School*, 304 N. Sheppard St., 23221. Tel: 804-342-1300; Fax: 804-342-1349. Email: info@benedictinehighschool.org. Web: www.benedictinehighschool.org. Very Rev. Michael Naughton, O.S.B., Pres. & Chm. Bd.; John B. McGinty, Headmaster. A Military High School in the Charge of the Benedictine Monks. Priests 2; Lay Teachers 33; Students 267.

Saint Gertrude High School, 3215 Stuart Ave., 23221. Tel: 804-358-9114; Fax: 804-355-5682. Email: sghs@saintgertrude.org. Web: www.saintgertrude.org. Sr. Charlotte Lange, O.S.B., Prin. Benedictine Sisters 1; Lay Teachers 29; Students 263.

WILLIAMSBURG. *Walsingham Academy Upper School*, (Grades 8-12), 1100 Jamestown Rd., 23185. Tel: 757-229-6026; Fax: 757-259-1401. Email: jcorrigan@walsingham.org. Web: www.walsingham.org. Jeffrey Corrigan, Prin. Private Day School for Boys and Girls. Sisters of Mercy 2; Lay Teachers 28; Students 302.

[C] ELEMENTARY SCHOOLS, DIOCESAN

RICHMOND. *All Saints Catholic School*, (Grades PreK-8), 3418 Noble Ave., 23222. Tel: 804-329-7524; Fax: 804-329-4201. Email: allsaintsric@juno.com. Web: www.allsaintsric.com. Lay Teachers 14; Total Staff 26; Total Enrollment 203.

St. Benedict School, (Grades K-8), 3100 Grove Ave., 23221. Tel: 804-254-8850. Email: ERossmoore@SaintBenedictSchool.org. Web: www.SaintBenedictSchool.org. Teachers 16; Total Staff 25; Total Enrollment 242.

St. Bridget School, (Grades K-8), 6011 York Rd., 23226. Tel: 804-288-1994; Fax: 804-288-5730. Email: information@saintbridget.org. Web: www.saintbridget.org. Priests 2; Lay Teachers 28; Total Staff 24; Total Enrollment 469.

St. Edward/Epiphany School, (Grades PreK-8), 10701 W. Huguenot Rd., 23235. Tel: 804-272-2881; Fax: 804-327-0788. Email: office@seeschool.com. Web: www.seeschool.com. Lay Teachers 29; Total Enrollment 476.

St. Mary's Catholic School, (Grades PreK-8), 9501 Gayton Rd., 23229. Tel: 804-740-1048; Fax: 804-740-1310. Email: jmregec@saintmary.org. Web: www.saintmary.org.

St. Patrick School, (Grades K-8), 2600 E. Grace St., 23222. Tel: 804-648-3621; Fax: 804-649-7717. Email: durban@richmonddiocese.org. Web: www.stpatricksschool.com. Mr. David Urban, Prin. Lay Teachers 12; Total Staff 17; Total Enrollment 79.

BLACKSBURG. *St. Mary's Preschool*, Formerly St. Mary Catholic School, 706 Harding Ave., N.E., 24060-3618. Tel: 540-951-0916; Fax: 540-953-2962. Lesley Lafon, Dir. (Ages 2 1/2 to 4 years of age). Lay Teachers 4; Students 38.

BRISTOL. *St. Anne School*, (Grades PreK-8), 300 Euclid Ave., 24201. Tel: 276-669-0048; Fax: 276-669-3523. Email: sas@stannes-bristol.org. Web: www.stannes-bristol.org. Dr. Jean Green, Prin. Lay Teachers 24; Total Staff 24; Total Enrollment 302.

CHARLOTTESVILLE. *Charlottesville Catholic Elementary School*, (Grades K-8), 1205 Pen Park Rd., 22901. Tel: 434-964-0400; Fax: 434-964-1373. Email: ddolan@cvillecatholic.com. Web: www.cvillecatholic.com. Dr. Grace Viere, Prin. Lay Teachers 23; Aides 5; Students 271.

HAMPTON. *St. Mary Star of the Sea*, (Grades PreK-8), 14 N. Willard Ave., 23663. Tel: 757-723-6358; Fax: 757-723-6544. Email: admin@SaintMaryStaroftheSea. Web: www.SaintMaryStaroftheSea.com. Sisters 4; Lay Teachers 15; Total Staff 27; Total Enrollment 206.

NEWPORT NEWS. *Our Lady of Mt Carmel*, (Grades PreK-7), 52 Harpersville Rd., 23601. Tel: 757-596-2754; Fax: 757-596-1570. Email: olmcdevelopment@ad.com. Web: www.olmc.org. Sisters 3; Lay Teachers 29; Total Staff 54; Total Enrollment 564.

NORFOLK. *Christ the King*, (Grades PreK-8), 3401 Tidewater Dr., 23509. Tel: 757-625-4951; Fax: 757-623-5212. Web: http://www.ctkparish.org. Priests 1; Lay Teachers 23; Total Staff 32; Total Enrollment 330.

Holy Trinity School, (Grades PreK-8), 154 W. Government Ave., 23503. Tel: 757-583-1873; Fax: 757-587-3677. Email: dnofplot@HolyTrinitySchoolVA.com. Web: www.HolyTrinitySchoolVA.com. Lay Teachers 13; Total Staff 24; Total Enrollment 201.

St. Pius X School, (Grades PreK-8), 7800 Halprin Dr., 23518. Tel: 757-588-6171; Fax: 757-587-6580. Email: stpiusoffice@yahoo.com. Web: www.rc.net/richmond/stpiusx/. Lay Teachers 26; Total Staff 39; Total Enrollment 408.

PETERSBURG. *St. Joseph School*, (Grades PreK-8), 123 Franklin St., 23803. Tel: 804-732-3931; Fax: 804-732-6479. Email: school@saintjosephschool.com. Web: www.saintjosephschool.com. Sisters 2; Lay Teachers 15; Total Staff 28; Total Enrollment 165.

PORTSMOUTH. *Portsmouth Catholic Elementary*, 2301 Oregon Ave., 23701. Tel: 757-488-6744; Fax: 757-465-8833. Email: pirates@pinn.net. Web: jbrown@portsmouthcatholic.com. Lay Teachers 14; Total Staff 22; Total Enrollment 251.

POWHATAN. *Blessed Sacrament/Huguenot School*, (Grades PreK-12), 2501 Academy Rd., 23139. Tel: 804-598-4211; Fax: 804-598-1053. Email: drhbsh@aol.com. Web: www.BlessedSacramentHuguenot.com. Dr. Lou Ross Hopewell, Pres.; Mr. John E. Talmadge Jr., Secondary Prin.; Mr. James Fortune, Elementary Prin. Religious 1; Lay Teachers 46; Students 500.

RICHMOND, HENRICO. *Our Lady of Lourdes School*, (Grades PreK-8), 8200 Woodman Rd., 23228. Tel: 804-262-1770; Fax: 804-262-1437. Email: ollofice@comcast.net. Web: www.oll-school.org. Total Staff 26; Total Enrollment 402.

STAUNTON. *Guardian Angels Regional School*, 410 W. Beverley St., 24401. Tel: 540-887-5900. Email: garcs24401@yahoo.com. Mrs. Mary Thompson, Prin.

VIRGINIA BEACH. *St. Gregory the Great School*, (Grades PreK-8), 5343 Virginia Beach Blvd., 23462. Tel: 757-497-1811; Fax: 757-497-7005. Email: podonne@stgregory.pvt.k12.va.us. Web: www.stgregory.pvt.k12va.us. Priests 1; Sisters 5; Teachers 44; Total Staff 48; Total Enrollment 760.

St. John the Apostle Catholic School, (Grades PreK-8), 1968 Sandbridge Rd., 23456. Tel: 757-821-1100; Fax: 757-821-1100. Email: sja.school@cov.net. Web: www.stjohnsandbridge.org. Charlene Feliton, Prin. Lay Teachers 15; Deacons 1; Total Staff 15; Total Enrollment 245.

St. Matthew School, (Grades PreK-8), 3316 Sandra Ln., 23464. Tel: 757-420-2455; Fax: 757-420-4880. Email: office@smsvb.net. Web: www.smsvb.net. Lay Teachers 32; Total Staff 66; Total Enrollment 625.

Star of the Sea School, (Grades PreK-8), 309 15th St., 23451. Tel: 757-428-8400; Fax: 757-428-2794. Email: information@sosschool.org. Web: www.sosschool.org. Lay Teachers 20; Total Staff 7; Total Enrollment 366.

[D] ELEMENTARY SCHOOLS, PRIVATE

WILLIAMSBURG. *Walsingham Academy Lower School*, (Grades PreK-7), 1100 Jamestown Rd., 23185. Tel: 757-229-2642 (Elementary); 757-229-6026 (Secondary); Fax: 757-259-1404. Email: walsingham@aol.com. Web: www.walsingham.org. Sr. Mary Jeanne Oesterle, R.S.M., Elementary Prin./Pres. Tel: 757-229-2642; Jeffrey Corrigan, Sec.Prin. Day School for Boys and Girls. Sisters 3; Lay Teachers 69; Students 703.

[E] GENERAL HOSPITALS

RICHMOND. *St. Mary's Hospital*, 5801 Bremo Rd., 23226. Tel: 804-285-2011; Fax: 804-627-5404. Web: www.bonsecours.com. Peter Bernard, Senior Vice Pres.; Rev. Joseph D'Aurora, Chap. Sisters of Bon Secours Sisters 3; Bed Capacity 391; Total Staff 1,544; Inpatients 20,386; Outpatients 255,222.

Bon Secours-Maryview Health Corporation Tel: 757-398-2200.

**Bon Secours-Maryview Foundation, Inc.* Tel: 757-398-2200.

Bon Secours-St. Mary's Health Care Foundation Tel: 804-342-1528; Fax: 804-287-7316.

Bon Secours-Stuart Circle Hospital Tel: 804-354-1121.

Bon Secours-Richmond Community Hospital Tel: 804-225-1701; Fax: 804-225-1725.

Bon Secours-Richmond Health System Tel: 804-281-8317; Fax: 804-282-1243.

NEWPORT NEWS. *Mary Immaculate Hospital*, 2 Bernardine Dr., 23602-4499. Tel: 757-886-6600; Fax: 757-886-6751. Web: www.bonsecourshamptonroads.com. Cynthia B. Farrand, Exec. Vice Pres. & Admin. Tel: 757-886-6768; Fax: 757-886-6751; Sr. Bernard Marie Magill, O.S.F., M.S., Dir. Pastoral Care Dept. The Bernardine Sisters of the Third Order of St. Francis 12; Bed Capacity 110; Nurses 303; Staff 629; Patients Assisted Annually 156,691.

Bernardine Franciscan Sisters Foundation, Inc., 3 Bernardine Dr., 23602. Tel: 757-886-6025; Fax: 757-886-6881.

NORFOLK. *Bon Secours De Paul Medical Center, Inc.*, 150 Kingsley Ln., 23505. Tel: 757-889-5000; Fax: 757-889-5837. Email: bonsecourshamptonroads.com. Susan Erickson, Exec. Vice Pres. & Admin.

Legal Title: *Bon Secours DePaul Medical Center*

Legal Title: *Bon Secours DePaul Health Foundation*

Legal Title: *Bon Secours Bayley Properties* Sisters of Bon Secours, Clinic is connected with hospital. Sisters 1; Staff 835; Bed Capacity 238; Patients Assisted Annually 6,954.

NORTON. *St. Mary's Hospital, Inc.*, P.O. Box 620, 24273. Tel: 540-679-9100; Fax: 540-679-7549. Email: office-lester@bshsl.org. Web: www.smhnorton.org. Luther E. Reeves, CEO. CBS Bon Secours Sisters Sisters 5; Bed Capacity 133; Patients Assisted Annually 74,816; Nurses 146; Staff 396.

PORTSMOUTH. *Maryview Behavioral Medicine Center*, 3636 High St., 23707. Tel: 757-398-2361; Fax: 757-398-2396. Web: www.BonSecoursHamptonRoads.com. Allan D. Erbe, Admin. Bed Capacity 54; Patients Assisted Annually 2,500; Total Staff 65.

Maryview Medical Center, 3636 High St., 23707. Tel: 757-398-2200; Fax: 757-398-2359. Web: http://www.bonsecourshamptonroads.com. Dominick Calgi, Exec. Vice Pres. & Admin.; Richard Chasse, Dir. Pastoral Care; Rita Hickey, Vice Pres. Mission; Rev. Pantaleon O. Manalo, Chap.; Sr. Grace Malonzo, Chap.; Kathy Kofron, Chap.

Legal Title: *Maryview Hospital* Sisters of Bon Secours Bed Capacity 341; Patients Assisted Annually 15,191; Total Staff 1,924.

[F] ORPHANAGES AND INFANT HOMES

RICHMOND. *St. Joseph's Villa*, 8000 Brook Rd., 23227-1338. Tel: 804-553-3200; Fax: 804-553-3259. Email: helpinghands@sjvmail.net. Web: www.stjosephsvilla.net. Mr. Ramon E. Pardue, CEO. Children in Residence 15; Children in Day Care 200; Children in Extended Day Services 15; Children in Special Education 50; Children in Alternative Education 30; Children in Transitional Housing 80; Total Staff 304.

NORFOLK. *St. Mary's Home for Disabled Children*, 317 Chapel St., 23504. Tel: 757-622-2208; Fax: 757-627-5314. William M. Jolly, Admin. Long term care for multiply handicapped children birth to eleven years old. Daughters of Wisdom 2; Bed Capacity 88; Total Staff 180.

ROANOKE. *DePaul Family Services, Inc.*, 5650 Hollins Rd., 24019. Tel: 540-265-8923; Fax: 540-265-7663. Email: info@DePaulFamilyServices.org. Web: www.DePaulFamilyServices.org. Herb Beskar, Exec. Dir. Treatment Foster Care. Total Assisted 525; Total Staff 200.

[G] CHILD LEARNING CENTERS

RICHMOND. *Holy Angels*, 1307 Lakeside Ave., 23228. Tel: 804-266-7200; Fax: 804-264-2906. Email: cmsusacommunity@mindspring.com. Sr. M. Bernadette Hilmer, C.M.S. Comboni Missionary Sisters 3; Lay Teachers 3; Children 44.

Sacred Heart Center, Inc., 1400 Perry St., 23224. Tel: 804-230-4399; Fax: 804-231-7247. Email: shcexecutive@mindspring.com. Naomi Chambers-Taylor, Exec. Dir. Neighboring Communities Day Care, After School Care, Adult

Education, Social Services.

NORFOLK. *Christ the King Extended Care*, 3401 Tidewater Dr., 23509. Tel: 757-627-0119; Fax: 757-623-5212. Email: ulrike@hamptonrds.com. Mrs. Uli Williford, Admin. Children 150.

POWHATAN. *St. John Neumann Family Life Center*, 2480 Batterson Rd., 23139. Tel: 804-598-3754; Fax: 804-598-1467. Email: sjn_powva@juno.com. Rev. J. Morton Biber, Board Pres.

ROANOKE. *The Achievement Center-St. Vincent's Home, Inc.* Tel: 540-982-0128; Fax: 540-982-3629. Email: tacenter@rev.net. Web: www.achievementcenter.org. P.O. Box 12368, 24025. Tel: 540-982-0128; Fax: 540-982-3629. 615 N. Jefferson St., 24016. Rebecca Clendenin, Dir. Private day school for children with learning disabilities. Total Assisted 140.

VIRGINIA BEACH. *Holy Family Day School*, 1279 N. Great Neck Rd., 23454-2117. Tel: 757-481-5702; Fax: 757-481-3989. Bernice Krauchak, Bookkeeper.

[H] HOMES FOR THE AGED

RICHMOND. *St. Francis Home, Inc.*, 2511 Wise St., 23225-3952. Tel: 804-231-1043; Fax: 804-231-1065. Email: davidcran@mindspring.com. Mr. David Cran, Dir. Total Staff 38; Bed Capacity 63.

St. Joseph's Home for the Aged, 1503 Michael Rd., 23229. Tel: 804-288-6245; Fax: 804-288-8906. Email: msrichesp@earthlink.net. Sr. Caroline John Pesartic, L.S.P., Supr. Attended by Rev. Donald F. Scales, O.S.B. Little Sisters of the Poor 9; Guests 96; Total Assisted Annually 70; Total Staff 96.

St. Mary Wood's, 1257 Marywood Ln., 23229. Tel: 804-741-8624; Fax: 804-740-7912. Email: stmw@mindspring.com. Web: www.stmaryswoods@worldnet.att.net. Randy Scott, Admin. Units 118; Independent Units 54; Total Staff 56; Total Assisted 64.

Marywood Apartments, 1261 Marywood Ln., 23229. Tel: 804-740-5567; Fax: 804-740-9016. Email: marywood@msn.com. Patricia Scott, Senior Mgr. Residents 129; Total Staff 7.

Our Lady of Hope Health Center, Inc., 13700 N. Gayton Rd., 23233. Tel: 804-360-1960; Fax: 804-364-0737. Email: gashley@ourladyofhope.com. Web: www.ourladyofhope.com. Gregory Ashley, Admin. Residents 133; Nursing Home Residents 60; Total Assisted Annually 77; Total Staff 150.

CHARLOTTESVILLE. *Our Lady of Peace*, 751 Hillsdale Dr., 22901. Tel: 434-973-1155; Fax: 434-973-3397. David L. Rawlings, Admin. Nursing Bed Capacity 30; Independent Units 32; Assisted Units 102.

HAMPTON. *Seton Manor*, 215 Marcella Rd., 23666. Tel: 757-827-6512; Fax: 757-827-0132. Victoria Harris, Mgr. Residents 112; Total Staff 5.

LYNCHBURG. *McGurk House Apartments*, 2425 Tate Springs Rd., 24501. Tel: 434-846-2425; Fax: 434-847-5046. Email: mcgurkhouse@lynchburg.net. Hannah Herward, Dir. Independent Living for adults 62 yrs. or older, or mobility impaired. Apartments 88; Total Staff 5.

NEWPORT NEWS. *St. Francis Nursing Center*, 4 Ridgewood Pkwy., 23602. Tel: 757-886-6500; Fax: 757-886-6539. Web: www.bshsihr.com. Lorraine Meadows, Admin. Tel: 757-886-6500. Bed Capacity 115; Total Assisted 1,339; Total Assisted Annually 108; Total Staff 118.

NORFOLK. *Madonna Home*, 814 W. 37th St., 23508. Tel: 757-623-6662; Fax: 757-623-4966. Charlene Davis, Dir. Total Staff 6; Residents 16; Total Assisted Annually 16.

ROANOKE. *Our Lady of the Valley Retirement Community*, 650 N. Jefferson St., 24016. Tel: 540-345-5111; Fax: 540-985-6561. Web: www.OurLadyoftheValley.com. Ms. Michele Crigger, Admissions Coord. Assisted Living Units 86; Skilled Nursing Facility Beds 70.

Sullivan House, Inc., 3333 Peter's Creek Rd., 24019. Tel: 540-563-4565; Fax: 540-362-2365. Email: jsink@csm.roacoxmail.com. Mary Ellen C. Cox, Pres. Tel: 804-227-3116; Fax: 804-227-3525; Jennifer Sink, Property Mgr. 67 units for very low income elderly.

SUFFOLK. *Bon Secours-Maryview Nursing Care*, 4775 Bridge Rd., 23435. Tel: 757-686-0488; Fax: 757-686-8211. Steven L. Minter, Admin. Bed Capacity 120.

Martha W. Davis Cancer Center
Maryview Employee Assistance Program
Maryview MedCare Centers (Urgent Care)
Maryview Wellspring Home Health Agency
Maryview Hospice Program

VIRGINIA BEACH. *Marian Manor*, 5345 Marian Ln., 23462. Tel: 757-456-5018; Fax: 757-497-7561. Email: mmanor@bellatlantic.net. Loryn Duncan-Marcil, Admin. Units 117; Total Assisted Annually 135; Total Staff 88.

Our Lady of Perpetual Help Health Center, Inc., 4560 Princess Anne Rd., 23462-7905. Tel: 757-495-4211; Fax: 757-495-7366. Email: olph1@bellatlantic.net. Web: www.OurLadyPerpetualHelp.com. Total Assisted Annually 120; Total Staff 145.

Russell House, 900 First Colonial Rd., 23454. Tel: 757-481-0770; Fax: 757-496-0859. Email: russellhouse@erols.com. Eleanor Olsen, Admin. Total Staff 6; Units 119; Residents 126.

The Sullivan House, 2033 General Booth Blvd., 23454. Tel: 757-437-0220. Mrs. Joanne Lindauer, Admin.

[I] HOME FOR HANDICAPPED ADULTS

RICHMOND. *St. Joseph's Villa Housing Corp.*, 7700 Brook Rd., 23227-1399. Tel: 804-553-3258; Fax: 804-553-3259. Email: sjvmail.net. Web: www.stjosephsvilla.net. Dr. Marty Muguira, Exec. Dir. Apartments for Adults with Disabilities and the Elderly. Apartments 30.

St. Joseph's Villa Housing Corp., II

[J] SERVICES FOR THE DISABLED

RICHMOND. *Hollybrook I & II* Apartments for adults with disabilities and the elderly. Tel 804-553-3283; Fax: 804-553-3259. Email: helpinghands@stjosephsvilla.net. Web: www.stjosephsvilla.net. *St. Joseph Villa*, 7700 Brook Rd., 23229. Tel: 804-553-3200; Fax: 804-553-3259. Dr. Marty Muguira, Exec. Dir Apartments 30.

Sean's Place, 713 N. First St., 23219. Tel: 804-344-8164; Fax: 804-233-3867. Web: www.hopeforhomeless.org. Mr. Pete Jones, Prog. Coord.

LYNCHBURG. *Nott Homes, Inc.*, 3009-3011 Roundelay Rd., 24502. Tel: 804-239-0722; Fax: 434-239-1042. Hallie Thaxton, Residential Mgr. Residents 8.

[K] SPECIALIZED SERVICES

RICHMOND. *Commonwealth Catholic Charities*, 1512 Willow Lawn Dr., 23230-0565. Tel: 804-285-5900; Fax: 804-285-9130. Email: agency@cccofvirginia.org. Web: www.cccofvirginia.org. Rev. David J. Bergner, S.D.S., Exec. Dir.

Satellite Offices:

820 Campbell Ave., S.W., Roanoke 24016. Tel: 540-344-5107; Fax: 540-344-2748.

Woodbrook Shopping Center, 1859-C3 Seminole Tr., Charlottesville, 22901. Tel: 434-974-6880; Fax: 434-974-4610.

Connections, 302 McClanahan St., S.W., Roanoke, 24014. Tel: 540-342-0411; Fax: 540-342-3307.

1024 Park Ave., N.W., Norton, 24273. Tel: 276-679-0967; Fax: 276-679-2719. Total Assisted 13,600.

VIRGINIA BEACH. *Catholic Charities of Hampton Roads, Inc.*, 4855 Princess Anne Rd., 23462. Tel: 757-437-7707; Fax: 757-495-3206. Email: administration@cc-hr.org. Web: www.cc-hr.org. Margaret M. Robertson, Exec. Dir.

Branch Offices:

12829 Jefferson Ave., Ste. 101, Newport News, 23608. Tel: 757-875-0060; Fax: 757-877-7883.

1301 Colonial Ave., Norfolk, 23517. Tel: 757-625-2568; Fax: 757-625-5684.

3804 Poplar Hill Rd., Ste. A, Chesapeake, 23321. Tel: 757-484-0703; Fax: 757-484-1096.

1315 Jamestown Rd., Suite 202, Williamsburg, 23185. Tel: 757-253-2847; Fax: 757-253-1296. Total Assisted 12,142.

121 S. Main St., Franklin, 23851. Tel: 757-562-6222; Fax: 757-652-3930.

Other Offices:

Catholic Charities Outreach Center, 269 Clearfield Ave., 23462. Tel: 757-490-4931; Fax: 757-490-7747.

[L] MONASTERIES AND RESIDENCES OF PRIESTS AND BROTHERS

RICHMOND. *Mary Mother of the Church Abbey*, 12829 River Rd., 23233. Tel: 804-784-3508; Fax: 804-784-2214. Email: abbots_office@richmondmonks.org. Web: www.richmondmonks.org. Rt. Rev. Benedict R. McDermott, O.S.B., Abbot (Retired); Very Rev. Michael Naughton, O.S.B., Admin.; Revs. Donald F. Scales, O.S.B., Prior; Adrian W. Harmening, O.S.B., Procurator; Theophile W. Brown, O.S.B.; Augustine W. Ludwig, O.S.B.; Anthony W. Morris, O.S.B.; Joseph M. Lukyamuzi, O.S.B.; Bros. David Owen, O.S.B.; Mark Purcell, O.S.B.; Barry Butler, O.S.B.; Jeffery Williams, O.S.B.; James Glass, O.S.B.; Robert Nguyen, O.S.B.; John Simes, O.S.B.; Gregory Gresko, O.S.B.; John Mary Lugemwa, O.S.B. Benedictine Monks Priests 8; Brothers 9.

WEST POINT. *Missionaries of the Holy Family, General Mission Office--M.S.F., Inc.*, P.O. Box 918, 23181. Tel: 804-843-2622; Fax: 804-843-3182. Rev. John Brieffies, M.S.F., Pres. & Dir.

[M] CONVENTS AND RESIDENCES FOR SISTERS

RICHMOND. *Benedictine Sisters of Virginia, Saint Gertrude Convent*, Formerly Benedictine Sisters of Virginia, St. Gertrude Convent, 200 N. Sheppard St., 23221. Tel: 804-342-1468. Sisters Anita Sherwood, O.S.B.; Charlotte Lange, O.S.B.; M. Gertrude Mueller, O.S.B. Sisters 3.

Comboni Missionary Sisters, Provincial House, 1307 Lakeside Ave., 23228. Tel: 804-266-2975; 804-262-8827; Fax: 804-264-2906. Email: combonisrs@ige.org. Web: www.combonisrs.com. Sr. Maria Teresa Goffi, C.M.S., Prov. Sisters 25.

BARHAMSVILLE. *Bethlehem Monastery of the Poor Clare Nuns*, 5500 Hollyfork Rd., 23011. Tel: 757-566-9081; Fax: 757-566-9082. Web: www.poor-clares.org. Sr. Mary Colette, Abbess. Observing the Primitive Rule of St. Clare, Constitutions of the Poor Clare Federation of Mary Immaculate (strictly cloistered, solemn vows). Solemnly Professed 12; Novices 3.

CROZET. *Our Lady of the Angels Monastery*, Cistercian Nuns of the Strict Observance (Virginia), 3365 Monastery Dr., 22932. Tel: 434-823-1452; Fax: 434-823-6379. Email: community@olamonastery.org. Web: www.olamonastery.org. Sr. Marion Rissetto, Prioress. Professed 8.

NEWPORT NEWS. *Bernardine Sisters of the Third Order of St. Francis*, 6E Ridgewood Pkwy., 23602. Tel: 757-886-6395; Fax: 757-886-6751. Email: kwieleba@cox.net. Web: www.bfranciscan.org. Sisters 11.

NORFOLK. *Sisters Servants of the Immaculate Heart of Mary*

St. Pius X Convent, 7813 Halprin Dr., 23518. Tel: 757-587-8657 Home; 757-588-6171 Work; Fax: 757-587-6580. Email: piusihmva@aol.com. Sr. Marie Renee Murphy, I.H.M., Supr. Sisters 5.

NORTON. *Poor Servants of the Mother of God*, P.O. Box 1080, 24273. Tel: 276-679-0477; Fax: 276-679-3581. Email: smgoo@bellatlantic.net. Web: www.poorservants.org. Sr. Loretta O'Connor, S.M.G., Sister in Charge. Sisters 5.

PETERSBURG. *Daughters of Charity of St. Vincent de Paul*, St. Joseph Convent, 127 Franklin St., 23803-3307. Tel: 804-732-8501; Fax: 804-862-9931. Email: stjpburg@juno.com. Web: www.daughtersofcharity-emmitsburg.org. Sr. Mary Beard, Local Supr. Sisters 5.

PORTSMOUTH. *Sisters of Bon Secours*, 412 West Rd., 23707. Tel: 757-397-3869. Email: rita_thomas@bshsi.com. Sr. Rita Thomas, Pres. Sisters 2.

ROCKVILLE. *Monastery of the Visitation Monte Maria*, 12221 Bienvenue Rd., 23146. Tel: 804-749-4885; Fax: 804-749-8606. Sr. Margaret Mary McGuire, Supr. Visitation Sisters 14.

VIRGINIA BEACH. *Sisters Servants of I.H.M.*, St. Gregory the Great, 5349 Virginia Beach Blvd., 23462. Tel: 757-497-7517; Fax: 757-490-1492. Email: helenek2@aol.com stgregsihms@aol.com Convent. Sr. Helene J. Kollar, Supr.

WILLIAMSBURG. *Sisters of Mercy*, Walsingham Academy, P.O. Box 8702, 1100 Jamestown Rd., 23187-8702. Tel: 757-229-2642; Fax: 757-259-1401. Email: larkrsm@hotmail.com. Web: www.walsingham. Sisters Kathleen Fox, Coord.; Carol Larkin, Treas.; Jean A. Burns; Berenice Eltz; Mary Jeanne Oesterle, R.S.M. Sisters 5.

[N] RETREAT HOUSES

RICHMOND. *Benedictine Retreat and Conference Center*, Mary Mother of the Church Abbey, 12829 River Rd., 23233. Tel: 804-784-3508; Fax: 804-784-2214. Email: retreat_director@richmondmonks.org. Web: www.richmondmonks.org. Bro. Jeffery Williams.

The Dwelling Place, 601 Holly Grove Ln., 23235. Tel: 804-323-3360.

Conducted by: Patricia Carreras; Audrey Stech.

Richmond Hill

Ecumenical Center, 2209 E. Grace St., 23235. Tel: 804-783-7903. Rev. Benjamin Campbell, Pastoral Dir.

ABINGDON. *Jubilee House Retreat Center*, 822 E. Main St., 24210-4415. Tel: 276-619-0919; Fax: 276-739-7753. Email: info@jubileeretreat.com. Web: www.jubileeretreat.com. Sr. Stephanie Ward, O.S.F., Dir.

HAMPTON. *Holy Family Retreat*, 1414 N. Mallory St., P.O. 3151, 23663. Tel: 757-722-3997; Fax: 757-723-2478. Email: holyfretreat@aol.com. Revs. Vincent Douglass, Supr. & Dir.; Charles J. Brinkmann, C.SS.R., Asst. Retreat Dir.; Vang C. Trang, C.S.R., Asst. Retreat Dir.

LYNCHBURG. *Tabor Retreat Center*, 2125 Langhorne Rd., 24501. Tel: 434-846-6475; Fax: 434-846-3047. Email: revgordonc@aol.com. Deacon Gordon Cartwright.

MONTPELIER. *Shalom House*

Retreat Center, P.O. Box 196, 23192. Tel: 804-883-6149; Fax: 804-883-5298. Ms. Catherine Cawley, Dir.

ROANOKE. *Madonna House*, 828 Campbell Ave., S.W., 24016. Tel: 540-343-8464. Web:

www.madonnahouse.org. Patricia Lawton, Dir.

SMITHFIELD. *The Well*, 18047 Quiet Way, 23430. Tel: 757-255-2366; Fax: 757-255-2366. Email: staff@thewellretreatcenter.org. Web: www.thewellretreatcenter.org. Sr. Nancy Healy, S.F.C.C., Co-Dir.; Diane Weymouth, Co-Dir.

[O] MISCELLANEOUS

RICHMOND. *The Catholic Foundation of the Diocese of Richmond*, 811 Cathedral Pl., 23220. Tel: 804-359-5661; Fax: 804-358-9159. Email: kbishop@richmonddiocese.org. Mrs. Karen Bishop, Contact Person.

St. Francis Home of Richmond Foundation, Ltd., 2511 Wise St., 23224. Tel: 804-231-1043; Fax: 804-231-1065. David Cran, Dir. Provides grants to subsidize cost of care for aged, infirm and disabled residents of limited means.

Shroud of Turin Center, Mary Mother of the Church Abbey, 12829 River Rd., 23233. Tel: 804-784-3366; Fax: 804-784-3431. Email: shroud@erols.com. Web: http://membersaol.com/turin99/shroud.htm. Bryan Walsh, Dir. Provides educational services and conducts historical research into the Shroud of Turin.

Transitional Housing

Flagler Home-St. Joseph's Villa, 8000 Brook Rd., 23227-1399. Tel: 804-553-3258; Fax: 804-553-3259. Email: helpinghands@stjosephsvilla.net. Web: www.st.josephsvilla.net. Brenda Bonuccelli-Puerto, Prog. Dir. Women & Children in residence 70.

CHARLOTTESVILLE. *Saint Anselm Institute for Catholic Thought*, P.O. Box 6432, 22906-6432. Tel: 434-924-6709; Fax: 434-924-1467. Email: rlw2w@virginia.edu. Web: www.stanselminstitute.org. Robert L. Wilken, Pres.

NORFOLK. **Barry Robinson Schools of Norfolk*, P.O. Box 1180, 23501. Tel: 757-455-7120. Charles V. McPhillips, Pres.

PORTSMOUTH. *Catholic Elementary Education Foundation of Hampton Roads*, 2301 Oregon Ave., 23701. Tel: 757-488-6744; Fax: 757-465-8833. Email: pces@pinn.net pirates@pinn.net. Web: www.portsmouthcatholic.com. Mr. Edward Williams, Prin.

ROANOKE. *Catholic Historical Society of the Roanoke Valley* (Museum & Religious Goods) , 400 W. Campbell Ave., 24016. Tel: 540-982-0152; Fax: 540-982-0152. Vernon E. Jolley, Pres.

St. Francis House, Inc., P.O. Box 2215, 24009. Tel: 540-345-9090. Email: feedthepoor@cox.net. Eileen Stone, Dir. Food Distribution & Social Svcs.

VIRGINIA BEACH. *Catholic Charities of Hampton Roads Foundation*, 4855 Princess Anne Rd., 23462. Tel: 757-467-7707. Email: mrobertson@cc-hr.org. Web: www.cc-hr.org. Margaret Robertson, Exec. Dir.

Catholic Diocese of Richmond Boy Scouts, Inc., 6300 Bucknell Cir., 23464. Tel: 757-424-2619. Email: tynwolf@aol.com. Paul Janka, Contact.

WILLIAMSBURG. **Little Sisters of St. Francis, United States and Canada Regional Center*, P.O. Box 1356, 23187. Tel: 757-564-7371; Fax: 757-564-0984. Email: lwangahouse@cox.net. Sisters Agnes Narocho, 2204 Jolly Pond Rd., 23188; Mary Grace Nasambu, 2204 Jolly Pond Rd., 23188; Rev. Philip Ghys, O.S.B., 2204 Jolly Pond Rd., 23188.

RELIGIOUS INSTITUTES OF MEN REPRESENTED IN THE DIOCESE

For further details refer to the corresponding bracketed number in the Religious Institutes of Men or Women section.

[0200]—*Benedictine Monks* (Latrobe, PA)—O.S.B.
[1350]—*Brothers of St. Francis Xavier*—C.F.X.
[0630]—*Congregation of the Missionaries of the Holy Family*—M.S.F.
[0570]—*The Glenmary Home Missioners*—Glmy.
[0690]—*Jesuits Fathers and Brothers*—S.J.
[0430]—*Order of Preachers (Dominicans)* (Province of St. Joseph)—O.P.
[1070]—*Redemptorist Fathers* (Baltimore Prov.)—C.SS.R.

RELIGIOUS INSTITUTES OF WOMEN REPRESENTED IN THE DIOCESE

[0230]—*Benedictine Sisters of Pontifical Jurisdiction*—O.S.B.
[1810]—*Bernardine Sisters of the Third Order of St. Francis*—O.S.F.
[0670]—*Cistercian Nuns of the Strict Observance*—O.C.S.O.
[0690]—*Comboni Missionary Sisters*—C.M.S.
[0270]—*Congregation of Bon Secours*—C.B.S.
[1070-09]—*Congregation of St. Catherine of Siena, Racine*—O.P.
[1070-07]—*Congregation of St. Cecelia, Nashville*—O.P.
[1070-13]—*Congregation of the Most Holy Rosary, Adrian*—O.P.
[1920]—*Congregation of the Sisters of the Holy Cross*—C.S.C.
[0760]—*Daughters of Charity of St. Vincent de Paul*—D.C.
[0820]—*Daughters of the Holy Spirit*—D.H.S.
[0960]—*Daughters of Wisdom*—D.W.
[1180]—*The Franciscan Sisters*—O.S.F.
[1840]—*Grey Nuns of the Sacred Heart*—G.N.S.H.
[2575]—*Institute of the Sisters of Mercy of the Americas*—R.S.M.
[2340]—*Little Sisters of the Poor*—L.S.P.
[2490]—*Medical Mission Sisters*—S.C.M.M.
[2490]—*Medical Mission Sisters*—M.M.S.
[2480]—*Medical Missionaries of Mary*—M.M.M.
[2790]—*Missionary Servants of the Most Blessed Trinity*—M.S.B.T.
[3760]—*Order of St. Clare*—P.C.C.
[3640]—*Poor Servants of the Mother of God*—S.M.G.
[3465]—*Religious of the Sacred Heart of Mary* (Eastern American Prov.)—R.S.H.M
[2970]—*School Sisters of Notre Dame*—S.S.N.D.
[1070-03]—*Sinsinawa Dominican Congregation of the Most Holy Rosary*—O.P.
[]—*Sisters for Christian Community*—S.F.C.C.
[0500]—*Sisters of Charity of Nazareth*—S.C.N.
[0590]—*Sisters of Charity of St. Elizabeth, Convent Station*—S.C.
[0990]—*Sisters of Divine Providence* (Our Lady of Divine Providence Prov.)—C.D.P.
[2990]—*Sisters of Notre Dame*—S.N.D.
[3000]—*Sisters of Notre Dame de Namur*—S.N.D.deN.
[1530]—*Sisters of St. Francis of the Congregation of Our Lady of Lourdes, Sylvania, Ohio*—O.S.F.
[3840]—*Sisters of St. Joseph of Carondelet*—C.S.J.
[2980]—*Sisters of the Congregation of Notre Dame*—C.N.D.
[1990]—*Sisters of the Holy Names of Jesus and Mary*—S.N.J.M.
[2110]—*Sisters of the Humility of Mary*—H.M.
[2170]—*Sisters, Servants of the Immaculate Heart of Mary* (Immaculata, PA)—I.H.M.
[4130]—*Ursuline Sisters of the Congregation of Tildonk, Belgium*—O.S.U.
[4190]—*Visitation Nuns*—V.H.M.

DIOCESAN CEMETERIES

RICHMOND. *Holy Cross*, First Ave. & Daniels St., 23222. Tel: 804-321-5936.

Mount Calvary, 1400 S. Randolph St., 23220. Tel: 804-355-5271.

LYNCHBURG. *Holy Cross*, 710 Clay St., 24504. Tel: 804-846-5245.

NORFOLK. *St. Mary's*, 722 E. 30th St., 23504. Tel: 757-627-2874.

PORTSMOUTH. *Portsmouth Catholic*, P.O. Box 155, 23705. Tel: 757-488-1723.

ROANOKE. *St. Andrew*, 3601 Salem Tpke., N.W., 24017. Tel: 540-342-9180.

NECROLOGY

† Cassidy, Patrick, (Retired)—Died Sept. 29, 2003
† Gloisten, Robert, Richmond, VA St. Patrick—Died Dec. 2, 2002
† Nolte, William, (Retired)—Died Nov. 17, 2002

Diocese of Rochester

(Dioecesis Roffensis)

Most Reverend

MATTHEW H. CLARK, D.D.

Bishop of Rochester; ordained December 19, 1962; appointed Bishop of Rochester April 23, 1979;consecrated May 27, 1979; installed June 26, 1979 *Res.: 1150 Buffalo Rd., Rochester, NY 14624.*

Pastoral Center: 1150 Buffalo Rd., Rochester, NY 14624-1890. Tel: 585-328-3210; 800-388-7177; Fax: 585-328-3149.

Web: www.dor.org

ESTABLISHED MARCH 3, 1868.

Square Miles 7,107.

Comprises the Counties of Cayuga, Chemung, Livingston, Monroe, Ontario, Schuyler, Seneca, Steuben, Tioga, Tompkins, Wayne and Yates in the State of New York.

Legal Title of Diocese: The Diocese of Rochester.

Legal Title: For legal titles of parishes and diocesan institutions, consult the Pastoral Center.

STATISTICAL OVERVIEW

Personnel	
Bishop	1
Abbots	2
Retired Abbots	1
Priests: Diocesan Active in Diocese	119
Priests: Diocesan Active Outside Diocese	7
Priests: Retired, Sick or Absent	88
Number of Diocesan Priests	214
Religious Priests in Diocese	57
Total Priests in Diocese	271
Extern Priests in Diocese	31
Ordinations:	
Diocesan Priests	1
Transitional Deacons	1
Permanent Deacons	5
Permanent Deacons in Diocese	141
Total Brothers	31
Total Sisters	588
Parishes	
Parishes	151
With Resident Pastor:	
Resident Diocesan Priests	92
Resident Religious Priests	8
Without Resident Pastor:	
Administered by Priests	34
Administered by Deacons	2
Administered by Religious Women	10
Administered by Lay People	5
Missions	6
Professional Ministry Personnel:	
Sisters	68
Lay Ministers	322
Welfare	
Catholic Hospitals	2
Total Assisted	235,000
Health Care Centers	2
Total Assisted	1,200
Homes for the Aged	4
Total Assisted	1,525
Residential Care of Children	1
Total Assisted	42
Day Care Centers	1
Total Assisted	180
Specialized Homes	8
Total Assisted	525
Special Centers for Social Services	54
Total Assisted	720,000
Residential Care of Disabled	10
Total Assisted	100
Educational	
Seminaries, Diocesan	1
Diocesan Students in Other Seminaries	6
Total Seminarians	6
High Schools, Diocesan and Parish	1
Total Students	124
High Schools, Private	6
Total Students	3,475
Elementary Schools, Diocesan and Parish	48
Total Students	9,962
Elementary Schools, Private	2
Total Students	370
Catechesis/Religious Education:	
High School Students	4,134
Elementary Students	23,345
Total Students under Catholic Instruction	41,416
Teachers in the Diocese:	
Priests	13
Scholastics	7
Sisters	47
Lay Teachers	1,027
Vital Statistics	
Receptions into the Church:	
Infant Baptism Totals	5,989
Adult Baptism Totals	287
Received into Full Communion	731
First Communions	4,536
Confirmations	4,094
Marriages:	
Catholic	1,163
Interfaith	449
Total Marriages	1,612
Deaths	4,124
Total Catholic Population	341,500
Total Population	1,485,837

Former Bishops—Rt. Rev. BERNARD J. MCQUAID, D.D., ord. Jan. 16, 1848; appt. March 31, 1868; consecrated July 12, 1868; died Jan. 18, 1909; Most Revs. THOMAS F. HICKEY, D.D., ord. March 25, 1884; consecrated May 24, 1905; succeeded to the See, Jan. 18, 1909; appt. assistant at the Pontifical Throne, May 4, 1925; made Archbishop of the Titular See of Viminacium, Oct. 30, 1928;; died Dec. 10, 1940; JOHN FRANCIS O'HERN, D.D., ord. Feb. 17, 1901; appt. Bishop of Rochester, Jan. 4, 1929; consecrated March 19, 1929; died May 22, 1933; His Eminence EDWARD CARDINAL MOONEY, appt. Aug. 28, 1922; transferred to Detroit, May 26, 1937; installed Archbishop of Detroit, Aug. 3, 1937; created Cardinal, Feb. 18, 1946; died Oct. 25, 1958; Most Revs. JAMES E. KEARNEY, D.D. (Retired), ord. Sept. 19, 1908; appt. Bishop of Salt Lake, Utah, July 1, 1932; consecrated Oct. 28, 1932; transferred to Rochester, July 31, 1937; installed Nov. 11, 1937; retired Oct. 26, 1966; died Jan. 12, 1977; FULTON J. SHEEN, D.D., ord. Sept. 20, 1919; appt. Titular Bishop of Cesariana and Auxiliary of New York, May 28, 1951; consecrated June 11, 1951; appt. to Rochester, Oct. 26, 1966; installed Dec. 15, 1966; resigned Oct. 15, 1969; appt. Titular Archbishop of Newport; died Dec. 9, 1979; JOSEPH L. HOGAN, S.T.D., D.D. (Retired), ord. June 6, 1942; appt. to Rochester, Oct. 15, 1969; consecrated and installed Nov. 28, 1969; retired Nov. 28, 1978; died Aug. 27, 2000.

Pastoral Center Administration

Pastoral Center—1150 Buffalo Rd., Rochester, 14624-1890. Tel: 585-328-3210; 800-388-7177 (Toll Free within Diocese); Fax: 585-328-3149. Web: www.dor.org.

Vicars General—Revs. JOSEPH A. HART, S.T.D.; JOHN M. MULLIGAN, V.G.

Moderator of the Pastoral Center—Rev. JOSEPH A. HART, S.T.D.

Chancellor—Rev. DANIEL J. CONDON, J.C.L.

Judicial Vicar—Rev. LOUIS A. SIRIANNI, J.C.L.

Vice Chancellor and Administrator of the Bishop's Office—Sr. MARY ANN BINSACK, R.S.M.

Secretary to the Bishop—Mrs. MARY MOORHOUSE.

Office of the Chancellor and Department of Legal Services

Chancellor and Director of the Department of Legal Services—Rev. DANIEL J. CONDON, J.C.L.

Judicial Vicar—Rev. LOUIS A. SIRIANNI, J.C.L.

Vice Chancellor—Sr. MARY ANN BINSACK, R.S.M.

Administrative Assistant—Ms. BARBARA FULLE.

Diocesan Archives—Sr. CONNIE DERBY, R.S.M., Dir. Archival Svcs.. Email: archives@dor.org; Rev. ROBERT F. MCNAMARA, Archivist (Retired), McAuley Residence, 1437 Blossom Rd., Rochester, 14610. Tel: 585-482-5442.

Censores Librorum—Revs. JOSEPH A. HART, S.T.D.; WILLIAM F. LAIRD, J.C.L.; Rev. Msgr. WILLIAM H. SHANNON (Retired); Revs. WILLIAM E. GRAF, D.Min.; PATRICK VAN DURME, S.T.L.; JOSEPH W. MARCOUX, S.T.L., 1150 Buffalo Rd., Rochester, 14624.

Conciliation Board—Rev. LANCE GONYO, 105 W. Main St., Sodus, 14551. Tel: 315-483-6111.

Tribunal—

Judges—Rev. LOUIS A. SIRIANNI, J.C.L., Judicial Vicar; Mr. RENATO AOANAN, J.C.L., Promoter of Justice & Defender of the Bond; Revs. R. RICHARD BRICKLER, Adjutant Judicial Vicar; DONALD J. CURTISS, J.C.L., Adjutant Judicial Vicar & Defender of the Bond; Rev. Msgr. GERARD C. KRIEG, J.C.L.; Ms. RENEE LISS-SIRACO, J.C.L.; Revs. JOHN A. LYNCH; JOHN M. MULLIGAN, V.G.; T. PIUS PATHMARAJAH, J.C.L.; Mr. JOHN G. SKVORAK, J.C.L.

Defenders of the Bond—Mr. RENATO AOANAN, J.C.L.; Revs. WILLIAM J. GORDINIER (Retired); DONALD A. CURTISS.

Staff—Ms. MARY ELLEN GOVERTS, Case Instructor & Notary; Rev. WILLIAM E. GRAF, D.Min., Advocate; Miss ANDREA IMBURGIA, Admin. Asst. & Notary; Deacon JAMES STEIGER, Auditor; Ms. ROSANNE WARNER, Case Monitor & Judicial Asst.

Consultative Bodies

Bishop's Stewardship Council—Most Rev. MATTHEW H. CLARK, D.D., Pres.; Ms. PATRICIA MALGIERI, Chm.

College of Consultors—Rev. DANIEL J. CONDON, J.C.L., Contact.

Priests' Council—Rev. CHARLES J. LATUS, Chm.

Regional Coordinators—Sr. MARY ANN BINSACK, R.S.M., Liaison.

Catholic Charities—

Catholic Charities of the Diocese of Rochester—1150 Buffalo Rd., Rochester, 14624. Tel: 585-328-3210. JACK BALINSKY, Diocesan Dir.; MAUREEN O'HARA,

Chm. Bd. Directors, (Refer to Catholic Charities section under Institutions Located in the Diocese for further listings).

Diocesan Newspaper "Catholic Courier"—Tel: 585-328-4340. KAREN FRANZ, Gen. Mgr. & Editor.

Board of Directors—Most Rev. MATTHEW H. CLARK, D.D., Pres.; Revs. JOSEPH HART, Vicar General & Vice Pres.; DANIEL J. CONDON, J.C.L., Sec.; MUSETTE CASTLE; Rev. PATRICK CONNOR; ROBERT FINNERTY; TIMOTHY FITZGERALD; WILLIAM H. KEDLEY; MARK HARE; RICHARD HARE; DAVID MACK; HELEN MCDERMOTT; GEORGE A. PARK JR.; JULIE THANEY.

Faith Development Ministry—

Department of Catholic Schools—Sr. ELIZABETH MEEGAN, O.P., Ph.D., Supt. Schools. Assistant Superintendents: Sisters PATRICIA CARROLL, S.S.J., Govt. Svcs. & Admin.; MARGARET MANCUSO, S.S.J., Curriculum & Instruction; Ms. PATRICIA JONES, Professional Devel.; Mrs. ANN FRANK, Assessment Coord.; Mr. GARY B. SMITH, Asst. Supt., Business; Sr. ELAINE ENGLERT, S.S.J., Dir., Catholic School Personnel & Recruitment.

Department of Evangelization and Catechesis—Ms. MARIBETH MANCINI, Dir.

Coordinator for Sacramental Catechesis—Sr. KAREN DIETZ, S.S.J.

AV Resource Librarian—Sr. CONNIE DERBY, R.S.M.

Director of Young Adult and Campus Ministry—SHANNON LOUGHLIN.

Program Specialist for Youth Ministry—SUE VERSLUYS.

Youth Minister for the City of Rochester—LYNETTE DEJESUS.

Director of Youth Ministry—MICHAEL THEISEN.

Office of Communications—

Director of Communications—Mr. DOUGLAS MANDELARO.

Director of School Communications—Mr. MICHAEL TEDESCO.

Office of Stewardship and Development—

Diocesan Director of Stewardship and Development—VACANT.

Associate Directors of Stewardship and Development—Mr. MARK J. CLARK; Mr. DAVID KELLY.

Administrative Assistant—Ms. LUCILLE BEARDEN.

Donor Relations Coordinator—VACANT.

Department of Financial Services—

Chief Financial Officer—Mr. JAMES M. RINEFIERD.

Assistant Director of Financial Services—Ms. MARY ZIARNIAK.

Buildings and Properties—Mr. ERIC PATCHKE, Mgr.

Information Systems And Research—

Diocesan Director—Ms. JOAN A. ZAIA.

AS/400 Coordinator—Mrs. LYNNE SUORSA.

Network Administrator—Mr. THOMAS VEEDER.

Associate Network Administrator—Mr. KEN MALETTE.

Parish Computer Coordinators—Mr. MARK DARLING; Mr. RICHARD BRAXTON; Mr. FRED STRINGER; Mr. RICHARD HARRINGTON, Coord., Catholic Charities Technology.

Human Resources—VACANT, Dir.; VACANT, Assoc. Dir.; Ms. JEAN WOOD, Admin. Asst.

Benefits Administration—Ms. PATRICIA HOSKING, Coord.; Ms. TRISH EMERSON, Benefits Asst.

Clergy Services—Mrs. SANDRA GROCKI, Coord.

Deacon Personnel—Deacon DAVID A. PALMA, Dir. & Contact, Deacon Personnel Board.

Department of Management and Staff Relations—Mrs. BARBARA PEDEVILLE, Dir.

Department of Priest Personnel—Rev. MICHAEL CONBOY, Dir.

Department of Catholic Schools and Diocesan Recruitment—Sr. ELAINE ENGLERT, S.S.J., Dir.

Ministry to Priests—Rev. WILLIAM GRAF, Coord., 63 Mason Rd., Fairport, 14450. Tel: 585-223-5500. Email: graf@dor.org.

Newly Ordained Priests—Rev. DANIEL CONDON, J.C.L., Dir.

Pension Committee (Lay and Priests)—VACANT, Contact.

Priests' Personnel Board—Rev. MICHAEL F. CONBOY, Chm.

Priests' Sabbatical Committee—Deacon THOMAS DRISCOLL, Chm.

Office of Seminarians—Rev. JAMES SCHWARTZ, D.Min., Dir., Becket Hall, 314 Gregory St., Rochester, 14620. Tel: 585-461-2890. Email: fschwartz@dor.org.

Office of Vocations—Rev. WILLIAM DONNELLY, Rector, Becket Hall, 314 Gregory St., Rochester, 14620. Tel: 585-461-2890. Email: fdonnelly@dor.org.

Office of Vocations Awareness—VACANT, Dir. Tel: 585-328-3210.

Vicar for Religious—Rev. DANIEL J. CONDON, J.C.L.

Parish Support Ministries—Tel: 585-328-3228, ext. 1337.

Director—Mr. BERNARD GRIZARD.

Associate Director—JOAN WORKMASTER.

Director of Liturgy—Ms. JOAN WORKMASTER; Ms. VIRGINIA MILLER, Assoc. Dir.

Ministry Offices—

Office of Asian Pacific Ministry—Ms. HA NGUYEN, Coord.

Health Care Ministry—Deacon JOHN NELSON.

Office Of Black Ministries—Rev. MICHAEL UPSON, Coord.

Office of Translations—Ms. LOURDES DECHATEAUVIEUX.

Office of Interdiocesan Hispanic Migrant Ministry—Rev. JESUS FLORES, Coord.; Sisters JUDITH JUSTINGER, Dir., Field Office, 152 Main St., Brockport, 14420. Tel: 585-637-3714; MARLENA ROEGER, S.S.J., Assoc. Dir., Field Office, 14 Ann St., Lockport, 14094. Tel: 585-433-3136.

Liturgical Commission—Rev. EDWARD L. PALUMBOS, Chm.

Office of Spanish Apostolate—VACANT, Dir.

Urban Subsidy Program—Ms. HA NGUYEN, Coord.

Ecumenical and Interreligious Services—Mr. BERNARD GRIZARD, Coord.

Jail Ministry Coordinator—Deacon JOHN BRASLEY.

Diocesan Missions—

The Society for the Propagation of the Faith—Rev. ROBERT C. BRADLER, Dir., 1150 Buffalo Rd., Rochester, 14624. Tel: 585-436-9200.

World and Diocesan Missions/Mission Awareness—Sr. JANET KORN, R.S.M., Coord.; JOSEPHINE C. CONLON, Sec. & Bookkeeper.

Pastoral Planning—Dr. WILLIAM PICKETT, Dir.. Email: pickett@dor.org; Mrs. MARY MOORHOUSE, Admin. Asst. Pastoral Planning Liaisons: Mr. CASEY LOPATA; Ms. KAREN RINEFIERD; Mr. ED BELL, Consultant.

Specialized Ministries—

Bishop Sheen Ecumenical Housing Foundation—935 East Ave., Ste. 300, Rochester, 14607. Tel: 585-461-4263; Fax: 585-461-5177. Email: sheen@netacc.net. Web: sheenhousing.org. ALLYNN SMITH, Exec. Dir.; PATRICK L. CUSATO, Pres. Bd. Directors, Subsidiaries: Brentland Woods, Inc., Bloomfield Meadows, Inc.

Mercy Center With The Aging—327 Warrington Dr., Rochester, 14618-1536. Tel: 716-244-5190. Sisters ANNE MALOY, R.S.M., M.S.W., Dir.; GRATIA L'ESPERANCE, R.S.M., M.Div., Asst. Dir.

Clergy Relief Society—Rev. WILLIAM E. GRAF, D.Min., Vice Pres., Church of the Resurrection, 63 Mason Rd., Fairport, 14450. Tel: 585-223-5500.

Diocesan Building Commission—ERIC PATCHKE, Contact.

Office of Ecumenical and Interreligious Affairs—Mr. BERNARD GRIZARD, Coord.

Commission of Women—JOAN WORKMASTER.

Diocesan Women's Commission—NORA SHANNON, Chm.

Holy Sepulchre Cemetery—Mr. JAMES WEISBECK, Dir. & Asst. Treas., 2461 Lake Ave., Rochester, 14612. Tel: 585-458-4110.

Victim Assistance Coordinators—Mrs. BARBARA PEDEVILLE. Tel: 585-328-3228, Ext. 1215. Email: pedeville@dor.org; Rev. ROBERT P. RING. Tel: 315-730-0882. Email: ring@dor.org.

CLERGY, PARISHES, MISSIONS AND PAROCHIAL SCHOOLS

METROPOLITAN ROCHESTER
(MONROE COUNTY)

1—SACRED HEART CATHEDRAL (1910), Revs. John M. Mulligan, V.G.; Joseph W. Marcoux, S.T.L.; Sr. Joan Hilbert, R.S.M., Pastoral Assoc. In Res., Most Rev. Matthew H. Clark, D.D.; Rev. Lawrence V. Murphy (Retired), (Senior Priest).
Res.: 296 Flower City Pk., 14615. Tel: 585-254-3221; Fax: 585-254-8970.
School— See separate listing under Monroe County School System in the Institution section.
Catechesis/Religious Program—Ms. Marianne Himmelsbach, D.R.E. Students 110.
Convent—287 Flower City Pk., 14615. Tel: 716-254-5048.

2—ST. AMBROSE (1921), Revs. Michael J. Schramel; John L. Dugan, C.S.B.; Sr. Gertrude Erb, R.S.M., Pastoral Assoc.; Laurie Maier, Business Mgr.
Res.: 25 Empire Blvd., 14609. Tel: 585-288-5000; Fax: 585-654-7658.
School— See separate listing under Monroe County School System in the Institution section.
Catechesis/Religious Program—Tel: 585-288-1620. Mary Kay Oberst, D.R.E.; Vicki Iannettone, D.R.E. Students 147.
Convent—61 Waldo Ave., 14609. Tel: 716-288-9149.

3—ST. ANDREW (1914), Rev. Michael A. Mayer; Sr. Anne Urquhart, S.S.J., Pastoral Assoc.
923 Portland Ave., 14621. Tel: 585-342-8686; Fax: 585-342-8686.
School— See separate listing under Monroe County School System in the Institution section.
Catechesis/Religious Program—Tel: 585-342-6665. Karen Fox Riordan, D.R.E. Students 34.

4—ST. ANNE (1930), [CEM] Revs. William B. Leone; Dominic Jung, C.PP.S., Korean Min.; Sr. Roberta Rodenhouse, R.S.M., Pastoral Assoc. In Res., Revs. Louis A. Sirianni, J.C.L.; Peter Abas; Dennis Bonsignore.
Res.: 1600 Mt. Hope Ave., 14620-4598. Tel: 585-271-3260; Fax: 585-271-7160.
Catechesis/Religious Program—Alice L. Leistman, D.R.E. Students 79.

5—ST. ANTHONY OF PADUA (1906), (Italian—Vietnamese), Revs. Paul J. Tomasso; Edward Golden; Louis Ha Pham, C.M.C., Vietnamese Min.; Barbara Smullen, Pastoral Assoc.; Deacons John Crego; Joseph Hac Thai Nguyen.
Res.: 60 Lorimer St., 14608. Tel: 585-458-1180; Fax: 585-458-7836.

6—ST. AUGUSTINE (1898), Consolidated, with Our Lady of Good Counsel and St. Monica to form Roman Catholic Community of the 19th Ward.

7—BLESSED SACRAMENT (1902), Rev. Robert J. Kennedy; Sr. Margaret Rose, Pastoral Assoc.; Deacon George Dardess; Jamie Fazio, Pastoral Assoc.; Beverly LaBelle, Pastoral Assoc.
Parish—534 Oxford St., 14607.
Res.: 259 Rutgers St., 14607. Tel: 585-271-7240; Fax: 585-442-7517.
Catechesis/Religious Program—Tel: 585-442-7240; Fax: 585-442-7517. Janette Roach, D.R.E. (PreK-6); Christopher Hood, D.R.E. (7-12). Students 67.

8—ST. BONIFACE (1860), (German), [CEM] Rev. R. Richard Brickler.
Res.: 330 Gregory St., 14620. Tel: 585-473-4271; Fax: 585-256-0868.
School— See separate listing under Monroe County School System in the Institution section.
Catechesis/Religious Program—Students 39.

9—ST. BRIDGET (1854), Rev. Anthony P. Mugavero; Deacon Charles R. Dispenza.
Res.: 8 Mark St., 14605.
Church: 14 Mark St., 14605. Tel: 585-454-4236; Fax: 585-454-0835.
Catechesis/Religious Program—Students 41.

10—ST. CECILIA (1949), [CEM] Rev. Kevin E. McKenna; Sr. Roberta Tierney, S.S.N.D., Parish Life Coord.; Michelle Cwiklinski, Business Mgr. In Res., Rev. Walter F. Cushing.
Res.: 2732 Culver Rd., 14622. Tel: 585-467-4286; Fax: 585-544-8889.
Catechesis/Religious Program—Tel: 585-338-1051. Ann G. Kubiak, D.R.E.; Mary Ann Noto, D.R.E. Students 152.

11—ST. CHARLES BORROMEO (1925), Rev. Timothy Brown; Deacon Thomas Schrage; Sharon Quattrociocchi, Business Mgr.; Sisters Barbara Baker, M.H.S.H., Pastoral Assoc.; Miriam Nugent, R.S.M., Pastoral Assoc. In Res., Revs. Elmer W. Heindl (Retired); Thomas R. Statt (Retired).
Res.: 3003 Dewey Ave., 14616. Tel: 585-663-3230; Fax: 585-663-8055.
School— See separate listing under Monroe County School System in the Institution section.
Catechesis/Religious Program—Tel: 585-663-8000; Fax: 585-663-8055. Christian Formation, D.R.E. Students 198.

12—CHRIST THE KING (1955), Revs. Norman C. Tanck, C.S.B.; Joseph A. Trovato, C.S.B.
Res.: 445 Kings Hwy., 14617. Tel: 585-266-1288; Fax: 585-266-1074.
School— See separate listing under Monroe County School System in the Institution section.
Catechesis/Religious Program—Tel: 585-338-1146. Mrs. Mary Ann Obark, D.R.E. Lay Teachers 62; Students 549.

13—CHURCH OF THE ANNUNCIATION (1917), (Italian), Rev. Emmanuel Nyong, Sacramental Min.; Sr. Marie Susanne Hoffman, S.S.J., Pastoral Admin.
Res.: 1754 Norton St., 14609. Tel: 585-544-1050; Fax: 585-544-5923.
Catechesis/Religious Program—Gerri Grandi, D.R.E. Students 19.

14—CORPUS CHRISTI (1888), Rev. Vincent P. Panepinto; Sr. Martha Teresa Gomez, O.L.C., Hispanic Pastoral Assoc.; Rosalee C. Magee, Business Mgr. & Pastoral Assoc.
Res.: 80 Prince St., 14605. Tel: 585-325-2424; Fax: 585-262-3576.
Church: 864 Main St. E., 14605.
School— See separate listing under Monroe County School System in the Institution section.
Catechesis/Religious Program—Tel: 585-232-3032; Fax: 585-262-3576. Janice Blodgett, D.R.E. Students 56.

15—EMMANUEL CHURCH OF THE DEAF OF THE DIOCESE OF ROCHESTER (1981), Rev. Raymond H. Fleming; Deacon Patrick A. Graybill.
Parish—75 Ernestine St., 14619.
Res.: 34 St. Monica St., 14619. Tel: 585-235-3244; 585-235-1812.

16—ST. FRANCIS ASSISI (1929), Closed., For inquiries for parish records, please contact: St. Anthony of Padua, 60 Lorimer St., Rochester, NY 14608; Tel: 585-548-1180.

17—ST. FRANCIS XAVIER, , (Canonically merged in 1985 and now known as Holy Redeemer-St. Francis Xavier). All inquiries should be directed to the listed address: 34 Teresa St., 14605-1696.

18—ST. GEORGE (1907), (Lithuanian), Rev. Dominic F. Mockevicius (Retired).
Res.: 545 Hudson Ave., 14605. Tel: 585-232-4111.

19—GUARDIAN ANGELS (1960), Rev. Louis Sirianni; Deacons Dean Condon, Pastoral Admin.; Anthony Mercadel; Mary Bills, Pastoral Assoc.
Res.: 2061 E. Henrietta Rd., 14623-3999. Tel: 585-334-1412; Fax: 585-334-7145.

20—ST. HELEN (1940), Rev. John A. Firpo; Deacon Richard Schuler, Pastoral Assoc.; Tracey Sheehan, Business Mgr.
Res.: 310 Hinchey Rd., 14624. Tel: 585-235-1210; Fax: 585-235-8018.
School— See separate listing under Monroe County School System in the Institution section.
Catechesis/Religious Program—Patricia Rodman, D.R.E.; Gina Jennison, D.R.E. Students 163.

21—HOLY APOSTLES (1884), Revs. Paul J. Tomasso; Edward Golden; Deacons John Crego; Salvador Otero; Carlos Vargas; Brunilda Martinez, Spanish Min.; Diane Grant, Business Mgr.
Parish—530 Lyell Ave., 14606.
Res.: 7 Austin St., 14606. Tel: 585-254-7170; Fax: 585-254-5813.

22—HOLY CROSS (1873), Revs. Thomas H. Wheeland; John Reif; Sisters Kathleen Mary O'Connell, Pastoral Assoc.; Rita Biel, Pastoral Visitor; Deacon Ed Giblin.
Res.: 4492 Lake Ave., 14612. Tel: 585-663-2244; Fax: 585-865-5379.
School— See Separate listing under Monroe County School System in the Institution section.
Catechesis/Religious Program—Tel: 585-621-8133. Karen Henrichs, D.R.E. Students 272.
Convent—4490 Lake Ave., 14612. Tel: 716-663-5351.

23—HOLY FAMILY (1864), (German), Revs. Paul J. Tomasso; Edward Golden; Deacons Robert Schrader; Angelo Coccia.
Res.: 415 Ames St., 14611. Tel: 585-328-3110; Fax: 585-328-3112.
School— See Separate listing under Monroe County School System in the Institution section.
Catechesis/Religious Program—Mr. Bernard Grizard, D.R.E.; Debbie Difilippo, D.R.E. Students 129.

24—HOLY GHOST (1875), [CEM] Rev. Albert Delmonte; Deacon David Cadregari; Gregory Allen, Pastoral Assoc.
Res.: 220 Coldwater Rd., 14624. Tel: 585-247-3535; Fax: 585-247-4223.
Catechesis/Religious Program—Tel: 585-426-1289. Rosanne Young, D.R.E.; Laurie Orman, D.R.E.

25—HOLY NAME OF JESUS (1964), Rev. Edwin Metzger (Retired); Michele Bertot, Pastoral Admin.
Res.: 15 St. Martin's Way, 14616. Tel: 585-621-4040; Fax: 585-621-6343; 585-621-1339.
Catechesis/Religious Program—Tel: 585-621-6343. Ms. Joann White, D.R.E. Students 302.

26—HOLY REDEEMER-ST. FRANCIS XAVIER (1867-1888), Merged, in 1985. Rev. Dennis J. Shaw; Sr. Zito Toto, O.L.C., Pastoral Assoc.; Deacon Agenol Rodriguez; Carmen Sanchez, Business Mgr.
Res.: 34 Teresa St., 14605. Tel: 585-482-3211; Fax: 585-325-1260.
Church: 300 Bay St., 14605.
Catechesis/Religious Program—Students 155.

27—HOLY ROSARY (1889), Rev. Gary L. Tyman; Rose Culligan Davis, Pastoral Assoc.; Deacon James Fitch.
414 Lexington Ave., 14613. Tel: 585-458-4422; Fax: 585-458-8209.
Res.: 219 Stenson St., 14606. Tel: 585-458-6079.
School— See separate listing under Monroe County School System in the Institution section.
Catechesis/Religious Program—Students 57.

28—IMMACULATE CONCEPTION (1849), Rev. Michael G. Upson.
Office:—445 Frederick Douglass St., 14608. Tel: 585-325-3893; Fax: 585-325-2082.

29—ST. JAMES (1949), Rev. John A. Lynch.
Res.: 109 Brockley Rd., 14609. Tel: 585-482-9796.
School— See separate listing under Monroe County School System in the Institution Section.
Catechesis/Religious Program—Students 51.

30—ST. JOHN THE EVANGELIST (1914), Rev. William V. Spilly; Anne-Marie Brogan, Pastoral Assoc.
Mailing Address: 150 Floverton St., 14610.
Res.: 549 Humboldt St., 14610. Tel: 585-482-6211; Fax: 585-482-8213.
School— See separate listing under Monroe County School System in the Institution section.
Catechesis/Religious Program—Students 150.

31—ST. JOHN THE EVANGELIST (1865), Revs. John V. Forni; Michael J. Volino.
Res.: 2400 Ridge Rd., W., 14626. Tel: 585-225-8980; Fax: 585-723-9825.
School— See separate listing under Monroe County School System in the Institution section.
Catechesis/Religious Program—Tel: 585-225-4200. Rose Battisto, D.R.E. Students 513.

32—ST. JOSEPH (1836), Closed., For inquiries for parish records contact Our Lady of Victory.

33—ST. JUDE THE APOSTLE (1968), Rev John J. Steger.
Res.: 4100 Lyell Rd., 14606. Tel: 585-247-4322; Fax: 585-429-5111.
Catechesis/Religious Program—Tel: 585-247-5275. Students 279.

34—ST. LAWRENCE (1959), Revs. Frank J. Falletta; Donald J Haycock, C.S.C.
Res.: 1000 N. Greece Rd., 14626. Tel: 585-723-1350; Fax: 585-723-1361.
School— See separate listing under Monroe County School System in the Institution section.
Catechesis/Religious Program—Tel: 585-225-7320. Mrs. Jamie O'Mara, D.R.E. Students 638.

35—ST. LUCY (1912), Closed., For inquiries for parish records contact Immaculate Conception Church.

36—ST. MARGARET MARY (1929), Rev. Timothy E. Horan; Deacon Gregory Sampson. In Res., Revs. Peter Bayer; John Rosse.
Res.: 401 Rogers Pkwy., 14617. Tel: 585-342-2100; Fax: 585-467-7694.
School— See separate listing under Monroe County School System in the Institution section.
Catechesis/Religious Program—Tel: 585-342-7114; Fax: 585-266-9322. Students 410.

37—ST. MARK (1964), Rev. Thomas M Erdle; Mary Chatterton, Pastoral Assoc.; Deacons James L. Chatterton; Thomas Kluchko. In Res., Rev. Frederick Bush.
Res.: 54 Kuhn Rd., 14612. Tel: 585-225-3710; Fax: 585-227-6824.
Catechesis/Religious Program—Tel: 585-227-6824; Fax: 585-225-8910. Charles Territo, D.R.E. Students 602.

38—ST. MARY (1834), Rev. William Donnelly; Deacon William Coffey; Richard Wolf, Pastoral Assoc.; Sr. Catherine Heverin, S.S.J., Pastoral Assoc.
Res.: 15 St. Mary's Pl., 14607. Tel: 585-232-7142; Fax: 585-232-6289.

39—ST. MICHAEL (1872), (German—Hispanic), Rev. Peter Deckman; Sr. Kay E. Schwenzer, R.S.M., Pastoral Assoc.; Deacon Jorge Malave.
Office & Res.: 124 Evergreen St., 14605-1016. Tel: 585-325-4040; Fax: 585-325-5771.
Church: 869 N. Clinton Ave., 14605-1196.
Catechesis/Religious Program—Students 116.

40—ST. MONICA (1898), (Irish), Consolidated, with Our Lady of Good Counsel and St. Augustine to form Roman Catholic Community of the 19th Ward.

41—MOST PRECIOUS BLOOD (1930), (Italian), Rev. Gary L. Tyman; Sr. Maura Wilson, Pastoral Assoc.; Deacon John Guigno.
Res.: 219 Stenson St., 14606.
Catechesis/Religious Program—Ms. Marianne Himmelsbach, D.R.E. Students 19.

42—OUR LADY OF GOOD COUNSEL (1928), Consolidated, with St. Augustine and St. Monica to form Roman Catholic Community.

43—OUR LADY OF LOURDES (1928), Revs. John L. O'Connor; Peter Mandina.
Res.: 150 Varinna Dr., 14618. Tel: 585-473-9656; Fax: 585-271-6472.
School— See separate listing under Monroe County School System in the Institution section.
Catechesis/Religious Program—Tel: 585-244-2361. Mrs. Suzanne Regan, D.R.E. Students 215.

44—OUR LADY OF MERCY (1957), Rev. Robert Beligotti; Deacon Dick Lombard.
Res.: 36 Armstrong Rd., 14616. Tel: 585-865-0775; Fax: 585-865-9403.
Catechesis/Religious Program—Tel: 585-865-2917; Fax: 585-865-9403. Geraldine Sauter, D.R.E.; Michell Andrews-Smith, D.R.E. Students 150.

45—OUR LADY OF MOUNT CARMEL (1909), Rev. Dennis Shaw; Sr. Julia Norton, R.S.M.; Deacon Felix Medero.
Res.: 53 Ontario St., 14605. Tel: 585-232-1133; Fax: 585-232-1554.
Catechesis/Religious Program—Tel: 585-325-4323. Yolanda Ortiz-Vargas, D.R.E. Students 139.
Convent—59 Ontario St., 14605. Tel: 716-454-6766.
St. Martin's Soup Kitchen—Tel: 716-325-6500.

46—OUR LADY OF PERPETUAL HELP (1905), Rev. Peter Deckman; Deacon John Brasley. In Res., Rev. Laurence C. Tracy.
Res.: 1089 Joseph Ave., 14621. Tel: 585-467-2725; Fax: 585-467-6841.
Catechesis/Religious Program—Students 50.

47—OUR LADY OF VICTORY-ST. JOSEPH (1848), Rev. Ronald A. Antinarelli; Carl J. Conde, Pastoral Assoc.
Res.: 210 Pleasant St., 14604. Tel: 585-454-2244; Fax: 585-454-2246.

48—OUR LADY QUEEN OF PEACE (1960), Very Rev. Joseph A. Hart, S.T.D., V.G.; Sr. Jacqulyn Reichart, R.S.M., Pastoral Admin.; Margaret Ostromecki, Pastoral Assoc. In Res., Rev. John T. Walsh, M.Div. (Retired).
Parish—601 Edgewood Ave., 14618-4329.
Res.: 18 Viennawood Dr., 14618. Tel: 585-244-3010; Fax: 585-242-7733.
Catechesis/Religious Program—Students 199.

49—OUR MOTHER OF SORROWS (1829), (Irish), [CEM] Rev. Alexander H. Bradshaw; Sr. Mary Doran, S.S.J., Pastoral Assoc. In Res., Revs. Winfried Kellner; Edwin Metzger (Retired); Deacon William Schmitz.
Res.: 5000 Mt. Read Blvd., 14612. Tel: 585-663-5432; Fax: 585-663-7683.
School— See separate listing under Monroe County School System in the Institution section.
Catechesis/Religious Program—Tel: 585-621-3495. Nancy Bentivegna, D.R.E.; Christian Formation, D.R.E. Students 455.

50—ST. PATRICK (1832), Closed., 1150 Buffalo Rd., 14624. (Old Cathedral). Records can be obtained from St. Anthony of Padua Church, 60 Lorimer St., Rochester, NY 14608. Tel: 585-458-1180.

51—SS. PETER AND PAUL (1843), Rev. Robert T. Werth; Sr. Patricia Flass, S.S.J., Pastoral Assoc.
Res.: 720 Main St., W., 14611. Tel: 585-436-3110; Fax: 585-436-0373.
Catechesis/Religious Program—Students 29.

52—ST. PHILIP NERI (1929), (Italian), Closed., For inquiries for parish records, refer to St. Andrew, 923 Portland Ave., Rochester, NY 14621. Tel: 585-342-8686.

53—ST. PIUS TENTH (1954), [CEM] Rev. Daniel F. Holland; Deacon Leo Aman; Mary Anne Bookman, C.S.J., Pastoral Assoc.
Mailing Address: 3010 Chili Ave., 14624.
Res.: 3032 Chili Ave., 14624. Tel: 585-247-2511; 585-247-2566 (Office); Fax: 585-247-8848.
School— See separate listing under Monroe County School System in the Institution section.
Catechesis/Religious Program—3000 Chili Ave., 14624. Tel: 585-247-5269; Fax: 585-247-7409; 585-247-5746. Ms. Ann Hastee, D.R.E.; Sr. Mary Cumbo, D.R.E. Students 482.

54—ROMAN CATHOLIC COMMUNITY OF THE 19TH WARD (1992),, Cluster of Our Lady of Good Counsel, St. Augustine, and St. Monica. Rev. Robert T. Werth; Mary Ellen Fischer, Pastoral Assoc.; Deacon Joseph Fiz H. Glasgow; Eileen Dillio, Business Mgr. In Res., Revs. Robert T. Werth; Raymond H. Fleming; Richard O'Connell.
Office & Res.: 34 Monica St., 14619. Tel: 585-235-3322; Fax: 585-235-3322.

55—ST. SALOME (1925), Rev. Richard J. Beligotti; Deacon Laurence Feasel.
Res.: 4282 Culver Rd., 14622. Tel: 585-323-1160; Fax: 585-544-4810.
Catechesis/Religious Program—Annette Truby, D.R.E. Students 85.

56—ST. STANISLAUS (1890), (Polish), Rev. Adam Ogorzaly; Deacon Raymond Mielcarek.
Res.: 34 St. Stanislaus St., 14621. Tel: 585-467-3068; Fax: 585-467-3072.
Catechesis/Religious Program—919 Norton St., 14621. Tel: 585-544-2614. Students 58.

57—ST. THEODORE (1924), Rev. George Okoth; Sisters Catherine Pfleger, R.S.M., Pastoral Assoc.; Mary Jean Smith, S.S.J., Pastoral Assoc.; Deacon Tony Caruso. In Res., Rev. Gerald T. Connor (Retired).
Res.: 168 Spencerport Rd., 14606. Tel: 585-429-6811; Fax: 585-429-7726.
Catechesis/Religious Program—Tel: 585-429-5650. Students 450.

58—ST. THERESA (1927), (Polish), Closed., For inquiries for parish records contact St. Stanislaus, Rochester.

59—ST. THOMAS MORE (1953), Rev. Lee P. Chase, S.T.L.; Sr. Ellen Galvin, S.S.J., Pastoral Assoc. In Res., Revs. William Amann; Daniel Condon; Otto J. Vogt (Retired).
Res.: 2617 East Ave., 14610. Tel: 585-381-4200; Fax: 585-381-6327.
School— See separate listing under Monroe County School System in the Institution section.
Catechesis/Religious Program—Tel: 585-381-0470. Deacon Don Smith, D.R.E. Students 102.

60—ST. THOMAS THE APOSTLE (1922), Rev. Robert C. Bradler; Deacon Thomas H. Beck; Mrs. Barbara Kelly, Business Mgr.
Res.: 4536 St. Paul Blvd., 14617. Tel: 585-342-2323;

Fax: 585-342-0356.
Catechesis/Religious Program—Tel: 585-342-1704. Students 109.

OUTSIDE METROPOLITAN ROCHESTER

ADDISON, STEUBEN CO., ST. CATHERINE OF SIENA (1854), [CEM] Rev. Gerald T. O'Connor.
Res.: P.O. Box 153, Bradford, 14815. Tel: 607-359-2115.
Church: 49 Maple St., 14801.
Catechesis/Religious Program—Tel: 607-359-2550. Students 72.

APALACHIN, TIOGA CO., ST. MARGARET MARY (1955), Merged, with St. Francis, Catatonk; St. John the Evangelist, Newark Valley; St. Pius the Tenth, Van Etten; and St. James, Waverly to form Blessed Trinity, Owego.

AUBURN, CAYUGA CO.
1—ST. ALOYSIUS, Closed., For inquiries for parish records please see Holy Family, Auburn.
2—ST. ALPHONSUS (1853), (German), [JC] Rev. Louis A. Vasile; Deacon Gregg Lawson; Jill A. Dello Stritto, Business Mgr. In Res., Revs. Paul J. Freemesser (Retired). Tel: 315-255-3159; Felicjan Sierotowicz.
Parish—85 E. Genesee St., 13021.
Mailing & Res.: 10 S. Lewis St., 13021. Tel: 315-252-7261; Fax: 315-252-7262.
School—St. Joseph's Elementary School and Primary School A consolidation of the parishes of Cayuga County. For detailed school information please see Category Schools outside Monroe County located in the Institution section.
Catechesis/Religious Program—Tel: 315-253-6147. Marie Venaglia, D.R.E. Students 140.
3—ST. FRANCIS OF ASSISI (1907), (Italian), [JC] Rev. Peter DeBellis. In Res., Rev. Ralph Fraats.
Res.: 299 Clark St., 13021. Tel: 315-252-7593; Fax: 315-252-2447.
Catechesis/Religious Program—Tel: 315-252-7594. Students 72.
4—HOLY FAMILY (1834), Rev. James C. Burke, Admin. In Res., Revs. Joseph McCaffrey; Ronald E. Gaesser (Retired).
Parish—85 N. St., 13021. Tel: 315-252-9576; Fax: 315-255-1506.
School—Cayuga County Catholic School, Tel: 315-253-8327; Fax: 315-253-2401.
Catechesis/Religious Program—Tel: 315-252-9578; 315-258-9317; Fax: 315-255-1506. Students 60.
5—ST. HYACINTH (1905), (Polish), [JC] Rev. Berard Dudek, O.F.M.Conv.
Res.: 61 Pulaski St., 13021. Tel: 315-252-7297; Fax: 315-255-3781.
School—St. Joseph School, Tel: 315-253-8327. A consolidation of the following parishes: Holy Family; Sacred Heart; St. Alphonsus; and St. Hyacinth.
Catechesis/Religious Program—Tel: 315-252-5132. Students 123.
6—ST. MARY (1868), (Irish), Rev. Robert J. Schrader. In Res., Revs. James C. Enright; Steven W. Lape.
Res.: 15 Clark St., 13021. Tel: 315-252-9545; Fax: 315-252-9546.
School—St. Joseph's, Tel: 315-253-8357. Also serving the parishes of Auburn.
Catechesis/Religious Program—90 Melrose Rd., 13021. Tel: 315-252-3439. Students 260.
7—SACRED HEART (1955), [JC] Rev. Felicjan Sierotowicz; Sr. Chris J. Treichel, O.S.F., Pastoral Admin.
Res.: 90 Melrose Rd., 13021. Tel: 315-252-7271; Fax: 315-255-0716.
School—St. Joseph Primary School, 17 Clymer St., 13021. Tel: 315-253-8327; Fax: 315-253-2401. A consolidation of the following parishes: Holy Family; Sacred Heart; and St. Alphonsus.
Catechesis/Religious Program—Tel: 315-253-2712. Sr. Nancy Emerick, O.S.F., D.R.E.; Maureen Collins, D.R.E.; Janis Schmidt, D.R.E. Students 409.
Mission—St. Ann (1912), 90 Melrose Rd., Owasco, Cayuga Co. 13021. Tel: 315-252-7271.

AURORA, CAYUGA CO.
1—GOOD SHEPHERD CATHOLIC COMMUNITY, [CEM] Rev. Donald J. Curtiss, J.C.L.; Deacon John Prave.
Mailing Address: P.O. Box 296, 13026-0296. Tel: 315-364-7197; Fax: 315-364-7197.
Catechesis/Religious Program—Sr. Mary Kay Ryan, S.S.J., D.R.E.
2—ST. PATRICK (1858), Closed., For inquiries for parish records contact Good Shepherd Catholic Community, Aurora.

AVON, LIVINGSTON CO., ST. AGNES (1866), [CEM] Rev. Gerald Appelby; Barbara Swiecki, Pastoral Admin.; Deacon Edward Mathis.
Res.: 108 Prospect St., 14414. Tel: 585-226-2100; Fax: 585-226-6436.
School— For detailed school information please see Category Schools outside Monroe located in the Institution section.
Catechesis/Religious Program—Tel: 585-226-3232. Michael Drexler, D.R.E. Students 134.

BATH, STEUBEN CO., ST. MARY (1860), [CEM] Rev. Pius Pathmarajah; Deacon Raymond Defendorf, Pastoral Admin.
Res.: 32 E. Morris St., 14810. Tel: 607-776-3327; Fax: 607-776-3409.
School—Tel: 607-776-4767.
Catechesis/Religious Program—36 E. Morris St., 14810. Tel: 607-776-4767; Fax: 607-776-3409. Students 130.

BRADFORD, STEUBEN CO., ST. STANISLAUS (1922), (Polish), Revs. Gerald T. O'Connor; Andrew J. Kalafsky (Retired).
Mailing Address: 49 Maple St., Addison, 14801.
Res.: Main St., P.O. Box 153, 14815-0153. Tel: 607-359-2115; Fax: 607-359-2121.
Catechesis/Religious Program—Students 103.
Mission—St. Joseph (1870), P.O. Box 153, Campbell, Steuben Co. 14815-0153.

BROCKPORT, MONROE CO., NATIVITY OF THE BLESSED VIRGIN MARY (1848), [CEM] Rev. Peter Enyan-Boadu; Cathy Cerame, Business Mgr.
Res.: 152 Main St., 14420-1972. Tel: 585-637-4500; Fax: 585-637-4232.
School— See separate listing under Monroe County School System in the Institution section.
Catechesis/Religious Program—Tel: 585-637-8490. Joan Tannous, D.R.E. Students 348.

CALEDONIA, LIVINGSTON CO., ST. COLUMBA (1885), [CEM] Rev. Walter J. Plominski, Admin.; Deacon David Paluskiewicz.
Res.: 198 North St., 14423. Tel: 585-538-2126.
Catechesis/Religious Program—Students 160.
Mission—St. Patrick (1854), Church St., Mumford, Monroe Co. 14511.

CANANDAIGUA, ONTARIO CO., ST. MARY (1844), [CEM] Revs. Thomas P. Mull; Mark Alan Brewer; Deacon Claude Lester, Pastoral Assoc. In Res., Rev. Emmett J. Halloran (Retired).
Res.: 95 N. Main St., Canadaigua, 14424. Tel: 585-394-1220; Fax: 585-396-3230.
School— For detailed school information please see Category Schools outside Monroe located in the Institution section.
Catechesis/Religious Program—16 Gibson St., 14424. Tel: 585-394-4590. Students 579.

CANISTEO, STEUBEN CO., ST. JOACHIM (1880), Revs. James Jeager; Elias Menuba; Audrey B. Tilden, Pastoral Assoc.
Mailing Address: P.O. Box 605, 14823.
Res.: 32 W. Main St., 14823. Tel: 607-324-5811; Fax: 607-324-5811.
Catechesis/Religious Program—Students 33.

CATO, CAYUGA CO., ST. PATRICK (1875), Rev. Malachy Nwosu.
Mailing Address & Res.: 2667 Hamilton St., Weedsport, 13166. Tel: 315-834-6266; Fax: 315-689-7090.
Parish—Mechanic St..
Catechesis/Religious Program—Tel: 315-834-9203. Walter Sheehan, D.R.E. Students 117.

CAYUGA, CAYUGA CO., ST. JOSEPH (1870), Closed., For inquiries for parish records contact Good Shepherd Catholic Community, Aurora.

CHURCHVILLE, MONROE CO., ST. VINCENT DE PAUL (1869), [CEM] Rev. Theodore J. Auble; Charlotte M. Bruney, Pastoral Admin.
Res.: 11 N. Main St., P.O. Box 609, 14428. Tel: 716-293-1400; Fax: 716-293-0531.
Catechesis/Religious Program—Tel: 585-293-1180. Kathleen Kuntz, D.R.E.; Patricia VerWeire, D.R.E. Students 156.

CLIFTON SPRINGS, ONTARIO CO.
1—ST. FELIX (1856), Merged, with St. Francis, Phelps to form St. Felix/St. Francis Parish Cluster, Clifton Springs.
2—ST. FELIX/ST. FRANCIS PARISH CLUSTER (1992), [CEM 2] Deacon Robert Cyrana; Sr. Joan Sobala, Pastoral Admin.
Office:—12 Hibbard Ave., 14432. Tel: 315-548-5331 (St.Francis); 315-548-9417 (St. Felix); Fax: 315-462-3608.
Catechesis/Religious Program—Students 124.

CLYDE, WAYNE CO., ST. JOHN THE EVANGELIST (1852), (Italian), [CEM] Rev. James E. Hewes.
Res.: 114 Sodus St., 14433. Tel: 315-923-3941; Fax: 315-923-3941.
Catechesis/Religious Program—Sr. Catherine Gibbons, D.R.E. Students 65.
Mission—St. Patrick (1875), Grand Ave., Savannah, Wayne Co. 13146. Tel: 315-365-3244.

COHOCTON, STEUBEN CO.
1—HOLY FAMILY CATHOLIC COMMUNITY, , Cluster of St. Mary's, Dansville; St. Joseph's, Wayland; Sacred Heart of Jesus, Perkinsville; and St. Pius V, Cohocton. Revs. Stephen Kraus; Stephen Karani; Gennaro J. Ventura (Retired); Deacons Dan Slattery; Michael Mahoney.
Mailing Address: 206 Fremont St., Wayland, 14572-1298. Tel: 585-728-2228; Fax: 585-728-2232.
Church: P.O. Box 387, 35 Maple Ave., 14826.
St. Mary's Rectory: 40 Elizabeth St., Dansville, 14437. Tel: 585-335-2700.
Catechesis/Religious Program—Sr. Virginia Taylor, R.S.M., D.R.E. Students 30.
2—ST. PIUS V (1861), (German), Consolidated, with St. Joseph's, Wayland; St. Mary's Danville; and Sacred Heart of Jesus, Perkinsville to form Holy Family Catholic Community, Cohocton.

CORNING, STEUBEN CO.
1—ALL SAINTS, Revs. Philip J. Billotte; Mark A. Miller; Sr. Joan Cawley, S.S.J., Pastoral Admin.; Deacon James Hankey; Mrs. Patricia LaFortune, Pastoral Assoc.; Ms. Susan Gruber, Pastoral Assoc.
Mailing Address: 222 Dodge Ave., 14830. Tel: 607-936-4689; Fax: 607-936-0222.
School— For detailed school information please see Category Schools outside Monroe located in the Institution section.
Catechesis/Religious Program—Arlene Goodman, D.R.E. Students 424.
2—ST. MARY (1848), Closed., For inquiries for parish records contact All Saints, Corning.
3—ST. PATRICK (1903), Closed., For inquiries for parish records contact All Saints, Corning.
4—ST. VINCENT DE PAUL (1913), Closed., For inquiries for parish records contact All Saints, Corning

DANSVILLE, LIVINGSTON CO., ST. MARY (1845), Consolidated, with St. Joseph's, Wayland; St. Pius V, Cohocton; and Sacred Heart of Jesus, Perkinsville to form Holy Family Catholic Community, Cohocton.

DRYDEN, TOMPKINS CO., HOLY CROSS (1962), Rev. Frank E. Lioi.
Parish—375 S.George Rd., Freeville, 13068. Tel: 607-844-8314; Fax: 607-844-8358.
Catechesis/Religious Program—Barbara Ivers, D.R.E. Students 156.

EAST BAY, WAYNE CO., ST. JOHN FISHER (1935), Closed., All inquiries for mission records can be made at St. Mary Magdalen, Wolcott.

EAST BLOOMFIELD, ONTARIO CO., ST. BRIDGET (1850), [CEM] Rev. Peter Mandina; Sisters Diane Dennie, Admin.; Deanna Gears, S.S.J., Pastoral Assoc.
Mailing Address: P.O. Box 248, 14443.
Res.: 15 Church St., 14443. Tel: 585-657-7626; Fax: 585-657-5349.
Catechesis/Religious Program—Students 128.

EAST ROCHESTER, MONROE CO., ST. JEROME (1905), Rev. Michael F. Conboy; Sr. Mary Ann Brunett, S.S.J., Pastoral Assoc.; Deacon Tom Ecker. In Res., Rev. Edward Steinkirchner.
Res.: 207 S. Garfield St., 14445. Tel: 585-586-3231; Fax: 585-586-0537.
Catechesis/Religious Program—206 West Ave., 14445. Tel: 585-586-1625. Students 249.

ELMIRA HEIGHTS, CHEMUNG CO., ST. CHARLES BORROMEO (1904), Rev. Eugene Dobosz, Admin.; Sr. Mary O'Brien, S.S.J., Pastoral Assoc.; Deacon William P. Dougherty, (Retired).
Res.: 130 Oakwood Ave., 14903. Tel: 607-734-1622.
Catechesis/Religious Program—Tel: 607-734-1622; Fax: 607-733-5870. Students 117.

ELMIRA, CHEMUNG CO.
1—ST. ANTHONY (1908), (Italian),, Clustered with St. Patrick's Church Rev. Walter L. Wainwright; Sr. Maureen Mylott, S.C., Pastoral Assoc.; Deacon I. Michael Mangione; Faith-Louise Eaton, Business Mgr.
Res.: 604 Park Pl., 14901. Tel: 607-733-0300; Fax: 607-733-3606.
School—Holy Family Catholic Schools, Tel: 607-737-0536. Serving the parishes in Elmira. See St. Mary, St. Casimir, and Our Lady of Lourdes for details. Lay Teachers 11; Students 42.
Catechesis/Religious Program—Rose Bennett, D.R.E. Clustered with St. Patrick. Students 41.
2—ST. CASIMIR (1890), (Polish), Rev. Eugene Dobosz, Admin.; Sr. Mary O'Brien, S.S.J., Pastoral Assoc.; Deacon William P. Dougherty, (Retired); Anne Bremer, Business Mgr.
Res.: 1012 Davis St., 14901. Tel: 607-734-1622; Fax: 607-733-5870.
School—Holy Family Jr. High For detailed school information please see Category Schools outside Monroe located in the Institution section.
Catechesis/Religious Program—Mrs. Maureen Donahue, R.E.C., D.R.E. Students 117.
3—ST. CECILIA OF EASTSIDE CATHOLIC PARISH (1904), Closed., For inquiries for parish records contact Sts. Peter and Paul of the Eastside Catholic, Elmira
4—ST. JOHN THE BAPTIST OF EASTSIDE CATHOLIC PARISH (1866), (German), Closed., For sacramental records, contact SS. Peter and Paul, Elmira
5—ST. MARY (1873), (Irish), [CEM] Rev. Richard T. Farrell; Deacon Robert Stowell; Jeannette Meck, Business Mgr. In Res., Rev. Patrick Connor.
Res.: 224 Franklin St., 14904. Tel: 607-734-6254; Fax: 607-733-8890.
School—Holy Family Primary For detailed school information please see Category Schools outside Monroe located in the Institution Section.
Catechesis/Religious Program—Tel: 607-734-5220; Fax: 607-733-8890. Donna Bennett, D.R.E.; Bonnie

Collins, D.R.E. Students 203.
6—OUR LADY OF LOURDES (1940), Rev. Jeremiah P. Moynihan; Lisa Rustici, Admin.
Parish—304 Demarest Pkwy., 14905.
Res.: 120 Fairmont Rd., 14905. Tel: 607-732-6261; Fax: 607-732-7256.
School—Holy Family Intermediate For detailed school information please see Category Schools outside Monroe located in the Institution section.
Catechesis/Religious Program—Tel: 607-734-0727. Margaret Johnson, D.R.E. Students 105.
7—ST. PATRICK (1871), (Irish), Rev. Walter L. Wainwright; Sr. Maureen Mylott, S.C., Pastoral Assoc.; Deacon I. Michael Mangione; Faith-Louise Eaton, Business Mgr.
Res.: 604 Park Pl., 14901. Tel: 607-733-0300; Fax: 607-733-3606.
School—Holy Family Catholic Schools, Tel: 607-734-4414. Serving the parishes in Elmira. See St. Mary, St. Casimir, and Our Lady of Lourdes for details. Lay Teachers 11; Students 45.
Catechesis/Religious Program—Tel: 607-737-0536; Fax: 607-733-3606. Rose Bennett, D.R.E. Students 45.
8—STS. PETER AND PAUL OF EASTSIDE CATHOLIC PARISH (1848), Rev. Patrick L. Connor; Sr. Kathleen Bayer, R.S.M., Pastoral Assoc.; Deacon George Welch.
Office—161 High St., 14901. Tel: 607-732-1994; Fax: 607-732-2629.
Res.: 950 Lake St., 14901. Tel: 607-732-2455; Fax: 607-732-2629.
School—Holy Family Catholic Schools Serving the parishes in Elmira. See St. Mary, St. Casimir, and Our Lady of Lourdes for details.
Catechesis/Religious Program—Cecilia Ryan, D.R.E. Clustered with St. Cecilia & St. John the Baptist. Students 68.

FAIRPORT, MONROE CO.
1—ASSUMPTION OF THE BLESSED VIRGIN MARY (1866), [CEM] Revs. Edward L. Palumbos; Sean McEntee, O.M.I. (GAL); Deni Mack, Pastoral Assoc.
Res.: 20 East Ave., 14450. Tel: 585-388-0040; Fax: 585-388-0248.
Catechesis/Religious Program—Assumption School of Religion, Tel: 585-223-0525; Fax: 585-223-5253. Cathy Tocci, D.R.E. Students 875.
2—CHURCH OF THE RESURRECTION (1973), Rev. William E. Graf, D.Min.
Res.: 52 Mason Rd., 14450. Tel: 585-223-6686; Fax: 585-223-6958.
Church: 63 Mason Rd., 14450. Tel: 585-223-5500; Fax: 585-223-6958.
Catechesis/Religious Program—Students 227.
3—ST. JOHN OF ROCHESTER (1962), Rev. James E. Boyle; Sr. Barbara Hesenius, Pastoral Assoc.; Deacons Thomas J. Cleary; Daniel M. Kinsky. In Res., Revs. John J. Phillips; Michael C. Hogan (Retired).
Ministry Bldg.: 8 Wickford Way, 14450. Tel: 585-248-5993; Fax: 585-387-0517.
Rectory—18 Wickford Way, 14450.
School— See separate listing under Monroe County School System in the Institution section.
Catechesis/Religious Program—Tel: 585-248-8850. Judith Swagler, D.R.E. Students 816.

FLEMING, CAYUGA CO., ST. ISAAC JOGUES (1946),, Mailing Address: 5043 State Rt. 34, Auburn, 13021.
Parish—Rt. 34.
Catechesis/Religious Program—Students 8.

GENESEO, LIVINGSTON CO., ST. MARY (1854), [CEM] Rev. Daniel T. McMullin.
Office—13 North St., 14454. Tel: 585-243-1100; Fax: 585-243-0240.
Res.: 4 Avon Rd., 14454. Tel: 585-243-1100; Fax: 585-243-0240.
Catechesis/Religious Program—Cathy Meyer, D.R.E. Students 210.

GENEVA, ONTARIO CO.
1—ST. FRANCIS DE SALES (1835), [CEM] [JC 2] Revs. Roy Kiggins; James Fennessy; Sr. Lucy Jean, C.S.C., Pastoral Assoc.; Miss Ruth A. Page, Pastoral Assoc.
Parish—130 Exchange St., 14456.
Res.: 48 Pultney St., 14456.
School—Consolidated School, Tel: 315-789-1828; Fax: 315-789-2186. See St. Stephen and St. Francis de Sales. Lay Teachers 12; Students 181; Preschool 11.
Catechesis/Religious Program—Tel: 315-789-0930; Fax: 315-781-1985. Students 154.
2—ST. STEPHEN (1904), [JC] Consolidated, with the following parishes: St. Francis de Sales and St. Stephen. Revs. Roy Kiggins; James Fennessy; Miss Ruth A. Page, Pastoral Assoc.; Sr. Lucy Jean, C.S.C., Pastoral Assoc.
Office—130 Exchange St., 14456.
Res. & Church Address: 48 Pulteney St., 14456. Tel: 315-789-1124; Fax: 315-781-1985.
School— For detailed school information please see Category Schools outside Monroe located in the Institution section.
Catechesis/Religious Program—110 Exchange St., 14456. Tel: 315-781-2624. Walter Savaria D.R.E. Students 413.

GROTON, TOMPKINS CO., ST. ANTHONY (1873), [CEM] Rev. Frank E. Lioi.
Res.: 312 Locke Rd., R.D. 2, 13073. Tel: 607-898-5135; Fax: 607-898-7608.
Catechesis/Religious Program—Students 60.

HAMLIN, MONROE CO., ST. ELIZABETH ANN SETON (1982), Rev. Paul J. Ryan; Deacons Klaus Schulz; Christopher Fisher.
Res.: 3747 Brick Schoolhouse Rd., 14464. Tel: 585-964-8627; Fax: 585-964-3352.
Catechesis/Religious Program—Tel: 716-964-3352. Cynthia Lazzaro, D.R.E. Students 233.

HAMMONDSPORT, STEUBEN CO., ST. GABRIEL (1845), [JC] Rev. Pius Pathmarajah; Sr. Anne Michelle McGill, Pastoral Admin.
Res.: 78 Shethar St., 14840. Tel: 607-569-3501; Fax: 607-569-3226.
Catechesis/Religious Program—Fax: 607-569-3501. Students 42.

HENRIETTA, MONROE CO., CHURCH OF THE GOOD SHEPHERD (1911), [CEM] Rev. Douglas DellaPietra; Walter Stacker, Business Mgr.; Susan Feed, Pastoral Assoc.
Res.: 3318 E. Henrietta Rd., 14467. Tel: 585-334-3518; Fax: 585-334-6015.
School— See separate listing under Monroe County School System in the Institution section.
Catechesis/Religious Program—Tel: 585-334-3023. Carolyn Hahn, D.R.E.; Margaret Churnetski, D.R.E. Students 554.

HILTON, MONROE CO., ST. LEO (1884), Rev. John J. Glogowski; Deacon James P. Steiger. In Res., Rev. Joseph F. D'Aurizio (Retired).
Res.: 167 Lake Ave., 14468. Tel: 585-392-2710; Fax: 585-392-9254.
Catechesis/Religious Program—Tel: 585-392-9694. Students 261.

HONEOYE FALLS, MONROE CO., ST. PAUL OF THE CROSS (1870), [CEM] Rev. Lawrence A. Gross; Sr. Yvonne Nadeau, S.S.N.D., Pastoral Assoc.; Deacon Albro C. Wilson Jr.
Res.: 29 Monroe St., 14472. Tel: 585-624-1443; Fax: 585-624-5169.
Catechesis/Religious Program—Students 231.

HONEOYE, ONTARIO CO., ST. MARY, OUR LADY OF THE HILLS (1868), [CEM] Rev. Richard J. Shatzel; Deacon Roger Loomis.
Parish—8961 Main St., 14471.
Res.: Rte. 20A, Box 725, 14471. Tel: 585-229-5007.
Catechesis/Religious Program—Students 82.

HORNELL, STEUBEN CO.
1—ST. ANN (1849), [CEM] [JC 2] Revs. James P. Jaeger; Elias Menuba; Deacon Robert W. McCormick; John Buchko, Business Mgr. In Res., Revs. Robert Kanka (Retired); Paul Schnacky (Retired).
Res.: 31 Erie Ave., P.O. Box 605, 14843. Tel: 607-324-0410; Fax: 607-324-6784.
School— For detailed school information please see Category Schools outside Monroe located in the Institution section.
Catechesis/Religious Program—Tel: 607-324-7121. Marianne Logan, D.R.E. Students 139.
2—ST. IGNATIUS LOYOLA (1931), Rev. James P. Jaeger, Temp. Admin.; John Buchko, Business Mgr.
Parish—343 Canisteo St., 14843.
Res.: 31 Erie Ave., 14843. Tel: 607-324-5811.
Catechesis/Religious Program—Tel: 607-324-7121. Students 84.

HORSEHEADS, CHEMUNG CO., ST. MARY OUR MOTHER (1866), [CEM] Rev. Christopher E. Linsler; Rosemary Bloise, Pastoral Assoc.; Deacon Daniel R. Hurley. In Res., Revs. Robert C. MacNamara (Retired); Gerard Kabarega.
Res.: 816 W. Broad St., 14845. Tel: 607-739-3817; Fax: 607-739-5628.
School—Mary Canali, Prin. For detailed school information please see Category Schools outside Monroe located in the Institution section.
Catechesis/Religious Program—Tel: 607-739-8214.

INTERLAKEN, SENECA CO., ST. FRANCIS SOLANUS (1875), Rev. William Winters, O.F.M.Cap.
Mailing Address: *c/o Holy Cross Church*, P.O. Box 337, Ovid, 14521.
Office—P.O. Box 357, Ovid, 14521-0337. Tel: 607-869-2261; Fax: 607-869-9825.
St. Fidelis Friary: 7790 County Rd. 153, 14847. Tel: 607-532-4432; Fax: 607-532-9271.
Church: Orchard St., 14847. Tel: 607-869-2261; Fax: 607-869-9825.

ITHACA, TOMPKINS CO.
1—ST. CATHERINE OF SIENA (1960), Rev. Michael J. Mahler; Mary Boris, Pastoral Assoc.; Patricia Marx, Pastoral Assoc.
Res.: 302 St. Catherine Cir., 14850. Tel: 607-257-2493; Fax: 607-257-5901.
Catechesis/Religious Program—Diane Schafer, D.R.E. Students 185.
2—IMMACULATE CONCEPTION (1848), [CEM 2] Rev. Leo J. Reinhardt; Deacons George Kozak; Daniel Hurley; Sr. Edna Slyck, R.S.M., Pastoral Assoc.; Mary Ann Kozak, Pastoral Assoc.; Gregory Wesley, Pastoral Assoc.
Res.: 113 N. Geneva St., 14850. Tel: 607-273-6121; Fax: 607-273-0185.
School— For detailed school information please see Category Schools outside Monroe located in the Institution section.
Catechesis/Religious Program—Tel: 607-273-0303. Students 162.

KING FERRY, CAYUGA CO., OUR LADY OF THE LAKE, KING FERRY (1868), Closed., For inquiries for parish records contact Good Shepherd Catholic Community, Aurora.

LANSING, ALL SAINTS (1913), Rev. Scott Kubinski.
Res.: 347 Ridge Rd., 14882. Tel: 607-533-7344.
Catechesis/Religious Program—Students 60.

LEICESTER, LIVINGSTON CO., ST. THOMAS AQUINAS (1897), Deacon George Spezzano.
Res.: 175 Main St. Box 195, 14481. Tel: 585-382-3400; Fax: 585-382-3349.
Catechesis/Religious Program—Students 58.
Mission—St. Lucy (1912), 2770 Retsof Ave., Retsof, Livingston Co. 14539. Tel: 585-243-4068.

LIMA, LIVINGSTON CO., ST. ROSE (1848), [CEM] Rev. Lawrence F. Gross; Deacon Eugene Edwards.
Mailing Address: P.O. Box 8A, 14485.
Church: 1985 Lake Ave., 14485.
Catechesis/Religious Program—Tel: 585-624-1005. Students 49.

LIVONIA CENTER, LIVINGSTON CO., ST. MICHAEL (1848), Closed., For inquiries for parish records contact St. Mary's, Honeoye.

LIVONIA, LIVINGSTON CO.
1—ST. JOSEPH (1911), Closed., For inquiries for parish records contact St. Matthew Catholic Church Society, Livonia
2—ST. MATTHEW CATHOLIC CHURCH SOCIETY, [CEM] Merged, with St. William, Conesus and St. Joseph, Livonia. Revs. John H. Hayes; Jerome F. Schifferli, Pastor Emeritus; Alice Miller Nation, Pastoral Assoc.
Res.: 14 Washington St., P.O. Box 77, 14487. Tel: 585-346-3815; Fax: 585-346-9445.
Catechesis/Religious Program—41 Spring St., 14487. Tel: 585-346-2500; Fax: 585-346-3723. Students 225.

LYONS, WAYNE, ST. MICHAEL (1852), (Italian), Ms. Deborah Housel, Pastoral Admin. In Res., Rev. Edward J. Dillon (Retired). Tel: 315-946-4299.
Res.: 3 Holley St., 14489-1505. Tel: 315-946-4182; Fax: 315-946-4736.
Catechesis/Religious Program—Students 58.

MACEDON, WAYNE CO., ST. PATRICK (1883), [CEM] Rev. Robert Scott Bourcy; Deacon Dominick N. Abballe.
Res.: 52 Main St., 14502. Tel: 315-986-5671; Fax: 315-986-4398.
Catechesis/Religious Program—Tel: 315-986-2021. Students 223.

MARION, WAYNE, ST. GREGORY (1914), Rev. Robert Gaudio; Donna Fitch, Pastoral Assoc.
Mailing Address: 136 Church St., Palmyra, 14522. Tel: 315-597-4571.
Office—3806 Union St., 14505. Tel: 315-926-4323.
Catechesis/Religious Program—Students 64.

MENDON, MONROE CO., ST. CATHERINE OF SIENA (1902), Rev. F. James Lawlor; Sr. Ruth Maier, S.S.J., Pastoral Assoc.
Res.: 26 Mendon-Ionia Rd., 14506. Tel: 585-624-4990; Fax: 585-624-4996.
Catechesis/Religious Program—Mrs. Gail Brooks, D.R.E. Students 386.
Convent—15 Mendon-Ionia Rd., 14506. Tel: 716-624-1538.

MONTEZUMA, CAYUGA CO., ST. MICHAEL (1865), Closed., For inquiries for parish records contact St. Joseph, Weedsport.

MORAVIA, CAYUGA CO., ST. PATRICK (1872), Closed., For inquiries for parish records contact Good Shepherd Catholic Community, Aurora.

MOUNT MORRIS, LIVINGSTON CO., ST. PATRICK (1869), [CEM] Rev. Michael R. Brown.
Res.: 46 Stanley St., 14510. Tel: 585-658-9591.
Parish Center—33 Murray St., Mt. Morris, 14510.
Catechesis/Religious Program—Students 96.

NAPLES, ONTARIO, OUR LADY OF THE LAKES CATHOLIC COMMUNITY, , (St. Januarius, Naples and St. Patrick's, Prattsburg) Revs. Robert P. Ring; John Gathenya; William McGrath; Deacons Michael E. McGuire; Claude Curtin.
Mailing Address: 180 N. Main St., 14512.
c/o St. Michael's Rectory: 312 Liberty St., Penn Yan, 14527. Tel: 585-374-2414; Fax: 585-374-2415.
Catechesis/Religious Program—Students 73.

NEWARK VALLEY, TIOGA COUNTY, ST. JOHN THE EVANGELIST (1880), Merged, with St. Francis of Assisi, Catatonk; St. Margaret Mary, Apalachin; St. Pius the Tenth, Van Etten and St. James, Waverly to form Blessed Trinity, Owego.

NEWARK, WAYNE CO., ST. MICHAEL (1863), Rev. Peter C. Clifford; Sr. Lucilla Romero Ponce, Rgnl. Hispanic Min.; Patricia Albrecht, Pastoral Admin.
Res.: 401 Main St., 14513. Tel: 315-331-6753; Fax: 315-331-2925.
School— For detailed school information please see Category Schools outside Monroe located in the Institution section.
Catechesis/Religious Program—Tel: 315-331-3408. Rose Leisenring, D.R.E. Tel: 315-331-6753; Jeanette Housecamp, D.R.E. Students 350.

NORTH CHILI, MONROE CO., ST. CHRISTOPHER (1968), Rev. Steven Kung'u; Sisters Maureen Mylott, S.C., Pastoral Assoc.; Barbara Stinard, R.S.M., Pastoral Admin.
Res.: 3350 Union St., P.O. Box 399, 14514. Tel: 585-594-1400.
Catechesis/Religious Program—Tel: 585-594-1441. Students 571.

NUNDA, LIVINGSTON CO., HOLY ANGELS (1854),, Clustered with St. Patrick's. Rev. Michael R. Brown.
Mailing Address: 46 Stanley St., Mount Morris, 14510. Tel: 585-658-2110; Fax: 585-658-9591.
Parish Address— Clustered with St. Patrick's. , c/o St. Patrick's Church, 46 Stanley St., Mount Morris, 14510.
Catechesis/Religious Program—21 Massachusetts St., 14517. Tel: 585-468-3450. Students 61.

ODESSA, SCHUYLER CO., ST. BENEDICT (1965), Rev. Paul Bonacci, Admin.; Deacons Daniel Hurley; Daniel Pavlina; David LaFortune, Pastoral Assoc.
Mailing Address: P.O. Box 289, Watkins Glen, 14891.
Res.: 1101 1/2 Tenth St., Watkins Glen, 14891. Tel: 607-535-2786; Fax: 607-535-2990.
Church: Speedway, 14869. Tel: 607-594-2226.
Catechesis/Religious Program—Tel: 607-387-5957. Students 24.

ONTARIO, WAYNE CO., ST. MARY OF THE LAKE (1869), [CEM] Sr. Doreen Glynn, C.S.J., Pastoral Admin.; Deacon Gerald J. Skerrett, Pastoral Assoc.; Lee Skerrett, Pastoral Assoc.
Res.: 5823 Walworth Rd., P.O. Box 499, 14519. Tel: 315-524-2611; Fax: 607-524-8353.
Catechesis/Religious Program—5823 Walworth Rd., 14519. Tel: 315-524-7421. Linda Moll, D.R.E. Students 300.

OVID, SENECA CO., HOLY CROSS (1849), [CEM] Rev. William H. Winters, O.F.M.Cap.
7239 Main St., P.O. Box 337, 14521-0337.
St. Fidelis Friary: 7790 County Rd. 153, Interlaken, 14847. Tel: 607-869-2261; Fax: 607-869-9825.
Catechesis/Religious Program—Students 31.

OWEGO, TIOGA CO.

1—BLESSED TRINITY (2003), Revs. William A. Moorby; Symon Peter Ntaiyia (Africa); Patrick VanDurme; Deacon Warren Rutan; Betty D'Arcy, Pastoral Assoc.; Helen Cooney, Pastoral Assoc.; William Cooney, Business Mgr.
Mailing Address: *Blessed Trinity and St. Patrick Parishes*, 300 Main St., 13827. Tel: 607-687-1068; Fax: 607-687-8122. Email: blessedtrinity@dor.org.

2—ST. PATRICK (1842), [CEM] Revs. William A. Moorby; Patrick Van Durme, S.T.L.; Symon Peter Ntaiyia (Africa); Betty D'Arcy, Pastoral Assoc.; Deacon Warren M. Rutan.
Res.: 300 Main St., 13827. Tel: 607-687-1068; Fax: 607-687-8122.
School—Tel: 607-687-0428. Gary Foote, Prin.; Linda Cvik, Prin. Lay Teachers 7; Students 99; Preschool 45.
Catechesis/Religious Program—Students 100.

PAINTED POST, STEUBEN CO., IMMACULATE HEART OF MARY (1952), Closed., For inquiries for parish records contact All Saints, Corning.

PALMYRA, WAYNE CO., ST. ANNE (1850), [CEM] Rev. Robert Gaudio; Donna Fitch, Pastoral Assoc.
Res.: 136 Church St., 14522. Tel: 315-597-4571; Fax: 315-597-4571.
Catechesis/Religious Program—Tel: 315-926-4323. Mrs. Pam McKechney, D.R.E. Students 155.

PENFIELD, MONROE CO.

1—HOLY SPIRIT (1965), Revs. P. Frederick Helfrich; Gerard J. McMahon.
Parish Address—1355 Hatch Rd., Webster, 14580. Tel: 585-671-5520; Fax: 585-671-7262.
Catechesis/Religious Program—Tel: 585-671-5680. Students 210.

2—ST. JOSEPH (1860), [CEM] Rev. Kevin P. Murphy; Deacons Ken Arnold; Don Germano. In Res., Rev. Robert G. Kreckel (Retired).
Parish—43 Gebhardt Rd., 14526.
Res.: 35 Gebhardt Rd., 14526. Tel: 585-586-8089; Fax: 585-586-0674.
School— See separate listing under Monroe County School System in the Institution section.
Catechesis/Religious Program—Patrick B. Fox, D.R.E. Students 1,091.

PENN YAN, YATES CO., ST. MICHAEL (1850), [CEM 2] Revs. Bob Ring; William McGrath; John Gathenya; Deacon Claude Curtin.
Mailing Address: 210 Keuka St., 14527.
Res.: 312 Liberty St., 14527. Tel: 315-536-7459; Fax: 315-536-6964.
School— For detailed school information please see Category Schools outside Monroe located in the Institution section.
Catechesis/Religious Program—210 Keuka St., 14527. Tel: 315-536-3794. Mary Tyrrell, D.R.E. Students 95.
Mission—St. Andrew (1877), Union St., Dundee, Yates Co. 14837.

PERKINSVILLE, STEUBEN CO., SACRED HEART OF JESUS, Consolidated, with St. Joseph's, Wayland; St. Mary's, Dansville; and St. Pius V, Cohocton to form Holy Catholic Community, Cohocton.

PHELPS, ONTARIO CO., ST. FRANCIS (1869), Merged, with St. Felix, Clifton Springs to form St. Felix/St. Francis Parish Cluster, Clifton Springs.

PITTSFORD, MONROE CO.

1—CHURCH OF THE TRANSFIGURATION (1983), Rev. Michael Bausch; Deacons Michael Piehler; Anthony Sciolino; Gloria Sciolino, Pastoral Assoc.
Res.: 50 W. Bloomfield Rd., 14534. Tel: 585-248-2427; Fax: 585-385-9870.
Catechesis/Religious Program—Tel: 585-248-2467; Fax: 585-248-3922. Mary Presutti-Lancto, D.R.E. Students 1,151.

2—ST. LOUIS (1911), Rev. James A. Schwartz; Sr. Judith Ann Kenrick, R.S.M., Pastoral Assoc.; Deacon John Payne. In Res., Rev. Msgr. Gerard C. Krieg, J.C.L., (Senior Priest); Revs. Raymond Booth, (Senior Priest); Bernard Munjalu (Kenya).
Res.: 60 S. Main St., 14534. Tel: 585-586-5675; Fax: 585-387-9888.
School— See separate listing under Monroe County School System in the Institution section.
Catechesis/Religious Program—64 S. Main St., 14534. Tel: 585-381-4455; Fax: 585-387-9888. Susan Payne, D.R.E. Students 403.

RED CREEK, WAYNE CO., ST. THOMAS THE APOSTLE (1882), [CEM] Rev. George P. Heyman.
Mailing Address: 11956 Washington St., Wolcott, 14590-1133. Tel: 315-594-9430.
Catechesis/Religious Program—Students 40.
Mission—St. Jude Chapel (1962), Wolcott. 11956 Washington St., Fair Haven, Cayuga Co. 14590.
All inquiries for sacramental records for St. Thomas and St. Jude prior to July 1, 1985 can be made at Cayuga Cluster 2667 Hamilton St., Weedsport, NY 13166. Telephone: 716-594-9430.

REXVILLE, STEUBEN CO., ST. MARY (1845), (Irish), [CEM 4] Revs. James P. Jaeger; Elias Menuba; Audrey B. Tilden, Pastoral Assoc.; John Buchko, Business Mgr.
Res.: 32 W. Main St., Canisteo, 14823. Tel: 607-324-5811; Fax: 607-324-5811.
Catechesis/Religious Program—Tel: 607-225-4426. Students 10.

RUSH, MONROE CO., ST. JOSEPH (1863), Rev. Pius Wekesa; Sr. Alice Cooney, S.S.J., Pastoral Admin.; Deacon Owen F. Bowers.
Res.: 1209 Rush West Rush Rd., 14543-0320. Tel: 585-533-1719.
Catechesis/Religious Program—Fax: 585-533-1790. Students 267.

SCIPIO CENTER, CAYUGA CO., ST. BERNARD (1867), Closed., For inquiries for parish records contact Good Shepherd Catholic Community, Aurora.

SCOTTSVILLE, MONROE CO., ST. MARY OF THE ASSUMPTION (1853), [CEM] Rev. William Endres; Irene Goodwin, Pastoral Admin.
Res.: 99 Main St., P.O. Box 23, 14546. Tel: 585-889-3100; Fax: 585-889-7806.
Catechesis/Religious Program—Tel: 585-889-8440; Fax: 585-889-7806. Students 145.

SENECA FALLS, SENECA CO., ST. PATRICK (1831), [CEM] Rev. William Laird; Deacon Robert Cyrana.
Res.: 97 W. Bayard St., 13148. Tel: 315-568-5203; Fax: 315-568-4893.
School— For detailed school information please see Category Schools outside Monroe located in the Institution section.
Catechesis/Religious Program—81 W. Bayard St., 13148. Tel: 315-568-2573. Students 153.

SHORTSVILLE, ONTARIO CO., ST. DOMINIC (1885), [CEM] Rev. John F. Gagnier; Maura L. Sweeney, Pastoral Assoc.; Deacon Edward A. Smith.
Res.: 6 Canandaigua St., 14548. Tel: 585-289-4164.
Catechesis/Religious Program—Andrea Record, D.R.E. Students 171.

SODUS, WAYNE CO., EPIPHANY (1922), Rev. Lance M. Gonyo; Deacon Edward R. Sergeant.
Parish—105 W. Main St., 14551.
Res.: 26 Orchard Park, 14551. Tel: 315-483-6111; Fax: 315-483-0325.
Catechesis/Religious Program—Ann Wilkins, D.R.E.; Mona Mattuzzi, D.R.E. Students 95.
Mission—St. Rose (1886), Sodus Point, Wayne Co.

SPENCERPORT, MONROE CO., ST. JOHN THE EVANGELIST (1867), [CEM] Rev. Dennis Sewar; Marnie Suss, Pastoral Admin.; Deacon Larry Van Etten. In Res., Revs. Paul G. Wohlrab (Retired); Pius Wekesa.
Parish—55 Martha St., 14559.
Res.: 60 Martha St., 14559. Tel: 585-352-5481; Fax: 585-352-3759.
School— See separate listing under Monroe County School System in the Institution section.
Catechesis/Religious Program—Tel: 585-352-0225; 585-352-7468 (Youth Min.); Fax: 585-352-3759. Shirley Curatolo, D.R.E. Students 475.

STANLEY, ONTARIO CO., ST. THERESA (1875), [CEM] Revs. Bob Ring; William McGrath; John Gathenya; Deacon Claude Curtin.
Mailing Address: c/o St. Michael's, 210 Keuka St., Penn Yan, 14527. Tel: 585-526-5566; Fax: 585-526-5566.
Res.: 312 Liberty St., Penn Yan, 14527. Tel: 315-536-7459; Fax: 315-536-6964.
Catechesis/Religious Program—Students 65.
Mission—St. Mary (1869), Gilbert St., Rushville, Ontario Co. 14561.

TRUMANSBURG, TOMPKINS CO., ST. JAMES THE APOSTLE (1857), [CEM] Rev. Eugene O'Hara, O.F.M.Cap.
Res.: 17 Whig St., P.O. Box 1, 14886. Tel: 607-387-6781; Fax: 607-387-3763.
Catechesis/Religious Program—Students 101.

UNION SPRINGS, CAYUGA CO., ST. MICHAEL'S (1851), Closed., For inquiries for parish records contact Good Shepherd Catholic Community, Aurora.

VAN ETTEN, CHEMUNG CO., ST. PIUS THE TENTH (1954), Merged, with St. Francis, Catatonk; St. Margaret Mary, Apalachin; St. John the Evangelist, Newark Valley; and St. James, Waverly to form Blessed Trinity, Owego. , Mailing Address: 3010 Chili Ave., 14624.

VICTOR, ONTARIO CO., ST. PATRICK (1856), (Irish), [CEM] Rev. Timothy L. Niven; Ruth Anne Dupre-Trippe, Pastoral Assoc.
Res.: 115 Maple Ave., 14564. Tel: 585-924-7111; Fax: 585-742-3296.
School—Preschool 68.
Catechesis/Religious Program—115 Maple Ave., 14564. Tel: 585-924-2800. Students 320.

WATERLOO, SENECA CO., ST. MARY (1868), [CEM] Rev. Eugene R. Weis; Patricia Albrecht, Pastoral Assoc.
Res.: 23 Center St., 13165. Tel: 315-539-2944; Fax: 315-539-8841.
School—Fred J. Smith, Prin. For detailed school information please see Category Schools outside Monroe located in the Institution section.
Catechesis/Religious Program—Tel: 315-539-8146. Lena Shipley, D.R.E. Students 163.

WATKINS GLEN, SCHUYLER CO., ST. MARY OF THE LAKE (1846), (Irish—Italian), [CEM 2] Rev. Paul Bonacci, Admin.; Deacons Dan Hurley; Fran Haber.
Parish—905 N. Decatur St., P.O. Box 289, 14891.
Res.: 110 1/2 Tenth St., 14891. Tel: 607-535-2786; Fax: 607-535-2990.
Parish Center—10th St., 14891.
Catechesis/Religious Program—Tel: 607-535-4367. Students 110.

WAVERLY, TIOGA CO., ST. JAMES (1881), [CEM] Merged, with St. Francis of Assisi, Catatonk; St. Margaret Mary, Apalachin; St. John the Evangelist, Newark Valley and St. Pius the Tenth, Van Etten to form Blessed Trinity, Owego.

WAYLAND, STEUBEN CO., ST. JOSEPH'S (1881), (German), Consolidated, with St. Pius V, Cohocton; St. Mary's, Dansville; and Sacred Heart of Jesus, Perkinsville to form Holy Family Catholic Community, Cohocton.

WEBSTER, MONROE CO.

1—HOLY TRINITY (1861), [CEM] Rev. William C. Michatek; Judith Kiehl, Pastoral Assoc.; Deacon Leo Kester.
Res.: 1460 Ridge Rd., 14580. Tel: 585-265-0391; Fax: 585-265-1627.
School— See separate listing under Monroe County School System in the Institution section.
Catechesis/Religious Program—Tel: 585-265-4750. Students 294.

2—ST. PAUL (1967), Rev. Stanley Kacprzak; Sheila Cody, Pastoral Assoc.; Deacon Robert Burke.
Res.: 783 Hard Rd., 14580. Tel: 585-671-2112; Fax: 585-787-8907.
Catechesis/Religious Program—Tel: 585-671-2110. Scott Rutan, D.R.E. Students 648.

3—ST. RITA (1950), Revs. Charles J. Latus; Joseph R. Catanise; Deacon Stan Douglas; Sr. Judith Whalen, S.S.J., Pastoral Assoc.
Res.: 1008 Maple Dr., 14580. Tel: 585-671-1100; Fax: 585-671-5446.
School— See separate listing under Monroe County School System in the Institution section.
Catechesis/Religious Program—Tel: 585-671-2079. Andrew Desmarais, D.R.E. Students 530.

WEEDSPORT, CAYUGA CO.

1—ST. JOHN (1865), Rev. Malachy Nwosu.
Parish—Rochester St., Port Byron, 13140.
Mailing & Res.: 2667 Hamilton St., P.O. Box 266, 13166. Tel: 315-834-6266; Fax: 315-834-6278.

Catechesis/Religious Program—Tel: 315-834-9203; Fax: 315-689-7090. Walter B. Sheehan, D.R.E. Students 92.

2—ST. JOSEPH (1854), [CEM] Rev. Malachy Nwosu. 111 S. Seneca St., 13166.

Res.: 2667 Hamilton St., 13166. Tel: 315-834-6266; Fax: 315-834-6278.

Catechesis/Religious Program—Tel: 315-834-9203; Fax: 315-689-7090. Walter Sheehan, D.R.E. Students 179.

WOLCOTT, WAYNE CO., ST. MARY MAGDALENE (1940), Rev. George P. Heyman.

Parish—Washington St. and Northup Ave., 14590-1133.

Mailing & Res.: 11956 Washington St., 14590-1133. Tel: 315-594-9430.

Catechesis/Religious Program—Students 50.

Chaplains of Public Institutions

ITHACA. *Cornell University*, G-22 Anabel Taylor Hall. Rev. Robert S. Smith, Interim Dir.

Health Care Facilities

ROCHESTER. *St. Ann's Home/Heritage*. Rev. Peter Bayer, Dir. Spiritual Care.

1500 Portland Ave., 14621. Tel: 716-342-1700. Rose-Marie Zlotnick, Pastoral Care Assoc.

Highland Hospital. Rev. William Endres.

1000 South Ave., 14620. Tel: 716-461-6890.

Monroe Community Hospital. Rev. Dennis Bonsignore, Mrs. Suzanne Shady.

435 E. Henrietta Rd., 14620. Tel: 716-760-6500.

Park Ridge Hospital/Unity Health System, 1555 Long Pond Rd., 14626. Betsy MacKinnon, Dir. Spiritual Care, Rev. Winfried Kellner, Jeanne Marie Jongen, Chap. Tel: 716-723-7969, Rev. Harriet McConnochie, Coord. Tel: 716-723-7967.

Rochester General Hospital/Via Health. (Vacant) 1425 Portland Ave., 14621. Tel: 716-338-4080.

Strong Health System. Revs. William Endres, Dennis Bonsignore.

601 Elmwood Ave., 14642. Tel: 716-275-2187.

Unity Health System, St. Mary's Genesee St. Campus. Rev. Winfried Kellner, Sr. Barbara Gulino, S.S.J., Chap.

89 Genesee St., 14611. Tel: 716-328-3268.

AUBURN, CAYUGA CO.. *Mercy Health and Rehabilitation Center*. Rev. Felicjan Sierotowicz, Sr. Mary Norbert, O.S.F. Cayuga Co.

3 St. Anthony St., 13021. Tel: 315-253-0351.

BATH, STEUBEN CO.. *Soliders' Home and Veterans' Hospital*, Tel: 607-776-2111, Ext. 1382. (Vacant)

CANANDAIGUA, ONTARIO CO.. *Veteran's Hospital*, Tel: 716-394-2000, Ext. 3052. Revs. Miecislaus I. Curzydio, William Cosgrove.

ELMIRA, CHEMUNG CO.. *St. Joseph Hospital*. Sr. Margot Mann, S.S.J., Deacon George Welch, Mary Ann Klee. Chemung Co.

555 E. Market St., 14902. Tel: 607-733-6541.

HORNELL, STEUBEN CO.. *St. James Mercy Hospital*. Rev. Brian Diffenbacher, Sr. Elaine Hollis, S.S.J., Chap. Steuben Co.

411 Canisteo St., 14843. Tel: 607-324-8153.

State Facilities

ROCHESTER. *Finger Lakes DDSO - Rochester Site*, 620 Westfall Rd., 14620. Tel: 716-461-8676. Deacon Edward Sergeant.

Rochester Psychiatric Center, 1111 Elmwood Ave., 14620. Tel: 716-473-3230. Deacon Brian McNulty, Chap.

AUBURN. *Auburn Correctional Facility*, 135 State St., 13021. Tel: 315-253-8401. Rev. James C. Enright, Chap.

ELMIRA. *Elmira Correctional Facility, Center and Camp Monterey*, P.O. Box 500, 14902. Tel: 607-734-3901. Rev. Richard Farrell, Mr. Peter G. Ladley, Mr. Michael Stanley.

Elmira Psychiatric Center, 100 Washington St., 14901. Tel: 607-737-4991. Deacon Michael Mangione, Chap.

GENESEO, LIVINGSTON CO.. *Finger Lakes DDSO - Geneseo Site*, 3 Park St., 14454-1217. Tel: 716-243-6405. Deacon Edward Sergent.

INDUSTRY. *State Agricultural & Industrial School, Div. of Youth* 14474. Tel: 716-533-1700. Vacant.

MORAVIA, CAYUGA CO.. *Cayuga Correctional*, P.O. Box 1150, 13118. Tel: 315-497-1110. Deacon Nick Valvo.

NEWARK, WAYNE CO.. *Finger Lakes DDSO - Newark Site*, 703 E. Maple Ave., 14513. Tel: 315-331-1700. Deacon Edward Sergeant.

PINE CITY. *Southport Correctional Facility*, P.O. Box 2000, 14871-2000. Tel: 607-737-0850. Rev. Richard T. Farrell, Chap., Mrs. Theresa Stanley, Chap.

RED CREEK. *Butler Correctional Facility*, P.O. Box 388, 13143. Tel: 315-754-6216, Ext. 288. (Vacant)

ROMULUS. *Five Points Correctional Facility*, State Rte. 96, 14541. Tel: 607-869-5111. Rev. P. Paul Brennan, Deacon Gregory Kiley, Chap.

SONYEA. *Livingston Correctional Facility and Seneca Correctional Facility*, Rt. 36, P.O. Box 49, 14556. Tel: 716-658-2731. Rev. Michael Brown, Deacon Nemesio Martinez.

SONYEA, LIVINGSTON CO.. *Groveland Correctional Facility*, Rt. 36, P.O. Box 50, 14556. Tel: 716-658-2871, Ext. 4003. Rev. Stephen Kraus, Deacon Paul Clement.

WILLARD, SENECA CO.. *Drug Treatment Center*, 7116 County Rd. 132, P.O. Box 303, 14588-0303. Tel: 607-869-5500, Ext. 4800. Rev. P. Paul Brennan.

County Jail Chaplains

ROCHESTER. *Livingston County Jail*. Vacant.

4 Church St.. Geneseo, 14454. Tel: 716-243-1100.

Monroe County Jail. Deacons William Baker, Brian Mahoney.

Tompkins County Jail. Vacant.

Yates County Jail. Vacant.

On Duty Outside the Diocese:

Revs.—

Bartollotta, Victor W., Jr., Bishop Lynch High School, 9750 Ferguson Rd., Dallas, TX 75228-3891.

Brown, Lewis, Naval District Washington, 2270 Enterprise Way SE, Ste. 134, Washinton, DC 20373-5804. Office of the Chaplain

Curran, Charles E., 4125 Woodcreek Dr., Dallas, TX 75220.

De Socio, John, The American College, Naamststraat 100, B-3000, Leuven, Belgium.

Fleming Terence K. (SP), St. Anthony's Hospital, 1200 Seventh Ave. N., St. Petersburg, FL 33705.

Valenti, Thomas J., Church of St. John the Baptist, 405 W. 114th St., Yonkers, 10710.

Zygadlo, Mitchell, United States Air Force, 422 ABS/HC Unit 5855,Box 11, Apo, AE 09494-5855.

Military Chaplains:

Revs.—

Brown Lewis E., CDR, CHC, USNR, Naval District Washington, 227 Enterprise Way S.W., Ste. 134, Washington, DC 20373-5804.

Zygadlo, Mitchell, United States Air Force, 422 ABS/HC Unit 5855, Box 11, Apo, AE 09494-5855.

Unassigned:

Revs.—

Celso Thomas B., 163 Patterson St., Newark, 14513.

Tracy, Laurence C., Our Lade ofPerpetual Help, 1089 Joseph Ave., 14621.

Absent on Leave::

Revs.—

Corriveau, Kip

Manning, Charles T.

Phillips, Eric

Retired

Rev. Msgrs.—

Gefell, Gerard J. (OG), 2332 Humphrey Rd., Cape Vincent, 13618.

Krieg, Gerard, St. Louis Rectory, 64 S. Main St., Pittsford, 14534.

Murphy, J. Emmett, Sisters of St. Joseph, 150 French Rd., 14618-3733.

Shannon, William H., Sisters of St. Joseph, 150 FrenchRd., 14618.

Revs.—

Amann, William, St. Thomas More Rectory, 2617 E. Ave., 14610.

Ammering, Bruce, Sisters of St. Joseph, 150 FrenchRd., 14618.

Appelby, Gerald J., 130 Southland Dr., 14623.

Barrett, William, 15 Washington St., Mayville, 14757.

Booth, Raymond, 60 S. Main St., Pittsford, 14534.

Brennan, Joseph P., 251 Bay Village Dr., 14609.

Brennan, Paul P., 345 Waters Edge, Auburn, 13021.

Bush, Frederick, St. Mark's Rectory, 54 Kuhn Rd., 14612.

Calimeri, Anthony F., P.O. Box 24, Phelps, 14532.

Cloonan, Paul F., 16608 Juarez Dr., San Diego, CA 92128.

Connor, Gerald T., 168 Spencerport Rd., 14606.

Cosgrove, William, 295 Chestnut Ridge Rd., 14624.

Cushing, Walter, St. Cecilia's Rectory, 2732 Culver Rd., 14622.

D'Aurizio, Joseph F., St. Leo's Rectory, 167 Lake Avenue, Hilton, 14468.

Davis, Francis R., St. Mary's Rectory, 155 State St., Corning, 14830.

Dillon, Edward J., St. Michael's Church, 3 Holley St., Lyons, 14489.

Dillon, John D., 19 Cady St., Auburn, 13021.

Dollen, Bernard, 4477 Buffalo Rd., North Chili, 14514.

Donovan, Robert, McAuley Residence, 1437 Blossom Rd., 14610. Tel: 716-342-8686

Downs, Robert, Southfield Apartments, Quill Ave. & Clymer St., Apt. D-13. Auburn, 13021.

Doyle, James, Chapel Oaks #1110, 1550 Portland Ave., 14621.

Egan, Robert, Auburn Nursing Home, 85 Thornton Ave., Auburn, 13021.

Eisemann, Frederick F., 151 Sheppler St., 14612.

Erb, Francis J., P.O. Box 665, Savona, 14879.

Falcone, Sabastian, 214 Alaimo Dr., 14625.

Fratts, Ralph J., St. Francis of Assisi Rectory, 299 Clark St., Auburn, 13021.

Freemesser, Paul J., St. Alphonsus Rectory, 10 S. Lewis St., Auburn, 13021.

Gaesser, Ronald E., Holy Family Rectory, 85 North St., Auburn, 13021.

Gardner, Clarence W., Sisters of St. Joseph, 150 French Rd., 14618.

Gordinier, William J., 20 E. Ave., Fairport, 14450.

Hafner, Gerard, 18800 Haywood Ter., Boca Ratan, FL 33496-2167.

Halloran, Emmett J., St. Mary's Rectory, 95 North Main St., Canandaigua, 14424.

Hanna, Austin B., McAuley Residence, 1437 Blossom Rd., 14610.

Hedges, L. John, McAuley Residence, 1437 Blossom Rd., 14610.

Heindl, Elmer W., St. Charles Borromeo Rectory, 3003 Dewey Ave., 14616.

Hoctor, Thomas D., P.O. Box506, Livonia, 14487.

Hogan, Michael C., St. John of Rochester Rectory, 8 Wickford Way, Fairport, 14450. Tel: 716-248-5993

Kalafsky, Andrew J., St. Stanislaus Church, Box153 Main St., Bradford, 14815.

Kanka, Robert, St. Ann's Rectory, 31 Erie Ave., P.O. Box 605, Hornell, 14843. Tel: 607-324-0410

Kreckel, Robert G., St. Joseph'sRectory, 35GebhardtRd., 14626.

MacNamara, Robert C., St. Mary Our Mother Rectory, 816 W. Broad St., Horseheads, 14845.

Mans, Leo J., 133Saratoga Rd. #110-I, Schenectady, 12302.

McDonald, Elmer J., 6145 Sun Blvd., #505B, St. Petersburg, FL 33715.

McDonnell, Joseph M., McAuley Residence, 1437 Blossom Rd., 14610.

McFarland, Eugene H., Chapel Oaks, #2306, 1500 Portland Ave., 14624.

McMahon, Gerald J., 1355 Hatch Rd., Webster, 14580.

McNamara, Joseph M., 3131 James St., Syracuse, 13206.

McNamara, Robert F., McAuley Center, 1437 Blossom Rd., 14610.

Meng, Robert A., 7 Harwood Ln.,, East Rochester, 14445.

Metzger, Edwin, Mother of Sorrows Rectory, 5000 Mt. Read Blvd., 14612.

Miller, Neil R., 2411 East Ridge Rd. Apt. 172, 14622.

Mockevicius, Dominic F., 1156 Plank Rd., Webster, 14580.

Morgan, John A., St. Mary Magdalen Rectory, 2532 Ventura Blvd., Camarillo, CA 93010.

Murphy, David M., 45 Smith Ave., Newton, MA 02165.

Murphy, Lawrence V., Sacred Heart Cathedral Rectory, 296 Flower City Park, 14615.

Murphy, Richard M., Chiropractic College, Box 800, Seneca Falls, 13148-0800.

Nacca, John J., 22 W. Church St., Fairport, 14450.

Nolan, Norbert L., 120 Holyoke St., Bldg. 4, Apt. 2, 14615.

Norris, John P., Sisters of St. Joseph, 150 French Rd., 14618.

Norton, George R., St. Ann's Home, 1500 Portland Ave., 14621.

O'Connell, Richard C., St. Monica Rectory, 34 Monica St., 14619.

Orlando, Richard J., Sisters of St. Joseph, 150 French Rd., 14618.

Phillips, John, 8 Wickford Way, Fairport, 14450.

Rosse, John, 401 Rogers Pkwy., 14616.

Sansom, Lawrence W., Sisters of St. Joseph, 150 French Rd., 14618.

Sasso, Joseph M., 8112 Oatka Tr., LeRoy, 14482.

Schifferli, Jerome F., 45 Washington St., Apt. 2, Box 311, Livonia, 14487.

Schmidt, Elmer J., McAuley Residence, 1437 Blossom Rd., 14610.

Schnacky, Paul, St. Ann's Rector;y, 31 Erie Ave., P.O. Box 605, Hornell, 14843.

Slattery, James F., Sisters of St. Joseph, 150 French Rd., 14618.

Smith, Robert, 9306 Blind Sodus Bay Rd., Red Creek, 13143.

Statt, Thomas R., P.O. Box 752, Honeoye, 14471.

Steinkirchner, Edward E., St. Jerome Rectory, 207 S. Garfield St., East Rochester, 14445.

Sundholm, Conrad, 3465 Treetop Cir., Spring Hill, FL 34606.

Tormey, Daniel, 48 Holiday Harbour, Canandaigua, 14424.

Ventura, Gennaro J., 8247 Dutch Hollow Rd.,

Wayland, 14572.
Vogt, Otto J., St. Thomas More Rectory, 2617 East Ave., 14610-3199.
Walsh, John T., M.Div., 18 Viennawood Dr., 14618.
Watts, Thomas H., 110 Washington St., Sayre, PA 18840.
Wiant, George, 5782 County Rd. 33, Canandaigua, 14424.
Wohlrab, Paul G., St. John the Evangelist Rectory, 60 Martha St., Spencerport, 14559.
Zenkel, Edward B., 4218 East Lake Rd., Livonia, 14487.

Permanent Deacons:
Abballe, Dominic, (Retired)
Almeter, Robert C., Diocese of Syracuse
Aman, Leo, St. Pius X, Chili
Antenucci, John, (On Leave of Absence)
Arnold, Kenneth, St. Joseph's Church, Penfield
Baker, William, Monroe County Jail Min.
Beck, Thomas, St. Thomas the Apostle, Rochester
Bergeron, Albert, (Retired)
Birx, Charles, Diocese of Richmond
Bowers, Owen F., St. Joseph's Church, Rush, 14543.
Brasley, John, Parish Support Ministries & Our Lady of Perpetual Help Church.
Burke, Robert, St. Paul's Church, Webster
Burnett, George, (Retired)
Cadregari, David, Holy Ghost, Gates
Campanelli, Michael, (Retired)
Carrol, Stephen, (Leave of Absence)
Caruso, Anthony, St. Theodore, Rochester
Casey, Lawrence B., Diocese of Atlanta
Cass, K. Thomas, Archdiocese of NY
Chatterton, James, St. Mark's, Rochester
Cleary, Thomas J., St. John of Rochester, Fairport
Clement, Paul F., Groveland Correctional Facility, Sonyea
Coccia, Angelo, Holy Family, Rochester; St. Francis House
Coffey, William, St. Mary's, Rochester
Condon, Dean, Guardian Angels Church, Henrietta
Crego, John, City West Parishes, Rochester
Cunningham, John, St. Christopher, North Chili
Curtin, Claude, St. Michael's, Penn Yan
Cyrana, Robert, St. Patrick's Church Seneca Falls, NY
Dardess, George, Blessed Sacrament Church
Datz, Ramon, Newman Center, Suny Brockport
Defendorf, Raymond, St. Mary's Church Bath, NY
DiLallo, Gary R., Archdiocese of NY
Dispenza, Charles, St. Bridget's, Rochester
Dizer, Robert, Leave of Absence
Dougherty, William P., (Retired)
Douglas, Stanley, St. Cecilia Irondequoit, NY
Doyle, Gregory J., Matt Talbot Ministry, Rochester
Driscoll, Joseph, St. Bernard's School of Theology & Ministry
Ecker, Thomas R., Bethany House, Rochester; St. Jerome's, East Rochester
Edwards, Eugene L., Jr., St. Rose, Lima
Erb, John, Our Lady of Mt. Carmel Church, Rochester
Feasel, Laurence, St. Salome's Church; Rochester Gen. Hospital
Federowicz, Joseph F., (Retired)
Fisher, Christopher, St. Elizabeth Ann Seton, Hamlin
Fitch, James E., Leave of Absence
Fuerst, Eugene C., (Retired)
Germano, Donald, St. Joseph, Penfield
Giblin, Edward, Holy Cross Church, Rochester
Giugno, John M, Most Precious Blood, Rochester
Glasgow, Joseph H., Fitz, RCC of the 19th Ward, Rochester
Graff, Stephen J., Diocese of Syracuse
Graybill, Patrick A., Emmanuel Church of the Deaf
Haber, Francis, (Retired) (Retired)
Hankey, James D., All Saints Parish, Corning
Hoerner, Gerard A., Diocese of Orlando
Holmes, John, Jr., Diocese of St. Augustine
Hurley, Daniel R., Cornell University Ithaca, NY
Jewell, Thomas, Leave of Absence
Kershner, Lynn W., Sacred Heart Cathedral
Kester, Leo A., (Retired)
Kiley, Gregory, St. John the Evangelist, Clyde
Kinsky, Daniel M., St. John of Rochester, Fairport
Kluchko, Thomas J., St. Mark, Rochester
Kohlmeier, Charles P., Holy Trinity Church
Kozak, George, Immaculate Conception, Ithaca
Krupiarz, Michael J., Ss. Peter and Paul Church
Lawson, Gregg K., St. Alphonsus, Auburn
Lebron, Juan, Leave of Absence
Lenhart, William, Good Shepherd Church, Henrietta
Lester, Claude E., St. Bridget/St. Joseph, Bloomfield
Lombard, Richard J., Our Lady of Mercy Church, Greece
Loomis, Roger, St. Mary's, Honeoye
Mahany, Richard E., (Retired)
Mahoney, Brian, Leave of Absence
Mahoney, I. Michael, (On Leave of Absence)
Malave, Jorge, St. Michael's, Rochester
Mangione, Michael, Elmira Psychiatric Hospital
Martinez, Nemesio, Livingston Correctional Facility
Mathis, Edward, Industry and Oatka Facilities, St. Agnes, Avon
Maune, William D., Diocese of Chicago
McCormick, Robert W., St. Ann's, Hornell
McGuire, Michael R., Assignment Pending
McNulty, Brian J., Rochester Psychiatric Center
Medero, Felix, Our Lady of Mt. Carmel, Rochester
Melendez, Eliseo, Diocese of Ponce, P.R.
Mercadel, Anthony J., Guardian Angels, Rochester
Mercado, Conrado, On Duty Outside the Diocese
Mielcarek, Raymond, St. Stanislaus, Rochester
Morin, Kenneth, Archdiocese of Boston
Nail, James, Catholic Community of Western Wayne County
Nelson, John, Christ the King Church and Parish Support Ministries
Nguyen, Hoc Thai, St. Anthony of Padua, Rochester
Ona, Fernando V., On Leave of Absence
Otera, Salvador, Holy Apostles Church and Monroe County Jail
Palma, David, Pastoral Center
Paluskiewicz, David L., St. Columba/ St. Patrick, Caledonia/Mumford
Pavlina, Daniel, Catholic Community of Schuyler County
Payne, John L., F.X., St. Louis, Pittsford
Piehler, Michael J., Transfiguration, Pittsford
Prave, John J., (Retired)
Rodriguez, Agenol, Holy Redeemer, Rochester
Roy, George, St. Catherine of Siena, Ithaca
Rutan, Warren, St. John the Evangelist, Newark Valley
Sampson, Gregory R., Leave ofAbsence, Diocese of Sioux City, IA
Scarciotta, Kenneth A., (Retired)
Schmitz, William F., Our Mother of Sorrows, Greece
Schrader, Robert, Holy Family Church, Rochester
Schrage, Thomas, St. Charles Borromeo, Rochester
Schuler, Richard, St. Helen, Rochester
Schultz, Klaus D., St. Elizabeth Ann Seton, Hamlin
Sciolino, Anthony, Transfiguration, Pittsford
Sergeant, Edward R., Newark Development Center, Newark; Church of the Epiphany, Sodus
Shanley, Patrick M., St. Boniface Church, Rochester
Skerrett, Jerry, St. Mary's of the Lake, Ontario
Slattery, Daniel P., St. Joseph's, Wayland
Smith, Edward A., St. Dominic's, Shortsville
Spezzano, George, Western Livingston Planning Group
Steiger, James P., Nativity of the Blessed Virgin Mary, Brockport
Stowell, Robert, St. Mary's, Elmira
Strode, Walter E., Diocese of Cincinnati
Tocci, Ronald, Church of the Assumption, Fairport
Tomandl, John D., Auburn Correctional & Butler Correctional Facililties
Valvo, Nicholas, Sacred Heart, Auburn
Van Etten, Laurence A., St. John the Evangelist, Spencerport
Vargas, Carlos H., St. Francis of Assisi, Rochester
Verkon, Ronald, Diocese of Scranton, Leave of Absence
Welch, George J., Eastside Catholic Community of Elmira & St. Joseph's Hospital, Elmira
Wight, Edward, St. Mary's, Bath
Wilson, Albro C., Jr., St. Paul of the Cross, Honeoye Falls
Yanaitis, Victor M., (Retired)
Yawman, Philip, St. Andrew / St. Philip Neri, Rochester
Zierle, John E., (Retired)

INSTITUTIONS LOCATED IN THE DIOCESE

[A] GRADUATE SCHOOL OF THEOLOGY

ROCHESTER. *St. Bernard's School of Theology & Ministry*, 120 French Rd., 14618. Tel: 585-271-3657; Fax: 585-271-2045. Email: lbarton@stbernards.edu. Web: www.stbernards.edu. Dr. Patricia A. Schoelles, S.S.J., Pres.; Dr. Joseph R. Piccolino, Dir. at Albany; Thomas McDade Clay, Dir. Admissions & Dir. of Certification; Deacon Thomas Driscoll, Dir. Community Education; Ms. Mary Ann LaCour, Dir. Business Affairs; Dr. Devadasan Premnath, Dean; Rebecca Plonsky, Registrar. Priests 2; Sisters 2; Lay Teachers 2; Total Staff 14; Total enrollment 196.

[B] HIGH SCHOOLS

ROCHESTER. *The Aquinas Institute*, 1127 Dewey Ave., 14613-9989. Tel: 585-254-2020; Fax: 585-254-7401. Email: jknapp@aquinasinstitute.com. Web: www.aquinasinstitute.com. Michael Daley, Pres.; Sally Cardilli, Prin. Lay Teachers 60; Students 850.

Bishop Kearney High School (Coed) , 125 Kings Hwy., 14617-5596. Tel: 585-342-4000; Fax: 585-342-4694. Email: principal@bkhs.org. Web: www.bkhs.org. Mark S. Peterson, Pres.; Louis D'Angelo, Prin.; Mrs. Donna Gmelin, Asst. Prin. Sponsored by the Congregation of Christian Brothers in association with the School Sisters of Notre Dame, Wilton Province. Sisters 1; Lay Teachers 32; Students 460.

McQuaid Jesuit High School, 1800 S. Clinton Ave., 14618. Tel: 585-473-1130; Fax: 585-256-6171. Email: jesuitres@mcquaid.org. Web: www.mcquaid.org. Revs. Edward F. Salmon, S.J., Supr.; James J. Fischer, S.J., Chancellor; Philip G. Judge, S.J., Prin.; John P. Carriero, S.J.; John M. Costello, S.J.; James R. Dolan, S.J.; Joseph DeMaio, O.Carm.; Jack Healy, O.Carm.; Leon J. Hogenkamp, S.J.; Richard D. Hunt, S.J. (BUF); Francis J. McNamara, S.J., Alumni Dir.; Brian Murphy, O.Carm.; James R. Van Dyke, S.J.; Lawrence J. Wroblewski, S.J. Jesuit Fathers Priests 3; Lay Teachers 52; Students 878.

Nazareth Schools: The Hall; The Academy, 1001 Lake Ave., 14613. Tel: 585-647-8733; Fax: 585-647-8737. Email: acollins@nazarethschools.org. Web: nazarethschools.org. Sr. Ann Collins, Pres. Sisters of St. Joseph 10; Lay Teachers 65; Students 665.

Our Lady of Mercy High School, (Grades 7-12), 1437 Blossom Rd., 14610. Tel: 585-288-7120; Fax: 585-288-7966. Email: mercyhs.com. Web: www.mercyhs.com. Mrs. Evelyn J. Kirst, Prin. Sisters of Mercy 10; Lay Teachers 59; Students 604.

ELMIRA. *Notre Dame High School*, 1400 Maple Ave., 14904. Tel: 607-734-2267; Fax: 607-737-8903. Email: kellyn@notredamehighschool.com. Web: www.notredamehighschool.com. Sr. Mary Walter Hickey, R.S.M., Prin.; Rev. Vincent McDonough, S.J., Chap. Priests 1; Sisters of Mercy 2; Lay Teachers 27; Students 405.

GENEVA. *De Sales High School* (Incorporated under the laws of the State of New York) , 90 Pulteney St., 14456. Tel: 315-789-5111; Fax: 315-789-8230. Email: mainoffice@desaleshs.org. Web: www.desaleshs.org. Dr. Karen M. Juliano, Ed.D., Prin. Priests 1; Lay Teachers 24; Students 125.

[C] MONROE COUNTY SCHOOL SYSTEM

ROCHESTER. *Catholic Schools of Monroe County*, 1150 Buffalo Rd., 14624. Tel: 585-328-3210; Fax: 585-328-3149. Email: rossetti@dor.org. Web: www.dor.org. Carole Rossetti, Contact. Priests 2; Sisters 35; Lay Teachers 832; Students 8,930.

Junior High Schools:

All Saints Catholic Academy (Grades 7-8), 170 Spencerport Rd., 14606-5217. Tel: 585-429-6010; Fax: 585-429-6761. Email: ascjhdsc@dor.org. William B. Davis, Prin.

Bishop Hogan Catholic Academy (Grades 7-8), 125 Kings Hwy. S., 14617-5502. Tel: 585-544-0560; Fax: 585-544-0411. Email: bhcadcs@dor.org. Vilma Goetting, Prin.

Elementary Schools:

Christ the King School (Grades PreK-6), 445 Kings Hwy. S., 14617-4138. Tel: 585-467-8730; Fax: 585-467-5392. Email: ctkdcs@dor.org. Mrs. Colleen D'Hondt, Prin.

Corpus Christi School (Grades PreK-6), 546 Oxford St., 14607. Tel: 585-473-3937; Fax: 585-422-0538. Email: ccdcs@dor.org. Sr. Eileen Daly, S.S.J., Prin.

Good Shepherd School (Grades PreK-6), 3288 E. Henrietta Rd., Henrietta, 14467-9701. Tel: 585-334-5100; Fax: 585-359-8962. Email: gsdcs@dor.org. Marie L. Arcuri, Prin.

Holy Cross School (Grades PreK-8), 4488 Lake Ave., 14612-4540. Tel: 585-663-6533; Fax: 585-621-4630. Email: hcdcs@dor.org. Mrs. Catherine H. Kress, Prin.

Holy Family School (Grades PreK-6), 899 Jay St., 14611-1219. Tel: 585-328-4800; Fax: 585-328-4728. Email: hfrdcs@dor.org. Mary Ellen Wagner, Prin.

Holy Rosary School (Grades PreK-6), 420 Lexington Ave., 14613-1997. Tel: 585-254-8180; Fax: 585-254-4604. Email: hrdcs@dor.org. Mary Beth Fuehrer, Prin.

Holy Trinity School (Grades PreK-6), 1456 Ridge Rd., Webster, 14580-3698. Tel: 585-265-2440; Fax: 585-265-3405. Email: htdcs@dor.org. Christopher Meagher, Prin.

Mother of Sorrows School (Grades K-8), 1777 Latta

Rd., 14612-3731. Tel: 585-663-1100; Fax: 585-663-5552. Email: mosdcs@dor.org. Mr. Samuel Zalacca, Prin.

Sacred Heart Cathedral School (Grades PreK-6), 311 Flower City Park, 14615-3614. Tel: 585-458-8088; Fax: 585-458-7155. Email: shcdcs@dor.org. Sr. Stephanine Riley, S.S.J., Prin.

Siena Catholic Academy (Grades 7-8), 2617 East Ave, 14610-3111. Tel: 585-381-1220; Fax: 585-381-1223. Email: scadcs@dor.org. Rev. Joseph A. Grasso, C.PP.S., Prin.

St. Ambrose School (Grades PreK-6), 31 Empire Blvd., 14609-4335. Tel: 585-288-0580; Fax: 585-288-2612. Email: sambdcs@dor.org. Rebecca Maloney, Prin.

St. Andrew School (Grades PreK-6), 901 Portland Ave., 14621-4194. Tel: 585-467-9201; Fax: 585-467-4191. Email: sstandre@dor.org. Tracy Nadler, Prin.

St. Boniface School (Grades PreK-6), 15 Whalin St., 14620-1399. Tel: 585-271-6370; Fax: 585-271-8099. Email: sbondcs@dor.org. Sr. Mary Smith, S.S.N.D., Prin.

St. Charles Borromeo School (Grades PreK-6), 64 Maiden Ln., 14616-4038. Tel: 585-663-1220; Fax: 585-663-2802. Email: scbdcs@dor.org. Mary E. Barrese-Frame, Prin.

St. Helen School (Grades PreK-6), 150 Lettington Dr., 14624-2910. Tel: 585-235-2391; Fax: 585-235-2417. Email: shelendcs@dor.org. Mary Beth Sullivan, Prin.

St. John of Rochester School (Grades PreK-6), 10 Wickford Way, Fairport, 14450-3132. Tel: 585-248-8836; Fax: 585-248-8839. Email: sjrdcs@dor.org. Mrs. Eileen O'Neill, Prin.

St. John the Evangelist School/Greece (Grades PreK-6), 2376 Ridge Rd. W., 14626-2998. Tel: 585-225-3450; Fax: 585-225-6301. Email: sjegdcs@dor.org. Ms. Eileen Preston, Prin.

St. John the Evangelist School/Humboldt St. (Grades PreK-6), 545 Humboldt St., 14610-1284. Tel: 585-654-9437; Fax: 585-654-8787. Email: sjehdcs@dor.org. Angela T. Fortunato, Prin.

St. John the Evangelist School/Spencerport (Grades PreK-6), 65 Martha St., Spencerport, 14559-1342. Tel: 585-352-4550; Fax: 585-349-2275. Email: sjesdcs@dor.org. Mrs. Linda Boone, Prin.

St. Joseph School (Grades PreK-6), 39 Gebhardt Rd., Penfield, 14526-1398. Tel: 585-586-6968; Fax: 585-586-4619. Email: sjpendcs@dor.org. Sr. Christina Marie Luczynski, C.S.S.F., Prin.

St. Lawrence School (Grades K-6), 1000 N. Greece Rd., 14626-1098. Tel: 585-225-3870; Fax: 585-225-1336. Email: slawrdcs@dor.org. Joseph Holleran, Prin.

St. Louis School (Grades PreK-6), 11 Rand Pl., Pittsford, 14534-2084. Tel: 585-586-5200; Fax: 585-586-4561. Email: slsdcs@dor.org. Ms. Kathleen Carroll, Prin.

St. Margaret Mary School (Grades PreK-6), 400 Rogers Pkwy., 14617-4799. Tel: 585-266-0413; Fax: 585-266-9322. Email: smmdcs@dor.org. Sr. Mary Alice O'Brien, R.S.M., Prin.

St. Monica School (Grades PreK-6), 841 Genesee St., 14611-3838. Tel: 585-235-4140; Fax: 585-235-4144. Email: smondcs@dor.org. Sr. Mary Marvin, R.S.M., Prin.

St. Pius X School (Grades PreK-6), 3000 Chili Ave., 14624-4598. Tel: 585-247-5650; Fax: 585-247-7409. Email: spxdcs@dor.org. Stephen Oberst, Prin.

St. Rita School (Grades PreK-6), 1008 Maple Dr., Webster, 14580-1726. Tel: 585-671-3132; Fax: 585-671-4562. Email: sritadcs@dor.org. Sr. Katherine Ann Rappl, R.S.M., Prin.

Seton Catholic School (Grades PreK-6), 165 Rhinecliff Dr., 14618-1525. Tel: 585-473-6604; Fax: 585-473-3347. Email: setondcs@dor.org. Sr. Kathleen Lurz, S.S.J., Prin.

[D] SCHOOLS OUTSIDE MONROE COUNTY

AUBURN. *St. Joseph School (Auburn)*, (Grades PreK-8), 89 E. Genesee St., 13021-4161. Tel: 315-253-8327; 315-252-8353; Fax: 315-789-9179. Email: sjadcs@dor.org. Stephen Miskell, Prin. Lay Teachers 23; Students 296; Preschool 98.

AVON. *St. Agnes*, (Grades PreK-6), 60 Park Pl., 14414-1053. Tel: 585-226-8500; Fax: 585-226-8500 (call first). Email: sagnesdcs@dor.org. Dr. Gerald E. Benjamin, Prin. Lay Teachers 8; Students 105; Preschool 46.

CANANDAIGUA. *St. Mary (Canandaigua)*, (Grades PreK-8), 16 Gibson St., 14424-1310. Tel: 585-394-4300; Fax: 585-396-3230. Email: smcdcs@dor.org. Ann Marie Deutsch, Prin. Lay Teachers 15; Students 205.

CORNING. *All Saints Academy*, (Grades 2-8), 158 State St., 14830-2594. Tel: 607-936-9234; Fax: 607-936-1797. Email: asastdcs@dor.org. Rose Ann Ewanyk, Prin.

All Saints Academy, (Grades PreK-1), 280 Denison Pkwy., E., 14830-2932. Tel: 607-962-6377; Fax: 607-962-0174. Email: asadendcs@dor.org. Rose Ann Ewanyk, Prin.

DANSVILLE. *St. Mary (Dansville)*, (Grades PreK-5), 43 Elizabeth St., 14437-1632. Tel: 585-335-6800; Fax: 585-335-9381. Email: smddcs@dor.org. Diane M. Sauerbier, Prin.

ELMIRA. *Holy Family Intermediate*, (Grades 4-6), 301 Demarest Pkwy., 14905-2143. Tel: 607-734-0841; Fax: 607-732-6638. Email: hfidcs@dor.org. Brenda L. Lisi, Prin. Sisters 1; Lay Teachers 10; Students 180.

Holy Family Junior High, (Grades 7-8), 1010 Davis St., 14901-1013. Tel: 607-734-0336; Fax: 607-734-4977. Email: hfjhdcs@dor.org. Elizabeth Berliner, Prin. Lay Teachers 20; Students 226.

Holy Family Primary, (Grades PreK-3), 421 Fulton St., 14904-1709. Tel: 607-732-3588; Fax: 607-732-1850. Email: hfpdcs@dor.org. Constance Brady, Prin. Lay Teachers 17; Students 278; Preschool 64.

GENEVA. *St. Francis Desales/St. Stephen*, (Grades PreK-8), 17 Elmwood Ave., 14456-2299. Tel: 315-789-1828 Fax: 315-789-9179. Email: sfssdcs@dor.org. Elaine Morrow, Prin. Sisters of St. Joseph 12; Lay Teachers 17; Students 181; Preschool 11.

HORNELL. *St. Ann*, (Grades PreK-8), 27 Erie Ave., 14843-1909. Tel: 607-324-0733; Fax: 607-324-0985. Email: sanndcs@dor.org. Sr. Dolores Ann Stein, R.S.M., Prin. Lay Teachers 13; Students 133; Preschool 33.

HORSEHEADS. *St. Mary Our Mother (Horseheads)*, (Grades PreK-6), 811 Westlake St., 14845-2099. Tel: 607-739-9157; Fax: 607-739-5628. Email: smomdcs@dor.org. Marilyn Zinn, Prin. Lay Teachers 14; Students 220; Preschool 30.

ITHACA. *Immaculate Conception*, (Grades PreK-8), 320 W. Buffalo St., 14850-4193. Tel: 607-273-2707; Fax: 607-272-8456. Email: icdcs@dor.org. Deacon Daniel Hurley, Prin. Lay Teachers 15; Students 184; Preschool 38.

NEWARK. *St. Michael (Newark)*, (Grades PreK-8), 320 S. Main St., 14513-1729. Tel: 315-331-2297; Fax: 315-331-2299. Email: smndcs@dor.org. David Doty, Prin. Lay Teachers 20; Students 301; Preschool 21.

PENN YAN. *St. Michael (Penn Yan)*, (Grades PreK-5), 214 Keuka St., 14527-1143. Tel: 315-536-6112; Fax: 315-536-6112. Email: smpydcs@dor.org. Jo Ann M. Struck, Prin. Lay Teachers 7; Students 93; Preschool 23.

SENECA FALLS. *St. Patrick (Seneca Falls)*, (Grades PreK-8), 81 W. Bayard St., 13148-1813. Tel: 315-568-6295; Fax: 315-568-6295. Email: spsfdcs@dor.org. Diana Oravec, Prin. Lay Teachers 16; Students 150; Preschool 25.

WATERLOO. *St. Mary (Waterloo)*, (Grades PreK-8), 35 Center St., 13165-1022. Tel: 315-539-3772; Fax: 315 539-4503. Email: smwdcs@dor.org. Fred Smith, Prin. Lay Teachers 13; Students 136; Preschool 34.

WAYLAND. *St. Joseph (Wayland)*, (Grades PreK-6), 209 Fremont St., 14572-1205. Tel: 585-728-5700; Fax: 585-728-3564. Email: sjwdcs@dor.org. Monette Mahoney, Prin.

[E] HOMES FOR AGED

ROCHESTER. *St. Ann's Home for the Aged*, 1500 Portland Ave., 14621. Tel: 585-697-6000; Fax: 585-342-9585. Email: info@stannscommunity.com. Web: www.stannscommunity.com. Betty Mullin-DiProsa, Pres. & CEO; Rev. Peter T. Bayer, Dir. of Pastoral Care; Rosemarie Zlotnick, Pastoral Care Coord.; Sheila Kinsky, Pastoral Care Coord. Residents 388.

St. Ann's Nursing Home Co., Inc. (The Heritage), 1450 Portland Ave., 14621. Tel: 585-697-6000; Fax: 585-342-9585. Email: info@stannscommunity.com. Web: www.stannscommunity.com. Betty Mullin-Di Prosa, Pres. & CEO; Rev. Peter T. Bayer, Dir. of Pastoral Care; Rosemarie Zlotnick, Pastoral Care Coord.; Sheila Kinsky, Pastoral Care Coord. Residents 203.

Chapel Oaks:, 1550 Portland Ave., 14621. Tel: 585-342-3052; Fax: 585-338-3453. Email: info@stannscommunity.com. Web: www.stannscommunity.com. Betty Mullin-DiProsa, Pres. & CEO; Rev. Peter T. Bayer, Dir. of Pastoral Care; Rosemarie Zlotnick, Pastoral Care Coord.; Sheila Kinsky, Pastoral Care Coord.

[F] CAMPS

LIVONIA. *Camp Stella Maris*, 4395 E. Lake Rd., 14487. Tel: 585-346-2243; Fax: 585-346-6921. Email: info@campstellamaris.org. Web: campstellamaris.org. Purpose: Residential camping under Catholic auspices, for boys and girls (ages 7-14) of all faiths. Encampment period: Eight weeks during summer (July/August). Rental of facility available September-June for family/youth development retreats. ACA accredited.; Day Camp Center for boys and girls (ages 5-10). Encampment period: Eight weeks during July/August in conjunction with resident camp. Adventure-Based Learning Experience (ABLE) high and low challenge ropes courses ideal for building trust, confidence, cooperation, teamwork, self-esteem, communication, and leadership skills. Total Staff 9.

Conesus Lake, 4395 E. Lake Rd., 14487. Tel: 585-346-2243; Fax: 585-346-6921. Matthew J. Flanigan, Exec. Dir.; Daniel O'Neill, Broad Pres.; Thomas Weaver, Camp Dir.

[G] GENERAL HOSPITALS

AUBURN. *Mercy Health & Rehabilitation Center Nursing Home Co., Inc.* (1972), St. Anthony St., 13021. Tel: 315-253-0351; Fax: 315-258-3904. Sr. Margaret Woods, Dir. Mission Svcs. & Spiritual Care; Mr. Robert C. Aims, Admin. Sisters of the Third Franciscan Order Nursing Facility Beds 297.

ELMIRA. *St. Joseph's Hospital*, 555 E. Market St., 14901. Tel: 607-733-6541; Fax: 607-737-7837. Email: srmarie@stjosephs.org. Web: www.stjosephs.org. Sr. Marie Castagnaro, Pres. Sisters of St. Joseph, Skilled Nursing Facility. Total Staff 1,028; Bed Capacity 224; Skilled Nursing Facility 71; Patients Assisted Annually 120,785.

St. Joseph's Hospital Foundation, Inc., 555 E. Market St., 14901. Tel: 607-737-7004; Fax: 607-271-3418. Email: dsullivan@stjosephs.org. David P. Sullivan, Pres.

HORNELL. *St. James Mercy Health System*, 411 Canisteo St., 14843. Tel: 607-324-8000; Fax: 607-324-8115. Email: tlaliberty@sjmh.org. Web: www.stjamesmercy.org. Clarence R. Laliberty Jr., Pres. & CEO; Corinne Francis, Vice Pres. Mission Svcs. Total Staff 1,000; Bed Capacity 296; Patients Assisted Annually 236,084.

[H] CATHOLIC CHARITIES

ROCHESTER. *Catholic Charities of the Diocese of Rochester, Inc.*, 1150 Buffalo Rd., 14624. Tel: 585-328-3210; Fax: 585-529-9534. Email: balinsky@dor.org. Web: www.dor.org/charities/index.htm. Jack Balinsky, Diocesan Dir. & Catholic Campaign for Human Devel.; Maureen O'Hara, Chm. Bd. of Directors; Judy Taylor, Catholic Relief Svcs. & Educ. and Advocacy Communications; Jann K. Armantrout, Life Issues; Sr. Janet Korn, R.S.M., Project Unity; Ruth Putnam, Works of Love Project.

Regional Offices:

Catholic Charities Community Services, 1945 E. Ridge Rd., Ste. 24, 14622. Tel: 585-339-9800; Fax: 585-339-9377. Paul T. Pickering, Exec. Dir.; Todd Gunther, Chm. Bd. of Directors; Barbara Poling, Human Resources Dir..; Jane Hallinen, AIDS Svcs. Dir.; Kathleen Termine, Devel. Disabilities Svcs. Dir.; Anne Sawyko, Devel. Dir.; James Crowley, Finances Dir.; Penny Coon, Quality Compliance Dir.; Tracy Columbo, Traumatic Brain Injury Dir.

Catholic Family Center, 87 N. Clinton Ave., 14604. Tel: 585-546-7220; Fax: 585-546-6396. Carolyn A. Portanova, Pres. & CEO; Irene Coveny, Vice Pres. Prog. Svcs.; Beverly Ludke, Vice Pres. Human Resources; Carl Hatch, Vice Pres. Chemical Dependency & Corp. Compliance; Brian Dwyer, Chm. Bd. of Directors.

Departments of Catholic Family Center:

Catholic Youth Organization (CYO) Tel: 585-262-7008; Fax: 585-262-7017. Deborah Cummings-Brown, Dir.

Children and Family Services Tel: 585-262-7102; Fax: 585-546-2611. Karen Emerton, Dir.

Elder Services Tel: 585-262-7053; Fax: 585-454-6286. Lou Ann Haney, Interim Dept. Dir.

Employee Assistance & Counseling Tel: 585-262-7029; Fax: 585-262-7036. Christine Spooner, Dir.

Homeless & Housing Services Tel: 585-423-9590; Fax: 585-546-7432. Lisa Lewis, Interim Dir.

Office of Social Policy & Research Tel: 585-262-7021; Fax: 585-262-7166. Marvin Mich, Dir.

Refugee Immigration Employment Services Tel: 585-262-7082; Fax: 585-262-7089. Patricia McCarthy, Interim Dir.

Restart Substance Abuse Services Tel: 585-546-1271; Fax: 585-546-2607. Carl A. Hatch, Vice Pres. Chemical Dependency & Corp. Compliance.

Fund Development & Community Relations Tel: 585-262-7056; Fax: 585-262-7166. William P. Keenan, Dir.

Wayne County Office Tel: 315-331-4867; Fax: 315-331-4918. I. Rojas, Dir.

Catholic Charities of the Finger Lakes Tel: 315-789-2686; Fax: 315-789-5785. (Serving Yates, Ontario, Wayne, Seneca, and Cayuga Counties)

Main Office:, 301 Franklin Sq., Geneva, 14456. Tel: 315-789-2686; Fax: 315-789-5785. Richard Fowler, Exec. Dir.; Scarlett Emerson, Dir. Parish & Community Devel. Coord.; D. Cole, Dir. CSW-R Svcs.;

L. Trojnor, Dir. Cayuga County Office. (Satellite Offices at: 33 William St., Auburn, NY 13021. Tel: 312-262-0018 and 4440 E. Ridge Rd., Williamson, NY 14589. Tel: 315-589-2600)

Catholic Charities of the Southern Tier, 215 E. Church St., Elmira, 14901. Tel: 607-734-9784; Fax: 607-734-6588.

Catholic Charities of Chemung/Schuyler Kathy Applin, Dir. of Gateways Community Living & Homeless Housing. Tel: 607-733-8274, Ext. 229; Fax: 607-734-3215; Joseph Bucci, Board Chairperson. Tel: 607-734-9787; Sarah Conley. Tel: 607-535-9161, Ext. 22; Fax: 607-535-7370 Schuyler Outreach; Marilyn Terkoski, First Time Homebuyer. Tel: 607-734-9784; Fax: 607-734-6588; Cindy Smith. Tel: 607-734-4898; Fax: 607-734-1213 Samaritan Center; Mary Nybeck, Office Coord. Tel: 607-734-9784; Fax: 607-734-6588.

Catholic Charities of Steuben Tel: 607-734-8085; Fax: 607-776-4092. Laura Opelt, Exec. Dir. Tel: 607-776-8085; Fax: 607-776-4092; Robert Turissini, Board Dir. Tel: 607-776-8085; Darcie Halifax, Day Care Svcs. Tel: 607-776-7387; Fax: 607-776-1220; Christine Wenzel, Prog. Coord. Tel: 607-776-8085; Fax: 607-776-4092.

Catholic Charities of Tompkins/Tioga George P. Ferrari, Exec. Dir. Tel: 607-272-5062; Fax: 607-272-4427; Carol Cooke, Chairman. Tel: 607-257-5443; Barbara Claussen. Tel: 607-272-5060 Samaritan Center.

Food Bank of the Southern Tier Paul A. Hesler, Exec. Dir. Tel: 607-796-6061; Fax: 607-796-6028; Anthony T. Barbaro, Board Chairman. Tel: 607-796-0784, Ext. 125; Natasha Thompson, Dir. Agency Svcs. Tel: 607-796-6061; Fax: 607-796-6028; Suzanne Peters, Admin. Svcs. Tel: 607-796-6061; Fax: 607-796-6028; Bernie Coon, Warehouse Mgr. Tel: 607-796-6061; Fax: 607-796-6028; Frank Carey, Development. Tel: 607-796-6061; Fax: 607-796-6028.

Regional Diocesan Administration Tel: 607-734-9847; Fax: 607-734-3764. Anthony T. Barbaro, Assoc. Diocesan Dir. Tel: 607-734-9784; Fax: 607-734-3764; Lee Randall, Dir. of Financial Svcs. Tel: 607-734-9784; Fax: 607-733-3614; Donna L. Rieker, Dir. of Human Resources. Tel: 607-734-9784, Ext. 165; Fax: 607-734-3764; Kathy Dubel, Dir. of Justice & Peace. Tel: 607-734-9784, Ext. 135; Fax: 607-734-6588.

Catholic Charities of Livingston County, 10 Chapel St., Mt. Morris, 14510. Tel: 716-658-4466; Fax: 585-658-2513. Timothy McMahon, M.S.W., Exec. Dir.

Departments: Sr. Nancy O'Brien, R.S.M., Rural Outreach; Christa Barrows, Faith in Action; Susan Bell, Youth Mentoring Program; Carol Gibson-Farley, Wheels for Work; Shadow Hill, Partnership for Success; Jackie Klube, Teen Services; Michelle Morris, Community of Caring; M. O'Hearn, Hispanic Latino Outreach; Mary Ann Thompson, Welfare to Work.

Kinship Family and Youth Services, 2 Bethesda Dr., Ste. 10, Hornell, 14843. Tel: 607-324-0909; Fax: 607-324-0983. Joseph Weider, Exec. Dir.; Dan Wenzel, Pres. Bd. of Directors.

Mercy Center With The Aging, 327 Warrinton Dr., 14618-1536. Tel: 585-244-5190; Fax: 585-244-3613. Sr. Anne Maloy, S.S.M., Dir.; Lucia Zeron-castillejo, Asst. Dir.

Providence Housing Development Corporation, 1136 Buffalo Rd., 14624. Tel: 585-328-3210; Fax: 585-529-9525. Maggie Bringewatt, Exec. Dir.; Jack Balinsky, Pres. Bd. of Directors; Donna Hall, Dir. Operations & Legal Devel.; Jane Lange, Project Devel. & Mktg. Dir.; Mary E. Mondo, Admin. Asst.; Mary Jo Carbonaro, Shelter & Care Prog. Dir.; Sheryl A. Hockey, Shelter & Care Program Coord.; Lisa Alcott, Homeownership, Monroe County Program Coord.

[I] MONASTERIES AND RESIDENCES OF PRIESTS AND BROTHERS

ROCHESTER. *Basilian Residence*, 3497 East Ave., 14618. Tel: 585-586-4600; Fax: 585-385-6383. Revs. Joseph M. Lanzalaco, C.S.B., Supvr.; Angelo D. Bovenzi, C.S.B., Councilor; T. Paul Broadhurst, C.S.B.; Albert W. Cylwicki, C.S.B.; John L. Dugan, C.S.B.; Leo A. Hetzler, C.S.B., Councilor; Richard C. Kinsky, C.S.B; John R. Lee, C.S.B.; Thomas M. Miller, C.S.B.; John C. Murray, C.S.B.; John A. Poluikis, C.S.B.; Donald J. Lococo, C.S.B.; Donald E. McCarthy, C.S.B. In Res. Revs. Steven Kung'u; Pius Wekesa.

Priests of the Region Serving Elsewhere:

Collegio San Clemente, Via Labicana, 95, 00184, Rome, Italy. Rev. William J. Sheehan, C.S.B.

c/o Companions of Christ the Lamb, P.O. Box 12, Paradise, MI 49768. Tel: 906-492-3647. Rev. George Kosicki, C.S.B.

16 Village Trail, Honeoye Falls, 14472. Rev. J. Gareth Poupore, C.S.B.

Basilian Fathers of Fisher House, 224 Fairport Rd., East Rochester, 14445. Tel: 585-381-9283. Rev. John R. Cavanaugh, Rector. Tel: 585-385-1353.

Becket Hall, 314 Gregory St., 14620. Tel: 585-461-2890; Fax: 585-244-5809. Email: beckethall@dor.org. Web: www.dor.org. Rev. William Donnelly. Residence for Pre-Theologate candidates. Students 3.

Missionaries of the Precious Blood, 1261 Highland Ave., 14620. Tel: 585-461-2750; Fax: 585-461-0318. Email: Jac56@rochester.rr.com. Revs. John A. Colacino, C.PP.S. Tel: 716-461-2750; Joseph A. Grasso, C.PP.S. Tel: 716-461-9250.

Whitefriars Priory, 625 Colebrook Dr., 14617. Tel: 585-266-2560. Revs. Brian Murphy, O.Carm.; Joseph DeMaio, O.Carm.; Jack Healy, O.Carm., Prior; Matthew Temple, O.Carm. Total in Residence 4.

INTERLAKEN. *St. Fidelis Friary*, 7790 County Rd. 153, 14847. Tel: 607-532-4423; Fax: 607-532-9271. Revs. Eugene O'Hara, O.F.M.Cap., Supr.; William H. Winters, O.F.M.Cap., Vicar; Carmine Funaro, O.F.M.Cap.; Terence Taft, O.F.M.Cap. Capuchin Friars-Province of St. Mary (Order of Friars Minor Capuchin). Priests 2.

PIFFARD. *Abbey of the Genesee* 14533. Tel: 585-243-0660; 585-243-2220 (Retreat House); Fax: 585-243-4816. Email: community@geneseeabbey.org. Web: www.geneseeabbey.org. Rt. Rev. John Eudes Bamberger, O.C.S.O., Retired Abbot (Retired); Revs. Francis R. Steger, O.C.S.O.; Thomas Aquinas Bond, O.C.S.O.; John J. Denburger, O.C.S.O., Abbot; Marcellus R. Earl, O.C.S.O.; Raymond J. Fournier, O.C.S.O.; Jerome J. Machar, O.C.S.O.; Robert J. Moore, O.C.S.O.; Justin R. Sheehan, O.C.S.O.; Gerard D' Souza, O.C.S.O. The Order of Cistercians of the Strict Observance (Trappists) Professed Monks 33; Priests 11; Total in Community (Piffard) 36.

Absent on Leave: Rev. Michael M. Hayden, O.C.S.O.

PINE CITY. *Mount Saviour Monastery*, 231 Monastery Rd., 14871-9787. Tel: 607-734-1688; Fax: 607-734-1689. Email: info@msaviour.org. Web: www.msaviour.org. Very Rev. Martin Boler, O.S.B., Prior; Revs. James Cronin, O.S.B.; James Kelly, O.S.B. Professed Monks 12; Professed Priests 3; Total in Community 14.

WATKINS GLEN. *St. Anthony of Padua Residence*, 225 Lakeview Ave. Ext., P.O. Box 41, 14891. Tel: 607-535-5035. Affiliated with the Assumption of the B.V.M. Province, with headquarters in Franklin, WI 53132

[J] CONVENTS AND RESIDENCES FOR SISTERS

ROCHESTER. *North American Union-Sisters of Our Lady of Charity, OLC Holy Angels Convent*, 1280 N. Winton Rd., 14609-5897. Tel: 585-654-8600; Fax: 585-654-8001. Sr. Martha Teresa Gomez, O.L.C., Supr.

Sisters of Mercy of the Americas Regional Community of Rochester, 1437 Blossom Rd., 14610. Tel: 585-288-2710; Fax: 585-288-2756. Email: mercy@mercyrochester.org. Web: www.mercyrochester.org. Sr. Sheila Stevenson, Pres. Professed Sisters & Perpetual Vows 191. In Res. Rev. Celesine Obi, Chap. Tel: 716-482-0553.

Sisters St. Joseph Motherhouse, 150 French Rd., 14618-3822. Tel: 585-641-8100; Fax: 585-586-1193. Email: cong@ssjrochester.org. Web: www.ssjvolunteers.org. Sr. Janice Morgan, Congregational Pres.; Rev. Msgr. William H. Shannon, Chap. (Retired); Rev. Bruce F. Ammering, Chap. Motherhouse Sisters of St. Joseph of Rochester, Inc. Professed Sisters in Community 350.

Spirit House, Inc., 72 Dorvid Rd., 14617. Tel: 585-544-5698; Fax: 585-266-2611. Email: spirithouse1@juno.com. Web: www.wounded-in-spirit.com. Sr. Mary Ann Ayers, R.S.M., Dir.

ELMIRA. *Monastery of Mary the Queen, Dominican Nuns*, 1310 W. Church St., 14905. Tel: 607-734-9506; Fax: 607-734-1452. Email: elmiraop@localnet.com. Web: www.op.org/maryqueen/default.htm. Sr. David Marie, O.P., Prioress. Solemn Vows 12; Perpetual Vows 1; In Formation 2.

PITTSFORD. *Monastery of Our Lady and St. Joseph Carmelite Monastery*, 1931 W. Jefferson Rd., 14534. Tel: 585-427-7094. Sr. John of the Cross, O.C.D., Prioress. Discalced Carmelite Nuns Professed Nuns with Solemn Vows 6; Externs with Simple Vows 1.

[K] RETREAT HOUSES

ROCHESTER. *Borromeo Prayer Center*, 3011 Dewey Ave., 14616. Tel: 585-663-5856; Fax: 585-663-8055. Email: bpc98@juno.com. Web: www.frontiernet.net/~stcharls. Patricia W. Scouten, Admin.

Mercy Prayer Center, 65 Highland Ave., 14620. Tel: 585-473-6893; Fax: 585-473-6414. Web: www.mercyprayercenter.org. Conducted and subsidized by Sisters of Mercy. Total in residence 2; Total Staff 6.

S.S.J. Spirituality Center, 402 Rogers Pkwy., 14617-4738. Tel: 585-336-4370; Fax: 585-336-4373. Email: mlhssj@juno.com. Mary Louise Heffernan, S.S.J., Dir. Total in residence 4; Total Staff 6.

CANANDAIGUA. *Notre Dame Retreat House*, Box 342, 5151 Foster Rd., 14424. Tel: 585-394-5700; Fax: 585-394-9215. Web: nortredameretreathouse.org. Revs. John G. Kingsbury, C.Ss.R., Dir.; Paul A. Miller, C.Ss.R.; Jack Jason Fiske, C.Ss.R.

[L] CAMPUS MINISTRY

ROCHESTER. *Campus Ministry* Pastoral Center, 1150 Buffalo Rd., 14624. Tel: 585-328-3210; Fax: 585-328-3149. Email: lough@dor.org. Shannon Loughlin, Dir. of Young Adult & Campus Ministry.

Catholic Newman Community at the University of Rochester Interfaith Chapel, 320 Wilson Blvd., 14627. Tel: 585-275-4321; Fax: 585-442-4279. Rev. Brian Cool; Sr. Kathleen Wayne, R.S.M., Contact Person.

Eastman School of Music Catholic Students Organization, c/o Rev. William Donnelly, St. Mary's Pl., 14607. Tel: 585-232-7140; Fax: 585-232-6289. Rev. William Donnelly, Contact Person; Helen Halligan, Contact Person.

Nazareth College of Rochester, 4245 East Ave., 14618. Tel: 585-389-2305; Fax: 585-389-2300. Lynne Boucher, Dir. of Campus Min. Tel: 585-389-2305.

Newman (Catholic Campus) Parish, RIT/NTID, Interfaith Center, 40 Lomb Memorial Dr., 14623. Tel: 585-475-2135; Fax: 585-475-5485. Email: dmhc@isc.rit.edu. Web: www.rit.edu/~newman/. Deirdre McKiernan Hetzler. Tel: 716-475-5172.

Monroe Community College - Office of the Chaplain, 1000 E. Henrietta Rd., 14623. Tel: 585-292-2558, Ext. 292; 585-328-3228, Ext. 292 (Contact); Fax: 585-292-2509.

St. John Fisher College, 3690 East Ave., 14618. Tel: 585-385-8368; Fax: 585-385-5209. Rev. Joseph Lanzalaco, C.S.B., Dir., Campus Min. Tel: 585-385-8367.

State University College at Brockport, the Newman Oratory of Brockport, NY, Inc., 101 Kenyon St., Brockport, 14420. Tel: 585-637-5036; Fax: 585-637-7866. Email: neuman@rpa.net. Margot Van Etten, Dir. of Campus Ministry.

State University College at Geneseo (Geneseo), Newman Catholic Community at the Interfaith Center, 11 Franklin St., Box 265, Geneseo, 14454. Tel: 585-243-1460. Email: neuman@geneseo.edu.

The Cornell Catholic Community, Inc. (Ithaca), Cornell University, G-22 Anabel Taylor Hall, Ithaca, 14853. Tel: 607-255-4228; Fax: 607-255-7793. Email: mjm48@cornell.edu. Rev. Michael Mahler, Chap. Dir. Tel: 607-255-6013.

The Catholic Community of Ithaca College, 100 Muller Chapel, Ithaca College, 453 Danby Rd., Ithaca, 14850. Tel: 607-274-3103; Fax: 607-274-1901. Rev. Scott M. Kubinski. Tel: 607-274-3184; Ms. Mary Humenay, Dir. Tel: 607-274-1117.

Elmira College, 1 Park Place, Elmira, 14901. Tel: 607-735-1824, Ext. 1824.

Finger Lakes Community College c/o St. Mary's Church, 95 N. Main St., Canandaigua, 14424. Tel: 585-394-1220; Fax: 585-396-3230.

Corning Community College, One Academic Dr., Corning, 14830. Tel: 607-962-9413; 585-328-3228 (Contact); Fax: 607-962-9548.

Hobart and William Smith College, c/o St. Stephen's Church, 48 Pulteney St., Geneva, 14456. Tel: 315-789-0930. Rev. Roy Kiggins. Tel: 315-789-1124.

Keuka College c/o St. Michael's Church, 312 Liberty St., Penn Yan, 14527. Tel: 315-536-7459; Fax: 315-536-6964.

Roberts Wesleyan College, 2301 Westside Dr., North Chili, 14514. Tel: 585-595-6830; 585-328-3228 (Contact).

Wells College, c/o St. Patrick Church, Main St., P.O. Box 296, Aurora, 13026-0296. Tel: 315-364-7197. Rev. Donald A. Curtiss, Contact.

Cayuga Community College, P.O. Box 1000, Auburn, 13021. Sr. Chris Lloyd, S.S.J., Contact. Tel: 315-255-1743.

New York Chiropractic College, c/o St. Patrick's Church, 97 W. Bayard St., Seneca Falls, 13148. Tel: 315-568-5203 (Rectory); 315-568-3124 (College); Fax: 315-568-4893. Rev. Richard Murphy.

[M] MISCELLANEOUS LISTINGS

ROCHESTER. *Apostleship of Prayer*, Diocesan Pastoral Center, 1150 Buffalo Rd., 14624. Tel: 716-328-3210. Rev. Thomas P. Mull.

Archivist (Diocese of Rochester Archives), 1150 Buffalo Rd., 14624. Tel: 585-328-3210, Ext. 204; Fax: 585-328-3149. Email: archive@dor.org. Sr. Connie Derby, R.S.M., Dir. of Archives and Records; Rev. Robert F. McNamara, Archivist (Retired).

1437 Blossom Rd., 14610. Tel: 585-288-2710, Ext. 180.

Catherine McAuley Housing dba Mercy Residential Services, 198 Oriole St., 14613-1923. Tel: 585-254-2175; Fax: 585-254-2229. Email: mercyresidential@mercyrochester.org. Susan B. Aiello, Exec. Dir. & Pres. Supportive Housing for Single Mothers and their Children. Total Staff 17; Families assisted 40.

Catholic Committee on Scouting, 1150 Buffalo Rd., 14624. Tel: 585-328-3210; Fax: 585-328-3149. Email: theisen@dor.org. Web: www.dor.org. Rev. William McGrath.

Catholic Gay & Lesbian Family Ministry, 1150 Buffalo Rd., 14624. Tel: 585-271-7363; Fax: 585-271-7363. Email: cglfm@aol.com. Karen Rinefierd, Diocesan Liaison.

Dunn Tower Apartments, Inc., 100 Dunn Tower Dr., 14606. Tel: 585-429-5520; Fax: 585-429-9720. Email: dt1@espernet. Web: www.dunntower.com. Housing for Seniors. Total Staff 6; Total in Residence 199.

Family Rosary For Peace, Inc., P.O. Box 11007, 14611. Tel: 585-254-7170; Fax: 585-254-5813. Rev. Paul J. Tomasso, Dir.; Dolores Mary Brien, Sec.

Holy Childhood Association, 1150 Buffalo Rd., 14624. Tel: 585-436-9200; Fax: 585-529-9501. Email: conlon@dor.org. Web: www.dor.org/missions. Rev. Robert C. Bradler, Dir.

St. Joseph's House of Hospitality (1941), 402 South Ave., 14620. Tel: 585-232-3262. Email: cathwork@frontiernet.net. P.O. Box 31062, 14603. Tel: 585-232-3262. Services provide soup kitchen, personal assistance to the needy, temporary housing and social justice advocacy. Total Staff 5; Total Assisted 120.

Marriage Encounter Apostolate (Worldwide) , 12 Parr Cir., 14617. Tel: 585-544-8896; Fax: 585-546-4486. Email: info@wwme-wny.org. Web: www.wwme-wny.org. Rev. John Murray, C.S.B.; Ed Knauf, Contact Person; Pam Knauf, Contact Person.

Mercy Center With The Aging, 327 Warrington Dr., 14618-1536. Tel: 585-244-5190; Fax: 585-244-3613. Email: mca@mercyrochester.org. Web: www.mercycenterwithaging.org. Sr. Anne Maloy, R.S.M., M.S.W., Dir.; Lucia Zeron-Castillejo, Asst. Dir.

Mercy Outreach Center, Inc., 142 Webster Ave., 14609. Tel: 585-288-2634; Fax: 585-288-0252. Email: skamoc@rochester.rr.com. Web: www.ggw.org/mercyoutreachcenter. Sr. Kathleen Ann Kolb, R.S.M., Exec. Dir. & Pres. Health and dental services for the uninsured and advocacy.

Providence Housing Development Corporation, 1136 Buffalo Rd., 14624. Tel: 585-328-3210; Fax: 585-529-9525. Email: bringewatt@dor.org. Programs offered: Property Management, Shelter & Care for the Homeless, First-time Homebuyers and Housing Information, Credit Repair and Housing Development. Units of Housing 260.

Rochester Catholic Worker Bethany House, 169 St. Bridget's Dr., 14605. Tel: 585-454-4197; Fax: 585-454-4197. Email: rbethan1@rochester.rr.com. Donna Ecker, Contact Person. Total staff 4.

St. Theodore's Apartment Housing Development Fund Co., Inc. (Dunn Tower II Apts.), 200 Dunn Tower Dr., 14606. Tel: 585-429-6840; Fax: 585-247-3723. Email: dt2@espernet.com. Web: www.dunntower.com.

Union Meadows Housing Development Fund Corp., 1136 Buffalo Rd., 14624. Tel: 585-328-3210; Fax: 585-529-9525. Email: bringewatt@dor.org. Maggie Bringewatt, Exec. Dir.; Jack Balinsky, Pres. & Board of Directors. Total Staff 2; Total in Residence 48.

CORNING. *Anawim Community Center*, 122 E. First St., 14830 Tel: 607-936-4965; Fax: 607-936-0207. Email: corning@anawim.com. Web: www.anawim.com. Rev. Daniel Healy (Philippines), Dir. Total In Residence 5; Total Staff 12.

FAIRPORT. *Catholic Charismatic Renewal*, 48 South Ave., 14450. Tel: 585-325-1670, Ext. 2939. Email: don_germano@mony.com. Deacon Donald Germano, Diocesan Liaison Team.

GENEVA. *DeSales Institution Foundation*, 90 Pulteney St., 14456. Tel: 315-789-5111; Fax: 315-789-8230. Email: hockpg@aol.com. Web: www.desales.org. Peter Koch, Pres.; Dr. Karen M. Juliano, Prin.; Edward Smaldone Jr., Sec. & Treas.

OWEGO. *Owego -Tioga Rural Ministry*, Formerly Oswego -Tioga Rural Ministry60 North Ave., 13827. Tel: 607-697-3021; Fax: 607-687-3033. Sr. Phyllis McGuire, R.S.M., Exec. Dir.. Email: phylrsm@juno.com. This ministry serves as a food pantry and an emergency outreach to the poor and elderly of the county. Total Staff 4; Total Assisted 2,496.

SENECA FALLS. *Patrician Fund Trust*, St. Patrick's Church, 97 W. Bayard St., 13148. Tel: 315-568-5203; Fax: 315-568-4893. Email: sstpatri@dor.org. Web: www.senecafallsonline.com/stpats/. Sean Anglim.

SPENCERPORT. *Legion of Mary*, 60 Martha St., 14559. Tel: 716-352-9052. Rev. Paul G. Wohlrab, Spiritual Dir. Rochester Comitium (Retired).

Rochester Comitium, 6 Martha St., 14559-1329. Tel: 716-266-8087. Mrs. Joan Stanton, Pres. 1381 Beach Ave., 14612. Tel: 716-663-0371.

RELIGIOUS INSTITUTES OF MEN REPRESENTED IN THE DIOCESE

For further details refer to the corresponding bracketed number in the Religious Institutes of Men or Women section.

[0170]—*Basilian Fathers*—C.S.B.
[0200]—*Benedictine Monks*—O.S.B.
[0470]—*The Capuchin Friars* (Province of St. Mary)—O.F.M.Cap.
[0270]—*Carmelite Fathers and Brothers*—O.Carm.
[0350]—*Cistercians Order of the Strict Observance (Trappists)*—O.C.S.O.
[0310]—*Congregation of Christian Brothers* (Eastern Prov.)—C.F.C.
[1140]—*Congregation of the Sacred Hearts of Jesus and Mary*—SS.CC.
[0480]—*Conventual Franciscans* (Buffalo & Immaculate Conception Provinces)—O.F.M.Conv
[0520]—*Franciscan Friars* (Assumption B.V.M. Prov.)—O.F.M.
[0690]—*Jesuit Fathers and Brothers* (New York Province)—S.J.
[0610]—*Priests of the Congregation of Holy Cross*—C.S.C.
[1070]—*Redemptorist Fathers* (Baltimore Province)—C.SS.R.
[0760]—*Society of Mary (Marianists)*—S.M.
[1060]—*Society of the Precious Blood*—C.PP.S.
[0560]—*Third Order Regular of Saint Francis*—T.O.R.

RELIGIOUS INSTITUTES OF WOMEN REPRESENTED IN THE DIOCESE

[3110]—*Congregation of Our Lady of the Retreat in the Cenacle*—R.C.
[0760]—*Daughters of Charity of St. Vincent de Paul*—D.C.
[0420]—*Discalced Carmelite Nuns*—O.C.D.
[1050]—*Dominican Contemplative Nuns*—O.P.
[1070-13]—*Dominican Sisters (Adrian, MI)*—O.P.
[1070-05]—*Dominican Sisters (Amityville, NY)*—O.P.
[]—*Franciscan Sisters of Alleghany, New York*—O.S.F.
[2575]—*Institute of the Sisters of Mercy of the Americas* (Rochester, NY)—R.S.M.
[2470]—*Maryknoll Sisters of St. Dominic*—M.M.
[]—*Misioneras Guadalupanas del Espiritu Santo*
[3070]—*North American Union Sisters of Our Lady of Charity*—N.A.U.-O.L
[3430]—*Religious Teachers Filippini*—M.P.F.
[2970]—*School Sisters of Notre Dame*—S.S.N.D.
[3950]—*Sisters of Saint Mary of Namur*—S.S.M.N.
[1800]—*Sisters of St. Francis of the Third Order Regular (Williamsville, New York)*—O.S.F.
[3840]—*Sisters of St. Joseph of Carondolet*—C.S.J.
[3830-14]—*Sisters of St. Joseph (Rochester)*—S.S.J.
[3730]—*Sisters of the Order of St. Basil the Great*—O.S.B.M.
[1490]—*Sisters of the Third Franciscan Order*—O.S.F.
[3620]—*Sisters, Servants of Mary Immaculate*—S.S.M.I.
[2160]—*Sisters, Servants of the Immaculate Heart of Mary*—I.H.M.

DIOCESAN CEMETERIES

ROCHESTER. *Holy Sepulchre*, 2461 Lake Ave., 14612. Tel: 585-458-4110; Fax: 585-458-3059. Web: www.holysepulchre.org.

REGIONAL CEMETERIES

AUBURN. *St. Joseph's*
CORNING. *St. Mary*
ELMIRA. *SS. Peter and Paul's*
GENEVA. *St. Mary's and St. Patrick's*

NECROLOGY

† Cirrincione, Rev. Msgr. Joseph, (Retired)—Died Nov. 21, 2002
† Duffy, Rev. Msgr. John F., (Retired)—Died Feb. 13, 2003
† Quinn, Rev. Msgr. Richard M., (Retired)—Died Sept. 17, 2003
† Burns, William A., (Retired)—Died Aug. 20, 2003
† Carges, Bernard, (Retired)—Died April 22, 2003
† Foy, Edward J., (Retired)—Died April 24, 2003
† Hempel, John L., (Retired)—Died Dec. 1, 2003
† O'Brien, Bartholomew J., (Retired)—Died Nov. 7, 2003
† Quinn, John J.—Died Dec. 27, 2002
† Shamon, Albert J.M.—Died Nov. 21, 2003

Diocese of Rockford

(Dioecesis Rockfordiensis)

Most Reverend

THOMAS G. DORAN

Bishop of Rockford; ordained December 20, 1961; appointed Bishop of Rockford April 19, 1994; consecrated and installed June 24, 1994 *Res.: 1243 N. Court St., Rockford, IL 61103.*

Most Reverend

ARTHUR J. O'NEILL, D.D., V.G.

Retired Bishop of Rockford; ordained March 27, 1943; appointed Bishop of Rockford August 19, 1968; consecrated and installed October 11, 1968; retired April 19, 1994 *Res.: 14 Country Club Beach, Rockford, IL 61103.* Tel: 815-877-5078; Fax: 815-877-2236.

Diocesan Chancery: 555 Colman Center Dr., P.O. Box 7044, Rockford, IL 61125. Tel: 815-399-4300; Fax: 815-399-4769.

Web: www.rockforddiocese.org

Email: chancery99@aol.com

ESTABLISHED SEPTEMBER 23, 1908.

Square Miles 6,457.

Comprises Jo Daviess, Stephenson, Winnebago, Boone, McHenry, Carroll, Ogle, DeKalb, Kane, Whiteside and Lee Counties in the State of Illinois.

Legal Title: For legal titles of parishes and diocesan institutions, consult the Chancery Office.

STATISTICAL OVERVIEW

Personnel	
Bishop	1
Retired Bishops	2
Abbots	1
Retired Abbots	2
Priests: Diocesan Active in Diocese	134
Priests: Diocesan Active Outside Diocese	8
Priests: Retired, Sick or Absent	44
Number of Diocesan Priests	186
Religious Priests in Diocese	61
Total Priests in Diocese	247
Extern Priests in Diocese	13
Ordinations:	
Diocesan Priests	12
Religious Priests	3
Transitional Deacons	3
Permanent Deacons	13
Permanent Deacons in Diocese	143
Total Brothers	15
Total Sisters	245
Parishes	
Parishes	105
With Resident Pastor:	
Resident Diocesan Priests	70
Resident Religious Priests	7
Without Resident Pastor:	
Administered by Priests	27
Administered by Deacons	1
Professional Ministry Personnel:	
Sisters	18
Lay Ministers	126
Welfare	
Catholic Hospitals	3
Total Assisted	520,794
Health Care Centers	13
Total Assisted	49,258
Homes for the Aged	8
Total Assisted	1,538
Day Care Centers	1
Total Assisted	69
Special Centers for Social Services	12
Total Assisted	321,487
Educational	
Diocesan Students in Other Seminaries	45
Total Seminarians	45
Colleges and Universities	1
Total Students	101
High Schools, Diocesan and Parish	6
Total Students	3,232
High Schools, Private	2
Total Students	913
Elementary Schools, Diocesan and Parish	41
Total Students	11,660
Catechesis/Religious Education:	
High School Students	4,157
Elementary Students	25,761
Total Students under Catholic Instruction	45,869
Teachers in the Diocese:	
Priests	8
Brothers	10
Sisters	21
Lay Teachers	1,035
Vital Statistics	
Receptions into the Church:	
Infant Baptism Totals	6,386
Adult Baptism Totals	201
Received into Full Communion	345
First Communions	6,626
Confirmations	4,482
Marriages:	
Catholic	915
Interfaith	389
Total Marriages	1,304
Deaths	2,034
Total Catholic Population	420,883
Total Population	1,374,899

Former Bishops—Most Revs. PETER J. MULDOON, D.D., ord. Dec. 18, 1886; consecrated Titular Bishop of Tamassus and Auxiliary Bishop of Chicago, July 25, 1901; appt. Bishop of Rockford, Sept. 28, 1908; made Assistant to the Pontifical Throne, June 8, 1921; died Oct. 8, 1927; EDWARD F. HOBAN, S.T.D., ord. July 11, 1903; consecrated Titular Bishop of Colonia and Auxiliary Bishop of Chicago, Dec. 21, 1921; appt. Bishop of Rockford, Feb. 10, 1928; appt. Assistant at the Pontifical Throne, Nov. 25, 1937; appt. Titular Bishop of Listra and Coadjutor Bishop of Cleveland, Nov. 16, 1942; succeeded to the See of Cleveland, Nov. 2, 1945; died Sept. 22, 1966; JOHN J. BOYLAN, D.D., Ph.D., ord. July 28, 1915; appt. Nov. 21, 1942; consecrated Feb. 17, 1943; died July 19, 1953; RAYMOND P. HILLINGER, D.D., ord. April 2, 1932; appt. Nov. 3, 1953; consecrated Dec. 29, 1953; appt. Titular Bishop of Derbe and Auxiliary Bishop of Chicago, June 27, 1956; died Nov. 13, 1971; Rt. Rev. DONALD M. CARROLL, D.D., appt. June 27, 1956; resigned Sept. 25, 1956; died Jan. 3, 2002; Most Rev. LORAS T. LANE, D.D., ord. March 19, 1937; appt. Titular Bishop of Bencenna and Auxiliary of Dubuque, May 29, 1951; consecrated Aug. 20, 1951; appt. to Rockford, Oct. 11, 1956; died July 22, 1968.

Diocesan Chancery—555 Colman Center Dr., P.O. Box 7044, Rockford, 61125. Tel: 815-399-4300; Fax: 815-399-5266. Address all official business to this office.; Office Hours: Mon.-Fri. 8:30-12, 1-4:30

Vicars General—Most Rev. ARTHUR J. O'NEILL, D.D., V.G.; Rev. Msgrs. THOMAS C. BRADY, P.A., V.G., Ph.D.; DAVID D. KAGAN, V.G., J.C.L.; GLENN L. NELSON, J.C.L., 555 Colman Center Dr., P.O. Box 7044, Rockford, 61125. Tel: 815-399-4300; Fax: 815-399-5266.

Moderator of the Curia—Rev. Msgr. DAVID D. KAGAN, V.G., J.C.L.

Vicar for Clergy and Religious—Rev. Msgr. ERIC R. BARR, S.T.L.

Parish Services and Directors—Mr. THOMAS MCKENNA, Dir. Social Svcs., 555 Colman Center Dr., P.O. Box 7044, Rockford, 61125; Mr. JASON CHRISTENSEN, Asst. Dir. Social Svcs., 850 N. Church St., Rockford, 61103; Rev. JOHN A. SLAMPAK, S.T.L., Dir. Pastoral Svcs., 555 Colman Center Dr., P.O. Box 7044, Rockford, 61125; LORRIE GRAMER, Asst. Dir. Pastoral Svcs., Bishop Lane Retreat Center, 7708 E. McGregor Rd., Rockford, 61102; Sr. PATRICIA DOWNEY, O.P., Dir. Educational Svcs., Catholic Education Office, 555 Colman Center Dr., P.O. Box 7044, Rockford, 61125; Mr. JOHN MCGRATH, Asst. Dir. Educational Svcs., Catholic Education Office, 555 Colman Center Dr., P.O. Box 7044, Rockford, 61125; Dr. WAYNE LENELL, Dir. Financial & Admin. Svcs., 555 Colman Center Dr., P.O. Box 7044, Rockford, 61125; Mrs. JODI RIPPON, Asst. Dir. Financial & Admin. Svcs., 555 Colman Center Dr., P.O. Box 7044, Rockford, 61125.

Chancellor—Rev. Msgr. GLENN L. NELSON, J.C.L.

Bishop's Secretary for Retired Priests—Rev. DANIEL J. DEUTSCH.

Secretary to the Bishop & Diocesan Master of Ceremonies—Rev. JOHN C. FRITZ.

Diocesan Tribunal—555 Colman Center Dr., P.O. Box 7044, Rockford, 61125. Tel: 815-399-4300; Fax: 815-399-4861. Address all official business to this office.

Judicial Vicar—Rev. Msgr. DAVID D. KAGAN, V.G., J.C.L.

Adjutant Judicial Vicar—Rev. MICHAEL KURZ, J.C.L.

Secretary and Director of the Tribunal—Sr. AUDREY STRAUB, S.S.N.D., J.C.L.

Secretary for Administrative Processes—Rev. ROBERT J. SWEENEY.

Promoter of Justice—Rev. Msgr. JOHN J. MITCHELL, V.F.

Defenders of the Bond—Sisters AUDREY STRAUB, S.S.N.D., J.C.L.; ELAINE KERSCHER, O.S.F., J.C.L.; BEVERLY JEANNE HOWE, O.P., J.C.L.

Pro Synodal Judges—Rev. Msgr. RAYMOND J. WAHL, P.A., J.C.D.; Revs. GERALD P. KOBBEMAN; WILLIAM A. KRIEGSMANN (Retired); FRANCIS E. MCDONNELL (Retired); Very Rev. ARQUIMEDES VALLEJO, J.C.D.

Advocates—Sisters MARGARET ANNE FLOTO, O.S.F.; JEANNINE WEIDNER, O.S.F.

Experts—Rev. THOMAS J. MONAHAN, Ph.D. (Retired); Mr. MICHAEL M. KAGAN, M.A.; Mr. DANIEL J. APPINO, M.S.Ed.

Notaries—Mrs. DENISE GEORGE; Mrs. DONNA HAYES; Mrs. BECKY ACKERMAN.

Diocesan Consultors—Rev. Msgrs. THOMAS E. BALES; THOMAS C. BRADY, P.A., V.G., Ph.D.; DAVID D. KAGAN, V.G., J.C.L.; DANIEL J. HERMES; JOHN J. MITCHELL, V.F.; WILLIAM H. SCHWARTZ; RAYMOND J. WAHL, P.A., J.C.D.; Revs. LEO J. BARTEL; JOHN W. CAHILL; DANIEL J. DEUTSCH; STEPHEN J. KNOX, S.T.L.; GEOFFREY D. WIRTH.

Deans—Rev. Msgrs. EDWARD S. WRIGHT, V.F., Aurora Deanery; WILLIAM J. CLAUSEN, DeKalb Deanery; ROBERT B. HOFFMAN, Elgin Deanery; P. WILLIAM MCDONNELL, Freeport Deanery; JAMES W. MCLOUGHLIN, McHenry County Deanery; JOHN J. MITCHELL, V.F., Rockford Deanery; THOMAS L. DZIELAK, Sterling Deanery.

Episcopal Delegate for Women Religious—Sr. JAMES MARIE O'CONNOR, S.S.N.D., 555 Colman Center Dr., P.O. Box 7044, Rockford, 61125. Tel: 815-399-4300; Fax: 815-399-5266.

Diocesan Offices and Directors

Accounting and Data Processing Office—JUDITH A. CROSS, Office Mgr., P.O. Box 7044, Rockford, 61125. Tel: 815-399-4300; Fax: 815-399-5657.

Catholic Campaign for Human Development—850 N. Church St., Rockford, 61103. Tel: 815-965-0623; Fax: 815-965-0628.

Catholic Charismatic Renewal Services—Mr. RON BERGMAN, Diocesan Liaison, 1910 Bracknel Blvd., Rockford, 61103. Tel: 815-654-4111.

Catholic Office of the Deaf—Rev. Msgr. GLENN L. NELSON, J.C.L., Dir., 555 Colman Center Dr., P.O. Box 7044, Rockford, 61125. Tel: 815-399-4300 (Voice); 815-962-2994 (TTY); Fax: 815-399-5266.

Catholic Relief Services—Mr. THOMAS MCKENNA, 555 Colman Center Dr., P.O. Box 7044, Rockford, 61125. Tel: 815-399-4300; Fax: 815-399-6303.

Catholic Social Services—Mr. THOMAS MCKENNA, Dir., P.O. Box 7044, Rockford, 61125. Tel: 815-399-4300; Fax: 815-399-6303.

Cemeteries—Rev. Msgr. THOMAS C. BRADY, P.A., V.G., Ph.D., Exec. Dir.; Dr. WAYNE LENELL, C.P.A., Ph.D., Admin.; CAROL GIAMBALVO, Dir., 8616 W. State St., Winnebago, 61088. Tel: 815-965-1450; Fax: 815-965-9632.

Censores Librorum—Rev. Msgr. CHARLES W. MCNAMEE, P.A., J.C.L. (Retired); Rev. FRANCIS E. MCDONNELL (Retired).

Charities—Mr. THOMAS MCKENNA, Acting Dir., Offices: 850 N. Church St., Rockford, 61103. Tel: 815-965-0623; Fax: 815-965-0628. 1700 N. Farnsworth Ave., Ste. 18, Aurora, 60505. 1315 Pleasant St., DeKalb, 60115. 566 Dundee Ave., Elgin, 60120. 1231 S. Walnut Ave., Freeport, 61032. 202 Summit St., Galena, 61036. 5215 W. Bull Valley Rd., McHenry, 60050. 801 W. 11th St., Sterling, 61081.

Satellite Offices—860 Biester Dr., #206 C, Belvidere, 61008. 315 S. Peoria Ave., Dixon, 61021.

Clergy Relief Society, Priests' Retirement Committee—Rev. DANIEL J. DEUTSCH, Exec. Sec., 2300 Main St., Batavia, 60510. Tel: 630-879-4750; Fax: 630-879-9502.

Communications—Dr. OWEN PHELPS, Dir., 555 Colman Center Dr., P.O. Box 7044, Rockford, 61125. Tel: 815-399-4300; Fax: 815-399-5225.

Conciliation and Arbitration Council—Sr. ELAINE KERSCHER, O.S.F., J.C.L., Exec. Sec., 555 Colman Center Dr., P.O. Box 7044, Rockford, 61125. Tel: 815-399-4300; Fax: 815-399-4861.

Council of Catholic Women, Diocesan—Rev. Msgr. THOMAS L. DZIELAK, Moderator, 708 10th Ave., Rock Falls, 61071. Tel: 815-625-4508; KATHY HOLT, 5005 N. Dunham Woods Rd., Harvard, 60033. Tel: 815-943-7158.

Cursillo Movement—Rev. ROBERT N. SHERRY, Dir., 5211 W. Bull Valley Rd., McHenry, 60050. Tel: 815-385-LORD.

Development Office—Mr. DAVID HOUGAN, Dir., 555 Colman Center Dr., P.O. Box 7044 Rockford, 61125. Tel: 815-399-4300; Fax: 815-399-5657.

Divine Worship, Office for— (and RCIA Resources)-- Rev. JOHN A. SLAMPAK, S.T.L., Dir., 555 Colman Center Dr., P.O. Box 7044, Rockford, 61125. Tel: 815-399-4300; Fax: 815-399-6303.

Ecumenism, Office of—Rev. ADDISON H. HART, Dir., Christ the Teacher, 512 Normal Rd., DeKalb, 60115. Tel: 815-787-7770; Fax: 815-758-2053.

Education—Sisters PATRICIA DOWNEY, O.P., Supt. Schools; EILEEN SULLIVAN, O.P., Asst. Supt. Schools; Mr. JOHN MCGRATH, Dir., Rel. Educ. & Formation, 555 Colman Center Dr., P.O. Box 7044, Rockford, 61125. Tel: 815-399-4300; Fax: 815-399-6278.

Ethicist for Health Care Issues, Diocesan—Rev. TIMOTHY L. DOHERTY, Ph.D., 555 Colman Center Dr., P.O. Box 7044, Rockford, 61125. Tel: 815-399-4300; Fax: 815-399-6303.

Family Life—LORRIE GRAMER, Dir., 7708 E. McGregor Rd., Rockford, 61102. Tel: 815-965-5011; Fax: 815-965-5811.

Finance and Administration—Dr. WAYNE LENELL, C.P.A., Ph.D., Dir. Fin. & Admin. Svcs., 555 Colman Center Dr., P.O. Box 7044, Rockford, 61125. Tel: 815-399-4300; Fax: 815-399-5591.

Hispanic Ministry Offices—Very Rev. ARQUIMEDES VALLEJO, J.C.D., 555 Colman Center Dr., P.O. Box 7044, Rockford, 61125. Tel: 815 399-4300; Fax: 815-399-6303. Offices for Diocese Aurora Deanery: Centro Cristo Rey, 115 State St. Aurora, 60505. DeKalb Deanery: Centro Cuerpo de Cristo, 308 Fisk Ave., Dekalb, 60115. Elgin Deanery: Centro Jesus Resucitado, 90 N. Kennedy Dr., Carpentersville, 60110. Freeport Deanery: Centro Jesus Galileo, 21 Burr Oaks Dr., E., Stockton, 61085. McHenry Deanery: Centro San Jose, 207 E. Brainard St., Harvard, 60033. Rockford Deanery: Centro Sembrador, 1536 S. Main St., Rockford, 61102. Sterling Deanery: Centro TU C.A.S.A., 202 W. Sixth St., Sterling, 61081.

Holy Childhood Association—Sr. PATRICIA DOWNEY, O.P., Dir., 555 Colman Center Dr., P.O. Box 7044, Rockford, 61125. Tel: 815-399-4300; Fax: 815-399-6278.

Immigration Services—Mrs. JEANNE LINDBERG, Dir., 300 N. Alpine Rd., Rockford, 61107. Tel: 815-399-1709; Fax: 815-399-1731.

Investment and Loan—Dr. WAYNE LENELL, C.P.A., Ph.D., 555 Colman Center Dr., P.O. Box 7044, Rockford, 61125. Tel: 815-399-4300; Fax: 815-399-5591.

Liturgical Commission, Diocesan—Rev. JOHN A. SLAMPAK, S.T.L., Dir., 555 Colman Center Dr., P.O. Box 7044, Rockford, 61125. Tel: 815-399-4300; Fax: 815-399-6303.

Ministry Formation, Office of—Mr. JOHN MCGRATH, Dir., 555 Colman Center Dr., P.O. Box 7044, Rockford, 61125. Tel: 815-399-4300; Fax: 815-399-6278.

Ministry to Priests Program—Rev. Msgr. ERIC R. BARR, S.T.L., Vicar, Clergy Sabbaticals and Diocesan Priests' Retreats, 555 Colman Center Dr., P.O. Box 7044, Rockford, 61125. Tel: 815-399-4300; Fax: 815-399-5962.

Newman-Campus Ministry—Rev. STEPHEN J. KNOX, S.T.L., Dir., 512 Normal Rd., DeKalb, 60115. Tel: 815-787-7770; Fax: 815-758-2053.

Newspaper—PENNY WIEGERT, Mng. Editor, 555 Colman Center Dr., P.O. Box 7044, Rockford, 61125. Tel: 815-399-4300; Fax: 815-399-6225. "The Observer"

Permanent Diaconate Program Diocesan—555 Colman Center Dr., P.O. Box 7044, Rockford, 61125. Tel: 815-399-4300; Fax: 815-399-6303.

Priests' Eucharistic League—Rev. THOMAS J. MONAHAN, Ph.D. (Retired), 2696 Aldersgate Dr., Rockford, 61103. Tel: 815-282-9972.

Priest Personnel—Rev. Msgr. ERIC R. BARR, S.T.L., Vicar, Clergy and Religious, 555 Colman Center Dr., P.O. Box 7044, Rockford, 61125. Tel: 815-399-4300; Fax: 815-399-5962.

Pro-Life Activities, Office of—Rev. DAVID A. PECK, Dir., 555 Colman Center Dr., P.O. Box 7044, Rockford, 61125. Tel: 815-877-LIFE; Fax: 815-282-5086.

Propagation of the Faith—Rev. ROBERT J. SWEENEY, Dir., 555 Colman Center Dr., P.O. Box 7044, Rockford, 61125. Tel: 815-399-4300; Fax: 815-399-4861.

Property Management Office—Mr. DAN LAUDER, Dir., P.O. Box 7044, Rockford, 61125. Tel: 815-399-4300; Fax: 815-399-5657.

Research and Planning—Dr. MICHAEL CIESLAK, Ph.D., Dir., 555 Colman Center Dr., P.O. Box 7044, Rockford, 61125. Tel: 815-399-4300; Fax: 815-399-6225.

Rural Life Conference—Mr. THOMAS MCKENNA, Dir., 555 Colman Center Dr., P.O. Box 7044, Rockford, 61125. Tel: 815-399-4300; Fax: 815-399-6303.

Scouts—Rev. Msgr. WILLIAM H. SCHWARTZ, Dir., 1243 N. Church St., Rockford, 61103. Tel: 815-965-2765; Fax: 815-965-0743.

Diocesan Administration Offices—Mr. RONALD DI TOMASSI, Building Mgr., 555 Colman Center Dr., P.O. Box 7044, Rockford, 61125. Tel: 815-399-4300; Fax: 815-399-6303.

Unemployment Insurance Office—JUDITH A. CROSS, Mgr., P.O. Box 7044, Rockford, 61125. Tel: 815-399-4300; Fax: 815-399-5657.

Victim Assistance Coordinator—Mr. DICK KUNNERT. Tel: 815-962-9347. Email: chancery99@aol.com.

Vocations—Revs. AARON R. BRODESKI, Dir.; MICHAEL G. BLACK, Asst. Dir.; STEVEN M. SABO, Asst. Dir., 555 Colman Center Dr., P.O. Box 7044, Rockford, 61125. Tel: 815-399-4300; Fax: 815-399-6085.

CLERGY, PARISHES, MISSIONS AND PAROCHIAL SCHOOLS

CITY OF ROCKFORD
(WINNEBAGO COUNTY)

1—ST. PETER CATHEDRAL (1922), Rev. Msgr. William H. Schwartz, Rector; Revs. Martins Emeh; Phillip Kaim; Steven Sabo; Deacons Charles Cooper; Martin Czerniewski; Randy Fast.
Res.: 1243 N. Church St., 61103. Tel: 815-965-2765; Fax: 815-965-0743.
School—1231 N. Court St. Tel: 815-963-3620; Fax: 815-963-0551. Mr. Michael Kagan, Prin. Lay Teachers 15; Students 291.
Catechesis/Religious Program—Mr. William Easton, D.R.E. Students 131.

2—ST. ANTHONY OF PADUA (1909), (Italian), Revs. Luke Poczworowski, O.F.M.Conv.; James Jankowski, O.F.M.Conv. In Res., Rev. Dominic Wisz, O.F.M-.Conv.; Deacon Sam Cassaro.
Res.: 1010 Ferguson St., 61102. Tel: 815-965-2761; Fax: 815-968-2798.
Catechesis/Religious Program—Tel: 815-965-3448. Students 136.

3—ST. BERNADETTE (1957), Revs. John L. Stringini; Pierre G. Polycarpe; Deacon Richard Gerdeman; Mary Trapani, Business Mgr.
Res.: 2400 Bell Ave., 61103. Tel: 815-968-0904; Fax: 815-987-9476.
Church: Rockton Ave. & Bell Ave., 61103. Tel: 815-968-0404; Fax: 815-987-9476.
School—2300 Bell Ave. Tel: 815-968-2288; Fax: 815-987-9453. Mrs. Elizabeth Adams-Young, Prin. Lay Teachers 23; Students 333.
Catechesis/Religious Program—2300 Bell Ave., 61103. Tel: 815-962-7345. Mrs. Judy Rossato, D.R.E. Students 70.

4—ST. EDWARD (1929), Rev. Msgr. Raymond J. Wahl, P.A., J.C.D.; Revs. James J. Murphy, Pastor Emeritus; Jerome P. Koutnik; Deacon Lambert Verstynen.
Parish Office—3004 11th St., 61109. Tel: 815-229-0282; Fax: 815-229-8912.
Res.: 3026 11th St., 61109. Tel: 815-398-1249.
School—3020 S. 11th St. Tel 815-398-2631; Fax: 815-398-3134. Mr. John Fitzsimmons, Prin. Lay Teachers 11; Students 249.
Catechesis/Religious Program—Tel: 815-229-8914. Linda S. Josephitis, D.R.E. Students 151.

5—HOLY FAMILY (1963), Rev. Msgr. Thomas E. Bales; Revs. Dennis D. Atto; Brian D. Grady; Michael E. Morrissey; Stephen Olutade Folorunso; Deacons Tom Welch; William Bronz; Patrick Moynihan; Robert Sweeney.
Office—4401 Highcrest Rd., 61107. Tel: 815-398-4280; Fax: 815-398-4287.
School—4407 Highcrest Rd. Tel: 815-398-5331; Fax: 815-398-5902. Mr. Anthony Smerko, Prin. Lay Teachers 28; Students 551.
Catechesis/Religious Program—Tel: 815-397-9395; Fax: 815-398-4287. Joellen Lansing, D.R.E. Students 208.

6—ST. JAMES (1853), [JC] Rev. David E. Beauvais; Deacons Ronald Magee; William Dean. In Res., Rev. William M. McKinstra (Retired).
Res.: 428 N. Second St., 61107. Tel: 815-962-1214; Fax: 815-962-1236.
School—409 N. First St. Tel: 815-962-8515. Ms. Margo Shifo, Prin. Lay Teachers 17; Students 228.
Catechesis/Religious Program—Tel: 815-962-5588. Cathy Becker, D.R.E. Students 120.

7—ST. MARY ORATORY, INSTITUTE OF CHRIST THE KING SOVEREIGN PRIEST (1997), Rev. Brian Bovee.
Res.: 517 Elm St., 61102. Tel: 815-965-5971; Fax: 815-965-6029.

8—ST. PATRICK (1919), [JC] Revs. Brian A. Geary; John Earl; Michael G. Black; Deacons Ron Graw; Frank Barone.
Res.: 2505 School St., 61101. Tel: 815-965-9539; Fax: 815-964-9705.
Catechesis/Religious Program—Students 200.

9—SS. PETER AND PAUL (1911), (Hispanic), Rev. Timothy Piasecki.
Res.: 617 Lincoln Ave., 61102. Tel: 815-962-7171; Fax: 815-962-5184.

Catechesis/Religious Program—Fax: 815-962-5184. Students 190.

10—ST. RITA (1914), Rev. Gerald P. Kobbeman; Deacons Gerald Savercool; Robert Martin. In Res., Rev. Michael Kurz.
Res.: 6254 Valley Knoll Dr., 61109-1898. Tel: 815-398-0853; Fax: 815-397-7499.
School—6284 Valley Knoll Dr., 61109-1898. Tel: 815-398-3466; Fax: 815-398-6104. Mrs. Diane Potts, Prin. Lay Teachers 14; Students 273.
Catechesis/Religious Program—Tel: 815-398-6483; Fax: 815-397-7499. Sr. Dorothy Bertsch, S.M.P., D.R.E. Students 300.

11—ST. STANISLAUS KOSTKA (1912), (Polish), Rev. John J. Mikula, O.F.M.Conv.; Deacon James Hudzinski.
Res.: 201 Buckbee, 61104. Tel: 815-965-3913; Fax: 815-965-3915.
Catechesis/Religious Program—Students 22.

OUTSIDE THE CITY OF ROCKFORD

ALBANY, WHITESIDE CO., ST. PATRICK, Rev. James R. Keenan.
Hwy. 84, 61230. Tel: 309-887-4072; 815-589-3542.

ALGONQUIN, MCHENRY CO., ST. MARGARET MARY (1954), Revs. Michael J. Tierney; Vicente Purgatorio; Ariel Valencia; Ricardo Hernandez; Deacons Howard Fischer; Simon Grossmayer; Patrick Maher.
Parish Office—111 S. Hubbard St., 60102. Tel: 847-658-7625; Fax: 847-658-7882.
School—(Grades PreK-8), 119 S. Hubbard St. Tel: 847-658-5313; Fax: 847-854-0501. Mrs. Kathleen McMahon, Prin. Lay Teachers 14; Students 354.
Catechesis/Religious Program—Tel: 847-658-9339; Fax: 847-854-0501. Mrs. Sharon Prykop, D.R.E.; Mrs. Teresa Chiappone, D.R.E. (Junior High & High School). Students 1,450.

AMBOY, LEE CO., ST. PATRICK (1857), [CEM] Rev. Aaron R. Brodeski; Deacon Kevin Prunty.
Res.: 32 N. Jones Ave., 61310. Tel: 815-857-2315; Fax: 815-857-3485.
Catechesis/Religious Program—Students 146.

APPLE RIVER, JO DAVIESS CO., ST. JOSEPH (1868), [CEM] Rev. Anthony Pantyra, Admin.
Mailing Address: *c/o St. Ann*, 608 E. Railroad St., P.O. Box 665, Warren, 61087. Tel: 815-745-2312; Fax: 815-745-2312.
Church: 107 Webster St., 61001. Tel: 815-745-2312; Fax: 815-745-2312.
Catechesis/Religious Program— Twinned with St. Ann, Warren. Students 45.

AURORA, KANE CO.

1—ANNUNCIATION OF THE BLESSED VIRGIN MARY (1875), [CEM] Rev. Mario Pedi, O.S.B.; Deacons Raymond Johnson; Harold Poss; Michael Giblin; Larry Motyka.
Res.: 1820 Church Rd., 60504. Tel: 630-851-1436; Fax: 630-851-2435.
School—1840 Church Rd. Tel: 630-851-4300; Fax: 630-851-4316. Mr. Paul Barton, Prin. Lay Teachers 10; Students 300.
Catechesis/Religious Program—Tel: 630-851-4300. Students 125.

2—HOLY ANGELS (1892), Revs. Martin G. Heinz; Victor H. Alcazar; Godwin Asuquo; Deacons Tim White; Tom Hawksworth.
Mailing Address: 180 S. Russell Ave., 60506.
Res.: 720 Hardin Ave., 60506-4997. Tel: 630-897-1194; Fax: 630-897-1370.
School—720 Kensington Pl., 60506. Tel: 630-897-3613; Fax: 630-897-8233. Dr. Mary-Margaret McHugh, Prin. Lay Teachers 50; Students 735.
Catechesis/Religious Program—Students 258.

3—ST. JOSEPH (1899), [CEM] Rev. Jerome I. Leake; Deacon Norbert Szudarski, Pastoral Assoc.
Mailing Address: P.O. Box 4395, 60507.
Res.: 405 St. Joseph Ave., 60505. Tel: 630-844-3780; Fax: 630-844-1338.
School—706 High St., 60507. Tel: 630-844-3781; Fax: 630-844-3656. Miss Marie Bockhaus, Prin. Lay Teachers 17; Students 360.
Catechesis/Religious Program—Tel: 630-844-3782. Students 50.

4—ST. MARY (1850), (Irish), Rev. Robert J. McClellan; Deacons William Rees; Bruce Watermann.
Res.: 430 E. Downer Pl., 60505-3475. Tel: 630-892-0480; Fax: 630-892-8664.
Catechesis/Religious Program—432 E. Downer Pl., 60505. Students 83.

5—ST. NICHOLAS (1862), (Hispanic), [CEM] Revs. David R. Engbarth; Cristian M. Trivino.
Res. & Mailing Address: 308 High St., 60505. Tel: 630-898-8707; Fax: 630-585-6423.
School—Archbishop Romero School, 312 N. High St. Tel: 630-898-8690; Fax: 630-898-8866. Mrs. Carol Kaspar, Prin. Lay Teachers 10; Students 179.
Catechesis/Religious Program—Tel: 630-898-8707; Fax: 630-585-6423. Sr. Clare Pardilla, R.S.M., D.R.E. Students 633.

6—OUR LADY OF GOOD COUNSEL (1909), Revs. Dean E. Russell; Antoni J. Kretowicz (Poland) (CHI); Deacons James J. Valesano; Ray Weaver.
Res.: 620 S. Fifth St., 60505. Tel: 630-851-1100; Fax: 630-851-4069.
School—601 Talma St.. Tel: 630-851-4400; Fax: 630-851-8220. Mrs. Susan Wallace, Prin. Students 347.
Catechesis/Religious Program—Tel: 630-851-1100; Fax: 630-851-4069. Students 100.

7—ST. PETER (1929), Rev. George R. Glover, O.S.B.; Deacon Carlos Navarro.
Res.: 925 Sard Ave., 60506. Tel: 630-896-6816; Fax: 630-896-2534.
School—915 Sard Ave.. Tel: 630-892-1283. Sr. Ann Brummel, O.P., Prin. Sisters 3; Lay Teachers 7; Students 80.
Catechesis/Religious Program—Students 40.

8—ST. RITA OF CASCIA (1927), Revs. Robert J. Willhite; Louis Busemeyer, S.J.
Res.: 750 W. Old Indian Trail Rd., 60506. Tel: 630-892-5918; Fax: 630-892-4236.
School—770 W. Old Indian Trail Rd., 60506. Tel: 630-892-0020; Fax: 630-892-4236. Ms. Elizabeth Faxon, Prin. Lay Teachers 18; Students 358.
Catechesis/Religious Program—Tel: 630-892-9507. Sr. Rita Mary Phalen, O.S.F., D.R.E. Students 431.

9—SACRED HEART (1861), (Hispanic), [CEM] Rev. Robert Camacho; Deacon Richard Groom.
Res.: 771 Fulton St., 60505. Tel: 630-898-4165; Fax: 630-898-4165.
School—Archbishop Romero School, Tel: 630-898-8690; Fax: 630-898-8866.
Catechesis/Religious Program—Tel: 630-499-4023; Fax: 630-898-3940. Carmen Rodriguez, D.R.E. Students 291.

10—ST. THERESE OF JESUS (1925), Rev. Joseph T. Muller, M.S.C.; Deacons Bruce M. Watermann; Julio Rosado.
Res.: 271 N. Farnsworth Ave., 60505. Tel: 630-898-5422; Fax: 630-898-5327.
School—255 N. Farnsworth Ave., 60505. Tel: 630-898-0620; Fax: 630-898-3087. Sr. Kathleen Gallagher, O.P., Prin. Lay Teachers 5; Students 81.
Catechesis/Religious Program—Tel: 630-898-5422; Fax: 630-898-5327. Students 320.

BATAVIA, KANE CO., HOLY CROSS (1857), [JC] Revs. Daniel J. Deutsch; James Parker; Deacons Raymond Martin; Edward Lober; Gregory Urban; William L. Jacobson, Business Mgr.
Res.: 2300 Main St., 60510-7625. Tel: 630-879-4750; Fax: 630-879-9502.
Catechesis/Religious Program—Tel: 630-879-4751. Mrs. Diane E. Downey, D.R.E.; Mrs. Laura M. Bretson, D.R.E. Students 1,378.

BELVIDERE, BOONE CO., ST. JAMES (1886), [CEM] Revs. Uriel Lopez; Lorenzo Gonzalez.
Office—535 Caswell St., 61008. Tel: 815-547-6397; Fax: 815-547-0607.
Res.: 514 Caswell St., 61008. Tel: 815-547-6397.
School—320 Logan Ave., 61008. Tel: 815-547-7633; Fax: 815-544-2294. Mr. William Murphy, Prin. Lay Teachers 13; Students 155.
Catechesis/Religious Program—Tel: 815-544-3698. Judith Cadie, D.R.E. Students 750.

BYRON, OGLE CO., ST. MARY (1895), [CEM] Rev. Timothy L. Doherty, Ph.D.; Deacon Bob Smits Jr.
Res.: 226 E. Second St., P.O. Box 1070, 61010. Tel: 815-234-7431; Fax: 815-234-2133.
Catechesis/Religious Program—Tel: 815-234-5349; Fax: 815-234-2133. Marilyn Herrmann, D.R.E.; Julie Weber, D.R.E. Tel: 815-234-7173. Students 317.

CARPENTERSVILLE, KANE CO., ST. MONICA (1957), (Hispanic), Revs. William R. Schuessler; Fabio H. Garzon, S.D.B.; Deacons John Bach; J. Michael Frazier; Dennis Garber.
Res.: 90 N. Kennedy Dr., 60110-1695. Tel: 847-428-2646; Fax: 847-428-0039.
Catechesis/Religious Program—Tel: 847-428-7562. Wilson Ramirez, D.R.E. Students 674.

CARY, MCHENRY CO., SS. PETER & PAUL (1904), Revs. Stephen St. Jules; Stephen Olutade Folorunso; Deacons Howard Ganschow II; Michael Boyce; Gregory Duffey.
Res.: 410 N. First St., 60013. Tel: 847-516-2636; Fax: 847-639-3474.
School—416 N. First St., 60013. Tel: 847-639-3041; Fax: 847-639-5329. Sr. Katrina Lamkin, O.P., Prin. Dominican Sisters 2; Lay Teachers 18; Students 376.
Catechesis/Religious Program—Tel: 847-639-0414; Fax: 847-639-3474. Terri Zbylut, D.R.E. Students 1,507.

CRYSTAL LAKE, MCHENRY CO.

1—ST. ELIZABETH ANN SETON (1978), Rev. Msgr. Thomas J. Dempsey; Revs. Perfecto Vasquez; Leonaldo M. Jacob; George Ross, Business Mgr.
Office—1023 McHenry Ave., 60014. Tel: 815-459-3033; Fax: 815-459-3040.
Res.: 991 McHenry Ave., 60014. Tel: 815-788-0062.
Catechesis/Religious Program—Tel: 815-459-3096; Fax: 815-459-3040. June Parisi, D.R.E. Students 1,538.

2—ST. THOMAS THE APOSTLE, Rev. Msgr. Daniel J. Hermes; Revs. Steven J. Lange; Kenneth Stachyra; Cesar C. Pajarillo; Mark Kreis, S.S.P. In Res., Rev. Hector Moreno.
Res.: 200 Washington St., 60014. Tel: 815-455-5407; Fax: 815-455-2733.
Pastoral Center—272 King St., 60014. Tel: 815-455-5400; Fax: 815-455-2733.
School—265 King St.. Tel: 815-459-0496; Fax: 815-459-0591. Mrs. Deanne Roy, Prin. Lay Teachers 25; Students 458.
Catechesis/Religious Program—Tel: 815-455-9787. Janet Kayser, D.R.E. Students 1,342.

DEKALB, DEKALB CO.

1—CHRIST THE TEACHER, UNIVERSITY PARISH OF NORTHERN ILLINOIS UNIVERSITY (1963), Revs. Stephen J. Knox, S.T.L.; Michael G. Black; Addison H. Hart; Deacon James Dombek.
Office—512 Normal Rd., 60115. Tel: 815-787-7770; Fax: 815-758-2053.
Catechesis/Religious Program— Dr. Laura Bird, D.R.E. Students 241.

2—ST. MARY (1861), [CEM] Revs. Karl P. Ganss; Kenneth J. Anderson. In Res., Revs. Anthony Vu Khac Long; Jose Luis Vazquez; Deacon Stephen Puscas.
Office—302 Fisk Ave., 60115. Tel: 815-758-5432; Fax: 815-758-2487.
Res.: 321 Pine St., 60115. Tel: 815-748-5654.
School—210 Gurler Rd.. Tel: 815-756-7905; Fax: 815-758-1459. Ms. Patricia Weis, Prin. Lay Teachers 27; Students 295.
Catechesis/Religious Program—Tel: 815-758-8504. Students 252.

DIXON, LEE CO.

1—ST. ANNE (1928), Rev. Michael E. Morrissey.
Res.: 1104 N. Brinton Ave., 61021. Tel: 815-288-3131; Fax: 815-288-3139.
School—1112 N. Brinton Ave.. Tel: 815-288-5619; Fax: 815-288-5820. Sr. Marcianne Bzdon, S.S.N.D., Prin. Lay Teachers 12; Students 113.
Catechesis/Religious Program—Students 56.

2—ST. PATRICK (1856), Revs. Robert W. Jones; Kenneth Wasilewski; Deacons Sam Berard; Terry Wagner.
Office—612 S. Highland, 61021. Tel: 815-284-7719; Fax: 815-284-4758.
School—St. Mary Elementary & Junior High, (Grades PreK-8), 704 Peoria Ave.. Tel: 815-284-6986; Fax: 815-288-2940. Mrs. Jean Spohn, Prin. Lay Teachers 16; Students 252.
Catechesis/Religious Program—Tel: 815-284-2867; Fax: 815-284-4758. Mrs. Jacqueline Schauff, D.R.E. Students 120.

DUNDEE, KANE CO., ST. CATHERINE OF SIENA (1914), Revs. Richard A. Rosinski; William R. Antillon; David Austin. In Res., Rev. Max Striedl Jr.
Office: 845 W. Main St., 60118. Tel: 847-426-2217; Fax: 847-426-1130.
School—Tel: 847-426-4808; Fax: 847-426-0437. Mrs. Magaret Sanders, Prin. Lay Teachers 16; Students 295.
Catechesis/Religious Program—Students 795.
Mission—St. Mary [CEM] West Dundee. c/o 845 W. Main St., Gilberts, Kane Co. 60136. Tel: 847-836-8315.

DURAND, WINNEBAGO CO., ST. MARY (1862), (Irish), [CEM 2] Rev. Msgr. Eric R. Barr, S.T.L.
Mailing Address: 606 W. Main St., 61024. Tel: 815-248-2490; Fax: 815-248-9100.
Catechesis/Religious Program—Students 179.
Mission—St. Patrick [CEM] Irish Grove Rd., Stephenson Co.

EAST DUBUQUE, JO DAVIESS CO., ST. MARY (1868), [JC] Rev. Timothy J. Seigel.
Res.: 170 Montgomery Ave., 61025. Tel: 815-747-3221; Fax: 815-747-3212.
School—701 Rte. 35 N., 61025. Tel: 815-747-3010; Fax: 815-747-6188. Sr. Maryann Tranel, O.P., Prin. Lay Teachers 7; Students 96.
Catechesis/Religious Program—Tel: 815-747-2038. Students 80.

ELBURN, KANE CO., ST. GALL (1870), (Irish), [CEM] Revs. Richard W. Paddock (Retired); Karl P. Ganss.
Res.: 120 W. Shannon, P.O. Box 8020, 60119. Tel: 630-365-6030; Fax: 630-365-5483.
Catechesis/Religious Program—Tel: 630-365-9166; Fax: 630-365-9166. Students 416.

ELGIN, KANE CO.

1—ST. JOSEPH (1887), (German—Spanish), Revs. Miroslaw Reikowski; Leonardo Maldonado; Manuel Mendez (YAK); Deacons John Sauceda; Armando Martinez.
Res.: 272 Division St., 60120. Tel: 847-931-2800; Fax: 847-931-2810.
School—274 Division St.. Tel: 847-931-2804; Fax: 847-931-2811. Janine M. Bolchazy, Prin. Lay Teachers 13; Students 225.
Catechesis/Religious Program—Tel: 847-931-2808. Students 827.

2—ST. LAURENCE (1929), Rev. Joseph F. Kulak.

Office—226 Orchard St., 60123. Tel: 847-468-6900; Fax: 847-468-6904.
Res.: 1213 Oakdale Dr., 60123. Tel: 847-468-6105.
School—572 Standish St., 60123. Tel: 847-468-6100; Fax: 847-468-6104. Mrs. Phyllis Jensen, Prin. Lay Teachers 13; Students 244.
Catechesis/Religious Program—Tel: 847-468-6900; Fax: 847-468-6104. Students 207.

3—St. Mary (1851), Rev. Edward J. Seisser; Deacon Henry Orlik.
Parish Office—397 Fulton St., 60120. Tel: 847-888-2828; Fax: 847-888-2883.
Res.: 390 Fulton St., 60120. Tel: 847-888-0502.
School—103 S. Gifford St.. Tel: 847-695-6609; Fax: 847-695-6623. Mrs. Mary Beth Mitchell, Prin. Lay Teachers 10; Students 236.
Catechesis/Religious Program—Tel: 847-888-2718; Fax: 847-888-2883. Lesli Wiseman, D.R.E. Students 257.

4—St. Thomas More (1959), [JC] Revs. Geoffrey D. Wirth; Andrew C. Hougan; Deacons William Joynt; Robert Plazewski; Gregory Stevens. In Res., Rev. Andrew J. Plesa (Retired).
Office—215 Thomas More Dr., 60123. Tel: 847-888-1682; Fax: 847-888-3198.
School—1625 W. Highland Ave.. Tel: 847-742-3959. Ms. Penelope Reid, Prin. Lay Teachers 13; Students 288.
Catechesis/Religious Program—Tel: 847-888-4887. Mr. Ron Becker, D.R.E. Students 600.

Elizabeth, Jo Daviess Co., St. Mary (1886), [CEM] Rev. Christopher J. Kuhn.
Res.: 112 E. Washington St., Box 246, 61028. Tel: 815-858-3422; Fax: 815-858-2622.
Catechesis/Religious Program—Students 71.

Freeport, Stephenson Co.

1—St. Catherine, Closed. For inquiries for parish records contact the chancery.

2—St. Joseph (1862), (German), [CEM] Revs. John W. Cahill; Donald M. Ahles; Victor H. Claros.
Res.: 229 W. Washington Pl., 61032. Tel: 815-232-7622; Fax: 815-235-4690.
School—Freeport Catholic Elementary School, 202 W. Pleasant St.. Tel: 815-232-6416. Mrs. Kathy Runte, Prin.; Mr. Randall Musser, Admin. & Prin. Lay Teachers 7; Students 196.
Catechesis/Religious Program—Tel: 815-235-4324. Students 61.

3—St. Mary (1846), [CEM] Revs. Raymond Guthrie; Victor H. Claros; Deacon Gary Klocke.
Office—704 S. State Ave., 61032. Tel: 815-235-7544; Fax: 815-233-0005.
Res.: 704 S. State Ave., 61032.
Catechesis/Religious Program— (Freeport Catholic School System) Students 50.

4—St. Thomas Aquinas (1921), Rev. Msgr. P. William McDonnell; Rev. Victor H. Claros; Deacons H. Donald Brunette; Richard Dinneen; Vincent Drees.
Res.: 1400 Kiwanis Dr., 61032. Tel: 815-232-3225; Fax: 815-232-3231.
Catechesis/Religious Program—Tel: 815-232-3225; Fax: 815-232-3231. Marie Dinneen, D.R.E.; Julie Dorsey, D.R.E. Students 172.

Fulton, Whiteside Co., Immaculate Conception (1863), Rev. James R. Keenan.
Res.: 703 12th Ave., 61252. Tel: 815-589-3542; Fax: 815-589-4915.
Catechesis/Religious Program—Students 66.

Galena, Jo Daviess Co.

1—St. Mary (1851), (German), [CEM] Rev. Daniel D. Tranel.
Res.: 406 Franklin St., 61036. Tel: 815-777-0134; Fax: 815-776-0138.
Catechesis/Religious Program—Tel: 815-777-2219. Patricia Schuler, D.R.E. Students 120.

2—St. Michael (1832), (Irish), [CEM] Rev. Daniel D. Tranel.
Res.: 227 S. Bench St., 61036. Tel: 815-777-2053; Fax: 815-777-1193.
Catechesis/Religious Program— Tricia Tranel, D.R.E. Students 97.

Geneva, Kane Co., St. Peter (1912), [JC] Rev. Msgr. Joseph F. Jarmoluk; Rev. Akan S. Simon; Deacon Michael Zibrun.
Office—1891 Kaneville Rd., 60134. Tel: 630-232-0124; Fax: 630-232-9262.
Res.: 1771 Kaneville Rd., 60134. Tel: 630-208-1625.
School—1881 Kaneville Rd.. Tel: 630-232-0476; Fax: 630-208-5681. Mrs. Deborah Bray, Prin. Lay Teachers 22; Students 503.
Catechesis/Religious Program— Mr. John N. Lamperis, D.R.E. Students 1,593.

Genoa, DeKalb Co., St. Catherine of Genoa (1912), [CEM] Revs. Aloysius J. Neumann; Harold L. Nilges, Pastor Emeritus (Retired); Deacons John Kohler; Robert Demming.
Res.: 340 S. Stott St., 60135. Tel: 815-784-2355; Fax: 815-784-2045.
Catechesis/Religious Program—Tel: 815-784-2045. Jeanette Strohmaier, D.R.E. Students 230.

Hampshire, Kane Co., St. Charles Borromeo (1878), [CEM] Rev. Joseph P. Nicolosi.
Res.: 297 E. Jefferson Ave., 60140-7646. Tel: 847-683-2391; Fax: 847-683-2396.
School—(Grades PreK-8), 288 E. Jefferson Ave., 60140. Tel: 847-683-3450; Fax: 847-683-3209. Mrs. Karen Behrns, Prin. Lay Teachers 11; Students 150.
Catechesis/Religious Program—295 E. Jefferson Ave., 60140. Tel: 847-683-1536. Linda O'Connor, D.R.E. Students 293.

Hanover, Jo Daviess Co., St. John the Evangelist (1925), [JC] Revs. Christopher J. Kuhn; Stanislaw Kos.
Res.: 103 Savanna Rd., 61041. Tel: 815-591-2258; Fax: 815-858-2622.
Catechesis/Religious Program—Tel: 815-591-2258. Students 14.

Harmon, Lee Co., St. Flannen (1898), (Irish), [CEM] Revs. Thomas P. Dolan (Retired); Kenneth Stachyra.
Res.: P.O. Box 130, 61042. Tel: 815-359-7819; Fax: 815-359-7819.
Catechesis/Religious Program—Tel: 815-359-7819; Fax: 815-359-7819. Students 3.

Hartland, McHenry Co., St. Patrick (1837), [CEM] Rev. Msgr. James W. McLoughlin; Rev. Joseph P. Naill; Deacons Arthur Holt; Joseph Kayser.
Parish Office—15012 St. Patrick Rd., Woodstock, 60098. Tel: 815-338-7883; Fax: 815-338-5570.
Catechesis/Religious Program—Tel: 815-338-5570. Students 41.

Harvard, McHenry Co., St. Joseph (1866), [CEM] Rev. Daniel E. Peters; Deacons Anthony Koss; Jack O'Leary; Phillip Emmert.
Res.: 206 E. Front St., 60033. Tel: 815-943-6406; Fax: 815-943-1604.
School—201 N. Division St.. Tel: 815-943-6933; Fax: 815-943-0549. Mr. Michael J. Shukis, Prin. Lay Teachers 7; Students 139.
Catechesis/Religious Program—Tel: 815-943-1644; Fax: 815-943-1604. Mrs. Beverly O'Leary, D.R.E. Students 197.

Huntley, McHenry Co., St. Mary (1873), [CEM] Revs. Robert M. Garrity; Mario Ronelo A. Meude; Deacons Thomas W. O'Brien; Anthony Schubert; John A. McPhee; Mr. Thomas O'Brien, Pastoral Assoc.
Mailing Address: 10307 Dundee Rd., 60142.
Res.: 10911 N. Woodstock St., 60142. Tel: 847-669-3137; Fax: 847-669-3138.
Catechesis/Religious Program—Students 740.

Johnsburg, McHenry Co., St. John the Baptist (1841), [CEM] Rev. Robert A. Balog.
Res.: 2302 W. Church St., McHenry, 60050. Tel: 815-385-1477; Fax: 815-363-3333.
School—Tel: 815-385-3959; Fax: 815-363-3337. Pamela Dvonch, Prin. Sisters 1; Lay Teachers 12; Students 207.
Catechesis/Religious Program—Tel: 815-385-4870. Marge Dickinson, D.R.E.; Joe Watkins, D.R.E. Students 412.

Lee, Lee Co., St. James (1878), [CEM 2] Rev. William D. Virtue (PEO).
Res.: P.O. Box 108, 60530. Tel: 815-824-2053; Fax: 815-824-8488.
Catechesis/Religious Program—Tel: 815-824-8389. Students 91.

Lena, Stephenson Co., St. Joseph (1870), [CEM] Revs. Michael A. Librandi (Retired); William R. Antillon; Deacon Edward Wendt.
Res.: 410 W. Lena St., 61048. Tel: 815-369-2810; Fax: 815-369-9137.
Catechesis/Religious Program—Tel: 815-443-2892. Louise Kloepping, D.R.E. Students 114.

Loves Park, Winnebago Co., St. Bridget (1946), Rev. Msgr. John J. Mitchell, V.F.; Deacons Philip Abel; William Dall. In Res., Very Rev. Arquimedes Vallejo.
Res.: 600 Clifford Ave., 61111. Tel: 815-633-6311; Fax: 815-633-6314.
School—604 Clifford Ave., 61111. Tel: 815-633-8255; Fax: 815-633-5847. Mrs. Roberta Gille, Prin. Religious 1; Lay Teachers 22; Students 471.
Catechesis/Religious Program—Tel: 815-633-4006. Students 354.

Maple Park, DeKalb Co., St. Mary (1850), [CEM 2] Rev. Msgr. William J. Clausen.
Mailing Address: 123 S. County Line Rd., 60151-8024. Tel: 815-827-3218; Fax: 815-827-3218.
Res.: 205 S. County Line Rd., 60151-8024. Tel: 815-827-3218; Fax: 815-827-3218.
Novak Center—211 S. County Line Rd., 60151-8024. Tel: 815-827-3205.
Catechesis/Religious Program—Tel: 815-827-3205. Students 128.

Marengo, McHenry Co., Sacred Heart (1902), [CEM] Rev. Msgr. Philip E. O'Neil (Retired); Rev. Richard M. Russo; Deacon Robert Anchor.
Res.: 323 N. Taylor St., 60152. Tel: 815-568-7878; Fax: 815-568-7929.
Catechesis/Religious Program—Tel: 815-568-6230; Fax: 815-568-7929. Robert Olsen, D.R.E.; Brenda Ramus, D.R.E. Students 398.

Maytown, Lee Co., St. Patrick (1840), [CEM] [JC 2] Revs. Thomas P. Dolan (Retired); Kenneth Stachyra.
Res.: P.O. Box 130, Harmon, 61042. Tel: 815-359-7819; Fax: 815-359-7819.
Catechesis/Religious Program—Students 21.

McHenry, McHenry Co.

1—Church of Holy Apostles (1989), [CEM] Revs. Robert N. Sherry; Jose Pancracio Seco; Deacons Joseph Phelan; Jack Roder; Timothy Adams; Mark Raz.
Church: 5211 W. Bull Valley Rd., 60050. Tel: 815-385-5673; Fax: 815-385-6045.
Catechesis/Religious Program—Tel: 815-385-4273. Jeanne Fraser, D.R.E. Students 800.

2—St. Mary (1894), (German), [CEM] Rev. Thomas E. Burr. School Sisters of St. Francis In Res., Rev. David Huber.
Res.: 1401 N. Richmond Rd., 60050. Tel: 815-385-0024; Fax: 815-385-7809.
School—Montini-Middle Grades, 1405 N. Richmond Rd., 60050. Tel: 815-385-1022; 815-385-0407; Fax: 815-363-7536. Lay Teachers 16; Students 272.
School—School Sisters of St. Francis, Tel: 815-385-0407. Mrs. Sheila Murphy, Prin.
Catechesis/Religious Program—Tel: 815-385-2959. Kristen Van Alystne, D.R.E. Students 65.

3—St. Patrick (1840), (Irish), [CEM 2] Revs. Stephen K. Potter; John A. Slampak.
Res.: 3425 W. Washington St., 60050. Tel: 815-385-0025; Fax: 815-385-0861.
School—Montini Primary Center, Tel: 815-385-5380; Fax: 815-385-5017. Mrs. Sheila Murphy, Prin.; Mrs. Marilyn Knapp, Asst. Prin. Sisters 1; Lay Teachers 25; Students 568.
Catechesis/Religious Program—Tel: 815-385-2959; Fax: 815-385-0861. Students 208.

Menominee, Jo Daviess Co., Nativity of the Blessed Virgin Mary (1864), (German), [CEM] Rev. Theodore V. Lewandowski.
Res.: 15406 W. Creek Valley Rd., Memominee, 61025. Tel: 815-747-3676; Fax: 815-747-2050.
School—15390 W. Creek Valley Rd.. Tel: 815-747-3670; Fax: 815-747-3670. Autumn Esch, Prin. Lay Teachers 5; Students 73.
Catechesis/Religious Program—Tel: 815-747-2389. Students 29.

Morrison, Whiteside Co., St. Mary (1904), Rev. Leo J. Bartel.
Office—13320 Garden Plain Rd., PO. Box 248, 61270. Tel: 815-772-3095; Fax: 815-772-4890.
Res.: 611 Greenwood Dr., 61270. Tel: 815-772-3095; Fax: 815-772-4890.
Catechesis/Religious Program—Tel: 815-772-4890. Students 89.

Mount Carroll, Carroll Co., SS. John and Catherine (1923), Attended by, Savanna. Rev. Moises Apostol.
Res.: 314 S. Main St., P.O. Box 193, 61053. Tel: 815-244-1835 (Church); Fax: 815-244-1835.
Catechesis/Religious Program—Fax: 815-244-1835. Students 48.

North Aurora, Kane Co., Blessed Sacrament (1970), Rev. Msgr. Edward S. Wright, V.F.
Res.: 801 Oak St., 60542-1063. Tel: 630-897-1029; Fax: 630-897-1062.
Catechesis/Religious Program—Tel: 630-897-4396. Sr. Rose Marie Weber, O.S.F., D.R.E. Students 341.

Oregon, Ogle Co., St. Mary (1862), [CEM] Revs. William A. Budden (Retired); Richard R. Kramer.
Mailing Address: P.O. Box 419, 61061. Tel: 815-732-7383; Fax: 815-732-4742.
Res.: 303 N. Fourth St., 61061. Tel: 815-732-2234; Fax: 815-732-6332.
Catechesis/Religious Program—Tel: 815-732-7383; Fax: 815-732-4742. Students 94.

Pecatonica, Winnebago Co., St. Mary (1872), (Irish—German), [CEM] Rev. Robert J. Sweeney; Deacon Warren LaMont.
Res.: 126 W. Fifth St., P.O. Box 656, 61063. Tel: 815-239-1271; Fax: 815-239-1271.
Catechesis/Religious Program—Students 141.

Polo, Ogle Co., St. Mary's (1854), [CEM] [JC] Rev. John A. Hanrahan.
Res.: 211 N. Franklin Ave., 61064. Tel: 815-946-2535; Fax: 815-946-9025.
Catechesis/Religious Program—Tel: 815-493-6227; Fax: 815-946-9025. Students 107.

Prophetstown, Whiteside Co., St. Catherine (1917), Rev. Carl E. Beekman.
Res.: 308 E. Third St., 61277. Tel: 815-537-2077; Fax: 815-537-5076.
Catechesis/Religious Program—Tel: 815-537-2077. Jan Halpin, D.R.E. Students 42.
Mission—St. Ambrose [JC] 5th & Main St., Erie, Whiteside Co. 61250. Tel: 309-659-2781; Fax: 815-537-5076.
Catechesis/Religious Program—Students 64.

Richmond, McHenry Co., St. Joseph (1930), (German), [CEM] Revs. Joseph W. Kaiser; Rodel Peji.

Res.: 10519 Main St., 60071. Tel: 815-678-7421; Fax: 815-678-6961.
Catechesis/Religious Program—Tel: 815-678-6961. Roberta Schroeder, D.R.E. Students 165.

ROCHELLE, OGLE CO., ST. PATRICK (1868), [CEM] Rev. David A. Peck; Deacon Higinio Perez.
Res.: 250 Kelley Dr., 61068. Tel: 815-562-2370; Fax: 815-562-5250.
Catechesis/Religious Program—Tel: 815-561-0079; Fax: 815-561-0239. Kalah Williams, D.R.E. Students 384.

ROCK FALLS, WHITESIDE CO., ST. ANDREW (1950), [JC] Rev. Msgr. Thomas L. Dzielak.
Res.: 708 10th Ave., 61071. Tel: 815-625-4508; Fax: 815-625-1569.
School—701 11th Ave., 61071. Tel: 815-625-1456; Fax: 815-625-1724. Mr. Philip D. Bellini, Prin. Lay Teachers 7; Students 129.
Catechesis/Religious Program—Tel: 815-625-4508. Students 70.

ST. CHARLES, KANE CO.

1—ST. JOHN NEUMANN (1977), Rev. Msgr. Robert B. Hoffman; Revs. Burt Absalon; Joel Lopez; Deacons Martin Hetzel; Paul Iwanski; Ronald Williams; Robert Wade.
Res.: 2900 E. Main St., 60174. Tel: 630-377-2797; Fax: 630-377-2834.
Catechesis/Religious Program—Tel: 630-377-2803. Jan Donovan, D.R.E. Students 1,645.

2—ST. PATRICK (1851), Revs. Joseph B. Linster; Bonaventure Okoro; David Finn.
Res. & Church Address: 408 Cedar St., 60174. Tel: 630-584-0092; Fax: 630-513-2246.
School—State St. & Fifth St.. Tel: 630-584-6367; Fax: 630-584-9759. Mr. Joseph Battisto, Prin. Sisters 2; Lay Teachers 29; Students 540.
Catechesis/Religious Program—Tel: 630-513-2247. Sr. Joelyn Hayes, D.R.E.; Patrice Spirou, D.R.E.; Alice Carney, D.R.E. Students 2,105.

SANDWICH, DEKALB CO., ST. PAUL (1925), [CEM] Rev. John T. Heraty.
Res.: 110 N. Eddy St., 60548. Tel: 815-786-9266; Fax: 815-786-2977.
Catechesis/Religious Program—Tel: 815-786-2004. Students 199.

SAVANNA, CARROLL CO., ST. JOHN THE BAPTIST (1884), [CEM] Rev. Moises Apostol.
Res.: 318 Chicago Ave., 61074. Tel: 815-273-3961; Fax: 815-273-3503.
Catechesis/Religious Program—Tel: 815-273-3582. Students 26.

SCALES MOUND, JO DAVIESS CO., HOLY TRINITY (1863), [CEM 2] Rev. Anthony F. Pantyra, Admin.
Mailing Address: *St. Ann*, 608 E. Railroad St., P.O. Box 665, Warren, 61087. Tel: 815-745-2312.
Church: 302 Franklin St., 61075.
Catechesis/Religious Program—Tel: 815-845-2347. Carol Bilgri, D.R.E. Students 76.

SHANNON, CARROLL CO., ST. WENDELIN (1870), [CEM] Rev. Michael J. Bolger.
18 S. Linn St., P.O. Box 23, 61078. Tel: 815-864-2548 (Church); Fax: 815-864-2729.
Catechesis/Religious Program—Students 50.

SOMONAUK, DEKALB CO., ST. JOHN THE BAPTIST (1865), [CEM] Rev. Donald D. DeSalvo.
Res.: 320 S. Depot St., Box 276, 60552. Tel: 815-498-2010; Fax: 815-498-2770.
Catechesis/Religious Program—Tel: 815-498-2627. Students 283.

SOUTH BELOIT, WINNEBAGO CO., ST. PETER (1909), Rev. Msgr. Thomas C. Brady, P.A., V.G., Ph.D.; Revs. Zdzislaw F. Wawryszuk; Jose Vicente Jimenez; Deacons Peter Calgaro; Michael Ryan.
Res.: 620 Blackhawk Blvd., 61080. Tel: 815-389-2024; Fax: 815-389-2274.
School—320 Elmwood Ave.. Tel: 815-389-3193; Fax: 815-389-2274. Rev. James Hoover (SAL), Prin. Lay Teachers 10; Students 105.
Catechesis/Religious Program—Tel: 815-389-9091. Jeanne Pulkrabek, D.R.E. Students 270.
Mission—Church of the Holy Spirit P.O. Box 478, Roscoe, Winnebago Co. 61073. Tel: 815-623-6930; Fax: 815-623-1890 9.
Catechesis/Religious Program—Fax: 815-623-1890. Kate Elliott, D.R.E. Students 56.

SPRING GROVE, MCHENRY CO., ST. PETER (1900), (German), [CEM] Rev. Steven J. Lange; Deacon Walter Freund.
Church: 2118 Main St., P.O. Box 129, 60081. Tel: 815-675-2288; Fax: 815-675-6774.
Catechesis/Religious Program—Tel: 815-675-2576. Students 403.

STERLING, WHITESIDE CO.

1—ST. MARY (1898), [CEM] Revs. Thomas E. Brantman; Jesus Dominguez; Deacons John Kellen; Daniel Goetz; James Lopez; Jane Olson, Pastoral Assoc.
Res.: 507 Ave. B, 61081. Tel: 815-625-0640; Fax: 815-625-1684.
School—6 W. Sixth St.. Tel: 815-625-2253; Fax: 815-625-8942. Mrs. Rebecca Scmitt. Lay Teachers 24; Students 324.
Catechesis/Religious Program—600 Ave. B, 61081. Tel: 815-625-6688; Fax: 815-625-8942. Students 209.

2—SACRED HEART (1870), (German), [CEM] Rev. Paul C. White. In Res., Rev. Paul M. Lipinski; Deacons Larry Zitkus; Ronald Szakatits.
Res.: 2224 Avenue J, 61081. Tel: 815-625-0631; 815-625-1134; Fax: 815-625-1138.
Catechesis/Religious Program—Tel: 815-625-4385; Fax: 815-625-1138. Students 103.

STOCKTON, JO DAVIESS CO., HOLY CROSS (1893), (German), [CEM] Rev. Dean M. Smith.
Res.: 223 E. Front Ave., 61085. Tel: 815-947-2545; Fax: 815-947-3705.
Catechesis/Religious Program—Students 106.

SUBLETTE, LEE CO., OUR LADY OF PERPETUAL HELP, [CEM] Rev. Edward R. Hughes.
Mailing Address: Box 80, West Brooklyn, 61378. Tel: 815-628-3901; Fax: 815-628-3901.
Catechesis/Religious Program—Students 84.

SYCAMORE, DE KALB CO., ST. MARY (1885), [CEM] Rev. Frank John Timar, M.S.C.; Deacon Lee Deatherage.
Res.: 244 Waterman St., 60178. Tel: 815-895-3275; Fax: 815-899-7890.
School—222 Waterman St.. Tel: 815-895-5215; Fax: 815-895-5295. Mrs. Roseann Feldmann, Prin. Lay Teachers 13; Students 189.
Catechesis/Religious Program—Tel: 815-895-3726; Fax: 815-895-4561. Students 250.

TAMPICO, WHITESIDE CO., ST. MARY (1875), [CEM] Rev. Thomas E. Brantman, Admin.; Deacon William Lemmer.
Res.: 105 Benton St., P.O. Box 159, 61283. Tel: 815-438-5425; Fax: 815-438-5425.
Catechesis/Religious Program—Students 37.

VIRGIL, KANE CO., SS. PETER AND PAUL (1909), [CEM] Rev. Les Suberi Echevia; Deacon Jim Newhouse.
Res.: 5 N. 939 Meredith Rd., 60182. Tel: 630-365-6618; Fax: 630-365-6659.
Catechesis/Religious Program—Students 105.

WALTON, LEE CO., ST. MARY (1913), [JC] Revs. Thomas P. Dolan (Retired); Kenneth Stachyra.
Res.: P.O. Box 130, Harmon, 61042. Tel: 815-359-7819.
Catechesis/Religious Program—Students 23.

WARREN, JO DAVIESS CO., ST. ANN (1914), [CEM] Rev. Anthony Pantyra, Admin.
Res.: 608 Railroad St., P.O. Box 665, 61087. Tel: 815-745-2312; Fax: 815-745-2312.
Catechesis/Religious Program—Students 70.

WEST BROOKLYN, LEE CO., ST. MARY, [CEM] Rev. Edward R. Hughes.
Mailing Address: P.O. Box 80, 61378. Tel: 815-628-3901; Fax: 815-628-3901.
Catechesis/Religious Program—Students 28.

WONDER LAKE, MCHENRY CO., CHRIST THE KING (1949), [CEM] Rev. Louis F. Tosto.
Res.: 5006 E. Wonder Lake Rd., 60097. Tel: 815-653-2561; Fax: 815-653-9401.
Catechesis/Religious Program—Tel: 815-653-2581. Ms. Maureen McLain, D.R.E. Students 113.

WOODSTOCK, MCHENRY CO.

1—ST. MARY (1853), [CEM] Rev. Msgr. James W. McLoughlin; Rev. Sylvester Nnaso; Deacons Louis Barone; Hans Rokus.
Res.: 312 Lincoln Ave., 60098. Tel: 815-338-3377; Fax: 815-338-3497.
School—313 Tryon St., 60098. Tel: 815-338-3598; Fax: 815-338-3408. Mr. Edward O'Brien, Prin. Lay Teachers 22; Students 349.
Catechesis/Religious Program—Tel: 815-338-3413; Fax: 815-334-4391. Mrs. Diane O'Donnell, D.R.E. Students 400.

2—RESURRECTION (1978), Rev. Jerzy Zieba, C.R.
Mailing Address: 2918 S. Country Club Rd., 60098. Tel: 815-338-7330; Fax: 815-338-7365.
Catechesis/Religious Program—Nancy Neumeister, D.R.E. Students 84.

Chaplains of Public Institutions
Graduate Studies

Revs. Phillip Kaim, Rome, Pontifical North American College, 00102 Vatican City State, EUROPE, Kenneth Wasilewski, Rome, Pontifical North American College, 00120 Vatican City State, EUROPE.

ELGIN. *Elgin State Hospital*, 750 S. State St., 60123. Vacant.

MOOSEHEART. *School of the Loyal Order of Moose*, 301 Fifth Ave., 60539. Vacant.

ST. CHARLES. *Illinois State Youth Center*, Chapel of the Immaculate Conception. Records kept at St. Patrick, St. Charles.

Special Assignment:
Rev. Msgrs.—
Barr, Eric R., S.T.L., Vicar for Clergy & Religious, 555 Colman Center Dr., P.O. Box 7044, 61125. Tel: 815-399-4300
Kagan, David D., V.G., J.C.L., Vicar Gen., Moderator of the Curia & Judicial Vicar, 555 Colman Center Dr., 61125. Tel: 815-399-4300
Nelson, Glenn L., J.C.L., Vicar Gen. & Chancellor, 555 Colman Center Dr., P.O. Box 7044, 61125. Tel: 815-399-4300
Revs.—
Brodeski, Aaron, Diocesan Dir. of Vocations, 555 Colman Center Dr., P.O. Box 7044, 61125. Tel: 815-399-4300
Fritz, John, Sec. to Bishop, Diocesan Master of Ceremonies, 555 Colman Center Dr., P.O. Box 7044, 61125. Tel: 815-399-4300
Fuller, Michael J.K., Mundelein, IL
Hart, Addison H., Diocesan Director of Ecumenism, Christ the Teacher Parish, 512 Normal Road, Dekalb, 60115.
Kurz, Michael, Adjutant Judicial Vicar, 555 Colman Center Dr., P.O. Box 7044, 61125. Tel: 815-399-4300
Long, Anthony Vu Khac, Vietnamese Catholic Ministry, St. Mary Parish, 321 Pine Street, Dekalb, 60115.
Moreno, Hector, Hispanic Ministry for McHenry County, 272 King St., Crystal Lake, 60014. Tel: 815-455-5400
Naill, Joseph P., Asst. Principal, Marian Central Catholic High School, 1001 McHenry Ave., Woodstock, 60098.
Slampak, John A., S.T.L., Office of Divine Worship, 555 Colman Center Dr., 61125. Tel: 815-399-4300
Very Rev.—
Vallejo, Arquimedes, Episocpal Vicar for Hispanic Ministry, 555 Colman Center Dr., P.O. Box 7044, 61125. Tel: 815-399-4300
Revs.—
Vasquez, Jose Luis, Hispanic Ministry for DeKalb Deanery, 302 Fisk Ave., DeKalb, 60115. Tel: 815-758-5432
Wentink, William R., Chaplain St. Anthony Hospital & Rockford Police & Fire Departments, St. Anthony Hospital and Rockford Police & Fire Departments, 5666 E. State St., 61108.

Active Outside the Diocese:
Revs.—
Donahugh, Donald E., 100 Gifford Pond Ln., Port Arthur, TX 77642.
Myers, William F., 17445 S.W. 254 St., Homestead, FL 33031.
Simonini, Michael F., St. Bernard, 1617 W. Pine St., Appleton, WI 54914. Tel: 414-739-0331
Wasilewski, Kenneth
Kaim, Phillip

On Disability Leave:
Revs.—
Joffe, William I.
Wagener, Donald

Absent on Leave:
Revs.—
Holdren, John C.
Tripodi, Frank J.
Wakitsch, Randall
Waser, Frank A.

Retired:
Rev. Msgrs.—
McNamee, Charles W., P.A., J.C.L., Unit 15, 4718 Covey Ridge Ct., Loves Park, 61111. Tel: 815-639-9690
O'Neil, Philip E., 2323 Rockton Ave., 61103. Tel: 815-962-7806
Revs.—
Becker, Anthony J., Oak Ridge Manor, 124 Liberty Court, Dixon, 61021.
Budden, William A., 4878 Ashelford Dr., Byron, 61010.
Collins, William P., Luther Center, 111 W. State St., Apt. 1303, 61101. Tel: 815-963-6997
Dolan, Thomas P., 3633 Park Center Blvd., Minneapolis, MN 55416. Tel: 952-926-0533
Falcone, Emilio, PSC2 Box 7192, APO, AE 09012.
Gillespie, Edward F., 6152 Wingate Dr., Lisle, 60532. Tel: 630-960-4838
Guagliardo, Salvatore J., Vianney Oaks, 7712 E. McGregor Rd., 61102. Tel: 815-963-5618
Hiller, Everett J., 2520 W. Council Hill Rd., Scales Mound, 61075.
Holmgren, Raymond O., 8020 N. Indian Ridge Rd., E., Dubuque, 61025. Tel: 815-747-2460
Jackson, Robert, Cor Marie Center, 3330 Maria Linden Dr., 61114. Tel: 815-282-5452
Knott, William P., 15528 W. Sky Hawk Dr., Sun City West, AZ 85375. Tel: 623-214-2520
Kraemer, John A., 6033 A Sheridan Rd., Apt. 32J, Chicago, 60660. Tel: 773-561-9857
Kriegsmann, William A., 1439 Rohde, Berkeley, 60163. Tel: 708-544-3039
Larson, James F., Provena Cor Marie, 3330 Maria

Linden Dr., 61114. Tel: 815-636-9387
Librandi, Michael A., 6419 Columbine Blvd., 61108. Tel: 815-226-1085
London, Lawrence, Vianney Oaks, 7712 E. McGregor Rd., 61102. Tel: 815-963-4820
Lutz, Joseph L., 1320 Brook St., #C, 60174. Tel: 630-587-9029
McDonnell, Francis E., 1801 Avenue G, Sterling, 61081. Tel: 815-626-0771
McKinstra, William M., Provena Cor Mariae, 61114. Tel: 815-282-6145
McKitrick, James V., N.1555 Shadow Ln., Fontana, WI 53125. Tel: 262-275-6711
Millen, Edwin F., 615 Gates Ave., Aurora, 60505. Tel: 630-906-6558
Monahan, Thomas J., Ph.D., 2696 Aldersgate Dr., 61103. Tel: 815-282-9972
Mullane, Bernard J., 253 Center St., PMB #192, Lake Geneva, WI 53147. Tel: 262-245-5592
Murphy, James L., 4449 Charles St., 61108. Tel: 815-397-8126
Neville, Thomas W., Vianney Oaks, 7712 E. McGregor Rd., 61102. Tel: 815-965-1108
Nilges, Harold L., 350 S. Stott St., Genoa, 60135. Tel: 815-784-4837
Paddock, Richard W., 1330 W. Indian Trail Rd., Apt. 8, Aurora, 60506. Tel: 630-801-9731
Peterson, William F., 147 Shadowood Dr., Martinez, GA 30907. Tel: 706-860-4738
Petit, Edmund P., 421 N. State St., #5060, Aurora, 60506. Tel: 630-897-8052
Plesa, Andrew J., 215 Thomas More Dr., Elgin, 60123. Tel: 847-888-1682
Ratazak, Bernard A., Vianney Oaks, 7712 E. McGregor Rd., 61102. Tel: 815-968-8126
Richter, Norbert M., 1230 Hillcrest Dr., Freeport, 61032. Tel: 815-232-6765
Rudden, Matthew T., 6102 Garrett Ln., 61107. Tel: 815-226-3605
Schlade, Joseph F., 1109 N. Ashland Ave., Chicago, 60622. Tel: 312-384-7967
Shindelar, Vincent J., 1508 E. State St., 61104. Tel: 815-962-2814
Tranel, Dorrance E., 8615 N. Tranel Rd., East Dubuque, 61025. Tel: 815-747-3792
Urbaniak, Lawrence M., 4210 W. Marshall Ave., Phoenix, AZ 85019.
Verstynen, Robert J., 4444 Brendenwood Rd., 61107. Tel: 815-394-0447
Vlasz, Melvyn J., 4060 Hidden Hollow Dr., Unit C, Gainsville, GA 30506. Tel: 770-297-0752

Permanent Deacons:
Abel, Philip, St. Bridget, Loves Park
Adams, Timothy, Church of Holy Apostles, McHenry
Anchor, Robert, Sacred Heart, Marengo
Bach, John, St. Monica, Carpentersville
Barone, Frank, St. Patrick, Rockford
Barone, Louis, St. Mary, Woodstock
Berard, Samuel, St. Parick, Dixon
Bondi, Allen, St. Thomas the Apostle, Crystal Lake
Boyce, Michael, SS. Peter & Paul, Cary
Bracken, Robert, (Retired)
Bronzi, William, Holy Family, Rockford
Brunette, Donald J., St. Thomas, Freeport
Calgaro, Peter, St. Peter, South Beloit; Church of the Holy Spirit, Roscoe;
Callahan, Donald J., (Retired)
Cassaro, Sam, St. Anthony of Padua, Rockford
Cooper, Charles, St. Peter Cathedral, Rockford
Czerniewski, Martin, St. Peter Cathedral, Rockford
Dall, William, St. Bridget, Loves Park
Dean, William, St. James, Rockford
Deatherage, Lee, St. Mary, Sycamore
Demming, Robert, St. Catherine of Genoa, Genoa
Dinneen, Richard, St. Thomas Aquinas, Freeport
Dombek, James, Christ the Teacher, DeKalb
Drees, Vincent, St. Thomas Aquinas, Freeport
Duffey, Gregory, SS. Peter & Paul, Cary
Ekstrom, Richard, St. Mary, McHenry
Emmert, Phillip, St. Joseph, Harvard
Fast, Randy, St. Peter Cathedral, Rockford
Felix, Ignacio, St. Rita of Cascia, Aurora
Ferrini, Armand, St. Mary, Huntley
Fischer, Howard, St. Margaret Mary, Algonquin
Frazier, J. Michael, St. Monica, Carpentersville
Freund, Walter, St. Peter, Spring Grove
Freund, Walter, St. Peter, Spring Grove
Gagnon, Charles, St. Elizabeth Ann Seton, Crystal Lake
Ganshow, Howard, SS. Peter & Paul, Cary
Garber, Dennis, St. Monica, Carpentersville
Gartland, William, St. Patrick, St. Charles
Gerdeman, Richard, St. Bernadette, Rockford
Giambalvo, Michael, St. Mary, Elgin
Giblin, Michael, Annunciation B.V.M., Aurora
Goetz, Daniel, St. Mary, Sterling
Graw, Ronald, St. Patrick, Rockford
Groom, Richard, Sacred Heart and St. Mary, Aurora
Grossmayer, Simon, St. Margaret Mary, Algonquin
Hainchek, Alex J., (Retired)
Hawksworth, Thomas, Holy Angels, Aurora
Hetzel, Martin, St. John Neumann, St. Charles
Holt, Arthur, St. Patrick, Hartland
Hudzinski, James, St. Stanislaus, Rockford
Hurley, Dan
Iwanski, Paul, St. John Neumann, St. Charles
Johnson Raymond R., Annunciation, Aurora
Johnson William, St. Patrick, St. Charles
Kayser, Joseph, St. Patrick, Hartland
Kellen, John, St. Mary, Sterling
Klocke, Gary, St. Mary, Freeport
Kocol, Theodore, St. Mary, Galena
Kohler, John, (Retired)
Koss, Anthony, St. Joseph, Harvard
Kulpin, John, St. Patrick, St. Charles
LaMont, Warren R., St. Mary, Pecatonica
Lemmer William, St. Mary, Tampico
Lober, Edward, Holy Cross, Batavia
Lopez, James, St. Mary, Sterling
Magee, Ronald, St. James, Rockford
Maher, Patrick, St. Margaret Mary, Algonquin
Martin, Raymond, Holy Cross, Batavia
Martin, Richard, St. Rita of Cascia, Aurora
Martin, Robert H., (Retired)
Martinez, Armando, St. Joseph, Elgin
McElroy Robert D., St. Rita of Cascia, Aurora
McPhee, John, St. Mary, Huntley
Milano, Robert, St. Mary, Oregon
Miller, William, St. Mary, Elgin
Morrison, Edward, St. Thomas the Apostle, Crystal Lake
Motyka, Larry, Annunciation, Aurora
Moynihan, Patrick, Holy Family, Rockford
Muehler, Gerald, (Retired)
Mulcahey, Richard, St. Mary, Durand
Murphy, Melvin J., (Retired)
Navarro, Carlos, St. Peter and St. Nicholas, Aurora
Newhouse, James, SS Peter & Paul, Virgil
O'Brien, Thomas, St. Mary, Huntley
O'Leary, Jack, St. Joseph, Harvard
Olson, James D., St. James, Belvidere
Perez, Higinio, St. Patrick, Rochelle
Petit, Thomas, St. Rita of Cascia, Aurora
Phelan, Joseph, Church of Holy Apostles, McHenry
Plazewski, Robert, St. Thomas More, Elgin
Poss, Harold, Annunciation of the B.V.M., Aurora
Prunty, Kevin, St. Patrick, Amboy
Puscas, Stephen, *St. Mary, DeKalb*
Raz, Mark, Church of Holy Apostles, McHenry
Real, Robert, St. Laurence, Elgin
Rees, William, St. Mary, Aurora
Roder, John, Holy Apostles, McHenry
Rokus, Hans, St. Mary, Woodstock
Rosado, Julio, St. Therese of Jesus, Aurora
Ryan, Michael, St. Peter, South Beloit
Sauceda, John, St. Joseph, Elgin
Savercool, Gerald, St. Rita, Rockford
Schubert, Anthony, St. Mary, Huntley
Skrade, Fred, St. Edward, Rockford
Smith, Daniel, St. James, Belvidere
Smits, Robert, St. Mary, Byron
Statter, Ralph, St. Thomas, Crystal Lake
Stevens, Greg, St. Thomas More, Elgin
Swearingen, Alvin, St. Mary, Morrison
Sweeney, Robert, Holy Family, Rockford
Szudarski, Norbert, St. Joseph, Aurora
Urban, Gregory, Holy Cross, Batavia
Valesano, James J., Our Lady of Good Counsel, Aurora
Verstynen, Lambert, St. Edward, Rockford
Wade, Robert, St. John Neumann, St. Charles
Wagner, Terrence, St. Patrick, Dixon
Watermann, Bruce, St. Therese, Aurora
Weaver, Raymond, Our Lady of Good Counsel, Aurora
Welch, Thomas, Holy Family, Rockford
Wendt, Edward, St. Joseph, Lena
White, Thomas, Holy Angels, Aurora
Whitehead, William, Jr., St. Catherine of Siena, Dundee
Wilbricht, David, St. John the Evangelist, Hanover
Williams, Ronald, St. John Neumann, St. Charles
Woeste, James, Crystal Lake
Zibrun, Michael, St. Peter, Geneva
Zitkus, Lawrence, Sacred Heart, Sterling
Orlik, Henry, St. Mary, Elgin
Cristoforo, Michael
Brandenburg, Robert, St. Patrick, Dixon
Szakatits, Ronald, Sacred Heart, Sterling

INSTITUTIONS LOCATED IN THE DIOCESE

[A] SEMINARIES, RELIGIOUS OR SCHOLASTICATES

AURORA. *Marmion Abbey*, 850 Butterfield Rd., 60504. Tel: 630-897-7215; Fax: 630-897-0393. Email: vbataille@marmion.org. Web: www.marmion.org. Rt. Rev. Vincent Bataille, O.S.B., Abbot; Very Rev. Kenneth Theisen, O.S.B., Prior. Priests 33; Brothers 15.

WOODSTOCK. *Resurrection Center Retreat House*, 2710 S. Country Club Rd., 60098. Tel: 815-338-1032; Fax: 815-338-1017. Email: info@resurrectioncenter.org. Web: www.resurrectioncenter.org. Mr. James F. Ivers, Exec. Dir.; Rev. Richard Grek, C.R. (CHI). Priests 1; Sisters 1; Lay Staff 6.

[B] HIGH SCHOOLS, DIOCESAN

ROCKFORD. *Boylan Central Catholic High School*, 4000 St. Francis Dr., 61103. Tel: 815-877-0531; Fax: 815-877-2544. Email: boylan@hughestech.net. Web: www.boylan.org. Sr. M. Anthony Marelli, O.P., Prin.; Mr. Vincent E. McGuire, Asst. Prin., Student Affairs; Rev. Msgr. William H. Schwartz, Asst. Prin., D.R.E. & Spiritual Dir.; Mr. William C. Thumm, Dean of Students; Mr. Dan Appino, Guidance Dir.; Mr. Dennis Hiemenz, Asst. Prin., Academic Affairs; Mrs. Mary Gavan, Admin. Asst. Priests 7; Sisters 2; Lay Teachers 84; Students 1,286.

AURORA. *Aurora Central Catholic High School*, 1255 N. Edgelawn Dr., 60506. Tel: 630-907-0095; Fax: 630-907-1076. Email: accpadre@prodigy.net. Web: www.auroracentral.com. Rev. F. William Etheredge, Prin.; Mr. Mark Krebs, Asst. Prin. Priests 1; School Sisters of St. Francis 1; Lay Teachers 30; Students 408.

ELGIN. *St. Edward Central Catholic High School*, 335 Locust St., 60123. Tel: 847-741-7535; Fax: 847-741-8658. Web: www.stedhs.org. Rev. Max J. Striedl, Supt. & Prin.; John Lucas, Asst. Prin.; Carl Koester, Dean of Students. Lay Teachers 37; Students 457.

FREEPORT. *Aquin Central Catholic Junior-Senior High School*, 1419 S. Galena Ave., 61032. Tel: 815-235-3154; Fax: 815-235-3185. Email: aquinhs@aeroinc.net. Kathleen Runte, Supt. Prin.; Rev. Raymond Guthrie, Asst. Prin. & Chm. Religious Studies Dept. Priests 2; Lay Teachers 18; Students 175.

STERLING. *Newman Central Catholic High School*, 1101 W. 23rd St., 61081-9002. Tel: 815-625-0500; Fax: 815-625-8444. Email: plipinski@newmancchs.org. Web: www.newmancchs.org. Revs. Paul M. Lipinski, Prin.; Paul C. White, Asst. Prin. & Spiritual Dir. Priests 2; Lay Teachers 24; Students 234.

WOODSTOCK. *Marian Central Catholic High School*, 1001 McHenry Ave., 60098. Tel: 815-338-4220; Fax: 815-338-4253. Email: tlanders@marian.com. Web: www.marian.com. Mr. Thomas E. Landers, Supt.; Mr. Charles Rakers, Prin.; Rev. Joseph P. Naill, Asst. Prin. & Spiritual Dir.; Mr. Charles Maveus Dean of Students; Mrs. Mary Ann Martinez, Devel. Dir. Priests 7; Lay Teachers 42; Students 735.

[C] HIGH SCHOOLS, PRIVATE

AURORA. *Marmion Academy*, 1000 Butterfield Rd., 60504. Tel: 630-897-6936; Fax: 630-897-7086. Email: jmilroy@marmion.org. Web: www.marmion.org. Rt. Rev. Vincent Bataille, O.S.B., Abbot & Pres.; Mr. John K. Milroy, Headmaster. Day School. Benedictines 16; Lay Teachers 32; Students 462.

Rosary High School, 901 N. Edgelawn Ave., 60506. Tel: 630-896-0831; Fax: 630-896-8372. Email: smfarrelly@rosaryhs.com. Web: www.rosaryhs.com. Sisters M. Megan Farrelly, O.P., Prin.; Patricia Burke, O.P., Asst. Prin.; Sandra Iwanski, Chm. Religious Studies. Sisters of St. Dominic 7; Lay Teachers 33; Girls 452.

[D] GENERAL HOSPITALS

ROCKFORD. *Saint Anthony College of Nursing*, 5658 E. State St., 61108. Tel: 815-395-5091; Fax: 815-395-2275. Email: Terriburch@sacn.edu. Web: www.sacn.edu. Terese A. Burch, Ph.D., R.N., Dean. Students 101.

Saint Anthony Medical Center, 5666 E. State St., 61108. Tel: 815-226-2000; Fax: 815-395-5449. Email: info@osfhealth.com. Web: osfhealth.com. Mr. David Schertz, Admin.; Rev. William R. Wentink, Chap. & Dir. of Pastoral Care. Sisters of the Third Order of St. Francis (East Peoria, IL) 4; Bed Capacity 254; Patients Assisted Annually 230,456; Total Staff 2,058.

AURORA. *Provena Mercy Center*, 1325 N. Highland Ave., 60506. Tel: 630-859-2222; Fax: 630-859-9014. Web: www.provenamercy.com. Jack Barto, Pres.; Mr. Michael Cook, Dir. Pastoral Care; Mrs. D. Van Dyke, Chap.

Legal Title: *Provena Hospitals dba Provena Mercy Center.* Bed Capacity 338; Patients Assisted

Annually 112,288; Total Staff 1,092.

ELGIN. *Provena St. Joseph Hospital*, 77 N. Airlite St., 60123. Tel: 847-695-3200; Fax: 847-931-5550. Email: edwardhunter@provenahealth.com. Web: www.provenahealth.com. Edward J. Hunter, Dir., Pastoral Care.
Legal Title: *Provena Hospitals dba Provena Saint Joseph Hospital.* Sisters 4; Bed Capacity 270; Patients Assisted Annually 178,050; Total Staff 1,040.

Provena Lake in the Hills Medical Center, Lake in the Hills Tel: 847-854-5511; Fax: 847-854-5531.

[E] SCHOOLS FOR EXCEPTIONAL ADOLESCENTS AND ADULTS

FREEPORT. *St. Vincent's Community Living Facility and Supported Living Arrangement*, 659 E. Jefferson St., 61032. Tel: 815-232-6181; Fax: 815-232-6143. Ms. Diane Cushman, Prog. Dir.; Rev. Raymond Guthrie, Chap. Sisters 1; Patients Assisted Annually 35.

[F] HOMES FOR AGED AND ADULT DAY CARE CENTERS

ROCKFORD. *St. Anne Place*, 4444 Brendenwood Rd., 61107. Tel: 815-399-6167; Fax: 815-399-6169. Email: eric@stanneplace.org. Web: www.stanneplace.org. Eric VandenBergh, Admin. Owned by the Rockford Diocese, managed by Provena Senior Services. Total Staff 38; Total in Residence 120.

Provena Cor Mariae Center, 3330 Maria Linden Dr., 61114. Tel: 815-877-7416; Fax: 815-877-4299. Email: cormariaectr@aol.com. Web: www.provenacormariae.com. Teresa Wester-Peters, Admin.
Legal Title: *Provena Senior Services dba Provena Cor Mariae Center.* Total Beds 152; Total Staff 126; Total Assisted 152.

Provena St. Anne Center, 4405 Highcrest Rd., 61107. Tel: 815-229-1999; Fax: 815-229-1560. Email: judylarson@provenahealth.com. Web: www.provenahealth.com. Ms. Judy K. Larson, Admin.
Legal Title: *Provena Senior Services dba Provena St. Anne Center.* Total Staff 365; Assisted 617.

Vianney Oaks, 7712 E. McGregor Rd., 61102. Tel: 815-399-4300; Fax: 815-399-5266. A retirement home for priests conducted by the Diocese of Rockford. Total in Residence 4.

AURORA. *Provena Fox Knoll*, 421 N. Lake St., 60506. Tel: 630-844-0380; Fax: 630-844-0702. Web: www.provenafoxknoll.com. Jennifer Roach, Admin.
Legal Title: *Provena Senior Services dba Provena Fox Knoll.* Total Staff 55; Total in Residence 167; Independent Living 90; Assisted Living 77.

Provena McAuley Manor, 400 W. Sullivan Rd., 60506. Tel: 630-859-3700; Fax: 630-264-1862.

FREEPORT. *Provena St. Joseph Adult Day Care Services*, 659 E. Jefferson St., 61032. Tel: 815-266-8067; Fax: 815-232-6143. Rev. Raymond Guthrie, Chap.; Ms. Eileen Ide, Prog. Dir. Sisters 1; Total Staff 10; Total Assisted 10,080.

Provena St. Joseph Center, 659 E. Jefferson St., 61032. Tel: 815-232-6181; Fax: 815-232-6143. Ms. Theresa Parsek, Admin.; Rev. Raymond Guthrie, Chap.
Legal Title: *Provena Senior Services dba Provena St. Joseph Center.* Sisters 1; Aged Residents 120; Total Staff 140.

GENEVA. *Provena Geneva Care Center*, 1101 E. State St., 60134. Tel: 630-232-7544; Fax: 630-232-4409. Email: JanelleLChadwick@provenahealth.com. Web: www.provenagenevacare.com. Janelle Chadwick, Admin.
Legal Title: *Provena Senior Services dba Provena Geneva Care Center.* Bed Capacity 107; Total Staff 105.

ST. CHARLES. *Provena Pine View Care Center*, 611 Allen Ln., 60174. Tel: 630-377-2211; Fax: 630-377-4352. Email: marypwright@provenahealth.com. Web: Provenahealth.com. Mary Wright, Admin.
Legal Title: *Provena Senior Services dba Provena Pine View Care Center.* Bed Capacity 120; Residents 102; Total Staff 97.

WHEATON. *Assisi Homes-Batavia Apartments, Inc.*, 1259 E. Wilson St., Batavia, 60510. Tel: 630-879-3117; Fax: 630-879-0665. Web: www.wfs-inc.org. 26 W. 171 Roosevelt Rd., P.O. Box 667, 60189-0667. Susan M. Dillberg, Contact.

[G] MONASTERIES AND RESIDENCES OF PRIESTS AND BROTHERS

AURORA. *Marmion Abbey*, Formerly Marmion Abbey-St. Augustine's Abbey, 850 Butterfield Rd., 60504. Tel: 630-897-7215; Fax: 630-897-0393. Email: vbataille@marmion.org. Web: www.marmion.org. Rt. Revs. Vincent Bataille, O.S.B., Abbot; Gerald Benkert, O.S.B., Abbot Emeritus; David J. Cyr, O.S.B., Abbot Emeritus; Very Rev. Kenneth Theisen, O.S.B., Prior; Revs. Barnabas Lundergan, O.S.B.; Andrew Wahmhoff, O.S.B.; Bede Stocker, O.S.B.; Alcuin Deck, O.S.B.; Luke Bohr, O.S.B.; Augustine Jones, O.S.B.; Martin Witting, O.S.B.; Hugh Schuck, O.S.B.; Matthias Zinkan, O.S.B.; Bernard Schaefer, O.S.B.; Gregory Obee, O.S.B.; Philip Kremer, O.S.B.; Mario Pedi, O.S.B.; Francis Daleiden, O.S.B.; David Palmatier, O.S.B.; Charles Reichenbacher, O.S.B.; Basil Yender, O.S.B.; Joel Rippinger, O.S.B.; Christian Pusateri, O.S.B.; Michael Burrows, O.S.B.; Orlando Perez Gomez, O.S.B.; John Brahill, O.S.B.; Rene Otzoy Colaj, O.S.B.; Cristobal Coche Quic; George Glover, O.S.B.; Frederick Peterson, O.S.B.
Legal Title: *Marmion.* Priests 33; Brothers 15.

Missionaries of the Sacred Heart Community, 305 S. Lake St., 6050. Tel: 630-892-2371; Fax: 630-892-1678. Email: provincial@misacor-usa.org. Web: www.misacor-usa.org. Very Rev. Joseph Jablonski, M.S.C., Prov. Supr.; Revs. Peter E. Campbell, M.S.C.; Raymond Diesbourg, M.S.C.; Howard Fath, M.S.C.; James Hall, M.S.C.; Ronald Leinen, M.S.C.; Joseph Muller, M.S.C.; Gerald Paul, M.S.C.; Luis Alfonso Segura, M.S.C.; Frank John Timar, M.S.C.; Norbert B. Weber, M.S.C.; Bros. George Farkas, M.S.C.; Nicholas Lanese, M.S.C. Provincial Administrative Office of the Missionaries of the Sacred Heart. Priests 11; Brothers 2.
Priests of the Province Serving Elsewhere - In Bogota, Colombia: Very Rev. German Barona, M.S.C., Sectional Supr.; Revs. Tito Medina, M.S.C.; Michael Miller, M.S.C.
In Papua New Guinea Revs. Hilary Fischer, M.S.C.; Richard Kennedy, M.S.C.; Bernard Miller, M.S.C.; Wilson Tascon, M.S.C.; Leon Weisenberger, M.S.C.; Bros. Anton Frietas, M.S.C.; James Miller, M.S.C.; Patrick O'Hara, M.S.C.; Daniel Rakow, M.S.C.; Joseph Tesar, M.S.C.
In Issoudun, France Rev. Mark McDonald, M.S.C.

MCHENRY. *Villa Desiderata Retreat House*, 3015 N. Bayview Ln., 60050. Tel: 815-385-2264. Rev. Daniel F. Reardon, C.S.V., Resident Priest; Bro. Patrick Drohan, C.S.V., Facilities Mgr.

[H] CONVENTS AND RESIDENCES FOR SISTERS

ROCKFORD. *The Poor Clares of Rockford*, Corpus Christi Monastery, 2111 S. Main St., 61102-3591. Tel: 815-963-7343; Fax: 815-963-7369. Web: www.poorclares.org/rockford/. Sr. Mary Regina Dice, P.C.C., P.C.C., Abbess; Rev. Christopher Henderson, C.P.M., Chap. Poor Clare Colettines Cloistered Sisters 20; Novices 2; Extern Sisters 1.

BATAVIA. *Holy Heart of Mary Novitiate*, 717 N. Batavia Ave., 60510. Tel: 630-879-1296; Fax: 630-879-7831. Email: hatton@inil.com. Web: www@inil.com/users/hatton. Sr. Linda K. Hatton, S.S.C.M., Supr. & Formation Dir. Servants of the Holy Heart of Mary Professed Sisters 7; Novices 2.

FREEPORT. *Congregation of the Sisters of the Immaculate Heart of Mary, Mother of Christ-Nigeria*, 1209 South Walnut St., 61032. Tel: 815-297-8287; Fax: 815-297-1786. Email: ihm@aeronic.com. Sr. M. Providentia Marinze, Regl. Supr.

ST. CHARLES. *Our Lady of Creek Bend*, 37 W. 584 Dean St., 60175. Tel: 630-584-5699; Fax: 630-587-0563. Email: sisteradria@juno.com. Felician Sisters Residence. Sisters 3.

[I] COMMUNITY SERVICES

ROCKFORD. *St. Elizabeth Catholic Community Center*, 1536 S. Main St., 61102. Tel: 815-969-6526; Fax: 815-969-0451. Email: saintel911@aol.com. Sr. M. Marcella Amaefule, I.H.M., Admin.; Mr. Thomas McKenna, Consultant. Total Staff 16; Total Assisted 15,028.

AURORA. *Hesed House, Inc.*, 659 S. River St., 60506. Tel: 630-897-2156; Fax: 630-801-9759. Email: rml@hesedhouse.org. Sr. Rose Marie Lorentzen, B.V.M., Exec. Dir. Ecumenical Center for ministry to the poor. Total Assisted 178,340.

Public Action to Deliver Shelter, Inc. (PADS), 659 S. River St., 60506. Tel: 630-897-2165; Fax: 630-801-9759. Email: rml@hesedhouse.org. Sr. Rose Marie Lorentzen, B.V.M., Exec. Dir. Ecumenical advocacy, overnight and transitional shelters and daytime drop-in center for homeless persons. Total Assisted 47,491.

[J] RETREAT HOUSES

ROCKFORD. *Bishop Lane Retreat Center*, 7708 E. McGregor Rd., 61102. Tel: 815-965-5011; Fax: 815-965-5811. Lorrie Gramer, Dir.; Don Gramer, Asst. Dir.

[K] FOUNDATIONS

ROCKFORD. *Boylan Educational Foundation, Inc.*, 4000 St. Francis Dr., 61103. Tel: 815-877-8008; Fax: 815-877-2544.

The Catholic Foundation for the People of the Diocese of Rockford, 555 Colman Center Dr., P.O. Box 7044, 61125-7044. Tel: 815-399-4300; Fax: 815-399-5657. Email: jpsentovich@rockforddiocese.org. Web: www.stewardshiprockford.com. Mr. John Sentovich, Exec. Dir.

AURORA. *Aurora Catholic Education Foundation*, P.O. Box 234, 60507. Tel: 630-898-2998; Fax: 630-898-0525.

Provena Mercy Center Foundation, 1325 N. Highland Ave., 60506. Tel: 630-801-2662; Fax: 630-801-5621. Email: PMCFoundation@Provenahealth.com. Web: provenamercy.com. Laura Stoney, Foundation President.

CRYSTAL LAKE. *St. Thomas the Apostle School Foundation, Inc.*, 272 King St., 60014. Tel: 815-455-5400; Fax: 815-455-2733. Email: vdefrisco@st-thomas-school.org.

DEKALB. *Newman Center of Northern Illinois University Educational Program*, 512 Normal Rd., 60115. Tel: 815-787-7770; Fax: 815-753-2053. Email: sknox1@niu.edu. Web: www.newman-niu.org.
Legal Title: *Newman Center of Northern Illinois University Educational Program and Development Fund, Inc.* Total Staff 9.

ELGIN. *St. Edward Central Catholic High School Education Foundation*, 335 Locust St., 60123. Tel: 847-695-4653; Fax: 847-695-4682. Email: Stedward@stedhs.org. Web: www.stedhs.org. Daniel Mollsen, Foundation Chm.

FREEPORT. *Education Through the 90's Foundation*, 1419 S. Galena Ave., 61032. Tel: 815-235-3154; Fax: 815-235-3185. Email: aquinhs@aeroinc.net. The foundation provides financial support for the Freeport Catholic School System.

Freeport Catholic Education Foundation, 1419 S. Galena Ave., 61032. Tel: 815-235-3154; Fax: 815-235-3185. Email: aquinhs@aeroinc.net. The foundation provides financial support for the Freeport Catholic School System.

STERLING. *Sauk Valley Catholic Education Foundation*, 1101 St. Mary's Rd., 61081. Tel: 815-626-5570; Fax: 815-626-5570. Email: mhenson@whitesideroe.org. Web: www.whitesideroe.org.

Sauk Valley Area Religious Education Center, 1101 St. Mary Rd., 61081. Tel: 815-626-5570; Fax: 815-626-5570.

SYCAMORE. *St. Mary's Educational Foundation, Ltd.*, 244 Waterman St., 60178. Tel: 815-895-3275; Fax: 815-899-7890. Email: fjtimar@juno.com.

[L] NEWMAN CENTERS

DEKALB. *Newman Foundation for Catholic Students of Northern Illinois University* 512 Normal Rd., 60115. Tel: 815-787-7770; Fax: 815-758-2053. Email: sknox1@niu.edu. Web: www.newman-niu.org. Revs. Stephen J. Knox, S.T.L., Dir. Campus Ministries; Addison H. Hart, Assoc. Dir. Campus Ministries; Michael Black, Assoc. Dir. Campus Ministries; Mr. Brian Kowalski, Pastoral Assoc.; Mrs. Pat Mulheran, Pastoral Assoc.

[M] MISCELLANEOUS

ROCKFORD. *Catholic Office of the Deaf*, 555 Colman Center Dr., P.O. Box 7044, 61125. Tel: 815-399-4300 (Voice); 815-962-2994 (TTY); Fax: 815-399-5266. Email: RockfordHI@aol.com. Web: www.members.aol.com/RockfordHI.

National Association of Diaconate Directors, 2136 - 12th St., Ste. 105, 61104. Tel: 815-399-4300; Fax: 815-399-6303. Email: NADD@Execpc.com. Web: www.NADD.fp.execpc.com.

Vineyard Books, Gifts & Church Supplies, Highcrest Centre, 1638 N. Alpine Rd., 61107. Tel: 815-398-4030; Fax: 815-398-8477; 800-587-9777. Email: books4cath@aol.com. Candice Daacon, Mgr. Total Staff 9.

AURORA. *Association of the Communications Congregation*, P.O. Box 1775, 60507. Tel: 630-859-3657; Fax: 630-859-3657. Email: evangelization@aol.com. Rev. Dennis Brown, Primary Supvr.

**Dominican Literacy Center, Aurora*, 260 Vermont Ave., 60505. Sr. Kathleen Ryan, Dir.

The J. Chevalier Charitable Trust, 305 S. Lake St., P.O. Box 270, 60507-0270. Tel: 800-807-0100, Ext. 2940; Fax: 630-378-2505. Email: Fran_Dyer@cbservices.org. Web: www.cbservices.org. Rev. Francis X. Dyer, O.P. (CHI), Co-Trustee.

**Joseph Corporation of Illinois, Inc.*, P.O. Box 525, 60507. Tel: 630-906-9400; Fax: 630-906-9406. Email: mary@josephcorp.org. Web: www.josephcorporation.org. Mary Tetzlaff, Exec. Dir.; Jerria Donelson, Prog. Asst.; Louise Ideran, Operations Coord.; Leticia Lara-Reyes, Dir. of Home Ownership Education; Jesus Fernandez, Dir. of Neighborhood Lending. (Ecumenical not-for-profit housing developer).

ST. CHARLES. *Cultivation Ministries*, P.O. Box 662, 60174. Tel: 630-513-8222; Fax: 630-513-8233. Email: info@cultivationministries.com. Web: www.cultivationministries.com. Frank Mercadante, Exec. Dir. To cultivate team-based, comprehensive, and disciple-making Catholic youth ministries by training, resourcing and supporting adult and student leaders.

Queen of Americas Guild, 345 Kautz Rd., P.O. Box 851, 60174. Tel: 630-584-1822; Fax: 630-587-2200. Email: staff@queenoftheamericasguild.org. Web: www.queenoftheamericasguild.org. Most Rev. Joseph J. Madera, M.Sp.S., Bishop for the Archdiocese for the Military Services, USA, Episcopal Moderator; Mr. Frank Smoczynski, Pres.; Mr. Stephen Banaszak, Vice Pres.; Beverly Smoczynski, Treas. & Dir.
Board of Directors: Revs. George M. Hastrich; Christopher Rengers, O.F.M.Cap.; Mrs. Ruth Sloan.

SAVANNA. *Mercy Homecare/Hospice*, 1125 N. 5th St., 61074. Tel: 815-273-2628; Fax: 815-273-7025. Email: johnsonv@mercyhealth.com. Web: www.mercyclinton.com. Vicki Johnson, R.N., B.S.N., Dir.; Joan Noe, Admin.; Tom Hesselmann, Pres. Sponsor: Mercy Health Services, Sisters of Mercy, Regional Community of Detroit

STERLING. *St. Vincent DePaul Society*, Tel: 815-625-0311; Fax: 815-625-1684. Email: dblum@stmary61081.org. Total Staff 16; Total Assisted 3,059.

St. Mary's Conference, 600 Ave. B, 61081. Tel: 815-625-0640; Fax: 815-625-1684.

STOCKTON. *Christ in the Wilderness*, 7500 S. Randecker Rd., 61085-8922. Tel: 815-947-2476; Fax: 815-947-2096. Email: citw@aeroinc.net. Web: www.citwretreat.com. Sr. Julia Marie Bathon, O.S.F., Dir., Center of Solitude and Prayer.

RELIGIOUS INSTITUTES OF MEN REPRESENTED IN THE DIOCESE

For further details refer to the corresponding bracketed number in the Religious Institutes of Men or Women section.

[0200]—*Benedictine Monks* (Marmion Abbey, Aurora)—O.S.B.
[1320]—*Clerics of St. Viator*—C.S.V.
[1080]—*Congregation of the Resurrection* (Chicago Prov.)—C.R.
[0480]—*Conventual Franciscans* (St. Bonaventure Province)—O.F.M.Conv
[]—*Institute of Christ the King Sovereign Priest (Provincial House-Italy)*
[1110]—*Missionaries of the Sacred Heart* (U.S. Province)—M.S.C.
[1190]—*Salesians of Don Bosco*—S.D.B.
[0690]—*Society of Jesus*—S.J.
[0820]—*The Fathers of Mercy*—C.P.M.

RELIGIOUS INSTITUTES OF WOMEN REPRESENTED IN THE DIOCESE

[0350]—*Carmelite Sisters (Corpus Christi)*—O.Carm.
[2100]—*Congregation of the Humility of Mary*—C.H.M.
[1920]—*Congregation of the Sisters of the Holy Cross*—C.S.C.
[1710]—*Congregation of the Third Order of St. Francis of Mary Immaculate*—O.S.F.
[1070-03]—*Dominican Sisters*—O.P.
[1070-13]—*Dominican Sisters*—O.P.
[1070-10]—*Dominican Sisters*—O.P.
[1070-01]—*Dominican Sisters of St. Catharine*—O.P.
[1170]—*Felician Sisters*—C.S.S.F.
[1430]—*Franciscan Sisters of Our Lady of Perpetual Help*—O.S.F
[1450]—*Franciscan Sisters of the Sacred Heart*—O.S.F.
[]—*Immaculate Heart of Mary*—I.H.M.
[2575]—*Institute of the Sisters of Mercy of the Americas* (Chicago, IL)—R.S.M.
[]—*Mexican Passionist Sisters*—C.F.P.
[2865]—*Missionaries of the Sacred Heart & Our Lady of Guadalupe*—M.S.C.Gpe.
[2790]—*Missionary Servants of the Most Blessed Trinity*—M.S.B.T.
[3760]—*Poor Clare Colettines*—P.C.C.
[2970]—*School Sisters of Notre Dame*—S.S.N.D.
[1680]—*School Sisters of St. Francis*—O.S.F.
[3520]—*Servants of the Holy Heart of Mary*—S.S.C.M.
[0430]—*Sisters of Charity of the Blessed Virgin Mary*—B.V.M.
[2360]—*Sisters of Loretto at the Foot of the Cross*—S.L.
[2450]—*Sisters of Mary of the Presentation*—S.M.P.
[3360]—*Sisters of Providence of Saint Mary-of-the-Woods, Indiana*—S.P.
[1705]—*The Sisters of St. Francis of Assisi*—O.S.F.
[1570]—*Sisters of St. Francis of the Holy Family*—O.S.F.
[3830-15]—*Sisters of St. Joseph*—C.S.J.
[3930]—*Sisters of St. Joseph of the Third Order of St. Francis*—S.S.J.-T.O.R.
[2183]—*Sisters of the Immaculate Heart of Mary Mother of Christ, Nigeria*—I. H. M.
[2350]—*Sisters of the Living Word*—S.L.W.
[1770]—*Sisters of the Third Order of St. Francis* (Peoria, Illinois)—O.S.F.

DIOCESAN CEMETERIES

ROCKFORD. *Calvary-St. Mary's/St. James*
AURORA. *Mount Olivet*
BATAVIA. *Geneva-St. Charles Resurrection*
ELGIN. *Mount Hope*
WINNEBAGO. *Calvary*

NECROLOGY

† McGowan, John J., (Retired)—Died Dec. 28, 2002
† Regnier, William H., (Retired)—Died May 23, 2003
† Thennes, Clarence J., (Retired)—Died Dec. 14, 2002

Diocese of Rockville Centre

(Dioecesis Petropolitana In Insula Longa)

Most Reverend

WILLIAM FRANCIS MURPHY, S.T.D., L.H.D.

Bishop of Rockville Centre; ordained December 16, 1964; appointed Auxiliary Bishop to the Archbishop of Boston and Titular Bishop of Saia Maggiore, November 21, 1995; consecrated December 27, 1995; appointed Fourth Bishop of Rockville Centre, June 26, 2001; installed September 5, 2001. *Diocesan Pastoral Center*, 50 N. Park Ave., Rockville Centre, NY 11570. Email: bishopsoffice@drvc.org.

Chancery Office: 50 N. Park Ave., Rockville Centre, NY 11570. Tel: 516-678-5800; Fax: 516-764-3316.

Web: www.drvc.org

Email: chancellor@drvc.org

Most Reverend

JAMES J. DALY

Retired Auxiliary Bishop of Rockville Centre; ordained May 22, 1948; appointed Titular Bishop of Castra Nova and Auxiliary to the Bishop of Rockville Centre February 28, 1977; ordained May 9, 1977; retired July 1, 1996. *Res.: 25 Lanes Rd., Blue Point, NY 11715*. Tel: 631-363-5150.

Most Reverend

EMIL A. WCELA

Auxiliary Bishop of Rockville Centre; ordained June 2, 1956; appointed Titular Bishop of Filaca and Auxiliary Bishop of Rockville Centre October 21, 1988; ordained December 13, 1988. *Res.: Eastern Vicariate - Diocese of Rockville Centre*, P.O. Box 780, Riverhead, NY 11901. Tel: 516-369-0071.

Most Reverend

JOHN C. DUNNE, D.D.

Auxiliary Bishop of Rockville Centre; ordained June 1, 1963; appointed Titular Bishop of Abercorn and Auxiliary Bishop of Rockville Centre October 21, 1988; ordained December 13, 1988. *Res.: Central Vicariate - Diocese of Rockville Centre*, P.O. Box 39, Farmingdale, NY 11735-0039. Tel: 516-249-1700.

Most Reverend

PAUL H. WALSH

Auxiliary Bishop of Rockville Centre; ordained June 9, 1966; appointed Auxiliary Bishop of Rockville Centre April 3, 2003; ordained May 29, 2003

..ESTABLISHED APRIL 6, 1957.

Square Miles 1,222.

The Roman Catholic Diocese of Rockville Centre, New York.

Comprises the Counties of Nassau and Suffolk (excepting Fishers Island) in the State of New York.

For legal titles of parishes and diocesan institutions, consult the Chancery Office.

STATISTICAL OVERVIEW

Personnel	
Bishop	1
Auxiliary Bishops	3
Retired Bishops	1
Priests: Diocesan Active in Diocese	256
Priests: Diocesan Active Outside Diocese	10
Priests: Diocesan in Foreign Missions	1
Priests: Retired, Sick or Absent	139
Number of Diocesan Priests	406
Religious Priests in Diocese	36
Total Priests in Diocese	442
Extern Priests in Diocese	43
Ordinations:	
Diocesan Priests	3
Religious Priests	1
Transitional Deacons	3
Permanent Deacons	14
Permanent Deacons in Diocese	255
Total Brothers	89
Total Sisters	1,368
Parishes	
Parishes	134
With Resident Pastor:	
Resident Diocesan Priests	130
Resident Religious Priests	4
Missions	1
Professional Ministry Personnel:	
Brothers	5
Sisters	135
Lay Ministers	343
Welfare	
Catholic Hospitals	5
Total Assisted	1,480,886
Homes for the Aged	5
Total Assisted	639,295
Residential Care of Children	4
Total Assisted	7,738
Day Care Centers	101
Total Assisted	3,792
Specialized Homes	8
Total Assisted	1,475
Special Centers for Social Services	37
Total Assisted	68,088
Residential Care of Disabled	23
Total Assisted	232
Other Institutions	121
Total Assisted	267,324
Educational	
Seminaries, Diocesan	1
Students from This Diocese	19
Students from Other Diocese	17
Total Seminarians	19
Colleges and Universities	2
Total Students	9,310
High Schools, Diocesan and Parish	5
Total Students	4,525
High Schools, Private	6
Total Students	7,449
Elementary Schools, Diocesan and Parish	59
Total Students	25,588
Elementary Schools, Private	4
Total Students	1,110
Non-residential Schools for the Disabled	1
Total Students	70
Catechesis/Religious Education:	
High School Students	2,711
Elementary Students	115,818
Total Students under Catholic Instruction	166,600
Teachers in the Diocese:	
Priests	10
Brothers	46
Sisters	129
Lay Teachers	1,947
Vital Statistics	
Receptions into the Church:	
Infant Baptism Totals	21,040
Adult Baptism Totals	703
Received into Full Communion	649
First Communions	21,905
Confirmations	18,703
Marriages:	
Catholic	4,424
Interfaith	951
Total Marriages	5,375
Deaths	13,606
Total Catholic Population	1,490,579
Total Population	2,781,159

Former Bishops—Most Revs. WALTER P. KELLENBERG, D.D. (Retired), first Bishop of Rockville Centre; ord. June 2, 1928; appt. Titular Bishop of Joannina and Auxiliary Bishop of New York, Aug. 25, 1953; consecrated Oct. 5, 1953; appt. Bishop of Ogdensburg, Jan. 19, 1954; appt. first Bishop of Rockville Centre, April 16, 1957; installed May 27, 1957; retired May 3, 1976; died Jan. 11, 1986; JOHN R. MCGANN, D.D. (Retired), second Bishop of Rockville Centre; ord. June 3, 1950; appt. Titular Bishop of Morosbisdus and Auxiliary to the Bishop of Rockville Centre, Nov. 12, 1970; consecrated Jan. 7, 1971; appt. second Bishop of Rockville Centre, May 3, 1976; installed June 24, 1976; retired Jan. 4, 2000; died Jan. 29, 2002; JAMES T. MCHUGH, S.T.D., third Bishop of Rockville Centre; ord. May 25, 1957; appt. Titular Bishop of Morosbisdo and Auxiliary Bishop of Newark, Nov. 20, 1987; consecrated Jan. 25, 1988; appt. Bishop of Camden, May 13, 1989; installed June 20, 1989; appt. Coadjutor Bishop of Rockville Centre, Dec. 7, 1998; installed Feb. 22, 1999; succeeded to the See, Jan. 4, 2000; died Dec. 10, 2000.

Diocesan Bishop—Most Rev. WILLIAM FRANCIS MURPHY, S.T.D., L.H.D.

Auxiliary Bishops—Most Revs. EMIL A. WCELA, D.D.; JOHN C. DUNNE, D.D.; JAMES J. DALY, D.D., Emeritus.

Secretary to the Bishop—Rev. ROBERT O. MORRISSEY, J.C.D., M.Div. Tel: 516-678-5800, Ext. 402; Fax: 516-678-3138. Email: rmorrissey@drvc.org.

Vicar General and Moderator of the Curia—Rev. Msgr. ROBERT J. BRENNAN, 50 N. Park Ave., Rockville Centre, 11570. Tel: 516-678-5800, Ext. 622. Email: rbrennan@drvc.org.

Vicar General—Rev. Msgr. JOHN A. ALESANDRO, S.T.L., J.C.D., J.D., Church of Saint Dominic, 93 Anstice St., Oyster Bay, 11771. Tel: 516-922-4488; Fax: 516-922-9491. Email: jalesandro@stdoms.org.

Episcopal Vicars—Western Vicariate: Most Rev. PAUL H. WALSH, D.D., Queen of the Most Holy Rosary Church, 196 W. Centennial Ave., Roosevelt, 11575-1937. Tel: 516-378-1315; Fax: 516-378-5754. Central Vicariate: Most Rev. JOHN C. DUNNE, D.D., P.O. Box 39, Farmingdale, 11735-0039. Tel: 516-249-1700; Fax: 516-249-1701. Email: dunnejc@worldnet.att.net. Eastern Vicariate: Most Rev. EMIL A. WCELA, D.D., P.O. Box 780, Riverhead, 11901. Tel: 631-369-0071; Fax: 631-727-8483. Email: wcela@drvc.org.

Chancery Office—

Chancellor—Sr. MARYANNE FITZGERALD, S.C. Tel: 516-678-5800, Ext. 583. Email: chancellor@drvc.org.

Vice Chancellors—Sr. LUCY BLYSKAL, C.S.J., J.C.D.. Email: dueprocess@drvc.org; Rev. ROBERT O. MORRISSEY, J.C.D., M.Div.. Email: rmorrissey@drvc.org.

Cabinet Secretaries—

Secretary for Administration—Mr. Kevin T. Murphy. Tel: 516-678-5800, Ext. 543. Email: ktmurphy@drvc.org.

Secretary for Communications—Joanne Novarro. Tel: 516-678-5800, Ext. 632. Email: jnovarro@drvc.org.

Secretary for Education and Formation—Sr. Joanne Callahan, O.S.U. Tel: 516-678-5800, Ext. 548. Email: jcallahan@drvc.org.

Secretary for Healthcare Services—Vacant.

Secretary for Ministerial Personnel—Rev. Msgr. Francis J. Caldwell, C.S.W. Tel: 516-678-5800, Ext. 585. Email: fcaldwell@drvc.org.

Secretary for Pastoral Ministries—Rev. Msgr. Donald M. Beckmann. Tel: 516-678-5800, Ext. 613. Email: dbeckmann@drvc.org.

Secretary for Social Services—Laura Cassell. Tel: 516-733-7013. Email: cassell.laura@catholiccharities.cc.

Censors of Books—Rev. Msgr. John A. Alesandro, S.T.L., J.C.D., J.D.; Rev. Charles Caccavale, S.T.D.; Rev. Msgrs. Francis X. Glimm, S.T.L. (Retired); George P. Graham, J.C.D., Ph.D. (Retired); Revs. James Massa, Ph.D.; Robert O. Morrissey, J.C.D., M.Div.; Rev. Msgr. Francis J. Schneider, J.C.D., M.Div.; Revs. Robert J. Smith, S.T.D.; Peter I. Vaccari, S.T.L.

Diocesan Tribunal—50 N. Park Ave., Rockville Centre, 11570. Tel: 516-678-5800; Fax: 516-594-1548.

Judicial Vicar—Rev. Msgr. Edward A. Sweeny, M.Div., J.C.D., Ph.D. Tel: 516-678-5800, Ext. 566.

Adjutant Judicial Vicars—Rev. Thomas V. Arnao, M.Div., J.C.D. Tel: 516-678-5800, Ext. 558; Rev. Msgr. Charles A. Guarino, J.C.D., M.A., M.Div. Tel: 516-678-5800, Ext. 568; Rev. James F. Pereda, M.Div., J.C.D. Tel: 516-678-5800, Ext. 565.

Diocesan Judges—Sr. Lucy Blyskal, C.S.J., J.C.D.; Deacon Thomas Rich, J.C.L. Tel: 516-678-5800, Ext. 559; Rev. Colvin F. Pulle, J.C.L.

Judges for Interdiocesan Tribunal—Rev. Msgrs. John A. Alesandro, S.T.L., J.C.D., J.D.; Richard C. Bauhoff, J.C.D., Ph.D.; Thomas D. Candreva, S.T.L., J.C.D.; George P. Graham, J.C.D., Ph.D. (Retired); Domenick T. Graziadio, M.A.; Richard P. Kopinski, M.S., M.A.; Francis S. Midura, M.Div., J.C.D.; Thomas E. Molloy; Rev. Robert O. Morrissey, J.C.D., M.Div.; Rev. Msgrs. John C. Nosser, M.S.; Francis J. Schneider, J.C.D., M.Div.; Rev. John J. Tutone, J.C.D., M.Div.

Promoter of Justice—Rev. Msgr. Charles A. Guarino, J.C.D., M.A., M.Div.

Defenders of the Bond—Sr. Lois Keller, R.S.M., J.C.L., Ph.D. Tel: 516-678-5800, Ext. 563; Rev. Antonio S. Pascual, J.C.L.

Notaries—Sr. Ruth Borgersen, R.S.M., M.A.; Mrs. Carol Gatz; Mrs. Nanno Hayes; Mrs. Helen Howe; Mrs. Grace Rohe; Mrs. Toni Tuzzolino.

In-Take Secretary—Mrs. Nanno Hayes. Tel: 516-678-5800, Ext. 571.

Medical Experts—Christopher Deeg, Ph.D.; Simeon Ryan, Ph.D.; Maureen Kaley, Ph.D.; William Van Ornum, Ph.D.; Ann Fahey, Psy.D.

Coordinator of Post-Annulment Counseling Program—Mrs. Barbara Butler. Tel: 631-754-9765.

Procurator & Advocates—Deacons Joseph T. Bartolotto; Edward Billia; Mrs. Marian Bopp; Rev. William G. Breslawski; Sisters Mary Jane Brustman, C.I.J.; Imelda Buetow, R.G.S.; Mrs. Barbara Butler; Sr. Helen Byrne, C.S.J.; Mrs. Gail Carton; Deacon Tony Cedrone; Mrs. Marcy Chapuisat; Mrs. Dolores Connors; Sr. Miriam Honora Corr, C.S.J.; Rev. Thomas C. Costa; Deacons Frank Cove; Anthony Cuseo; Ms. Mary Anne Dejewski; Rev. John Derasmo; Dr. Joan B. Dorr; Ms. Anita Dos Santos; Rev. Msgr. John R. Dreasen; Rev. Lawrence T. Duncklee; Sr. Judy Enterlin, C.S.J.; Mr. Thomas J. Evrard; Mrs. Kathleen Forbes; Mr. Thomas Forbes; Deacon Andrew Gargiulo; Sr. Margaret Gerard von Achen, O.P.; Deacon Ronald J. Gillette; Mr. John E. Glynn; Rev. Thomas Haggerty; Ms. Valerie Haug; Mrs. Nanno E. Hayes; Sisters Bonnie Kelly, C.S.J.; Jane Lyons, C.I.J.; Rev. James P. Mannion Jr.; Deacon Salvatore Marino; Mr. James J. Maune; Rev. Msgr. James McDonald; Mr. Steve McGiff; Deacon James McQuade; Rev. Joseph A. Mirro; Mr. Christopher J. Murano; Deacons Charles Muscarnera; Montford D. Nayler; Mrs. Mary Ann O'Connor; Mr. Thomas O'Connor; Dr. Mary O'Grady; Deacon Phil Paolicelli; Mr. Joseph Paradise; Rev. Vitalis Pedzik; Mr. John P. Reali; Ms. Vilma Rivera; Rev. Robert Romeo; Sr. Mary Ronald, C.S.F.N.; Ms. Carmen Roncal; Rev. Thomas J. St. Pierre; Ms. Jane Smith; Deacon Neil Squitieri; Sr. Maria Stapleton, C.S.J.; Rev. Joseph W. Staudt; Mrs. Ann Mary Strieder; Ms. Joan Sullivan; Sr. Kathleen T. Sullivan, C.S.J.; Eileen Tracy; Sr. Eugenia M. Travers, O.P.; Rev. Msgr. Edmond J. Trench (Retired); Sr. Patricia Turley, C.S.J.; Rev. Michael Vetrano; Sr. Ellen Zak, C.S.F.N.; Revs. Kenneth Zach; Andrzej Zglejszewski.

Senate of Priests (Presbyteral Council/College of Consultors)—Most Revs. John C. Dunne, D.D.; Paul H. Walsh, D.D.; Emil A. Wcela, D.D.; Rev. Msgrs. Robert J. Brennan; John A. Alesandro; John F. Bennett; Revs. William G. Breslawski; Thomas Cardone, S.M.; Thomas M. Coogan; Thomas C. Costa; James M. Kissane; Rev. Msgr. William E. Costello; Rev. William J. Gomes; Rev. Msgr. James M. McDonald; Revs. Brian J. McNamara; Robert O. Morrissey, J.C.D., M.Div., Exec. Sec.; Rev. Msgr. Pablo M. Rodriquez; Rev. Gregory Semeniuk, C.M.; Rev. Msgr. Edmond J. Trench; Rev. Thomas L. Spadaro.

Deans—Rockville Centre Deanery: Rev. Msgr. John Bennett. North Hempstead Deanery: Rev. Msgr. John J. McCann. Oyster Bay Deanery: Rev. Msgr. Richard P. Kopinski, M.S., M.A. Belmont Deanery: Rev. John D. Gilmartin. Hicksville Deanery: Rev. Donald Hanson. Five Towns Deanery: Rev. Msgr. William W. Jablonski. Seaford Deanery: Rev. Msgr. Robert E. Guglielmone. Huntington Deanery: Rev. Msgr. T. Peter Ryan. Smithaven Deanery: Rev. Msgr. Ellsworth R. Walden. Babylon Deanery: Rev. Msgr. Francis X. Gaeta. Islip Deanery: Rev. Steven J. Peterson. North Brookhaven Deanery: Rev. Christopher J. Heller. South Brookhaven Deanery Rev. Thomas L. Spadaro. Peconic Deanery Rev. Donald J. Desmond.

Diocesan Offices

Pastoral Center—50 N. Park Ave., Rockville Centre, 11570. Tel: 516-678-5800; Fax: 516-678-1786.

Director of Administration—Mr. Kevin T. Murphy, Dir. Admin. & Corporate Chancellor. Tel: 516-678-5800; Fax: 516-536-6554. Email: ktmurphy@drvc.org; Ms. Ellen R. Huling, Internal Auditor. Email: ehuling@drvc.orgTel: 516-678-5800, Ext. 291.

Archives—Ms. Jean Walsh, Archivist, Seminary of the Immaculate Conception, 440 W. Neck Rd., Huntington, 11743. Tel: 631-423-0483; Fax: 631-423-7922. Email: archives@drvc.org.

Bishop's Annual Appeal—Mrs. Kathy Mulvey, Dir., 200 W. Centennial Ave., Roosevelt, 11575. Tel: 516-379-5210, Ext. 210; Fax: 516-379-5043. Email: bishopappeal@drvc.org.

Building Office—Mr. Chester J. Strzepek, Dir. Tel: 516-678-5800, Ext. 603; Fax: 516-594-1128. Email: strzepek@drvc.org.

Campus Ministry—Rev. Joseph J. D'Angelo, M.A.C., M.Div., M.S., C.A.S.A.C., Campus Ministry Dir. Tel: 516-678-5800, Ext. 614; Fax: 516-763-1078. Email: CHAJJD@hofstra.edu.

Catechesis—Mr. George Rand, Dir. Tel: 516-678-5800, Ext. 506; Fax: 516-255-3786; Sisters Anne Marie Dean, C.S.J. Western Vicariate Catechetical Coord., Personnel Svcs., Textbook ConsultantTel: 516-678-5800, Ext. 502; Joan Mary Finn, O.P., Coord. Pastoral Ministry for the Deaf. Tel: 516-678-5800, Ext. 205; Sally Ryan, R.S.M. Pastoral Ministry for Persons with Disabilities, Eastern Vicariate Catechetical Coord.Tel: 516-678-5800, Ext. 540; Mr. Timothy Carroll Adult Catechesis, Catechetical Svc. Awards, Central Vicariate Catechetical Coord.Tel: 516-678-5800, Ext. 542; Sr. Judith O'Brien, I.H.M., Coord. Human Sexuality Education. Tel: 516-678-5800, Ext. 229.

Catholic Charities—Ms. Laura A. Cassell, Exec. Dir., 90 Cherry Ln., Hicksville, 11801. Tel: 516-733-7013 See separate listing below.

Catholics of African Ancestry—Mrs. Vanessa Baird-Streeter, Dir. Tel: 516-678-5800, Ext. 239; Fax: 516-255-3780. Email: elvan@aol.com.

Cemeteries—Mr. Neal S. Barlin, Dir., Catholic Cemeteries, Diocese of Rockville Centre, P.O. Box 182, Westbury, 11590. Tel: 516-334-7990; Fax: 516-334-4383. Email: director@holyroodcemetery.org. Web: www.holyroodcemetery.org; Holy Rood Cemetery, 111 Old Country Rd., Box 182, Westbury, 11590-0182. Tel: 516-334-7990; Fax: 516-334-4383. Holy Sepulchre Cemetery, 3442 Rte. 112, Coram, 11727. Tel: 631-732-3460; Fax: 631-732-3476. Queen of All Saints Cemetery, 115 Wheeler Rd., Central Islip, 11722. Tel: 631-234-8297; Fax: 631-234-8632.

Chaplains (Uniformed)—

Co-Chaplains of the Nassau County Firemen's Association—Rev. Msgr. John F. Bennett, St. Christopher, Baldwin; Rev. Kevin Smith, St. Francis de Sales, Patchogue.

Chaplains of the Nassau County Police Department—Rev. Msgr. John A. Alesandro, St. Dominick, Oyster Bay; Rev. Joseph D'Angelo, Dir. Campus Ministry; Rev. Msgr. Thomas Hartman, Dir. Telecare.

Chaplains of the Suffolk County Police Department—Revs. James Kissane, Pastor, St. John of God, Central Islip; Bruce Powers, Pastor, St. Elizabeth, Melville.

Charismatic Renewal—Sr. Marcella Purpura, C.S.J.; Deacon Filipe J. Sin, Hispanic Charismatic Renewal, P.O. Box 1301, Brentwood, 11717. Tel: 631-952-7400; Fax: 631-952-7403.

Consultation Service for Religious Personnel—Sr. Mildred Schubert, S.C., Exec. Dir., P.O. Box 467, Rockville Centre, 11571. Tel: 516-678-2135.

Deacons—Deacon James W. Flannery, Dir., Seminary of the Immaculate Conception, Office of Deacons, 440 W. Neck Rd., Huntington, 11743. Tel: 631-424-8360; Fax: 631-424-8361. Email: jflannery@drvc.org.

Diocesan Attorney—Mr. George Rice, Spellman, Walsh, Rice, Schure and Markus, LLP, 229 Seventh St., P.O. Box 7775, Garden City, 11530. Tel: 516-747-1640; Fax: 516-747-0825. Email: grice@spellmanlaw.com.

Diocesan Services, Inc.—Mr. Kevin T. Murphy, Dir. Tel: 516-678-5800, Ext. 543.

Due Process (Conciliation-Arbitration)—Sr. Lucy Blyskal, C.S.J., J.C.D., Admin., St. Joseph Renewal Center, 1725 Brentwood Rd., Brentwood, 11717-5587. Tel: 631-273-1187, Ext. 32; Fax: 631-273-1451. Email: dueprocess@drvc.org.

Ecumenical & Interreligious Affairs—Rev. Msgr. Donald M. Beckmann, Dir. Tel: 516-678-5800, Ext. 613; Fax: 516-763-1078.

Education—Sr. Joanne Callahan, O.S.U., M.S., P.D., Supt. Tel: 516-678-5800, Ext. 548; Fax: 516-678-7362. Email: education@edrvc.org; Dr. Joanne O'Brien, M.A., M.Ed., Ed.D., Assoc. Supt. Tel: 516-678-5800, Ext. 546; Sisters Lorraine McDonald, O.P., M.S., P.D., Asst. Supt. Elementary Schools. Tel: 516-678-5800, Ext. 545; Kathleen Egan, C.S.J., M.A., Asst. Supt. Public Policy & Govt. Programs. Tel: 516-678-5800, Ext. 555; Mr. Biagio Arpino, M.S., P.D., Dir. Teacher Personnel. Tel: 516-678-5800, Ext. 553; Ms. Rosemary Damm, M.A., Dir. Curriculum & Instruction. Tel: 516-678-5800, Ext. 551; Sisters Catherine Stare, S.C., M.S., M.A., Dir. Curriculum & Testing. Tel: 516-678-5800, Ext. 550; Antoinette De Aveiro, O.P., M.S., Dir. Early Childhood Programs. Tel: 516-678-5800, Ext. 277; Mrs. Penny Curry, M.S., Dir. Technology. Tel: 516-678-5800, Ext. 404.

Financial Affairs—

Chief Fiscal Officer, Corporate Chancellor and Diocesan Finance Officer—Mr. Kevin T. Murphy. Tel: 516-678-5800, Ext. 543; Fax: 516-536-6554. Email: ktmurphy@drvc.org.

Controller's Office—Mr. Raymond J. Calame, Controller. Tel: 516-678-5800, Ext. 534; Fax: 516-536-6554. Email: rcalame@drvc.org.

Diocesan Services, Inc.—Mr. Kevin T. Murphy, Sec. & Treas. Tel: 516-678-5800, Ext. 543.

Facilities and Risk Management—Mr. William G. Chapin, Dir. Tel: 516-678-5800, Ext. 261; Fax: 516-763-2606. Email: wgchapin@drvc.org.

Human Resources—Mr. Raymond J. Calame, Interim Dir. Tel: 516-678-5800, Ext. 534; Fax: 516-678-9566.

Treasury Operations—Mrs. Maureen T. Scaduto, Dir. Tel: 516-678-5800, Ext. 526; Fax: 516-536-6554. Email: mtscaduto@drvc.org.

Haitian-American Apostolate Ministry—Rev. Moise Aime, Dir.; Ms. Maryse Emmanuel-Garcy, Coord.; Ms. Maryse Sajous, Sec., 333 N. Main St., Freeport, 11520. Tel: 516-868-8076; Fax: 516-868-0075.

Health Care Apostolate—Catholic Health Services of Long Island, 992 N. Village Ave., Rockville Centre, 11570. Tel: 516-705-3700. Mr. Patrick Scollard, Interim CEO, Catholic Health Svcs.; Mrs. Cathy Grandjean, 1010 Rte. 112, Port Jefferson Station, 11776. Tel: 631-474-5663; Fax: 631-331-0586 For individual hospitals and other healthcare institutions see separate listings below.

Information Bureau—Mrs. Joanne C. Novarro, Dir., Office Public Information. Tel: 516-678-5800, Ext. 632; Fax: 516-594-0984. Email: rvcinfo@drvc.org.

Information Technology—Mrs. Maureen T. Scaduto, Dir. Tel: 516-678-5800, Ext. 526; Fax: 516-536-6554. Email: mtscaduto@drvc.org; Eva Casale, Information Systems Mgr. Tel: 516-678-5800, Ext. 515. Email: ecasale@drvc.org; Eugene Lyktey, IT Technician. Tel: 516-678-5800, Ext. 514. Email: elyktey@druc.org; Brian Wasson, Training Specialist. Tel: 516-678-5800, Ext. 528. Email: bwasson@drvc.org; Edward Tomczyk, Level II - Help Desk Support. Tel: 516-678-5800, Ext. 292. Email: etomczyk@drvc.org.

Institutional Advancement—Mr. Jeff Turocy, Dir., 200 W. Centennial Ave., Roosevelt, 11575. Tel: 516-379-5210, Ext. 226; Fax: 516-379-5043. Email:

jturocy@drvc.org.

Laity and Family—Sr. LAUREN HANLEY, C.S.J., Dir. Tel: 516-678-5800, Ext. 539; Fax: 516-594-8385; 516-535-3473. Email: lhanley@drvc.org. Assistant Directors: Sr. MAUREEN JESSNIK, R.S.M., Ministry Formation. Tel: 516-678-5800, Ext. 210; Mrs. CLAIRE STIGLIC, Pastoral Formation Institute. Tel: 516-678-5800, Ext. 596; Mrs. LINDA REICH, Ministry to Families. Tel: 516-678-5800, Ext. 538. Coordinators: Mrs. ALYCIA GORMAN, Marriage Preparation. Tel: 516-678-5800, Ext. 223; Ms. DIANE VELLA, Curriculum. Tel: 516-678-5800, Ext. 222; Mrs. CAROL CELLA, Collaborative Formation. Tel: 516-678-5800, Ext. 592; Deacon FRED QUINONES, Multi-Cultural Ministry. Tel: 516-678-5800, Ext. 200; Mrs. ELAINE STILLWELL, Bereavement. Tel: 516-678-5800, Ext. 628; Mrs. MARGE TORCHIA, Golden Wedding. Tel: 516-678-5800, Ext. 224. Regional Directors: Mrs. CAROL CALLAN, Eastern Suffolk; Mrs. PATRICIA CHAPIN, Western Suffolk; Mrs. MARCIA JOHNSON, Central; Mrs. ELENA SANCHEZ, Nassau. Consultants: Mrs. PATRICIA MEGALE; Rev. Msgr. VINCENT RUSH.

Marian Renewal—Sr. MARCELLA PURPURA, C.S.J., Coord., P.O. Box 1301, Brentwood, 11717. Tel: 631-952-7400; Fax: 631-952-7403.

Migration Office—Mr. JOHN K. BINGHAM, Dir. Immigrant Svcs. Catholic Charities, 143 Schleigel Blvd., Amityville, 11701. Tel: 631-789-5210; Fax: 631-789-5245.

Mission Office— Society for the Propagation of the Faith, Holy Childhood Association, Catholic Relief Services, Diocesan Mission in the Dominican Republic, American Home Missions, Secretariat for Latin America. Bro. WILLIAM BOSLET, O.S.F., Dir. Tel: 516-678-5800, Ext. 513; Fax: 516-594-0064. Email: wboslet@drvc.org.

Newspaper - "The Long Island Catholic"— (published by the Catholic Press Association of the Diocese of Rockville Centre, Inc.) Ms. ELIZABETH O'CONNOR, Assoc. Publisher & Editor, 200 W. Centennial Ave., Ste. 201, P.O. Box 9000, Roosevelt, 11575. Tel: 516-594-1000; Fax: 516-594-1092. Email: editor@licatholic.org (editorial). Web: www.licatholic.org. Email: adstlic@licatholic.org (advertisements).

Office for the Protection of Children & Young People—EILEEN PUGLISI, Dir. Tel: 516-678-5800, Ext. 573; Fax: 516-887-1584. Email: epuglisi@drvc.org.

Parish Stewardship—200 W. Centennial Ave., Ste. 202, Roosevelt, 11575. Tel: 516-379-4055; Fax: 516-379-3234. Email: stewardship@prodigy.net. Web: www.stewardshipli.org. Mr. ROBERT P. CAMMARATA, Dir.; Ms. LAURIE WHITFIELD, Assoc. Dir.; Mr. JOHN RAVICH, Training & Support Specialist; Mrs. GEORGENA MCCANDLESS, Program Svcs. Coord.

Priest Personnel—Rev. Msgr. FRANCIS J. CALDWELL, C.S.W., Dir. Tel: 516-678-5800, Ext. 585; Fax: 516-764-3467. Email: fcaldwell@drvc.org.

Priestly Life and Ministry—Rev. THOMAS F. MULVANERTY, Dir., St. Pius X Residence, 11220 Front St., Uniondale, 11553. Tel: 516-485-4200; Fax: 516-485-0596.

Priests' Personnel Assignment Board—Most Revs. JOHN C. DUNNE, D.D.; PAUL H. WALSH, D.D.; EMIL A. WCELA, D.D.; Rev. Msgrs. ROBERT J. BRENNAN; FRANCIS J. CALDWELL, C.S.W., Chm.; Revs. WILLIAM G. BRESLAWSKI; THOMAS W. GROENEWOLD; WILLIAM E. KOENIG; JOSEPH W. STAUDT; Mrs. PATRICIA FERGUS, Sec.

Priests' Personnel Policy Board—Rev. Msgr. FRANCIS J. CALDWELL, C.S.W.; Rev. EDWARD R. D'ANDREA, M.Div.; Rev. Msgr. JOHN BENNETT; Revs. BRIAN J. MCNAMARA; THOMAS F. MULVANERTY; THOMAS G. SALOY; JOSEPH M. SCHLAFER.

Priests' Retirement Board—Most Rev. JOHN C. DUNNE, D.D.; Rev. THOMAS F. MULVANERTY; Rev. Msgr. FRANCIS J. CALDWELL, C.S.W.; Rev. ROBERT J. CLERKIN; Rev. Msgrs. GEORGE P. GRAHAM, J.C.D., Ph.D. (Retired); ROBERT E. GUGLIELMONE; JOHN P. MARTIN; THADDEUS ROONEY (Retired); JAMES P. SWIADER.

Prison Ministry and Criminal Justice Affairs—26 S. Saxon Ave., Bay Shore, 11706-8920. Tel: 631-969-0837; Fax: 631-666-5073. Bro. JACK MOYLAN, O.S.F., D.Min., Dir.; SUZANNE D. JONES, Coord. Ministerial Svcs.

Nassau County Correctional Center—100 Carman Ave., East Meadow, 11554-1146. Tel: 516-572-4145; 516-572-3622. Chaplains: Rev. RALPH FERRO; Sr. VIRGINIA WATERS, F.S.P.; Bro. BILL CAWLEY, S.C.

Nassau County Juvenile Detention Center—61 Carman Ave., Westbury, 11590. Tel: 516-571-9153. Bro. JACK MOYLAN, O.S.F., D.Min., Chap.

Suffolk County Correctional Facility—100 Center Dr., Riverhead, 11901. Tel: 631-852-2294; 631-852-2728. Chaplains: Sr. MICHELLE BREMER, C.S.F.N.; Deacon CHRIS VIGLIOTTA.

Suffolk County Minimum Security Facility—P.O. Box 69, Yaphank, 11980. Tel: 631-852-4713. Chaplains: Sr. MICHELLE BREMER, C.S.F.N.; Deacon JOHN SULLIVAN.

Religious—Vicars for Religious: Sr. MARYANNE FITZGERALD, S.C. Tel: 516-678-5800, Ext. 589. Email: mfitzgerald@drvc.org; Bro. WILLIAM BOSLET, O.S.F. Tel: 516-678-5800, Ext. 588.

Religious Retirement Fund—Mrs. KATHLEEN MULVEY, Dir. Tel: 516-379-5210, Ext. 210; Fax: 516-379-5043. Email: bishopappeal@drvc.org.

Respect Life—Co-Directors: Mrs. MARY BOSSART; Mrs. MADELINE WILLI, 200 W. Centennial Ave., Roosevelt, 11575. Tel: 516-379-8292, Ext. 224 &; Fax: 516-379-0041.

Spanish Apostolate—Rev. Msgr. PABLO M. RODRIQUEZ, Vicar for Hispanics. Tel: 516-489-3675.

Office of Hispanic Ministry—Mr. MANUAL J. RAMOS, Dir. Tel: 516-678-5800, Ext. 617; Deacon LUIS GIRALDO, Youth Coord. Tel: 516-678-5800, Ext. 636; Mr. MIGUEL LEON, Formation Coord. Tel: 516-678-5800, Ext. 617; Ms. MARTA G. MOSCOSO, Editor Hispanic Newspaper. Tel: 516-594-1000, Ext. 38; Mr. CESAR GONZALEZ, Producer Spanish TV Program. Tel: 516-538-8704, Ext. 128. Brookhaven: Revs. ANDREW CONNOLLY, Coord.; FREDDY LOZANO. Tel: 631-475-3847. North Fork: Sr. MARGARET SMYTH, O.P., Coord. Tel: 631-369-4601. South Fork: Revs. ORLANDO CARDONA, C.M.; AUGUSTO CORTEZ, C.M.; Mrs. ANA MARIA BENITEZ. Tel: 631-286-9647. Hampton Bays Ministry: Sisters FRANCES LANE, Coord.; MARY LANG; ELIZABETH MEEHAN. Tel: 631-728-5558.

Synod Office—Tel: 516-678-5800, Ext. 242. Email: synod@drvc.org.

Television (Telecare/TV 29)—1200 Glenn Curtiss Blvd., Uniondale, 11553. Tel: 516-538-8700; Fax: 516-489-9701. Email: info@telecaretv.org. Rev. Msgr. THOMAS J. HARTMAN, Dir.; VERONICA ALLOCCA, Vice Pres. Devel.; KATHY DULANTO, Vice Pres. Sponsorship; RICHARD HAEMMERLE, Station Mgr.

Victim Assistance Coordinator—EILEEN PUGLISI. Tel: 516-678-5800, Ext. 573. Email: epuglisi@drvc.org.

Vocations—Rev. THOMAS COOGAN, Dir., Vocation Office, 440 W. Neck Rd., Huntington, 11743. Tel: 631-242-9888; Fax: 631-242-9889. Email: vocations@drvc.org. Web: www.drvc.org/vocations. Associate Vocation Directors: Revs. DOUGLAS R. ARCOLEO; BRIAN P. BARR; ROBERT J. BATULE; GERALD CESTARE; GERARD GENTLEMAN, M.A., M.Div.; CHARLES N. MANGANO; Rev. Msgr. JAMES M. MCDONALD; Revs. BRIAN J. MCNAMARA; JOSEPH J. NIXON, M.A., M.Div.; MICHAEL J. RIEDER; Rev. Msgr. EDMOND J. TRENCH (Retired); Rev. JAMES C. VLAUN; Mrs. ROSEMARY C. SULLIVAN, Vocation Program Coord.. Email: vocations@drvc.org rsullivan@drvc.org.

Women in the Church and in Society, Diocesan Commission—Rev. Msgr. VINCENT RUSH, Sec. Commission, 50 N. Park Ave., Rockville Centre, 11570.

Worship—Rev. Msgr. RONALD HAYDE, Dir. Tel: 516-678-5800, Ext. 503; Fax: 516-255-3786. Email: worship@drvc.org; Sr. SHEILA BROWNE, R.S.M., Coord., Catechumenate. Tel: 516-678-5800, Ext. 231.

Youth and Young Adult Ministry—Mr. MICHAEL G. MCCARTHY, Dir. Tel: 516-678-5800, Ext. 522. Email: youth@drvc.org; Mrs. MARIANNE COLLINS, CYO. Tel: 516-678-5800, Ext. 238. Email: cyo@drvc.org; Mr. AUSTIN CANNON, Scouting. Tel: 516-678-5800, Ext. 245. Email: scouting@drvc.org.

Diocesan Organizations

Apostleship of Prayer—Rev. Msgr. JAMES M. MCDONALD, Dir., 35 N. Service Rd., Dix Hills, 11746. Tel: 631-499-8520; Fax: 631-499-1530.

Catholic Accountants' Guild—Miss MARY R. GOELLER, Contact Person, 155 Garfield Ave., Mineola, 11501. Tel: 516-746-1223.

Catholic Lawyer's Guild—Rev. Msgr. GEORGE P. GRAHAM, J.C.D., Ph.D., Chap. (Retired), 3100 Hempstead Turnpike, Levittown, 11756. Tel: 516-731-4220.

Catholic Youth Organization of Nassau and Suffolk—Ms. MARGARET JOHNSON, Dir.; Rev. WILLIAM E. KOENIG, Moderator, 20 E. Cherry St., Hicksville, 11801. Tel: 516-433-1145; Fax: 516-433-1238.

Nocturnal Adoration Society—Rev. Msgr. JAMES M. MCDONALD, Dir., 35 N. Service Rd., Dix Hills, 11746. Tel: 631-499-8520; Fax: 631-499-1530.

Legion of Mary—Rev. JAMES MANNING, S.M.M., Dir., 26 S. Saxon Ave., Bayshore, 11706. Tel: 631-666-7500; Fax: 631-665-4349.

Society of St. Vincent de Paul—249 Broadway, Bethpage, 11714. Tel: 516-822-3132; Fax: 516-822-2728.

Sophia Center—Rev. ROBERT S. SMITH, Dir. (Retired), 440 W. Neck Rd., Huntington, 11743. Tel: 631-423-0483, Ext. 100.

CLERGY, PARISHES, MISSIONS AND PAROCHIAL SCHOOLS

VILLAGE OF ROCKVILLE CENTRE
(NASSAU COUNTY)

1—ST. AGNES CATHEDRAL (1894), Rev. Msgr. James P. Kelly, Rector; Revs. German Villabon, O.S.A.; Gerald Cestare; Augustine Asare Addai (Ghana); Deacon Thomas McDaid. In Res., Rev. Msgrs. Frank J. Caldwell; Ronald E. Hayde; Robert J. Brennan.
Res.: 29 Quealy Pl., 11570. Tel: 516-766-0205; Fax: 516-763-0745.
School—Tel: 516-678-5550; Fax: 516-678-0437. Sr. Kathleen Carlin, Co-Prin.; Helen Newman, Co-Prin. Sisters of St. Dominic 3; Sisters of Charity 1; Lay Teachers 44; Students 893.
Catechesis/Religious Program—Tel: 516-678-2306. Mrs. Donna Eschenauer, D.R.E. Students 1,330.

2—CAMPUS PARISH OF LONG ISLAND (1972), Rev. Joseph J. D'Angelo, M.A.C., M.Div., M.S., C.A.S.A.C. Office: 50 N. Park Ave., 11570. Tel: 516-678-5800, Ext. 614; Fax: 516-763-1078. (For details, please refer to Campus Ministries and Newman Centers under the Institution section).

OUTSIDE VILLAGE OF ROCKVILLE CENTRE

AMITYVILLE, SUFFOLK CO., ST. MARTIN'S (1897), Revs. Richard T. Stelter; Robert J. Batule; Deacons John Sheehan; Richard Ferri.
Res.: 37 Union Ave., 11701. Tel: 631-264-0124; Fax: 631-264-0139.
School—Tel: 631-264-7166; Fax: 631-264-0136. Sisters of St. Dominic (Union Ave.) 1; Lay Teachers 25; Students 515.
Catechesis/Religious Program—Tel: 631-691-1617. Students 351.

BABYLON, SUFFOLK CO., ST. JOSEPH'S (1877), [CEM] Revs. John J. Barrett; Richard F. Kammerer; Francis A. Samuel, O.C.I.; Thomas P. Maloney; Deacons Michael J. Leyden; John F. Sullivan; Barry P. Croce; George F. Nealis. In Res., Rev. John J. Gorman (Retired); Joseph Milazzo, Pastoral Assoc.
Res.: 39 N. Carll Ave., 11702-2701. Tel: 631-669-0068; Fax: 631-669-9175.
Catechesis/Religious Program—Tel: 631-587-4717. Marianne Mione, D.R.E. Students 1,427.
Mission— Oak Beach, Suffolk Co. 11702. (Summer)
Mission— West Gilgo Beach, Suffolk Co. 11702. (Summer)

BALDWIN, NASSAU CO., ST. CHRISTOPHER (1915), Rev. Msgrs. John F. Bennett; Joseph F. Lawlor, Pastor Emeritus (Retired); Rev. Brian McQuade; Deacons Charles Muscarnera; Joseph Pellegrino; Anthony Banno; James Carroll. In Res., Revs. Michael A. Carroll; R. Michael Reid.
Res.: 11 Gale Ave., 11510-3202. Tel: 516-223-0723; Fax: 516-867-5678.
School—21 Pershing Blvd., 11510. Tel: 516-223-4404; Fax: 516-223-1409. Sr. Dolores McLaughlin, Prin.; Miss Joan Hanlon, Asst. Prin. Sisters of St. Joseph 4; Lay Teachers 23; Students 428.
Catechesis/Religious Program—Tel: 516-223-5813; Fax: 516-223-5609. Ms. Marguerite Cassidy, D.R.E.; Mrs. Gail Milne, D.R.E. Students 1,109.

BAY SHORE, SUFFOLK CO., ST. PATRICK'S (1883), [CEM] Rev. Msgr. John C. Nosser, M.S.; Revs. Charles N. Mangano; Gregory Yacyshyn; Deacons Joseph Peralta; Michael Mahoney; Frank Keach. In Res., Rev. Msgr. James F. Coffey, Pastor Emeritus (Retired).
Res.: 9 N. Clinton Ave., 11706. Tel: 631-665-4911; Fax: 631-665-8388.
School—Tel: 631-665-0569; Fax: 631-665-1456. Ms. Cathleen Quinn, Prin. Lay Teachers 33; Students 480.
Catechesis/Religious Program—Tel: 631-665-4914; Fax: 631-665-9009. Students 1,481.

BAYVILLE, NASSAU, ST. GERTRUDE'S (1959), Rev. Peter Kaczmarek.
Res.: 28 School St., 11709. Tel: 516-628-1113; Fax: 516-628-9032.
Catechesis/Religious Program—Tel: 516-628-2432; Fax: 516-628-0224. Students 500.

BELLMORE, NASSAU CO., ST. BARNABAS THE APOSTLE (1912), Revs. Peter C. Dooley; Edward J. Muhs, Pastor Emeritus (Retired); Gilbert D. Lap; Anthony Iaconis; Deacons Bernard Sherlock; Thomas Coleman. In Res., Rev. Msgr. Charles A. Guarino, J.C.D., M.A., M.Div.
Res.: 2320 Bedford Ave., 11710. Tel: 516-785-0054;

Fax: 516-221-7789.
School—St. Elizabeth Ann Seton Regional School, Tel: 516-785-5709; Fax: 516-785-4468. See Regional Schools under Institutions Located in the Diocese.
Catechesis/Religious Program—Tel: 516-785-0130. Students 1,895.

BELLPORT, SUFFOLK CO., MARY IMMACULATE (1905), Rev. Gennaro J. DiSpigno. In Res., Rev. Patrick Fitzgerald.
Res.: 16 Brown's Ln., 11713. Tel: 631-286-0154; Fax: 631-286-2937.
School—Holy Angels Regional School, Patchogue, Tel: 631-475-0422; Fax: 631-475-2641. See Regional Schools under Institutions Located in the Diocese.
Catechesis/Religious Program—Tel: 631-286-3504; Fax: 631-286-2937. Students 549.

BETHPAGE, NASSAU CO., ST. MARTIN OF TOURS (1923), Revs. Thomas J. Siconolfi, C.SS.R.; Thomas Schmidt, C.SS.R.; John McKenna, C.SS.R.; Vincent Crotty, C.SS.R.; Deacons James A. Biggin; Eugene Capobianco; Frank Carrello; Thomas Hennessy
Res.: 40 Seaman Ave., 11714. Tel: 516-931-0818; Fax: 516-931-0559.
School—St. John Baptist de LaSalle Regional School, Bethpage/Farmingdale, Tel: 516-931-0983. Elizabeth F. Ceccarini, Prin. See Regional Schools under Institutions Located in the Diocese.
Catechesis/Religious Program—208 Broadway, 11714. Tel: 516-822-9768; Fax: 516-932-8454. Annemarie Ryan, D.R.E. Students 250.

BLUE POINT, SUFFOLK CO., OUR LADY OF THE SNOW (1917), Revs. Diarmuid F. McGann; Richard M. Scanlon, Pastor Emeritus (Retired); Deacons Robert Gronenthal; Steve Kramer; Frank Hartmann.
Res.: 175 Blue Point Ave., 11715. Tel: 516-363-6385; Fax: 516-363-7394.
School—Prince of Peace Regional School, Sayville, Tel: 516-589-3426. See Regional Schools under Institutions Located in the Diocese.
Catechesis/Religious Program—Tel: 516-363-6394; Fax: 516-589-3426. Students 1,109.

BOHEMIA, SUFFOLK CO., ST. JOHN NEPOMUCENE (1919), [CEM] Revs. James L. Wood; Louis L. Reuss, Pastor Emeritus (Retired); Kevin W. Gruber; Sr. Phyllis Esposito, C.S.J., Pastoral Assoc.; Deacons James Bohuslaw; Anthony Cusumano; George Reich; Roger Mott.
Res.: 1140 Locust Ave., 11716. Tel: 631-589-0540; Fax: 631-244-8086.
School—Prince of Peace Regional School, Sayville, Tel: 631-589-0422. See Regional Schools under Institutions Located in the Diocese.
Catechesis/Religious Program—1150 Locust Ave., 11716. Tel: 631-567-1765. Mrs. Cathy Roberts, D.R.E.; Ms. Mary Lou Razzagone, D.R.E. Students 1,762.

BRENTWOOD, SUFFOLK CO.
1—ST. ANNE'S (1895), Revs. Thomas J. St. Pierre, Co-Pastor; Gerald S. Twomey, Co-Pastor; James J. Hannon; Deacons Juan Diaz, Pastoral Assoc.; Terence A. Rasanen; Thomas R. Samson; John E. Walters.
Res.: 88 Second Ave., 11717. Tel: 631-273-8113; Fax: 631-436-7914.
School—Our Lady of Providence Regional School, Central Islip, Tel: 631-234-6324; Fax: 631-234-6360. See Regional Schools under Institutions Located in the Diocese.
Catechesis/Religious Program—Tel: 631-231-7344. Students 763.
2—ST. LUKE (1965), (Hispanic), [JC] Rev. Lawrence Duncklee; Deacons John Trodden; Richard A. Luken; Wenceslao Rivera.
Res.: 266 Wicks Rd., 11717. Tel: 631-273-1110; Fax: 631-951-2779.
School—Our Lady of Providence Regional School, Central Islip, Tel: 631-234-6535. See Regional Schools under Institutions located in the Diocese.
Catechesis/Religious Program—Tel: 631-273-4333. Students 686.

BRIDGEHAMPTON, SUFFOLK CO., QUEEN OF THE MOST HOLY ROSARY (1922), Rev. Msgr. Ronald Richardson.
Mailing Address: P.O. Box 3035, 11932. Tel: 631-537-0156; Fax: 631-537-7116.
School—Stella Maris Regional School, Sag Harbor, Tel: 631-725-2525; Fax: 631-725-4587.

See Regional Schools under Institutions Located in the Diocese.

BROOKVILLE, NASSAU CO., ST. PAUL THE APOSTLE (1962), Rev. Robert J. Clerkin.
Res.: Cedar Swamp Rd., Brookville, Glen Head, 11545. Tel: 516-935-1880; Fax: 516-938-3683.
Catechesis/Religious Program—Tel: 516-938-4531. Sr. Regina Kraft, O.P., D.R.E.; Bro. Joseph Bellizzi, S.M., D.R.E. Students 550.

CARLE PLACE, NASSAU CO., CHURCH OF OUR LADY OF HOPE (1987), Rev. Donald M. Hanson; Deacons John T. Hickey; Thomas B. Rich; Raymond J. Tirelli; Patrick J. Dunphy.
Church: 534 Broadway, 11514-1712. Tel: 516-334-6288; Fax: 516-997-4622.
School—St. Brigid/ Our Lady of Hope Regional School, 101 Maple Ave., Westbury, 11590. Tel: 516-333-0580; Fax: 516-333-0590.
Catechesis/Religious Program—Tel: 516-334-4781. Donna Manley, D.R.E. Students 584.

CEDARHURST, NASSAU CO., ST. JOACHIM (1894), Rev. Paul Rahilly; Deacon Frank J. Bono.
Res.: 614 Central Ave., 11516. Tel: 516-569-1845; Fax: 516-569-0117.
School—620 Central Ave., 11516. Tel: 516-569-2290; Fax: 516-374-5158. Sisters of St. Joseph 2; Lay Teachers 13; Students 175.
Catechesis/Religious Program—Tel: 516-295-0878. Students 199.

CENTER MORICHES, SUFFOLK CO., ST. JOHN THE EVANGELIST (1898), Revs. Joseph C. Coschignano; John J. Corcoran, Pastor Emeritus; John J. McCartney; Deacons Galvin Murphy; Chris Vigliotta; Mark Herrmann.
Res.: 25 Ocean Ave., 11934. Tel: 631-878-0009; Fax: 631-874-2466.
School—Our Lady, Queen of Apostles Regional School, Center Moriches, Tel: 631-878 1033; Fax: 631-878-1059. See Regional Schools under Institutions Located in the Diocese.
Catechesis/Religious Program—Tel: 631-878-4141. Students 1,900.

CENTEREACH, SUFFOLK CO., ASSUMPTION OF THE BLESSED VIRGIN MARY (1955), Rev. Msgr. Joseph K. Curley; Revs. William F. Shean; Charles N. Srion.
Res.: 20 Chestnut St., 11720. Tel: 631-585-8760; Fax: 631-585-3601.
Catechesis/Religious Program—Tel: 631-588-6408. Mrs. Jeanne Flynn, D.R.E. Students 1,350.

CENTERPORT, SUFFOLK CO., OUR LADY QUEEN OF MARTYRS (1966), Rev. Msgr. T. Peter Ryan; Sr. Eileen Corcoran, O.P., Pastoral Assoc.; Deacons Joseph Montesano; James Butler. In Res., Rev. Msgr. Joseph F. Colligan, Pastor Emeritus (Retired).
Res.: Prospect and Mill Dam Rds., P.O. Box 609, 11721. Tel: 631-757-8184; Fax: 631-262-0155.
School—Trinity Regional School, East Northport, Tel: 631-261-5130; Fax: 631-266-5345. See Regional Schools under Institutions Located in the Diocese.
Catechesis/Religious Program—Tel: 631-757-0720; Fax: 631-757-3512. Margaret Dritto, D.R.E. Students 1,100.

CENTRAL ISLIP, SUFFOLK CO., ST. JOHN OF GOD (1904), [CEM] Revs. Joseph P. Granata; Michael J. Rieder; Sisters Catherine Peluso, O.P., Pastoral Assoc.; Agnes Claudia Allen, C.S.J., Pastoral Assoc. (Spanish Apostolate); Deacons Ronald J. Gillette, Pastoral Assoc.; Frank Gariboldi, Pastoral Assoc. In Res., Rev. Marc-Arthur Jerome.
Res.: 84 Carleton Ave., 11722. Tel: 631-234-6535; Fax: 631-234-7474.
School—Our Lady of Providence Regional School, Central Islip, Tel: 631-234-6324; Fax: 631-234-6360. See Regional Schools under Institutions Located in the Diocese.
Catechesis/Religious Program—Tel: 631-234-4040. Sr. Diane Morgan, O.P., D.R.E. Students 680.
Parish Outreach Office—Tel: 631-234-1884. Sr. Julianne Spiess, S.S.N.D.
Convent—Sisters of St. Joseph, 330 St. John St., 11722. Tel: 631-234-6533.

COMMACK, SUFFOLK CO., CHRIST THE KING (1959), Revs. Joseph W. Staudt; Simon Fernando; Sean Gann; Sr. Joy Castiglione, O.P., Pastoral Assoc.; Deacon Anthony M. Giambalvo. In Res., Rev. Msgr. Dennis M. Regan.
Res.: 2 Indian Head Rd., 11725. Tel: 631-864-1623; Fax: 631-864-8891.
School—Holy Family Regional School, Commack, Tel: 631-543-0202; Fax: 631-543-0203. See Regional Schools under Institutions Located in the Diocese.
Catechesis/Religious Program—Tel: 631-864-3696; Fax: 631-864-1623. Mrs. Margaret Marconi, D.R.E. Students 1,213.

COPIAGUE, SUFFOLK CO., OUR LADY OF THE ASSUMPTION (1928), Revs. Michael Flynn; Paul Mikas (Poland); Camillo Lugo (Colombia); Deacon Philip Mills Jr.
Res.: Molloy St., 11726. Tel: 631-842-5211; 631-842-5476; Fax: 631-789-5326.
Catechesis/Religious Program—Tel: 631-842-3545. Ruth Durago, D.R.E. Students 1,115.

CORAM, SUFFOLK CO., ST. FRANCES CABRINI (1953), Rev. Nicholas J. Figliola; Deacons Fred Molina; Carmen L. Pagrotta.
Res.: 134 Middle County Rd., 11727. Tel: 631-732-8445; Fax: 631-732-8978.
School—Holy Angels Regional School, Patchogue, Tel: 631-475-0422. See Regional Schools under Institutions Located in the Diocese.
Catechesis/Religious Program—Tel: 631-698-3149. Vincent J. Whitfield, D.R.E. Students 717.

CUTCHOGUE, SUFFOLK CO.
1—OUR LADY OF OSTRABRAMA (1909), (Polish), [JC] Rev. Wladyslaw Rudnicki, Admin.
Res.: 3000 Depot Ln., Box 997, 11935. Tel: 631-734-6446; Fax: 631-734-4117.
School—North Fork Regional Catholic School, Cutchogue, Tel: 631-734-5166. See Regional Schools under Institutions Located in the Diocese.
Catechesis/Religious Program—Students 102.
2—SACRED HEART (1901), [CEM] Revs. Peter A. Allen; John P. Henry, Pastor Emeritus (Retired); Sr. Anne Lynch, R.S.M., Pastoral Assoc.; Deacon John Bopp.
Res.: 27905 Main Rd., P.O. Box 926, 11935-0926. Tel: 631-734-6722; Fax: 631-734-7906.
School—Our Lady of Mercy Regional School, Tel: 631-734-5166. See Regional Schools under Institutions Located in the Diocese.
Catechesis/Religious Program—Tel: 631-734-2568. Sr. Ann Lynch, D.R.E. Students 460.
Mission—Our Lady of Good Counsel Main Rd., Mattituck, Suffolk Co. 11952.

DAVIS PARK, FIRE ISLAND SUFFOLK CO., MOST PRECIOUS BLOOD (1962),, (Summer Mission) Rev. Francis Pizzarelli, S.M.M.
Mailing Address: P.O. Box 358, Port Jefferson, 11777. Tel: 631-928-2377; Fax: 631-473-5210.
Res.: Spindrift Walk, Fire Island, 11728. Tel: 631-597-6525.

DEER PARK, SUFFOLK CO., SS. CYRIL AND METHODIUS (1956), Rev. Msgr. Francis X. Gaeta; Revs. Brian Barr; Caetano F. Costa (India); Francis D. Sang (Vietnam); Frank M. Grieco; Deacons John Fitzpatrick; Charles F. Huber. In Res., Rev. Msgr. Thaddeus Rooney (Retired).
Res.: 125 Half Hollow Rd., 11729-4288. Tel: 631-667-4044; Fax: 631-667-6237.
School—Tel: 631-667-6229; Fax: 631-667-0093. Lay Teachers 26; Students 368; Preschool 34.
Catechesis/Religious Program—Tel: 631-667-6264; Fax: 631-667-7767. Virginia Conzo, D.R.E. Students 1,819.

DIX HILLS, SUFFOLK CO., ST. MATTHEW (1965), Rev. Msgr. James M. McDonald; Revs. Lawrence A. Chadwick; Steven Scarmozzino; Bonaventure Thekkeveetil; Francis B. Nuss; Robert Kayser; Deacons James M. McQuade; James Hanly; Carmine DeStefano.
Res.: 35 N. Service Rd., 11746. Tel: 631-499-8520; Fax: 631-499-1530.
School—Holy Family Regional School, Tel: 631-453-0202. See Regional Schools under Institutions Located in the Diocese.
Catechesis/Religious Program—Tel: 631-499-8521. Theresa Costello, Temp. D.R.E. Students 1,711.

EAST HAMPTON, SUFFOLK CO., MOST HOLY TRINITY (1894), [CEM] Rev. Donald J. Desmond, Pastor.
Res.: 57 Buell Ln., 11937. Tel: 631-324-0134; Fax: 631-329-3552.
Business: 79 Buell Ln., 11937. Tel: 631-324-1444.
School—Stella Maris Regional School, Sag Harbor, Tel: 631-725-2525; Fax: 631-725-4587. See Regional Schools under Institutions Located in the Diocese.
Catechesis/Religious Program—Tel: 631-324-7994. Sharon Burns, D.R.E. Students 407.
Mission—St. Peter the Apostle Main St., Amagansett, Suffolk Co. 11930.

EAST ISLIP, SUFFOLK CO., ST. MARY'S (1898), Rev. Steven J. Peterson; Rev. Msgr. Peter A. Chiara, Pastor Emeritus (Retired); Revs. John Whalen; John R. Moore; Sr. Pat Tippen, Pastoral Assoc.; Kevin Wilson, Pastoral Assoc.
Res.: 20 Harrison Ave., 11730. Tel: 631-581-4266; Fax: 631-581-0112.
School—Tel: 631-581-3423; Fax: 631-581-7509. Biagio Arpino, Prin. Lay Teachers 40; Students 780.
Catechesis/Religious Program—Tel: 631-581-3304. Students 1,599.

EAST MEADOW, NASSAU CO., ST. RAPHAEL (1941), Revs. Thomas J. Haggerty; Michael Rieder; Antony Asir; Deacons Robert Mongillo; Christopher Sisinni; Angelo D'Aversa; Victor Costa; Sr. Judith Enterlin, C.S.J., Pastoral Assoc.; MaryAnn O'Brien, Business Mgr.
Res.: 600 Newbridge Rd., 11554. Tel: 516-785-0236; Fax: 516-783-9578.
School—St. Elizabeth Ann Seton Regional School, East Meadow Campus, Tel: 516-785-7006; Fax: 516-785-7008. See Regional Schools under Institutions Located in the Diocese.
Catechesis/Religious Program—Tel: 516-221-9096. Mrs. Arlene Vosilla, D.R.E. Students 973.

EAST NORTHPORT, SUFFOLK CO., ST. ANTHONY OF PADUA (1951), Rev. Msgr. John R. Dreasen; Revs. John V. O'Farrell; James M. Kissane; Rudy Pesongco; Deacon Robert Braun.
Res.: 20 Cheshire Pl., 11731-2591. Tel: 631-261-1077; Fax: 631-757-0572.
School—Trinity Regional School, East Northport, Tel: 631-261-5130. See Regional Schools under Institutions Located in the Diocese.

Catechesis/Religious Program—Tel: 631-261-1306. Mrs. Judith Corbellini, D.R.E.; Mrs. Eileen Schlee, D.R.E.; Mrs. Patricia Seibert, D.R.E. Students 1,800.

EAST PATCHOGUE, SUFFOLK CO., ST. JOSEPH THE WORKER (1955), Revs. John McHugh, O.F.M.Cap.; Philip Bohan, O.F.M.Cap.; Philip Fabiano, O.F.M.Cap. (MIA).
Res.: 510 Narragansett Ave., 11772. Tel: 631-286-9133; Fax: 631-286-9145.
School—Holy Angels Regional School, Patchogue, Tel: 631-475-0422; Fax: 631-475-2036. See Regional Schools under Institutions Located in the Diocese.
Catechesis/Religious Program—Tel: 631-286-2550. Mrs. Mary Mensch, D.R.E. Students 612.

EAST ROCKAWAY, NASSAU CO., ST. RAYMOND'S (1909), Rev. Msgr. William W. Jablonski; Rev. William V. Singleton, Pastor Emeritus (Retired); Rev. Msgr. Thomas D. Candreva, S.T.L., J.C.D., Pastoral Assoc.; Rev. Francis X. Eisele, Pastoral Assoc.; Deacons Richard W. LaRossa, Pastoral Assoc.; Robert C. Campbell; Thomas Wm. Connolly; Guy Donza, Pastoral Assoc.
Res.: 263 Atlantic Ave., 11518. Tel: 516-593-5000; Fax: 516-887-0554.
School—Tel: 516-593-9010; Fax: 516-593-0986. Sisters, Servants of the Immaculate Heart of Mary 4; Lay Teachers 21; Students 403.
Catechesis/Religious Program—Tel: 516-593-9075. Mrs. Evelyn Contaldi, D.R.E. Students 1,011.

ELMONT, NASSAU CO.

1—ST. BONIFACE (1852), [CEM] Rev. William J. Gomes; Sr. Evelyn Lamoureux, D.W., Human Svcs. In Res., Rev. George Punti.
Res.: 631 Elmont Rd., 11003. Tel: 516-354-0715; Fax: 516-354-0446.
School—Tel: 516-354-6084; Fax: 516-437-5554. Mrs. Kathleen Spollen, Prin. Sisters of St. Dominic 1; Lay Teachers 18; Students 175.
Catechesis/Religious Program—Tel: 516-437-7112. Sr. Peggy Fanning, C.S.J., D.R.E. Students 565.

2—ST. VINCENT DE PAUL (1951), Rev. Donald E. Babinski, M.Div.
Res.: 1500 DePaul St., 11003. Tel: 516-352-2127; Fax: 516-352-2358.
Catechesis/Religious Program—Tel: 516-352-2265. Ms. Mary Alice Burchell, M.A., D.R.E. Students 535.

FARMINGDALE, NASSAU CO., ST. KILIAN (1896), Rev. Msgr. James P. Swiader; Revs. Augustine Fernando (India); Todd C. Saccoccia; Deacons Frank D. Barone; Lucio Cotone; William Griffin; Herman Rodenburg; Vacant (GB); Deacon George Owen; Frank Shanley, Business Mgr. In Res., Most Rev. John C. Dunne, D.D.
Res.: 485 Conklin St., 11735. Tel: 516-249-0127; Fax: 516-249-7131.
School—St. John Baptist de LaSalle Regional School, Bethpage/Farmingdale, Tel: 516-931-0983 (Bethpage); 516-694-3610 (Farmingdale); Fax: 516-931-1502 (Bpg); 516-694-7296 (Fmdl). See Regional Schools under Institutions Located in the Diocese.
Catechesis/Religious Program—Tel: 516-694-0633; Fax: 516-454-8612. Ms. Maryanne Trezza, D.R.E. Students 1,654.
Parish Social Ministy/Outreach—Tel: 516-756-9656. Lisa Molluso, Dir.

FARMINGVILLE, SUFFOLK CO., CHURCH OF THE RESURRECTION (1988), Rev. John M. Derasmo; Deacon Daniel Macellaro.
Church: 50 Granny Rd., 11738. Tel: 631-696-0232; Fax: 631-696-0271.
Catechesis/Religious Program—Tel: 631-696-0270. Rosemarie Hayman, D.R.E. Students 950.

FLORAL PARK, NASSAU CO.

1—ST. HEDWIG'S (1902), (Polish), Revs. Francis E. Filmanski; Chester Diadia; Lejzek Wiecaszek.
Res.: One Depan Ave., 11001. Tel: 516-354-0042; Fax: 516-327-2458.
Catechesis/Religious Program—Students 240.

2—OUR LADY OF VICTORY (1921), Rev. Msgr. Charles J. Nosser; Revs. Thomas Moriarty; John Hein (Vietnam); Deacon Lawrence P. Mulligan.
Res.: 2 Floral Pkwy., 11001-3198. Tel: 516-354-0482; 516-354-0479; Fax: 516-354-7450.
School—2 Bellmore St., 11001. Tel: 516-352-4466; 516-354-2150; Fax: 516-352-2998. Margaret M. Augello, Prin. Religious 3; Lay Teachers 23; Students 487.
Catechesis/Religious Program—Tel: 516-352-0510. Sr. Barbara Kaiser, C.S.J., D.R.E. Students 1,115.

FRANKLIN SQUARE, NASSAU CO., ST. CATHERINE OF SIENNA (1908), Rev. Thomas W. Groenewold; Rev. Msgr. William F. Costello, Pastor Emeritus (Retired); Revs. William D. O'Rourke; Walter F. Kedjierski; Dennis Whelan; Deacons John Fodale; Joseph Benincasa; Douglas Ferreiro.
Res.: 33 New Hyde Park Rd., 11010. Tel: 516-352-0146; Fax: 516-326-7427.
School—990 Holzhimer. Tel: 516-437-2733. Mrs. Diane Staudinger, Prin. Sisters of St. Dominic 1; Lay Teachers 25; Students 440.
Catechesis/Religious Program—Tel: 516-354-4554. Helen Giordano, D.R.E. Students 1,550.

FREEPORT, NASSAU CO., OUR HOLY REDEEMER (1903), (Hispanic), Revs. Richard M. Figliozzi; Joseph Arevalo. In Res., Rev. William Delaney; Deacons James Dunne; Francisco Cales; Bruce A. Burnham; Cristobal Sanchez; Gregory La Freniere.
Res.: 37 S. Ocean Ave., 11520. Tel: 516-378-0665; Fax: 516-546-1416.
Catechesis/Religious Program—Tel: 516-546-1057; Fax: 516-546-0526. Students 725.

GARDEN CITY, NASSAU CO.

1—ST. ANNE (1929), Revs. John D. Gilmartin; Patrick M. Riegger; Deacons Edward Cunningham; Jack McGowan; George Browne; James O'Brien. In Res., Rev. Msgr. William F. Costello (Retired); Rev. Isaac Mensah.
Res.: 35 Dartmouth St., 11530. Tel: 516-352-5904; Fax: 516-352-1360.
School—25 Dartmouth St., 11530. Tel: 516-352-1205; Fax: 516-352-5969. Mr. Robert Parry, Prin. Religious of the Sacred Heart of Mary 2; Lay Teachers 25; Students 479.
Catechesis/Religious Program—Tel: 516-488-1032; Fax: 516-328-8826. Dr. Mary O'Grady, D.R.E. (Grades 1-4); Mrs. Paula Tusiani, D.R.E. (Grades 5-8). Students 1,040.

2—ST. JOSEPH'S (1901), Revs. Joseph M. Schlafer; Laurence Behan.
Res.: 130 Fifth St., 11530. Tel: 516-747-3535; Fax: 516-746-0719.
School—450 Franklin Ave., 11530. Tel: 516-747-2730; Fax: 516-747-2854. Miss Patricia Devine, Prin.; Ms. Florence Puff, Asst. Prin. Lay Teachers 30; Students 442.
Catechesis/Religious Program—Tel: 516-741-7787; Fax: 516-741-5049. Susan Mirabella, D.R.E. Students 962.

GLEN COVE, NASSAU CO.

1—ST. PATRICK'S (1856), [CEM] Revs. Thomas C. Costa; Marian Bicz; Rolando Ticllasuca, M.R.S.M. (Peru); Martin L. Klein; Henry I. Benack (Retired); Mr. Cantalicio Gamarra, Spanish Min.; Deacons Frank Borchardt; Juan Guilfu.
Res.: 235 Glen St., 11542. Tel: 516-676-0276; Fax: 516-674-9137.
For Hispanic Ministry—Tel: 516-759-6039.
School—All Saints Regional Catholic School, Glen Cove, Tel: 516-676-0762; Fax: 516-676-0660. See Regional Schools under Institutions Located in the Diocese.
Catechesis/Religious Program—Tel: 516-671-7223. Sr. Teresa Raftery, I.H.M., D.R.E. Students 640.
Convent—Sisters of St. Dominic, Amityville. Tel: 516-671-0501. Sisters 3.

2—ST. ROCCO (1937), (Italian), Rev. Aaron T. Vellaramparampil. In Res., Rev. Juniper J. Thomas.
Res.: 18 Third St., 11542. Tel: 516-676-2482; Fax: 516-676-2117.
School—All Saints Regional Catholic School, Glen Cove, Tel: 516-676-0762; Fax: 516-676-0660. Sr. Maureen Zellon, R.S.H.M., Prin. See Regional Schools under Institutions Located in the Diocese.
Catechesis/Religious Program—Students 290.

GLEN HEAD, NASSAU CO., ST. HYACINTH (1909), (Polish), Revs. Richard Kopinski; Janusz Lipski; Joseph P. Kozlowski, Pastor Emeritus (Retired); Deacon Robert J. Heintz, (Retired).
Res.: 319 Cedar Swamp Rd., 11545. Tel: 516-676-0361; Fax: 516-674-4728.
School—All Saints Regional Catholic School, Glen Cove, Tel: 516-671-3033. See Regional Schools under Institutions Located in the Diocese.
Catechesis/Religious Program—Tel: 516-676-0361, Ext. 37. Miss Eileen Meserole, D.R.E. Students 200.

GREAT NECK, NASSAU CO., ST. ALOYSIUS (1876), (Hispanic—Korean), Rev. Msgr. Brendan P. Riordan; Revs. Benedict DoHa Bae (Korea, South); Basil C. Colasito (Philippines), Hispanic Ministry. In Res., Rev. Msgr. Alan J. Placa.
Res.: 592 Middle Neck Rd., 11023. Tel: 516-482-2770; Fax: 516-829-3504.
Catechesis/Religious Program—Tel: 516-482-5660; Fax: 516-829-4054. Students 261.

GREENLAWN, SUFFOLK CO., ST. FRANCIS OF ASSISI (1966), (Hatian), Rev. Msgr. Patrick J. Armshaw; Deacon Allan Longo.
Res.: 29 Northgate Dr., 11740. Tel: 631-757-7435; Fax: 631-757-0469.
School—Trinity Regional School, East Northport, Tel: 631-261-5130; Fax: 631-266-5345. See Regional Schools under Institutions Located in the Diocese.
Catechesis/Religious Program—Tel: 631-754-6436. Mrs. Theresa DeMayo, D.R.E. Students 605.

GREENPORT, SUFFOLK CO., ST. AGNES (1886), (Hispanic), [CEM] Rev. Thomas P. Murray.
Res.: Front St., 11944. Tel: 631-477-0048; Fax: 631-477-8519.
School—Our Lady of Mercy, Cutchogue, Tel: 631-734-5166; Fax: 631-734-4266. See Regional Schools under Institutions Located in the Diocese.
Catechesis/Religious Program—Tel: 631-477-1422. Students 163.

HAMPTON BAYS, SUFFOLK CO., ST. ROSALIE'S (1901), Revs. William J. Gill; Sabbas Rodrigues.
Res.: 31 Montauk Hwy., 11946. Tel: 631-728-9461; Fax: 631-728-2559.
School—Our Lady of the Hamptons Regional School, Tel: 631-283-9140; Fax: 631-287-3958. See Regional Schools under Institutions Located in the Diocese.
Catechesis/Religious Program— Sarah Cunliffe, D.R.E. Students 595.
Mission— 31 Montauk Hwy., East Quogue, Suffolk Co. 11946. Tel: 631-653-4471.

HAUPPAUGE, SUFFOLK CO., ST. THOMAS MORE (1967), Rev. Msgr. Francis S. Midura, M.Div., J.C.D.; Joan Dorr, Pastoral Assoc.; Deacon Robert Weisz.
Res.: 115 Kings Hwy., 11788. Tel: 631-234-5551; Fax: 631-234-6412.
School—Holy Family Regional School, Commack, Tel: 631-678-5800; Fax: 631-678-7362. See Regional Schools under Institutions Located in the Diocese.
Catechesis/Religious Program—119 Kings Hwy., 11788. Tel: 631-234-0397; Fax: 631-234-1199. Mrs. Mary Ellen Carroll, D.R.E.; Mrs. Patricia Chapin, D.R.E. Students 1,343.

HEMPSTEAD, NASSAU CO.

1—ST. JOHN CHRYSOSTOM MALANKARA MISSION (1999), Rev. Saji M. George, Admin.
115 Greenwich St., 11550. Tel: 516-539-0414; Fax: 516-568-1906.

2—ST. LADISLAUS (1915), (Polish), Rev. Msgr. Edward Wawerski. In Res., Rev. John Siebor.
Res.: 18 Richardson Pl., 11550. Tel: 516-489-0368; Fax: 516-292-9193.
School—St. Martin de Porres Regional School, Uniondale See Regional Schools under Institutions Located in the Diocese.

3—OUR LADY OF LORETTO (1870), Rev. Msgr. Pablo M. Rodriguez; Rev. Fruto Rosales; Sr. Winifred Cunniff, S.C., Pastoral Assoc.; Deacons Jose Roa; Juan Perez; Mrs. Rosemary Viola.
Res.: 104 Greenwich St., 11550. Tel: 516-489-3675; Fax: 516-485-8371.
School—St. Martin de Porres Regional School, Uniondale, Tel: 516-481-3303; Fax: 516-483-4138. See Regional Schools under Institutions Located in the Diocese.
Catechesis/Religious Program—Tel: 516-483-3643. Students 314.

HEWLETT, NASSAU CO., ST. JOSEPH'S (1872), Rev. Msgr. Charles R. Fink; Deacons Thomas Costello; Joseph Byrne.
Res.: 1346 Broadway, 11557. Tel: 516-374-0290; Fax: 516-374-2598.
Catechesis/Religious Program—1355 Noel Ave., 11557. Tel: 516-569-6080; Fax: 516-374-3664. Frances Acquafredda, D.R.E. Students 443.

HICKSVILLE, NASSAU CO.

1—HOLY FAMILY (1951), (Irish—Italian), Rev. Msgr. Edward J. Donnelly; Revs. Vincent Schifano; Varghese Kocherry, C.Ss.R.; Deacon Joseph G. McNicholas.
Res.: 5 Fordham Ave., 11801. Tel: 516-938-3846; Fax: 516-938-6241.
School—Tel: 516-938-3881; Fax: 516-938-5041. Mrs. Janice Vetter, Prin.; Ms. Jacqueline Lucarelli, Asst. Prin. Sisters of Saint Dominic 2; Lay Teachers 25; Students 550.
Catechesis/Religious Program—Tel: 516-938-3854; Fax: 516-938-3875. Mrs. Carol Nealon, D.R.E. Students 975.

2—ST. IGNATIUS LOYOLA (1859), Rev. Msgr. Donald T. Bennett; Revs. James Carmody; Douglas R. Arcoleo; Frederic J. Harrer, Pastor Emeritus (Retired); Rev. Msgr. Edward L. Tarrant, Pastor Emeritus (Retired). In Res., Rev. Jose Quilcate (Peru).
Res.: 129 Broadway, 11801. Tel: 516-931-0056; Fax: 516-939-0852.
School—30 E. Cherry St., 11801. Tel: 516-931-0831; Fax: 516-933-6528. Sisters Mary Ann Noonan, R.S.M., Prin.; Mary F. O'Donnell, O.P., Prin. Lay Teachers 19; Students 284.
Catechesis/Religious Program—Tel: 516-935-6873. Mary Jane Mastrodomenico, D.R.E.; Sr. Kathleen Corr, O.P., D.R.E. Students 728.

3—OUR LADY OF MERCY (1953), Rev. Robert Y. Blyman; Rev. Msgr. James E. Boesel (Retired); Revs. Charles A. Gartner (Retired); Jose Simon Palliparambil; Thomas P. Tuite Jr.; Sr. Suzanne Le Pre, Pastoral Assoc.
Res.: 500 S. Oyster Bay Rd., 11801. Tel: 516-931-4351; Fax: 516-433-8702.
School—Tel: 516-433-7040; Fax: 516-433-8286. Sr. Mary Joanne Deegan, R.S.M., Prin. Sisters of Mercy 8; Lay Teachers 26; Students 585.

Catechesis/Religious Program—Tel: 516-681-1228. Mrs. Linda Ward, D.R.E. Students 816.
Youth Ministry—Tel: 516-935-2444. Lay Teachers 7; Students 43.

HOLBROOK, SUFFOLK CO., GOOD SHEPHERD (1970), Rev. Thomas L. Spadaro; Rev. Msgr. Thomas S. Kane; Rev. Robert C. Scheckenback; Deacons Robert Hernandez; Paul Chedda.
Res.: 1370 Grundy Ave., 11741. Tel: 631-588-7689; Fax: 631-588-7603.
School—Prince of Peace Regional School, Sayville, Tel: 631-589-3426; Fax: 631-589-4523. See Regional Schools under Institutions Located in the Diocese.
Catechesis/Religious Program—Tel: 631-981-3889. Sisters Lillian Delorme, O.P., D.R.E.; Ellen Zak, C.S.F.N., D.R.E.; Jeanne Cook, D.R.E. Students 2,300.

HUNTINGTON STATION, SUFFOLK CO., ST. HUGH OF LINCOLN (1913), Rev. Msgr. Vincent Rush; Rev. Christopher Nowak, O.S.A.; Deacons Edward W. Billia; Vito B. Taranto; Thomas Reilly; Luis Giraldo; Luis Florces.
Res.: 21 E. Ninth St., 11746. Tel: 631-427-0638; Fax: 631-427-1319.
Parish Center—1450 New York Ave., 11746.
School—Trinity Regional School, East Northport, Tel: 631-261-5130; Fax: 631-266-5345. See Regional Schools under Institutions Located in the Diocese.
Catechesis/Religious Program—Tel: 631-271-6081. Miss Eileen McNamara, D.R.E. Students 1,064.

HUNTINGTON, SUFFOLK CO., ST. PATRICK'S (1849), [CEM] Rev. John Denniston; Rev. Msgr. James B. Richter (Retired); Rev. Steven A. Berbig; Deacon Jules Gagnon; Alan Jones, Business Mgr. In Res., Rev. Thomas Edamattan (India).
Res.: 400 Main St., 11743-3298. Tel: 631-673-5320; Fax: 631-673-4102.
School—360 Main St., 11743-3298. Tel: 631-673-5325; Fax: 631-673-4609. Sr. Maureen McDade, Prin. Sisters 2; Lay Teachers 34; Students 684.
Catechesis/Religious Program—Tel: 631-673-5323. Sisters Frances Viola, D.R.E.; Peggy Ford, D.R.E.; Robert Mahoney, D.R.E. Students 1,824.

INWOOD, NASSAU CO., OUR LADY OF GOOD COUNSEL (1910), Rev. Richard Nilsson; Deacons George Bruck; Hugh Mills.
Res.: 68 Wanser Ave., 11096. Tel: 516-239-0953; Fax: 516-239-0386.
Catechesis/Religious Program—Tel: 516-239-0662. Sr. Kathryn Slevin, C.S.J., D.R.E. Students 351.

ISLAND PARK, NASSAU CO., SACRED HEART (1938), Rev. John J. Tutone, J.C.D., M.Div.
Res.: 282 Long Beach Rd., 11558. Tel: 516-432-0655; Fax: 516-897-7567.
Catechesis/Religious Program—Tel: 516-431-7877. Mrs. Carmel Caracciolo, D.R.E. Students 331.

ISLIP TERRACE, SUFFOLK CO., ST. PETER THE APOSTLE (1962), Rev. Hugh D. Cannon; Deacon Joseph Marfoglio.
Res.: 94 Valley Stream St., 11752. Tel: 631-277-9448; Fax: 631-224-1594.
School—Our Lady of Providence Regional School, Central Islip, Tel: 631-234-6324; Fax: 631-234-6360. See Regional Schools under Institutions Located in the Diocese.
Catechesis/Religious Program—Tel: 631-581-5715. Mrs. Eileen C. Will, D.R.E. Students 196.

KINGS PARK, SUFFOLK CO., ST. JOSEPH'S (1888), Rev. Msgr. Alex F. Manly; Revs. Francis P. Vattakudiyil; Joseph V. Davanzo; Deacons John E. Trodden; Roy Smith.
Parish Center—59 Church St., 11754. Tel: 631-269-6635; Fax: 631-269-7508.
School—Holy Family Regional School, Commack, Tel: 631-543-0202; Fax: 631-543-0203. See Regional Schools under Institutions Located in the Diocese.
Catechesis/Religious Program—Tel: 631-269-4383. Students 1,828.

LAKE RONKONKOMA, SUFFOLK CO., ST. ELIZABETH ANN SETON (1988), Rev. Patrick J. Whitney; Deacons Joseph Maffeo; Robert Gaudioso.
Res.: 800 Portion Rd., 11779. Tel: 631-737-4388; Fax: 631-737-4389.
Catechesis/Religious Program—Tel: 631-737-8915. Mrs. Mary DellaVecchia, D.R.E. Students 1,200.

LEVITTOWN, NASSAU CO., ST. BERNARD (1948), Revs. Gerard A. Ringenback, M.S.Ed., M.A.; Vincent Ritchie, M.S.W., S.J., M.B.A., M.Div., S.T.M. In Res., Rev. Msgr. George P. Graham, J.C.D., Ph.D. (Retired); Revs. Martin J. Hall, M.A. (Retired); Gerard Gentleman, M.A., M.Div.
Res.: 3100 Hempstead Tpke., 11756. Tel: 516-731-4220; Fax: 516-731-4355.
School—Tel: 516-731-4322; Fax: 516-735-0332. Lay Teachers 18; Students 249.
Catechesis/Religious Program—Tel: 516-731-8511; Fax: 516-731-7860. Students 1,600.

LINDENHURST, SUFFOLK CO., OUR LADY OF PERPETUAL HELP (1871), Rev. Msgr. Daniel S. Hamilton; Revs. Vitalis B. Pedzik, Pastoral Assoc.; James T. Stachacz, Pastoral Assoc.; John C. Vatakkummoolayil (India), Pastoral Assoc.; Deacons George P. Connolly, (Retired); Andrew T. Gargiulo; Frank A. Odin.
Res.: 210 S. Wellwood Ave., 11757-4989. Tel: 631-226-7725; Fax: 631-225-9597.
School—Tel: 631-226-0208; Fax: 631-226-4221. Sisters of St. Dominic 1; Lay Teachers 25; Students 540.
Catechesis/Religious Program—Tel: 631-226-2384. Diana Castellano, Coord. Prog. Admin.; Biagio Arpino, Coord. Teaching Training & Curriculum Planning Students 1,850.

LONG BEACH, NASSAU CO.

1—ST. IGNATIUS MARTYR (1926), Rev. William R. Logan; Deacon Thomas J. Evrard. In Res., Rev. Msgr. Edward A. Sweeny, M.Div., J.C.D., Ph.D.
Res.: 721 W. Broadway, 11561. Tel: 516-432-0045; Fax: 516-432-0358.
School—Long Beach Regional Catholic School, Long Beach, Tel: 516-432-8900; Fax: 516-432-8926. See Regional Schools under Institutions Located in the Diocese.
Catechesis/Religious Program—Tel: 516-432-6788. Pam Shannon, D.R.E. Students 541.

2—ST. MARY OF THE ISLE (1915), (Spanish), Rev. Thomas E. Donohoe; Deacons John P. Dunlop; Nelson Laza; Sr. Frances Monuszko, O.P., Pastoral Assoc. & Dir. St. Mary of the Isle Community Center.
Res.: 315 E. Walnut St., 11561. Tel: 516-432-0157; Fax: 516-897-0566.
School—Long Beach Regional Catholic School, Long Beach, Tel: 516-432-8900. See Regional Schools under Institutions Located in the Diocese.
Catechesis/Religious Program—Tel: 516-432-1320. Maryann Specht, D.R.E. Students 425.

LYNBROOK, NASSAU CO., OUR LADY OF PEACE (1941), Rev. William G. Breslawski; Deacons Aniello Squitieri; Thomas Bast. In Res., Revs. Gabriel Miah; Sriyananda Fernando.
Res.: 25 Fowler Ave., 11563. Tel: 516-599-6414; Fax: 516-596 1847.
School—Tel: 516-593-4884; Fax: 516-593-9861. Sisters of Mercy 1; Lay Teachers 17; Students 320.
Catechesis/Religious Program—Tel: 516-593-5150. Students 585.

MALVERNE, NASSAU CO., OUR LADY OF LOURDES (1926), Revs. Donald M. Baier; Edwin J. Collins, Pastor Emeritus (Retired); Richard R. Donovan; John F. Wymes, M.M.; Chux Okochi, Chap. Mercy Medical Center; Deacons Frank Cove; Theodore J. Van De Ven.
Res.: 65 Wright Ave., 11565. Tel: 516-599-1269; Fax: 516-887-9517.
School—76 Park Blvd., 11565. Tel: 516-599-7328; Fax: 516-599-3813. Mr. John A. McQuillan, Prin. Lay Teachers 19; Students 334.
Catechesis/Religious Program—Tel: 516-599-7222; Fax: 516-599-2256. Miss Anne Coghlan, D.R.E. Students 463.

MANHASSET, NASSAU CO., ST. MARY'S (1853), Rev. Msgrs. John J. McCann; John J. Skelly, Pastor Emeritus (Retired); John J. Wiest, Pastor Emeritus (Retired); Rev. Nicholas A. Zientarski. In Res., Rev. Lawrence Vareedayah.
Res.: 1300 Northern Blvd., 11030. Tel: 516-627-0385; Fax: 516-627-6070.
School—1340 Northern Blvd., 11030. Tel: 516-627-0184; Fax: 516-627-3795. Lay Teachers 30; Students 423.
High School—25 Second St., 11030. Tel: 516-627-2092; Fax: 516-627-4383. (Coed)
High School—51 Clapham Ave., 11030. Tel: 516-627-2711; Fax: 516-627-3209. Sisters of the Immaculate Heart of Mary 1; Dominican Sisters 2; Marist Brothers 2; Lay Teachers 59; Students 972.
Catechesis/Religious Program—Tel: 516-627-4028; Fax: 516-627-5543. Students 1,004.

MANORHAVEN, NASSAU CO., OUR LADY OF FATIMA (1948), Rev. Joseph P. Granata.
Res.: 6 Cottonwood Rd., Port Washington, 11050. Tel: 516-767-0781; Fax: 516-767-298_.
Catechesis/Religious Program—Tel: 516-944-8322. Students 163.

MANORVILLE, SUFFOLK CO., ST. PETER & PAUL (1912), Rev. John J. McGratty; Deacon Robert Dejewski.
Res.: 781 Wading River Rd., P.O. Box 207, 11949. Tel: 631-369-1273; Fax: 631-369-7141.
Catechesis/Religious Program—Tel: 631-208-1978. Students 468.

MASSAPEQUA PARK, NASSAU CO., OUR LADY OF LOURDES (1955), Revs. Robert E. Mason; Anthony J. Heinlein; Augustine Pizhayakatt; Deacon Domenick Valdano.
Res.: 855 Carmans Rd., 11762. Tel: 516-541-3270; Fax: 516-797-9851.
School—Tel: 516-798-7926; Fax: 516-798-8159. Lay Teachers 17; Students 264.
Catechesis/Religious Program—379 Linden St., 11762. Tel: 516-799-5179. Students 612.

MASSAPEQUA, NASSAU CO., ST. ROSE OF LIMA (1952), Rev. Msgr. Daniel J. Hurley; Revs. Lawrence A. Sheehan, S.J.; Aloysius Pakianather (Sri Lanka); Andrzej Zglejszewski (Poland); Belevendiram S. Rathinam (India); Deacons Thomas J. Forbes; Frank J. Flood; Francis B. McGuiness; Dennis R. O'Connor.
Res.: 2 Bayview Ave., 11758-7299. Tel: 516-798-4992; Fax: 516-795-7836.
School—Tel: 516-541-1546; Fax: 516-797-0351. Sr. Kathleen Gallina, Prin. Sisters of St. Dominic 1; Lay Teachers 26; Students 443.
Catechesis/Religious Program—Tel: 516-541-1712. Students 2,750.

MASTIC BEACH, SUFFOLK CO., ST. JUDE (1949), Revs. James Atkins; Joseph Baidoo; Rev. Msgr. Ivan Gonzalez; Deacons Thomas Gillen; Kenneth Geoghan.
Res.: 89 Overlook Dr., 11951. Tel: 631-281-5743; Fax: 631-395-5786.
School—Our Lady, Queen of Apostles Regional School, Center Moriches, Tel: 631-878-1033; Fax: 631-874-2466. See Regional Schools under Institutions Located in the Diocese.
Catechesis/Religious Program—Tel: 631-281-2835. Theresa Amorese, D.R.E. Students 1,910.
Parish Human Services Center—89 Overlook Dr., 11951. Tel: 631-281-5634. Laura De Guiseppe, Assoc.Coord.

MEDFORD, SUFFOLK CO., ST. SYLVESTER (1948), Revs. Michael F. Holzmann; Edward J. Kealey; Deacons George J. Riegger; Frank Rivera.
Res.: 68 Ohio Ave., 11763. Tel: 631-475-4506; Fax: 631-475-1057.
School—Holy Angels Regional School, Patchogue, Tel: 631-475-0422; Fax: 631-475-2038. See Regional Schools under Institutions Located in the Diocese.
Catechesis/Religious Program—Tel: 631-475-8191. Students 1,600.

MELVILLE, SUFFOLK CO., ST. ELIZABETH (1962), Revs. Bruce J. Powers; John Thoonunkaparambil (India); Deacon Joseph Mercolino.
Res.: 181 Wolf Hill Rd., 11747. Tel: 631-271-4455; Fax: 631-271-1415.
School—Trinity Regional School, East Northport, Tel: 631-261-5130; Fax: 631-266-5345. See Regional Schools under Institutions Located in the Diocese.
Catechesis/Religious Program—Students 898.

MERRICK, NASSAU CO., CURE OF ARS (1926), Revs. James-Patrick Mannion; Zachary Callahan; Sisters Miriam Michael Joos, O.P., Pastoral Assoc.; Peggy Tully, O.P., Pastoral Assoc.
Res.: 2323 Merrick Ave., 11566. Tel: 516-623-1400; Fax: 516-623-1107.
School—St. Elizabeth Ann Seton Regional School, Bellmore, Tel: 516-785-5709. See Regional Schools under Institutions Located in the Diocese.
Catechesis/Religious Program—Tel: 516-223-3878. Students 944.

MINEOLA, NASSAU CO., CORPUS CHRISTI (1901), (Spanish—Portuguese), Revs. James C. Bowman; Tomaz Gomide; Paul A. Dolan; Deacons John C. Reinhart; Brian J. Mannix. In Res., Rev. Msgrs. Edward L. Tarrant (Retired); Eugene F. Murphy (Retired); Revs. Antony Arulsamy (India), Hospital Chap.; James L. Maltese, Hospital Chap.
Res.: 155 Garfield Ave., 11501. Tel: 516-746-1223; Fax: 516-294-5311.
School—(Grades N-8), 120 Searing Ave., 11501. Tel: 516-746-2966; Fax: 516-739-3363. Mrs. Susan Anaischik, Prin. Sisters of St. Dominic 2; Lay Teachers 15; Students 295.
Catechesis/Religious Program—Tel: 516-294-0631; Fax: 516-294-0352. Mrs. Ursula Bordonaro, D.R.E. Students 632.

MONTAUK, SUFFOLK CO., ST. THERESE OF LISIEUX (1950), Rev. Peter Libasci.
Res.: 55 S. Etna Ave., P.O. Box 5027, 11954. Tel: 631-668-2200; Fax: 631-668-2384.
School—Stella Maris Regional School, Sag Harbor, Tel: 516-725-2525. See Regional Schools under Institutions Located in the Diocese.
School—Day Care/Nursery School, Tel: 631-668-5353. (3 & 4 years old) Children 43.
Catechesis/Religious Program—Tel: 631-668-2460. Students 201.

NESCONSET, SUFFOLK CO., CHURCH OF THE HOLY CROSS (1988), Rev. James McNamara; Sr. Marion Snow, C.S.J., Pastoral Assoc.; Deacons Gerard K. Steffens, Pastoral Team; Owen E. Farley Jr., Pastoral Team.
Res.: 95 Old Nichols Rd., 11767. Tel: 631-265-2200; Fax: 631-265-2229.
Catechesis/Religious Program—Tel: 631-265-2200, Ext. 12. Mrs. Judith Pickel, D.R.E. Students 1,240.

NEW HYDE PARK, NASSAU CO.

1—HOLY SPIRIT (1893), Rev. Anthony M. Stangnelli. In Res., Rev. Ralph Ferro; Deacons Richard Garcia;

Lachlan Cameron.
Res.: 16 S. Sixth St., 11040. Tel: 516-354-0359; Fax: 516-354-2611 (Rectory).
School—13 S. Sixth St., 11040. Tel: 516-354-5566; Fax: 516-354-0325. Mrs. Denise Carlin Seck, Prin. Sisters of St. Dominic (Amityville) 4; Lay Teachers 15; Students 220.
Catechesis/Religious Program—13 S. 6th St., 11040. Tel: 516-354-2363. Students 540.

2—NOTRE DAME (1941), Rev. Msgr. John P. Martin; Revs. John Murray, Pastor Emeritus; William T. Slater; Sisters Judith A. Golden, O.P., Pastoral Assoc.; Margaret Ann Hartigan, R.S.M., Pastoral Assoc.
Res.: 45 Mayfair Rd., 11040. Tel: 516-352-7203; Fax: 516-326-7988.
School— 11040. Tel: 516-354-5618; Fax: 516-354-5373. Mrs. Margaret Moss, Prin. Sisters of St. Dominic (Amityville) 3; Lay Teachers 29; Students 514.
Catechesis/Religious Program—25 Mayfair Rd., 11040. Tel: 516-437-5604. Sr. Mary Jane Coleman, R.S.M., D.R.E. Students 1,002.

NORTH MERRICK, NASSAU CO., SACRED HEART (1952), Rev. Thomas G. Gallagher.
Res.: 720 Merrick Ave., 11566. Tel: 516-379-1356; Fax: 516-379-1610.
School—Merrick, 11566. Tel: 516-378-5797; Fax: 516-378-5797. Sr. Mary Morrin, C.S.J., Prin. Sisters of St. Joseph 4; Lay Teachers 20; Students 330.
Catechesis/Religious Program—Tel: 516-868-9406. Mrs. Cecelia Lerro, D.R.E. Students 1,100.

NORTHPORT, SUFFOLK CO., ST. PHILIP NERI (1894), [CEM] Rev. Peter J. Garry; Deacons John F. Burkart; Andrew Schneider; Sr. Grace Vagnini, C.S.J., Pastoral Assoc. In Res., Rev. Thomas J. Colgan (Retired).
Res.: 344 Main St., 11768. Tel: 631-261-7753; Fax: 631-261-7420.
School—Trinity Regional School, East Northport, Tel: 631-261-5130 (Main); 631-261-8520; Fax: 631-261-8560. See Regional Schools under Institutions Located in the Diocese.
Catechesis/Religious Program—Tel: 631-261-2485; Fax: 631-261-7836. Kathleen Reid, D.R.E.; Carol Arote, D.R.E. Students 876.

OCEAN BEACH, (FIRE ISLAND) SUFFOLK CO., OUR LADY OF THE MAGNIFICAT (1921), Rev. Msgr. Ronald E. Hayde, Co-Admin.; Rev. Robert O. Morrissey, J.C.D., M.Div., Co-Admin.
Mailing Address: P.O. Box 445, 11770. Tel: 631-583-5868.

OCEANSIDE, NASSAU CO., ST. ANTHONY (1927), Revs. Carsten Martensen, S.J.; Claudio Burgaleta, S.J.; Rev. Msgr. Conrad R. Dietz; Revs. Michael A. Guzik, S.J.; Pierce A. Brennan, S.J.; Matthew F. Roche, S.J.; Deacons James W. Flannery; James O'Neill; Anna Maria Sirianni, C.S.W., Parish Outreach Coord. Tel: 516-764-9257.
Res.: 110 Anchor Ave., 11572. Tel: 516-764-0048; 516-764-0665; Fax: 516-764-7726.
Catechesis/Religious Program—Tel: 516-678-3388. Kathy Logan, D.R.E. Students 1,608.

OYSTER BAY, NASSAU CO., ST. DOMINIC'S (1894), Rev. Msgr. John A. Alesandro; Rev. Malcolm J. Burns. In Res., Rev. Msgr. Donald Beckmann, D.Min.
Res.: 93 Anstice St., 11771. Tel: 516-922-4488; Fax: 516-922-9491.
School—35 School St., 11771. Tel: 516-922-4233; Fax: 516-624-7613. Sisters of the Immaculate Heart of Mary 2; Lay Teachers 21; Students 322.
High School—110 Antice St., 11771. Tel: 516-922-4888; Fax: 516-922-4898. Sisters 1; Lay Teachers 37; Students 530.
Catechesis/Religious Program—Tel: 516-922-7788. Students 755.

PATCHOGUE, SUFFOLK CO.

1—ST. FRANCIS DE SALES (1888), [CEM] Rev. Kevin M. Smith; Deacons Martin McIndoe; Fernando J. Quinones; Francisco Diaz-Granados; Sr. Joanna Ohlandt, C.S.J.; Mrs. Anne Boyce, Pastoral Assoc. In Res., Rev. Andrew P. Connolly.
Res.: 7 Amity St., P.O. Box 71, 11772. Tel: 631-475-0161; Fax: 631-475-1481.
School—Holy Angels Regional School, Patchogue, Tel: 631-475-0422; Fax: 631-475-2036. See Regional Schools under Institutions Located in the Diocese.
Catechesis/Religious Program—Tel: 631-289-4339; Fax: 631-475-0161. Elaine Heschl, D.R.E. Students 450.

2—OUR LADY OF MT. CARMEL (1925), (Italian), Revs. Robert J. O'Connell; Alexander L. Sledzaus, Pastor Emeritus (Retired); Deacons Joseph Mystkowski; Bela Kalman; Barbara Cotsifas, Business Mgr.
Res.: 495 New North Ocean Ave., 11772. Tel: 631-475-4739; Fax: 631-447-1030.
School—Holy Angels Regional School, Patchogue, Tel: 631-475-0422; Fax: 631-475-2036. See Regional Schools under Institutions Located in the Diocese.
Catechesis/Religious Program—Tel: 631-289-7327. Frances McMahon, D.R.E. Students 790.

PLAINVIEW, NASSAU CO., ST. PIUS X (1955), Rev. Msgr. Domenick T. Graziadio, M.A. In Res., Elaine D. Hallisey, Pastoral Assoc.; Saivatore Spano, Pastoral Assoc.
Res.: One St. Pius Ct., 11803. Tel: 516-938-3959; Fax: 516-433-6138.
School—St. John Baptist de LaSalle Regional School, Bethpage/Farmingdale, Tel: 516-931-0983 (Bethpage); 516-694-3610 (Farmingdale); Fax: 516-931-1502 (Bthpg.); 516-694-3614 (Fmgdl.). See Regional Schools under Institutions Located in the Diocese.
Catechesis/Religious Program—Tel: 516-822-8348. Students 385.
Spirit Life Center—300 Washington Ave.. Tel: 516-938-7119; Fax: 516-938-7225. Rev. Robert A. McGuire, S.J.

POINT LOOKOUT, NASSAU CO., OUR LADY OF THE MIRACULOUS MEDAL (1937), (Irish), Revs. Patrick J. Callan; Andrew J. Gallagher, Pastor Emeritus (Retired).
Res.: 75 Parkside Dr., 11569. Tel: 516-431-2772; Fax: 516-432-8669.
School—Long Beach Regional Catholic School, Long Beach, Tel: 516-432-8900; Fax: 516-432-8926. See Regional Schools under Institutions Located in the Diocese.
Catechesis/Religious Program—Tel: 516-432-8074. Students 100.

PORT JEFFERSON, SUFFOLK CO.

1—ST. GERARD MAJELLA (1968), Revs. William A. Hanson, Co-Pastor; Christopher J. Heller, Co-Pastor; Deacon Thomas O'Connor, Co-Pastor.
Res.: 300 Terryville Rd., Port Jefferson Station, 11776. Tel: 631-473-2900; Fax: 631-473-0015.
School—Our Lady of Wisdom Regional School, Port Jefferson, Tel: 631-473-1211; Fax: 631-473-1064. See Regional Schools under Institutions Located in the Diocese.
Catechesis/Religious Program—Tel: 631-928-2550. Fran Bursztyn, D.R.E. Students 1,430.

2—INFANT JESUS (1903), Revs. Charles Romano; Andrew Nierengarten; Eric Dadson; Deacons William J. Powers; Richard E. Waldmann.
Res.: 110 Myrtle Ave., 11777. Tel: 631-473-0165; Fax: 631-331-8094.
School—Our Lady of Wisdom Regional School, Port Jefferson, Tel: 631-473-1211; Fax: 631-473-1064. See Regional Schools under Institutions Located in the Diocese
Catechesis/Religious Program— 11777. Tel: 631-928-0447. Mrs. Barbara Saulino, D.R.E. Students 1,400.

PORT WASHINGTON, NASSAU CO., ST. PETER OF ALCANTARA (1901), Rev. Msgrs. Daniel A. Picciano; Walter E. Simmons, Pastor Emeritus (Retired); Rev. Robert A. Romeo; Deacons Frank G. D'Angelo; Francis B. McGuinness, Business Mgr.
Res.: 1327 Port Washington Blvd., 11050. Tel: 516-883-6675; Fax: 516-944-7461.
School—Tel: 516-944-3772; Fax: 516-767-8075. Dr. Robert Fredericks, Prin. Sisters 4; Lay Teachers 26; Students 568.
Catechesis/Religious Program—Tel: 516-883-5584. Dr. Timothy B. Kunz, D.R.E. Students 500.
Convent—Sisters, Servants of the Immaculate Heart of Mary (Scranton, PA), 1317 Port Washington Blvd., 11050. Tel: 516-762-1282.

RIVERHEAD, SUFFOLK CO.

1—ST. ISIDORE'S (1903), (Polish), [CEM] Rev. Msgr. John J. Mirecki, Riverhead, NY St. Isidore; Revs. Kenneth M. Zach; Joseph Walas (Poland), Pastoral Assoc.
Res.: 622 Pulaski St., 11901. Tel: 631-727-2114; Fax: 631-369-3566.
School—515 Marcy Ave., 11901. Tel: 631-727-1650; Fax: 631-727-3945. Sr. Linda Joseph Chichi, C.S.F.N., Prin. Sisters of the Holy Family of Nazareth 2; Lay Teachers 17; Students 282.
Catechesis/Religious Program—Students 121.

2—ST. JOHN THE EVANGELIST (1861), [CEM] Rev. Thomas W. Coby. In Res., Most Rev. Emil A. Wcela, D.D.; Deacon John Lovett.
Res.: 546 St. John's Pl., 11901. Tel: 631-727-2030; Fax: 631-369-5228.
Catechesis/Religious Program—Tel: 631-727-6774. Students 525.

ROCKY POINT, SUFFOLK CO., ST. ANTHONY OF PADUA (1948), Revs. Richard P. Hoerning; Michael T. Maffeo.
Res.: 614 Rte. 25A, 11778. Tel: 631-744-2609; Fax: 631-744-5782.
Catechesis/Religious Program—Tel: 631-821-0872. Sr. Phylis O'Dowd, O.P., D.R.E. Students 1,657.

RONKONKOMA, SUFFOLK CO., ST. JOSEPH'S (1910), Revs. Michael T. Maffeo; Paul F. Butler; Peter Devaraj; Peter T. Liu (Retired); Deacons James Altonji; Michael J. DeBellis; Joseph Dougherty; Joseph Califano; Michael DeVenney.
Res.: 45 Church St., 11779-3300. Tel: 631-588-8456; Fax: 631-471-2569.
School—25 Church St., 11779. Tel: 631-588-4760; Fax: 631-588-0543. Mrs. Marie Salvietti, Prin. Lay Teachers 24; Students 403.
Catechesis/Religious Program—Tel: 631-981-1805. Students 1,312.

ROOSEVELT, NASSAU CO., QUEEN OF THE MOST HOLY ROSARY (1919), Most Rev. Paul H. Walsh, D.D.; Very Rev. Francis E. Peluso, O.A.R. (NY); Sr. Kathleen O'Donnell, S.C., Pastoral Assoc.; Deacons Clinton Lewis; Thomas Jackson.
Res.: 196 W. Centennial Ave., 11575. Tel: 516-378-1315; Fax: 516-378-5754.
Catechesis/Religious Program—200 W. Centennial Ave., 11575. Tel: 516-623-1391. Students 200.

ROSLYN, NASSAU CO., ST. MARY'S (1871), Rev. Msgr. Richard C. Bauhoff, J.C.D., Ph.D.; Deacons Edward M. Case; Jorge Coyoy; James DiGiovanna.
Res.: 110 Bryant Ave., P.O. Box 387, 11576-0387. Tel: 516-621-2222; Fax: 516-621-7892.
School—All Saints Regional Catholic School, Glen Cove, Tel: 516-676-0762; Fax: 516-676-0660. See Regional Schools under Institutions Located in the Diocese.
Catechesis/Religious Program—Tel: 516-621-6798. Nora Toal, D.R.E. Students 306.

ST. JAMES, SUFFOLK CO., SS. PHILIP AND JAMES (1907), Revs. Brian J. McNamara; Martin J. Bancroft Jr., Parochial Vicor; Deacons Charles Brown; Kenneth Maher; Frank Crivello; Robert Heschl; John Keenan; Anthony Chamberlain; Gerard Reda.
Res.: One Carow Pl., 11780. Tel: 631-584-5454; Fax: 631-862-9675.
School—(Grades PreK-8) 11780. Tel: 631-584-7896; Fax: 631-584-3258. Mr. Anthony Giordano, Prin. Lay Teachers 20; Students 420.
Catechesis/Religious Program—Tel: 631-584-5486; Fax: 631-584-3204. Students 1,584.

SAG HARBOR, SUFFOLK CO., ST. ANDREW'S (1859), [CEM] Rev. Msgr. Ronald A. Richardson. In Res., Rev. Andrew P. Blake, Pastor Emeritus (Retired).
Res.: 122 Division St, 11963-3154. Tel: 631-725-0123; Fax: 631-725-3310.
School—Stella Maris Regional School, Sag Harbor, Tel: 631-725-2525; Fax: 631-725-4587. See Regional Schools under Institutions Located in the Diocese.
Catechesis/Religious Program—Tel: 631-725-0123, Ext. 22. Students 245.

SALTAIRE, SUFFOLK CO., OUR LADY STAR OF THE SEA, MISSION CHAPEL, , (Summer Mission) Rev. Richard R. Viladesau, S.T.D., Admin.
Res.: 1500 de Paul St., Elmont, 11003. Tel: 516-352-2127; Fax: 516-352-2358.
Church: Lighthouse and Pilot Walks, 11706. Tel: 631-583-7613; Fax: 631-583-7613.

SAYVILLE, SUFFOLK CO., ST. LAWRENCE THE MARTYR (1895), [CEM] Rev. Msgrs. John Rowan; John T. Heinlein; Deacon Patrick LaBella.
Res.: 27 Handsome Ave., 11782. Tel: 631-589-0042; 631-589-8135; 631-589-3887; Fax: 631-589-5318.
School—Prince of Peace Regional School, Sayville, Tel: 631-589-3926. See Regional Schools under Institutions Located in the Diocese.
Catechesis/Religious Program—Tel: 631-589-3160. Mrs. Lorraine Gallagher, D.R.E. Students 1,600.

SEA CLIFF, NASSAU CO., ST. BONIFACE MARTYR (1898), Rev. Michael J. Torpey; Deacon Theodore Kolakowski.
Res.: 145 Glen Ave., 11579. Tel: 516-676-0676; Fax: 516-674-6742.
School—All Saints Regional Catholic School, Glen Cove See Regional Schools under Institutions Located in the Diocese.
Catechesis/Religious Program—Tel: 516-671-0418. Julia Byrne, D.R.E. Students 360.

SEAFORD, NASSAU CO.

1—ST. JAMES (1951), Revs. Robert S. Hewes; James Calledo (Philippines); Paul G. Driscoll; Deacons James G. Beirne; John G. Leahy; John J. Lynch; Allan J. Helmbrecht, Business Mgr.
Res.: 80 Hicksville Rd., 11783. Tel: 516-731-3710; Fax: 516-731-4828.
School—St. John Baptist de LaSalle Regional School, Bethpage/Farmingdale, Tel: 516-931-0983; Fax: 516-931-1502. See Regional Schools under Institutions Located in the Diocese.
Catechesis/Religious Program—Tel: 516-796-2979; Fax: 516-731-4828. Sr. Rosemary Traynor, C.P., D.R.E. Students 1,810.

2—MARIA REGINA (1954), Rev. Msgr. Peter J. Pflomm; Rev. Joseph E. Nohs; Deacons Gerald F. Whitfield; John A. Weigel; John R. Nuzzi.
Res.: 3945 Jerusalem Ave., 11783. Tel: 516-798-2415; Fax: 516-798-7493.
School—4045 Jerusalem Ave., 11783. Tel: 516-541-1229; Fax: 516-541-1235. John Callow, Prin.; Leona Arpino, Asst. Prin. Lay Teachers 27; Students 612.
Catechesis/Religious Program—3945 Jerusalem

Ave., 11783. Tel: 516-541-0921; Fax: 516-795-2510. Carol Tannehill, D.R.E. Students 1,810.

3—St. William, the Abbot (1928), Rev. William E. Koenig; Rev. Msgr. Thomas G. Leavey, Pastor Emeritus (Retired); Revs. Steven Camp; Eric R. Fasano; Deacon Thomas Buchenberger.
Res.: 2000 Jackson Ave., 11783. Tel: 516-785-1266; Fax: 516-785-4824.
School—2001 Jackson Ave., 11783. Tel: 516-785-6784; Fax: 516-785-2752. Mrs. Anna Guardino, Prin. Lay Teachers 27; Students 585.
Catechesis/Religious Program—Tel: 516-679-9558; Fax: 516-679-1649. Mrs. Georgette Levesque, D.R.E.; Mrs. Mary Calabrese, D.R.E. Students 1,676.

Selden, Suffolk Co., St. Margaret of Scotland (1948), Revs. Christopher Aridas; Joseph Alenchery (India); Deacons William E. Kogler; Biagio Muratore; Phil Paolicelli; Joseph Scollan.
Res.: 81 College Rd., 11784. Tel: 631-732-3131; Fax: 631-732-8827.
School—Holy Angels Regional School, Patchogue, Tel: 631-475-0422; Fax: 631-475-2036. See Regional Schools under Institutions Located in the Diocese.
Catechesis/Religious Program— 11784. Tel: 631-698-0798. Barbara Mahon, D.R.E.; Marilynne Schaefer, D.R.E.; Peggy Scheiner, D.R.E. Students 1,300.

Setauket, Suffolk Co., St. James (1949), [CEM] Revs. Robert J. Smith, S.T.L., S.T.D.; Mathew Kottaram; James Drew; Deacons Thomas Owens; Joseph Ingulli. In Res., Rev. John J. Fitzgerald (Retired).
Res.: 429 Rte. 25-A, 11733. Tel: 631-941-4141; Fax: 631-751-6607.
School—Our Lady of Wisdom Regional School, Port Jefferson, Tel: 631-473-1211. See Regional Schools under Institutions Located in the Diocese.
Catechesis/Religious Program—Tel: 631-751-7287. Louise DiCarlo, D.R.E. Students 1,361.

Shelter Island, Suffolk Co., Our Lady of the Isle (1907), [CEM] Rev. Charles Dougherty, C.P. Shelter Island Heights, Box 3027, Shelter Island Heights, 11965. Tel: 631-749-0001; Fax: 631-749-4218.
School—Stella Maris Regional School, Sag Harbor, Tel: 631-725-2525; Fax: 631-725-4601. See Regional Schools under Institutions Located in the Diocese.
Catechesis/Religious Program—Students 50.

Shoreham, Suffolk Co., St. Mark (1973), Revs. Theodore J. Howard; Felix Weerasinghe (Sri Lanka); Deacon Patrick Gerace.
Res.: 105 Randall Rd., 11786. Tel: 631-744-2800; Fax: 631-821-1628.
Catechesis/Religious Program— 11786. Tel: 631-821-0550. Mrs. Lynn Fein, D.R.E. Students 1,195.

Smithtown, Suffolk Co., St. Patrick (1952), (Irish—Italian), [CEM] Rev. Msgr. Ellsworth R. Walden; Revs. Jilson George (India); Frank J. Parisi; Deacons Richard Sanders; Fred Jackman; John Chott; Vincent Abrahams. In Res., Revs. Vincent Liu; Frederick Hill.
Res.: 280 E. Main St., 11787. Tel: 631-265-2271; Fax: 631-863-1586.
School—Tel: 631-724-0285; Fax: 631-265-4841. Mrs. Eileen Sadicario, Prin. Sisters of St. Joseph 2; Lay Teachers 31; Students 613.
Catechesis/Religious Program—Tel: 631-724-7454; Fax: 631-265-1250. Paula Billyard, D.R.E. Students 2,297.

Sound Beach, Suffolk Co., St. Louis de Montfort (1971), Rev. Charles E. Papa; Rev. Msgr. John A. McGuire, Pastor Emeritus (Retired); Rev. Stephen H. Donnelly; Deacons Joseph T. Bartolotto; Peter F. Schultz; Gary F. Swane.
75 New York Ave., 11789-2506. Tel: 631-744-8566; Fax: 631-744-8611.
School—Our Lady of Wisdom Regional School, Port Jefferson, Tel: 631-473-1211; Fax: 631-473-1064. See Regional Schools under Institutions Located in the Diocese.
Catechesis/Religious Program—Tel: 631-744-9515; Fax: 631-821-6089. Mr. John McNamara, D.R.E. Students 2,022.

Southampton, Suffolk Co.

1—Our Lady of Poland (1918), (Polish), Rev. Stanley Kondeja; Deacon James Ashe.
Res.: 35 Maple St., 11968. Tel: 631-283-0667; Fax: 631-287-4146.
School—Our Lady of the Hamptons Regional School, Tel: 631-283-9140; Fax: 631-287-3958. See Regional Schools under Institutions Located in the Diocese.
Catechesis/Religious Program—Tel: 631-283-5230; Fax: 631-283-5230. Students 400.

2—Sacred Hearts of Jesus and Mary (1896), [CEM] Rev. Jeffrey J. Madley; Rev. Msgr. Edmond J. Trench, Pastor Emeritus (Retired); Deacon John P. Moran.
Res.: 168 Hill St., 11968. Tel: 631-283-0097; Fax: 631-283-3836.
School—Our Lady of the Hamptons Regional School, Tel: 631-283-9140; Fax: 631-287-3958. See Regional Schools under Institutions Located in the Diocese.
Catechesis/Religious Program—Tel: 631-283-0508. Students 350.

Southold, Suffolk Co., St. Patrick's (1855), [CEM] Revs. George J. Michell; Martin J. Osborne, Pastor Emeritus (Retired).
Res.: Main Rd., P.O. Box 1117, 11971 1401. Tel: 631-765-3442; Fax: 631-765-9631.
School—Our Lady of Mercy, Cutchogue, Tel: 631-734-5166. See Regional Schools under Institutions Located in the Diocese.
Catechesis/Religious Program—Tel: 631-765-2338. Students 290.

Syosset, Nassau Co., St. Edward Confessor (1952), Revs. Thomas M. Fusco; Roland Fahey, T.O.R.; Deacon James Murphy.
Res.: 205 Jackson Ave., 11791-4218. Tel: 516-921-0756 (Rectory Office); Fax: 516 921-4549.
School—2 Teibrook Ave., 11791. Tel: 516-921-7767; Fax: 516-496-0001. Mrs. Anne Schaefer, M.S., Prin. Sisters of Mercy (Brooklyn) 1; Lay Teachers 20; Students 262.
Parish Social Ministry Office—Tel: 516-921-5628; Fax: 516-364-7326. Sr. Anne Carron, R.S.M., Dir.
Youth Ministry Office—Tel: 516-921-7631; Fax: 516-921-3035. Gerard Giglio, Dir.
Catechesis/Religious Program—Tel: 516-364-1790 (Grades 1-5); 516-364-6803 (Grades 6-8). Mrs. Dorothy Kuchler, D.R.E. Students 900.

Uniondale, Nassau Co., St. Martha (1949), Revs. Edward C. Fitzpatrick; Edward G. Sullivan (Retired); Deacons Miguel Angel Romero; Trevor St. Ives Machurin.
Res.: 546 Greengrove Ave., 11553. Tel: 516-481-2550; Fax: 516-564-4552.
School—St. Martin de Porres Regional School, Uniondale, Tel: 516-481-3303; Fax: 516-483-4138. See Regional Schools under Institutions Located in the Diocese.
Catechesis/Religious Program—Tel: 516-481-6608. Sr. Eileen Curley, R.S.M., D.R.E. Students 251.

Valley Stream, Nassau Co.

1—Blessed Sacrament (1950), Revs. Gregory J. Cappuccino; Frank M. Nelson; Deacons John Coughlin; Salvatore A. Marino; Kevin McCormick.
Res.: 201 N. Central Ave., 11580. Tel: 516-568-1027; Fax: 516-872-1499.
School—50 Rose Ave., 11580. Tel: 516-825-7334; Fax: 516-825-4376. Mr. William Fahey, Prin. Sisters of St. Joseph 1; Lay Teachers 18; Students 332.
Catechesis/Religious Program—Tel: 516-561-1407. Lucille Vavosa, D.R.E. Students 718.

2—Holy Name of Mary (1902), Revs. Thomas J. Harold; Theodore J. LeTure, Pastor Emeritus (Retired); James L. Maltese; Saji George; Deacons Anthony W. Cuseo; James O'Hara; Clyde Ruggieri; Richard F. Raad.
Res.: 55 E. Jamaica Ave., 11580. Tel: 516-825-1450; Fax: 516-568-1906.
School—90 S. Grove St., 11580. Tel: 516-825-4009. Sr. Elizabeth Marie Lynch, C.S.J., Prin. Lay Teachers 17; Students 262.
Catechesis/Religious Program—90 S. Grove St., 11580. Tel: 516-825-1810. Sr. Barbara Shea, O.P., D.R.E. Students 966.
Parish Outreach—Tel: 516-825-0177; Fax: 516-825-5092. Sr. Margie Kelly, C.S.J., Dir.

Wading River, Suffolk Co., St. John Baptist (1922), Rev. Msgr. John P. Sullivan; Sr. Sheila Molloy, O.S.U., Pastoral Assoc.; Deacons Frederick Finter; Gregory Senholzi.
Res.: 1488 North Country Rd., 11792. Tel: 631-929-4339; Fax: 631-369-6961.
Catechesis/Religious Program—Students 713.

Wantagh, Nassau Co., St. Frances de Chantal (1952), Rev. Msgr. Robert E. Guglielmone; Revs. Steven J. Hannafin; Antonio S. Pascual, J.C.L.; Sr. Jocelyn Panzetta, C.I.J.; Deacons Robert O'Donovan; Joseph Torres. In Res., Rev. Thomas Coogan.
Res.: 1309 Wantagh Ave., 11793. Tel 516-785-2333; Fax: 516-826-7645.
School—St. Elizabeth Ann Seton Regional School, Bellmore/East Meadow, Tel: 516-785-5709; Fax: 516-785-4468. See Wantagh Regional Schools under Institutions Located in the Diocese.
Catechesis/Religious Program—Tel: 516-785-2333, Ext. 205. Judith Brady, D.R.E. Students 2,168.

West Babylon, Suffolk Co., Our Lady of Grace (1965), Revs. Lawrence Duncklee; Thomas Saloy; Edward H. Koch; Deacons Peter DiGiuseppe, Pastoral Assoc.; John Morrow; Charles Graff; William Austin; Brian Miller.
Res. 666 Albin Ave., 11704. Tel: 631-587-5185; Fax: 631-587-1427.
Catechesis/Religious Program—Tel: 631-661-9353; Fax: 631-422-8607. Mrs. Lee Ann Abseck, D.R.E.; Mrs Barbara McGrellis, D.R.E. Mrs. Patricia Callahan, D.R.E. Students 3,039.

West Hempstead, Nassau Co., St. Thomas, the Apostle (1931), Rev. Msgr. James P. Lisante; Revs. Andrzej Zglejszewski (Poland); Paul R. Bie; Deacon John E. Ford.
Res.: 24 Westminster Rd., 11552. Tel: 516-489-8585; Fax: 516-292-2651.
School—12 Westminster Rd., 11552. Tel: 516-481-9310; Fax: 516-481-8769. Mrs. Christina Teisch, Prin. Sisters 3; Lay Teachers 24; Students 689.
Catechesis/Religious Program—Tel: 516-538-7460. Mrs. Mary Ann Pellegrino, D.R.E. Students 997.
Mission—Chapel Nassau Blvd. & Hempstead Ave., Lakeview, Nassau Co. 11552. Tel: 516-483-4091.

West Islip, Suffolk Co., Our Lady of Lourdes (1956), Revs. Michael A. Vetrano; Stephen J. Brigandi; Deacons Stephen M. Behar; John Teufel; John DeGuardi; Jack Meehan.
Res.: 455 Hunter Ave., 11795. Tel: 631-661-3224; Fax: 631-661-7143.
School—44 Toomey Rd., 11795. Tel: 631-587-7200; Fax: 631-587-4531. Regina A. Cioffi, Prin. Lay Teachers 18; Students 355.
Catechesis/Religious Program—Tel: 631-661-5440; Fax: 631-661-3606. Sisters Diane Liona, D.R.E.; Nancy Campkin, D.R.E. Students 2,600.

Westbury, Nassau Co., St. Brigid (1850), Revs. Ralph Sommer; Syriaque Cine, S.M.M.; Leonard Ogbonna; Kevin J. Dillon; George Onida, S.M.; Deacons Manuel J. Ramos; Michael Metzdorff; James Morris; Frank Pesce.
Res.: 75 Post Ave., 11590. Tel: 516-334-0021; Fax: 516-334-0082.
School—St. Brigid/ Our Lady of Hope Regional School, 101 Maple Ave., 11590. Tel: 516-333-0580; Fax: 516-333-0590. Paul P. Clagnaz, Prin. School Sisters of Notre Dame 1; Lay Teachers 29; Students 431.
Catechesis/Religious Program—Tel: 516-333-9434. Sr. Ann Horn, O.P., D.R.E.; Kelly Kraemer, D.R.E. Students 1,600.

Westhampton Beach, Suffolk Co., Immaculate Conception (1891), Rev. Joseph Mirro.
Res.: 580 Main Rd., 11978. Tel: 631-288-1423; Fax: 631-288-5498.
School—Our Lady, Queen of Apostles Regional School, Center Moriches, Tel: 631-878-1033; Fax: 631-878-1059. See Regional Schools under Institutions Located in the Diocese.
Catechesis/Religious Program—Tel: 631-288-4188; Fax: 631-288-8215. Sr. Virginia Baeder, D.R.E. Students 585.

Williston Park, Nassau Co., St. Aidan's Church (1928), Revs. Robert L. Hayden; Stephen Pietrowski; Bruno Dekrem; Rev. Msgr. Robert J. Kirwin, Pastor Emeritus (Retired); Deacons Herman J. Determann; Francis J. Love; Salvatore Villani; Ms. Claire Jo Schirtzer, Pastoral Assoc. In Res., Rev. James Nunes.
Res.: 505 Willis Ave., 11596. Tel: 516-746-6585; Fax: 516-746-6055.
School—(Grades N-3), 525 Willis Ave., 11596. Tel: 516-746-6585, Ext. 202; Fax: 516-746-8817.
School—(Grades 4-8), 510 Willis Ave., 11596. Tel: 518-747-6585, Ext. 302; Fax: 516-746-3086. Eileen Oliver, Prin.; Jo Anne Rowan, Asst. Prin. Sisters 2; Lay Teachers 28; Students 597.
Catechesis/Religious Program—Tel: 516-746-6585, Ext. 404. Mrs. Elaina Kedjierski, D.R.E. Students 1,231.
Convent—Sisters of Charity, 16 Pembroke St., 11596. Tel: 516-741-6869.

Woodbury, Nassau Co., Holy Name of Jesus (1962), Rev. Msgr. Lawrence B. Rafferty.
Res.: 690 Woodbury Rd., 11797-2504. Tel: 516-921-2334; Fax: 516-682-8161.
Catechesis/Religious Program—Tel: 516-921-2347. Students 200.

Wyandanch, Suffolk Co., Our Lady of the Miraculous Medal (1932), Rev. William F. Brisotti; Deacon Donald Zirkel.
Res.: 1434 Straight Path, 11798. Tel: 631-643-7568; Fax: 631-643-5935.
Gerald Ryan Outreach Center, Inc.—Tel: 631-643-7591. Mrs. Ann Druckenmiller, Dir.; Sr. Elizabeth Myles, C.S.J., Religious Education & Youth Ministry. Tel: 631-643-3364.
Catechesis/Religious Program—Tel: 631-643-3364. Students 240.

Chaplains of Public Institutions

Rockville Centre. *Mercy Medical Center*, 50 North Park Ave.. Tel: 516-678-5800, Ext. 521. Revs. Valentine Rebelo, Chux Okochi, Chap., Sisters Mary Alice Aschenbach, C.I.J., Chap. & Dir., Mary Morrow, D.W., Chap., Norma Jean Lokcinski, C.I.J., Chap., Elizabeth Scanlan, R.S.M., Chap., Mary Ellen Eichman, Chap.
Good Shepherd Hospice (Nassau). Tel: 516-876-8485. Sr. Mary Lou Kelly, Dir., Mrs. Shevawn O'Connor.

Amityville. *Brunswick Hospital*, 366 Broadway,

11701. Tel: 631-789-7000; 631-264-0124; 631-842-8488. (Vacant)

South Oaks Psychiatric Hospital, Sunrise Hwy., 11701. Tel: 631-264-4000. Rev. Robert A. Hyatt (Retired).

BAY SHORE. *Southside Hospital*, Montauk Hwy., 11706. Tel: 631-968-3000. Bro. Christopher Golla, Revs. Peter J. McCrann, S.M.M., Theodore Murphy, S.M.M.

BETHPAGE. *New Island Hospital*, Tel: 516-520-2706. Deacons Frank Carrello, John Audia.

EAST MEADOW. *Nassau County Police Department*. Rev. Msgr. John A. Alesandro, Rev. Joseph J. D'Angelo, M.A.C., M.Div., M.S., C.A.S.A.C., Rev. Msgr. Thomas Hartman.

Nassau County, Fire Chiefs, Council of. Rev. Kevin M. Smith, Rev. Msgr. John F. Bennett.

Nassau University Medical Center, 2201 Hempstead Tpke., 11554. Tel: 516-572-3195; 516-572-6069. Revs. Gabriel Miah, Anthony Bonsu, Sr. Maureen Chase, Dir. Pastural Care.

GLEN COVE. *North Shore Community Hospital at Glen Cove*, Tel: 516-674-7300. Rev. Juniper J. Thomas.

HUNTINGTON. *Huntington Hospital* 11743. Tel: 631-351-2000. Rev. Thomas Edamattan, Deacon Edward Billia.

MANHASSET. *North Shore Univ. Hospital*, 1554 Community Dr., 11030. Tel: 516-562-0100. Revs. Antony Xavier, Isaac Mensah, Jon Overvold, Dir.

North Shore Hospital: Tel: 516-562-4713.

MELVILLE. *Catholic Health Services of Long Island*, 992 N. Village Ave., 11747. Tel: 631-454-2234. Mrs. Cathy Grandjean, Dir. Chaplaincy.

Long Island Developmental Center, Box 788, 11747. Tel: 516-385-2700. (Vacant)

MINEOLA. *Winthrop Hospital*, First St., 11501. Tel: 516-663-0333. Revs. James L. Maltese, Antony Arulsamy, Jane Mather, Dir.

Corpus Christi: 155 Garfield Ave., 11501-2583. Tel: 516-746-1223.

NESCONSET. *Nesconset Nursing Home* 11767. Tel: 516-361-8800. Vacant.

NORTHPORT. *Veteran's Administration Hospital* 1176. Tel: 631-261-4400. Revs. John S. Malone, C.S.C., John Rich, George Lutz, Chap., Harold Story, Chap.

OCEANSIDE. *Brookhaven Hospice*, Tel: 631-687-2960. Deacon Bob Groenwold.

South Nassau Communities Hospital, Tel: 516-763-2030. Deacon Charles Muscarnera.

PATCHOGUE. *Brookhaven Memorial Hospital*, 100 Hospital Rd., 11772. Tel: 631-654-7100. Bro. James Maloney, O.F.M.Cap.

PLAINVIEW. *North Shore Hospital at Plainview*, 888 Old Country Rd., 11083. Tel: 516-681-8900. Rev. Jose Simon Palliparambil.

St. Pius X: 1 St. Pius Ct., 11803-4023. Tel: 516-938-3959.

PORT JEFFERSON. *St. Charles Hospital, Port Jefferson, New York* 11777. Tel: 631-474-6411. Revs. Eric Dadson, Jose Mappilamattel, Deacon Joseph Scollan, Sisters Mary Jo O'Connor, D.W., Josefita Rodriguez, Dir.

Maryhaven Center of Hope 11777. Tel: 631-474-3400. Sisters Maryaline Zierle, O.P., Cathy Smith.

Mather Memorial Hospital 11777. Tel: 631-473-1320, Ext. 4007. Sr. Maeve O'Connor, R.S.H.M.

ROSLYN. *St. Francis Hospital* 11576. Sr. Lois Ann Van Delft, F.M.M., Dir., Revs. John Ofosu-Mireku, Patrick Geo, Sisters Rita Sculti, O.P., Elizabeth Burke, P.B.V.M., Minda Castrillo, F.M.M., Claire MacDonald, O.P., Anna Tarnauskas, F.M.M., Christina Sanchez, Gina Chua, F.M.M., Elisa Fernando, F.M.M., Ms. Barbara Ludeman.

SAYVILLE. *Good Samaritan Nursing Home*. 11782. Tel: 631-244-2400. Sr. Doris Marie Deane, S.C., Rev. Francis B. Nuss.

SMITHTOWN. *St. Catherine of Siena Hospital* 11787. Tel: 631-360-2000. Revs. Frederick Hill, Mark Applewhite.

St. Patrick: 280 E. Main St., 11787. Tel: 631-862-3000; 631-979-1292. Sr. Patricia McDonnell, O.P., Dir.

STONY BROOK. *L.I. State Veterans' Home*, Tel: 631-444-8737. Rev. Charles F. Kohli (Retired).

Stony Brook University Hospital, SUNY at Stony Brook, 11790. Tel: 631-444-8157. Revs. Steve Unger, Dir. Pastoral Care, Anthony Ewherido, Thomas Aidoo, Micael Ufok-Udoekpo, Sr. Lynn Queck, Mrs. Anne Coulehan.

UNIONDALE. *Holly Patterson Geriatric Center*, 875 Jerusalem Ave., 11553. Tel: 516-572-1500. Rev. R. Michael Reid.

Res.: *Holy Trinity High School*, Hicksville. Tel: 516-433-2900.

VALLEY STREAM. *Franklin Medical Center Hospital* 11580. Tel: 516-256-6000. Revs. Augustine Okochi, Tim Stansberry, Dir. Pastoral Care, Kathryn Martino.

St. Boniface Rectory: 631 Elmont Rd., Elmont, 11003-4028. Tel: 516-825-8800.

WEST BRENTWOOD. *Pilgrim Psychiatric Center*, P.O. Box A, 11717. Tel: 631-761-2828. Rev. Lawrence J. O'Leary, Sr. Mary Summerville, C.S.J.

WEST ISLIP. *Consolation Nursing Home* 11795. Tel: 631-587-1600. Rev. William Dailey, Sr. Dorothy Egan, Peggy Nixdorf, Sr. Janet Jeffers, Mr. John Murdoch.

Good Samaritan Hospital Medical Center 11795. Tel: 631-376-3000. Revs. Vincent P. Cunningham, S.M.M., Jerome Madumelu, Paul Nwobi, Paul J. Dahm (Retired), Douglas Dower, Sisters Gertrude O'Brien, D.W., Ellen Moore, O.P., Betty Keegan, F.M.M., Ann Marie Pierce, Rosemary Jermusryk, Mary Anna Euring, O.P., Monica Belber, Mrs. Vivian Badami.

Good Shepherd Hospice Program. Babylon. Tel: 631-376-3850. Sr. Rita Mileti, Mr. Raymond Townsend.

Good Shepherd Hospice Program. Port Jefferson. Tel: 631-474-4040. Sisters Joyce Osgood, O.P., Marylou Kelly, Lorraine Liebold, O.P., Vivi Tsouris, Mrs. Shevawn O'Connor.

Good Samaritan Home Health Agency, Tel: 631-376-4300. (Vacant)

Prison Ministry

BAY SHORE. *Office of Prison Ministry and Criminal Justice Affairs*, 26 S. Saxon Ave., 11706-8920. Tel: 631-969-0837; Fax: 631-666-5073. Bro. John Moylan, O.S.F., D. Min., Dir., Suzanne D. Jones, Coord. of Ministerial Svcs.

EAST MEADOW. *Nassau County Correctional Center*, 100 Carman Ave., 11554-1146. Tel: 516-572-4145. Rev. Ralph Ferro, Chap., Sr. Virginia Waters, F.S.P., Chap., Bro. Bill Cawley, S.C., Chap.

RIVERHEAD. *Suffolk County Correctional Facility*, 100 Center Dr., 11901. Tel: 631-852-2294; 631-852-2728. Sr. Michelle Bremer, C.S.F.N., Chap., Deacon Chris Vigliotta, Chap.

WESTBURY. *Nassau County Juvenile Detention Center*, 61 Carman Ave., 11590. Tel: 516-571-9153. Bro. Jack Moylan, O.S.F., D.Min., Chap.

YAPHANK. *Suffolk County Minimum Security Facility*, P.O. Box 69, 11980. Tel: 631-852-4713. Sr. Michelle Bremer, C.S.F.N., Chap., Deacon John Sullivan, Chap.

Absent on Leave:

Revs.—

Ball, Matthew J.
Bastian, Thomas
Boyle, Michael
Carroll, Michael A.
Donovan, William
Gabriele, John J.
Houghton, Timothy
Kennedy, Glenn C.
Lennon, Charles
Lubrano, Robert
Miller, James
Mundy, Joseph
Parkinson, Todd
Passamonte, Philip B.
Rebaldo, Ronald
Reed, Bruce
Rogers, John
Rogers, Paul
Walsh, Edward
White, John
Whitney, Richard

Priests Released from Diocesan Assignment:

Rev. Msgrs.—

Boccafola, Kenneth
Cervini, John
Maniscalco, Francis

Revs.—

Bogert, James (Retired)
Coyle, Robert
D'Souza, Claude
Ehrhart, Charles M., Chap. Major
McMullen, Francis R. (Retired)
Morris, Stephen
Trapani, Anthony M., Lt., CHC, USNR
Viladesau, Richard R., S.T.D.

Military Chaplains:

Revs.—

Erhart, Charles M., U.S.M.C.A.-N.B.G.
Rowan, Mark P.
Trapani, Anthony

Retired:

Most Rev.—

Daly, James, Diocese of Rockville Centre, 50 N. Park Ave., 11570.

Rev. Msgrs.—

Ballweg, Lawrence F., Church of St. Thomas Moore, 115 Kings Highway, Hauppauge, 11788.
Boesel, James E., Church of Our Lady of Mercy, 500 S. Oyster Bay Rd., Hicksville, 11801.
Brassil, James A., Church of the Sacred Heart, 720 Merrick Ave., North Merrick, 11566.
Chiara, Peter A., St. Mary, 20 Harrison Ave., East Islip, 11730-2314.
Coffey, James F., St. Patrick, Nine North Clinton Ave., Bay Shore, 11706-7899.
Colligan, Joseph F., Our Lady Queen of Martyrs, P.O. Box 0609, Centerport, 11721-1130.
Costa, Mario C., Church of St. Paul the Apostle, Cedar Swamp Rd., Glen Head, 11545.
Costello, William F., St. Anne, 35 Dartmouth St., Garden City, 11530-5109.
Glimm, Francis X., S.T.L., St. Joseph Guest House, 350 Cuba Hill Rd., Huntington, 11743-4896.
Graham, George P., J.C.D., Ph.D., St. Bernard, 3100 Hempstead Tpke., Levittown, 11756.
Kirwin, Robert J., St. Aidan, 505 Willis Ave., Williston Park, 11596-1786.
Lawlor, Joseph F., St. Joseph Guest House, 350 Cuba Hill Rd., Huntington, 11743-4896.
Leavey, Thomas G., St. William the Abbot, 2000 Jackson Ave., Seaford, 11783-2688.
McCarren, Edgar, Our Lady of Peace Church, Santa Clara, CA.
McGuire, John A., St. Louis de Montfort, 75 New York Ave., Sound Beach, 11789-0810.
Murphy, Eugene F., Diocese of Corpus Christi, 155 Garfield Ave., Mineola, 11501.
Murray, Joseph M., 51 Merrion Village, Merrion Rd., Ballsbridge, Dublin 4 Ireland.
Ribaudo, Charles A., 18 Monitor Rd., Smithtown, 11787.
Richter, James B., St. Patrick, 400 Main St., Huntington, 11743-3298.
Rooney, Thaddeus, Ss. Cyril & Methodius, 125 Half Hollow Rd., Deer Park, 11795-4288.
Saccacio, Robert J., 3102 Bludds Dr. S., Baiting Hollow, 11933.
Savastano, Anthony J., 80 Park Ave., Manhasset, 11030.
Simmons, Walter E., St. Peter of Alcantara, 1327 Port Washington Blvd., Port Washington, 11050-3096.
Skelly, John J., P.O. Box 5217, Rocky Point, 11778.
Tarrant, Edward L., Corpus Christi, 155 Garfield Ave., Mineola, 11501.
Trench, Edmond J., P.O. Box 1503, East Quogue, 11942.
Villar, Demetrio L., 8528 Riverside Rd., Alexandria, VA 22308.
Wiest, John J., St. Mary, 1300 Northern Blvd., Manhasset, 11030-3020.

Revs.—

Alarcon, Felix, Church of St. Andrew, 2628 Del Prado Blvd., Cape Coral, FL 33904.
Anderson, Arthur C., 245 Alphano Rd., Great Meadows, NJ 07838.
Barry, Ronald A., P.O Box 1708, Chandler, AZ 85244-1708.
Benack, Henry I., St. Patrick, 235 Glen St., Glen Cove, 11542-3091.
Blake, Andrew P., St. Andrew, 122 Division St., Sag Harbor, 11963-3154.
Bogert, James, 721 S.W. Lake Court #104, Boynton Beach, FL 33426.
Buckley, Harold P., St. Rose of Lima, Two Bayview Ave., Massapequa, 11758-7299.
Callahan, Zachary, Church of Cure of Ars, 2323 Merrick Ave., Merrick, 11566.
Casey, Francis M., St. Pius X Residence, 1220 Front St., Uniondale, 11553.
Colgan, Thomas J., St. Philip Neri, 344 Main St., Northport, 11768-1779.
Collins, Edwin J., 14295 Aster Ave., Wellington, FL 33414.
Corali, Serafino A., St. Pius X Residence, 1220 Front St., Uniondale, 11553-2097.
Cser, Ladislaus, S.J., 17 Lanier Ln., Bay Shore, 11706.
Curley, Martin W., Jennings Hall at Broadlawn, 397 County Line Rd., Amityville, 11701.
Curry, Thomas P. (BRK), Queen of Peace Residence, 110-30 221 St., Queens Village, 11429.
Dahm, Paul J., 176 Montauk Hwy., Southampton, 11968.
Dailey, William, 1016 Bishop's Rd., Smithtown, 11787.
De Vita, James C., C.V.E., Grantham B., 331, Deerfield Beach, FL 33442.
Delaney, Richard, St. Pius X Residence, 1220 Front St., Uniondale, 11553.
Delaney, William I., Church of Our Holy Redeemer, 37 S. Ocean Ave., Freeport, 11520.
Diederich, Donald F., J.C.D., Founders Village Apt. 1813, 2555 Youngs Ave., Southold, 11971.
Dineros, Santiago A., Church of St. Raphael, 600 Newbridge Rd., East Meadow, 11554.
Dolan, James J., St. Pius X Residence, 1220 Front St., Uniondale, 11553-2097.
Drab, John P., 24 Pheasant Rd., Noyac, 11963-2908.

Duvelsdorf, Peter L., St. Pius X Residence, 1220 Front St., Uniondale, 11553-2097.
Fitzgerald, John J., Church of St. James, 429 Route 25A, East Setauket, 11733.
Gallagher, Andrew J., Our Lady of Miraculous Medal, 75 Parkside Dr., Point Lookout, 11569-9999.
Gallagher, William G., 9949 Shore Rd., Brooklyn, 11209.
Gartner, Charles A., Our Lady of Mercy, 500 South Oyster Bay Rd., Hicksville, 11801-3570.
Gfroerer, Gerard J., St. Pius X Residence, 1220 Front St., Uniondale, 11553-2097.
Gorman, John J., St. Joseph, 39 N. Carll Ave., Babylon, 11702-2701.
Govern, William H., Maria Regina Convent, Brentwood Rd., Brentwood, 11717-5589.
Hall, Martin J., M.A., St. Bernard, 3100 Hempstead Tpke., Levittown, 11756-1339.
Harrer, Frederic J., St. Pius X Residence, 1220 Front St., Uniondale, 11553.
Heenan, Michael F., 2021 Bonisle Cir., Palm Beach Gardens, FL 33418.
Henry, John P., St. Ignatius, 715 E. Orange St., Tarpon Springs, FL 34689.
Hourihane, Francis, 8170 Summerlin Village, Unit 602, Fort Myers, FL 33919.
Hyatt, Robert A., 298 Elton St., Riverhead, 11901.
Kayser, Robert, Manor Park, 215 Carll's Path, Apt. 4C, Deer Park, 11729.
Kohli, Charles F., 80 Hallock Ave., Smithtown, 11787.
Korycki, Walter R., 7 Susan Dr., Northport, 11768.
Kozlowski, Joseph P., St. Hyacinth, 319 Cedar Swamp Rd., Glen Head, 11545-2296.
LeTure, Theodore J., 2443 S.W. Sansome Ln., Port St. Lucie, FL 34953.
Liu, Peter T., 2886 Fernley Dr. E. #75, West Palm Beach, FL 33417.
Liu, Vincent, St. Patrick, 280 E. Main St., Smithtown, 11787-2920.
McCabe, John H., St. Pius X Residence, 1220 Front St., Uniondale, 11553.
McCarthy, Thomas, 215 W. Santa Barbara Rd., Lindenhurst, 11757.
McCarthy, William E., M.M., St. Teresa's Residence, P.O. Box 321, Maryknoll, 10545.
McComiskey, Joseph C., 137 Brookside Dr., Smithtown, 11787.
McMullen, Francis R., 14415 Capt. John Smith Dr., Accokeek, MD 20607.
Meade, James C., Queen of Peace Residence, 110-30 221 St., Queens Village, 11429-1655.
Millar, Andrew, Diocese of Rockville Centre, 50 N. Park Ave., 11570.
Minturn, Joseph, 107 Colonial Pkwy., Manhasset, 11030.
Muhs, Edward J., St. Barnabas the Apostle, 2320 Bedford Ave., Bellmore, 11710-3617.
Murphy, William T., 288 Court House Rd., Franklin Square, 11010.
Murray, John E., Notre Dame, 45 Mayfair Rd., New Hyde Park, 11040-2094.
Murray, John P., 19 Redfield Rd., Island Park, 11558.
Navarroli, Frederick, 3900 Forest Grove Dr., Annandale, VA 22003.
Navarroli, Frederick, 3900 Forest Grove Dr., Annandale, VA 22003.
Nee, Kenneth T., St. Pius X Residence, 1220 Front St., Uniondale, 11553.
Newman, Louis I., St. Columba's Rectory, 3327 Glencolum Dr., San Diego, CA 92123.
Nieva, Constantino S., St. Pius X Residence, 1220 Front St., Uniondale, 11553.
Niewczas, Taddeus, 84 Berry St. Apt. 1L, Brooklyn, 11211.
Nugent, Raymond H., 745 Pinewood Rd., Cutchogue, 11935.
O'Brien, Denis J., St. Anthony's Friary, 275 Wolf Hill Rd., South Huntington, 11743-1363.
Osborne, Martin J., St. Patrick, P.O. Box 117, Southold, 11971.
Pai, Simon, Nathan Hale Senior Village, 30 Doxsey Pl., Apt. 231, Lynbrook, 11563.
Pazo, John T., P.O. Box 525, Clairton, PA 15025-0525.
Punti, George, St. Boniface, 631 Elmont Road, Elmont, 11003-4028.
Reuss, Louis L., St. John Nepomucene, 1140 Locust Ave., Bohemia, 11716-2139.
Scanlon, Richard M., Consolation Nursing Home, 111 Beach Dr., West Islip, 11795-4860.
Serrano, John J., St. Pius X Residence, 1220 Front St., Uniondale, 11553-2097.
Sheehan, Augustine J., Department of Veterans Affairs, Medica, 79 Middleville Rd., Northport, 11768.
Sheridan, Denis J., St. Pius X Residence, 1220 Front St., Uniondale, 11553-2097.
Singleton, William V., St. Raymond, 263 Atlantic Ave., East Rockaway, 11518-1117.
Sledzaus, Alexander L., Our Lady of Mount Carmel, 495 New N. Ocean Ave., Patchogue, 11772-1793.
Smith, Robert S., Immaculate Conception Seminary, 440 W. Neck Rd., Huntington, 11743.
Sullivan, Edward G., Church of St. Martina, 546 Greengrove Ave., Uniondale, 11553.
Swiatocha, Bruno, 34 Country Club Dr. Shallotte, NC 28470.
Traynor, John J., 25 Pitch Pine Pl., Medford, 11763.
Wickman, Robert T., 14 Abergele Dr., Toms River, NJ 08757.
Wilutis, John P., St. Pius X Residence, 1220 Front St., Uniondale, 11553-2097.
Wodziak, Michael, c/o Mrs. R. Sircovics, 1148 5th Ave., Berwick, PA 18603.

Permanent Deacons:
Abrahams, Vincent, St. Patrick, Smithtown
Altonji, James F., St. Joseph, Ronkonkoma
Alvarado, Jesus, Florida
Ashe, James C., Our Lady of Poland, Southampton
Audia, John P., Maria Regina, Seaford
Austin, William, Our Lady of Grace, West Babylon
Banno, Anthony, St. Christopher, Baldwin
Barone, Frank D., St. Kilian, Farmingdale
Bartolotto, Joseph T., St. Louis De Montfort, Sound Beach
Bast, Thomas J., Our Lady of Peace, Lynbrook
Bedell, Paul, Campus Parish
Behar, Stephen, Our Lady of Lourdes, West Islip
Beirne, James G., St. James, Seaford
Benincasa, Joseph, St. Catherine of Sienna, Franklin Square
Bennettson, Donald W., St. Joseph's, Kings Park
Biggin, James A., St. Martin of Tours, Bethpage
Billia, Edward W., St. Hugh of Lincoln, Huntington Station
Blasius Ronald, Ss. Philip & James, St. James
Bohuslaw, James, St. John Nepomucene, Bohemia
Bono, Frank J., St. Joachim, Cedarhurst
Bopp, John T., Sacred Heart, Cutchogue
Borchardt, Frank, St. Patrick, Glen Cove
Bowe, Martin J., (On Leave of Absence)
Braun, Robert G., St. Anthony of Padua, East Northport
Brown, Charles, SS. Philip & James, St. James
Browne, George J., St. Anne, Garden City
Bruck, George P., Our Lady of Good Counsel, Inwood
Buchenberger, Thomas E., St. William the Abbot, Seaford
Burkart, John F., St. Philip Neri, Northport
Burnham, Bruce A., Our Holy Redeemer, Freeport
Byrne, Joseph, St. Joseph, Hewlett
Cales, Francisco, Our Holy Redeemer, Freeport
Califano, Joseph, St. Joseph, Ronkonkoma
Campbell, Robert, St. Raymond, East Rockaway
Capobianco, Eugene, St. Martin of Tours, Bethpage
Carrello, Frank, St. Martin of Tours Bethpage
Carroll, James P., St. Christopher, Baldwin
Case, Edward M., St. Mary, Roslyn
Cedrone, Anthony M., Blessed Sacrament, Valley Stream
Cepeda, Jose A., Our Lady of Assumption, Copiague
Chamberlain, Anthony J., SS. Philip & James, St. James
Chedda, Paul, The Good Sheperd, Holbrook
Chott, John, St. Patrick, Smithtown
Coleman, Thomas, St. Barnabas the Apostle, Bellmore
Connolly, George P., Our Lady of Perpetual Help, Lindenhurst
Connolly, Thomas, St. Raymond, East Rockaway
Costa, Victor, St. Raphael, East Meadow
Costello, Thomas P., St. Joseph, Hewlett
Cotone, Louis, St. Kilian, Farmingdale
Coughlin, John, Blessed Sacrament, Valley Stream
Cove, Francis K., Our Lady of Lourdes, Malverne
Coycy, Jorge, (On Leave of Absence)
Crivello, Frank, Sts. Philip & James, St. James
Croce, Barry, St. Joseph, Babylon
Cunningham, Edward F., St. Anne Garden City
Cuseo, Anthony W., Holy Name of Mary, Valley Stream
Cusumano, Anthony P., St. John Nepomucene, Bohemia
D'Angelo, Frank G., St. Peter of Alcantara, Port Washington
D'Averse, Angelo D., St. Raphael, East Meadow
Daza, H. Nelson, St. Mary of the Isle, Long Beach
DeBellis, Michael J., St. Joseph, Ronkonkoma
DeGuardi, John P., Our Lady of Lourdes, Islip
Deignan, Thomas F., Maine
Dejewski, Robert, Ss. Peter & Paul, Manokville
DeStefano, Carmine E., St. Matthew, Dix Hills
Determann, Herman J., St. Aidan, Williston Park
Devenney, Michael L., St. Joseph Kings Park
Diaz, Juan, St. Anne, Brentwood
Diaz-Granados, Francisco, St. Francis de Sales, Patchogue
DiGiovanna, James R., St. Mary, Roslyn
DiGiuseppe, Peter A., Our Lady Grace, West Babylon
Donza, Gaetano, St. Raymond, East Rockaway
Dougherty, Joseph M., St. Joseph, Ronkonkoma
Dunlop, John P., St. Mary of the Isle, Long Beach
Dunne, James A., Our Holy Redeemer, Freeport
Dunphy, Patrick J., Our Lady of Hope, Carle Place
Earley, George G., (On Leave of Absence)
Evrard, Thomas J., St. Ignatius Martyr, Long Beach
Farley, Owen, Holy Cross, Nesconset
Ferreiro, Douglas, St. Catherine of Sienna, Franklin Square
Ferri, Richard, St. Martin of Tours, Amityville
Finter, Frederick E., St. John the Baptist, Wading River
Fitzpatrick, John, Ss. Cyril & Methodius, Deer Park
Flannery, James W., St. Anthony, Oceanside
Flood, Frank J., St. Rose of Lima, Massapequa
Flores, Luis, St. Hugh of Lincoln, Huntington Station
Fodale, John E., St. Catherine of Siena, Franklin Square
Forbes, Thomas J., St. Rose of Lima, Massapequa
Ford, John E., St. Thomas the Apostle, West Hempstead
Fox, Thomas, St. Boniface Martyr, Sea Cliff
Fullam, William F., Jr., St. Lawrence the Martyr, Sayville
Gagnon, Jules O. A., St. Patrick, Huntington
Garcia, Ricardo L., Holy Spirit, New Hyde Park
Gargiulo, Andrew T., Our Lady of Perpetual Help, Lindenhurst
Gariboldi, Frank, St. John of God, Central Islip
Gaudioso, Robert, St. Elizabeth Ann Seton, Lake Ronkonkoma
Geoghan, Kenneth, St. Jude, Mastic Beach
Gerace, Patrick C., St. Mark, Shoreham
Giambalvo, Anthony M., Christ the King, Commack
Gillen, Thomas J., St. Jude's, Mastic Beach
Gillette, Ronald J., St. John of God, Central Islip
Giraldo, Luis D., St. Hugh of Lincoln, Huntington Station
Graff, Charles J., Our Lady of Grace, West Babylon
Griffin, William, St. Kilian, Farmingdale
Gronenthal, Robert W., Our Lady of Snow, Blue Point
Guilfo, Juan, St. Patrick, Glen Cove
Guntert, Joseph F., (On Leave of Absence)
Hanly, James, St. Matthew, Dix Hills
Hartmann, Frank C., Our Lady of the Snow, Bluepoint
Hennessy, Thomas R., St. Martin of Tours, Amityville
Hernandez, Robert, Good Shepherd, Holbrook
Herrmann, Mark, St. John the Evangelist, Center Moriches
Heschl, Robert J., Sts. Philip & James, St. James
Hickey, John, Our Lady of Hope, Carle Place
Huber, Charles F., SS. Cyril & Methodius, Deer Park
Ingulli, Joseph, St. James, Setauket
Jackman, Frederick, St. Patrick, Smithtown
Jackson, Thomas H., Queen of the Most Holy Rosary, Roosevelt
Keach, Frank, St. Patrick, Bay Shore
Keenan, John, Sts. Philip & James, St. James
Kogler, William E., St. Margaret of Scotland, Selden
Kolakowski, Theodore, St. Boniface Martyr, Sea Cliff
Kramer, Steven L., Our Lady of the Snow, Blue Point
La Freniere, Gregory, Our Holy Redeemer, Freeport
LaBella, Patrick, St. Lawrence the Martyr, Sayville
Lachlan, Cameron, Holy Spirit, New Hyde Park
Lamb, Richard W., Our Lady of the Miraculous Medal, Wyandanch
LaRossa, Richard W., St. Raymond, East Rockaway
Leahy, John G., St. James, Seaford
Lewis, Clinton, Queen of the Most Holy Rosary, Roosevelt
Leyden, Michael J., St. Joseph, Babylon
Logan, George, Most Holy Trinity, East Hampton
Logsdon, Patrick B., St. Vincent de Paul Society
Longo, Allan D., St. Francis of Assisi, Greenlawn
Love, Francis J., St. Aidan, Williston Park
Lovett, John J., St. John the Evangelist, Riverhead
Luken, Richard A., St. Luke, Brentwood
Lynch, John, St. James, Seaford
Macellaro, Daniel A., Resurrection, Farmingdale
Maffeo, Joseph R., St. Elizabeth Ann Seton, Ronkonkoma
Maher, Kenneth, SS. Philip & James, St. James
Mahoney, Michael A., St. Patrick, Bay Shore

Mannix, Brian, Corpus Christi, Mineola
Marfoglio, Joseph, St. Peter the Apostle, Islip Terrace
Marino, Francis, St. Kilian, Farmingdale
Marino, Salvatore A., Blessed Sacrament, Valley Stream
Matheis, Felix J., St. Brigid, Westbury
Mathurin, Trevor S., St. Martha, Uniondale
McCormack, Kevin, Blessed Sacrament, Valley Stream
McDaid, Thomas P., St. Agnes, Rockville Centre
McGauvran, John W., Queen of the Mast Holy Rosary, Bridghampton
McGowan, John, St. Anne, Garden City
McGuinness, Francis B., St. Rose of Lima, Massapequa
McIndoe, Martin B., St. Francis de Sales, Patchogue
McKenna, John J., St. Joseph, Garden City
McKenna, Michael A., St. Boniface, Elmont
McLaughlin, James, Sts. Peter & Paul, Manorville
McNicholas, Joseph G., Holy Family, Hicksville
McQuade, James J., St. Matthew, Dix Hills
Meehan, John J., Our Lady of Lourdes, East Islip
Mercolino, Joseph T., St. Elizabeth, Melville
Metzdorff, Michael C., St. Brigid, Westbury
Micucci, Raymond R., St. Boniface, Elmont
Mildeberger, William H., Jr., St. Boniface, Elmont
Miller, Brian, Our Lady of Grace, West Babylon
Mills, Hugh, Our Lady of Good Counsel, Inwood
Mills, Philip, Jr., Our Lady of the Assumption, Copiague
Molina, Fernando, St. Frances Cabrini, Coram
Mongillo, Robert, St. Raphael, East Meadow
Montesano, Joseph A., Our Lady Queen of Martyrs, Centerport
Moran, John, Sacred Hearts of Jesus and Mary, Southampton
Morris, James P., St. Brigid, Westbury
Morrow, John W., Our Lady of Grace, West Babylon
Mott, Roger P., St. John Nepomucene, Bohemia
Mulligan, Lawrence P., Our Lady of Victory, Floral Park
Muratore, Biagio V., St. Margaret of Scotland, Selden
Murphy, Galvin C., St. John the Evangelist, Center Moriches
Murphy, James, St. Edward the Confessor, Syosset
Muscarnera, Charles, Chaplain, S. Nassau Hospital
Mystkowski, Joseph J., Our Lady of Mt. Carmel, Patchogue
Naylor, Montford D., St. Francis Cabrini, Coram
Nealis, George F., St. Joseph, Babylon
Nuzzi, John, Maria Regina, Seaford
O'Brien, James J., St. Anne, Garden City
O'Connor, Dennis R., St. Rose of Lima, Massapequa
O'Connor, Thomas F., St. Gerard Majella, Port Jefferson Station
O'Donovan, Robert S., St. Frances de Chantal, Wantagh
O'Hara, James, Holy Name of Mary, Valley Stream
O'Neill, James, St. Anthony, Oceanside
Odin, Frank A., Our Lady of Perpetual Help, Lindenhurst
Owen, George, St. Kilian, Farmingdale
Owens, Thomas F., St. James, Setauket
Pagnotta, Carmen, St. Frances Cabrini, Coram
Paolicelli, Philip, St. Margaret of Scotland, Selden
Pellegrino, Joseph C., St. Christopher, Baldwin
Peralta, Joseph F., St. Patrick, Bay Shore
Perez, Juan, Our Lady of Loretto, Hempstead
Pesce, Frank V., St. Brigid, Westbury
Pettorino, John C., SS. Peter and Paul, Manorville
Pickel, James D., Campus Ministry
Powers, William J., Infant Jesus, Port Jefferson
Quinn, Thomas J., St. Rose of Lima, Massapequa
Quinones, Fernando J., St. Francis de Sales, Patchogue
Raad, Richard, Holy Name of Mary, Valley Stream
Ramos, Manuel J., St. Brigid, Westbury
Rasanen, Terence A., St. Anne, Brentwood
Reda, Gerard, Ss. Philip & James, St James
Reich, George F., St. John Nepomucene, Bohemia
Reilly, Thomas J., St. Hugh of Lincoln, Huntington Station
Reinhart, John C., Corpus Christi, Mineola
Rich, Thomas B., Our Lady of Hope, Carle Place
Riegger, George J., St. Sylvester, Medford
Rivera, Franklin, St. Sylvester, Medford
Rivera, Wenceslao, St. Luke, Brentwood
Roa, Jose, Our Lady of Loretto, Hempstead
Rodenburg, Herman I., St. Kilian, Farmingdale
Roettinger, Francis P., St. Sylvester, Medford
Romero, Miguel A., St. Martha, Uniondale
Ruggieri, Clyde, Holy Name of Mary, Valley Stream
Samson, Thomas R., St. Anne, Brentwood
Sanchez, Cristobal, Our Holy Redeemer, Freeport
Sanders, Richard W., St. Patrick's, Smithtown
Schneider, Andrew M., St. Philip Neri, Northport
Schultz, Peter F., St. Louis de Montfort, Sound Beach
Scollan, Joseph M., St. Margaret of Scotland, Selden
Senholzi, Gregory B., St. John the Baptist, Wading River
Severe, Max, (On Leave of Absence)
Sheehan, John W., St. Martin of Tours, Amityville
Sherlock, Bernard F., St. Barnabas Apostle, Bellmore
Sisinni, Christpher, St. Raphael, East Meadow
Smith, Robert, St. Rosalie, Hampton Bays
Smith, Roy, St. Joseph, Kings Park
Squiteri, Aniello, Our Lady of Peace, Lynbrook
Steffens, Gerard K., Holy Cross, Nesconset
Sullivan, John F., St. Joseph, Babylon
Sullivan, Kenneth R., St. Martha, Uniondale
Swane, Gary, St. Souis de Montfort, Sound Beach
Taranto, Vito, St. Hugh, Huntington Station
Teufel, John G., Our Lady of Lourdes, West Islip
Tirelli, Raymond J., Our Lady of Hope, Carle Place
Torres, Joseph, St. Frances de Chantal, Wantagh
Trodden, John E., St. Luke, Brentwood
Valdaro, Dominick, Our Lady Lourdes, Massapequa Park
Van De Ven, Theodore, Our Lady of Lourdes, Malverne
Vargas, Daniel E., Our Lady of Assumption, Copiague
Vigliotta, Albert C., (Retired)
Vigliotta, Crescenzo T., St. John the Evangelist, Center Moriches
Villani, Salvatore B., St. Aidan, Williston Park
Voegele, Richard, St. Rosalie, Hampton Bays
Waldmann, Richard E., Infant Jesus, Port Jefferson
Walters, John, St. Anne, Brentwood
Weigel, John A., Maria Regina, Seaford
Weisz, Robert D., St. Thomas More, Hauppauge
Wetzel, Edward V., Sacred Heart, Cutohogue
Whitfield, Gerald F., Maria Regina, Seaford

INSTITUTIONS LOCATED IN THE DIOCESE

[A] SEMINARIES, DIOCESAN

HUNTINGTON. *Diocesan Seminary of the Immaculate Conception*, 440 West Neck Rd., 11743. Tel: 631-423-0483; Fax: 631-423-2346. Web: www.icseminary.edu. Most Rev. William Murphy, S.T.D., L.H.D., Chm., Bd. of Governors; Rev. Msgr. Francis J. Schneider, J.C.D., M.Div., Rector; Bro. Jeffrey Pedersen, O.S.F., M.A., Academic Dean; Revs. Edward R. D'Andrea, M.Div., Dir. Spiritual Formation; Joseph J. Nixon, M.A., M.Div., Dir. Pastoral Formation & Dean of Seminarians; Sr. Mary Louise Brink, S.C., Ph.D., Assoc. Dean, Dir. Graduate Studies; Elyse B. Hayes, M.L.S., Library Dir.; Mrs. Bernadette M. Grodman, Business Officer; Mrs. Joan Innvar, Registrar; Rev. Patrick J. Griffin, C.M., Ph.D.; Katherine M. Hayes, Ph.D.; Rev. Gerard H. Luttenberger, C.M., S.T.D.; Rev. Msgr. Peter I. Vaccari, S.T.L. (BRK); Rev. Richard G. Henning, M.A., M.Div.; James Massa, Ph.D.; Charles Caccavale, S.T.L., S.T.D. Priests 10; Brothers 1; Sisters 1; Lay Professor 1; Support Lay Staff 34; Seminarians 41; M.A. Students 107; D.Min. Students 7.

[B] COLLEGES AND UNIVERSITIES

ROCKVILLE CENTRE. *Molloy College*, 1000 Hempstead Ave., 11571-5002. Tel: 516-678-5000; 888-466-5569; Fax: 516-678-7295. Email: mharrison@molloy.edu. Web: www.molloy.edu. Dr. Drew Bogner, Pres.; Sisters Dorothy Anne Fitzgibbons, O.P., Ed.D., Vice Pres. for Mission; Joan Garvey, O.P., Dir. Campus Ministries; Michail Allen Harrison, Dir. of Communications; Edward J. Thopson, Vice Pres. for Advancement; Dr. Joan Marlo, Vice Pres. for Technology; Linda Albanese, Vice Pres. for Enrollment Management; Vincent Tunstall, Dir. of Financial Aid; Sr. Doris Nevitt, O.P., M.A., Dir. Student Financial Svcs.; Rev. John A. Madigan, O.P., M.A., Chap. Priests 2; Brothers 1; Ministers 4; Sisters of St. Dominic (Amityville Community) 29; Lay Teachers 309; Students 2,500.

PATCHOGUE. **St. Joseph's College*, 155 W. Roe Blvd., 11772-2399. Tel: 631-447-3200; Fax: 631-654-1782. Email: lmcgrann@sjcny.edu. Web: www.sjcny.edu. 245 Clinton Ave., Brooklyn, 11205-3688. Sr. Loretta McGrann, C.S.J.; Rev. Frank Pizzarelli, S.M.M., Part-time. Sisters 13; Lay Teachers 77; Students 3,804.

[C] HIGH SCHOOLS, DIOCESAN

NASSAU COUNTY

HICKSVILLE
Holy Trinity, 98 Cherry Ln., 11801. Tel: 516-433-2900; Fax: 516-433-2827. Email: hths98@holytrinityhs.org. Web: www.holytrinityhs.org. Mr. James J. Boglioli, Prin.; Rev. Gerard Gentleman, M.A., M.Div., Chap. Sisters 7; Lay Teachers 99; Students 1,665. In Res. Rev. Msgr. Thomas J. Hartman.

SUFFOLK COUNTY

WEST ISLIP
St. John the Baptist, 1170 Montauk Hwy., 11795. Tel: 631-587-8000; Fax: 631-587-8996. Walter D. Lace, Prin.; Rev. James C. Vlaun, Chap. Sisters 5; Priests 1; Lay Teachers 79; Students 1,250.

[D] HIGH SCHOOLS, PRIVATE

BRENTWOOD. *Academy of St. Joseph* Independent; (Coed school grades K-6; Girl's school grades 7-12) , 1725 Brentwood Rd., 11717. Tel: 631-273-2406; Fax: 631-231-4155. Email: asjli@asjli.org. Web: www.asjli.org. Sisters Valerie Scholl, C.S.J., Dir.; Joanne Forker, C.S.J., Prin. Directed by the Sisters of St. Joseph Sisters of St. Joseph 11; Lay Teachers 32; Students 340.

FREEPORT. *The De La Salle School*, 87 Pine St., 11520-3615. Tel: 516-379-8660; Fax: 516-379-8806. Email: DeLaSalleLI@hotmail.com. Bro. Thomas P. Casey, F.S.C., Exec. Dir. Brothers 2; Lay Teachers 2; Total Enrollment 25.

HEMPSTEAD. *Sacred Heart Academy* College preparatory-girls , 47 Cathedral Ave., 11550. Tel: 516-483-7383; Fax: 516-483-1016. Email: sha@sacredheartacademyhempstead.org. Web: www.sacredheartacademyhempstead.org. Sr. Jeanne Marie Ross, C.S.J., Prin. Sisters 17; Lay Teachers 58; Students 775.

MINEOLA. *Chaminade High School (Boys)* Directed by the Society of Mary (Marianists) , 340 Jackson Ave., 11501. Tel: 516-742-5555; Fax: 516-742-1989. Email: flyers@chaminade-hs.org. Web: www.chaminade-hs.org. Rev. James C. Williams, S.M., Pres.; Bro. Joseph D. Bellizzi, S.M., Prin.; Mr. Salvatore Trentacoste, Asst. Prin.; Mr. Daniel Petruccio, Dir. of Guidance; Bros. Thomas J. Cleary, S.M., Dean of Students; James W. Conway, S.M., Dir. Student Svcs.; Rev. Garrett J. Long, S.M., Chap.; Bro. Peter H. Heiskell, S.M., Dir. of Apostolic Action. Brothers 18; Priests 3; Lay Teachers 48; Students 1,600.

RIVERHEAD. *Bishop McGann Mercy High School*, 1225 Ostrander Ave., 11901. Tel: 631-727-5900; Fax: 631-727-8483; 631-369-7328. Web: www.mcgann-mercy.org. Mr. Steven F. Cheeseman, Prin.; Ms. Kathleen Venable; Deacon Cletus Burke, O.S.F., Dean of Students, Asst. Prin. Directed by the Diocese of Rockville Centre/Sisters of Mercy, (Coed) Sisters of Mercy (Brooklyn) 5; Other Sisters 1; Lay Teachers 35; Students 340.

SOUTH HUNTINGTON. *St. Anthony's High School* College Prep. , 275 Wolf Hill Rd., 11747-1394. Tel: 631-271-2020; Fax: 631-547-6820. Email: administration@stanthonyshs.org. Web: www.stanthonyshs.org. Bro. Gary Cregan, O.S.F., Prin. Directed by the Franciscan Brothers of Brooklyn Priests 1; Brothers 18; Permanent Deacon 1; Intercommunity Sisters 7; Lay Teachers 107; Students 2,162.

SYOSSET. *Our Lady of Mercy Academy* Girls-day students. , 815 Convent Rd., 11791-3895. Tel: 516-921-1047; Fax: 516-921-3634. Email: olma1@yahoo.com. Web: www.OLMA.org. Sr. Margaret M. Conway, C.S.J., Prin. Directed by the Sisters of Mercy Sisters of Mercy 7; Sisters of St. Joseph 1; Sisters of St. Dominic 3; Lay Teachers 42; Students 460; Sisters of St. Ursula 1.

UNIONDALE. *Kellenberg Memorial High School*, 1400 Glenn Curtiss Blvd., 11553. Tel: 516-292-0200; Fax: 516-292-0877. Email: kmhs@li.net. Web: www.kellenberg.org. Rev. Philip K. Eichner, S.M., Pres.; Bros. Kenneth M. Hoagland, S.M., Prin.; Richard Hughes, S.M., Asst. Prin. for Academics; Mr. Kenneth Conrade, Asst. Prin. for School Personnel; Rev. Albert Bertoni, S.M., Asst. Prin. Guidance; Ms. Maria Korzekwinski, Asst. Prin. Latin School; Bro. Roger Poletti, S.M., Asst. Prin. Activities; Rev. Thomas A. Cardone, S.M., Chap.; Mrs. Marina Trentacoste, Dean of Students; Mr. Edward Solosky, Dean of Men; Mr. Edward Dunn, Athletic Dir.; Mr. Richard Kotlarz, Supvr. of Building Maintenance & Landscaping; Bro. Donald Nussbaum, S.M., Suprv. New Construction, Vehicles; Mr. Jim Payne, Supvr. Cleaning Maintenance; Mrs. Catherine Zabrouski, Financial Supvr. Directed by the Society of Mary Priests 4; Brothers 10; Lay Teachers 112; Students 2,458.

[E] REGIONAL SCHOOLS

BELLMORE. *St. Elizabeth Ann Seton Regional School* Tel: 516-785-5709; Fax: 516-785-4468. Email: etk@seas.edrvc.org. Supported by the following parishes: St. Barnabas, Bellmore; St. Raphael,

East Meadow; Cure of Ars, Merrick; St. Frances de Chantal, Wantagh.

Bellmore Campus, 2341 Washington Ave., 11710. Tel: 516-785-5709; Fax: 516-785-4468. Dr. Eileen Kilbride, Prin. Sisters 1; Lay Teachers 31; Students 450.

East Meadow Campus, 600 Newbridge Ave., East Meadow, 11554. Tel: 516-785-7006; Fax: 516-785-7008. Mrs. Jane Harrigan, Prin. Sisters 1; Lay Teachers 12; Students 200.

Wantagh Campus, 1309 Wantagh Ave., Wantagh, 11793. Tel: 516-826-3882; Fax: 516-679-2082. N-K Early Childhood Center Lay Teachers 7; Students 230.

BETHPAGE. *St. John Baptist de LaSalle Regional School* Tel: 516-931-0983; Fax: 516-931-1502. Email: LSReg220B@aol.com. Supported by the following parishes: St. Martin of Tours, Bethpage; St. Kilian, Farmingdale; St. Pius X, Plainview; St. James, Seaford.

Bethpage Campus, 220 Central Ave., 11714. Tel: 516-931-0983; Fax: 516-931-1502. Elizabeth F. Ceccarini, Prin. Lay Teachers 19; Students 236.

Farmingdale Campus, 50 Cherry St., Farmingdale, 11735. Tel: 516-694-3610; Fax: 516-694-7296. Diane Ragonnet, Prin. Sisters 1; Lay Teachers 19; Students 224.

CENTER MORICHES. *Our Lady, Queen of Apostles Regional School*, 2 St. Johns Pl., 11934. Tel: 631-878-1033; Fax: 631-878-1059. Email: sreileen@olqa.edruc.org. Sr. Eileen Martin, S.C., Prin. Supported by the following parishes: St. John Evangelist, Center Moriches; St. Jude, Mastic Beach; Immaculate Conception, Westhampton Beach; Ss. Peter & Paul, Manorville. Sisters 2; Lay Teachers 19; Students 294.

CENTRAL ISLIP. *Our Lady of Providence Regional School*, 82 Carleton Ave., 11722. Tel: 631-234-1113; 631-234-6324; Fax: 631-234-6360. Email: provcsj@aol.com. Sisters Kerry Handal, C.S.J., Prin. Upper School; Stephen Mary Puglisi, C.S.J., Prin. Lower School. Supported by the following parishes: St. Anne, Brentwood; St. Luke, Brentwood; St. John of God, Central Islip; St. Peter the Apostle, Islip Terrace. Sisters 1; Lay Teachers 29; Students 470.

COMMACK. *Holy Family Regional School*, Indian Head Rd., P.O. Box 729, 11725. Tel: 631-543-0202; Fax: 631-543-0203. Email: hfrs@aol.com. Ms. Agatha Cavoli, Prin. Supported by the following parishes: Christ the King, Commack; St. Matthew, Dix Hills; St. Thomas More, Hauppauge; St. Joseph, Kings Park. Sisters 4; Lay Teachers 21; Students 424.

CUTCHOGUE. *Our Lady of Mercy Regional School*, P.O. Box 970 - Main St., 11935. Tel: 631-734-5166; Fax: 631-734-4266. Email: olmcutho@optonline.net. Web: www.myschoolonline.com. Sr. Mary Christi, Prin. Supported by the following parishes: Sacred Heart, Cutchogue; Our Lady of Ostrabrama, Cutchogue; St. Agnes, Greenport; and St. Patrick, Southold. Lay Teachers 8; Students 250.

EAST NORTHPORT. *Trinity Regional School*, 1025 Fifth Ave., 11731. Tel: 631-261-5130; Fax: 631-266-5345. Email: tregion@optonline.net. Ms. Jeanne Morcone, Prin. Supported by the following parishes: Our Lady Queen of Martyrs, Centerport; St. Anthony of Padua, East Northport; St. Francis of Assisi, Greenlawn; St. Hugh of Lincoln, Huntington Station; St. Elizabeth, Melville; St. Philip Neri, Northport. Sisters 2; Lay Teachers 40; Students 800.

Satellite campuses exist at:

1450 New York Ave., Huntington Station, 11746. Tel: 631-549-7450; Fax: 631-549-7454.

364 Main St., Northport, 11768. Tel: 631-261-8520; Fax: 631-261-8560.

GLEN COVE. *All Saints Regional Catholic School*, 12 Pearsall Ave., 11542-3052. Tel: 516-676-0762; Fax: 516-676-0660. Web: www.asrcatholic.com. Supported by the following parishes: St. Boniface, Sea Cliff; St. Hyacinth, Glen Head; St. Mary, Roslyn; St. Patrick, Glen Cove; St. Rocco, Glen Cove. Lay Teachers 28; Students 442.

Primary Campus (Grades N-PreSchool), 319 Cedar Swamp Rd., Glen Head, 11545-2298. Tel: 516-671-4247; Fax: 516-671-4247.

Upper Campus (Grades K-8), 12 Pearsall Ave., 11542-3052. Tel: 516-676-0762; Fax: 516-676-0660. Rev. James W. Thompson (L), Prin. (Retired).

LONG BEACH. *Long Beach Catholic Regional School*, (Grades PreK-8), 735 W. Broadway, 11561. Tel: 516-432-8900; Fax: 516-432-3841. Mrs. Veronica Danca, Prin. Supported by the following parishes: St. Ignatius, Long Beach; St. Mary of the Isle, Long Beach, and Our Lady of the Miraculous Medal, Point Lookout. Sisters 2; Lay Teachers 20; Students 455.

PATCHOGUE. *Holy Angels Regional School*, (Grades K-8), Division St., 11772. Tel: 631-475-0422; Fax: 631-475-2036. Email: smelise@holyangels.edrvc.org. Web: http://myschoolonline.com/ny/HolyAngelsSchool. Sr. Elise Bier, R.S.M., Prin. Supported by the following parishes: Mary Immaculate, Bellport; St. Frances Cabrini, Coram; St. Joseph the Worker, E. Patchogue; St. Sylvester, Medford; Our Lady of Mount Carmel, Patchogue; St. Frances de Sales, Patchogue, and St. Margaret of Scotland, Selden. Sisters 2; Lay Teachers 18; Students 370.

PORT JEFFERSON. *Our Lady of Wisdom Regional School*, 114-116 Myrtle Ave., 11777. Tel: 631-473-1211; Fax: 631-473-1064. Email: ninaed@optonline.net. Web: www.ourladyofwisdom.com. Mrs. Nina Edwards, Prin. Supported by the following parishes: Infant Jesus, Port Jefferson; St. Louis de Montfort, Sound Beach; St. James, Setauket; St. Gerard Majella, Port Jefferson Station. Lay Teachers 14; Students 225; Total Staff 25.

SAG HARBOR. *Stella Maris Regional School*, 135 Division St., 11963. Tel: 631-725-2525; Fax: 631-725-0563. Web: www.StellaMarisSchool.org. Susan Norbeck, Prin. Supported by the following parishes: St. Therese of Lisieux, Montauk; Most Holy Trinity, East Hampton; St. Andrew, Sag Harbor; Queen of the Most Holy Rosary, Bridgehampton; Our Lady of the Isle, Shelter Island. Sisters 1; Lay Teachers 14; Students 220.

SAYVILLE. *Prince of Peace Regional School*, 200 Main St., 11782. Tel: 631-589-3426; Fax: 631-589-4523. Jane F. Harrigan, Prin. Supported by the following parishes: Our Lady of Snow, Blue Point; St. John Nepomucene, Bohemia; Good Shepherd, Holbrook; St. Lawrence, Sayville. Lay Teachers 13; Students 230.

SOUTHAMPTON. *Our Lady of the Hamptons Regional School*, (Grades K-8), 160 N. Main St., 11968. Tel: 631-283-9140; Fax: 631-283-3958. Email: sks@hamptons.com. Web: www.olh.org. Nursery and PreK.; Supported by the following parishes: St. Rosalie, Hampton Bays; Our Lady of Poland, Southampton, and Sacred Hearts Jesus Mary, Southampton. Sisters 3; Lay Teachers 24; Total Enrollment 400.

31 Montauk Hwy., Hampton Bays, 11946. Tel: 631-723-3740; Fax: 631-728-2559. Sr. Kathryn Schlueter, C.S.J., Prin. Sisters 3; Lay Teachers 22; Students 401.

UNIONDALE. *St. Martin de Porres Regional School*, 530 Hempstead Blvd., 11553. Tel: 516-481-3303; Fax: 516-483-4138. Email: wkemmerer@stmarndep.edrvc.org. Supported by the following parishes: Our Lady of Loretto, Hempstead; St. Ladislaus, Hempstead; St. Martha, Uniondale. Lay Teachers 18; Students 231; Total Enrollment 231.

[F] ELEMENTARY SCHOOLS, PRIVATE

MANHASSET. *Our Lady of Grace Montessori School and Center*, (Grades PreK-3), 29 Shelter Rock Rd., 11030. Tel: 516-365-9832; Fax: 516-365-9329. Sisters, Servants of the Immaculate Heart of Mary 4; Lay Teachers 17; Students 230.

OLD WESTBURY. *Old Westbury School of the Holy Child*, (Grades N-8), 25 Store Hill Rd., 11568. Tel: 516-626-9300; Fax: 516-626-7814. Email: mmod7@hotmail.com. Web: www.oldwestburyschoolhc.com. Mr. Michael O'Donoghue, Head of School; Palma Gartland, Asst. to Head; Gail Walker, Asst. to Head. Lay Teachers 25; Students 175.

[G] SPECIALIZED CHILD CARE AGENCIES

NESCONSET. *Cleary Deaf Child Center, Inc.*, 301 Smithtown Blvd., 11767. Tel: 631-588-0530 (Voice and TTY); Fax: 631-588-0016. Email: catherinef@clearyschool.org. Web: www.clearyschool.org. Sr. Catherine Fitzgibbon, C.S.J., Supt. Directed by Catholic Charities., Day School (Infants thru 21 years). Students 70.

PORT JEFFERSON STATION. *Maryhaven Center of Hope*, Administrative Offices, 1010 Rte. 112, 11776. Tel: 631-474-4120; Fax: 631-474-4110. Email: LGrossman@maryhaven.org. Web: www.maryhaven.org. Mr. Lewis Grossman, CEO. Maryhaven provides services to approximately 2,000 mentally and physically challenged children and adults. Total Assisted Annually 2,000; Total Staff 1,100.

Adult Day Services (over age 18):

Vocational Training/Supported Work/Sheltered Workshop Tel: 631-924-5900; Fax: 631-924-2464.

Day Habilitation Tel: 631-474-4100; Fax: 631-474-4156.

Adult Residential Services:

Adult Residences Tel: 631-474-4100; Fax: 631-474-9014.

Home Touch Tel: 631-474-4100; Fax: 631-474-9014.

Mental Health Services:

Case Management Tel: 631-474-4100; Fax: 631-474-4156.

Continuing Day Treatment/Intensive Psychiatric Rehabilitation Treatment Tel: 631-727-4044; Fax: 631-727-6531.

Children Services (Ages 5-21):

Maryhaven School Tel: 631-474-3400; Fax: 631-474-4181.

Children's Residences Tel: 631-474-3400; Fax: 631-474-4181.

SYOSSET. *St. Mary's Children and Family Services*, 525 Convent Rd., 11791-3864. Tel: 516-921-0808; Fax: 516-921-4542. Email: stmlg@cs.com. Web: www.stmaryscfs.com. Liz Giordano, CEO. Under the sponsorship of the Sisters of Mercy, Residential treatment center, non-secure detention, group homes, supervised independent living apartments, foster boarding homes, diagnostic assessment prog., preventive svc. prog. in Nassau Co. and Queens. Residential treatment facility for mentally ill children. Abuse treatment & prevention program, hard to place (JD) program for males. Total Staff 643; Total Assisted 4,420.

WADING RIVER. *Little Flower Children's Services of New York* 11792. Tel: 631-929-6200; Fax: 631-929-6121. Web: www.LittleFlowerNY.org. Rev. Msgr. John T. Fagan, Honorary Chmn. of Advisory Board (Retired); Hon. Herbert W. Stupp, Exec. Vice Pres.; Sr. Rita Wasilewski, C.S.F.N., Supr. Sisters of the Holy Family of Nazareth, Directed by the Diocese of Brooklyn. Foster care, adoption & post-adoption svcs., intermediate care facilities, residential treatment center, Special Act school district, family day care, family care for MR/DD clients, foster homes for teen mothers & their babies. Therapeutic foster boarding homes. Total Assisted 2,119; Total Staff 717.

[H] CATHOLIC CHARITIES

HICKSVILLE. *Catholic Charities*, 90 Cherry Ln., 11801-6299. Tel: 516-733-7000; Fax: 516-733-7099. Web: www.catholiccharities.cc. Laura A. Cassell, CEO. Tel: 516-733-7013; Paul Englehart, Chief Prog. Officer. Tel: 516-733-7012; Fax: 516-733-7099; Robert J. Manfredi, MIS Admin. Tel: 516-733-7003; Fax: 516-733-7098; John Gonta, Purchasing & Facilities Admin. Tel: 516-733-7090; Fax: 516-733-7099; Mr. John K. Bingham, Dir. of Capital Projects & Law. Tel: 516-733-7040.

Human Resources, 90 Cherry Lane, 11801-6299. Tel: 516-733-7000; Fax: 516-733-7038. Edward Moore, Human Resource Admin. Tel: 516-733-7005; Fax: 516-733-7038; Carol Ann Radziewicz, Human Resource Coord. Tel: 516-733-7006; Fax: 516-733-7099.

Finance, 90 Cherry Ln., 11801-6299. Tel: 516-733-7015; Fax: 516-733-7099. Edwin M. Kennedy, Dir. Finance; Jo Ann Parda, Financial Admin. Tel: 516-733-7017; Maureen Angelillo, Payroll Coord. Tel: 516-733-7031.

Office of Mental Health Residences Tel: 631-665-5902; Fax: 631-665-3890. Howard G. Duff, Prog. Coord.

Residence for people who are psychiatrically impaired:

Siena Residence, 12 Mechanicsville Rd., Bay Shore, 11706. Tel: 631-968-8007; Fax: 631-968-8009.

Residences for children who are seriously emotionally disturbed:

Teaching Family Home Program

269 W. Main St., Bay Shore, 11706. Tel: 631-665-5902; Fax: 631-665-3890. Howard G. Duff, Prog. Coordinator.

Maternity Services, 29 Kirkwood Ave., Merrick, 11566. Tel: 516-223-7888; Fax: 516-223-2752. Kathleen Ryan, Prog. Admin.; Carole Hendler, Mentoring of Moms Contact.

Residence for Pregnant Women:

Regina Residence, 29 Kirkwood Ave., Merrick, 11566. Tel: 516-223-7888; Fax: 516-223-2752. Kathleen Ryan, Prog. Admin.

Residence for Mothers and Babies:

Malta House Tel: 516-223-7888; Fax: 516-223-2752. Kathleen Ryan, Prog. Admin.

Alcohol & Substance Abuse Services, 155 Indian Head Rd., Commack, 11725. Tel: 631-543-6200; Fax: 631-543-6203. Kathleen Ayers-Lanzilotta, Prog. Admin.; David Emeritz, Outpatient Clinic Contact.

Outpatient Clinics:

31 E. Main St., P.O. Box 758, Hampton Bays, 11956-0701. Tel: 631-723-3362; Fax: 631-723-3365.

St. Therese of Lisieux Parish House, South Etna Ave., Montauk, 11954. Tel: 631-537-1159.

St. Ann's Episcopal Church Parish House: 2463 Main St., Bridgehampton, 11932. Tel: 631-723-3362; Fax: 631-723-3365. Wayne Cavaliere, Contact.

Talbot House Alcohol Crisis Center, 30-C Carlough Rd., Bohemia, 11716. Tel: 631-589-4144; Fax: 631-589-3281. Brian Nichols, Contact.

Mental Health Services, 1729 N. Ocean Ave., Medford, 11763. Tel: 631-654-2944; Fax: 631-654-2966. Denis Demers, Mental Health Services Admin.

Mental Health Clinics (Suffolk):
9 Fourth Ave., Bay Shore, 11706. Tel: 631-665-6707; Fax: 631-665-3564. Adelaide Corvelle, Contact.
1727 N. Ocean Ave., Medford, 11763. Tel: 631-654-1919; Fax: 631-475-8407. Joan England, Contact.
Mental Health Clinics (Nassau):
259 Mineola Blvd., Mineola, 11501. Tel: 516-248-7100; Fax: 516-877-0717.
333 N. Main St., Freeport, 11520. Tel: 516-623-3322; Fax: 516-623-3526. Patricia Quinn, Contact.
HIV/AIDS Services, 333 N. Main St., Freeport, 11520. Tel: 516-623-7400; Fax: 516-623-9607.
Special Dental Services Program, 333 N. Main St., Freeport, 11520. Tel: 516-623-4420; Fax: 516-623-1313. Dr. Samantha Ifill, Dental Dir.
AIDS Adult Day Health Care Program, 333 N. Main St., Freeport, 11520. Tel: 516-623-7400; Fax: 516-623-9607. Michael Ingrassea, Prog. Coord.
Housing Services, 90 Cherry Ln., 11801-6299. Tel: 516-733-7076; Fax: 516-733-7098. Paul A. Chedda, Dir. Tel: 516-733-7075; Robert Lulley, Pastoral Care Coord. (Suffolk Co.). Tel: 516-733-7076; Lynn Reddy, Pastoral Care Coord. (Nassau Co.). Tel: 516-733-7076.
Senior Housing: Tel: 516-733-7076.
St. Agnes Village, 100 St. Agnes Rd., Uniondale, 11553. Tel: 516-485-4721. Virginia Schultz, Contact.
St. Joseph's Village, 2000 Boyle Rd., Selden, 11784. Tel: 631-736-0524. Angela Cammarata, Contact.
Bishop Kellenberg Gardens, 2477 Long Beach Rd., Oceanside, 11572. Tel: 516-766-0777. Eileen Frost, Contact.
Peternana Terrace, 45 Wallace St., Freeport, 11520. Tel: 516-378-4072. Nancy Turner, Contact.
Bishop Ryan Village, 10 Squiretown Rd., Hampton Bays, 11946. Tel: 631-728-2413.
St. Paul's Gardens, 702 St. Paul's Ct., Brentwood, 11717. Tel: 631-436-9074. Eileen Grabow, Contact.
George Link Jr. Apts., George Link Jr. Cir., Coram, 11727. Tel: 631-732-6878. Cathy Sileo, Contact.
Mary's Manor, 60 Doughty Blvd., Inwood, 11696. Tel: 516-239-4291. Juanita Warren, Contact.
Msgr. Henry J. Reel, 590 Christopher Ct., Medford, 11763. Tel: 631-475-6504. Deborah Chilcott, Contact.
St. Hedwig's Gardens, 8 Linden Ave., Floral Park, 11001. Tel: 516-616-9023. Fern M. Shakespeare, Contact.
Bishop McGann Village, 200 Bishop McGann Dr., Central Islip, 11722. Tel: 631-232-9356. Eileen Donaldson, Contact.
Thea Bowman Residence, 100 Schleigel Ct., Amityville, 11701. Tel: 631-789-4573. Celeste Martin, Contact.
Food and Nutrition (FAN) Program, 143 Schleigel Blvd., Amityville, 11701. Tel: 516-789-9533; Fax: 516-789-9542. Liivia Westervelt, Prog. Admin. Tel: 631-789-0520; Fax: 516-789-3844.
Food Center Locations:
66 N. 19th St., Wyandanch, 11798. Tel: 631-491-4166; Fax: 631-491-4950.
61-C Brightside Ave., Central Islip, 11722. Tel: 631-232-2797.
38 St. John's Pl., Freeport, 11520. Tel: 516-623-4568; Fax: 516-623-2125.
Health Services:
Office for Persons with Disabilities, 143 Schleigel Blvd., Amityville, 11701. Tel: 631-789-5219; Fax: 631-789-3844. Lori Scharff, Cood. Tel: 516-789-5219 Lavelle Fund for the Blind.
Services for Persons Blind/Visually Impaired Tel: 631-789-5213; Fax: 631-789-3844.
Services for Persons Deaf and Hard of Hearing Tel: 631-789-5219; Fax: 631-789-3844. Bro. Alan J. Thomas, O.F.M., Contact.
Residential Services, 269 W. Main St., Bay Shore, 11706. Tel: 631-665-3434; Fax: 631-665-3586. Diane Ammirati, Prog. Admin.
Community residences for people who are developmentally disabled:
Alhambra House, 3 Forest Pl., Huntington Station, 11746. Tel: 631-673-5240; Fax: 631-425-9628. Jeannette Morris, Contact.
Caritas Residence, P.O. Box 2383, 4 Hilton Ct., Aqueboque, 11931. Tel: 631-722-5366; Fax: 631-722-5366. Kelly McLaren, Contact.
Christopher Residence, 70 McKeon Ave., Valley Stream, 11580. Tel: 516-825-8282; Fax: 516-825-5383. Kathleen O'Mahony, Contact.
Msgr. R. Emmet Fagan Residence, 1504 DePaul St., Elmont, 11003. Tel: 516-358-2559; Fax: 516-616-0304. Donna Maria Castanedo, Contact.
Mako Residence, 380 Ed's Rd., Southold, 11971. Tel: 631-765-1783; Fax: 631-765-1783. Kelly McLaren, Contact.
Neumann Residence (For Deaf Adults) , 30 Brinkerhoff Ln., Manhassett, 11030. Tel: 516-627-5038; Fax: 516-869-0709. Marlowe Morrison, Contact.
Bishop Ryan Residence, 258 Deauville Blvd., Copiague, 11726. Tel: 631-691-2126; Fax: 631-691-0860. Denise O'Halloran, Contact.
Seton Residence, 3 Lombardi Pl., Amityville, 11701. Tel: 631-598-8216; Fax: 631-264-7967. Sr. Margaret Stadelman, Contact.
Ted Hansler Residence, 24 Gardiners Ln., Hampton Bays, 11946. Tel: 631-728-8125; Fax: 631-728-0861. Amy Goff, Contact.
Joseph Virdone Residence, 27 North Carll Ave., Babylon, 11702. Tel: 631-661-2826; Fax: 631-661-2952. James Kelly, Contact.
Senior Services, 147 Schleigel Blvd., Amityville, 11701. Tel: 631-789-0520; Fax: 631-789-3844. Livia Westervelt, Prog. Admin. Tel: 631-789-0520.
Bi-County Alliance of Senior Clubs Tel: 631-789-0520; Fax: 631-789-3844. Liivia Westervelt, Contact.
Link-Age Case Management, 90 Cherry Ln., 11801-6299. Tel: 516-733-7064; Fax: 516-733-7098. John Sheridan, Contact.
Meals-On-Wheels (Nassau) (For Seniors and People with AIDS) , 131 Fulton St., Ste 100, Hempstead, 11550. Tel: 516-485-7555; Fax: 516-485-7598. Jackie Blount, Contact.
Meals-On-Wheels (Suffolk), 147 Schleigel Blvd., Amityville, 11701. Tel: 631-842-4123. MaryAnn McGrenra, Contact.
Senior Community Service Centers:
145 Schleigel Blvd., Amityville, 11701. Tel: 631-842-7331; 631-842-7332. Dennis Sullivan, Contact.
379 Linden St., Massapequa Park, 11762. Tel: 516-797-5357; Fax: 516-797-5529. Marline Evangelista, Contact.
619 Fenworth Blvd., P.O. Box 183, Franklin Square, 11010. Tel: 516-481-3322; Fax: 516-481-3236. Sue Bouffier, Contact.
P.O. Box 243, 25 Nassau Ln., Island Park, 11558. Tel: 516-432-3388; Fax: 516-432-3958. Marie Frangella, Contact.
80 Anchor Ave., Oceanside, 11572. Tel: 516-764-9792; Fax: 516-764-9853. Margaret Keffel, Contact.
P.O. Box 524, 2197 Jackson Ave., Seaford, 11783. Tel: 516-679-8373; Fax: 516-679-8374. Patricia Nadeau, Contact.
Immigrant Services, 143 Schleigel Blvd., Amityville, 11701. Tel: 631-789-5210; Fax: 631-789-5245. Carmen Maquilon, Dir. of Immigrant Services. Tel: 631-789-5225.
Parish Social Ministry, 90 Cherry Ln., 11801. Tel: 516-733-7078; Fax: 516-733-7098. Anthony Mullen, Dir. of Parish and Community Services. Tel: 516-733-7084; Richard Koubek, Public Policy Education Network Coord. Tel: 516-733-7077; Judy Mazzarella. Tel: 631-654-2979 Special Projects, Parish Outreach; Brian Paradine. Tel: 516-733-7050 Volunteer Lawyers Initiative & Special Projects; George Reich, Developer, Parish Outreach. Tel: 516-733-7048; Patricia Oliviero, Developer, Parish Outreach. Tel: 631-654-0365; Kathy McIntyre, Developer; Connie Loos, Parish Outreach, Catholic Campaign for Human Development. Tel: 516-733-7054; Louise Simon, Developer, Parish Outreach. Tel: 516-733-7054.
Central Intake Coords. Tel: 516-733-7045, Ext. 46; Fax: 516-733-7098.
Public Affairs and Development, 90 Cherry Ln., 11801. Tel: 516-733-7042; Fax: 516-733-7098. Scott A. Stepp, Coord. Tel: 516-733-7042; Helene A. Canberg, Communications & Public Rels. Specialist. Tel: 516-733-7043; Watson Jean-Baptiste, Development Assoc. Tel: 516-733-7082.

UNIONDALE. *Bishop Daly Gardens*, Greengrove Ave. & Jerusalem Ave., 11553.

[I] CATHOLIC HEALTHCARE APOSTOLATE NASSAU COUNTY

ROCKVILLE CENTRE
Catholic Health Services of Long Island, 992 N. Village Ave., 11570. Tel: 516-705-3700; Fax: 516-705-3730. Web: chsli.org.
Legal Title: *Catholic Health Systems of Long Island, Inc.*
Catholic Healthcare Network of Long Island, 992 N. Village Ave., 11570. Tel: 516-705-3700; Fax: 516-705-3730. Mr. Patrick Scollard, Interim CEO; Richard J.J. Sullivan Jr., Bd. Chair; Sr. Evelyn Eckhardt, D.W., Vice Chair; Thomas F. Christman, Treas.; Robert Z. Gussin, Ph.D., Corp. Sec.; Donna M. O'Brien, Exec. Vice Pres. & CAO; Rev. Msgr. Dennis M. Regan, Senior Vice Pres. Mission & Ethics; Terence G. Daly, Senior Vice Pres. Finance & Chief Fin. Officer.
Hospitals:
St. Charles Hospital and Rehabilitation Center, 200 Belle Terre Rd., Port Jefferson, 11777. Tel: 631-474-6600; Fax: 631-474-6884. William Casey, Pres. & CEO.
Mercy Medical Center, 1000 N. Village Ave., 11570. Tel: 516-705-1401; Fax: 516-705-1406. Martin A. Bieber, Interim Pres. & CEO.
St. Francis Hospital, 100 Port Washington Blvd., Roslyn, 11576. Tel: 516-562-6901; Fax: 516-562-6909. Alan D. Guerci, M.D., Pres. & CEO.
St. Catherine of Siena Medical Center, 50 Rte. 25A, Smithtown, 11787. Tel: 631-862-3000; Fax: 631-862-3105. Vincent DiRubbio, Pres. & CEO.
Good Samaritan Hospital Medical Center, 1000 Montauk Hwy., West Islip, 11795. Tel: 631-376-4001; Fax: 631-376-4208. Richard J. Murphy, Pres. & CEO.
Nursing Homes and Sub-Acute Care:
Good Samaritan Nursing Home, 101 Elm St., Sayville, 11782. Tel: 631-244-2400; Fax: 631-244-2405. Michael Quartararo, Admin. Operating as a part of Good Samaritan Hospital Medical Center
St. Catherine of Siena Nursing Home, 52 Rte. 25A, Smithtown, 11787. Tel: 631-862-3905; Fax: 631-862-3983. Jeffrey Rogoff, Admin. Operating as apart of St. Catherine of Siena Medical Center
Our Lady of Consolation Nursing & Rehabilitative Care Center, 111 Beach Dr., West Islip, 11795. Tel: 631-587-1600; Fax: 631-587-5960. Mr. Dennis J. Verzi, Pres. & CEO.
Hospice and Palliative Care Services:
Good Shepherd Hospice, 4747-20 Nesconset Hwy., Port Jefferson, 11776. Tel: 631-474-5500; Fax: 631-474-2568. Marianne Gillan, Pres. Operating Under Nursing Sisters Home Care
Community-Based Programs:
Maryhaven Center of Hope, 1010 Rte. 112, Port Jefferson Station, 11776. Tel: 631-474-4120; Fax: 631-474-4110. Mr. Lewis Grossman, Pres. & CEO.
Maryhaven School, 1010 Rte. 112, Port Jefferson Station, 11776. Tel: 631-474-4120; Fax: 631-474-4110. Robin Dwyer, Contact. Operating Under Maryhaven Center of Hope
Maryhaven Transportation Services, Inc., 51 Terryville Rd., Port Jefferson Station, 11776. Tel: 631-474-4100; Fax: 631-474-4110. Alice Stanek, Contact. Operating Under Maryhaven Center of Hope
Home Care Agency:
Nursing Sisters Home Care, 190 Motor Pkwy., Hauppauge, 11788. Tel: 631-940-3390; Fax: 631-940-3419. Keith Kertland, Pres. & CEO.
Miscellaneous Entities:
CHS Services, Inc., 992 N. Village Ave., 11570. Tel: 516-705-2900; Fax: 516-705-1997. Donna M. O'Brien, Pres.
Riverhead Hostel Holding Corporation, 1010 Rte. 12, Port Jefferson Station. Tel: 631-474-4120; Fax: 631-474-4110. Under the auspices of Maryhaven Center of Hope.
Suffolk Hearing & Speech Center, Inc., 369 E. Main St., East Islip, 11730. Tel: 631-376-4001; Fax: 631-376-4208. Under the auspices of Good Samaritan Hospital Medical Center.
The Samaritan Corporation, 992 N. Village Ave., 11570. Tel: 516-705-3700; Fax: 516-705-3730.
St. Charles Corporation, 992 N. Village Ave., 11570. Tel: 516-705-3700; Fax: 516-705-3730.
CHS Home Support Services, 15 Power Dr., Hauppauge. Tel: 631-940-3390; Fax: 631-940-3419. Operating under Nursing Sisters Home Care
St. Francis Research and Educational Corporation, 100 Port Washington Blvd., Roslyn, 11576. Tel: 516-562-6901; Fax: 516-562-6909. Operating under St. Francis Hospital
St. Francis-Mercy Corporation, 992 N. Village Ave., 11570. Tel: 516-705-3700; Fax: 516-705-3730.
Siena Village, Inc., 2000 Bishop's Rd., Smithtown, 11787. Tel: 631-360-6000; Fax: 631-360-6006. Jane Zorn, Admin. Operating under St. Catherine of Siena Medical Center
Wisdom Gardens Housing Development Fund Company, Inc., 1010 Rte. 112, Port Jefferson Station, 11776. Tel: 631-474-4120; Fax: 631-474-4110. Operating under Maryhaven Center of Hope
Foundations:
The St. Francis Hospital Foundation, 100 Port Washington Blvd., Roslyn, 11576. Tel: 516-562-6901; Fax: 516-562-6909. Alan D. Guerci, M.D., Pres. & CEO. Operating under St. Francis Hospital
The Good Samaritan Hospital Foundation, 1000 Montauk Hwy., West Islip, 11795. Tel: 631-376-4001; Fax: 631-376-4208. Richard J. Murphy, Pres. & CEO. Operating under Good Samaritan Hospital
St. Charles Hospital Foundation, 200 Belle Terre Rd., Port Jefferson, 11777. Tel: 631-474-6600; Fax: 631-474-6884. William Casey, Pres. & CEO. Operating under St. Charles Hospital & Rehabilitation Center.
Mercy Medical Center Foundation, 1000 N. Village Ave., 11570. Tel: 516-705-1401; Fax: 516-705-1406. Martin A. Bieber, Interim Pres. & CEO(2). Operating under Mercy Medical Center
St. Catherine of Siena Medical Center Foundation, 52 Rte. 25 A, Smithtown, 11787. Tel: 631-862-3905; Fax: 631-862-3983. Vincent DiRubbio, Pres. & CEO(2). Operating under St. Catherine of Siena Medical Center
Our Lady of Consolation Nursing & Rehabilitative Care Center Foundation, 111 Beach Dr., West Islip,

11795. Tel: 631-587-1600; Fax: 631-587-5960. Mr. Dennis J. Verzi, Pres. & CEO. Operating under Our Lady of Consolation Geriatric Care Center

The Catholic Health Services Home Care and Hospice Foundation, 190 Motor Pkwy., Hauppauge, 11788. Tel: 631-940-3390; Fax: 631-940-3419. Keith Kertland, Pres. & CEO. Operating under Nursing Sisters Home Care Bed Capacity 1,697; Total Annually Assisted 740,000; Total Staff 14,125; Nursing Home 790.

[J] RESIDENCES FOR AGED

AMITYVILLE. *Dominican Village, Inc.*, 565 Albany Ave., 11701. Tel: 631-842-6091; Fax: 631-842-6131. Email: dv@dominicanvillage.org. Sisters Helen Butler, O.P., Pres. & CEO; Christine Sammons, O.P., Vice Pres. Operations; Elizabeth Stringer, O.P., Vice Pres. Environment. Housing Units 266; Total Assisted 66; Total Staff 115.

HUNTINGTON. *St. Joseph's Guest Home for the Aged, Inc.*, 350 Cuba Hill Rd., 11743. Tel: 631-368-9528; Fax: 931-266-1015. Email: mssb350@aol.com. Web: www.missionarysistersofstbenedict.org. Sr. M. Joachima Mystkowska, O.S.B., Admin. Missionary Sisters of St. Benedict In Res. Rev. Msgrs. Francis X. Glimm, S.T.L. (Retired); Joseph Lawlor; Revs. Malachy C. Flacherty, O.F.M.Cap.; Robert J. Giuntini.

WEST ISLIP. *Our Lady of Consolation Nursing & Rehabilitative Care Center*, 111 Beach Dr., 11795. Tel: 631-587-1600; Fax: 631-587-5960. Web: www.olc.chsli.org. Mr. Dennis J. Verzi, Pres. & CEO; Rev. William Dailey, Chap. (Retired). Under the supervision of the Sisters of St. Dominic, Member of Catholic Health Services of LI.; Conducted in the tradition of the Sisters of St. Dominic Bed Capacity 450; Total Assisted 994; Total Staff 850.

[K] SOCIETY OF ST. VINCENT DE PAUL

BETHPAGE. *Central Council*, Diocese of Rockville Centre, 249 Broadway, 11714. Tel: 516-822-3132; Fax: 516-822-2728. Email: jdilts@svdprvc.org. Web: svdprvc.org. Rev. Msgr. Patrick J. Armshaw, Spiritual Dir.; Patrick O'Dea, Pres.; James T. Dilts, Exec. Dir. Total Assisted 130,754; Total Staff 114; Volunteers 1,219.

[L] HOME HEALTH SERVICES

HAMPTON BAYS. *Dominican Sisters Family Health Service*, 103-6 W. Montauk Hwy., 11946. Tel: 631-728-0181; Fax: 631-723-0866. Email: hamptons@dsfhs.org. Web: www.dsfhs.org. Pamella Ash, R.N., M.A., Admin. Suffolk Offices.

360 Montauk Hwy., P.O. Box 678, Wainscott, 11975. Tel: 631-537-6759; Fax: 631-537-7187.

1729A N. Ocean Ave., Medford, 11763. Tel: 631-207-1170; Fax: 631-207-0149.

DSFHS Special Programs, P.O. Box 1028, 11946. Tel: 631-728-0937; Fax: 631-728-7162.

HAUPPAUGE. *Nursing Sisters Home Care* Administrative Office , 15 Power Dr., 11788. Tel: 631-940-3390; Fax: 631-940-3419. Keith Kertland, Pres. & CEO.

Administrative Office, 1600 Stewart Ave., Westbury, 11590. Tel: 631-940-3390; Fax: 631-940-3419. Nursing Service Offices:

Kings County, 500 19th St., Brooklyn, 11215. Tel: 718-768-7271; Fax: 718-484-2225.

Nassau County, 1600 Stewart Ave., Westbury, 11590. Tel: 516-683-1300; Fax: 516-683-1367.

Suffolk County, 3241 Rte. 112, Medford, 11763. Tel: 631-696-1002; Fax: 631-696-1007. Medford Office

Commack Office, 2171 Jericho Tpke., Ste. 100, Commack, 11725. Tel: 631-462-9000; Fax: 631-462-6947.

Riverhead Office, 1380 Roanoke Ave., Riverhead, 11901. Tel: 631-940-3344; Fax: 631-940-3320.

[M] MONASTERIES AND RESIDENCES OF PRIESTS AND BROTHERS

BAY SHORE. *Montfort Missionaries*, 26 S. Saxon Ave., 11706. Tel: 631-666-7500; 631-665-4349; Fax: 631-665-4349. Email: PRETRE@worldnet.att.net. Revs. Roger M. Charest, S.M.M., Mng. Editor; J. Patrick Gaffney, S.M.M., Assoc. Edit. & Preaching Team; George J. Werner, S.M.M., Supr., Preaching Team; Bernard M. Blood, S.M.M., Preaching Team; William M. Dilgen, S.M.M., Marriage Encounter; Maurice A. Landry, S.M.M.; Francis J. Allen, S.M.M., Preaching Team; Francis Pizzarelli, S.M.M., Hope House Ministry; Vincent P. Cunningham, S.M.M., Hospital Chap.; Harold E. McBride, S.M.M., Hospital Chap.; Peter J. McCrann, S.M.M., Hospital Chap.; Theodore Murphy, S.M.M., Hospital Chap.; Deacon Christopher Golla, S.M.M., Hospital Chap. Montfort Spiritual Center and Headquarters of magazine "Queen of All Hearts" and "Montfort Publications" Priests 11; Brothers 1.

Montfort Missionaries - Retreat Center, 26 S. Saxon Ave., 11706. Tel: 631-666-7500; Fax: 631-666-4349.

EASTPORT. *Shrine of Our Lady of the Island* Montfort Missionaries; Eastport-Manor Rd., 11941. Tel: 631-325-0661; Fax: 631-325-5592. Revs. William J. Vigliotta, S.M.M., Dir.; Raymond Graham, S.M.M.; James J. Manning, S.M.M.

GLEN COVE. *St. Josaphat's Monastery, Novitiate and Retreat House*, East Beach Dr., 11542 Tel: 516-671-0545; Fax: 516-676-7465. Email: sjmosbm@aol.com. Revs. Cyril Iseszczuk, O.S.B.M. (Brazil), Supr. & Master of Novices; Hilarion Benedik, O.S.B.M.; Januario Lucavei, O.S.B.M., Asst. Master of Novices; Athanasius B. Pekar, O.S.B.M. Taras Prokopiw, O.S.B.M.; Bros. Josaphat Oribka, O.S.B.M.; Samuel Basniak, O.S.B.M. Basilian Fathers

MINEOLA. *Provincial Residence and Novitiate*, 240 Emory Rd., 11501. Tel: 516-742-5555 Fax: 516-742-1989. Email: frthomas@kellenberg.org. Rev. Thomas A. Cardone, S.M., Prov. & Asst. for Religious Life; Bro. Kenneth M. Hoagland, S.M., Asst. Prov. & Asst. Education; Rev. James C. Williams, S.M., Councilor; Bro. Richard J. Hughes, S.M., Asst. Temporalities; Rev. Philip K. Eichner, S.M., Councilor; Bros. Michael J. Gillen, S.M., Councilor; Thomas J. Clearly, S.M., Councilor. Society of Mary (Marianists) In Res. Revs. Garrett J. Long, S.M.; Ernest P. Lorfanfant, S.M.

OYSTER BAY. *Vincentian Community*, 104 Anstice St., 11771. Tel: 516-922-3494; Fax: 516-922-5715. Email: vinchouse@aol.com. Revs. Gerard H. Luttenberger, C.M., S.T.D.; Patrick J. Griffin, C.M., Ph.D.

POINT LOOKOUT. *Franciscan Friars*, 128 Hewlett Ave., P.O. Box 211, 11569. Tel: 516-432-3719; Fax: 516-432-1377.

UNIONDALE. *St. Pius X Residence*, 1220 Front St., 11553. Tel: 516-485-4200; Fax: 516-485-0596. Rev. Thomas F. Mulvanerty, Vicar for Senior Priests, Dir. of Priestly Life & Ministry; Deacon Patrick Murphy, O.S.F., Pastoral Assoc. In Res. Revs. Brian J. Brinker; Francis M. Casey (Retired); Serafino A. Corali (Retired); Richard F. Delaney; Angelo J. Ditta; James J. Dolan (Retired); Peter L. Duvelsdorf (Retired); Gerard J. Gfroerer; Frederic J. Harrer (Retired); John H. McCabe (Retired); Thomas F. Mulvanerty; Kenneth T. Nee (Retired); Constantino S. Nieva Ernest E. Robinson; Denis J. Sheridan (Retired); John P. Wilutis (Retired).

[N] CONVENTS AND RESIDENCES FOR SISTERS

ROCKVILLE CENTRE. *Villa St. Joseph*, 984 N. Village Ave., 11570. Tel: 516-823-3800; Fax: 516-594-0412. Email: bsd@earthlink.net. Web: www.cijnssp.org. Congregation of the Infant Jesus (Nursing Sisters of the Sick Poor) Professed Sisters 31.

AMITYVILLE. *Queen of the Rosary, Motherhouse*, 555 Albany Ave., 11701-1197. Tel: 631-842-6000; Fax: 631-842-0240. Email: prioress@aol.com. Web: www.amityvilleop.org. Sisters Virginia Maguire, O.P., Prioress; Mary Arline Hornidge, O.P., Admin.; Rev. Msgr. Dominick J. Adessa, Chap.

Legal Title: *Dominican Sisters Community Support Corporation*

Legal Title: *Amityville Dominican Sisters, Inc.* Sisters of St. Dominic Total in Residence 97.

BAY SHORE. *New Jerusalem*, 106 N. Penataquit Ave., 11706-6939. Tel: 631-968-8859. Sisters 6.

BLUE POINT. *St. Ursula Center*, Formerly Ursuline Sisters, St. Ursula Center, 186 Middle Rd., 11715. Tel: 631-363-2422; Fax: 631-363-7403. Email: retreatcenter@ursulinesofbluepoint.org. Web: www.ursulinesofbluepoint.org. Sisters Mary Elizabeth Preston, O.S.U., Dir., St. Ursula R. Center; Agnes Seebach, O.S.U., Coord., St. Ursula Convent. Ursuline Sisters, Congregation of Tildonk

BRENTWOOD. *Saint Joseph Convent*, Motherhouse, Brentwood Rd., 11717. Tel: 631-273-4531; Fax: 631-273-1451. Email: BrentCSJ@aol.com. Web: www.csjbrentwoodny.org. Sisters Jean Amore, Pres.; Miriam Lucille Montella, Gen. Sec.; Joanne Feulner, Gen. Treas.; Edna McKeever, C.S.J., Community Archivist. Sisters of Saint Joseph Generalate Sisters 799.

Saint Joseph Novitiate, 1725 Brentwood Rd., 11717. Tel: 631-273-1187, Ext. 42; Fax: 631-273-1451. Email: brentcsj@aol.com. Sr. Maryann Rogers, C.S.J., Coord.

Maria Regina Residence, Inc. Sisters of St. Joseph , 1725 Brentwood Rd., Bldg. 1, 11717-5589. Tel: 631-273-4500; Fax: 631-952-2378. Email: mrr@mariareginaresidence.org. Web: www.mariareginaresidence.org.

DIX HILLS. *Contemplative Sisters of the Good Shepherd*, 151 Burrs Ln., P.O. Box 8020, 11746-9020. Tel: 631-643-1071; Fax: 631-643-9563. Email: torrie318@aol.com. Web: www.goodshepardsisters.org. Sr. Virginia Agnes Turinese, Supr. Sisters 16.

Sisters of the Good Shepherd, 151 Burrs Ln., P.O. Box 8020, 11746-9020. Tel: 631-491-6850; Fax: 631-643-9199. Sr. Mary Michael Kennedy, Supr.

Legal Title: *Sisters of the Good Shepherd, Huntington, NY, Inc.* Sisters 19.

FRANKLIN SQUARE. *Spiritual Life Center*, 1031 Mosefan St., 11010. Tel: 516-328-7438. Email: Kathleen.L.Murphy@att.net. Sr. Kathleen Murphy, O.P., Dir. Sisters of St. Dominic Sisters 2.

HAMPTON BAYS. *St. Joseph's Villa Retreat and Renewal Center*, 81 Lynn Ave., 11946. Tel: 631-728-6074; Fax: 631-273-1451. Email: brentcsj@aol.com. Web: www.csjbrentwoodny.org. Sisters of St. Joseph 2.

HUNTINGTON. *Missionary Sisters of St. Benedict*, 350 Cuba Hill Rd., 11743. Tel: 631-368-9528; Fax: 631-266-1015. Email: MSSB350@aol.com. Web: www.missionarysistersofstbenedict.org. Sr. M. Serafina Sarnowska, O.S.B., Supr. Sisters 29.

ISLIP. *Daughters of Wisdom (Administration)*, 385 Ocean Ave., 11751. Tel: 631-277-2660; Fax: 631-277-3274. Email: wisdomsisters@cs.com. Web: www.daughtersofwisdom.org. Sr. Evelyn Eckhardt, D.W., Prov. Administration Offices. Sisters 3.

OCEANSIDE. *St. Anthony's Parish House*, 111 Anchor Ave., 11572. Tel: 516-536-3308. Email: oceansideop@att.net. Dominican Sisters (Amityville) 0.

POINT LOOKOUT. *St. Clare Convent-Franciscan Sisters of Allegany*, 104 Ocean Blvd., 11569. Tel: 718-842-2615. Sr. Catherine Moran, O.S.F., Contact Person.

St. Elizabeth Convent-Franciscan Sisters of Allegany, 29 Ocean Blvd., 11569. Tel: 718-842-2615. Sr. Catherine Moran, O.S.F., Contact Person.

RONKONKOMA. *Religious of Our Lady of the Retreat in the Cenacle*, 310 Cenacle Rd., 11779-2203. Tel: 631-588-8366; Fax: 631-588-1729. Web: www.cenaclesisters.org.

Cenacle Retreat House Tel: 631-588-8366; Fax: 631-588-1729. Sr. Marie T. Halligan, Supr. Professed Sisters in Residence 35.

St. Therese Couderc Community, 312 Cenacle Rd., 11779-2203. Tel: 631-737-8491; Fax: 631-737-3375. Sr. Elenore Woronick, R.C., Contact. Professed Sisters 3.

Maude Adams House, 310 Cencale Rd., 11779. Tel: 631-471-3709; Fax: 631-471-4745. Sr. Kathleen O'Brien, Contact. Sisters 5.

Cenacle Sisters at Brentwood (Maria Regina Convent) Tel: 631-273-4500. Sisters 9.

ROOSEVELT. *Oblate Sisters of the Most Holy Redeemer*, Mother of Good Counsel Home, 290 Babylon Tpke., P.O. Box 329, 11575-0329. Tel: 516-223-1013; Fax: 516-223-4254. Email: ossr290@earthlink.net. Sr. Matilde Murillo, O.SS.R., Dir. Mother of Good Counsel Home is a small group home for pregnant and parenting teenage mothers and their infants.

SEAFORD. *Sisters of St. Joseph*, 2316 Hampton Ave., 11783. Tel: 516-826-1773. Email: murphkath@aol.com. Sisters 5.

SELDEN. *Providence Newman Center*, 76 College Rd., 11784. Tel: 631-696-6129. Email: opselden@aol.com. Web: www.drvc.org/campusministry.

SOUND BEACH. *Our Lady of Perpetual Help Convent*, 49 Convent Dr., 11789. Tel: 631-744-2477; Fax: 631-744-2515. Email: DwSndBea@aol.com. Sr. Edna Butler, D.W., Coord. Daughters of Wisdom 23.

[O] RETREAT HOUSES

BLUE POINT. *St. Ursula Retreat Center, Inc.*, 186 Middle Rd., 11715-0086. Tel: 631-363-6544 (Convent); 631-363-2422 (Retreat Center); Fax: 631-363-0319. Email: retreatcenter@ursulinesofbluepoint.org. Web: www.ursulinesofbluepoint.org. Sisters Mary Elizabeth Preston, O.S.U., Retreat Dir.; Agnes Seebach, O.S.U., Coord. of Sisters Ursuline Convent. Directed by Ursuline Sisters of Tildonk, Weekend retreats; private retreats; directed retreats; days and evenings of prayer. Total in Residence 15.

CENTERPORT. *St. Francis Center, Inc.*, P.O. Box 301, 11721. Tel: 631-261-5730; Fax: 631-754-4204. Email: alvernia@juno.com. Web: www.alvernia.org. Directed by Franciscan Bros. of Brooklyn

MANHASSET. *St. Ignatius Retreat House, Inisfada*, 251 Searingtown Rd., 11030. Tel: 516-621-8300; Fax: 516-521-7201. Email: inisfada@inisfada.net. Web: www.inisfada.net. Revs. Joseph S. Costantino, S.J., Dir.; Damian O. Halligan, S.J.; William P.

Walsh, S.J.; David C. McCallum, S.J.; Peter K. Arabia, S.J. The Society of Jesus Sisters 1; Total Staff 6.

MOUNT SINAI. *House of the Holy Innocents, Inc.*, 722 Mt. Sinai-Coram Rd., Box 174, 11766. Tel: 516-331-1745. Email: monkpeace@yahoo.com.

PATCHOGUE. *St. Joseph's Prayer Center*, 312 Maple Ave., 11772. Tel: 631-207-3751; Fax: 631-764-3316. Mrs. Suzanne Reilly, Dir.; Rev. James J. Wheeler, S.J., Apostolic Dir. Total Staff 15.

RONKONKOMA. *Cenacle Retreat Center*, 310 Cenacle Rd., 11779-2203. Tel: 631-588-8366; Fax: 631-585-8485. Email: retreat@cenaclesisters.org. Web: www.cenaclesisters.org. Sisters Madeline Birmingham, R.C., Co-Coord. of Ministry; Mary Spratt, R.C., Co-Coord. of Ministry. Religious of the Cenacle Ministry Staff 6.

SAG HARBOR. *Cormaria Retreat House* 11963. Tel: 631-725-4206; Fax: 631-725-1837. Email: cormaria@aol.com. Web: www.cormaria.org. Sr. Ann Thaddeus Marino, R.S.H.M., Retreat Dir. Directed by the Religious of the Sacred Heart of Mary Religious of the Sacred Heart of Mary 6; Total Staff 12.

SHELTER ISLAND HEIGHTS. *St. Gabriel's Spiritual Center for Youth* A youth retreat ministry directed by the Passionists. Retreats available for youth, young adults, women, men and married couples. , P.O. Box 3015/64 Burns Rd., 11965. Tel: 631-749-0850; Fax: 631-749-3154. Email: stgabes@aol.com. Revs. Christopher Cleary, C.P., Admin.; Leo O'Boyle, C.P., Retreat Team; Kathleen LaPlant, Retreat Team.

WATER MILL. *Siena Spirituality Center*, 615 Montauk Hwy., 11976. Tel: 631-726-4740; Fax: 631-726-1930. Web: www.sienawatermill.org. P.O. Box 660, 11976. Sr. Honora Nolty, O.P., Exec. Dir.; James Coomey, M.A., Prog. Dir. Center offers private/directed retreats, recollection days, special interest programs and hosts business conferences. Also, Sabbatical (100 days) in Dominican tradition. Dominican Sisters O.P. 3.

[P] CAMPUS MINISTRIES AND NEWMAN CENTERS

ROCKVILLE CENTRE. *The Campus Parish of Long Island* Office of Campus 50 N. Park Ave., 11570. Tel: 516-678-5800, Ext. 614; Fax: 516-763-1068. Email: CHAJJD@hofstra.edu. Web: www.drvc.org/campusparish. Rev. Joseph J. D'Angelo, M.A.C., M.Div., M.S., C.A.S.A.C., Pastor & Dir., Canonical Institute of Nonterritorial Campus Parishes. Canonical Institute of Non-territorial Campus Parishes

Adelphi University, Rm. 302, University Center, Chaplain's Center, Garden City, 11530. Tel: 516-877-3116; Fax: 516-877-3148. Sr. Eileen M. Connor, O.P.

Hofstra University Tel: 516-463-6920; Fax: 516-463-5921.

Chaplains' Office, Student Center 213, 200 Hofstra University, Hempstead, 11549. Tel: 516-463-6814; Fax: 516-463-5921. Rev. Joseph J. D'Angelo, M.A.C., M.Div., M.S., C.A.S.A.C., Pastor & Dir., Newman Apostolate; Sr. Kathleen Riordan, O.P.

Nassau Community College Tel: 516-572-8064.

Stewart Avenue-College Union, Rm. 300, Garden City, 11530-6793. Tel: 516-572-8064. Deacon George Browne.

NY Institute of Technology, Student Activities Center, P.O. Box 8000, Old Westbury, 11548. Tel: 516-686-7794.

LIU/C.W. Post College (Brookville) Tel: 516-299-2229; Fax: 516-299-2228.

Interfaith Center 720 Northern Blvd., Brookville, 11548. Tel: 516-299-2229; Fax: 516-299-2228. Rev. Edward J. Brown, M.S.

Southampton Campus of Long Island University Tel: 516-287-8110.

Student Activities Center, Wood Hall, 239 Montauk Hwy., Southampton, 11968. Tel: 631-287-8110.

Office of the Catholic Chaplain, Southampton, 11968. Tel: 516-287-8110. Deacon George Logan.

Suffolk Community College Tel: 631-451-4765.

Riverhead Bldg., Rm. 349 533 College Rd., Selden, 11784. Tel: 631-451-4765. Ms. Regina Keller.

SUNY at Farmingdale Tel: 631-420-2134; Fax: 631-420-2692.

Laffin Hall, Rm. 310 Melville Rd., Farmingdale, 11735. Tel: 631-420-2134; Fax: 631-420-2692. Sr. Elizabeth McGarvey, O.P.

SUNY at Old Westbury Tel: 516-876-3031; Fax: 516-876-3142.

Interfaith Chaplaincy Student Union 313G, Old Westbury, 11568-0219. Tel: 516-876-3031; Fax: 516-876-3142. Rev. Roy Tvrdik, S.M.M.

SUNY at Stony Brook - Catholic Campus Ministry Tel: 631-632-6562; Fax: 631-632-6524.

Interfaith Center Union 272B, Stony Brook, 11794-8033. Tel: 631-632-6562; Fax: 631-632-4542. Sr. Margaret Ann Landry, R.S.H.M.; Rev. Robert J. Smith, S.T.D.

Dowling College Tel: 631-244-5034.

Chateau 64 Ste. 116, Oakdale, 11769-1999. Tel: 516-244-5034. Deacon James Pickel.

[Q] MISCELLANEOUS

AMITYVILLE. *Amityville Dominican Sisters, Inc.*, 555 Albany Ave., 11701. Tel: 631-842-6000; Fax: 631-842-0240. Email: prioress@aol.com. Web: www.amityvilleop.org. Sisters Virginia Maguire, O.P., Pres.; Diane Morgan, O.P., Vice Pres.; Kathleen McGinn, O.P., Sec. & Treas.

Benincasa Family Services, Inc., 555 Albany Ave., 11701. Tel: 631-842-6000, Ext. 351; Fax: 631-842-1596. Email: mkbenin555@aol. Sr. Margaret A. Krajci, O.P., Contact.

Dominican Sisters Community Support Corp., 555 Albany Ave., 11701. Tel: 631-842-6000; Fax: 631-842-0240. Email: prioress@aol.com. Web: www.amityvilleop.org. Sisters Virginia Maguire, O.P., Pres.; Diane Morgan, O.P., Vice Pres.; Kathleen McGinn, O.P., Sec. & Treas.

Siena Spirituality Center, Inc., c/o Sisters of the Order of St. Dominic, 555 Albany Ave., 11701. Tel: 631-842-6043; Fax: 631-842-1347. Email: sistersop@aol.com. Web: www.amityvilleop.org. Sr. Kathleen McGinn, O.P., Sec. & Treas.

BAY SHORE. *Pronto of Long Island, Inc.*, 128 Pine Aire Dr., 11706. Tel: 631-231-8290; Fax: 631-231-8390. Mrs. Nilda Alvarez, Contact Person.

BRENTWOOD. *CSJ Learning Connection for Education, Inc.*, 1725 Brentwood Rd., 11717. Tel: 631-951-4783; Fax: 631-951-0642. Email: SCJTLC@optonline.net. Sr. Kathleen Carberry, C.S.J., Contact.

Thomas I. Conerty Outreach Center of Brentwood, Inc., 88 Second Ave., 11717. Tel: 631-273-8113; Fax: 631-435-3575. Ligia Guerrero, Contact Person.

CENTERPORT. *Mt. Alvernia, Inc.*, Prospect Rd., P.O. Box 301, 11721. Tel: 631-261-5730; Fax: 631-754-4204. Email: alvernia@juno.com. Web: www.alvernia.org. Directed by the Franciscan Brothers

Camp Alvernia Tel: 631-261-5730; Fax: 631-754-4204.

Mt. Alvernia Center for Retreats Tel: 631-261-5730; Fax: 631-754-4204.

FARMINGVILLE. *Religious Computer Systems*, P.O. Box 508, 11738-0508. Tel: 631-732-7270; Fax: 631-732-6591. Email: rcsjane@cs.com. Web: www.rcswebsite.org. Sr. Jane Muller, O.P. Social Security and computer services for Religious institutions under sponsorship of the Amityville Dominicans

ISLIP. *Wisdom Charitable Trust*, 385 Ocean Ave., 11751. Tel: 631-277-2660; Fax: 631-277-3274. Email: wisdomsisters@cs.com.

OAKDALE. *Saint John Baptist De La Salle of New York, Inc.*, P.O. Box 538, 11769. Tel: 401-789-0244; Fax: 401-783-5303. Email: cbcdcasey@aol.com. Bro. Daniel Casey, F.S.C.

RONKONKOMA. *Catholic Press Association of the United States and Canada, Inc.*, 3555 Veterans Memorial Hwy., Unit O, 11779. Tel: 631-471-4730; Fax: 631-471-4804. Email: CathJourn@aol.com. Web: www.catholicpress.org. Dennis Heaney, Pres.; Mr. Owen P. McGovern, Exec. Dir.

ROOSEVELT. *Friends of Mother of Good Counsel Home, Inc.*, 290 Babylon Tpke., 11575. Tel: 516-223-1013; Fax: 516-223-4254. Email: ossr290@earthlink.net. Sr. Matilde Murillo, O.SS.R., Dir.

UNIONDALE. *TELEcare of the Diocese of Rockville Centre*, Tel: 516-538-8700; Fax: 516-489-9701. Email: info@telecaretv.org. Web: www.telecaretv.org. 1200 Glenn Curtiss Blvd., 11553. Richard Haemmerle, Vice Pres. & Business Mgr.

WEST BABYLON. *Christa House, Inc.*, 720 Albin Ave., 11704. Tel: 631-376-0114; Fax: 631-376-0115. Email: christahouse@yahoo.com. Web: www.ChristaHouse.org. Sr. Patricia A. Ryan, C.S.J.

WESTBURY. *Sisters, Lovers of the Holy Cross*, Tel: 516-333-9464; Fax: 516-333-9464. Email: theresamartin@worldnet.att.net.

St. Theresa Convent, 43 Crown Ln., 11590. Tel: 516-333-9464; Fax: 516-333-9464. Sr. Theresa Nguyen, Pres.

WYANDANCH. *Gerald J. Ryan Outreach Center, Inc.*, 1434 Straight Path, 11798. Tel: 631-643-7591; Fax: 631-643-5935. Total Assisted 16,000; Total Staff 3.

The Opening Word Program, Inc., 1434 Straight Path, 11798. Tel: 631-643-0541; Fax: 631-643-0541. Email: opword@optonline.net. Sisters Mary Ryan, O.P., Exec. Dir.; Leonore Toscano, O.P., Treas.; Virginia Maguire, O.P., Chairperson. Directed by the Sisters of St. Dominic

RELIGIOUS INSTITUTES OF MEN REPRESENTED IN THE DIOCESE

For further details refer to the corresponding bracketed number in the Religious Institutes of Men or Women section.

[0330]—*Brothers of the Christian Schools*—F.S.C.
[1100]—*Brothers of the Sacred Heart* (Province of New York)—S.C.
[0470]—*The Capuchin Friars* (St. Mary Prov.)—O.F.M.Cap.
[1330]—*Congregation of the Mission-Vincentians* (Eastern Prov.)—C.M.
[1000]—*Congregation of the Passion* (Prov. of St. Paul of the Cross)—C.P.
[0490]—*Franciscan Brothers of Brooklyn*—O.S.F.
[0690]—*Jesuit Fathers and Brothers* (NY Prov.)—S.J.
[0770]—*The Marist Brothers*—F.M.S.
[0800]—*Maryknoll*—M.M.
[0720]—*Missionaries of Our Lady of La Salette*—M.S.
[0870]—*Montfort Missionaries*—S.M.M.
[0430]—*Order of Preachers-Dominicans*—O.P.
[1070]—*Redemptorist Fathers*—C.SS.R.
[0760]—*Society of Mary* (Provs. of NY; Meribah)—S.M.

RELIGIOUS INSTITUTES OF WOMEN REPRESENTED IN THE DIOCESE

[3110]—*Congregation of Our Lady of the Retreat in the Cenacle*—R.C.
[1920]—*Congregation of the Sisters of the Holy Cross*—C.S.C.
[]—*Daughters of Mary* (Haiti)—F.de M.
[0960]—*Daughters of Wisdom*—D.W.
[1070-05]—*Dominican Sisters* (Amityville)—O.P.
[1070-15]—*Dominican Sisters* (Blauvelt)—O.P.
[1070-16]—*Dominican Sisters* (Hope)—O.P.
[1070-11]—*Dominican Sisters* (Sparkill)—O.P.
[1370]—*Franciscan Missionaries of Mary*—F.M.M.
[1180]—*Franciscan Sisters of Allegany, New York*—O.S.F.
[1425]—*Franciscan Sisters of Peace*—F.S.P.
[1840]—*Grey Nuns of the Sacred Heart*—G.N.S.H.
[2070]—*Holy Union Sisters*—S.U.S.C.
[2575]—*Institute of the Sisters of Mercy of the Americas* (Brooklyn, NY)—R.S.M.
[0210]—*Missionary Benedictine Sisters*—O.S.B.
[3030]—*Oblate Sisters of M.H. Redeemer*—O.S.S.R.
[3465]—*Religious of the Sacred Heart of Mary*—R.S.H.M.
[2970]—*School Sisters of Notre Dame*—S.S.N.D.
[0640]—*Sisters of Charity of St. Vincent de Paul* (Halifax)—S.C.
[0650]—*Sisters of Charity of St. Vincent de Paul, of New York*—S.C.
[0430]—*Sisters of Charity of the Blessed Virgin Mary*—B.V.M.
[2575]—*Sisters of Mercy of the Americas* (Dallas Region)—R.S.M.
[2575]—*Sisters of Mercy of the Americas* (NY Region)—R.S.M.
[2990]—*Sisters of Notre Dame de Namur*—S.N.D.
[3000]—*Sisters of Notre Dame de Namur* (Baltimore & Base Communities Provinces)—S.N.D.deN.
[3830-05]—*Sisters of St. Joseph* (Brentwood, NY)—C.S.J.
[3840]—*Sisters of St. Joseph of Carondelet* (Province of Albany)—C.S.J.
[3393]—*Sisters of St. Joseph of Chestnut Hill* (Philadelphia, PA)—S.S.J.
[3830-11]—*Sisters of St. Joseph of Nazareth*—S.S.J.
[3180]—*Sisters of the Cross and the Passion*—C.P.
[1830]—*Sisters of the Good Shepherd*—R.G.S.
[1970]—*Sisters of the Holy Family of Nazareth*—C.S.F.N.
[2240]—*Sisters of the Infant Jesus*—C.I.J.
[3320]—*Sisters of the Presentation of the BVM* (New Windsor, N.Y.)—P.B.V.M.
[2392]—*Sisters, Lovers of the Holy Cross* (Brookville, N.Y.)—L.H.C.
[2160]—*Sisters, Servants of the Immaculate Heart of Mary*—I.H.M.
[2150]—*Sisters, Servants of the Immaculate Heart of Mary* (Monroe, MI)—I.H.M.
[4130]—*Ursuline Sisters of the Congregation of Tildonk, Belgium*—O.S.U.

DIOCESAN CEMETERIES

CENTRAL ISLIP. *Queen of All Saints*, 115 Wheeler Rd., 11722. Tel: 631-234-8297.

CORAM. *Holy Sepulchre*, 3442 Rte. 112, 11727. Tel: 631-732-3460.

WESTBURY. *Holy Rood*, 111 Old Country Rd., Box 182, 11590. Tel: 516-334-7990.

NECROLOGY

† Bermingham, Rev. Msgr. Charles E., (Retired)—Died Dec. 21, 1903
† Hendel, Rev. Msgr. Richard P., (Retired)—Died April 30, 2003
† Ryan, Rev. Msgr. Bernard J.—Died April 13, 2003
† Gfroerer, Rev. Gerard J., (Retired)—Died Feb. 18, 2003
† Henesy, William P., (Retired)—Died Aug. 5, 2003
† McGlade, Thomas F., (Retired)—Died May 22, 2003
† Shane, Donald R., (Retired)—Died May 13, 2003
† Yang, Paul, (Retired)—Died Dec. 31, 2002

Diocese of Sacramento

(Dioecesis Sacramentensis)

Most Reverend

WILLIAM K. WEIGAND, D.D.

Bishop of Sacramento; ordained May 25, 1963; appointed Bishop of Salt Lake City September 3, 1980; ordained and installed November 17, 1980; appointed Bishop of Sacramento November 30, 1993; installed January 27, 1994 *Diocesan Pastoral Center, Office of the Bishop: 2110 Broadway, Sacramento, CA 95818-2541.* Tel: 916-733-0202; Fax: 916-733-0215.

Most Reverend

RICHARD J. GARCIA, D.D.

Auxiliary Bishop of Sacramento; ordained June 15, 1973; appointed Titular Bishop of Bapara and Auxiliary Bishop of Sacramento November 25, 1997; ordained January 28, 1998 *Office: 2110 Broadway, Sacramento, CA 95818-2541.* Tel: 916-733-0203.

Diocesan Pastoral Center: 2110 Broadway, Sacramento, CA 95818-2541. Tel: 916-733-0100; Fax: 916-733-0195.

Web: www.diocese-sacramento.org

Most Reverend

FRANCIS A. QUINN, D.D., ED.D.

Retired Bishop of Sacramento; ordained June 15, 1946; appointed Titular Bishop of Numana and Auxiliary Bishop of San Francisco April 28, 1978; Episcopal ordination June 29, 1978; appointed Bishop of Sacramento December 18, 1979; retired November 30, 1993 *Office: 2110 Broadway, Sacramento, CA 95818-2541.* Tel: 916-733-0200.

Square Miles 42,597.

Erected by His Holiness, Leo XIII, May 28, 1886.

Comprises the Counties of Amador, Butte, Colusa, El Dorado, Glenn, Lassen, Modoc, Nevada, Placer, Plumas, Sacramento, Shasta, Sierra, Siskiyou, Solano, Sutter, Tehama, Trinity, Yolo and Yuba in the State of California.

Co-Patrons of Diocese: St. Patrick; Our Lady of Guadalupe.

Legal Title: "Roman Catholic Bishop of Sacramento, A Corporation Sole."
Legal Title: *For legal titles of parishes and diocesan institutions, consult the Diocesan Pastoral Center.*

STATISTICAL OVERVIEW

Personnel	
Bishop	1
Auxiliary Bishops	1
Retired Bishops	1
Abbots	1
Retired Abbots	1
Priests: Diocesan Active in Diocese	117
Priests: Diocesan Active Outside Diocese	5
Priests: Retired, Sick or Absent	49
Number of Diocesan Priests	171
Religious Priests in Diocese	53
Total Priests in Diocese	224
Extern Priests in Diocese	37
Ordinations:	
Diocesan Priests	8
Transitional Deacons	6
Permanent Deacons	27
Permanent Deacons in Diocese	138
Total Brothers	22
Total Sisters	180
Parishes	
Parishes	98
With Resident Pastor:	
Resident Diocesan Priests	85
Resident Religious Priests	8
Without Resident Pastor:	
Administered by Priests	1
Administered by Deacons	2
Administered by Religious Women	3
Administered by Pastoral Teams, etc.	1
Missions	42
Pastoral Centers	3
Professional Ministry Personnel:	
Sisters	24
Lay Ministers	96
Welfare	
Catholic Hospitals	6
Total Assisted	492,719
Homes for the Aged	1
Total Assisted	118
Residential Care of Children	1
Total Assisted	32
Day Care Centers	4
Total Assisted	1,713
Specialized Homes	1
Total Assisted	23
Special Centers for Social Services	10
Total Assisted	154,057
Educational	
Diocesan Students in Other Seminaries	26
Seminaries, Religious	2
Students Religious	3
Total Seminarians	29
High Schools, Diocesan and Parish	4
Total Students	1,867
High Schools, Private	3
Total Students	2,631
Elementary Schools, Diocesan and Parish	47
Total Students	12,436
Catechesis/Religious Education:	
High School Students	3,048
Elementary Students	15,029
Total Students under Catholic Instruction	35,040
Teachers in the Diocese:	
Priests	11
Brothers	6
Sisters	19
Lay Teachers	832
Vital Statistics	
Receptions into the Church:	
Infant Baptism Totals	9,728
Adult Baptism Totals	660
Received into Full Communion	1,018
First Communions	7,278
Confirmations	5,960
Marriages:	
Catholic	1,075
Interfaith	344
Total Marriages	1,419
Deaths	2,600
Total Catholic Population	520,301
Total Population	3,229,945

Former Bishops—Rt. Revs. EUGENE O'CONNELL, D.D., consecrated Titular Bishop of Flaviopolis and appt. Vicar Apostolic of Marysville, Feb. 3, 1861; appt. First Bishop of Grass Valley, March 22, 1868; resigned March 17, 1884 and appt. Titular Bishop of Joppa; died Dec. 4, 1891; PATRICK MANOGUE, D.D., consecrated Titular Bishop of Ceremos, Coadjutor to Bishop O'Connell of Grass Valley, Jan. 16, 1881; succeeded to the See of Grass Valley on Bishop O'Connell's resignation, March 17, 1884; became the first Bishop of Sacramento, May 1886; died Feb. 27, 1895; THOMAS GRACE, D.D., consecrated June 16, 1896; died Dec. 27, 1921; PATRICK J. KEANE, D.D., ord. June 20, 1895; consecrated Bishop of Samaria, Dec. 14, 1920; appt. to See of Sacramento, March 17, 1922; died Sept. 1, 1928; Most Revs. ROBERT J. ARMSTRONG, D.D., Litt.D., ord. Dec. 10, 1910; consecrated March 12, 1929; died Jan. 14, 1957; JOSEPH T. MCGUCKEN, D.D., S.T.D., LL.D., ord. Jan. 16, 1928; consecrated Titular Bishop of Sanavo and Auxiliary Bishop of Los Angeles, March 19, 1941; Coadjutor Bishop of Sacramento, Oct. 26, 1955; succeeded to Jan. 14, 1957, as Bishop of Sacramento; promoted to the See of San Francisco, Feb. 21, 1962; died Oct. 6, 1983; ALDEN J. BELL, D.D., M.S.S.W. (Retired), ord. May 14, 1932; appt. Titular Bishop of Rhodopolis and Auxiliary Bishop of Los Angeles, April 18, 1956; consecrated June 4, 1956; appt. Bishop of Sacramento, March 30, 1962; retired March 15, 1979; died Aug. 28, 1982; JOHN S. CUMMINS, D.D., ord. Jan. 24, 1953; appt. Titular Bishop of Lambesi and Auxiliary Bishop of Sacramento, Feb. 26, 1974; consecrated May 26, 1974; appt. Bishop of Oakland, May 3, 1977; FRANCIS A. QUINN, D.D., Ed.D. (Retired), ord. June 15, 1946; appt. Titular Bishop of Numana and Auxiliary Bishop of San Francisco, April 28, 1978;; Episcopal Ordination, June 29, 1978;; appt. Bishop of Sacramento, Dec. 18, 1979; retired Nov. 30, 1993; ALPHONSE GALLEGOS, O.A.R., D.D., ord. May 24, 1958; appt. Titular Bishop of Sassabe and Auxiliary Bishop of Sacramento, Sept. 1, 1981; consecrated Nov. 4, 1981; died Oct. 6, 1991.

Auxiliary Bishop, Moderator of the Curia—Most Rev. RICHARD J. GARCIA, D.D. Tel: 916-733-0203; Fax: 916-733-0215.

Vicar General and Vicar for Temporalities & Administration—Rev. Msgr. ROBERT P. WALTON. Tel: 916-733-0216; Fax: 916-733-0215.

Vicar for Pastoral Ministry—Sr. EILEEN ENRIGHT, R.S.M. Tel: 916-733-0190; Fax: 916-733-0195.

Co-Vicar for Clergy & Religious and Personnel Director for Priests—Rev. THOMAS A. BLAND. Tel: 916-733-0216; Fax: 916-733-0215.

Co-Vicar for Clergy & Religious—Sr. PAULINA HURTADO, O.P. Tel: 916-733-0244; Fax: 916-733-0224.

Vicar for Social Services—Rev. MICHAEL F. KIERNAN. Tel: 916-733-0253; Fax: 916-733-0224.

Vicar for Canonical Affairs—Rev. DAVID DEIBEL, J.D., J.C.L. Tel: 916-733-0225; Fax: 916-733-0224.

Chancellor and Vicar Episcopal for Theological Affairs—Rev. CHARLES S. MCDERMOTT, S.T.D. Tel: 916-733-0204; Fax: 916-733-0215.

Vice Chancellor and Secretary to the Bishop—Rev. BLAISE R. BERG, S.T.D. Tel: 916-733-0211; Fax: 916-733-0215.

Coordinator for Retired Priests—Rev. RONAN BRENNAN. Tel: 530-887-8842.

Delegate for Deacons—Deacon THOMAS MCGILL, 2110 Broadway, Sacramento, 95818-2541. Tel: 916-733-0256; Fax: 916-733-0224.

Vicars Forane—Revs. AIDAN O'REILLY, (Siskiyou); MICHAEL HEBDA, (Shasta); BENEDICT DELEON,

(North Valley); Manuel Soria, (South Valley); Andrzej Koziczuk, (Ridge); Patrick O'Connor, (Northern Mines); John P. Sullivan, (Southern Mines) (Retired); John E. Boll, (Yolo); Leon Juchniewicz, (Solano); Rev. Msgr. Albert O'Connor, (Southern Suburbs); Revs. T. Brendan O'Sullivan, (City); Gerald Robinson, S.J., (American River); Troy Powers, (Northern Suburbs).

Diocesan Tribunal— Please direct all requests to the Tribunal. *2110 Broadway, Sacramento, 95818-2541*. Tel: 916-733-0225; Fax: 916-733-0224.

Judicial Vicar—Rev. David L. Deibel, J.D., J.C.L.

Adjutant Judicial Vicar—Rev. Mark R. Richards, J.C.L.

Canonical Affairs—Rev. David L. Deibel, J.D., J.C.L.

Pro-Synodal Judges—Rev. Msgr. Patrick M. Nolan (Retired); Revs. Rodolfo Delgado, J.C.L.; Joseph Huyen Nguyen, J.C.L.; Liam MacCarthy; Mark Richards.

Promoter of Justice—Rev. Charles S. McDermott, S.T.D.

Defenders of the Bond—Rev. Msgr. James C. Kidder; Revs. John Boll; Brendan McKeefry; John Folmer, J.C.D.; Deborah A. Barton, J.C.L.

Approved Advocates—Susan Boone; Carol Scott; Joanne Fankhauser; Nancy Milton, J.D.

Notaries—Marisa Menendez; Maureen Kubasak; Carmen Diaz-Lawson.

Civil Law—Edward G. Heidig Esq., Diocesan Attorney.

College of Consultors—Most Rev. Richard Garcia; Rev. Msgr. James Church; Revs. Michael Hebda; Liam MacCarthy; Polycarpo Gumapo; Sylvester McDermott; Manuel Soria; Rev. Msgr. Robert P. Walton.

Diocesan Offices and Directors

AIDS, Ministry to—Rev. John Healy, Coord., Mercy General Hospital, 4001 J St., Sacramento, 95819. Tel: 916-453-4753.

Alcoholism Advisory Board—Most Rev. Richard J. Garcia, D.D. Tel: 916-733-0200; Rev. Thomas Maguire. Tel: 916-985-2561, Ext. 4206.

Archives—Rev. William Breault, S.J., Archivist, 2110 Broadway, Sacramento, 95818-2541. Tel: 916-733-0299; 916-480-2165.

Black Catholic Council—Brenda Elazier, Office, 2110 Broadway, Sacramento, 95818-2541. Tel: 916-733-0160; 916-227-2288; Fax: 916-733-0195.

Building Committee— Direct inquiries to: Mr. Thomas McNamara, Staff, Diocesan Pastoral Center, 2110 Broadway, Sacramento, 95818-2541. Tel: 916-733-0277; Fax: 916-733-0295.

Catholic Faith Formation—Mr. John Rieschick, Dir., 2110 Broadway, Sacramento, 95818-2541. Tel: 916-733-0123; Fax: 916-733-0195; Mrs. Linda Shumate, Consultant for Catechesis; Deacons Antonio Ramirez, Consultant for Hispanic Catechesis; Ray Helgeson, Coord. for Adult Faith Formation; Kathy Conner, Respect Life/NFP Coord.; Mr. Stephen Tholcke, Pendola Center; Mrs. Gloria Soto, Coord. Family Life; Mrs. Margaret Walrath, Coord. Deaf Ministry; Mr. Feliciano Tapia, Hispanic Institute; Jeannette Holmes, Master Catechist; Adolfo Mercado, Youth & Young Adult Coord.; Mrs. Michelle Hendricks, Catechesis, Persons with Special Needs; Mr. John Donahoe, Coord. for Camp Recreation.

Office of Evangelization—Sr. Susan McCarthy, R.S.M., Dir., 2110 Broadway, Sacramento, 95818. Tel: 916-733-0154.

Catholic Charities of Sacramento, Inc.—Vacant, Pres. & Chm. Bd. of Directors; Rev. Michael Kiernan, Exec. Dir., 2110 Broadway, Sacramento, 95818. Tel: 916-733-0253; Fax: 916-733-0224.

Cemeteries—Mr. Philip Niederberger, Dir., 2110 Broadway, Sacramento, 95818. Tel: 916-733-0247; Fax: 916-733-0224.

Censor Librorum—Rev. Charles S. McDermott, S.T.D., 2110 Broadway, Sacramento, 95818-2541. Tel: 916-733-0200; Fax: 916-733-0215.

Communications and Media—Rev. James T. Murphy, Dir., 1017 11th St., Sacramento, 95814. Tel: 916-444-3071; Fax: 916-443-2749.

Council of Priests—Rev. Daniel Looney, Chm. Tel: 530-673-1573; Most Revs. William K. Weigand, D.D., Pres.; Richard Garcia; Revs. Philip Wells; Timothy Nondorf; Benedict DeLeon; Ronan Brennan; Charles S. McDermott, S.T.D.; Michael Carroll; Thomas Bland; Michael Newman; Brendan O'Sullivan; Michael Hebda; Vincent O'Reilly; Simon Twomey; Ambrose Ugwuegbu; Rodolfo Delgado; Rev. Msgrs. Robert P. Walton; James Church, Direct all correspondence to: 2110 Broadway, Sacramento, 95818-2541.

Development—Vacant, Diocesan Dir., 2110 Broadway, Sacramento, 95818-2541. Tel: 916-733-0266; Fax: 916-733-0295.

Diocesan Pastoral Council— Please direct all inquiries to: Sr. Eileen Enright, R.S.M., Staff, Office of the Bishop. Tel: 916-733-0200.

Diocesan Priests' Trust Fund—Most Rev. William K. Weigand, D.D., Pres. Ex Officio. Please direct all inquiries to:: Rev. Msgr. Murrough Wallace, Treas., St. Theresa Church, 1041 Lyons Ave., South Lake Tahoe, 96150. Tel: 530-544-3533; Fax: 916-544-4662.

Divorced and Separated, Ministry to—Direct inquiries to: Catholic Faith Formation, 2110 Broadway, Sacramento, 95818-2541. Tel: 916-733-0123; Fax: 916-733-0195.

Due Process— Direct inquiries to: Rev. David L. Deibel, J.D., J.C.L., 2110 Broadway, Sacramento, 95818-2541. Tel: 916-733-0225; Fax: 916-733-0224.

Eastern Catholic Churches—Rev. Charles S. McDermott, S.T.D., Liaison Officer, 2110 Broadway, Sacramento, 95818-2541. Tel: 916-733-0200.

"Ecclesia Dei" Community (Latin Mass)—Rev. John Berg, F.S.S.P., P.O. Box 5382, Sacramento, 95817. Tel: 916-446-5908; Fax: 916-446-5702.

Ecumenical & Interreligious Affairs—Rev. Blaise R. Berg, S.T.D., 2110 Broadway, Sacramento, 95818-2541. Tel: 916-733-0200; Fax: 916-733-0215.

Finance Council—Members: Rev. Brendan McKeefry; Robert Granucci Esq.; Anne Heck Long; Mr. Michael Profumo; Robert Slakey; Mr. Charles Sylva; Rev. Mark R. Richards, J.C.L.; Ms. Julie Nauman. Ex Officio: Rev. Msgr. Robert P. Walton; Mr. Thomas J. McNamara, Chancery Office, 2110 Broadway, Sacramento, 95818-2541. Tel: 916-733-0277.

Investment Review Committee— Direct inquiries to: Mr. Thomas McNamara, 2110 Broadway, Sacramento, 95818-2541. Tel: 916-733-0277; Fax: 916-733-0295.

Finance Office—Mr. Thomas McNamara, Dir., 2110 Broadway, Sacramento, 95818-2541. Tel: 916-733-0277; Fax: 916-733-0295.

Hispanic Apostolate—Deacon German Toro, 2110 Broadway, Sacramento, 95818-2541. Tel: 916-733-0177; Fax: 916-733-0195.

Holy Childhood Association—2110 Broadway, Sacramento, 95818-2541. Tel: 916-733-0110; Fax: 916-733-0120.

Hospitals, Diocesan Liaison for Catholic—Rev. John J. Healy, Mercy General Hospital, 4001 J St., Sacramento, 95819. Tel: 916-453-4753.

Lay Personnel—Mr. John Hale, Dir., 2110 Broadway, Sacramento, 95818-2541. Tel: 916-733-0240; Fax: 916-733-0295.

Marriage Preparation—John Rieschick, Dir., Catholic Faith Formation, 2110 Broadway, Sacramento, 95818-2541. Tel: 916-733-0123.

Newspapers—Ms. Julie Sly, Editor, Catholic Herald; Ricardo Olvera, Editor, El Heraldo, Office, 5890 Newman Ct., Sacramento, 95819-2608. Tel: 916-452-3344; Fax: 916-452-2945. "Catholic Herald" and "El Heraldo Catolico"

Ongoing Education of Clergy—Rev. T. Brendan O'Sullivan, Dir., St. Anthony Church, 660 Florin Rd., Sacramento, 95831. Tel: 916-428-5678.

Opus Sanctorum Angelorum—Rev. J. Dermot Dwyer, Spiritual Dir., P.O. Box 752, Colfax 95713. Tel: 916-346-2286.

Permanent Diaconate Program—Sr. Paulina Hurtado, O.P., Dir. Asst. Directors:: Deacon Lou Del Gaudio; Mrs. Susan Del Gaudio, Office, 2110 Broadway, Sacramento, 95818-2541. Tel: 916-733-0244.

Priests' Diocesan Aid Society—Rev. Msgr. James F. Church, Sec. & Treas., 7584 Center Pkwy., Sacramento, 95823. Tel: 916-421-5177; Fax: 916-392-4821. Ex Officio Officer: Most Rev. William K. Weigand, D.D. Please direct all inquiries to:.

Priests' Personnel Board, Diocesan—Please direct all inquiries to: Priest Personnel, Office of the Bishop, 2110 Broadway, Sacramento, 95818. Tel: 916-733-0200. Revs. Daniel Looney; Francisco Hernandez-Gomez; Thomas Bland; Polycarp Gumapo; Michael Kiernan; Eric Lofgren; Philip Wells; Brendan T. O'Sullivan, Chm.; Rev. Msgr. Robert P. Walton.

Propagation of the Faith—Rev. Msgr. James Church, Dir., 2110 Broadway, Sacramento, 95818-2541. Tel: 916-733-0200; Fax: 916-733-0215.

Properties Committee— Please direct all inquiries to: Mr. Thomas McNamara, Staff, 2110 Broadway, Sacramento, 95818-2541. Tel: 916-733-0277.

Radio and Television— See Communications and Media

Research and Planning—Sr. Eileen Enright, R.S.M., Chancellor, 2110 Broadway, Sacramento, 95818 2541. Tel: 916-733-0200; Fax: 916-733-0215.

Respect Life/NFP—Kathy Conner, Diocesan Coord., Catholic Faith Formation, 2110 Broadway, Sacramento, 95818-2541. Tel: 916-733-0123.

Schools—Mr. Dominic Puglisi, Interim Supt., 2110 Broadway, Sacramento, 95818-2541. Tel: 916-733-0110; Fax: 916-733-0120.

Victim Assistance Coordinator—Nancy J. Milton. Tel: 916-733-0227. Email: nmilton@diocese-sacramento.org.

Vocations—Sr. Maria Campos, R.S.M., Assoc. Dir., 2110 Broadway, Sacramento, 95818-2541. Tel: 916-733-0258. Co Directors:: Revs. Mark Richards; Humberto Gomez.

Worship, Office of—Mr. Jackson Schoos, Dir., 2110 Broadway, Sacramento, 95818-2541. Tel: 916-733-0220; Fax: 916-733-0295.

Lay Organizations—

Beginning Experience—Roberta Morris, Pres. Tel: 916-536-9791; Linda Dickinson, Public Rels. Tel: 916-774-9513.

Catholic Alumni Club—Jerry Nelson, Pres., P.O. Box 1777, Carmichael, 95609-1777. Tel: 916-863-3040 (Hotline).

Catholic Daughters of the Americas—Shirley Godfrey, 6600 Greenhaven Dr., Sacramento, 95831. Tel: 916-428-5044.

Charismatic Renewal—Rev. Msgr. Andrew V. Coffey, Diocesan Liaison (Retired); Deacon Jerry Pauly, Assoc. Diocesan Liaison. Tel: 916-451-3738; Mr. Michael Doneen, Treas.

Cursillo Movement—Office, 2110 Broadway, Sacramento, 95818-2541. Tel: 916-733-0181.

Daughters of Isabella—Carolyn Hadden, Regent, P.O. Box 276, Galt, 95632. Tel: 209-744-1802.

Diocesan Council of Catholic Nurses—Mrs. Eleanor Havey, 4935 61st St., Sacramento, 95820. Tel: 916-457-8649.

Diocesan Council of Catholic Women—Rev. Msgr. Edward J. Kavanagh, Moderator; Sue Westerfeld, 97 Dean Rd., Sacramento, 95815. Tel: 916-657-0366.

Handicapables—Mrs. Michelle Hendricks. Tel: 916-733-0123.

Italian Catholic Federation—Vacant, Chap.; Ricki Zarelli-Duggan, Dist. Pres., 3337 Bristol Rd., Sacramento, 95864. Tel: 916-489-6213.

Knights of Peter Claver and Ladies Aux.—Mr. Fred McLaurin, Sacramento, Area Deputy, P.O. Box 13471, Sacramento, 95813. Tel: 916-971-4954; Mrs. Albertine Taylor, Area Deputy, Ladies Div., 2606 Escobar Way, Sacramento, 95827. Tel: 916-362-8426.

Knights of Columbus—Mr. Danny J. Thompson, Northern California Chapter Pres., 5843 Wildwood Way, Marysville, 95901-7337. Tel: 530-743-8324.

Legion of Mary—Rev. William Dohman, 5972 Via Casitas Ave., Carmichael, 95608. Tel: 916-332-9747; Betty Friez, Pres., 6090 S. Southland Park Dr., #2, Sacramento, 95822. Tel: 916-422-7437 Three Curiae attached: Marysville-Yuba City, North Sacramento, Solano.

Marriage Encounter Worldwide—2110 Broadway, Sacramento, 95818-2541. Tel: 916-733-0123. Contact Catholic Faith Formation

Scouting, Catholic Committee on—Rev. Mark Richards, 2110 Broadway, Sacramento, 95818. Tel: 916-733-0258.

Secular Franciscan Order—

Grass Valley-St. Patrick Parish—Liz Hengesbach, SFO. Tel: 530-273-0787. San Damiano Fraternity

Sacramento-St. Francis of Assisi Parish— Fraternidad De San Juan Bautista (Spanish) Genaro Gonzalez, SFO. Tel: 916-392-9632 St. Francis of Assisi Fraternity (English); John Schroeder, SFO. Tel: 916-967-4233.

Secular Order of Discalced Carmelites—Harold Hunt, Pres., P.O. Box 25, Rancho Cordova, 95741. Tel: 916-362-5631.

Serra Club of Sacramento—Ronald Wood, Pres., 2029 Farmgate Lane, Lincoln, 95648-8600. Tel: 916-434-0378; Fax: 916-434-0815.

Young Ladies Institute—Mrs. Patricia Carvo, District Deputy, 2768 Lincoln Rd., Yuba City, 95993. Tel: 530-673-7147.

St. Thomas More Society—Herb Bolz, Pres. Tel: 530-753-6094; Rev. Charles S. McDermott, S.T.D. Tel: 916-733-0200.

CLERGY, PARISHES, MISSIONS AND PAROCHIAL SCHOOLS

CITY OF SACRAMENTO
(SACRAMENTO COUNTY)

1—CATHEDRAL OF THE BLESSED SACRAMENT (1889),, Catechetical Center Cathedral Parish Hall Conducted by parish CCD and Daughters of Charity of Canossa. Most Rev. William K. Weigand, D.D.; Revs. James Murphy, Rector; Nicholas Ho; Deacons Don De Haven; Raul Leon; Allen Pierre.
Res.: 1017 Eleventh St., 95814. Tel: 916-444-3071; Fax: 916-443-2749.
Res.: 1949 North Ave., 95838. Tel: 916-925-4001; Fax: 916-925-8897.
Catechesis/Religious Program—Tel: 916-444-5364. Students 469.

2—ALL HALLOWS (1942), Revs. Rodolfo Llamas, Co-Pastor; Erwin C. Mesiona, Co-Pastor; Deacons Michael Donovan; George Kriske; Gilberto Miranda.
Res.: 5500 13th Ave., 95820. Tel: 916-456-7206; Fax: 916-456-7325.
School—5700 13th Ave., 95820. Tel: 916-457-5621. Patricia Peterson, Prin. Lay Teachers 10; Students 219.
Catechesis/Religious Program—Tel: 916-736-0204. Students 105.
Station—California State Youth Authority Center 3001 Ramona Ave., 95820. Tel: 916-733-2350; Fax: 916-227-2511. Rev. Humberto Gomez, Chap.

3—ST. ANNE (1961), Rev. Januarius E. Rodrigues; Deacon Pedro Manriquez.
Res.: 7724 24th St., 95832. Tel: 916-422-8380; Fax: 916-422-7538.
School—7720 24th St., 95832. Tel: 916-422-3142. Mrs. Donna Nelson, Prin. Lay Teachers 6; Students 134.
Catechesis/Religious Program—Tel: 916-422-2419. Students 150.

4—ST. ANTHONY (1974), Revs. T. Brendan O'Sullivan; Joselito Vibandor; Deacons James Healy; Richard Koppes; Michael Crowley.
Res.: 660 Florin Rd., 95831. Tel: 916-428-5678; Fax: 916-428-0312.
Catechesis/Religious Program—Tel: 916-392-6362. Students 337.

5—ST. CHARLES BORROMEO (1960), (Spanish), Rev. Msgr. James Church; Revs. Felipe Paraguya; Fernando Meza; Deacons Manuel Ocon; Don DeHaven.
Res.: 7584 Center Pkwy., 95823. Tel: 916-421-5177; Fax: 916-392-4831.
School—7580 Center Pkwy., 95823. Tel: 916-421-6189; Fax: 916-421-3954. Thomas Yurkovic, Prin. Lay Teachers 13; Students 272.
Catechesis/Religious Program—Tel: 916-421-1063. Students 568.

6—ST. ELIZABETH (1909), (Portuguese), Rev. Eduino Silveira.
Res.: 1817 12th St., 95814. Tel: 916-442-2333; Fax: 916-498-0676.
Catechesis/Religious Program—Students 47.

7—ST. FRANCIS OF ASSISI (1894), Rev. Evan Howard, O.F.M. (PHX); Bro. Anthony Garibaldi, O.F.M.
1066 26th St., 95816. Tel: 916-443-8084; Fax: 916-443-7356.
School—2500 K St., 95816. Tel: 916-442-5494; Fax: 916-442-1390. Ms. Barbara O'Donnell, Prin. Lay Teachers 18; Students 287.
Catechesis/Religious Program—Tel: 916-443-8084, Ext. 105. Students 135.

8—HOLY SPIRIT (1940), Rev. Charles Brady; Deacon Ray Helgeson.
Res.: 3159 Land Park Dr., 95818. Tel: 916-443-5442; Fax: 916-446-9015.
School—3920 W. Land Park Dr., 95822. Tel: 916-448-5663; Fax: 916-444-9631. Jude Mikal, Prin. Lay Teachers 20; Students 303.
Catechesis/Religious Program—Tel: 916-448-8257. Students 137.
Convent—Sisters of Mercy (Auburn, CA), Tel: 916-448-3578.

9—ST. IGNATIUS OF LOYOLA (1954), Revs. Gerald H. Robinson, S.J.; David W. MacDonald, S.J.; Thomas G. Piquado, S.J. (HON); Robert Glynn, S.J.; Deacon Jackson Gualco.
Res.: 3235 Arden Way, 95825-2014. Tel: 916-482-9666; Fax: 916-482-6573.
School—3245 Arden Way, 95825. Tel: 916-488-3907; Fax: 916-488-0569. Patricia Lane, Prin. Lay Teachers 15; Students 331.
Catechesis/Religious Program—Tel: 916-482-9666, Ext. 238; Fax: 916-482-4869. Fatima Avila-Ohlsen, D.R.E. Students 230.
Ignatian Institute for Family Life—Tel: 916-482-9666, Ext. 205.

10—IMMACULATE CONCEPTION (1909), Rev. Roberto Jaramillo (Colombia); Deacon Gerald Pauly, Parish Steward. In Res., Rev. William Feeser.
Parish Office—3263 First Ave., 95817. Tel: 916-452-6866; Fax: 916-452-3879.
Catechesis/Religious Program—Tel: 916-682-9860. Students 120.

11—ST. JEONG-HAE ELIZABETH (1993), (Korean), Rev. Josephus Hee Jung Lee.
Res.: 9354 Kiefer Blvd., 95826. Tel: 916-368-9204; Fax: 916-368-8304.
Catechesis/Religious Program—Students 65.

12—ST. JOSEPH'S (1924), Revs. Cesar Ageas; Joseph Nguyen; Enrique Alvarez; Sr. Rose Ereba, H.H.C.J., Parish Min.; Deacon Henry Garcia. In Res., Rev. Blaise Berg.
Res.: 1717 El Monte Ave., 95815. Tel: 916-925-3584; Fax: 916-925-1045.
School—1718 El Monte Ave., 95815. Tel: 916-925-1465; Fax: 916-925-0963. Mrs. Jeannie Venturini, Prin. Sisters of Mercy (Auburn, CA) 1; Lay Teachers 10; Students 232.
Catechesis/Religious Program—Tel: 916-419-3216. Sr. Soledad Castillo, H.R.F., D.R.E. (Spanish). Tel: 916-922-7354; Irene Ogbonna, D.R.E. Students 497.

13—ST. MARY (1906), Rev. Francisco Valazquez, V.D.F.M.; Deacon Luigi Del Gaudio.
Res.: 1333 58th St., 95819. Tel: 916-452-0296; Fax: 916-452-3908.
School—1351 58th St., 95819. Tel: 916-452-1100; Fax: 916-453-2750. Laura Allen, Prin. Tel: 916-452-1100, Ext. 11. Lay Teachers 17; Aides 5; Students 327.
Catechesis/Religious Program—Tel: 916-452-4115. Students 105.

14—OUR LADY OF GUADALUPE SHRINE (1958), (Hispanic), Revs. Salvador Gomez, L.C.; Lino Otero, L.C.; Robert Presutti, L.C.; Jeffrey Jambon, L.C.
Res.: 711 T St., 95814. Tel: 916-442-3211; Fax: 916-442-3679.
Catechesis/Religious Program—730 S St., 95814. Tel: 916-446-3500. Students 480.

15—OUR LADY OF LOURDES (1957), Rev. Anthony Traynor; Deacon James Lalonde.
Res.: 1951 North Ave., 95838. Tel: 916-925-5313; Fax: 916-922-0625.
Catechesis/Religious Program—Tel: 916-925-4001. Students 165.
Convent—Daughters of Charity of Cannosa, 1949 North Ave., 95838. Tel: 916-925-4001; Fax: 916-925-8897.

16—ST. PAUL (1958), Rev. Nicholas Duggan (Retired); Deacons Charles Morrison; Thomas Ferreira.
Res.: 7200 Gardner Ave., P.O. Box 292280, 95829. Tel: 916-381-5200; Fax: 916-381-0332.
Catechesis/Religious Program—Students 250.

17—ST. PETER (1955), Revs. Erwin C. Mesiona; Rodolfo Llamas; Deacons Deogracia "Ray" Ramos; Gilberto Miranda; Tou Moua.
Res.: 6210 McMahon Dr., 95824. Tel: 916-455-3001; Fax: 916-455-4721.
School—6200 McMahon Dr., 95824. Tel: 916-455-2915; Fax: 916-455-2915. Sisters 4; Lay Teachers 9; Students 185.
Convent—Sisters Servants of the Blessed Sacrament (Guadalajara, Mexico), 5929 61st St., 95824. Tel: 916-457-0182.

18—ST. PHILOMENE (1948), Rev. John Hannan; Rev. Msgr. Patrick M. Nolan, Pastor Emeritus (Retired); Rev. Tim Nondorf; Deacons Charles Cheever; Martin Rodriguez. In Res., Rev. Thomas Bland.
Res.: 2428 Bell St., 95825. Tel: 916-481-6757; Fax: 916-481-1603.
School—2320 El Camino Ave., 95825. Tel: 916-489-5466; Fax: 916-489-2642. Debra Mosbrucker, Prin. Lay Teachers 13; Students 243.
Catechesis/Religious Program—Students 211.

19—PRESENTATION OF THE BLESSED VIRGIN MARY (1961), Rev. Michael Carroll.
Mailing Address: P.O. Box 214208, 95821-0208. In Res., Rev. Bernardin Mugabowakigeri (Rowanda).
Res.: 4123 Robertson Ave., 95821. Tel: 916-481-7441; Fax: 916-481-2841.
School—3100 Norris Ave., 95821. Tel: 916-482-0351; Fax: 916-482-0377. Patrick O'Neill, Prin. Lay Teachers 14; Students 265.
Parish Center—3110 Norris Ave., 95821. Tel: 916-428-8883.
Catechesis/Religious Program—Tel: 916-482-8883. Sr. Juliana Clancy. Students 160.

20—ST. ROBERT (1955), Rev. Kieran M. McMahon.
Res.: 2243 Irvin Way, 95822. Tel: 916-451-1475, Ext. 10,11; Fax: 916-451-0534.
School—2251 Irvin Way, 95822. Tel: 916-452-2111; Fax: 916-452-5765. Brian James, Prin. Lay Teachers 10; Students 291.
Catechesis/Religious Program—Tel: 916-454-1747. Students 81.

21—ST. ROSE (1942), Rev. Msgr. Edward J. Kavanagh; Rev. Francis Lawlor. In Res., Rev. Charles S. McDermott, S.T.D.
Res.: P.O. Box 5037, Oak Park Station, 95817. Tel: 916-421-1414; Fax: 916-421-0460.
School—St. Patrick, 5945 Franklin Blvd., 9582. Tel: 916-421-4963; Fax: 916-421-3849. Dave Hoffman, Prin. Lay Teachers 16; Students 303.
Catechesis/Religious Program—Tel: 916-392-5679. Students 640.

22—SACRED HEART OF JESUS (1926), Rev. Msgr. Robert P. Walton; Rev. Sylvester Kwiatkowski; Sr. Mary Martin, R.S.M., Pastoral Assoc. Tel: 916-452-4830; Deacons Gilbert Parra; William Riehl.
Res.: 1040 39th St., 95816. Tel: 916-452-4136; Fax: 916-457-9361.
School—Sacred Heart, 3933 I St., 95816. Tel: 916-456-1576; Fax: 916-456-4773. Raymond Burnell, Prin. Sisters of Mercy (Auburn, CA) 1; Lay Teachers 13; Students 305.
Catechesis/Religious Program—Tel: 916-454-3640. Sr. Mary O'Meara, R.S.M., D.R.E. Students 70.

23—ST. STEPHEN THE FIRST MARTYR CHURCH (2002),, (Tridentine Latin Mass) Revs. John Berg, F.S.S.P., Chap.; Stephane Dupre, F.S.S.P., Asst. Chap.
5461-44th St., 95817. Tel: 916-446-5908; Fax: 916-446-5702.
Catechesis/Religious Program—Students 70.

24—VIETNAMESE CATHOLIC MARTYRS (1976), (Vietnamese), Rev. Jude Ban Nguyen, C.M.C.; Deacon Anthony Huy Nguyen.
Res.: 10371 Jackson Rd., 95827. Tel: 916-383-4276; Fax: 916-383-4276.
Catechesis/Religious Program—Students 450.

OUTSIDE THE CITY OF SACRAMENTO

ALTURAS, MODOC CO., SACRED HEART (1883), Rev. Patrick J. Henry.
Res.: 507 E. Fourth St., 96101-3406. Tel: 530-233-2119.
Mission—St. James Bonner St. & Garfield St., Cedarville, Modoc Co. 96104.

ANDERSON, SHASTA CO., SACRED HEART (1949), Revs. Eric Lofgren; Efren Garcia; Deacons Michael Evans; Anthony Short; Ray Hemenway.
Res.: 3141 St. Stephen's Dr., 96007. Tel: 530-365-8573; Fax: 530-365-9544.
School—(Grades PreK-5), 3167 St. Stephen's Dr., 96007. Tel: 530-365-1429; Fax: 530-365-3039. Jennifer Bragg, Prin. Lay Teachers 6; Students 85.
School—St. Francis Middle School, 21945 Old 44 Dr., Palo Cedro, 96073. Tel: 530-547-2900; Fax: 530-547-5439. Students 194.
Catechesis/Religious Program—Students 90.
Mission—St. Anne 2nd St. & Main St., Cottonwood, Shasta Co. 96022.
Mission—Mary Queen of Peace Shingletown Ridge Rd., Shingletown, Shasta Co. 96088. Tel: 916-474-1870.

ANTELOPE, SACRAMENTO CO., ST. CLARE (1992), [JC] Revs. Colin Macdonald; Vincent Juan.
Res.: 1950 Junction Blvd., Roseville, 95747. Tel: 916-772-4717; Fax: 916-772-4152.
Catechesis/Religious Program—Tel: 916-339-2457; 916-722-0559. Students 404.

AUBURN, PLACER CO., ST. JOSEPH (1861), [CEM] Revs. Noel T. Lynch (Retired); Juan Manuel Ponce; Deacon Ed Morgado.
Res.: 1162 Lincoln Way, 95603. Tel: 530-885-2956; Fax: 530-823-6676.
School—11610 Atwood Rd., 95603. Tel: 530-885-4490; Fax: 530-885-0182. Mrs. Joan Walthers, Prin. Lay Teachers 11; Students 255.
Catechesis/Religious Program—Tel: 530-885-0362. Students 315.
Mission—St. Teresa of Avila (1994), 11600 Atwood Rd., Placer Co. 95603.
Station— Forest Hill.

BENICIA, SOLANO CO., ST. DOMINIC (1854), [CEM] Revs. David J. Farrugia, O.P.; Victor Cavalli, O.P.; Eugene W. Sousa, O.P.; Bartholomew de la Torre, O.P.; Deacons Ed Lazarek; John Flanagan; Juvencio Vela.
Mailing Address: P.O. Box 756, 94510-0756.
Res. & Church: 475 E. I St., 94510. Tel: 707-747-7220; Fax: 707-745-5642.
School—935 E. 5th St., 94510. Tel: 707-745-1266. Sr. Elizabeth Curtis, C.H.F., Prin. Lay Teachers 10; Students 300.
Catechesis/Religious Program—433 E. I St., 94510. Tel: 707-747-7240. Students 588.

BURNEY, SHASTA CO., ST. FRANCIS OF ASSISI (1949), Rev. Alfredo L. Tamayo.
Mailing Address: P.O. Drawer 160, 96013.
Res. & Church: 37464 Juniper Ave., 96013. Tel: 530-335-2372; Fax: 530-335-2306.
Catechesis/Religious Program—Tel: 530-294-5290. Students 50.
Mission—St. Stephen Hwy. 299, Bieber, Lassen Co. 96009.
Mission—Our Lady of the Valley 43434 Main St., Fall River Mills, Shasta Co. 96028. Tel: 530-336-6212.

CARMICHAEL, SACRAMENTO CO.

1—ST. JOHN THE EVANGELIST (1960), Revs. John Lagomarsino, S.S.C., Parochial Admin.; Ambrose

Ugwuegbu; Deacons James Weeks, (Retired); Floyd Shields.
Res.: 5751 Locust Ave., 95608. Tel: 916-483-8454; Fax: 916-481-8326.
School—5701 Locust Ave., 95608. Tel: 916-481-8845; Fax: 916-481-1319. Mrs. Ellen Gemma. Lay Teachers 14; Students 270.
Catechesis/Religious Program—Tel: 916-483-4628. Sr. Hannah O'Donoghue, D.R.E. Students 191.

2—OUR LADY OF THE ASSUMPTION (1952), Rev. Leo McAllister; Deacons Michael Tateishi; Richard Driggs. In Res., Revs. William Broderick (Retired); Jose Karikattil.
Res.: 5057 Cottage Way, 95608. Tel: 916-481-5115; Fax: 916-481-4026.
School—2141 Walnut Ave., 95608. Tel: 916-489-8958; Fax: 916-489-3237. Theresa Sparks, Prin. Lay Teachers 13; Students 305.
Catechesis/Religious Program—Tel: 916-488-4626. Students 325.
Convent—Ladies of Loretto (Toronto, Canada), Tel: 916-488-8188.

CHICO, BUTTE CO.

1—ST. JOHN THE BAPTIST (1878), Revs. Terry Fulton; Paul Schloeder; Guillermo Rodriguez; Deacons Jesus Campos Padilla; Stephen Schwartz.
Res.: 435 Chestnut St., 95928. Tel: 530-343-8741; Fax: 530-345-8602.
School—(Grades K-8), 435 Hazel St., 95928. Tel: 530-342-2502; Fax: 530-342-6292. Colleen Waugh, Prin. Lay Teachers 10; Students 239.
Catechesis/Religious Program—Students 515.
Mission—St. James [JC] P.O. Box 562, Durham, Butte Co. 95938.

2—OUR DIVINE SAVIOR (1967), Rev. Edward Pepka.
Office—566 E. Lassen Ave., 95973. Tel: 530-343-4248; Fax: 530-343-3538.
Catechesis/Religious Program—Tel: 530-345-6201. Students 25.

CITRUS HEIGHTS, SACRAMENTO CO., HOLY FAMILY (1949), Rev. Troy Powers; Rev. Msgr. Vito F. Mistretta, Pastor Emeritus (Retired); Revs. Christian Paul Egege; Santiago Raudes.
Res.: 7817 Old Auburn Rd., 95610. Tel: 916-723-2494; Fax: 916-723-0199.
School—Tel: 916-722-7788; Fax: 916-722-5297. Sr. Arlene Connelly, I.B.V.M., Prin. Lay Teachers 45; Students 550.
School—Preschool, Tel: 916-722-4620; Fax: 916-722-4509. Patricia Peterson, Preschool Dir. Tel: 916-722-4620. Lay Teachers 7; Students 100.
Catechesis/Religious Program—Tel: 916-726-7217; Fax: 916-721-3292. Shawnmarie Allen, D.R.E. Students 365.

CLARKSBURG, YOLO CO., ST. JOSEPH (1893), Rev. Daniel Madigan.
Res. & Church Address: 32890 S. River Rd., 95612. Tel: 916-665-1132; Fax: 916-665-9264.
Catechesis/Religious Program—Students 29.

COLFAX, PLACER CO., ST. DOMINIC (1951), [CEM] Unassigned., Mailing Address: c/o P.O. Box 752, 95713.
Res. & Church: 58 E. Oak St., 95713. Tel: 530-346-2286; Fax: 530-346-2286.
Catechesis/Religious Program—Tel: 530-346-2915. Students 140.

COLUSA, COLUSA CO., OUR LADY OF LOURDES (1870), Revs. Roy Doner; Francisco Hernandez-Gomez; Deacon Miguel Fernandez.
Res.: 745 Ware Ave., 95932. Tel: 530-458-4170; Fax: 530-458-8728.
Church: 345 Oak St., 95932. Tel: 530-458-7901.
School—(Grades PreK-8) Tel: 530-458-8208; Fax: 530-458-8657. Mrs. Barbara Genera, Prin. Lay Teachers 5; Students 109.
Catechesis/Religious Program—Tel: 530-458-2515. Students 125.
Mission—St. Joseph 1st St. & Center St., Princeton, Colusa Co. 95970.
Station—Our Lady of Sorrows [CEM] [JC] Sycamore.

CORNING, TEHAMA CO., IMMACULATE CONCEPTION (1946), [JC] Rev. Miguel Silva.
Res.: 814 Solano St., 96021. Tel: 530-824-5879; Fax: 530-824-6534.
Catechesis/Religious Program—Tel: 530-824-2477. Students 154.
Mission—St. Stanislaus 4th St. & D St., Tehama, Tehama Co. 96090.

DAVIS, YOLO CO., ST. JAMES (1912), [JC] Rev. Daniel A. Looney; Rev. Msgr. Andrew V. Coffey, Pastor Emeritus (Retired); Rev. Richard J. Blinn, S.J.; Deacons Paul Taloff; Sam Colenzo; Clark Goecker. In Res., Rev. David O. Fontaine, O.Carm. (STO).
Res.: 200 W. 14th St., 95616. Tel: 530-756-3636; Fax: 530-756-5342.
School—1215 B St., 95616. Tel: 530-756-3946; Fax: 530-753-9765. Mary Kay Bolz, Prin. Lay Teachers 16; Students 302.
Catechesis/Religious Program—Tel: 530-758-9000. Linda O'Hara, D.R.E. Students 415.
Newman Center—514 C St., 95616. Tel: 530-753-7393; Fax: 530-753-2794.

DIXON, SOLANO CO., ST. PETER (1877), Revs. Maurice O'Brien; John J. Kyne, Pastor Emeritus; Deacons Robert H. Ikelman; John King; Felix Lupercio.
Res.: 105 S. 2nd St., 95620. Tel: 707-678-9424; Fax: 707-678-9432.
Catechesis/Religious Program—Students 370.

DOWNIEVILLE, SIERRA CO., IMMACULATE CONCEPTION (1853), [CEM] [JC] Rev. Godwin Xavier.
Mailing Address: P.O. Box 48, North San Juan, 95960.
Office—Flume St., North San Juan, 95960. Tel: 530-292-3227; Fax: 530-292-3560.
Church: Church St., 95936.
Mission—St. John 10047 Flume St., North San Juan, Nevada Co. 95960.

DUNSMUIR, SISKIYOU CO., ST. JOHN THE EVANGELIST (1899), [JC] Rev. Aidan O'Reilly.
P.O. Box 298, Mount Shasta, 96067.
Church: 5605 Shasta Ave., 96025. Tel: 530-926-4477; Fax: 530-926-4234.
Catechesis/Religious Program—Tel: 530-235-4705; Fax: 530-235-4759. Students 26.

EL DORADO HILLS, EL DORADO CO., HOLY TRINITY (1992), Rev. Msgr. James C. Kidder; Greg McAvoy-Jensen, M.Div., Pastoral Assoc.; Deacon Neil Zachary. In Res., Rev. John P. Sullivan (Retired)
Church: 3111 Tierra de Dios Dr., 95762-8008. Tel: 530-677-3234; Fax: 530-677-3570.
School—3115 Tierra de Dios Dr., 95762-8008. Tel: 530-677-3591. Marsha Cornelius, Prin.
Catechesis/Religious Program—Tel: 530-677-3234, Ext. 133. Students 907.

ELK GROVE, SACRAMENTO CO.

1—GOOD SHEPHERD CATHOLIC CHURCH (1993), Revs. Brendan McKeefry; Mervin Concepcion.
Res.: 9539 Racquet Ct., 95758. Tel: 916-684-5722; Fax: 916-684-4472.
School—St. Elizabeth Ann Seton Elementary School, 9539 Racquet Ct., 95758. Tel: 916-684-7903; Fax: 916-691-4064. Thomas M. Butler, Prin. Students 324.
Catechesis/Religious Program—Tel: 916-683-2963, Ext. 30. Students 500.

2—ST. JOSEPH (1962), Rev. Msgr. Albert G. O'Connor; Rev. Brian Joseph Cabrera Atienza; Deacon Paul Imrisek.
Res.: 9961 Elk Grove-Florin Rd., 95624. Tel: 916-685-3681; Fax: 916-685-7254.
Catechesis/Religious Program—Tel: 916-685-5636. Students 860.
Mission— 14673 Cantova Way, Rancho Murieta, Sacramento Co. 95683. Tel: 916-354-2[illegible]03.

FAIR OAKS, SACRAMENTO CO., ST. MEL (1948), Revs. Richard Doheny; Carroll Keating, S.J.; Deacons Patrick Henning; David Lehman.
Mailing Address: c/o P.O. Box 1180, 95628.
Res. & Church: 4745 Pennsylvania Ave., 95628. Tel: 916-967-1229; Fax: 916-967-5659.
School—Tel: 916-967-2814; Fax: 916-967-0705. Janet Nagel, Prin. Lay Teachers 15; Students 314.
Catechesis/Religious Program—Tel: 916-966-4314. Students 250.

FAIRFIELD, SOLANO CO.

1—HOLY SPIRIT (1950), [CEM] Revs. Michael Downey; Stephen Olario; Luis Urrego (Colombia).
Mailing Address: c/o P.O. Box X, 94533.
Res. & Church: 1050 N. Texas St. 94533. Tel: 707-425-3138; Fax: 707-425-2029.
School—(Grades K-8) Tel: 707-422-5016; Fax: 707-422-0874. Sr. Mairead Langley, C.H.F., Prin. Sisters 4; Lay Teachers 14; Students 357.
Catechesis/Religious Program—Tel: 707-425-9042. Suselia Hernandez, D.R.E. Students 1,100.
Convent—Sisters of the Holy Faith (Dublin, Ireland), Tel: 707-425-3572.

2—OUR LADY OF MOUNT CARMEL (1979),, (Carmelite Fathers) Revs. Sebastian Meyer, O.Carm.; James H. Mueller, O.Carm.; Deacon Phil Verba.
Parish Office—Tel: 707-422-7767; Fax: 707-422-7946.
Res.: 2700 Dover Ave., 94533. Tel: 707-426-3639.
Church: 2700 Dover Ave., 94533.
Catechesis/Religious Program—Tel: 707-422-2814. Students 334.

FOLSOM, SACRAMENTO CO., ST. JOHN THE BAPTIST (1857) [CEM] Revs. Ignatius Harang; Vicente Teneza; Cormac Lacre; Deacons Dennis Merino; Jim Meucci.
Mailing Address: *Office*, 307 Montrose Dr., 95630. Tel: 916-985-2065; Fax: 916-985-7579. Mailing Address: *Folsom State Prison*, P.O. Box 29, Represa, 95671. Tel: 916-985-8610, Ext. 6425; Fax: 530-647-0763.
Res.: 107 Joseph Way, 95630. Tel: 916-351-1939.
School—St. John's-Notre Dame, Tel: 916-985-4129; Fax: 916-985-7958. Sue Halfman, Prin. Lay Teachers 15; Students 320.
Catechesis/Religious Program—Tel: 916-985-7338. Students 750.
Station—Folsom State Prison P.O. Box W, Represa, 95671. Tel: 916-985-2561; Fax: 916-351-3070. Rev. Thomas Maguire, Chap. Tel: 916-989-6564; Deacon Dennis Merino, Chap.
Station—California State Prison P.O. Box 29, 95671. Tel: 916-985-8610; Fax: 916-985-6425.

FORT JONES, SISKIYOU CO., SACRED HEART (1921), [CEM] Rev. John M. Lawrence.
Res.: 101 Carlock St., P.O. Box 126, 96032-0126. Tel: 530-468-2605; Fax: 530-468-5577.
Catechesis/Religious Program—Students 59.
Mission—St. Mary's Etna. 386 Center St., Etna, Siskiyou Co. 96027. Tel: 530-467-3561.
Mission—All Saints 1321 Indian Creek Rd., Happy Camp, Siskiyou Co. 96093. Tel: 530-493-2657.
Mission—St. Joseph Etna. Sawyer's Bar Rd., Sawyer's Bar, Siskiyou Co. 96027.

GALT, SACRAMENTO CO., ST. CHRISTOPHER (1885), Rev. Gerald Ryle; Deacon Thomas McGill; Rev. Adolfo Rivera.
Mailing Address: 950 S. Lincoln Way, 95632.
Res.: 211 Sterling Grove, P.O. Box 276, 95632. Tel: 209-745-1389; Fax: 209-744-2183.
Catechesis/Religious Program—Tel: 209-745-1389, Ext. 304. Students 322.

GRASS VALLEY, NEVADA CO., ST. PATRICK (1855), [CEM] Revs. Nicholas Phelan, Pastor Emeritus; Simon D. Twomey; Deacons Carlos Astesana; James Chatigny; Brian Moore.
Res.: 235 Chapel St., 95945. Tel: 530-273-2347; Fax: 530-272-9681.
School—Mt. St. Mary's, Tel: 530-273-4694; Fax: 530-273-1724. Judy Schank, Prin. Lay Teachers 11; Students 140.
School—Preschool/Day Care, Tel: 530-273-6244; Fax: 530-273-1724. Students 24.
Catechesis/Religious Program—Tel: 530-273-2336. Students 280.

GRIDLEY, BUTTE CO., SACRED HEART (1926), Rev. Rodolfo Delgado.
Res. & Church: 1560 Hazel St., 95948. Tel: 530-846-2140; Fax: 530-846-5077.
Catechesis/Religious Program—Students 300.
Mission—Our Lady of Guadalupe 9660 Broadway, Live Oak, Sutter Co. 95953.

IONE, AMADOR CO., SACRED HEART (1932), [CEM] [JC] Rev. Thomas Relihan.
Res.: Church and Washington Sts., P.O. Box 4, 95640. Tel: 209-274-2158.
Catechesis/Religious Program—Students 55.
Mission—Preston School of Industry, California Youth Authority 201 Waterman Rd., Amador Co. 95640. Tel: 209-274-4771, Ext. 250. Rev. Adolfo Rivera.
Mission—Mule Creek State Prison P.O. Box 409099, Amador Co. 95640. Tel: 209-274-4911. Rev. Diego Baptista.

ISLETON, SACRAMENTO CO., ST. THERESE'S (1953), Deacon Jose R. Revelo.
Res.: P.O. Box 697, 95641. Tel: 916-777-6871; Fax: 916-777-6871.
Church: 4th St. & Jackson Blvd., 95641.
Catechesis/Religious Program—Students 80.

JACKSON, AMADOR CO., ST. PATRICK'S (1864), [CEM 2] Rev. Thomas L. Seabridge; Jeannine Crew, Pastoral Assoc.; Deacon William Thompson, (Retired).
Res.: 115 Court St., 95642. Tel: 209-223-0168; Fax: 209-223-2548.
Catechesis/Religious Program—Students 100.
Mission—Our Lady of the Pines Pioneer. 26750 Tiger Creek Rd., Buckhorn, Amador Co. 95666. Tel: 209-295-4909.
Mission—St. Bernard Plug-Emigrant St., Volcano, Amador Co. 95689.

KNIGHTS LANDING, YOLO CO., ST. PAUL (1949), Rev. Joseph Huong Nguyen; Deacon Antonio Gonzalez.
Res.: 222 Sycamore Way, P.O. Box 176, 95645. Tel: 530-735-6478; Fax: 530-735-9498.
Catechetical Center—6th St. & Locust St., 95645.
Catechesis/Religious Program—Students 80.
Mission—St. Agnes 9865 Main St., Zamora, Yolo Co. 95645.

LINCOLN, PLACER CO., ST. JOSEPH (1892), [CEM] [JC] Revs. Polycarpo Gumapo; James Rockenstein, O.F.M.; Eduardo Toscano; Deacons Jesus Rodriguez; Roberto Ruiz; Kenneth Boone.
Res.: 585 D St., 95648. Tel: 916-645-2102; Fax: 916-645-1422.
Catechesis/Religious Program—Tel: 916-645-7754; Fax: 916-645-2144. Students 280.
Mission—St. Boniface 1028 Marcum Rd., Nicolaus, Sutter Co. 95659. Tel: 916-656-2368.
Mission—St. Daniel 214 Main St., Wheatland, Yuba Co. 95692. Tel: 916-633-0344.
Shrine—Our Lady of Guadalupe 3rd St. & K St., 95648.

MARYSVILLE, YUBA CO., ST. JOSEPH (1852), [CEM] Revs. Robert A. Copsey; Heriberto Serrano; Deacons Jesus Munoz; David Perez.
Office & Mailing Address: 223 Eighth St., 95901.
Res.: 319 Seventh St., 95901. Tel: 530-742-6461;

Fax: 530-742-0346.
School—(Grades K-8), 715 C St., 95901. Tel: 530-743-4484; Fax: 530-743-4485. Anthony Hinojosa, Prin. Lay Teachers 9; Students 168.
Catechesis/Religious Program—Tel: 530-742-7100. Students 168.
Mission—Sacred Heart Church P.O. Box 208, Dobbins, Yuba Co. 95953.

MAXWELL, COLUSA CO., SACRED HEART (1881), [CEM] Revs. John Myles; Francisco Hernandez.
Mailing Address: c/o P.O. Box 607, 95955.
Res. & Church: 45 Elm St., 95955. Tel: 530-438-2432; Fax: 530-438-2432.
Mission—Holy Cross 408 Laurel St., Arbuckle, Colusa Co. 95912.
Mission—Annunciation 617 8th St., Williams, Colusa Co. 95987. Tel: 530-473-2925.
Mission—St. Mary of the Mountain 2nd St. & Geary St., Stonyford, Colusa Co. 95979.
Catechesis/Religious Program—Students 175.

MCCLOUD, SISKIYOU CO., ST. JOSEPH (1933), (Italian), [JC] Rev. Philip Wells.
Church & Mailing Address: 213 Colombero Dr., P.O. Box 518, 96057. Tel: 530-235-4705; Fax: 530-235-4759.
Res.: 1051 N. David Ave., Weed, 96094. Tel: 530-938-2076; Fax: 530-938-3837.
Catechesis/Religious Program—Students 20.

MOUNT SHASTA, SISKIYOU CO., ST. ANTHONY (1954), Rev. Aidan O'Reilly.
Res.: P.O. Box 298, 96067. Tel: 530-926-4477; Fax: 530-926-4234.
Church: Pine St. & Alma St., 96067. Tel: 530-926-4477.
Catechesis/Religious Program—Tel: 530-926-3061. Students 93.

NEVADA CITY, NEVADA CO., ST. CANICE (1851), [CEM] Rev. James McKnight (Retired).
Mailing Address: c/o P.O. Box 1597, 95959.
Res.: 317 Washington St., 95959. Tel: 530-265-2049; Fax: 530-265-3697.
Church: Coyote St., 95959.
Catechesis/Religious Program—Tel: 530-265-2712. Students 62.

NORTH HIGHLANDS, SACRAMENTO CO., ST. LAWRENCE (1955), Rev. Joseph P. Ternullo. In Res., Rev. Michael F. Kiernan.
Res.: 4325 Don Julio Blvd., 95660. Tel: 916-332-4777; Fax: 916-332-8325.
School—(Grades K-8), 4325 Don Julio Blvd., 95660. Tel: 916-332-4779. Mrs. Marilyn Fleming, Prin. Lay Teachers 10; Students 204.
Catechesis/Religious Program—Tel: 916-332-4777. Students 248.

ORANGEVALE, SACRAMENTO CO., DIVINE SAVIOR (1987), Revs. Thomas Tureman, S.D.S.; Jeffrey Wocken, S.D.S., Vicar.
Mailing Address: 9079 Greenback Ln., 95662-4703. Tel: 916-989-7400; Fax: 916-989-7410.
Res.: 8680 Hickory Leaf Pl., 95662-3444. Tel: 916-989-5425.
Catechesis/Religious Program—Students 440.
Counseling Center—Tel: 916-989-7414.

ORLAND, GLENN CO., ST. DOMINIC (1919), Revs. Michael O'Reilly; Eduardo Toscano.
Mailing Address: c/o Box 816, 95963.
Res. & Church: 822 A St., 95963. Tel: 530-865-4550; Fax: 530-865-8451.
Catechesis/Religious Program—Tel: 530-865-7115. Students 178.
Mission—St. Mary 400 Los Robles, Hamilton City, Glenn Co. 95951.

OROVILLE, BUTTE CO., ST. THOMAS THE APOSTLE (1857), Rev. Benedict DeLeon.
Res.: 1330 Bird St., 95965. Tel: 530-533-0262; Fax: 530-533-1148.
School—1380 Bird St., 95965. Tel: 530-534-6969; Fax: 530-534-9374. Joani Briggs, Prin. Lay Teachers 9; Students 86.
Catechesis/Religious Program—Students 60.

PARADISE, BUTTE CO., ST. THOMAS MORE (1949), Rev. Steven Eugene Foppiano.
Res.: 767 Elliott Rd., 95969. Tel: 530-877-4501; Fax: 530-877-5633.
School—771 Elliott Rd., 95969. Tel: 530-877-5328; Fax: 530-877-3114. Mr. Richard Priest, Interim Prin. Lay Teachers 6; Students 50.
Catechesis/Religious Program—Tel: 530-877-6023. Students 50.

PLACERVILLE, EL DORADO CO., ST. PATRICK'S (1854), [CEM] Revs. John Cantwell; Eugenio Lopez-Restrepo; Deacon Stan S. Rudger.
Res.: 3109 Sacramento St., 95667. Tel: 530-622-0373; Fax: 530-621-7770.
Catechesis/Religious Program—Tel: 530-622-7692; Fax: 530-621-7771. Students 357.
Mission—St. James 2831 Harkness St., Georgetown, El Dorado Co. 95634. Tel: 530-333-9432.

PORTOLA, PLUMAS CO., HOLY FAMILY (1929), Rev. Glenn O. Dare.
Mailing Address: c/o P.O. Box 1077, 96122.
Res. & Church: 108 Taylor Ave., 96122. Tel: 530-832-5006; Fax: 530-832-5520.
Catechesis/Religious Program—Students 60.
Mission—Holy Rosary 4th St., Loyalton, Sierra Co. 96118.

QUINCY, PLUMAS CO., ST. JOHN (1947), [JC 6] Rev. Andrzej A. Koziczuk.
Mailing Address: c/o Box 510, 95971.
Res. & Church: 170 Lawrence St., 95971. Tel: 530-283-0890; Fax: 530-283-4204.
Catechesis/Religious Program—Tel: 530-283-4936. Students 55.
Mission—St. Anthony 209 Jesse St., Greenville, Plumas Co. 95947. Tel: 530-284-6882.
Station—Quincy Buck's Lake.

RANCHO CORDOVA, SACRAMENTO CO., ST. JOHN VIANNEY (1958), Revs. Martin J. Moroney; Perlito de la Cruz; Deacons Walter Little; Phil Moseley.
Res.: 10497 Coloma Rd., 95670. Tel: 916-362-1385; Fax: 916-361-8102.
School—10499 Coloma Rd., 95670. Tel: 916-363-4610; Fax: 916-363-3243. Mrs. Vicky Andrews, Prin. Lay Teachers 11; Students 290.
Catechesis/Religious Program—Tel: 916-362-3827. Students 320.

RED BLUFF, TEHAMA CO., SACRED HEART (1867), [CEM] Revs. Michael J. Hebda; Juan Manual Ponce.
Parish Hall—2355 Monroe St., 96080. Tel: 530-527-1351; Fax: 530-529-2586.
School—2255 Monroe St., 96080. Tel: 530-527-6727; Fax: 530-527-5026. Mrs. Kate Grimes, Prin. Lay Teachers 9; Students 163.
Catechesis/Religious Program—Students 75.

REDDING, SHASTA CO.

1—ST. JOSEPH (1907), [CEM] Rev. Msgr. Russell G. Terra; Rev. Bernard Tape; Deacons David Gasman; Frank Lopez; Michael Mangas.
Res.: 2040 Walnut Ave., 96001. Tel: 530-243-3463; Fax: 530-243-7999.
School—2460 Gold St., 96001. Tel: 530-243-2302; Fax: 530-243-2747. Mr. Tom Schwerdt, Prin. Lay Teachers 11; Students 254.
School—St. Francis Middle School, 21945 Old 44 Dr., Palo Cedro, 96073. Tel: 530-547-2900; Fax: 530-547-5349. Students 167.
Catechesis/Religious Program—Students 119.
Mission—St. Michael 3440 Shasta Dam Blvd., Shasta Lake City, Shasta Co. 96019.

2—OUR LADY OF MERCY (1980), Rev. Michael Canny.
Office—2600 Shasta View Dr., 96002. Tel: 530-222-3424; Fax: 530-221-5717.
School—St. Francis Middle School, 21945 Old 44 Dr., Palo Cedro, 96073. Tel: 530-547-2900; Fax: 530-547-5349. Lay Teachers 14; Students 196.
Catechesis/Religious Program—Tel: 530-222-3424, Ext. 12. Students 268.

RIO VISTA, SOLANO CO., ST. JOSEPH (1885), [CEM 2] Revs. Julian Medina; William K. Walsh, Pastor Emeritus (Retired).
Res.: 130 S. 4th St., 94571. Tel: 707-374-2155; Fax: 707-374-5071.
Catechesis/Religious Program—Students 147.

ROCKLIN, PLACER CO., SS. PETER AND PAUL (1981), Rev. Michael J. Dillon.
Mailing Address: c/o Box 824, 95677.
Res. & Church: 4450 Granite Dr., 95677. Tel: 916-624-5827; Fax: 916-624-5924.
Catechesis/Religious Program—Tel: 916-624-5827, Ext. 210; Fax: 916-624-5925. Students 1,164.

ROSEVILLE, PLACER CO., ST. ROSE OF LIMA (1907), (Mexican), Revs. Michael McKeon; Gary Norman (GF); Deacons William H. Boudier; Peter M. Silott; Mark Van Hook; Don Waldemar. In Res., Rev. Michael J. Cormack, Pastor Emeritus (Retired).
Res.: 615 Vine Ave., 95678. Tel: 916-783-5211; Fax: 916-783-5212.
School—633 Vine Ave., 95678. Tel: 916-782-1161; Fax: 916-782-7862. Charles Suarez, Prin. Sisters 1; Lay Teachers 14; Students 311.
Catechesis/Religious Program—Tel: 916-786-0650. Students 550.

SOUTH LAKE TAHOE, EL DORADO CO., ST. THERESA (1951), Revs. Mark R. Richards, J.C.L.; Oscar Gomez Medina; Rev. Msgr. Murrough C. Wallace, Pastor Emeritus (Retired); Rev. John J. Grace, Pastor Emeritus (Retired).
Res.: 1041 Lyons Ave., 96150. Tel: 530-544-3533; Fax: 530-544-4662.
School—1081 Lyons Ave., 96150. Tel: 530-544-8944; Fax: 530-544-8909. Danette Winslow, Prin. Lay Teachers 8; Students 167.
Catechesis/Religious Program—Tel: 530-544-4788; Fax: 530-544-8909. Students 385.
Mission—Our Lady of the Sierra Camp Sacramento, El Dorado Co.

SUSANVILLE, LASSEN CO., SACRED HEART (1912), Rev. Robert E. Brooks.
Mailing Address: c/o P.O. Box 501, 96130.
Res. and Church: 120 N. Union St., 96130. Tel: 530-257-3230; Fax: 530-257-9213.
Catechesis/Religious Program—Msgr. Moran Hall, 140 N. Weatherlow St., 96130. Tel: 530-257-8008.
Station— Herlong.

SUTTER CREEK, AMADOR CO., IMMACULATE CONCEPTION (1864), [CEM 4] Revs. Liam MacCarthy; Ronan P. Brennan, Pastor Emeritus (Retired); Deacon Ed Pogue.
Res.: P.O. Box 127, 95685. Tel: 209-267-5602; Fax: 209-267-1278.
Catechesis/Religious Program—Spanish St. & Amelia St., 95685. Students 85.
Mission—St. Mary of the Mountains Church St., Plymouth, Amador Co. 95669.

TAHOE CITY, PLACER CO., CORPUS CHRISTI (1961), Rev. Patrick J. O'Connor.
Mailing Address: P.O. Box 1878, 96145.
Church & Res.: 905 W. Lake Blvd., 96145. Tel: 530-583-4409; Fax: 530-583-1408.
Catechesis/Religious Program—Tel: 530-581-4637. Students 72.
Mission—Queen of the Snows 1550 Squaw Valley Rd., Olympic Valley, Placer Co. 96146.
Station— Tahoma.

TRUCKEE, NEVADA CO., ASSUMPTION OF THE BLESSED VIRGIN MARY (1870), Rev. Stanley Poltorak; Deacon Ray Craig.
Mailing Address: P.O. Box 34014, 96160.
Res. & Church: 10124 E. St., 96160. Tel: 530-587-3595; Fax: 530-582-8648.
Catechesis/Religious Program—Students 265.
Mission—Our Lady of the Lake 8363 Steelhead, Kings Beach, Placer Co. 96143.

TULELAKE, SISKIYOU CO., HOLY CROSS (1949), Rev. Brent C. Nall.
Mailing Address: P.O. Box 266, 96134. Fax: 530-667-2818.
Res. & Church: 765 First St., 96134. Tel: 530-667-2727.
Catechesis/Religious Program—Students 35.
Mission—Our Lady of Good Counsel W. 3rd St., Dorris, Siskiyou Co. 96023.

VACAVILLE, SOLANO CO.

1—ST. JOSEPH (1992), [JC] Rev. Vincent O'Reilly.
Res.: 1771 Marshall Rd., 95687. Tel: 707-447-2354; Fax: 707-447-9322.
School—Notre Dame, 1781 Marshall Rd., 95687. Tel: 707-447-1460; Fax: 707-447-1498. Karen Dietrich, Prin. Lay Teachers 12; Students 338.
Catechesis/Religious Program—Students 230.

2—ST. MARY (1947), Revs. Michael McFadden; Oscar Gutierrez; Paul Ricks; Deacons Domingo Cabrera, (Retired); Ernesto Vitae.
Res.: 350 Stinson Ave., 95688. Tel: 707-448-2390; Fax: 707-448-2818.
Catechesis/Religious Program—Tel: 707-446-1881. Students 674.
Catechetical Center—300 Hemlock St., 95688. Tel: 707-446-1881. Students 25.

VALLEJO, SOLANO CO.

1—ST. BASIL (1941), Revs. Leon Juchniewicz; Joel Genabia; Deacon Mike Urick.
Res.: 1200 Tuolumne St., 94590. Tel: 707-644-5251; Fax: 707-644-1423.
School—1230 Nebraska St., 94590. Tel: 707-642-7629; Fax: 707-642-8635. Mrs. Susan M. Hill, Prin. Lay Teachers 12; Students 353; Preschool 93.
Catechesis/Religious Program—Tel: 707-644-8309. Students 300.

2—ST. CATHERINE OF SIENA (1964), Revs. Jesus T. Soriano; Francisco Hernandez Tovar; Stephen Olario; Deacons Pete Lobo; Rudy David; Bobby Peregrino.
Mailing Address & Res.: 3450 Tennessee St., 94591. Tel: 707-553-1355; Fax: 707-557-6896.
School—(Grades K-8), 3460 Tennessee St., 94591. Tel: 707-643-6691; Fax: 707-647-4441. Mrs. Lee Roark, Prin. Lay Teachers 14; Students 327.
Catechesis/Religious Program—Tel: 707-647-4445. Students 310.

3—ST. VINCENT FERRER (1855), Revs. Stephen M. Borlang; Filomeno Cabulosan; Hernando Gomez Amaya.
Res.: 925 Sacramento St., 94590. Tel: 707-644-8396; Fax: 707-644-1330.
School—420 Florida St., 94590. Tel: 707-642-4311; Fax: 707-642-1329. Mrs. Susan Fulton, Prin. Lay Teachers 12; Students 349.
Catechesis/Religious Program—Tel: 707-643-0188. Students 784.
Mission—St. Louis Bertrand 643 Sonoma Blvd., South Vallejo, Solano Co. 94590.

WALNUT GROVE, SACRAMENTO CO., ST. ANTHONY (1931), Rev. William J. Dinelli.
Mailing Address: P.O. Box 436, 95690.
Res. & Church: 14012 Walnut Ave., 95690. Tel: 916-776-1330.
Catechesis/Religious Program—Students 60.

WEAVERVILLE, TRINITY CO., ST. PATRICK (1853), [CEM] Rev. Keith Canterbury; Deacon Everett Layne.
Res.: P.O. Box 1219, 96093-1219. Tel: 530-623-4383.
Church: 102 Church St., 96093.

Catechesis/Religious Program—Students 29.
Mission—Holy Trinity Hayfork, Trinity Co.
Mission—St. Gilbert Lewiston, Trinity Co.
Station— Mad River.

WEED, SISKIYOU CO., HOLY FAMILY (1933), Rev. Philip Wells.
Res.: 1051 N. Davis Ave., 96094. Tel: 530-938-2076; Fax: 530-938-3837.
Catechesis/Religious Program—Tel: 530-459-5124. Students 77.

WEST SACRAMENTO, YOLO CO.

1—HOLY CROSS (1913), Rev. Chad C. Puthoff, S.D.S.; Bro. William Hoefgen, S.D.S.; Deacon Raul Leon. In Res., Rev. Sidney Peter Hall.
Res.: 1321 Anna St., 95605. Tel: 916-371-1211; Fax: 916-371-9277.
School—800 Todhunter Ave., 95605. Tel: 916-371-1313. Sr. Jane Golden, R.S.M., Prin. Sisters 3; Lay Teachers 8; Students 151.
Catechesis/Religious Program—Tel: 916-371-5884. Students 205.
Convent—Sisters of Mercy (Auburn, CA), Tel: 916-371-1931; 916-933-0971.

2—OUR LADY OF GRACE (1949), Rev. J. B. Walsh (Ireland).
Res.: 911 Park Blvd., 95691. Tel: 916-371-4814.
School—1990 Linden Rd., 95691. Tel: 916-371-9416; Fax: 916-371-1319. Sr. Michael Henry Moulin, D.H.S., Prin. Sisters 1; Lay Teachers 11; Students 225.
Catechesis/Religious Program—Fax: 916-371-4816. Students 183.
Convent—Tel: 916-371-9416.

WESTWOOD, LASSEN CO., OUR LADY OF THE SNOWS (1929), Rev. Mathew M. Marankulam Rappuzha (India).
Res.: 307 Fifth St., P.O. Box 905, 96137. Tel: 530-256-3344; Fax: 530-256-3344.
Church: 425 Cedar St., 96137.
Catechesis/Religious Program—Students 32.
Mission—Christ the King Melissa St., Chester, Plumas Co. 96020. Tel: 530-258-3231.

WILLOWS, GLENN CO., ST. MONICA (1877), [CEM] Revs. Matthias J. O'Callaghan; Juan Ponce-Red Bluff.
Res.: 1129 W. Wood St., 95988. Tel: 530-934-3314; Fax: 530-934-3205.
Catechesis/Religious Program—Tel: 530-934-3293. Students 190.
School—Catechetical School, 1151 W. Wood St., 95988. Tel: 530-934-5916; Fax: 530-934-3205. Students 185.

WINTERS, YOLO CO., ST. ANTHONY (1913), [JC] Rev. Charles Kelly; Deacon Alejandro Arroyo.
Mailing Address: 511 Main St., 95694.
Res.: 303 Main St., 95694. Tel: 530-795-2230; Fax: 530-795-5470.
Church: 301 Main St., 95694.
Catechesis/Religious Program—Dawn Barrera, D.R.E. Students 125.
Mission—St. Martin 25633 Grafton Rd., Esparto, Yolo Co. 95627. Tel: 530-787-3750.

WOODLAND, YOLO CO., HOLY ROSARY (1870), [CEM] Revs. John E. Boll; Colm O'Kelly; Juan Perez; Deacons Edward Kull; Gonzalo Chavez; Antonio Fernandez.
Mailing Address: 503 California St., 95695. Tel: 530-662-2805.
(Corner of Walnut & Court Sts.) , Church: 301 Walnut St., 95695. Fax: 530-662-0796.
School—505 California St., 95695. Tel: 530-662-3494; Fax: 530-668-2442. Suzanne Hughes, Prin. Lay Teachers 15; Students 243.
Catechesis/Religious Program—Tel: 530-662-5394; Fax: 530-662-1310. Nancy Johnson, Coord. (English); Patricia Arriaga, Coord. (Spanish). Tel: 530-662-2894.
Mission—Our Lady of Guadalupe Sacramento St., Yolo, Yolo Co. 95697.

YREKA, SISKIYOU CO., ST. JOSEPH (1855), Rev. John M. Lawrence.
Res.: 314 Fourth St., 96097. Tel: 530-842-3842; Fax: 530-842-7076.
Catechetical Center—310 Fourth St., 96097. Tel: 530-842-4874.
Catechesis/Religious Program—Tel: 530-842-4874. Students 45.
Mission—Immaculate Conception Hawkinsville, Siskiyou Co.

YUBA CITY, SUTTER CO., ST. ISIDORE (1952), Rev. Manuel B. Soria.
Res.: 222 Clark Ave., 95991. Tel: 530-673-1573; Fax: 530-673-2512.
School—200 Clark Ave., 95991. Tel: 530-673-2217; Fax: 530-673-2217. Mr. Anthony Hinososa, Prin. Lay Teachers 10; Students 200.
Catechesis/Religious Program—Tel: 530-673-1573, Ext. 221. Students 770.

Chaplains of Public Institutions

SACRAMENTO. *California Youth Authority*, Northern Reception Center-Clinic, 3001 Ramona Ave., 95826. Tel 916-733-2350. Rev. Humberto Gomez.
Mule Creek State Prison.
P.O. Box 409099, Ione, 95640. Tel: 209-274-4911. Rev. Diogo Bapcista.
Sacramento International Airport. Rev. Anthony Traynor. Tel: 916-925-5313.
Sacramento Juvenile Hall, 9601 Kiefer Blvd., 95827. Tel: 916-875-5083. Matt Sanders, Youth Chap. & Contact Person. Tel: 916-489-3394.
Sutter General Hospital, 2801 L St., 95816. Rev. James P. Sheets.
Sutter Memorial Hospital, 52nd & F Sts., 95819. Tel: 916-454-3333. Rev. James P. Sheets.
University of California, Davis Medical Center, 2315 Stockton Blvd., 95817. Tel: 916-453-2011. Rev. William Feeser.

ELK GROVE. *Rio Consumnes Correctional Center*, 12500 Bruceville Rd, 95758. Tel: 916-384-2001. (Vacant)

FOLSOM. *California State Prison*, Tel: 916-985-8610, Ext. 6025.
P.O. Box 29, Represa, 95671. Deacon Dennis Merino.
Folsom State Prison, Tel: 916-985-2561, Ext. 4206.
P.O. Box 71, Represa, 95671. Tel: 916-985-2561. Rev. Thomas Maguire.

PRESTON. *School of Industry*, California Youth Authority. Tel: 209-274-8250. Deacon Adolfo Rivera.

SUSANVILLE. *California Correctional Center*, P.O. Box 790, 96130. Tel: 530-257-2181, Ext. 1180. Rev. Anthony B. Warnakula, C.H.S.P.
High Desert State Prison, P.O. Box 750, 96130. Tel: 916-251-5100, Ext. 6722. Deacon William Goeke.
Sierra Army Depot. Attended by Army & Navy Chaplains and Sacred Heart Parish.

VACAVILLE. *California Medical Facility*, P.O. Box 2000, 95688. Tel: 707-448-6841, Ext. 2976. Rev. Innocent Emechete (Nigeria), Chap.
California State Prison, Solano, P.O. Box 4000, 95696. Tel: 707-451-0182, Ext. 5474. Rev. R. Francis Stevenson. (Vacant)

Special Assignment:
Revs.—
Silveira Eduino, Chap. to Sheriff Deputies, St. Elizabeth Church, 1817 12th St., 95814. Tel: 916-442-2333
Traynor, Anthony, Chap. to Firefighters & Sacramento Metro Airport, Our Lady of Lourdes Church, 1951 North Ave., 95838. Tel: 916-925-5313

On Duty Outside the Diocese:
Revs.—
Figueroa, Oscar, North American College, Vatican City
Leslie, Patrick J., S.A.C. (SR), Santa Rosa Diocese
McGrath, Patrick, Limerick, Ireland
Rojas, Loretto, North American College, Vatican City

Military Chaplains:
Rev.—
Higgins, Richard B., U.S. Air Force

Absent on Leave:
Revs.—
Brusasco, Martin
Conway, Malachy
Lewis Edward
McCarthy, D. Joseph
Nguyen, Charles
Valenzuela, Louis

Retired and in Senior Ministry:
Rev. Msgrs.—
Coffey, Andrew V., 200 West 14th St., Davis, 95616.
Mennis, James F., 1601 Ocean Dr. S. #203, Jacksonville, FL 32250.
Mistretta, Vito F., 7760 Woodchuck Way, Citrus Heights, 95610.
Nolan, Patrick M., P.O. Box 215231 95821.
O'Neill, Patrick J., 350 Locust Dr., Apt. #L-104, Vallejo, 94591.
Peters, Roy V., 469 Ena Rd. #3010, Honolulu, HI 96815.
Schons, Gerard, c/o St. Rose Parish 5961 Franklin Blvd., 95817.
Wallace, Murrough C., P.O. Box 612043, South Lake Tahoe, 96152.
Revs.—
Albrecht, Walter H., 722 State St., Aberdeen, WA 98520.
Batch, Thomas A., 223 Hooper Rd., Yuba City, 95993.
Brennan, Ronan P., 122 Pacific, Auburn, 95603.
Burke, Walter Dev, Courhill Rd., Kincon Ballina, Mayo Ireland.
Burns, Bernard J., Swellan, Co. Cavan Ireland.
Carrigan, Thomas C., Clarabricken House, Kilkenny, Clifden Co. Ireland.
Casey, Daniel, P.O. Box 5006 Fair Oaks, CA
Cormack, Michael J., 7413 Timberrose, Roseville, 95747.
Delahunty, Thomas P., 3247 Sandhurst Ct., Cameron Park, 95682.
Dermody, Michael, Rocklin, 95765.
Dermody, Thomas, P.O. Box 1151, Brawley, 92227.
Duggan, Nicholas, C/o St. Paul Parish, P.O. Box 292280, 95829.
Dwyer, Dermot, 4801 "T" St., 95819.
Grace, John J., 3035 Berkeley Ave., South Lake Tahoe, 96150.
Gurnell, Anthony, P.O. Box 437, Cayucos, 93430.
Hall, Rodney, P.O. Box 144, Gerlach, NV 89412.
Hall, Sidney, Holy Cross Parish, 1321 Anna St., West Sacramento, 95605.
Hold, William, 873 Colombine Way, Central Pointe, OR 97502.
Lanigan, Patrick J., 1182 Hartford Pl., Fairfield, 94533.
Lenehan, Vincent, 2252 Westfield Ave., Reno, NV 89509-1822.
Lynch, Noel T., Garnavilla, Tipperary, Ireland.
Maio, Anthony V., 110 Village Ct., 95687.
McKnight, James, 5 Loretto Park, Dublin Rd., Down BT3585A Ireland.
O'Hara, Edward, Kilsonna, Longford, Granard Ireland.
O'Leary, Sean, Bunowen Rd., Louisburgh, Co. Mayo Ireland.
O'Rafferty, Patrick, 39100 Orchard Ave., Cherry Valley, 92223-3797.
Phelan, Nicholas, Vicar for Retired Priests, 439 Mill St. Apt. A, Grass Valley, 95945.
Ramos, Cipriano, P.O. Box 684, Roseville, 95678.
Ryan, Lawrence A., St. Bartholomew Parish Community, 600 Columbia Dr., San Mateo, 94402.
Storan, William, P.O. Box 1675, Paradise, 95967.
Sullivan, John P., 3111 Tierra de Dios Dr., El Dorado Hills, 95762.
Walsh, William K., 50 River Rd., #30, Rio Vista, 94571.
Wdowiak, Boleslaw, 2404 Ruby Ct., Rocklin, 95677.

Permanent Deacons:
Arroyo, Alejandro, St. Anthony, Winters
Astesana, Carlos, St. Patrick's, Grass Valley
Boone, Kenneth, St. Joseph, Lincoln
Boudier, William, St. Rose of Lima, Roseville
Burke, Keith, St. Philomene, Sacramento
Burkett, James, Our Divine Savior Parish, Chico
Cabrera, Domingo, St. Mary, Vacaville
Cavanagh, Paul, St. Vincent Ferrer, Vallejo
Chatigny, James, St. Patrick, Grass Valley
Chavez, Gonzalo, Holy Rosary, Woodland
Cheever, Charles, St. Philomene, Sacramento
Colenzo, Sam, St. James, Davis
Craig, Ray, Assumption, Truckee
Crowley, Michael, St. Anthony, Sacramento
David, Rudy, St. Catherine of Siena, Vallejo
DeHaven, Donald, St. Charles Borromeo, Sacramento
Del Gaudio, Lou, St. Mary, Sacramento
Donovan, Michael, All Hallows, Sacramento
Driggs, Richard, Our Lady of Assumption, Carmichael
Dufault, Duane, St. Anthony, Mount Shasta
Espinoza, Adrian, St. Robert, Sacramento
Evans, Michael, Sacred Heart, Anderson
Fernandez, Antonio, Holy Rosary, Woodland
Fernandez, Miguel, Our Lady of Lourdes, Colusa
Ferreira, Thomas, St. Paul, Sacramento
Flanagan, John, St. Dominic, Benicia
Fracolli, Gary, St. Lawrence, North Highlands
Garcia, Henry, St. Joseph, Sacramento
Gasman, David H., St. Joseph, Redding
Godinez, Rafael, (Unassigned)
Goecker, Clark, St. James, Davis
Gonzalez, Antonio, St. Paul, Knights Landing
Gualco, Jack, St. Ignatius of Loyola, Sacramento
Haproff, David, SS. Peter & Paul, Rocklin
Healy, James, St. Anthony's, Sacramento
Helgeson, Raymond, Holy Spirit, Sacramento
Hemenway, Raymond, Sacred Heart, Anderson
Henning, Patrick, St. Mel, Fair Oaks
Hernandez, Jesus, Holy Spirit, Fairfield
Ikelman, Robert, St. Peter, Dixon
Imrisek, Paul, St. Joseph, Elk Grove
King, John, St. Peter, Dixon
Koppes, Richard, St. Anthony, Sacramento
Kriske, George, All Hallows, Sacramento
Kull, Edward, Holy Rosary, Woodland
Layne, Everett H., St. Patrick, Weaverville
Lazarek, Edward, St. Dominic, Benicia
Lehman, David, St. Mel, Fair Oaks
Leon, Raul, Holy Cross, West Sacramento; Cathedral of the Blessed Sacrament
Link, Robert, Sacramento
Little, Walter, St. John Vianney, Rancho Cordova

Lobo, Pete, St. Catherine of Siena, Vallejo
Lopez, Frank, St. Joseph, Redding
Lucas, George, Immaculate Conception, Downieville
Lupercio, Felix, St. Peter, Dixon
Mangas, Michael, St. Joseph, Redding
Mangoba, Leo, St. Vincent Ferrer, Vallejo
Manriquez, Pedro, St. Anne, Sacramento
Marchese, Charles, Jr., Divine Savior, Orangevale
McGill, Thomas, St. Christopher, Galt
Merino, Dennis, St. John the Baptist, Folsom
Meucci, James, Our Lady of the Assumption, Carmichael
Miranda, Gilberto, All Hallows, Sacramento; St. Peter, Sacramento
Moore, Brian, St. Patrick, Grass Valley
Morgado, Edwin, St. Joseph, Auburn
Morrison, Charles, St. Paul, Sacramento
Moseley, Philip, St. John Vianney, Rancho Cordova; St. Paul, Sacramento
Moua, Tou, St. Peter, Sacramento
Munoz, Jesus, St. Joseph, Marysville
Nguyen, Anthony, Vietnamese Catholic Martyrs, Sacramento
Niekamp, Lawrence, Our Divine Savior, Orangevale
Ocon, Manuel, St. Charles, Sacramento
Padilla, Jesus, St. John the Baptist, Chico
Parra, Gilbert, Sacred Heart, Sacramento
Pauly, Gerald, Immaculate Conception, Sacramento
Peregrino, Bobby, St. Catherine of Siena, Vallejo
Perez, David, St. Joseph's, Marysville
Pierre, Allen, St. Francis, Sacramento; Cathedral of the Blessed Sacrament, Sacramento
Pogue, Edwin, Immaculate Conception, Sutter Creek
Quigley, Ned, Avenal State Prison
Ramirez, Antonio, St. Joseph, Elk Grove
Ramirez, Jose, Sacramento
Ramos, Ray, St. Peter, Sacramento
Revelo, Jose R., St. Therese, Isleton
Reyna, Pedro, Sacred Heart, Maxwell
Reynoso, Alejandro, St. Peter, Sacramento
Riehl, William, Sacred Heart, Sacramento
Rivera, Adolfo, St. Christopher, Galt
Rodriguez, Jesus, St. Joseph, Lincoln
Rodriguez, Martin, St. Philomene, Sacramento
Rojo, Ruben, St. Isidore, Yuba City
Rudger, Stanley, St. Patrick, Placerville
Ruiz, Roberto, St. Joseph, Lincoln
Schaeffer, William, Abbey of New Clairvaux, Vina
Schwartz, Steve, St. John the Baptist, Chico
Shields, Floyd, St. John the Evangelist, Carmichael
Short, Anthony, Sacred Heart, Anderson
Silott, Peter, St. Rose of Lima, Roseville
Smith, Colby, High Desert State Prison, Susanville
Sousa, William, Good Shepherd, Elk Grove
Stackhouse, Milton, St. Patrick, Grass Valley
Symkowick, Joseph, Newman Catholic Community, CSUS, Sacramento
Taloff, Paul, St. James, Davis
Tateishi, Michael, Our Lady of the Assumption, Carmichael
Thompson, William, St. Patrick, Jackson
Toro, German, Hispanic Ministry for the Diocese, Sacramento
Urick, Michael, St. Basil, Vallejo
Van Hook, Mark, St. Rose of Lima, Roseville
Vela, Juvencio, St. Dominic, Benecia; St. Vincent Ferrer, Vacaville
Venegas, Jesus, Sacred Heart, Gridley
Verba, Phil, Jr., Our Lady of Mt. Carmel, Fairfield
Vignery, Eldon, St. Isidore, Yuba City
Vital, Ernesto, St. Mary, Vacaville
Waldemar, Don, St. Rose of Lima, Roseville
Weeks, James, St. John the Evangelist, Carmichael
Young, Gnia, St. Peter, Sacramento
Young, Michael, St. Joseph, Auburn
Zachary, Neil, Holy Trinity, El Dorado Hills

INSTITUTIONS LOCATED IN THE DIOCESE

[A] SEMINARY, RELIGIOUS

LOOMIS. *Mount St. Joseph Novitiate and Seminary*, 6530 Wells Ave., P.O. Box 547, 95650. Tel: 916-652-6336; Fax: 916-652-0620. Email: fbrian@osjoseph.org. Web: www.osjoseph.org. Revs. Arnold Ortiz, O.S.J., Rector; Mariusz Beczek, O.S.J.; Bro. Mathew Chipp, O.S.J. Novitiate of Oblates of St. Joseph Priests 2; Brothers 1; Seminarians 3.

VINA. *Abbey of New Clairvaux, Trappist Seminary*, P.O. Box 80, 96092. Tel: 530-839-2161; Fax: 530-839-2332. Email: txd@maxinet.com. Web: www.maxinet.com/trappist/. Rt. Rev. Thomas X. Davis, O.C.S.O., J.C.L., Abbot. Priests 8. In Res. Rt. Rev. Bernard Johnson, O.S.C.O. J.C.L., J.C.L., Abbot Emeritus; Revs. Anthony R. Bellesorte, O.C.S.O.; Lawrence A. Glaser, O.C.S.O.; Paul Jerome Konkler, O.C.S.O.; Harold K. Meyer, O.C.S.O.; Paul Mark Schwan, O.C.S.O.; Dominic Tran, O.Cist.

[B] COLLEGES AND UNIVERSITIES

De La Salle University, c/o 2110 Broadway, 95818-2541. Tel: 707-252-3726. Bro. Louis De Thomasis, F.S.C., Pres.

University of Sacramento, 915 L St., #C404, 95814. Tel: 916-443-4760; Fax: 916-443-4765. Email: info@universityofsacramento.org. Web: www.universityofsacramento.org. Rev. Robert Presutti, L.C., Gen. Coord.; Dr. Barry Sugarman, Vice Pres., Inst. Devel. Founded by the Legionaries of Christ.

[C] HIGH SCHOOLS, DIOCESAN

SACRAMENTO. *St. Francis High School* (Girls) , 6051 M St., 95819. Tel: 916-452-3461; Fax: 916-452-1591. Email: sfhsinfo@stfrancishs.org. Web: www.stfrancishs.org. Marion L. Bishop, Pres.; Kathleen Gaines, Prin. Lay Teachers 61; Girls 853.

PALO CEDRO. *Bishop Quinn High School*, 21893 Old 44 Dr., 96073. Tel: 530-547-2900; Fax: 530-547-5349. Email: ckoestner@diocese-sacramento.org. Web: www.stfrancis-bquinn.org. Mr. Carl Koestner, Prin. Lay Teachers 16; Students 186.

RED BLUFF. *Mercy Catholic High School*, 233 Riverside Way, 96080. Tel: 530-527-8313; Fax: 530-527-3058. Email: cramirez@mercy-high.org. Web: www.mercy-high.org. Cheryl Ramirez, Prin. Lay Teachers 13; Students 183.

VALLEJO. *St. Patrick-St. Vincent High School*, 1500 Benicia Rd., 94591. Tel: 707-644-4425; Fax: 707-644-3107. Email: spixley@diocese-sacramento.org. Web: www.ca.campusgrid.net. Sr. Sue Pixley, O.P., Prin. Sisters 1; Lay Teachers 47; Students 642.

[D] HIGH SCHOOLS, PRIVATE

SACRAMENTO. *Christian Brothers High School of Sacramento, Inc.*, 4315 Martin Luther King Jr. Blvd., 95820. Tel: 916-733-3600; Fax: 916-733-3624. Web: www.cbhs-sacramento.org. Mr. Mark L. Warren, Pres.; Schulze Rudolf, Prin. Brothers 5; Sisters 2; Lay Teachers 66; Students 1,044.

Jesuit High School Tel: 916-482-6060; Fax: 916-482-2310. Email: leidichk@jhssac.org. Web: www.jhssac.org. P.O. Box 254647, 95865-4647. Tel: 916-482-6060. 1200 Jacob Ln., Carmichael, 95608-6024. Tel: 916-482-6060; Fax: 916-482-2310. Revs. Gregory R. Bonfiglio, S.J., Pres.; James A. Doogan, S.J.; Francis G. Hernandez, S.J.; David F. Klein, S.J.; Kevin A. Leidich, S.J., Supr.; Richard L. McCurdy, S.J.; John P. McGarry, S.J., Prin.; John D. Nguyen, S.J.; Charles R. Olsen, S.J.; Lorenzo J. Palafox, S.J.; William K. Stolz, S.J.; George V. Wanser, S.J.; Edward S. Fassett, S.J. (SFR); Edward Callanan, S.J. (Boys) Jesuit Priests 15; Brothers 1; Lay Teachers 74; Boys 1,000.

Loretto High School (Women) , 2360 El Camino Ave., 95821. Tel: 916-482-7793; Fax: 916-482-3621. Email: LorettoHS@aol.com. Web: www.Loretto.net. Sisters Helen Timothy, I.B.V.M., Pres.; Barbara Nelson, I.B.V.M., Prin. Religious of the Institute of the Blessed Virgin Mary Sisters 2; Lay Teachers 58; Women 550.

[E] ELEMENTARY SCHOOLS

ELK GROVE. *St. Elizabeth Ann Seton Elementary*, 9539 Racquet Ct., 95758. Tel: 916-684-7903; Fax: 916-691-4064. Email: seascs@stelizabetheg.org. Web: www.stelizabetheg.org. Thomas Butler, Prin. Lay Teachers 9; Students 315; Total Staff 27.

[F] DAY NURSERY AND CHILD CARE HOMES

SACRAMENTO. *Grace Day Home*, 1909 7th St., 95814. Tel: 916-442-6557; Fax: 916-442-0924. Email: gracedayhome@aol.com. Katriona McLean-Lucas, Exec. Dir.; Gina Queral, Prog. Dir. Lay Staff 34; Children 1,488.

St. Patrick Children's Home, Inc., 5945 Franklin Blvd., 95824. Tel: 916-421-1620; Fax: 916-421-3849. Email: maloney@saintpatricks.net. Web: www.saintpatricks.net. Rev. Msgr. Edward J. Kavanagh, Exec. Dir.; Colleen Maloney, Financial Officer.

Two Residential Group Homes for Girls: Veda Cannon, Dir.

Lopresti, 5036 Lemon Hill Ave., 95828. Tel: 916-421-1620; Fax: 916-421-3729.

McMahon, 8529 Florin Rd., 95828. Tel: 916-421-1620; Fax: 916-421-3729. Total Residents 16; Total Assisted 32; Total Staff 41.

St. Patrick's Child Care Centers, 5945 Franklin Blvd., 95824. Tel: 916-422-0123; Fax: 916-421-3849. Erin Young, Dir. Children (ages 2-5) 68; Children in after school care program 34; Total Assisted 119.

St. Patrick's Infant Toddler Program, 5945 Franklin Blvd., 95824. Tel: 916-422-0123; Fax: 916-421-3849. Children (ages 6 weeks-2 years) 26; Total Assisted 36.

St. Patrick's Infant-Toddler Program, 8201 Florin Rd., 95828. Tel: 916-383-3254; Fax: 916-421-3849. Erin Young, Dir. Children (ages 6 weeks-2 years 9 months) 34; Total Assisted 70.

St. Patrick's Foster Care Program Tel: 916-386-1603; Fax: 916-386-0654. Stephen Isbell, Dir. Tel: 916-386-1603. Families providing care 49; Children 128; Total Staff 11.

[G] HOMES FOR SENIOR CITIZENS

SACRAMENTO. *Mercy-McMahon Terrace*, 3865 J St., 95816. Tel: 916-733-6510; Fax: 916-733-6515. Email: mfgexcalibur@earthlink.net. Web: www.mercymcmahonterrace.org. Mary Francis Giammona, Admin. Licenced Units 118; Total Assisted 85; Total Staff 58.

[H] GENERAL HOSPITALS

SACRAMENTO. *Mercy General Hospital* dba Mercy Healthcare Sacramento , 4001 J St., 95819. Tel: 916-453-4545; Fax: 916-453-4587. Web: www.mercygeneral.org. Denny Powell, Pres. Sponsored by Auburn Regional Community of the Sisters of Mercy Sisters of Mercy 7; Patients Assisted Annually 115,664; Beds 415; Total Staff 1,681.

CARMICHAEL. *Mercy San Juan Medical Center* dba Mercy Healthcare Sacramento , 6501 Coyle Ave., 95608. Tel: 916-537-5000; Fax: 916-537-5111. Web: www.mercysanjuan.org. Michael Uboldi, Pres. Sponsored by Auburn Regional Community of Sisters of Mercy Sisters of Mercy 6; Beds 267; Patients Assisted Annually 110,975; Total Staff 1,672.

FOLSOM. *Mercy Hospital of Folsom* dba Mercy Healthcare Sacramento , 1650 Creekside Dr., 95630. Tel: 916-983-7400; Fax: 916-983-7406. Web: www.mercyfolsom.org. Don Hudson, Pres. Sponsored by Auburn Regional Community of the Sisters of Mercy Sisters of Mercy 3; Beds 91; Total Staff 433; Patients Assisted Annually 42,854.

MT. SHASTA. *Mercy Medical Center Mt. Shasta* dba Catholic Healthcare West , 914 Pine St., 96067. Tel: 530-926-6111; Fax: 530-926-0517. Web: www.mercy.org. Chuck H. Gersdorf, Pres. Sponsored by Auburn Regional Community of the Sisters of Mercy Sisters 1; Bed Capacity 84; Patients Assisted Annually 39,158; Total Staff 352.

RED BLUFF. *St. Elizabeth Community Hospital* dba Catholic Healthcare West , 2550 Sr. Mary Columba Dr., 96080-4397. Tel: 530-529-8000; Fax: 530-529-8009. Web: www.mercy.org. Jon Halfhide, Pres. Sponsored by Auburn Regional Community of the Sisters of Mercy Sisters 1; Bed Capacity 82; Patients Assisted Annually 64,316; Total Staff 439.

REDDING. *Mercy Medical Center Redding*, 2175 Rosaline Ave., 96001. Tel: 530-225-6000; Fax: 530-225-6125. Web: www.mercy.org. Rick Barnett, Pres. Sponsored by Auburn Regional Community of the Sisters of Mercy; Catholic Healthcare West Sisters of Mercy 1; Beds 293; Total Staff 1,388; Patients Assisted Annually 119,752.

[I] MONASTERIES AND RESIDENCES OF PRIESTS AND BROTHERS

CARMICHAEL. *Jesuit High School Community of Sacramento* Tel: 916-482-6060; Fax: 916-972-8037. Email: leidichk@jhssac.org. Web: www.jhssac.org. P.O. Box 254647, 95865. Tel: 916-482-6060. 1200 Jacob Ln., 95608. Tel: 916-482-6060; Fax: 916-972-8037. Revs. Gregory R. Bonfiglio, S.J.; William F. Breault, S.J.; James A. Doogan, S.J.; Francis G. Hernandez, S.J.; David F. Klein, S.J.; Kevin Leidich, S.J., Supr.; Richard L. McCurdy, S.J.; John P. McGarry, S.J.; Phong Nguyen, S.J.; Charles R. Olsen, S.J.; Lorenzo J. Palafox, S.J.; William K. Stolz, S.J.; George V. Wanser, S.J.; Edward Callanan, S.J.; Edward S. Fassett, S.J. (SFR); Bro. Justin DeChance, S.J. (California Prov., Los Gatos) Priests 15; Brothers 1.

CITRUS HEIGHTS. *Christ the King Retreat*, 6520 Van Maren Ln., 95621. Tel: 916-723-5162; Fax: 916-723-6368. Email: christtheking@passionist.org. Web: www.passionist.org. Revs. Neil J. Parsons, C.P.; Thomas More Newbold, C.P.; James G. Strommer, C.P.; San Juan Alfonso, C.P.; Christopher Gibson; Ronald Corl, C.P.; Richard L. Parks, C.P.; Bro. Kurt Wernert, C.P. The Passionists (Chicago, IL), A community residence for the Passionist priests and brothers who conduct missions and retreats. Priests 7; Brothers 1.

VINA. *Abbey of New Clairvaux, Trappist*, P.O. Box 80, 96092. Tel: 530-839-2161; Fax: 530-839-2332. Email: txdavis@maxinet.com. Web: www.maxinet.com/trappist/. Rt. Revs. Thomas X. Davis, O.C.S.O., J.C.L., Abbot; Bernard Johnson, O.S.C.O. J.C.L., J.C.L., Abbott Emeritus; Revs. Harold K. Meyer, O.C.S.O., Prior; Lawrence A. Glaser, O.C.S.O.; Paul Jerome Konkler, O.C.S.O.; Anthony R. Bellesorte, O.C.S.O.; Paul Mark Schwan, O.C.S.O.; Dominic Tran, O.Cist. Cistercian Abbey, Cistercians of the Strict Observance Priests 8; Professed Brothers 12.

[J] CONVENTS AND RESIDENCES FOR SISTERS

SACRAMENTO. *Canossian Daughters of Charity*, Our Lady of Lourdes Convent, 1949 North Ave., 95838. Tel: 916-925-4001; Fax: 916-925-8897. Email: fdcc_sac@yahoo.com. Sisters 4.

St. Charles Borromeo Convent, 7580 Center Pkwy., 95823. Tel: 916-421-7174; Fax: 916-421-3954. Email: sactorum@netzero.net.

Religious of the Virgin Mary, 7580 Center Pkwy., 95823. Tel: 916-421-7174. Sisters 4.

Sister Servants of the Blessed Sacrament, St. Peter's Convent, 5929 61st St., 95824. Tel: 916-457-0182; Fax: 916-453-8950. Email: sisbs@pacbell.net. Sisters 4.

Sisters Catechists of Jesus Crucified, Ave Maria House, 1123 W St., 95818. Tel: 916-443-7626; Fax: 916-442-1748. Email: hermanascjc@aol.com. Sisters 5.

Sisters of Social Service Tel: 916-489-3714; Fax: 916-485-0363. 5349 Sedona Ct., Carmichael, 95608. Tel: 916-489-3714; Fax: 916-485-0363.

Sisters of the Holy Rosary of Fatima, 1708 U St., 95818. Tel: 916-442-8646. Email: vlemus@diocese-sacramento.org. Sisters 4.

Sisters of the Sacred Hearts of Jesus & Mary, St. Paul's Convent, P.O. Box 292280, 95829. Tel: 916-381-5200; Fax: 916-381-0332. Sisters 2.

AUBURN. *Institute of the Sisters of Mercy of the Americas* Tel: 530-887-2000; Fax: 530-887-0789. Email: auburn@mercysisters.org. Web: www.mercysisters.org. Auburn Regional Community.

Motherhouse:, 535 Sacramento St., 95603-5699. Tel: 530-887-2000; Fax: 530-887-0789. Sr. Sheila Browne, R.S.M., Pres. Sisters in Community 20; Sisters in Diocese 78.

Russell House, 2223 L St., 95816-4926. Tel: 916-446-9251. Sisters 4.

McAuley Convent, 3846 H St., 95816-4613. Tel: 916-455-2843. Sisters 4.

Sisters of Mercy, 5625 Frontier Way, Carmichael, 95608. Tel: 916-489-0844. Sisters 4.

Our Lady of Fatima Convent, 2240 Hawthorne St., 95815-2910. Tel: 916-924-8541. Sisters 4.

Holy Spirit Convent, 3920 W. Land Park Dr., 95822-1123. Tel: 916-448-3578. Sisters 6.

Mercy Convent, 750 41st St., 95819-2738. Tel: 916-457-8274. Sisters 7.

Mercy San Juan, 6620 Oakbrook Dr., Fair Oaks, 95628. Tel: 916-962-7144. Sisters 6.

Holy Cross Convent, 800 Todhunter Ave., West Sacramento, 95605-2299. Tel: 916-371-1931. Sisters 4.

Sisters of Mercy, 212 Bittercreek Dr., Folsom, 95630-2353. Tel: 916-983-9268. Sisters 3.

Coolock Community, 848 39th St., 95816. Tel: 916-454-1723. Sisters 2.

Trocaire Cottage, 319 Elk Dr., Redding, 96003-3431. Tel: 530-244-1058. Sisters 2.

Kinsale Convent, 5256 H St., 95819-3539. Tel: 916-455-2715. Sisters 4.

CARMICHAEL. *Religious of the Institute of the Blessed Virgin Mary*, Assumption Convent, 5055 Cottage Way, 95608. Tel: 916-488-8188; Fax: 916-488-6983. Email: olanuns@msn.com. Sisters 5.

Other Locations:

3606 Chadsworth Way, 95821. Tel: 916-485-6384; Fax: 916-485-6385. Sisters 4.

9190 Sebastiani Way, 95829. Tel: 916-681-2016; Fax: 916-739-1178.

3632 Ardmore Rd., 95821. Tel: 916-489-8931. Sisters 2.

FAIR OAKS. *Sisters of Mercy of Cashel*, St. Mel's Convent, P.O. Box 1180, 95628. Tel: 916-967-9504; Fax: 916-967-9504. Sisters 2.

FAIRFIELD. *Sisters of the Holy Faith*, Holy Spirit Convent, 1050 N. Texas St., 94533. Tel: 707-425-3572. Email: hssf@aol.com. Web: www.hsschool.org. Sisters 4.

GEORGETOWN. *Discalced Carmelite Nuns*, P.O. Box 1720, 95634. Tel: 530-333-1617; Fax: 530-333-1617. Web: www.carmelitemonastery.com. Carmel of the Holy Family and Saint Therese Sisters 16.

WEST SACRAMENTO. *Daughters of the Holy Spirit*, Our Lady of Grace Convent, 1990 Linden Rd., 95691. Tel: 916-371-9416; Fax: 916-371-1319. Email: olglab@aol.com.

[K] RETREAT HOUSES

SACRAMENTO. *Pendola Center*, 2110 Broadway, 95818-2541. Tel: 916-736-3652; Fax: 916-733-0195. Email: campendola@aol.com. Web: www.pendola.org. Center located in Sierra-Nevada foothills near Camptonville. Summer camp for boys and girls 6-16. Available for teenage and young adult retreats, school midweek retreats, field trips. Contact: Stephen Tholcke, Dir. of Pendola Center.

APPLEGATE. *Our Lady of the Oaks Villa*, P.O. Box 128, 95703. Tel: 530-878-2776; Fax: 530-878-1615. Email: appvillia@pacbell.net. Rev. Gerald H. Robinson, S.J., Dir. Tel: 916-482-9666; Bro. James Sanders, S.J., Asst. Dir. Tel: 916-482-6050; Ronald W. Weingart, Resident Mgr. Tel: 530-878-2776. Available for retreats and conferences from September 1 to May 15

AUBURN. *Mercy Center Auburn*, 535 Sacramento St., 95603-5699. Tel: 530-887-2019; Fax: 530-887-1154. Email: mercycenter@mercyauburn.com. Web: www.mercyauburn.org.

CITRUS HEIGHTS. *Christ the King Passionist Retreat Center*, 6520 Van Maren Ln., 95621. Tel: 916-725-4720; Fax: 916-725-4812. Email: christtheking@passionist.org. Web: www.passionist.org. Rev. Ronald Corl, C.P., Dir.; Sr. Marcella Fabing, C.S.J., Assoc. Dir.; Bro. Kurt Werner, C.P.; Mr. Thomas Borkowski, Admin.

Christ the King Institute for Counseling & Spiritual Direction, 6520 Van Maren Ln., 95621. Tel: 916-783-9005; Fax: 916-723-6368. Rev. Jim Strommer, C.P., Dir.; Elizabeth Evans, M.A., Assoc.

Spiritual Life Institute at Christ the King Retreat Center, 6520 Van Maren Ln., 95621. Tel: 916-725-4720; Fax: 916-725-4812. Sr. Marcella Fabing, C.S.J., Coord. Programs and courses in contemporary spirituality.

[L] CAMPUS MINISTRIES AND NEWMAN CENTERS

CHICO. *California State University (Chico), Newman Catholic Community* 346 Cherry St., 95928-5113. Tel: 530-342-5180; Fax: 530-342-3016. Email: mikenewsds@aol.com. Web: www.now2000.com/newman. Rev. Michael J. Newman, S.D.S., Dir.; Ms. Marge Flynn, Sec.

California State University (Sacramento), Newman Catholic Community Tel: 916-454-4188; Fax: 916-454-4180.

5900 Newman Ct., 95819. Tel: 916-454-4188; Fax: 916-454-4180. Rev. George Wanser, S.J., Dir.; Deacon Joseph Symkowick; Ms. Mary Ann Williams, Business Mgr.

University of California (Davis), Newman Catholic Community, 514 C St., Davis, 95616. Tel: 530-753-7393; Fax: 530-753-2794. Deacon Clark Goecker, Dir., Pro Tem; Ms. Gayla Ponce, Sec.

[M] CATHOLIC SOCIAL WELFARE ACTIVITIES

SACRAMENTO. *Catholic Charities of Sacramento, Inc.*, 2110 Broadway, 95818. Tel: 916-733-0253; Fax: 916-733-0224. Email: mkiernan@diocese-sacramento.org. Michael F. Kiernan, Chm. Bd. of Directors & Exec. Dir.

Member Agencies of Catholic Charities of Sacramento, Inc.:

Catholic Social Service of Sacramento, 5890 Newman Ct., 95819-2608. Tel: 916-452-7481; Fax: 916-736-0282. Rev. Michael F. Kiernan, Chm. Bd. of Dir.; Kurt Chismark, Exec. Dir. Total Staff 20; Total Assisted 23,500.

Northern Valley Catholic Social Service, 1020 Market St., Redding, 96001. Tel: 530-241-0552; Fax: 530-247-3354. David Gasman, Chm. Bd. of Directors; Jan Maurer Watkins, Exec. Dir. Total Staff 180; Total Served 9,500.

Catholic Social Service of Solano County, 745 Georgia St., Vallejo, 94590. Tel: 707-644-8909; Fax: 707-644-6314. Robert C. Fracchia Chm. Bd. of Directors; Kurt Chismark, Exec. Dir Total Staff 14; Total Assisted 8,000.

Subsidiaries of Catholic Charities of Sacramento:

Sacramento Food Bank Services, 3333 Third Ave., 95817. Tel: 916-456-1980; Fax: 916-451-5920. Charles Sylva, Chm. Bd. of Directors; Peter Bergquis, Exec. Dir. Total Staff 25; Total Served 30,000.

Administrative Project of Catholic Charities of Sacramento:

Mother Teresa Maternity Home, 3109 Sacramento St., Placerville, 95667. Tel: 530-662-0373. Lucille Mosbacher, Chm. Bd. of Directors. Total Staff 3; Total Served 23.

Cathedral Neighborhood Senior Center, 711 J St., 95814. Tel: 916-442-9014. Elizabeth White, Prog. Dir. Total Staff 3; Total Assisted 25,075.

Centro Guadalupe, 730 S St., 95814. Tel: 916-443-5367; Fax: 916-443-5845. Elizabeth White, Prog. Dir. Total Staff 2; Total Assisted 18,152.

Mercy Education Resource Center, 6007 Folsom Blvd. #200, 95819. Tel: 916-737-6026; Fax: 916-737-6507. Email: terry@mercyeducation.com. Web: www.mercyeducation.com. Sponsored by the Sisters of Mercy Auburn Regional Community, Provides marriage counseling and individual counseling, and psycho-educational assessment. Total Staff 17; Total Assisted 2,700.

Society of St. Vincent de Paul, Sacramento District Council Main Office: , P.O. Box 661715, 95866-1715. Tel: 916-719-4168; Fax: 916-972-1255. Email: svdp2620@pacbell.net. Web: www.stvincentdepaul-sacramento.net. Bill Hallerman, Pres.

Society St. Vincent de Paul, Sacramento District Council. Tel: 916-719-4168; Fax: 916-972-1255.

MARYSVILLE. *Grand Council, Catholic Ladies Relief Society of the Diocese of Sacramento*, 2074 Virgilia Ln., 95901. Tel: 530-742-9377. Doris Bitterman, Grand Pres. Tel: 530-742-9377; Rev. Leon Juchniewicz, Chap.

223 8th S.W. St., 95901.

ROSEVILLE, PLACER CO.. *Society of St. Vincent DePaul*, 139 Riverside Ave., 95678. Tel: 916-781-3303 (Dining Room/Office. Hours: 10am-3pm M-F); 916-781-3368 (Thrift Store. Hours: 10am-4pm, M-Sat.); 916-781-3335 (Food Locker. Hours: 9am-11:30am, Tues-Sat.); Fax: 916-781-8105 (Office Fax). Mr. Ray Daniels, Pres. Emergency Services, Motel Vouchers, Clothing Vouchers, Food Assistance, Dining Room, Thrift Store, 6 Transitional Housing Units, Mail Service, SSI Payee, etc. Total Assisted 24,130.

VALLEJO. *Society of St. Vincent de Paul*, 1225 Tuolumne St., 94590. Tel: 707-644-5251; Fax: 707-644-1423. Rene Perryman, Pres.

[N] YOUTH AND YOUNG ADULT MINISTRIES

SACRAMENTO. *Catholic Committee on Scouting*, 2110 Broadway, 95818. Tel: 916-733-0258; Fax: 916-733-0224. Email: mrichard@diocese-sacramento.org. Web: www.oharanetworks.com/dccs.htm. Rev. Mark R. Richards, J.C.L., Diocesan Chap.

Department of Catholic Faith Formation, 2110 Broadway, 95818. Tel: 916-733-0123; Fax: 916-733-0195. Email: jrieschi@diocese-sacramento.org. Web: www.diocese-sacramento.org. John Rieschick, Dir.; Linda Shumate, Consultant for Catechetics; Deacon Antonio Ramirez, Consultant, Hispanic Catechesis; Jeannette Holmes, Master Catechist, Pendola Center; Mrs. Margaret Walrath, Coord. Deaf Ministry; Mr. Feliciano Tapia, Hispanic Institute; Mrs. Michelle Hendricks, Coord. Catechesis with Special Needs Persons; Mr. John Donahoe, Coord. Camp Recreation; Deacon Ray Helgeson, Coord. Adult Faith Formation; Kathy Conner, Respect Life Coord.; Mrs. Gloria Soto, Family Life Coord.; Adolfo Mercado, Youth & Young Adult Coord.

[O] CAMPS

SACRAMENTO. *Pendola Center*, Office, 2110 Broadway, 95818-2541. Tel: 916-733-0127; 916-736-3652; Fax: 916-733-0195. Email: campendola@aol.com. Web: www.pendola.org. Mr. Stephen F. Tholcke, Dir. Located at Camptonville, Yuba County.; Diocesan youth & young adult retreat center (September-April). Summer camp for boys and girls 6-16 (June, July, August). Outdoor school (September, October, November), available for parish youth and young adult retreats, school field trips and retreats.

[P] MISCELLANEOUS

SACRAMENTO. *California Catholic Conference*, 1119 K St., 95814. Tel: 916-443-4851; Fax: 916-443-5629. Web: www.cacatholic.org. Most Revs. Sylvester D. Ryan, Pres.; William K. Wiegand, Vice Pres.; Stephen E. Blaire, D.D. (STO), Sec. & Treas.; Mr. Edward "Ned" E. Dolejsi, Exec. Dir.; Mr. Robert Teegarden, Assoc. Dir. for Education; Carol Hogan, Dir. Pastoral Projects & Communication; Mr. Al Santana Hernandez, Assoc. Dir. for Hispanic Affairs; Mrs. Linda Wanner, Assoc. For Governmental Relations; Mr. Rick Mockler, Exec. Dir., Catholic Charities of CA.

Catholic Charities of California, Inc., 1119 K St., 2nd Flr., 95814. Tel: 916-313-4005; Fax: 916-443-4731. Email: rmockler@cacatholic.org. Web: www.cccalifornia.org. Richard Mockler, Exec. Dir.; Martina O'Sullivan, Pres.; Maureen Shaw, Vice Pres.; Brian Cahill, Sec. & Treas.

Catholic Professional & Business Breakfast Club, P.O. Box 254848, 95865-4848. Tel: 916-481-5222; Fax: 916-481-5222. Web: www.catholicbreakfastclub.com.

The Manogue Perpetual Endowment Foundation,

Inc., P.O. Box 188066, 95818. Tel: 916-733-0277; Fax: 916-733-0295. Thomas L. McNamara, Treas.

Mercy Senior Housing dba Mercy McMahon Terrace, 3865 J St., 95819. Tel: 916-733-6510; Fax: 916-733-6515.

The Parochial Fund, P.O. Box 189666, 95818. Tel: 916-733-0277; Fax: 916-733-0295. Thomas McNamara, Treas.

The Preserving Our Past, Building Our Future Foundation of Northern California, Inc., P.O. Box 188617, 95818. Tel: 916-733-0277; Fax: 916-733-0295. Thomas McNamara, Treas.

**Stanford Settlement*, 450 W. El Camino, 95833-2299. Tel: 916-927-1303; Fax: 916-922-1694. Email: srjfelion@aol.com. Web: www.stanfordsettlement.org. Sr. Jeanne Felion, S.S.S., Dir. Assisted annually 10,000.

RANCHO CORDOVA. *Catholic Healthcare West - Sacramento Office*, 3400 Data Dr., 95670. Tel: 916-851-2000; Fax: 916-851-2727. Web: www.chwhealth.org/sacramento.

Corporate Headquarters, Catholic Healthcare West, San Francisco. Tel: 415-438-5500; Fax: 415-438-5726.

Mercy Foundation, 3400 Data Dr., 95670. Tel: 916-851-2700; Fax: 916-851-2724. Email: mthoman@chw.edu. Web: www.chwhealth.org/sacramento. Mr. H. John Shaw III, Pres.

Mercy Healthcare Sacramento, 3400 Data Dr., 95670. Tel: 916-851-2000; Fax: 916-851-2727. Web: www.chwhealth.org/sacramento. William Hunt, CEO. This organization holds licenses for and provides management and support functions for the following hospitals: Mercy General Hospital in Sacramento; Mercy San Juan Medical Center in Carmichael; Mercy Hospital of Folsom. In addition, it is the corporate member and sponsor of Mercy Senior Housing dba Mercy McMahon Terrace.

Corporate Office, 1700 Montgomery St., Ste. 300, San Francisco, 94111. Tel: 415-397-9000; Fax: 415-438-5724. Lloyd Dean, Pres. & CEO.

RELIGIOUS INSTITUTES OF MEN REPRESENTED IN THE DIOCESE

For further details refer to the corresponding bracketed number in the Religious Institutes of Men or Women section.

[]—*Augustinian Assumptionist Fathers*—A.A.
[0330]—*Brothers of the Christian Schools* (Napa, CA)—F.S.C.
[0270]—*Carmelite Fathers & Brothers* (Barrington, IL)—O.Carm.
[0350]—*Cistercians Order of the Strict Observance-Trappists* (Rome, Italy)—O.C.S.O.
[0370]—*Columban Fathers*—S.S.C.
[]—*Congregation of Mother Coredemptrix*—C.M.C.
[1000]—*Congregation of the Passion* (Chicago, IL)—C.P.
[]—*Crusade of the Holy Spirit*
[0520]—*Franciscan Friars* (Prov. of St. Barbara)—O.F.M.
[]—*Franciscan Order of the Atonement*—S.A.
[]—*Hermits of the Most Blessed Virgin Mary of Mt. Carmel*—H.O.C.
[0690]—*Jesuit Fathers and Brothers* (California Prov., Los Gatos, CA)—S.J.
[0730]—*Legionaries of Christ*—L.C.
[0930]—*Oblates of St. Joseph* (Santa Cruz, CA)—O.S.J.
[]—*Oratorians* (Colombia)
[0950]—*Oratorians*—C.O.
[0430]—*Order of Preachers-Dominicans*—O.P.
[1065]—*Priestly Fraternity of St. Peter*—F.S.S.P.
[1200]—*Society of the Divine Savior* (Milwaukee, WI)—S.D.S.
[]—*Society of the Divine Word*—S.V.D.

RELIGIOUS INSTITUTES OF WOMEN REPRESENTED IN THE DIOCESE

[1940]—*Congregation of the Sisters of the Holy Faith*—C.H.F.
[0730]—*Daughters of Charity of Canossa* (Rome, Italy)—Fd.CC.
[]—*Daughters of Divine Love*
[0820]—*Daughters of the Holy Spirit* (Putnam, CT)—D.H.S.
[0420]—*Discalced Carmelite Nuns*—O.C.D.
[1070-03]—*Dominican Sisters* (Sinsinawa, WI)—O.P.
[1070-04]—*Dominican Sisters* (San Rafael, CA)—O.P.
[]—*Dominican Sisters of Charity of the Presentation of the Blessed Virgin Mary*—O.P.
[]—*Handmaids of the Holy Child Jesus*—H.H.C.J.
[2370]—*Institute of the Blessed Virgin Mary (Loretto Sisters)*—I.B.V.M.
[2575]—*Institute of the Sisters of Mercy of the Americas*—R.S.M.
[]—*Religious of the Virgin Mary* (Quezon City, Philippines)—R.V.M.
[3499]—*Sister Servants of the Blessed Sacrament*—S.S.B.S.
[]—*Sisters Catechists of Jesus Crucified* (Mexico)—S.J.C.
[]—*Sisters of Mercy* (Omaha)—R.S.M.
[]—*Sisters of Mercy of Cashel* (U.S. Province)—R.S.M.
[]—*Sisters of Social Service*—S.S.S.
[4080]—*Sisters of Social Service of Los Angeles, Inc.*—S.S.S.
[1630]—*Sisters of St. Francis of Penance and Christian Charity* (Redwood City, CA)—O.S.F.
[]—*Sisters of St. Joseph of Carondelet*—C.S.J.
[1960]—*Sisters of the Holy Family* (San Jose, CA)—S.H.F.
[]—*Sisters of the Holy Rosary of Fatima* (Salvatierra, Mexico)—H.R.F.
[3680]—*Sisters of the Sacred Hearts of Jesus and Mary* (Essex)—S.H.J.M.
[4110]—*Ursuline Nuns of the Congregation of Paris*—O.S.U.
[]—*Visitation Sisters of Alleppey*—S.V.C.

DIOCESAN CEMETERIES

SACRAMENTO. *St. Joseph Catholic Cemetery*, 2615 21st St., 95818. Tel: 916-452-4831.

St. Mary's Catholic Cemetery & Mausoleum, 6700 21st Ave., 95820. Tel: 916-452-4831.

CITRUS HEIGHTS. *Calvary Catholic Cemetery & Mausoleum*, 7101 Verner Ave., 95841. Tel: 916-726-1232.

COLUSA. *Holy Cross Catholic Cemetery*, 745 Ware Ave., 95932. Tel: 530-458-3693.

FAIRFIELD. *St. Alphonsus Catholic Cemetery*, 1707 Union Ave., 94533. Tel: 707-425-3111.

GRASS VALLEY. *St. Patrick Catholic Cemetery*, Rough & Ready Hwy., 95945. Tel: 530-277-6451.

RANCHO MURIETA. *St. Vincent DePaul Catholic Cemetery*, Jackson Hwy., 95683. Tel: 916-452-4831.

VALLEJO. *All Souls Catholic Cemetery & Mausoleum*, 550 Glen Cove Rd., 94591. Tel: 707-644-5209.

St. Vincent, 550 Glen Cove Rd., 94591. Tel: 707-644-5209.

WOODLAND. *St. Joseph Catholic Cemetery & Mausoleum*, 503 California St., 95695. Tel: 530-662-8645.

NECROLOGY

† Broderick, William—Died 2003
† Connelly, Robert J.—Died 2003
† O'Dowd, Brendan, (Retired)—Died Oct. 10, 2003

Diocese of Saginaw

(Dioecesis Saginavensis)

ESTABLISHED FEBRUARY 26, 1938.

Square Miles 6,955.

Comprises the following Counties in the State of Michigan: Arenac, Bay, Clare, Gladwin, Gratiot, Huron, Isabella, Midland, Saginaw, Sanilac and Tuscola.

For legal titles of parishes and diocesan institutions, consult the Chancery Office.

(VACANT SEE)

Chancery: 5800 Weiss St., Saginaw, MI 48603-2799. Tel: 989-799-7910; Fax: 989-797-6670.

Web: www.dioceseofsaginaw.org

STATISTICAL OVERVIEW

Personnel	
Bishop	1
Priests: Diocesan Active in Diocese	65
Priests: Diocesan Active Outside Diocese	1
Priests: Diocesan in Foreign Missions	1
Priests: Retired, Sick or Absent	35
Number of Diocesan Priests	102
Religious Priests in Diocese	11
Total Priests in Diocese	113
Extern Priests in Diocese	7
Ordinations:	
Diocesan Priests	1
Permanent Deacons in Diocese	15
Total Brothers	1
Total Sisters	124
Parishes	
Parishes	108
With Resident Pastor:	
Resident Diocesan Priests	61
Resident Religious Priests	14
Without Resident Pastor:	
Administered by Priests	10
Administered by Deacons	1
Administered by Religious Women	14
Administered by Lay People	4
Administered by Pastoral Teams, etc.	4
Professional Ministry Personnel:	
Brothers	1
Sisters	38
Lay Ministers	18
Welfare	
Catholic Hospitals	1
Total Assisted	258,427
Health Care Centers	1
Total Assisted	10,850
Homes for the Aged	1
Total Assisted	100
Residential Care of Children	4
Total Assisted	201
Day Care Centers	9
Total Assisted	341
Educational	
Students from Other Diocese	6
Total Seminarians	6
High Schools, Diocesan and Parish	3
Total Students	854
Elementary Schools, Diocesan and Parish	24
Total Students	3,524
Catechesis/Religious Education:	
High School Students	1,506
Elementary Students	8,990
Total Students under Catholic Instruction	14,880
Teachers in the Diocese:	
Priests	1
Sisters	7
Lay Teachers	208
Vital Statistics	
Receptions into the Church:	
Infant Baptism Totals	1,653
Adult Baptism Totals	213
Received into Full Communion	368
First Communions	1,831
Confirmations	2,107
Marriages:	
Catholic	422
Interfaith	264
Total Marriages	686
Deaths	1,714
Total Catholic Population	131,937
Total Population	724,142

Former Bishops—Most Revs. WILLIAM F. MURPHY, S.T.D., J.C.L., LL.D., ord. June 13, 1908; appt. first Bishop of Saginaw, March 17, 1938; consecrated May 17, 1938; died Feb. 7, 1950; STEPHEN S. WOZNICKI, D.D., second Bishop; ord. Dec. 22, 1917; appt. Titular Bishop of Pelte and Auxiliary Bishop of Detroit, Dec. 13, 1937; consecrated Jan. 25, 1938; transferred to Saginaw, March 28, 1950; Assistant at the Pontifical Throne, Dec. 22, 1967;; resigned and transferred to the Titular See of Tiava, Oct. 30, 1968; died Dec. 10, 1968; FRANCIS F. REH, S.T.L., J.C.D. (Retired), third Bishop; ord. Dec. 8, 1935; appt. Bishop of Charleston, June 4, 1962; consecrated June 29, 1962;; transferred to the Titular See of Macrinna in Maurentania; Rector Pontifical North American College in Rome, Sept. 5, 1964; transferred to Saginaw, Dec. 18, 1968; installed Feb. 26, 1969; retired April 29, 1980; died Nov. 14, 1994; KENNETH E. UNTENER, ordained June 1, 1963; ordained and installed as Bishop of Saginaw November 24, 1980; died March 27, 2004.

Delegate to Senior Priests—Rev. ROBERT S. GOHM, 5800 Weiss St., Saginaw, 48603. Tel: 989-799-7910.

Vicars General—Revs. JAMES F. GAVIT, J.C.D., 2872 N. Euclid Ave., Bay City, 48706-1342. Tel: 989-684-1523; THOMAS E. SUTTON, J.C.L., 84 W. Midland Rd., Auburn, 48611. Tel: 989-662-6861.

Episcopal Vicars—

Vicar for Hispanics—MARIA CEPEDA, Pastoral Minister, Coord., Our Lady of Guadalupe Chapel & Center, 1619 Broadway, Bay City, 48708-8538. Tel: 989-894-0661.

Vicar for Religious—Sr. JANET FULGENZI, O.P., Ph.D., 5800 Weiss St., Saginaw, 48603-2799. Tel: 989-799-7910.

Vicar of Administration—Rev. THOMAS E. SUTTON, J.C.L., c/o 5800 Weiss St., Saginaw, 48603-2799.

Vicar for Canonical Affairs—Rev. JAMES F. GAVIT, J.C.D., c/o 5800 Weiss St., Saginaw 48603-2799.

Vicars for Vicariates—Revs. ROBERT PARE, Vicariate 1; T. J. FLEMING, Vicariate 2; RICHARD BOKINSKIE, Vicariate 3; STEVE FILLION, Vicariate 4; JAMES R. CARLSON, Vicariate 5; RONALD WAGNER, Vicariate 6; DAVID PARSCH, Vicariate 7; JAMES HELLER, Vicariate 8; JOSEPH GRIFFIN, Vicariate 9; JEFFREY DONNER, Vicariate 10; RICHARD M FILARY, J.C.L., Vicariate 11; THOMAS KOWALCZYK, Vicariate 12.

Chancery—5800 Weiss St., Saginaw, 48603-2799. Tel: 989-799-7910; Fax: 989-797-6670.

Chancellor—Rev. THOMAS E. SUTTON, J.C.L.

Administrative Assistant to the Chancellor—CONNIE HUISKENS WOJDA.

Administrative Assistant to the Bishop—LEONA JONES.

Director of Finance—Mr. BRIAN BUCKINGHAM.

Administrative Assistant—KAREN SCHULTZ.

General Accountants—MARY JANE TACEY; NANCY SCHULTZ.

Accounting Assistant—JOSEPHINE MENDOZA.

Finance Council—ANNETTE MCTAGGART, Chm.

Catholic Services Appeal—ADRIENNE JESCHKE, Coord., 5800 Weiss St., Saginaw, 48603-2799. Tel: 989-799-7910.

Diocesan Building Commission—GREG BATOR, Chm., 5800 Weiss St., Saginaw, 48603-2799. Tel: 989-799-7910.

Tribunal—MAUREEN MCPARTLAND, O.P., Dir., 5800 Weiss St., Saginaw, 48603-2799. Tel: 989-799-7910.

Judicial Vicar—Rev. ROBERT DELAND, J.C.L.

Defenders of the Bond—Revs. JAMES F. GAVIT, J.C.D.; ROBERT J. DELAND, J.C.L.

Judges—Rev. THOMAS E. SUTTON, J.C.L.; Rev. Msgr. EUGENE A. FORBES, J.C.D., V.G., P.A. (Retired); Revs. ROBERT J. MEISSNER; ROBERT W. DAVEY, M.A.; RICHARD M. FILARY, J.C.L.; MAUREEN MCPARTLAND, O.P.

Promoter of Justice—Rev. JAMES F. GAVIT, J.C.D.

Notary—PATRICIA D. PRESTON.

Advocate—Rev. ROBERT W. DAVEY, M.A.

Diocesan Pastoral Advisory Council—Sr. JANET FULGENZI, O.P., Ph.D., Interim Coord., 5800 Weiss, Saginaw, 48603-2799. Tel: 989-799-7910.

Diocesan Presbyteral Council—Rev. ROBERT BYRNE, Chm., 302 S. Kinney Blvd., Mt. Pleasant, 48858-2773.

Diocesan Consultors—Revs. RICHARD BOKINSKIE; WILLIAM RUTKOWSKI; LOREN KALINOWSKI; JERRY KUKLA; FREDERICK J. KAWKA.

Clergy Personnel Board—Rev. WILLIAM TAYLOR, Chm., 1525 S. Washington, Saginaw, 48601-2895. Tel: 989-755-8020.

Diocesan Council of Catholic Women—RITA FAITH MAHER, Pres., 3028 McGill St., Marlette, 48453; Rev. DONALD J. EPPENBROCK, Moderator, 5366 Main St., Box 399, Lexington, 48450-0399. Tel: 810-359-8101.

Office of Communication—Mrs. CATHERINE HAVEN, Dir., 5800 Weiss St., Saginaw, 48603-2799. Tel: 989-797-6666.

Mission Office—Sr. CORRINE WEISS, S.J., Dir. for Missions, 5800 Weiss St., Saginaw, 48603-2799. Tel: 989-797-6633.

Office of Education-Formation—BARBARA GEARY, Supt. of Schools, 5800 Weiss St., Saginaw, 48603-2799. Tel: 989-797-6651; BARBARA MINCZENSKI, Dir. Rel. Educ. Formation; MARY JANE SPIRK, Catechetical

Ministry Dir.

Director of Family-Youth Ministry—PEGGY MCCOURTNEY.

Family Life Ministry— Refer to: Catholic Family Service, *5800 Weiss St., Saginaw, 48603-2799.* Tel: 989-797-6638.

Evangelization Ministry— Contact Office of Education

Ecumenism Ministry—Rev. GEORGE SEROUR (Retired), 8370 Unionville Rd., Sebewaing, 48759-9553. Tel: 989-883-2746.

Ministry to Charismatic Renewal—MARGE FOBEAR, Dir., Charismatic Renewal Center, 1110 State St., Bay City, 48706. Tel: 989-686-4640.

Ministry to Priests—Rev. RICHARD BOKINSKIE, 5800 Weiss St., Saginaw, 48603-2799. Tel: 989-799-7910 Saginaw Diocesan Center,.

Financial Council—ANNETTE MCTAGGART.

Diocesan Building Commission—GREG BATOR.

Office of Church Ministries—Sr. MARY ANN FLANAGAN, I.H.M., Dir. Church Ministries Office; Rev. THOMAS MOORE, O.S.F.S., Dir. Seminarians & Vocations; Sisters ROBERTA KOLASA, S.J., Dir., Center for Ministry; JOSEPHINE GAUGIER, O.P., English Language Lay Ministry Program; Revs. RICHARD BOKINSKIE, Ministry to Priests, Continuing Education for Priests; ROBERT GOHM, Ministry to Senior Priests.

Office of Christian Service—THOMAS CONKLIN, Dir.; DIANE BELKNAP, Sec. Outreach Workers: TERRI GRIERSON, Vic. 3, 4, 7, 10; SANDY BUZA, Vic. 1, 2, 8, 11; JENNIFER SANNAN, Vic. 5, 6, 9, 12, 5800 Weiss St., Saginaw, 48603-2799. Tel: 989-797-6672.

Office of Liturgy—MARY SELLARS MALLOY, Dir.; ELIZABETH GRZEMKOWSKI, Sec., 5800 Weiss St., Saginaw, 48603-2799. Tel: 989-797-6664.

Catholic Family Services—THOMAS CONKLIN, Exec. Dir., 5800 Weiss St., Saginaw, 48603-2799. Tel: 989-797-6636.

Saginaw Counseling Center—THOMAS CONKLIN, Dir., 710 N. Michigan Ave., Saginaw, 48602-4372. Tel: 989-753-8446.

Bad Axe Counseling Center—123 Scott St., Bad Axe, 48413-1329. Tel: 989-269-7931.

Bay City Counseling Center—915 Columbus Ave., Bay City, 48708. Tel: 989-892-2504.

Midland Counseling Center—220 W. Main St., Midland, 48640-5165. Tel: 989-631-4711.

Mt. Pleasant Counseling Center—118 S. Washington, Mt. Pleasant, 48858. Tel: 989-773-9328.

Sandusky Counseling Center—119 E. Sanilac, Sandusky, 48471-1147. Tel: 810-648-2304.

Hispanic Ministries Cultural Center—MARIA CEPEDA, Dir.; Mr. GILBERTO GUEVARA, Dir. of Social Awareness, Youth & Immigration, 5800 Weiss, Saginaw, 48603-2799. Tel: 989-797-6646; MIGUEL MORENO, Dir. Hispanic Lay Ministry.

St. Francis Home (for elderly)—Sr. JANE MARIE LEBIEDZINSKI, C.S.S.F., Admin., 915 N. River Rd., Saginaw, 48609-6865. Tel: 989-781-3150.

St. Vincent Home-Boysville of Michigan (for children)—Mr. RICK L. BOONE, M.S.W., North Regl. Dir., 925 N. River Rd., Saginaw, 48609-6866. Tel: 989-781-0490.

Partnership Center—GEORGANN HEMKER, Dir.; Mr. THOMAS M. SCHREMS, Mgr., 122 S. Hamilton St., Saginaw, 48602-2013. Tel: 989-249-4290.

Organizations and Services—

Association of Saginaw Priests—Rev. JOHN A. EDERER, Pres.

Catholic Cemeteries—KENNETH GROYA, Dir.; ANDREA SALDANA, Sec., 5800 Weiss St., Saginaw, 48603-2799. Tel: 989-797-6627.

Catholic Newspaper—MARK A. MYCZKOWIAK, Gen. Mgr., 1520 Court St., P.O. Box 1405, Saginaw, 48605-1405. Tel: 989-793-7661; Fax: 989-793-7663.

Censor—Rev. Msgr. FRANCIS J. MURRAY, 915 N. River Rd., Saginaw, 48609. Tel: 989-781-4209.

Clergy Benefit Society—Rev. ROBERT MEISSNER, 2956 E. North Union Rd., Bay City, 48706-9246. Tel: 989-684-1170.

Conciliation-Arbitration—ANN M. SCHULTE, Conciliation Clerk, 5800 Weiss, Saginaw, 48603.

Holy Childhood Association—Sr. CORINNE WEISS, S.J., 5800 Weiss St., Saginaw, 48603-2799.

Marriage Encounter—Rev. JOSEPH A. SCHABEL, Spiritual Dir. (Retired). Tel: 989-753-8446.

St. Vincent de Paul Society—Mr. THOMAS LEFEVRE, Pres., 523 Michigan Ave., Bay City, 48708. Tel: 989-893-5772.

Office of Stewardship/Development—ANNETTE O'BRIEN, 5800 Weiss St., Saginaw, 48603-2799. Tel: 989-797-6679.

Victim Assistance Coordinator—Sr. JANET FULGENZI, O.P., Ph.D. Tel: 989-797-6682. Email: janet@dioceseofsaginaw.org.

CLERGY, PARISHES, MISSIONS AND PAROCHIAL SCHOOLS

CITY OF SAGINAW
(SAGINAW COUNTY)

1—ST. MARY CATHEDRAL (1853), Rev. Ronald F. Wagner.
Res.: 615 Hoyt Ave., 48607-1713. Tel: 989-752-8119; Fax: 989-752-2165.
Catechesis/Religious Program—Carmen de Jesus Mora, D.R.E. Students 181.

2—ST. ANDREW, Rev. Donald L. Christensen.
Res.: 612 N. Michigan Ave., 48602-4387. Tel: 989-754-0487; Fax: 989-754-0308.
Catechesis/Religious Program—Sr. Anne Cenci, O.P., D.R.E.; Michele Olvera, D.R.E. Students 86.

3—ST. ANTHONY OF PADUA, [JC] Rev. Francis Voris, O.F.M.Cap.
Res.: 3680 S. Washington Rd., 48601-4997. Tel: 989-752-1971; Fax: 989-752-1441.
Catechesis/Religious Program—Sr. Sharon Haskins, D.C., D.R.E. Students 68.

4—ST. CASIMIR, [JC] Rev. John S. Sarge.
Res.: 2122 S. Jefferson Ave., 48601-3498. Tel: 989-752-6648; Fax: 989-752-6691.
Catechesis/Religious Program—Maria C. Rodriguez, D.R.E.

5—ST. GEORGE, [JC] Rev. John S. Sarge; Nanette Navarre, Pastoral Assoc.
Res.: 2120 Erie St., 48601-4497. Tel: 989-753-3865; Fax: 989-753-6903.
Catechesis/Religious Program—Connie Rodriguez, D.R.E. Students 49.

6—ST. HELEN, [JC] Rev. Emmet L. Marceau.
Res.: 2445 N. Charles St., 48602-5096. Tel: 989-793-0618; Fax: 989-793-5487.
School—Joyce DeKarske, Prin. Lay Teachers 11; Students 190.
Catechesis/Religious Program—Chris Platko, D.R.E. Students 104.

7—HOLY FAMILY, [CEM] Rev. William R. Taylor.
Res.: 1525 S. Washington Ave., 48601-2895. Tel: 989-755-8020; Fax: 989-755-7193.
Catechesis/Religious Program—Anne Hamilton, D.R.E. Students 9.

8—HOLY ROSARY, Closed., For inquiries for parish records contact SS. Simon and Jude Parish, Saginaw.

9—ST. JOHN VIANNEY, Rev. Loren M. Kalinowski.
Church: 6400 McCarty Rd., 48603-9621. Tel: 989-790-5086; Fax: 989-790-1681.
Res.: 4477 McCarty Rd., 48603. Tel: 517-792-6582.
Catechesis/Religious Program—Kathy Bronz, D.R.E. Students 161.

10—ST. JOSEPH, Rev. Leo Petrimoulx, O.F.M.Cap.
Res.: 910 N. Sixth Ave., 48601-1103. Tel: 989-753-4418; Fax: 989-755-1090.
Catechesis/Religious Program—Christina Gayton, D.R.E. Students 145.

11—OUR LADY HELP OF CHRISTIANS, Closed., For inquiries for parish records contact SS. Simon and Jude Parish, Saginaw.

12—OUR LADY OF MOUNT CARMEL, Closed., For inquiries for parish records contact SS. Simon and Jude Parish, Saginaw.

13—SS. PETER AND PAUL, Rev. Robert J. DeLand; Janel Esker, Pastoral Assoc.
Res.: 4735 W. Michigan Ave., 48603-6370. Tel: 989-799-5448; Fax: 989-799-1495.
School—Sr. James Nyquist, Prin. Sisters 1; Lay Teachers 11; Students 170.
Catechesis/Religious Program—Amy Kloff, D.R.E. Students 128.

14—ST. RITA, Closed., For inquiries for parish records contact SS. Simon & Jude Parish, Saginaw.

15—SACRED HEART, Closed., For inquiries for parish records contact SS. Simon and Jude Parish, Saginaw.

16—SS. SIMON AND JUDE, Pastoral Team, Revs. Robert Schramm, O.S.F.S.; John S. Mancini, O.S.F.S.; Thomas M. Moore, O.S.F.S.; Sr. Ellen Rinke, I.H.M.; Joan LaPointe.
Res.: 2395 S. Outer Dr., 48601-6643. Tel: 989-752-7424; Fax: 989-753-8601.
Catechesis/Religious Program—Students 18.

17—ST. STEPHEN, Revs. Patrick C. O'Connor; Brian Spencer; Sr. Marcia Andrews, I.H.M., Pastoral Assoc.; Hank J. Messing, Pastoral Assoc.
Res.: 2711 Mackinaw St., 48602-3146. Tel: 989-799-2334; Fax: 989-793-3611.
School—Tel: 989-793-2811; Fax: 989-793-8463. Susan Nash, Prin. Lay Teachers 23; Students 445.
Catechesis/Religious Program—Sharon Wahl, D.R.E. Students 87.

18—ST. THOMAS AQUINAS, [JC] Revs. Robert Konopa, O.F.M.; Leonard Stunek, O.F.M.
Res.: 5376 State Rd., 48603-3771. Tel: 989-799-2460; Fax: 989-799-0207.
School—Bernardine Sisters of Third Order of St. Francis Sr. Ann De Guise, O.S.F., Prin. (Farmington, MI) Sisters 2; Lay Teachers 20; Students 490.
Catechesis/Religious Program—Patricia Michalski, D.R.E. Students 164.

OUTSIDE THE CITY OF SAGINAW

ALBEE, SAGINAW CO., ST. MARY, Rev. Robert W. Shine.
Catechesis/Religious Program—Joy Tanner, D.R.E. Students 54.
Res.: 5661 Fergus Rd., Rte. 2, St. Charles, 48655-9624. Tel: 989-770-4453; Fax: 989-770-5111.

ALMA, GRATIOT CO., ST. MARY, Rev. Charles Hammond.
Res.: 517 N. Prospect Ave., 48801-1694. Tel: 989-463-5370; Fax: 989-463-8297.
School—220 W. Downie St., 48801. Tel: 989-463-4579. Cynthia Araway, Prin. Lay Teachers 9; Students 148.
Catechesis/Religious Program—Marilyn Lorenz, D.R.E. Students 89.

ARGYLE, SANILAC CO., ST. JOSEPH, [CEM] Rev. Thomas J. Fleming.
Res.: 4960 N. Ubly Rd., 48410-0007. Tel: 989-658-8145; Fax: 989-658-8105.
Mission—St. Ignatius Freiburg, Sanilac Co.
Catechesis/Religious Program—Edith Izydorek, D.R.E. Students 54.

AUGRES, ARENAC CO., ST. MARK, Rev. James E. Falsey.
Res.: 415 S. Court St., 48703-9598. Tel: 989-876-7925; Fax: 989-876-7778.
Catechesis/Religious Program—Angie Sweeney, D.R.E.; Nancy LaLonde, D.R.E. Students 39.

AUBURN, BAY CO., ST. ANTHONY/ST. JOSEPH, Formerly St. Joseph, Operates jointly with St. Anthony, Fisherville. Rev. Thomas E. Sutton, J.C.L.
Res.: 84 W. Midland Rd., 48611. Tel: 989-662-6861; Fax: 989-662-0064.
School—Area School Lee Ann Berg, Prin. Students 117.
Catechesis/Religious Program—Jenny Geneseo, D.R.E. Students 144.

BAD AXE, HURON CO., SACRED HEART, [CEM] Rev. James R. Carlson.
Res.: 311 Whitelam St., 48413-1205. Tel: 989-269-7729; Fax: 989-269-4010.
Catechesis/Religious Program—Mickey Gavitt, D.R.E. Students 163.

BANNISTER, GRATIOT CO., ST. CYRIL, Rev. Wolfgang Streichardt.
Res.: 517 E. Main St., 48807-9762. Tel: 989-862-5270; Fax: 989-862-4534.
Catechesis/Religious Program—James Ginther, D.R.E.; Theresa Ginther, D.R.E. Students 88.

BAY CITY, BAY CO.

1—ST. BONIFACE, Rev. Dale A. Orlik.
Res.: 510 N. Lincoln Ave., 48708-6694. Tel: 989-893-4851; Fax: 989-893-1781.
Catechesis/Religious Program—Diane Seidel, D.R.E. Students 124.

2—ST. HEDWIG, Sr. Joann Plumpe, O.P., Pastoral Admin.
Res.: 1504 S. Kiesel, 48706-5240. Tel: 989-893-1072; Fax: 989-893-4710.
Catechesis/Religious Program—Mary Dierich, D.R.E. Students 51.

3—HOLY TRINITY, Rev. Robert S. Gohm. In Res., Rev. Kevin Kerbawy.
Res.: 1008 S. Wenona Ave., 48706-5094. Tel: 989-893-4073; Fax: 989-893-7087.
School—Tel: 517-892-3018. Sally Preston, Prin. Lay Teachers 7; Students 134.
Catechesis/Religious Program—Sisters Jean Jeziolkowski, O.P., D.R.E.; Joanne Gwizdala, O.P., Youth Minister. Students 158.

4—ST. HYACINTH, [CEM] Rev. Edward J. Konieczka.
Res.: 1515 Cass Ave., 48708-8740. Tel: 989-895-5581; Fax: 989-895-5583.
Catechesis/Religious Program—Susana Roznowski, D.R.E. Students 89.
Convent—912 S. Farragut St., 48708.

5—ST. JAMES (1983), [CEM] Rev. John R. Johnson.
Res.: 710 Columbus Ave., 48708-6483. Tel: 989-893-4693; Fax: 989-893-1504.
School—Tel: 989-892-4371. Sr. Julie Gatza, S.C., Prin. Sisters of Charity of Cincinnati, OH 3; Lay Teachers 11; Students 143.
Catechesis/Religious Program—Susana Roznowski, D.R.E. Students 104.
Convent—200 S. Farragut St., 48708.

6—ST. JOSEPH, Sr. Gail Addis, I.H.M., Pastoral Admin.
Res.: 1005 Third St., 48708-6006. Tel: 989-895-5783; Fax: 989-895-8837.

Catechesis/Religious Program—Ruth Nietzel, D.R.E. Students 99.
7—ST. MARIA GORETTI, Rev. James F. Gavit, J.C.D.
Res.: 2872 N. Euclid Rd., 48706-1342. Tel: 989-684-1523; Fax: 989-684-8286.
Catechesis/Religious Program—Rita Narlock, D.R.E. Students 119.
8—ST. MARY, Rev. James Heller.
Res.: 607 E. S. Union St., 48706. Tel: 989-892-6031; Fax: 989-892-4005.
Catechesis/Religious Program—Marlene Sajdak, D.R.E. Students 102.
9—OUR LADY OF GUADALUPE CHAPEL AND CENTER, Mrs. Maria Cepeda, Vicar for Hispanics.
Res.: 1619 Broadway, 48708-8538. Tel: 989-894-0661; Fax: 989-894-0771.
Catechesis/Religious Program—Josephine Perez, D.R.E. Students 32.
10—OUR LADY OF THE VISITATION, Rev. Gerald E. Balwinski.
Res.: 1106 State St., 48706-3697. Tel: 989-684-5184; Fax: 989-684-5189.
Catechesis/Religious Program—Gerald Hegenauer, D.R.E. Students 47.
11—ST. STANISLAUS, Rev. William J. Rutowski.
Res.: 1503 Kosciuszko Ave., Ste. 100, 48708-8027. Tel: 989-893-6421; Fax: 989-893-3985.
School—Sr. Annette Marie Myrand, C.S.S.F., Prin. Felician Sisters (Livonia, MI) 2; Lay Teachers 10; Students 135.
Catechesis/Religious Program—Jan Musinski, D.R.E. Students 259.
12—ST. VINCENT DE PAUL, Rev. Robert J. Meissner.
Res.: 2956 E. North Union Rd., 48706-9246. Tel: 989-684-1170; Fax: 989-684-4925.
Catechesis/Religious Program—Sandy DesJardins, D.R.E. Students 190.

BEAL CITY, ISABELLA CO., ST. JOSEPH THE WORKER, [CEM] Rev. John F. Cotter.
Res.: 2163 N. Winn Rd., Mount Pleasant, 48858-9730. Tel: 989-644-2041; Fax: 989-644-2026.
School—Tel: 989-644-6968. Mrs. Mary Hauck, Prin. Lay Teachers 6; Students 131.
Catechesis/Religious Program—Sr. Helen Settersten, S.S.N.D., D.R.E. Students 92.

BEAVER, BAY CO., ST. VALENTINE, [CEM] Rev. Richard C. Ratajczak.
Res.: 999 S. 9 Mile Rd., Kawkawlin, 48631-9756. Tel: 989-662-6843; Fax: 989-662-0152.
School—1010 S. 9 Mile Rd., Kawkawlin, 48631. Tel: 989-662-6966; Fax: 989-662-0152. Sr. James Fielbrandt, Prin. Lay Teachers 3; Students 54.
Catechesis/Religious Program—Charlene Fisher, D.R.E. Students 45.

BIRCH RUN, SAGINAW CO., SACRED HEART, Pastoral Team, Revs. Robert Schramm, O.S.F.S.; John Mancini, O.S.F.S.; Thomas Moore, O.S.F.S.; Sr. Ellen Rinke, I.H.M.; Joan LaPointe.
Res.: 12157 Church St., 48415-8706. Tel: 989-624-9098; Fax: 989-624-9427.
Catechesis/Religious Program—Ginger Scheffler, D.R.E. Students 198.

BRIDGEPORT, SAGINAW CO.
1—ASSUMPTION OF THE BLESSED VIRGIN MARY, Pastoral Team, Revs. Robert Schramm, O.S.F.S.; John Mancini, O.S.F.S.; Thomas M. Moore, O.S.F.S.; Sr. Ellen Rinke, I.H.M.; Joan LaPointe.
Res.: 7945 Bell Rd., P.O. Box 602, 48722-0602. Tel: 989-777-1200; Fax: 989-777-6280.
Catechesis/Religious Program—Norma Fackler, D.R.E. Students 66.
2—ST. CHRISTOPHER, Pastoral Team, Revs. Robert Schramm, O.S.F.S.; John Mancini, O.S.F.S.; Thomas Moore, O.S.F.S.; Sr. Ellen Rinke, I.H.M.; Joan LaPointe.
Res.: 3926 Williamson Rd., 48601-5839. Tel: 989-777-2605; Fax: 989-777-9691.
Catechesis/Religious Program—Arlene Patelski, D.R.E. Students 53.

CARO, TUSCOLA CO., SACRED HEART, [CEM] Rev. Dennis H. Kucharczyk.
Res.: 140 Atwood, 48723-1742. Tel: 989-673-2346; Fax: 989-673-5669.
Catechesis/Religious Program—Lisa Bednarski, D.R.E.; Karen Cody; Ann Reinelt. Students 212.

CARROLLTON, SAGINAW CO.
1—ST. JOHN THE BAPTIST, Rev. Richard T. Szafranski; Sr. Honora Remes, D.C., Pastoral Admin.
Res.: 3160 Carla Dr., 48604-1749. Tel: 989-752-9350; Fax: 989-753-4943.
Catechesis/Religious Program—Mary Jo Hudson, D.R.E. Students 64.
2—ST. JOSAPHAT, Rev. Ronald J. Dombrowski.
Res.: 469 Shattuck Rd., 48604-2391. Tel: 989-753-2497; Fax: 989-753-2498.
Catechesis/Religious Program—Sr. Dorthy Ann Blasko, O.P., D.R.E. Students 26.

CASEVILLE, HURON CO., ST. ROCH, Rev. Kenneth Yaroch.
Res.: 6253 Main St., 48725. Tel: 989-856-4933; Fax: 989-856-2861.
Catechesis Religious Program—Susan Grates, D.R.E. Students 55.

CASS CITY, TUSCOLA CO., ST. PANCRATIUS, Rev. Stephen Fillion.
Res.: 4292 S. Seeger St., 48726-1423. Tel: 989-872-3336; Fax: 989-872-1852.
Catechesis Religious Program—Students 108.

CHESANING, SAGINAW CO., OUR LADY OF PERPETUAL HELP, [CEM] Rev. Joseph M. Griffin.
Res.: 404 S. Wood, 48616-1399. Tel: 989-845-6894; Fax: 989-845-7787.
School—802 Lockwood St., 48616. Keith Valentine, Prin. Lay Teachers 7; Students 80.
Catechesis/Religious Program—Alden Sharon, D.R.E. Students 131.

CLARE, CLARE CO., ST. CECILIA, [CEM] Rev. Joseph Ryan.
Res.: 106 E. Wheaton St., 48617-1297. Tel: 989-386-7681; Fax: 989-386-3550.
School—Yvonne Bower, Prin. Lay Teachers 6; Students 31.
Catechesis/Religious Program—Ann Strick, D.R.E. Students 55.

COLEMAN, MIDLAND CO., ST. PHILIP NERI, Sr. Mary Ellen McDonald, O.P.
Res.: 5199 W. Shaffer Rd., P.O. Box 512, 48618-0512. Tel: 989-465-1768; Fax: 989-465-6311.
Catechesis/Religious Program—Judie Kumkiewicz, D.R.E. Students 37.
Mission—St. Anne Edenville, Gladwin Co.
Catechesis/Religious Program—Students 35.

CROSWELL, SANILAC CO., ST. PATRICK, [CEM] Rev. Donald G. Dueweke.
Res.: 105 W. Sanborn Ave., 48422-1399. Tel: 810-679-3849; Fax: 810-679-3903.
Catechesis/Religious Program—Christina Lowry, D.R.E. Students 88.
Mission—St. John [CEM] Peck, Sanilac Co.
Catechesis/Religious Program—Students 10.

ESSEXVILLE, BAY CO., ST. JOHN THE EVANGELIST, Rev. Thomas J. McNamara. In Res., Rev. Michael H. Wolf (Retired).
Res.: 1600 Hudson St., 48732-1377. Tel: 989-892-1893; Fax: 989-894-5558.
School—619 Main St., 48732. Sue Grzegorczyk, Prin. Lay Teachers 8; Students 133.
Catechesis/Religious Program—Barbara Walkley, D.R.E.; Judith Klimkiewicz. Students 216.

FISHERVILLE, BAY CO., ST. ANTHONY/ST. JOSEPH, [CEM], Operates jointly with St. Joseph, Auburn. Rev. Thomas E. Sutton, J.C.L.
Church: 4699 S. 11 Mile Rd., Auburn, 48611-9535. Tel: 989-662-6480; Fax: 989-662-4335.
School—Auburn Area Catholic, West Campus, 1492 W. Midland Rd., Auburn, 48611-9560 Tel: 989-662-6581; Fax: 989-662-4335.
Catechesis/Religious Program—Students 106.

FRANKENMUTH, SAGINAW CO., BLESSED TRINITY, Rev. Frederick J. Kawka.
Res.: 958 E. Tuscola Rd., 48734-9770. Tel: 989-652-3259; Fax: 989-652-2206.
Catechesis/Religious Program—Carol Fox, D.R.E. Students 283.

FREELAND, SAGINAW CO., ST. AGNES, Rev. Lawrence M. Pashak.
Res.: 335 Johnson, 48623-9006. Tel: 989-695-5652; Fax: 989-695-6275.
Catechesis/Religious Program—Connie Juegner. Students 193.

GAGETOWN, TUSCOLA CO., ST. AGATHA, Joan Wyskiel, Pastoral Administrator.
Res.: 4618 South St., Box 139, 48735-0139. Tel: 989-665-9966.

GLADWIN, GLADWIN CO., SACRED HEART, Rev. Patrick Jankowiak.
Res.: 300 N. Silverleaf St., 48624-1697. Tel: 989-426-7154; Fax: 989-426-0896.
School—Susan Mansfield, Prin. Lay Teachers 5; Students 87.
Catechesis/Religious Program—Joan Turner, D.R.E. Students 53.

HARBOR BEACH, HURON CO., OUR LADY OF LAKE HURON, [CEM] Rev. Gerald F. Kukla; Sr. Eileen Houlihan, I.H.M., Pastoral Assoc.
Res.: 413 S. First St., 48441-1325. Tel: 989-479-3393; Fax: 989-479-3335.
School—Mr. Lawrence E. Kish II, Prin. Lay Teachers 10; Students 155.
Catechesis/Religious Program—Jean Winkel, D.R.E. Students 105.
Convent—406 S. First St., 48441.

HARRISON, CLARE CO., ST. ATHANASIUS, Rev. Noel Rudy, Sacramental Min.; Sr. Rosemary Wrinn, C.S.J., Pastoral Admin.
Res.: 310 S. Broad St., P.O. Box 528, 48625-0528. Tel: 989-539-6232; Fax: 989-539-4129.
Catechesis/Religious Program—Theresa Borawski, D.R.E. Students 44.

HELENA, HURON CO., ST. ANTHONY, [CEM] Rev. Andrzej Boroch.
Res.: 4190 Parisville Rd., Ruth, 48470-9759. Tel: 989-479-6781; Fax: 989-864-3164.
Catechesis/Religious Program—Students 47.

HEMLOCK, SAGINAW CO., ST. MARY, [CEM] Sr. Mary Garascia, C.P.P.S., P.A.
Res.: 151 St. Mary's Dr., 48626-9614. Tel: 989-642-5606; Fax: 989-642-5240.
St. Mary Center—245 St. Mary's Dr., 48626.
Catechesis/Religious Program—Judy Horny, D.R.E.; Marjorie Morrison, D.R.E. Students 147.

ITHACA, GRATIOT CO., ST. PAUL THE APOSTLE, Rev. Julius A. Spleet, Sacramental Min. (Retired); Sr. Margo Tafoya, M.S.Sp., Pastoral Admin.
Res.: 121 N. Union St., 48847-1596. Tel: 989-875-2852; Fax: 989-875-7027.
Catechesis/Religious Program—Sharon Spitzley, D.R.E. Students 70.
Mission—St. Martin De Porres Perrinton, Gratiot Co.
Catechesis/Religious Program—Students 46.

KAWKAWLIN, BAY CO., SACRED HEART, Rev. Chester J. Pilarski.
Res.: 2510 S. Fraser Rd., 48631-9115. Tel: 989-684-1402; Fax: 989-684-0038.
Catechesis/Religious Program—Leoma Bujalski, D.R.E. Students 151.

KINDE, HURON CO., ST. MARY-ST. EDWARD, Rev. Mieczyslaw Oniskiewicz; Sr. Judy O'Brien, I.H.M., Pastoral Assoc.
Res.: 1709 Moeller Rd., P.O. Box 68, 48445-0068. Tel: 989-874-4744; Fax: 989-874-4010.
Catechesis/Religious Program—St. Edward 51; St. Mary 78.

LEXINGTON, SANILAC CO., ST. DENIS, [CEM] Rev. Donald J. Eppenbrock.
Res.: 5366 Main St., P.O. Box 399, 48450-0399. Tel: 810-359-5400; Fax: 810-359-5833.
Catechesis/Religious Program—Sr. John Marie Charniga, D.R.E. Students 52.

LINWOOD, BAY CO., ST. ANNE, Rev. Thomas M. Kowalczyk.
Res.: 315 W. Center St., 48634-9813. Tel: 989-697-4443.
School—Tel: 989-697-3100. Sr. Rose Ellen Dzwieleski, O.S.F., Prin. Bernardine Sisters of Third Order of St. Francis (Farmington, MI) 3; Lay Teachers 8; Students 150.
Catechesis/Religious Program—Students 54.

MAPLE GROVE, SAGINAW CO., ST. MICHAEL, [CEM] Rev. Randy J. Kelly.
Res.: 17994 Lincoln Rd., New Lothrop, 48460-9600. Tel: 989-845-7011; Fax: 989-845-4729.
Catechesis/Religious Program—Nancy Ebenhoeh, D.R.E. Students 333.

MARLETTE, SANILAC CO., ST. ELIZABETH, Rev. Richard Bokinskie.
Res.: 6785 W. Marlette St., 48453-1296. Tel: 989-635-7581; Fax: 989-635-5808.
Catechesis/Religious Program—Barbara Davis, D.R.E.; Roxann Ross, D.R.E. Students 68.

MAYVILLE, TUSCOLA CO., ST. JOSEPH, Rev. Richard Bokinskie, Sacremental Min.; Sr. Riccardina Silvestri, M.C., Pastoral Administrator.
Mailing Address: 315 Ohmer Rd., P.O. Box 283, 48744-0283. Tel: 989-843-6565; Fax: 989-683-2556.
Catechesis/Religious Program—Kathy Waldorf, D.R.E. Students 62.

MERRILL, SAGINAW CO., SACRED HEART, [CEM] Rev. Craig L. Albrecht.
Res.: 419 S. Midland St., 48637-0099. Tel: 989-643-5366; Fax: 989-643-5171.
Catechesis/Religious Program—Mary Miller, D.R.E. Students 107.

MIDLAND, MIDLAND CO.
1—ASSUMPTION BLESSED VIRGIN MARY, Rev. Richard M. Filary, J.C.L.
Res.: 3516 Monroe, Rd. 8, 48642. Tel: 989-631-4447; Fax: 989-631-4323.
Catechesis/Religious Program—Norbert Bufka, D.R.E.; Mary Fey, D.R.E. Students 176.
2—BLESSED SACRAMENT, Revs. Peter J. Gaspeny; Kevin Maksym.
Res.: 3109 Swede Ave., 48642-3888. Tel: 989-835-6777; Fax: 989-835-2451.
School—Michael J. Knoff, Prin. Lay Teachers 13; Students 236.
Catechesis/Religious Program—Janet Martyn, Director of Faith Formation. Students 856.
3—ST. BRIGID, Rev. James Bessert.
Res.: 207 Ashman St., 48640-5185. Tel: 989-835-7121; Fax: 989-835-9141.
School—130 W. Larkin St., 48640-6579. Tel: 989-835-9481; Fax: 989-835-9141. Sandy Slicker, Co-Prin.; Maureen Belker, Co-Prin. Lay Teachers 14; Students 95.
Catechesis/Religious Program—Richard Meyette, D.R.E. Students 204.

MOUNT PLEASANT, ISABELLA CO.
1—ST. MARY UNIVERSITY PARISH, Rev. Jeffrey Donner.
Res.: 1405 S. Washington, 48858-4280. Tel: 989-773-3931; Fax: 989-772-2745.
Catechesis/Religious Program—Joseph

Frankenfield, D.R.E. Students 56.
2—SACRED HEART, [CEM] Revs. Robert H. Byrne; Donald E. Henkes (MEM).
Res.: 302 S. Kinney, 48858-2773. Tel: 989-772-1385; Fax: 989-773-9118.
School—(Grades PreK-6), 200 S. Franklin St., 48858-2529. Eileen Ball, Prin. Sisters 1; Lay Teachers 15; Students 241.
High School—Sacred Heart Academy, (Grades 7-12), 316 E. Michigan, 48858-2640. Tel: 989-772-1457. Nancy English, Prin. Priests 1; Sisters 1; Lay Teachers 19; Students 208.
Catechesis/Religious Program—Mary Kay Gagnon, D.R.E. Students 187.

MUNGER, BAY CO., ST. NORBERT, Rev. William J. Gruden; Sr. Tereska Wozniak, O.P., Pastoral Assoc.
Res.: 126 W. Munger Rd., 48747-9767. Tel: 989-659-2193; Fax: 989-659-3417.
Catechesis/Religious Program—Maryanne Adams, D.R.E. Students 82.

NINE MILE, BAY CO., ST. MARY, [CEM] Rev. Joseph K. Miller.
Res.: 739 W. Cody-Estey Rd., Pinconning, 48650-8925. Tel: 989-879-5596; Fax: 989-879-6151.
Catechesis/Religious Program—Students 101.
Station—St. Agnes 216 E. Fifth St., Piconning, 48650.

OAKLEY, SAGINAW CO., ST. MICHAEL, [CEM] Rev. Joseph Griffin, Sacremental Min.; M. Katherine Paul, M.Div., Pastoral Admin.
Res.: Box 75, 48649-0075. Tel: 989-845-3545; Fax: 989-845-5499.
Catechesis/Religious Program—Students 51.

PALMS, SANILAC CO., ST. PATRICK, Rev. Steven M. Gavit, Sacramental Min.; Sr. Betty Zeestratten, O.S.F., Pastoral Admin.
Res.: 1801 Palms Rd., 48465. Tel: 810-376-4853; Fax: 989-864-3526.
Catechesis/Religious Program—Students 74.

PARISVILLE, HURON CO., ST. MARY, Rev. Andrzej Boroch.
Res.: 4190 Parisville Rd., Ruth, 48470-9759. Tel: 989-864-3523; Fax: 989-864-3164.
Catechesis/Religious Program—Brenda Plester, D.R.E. Students 45.

PIGEON, HURON CO., ST. FRANCIS BORGIA, [CEM] Rev. John Weis; Sr. Theresa Fox, O.P., P.A.
Res.: 25 Moeller St., Box U, 48755. Tel: 989-453-2151; Fax: 989-453-2156.
Catechesis/Religious Program—Students 59.

PINCONNING, BAY CO., ST. MICHAEL, Rev. Steven S. Killey.
Res.: 225 Jennings St., 48650-9408. Tel: 989-879-2141; Fax: 989-879-6633.
School—Celeste DeLano, Prin. Lay Teachers 9; Students 113.
Catechesis/Religious Program—Mary Warren, D.R.E. Students 60.

PINNEBOG, HURON CO., ST. FELIX, [CEM] Rev. Kenneth Yaroch, Sacramental Min.; Sr. Mary Schwartz, S.S.J., Pastoral Admin.
Res.: 3515 Limerick, Kinde, 48445-9723. Tel: 989-874-5833.
Catechesis/Religious Program—Students 43.

PORT AUSTIN, HURON CO., ST. MICHAEL, [CEM] Rev. Robert Pare.
Res.: 8637 Garfield, P.O. Box 355, 48467-0355. Tel: 989-738-7521; Fax: 989-738-5886.
Parish Center—8661 Independence Ave., P.O. Box 350, 48467.
Catechesis/Religious Program—Sr. Margaret Ann Roggenbuck, O.P., D.R.E. Students 49.

PORT SANILAC, SANILAC CO., ST. MARY, [CEM] Rev. Paul Bala.
Res.: 7066 W. Main St., P.O. Box 467, 48469-0467. Tel: 810-622-9904; Fax: 810-622-7953.
Catechesis/Religious Program—Sr. Joan Maher, M.S.Sp., D.R.E. Students 49.
Mission—St. John Chrysostom Forestville, Sanilac Co.

RAPSON, HURON CO., ST. JOSEPH, [CEM] Rev. John Killop.
Res.: 3455 Rapson Rd., Rte. 3, Bad Axe, 48413-9149. Tel: 989-269-8084.
Catechesis/Religious Program—Maryanne Adams, D.R.E. Students 63.
Mission—Holy Trinity [CEM] Smiths Corners, Huron Co.
Catechesis/Religious Program—Students 25.

REESE, TUSCOLA CO., ST. ELIZABETH, [CEM] Rev. William J. Gruden; Sr. Tereska Wozniak, O.P., Pastoral Assoc.
Res.: 12835 E. Washington, P.O. Box 392, 48757-9712. Tel: 989-868-4081; Fax: 989-868-9785.
School—Dr. Angela Radlinski, Prin. Lay Teachers 6; Students 70.
Catechesis/Religious Program—Valerie Sulfaro, D.R.E. Students 46.

ROSEBUSH, ISABELLA CO., ST. HENRY, [CEM] Lorraine McGuinness, Pastoral Admin.; Rev. Jeffrey Donnar, Sacramental Min.
Res.: 4079 E. Vernon Rd., 48878-0067. Tel: 989-433-2229; Fax: 989-433-2229.
Catechesis/Religious Program—Theresa Borawski, D.R.E. Students 70.
Mission—St. Charles Leaton, Isabella Co.

RUTH, HURON CO., SS. PETER AND PAUL, [CEM] Rev. Steven W. Gavit.
Res.: 7115 Atwater Dr., P.O. Box 55, 48470-0055. Tel: 989-864-3650; Fax: 989-864-8600.
School—Sr. Patricia Hejna, O.S.F., Prin. Lay Teachers 4; Students 57.
Catechesis/Religious Program—Students 40.

RYAN, MIDLAND CO., ST. PATRICK, [CEM] Sr. Janet Brown, O.P., Pastoral Admin.; Rev. Craig L. Albrecht, Sacramental Min.
Res.: 4708 N. Meridian Rd., Rte. 2, Merrill, 48637-9546. Tel: 989-643-5652; Fax: 989-643-5652.
Catechesis/Religious Program—Sheila Bugbee, D.R.E. Students 24.

ST. CHARLES, SAGINAW CO., IMMACULATE CONCEPTION, [CEM] Rev. Todd Arnberg.
Res.: 708 Sanderson St., 48655-1895. Tel: 989-865-9460; Fax: 989-865-9460.
Catechesis/Religious Program—Rita Chad, D.R.E. Students 54.

ST. LOUIS, GRATIOT CO., ST. JOSEPH, Rev. Charles Hammond.
Office—605 S. Franklin, 48880-1747. Tel: 989-681-5080; Fax: 989-681-2887.
Catechesis/Religious Program—Kathy Fairchild, D.R.E. Students 67.

SANDUSKY, SANILAC CO., ST. JOSEPH, Rev. R. Keith LeFleur.
Res.: 511 N. Sandusky Rd., P.O. Box 249, 48471-0249. Tel: 810-648-4293; Fax: 810-648-4293.
Catechesis/Religious Program—Students 142.

SANFORD, MIDLAND CO., ST. AGNES, Rev. James Hast, O.F.M.Cap.
Res.: 2500 W. River Rd., 48657-9497. Tel: 989-687-5657; Fax: 989-687-2450.
Catechesis/Religious Program—Ann M. Schoren, D.R.E. Students 171.

SEBEWAING, HURON CO., HOLY FAMILY, [CEM] Rev. John Weis.
Res.: 8370 Unionville Rd., 48759-9553. Tel: 989-883-2746; Fax: 989-883-3117.
Catechesis/Religious Program—Students 52.

SHEPHERD, ISABELLA CO., ST. VINCENT DE PAUL, [CEM] Rev. Robert J. Howe.
Res.: 168 Wright, 48883-9079. Tel: 989-828-5720; Fax: 989-828-4652.
Catechesis/Religious Program—Sue Wieferich, D.R.E. Students 66.
Mission—St. Leo [CEM] Winn, Isabella Co.
Catechesis/Religious Program—Beverly Kalmar, D.R.E. Students 23.
Mission—St. Patrick Irishtown, Gratiot Co.
Catechesis/Religious Program—Kathy Duffy, D.R.E. Students 36.

SHIELDS, SAGINAW CO., HOLY SPIRIT, Rev. David L. Parsch.
Res.: 1035 N. River Rd., 48609-6864. Tel: 989-781-2457; Fax: 989-781-5518.
Catechesis/Religious Program—Nancy Ruh, D.R.E. Students 293.

STANDISH, ARENAC CO., RESURRECTION OF THE LORD, [CEM] Rev. James M. Fitzpatrick.
Res.: 423 Cedar, Box 306, 48658-0306. Tel: 989-846-9565; Fax: 989-846-9566.
Catechesis/Religious Program—Sharon Dupuis, D.R.E. Students 112.

UBLY, HURON CO.
1—ST. COLUMBKILLE, [CEM] Rev. Thomas J. Fleming.
Res.: 4470 Washington St., 48475. Tel: 989-658-8824; Fax: 989-658-2088.
Catechesis/Religious Program—Audean Vatter, D.R.E. Students 79.
2—ST. JOHN THE EVANGELIST, [CEM] Rev. Thomas J. Fleming.
Res.: 4470 Washington St., 48475. Tel: 989-658-8824; Fax: 989-658-2088.
Catechesis/Religious Program—Audean Vatter, D.R.E. Students 135.

VASSAR, TUSCOLA CO., ST. FRANCES XAVIER CABRINI, Rev. John Ederer.
Res.: 165 W. Maple St., 48768-1203. Tel: 989-823-2911; Fax: 989-823-2999.
Catechesis/Religious Program—Students 52.
Mission—St. Bernard Millington, Tuscola Co. Closed.

WILMOT, TUSCOLA CO., ST. MICHAEL, [CEM] Rev. Richard Bokinskie, Sacramental Min.; Sr. Riccardina Silvestri, M.C., Pastoral Admin.
Res.: 1951 Kingston Rd., Deford, 48729. Tel: 989-683-2475; Fax: 989-683-2556.
Catechesis/Religious Program—Students 22.

ZILWAUKEE, SAGINAW CO., ST. MATTHEW, Rev. Richard T. Szafranski.
Res.: 511 W. Cornell, 48604-1311. Tel: 989-755-7336; Fax: 989-755-4228.
Catechesis/Religious Program—Sally Macomber, D.R.E. Students 105.

Chaplains of Public Institutions

BAY CITY. *Bay Medical Center and Bay Osteopathic Hospital*, 1201 S. Erie, 48706. Sr. Beth Pero, S.S.J.

On Duty Outside the Diocese:
Revs.—
Friske, Joseph P. (Retired), Damaschkestr. 20, 8000 Munchen 82, Germany.
Loos, Frederick C., Ave. Naucalpan #84, Col. La Canada, Naucalpan 53570 Mexico.
Mullet, John, Pompano Beach, FL

Retired:
Rev. Msgrs.—
Forbes, Eugene A., J.C.D., V.G., P.A.
Murdick, Olin J.
Murray, Francis
Revs.—
Boucher, Edward F.
Davey, Robert
Eickholt, Henry C.
Favara, Joseph F.
Frego, Max
Friske, Joseph P.
Ganley, Charles
Greiner, Lawrence
Janowicz, Barney J.
Jozwiak, Richard
Kearns, Joseph J.
Klimas, George H.
LaMarre, Theodore E.
Maher, Michael L.
Matuszewski, Ramon
Moeggenberg, Raymond
Navarre, Robert G.
Roach, Joseph W., S.A.G.
Rudy, Noel T.
Schabel, Joseph A.
Serour, George J.
Sierminski, Vernon
Sikorski, Harold R.
Skornia, Bernard L.
Spleet, Julius A.
Surman, Stanley
Thome, John J.
Van Mullekom, Richard
Vaughn, Mason
Welna, Floyd
Welsmiller, Francis F.
Wolf, Michael H.

Permanent Deacons:
Alex, Frank, St. Anne, Edenville; & St. Philip Neri, Coleman
Arnold, Michael, St. Valentine Church, Beaver
Belanger, Stanley, (Retired)
Cremin, John J., St. Mary, Alma
DeNeut, Gerard H., St. Matthew, Zilwaukee
Detwiler, Russell, Jail Ministry
Emmeot, Dale, Blessed Sacrament Church, Midland
Fussman, Lawrence, Sacred Heart Church, Mount Pleasant
Hudson, Francis W., St. Brigid, Midland
Jankowiak, Michael, Blessed Sacrament, Midland
Kasprzyk, David, On Duty Outside the Diocese
Kebblish, Edward, St. Agnes, Sanford
Keller, George, Bay County Jail Ministry
Kuhr, Lambert, Jr., (Retired), Out of the Diocese
Masserang, Lawrence, Blessed Trinity, Frankenmuth
Middleton, Allan, St. Cecilia, Clare
Moeggenberg, John, On Duty Outside the Diocese
Stilwell, Lee, St. John The Evangelist, Essexville
Wilberding, John, St. Vincent dePaul, Shepherd
Winkler, Frank, (Retired)

INSTITUTIONS LOCATED IN THE DIOCESE

[A] HIGH SCHOOLS, INTER-PAROCHIAL

SAGINAW. *Nouvel Catholic Central High School*, 2555 Wieneke Rd., 48603. Tel: 989-791-4330; Fax: 989-787-6603. Email: msullivan@nouvel.org. Web: www.nouvel.org. Ronald Szewczyk, Prin.; Dave Szymanowskt, Asst. Prin.; Kathy Myles, Campus Min. Lay Teachers 41; Students 503.

BAY CITY. *All Saints Central High School*, 217 S. Monroe St., 48708. Tel: 989-892-2533; Fax: 989-892-7188. Email: vwelter@bayareacatholicschools.org. Web: www.bayareacatholicschools.org. Veronica Welter,

Prin. Priests 1; Sisters 1; Lay Teachers 15; Students 188.

[B] MIDDLE SCHOOLS

BAY CITY. *Holy Family Middle School*, 2307 S. Monroe St., 48708. Tel: 989-892-8727. Email: holyfamilyms@hotmail.com. Barbara Rakowski, Prin.; Sr. Irene Chrusciel, O.P., Pastoral Counselor. Sisters 1; Lay Teachers 11; Students 166.

[C] ELEMENTARY SCHOOLS, PRIVATE

AUBURN. *Auburn Area Catholic Schools*, East Campus: W. 114 Midland Rd., 48611. Tel: 517-662-6431; Fax: 989-662-3391. Email: aacs@vsol.com. Lee Ann Berg, Prin. Lay Teachers 7; Students 112.

[D] CHILDREN'S HOMES

SAGINAW. *St. Vincent Home-Boysville of Michigan, Inc.*, 925 N. River Rd., 48609. Tel: 989-781-2780; Fax: 989-781-5422. Rick Boone, M.S.W., C.S.W., Regl. Dir.; Mr. Joe Martinus, Pastoral Min. Residential and community based treatment programs for troubled youth and families with facilities located throughtout the state of Michigan, under the auspices of the Brothers of the Holy Cross at Notre Dame. Youth 60.

Holland House, 614 E. Holland Ave., 48601. Tel: 989-755-5396; Fax: 989-755-1616. Boys 14.

Boysville's Family & Community Support Program, 705 Hoyt St., 48601. Tel: 989-752-5622; Fax: 989-752-6033. Includes Specialized Foster Care, Supervised Independent Living, In-Home Treatment, Families First, and Nokomis Challenge.

Curtis House, P.O. Box 309, Frankenmuth, 48734. Tel: 517-652-3212; Fax: 989-652-3214. Boys 14.

[E] GENERAL HOSPITALS

SAGINAW. *St. Mary's Medical Center of Saginaw, Inc.*, 800 S. Washington Ave., 48601-2524. Frederic L. Fraizer, Pres. & CEO; Sr. Dinah White, D.C., Vice Pres. Mission Svcs.; Revs. James Martin, Sacramental Min. & Chap.; Timothy Hastings, Sacramental Min. & Chap.; Sr. Barbara Rieley, D.C., Patient Representative & Chap.; Delmar Smolinski, Chap.; William Rabior, Chap.; Diane Smiley, Chap. Daughters of Charity of St. Vincent de Paul, East Central Province, Evansville, IN Sisters 3; Bed Capacity 268; Patients assisted annually 258,427.

Field Neurosciences Institute, 800 S. Jefferson Ave., 48601-2524. Frederic L. Fraizer, Registered Agent.

[F] HOMES FOR AGED

SAGINAW. *St. Francis Nursing Home*, 915 N. River Rd., 48609. Fax: 989-781-3791. Sr. Jane Marie Lebiedzinski, C.S.S.F., Admin. Felician Sisters (Livonia, MI) 3; Total Staff 150; Residents 100.

[G] MONASTERIES AND RESIDENCES OF PRIESTS AND BROTHERS

SAGINAW. *Queen of Angels Friary and Retreat House*, 3400 S. Washington Rd., P.O. Box 2026, 48605. Tel: 989-755-2149; Fax: 989-755-1640. Web: www.rc.net/saginaw/retreat. Priests 5.
Retreat Team: Revs. Wally Balouck, O.F.M.Cap.; Malcolm Maloney, O.F.M.Cap.

[H] CONVENTS AND RESIDENCES FOR SISTERS

SAGINAW. *Franciscan Poor Clare Nuns, O.S.C.*, 4875 Shattuck Rd., 48603-2962. Tel: 989-797-0593. Email: srsclare@saginaw.org. Web: www.rc.net/saginaw/srsclare. Sr. Dianne Doughty, O.S.C., Abbess. Solemnly Professed 4.

Motherhouse and Novitiate of the Mission Sisters of the Holy Spirit, 1030 N. River Rd., 48609. Tel: 989-781-0934. Sr. Mary Lou Owczarak, M.S.Sp., Community Coord. Sisters 11.

ALMA. *Motherhouse and Novitiate of the Religious Sisters of Mercy of Alma, Michigan*, 1965 Michigan Ave., 48801. Tel: 989-463-6035; Fax: 989-463-5811. Sr. Mary McGreevy, R.S.M., Vicar. Sisters 14.

[I] CATHOLIC EDUCATION ENDOWMENT FUNDS

SAGINAW. *St. Helen Catholic School Foundation Endowment Fund*, 2415 N. Charles St., 48602-5009. Tel: 989-792-7781.

Nouvel Catholic Central Educational Foundation Catholic School Foundation Endowment Fund, 2555 Wieneke Rd., 48603-2897. Tel: 989-791-4330.

SS. Peter and Paul Catholic School Foundation Endowment Fund, 4735 W. Michigan Ave., 48603-6370. Tel: 989-799-9006.

Roman Catholic Diocese of Saginaw Catholic School Foundation, 5800 Weiss St., 48603-2799. Tel: 989-797-6679. Annette M. O'Brien, Contact Person.

St. Stephen Catholic School Foundation Endowment Fund, 1300 Malzahn St., 48602. Tel: 989-793-2811.

St. Thomas Aquinas Catholic School Foundation Endowment Fund, 2136 Berbercvich St., 48603-3699. Tel: 989-792-2361.

AUBURN. *Auburn Area Catholic Schools Catholic School Foundation Endowment Fund*, 1492 W. Midland Rd., 48611-9560. Tel: 989-662-6581.

BAY CITY. *All Saints Central High Catholic School Foundation Endowment Fund*, 217 S. Monroe St., 48708-7298. Tel: 989-892-2533.

Bay Catholic Educational Foundation Catholic School Foundation Endownment Fund, 2306 S. Monroe St., 48708-8786. Tel: 989-894-8777.

Holy Family Middle School Catholic School Foundation Endowment Fund, 1503 Kosciuszko Ave., Ste. 200, 48708-8027. Tel: 989-892-8332.

St. James Catholic School Foundation Endowment Fund, 715 14th St., 48708-7288. Tel: 989-892-4371.

St. Stanislaus Catholic School Foundation Endowment Fund, 900 S. Grant St., 48708-7393. Tel: 989-893-5085.

BEAL CITY. *St. Joseph the Worker Catholic School Foundation Endowment Fund*, 2091 N. Winn Rd., Mt. Pleasant, 48858-9730. Tel: 989-644-3970.

CLARE. *St. Cecilia Catholic School Foundation Endowment Fund*, 106 E. Wheaton St., 48617-1398. Tel: 989-386-9862.

ESSEXVILLE. *St. John the Evangelist Catholic School Foundation Endowment Fund*, 619 Main St., 48732-1398. Tel: 989-892-0363.

GLADWIN. *Sacred Heart Catholic School Foundation Endowment Fund*, 330 N. Silverleaf St., 48624-1326. Tel: 989-426-8574.

HARBOR BEACH. *Our Lady of Lake Huron Catholic School Foundation Endowment Fund*, 222 Court St., 48441-1361. Tel: 989-479-3427.

KAWKAWLIN. *St. Valentine Catholic School Foundation Endowment Fund*, 1010 S. 9 Mile Rd., 48631. Tel: 989-662-3100.

LINWOOD. *St. Anne Catholic School Foundation Endowment Fund*, P.O. Box 548, 48634-0548. Tel: 989-697-3100.

MIDLAND. *Blessed Sacrament Catholic School Foundation Endowment Fund*, 3109 Swede Ave., 48642-3888. Tel: 989-832-8283.

The James Cardinal Hickey Educational Endowment Fund for St. Brigid Catholic School, 130 W. Larkin St., 48640-6579. Tel: 517-835-9481. Rev. James W. Bessert, Pastor.

PINCONNING. *St. Michael Catholic School Foundation Endowment Fund*, 310 E. 2nd St., 48650-9409. Tel: 517-879-3063.

REESE. *St. Elizabeth Catholic School Foundation Endowment Fund*, P.O. Box 392, 48757-9547. Tel: 517-868-4108.

RUTH. *SS. Peter & Paul Catholic School Foundation Endowment Fund*, 7135 E. Atwater Rd., 48470-9777. Tel: 517-864-3649.

SHEPHERD. *St. Vincent de Paul Catholic School Foundation Endowment Fund*, 205 E. Maple St., 48883-9007. Tel: 517-828-5970.

[J] MISCELLANEOUS LISTINGS

SAGINAW. *Holy Spirit Sisters Charitable Trust*, 1030 N. River Rd., 48609. Sr. Mary Lou Owczarak, M.S.Sp., Pres.

St. Mary's Medical Center of Saginaw, Inc., 800 S. Washington Ave., 48601.

Seton Health Corporation of East Central Michigan, 800 S. Washington Ave., 48601. Tel: 989-776-8176; Fax: 989-776-1704. Email: ffraizer@saintmarys-saginaw.org. Web: www.saintmarys-saginaw.org. Fred Fraizer, Pres. & CEO.

ALMA. *Religious Sisters of Mercy of Alma Corporation*, 1835 Michigan Ave., 48801. Tel: 989-463-6035. Sisters Mary Quentin Sheridan, R.S.M., Pres.; Mary McGreevy, R.S.M., Vice Pres.

Sacred Heart Mercy Health Care Center, 7320 N. Alger Rd., 48801. Tel: 989-463-3451; 989-463-8464. Sr. Mary Judith O'Brien, R.S.M.

BAY CITY. *Society of St. Vincent de Paul*, 523 Michigan Ave., 48708. Mr. Thomas Lefevre, Pres. Member Conferences: Bay City-Holy Trinity, St. Hyacinth, St. James, St. Joseph's, St. Mary, St. Stanislaus, Visitation, St. Vincent de Paul; Essexville-St. John.

RELIGIOUS INSTITUTES OF MEN REPRESENTED IN THE DIOCESE

For further details refer to the corresponding bracketed number in the Religious Institutes of Men or Women section.

[0470]—*The Capuchin Friars* (St. Joseph Prov.)—O.F.M.Cap.
[0480]—*Conventual Franciscans*—O.F.M.
[0520]—*Franciscan Friars* (Assumption Prov.)—O.F.M.
[0920]—*Oblates of St. Francis De Sales*—O.S.F.S.

RELIGIOUS INSTITUTES OF WOMEN REPRESENTED IN THE DIOCESE

[1810]—*Bernadine Sisters of Third Order of St. Francis*—O.S.F.
[0760]—*Daughters of Charity of St. Vincent de Paul* (Evansville)—D.C.
[1070-03]—*Dominican Sisters* (Sinsinawa, WI)—O.P.
[1070-09]—*Dominican Sisters* (Racine, WI)—O.P.
[1070-13]—*Dominican Sisters* (Adrian, MI)—O.P.
[1070-26]—*Dominican Sisters* (Oxford, MI)—O.P.
[1070-14]—*Dominican Sisters* (Grand Rapids)—O.P.
[1170]—*Felician Sisters*—C.S.S.F.
[]—*Franciscan Poor Clare Nuns*—O.S.C.
[2740]—*Mission Sisters of the Holy Spirit*—M.S.Sp.
[3130]—*Our Lady of Victory Missionary Sisters* (Huntington, IN)—O.L.V.M.
[3560]—*Servants of Jesus*—S.J.
[0440]—*Sisters of Charity of Cincinnati, Ohio*—S.C.
[2519]—*Sisters of Mercy of Alma, Michigan*—R.S.M.
[2575]—*Sisters of Mercy of the Americas* (Detroit, MI)—R.S.M.
[3000]—*Sisters of Notre Dame de Namur* (Boston, MA; Cincinnati, OH)—S.N.D.deN.
[1570]—*Sisters of St. Francis of the Holy Family* (Dubuque, IA)—O.S.F.
[3830-11]—*Sisters of St. Joseph* (Nazareth, MI)—S.S.J.
[1030]—*Sisters of the Divine Savior* (Milwaukee, WI)—S.D.S.
[1990]—*Sisters of the Holy Name of Jesus and Mary* (Spokane, WA)—S.N.J.M.
[3260]—*Sisters of the Precious Blood (Dayton, Ohio)*—C.PP.S.
[2150]—*Sisters, Servants of the Immaculate Heart of Mary* (Monroe)—I.H.M.

DIOCESAN CEMETERIES

SAGINAW. *St. Andrew's, Mt. Olivet & Calvary*
BAY CITY. *St. Patrick's, Calvary & St. Stanislaus*
LINWOOD. *St. Anne*
MIDLAND. *Calvary*

NECROLOGY

✠ Untener, Most Rev. Kenneth E., Bishop of Saginaw.—Died March 27, 2004
† Fron, Raymond S., Bay City, MI St. Joseph—Died Dec. 14, 2002
† Hoogterp, Richard P., (Retired)—Died Sept. 27, 2002
† McEachin, Cornelius, (Retired)—Died May 16, 2003
† Rabideau, Richard L.—Died Aug. 24, 2002

Diocese of St. Augustine

(Dioecesis Sancti Augustini)

Most Reverend

VICTOR BENITO GALEONE

Bishop of St. Augustine; ordained December 18, 1960; appointed Bishop of St. Augustine June 26, 2001; ordained August 21, 2001. *Office: P.O. Box 24000, Jacksonville, FL 32241-4000.*

Catholic Center: P.O. Box 24000, Jacksonville, FL 32241-4000. Tel: 904-262-3200; Fax: 904-262-0698.

Web: www.dosafl.com

Square Miles 11,032.

Florida, east of the Apalachicola River, was erected by Pope Pius IX into a Vicariate-Apostolic in the year 1857, and in 1870 into the Diocese of St. Augustine.

Comprises all of the northeastern Counties of the State of Florida including Alachua, Baker, Bradford, Clay, Columbia, Dixie, Duval, Flagler, Gilchrist, Hamilton, Lafayette, Levy, Nassau, Putnam, St. Johns, Suwannee and Union Counties.

For legal titles of parishes and diocesan institutions, consult the Catholic Center.

STATISTICAL OVERVIEW

Personnel	
Bishop	1
Retired Bishops	1
Priests: Diocesan Active in Diocese	65
Priests: Diocesan Active Outside Diocese	6
Priests: Retired, Sick or Absent	20
Number of Diocesan Priests	91
Religious Priests in Diocese	23
Total Priests in Diocese	114
Extern Priests in Diocese	23
Ordinations:	
Diocesan Priests	3
Permanent Deacons in Diocese	32
Total Brothers	3
Total Sisters	115
Parishes	
Parishes	51
With Resident Pastor:	
Resident Diocesan Priests	47
Resident Religious Priests	3
Without Resident Pastor:	
Administered by Deacons	1
Missions	8
Welfare	
Catholic Hospitals	1
Total Assisted	170,369
Homes for the Aged	2
Total Assisted	43,548
Special Centers for Social Services	9
Total Assisted	73,000
Residential Care of Disabled	4
Total Assisted	21
Other Institutions	5
Total Assisted	275
Educational	
Diocesan Students in Other Seminaries	13
Students Religious	6
Total Seminarians	19
High Schools, Diocesan and Parish	3
Total Students	1,915
Elementary Schools, Diocesan and Parish	27
Total Students	8,335
Non-residential Schools for the Disabled	1
Total Students	114
Catechesis/Religious Education:	
High School Students	1,384
Elementary Students	8,600
Total Students under Catholic Instruction	20,367
Teachers in the Diocese:	
Priests	2
Sisters	21
Lay Teachers	684
Vital Statistics	
Receptions into the Church:	
Infant Baptism Totals	2,310
Adult Baptism Totals	410
Received into Full Communion	557
First Communions	2,504
Confirmations	2,143
Marriages:	
Catholic	436
Interfaith	295
Total Marriages	731
Deaths	1,079
Total Catholic Population	160,479
Total Population	1,749,106

Former Bishops—Rt. Revs. AUGUSTIN VEROT, S.S., D.D., consecrated April 25, 1858; Vicar-Apostolic of Florida; translated to the See of Savannah in July, 1861;; appt. Bishop of St. Augustine March, 1870; died June 10, 1876; JOHN MOORE, D.D., consecrated May 13, 1877; died July 30, 1901; WILLIAM JOHN KENNY, D.D., ord. Jan. 15, 1879; consecrated May 18, 1902; died Oct. 23, 1913; M. J. CURLEY, D.D., consecrated June 30, 1914; promoted to See of Baltimore Aug. 10, 1921; died May 16, 1947; Most Revs. PATRICK BARRY, D.D., ord. June 9, 1895; appt. Feb. 22, 1922; consecrated May 3, 1922; died Aug. 13, 1940; JOSEPH P. HURLEY, D.D., ord. May 25, 1919; appt. Aug. 16, 1940; consecrated Oct. 6, 1940; Received Personal title of Archbishop Aug. 18, 1950;; died Oct. 30, 1967; PAUL F. TANNER, D.D. (Retired), ord. May 30, 1931; appt. Titular Bishop of Lamasba, Oct. 18, 1965; appt. Bishop of Saint Augustine, Feb. 21, 1968; retired April 21, 1979; Remained as Administrator to Dec. 4, 1979;; died July 29, 1994; JOHN J. SNYDER, D.D. (Retired), ord. June 9, 1951; appt. Titular Bishop of Forlimpopuli Dec. 19, 1972; consecrated Feb. 2, 1973; appt. Bishop of St. Augustine Oct. 2, 1979; installed Dec. 5, 1979; retired Dec. 12, 2000; Remained as Administrator to Aug. 21, 2001;.

Catholic Center—11625 Old St. Augustine Rd., Jacksonville, 32258. Mailing Address, P.O. Box 24000, Jacksonville, 32241-4000. Tel: 904-262-3200; Fax: 904-262-0698. Office Hours: Mon.-Fri. 9-4:30

Vicar General and Moderator of Curia—Rev. Msgr. VINCENT J. HAUT, V.G., M.S.W.

Chancellor—Rev. KEITH R. BRENNAN, J.C.D.

Secretary to the Bishop—Ms. NANCY MADDEN.

Secretary to the Chancellor—JUDY T. PINSON.

Fiscal Office—VACANT.

Diocesan Tribunal—P.O. Box 24000, Jacksonville, 32241-4000. Tel: 904-262-3200.

Judicial Vicar—Rev. RALPH L. BESENDORFER, J.C.D.

Associate Judges—Rev. Msgr. DANIEL B. LOGAN; Rev. PETER H. COLASURDO, J.C.L.

Defender of the Bond—Rev. JAMES R. BODDIE JR.

Advocates—Revs. TIMOTHY LINDENFELSER; MICHAEL MORGAN.

Promoter of Justice—Administrative Assistants: MARY C. SLEEPER; VERONICA DOSKOCIL.

Diocesan Consultors—Revs. KEITH R. BRENNAN, J.C.D.; ALAN E. BOWER; Rev. Msgr. VINCENT HAUT, V.G., M.S.W.; Revs. WILLIAM A. KELLY, V.F.; TIMOTHY LINDENFELSER; JOSEPH MEEHAN; VICTOR Z. NARIVELIL, C.M.I.

Diocesan Pastoral Council—EDWARD TRENT, Chm., Diocese of St. Augustine Catholic Center, P.O. Box 24000, Jacksonville, 32241-4000. Tel: 904-262-3200; Fax: 904-262-0698.

Presbyteral Council—Most Rev. VICTOR GALEONE, Pres.; Revs. ALAN BOWER, Chm.; JASON TRULL, Vice Chm.; TIMOTHY LINDENFELSER; KEITH R. BRENNAN, J.C.D., Treas.; VICTOR NARIVELIL, C.M.I., Sec.; Rev. Msgr. VINCENT J. HAUT, V.G., M.S.W.; Revs. MICHAEL MORGAN; JOSEPH MEEHAN; WILLIAM A. KELLY, V.F.; ROLAND M. JULIEN, V.F.; JAMES R. BODDIE JR.; TONY SEBRA; THANH THAI NGUYEN.

Deans—Revs. DONAL SULLIVAN, St. Augustine Deanery; ROLAND M. JULIEN, V.F., Gainesville Deanery; ANTHONY G. SEBRA, V.F., North Jacksonville Deanery; WILLIAM A. KELLY, V.F., South Jacksonville Deanery.

Building Commission—Most Rev. VICTOR GALEONE, Chm.; Rev. Msgr. VINCENT J. HAUT, V.G., M.S.W.; Rev. KEITH R. BRENNAN, J.C.D., Chancellor; Rev. Msgr. DANIEL B. LOGAN; Revs. MICHAEL J. LARKIN; GREGORY J. FAY.

Catholic Foundation of Diocese of St. Augustine—Most Rev. VICTOR GALEONE, Pres.; ANNE CONNOLLY, Chm. Bd., P.O. Box 24000, Jacksonville, 32241-4000. Tel: 904-262-3200.

Finance Committee—Rev. Msgr. VINCENT J. HAUT, V.G., M.S.W., Chm., P.O. Box 24000, Jacksonville, 32241-4000. Tel: 904-262-3200.

Insurance Committee, Diocesan—Rev. Msgr. VINCENT J. HAUT, V.G., M.S.W., Chm., P.O. Box 24000, Jacksonville, 32241-4000. Tel: 904-262-3200.

Stewardship Council, Diocesan—Most Rev. VICTOR BENITO GALEONE, P.O. Box 24000, Jacksonville, 32241-4000. Tel: 904-262-3200.

Diocesan Offices and Directors

Apostleship of the Sea—Deacon GJET BAJRAKTARI, Providence Center, 134 E. Church St., Jacksonville, 32202-3130. Tel: 904-356-3104.

Archives of Diocese—VACANT, P.O. Box 24000, Jacksonville, 32241-4000. Tel: 904-262-3200.

Bioethics Commission—Mr. WILLIAM J. TIERNEY, Chm., P.O. Box 24000, Jacksonville, 32241-4000. Tel: 904-262-3200.

African and Native American Ministries—Rev. CLETUS M.S. WATSON, T.O.R., Vicar of the Black Apostolate; ELLA SIMMONS, Dir., 134 E. Church St., Jacksonville, 32202. Tel: 904-854-8205; Fax: 904-854-8207.

Campaign for Human Development—Rev. EDWARD K. ROONEY, Dir., 1606 Blanding Blvd., Middleburg, 32068. Tel: 904-282-0439.

Campus Ministry—PETER W. MORGAN, Campus Min., Jacksonville University, 2800 University Blvd., W., Jacksonville, 32211. Tel: 904-744-3950,; 904-646-2638.

Christian Formation—Sr. LUCILLE CLYNES, D.W, Dir., P.O. Box 24000, Jacksonville, 32241-4000. Tel: 904-262-3200.

Catholic Burse Endowment Fund, Inc.— (Education of Priests), *P.O. Box 24000, Jacksonville, 32241-4000.* Tel: 904-262-3200.

Catholic Charities Bureau, Inc.—Mr. WILLIAM J. TIERNEY, Exec. Dir., P.O. Box 24000, Jacksonville, 32241-4000. Tel: 904-262-3200 See Separate Listing for more details.

Catholic Relief Services—Mr. WILLIAM J. TIERNEY, Dir., P.O. Box 24000, Jacksonville, 32241-4000. Tel: 904-262-3200.

Catholic Women, Council of—Rev. LUKE MCLOUGHLIN, Spiritual Moderator, St. Matthew Church, 1773 Blanding Blvd., Jacksonville, 32210. Tel: 904-388-8698.

Charismatic Renewal—Rev. Msgr. HAROLD F. JORDAN, Liaison (Retired); KATHERINE A. PERNINI, Sec., P.O. Box 13888, Gainesville, 32604. Tel: 352-371-2185.

Civil Institutions—Rev. JOSE MANIYANGAT, St. Mary Parish, P.O. Box 1120, Macclenny, 32063. Tel: 904-259-6414.

Communications Commission—ART MARSHALL, Chm., P.O. Box 24000, Jacksonville, 32241-4000. Tel: 904-262-3200.

Communications, Office of—KATHLEEN BAGG-MORGAN, Dir., P.O. Box 24000, Jacksonville, 32241-4000. Tel: 904-262-3200.

Continuing Education for Priests—Directors: Revs. JOHN GILLESPIE; GUY NOONAN, P.O. Box 13888, Gainesville, 32604. Tel: 352-372-3533.

Cursillos de Cristiandad—Revs. ROBERT L. NAPIER, Spiritual Dir., P.O. Box 207, Interlachen, 32148. Tel: 386-684-2528; TIMOTHY R. LOZIER, Asst. Spiritual Dir., St. Augustine Parish, P.O. Box 13888, Gainesville, 32604. Tel: 904-372-3533; Deacon HAROLD BRODEUR, Asst. Spiritual Dir., P.O. Drawer 330005, Atlantic Beach, 32233. Tel: 904-246-6014.

Disabilities, Ministry of Persons with—PATRICK KENNEDY, Dir., Providence Center, 134 E. Church St., Jacksonville, 32202-3130. Tel: 904-356-0810; Fax: 904-358-7302.

Ecumenism—Rev. Msgr. DANIEL B. LOGAN, Chm., 545 A1A North, Ponte Vedra Beach, 32082. Tel: 904-285-2698.

Educational Services—PATRICIA A. TIERNEY, M.S.Ed., Supt. Schools, P.O. Box 24000, Jacksonville, 32241-4000. Tel: 904-262-3200.

The Guardian of Dreams—Mr. JIM SELZER, Exec. Dir., Providence Center, 134 E. Church St., Jacksonville, 32202-3130. Tel: 904-354-4788; Fax: 904-358-7302.

Family Life, Diocesan Center for—Mr. JOSEPH C. PAYNE, Dir.; Rev. DANIEL CODY, Consultant, P.O. Box 24000, Jacksonville, 32241-4000. Tel: 904-262-3200. Regional Office: St. Vincent's Health System. Tel: 904-308-7474.

Farmworker Services Program—Mrs. CHIQUI MALDONADO, Dir., 40 Sanford St., St. Augustine, 32084. Tel: 904-829-6300.

Florida Catholic Conference—D. MICHAEL MCCARRON, Ph.D., Exec. Dir., 313 S. Calhoun St., Tallahassee, 32301-1807. Tel: 850-222-3803.

Health Care Task Force—Mr. WILLIAM J. TIERNEY, Chm., P.O. Box 24000, Jacksonville, 32241-4000. Tel: 904-262-3200.

Hispanic Ministry—Rev. LUIS FLOREZ, Dir. Ms. ALBA OROZCO, Coord., 134 E. Church St., Jacksonville, 32202. Tel: 904-262-3200; 904-353-3243.

Holy Childhood Association, The—Rev. BRIAN EBURN, Dir., P.O. Box 6310, Fernandina Beach, 32035-6310. Tel: 904-261-3472.

Holy Name Societies—VACANT.

Investment Committee—Rev. Msgr. VINCENT J. HAUT, V.G., M.S.W., Chm.

Justice and Peace Commission—ELIZABETH O'BRIEN, Chm., Providence Center, 134 E. Church St., Jacksonville, 32202-3130. Tel: 904-358-7410; 904-358-7409; Fax: 904-358-7302.

Justice and Reconciliation, Ministry for—Sr. DOROTHEA MURPHY, R.S.M., Dir. Advocacy Office, 1717 N.E. 9th, Suite 123, Gainesville, 32609-3719. Tel: 352-372-6006; Fax: 352-379-9670. Email: justice@gru.net.

Legalization—NANCY VALDIVIESO, Dir., Providence Center, 134 E. Church St., Rm. D-21, Jacksonville, 32202. Tel: 904-354-5904; Fax: 904-356-2092.

Legion of Mary—Rev. JOSE MANIYANGAT, Spiritual Dir., P.O. Box 1120, Macclenny, 32063. Tel: 904-259-6414.

Office of Liturgy—Rev. THOMAS WILLIS, Dir., 8523 Normandy Blvd., Jacksonville, 32221-6701. Tel: 904-786-1192; Fax: 904-786-4224.

Planned Giving Office—Ms. NANCY GEARY, Dir., P.O. Box 24000, Jacksonville, 32241-4000. Tel: 904-262-3200.

Parish Social Ministry—Sr. MARLENE PAYETTE, S.S.J., Dir., Providence Center, 134 E. Church St., Jacksonville, 32202-3130. Tel: 904-354-3416.

Priests' Spirituality Committee—Rev. JOSEPH MEEHAN, P.O. Drawer 330005, Atlantic Beach, 32233. Tel: 904-246-6014.

Propagation of the Faith—Rev. BRIAN EBURN, Dir., P.O. Box 6310, Fernandina Beach, 32035-6310. Tel: 904-261-3472.

Refugee Resettlement—WILLIAM C. BEITZ, Dir., Providence Center, 134 E. Church St., Jacksonville, 32202-3130. Tel: 904-354-3416.

Respect Life Activities—BONNIE SEAVER, Dir.; Rev. THOMAS S. WILLIS, Spiritual Moderator, P.O. Box 24000, Jacksonville, 32241-4000. Tel: 904-262-3200.

Rural Life Director—Rev. MICHAEL PENDERGRAFT, P.O. Box 1179, Live Oak, 32064. Tel: 904-364-1108.

St. Vincent de Paul Societies—Tel: 904-262-3200.

Scouts—Revs. JAMES R. BODDIE JR., Chap.; EDWARD MURPHY, Asst. Chap., P.O. Box 24000, Jacksonville, 32241-4000. Tel: 904-262-3200.

Seminarians—Rev. JOHN H. TETLOW, Dir., P.O. Box 24000, Jacksonville, 32241-4000. Tel: 904-262-3200.

Stewardship, Office of—P.O. Box 24000, Jacksonville, 32241-4000. Tel: 904-262-3200.

Vicar for Clergy—Rev. DONAL P. SULLIVAN, V.F., P.O. Box 24000, Jacksonville, 32241-4000. Tel: 904-262-3200.

Vicar for Religious—Sr. MAUREEN KELLEY, O.P., P.O. Box 24000, Jacksonville, 32241-4000. Tel: 904-262-3200.

Vicar for Senior Priests—Rev. Msgr. EUGENE C. KOHLS, P.A., J.C.D. (Retired), 5201 Atlantic Blvd., #228, Jacksonville, 32207. Tel: 904-348-3983.

Victim Assistance Coordinator—JUDY PINSON. Tel: 904-262-3200. Email: jpinson@dosafl.com.

Vocations—Rev. JOHN H. TETLOW, Dir., P.O. Box 24000, Jacksonville, 32241-4000. Tel: 904-262-3200.

Youth and Young Adult Ministry—134 E. Church St., Jacksonville, 32202. Tel: 904-355-1100; Fax: 904-358-7302.

CLERGY, PARISHES, MISSIONS AND PAROCHIAL SCHOOLS

CITY OF ST. AUGUSTINE
(ST. JOHN'S COUNTY)

1—CATHEDRAL - BASILICA OF ST. AUGUSTINE (1565), [CEM] [JC] Revs. D. Terrence Morgan; Timothy M. Lindenfelser; James Orumpakkatt, C.M.I.; Daniel Shashy (Retired); Deacons Thomas Richards; John Pelletier. In Res., Rev. Msgr. Harold F. Jordan (Retired).
Res.: 35 Treasury St., St. Augustine, 32084. Tel: 904-824-2806; Fax: 904-824-0761.
School—Cathedral Parish School, (Grades K-8), 259 St. George St., St. Augustine, 32084. Tel: 904-824-2861; Fax: 904-829-2059. Sr. Mary Victor Azar, S.S.J., Prin. Sisters 1; Lay Teachers 26; Students 410.
Cathedral Parish Early Education Center—10 San Sabastian Ave., St. Augustine, 32084. Tel: 904-829-2933; Fax: 904-829-9339. Jill Valley, Dir. (Preschool with Before and After School Care) Lay Teachers 15; Students 106.
Catechesis/Religious Program—Tel: 904-829-3338. Sr. Marilyn Dingman, S.S.J., Dir. Students 118.
Mission—Prince of Peace San Marco Ave., St. Augustine, St. Johns Co. 32084.
Mission—St. Benedict the Moor Martin Luther King Ave., St. Augustine, St. Johns Co. 32084.

2—ST. ANASTASIA (1988), Rev. Seamus O'Flynn; Sr. Enda Egan, R.S.M., Pastoral Assoc.; Deacons Bob Lucian; Ron Gagne; Paul Pettie; George Murati.
Mailing Address: 5205 A1A S., St. Augustine, 32080-8006.
Res.: 5319 Fifth St., St. Augustine, 32084. Tel: 904-471-5364 (Office); Fax: 904-471-7448.
Catechesis/Religious Program—Sr. Enda Egan, R.S.M., D.R.E. Students 175.

3—MISSION OF NOMBRE DE DIOS AND SHRINE OF OUR LADY OF LA LECHE (1565), Eric P. Johnson, Dir.
Office—27 Ocean Ave., St. Augustine, 32084. Tel: 904-824-2809; Fax: 904-829-0819.

4—SAN SEBASTIAN (1968), Rev. Thomas P. Walsh; Deacon James Swanson. In Res., Rev. Rene Robert.
Res.: 1112 State Rd. 16, St. Augustine, 32084. Tel: 904-824-6625; Fax: 904-829-0459.
Catechesis/Religious Program—Students 91.

OUTSIDE THE CITY OF ST. AUGUSTINE

ATLANTIC BEACH, DUVAL CO., ST. JOHN THE BAPTIST (1967), Rev. Joseph Meehan; Deacon Harold Brodeur.
Mailing Address: P.O. Drawer 330005, 32233. Tel: 904-246-6014; Fax: 904-246-1219.
Catechesis/Religious Program—Carole Fuchs, D.R.E. Students 208.

BRANFORD, SUWANNEE CO., SAN JUAN MISSION (1976), Rev. Edward W. Murphy.
Mailing Address: P.O. Box 949, 32008. Tel: 386-935-2632; Fax: 386-935-4050.
Catechesis/Religious Program—Students 37.

BUNNELL, FLAGLER CO., ST. STEPHEN (1957), Rev. Mark S. Waters.
Mailing Address: 4600 Belle Terre Pkwy., Palm Coast, 32164.
Res.: Rte. 100, 32110. Tel: 904-445-2246; Fax: 904-445-7808.

CALLAHAN, NASSAU CO., OUR LADY OF CONSOLATION (1974), Rev. Ralph L. Besendorfer, J.C.D.
Res.: 541668 U.S. Hwy. One, P.O. Box 692, 32011. Tel: 904-262-3200.
Catechesis/Religious Program—Tel: 904-879-3662. Sr. Helen Marie Kling, D.C., D.R.E. Students 64.

CHIEFLAND, LEVY CO., ST. JOHN THE EVANGELIST (1981), (Hispanic), Rev. Joseph Maniangat.
Res.: P.O. Box 863, 32644-0863. Tel: 352-493-1561; 352-493-9723 (Office); Fax: 352-493-9258.
Catechesis/Religious Program—Students 45.
Mission—Holy Cross 2090 S.W. Hwy. 19, Cross City, Dixie Co. 32628. Tel: 352-498-5671.

CRESCENT CITY, PUTNAM CO., ST. JOHN THE BAPTIST (1910), [CEM] [JC] Rev. James May.
Res.: P.O. Box 908, 32112. Tel: 386-698-2055; Fax: 386-698-4146. Rev. Justo P. Buitrago Franco.
Catechesis/Religious Program—Students 108.

ELKTON, ST. JOHN CO., ST. AMBROSE (1875), (Minorcan), [CEM] Rev. Patrick Carroll, C.S.Sp., Admin.
Res.: 6070 Church Rd., 32033. Tel: 904-692-1366; Fax: 904-692-1136.
Catechesis/Religious Program—Students 25.
Mission—Our Lady of Good Counsel [CEM] St. Augustine. 5950 SR16, Millcreek, St. Johns Co. 32092. Tel: 940-904-1023.

FERNANDINA BEACH, AMELIA ISLAND, NASSAU CO., ST. MICHAEL'S (1872), [JC] Revs. Brian Eburn; Neil Cornelli.
Res.: 505 Broome St., 32034. Tel: 904-261-3472; Fax: 904-321-1901.
School—St. Michael's Academy, (Grades PreK-8) Tel: 904-321-2102; Fax: 904-321-2330. Sr. Elizabeth Dunn, O.P., Prin.
Catechesis/Religious Program—Lori Kennedy, D.R.E. Students 204.

FLAGLER BEACH, FLAGLER CO., SANTA MARIA DEL MAR (1970), Rev. John H. Tetlow.
Res.: 1618 N. Central Ave., P.O. Box 130, 32136. Tel: 386-439-2791; Fax: 386-439-1362.
Catechesis/Religious Program—Students 142.
Mission—St. Mary's - Korona P.O. Box 1537, Bunnell, 32110. Tel: 386-437-5098.

GAINESVILLE, ALACHUA CO.

1—ST. AUGUSTINE (1923),, (Student Center) Revs. John D. Gillespie; Guy F. Noonan; Timothy R. Lozier. In res., Rev. Jose L. Mesa, S.J. (Dominican Republic).
Res.: 1738 W. University Ave., P.O. Box 13888, 32604. Tel: 352-372-3533; Fax: 352-378-9010.
Catechesis/Religious Program—Thomas Rinkoski, Dir. Youth Min. Students 200.

2—HOLY FAITH (1973), Revs. John M. Phillips; Ignatius J. Plathanam, C.M.I. (India).
Res.: 700 N.W. 39 Rd., 32607. Tel: 352-376-5405; Fax: 352-375-7568.
Catechesis/Religious Program—Tel: 352-376-5405; Fax: 352-375-7568. Carmen M. McMahon, D.R.E. Students 287.

3—ST. PATRICK'S (1887), Revs. Roland M. Julien, V.F.; Jose Paruvanani. In Res., Revs. Robert J. McDermott; Conrad Cowart.
Res.: 500 N.E. 16th Ave., 32601. Tel: 352-372-4641; 352-376-0575; Fax: 352-376-0575.
School—Tel: 352-376-9878; Fax: 352-371-6177. Elaine Baumgartner, Prin. Lay Teachers 28; Students 548.
Catechesis/Religious Program—Tel: 352-376-9878, Ext. 60. Diane St. Onge, D.R.E. Students 81.
Mission—St. Philip Neri U.S. 301 S., Hawthorne, Alachua Co. 32640.

4—QUEEN OF PEACE (1987), [JC] Revs. Jeffrey A. McGowan; Alberto Esposito.
Church: 10900 S.W. 24th Ave., 32607. Tel: 352-332-6279; Fax: 352-331-7347.
School—Tel: 352-332-8808. Sr. Nancy Elder, I.H.M., Prin. Students 141.
Catechesis/Religious Program—Tel: 352-332-6279, Ext. 17. Sr. Beatrice Caulson, I.H.M., D.R.E. Students 491.

GREEN COVE SPRINGS, CLAY CO., SACRED HEART (1874), [CEM] Revs. Donal Sullivan; John Guarnizo.
Res.: 7190 Hwy. 17 S., P.O. Box 276, 32043. Tel: 904-284-3811; Fax: 904-529-8845.
Catechesis/Religious Program—Tel: 904-284-9983; Fax: 904-284-1929. Mrs. Sherry Latta-Raines, D.R.E. Students 575.

HIGH SPRINGS, ALACHUA CO., ST. MADELEINE SOPHIE PARISH (1925), Rev. Edward W. Murphy.

Mailing Address: P.O. Box 3220, 32655-3220. Tel: 386-454-2358; Fax: 386-454-4985.
Res.: 3210 NE Santa Fe Blvd., 32643. Tel: 386-454-2358; Fax: 386-454-4985.
Catechesis/Religious Program—Students 81.

INTERLACHEN, PUTNAM CO., ST. JOHN'S MISSION (1968), [JC] Rev. Robert L. Napier. In Res., Rev. Richard J. Powers, S.J. (New York).
Res.: P.O. Box 207, 32148. Tel: 386-684-2528; Fax: 386-684-3819.
Catechesis/Religious Program—Students 37.

JACKSONVILLE BEACH, DUVAL CO., ST. PAUL'S (1930), Revs. William A. Kelly, V.F.; Lawrence Mulinda; Dung Quang Bui.
Res.: 224 N. Fifth St., 32250. Tel: 904-249-2600; Fax: 904-249-3635.
School—Tel: 904-249-5394; Fax: 904-241-2911. Mrs. Katherine Boice, Prin. Lay Teachers 30; Students 550.
Catechesis/Religious Program—Tel: 904-249-2660; Fax: 904-249-8085. Mary Coleman, D.R.E. Students 670.

JACKSONVILLE, DUVAL CO.

1—ASSUMPTION (South Jacksonville) (1913), Revs. Frederick R. Parke; Anthony Dai Viet Mai; Jan Ligeza. In Res., Rev. Luis Florez, Dir., Hispanic Apostolate.
Res.: 2403 Atlantic Blvd., 32207. Tel: 904-398-1963; Fax: 904-398-6115.
School—Tel: 904-398-1774; Fax: 904-398-6712. Dr. William E. Howes, Prin. Lay Teachers 33; Students 600.
Catechesis/Religious Program—Mrs. Kathleen K. Lyons, D.R.E. Students 69.

2—BLESSED TRINITY (1957), Revs. Keith R. Brennan, J.C.D.; Jason Trull.
Res.: 10472 Beach Blvd., P.O. Box 16466, 32246. Tel: 904-641-1414; Fax: 904-641-8171.
School—(Grades PreK-6) Tel: 904-641-6458; Fax: 904-645-3762. Marie Davis, Prin. Students 212.
Catechesis/Religious Program—Tel: 904-646-4320. Mrs. Aixa Feliciano, D.R.E. Students 189.

3—CHRIST THE KING (1954), Revs. Thanh T. Nguyen; Rouville Fisher; Cornelius J. Carr, S.J.; Deacon David MacNamara.
Res.: 742 Arlington Rd., 32211. Tel: 904-724-0080; Fax: 904-724-3340.
School—Tel: 904-724-2954; Fax: 904-721-8004. Mrs. Janet Morton, Prin. Lay Teachers 31; Teachers Aids 4; Students 509.
Catechesis/Religious Program—Tel: 904-724-9617; Fax: 904-721-8585. Lucille Guzzone, D.R.E. & Dir.. Students 252.

4—CHURCH OF THE CRUCIFIXION (1974), (African American), Rev. Cletus M. Watson, T.O.R.
Rectory—Mailing Address & Rectory: 6079 Bagley Rd., 32209-1805. Tel: 904-765-5284; Fax: 904-765-1680.
Catechesis/Religious Program—Tel: 904-765-2851. Students 31.

5—ST. FRANCIS CHOE CHAPEL (1997), (Korean), Unassigned.
Res.: 8051 Rampart Rd., 32244. Tel: 904-573-1833; Fax: 904-573-1833.

6—HOLY FAMILY (1974), Revs. Gregory Fay; John O'Hara.
Office—9800 Baymeadows Rd., 32256. Tel: 904-641-5838; Fax: 904-641-9704.
School—Tel: 904-645-9875; Fax: 904-899-6060. Michael P. Corrigan, Prin. Lay Teachers 16; Students 247.
Catechesis/Religious Program—Lisa Wilson, D.R.E. Students 260.

7—HOLY ROSARY (1921), Revs. Michael Koncik, C.SS.R.; William Spillane, C.SS.R.; Bro. Martin Smith, C.SS.R.
Res.: 746 W. 41st St., 32206. Tel: 904-764-3241; Fax: 904-765-4995.
School—Sisters of Notre Dame, 4631 Brentwood Ave., 32206. Tel: 904-765-6522; 904-353-6933; Fax: 904-765-9486. Sr. Dianne Rumschlag, S.N.D., Prin. (Toledo Prov.) Sisters 4; Lay Teachers 10; Students 174.
Catechesis/Religious Program—Students 25.

8—HOLY SPIRIT (1966), Rev. Msgr. James J. Heslin; Deacon Gjet Bajraktari.
Res.: 11665 Fort Caroline Rd., 32225. Tel: 904-641-7244; Fax: 904-641-7266.
School—(Grades PreK-8) Tel: 904-642-9165. John Luciano, Prin. Lay Teachers 17; Students 267.
Catechesis/Religious Program—Judy Altmiller, D.R.E. Students 323.

9—IMMACULATE CONCEPTION (1854), [CEM] [JC] Revs. Antonio Leon; Warren Keene.
Res.: 121 E. Duval St., P.O. Box 100, 32201. Tel: 904-359-0331; Fax: 904-356-8133.
Catechesis/Religious Program—Students 42.

10—ST. JOSEPH'S (1883), [CEM] Revs. Daniel Cody; Ananda Prasad, M.S.F.S. (India).
Res.: 11730 Old St. Augustine Rd., 32258-2002. Tel: 904-268-5422; Fax: 904-292-0248.
School—Tel: 904-268-6688; Fax: 904-268-8989. Mrs. Rhonda Rose, Prin. Lay Teachers 26; Students 600.
Catechesis/Religious Program—Maria Daidone, D.R.E. Students 517.

11—MARY QUEEN OF HEAVEN (1988), Rev. Caesar Russo.
Res.: 9401 Staples Mill Dr., 32244. Tel: 904-777-1272; Fax: 904-778-7691.
Catechesis/Religious Program—Tel: 904-777-3168. Students 115.

12—ST. MATTHEW'S (Lake Shore) (1949), Revs. Luke McLoughlin; Daniel B. Devore.
Res.: 1773 Blanding Blvd., 32210. Tel: 904-388-8698; Fax: 904-384-1233.
School—Tel: 904-387-4401; Fax: 904-388-4404. Mrs. Cathy Tuerk, Prin. Lay Teachers 23; Students 291.
Catechesis/Religious Program—Tel: 904-388-1207. Onie Lee, D.R.E. Students 165.

13—MOST HOLY REDEEMER (1962), Rev. Thomas S. Willis.
Res.: 8523 Normandy Blvd., 32221-6701. Tel: 904-786-1192; Fax: 904-786-4224.
Catechesis/Religious Program—Sharon Tomore, D.R.E. Students 116.

14—OUR LADY OF THE ANGELS (1917), [CEM] Rev. Joseph Notarpole.
Res.: 430 Crystal St., 32254. Tel: 904-389-4878; Fax: 904-389-4878.

15—ST. PATRICK (1959), Rev. Ronald A. Camarda.
Res.: 1429 Broward Rd., 32218. Tel: 904-768-2593; Fax: 904-768-2251.
School—Sisters of Mercy, (Grades K-8) Tel: 904-768-6323; Fax: 904-768-2144. Sr. Carmel O'Callahan, R.S.M., Prin. Lay Teachers 14; Students 196.
Catechesis/Religious Program—Students 140.

16—ST. PAUL'S (1923), Revs. Thomas K. Sullivan; James J. Corry, C.S.Sp.
Res.: 2609 Park St., 32204. Tel: 904-387-2554; Fax: 904-388-6871.
School—Tel: 904-387-2841; Fax: 904-387-1781. Mr. John C. Lippincott, Prin. Lay Teachers 21; Students 215.
Catechesis/Religious Program—Students 240.

17—ST. PIUS THE FIFTH (1919), (African American), Rev. Cletus M. Watson, T.O.R.; Deacon Michael Leahy, Admin.
Res.: 2110 Blue Ave., 32209. Tel: 904-354-1501; Fax: 904-354-7240.
School—1470 W. 13th St., 32209. Tel: 904-354-2613; Fax: 904-356-4522. Sr. Elise Kennedy, S.S.J., Prin. Sisters 3; Lay Teachers 14; Students 181.
Catechesis/Religious Program—Tel: 904-354-1501; Fax: 904-354-7240. Students 33.

18—PRINCE OF PEACE (1970), Rev. Michael J. Larkin.
Res.: 6320 Bennett Rd., 32216. Tel: 904-733-6860; Fax: 904-367-0215.
Catechesis/Religious Program—Tel: 904-733-6011. Students 73.

19—RESURRECTION (1959), Rev. Msgr. Vincent J. Haut, V.G., M.S.W.; Rev. Michael Thompson; Deacon Stan Grenn.
Res.: 3383 University Blvd. N., 32277. Tel: 904-744-0833; Fax: 904-744-7235.
School—Tel: 904-744-1266; Fax: 904-744-5800. Rosemary Nowotny, Prin. Lay Teachers 16; Students 257.
Catechesis/Religious Program—Tel: 904-744-5800. Noreen Thurson, D.R.E. Students 116.

20—SACRED HEART (1959), Revs. Anthony G. Sebra, V.F.; Victor Z. Narivelil, C.M.I.
Res.: 5752 Blanding Blvd., 32244. Tel: 904-771-2152; Fax: 904-573-8816.
School—Sisters of Mercy (Clonakilty, Ireland), Tel: 904-771-5800; Fax: 904-771-5323. Sr. Josephine O'Leary, R.S.M., Prin. Sisters 1; Lay Teachers 30; Students 557.
Catechesis/Religious Program—Tel: 904-771-2152, Ext. 23; Fax: 904-771-5323. Sr. Mary of Mercy, D.R.E. Students 222.

21—SAN JOSE (1959), Revs. James Moss; Rodolfo Godinez.
Res.: 3619 Toledo Rd., 32217. Tel: 904-733-1630; Fax: 904-731-4335.
School—Sisters of Mercy, Tel: 904-733-2510; Fax: 904-733-2510. Mrs. Jan Magiera, Prin. Sisters 1; Lay Teachers 28; Students 510.
Catechesis/Religious Program—Tel: 904-733-1630, Ext. 18; Fax: 904-731-4335. Sr. Ambrose Cruise, R.S.M., D.R.E. Students 150.

22—SYRIAC ANTIOCHIAN-RITE MISSION ST. EPHREM (1986), Closed. For inquiries for parish records contact the chancery.

KEYSTONE HEIGHTS, CLAY CO., ST. WILLIAM (1948), [JC] Rev. Michael S. Williams.
Res.: P.O. Box 721, 32656. Tel: 352-473-4136; Fax: 352-473-4119.
Catechesis/Religious Program—Tel: 352-473-4223. Students 85.

KORONA, FLAGLER CO., ST. MARY'S (1914), (Polish), Rev. Slawomir S. Podsiedlik, O.C.D.
Mailing Address: P.O. Box 1537, Bunnell, 32110-1537. Tel: 386-437-5098; 386-439-2791; Fax: 386-437-5098; 386-439-1362.
Res.: 801 N. Central Ave., P.O. Box 130, Flagler Beach, 32136. Tel: 386-439-2791; Fax: 386-439-1362.

LAKE CITY, COLUMBIA CO., EPIPHANY (1965), Revs. Michael Morse; George Kuruvilla, C.M.I.
Res.: 1905 SW Epiphany Ct., 32025. Tel: 386-752-4470; Fax: 386-752-4652.
School—Tel: 386-752-2320; Fax: 386-752-2364. Ms. Carol Chionzoli, Prin. Lay Teachers 13; Students 127.
Catechesis/Religious Program—Tel: 386-752-3893. Students 93.

LIVE OAK, SUWANNEE CO., ST. FRANCIS XAVIER (1979), Rev. W. Michael Pendergraft.
Res.: P.O. Box 1179, 32064. Tel: 386-364-1108; Fax: 386-364-1836.
Catechesis/Religious Program—Tel: 386-362-7287. Nancy Roberts, D.R.E. Students 49.
Mission—St. Therese of Jesus P.O. Box 890, Jasper, Hamilton Co. 32052. Tel: 386-364-1108.

MACCLENNY, BAKER CO., ST. MARY'S (1960), (Vietnamese-Filipino), [JC] Rev. Jose Maniyangat.
Res.: 104 Jacqueline Cir., P.O. Box 1120, 32063. Tel: 904-259-6414; Fax: 904-259-9712.
Catechesis/Religious Program—Angela Boyette, D.R.E. Students 60.
Chaplaincy—Tel: 904-964-8125. Northeast Florida State Hospital, Macclenny; Union Correctional Institute, Raiford; and Florida State Prison, Starke.

MIDDLEBURG, CLAY CO., ST. LUKE'S (1982), Rev. Edward Rooney.
Res.: 1606 Blanding Blvd., 32068. Tel: 904-282-0439; Fax: 904-291-9711.
Catechesis/Religious Program—Linda Kidwell, D.R.E. Students 327.

ORANGE PARK, CLAY CO., ST. CATHERINE'S (1877), Revs. James R Boddie Jr.; Jose Kulathinal, C.M.I. (India).
Res.: 1649 Kingsley Ave., 32073. Tel: 904-264-0577; Fax: 904-264-7999.
Catechesis/Religious Program—Tel: 904-264-2470. Bro. Dominic M. O'Brien, F.M.S., D.R.E. Students 669.
Mission—Moosehaven Chapel 1700 Park Ave., Clay Co. 32073. Tel: 904-278-1210.

PALATKA, PUTNAM CO., ST. MONICA'S (1858), [CEM] Rev. Joseph F. Finlay.
Office:—114 S. 4th St., 32177. Tel: 386-325-9777; Fax: 386-329-1960.
Catechesis/Religious Program—Tel: 386-325-7777; Fax: 386-325-9777. Rev. Joseph F. Finlay, D.R.E. Students 75.

PALM COAST, FLAGER CO., ST. ELIZABETH ANN SETON (1978), [CEM] Revs. Mark S. Waters; Michael Morgan; Sebastian Kaithamatton, C.M.I.; Deacons John Holmes, Pastoral Min.; James Casapulla, Pastoral Min.; W. Mike Moody, Pastoral Min.
Res.: 4600 Belle Terre Pkwy., 32164. Tel: 386-445-2246; Fax: 386-445-7808.
Catechesis/Religious Program—Tel: 386-446-5854. Mrs. Rosaire Downey, D.R.E.; Mrs. Dee Casapulla, D.R.E. Students 55; Students 655.

PONTE VEDRA BEACH, ST. JOHN CO., OUR LADY STAR OF THE SEA (1972), Rev. Msgr. Daniel B. Logan; Rev. Christopher Liguori; Deacons Anthony Marini; Frank Harla.
Mailing Address: 545 Hwy. A1A N., 32082. Tel: 904-285-2698; Fax: 904-285-2502.
School—Preschool, Tel: 904-285-2698, Ext. 2; Fax: 904-273-9740. Mrs. Laurie Kelley, Dir.
School—Palmer Catholic Academy, Tel: 904-543-8515; Fax: 904-543-8750. Mrs. Linda Earp, Prin.
Catechesis/Religious Program—Tel: 904-285-2698, Ext. 5; Fax: 904-273-0590. Students 467.

ST. AUGUSTINE SHORES, ST. JOHN CO., CORPUS CHRISTI (1975), [CEM] Rev. William C. Mooney.
Res.: P.O. Box 3064, 32085. Tel: 904-797-4842; Fax: 904-797-2746.
Catechesis/Religious Program—Students 131.

STARKE, BRADFORD CO., ST. EDWARD'S (1941), Unassigned.
Res.: 441 N. Temple Ave., 32091-3207. Tel: 904-964-6155; Fax: 904-964-1411.
Catechesis/Religious Program—Students 8.

SWITZERLAND, ST. JOHN CO., SAN JUAN DEL RIO (1977), Rev. Edward Booth; Deacons James Fugit; Stan Barrows; Lawrence Geinosky.
Res.: 1714-3 State Rd., No. 13, 32259. Tel: 904-287-1589; 904-287-0519 (Office); Fax: 904-287-1504.
School—1714-2 State Rd. 13, 32259. Tel: 904-287-8081; Fax: 904-287-4574. Lay Teachers 17; Students 207.
Catechesis/Religious Program—Tel: 904-287-2801. Students 550.

WILLISTON, LEVY CO., HOLY FAMILY (1970), Rev. Alan E. Bower.
Res.: 17353 N.E. 27 A, 32696. Tel: 352-528-2893; Fax: 352-528-6002.
Catechesis/Religious Program—Students 98.

Mission—St. Anthony the Abbot P.O. Box 1070, Inglis, Levy Co. 34449. Tel: 352-447-4573; Fax: 352-447-4573.

Special Assignment:
Revs.—
Brennan, Keith R., J.C.D., Chancellor
Cowart, Conrad, Chap., Shands Hospital, 500 North East 16th Ave., Gainesville, 32601.
Gagan, Philip R., Pastoral Care/St. Vincent's Medical Center, 1800 Barrs St., 32254.
Houle, Michael R., M.A., M.Ed., M.Div., Pres., Bishop Kenny High School, P.O. Box 5544, 32247.
McDermott, Robert, Chap., Prison Ministry, Shands Hospital, 500 North East 16th Ave., Gainesville, 32601.
Palazzolo, Anthony P., 101 Marsh Cove Ln., Ponte Vedra Beach, 32082. Tel: 904-280-5422 Diocese of Mandeville, Jamaica
Young, Dennis M., V.A. Medical Center, 1601 S.W. Archer Rd., Gainesville, 32608-1197.

On Duty Outside the Diocese:
Revs.—
Cusick, Timothy S., St. Patrick's Seminary, 320 Middlefield Rd., Menlo Park, CA 94025
Dux, John H., 311 Ayers Cir., Summerville, SC 29485.
Glisson, Nicholas J., P.O. Box 817, Pleasanton, CA 94566.
Moore, Frederick Thomas, Pensacola, FL
O'Neal, James E., P.O. Box 10321, Fort Jackson, SC 29207
Walsh, Flannan J.

Absent on Sick Leave:
Revs.—
Cody, Thomas
Palaroan, Moises
Pollard, John L.
Rene, Robert
Reynolds, John

Retired:
Rev. Msgrs.—
Conesa, Diego
Danaher, Mortimer, 7843 Fawn Oaks Ct., 32256.
Danaher, T. Leo, P.O. Box 330929, Atlantic Beach, 32233.
Jordan, Harold F., 35 Treasury St., St. Augustine, 32084.
Kohls, Eugene C., P.A., J.C.D., 5201 Atlantic Blvd., # 228, 32207.
Lenihan, John J., 102 Hammock Circle, St. Augustine, 32095.
Madden, Patrick M., 4 Casa San Pedro, 1714 State Rd. 13, Ste. 6, Jacksonville 32259.
Revs.—
Colasurdo, Peter, 3800 Michael's Landing East, 32224.
Couture, Fernand, Hwy. 17, Orange Park, 32073.
Ducci, Alex, Poste Italiane BG Centro, C.P. 127, 24100 Bergamo, Italy.
Haryasz, Francis S., 244 St. Thomas St., St. Augustine, 32095.
Hochheim, William A., Casa San Pedro, 1714 State Rd. 13 Ste. 6, 32259.
O'Flaherty, John P., P.O. Box 1942, Flagler Beach, 32136.
O'Regan, Denis, The Overlook, 10550 Baymeadows Rd., # 718, 32256.
Revilla, Francisco, Suecia 100-3-3B, 28022 Madrid, Spain.
Shashy, Daniel, 35 Treasury St., St. Augustine, 32084.

INSTITUTIONS LOCATED IN THE DIOCESE

[A] HIGH SCHOOLS, DIOCESAN

ST. AUGUSTINE. *St. Joseph Academy*, 155 State Rd. 207, 32084. Tel: 904-824-0431; Fax: 904-826-4477. Email: sjaweb.org. Web: www.sjaweb.org. Mike Heubeck, Prin. Day School. Sisters 2; Lay Teachers 24; Students 285.

JACKSONVILLE. *Bishop John J. Snyder High School*, 5001 Samaritan Way, 32221. Tel: 904-771-1029; Fax: 904-908-8988. Email: yazdiya@bellsouth.net. Web: www.bishopsnyder.org. David Yazdiya, Prin. Lay Teachers 12; Students 162; Total Staff 24.

Bishop Kenny High School, 1055 Kingman Ave., P.O. Box 5544, 32247. Tel: 904-398-7545; Fax: 904-398-5728. Rev. Michael R. Houle, M.A., M.Ed., M.Div., Pres.; Mr. Todd Orlando, M.Ed., Prin.; Robert West, M.Ed., Vice Prin. & Athletic Dir.; Mrs. Mary DeSalvo, M.Ed., Vice Prin.; Dave Williams, M.Ed., Dean of Students. Priests 1; Sisters 1; Lay Teachers 93; Students 1,550.

[B] ELEMENTARY SCHOOLS, INTERPAROCHIAL

MIDDLEBURG. *Annunciation School*, (Grades PreK-8), 1610 Blanding Blvd., 32068. Tel: 904-282-0504; Fax: 904-282-6808. Email: suea@annunciationcatholic.org. Web: www.annunciationcatholic.org. Susan Altieri, Prin. Interparish school composed of students from Sacred Heart, Green Cove Springs; St. Catherine's, Orange Park; and St. Luke, Middleburg. Lay Teachers 21; Students 375.

[C] CATHOLIC CHARITIES

ST. AUGUSTINE. *Catholic Charities Regional Office*, 225 W. King St., P.O. Box 543, 32085. Tel: 904-829-6300; Fax: 904-829-0494. Email: info@ccbstaug.org. Web: ccbstaug.org. Rebecca Stringer, COO.

GAINESVILLE. *Catholic Charities Regional Office* Emergency services, counseling, respite care, and adoptions. , 1717 N.E. 9th St., 32609. Tel: 352-372-0294; Fax: 352-371-3157. Email: cathchar@juno.com. Web: www.ccbgainesville.org. Gwain Davis, Dir.

JACKSONVILLE. *Catholic Charities Bureau, Inc.*, 11625 Old St. Augustine Rd., P.O. Box 24000, 32241-4000. Tel: 904-262-3200; Fax: 904-262-0372. Email: btierney@dosafl.com. Web: www.ccbjax.org. Mr. William J. Tierney, Diocesan Dir. Tel: 904-262-3200. Total Assisted 60,000; Total Staff 200.

Catholic Charities Regional Office, 134 E. Church St., 32202. Tel: 904-354-4846, Ext. 233; Fax: 904-354-4718. Email: bbeitz@ccbjax.org. Web: www.ccbjax.org. William C. Beitz, COO. Provides counseling services for substance abuse, marriage, families, maternity & aging. Also, emergency financial assistance for housing/utilities, food pantry, adoption programs, & financial assistance for housing opportunities for persons with AIDS, and refugee resettlement.

New Hope Program, 134 East Church St., 32202. Tel: 904-354-3464; Fax: 904-358-7302. Email: sgrenn@ccbjax.org. Deacon Stanley Grenn, Dir. Total Assisted Annually 700; Total Staff 2.

Office of Aging Services, 134 E. Church St., 32202-3130. Tel: 904-354-4846; Fax: 904-354-4718. Email: kstrayer@ccbjax.org. Ms. Kathryn Strayer, L.C.S.W., Dir.

Office of AIDS Ministry, 134 E. Church St., 32202-3130. Tel: 904-354-4846, Ext. 229; Fax: 904-354-4718. Email: mpayette@ccbjax.org. Sr. Marlene Payette, S.S.J., Dir.

Office of Justice and Peace, 134 E. Church St., 32202-3130. Tel: 904-358-7409; 904-358-7410; Fax: 904-358-7302. Email: dstephen@ccbjax.org.

[D] SPECIAL APOSTOLATES

ST. AUGUSTINE. *Religious Education for Catholic Deaf and Blind*, 30 Ocean Ave., 32084-2813. Tel: 904-825-4272 (Voice/TDD); Fax: 904-825-4272. Email: cathdb@juno.com. Web: www.catholicdeaf.org; www.catholicblind.org. Florida School for the Deaf and Blind.

JACKSONVILLE. *L'Arche Harbor House I, II, III and IV*, 700 Arlington Rd., 32211. Tel: 904-721-5992; Fax: 904-721-7143. Email: larchfl@aol.com. Patrick J. Mayhew, Exec. Dir. A community residence for mentally retarded adults. Total Staff 17; Total in Residence 21.

Morning Star School, 725 Mickler Rd., 32211. Tel: 904-721-2144; Fax: 904-721-1040. Email: taschliman@juno.com. Web: www.morningstar-jax.com. Dr. Teri Aschliman, Prin. A school for exceptional children. Lay Teachers 11; Students 114.

[E] GENERAL HOSPITALS

JACKSONVILLE. *St. Vincent's Health System, Inc.*, 1801 Barrs St., Ste. 600, 32204. Tel: 904-308-4001. John J Maher, Pres. & CEO. Statistics are reported under St. Vincent's Medical Center, Inc.

St. Vincent's Medical Center, Inc., 1800 Barrs St., P.O. Box 2982, 32203. Tel: 904-308-7300; Fax: 904-308-7326. Email: jnorman@stvincentshealth.com. Jeffrey K. Norman, Exec. V.P. & COO. Daughters of Charity of St. Vincent de Paul, Member St. Vincent's Health System, Inc. Nurses 818; Total Staff 3,712; Bed Capacity 528; Bassinets 30; Outpatients 146,191; Inpatients 24,178.

St. Vincent's Foundation, Inc. Tel: 904-308-7306; Fax: 904-308-7573.

St. Vincent's Ambulatory Care, Inc. Tel: 904-308-2110; Fax: 904-396-3646.

St. Catherine Laboure Manor, Inc. Tel: 904-308-4702; Fax: 904-308-2987.

[F] HOMES FOR AGING

JACKSONVILLE. *All Saints Nursing Home & Rehabilitation Center, Inc.*, 5888 Blanding Blvd., 32244. Tel: 904-772-1220; Fax: 904-772-6334. Email: codonnell@allsaintsnursing.org. Web: www.allsaintsnursing.org. Connie O'Donnell, Admin.; Deacon Joe Johnson, Chap. Physical Therapy, Speech Therapy & Occupational Therapy Available. Total Assisted 42,664.

Casa San Pedro, 1714 State Rd. 13, Ste. 6, 32259. Tel: 904-230-2562; Fax: 904-230-2563. Email: csanpedr@bellsouth.net. Sr. Mary Ruth Mustonen, O.S.B.

St. Catherine Laboure Manor, 1750 Stockton St., 32204 Tel: 904-308-4700; Fax: 904-308-2987. Email mgartlan@jaxhealth.com. Web: www.stvincentshealth.com. Long term health care Skilled Nursing Facility. Bed Capacity 240; Sisters 3; Total Staff 239; Patients Assisted Annually 884.

[G] CATHOLIC CHARITIES OFFICE OF HOUSING

JACKSONVILLE. *Jacksonville, Family Housing Management Co.*, 134 E. Church St., 32202. Tel: 904-632-1255; Fax: 904-632-2135. Email: fahomaco@aol.com. Alma C. Ballard, Exec. Dir.

Jacksonville, Office of Housing Development, 134 E. Church St., 32202. Tel: 904-632-1255; Fax: 904-632-2135. Alma C. Ballard, Exec. Dir.

Hurley Manor I, 3333 University Blvd. N., 32277. Tel: 904-744-6022; Fax: 904-744-6037. Joyce Sommers, Mgr. Parent Co., Catholic Charities Housing Association of Jacksonville, Inc.

Hurley Manor II, 3335 University Blvd. N., 32277. Tel: 904-744-6022; Fax: 904-744-6037. Joyce Sommers, Mgr. Parent Co., Diocesan Housing Bureau, Inc.

Barry Manor, 1000 Husson Ave., Palatka, 32177. Tel: 386-328-5137; Fax: 386-328-5138. Marilyn Canup, Mgr. Parent Co., Palatka Retirement Villas, Inc.

Providence Center, 134 E. Church St., 32202. Tel: 904-632-1255; Fax: 904-632-2135.

San Jose Manor I, 3630 Galicia Rd., 32217. Tel: 904-739-0555; Fax: 904-739-0559. T. William Glocker, Pres.; Kathleen Garrett, Mgr. (Parent Company: Housing Association of the Diocese of St. Augustine.)

San Jose Manor II, 3622 Galicia Rd., 32217. Tel: 904-739-0555; Fax: 904-739-0559. Ruby Peters, Pres.; Kathleen Garrett, Mgr. (Parent Company: San Jose Catholic Housing Assoc., Inc.)

[H] MONASTERIES AND RESIDENCES OF PRIESTS AND BROTHERS

JACKSONVILLE. *Maryknoll Fathers & Brothers*, 2243 Saragossa Ave., 32217-2685. Tel: 904-739-1112; Fax: 904-739-9083. Email: mklflorida@aol.com. Web: maryknoll.org. Total in Residence 2. In Res. Revs. Lawrence F. McCulloch, M.M.; Michael J. Sloboda, M.M.

[I] CONVENTS AND RESIDENCES FOR SISTERS

ST. AUGUSTINE. *Motherhouse of the Sisters of St. Joseph of St. Augustine, Florida*, 241 St. George St., P.O. Box 3506, 32085. Tel: 904-824-1752; Fax: 904-826-0949. Email: ssjfl@aol.com. Web: ballingerr.xray.ufl.edu/sisters.html. Sr. Ann Kuhn, S.S.J., Gen. Supr. Professed Sisters 97.

The Sisters of St. Joseph Continuing Community Support Trust Fund. Tel: 904-824-1752; Fax: 904-826-0949.

[J] RETREAT HOUSES

BUNNELL. *Discalced Carmelite Fathers of Florida*, 141 Carmelite Dr., 32110. Tel: 386-437-2910; Fax: 386-437-5125. Revs. Joseph F. Zawada, O.C.D.; Benedict Jurkiewicz; Slawomir S. Podsiedlik, O.C.D., Prior; Bro. Anthony Gemmato, O.C.D. Total Staff 4.

JACKSONVILLE. *Marywood Center for Spirituality and Ministry*, 1714-5 State Rd. 13, 32259. Tel: 904-287-2525; Fax: 904-287-9738. Email: info@marywoodcenter.org. Web: www.marywoodcenter.org. Sr. Kathleen Power, Prog. Coord. Total Staff 16.

[K] MISCELLANEOUS

ST. AUGUSTINE. *Nombre de Dios House of Prayer*, 34 Ocean Ave., 32084. Tel: 904-824-4831; Fax: 904-824-7205. Rev. Msgr. Harold Jordan, Spiritual Dir.

Sisters of St. Joseph's Architectural Stained Glass, 2745 Industry Center Rd., #6, 32084. Tel: 904-823-1918; Fax: 904-823-1918. Email: liteart@aol.com. Web: www.ssjstainedglass.com. Sr. Diane Couture, S.S.J., Dir.

GAINESVILLE. *The Center for the Study of the Passion of Christ and the Holy Shroud,* 1738 W. University, 32603. Tel: 352-372-3533; Fax: 352-378-0435. Mrs. Gerry DeGraff, Exec. Sec.

Spirit Radio of North Florida, Inc., 500 N.E. 16th Ave., 32601. Tel: 352-372-4641; Fax: 352-376-0575. Email: rolandjulien@hotmail.com. Web: www.wwlc.org. Rev. Roland M. Julien, V.F.

JACKSONVILLE. *The Florida Catholic AIDS Network,* Catholic Charities, 134 E. Church St., 32202-3130. Tel: 904-354-4846, Ext. 229; Fax: 904-354-4718. Email: mpayette@ccbjax.org.

[L] NEWMAN CENTERS

ST. AUGUSTINE. *Flagler College Newman Center* c/o Cathedral of St. Augustine, 35 Treasury St., 32084. Tel: 904-461-5795. Email: ccfis@juno.com. Rev. D. Terrence Morgan.

JACKSONVILLE. *Jacksonville Univ. & Univ. of North Florida Catholic Campus Ministry* 4567 St. Johns Bluff Rd. S., 32224. Tel: 904-620-2837, Ext. 7258; Fax: 904-620-1057. Email: pmorgan@unf.edu. Web: www.catholiccampusmin.com. Mr. Pete Morgan, Dir. Catholic Campus Ministry.

RELIGIOUS INSTITUTES OF MEN REPRESENTED IN THE DIOCESE

For further details refer to the corresponding bracketed number in the Religious Institutes of Men or Women section.

[0275]—*Carmelites of Mary Immaculate*—C.M.I.
[1330]—*Congregation of the Mission*—C.M.
[0260]—*Discalced Carmelite Friars*—O.C.D.
[0650]—*Holy Ghost Fathers*—C.S.Sp.
[0690]—*Jesuit Fathers and Brothers*—S.J.
[0780]—*Marist Fathers*—S.M.
[0800]—*Maryknoll*—M.M.
[0920]—*Oblates of St. Francis de Sales*—O.S.F.S.
[1070]—*Redemptorist Fathers*—C.SS.R.
[0560]—*Third Order Regular of St. Francis*—T.O.R.

RELIGIOUS INSTITUTES OF WOMEN REPRESENTED IN THE DIOCESE

[0230]—*Benedictine Sisters of Pontifical Jurisdiction*—O.S.B.
[0685]—*Claretian Missionary Sisters*—R.M.I.
[3110]—*Congregation of Our Lady of Retreat in the Cenacle*—R.C.
[1730]—*Congregation of the Sisters of the Third Order of St. Francis, Oldenberg, Indiana*—O.S.F.
[0760]—*Daughters of Charity of St. Vincent de Paul* (Eastern Prov.)—D.C.
[0960]—*Daughters of Wisdom*—D.W.
[1070-13]—*Dominican Sisters*—O.P.
[0410]—*Institute of The Sisters of Our Lady of Mount Carmel*—O.Carm.
[]—*Order of Carmelites*
[2170]—*Servants of the Immaculate Heart of Mary*—I.H.M.
[]—*Sisters for Christian Community*—S.F.C.C.
[]—*Sisters of Mercy of Ireland*—R.S.M.
[2575]—*Sisters of Mercy of the Americas*—R.S.M.
[2990]—*Sisters of Notre Dame* (Toledo Prov.)—S.N.D.
[3890]—*Sisters of St. Joseph of Peace*—C.S.J.P.
[3900]—*Sisters of St. Joseph of St. Augustine, FL*—S.S.J.
[]—*Trinitarian Handmaids of the Divine Word*—T.H.W.D.

DIOCESAN CEMETERIES

ST. AUGUSTINE. *San Lorenzo Cemetery*, 35 Treasury St., 32084. Tel: 904-824-2806. Francis F. Elliott, Exec. Dir. Diosesan Cemeteries.

NECROLOGY

† James, Rev. Msgr. R. Joseph, Jacksonville, FL Mary, Queen of Heaven—Died May 7, 2003

Diocese of St. Cloud

(Dioecesis S. Clodoaldi)

Most Reverend

JOHN F. KINNEY, D.D., J.C.D.

Bishop of St. Cloud; ordained February 2, 1963; appointed Titular Bishop of Caorle and Auxiliary Bishop of St. Paul and Minneapolis November 16, 1976; consecrated January 25, 1977; appointed Bishop of Bismarck June 28, 1982; installed August 23, 1982; appointed Bishop of St. Cloud May 9, 1995; installed July 6, 1995 *Office: 214 Third Ave. S., P.O. Box 1248, St. Cloud, MN 56302-1248*. Tel: 320-251-2340.

Chancery: 214 Third Ave. S., P.O. Box 1248, St. Cloud, MN 56302. Tel: 320-251-2340; Fax: 320-251-0470.

Web: www.stcdio.org

Square Miles 12,251.

Corporate Title: "The Diocese of St. Cloud."

Erected as the Vicariate of Northern Minnesota, February 12, 1875.

Created as the Diocese of St. Cloud, September 22, 1889.

Comprises the Counties of Stearns, Sherburne, Benton, Morrison, Mille Lacs, Kanabec, Isanti, Pope, Stevens, Traverse, Grant, Douglas, Wilkin, Otter Tail, Todd and Wadena in the State of Minnesota.

Legal Title: For legal titles of parishes and diocesan institutionss, consult the Chancery Office.

STATISTICAL OVERVIEW

Personnel	
Bishop	1
Retired Bishops	2
Abbots	1
Retired Abbots	2
Priests: Diocesan Active in Diocese	76
Priests: Diocesan Active Outside Diocese	2
Priests: Retired, Sick or Absent	53
Number of Diocesan Priests	131
Religious Priests in Diocese	109
Total Priests in Diocese	240
Extern Priests in Diocese	4
Ordinations:	
Diocesan Priests	2
Religious Priests	1
Permanent Deacons	5
Permanent Deacons in Diocese	44
Total Brothers	67
Total Sisters	583
Parishes	
Parishes	138
With Resident Pastor:	
Resident Diocesan Priests	70
Resident Religious Priests	12
Without Resident Pastor:	
Administered by Priests	56
Professional Ministry Personnel:	
Sisters	7
Lay Ministers	76
Welfare	
Catholic Hospitals	4
Total Assisted	247,892
Homes for the Aged	14
Total Assisted	1,181
Residential Care of Children	1
Total Assisted	241
Special Centers for Social Services	66
Total Assisted	39,405
Residential Care of Disabled	7
Total Assisted	51
Other Institutions	12
Total Assisted	735
Educational	
Diocesan Students in Other Seminaries	15
Seminaries, Religious	1
Students Religious	7
Total Seminarians	22
Colleges and Universities	2
Total Students	4,045
High Schools, Diocesan and Parish	1
Total Students	792
High Schools, Private	1
Total Students	320
Elementary Schools, Diocesan and Parish	31
Total Students	4,977
Catechesis/Religious Education:	
High School Students	7,012
Elementary Students	13,445
Total Students under Catholic Instruction	30,613
Teachers in the Diocese:	
Priests	17
Brothers	6
Sisters	28
Lay Teachers	723
Vital Statistics	
Receptions into the Church:	
Infant Baptism Totals	2,211
Adult Baptism Totals	76
Received into Full Communion	195
First Communions	2,645
Confirmations	2,599
Marriages:	
Catholic	665
Interfaith	316
Total Marriages	981
Deaths	1,420
Total Catholic Population	147,748
Total Population	516,755

Former Bishops—Rt. Revs. RUPERT SEIDENBUSCH, O.S.B., D.D., consecrated Bishop of Halia, Vicar-Apostolic of Northern Minnesota, May 30, 1875; resigned Nov. 15, 1888; died June 2, 1895; OTTO ZARDETTI, D.D., consecrated Oct. 20, 1889; transferred to Bucharest, Romania, and raised to the Archiepiscopal Dignity, Feb. 23, 1894; died May 9, 1902; MARTIN MARTY, O.S.B., D.D., consecrated Bishop of Tiberias, Feb. 1, 1880; Bishop of Sioux Falls, 1889; transferred to St. Cloud, Jan. 21, 1895; died Sept. 19, 1896; JAMES TROBEC, D.D., ord. Sept. 8, 1865; consecrated Bishop of St. Cloud, Sept. 21, 1897; resigned April 15, 1914; appt. Titular Bishop of Lycopolis; died Dec. 14, 1921; Most Revs. JOSEPH F. BUSCH, D.D., ord. July 28, 1889; appt. Bishop of Lead, S. D., April 9, 1910; consecrated May 19, 1910; transferred to See of St. Cloud, Jan. 19, 1915; died May 31, 1953; PETER W. BARTHOLOME, D.D., ord. June 12, 1917; appt. Titular Bishop of Lete and Coadjutor Bishop of St. Cloud "cum jure successionis", Dec. 6, 1941; consecrated March 3, 1942; succeeded to See May 31, 1953; appt. Assistant at the Pontificial Throne July 23, 1954; resigned Jan. 31, 1968; died June 17, 1982; GEORGE H. SPELTZ, D.D., Ph.D., appt. Auxiliary Bishop of Winona and Titular Bishop of Claneus February 13, 1963; consecrated March 25, 1963; appt. Coadjutor of St. Cloud April 4, 1966; succeeded Jan. 31, 1968;; resigned Jan. 13, 1987; died Feb. 1, 2004; JEROME HANUS, O.S.B., D.D., appt. Bishop of St. Cloud, July 6, 1987; ord. and installed Aug. 24, 1987; appt. Coadjutor Archbishop of Dubuque, IA, Aug. 23, 1994.

Chancery—P.O. Box 1248, 214 Third Ave. S., St. Cloud, 56302. Tel: 320-251-2340; 320-259-5227 (after hours); Fax: 320-251-0470. Office Hours: Mon.-Fri. 8:30-12 & 1-4:30

Vicar General—Rev. MARVIN ENNEKING, J.C.L.

Chancellor—Rev. ROBERT ROLFES, J.C.L.

Vice Chancellor—Sr. NANCY BAUER, O.S.B.

Assistant Chancellor—Sr. MARY MANDERNACH, O.S.B.

Diocesan Tribunal—305 Seventh Ave. N., St. Cloud, 56303. All marriage cases are to be directed to: The Tribunal, Box 576, St. Cloud, 56302. Tel: 320-251-6557.

Judicial Vicar—Rev. VIRGIL HELMIN, J.C.L.

Adjutant Judicial Vicar—Rev. ROBERT ROLFES, J.C.L.

Promoter Justitiae—Rev. Msgr. DANIEL J. TAUFEN, S.T.L.

Defensor Vinculi—Revs. NICHOLAS LANDSBERGER, S.T.L.; GREGORY LIESER; THOMAS OLSON; Deacon JOHN SALCHERT.

Judges—Revs. ROBERT LANDSBERGER (Retired); JONATHAN LICARI, O.S.B.; MARVIN ENNEKING, J.C.L.; ROBERT HARREN, J.C.L.; ROBERT ROLFES, J.C.L.; THERESA A. WYBURN, J.C.L.

Notaries—Revs. VIRGIL HELMIN, J.C.L.; ROBERT ROLFES, J.C.L.; THERESA A. WYBURN, J.C.L.; DIANA SKAJA.

Advocates—Revs. JOSEPH KORF; LEON SLOMINSKI (Retired); ROGER KLASSEN, O.S.B.; MARK INNOCENTI; Deacons DONALD TZINSKI; JOHN WOODS; Mrs. DOLORES SALCHERT.

Marriage Counseling—Pastoral Center, Diocese of St. Cloud, 911 18th St. N., St. Cloud, 56303. Tel: 320-650-1660. Caritas Family Services,

Diocesan Consultors—Revs. KEVIN ANDERSON; THOMAS BECKER; JOHN CASKEY; MARVIN ENNEKING; BERNARD GRUENES; GREGORY MILLER, O.S.B.; JEROME NORDICK; THOMAS OLSON; LAURN VIRNIG; STANLEY WIESER.

Deans—Revs. KEVIN ANDERSON, St. Cloud; RONALD DOCKENDORF, Melrose; THOMAS BECKER, Alexandria; CLETUS CONNORS, O.S.B., Cold Spring; ROBERT KIEFFER, Fergus Falls; THOMAS OLSON, Foley; MARK INNOCENTI, Little Falls; GERALD MISCHKE, St. Joseph; STANLEY WIESER, Morris; JOSEPH VANDEBERG, Princeton; JAMES STATZ, Sauk Centre; JEROME NORDICK, Wadena.

Diocesan Corporate Board—Most Rev. JOHN KINNEY, Pres.; Revs. MARVIN ENNEKING, J.C.L., Vice Pres.; ROBERT ROLFES, J.C.L., Sec.; TIMOTHY BALTES; GREGORY LIESER.

Diocesan Finance Council—Most Rev. JOHN F. KINNEY, D.D., J.C.D.; Mr. DAVID EICKHOFF, Finance Officer; Revs. MARVIN ENNEKING, J.C.L.; JOSEPH KORF; Sr. RITA KRAEMER, O.S.F.; Mr. ALEX DIDIER; Mr. PETER FUCHSTEINER; Mr. JAMES MEGEL; Mr. HUB LEVANDOWSKI; Mrs. LUANN POPP; Mr. LOREN LIESEMEYER; Ms. MARGARET ARNOLD.

Due Process Service—Sr. NANCY BAUER, O.S.B., P.O. Box 1248, St. Cloud, 56302.

Presbyteral Council—Revs. THOMAS BECKER, Chm.; ROBERT KIEFFER, Vice Chm.; JEROME NORDICK, Sec.; GERALD MISCHKE; JAMES STATZ; RONALD DOCKENDORF; MARK INNOCENTI; MARVIN ENNEKING; CLETUS CONNORS, O.S.B.; THOMAS OLSON; KEVIN ANDERSON; STANLEY WIESER; JOSEPH VANDEBERG; GREGORY MILLER, O.S.B.; PAUL ZYLLA (Retired), Address correspondence to: Church of the Sacred Heart, 105 N. Franklin, Glenwood, 56334-1122.

Pastoral Council—Mrs. LEMAY BECHTOLD, Exec. Sec.; Revs. RONALD DOCKENDORF; BLANE WASNIE, O.S.B.; Deacon DAVID LINDMEIER; JEFF KUHN; ANN JONAS; LINDA STUMVOLL; PATRICK E. CUNNINGHAM; LYNN ANDREWS; EVA KOEP; PAM PONTIUS; SUSAN

WARD; CHRISTA MEYER; RAMONA STEINKE; JONELLE KIRCHNER; ROSELYN GIESE; CHUCK AUSTING; MARY KESKE; Sisters CLARA STANG, O.S.F.; MARLENE MEIERHOFER, O.S.B.

Diocesan Offices and Programs

Archives—LOUISE THEISEN, Archivist. Tel: 320-251-2340. Email: ltheisen@gw.stcdio.org.

Boy Scouts—Rev. LEROY SCHEIERL, Dir., St. Francis DeSales, P.O. Box 69, Belgrade, 56312-0069.

Catholic Campaign for Human Development—JANE MARRIN, Dir., P.O. Box 1248, St. Cloud, 56302.

Campus Ministry—Rev. KEVIN ANDERSON, Newman Center, 396 First Ave. S., St. Cloud, 56301.

Catholic Charities—Mr. STEVEN BRESNAHAN, Exec. Dir., 911 18th St. N., P.O. Box 2390, St. Cloud, 56302. Tel: 320-650-1510; Fax: 320-650-1528 Aging Services (Central Minnesota Foster Grandparent Program, Senior Dining); Caritas Family Services (Adoption, Counseling, Emergency Services -Food- Clothing-Financial, Financial Counseling, In Home Family Services, Life Transitions Services, Caritas Mental Health Clinic, Pregnancy Counseling); Housing Services (Housing Management Services and Transitional Housing); Residential and Day Services (Bethany Home, Day Programs, Hope Community Support, Intensive Treatment Unit, Mother Teresa Home, St. Anne's Home, St. Cloud Children's Home, St. Elizabeth Residential Care, St. Francis Home, St. Luke's Home, St. Michael's Home, Semi-Independent Living Services, Waivered Services for Mental Retardation and Related Conditions, St. Margaret's Home). Web: www.ccstcloud.org.

Catholic Foundation of the Diocese of St. Cloud—CATHERINE M. COGHLAN, Exec. Dir., 325 7th Ave. N., St. Cloud, 56303. Tel: 320-258-0390.

Catholic Relief Services—Rev. WILLIAM VOS, Dir., 11 Eighth Ave. S., St. Cloud, 56301. Tel: 320-251-1100; Fax: 320-251-2061.

Catholic Women, Council of—Rev. THOMAS KNOBLACH, Moderator, P.O. Box 158, Bertha, 56437; EVA KOEP, Pres., 24426 Liberty Dr., Henning, 56551.

Cemeteries Assumption-Calvary—2341 Roosevelt Rd., St. Cloud, 56301. Tel: 320-251-5511.

Censores Librorum—Revs. PAUL ZYLLA (Retired); ROBERT C. HARREN, J.C.L.; Rev. Msgr. DANIEL J. TAUFEN, S.T.L.

Clerical Aid Association—Most Rev. JOHN F. KINNEY, D.D., J.C.D., Pres.; Revs. MARK WILLENBRING, Treas.; ROBERT ROLFES, J.C.L., Sec. Directors: Revs. GERALD DALSETH; MARVIN ENNEKING, J.C.L.; BERNARD GRUENES; EDWIN KRAEMER; KENNETH RIEDEMANN; JOSEPH VANDEBERG, Address Mail to: The Chancery, P.O. Box 1248, St. Cloud, 56302.

Communications Office— (Radio, Television, Public Information), STEVE GOTTWALT, Dir., Pastoral Center, Diocese of St. Cloud, 305 N. Seventh Ave., St. Cloud, 56303. Tel: 320-251-0558.

Continuing Formation of Priests—Rev. RALPH ZIMMERMAN, Dir., Church of Our Lady of the Lake, Box 100, Big Lake, 55309-0100.

Development Office—CATHERINE M. COGHLAN, Dir. Devel., 325 7th Ave. N., St. Cloud, 56303. Tel: 320-258-0390.

Diocesan Education Council—Sr. CATHERINE KALLHOFF, S.S.N.D.; Rev. JOHN CASKEY; Deacon VERN SCHMITZ; Sr. CHRISANN MORTENSEN, S.S.N.D.; LINDA ARNOLD; LINDA KAISER; BRENDA KRESKY; ELMER KOBBERMANN; KATHY LANGER; MARGE LELWICA; SCOTT FRIELER; PATRICK MURPHY; JOHN STOKMAN; PEGGY STOKMAN; TIMOTHY WELCH.

Office of Catholic Education Ministries—Sr. CATHERINE KALLHOFF, S.S.N.D., Supt. Educ.; LINDA KAISER, School Consultant; Sr. CHRISANN MORTENSEN, S.S.N.D., Consultant for Disabilities & Catechist Formation; TIMOTHY WELCH, Consultant Media/Computer & Ministry Formation Program; BARBARA SIMON-JOHNSON, Office Coord.; LISA NEU, Consultant for the Formation of Youth; BRENDA KRESKY, Consultant for Adult Faith Formation; MATTHEW VAN DE VOORT, Media Coord.; JULIE TSCHIDA, Receptionist/ Sec., Address all correspondence to: Catholic Education Ministries, Pastoral Center, Diocese of St. Cloud, 305 Seventh Ave., N., St. Cloud, 56303. Tel: 320-251-0111.

Diocesan Ecumenical Commission—Rev. GERALD DALSETH, Chm., Address all correspondence to: P.O. Box 428, Pierz, 56364-0428.

Diocesan Planning Council—Mrs. JANE MARRIN, Dir.; Revs. RALPH ZIMMERMAN, Chm.; ROBERT KIEFFER; JOSEPH HERZING; JAMES REMMERSWAAL, O.S.C.; Sr. GEN MAIERS, O.S.B.; Ms. RITA CLASEMANN; Mr. BRUCE MANCINI; RAMONA STEINKE; Mr. JOE WOOD; Mr. GERALD KRITZECK; Sr. MARY ZIRBES, O.S.F.; Mr. VICTOR KLIMOSKI.

Diocesan Priests Pension Plan Trustees—Most Rev. JOHN KINNEY; Revs. MARVIN ENNEKING, J.C.L.; KENNETH BRENNY; BERNARD GRUENES; ROBERT HARREN, J.C.L.; RICHARD LEISEN; ALEXANDER LUDWIG; ROBERT ROLFES, J.C.L.; SEVERIN SCHWIETERS.

Director of Retired Priests—Rev. Msgr. DANIEL J. TAUFEN, S.T.L.

Family Life Bureau—CHRISTINE CODDEN, Dir., Pastoral Center, Diocese of St. Cloud, 305 N. Seventh Ave., St. Cloud, 56303. Tel: 320-252-4721.

Health Ministry—Sr. MICHAEA BYRON, O.S.F., Coord., 214 3rd Ave. S., St. Cloud, 56301. Tel: 320-252-7644; Rev. THOMAS KNOBLACH, Consultant for Healthcare Ethics.

Holy Childhood Association—Rev. WILLIAM VOS, Dir., 11-Eighth Ave., S., St. Cloud, 56301.

Koinonia Program of Central Minnesota—Rev. DAVID MACIEJ, P.O. Box 188, Rice, 56367.

Legion of Decency—Rev. ROBERT E. ROLFES, P.O. Box 1248, St. Cloud, 56302.

Legion of Mary—Rev. RAYMOND STEFFES, O.S.C., Crosier Monastery, Onamia, 56359.

Multicultural Ministry—Sr. ADELA GROSS, O.S.F., Consultant, 116 8th Ave., S.E., Little Falls, 56345. Tel: 320-632-2981; Fax: 320-632-6313.

Natural Family Planning—Mrs. KAY EK, Dir., 305 Seventh Ave. N., St. Cloud, 56303. Tel: 320-252-2100.

Newspaper "St. Cloud Visitor"—JOE TOWALSKI, Editor & Business Mgr., Pastoral Center, Diocese of St. Cloud, 305 N. Seventh Ave., Box 1068, St. Cloud, 56302. Tel: 320-251-3022.

Office of Diaconate—Deacon VERNON SCHMITZ, Dir.; Rev. RALPH ZIMMERMAN, Vicar for Permanent Deacons, Church of Our Lady of the Lake, P.O. Box 100, Big Lake, 55309-0100; Deacon DONALD TZINSKI, Pres. Diaconal Community, 305 Seventh Ave. N., St. Cloud, 56303. Tel: 612-252-4721.

Personnel Committee—Revs. MARVIN ENNEKING, J.C.L., Dir.; MARK INNOCENTI; PETER KIRCHNER; DAVID RIEDER; MEINRAD DINDORF, O.S.B.; JANE MARRIN, P.O. Box 1248, St. Cloud, 56302.

Respect Life Program—CHRISTINE CODDEN, 305 7th Ave N., Ste. 102, St. Cloud, 56303. Tel: 320-650-1676; Fax: 320-650-1675.

Propagation of the Faith—Rev. WILLIAM VOS, Dir., 11 Eighth Ave. S., St. Cloud, 56301. Tel: 320-251-1100; Fax: 320-251-2061.

Rural Life Program—214 3rd Ave. S., St. Cloud, 56301. Tel: 320-251-2340.

TEC (Central Minnesota TEC) (Together Encountering Christ)—Rev. KENNETH OPAT, O.S.C., Coord., 516 School St., Anoka, 55303. Tel: 763-323-8178; Fax: 763-421-4230.

Victim Assistance Coordinator—MAXINE BARNETT. Tel: 320-253-6900. Email: maxine@annamaries.org.

Vocations—Rev. GREGORY MASTEY, Dir., 305 Seventh Ave. N., Ste. 102B, St. Cloud, 56303-3633. Tel: 320-251-5001; Fax: 320-251-0424. Email: gmastey@gw.stcdio.org.

Worship, Office of—ANITA FISCHER, Dir., Pastoral Center, Diocese of St. Cloud, 305 N. Seventh Ave., St. Cloud, 56303. Tel: 320-255-9068.

CLERGY, PARISHES, MISSIONS AND PAROCHIAL SCHOOLS

CITY OF ST. CLOUD

(BENTON, STEARNS, SHERBURNE COUNTIES)

1—ST. MARY'S CATHEDRAL OF ST. CLOUD, Rev. Steven Binsfeld; Deacon Leo Kosiba. In Res., Rev. Thomas Assenga.
Res.: 25 Eighth Ave. S., 56301-4279. Tel: 320-251-1840; Fax: 320-251-1840.
School— See St. Augustine's for details.

2—ST. ANTHONY OF PADUA, Rev. Tiomthy Wenzel; Deacon Carl S. Nord.
Office: 2405 1st St. N., 56303. Tel: 320-251-5966; Fax: 320-251-0664.
School—St. Elizabeth Ann Seton Inter-Parochial School See separate listing.

3—ST. AUGUSTINE, Rev. Geoffrey Fecht, O.S.B.; Deacon Richard Scheierl.
Office—442 Second St., S.E., 56304. Tel: 320-251-8335; Fax: 320-529-3231.
Res.: 210 Fifth Ave., S.E., 56304.
School—St. Augustine's/St. Mary's Cathedral, Tel: 320-251-2376; Fax: 320-529-3222. Lay Teachers 20; Students 217.
Catechesis/Religious Program—Tel: 320-252-6042; Fax: 320-529-3236. Helen Bettendorf, D.R.E. Students 260.

4—CHRIST CHURCH, Rev. Kevin Anderson.
Res.: 396 First Ave. S., 56301. Tel: 320-251-2712; Fax: 320-252-3930.
Catechesis/Religious Program—Tel: 320-251-3260.

5—HOLY ANGELS, Closed., For inquiries for parish records contact St. Mary's Cathedral, St. Cloud.

6—HOLY SPIRIT, Revs. Virgil A. Helmin; Michael Kellogg; Deacon Vernon Schmitz.
Office—2405 Walden Way, 56301. Tel: 320-251-3764; Fax: 320-252-5143.
School—St. Elizabeth Ann Seton Inter-Parochial school. See separate listing.
Catechesis/Religious Program—Thomas Toohey, D.R.E. Students 300.

7—ST. JOHN CANTIUS, Rev. Marvin Enneking; Deacon Fred Reker. In Res., Rev. Adaikalam Maria Mariadoss (India).
Res.: 1515 Third St. N., 56303. Tel: 320-251-4455; Fax: 320-240-1238.

8—ST. MICHAEL, Rev. Bernard Gruenes.
Res.: 1036 Co. Rd. 4, 56303. Tel: 320-251-6923; Fax: 320-202-1104.
School—Sts. Peter & Paul & Michael Inter-Parochial School See separate listing.
Catechesis/Religious Program—Students 225.

9—ST. PAUL, Rev. Timothy Baltes; Deacons Todd Warren; David Lindmeier.
Res.: 1125 11th Ave. N., 56303. Tel: 320-251-4831; Fax: 320-251-2648.
School—Sts. Peter & Paul & Michael Inter-Parochial School See separate listing.

10—ST. PETER, Rev. Gregory Lieser; Deacons William Ritchie; John Woods.
Res.: 930 31st Ave. N., 56303. Tel: 320-252-2113; Fax: 320-529-0796.
School—Sts. Peter & Paul & Michael Inter-Parochial School See separate listing.
Catechesis/Religious Program—Tel: 320-253-5768. Linda Arnold, D.R.E.; Laurie Mullin, D.R.E. Students 164.

OUTSIDE THE CITY OF ST. CLOUD

ALBANY, STEARNS CO., SEVEN DOLORS, [CEM] Rev. Corwin Collins, O.S.B.
Res.: Box 277, 56307. Tel: 320-845-2705; Fax: 320-845-2705.
School—Holy Family, Tel: 320-845-2011; Fax: 320-845-7380. Lay Teachers 8; Students 132.
Catechesis/Religious Program—Tel: 320-845-4335. Sr. Alice Imdieke, O.S.B., D.R.E. Students 336.

ALEXANDRIA, DOUGLAS CO., ST. MARY'S, [CEM] Rev. Alexander P. Ludwig.
Res.: 411 Hawthorne St., P.O. Box 669, 56308. Tel: 320-763-5781; Fax: 320-763-4833.
School—Tel: 320-763-5861; Fax: 320-763-7992. Lay Teachers 11; Students 165.
Catechesis/Religious Program—Tel: 320-763-9202. Paulette Baumgartner, D.R.E. Students 709.

AVON, STEARNS CO., ST. BENEDICT'S, [CEM] Rev. Blane Wasnie, O.S.B.
Church: P.O. Box 98, 56310. Tel: 320-356-7121; Fax: 320-356-9203.

BATTLE LAKE, OTTER TAIL CO., OUR LADY OF THE LAKE, Rev. Paul Folsom.
Res.: 409 Lake Ave. N., P.O. Box 671, 56515. Tel: 218-864-5619; Fax: 218-864-5747.
Catechesis/Religious Program—Students 104.

BECKER, SHERBUNE CO., IMMACULATE CONCEPTION, [CEM] Rev. Eberhard Schefers; Deacon Gregory Steele.
Res.: 12100 Sherburne Ave., Box 426, 55308. Tel: 763-261-4242; Fax: 763-261-4314.
Catechesis/Religious Program—Fax: 763-261-5920. Sr. Julie Schleper, O.S.B., D.R.E. Students 339.

BELGRADE, STEARNS CO., ST. FRANCIS DE SALES, [CEM] Rev. LeRoy Scheierl.
Res.: 541 Martin Ave., P.O. Box 69, 56312. Tel: 320-254-8218; Fax: 320-254-3239.
Catechesis/Religious Program—JoAnn Braegelman, D.R.E. Students 94.

BELLE PRAIRIE, MORRISON CO., HOLY FAMILY, [CEM] Revs. Nicholas Landsberger; Mark Innocenti; William Vouk III.
Res.: 18777 Riverwood Dr., Little Falls, 56345. Tel: 320-632-5720.
Catechesis/Religious Program—Tel: 320-632-5754. Anna Moran, D.R.E. Students 113.

BELLE RIVER, DOUGLAS CO., ST. NICHOLAS, [CEM] Rev. Jeffrey D. Ethen.
Church: 9473 County Rd. 3, N.E., Box 339, Carlos, 56319. Tel: 612-852-7041.
Catechesis/Religious Program—Tel: 612-852-7912. Tonya Beulke, D.R.E. Students 47.

BERTHA, TODD CO., ST. JOSEPH'S, [CEM] Rev. Thomas Knoblach.
Res.: P.O. Box 158, 56437-0158. Tel: 218-924-2605; Fax: 218-924-2144.
Catechesis/Religious Program—Tel: 218-924-2144. Students 66.

BIG LAKE, SHERBURNE CO., OUR LADY OF THE LAKE, [CEM] Rev. Ralph Zimmerman; Deacon Steven DuPay.
Res.: 440 North Lake St., Box 100, 55309. Tel:

763-263-2863; Fax: 763-263-3187.
Catechesis / Religious Program—Students 450.

BLUEGRASS, WADENA CO., ST. HUBERT'S, [CEM] Revs. Albert Holmes; Ronald Schmelzer.
Res.: 20 Brown St. N., P.O. Box C, Verndale, 56481. Tel: 218-445-5786.
Catechesis / Religious Program—Tel: 218-631-1836. Vera Malone, D.R.E. Students 89.

BLUFFTON, OTTER TAIL CO., ST. JOHN THE BAPTIST, [CEM] Revs. Albert Holmes; Ronald Schmelzer.
Res.: P.O. Box 36, 56518. Tel: 218-385-2608; Fax: 218-385-2608.
Catechesis / Religious Program—Students 153.

BOWLUS, MORRISON CO., ST. STANISLAUS KOSTKA, [CEM] Revs. Donald Wagner; LeRoy Schik.
Office: P.O. Box 8, 56314. Tel: 320-584-5313; Fax: 320-584-8231.

BRAHAM, ISANTI CO., ST. PETER & PAUL, [CEM] Rev. Leroy Kremer; Deacon Donald Tzinski.
Res.: P.O. Box 483, 55006. Tel: 320-396-3105.
Catechesis / Religious Program—Jan Neville, D.R.E. Students 175.

BRANDON, DOUGLAS CO., CHURCH OF ST. ANN, [CEM] Rev. Eugene Lemm. In Res., Rev. Richard J. Heid (Retired).
Res.: P.O. Box 256, 56315. Tel: 320-524-2462; 320-834-5095.
Catechesis / Religious Program—Students 93.

BRECKENRIDGE, WILKIN CO., ST. MARY OF THE PRESENTATION, [CEM 2] Rev. Kenneth Popp.
Res.: 221 Fourth St. N., 56520-1496. Tel: 218-643-5173; Fax: 218-643-1881.
School—Tel: 218-643-5443; Fax: 218-643-5443. Lay Teachers 11; Students 120.
Catechesis / Religious Program—Students 185.

BRENNYVILLE, BENTON CO., ST. ELIZABETH, [CEM] Rev. Thomas F. Olson.
Res.: 16426 125th Ave., N.E., Foley, 56329. Tel: 320-355-2454; Fax: 320-355-2819.
Catechesis / Religious Program—Tel: 320-387-3332. Students 79.

BROOTEN, STEARNS CO., ST. DONATUS, [CEM] Rev. LeRoy Scheierl.
Office and Mailing: P.O. Box 159, 56316.
Res.: St. Francis De Sales, Belgrade, 56312. Tel: 320-346-2431; Fax: 320-346-2431.
Catechesis / Religious Program—Audrey Rademacher, D.R.E. Students 55.

BROWERVILLE, TODD CO., CHRIST THE KING, [CEM] Rev. John Caskey.
Res.: P.O. Box 83, 56438. Tel: 320-594-2291.
School—Tel: 320-594-6114; Fax: 320-594-6114. Lay Teachers 4; Students 48.
Catechesis / Religious Program—Beverly Geraets, D.R.E. Tel: 320-594-2441; Kimberly Marstein, D.R.E. Tel: 320-594-7149. Students 157.

BROWN'S VALLEY, TRAVERSE CO., ST. ANTHONY'S, [CEM] Revs. Stanley Wieser; David Trujillo (Venezuela).
Res.: Box 359, 56219. Tel: 320-695-2621.
Catechesis / Religious Program—Students 65.

BUCKMAN, MORRISON CO., ST. MICHAEL'S, [CEM] Rev. Gerald Dalseth; Deacon Guy Beck.
Res.: P.O. Box 428, Pierz, 56364. Tel: 320-468-6033; Fax: 320-468-2296.
Catechesis / Religious Program—Tel: 320-468-2640. Students 128.

BUTLER, OTTER TAIL CO., HOLY CROSS, [CEM] Revs. David Rieder; Jerome Nordick.
Res.: County Hwy. 62, New York Mills, 56567. Tel: 218-385-2608.

CAMBRIDGE, ISANTI CO., CHRIST THE KING, [CEM] Rev. James David Hahn.
Res.: 230 Fern St. N., 55008-1094. Tel: 763-689-1221; Fax: 763-689-8950.
Catechesis / Religious Program—Students 228.

CHOKIO, STEVENS CO., ST. MARY'S, [CEM] Rev. Nathan Packard.
Res.: P.O. Box 187, 56221. Tel: 320-324-2680; Fax: 320-324-2732. Jeri Erickson, D.R.E.
Catechesis / Religious Program—Students 66.

CLARISSA, TODD CO., ST. JOSEPH, [CEM] Rev. John Caskey.
Res.: Box 83, Browerville, 56438. Tel: 320-594-2291; Fax: 320-594-6114.
Office: 107 John St. S., 56440.
Catechesis / Religious Program—Tel: 218-756-2205; Fax: 218-756-2203. Eileen Uhlenkamp, D.R.E. Tel: 218-756-3614; Kathryn Harren, D.R.E. Tel: 218-738-3558. Students 87.

CLEAR LAKE, SHERBURNE CO., ST. MARCUS, [CEM] Rev. Joseph Vandeberg.
Res.: P.O. Box 237, 55319. Tel: 320-743-2481; Fax: 320-743-3346.
Catechesis / Religious Program—Tel: 320-743-3346. Students 197.

COLD SPRING, STEARNS CO., ST. BONIFACE, [CEM] Rev. Cletus Connors, O.S.B.; Deacon John Salchert.
Res.: 418 Main St., 56320. Tel: 320-685-3280; Fax: 320-685-7792.
School—Tel: 320-685-3541; Fax: 320-685-8194. Lay Teachers 14; Students 224.
Catechesis / Religious Program—Tel: 320-385-8222, Ext. 103. Karen Neu, D.R.E. Students 598.

COLLEGEVILLE, STEARNS CO., ST. JOHN THE BAPTIST, [JC] Rev. Eugene J. McGlothlin, O.S.B.
Res.: P.O. Box 2015, 56321. Tel: 320-363-2765.
Catechesis / Religious Program—Julie Orthoff, D.R.E. Students 113.

DENT, OTTER TAIL CO., SACRED HEART, [CEM] Revs. Jerome Nordick; David Rieder.
Res.: 36363 State Hwy. 108, 56528. Tel: 218-758-2700.
Catechesis / Religious Program—Joe Sazama, D.R.E.; Diane Sazama, D.R.E. Students 103.

DONNELLY, STEVENS CO., ST. THERESIA, Closed., For inquiries for parish records contact St. Charles, Herman.

DUELM, BENTON CO., ST. LAWRENCE'S, [CEM] Rev. Bernard Kahlhamer.
Res.: 10915 Duelm Rd., N.E., Foley, 56329. Tel: 320-968-7502; Fax: 320-968-7252.
Catechesis / Religious Program—Tel: 320-968-6595. Betty Pundsach, D.R.E. Students 210.

DUMONT, TRAVERSE CO., ST. PETER'S, Revs. Stanley Wieser; David Trujillo (Venezuela).
Res.: 201 Ninth St. S., Wheaton, 56296. Tel: 320-563-4421.
Catechesis / Religious Program—Tel: 320-563-8875. Marilyn Mathias, D.R.E. Students 28.

EDEN VALLEY, STEARNS CO., THE CHURCH OF THE ASSUMPTION, [CEM 2] Rev. Virgil R. Braun.
Res.: P.O. Box 9, 55329. Tel: 320-453-2788.
Catechesis / Religious Program—Tel: 320-453-7388. Rose Fink, D.R.E.; Anna Mae Gruenes, D.R.E. Students 217.

ELBOW LAKE, GRANT CO., ST. OLAF, [CEM] Rev. Andrew Marthaler.
Res.: 18 Sixth Ave. N., 56531. Tel: 218-685-4318.

ELIZABETH, OTTER TAIL CO., ST. ELIZABETH, [CEM] Rev. Richard Walz.
Res.: 706 W. Pleasant Ave., 56533. Tel: 218-736-5230.
Catechesis / Religious Program—Julie Ludke, D.R.E. Students 92.

ELK RIVER, SHERBURNE CO., THE CHURCH OF ST. ANDREW, [CEM] Revs. Joseph Korf; Daniel Walz, 566 Fourth St., 55330; Deacon Frederick St. Jean.
Res.: 566 Fourth St., 55330. Tel: 763-441-1483; Fax: 763-441-1485.
School—Tel: 763-441-2216; Fax: 763-441-1146. Sisters 1; Lay Teachers 15; Students 329.
Catechesis / Religious Program—Students 1,486.

ELMDALE, MORRISON CO., ST. EDWARD'S, [CEM] Revs. Donald Wagner; LeRoy Schik.
Office: P.O. Box 8, Bowlus, 56314. Tel: 320-584-5313; Fax: 320-584-8231.
Catechesis / Religious Program—308 S. Main St., Upsala, 56384. Tel: 320-573-2132. Students 43.

ELROSA, STEARNS CO., SS. PETER AND PAUL, [CEM] Rev. LeRoy Scheierl.
Res.: P.O. Box 95, 56325. Tel: 320-697-5541; Fax: 320-254-3239.
Catechesis / Religious Program—Tel: 320-254-8218; Fax: 320-254-8218. Jo Braegelman, D.R.E. Students 74.

FARMING, STEARNS CO., ST. CATHERINE'S, [CEM] Rev. Julian Schmiesing, O.S.B.
Res.: Rte. 1, Richmond, 56368. Tel: 320-548-3550.
Catechesis / Religious Program—Tel 320-597-3033. Mary Brinkman, D.R.E. Students 62.

FERGUS FALLS, OTTER TAIL CO., OUR LADY OF VICTORY [JC] Rev. Robert Kieffer.
Res.: 207 Vine St. N., 56537. Tel 218-736-2429; Fax: 218-736-4407.
School—Tel: 218-736-6661; Fax: 218-736-4407. Lay Teachers 8; Students 120.
Catechesis / Religious Program—Tel: 218-736-6837; Fax: 218-736-6837. Susan Roberts, D.R.E.; Mary Loreno, D.R.E. Students 250.

FLENSBURG, MORRISON CO., SACRED HEART, [CEM 2] Rev. Leo Moenkedick.
Mailing Address: 18 Pine St., 56328. Tel: 320-632-5086; Fax: 320-616-6886.

FOLEY, BENTON CO., ST. JOHN'S, [CEM] Rev. Gregory Paffel.
Res.: Box 337, 56329. Tel: 320-968-7913.
School—St. John's Area School, Tel: 320-968-7972; Fax: 320-968-9956. Lay Teachers 9; Students 135.
Catechesis / Religious Program—Tel: 320-968-6836. Catherine Herbst, D.R.E. Students 256.

FORESTON, MILLE LACS CO., ST. LOUIS BERTRAND, [CEM] Rev. James Cashman, O.S.C.
Res.: 187 First St. S., P.O. Box 128, 56330. Tel: 320-294-5460; Fax: 320-294-5588.

FOXHOME, WILKIN CO., ST. JOSEPH, Closed., For inquiries for parish records contact St. Mary of the Presentation, Breckenridge.

FREEPORT, STEARNS CO., SACRED HEART, [CEM] Revs. Roger Klassen, O.S.B.; Julius Beckermann, O.S.B.; Deacon Richard Scherping.
Res.: P.O. Box 155, 56331-0155. Tel: 320-836-2143; Fax: 320-836-2142.
School—Tel: 320-836-2591; Fax: 320-836-2514. Lay Teachers 3; Students 47.
Catechesis / Religious Program—Kathy Well, D.R.E. Students 86.

GILMAN, BENTON CO., SS. PETER AND PAUL, [CEM] Rev. Thomas Olson.
Res.: P.O. Box 86, 56333. Tel: 320-387-2255; Fax: 320-355-2819.
School—St. John's, Tel: 320-968-7972. (Foley) Area School
Catechesis / Religious Program—P.O. Box 87, 56333. Tel: 320-387-3332; 320-387-3332. Students 185.

GLENWOOD, POPE CO., SACRED HEART, [CEM 2] Rev. Thomas G. Becker; Deacon Frank Schmainda.
Res.: 105 Franklin St. N., 56334. Tel: 320-634-3813; Fax: 320-634-0590.
Catechesis / Religious Program—Tel: 320-634-4828. Diane Mrnak, D.R.E. Students 235.

GREENWALD, STEARNS CO., ST. ANDREW'S, [CEM] Rev. Ronald Dockendorf.
Res.: P.O. Box 120, 56335. Tel: 320-987-3160; Fax: 320-987-3306.
School—Tel: 320-987-3133. Sisters 1; Lay Teachers 2; Students 26.
Catechesis / Religious Program—Tel: 320-987-3200; Fax: 320-987-3200. Bonnie Schulzetenberg, D.R.E. Students 46.

GREY EAGLE, TODD CO., ST. JOSEPH'S, [CEM 2] Rev. Arlie Sowada.
Res.: P.O. Box 366, 56336. Tel: 320-285-2545; Fax: 320-285-5255.
Catechesis / Religious Program—Students 133.

HARDING, MORRISON CO., HOLY CROSS, [CEM] Rev. Roger Thoennes.
Res.: 29482-243 St., Pierz, 56364. Tel: 320-277-3701.

HENNING, OTTER TAIL CO., CHURCH OF ST. EDWARD OF HENNING, [CEM] Rev. Thomas Knoblach.
Res.: P.O. Box 314, 56551. Tel: 218-583-2490.
Catechesis / Religious Program—Marilyn Bolland, D.R.E. Students 62.

HERMAN, GRANT CO., ST. CHARLES, [CEM] Rev. Nathan Packard.
Res.: P.O. Box 187, Chokio, 56221. Tel: 320-677-2433; Fax: 320-324-2732.
Catechesis / Religious Program—Students 40.

HILLMAN, MORRISON CO., ST. RITA'S, [CEM] Rev. Raymond Steffes, O.S.C.
Mailing Address: 16691 371st Ave., 56338. Tel: 320-277-3807.
Catechesis / Religious Program—Steve Kummet, D.R.E.; Marie Kummet, D.R.E. Students 50.

HOLDINGFORD, STEARNS CO.

1—ST. HEDWIG'S, [CEM] Revs. Gerald Mischke, Co-Pastor; Joseph Herzing, Co-Pastor; Deacons Jeffrey Fromm; Jerome Schwarzbauer.
Res.: P.O. Box 308, 56340. Tel: 320-746-2231; Fax: 320-746-2449.
Catechesis / Religious Program—Students 80.

2—ST. MARY'S, [CEM] Revs. Gerald Mischke, Co-Pastor; Joseph Herzing, Co-Pastor; Deacons Jeffrey Fromm; Jerome Schwarzbauer.
Res.: P.O. Box 308, 56340. Tel: 320-746-2231; Fax: 320-746-2449.
Catechesis / Religious Program—Students 143.

ISANTI, ISANTI CO., ST. ELIZABETH ANN SETON, [CEM] Rev. Jose Edayadiyil (India), Admin.
Res.: 109 Fifth Ave. S., 55040. Tel: 763-444-5226; Fax: 763-444-5226.
Catechesis / Religious Program—Mary Mack, D.R.E. Tel: 763-444-5226; Fax: 763-444-5226. Students 185.

JACOB'S PRAIRIE, WAKEFIELD TOWNSHIP, STEARNS CO., ST. JAMES, [CEM] Rev. Mathias Spier, O.S.B.
Res.: 25042 County Rd. 2, Cold Spring, 56320. Tel: 320-685-3479.

KENSINGTON, GRANT CO., OUR LADY OF THE RUNESTONE, [CEM] Rev. Kenneth Riedemann.
Res.: 25890 110th St., Lowry, 56349-4580. Tel: 320-283-5273; Fax: 320-283-5253.
Catechesis / Religious Program—Students 52.

KENT, WILKIN CO., ST. THOMAS, [CEM] Rev. Anthony Kroll.
Res.: P.O. Box 23, 56553. Tel: 218-557-8312.
Catechesis / Religious Program—Tel: 218-557-9226. Nancy Grotluschen, D.R.E. Students 34.

KIMBALL, STEARNS CO., CHURCH OF SAINT ANNE, [CEM] Rev. David Grundman.
Church: 441 Hazel Ave. E., 55353. Tel: 320-398-3860.
Res.: 22714 State Hwy. 15, 56301.
Catechesis / Religious Program—Students 176.

LAKE HENRY, STEARNS CO., ST. MARGARET'S, [CEM] Rev. Leo Leisen. In Res., Rev. Walter Bednark.
Res.: 100 Lillie Ave., Roscoe, 56371. Tel: 320-243-4574.
Catechesis / Religious Program—Tel: 320-243-4378. Mary Jane Lenzmeier, D.R.E. Students 77.

LAKE RENO, POPE CO., ST. JOHN NEPOMUK, [CEM] Rev. Kenneth Riedemann.
Res.: 25890 110th St., Lowry, 56349-4580. Tel: 320-283-5273; Fax: 320-283-5253.

Catechesis/Religious Program—Students 44.
LASTRUP, MORRISON CO., ST. JOHN NEPOMUK, [CEM] Rev. Roger Thoennes.
Res.: P.O. Box 38, 56344. Tel: 320-468-2111.
LITTLE FALLS, MORRISON CO.
1—ST. MARY, [CEM 3] Revs. Nicholas Landsberger; William Vouk III.
Res.: 305 Fourth St., S.E., 56345. Tel: 320-632-5640; Fax: 320-632-6002.
School— See Inter-Parochial Schools under Institutoins Located in the Diocese.
Catechesis/Religious Program—Tel: 320-632-3911. Brenda Przybilla, D.R.E. Students 214.
2—OUR LADY OF LOURDES, [CEM] Revs. Mark Innocenti; William Vouk III; Deacon Bruce Geyer.
Res.: 208 W. Broadway, 56345. Tel: 320-632-8243; Fax: 320-616-2129.
School— See Inter-Parochial Schools under Institutoins Located in the Diocese.
Catechesis/Religious Program—Tel: 320-616-9689. Linda Benson, D.R.E. Students 293.
LONG PRAIRIE, TODD CO., ST. MARY OF MT. CARMEL, [CEM] [JC] Rev. Mark Stang; Deacon Mark Zenner.
Res.: 409 Central Ave., 56347. Tel: 320-732-2635; Fax: 320-732-2025.
School—Tel: 320-732-3478; Fax: 320-732-3894. Lay Teachers 9; Students 99.
Catechesis/Religious Program—Tel: 320-732-6590. Mrs. Tami Westerberg, D.R.E. Students 316.
LUXEMBURG, STEARNS CO., ST. WENDELIN'S, [CEM] Revs. Leon Slominski (Retired); David Grundman.
Res.: 22714 State Hwy. 15, 56301. Tel: 320-251-6944.
School—Tel: 612-251-9175. Sisters 1; Lay Teachers 6; Students 101.
Catechesis/Religious Program—Students 80.
MAINE, OTTER TAIL CO., CHURCH OF SAINT JAMES AT MAINE, [CEM] Rev. Paul Folsom.
Res.: 32009 County Hwy. 74, Underwood, 56586. Tel: 218-495-2184.
Catechesis/Religious Program—Students 60.
MAYHEW LAKE, BENTON CO., ANNUNCIATION, [CEM] Rev. Francis Britz.
Res.: 9965 Mayhew Lake Rd., N.E., Sauk Rapids, 56379. Tel: 320-252-1729.
Catechesis/Religious Program—Tel: 320-259-4941. Shirley Scapanski, D.R.E. Students 171.
MEIRE GROVE, STEARNS CO., ST. JOHN'S, [CEM] Rev. Ronald Dockendorf.
Res.: P.O. Box 120, Greenwald, 56335. Tel: 320-987-3160; Fax: 320-987-3306.
School—Tel: 320-987-3491. Lay Teachers 2; Students 39.
Catechesis/Religious Program—Tel: 320-256-3498. Ruth Klaphake, D.R.E. Students 20.
MELROSE, STEARNS CO., ST. MARY'S, [CEM 2] Rev. Vincent Lieser; Deacon Richardo de la Garza; Stephen Arnold, Pastoral Assoc.
Res.: 211 S. Fifth Ave. E., 56352-1427. Tel: 320-256-4207; Fax: 320-256-4208.
School—Tel: 320-256-4257. Lay Teachers 12; Students 163.
Catechesis/Religious Program—Tel: 320-256-4258. Vern Hollermann, D.R.E. Students 366.
MENAHGA, WADENA CO., THE CHURCH OF THE ASSUMPTION OF OUR LADY OF MENAHGA, [CEM] Revs. Ronald Schmelzer; Albert Holmes.
Res.: St. John the Baptist, P.O. Box 36, Bluffton, 56518. Tel: 218-385-2608.
MILACA, MILLE LACS CO., ST. MARY'S, [CEM] Rev. Charles Kunkel, O.S.C.
Res.: 625 3rd Ave., S.E., 56353. Tel: 320-983-3255; Fax: 320-983-6564.
Catechesis/Religious Program—Students 184.
MILLERVILLE, DOUGLAS CO., SEVEN DOLORS, [CEM] Rev. Eugene Lemm.
Res.: 16921 County Rd. 7, N.W., Brandon, 56315. Tel: 320-876-2240.
Catechesis/Religious Program—Students 51.
MORA, KANABEC CO., ST. MARY'S, [CEM] Rev. William Vos.
Res.: 201 Forest Ave. E., 55051. Tel: 320-679-1593; Fax: 320-679-6896.
Catechesis/Religious Program—Sue Grabowski, D.R.E. Students 179.
MORAN, TODD CO., ST. ISIDORE, [CEM] Rev. John Caskey; Deacon Robert Shaffer.
Mailing Address: P.O. Box 83, Browerville, 56438. Tel: 320-594-2291; Fax: 320-594-6114.
Catechesis/Religious Program—Tel: 218-894-2199. Gina Dreher, D.R.E. Students 45.
MORRILL, MORRISON CO., ST. JOSEPH'S, [CEM] Rev. Thomas F. Olson.
Res.: 16454 125th Ave., N.E., Foley, 56329. Tel: 320-355-2454; Fax: 320-355-2819.
Catechesis/Religious Program—P.O. Box 87, Elizabeth, 56533. Tel: 320-387-3332. Students 104.
MORRIS, STEVENS CO., ASSUMPTION OF THE BLESSED VIRGIN MARY, [CEM] Rev. Alan Wielinski; Deacon Stanley Hennen.
Res.: 207 E. Third, Box 287, 56267. Tel: 320-589-3003; Fax: 320-589-1822.
School—Tel: 320-589-1704. Lay Teachers 7; Students 99.
Catechesis/Religious Program—Kim Gullickson, D.R.E. Students 171.
MOTLEY, MORRISON CO., ST. MICHAEL'S, Rev. Peter Kirchner.
Res.: P.O. Box 218, 56466. Tel: 218-352-6143.
Catechesis/Religious Program—Tel: 218-352-6782. Donald Westfall, D.R.E. Students 120.
NEW MUNICH, STEARNS CO., IMMACULATE CONCEPTION, [CEM] Revs. Roger Klassen, O.S.B.; Julius Beckermann, O.S.B.; Deacon Richard Scherping.
Res.: P.O. Box 155, Freeport, 56331-0155. Tel: 320-836-2143; Fax: 320-836-2142.
NORTH PRAIRIE, MORRISON CO., HOLY CROSS, [CEM] Rev. Laurn Virnig.
Res.: P.O. Box 258, Royalton, 56373. Tel: 320-584-5484; Fax: 320-584-0028.
Catechesis/Religious Program—Students 47.
OGILVIE, KANABEC CO., ST. KATHRYN'S, [CEM] Rev. William Vos.
Res.: 201 Forest Ave. E., Mora, 55051. Tel: 320-679-1593; Fax: 320-679-6896.
Catechesis/Religious Program—Students 78.
ONAMIA, MILLE LACS CO., THE CHURCH OF THE HOLY CROSS OF ONAMIA, [CEM] Rev. William T. McNiff, O.S.C.
Res.: P.O. Box 500, 56359. Tel: 320-532-3122.
OPOLE, STEARNS CO., OUR LADY OF MT. CARMEL, [CEM] Revs. Gerald Mischke, Co-Pastor; Joseph Herzing, Co-Pastor; Deacons Jeffrey Fromm; Jerome Schwarzbauer.
Res.: St. Mary's Rectory, P.O. Box 308, Holdingford, 56340. Tel: 320-746-2231; Fax: 320-746-2449.
Catechesis/Religious Program—Students 130.
OSAKIS, DOUGLAS CO., IMMACULATE CONCEPTION, [CEM] Rev. Richard McGuire.
Res.: 316 Third Ave. W., P.O. Box F, 56360. Tel: 320-859-2390.
School—St. Agnes, Tel: 320-859-2130; Fax: 320-859-5850. Sisters 1; Lay Teachers 5; Students 54.
Catechesis/Religious Program—Steve Bogenrief, D.R.E. Students 156.
PADUA, STEARNS CO., CHURCH OF ST. ANTHONY OF PADUA, Closed., For inquiries for parish records contact St. Donatus Church, Brooten.
PARKERS PRAIRIE, OTTER TAIL CO., CHURCH OF ST. WILLIAM, [CEM] Rev. Jeff Ethen.
Res.: P.O. Box 339, 56361. Tel: 218-338-2761.
PAYNESVILLE, STEARNS CO., ST. LOUIS, [CEM] Rev. Richard Leisen.
Res.: 505 Burr St., Box 39, 56362. Tel: 320-243-4413.
Catechesis/Religious Program—Phyllis Gardner, D.R.E. Students 331.
PEARL LAKE, STEARNS CO., HOLY CROSS, [CEM] Rev. Msgr. Daniel J. Taufen, S.T.L.; Deacon Andrew Kunkel.
Res.: 10651 County Rd. 8, Kimball, 55353. Tel: 320-398-7986; Fax: 320-398-7873.
School—Tel: 320-398-7885; Fax: 320-398-7873. Lay Teachers 5; Students 72.
Catechesis/Religious Program—Students 27.
PELICAN RAPIDS, OTTER TAIL CO., ST. LEONARD'S, [CEM] Rev. Richard Walz; Deacon Joseph Hilber.
Res.: P.O. Box 378, 56572. Tel: 218-863-5161.
Catechesis/Religious Program—Julie Morgan, D.R.E. Students 91.
PERHAM, OTTER TAIL CO.
1—ST. HENRY'S, [CEM] Rev. David J. Rieder.
Res.: Box 216, 56573. Tel: 218-346-4240; Fax: 218-346-4240.
School—Area School, Tel: 218-346-6190; Fax: 218-346-6190. Lay Teachers 8; Students 94.
Catechesis/Religious Program—Tel: 218-346-7030. Students 208.
2—ST. STANISLAUS, [CEM] Revs. David J. Rieder; Jerome Nordick.
Res.: P.O. Box 216, 56573. Tel: 218-346-4240; Fax: 218-346-4240.
Catechesis/Religious Program—Students 29.
PIERZ, MORRISON CO., ST. JOSEPH'S, [CEM] Rev. Gerald Dalseth; Deacon Guy Beck.
Res.: 68 Main St., P.O. Box 428, 56364. Tel: 320-468-6033; Fax: 320-468-2296.
School— See Inter-Parochial School under Institutions Located in the Diocese.
Catechesis/Religious Program—P.O. Box 205, 56364. Tel: 320-468-2640. Students 225.
PRINCETON, MILLE LACS CO., ST. EDWARD'S, [CEM] Rev. Leroy Kremer.
Res.: 804 7th Ave. S., 55371. Tel: 763-389-2115; Fax: 763-389-5137.
Catechesis/Religious Program—Sarah McIntosh, D.R.E. Students 288.
RANDALL, MORRISON CO., ST. JAMES, [CEM] Rev. Leo Moenkedick.
Mailing Address: P.O. Box 225, 56475.
RICE, BENTON CO., IMMACULATE CONCEPTION, [CEM] Rev. David Maciej; Deacon Russell Hackett.
Res.: 130 First Ave., N.E., P.O. Box 189, 56367. Tel: 320-393-2725; Fax: 320-393-7507.
Catechesis/Religious Program—Tel: 320-393-2826. Sr. Carol Ann Gosse, D.R.E. Students 190.
RICHMOND, STEARNS CO., SS. PETER AND PAUL'S, [CEM] Rev. Stephen Beauclair, O.S.B.
Res.: P.O. Box 69, 56368. Tel: 320-597-2575; Fax: 320-597-5231.
School—Tel: 320-597-2565; Fax: 320-597-4385. Lay Teachers 7; Students 122.
Catechesis/Religious Program—Tel: 320-597-3720. Teri Krowka-Ansberry, D.R.E. Students 224.
ROCKVILLE, STEARNS CO., MARY OF THE IMMACULATE CONCEPTION, [CEM] Rev. Gregory Mastey.
Res.: 113 Broadway, P.O. Box 7, 56369. Tel: 320-251-7801.
Catechesis/Religious Program—Students 296.
ROSCOE, STEARNS CO., ST. AGNES, [CEM] Rev. Leo Leisen.
Res.: 100 Lillie Ave., 56371. Tel: 320-243-4574.
Catechesis/Religious Program—Students 46.
ROYALTON, MORRISON CO., HOLY TRINITY, [CEM] Rev. Laurn Virnig.
Res.: P.O. Box 258, 56373. Tel: 320-584-5484; Fax: 320-584-0028.
Catechesis/Religious Program—Students 210.
RUSH LAKE, OTTER TAIL CO., ST. LAWRENCE, [CEM] Revs. Jerome Nordick; David J. Rieder. In Res., Rev. Kevin Schwartz.
Res.: 46404 County Hwy. 14, Perham, 56528. Tel: 218-346-5944; Fax: 218-346-5946.
Catechesis/Religious Program—Students 115.
ST. ANNA, STEARNS CO., IMMACULATE CONCEPTION, [CEM] Revs. Gerald Mischke, Co-Pastor; Joseph Herzing, Co-Pastor; Deacons Jeffrey Fromm; Jerome Schwarzbauer.
Res.: St. Mary's Rectory, P.O. Box 308, Holdingford, 56340. Tel: 320-746-2231; Fax: 320-746-2449.
Catechesis/Religious Program—Students 105.
ST. ANTHONY, STEARNS CO., ST. ANTHONY'S, [CEM] Revs. Donald Wagner; LeRoy Schik.
Res.: 24328 Trobec St., Albany, 56307. Tel: 320-845-2416; Fax: 320-845-2414.
Catechesis/Religious Program—Lou Ann Goebel, D.R.E. Students 58.
ST. AUGUSTA, STEARNS CO., ST. MARY HELP OF CHRISTIANS, [CEM] Rev. Robert E. Rolfes.
Res.: 24588 County Rd. 7, 56301. Tel: 320-252-1799; Fax: 320-252-1992.
School—Tel: 320-251-3937. Sisters of St. Benedict 1; Lay Teachers 10; Students 122.
Catechesis/Religious Program—Karen Thole, D.R.E. Students 275.
ST. FRANCIS, STEARNS CO., ST. FRANCIS OF ASSISI, [CEM] Revs. Donald Wagner; LeRoy Schik.
Res.: 44055 State Hwy. 238, Freeport, 56331. Tel: 320-573-2203; Fax: 320-573-2205.
Catechesis/Religious Program—Students 102.
ST. JOSEPH, STEARNS CO., ST. JOSEPH'S, [CEM] Rev. Gregory Miller, O.S.B.; Deacon Thomas Murray.
Res.: 12 W. Minnesota St., 56374. Tel: 320-363-7505; Fax: 320-363-0710.
School—Fax: 320-363-7760. Lay Teachers 11; Students 184.
Catechesis/Religious Program—Students 300.
ST. MARTIN, STEARNS CO., ST. MARTIN'S, [CEM] Rev. Julian Schmiesing, O.S.B.
Res.: 119 Maine St., Box 290, 56376. Tel: 320-548-3550.
Catechesis/Religious Program—Tel: 320-548-3209. Joan Rothstein, D.R.E. Students 154.
ST. NICHOLAS, STEARNS CO., ST. NICHOLAS, [CEM] Rev. Msgr. Daniel J. Taufen, S.T.L.
Res.: 15862 County Rd. 165, Watkins, 55389. Tel: 320-764-7345; Fax: 320-764-7345.
Catechesis/Religious Program—Students 31.
ST. ROSA, STEARNS CO., ST. ROSE OF LIMA, [CEM] Revs. Roger Klassen, O.S.B.; Julius Beckermann, O.S.B.; Deacon Richard Scherping.
Res.: P.O. Box 155, Freeport, 56331-0155. Tel: 320-836-2143; Fax: 320-836-2142.
ST. STEPHEN, STEARNS CO., ST. STEPHEN'S, [CEM] Rev. Robert C. Harren, J.C.L.
Res.: 103 Central Ave. S., 56375. Tel: 320-251-1520.
Catechesis/Religious Program—Tel: 320-251-5066. Andrew Case, D.R.E. Students 168.
ST. WENDEL, STEARNS CO., ST. COLUMBKILLE'S, [CEM] Revs. Gerald Mischke, Co-Pastor; Joseph Herzing, Co-Pastor; Deacons Jeffrey Fromm; Jerome Schwarzbauer.
St. Mary's Rectory: P.O. Box 308, Holdingford, 56340. Tel: 320-746-2231; Fax: 320-746-2449.
Catechesis/Religious Program—Students 90.
SARTELL, STEARNS CO., ST. FRANCIS XAVIER, [CEM] Rev. Lauren Germann; Deacon Dirck Curry.
Res.: P.O. Box 150, 56377. Tel: 320-252-1363; Fax: 320-259-7090.
School—Tel: 320-252-9940. Lay Teachers 15; Students 193.
Catechesis/Religious Program—Students 955.
SAUK CENTRE, STEARNS CO.
1—OUR LADY OF THE ANGELS, [CEM] Rev. James Statz; Deacon Lawrence Kaas.

Res.: 211 Seventh S., 56378-1505. Tel: 320-352-3502; Fax: 320-351-3502.
Catechesis/Religious Program—Tel: 320-352-5580. Students 232.
2—ST. PAUL'S, Rev. Todd Schneider; Deacon Thomas McFadden.
Res.: 304 Sinclair Lewis Ave., 56378. Tel: 320-352-2196; Fax: 320-351-8475.
School—Holy Family School, 231 Sinclair Lewis Ave., 56378. Tel: 320-352-6535; Fax: 320-352-6537. Inter-Parochial School: St. Paul's Sauk Centre, Our Lady of Angels, Sauk Center. Lay Teachers 16; Students 226.
Catechesis/Religious Program—220 S. Birch, 56378. Tel: 320-352-5580. Students 275.
SAUK RAPIDS, BENTON CO.
1—ST. PATRICK, [CEM] Rev. Bernard Kahlhamer.
Res.: 7286 Duelm Rd., N.E., 56379. Tel: 320-252-2069.
2—SACRED HEART, [CEM] Rev. Eugene Doyle; Deacon Kirk Kedrowski.
Res.: 216 Third Ave. S., 56379. Tel: 320-251-8115; Fax: 320-252-0710.
School—324 Third Ave. S., 56379. Tel: 320-251-2854; Fax: 320-251-0705. Lay Teachers 14; Students 185.
SEDAN, POPE CO., IMMACULATE CONCEPTION, Closed., For inquiries for parish records contact Sacred Heart, Glenwood.
SOBIESKI, MORRISON CO., ST. STANISLAUS, [CEM] Rev. Leo Moenkedick.
Res.: 9406 Church Cir., Little Falls, 56345-9803. Tel: 320-632-5086; Fax: 320-632-5644.
SPRING HILL, STEARNS CO., ST. MICHAEL'S, [CEM] Rev. Leo Leisen. In Res., Rev. Edward Ramacher.
Res.: 100 Lillie Ave., Roscoe, 56371. Tel: 320-243-4574.
Catechesis/Religious Program—Students 84.
STAPLES, TODD CO., SACRED HEART, [JC] Rev. Peter Kirchner.
Res.: 310 Fourth St. N.E., Box 177, 56479. Tel: 218-894-2296; Fax: 218-894-2994.
School—Tel: 218-894-2077. Lay Teachers 7; Students 79.
Catechesis/Religious Program—Tel: 218-894-1095. Students 175.
SWANVILLE, MORRISON CO., ST. JOHN THE BAPTIST, [CEM] Rev. Arlin Sowada.
Res.: P.O. Box 366, Grey Eagle, 56336. Tel: 320-285-2545; Fax: 320-547-2578.
Catechesis/Religious Program—P.O. Box 68, 56382. Tel: 320-547-2920. Students 134.
TINTAH, TRAVERSE CO., ST. GALL'S, [CEM] Rev. Andrew Marthaler.
Res.: P.O. Box 127, 56583. Tel: 218-369-2188. Email: stgall@runestone.net.
Catechesis/Religious Program—Students 30.
UPSALA, MORRISON CO., ST. MARY, [CEM] Revs. Donald Wagner; LeRoy Schik.
Res.: P.O. Box 8, Bowlus, 56314. Tel: 320-584-5313; Fax: 320-584-8231.
Catechesis/Religious Program—Students 72.
URBANK, OTTER TAIL CO., SACRED HEART, [CEM] Rev. Jeff Ethen.
Res.: 60 Central Ave. N., Parkers Prairie, 56361. Tel: 218-267-2661.
Catechesis/Religious Program—Students 44.
VERNDALE, WADENA CO., ST. FREDERICK'S, [CEM] Revs. Albert Holmes; Ronald Schmelzer.
Res.: 20 Brown St. N., P.O. Box C, 56481. Tel: 218-445-5786.
Catechesis/Religious Program—23764 U.S. Hwy. 71, Sebeka, 56477. Tel: 218-631-1832. Vera Malone, D.R.E. Students 87.
VILLARD, POPE CO., ST. BARTHOLOMEW'S, [CEM] Rev. Thomas Becker.
Sacred Heart Church: Glenwood, 56334. Tel: 320-634-3813; Fax: 320-634-0590.
Catechesis/Religious Program—Leonard Heidelberger, D.R.E. Students 22.
VINELAND, MILLE LACS CO., ST. THERESE, LITTLE FLOWER INDIAN MISSION, [CEM] [JC] Rev. David Gallus, O.S.C.
Mailing Address: P.O. Box 500, Onamia, 56359. Tel: 320-532-3601; Fax: 320-532-5222.
WADENA, WADENA CO., ST. ANN'S, [CEM] Revs. Albert Holmes; Ronald Schmelzer.
Res.: 514 First St., S.E., 56482. Tel: 218-631-1593; Fax: 218-631-7149.
School—Tel: 218-631-2631; Fax: 218-632-5612. Lay Teachers 7; Students 65.
Catechesis/Religious Program—Students 124.
WAHKON, MILLE LACS CO., SACRED HEART, [CEM] Rev. Raymond Steffes, O.S.C.
Mailing Address: *Crosier Community*, P.O. Box 500, Onamia, 56359. Tel: 320-532-3103; Fax: 320-532-3103.
Catechesis/Religious Program—Tel: 320-495-3324. Lola Larson, D.R.E. Students 31.
WAITE PARK, STEARNS CO., ST. JOSEPH'S, [CEM] Rev. Ronald Weyrens; Deacon Richard Midas.
Res.: 106 Seventh Ave. N., 56387. Tel: 320-251-5231; Fax: 320-251-3010.
School—Tel: 320-251-4741, Ext. 1; Fax: 320-230-2161. Lay Teachers 9; Students 153.
Catechesis/Religious Program—Tel: 320-251-4771, Ext. 3. Students 93.
WARD SPRINGS, TODD CO., ST. BERNARD'S, Closed., For inquiries for parish records contact St. Joseph, Grey Eagle.
WEST UNION, TODD CO., ST. ALEXIUS, [CEM] Rev. James Statz.
Res.: 211 S. 7th St., Sauk Centre, 56378. Tel: 320-352-3502.
Catechesis/Religious Program—Box 4A, 56389. Tel: 320-352-2563; Fax: 320-352-2930. Students 54.
WHEATON, TRAVERSE CO., AVE MARIA, [JC] Revs. Stanley Wieser; David Trujillo (Venezuela).
Res.: 201 Ninth St. S., 56296. Tel: 320-563-4421.
ZIMMERMAN, SHERBURNE CO., ST. PIUS X, [CEM] Rev. Antonio Marfori.
Res.: Box 152, 55398. Tel: 763-856-4401; Fax: 763-856-4401.
Catechesis/Religious Program—Tel: 763-856-2400. Noreen Olson, D.R.E. Students 303.

Chaplains of Public Institutions

ST. CLOUD. *Minnesota State Reformatory for Men*. Rev. Joel Kelly, O.S.B.
St. John's Abbey: P.O. Box 2015, Collegeville, 56321.
U.S. Veteran's Hospital 56301. Rev. Alfred Stangl.
CAMBRIDGE. *Cambridge State School and Hospital* 55008. (Vacant)
FERGUS FALLS. *State Hospital Chapel* 56537. (Vacant)

Special Assignment:
Revs.—
Belland, David
Oelrich, Anthony
Ostendorf, Mark
Stangl, Alfred
Trussel, Christopher

Retired:
Most Rev.—
Sowada, Alphonse
Revs.—
Bednark, Walter, 23189 State Hwy. 4, Paynesville, 56362.
Belair, Eugene, 511 S. Fourth Ave., Princeton, 55371.
Brenny, Kenneth, P.O. Box 608, Buckman, 56317.
Donnay, Raymond, 808 Ann Marie Cir., # 701, Little Falls, 56345.
Ebner, Frank, 1810 Minnesota Blvd., S.E., 56304.
Eccleston, John, 116-8th Ave., SE Little Falls, 56345.
Fadrowski, Stanislaus, 1934 Michigan Ave., Englewood, FL 34224.
Fehrenbacher, Henry, 371-7th Ave. #24D, New York, NY 10001.
Finnegan, Roscoe L., 715 Farney Rd., Las Cruces, NM 88005.
Furlan, William, 320 Fourth Ave. S., Sauk Rapids, 56379.
Gall, Sylvester, 520 First St., N.E., Apt. 80, Sartell, 56377.
Haupt, Lloyd, 929 Brenda Lee Dr., 56303.
Heid, Richard J., Box 256, Brandon, 56315.
Hoppe, Arthur, 28905 County Rd. 17, Freeport, 56331.
Kalkman, Richard, 23 Diaz Ave., San Francisco, CA 94132.
Kinzer, Victor, 321 Jefferson St., Apt. 6, Alexandria, 56308.
Kleinschmidt, Sylvester, 412 First St. S., Apt. 1, Sauk Centre, 56378.
Kraemer, Edwin, 828 Village Ave., Sartell, 56377.
Landsberger, Robert, 12536 County Rd. 4, Avon, 56310.
Lang, Raymond, 35-1st Ave., N # 110, Waite Park, 56387.
Maierus, Daniel, 8722 Timberbriar, San Antonio, TX 78250.
Maus, Le Roy, 11367 Phoenix Dr. # 175, Yuma, AZ 85367.
Meemken, Eugene A., P.O. Box 124, Clarissa, 56440.
Miller, John, 31 Pine Tree Ct., Sartell, 56377.
Minette, James, 101 Enterprise Dr., Apt. 163, Rohnert Park, CA 94928.
Otto, Leo, R.R. 3, Box 118, Perham, 56573.
Pavelis, Harold, Box 88, Concord, CA 94522.
Pecovnik, Karel, McCornell Ct. # 207, 212 W. Soo St., Parkers Prairie, 56361.
Podrosky, Alfred, 117 Bechwood Dr., Monongahela, PA 15063.
Poncelet, Frank, Institute of Christ the King, P.O. Box 12, Glenwood, 56334.
Quade, Alvin, P.O. Box 225, Randall, 56475.
Ramacher, Edward, 102 St. Michael Ave. N. Spring Hill, Melrose, 56352.
Rieder, Donald, 213-3rd St. S., 56301.
Riley, Patrick, 3034 Fulton Cir., Clearwater, 55320.
Sauer, Alban, 1525 24th Ave. N., 56303.
Schmitt, Silverius, 5290-175th St., N.W., Box 353, Royalton, 56373.
Schwieters, Severin, 207-3rd. St. S., 56301.
Schwinghammer, Claude, Park Gardens, 114 First St. N., Apt. 219, Waite Park, 56387.
Slominski, Leon, 10651 County Rd. 8, Kimball, 55353.
Snyers, Peter, 1305 15th St., N.E. # 101, Sauk Rapid, 56379.
Thielman, Kenneth, Park View Center, 125 N. Fifth Ave. W., Melrose, 56352.
Tomasiewicz, Frank, 27240 Lakewood Dr. NW, Isanti, 55040.
Torborg, Elmer, P.O. Box 308, Holdingford, 56340.
Vogel, Arthur, 617 Pinecone Rd., Apt. 308, Sartell, 56377.
Wey, Richard, 89 Greenstone Ln., Waite Park, 56387.
Wiersgalla, Joseph, St. Benedict's Senior Community, 1810 S.E. Minnesota Blvd., 56304.
Willenbring, Mark W., P.O. Box 147, Kimball, 55353.
Zimmer, Nicholas, Elmhurst Commons, 400 3rd St., S.W., Apt. 211, Braham, 55006.
Zylla, Paul, 1615-15th Ave., S.E. #251, 56304.

Permanent Deacons:
Adams, Cecil, St. Henry's Monticello
Anderberg, George, Owatonna
Bates, Kenneth, (Retired)
Beck, Guy, St. Michael, Buckman; St. Joseph, Pierz
Bobertz, Charles
Curry, Dirck, St. Francis Xavier, Sartell
DuPay, Steven, Our Lady of the Lake, BigLake
Eichers, Elmer, (Retired)
Fromm, Jeffrey, St. Mary's, Holdingford
Geyer, Bruce, Our Lady of Lourdes, Little Falls
Hackett, Russell, Immaculate Conception, Rice
Hennen, Stanley, Assumption, Morris
Hennes, James C., (Retired)
Kaas, Lawrence, Our Lady of the Angels, Sauk Centre
Keable, Michael, St. John Baptist, Collegeville
Kedrowski, Kirk, Sacred Heart, Sauk Rapids
Kosiba, Leo, St. Mary, St. Cloud
Krebs, Brian
Kruchten, Kenneth R., (Retired)
Kunkel, Andrew, Holy Cross, Pearl Lake
Lindmeier, David, St. Paul, St. Cloud
Maltzen, Bruce
McFadden, Thomas, St. Paul's Sauk Center
Midas, Richard, St. Joseph, Waite Park
Murray, Thomas, St. Joseph, St. Joseph.
Nord, Carl, St. Anthony, St. Cloud
Reker, Fred, St. John Cantius, St. Cloud
Ritchie, William, St. Peter, St. Cloud
Roth, Jerome, (Retired)
Salchert, John, St. Boniface, Cold Spring
Scheierl, Richard, St. Augustine, St. Cloud
Scherping, Richard, Sacred Heart, Freeport
Schmainda, Frank, Sacred Heart, Glenwood
Schmitz, Vernon, Holy Spirit, St. Cloud
Schwarzbauer, Jerome, St. Mary's, Holdingford
Scott, John W., (Retired)
Sell, Lawrence, St. Boniface, Cold Spring
Shaffer, Robert, St. Isidore, Moran
St. Jean, Fred, St. Andrew, Elk River
Steele, Gregory J., Immaculate Conception, Becker
Tzinski, Donald, Sts. Peter & Paul, Braham
Warren, Todd, St. Paul, St. Cloud
Wolak, John, Sacred Heart, Staples
Woods, John, St. Peter, St. Cloud
Yanish, Stephen
Zenner, Mark, Mary of Mt. Carmel, Long Prairie

INSTITUTIONS LOCATED IN THE DIOCESE

[A] SEMINARIES, RELIGIOUS OR SCHOLASTICATES

COLLEGEVILLE. *St. John's School of Theology and Seminary*, Formerly St. John's Seminary, P.O. Box 7288, 56321. Tel: 320-363-2100; Fax: 320-363-3145. Email: cclement@csbsju.edu. Web: www.csbsju.edu/sot. Rev. John Klassen, O.S.B., Ph.D.; Dr. William Cahoy, Dean.
Legal Title: *St. John's School of Theology and Seminary*

[B] COLLEGES AND UNIVERSITIES

COLLEGEVILLE. *St. John's University* (1857), (Men) , 56321-2000. Tel: 320-363-2011; Fax: 320-363-2504. Email: nthorburn@csbsju.edu. Web: www.csbsju.edu. Rev. John Klassen, O.S.B., Ph.D., Abbot & Chancellor. Sponsored by the Collegeville Benedictine Monks as a division of the corporate Order of St. Benedict, Collegeville, MN.; The Graduate School of Theology (Coed)/Saint John's Seminary (Men): M.A. in Theology, Liturgical Studies, Liturgical Music, Pastoral Ministry and a Master of Divinity. The Undergraduate College of Liberal Arts and Sciences (Men), in full coordinate academic relation with the College of St. Benedict, St. Joseph (Women), offers forty departments, ten pre-professional and ten special academic programs.; Sponsored Programs: The Hill Monastic Manuscript Library and the Saint John's Pottery. Priests 14; Brothers 4; Sisters 4; Lay Teachers 130; Administrators 180; Students 2,054.

Officers Group: Bros. Benedict Leuthner, O.S.B., Corp. Treas.; Dietrich Reinhart, O.S.B., Pres.; Dr. William Cahoy, Dean, School of Theology; Mr. Rob Culligan, Vice Pres., Institutional Advancement; Dr. Gar Kellom, Vice Pres., Student Devel.; Rita Knuesel, Dean of the College; Mary Milbert, Dean of Admissions & Financial Aid; Dr. Henry Smorynski, Provost, Academic Affairs.

Administrative Group: Revs. John Klassen, O.S.B., Ph.D., Rector, St. John's Seminary; Timothy Backous, O.S.B., Dir. Athletics; Robert Pierson, O.S.B., Dir. Campus Ministry; Columba Stewart, O.S.B., Dir. Hill Monastic Manuscript Library; Bros. Linus Ascheman, O.S.B., Dir. Buildings and Grounds; David Klingeman, O.S.B., Archivist; Dr. Annette Atkins, The Michael Blecker Professorship; Dr. David Bennetts, Dir. Summer Academic Prog.; Mr. Ronald Bosrock, The John & Elizabeth Myers Chair in Mgmt.; Mr. Richard Bresnahan, Potter, The St. John's Pottery; Barry Cytron, Rabbi, The Jay Phillips Center for Jewish-Christian Learning; Patti Epsky, Exec. Asst.; Dr. Bernard Evans, The Butler Family's Virgil Michel Ecumenical Chair in Rural Social Ministries; Dr. Daniel Rush Finn, The William & Virginia Clemens Chair in Economics & the Liberal Arts; Ms. Julie Gruska, Registrar; Dr. Nicholas P. Hayes, Univ. Chair in Critical Thinking; Mr. Gregory Hoye, Exec. Dir. Communications & Mktg.; Mr. Michael Kathman, Dir. Libraries and Media; Mr. James Koenig, Dir. Computing Svcs.; Mr. Jason Laker, Dean of Campus Life; Ms. Theresa McNutt, Dir. of Intercultural Programs; Mr. Stuart Perry, Dir. Financial Aid; Mr. Herb Trenz, Dir. Human Resources; Mr. John Young, Exec. Devel. & Univ. Rels.

ST. JOSEPH. *College of St. Benedict* (1913), (Women) , 37 College Ave. S., 56374-2099. Tel: 320-363-5407 (Communications & Mktg. Svcs.); Fax: 320-363-5136 (Inst. Mktg. & Communication & Mktg. Svcs.). Email: cms@csbsju.edu. Web: www.csbsju.edu.

Legal Title: *College of Saint Benedict* Sisters of the Order of St. Benedict, Affiliation: Roman Catholic, established for the undergraduate education of women by the Sisters of the Order of Saint Benedict.; Partnership: The College of St. Benedict is a private, nationally recognized women's, residential, liberal arts, Catholic, Benedictine college, located in St. Joseph, Minn. joined in a coeducational mission with St. John's University for men. As the only Catholic all women's Baccalaureate I college, St. Benedict's is unique in its commitment to gender specfic education within a coeducational environment. Sisters 17; Faculty 160; Administrators 128; Students 1,991.

Officers Group: Mary Geller, Vice Pres. Student Devel.; Carol Guardo, Pres.; Rita Knuesel, Assoc. Provost & Academic Dean; Mary Milbert, Dean of Admissions; Colman O'Connell, O.S.B., Vice Pres. Institutional Advancement; Susan Palmer, Fincial Chief. & Admin.; Henry Smorynski, Provost, Academic Affairs.

Administrative Group: Kay Buytaert, Assoc. Dir. of Publications & Graphics; Susan Douma, Dir. of Academic Advising; Mike Durbin, Dir. of Sports Information; Jim Fredricks, Chief Physical Plant & Facilities Mgr.; Mary Geller, Vice Pres. of Students Devel.; Ms. Julie Gruska, Registrar; Mary Harlander-Locke, Dir. of Career Svcs.; Jane Haugen, Exec. Dir. of Financial Aid; Carol Howe-Veenstra, Dir. of Athletics; Greg Hoye, Exec. Dir. Communication & Mktg. Svc.; Mr. Michael Kathman, Dir. of Libraries & Media; James Koenig, Dir., Information Technology Svc.; Jon McGee, Vice Pres. Inst. Planning, Research & Comm.; Frank Rioux, Dir. of International Education; JoAnn Shroyer, Dir. Communications & Mktg. Svcs.; Jody Terhaar, Dean of Students; Herb Trenz, Dir. Human Resources.

[C] HIGH SCHOOLS, DIOCESAN

ST. CLOUD. *Cathedral High and John XXIII Middle School*, P.O. Box 1579, 56302. Tel: 320-251-3421; Fax: 320-253-5576. Email: rstewart@chsj23.org. Mr. Robert Stewart, Pres.; Ms. Lynn Grewing, Prin.; Rev. Christopher Trussel. Priests 1; Sisters 2; Lay Teachers 50; Students 792.

Cathedral High School Education Foundation, P.O. Box 1579, 56302. Tel: 320-251-3421; Fax: 320-253-5576. Bob Kovell, Pres.

[D] HIGH SCHOOLS, PRIVATE

COLLEGEVILLE. *St. John's Preparatory School* College Preparatory. , P.O. Box 4000, 56321. Tel: 320-363-3315; Fax: 320-363-3513. Email: gtavis@csbsju.edu. Web: www.sjprep.net. Rev. Gordon Tavis, O.S.B., Pres. Priests 2; Students 320; Brothers 2; Lay Teachers 32.

[E] INTER-PAROCHIAL SCHOOLS

ST. CLOUD. *St. Elizabeth Ann Seton School*, (Grades K-3), Primary: 1615 Eleventh Ave. S., 56301. Tel: 320-251-1988; Fax: 320-229-2149. Email: bonniemassmann@hotmail.com. Bonnie Massmann, Prin. Consolidation of schools of the following parishes: Holy Spirit, St. Anthony and St. John Cantius, St. Cloud. Lay Teachers 12; Students 172.

Middle: (Grades 4-6), 2410 First St. N., 56303. Tel: 320-251-6231; Fax: 320-251-7396. Dan Hollenhorst, Prin. Lay Teachers 7; Students 115.

Sts. Peter, Paul and Michael School, (Grades K-4), Primary: 925 30th Ave. N., 56303. Tel: 320-251-4737; Fax: 320-253-7110. Email: sppm945@astound.net. Mrs. Sharon Bichler, Prin. Consolidation of the following parishes: St. Michael; St. Paul; St. Peter, St. Cloud. Lay Teachers 20.

Preschool, 1036 County Rd. 4, 56303. Lay Teachers 1; Students 34.

Middle (Grades 5-8), 1215 N. 11th Ave., 56303. Tel: 320-251-5295; Fax: 320-251-7014. Email: sppmmiddle@astound.net. Lay Teachers 18; Students 526.

FOLEY. *St. John's Area School*, (Grades PreK-6), 215 7th Ave. S., 56329. Tel: 320-968-7972; Fax: 320-968-9956. Email: sjasfm@cloudnet.com. Web: www.cloudnet.com~sjasfm. Mary Sabin, Prin. Consolidation of the following parishes: St. John of Foley; St. Lawrence, Duelm; St. Elizabeth, Brennyville; St. Joseph, Morrill; SS. Peter and Paul, Gilman; St. Louis, Foreston; St. Patrick of Minden Township Lay Teachers 9; Students 146.

LITTLE FALLS. *Mary of Lourdes Elementary and Middle School*, (Grades K-4), Primary: 307 Fourth St., S.E., 56345. Tel: 320-632-5408; Fax: 320-632-5409. Email: pschieffert@molschool.org. Web: www.molschool.org. Paul Schieffert, Prin. Consolidation of following parishes: St. Mary and Our Lady of Lourdes, Little Falls Lay Teachers 15; Students 203; Preschool Students 39.

Middle: (Grades 5-8), 205 N.W. Third St., 56345. Tel: 320-632-6742; Fax: 320-632-3556. Debra J. Meyer, Prin. Lay Teachers 10; Students 147.

PIERZ. *Holy Trinity School*, 80 Edward St. S., Box 427, 56364. Tel: 320-468-6446; Fax: 320-468-6446. Email: holytrinity@pierz.net. Web: holytrinitypierz.org. Consolidation of the following parishes: St. Michael's, Buckman; Holy Cross, Harding; St. John Nepomuk, Lastrup; St. Joseph, Pierz. Lay Teachers 13; Students 185.

SAUK CENTRE. *Holy Family School*, (Grades K-6), 231 Sinclair Lewis Ave., 56378. Tel: 320-352-6535; Fax: 320-352-6537. Email: hfs@isd743.k12.mn.us. Web: www.rc.net/stcloud/hfs. Lynn Peterson, Prin. Consolidation of the following parishes: St. Paul's and Our Lady of the Angels, Sauk Centre. Lay Teachers 16; Students 226.

[F] HOMES FOR EMOTIONALLY DISTURBED AND HANDICAPPED

ST. CLOUD. *St. Cloud Children's Home of the Diocese of St. Cloud*, 1726 Seventh Ave. S., 56301. Tel: 320-650-1500; Fax: 320-650-1508. Mr. Steven P. Bresnahan, Exec. Dir.; John Krueger, Dir. Residential Svcs. Children 78.

St. Elizabeth Home Contact John Krueger at Catholic Charities. , 306 15th Ave. N., 56303. Tel: 320-240-3350. Email: rhanish@gw.stcdio.org. Mr. Steven P. Bresnahan, Exec. Dir.; John Krueger, Dir. of Residential Day Svcs. Board and Lodging Home for Functionally Impaired Adults. Residents 18.

LaPaz Community Inc., Catholic Charities Housing Services, 157 Roosevelt Rd., Ste. 200, 56301. 1730 Seventh Ave. S., 56301. Tel: 320-253-9470; Fax: 320-253-7464. Mr. Steven P. Bresnahan, Exec. Dir.; Harvey Schmitt, Dir. Housing Svcs.

COLD SPRING. *St. Anne's Home* Contact Catholic Charities. , 103 10th Ave. N., 56320. Tel: 320-685-7898; Fax: 320-685-8626. Mr. Steven P. Bresnahan, Exec Dir.; John Krueger, Dir. Residential Day Svcs. Supervised Living Situation for Persons with Developmental Disabilities Residents 4.

Bethany Home Contact John Krueger at Catholic Charities. , 13 Eighth Ave. S., 56320. Tel: 320-685-7899; Fax: 320-685-9808. Email: jkrueger@gw.stcdio.org. Mr. Steven P. Bresnahan, Exec Dir.; John Krueger, Dir. Residential Day Svcs. Supervised Living Situation for Persons with Developmental Disabilities Residents 4.

St. Luke's Home Contact Catholic Charities. , 411 Eighth Ave. N., 56320. Tel: 320-685-7750. Mr. Steven P. Bresnahan, Exec. Dir.; John Krueger, Dir. Residential Svcs. Adults with mild to moderate developmental disabilities. Residents 4.

Mother Teresa Home Contact Catholic Charities. , 101 Tenth Ave., 56320. Tel: 320-685-8626; Fax: 320-685-8626. Mr. Steven P. Bresnahan, Exec. Dir.; John Krueger, Dir. Residential Day Svcs. Supervised Living Situation for Persons with Developmental Disabilities Residents 4.

FERGUS FALLS. *Catholic Charities Intensive Treatment Unit*, P.O. Box 1006, 56538-1006. Tel: 218-739-9325; Fax: 218-739-2242. Mr. Steven Bresnahan, Exec. Dir.; John Krueger, Dir. Residential Day Svcs. Children 19; Total Persons 57.

LITTLE FALLS. *St. Camillus Place*, 1100 S.E. Fourth St., 56345. Tel: 320-632-1212; Fax: 320-632-1383. Cory Glad, Admin.; Barbara A. Miller, Dir.; Bea Britz, Chap. Bed Capacity 13.

WAITE PARK. *St. Francis Home*, P.O. Box 326, 56387. Tel: 320-251-7630; Fax: 320-240-8097. Mr. Steven P. Bresnahan, Exec. Dir.; John Krueger, Dir. Residential Day Svcs. Supervised Living Situation for Persons with Developmental Disabilities Residents 4.

[G] GENERAL HOSPITALS

ST. CLOUD. *St. Cloud Hospital*, 1406 Sixth Ave. N., 56303. Tel: 320-251-2700; Fax: 320-255-5711. Web: www.stcloudhospital.com. Craig Broman, Pres.; Bret Reuter, Dir. Mission and Spiritual Care; Rev. Roger Botz, O.S.B., Chap.; Sisters Joyce Iten, O.S.B., Chap.; Joan Felling, O.S.B., Chap. Sisters of St. Benedict 3; Bed Capacity 489; Bassinets 40; Patients Assisted Annually 180,538.

ALBANY. *Albany Area Hospital*, 300 Third Ave., 56307. Tel: 320-845-2121; Fax: 320-845-4707. Web: www.albanyareahospital.com. Ben Koppelman, Admin.; Deborah Robinson, Chap. Sisters of St. Francis 2; Bed Capacity 17; Patients Assisted Annually 9,000.

BRECKENRIDGE. *St. Francis Medical Center*, 415 Oak St., 56520. Tel: 218-643-3000; Fax: 218-643-7502. Email: davidnelson@catholichealth.net. Web: www.sfcare.org. David Nelson, Pres.; Ann Trebsch, Vice Pres. Mission; Rev. Anthony Kroll, Chap. Bed Capacity 47; Patients Assisted Annually 27,866.

LITTLE FALLS. *St. Gabriel's Hospital*, 815 S.E. Second St., 56345. Tel: 320-632-5441; Fax: 320-632-1190. Carl P. Vaagenes, Pres. & CEO; Bea Britz, Chap. Sisters 1; Bed Capacity 49; Bassinets 10; Patients Assisted Annually 30,488.

[H] HOMES FOR AGED

ST. CLOUD. *St. Benedict's Senior Community*, 1810 Minnesota Blvd., S.E., 56304. Tel: 320-252-0010; Fax: 320-654-2351. Linda Doerr, Exec. Dir.; Doug Aretz, Admin. Care Center; Sr. Susan Rudolph, O.S.B., Chap. & Dir. of Pastoral Care; Rev. Meinrad Dindorf, O.S.B., Chap. Corporate Division of the St. Cloud Hospital. Operated under the auspices of the local Catholic Church of St. Cloud.; Care Center managed by St. Benedict's Senior Community. A division of the St. Cloud Hospital. Operated under the auspices of the local Catholic Church of St. Cloud. Residents 198; Sub-Acute Unit Beds 24.

Benedict Village: 2000 15th Ave., S.E., 56304. Tel: 320-252-4380; Fax: 320-654-2351. Linda Doerr, Exec. Dir.; Robin Theis, Admin., Housing and Community Svcs. Managed by St. Benedict's Senior Community. A Division of the St. Cloud Hospital. Operated under the auspices of the local Catholic Church of St. Cloud. Residents 115.

Benedict Homes (4), 1342 Minnesota Blvd., S.E., 56304. Tel: 320-252-0010. Residential Homes for residents with Alzheimers. All Benedict Homes are managed by St. Benedict's Senior Community. A division of the St. Cloud Hospital. Operated under the auspices of the local Catholic Church of St. Cloud. Residents 20.

Benedict Court, 1980 15th Ave., S.E., 56304. Tel: 320-252-0010; Fax: 320-654-2351. Linda Doerr, Exec. Dir.; Robin Theis, Admin., Housing and Community Svcs. 39 assisted living apartments; Managed by St. Benedict's Senior Community. A Division of the St. Cloud Hospital. Operated under the auspices of the local Catholic Church of St.

Cloud. Residents 40.
Benet Place, 1420 Minnesota Blvd., S.E., 56304. Tel: 320-252-2557; Fax: 320-654-2351. Subsidized apartments with supportive services for older adults only. Managed by St. Benedict's Senior Community. Tenants 40.
Benet Place South, 1975 15th Ave., S.E., 56304. Tel: 320-529-8700; Fax: 320-654-2351. Tenants 36.

ALBANY. *Mother of Mercy Campus of Care*, Formerly Mother of Mercy Nursing Home and Retirement Center, Box 676, 56307. Tel: 320-845-2195; Fax: 320-845-7092. Email: bwikan@momnursinghome.com. Bob Wikan, Admin. Guests 169.

BRECKENRIDGE. *Apple Tree Court*, 601 Oak St., 56520. Tel: 218-643-7667; Fax: 218-743-7279. Email: jolyndohman@catholic.net. David Nelson, CEO. Residents 20.
St. Francis Home, 415 Oak St., 56520. Tel: 218-643-7661; Fax: 218-643-7655. Email: davidnelson@chi-midwest.org. Web: www.sfcare.org. David Nelson, CEO; Rev. Anthony Kroll, Chap. Residents 120.

COLD SPRING. *Assumption Court*, 615 First St. N., 56320. Tel: 320-685-4110; Fax: 320-685-7044. Jan Luthens, Admin.; Rev. Mathias Spier, O.S.B., Chap. Apparments 34.
Assumption Home, 715 First St. N., 56320. Tel: 320-685-3693; Fax: 320-685-7044. Email: assumpt@cloudnet.com. Jan Luthens, Admin.; Rev. Mathias Spier, O.S.B. Sisters of St. Benedict 1. Residents 89.
John Paul Apartments, 200 Eighth Ave. N., 56320. Tel: 320-685-4429; Fax: 320-685-7044. Email: jpa@cloudnet.com. Jan Luthens, Admin.; Rev. Mathias Spier, O.S.B., Chap. Pioneer Housing Development, Inc. Apartments 61.

LITTLE FALLS. *Alverna Apartments* (An Affiliate of Catholic Health Initiatives.) , 300 Eighth Ave., S.E., 56345. Tel: 320-632-1246; Fax: 320-632-1190. Bea Britz, Chap. Residents 60.
St. Otto's Care Center, 920 S.E. 4th St., 56345. Tel: 320-632-9281; Fax: 320-632-1120. Cory Glad, Vice Pres.; Sharon Ruhland, Chap. Residents 150.

MORRIS. *West Wind Village*, 1001 Scott Ave., 56267. Tel: 320-589-1133; Fax: 320-589-3005. Email: vosf@info.link.net. Carol Abele, Admin. Guests 104.

PARKERS PRAIRIE. *St. William's Living Center*, P.O. Box 30, 56361. Tel: 218-338-4671; Fax: 218-338-5917. Email: pbaer@midwestinfo.net. Paul Baer, Admin. Bed Capacity 85.

STAPLES. *Mary Rondorf Retirement Home of Sacred Heart Parish*, 222-5th St., N.E., 56479. Tel: 218-894-2124; Fax: 218-894-3067. Email: mrrh@arvig.net. Mrs. Virginia Rollins, Admin. Assisted 20.

[I] MONASTERIES AND RESIDENCES OF PRIESTS AND BROTHERS

COLLEGEVILLE. *St. John's Abbey, of the Order of St. Benedict* and St. John's University, School of Theology, Seminary, Preparatory School and Novitiate. , P.O. Box 2015, 56321-2015. Tel: 320-363-2011; Fax: 320-363-2504. Web: www.sja.osb.org. Rev. John Klassen, O.S.B., Ph.D., Abbot & Chancellor; Very Revs. Raymond Pedrizetti, O.S.B., Prior; Paul Richards, O.S.B., Subprior; Revs. Henry Anderl, O.S.B.; Knute Anderson, O.S.B.; Thomas Andert, O.S.B.; Alexander Andrews, O.S.B.; Burkard Arnheiter, O.S.B.; Timothy Backous, O.S.B.; Stephen Beauclair, O.S.B.; Michael Bik, O.S.B.; Simon Bischof, O.S.B.; Burton Blums, O.S.B.; Roger Botz, O.S.B.; Allan Bouley, O.S.B.; Silvan Bromenshenkel, O.S.B.; Alto Butkowski, O.S.B.; Jerome Coller, O.S.B.; Corwin Collins, O.S.B.; Cletus Connors, O.S.B.; David Cotter, O.S.B.; Alberic Culhane, O.S.B.; Cosmas Dahlheimer, O.S.B.; Meinrad Dindorf, O.S.B.; Ian Dommer, O.S.B.; Daniel Durken, O.S.B.; John Patrick Earls, O.S.B., Formation Dir.; Richard Eckroth, O.S.B.; John Eidenschenk, O.S.B.; Geoffrey Fecht, O.S.B.; Joseph Feders, O.S.B.; Jonathan Fischer, O.S.B.; Melchior Freund, O.S.B.; Thomas Gillespie, O.S.B.; Cyril Gorman, O.S.B.; Thomas Hallsten, O.S.B.; Nathanael Hauser, O.S.B.; Henry Bryan Hays, O.S.B.; Francis Hoefgen, O.S.B.; Eric Hollas, O.S.B.; Roger Kasprick, O.S.B.; Philip Kaufman, O.S.B.; Joel Kelly, O.S.B.; Timothy Kelly, O.S.B.; Chrysostom Kim, O.S.B.; Roger Klassen, O.S.B.; Robert Koopmann, O.S.B.; John Kulas, O.S.B.; Michael Kwatera, O.S.B.; Nathan Libaire, O.S.B.; Dale Launderville, O.S.B.; Donald LeMay, O.S.B.; Jonathan Licari, O.S.B.; Brennan Maiers, O.S.B.; Luke Mancuso, O.S.B.; Paul Marx, O.S.B.; Omer Maus, O.S.B.; J. Patrick McDarby, O.S.B.; Finian McDonald, O.S.B.; Kilian McDonnell, O.S.B.; Eugene J. McGlothlin, O.S.B.; Rene McGraw, O.S.B.; Gregory Miller, O.S.B.; Dustan Moorse, O.S.B.; Florian Muggli, O.S.B.; Virgil O'Neill, O.S.B.; Michael Patella, O.S.B.; Roman Paur, O.S.B.; Robert Pierson O.S.B., College Chap.; Martin Rath, O.S.B.; Rev. Msgr. James Reichert, O.S.B.; Revs. Stanley Roche, O.S.B.; Landelin A. Robling, O.S.B., Guestmaster; Gunther Rolfson; Anthony Ruff, O.S.B.; Dominic Ruiz, O.S.B.; Bartholomew Sayles, O.S.B.; William Schipper, O.S.B.; Julian Schmiesing, O.S.B.; Mark Schneider, O.S.B.; Francisco Schulte, O.S.B.; Kevin Seasoltz, O.S.B.; Gregory Sebastien, O.S.B.; William Skudlarek, O.S.B.; Mathias Spier, O.S.B.; Luke Steiner, O.S.B.; Columba Stewart, O.S.B., HMML Dir.; Edwin Stueber, O.S.B.; Don Talafous, O.S.B.; Allen Tarlton, O.S.B.; Donald Tauscher, O.S.B.; Gordon Tavis, O.S.B., Pres., St. John's Preparatory School; Vincent Tegeder, O.S.B.; Mark Thamert, O.S.B.; Wilfred Theisen, O.S.B.; Hilary Thimmesh, O.S.B.; Simeon J. Thole, O.S.B.; Thomas Thole, O.S.B.; Jerome Tupa, O.S.B.; Blane Wasnie, O.S.B.; Arnold Weber, O.S.B.; Magnus Wenninger, O.S.B.; Robert Wieber, O.S.B.; Hugh Witzmann, O.S.B.; Bruce Wollmering, O.S.B.; Angelo Zankl, O.S.B.
On Special Assignments:
St. Leo Abbey, St. Leo, FL 33574-9999. Tel: 352-588-8623; Fax: 352-588-5217. Very Rev. James Tingerthal, O.S.B., Admin.
Sant' Anselmo, Piazza Cavalieri di Malta, 5, Rome 1-00153 Italy. Tel: 3906-5791-264. Rev. Luigi Bertocchi, O.S.B.
2613 Woodege Rd., Silver Springs, MD 20906. Tel: 301-933 0447; Fax: 301-589-2897. Rev. Daniel Ward, O.S.B.
St. Bernardine Hospital, 2101 N. Waterman Ave., San Bernardino, CA 92404. Tel: 909-883-8711. Rev. Barnabas Laubach, O.S.B.
Mary Mother of the Church Abbey, 12829 River Rd., Richmond, VA 23233-7206. Tel: 804-784-2040; Fax: 804-784-2214. Very Rev. Michael Naughton, O.S.B., Admin.
Priests of the Abbey Serving Abroad:
St. Augustine Monastery, Box N-3940, Nassau, Bahamas. Tel: 242-364-1331; Fax: 242-364-8929. Very Rev. Mel Taylor, O.S.B.; Revs. Fintan Bromenshenkel, O.S.B.; George Wolf, O.S.B.
St. Augustine Monastery, Box N-3940, Nassau, Bahamas. Tel: 242-364-1511; Fax: 242-364-8929. Revs. Neal Henry Lawrence, O.S.B.; Aloysius Michels, O.S.B.; Kieran Nolan, O.S.B.; Very Rev. Thomas Wahl, O.S.B., Prior; Rev. Peter Kawamura, O.S.B.
Holy Trinity Benedictine Monastery, 3110 Fujimi-Fujimi Machi, Nagano Ken 399-0211 Japan. Tel: 011-81-266-62-8770; Fax: 011-81-266-62-8765. Rev. Cyprian Weaver, O.S.B.
Benedictine Wimmer Priory, 1 Lane 96, Ming Chih Rd., Sec. 3, Taishan, Taipei, Hsien Republic of China 24302 Taiwan. Tel: 011-886-2-2901-8343; Fax: 011-886-2-2904-3944. Community Priests 121; Professed Brothers 55; Novices 1; Claustral Oblate 1.

ONAMIA. *Crosier Monastery*, P.O. Box 500, 56359. Tel: 320-532-3103; Fax: 320-532-5222. Email: info@crosiers.org. Web: www.crosiers.org. Very Rev. James H. Remmerswaal, O.S.C., Prior; Revs. Joseph Brennan, O.S.C.; David Gallus, O.S.C.; Edward Greiwe, O.S.C.; Charles Kunkel, O.S.C.; Gregory Poser, O.S.C.; William T. McNiff, O.S.C.; Henry Miller, O.S.C.; Bernard Mischke, O.S.C.; James Moeglein, O.S.C.; Raymond Steffes, O.S.C.
Legal Title: *Crosier Fathers of Onamia*. The National Shrine of St. Odilia is sponsored and maintained by the Crosier Fathers of Onamia Priests in Residence 11; Priests Elsewhere 3; Brother in Residence 12.
Priests Elsewhere: Revs. James H. Cashman, O.S.C., Foreston; John J. Fleischhacker, O.S.C. (DUL), McGregor; Clement N. Gustin, O.S.C., Hibbing.

[J] CONVENTS AND RESIDENCES FOR SISTERS

LITTLE FALLS. *St. Francis Convent*, 116 Eighth Ave., S.E., 56345. Tel: 320-632-2981; Fax: 320-632-6313. Email: info@fslf.org. Web: www.fslf.org. Sr. Beatrice Eichten, Community Min. Motherhouse of Franciscan Sisters of Little Falls, MN Sisters 78. Total in Community 219.

ST. JOSEPH. *St. Benedict's Monastery*, 104 Chapel Ln., 56374-0220. Tel: 320-363-7100; Fax: 320-363-7130. Email: bkort@csbsju.edu. Web: www.sbm.osb.org. Sisters Ephrem Hollermann, O.S.B., Prioress; Elaine Schroeder, O.S.B., Coord. Eucharistic Presiders. Motherhouse and Formation House for Sisters of the Order of Saint Benedict. Sisters 180; Total in Community 343.

SAUK RAPIDS. *St. Clare's Monastery* Major Papal Cloister , 421 4th St. S., 56379. Tel: 320-251-3556. Sr. Mary Peter, O.S.C., Abbess. Franciscan Poor Clare Nuns Cloistered Nuns: Solemn Professed 15; Simple Professed 1; Extern Sisters: Perpetual Professed 3; Novices 1; Postulants 2.

[K] RETREAT HOUSES

ST. FRANCIS. *Pacem in Terris Center for Spirituality*, Hermitage Retreats, P.O. Box 418, 55070. Tel: 763-444-6408; Fax: 763-444-9649. Email: jeffrey@paceminterris.org. Jeffrey Wanchena, Dir.

[L] NEWMAN CENTERS

ST. CLOUD. *Newman Center, Inc.* 396 First Ave. S., 56301. Tel: 320-251-3260; 320-251-2712 (Home); Fax: 320-252-3930. Email: newman@stcloudstate.edu. Web: studentorg.stcloudstate.edu/newman. Rev. Kevin Anderson.

MORRIS. *Newman Catholic Student Center* 306 E. Fourth St., 56267. Tel: 320-589-1947. Email: newmanha@info-link.net. Web: www.mrs.umn.edu/~catholic/. Patrick Murphy, Dir. Campus Ministry.

[M] MISCELLANEOUS

ST. CLOUD. *Affordable Community Housing, Inc.*, P.O. Box 2390, 56302. 911-18th St. N., 56303. Tel: 320-229-4576. Harvey Schmitt, Dir. Housing & Contact Person; Mr. Steven P. Bresnahan, Exec. Dir.
Domus Transitional Housing Catholic Charities Housing Services, 157 Roosevelt Rd., Ste. 200, 56301. Tel: 320-229-4576; Fax: 320-253-7464. Mr. Steven P. Bresnahan, Exec. Dir.; Harvey Schmitt, Contact Person.
Key Row Community, Inc., 157 Roosevelt Rd., Ste. 200, 56301. Tel: 320-229-4576; Fax: 320-253-7464. Mr. Steven P. Bresnahan, Exec. Dir.; Harvey Schmitt, Dir. Housing & Contact Person. Providing low-cost housing to Elderly and Families in Morris, and St. Cloud.
Munich Manor Apartments, c/o Catholic Charities Housing Services, 157 Roosevelt Rd., Ste. 200, 56301. Tel: 320-229-4576; Fax: 320-253-7464. Steven Bresnahan, Exec. Dir.; Harvey Sehmitt, Dir. Housing.
St. Joseph's Apartment, Inc. Contact Catholic Charities. , 410 W. Minnesota St., St. Joseph, 56374. *Catholic Charities Housing Services*, 157 Roosevelt Rd., Ste. 200, 56301. Tel: 320-229-4576; Fax: 320-253-7464. Mr. Steven P. Bresnahan, Exec. Dir.; Harvey Schmitt, Dir. Housing Svcs.
410 W. Minnesota St., St. Joseph, 56374.
217 Railroad Avenue Ct., Sauk Centre, 56378.
Sauk Centre Apts., Catholic Charities Housing Services, 157 Roosevelt Rd., Ste. 200, 56301. Tel: 320-229-4576; Fax: 320-253-7464. Mr. Steven P. Bresnahan, Exec. Dir.; Harvey Schmitt, Dir. Housing Svcs. & Contact Person.
St. Therese Center for Special Ministry, 2056 15th Ave., S.E., 56304. Tel: 320-251-8064; Fax: 320-229-7679. Email: st.theresecenter@juno.com. Rev. John H. McManus, O.M.I.; Sr. Georganne Burr, O.S.B.; Nan Figge; Bernadette Stein.
Valley Vista Apartments of Browns Valley Inc., 157 Roosevelt Rd., Ste. 200, 56219. Tel: 320-229-4576; Fax: 320-253-7464.

ALEXANDRIA. *Carmelite Hermits of Adoration, Inc.*, 7005 State Hwy. 27 E., 56308. Tel: 320-762-0341. Sr. Imelda, Prioress. Sisters 2.

BROWNS VALLEY. **Browns Valley Health Center*, 114 Jefferson St. S., 56219. Tel: 320-695-2165; Fax: 320-695-2166. Email: bvhc@info-link.net.

CAMBRIDGE. *Benedictine Care Centers of the Benedictine Health System*, 1995 E. Rum River Dr. S., 55008. Tel: 763-689-1162; Fax: 763-689-1197. Dale M. Thompson, CEO.
Benedictine Health Dimensions, Inc., 1995 E. Rum River Dr., S., 55008. Tel: 763-689-1162; Fax: 763-689-1197. Email: webmaster@bhshealth.org. Web: www.bhshealth.org. Dale M. Thompson, Pres. & CEO.
Cambridge Benedictine Health Dim, Inc., 1995 E. Rum River Dr. S., 55008. Tel: 763-689-1162; Fax: 763-689-1197. Web: www.bhshealth.org. Dale M. Thompson, Pres. & CEO.

LITTLE FALLS. *Franciscan Sisters of Little Falls, MN Charitable Trust*, 116 Eighth Ave., S.E., 56345. Tel: 320-632-2981; Fax: 320-632-6313. Email: info@fslf.org. Web: www.fslf.org.
Key Row Little Falls, Inc., 905 N.E. 6th Ave., 56345. Harvey Schmitt, Dir. Housing & Contact Person.

LONG PRAIRE. *Central Minnesota Residents Encountering Christ*, 525 2nd Ave., S.E., Long Prairie, 56347. Tel: 320-732-6493. Email: longhorns2002@hotmail.com. Michael Ambrosius, Prog. Dir.

MELROSE. *Rose Mills Apartments, LLC*, 157 Roosevelt Rd., Ste. 200, 56301. Tel: 320-229-4576. Mr. Steven P. Bresnahan, Exec. Dir.; Harvey Schmitt, Dir. Housing Svcs.

MILACA. *Key Row Milaca, Inc.*, 410 N.W. 4th Ave., 56353. Tel: 320-229-4576; Fax: 320-253-7464. Harvey Schmitt, Dir. Housing & Contact Person.

MORRIS. *St. Francis Health Services*, 801 Nevada, Ste.

100, 56267. Tel: 320-589-2004; Fax: 320-589-1270. Email: lhoffman@sfhs.org. Web: www.sfhs.org.

Prairie Community Services, 801 Nevada Ave., P.O. Box 468, 56267. Tel: 320-589-3077; Fax: 320-589-2543. Web: www.pcs.sfhs.org.

ONAMIA. *National Shrine of St. Odilia*, P.O. Box 500, 56359. Tel: 320-532-3103; Fax: 320-532-5222. Email: info@crosiers.org. Web: www.crosiers.org. Bro. Albert Becker, O.S.C., Contact Person. Sponsored and maintained by The Crosiers of Onamia.

RICHMOND. *Maple Apartments of Richmond , Inc.*, 488 1st St., N.E., 56368. Tel: 320-229-4576; Fax: 320-253-7464. Mr. Steven P. Bresnahan, Exec. Dir.; Harvey Schmitt, Dir. of Housing Svcs.

ST. JOSEPH. *Monastic Interreligious Dialogue*, St. Benedict's Monastery, 104 Chapel Ln., 56374-2020. Tel: 320-363-7187; Fax: 320-363-7173. Email: khoward@csbsju.edu. Web: www.monasticdialog.org. Sr. Katherine Howard, O.S.B., Contact Person.

RELIGIOUS INSTITUTES OF MEN REPRESENTED IN THE DIOCESE

For further details refer to the corresponding bracketed number in the Religious Institutes of Men or Women section.

[0200]—*Benedictine Monks* (Collegeville, MN)—O.S.B.

[0400]—*Canons Regular of the Order of the Holy Cross* (Province of St. Odilia)—O.S.C.

RELIGIOUS INSTITUTES OF WOMEN REPRESENTED IN THE DIOCESE

[0230]—*Benedictine Sisters of Pontifical Jurisdiction*—O.S.B.

[1920]—*Congregation of the Sisters of the Holy Cross*—C.S.C.

[1310]—*Franciscan Sisters of Little Falls, Minnesota*—O.S.F.

[3760]—*Order of St. Clare*—O.S.C.

[2970]—*School Sisters of Notre Dame* (Northwestern Prov.)—S.S.N.D.

[1710]—*Sisters of St. Francis of Mary Immaculate*—O.S.F.

NECROLOGY

✠ Speltz, Most Rev. George H., Former Bishop of St. Cloud—Died Feb. 1, 2004

† Illies, Wilfred, (Retired)—Died March 25, 2003

† Kloeckner, William, (Retired)—Died Sept. 2, 2003

Archdiocese of St. Louis

(Archidioecesis S. Ludovici)

Most Reverend

RAYMOND L. BURKE, D.D., J.C.D.

Archbishop of St. Louis; ordained June 29, 1975; appointed to the Residential See of La Crosse December 10, 1994; consecrated January 6, 1995; installed as Eighth Bishop of La Crosse February 22, 1995; appointed Archbishop of St. Louis December 2, 2003; installed January 26, 2004 *Office: 4445 Lindell Blvd., St. Louis, MO 63108-2497.*

The Catholic Center: 4445 Lindell Blvd., St. Louis, MO 63108-2497. Tel: 314-633-2222; Fax: 314-633-2333.

Web: www.archstl.org

Email: stika@archstl.org

Most Reverend

ROBERT J. HERMANN

Auxiliary Bishop of St. Louis; ordained March 30, 1963; appointed Auxiliary Bishop of St. Louis October 16, 2002; ordained December 12, 2002 *Office: 4445 Lindell Blvd., St. Louis, MO 63108-2497.*

Square Miles 5,968.

Diocese July 18, 1826; Archdiocese July 20, 1847.

Comprises that portion of the State of Missouri bounded on the north by the northern line of the County of Lincoln; on the west by the western lines of the Counties of Lincoln, Warren, Franklin and Washington; on the south by the southern lines of the Counties of Washington, St. Francois and Perry; on the east by the Mississippi River.

Heavenly Patrons--Saint Louis, King, Saint Vincent de Paul and Saint Rose Philippine Duchesne.

Legal Title: For legal titles of parishes and archdiocesan institutions, consult the Catholic Center.

STATISTICAL OVERVIEW

Personnel	
Archbishops	1
Auxiliary Bishops	2
Retired Bishops	1
Abbots	1
Retired Abbots	2
Priests: Diocesan Active in Diocese	313
Priests: Diocesan Active Outside Diocese	5
Priests: Diocesan in Foreign Missions	6
Priests: Retired, Sick or Absent	68
Number of Diocesan Priests	392
Religious Priests in Diocese	345
Total Priests in Diocese	737
Extern Priests in Diocese	9
Ordinations:	
Diocesan Priests	8
Religious Priests	2
Transitional Deacons	4
Permanent Deacons	14
Permanent Deacons in Diocese	253
Total Brothers	153
Total Sisters	1,647
Parishes	
Parishes	214
With Resident Pastor:	
Resident Diocesan Priests	200
Resident Religious Priests	25
Without Resident Pastor:	
Administered by Priests	14
Missions	8
New Parishes Created	2
Closed Parishes	5
Welfare	
Catholic Hospitals	10
Total Assisted	2,030,576
Homes for the Aged	33
Total Assisted	41,258
Residential Care of Children	6
Total Assisted	4,890
Day Care Centers	12
Total Assisted	22,902
Specialized Homes	11
Total Assisted	5,518
Special Centers for Social Services	35
Total Assisted	126,478
Educational	
Seminaries, Diocesan	2
Students from This Diocese	36
Students from Other Diocese	53
Diocesan Students in Other Seminaries	1
Seminaries, Religious	2
Students Religious	15
Total Seminarians	52
Colleges and Universities	2
Total Students	14,617
High Schools, Diocesan and Parish	11
Total Students	5,701
High Schools, Private	16
Total Students	8,296
Elementary Schools, Diocesan and Parish	126
Total Students	33,920
Elementary Schools, Private	10
Total Students	2,136
Non-residential Schools for the Disabled	9
Total Students	257
Catechesis/Religious Education:	
High School Students	865
Elementary Students	22,889
Total Students under Catholic Instruction	88,733
Teachers in the Diocese:	
Priests	110
Scholastics	4
Brothers	21
Sisters	171
Lay Teachers	5,179
Vital Statistics	
Receptions into the Church:	
Infant Baptism Totals	6,572
Adult Baptism Totals	624
Received into Full Communion	958
First Communions	7,450
Confirmations	7,114
Marriages:	
Catholic	1,812
Interfaith	792
Total Marriages	2,604
Deaths	4,253
Total Catholic Population	550,000
Total Population	2,114,497

Former Bishops—Most Rev. LOUIS WILLIAM VALENTINE DUBOURG, Archbishop of the Cardinalatial See of Besancon; consecrated in Rome, Sept. 24, 1815, Bishop of Louisiana, Upper and Lower, took his first residential seat in St. Louis, Jan. 6, 1818. On July 18, 1826, the Diocese of Louisiana was divided and the Sees of St. Louis and New Orleans erected. Bishop DuBour having resigned the See of Louisiana, was transferred to the Diocese of Montauban in France, Aug. 13, 1826, and made Archbishop of the Cardinalatial See of Besancon, Feb. 15, 1833, where he died Dec. 12 of the same year; Rt. Rev. JOSEPH ROSATI, C.M., Bishop of St. Louis; consecrated Bishop of the Titular See of Tenagra and constituted Coadjutor of Bishop DuBourg of Louisiana at Donaldsville, LA, March 25, 1824. When the See of Louisiana was divided Bishop Rosati was made Bishop of St. Louis and Administrator of New Orleans. He died while on business in Rome on September 25, 1843; Most Revs. PETER RICHARD KENRICK, D.D., Archbishop of St. Louis; consecrated Nov. 30, 1841, Bishop of Drasa and Coadjutor to Bishop of St. Louis; Succeeded as Bishop Sept. 25, 1843; appt. Archbishop of St. Louis July 12, 1847; retired May 21, 1895; died March 4, 1896; JOHN JOSEPH KAIN, D.D., Archbishop of St. Louis; consecrated Bishop of Wheeling, WV on May 23, 1875; Titular Archbishop of Oxyrynchia and Coadjutor "cum jure successionis" of Archbishop of St. Louis, 1893; Administrator of Archdiocese of St. Louis, Dec. 14, 1893; created Archbishop of St. Louis on May 21, 1895; died Oct. 13, 1903; His Eminence JOHN CARDINAL GLENNON, D.D., Archbishop of St. Louis; born June 14, 1862; ord. Dec. 20, 1884; appt. Titular Bishop of Pinara and Coadjutor to the Bishop of Kansas City, March 14, 1896; consecrated June 29, 1896; transferred to St. Louis, April 27, 1903, as Coadjutor to the Archbishop of St. Louis "cum jure successionis"; Archbishop of St. Louis, Oct. 13, 1903; Pallium received May 14, 1905; Assistant at the Pontifical Throne, June 21, 1921; created Cardinal Priest, Feb. 18, 1946; died March 9, 1946; JOSEPH CARDINAL RITTER, D.D., Archbishop of St. Louis; born July 20, 1892; ord. May 30, 1917; appt. Titular Bishop of Hippo, Feb. 3, 1933 and Auxiliary Bishop of Indianapolis; consecrated March 28, 1933; appt. Archbishop of Indianapolis, Nov. 11, 1944; appt. Archbishop of St. Louis, July 20, 1946 assistant at the Pontifical Throne, Oct. 5, 1956; created Cardinal, Priest Jan. 16, 1961; died June 10, 1967; JOHN JOSEPH CARDINAL CARBERRY, D.D., S.T.D., J.C.D., Ph.D. (Retired), Archbishop of St. Louis; ord. July 28, 1929; appt. Titular Bishop of Elis and Coadjutor of Lafayette in Indiana, May 3, 1956; consecrated July 25, 1956; Succeeded to See, Nov. 20, 1957; transferred to Columbus, Jan. 16, 1965; appt. Archbishop of St. Louis, Feb. 17, 1968; installed March 25, 1968; created Cardinal, April 28, 1969; retired July 31, 1979; died June 17, 1998; Most Revs. JOHN L. MAY, D.D., Archbishop of St. Louis; ord. May 3, 1947; appt. Auxiliary Bishop of Chicago, June 21, 1967; consecrated Aug. 24, 1967; transferred to Mobile, Oct. 8, 1969; installed as Bishop of

Mobile, Dec. 10, 1969; appt. Archbishop of St. Louis, Jan. 29, 1980; installed March 25, 1980; resigned Dec. 9, 1992; died March 24, 1994; JUSTIN F. RIGALI, J.C.D., Archbishop of St. Louis; born April 19, 1935; ord. April 25, 1961; appt. Titular Archbishop of Bolsena, June 8, 1985; consecrated Sept. 14, 1985; appointed Archbishop of St. Louis, Jan. 25, 1994; installed Mar. 15, 1994; Pallium received June 29, 1994; transferred to Archdiocese of Philadelphia, July 15, 2003; created Cardinal, Sept. 28, 2003; installed as Archbishop of Philadelphia, Oct. 7, 2003.

The Catholic Center—4445 Lindell Blvd., St. Louis, 63108-2497. Tel: 314-633-2222; Fax: 314-633-2333. Office Hours: Mon.-Fri. 8:30-4

Vicars General—Most Rev. ROBERT J. HERMANN, V.G.; Rev. Msgrs. VERNON E. GARDIN, Ph.D., V.G.; RICHARD F. STIKA, V.G.

Moderator of the Curia—Rev. Msgr. DENNIS M. DELANEY.

Chancellor—Rev. Msgr. RICHARD F. STIKA, V.G., 4445 Lindell Blvd., St. Louis, 63108-2497. Tel: 314-633-2273; Fax: 314-633-2306.

Vice Chancellor for Special Projects—Mrs. JENNIFER STANARD.

Secretary to the Archbishop—Rev. HENRY J. BREIER.

Masters of Ceremonies to the Archbishop—Revs. HENRY J. BREIER; MARK S. RIVITUSO, J.C.L., M.C.L., M.A., M.Div.

Archdiocesan Master of Ceremonies—Rev. THOMAS G. KELLER.

Chief Financial Officer—Deacon C. FRANK CHAUVIN.

Metropolitan Tribunal—4445 Lindell Blvd., St. Louis, 63108. Tel: 314-633-2280; Fax: 314-633-2301.

Judicial Vicar—Rev. JOHN B. SHAMLEFFER, J.C.L., M.C.L., M.A., M.Div.

Adjutant Judicial Vicars—Rev. MARK S. RIVITUSO, J.C.L., M.C.L., M.A., M.Div.; Very Rev. JOHN A. BROCKLAND, V.F., J.C.L., M.A., M.Div.

Judges—Revs. PHILIP J. BENE, J.C.D.; DENNIS M. DOYLE, J.C.L.

Defender of the Bond—Rev. JEROME D. BILLING, J.C.L., S.T.L.

Director of Advocate Services—Very Rev. JOHN A. BROCKLAND, V.F., J.C.L., M.A., M.Div.

Auditor—Deacon ROBERT RIEGEL.

Promoter of Justice—Rev. JEROME D. BILLING, J.C.L., S.T.L.

Notaries—Mrs. JOYCE KOETTING; Mrs. PATRICIA LANASA.

Missouri Appellate Tribunal—20 Archbishop May Dr., St. Louis, 63119.

Archdiocesan Consultors—Most Revs. JOSEPH F. NAUMANN, V.G.; ROBERT J. HERMANN, V.G.; Rev. Msgrs. DENNIS DELANEY; RICHARD F. STIKA, V.G.; Rev. PETER BLAKE; Rev. Msgr. KEVIN CALLAHAN; Rev. MICHAEL DIECKMANN; Rev. Msgr. PATRICK K. HAMBROUGH; Rev. JOHN G. DEMPSEY.

Deaneries/Deans—Very Rev. MARK C. ULLRICH, M.Div., M.S.W., V.F., North St. Louis; Rev. Msgr. DENNIS E. DOERHOFF, V.F., South St. Louis; Very Revs. JOHN A. BROCKLAND, V.F., J.C.L., M.A., M.Div., Northeast County; JOHN J. LEYKAM, V.F., Northwest County; JOSEPH E. WORMEK, V.F., Southwest County; DENNIS STEHLY, V.F., Southeast County; PAUL J. NIEMANN, V.F., Festus; JAMES P. CALLAHAN, V.F., St. Charles; JAMES W. SCHAEFER, V.F., Ste. Genevieve; JEFFREY N. KNIGHT, V.F., Washington.

Vicar for Administration—Rev. Msgr. JOHN R. MAGUIRE.

Vicar for Pastoral Planning—Rev. Msgr. DENNIS M. DELANEY.

Co-Vicar for Religious—Sr. EVA-MARIA ACKERMAN, F.S.G.M., 20 Archbishop May Dr., St. Louis, 63119-5004. Tel: 314-792-7250.

Archdiocesan Offices and Directors

Archdiocesan Archives—Rev. Msgr. RICHARD F. STIKA, V.G., Chancellor; AUDREY POWDERLY-NEWCOMER, Archivist; HELEN GOLLIHUR, Archivist Asst.; ELAINE SNYDER, 20 Archbishop May Dr., St. Louis, 63119. Tel: 314-792-7020; Fax: 314-792-7029.

Archdiocesan Building and Boundary Commission—Rev. Msgr. RICHARD J. GALLAGHER, Exec. Sec.

Catholic Family Counseling—Dr. JERRY MARKS, D.S.W., A.C.S.W., Exec. Dir., 20 Archbishop May Dr., St. Louis, 63119. Tel: 314-792-7030; Fax: 314-792-7059 See MISCELLANEOUS section for more information.

Catholic Family Tuition—20 Archbishop May Dr., St. Louis, 63119.

Archdiocesan Development Appeal— See MISCELLANEOUS section for more information Mr. FRANK COGNATA JR., Chief Devel. Officer; TERESA MANNA, Dir., 20 Archbishop May Dr., St. Louis, 63119. Tel: 314-792-7680; Fax: 314-792-7699.

Catholic Information Center—Rev. VALENTINE YOUNG, O.F.M.Cap., Dir. Tel: 314-621-6555; 314-231-9991 See MISCELLANEOUS section for more information.

Catholic Office of Disability Ministry—JANE WALKER, Dir., 20 Archbishop May Dr., St. Louis, 63119. Tel: 314-792-7050; Fax: 314-792-7159 Also see MISCELLANEOUS section.

Catholic Relief Services—VACANT, Dir., 20 Archbishop May Dr., St. Louis, 63119. Tel: 314-792-7655; Fax: 314-792-7669.

Catholic Cemeteries of St. Louis—Rev. Msgr. ROBERT MCCARTHY, Dir., 6901 Mackenzie Rd., St. Louis, 63123. Tel: 314-381-1313 See CEMETERIES section for more information.

Central Purchasing—Mrs. EDITH TIERNEY, Dir., 20 Archbishop May Dr., St. Louis, 63119. Tel: 314-792-7065; Fax: 314-792-7019.

Charismatic Renewal—8300 Morganford Rd., St. Louis, 63123-6815. Tel: 314-633-2572.

Tree House Ministry—St. Louis, 63123-6815. Tel: 314-633-2572.

Compliance Office—20 Archbishop May Dr., St. Louis, 63119-5738. Tel: 314-792-7085.

Finance Office—20 Archbishop May Dr., St. Louis, 63119-5738. Tel: 314-792-7100.

Catholic Charities—Mr. JAMES STUTZ, Pres.; NETTA KOWALSKI, Dir., Finance, 4532 Lindell Blvd., St. Louis, 63108. Tel: 314-367-5500; Fax: 314-367-2982. Web: www.ccstl.org. See MISCELLANEOUS section for more information.

Cardinal Ritter Institute-Archdiocesan Office for Services to the Elderly—Sr. SUZANNE WESLEY, C.S.J., COO, 7601 Watson Rd., St. Louis, 63119. Tel: 314-961-8000; Fax: 314-961-1934. Email: swesley@ccstl.org. See SERVICES FOR THE ELDERLY section for more information.

Catholic Commission on Housing—KAREN WALLENSAK, Exec. Dir., 800 N. Tucker Blvd., St. Louis, 63101. Tel: 314-241-5600; Fax: 314-241-5608 See MISCELLANEOUS section for more information.

Catholic Community Services—Dr. JERRY MARKS, D.S.W., A.C.S.W., Exec. Dir.; ED BARNI, Coord., 20 Archbishop May Dr., St. Louis, 63119. Tel: 314-792-7300; Fax: 314-792-7399. Email: jmarks@ccstl.org. See MISCELLANEOUS section for more information.

Archdiocesan Deaf Ministry—Rev. VICTOR A. BARNHART, Dir., 8300 Morganford Rd., St. Louis, 63123. Tel: 314-633-2540; Fax: 314-633-2549 See MISCELLANEOUS section for more information.

Archdiocesan Orphan Board (Managers of the Roman Catholic Orphan Asylums)—DAN VALLEROY, Exec. Dir., St. Joseph's Home and Family Support Services, 20 Archbishop May Dr., St. Louis, 63119. Tel: 314-792-7815; Fax: 314-792-7438. Email: dvalleroy@ccstl.org.

Catholic Services for Children and Youth—Mr. RICHARD L. KING, A.C.S.W, Exec. Dir., 20 Archbishop May Dr., St. Louis, 63119. Tel: 314-792-7400; Fax: 314-792-7438. Email: rking@ccstl.org. See MISCELLANEOUS section for more information.

Archdiocesan Data Center—Mr. GERALD F. LAWLER, Dir. Mgmt. Information Systems, 20 Archbishop May Dr., St. Louis, 63119. Tel: 314-792-7570; Fax: 314-792-7579.

Office for Ecumenical & Interreligious Affairs—Rev. VINCENT A. HEIER, Dir., 20 Archbishop May Dr., St. Louis, 63119. Tel: 314-792-7060; Fax: 314-792-7164.

Fleur de Lis—20 Archbishop May Dr., St. Louis, 63119.

Archdiocesan Office of Worship—Rev. WILLIAM MCCUMBER, 20 Archbishop May Dr., St. Louis, 63119. Tel: 314-792-7230; Fax: 314-792-7019.

Archdiocesan Commission for Sacred Liturgy—Sr. CATHY DOHERTY, S.S.N.D., Chm.; Deacon GEORGE BEINKE; Mrs. ELIZABETH COFFMAN; Deacon RICHARD COFFMAN; Mr. JIM COMBS; Ms. RUBY DOUTHET; Mrs. KATHY GIBLER; Revs. THOMAS KELLER; WILLIAM MCCUMBER; Mrs. SHARON MCGINNIS; Mrs. MARGE MEYER.

Archdiocesan Commission for Sacred Music—Mr. JEFF BUSH, Chm.; Mrs. MARY KAY CHRISTIAN; Mr. PHIL BARRECA; Mr. CHRISTOPHER ORF; Mr. DAVID BRINKER; Dr. JOHN A. ROMERI; Dr. MARIE KREMER; Ms. TINA MOWRER.

Archdiocesan Commission for Sacred Art and Architecture—Mr. ROBERT BARRINGER, Chm.; Ms. BETH PILARSKI; Sr. GABRIELLA ROGENSKI, C.D.P.; Mr. DARREN STROSS; Sr. JOSEPHINE NIEMANN; Ms. LEA KOESTERER.

Archdiocesan Human Rights Office/HRO System—Ms. LEODIA GOOCH, Dir., 20 Archbishop May Dr., St. Louis, 63119. Tel: 314-792-7640; Fax: 314-792-7654.

Commission on Human Rights

Capitol Punishment Opposition

Black & Native American Missions Program

Catholic Campaign for Human Development

Committee on Women in the Church

National Black Catholic Congress

Council of Catholic Youth—Mr. MICHAEL P. KALIST, Exec. Dir., 20 Archbishop May Dr., St. Louis, 63119. Tel: 314-792-7600; Fax: 314-792-7619.

Holy Childhood, Pontifical Association—Rev. Msgr. BERNARD H. SANDHEINRICH, Dir., 20 Archbishop May Dr., St. Louis, 63119. Tel: 314-792-7655; Fax: 314-792-7669.

Catholic Legal Assistance Ministry—MARIE KENYON, J.D., Dir., 321 N. Spring, St. Louis, 63108. Tel: 314-977-3993; Fax: 314-977-3334.

Holy Name Society—Mr. NICK PFISTER, Archdiocesan Pres., Holy Name Society, P.O. Box 190435, St. Louis, 63119-6435. Tel: 314-428-9073.

Human Resources—20 Archbishop May Dr., St. Louis, 63119.

Latin American Apostolate, Archdiocese of St. Louis—VACANT, Dir., 20 Archbishop May Dr., St. Louis, 63119. Tel: 314-792-7655; Fax: 314-792-7669.

The Legion of Mary—Mrs. MARY BUDDE, Pres., P.O. Box 1313, St. Louis, 63188. Tel: 314-631-3447. Spiritual Directors: Revs. DAVID WICHLAN; EDWARD HILGEMAN.

Pan y Amor—VACANT, Dir., 20 Archbishop May Dr., St. Louis, 63119. Tel: 314-792-7655; Fax: 314-792-7669.

Archdiocesan Newspaper "The St. Louis Review"—VACANT, Editor; Mr. JIM RYGELSKI, Mng. Editor; Mr. THOMAS L. COURTAWAY, Business Mgr., 20 Archbishop May Dr., St. Louis, 63119. Tel: 314-792-7500; Fax: 314-792-7534.

Archdiocesan Office of Stewardship & Development—Mr. FRANK J. COGNATA JR., Chief Devel. Officer, 20 Archbishop May Dr., St. Louis, 63119-5004. Tel: 314-792-7210.

Archdiocesan Planned Giving and Endowment Council— See MISCELLANEOUS section for more information

Priests' Mutual Benefit/Risk Management—VACANT, Pres.; Rev. JOSEPH WORMEK, Exec. Sec., 20 Archbishop May Dr., St. Louis, 63119. Tel: 314-792-7200; Fax: 314-792-7209.

Priests' Purgatorial Society—Rev. Msgr. RICHARD F. STIKA, V.G., Pres.

Pro-Life—Mrs. MOLLY CORCORAN KERTZ, Dir. & Coord., 20 Archbishop May Dr., St. Louis, 63119. Tel: 314-792-7555; Fax: 314-792-7569.

Project Rachel—20 Archbishop May Dr., St. Louis, 63119.

Regina Cleri—Sr. GERALDINE VOGEL, Admin., 10 Archbishop May Dr., St. Louis, 63119. Tel: 314-968-2240; Fax: 314-968-1049.

Society for the Propagation of the Faith—VACANT, Dir., 20 Archbishop May Dr., St. Louis, 63119. Tel: 314-792-7655; Fax: 314-792-7669.

Special Facilities Projects—20 Archbishop May Dr., St. Louis, 63119.

Today and Tomorrow Education Foundation—Ms. MARTI OCHS, Exec. Dir., 20 Archbishop May Dr., St. Louis, 63119. Tel: 314-792-7620; Fax: 314-792-7629.

Criminal Justice Ministry—1408 S. Tenth St., St. Louis, 63104. Tel: 314-241-8062; Fax: 314-241-1307.

Office of Communications—Mr. JIM ORSO, Exec. Dir., 20 Archbishop May Dr., St. Louis, 63119. Tel: 314-792-7630; Fax: 314-792-7639.

Society of St. Vincent de Paul, Council of St. Louis—Rev. JAMES CORMACK, C.M., Spiritual Advisor; RICHARD J. KLOHR III, Pres.; LAURA ELLER, Acting Interim Exec. Dir., 4141 Forest Park Ave., St. Louis, 63108. Tel: 314-521-2183; Fax: 314-531-6712 See MISCELLANEOUS section for more information.

Society of St. Vincent de Paul, Council of the United States--(Territory: United States)—Most Rev. EDWIN M. CONWAY, D.D., Auxiliary Bishop of Chicago, Spiritual Advisor; EUGENE B. SMITH, Pres.; RICHARD E. HENNICKE, Exec. Dir., 58 Progress Pkwy., St. Louis, 63043-3706. Tel: 314-576-3993; Fax: 314-576-6755 See MISCELLANEOUS section for more information.

Schools/Catholic Education Office—Mr. GEORGE HENRY, Supt., 20 Archbishop May Dr., St. Louis, 63119. Tel: 314-792-7300; Fax: 314-792-7399 See SCHOOLS section for more information.

St. Louis Roman Catholic Theological Seminaries, Inc.—Rev. Msgr. RICHARD F. STIKA, V.G., Sec., 4445 Lindell Blvd., St. Louis, 63108. Tel: 314-633-2273.

Kenrick-Glennon Seminary— (St. Louis Roman Catholic Theological Seminary-Kenrick School of Theology) Rev. Msgr. TED WOJCICKI, Pres. & Rector.

Cardinal Glennon College—Rev. TIMOTHY P. CRONIN,

Dir., 5200 Glennon Dr., St. Louis, 63119. Tel: 314-792-6100; Fax: 314-792-6500 See SEMINARIES section for more information.

Office of Vocations—Rev. MICHAEL T. BUTLER, Dir., 5200 Glennon Dr., St. Louis, 63119. Tel: 314-792-6460; Fax: 314-792-6502.

Archdiocesan Council of Priests—Most Revs. RAYMOND L. BURKE; ROBERT J. HERMANN, V.G.; Rev. Msgrs. RICHARD F. STIKA, V.G.; JAMES T. TELTHORST, South City Deanery, Interim Sec.; Very Rev. JOSEPH E. WORMEK, V.F., Southwest Deanery; Rev. Msgr. PATRICK K. HAMBROUGH, Southeast Deanery; Revs. JOHN J. BORCIC, Washington Deanery; C. ROBERT MANNING, Northwest Deanery; ERIC A. FECHNER, Northeast Deanery; LARRY T. HUBER, St. Charles Deanery; JOHN H. SCHNEIDER, Ste. Genevieve Deanery; DENNIS C. SCHMIDT, Festus Deanery; Rev. Msgr. TED L. WOJCICKI, Ed.D., Ex Officio, Rector/Kenrick-Glennon Seminary; Very Rev. JAMES P. CALLAHAN, V.F., Ex Officio, Dir. Priests' Personnel; Revs. RICHARD O. BUHLER, S.J., Religious-Other; MICHAEL JOYCE, C.M., Religious-Parish; MICHAEL K. MAY, S.J., Religious-Teaching.

Archdiocesan Pastoral Council—Most Revs. RAYMOND L. BURKE; ROBERT J. HERMANN; Rev. Msgrs. RICHARD F. STIKA, V.G.; DENNIS M. DELANEY, Vicar for Pastoral Planning; Sr. MARY ANTONA EBO, F.S.M.; Bro. LAWRENCE HUMPHREY, F.S.C. North: Very Rev. MARK C. ULLRICH, M.Div., M.S.W., V.F.; Mr. JERRY HALL. South: Rev. Msgr. DENNIS DOERHOFF, V.F.; Mrs. JAN GODEFROID. Northeast: Very Rev. JOHN A. BROCKLAND, V.F., J.C.L., M.A., M.Div.; Mrs. DENISE SAUSER. Northwest: Rev. Msgr. JOHN LEYKAM, V.F.; Mr. STEPHEN BOLLINGER. Southwest: Very Rev. JOSEPH E. WORMEK, V.F.; Mrs. PATRICIA KOZARITIS. Southeast: Very Rev. DENNIS R. STEHLY, V.F.; Mr. PAUL GOLDAK. Festus: Very Rev. PAUL J. NIEMANN, V.F.; Judge TIMOTHY PATTERSON. St. Charles: Very Rev. JAMES P. CALLAHAN, V.F.; Mrs. SHARON GIETL. Ste. Genevieve: Very Rev. JAMES W. SCHAEFER, V.F.; Mrs. LYNN DAVIS. Washington: Very Rev. JEFFREY N. KNIGHT, V.F.; Mr. DANNY HILLERMAN.

Office of Priests' Personnel and Continuing Formation of Priests—Rev. Msgr. KEVIN G. CALLAHAN, Dir., 20 Archbishop May Dr., St. Louis, 63119. Tel: 314-792-7550; Fax: 314-792-7554.

Archdiocesan Priests' Personnel Board—Most Rev. ROBERT J. HERMANN, V.G.; Rev. Msgrs. RICHARD F. STIKA, V.G.; KEVIN G. CALLAHAN, Personnel Dir.; EDWARD W. REILLY; RICHARD A. BUCHHEIT; JOHN T. RONQUEST (Retired); Revs. H. JOHN REIKER; JOHN B. SHAMLEFFER, J.C.L., M.C.L., M.A., M.Div.; Rev. Msgr. NORBERT A. ERNST; Rev. THOMAS C. MILLER.

Archdiocesan Office of Urban and Community Affairs—Rev. Msgr. SALVATORE E. POLIZZI, Dir.; LOUIS G. BERRA, Consultor, 6052 Waterman, St. Louis, 63112. Tel: 314-721-6340; Fax: 314-721-1656.

Archdiocesan Office of the Permanent Diaconate—Deacons GEORGE MILLER, Dir., 8300 Morganford Rd., St. Louis, 63123. Tel: 314-633-2530; Fax: 314-633-2539; THOMAS FORSTER, Dir., Life & Ministry; J. GERARD QUINN, Dir., Formation; Mrs. PATRICIA MCVEY, Sec.

Archdiocesan Office of Laity and Family Life—Mrs. SUSAN EDWARDS, Exec. Dir., 20 Archbishop May Dr., St. Louis, 63119-5738. Tel: 314-792-7170; Fax: 314-792-7199.

Blessed John XXIII Center—Deacon ROBERT SNYDER, Bldg. Admin., 8300 Morganford Rd. St. Louis, 63123-6815. Tel: 314-633-2600; Fax: 314-633-2529; Rev. Msgr. CHARLES MOTTIN, Chap. Tel: 314-638-4099.

Archdiocesan Pastoral Center—MARY DE FRANK, Bldg. Admin., 20 Archbishop May Dr., St. Louis, 63119. Tel: 314-792-7000; Fax: 314-792-7019.

Office of Youth Ministry—Rev. ROBERT SMOOT, Dir.; Sr. M. CONSOLATA CREWS, F.G.S.M., Contact Person, 8300 Morganford Rd., St. Louis, 63123-6815. Tel: 314-633-2500; Fax: 314-633-2525.

Victim Assistance Coordinator—NANCY BROWN, Ph.D. Tel: 314-633-2279. Email: nancybrown@archstl.org.

Franklin County Catholic Church Real Estate Corporation—Rev. JOHN M. COSTELLO, Contact Person 311 W. Second St., Washington, 63090. Tel: 636-239-6701.

Jefferson County Catholic Church Real Estate Corporation—Very Rev. PAUL J. NIEMANN, V.F., Contact Person, 2300 Church St., Arnold, 63010. Tel: 636-296-5289.

Lincoln County Catholic Church Real Estate Corporation—Rev. FRANK A. D'AMICO, Contact Person, 29 St. Alphonsus Rd., Silex, 63377. Tel: 573-384-6223.

Perry County Catholic Church Real Estate Corporation—Rev. KEVIN P. FAUSZ, C.M., Contact Person, 1000 Rosati Court, Perryville, 63775. Tel: 573-547-2678.

St. Charles County Catholic Church Real Estate Corporation—Rev. RICHARD J. TILLMAN, Contact Person, 601 N. Fourth St., St. Charles, 63301. Tel: 636-946-6370.

St. Francois County Catholic Church Real Estate Corporation—Rev. JOHN H. SCHNEIDER, Contact Person, 15 St. Joseph St., Bonne Terre, 63628. Tel: 573-358-2112.

Ste. Genevieve County Catholic Church Real Estate Corporation—Rev. DANIEL E. MOSLEY, Contact Person, 49 DuBourg Pl., Sainte Genevieve, 63670.

St. Louis City Catholic Church Real Estate Corporation—Rev. Msgr. RICHARD F. STIKA, V.G., Contact Person, 4445 Lindell Blvd., St. Louis, 63108. Tel: 314-633-2273.

St. Louis County Catholic Church Real Estate Corporation—GERARD J. HOEING, Contact Person, 20 Archbishop May Dr., St. Louis, 63119. Tel: 314-792-7111.

Warren County Catholic Church Real Estate Corporation—Rev. JOHN J. BORCIC, Contact Person, 7602 South Hwy. 94, Marthasville, 63357. Tel: 636-433-2678.

Washington County Catholic Church Real Estate Corporation—Rev. THEODORE X. PIEPER, Contact Person, Rte. 1, Box 1110, Cadet, 63630. Tel: 573-438-6181.

CLERGY, PARISHES, MISSIONS AND PAROCHIAL SCHOOLS

CITY OF ST. LOUIS

ST. LOUIS COUNTY

1—CATHEDRAL BASILICA OF SAINT LOUIS (1896), Rev. Msgr. Vernon E. Garoin, Ph.D.; Deacons John A. Curtin; T. Michael Kenney; Raymond McKeever, Business Mgr.; Mary Wainscott, Ph.D., Pastoral Assoc. In Res., Most Rev. Joseph F. Naumann, V.G.; Revs. Thomas G. Keller; Nicholas W. Smith.
Res.: 4431 Lindell Blvd., 63108. Tel: 314-533-2824; Fax: 314-533-2844.
School—Tel: 314-531-3375. Michel Wendell, Prin. Lay Teachers 12; Students 207.

2—ST. ALOYSIUS GONZAGA (1892), (Italian), Rev. John Blomberg; Deacon Richard C. Lake.
Res.: 5608 N. Magnolia Ave., 63139. Tel: 314-647-2541; Fax: 314-647-2011.
School—Preschool, 5625 S. Magnolia, 63139. Tel: 314-645-2363.
Extended Day Care—Tel: 314-645-2363. Lay Teachers 2; Students 15.
Catechesis/Religious Program—Students 104.

3—ST. ALPHONSUS LIGUORI (1867), (African American), Rev. Richard Potts, C.SS.R.; Deacons Matthew Bonk; Leslie A. Johnson. In Res., Revs. Bill Parker; David Polek, C.S.S.R.; Gary Ziuraitis, C.SS.R.
Res.: 1118 N. Grand Blvd., 63106. Tel: 314-533-0304; Fax: 314-533-4260.
Catechesis/Religious Program—Tel: 314-533-3103. Ms. Donna Grant, D.R.E. Students 412.

4—ST. AMBROSE (1903), (Italian), Revs. Vincent R. Bommarito; Dennis M. Doyle, J.C.L.; Deacons John J. Stoverink; Daniel J. Tracy Sr.
Res.: 5130 Wilson Ave., 63110. Tel: 314-771-1228; Fax: 314-771-0454.
School—5110 Wilson Ave., 63110. Tel: 314-772-1437; Fax: 314-771-4560. S. Maureen Martin, A.S.C.J., Prin. Apostles of the Sacred Heart of Jesus 4; Lay Teachers 19; Students 332.
Catechesis/Religious Program—Tel: 314-771-5298. Students 332.

5—ST. ANN, MOTHER B.V.M., Closed. For inquiries for parish records contact the chancery.

6—ST. ANTHONY OF PADUA (1863), Revs. Robert C. Sieg, O.F.M.; Robert Behnen, O.F.M.; Lisa Sieve, Parish Mgr.
Res.: 3140 Meramec St., 63118. Tel: 314-353-7470; Fax: 314-655-0573.
School—4235 Compton Ave., 63118. Tel: 314-752-3397; Fax: 314-752-4384. Sue Goldmacher, Prin. Lay Teachers 10; Students 161.
Catechesis/Religious Program—Tel: 314-752-9908. Students 9.

7—ST. AUGUSTINE (1992), (African American), [JC], Consolidation of St. Barbara, St. Rose of Lima, St. Edward, St. Mark, and Notre Dame de Lourdes (Wellston). Rev. Msgr. Robert J. Gettinger; Deacon Perez Eric Maxwell.
1371 Hamilton Ave., 63112. Tel: 314-385-1934; Fax: 314-385-2949.
Catechesis/Religious Program—Students 214.

8—ST. BARBARA, Closed., See St. Augustine for details.

9—BASILICA OF ST. LOUIS, KING OF FRANCE (1770), Rev. Msgr. Bernard H. Sandheinrich; Rev. Richard J. Quirk. In Res., Rev. William W. McCumber.
Res.: 209 Walnut St., 63102. Tel: 314-231-3250; Fax: 314-231-4280.

10—ST. BONIFACE (1859), (German), Rev. James C. Gray Admin.; Deacon Richard Stevens.
Res.: 7622 Michigan Ave., 63111. Tel: 314-638-1438; Fax: 314-638-1460.
Catechesis/Religious Program—Students 28.

11—ST. BRIDGET OF ERIN (1853), Closed., For inquiries for sacramental records, contact Sts. Teresa and Bridget, St. Louis.

12—ST. CECILIA (1906), Rev. Msgr. Francis X. Blood; Deacon Michael Suden. In Res., Rev. Cajetan Ihewulezi, O.P.
Res. 5418 Louisiana Ave., 63111. Tel: 314-351-1318; Fax: 314-351-3372.
Church: Eiler & Alaska Ave., 63111.
School—906 Eichelberger Ave., 63111. Tel: 314-353-2455; Fax: 314-353-2411. Jim Ford, Prin. Lay Teachers 11; Students 150.

13—ST. CRONAN (1878), Rev. Gerald J. Kleba.
Res.: 1203 S. Boyle Ave., 63110. Tel: 314-289-9545; Fax: 314-289-9546.
Catechesis/Religious Program—Students 22.

14—ST. EDWARD, KING, Closed., See St. Augustine for details.

15—ST. ELIZABETH, MOTHER OF JOHN THE BAPTIST (1891), (African American), Revs. Carl J. Scheble; Mike Freymuth; Deacons Jesse Bell; Allen Conley.
Res.: 4330 Shreve Ave., 63115. Tel: 314-381-4145; Fax: 314-381-2212.
School—St. Engelbert "FOCUS" Consolidated School, 4720 Carter Ave., 63115. Tel: 314-389-0401; Fax: 314-389-7042. Mrs. Sybill Seefe, Prin. Religious 1; Lay Teachers 13; Students 190.
School—St. Engelbert "FOCUS" Day Care Center, 4746 Carter Ave., 63115. Tel: 314-389-0720. Ms. Belinda Palmer, Dir. Lay Teachers 18; Students 105.

16—EPIPHANY OF OUR LORD (1911), Rev. Dale P. Wunderlich; Deacon Chris Winkelmann; Terry Signaigo, Business Mgr.
Res.: 6596 Smiley Ave., 63139. Tel: 314-781-1199; Fax: 314-645-8760.
School—Tel: 314-781-5626; Fax: 314-645-7166. Sharon Morgenthaler, Prin. Lay Teachers 16; Students 278.
Catechesis/Religious Program—Students 427.

17—ST. FRANCIS DE SALES (1867), (German), Rev. Paul Otto Schneebeck, C.M.; Deacon Thomas A. Buhr. In Res., Rev. Romain G. Morales, C.M.
Res.: 2653 Ohio Ave., 63118. Tel: 314-771-3100; Fax: 314-771-3295.
School—3022 Oregon, 63118. Tel: 314-776-0883; Fax: 314-776-4912.
Catechesis/Religious Program—Students 35.

18—ST. FRANCIS XAVIER (1841),, (College) Revs. Leonard E. Kraus, S.J.; James J. Costello, S.J.; Deacon Louis A. Menard.
3628 Lindell Blvd., 63108. Tel: 314-977-7300; Fax: 314-977-7315.
Catechesis/Religious Program—Tel: 314-977-7302. Students 126.

19—ST. GABRIEL THE ARCHANGEL (1934), Revs. Charles E. Burgoon; Thomas C. Miller; Edwin J. Burmester (Retired); Deacons Phillip Gerdes; James Volansky.
Res.: 6303 Nottingham Ave., 63109. Tel: 314-353-6303; Fax: 314-353-7704.
School—4711 Tamm Ave., 63109. Tel: 314-353-1229; Fax: 314-353-6737. Lay Teachers 39; Students 520.
Catechesis/Religious Program—Students 835.

20—ST. HEDWIG (1904), (Polish), Rev. Msgr. Joseph W. Baker.
Res.: 3202 Pulaski St., 63111. Tel: 314-481-2486; Fax: 314-353-2454.

21—HOLY FAMILY (1898), Rev. Rickey J. Valleroy.
Res.: 4125 Humphrey St., 63116. Tel: 314-772-8292; Fax: 314-773-2283.
School—Tel: 314-771-2007. Mary Ann Kauffman, Prin. Lay Teachers 13; Students 260; Preschool 50.
Catechesis/Religious Program—Students 365.

22—HOLY GUARDIAN ANGELS, Closed. For inquiries for parish records contact the chancery.

23—HOLY INNOCENTS (1893), Rev. James P. Grady.
Res.: 4923 Odell St., 63139. Tel: 314-776-6440; Fax: 314-776-6441.

24—IMMACULATE CONCEPTION-ST. HENRY (1865), Rev. John Gavin, O.S.A. In Res., Rev. Francis Lawlor, O.S.A.
Res.: 3120 Lafayette Ave., 63104. Tel: 314-776-1333; Fax: 314-776-0642.
Catechesis/Religious Program—Students 138.

25—IMMACULATE HEART OF MARY (1951), Revs. John

Reiker; Mark Whitman.
Res.: 4092 Blow St., 63116. Tel: 314-481-7543; Fax: 314-481-6316.
School—4070 Blow St., 63116. Tel: 314-832-1678; Fax: 314-832-1627. Mrs. Pam Brown, Prin. Lay Teachers 21; Students 304.
Catechesis/Religious Program—Students 27.
26—ST. JAMES THE GREATER (1860), (Irish), Rev. John J. Johnson.
Res.: 6401 Wade Ave., 63139. Tel: 314-645-0167; Fax: 314-645-0168.
School—1360 Tamm Ave., 63139. Tel: 314-647-5244; Fax: 314-647-8237. Ms. Karen Battaglia, Prin. Lay Teachers 14; Students 165.
Catechesis/Religious Program—Students 165.
27—ST. JOAN OF ARC (1941), Rev. Msgr. Michael E. Turek; Rev. Kenneth J. Etter; Deacon Daniel H. Henroid. In Res., Rev. Msgr. Richard J. Gallagher.
Res.: 5800 Oleatha St., 63139. Tel: 314-832-2838; Fax: 314-352-9350.
School—Tel: 314-752-4171; Fax: 314-351-8562. Mrs. Debra Dalay, Prin. Lay Teachers 21; Students 325.
28—ST. JOHN NEPOMUK (1854), (Czech), Rev. Paul Spielmann.
Res.: 1625 S. 11th St., 63104. Tel: 314-231-0141; Fax: 314-231-0141.
29—ST. JOHN THE APOSTLE AND EVANGELIST (1847), Rev. Msgr. Dennis Delaney.
Res.: 15 Plaza Sq., 63103. Tel: 314-421-3467; Fax: 314-588-9544.
Catechesis/Religious Program—Students 3.
30—ST. JOHN THE BAPTIST (1914), (German), Revs. Edward M. Rice; Leo J. Spezia.
4200 Delor St., 63116. Tel: 314-353-1255; Fax: 314-752-3154.
School—4170 Delor St., 63116. Tel: 314-481-6654; Fax: 314-481-3179. Sisters of the Most Precious Blood, O'Fallon 1; Lay Teachers 16; Students 260.
High School—5021 Adkins St., 63116. Tel: 314-351-5604; Fax: 314-351-3050. Dr. John Kosash, Prin. Sisters 2; Lay Teachers 22; Students 221.
Catechesis/Religious Program—Students 481.
31—ST. JOSEPH (1904), (Croatian), Revs. Joseph M. Abramovic, O.F.M.; Robert Galinac, O.F.M.
Res.: 2112 S. 12th St., 63104. Tel: 314-771-0958; Fax: 314-771-0958.
Catechesis/Religious Program—Students 38.
32—ST. LIBORIUS, Closed. For inquiries for parish records contact the chancery.
33—ST. MARGARET OF SCOTLAND (1899), Rev. Kenneth Brown.
Res.: 3854 Flad Ave., 63110. Tel: 314-776-0363; Fax: 314-776-0364.
School—3964 Castleman, 63110. Tel: 314-776-7837. Sisters 2; Lay Teachers 17; Students 245.
Catechesis/Religious Program—Students 245.
34—ST. MARK, Rev. Patrick K. Hambrough.
8300 Morganford Rd., 63123. Tel: 314-743-8600; Fax: 314-743-8619.
35—ST. MARK, EVANGELIST, Closed., See St. Augustine for details.
36—STS. MARY AND JOSEPH (1821), Rev. Robert L. Szydlowski.
Res.: 6304 Minnesota Ave., 63111. Tel: 314-481-6304; Fax: 314-481-6337.
Catechesis/Religious Program—Students 3.
37—ST. MARY MAGDALEN (1919), Rev. Msgr. Dennis E. Doerhoff, V.F.; Rev. Bradley E. Modde. In Res., Rev. Mark Rivituso; Deacons Gerry Quinn; Kenneth Inman.
Res.: 4924 Bancroft Ave., 63109. Tel: 314-352-2111; Fax: 314-481-7661.
School—4911 Sutherland Ave., 63109. Tel: 314-832-3360; Fax: 314-481-7661. Lay Teachers 15; Students 193.
Catechesis/Religious Program—Southside Regional Parish School of Religion, Tel: 314-752-9908. Students 11.
38—ST. MARY OF VICTORIES (1843), (Hungarian), Rev. Paul E. Spielman.
Res.: 744 S. 3rd St., 63102. Tel: 314-231-8101; Fax: 314-231-0141.
39—ST. MATTHEW, APOSTLE (1893), (African American), [CEM] Revs. Mark D. McKenzie, S.J.; Jeffrey D. Harrison, S.J.; William J. Hutchison, S.J.
Res.: 2715 N. Sarah St., 63113. Tel: 314-531-6443; Fax: 314-533-7318.
Catechesis/Religious Program—Students 39.
40—MOST BLESSED SACRAMENT (1907), Closed. For inquiries for parish records contact the chancery.
41—MOST HOLY NAME OF JESUS, Merged, with Most Holy Trinity.
42—MOST HOLY ROSARY (1891), Closed., See St. Elizabeth, Mother of John the Baptist.
43—MOST HOLY TRINITY (1848), Rev. Richard H. Creason; Sr. Joyelle Proot, S.S.N.D., Pastoral Assoc.
Res.: 3519 N. Fourteenth St., 63107-3796. Tel: 314-241-9165; Fax: 314-436-9291.
School—1435 Mallinckrodt St., 63107-3796. Tel: 314-231-9014; Fax: 314-436-9291. Carol Werner, Prin. Sisters 4; Lay Teachers 6; Students 88.
Convent—Tel: 314-621-6835. Sisters 1.
44—ST. NICHOLAS (1865), (African American), Revs. George Kintiba, S.V.D. (TR); Yoo Yong Duc Odilon, S.V.D.; Sr. Antona Ebo, F.S.M., Pastoral Assoc.; Deacon Stanley Peterson; Ms. Ella L. Scott, Pastoral Assoc. In Res., Rev. Vincent Burke.
Res.: 701 N. 18th St., 63103. Tel: 314-231-2860; Fax: 314-231-9823.
School—Central Catholic/St. Nicholas School, 1805 Lucas St., 63103. Tel: 314-421-1822. Lay Teachers 40; Students 300.
Catechesis/Religious Program—Students 9.
Chapel—Christ the King
45—OUR LADY OF MOUNT CARMEL, Closed. For inquiries for parish records contact the chancery.
46—OUR LADY OF PERPETUAL HELP, Merged, with Most Holy Trinity.
47—OUR LADY OF SORROWS (1907), Rev. Msgr. James T. Telthorst; Revs. Bradley E. Modde; John Schweitzer; Jack Heil; Timothy M. Foley; Most Rev. Robert Hermann, V.G.; Deacons Robert Wertz; Robert H. Schnable; Ed Auer.
Res.: 5020 Rhodes Ave., 63109. Tel: 314-351-1600; Fax: 314-351-1602.
School—5831 S. Kingshighway, 63109. Tel: 314-353-1451; Fax: 314-351-8464. Sisters of Notre Dame 2; Lay Teachers 46; Students 440.
Catechesis/Religious Program—Students 509.
48—OUR LADY OF THE HOLY CROSS (1864), Very Rev. Mark C. Ullrich, M.Div., M.S.W., V.F.; Deacon Donald Driscoll.
Res.: 8115 Church Rd., 63147. Tel: 314-381-0323; Fax: 314-381-4828.
School—1018 Baden Ave., 63147. Tel: 314-383-4782; Fax: 314-383-5982. Sisters 3; Lay Teachers 8; Students 70.
49—ST. PATRICK (1981), Revs. Valentine Young, O.F.M.Cap.; Simon R. Conrad, O.F.M.Cap.; Canice Froelich, O.F.M.Cap.; Simeon Gallagher, O.F.M-.Cap.; Earl Meyer, O.F.M.Cap.
Res.: 1000 N. 7th St., 63101. Tel: 314-231-9991; Fax: 314-231-9289.
Shrine—Shrine of St. Joseph, Tel: 314-231-9407.
50—STS. PETER AND PAUL (1849), Rev. Bruce H. Forman; Deacons Joseph T. Haefner; Thomas Gorski.
Res.: 1919 S. 7th St., 63104. Tel: 314-231-9923; Fax: 314-231-7464.
51—ST. PIUS THE FIFTH (1905), Rev. Michael J. Lydon; Mrs. Barbara Loeb, Business Mgr.; Deacon Walter W. Christ; Sisters Paulette Weindell, C.PP.S., Pastoral Assoc.; Dorothy Ann Katke, C.PP.S., Pastoral Assoc. In Res., Rev. Joseph Kaberia (Kenya).
Res.: 3310 S. Grand Blvd., 63118. Tel: 314-772-1525; Fax: 314-772-5615.
School— For further information please see St. Frances Cabrini Academy at St. Wenceslaus, St. Louis
52—ST. RAPHAEL THE ARCHANGEL (1950), Rev. Msgr. William A. Drennan; Rev. Joseph R. Monahan. In Res., Rev. Richard H. Suren (Retired); Deacons Gerald Geiser; Roger Kreitler.
Res.: 6047 Bishops Pl., 63109. Tel: 314-352-8100; Fax: 314-353-6603.
School—Tel: 314-352-9474; Fax: 314-352-7285. Mrs. Susan Brown, Prin. Lay Teachers 13; Students 175.
Catechesis/Religious Program—Students 288.
53—RESURRECTION OF OUR LORD (1930), Revs. Thomas W. Wyrsch; Robert W. Argent.
3900 Meramec St., 63116. Tel: 314-832-7023; Fax: 314-832-7024.
School—3880 Meramec St., 63116. Tel: 314-772-6745; Fax: 314-772-6745. Sr. Bernadette Miller, Prin. Sisters 2; Lay Teachers 9; Students 139.
54—ST. ROCH (1911), Rev. Msgr. Salvatore E. Polizzi; Rev. Lawrence A. Herzog.
Res.: 6052 Waterman Blvd., 63112. Tel: 314-721-6340; Fax: 314-721-1656.
School—6040 Waterman Blvd., 63112. Tel: 314-721-2595. Gloria Openlander, Prin. Lay Teachers 13; Students 198.
55—ST. ROSE OF LIMA, Closed., See St. Augustine for details.
56—ST. SEBASTIAN (1953), Rev. Robert L. Banken; Deacons Herbert L. Ehrhard; Ralph Hayes.
Res.: 9950 Glen Owen Dr., 63136. Tel: 314-868-0730; Fax: 314-868-0731.
Catechesis/Religious Program—Students 62.
57—THE SHRINE OF ST. JOSEPH, CAPUCHIN FATHERS (1844), (German), Unassigned. Rev. Valentine Young, O.F.M.Cap.
Res.: 1220 N. 11th St., 63106. Tel: 314-231-9407; Fax: 314-231-0802.
58—ST. SIMON OF CYRENE (1993), (African American), Rev. Steven P. Robeson; Deacon Fred Dodson.
Res.: 5076 Durant Ave., 63115. Tel: 314-385-0068; Fax: 314-385-5339.
Catechesis/Religious Program—Students 1.
59—ST. STANISLAUS KOSTKA (1880), (Polish), Rev. Philip J. Bene, J.C.D., Admin. In Res., Rev. Adam Hurbanczuk.
Res.: 1413 N. 20th St., 63106. Tel: 314-421-5948; Fax: 314-588-8688.
60—ST. STEPHEN, PROTOMARTYR (1926), Revs. Charles Barthel; Ronald Chochol, Senior Assoc.; Deacons Leo Esswein; Bill Casseau.
Res.: 3949 Wilmington Ave., 63116. Tel: 314-481-1133; Fax: 314-481-6036.
School—3923 Wilmington Ave., 63116. Tel: 314-752-4700; Fax: 314-752-5165. Dennis Moorehead, Prin. Lay Teachers 15; Students 206.
Catechesis/Religious Program—Students 7.
61—STS. TERESA AND BRIDGET (2003), Rev. Timothy R. Cook.
3636 N. Market.
62—ST. TERESA OF AVILA (1865), Closed., For inquiries for sacramental records, contact Sts. Teresa and Bridget, St. Louis.
63—ST. THOMAS OF AQUIN (1882), Revs. Chau Pham, S.V.D.; Andrew Biller, S.V.D.
Res.: 3949 Iowa Ave., 63118. Tel: 314-772-2644; Fax: 314-776-4639.
Catechesis/Religious Program—Students 117.
64—ST. VINCENT DE PAUL (1841), Rev. Joseph S. Williams, C.M.; Sr. Jackie Toben, S.S.N.D., Pastoral Assoc.; Deacon Joe Cox; Mr. Dennis Wells, Pastoral Assoc.
Res.: 1408 S. Tenth St., 63104. Tel: 314-231-9328; Fax: 314-621-2232.
Catechesis/Religious Program— Linda Mertz, D.R.E. Students 54.
65—VISITATION-ST. ANN'S SHRINE (1881), (African American), Rev. Timothy R. Cook; Rev. Msgr. Richard A. Buchheit.
Res.: 4515 Evans Ave., 63113. Tel: 314-535-8804; Fax: 314-531-8486.
66—ST. WENCESLAUS (1895), (Bohemian), Revs. James E. Wuerth, M.S.F.; John Carl Lombardi, M.S.F.; Deacons George W. Miller; John Griffin, M.S.F.
Res.: 3014 Oregon Ave., 63118-1498. Tel: 314-865-1020; Fax: 314-664-8260.
Catechesis/Religious Program—St. Frances Cabrini Academy, 3022 Oregon Ave., 63118-1498. Tel: 314-776-0883; Fax: 314-776-4912. Students 135.

CHURCHES IN ST. LOUIS COUNTY

AFFTON
1—ST. DOMINIC SAVIO (1956), [CEM] Revs. John S. Siefert; David A. Novak; Deacons James L. Murphy; John W. Beckmann.
Res.: 6120 Pebble Hill Dr., 63123. Tel: 314-353-7629; Fax: 314-481-2908.
Church: 7748 MacKenzie Rd., 63123.
School—Tel: 314-832-4161. Mrs. Susan E. Hooker, Prin. Lay Teachers 16; Students 214.
Catechesis/Religious Program—Students 78.
2—SEVEN HOLY FOUNDERS (1927), Revs. Michael Doyle, O.S.M.; Joseph Chamblain, O.S.M.; John Fontana, O.S.M.; Deacons Charles Lombardo; Ted Rodis.
Office—6820 Aliceton Ave., 63123. Tel: 314-638-3938; Fax: 314-638-0613.
Church: 6741 Rock Hill Rd., 63123. Tel: 314-631-3938.
School—6737 Rock Hill Rd., 63123. Tel: 314-631-8149. Mr. Richard Muth, Prin. Lay Teachers 23; Students 452.
Catechesis/Religious Program—Tel: 314-638-3938. Students 175.
3—ST. TIMOTHY (1958), Closed., For inquiries for sacramental records, contact St. Mark, St. Louis.
BALLWIN, HOLY INFANT (1954), Rev. Msgr. Thomas J. Dempsey; Revs. Joseph J. Welschmeyer; William F. Vatterott; Deacon Kenneth C. Clemens.
Res.: 627 Dennison Dr., 63021. Tel: 636-227-7440; Fax: 636-227-4548.
School—Tel: 636-227-0802; Fax: 636-227-9184. Sr. Rosario Delaney, R.S.M., Prin. Sisters of Mercy (Meath Mercy Generalate, Ireland) 3; Lay Teachers 44; Students 938.
Catechesis/Religious Program—Tel: 636-779-0002; Fax: 636-227-9184. Students 648.
BEL-RIDGE, ST. THOMAS MORE (1955), Closed. For inquiries for parish records contact the chancery.
BELLEFONTAINE NEIGHBORS, OUR LADY OF GOOD COUNSEL (1951), Rev. Donald R. Wester.
Res.: 1160 St. Cyr Rd., 63137. Tel: 314-867-1441; Fax: 314-867-1442.
School—Pope John Paul II Catholic Elementary School, 1134 St. Cyr Rd., 63137. Tel: 314-867-2400; Fax: 314-867-3776. Sr. Barbara Thomas, A.S.C.J., Prin. Sisters 5; Lay Teachers 22; Students 405.
Convent—1142 St. Cyr Rd., 63137. Tel: 314-868-3067.
BERKELEY, HOLY GHOST (1923), Closed., For inquiries for parish records please see St. Bartholomew, Hazelwood.
BISSELL HILLS, ST. JEROME (1952), Rev. Mark A. Dolan.
Res.: 10235 Ashbrook Dr., 63137. Tel: 314-868-2310; Fax: 314-868-3919.
School—Pope John Paul II Catholic Elementary School, Tel: 314-867-2400; Fax: 314-867-3776. (See

Our Lady of Good Counsel, Bellefontaine Neighbors.)

BRENTWOOD, ST. MARY MAGDALEN (1912), Revs. Bernard J. Wilkins; Michael Witt; Deacon Leroy Martin.
Res.: 2618 Brentwood Blvd., 63144. Tel: 314-961-8400; Fax: 314-961-7019.
School—8762 Magdalen Ave., 63144. Tel: 314-961-0149; Fax: 314-961-7208. Ms. Julie Hesed, Prin. Lay Teachers 16; Students 180.
Catechesis/Religious Program—Students 180.

BRIDGETON

1—ST. LAWRENCE THE MARTYR (1960), Rev. C. Robert Manning; Deacons Wm. Walbridge; Charles Georges.
Res.: 4335 DuPage Dr., 63044. Tel: 314-739-0496; Fax: 314-739-2768.
School—4329 DuPage Dr., 63044. Tel: 314-739-3123; Fax: 314-739-2648.
Catechesis/Religious Program—Students 155.

2—ST. MARY (1852), Closed. For inquiries for parish records contact the chancery.

CHESTERFIELD

1—ASCENSION (1923), Rev. Msgr. Joseph Pins; Revs. Richard Nelke; Christopher F. Holtmann; Deacons Larry Hutti; Frank Chauvin; William P. Wunderlich; Robert Keeney.
Res.: 230 Santa Maria Dr., 63005. Tel: 636-532-3304; Fax: 636-532-3518.
School—Preschool, Ascension Early Childhood Center, 238 Santa Maria Dr., 63005. Tel: 636-532-3375.
School—238 Santa Maria Dr., 63005. Tel: 636-532-1151; Fax: 636-532-6502. Mrs. Cathie Wayland, Prin. Lay Teachers 33; Students 678.
Catechesis/Religious Program—Tel: 636-532-1136. Students 767.

2—INCARNATE WORD (1965), Revs. G. Timothy Vowels; Eugene E. Utrup; Joseph F. Classen; Deacons James Russell; Larry Stallings.
Res.: 13416 Olive Blvd., 63017. Tel: 314-576-5366; Fax: 314-576-2046.
School—Tel: 314-576-5366, Ext. 11. C. Michael Welling, Prin. Lay Teachers 23; Students 470.
Catechesis/Religious Program—Tel: 314-576-5366, Ext. 26. Mrs. Jane Schwendeman, D.R.E. Students 350.

CLAYTON, ST. JOSEPH (1842), Rev. Msgr. John B. Shamleffer, J.C.L., M.C.L.; Rev. Martin J. Mulvihill; Deacon Albert Williams.
Res.: 106 N. Meramec Ave., 63105. Tel: 314-726-1221; Fax: 314-721-5110.
Catechesis/Religious Program—Tel: 314-727-9059. Mrs. Terri Venneman, D.R.E. Students 190.

CRESTWOOD

1—ST. ELIZABETH OF HUNGARY (1956), Deacon Robert Snyder; Rev. James T. Edwards. In Res., Rev. John P. Comer.
Res.: 1420 S. Sappington Rd., 63126. Tel: 314-968-0760; Fax: 314-968-8023.
School—1414 S. Sappington Rd., 63126. Tel: 314-962-9698; Fax: 314-918-1976. Mr. Kenneth Weis, Prin. Sisters 1; Lay Teachers 13; Students 126.
Catechesis/Religious Program—Tel: 314-962-0834. Students 95.
Convent—1405 S. Sappington Rd., 63126. Tel: 314-961-2630.

2—OUR LADY OF PROVIDENCE (1954), Revs. David E. Rauch; Glennon C. Doherty; Deacons Gerald Prives; David Amelotti.
Res.: 8866 Pardee Rd., 63123. Tel: 314-843-3570; Fax: 314-843-8033.
School—8874 Pardee Rd., 63123. Tel: 314-842-2073. Mary Jo Masterson, Prin. Lay Teachers 14; Students 225.
Catechesis/Religious Program—Students 68.

CREVE COEUR

1—ST. ANSELM (1966), Revs. Gerard Garrigan, O.S.B.; R. Benedict Allin, O.S.B.; Deacon Steven H. Wohlert, Pastoral Assoc.
Res.: 530 S. Mason Rd., 63141. Tel: 314-878-2120; Fax: 314-878-2199.
Catechesis/Religious Program—Students 196.

2—ST. JOHN BOSCO (1972), Rev. Gerard R. Welsch. In Res., Rev. Msgr. Jerome F. Wilkerson, Ph.D. (Retired); Rev. David T. Thomas (Retired).
Res.: 12934 Marine Ave., 63146. Tel: 314-434-1312; Fax: 314-514-0478.
Catechesis/Religious Program—Tel: 314-878-6492. Students 180.

3—ST. MONICA (1872), [CEM] Rev. Msgr. Nicholas A. Schneider; Rev. George P. Brennan; Deacons Robert K. Gamache; Robert Birkenmaier; Millard R. Miller; James P. Martin; Thomas K. Coerver, Dir. Business Admin.
Res.: 12136 Olive Blvd., 63141-6629. Tel: 314-434-4211; Fax: 314-434-5978.
School—12132 Olive Blvd., 63141-6698. Tel: 314-434-2173; Fax: 314-434-7689. Mr. James J. Spies, Prin. Lay Teachers 28; Students 396.
Catechesis/Religious Program—Students 89.

4—OUR LADY OF THE PILLAR (1938), Rev. James M. Tobin, S.M.; Deacon Norman B. Werner. In Res., Rev. J. Donald Cahill, S.M.
Res.: 401 S. Lindbergh Blvd., 63131. Tel: 314-993-2280; Fax: 314-993-6462.
School—Tel: 314-993-3353; Fax: 314-993-2172. Franciscan Sisters of Our Lady of Perpetual Help 3; Lay Teachers 22; Students 215.
Catechesis/Religious Program—Students 105.
Convent—403 S. Lindbergh Blvd., 63131. Tel: 314-993-3666.

5—ST. RICHARD (1963), Rev. C. Robert Dochauer. In Res., Rev. Phil Krahman; Deacon Jerry N McGuire.
Res.: 11223 Schuetz Rd., 63146. Tel: 314-432-6224; Fax: 314-432-6030.
School—11211 Schuetz Rd., 63146. Tel: 314-872-3152; Fax: 314-872-7326. Mrs. Julie Blow, Prin. Sisters 1; Lay Teachers 15; Students 16[illegible].
Catechesis/Religious Program—Students 102.

DES PERES, ST. CLEMENT (1951), Rev. Msgrs. James E. Pieper; Robert McCarthy; Rev. Stephen P. Giljum; Deacon Richard Vehige.
Res.: 1510 Bopp Rd., 63131. Tel: 314-965-0709; Fax: 314-965-1486.
School—1508 Bopp Rd., 63131. Tel: 314-822-1903; Fax: 314-822-8371. Mary Christina Reichardt, Prin. Lay Teachers 35; Students 435.
Catechesis/Religious Program—Students 120.

ELLISVILLE, ST. CLARE OF ASSISI (1963), Revs. Richard E. Hanneke; Michael J. Esswein; Brian R. Fischer; Deacons Dennis K. Stovall; W. Alan Whitson.
Res.: 15642 Clayton Rd., 63011. Tel: 636-394-7307; Fax: 636-394-6264.
School—Tel: 636-227-8654; Fax: 636-394-0359. Mrs. Marie Sinnett, Prin. Lay Teachers 24; Students 485.
Catechesis/Religious Program—Tel: 636-394-4368; Fax: 636-394-4397. Students 565.

EUREKA, SACRED HEART (1889), Rev. Alexander R. Anderson.
Res.: 350 E. Fourth St., 63025. Tel: 636-938-5048; Fax: 636-587-2736.
School—Tel: 636-938-4602. Michael Talleur, Prin. Lay Teachers 13; Students 266.
Catechesis/Religious Program—Tel: 636-938-9507. Students 352.

FENTON, ST. PAUL (1878), [CEM] Revs. Michael Dieckmann; John Wetmore; Jack Suren; Deacons John Weatherholt; Paul Crafts.
Res.: 15 Forest Knoll, 63026. Tel: 636-343-1234; Fax: 636-343-4809.
School—465 New Smizer Mill Rd., 63026. Tel: 636-343-4333; Fax: 636-343-1769. Religious 2; Lay Teachers 22; Students 475.
Catechesis/Religious Program—Tel: 636-343-1678. Students 452.

FERGUSON

1—GOOD SHEPHERD (1958), Rev. Gregory R. Mikesch; Deacon Edward Beirne.
Res.: 921 Smith Ave., 63135. Tel: 314-521-1008; Fax: 314-521-1034.
School—1050 Smith Ave., 63135. Tel: 314-524-4332. Sisters 1; Lay Teachers 13; Students 196.

2—STS. JOHN AND JAMES (1882), Rev. Richard J. Schilli Deacon L. Jerome Marren; Jeffrey Finnegan, Pastoral Assoc.
Res.: 140 N. Elizabeth Ave., 63135. Tel: 314-522-0275; Fax: 314-522-9404.
School—150 N. Elizabeth Ave., 63135. Tel: 314-522-3888; Fax: 314-595-9274.
Catechesis/Religious Program—Students 199.

3—OUR LADY OF GUADALUPE (1954), (Hispanic), Revs. A. John Schuler; Dick Vogt, S.J.; Sr. Cathy Doherty, Pastoral Assoc.
Res.: 17 Hawkesbury Dr., 63121. Tel: 314-522-9264; Fax: 314-522-8461.
School—1115 S. Florissant Rd., 63121. Tel: 314-524-1948. Jane Dowd, Prin. Lay Teachers 10; Students 176.
Catechesis/Religious Program—Students 24.

FLORISSANT

1—ST. ANGELA MERICI (1962), Revs Ferdinand J. Welsh; Vincent Nyman.
Res.: 14005 Davey Dr., 63034. Tel 314-838-6565; Fax: 314-838-6566.
School—3860 N. Hwy. 67, 63034. Tel: 314-831-8012. Lay Teachers 21; Students 300.
Catechesis/Religious Program—Students 60.

2—ST. CHRISTOPHER (1967), Rev. Thomas J. Schaab; Deacons Kenneth M. Potzman; George A. Graham; George Blase.
Res. 11575 Old Halls Ferry Rd., 63033. Tel: 314-839-2427; Fax: 314-839-2428.
Catechesis/Religious Program—Students 38.

3—ST DISMAS (1956), Rev. Robert W. Burkemper.
Res.: 2650 Parker Rd., 63033. Tel: 314-837-3410; Fax: 314-837-6628.
School—1220 Paddock Dr., 63033. Tel: 314-837-0369; Fax: 314-837-8956. Lay Teachers 12; Students 167
Catechesis/Religious Program—St. Dismas School, 2650 Parker Rd., 63033. Tel: 314-837-0369. Students 110.

4—ST. FERDINAND (1788), Revs. John G. Dempsey; Eugene G. Robertson. In Res., Deacon Joseph Kroutil.
Res.: 1765 Charbonier Rd., 63031. Tel: 314-837-3165; Fax: 314-837-5799.
School—Tel: 314-921-2201; Fax: 314-921-2253. Sisters of the Most Precious Blood 1; Lay Teachers 20; Students 285.
Catechesis/Religious Program—Tel: 314-831-5273. Students 345.

5—ST. NORBERT (1965), Revs. Patrick D. Ryan, D.Min.; Charles P. Tichacek; Deacons Robert Klostermann, Pastoral Assoc.; Leonard Sisol.
Res.: 16455 New Halls Ferry Rd., 63031. Tel: 314-831-3874; Fax: 314-831-3875.
School—Tel: 314-839-0948; Fax: 314-839-0948. Mrs. Pam Gilbert, Prin. Sisters 1; Lay Teachers 24; Students 416.
Catechesis/Religious Program—Tel: 314-830-0841. Deacon Leonard Sisul, D.R.E. Students 150.

6—NORTH AMERICAN MARTYRS (1955), Rev. James J. Byrnes; Deacons Robert J. Powers; Peter Gounis.
Res.: 1400 S. Lafayette St., 63031-7997. Tel: 314-837-9304; Fax: 314-972-0091.
Catechesis/Religious Program—Students 62.

7—OUR LADY OF FATIMA (1950), Rev. Donald L. Buhr; Deacon Robert J. Mayo II.
Res.: 4550 Washington St., 63033. Tel: 314-837-9366; Fax: 314-837-9367.
School—4500 Washington St., 63033. Tel: 314-921-0437; Fax: 314-921-2044. Lay Teachers 12; Students 169.
Catechesis/Religious Program—Tel: 314-921-9814. Students 220.

8—ST. SABINA (1960), Rev. Robert J. Samson; Deacons Harold A. Strauss; Alvin Dietz.
Res.: 1365 Harkee Dr., 63031. Tel: 314-837-1365; Fax: 314-837-7680.
School—1625 Swallow Dr., 63031. Tel: 314-837-6524; Fax: 314-837-3162. Sr. Joan Galli, C.S.J., Prin. Sisters 2; Lay Teachers 15; Students 215.
Catechesis/Religious Program—Tel: 314-837-6524. Students 194.

9—SACRED HEART (1866), (German), Rev. Edward J. Stanger; Rev. Msgr. Arthur F. Bromschwig; Deacons James Griffard; Bruce A. Burkhard.
Res.: 751 N. Jefferson St., 63031. Tel: 314-837-3757; Fax: 314-837-8897.
School—501 St. Louis St., 63031. Tel: 314-831-3372. Ms. Clare Ortmeier, Prin. Lay Teachers 23; Students 345.
Catechesis/Religious Program—Tel: 314-837-3757, Ext. 232. Students 90.

10—ST. THOMAS THE APOSTLE (1960), Rev. Timothy M. Foley; Deacons Joseph Morris; Charles Holmes.
Res.: 500 Clemens Dr., 63033. Tel: 314-838-4017; Fax: 314-921-6724.
School—3500 St. Catherine St., 63033. Tel: 314-921-7313. Ann Allen, Prin. Religious 1; Lay Teachers 21; Students 251.
Catechesis/Religious Program— Twinned with St. Dismas, Florissant

11—TRANSFIGURATION (1965), Rev. Joseph W. Banden.
Res.: 6685 Lakeside Hills Dr., 63033. Tel: 314-741-2309; Fax: 314-355-7527.
Catechesis/Religious Program—1650 Redman Ave., 63138. Tel: 314-741-0400; Fax: 314-741-2583. Students 23.
Convent—12613 Partridge Run Dr., 63033. Tel: 314-741-6568.

GARDENVILLE, ST. GEORGE (1915), Revs. Thomas Haley; Joseph J. Adragna; Ralph E. Stroot (Retired); Deacons Roy E. Schulze; Robert Penberthy.
Res.: 4980 Heege Rd., 63123. Tel: 314-352-3544; Fax: 314-832-6916.
School—4974 Heege Rd., 63123. Tel: 314-832-6432; Fax: 314-832-0561. Lay Teachers 14; Students 142.
Catechesis/Religious Program—Students 180.

GLASGOW VILLAGE, ST. PIUS X (1954), Rev. James C. Marshall.
Res.: 335 Shepley Dr., 63137. Tel: 314-867-1139; Fax: 314-867-7083.
School—Pope John Paul II Catholic Elementary School, Tel: 314-867-2400; Fax: 314-867-3776. (See Our lady of Good Counsel, Bellefontaine Neighbors.)

GLEN OWEN, ST. SEBASTIAN, , See St. Sebastian, St. Louis County.

GRANTWOOD

GREEN PARK, ST. SIMON THE APOSTLE (1959), Revs. Mark S. Ebert; James B. Wilke; Deacon Paul F. Stackle. In Res., Rev. Msgr. John T. Ronquest (Retired).
Res.: 11011 Mueller Rd., 63123. Tel: 314-842-3848; Fax: 314-842-9829.
School—Preschool, 11015 Mueller Rd., 63123. Tel: 314-842-3435.
School—11019 Mueller Rd., 63123. Tel: 314-842-0181; Fax: 314-849-6355. Lay Teachers 25; Students 455.
Catechesis/Religious Program—Students 130.

HATHAWAY MANOR, ST. CASIMIR, Closed. For inquiries for parish records contact the chancery.

HAZELWOOD

1—ST. BARTHOLOMEW (1959), Very Rev. John Brockland, J.C.L., V.F.; Deacon Charles Davanzo.
Res.: 8370 Latty Ave., 63042. Tel: 314-524-4422; Fax: 314-524-7036.
Catechesis/Religious Program—Students 31.

2—ST. MARTIN DE PORRES (1962), Rev. Patrick Christopher.
Res.: 615 Dunn Rd., 63042-1799. Tel: 314-895-1100; Fax: 314-895-5992.
School—631 Undercliff, 63042. Tel: 314-895-3600; Fax: 314-895-3601. Lay Teachers 13; Students 142.
School—Kinderhaus, 627 Undercliff, 63042.
Catechesis/Religious Program—Tel: 314-895-4631. Students 117.

3—OUR LADY OF MERCY (1964), Rev. James M. Sullivan; Deacon David Pacino.
Res.: 1607 Ville Maura Ln., 63042. Tel: 314-739-9369; Fax: 314-739-1242.
Catechesis/Religious Program—Students 50.

JENNINGS

1—CORPUS CHRISTI (1915), Revs. James J. Foster; Edward Schramm; Deacons Raymond Audrain; Frank E. Nesbitt.
Res.: 8449 Jennings Station Rd., 63136. Tel: 314-388-0123; Fax: 314-868-2401.
School—2120 Switzer Ave., 63136. Tel: 314-388-0468; Fax: 314-388-3855. Lay Teachers 13; Students 171.

2—ST. FRANCES XAVIER CABRINI (1965), Merged, with Coprus Christi, Jennings.

3—ST. LOUISE DE MARILLAC (1935), Merged, with Corpus Christi to form Corpus Christi, Jennings.

4—ST. LUCY, , See Corpus Christi for details.

KINLOCH, HOLY ANGELS (1931), (African American), Closed. For inquiries for parish records contact the chancery.

KIRKWOOD

1—ST. GERARD MAJELLA (1955), Revs. Herbert C. Hauck; Thomas C. Bryon; Deacons Timothy Dolan; James Burton; Donald Denham; Leslie Walrath, Pastoral Assoc.
Res.: 1969 Dougherty Ferry Rd., 63122. Tel: 314-965-3985; Fax: 314-965-7650.
School—2005 Dougherty Ferry Rd., 63122. Tel: 314-822-8844; Fax: 314-822-8588. Jane Koberlein, Prin. Lay Teachers 26; Students 372.
Catechesis/Religious Program—Students 310.

2—ST. PETER (1832), [CEM] Revs. John J. Brennell; Gary Meier; Deacons Joseph Sulze; Jimmy Broyles. In Res., Rev. Theodore Burghoff.
Res.: 243 W. Argonne Dr., 63122. Tel: 314-966-8600; Fax: 314-966-5721.
School—215 N. Clay St., 63122. Tel: 314-821-0460. Lay Teachers 25; Students 439.
Catechesis/Religious Program—Tel: 314-822-1347. Linda Doyle, D.R.E.; Jan Hartman, D.R.E. Students 232.

LADUE, CHURCH OF THE ANNUNZIATA (1929), Rev. Msgr. Robert M. Krawinkel; Christie Murphy, Pastoral Assoc.
Res.: 925 Cella Rd., 63124. Tel: 314-993-4422; Fax: 314-994-7877.
Catechesis/Religious Program—Students 135.

LEMAY

1—ST. ANDREW (1905), Revs. Joseph A. Weber; Albert F. Danter (Retired); Deacons Robert Karsznia; C. Allen Boedeker.
Res.: 309 Hoffmeister Ave., 63125-1609. Tel: 314-631-0691; Fax: 314-631-0692.
Catechesis/Religious Program—317 Hoffmeister Ave., 63125. Tel: 314-631-5135; Fax: 314-631-5633. Mrs. Mary Boedeker, D.R.E.; Mrs. Karen Freese, D.R.E. Students 25.
Convent—Sisters of Notre Dame, 232 Hoffmeister Ave., 63125. Tel: 314-631-2010.

2—ST. BERNADETTE (1947), Rev. Gary J. Faust, M.A., M.Div.; Deacons Michael Coppage; Michael Buckley.
Res.: 68 Sherman Rd., Jefferson Barracks, 63125. Tel: 314-892-6882; Fax: 314-892-7716.
Catechesis/Religious Program—Tel: 314-892-8379. Students 21.

3—ST. MARTIN OF TOURS (1939), Rev. Msgr. Kevin G. Callahan; Revs. Terry J. Borgerding; Norbert A. Mersinger (Retired); James J. Ramacciotti; Deacons Terrance McNamee; Edward Fronick; Sr. Pat Kofron, A.S.C.J., Pastoral Assoc.
Res.: 610 W. Ripa Ave., 63125. Tel: 314-544-5664; Fax: 314-631-3118.
School—618 W. Ripa Ave., 63125. Tel: 314-544-5793; Fax: 314-544-1892. Mr. Greg Sturgill, Prin. Lay Teachers 12; Students 206.
Catechesis/Religious Program—Students 58.

4—MARY, QUEEN OF THE UNIVERSE (1955), Closed., For inquiries for sacramental records, contact St. Mark, St. Louis.

5—ST. MATTHIAS (1959), Revs. William J. Kester; Didacus Dunn; Deacon Joseph Hercules.
Res.: 796 Buckley Rd., 63125. Tel: 314-892-5109; Fax: 314-892-0629.
School—800 Buckley Rd., 63125. Tel: 314-892-7500. Lay Teachers 13; Students 183.
Catechesis/Religious Program—Students 84.

6—MOST PRECIOUS BLOOD (1961), Closed., For inquiries for sacramental records, contact St. Mark, St. Louis.

MANCHESTER

1—CHRIST, PRINCE OF PEACE (1971), Very Rev. Joseph E. Wormek, V.F.; Rev. Robert Corbett; Deacons Thomas L. Eultgen; Joseph M. Kennedy.
Res.: 415 Weidman Rd., 63011. Tel: 636-391-1307; Fax: 636-391-1319.
School—417 Weidman Rd., 63011. Tel: 636-394-6840; Fax: 636-394-3860. Mrs. Chris Einig, Prin. Lay Teachers 29; Students 372.
Catechesis/Religious Program—Tel: 636-391-1560. Students 195.

2—ST. JOSEPH (1865), [CEM] Revs. Thomas J. Santen; Robt. Boisaubin; James Krings.
Res.: 567 St. Joseph Ln., 63021. Tel: 636-227-5247; Fax: 636-391-8393.
School—555 St. Joseph Ln., 63021. Tel: 636-391-1253; Fax: 636-391-1462. Jeannie Dandino, Prin.; Michael Larson, Asst. Prin. Sisters 1; Lay Teachers 36; Students 566.
Catechesis/Religious Program—Tel: 636-391-1404. Students 515.

MAPLEWOOD, IMMACULATE CONCEPTION (1904), [JC] Rev. Terry Niziolek, M.S.; Sr. Georgeann Hanson, S.L., Pastoral Assoc.; Deacon Clyde McEntire.
Res.: 2900 Marshall Ave., 63143. Tel: 314-645-3307; Fax: 314-645-0672.
Additional Residence for Priests—2900 Marshall, 63143. Tel: 314-645-5904; Fax: 314-781-8907. Rev. Dennis J. Meyer, M.S.
Catechesis/Religious Program—Tel: 314-644-6787. Students 10.

MARYLAND HEIGHTS, ST. BLAISE (1961), Revs. Richard J. Bockskopf; John Patrick Day, C.P.; Deacons Jacob W. Dorhauer; Eugene Naumann.
Res.: 3130 Parkwood Ln., 63043. Tel: 314-739-0230; Fax: 314-739-0237.
School—Tel: 314-739-1934; Fax: 314-739-7703. Sisters 2; Lay Teachers 12; Students 217.
Catechesis/Religious Program— Ree Gerdes, D.R.E.; Donna Wright, D.R.E. Students 215.

MATTESE

1—ASSUMPTION (1839), [CEM] Revs. Peter M. Blake; Edward Ramatowski; Bob Smoot; Deacon Richard B. Levac.
Res.: 4725 Mattis Rd., 63128. Tel: 314-487-7970; Fax: 314-892-5513.
School—Tel: 314-487-6520; Fax: 314-487-3598. Lay Teachers 24; Students 486.
Catechesis/Religious Program—Tel: 314-487-7970, Ext. 218. Evelyn Tucker, D.R.E.; Donna Koppy, D.R.E. Students 186.

2—MARY, MOTHER OF THE CHURCH (1971), Rev. Msgrs. Edward Reilly; Edward Deutschmann (Retired); Deacons Richard Coffman; Richard Bub.
Res.: 5901 Kerth Rd., 63128. Tel: 314-894-1373; Fax: 314-894-3801.
Catechesis/Religious Program— Ed Lewandowski, D.R.E. Students 372.

MEHLVILLE, ST. MARGARET MARY ALACOQUE (1962), Very Rev. Dennis R. Stehly, V.F.; Rev. Kristian C. Teater; Deacon Andrew Daus.
4900 Ringer Rd., 63129. Tel: 314-487-4475. In Res., Rev. Alan J. Knaup (Retired).
Res.: 5056 Faust Ct., 63129. Tel: 314-487-2522.
School—Tel: 314-487-1666. Lay Teachers 35; Students 709.
Catechesis/Religious Program—Students 400.

NORMANDY

1—ST. ANN (1856), [CEM] Revs. William G. Kempf; Victor Barnhart.
Res.: 7530 Natural Bridge Rd., 63121. Tel: 314-385-5090; Fax: 314-385-6527.
School—Tel: 314-381-0113; Fax: 314-381-1367. Sr. Dawn Achs, Prin. Lay Teachers 13; Students 204.

2—ASCENSION-ST. PAUL (1995), Rev. Mitchell S. Doyen; Deacon Albert Bernsen.
Res.: 7005 Ascension Dr., 63121. Tel: 314-385-6750; Fax: 314-385-6965.
School—3801 Nelson Dr., 63121. Tel: 314-261-1592; Fax: 314-385-9095. Kathy Rauschenbach, Prin.; Jessie Joiner, Prin. Lay Teachers 14; Students 128.
Catechesis/Religious Program—Students 7.

OAKVILLE

1—ST. FRANCIS OF ASSISI (1927), Revs. Gary M. Gebelein; Nicholas E. Kastenholz; Deacons George R. Fink; Lawrence Kelly; Alan Ecker.
Res.: 4556 Telegraph Rd., 63129. Tel: 314-487-5736; Fax: 314-487-3701.
School—4550 Telegraph Rd., 63129. Fax: 314-416-7118. Wayne Schiefelbein, Prin. Franciscan Sisters of Our Lady of Perpetual Help 1; Lay Teachers 22; Students 395.
Catechesis/Religious Program—Tel: 314-487-5736, Ext. 125. Students 140.

2—QUEEN OF ALL SAINTS (1972), Rev. Msgr. Robert P. Jovanovic, M.Ed.; Revs. John L. Hallemann, Senior Assoc.; John R. Vien; Deacons William Sinak; Richard Schellhase.
Res.: 6603 Christopher Dr., 63199. Tel: 314-846-8207; Fax: 314-846-0636.
School—6611 Christopher Dr., 63199. Tel: 314-846-0506; Fax: 314-846-4939. Mrs. Mary Price, Prin. Students 690.
Catechesis/Religious Program—Tel: 314-846-8126. Ms. Marge Schumer, D.R.E. Students 480.

OVERLAND

1—ALL SOULS (1906), Rev. Paul J. Rothschild; Deacons Arnold Krieger; Jack Shannon.
Res.: 9550 Tennyson Ave., 63114. Tel: 314-427-0442; Fax: 314-427-3872.
Catechesis/Religious Program—Tel: 314-427-5319. Students 90.

2—OUR LADY OF THE PRESENTATION (1915), Rev. Dennis R. Port; Deacons Singleton Harris; Gerry Lauterwasser.
Res.: 8860 Tudor Ave., 63114. Tel: 314-427-0486; Fax: 314-423-3020.
School—8840 Tudor Ave., 63114. Tel: 314-428-8191; Fax: 314-423-1213. Lay Teachers 16; Students 175.
Catechesis/Religious Program—Students 104.

PAGEDALE, ST. CATHERINE OF SIENA (1909), Closed. For inquiries for parish records contact the chancery.

PINE LAWN, ST. PAUL THE APOSTLE, Merged, to form Ascension-St. Paul, Normandy.

RICHMOND HEIGHTS

1—IMMACOLATA (1945), Revs. John M. Seper; Robert T. Evans; Robert L. Roedig; Deacons Joseph LaMartina; Edward Grotpeter.
Church: 8900 Clayton Rd., 63117. Tel: 314-991-5700; Fax: 314-991-4769.
School—8910 Clayton Rd., 63117. Tel: 314-991-1924. Mr. Salvatore Latragna, Prin. Lay Teachers 22; Students 279.
Catechesis/Religious Program—Tel: 314-991-1832. Students 120.

2—LITTLE FLOWER, ST. TERESA OF THE INFANT JESUS (1925), Rev. James J. Benz; Deacons Stephen L. Murray; William G. Weiss. In Res., Rev. Gregory G. Kirsch.
Res.: 1264 Arch Terrace, 63117. Tel: 314-645-1445; Fax: 314-645-3258.
School—1275 Boland Pl., 63117. Tel: 314-781-4995; Fax: 314-781-9177. Mrs. Deborah Marino, Prin. Sisters 2; Lay Teachers 11; Students 227.

3—ST. LUKE THE EVANGELIST (1914), Rev. Stephen F. Bauer.
Res.: 7230 Dale Ave., 63117. Tel: 314-644-2144; Fax: 314-644-4624.
School—1414 Bellevue Ave., 63177. Tel: 314-781-2072; Fax: 314-781-7411. Lay Teachers 13; Students 124.

RIVERVIEW GARDENS, ST. CATHERINE OF ALEXANDRIA (1921), Rev. Thomas M. Robertson; Deacon Edwin Schulte.
Res.: 351 Chambers Rd., 63137. Tel: 314-867-8515; Fax: 314-867-3751.
School—Pope John Paul II Catholic Elementary School See Our Lady of Good Counsel, Bellefontaine Neighbors. Tel: 314-867-2400.

SAPPINGTON, ST. CATHERINE LABOURE (1953), Revs. James B. Cormack, C.M.; Otto Schneebeck, C.M.; Ignatius M. Melito, C.M.; Raymond Ross, C.M.; Deacons George Tichacek; Charles Ryder.
Res.: 9740 Sappington Rd., 63128. Tel: 314-843-3245; Fax: 314-843-3196.
School—9750 Sappington Rd., 63128. Tel: 314-843-2819; Fax: 314-843-7687. Sr. Carol Sansone, A.S.C.J., Prin. Lay Teachers 26; Students 475.
Catechesis/Religious Program—Tel: 314-843-2996. Peggy Brinkmann, D.R.E. Students 148.

SHREWSBURY

1—CURE' OF ARS (1966), Rev. Msgr. Kevin G. Callahan; Deacons Thomas Murphy; Herbert Luke, M.D. In Res., Rev. Msgr. John R. Maguire.
Res.: 670 S. Laclede Station Rd., 63119. Tel: 314-962-5883; Fax: 314-968-3554.

2—ST. MICHAEL (1895), Revs. Edmond J. Fitzgibbon; Jerome D. Billing, J.C.L., S.T.L.; Deacons Stephen Arnold; William O. Murphy.
Res.: 7622 Sutherland Ave., 63119. Tel: 314-647-5611; Fax: 314-781-9211.
School—7630 Sutherland Ave., 63119. Tel: 314-647-7159; Fax: 314-644-1433. Lay Teachers 18; Students 216.
Catechesis/Religious Program—Students 78.

SPANISH LAKE

1—ST. ALOYSIUS (1871), Rev. Gerald T. Nienhaus; Deacon Walter J. Ruegg.
Res.: 12110 Larimore Rd., 63138. Tel: 314-741-3690; Fax: 314-741-6468.
School—St. John Neumann, 1650 Redman Rd., 63138. Tel: 314-741-0400; Fax: 314-653-2531. Sr. Mary Lawrence, S.S.N.D., Prin. Sisters 1; Lay Teachers 13; Students 219.

Catechesis/Religious Program—Trinity School of Religion (Combined with Our Lady of Loretto and Transfiguration), Fax: 314-741-2531. Students 68.
2—OUR LADY OF LORETTO (1959), Rev. Ted Sosnowski, C.R.; Deacons James Michael Buckley; Dave Harpring.
Res.: 11725 Bellefontaine Rd., 63138. Tel: 314-741-7700; Fax: 314-741-7700.
School—St. John Neumann, 1650 Redman Ave., 63138. Tel: 314-741-0400. Ms. Ann Cleeland, Prin. Lay Teachers 15; Students 201.
Catechesis/Religious Program—Tel: 314-741-2583. Students 45.

ST. ANN
1—ST. GREGORY (1942), Merged, with St. Kevin, St. Ann to form Holy Trinity, St. Ann
2—HOLY TRINITY (2002), Rev. Msgrs. John J. Leykam, V.F.; Donald C. Schramm; Deacons William F. Priesmeyer; David Bolderson.
Res.: 3500 St. Luke Ln., 63074. Tel: 314-733-1463; Fax: 314-426-7584.
School—10901 St. Henry Ln., 63074. Tel: 312-426-8966; Fax: 314-428-7084. Margaret Ahle, Prin.
Catechesis/Religious Program—Students 470.
3—ST. KEVIN (1953), (Irish), Merged, with St. Gregory, St. Ann to form Holy Trinity, St. Ann

SUNSET HILLS, ST. JUSTIN MARTYR (1964), Revs. Bernard J. Schloemer; John L. Mayer; Deacon Thomas J. Gottlieb.
Res.: 11910 Eddie and Park Rd., 63126-2908. Tel: 314-843-8482; Fax: 314-843-8507.
School—11914 Eddie and Park Rd., 63126. Tel: 314-843-6447; Fax: 314-843-9257. Mrs. Judy Talleur, Prin. Lay Teachers 13; Students 194.
Catechesis/Religious Program—Tel: 314-843-6447, Ext. 2. Students 85.

UNIVERSITY CITY
1—ALL SAINTS (1901), Rev. Vincent A. Heier; Deacons Glennon Bourbon; Dennis Chitwood.
Res.: 6403 Clemens Ave., 63130. Tel: 314-721-6403; Fax: 314-659-9799.
Catechesis/Religious Program—Students 12.
2—ST. ANDREW KIM (2001), (Korean), Rev. John Youn Ki-Kuk.
Church: 8665 Olive Blvd., 63132. Tel: 314-993-1277; Fax: 314-993-2031.
3—CHRIST THE KING (1927), Rev. John A. Ditenhafer. In Res., Rev. John Jay Hughes; Deacon E. Ray Kiely.
Res.: 7316 Balson Ave., 63130. Tel: 314-721-8737; Fax: 314-721-8738.
School—7324 Balson Ave., 63130. Tel: 314-725-5855; Fax: 314-725-5981. Sr. Rosella McNamee, R.S.M., Prin. Sisters of Mercy 1; Lay Teachers 14; Students 200.
4—OUR LADY OF LOURDES (1916), Rev. Msgrs. Edward J. Sudekum; Norbert J. Dietz (Retired); Rev. Matthew L. O'Toole; Deacon Albert X. Vaughn.
Res.: 7148 Forsyth Blvd., 63105. Tel: 314-726-6200; 314-726-6201; Fax: 314-726-1602.
School—7157 Northmoor Dr., 63105. Tel: 314-726-3352; Fax: 314-726-0503. Lay Teachers 22; Students 243.
5—ST. PATRICK (1940), Closed. For inquiries for parish records contact the chancery.

VALLEY PARK, SACRED HEART (1903), [CEM] Revs. Robert T. Rosebrough; David A. Novak; Thomas J. Pastorius; Sr. Donna Fischer, S.S.N.D., Pastoral Assoc.; Deacons Dave Lemoine; Larry Damato; Allen F. Love.
Res.: 17 Ann Ave., 63088. Tel: 636-225-5268; Fax: 636-225-6969.
School—12 Ann Ave., 63088. Tel: 636-225-3824; Fax: 636-225-8941. Joan Wojciechowski, Prin. Lay Teachers 27; Students 384.
Catechesis/Religious Program—Tel: 636-225-0341. Sr. Lynne Schmidt, S.S.N.D., D.R.E. Students 516.

VINITA PARK, ST. RITA (1919), Rev. David L. Wichlan; Deacon Louis J. Reynoso.
Res.: 8240 Washington St., 63114. Tel: 314-428-4845; Fax: 314-428-4845.

WARSON WOODS, STE. GENEVIEVE DU BOIS (1956), Rev. Msgrs. Paul G. Anthony; John M. Unger; Deacon Donald Heitert.
Res.: 1575 N. Woodlawn Ave., 63122. Tel: 314-966-3780; Fax: 314-966-4687.
School—Tel: 314-821-4245; Fax: 314-822-4881. Mrs. Claudia Dougherty, Prin. Lay Teachers 13; Students 203.
Catechesis/Religious Program—Tel: 314-822-1347. Students 17.

WEBSTER GROVES
1—ANNUNCIATION (1950), Rev. Denny M. Schaab; Deacon Tom Forster, Pastoral Assoc. Tel: 314-631-5440. In Res., Rev. Mark Fuller.
Res.: 12 W. Glendale Rd., 63119. Tel: 314-962-5955; Fax: 314-961-0643.
School—16 W. Glendale, 63119. Tel: 314-961-7712. Mrs. Catherine Davis, Prin. Lay Teachers 15; Students 154.
Catechesis/Religious Program—Students 144.
2—HOLY REDEEMER (1886), Rev. Joseph M. Simon; Deacons Richard Wessels; John P. Flanigan. In Res., Rev. Msgr. Robert W. Finn.
Res.: 17 Joy Ave., 63119. Tel: 314-962-8038; Fax: 314-962-2084.
School—341 E. Lockwood, 63119. Tel 314-962-8989; Fax: 314-962-6519. Susan Fritz, Prin. Lay Teachers 16; Students 217.
Catechesis/Religious Program—Tel: 314-962-1487. Students 172.
3—MARY, QUEEN OF PEACE (1922), Rev. Gerald A. Meier; Rev. Msgr. Richard J. Lubeley, Senior Priest (Retired); Deacons Robert C. Riegel; Paul McKee.
Res.: 676 W. Lockwood Blvd., 63119. Tel: 314-962-2311; Fax: 314-968-9885.
School—680 W. Lockwood Ave., 63119. Tel: 314-961-2891; Fax: 314-961-7469. Mr. Michael Biggs, Prin. Dominican Sisters 1; Sisters of Loretto at the Foot of the Cross 1; Lay Teachers 33; Students 636.
Catechesis/Religious Program— Sr. Charlotte Flarlong, D.R.E. Students 93.

WELLSTON, NOTRE DAME DE LOURDES, Closed., See St. Augustine, St. Louis for details.

WEST OVERLAND, ST. JUDE (1953), Rev Joseph L. Parisi.
Res.: 2218 N. Warson Rd., 63114. Tel: 314-428-2262; Fax: 314-890-2257.
Catechesis/Religious Program—Students 21.

WILDWOOD, ST. ALBAN ROE (1980), Revs. Dennis B. Zacheis; Charles F. Ferrara, S.J.; Eugene P. Selzer; Deacon Norman Nuelle.
Res.: 2001 Shepard Rd., 63038. Tel: 636-458-2977; Fax: 636-405-1276.
School—2005 Shepard Rd., 63038. Tel: 636-458-6084. Patricia Brady, Prin.
Catechesis/Religious Program—Tel: 636-458-2460; Fax: 636-405-3026. Sarah Lowery, D.R.E. Students 1,301.

WOODSON TERRACE, ST. WILLIAM (1953) Closed. For inquiries for parish records contact the chancery.

CHURCHES OUTSIDE ST. LOUIS CITY AND ST. LOUIS COUNTY

APPLE CREEK, PERRY CO., ST. JOSEPH (1828), (German), [CEM] [JC 2] Rev. Anthony A. Dattilo.
Res.: 138 St. Joseph Ln., 63775. Tel: 573-788-2330; Fax: 573-788-2351.
Catechesis/Religious Program—Tel: 573-547-5246. Students 21.

ARNOLD, JEFFERSON CO.
1—ST. DAVID (1963), Rev. Richard J. Rath; Deacons Thomas G. Politte; Diosdado Maranan, M.D.
Res.: 2334 Tenbrook Rd., 63010. Tel: 636-296-5485; Fax: 636-296-5526.
School—Holy Child Consolidated School See Immaculate Conception for details. Tel: 636-296-0055.
Catechesis/Religious Program—Students 200.
2—IMMACULATE CONCEPTION (1840), [CEM] Very Rev. Paul J. Niemann, V.F.; Rev. Richard J. Heman; Deacons Joseph C. Streckfuss; Bradford M. Buchek.
Res.: 2300 Church Rd., P.O. Box 217, 63010. Tel: 636-296-5289; Fax: 636-287-9035.
School—Holy Child School Consolidated with St. David, Arnold. Tel: 636-296-0055; Fax: 636-296-5639. Mrs. Joann O. Coyle, Prin. Lay Teachers 14; Students 275.
Catechesis/Religious Program—Tel 636-296-0066. Mary Winkelmann, D.R.E. Students 401.

AUGUSTA, ST. CHARLES CO., IMMACULATE CONCEPTION (1851), [CEM] Rev. Edward L. Heim.
Res.: 5912 Hwy. 94 S., 63332. Tel: 636-482-4455; Fax: 636-228-4529.
Catechesis/Religious Program—Students 42.

BELGIQUE, PERRY CO., NATIVITY OF THE BLESSED VIRGIN MARY, Closed. For inquiries for parish records contact the chancery.

BERGER, FRANKLIN CO., ST. PAUL (1853), (German), [CEM] Rev. John C. Deken.
Res.: 603 Miller St., New Haven, 63068. Tel: 573-237-3372; Fax: 573-237-3372.
Catechesis/Religious Program—Students 7.

BIEHLE, PERRY CO., ST. MAURUS (1870), (German), [CEM] [JC] Rev. Anthony A. Dattilo.
Res.: 10198 Hwy. B, Perryville, 63775. Tel: 573-788-2330; 573-547-5246; Fax: 573-788-2351.
Catechesis/Religious Program—Students 74.

BLOOMSDALE, STE. GENEVIEVE CO., ST. AGNES (1835), [CEM] Rev. Raymond J. Oge; Deacon James Basler.
Res.: P.O. Box 124, 63627. Tel: 573-483-2555; Fax: 573-483-9497.
School—Tel: 573-483-2506. Sr. Donna Marie Kist, C.PP.S., Prin. Sisters of the Most Precious Blood (O'Fallon, MO) 1; Lay Teachers 11; Students 172.
Catechesis/Religious Program—Students 26.

BONNE TERRE, ST. FRANCOIS CO., ST. JOSEPH'S (1872), [CEM] Rev. John H. Schneider; Deacon Ronald Kreft.
Res.: 15 St. Joseph St., 63628. Tel: 573-358-2112; Fax: 573-358-4233.
School—(Grades K-6) Tel: 573-358-5947. Barbara Monahan, Admin. Lay Teachers 4; Students 44.
Catechesis/Religious Program—Students 38.
Mission—St. Anne 5425 Brickey Rd., P.O. Box 307, French Village, St. Francois Co. 63036. Tel: 573-358-2112.

BREWER, PERRY CO., CHRIST THE SAVIOR (1907), [CEM] Rev. Felipe J. Martinez, C.M.
Res.: 57 Shady Ln., Perryville, 63775. Tel: 573-547-2677; Fax: 573-547-7556.
Catechesis/Religious Program—Students 51.

CATAWISSA, FRANKLIN CO., ST. JAMES (1913), [CEM] Rev. Mark S. Bozada; Deacon Harvey Dubbs.
Res.: 1107 Summit Dr., 63015. Tel: 636-271-6038; Fax: 636-257-2235.
Catechesis/Religious Program—Students 28.
Mission—St. Patrick [CEM] Hwy. NN & Rock Church Rd., Armagh, Franklin Co. 63015. Tel: 636-257-2227.

CLOVER BOTTOM, FRANKLIN CO., ST. ANN (1883), (Polish—German), [CEM] Rev. Timothy J. Toohey.
Clover Bottom: 7851 State Rd. YY, Washington, 63090-9627. Tel: 636-239-3222; Fax: 636-390-2849.
Catechesis/Religious Program—Students 58.

COFFMAN, STE. GENEVIEVE CO., ST. CATHERINE OF ALEXANDRIA (1929), [CEM] [JC] Attended by, River Aux Vases Rev. F. Joseph Reilly.
Res.: 18411 RAV Church Rd., Ste. Genevieve, 63670. Tel: 573-883-2923; Fax: 573-883-9605.

CONCORD HILL, WARREN CO., ST. IGNATIUS (1857), (German), [CEM 3] Rev. Finbarr Dowling, O.S.B.
Res.: 701 Mill Rd., Marthasville, 63357. Tel: 636-932-4445; Fax: 636-932-4032.
School—691 Mill Rd., 63357. Tel: 636-932-4444. Jennifer Fregalette, Prin. Lay Teachers 5; Students 52.

COTTLEVILLE, ST. CHARLES CO., ST. JOSEPH (1873), [CEM] Rev. Msgr. Walter M. Whited; Revs. Brian A. Kennebeck; Larry T. Huber; Sr. Mary Pezold, C.C.V.I., Pastoral Assoc.; Deacons Ronald Bachista, Pastoral Assoc.; George A. Beinke, Pastoral Assoc.; Mrs. Judy Powers, Pastoral Assoc.; Deacons Gary Meyerkord, Pastoral Assoc.; Glennon Schultheis, Pastoral Assoc.
Res.: 1355 Motherhead Rd., St. Charles, 63304. Tel: 636-441-0055; Fax: 636-926-7341.
School—1351 Motherhead Rd., St. Charles, 63304. Fax: 636-441-9932. Ms. Mary Ellen Schrader, Prin.; Mrs. Charlotte Litzinger, Asst. Prin. Lay Teachers 49; Students 852.
Catechesis/Religious Program—Tel: 636-441-0055, Ext. 104. Dr. Barbara Blackburn, D.R.E.; Mrs. Laura Lucas, D.R.E. Tel: 636-441-0055, Ext. 300. Students 1,212.

CRYSTAL CITY, JEFFERSON CO., SACRED HEART (1881), [CEM] Rev. Michael L. Donald; Deacon Gerard G. Stoverink.
Res.: 555 Bailey Rd., 63019-1798. Tel: 636-937-4662; Fax: 636-931-5507.
School—Tel: 636-931-5701; 636-937-5298; Fax: 636-931-0422. Lay Teachers 12; Students 133.
Catechesis/Religious Program—Tel: 636-937-5298; Fax: 636-931-0422. Students 165.

DARDENNE, ST. CHARLES CO., IMMACULATE CONCEPTION (1880), [CEM] Revs. Robert J. Reiker; Gregory S. Klump; John I. Caffe; Deacons Don Schiffman; Russ Butler.
Res.: 7701 Hwy. N, O'Fallon, 63366. Tel: 636-561-6611; Fax: 636-561-3883.
School—Tel: 636-561-4450. Lay Teachers 23; Students 504.
Catechesis/Religious Program—Tel: 636-561-1974. Students 1,022.

DE SOTO, JEFFERSON CO., ST. ROSE OF LIMA (1885), [CEM] Rev. Ronald J. Hopmeir; Deacon Edward J. Boyer.
Res.: 504 S. Third St., 63020. Tel: 636-337-2212; Fax: 636-337-2394.
School—Tel: 636-586-3594; 636-337-7855. Barbara Donner, Prin. Lay Teachers 10; Students 165.
Catechesis/Religious Program—Students 114.

DUTZOW, WARREN CO., ST. VINCENT DE PAUL (1856), [CEM] Rev. John J. Borcic.
Res.: 7602 S. Hwy. 94, Marthasville, 63357. Tel: 636-433-2678; Fax: 636-433-2924.
School—Tel: 636-433-2466. Sisters 3; Lay Teachers 9; Students 129.

ELSBERRY, LINCOLN CO., SACRED HEART (1905), (German—Irish), Rev. William J. Baier.
Res.: 714 Lincoln St., 63343. Tel: 573-898-2202; Fax: 573-898-2652.
Catechesis/Religious Program—Students 87.

FARMINGTON, ST. FRANCOIS CO., ST. JOSEPH (1890), [JC 2] Revs. James M. Mitulski; James W. Dyer; Deacons William J. Greif; Albin A. Gegg.
Res.: 5 S. Carleton, 63640. Tel: 573-756-4250; Fax: 573-756-6938.
School—501 Ste. Genevieve Ave., 63640. Tel: 573-756-6312; Fax: 573-756-0738. Students 139.
Catechesis/Religious Program—Students 65.

FESTUS, JEFFERSON CO., OUR LADY (1956), Rev. John V. Kerber; Sr. Pat Murray, O.S.F., Pastoral Min.
Res.: 1550 St. Mary Ln., 63028. Tel: 636-937-5513; 636-931-4702 (toll-free); Fax: 636-931-5875.

School—Tel: 636-937-5008. Lay Teachers 15; Students 252.
Catechesis/Religious Program—Students 145.

FLINT HILL, ST. CHARLES CO., ST. THEODORE (1883), [CEM] Rev. Albert A. Mattler; Deacon Patrick Rankin.
Res.: P.O. Box 246, 63346. Tel: 636-332-9269; Fax: 636-639-1385. Email: sttheodore_church@centurytel.net.
School—Tel: 636-332-9269, Ext. 4; Fax: 636-327-5115. Lay Teachers 8; Students 147.
Catechesis/Religious Program—Students 141.

GILDEHAUS, FRANKLIN CO., ST. JOHN THE BAPTIST (1839), [CEM] Very Rev. Jeffrey N. Knight, V.F.
Res.: 5567 Gildehaus Rd., Villa Ridge, 63089. Tel: 636-583-2488; Fax: 636-583-6114.
School—Tel: 636-583-2392; Fax: 636-583-6112. Marian Schelich, Prin. Lay Teachers 13; Students 139.
Catechesis/Religious Program—Students 77.

HAWK POINT, LINCOLN CO., ST. MARY (1919), (Bohemian), [CEM 2] Rev. Francis F. Koeninger.
Res.: P.O. Box 205, 63349. Tel: 636-338-4331; Fax: 636-338-4007.
Catechesis/Religious Program—Fax: 636-338-4331. Students 68.

HERCULANEUM, JEFFERSON CO., CHURCH OF THE ASSUMPTION OF B.V.M. (1916), [CEM] Rev. Robert V. Fleiter; Deacon Steven M. Schisler.
Res.: 329 Station St., 63048-1328. Tel: 636-475-5305; Fax: 636-475-5305.
Catechesis/Religious Program—Students 20.

HIGH RIDGE, JEFFERSON CO., ST. ANTHONY OF PADUA (1921), Rev. Eugene R. Sinz; Deacons William Gearon; David Camden; Richard Shelby.
Res.: 3009 High Ridge Blvd., 63049. Tel: 636-677-4868; Fax: 636-677-2781.
School—3005 High Ridge Blvd., 63049. Tel: 636-677-3585. Mrs. Pat Kohn, Prin. Lay Teachers 11; Students 138.
Catechesis/Religious Program—Students 156.

HILLSBORO, JEFFERSON CO., CHURCH OF THE GOOD SHEPHERD (1934), [CEM] Rev. Dennis C. Schmidt.
Res.: 703 Third St., 63050-4342. Tel: 636-789-3356; Fax: 636-789-9986.
School—Tel: 636-797-2300; Fax: 636-789-5798. Mrs. Peggy Visconti, Prin. Lay Teachers 9; Students 90.
Catechesis/Religious Program—Students 112.

HOUSE SPRINGS, JEFFERSON CO., OUR LADY, QUEEN OF PEACE (1961), [CEM 2] Rev. Msgr. Norbert A. Ernst; Rev. Donald F. Molitor; Deacons Thomas Gerling; Paul Turek.
Res.: 4696 Notre Dame Ln., 63051. Tel: 636-671-3062; Fax: 636-671-0003.
School—Tel: 636-671-0247; Fax: 636-671-0418. Mrs. Debbi Clark, Admin. Sisters 2; Lay Teachers 11; Students 200.
Catechesis/Religious Program—Students 187.

IMPERIAL, JEFFERSON CO.

1—ST. JOHN LATERAN (1869), [CEM] Rev. Michael G. Murphy; Deacon Norbert Gawedzinski.
Res.: 4525 Old Hwy. 21, 63052. Tel: 636-296-8061; Fax: 636-296-8067.
School—Tel: 636-296-8112; Fax: 636-296-4172. Mrs. Vicky Meadows Yochum, Prin. Lay Teachers 9; Students 120.
Catechesis/Religious Program—Students 165.

2—ST. JOSEPH (1905), [CEM] Revs. Andrew J. Sigmund; Edward R. Goldian, S.J., Senior Assoc.; Deacon Glennon P. Politte Sr.
Res.: 6020 Old Antonia Rd., 63052-0968. Tel: 636-464-1013; Fax: 636-461-0411.
School—6024 Old Antonia Rd., 63052. Tel: 636-464-9027; Fax: 636-464-3574. Pat Kirk, Prin. Students 360.
Catechesis/Religious Program—Students 239.

JOSEPHVILLE, ST. CHARLES CO., ST. JOSEPH (1852), [CEM] Rev. Timothy P. Elliott; Deacon Fielding Harrison.
Res.: 1390 Josephville Rd., Wentzville, 63385. Tel: 636-332-6676; Fax: 636-332-8648.
School—1410 Josephville Rd., Wentzville, 63385. Tel: 636-327-7174. Barbara Rygelski, Prin. Lay Teachers 6; Students 104.

KRAKOW, FRANKLIN CO., ST. GERTRUDE (1845), [CEM] Rev. Richard V. Coerver; Deacon Charles Gildehaus.
Res.: 6535 Hwy. YY, Washington, 63090. Tel: 636-239-4216; Fax: 636-239-3590.
School—Tel: 636-239-2347; Fax: 636-239-3550. Mike Newbanks, Prin. Lay Teachers 18; Students 288.
Catechesis/Religious Program—Students 48.

LAWRENCETON, STE. GENEVIEVE CO., ST. LAWRENCE (1872), [CEM] Attended by, St. Agnes Rectory. Rev. Raymond J. Oge.
Bloomsdale, 63627. Tel: 573-483-2555; Fax: 573-483-9497.
Catechesis/Religious Program—Students 11.

LUEBBERING, FRANKLIN CO., ST. FRANCIS OF ASSISI (1874), [CEM] Rev. John B. McEntee.
Res.: 1000 Luebbering Rd., 63061-9705. Tel: 636-629-1717; Fax: 636-629-8408.
Catechesis/Religious Program—Students 73.

MILLWOOD, LINCOLN CO., ST. ALPHONSUS (1850), [CEM] Rev. Frank A. D'Amico.
Res.: 29 St. Alphonsus Rd., Silex, 63377. Tel: 573-384-6223; Fax: 573-384-5981.
School—Tel: 573-384-5305. Lay Teachers 5; Students 60.
Catechesis/Religious Program—Students 35.

MOSELLE, FRANKLIN CO., ST. MARY OF PERPETUAL HELP (1905), [CEM] Rev. Mark Bozada; Deacon Harvey Dubbs.
Res.: 1587 Hwy. AM, Villa Ridge, 63089. Tel: 636-451-4685; Fax: 636-742-4820.

NEIER, FRANKLIN CO., ST. JOSEPH (1881), [CEM] Rev. Kevin V. Schmittgens.
Res.: 2401 Neier Rd., Union, 63084. Tel: 636-583-2806; Fax: 636-583-0627.
Catechesis/Religious Program—Students 50.

NEW HAVEN, FRANKLIN CO., ASSUMPTION (1892), (German), [CEM] Revs. Daniel E. Mosley; John C. Deken.
Res.: 603 Miller St., 63068. Tel: 573-237-3372; Fax: 573-237-3372.
Catechesis/Religious Program—Students 100.

NEW MELLE, ST. CHARLES CO., IMMACULATE HEART OF MARY (1945), [CEM] Rev. Richard L. Stoltz; Deacon Lonnie Weishaar.
Res.: 26 W. Hwy. D, Box 100, 63365-0100. Tel: 636-398-5270; Fax: 636-398-5577.
Catechesis/Religious Program— Susie Chenot, D.R.E. Students 255.

O'FALLON, ST. CHARLES CO.

1—ASSUMPTION (1871), (German), [CEM] Revs. Joseph G. Kempf; Ronald J. Rubbelke; Eugene F. Bendel; Deacons Fred Volansky; Howard Vanbooven.
Res.: 115 W. Third St., 63366. Tel: 636-240-3721; Fax: 636-240-3722.
School—Tel: 636-240-4474. Robert Cowell, Prin. Lay Teachers 22; Students 471.
Catechesis/Religious Program—Tel: 636-978-3857. Students 531.

2—ST. BARNABAS (1961), Rev. Msgr. Daniel M. Hogan.
Res.: 1400 N. Main St., 63366. Tel: 636-240-4556; Fax: 636-978-3358.
Catechesis/Religious Program—Tel: 636-281-3211. Students 80.

OLD MINES, WASHINGTON CO., ST. JOACHIM (1723), [CEM 3] Rev. Theodore X. Pieper; Deacon Steven Politte.
Res.: Rte. 1, Box 1110, Cadet, 63630. Tel: 573-438-6181; Fax: 573-438-3685.
School—Tel: 573-438-3973; Fax: 573-438-3161. Joyce Politte, Prin. Lay Teachers 6; Students 72.
Catechesis/Religious Program—Students 25.

OLD MONROE, LINCOLN CO., IMMACULATE CONCEPTION (1867), [CEM] Rev. Msgr. Gregory L. Schmidt; Deacon Anthony Trautman.
Res.: 110 Maryknoll Rd., 63369. Tel: 636-661-5002; Fax: 636-665-5943.
School—120 Maryknoll Rd., 63369. Tel: 636-661-5156. Susan Schutz, Prin. Sisters of the Third Order Regular of St. Francis (Oldenburg, IN) 1; Lay Teachers 9; Students 185.
Catechesis/Religious Program—Students 55.
Convent—122 Maryknoll Rd.. Tel: 636-661-5177.

OZORA, STE. GENEVIEVE CO., SACRED HEART (1898), [CEM] Very Rev. James W. Schaefer, V.F.
Res.: 17742 State Rte. N., St. Mary, 63673. Tel: 573-543-2209; Fax: 573-543-2209.
School—Tel: 573-543-2997. Sr. Agnes Keena, B.V.M., Prin. Sisters of Charity 1; Lay Teachers 2; Students 24.
Catechesis/Religious Program—Students 24.

PACIFIC, FRANKLIN CO., ST. BRIDGET CHURCH (1841), [CEM 2] Rev. John A. Keenoy.
Res.: 111 W. Union St., 63069. Tel: 636-271-3993; Fax: 636-257-6265.
School—Tel: 636-257-4533; Fax: 636-257-2504. Lay Teachers 10; Students 155.

PARK HILLS, ST. FRANCOIS CO., IMMACULATE CONCEPTION (1903), [CEM] [JC] Rev. James R. French; Deacon Walter Roderick, (Retired).
Res.: 1020 W. Main St., Box 66, 63601-0066. Tel: 573-431-2427; Fax: 573-431-4060.
Catechesis/Religious Program—Students 83.
Mission—St. John (1879), [CEM] [JC] Maple St. & Walnut St., Bismarck, St. Francois Co. 63624.

PERRYVILLE, PERRY CO., ST. VINCENT DE PAUL (1818), [CEM 4] Rev. Kevin P. Fausz, C.M.
Res.: 1000 Rosati Court, 63775. Tel: 573-547-4591; Fax: 573-547-4145.
Parish Center—1010 Rosati Ct., 63775.
School—Tel: 573-547-6503. Robert Rousseau, Prin. Lay Teachers 23; Students 343.
School—Junior-Senior High School, Tel: 573-547-2560. Lisa Best, Prin. Lay Teachers 23; Students 272.
Catechesis/Religious Program—Parish School of Religion Students 180.
Mission—St. Joseph 1701 W. St. Joseph, Highland, Perry Co. 63775. Tel: 314-547-6533; Fax: 573-547-2204.
Mission—St. James c/o St. Vincent De Paul Parish, Crosstown, Perry Co. 63775.

PORT HUDSON, FRANKLIN CO., HOLY FAMILY (1872), [CEM] Rev. Robert G. Leibrecht.
Res.: 124 Holy Family Church Rd., New Haven, 63068. Tel: 573-459-6441; Fax: 573-459-2257.
Catechesis/Religious Program—Tel: 573-459-6594; 573-764-3292. Students 88.
Mission—St. Gerald 124 Holy Family Church Rd., New Haven, Franklin Co. 63068.

PORTAGE DES SIOUX, ST. CHARLES CO., ST. FRANCIS OF ASSISI (1799), (French—German), [CEM 2] Rev. Michael J. Sandweg, Ph.D.
Res.: P.O. Box 128, 63373. Tel: 636-899-0906; Fax: 636-899-0909.
Mission—Immaculate Conception 14060 Hwy. 94 N., P.O. Box 147, West Alton, St. Charles Co. 63386.

POTOSI, WASHINGTON CO., ST. JAMES (1829), [CEM 2] Rev. George Galovich.
Res.: 201 N. Missouri Ave., 63664. Tel: 573-438-4686; 888-868-8188 (toll-free); Fax: 573-438-2100.
Catechesis/Religious Program—Students 120.

RICHWOODS, WASHINGTON CO., ST. STEPHEN'S (1841), [CEM] Rev. Robert C. Liss.
Res.: H.C.R. 63, Box 1, 63071-9701. Tel: 573-678-2207; 573-678-2203 (Hall); Fax: 573-678-2380.

RIVER AUX VASES, STE. GENEVIEVE CO., SS. PHILIP AND JAMES (1840), [CEM] [JC] Rev. F. Joseph Reilly.
Res.: 18411 RAV Church Rd., Ste. Genevieve, 63670. Tel: 573-883-2923; Fax: 573-883-9605.
Catechesis/Religious Program—Students 32.

ST. CHARLES, ST. CHARLES CO.

1—ST. CHARLES BORROMEO (1792), Revs. Richard J. Tillman; Eugene P. Brennan; Deacon Michael Piva.
Res.: 601 N. 4th St., 63301. Tel: 636-946-6370; 636-946-1893; Fax: 636-946-1893.
School—431 Decatur, 63301. Tel: 636-946-2713; Fax: 636-946-3096. Sisters of Notre Dame 1; Lay Teachers 23; Students 281.
Catechesis/Religious Program—Tel: 636-946-2916. Students 168.
Chapel—Convent of the Sacred Heart, Regis Hall, Tel: 636-946-6456.

2—ST. CLETUS (1965), Very Rev. James P. Callahan, V.F.; Rev. Jeffrey G. Vomund; Deacons Frank Olmsted; Mark McCarthy.
Res.: 2705 Zumbehl Rd., 63301. Tel: 636-946-6327; Fax: 636-946-6466.
School—Tel: 636-946-7756; Fax: 636-946-6526. Lay Teachers 24; Students 305.
Catechesis/Religious Program—Tel: 636-946-5936. Students 393.

3—ST. ELIZABETH ANN SETON (1975), Revs. Kevin J. Mahoney; Donald L. Neuner; Clark B. Maes; Deacons Gerald Hurlbert; Joseph Fugere.
Res.: 2 Seton Ct., 63303. Tel: 636-946-6717; Fax: 636-946-9263.
School—Tel: 636-946-6716; Fax: 636-946-2670. Sisters 1; Lay Teachers 36; Students 582.
Catechesis/Religious Program—Tel: 636-949-3833. Nancy Burian, D.R.E. Students 400.

4—STS. JOACHIM AND ANN (1981), Revs. Dennis J. Doyle; James L. Gahan; Jeffrey A. Maassen.
Mailing Address: 4112 McClay Rd., 63304. Tel: 636-441-7503; Fax: 636-441-6574.
School—(Grades K-8), 4110 McClay Rd., 63304-7915. Tel: 636-441-4835; Fax: 636-441-9534. Mrs. Debbie Johnson, Prin. Sisters 1; Lay Teachers 24; Students 564.
Catechesis/Religious Program—Tel: 314-926-0021. Students 668.

5—ST. PETER (1850), [CEM] Revs. John J. Ghio; William Leach; Deacons Thomas J. Willbrand; Donald A. Wussler. In Res., Rev. Msgr. Raymond A. Hampe.
Res.: 324 S. Third St., 63301-3413. Tel: 636-946-6641; Fax: 636-946-9789.
School—222 Jackson St., 63301. Tel: 636-947-9669. Lay Teachers 20; Students 260.
Catechesis/Religious Program—Students 120.

6—ST. ROBERT BELLARMINE (1964), Rev. Fred A. Meyer.
Res.: 1424 First Capitol Dr. S., 63303. Tel: 636-946-6799; Fax: 636-946-0380.
School—Tel: 636-946-1474. Dr. Phyllis Frederickson, Prin.; Melissa Hildebrand, Asst. Prin. Lay Teachers 10; Students 189.
Catechesis/Religious Program—Tel: 636-946-6401; Fax: 636-946-0380. Students 155.

ST. CLAIR, FRANKLIN CO., ST. CLARE (1916), [CEM] Rev. Paul E. Telken.
Res.: Box 526, 63077. Tel: 636-629-0315; Fax: 636-629-2327.
School—Tel: 636-629-0413. Lay Teachers 6; Students 60.
Catechesis/Religious Program—Students 57.

ST. MARY, STE. GENEVIEVE CO., IMMACULATE CONCEPTION (1869), [CEM] Rev. Richard C. Kasznel.
Res.: P.O. Box 27, 63673. Tel: 573-543-2536.

ST. PAUL, ST. CHARLES CO., ST. PAUL (1850), [CEM] Rev. Msgr. John J. Hickel.

Res.: P.O. Box 66069, 63366. Tel: 636-978-1400 (Rectory); 636-978-1900 (Parish Center Offices); Fax: 636-980-2722 (Parish Center Offices)
School—P.O. Box 66070, 63366. Tel: 636-978-1900, Ext. 230; Fax: 636-272-4469. Lay Teachers 16; Students 225.
Catechesis/Religious Program—Tel: 636-978-1900. Students 155.

ST. PETERS, ST. CHARLES CO., ALL SAINTS (1815), [CEM] Revs. Michael L. Henning; Gary L. Vollmer; Robert C. Lane; Deacon Gerald Knobbe.
Res.: 7 McMenamy Rd., 63376. Tel: 636-397-1440; Fax: 636-397-1421.
School—Tel: 636-397-1477; Fax: 636-970-3735. Rae Ann Kielty, Prin. Religious Teachers 2; Lay Teachers 22; Students 434.
Catechesis/Religious Program—Tel: 636-397-6995. Ms. Marya Pohlmeier, D.R.E. Students 465.

SERENO, PERRY CO., OUR LADY OF VICTORY (1908), [JC] Rev. Francis H. Agnew, C.M.
Res.: 172 PCR 920, Perryville, 63775. Tel: 573-547-6812; Fax: 573-547-6812.
Catechesis/Religious Program—Students 58.

SILVER LAKE, PERRY CO., ST. ROSE OF LIMA (1885), [CEM] Rev. Kevin P. Fausz, C.M.
Res.: 1010 Rosati Ct., Perryville, 63775. Tel: 573-547-4591; Fax: 573-547-4145.

STE. GENEVIEVE, STE. GENEVIEVE CO., STE. GENEVIEVE (1759), [CEM] Revs. Daniel E. Mosley; Raymond Hager.
Res.: 49 Du Bourg Pl., 63670. Tel: 573-883-2731.
School—40 N. Fourth St., 63670. Tel: 573-883-2403. Lay Teachers 20; Students 298.
High School—Valle High School, Tel: 573-883-7496; Fax: 573-883-9142. Lay Teachers 16; Students 149.
Catechesis/Religious Program—Students 90.

SULLIVAN, FRANKLIN CO.
1—ST. ANTHONY (1891), [CEM] Rev. Theodore J. Brunnert.
Res.: 201 W. Springfield Ave., 63080. Tel: 573-468-6101; Fax: 573-468-8584.
School—119 W. Springfield Ave., 63080. Tel: 573-468-4423. E. Anne Hanneken, Prin. Lay Teachers 7; Students 110.
Catechesis/Religious Program—Students 75.
2—CHURCH OF THE HOLY MARTYRS OF JAPAN (1879), [CEM 2] Unassigned.
Church: 8244 Hwy. AE, 63080-3229. Tel: 573-627-3378.
Catechesis/Religious Program—Students 50.

TIFF, WASHINGTON CO., ST. JOSEPH (1905), [CEM] Rev. Theodore X. Pieper, Admin.
Res.: R.R.I. Box 1110, Cadet, 63630. Tel: 573-438-6181; Fax: 573-438-3685.

TROY, LINCOLN CO., SACRED HEART (1891), [CEM] Rev. Thomas Wissler; Sr. Mary Ann Fisher, C.S.J., Pastoral Min.; Deacon Thomas Burkemper.
Res.: 100 Thompson Dr., 63379. Tel: 636-528-8219; Fax: 636-528-3983.
School—Tel: 636-528-6684; Fax: 636-528-3923. Sr. Jeannette Fennewald, S.S.N.D., Prin. Lay Teachers 13; Students 294.
Catechesis/Religious Program—Students 262.

UNION, FRANKLIN CO., IMMACULATE CONCEPTION (1866), [CEM] Rev. Matthew M. Mitas.
Res.: 100 N. Washington Ave., 63084. Tel: 636-583-5144; Fax: 636-583-7784.
School—6 W. State St., 63084. Tel: 636-583-2641; Fax: 636-583-3073. Sisters 2; Lay Teachers 18; Students 304.
Catechesis/Religious Program—Tel 636-583-4520. Students 142.

WARRENTON, WARREN CO., HOLY ROSARY (1868), [CEM] Rev. Erich A. Fechner; Deacons Bob Roberson; Ray Burle; Sr. Carol Ditto, M.P.S., Pastoral Assoc.
Res.: 724 E. Booneslick Rd., 63383. Tel: 636-456-3698; Fax: 636-456-5560.
School—Tel: 636-456-2882; Fax: 636-456-2882. Mrs. Margaret Burrus, Prin. Sisters of Notre Dame 1; Permanent 1; Lay Teachers 9; Students 166.
Catechesis/Religious Program—Students 95.

WASHINGTON, FRANKLIN CO.
1—ST. FRANCIS BORGIA (1834), (German), [CEM] Revs. John M. Costello; Michael P. Boehm; Deacons Gilbert Holtmeyer; Leon Noelker.
Res.: 311 W. Second St., 63090. Tel: 636-239-6701; Fax: 636-239-9499.
School—225 Cedar St., 63090. Tel: 636-239-2590; Fax: 636-316-9384. Lay Teachers 33; Students 446.
Catechesis/Religious Program—Students 120.
2—OUR LADY OF LOURDES (1958), Rev. Robert L. Heimos; Deacon Richard J. Boland.
Res.: 1014 Madison Ave., 63090. Tel: 636-239-3520; Fax: 636-239-7682.
School—950 Madison Ave., 63090. Tel: 636-239-5292; Fax: 636-239-7682. Lay Teachers 21; Students 271.
Catechesis/Religious Program—Students 101.

WEINGARTEN, STE. GENEVIEVE CO., OUR LADY HELP OF CHRISTIANS (1872), [CEM] Rev. William Wigand.
Res.: 13370 Hwy. 32, Ste. Genevieve, 63670-9402. Tel: 573-883-3796; Fax: 573-883-8871.
Catechesis/Religious Program—Students 15.

WENTZVILLE, ST. CHARLES CO., ST. PATRICK (1905), [CEM] [JC] Revs. Patrick J. O'Laughlin; Donald A. Glastetter; Deacons Paul H. Chavaux; Bernard A. Buckman.
Res.: 405 S. Church St., 63385. Tel: 636-332-9225; Fax: 636-332-6998.
School—701 Church St., 63385. Tel: 636-332-9913; Fax: 636-332-4877. Mrs. Janice Ward, Prin. Lay Teachers 21; Students 422.
Catechesis/Religious Program—Tel: 636-332-9036; Fax: 636-332-4877. Students 296.

ZELL, STE. GENEVIEVE CO., ST. JOSEPH (1845), [CEM] Rev. Msgr. James E. Hanson.
Res.: 11824 Zell Rd., Ste. Genevieve, 63670. Tel: 573-883-5481; Fax: 573-883-7829.
School—Tel: 573-883-5097. Adorers of the Blood of Christ (Ruma, IL) 1; Lay Teachers 4; Students 55.
Catechesis/Religious Program—Students 87.

Chaplains of Public Institutions

ST. LOUIS. *St. Anthony's Medical Center*, Tel: 314-525-1000.
Barnes - Jewish Hospital. Rev. James C. Gray. Tel: 314-747-3000.
Christian Hospital Northeast-Northwest, 11133 Dunn Rd., 63136. Tel: 314-653-5000 (Northeast); 314-953-6000 (Northwest). Rev. Thomas M. Begley.
DePaul Health Center. Rev. Lawrence Asma, C.M.
St. John's Mercy Medical Center, Tel: 314-569-6000. Rev. Philip G. Krahman, David Sullivan.
Lambert - St. Louis International Airport. Rev. Msgr. Louis F. Meyer (Retired), Deacon Arnold Krieger. Tel: 314-427-8787.
St. Mary's Health Center, Tel: 314-768-8000. Gregory G. Kirsch. Tel: 314-289-9545.

KIRKWOOD. *St. Joseph Hospital*, Tel: 314-966-1500. Rev. Mark L. Fuller. Tel: 314-962-5955.

ST. CHARLES. *St. Joseph Health Center*, Tel: 636-946-6641. Rev. Msgr. Raymond H. Hampe. Tel: 636-947-5000.

WASHINGTON. *St. John's Mercy Hospital*, Tel: 636-239-8000. Rev. Timothy J. Toohey.

Special Assignment:
Rev. Msgrs.—
Callahan, Kevin G., Dir. Personnel & Continuing Formation, 20 Archbishop May Dr., 63119.
Lyons William J., S.T.L., North American College, Rome, Faculty
Stika, Richard F., V.G., Chancellor & Vicar Gen., 4510 Lindell, 63108. Tel: 314-367-1437
Revs.—
Aten, Robert L., Heart of Mary Hermitage, Lesterville. Tel: 573-648-2467
Breier, Henry, Sec. to the Bishop
Dalton, Donald T., Ursuline Provincialate, 210 Glennon Heights Rd., Crystal City, 63019. Tel: 636-937-6206; Fax: 636-937-7627
Henke, Donald E., North American College, Rome, Italy.

On Duty Outside the Archdiocese:
Rev. Msgr.—
Ratermann, David A., Cochabamba, Bolivia
Revs.—
Blattner, Joseph H., Burlington, VT
Bolderson, John D., Kansas City, MO
Hayden, Patrick T., La Paz, Bolivia
Hederman, Kevin F., Belmopan, Belize
Koch, Donald J., Delray Beach, FL.
Kopfensteiner, Thomas R., Fordham University, Bronx, NY.
Lampert, Robert E., Christus Health, Irving, TX
Lockwood, Gregory J. (CIN)
Means, David A., Anchorage, AK
Menner, Robert J., La Paz, Bolivia
Michler, James R., La Paz, Bolivia
Rauch, David E., England.
Rutkowski, James, San Antonio, TX
Siebert, Anthony G., Dangriga, Belize

Military Chaplains:
Revs.—
Breig, Gary R.
Kirchhoefer, Thomas A.
Kovalcin, John A.
Swetnam, William R.

On Medical Leave:
Revs.—
Everding, Richard F.
Walter, David A.

Retired:
Most Rev.—
O'Donnell, Edward Joseph, D.D. (LAF), Bishop Emeritus of Lafayette, LA, 7500 Cromwell, 63105.
Rev. Msgrs.—
Behrmann, Elmer H., 2012 Clermont Crossing Dr., Apt. G, 63146.
Buchheit, Jerome J., 3293 Old County Rd., DeSoto, 63020.
Byrne, Henry L., St. Agnes Home, 10341 Manchester Rd., Kirkwood, 63122.
Chiodini, Jasper J., Regina Cleri, 10 Archbishop May Dr., 63119.
Clavenna, Charles G., Regina Cleri, 10 Archbishop May Dr., 63119.
Deutschmann, Edward, Mary, Mother of the Church, 5901 Kerth Rd., 63119.
Dietz, Norbert J., 7148 Forsyth, 63105.
Forst, Charles J., Saint Mark, 4230 Ripa, 63125.
Glynn, Gerard N., Regina Cleri, 10 Archbishop May Dr., 63119.
Kennedy, John J., Regina Cleri, 10 Archbishop May Dr., 63119.
Krieger, Wilfred L., 4286 Putting Green Dr., San Antonio, TX 78217.
Lubeley, Richard J., 676 W. Lockwood Blvd., 63119.
Marschner, Aloysius J., Mother Good Counsel Home, 6825 Natural Bridge Rd., 63121.
Meyer, Louis F., 4908 Sutherland, 63109.
Molloy, Patrick J., Regina Cleri, 10 Archbishop May Dr., 63119.
Mottin, Charles A., 125 Union Rd., 63119.
Muesenfechter, Robert J., 9401 Easy St., Hillsboro, 63050.
O'Connell, James P., Mother of Good Counsel Home, 6825 Natural Bridge Rd., 63121.
Overman, Robert F., 1711 Parhaven, San Antonio, TX 78232.
Ronquest, John T., St. Simon Rectory, 11011 Mueller Rd., 63123.
Sommer, Jerome, Regina Cleri, 10 Archbishop May Dr., 63119.
Sullivan, Leo F., 6825 Natural Bridge Rd., 63121.
Walsh, Lawrence J., Regina Cleri, 10 Archbishop May Dr., 63119.
Wilkerson, Jerome F., Ph.D., St. John Bosco, 12934 Marine Ave., 63146.
Woracek, Thomas J., Regina Cleri, 10 Archbishop May Dr., 63119.
Revs.—
Ahrens, William B., 7655 Watson Rd., 63119.
Albert, Xavier, Regina Cleri, 10 Archbishop May Dr., 63119.
Althoff, Arthur J., Regina Cleri, 10 Archbishop May Dr., 63119.
Britt, William J., Regina Cleri, 10 Archbishop May Dr., 63119.
Bukauskas, Anthony, 10 Archbishop May Dr., 63119.
Burghoff, Theodore H., 243 W. Aragonne Dr., 63122.
Burmester, Edwin J., St. Gabriel, 6303 Nottingham, 63109.
Danter, Albert F., St. Andrew Rectory, 309 Hoffmeister Ave., 63125.
Deutsch, Bernard F., 3729 Tamarron Dr., Bloomington, IN 47408.
Deutschmann, Edward J., 5901 Kerth Rd., St.Louis, 63128.
Ditch, Robert G., Regina Cleri, 10 Archbishop May Dr., 63119.
Forst, Aloysius A., 4141 Germania, Apt. 2B, 63116.
Gambon, John A., 300 E. Lane Dr., 63090.
Geoghegan, John F., Regina Cleri, 10 Archbishop May Dr., 63119.
Goellner, Glennon J., Regina Cleri, 10 Archbishop May Dr., 63119.
Good, Clarence P., Regina Cleri, 10 Archbishop May Dr., 63119.
Haar, George B., Regina Cleri, 10 Archbishop May Dr., 63119.
Hilgeman, Edward J., 8728 Magdalen Ave., 63144.
Horrigan, Kevin D., St. Agnes Home, 10341 Manchester Rd., 63122.
Julius, James A., 29 Pecan Dr., Long Beach, MS 39560.
Kersgieter, Paul J., 2605 Mullanphy Ln., Florissant, 63031.
Knaup, Alan J., 4900 Ringer Rd., 63129.
Knoll, Urban H., 629 S. Fourth St., St. Charles, 63301.
Komaska, James R., Regina Cleri, 10 Archbishop May Dr., 63119.
Kraus, Robert J., 1306 W. Main, #214, Jefferson City, 65109.
Lewis, Leo T., 9100 Cherry Brook Ln., 63126.
Liermann, Raymond B., 910 Hackman Rd., St. Paul, 63366.
Matyas, Francis B., Regina Cleri, 10 Archbishop May Dr., 63119.
Mersinger, Norbert A., St. Martin of Tours, 610 W. Ripa Ave., 63125.
Murphy, James E., 16 Tournament Tee Dr., O'Fallon, 63366.

Noser, J. Homer, Regina Cleri, 10 Archbishop May Dr., 63119.
Palmer, Michael J., Regina Cleri, 10 Archbishop May Dr., 63119.
Portucheck, Joseph J., Regina Cleri, 10 Archbishop May Dr., 63119.
Rehme, Albert A., 810 Napoleon Dr. (TDL), Bonne Terre, 63628.
Ruff, Charles R., Regina Cleri, 10 Archbishop May Dr., 63119.
Ryan, Joseph J., 5910 Majestic Way, Palmetto, FL 34221.
Schieber, Lawrence J., 700 W. Union, Apt. # 1, Pacific, 63069.
Schneider, John G., Regina Cleri, 10 Archbishop May Dr., 63119.
Stolzer, Vincent A., 1011A Cy Ann Dr., Town & Country, 63017.
Stroot, Ralph E., 4980 Heege Rd., 63123.
Suellentrop, Bernard A., Regina Cleri, 10 Archbishop May Dr., 63119.
Suren, Richard H., 6047 Bishops Pl., 63109.
Thomas, David T., 12934 Marine Ave., 63146.
Tiefenbrunn, Ronald R., 2403 Albert Rasche Dr., Cape Girardeau, 63701.
Voelker, Harold H., 7655 Watson Rd., Apt. # 162, 63119.
Winzerling, James L., 12685 Dorsett Rd., #228, Maryland Heights, 63043.
Wolf, Joseph B., 1970 Greenpoint Dr., Apt. 103, 63122.
Zinzer, Walter W., 3605 Hidden Rd., #B-4, San Antonio, TX 78217.

Permanent Deacons:
Amelotti, David
Arnold, Steven J.
Audrain, Raymond J.
Auer, Edward J.
Bachista, Ronald J.
Baker, John H., M.D., (On Duty Outside the Archdiocese)
Bansbach, Paul, (Retired)
Basler, James H.
Becker, Gerald H.
Beckmann, John W.
Beinke, George A.
Beirne, Edward R.
Bell, Jesse H.
Bernsen, Albert B.
Birkenmaier, Robert G.
Blase, George A.
Boedeker, C. Allen
Boland, Richard J.
Bolderson, David A.
Bourbon, Glennon L., Sr.
Boyer, Edward J.
Broyles, Jimmy D.
Bryant, Wayne T.
Bub, Richard F.
Buchek, Bradford M.
Buckley, James Mike
Buckley, John
Buckley, Michael L.
Buckman, Bernard A.
Buhr, Thomas A.
Burkard, Bruce A.
Burkemper, Thomas B.
Burle, Raymond J., Jr.
Burton, James L.
Butler, James R.
Butler, Russ, Immaculate Conception, Dardenne
Camden, David M.
Caruana, Philip P.
Casseau, William U.
Chauvin, C. Frank
Chavaux, Paul H.
Chitwood, Dennis M.
Christ, Walter W.
Clemens, Kenneth C.
Coffman, Richard W.
Conley, Allen M.
Coppage, Michael J., Jr.
Cox, Joseph E.
Crafts, R. Paul
Craska, Paul D.
Curtin, John A.
Czarnecki, Eugene J.
Damato, Larry
Danna, Frank, (On Duty Outside the Archdiocese)
Daus, Andrew C.
Davanzo, Charles R.
Denham, Donald C.
DePyper, Robert R., (On Duty Outside the Archdiocese)
Dickerson, Raymond A.
Dietz, Alvin J.
Dingman, Edwin H.
Dobelmann, Vernon L.
Dodson, Fred
Dolan, Timothy C.
Dorhauer, Jacob W.
Dowd, Thomas L.
Driscoll, Donald L.
Dubbs, Harvey
Ecker, Alan E.
Ehrhard, Herbert L.
Esswein, Leo F.
Eultgen, Thomas L.
Fink, George Russ
Flanigan, John P.
Flint, Edward G.
Forster, Thomas E.
Fronick, Edward C.
Fugere, Joseph H., (On Duty Outside the Archdiocese)
Gabbert, William L.
Gamache, Robert K.
Gawedzinkski, Norbert L.
Gearon, William A.
Gegg, Albin A.
Geiser, Gerald J.
Georges, Charles W.
Gerdes, Philip J.
Gerling, Thomas J.
Gettemeier, Herbert B., (Retired)
Ghiglione, James J., (On Duty Outside the Archdiocese)
Gholston, Clifford
Gildehaus, Charles R.
Gorski, Thomas
Gottlieb, Thomas J.
Gounis, Peter E.
Graham, George A.
Greif, William J.
Griffard, James M.
Grotpeter, Edward R.
Gunsaullus, Roland J.
Haefner, Joseph Tom
Hanses, Eugene J.
Harpring, David I.
Harris, Singleton L.
Harrison, R. Fielding
Hayes, Ralph
Heitert, Donald C.
Hengen, Philip R.
Hennicke, Raymond C.
Henning, Kenneth A.
Henroid, Daniel H.
Hercules, Joseph E.
Hoffmann, Eugene A.
Holmes, Charles E.
Holtmeyer, Gilbert C.
Hurlbert, Gerald R.
Hutti, Lawrence J., Jr.
Inman, Kenneth A.
Janson, Norman F.
Johnson, Leslie A.
Jurek, Thomas F., (On Duty Outside the Archdiocese)
Karsznia, Robert A.
Keeney, Robert J.
Kelly, Lawrence C.
Kennedy, Joseph M.
Kenney, T. Michael, III
Kieffer, William A., (On Duty Outside the Archdiocese)
Kiely, E. Ray
Klempert, Michael L.
Klostermann, Robert A., Sr.
Knobbe, Gerald E.
Kreft, Ronald J.
Kreitler, Roger A.
Krieger, Arnold F.
Kroutil, Joseph C.
Kuenz, Gary J.
La Martina, Joseph A.
Lake, Richard C.
Lauterwasser, Gerard M.
LeFors, Ronald S.
Lemoine, David E.
Leonardo, Delfin S.
Levac, Richard B.
Lombardo, Charles W.
Longmeyer, Harold
Love, Allen F., (On Duty Outside the Archdiocese)
Luke, Herbert, M.D.
Macauley, Edward C.
Maranan, Diosdado L.
Marren, L. Jerome
Martin, James P.
Martin, Leroy A., Jr.
Maxwell, Perez E.
Mayo, Robert J., II
McCarthy, Mark J.
McEntire, Clyde W.
McGuire, Jerry N.
McKee, Paul R., Ph.D.
McKenna, William J.
McNamee, Terrance M.
Menard, Louis A.
Meyerkord, Gary A.
Miller, George W.
Miller, Millard Ray
Morris, Joseph C.
Mroczkowski, R. V.
Mueller, Frederick J.
Murphey, James W., Jr.
Murphy, James L.
Murphy, Thomas P.
Murphy, William O.
Murray, Stephen L.
Naumann, Eugene J.
Nesbitt, Frank E.
Noelker, Leon R.
Nuelle, Norman C.
Olmsted, Francis J.
Otzenberger, Joseph M.
Pacino, David
Peacock, Joseph C.
Penberthy, Robert S.
Peterson, Stanley M., Jr.
Piva, Michael J.
Politte, Glennon P., Sr.
Politte, Stephen A.
Politte, Thomas G.
Porterfield, Paul D.
Potzman, Kenneth M.
Powers, Robert J.
Prideaux, Frank W.
Priesmeyer, W., Jr.
Prives, Gerald J.
Quinn, J. Gerard
Rankin, Patrick J.
Reynoso, Louis J.
Riegel, Robert C.
Roberson, Robert L.
Roderick, Walter L.
Rodis, Theodore J.
Ruegg, Walter J.
Russell, James W.
Ryder, Charles T.
Schellhase, Richard H.
Schiffman, Don, Immaculate Conception, Dardenne
Schiffman, Donald J.
Schisler, Steven M.
Schmidt, Donald J.
Schnable, Robert H.
Schulte, Edwin
Schultheis, Glennon J.
Schultz, Timothy
Schulze, Roy E.
Shannon, John R.
Shelby, Richard L.
Sinak, William S.
Sisul, Leonard A.
Smerek, Robert S., (On Duty Outside the Archdiocese)
Smith, John F.
Snyder, Robert J.
Snyder, Robert C.
Stackle, Paul F.
Stallings, Larry J.
Stevens, Richard L.
Stigall, Donald R.
Stovall, Dennis K.
Stoverink, Gerard G.
Stoverink, John J.
Strauss, Harold A.
Streckfuss, Joseph C.
Suden, Michael E., D.D.S.
Sulze, Joseph W.
Sutton, Ronald L.
Tichacek, George A.
Towey, Martin G., Ph.D., (On Duty Outside the Archdiocese)
Tracy, Daniel J., Sr.
Trautman, Anthony G.
Turek, Paul J., Sr.
Van Booven, Howard J.
Vaughn, Albert X.
Vehige, Richard J.
Volansky, Fred N.
Volansky, James M.
Walbridge, William F.
Weatherholt, Harold J.
Weishaar, Lonnie G.
Weiss, William G.
Werner, Norman B.
Wertz, Robert E.
Wessels, Richard H., (Retired)
White, Otis D.
Whitson, Alan W.
Willbrand, Thomas J.
Williams, Albert C.
Winkelmann, Christian H.
Wohlert, Steven H.
Wood, George F.
Wunderlich, William P.
Wussler, Donald A.

INSTITUTIONS LOCATED IN THE ARCHDIOCESE

[A] SEMINARIES, ARCHDIOCESAN

ST. LOUIS. *Kenrick-Glennon Seminary* (St. Louis Roman Catholic Theological Seminary) Tel: 314-792-6100; Fax: 314-792-6500. Email: info@kenrick.edu. Web: www.kenrick.edu.

Kenrick School of Theology, 5200 Glennon Dr., 63119. Tel: 314-792-6100; Fax: 314-792-6500. Web: www.kenrick.edu. Revs. John M. Hunthausen; Raul Salas, O.M.I.; Gregory Lockwood; Gregory J. Mansour; Steven Thoma, C.R.; Rev. Msgr. Ted L. Wojcicki, Ed.D., Rector; Revs. Thomas M. Molini, M.A., Vice Rector & Dean Students; Edward J. Richard, M.S., Academic Dean; Rev. Msgr. Edmund O. Griesedieck, Assist. Spiritual Dir.; Revs. Lawrence C. Brennan, S.T.D.; John F. Clark, C.M., M.A.; Glennon C. Doherty; Damien R. Dougherty, O.F.M., S.T.D.; Matthew J. Gutowski, S.T.L.; John P. Heil; James J. Ramacciotii; Michael J. Witt, Ph.D.; Rev. Msgr. Edward C. Eichor, M.A.; Sr. Zoe Glenski, D.C., Ph.D.; Susanne M. Harvath, Ph.D.; Peter F. Hesed, M.A.; Anne Marie Kitz, Ph.D.; Dr. John L. Gresham, Ph.D.; Lucius Hernandez, M.A..; Andrew J. Sopko, Ph.D.; Sebastian Mahfood; Lawrence J. Welch, Ph.D. Priests 12; Sisters 1; Students 64; St. Louis Students 16; Permanent Staff: Priests 12; Sisters 2; Lay Staff 8.

Cardinal Glennon College, 5200 Glennon Dr., 63119. Tel: 314-792-6100; Fax: 314-792-6500. Revs. Timothy P. Cronin, Dir.; C. Eugene Morris, S.T.L., Dir of Worship; Sr. Elizabeth Ann Buscher, S.C.C., Academic Advisor; Rita Altmann, R.N. Priests 3; Sisters 2; Lay Teachers 1; Students 25; St. Louis Students 20; Belize, AL Students 2; Jefferson City, NE Students 1; Springfield, IL Students 1; Permanent Staff: Priests 3; Sisters 2; Lay Teachers 1.

[B] SEMINARIES, RELIGIOUS, OR SCHOLASTICATES

ST. LOUIS. *Aquinas Institute of Theology*, 3642 Lindell Blvd., 63108. Tel: 314-977-3882; Fax: 314-977-7225. Email: aquinas@slu.edu. Web: www.ai.edu. Rev. Charles E. Bouchard, O.P., Pres.; Sr. Mary Kate Oosdykr, O.P., Ph.D., Dean; Rev. Albert G. Glade, O.P., Business Mgr. & Dir. Student Affairs; Marcus Watson, Institutional Advancement; Ron Knapp, Admissions; Kristi Ruggles, Communications Dir.; Revs. Richard A. Peddicord, O.P.; Sean Martin; Gregory J. Heille, O.P.; Thomas E. Esselman, C.M.; Harry M. Byrne, O.P.; Frank C. Quinn, O.P.; George R. Boudreau, O.P.; Sisters Marygrace Peters, O.P.; Jean deBlois, C.S.J.; Janet Schlictiong, O.P.; Carla Mae Streeter, O.P.; Catherine Vincie, R.S.H.M.; Patricia Walter, O.P. Priests 9; Sisters 7; Lay Teachers 2.

St. John Neumann House Redemptorist College Seminary Residence , 3737 Washington Blvd., 63108. Tel: 314-531-2777; Fax: 314-531-5726. Web: www.redemptorists-denver.org. Revs. Richard Boever, C.Ss.R., Dir. Formation Supr. Tel: 314-531-2777, Ext. 215; Gary Lauenstean, C.Ss.R., Vocation Dir.; Edward Vella, C.Ss.R., Vocation Dir.; Wm. Emmett Collins, C.Ss.R.; Jack Hacker, C.Ss.R.; Bro. Anthony Nguyen, C.S.S.R. Priests 6; Seminarians 5.

[C] COLLEGES AND UNIVERSITIES

ST. LOUIS. *Fontbonne University*, 6800 Wydown Blvd., 63105. Tel: 314-862-3456; Fax: 314-889-1451. Email: mjohnson@fontbonne.edu. Web: www.fontbonne.edu. Dennis C. Golden, Ed.D., Pres. Sisters 7; Lay Teachers 54; Students 2,344.

Saint Louis University Corporate Title: Saint Louis University , 221 N. Grand Blvd., 63103-2097. Tel: 314-977-2222; Fax: 314-977-3874. Email: admitme@slu.edu. Web: www.slu.edu. Mr. J. Joseph Adorjan, Chm. Bd. of Trustees; Rev. Lawrence H. Biondi, S.J., Pres.; Joseph Weixlmann, Ph.D., Provost. Priests 46; Brothers 1; Brothers 1; Sisters 6; Lay Teachers 1,563; Total Staff 4,181; Total Enrollment 11,217.

Vice Presidents: Robert Altholz, M.B.A., Vice Pres. Business & Finance; Donald J. Whelan Jr., Vice Pres. Devel. & Univ. Rels.; Kathleen T. Brady, Vice Pres. Facilities Mgmt. & Civic Affairs; William R. Kauffman, J.D., Vice Pres. & General Counsel; Kathy G. Hagedorn, Vice Pres. Human Resource Mgmt.; Kathy Humphrey, Vice Pres. Student Devel.; Carl Starkloff, S.J., Vice Pres. Univ. Mission & Ministry; Ms. Ellen Watson, Vice Pres., Chief of Info. Officer; Marla Berg-Weger, Ph.D., Assoc. Provost; Rev. Edwin B. Harris, S.J. (SJ), Assoc. Provost; Patricia A. Hagen, Ph.D.; Paul K. Jackson, Asst. Provost; Julie Weissman, Ph.D., Asst. Provost.

Deans:

Allied Health Professions, Doisy School of Tel: 314-577-8501; Fax: 314-577-8503. Charlotte Brasic Royeen, Ph.D., Dean.

Arts and Sciences, College of Tel: 314-977-2705; Fax: 314-977-3649. Rev. Michael May, S.J., Interim Dean.

John Cook School of Business Tel: 314-977-3833; Fax: 314-977-3897. Ellen F. Harshman, J.D., Ph.D., Dean.

Graduate School Tel: 314-977-2244; Fax: 314-977-3943. Donald G. Brennan, Ph.D., Dean.

Law, School of Tel: 314-977-8172; Fax: 314-977-3332. Jeffrey E. Lewis, J.D., Dean.

Medicine, School of Tel: 314-577-8201; Fax: 314-577-8645. Patricia L. Monteleone, M.D., Dean.

Nursing, School of Tel: 314-577-8910; Fax: 314-577-8949. Joan Hrubetz, Ph.D., R.N., Dean.

Parks College of Engineering and Aviation Tel: 314-977-8203; Fax: 314-977-8403. Bjong Wolf Yeigh, Ph.D., Dean.

Philosophy and Letters, College of Tel: 314-977-2701; Fax: 314-977-7211. Rev. Garth L. Hallett, S.J., Dean.

Professional Studies, School of Tel: 314-977-7234; Fax: 314-977-1482. Jennifer Kohler, Interim Dean.

Public Health, School of Tel: 314-977-8111; Fax: 314-977-8150. E. Andrew Balas, M.D., Ph.D., Dean.

College of Public Service Tel: 314-977-3292; Fax: 314-977-3290. James F. Gilsinan, Ph.D., Dean.

Social Service, School of Tel: 314-977-2730; Fax: 314-977-2731. Susan C. Tebb, Ph.D., Dean.

Academic Services Tel: 314-977-2370; Fax: 314-977-1424. Denise Sleet, Ph.D., Dir.

Pius XII Memorial Library Tel: 314-977-3100; Fax: 314-977-3108. Frances Benham, Ph.D., Univ. Librarian.

Student Educational Services Center Tel: 314-977-2930; Fax: 314-977-3315. Celerstine B. Johnson, Ed.D., Asst. Provost & Dir.

Other Jesuits Associated with the University: Revs. Steven J. Agostino, S.J.; Bernard J. Berry, S.J.; Francis C. Brennan, S.J.; Stephen C. Koitharayil; Donald F. Rauscher, S.J.; J. David Corrigan, S.J.; James H. Baker, S.J.; Michael D. Barber, S.J.; R. Bentley Anderson, S.J.; Stephen M. Belt, S.J.; Anthony C. Daly, S.J.; Denis E. Daly, S.J.; Terrence E. Dempsey, S.J.; Yoshio Ignatius Fuko, S.J.; James F. Goeke, S.J., M.Ed., M.Div., B.C.; Martin D. O'Keefe, S.J.; Carl F. Starkloff, S.J.; William V. Stauder, S.J.; Michael J. Doody, S.J. BO); David L. Fleming, S.J.; Robert S. Flack, S.J.; John B. Foley, S.J.; Garth L. Hallett, S.J.; W. Charles Heiser, S.J.; John J. Kavanaugh, S.J.; Thomas F. J. Kelly, S.J.; Edwin Lisson, S.J.; Michael K. May, S.J.; Frederick G. McLeod, S.J.; John J. Mueller, S.J.; Claude N. Pavur, S.J.; Robert L. Phillips, S.J.; Donald W. Reck, S.J.; Bro. William R. Rehg, S.J.; Revs. James A. Sebesta, S.J.; James V. Veltrie, S.J.; James K. Voiss, S.J.; Daniel P. Viegas, S.J.

Pastoral Care Dept. of Saint Louis University Hospital: Sandra Spencer, Dir., MFHC, BCC.

[D] RELIGIOUS EDUCATION

ST. LOUIS. *Paul VI Institute of Catechetical and Pastoral Studies*, 8300 Morganford Rd., 63123-6815. Tel: 314-633-2550; Fax: 314-633-2559. Email: paul6@archstl.org. Web: www.archstl.org. Rev. Edward J. Richard, M.S., Dir.; Dr. John L. Gresham, Ph.D., Curriculum & Technology Coord.; Sr. Catherine Marie Stewart, S.D.S.H., Coord. of Sacramental/Catechetical Retreats; Mary L. Beier, Registrar - Business Manager; Marisol D. Pfaff, Admin. Asst.- Online Course System Admin.; Dr. Shawn McCauley Welch, Assoc. Dean; Mary L. Beier, Registrar. Priests 16; Sisters 4; Lay Teachers 14; Total Enrollment 1,550.

[E] HIGH SCHOOLS, ARCHDIOCESAN

ST. LOUIS. *Bishop DuBourg High School*, 5850 Eichelberger St., 63109. Tel: 314-832-3030; Fax: 314-832-0529. Email: info@bishopdubourg.org. Web: www.bishopdubourg.org. Dr. Donna A. Payne, Prin.; Dr. Gerald Gruszka, Assoc. Prin.; Miss Bridget Timoney, Assoc. Prin. A Co-Educational School Staffed by Diocesan Priests, Religious and Lay Teachers. Priests 2; Sisters 3; Lay Teachers 48; Students 670.

Cardinal Ritter College Prep, 701 N. Spring, 63108. Tel: 314-446-5500; Fax: 314-446-5570. Email: crhall@archstl.org. Web: info.csd.org/ritter.htm. Leon Henderson, Pres.; Michawl Salsich, Vice Pres.; Mrs. Carmele U. Hall, Prin. Co-Educational High School Staffed by Religious and Laity. Priests 2; Sisters 1; Lay Teachers 26; Students 341.

Saint Mary's High School, 4701 S. Grand Blvd., 63111. Tel: 314-481-8400; Fax: 314-481-3670. Email: mainoffice@stmaryshs.com. Web: www.stmaryshs.com. Mr. Kevin Hacker, B.A., M.Ed., Prin. For Boys, Staffed by Brothers of Mary and Archdiocesan Priests. Priests 1; Lay Teachers 35; Total Enrollment 488.

Rosati-Kain High School, 4389 Lindell Blvd., 63108. Tel: 314-533-8513; Fax: 314-533-1618. Email: rkoffice@rosati-kain.org. Web: www.rosati-kain.org. Sr. Joan Andert, S.S.N.D., Prin.; Nancy P. Lydon, Assoc. Prin. Conducted for Girls by the Archdiocese of St. Louis, the Sisters of St. Joseph and the School Sisters of Notre Dame. Priests 1; Sisters 6; Lay Teachers 26; Girls 401.

Trinity High School, 1720 Redman Rd., 63138. Tel: 314-741-1333; Fax: 314-741-1335. Email: office@trinitycatholichighschool.org. Web: www.trinitycatholichighschool.org. Kirk Boschert, Prin.; Dr. Christine Vonder Harr, Assoc. Prin.; Mr. Richard Barrett, Assoc. Prin. Priests 1; Sisters 2; Brothers 1; Lay Teachers 40.

FESTUS. *St. Pius X High School*, 1030 St. Pius Dr., 63028. Tel: 636-937-3695; 636-931-7487; Fax: 636-931-7487. Email: lancer@stpius.com. Web: stpius.com. Mr. Charles Nolan, Pres.; Ms. Norma Overberg, Assoc. Prin. A Co-Educational High School Conducted by Diocesan Priests and Lay Faculty. Priests 1; Lay Teachers 32; Students 402.

MANCHESTER. *John F. Kennedy Catholic High School*, 500 Woods Mill Rd., 63011. Tel: 636-227-5900; Fax: 636-227-0298. Email: admin@JFK-Catholic-high.org. Web: www.jfk-catholic-high.org. Christine A. Bolesta, Prin. A Co-Educational High School Staffed by Lay Faculty. Priests 1; Lay Teachers 40; Students 500.

O'FALLON. *St. Dominic High School*, 31 St. Dominic Dr., 63366. Tel: 636-240-8303; Fax: 636-240-9884. Email: mainoffice@stdominichs.org. Web: www.stdominichs.org. Sisters Mary H. Bender, S.S.N.D., Admin.; Carolyn, O.P., Prin. A Co-Educational High School Conducted by Diocesan Priests and Sisters of the Third Order of St. Dominic and laymen and laywomen. Priests 1; Sisters 3; Lay Teachers 50; Students 736.

ST. CHARLES. *Duchesne High School*, 2550 Elm St., 63301-1494. Tel: 636-946-6767; Fax: 636-946-6267. Email: tgravemann@duchesne-hs.com. Web: www.duchesne-hs.org. Terry W. Gravemann, Admin.; Mr. Donald C. Burkhart, Prin.; Rev. James L. Gahan. A Co-Educational College Prep High School Conducted by Archdiocesan Priests and Catholic Lay Staff. Under the Auspices of the Catholic Education Office. Sponsored by Seven Parishes in and around St. Charles, MO and its surrounding counties and its surrounding counties. Priests 1; Lay Teachers 53; Students 718.

WASHINGTON. *St. Francis Borgia Regional High School*, 1000 Borgia Dr., 63090. Tel: 636-239-7871; Fax: 636-239-1198. Email: mtraffas@borgia.com. Web: www.borgia.com. Marilyn Traffas, Admin.; Mr. George Wingbermuehle, Prin. A Co-Educational High School Staffed by Diocesan Priests and School Sisters of Notre Dame and dedicated lay faculty Priests 1; Sisters 1; Lay Teachers 44; Students 593.

[F] HIGH SCHOOLS, PRIVATE

ST. LOUIS. *Christian Brothers College High School (C.B.C.)*, 1850 De La Salle Dr., 63141. Tel: 314-985-6100; Fax: 314-985-6115. Email: admin@cbchs.org. Web: www.cbchs.org. Rev. Matthew O'Toole, Chap.; Bro. Lawrence Humphrey, F.S.C., Pres.; Mr. James B. Gerdes, Prin. Brothers 7; Lay Teachers 69; Students 1,012.

Cor Jesu Academy, 10230 Gravois, 63123. Tel: 314-842-1546; Fax: 314-842-6061. Email: principal@corjesu.org. Web: www.corjesu.org. Sr. Sheila O'Neill, A.S.C.J., Prin. Apostles of the Sacred Heart Priests 1; Sisters 5; Lay Teachers 41; Students 540.

De Smet Jesuit High School, 233 N. New Ballas Rd., 63141. Tel: 314-567-3500; Fax: 314-567-1519. Web: www.desmet.org. Dr. Gregory A. Densberger, Ph.D., Prin.; Rev. John D. Arnold, S.J., Pres. Priests 7; Sisters 2; Brothers 2; Lay Teachers 79; Students 1,248.

St. Elizabeth Academy, 3401 Arsenal St., 63118. Tel: 314-771-5134; Fax: 314-771-3528. Email: rjhenry@stelizabethacademy.org. Web: stelizabethacademy.org. Mrs. Rosalie Henry, Prin. Sisters of the Most Precious Blood Sisters 4; Lay Teachers 25; Students 208.

Incarnate Word Academy, 2788 Normandy Dr., 63121. Tel: 314-725-5850; Fax: 314-725-2308. Email: rmikolas@iwacademy.org. Web: www.iwacademy.org. Randy Berzon-Mikolas, Ph.D. Sisters of Charity of Incarnate Word of San Antonio Lay Teachers 48; Support Staff 14; Students 540.

St. Joseph's Academy, 2307 S. Lindbergh Blvd., 63131. Tel: 314-965-7205; Fax: 314-965-9114. Email: sjaprin@stjosephacad.org. Web:

www.stjosephacad.com. Mrs. Nancy Repking, Prin. Sisters of St. Joseph of Carondelet 5; Lay Teachers 51; Girls 615.

St. Louis University High School, George H. Backer Memorial, 4970 Oakland Ave., 63110. Tel: 314-531-0330; Fax: 314-534-3441. Web: www.sluh.org. Revs. Richard E. Hadel, S.J.; Paul G. Sheridan, S.J., Pres.; Martin Hagan, S.J.; Jeffrey D. Harrison, S.J.; James G. Knapp, S.J., Supr.; Ralph D. Houlihan, S.J.; Brian J. Christopher, S.J., Scholastics; Nhan An Pham, S.J., Scholastics. Priests 8; Scholastics 2; Admin. 5; Lay Teachers 85; Students 1,039. In Res. Very Revs. Timothy M. McMahon, S.J.; Frank E. Reale, S.J.

Notre Dame High School, 320 E. Ripa Ave., 63125. Tel: 314-544-1015; Fax: 314-544-8003. Email: archstl875@connectinc.com. Web: www.ndhs.net. Sr. Michelle Emmerich, S.S.N.D., Prin. Sisters 11; Lay Teachers 44; Girls 450.

CREVE COEUR. *Chaminade College Preparatory School Inc.*, 425 S. Lindbergh Blvd., 63131-2799. Tel: 314-993-4400; Fax: 314-993-4403. Email: archstl851@impresso.com. Web: www.chaminademo.com. Rev. Ralph A. Siefert, S.M., Pres.; James E. Gerker, Prin.; Michael Thro, Campus Min. Society of Mary, Residents and Day Students. Priests 1; Brothers 2; Sisters 1; Lay Teachers 80; Students 600.

St. Louis Priory School, 500 S. Mason Rd., 63141-8500. Tel: 314-434-3690; Fax: 314-576-7088. Web: www.priory.org. Rev. J. Gregory Mohrman, O.S.B., Headmaster; Rt. Rev. Thomas Frerking, O.S.B.; Revs. Christopher Hanson, O.S.B.; M. Paul Kidner, O.S.B.; J. Laurence Kriegshauser, O.S.B.; Dominic Lenk, O.S.B.; D. Ralph Wright, O.S.B. Priests 7; Brothers 4; Lay Teachers 38; High School Students 253; Students (Grades 7-8) 138.

FRONTENAC. *Villa Duchesne/Oak Hill*, 801 S. Spoede Rd., 63131. Tel: 314-432-2021; Fax: 314-432-7713. Email: vdoh@vdoh.org. Web: www.vdoh.org. Mrs. Renee Allen, Prin. (7-12); Margaret Karl, Prin. (PreK-6); Dr. Sam Sciortino, Head of School. Religious of the Sacred Heart, (Girls: PreK-12; Boys: PreK-6) Sisters 4; Lay Faculty 113; Elementary School Students (PreK-6) 373; High School Students (7-12) 417.

KIRKWOOD. *St. John Vianney High School*, 1311 S. Kirkwood Rd., 63122. Tel: 314-965-4853; Fax: 314-965-1950. Email: lkeller@vianney.com. Web: www.vianney.com. Revs. Robert R. Osborne, S.M., Pres.; William R. Wightman, S.M. Conducted for Boys by the Society of Mary (Marianists) Priests 2; Brothers 3; Sisters 1; Lay Teachers 56; Students 751.

Ursuline Academy, 341 S. Sappington Rd., 63122. Tel: 314-966-4556; Fax: 314-965-4443. Email: mohara@ursulinest1.org. Web: www.ursulinestl.org. Sr. Madonna O'Hara, Pres.; Dr. Patricia Hensley, Prin. Ursuline Nuns of the Roman Union Sisters 4; Lay Teachers 48; Students 630.

TOWN AND COUNTRY. *Visitation Academy*, 3020 N. Ballas Rd., 63131. Tel: 314-432-5353; Fax: 314-432-7210. Web: www.visitationacademy.org. Cynthia Vives, S.H.C.J., Head of School; Barbara McMullen, Acting US Prin. (Grades 7-12). Visitation Sisters 1; Lay Teachers 46; Students 443.

WEBSTER GROVES. *Nerinx Hall High School*, 530 E. Lockwood, 63119. Tel: 314-968-1505; Fax: 314-968-0604. Email: jkosash@nerinxhs.org. Web: www.nerinxhs.org. Sr. Barbara Roche, S.L., Pres.; Mrs. Jane W. Kosash, Prin.; Mrs. Teresa R. Corley, Assoc. Prin. Sisters of Loretto at the Foot of the Cross 4; Religious 7; Lay Teachers 56; Students 594.

[G] ELEMENTARY SCHOOLS, PRIVATE

ST. LOUIS. **De La Salle Middle School, Inc.*, 4145 Kennerly Ave., 63113. Tel: 314-368-3290. Bro. David Poos, F.S.C., Contact Person.

Loyola Academy of St. Louis, 3854 Washington Blvd., 63108. Tel: 314-531-9091; Fax: 314-531-3603. Email: tom@loyolaacademy.org. Web: www.loyolaacademy.org. Thomas M. Nolan, Dir. Lay Teachers 6; Students 60.

Marian Middle School, 3112 Meramec St., 63118-4339. Tel: 314-351-7674; Fax: 314-351-5496. Email: director@marianmiddleschool.org. Mrs. Susan Rothweil, Contact Person.

CHESTERFIELD. *Linda Vista Catholic School*, 1633 Kehrs Mill Rd., 63005. Tel: 636-532-3315; Fax: 636-532-2578. Email: info@lvcsstl.org. Web: www.lvcsstl.org. Conducted by the Sisters of the Most Precious Blood, Preschool Classes for 3-6 Year Olds, Grades 1-8. Lay Teachers 31; Students 202.

CREVE COEUR. *Chaminade College Preparatory*, (Grades 6-12), 425 S. Lindbergh Blvd., 63131. Tel: 314-993-4400; Fax: 314-993-4403. Email: archstl851@impresso.com. Web: www.chaminademo.com. Rev. Ralph A. Siefert, S.M., Pres.; Mr. Michael T. Bander, Prin. Society of Mary, (Middle School), Residents and Day Students (Boys) Lay Teachers 27; Students 350.

St. Louis Priory School, (Grades 7-8), 500 S. Mason Rd., 63141-8500. Tel: 314-434-3690; Fax: 314-576-7088. Web: www.priory.org. (Boys) Priests 2; Brothers 2; Lay Teachers 25; Students 138.
Corporate Title: The Abbey of St. Mary and St. Louis Rev. J. Gregory Mohrman, O.S.B., Headmaster.

FRONTENAC. *Villa Duchesne*, (Grades 7-12) Tel: 314-432-2021; Fax: 314-432-7713. Email: rallen@udoh.org. Web: www.udoh.org. 801 S. Spoede Rd., 63131-2699. Tel: 314-432-2021; Fax: 314-432-7713. Email: rallen@vdoh.org. Web: www.vdoh.org. Mrs. Renee Allen, Prin.; Sr. Sam Sciortine, Head of School. (Girls) Sisters 1; Lay Teachers 48; Girls 410.

ST. CHARLES. *Academy of the Sacred Heart* (Coed), 619 N. 2nd St., 63301. Tel: 636-946-6127; Fax: 636-949-6659. Email: mcaire@ash1818.org. Web: www.ash1818.org. Sr. Margaret Caire, Headmistress; Mrs. Kathy Hopper, Prin. Sisters 11; Lay Teachers 47; Students 672.

TOWN AND COUNTRY. *Visitation Academy*, (Grades PreK-6), 3020 N. Ballas Rd., 63131. Tel: 314-432-5353; Fax: 314-432-5355. Email: jnowak@visitationacademy.org. Web: www.visitationacademy.org. Sr. Cynthia H. Vives, S.H.C.J., Head of School; Mimi Kueneke, Prin. (PreK-6). Visitation Sisters 4; Lay Teachers 66; Students 694.

[H] DEPARTMENT OF SPECIAL EDUCATION

ST. LOUIS. *Catholic Guidance Center*, 4472 Lindell Blvd., 63108. Tel: 314-533-3454; Fax: 314-533-0140. Email: special-education@att.net. Web: www.special-education.org. Rev. Msgr. Vernon E. Gardin, Ph.D., V.G., Exec. Dir. Psycho-Educational Testing Facility and also Administrative Office for the Archdiocesan Department of Special Education, Serving Children with Developmental Disabilities, Mental Retardation, Learning Disabilities or Attention Deficit Disorder.; Special Ungraded Day Classes, Schools, Preschool, PSR for Disabled children with Mental Retardation or Major Learning Disabilities (ages 5-16). Located in the Following Parish Schools: Epiphany of Our Lord (2 LD Classes); Sacred Heart (1 MR Classes); St. Christopher (5 LD Classes); Annunziata (6 LD Classes); St. John the Baptist (3 LD Classes); Our Lady of the Presentation (2 LD Classes); Ascension, Chesterfield (2 LD Classes). Sisters 1; Teachers 34; Total Number of Children Served 750.

St. Mary's Special Services, 1724 Redman Ave., 63138. Tel: 314-261-8533; Fax: 314-653-2591. Web: www.special-education.org. Rev. Msgr. Vernon E. Gardin, Ph.D., V.G., Exec. Dir.
Legal Title: *St. Mary's Special School for Exceptional Children*, Early Intervention therapies and child care for preschool children (ages 6 months-5 years) developmentally disabled in a normalized mainstream setting (capacity 80).; Inclusionary early childhood education for children ages 3-6 years (capacity 20). Lay Staff 31; Clients 97.

Special Religious Education Ministry, 4472 Lindell Blvd., 63108. Tel: 314-533-3454, Ext. 231; Fax: 314-533-0140. Email: SpecRelEdu@aol.com. Web: www.special-educationstl.org. Mary Beth Schulte, Coord. Department of Special Education.; Provides Catholic religious education for children with disabilities in public special programs. (ages 7-21) & for adults with disabilities living in institutions or in their own homes. Priests 2; Lay Teachers 33; Total Enrollment 100.

CHESTERFIELD. *St. Joseph Institute for the Deaf*, 1809 Clarkson Rd., 63017-5065. Tel: 636-532-3211 (Voice/TTY); Fax: 636-532-4560. Email: info@sjid.org. Web: www.sjid.org. Mary Tumbrink Gannon, M.A.Ed., Prin. School for the Deaf; Auditory-oral day & residential school for hearing-impaired children from birth-8th grade. Early intervention therapy for children 0-5; pre- & elementary school offering intense speech & academic prog. Sisters 3; Lay Teachers 37; Students 100.

[I] SERVICES FOR THE ELDERLY

ST. LOUIS. *Cardinal Ritter Institute*, 7601 Watson Rd., 63119. Tel: 314-961-8000; Fax: 314-961-1934. Email: swesley@ccstl.org. Web: www.ccstl.org. Sr. Suzanne Wesley, CEO.
Legal Title: *Cardinal Ritter Institute, Inc.*, Catholic Charities network of agencies provides social services, in home services, residences, adult day care, employment and volunteer services for the elderly. Total Staff 263; Total Housing Units 2,047; Total Clients Served 40,002.

Cardinal Ritter Institute - Adult Day Care Program, 7663 Watson Rd., 63119. Tel: 314-962-7501; Fax: 314-962-7140.

Cardinal Ritter Institute Residential Services, Inc., 4483 Lindell Blvd., 63108. Tel: 314-652-3600; Fax: 314-652-8840. Kevin Klingerman, Dir. Provides housing Mgmt. & other svcs. for residential facilities for the elderly.

Alexian Court Apartments, 2636 Chippewa St., 63118. Tel: 314-771-5604; Fax: 314-771-7629. (Legal Title: Alexian Brothers Services, Inc.); Sponsored by Alexian Brothers of Missouri, Inc., Managed by Cardinal Ritter Institute.

St. John Neumann Apartments, Inc., 8424 Lucas Hunt Rd., 63136. Tel: 314-385-0707; Fax: 314-385-5299.

St. Joseph Apartments, Inc., 7677 Watson Rd., 63119. Tel: 314-962-0969; Fax: 314-962-1393.

St. Patrick Apartments, Inc., 555 Bluff Parks Dr., 63031. Tel: 314-839-3212; Fax: 314-839-7537.

St. Patrick's Apartments II, Inc., 583 Bluff Parks Dr., Florissant, 63031. Tel: 314-837-4101; Fax: 314-837-4389.

San Luis Apartments, Inc., 4483 Lindell Blvd., 63108. Tel: 314-534-4730; Fax: 314-534-0567.

Santa Ana Apartments, Inc., 3737 Ashby Rd., 63074. Tel: 314-428-7385; Fax: 314-428-6541.

Visitation Senior Apartments, Inc., 1911 N. Taylor Ave., 63113. Tel: 314-961-8000; Fax: 314-961-1934.

Holy Infant Apartments, Inc., 7663 Watson Rd., 63119. Tel: 314-962-7878; Fax: 314-962-1393.

St. Agnes Apartments, Inc., 2840 Wisconsin, 63118. Tel: 314-664-1255; Fax: 314-664-1192.

Santa Maria Apartments, 12565 Santa Maria Ct., Hazelwood, 63042. Tel: 314-739-7220; Fax: 314-739-2950.

Pope John Paul II Apartments, Inc., 6325 Waterways Dr., 63033. Tel: 314-653-0400, Ext. 294; Fax: 314-653-2840.

St. Ann Assisted Living, 10441 International Plaza Dr., St. Ann, 63074. Tel: 314-423-0600; Fax: 314-423-4842.

St. Elizabeth Hall, 325 N. Newstead, 63108. Tel: 314-652-9525; Fax: 314-652-8879.

Du Bourg House, 8590 Eichelberger, 63109. Tel: 314-752-1901; Fax: 314-752-0572.

Cardinal Carberry Senior Living Center Tel: 314-961-8000; Fax: 314-961-1934. Sr. Suzanne Wesley, C.S.J., CEO.

Our Lady of Life Apartments, 7655 Watson Rd., 63119. Tel: 314-968-9447; Fax: 314-968-1758.

Mother of Perpetual Help Residence, 7609 Watson Rd., 63119. Tel: 314-961-8000; Fax: 314-961-3061.

Mary, Queen and Mother Center, 7601 Watson Rd., 63119. Tel: 314-961-8000; Fax: 314-961-1548.

Holy Angels I, 3455 DePaul Ln., Bridgeton, 63044.

Holy Angels II, 3499 DePaul Ln., Bridgeton, 63044.

Warrington Senior Village dba St. Clare of Assisi Senior Village, c/o 4112 McClay St., St. Charles, 63304.

Corporate Action for the Care of the Elderly, Inc., 335 S. Kirkwood Rd., 63122. Tel: 314-965-3700; Fax: 314-965-3710. Sr. Cathy Vetter, C.C.V.I., Pres. Association Composed of Representatives of 14 Religious Communities. Grants offered to assist those who work with the elderly.

St. Elizabeth Adult Day Care Center, 3401 Arsenal St., 63118. Tel: 314-772-5107; Fax: 314-772-3674. Email: sjamiller@juno.com. Web: www.cpps-ofallon.org. Sr. John Antonio Miller, C.PP.S., Dir. Conducted by the Sisters of the Most Precious Blood to Provide Day Care for the Elderly and Handicapped.

St. Elizabeth East Adult Day Care Center, 3227 S. Ninth St., 63118. Tel: 314-771-1591; Fax: 314-771-1591.

St. Elizabeth North Adult Day Care Center, 2142 Switzer, 63136. Tel: 314-867-6511; Fax: 314-867-6511.

St. Elizabeth/Visitation Adult Day Care Center, 1421 N. Taylor, 63113. Tel: 314-531-2985; Fax: 314-531-2985.

St. Elizabeth/Visitation Adult Day Care Center, 2000 El Lago, Arnold, 63010. Tel: 636-461-0730; Fax: 636-461-0730.

St. Elizabeth Adult Day Care Center of Washington, 1202 W. 5th St., Washington, 63090. Tel: 636-239-7100; Fax: 636-239-7100. For all: Total Assisted 219; Total Staff 48.

[J] GENERAL HOSPITALS

ST. LOUIS. *St. Anthony's Medical Center*, 10010 Kennerly Rd., 63128. Tel: 314-525-1000; Fax: 314-525-4485. Email: mcshrs@samcstl.org. Web: www.stanthonysmedcenter.com. Rita S. McShea, Dir. Pastoral Care Dept.; Revs. Nathan McNally, Chap.; William Candy, Chap. Bed Capacity 821; Patients Assisted Annually 374,382; Staff 3,789.

SSM St. Mary's Health Center, 6420 Clayton Rd., 63117. Tel: 314-768-8000; Fax: 314-768-8011.

Email: tim_blackmore@ssmhc.com. Web: www.stmarys-stlouis.com. Kenneth W. Lukhard, Pres.; Rev. Gregory Kirsch, Dir.-Spiritual Care Mission. Member of SSM Health Care Franciscan Sisters of Mary 5; Bed Capacity 582; Patients Assisted Annually 161,410; Total Staff 2,026.

BRIDGETON. *SSM De Paul Health Center*, 12303 De Paul Dr., 63044. Tel: 314-344-6000. Web: www.ssmdphc.com. Melinda Clark, Pres.; Revs. Lawrence F. Asma, C.M., Chap.; David Boule, Chap.; Sr. Joann Lukefahr, Chap.; Charlene Raitt, Chap.; Angie Vorholt, Chap. Member of SSM Health Care.

DePaul General Hospital Division (Operating) Excluding Nursery-Including 14 Bed Acute Rehabilitation Unit 345; (Licensed) Excluding Nursery-Including 14 Bed Acute Rehabilitation Unit 440; Sisters 3; Patients Assisted Annually 158,777; Staff 4,849.

St. Vincent Division, 12303 De Paul Dr., 63044. Tel: 314-344-7135. Pre-Adolescent, Adolescent, Adult & Gero Psychiatric Care and Chemical Dependency. Operating 98; Licensed 98.

CREVE COEUR. *St. John's Mercy Medical Center*, 615 S. New Ballas Rd., 63141. Tel: 314-569-6000; Fax: 314-569-6910. Mr. Michael Morgan, Pres. & CEO; Revs. David D. Sullivan, Chap.; Philip G. Krahman, Chap.; Deacon Ken Potzman, Chap. Conducted by the Religious Sisters of Mercy of the Americas-St. Louis Region, (See Branch Unit under Washington, MO) Sisters 25; Other Nurses 1,500; Bed Capacity 1,125; Patients Assisted Annually 700,000; Capacity Includes: Chemical Dependency Unit of 35; Skilled Nursing facility of 120; Total Staff 7,200.

KIRKWOOD. *SSM St. Joseph Hospital of Kirkwood*, 525 Couch Ave., 63122. Tel: 314-966-1601; Fax: 314-966-1681. Web: www.stjosephkirkwood.com. Carla S. Baum, Pres.; Revs. Mark L. Fuller, Supr. & Chap.; James A. Krings, Dir. Mission Svcs. Member of SSM Health Care. Bed Capacity 263; Sisters 2; Nurses 279; Patients Assisted Annually 115,028.

LAKE ST. LOUIS. *SSM St. Joseph Hospital West*, 100 Medical Plaza, 63367. Tel: 314-625-5200; Fax: 314-625-5314. Web: www.ssmstjoseph.com. Kevin F. Kast, Pres.; Sisters Donna Olson, Pastoral Care; Charlotte Lehman, Pastoral Care. Member of SSM Health Care. Bed Capacity 88; Patients Assisted Annually 90,358; Staff 587.

ST. CHARLES. *SSM St. Joseph Health Center*, 300 First Capitol Dr., 63301. Tel: 314-947-5000; Fax: 314-947-5090. Email: kevin_kast@ssmhc.com. Web: www.ssmstjoseph.com. Kevin F. Kast, Pres.; Mr. David Fitzgerald, Dir. Pastoral Care; Rev. Ray Hampe. Member of SSM Health Care. Sisters 3; Bed Capacity 363; Patients Assisted Annually 178,507; Staff 1,621.

WASHINGTON. *St. John's Mercy Hospital*, 901 E. 5th St., 63090. Tel: 636-239-8010; Fax: 636-239-8010. Web: www.smhs.com. Michael Zilm, Admin.; Sr. Louise Eggen, O.S.B., Mgr.; Rev. Timothy J. Toohey, Chap.; Sr. Michaelanne Estoup, R.S.M., Chap.; Rev. Tom Haller, Chap. (Protestant); Melba Peters, Chap.; Deacon Harvey Dubbs, Chap. (See Listing Under Creve Coeur, MO) Bed Capacity 187; Total Assisted 20,403; Staff 809.

[K] SPECIAL HOSPITALS

ST. LOUIS. *SSM Cardinal Glennon Children's Hospital*, 1465 S. Grand Blvd., 63104. Tel: 314-577-5600; Fax: 314-268-6468. Email: Doug_Ries@ssmhc.com. Web: www.cardinalglennon.com. Mr. Douglas A. Ries, Pres. Member of SSM Health Care. Sisters 3; Bed Capacity (for Children) 190; Patients Assisted Annually 213,570; Total Staff 1,504.

SSM Rehab, 6420 Clayton Rd., Exec. Offices, 63117-1861. Tel: 314-768-5300; Fax: 314-768-5355. Web: www.ssmrehab.com. Steven P. Johnson, Pres. Member of SSM Health Care.; For rehabilitation of pediatrics, adolescents and adults Bed Capacity: SSM St. Mary's Health Center, St. Louis 80; SSM St. Joseph Health Center, St. Charles 20; SSM DePaul Health Center, Bridgeton 22; Outpatient Locations 17.

[L] PROTECTIVE INSTITUTIONS
Day Care Centers

ST. LOUIS

Child Center of Our Lady, 7900 Natural Bridge Rd., 63121. Tel: 314-383-0200; Fax: 314-383-6334. Email: ekoszykowski@ccstl.org. Edward S. Koszykowski, Exec. Dir.

Legal Title: *Child Center of Our Lady of Grace, Inc.*, Psychiatric Treatment Center. Patients Assisted Annually 139; Total Staff 52.

Guardian Angel Settlement Association, Mailing Address: P.O. Box 2055, 63158. Tel: 314-231-3188; Fax: 314-231-8126. Email: efmurphy@guardianangelsettlement.org. Web: www.guardianangel.org. Rev. Edward F. Murphy, C.M., Exec. Dir. Founded by the Daughters of Charity of St. Vincent de Paul, Child Day Care Services and Social Services.

DeSales Child Care, 2652 Ohio, 63118. Tel: 314-771-6417; Fax: 314-231-8126.

Gabriel Child Care, 818 Cass Ave., 63106. Tel: 314-621-2898; Fax: 314-231-8126.

Guardian Angel at Hosea House, 2635 Gravois Ave., 63118. Tel: 314-773-5438; Fax: 314-773-6140.

Guardian Angel, 1401 La Salle St., 63104. Tel: 314-231-3188; Fax: 314-231-8126. Casework & Case Mgmt.; Emergency Svcs.; Senior Prog., Summer Youth Employment Prog.; Neighborhood Activities; Art, Gardening & Environmental Prog.; Paralegal on staff. For all: Total Assisted 22,214; Total Staff 53.

Sacred Heart Villa, 2108 Macklind Ave., 63110. Tel: 314-771-2224; Fax: 314-771-1262. Email: SHVilla@aol.com. Web: hometown.aol.com/shvilla. Sr. John Catherine Coleman, A.S.C.J., Dir. Conducted by the Apostles of the Sacred Heart of Jesus, Full-Time Care From 6:30-5:30 for children 3-5 years old. Total Assisted 125; Total Staff 26.

Stella Maris Child Center, 5654 Delmar Blvd., 63112-2547. Tel: 314-367-7950; Fax: 314-367-8849. Email: stellamaris2_2000@yahoo.com. Web: www.stellamariscc.org. Bonnie Shearin, Exec. Dir. Conducted by a Board of Directors and Staff of Lay Teachers. Licensed Capacity 132; Total Assisted 163; Total Staff 40.

BERKELEY

St. Martin's Child Center, 6315 Garfield, P.O. Box 34103, 63134. Tel: 314-524-4719; Fax: 314-524-5969. Email: fern.fergusonBush@sbcglobal.net. Web: www.smccinc.org. Fern Y. Ferguson Bush, Exec. Dir.

Legal Title: *St. Martin Child Center, Inc.*, Day care for children 6 weeks-14 years old. Bed Capacity 99; Infant Daycare 16; Total Assisted 100; Total Staff 21.

IMPERIAL

Queen of Apostles Center, 800 Montebello Camp Rd., 63052. Tel: 636-464-0163; Fax: 636-464-1136. Email: sam1916@aol.com. Days of Recollection, conferences and private weekend retreats. Apostles of the Sacred Heart of Jesus 3; Total Staff 8; Children 40.

KIRKWOOD

Carmelite Child Development Center, 1111 N. Woodlawn Ave., 63122. Tel: 314-822-0058; Fax: 314-822-3573 Email: vocations@carmelitedcj.org. Web: www.carmelitedcj.org. Joan Kletzker, Dir. Operated by the Carmelite Sisters of the Divine Heart of Jesus. Provides child development, child care and services. Full Day 106; Total Staff 15.

[M] HOMES FOR CHILDREN

ST. LOUIS. *Boys Hope/Girls Hope of St. Louis, Inc.*, 755 S. New Ballas Rd., Ste. 120, 63141. Tel: 314-692-7477; Fax: 314-692-7810. Email: hopestlouis@bhgh.org. Web: www.hopestlouis.org. Julie Sheridan, Exec. Dir. Residential Care for Adolescent Boys and Girls, Troubled by Family Disruptions, who are Capable of College Preparatory High School Work. Ages 7-18. Total Assisted 20; Total Staff 9.

Marian Hall Agencies, 1340 Partridge Ave., 63130. Tel: 314-726-3339; Fax: 314-726-3470. Email: sking@ccstl.org. Suzanne King, Exec. Dir.

Legal Title: *Managers of the Roman Catholic Orphan Asylums of St. Louis*, Residential Care to Homeless, Neglected and Abused Adolescent Girls (ages 11-18) with Emotional and/or Behavioral Problems. Lay Staff 24; Capacity 26; Total Assisted 43.

Marian Hall Emergency Shelter, 1340 Partridge, 63130. Tel: 314-531-7233; Fax: 314-531-2993. Email: snewberry@ccstl.org.

Legal Title: *Managers of the Roman Catholic Orphan Asylums of St. Louis*, Emergency Shelter in a Residential Setting for Runaway, Homeless or Abused Adolescent Girls (ages 11-18), with Emotional and/or Behavioral Problems. Total Staff 10; Capacity 10; Total Assisted 150.

FLORISSANT. *Father Dunne's News Boys Home*, 853 Dunn Rd., 63031. Tel: 314-837-0513; Fax: 314-837-0883. Email: kpipkins@ccstl.org. Web: www.fatherdunnes.com. Monthly Residents 20; Total in Residence 19; Total Assisted Annually 54; Total Staff 26.

Corporate Title: Father Dunnes Newsboys' Home and Protectorate Kelly Pipkins LPC, Exec. Dir.

Marygrove, 2705 Mullanphy Ln., 63031. Tel: 314-837-1702; Fax: 314-830-6268. Email: hnegri@ccstl.org. Web: www.marygroveonline.org. Sr. Helen Negri, D.C., Admin. Owned and operated under the auspices of Catholic Charities.; Residential treatment for emotionally disturbed males and females (ages 6-21). Special education, therapy and medical services. Overnight emergency care: and crisis nursery males and females (Birth-21). Bed Capacity 103; Total Assisted 4,057; Total Staff 160.

Sequoia House - Mullanphy Tel: 314-837-1702; Fax: 314-830-6260. Group Home for Females Ages 17-21. Bed Capacity 10.

Sequoia Apartment Services Tel: 314-837-1702.

Sycamore House Tel: 814-830-1329. Bed Capacity 3; Overnight Emergency Care: Bed Capacity 8; Crisis Nursery 6.

NORMANDY. *St. Vincent Home for Children*, 7401 Florissant Rd., 63121. Tel: 314-261-6011; Fax: 314-385-1467. Email: cblake@saintvincenthome.org. Web: www.saintvincenthome.org. Christopher M. Blake, Exec. Dir.

Legal Title: *The German St. Vincent Orphan Association*, Chapel of the Sacred Heart. Children 36; Total Assisted 486; Total Staff 87.

[N] HOMES FOR AGED

ST. LOUIS. *Alexian Brothers Lansdowne Village*, 4624 Lansdowne, 63116. Tel: 314-351-6888; Fax: 314-351-5825. Web: ablv.org. Tony Altobella, Admin. Total Assisted 162; Total Staff 193.

Alexian Brothers Sherbrooke Village, 4005 Ripa Ave., 63125. Tel: 314-544-1111; Fax: 314-544-5134. Email: mroth@aol.com. C. Michael Roth, Pres. Total in Residence (Assisted Living) 42; Total Assisted (Nursing Care) 115; Total Staff 164.

Fusz Pavilion A Retirement Home for Jesuits. , 3601 Lindell Blvd., 63108. Tel: 314-977-2591; Fax: 314-977-7910. Rev. Gregg H. Grovenburg, S.J., Dir.; Bro. Robert L. Aug, S.J., Aide to Dir.; Revs. Philip D. Kraus, S.J., Aide to Dir.; Lawrence E. Barry, S.J.; Donald J. Murphy, S.J.; Lucius F. Cervantes, S.J.; Francis X. Cleary, S.J.; Jules M. Brady, S.J.; John C. Choppesky, S.J.; Daryl G. Cornish, S.J.; Chester E. Gaiter, S.J.; John G. Flannigan, S.J.; Robert A. Simms, S.J.; Edward D. Harris, S.J.; William J. Kane, S.J.; Frederick E. Schuller, S.J.; Thomas F. Denzer, S.J.; Bro. Lawrence W. Eilert, S.J.; Deacon Clyde C. Croy, S.J.; Bro. C. Thomas Thornton, S.J.; Revs. John J. Walsh, S.J.; John J. Killoren, S.J.; John C. Ruoff, S.J.; Francis J. Murphy, S.J.; Pablo E. Hernandez, S.J. Priests 18; Brothers 4; Total Assisted 22; Total Staff 3.

Little Sisters of the Poor, Home for the Aged, 3225 N. Florissant Ave., 63107. Tel: 314-421-6022; Fax: 314-436-9069. Sr. Loraine Maguire, L.S.P., Supr.; Rev. Alberto Travino, M.S.F., Chap. Sisters 14; Residents 100; Total Assisted 112; Total Staff 115.

Mary, Queen and Mother Center, 7601 Watson Rd., 63119. Tel: 314-961-8000; Fax: 314-961-1548. Email: rmantia@archstl.org. Web: cardinalcarberry.org. Ronald Mantia, Admin. Skilled Nursing Facility.; A part of Cardinal Carberry Living Center Total Staff 158; Total in Residence 230.

Mother of Good Counsel Home, 6825 Natural Bridge Rd., (St. Louis Co.), 63121. Tel: 314-383-4765; Fax: 314-383-7256. Email: mogch@catholic.org. Web: mogch.com. Sr. M. Stephanie Belgeri, O.S.F., Admin. Conducted by Sisters of St. Francis of the Martyr St. George, Skilled Nursing Facility for Men and Women. Sisters 12; Residents 114; Total Staff 156.

Mother of Perpetual Help Residence, 7609 Watson Rd., 63119. Tel: 314-918-2260; Fax: 314-961-3061. Email: swesley@ccstl.org. Web: cardinalcarberry.org. Sr. Suzanne Wesley, CEO; Karen Ledbetter, Admin. A part of Cardinal Carberry Living Center Total Assisted 112; Total Staff 39.

Nazareth Living Center, 2 Nazareth Ln., 63129. Tel: 314-487-3950; Fax: 314-487-8001. Email: lwesthoff@nlccsj.com. Web: www.nazarethlivingcenter.com. Sr. Kathleen Karbowski, C.S.J., Supr.; Rev. Henry J. Garavaglia, Chap.; Lola J. Westhoff, Exec. Dir. Skilled & Assisted Living. Sisters of St. Joseph of Carondelet and General Public, Residential and Skilled Nursing Care Facility. Total Assisted 272; Total Staff 279.

Our Lady of Life Apartments, Inc., 7655 Watson Rd., 63119. Tel: 314-968-9447. Email: twalther@archstl.org. A part of Cardinal Carberry Living Center. Total Independent Living Apartments 207; Total Staff 67.

Regina Cleri Residence, 10 Archbishop May Dr., 63119. Tel: 314-968-2240; Fax: 314-968-1049. Email: reginacleri@earthlink.net. Sr. Geraldine Vogel, C.PP.S., Admin. A Residence for Retired Diocesan Priests of the Archdiocese of St. Louis. Conducted by the Archdiocese of St. Louis. Sisters of the Most Precious Blood of O'Fallon, MO 4; Franciscan Sisters of Our Lady of Perpetual Help 3; Siters of St. Joseph of Carondelet 1; Priests 38; Total Staff 20; Total Assisted 43.

EUREKA. *St. Joseph Hill Infirmary, Inc.* dba St. Joseph Hill Infirmary , St. Joseph Rd., 63025. Tel: 636-587-3661; Fax: 636-938-6398. Bro. Bernardo Trosa, O.S.F., Admin. A skilled nursing facility conducted by the Franciscan Missionary Brothers of the Sacred Heart of Jesus. Brothers 8; Residents 126; Total Assisted 120; Total Staff 55.

Price Memorial, Forby Rd., P.O. Box 476, 63025. Tel: 636-587-3200; Fax: 636-938-5266. Email: pricesnf@mindspring.com. Bro. John Spila, O.S.F., Admin. A skilled nursing facility conducted by the Franciscan Missionary Brothers of St. Joseph's Hill Infirmary. Brothers 3; Residents 120.

KIRKWOOD. *St. Agnes Home for the Elderly*, 10341 Manchester Rd., 63122. Tel: 314-965-7616; Fax: 314-965-3179. Yvonne C. Walker, Admin.; Rev. Msgr. Bernard Granich.

Legal Title: *Carmelite Sisters of the Divine Heart of Jesus of Missouri*, Conducted for Elderly Ladies, Gentlemen and Couples by the Carmelite Sisters of the Divine Heart of Jesus. Sisters 28; Guests 120; Total Staff 115; Total Assisted Annually 120.

[O] MONASTERIES AND RESIDENCES OF PRIESTS AND BROTHERS

ST. LOUIS. *The Abbey of St. Mary and St. Louis*, 500 S. Mason Rd., 63141-8500. Tel: 314-434-2557; Fax: 314-434-0795. Web: www.priory.org. Rt. Rev. Thomas Frerking, O.S.B., Abbot; Rev. M. Paul Kidner, O.S.B., Prior; Rt. Rev. J. Luke Rigby, O.S.B.; Very Rev. Timothy Horner, O.S.B.; Revs. D. Ralph Wright, O.S.B.; R. Benedict Allin, O.S.B.; P. Finbarr Dowling, O.S.B.; J. Laurence Kriegshauser, O.S.B.; J. Gregory Mohrman, O.S.B.; Gerard Garrigan, O.S.B.; Christopher Hanson, O.S.B.; Dominic Lenk, O.S.B.; Bede Price, O.S.B. Benedictines of the English Congregation Priests 13; Brother Monks 12; Total Staff 25.

Bellarmine House of Studies, 3737 Westminster Pl., 63108-3407. Tel: 314-652-8862; Fax: 314-535-4597. Revs. Ralph G. Huse, S.J., Rector & Treas.; James J. Burshek, S.J.; Christopher P. Pinne, S.J.; David J. Suwalsky, S.J.; Thomas G. Cwik, S.J., Asst. Rector; Very Rev. Frank E. Reale, S.J. Jesuit Residence for Students in the College of Philosophy and Letters of St. Louis University. Priests 6; Brothers 2; Students 14; Total Staff 2.

St. Crispin's Friary, 3731 Westminster Pl., 63108. Tel: 314-531-4506; Fax: 314-531-5494. Email: blaineb@slu.edu. Web: www.midamcaps.org. Revs. Blaine Burkey, O.F.M.Cap., Guardian; Francis Xavier Grinko, O.F.M.Cap., Vicar; Didacus Joseph Dunn, O.F.M.Cap.; Christopher Popravak, O.F.M.Cap.; Bro. Benignus Scarry, O.F.M.Cap. Priests 4; Lay Brothers 1; Postulants 3.

De Smet Jesuit High School Community, 233 N. New Ballas Rd., 63141. Tel: 314-567-3500; Fax: 314-567-1519. Email: mhdurso@hotmail.com. Revs. Michael H. Durso, S.J., Supr.; John D. Arnold, S.J.; Richard L. Bailey, S.J.; John J. Bergin, S.J.; Robert E. Bosken, S.J.; John V. Craig, S.J.; Bro. Donald E. Lee, S.J.; Rev. Michael A. Marchlewski, S.J.; Bro. Henry E. Welch, S.J. Jesuits 9.

St. Dominic Priory, 3601 Lindell Blvd., 63108. Tel: 314-977-2588; Fax: 314-977-7225. Email: joachimop@yahoo.com. Web: www.op.org/stlouis. Revs. Joachim N. Culotta, O.P., Prior; Benedict M. Ashley, O.P.; Vincent W. Bryce, O.P.; James R. Motl, O.P.; David L. Delich, O.P., Subprior; Arthur L. Kinsella, O.P. (CHI); Albert G. Glade, O.P.; Gregory J. Heille, O.P.; Richard A. Peddicord, O.P., Student Master. Total in Residence 19.

Dominican Community of St. Louis St. Louis Bertrand Priory - Province of St. Albert the Great. , 97 Waterman Pl., 63112-1820. Tel: 314-361-4445; Fax: 314-977-7225. Revs. Frank C. Quinn, O.P.; Charles E. Bouchard, O.P.; Harry M. Byrne, O.P., Prior; Charles E. Bouchard, O.P., Subprior.

Franciscan Friary of St. Anthony of Padua (Franciscan Province of the Sacred Heart-Provincial Headquarters) , 3140 Meramec St., 63118-4339. Tel: 314-353-7470; Fax: 314-353-0935. Email: provoff@aol.com. Web: www.thefriars.org. Bros. Patrick Darnell, O.F.M., Household Staff; Loyola Freightman, O.F.M., Volunteer Ministry; Leo Geurts, O.F.M., Dir. Franciscan Connection; Patrick Hanrahan, O.F.M., (Sabbatical); Herman Joseph James, Cord Machine; Christopher Lambert, O.F.M., Province Sec.; Joseph Rogenski, Dir. Franciscan Missionary Union; Revs. Andrew Lewandowski, O.F.M., Chap. for Franciscan Sisters of Mary; Elvan Maschmann, O.F.M. (Retired); John Rausch, O.F.M., Chap., St. Louis University Hospital; Bros. Nathan McNally, O.F.M., Chap. St. Anthony Hospital; Robert Gross, O.F.M., Software Eng.; Damian Pfeifer, O.F.M., Maintenance; David Schulte, O.F.M., Maintenance; William Schulte, O.F.M., Dir. Office of Public Rels. & Devel., St. Anthony Bread for the Poor & Franciscan Charities; Revs. Alois Gabrus; Robert Sieg, O.F.M., Pastor of St. Anthony's Church; Henry Willenborg, O.F.M., Dir. Office Friar Formation; Robert Behnen, O.F.M.; William Cardy, O.F.M., Chap. St. Anthony's Hosp.; Bernardine Hahn, Chap. Poor Clares; Bro. Patrick Shea, Provincial Policies; Revs. Jason Kommer (Retired), (Retired); Ladislas Siekaniec (Retired).

Legal Title: *The Franciscan Friars of the State of Missouri*, Co-sponsor of the 8th Day Center for Justice in Chicago Priests 16; Brothers 12.

106B Magnolia Ave., Berryvile, AR 72616. Tel: 870-423-4362. Rev. Martin Wolter, O.F.M., Supply Min. (Retired).

Military Chaplains: Revs. Richard Bendorf, O.F.M., South Korea; Joseph Carlos, O.F.M., CHC, USNR, Sicily, Italy.

Friars of Sacred Heart Province Serving Abroad: People's Republic of China , Guangqumen Wai Ave., West Lodge, Apt. 8D, Beijing 100022, China. Tel: 86--0-6-79-2, Ext. 10804. Rev. Albert Haase, O.F.M. Century Towers, Chao Yang District, No. 18

Foreign Experts Building, Jinan University, Shi Pai, Guangzhou 510632 China. Tel: 86-020-8522-0093. Bro. Jettery Haller, O.F.M.

Curia Generalizia dei Frati Minori, Via Santa Maria Mediatrice, 25, Rome, Italy. Tel: 390--68-91-9. Rev. James Perluzzi, O.F.M.

51 Rue Driba, Meknes-Median 50004 Morocco. Tel: 212-553-0036. Rev. Jesus Aguirre-Garza, O.F.M.

Franciscan Friars, 2-oj pereulok Mira, 10, Novosibirsk, Russia. Tel: 011-7-3832-53-53-90. Rev. James Edmiston, O.F.M.

Friars Attached to the Province but Residing Elsewhere:

Frene Valley Geriatric Center, P.O. Box 438, Hermann, 65041. Rev. Ambrose German, O.F.M. (Retired).

1782 Troy Ln., Oceanside, CA 92054. Rev. Kenneth Kieffer, O.F.M.

St. Joseph, 125 E. Broadway, Shelbyville, IN 46176. Tel: 317-398-8227. Rev. Leon Reuter, O.F.M.

1475 Upper 55th St. East, Apr. #304, Inver Grove Heights, MN 55077. Rev. Edmund Mundwiller, O.F.M.

St. Clare Villa, 915 E. 5th St., Alton, IL 62002. Tel: 618-463-9000. Rev. Finian McMullin, O.F.M.

422 S. Moody Rd., St. Croix Falls, WI 54024. Rev. Raymond Rickles, O.F.M., Counselor.

International Fraternity, Brussels, Belgium.

St. Bonaventure University, St. Bonaventure, NY 14778. Rev. Allan Wolter, O.F.M.

1215 E. Union, Litchfield, IL 62056. Rev. Theodosius A. Schelich, O.F.M., Chap. St. Francis Hospital.

Friars Associated with the Friary but Residing Elsewhere: Rev. Larry Nickels, Prov. Councilor & Interim Dir, Office of Ministries.

Hallahan House, 4511 W. Pine Blvd., 63108-2191. Tel: 314-361-7765 (day); 314-758-7125 (night); Fax: 314-758-7166. Email: rweiss@jesuits-mis.org. Web: www.jesuits-mis.org. Revs. Robert F. Weiss, S.J., Supr.; William K. Kellett, S.J., Min.; J. David Corrigan, S.J.; Thomas J. Hogan, S.J.; Thomas N. Lay, S.J.; L. Gene Martens, S.J.; Daniel C. O'Connell, S.J.; Paul C. Pilgram, S.J.; Ralph E. Vonderhaar, S.J.; Bros. Julius F. Petrk, S.J.; Richard H. Witzofsky, S.J. Total in Residence 11; Total Staff 4.

Jesuit Community Corporation at St. Louis University - Jesuit Hall, 3601 Lindell Blvd., 63108-3393. Tel: 314-977-2588; Fax: 314-977-7211. Email: comboyr@slu.edu. Revs. John W. Padberg, S.J., Rector; James H. Baker, S.J.; Lawrence H. Biondi, S.J.; Francis C. Brennan, S.J.; Joseph E. Brown, S.J.; Robert A. Brungs, S.J.; J. Richard Burtschi, S.J.; J. Eugene Coomes, S.J.; Anthony C. Daly, S.J.; Denis E. Daly, S.J.; Terrence E. Dempsey, S.J.; Everett A. Diederich, S.J.; Michael J. Doody, S.J. (BO); William B. Faherty, S.J.; Philip C. Fischer, S.J.; Robert S. Flack, S.J.; David L. Fleming, S.J.; John B. Foley, S.J.; William B. Foley, S.J. (BO); Yoshio Ignatius Futo, S.J.; Eugene E. Grollmes, S.J.; Francis J. Guentner, S.J.; Martin Hagan, S.J.; Garth L. Hallett, S.J.; W. Charles Heiser, S.J.; Harry H. Hoormann, S.J.; John F. Kavanaugh, S.J.; George V. Kennard, S.J.; John J. Killoren, S.J.; Leonard E. Kraus, S.J.; Gerhardt B. Lehmkuhl, S.J.; Edwin Lisson, S.J.; Michael W. Maher, S.J.; Michael K. May, S.J.; John L. McCarthy, S.J.; Frederick G. McLeod, S.J.; Maurice B. McNamee, S.J.; John J. Mueller, S.J.; William L. Mugan, S.J.; Edward C. O'Brien, S.J.; Martin D. O'Keefe, S.J.; Claude N. Pavur, S.J.; Frank L. Pedrotti, S.J.; Robert L. Phillips, S.J.; Donald F. Rauscher, S.J.; Raymond H. Reis, S.J.; Ralph C. Renner, S.J.; Anthony J. Rochel, S.J.; R. Bentley Anderson, S.J.; Bernard J. Barry, S.J.; Thomas Joseph Casey, S.J.; James. J. Costello; Stephen F. Mitten, S.J.; Walter G. Nesbit, S.J.; John J. Walsh, S.J.; John C. Ruoff, S.J.; James A. Sebesta, S.J.; John F.X. Sheehan, S.J.; John F. Snyder, S.J.; Carl F. Starkloff, S.J.; William V. Stauder, S.J.; John G. Valenta; James V. Veltrie, S.J.; Richard J. Vogt, S.J.; James K. Voiss, S.J.; Raymond L. Windle, S.J.; Steven J. Agostino, S.J.; Richard Comboy, S.J.; Carl A. Dehne, S.J.; John M. Hunthausen; Stephen C. Koitharayil; Robert E. O'Toole, S.J.; Patrick Viegas, S.J.; Lawrence E. Barry, S.J.; Jules M. Brady, S.J.; Lucius F. Cervantes, S.J.; John C. Choppesky, S.J.; Francis X. Cleary, S.J.; Daryl G. Cornish, S.J.; Thomas F. Denzer, S.J.; John G. Flannigan, S.J.; Joseph C. Fortier, S.J.; Chester E. Gaiter, S.J.; Gregg H. Grovenburg, S.J.; Edward D. Harris, S.J.; William J. Kane, S.J.; Philip D. Kraus, S.J.; Robert C. Luchi, S.J.; Donald J. Murphy, S.J.; Francis J. Murphy, S.J.; Albert C. Rotola, S.J.; John F. Schroder, S.J.; Frederick E. Schuller, S.J.; Robert A. Simms, S.J.; Bro. Robert L. Aug, S.J.; Deacon Clyde C. Croy, S.J.; Bro. Lawrence W. Eilert, S.J.; Rev. Pablo E. Hernandez, S.J.; Bro. C. Thomas Thornton, S.J.; Deacons William E. Biernatzki, S.J.; Kei Nishiyama, S.J.; Robert C. Snyder. Priests 90; Brothers 7; Scholastics 2.

The Jesuits of the Missouri Province, 4511 W. Pine Blvd., 63108-2191. Tel: 314-361-7765; Fax: 314-758-7164. Email: moprov@jesuits-mis.org. Web: www.jesuits-mis.org. Very Rev. Timothy M. McMahon, S.J.; Revs. Philip G. Steele, S.J., Socius & Asst. For Communications; James J. Burshek, S.J., Treas.; Thomas G. Cwik, S.J., Asst. for Social Ministries; David L. Fleming, S.J., Asst. for Formation; Christopher P. Pinne, S.J., Asst. for Vocations & Asst. Dir. Devel.; Mr. Paul Owens, Dir. Devel.; Revs. Joseph Damhorst, S.J., Delegate for Pastoral Min.; L. Gene Martens, S.J., Assoc. Dir. Devel.; David L. Fleming, S.J., Dir. Publications & Editor of the Jesuit Bulletin; Gerard E. Menard, S.J., Delegate for Sec. Educ.; William L. Mugan, S.J., Archivist; William B. Faherty, S.J., Archivist Emeritus; Robert F. Weiss, S.J., Delegate for Higher Educ. Missouri Province of the Society of Jesus Priests 236; Students in Major Seminary 15; Novices 6; Brothers 24.

Missouri Province Jesuit Priests Not Listed Elsewhere: Rev. James J. White, S.J.

12600 Hollingsworth, Kansas City, KS 66109-3821. Tel: 913-721-3966.

Lazarist Residence, 13245 Tesson Ferry Rd., 63128-3888. Tel: 314-843-0108; Fax: 314-849-1267. Revs. John F. Clark, C.M., M.A.; Joseph E. Begue, C.M.; Wilbert H. Bruns, C.M.; Robert F. Coerver, C.M.; Martin J. Culligan, C.M.; Ray Van Dorpe, C.M.; Thomas Kloppenborg, C.M.; Richard L. Lause, C.M.; Bro. Stanley Conner, C.M.; Revs. Ronald W. Ramson, C.M., Supr.; Paul Otto Schneebeck, C.M., Admin.; James E. Swift, C.M.; Jules G. Yallaly, C.M.; Gerald Brown, C.M.; Patrick J. Keeley, C.M. (SPC); Ignatius M. Melito, C.M.; Raymond Ross, C.M.; Daniel Schulte, C.M. Priests 17; Brothers 1.

Leo Brown Jesuit Community, 5047 Washington Pl., 63108. Tel: 314-367-8013; Fax: 314-367-1478. Email: psteele@jesuits-mis.org. Revs. Philip G. Steele, S.J., Supr.; Michael D. Barber, S.J.; Thomas E.J. Kelly, S.J., Supr.; Very Rev. Timothy M. McMahon, S.J.; Revs. Donald W. Reck, S.J.; Gary G. Seibert, S.J.; Robert L. Poirier, S.J. Total in Residence 7.

St. Louis University High School Jesuit Community, #3 Lawn Pl., 63110. Tel: 314-652-5425; Fax: 314-652-7028. Email: sluh.org. Revs. Thomas W. Cummings, S.J., Supr.; Richard E. Hadel, S.J.; Ralph D. Houlihan, S.J.; James J. Dougherty, S.J.; Paul G. Sheridan, S.J.; Michael D. Kurimay, S.J. Priests 6.

Marianist Community Tel: 636-938-5470; Fax: 636-938-3493. Email: mcmrcc@aol.com.

P.O. Box 718, Eureka, 63025. Tel: 636-938-5470; Fax: 636-938-3493. Email: macmrcc@aol.com. Revs. Herbert Pieper, S.M.; Jose Ramirez, S.M.; Bros. James Droste, S.M., Dir.; Fred Hausch, S.M.; Robert Massa, S.M.; Joseph Markel, S.M.; Irwin Wachtel, S.M. Priests 1; Brothers 5.

Maryknoll House, 4542 W. Pine Blvd., 63108. Tel: 314-361-7729. Email: mklstl@igc.org. Web: maryknoll.org. Revs. Stephen L. Schroeppel, M.M.; John C. Ganly, M.M.

St. Matthew Jesuit Community, 2715 N. Sarah St., 63113-2940. Tel: 314-531-6443; Fax: 314-533-7318. Email: stmatthews@sbcglobal.net. Web: www.catholic-forum.com/churches/338stmatthew. Revs. Mark D. McKenzie, S.J., Pastor; Jeffrey D. Harrison, S.J.; William Hutchison, S.J.

Missionaries of LaSalette, Province of Mary, Mother of the Americas, 4650 S. Broadway, 63111-1398. Tel: 314-353-5000; Fax: 314-353-4582. Email: lasalettestl@juno.com. Web: www.lasalette.org. Rev. Paul Mandziuk, M.S., Supr.

Legal Title: *Missionaries of La Salette Corp. of Missouri*

LaSalette Spirituality Center Tel: 314-752-0760; Fax: 314-353-4582. Rev. Dennis J. Meyer, M.S., Dir.

La Salette Communications Center Tel: 314-353-5251; Fax: 314-353-4582. Email: lasalettecom@aol.com. Revs. James R. Dunphy, M.S.; Edward Richard, M.S.; Paul Mandziuk, M.S.; Patrick McCarthy, M.S.; Thomas Ripper, M.S.; Bro. Roman Wilbers, M.S.

Rome, Italy:

Generalate, Missionari di N.S. de La Salette, Piazza Madonna della Salette, 3. Tel: -06-532-701- (39); Fax: -06-534-6218 (39). Very Rev. Isidro Perin, M.S.; Revs. Roland Nadeau, M.S., Vicar Gen.; James Staijkowski, M.S., Gen. Councillor; Andre Ravelojaona, M.S., Gen. Councillor & Treas.; Henry Kuman, M.S., Gen. Councillor; Rene Butler, M.S., Procurator to Holy See & Gen. Sec.

St. Patrick Friary, 1000 N. 7th St., 63101. Tel: 314-231-9991; Fax: 314-231-9289. Revs. Valentine Young, O.F.M.Cap., Supr.; Simon R. Conrad, O.F.M.Cap.; Canice Froehlich, O.F.M.Cap.; Simeon Gallagher, O.F.M.Cap.; Bro. Felix Shinrsy, O.F.M.Cap.; Rev. Earl Meyer, O.F.M.Cap. Priests 5.

Provincialate of the Society of Mary, Province of the United States, 4425 W. Pine, 63108-2301. Tel: 314-533-1207; Fax: 314-533-0778. Email: sglodek@sm-usa.org. Bros. Stephen Glodek, S.M., Prov.; Richard Dix, S.M., Councilor; Revs. Timothy Dwyer, S.M., Councilor; James Fitz, S.M., Asst. Prov.; Joseph Lackner, S.M., Councilor; Timothy Kenney, S.M., Asst. Education & Councilor. Total Staff 20.

Priests of the Province on Special Assignment:

St. Agatha Rectory, 1860 Northam Rd., Columbus, OH 43221-3299. Tel: 614-488-6149. Rev. John L. Bakle, S.M.

461 Montery Ave., Los Gatos, CA 95030-5302. Tel: 408-395-1816. Rev. Jorge de Silva, S.M.

8 Wildwood Gardens, F-2, Port Washington, NY 11050. Tel: 516-883-3694. Rev. Thomas J. Doyle, S.M.

Casa San Juan, 1701 Alametos, San Antonio, TX 78201. Tel: 201-734-6727. Rev. Robert E. Hogan, S.M.

25149 Hanover St., Dearborn Heights, MI 48125-1831. Tel: 313-292-0629. Rev. Raymond J. KacirkMontague, S.M.

4619 Country Ln., Apt. D, 63074-1254. Tel: 314-428-7990. Rev. James F. Kunes, S.M.

1922 Churchill Dr., South Bend, IN 46617. Tel: 219-287-2263. Rev. John A. Melloh, S.M.

5700 Blanco Rd., San Antonio, TX 78216. Tel: 201-349-4173; Fax: 201-349-4281. Rev. William Meyer, S.M.

1184 Bishop St., Honolulu, HI 96813-2857. Tel: 808-536-7036. Rev. Francis Nakagawa, S.M.

St. William the Abbott, 2000 Jackson Ave., Seaford, NY 11783. Tel: 516-785-1266; 516-785-5182 (Personal). Rev. George F. Onida, S.M.

7734 Santiago Canyon Rd., Orange, CA 92869-1829. Tel: 714-633-2698. Rev. Patrick Philibin, S.M.

5306 S. Hyde Park Blvd., Apt. 3F, Chicago, IL 60615-5749. Tel: 773-955-1817. Rev. Jemes Schimelpfening, S.M.

5440 Moeller Ave., Cincinnati, OH 45212. Tel: 513-351-3204. Rev. Kenneth J. Sommer, S.M.

5306 S. Hyde Park Blvd., Apt. 3F, Chicago, IL 60615-5749. Tel: 773-955-1817. Rev. Rudy Vela, S.M.

Jesuit Hall, 3601 Lindell Blvd., 63108. Tel: 314-977-2588. Rev. Richard Wosman, S.M.

Priests of the Province Serving Outside the USA:

St. Colmba's, Church Ave., Ballybrack, Dublin Ireland. Tel: 011-353-1285-8301; Fax: 011-353-1235-2789. Rev. Michael R. Reaume, S.M.

Priests of the Province Serving in the Missions:

Marianist Community, P.O. Box 32494, Lusaka 10101 Zambia. Tel: 011-260-124-07-45; Fax: 011-260-124-07-45. Rev. Anthony G. Jansen, S.M.

Chaminade Marianist Community, P.O. Box 100, Karonga, Malawi. Tel: 011-873-762-095059. Rev. Richard A. Loehrlein, S.M.

Marianist Novitiate, P.O. Box 210, Limuru, Kenya. Tel: 011-254-015473158. Rev. Michael F. Nartker, S.M.

Bro. Vincent House, P.O. Box 25156, Nairobi, Kenya. Tel: 011-254-2566644. Rev. Maritn A. Solma, S.M.

Special Status: Revs. John Moder, S.M.; Paul Donoghue, S.M.

Marycliff Marianist Community, 4000 Hwy. 109, Box 718, Eureka, 63025-0178. Tel: 636-938-3493. Bros. James Droste, S.M., Dir.; Fred Hausch, S.M.; Joseph Markel, S.M.; Robert Massa, S.M.; Irwin Wachtel, S.M.; Rev. Jose Ramirez, S.M. Priests 1; Brothers 5.

Chaminade-Waldron Marianist Community, 425 S. Lindbergh Blvd., 63131-2799. Tel: 314-997-4336; Fax: 314-997-4762. Rev. Ralph Siefert, S.M.; Bros. Anthony Pistone, S.M.; James Moran, S.M.; Deacons James Eppy; Kenneth Jung; Richard Middleton; Louis Pinckert, Dir. Priests 1; Brothers 6.

Maryland Avenue Marianist Community, 4528 Maryland Ave. 63108. Tel: 314-367-0390. Bro. Arthur Cherrier, S.M.; Deacon Richard M. Dix, Dir.; Bro. Arthur Cherrier, S.M.; Deacon Stephen Erspamer; Bro. Stephen Glodek, S.M.; Deacon Francis Heyer; Bros. Thomas Payne, S.M.; Robert Resing, S.M.; Deacon Kenneth Straubinger; Revs. Timothy Dwyer, S.M.; Timothy Kenney, S.M., Dir.; Alvin McMenamy, S.M. Priests 3; Brothers 7.

Marianist Community, Our Lady of the Pillar Parish, 401 S. Lindbergh Blvd., 63131-2729. Tel: 314-993-2282; Fax: 314-993-6462. Revs. J. Donald Cahill, S.M., Dir.; James Tobin, S.M.; Deacon William O'Leary, S.M. Priests 2; Brothers 1.

Marianist Community, 4314 Lindell Blvd., 63108. Tel: 314-533-3047. Bros. Charles J. Johnson, S.M., Dir.; Robert Metzger, S.M.; Jack Ventura, S.M.; Brian Zampier, S.M.; Rev. Joseph Lackner, S.M. Brothers 4; Priests 1.

Cure of Ars Marianist Community, 1311 S. Kirkwood Rd., 63122-7299. Tel: 314-965-0727; Fax: 314-835-1342. Revs. William Wightman, Dir.; Richard O'Shaughnessy, S.M.; Joseph Uvietta, S.M.; Alvin McMenamy, S.M.; Robert Osborne, S.M.; Bros. Chester Burnog, S.M.; Arthur Dofing, S.M.; Walter Ebbesmeyer, S.M.; Louis Fournier, S.M.; Francis Haug, S.M.; Gerald Hyland, S.M.; Melvin Meyer, S.M.; Eugene Meyerpeter, S.M.; Robert Minges S.M.; Joseph O'Meara, S.M.; Leonard Rudy, S.M.; Leo Slay, S.M. Priests 5; Brothers 12.

Redemptorist Fathers, 1118 N. Grand Blvd., 63106. Tel: 314-533-0304; Fax: 314-533-4260. Email: therock@saintly.com. Web: www.stalphonsusrock.org. Rev. Richard Potts, C.SS.R. Total Staff 6. In Res. Revs. William Parker, C.SS.R.; David Polek, C.SS.R.; Gary Ziuraitis, C.SS.R.; Bro. Terrance Burke, C.SS.R.; Deacon Matthew Bock.

Servants of the Paraclete, St. Michael's Community, 13270 Maple Dr., 63127. Tel: 314-965-0860; Fax: 314-965-7202. Email: manilasp@aol.com. Web: www.theservants.org. Rev. Peter Lechner, S.P.; Deacon Bernard Scollon, S.P.; Bro. John Paul Pelletier, S.P.

Vianney Renewal Center, 6476 Eime Rd., 63023. Tel: 314-274-5226; Fax: 314-274-1430.

Vincentian Community, St. Francis de Sales Rectory, 2653 Ohio Ave., 63118. Tel: 314-771-3100; Fax: 314-771-3295. Email: sfdsparish@birch.net. Revs. Paul Otto Schneebeck, C.M., Supr.; Romain G. Morales, C.M. Attached But Not In Residence:

Vincentian Residence, 10336 Corbeil Dr., 63146-5928. Tel: 314-997-5645; 314-872-2990. Revs. Lawrence F. Asma, C.M.; James T. Beighlie, C.M.

Vincentian Residence, 2912 Arsenal St., 63118. Tel: 314-771-1869; Fax: 314-771-2410. Bros. James E. Donlevy, C.M.; David Nations, C.M.; Derek Swanson, C.M.; Rev. Thomas E. Esselman, C.M.

Vincentian Residence, 2904 Arsenal St., 63118. Tel: 314-773-7633; Fax: 314-773-0882. Revs. Daniel A. Ricci, C.M.; Edward F. Murphy, C.M., Supr.; David G. Nations, C.M.; William Hartenbach, C.M.; Thomas E. Esselman, C.M.; Romain G. Morales, C.M.; Bro. David P. Goodman, C.M. Priests 4; Brothers 1.

Attached But Not In Residence: Revs. Lawrance Asma; James Beighlie; Daniel E. Harris, C.M., St. John's Seminary Theologate, Camarillo, CA 93012; P. Vincent Aherne, C.M., Carlsbad, CA; Philip M. Floersh, C.M., Tucson, AZ.

White House Retreat Jesuit Community, 7400 Christopher Dr., 63129-5799. Tel: 314-846-2575; Fax: 314-846-2575. Email: whretreat@whretreat.org. Web: www.whretreat.org.

Office, 3601 Lindell Blvd., 63108-3393. Tel: 314-533-8903; 800-643-1003; Fax: 314-533-8428. Revs. Richard O. Buhler, S.J., Dir. & Supr.; Donald M. Cunningham, S.J., Assoc. Dir.; David W. Koesterer, S.J., Assoc. Dir.; Edward C. O'Brien, S.J., Assoc. Dir.; William H. Runde, S.J., Assoc. Dir.; Bro. John Fava, S.J., Assoc. Dir.

CENTERVILLE. *Contemplative Heart of Mary Hermitage* Tel: 573-648-2467. R.R. #1 309-C, Lesterville, 63654. Tel: 573-648-2467. Rev. Robert L. Aten.

EARTH CITY. *Congregation of the Mission Midwest Province (Vincentians)*, 13663 Rider Tr. N., 63045-1512. Tel: 314-344-1184; Fax: 314-344-2989. Email: cmstlouis@aol.com. Web: www.vincentian.org. Revs. James E. Swift, C.M., Prov.; Joseph C. Geders, C.M. (CHI), Treas.

Vincentian Foreign Mission Society, 13663 Rider Tr. N., 63045-1512. Tel: 314-344-1184; Fax: 314-344-2989. Rev. James P. Graham, C.M., Dir. Office for Vincentian Foreign Missions' Personnel and Projects.

EUREKA. *Franciscan Brothers House of Studies*, Forby Rd., P.O. Box 129, 63025. Tel: 636-938-5539. Bro. John Spila, O.S.F., Dir. House of Studies of Franciscan Missionary Brothers of the Sacred Heart of Jesus Total in Residence 2; Total Staff 1.

Our Lady of the Angels Monastery, St. Joseph Rd., 63025. Tel: 636-587-3661; Fax: 636-938-4960. Web: www.franciscancaring.org. Bros. Bernardo Trosa, O.S.F., Dir. General; John Spils, O.S.F., Asst. Dir.; Rev. Josef Lukaszczyk, Chap. Generalate of Franciscan Missionary Brothers of the Sacred Heart of Jesus, Apostolate: Price Memorial Nursing Home and St. Joseph's Hill Infirmary/Black Madonna Shrine, Adult Boarding Facility at Camilus Hall Boarding Home, Merkle Knipprath Nursing home, Joliet Diocese and Countryside Villas Retirement Center, Clifton, IL 60927. Professed Brothers 12.

HIGH RIDGE. *Society of Our Mother of Peace*, Sons of Our Mother of Peace, Mary the Font Solitude, 6150 Antire Rd., 63049-2135. Tel: 636-677-3235; Fax: 636-677-0644. Email: motherofpeace@netzero.net. Rev. Placid Guste, S.M.P., Supr. Priests 1; Brothers 7; Total in Residence 8; Total Staff 2.

LIGUORI. *Alphonsian Foundation*, One Liguori Dr., 63057-9999. Tel: 636-296-3500, Ext. 21; Fax: 636-282-3272. Email: foundation@alfonsiana.edu. Web: www.alfonsiana.edu. Rev. John C. Vargas, C.SS.R., Exec. Dir.; Victor L. Ottenlips, Devel. Dir. Purpose: to provide public relations and financial support for the Alphonsian Academy of Moral Theology in Rome.

St. Clement Health Care Center, 300 Liguori Dr., 63057. Tel: 636-464-3666; Fax: 636-464-4717. Revs. Gary L. Heinecke, C.Ss.R., Rector & Admin.; John E. Bellon, C.Ss.R.; Thomas H. Cosgrove, C.Ss.R.; Joseph J. Elworthy, C.Ss.R; Wallis W. George, C.Ss.R.; Joseph M. Greenwell, C.Ss.R; Gerald B. Heim, C.Ss.R.; Bruno V. Lischwe, C.Ss.R.; John R. McPhee, C.Ss.R.; Bernard P. Mulligan, C.Ss.R.; Francis G. Novak, C.Ss.R.; James J. Nugent, C.Ss.R.; Gerard J. Pecht, C.Ss.R.; Gerard F. Resch, C.Ss.R.; J. Robert Rossbach, C.Ss.R.; Arthur R. Rossie, C.Ss.R.; Carl V. Schwarz, C.Ss.R.; Robert C. Simon, C.Ss.R.; Anthony P. Slane, C.Ss.R.; William H. (Carlos) Steiner, C.Ss.R.; Harold J. Thiel, C.Ss.R.; Ronald J. Weninger, C.Ss.R.; Deacon Richard W. Fischer, C.SS.R.; Bros. Daniel Hall, C.Ss.R.; Harry Jadczak, C.Ss.R.; Martin Shields, C.Ss.R.; Martin Temple, C.Ss.R. The Redemptorists Total in Residence 26; Total Staff 2.

Liguori Mission House/Redemptorists, Ten Liguori Dr., 63057. Tel: 314-464-6999; Fax: 314-464-6765. Email: vkliguori.org. Web: www.jcnl.com/william. Revs. Charles C. Bueche, C.SS.R.; Thomas H. Cosgrove, C.Ss.R.; Thomas Duggan, C.SS.R.; Paul Farrell, C.SS.R.; James Gleason; William Hogan, C.SS.R.; Victor Karls, C.SS.R., Supr.; Harry A. Grile, C.SS.R.; Matt Kessler, C.SS.R.; Joseph Nolen, C.SS.R.; Andrew Meiners, C.SS.R.; William McKee, C.SS.R.; Bro. Gabriel Medic, C.SS.R.; Deacon William Roberts, C.SS.R.; Revs. Thomas Danielsen, C.SS.R.; Norman J. Muckerman, C.SS.R.; James Patterson, C.SS.R.; Allan Weinert, C.SS.R.; Henry McKeever, C.SS.R. Priests 17; Brothers 2.

Redemptorists Foundation Office, One Liguori Dr., 63057-9999. Tel: 636-296-3500, Ext. 21; 800-436-0334, Ext. 21; Fax: 636-282-3272. Email: denverfoundation@sbcglobal.net. Web: www.redemptorists-denver.org. Victor L. Ottenlips, Exec. Dir. Conducted by the Redemptorist/Denver Province in the Archdiocese of St. Louis., Purpose: supports the religious and charitable purposes of the Redemptorists.

PERRYVILLE. *Congregation of the Mission*, St. Mary's Seminary, 63775-1599. Tel: 573-547-6533; Fax: 573-547-2204. Revs. John F. Gagnepain, C.M., Supr.; Robert J. Brockland, C.M.; Clarence J. Bogetto, C.M.; James A. Fischer, C.M., (Fayetteville, AR); Walter J. Reisinger, C.M., (Dixon, MO); Patrick V. Harrity, C.M., (Evansville, IN); Alphonse X. Hoernig, C.M.; Charles F. Shelby, C.M.; Charles D. Saunders, C.M.; Kenneth E. Grass, C.M.; Francis Germovnik, C.M.; Nicholas E. Persich, C.M.; Robert J. Zimney, C.M.; Louis J. Derbes, C.M.; James P. Graham, C.M.; Oscar Lukefahr, C.M.; Edward J. Mullin, C.M.; Francis H. Agnew, C.M.; Bros. Peter Baxter, C.M.; Harvey Goertz, C.M.; Richard A. Hermann, C.M.; Mark Howard Argus, C.M.; John Mangogna, C.M.; Matthew J. Teel, C.M.; Richard Zoellner, C.M. U.S. Motherhouse of the Congregation of the Mission (Vincentian Fathers, Prov. of the Midwest) Fathers 18; Professed Brothers 7; Total Staff 3.

[P] PERSONAL PRELATURES

KIRKWOOD. *Prelature of the Holy Cross and Opus Dei*, Wespine Study Center, 100 E. Essex Ave., 63122.

Tel: 314-821-1608; Fax: 314-821-4722. Email: info@wespine.org. Web: www.opusdei.org. Revs. Michael Giesler; John J. Alvarez.

[Q] CONVENTS AND RESIDENCES FOR SISTERS

ST. LOUIS. *Adorers of the Blood of Christ, United States Province*, 721 Emerson Rd., Ste. 685, 63141. Tel: 314-991-5400; Fax: 314-989-9164. Email: franklinb@adorers.org. Web: www.adorers.org. Sr. Barbara Jean Franklin, A.SC., Prin.

Carmelite Religious of Trivandrum, 4172 Delor, 63116. Sr. Vivienne Gemma Mendonca, C.C.R., Contact Person.

Congregation of Mary, Queen, 3811 Westminster Pl., 63108. Tel: 314-371-1294. Email: Dongtrinhvuong@juno.com. Web: www.trinhvuong.org. Sr. Marcianna Dinh, C.M.R., Local Supr.

Daughters of Our Mother of Peace, 5587 Page Blvd., 63112. Tel: 314-382-2592. Email: smpconvent@yahoo.com. Sr. Maryjoy Lambert, S.M.P., Supr. Sisters 3.

Daughters of St. Paul Convent, 9804 Watson Rd., 63126. Tel: 314-965-3512; Fax: 314-821-8401. Email: stlouis@pauline.org. Web: www.pauline.org. Sisters 7.

Eucharistic Missionaries of St. Theresa, 12934 Marine Ave., 63146. Tel: 314-434-1312.

Franciscan Sisters of Mary Administration, 1100 Bellevue Ave., 63117-1883. Tel: 314-768-1824; Fax: 314-768-1880. Email: jmotzel@fsmonline.org. Web: www.fsmonline.org. Jacqueline Motzel, F.S.M., Pres.; Rev. Andrew Lewandowski, O.F.M., Chap. Offices of the Franciscan Sisters of Mary & Convent. Professed Sisters in Archdiocese 123; In Residence 76.

Franciscan Sisters of Mary Novitiate, 1100 Bellevue Ave., 63117-1883. Tel: 314-768-1826; Fax: 314-768-1880. Email: scoleman@fsmonline.org. Web: www.fsmonline.org.

Franciscan Sisters of Our Lady of Perpetual Help, 335 S. Kirkwood Rd., 63122. Tel: 314-965-3700; Fax: 314-965-3710. Email: srmonica@fsolph.org. Web: www.franciscansisters-olph.org. Sr. Monica Marie Laws, O.S.F., Supr. Gen. Motherhouse and Novitate of Franciscan Sisters of Our Lady of Perpetual Help Total Sisters in the Community 127; Total Staff 4.

Heart of Mary Center, 6220 Westway Pl., 63109. Tel: 314-752-4459; Fax: 314-457-1170. Sr. Loretta Elfrink, D.H.M., Supr. Daughters of the Heart of Mary 4; Novices 1.

St. Joseph's Convent of Mercy, 611 S. New Ballas Rd., 63141. Tel: 314-569-6800; Fax: 314-569-6910. Email: cacallahan@rsm-stl.org. Sr. Carol Ann Callahan, R.S.M., Coord. Sisters of Mercy of the Americas Sisters 45.

St. Joseph's Provincial House, 6400 Minnesota Ave., 63111-2899. Tel: 314-481-8800; Fax: 314-481-2366. Email: mhadican@csjsl.org. Web: www.csjsl.org. Sisters Mary Kay Hadican, C.S.J.; Mary Kay Liston, C.S.J.; Sandra Struab, C.S.J., Province Leadership Team; Marion Renkens, C.S.J., Admin. Prov. House of the Sisters of St. Joseph of Carondelet Sisters in Province 505; In Archdiocese 351.

Loretto Center, 590 E. Lockwood, 63119-3279. Tel: 314-968-1887; Fax: 314-968-7527. Sisters 32; Total Staff 24.

Marillac Provincialate, 4330 Olive St., 63108-2622. Tel: 314-533-3004. Email: rdowney@dcwcp.org. Web: www.daughters-of-charity.org. Daughters of Charity of St. Vincent de Paul, Provincial House for Daughters of Charity.

Provincial Offices, 4330 Olive St., 63108-2622. Fax: 314-533-3226. Email: rdowney@dcwcp.org. Sr. Marie Therese Sedgwick, D.C., Visitatrix; Rev. John F. Clark, C.M., M.A., Dir. Sisters in Archdiocese 77.

Missionaries of Charity, 3629 Cottage Ave., 63113-3539. Tel: 314-533-2777. Sr. M. Rochelle, M.C., Regl. Supr. Missionaries of Charity also in: Peoria, IL; Chicago, IL; Detroit, MI; Memphis, TN; Dallas, TX; Little Rock, AR; Baton Rouge, LA; Lafayette, LA; Jenkins, KY; Atlanta, GA; Charlotte, NC; Gary, IN; Indianapolis, IN., Houston, TX; Minneapolis, MN. Sisters 6; Total Assisted 20,881.

Monastery of St. Clare of the Immaculate Conception, 200 Marycrest Dr., 63129-4813. Tel: 314-846-2618. Sr. Mary Leo Hoffman, O.S.C., Abbess. Poor Clare Nuns Cloistered Nuns 9.

Mount Grace Convent and Chapel of Perpetual Adoration, 1438 E. Warne Ave., 63107. Tel: 314-381-2654; Fax: 314-381-8869. Email: sspsap@inlink.com. Web: www.mountgraceconvent.org. P.O. Box 470219, 63147. Sr. Mary Gemma, Supr. Sister Servants of the Holy Spirit of Perpetual Adoration (Generalate, Bad Driburg, Germany)Attended by Divine Word Fathers. Sisters 26.

1438 E. Warne Ave., 63107. Tel: 314-381-2654; Fax: 314-381-8869.

1446 E. Warne Ave., 63107. Tel: 314-381-0219; Fax: 314-381-8521. Sisters 25.

Provincial House, Society of the Sacred Heart-United States Province, 4389 W. Pine Blvd., 63108. Tel: 314-652-1500; Fax: 314-534-6800. Email: provincialhouse@rscj.org. Web: www.rscj.org. Kathleen Hughes, Prov. Province Corporations: California Province of the Society of the Sacred Heart, Inc.; Ladies of the Sacred Heart of St. Louis, Missouri; Society of the Sacred Heart, Chicago Province, Inc.; Religious of the Sacred Heart, Washington Province, Inc.; Religious of the Sacred Heart, New York Province, Inc.; Religious of the Sacred Heart in Massachusetts, Inc. Total in Residence 8; Total Staff 5.

School Sisters of Notre Dame, Sancta Maria in Ripa, 320 E. Ripa Ave., 63125-2897. Tel: 314-544-0455; Fax: 314-544-6754. Email: jberkel@ssnd-sl.org. Web: www.ssnd.org. Sr. Joanne Hanrahan, Prov. Leader; Rev. Charles C. Deister, Chap.; Rev. Msgr. John M. Unger, Chap. Motherhouse of the School Sisters of Notre Dame, St. Louis Province Sisters in Diocese 344.

Interprovincial Novitiate for School Sisters of Notre Dame, 4950 Heege Rd., 63123. Tel: 314-481-8634; Fax: 314-481-8643. Sisters 5.

Liturgical Fabric Arts Tel: 314-544-0455; 314-633-7030; Fax: 314-544-6754.

Maria Center Tel: 314-544-6757; 314-633-7050; Fax: 314-544-6754.

Resource Development Tel: 314-631-3530; Fax: 314-633-7056.

Sisters of Good Shepherd Province of Mid North America, 7654 Natural Bridge Rd., 63121. Tel: 314-381-3400; Fax: 314-381-7102. Email: bbeasley@gspmna.org. Web: goodshepherdsisters.org. Sr. Barbara Beasley, R.G.S., Contact Person.

Sisters of Mercy of the Americas, Regional Community of St. Louis, 2039 N. Geyer Rd., 63131-3399. Tel: 314-966-4313; Fax: 314-909-4600. Email: jarvin@corp.mercy.net. Web: www.sistersofmercy.org. Sr. Richard Mary Burke, R.S.M., Regl. Pres. Regional Sisters in Archdiocese 70.

Convent Corporations:

Sisters of Mercy of the St. Louis Regional Community, Inc. Tel: 314-966-4313; Fax: 314-909-4600.

Other: Mercy Center, Conference Retreat Ministry Tel: 314-966-4686; Fax: 314-909-4631.

St. Joseph's Convent of Mercy of St. Louis Tel: 314-569-6800; Fax: 314-569-6910.

Education Institutions:

Begin Literacy Program Tel: 601-362-9024; Fax: 601-206-1271.

Health Institutions:

Sisters of Mercy Health System Tel: 314-965-6100; Fax: 314-957-0466.

Sisters of St. Francis of the Martyr St. George Tel: 314-383-4765; Fax: 314-383-7256. Email: srmangela@catholic.org. Web: mogch.com.

Mother of Good Counsel Home, 6825 Natural Bridge Rd., 63121. Tel: 314-383-4765; Fax: 314-383-7256. Sisters 11.

Sisters of the Good Shepherd, 7654 Natural Bridge Rd., 63121. Tel: 314-381-3400; Fax: 314-381-6449. Email: mckirst@gspmna.org. Web: www.goodshepherdsisters.org. Sr. Mary Charlotte Kirst, R.G.S., Contact Person. Sisters 12; Total Staff 10.

Society of Helpers, 2800 Olive St., Apt 12K, 63103. Tel: 314-535-2622. Sr. Patricia A. Hottinger, S.H., Contact.

Legal Title: *Society of the Helpers of the Holy Souls.*, Spiritual Direction, Parish Weeks of Guided Prayer, Seceretarial work, Visiting homebound and frail elders.; Spiritual direction, Parish Weeks of Guided Prayer, Prison Ministry.

3817 McDonald Ave., 63116. Tel: 314-776-6917. Email: Mary_Funge@claret.org.

BRIDGETON. *Cenacle Sisters*, 3437 Bridgeland Dr., 63044-2604. Tel: 314-387-2211; Fax: 314-739-5533. Sr. Mary Westhues, R.C., Local Leader. Congregation of Our Lady of the Retreat in the Cenacle Sisters 7.

Naomi House - 211, 3393 McKelvey Rd., 63044-2544.

Incarnate Word Sisters, 3393 McKelvey Rd., Apt. 326, 63044. Tel: 314-387-3326. Email: mseeker314@aol.com. Web: www.ccrtsantonio.org. Sisters Bette Bluhm, C.C.V.I., Prov. Coord.; Mary Ann Seeker, C.C.V.I., Contact. Sisters 24.

Providence Center Sisters of Divine Providence, 3415 Bridgeland Dr., 63044. Tel: 314-209-9181; Fax: 314-209-9207. Email: mjcoultas@yahoo.com. Web: www.divineprovidence-cdpmo.org. Sr. Mary Joan Coultas, C.D.P., Prov.

Legal Title: *Sisters of Divine Providence of Missouri*

Legal Title: *Sisters of Divine Providence of Missouri Charitable Trust* Offices of the Sisters of Divine Providence Sisters 48.

CHESTERFIELD. *Missionary Sisters of St. Peter Claver*, 667 Woods Mill Rd. S., P.O. Box 6067, 63006-6067. Tel: 314-434-8084; Fax: 314-469-0869. Email: Chesclaver@aol.com. Sr. M. Irene Brahmakulath, S.S.P.C., Supr. Sisters 5.

CRYSTAL CITY. *Ursuline Provincialate*, 210 Glennon Heights Rd., 63019. Tel: 636-937-6206; Fax: 636-937-7627. Email: ursulines@osucentral.org. Web: www.osucentral.org. Sr. Margaret Mary Moore, O.S.U., Prov. Prioress. Central Province of the Ursuline Nuns of the Roman Union Sisters: In Province 158; In the Archdiocese 32; In residence 9.

Other Locations:

512 S. Third St., DeSoto, 63020. Tel: 636-337-2854. Sisters 2.

353 S. Sappington Rd., 63122. Tel: 314-821-2150; Fax: 314-821-5827. Sr. Mary Ann Dooling, O.S.U., Prioress. Sisters 10.

4900 Reber Pl., 63139. Tel: 314-773-4829; Fax: 314-773-3982. Sr. Marietta Boyd, O.S.U., Prioress. Sisters 6.

1210 Paddock Dr., Florissant, 63033. Tel: 314-839-2803; Fax: 314-839-1533. Sr. Mary Lapping, O.S.U., Prioress. Sisters 3.

ELLISVILLE. *Passionist Nuns Monastery*, 15700 Clayton Rd., 63011-2300. Tel: 636-527-6867. Sr. Mary Veronica, C.P., Supr. Cloistered Contemplatives Professed Religious 10.

FLORISSANT. *Contemplative Sisters of the Good Shepherd*, 2711 Mullanphy Ln., 63031. Tel: 314-837-1719; Fax: 314-837-5925. Email: cgsflo@mindspring.com. Web: www.archstl.org. Sr. Sharon Rose Authorson, C.G.S., Supr. Sisters 19.

Pallottine Missionary Sisters-Queen of Apostles Province, 15270 Old Halls Ferry Rd., 63034-1661. Tel: 314-837-7100; Fax: 314-837-1041. Email: Pall4@juno.com. Web: www.geocities.com/pallottinerenewal. Sr. Elisabeth Heptner, S.A.C., Prov. Provincialate, novitiate & renewal center of the Missionary Sisters of the Catholic Apostolate. Professed Sisters 6; Total Staff 13.

Frascati Community and Windridge Solitude, 1932 W. Linda Ln., Lonedell, 63060-9739. Tel: 636-629-5610; Fax: 636-629-5877. Professed Sisters 3; Total Staff 6.

FRONTENAC. *Congregational Office of the Sisters of St. Joseph of Carondelet*, 2311 S. Lindbergh Blvd., 63131. Tel: 314-966-4048; Fax: 314-966-5041. Email: congtcrcsj@attglobal.net. Web: www.csjcongregation.org. Sisters Joan Henehan, C.S.J., Congregational Leadership Team; Karen Kennelly, C.S.J., Congregational Leadership Team; Theresa Kvale, C.S.J., Congregational Leadership Team; Joan Lescinski, C.S.J., Congregational Leadership Team; Barbara Moore, C.S.J., Congregational Leadership Team. Sisters 5.

Religious of the Sacred Heart Convent, Villa Duchesne, 801 S. Spoede Rd., 63131. Tel: 314-432-2021; Fax: 314-432-7713. Email: nghio@rscj.org. Sisters 4.

HIGH RIDGE. *Society of Our Mother of Peace, Daughters of Our Mother of Peace*, Mary the Fonte Solitude, 6150 Antire Rd., 63049-2135. Tel: 636-677-3235; Fax: 363-677-0644. Email: motherofpeace@netzero.com. Sr. Mary Catherine Snyder, S.M.P., Supr. Sisters 18; Total in Residence 6.

KIRKWOOD. *Carmelite Sisters of the Divine Heart of Jesus Provincial House and Novitiate* of the Central Province (St. Agnes), 10341 Manchester Rd., 63122. Tel: 314-965-1638; Fax: 314-822-3154. Email: vocations@carmelitedcj.org. Web: carmelitedcj.org. Sr. Mary Joseph Heisler, Prov. Superior. The Sisters own and operate three nursing homes and one day care center in their Province. Final Professed 17; Junior Professed 3; Novices 1; Postulants 3.

LADUE. *Carmel of St. Joseph*, 9150 Clayton Rd., 63124-1898. Tel: 314-993-6899; Fax: 314-993-5039. Email: sr-maryjoseph@mindspring.com. Web: www.stormpages.com/mtcarmel. Sr. Stella Maris, O.C.D., Prioress. Discalced Carmelites, Chapel of the Precious Blood. Professed 7; Extern Sisters 1; Temporary Professed 3.

LIGUORI. *Monastery of St. Alphonsus*, 200 Liguori Dr., 63057-9999. Tel: 636-464-1093; Fax: 636-464-9446. Email: rednun@jcnl.com. Sisters Joan E. Calver, Prioress; Mary Gerard Armstrong, Sub-Prioress; Mary Supawadee Khamsamran, Novice; Weena Suttinavin, Novice. Order of the Most Holy Redeemer (Redemptoristine Nuns) Professed 15.

LONEDELL. *Pallottine Missionary Sisters-Frascati Community and Windridge Solitude*, 1932 W. Linda Ln., 63060-9739. Tel: 636-629-5610; Fax: 636-629-5877. Email: pallotti@yhtl.net. Sr. Carolyn Callahan, Supr. Sisters 6.

NORMANDY. *Convent of the Immaculate Heart*, 7626 Natural Bridge Rd., 63121. Tel: 314-383-0300; Fax: 314-383-6523. A residence for aged & infirm Good Shepherd Sisters of the Mid-North America Prov. Total Staff 40; Total in Residence 27.

O'FALLON. *St. Mary's Institute of O'Fallon*, 204 N. Main St., 63366-2299. Tel: 636-240-3420; 636-240-6010; Fax: 636-272-5031. Email: susanb@cpps-ofallon.org. Web: www.cpps-ofallon.org. Sr. Susan Borgel, C.PP.S., Supr. Gen. Motherhouse of the Sisters of the Most Precious Blood, Chapel of St. Joseph. Sisters in Archdiocese 202.

ST. CHARLES. *Franciscan Sisters of Mary*, 320 Jackson St., 63301-3496. Tel: 636-946-7258; 636-255-0194; Fax: 636-947-5090. Email: mvehige@accessus.net.

Religious of the Sacred Heart, 301 Decatur St., 63301-2089. Tel: 636-946-7276; Fax: 636-949-6659. Email: mmmunch@rscj.org. Sisters 4.

Religious of the Sacred Heart, 800 N. 5th St., 63301. Tel: 636-946-6148. Web: www.rscj.org. Sisters 2.

Religious of the Sacred Heart-Regis, 221 Decatur St., 63301. Tel: 636-946-6456; Fax: 636-946-4425. Email: regis211@aol.com. Sisters 4.

ST. LOUIS COUNTY. *Religious of the Sacred Heart*, 13644 Conway Rd., 63141. Tel: 314-434-7687. Email: hpadberg@rscj.org. Sisters 2.

Religious of the Sacred Heart, 541 S. Mason Rd., 63141-8550. Tel: 314-878-6705. Email: lnordmann@rscj.org. Web: www.rscj.org. Sisters 6.

TOWN AND COUNTRY. *Monastery of the Visitation, St. Louis*, 3020 N. Ballas Rd., 63131. Tel: 314-432-5353; Fax: 314-432-5354. Email: sramgodefroy@visitationacademy.org. Web: www.visitationmonastery.org/stlouis. Sr. Anne Madeleine Godefroy, V.H.M., Supr. Residence of Visitation Nuns Teaching or Living at the Monastery of the Visitation. Sisters 23.

[R] HOMES FOR MEN AND WOMEN

ST. LOUIS. *Cathedral Tower*, 325 N. Newstead Ave., 63108. Tel: 314-367-5500; Fax: 314-652-2139. Email: dfagin@ccstl.org. Web: www.ccstl.org. Building which houses several agencies of Catholic Charities: Queen of Peace Center; St. Elizabeth Hall; Marian Hall; Emergency Shelter, Dial Help and Peace for Kids, Inc. Residents 150.

Father Dempsey's Hotel, Inc., 3427 Washington Ave., 63103. Tel: 314-535-7221; Fax: 314-535-7289. Email: maboussie@archstl.org. Martie Aboussie, Exec. Dir. Total in Residence 41; Total Staff 5.

Father Jim's Home, 3427 Washington Ave., 63103. Tel: 314-535-7221; Fax: 314-535-7289. Email: maboussie@archstl.org. Martie Aboussie, Exec. Dir. Total in Residence 41; Total Staff 5.

St. Martha's Hall, P.O. Box 4950, 63108. Tel: 314-533-1313; Fax: 314-533-2035. Email: stmarthas@igateway.net. Web: www.saintmarthas.org; www.ccstl.org. Michelle Schiller-Baker, Dir. Provides Shelter, Advocacy and Support to Abused Women & their Children. Capacity 25; Total Assisted Annually 300; Total Staff 12.

St. Philippine Home, 1015 Goodfellow Blvd., 63112. Tel: 314-454-1012; Fax: 314-367-7455. Lavonne McClain, Contact Person. Transitional housing for drug affected homeless city women and their children. Total Assisted 25; Total Staff 7.

Queen of Peace Center, 325 N. Newstead Ave., 63108. Tel: 314-531-0511; Fax: 314-531-1458. Email: cneumann@ccstl.org. Web: www.ccstl.org. Constance S. Neumann, Admin. Comprehensive substance abuse treatment and rehabilitation for women and their children, including in-patient/outpatient. Licensed by DMH and accredited by COA. Licensed day care, infant care, development center and licensed comprehensive psychiatric services, licensed by SMH, St. Louis City Health Department, Missouri Department of Health and accredited by COA. Transitional housing and therapeutic services for drug-affected, homeless city women and their children, accredited by COA. Housing subsidy for the disabled homeless. Bed Capacity 94; Outpatient 250; Total Assisted 5,000; Total Staff 65.

Rosati Group Home, Inc., 4218 N. Grand Blvd., 63107. Tel: 314-534-6624; Fax: 314-535-4394. Email: nboland@stpatrickcenter.org. Web: stpatrickcenter.org. Nora Boland, Admin. Group Home and Stabilization Center for homeless mentally ill adults. Total Assisted 140; Total Staff 25.

Rosati Stabilization Center, 4224 N. Grand Ave., 63107. Tel: 314-534-6624; Fax: 314-535-4394. Residential Transitional Facility for Mentally Ill Homeless.; Managed by the St. Patrick Center. Capacity 15; Total Assisted 83; Total Staff 12.

Villa Maria Center, 2647 Ohio Ave., 63118. Tel: 314-664-4715; Fax: 314-664-4970. Email: tcrumble@ccstl.org. Tammie Crumble, Site Dir. Under the Auspices of Catholic Services for Children and Youth. Comprehensive Residential Program for Pregnant and Parenting Teenage Girls; Provides Individual, Family and Group Counseling, Arranges Obstetrical and Pediatric Care, Provides Educational Services Including Academic and Personal Growth and Development, Training in Parenting and Living Skill. Capacity 15 Teens and 12 Children 0; Total Assisted 50; Total Staff 26.

NORMANDY. *Maria Droste Residence*, 7660 Natural Bridge Rd., 63121. Tel: 314-383-5553; Fax: 314-382-5294. Web: goodshepherdsisters.org. Sisters of the Good Shepherd, For Women in Need. Capacity 10; Total Assisted 70; Total Staff 6.

[S] RETREAT HOUSES

ST. LOUIS. *Mercy Center*, 2039 N. Geyer Rd., 63131. Tel: 314-966-4686; Fax: 314-909-4631. Email: mkaletta@somh.smhs.com. Mary Ann Kaletta, Admin. Operated by the Sisters of Mercy of the Americas Province St. Louis, Conference and Renewal Ministry.

White House Retreat, Office: 3601 Lindell Blvd., Ste. 204, 63108. Tel: 314-533-8903; Fax: 314-293-0931. Email: whretreat@whretreat.org. Web: www.whretreat.org.

Retreat House, 7400 Christopher Dr., 63129. Tel: 314-846-2575; Fax: 314-846-2575. Revs Richard O. Buhler, S.J., Dir.; William H. Runde, S.J., Assoc. Dir.; David W. Koesterer, S.J., Assoc. Dir.; Edward C. O'Brien, S.J.; Donald M. Cunningham, S.J., Assoc. Dir.; Bro. John Fava, S.J., Assoc. Dir. Total in Residence 6; Total Staff 6.

DITTMER. *Il Ritiro-The Little Retreat*, Eime Rd., P.O. Box 38, 63023. Tel: 636-285-3759; 636-274-0554 (Toll Free from St. Louis); Fax: 636-274-2380. Email: gpeter@nightowl.net. 7935 St. Francis Lane, 63023. Revs. Bertin Miller, O.F.M., Exec. Dir.; Michael Crosby, O.F.M.; Dismas Bonner, O.F.M.; Dennis Schafer, O.F.M.; Damien R. Dougherty, O.F.M., S.T.D.; Deacon Joe Middleton, O.F.M., Retreat Co-Dir.; Bro. Patrick Kendrick, O.F.M.; Rev. Andre Schludecker, O.F.M. Operated by the Franciscan Friars Total in Residence 8; Total Staff 6.

Vianney Renewal Center, 6476 Eime Rd., P.O. Box 130, 63023. Tel: 636-274-5226; Fax: 636-274-1430. Web: www.theservants.org. Revs. Peter Lechner, s.P., Dir. of Prog.; Edward Ralph, s.P., Father Servant; Deacon John Paul Pelletier s.P.; Dr. Rob Furey. Operated by the Servants of the Paraclete Total in Residence 17; Total Staff 5.

EUREKA. *Marianist Retreat & Conference Center*, P.O. Box 718, 63025. Tel: 636-938-5390; Fax: 636-938-3493. Email: macmrcc@aol.com. Web: www.mretreat.org. Revs. Joseph Uvietta, S.M., Dir.; Jose Ramirez, S.M. Conducted by the Society of Mary, Center for Formation and Growth in the Christian Life. Total in Residence 7; Total Staff 18.

FLORISSANT. *Pallottine Renewal Center*, 15270 Old Halls Ferry Rd., 63034. Tel: 314-837-7100; Fax: 314-837-1041. Email: Pall4@juno.com. Web: www.geocities.com/pallottinerenewal. Sr. Bernadita Peterson, S.A.C., Admin. Pallottine Missionary Sisters Total in Residence 6; Total Staff 13.

HIGH RIDGE. *Society of Our Mother of Peace Mary the Font Solitude*, 6150 Antire Rd., 63049-2135. Tel: 636-677-3235; Fax: 636-677-0644. Email: motherofpeace@netzero.net. Sr. Mary Catherine, S.M.P.; Rev. Placid Guste, S.M.P.

PEVELY. *Vision of Peace Ministries*, Abby Ln., P.O. Box 69, 63070. Tel: 636-475-3697; Fax: 636-475-3697. Email: visofpeace@juno.com. Web: www.dogbird.com/vision_of_peace. Mrs. James Ruth Muskopf. Total in Residence 2; Total Staff 2.

WILDWOOD. *La Salle Institute - Retreat and Conference Center*, 2101 Rue De La Salle, 63038-2299. Tel: 636-938-5374; Fax: 636-587-9792. Email: CBLaSalle@sbcglobal.net.

Community:, De La Salle Christian Brothers (FSC). Tel: 636-938-6142; Fax: 636-587-9792. Bro. Joseph Zastrow, Dir. Community 4; Total in Residence 4; Total Staff 7.

[T] NEWMAN CENTERS

ST. LOUIS. *University of Missouri, St. Louis, Catholic Newman Center* 8200 Natural Bridge Rd., 63121. Tel: 314-385-3455; Fax: 314-385-1523. Email: cnumsl@aol.com. Web: www.umsl.edu/~newman. Rev. William Kempf, Dir.

Washington University Newman Centers, Washington University Newman Chapel, 6352 Forsyth Blvd., 63105-2269. Tel: 314-935-9191; Fax: 314-727-6053. Email: newman@washucsc.org. Web: www.washucsc.org. Rev. Gary G. Braun, Archdiocesan Dir. of Campus Ministries. Total in Residence 1 Total Staff 15.

[U] MISCELLANEOUS

ST. LOUIS. *Alexian Brothers of Missouri, Inc., Alexian Brothers (Residence)*, 3910 Ohio, 63118-4697.

Alexian Brothers of St. Louis, Inc., Alexian Brothers (Residence), 3910 Ohio, 63118-4697.

Alexian Brothers Salus Place, 2703 Keokuk Ave., 63118. Tel: 314-771-5400; Fax: 314-771-5454. Email: dboyer@salusplace.org. Web: www.salusplace.org. Dale Wrigley, Exec. Dir. Congregation of Alexian Brothers, Immaculate Conception Province: Operated by Alexian Brothers Bonaventure House. Residence for persons with HIV/AIDS.

Almost Home, 3200 St. Vincent Ave., 63104-1336. Tel: 314-771-4663; Fax: 314-865-4692. Email: smukhtiar@almosthomestl.org. Web: www.fsmonline.org. Sheroo Mukhtair, Exec. Dir. Transitional living program for teenage mothers and their children who are homeless. Total Assisted 800; Total Staff 18.

American Academy of FertilityCare Professionals, 11700 Studt Ave., Ste. C, 63141. Tel: 314-991-0327; Fax: 314-692-8097. Email: dalydk@stlo.smhs.com. Web: aafcp.org. Mrs. Diane Daly.

Anna Trust, 6400 Minnesota Ave., 63111. Tel: 314-481-8800; Fax: 314-481-2366. A Charitable Trust Fund Established to Support the Religious and Charitable Purposes of the Sisters of St. Joseph of Carondelet, St. Louis Province.

Archdiocesan Development Appeal, 20 Archbishop May Dr., 63119. Tel: 314-792-7681, Ext. 166; Fax: 314-792-7229. Email: manna@archstl.org. Web: www.archstl.org. Teresa Manna, Dir.

Archdiocesan Planned Giving & Endowment Council, 4445 Lindell Blvd., 63108. Tel: 314-633-2222; Fax: 314-633-2333. Web: www.archstl.org. Mr. Frank J. Cognata Jr., Chief Devel. Officer; Mr. John Lenzini, Dir. Major Gifts; Mr. John A. Lally, Chair, Planned Giving & Endowment Council; Mr. Rudy Beck; Mr. George T. Bidleman Jr.; Deacon Frank Chauvin; Mr. William Drennan; Mr. David Fairchild; Rosemary Fairhead; Mr. Ron Gagnepain; Mr. Daniel Gunn; Very Rev. Robert Hermann; Mr. Jonathan W. Igoe; William Jochens; Marie Kenyon, J.D.; Joan D. Malloy; Mr. Michael Niemann; William O'Connor; Anthony O'Connor; Timothy Prosser; Charles A. Redd; Jeanne Rudolph; Sharon Sanders; Dan Shasserre; Anthony E. Veith; Daniel D. Watt; Michael Weisbrod.

Archdiocesan Stewardship Education Committee, 20 Archbishop May Dr., 63119. Tel: 314-792-7215; Fax: 314-792-7229. Email: erschen@arstl.org. Web: www.archstl.org/stewardship. Mr. Frank J. Cognata Jr., Chief Devel. Officer; Susan Erschen, Dir. Stewardship Education; Anne Carleton; Mary Reichenbach; Mr. Jim Richter; Mr. Kevin Conway; Timothy P. Killion; Craig L. Wentworth; Revs. Michael P. Boehm; Michael L. Henning; Dale P. Wunderlich; Thomas W. Wyrsch.

Ascension Health, 4600 Edmundson Rd., 63134. Tel: 314-733-8000; Fax: 314-733-8013. Email: dfrench@ascensionhealth.org. Web: www.ascensionhealth.org. Douglas D. French, Pres. & CEO. Co-sponsored by four of the United States Provinces of the Daughters of Charity: Northeast Prov., Albany, NY; Southeast Prov., Emmitsburg, MD; East Central Prov., Evansville, IN; West Central Prov., St. Louis, MO and by the Congregation of the Sisters of St. Joseph of Nazareth, Nazareth, MI and the Congregation of the Sister of St. Joseph of Carondelet.

Aware, Inc., St. Anthony's Medical Center, 10016 Kennerly Rd., 63128. Tel: 314-525-1622. Karen Molner, Pres.

B.R.E.M. Catholic Social Ministry, 1371 Hamilton Ave., 63112. Tel: 314-383-4666; Fax: 314-383-0334. Janese Prince, Interim Dir. Provides Employment Counseling and Referrals, Health Outreach, and Referrals for Food and Clothing. Also Provides Community Education, Leadership Development, Family Support and Community Development Services. Total Assisted 3,000; Total Staff 2.

Birthright, 2206 S. Brentwood Blvd., 63144. Tel: 314-962-5300; Fax: 314-962-7606. Web: www.birthrightstlouis.org. Shirley E. Ducey, Admin. Dir. Total Assisted 7,000; Total Staff 20.

Branch Offices:

170 Clarkson Exec. Park, 63011. Tel: 636-227-2266; Fax: 636-227-2012.

6680 Chippewa, 63109. Tel: 314-962-3653; Fax: 314-351-4531.

3435A Bridgeland, 63044. Tel: 636-227-8775; Fax: 314-298-0813.

205 N. 5th St., St. Charles, 63301. Tel: 636-724-1200; Fax: 636-946-0447.

625 N. Euclid, 63108. Tel: 636-946-4900.

Cardinal Carberry Senior Living Center, 7609 Watson Rd., 63119. Tel: 314-961-8000; Fax: 314-961-1934. Email: swesley@ccstl.org. Web: www.cardinalcarberry.org; www.ccstl.org. Sr. Suzanne Wesley, Contact Person.

Cardinal Glennon Children's Hospital Foundation,

1465 S. Grand Blvd., 63104. Tel: 314-577-5605; Fax: 314-268-6416. Email: info@glennon.org. Web: www.glennon.org. Member of SSM Health Care

The Caroline Trust, 320 E. Ripa Ave., 63125-2897. Tel: 314-633-7021; Fax: 314-633-7057. Email: lindajansen@ssnd-sl.org. Supports the Religious and Charitable Purposes of the School Sisters of Notre Dame and Provides Support for the Aged, Infirm and Disabled Sisters of the Province.

Carondelet Health Association, 4600 Edmundson Rd., 63134. Tel: 314-770-0333; Fax: 314-770-0444. Email: atersign@ascensionhealth.org. Web: chs-stl.com. Anthony R. Tersigni, Board Chair. Tel: 314-770-0333.

Catholic Charities Dial Help, 325 N. Newstead, 63108. Tel: 314-371-4357; Fax: 314-652-2139. Email: dfaginccstl.org. Debbie Fagin, Dir. Information/Referral Svcs. Information and Referral Service Operated by Catholic Charities. Total Assisted 32,869; Total Staff 3.

Catholic Charities Foundation, 4532 Lindell Blvd., 63108. Tel: 314-367-5500; Fax: 314-367-2982. Email: jstutz@ccstl.org. Web: www.ccstl.org. James C. Stutz, Pres. A Charitable Fund Established to Support the Activities of Catholic Charities.

Catholic Charities Refugee Services, 2840 Wisconsin Ave., 63118. Tel: 314-771-2570; Fax: 314-771-6406. Email: ccrs@prodigy.net. To Facilitate the Resettlement of Refugees. Total Staff 8; Total Assisted 264.

Catholic Charities Volunteer Department, 4532 Lindell Blvd., 63108. Tel: 314-367-5500, Ext. 155; Fax: 314-367-2982. Email: mcunningham@ccstl.org. Web: www.ccstl.org. Recruiting and referral office for volunteers serving the Catholic Charities Foundation within some 125 programs offering assistance to children, adolescents, families, olderpersons, and other vulnerable people. Full time lay volunteers in conjunction with the St. Vincent Pallotti Center.

Catholic Commission on Housing, 800 N. Tucker Blvd., 63101. Tel: 314-241-5600; Fax: 314-241-5608. Email: ccoh@ccstl.org. Web: www.ccstl.org. Karen Wallensak, Exec. Dir. An Agency of the Catholic Charities Federation that helps low and moderate-income families purchase their first home; maintain and repair their property; avoid foreclosure; and achieve financial stability. Total Staff 7; Total Assisted 1,563.

Catholic Community Services Administration, 20 Archbishop May Dr., 63119. Tel: 314-792-7054; Fax: 314-792-7056. Email: jmarks@ccstl.org. Web: www.ccsach.org. Dr. Jerry Marks, D.S.W., A.C.S.W., Exec. Dir. A Consolidation of Catholic Charities Out neighborhood outreach centers, and the Archbishop's Commission on Community Health.

Midtown Catholic Community Services, 1202 S. Boyle Ave., 63110-3814. Tel: 314-534-1180; Fax: 314-534-3727.

Jefferson County Catholic Community Services, P.O. Box 668, Festus, 63028-0668. Tel: 636-931-1912; Fax: 636-933-5148.

Father Tolton Catholic Community Services, 4746 Carter Ave., 63115. Tel: 314-385-3445; Fax: 314-385-4479.

St. Jane Catholic Community Services, 7005 Ascension Dr., 63121-3427. Tel: 314-383-6539; Fax: 314-383-6591.

St. Joseph Catholic Community Services, 6322 Minnestoa, 63111-2553. Tel: 314-351-6407; Fax: 314-752-3896.

Southside Catholic Community Services, 2647 Ohio, 63118. Tel: 314-773-6100; Fax: 314-773-2346.

St. Charles Catholic Community Services, 6055 Mexico Rd., St. Peters, 63376-1632. Tel: 636-498-2273; Fax: 636-498-0390.

Catholic Community Services-Vietnamese Center, 2647 Ohio Ave., 63118-1533. Tel: 314-664-8990; Fax: 314-773-2346.

Catholic Community Services - Friends of Moms, 2647 Ohio Ave., 63118-1533. Tel: 314-771-7423; Fax: 314-771-2346.

Language Access Metro Project (LAMP), 2647 Ohio Ave., 63118-1533. Tel: 314-865-5267; Fax: 314-772-2369.

Catholic Charities Refugee Services, 2840 Wisconsin Ave., 63118-1656. Tel: 314-771-2570; Fax: 314-771-6406. For all: Total Families Assisted 29,000; Total Staff 81.

Catholic Deaf Ministry, Blessed John XXIII Center, 8300 Morganford Rd., 63123-6815. Tel: 314-633-2540; 314-633-2548 (TDD). Email: vbarnhart@archstl.org. Provides Services for Deaf and Hearing Impaired Persons.

Catholic Family Services dba Catholic Family Counseling, 20 Archbishop May Dr., 63119. Tel: 314-792-7030; Fax: 314-792-7059. Email: jmarks@ccstl.org. Web: www.ccstl.org. Dr. Jerry Marks, D.S.W., A.C.S.W., Exec. Dir. Provides professional counseling (individual & small groups) to individuals, couples & families experiencing stress. Family Life Education and Outreach available. Fees based on ability to pay.

District Offices:

South, 20 Archbishop May Dr., 63119. Tel: 314-792-7030; Fax: 314-792-7059.

Northwest, 4450 Washington, Florissant, 63033. Tel: 314-831-1533; Fax: 314-831-5478.

West County, 498 Woods Mill Rd., Manchester, 63011. Tel: 636-391-9966; Fax: 636-394-4678.

St. Charles/Troy, 6055 Mexico Rd., St. Peters, 63367. Tel: 636-498-2273; Fax: 636-498-0390.

North City, 2405 N. Grand, 63113. Tel: 314-535-0017; Fax: 314-535-3155.

Crystal City/Festus/Perryville, 109 N. Mill, Festus, 63028. Tel: 636-937-2157; 636-937-2163; 800-652-8055; Fax: 636-937-3172.

Franklin/Warren Counties, 119 W. Locust, Union, 63084. Tel: 636-583-1800; 800-583-8355; Fax: 636-583-0836.

St. Vincent Church: De Paul Bldg., 1010 Rosati Ct., Perryville, 63775. Tel: 573-547-4591; 800-652-8055. For all: Total Assisted 9,615; Total Staff 46.

The Catholic Health Association of the United States, 4455 Woodson Rd., 63134-3797. Tel: 314-427-2500; Fax: 314-427-0029. Web: www.chausa.org. Rev. Michael D. Place, S.T.D., Pres. & CEO. Established June 24, 1915.

Catholic High School Association, 20 Archbishop May Dr., 63119. Tel: 314-792-7300; Fax: 314-792-7399. Email: stlsupt@archstl.org. Web: www.archstl.org/education/. Mr. George Henry, Supt.

Catholic Education Office, Archdiocesan Pastoral Center, 20 Archbishop May Dr., 63119-5004. Tel: 314-792-7300; Fax: 314-792-7399. Mr. George Henry, Supt.

Catholic Information Center, 1000 N. Seventh St., 63101. Tel: 314-621-6555; 314-231-9991; Fax: 314-231-9289. Rev. Valentine Young, O.F.M.Cap., Dir.

Catholic Kolping Society of America, 4035 Keokuk St., 63116. Tel: 314-776-5312. Otto J. Eichhorn, Treas.

Catholic Office of Disability Ministry, 20 Archbishop May Dr., 63119. Tel: 314-792-7150; 314-792-7158 (TDD); Fax: 314-792-7159. Email: dministry@archstl.org. Web: www.archstl.org. Jane Walker, Dir.

Catholic Services for Children & Youth, 20 Archbishop May Dr., Ste. 2200, 63119. Tel: 314-792-7400; Fax: 314-792-7438. Email: RKing@ccstl.org. Web: www.ccstl.org. Mr. Richard L. King, A.C.S.W, Exec. Dir. Child Welfare Agency Providing Adoption, Post Adoption Services, Foster Family Care, Expectant Parent Service and Intake and Referral Services. Total Staff 25.

Central Bureau of the CCUA, 3835 Westminster Pl., 63108-3472. Tel: 314-371-1653; Fax: 314-371-0889. Email: centbur@juno.com. Web: www.socialjusticereview.org. Rev. John H. Miller, C.S.C., Dir. & Editor of the Social Justice Review.

St. Charles Lwanga Center, 4746 Carter Ave., 63115-2238. Tel: 314-367-7929; Fax: 314-367-4134. Email: info@lwangacenter.org. Jane Wexler Brown, Exec. Dir. A spiritual formation Center that focuses primarily on the African American Catholic Community, in the Archdiocese of St. Louis and throughout the United States. Provides leadership and development for junior high and teenage youth. In collaboration with all Christians, conducts weekend marriage preparation workshops. Specialized evangelization outreach is arranged according to the expressed needs of the pastors. Total Staff 6.

Chiara Corporation, 1100 Bellevue Ave., 63117-1883. Tel: 314-768-1817; Fax: 314-768-1803. Email: joshaughnessy@fsmonline.org. Mr. John O'Shaughnessy, Contact Person. Ministries that promote, enhance and provide for the spiritual, religious, physical or mental well-being of members of society in accordance with the religious and charitable purposes of the Franciscan Sisters of Mary.

Child Center Foundation, 7900 Natural Bridge Rd., 63121. Tel: 314-383-0200; Fax: 314-383-6334. Email: ekoszykowski@ccstl.org. Andrew Condie, Pres., Bd. of Directors. Child Center Foundation provides financial support to the Child Center of Our Lady, a residential and day treatment facility serving severely emotionally disturbed children and their families.

Collaborative Daminican Novitiate, 4928 Washington Blvd., 63108. Tel: 314-454-0664; Fax: 314-454-3849. Email: awalters@grdominicans.org. Maria Beesing, O.P., Contact Person; Ann Walters, O.P., Contact Person.

CSJ Ministries, 6400 Minnesota Ave., 63111. Tel: 314-481-8800; Fax: 314-481-2366.

Daughters of Charity Foundation, 231 S. Bemiston, Ste. 350, 63105. Tel: 314-802-2060; Fax: 314-802-2051. Email: jkuester@docfdn.org. Web: www.daughtersofcharityfdn.org. Sr. Joan Kuester, D.C., Pres. Provides funds for the poor & underserved; will fund projects related to health education & wellness primary/preventive medical svcs. & social svcs.

Daughters of Charity Healthcare Foundation of St. Louis, 231 S. Bemiston, Ste. 350, 63105. Tel: 314-802-2060; Fax: 314-802-2051. Web: www.daughtersofcharityfdn.org. Email: jkuester@docfdn.org. Sr. Joan Kuester, D.C., Pres.

Daughters of Charity National Health System, Inc., 4600 Edmundson Rd., 63134. Tel: 314-733-8000; Fax: 314-733-8013. Email: dfrench@ascensionhealth.org. Douglas D. French, Pres. & CEO.

De Mattias Jubilee Corporation, 721 Emerson Rd., Ste. 685, 63141. Tel: 314-991-5400; Fax: 314-989-9164. Email: reidk@adorers.org. Sr. JoAnn Mark, A.S.C., Chairperson.

Dismas House of St. Louis, 5025 Cote Brilliante Ave., 63113. Tel: 314-361-2802; Fax: 314-367-0604. John R. Flatley, Exec. Dir. Total in Residence 170; Total Staff 60.

Equestrian Order of the Holy Sepulchre of Jerusalem, 7 Huntleigh Trails Ln., 63131. Tel: 314-966-8660; Fax: 314-909-9454. Email: vinceshaw@hotmail.com. Mr. Vincent E. Shaw, Lieutenant.

St. Francis de Sales Association, 10140 Chaucer, Apt. #3, 63114-2340. Tel: 314-428-8542. Email: priggelja@att.net. JoAnn Priggel, Valley Regl. Dir. A call to the laity to live their individual vocation in the spirit of Jesus, using the writings of St. Francis de Sales as a means to see and do God's will and grow in holiness.; Private Universal Association of the Faithful.

The Franciscan Connection, 2903 Cherokee St., 63118. Tel: 314-773-8485; Fax: 314-353-0958; 314-773-8573. Bro. Leo Geurts, O.F.M., Contact Person.

Friends of the Archbishop, 4445 Lindell Blvd., 63108. Tel: 314-633-2273; Fax: 314-633-2306. Todd Schnuck, Chm.; Rev. Msgr. Richard F. Stika, V.G., Incorporator. Purpose: To Raise Funds to Support the Roman Catholic Archdiocese of St. Louis.

Good Shepherd Programs, Inc., 7654 Natural Bridge Rd., 63121. Tel: 314-381-3400; Fax: 314-382-5294. Web: goodshepherdsisters.org. Operates the Maria Droste Residence. Total Staff 6; Total Assisted 70.

Hispanic Ministry of the Archdiocese of St. Louis, 20 Archbishop May Dr., 63119. Tel: 314-792-7890; Fax: 314-792-7898. Email: hmolina@archstl.org. Mr. Hector Antonio Monlina Jr., Dir.; Mrs. Sylvia Ledesma Ortiz, Youth Minister. Total Staff 2.

Holy Angels Apartments, Inc., 7601 Watson Rd., 63119. Tel: 314-652-3600, Ext. 291; Fax: 314-652-8840. Email: bperrone@ccstl.org. Web: www.ccstl.org/cri/independent.html.

Incarnate Word Foundation, Missouri, 5257 Shaw Ave., Ste. 309, 63110. Tel: 314-773-5100; Fax: 314-773-5102. Email: iwfdn@swbell.net. Web: www.incarnatewordfund.com. Bridget M. Flood, Exec. Dir.

Institute for Theological Encounter with Science & Technology (ITEST), 3601 Lindell Blvd., 63108. Tel: 314-977-2703; Fax: 314-977-7211. Email: postigm@slu.edu. Web: ITEST.slu.edu. Rev. Robert A. Brungs, S.J., Dir.

Institute of Jesuit Sources, 3601 Lindell Blvd., 63108. Tel: 314-977-7257; Fax: 314-977-7263. Email: ijs@slu.edu. Web: www.jesuitsource.com. Rev. John W. Padberg, S.J., Dir.

Intercommunity Housing Association, 3407 Lafayette Ave., Ste. 204, 63104-1313. Tel: 314-664-6811; Fax: 314-664-7189. Email: intercomm.housing@aol.com. Web:. Provides safe, affordable housing & supportive svcs. for economically disadvantaged & working poor families in St. Louis operates Pillar Place Apartments, Compton Place Apartments. Total Staff 3; Total Assisted 126.

Jesuit Community - Ministries, 3601 Lindell Blvd., 63108. Tel: 314-977-2588; Fax: 314-977-7211. Email: comboyr@slu.edu. Rev. John W. Padberg, S.J., Rector. Total in Residence 99.

The Jesuits of the Missouri Province, Office of Development: 4517 W. Pine Blvd., 63108. Tel: 314-361-7765; Fax: 314-758-7163. Email: development@jesuits-mis.org. Web: www.jesuits-mis.org. Mr. Paul Owens, Dir.; Revs. L. Gene Martens, S.J., Assoc. Dir.; Christopher P. Pinne, S.J., Assoc. Dir.

Legal Title: *The Jesuits of the Missouri Prov.*

St. John's Mission, 4517 W. Pine Blvd., 63108. Tel: 314-361-7765; Fax: 314-758-7163. Email: development@jesuits-mis.org. Web: www.jesuits-mis.org.

Ladies of Charity of St. Catherine Laboure, 12160 Leelaine Dr., 63126. Susan Tumminia, Pres.

Affiliate with Ladies of Charity of the United States & the Assoc. of Intl. Charities of St. Vincent de Paul.

Ladies of Charity of St. Vincent-Guardian Angel, Tel: 314-231-9328; Fax: 314-621-2232. Email: stvstl@swbell.net. Affiliate with Ladies of Charity of the United States & the Assoc. of Intl. Charities of St. Vincent de Paul.

St. Vincent's Church: 1408 S. Tenth St., 63104. Tel: 314-231-9328; Fax: 314-621-2232.

Ladies of Charity of the United States of America, P.O. Box 31697, 63131-0697. Tel: 314-344-1184; Fax: 314-344-2989. Email: lcstlouis@aol.com. Web: www.famvin.org/lcusa. Margaret Hanson, Pres. LCUSA continues, expands, and improves the charitable works of the local associations of the LCUSA, which number 79.

Ladies of Charity Service Center, 7500 Natural Bridge Rd., 63121. Tel: 314-383-4207; Fax: 314-383-0605. Cindy Barry, Coord.

Legal Title: *Ladies of Charity Service Center*, Ladies of Charity Service Center; Thrift Store & Food Pantry Total Assisted 28,910; Total Staff 60.

St. Louis Catholic Charismatic Renewal, 8300 Morganford Rd., 63123. Tel: 314-633-2570, Ext. 418; Fax: 314-633-2584. Email: dennis@stlcharismatic.org. Web: stlcharismatic.org. Deacon Dennis Chitwood, Liaison & Dir.; Robert Gleason, Admin.

Abiding Bible Companion Tel: 314-725-6527.

Healing & Deliverance Ministry Tel: 314-633-2577; Fax: 314-633-2584.

Jonah Teams Tel: 314-633-2578; Fax: 314-633-2584.

Overflowing Joy Ministry Tel: 314-633-2570; Fax: 314-633-2584.

Genesis Tel: 314-633-2570; Fax: 314-633-2584.

Tree House Healing Ministry Tel: 314-633-2574; Fax: 314-633-2584.

Theotokos Ministry, 4311 S. Compton, 63111. Tel: 314-351-6061. Center with books & tapes, prayer time, ministry times, retreats for parishes, leaders training, small faith groups, conferences, special events & days of renewal.

Mary and Joseph Trust, 1100 Bellevue Ave., 63117-1883. Tel: 314-768-1817; Fax: 314-768-1803. Email: joshaughnessy@fsmonline.org.

Mary Queen Charitable Trust Fund, LaSallette Missionaries, 4650 South Broadway, 63111. Tel: 314-353-5000.

St. Mary's Health Center Foundation, 6420 Clayton Rd., 63117. Tel: 314-768-8067; Fax: 314-768-8011. Email: Karen_harriman@ssmhc.com. Web: www.stmarys-stlouis.com. Member of SSM Health Care.

McAuley Charitable Trust, 2039 N. Geyer Rd., 63131-3399. Tel: 314-909-4617; Fax: 314-909-4622. Email: kglosenger@corp.mercy.net. Sr. Katherine Marie Glosenger, R.S.M., Contact Person. The Sisters of Mercy of the Americas, Regional Community of St. Louis

National Christian Life Community of the United States of America (CLC), 3601 Lindell Blvd., Rm. 202 (Jesuit Hall), 63108-3393. Tel: 314-977-7370; Fax: 314-977-7211. Web: www.clc-usa.org. Lois Campbell, Pres. Founded c. 1540 & approved 1584, a public, intl. assn. of the Faithful of Pontifical Right which builds small Faith-Communities for mission & Svc. to the church. It uses the Spiritual Exercises of Saint Ignatius of Loyola as its specific source & characteristic instrument for its spirituality. Membership equally open to primarily catholic christian men, women, youth & young adults, clergy, brothers & sisters.

Network of Sacred Heart Schools, Inc., 4389 W. Pine Blvd., 63108. Tel: 314-652-1500; Fax: 314-534-6800. Email: nshoffice@sofie.org. Web: www.sofie.org. Madeleine Ortman, Dir.

Notre Dame Ministry Corporation, 320 Ripa Ave., 63125. Tel: 314-544-0455; Fax: 314-544-6754. Includes: Notre Dame High School, Notre Dame Preschool, Notre Dame Tutorial Center, Immigrant & Refugee Women's Program, & The Family Center.

Our Lady's Inn, 4223 S. Compton, 63111. Tel: 314-351-4590; Fax: 314-351-2119. Email: glee@ourladysinn.org. Web: www.ourladysinn.org. Gloria Lee, Contact Person. A residential shelter for pregnant women who have no home, who are being abused, who have no one who cares, and/or who are being pressured to abort their baby. We provide living facilities, food, clothing, counseling, vocational guidance and followup care. Total Assisted 350; Total Staff 18.

St. Patrick Center, 800 N. Tucker, 63101. Tel: 314-802-0700; Fax: 314-802-1981. Email: gvogelweid@stpatrickcenter.org. Web: stpatrickcenter.org. An Agency in Downtown St. Louis, Housing a Wide Range of Social Services for Mentally Ill and/or Chemically Dependent Homeless Persons and for Residents in the Area at Risk of Becoming Homeless. Total Assisted 10,000; Total Staff 125.

Pauline Books and Media, 9804 Watson Rd., 63126. Tel: 314-965-3512; Fax: 314-821-8401. Email: stlouis@pauline.org. Web: www.pauline.org. Daughters of St. Paul

Pelletier Trust, a Charitable Trust of the Sisters of the Good Shepherd 63121. Tel: 314-381-3400; Fax: 314-381-6449.

Perpetual Help Retirement Corporation, 335 S. Kirkwood Rd., 63122. Tel: 314-965-3700; Fax: 314-965-3710. Email: srmonica@fsolph.org. Web: www.franciscansisters-olph.org. Established by the Franciscan Sisters of Our Lady of Perpetual Help to Support the Religious and Charitable Purposes of the Franciscan Sisters of Our Lady of Perpetual Help.

Redemptorist of Mattese, 1118 N. Grand Blvd., 63106. Tel: 314-533-0304; Fax: 314-533-4260. Bro. Terrance Burke, C.SS.R.

Review for Religious, 3601 Lindell Blvd., Rm. 428, 63108. Tel: 314-977-7363; Fax: 314-977-7362. Email: review@slu.edu. Web: www.reviewforreligious.org. Rev. David L. Fleming, S.J., Editor. Total Staff 6.

Sacred Heart Program, Inc., 3900 Westminster Pl., 63108. Tel: 314-533-0320; Fax: 314-533-0335. Email: gkolarcik@sacredheartprogram.org. Web: www.sacredheartprogram.org. Gary Kolarcik, Exec. Dir. The Sacred Heart Program produces "Contact", an international radio broadcast featuring real-life stories of people dealing with the issues and challenges of everday life. Topics reflect the principles of Catholic social teaching. It also produces "Contact Minutes", a series of one-minute radio spots dealing with basic human needs and family values. The organization also fosters devotion to the Sacred Heart and offers a number of devotional items. Total Staff 8.

The Sarah Community, 1100 Bellevue Ave., 63117-1883. Tel: 314-768-1833; Fax: 314-768-1880. Email: jmotzel@fsmonline.org. Purpose: provides retirement housing and services to members of religious congregations and laity. Operates the following: Anna House, a skilled nursing facility; Veronica House, a residential care facility; Naomi House, an independent living facility.

The Sarah Community Foundation, 1100 Bellevue Ave., 63117-1883. Tel: 314-768-1833; Fax: 314-768-1880. Email: jmotzel@fsmonline.org. Jacqueline Motzel, F.S.M., Contact Person.

Sisters of the Good Shepherd Province of Mid-North America Foundation, 7654 Natural Bridge Rd., 63121 Tel: 314-381-3400; Fax: 314-381-7102. Email cmcquaid@gspmna.org. Web: goodshepherdsisters.org. Sr. Mary Caroline McQuaid, R.G.S.

Society of St. Vincent De Paul, Council of St. Louis, 4127 Forest Park Ave., 63108-2808. Tel: 314-531-2183; Fax: 314-531-6712. Email: debbiem@svdpstl.org. Web: www.svdpstl.org. Lay-based volunteer organization which provides both direct aid and program services to all eleven counties of the Archdiocese. Affiliated with 167 parishes.; Car donation program whose proceeds benefit agency programs and services.; Serves the incarcerated, their families, and victims through a three-fold approach of direct service, public education, and advocacy for systemic change within the judicial and corrections systems.; Provides referrals for people seeking work, for those addicted to drugs or alcohol, and for those with emotional problems.; Archdiocesan outreach program targeting hunger and utility relief, administered by the Society of St. Vincent De Paul.; Provides direct assistance to domestic abuse victims treated by St. Martha's Hall and Kathy J. Weinman Shelter.; Provides household resources to members attempting to help needy individuals. Offers low-cost items for sale to the public. Proceeds benefit agency programs and services. Total Assisted 245,000; Total Staff 35; Volunteer Members 2,500.

Cars For A Cause, 4127 Forest Park Ave., 63108-2808. Tel: 800-240-4225; Fax: 314-531-6712.

Criminal Justice Ministry, 1408 S. 10th St., 63104. Tel: 314-241-8062; Fax: 314-241-1307.

1st STEP Support Ministry, 4127 Forest Park Ave., 63108. Tel: 314-531-2183; Fax: 314-531-6712.

Food and Fuel for Life, 4127 Forest Park Ave., 63108-2808. Tel: 314-531-2183; Fax: 314-531-6712. Richard J. Klohr III, Pres.

Susanna Family Violence Ministry, 4127 Forest Park Ave., 63108-2808. Tel: 314-531-2183; Fax: 314-531-6712.

St. Vincent De Paul Thrift Store, 4127 Forest Park Ave., 63108. Tel: 314-531-2183; Fax: 314-531-6712. Provides household resources to members helping needy individuals. Offers low-cost ites for sale to the public. Proceeds benefit agency programs and services.

Society of St. Vincent DePaul, Council of the United States, 58 Progress Pkwy., 63043-3706. Tel: 314-576-3993; Fax: 314-576-6755. Email: usacouncil@svdpusa.org. Web: www.svdpusa.org. Most Rev. Edwin M. Conway, D.D., Auxiliary Bishop of Chicago, Episcopal Advisor; Eugene B. Smith, Pres.; Roger T. Playwin, Exec. Dir.

SSM Health Businesses, 477 N. Lindbergh, 63141. Tel: 314-994-7900; Fax: 314-994-7900. Email: june_pickett@ssmhc.com. Member of SSM Health Care.

SSM Health Care Corporation, 477 N. Lindbergh, 63141. Tel: 314-994-7800; Fax: 314-994-7782. Email: june_pickett@ssmhc.com. Member of SSM Health Care.

SSM Health Care Portfolio Management Company, 447 N. Lindbergh Blvd., 63141. Tel: 314-994-7800; Fax: 314-994-7900. Email: june_pickett@ssmhc.com. Member of SSM Health Care

SSM Health Care St. Louis, 1173 Corporate Lake Dr., 63132. Tel: 314-989-2020; Fax: 314-989-2400. Web: www.ssmhealth.com. Email: judy_gartland@ssmhc.com. Member of SSM Health Care

SSM Hospice and Home Care Foundation, 477 N. Lindbergh Blvd., 63141. June L. Pickett, Contact Person.

SSM Regional Health Services, 477 N. Lindbergh Blvd., 63141. Tel: 314-994-7800; Fax: 314-994-7900. Email: june_pickett@ssmhc.com. Member of SSM Health Care.

SSM Rehab Foundation, 6420 Clayton Rd., Exec. Offices, 63117. Tel: 314-768-5358; Fax: 314-768-5355. Email: peg_dube@ssmhc.com. Web: www.ssmrehab.com. Member of SSM Health Care.

St. Louis City Catholic Church Real Estate Corporation, 4445 Lindell Blvd., 63108. Rev. Msgr. Richard F. Stika, V.G., Registered Agent.

St. Louis County Catholic Church Real Estate Corporation, 20 Archbishop May Dr., 63119. Gerard J. Hoeing, Registered Agent.

Saint Stanislaus Historical Mission Society, #1 St. Francois P.O. Box 1095, 63031. Tel: 314-361-5122; Fax: 314-758-7166. Email: pastoral@jesuits-mis.org. Dr. Edwin Benton, Curator; Lynn Cocks, Pres.; Robert Gronemeyer, Treas.; Jean Frett, Sec. Total in Residence 1; Total Staff 10.

Theology Digest, 3800 Lindell Blvd., 63156-0907. Tel: 314-977-3410; Fax: 314-977-3704. Email: thdigest@slu.edu. Total Staff 3.

St. Vincent Pallotti Center for Apostolic Development, 4532 Lindell Blvd., 63108. Tel: 314-367-5500, Ext. 155; Fax: 314-361-5099. Web: pallotticenter.org. Email: mcunningham@ccstl.org. Develop, enhance and support lay, full-time volunteer ministries by bringing together Clergy, Religious and Laity; (See Catholic Charities Volunteer Department)

The Vincentian Press Religious Supply, 1405 S. Ninth St., 63104. Tel: 314-421-2834; Fax: 314-421-0684. Rev. Joseph E. Begue, C.M., Dir. Total Staff 3.

We & God Spirituality Center, 3601 Lindell Blvd., 63108. Tel: 314-977-2696; Fax: 314-977-7211. Email: wgsc@slu.edu. Web: www. slu.edu/orginazations/wgsc.

**Women for Faith and Family*, P.O. Box 8326, 63132. Tel: 314-863-8385; Fax: 314-863-5858. Email: editor@wf-f.org. Web: www.wf-f.org. Mrs. Helen Hull Hitchock, Pres.

Women of Providence in Collaboration, 3415 Bridgeland Dr., 63044. Tel: 314-209-9181; Fax: 314-209-9207. Email: bmcmullen6650@aol.com. Sr. Barbara McMullen, C.D.P., Contact Person.

ARNOLD. *Jefferson County Catholic Church Real Estate Corporation*, 2300 Church St., 63010. Rev. Paul J. Nieman, Registered Agent.

BONNE TERRE. *St. Francois County Catholic Church Real Estate Corporation*, 15 St. Joseph St., 63628. Rev. John H. Schneider, Registered Agent.

BRIDGETON. *Boys Hope Girls Hope*, 12120 Bridgeton Square Dr., 63044. Tel: 314-298-1250; Fax: 314-298-1251. Email: hope@bhgh.org. Web: www.boyshopegirlshope.org. Paul A. Minorini, Pres. & CEO. A College Prepatory Residential Child Care Agency Serving Abandoned, Abused and Neglected Children. Founded in 1977; With affiliated programs in: Baton Rouge; Chicago; Cincinnati; Denver; Detroit; Jacksonville; Nevada; New Orleans; New York; Northeast Ohio; Orange County, CA; Phoenix; Pittsburgh; St. Louis; San Antonio; San Francisco, Baltimore, Kansas City. Total Assisted 5,000; Total Staff 130.

DePaul Health Center Foundation, 12303 DePaul Dr., 63044. Tel: 314-344-7477; Fax: 314-344-6172. Email: sherry_weber@ssmhc.com. Web: www.ssmdepaul.com. Member of SSM Health Care.

Providence Ministry Corporation, 3415 Bridgeland Dr., 63044. Tel: 314-209-9181; Fax: 314-209-9207. Email: mjcoultas@aol.com. Web: www.divineprovidence-cdpmo.org. Sr. Mary Joan

Coultas, C.D.P., Contact Person.

CADET. *Rural Parish Workers of Christ the King*, R.R. 1, Box 1667, 63630. Tel: 636-586-5171; Fax: 636-586-5918. Email: rpwck@jcn.net. Web: web.jcn.net/rpwck. Miss Natalie Villmer, Gen. Dir. A Secular Institute of the Archdiocese of St. Louis. Workers 5; Total Assisted 2,500; Total in Residence 5; Total Staff 6.

Washington County Catholic Church Real Estate Corporation, Rte. 1, Box 1110, 63630. Rev. Theodore X. Pieper.

CHESTERFIELD. *Gareway Educational Foundation, Inc.*, 69 Graymore Dr., 63017. Tel: 914-773-1368. Rev. Juan Sabadell, L.C., Sec. & Treas.

Saint Louis LaSalle Leadership, Inc., 645 Clovertrail Dr., 63017-2612. Tel: 314-434-8789; Fax: 314-434-8789. Email: stl3i@aol.com. Waldemar E. Bode, Pres.; John J. Hall, Sec.; Staunton E. Boudreau, Treas.

CRYSTAL CITY. *St. Louis Area Women Religious Collaborative Ministries*, 210 Glennon Heights Rd., 63019. Tel: 636-937-6206; Fax: 636-937-7627. Email: peggy.moore@osucentral.org. Sr. Margaret Mary Moore, O.S.U., Contact Person.

Ursuline Sisters Trust Fund, 210 Glennon Heights Rd., 63019. Tel: 636-937-6206; Fax: 636-937-7627. Email: carolyn@osucentral.org. Web: http://www.osucentral.org. Sr. Carolyn Marie Brockland, O.S.U.

EARTH CITY. *Congregation of the Mission International Fund*, 13663 Rider Tr. N., 63045-1512. Tel: 314-344-1184; Fax: 314-344-2989. Email: cmstlouis@aol.com.

Lazarist Trust Fund, 13663 Rider Tr. N., 63045-1512. Tel: 314-344-1184; Fax: 314-344-2989. Email: cmstlouis@aol.com.

EUREKA. *Providence Trust*, Our Lady of the Angels Monastery, St. Joseph Rd., 63025. Fax: 636-938-4960. Web: www.franciscancaring.org. Purpose: To support the religious and charitable purposes of the Franciscan Missionary Brothers of the Sacred Heart.

FLORISSANT. *Marygrove Services, Inc.*, 2705 Mullanphy, 63031. Tel: 314-837-1702; Fax: 314-830-6263. Email: hnegri@csstl.org. Web: www.marygroveonline.org. Total Assisted 91; Total Staff 10.

Pope John Paul II Apartments, Inc., 6325 Waterways Dr., 63033. Tel: 314-653-0400; Fax: 314-653-2840. Email: bperrone@ccstl.org. Web: www.ccstl.org/cri/independent.html. Purpose: to provide facilities and services specifically designed to meet the physical, social, spiritual and psychological needs of elderly persons.

STE. GENEVIEVE. *Ste. Genevieve County Catholic Church Real Estate Corporation*, 49 DuBourg Pl., Sainte Genevieve, 63670. Rev. Daniel E. Mosely, Registered Agent.

KIRKWOOD. *St. Joseph Hospital of Kirkwood Foundation*, Tel: 314-966-1644; Fax: 314-966-1681. Email: arlene_sullivan@ssmhc.com. Web: www.stjosephkirkwood.com. 525 Couch Ave., 63122. Tel: 314-966-1644; Fax: 314-966-1681. Member of SSM Health Care.

LIGUORI. *Redemptorist Fathers dba Liguori Publications*, One Liguori Dr., 63057. Tel: 636-464-2500; Fax: 636-464-8449. Email: hgrile@liguori.org. Web: www.liguori.org. Rev. Harry A. Grile, C.SS.R., Pres. & Publisher.

MARTHASVILLE. *Warren County Catholic Church Real Estate Corporation*, 7602 S. Hwy. 94, 63357. Rev. John J. Borcic, Registered Agent.

O'FALLON. *Centers for Professional and Pastoral Services*, 204 N. Main St., 63366-2299. Tel: 636-240-6010; Fax: 636-272-5031. Email: ruthk@cpps-ofallon.org. Sr. Susan Borgel, C.PP.S. Sponsored by Sisters of the Most Precious Blood of O'Fallon, MO Centers 4; Total Assisted 400; Total Staff 5.

Charitable Trust, Sisters of the Most Precious Blood of O'Fallon, MO, 204 N. Main St., 63366-2299. Tel: 636-240-6010; Fax: 636-272-5031. Email: nadinef@cpps-ofallon.org. Web: www.cpps-ofallon.org. Trust fund for support of retired Sisters of the Most Precious Blood.

St. Dominic Endowment Fund, St. Dominic High School, 31 St. Dominic Dr., 63366. Tel: 314-240-8303; Fax: 314-240-9884. Email: mainoffice@stdominichs.org. Web: www.stdominichs.org. Sr. Mary H. Bender, S.S.N.D., Treas.

PERRYVILLE. *Association of the Miraculous Medal*, 1811 W. St. Joseph St., 63775. Tel: 573-547-8343; Fax: 573-547-1389. Email: amm1@amm.org. Web: www.amm.org. Rev. Charles F. Shelby, C.M., Pres.

Catholic Home Study Service, P.O. Box 363, 63775. Tel: 573-547-4084. Email: chss@ldd.net. Web: www.amm.org/chss.htm. Rev. Oscar Lukefahr, C.M., Dir.

Offers free correspondence courses on the Catholic Faith.

Ladies of Charity of St. Vincent de Paul Parish, 1010 Rosati Ct., 63775. Tel: 573-547-4591; Fax: 573-547-4145. Email: svdepaul@svdepaul.org. Dorothy Barry, Pres. Affiliate with Ladies of Charity of the United States & the Assoc. of Intl. Charities of St. Vincent de Paul. Total Assisted 790.

Perry County Catholic Church Real Estate Corporation, 1000 Rosati Ct., 63775. Rev. Kevin P. Fausz, C.M., Registered Agent.

St. Vincent De Paul Educational Foundation, 1010 A Rosati Ct., 63775. Tel: 573-547-4591; Fax: 573-547-4145. Email: svdepaul@svdepaul.org. Web: www.svdepaul.org. Rev. Kevin P. Fausz, C.M., Moderator. Develops, Promotes and Sustains Catholic Education in Perry County.

SILEX. *Lincoln County Church Real Estate Corporation*, 29 St. Alphonsus Rd., 63377. Rev. Frank A. D'Amico, Registered Agent.

ST. CHARLES. *Academy of the Sacred Heart of St. Charles, Missouri Endowment Trust Fund*, 619 N. 2nd St., 63301. Tel: 636-946-5632; Fax: 636-949-6659. Email: mcaire@ash1818.org. Web: www.ash1818.org.

Duchesne High School Endowment Fund Inc., 2550 Elm St., 63301. Tel: 636-946-6767; Fax: 636-946-6267. Email: tgravemann@duchesne-hs.com. Web: www.duchesne-hs.org. Terry W. Gravemann, Admin. Receives Bequests and Gifts from Various Donors for the Express Purpose of Aiding and Benefitting Duchesne High School, St. Charles, and by Investment and Use of Such Bequests and Gifts and Income therefrom Aids and Benefits the High School in Fulfilling its Educational Purposes.

Sts. Joachim and Ann Care Service, 4112 McClay Rd., 63304. Tel: 636-441-1302; Fax: 636-447-6283. Email: jacares@sbcglobal.net. Miriam Mahan, Exec. Dir.

St. Joseph Health Center and St. Joseph Hospital West Foundation, 300 First Capitol Dr., 63301. Tel: 314-947-5612; Fax: 314-947-5090. Web: www.ssmstjoseph.com. Member of SSM Health Care.

St. Charles County Catholic Church Real Estate Corporation, 601 N. Fourth St., 63301. Rev. Richard J. Tillman, Registered Agent.

Warrenton Senior Village, Inc., Hwy. U & Woolf Rd., Warrenton, 63383.

WASHINGTON. *Franklin County Catholic Church Real Estate Corporation*, 311 W. Second St., 63090. Rev. John M. Costello, Registered Agent.

RELIGIOUS INSTITUTES OF MEN REPRESENTED IN THE ARCHDIOCESE

For further details refer to the corresponding bracketed number in the Religious Institutes of Men or Women section.

[0120]—*Alexian Brothers* (Chicago)—C.F.A.
[0140]—*The Augustinians. (Prov. of Our Mother of Good Counsel)*—O.S.A.
[0200]—*Benedictine Monks. (English, Swiss American Congregation)*—O.S.B.
[]—*Brothers of St. Charles Lwanga*—B.S.C.L.
[0330]—*Brothers of the Christian Schools. (St. Louis Prov.)*—F.S.C.
[0470]—*The Capuchin Friars* (Kansas City, MO)—O.F.M.Cap.
[1330]—*Congregation of the Mission. (Midwest Prov.)*—C.M
[0630]—*Congregation of the Missionaries of the Holy Family* (Europe)—M.S.F.
[1000]—*Congregation of the Passion (Eastern Prov. of Holy Cross)*—C.P.
[1000]—*Congregation of the Passion (Western Prov. of Holy Cross)*—C.P.
[1130]—*Congregation of the Priests of the Sacred Heart*—S.C.J.
[1080]—*Congregation of the Resurrection* (Rome, Italy)—C.R.
[0480]—*Conventual Franciscans. (Our Lady of Consolation Prov.)*—O.F.M.Conv
[0520]—*Franciscan Friars. (Croatian Franciscan Commissariat, Sacred Heart Prov.)*—O.F.M.
[0540]—*Franciscan Missionary Brothers of the Sacred Heart of Jesus* (Eureka, MO)—O.S.F.
[0690]—*Jesuit Fathers and Brothers* (Missouri Prov.)—S.J.
[0730]—*Legionaries of Christ*—L.C.
[0800]—*Maryknoll*—M.M.
[0720]—*The Missionaries of Our Lady of La Salette*—M.S.
[0870]—*Monfort Missionaries*—S.M.M.
[0430]—*Order of Preachers*—O.P.
[0610]—*Priests of the Congregation of Holy Cross*—C.S.C.
[1070]—*Redemptorist Fathers* (Denver Prov.)—C.SS.R.
[1230]—*Servants of the Paraclete*—s.P.
[1240]—*Servites* (Chicago)—O.S.M.
[0760]—*Society of Mary* (St. Louis Prov.)—S.M.
[0975]—*Society of Our Lady of the Most Holy Trinity*—S.O.L.T.
[0420]—*Society of the Divine Word* (Northern Prov.)—S.V.D.
[]—*Sons of Our Mother*—S.M.P.

RELIGIOUS INSTITUTES OF WOMEN REPRESENTED IN THE ARCHDIOCESE

[0100]—*Adorers of the Blood of Christ* (U.S. Prov.)—A.S.C.
[0130]—*Apostles of the Sacred Heart of Jesus*—A.S.C.J.
[0360]—*Carmelite Sisters of the Divine Heart of Jesus* (Carmel)—D.C.J.
[3110]—*Congregation of Our Lady of the Retreat in the Cenacle*—R.C.
[]—*Congregation of Our Lady of the Rosary*
[]—*Congregation of Our Lady of the Sacred Heart*
[]—*Congregation of St. Catherine of Siena*
[]—*Congregation of the Most Holy Rosary*
[0460]—*Congregation of the Sisters of Charity of the Incarnate Word*—C.C.V.I.
[1730]—*Congregation of the Third order of St. Francis Oldenburg, IN*—O.S.F.
[1830]—*Contemplatives of the Good Shepherd*—C.G.S.
[0760]—*Daughters of Charity of St. Vincent de Paul*—D.C.
[]—*Daughters of Our Mother of Peace*—S.M.P.
[0810]—*Daughters of the Heart of Mary*—D.H.M.
[0420]—*Discalced Carmelite Nuns*—O.C.D.
[1070-19]—*Dominican Sisters* (of Houston, TX)—O.P.
[]—*Eucharist Missionaries of St. Theresa*—M.E.S.T.
[1370]—*Franciscan Missionaries of Mary*—F.M.M.
[1310]—*Franciscan Sisters of Little Falls, Minnesota*—O.S.F.
[1415]—*Franciscan Sisters of Mary*—F.S.M.
[1430]—*Franciscan Sisters of Our Lady of Perpetual Help*—O.S.F.
[]—*Franciscan Sisters, Daughters of the Sacred Hearts of Jesus and Mary*
[2340]—*Little Sisters of the Poor*—L.S.P.
[2490]—*Medical Mission Sisters*—M.M.S.
[2710]—*Missionaries of Charity*—M.C.
[0390]—*Missionary Carmelites of St. Teresa*—C.M.S.T.
[3990]—*Missionary Sisters of St. Peter Claver*—S.S.P.C.
[3760]—*Order of St. Clare*—O.S.C.
[2010]—*Order of the Most Holy Redeemer*—O.SS.R.
[0950]—*Pius Society Daughters of St. Paul*—F.S.P.
[3170]—*Religious of the Passion of Jesus Christ*—C.P.
[3465]—*Religious of the Sacred Heart of Mary*—R.S.H.M.
[2970]—*School Sisters of Notre Dame*—S.S.N.D.
[]—*Sinsinawa Dominican Congregation of the Most Holy Rosary*
[0430]—*Sisters of Charity of the Blessed Virgin Mary*—B.V.M.
[0460]—*Sisters of Charity of the Incarnate Word* (San Antonio, TX)—C.C.V.I.
[0660]—*Sisters of Christian Charity*—S.C.C.
[0990]—*Sisters of Divine Providence*—C.D.P.
[2360]—*Sisters of Loretto at the Foot of the Cross* (St. Louis Prov.)—S.L.
[2570]—*Sisters of Mercy*—R.S.M.
[2580]—*Sisters of Mercy of the Americas*—R.S.M.
[1540]—*Sisters of Saint Francis, Clinton, Iowa*—O.S.F.
[1600]—*Sisters of St. Francis of the Martyr St. George*—F.S.G.M.
[3830]—*Sisters of St. Joseph*—C.S.J.
[1830]—*Sisters of the Good Shepherd*—R.G.S.-C.G
[3270]—*Sisters of the Most Precious Blood* (O'Fallon, MO)—C.PP.S.
[3150]—*Sisters of the Pallottine Missionary Society*—S.A.C.
[3540]—*Sisters Servants of the Holy Spirit of Perpetual Adoration*—S.Sp.S.deA
[2150]—*Sisters, Servants of the Immaculate Heart of Mary*—I.H.M.
[1890]—*Society of Helpers of the Holy Souls*—S.H.
[4070]—*Society of the Sacred Heart*—R.S.C.J.
[4110]—*Ursuline Nuns*—O.S.U.
[4190]—*Visitation Nuns*—V.H.M.

ARCHDIOCESAN CEMETERIES

ST. LOUIS. *Calvary*, 5239 W. Florissant Ave., 63115. Tel: 314-381-1313.

SS. Peter and Paul, 7030 Gravois Ave., 63116. Tel: 314-352-5300.

Resurrection, 6901 Mackenzie Rd., 63123. Tel: 314-352-5300.

ARNOLD. *St. Vincent Cemetery*, Romaine Creek Rd., 63010. Tel: 314-352-5300. Rev. Msgr. Robert

McCarthy, Dir.

CREVE COEUR. *St. Monica*, 12136 OLive Blvd., 63141. Tel: 314-352-5300.

FLORISSANT. *Sacred Heart*, Graham Rd., 63033. Tel: 314-381-1313.

GLENCOE. *Holy Cross*, 16200 Manchester Rd., 63038. Tel: 314-352-5300.

HAZELWOOD. *St. Ferdinand*, Graham Rd., 63042. Tel: 314-381-1313.

St. Mary, 5200 Fee Fee Rd., 63042. Tel: 314-381-1313.

KIRKWOOD. *St. Peter*, 520 W. Monroe Ave., 63122. Tel: 314-381-1313.

LAKE ST. LOUIS. *Cemetery of Our Lady*, Freymuth & Orf Rd., 63366. Tel: 314-381-1313.

LEMAY. *Mount Olive*, 3906 Mount Olive Rd., 63125. Tel: 314-352-5300.

ST. CHARLES. *St. Charles Borromeo*, Randolph St., 63301. Tel 314-381-1313.

Ste. Philippine Cemetiere, 4057 Towers Rd., 63304. Tel: 314-381-1313. Rev. Msgr. Robert McCarthy, Dir.

WAHINGTON. *Ascension*, 5563 Country Club Rd., Washington, 63090. Tel: 314-352-5300.

NECROLOGY

† Dwyer, Rev. Msgr. Adrian I., St. Louis, MO St. Roch Rectory—Died June 5, 2003

† Peet, Rev. Msgr. Arthur V., (Retired)—Died Nov. 22, 2002

† Regan, Rev. Msgr. Michael F., (Retired)—Died Jan. 14, 2003

† Shocklee, Rev. Msgr. John A.—Died Feb. 6, 2003

† Carey, Donald D., (Retired)—Died Nov. 14, 2003

† Eilers, Joseph B., (Retired)—Died Nov. 15, 2003

† Hemkens, Edward B., (Retired)—Died March 18, 2003

† Hoffman, Donald J., (Retired)—Died Oct. 27, 2003

† Hrdlicka, Lambert A., (Retired)—Died June 9, 2003

† Keutzer, Walter J., (Retired)—Died April 29, 2003

Archdiocese of St. Paul and Minneapolis

(Archidioecesis Paulopolitana et Minneapolitana)

Most Reverend

HARRY J. FLYNN, D.D.

Archbishop of Saint Paul and Minneapolis; ordained May 28, 1960; appointed Coadjutor of Lafayette April 19, 1986; consecrated June 24, 1986; appointed Bishop of Lafayette May 13, 1989; appointed Coadjutor Archbishop of Saint Paul and Minneapolis February 22, 1994; appointed Archbishop of Saint Paul and Minneapolis September 8, 1995.

Chancery: 226 Summit Ave., St. Paul, MN 55102. Tel: 651-291-4400; Fax: 651-290-1629.

Web: www.archspm.org

Email: archcom@archspm

Most Reverend

FREDERICK F. CAMPBELL, D.D.

Auxiliary Bishop of Saint Paul and Minneapolis; ordained May 31, 1980; appointed Titular Bishop of Afufenia and Auxiliary Bishop of St. Paul and Minneapolis March 2, 1999; consecrated May 14, 1999 *Office: 226 Summit Ave., St. Paul, MN 55102.* Tel: 651-291-4400.

Most Reverend

RICHARD E. PATES

Auxiliary Bishop of Saint Paul and Minneapolis; ordained December 20, 1968; appointed Titular Bishop of Suacia and Auxiliary Bishop of Saint Paul and Minneapolis December 22, 2000; ordained March 26, 2001. *Office: 226 Summit Ave., St. Paul, MN 55102.* Tel: 651-291-4400.

Square Miles 6,187.

Diocese Established, July 19, 1850. Archdiocese Established, May 4, 1888.

Comprises the following twelve Counties of the State of Minnesota: Ramsey, Hennepin, Anoka, Carver, Chisago, Dakota, Goodhue, Le Sueur, Rice, Scott, Washington and Wright.

Corporate Title: The Archdiocese of Saint Paul and Minneapolis.

For legal titles of parishes and archdiocesan institutions, consult the Chancery.

STATISTICAL OVERVIEW

Personnel	
Archbishops	1
Auxiliary Bishops	2
Priests: Diocesan Active in Diocese	220
Priests: Diocesan Active Outside Diocese	8
Priests: Diocesan in Foreign Missions	2
Priests: Retired, Sick or Absent	91
Number of Diocesan Priests	321
Religious Priests in Diocese	128
Total Priests in Diocese	449
Extern Priests in Diocese	44
Ordinations:	
Diocesan Priests	7
Transitional Deacons	6
Permanent Deacons	7
Permanent Deacons in Diocese	210
Total Brothers	65
Total Sisters	991
Parishes	
Parishes	220
With Resident Pastor:	
Resident Diocesan Priests	169
Resident Religious Priests	25
Without Resident Pastor:	
Administered by Priests	14
Administered by Deacons	2
Administered by Lay People	5
Missions	5
Pastoral Centers	4
New Parishes Created	1
Closed Parishes	1
Professional Ministry Personnel:	
Brothers	2
Sisters	70
Welfare	
Catholic Hospitals	5
Total Assisted	187,000
Health Care Centers	1
Total Assisted	175
Homes for the Aged	7
Total Assisted	1,084
Residential Care of Children	1
Total Assisted	2,400
Specialized Homes	4
Total Assisted	1,200
Special Centers for Social Services	19
Total Assisted	10,000
Residential Care of Disabled	3
Total Assisted	150
Educational	
Seminaries, Diocesan	2
Students from This Diocese	67
Students from Other Diocese	76
Diocesan Students in Other Seminaries	3
Seminaries, Religious	1
Students Religious	23
Total Seminarians	93
Colleges and Universities	3
Total Students	16,835
High Schools, Diocesan and Parish	10
Total Students	8,245
High Schools, Private	3
Total Students	551
Elementary Schools, Diocesan and Parish	92
Total Students	29,483
Elementary Schools, Private	3
Total Students	499
Catechesis/Religious Education:	
Elementary Students	66,500
Total Students under Catholic Instruction	122,206
Teachers in the Diocese:	
Priests	19
Brothers	10
Sisters	39
Lay Teachers	1,847
Vital Statistics	
Receptions into the Church:	
Infant Baptism Totals	10,022
Adult Baptism Totals	401
Received into Full Communion	1,304
First Communions	10,290
Confirmations	7,922
Marriages:	
Catholic	1,789
Interfaith	1,042
Total Marriages	2,831
Deaths	4,633
Total Catholic Population	730,989
Total Population	2,949,643

Former Bishops—Rt. Rev. JOSEPH CRETIN, D.D., consecrated Jan. 26, 1851; died Feb. 22, 1857; Most Revs. THOMAS L. GRACE, O.P., D.D., consecrated July 24, 1859; resigned July 31, 1884; named Titular Bishop of Menith, and later, Titular Archbishop of Siunia; died Feb. 22, 1897; JOHN IRELAND, D.D., cons. Dec. 21, 1875; Bishop of Maronea, and Coadjutor to; THOMAS L. GRACE, O.P., D.D., succeeded to the See of St. Paul, July 31, 1884; appt. Archbishop, May 15, 1888; died Sept. 25, 1918; AUSTIN DOWLING, D.D., Archbishop of St. Paul; ord. June 24, 1891; appt. Bishop of Des Moines, Iowa, Jan. 31, 1912; consecrated April 25, 1912; Nominated Archbishop of St. Paul, Feb. 1, 1919;; died Nov. 29, 1930; JOHN GREGORY MURRAY, S.T.D., ord. April 14, 1900; appt. Titular Bishop of Flavias, Auxiliary to the Bishop of Hartford, Nov. 15, 1919; consecrated April 28, 1920; transferred to the Diocese of Portland, May 29, 1925; appt. Archbishop of St. Paul, Oct. 29, 1931; died Oct. 11, 1956; WILLIAM O. BRADY, D.D., Archbishop of St. Paul; ord. Dec. 21, 1923; appt. Bishop of Sioux Falls, June 10, 1939; consecrated Aug. 24, 1939; appt. Titular Archbishop of Selymbria and Coadjutor "cum jure successionis" of St. Paul, June 16, 1956; succeeded to See, Oct. 11, 1956; died Oct. 1, 1961; LEO C. BYRNE, D.D. Coadjutor Archbishop "cum jure successionis" of Saint Paul and Minneapolis ord. June 10, 1933; appt. titular Bishop of Sabidia and Auxiliary of St. Louis, May 21, 1954; consecrated June 29, 1954; transferred to Wichita, "cum jure successionis" 1961; appt. Apostolic Administrator of Wichita, Feb. 25, 1963; promoted to St. Paul and Minneapolis, Aug. 2, 1967; died Oct. 21, 1974; LEO BINZ, D.D., ord. March 15, 1924; appt. Titular Bishop of Pinara and Coadjutor Bishop of Winona, Nov. 21, 1942; consecrated Dec. 21, 1942; Titular Archbishop of Silyum and Coadjutor to the Archbishop of Dubuque "cum jure successionis," Oct. 15, 1949; Archbishop of Dubuque, Dec. 2, 1954; appt. Archbishop of Saint Paul, Dec. 16, 1961; resigned May 21, 1975; died Oct. 9, 1979; JOHN R. ROACH, D.D., Archbishop of St. Paul and Minneapolis; ord. June 8, 1946; appt. Titular Bishop of Cenae and Auxiliary Bishop of St. Paul and Minneapolis, July 12, 1971; consecrated Sept. 8, 1971; appt. Archbishop of St. Paul and Minneapolis, May 21, 1975; resigned Sept. 8, 1995; died July 11, 2003.

Chancery—226 Summit Ave., St. Paul, 55102. Tel: 651-291-4400; Fax: 651-290-1629. Office Hours: Mon.-Fri. 9-5; All Official business should be directed to this office.

Vicar General and Moderator of the Curia—Rev. KEVIN M. MCDONOUGH, J.C.D.

Chancellor for Civil Affairs—Mr. WILLIAM S. FALLON, J.D.

Chancellor for Canonical Affairs—Sr. M. DOMINICA BRENNAN, O.P., J.C.L.

Episcopal Vicars—

For Catholic Teaching—Most Rev. FREDERICK F. CAMPBELL, D.D.

For Clergy; For Evangelization; For Youth and Young Adults—Most Rev. RICHARD E. PATES.

For Canonical Affairs; For African-American

Catholics; For Hispanic Ministry—Rev. KEVIN M. McDONOUGH, J.C.D.
For Marriages—Rev. KEVIN M. McDONOUGH, J.C.D.
For Retired Priests—Rev. RICHARD J. MAHONEY (Retired).
Co-Vicars for Religious—Sisters DOMINICA BRENNAN, O.P.; FRAN DONNELLY, B.V.M.
Archdiocesan Divisions—
Administration and Financial Services—VACANT, Dir.
Christian Formation and Education—THOMAS McCARVER, Dir.
Ministry Personnel—Sr. FRAN DONNELLY, B.V.M., Dir.
Outreach—Rev. KEVIN M. McDONOUGH, J.C.D., Interim Dir.
Community Services—Rev. LARRY J. SNYDER, Dir.
Resource Development—Ms. MICKEY NICKELSON, Dir.
Conciliation Office—Sr. M. DOMINICA BRENNAN, O.P., J.C.L.
Administrative Asst. to the Vicar General and to the Moderator of the Curia—Ms. JUDY DELANEY.
Special Asst. to Archbishop Flynn—Sr. ANN GANLEY, S.S.N.D.
Archivist—Mr. STEVEN T. GRANGER; Mr. PATRICK ANZELC, Asst.
Controller—Mr. THOMAS J. BAKER.
Assistant Controller—Mr. SCOTT J. DOMEIER.
Human Resources—Mr. LARRY VANDENPLASS.
Pension Plan—Ms. MARY LYNN VASQUEZ.
Personnel Director—Rev. PAUL JAROSZESKI.
Metropolitan Tribunal—*328 W. Kellogg Blvd., St. Paul, 55102-1997*. Tel: 651-291-4466; Fax: 651-291-4467. Email: tribunal@archspm.org.
Judicial Vicar—Rev. DANIEL C. CONLIN, J.C.D.
Adjutant Judicial Vicars—Revs. RONALD J. BOWERS, J.C.D.; KEVIN M. McDONOUGH, J.C.D.
Associate Judges—Revs. TIMOTHY D. CLOUTIER, J.C.L.; NATHAN ALLEN; THOMAS J. WALKER, J.D.; RICHARD KLISH; GERALD A. SCHERKENBACH, M.A.; Sr. DOMINICA BRENNAN, O.P., J.C.L.; Revs. MERLIN N. ROERS, M.Div.; DAVID McCAULEY; Mrs. MARILIES YOUNG, J.U.D.
Defenders of the Bond—Revs. JEROME W. FEHN; JEROME PAULSON, J.C.L.; JAMES P. BURNS; JAY CONZIEMUS, J.C.L.; MICHAEL REISLING.
Auditor—Mr. EUGENE E. BURKE, M.A.
Ecclesiastical Notaries—Mrs. LINDA BOTKIN; Mrs. MICHELLE GERLACH; Ms. LISA BENNETT.
Archdiocesan Consultors—Most Revs. FREDERICK F. CAMPBELL, D.D.; RICHARD E. PATES; Revs. JOSEPH J. ARACKAL, V.C.; KEVIN M. McDONOUGH, J.C.D.; ROBERT T. CASSIDY; GEORGE J. GRAFSKY; A. MICHAEL SAUBER; PETER C. WITTMAN.
Presbyteral Council—Most Revs. HARRY J. FLYNN, D.D.; RICHARD E. PATES; FREDERICK CAMPBELL; Revs. JAMES C. ZAPPA JR., Exec. Dir.; MARK J. UNDERDAHL; THOMAS J. GARVEY (Retired); MICHAEL ERLANDER; JOHN KLOCKMAN; DAVID BARRETT; ROBERT H. HART; PATRICK J. HIPWELL; LAWRENCE R. JOHNSON; LEO J. TIBESAR; MICHAEL TEGEDER; DANIEL F. GRIFFITH; BRYAN A. O'ROURKE; STEPHEN J. ADRIAN; A. MICHAEL SAUBER; JAMES M. PERKL; THOMAS RAYAR; EUGENE W. TIFFANY; WILLIAM DEZIEL, O.S.C.; CHARLES L. FROEHLE; TERRENCE M. HAYES; JOHN L. UBEL; RICHARD J. MAHONEY (Retired); PAUL A. LAFONTAINE; BRIAN J. FIER; MICHAEL C. SKLUZACEK.
Corporate Board—Most Revs. HARRY J. FLYNN, D.D.; FREDERICK F. CAMPBELL, D.D.; RICHARD E. PATES; Rev. KEVIN M. McDONOUGH, J.C.D.; THOMAS HOLLORAN; MARY FREY; Mr. WILLIAM S. FALLON, J.D.; THOMAS SCHREIER; STEVEN HEMSLEY.
Censores Librorum—Rev. GEORGE A. WELZBACHER, Chm. Bd. (Retired), Church of St. Agnes, 548 Lafond Ave., St. Paul, 55103; Rev. Msgr. RICHARD J. SCHULER (Retired); Revs. DENNIS J. DEASE; CHARLES L. FROEHLE; JAMES A. LAVIN; DAVID W. SMITH; MARK B. DOSH; JOSEPH R. JOHNSON; Dr. DON J. BRIEL.

Archdiocesan Offices and Directors

Advisory Board on Natural Family Planning—Deacon JAMES F. BASKFIELD, Liaison, 328 W. Kellogg Blvd., St. Paul, 55102. Tel: 612-291-4438.
Allocations Committee—Mr. SCOTT J. DOMEIER, Dir., 226 Summit Ave., St. Paul, 55102. Tel: 612-291-4400.
Archbishop Ireland Educational Fund, Inc.—Most Rev. HARRY J. FLYNN, D.D., Pres., 226 Summit Ave., St. Paul, 55102.
Archdiocesan AIDS Ministry Office—Sr. JOANNE LUCID, B.V.M., Dir., Riverside Medical Center, Riverside at 25th Ave. S., Minneapolis, 55454. Tel: 612-672-4345.
Archdiocesan Council of Catholic Women—Rev. Msgr. JAMES D. HABIGER, Moderator; OLIVE HUPF, Pres., 328 W. Kellogg Blvd., St. Paul, 55102. Tel: 651-291-4545.
Archdiocesan Finance Council—LAURA KING, Chm.; PHILIP PACUETTE, 5826 Blackshire Path, Inver Grove Heights, 55076. Tel: 651-389-1070.
Building Commission—Rev. JOHN ESTREM, Chm., 226 Summit Ave., St. Paul, 55102.
Campus Ministry—Rev. JEFFREY H. HUARD, Dir., University of St. Thomas, 2115 Summit Ave., P.O. Box 5028, St. Paul, 55105.
Catholic Center for the Separated and Divorced—STEVE KING, Dir., 215 Old Sixth St., St. Paul, 55102. Tel: 651-222-3001.
Catholic Charities—Rev. LARRY SNYDER, Dir., 1200 2nd Ave., S., Minneapolis, 55403. Tel: 612-664-8500.
Catholic Commission on Social Justice—JULIE SMENDZIOL-O'BRIEN, Chm.; RON KRIETEMEYER, Dir., 328 W. Kellogg Blvd., St. Paul, 55102. Tel: 651-291-4477.
Catholic Committee on Scouting—Deacon DONALD RINKENBERGER, Church of St. Joseph the Worker, Maple Grove, 55369. Tel: 612-559-9178.
Catholic Education and Formation Ministries—THOMAS McCARVER, Dir., 328 W. Kellogg Blvd., St. Paul, 55102. Tel: 651-291-4500.
Cemeteries—Mr. JOHN CHEREK, Dir., 2105 Lexington Ave. S., Mendota Heights, 55120. Tel: 651-228-9991.
Center for Diaconate—Deacon RIP RIORDAN, Dir., 226 Summit Ave., St. Paul, 55102. Tel: 651-291-4400; JOSEPH MICHALAK, Dir. Formation, 226 Summit Ave., St. Paul, 55102. Tel: 651-251-7722.
Center for Ministry—Sr. FRAN DONNELLY, B.V.M., Dir., 244 Dayton Ave., St. Paul, 55102. Tel: 651-290-1616.
Charismatic Renewal Office—COLIN LAVERGNE, Dir., 3927 E. Lake, Minneapolis, 55406. Tel: 612-721-2543.
Christ Child Services, Inc.—*226 Summit Ave., St. Paul, 55102*. Tel: 612-291-4400.
Christian Sharing Fund—SARA McGRATH JOHNSON, 328 W. Kellogg Blvd., St. Paul, 55102. Tel: 651-291-4477.
Clergy Review Board—ED FOX, Chair, 226 Summit Ave., St. Paul, 55102. Tel: 651-291-4400.
Commission on Bio-Medical Ethics—Dr. PAUL WOJDA, Chm., University of St. Thomas, 2115 Summit Ave., St. Paul, 55105. Tel: 651-647-5000.
Commission on Chemical Health—Rev. BRYAN O'ROURKE, Chm., Church of St. Mark, 2001 Dayton Ave., St. Paul, 55104. Tel: 651-645-5717.
Commission on Women—PHYLLIS A. WILLERSCHEIDT, Exec. Coord., 328 W. Kellogg Blvd., St. Paul, 55102. Tel: 651-291-4495.
Commission for Black Catholics—Co-Chm.: GWENDOLYN JEFFERSON; TERESA EVANS-ROSS; Sr. SHARON M. HOWELL, C.S.J., Exec. Sec., 2115 Summit Ave., Mail #5006, St. Paul, 55105. Tel: 651-962-6462.
Commission for Ecumenism and Interreligious Affairs—Rev. LEE PICHE, Chm., Church of St. Joseph, 1154 Seminole Ave., West St. Paul, 55118. Tel: 651-457-2781.
Commission on Pastoral Health Care—Rev. PAUL JAROSZESKI, Chm., 1884 Randolph Ave., St. Paul, 55105. Tel: 651-690-7028.
Commission on Ministry—MARLENE PALKOVICH, Chm., 244 Dayton Ave., St. Paul, 55102. Tel: 651-290-1616.
Common Bond Communities—Mr. JOSEPH A.L. ERRIGO JR., Pres., 328 W. Kellogg Blvd., St.Paul, 55102. Tel: 651-291-1750.
Communications Office—DENNIS McGRATH, Dir., 226 Summit Ave., St. Paul, 55102. Tel: 651-291-4411.
Council of Religious—Sr. FRAN DONNELLY, B.V.M., Ex Officio, 244 Dayton Ave., St. Paul, 55102. Tel: 651-290-1616.
Cursillo—Rev. WILLIAM F. MARTIN, Spiritual Advisor. Lay Directors:: LARRY PRESSELLER; MARILYN PRESSELLER, 2933 16th St., N.W., New Brighton, 55112. Tel: 651-635-0760.
Deacon Assembly—Deacon TONY PASKO, Pres., 226 Summit Ave., St. Paul, 55102. Tel: 651-251-7722.
Hispanic Ministry—ANNE "ANITA" ATTEA, Coord., 840 E. 6th St., St. Paul, 55106. Tel: 651-793-9791.
Holy Childhood, Pontifical Association, Society for the Propagation of the Faith—MICKEY FRIESEN, Dir., 328 W. Kellogg Blvd., St. Paul, 55102.
Institute for Christian Life & Ministry—Deacon RIP RIORDAN, Dir.; JOSEPH MICHALAK Dir. Formation, 226 Summit Ave., St. Paul, 55102. Tel: 651-251-7722.
Legion of Mary— St. Paul Curia and Comitium, Rev. Msgr. RICHARD J. SCHULER (Retired), 548 Lafond Ave., St. Paul, 55103. Tel: 651-293-1710.
Marriage Encounter—JEANNE STOESSEL, Exec. Dir., 953 Lake Dr., St. Paul, 55120. Tel: 651-454-3238.
Marriage and Family Life Office—KATHLEEN M. LAIRD, Dir., 328 W. Kellogg Blvd., St. Paul, 55102. Tel: 651-291-4438.
Migration and Refugee Services—Mr. THOMAS KOSEL, Admin., 215 Old Sixth St., St. Paul, 55102. Tel: 651-222-3001.
Ministry to Hmong—Rev. ROBERT GRABNER; Deacon VA THAI LO, Twin Cities Hmong Catholic Community, Church of St. Vincent De Paul, 651 Virginia St., St. Paul, 55103. Tel: 651-488-6737.
Ministry to Koreans—Rev. DO DONG ANDREW BAE, Church of St. Andrew Kim, 1449 Cleveland Ave., St. Paul, 55108. Tel: 651-642-9822.
Ministry to Vietnamese—Rev. MATTHIAS CHUONG, C.M.C., Church of St. Joseph Hien, 1800 Dupont Ave. N., Minneapolis, 55411. Tel: 612-522-5006.
Nazareth Hall College and Seminary, Inc.—Most Rev. HARRY J. FLYNN, D.D., Pres.
Newman Centers—Revs. JOHN J. BEHNKE, C.S.P., Dir., 1201 5th St., S.E., Minneapolis, 55414. Tel: 612-331-7941 Macalester College; PETER ETZEL, S.J., Campus Min., 1550 Summit Ave., St. Paul, 55105. Tel: 651-644-9041.
Newspaper—Mr. ROBERT ZYSKOWSKI, Assoc. Publisher; Mr. MIKE KROKOS, Editor, 244 Dayton Ave., St. Paul, 55102. Tel: 651-291-4444. "The Catholic Spirit"
Office of the Deaf—MARGERY E. POWERS, 701 Fillmore St., N.E., Minneapolis, 55413. Tel: 612-623-4019; 612-378-1344 (TTD).
Office of Indian Ministry—Rev. JAMES C. NOTEBAART, Dir., 3045 Park Ave., Minneapolis, 55407. Tel: 612-824-7616.
Office for Social Justice—KATHLEEN TOMLIN, Admin., 328 W. Kellogg Blvd., St. Paul, 55102. Tel: 651-291-4477.
Office of Conciliation—Sr. M. DOMINICA BRENNAN, O.P., J.C.L., Dir., 226 Summit Ave., St. Paul, 55102. Tel: 651-291-4437.
Office of Ecumenism—Rev. LEE PICHE, Ecumenical Officer, Church of St. Joseph, West Saint Paul, 55118. Tel: 651-457-2781.
Office of Evangelization—PHILIP SOUCHERAY, Exec. Dir., 226 Summit Ave., St. Paul, 55102. Tel: 651-291-7727.
Office of Human Resources—LARRY VANDENPLAS, 328 W. Kellogg Blvd., St. Paul, 55102. Tel: 651-291-4499.
Office of Presbyteral Personnel Resources—Revs. PAUL JAROSZESKI, Exec. Sec.; LAWRENCE BLAKE, 226 Summit Ave., St. Paul, 55102. Tel: 651-291-4430.
Parish Pastoral Council Assistance Center—VACANT, Dir., 328 W. Kellogg Blvd., St. Paul, 55102. Tel: 651-291-4544.
Pastoral Council—Most Rev. HARRY J. FLYNN, D.D., Chm.
Promotion of Ministerial Standards—Deacon SHERMAN H. OTTO, Dir., 226 Summit Ave., St. Paul, 55102. Tel: 651-291-4400.
Presbyteral Council—Rev. JAMES C. ZAPPA JR., Exec. Dir., 226 Summit Ave., St. Paul, 55102. Tel: 651-291-4400.
Propagation of the Faith—MICKEY FRIESEN, Dir., 328 W. Kellogg Blvd., St. Paul, 55102. Tel: 651-222-6556.
Records Management—SUSAN STEPKA, Mgr., 226 Summit Ave., St. Paul, 55102. Tel: 651-291-4481.
Resource Development Office—Ms. MICKEY NICKELSON, Dir., 328 W. Kellogg Blvd., St. Paul, 55102. Tel: 651-290-1610.
Annual Catholic Appeal—Ms. MICKEY NICKELSON, Dir., 328 Kellogg Blvd., St. Paul, 55102. Tel: 651-290-1649.
Respect Life—Mrs. SHARON SODERLUND, Dir., 328 W. Kellogg Blvd., St. Paul, 55102. Tel: 651-291-4505.
Rural Life Conference—Mr. DALE R. HENNEN, 105 3rd St., N.W., Montgomery, 56069. Tel: 612-364-7323.
Sacerdotal Union of Daily Adoration—Rev. ALBERT F. BYRNE (Retired), 2590 Margaret St., North St. Paul, 55109.
Seton Center—MICHELLE BAILEY, Admin., Spruce Tree Center, Ste. 400, 1600 University Ave., St. Paul, 55104. Tel: 651-641-1180 Outpatient social and medical services for unwed women and young couples.
To Encounter Christ (TEC)—PAM GEEMSCHEID DEMORETT, Coord., 1201 S.E. 5th St., Minneapolis, 55414. Tel: 612-331-3644.
Venezuelan Missions—Revs. TIMOTHY L. NORRIS; GREGORY J. SCHAFFER, El Buen Pastor Parroquia San Francisco de Asis, Apartado 272, Puerto Ordaz, Estado Bolivar, Ve 8015.
Victim Assistance Coordinator—PHYLLIS A. WILLERSCHEIDT. Tel: 651-291-4497. Email: willerscheidtp@archspm.org.
Vocation Office—Rev. THOMAS WILSON, Dir., Vocations, 2260 Summit Ave., St. Paul, 55105. Tel: 651-962-6890.
Worship Board—Ms. ANNA OTTO, Chm., 244 Dayton Ave., St. Paul, 55102. Tel: 651-290-1625.
Worship Center—VICKI KLIMA, Dir.; Mr. MICHAEL

SILHAVY, Assoc. Dir., Music, 244 Dayton Ave., St. Paul, 55102. Tel: 651-290-1625.

CLERGY, PARISHES, MISSIONS AND PAROCHIAL SCHOOLS

METROPOLITAN ST. PAUL
(RAMSEY COUNTY)

1—CATHEDRAL OF ST. PAUL (1850), Revs. John Estrem, Rector; John Estrem, Rector; Joseph A. Williams; Nathan Allen; Deacon James Hepp.
Res.: 239 Selby Ave., 55102. Tel: 651-228-1766; Fax: 651-228-9942.

2—ST. ADALBERT (1881), (Vietnamese—Polish), Rev. Minh Vu.
Res.: 265 Charles Ave., 55103. Tel: 651-228-9002; Fax: 651-225-0902.
Catechesis/Religious Program—Students 105.

3—ST. AGNES (1887), (Austrian), Rev. George Welzbacher; Rev. Msgr. Richard J. Schuler, Pastor Emeritus (Retired); Rev. Robert J. Altier; Deacons Harold Hughesdon; Bernard Pedersen.
Res.: 548 Lafond Ave., 55103. Tel: 651-293-1710; Fax: 651-227-4229.
School—530 Lafond Ave., 55103. Tel: 651-227-1886; Fax: 651-228-1158. Mr. Jeffrey Brengman, Headmaster (Elementary and High Schools). Lay Teachers 16; Students 185.
High School—Tel: 651-228-1161. Lay Teachers 28; Students 229.
Catechesis/Religious Program—Students 64.

4—ST. ANDREW (1895), Rev. Patrick Ryan.
Res.: 1051 Como Ave., 55103. Tel: 651-488-6775; Fax: 651-488-4461.
School—Maternity of Mary/St. Andrew, Tel: 651-489-1459; Fax: 651-489-3560. Consolidated. See Maternity of the Blessed Virgin for details.
Catechesis/Religious Program—Tel: 651-489-8827; Fax: 651-488-4055. Twinned with Maternity of Mary, St. Paul. Students 23.

5—ST. ANDREW KIM (1990), (Korean), [JC] Rev. Do Dong Andrew Bae (Korea, South).
Res.: 1449 N. Cleveland Ave., 55108. Tel: 651-642-9822 (Rectory); Fax: 651-642-0140.
Catechesis/Religious Program—Tel: 651-644-1605; Fax: 651-644-4908. Students 76.

6—ASSUMPTION (1856), (German), Revs. John M. Malone; David A. Barrett; Deacon Jerome Ciresi.
Res.: 51 W. Seventh St., 55102. Tel: 651-224-7536; Fax: 651-224-8514.
Catechesis/Religious Program—261 E. 8th St., 55101. Tel: 651-222-2619. Students 21.

7—ST. BERNARD (1890), (German), Revs. Michael F. Anderson; Anthony G. VanderLoop; Deacon Sonny Laqui.
Mailing Address: 1160 Woodbridge St., 55117-4491. Tel: 651-488-6733; Fax: 651-489-9203.
Res.: 197 W. Geranium Ave., 55117-4437. Tel: 651-488-6733.
School—(Grades K-12), 170 W. Rose Ave., 55117-4437. Tel: 651-489-1338; Fax: 651-488-9466. Jennifer Cassidy, Pres. (K-12); Mark Lenihan, Prin. (K-12). Lay Teachers 33; Students 442.
Catechesis/Religious Program—Students 442.

8—BLESSED SACRAMENT (1916), Rev. Jerry F. Fenton.
Res.: 1801 La Crosse Ave., 55119. Tel: 651-735-3707; Fax: 651-578-1125.
School—1800 Ames Ave., 55119. Tel: 651-735-3676; Fax: 651-264-0647. Lay Teachers 10; Students 80.
Catechesis/Religious Program—Students 78.

9—ST. CASIMIR (1892), Revs. Greg Gallagher, O.M.I.; James D. Deegan, O.M.I. In Res., Bros. Will Upson, O.M.I.; Andrew Wieser, O.M.I.
Res.: 934 E. Geranium Ave., 55106. Tel: 651-774-0365; Fax: 651-774-0508.
School—Trinity Catholic School, 835 E. Fifth St.. Tel: 651-776-2763; Fax: 651-776-2764. Collaborative School with St. Patrick & Sacred Heart Parishes in St. Paul. Students 198; Preschool 25.
Catechesis/Religious Program—Students 35.

10—ST. CECILIA (1912), Rev. Paul A. Jaroszeski.
Res.: 2357 Bayless Pl., 55114. Tel: 651-644-4502; Fax: 651-647-1445.
Catechesis/Religious Program—Students 135.

11—ST. COLUMBA (1914), (Irish), Revs. Dan Conlin; Thomas Tam (Vietnam); Deacon Thomas Stiles.
Res.: 1327 Lafond Ave., 55104. Tel: 651-645-9179; Fax: 651-645-9170.
School—1330 Blair Ave., 55104. Tel: 651-644-1807; Fax: 651-644-9078 (Call First). Lay Teachers 11; Students 125.
Catechesis/Religious Program—Tel: 651-644-9078. Students 38.

12—ST. FRANCIS DE SALES (1884), (German), Rev. Dennis Dempsey; Deacon James Clasen.
Res.: 650 Palace Ave., 55102-3593. Tel: 651-228-1169; Fax: 651-224-7744.
School—St. Francis-St. James United School, 426 S. Osceola St., 55102. Tel: 651-228-1167; Fax: 651-228-0169. Sisters of Notre Dame 1; Lay Teachers 9; Students 143.
Catechesis/Religious Program—Students 50.

13—ST. GREGORY THE GREAT (HIGHLAND CATHOLIC COMMUNITY) (1951),, (A formation of the following: St. Gregory the Great, St. Paul; St. Leo, St. Paul and St. Therese, St. Paul) Revs. John M. Bauer; Scott M. Carl.
Mailing Address: 2055 Bohland Ave., 55116.
Church: 1668 Montreal Ave., 55116-2499. Tel: 651-698-3767.
Parish Center—Tel: 651-698-5581; Fax: 651-698-9526.
School—Highland Catholic School, Tel: 651-690-2477; Fax: 651-699-1869. See separate listing under Institutions Located in the Archdiocese for details.
Catechesis/Religious Program—Highland Catholic Community, Tel: 651-698-5583. Students 282.

14—HOLY CHILDHOOD (1946), Rev. James G. Wolnik.
Res.: 1435 Midway Pkwy., 55108. Tel: 651-644-7495.
School—1435 Midway Pkwy., 55108. Tel: 651-644-2791; Fax: 651-917-8797. Lawrence Gallatin, Prin. Sisters 1; Lay Teachers 12; Students 119.
Catechesis/Religious Program—Tel: 651-644-5645. Rev. James G. Wolnik, D.R.E. Students 13.

15—HOLY SPIRIT (1936), Rev. Michael L. Papesh; Deacon William Umphress.
Res.: 515 S. Albert St., 55105. Tel: 651-698-3353; Fax: 651-698-1605.
School—Joy Biedrzycki, Pastoral Assoc.
Catechesis/Religious Program—Tel: 651-698-3353; Fax: 651-698-1605. Students 66.

16—THE IMMACULATE HEART OF MARY (1949), Rev. Charles F. Burns, S.J.
Mailing Address: 1550 Summit Ave., 55105-2290. Tel: 651-699-7722; Fax: 651-690-9729.
School—IHM-St. Luke, Tel: 651-224-4836; Fax: 651-224-0097. See St. Luke, St. Paul for details.
Catechesis/Religious Program—Students 37.

17—ST. JAMES (1887), Rev. Dennis Dempsey.
Res.: 650 Palace Ave., 55102. Tel: 651-227-7029.
School—St. Francis-St. James United School, (Grades K-8) Tel: 651-228-1167; Fax: 651-228-0169. See St. Francis De Sales for details.
Catechesis/Religious Program—Tel: 651-228-1169; Fax: 651-224-7744. Students 75.

18—ST. JOHN OF ST. PAUL (1886), Rev. Thomas Pingatore.
Res.: 977 E. Fifth St., 55106. Tel: 651-771-3690; Fax: 651-771-7919.
Catechesis/Religious Program—Tel: 651-771-3690. Students 42.

19—ST. LEO (HIGHLAND CATHOLIC COMMUNITY) (1945),, (A formation of the following: St. Gregory the Great, St. Paul; St. Leo, St. Paul; St. Therese, St. Paul) Revs. John M. Bauer; Scott M. Carl.
Office:—2055 Bohland Ave., 55116. Tel: 651-698-5581; Fax: 651-698-9526.
School—Highland Catholic School, Tel: 651-690-2477; Fax: 651-699-1869. See separate listing under Institutions Located in the Archdiocese for details.
Catechesis/Religious Program—Highland Catholic Community, Tel: 651-698-5583; Fax: 651-698-9526. Students 435.

20—ST. LOUIS KING OF FRANCE (1868), (French), Revs. Paul F. Morrissey, S.M.; Ronald J. Nikodem, S.M.
Res.: 506 Cedar St., 55101-2280. Tel: 651-224-3379; Fax: 651-224-0017.
Catechesis/Religious Program—Students 20.

21—ST. LUKE (1888), Revs. Charles F. Burns, S.J., Admin.; Patrick Malone, S.J.; Deacon Thomas Dzik.
Center—1079 Summit Ave., 55105. Tel: 651-227-7669; Fax: 651-227-0847.
School—IHM-St. Luke, 1065 Summit Ave., 55105. Tel: 651-224-4836; Fax: 651-224-0097. Sisters 2; Lay Teachers 29; Students 394.
Catechesis/Religious Program—Students 109.

22—ST. MARK (1889), Rev. Bryan O'Rourke; Deacon Scott Wright.
Res.: 2001 Dayton Ave., 55104. Tel: 651-645-5717; Fax: 651-644-0011.
School—1983 Dayton Ave., 55104. Tel: 651-644-3380; Fax: 651-644-1923. Sisters 2; Lay Teachers 25; Students 382.
Catechesis/Religious Program—Fax: 651-645-5717. Students 105.

23—ST. MARY (1865), Revs. George Jacob Manjankal (India); Shaji Joseph Pazzhukkathara (India); Bros. Ronald Generao (Philippines); Alejandro Serrano (Argentina), In Seminary; Carlos Salazar (Bolivia), In Seminary. In Res., Rev. Robert Allie, O.M.I.
Res.: 261 E. 8th St., 55101. Tel: 651-222-2619; Fax: 651-224-1190.
Catechesis/Religious Program—Students 24.

24—MATERNITY OF THE BLESSED VIRGIN (1949), Rev. Paul D. Sirba.
Res.: 1414 N. Dale St., 55117. Tel: 651-489-8825; Fax: 651-488-4055.
School—Maternity of Mary-St. Andrew, 592 Arlington Ave., 55117. Tel: 651-489-1459; Fax: 651-489-3560. Sisters 2; Lay Teachers 26; Students 332.
Catechesis/Religious Program—Tel: 651-489-8825; Fax: 651-488-4055. Mary Weyandt, D.R.E. Students 139.

25—ST. MATTHEW (1886), (German), Revs. Stephen J. Adrian; Martin L. Warren (England); Deacon John Murphy.
Office:—490 Hall Ave., 55107. Tel: 651-224-9793.
Church: 510 Hall Ave, 55107. Tel: 651-224-9793; Fax: 651-228-9448.
Res.: 507 Hall Ave., 55107. Tel: 651-224-1037; Fax: 651-292-0925.
School—497 Humboldt Ave., 55107. Tel: 651-224-6912. Sisters 1; Lay Teachers 12; Students 206.
Catechesis/Religious Program—Students 130.

26—THE NATIVITY OF OUR LORD (1922), Revs. Peter Christensen; Christopher T. Wenthe.
Office:—1900 Wellesley, 55105. Tel: 651-698-0309; Fax: 651-696-5458.
School—1900 Stanford Ave., 55105. Tel: 651-699-1311; Fax: 651-696-5420. Mrs. Margo Weiberg, Prin.; Ms. Kate Wollan, Prin. Sisters of St. Joseph 1; Lay Teachers 41; Students 776.
Catechesis/Religious Program—Tel: 651-696-5454; Fax: 651-696-5458. Students 77.

27—OUR LADY OF GUADALUPE (1931), (Hispanic), Rev. Thomas Merrill, O.F.M.Conv.
Res.: 401 Concord Street, 55107. Tel: 651-228-0506; Fax: 651-224-5162.
Catechesis/Religious Program—Students 90.

28—ST. PASCAL BAYLON (1946), Rev. David F. McCauley; Deacon Richard Pashby.
Res.: 1757 Conway St., 55106. Tel: 651-774-1585; Fax: 651-774-9152.
School—Tel: 651-776-0092. Lay Teachers 24; Students 350.
Catechesis/Religious Program—Tel: 651-774-0655. Students 111.

29—ST. PATRICK (1884), (Irish), Rev. Jerome B. Hackenmueller.
Res.: 1095 De Soto St., 55101. Tel: 651-774-8675; Fax: 651-774-9106.
School—Trinity Catholic School, Tel: 651-776-2763; Fax: 651-774-9943. Collaborative School with St. Patrick, St. Casimir & Sacred Heart Parishes in St. Paul.
Catechesis/Religious Program—Tel: 651-776-7686. Students 145.

30—ST. PETER CLAVER (1892), (African American), Rev. Kevin M. McDonough; Deacon Fred L. Johnson.
Res.: 375 N. Oxford St., 55104. Tel: 651-646-1797; Fax: 651-647-5341.
Catechesis/Religious Program—Students 180.

31—SACRED HEART (1881), (German), Rev. Eugene Michel; Deacons Wayne Wittman; Gregg Sroder. In Res., Revs. Valerius Messerich, O.F.M.; Nicholas W. Meyer, O.F.M.; Bro. Leonard Lawrence, O.F.M.
Res.: 840 E. Sixth St., 55106. Tel: 651-776-2741; Fax: 651-776-2759.
School—Trinity Catholic School, 835 E. Fifth St., 55106. Tel: 651-776-2763; Fax: 651-776-2764. Collaborative School with St. Patrick & St. Casimir Parishes in St. Paul.
Catechesis/Religious Program—Tel: 651-774-7505. Kim Roering, D.R.E. Students 98.

32—ST. STANISLAUS (1872), (Czech), Rev. John C. Clay.
Office—398 Superior St., 55102. Tel: 651-292-0303; Fax: 651-292-1098.
Catechesis/Religious Program—395 Superior St., 55102. Tel: 651-292-1913. Students 245.

33—ST. THERESE (HIGHLAND CATHOLIC COMMUNITY) (1926),, (A consolidation of the following: St. Gregory the Great, St. Paul; St. Leo, St. Paul; and St. Therese, St. Paul) Revs. John M. Bauer; Scott M. Carl.
Mailing Address & Office: 2055 Bohland Ave., 55116.
Parish Center—Tel: 651-698-5581; Fax: 651-698-9526.
School—Highland Catholic School, Tel: 651-690-2477; Fax: 651-699-1869. See separate listing under Institutions Located in the Archdiocese for details.
Catechesis/Religious Program—Highland Catholic Community, Tel: 651-698-5583. Students 274.

34—ST. THOMAS THE APOSTLE (1954), Rev. Joseph Anthony Andrade; Deacon Richard Moore.
Res.: 2119 Stillwater Ave., 55119. Tel: 651-738-0677; Fax: 651-738-6492.
Catechesis/Religious Program—Students 130.

35—ST. VINCENT DE PAUL (1888), [CEM] Rev. Robert J. Grabner; Deacon Va Thai Lo, Admin.
Res.: 651 Virginia St., 55103. Tel: 651-488-6737;

Fax: 651-487-6790.
Catechesis/Religious Program—Students 55.

OUTSIDE METROPOLITAN ST. PAUL

COTTAGE GROVE, WASHINGTON CO., ST. RITA (1966), Rev. James M. Grogan; Deacons Jack Nicklay; Steve Koop.
8694 80th St. S., 55016. Tel: 651-459-4596; Fax: 651-459-5364.
Catechesis/Religious Program—Students 1,533.

LITTLE CANADA, RAMSEY CO., ST. JOHN THE EVANGELIST (1851), [CEM] Revs. Robert J. Fitzpatrick; George Kallumkalkudy, C.M.I.; Marie Winn, Pastoral Assoc.; Suzanne Laddusire, Dir. Pastoral Ministry; Deacon R. Thomas Keyes.
Res.: 380 Little Canada Rd., 55117. Tel: 651-484-2708; Fax: 651-484-0567.
School—Preschool Lay Teachers 2; Students 40.
School—2621 McMenemy St., 55117. Tel: 651-484-3038; Fax: 651-481-1355. Mary Kay Rowan, Prin. Lay Teachers 18; Students 254.
Catechesis/Religious Program—Tel: 651-484-0048; Fax: 651-288-3233. Jean Conant Winter, D.R.E. Students 560.

MAHTOMEDI, WASHINGTON CO., ST. JUDE OF THE LAKE (1939), Rev. Jon P. Shelley.
Res.: 700 Mahtomedi Ave., 55115. Tel: 651-426-3245; Fax: 651-653-3554.
School—600 Mahtomedi Ave., 55115. Tel: 651-426-2562; Fax: 651-653-3662. Ann Austin McCormick, Prin. Lay Teachers 15; Students 300.
Catechesis/Religious Program—Students 600.

MAPLEWOOD, RAMSEY CO.
1—HOLY REDEEMER (1880), (Italian),
Res.: 2555 Hazelwood Ave., 55109. Tel: 651-777-1321.
Catechesis/Religious Program—Tel: 651-777-1231. Students 55.

2—ST. JEROME (1940), Rev. Kenneth F. Ludescher.
1894 McMenemy Rd., 55117. Tel: 651-771-1928.
Church: 380 Roselawn Ave. E., 55117. Tel: 651-771-1209; Fax: 651-771-3623.
School—384 E. Roselawn Ave., 55117. Tel: 651-771-8494; Fax: 651-771-3466. Lay Teachers 13; Students 185.
Catechesis/Religious Program—Students 185.

3—PRESENTATION OF THE BLESSED VIRGIN MARY (1946), Rev. Phillip J. Rask; Deacons Jack Veiman; James Saumweber.
Res.: 1725 Kennard St., 55109. Tel: 651-777-8116; Fax: 651-777-8743.
School—1695 Kennard St., 55109. Tel: 651-777-5877; Fax: 651-777-8283. Lay Teachers 20; Students 325.
Catechesis/Religious Program—Tel: 651-777-6041; Fax: 651-777-8743. Students 163.

MENDOTA, DAKOTA CO., ST. PETER (1840), (Native American—French), [CEM] Rev. Kevin I. Clinton; Deacon Martin Shanahan.
Res.: P.O. Box 50679, 55150. Tel: 651-452-4030; Fax: 651-456-0646.
Catechesis/Religious Program—Tel: 651-452-4550; Fax: 651-456-0646. Kathy Raible, D.R.E. Students 251.

NEW BRIGHTON, RAMSEY CO., ST. JOHN THE BAPTIST (1906), (Polish), [CEM] Revs. William Murtaugh; Michael J. Keating; Deacon Michael Winn.
Parish Center—835 2nd Ave., N.W., 55112. Tel: 651-633-8333; Fax: 651-633-7404.
Res.: 812 1st Ave., N.W., 55112.
School—845 2nd Ave., N.W., 55112. Tel: 651-633-1522; Fax: 651-633-1522. Lay Teachers 19; Students 440.
Catechesis/Religious Program—Tel: 651-633-1540; Fax: 651-633-7404. Students 529.

NORTH ST. PAUL, RAMSEY CO., ST. PETER (1888), [CEM] Rev. John R. Estram; Deacon William Umphress, Parish Life Admin.
Res.: 2590 N. Margaret St., 55109. Tel: 651-777-8304; Fax: 651-777-0497.
School—Preschool, Tel: 651-777-5282. Lay Teachers 2; Students 61.
School—2602 N. Margaret St., 55109. Tel: 651-777-3091; Fax: 651-777-7750. Lay Teachers 22; Students 440.
Catechesis/Religious Program—Students 455.

OAKDALE, WASHINGTON CO.
1—GUARDIAN ANGELS (1885), [CEM] Revs. William F. Martin; Stanley Maslowski; Sr. Dorothy Mrock, O.S.F.; Deacon Terry Beer.
Res.: 8260 Hudson Blvd., 55128. Tel: 651-738-2223; Fax: 651-738-2453.
Catechesis/Religious Program—Students 865.

2—TRANSFIGURATION (1939), Rev. Robert H. Hart; Deacon Phillip Stewart.
Res.: 6133 15th St. N., 55128. Tel: 651-738-2646; Fax: 651-501-2230.
School—935 Ferndale Ave., Maplewood, 55119. Tel: 651-501-2220; Fax: 651-501-2258. Ted Zarembski, Prin. Lay Teachers 21; Students 404.
Catechesis/Religious Program—Tel: 651-501-2204. Carole Zempel, D.R.E. Students 644.

ROSEVILLE, RAMSEY CO.
1—CORPUS CHRISTI (1939), Rev. Francis L. Fried.
Res.: 2131 N. Fairview Ave., 55113-5499. Tel: 651-639-8888; Fax: 651-639-8288.
Catechesis/Religious Program—Colleen Ciaccio, D.R.E.; Alisa Weber, D.R.E. Students 279.

2—ST. ROSE OF LIMA (1939), Rev. Walter L. Sochacki.
Res.: 2048 N. Hamline Ave., 55113. Tel: 651-645-9389; Fax 651-646-4187.
School—2072 Hamline Ave. N., 55113. Tel: 651-646-3832; Fax: 651-647-6437. Sisters 2; Lay Teachers 29; Students 438.
Catechesis/Religious Program—Tel: 651-646-8029. Deb McPherson, D.R.E. Students 175.

SHOREVIEW, RAMSEY CO., ST. ODILIA (1960), Revs. Richard McGuire, O.S.C.; Jerome Schik, O.S.C.; Marven Tellers, O.S.C.; Dave Donnay, O.S.C.; Deacons John Flood; Gabriel Gregory.
3495 N. Victoria St., 55126. Tel: 651-484-6681; Fax: 651-484-0780.
School—(Grades K-8) Tel: 651-484-3364; Fax: 651-415-3395 Mr. Robert Grose, Prin. Lay Teachers 36; Students 710.
Catechesis/Religious Program—Tel: 651-484-2777. Sr. Penny Dunn, O.S.F., D.R.E. Students 1,042.

WEST ST. PAUL, DAKOTA CO.
1—ST. JOSEPH (1942), Revs. Lee A. Piche; Curtis C. Wehmeyer.
Res.: 1154 Seminole Ave., 55118. Tel: 651-457-2781; Fax: 651-451-1272.
School—1138 Seminole Ave., 55118. Tel: 651-457-8550; Fax: 651-457-0780. Lay Teachers 49; Students 750.
Catechesis/Religious Program—Tel: 651-457-8841. Students 300.

2—ST. MICHAEL (1879), Rev. Kenneth L. O'Hotto.
Res.: 337 E. Hurley, 55118. Tel: 651-457-2334; Fax: 651-451-1668.
School—E. Haskell & Sperl, 55118. Tel: 651-457-2510; Fax: 651-457-5049. Sisters 2; Lay Teachers 13; Students 147.
Catechesis/Religious Program—Tel: 651-457-0172. Students 54.

WHITE BEAR LAKE, RAMSEY CO.
1—ST. MARY OF THE LAKE (1881), [CEM] Revs. Rodger Bauman; Roger P. Pierre; Deacon Sherm Stromen.
Res.: 4690 Bald Eagle Ave., 55110. Tel: 651-429-7771; Fax: 651-429-9539.
School—4690 Bald Eagle Ave., 55110. Lay Teachers 21; Students 308.
Catechesis/Religious Program—Tel: 651-429-8001. Helen Welter, D.R.E.; Mary Beth Jambor, D.R.E. Students 468; Students 578.

2—ST. PIUS X (1954), Rev. Michael J. Krenik; Deacon Thomas L. Semlak.
Mailing Address: 3878 Highland Ave., 55110. Tel: 651-429-5337; Fax: 651-429-9359.
School—Tel: 651-429-5338. Lay Teachers 24; Students 364.
Catechesis/Religious Program—Tel: 651-429-5994. Students 398.

WOODBURY, CARLTON CO., SAINT AMBROSE OF WOODBURY (1998), Revs. Thomas J. Walker, J.D.; Paul Keller; Deacon J. Neil Tift.
Mailing Address: 4125 Woodbury Dr., 55129-9627. Tel: 651-714-1058; Fax: 651-714-9257.
Catechesis/Religious Program—Tel: 651-768-3011. Students 1,353.

METROPOLITAN MINNEAPOLIS
(HENNEPIN COUNTY)

1—ST. ALBERT THE GREAT (1935), Rev. Thomas R. Poulsen, O.P. In Res., Revs. Brendan J. McMullen, O.P.; C. A. Kilroy, O.P.; Joseph P. Gillespie, O.P.; Joseph E. Bidwill, O.P.; Jose M. Santiago, O.P.; Cletus J. Wessels, O.P.; Jerry C. Vandrovec; Dan H. Ostdiek, O.P. (CHI); Bros. Vincent H. Champine, O.P. Kevin W. Carroll, O.P.
Mailing Address & Parish Center 2836-33rd Ave. S., 55406. Tel: 612-724-3643; Fax: 612-722-9726.
Res.: 2833 32nd Ave. S., 55406. Tel: 612-724-3644; Fax: 612-724-5057.
Catechesis/Religious Program—Students 35.

2—ALL SAINTS (1916), (Polish), Rev. George J. Kovalik.
Res.: 435 4th St., N.E., 55413. Tel: 612-379-4996.
School—Pope John Paul II Catholic School, Tel: 612-789-8851. See Elementary Schools, Consolidated, Parochial under Institutions Located in the Archdiocese for details.
Catechesis/Religious Program—Tel: 612-379-2761; Fax: 612-676-1532.

3—ST. ANNE (1884), (French), Rev. Michael G. Monogue.
Res.: 2627 Queen Ave. N., 55411. Tel: 612-529-0503; Fax: 612-529-5860.
School—St. Elizabeth Seton, 5140 Fremont Ave. N., 55430-3496. Tel: 612-529-7781; Fax: 612-529-3343. (Consolidated).
Catechesis/Religious Program—Tel: 612-521-7454. Students 4.

4—ANNUNCIATION (1922), Rev. Timothy Dolan.
Res.: 509 W. 54th St., 55419. Tel: 612-824-0787; Fax: 612-823-8467.
School—525 W. 54th St., 55419. Tel: 612-823-4394; Fax: 612-824-0998. Lay Teachers 25; Students 412.
Catechesis/Religious Program—Tel: 612-824-9993, Ext. 260. Students 85.

5—ST. ANTHONY OF PADUA (1849), Rev. Joseph G. Kivel.
Res.: 804 Second St., N.E., 55413. Tel: 612-379-2324; Fax: 612-379-2325. Email: stanthonychrch@msn.com.
School—Pope John Paul II Catholic School, Tel: 612-789-8851; Fax: 612-379-2225. Please refer to the listing under Elementary Schools, Consolidated, Parochial in the Institutions section.
Catechesis/Religious Program—Students 20.

6—ASCENSION (1890), Rev. Michael O'Connell.
Res.: 1723 Bryant Ave. N., 55411. Tel: 612-529-9684; Fax: 612-529-7618.
School—1726 Dupont Ave. N., 55411. Tel: 612-521-3609; Fax: 612-522-3862. Students 265.
Catechesis/Religious Program—Tel: 612-521-7454; Fax: 612-529-3343. Students 9.

7—ST. AUSTIN (1937), (Polish), Rev. Gregory T. Welch; Sr. Anne Becker, S.S.N.D., Pastoral Assoc.
Res.: 4050 Upton Ave. N., 55412. Tel: 612-529-9561; Fax: 612-529-8787.
School—St. Elizabeth Seton, 5140 Fremont Ave. N., 55430. Tel: 612-529-7781; Fax: 612-529-3343. Lay Teachers 14; Students 230.
Catechesis/Religious Program—Students 52.

8—THE BASILICA OF ST. MARY CO-CATHEDRAL (1907), Revs. Michael O'Connell, Rector; Joseph P. Gillespie, O.P.; Deacons David Ingwell; Del Ferguson; Roger Carlson.
Mailing Address: P.O. Box 50010, 55405-0010.
Res.: 88 N. 17th St., 55403-1295. Tel: 612-333-1381; Fax: 612-333-7230.
Catechesis/Religious Program—Tel: 612-317-3473. Students 305.

9—ST. BONIFACE (1858), (German), Unassigned.
Res.: 629 Second St., N.E., 55413. Tel: 612-379-2761; Fax: 612-676-1532.
School—Pope John Paul II Catholic School Please refer to the listing under Elementary Schools, Consolidated, Parochial in the Institutions section.
Catechesis/Religious Program—Tel: 612-379-2451. Students 14.

10—ST. BRIDGET (1915), Very Rev. Anthony M. Criscitelli, T.O.R.; Deacon Richard Heineman. In Res., Revs. Vincent J. Spinos, T.O.R.; J. Patrick Quinn, T.O.R.
Res.: 3811 Emerson Ave. N., 55412. Tel: 612-529-7779; Fax: 612-529-8451.
School—5140 Fremont Ave. N., 55430-3497. Tel: 612-529-7781; Fax: 612-529-3343. Joyce Klevence, Prin. (Consolidated) Lay Teachers 20; Students 180.
Catechesis/Religious Program—555 Emerson Ave., North Minneapolis, 55430. Tel: 612-521-7454. Students 40.

11—ST. CHARLES BORROMEO (1938), Revs. Paul A. LaFontaine; Rolf R. Tollefson.
Res.: 2739 Stinson Blvd. N.E., 55418. Tel: 612-781-6529; Fax: 612-781-9723.
School—2727 Stinson Blvd., 55418. Tel: 612-781-2643; Fax: 612-788-7768. Lay Teachers 25; Students 347.
Catechesis/Religious Program—Students 140.

12—CHRIST THE KING (1938), [JC] Rev. Dale J. Korogi.
5029 Zenith Ave. S., 55410. Tel: 612-920-5030; Fax: 612-920-1179.
School—Tel: 612-927-8673; 612-920-9075; Fax: 612-927-7426. Cooperative program with St. Thomas the Apostle, Minneapolis.
Catechesis/Religious Program—Students 242.

13—ST. CLEMENT (1902), Rev. Earl C. Simonson.
Res.: 911 24th Ave., N.E., 55418. Tel: 612-789-3533.
School—Pope John Paul II Catholic School Please refer to the listing under Elementary Schools, Consolidated, Parochial in the Institutions section.

14—SS. CYRIL & METHODIUS (1891), (Slovak—Hispanic), In Res., Rev. Edison Galarza, O.C.C.S.S.
Res.: 1315 2nd St., N.E., 55413-1905. Tel: 612-379-9736.
Catechesis/Religious Program—629 2nd St., N.E.. Tel: 612-379-2761. Students 30.

15—ST. FRANCES CABRINI (1946), Rev. Leo J. Tibesar; Marie Rossa, Admin.
Res.: 1500 Franklin Ave., S.E., 55414-3697. Tel: 612-339-3023; Fax: 612-339-0734.
Catechesis/Religious Program—Students 116.

16—ST. HEDWIG (1914), (Polish), Rev. Donald Schwalm.
Res.: 129 29th Ave., N.E., 55418. Tel: 612-789-4830; Fax: 612-789-1985.
School—Pope John Paul II Catholic School See Elementary Schools, Consolidated, Parochial under the Institutions Located in the Archdiocese for details.
Catechesis/Religious Program—Students 59.

17—ST. HELENA (1913), Rev. Richard R. Villano. 3204 E. 43rd St., 55406. Tel: 612-729-7344.
Res.: 4320 33rd Ave. S., 55406. Tel: 612-729-2252; Fax: 612-724-8695.
School—3200 E. 44th St., 55406. Tel: 612-729-9301; Fax: 612-729-6016. Lay Teachers 13; Students 167.
Catechesis/Religious Program—Tel: 612-729-7321. Students 56.

18—HOLY CROSS (1886), (Polish), Revs. David T. Ostrowski; Andrzej Salapata, S.Ch. (Poland) (CHI).
Res.: 1621 University Ave., N.E., 55413. Tel: 612-789-7238; Fax: 612-789-5769.
School—Pope John Paul II Catholic School Please refer to the listing under Elementary Schools, Consolidated, Parochial in the Institutions section.
Catechesis/Religious Program—Tel: 612-789-9168. Students 107.

19—HOLY NAME (1916), Rev. Leo J. Schneider.
Res.: 3637 11th Ave. S., 55407. Tel: 612-724-5465; Fax: 612-724-5466.
School—Risen Christ Catholic School, Tel: 612-822-5329; Fax: 612-822-5903. See Elementary Schools, Consolidated, Parochial under Institutions Located in the Archdiocese for details.
Catechesis/Religious Program—Students 40.

20—HOLY ROSARY (1878), (Hispanic), Rev. Jose Santiago, O.P.; Bro. Kevin W. Carroll, O.P., Pastoral Assoc.
Res.: 2424 18th Ave. S., 55404. Tel: 612-724-3651; Fax: 612-728-8944.
School—Risen Christ Catholic School, Tel: 612-822-5329; Fax: 612-729-2336. See Elementary Schools, Consolidated, Parochial under Institutions Located in the Archdiocese for details.
Catechesis/Religious Program—Students 180.
Convent—1614 E. 24th St., 55404. Tel: 612-724-2620. Dominican Sisters (Sinsinawa, WI) 6.

21—INCARNATION (1909), Rev. Robert Monaghan.
Res.: 3817 Pleasant Ave., 55409-1296. Tel: 612-822-2101; Fax: 612-822-7928.
School—Risen Christ Catholic School, Tel: 612-822-5329; Fax: 612-822-5903. See Elementary Schools, Consolidated, Parochial under Institutions Located in the Archdiocese for details.
Catechesis/Religious Program—Students 105.

22—ST. JOAN OF ARC (1946), Rev. George P. Wertin.
Res.: 4537 3rd Ave. S., 55409. Tel: 612-823-8205; Fax: 612-825-7028.
Catechesis/Religious Program—Kathy Itzin, D.R.E. Students 708.

23—ST. JOSEPH HIEN (1987), (Vietnamese), [JC] Revs. Jim N. Khoi, C.M.C.; Andrew Dolinh Sang, C.M.C.; Andrew Nguyen-Hong-Aw, C.M.C.
Res.: 1814 Dupont Ave. N., 55411. Tel: 612-522-5006; Fax: 612-522-5006.
Catechesis/Religious Program—Tel: 612-513-9112. Students 450.
Mission—Mission of the Mother-Coredemptrix

24—ST. LAWRENCE-NEWMAN (1887), In Res., Revs. Richard Chilson, C.S.P.; John J. Behnke, C.S.P.; Michael Martin, C.S.P.; Donald A. Andrie, C.S.P.; Deacon Paul Carlson.
Res.: 1201 5th St., S.E., 55414. Tel: 612-331-7941; 612-331-3437; Fax: 612-378-1771.
Catechesis/Religious Program—Students 43.

25—ST. LEONARD OF PORT MAURICE (1941), (African American), Rev. James R. DeBruycker.
Res.: 3949 Clinton Ave., 55409. Tel: 612-825-5811; Fax: 612-825-5811.
Catechesis/Religious Program—Students 16.

26—ST. OLAF (1941), [JC] Revs. John E. Forliti; Mark L. Pavlik; Leon F. Klimczyk, S.J.; Deacons Stephen Boatwright; Clarence Shallbetter.
Res.: 215 S. 8th St., 55402. Tel: 612-332-7471; Fax: 612-332-3412.

27—OUR LADY OF LOURDES (1877), (French-Canadian), Rev. Charles L. Froehle.
Res.: One Lourdes Pl., 55414. Tel: 612-379-2259; Fax: 612-379-0165.
Catechesis/Religious Program—Students 86.

28—OUR LADY OF MOUNT CARMEL (1938), (Italian), Rev. William J. Kenney (Retired); Deacon Michael D. Powers; Margery E. Powers, Parish Life Admin.
Res.: 701 Fillmore St., N.E., 55413. Tel: 612-623-4019; Fax: 612-331-3407.
School—Pope John Paul II Catholic School Please refer to the listing under Elementary Schools, Consolidated, Parochial in the Institutions section.
Catechesis/Religious Program—Students 14.

29—OUR LADY OF PEACE (1991), Rev. Kevin T. Kenney.
Res.: 5425 11th Ave. S., 55417. Tel: 612-823-8253; Fax: 612-823-5102.
School—5435 11th Ave. S., 55417. Tel: 612-824-3455; Fax: 612-824-7328. Lay Teachers 23; Students 361.
Catechesis/Religious Program—Students 176.

30—OUR LADY OF PERPETUAL HELP, Closed. For inquiries for parish records contact the chancery.

31—OUR LADY OF VICTORY (1945), Rev. Terrence M. Hayes.
Res.: 5155 Emerson Ave. N., 55430. Tel: 612-529-7788; Fax: 612-529-3343.
Church: 52nd and Fremont Aves., 55430.
School—St. Elizabeth Seton, 5140 Fremont Ave. N., 55430. Tel: 612-529-7781. Lay Teachers 16; Students 170.
Catechesis/Religious Program—Tel: 612-521-7454. Students 45.

32—ST. PHILIP (1906), (Polish), [CEM] Deacon Dale Timmerman.
Res.: 2507 Bryant Ave. N., 55411. Tel: 612-529-3125; Fax: 612-287-9133.
Catechesis/Religious Program—Students 27.

33—ST. STEPHEN (1885), Rev. Patrick E. Griffin.
Parish Center—2211 Clinton Ave., 55404. Tel: 612-874-0311; Fax: 612-874-0313.
School—Risen Christ Catholic School, Tel: 612-822-5329. See Elementary Schools, Consolidated, Parochial under Institutions Located in the Archdiocese for details.
Catechesis/Religious Program—Students 75.

34—ST. THOMAS THE APOSTLE (1908), Rev. Stephen R. O'Gara.
Res.: 2914 W. 44th St., 55410. Tel: 612-922-0041; Fax: 612-922-1921.
School—2900 W. 44th St., 55410. Tel: 612-920-9075; Fax: 612-927-7426. Combined program with Christ the King, Minneapolis. Lay Teachers, Both Campuses 35; Students 470.
Catechesis/Religious Program—Students 250.

35—VISITATION (1946), Rev. Francis A. Pouliot; Deacon Peter A. D'Heilly.
Res.: 4500 Lyndale Ave. S., 55409. Tel: 612-822-3139.
School—4530 Lyndale Ave. S., 55409. Tel: 612-827-3861; Fax: 612-824-3515. Lay Teachers 11; Students 89.
Catechesis/Religious Program—Students 27.

OUTSIDE METROPOLITAN MINNEAPOLIS

BLAINE, ANOKA CO., ST. TIMOTHY'S (1943), Rev. Harold J. Tasto; Deacons Jerry Devine; Kevin Jents.
Res.: 707 89th Ave., N.E., 55434. Tel: 763-784-1329; Fax: 763-784-0652.
Catechesis/Religious Program—Students 840.

BLOOMINGTON, HENNEPIN CO.

1—ST. BONAVENTURE (1959), Revs. Bernard Zajdel, O.F.M.Conv.; Robert St. Martin, O.F.M.Conv.; Deacons Jack Herzog; Jon DeLuney. In Res., Revs. Thomas Merrill, O.F.M.Conv.; Steve McMichael, O.F.M.Conv.
Res.: 901 E. 90th St., 55420. Tel: 952-854-4733; Fax: 952-851-9690.
Catechesis/Religious Program—Tel: 952-854-4753. Students 313.

2—ST. EDWARD (1967), Rev. Michael Tegeder; Deacon Willard F. Dornfeld.
Res.: 9401 Nesbitt Ave. S., 55437. Tel: 952-835-7101; Fax: 952-835-0156. Web: www.StEdwardsChurch.org.
Catechesis/Religious Program—Students 540.

3—NATIVITY OF THE BLESSED VIRGIN MARY (1949), Rev. Robert E. Johnson; Deacons James McLaughlin; Rob Warhol.
Office—9900 Lyndale Ave. S., 55420. Tel: 612-881-8671; Fax: 612-881-8692.
School—9901 Bloomington Fwy., 55420. Tel: 612-881-8160; Fax: 612-881-3032. Lay Teachers 21; Students 398.
Catechesis/Religious Program—Tel: 612-881-1451; Fax: 612-881-8671. Christie Burke, D.R.E. Students 180.

BROOKLYN CENTER, HENNEPIN CO., ST. ALPHONSUS (1959), Revs. Patrick Grile, C.SS.R.; Martin Stillmock, C.SS.R.; Joseph Stenger, C.SS.R.; Wil Lowery, C.SS.R.; Tuan Pham, C.SS.R.; Bro. Raymond Bowersox, C.SS.R., (Retired); Deacons Jerome H. Bisek; Bobby May; David Holst; John Winkelman. In Res., Rev. David Shannon, C.SS.R.
Res.: 7025 Halifax Ave. N., 55429. Tel: 763-561-5100; Fax: 763-561-0336.
School—7031 Halifax Ave., N., 55429. Tel: 763-561-5101. Lay Teachers 19; Students 297.
Catechesis/Religious Program—4111 71st Ave. N., 55429. Tel: 612-561-5102. Barbara Walhood, D.R.E. Students 661.

BROOKLYN PARK, HENNEPIN CO., ST. GERARD (1970), [JC] Very Rev. Giles A. Schinelli, T.O.R.; Rev. Terrence T. Smith.
Res.: 9600 Regent Ave. N., 55443. Tel: 763-424-8770; Fax: 763-424-4327.
Catechesis/Religious Program—Tel: 763-424-8600; Fax: 763-424-4327. Students 710.

BURNSVILLE, DAKOTA CO.

1—CHURCH OF THE RISEN SAVIOR (1970), Revs. Tim Wozniak; James Gorman; Deacon Richard Stevens; Mary Woida, Admin.
Office—1501 E. County Rd. 42, 55306. Tel: 952-431-5222; Fax: 952-431-5221.
Catechesis/Religious Program—Mary Anne Schaenzer, S.S.N.D., D.R.E.; Mary Ann Zervas, D.R.E.; Desire Sobiech, D.R.E. Students 857.

2—MARY, MOTHER OF THE CHURCH (1965), Revs. James C. Zappa Jr.; Cletus Basekela; Deacon Peter Huberty; Barry Haller, Business Admin.
Church: 3333 Cliff Rd., 55337. Tel: 952-890-0045; Fax: 952-890-0789.
Catechesis/Religious Program—Al Rocklage, D.R.E. Students 830.

COLUMBIA HEIGHTS, ANOKA CO., IMMACULATE CONCEPTION (1923), Rev. Albert P. Backmann; Deacon Larry Palkert.
Res.: 4030 Jackson St., N.E., 55421. Tel: 763-788-9062; Fax: 763-788-0202.
School—4030 Jackson Street N.E., 55421. Tel: 763-788-9065; Fax: 763-788-9066. Sisters of St. Francis 3; Lay Teachers 15; Students 260.
Catechesis/Religious Program—Tel: 763-788-9067. Students 143.

COON RAPIDS, ANOKA CO., CHURCH OF THE EPIPHANY (1964), [CEM] Revs. Patrick Kennedy; Bernard A. Reiser, Pastor Emeritus (Retired); Joel Cyenas; Thomas Kunnel, T.O.R. (India); James L. Lamm, Admin.
Res.: 1900 111th Ave., N.W., 55433. Tel: 763-755-1020; Fax: 763-862-4303.
School—11001 Hanson Blvd., 55433. Tel: 763-754-1750; Fax: 763-862-4350. Michael Strauss, Prin. Lay Teachers 44; Students 800.
Catechesis/Religious Program—11001 Hanson Blvd., 55433. Tel: 763-755-5010; Fax: 763-862-4354. Students 1,258.

CRYSTAL, HENNEPIN CO., ST. RAPHAEL (1951), Revs. Mark R. Juettner; Bryan J. Pederson.
Res.: 7301 Bass Lake Rd., 55428. Tel: 763-537-8401; Fax: 763-537-4878.
School—Tel: 763-504-9450; Fax: 763-504-9460. Sisters 1; Lay Teachers 30; Students 378.
Catechesis/Religious Program—Tel: 763-537-8401, Ext. 211; Fax: 763-537-4878. Paulette Schatz, D.R.E. Students 295.

EAGAN, DAKOTA CO.

1—ST. JOHN NEUMANN (1977), Revs. Charles V. Lachowitzer; Cory J. Rohlfing; Richard Klish.
Res.: 4030 Pilot Knob Rd., 55122. Tel: 651-454-2079; Fax: 651-454-0860.
Catechesis/Religious Program—Students 2,136.

2—ST. THOMAS BECKET (1989), Rev. Thomas H. Brioschi; Deacons Paul Tatone; Bob Kelly.
Res.: 4455 S. Robert Tr., 55123. Tel: 651-683-0689; 651-683-9808 (Parish Center); Fax: 651-683-0361.
Catechesis/Religious Program—Students 200.

EDEN PRAIRIE, HENNEPIN CO., PAX CHRISTI (1981), Revs. J. Timothy Power; Douglas E. Dandurand, Ph.D.; Deacon Al Schroeder.
Res.: 12100 Pioneer Tr., 55347-4208. Tel: 952-941-3150; Fax: 952-941-7942.
Catechesis/Religious Program—Tel: 952-941-6007; Fax: 952-941-7942. Students 1,526.

EDINA, HENNEPIN CO.

1—OUR LADY OF GRACE (1946), Revs. Robert M. Schwartz; Kevin P. Magner; Kevin P. Manger; Deacon Anthony Pasko. In Res., Revs. Jerome W. Fehn; Robert T. Cassidy.
Res.: 5051 Eden Ave., 55436. Tel: 952-929-3317; Fax: 952-929-4612.
School—5071 Eden Ave., 55436. Tel: 952-929-5463; Fax: 952-929-8170. Lay Teachers 34; Students 673.
Catechesis/Religious Program—Students 737.

2—ST. PATRICK (1857), Rev. Thomas H. Sieg; Deacon Byron Rudolphi.
Res.: 6820 St. Patrick's Ln., 55439. Tel: 952-941-3164; Fax: 952-941-7371.
Catechesis/Religious Program—Patricia Brady, D.R.E.; Cheryl Wood, D.R.E.; Brenda Latterell, D.R.E. Students 583.

FRIDLEY, ANOKA CO., ST. WILLIAM (1963), Rev. Joseph Whalen; Deacon Jim Wagner.
Admin. Center—6120 5th St., N.E., 55432. Tel: 763-571-5600; Fax: 763-571-6924.
Catechesis/Religious Program—Students 211.

GOLDEN VALLEY, HENNEPIN CO.

1—GOOD SHEPHERD (1946), [JC] Rev. Theodore C. Campbell.
Res.: 145 Jersey Ave. S., 55426. Tel: 763-544-0416; Fax: 763-544-9896.
School—Tel: 763-545-4285; Fax: 763-545-1896. Lay Teachers 20; Students 315.
Catechesis/Religious Program—Tel: 763-544-0416. Students 183.

2—ST. MARGARET MARY (1946), Rev. Paul Moudry.
Res.: 2301 Zenith Ave., N., 55422. Tel: 763-588-9466; Fax: 763-588-0190.
Catechesis/Religious Program—Students 40.

HAM LAKE, ANOKA CO., SAINT PAUL (1981), Rev. Timothy F. Nolan; Deacon Bill Beck.
Res.: 1740 Bunker Lake Blvd., N.E., 55304. Tel: 763-757-6910; Fax: 763-757-6920.
Catechesis/Religious Program—Tel: 763-757-1148. Trudy Swanson, D.R.E. Students 635.

LINO LAKES, ANOKA CO., ST. JOSEPH (1891), [CEM] Revs. Timothy Morin; Thomas Konkel.
Office—171 Elm St., 55014. Tel: 651-784-3015; Fax:

651-784-3699.
Catechesis/Religious Program—Shirley Gormley, D.R.E.; Denise Walsh, D.R.E.; Jeanne Degerstrom, D.R.E.; Michael Lentz, Admin.; Judy Doonan-Twoh, D.R.E. Students 1,458.

NEW HOPE, HENNEPIN CO., ST. JOSEPH (1858), [CEM] Rev. Robert Hazel.
Res.: 8701 36th Ave. N., 55427. Tel: 763-544-3352; Fax: 763-544-3435.
Parish Center & Office—Tel: 763-544-3352; Fax: 763-544-3435.
Catechesis/Religious Program—Mary Greving, D.R.E., (Catechetics). Tel: 763-544-3352, Ext. 111; Christopher Briggs. Tel: 763-544-3352, Ext. 138 (High School); Larry Thomas. Tel: 763-544-3352, Ext. 139 (Middle School). Students 603.

PLYMOUTH, HENNEPIN CO., ST. MARY OF THE LAKE (1935), Rev. Curtis F. Lybarger.
Res.: 105 Forestview Ln. N., 55441. Tel: 763-545-1443; Fax: 763-797-0996.
Catechesis/Religious Program—Students 188.

RICHFIELD, HENNEPIN CO.
1—THE CHURCH OF THE ASSUMPTION (1876), (German), [CEM] Rev. Michael Tix; Deacons Robert Smith; Carl Valdez; James Meyer.
Res.: 305 E. 77th St., 55423. Tel: 612-866-5019; Fax: 612-866-5274.
School—Blessed Trinity Nicollet & Penn Campus, Tel: 612-869-5200 (Nicollet); 612-866-6906 (Penn); Fax: 612-869-0277; 612-866-5080. Students 458.
Catechesis/Religious Program—Students 120.
2—ST. PETER (1943), Rev. Eugene A. Pouliot; Deacon Mark Johanns.
Res.: 6740 Nicollet Ave. S., 55423. Tel: 612-866-5089; Fax: 612-866-5080.
School—6720 Nicollet Ave. S., 55423. Tel: 612-869-5200. Consolidation of Assumption, St. Peter & St. Richard. Lay Teachers 23; Students 453.
Catechesis/Religious Program—Students 41.
3—ST. RICHARD (1952), Rev. Thomas Krenik; Deacon William J. Berghoff.
Office:—7540 Penn Ave. S., 55423. Tel: 612-869-2426; Fax: 612-869-0277.
School—Blessed Trinity Catholic School, Tel: 612-866-6906. Consolidation of Assumption, St. Peter & St. Richard. Lay Teachers 25; Students 459.
Catechesis/Religious Program—Students 170.

ROBBINSDALE, HENNEPIN CO., SACRED HEART (1910), Rev. Michael Creagan; Deacons Thomas Coleman; James Ramsey, Ph.D.
Office:—4087 W. Broadway, 55422. Tel: 763-537-4561; Fax: 763-537-5426.
Res.: 4510 40-1/2 Ave. N., 55422.
School—4050 Hubbard, 55422. Tel: 763-537-1329; Fax: 763-537-1486. Lay Teachers 20; Students 262.
Catechesis/Religious Program—Cyrilene Brouillard, D.R.E. Students 131.

ST. LOUIS PARK, HENNEPIN CO.
1—HOLY FAMILY (1926), Rev. Thomas W. Dufner.
Res.: 5900 W. Lake St., 55416. Tel: 612-929-0113; Fax: 612-915-1474.
Catechesis/Religious Program—Tel: 612-929-0113. Students 90.
2—MOST HOLY TRINITY (1943), Rev. Paul F. Feela, M.A.
Parish Center—4017 Utica Ave., 55416. Tel: 952-926-7516; Fax: 952-926-6069.
School—3946 Wooddale Ave., 55416. Tel: 952-926-2222; Fax: 952-926-2222. Lay Teachers 11; Students 100.
Catechesis/Religious Program—Tel: 952-926-7516, Ext. 201. Students 125.

OUTSIDE TWIN-CITY METROPOLITAN AREA

ALBERTVILLE, WRIGHT CO., ST. ALBERT (1902), [CEM] Revs. Peter Richards; James McConville, Pastoral Assoc.
Mailing Address: P.O. Box 127, 55301. Tel: 763-497-2474; Fax: 763-497-7678. In Res., Rev. Mark W. Willenbring (Retired).
Catechesis/Religious Program—P.O. Box 67, 55301. Tel: 612-497-3782. Students 261.

ANNANDALE, WRIGHT CO., ST. IGNATIUS (1882), [CEM] Rev. Victor Valencia.
Res.: 55302. Tel: 320-274-8828.
Catechesis/Religious Program—Tel: 320-274-5064; Fax: 320-274-3961. Students 245.

ANOKA, ANOKA CO., ST. STEPHEN (1856), [CEM] Revs. Michael Van Sloun, O.S.C.; William Deziel, O.S.C.; Adrian Piotrowski, O.S.C.; Deacons Peter Bednarczyk; Dominic Ehrmantraut; Daniel Nalezny; Charles Waugh. In Res., Revs. Kenneth Opat, O.S.C.; Eugene D. Plaisted, O.S.C.; Oscar Schoenberg, O.S.C.; Richard John, O.S.C.
Office:—525 Jackson St., 55303. Tel: 763-421-2471; Fax: 763-421-4230.
Rectory—516 School St.. Tel: 763-421-7115 (Res.).
School—506 Jackson St., 55303. Tel: 763-421-3236; Fax: 763-712-7433. Lay Teachers 24; Students 438.
Catechesis/Religious Program—Students 983.

BAYPORT, WASHINGTON CO., ST. CHARLES (1943), [CEM] Rev. Mark J. Underdahl; Deacon Roger B. Carlson.
Res.: 409 N. 3rd St., 55003. Tel: 651-439-4511; Fax: 651-430-9717.
School—St. Croix Catholic School, 621 S. 3rd St., Stillwater, 55082. Tel: 651-439-5581; Fax: 651-439-8360. See Elementary Schools, Consolidated, Parochial under Institutions Located in the Archdiocese for details.
Catechesis/Religious Program—Tel: 651-439-7142; Fax: 651-439-7705. Students 141.

BELLE CREEK, GOODHUE CO., ST. COLUMBKILL (1860), (Irish), [JC] Rev. Bruce Peterson.
Res.: 311 N. 6th St., Goodhue, 55027. Tel: 651-923-4184.
Catechesis/Religious Program—Students 132.
Mission—Holy Trinity 308 4th St. N. Goodhue, Goodhue Co. 55027. Tel: 651-923-4472.

BELLE PLAINE, SCOTT CO., OUR LADY OF THE PRAIRIE (1972), [CEM 2] Rev. Thomas McCabe.
Res.: 215 N. Chestnut St., 56011. Tel: 952-873-2323; Fax: 952-873-6717.
School—Tel: 612-873-6564. Lay Teachers 6; Students 73.
Catechesis/Religious Program—Mrs. Janice Teal, D.R.E. Students 242.

BELLECHESTER, GOODHUE CO., ST. MARY (1859), (Luxembourgian), [CEM] Rev. Bruce Peterson, Admin.
Res.: 223 Chester Ave., 55027. Tel: 651-923-4305.
Catechesis/Religious Program—Students 33.

BROOKLYN PARK, HENNEPIN CO., ST. VINCENT DE PAUL (1855), (French), [CEM] Revs. John Long; Mark Ostendorf; Deacon Sherman H. Otto.
Res.: 9100 93rd Ave. N., 55445-1407. Tel: 763-425-2210; Fax: 763-425-7898.
School—Tel: 763-425-3970; Fax: 763-425-2674. Lay Teachers 20; Students 418.
Catechesis/Religious Program—Arlys Lingen, D.R.E.; Renee Paske, D.R.E. (Elementary Coord.); Suzanne Giese, D.R.E., (Elementary Coord.); Joe Cassady; Kathleen Pommerlau, D.R.E., (Preschool Coord.); Sandra Wheeler, D.R.E., (Junior High School Coord.). Students 1,405.

BUFFALO WRIGHT CO., ST. FRANCIS XAVIER (1888), [CEM 2] Rev. Thomas Rayar; Deacon Richard Boisclair.
Res.: 9 N.W. 3rd St., 55313. Tel: 763-682-1183; Fax: 763-682-0485.
School—Tel: 763-682-1295; Fax: 763-684-5377. Leighton Johnson, Prin. Lay Teachers 14; Students 203.
Catechesis/Religious Program—Tel: 763-684-5326. Sharon Kelly, D.R.E. Students 580.

CANNON FALLS, GOODHUE CO., ST. PIUS V (1856), [CEM] Rev. Roger J. Hessian, Admin.; Deacon Patrick Evans.
Res.: 410 W. Colvill Ave., P.O. Box 367, 55009-0367. Tel: 507-263-2578; Fax: 507-263-8005. Email: stpius@rconnect.com.
Catechesis/Religious Program—Tel 507-263-4800 (Grades PreK-6); 507-263-4680 (Grades 7-12); Fax: 507-263-8005. Students 285.

CARVER, CARVER CO., ST. NICHOLAS (1868), (German), [CEM 2] Rev. William J. Paron.
Res.: 412 W. Fourth St., Box 133, 55315. Tel: 952-448-2345; Fax: 952-368-0502.
Catechesis/Religious Program—Tel 952-448-7015. Students 98.

CEDAR LAKE, SCOTT CO., ST. PATRICK (1856), (Czech), [CEM] Rev. Orlando Tatel.
Res.: Cedar Lake Twp., 24425 Old Hwy. 13 Blvd., Jordan, 55352. Tel: 612-492-6276; Fax: 612-492-6290.
Catechesis/Religious Program—Tel: 612-492-6290. Students 120.
Mission—St. Catherine (1865), [CEM] Prior Lake. 4500 E. 220th St., Spring Lake Twp., Scott Co. 55372. Tel: 612-447-2180.

CEDAR, ANOKA CO., ST. PATRICK (1894), (Irish), [CEM] Rev. Michael J. Kennedy; Thomas Patricia Orzechowski, Parish Admin.; Deacon Terry Scherer.
Res.: 19921 Nightingale St., N.W., Oak Grove, 55011-9243. Tel: 763-753-2011; Fax: 763-753-9803.
Catechesis/Religious Program—Emilie Bauer, D.R.E. Students 1,400.

CENTERVILLE, ANOKA CO., ST. GENEVIEVE (1854), (French-Canadian), [CEM] Rev. Thomas P. Fitzgerald.
Res.: 7087 Goiffon Ave., 55038. Tel: 651-429-7937; Fax: 651-653-0071.
Catechesis/Religious Program—Tel: 612-426-1818. Students 280.

CHANHASSEN, CARVER CO., ST. HUBERT (1865), (German), [CEM] Revs. Stephen L. Ulrick; Lawrence R. Blake; Deacons Timothy Helmeke; Robert Wagner.
Res.: 8201 Main St., 55317. Tel: 952-934-9106; Fax: 952-934-8209.
School—Tel: 952-934-6003; Fax: 952-906-1229. Lay Teachers 37; Students 634.
Catechesis/Religious Program—Students 1,143.

CHASKA, CARVER CO., GUARDIAN ANGELS (1858), [CEM] Rev. Lawrence R. Johnson.
Res.: 215 W. 2nd St., 55318. Tel: 952-448-4100; Fax: 952-448-3076.
School—Tel: 952-448-2562; Fax: 952-448-3281. Lay Teachers 21; Students 334.
Catechesis/Religious Program—Tel: 952-227-4007. Students 240.

CLEARWATER, WRIGHT CO., ST. LUKE (1870), [CEM] Rev. Jacob Yali (Nigeria).
Mailing Address: P.O. Box 249, 55320-0249. Tel: 320-558-2124; Fax: 320-558-2875.
Res.: 425 Spring St., 55320. Tel: 320-558-9001.
Catechesis/Religious Program—Students 126.

CLEVELAND, LE SUEUR CO., CHURCH OF THE NATIVITY OF THE BLESSED VIRGIN MARY (1865), (Irish—German), [CEM] Rev. Edwin Savundra.
Mailing Address: P.O. Box 187, 56017-0187. Tel: 507-243-3166; Fax: 507-243-3849.
Res.: 56017-0187. Tel: 507-931-5409.
Catechesis/Religious Program—Students 67.

COATES, DAKOTA CO., ST. AGATHA (1870), [CEM] Unassigned., 3700 160th St. E., Rosemount, 55068. University of St. Thomas: 2115 Summit Ave., 55105. Tel: 651-645-2400; Fax: 651-962-6360.
Catechesis/Religious Program—Students 67.

COLOGNE, CARVER CO., ST. BERNARD (1859), [CEM] [JC] Rev. George Thoomkuzhy (India) (Ujjain).
Res.: 212 Church St. E., 55322. Tel: 952-466-2031; Fax: 952-466-2031.
School—300 Church St. E., 55322. Tel: 952-466-5917. Lay Teachers 6; Students 75.
Catechesis/Religious Program—Students 84.

CORCORAN, HENNEPIN CO., ST. THOMAS THE APOSTLE (1896), [CEM 4] [JC 4] Rev. George R. Kinney.
Res.: 20,000 County Rd. 10, Hamel, 55340. Tel: 612-420-2385; Fax: 612-420-4710.
Catechesis/Religious Program—Tel: 612-420-2385; Fax: 612-420-4710. Brenda Dalman, D.R.E.; Susan Wieneke, D.R.E.; Linda Stanton, D.R.E. Students 336.

DAYTON, HENNEPIN CO., ST. JOHN THE BAPTIST (1862), (French-Canadian), [CEM 2] Rev. Peter Richards; Rev. Msgr. Michael Becker.
Res.: P.O. Box 201, 55327. Tel: 763-428-2828; Fax: 763-428-6462.
Catechesis/Religious Program—Students 175.

DEEPHAVEN, HENNEPIN CO., ST. THERESE (1946), Rev. Martin Shaiibetter; Deacon James F. McDonald.
Res.: 18323 Minnetonka Blvd., 55391. Tel: 952-473-4422; Fax: 952-261-0585.
School—18325 Minnetonka Blvd., 55391. Tel: 952-473-4355; Fax: 952-261-0630. Sisters 5; Lay Teachers 22; Students 381; Pre-school 29.
Catechesis/Religious Program—Laurie Acker, D.R.E. Students 635.

DELANO, WRIGHT CO.
1—ST. JOSEPH (1902), (Polish), [CEM] Rev. Michael J. Miller; Deacon Joseph Kittok.
Church: 401 River St., P.O. Box 470, 55328-0470. Tel: 763-972-2077; Fax: 763-972-6177.
School—St. Peter School, Tel: 763-972-2528; Fax: 763-972-6177.
Catechesis/Religious Program—Tel: 763-972-2976. Clustered with St. Peter, Delano. Students 106.
2—ST. MARY OF CZESTOCHOWA (1884), (Polish), [CEM] Rev. Joseph G. Gallatin.
Office & Res.: 1867 95th St., S.E., 55328. Tel: 952-955-1139.
Catechesis/Religious Program—Tel: 952-955-1180. Students 62.
3—ST. PETER (1865), (German), [CEM 2] Rev. Michael J. Miller; Deacon Joseph Kittok.
Offices:—204 River St., P.O. Box 470, 55328. Tel: 763-972-2077; Fax: 763-972-6177.
School—St. Peter, Tel: 763-972-2528. Lay Teachers 10; Students 123.
Catechesis/Religious Program—235 S. 2nd St., 55328. Tel: 763-972-2976; Fax: 763-972-6177. Clustered with St. Joseph, Delano. Students 248.

ELYSIAN, LE SUEUR CO., ST. ANDREW, WATERVILLE, MN (1894), Rev. Michael W. Ince, Admin.
Church: Box 261, 56028. Tel: 507-267-4928.
Catechesis/Religious Program—Students 59.

EXCELSIOR, HENNEPIN CO., ST. JOHN THE BAPTIST (1903), [CEM] Rev. Mark B. Dosh; Deacon Gary Hoffman.
Res.: 680 Mill St., 55331-3243. Tel: 952-474-8868; Fax: 952-474-5962.
School—Tel: 952-474-5812; Fax: 952-401-8778. Lay Teachers 14; Students 179.
Catechesis/Religious Program—Students 180.

FARIBAULT, RICE CO.
1—DIVINE MERCY CATHOLIC CHURCH (2002), [CEM 2] Revs. J. Kevin Finnegan; Jay K. Kythe; Vicente Miranda (Ecuador); Deacons R. Daniel Wesley; Steven Moses.
Res.: 4 Second Ave., S.W., 55021-6029. Tel: 507-334-2266; Fax: 507-334-3895.
School—Catholic School of Faribault, Tel: 507-334-7706; Fax: 507-332-2669. See Elementary Schools,

Consolidated, Parochial under Institutions Located in the Archdiocese for details.
Catechesis/Religious Program—Students 509.
2—IMMACULATE CONCEPTION (1856), Merged, with Sacred Heart and St. Lawrence, Faribault to form Divine Mercy Catholic Church, Faribault.
3—ST. LAWRENCE (1869), (German), Merged, with Sacred Heart and Immaculate Conception, Faribault to form Divine Mercy Catholic Church, Faribault.
4—SACRED HEART, (French—German), Merged, with St. Lawrence and Immaculate Conception, Faribault to form Divine Mercy Catholic Church, Faribault.
5—SACRED HEART - ST. LAWRENCE OF FARIBAULT, Merged, with Immaculate Conception, Faribault to form Divine Mercy Catholic Church, Faribault.

FARMINGTON, DAKOTA CO., ST. MICHAEL (1854), [CEM] Rev. Dennis Thompson.
Church and Center: 22120 Denmark Ave., P.O. Box 227, 55024. Tel: 651-463-3360; Fax: 651-463-2339.
Catechesis/Religious Program—Students 480.

FOREST LAKE, WASHINGTON CO., ST. PETER (1904), [CEM] Revs. Robert J. Sipe; Clement Kabuk (Nigeria); Deacons Gary Houle; Ralph L'Allier, Pastoral Min.; Mylo Shoberg; Terrence Moravec.
Res.: 1250 S. Shore Dr., 55025. Tel: 651-982-2200; Fax: 651-982-2220.
School—Tel: 651-982-2215; Fax: 651-982-2230. John G. Mooney, Prin. Lay Teachers 20; Students 376.
Catechesis/Religious Program—Tel: 651-464-7557; Fax: 651-464-1924. Susan Fast, D.R.E. Students 596.

HAMEL, HENNEPIN CO., ST. ANNE (1879), [CEM] Rev. Robert A. Patterson.
Res.: 200 Hamel Rd., Box 256, 55340-0256. Tel: 763-478-6644; Fax: 763-478-9141.
Catechesis/Religious Program—Students 69.

HAMPTON, DAKOTA CO., ST. MATHIAS (1900), [CEM] Arthur Bowman, Parish Life Admin.
Office—23325 Northfield Blvd., 55031.
Res.: 23315 Northfield Blvd., 55031-9667. Tel: 651-437-9030; Fax: 651-437-3427.
School—(Grades K-5) Tel: 651-437-5282. Lay Teachers 8; Students 70.
Catechesis/Religious Program—Students 117.

HANCOCK TOWNSHIP, CARVER CO., ASSUMPTION, Closed. For inquiries for parish records contact the chancery.

HASSAN TOWNSHIP, HENNEPIN CO., ST. WALBURGA (1857), Closed. For inquiries for parish records contact the chancery.

HASTINGS, DAKOTA CO., ST. ELIZABETH ANN SETON (1987), [CEM] [JC] Revs. James M. Perkl; Jose Kirianthan (India); Deacon Michael Humbert.
Res.: 2035 W. Fifteenth St., 55033. Tel: 651-437-4254; Fax: 651-438-2948.
School—Tel: 651-437-3098; Fax: 651-438-3377. Rita Humbert, Prin. Lay Teachers 32; Students 381; Preschool 60.
Catechesis/Religious Program—Tel: 651-437-9191. Students 359.

HAZELWOOD, RICE CO., ANNUNCIATION OF THE B.V.M. (1863), [CEM] Rev. Dennis D. Evenson.
Res.: 4996 Hazelwood Ave., Northfield, 55057. Tel: 952-652-2625; Fax: 952-652-2625.
Catechesis/Religious Program—Students 65.

HEIDELBERG, LE SUEUR CO., ST. SCHOLASTICA (1856), (German—Czech), [CEM] Rev. Richard P. Roedel.
Res.: 31525 181st Ave., New Prague, 56071. Tel: 612-758-4292.
Catechesis/Religious Program—Students 4.

HOPKINS, HENNEPIN CO.
1—ST. JOHN THE EVANGELIST (1950), Rev. Ralph J. Goman.
Res.: 6 Interlachen Rd., 55343. Tel: 952-935-5536; Fax: 952-938-2724.
School—John Ireland Schools, Tel: 952-938-3442. See Elementary Schools, Consolidated, Parochial under Institutions Located in the Archdiocese for details.
Catechesis/Religious Program—Tel: 952-935-4696. Students 75.
2—ST. JOSEPH'S (1926), [CEM] Rev. Gerald Dvorak; Deacon Francis J. Tangney. In Res., Rev. Gerald E. Keefe (Retired).
Res.: 1310 Main St., 55343. Tel: 952-935-0111; Fax: 952-935-4539.
School—John Ireland Schools, Tel: 952-938-3442; Fax: 952-938-3457. See Elementary Schools, Consolidated, Parochial under Institutions Located in the Archdiocese for details.
Catechesis/Religious Program—Tel: 952-935-7004; 952-935-5059. Students 248.

HUGO, WASHINGTON CO., ST. JOHN THE BAPTIST (1902), (French), [CEM] Rev. Sebastien Bakatu.
Res.: 14383 N. Forest Blvd., 55038. Tel: 651-429-9170; Fax: 651-429-3190.
Catechesis/Religious Program—Tel: 651-762-4676. Karlene Feidt, D.R.E. Students 262.

INVER GROVE HEIGHTS, DAKOTA CO., ST. PATRICK (1856), (Irish), [CEM] Rev. Michael M. Arms; Deacon Harlan Christensen.
Res.: 3535 72nd St. E., 55076. Tel: 651-455-6624; Fax: 651-455-8984.
Catechesis/Religious Program—Students 446.

JORDAN, SCOTT CO., ST. JOHN THE BAPTIST (1858), [CEM] [JC] Rev. John J. Mitchell.
Res.: 313 E. 2nd St., 55352. Tel: 952-492-2640; Fax: 952-492-5683.
School—215 E. 2nd St., 55352. Tel: 612-492-2030; Fax: 612-492-3211. Lay Teachers 15; Students 135.
Catechesis/Religious Program—Tel: 952-492-5827. Students 358.

KENYON, GOODHUE CO., ST. MICHAEL (1944), [CEM] Rev. Peter Njoku (Nigeria), Admin.
Church & Office: 108 Bullis St., 55946. Tel: 507-789-6120.
Res.: 590 Sequoia Ln., Zumbrota, 55992. Tel: 507-732-4396.
Catechesis/Religious Program—Students 111.

KILKENNY, LE SUEUR CO., ST. CANICE (1858), (Irish), [CEM] Rev. Ronald W. Dahlheimer.
Res.: 183 W. Maple St., Box 38, 56052. Tel: 507-595-2561.
Catechesis/Religious Program—Students 115.

LAKE ST. CROIX BEACH, WASHINGTON CO., ST. FRANCIS OF ASSISI (1938), Rev. Jerome F. Keiser; Deacon Rip Riordan.
Res.: 16770 13th St., 55043. Tel: 651-436-7817; Fax: 651-436-6524.
Catechesis/Religious Program—Tel: 651-436-8312. Students 236.

LAKEVILLE, DAKOTA CO., ALL SAINTS (1877), [CEM] Revs. Eugene W. Tiffany; Daniel F. Griffith; Deacons James Marschall; George Nugent.
Res.: 19795 Holyoke Ave., 55044. Tel: 952-469-4481; Fax: 952-469-5752.
School—Tel: 952-469-3332; Fax: 952-469-4484. Jan Heuman, Prin. Lay Teachers 25; Students 334.
Catechesis/Religious Program—19795 Holyoke Ave., 55044. Tel: 952-469-6461. Students 1,938.

LE CENTER, LE SUEUR CO., ST. MARY (1899), [CEM] Rev. Raymond G. Monsour.
Res.: 165 N. Waterville Ave., 56057. Tel: 507-357-4838; Fax: 507-357-4838.
Catechesis/Religious Program—Tel: 507-357-6633. Students 276.

LE SUEUR, LE SUEUR CO., ST. ANNE (1852), [CEM 2] Rev. George J. Grafsky.
Res.: 217 N. 3rd St., 56058. Tel: 507-665-2047; Fax: 507-665-3811.
School—Tel: 507-665-2489; Fax: 507-665-6186. Lay Teachers 9; Students 101.
Catechesis/Religious Program—503 N. 4th St., 56058. Tel: 507-665-3811. Students 130.

LEXINGTON, LE SUEUR CO., ST. JOSEPH (1903), (Polish), [CEM] Rev. Richard P. Roedel.
Res.: 31525 181st Ave., New Prague, 56071. Tel: 952-758-4292.
Catechesis/Religious Program—Students 8.

LINDSTROM, CHISAGO CO., ST. BRIDGET OF SWEDEN (1948), Rev. Charles A. Brambilla.
Res.: Box 754, 55045. Tel: 651-257-2474; Fax: 651-257-1498.
Catechesis/Religious Program—Tel: 651-257-0694. Students 575.

LONG LAKE, HENNEPIN CO., ST. GEORGE (1917), [CEM] Rev. Ralph Huar; Deacon Walter Haselhuhn.
Mailing Address: 133 N. Brown Rd., 55356-9560. Tel: 952-473-1247; Fax: 952-404-0129.
Res.: Tel: 952-476-0170; Fax: 952-404-0129.
Catechesis/Religious Program—Tel: 952-475-3739. Students 130.

LONSDALE, RICE CO., IMMACULATE CONCEPTION (1903), [CEM 2] Rev. A. Michael Sauber.
Res.: P.O. Box 169, 55046-0169. Tel: 507-744-2829.
School—Tel: 507-744-2394; Fax: 507-744-2395. For details, please see Holy Cross LNMV Catholic Schools under Elementary Schools, Consolidated, Parochial in the Institution section.
Catechesis/Religious Program—Students 95.

LORETTO, HENNEPIN CO., SS. PETER AND PAUL (1867), [CEM] Unassigned., Mailing Address: P.O. Box 96, 55357. Tel: 763-479-0535; Fax: 763-479-4383.
Res.: 145 Railway St., E., 55357. Tel: 763-479-0537.
School—Tel: 763-479-0540; Fax: 763-479-4046. Lay Teachers 15; Students 180.
Catechesis/Religious Program—Tel: 763-479-0538. Students 150.

MAPLE GROVE, HENNEPIN CO., ST. JOSEPH THE WORKER (1870), Rev. Michael Sullivan; Deacons Donald S. Rinkenberger; Joseph Smith.
Church: 7180 Hemlock Ln., 55369-5597. Tel: 763-425-6505; Fax: 763-425-6587.
Catechesis/Religious Program—Tel: 763-425-9801. Stephen R. Robach, D.R.E. Students 1,099.

MAPLE LAKE, WRIGHT CO., ST. TIMOTHY (1882), [CEM 3] Rev. Mark A. Huberty; Deacons Ron Freeman; Michael Medley.
Res.: 8 N. Oak Ave., Box 281, 55358. Tel: 320-963-3726; Fax: 320-963-2008.
School—Tel: 320-963-3417; Fax: 320-963-8804. Mr. Frank Mazzuca Sr., Prin. Lay Teachers 7; Students 114.
Catechesis/Religious Program—Students 230.

MARYSBURG, LE SUEUR CO., IMMACULATE CONCEPTION (1857), (Irish), [CEM] Rev. Edwin Savandra.
Res.: 27528 Patrick St., Madison Lake, 56063. Tel: 507-243-4157.
Catechesis/Religious Program—Tel: 507-243-3166; Fax: 507-243-3849. Students 67.

MARYSTOWN, SCOTT CO., ST. MARY OF THE PURIFICATION (1855), (German), [CEM] Deacon Jack Weiland, Parish Life Admin.
15850 Marystown Rd., Shakopee, 55379-9556. Tel: 952-445-3469; Fax: 952-403-9330.
Parish Center:—Tel: 952-445-2647; Fax: 952-403-9330.
School—Shakopee Area Catholic School, Tel: 952-445-3387; Fax: 952-445-7256. See Elementary Schools, Consolidated, Parochial under Institutions Located in the Archdiocese for details.
Catechesis/Religious Program—Shakopee Area Religious Education (SARE), 2700 17th Ave. W., Shakopee, 55379. Tel: 952-445-3387. Students 88.

MIESVILLE, DAKOTA CO., ST. JOSEPH (1873), (German—Irish), [CEM], Mailing Address: *Office*, 23955 Nicolai Ave. E., 55033-9650. Tel: 651-437-3526; Fax: 651-437-3526. In Res., Rev. Michael F. O'Connor (Retired).
Catechesis/Religious Program—Tel: 651-437-3506. Students 179.

MINNETONKA, HENNEPIN CO., IMMACULATE HEART OF MARY (1946), Revs. Patrick J. Hipwell; Daniel C. Haugan; Deacon David Huibregtse.
Res.: 13505 Excelsior Blvd., 55345-4999. Tel: 952-935-1432; Fax: 952-935-0474.
Catechesis/Religious Program—Tel: 612-935-7077. Students 306.

MONTGOMERY, LE SUEUR CO., HOLY REDEEMER (1881), [CEM 2] Rev. George J. Grafsky.
Res.: 206 Vine Ave. W., 56069. Tel: 507-364-7981; Fax: 507-364-8660.
School—205 Vine Ave. W., 56069. Tel: 507-364-7383. Sisters of St. Benedict 1; Sisters of Dominican 1; Lay Teachers 12; Students 148.
Catechesis/Religious Program—Students 152.

MONTICELLO, WRIGHT CO., ST. HENRY (1904), [CEM] Rev. Timothy C. Rudolphi; Deacon Greg Woznick.
Office:—1001 E. 7th St., 55362. Tel: 763-295-2402; Fax: 763-295-6333.
Catechesis/Religious Program—Tel: 763-271-3079. Mark Barder, D.R.E. Students 698.

MOUND, HENNEPIN CO., OUR LADY OF THE LAKE (1909), [CEM] Rev. Stan P. Mader.
Res.: 2385 Commerce Blvd., 55364. Tel: 952-472-1284; Fax: 952-472-1216.
School—Preschool, Tel: 952-472-1284, Ext. 172. Students 56.
School—Tel: 952-472-1284, Ext. 151; Fax: 952-472-9152. Dorothy Bialke. Lay Teachers 16; Students 183.
Catechesis/Religious Program—Tel: 952-472-1284, Ext. 144; Fax: 952-472-1216. Students 250.

NEW MARKET, SCOTT CO., ST. NICHOLAS (1893), (German), [CEM] Rev. Glen T. Jenson.
Res.: 51 Church St., P.O. Box 9, 55054-0009. Tel: 952-461-2403; Fax: 952-461-2403.
School—Tel: 507-744-2394; Fax: 507-744-4117. For details, please see Holy Cross LNMV under Elementary Schools, Consolidated, Parochial under the Institution section.
Catechesis/Religious Program—Tel: 952-461-3358. Students 99.

NEW PRAGUE, SCOTT CO., ST. WENCESLAUS (1857), [CEM] Rev. George J. Freeman; Deacons Leonard J. Shanbour; Robert Raleigh.
Res.: 215 Main St. E., 56071-1837. Tel: 952-758-3225; Fax: 952-758-2960.
School—Tel: 952-758-3133; Fax: 952-758-2958. Sarah Mueller, Prin. Lay Teachers 22; Students 377.
Catechesis/Religious Program—Tel: 952-758-2276. Margaret Benson, D.R.E. Students 434.

NEW TRIER, DAKOTA CO., ST. MARY (1856), [CEM] Unassigned. In Res., Rev. Marvin J. Klaers (Retired).
Res.: 8433 239th St. E., Hampton, 55031. Tel: 651-437-5520.
School—Tel: 651-437-5546; Fax: 651-437-5546. Lay Teachers 3; Students 31.
Catechesis/Religious Program—(Grades 6-12) Students 42.

NORTH BRANCH, CHISAGO CO., ST. GREGORY (1874), [CEM] Rev. John F. Parkos; Deacon Thomas P. Langlois; Elizabeth R. Langlois, Pastoral Min.
Res.: P.O. Box 609, 55056. Tel: 651-674-4056; Fax: 651-277-4563.
Catechesis/Religious Program—(Grades 2-8) Tel: 651-674-7382. Students 275.

NORTHFIELD, RICE CO., ST. DOMINIC (1869), [CEM] Rev. Jon Vander Ploeg; Deacon Len Gruber.

Office & Mailing Address: 216 N. Spring St., 55057-1431. Tel: 507-645-8816; Fax: 507-645-8818.
Res.: 116 N. Linden St., 55057. Tel: 507-663-0154.
School—Tel: 507-645-8136. School Sisters of Notre Dame 1; Students 196.
Catechesis/Religious Program—Students 441.

NORWOOD, CARVER CO., ASCENSION (1859), (German), [CEM 2] Rev. Paul C. Ardolf.
Res.: 323 Reform St., N., 55368. Tel: 952-467-3351.
Catechesis/Religious Program—Students 123.

PINE ISLAND, GOODHUE CO., ST. MICHAEL (1878), [CEM] Rev. Peter Njoku (Nigeria).
P.O. Box 368, 55963-0368.
Res.: 590 Sequoia Ln., Zumbrota, 55992. Tel: 507-732-4396; Fax: 507-356-2080.
Catechesis/Religious Program—Tel: 507-356-4280; Fax: 507-356-4280. Students 174.

PRIOR LAKE, SCOTT CO., ST. MICHAEL (1912), [CEM 2] Rev. Richard A. Banker; Deacon Russell D. Shupe.
Res.: 16311 Duluth Ave., S.E., 55372. Tel: 952-447-2491; Fax: 952-447-2489.
School—Preschool, Tel: 952-447-2483; Fax: 952-447-2182. Lay Teachers 2; Students 80.
School—(Grades K-8) Tel: 952-447-2124; Fax: 952-447-2132 (Primary); 952-447-2348 (Middle School). Sisters 1; Lay Teachers 33; Students 567.
Catechesis/Religious Program—Tel: 612-447-2486; Fax: 612-447-2489. Janel Boegeman, D.R.E. (Elementary); Gina Tupy, D.R.E. (Senior High); Nate Lamusga, D.R.E.; Laura Shupe, D.R.E. Students 654; Students 873.

RED WING, GOODHUE CO., ST. JOSEPH (1865), [CEM] Rev. Thomas M. Kommers.
Res.: 426 8th St., 55066. Tel: 651-388-1133; Fax: 651-388-5294.
School—Tel: 651-388-9493; Fax: 651-385-0769. Marion Willis, Prin. Religious 1; Lay Teachers 8; Students 125.
Catechesis/Religious Program—Tel: 651-388-6000. Students 528.

ROGERS, HENNEPIN CO.
1—ST. MARTIN (1912), Closed. For inquiries for parish records contact the chancery.
2—THE CATHOLIC CHURCH OF MARY QUEEN OF PEACE, Rev. Mark D. Moriarty.
21304 Church Ave., 55374. Tel: 763-428-2585.

ROSEMOUNT, DAKOTA CO., ST. JOSEPH (1865), [CEM 2] Rev. Thomas F. Hill, O.F.M.Cap.
Church & Office: 13900 Biscayne Ave., 55068.
Res.: 14375 S. Robert Tr., 55068. Tel: 651-423-4402; Fax: 651-423-6616.
School—Tel: 651-423-1658. Sisters 2; Lay Teachers 8; Students 229.
Catechesis/Religious Program—Tel: 651-423-3131; Fax: 651-423-1855. Sr. Mary Louise McKenna, D.R.E. Students 775.

RUSH CITY, CHISAGO CO., SACRED HEART (1872), (Irish), [CEM] Rev. Xavier Thelakkatt (India).
Res.: P.O. Box 45, 55069. Tel: 320-358-4370; Fax: 320-358-4452.
Catechesis/Religious Program—Students 101.

ST. BENEDICT, SCOTT CO., ST. BENEDICT, (German), [CEM] [JC] Rev. Elgar Bockenfeld, O.F.M.
Res.: 20087 Hub Dr., New Prague, 56071. Tel: 952-738-4642.
Catechesis/Religious Program—Students 20.

ST. BONIFACIUS, HENNEPIN CO., ST. BONIFACE (1859), (German), [CEM] Rev. Joseph G. Gallatin.
Res.: 4025 Main St., P.O. Box 68, 55375. Tel: 612-446-1054; Fax: 612-446-1158.
Catechesis/Religious Program—8801 Wildwood Ave., P.O. Box 276, 55375. Tel: 952-446-1224. Students 103.

ST. HENRY, LE SUEUR CO., CHURCH OF ST. HENRY, [CEM] Rev. Frederick C. Meyer.
Mailing Address: P.O. Le Sueur, 38807-261 Ave., 56058. Tel: 507-357-4990.
Catechesis/Religious Program—Students 33.

ST. MICHAEL, WRIGHT CO., ST. MICHAEL (1857), [CEM 2] Rev. Msgr. Michael Becker; Deacons Maynard Warne; Don Fidler; Donald Becker.
Res.: P.O. Box 180, 55376. Tel: 612-497-2745; Fax: 763-497-5273.
School—Tel: 763-497-3887; Fax: 763-497-9159. Lay Teachers 19; Students 276.
Catechesis/Religious Program—Students 742.

ST. PAUL PARK, WASHINGTON CO., ST. THOMAS AQUINAS (1885), [CEM] Rev. Gregory L. Esty.
Res.: 920 Holly Ave., 55071. Tel: 651-459-2131; Fax: 651-459-8765.
Catechesis/Religious Program—Fax: 651-459-8756. Students 302.

ST. THOMAS, LE SUEUR CO., ST. THOMAS (1858), (Irish), [CEM] Rev. Richard P. Roedel.
Res.: 31525 181st Ave., New Prague, 56071. Tel: 612-758-4292.
Catechesis/Religious Program—Students 43.

SAVAGE, SCOTT CO., ST. JOHN THE BAPTIST (1854), [CEM] Revs. Peter C. Wittman; Rinaldo B. Custodio; Deacons Tom Michaud; Jerry Little.
Res.: 4625 W. 125th St., 55378-1357. Tel: 952-890-9465; Fax: 952-890-3006.
School—Tel: 952-890-6604; Fax: 952-890-9481. Lay Teachers 38; Students 842.
Catechesis/Religious Program—Tel: 952-890-9434; Fax: 952-890-9481. Amy Kusber, D.R.E.; Andi Little, D.R.E.; Jan Jirik, D.R.E. Students 913; Students 910.

SHAKOPEE, SCOTT CO.
1—ST. MARK (1856), (German), [JC 2] Rev. William F. Stolzman; Deacon Allan A. Schroeder.
Res.: 350 S. Atwood St., 55379-1238. Tel: 952-445-1229; Fax: 952-445-9639.
School—Shakopee Area Catholic School Please refer to the listing under Elementary Schools, Consolidated, Parochial in the Institutions section.
Catechesis/Religious Program—2700 17th Ave. E., 55379.
2—ST. MARY (1865), (Irish), [CEM] [JC] Rev. Joseph Fink; Deacon James L. Thornton.
Res.: 535 S. Lewis St., 55379. Tel: 952-445-1319; Fax: 952-445-0511.
School—Shakopee Area Catholic School, Tel: 952-445-3387; 952-445-3159; Fax: 952-445-7256. See Elementary Schools, Consolidated, Parochial under Institutions Located in the Archdiocese for details.
Catechesis/Religious Program—Shakopee Area Religious Education, 2700 17th Ave. W., 55379. Tel: 952-445-3387. Mary Luxem, D.R.E. This is a consolidation of three parish programs. Students 419.

SHIELDSVILLE, RICE CO., ST. PATRICK (1856), (Irish—Czech), [CEM] Revs. George J. Grafsky; Barry L. Schneidek, O.F.M., Pastoral Admin.
Res.: 7525 Dodd Rd., 55021. Tel: 507-334-6002; Fax: 507-334-6002. Web: www.stpatrick-church.org.
Catechesis/Religious Program—Students 67.

SOUTH ST. PAUL, DAKOTA CO.
1—ST. AUGUSTINE (1896), Revs. John M. LeVoir; Mark H. Wehmann.
Res.: 302 5th Ave. N., 55075. Tel: 651-451-1212.
Catechesis/Religious Program—Tel: 651-451-1560; 651-451-0685; Fax: 651-451-1560. Sr. Bernadine Frischmon, O.S.B., D.R.E. Students 178.
2—HOLY TRINITY (1918), (Polish), Revs. John M. LeVoir; Mark H. Wehmann.
Res.: 752 5th Ave. S., 55075. Tel: 651-455-1228; Fax: 651-455-7600.
Office:—749 6th Ave. S., 55075. Tel: 651-455-1302; Fax: 651-455-6004.
School—745 6th Ave. S., 55075. Tel: 651-455-8557; Fax: 651-455-9696. Lay Teachers 25; Students 349.
Catechesis/Religious Program—Tel: 651-455-6004; Fax: 651-455-7600. Students 187.
3—ST. JOHN VIANNEY (1946), [CEM] Rev. Thadeus Aravindathu; Deacon Fred de los Reyes.
Res.: 789 17th Ave. N., 55075. Tel: 651-451-1863; Fax: 651-451-1864.
School—1815 Bromley, 55075. Tel: 651-451-8395. Lay Teachers 14; Students 187.
Catechesis/Religious Program—Students 220.

STILLWATER, WASHINGTON CO.
1—ST. MARY (1865), (German), [JC] Revs. Michael C. Skluzacek; Corey Belden. In Res., Rev. Robert L. Valit (Retired).
Church & Mailing Address: 423 S. Fifth St., 55082.
Res. 407 S. 5th St., 55082. Tel: 651-439-1270; Fax: 651-439-7705.
School—St. Croix Catholic School, Tel: 651-439-5581; Fax: 651-439-8360. See Elementary Schools, Consolidated, Parochial under Institutions Located in the Archdiocese for details.
Catechesis/Religious Program—Tel: 651-439-7142. Students 40.
2—ST. MICHAEL (1853), [JC] Revs. Michael C. Skluzacek. Corey Belden; Deacons Roger Carlson; Greg Glover.
Res.: 611 S. Third St., 55082-4998. Tel: 651-439-4400; Fax: 651-430-3271.
School—St. Croix Catholic School, Tel: 651-439-5581; Fax: 651-439-8360. Cressy Epperly, Prin. See Elementary Schools, Consolidated, Parochial under Institutions Located in the Archdiocese for details.
Catechesis/Religious Program—Tel: 651-439-7142; Fax: 651-439-7705. William Klein, D.R.E. Students 453.

TAYLORS FALLS, CHISAGO CO., ST. JOSEPH'S (1873), [CEM] [JC] Rev. Albert J. Sharkey, M.S.; Deacon Frank J. Thell; Ms. Nancy Madden, Parish Life Coord.
Res.: Box 234, 55084. Tel: 651-465-7345.
Catechesis/Religious Program—Tel: 651-433-3951. Students 220.
Mission—St. Francis Xavier Franconia, Chisago Co. Tel: 651-433-3951.

UNION HILL, LE SUEUR CO., ST. JOHN THE EVANGELIST, [CEM] Rev. Elgar Bockenfeld, O.F.M.
Res.: 20087 Hub Dr., New Prague, 56071. Tel: 952-758-4642.
Catechesis/Religious Program—Students 120.

VERMILLION, DAKOTA CO., ST. JOHN THE BAPTIST (1881), [CEM] Rev. Joseph J. Arackal, V.C. (SYM).
Res.: 106 W. Main St., 55085. Tel: 651-437-5652; Fax: 651-437-1933.
School—111 W. Main St., 55085. Tel: 651-437-2644; Fax: 651-437-2644. Franciscan Clarist Sisters 2; Lay Teachers 6; Students 80.
Catechesis/Religious Program—Fax: 651-437-5652. Students 118.

VESELI, RICE CO., MOST HOLY TRINITY (1874), (Czech), [CEM 2] Rev. John G. Lapensky.
Res.: 9845 Main St., 55046. Tel: 507-744-2823; Fax: 507-744-2823.
School—Tel: 507-744-2394; Fax: 507-744-2395. For details, please see Holy Cross LNMV Catholic School under Elementary Schools, Consolidated, Parochial in the Institution section.
Catechesis/Religious Program—Students 99.

VICTORIA, CARVER CO., ST. VICTORIA (1856), (German), [CEM] Rev. Robert L. White; Deacon Ray Ortman.
Res.: 8228 Victoria Dr., 55386. Tel: 952-443-2661; Fax: 952-443-3866.
Catechesis/Religious Program—Tel: 952-443-3536. Students 231.

WACONIA, CARVER CO., ST. JOSEPH (1859), [CEM] Rev. James R. Himmelsbach.
Res.: 41 E. 1st St., 55387. Tel: 952-442-2384 (Office); Fax: 952-442-3719.
School—Tel: 952-442-4500. Lay Teachers 20; Students 321.
Catechesis/Religious Program—Tel: 952-442-4871. Students 280.

WATERTOWN, CARVER CO., IMMACULATE CONCEPTION (1863), (German—Irish), [CEM] Rev. Frank J. Wampach.
Res.: 109 Angel Ave., N.W., P.O. Box 548, 55388. Tel: 952-955-1458; Fax: 952-955-1777.
Catechesis/Religious Program—109 Angel Ave., N.W.. Tel: 952-955-1777. Patti Pokorney, D.R.E. Students 260.

WATERVILLE, LE SUEUR CO., HOLY TRINITY (1892), [CEM] Rev. Michael W. Ince.
Res.: 506 Common St., 56096. Tel: 507-362-4311.
Catechesis/Religious Program—Tel: 507-362-8396. Students 107.

WAVERLY, WRIGHT CO., ST. MARY (1884), [CEM] [JC 3] Rev. Timothy Cloutier, J.C.L.
Res.: P.O. Box 278, 55390. Tel: 763-658-4319; Fax: 763-658-3519.
Catechesis/Religious Program—Tel: 763-658-4118. Students 229.

WAYZATA, HENNEPIN CO.
1—ST. BARTHOLOMEW (1916), Rev. Michael A. Reding.
Office:—630 E. Wayzata Blvd., 55391. Tel: 952-473-6601; Fax: 952-473-0980.
School—(Grades PreK-6) Tel: 952-473-6189. Lay Teachers 18; Students 311.
Catechesis/Religious Program—Students 317.
2—HOLY NAME (1865), [CEM] Revs. Jonathan Licari, O.S.B.; Joseph Feders, O.S.B. (SCL); Deacons Joe Wierschem; Nelson Hickman; Terry Schneider; Sam Catapano; Dennis Hanson.
Res.: 155 County Rd., 24, 55391. Tel: 763-473-9620; Fax: 763-745-3488.
School—Tel: 763-473-3675; Fax: 763-745-3499. Lay Teachers 25; Students 341.
Catechesis/Religious Program—Tel: 763-473-7901. Students 1,200.

ZUMBROTA, GOODHUE CO., ST. PAUL (1900), [CEM] [JC] Rev. Peter Njoku (Nigeria).
Office & Mailing Address: 749 S. Main St., 55992-1608. Tel: 507-732-5324; Fax: 507-732-5324.
Res.: 590 Sequoia Ln., 55992. Tel: 507-732-4396.
Catechesis/Religious Program—Tel: 507-732-5501; Fax: 507-732-5501. Students 101.

Chaplains of Public Institutions

ST. PAUL. *Bethesda Medical Center*. Revs. Gerald Onuoha, Daniel Ostdiek.
Gillette Children's Hospital. Rev. George Jacob Manjankal (India).
HealthEast, Inc.. Rev. Gerald K. Foley (CR).
St. Joseph's Hospital. Revs. Steve La Canne, Dir. Spiritual Care, Michael Erlander, Chap.
Ramsey County Correctional Facilities. Rev. Stanley Sledz.
Regions Medical Center. Rev. George Jacob Manjankal (India).
United Hospitals, Inc.. Rev. Shaji Joseph Pazzhukkathara (India).

MINNEAPOLIS. *Abbot-Northwestern Hospital*, 3617 38th Ave. S., 55066. Revs. Clement J. Burke (DUB), Jerry C. Vandrovec.
Fairview University Medical Center. Rev. Leo J. Tibesar.
Hennepin County Courts. (Vacant)
Hennepin County Medical Center, 2421 Third Ave. S., 55404. Rev. James R. DeBruycker.
Metropolitan Medical Center. Rev. James Cassidy, Chap.
Minneapolis Children's Medical Center, 3617 38th Ave. S., 55406. Rev. Robert A. Patterson.

Veterans Administration Medical Center. Rev. Damien Schill.
EDINA. *Fairview-Southdale Hospital*. Rev. Gerald Onvoha, Chap.
COON RAPIDS. *Mercy Hospital*. Rev. Jose Puthenparambil.
FARIBAULT. *Faribault State School and Hospital*. Attended by Immaculate Conception Parish.
GOLDEN VALLEY. *North Memorial Hospital*. Rev. Dale J. Korogi.
HASTINGS. *Regina Medical Center*. Rev. John Marley, S.S.C.
LINO LAKES. *Minnesota Correctional Facility*. Rev. Msgr. J. Jerome Boxleitner, Chap. (Retired). 1121 E. 46th St., 55407.
MAPLEWOOD. *St. John's Hospital*, 1575 Beam Ave., 55109. Rev. Fabian F. Burdiek, O.F.M. (Lutheran)
SHAKOPEE. *Women's State Reformatory*. Rev. James T. Schoenberger.
ST. LOUIS PARK. *Methodist Hospital*. Revs. Gerald Onuoha, Daniel Ostdiek.
STILLWATER. *Minnesota State Prison*. Rev. Gregory A. Skrypek.

Special Assignment:
Revs.—
Conlin, Daniel C., J.C.D., Tribunal
Corbley, Timothy L., Chancery Pro Tem
Gamber, William K., Chap. (Retired), V.A. Medical Center
Hubbard, Lawrence E., Hispanic Ministry
Knaup, Daniel, Chancery Pro Tem
Lepak, Roy C. (Retired), Hermit, Cotton, MN
Magee, Paul L., Chancery Pro Tem
Maus, Mark T., Chancery Pro Tem
McDonough, Thomas R.
McDonough, William C., Chancery Pro Tem
Montero, Hugo L., Chancery Pro Tem
Notebaart, James C., Office of Indian Ministry
Pelant, William, Chancery Pro Tem
Piche, Donald J., Chancery Pro Tem
Smith, James D., Chancery Pro Tem
Snyder, Larry J., Catholic Charities
Wajda, Joseph L., Tribunal
Walsh, Harry A., Chancery Pro Tem
Wilson, Thomas, Vocations Office
Ying, Vang Chue

On Duty Outside the Archdiocese:
Revs.—
Brandes, John F. (Retired), Parroquia San Lucas Toliman, Dept. Solola 07013, Guatemala.
Bury, Harold J. (Retired), P.O. Box 20310, Cleveland, OH 44120.
Hogan, Richard, Archdiocese of Oklahoma City
Norris, Timothy L., Apartado 272,, Puerto Ordaz, Estado Bolivar 8050 Venezuela.
O'Connell, Marvin R. (Retired), University of Notre Dame, IN
Schaffer, Gregory J., El Buen Pastor Parroquia San Francisco de Asis, Apartado 22, Puerto Ordaz, Estado Bolivar 8015 Venezuela.
Slusser, Michael S., Dept. of Theology, Duquesne Univ., Pittsburgh, PA 15282.
Wasinger, Shane (DEN), St. Rafka Mission, 4950 S. Logan St., Englewood, CO 80110.

Military Chaplains:
Revs.—
Echert, John, S.S.L.
Fehn, Jerome W.
Himmelsbach, James R., U.S. Army
Thiesen, Eugene
Vakoc, Henry T., U.S. Army

Graduate Studies:
Revs.—
Beaudet, Christopher J., Washington, D.C.
Burns, James P., Waltham, MA.
Cozzens, Andrew, Rome
Johnson, Joseph R., Rome, Italy.
Laird, Peter A., Rome, Italy.
Margevicius, Thomas, Washington, D.C.

Retired:
Rev. Msgrs.—
Baumgaertner, William L., 60 S. Miss. River Blvd., 55105.
Boxleitner, J. Jerome, 1001 E. 46th St., 55407.
Fleming, Francis J., #4 Edgecumbe Pl., 55116.
Hessian, Patrick J., 8066 Timber Lake Dr., Eden Prairie, 55347.
Kneal, Ellsworth, 2260 Summit Ave., 55105.
Lavin, James M., 2115 Summit Ave., 55105.
Murphy, Terrance J., 2115 Summit Ave., 55105.
Probst, Robert L., College of St. Thomas, 60 S. Miss River Blvd., 55105.
Sankovitz, John P., 60 S. Miss. River Blvd., 55105.
Schuler, Richard J., St. Agnes (In Res.), 55103.
Srnec, Stanley J., 60 S. Miss. River Blvd., 55105.
Sweeney, John A., 60 S. Mississippi River Blvd., #227, 55105.
Revs.—
Abbott, Eugene J., 1241 Edgcumbe Rd., 55105.
Beckman, Martin A., P.O. Box 1751, Minnetonka, 55345.
Berg, Richard V., 60 S. Mississippi River Blvd., 55105.
Blais, Melvin J., 1305, 26 W. 10th St., 55102.
Boller, Robert J., 16205 36th Ave. N. Plymouth, 55447.
Brandes, John F., Parroquia San Lucas Toliman, DeptoSola La 07013 Guatemala.
Bury, Harold J., 60 S. Miss. River Blvd., 55105.
Byrne, Albert F., 330 Exchange St., 55102.
Carroll, Roger, 60 S. Miss. River Blvd., 55105.
Cassidy, Robert, 5051 Eden Ave., Edina, 55436.
Clubb, Ronald E., S.T.P. (HON), 4300 W. River Pkwy., 55406.
Cody, Nicholas A., P.O. Box 22, Cross Lake, 56442.
Colon, Vincent A., 2350 Springside Dr., Maplewood, 55119.
Conroy, Thomas J., 60 S. Miss. River Blvd., 55105.
Dobihal, Robert F., 60 S. Miss. River Blvd., 55116.
Doffing, Gordon M., 5820 E. Marlin St., Mesa, AZ 85215.
Dolan, Leo A., 200 Earl St., 55106.
Donahue, John G., 423 5th, 55082.
Dufresne, Oliver J., 26262 Hwy. 65, N.E., Isanti, 55040.
Egan, Harvey F., 121 S. Washington, No. 512, 55401.
Endres, Gilbert J., 652 Ellsworth Rd., Mesa, AZ 85208.
Fitzpatrick, John P., 642 Monna Ave., Vadnais Heights, 55127.
Flahavan, Edward J., 811 Portland Ave., 55104.
Fleming, Martin M.P., 383 Portland Ave., 55102.
Friberc, Daniel, 2021 Wentworth, South St. Paul, 55075.
Gamber, William K., 133 S. Mill St., #205, Fergus Falls.
Gannon, Joseph T., 60 S. Miss. River Blvd., 55105.
Garvey, Thomas J., 1041 16th Ave., S.E., 55414.
Grieman, Gerald G., 264 Ashurst Dr., Phoenix, AZ.
Grzeskowiak, Edward S., 330 Exchange St., 55102.
Gutierrez, Jose, 60 S. Miss. River Blvd., 55105.
Hamel, Robert F., 225 Frank St., 55106.
Hermes, Roger J., 2329 N. Recker Rd., #117, Mesa, AZ.
Holl, James E., 86 Wilkin St., 55102.
Huber, Leo R., 710 19th Ave. N., South St. Paul, 55075.
Huntstiger, Thomas, 625 Oaks Dr., Pompano Beach, FL 33069.
Janski, Jerome J., 10419 El Captain Cir., Sun City, AZ 85351.
Jenniges, Leonard J., 18760 City Hwy 17, Sanborn, 56083.
Jude, Robert J., 332 2nd St. W #7, Maple Lake, 55358.
Karels, Agdus S., 513 N.W. 4th St., Ortonville, 56278.
Keane, Robert E., 5921 14th Ave. S., 55417.
Keefe, Gerald E., 1310 Main St., Hopkins, 55343.
Keller, Lawrence E., 1212 Larpenteur Ave. E., 55109.
Kenney, William J., 1690 McKnight Lane, Maplewood, 55109.
Kittock, Francis R., 60 S. Miss River Blvd., 55102.
Klaers, Marvin J., 8433 239th St. E., Hampton, 55031.
Klein, Bernard C., 86 Wilkin St., #203, 55102.
Kozlak, Stanley, P.O. Box 101, Annandale, 55302.
Kubat, Alphonse M., 60 S. Miss. River Blvd., 55105.
Larkin, Richard, 2099 Silver Bell Rd., Eagan, 55122.
LaVan, Kenneth G., 1657 Granada, Oakdale, 55128.
Lepak, Roy C., 8830 Strand Lake Rd. N., Cotton, 55724.
Mahon, Ambrose J., 1010 Coventry Pl., Edina, 55435.
Mahoney, Richard J., 60 S. Miss. River Blvd., 55105.
McIntyre, Allen J., 60 S. Miss. River Blvd., 55105.
Mitchell, John E., 1824 Eleanor Ave., 55116.
Moorman, Raymond J., 3220 S. Yosemite Ave. S., St. Louis Park, 55416.
Moudry, Richard P., 11113 Hyland Ter., Eden Prairie, 55344.
Namie, James B., 4010 Galt Ocean Dr., Apt. # 1203, Fort Lauderdale, FL.
O'Connell, Marvin R., 15625 Hearthstone Dr., Mishawaka, IN 46545.
Pierre, Kenneth J., 894 Hoyt Ave., 55117.
Pingatore, Thomas J., 7587 Newbury Rd., Woodbury, 55125.
Reidy, James E., 60 S. Miss. River Blvd., 55105.
Reiser, Bernard A., 1900 111th Ave. N.W., Coon Rapids, 55433.
Riley, John F., 60 S. Miss. River Blvd., 55105.
Roach, Francis J., 2132 Bard Ct., P.O. Box 1064, Faribault, 55021.
Schoenberger, James T., 60 S. Miss. River Blvd., 55105.
Siebenaler, John M., Leo Byrne Residence.
Siebenaler, Leonard, 325 Hillcrest Dr., St. Michael, 55376.
Siebenaler, Martin, 122 Farm St., Hastings, 55033.
Skluzacek, Richard F., 1903 Silver Bell Rd., Eagan, 55122.
Smith, John B., 5312 Twin Creek Dr., Valrico, FL 33594.
Stromberg, James S., 60 S. Miss. River Blvd., 55105.
Valit, Robert L., 423 5th St., 55082.
Whittier, William O., St. Mary of the Lake, 2801 Flag Ave. No., New Hope, 55427.
Wirth, John J., 330 S. Exchange, 55102.
Wirth, Richard P., 2350 Stillwater Ave. #212, 55117.
Wittman, Karl M., Leo Byrne Residence.
Wolter, Richard J., 60 S. Miss. River Blvd., 55105.
Zweber, Clement J., P.O. Box 962, Lakeville, 55044.

Permanent Deacons:
Scherkenbach, Gerald A., M.A., Tribunal; St. Joseph, West St. Paul
Allen, Nathan, Cathedral of St. Paul & Tribunal
Asenbrenner, Francis, Maternity of Mary, St. Paul
Babcock, George H., (Retired)
Backmann, Howard, St. Anthony of Padua, MN
Barrett, Ervin F., (Retired)
Barrett, Thomas F., (Retired)
Baskfield, James F., Diocese of Duluth
Beck, William E., St. Paul, Ham Lake
Becker, Donald L., St. Michael, St. Michael
Bednarczyk, Peter, St. Stephen, Anoka
Beer, Terry, Guardian Angels
Bellavance, Peter G., On Leave of Absence
Berghoff, William J., St. Richard, Richfield
Bernard, Charles V., (Retired)
Bisek, Jerome H., On Leave of Absence
Blissenbach, Gerald, (Retired)
Boatwright, Stephen, St. Olaf, Minneapolis
Boisclair, A. Richard, St. Francis, Buffalo
Bramwell, Robert, St. Thomas, Corcoran
Broich, Richard, Chap., Fairview Hospital
Brown, Fredrick L., (Retired)
Campbell, Kevin A., On Leave of Absence
Carlson, Paul, St. Lawrence, Minneapolis and Metropolitan Tribunal
Carlson, Roger B., Michaels, Stillwater
Catapano, Salvatore, Holy Name of Jesus
Christensen, Harlan L., St. Patrick, Inver Grove Heights
Ciresi, Jerome D., Assumption, Richfield
Clasen, James, St. Francis de Sales and United Hosp.
Coffey, Thomas, (Unassigned)
Coleman, Thomas F., Sacred Heart, Robbinsdale
Courrier, Darrel, Ss. Peter & Paul, Loretto
Crowley, John, St. Francis Xavier, St. Rose of Lima and Aids Ministry
Curtan, Sean, Annunciation Mpls
D'Heilly, Peter, (Retired)
DeFrank, Frank, On Leave of Absence
DeLosReyes, Alfredo L., St. John Vianney, South St. Paul
DeLuney, Jon, St. Bonaventure, Bloomington; Minneapolis Police Dept.
DeShane, James, Most Holy Trinity
Devine, Gerald L., St. Timothy, Blaine
Dolan, Thomas E., (Retired)
Dols, Bernard R., St. Gerard, Brooklyn Park
Dondelinger, James, (Retired)
Dornfeld, Willard, St. Edward, Bloomington
Dzik, Thomas W., St. Luke, St. Paul
Ehrmantraut, Dominic, St. Stephen, Anoka and St. Walburga, Fletcher
Erpenbach, William L., (Retired)
Evans, Patrick, St. Pius V, Cannon Falls
Evans, Russell, (Unassigned)
Falvey, William E., (Retired)
Feffer, Edward F., (Retired)
Ferguson, Delmar F., (Retired)
Fidler, Donald, St. Michael, St. Michael
Flood, John J., (Retired)
Frederick, Joseph J., Basilica of St. Mary
Freeman, Ronald, St. Timothy, Maple Lake
Friesen, Michael, St. Francis Cabrini, Minneapolis
Gerdts, Michael G., (Retired)
Getz, Ronald L., (Retired)
Glover, Guy, St. Michael/St. Mary, Stillwater
Gregory, Gabriel, (Retired)
Gruber, Leonard L., St. Dominic, Northfield
Hamilton, Donald, St. Rose of Lima, Roseville
Hanson, Dennis, Holy Name, Wayzata
Harrer, Timothy, St. Joseph, Waconia
Haselhuhn, Walter, St. George, Long Lake
Hathaway, Donald F., (Retired)
Heidenreich, Michael, Diocese of Las Vegas, NV

Heiman, William, St. John Vianny Seminary
Heineman, Richard, St. Bridget and Catholic Eldercare
Helmeke, Timothy, St. Hubert, Chanhassen
Hepp, James E., St. Peters, St. Paul
Herzog, Jack, St. Bonaventure, Bloomington
Hickman, Nelson, (Retired)
Hoffman, Gary, St. John Excelsior
Holst, David, St. Alphonsus, Brooklyn Park
Houle, Gary J., St. Peter, Forest Lake
Huber, James, On Leave of Absence
Huberty, Peter J., (Retired)
Hughesdon, Harold, St. Agnes, St. Paul
Huibregtse, David, Immaculate Heart of Mary, Minnetonka, AIDS Ministry
Humbert, Michael, St. Elizabeth Ann Seton
Ingwell, David, Leave of Absence
Janes, Edward, (Retired)
Jaques, Martin, Sacred Heart
Jents, Kevin, St. Timothy, Blaine
Johanns, Mark, St. Peter, Richfield
Johnson, Fred, St. Peter Claver, St. Paul
Kasbohm, Thomas F., (Retired)
Kelly, Robert, St. Thomas Becket and Our Lady of Good Council Home
Kenney, Joseph G., (Retired)
Keyes, Thomas, St. John the Evangelist, Little Canada
Kirchoffner, Daniel D., St. Genevieve, Centerville & Good Shepard, Golden Valley
Kittok, Joseph, Delano Cathlic Community
Klish, Richard, St. John Neumann, Eagan & Tribunal
Konkel, Thomas A., St. Joseph, Lino Lakes
Koop, Steven E., St. Rita, Cottage Grove
Kuebler, Myon, On leave
L'Allier, Ralph, St. Peter, Forest Lake
Langlois, Thomas, St. Gregory the Great, North Branch
Laqui, Marciano I., St. Bernard, St. Paul
Lee, Joseph, Office of Indian Ministry, National Korean Evangelization
Little, Gerald, St. John the Baptist and Catholic Charities in Frogtown
Lo, Va Thai, Hmong Community, St. Vincent de Paul, St. Paul
Lukach, George, Diocese of Spokane
MacKenzie, John M., St. John the Baptist, Excelsior
Maltzen, Bruce, Epiphany, Coon Rapids - incardinating
Mangan, John T., Minnesota Veteran's Home
Mann, George A., (Retired)
Marshall, James, All Saints, Lakeville
Masla, John, (Retired)
May, Bobby, St. Alphonsus, Brooklyn Center
McDonald, James F., St. Therese, Deephaven
McLaughlin, James, Nativity, Bloomington
McPherson, Joseph T., On Loan to Montana
Medley, Michael, St. Timothy Maple Lake
Medlicott, James V., (Retired)
Meyer, James, Assumption, Richfield
Michaud, Thomas P., St. John, Savage
Moore, Richard, St. Thomas the Apostle and Net Ministry
Moravec, Terry, St. Peter, Forest Lake
Moses, Steven, Fairbault Catholic Community
Murphy, John L., St. Matthew, St. Paul
Murphy, John W., Jr., St. John, Hopkins
Murphy, Lawrence J., Diocese of Superior
Najarian, Stephen, St. Charles Borromeo
Nalezny, Daniel, St. Stephen, Anoka
Nelson, Ronald, Sacred Heart/St. Lawrence, Faribault
Neumann, Dennis J., (Retired)
Nicklay, John, St. Rita, Cottage Grove
Nowak, David, Highland Catholic Community and Catholic Charities in Frogtown
Nugent, George J., All Saints, Lakeville
O'Connor, Robert, (Retired)
O'Keefe, Clyde, (Retired)
Ortman, Raymond, St. Victoria and Carver County Prison
Otto, Sherman H., St. Vincent de Paul, Brooklyn Park
Palkert, Lawrence, Immaculate Conception, Columbia Heights
Palmer, Rodney, St. John the Baptist, New Brighton
Pashby, Richard E., St. Pascal, St. Paul
Pasko, Anthony, Our Lady of Grace, Edina
Pederson, Bernard A., St. Agnes, St. Paul
Pendergast, Donald, (Retired)
Powers, Michael, Our Lady of Mt. Carmel, Minneapolis
Quayle, Thomas, St. John the Baptist, New Brighton & Hennepin County Juvenile Center
Rajcich, G. Michael, On loan to New Ulm Diocese
Raleigh, Robert, St. Wenceslaus, New Prague/ Minnesota Correctional Facility
Ramsey, James, Sacred Heart, Robbinsdale
Reed, John A., Diocese of Duluth
Rinkenberger, Donald, St. Joseph the Worker, Maple Grove
Riordan, Ripperton W., Dir. Center for Diaconate and St. Francis of Assisi
Rollings, Virgil, (Retired)
Rudolphi, Byron W., Jr., St. Patrick, Edina
Saumweber, James, Presentation, Maplewood
Scherer, Terrance P., St. Patrick, Oak Grove
Schmitz, Joseph, (Retired)
Schneider, Frank J., (Retired)
Schneider, Terrence, Wayzata
Schramer, Joseph J., (Retired)
Schroeder, Allan, St. Mark, Shakopee
Schroeder, Alphonse, Pax Christi, Eden Prairie
Seaton, James B., (Retired)
Semlak, Thomas L., St. Pius X, White Bear Lake
Shallbetter, Clarence, St. Olaf, Minneapolis
Shambour, Leonard, St. Wenceslaus, New Prague
Shoberg, Mylo, St. Peter, Mendota
Shupe, Russell, St. Michael, Prior Lake
Skala, Mark
Smith, James, (Retired)
Smith, Joseph, St. Joseph the Worker, Maple Grove
Smith, Robert B., Assumption, Richfield
Sroder, Gregory, Sacred Heart, St. Paul
Stevens, Richard, Risen Savior, Burnsville
Stewart, Phillip, Transfiguration and with Franciscan Brothers of Peace working with torture victims
Stickney, Stephen S., (Retired)
Stiles, Thomas G., St. Columba, St. Paul
Stipe, Bruce
Straub, Art, On loan to New Ulm
Stromen, Sherman, St. Mary of the Lake, White Bear Lake
Swirtz, Lawrence, (Retired)
Tangney, Francis J., St. Joseph, Hopkins
Tatone, Paul M., St. Thomas Becket, Eagan
Thell, Frank J., St. Paul Police Chap.
Thoennes, Michael, St. Mary, Waverly
Thornton, James, (Retired)
Tift, J. Neil, St. Ambrose, Woodbury
Timmerman, Dale, St. Philip, Minneapolis
Umphress, William G., Holy Spirit, St. Paul
Urbanski, Roger G., (Retired)
Valdez, Carl R., Assumption, Richfield
Veiman, John, Presentation, Maplewood
Wagner, James M., St. Hubert, Chanhassen
Wagner, Robert C., St. Hubert, Chanhassen
Walker, Lawrence, St. Bridget of Sweden, Lindstrom
Warhol, Robert W., Nativity of B.V.M., Bloomington
Warne, Maynard E., St. Michael, St. Michael
Waugh, Charles, St. Stephen, Anoka
Weiland, John D., St. Mary, Shakopee
Wesley, R. Daniel, Immaculate Conception, Fairbault
Wierschem, Joseph G., Holy Name, Medina
Wilkenson, Del, Leave of Absence
Winkelman, John W., Ascension, Minneapolis
Winn, Luther E., (Retired)
Winn, Michael, Holy Name, Medina
Winnhelman, John, St. Alphnsus, Brooklyn Center
Wirtz, Howard, Archdiocese of Milwaukee
Wittman, Wayne C., Sacred Heart, St. Paul
Witucki, Richard P., St. Bartholomew, Wayzata
Woznick, Greg, St. Henry, Monticello
Wright, Scott, St. Mark & St. Paul
Wurdock, Mike, Our Lady of Lourdes
Yaeger, Loren, (Retired)
Yang, Naokao, St. Adalbert, St. Paul
Yekaldo, Fred, Medical Leave

INSTITUTIONS LOCATED IN THE ARCHDIOCESE

[A] SEMINARIES, ARCHDIOCESAN

ST. PAUL. *St. John Vianney Seminary*, 2115 Summit Ave., #5024, 55105. Tel: 651-962-6825; Fax: 651-962-6835. Email: sjv@stthomas.edu. Web: www.stthomas.edu/sjv. Rev. William J. Baer, Rector. Priests 4; Lay Teachers 2; Students 80. Spiritual Directors & Counselors: Revs. Donald E. DeGrood; Thomas Thakadipuram; John A. Klockeman; Deacon William Heiman, Apostolic Outreach Dir.; Mr. John Daniewicz, D.R.E.

The Saint Paul Seminary, School of Divinity of the University of St. Thomas, 2260 Summit Ave., 55105. Tel: 651-962-5050; Fax: 651-962-5790. Email: amserdar@stthomas.edu. Web: www.stthomas.edu/sod. Most Rev. Frederick J. Campbell, D.D., Ph.D., Rector; Revs. David W. Kohner, Dir. Spiritual Formation; Jerome M. Dittberner, S.T.D.; Andrew Cozzens; J. Patrick Quinn, T.O.R.; Ronald Bowers, J.C.D., Vice Rector; J. Michael Byron, S.T.D.; Thomas Margevicius; John L. Ubel; Thomas Fisch, Ph.D.; Jeanne P. McLean, Ph.D., Academic Dean; Rev. John Echert, S.S.L.; Kenneth D. Synder, Ph.D.; Gene Scapanski, S.T.D.; Charlotte Berres, D.Min., Dir. Field Education; David Jenkins, D.Mus., Dir. Liturgical Music; Sisters Paul Therese Saiko, S.S.N.D., M.A.; Katarina Schuth, O.S.F., Ph.D.; Rev. Douglas E. Dandurand, Ph.D.; Walter D. Ray, Ph.D.; Jan Viktora, Ph.D.; Rev. Peter Laird, M.A.; Deborah A. Organ, D.Min.; Seung Ai Yang, Ph.D. Legal Title: *The Saint Paul Seminary* M.Div./Seminarians 62; Pastoral Studies Division 56; Pastoral Studies (non-degree) 16; Doctor of Ministry 11; Priests 11; Sisters 2; Lay Staff 9.

[B] SEMINARIES, RELIGIOUS, OR SCHOLASTICATES

ST. PAUL. *Jesuit Novitiate*, 1035 Summit Ave., 55105-3034. Tel: 651-224-5593; Fax: 651-224-4734. Email: sjstpaul@aol.com. Revs. Kevin Cullen, S.J., Novice Dir.; Matthew L. Linn, S.J., Retreat Dir.; John P. Fitzgibbons, S.J., Novice Dir.; Bro. John J. Masterson, S.J., Asst. to Novice Dir. Priests 3; Brothers 1; Novices 18.

[C] COLLEGES AND UNIVERSITIES

ST. PAUL. *College of St. Catherine*, 2004 Randolph Ave., 55105. Tel: 651-690-6000; Fax: 651-690-6024. Email: admissions@stkate.edu. Web: www.stkate.edu. Andrea J. Lee, I.H.M., Pres.; Mary Margaret Smith, Ph.D., Vice Pres. Academic Affairs & Dean of Faculty; Mary Desroches, Vice Pres. Fin. & Business Operations; Patricia Hvidstun, Vice Pres. Devel. & External Rels.; Colleen Hegranes, Vice Pres. Student Affairs; Jan Czechowski, Dean of Arts & Sciences; Susan Eames, C.S.J., Co-Dir. Campus Ministry; Cathy Steffens, C.S.J., Co-Dir. Campus Ministry; Susan Cochrane, Dean of Professional Studies; Margaret McLaughlin, Dean of Health Professions; Brian Bruess, Dean of Students. Sisters of St. Joseph of Carondelet 13; Total Staff 947; Students 4,807.

University of St. Thomas, 2115 Summit Ave., 55105. Tel: 651-962-5000; Fax: 651-962-6504. Web: www.stthomas.edu. Rev. Dennis J. Dease, Pres.; Rev. Msgr. Terrence J. Murphy, Chancellor; Dr. Thomas Rochon, Exec. Vice Pres. & Chief Academic Officer; Dr. Nancy H. Zingale, Exec. Asst. to the Pres.; Dr. Thomas Connery, Dean of the College of Arts & Sciences; Dr. Angeline Barreta-Herman, Assoc. Vice Pres. Academic Affairs (Interim); Dr. Joseph Kreitzer, Assoc. Vice Pres. for Academic Affairs; Mr. Terrence O'Connor, Vice Pres., Finance & Admin.; Ms. Mary Ann Ryan, Vice Pres. Student Affairs; Dr. Gene Scapanski, Vice Pres. for Mission; Mr. Quentin J. Hietpas, Senior Vice Pres. External Affairs Emeritus; Dr. Mark Dienhart, Exec. Vice Pres. & Chief Admin. Officer; Dr. Christopher Puto, Dean College of Business; Dr. Nona Mason, Dir. Masters in Business Communications; Dr. Bhabani Misra, Interim Dir. Graduate Program in Software Design; Ms. Karen Lange, Dean of Student Life; Dr. Ronald Bennett, Dir. Programs in Engrg. & Technology Mgmt.; Dr. Samuel Levy, Vice Pres. for Info. Svcs. & Technologies; Mr. Doug Hennes, Vice Pres. for Univ. & Govt. Rels.; Mr. Thomas Mengler, Dean School of Law; Most Rev. Frederick Campbell, Vice Pres. & Rector of St. Paul Seminary School of Divinity; Dr. Jeanne McLean, Dean St. Paul Seminary School of Divinity; Dr. Miriam Q. Williams, Dean School of Education; Dr. Barbara Shank, Dean School of Social Work; Dr. Jean Birbilis, Interim Dean Graduate Prog. in Professional Psychology; Rev. Msgrs. William L. Baumgaertner, Prof. Emeritus, School of Divinity (Retired); James Habiger, Campus Ministry; Ellsworth Kneal, Prof. Emeritus School of Divinity; James M. Lavin, Alumni Affairs (Retired); Robert L. Probst, Computing & Communication Svcs. (Retired); John P. Sankovitz, Theology Dept. (Retired); Revs. Ronald Bowers, J.C.D., Assoc. Prof. of Canon Law, Vice Rector; William J. Baer, Rector, St. John Vianney Seminary; Michael Byron, Asst. Prof. of Systematic Theology, School of Divinity; Thomas J. Conroy, Asst. Prof. Theology (Retired); Andrew Cozzens, (On study leave); Douglas E. Dandurand, Ph.D., Assoc. Dir. Spiritual Formation; Jerome M. Dittberner, S.T.D., Prof. Dogmatic Theology; John P. Echert, S.S.L., Asst. Prof. Sacred Scripture; Paul F. Feela, M.A., Instructor, Sacramental Theology & Liturgy; Dir. Worship; Peter E. Feldmeier, Ph.D., Asst. Prof. Spirituality; Jeffrey Huard, Dir. Campus Ministry; Leo R. Huber (Retired); Jan Michael Joncas, Assoc. Prof. Theology, Catholic Studies; Arthur L. Kennedy (BO), Prof. Theology, (On leave); David W. Kohner, Dir. Spiritual Formation; Peter Laird, M.Div., Instructor in Moral Theology, (On study leave); Roy Lepak (Retired), Philosophy; John M. Malone, Development; James R. Motl, O.P., Ph.D., Assoc. Prof. Emeritus Homiletics, (Retired);

William O'Neill, C.PP.S., Ph.D. (Retired), Assoc. Prof. Psychology; Thadeus J. Posey, O.F.M.Cap., Assoc. Prof. of Theology; Patrick Quinn, T.O.R., Asst. Prof. of Dogmatic Theology; James E. Reidy (Retired), English Dept.; John F. Riley, Theology Dept. (Retired); Rev. Msgr. John A. Sweeney, Prof., Liturgical Music (Retired); Revs. Donald E. DeGrood, Spiritual Dir. St. John Vianney Seminary; David W. Smith, Prof. Theology; James S. Stromberg, Philosophy Dept. (Retired); Thomas Thakadipuram, St. John Vianney Seminary; Martin L. Warren (England), Asst. Prof. of English; Robert B. Wellisch, Assoc. Prof. English; George A. Welzbacher (Retired), Dept. of History; Dwight Reginald Whitt, O.P., Prof. Law. Priests 11; Sisters 2; Brothers 1; Lay Teachers 389; Students 11,084; Total Faculty & Staff 1,327.

MINNEAPOLIS. *The College of St. Catherine-Minneapolis*, 601 25th Ave. S., 55454. Tel: 651-690-7702; Fax: 651-690-7849. Email: mkmclaughlin@stkate.edu. Web: www.stkate.edu. Margaret McLaughlin, Ph.D., Dean Health Professions; Andrea Lee, IHM Pres. Coed Health Occupation Human Service and Continuing Education Programs. Total Staff 100; Students 944.

[D] HIGH SCHOOLS, ARCHDIOCESAN

ST. PAUL. *The Saint Thomas Academy* (Boys) Tel: 651-454-4570; Fax: 651-454-4574. Email: sta@cadets.com. Web: www.cadets.com. 949 Mendota Heights Rd., Mendota Heights, 55120-1496. Mr. Bob Ostlund, Interim Headmaster; Rev. John L. Ubel, Chap. Priests 1; Lay Teachers 59; Students 657.

[E] HIGH SCHOOLS, PRIVATE

ST. PAUL. *Cretin-Derham Hall*, 550 S. Albert St., 55116. Tel: 651-690-2443; Fax: 651-696-3394. Email: rengler@cretin-derhamhall.org. Web: www.cretin-derhamhall.org. Richard Engler, Pres. & Prin. Co-Sponsors: Brothers of the Christian Schools and Sisters of St. Joseph of Carondelet Priests 1; Sisters 4; Brothers 3; Lay Teachers 102; Students 1,307; Total Staff 162.

MINNEAPOLIS. *DeLaSalle High School*, Christian Brothers, One DeLaSalle Dr., 55401. Tel: 612-676-7600; Fax: 612-362-9641. Email: principal@delasalle.com. Web: www.delasalle.com. Bro. Michael Collins, F.S.C., Pres.; Barry C. Lieske, Prin. Brothers 5; Sisters 1; Lay Teachers 35; Students 608.

Totino-Grace High School, 1350 Gardena Ave., N.E., Fridley, 55432-5899. Tel: 763-571-9116; Fax: 763-571-9118. Email: kmurphy@totinograce.org. Web: www.totinograce.org. Bro. Milton Barker, F.S.C., Pres.; Julie Michels, Prin. Brothers 1; Lay Teachers 57; Students 1,125.

FARIBAULT. *Bethlehem Academy* 55021. Tel: 507-334-3948; Fax: 507-334-3949. Email: principal@bacards.pvt.k12.mn.us. Web: www.bacards.pvt.k12.mn.us. Sisters 1; Lay Teachers 16; Students 236.

Faribault B.A., Inc., 105 3rd Ave., S.W., 55021-6096. Tel: 507-334-3948; Fax: 507-334-3949. Email: principal@bacards.pvt.k12.mn.us. Web: www.bacards.pvt.k12.mn.us. Sisters of St. Dominic (Sinsinawa, WI) Sisters 1; Lay Teachers 12; Total Enrollment 236; Total Staff 21.

MAPLEWOOD. *Hill-Murray School*, 2625 Larpenteur Ave. E., 55109-5098. Tel: 651-777-1376; Fax: 651-748-2444. Email: jpescheges@hill-murray.org. Web: www.hill-murray.org. Joseph M. Peschges, Pres. Lay Teachers 70; Students 950.

MENDOTA HEIGHTS. *Convent of the Visitation School* Day School for Girls grades 7-12; coed grades PreK-6. , 2455 Visitation Dr., 55120. Tel: 651-683-1700; Fax: 651-454-7144. Email: ksteiner@vischool.org. Web: www.visitation.net. Dawn Nichols, Head of School. Sisters 16; Lay Teachers 53; Students 584.

RICHFIELD. *Academy of Holy Angels*, 6600 Nicollet Ave. S., 55423-2498. Tel: 612-798-2600; Fax: 612-798-2610. Email: jreilly@ahastars.org. Web: www.ahastars.org. Dr. Jill M. Reilly, Pres. & Prin. Priests 1; Sisters 1; Lay Teachers 70; Students 843.

ST. LOUIS PARK. *Benilde-St. Margaret's School*, 2501 Hwy. 100 S., 55416. Tel: 612-927-4176; Fax: 612-920-8889. Web: www.bsm-online.org. James F. Hamburge, Pres.; Mr. Robert C. Tift, Prin.; Mary Andersen, Asst. Prin. Priests 1; Sisters 1; Lay Teachers 72; Students 1,123.

VICTORIA. *Holy Family Catholic High School*, 8101 Kochia Ln., 55386. Tel: 952-443-4659; Fax: 952-443-1822. Email: communications@holyfamilycatholichs.org. Web: www.holyfamilycatholichs.org. Patrick Peyton, Chm.; Tom Burke, Vice Chm.; Mary Fafinski, Sec.; Frank Miley, Pres. Lay Teachers 28; Students 398.

[F] ELEMENTARY SCHOOLS, PRIVATE

MINNEAPOLIS. **San Miguel Middle School of Minneapolis*, 3800 Pleasant Ave. S., 55409-1229. Tel: 612-870-1109; Fax: 612-870-1224. Email: sanmiguel-mpls@hutman.net. Web: www.sanmiguel-mpls.org. Sr. Mary Willette, S.S.N.D., Prin. Lay Teachers 4; Students 37; Total Staff 15.

MENDOTA HEIGHTS. *Convent of the Visitation School*, 2455 Visitation Dr., 55120. Tel: 651-683-1700; Fax: 651-454-7144. Email: vischool@vischool.org. Web: www.visitation.net. Dr. Dawn Nichols, Head of School. (Montessori-Grade 12) Sisters of The Visitation of Holy Mary 15; Lay Teachers 56; Students 596.

[G] ELEMENTARY SCHOOLS, CONSOLIDATED, PAROCHIAL

ST. PAUL. *Highland Catholic School*, (Grades K-8), 2017 Bohland Ave., 55116. Tel: 651-690-2477; Fax: 651-699-1869. Email: jschmidt@highlandcatholic.org. Web: www.highlandcatholic.org. Serving the parishes of Highland Catholic Community. Lay Teachers 30; Students 481.

IHM-St. Luke's School, (Grades K-8), 1065 Summit Ave., 55105. Tel: 651-224-4836; Fax: 651-224-0097. Email: dyann-witucki@ihm-stlukes.org. Web: www.ihm-stlukes.org. Serving the parishes of Immaculate Heart of Mary and St. Luke. Sisters 2; Lay Teachers 26; Students 387.

Maternity of Mary/St. Andrew School, 592 Arlington Ave. W., 55117. Tel: 651-489-1459; Fax: 651-489-3560. Email: florence@cpinternet.com. Web: www.mmsaschool.org. Serving the parishes of Maternity of Mary and St. Andrew. Sisters 2; Lay Teachers 27; Students 369.

Trinity Catholic School, 835 E. Fifth St., 55106. Tel: 651-776-2763; Fax: 651-772-4847. Email: skrekeler@www.trinity-catholic.org. Web: www.trinity-catholic.org. Serving the parishes of Sacred Heart, St. Casimir and St. Patrick. Sisters 4; Lay Teachers 13; Students 201.

MINNEAPOLIS. *Pope John Paul II Catholic School*, 1630 Fourth St, N.E., 55413. Tel: 612-789-8851; Fax: 612-789-8773. Web: www.popejohnpaul2.org. Serving the parishes of St. Cyril & Methodius, Holy Cross, St. Anthony, All Saints, Our Lady of Lourdes, St. Hedwig, St. Clement, St. Boniface, St. Maron, Our Lady of Mt. Carmel and St. Lawrence. Sisters 3; Lay Teachers 10; Students 141; Total Staff 26.

Risen Christ Catholic School, (Grades K-8), 1120 E. 37th St., 55407. Tel: 612-822-5329; Fax: 612-729-2336. Email: hdahlman@risenchristschool.org. Web: risenchristschool.org. Serving the parishes of Holy Name, Holy Rosary, Incarnation, St. Albert the Great and St. Stephen.

EAGAN. *Faithful Shepherd Catholic School*, 3355 Columbia Dr., 55121. Tel: 651-406-4747; Fax: 651-406-4743. Email: info@faithfulshepherd.org. Web: www.faithfulshepherd.org. Revs. Kevin I. Clinton; Charles V. Lachowitzer, Cononical Admin.; Thomas H. Brioschi; Sr. Patricia Beckman, O.P., Prin. Serving the parishes of St. Peter, St. John Neumann and St. Thomas Becket. Lay Teachers 36; Total Staff 45; Total Enrollment 535.

FARIBAULT. *Consolidated Catholic School of Faribault*, (Grades PreK-6), 15 S.W. Third Ave., 55021. Tel: 507-334-7706; Fax: 507-332-2669. Email: lyouso@faribaultcatholics.com. Web: www.faribaultcatholics.com. Serving the parish of Divine Mercy Catholic Church. Lay Teachers 20; Students 421.

HASTINGS. *St. Elizabeth Ann Seton School*, 600 Tyler St., 55033. Tel: 651-437-3098; Fax: 651-438-3377. Web: www.seasparish.org. Rita Humbert, Admin. Lay Teachers 24; Students 381.

HOPKINS. *John Ireland Schools*, (Grades PreK-8), 1320 Main Street, 55343. Tel: 952-938-3442; Fax: 952-938-0642. Email: jisprincipal@johnireland.org. Web: www.johnireland.org. Serving the parishes of St. John the Evangelist, St. Joseph and Immaculate Heart of Mary. Lay Teachers 41; Students 470.

LONSDALE. *Holy Cross LNMV Catholic School*, 108 First Ave., S.E., P.O. Box 10, 55046. Tel: 507-744-2394; Fax: 507-744-4117. Email: vickim@holycrossschool.net. Web: www.holycrossschool.net. Serving the parishes of Lonsdale, New Market and Veseli. Lay Teachers 11; Students 193; Total Staff 23.

RICHFIELD. *Blessed Trinity Catholic School of Richfield, Minnesota*, 6720 Nicollet Ave., 55423. Tel: 612-869-5200; Fax: 612-866-5080. Email: doylek@btcsmn.org. Web: www.btcsmn.org. Serving the parishes of Assumption, St. Peter's and St. Richard's. Lay Teachers 26; Students 453.

SHAKOPEE. *Shakopee Area Catholic School*, (Grades PreK-8), 2700 17th Ave. E., 55379. Tel: 952-445-3387; Fax: 952-445-7256. Email: dlee@sacsschools.org. Serving the parishes of St. Mark, St. Mary, St. Mary of the Purification. Lay Teachers 35; Students 775; Total Staff 80.

STILLWATER. *St. Croix Catholic Educational Programs*, 611 S. 3rd St., 55082. Tel: 651-439-4400; Fax: 651-439-8360. Email: cepperly@stccs.com. Rev. Michael C. Skluzacek, Pres. Serving the parishes of St. Michael's, St. Mary's, and St. Charles. Priests 3; Sisters 4; Lay Teachers 25; Students 518; Total Staff 32.

St. Croix Catholic School, (Grades K-8), 621 S. Third St., 55082. Tel: 612-439-5581; Fax: 651-439-8360. Email: cepperly@stccs.com. Web: www.stcroixcatholic.com. Mr. Marty Weisbeck, Prin. Serving the parishes of St. Charles, Bayport; St. Mary, Stillwater; St. Michael, Stillwater. Lay Teachers 27; Students 523; Sisters 3.

[H] HOMES FOR CHILDREN

MINNEAPOLIS. *St. Joseph's Home for Children*, 1121 E. 46th St., 55407. Tel: 612-827-6241; Fax: 612-827-9321. Web: www.ccspm.org. Mr. Edward McBrayer, Admin. Intake; Emergency Shelter; Diagnostic and Assessment; Serving 2400 Children Yearly; Residential Treatment (services 24); Day Treatment (services 24). Lay persons 205; Total Assisted Annually 2,400; Total Staff 180. In Res. Rev. Msgr. J. Jerome Boxleitner (Retired).

[I] GENERAL HOSPITALS

ST. PAUL. **HealthEast St. Joseph's Hospital*, 69 W. Exchange St., 55102. Tel: 651-232-3611; Fax: 651-232-3518. Email: sbatulis@healtheast.org. Scott Batulis, Contact Person; Revs. Stephen J. LaCanne, Dir., Spiritual Care. Tel: 651-232-3060; Fax: 651-232-4155; Michael Erlander; Jonathan Fischer, O.S.B. (SCL). Bed Capacity 401; Total Staff 1,150.

HASTINGS. *Regina Medical Center*, 1175 Nininger Rd., 55033. Tel: 651-480-4100; Fax: 651-480-4212. Email: kochendorfer@reginamedical.org. Web: www.reginamedical.org. Mark D. Wilson, CEO; Rev. John Marley, S.S.C., Chap. A part of Regina Healthcare. Other Sister Personnel 1; Patients Assisted Annually 33,637; Total Staff 653; Bed Capacity 57.

NEW PRAGUE. *Queen of Peace Hospital*, 302 Second St., N.E., 56071. Tel: 612-758-4431; Fax: 612-758-5009. Email: sjean@qofp.org. Web: www.np.k12.mn.us/~qofp.htm. Sr. Jean Juenemann, O.S.B., Admin.; Ann Schoenbauer, Chap. Sisters 2; Bed Capacity 56; Bassinets 6; RNs 56; LPNs 12; Other Personnel 217; Patients Assisted Annually 96,000.

SHAKOPEE. *St. Francis Regional Medical Center*, 1455 St. Francis Ave., 55379-3380. Tel: 952-403-3000; Fax: 952-403-2767. Email: diana.mckee@allina.com. Web: www.stfrancis-shakopee.com. Tom O'Connor, CEO & Pres.; Diana McKee, Chap. Subsidiary of Benedictine Health System. Benedictine, Allina and Park Nicollet Sponsorship. Nurses 263; Bed Capacity 93; Patients Assisted Annually 68,139; Total Staff 702.

[J] SPECIAL HOSPITALS AND SANATORIA FOR INVALIDS

ST. PAUL. *Our Lady of Good Counsel Home*, 2076 St. Anthony Ave., 55104-5096. Tel: 651-646-2797; Fax: 651-646-7884. Email: sam@ourladyhome.org. Web: www.hawthorne-dominicans.org. Sisters Anne Marie, O.P., Supr.; Mary Denise, O.P., Admin.; Rev. James W. Jackson. Sisters of St. Dominic. Servants of Relief for Incurable Cancer Nursing Sisters 7; Bed capacity 40; Patients Assisted Annually 175; Total Assisted 116; Total Staff 35.

[K] SOCIAL SERVICE AGENCIES

ST. PAUL. *Home of the Good Shepherd*, 5100 Hodgson Rd., 55126. Tel: 651-484-0221; Fax: 651-486-1616. Email: carmelrgs@hgsmn.net. Sr. Carmel Therese Irving, Admin. Transitional housing and case-management services for at-risk, homeless women Sisters 3; Lay Staff 7.

[L] HOMES FOR AGED

ST. PAUL. *Bethany Convent for Retired Sisters*, 1870 Randolph, 55105. Tel: 651-696-2500; Fax: 651-696-2501. Email: aschreiber@csjstpaul.org. Sisters Angela Schreiber, C.S.J., Dir. of Community; George Ann Bohl, C.S.J., Assoc. Dir. of Community. Sisters of St. Joseph of Carondelet Total Staff 180; Total in Residence 136; Total Assisted Annually 20.

Franciscan Health Community, 1925 Norfolk Ave., 55116. Tel: 651-696-8400; Fax: 651-696-8404. Email: jstan@mtn.org. Web: www.franciscancare.org. Joseph Stanislav, Pres. &

CEO. Sisters 4; Aged Residents 719; Total Assisted Annually 798; Total Staff 129.

Good Shepherd Care Center, Inc., 324 Johnson Pkwy., 55106. Tel: 651-774-4000; Fax: 651-774-9641. Mary Roy, Admin. & CEO. Patients Assisted Annually 330; Total Staff 160.

Holy Family Residence, 330 S. Exchange St., 55102. Tel: 651-227-0336; Fax: 651-227-7321. Email: mslspsp@hotmail.com. Sr. Mary Sylvia Karl, Supr. Little Sisters of the Poor 11; Aged Residents 72; Apartments 32; Total Staff, all facilities 102.

MINNEAPOLIS. *City of Lakes Care Center*, 110 E. 18th St., 55403. Tel: 612-879-2800. Mr. David Brennan, Admin. & CEO.

HASTINGS. *Regina Retirement Center*, 1175 Niningar Rd., 55033. Tel: 651-480-4100; Fax: 651-480-4212. Email: kochendorfer@reginamedical.org. Web: www.reginamedical.org. Rev. John Marley, S.S.C., Resident Chap. Total Assisted Annually 290; Total Staff 135.

Regina Medical Center Tel: 651-480-4100; Fax: 651-480-4212. A part of Regina Healthcare. Number under care 181; Nursing Care 61; Assisted living 134; Total Staff 134.

SHAKOPEE. *St. Gertrude's Health and Rehabilitation Center*, 1850 Sarazin St., 55379. Tel: 952-233-4400; Fax: 952-233-4476. Lee Larson, Admin.; Marge Henderson, Chairperson; Kevin Rymanowski, Treas. Total Staff 129.

[M] MONASTERIES AND RESIDENCES OF PRIESTS AND BROTHERS

ST. PAUL. *Franciscan Brothers of Peace*, Queen of Peace Friary, 1289 Lafond Ave., 55104-2035. Tel: 651-646-8586; Fax: 651-646-9083. Web: www.brothersofpeace.org. Bros. Paul O'Donnell, F.B.P., Guardian Overall; Anthony Sweere, F.B.P., Vicar; Michael Gaworski, F.B.P.; Hilary McGee, F.B.P.; Conrad Richardson, F.B.P.; Joseph Katzmarek, F.B.P.; John Mary Kaspari, F.B.P.; Pio King, F.B.P; James Voeller, F.B.P.

Maryknoll Fathers and Brothers, Catholic Foreign Mission Society of America, P.O. Box 16538, 55116. Tel: 651-222-5530; Fax: 651-222-2367. Email: minneapolis@maryknoll.org. Web: www.maryknoll.org. Mr. Gregory Darr, Dir.

Oblate Residence, 104 N. Mississippi River Blvd., 55104-2374. Tel: 651-645-3560; Fax: 651-645-3704. Bro. Paul Daly, O.M.I., Dir. of House In Res. Revs. Robert Allie, O.M.I.; Donald Dummer, O.M.I.; Ronald Harrer, O.M.I.; Joseph H. Hitpas, O.M.I., Area Supr.; Paul Ischler, O.M.I.; Andrew Knop, O.M.I., Vocation Dir.; William Mason, O.M.I.; Joseph Menker, O.M.I.; John E. Pilaczynski, O.M.I.

MINNEAPOLIS. *St. Albert the Great Priory*, 2833 32nd Ave. S., 55406. Tel: 612-724-3644; Fax: 612-724-5057. Email: dommpls@mn.rr.com. Rev. Cletus J. Wessels, O.P., Prior. Order of Preachers (Dominicans). Province of St. Albert the Great Total in Residence 10.

St. Bridget Friary, 3811 Emerson Ave. N., 55412-2038. Tel: 612-588-9078; Fax: 612-588-8777. Web: www.franciscanfriarstor.com. Revs. J. Patrick Quinn, T.O.R.; Vincent J. Spinos, T.O.R.; Bros. Robert Juroszek, T.O.R.; David Kaczmarek, T.O.R.; John Kerr, T.O.R.; David Liedl, T.O.R.; Tello Truong Vu, T.O.R. Third Order Regular of St. Francis, Province of the Immaculate Conception.

St. Gerard Friary, 9600 Regent Ave. N., 55443-1499. Tel: 763-424-7659. Very Rev. Giles A. Schinelli, T.O.R.

Paulist Fathers, 1201 5th St., S.E., 55414. Tel: 612-331-7941; Fax: 612-378-1771. Email: nccampus@stlawrencenewman.org. Web: www.stlawrencenewman.org/. Revs. John J. Behnke, C.S.P.; Donald A. Andrie, C.S.P.; Michael Martin, C.S.P.; Richard Chilson, C.S.P. Total in Residence 4.

ANOKA. *Crosier Community of Anoka*, 516 School St., 55303-2349. Tel: 763-421-7115; Fax: 763-421-4230. Email: crosier@ststephenchurch.org. Web: www.crosier.org. Rev. Kermit Holl, O.S.C., Temp. Admin. Total in Residence 7; Total Staff 10. In Res. Revs. William Deziel, O.S.C.; Richard John, O.S.C.; Kenneth Opat, O.S.C.; Adrian Piotrowski, O.S.C.; Eugene D. Plaisted, O.S.C.; Oscar Schoenberg, O.S.C.; Michael Van Sloun, O.S.C.

St. Mary's International School, 1-6-19, Seta Setagaya-Ku, Tokyo, 158-8668, Japan. Tel: 81-3-3709-3416; Fax: 81-3-3707-1950. In Res. Revs. Lyle Ehmke, O.S.C.; Jim Herrmann, O.S.C.

BROOKLYN CENTER. *Redemptorist Fathers of Hennepin County*, 7025 Halifax Ave. N., 55429-1394. Tel: 763-561-5100; Fax: 763-561-0336.

LAKE ELMO. *Carmelite Hermitage of the Blessed Virgin Mary*, 8249 De Montreville Tr. N., 55042-9545. Tel: 651-779-7351; Fax: 651-779-7351. Email: carmelus@earthlink.net. Web: www.decorcarmeli.com. Revs. John M. Burns, O. Carm., Prior; Joseph V. Vaccaro, O. Carm. Carmel of the Blessed Virgin Mary Priests 2; Brothers 3.

SHOREVIEW. *Crosier Community of Shoreview*, 3500 Vivian Ave., 55126-3852. Tel: 651-486-7456; Fax: 651-287-1130. Email: shoreview@crosier.org. Revs. Jerome Schik, O.S.C.; Tom Enneking, O.S.C.; David Donnay, O.S.C.; Marven Tellers, O.S.C.; Richard McGuire, O.S.C.; Kermit Holl, O.S.C., Prior; Stephan Bauer, O.S.C.; Steven Henrich, O.S.C.; John Neville, O.S.C. (CHI); Bros. Timothy Tomczak, O.S.C.; Jim Lewandowski, O.S.C.; Greg Madigan, O.S.C.; Bob Mandernach, O.S.C.; David Johnson, O.S.C.

Crosier Provincial House Province of St. Odilia, 3470 Vivian Ave., 55126-3853. Tel: 651-486-7456; Fax: 651-287-1130. Email: provincial@crosier.org. Web: www.crosierhome.org. In Res. Very Rev. Thomas E. Carkhuff, O.S.C., Prov.; Revs. Michael Cotone, O.S.C.; Dale Ehrman, O.S.C.; Joseph Hennen, O.S.C; Michael Paquet, O.S.C.; Philip Suehr, O.S.C.

[N] CONVENTS AND RESIDENCES FOR SISTERS

ST. PAUL. *Contemplative Sisters of the Good Shepherd*, 5104 Hodgson Rd., 55126-1229. Tel: 651-482-5240; Fax: 651-486-1600. Email: cgsstpaul@isd.net. Sr. Ann J. Dye, Coord. Sisters 16.

Convent of the Good Shepherd, 5100 Hodgson Rd., 55126-1297. Tel: 651-484-0221; Fax: 651-486-1600. Email: vocations@goodshepherdsisters.org. Web: www.goodshepherdsisters.org. Sisters of the Good Shepherd 36.

Contemplative Sisters of the Good Shepherd, 5104 Hodgson Rd., 55126-1229. Tel: 651-482-5240; Fax: 651-486-1600. Sisters 9.

Franciscan Sisters of Little Falls, MN (O.S.F.), 727 E. Margaret St., 55106. Tel: 651-772-1740. Web: www.fslf.org. Professed 5.

Franciscan Sisters of St. Paul, Franciscan Regional Center, 1388 Prior Ave. S., 55116. Tel: 651-690-1501; Fax: 651-690-2509. Email: spfranci@cpinternet.com. Web: www.askmotherrose.org. Sr. Mary Lucy Scheffler, O.S.F., Regl. Dir. Sisters 13.

St. Mary's Mission House, 265 Century Ave., 55125. Tel: 651-738-9704; Fax: 651-738-9704. Email: sspsmain@cpinternet.com. Sr. Danuta Stepak, S.S.P.C., Supr. Missionary Sisters of St. Peter Claver Sisters 7.

Monastery of the Visitation, 2455 Visitation Dr., 55120. Tel: 651-683-1700; Fax: 651-454-0602. Sr. Marie Therese Conaty, Supr. Visitation Nuns 19.

St. Paul's Monastery, 2675 Larpenteur Ave. E., 55109-5097. Tel: 651-777-8181; Fax: 651-777-4442. Email: srmarie@stpaulsmonastery.org. Web: www.osb.org/spm. Sisters Marie Fujan, O.S.B., Prioress; Annette Esboldt, O.S.B., Subprioress. Benedictine Sisters of Pontifical Jurisdiction Sisters 64.

Sisters of St. Joseph of Carondelet 1884 Randolph Ave., 55105. Tel: 651-690-7000; Fax: 651-690-7039. Web: www.csjstpaul.org. Sisters of Province 389; Total Staff 91.
Province Leadership Team: Sisters Christine Ludwig, C.S.J.; Susan Oeffling, C.S.J.; Dolore Rochon, C.S.J.

MINNEAPOLIS. *St. Clare's Monastery of the Infant Jesus*, 8650 Russell Ave. S., 55431-1998. Tel: 612-881-4766; Fax: 612-881-0358. Email: mplsclares@juno.com. Web: www.poorclare.com/minneapolis. Sr. Mary Catherine Martin, O.S.C., Abbess. Franciscan Poor Clare Nuns Professed Nuns 11.

Visitation Monastery of Minneapolis, 1527 Fremont Ave. N., 55411. Tel: 612-521-6113; Fax: 612-521-4020. Email: vmonastery@aol.com. Web: www.visitationmonastery.org/minneapolis. Sr. Mary Margaret McKenzie, V.H.M., Supr.

LAKE ELMO. *Carmel of Our Lady of Divine Providence*, 8251 De Montreville Tr. N., 55042-9547. Tel: 651-777-3882. Sr. Rose of the Sacred Heart, O.C.D., Prioress; Rev. John M. Burns, O. Carm., Chap. Discalced Carmelite Nuns Professed 11; Novices 3; Postulants 1.

WAYZATA. *Franciscan Clarist Congregation, F.C.C.*, Vimala Province, Convent of St. Therese House, 17931 Minnetonka Blvd., 55391. Tel: 651-438-8680; Fax: 651-438-8680. Email: srtresamargret@yahoo.com. Total in Residence 14.

[O] SECULAR INSTITUTES

ST. PAUL. *Missionaries of the Kingship of Christ*, The Chancery, 226 Summit Ave., 55102. Tel: 612-291-4400. Sr. M. Dominica Brennan, O.P., J.C.L. Secular Institute of Pontifical Right for women and men founded in Italy in 1919.

[P] RETREAT HOUSES AND CENTERS OF SPIRITUALITY

ST. PAUL. *Benedictine Center - St. Paul's Monastery*, 2675 E. Larpenteur Ave., 55109. Tel: 651-777-7251; Fax: 651-773-5124. Email: info@benedictctr.org. Web: www.osb.org/spm. Carol Rennie, Dir. Total Staff 5.

Loyola, 389 N. Oxford St., 55104. Tel: 612-641-0008; Fax: 651-641-0554. Email: loyosrr@attglobal.net. Web: www.loydasrr.org. Revs. Richard M. Rice, S.J.; Frederic A. Maples, S.J.; Sr. Elizabeth Kerwin, C.S.J., Dir. Total Staff 8.

Maryhill, 1988 Summit Ave., 55105. Tel: 651-696-2970; Fax: 651-696-1190. Email: maryhillsd@earthlink.net. Web: www.dhmna.org. Daughters of the Heart of Mary Sisters 9; Total in Residence 1; Total Staff 3.

BUFFALO. *Christ the King Retreat Center*, 621 First Ave. S., 55313. Tel: 763-682-1394; Fax: 763-682-3453. Email: christtheking@kingshouse.com. Web: www.kingshouse.com. Revs. Aloysius Svobodny, O.M.I.; John H. McManus, O.M.I.; Raymond R. Kirtz, O.M.I.; John Mark Ettensohn, O.M.I., Dir.; Randy Oswald, O.M.I.; John Lau, O.M.I.; Bro. Anthony Szklarski, O.M.I., Business Mgr. Total in Residence 7; Total Staff 25.

FRONTENAC. *Villa Maria Retreat and Conference Center*, 29847 County Blvd. 2, 55026. Tel: 651-345-4582; Fax: 651-345-3457. Email: villamaria_retreats@yahoo.com. Web: villamariaretreats.org. Sisters Rita Ann Bregenhorn, O.S.U., Prioress; Rose Elsbernd, F.S.P.A., Dir. Ursuline Sisters of the Roman Union 8.

LAKE ELMO. *Jesuit Retreat House*, 8243 Demontreville Tr. N., 55042-9546. Tel: 651-777-1311. Revs. Gerald E. Goetz, S.J., Dir.; Edward S. Sthokal, S.J., Asst.; Patrick M. McCorkell, S.J. Total in Residence 3; Total Staff 6.

MARINE ON ST. CROIX. *Christian Brothers Retreat Center*, 15525 St. Croix Tr. N., 55047. Tel: 651-433-2486; Fax: 651-433-5755. Email: dunrovin@dunrovin.org. Web: www.dunrovin.org. Jerome Meeds, Dir. Total in Residence 10; Total Staff 15.

PRIOR LAKE. *Franciscan Retreats*, 16385 Saint Francis Ln., 55372. Tel: 952-447-2182; Fax: 952-447-2170. Email: director@franciscanretreats.net. Web: www.franciscanretreats.net. Revs. Ken Bartsch, O.F.M.Conv., Guardian & Retreat Dir.; Mark F. Mindrup, O.F.M.Conv.; Camillus Gott, O.F.M.; Howard Hansen, O.F.M.Conv.

[Q] HOMES FOR DISABLED

ST. PAUL. *Our House of Minnesota, Inc. I*, 1846 Dayton Ave., 55104. Tel: 651-644-6650; Fax: 651-646-1104. Staff 20; Mentally Handicapped Adults 6; Total Assisted 12.

Office Tel: 615-646-1104; Fax: 615-646-1104. Dennis Holman, Admin.

Our House of Minnesota, Inc. II, 1846 Portland, 55104. Tel: 651-644-2411; Fax: 651-646-1104. Staff 21; Mentally Handicapped Adults 6; Total Assisted Annually 12.

Office Tel: 615-646-1104; Fax: 615-646-1104. Dennis Holman, Admin.

WEST ST. PAUL. *Guild Incorporated*, 1025 Dodd Rd., 55118. Tel: 651-450-2220; Fax: 651-450-2221. Email: info@guildincorporated.org. Web: www.guildincorporated.org. Programs formed by The Guild of Catholic Women. A variety of housing and support services for adults who have serious and persistant mental illness. Apartments and group living available. Capacity for Clients: St. Paul 200; Total Assisted Annually 435; Total Staff 52.

[R] MINNESOTA CATHOLIC CONFERENCE (M.C.C.)

ST. PAUL. *Minnesota Catholic Conference*, 475 University Ave. W., Ste. B, 55103. Tel: 651-227-8777; Fax: 651-227-2675. Email: info@mncc.org. Web: www.mncc.org. Christopher Leifeld, Exec. Dir.; Kate Krisik, Social Concerns Dir.; Dr. Peter A. Noll, Dir. Education. The M.C.C. is a Minnesota Corporation, the purpose of which is to promote the general welfare of the people of the State of Minnesota. All Catholic Bishops of the State of Minnesota constitute Ex Officio the Board of Directors. Total Staff 5.

[S] ASSOCIATIONS OF THE FAITHFUL

ST. PAUL. *The Companions of Christ*, 2137 Marshall Ave., 55104. Tel: 651-642-5933. Email: contact@companionsofchrist.org. Web: www.CompanionsOfChrist.org. Rev. Jeffrey Huard, Moderator. Total in Residence 13.

Franciscan Brothers of Peace, Queen of Peace Friary, 1289 Lafond Ave., 55104-2035. Tel: 651-646-8586; Fax: 651-646-9083. Email: anthony@brothersofpeace.org. Web: www.brothersofpeace.org. Bros. Paul O'Donnell, F.B.P., Guardian Overall; Anthony Sweere, F.B.P., Vicar; Joseph Katzmarek, F.B.P.; Hilary McGee, F.B.P.; Conrad Richardson, F.B.P.; James Voeller,

F.B.P.; John Mary Kaspari, F.B.P.; Pio King, F.B.P. Total in Residence 8; Total Staff 1.

WEST ST. PAUL. *Community of Christ the Redeemer*, 110 Crusader Ave. W., 55118. Tel: 651-451-6114; Fax: 651-453-0810. Email: ccrspo@juno.com. Web: www.ccredeemer.org. Dr. James C. Kolar, Pres.

NET Ministries, Inc., 110 Crusader Ave. W., 55118-4427. Tel: 651-450-6833; Fax: 651-450-9984. Email: ministry@netusa.org. Web: www.netusa.org. Mr. Mark Berchem, Exec. Dir. Total Staff 28.

[T] CAMPS AND COMMUNITY CENTERS

MCGREGOR. *Catholic Youth Camps, Inc.*, Administrative Offices: 2131 Fairview Ave. N., Roseville, 55113. Tel: 651-636-1645; Fax: 651-628-9323. Email: office@cycamp.org. Web: www.cycamp.org. Camp location: 19590 520th Ln., 55760. Tel: 218-426-3383; Fax: 218-426-4675. Bob Braun, Co-Exec. Dir.; Maggie Braun, Co-Exec. Dir. Total Assisted 1,535; Total Staff 55.

[U] NEWMAN CENTERS

MINNEAPOLIS. *Newman Center at St. Lawrence* 1201 5th St., S.E., 55414. Tel: 612-331-7941; Fax: 612-378-1771. Email: nccampus@stlawrencenewman.org. Web: www.stlawrencenewman.org/~nccampus. Revs. John J. Behnke, C.S.P., Dir.; Donald A. Andrie, C.S.P.; Michael Martin, C.S.P. Total Staff 3.

[V] MISCELLANEOUS LISTINGS

ST. PAUL. *Carondelet LifeCare Ministries/St. Mary's Health Clinics*, 1884 Randolph Ave., 55105-1700. Tel: 651-690-7020; Fax: 651-690-7075. Email: bdickie@stmarysclinics.org. Barbara L. Dickie, Exec. Dir. Neighborhood Clinics 11; Patients Assisted Annually 4,852; Total Staff 11.

**Catholic Community Foundation*, 328 W. Kellogg Blvd., 55102. Tel: 651-290-1613; Fax: 651-291-4547. Email: info@catholiccommunityfoundation.org. Web: www.catholiccommunityfoundation.org. Mr. James Mullin, Pres.

Christian Brothers Youth Home, 1540 Lincoln Ave., 55105. Tel: 651-699-0736. Bro. Michael Lee Anderson, F.S.C., Dir.; Mr. Bob Paradise, Pres. Total Assisted 3; Total Staff 1.

Crosier Missions, 3510 Vivian Ave., 55126-3852. Tel: 651-486-7456; Fax: 651-287-1130. Email: dkostik@crosier.org. Web: www.crosierhome.org. Mr. David Kostik, Mission Coord. Total Staff 1.

Growing in Faith Capital Campaign, 328 W. Kellogg Blvd., 55102. Tel: 651-290-1610; Fax: 651-290-1609. Email: growinginfaith@archspm.org. Ms. Mickey Nickelson, Chief Campaign Officer.

The Highland Catholic Community, 2055 Bohland Ave., 55116. Tel: 651-698-5581; Fax: 651-698-9526. Revs. John M. Bauer, Pres.; Thomas P. Hunstiger, Vice Pres.; Mr. John Hannahan, Sec.; Sr. Janet Wermerskirchen, Pastoral Min.; Lynn Johnson, D.R.E.; Chuck Lenz, Liturgist.

Highland Catholic School (Grades K-8) Tel: 651-690-2477.

**Mary Mother of God Mission Society*, 1854 Jefferson Ave., 55105-1662. Tel: 651-227-0208; Fax: 651-227-0208. Email: usoffice@vladmission.org. Web: www.vladmission.org. Ms. Sandra Sonnen, Contact Person.

**Minnesota Catholic Education Association*, 475 University Ave., 55103-1996. Tel: 651-227-8777; Fax: 651-227-2675. Email: pnoll@mncc.org. Web: www.mncc.org. Dr. Peter Noll, Exec. Dir.

Missionary Oblates of Mary Immaculate, 104 N. Mississippi River Blvd., 55104-5698. Tel: 651-645-3560; Fax: 651-645-3702. Rev. Joseph H. Hitpas, O.M.I., Area Supr.

Legal Title: *Missionary Oblates of Mary Immaculate U.S. Prov.*

Members Attached to the Office of the Area Superior Revs. James Pillar, O.M.I., 555 S. Rockrimmon Blvd., #224, Colorado Springs, CO 80919. Tel: 719-531-0113; Eugene Tremblay, O.M.I., 1614 S. 17th St., Manitowoc, WI 54220. Tel: 920-683-9860; Raymond Quesnel, O.M.I. (WIN) (Retired), Madonna Towers, 4001 19th Ave., N.W., #202, Rochester, 55901. Tel: 507-285-0781.

Nativity of Our Lord Endowment Fund, 1900 Wellesley Ave., 55105. Tel: 612-699-0309; Fax: 612-696-5458. Email: info@nativity-mn.org. Web: www.nativity-mn.org. Total Assisted 5,000; Total Staff (Finance Council) 8.

Oblate Media and Communication Corporation, 104 N. Mississippi River Blvd., 55104. Tel: 651-645-3560. Rev. David A. Kalert, O.M.I., Pres. Oblates of Mary Immaculate, U.S. Province

Sisters of St. Joseph of Carondelet Ministries Foundation, St. Paul Province, 1884 Randolph Ave., 55105. Tel: 651-690-7026; Fax: 651-690-7039. Email: ioneill@csjstpaul.org. Web: www.csjstpaul.org. Sr. Irene O'Neill, C.S.J., Exec. Dir.

To Encounter Christ of the Archdiocese of St. Paul-Minneapolis, Minnesota, Inc. (Twin Cities TEC), (Twin Cities TEC): 76 Crusader Ave. W., 55118. Tel: 651-281-0085; Fax: 651-225-1885. Email: retreats@twincitiestec.org. Web: www.twincitiestec.org. Shelley Anderson, Admin. Dir.; Nathan Metzinger, Prog. Dir. Total Staff 2.

WomanWell, 1784 La Crosse Ave., 55119-4808. Tel: 651-739-7953; Fax: 651-739-7475. Email: seeking@WomanWell.org. Web: www.womanwell.org. Sr. Delmarie Gibney, F.S.P.A., Dir.

MINNEAPOLIS. *Catholic Eldercare, Inc.*, 817 Main St., N.E., 55413. Tel: 612-379-1370; Fax: 612-362-2486. Email: mshasky@catholiceldercare.org. Web: www.catholiceldercare.org. Mary Broderick, Pres. & CEO. Total Assisted 300; Total Staff 280.

Skilled Nursing Facility Tel: 612-379-1370; Fax: 612-379-2486. Bed Capacity 150.

Assisted Living Apartments for Elderly Adults Tel: 612-362-2405; Fax: 612-362-2449. Units 52.

Adult Day Program Tel: 612-362-2405; Fax: 612-379-2486. Assisted 80.

Safe Place for Newborns, 120 S. 6th St., Ste. 1150, 55402. Tel: 612-317-2895; 877-440-2229 24/7 Crisis Line; Fax: 612-317-2899. Email: safeplace@safeplacefornewborns.com. Web: www.safeplacefornewborns.com. Laure L. Krupp, Exec. Dir.

Sagrado Corazon de Jesus, 2645 1st Ave., S., 55408. Tel: 612-874-7169; Fax: 612-870-0408. Email: sagradocorazonl@msn.net. Rev. Lawrence E. Hubbard, Pres.; Bradley Capouch, Vice Pres.; Hugo Artola, Sec.; Armando Blas Garcia, Treas.

Society of St. Vincent De Paul, Archdiocesan Council, 2939 12th Ave., S., 55407. Tel: 612-772-7882. Ed Koerner, Dir.

Twin Cities Catholic Alumni Club, Mailing Address: P.O. Box 581321, 55458-1321. Tel: 651-603-1412. Carl Berstrom, Club Pres.

Youth and Family Center Inc., 4405 E. Lake St., 55406. Tel: 612-722-9612. Sisters Martha Merriman, C.S.J., Dir.; Betty Wurm, C.S.J., Dir. Counseling Center. Total Assisted 50; Total Staff 2.

HASTINGS. *Regina Foundation*, 1175 Nininger Rd., 55033. Tel: 651-480-4104; Fax: 651-480-4212. Email: kochendorferp@reginamediacal.org. Web: www.reginamedical.org. Mark W. Wilson, Pres. & CEO; Pam Kochendorfer, Corp. Sec.

INVER GROVE HEIGHTS. *Catholic Finance Corporation*, 5826 Blackshire Path, 55076. Tel: 651-389-1070; Fax: 651-389-1071. Email: mpschaefer@catholicfinance.org. Michael P. Schaefer, Contact.

MAPLEWOOD. *Maple Tree: Monastery Childcare Center*, 1695 Century Ave. N., 55109. Tel: 651-770-0766. Email: jschlauch2@aol.com. Sisters Marie Fujan, O.S.B., Prioress - St. Paul Priory; Annette Esboldt, Vice Pres. Total Assisted 70; Total Staff 20.

NEW BRIGHTON. *Preferred Choice Pharmacy, Inc.*, 900 Long Lake Rd., Ste. 150, 55112. Tel: 651-636-3919; Fax: 651-582-0290. Email: sandy.smilanich@bhshealth.org. Sandra A. Smilanich, Pres. & Corp. Dir. Pharmacy Svcs.

OSSEO. *Steeple Pointe Senior Living Community*, 625 Central Ave., 55369. Tel: 763-425-4440; Fax: 763-391-0747. Email: bobbie.guidry@bhshealth.org. Roberta Guidry, Resident Svcs. Admin.

SCANDIA. *The Brothers and Sisters of Penance of St. Francis*, 20939 Quadrant Ave. N., 55073. Tel: 651-433-2753. Email: bspenance@yahoo.com. Bruce A. Fahey, Dir.

WEST ST. PAUL. *St. Paul's Outreach, Inc.*, 110 Crusader Ave., 55118. Tel: 651-451-6114; Fax: 651-453-0810. Email: info@spoweb.org. Web: www.spoweb.org. Mr. Gordon C. DeMarais, Exec. Dir.; Dr. James C. Kolar, Board Pres.

RELIGIOUS INSTITUTES OF MEN REPRESENTED IN THE ARCHDIOCESE

For further details refer to the corresponding bracketed number in the Religious Institutes of Men or Women section.

[0200]—*Benedictine Monks* (St. John's Abbey)—O.S.B.
[0330]—*Brothers of the Christian Schools* (Midwest Prov.)—F.S.C.
[0400]—*Canons Regular of the Order of the Holy Cross*—O.S.C.
[0470]—*The Capuchin Fathers* (Prov. of St. Joseph)—O.F.M.Cap.
[0270]—*Carmelite Fathers and Brothers*—O.Carm.
[0270]—*Carmelite Hermitage of the Blessed Virgin Mary*—O.Carm.
[0480]—*Conventual Franciscans* (Prov. of Our Lady of Consolation)—O.F.M.Conv
[0520]—*Franciscan Friars* (Prov. of Sacred Heart)—O.F.M.
[0690]—*Jesuit Fathers and Brothers* (Wisconsin Prov.)—S.J.
[0780]—*Marist Fathers* (American Prov.)—S.M.
[0800]—*Maryknoll*—M.M.
[0720]—*The Missionaries of Our Lady of La Salette*—M.S.
[0910]—*Oblate Fathers of Mary Immaculate* (Central Prov.)—O.M.I.
[0430]—*Order of Preachers (Dominicans)* (Prov. of St. Albert the Great)—O.P.
[1030]—*Paulist Fathers*—C.S.P.
[1070]—*Redemptorist Fathers* (St. Louis Prov.)—C.SS.R.
[1060]—*Society of the Precious Blood* (Cincinnati Prov.)—C.PP.S.
[0560]—*Third Order Regular of St. Francis* (Prov. of the Immaculate Conception)—T.O.R.
[]—*Vincentian Congregation* (India)—V.C.

RELIGIOUS INSTITUTES OF WOMEN REPRESENTED IN THE ARCHDIOCESE

[0230]—*Benedictine Sisters of Pontifical Jurisdiction* (Crookston, St. Paul, St. Joseph, Duluth, MN)—O.S.B.
[3110]—*Congregation of Our Lady of the Retreat in the Cenacle*—R.C.
[3710]—*Congregation of the Sisters of St. Agnes*—C.S.A.
[1780]—*Congregation of the Sisters of the Third Order of St. Francis of Perpetual Adoration* (Eastern Region)—F.S.P.A.
[0810]—*Daughters of the Heart of Mary*—D.H.M.
[0420]—*Discalced Carmelite Nuns*—O.C.D.
[1070-03]—*Dominican Sisters*—O.P.
[1070-10]—*Dominican Sisters*—O.P.
[1070-23]—*Dominican Sisters*—O.P.
[1170]—*Felician Sisters*—C.S.S.F.
[1310]—*Franciscan Sisters of Little Falls, Minnesota*—O.S.F.
[1485]—*Franciscan Sisters of St. Paul, MN*—O.S.F.
[2575]—*Institute of the Sisters of Mercy of the Americas* (Dubuque, IA; Detroit, MI; Omaha, NE)—R.S.M.
[2340]—*Little Sisters of the Poor*—L.S.P.
[3990]—*Missionary Sisters of St. Peter Claver*—S.S.P.C.
[3760]—*Order of St. Clare*—O.S.C.
[3230]—*Poor Handmaids of Jesus Christ*—P.H.J.C.
[2970]—*School Sisters of Notre Dame*—S.S.N.D.
[1680]—*Schools Sisters of St. Francis*—O.S.F.
[3590]—*Servants of Mary (Servite Sisters)*—O.S.M.
[3520]—*Servants of the Holy Heart of Mary*—S.S.C.M.
[0520]—*Sisters of Charity of Our Lady, Mother of Mercy*—S.C.M.M.
[0430]—*Sisters of Charity of the Blessed Virgin Mary*—B.V.M.
[0660]—*Sisters of Christian Charity*—S.C.C.
[1705]—*The Sisters of St. Francis of Assisi*—O.S.F.
[1530]—*Sisters of St. Francis of the Congregation of Our Lady of Lourdes, Sylvania, Ohio*—O.S.F.
[1570]—*Sisters of St. Francis of the Holy Family*—O.S.F.
[3840]—*Sisters of St. Joseph of Carondelet*—C.S.J.
[3880]—*Sisters of St. Joseph of Medaille*—C.S.J.
[3930]—*Sisters of St. Joseph of the Third Order of St. Francis*—S.S.J.-T.O
[1020]—*Sisters of the Divine Redeemer*—S.D.R.
[1830]—*The Sisters of the Good Shepherd*—R.G.S.
[3320]—*Sisters of the Presentation of the B.V.M.* (Dubuque, IA; Sioux Falls, SD)—P.B.V.M.
[1720]—*Sisters of the Third Order Regular of St. Francis of the Congregation of Our Lady of Lourdes*—O.S.F.
[2150]—*Sisters, Servants of the Immaculate Heart of Mary*—I.H.M.
[4110]—*Ursuline Nuns (Roman Union)*—O.S.U.
[4190]—*Visitation Nuns*—V.H.M.

ARCHDIOCESAN CEMETERIES

ST. PAUL. *Calvery*

The Catholic Cemeteries, 400 Selby Ave., Ste. S, 55102. Tel: 612-228-9991.

MINNEAPOLIS. *St. Anthony & St. Mary*

MENDOTA HEIGHTS. *Resurrection*

NEW HOPE. *Assumption & Gethsemane*

PARISH CEMETERIES

SHAKOPEE. *Catholic Cemeteries of Shakapee, Minnesota, Inc.*, 535 S. Lewis St., 55379. A corporation formed by the Church of St. Mark and the Church of St. Mary, both of Shakopee, to consolidate separate cemeteries.

NECROLOGY

✠ Roach, Most Rev. John R., Retired Archbishop of Saint Paul and Minneapolis—Died July 11, 2003

† Eggert, Charles M., (Retired)—Died June 20, 2003
† Guminga, Theodore C., (Retired)—Died April 3, 2003
† Kolath, George, Minneapolis, MN St. Timothy's—Died Aug. 24, 2003
† Mertz, William H., (Retired)—Died July 19, 2003
† Mycue, Gordon E., (Retired)—Died Feb. 14, 2003
† Russell, J. Christopher, (Retired)—Died Feb. 7, 2003
† Seefeldt, Wilbert T., (Retired)—Died Feb. 7, 2003
† Tolaas, Gregory, Minneapolis, MN St. Philip—Died Sept. 7, 2003
† Vrano, Francis R., (Retired)—Died Oct. 16, 2003
† Ward, Austin T., Maplewood, MN Holy Redeemer—Died Sept. 6, 2003
† Wellisch, Robert, St. Paul, MN St. Vincent de Paul—Died May 24, 2003
† Whalen, James W., (Retired)—Died April 8, 2003

Diocese of St. Petersburg

(Dioecesis Sancti Petri in Florida)

Most Reverend

ROBERT N. LYNCH

Fourth Bishop of St. Petersburg; ordained May 13, 1978; appointed Fourth Bishop of St. Petersburg December 5, 1995; consecrated and installed January 26, 1996. *Office: P.O. Box 40200, St. Petersburg, FL 33743-0200.*

Most Reverend

W. THOMAS LARKIN, D.D.

Retired Bishop of St. Petersburg; ordained May 15, 1947; appointed Second Bishop of St. Petersburg April 24, 1979; ordained Bishop May 27, 1979; installed June 28, 1979; retired November 28, 1988.

ESTABLISHED JUNE 17, 1968.

Square Miles 3,177.

Comprises the Counties of Citrus, Hernando, Hillsborough, Pasco and Pinellas in the State of Florida.

Legal Title: For legal titles of parishes and diocesan institutions, consult the Chancery.

Pastoral Center: P.O. Box 40200, St. Petersburg, FL 33743-0200. Tel: 727-344-1611; Fax: 727-345-2143.

Web: www.dioceseofstpete.org

Email: comdosp@aol.com

STATISTICAL OVERVIEW

Personnel	
Bishop	1
Retired Bishops	2
Priests: Diocesan Active in Diocese	88
Priests: Diocesan Active Outside Diocese	6
Priests: Retired, Sick or Absent	28
Number of Diocesan Priests	122
Religious Priests in Diocese	111
Total Priests in Diocese	233
Extern Priests in Diocese	81
Ordinations:	
Religious Priests	1
Transitional Deacons	2
Permanent Deacons in Diocese	107
Total Brothers	44
Total Sisters	321
Parishes	
Parishes	73
With Resident Pastor:	
Resident Diocesan Priests	61
Resident Religious Priests	11
Without Resident Pastor:	
Administered by Priests	1
Missions	4
Pastoral Centers	1
Professional Ministry Personnel:	
Brothers	10
Sisters	84
Welfare	
Catholic Hospitals	2
Total Assisted	500,163
Health Care Centers	7
Total Assisted	35,000
Homes for the Aged	9
Total Assisted	950
Residential Care of Children	55
Total Assisted	11,000
Day Care Centers	12
Total Assisted	2,200
Specialized Homes	4
Total Assisted	650
Special Centers for Social Services	11
Total Assisted	20,768
Educational	
Diocesan Students in Other Seminaries	21
Total Seminarians	21
Colleges and Universities	1
Total Students	12,190
High Schools, Diocesan and Parish	4
Total Students	1,977
High Schools, Private	2
Total Students	969
Elementary Schools, Diocesan and Parish	28
Total Students	9,371
Elementary Schools, Private	3
Total Students	1,040
Non-residential Schools for the Disabled	2
Total Students	130
Catechesis/Religious Education:	
High School Students	2,898
Elementary Students	19,380
Total Students under Catholic Instruction	47,976
Teachers in the Diocese:	
Priests	6
Brothers	4
Sisters	30
Lay Teachers	780
Vital Statistics	
Receptions into the Church:	
Infant Baptism Totals	4,788
Adult Baptism Totals	668
Received into Full Communion	630
First Communions	5,125
Confirmations	3,814
Marriages:	
Catholic	944
Interfaith	525
Total Marriages	1,469
Deaths	4,244
Total Catholic Population	398,702
Total Population	2,660,220

Former Bishops—Most Revs. CHARLES B. MCLAUGHLIN, D.D., ord. June 6, 1941; appt. Titular Bishop of Risinium and Auxiliary of Raleigh, Jan. 13, 1964; appt. First Bishop of St. Petersburg, May 8, 1968; installed June 17, 1968; died in Office, Dec 14, 1978; W. THOMAS LARKIN, D.D. (Retired), ord. May 15, 1947; Second Bishop of St. Petersburg; appt. April 24, 1979; ord. Bishop, May 27, 1979; installed June 28, 1979; retired Nov. 28, 1988; JOHN C. FAVALORA, D.D., Third Bishop of St. Petersburg; ord. Dec. 20, 1961; appt. Bishop of Alexandria, June 16, 1986; ord. and installed July 29, 1986; appt. Third Bishop of St. Petersburg, March 7, 1989; installed May 16, 1989; installed Third Archbishop of Miami, Dec. 20, 1994.

Diocesan Offices

Pastoral Center—6363 Ninth Ave. N., St. Petersburg, 33710. Tel: 727-344-1611; Fax: 727-345-2143. *Mailing Address, P.O. Box 40200, St. Petersburg, 33743-0200.*

Tribunal—905 S. Prospect Ave., Clearwater, 33756. Tel: 727-446-2326; 727-442-8884; Fax: 727-446-4287.

WBVM 90.5 FM, Inc.—3816 Morrison Ave., Tampa, 33629. Tel: 813-289-8040. *Mailing Address, P.O. Box 18081, Tampa, 33679.*

Office of the Bishop

Office of the Bishop—Most Rev. ROBERT N. LYNCH.

Executive Secretary—Mrs. ANGELICA "VIVI" IGLESIAS.

Diocesan Curia

Vicars General—Rev. Msgr. BRENDAN MULDOON, V.G.; Rev. ALAN WEBER, V.G.

Moderator of the Curia—Rev. ALAN WEBER, V.G.

Chancellor—Rev. ROBERT C. GIBBONS, J.C.L.; Mrs. CECILIA SVAB, Exec. Sec.; Mrs. LISA MOBLEY, Archivist & Notary.

Vice Chancellor—Mrs. JOAN MORGAN, Notary.

Director of Priest Personnel—Rev. ROBERT MORRIS.

Secretary for Pastoral Programs—Rev. ALAN WEBER, V.G.

Secretary for Administration—Mrs. ELIZABETH DEPTULA; Miss BARBARA STUTTS, Exec. Sec. & Notary.

The Tribunal—

Judicial Vicar—Rev. Msgr. DACIAN DEE, J.C.D.

Tribunal Staff—

Judges—Rev. Msgr. DACIAN DEE, J.C.D.; Revs. ROBERT C. GIBBONS, J.C.L.; RONALD AUBIN, J.C.L.; WILLIAM SWENGROS, J.C.D.; Mr. ANTHONY ELLUL, J.C.D.

Promoter of Justice—Rev. STEPHEN DAMBRAUSKAS, J.C.L.

Defenders of the Bond—Rev. STEPHEN DAMBRAUSKAS, J.C.L.; Mr. DAVID RIDENOUR, J.D., J.C.L.

Auditor—Mr. KAZ MIELCAREK, Ph.D.

Notaries—Mrs. SARAH DURST; Mrs. LOUISE KNOCHELMANN; Mrs. MARY SUE OLIVER.

Secretary and Receptionist—Ms. ANA RIVERA.

Priests Personnel Board—Very Rev. DESMOND DALY, V.F.; Revs. JOHN MCEVOY; LEONARD PIOTROWSKI; Very Rev. GREGG TOTTLE. Ex Officio: Rev. Msgr. BRENDAN MULDOON, V.G.; Revs. ALAN WEBER, V.G.; ROBERT C. GIBBONS, J.C.L.; ROBERT MORRIS; Mrs. ELIZABETH DEPTULA; Mrs. JOAN MORGAN.

Incardination Commission—Revs. ROBERT C. GIBBONS, J.C.L., Exec. Sec.; JOHN GERTH; ROBERT DONLAN; FELIX SANCHEZ; Rev. Msgrs. AIDEN FOYNES; BRENDAN MULDOON, V.G.; Revs. ALAN WEBER; ROBERT MORRIS.

Vocations Office—Rev. LEONARD PLAZEWSKI, Dir. Vocations; Mrs. ELAINE THELEN, Admin. Asst.

Permanent Diaconate Office—Rev. ALAN WEBER, V.G., Dir.; Deacon LIONEL ROBERTS, Admin. Asst.; Mrs.

HEIDI SUMNER, Sec.
Vicar for Religious—Sisters GERMAINE BEVANS, O.S.B.; EUGENE MARIE SCHNEIDER, O.S.F., Sec.

Department of Pastoral Programs

Sea, Apostleship of the—
Port of St. Petersburg—515 4th St., St. Petersburg, 33701. Tel: 727-896-2191.
Tampa Port Ministry-Seafarers Center—Deacon MAXIMO MONTAYRE, Chap., 2790 Maritime Dr., Tampa, 33610.
Black Catholic Ministries, Office for—Ms. YVONNE NELLUM, Asst. Dir.
Spanish Speaking Spiritual Monitor—Rev. Msgr. ANTONIO DIEZ, 6819 Krycul Ave., P.O. Box 418, Riverview, 33569. Tel: 813-677-2175.
Cursillo, English—Ms. KITTY MCKIERMAN, Lay Coord., 1772 S. Cove Walk, Inverness, 34450-5066. Cursillo, Spiritual Advisors: Rev. JEAN C. ROBITAILLE, M.Afr., Missionaries of Africa Residence, 5757 7th Ave. N., St. Petersburg, 33710. Tel: 727-343-1001; Deacon JOHN EDGERTON, St. Luke the Evangelist Church, 2757 Alderman Rd., Palm Harbor, 34684. Tel: 727-786-3648.
Cursillo, Spanish—Rev. KAZIMIERZ DOMEK, Dir., Nativity Church, 705 E. Brandon Blvd., Brandon, 33511. Tel: 813-681-4608.
Ecumenical and Inter-Religious Affairs—Rev. Msgr. J. BERNARD CAVERLY, St. Raphael Church, 1376 Snell Isle Blvd., N.E., St. Petersburg, 33704. Tel: 727-821-7989.
Hispanic Apostolate—Mrs. SANDRA BONILLA, Dir.; Rev. RAMON HERNANDEZ, Spiritual Moderator.
Lay Pastoral Ministry Institute—ANNE MARIE WINTERS, Ph.D., Dir.
Our Lady of Good Counsel Camp—Rev. JAMES JOHNSON, Dir., 8888 E. Gobbler Dr., Floral City, 34436. Tel: 352-726-2198. Email: gcccamp@infi.net.
Prison Ministry—Deacon JOHN ALVAREZ, Dir. Tel: 727-812-4838.
Propagation of the Faith—Rev. Msgr. JOHN SCULLY, P.A., Diocesan Dir.
Small Christian Communities and Evangelization, Office for—Mrs. DIANE KLEDZIK, Dir.
St. Casimir Lithuanian Apostolate—Rev. BERNARDAS TALAISIS, 555 68th Ave., St. Petersburg Beach, 33706. Tel: 727-367-2408.
Victim Assistance Coordinator—Ms. MARTI ZEITZ, M.A., 1213 16th St. N., St. Petersburg, 33705. Tel: 866-407-4505 (Toll Free). Email: mzeitz@ccdosp.org.
Worship, Office of—Mr. DOUGLAS REATINI, Dir.; Mrs. KATHY PROEFKE, Assoc. Dir.
Catholic Schools Office—Bro. JOHN CUMMINGS, F.M.S., Supt.; Ms. MARY BRYAN, Assoc. Supt. for Administrative Svcs.; Ms. KAY RIZZO, Assoc. Supt. for Curriculum and Instruction.
Family Life Office—Deacon JOSEPH GROTE, Dir.
Father William F. Balfe Memorial Library—Mrs. CLARA BLOWERS, Dir.
Religious Education Office—Mr. BRIAN A. LEMOI, Dir.; Mrs. PAT WIAND, Catechist Certification Program Coord.
Respect Life Office—Mrs. SHARON ILER, Dir.
Scouting Office, Girls—Rev. Msgr. ANTON DECHERING, Dir., 1600 54th Ave. S., St. Petersburg, 33712. Tel: 727-867-3663.
Scouting Office, Boys—Rev. ANTHONY COPPOLA, Diocesan Chap. Tel: 727-584-2318; Mr. MICHAEL KOSIBA, Diocesan Chm. Tel: 813-839-4644.
Youth Ministry Office—Bro. GERALD D. MEEGAN, S.D.B., Dir.

Communications

Communications Office—Mrs. MARY JO MURPHY, Dir.
Diocesan Radio - WBVM 90.5 FM & WLMS 88.3 FM—Mr. JOHN MORRIS, Station Mgr., P.O. Box 18081, Tampa, 33679. 3816 Morrison Ave., Tampa, 33629. Tel: 813-289-8040; 800-223-9286 (800-223-WBVM); Fax: 813-282-3580.
"The Florida Catholic" Newspaper—Mrs. JANET SHELTON, Diocesan Editor.
Circulation & Subscription—P.O. Box 609512, Orlando, 32802-9512. Tel: 888-275-9953. Email: RNOVAK@thefloridacatholic.org.

Department of Temporal Affairs

Department of Temporal Affairs—Rev. ALAN WEBER, V.G., Chief Fin. Officer; Mrs. ELIZABETH DEPTULA, Sec. for Admin.; Mr. PAUL A. WARD JR., Exec. Dir., Finance Office.
Calvary Catholic Cemetery and Miserere Guild—Rev. Msgr. NORMAN BALTHAZAR, Dir. Cemeteries, 11801 U.S. Hwy. 19 N., Clearwater, 33764-7407. Tel: 727-572-4355; Fax: 727-592-9241.
Finance and Accounting—Mr. PAUL A. WARD JR., Exec. Dir.; Mr. JOSEPH CORSETTI, Dir., Parish Accounting.
Diocesan Finance Council—Mrs. LAURA KRUEGER BROCK, Chm.; Mr. C. DAVID CARLEY; Rev. Msgr. BRENDAN MULDOON, V.G.; Revs. ROBERT C. GIBBONS, J.C.L.; ALAN WEBER, V.G.; Mr. MICHAEL CARRERE; Mr. FRED DOBBINS; Mr. GREG KIELER; Ms. RETIA MCADORY; Mrs. NANCY RIDENOUR; Mr. WILLIAM G. TAPP; Rev. Msgr. FRANK MOUCH; Very Rev. GREGG TOTTLE; Mrs. ELIZABETH DEPTULA; Mr. MARK BARHONOVICH; Mr. DONALD F. DUNN.
Diocesan Legal Council— DiVito & Higham, P.A. JOSEPH A. DIVITO; FREDERICK A. HIGHAM JR., 4514 Central Ave., St. Petersburg, 33711-1041. Tel: 727-321-1201 Fax: 727-321-5181. DiVito & Higham, P.A.
Insurance, Health & Welfare Administration, Risk Management—Mr. RICARDO OSORIO, Dir.; Mrs. MONITA BONCZEK, Admin. Asst.
Real Estate—Mr. RONALD G. BENTO, Real Estate Mgr.; Mr. STEVE B. ZIENTEK, Real Estate Planning Mgr.
Information Technology—Mr. JOSEPH SCHORR, Dir.; Mrs. CAROL PILARSKI, Asst. Dir.
Office of Construction Management—Mr. RICK KOLHOFF, Exec. Dir.
Human Resources—Mr. THOMAS SCHROEDER, Exec. Dir.; Mrs. CHARLOTTE MYERS, Personnel Asst.
Internal Services Administration—Mrs. WANDA BIDWELL, Dir.
Diocesan Development Office—
Bishop's Annual Appeal—Ms. MEEGAN WRIGHT, Dir. Campaign & Devel.
The Catholic Foundation—JOSEPH CITRO, Dir.

Pastoral Offices and Consultative Bodies to the Diocesan Curia

Presbyteral Council—Most Rev. ROBERT N. LYNCH, Pres.; Rev. ALAN WEBER, V.G., Vice Pres.; Very Rev. JOSEPH WATERS, V.F., Chm.; Rev. ROBERT GIBBONS, J.C.L.; Rev. Msgrs. BRENDAN MULDOON, V.G.; DACIAN DEE, J.C.D.; Very Revs. JAMES BUCARIA, V.F.; DESMOND DALY, V.F.; Rev. Msgr. ANTON DECHERING, V.F.; Very Rev. JACOB MONTELEONE, V.F.; Revs. VINCENT MORTON, V.F.; GEORGE ROZYCKI; Rev. Msgr. J. BERNARD CAVERLY; Revs. LEONARD PLAZEWSKI; ARTHUR PROULX; RICHARD JANKOWSKI; Very Rev. GREGG TOTTLE; Revs. JOHN BLUM; THOMAS ANASTASIA; LEONARD PIOTROWSKI; TIM SHERWOOD; ROBERT SCHNEIDER; LOUIS MOLINELLI, S.D.B.; THOMAS MORGAN; ROBERT MORRIS.
College of Consultors—Rev. ALAN WEBER, V.G.; Rev. Msgr. BRENDAN MULDOON, V.G.; Revs. ROBERT C. GIBBONS, J.C.L., Sec.; ROBERT MORRIS; Rev. Msgr. DACIAN DEE, J.C.D.; Very Rev. JAMES BUCARIA, V.F.; Rev. DESMOND DALY, V.F.; Rev. Msgr. ANTON DECHERING, V.F.; Very Rev. JACOB MONTELEONE, V.F.; Revs. VINCENT MORTON, V.F.; GEORGE ROZYCKI; Very Rev. JOSEPH WATERS, V.F.; Rev. ARTHUR PROULX.
Diocesan Review Board—Mrs. SUE BRETT, Chm. Tel: 727-384-0730; Fax: 727-344-4060.
Vicars Forane—Very Revs. JOSEPH WATERS, V.F., East Hillsborough Deanery; JACOB MONTELEONE, V.F., Upper Pinellas Deanery; Rev. Msgr. ANTON DECHERING, V.F., Lower Pinellas Deanery; Very Rev. DESMOND DALY, V.F., West Hillsborough Deanery; Revs. GEORGE ROZYCKI, Pasco Deanery; JAMES BUCARIA, V.F., Hernando Deanery; VINCENT MORTON, V.F., Citrus Deanery.

Organizations Serving the Diocese

Archdiocese of Miami, Diocese of St. Petersburg, and Diocese of Venice Pension Plan—
Pension Plan Administrator—Gabriel, Roeder, Smith & Co., 301 E. Las Olas Blvd., Ste. 200, Fort Lauderdale, 33301. Tel: 954-527-1616; Fax: 954-525-0083.
Catholic Charities, Diocese of St. Petersburg, Inc.—
Central Services—1213 16th St., N., St. Petersburg, 33705. Tel: 727-893-1314; Fax: 727-893-1307. Web: www.ccdosp.org. Mr. ARNOLD ANDREWS, Exec. Dir.

Pious Foundations

Catholic Education Foundation, Inc.—6363 Ninth Ave. N., St. Petersburg, 33710. Tel: 727-344-1611. *Mailing Address, P.O. Box 40200, St. Petersburg, 33743-0200.*
Emmaus Foundation, Inc.—6363 Ninth Ave. N., St. Petersburg, 33710. Tel: 727-344-1611. *Mailing Address, P.O. Box 40200, St. Petersburg, 33743-0200.*

Organizations of the Catholic Faithful

Catholic Daughters of America—Ms. GRACE DICAIRANO, Natl. Regent, Manasquan, NJ; Ms. DAHLIA PEREZ, State Regent. Tel: 813-876-7100. National Office. Tel: 212-877-3041.
Diocesan Council of Catholic Women—Rev. ROBERT SCHNEIDER, Diocesan Moderator. Tel: 727-526-5783.
Family of St. Jerome, "Familian Sancti Hieronymi"—Mr. JAN G. HALISKY, P.A., Praeses Generalis, 507 S. Prospect Ave., Clearwater, 33756.
Knights of Columbus—Rev. PAUL HERVEY, Diocesan Chap. Tel: 727-786-3648.
Society of St. Vincent de Paul—
Central Council of St. Petersburg Diocese—19111 Vista Bay Dr., #415, Indian Shore, 33785. Tel: 727-595-3876. JOHN ALLEN, Pres.; Mr. MARVIN ROPERT, Exec. Dir. Tel: 813-832-5486.
Hernando/Citrus St. Vincent de Paul Society District Council—Mr. BOB FRANK, Pres. Tel: 352-686-8584.
Hillsborough District Council—Mr. TIM CASEY, Pres. Tel: 813-933-9729.
Ozanam District Council (Pasco Deanery)—Mr. ED MCCOY, Pres. Tel: 727-819-0444.
Lower Pinellas District Council—Mrs. SOPHIE SAMPSON, Pres. Tel: 727-823-2516.
Upper Pinellas District Council—THOMAS RYAN, Pres. Tel: 727-442-5306.

CLERGY, PARISHES, MISSIONS AND PAROCHIAL SCHOOLS

CITY OF ST. PETERSBURG
(PINELLAS COUNTY)

ST. PETERSBURG

1—CATHEDRAL OF ST. JUDE THE APOSTLE (1950), Very Rev. Gregg Tottle, Rector; Revs. Craig Morley; Leonard Plazewski; Michael Perry, O.de.M.; Deacon David Sirrianna.
Res.: 5815 Fifth Ave. N., 33743. Tel: 727-347-9702; Fax: 727-343-8370.
School—Tel: 727-347-8622; Fax: 727-343-0305. Mr. Larry Lopez, Prin. Lay Teachers 33; Students 519.
Catechesis/Religious Program—Tel: 727-247-9702; Fax: 727-343-8370. Ms. Dorothy Sanderson, D.R.E. Students 229.

2—BLESSED TRINITY (1960), Rev. Msgr. Anton Dechering; Revs. J. Frederick McGuire (CIN); Paul Bondi (ALB) (Retired); Sr. Jean Barrett, O.S.F., Pastoral Assoc.; Deacon Lionel Roberts.
Res.: 1600 54th Ave. S., 33712. Tel: 727-867-3663; Fax: 727-864-2679.
School—St. Paul Interparochial School, Tel: 727-823-6144; Fax: 727-896-0609. See Elementary Schools, Interparochial under Institutions Located in the Diocese
Catechesis/Religious Program—Tel: 727-867-3663; Fax: 727-864-2679. Mrs. Sonya Ackins, D.R.E. Students 114.

3—HOLY CROSS (1965), Rev. Thomas Anastasia; Deacons Richard Brady; Richard Nagle Jr.; Lowell Hecht.
Res.: 7851 54th Ave. N., 33709. Tel: 727-546-3315; 727-541-2242; Fax: 727-547-2005.
Catechesis/Religious Program—Tel: 727-547-2004; Fax: 727-547-2005. Students 230.

4—HOLY FAMILY (1959), Rev. John Tapp; Sr. Jamesann McCue, I.H.M., Dir., Pastoral Assoc.; Deacon Michael Columbus; David J. Koval, Admin.
Res.: 200 78th Ave., N.E., 33702. Tel: 727-526-5783; Fax: 727-521-2545.
School—250 78th Ave., N.E., 33702. Tel: 727-526-8194; Fax: 727-527-6567. Sr. Florence Ann Marino, I.H.M., Prin. Sisters 1; Lay Teachers 15; Students 220.
Catechesis/Religious Program—Tel: 727-526-5783, Ext. 21; Fax: 727-521-2545. George Pioli, D.R.E. (Adult & Elementary). Students 185.

5—ST. JOSEPH (1926), Rev. Timothy E. Sherwood. Mailing Address: 2025-22 Ave. S., 33712. Tel: 727-822-2153; Fax: 727-823-5820.
School—Preschool, Immaculate Conception. Tel: 727-822-2156; Fax: 727-553-9133. Lay Teachers 17; Students 142.
Catechesis/Religious Program—Students 56.

6—ST. MARY OUR LADY OF GRACE (1921), Revs. Luke Robertson, T.O.R.; Brian J. Miller, T.O.R.; Patrick George, T.O.R.; Raymond Nedimyer, T.O.R.
Res.: 515 Fourth St. S., 33701. Tel: 727-896-2191; Fax: 727-895-6279.
Catechesis/Religious Program—Students 73.

7—ST. PAUL (1929), Revs. Robert C. Gibbons, J.C.L.; Michael Robert Cormier.
Res.: 1800 12th St. N., 33704. Tel: 727-822-3481; Fax: 727-822-1754.
School—St. Paul Interparochial School, Tel: 727-823-6144; Fax: 727-896-0609. See Elementary Schools, Interparochial under Institutions Located in the Diocese
Catechesis/Religious Program—Tel: 727-822-3481; Fax: 727-822-1754. Students 121.
Mission—The Mercy of God Polish Mission 1358 20th Ave. N., Pinellas Co. 33704. Tel: 727-823-6997; Fax: 727-821-8242. Rev. Janusz Burzawa (Poland).

8—ST. RAPHAEL (1961), Rev. Msgr. J. Bernard Caverly; Rev. Michel Robert Smith; Deacon Joseph Grote. In Res., Rev. Jose G. Gonzalez.
Res.: 1376 Snell Isle Blvd., N.E., 33704. Tel: 727-821-8270; Fax: 727-896-9619.
School—Tel: 727-821-9663; Fax: 727-821-9665. Mrs. Caryl Nolan, Prin. Lay Teachers 19; Students 272.
Catechesis/Religious Program—Tel: 727-821-0155. Rhona Beettam, D.R.E. Students 364.

9—TRANSFIGURATION (1959), Rev. Msgr. John F. Bolger, Pastor Emeritus (Retired); Revs. Anthony M. Fortunato, O.de.M.; Jerome P. Laubacker, O.de.M.; Oscar Z. Kozyra, O.de.M. (Argentina).
Church: 4000 43rd St. N., 33714.
Res.: 5650 7th Ave N., 33710. Tel: 727-345-4766; Fax: 727-347-5345.
School—Tel: 727-527-2880; Fax: 727-522-1328. Sr. Bridget Cedji, S.O.L.M., Prin. Religious 3; Lay Teachers 15; Students 220.
Catechesis/Religious Program—Tel: 727-525-0262. Mary Holmes, D.R.E. Students 56.
Convent—4000-43 St. N., 33714-4335. Tel: 727-521-6394; Fax: 727-526-7794.

OUTSIDE THE CITY OF ST. PETERSBURG

BEVERLY HILLS, CITRUS CO., OUR LADY OF GRACE (1966), Rev. Paul Mizener; Deacon Heiberto Lopez.
Res.: 6 Roosevelt Blvd., 34465. Tel: 352-746-2144; Fax: 352-746-6892.
School—Pope John Paul II, Lecanto, Tel: 352-746-2020; Fax: 352-746-3448. See Elementary Schools, Interparochial under Institutions Located in the Diocese.
Catechesis/Religious Program—Tel: 352-746-2144; Fax: 352-746-6892. Students 87.

BRANDON, HILLSBOROUGH CO., CHURCH OF THE NATIVITY (1960), [JC] Rev. Msgr. James C. Lara, Pastor Emeritus; Revs. Ralph J. Argentino; Gary Dowsey; Kasimierz Domek; Deacons Jim Pescatore; Luis Zayas.
Church: 705 E. Brandon Blvd., 33511. Tel: 813-681-4608; Fax: 813-653-9482.
Res.: 805 Westbrook, 33511. Tel: 813-684-0256.
School—Tel: 813-689-3395; Fax: 813-681-5406. Sr. Irene St. Jean, C.S.C., Prin. Sisters of Holy Cross (Pittsfield, NH) 2; Lay Teachers 33; Students 683.
Catechesis/Religious Program—Tel: 813-689-3395; Fax: 813-681-5406. Vicki Hawkins, D.R.E. Students 1,081.

BROOKSVILLE, HERNANDO CO., ST. ANTHONY (1892), Rev. Robert R. Donlan; Deacon Manuel Carreiro; Sr. Loretta Lonsdorf, O.S.M., Pastoral Assoc.
Res.: 20428 Cortez Blvd., 34601-5601. Tel: 352-796-2096; Fax: 352-796-7144.
School—Notre Dame Interparochial School, Tel: 352-683-0755; Fax: 352-683-3924. See Elementary Schools, Interparochial under Institutions Located in the Diocese.
Catechesis/Religious Program—Tel: 352-796-2096; Fax: 352-796-7144. Sr. Patricia Saunders, O.P., D.R.E. Students 218.

CITRUS SPRINGS, CITRUS CO., ST. ELIZABETH ANN SETON (1976), Rev. Eric Peters; Rev. Msgr. George Cummings, Pastor Emeritus; Deacon T. Eric Makoid.
Office & Mailing Address: 1460 W. St. Elizabeth Pl., 34434. Tel: 352-489-4889; 352-489-5226; Fax: 352-489-4770.
Res.: 9037 N. Bertin Dr., 34434. Tel: 352-465-5298.
School—Pope John Paul II, Lecanto. Tel: 352-746-2020; Fax: 352-746-3448. See Elementary Schools, Interparochial under Institutions Located in the Diocese.
Catechesis/Religious Program—Tel: 352-489-4889. Deacon T. Eric Makoid, D.R.E. Students 45.

CLEARWATER, PINELLAS CO.

1—ALL SAINTS (1987), Rev. Callist N. Nyambo; Deacon Jack Lyons.
Office—2801 Curlew Rd., 33761. Tel: 727-789-1025; Fax: 727-784-8025.
School—Guardian Angels Interparochial School, Tel: 727-799-6724; Fax: 727-724-9018. See Elementary Schools, Interparochial under Institutions Located in the Diocese.
Catechesis/Religious Program—Tel: 727-789-1025; Fax: 727-764-8025. Students 208.

2—ST. BRENDAN (1978), Rev. Msgr. Michael F. Devine; Deacon James Grevenites.
Res.: 245 Dory Passage, 33767. Tel: 727-443-5485; Fax: 727-442-5896.
School—St. Cecelia Interparochial School, Tel: 727-461-1200; Fax: 727-446-9140. See Elementary Schools, Interparochial Under Institutions Located in the Diocese.

3—ST. CECELIA (1924), Rev. Msgr. Aiden Foynes; Revs. Robert Gomes; Francis X. Sarjeant, S.J. In Res., Rev. Eduardo Wal.
Res.: 820 Jasmine Way, 33756. Tel: 727-447-3494; Fax: 727-442-4810.
School—St. Cecelia Interparochial School, Tel: 727-461-1200; Fax: 727-446-9140. See Elementary Schools, Interparochial under Institutions Located in the Diocese.
Catechesis/Religious Program—Mrs. Mary M. Thomas, D.R.E. Students 295.

4—LIGHT OF CHRIST (1966), Very Rev. Jacob Monteleone, V.F.; Rev. Robert J. Kuzmann; Deacon James Hassett.
Res.: 2176 Marilyn St., 33765. Tel: 727-441-4545; Fax: 727-441-8771.
School—St. Cecelia Interparochial School, Tel: 727-461-1200; Fax: 727-446-9140. See Elementary Schools, Interparochial under Institutions Located in the Diocese.
Pre-School—Tel: 727-442-4797; Fax: 727-441-8771. Mrs. Rebecca Daschbach, Dir. Lay Teachers 6; Students 87.
Catechesis/Religious Program—Tel: 727-442-7081. William Woodard, D.R.E. Students 334.

5—ST. MICHAEL THE ARCHANGEL (1980), Revs. Colman M. Cooke; Ted Costello; Sr. Theresa Betz, S.N.D., Pastoral Assoc.
2281 State Rd. 580, 33763. Tel: 727-797-2375; Fax: 727-791-8287.
Catechesis/Religious Program—Tel: 727-797-7083. Mrs. Katie White, D.R.E. Students 274.

CRYSTAL RIVER, CITRUS CO., ST. BENEDICT (1953), Very Rev. Vincent R. Morton, V.F.; Rev. Evaristus Mushi; Deacons James Pullar; James Kennedy.
Mailing Address: 455 S. Suncoast Blvd., 34429. Tel: 352-795-4478; 352-795-4479; Fax: 352-795-6638.
School—Pope John Paul II, Lecanto. Tel: 352-746-2020; Fax: 352-746-3448. See Elementary Schools, Interparochial under Institutions Located in the Diocese.
Catechesis/Religious Program—Tel: 352-795-4479; Fax: 352-795-6638. Students 88.

DADE CITY, PASCO CO., ST. RITA (1912), (Hispanic), Revs. Ramon Hernandez; Edwin Palka; Anselm Harry Morrison, A.A.
Office & Mailing Address: 14404 14th St., 33523. Tel: 352-567-2894; Fax: 352-567-2777.
Res.: 14325 13th St., 33523. Tel: 352-521-3145.
School—St. Anthony Interparochial School, San Antonio. Tel: 352-588-3041; Fax: 352-588-3142. See Elementary Schools, Interparochial under Institutions Located in the Diocese.
Catechesis/Religious Program—Sr. Eugenia Aguilar, O.P., D.R.E. Students 373.

DUNEDIN, PINELLAS CO., OUR LADY OF LOURDES (1958), Revs. Thomas L. Madden; Thomas Spillett; Charles Banda (Malawi). In Res., Rev. Denis Kitenge (Congo).
Res.: 750 San Salvador Dr., 34698. Tel: 727-733-3606; Fax: 727-733-8305.
School—Tel: 727-733-3776; Fax: 727-733-3776. Mrs. Janice Metz. Lay Teachers 15; Students 309.
Catechesis/Religious Program—Tel: 813-733-0872; Fax: 813-733-8305. Sr. Kathleen Dede, S.P., D.R.E. Students 561.

GULFPORT, PINELLAS CO., MOST HOLY NAME OF JESUS (1960), Revs. William J. Swengros; Vladimir Dziadek; Deacon Glenn Pickart.
Res.: 5800 15th Ave. S., 33707. Tel: 727-347-9989; Fax: 727-343-6420.
School—Tel: 727-347-1774; Fax: 727-381-7225. Lynn Yakes, Dir. Lay Teachers 16; Students 159.
Catechesis/Religious Program—Lyn Folsom, D.R.E. Students 32.

HOLIDAY, PASCO CO., ST. VINCENT DE PAUL (1969), Revs. Robert Chabot, S.S.S.; Mario Marzocchi, S.S.S. (CLV); Edward Stapleton, S.S.S.; Sr. Madeleine Donnelly, O.S.C.; Deacons Frank Longo; Gerard White. In Res., Rev. Julian Rousseau, S.S.S.
Res.: 4843 Mile Stretch Dr., P.O. Box 3865, 34690. Tel: 727-938-1974; Fax: 727-938-1975.
School—Bishop Larkin Interparochial School, Hudson. Tel: 727-862-6981. See Elementary Schools, Interparochial under Institutions Located in the Diocese.
Catechesis/Religious Program—Tel: 727-934-8035. Jane Etzel, D.R.E. Students 225.

HOMOSASSA, CITRUS CO., ST. THOMAS THE APOSTLE (1987), Rev. David A. Banks; Deacon Richard Meyer.
Res.: 7040 S. Suncoast Blvd., 34446. Tel: 352-628-7000; Fax: 352-628-4723.
School—Pope John Paul II, Lecanto. Tel: 352-746-2020; Fax: 352-746-3448. See Elementary Schools, Interparochial under Institutions Located in the Diocese.
Catechesis/Religious Program—Sharon Bassing, D.R.E. Students 63.

HUDSON, PASCO CO., ST. MICHAEL (1971), Revs. Paul Goudreau; Emil Styczen; Seamus Collins, O.P.; Tomy John (India); Deacons Robert Simpson; Howard Page.
Res.: 8014 State Rd. #52, 34667. Tel: 727-868-5276; Fax: 727-862-9187.
Catechesis/Religious Program—Tel: 727-863-9742. Mary Alber, D.R.E. Students 386.

INDIAN ROCKS BEACH, PINELLAS CO., ST. JEROME (1956), Rev. Msgr. Brendan Muldoon, V.G.; Rev. Hugh Chikawe; Sisters Lucia Brady, O.S.C., Pastoral Assoc.; Cecilia McDonnell, O.S.C., Pastoral Assoc.; Deacon William Mahood.
Mailing Address: P.O. Box 100, 33785. In Res., Rev. Msgr. Dacian Dee, J.C.D., V.E.
Res.: 10895 Hamlin Blvd., Largo, 33774. Tel: 727-595-4610; Fax: 727-596-6792.
School—Early Childhood Center, Tel: 727-596-9491; Fax: 727-596-8953. Denise Roach, Dir.
Catechesis/Religious Program—Tel: 727-595-3100. Tamara Gildea, D.R.E. Students 520.

INVERNESS, CITRUS CO., OUR LADY OF FATIMA (1955), Revs. James B. Johnson; Charles Leke; Desmond Gill, Pastor Emeritus; Deacon Romy Postadan.
Mailing Address: 550 U.S. Hwy. 41 S., 34450. Tel: 352-726-1670; Fax: 352-344-8384.
Res.: 518 Desota Ave., 34450. Tel: 352-726-1670.
School—Pope John Paul II, Tel: 352-746-2020; Fax: 352-746-3448. See Elementary Schools, Interparochial under Institutions Located in the Diocese
Catechesis/Religious Program—Rebecca Pound, D.R.E.; Annette Tremante, D.R.E. Students 247.

LAND O'LAKES, PASCO CO., OUR LADY OF THE ROSARY (1952), Revs. Ronald B. Aubin; Raphael Kilumanga; Deacons Augustin Ortiz; Eric Wells.
P.O. Box 1229, 34639.
2348 Collier Pkwy., Land O Lakes, 34639. Tel: 813-949-4565; Fax: 813-948-1981.
School—Most Holy Redeemer Interparochial School, Tampa. Tel: 813-933-4750; Fax: 813-933-3181. See Elementary Schools, Interparochial under Institutions Located in the Diocese.
Catechesis/Religious Program—Tel: 813-949-2699; Fax: 813-948-1981. Miriam Melfy, D.R.E. Students 919.

LARGO, PINELLAS CO.

1—ST. CATHERINE OF SIENA (1976), Revs. Michael J. Finnegan; John O'Donovan (Ireland); Sisters Kathleen Beatty, S.S.J., Pastoral Assoc.; Marie Cella, S.S.J., Pastoral Assoc.
Res.: 1955 S. Belcher Rd., Clearwater, 33764. Tel: 727-531-7721; 531-169-; Fax: 727-531-7723.
School—St. Cecelia Interparochial School, Tel: 727-461-1200; Fax: 727-442-4810. See Elementary Schools, Interparochial under Institutions Located in the Diocese.
Catechesis/Religious Program—Tel: 727-531-7721; Fax: 727-531-7723. Paula Sikora, D.R.E. Students 244.

2—ST. JUSTIN MARTYR (1987), Rev. Michael O'Brien.
Res.: 10725 Ridge Rd., Seminole, 33778. Tel: 727-397-3312; Fax: 727-392-6653.
Catechesis/Religious Program—Tel: 727-397-3312, Ext. 307. Rosemary Mandery, D.R.E. Students 70.

3—ST. MATTHEW (1985), Rev. John Gerth; Deacons John DiVito; John Buckley; Bernard Braun.
Mailing Address: P.O. Box 10097, 33773-0097.
Office—9111 90th Ave. N., 33777. Tel: 727-393-1288; Fax: 727-398-2683.
Catechesis/Religious Program—Tel: 727-398-6618, Ext. 207. Ruth Appel, D.R.E. Students 210.
Mission—Holy Martyrs of Vietnam 8928 91st Ter. N., Pinellas Co. 33777.

4—ST. PATRICK (1958), Revs. Arthur J. Proulx; Anthony Coppola; Deacons Richard Brady; Ken Spaulding.
Res.: 2121 16th Ave., S.W., P.O. Box 167, 33779. Tel: 727-584-2318; Fax: 727-586-5413.
School—Tel: 727-581-4865; Fax: 727-581-7842. Therese Hernandez, Prin. Lay Teachers 17; Students 240.
Catechesis/Religious Program—Tel: 727-584-6697. Kathy Filippelli, D.R.E.; Lynn Edmonds, D.R.E. Students 155.

LECANTO, CITRUS CO., ST. SCHOLASTICA (1987), Rev. Richard Jankowski; Deacons Terrence E. Knox; Stephen Sablone. In Res., Rev. James Hoge, O.S.B.
Res.: 4301 W. Homosassa Tr., 34461-9106. Tel: 352-746-9422; 352-563-2296; Fax: 352-746-2335.
School—Pope John Paul II, Tel: 352-746-2020; Fax: 352-746-3448. See Elementary Schools, Interparochial under Institutions Located in the Diocese.
Catechesis/Religious Program—Tel: 352-746-9422; Fax: 352-746-2335. Judi Bescher, D.R.E. Students 389.

MASARYKTOWN, PASCO CO., ST. MARY, OUR LADY OF SORROWS (1931), Very Rev. James A. Bucaria, V.F.; Deacon Leonard Iverson.
Mailing Address: P.O. Box 9250, 34604. Tel: 352-796-2792; Fax: 352-544-0398.
School—Notre Dame Interparochial School, Spring Hill. Tel: 352-683-0755; Fax: 352-683-3924. See Elementary Schools, Interparochial under Institutions Located in the Diocese.
Catechesis/Religious Program—Students 20.

NEW PORT RICHEY, PASCO CO.

1—OUR LADY QUEEN OF PEACE (1913), (Hispanic), Revs. Kenneth Slattery; Jairo Atehortua; Augustine Shayo; John Anoia (SPR); Joseph A. Pastick (Retired); Deacons Roger F. Lind; John Liggan; Jose Morales; Carol Passenti, Parish Mgr.
Res.: 5340 High St., 34652. Tel: 727-849-7521; Fax:

727-849-4814.
School—Bishop Larkin Interparochial School, Hudson. Tel: 727-862-6981; Fax: 727-869-9893. See Elementary Schools, Interparochial under Institutions Located in the Diocese.
Catechesis/Religious Program—Tel: 727-842-9396; Fax: 727-841-6601. Alex Groppe, D.R.E. Students 175.

2—ST. THOMAS AQUINAS (1980), Revs. Michael Lydon; Joseph Sojan Punnakkattu.
Res.: 8320 Old C.R. #54, 34653. Tel: 727-372-8600; Fax: 727-376-7204.
St. Thomas Early Childhood Development Center—Tel: 727-376-2330; Fax: 727-372-5712.
School—Bishop Larkin Interparochial School, Hudson. Tel: 727-862-6981; Fax: 727-862-9187. See Elementary Schools, Interparochial under Institutions Located in the Diocese.
Catechesis/Religious Program—Tel: 727-376-1622; Fax: 727-372-5712. Jeanne Schneider, D.R.E. Students 671.

PALM HARBOR, PINELLAS CO., ST. LUKE THE EVANGELIST (1985), Revs. Ronald J. Poirier; Paul Hervey; Sr. Bridget Mulligan, O.S.C., Pastoral Assoc.; Deacon James Blaney, Pastoral Assoc.
Res.: 2757 Alderman Rd., 34684. Tel: 727-786-3648; Fax: 727-789-9556. Web: www.stlukepalmharbor.org.
St. Luke Early Childhood Center—Tel: 727-787-2914; Fax: 727-786-8648.
School—Guardian Angels Interparochial School, Clearwater. Tel: 727-799-6724; Fax: 727-724-9018. See Elementary Schools, Interparochial under Institutions Located in the Diocese. Students 149.
Catechesis/Religious Program—Tel: 727-787-2845; Fax: 727-786-8648. Linda Gies, D.R.E. Students 680.

PINELLAS PARK, PINELLAS CO., SACRED HEART (1910), Revs. James Merkel; Theobold Weria, A.L.C.P.; Deacons Louis Izzo; L. Roger Cartier.
Res.: 8001 46th St. N., 33781. Tel: 727-541-4447; Fax: 727-541-2073.
School—7951 46th Way N., 33781. Tel: 727-544-1106; Fax: 727-541-2073. Ms. Penelope Howell, Prin. Lay Teachers 14; Students 185.
Catechesis/Religious Program—Mrs. Cris Quinn, D.R.E. Students 89.

PLANT CITY, HILLSBOROUGH CO., ST. CLEMENT (1912), Revs. Thomas Morgan; Gilberto Quintero.
Res.: 1104 Alexander St., 33563. Tel: 813-752-8251; Fax: 813-759-2721.
School—St. Clement Early Childhood Center, Formerly St. Clement Catholic School, 1104 N. Alexander St., 33563-2259.
Catechesis/Religious Program—Jo Ann Parolini, D.R.E. Students 408.

PORT RICHEY, PASCO CO., ST. JAMES THE APOSTLE (1984), Revs. Dennis E. Hughes; Michael Suszynski; Deacon Paul G. Metilly.
Res.: 8400 Monarch Dr., 34668. Tel: 727-869-3130; Fax: 727-869-8886.
School—Bishop Larkin Interparochial School, Hudson. Tel: 727-862-6981; Fax: 727-869-9893. See Elementary Schools, Interparochial under Institutions Located in the Diocese.
Catechesis/Religious Program—Sr. M. Bernadette Wyman, O.S.F., D.R.E. Students 400.

RIDGE MANOR, HERNANDO CO., ST. ANNE (1960), Rev. Ronald Marecki.
Res.: 4142 Treiman Blvd., Hwy. 301, 33525. Tel: 352-583-2550; Fax: 352-583-0300.
Catechesis/Religious Program—Students 14.

RIVERVIEW, HILLSBOROUGH CO., RESURRECTION (1983), Rev. Msgr. Antonio Diez.
Mailing Address: P.O. Box 418, 33568.
Res.: 6819 Krycul Ave., 33569. Tel: 813-677-2175; Fax: 813-671-7844.
Catechesis/Religious Program—Anna May Lovejoy, D.R.E. Students 200.

RUSKIN, HILLSBOROUGH CO., ST. ANNE (1956), Revs. John McEvoy; Rafael E. Martos.
Office—106 11th Ave., N.E., 33570. Tel: 813-645-1714; Fax: 813-645-5570.
Catechesis/Religious Program—Sr. Marian Stenken, S.C.N., D.R.E.; Mrs. Cindy Cyman, D.R.E. Students 208.

ST. JOSEPH, PASCO CO., SACRED HEART (1888), [CEM] Rev. Patrick M. Rebel; Deacon William Connors.
Res.: 32145 St. Joe Rd., Dade City, 33525. Tel: 352-588-3641; Fax: 352-588-5299.
School—St. Anthony Interparochial School, San Antonio. Tel: 352-588-3041; Fax: 352-588-3142. See Elementary Schools, Interparochial under Institutions Located in the Diocese.
Catechesis/Religious Program—Tel: 352-588-3641; Fax: 352-588-5299. Students 100.
Sacred Heart Child Care Center—32245 St. Joe Rd., Dade City, 33525. Tel: 352-588-4060; Fax: 352-588-4871. Mrs. Toni Watkins.

ST. PETE BEACH, PINELLAS CO., ST. JOHN (1939), Revs. John C. Murphy; Kevin Molloy; Deacon Karl A. Boehme. In Res., Rev. Msgr. Patrick Trainor, P.A.
Res.: 445 82nd Ave., 33706. Tel: 727-360-1147; Fax: 727-360-5267 (Rectory); 727-367-4418 (Office).
School—500 84th Ave., 33706. Tel: 727-360-1113; Fax: 727-367-8734. Sr. Joan Brennan, S.C., Prin. Sisters 1; Lay Teachers 18; Students 250
Catechesis/Religious Program—Tel: 727-360-1147, Ext. 101; Fax: 727-367-4418. Michelle Robinson. Students 160.

SAFETY HARBOR, PINELLAS CO., ESPIRITU SANTO (1960), Revs. Robert Schneider; James Ruhlin; Sisters Phyllis Shaughnessy, O.S.C., Pastoral Assoc.; Paulamarie Lacy, S.N.D., Pastoral Assoc.; Deacons Dominic P. Friscia, Pastoral Assoc.; Vincent Alterio, Pastoral Assoc.
Res.: 2405 Philippe Pkwy., P.O. Box 176, 34695. Tel: 727-726-8477; Fax: 727-799-2062.
School—Espiritu Santo Catholic School Tel: 727-812-4650; Fax: 727-812-4658. See Elementary Schools, Interparochial under Institutions Located in the Diocese.
Catechesis/Religious Program—Tel: 727-812-4650, Ext. 205; Fax: 727-812-4658. Students 860.

SAN ANTONIO, PASCO CO., ST. ANTHONY OF PADUA (1884), [CEM] Rev. Henry J. Riffle; Deacon Barry Wallace.
Res.: 32832 Massachusetts Ave., P.O. Box 875, 33576. Tel: 352-588-3081; Fax: 352-588-5070.
School—St. Anthony Interparochial School, Tel: 352-588-3041; Fax: 352-588-3142. See Elementary Schools, Interparochial under Institutions Located in the Diocese.
Catechesis/Religious Program—Tel: 352-588-3081; Fax: 352-588-5070. Students 106.

SEFFNER, HILLSBOROUGH CO., ST. FRANCIS OF ASSISI (1987), Revs. Christopher Fitzgerald, I.C.; Michael O'Neill, I.C.; Deacons Jerome Thomas; Richard Beauolry.
Res.: P.O. Box 1218, 33583. Tel: 813-681-9115; Fax: 813-689-4148.
Catechesis/Religious Program—Joan McCollum, D.R.E. Students 256.

SEMINOLE, PINELLAS CO., BLESSED SACRAMENT (1959), Revs. James Gordon, I.C.; G. Richard Filger, I.C.
Res.: 11565 66th Ave. N., 33772. Tel: 727-391-4661.
School—Tel: 727-391-4060; Fax: 727-391-5638. Lay Teachers 24; Students 240.
Catechesis/Religious Program—Tel: 727-391-4661; Fax: 727 391-5638. Students 208.

SPRING HILL, HERNANDO CO.

1—ST. FRANCES XAVIER CABRINI (1980), Rev. Msgr. John A. Cippel; Rev. John Blum.
Mailing Address: 5030 Mariner Blvd., 34609. Tel: 352-683-9666; Fax: 352-688-2660. In Res., Rev. Andrew Beaudoin, S.S.S.; Deacons Roland Desjardins; Edward Lyczak; Gregorio Lugo; Edward Smith.
School—Notre Dame Interparochial School, Tel: 352-683-0755; Fax: 352-683-3924. See Elementary Schools, Interparochial under Institutions Located in the Diocese.
Catechesis/Religious Program—Tel: 352-683-6214; Fax: 352-688-2660. Sherri Collinsworth, D.R.E. Students 775.

2—SAINT JOAN OF ARC (1988), Rev. Raymond F. O'Neill.
Res.: 13485 Spring Hill Dr., 34609. Tel: 352-688-0663; Fax: 352-686-7937.
School—Notre Dame Interparochial School, Tel: 352-683-0755; Fax: 352-683-3924. See Elementary Schools, Interparochial under Institutions Located in the Diocese.
Catechesis/Religious Program—Tel: 352-688-0663; Fax: 352-686-7937. Sr. Mary Gracia Klech, S.S.N.D., D.R.E. Students 235.

3—ST. THERESA (1969), Revs. James McAteer, I.C.; Frank Oman, I.C.; Deacons Abraham Rosa; Jose Rios.
Res.: 1107 Commercial Way, 34606. Tel: 352-683-2849; Fax: 352-683-3437.
School—Notre Dame Interparochial School, Tel: 352-683-0755; Fax: 352-683-3924. See Elementary Schools, Interparochial under Institutions Located in the Diocese.
Catechesis/Religious Program—Dorothy Siegrist, D.R.E. Students 181.

SUN CITY CENTER, HILLSBOROUGH CO., PRINCE OF PEACE (1970), Rev. Msgr. Harold Bumpus; Rev. Austin Mullen; Deacon Angelo Pignataro.
Mailing Address: 702 Valley Forge Blvd., 33573-5353. Tel: 813-634-2328; Fax: 813-633-6670. In Res., Rev. Desmond Gill.
Res.: 1002 Fordham Dr., 33573. Tel: 813-634-2328; Fax: 813-633-9244.
Catechesis/Religious Program—Eileen O'Leary, D.R.E. Students 66.

TAMPA, HILLSBOROUGH CO.

1—BLESSED SACRAMENT (1959), (Spanish), Rev. Jose Furtado, Admin.
Res.: 1205 Windermere Way, 33619-4601. Tel: 813-626-2984; Fax: 813-626-2842.
Church: 7001 12th Ave. S., 33619-4649.
Catechesis/Religious Program—Students 70.

2—CHRIST THE KING (1941), Revs. Desmond Daly; Terrance Sowada; Deacons William E. Diaz; Michael Solomon.
Res.: 821 S. Dale Mabry Hwy., 33609. Tel: 813-876-5841; Fax: 813-873-2426.
School—Tel: 813-876-8770; Fax: 813-879-0315. Sr. Karen Dunn, F.M.A., Prin. Daughters of Mary Help of Christians 3; Lay Teachers 28; Students 505.
Catechesis/Religious Program—Tel: 813-870-2509. Jackie Peterson, D.R.E.; Linda B. Edge, D.R.E. (Adult). Students 791.

3—EPIPHANY (1963), Rev. Ignatius Tuoc; Deacon Maximo E. Montayre.
Mailing Address: P.O. Box 11246, 33680. Tel: 813-234-8693; Fax: 813-238-5060. In res., Rev. Fracilus Petit Lomme.
Res.: 2510 E. Hanna Ave., 33610. Tel: 813-238-5060; 813-234-8693.
Catechesis/Religious Program—Tel: 813-238-1751. Students 85.
Mission—St. Joseph Vietnamese Mission 2510 E. Hanna Ave., Hillsborough Co. 33610. Tel: 813-238-5060.

4—GOOD SHEPHERD (1966), Revs. Donald Zarkoski, S.D.B.; Bernard Lee, S.D.B.; Deacon Edmond Anctil.
Res.: 6410 E. Hillsborough Ave., 33610. Tel: 813-626-7588; Fax: 813-626-5882.
Catechesis/Religious Program—Tel: 813-626-9991 (Sundays). Students 65.

5—INCARNATION (1962), Revs. Eric Hunter; Jude Vera; Rev. Msgr. John Vargas; Rev. Eugeniusz Gancarz; Deacons Joseph Krzanowski; Andres Maldonado; Julio Vasquez.
Res.: 5124 Gateway Dr., 33615. Tel: 813-885-7861; Fax: 813-884-3624.
School—Tel: 813-884-4502; Fax: 813-885-3743. Mrs. Carolyn Goslee, Prin. Lay Teachers 29; Students 465.
Catechesis/Religious Program—Tel: 813-887-5110; Fax: 813-884-3624. Janet Foxenberger, D.R.E. Students 950.

6—ST. JOSEPH (1896), Rev. Felix Sanchez.
Mailing Address: P.O. Box 4298, 33677.
Res.: 3012 Cherry St., 33607. Tel: 813-877-5729; Fax: 813-877-5720.
School—Tel: 813-879-7720; Fax: 813-873-0804. Daughters of Mary Help of Christians (Paterson, NJ) 3; Lay Teachers 15; Students 250.
Catechesis/Religious Program—Students 251.

7—ST. LAWRENCE (1959), Rev. Msgr. Laurence E. Higgins, P.A.; Rev. Edward C. Keating, O.F.M.
Res. and Mailing: 5225 N. Himes Ave., 33614. Tel: 813-875-4040; Fax: 813-876-0491.
School—Tel: 813-879-5090; Fax: 813-879-6886. Lay Teachers 40; Students 645.
Catechesis/Religious Program—Tel: 813-875-4040, Ext. 206; Fax: 813-876-0491. Students 325.

8—ST. MARK THE EVANGELIST (1996), Revs. David DeJulio; John D'Antonio.
Mailing Address: 9724 Cross Creek Blvd., 33647-7556.
Res.: 17531 Edinburgh Dr., 33647. Tel: 813-907-9517; Fax: 813-907-9617.
Catechesis/Religious Program—Tel: 813-907-7746; Fax: 813-907-7556. Students 870.

9—ST. MARY (1966), Revs. Robert F. Morris; Kzimierz Nawalaniec (Poland); Paul Damien, Eparchy of St. Maron of Brooklyn; Sr. Nancy Christopher, O.S.F., Pastoral Assoc.
Res.: 15520 North Blvd., 33613. Tel: 813-961-1061; Fax: 813-961-3782.
School—Most Holy Redeemer Interparochial School, Tel: 813-933-4750; Fax: 813-933-3181. See Elementary Schools, Interparochial under Institutions Located in the Diocese.
Catechesis/Religious Program—Tel: 813-963-2079. Sabrina Burton, D.R.E. Students 354.

10—MOST HOLY REDEEMER (1937), Revs. Peter Nicosia, O.F.M.Cap.; Alfonso D. Pagliara, O.F.M.Cap.; Remo DiSalvatore, O.F.M.Cap.; Bro. John Paul Russo, O.F.M.Cap., Pastoral Assoc.; Deacon Leocadio Nova, Pastoral Assoc.
Res.: 10110 Central Ave., 33612. Tel: 813-933-2859; Fax: 813-932-6153.
School—Tel: 813-933-4750; Fax: 813-933-3181. See Elementary Schools, Interparochial under Institutions Located in the Diocese.
Catechesis/Religious Program—Bro. John Paul Russo, O.F.M.Cap., D.R.E. Students 105.

11—OUR LADY OF PERPETUAL HELP (1890), (Hispanic—Haitian), [JC] Revs. Thomas A. Stokes, S.M.; John Jazwiecki, S.M. (Retired).
Res.: 1711 11th Ave., 33605. Tel: 813-248-5701; Fax: 813-241-4128.
Catechesis/Religious Program—Debbie Toth, D.R.E. Students 47.

12—ST. PATRICK (1958), [JC] Revs. Angelus Migliore, T.O.R.; Joseph Chancler, T.O.R.; Bro. Edward Bennett, T.O.R.; Mrs. Maureen Connelly, Parish Mgr. In Res., Rev. Colman McGarrill, T.O.R.

Parish Office—4212 Fair Oaks Ave., 33611. Tel: 813-839-5337; Fax: 813-831-2778.
School—4518 S. Manhattan Ave., 33611. Tel: 813-839-5056; Fax: 813-832-5907. Mr. Thom Laux, Interm Prin. Lay Teachers 25; Students 336.
Catechesis/Religious Program—Tel: 813-839-4958. Mrs. Jackie Mallory, D.R.E. Students 138.

13—ST. PAUL (1963), Revs. Leonard Piotrowski; Bill Wilson; Jose Colina; Deacons Greg Kovalesky, Pastoral Assoc.; John Alvarez; Greg Lambert; Juan Sierra; Ron Rojas; Winston McDonald.
Mailing Address: 12708 N. Dale Mabry, 33618. Tel: 813-961-3023; Fax: 813-962-8780.
School—Most Holy Redeemer Interparochial School, Tel: 813-933-4750; Fax: 813-933-3181. See Elementary Schools, Interparochial under Institutions Located in the Diocese.
Catechesis/Religious Program—Tel: 813-264-3309; Fax: 813-962-8780. Mrs. Haydee Grillo, D.R.E. Students 1,130.

14—ST. PETER CLAVER (1893), (African American), Rev. Paul Kochu.
Res.: 1203 N. Nebraska Ave., 33602. Tel: 813-223-7098; Fax: 813-223-6520.
School—(Grades PreK-8) Tel: 813-224-0865; Fax: 813-223-1982. Sr. Catherine Bitzer, S.S.J., Prin. Lay Teachers 9; Students 124.
Catechesis/Religious Program—Students 54.

15—SACRED HEART (1860), Revs. Paul V. Osterle, S.J.; Dwayne A. Varas, S.J.
Mailing Address: P.O. Box 1524, 33601. Tel: 813-229-1595; Fax: 813-221-2350.
School—Tel: 813-229-0618; Fax: 813-223-7667. Mrs. Margaret Ruiz Carus, Prin. Lay Teachers 16; Students 200.
Catechesis/Religious Program—Students 66.

16—ST. TIMOTHY (1985), Rev. Patrick Kennedy; Deacons Jerry L. Crall; John Iadanza.
Res.: 17512 Lake Shore Rd., Lutz, 33558-4802.
School—Most Holy Redeemer Interparochial School, Tel: 813-933-4750; Fax: 813-933-3181. See Elementary Schools, Interparochial under Institutions Located in the Diocese.
Catechesis/Religious Program—Tel: 813-961-1716. Judy Anderson, D.R.E.; Jean Gadoury, D.R.E. Students 785.

TARPON SPRINGS, PINELLAS CO., ST. IGNATIUS (1889), Revs. Joseph A. Pellegrino; Joel Kovanis; Thomas Kumblanthanath, M.S.T.
Mailing Address: P.O. Box 1306, 34688-1306. In Res., Rev. John P. Henry (RVC) (Retired).
Res.: 715 E. Orange St., 34689. Tel: 727-937-4050; Fax: 727-943-0676.
School—Guardian Angels Interparochial School, Clearwater, Tel: 727-799-6724; Fax: 727-724-9018. See Elementary Schools, Interparochial under Institutions Located in the Diocese.
Catechesis/Religious Program—Tel: 727-934-4163, Ext. 223; Fax: 727-942-2331. Diane Magoulis, D.R.E. Students 765.

TEMPLE TERRACE, HILLSBOROUGH CO., CORPUS CHRISTI (1958), Revs. Joseph L. Waters; Ryszard Stradomski (Poland).
Mailing Address: 9715 N. 56th St., 33617. Tel: 813-988-1593; Fax: 813-985-3583.
School—Tel: 813-988-1722; Fax: 813-989-2665. Margaret A. Penn, Prin. Lay Teachers 16; Students 295.
Catechesis/Religious Program—Lily Hughson, D.R.E. Students 422.

VALRICO, HILLSBOROUGH CO., ST. STEPHEN (1987), Revs. Patrick Irwin; Paul Pecchie; Rev. Msgr. Mariano Madrid.
Church: 5049 Bell Shoals Rd., 33594. Tel: 813-689-4900; Fax: 813-689-7492.
Catechesis/Religious Program—Tel: 813-671-4434; Fax: 813-671-2994. Joyce Morgan, D.R.E. Students 1,130.

ZEPHYRHILLS, PASCO CO., ST. JOSEPH (1912), Revs. George Rozycki; John Hays; Jayanna Kanna; Deacon Raymond A. Haberle; Mrs. Patricia Hennessy, Business Admin.
Church: 5316 11th St., 33540. Tel: 813-782-2813; Fax: 813-788-1036.
School—St. Anthony Interparochial School, San Antonio, Tel: 352-588-3041; Fax: 352-588-3142. See Elementary Schools, Interparochial under Institutions Located in the Diocese.
Catechesis/Religious Program—Tel: 813-788-2510. Mrs. Annetta Wallace, D.R.E. Students 125.

On Duty Outside the Diocese:
Revs.—
Garcia, Avelino R.
Lamp, Edward
McDonagh, Donat Michael
Scott, Philip
Toups, David
Young, Robert

Military Chaplains:
Rev. Msgr.—
McCahon, Joseph F.S., U.S.A.F.

Retired:
Rev. Msgrs.—
Bolger, John F.
Cummings, George
DuBois, William
Earner, Thomas
Lara, Jaime C.
McCall, John
McNulty, John
Mulligan, Edward
Neff, John
Scully, John
Trainor, Patrick
Revs.—
Colgan, John
Cottrell, James
D'Angelo, Rocco
Dambrauskas, Stephen
Dauss, Francis
Dionne, Francis
Estibalez, Inocencio
Gill, Desmond
Kane, John
Kearney, William
Lagan, Hugh
Lawlor, Brendan
Leininger, Donald
Lettre, Raymond
Mahony, John
Villemaire, Arthur

Permanent Deacons:
Alterio, Vincent
Alvarez, John
Anctil, Edmond
Andre, Peter
Arsenault, Richard
Beaudry, Richard
Bevvino, Frank, On Duty Outside of Diocese
Blaney, James
Boehme, Karl
Brady, Richard
Braun, Bernard
Brennan, Lee
Brown, Joseph
Carreiro, Manuel
Cartier, Roger L.
Cavaliere, Frank, (Philadelphia)
Ciarciaglino, Joseph
Columbus, Michael
Connors, William
Crall, Jerry
D'argis, Leo
Desjardins, Roland
Diaz, William
DiVito, John
Dunphy, Melvin
Edgerton, John
Evans, Forrest, On Duty Outside the Diocese
Friscia, Dominic
Gagne, Gerard
Gould, Stanley, On Duty Outside of Diocese
Grevenites, James
Grote, Joseph
Haberle, Raymond
Hassett, James
Hecht, Lowell
Hewitt, Wesley
Hinderscheid, Lee
Iadanza, John
Iverson, Leonard, Peoria
Izzo, Louis
Kennedy, Frank, (Brooklyn)
Knox, Terrence
Koppenaal, John, On Duty Outside of Diocese
Kovalesky, Gregory
Krzanowski, Joseph
Kurylowicz, Stephen
Lambert, Greg
Lamothe, Allan
Liggan, John
Lind, Roger F.
Longo, Frank
Lopez, Heriberto
Lugo, Gregorio
Lyczak, Edward
Lyons, John
Mahood, William
Makoid, Eric, (Philadelphia)
Maldonado, Andres, (Ponce, Puerto Rico)
Mathias, James
McDonald, Winston
McGory, Gerald
Metilly, Paul
Meyer, Richard
Montayre, Maximo
Morales, Jose A.
Morales, Jose
Morales, Julio
Moschetto, Samuel
Nagle, Richard, Jr.
Nova, Leocadia
Ortiz, Augustin
Page, Howard
Pescatore, James
Pickart, Glenn
Pignataro, Angelo
Polcari, Joseph
Postadan, Romulo, (Newark)
Powell, Eugene
Pullar, James
Quiles, Rafael
Rios, Jose
Roberts, Lionel
Rodriguez, Manuel
Rojas, Ronald
Rosa, Abraham
Sablone, Stephen
Schott, Thomas
Shiel, Thomas
Sierra, John
Simpson, Robert C.
Sirrianna, David
Smith, Edward
Solomon, Michael
Sparks, Robert, Toronto, Canada
Spaulding, Ken, Lansing
Stahl, Raymond
Thomas, Jerome
Tibbetts, Albert
Uzzi, Gerard
Vance, Ronald, On Duty Outside the Diocese
Vasquez, Julio
Wallace, Barry
Wells, Eric
White, Gerard
Yarawsky, William S.
Zayas, Luis
Zeitler, Richard

INSTITUTIONS LOCATED IN THE DIOCESE

[A] COLLEGES

SAINT LEO. *Saint Leo University, Institutional Research*, Formerly Saint Leo University, University Ministry, P.O. Box 6665, MC 2219, St. Leo, 33574-6665. Tel: 352-588-8200; 352-588-8331; Fax: 352-588-8885. Email: michael.coopersj@saintleo.edu. Web: www.saintleo.edu. Dr. Arthur F. Kirk Jr., Pres.; Revs. Michael Cooper, S.J., S.T.D., Asst. to Pres. for Univ. Ministry; Anthony Kissel, Ph.D., S.T.D., Assoc. Prof. Rel. Studies; Sisters Caroline Cerveny, SSJ-TOSF, Assoc. Dir. Univ. Min. & Asst. Dir. Academic Tech.; Mary Dorothy Neuhofer, O.S.B., Prof., Archivist, Dir. of Library Services.
Legal Title: *Saint Leo University, Inc.*
Legal Title: *Saint Leo University Educational Fund, Inc.*, An Independent and Catholic Coeducational Liberal Arts University Priests 2; Lay Teachers 89; Total Enrollment 12,190.

[B] HIGH SCHOOLS, DIOCESAN

ST. PETERSBURG. *St. Petersburg Catholic High School*, 6333 Ninth Ave. N., 33710. Tel: 727-344-4065; Fax: 727-343-9311. Email: info@spchs.org. Web: spchs.org. Revs. John Grinsell, S.D.B., Dir.; Louis J. Molinelli, S.D.B., Prin.; Ms. Barbara A. Rusin, Asst. Prin. for Academics; Mr. Michael Shelby, Asst. Prin. for Student Life; Rev. Gregory Fishel, S.D.B., Coord. Youth Ministry; Bro. William Hanna, S.D.B. Salesians of St. John Bosco (New Rochelle, NY) 4; Sisters of the Third Franciscan Order (Syracuse, NY) 2; Sisters of Our Lady of Kilimanjaro 2; Brothers 1; Lay Teachers 43; Students 662.

CLEARWATER. *Clearwater Central Catholic High School*, 2750 Haines Bayshore Rd., 33760. Tel: 727-531-1449; Fax: 727-535-7034. Email: dhorrigan@cchs.org. Web: www.cchs.org. Sr. Mary Dion Horrigan, S.N.D., Prin. Sisters of Notre Dame (Chardon, Ohio) 2; Lay Teachers 40; Students 584.

SPRING HILL. *Bishop McLaughlin Catholic High School*, 13651 Hays Rd., 34610. Tel: 727-857-2600; Fax: 727-857-2610. Email: bmchs.com. Jane Moerschbacher, Prin. Order of St. Benedict 1; Lay Teachers 5; Students 47.

TAMPA. *Tampa Catholic High School*, 4630 N. Rome Ave., 33603. Tel: 813-870-0860; Fax: 813-877-9136.

Email: contactperson@tampacatholic.org. Web: www.tampacatholic.org. Ms. Patricia A. Landry, Prin. Congregation of Christian Brothers (New Rochelle, NY) 2; Sisters 1; Lay Teachers 53; Students 692.

[C] HIGH SCHOOLS, PRIVATE

TAMPA. *Academy of the Holy Names High School*, 3319 Bayshore Blvd., 33629. Tel: 813-839-5371; Fax: 813-839-1486. Email: sregan@holynamestpa.org. Web: holynamestpa.org. Ms. Colleen Brady, Pres.; Ms. Sarah Regan, Prin.; Sisters Mary Glavin, Asst. Prin. of Academic Affairs; Mary Patricia Plumb, Asst. Prin. for Student Life.
Legal Title: *Academy of the Holy Names of Florida, Inc.*
Legal Title: *Academy of the Holy Names Foundation, Inc.* Sisters 4; Lay Teachers 28; Students 338.

Jesuit High School, 4701 N. Himes Ave., 33614. Tel: 813-877-5344; Fax: 813-872-1853. Email: jhscomm@aol.com. Web: www.jesuittampa.org. Revs. Peter J. Callery, S.J., Rector; Joseph Doyle, S.J., Chap. & Pres.; Douglas Hypolite, S.J., Head Counseling Dept.
Legal Title: *Jesuit High School of Tampa, Inc., FKA*
Legal Title: *St. Louis Catholic, Benevolent and Educational Association, Inc.*
Legal Title: *Jesuit High School Foundation, Inc.* Priests 3; Sisters 1; Lay Teachers 47; Students 630.

[D] ELEMENTARY SCHOOLS, INTERPAROCHIAL

ST. PETERSBURG. *St. Paul Interparochial School*, (Grades PreK-8), 1900 12th St. N., 33704. Tel: 727-823-6144; Fax: 727-896-0609. Email: efulham@mail.stpanicatholicschool.org. Web: www.webcoast.com/stpaulcs. Elizabeth Fulham, Prin. Serving Blessed Trinity and St. Paul. Sisters 2; Lay Teachers 15; Students 329.

CLEARWATER. *St. Cecelia Interparochial School*, (Grades K-8), 400 S. Hillcrest Ave., 33756. Tel: 727-461-1200; Fax: 727-446-9140. Email: hmarston@st-cecelia.org. Web: www.st-cecelia.org. Mrs. Helen S. Marston, Prin. Serving Light of Christ, St. Brendan, St. Catherine of Siena and St. Cecelia. Sisters 1; Deacons 1; Lay Teachers 43; Students 760.

Guardian Angels Catholic School, (Grades K-8), 2270 Evans Rd., 33763. Tel: 727-799-3724; Fax: 727-724-9018. Email: gacs_cmalinski@lycos.com. Web: www.gacsfl.com. Robert Yarnell, Prin. Serving All Saints, St. Ignatius, St. Luke and St. Michael the Archangel. Sisters 1; Lay Teachers 26; Students 463.

LECANTO. *Pope John Paul II Catholic School*, 4341 W. Homosassa Tr., 34461. Tel: 352-746-2020; Fax: 352-746-3448. Email: tpetersen@pjp2.com. Web: www.pjp2.com. Tom Petersen, Prin. Serving Our Lady of Fatima, Our Lady of Grace, St. Benedict, St. Elizabeth Ann Seton, St. Scholastica and St. Thomas the Apostle. Lay Teachers 17; Students 210.

PORT RICHEY. *Bishop Larkin Interparochial School*, (Grades PreK-8), 8408 Monarch Dr., 34668. Tel: 727-862-6981; Fax: 727-869-9893. Email: bishop4@microd.com. Sr. Regina Ozuzu, H.H.C.J., Prin. Serving Our Lady Queen of Peace, St. James, St. Michael the Archangel, St. Thomas Aquinas and St. Vincent de Paul. Lay Teachers 18; Sisters 3; Students 262.

RIVERVIEW. *St. Stephen Catholic School* 3-3, Extended Day , 10424 Saint Stephen Cir., 33569. Tel: 813-741-9203; Fax: 813-741-9622. Email: mliddy@tampabay.rr.com. Web: www.ststephencatholicschool.org. Mary Liddy, Prin. Lay Teachers 15; Students 253.

SAFETY HARBOR. *Espiritu Santo Catholic School*, (Grades PreK-8) , Formerly Espiritu Santo Early Childhood Center. , 2405 A Philippe Pkwy., 34695-2047. Tel: 727-812-4650; Fax: 727-812-4658. Email: bsolinsky2001@yahoo.com. Bonnie Solinsky, Prin. Lay Teachers 26; Students 489.

SAN ANTONIO. *St. Anthony Interparochial Catholic School*, (Grades PreK-8), 32902 Massachusetts Ave., P.O. Box 847, 33576-0847. Tel: 352-588-3041; Fax: 352-588-3142. Email: sasadmin@saintleo.edu. Serving Sacred Heart, St. Anthony, St. Joseph and St. Rita, St. Mark's, St. Anne's, Corpus Christi, St. Mary's, St. Anthony, Brooksville. Sisters 2; Lay Teachers 13; Students 254.

SPRING HILL. *Notre Dame Interparochial School*, (Grades PreK-8), 1117 Suzanne Dr. 34607. Tel: 352-683-0755; Fax: 352-683-3924. Email: notredame@ndischool.org. Web: www.ndischool.org. Sr. Eileen Marie Woodbury, F.S.S.E., Prin. Serving St. Anne, St. Anthony, St. Frances Xavier Cabrini, St. Joan of Arc, St. Mary and St. Theresa. Lay Teachers 15; Students 225.

TAMPA. *Most Holy Redeemer Interparochial School*, (Grades K-8), 302 E. Linebaugh Ave., 33612. Tel: 813-933-4750; Fax: 813-933-3181. Email: mhrtampa@dosp.org. Web: www.mhr-tampa.org. Fred Coffaro, Prin.; Dr. Jo Ann Quinn, Asst. Prin. Serving Most Holy Redeemer, Our Lady of the Rosary, St. Mary, St. Paul and St. Timothy. Lay Teachers 26; Students 459.

[E] ELEMENTARY SCHOOLS, PRIVATE

TAMPA. *Academy of the Holy Names*, (Grades PreK-12), 3319 Bayshore Blvd., 33629. Tel: 813-839-5371; Fax: 813-837-5710. Email: webmaster@holynamestpa.org. Web: www.holynamestpa.org. Colleen K. Brady, Pres.; Dr. Carmen Caltagirone, Prin. (Elementary); Ms. Sarah Regan, Prin. (High School).
Legal Title: *Academy of the Holy Names of Florida, Inc.*
Legal Title: *Academy of the Holy Names Foundation, Inc.* Sisters of the Holy Names of Jesus and Mary (Albany) 7; Lay Teachers 75; Students 345.

Mary Help of Christians School, (Grades 6-8) , (Boys & Girls) 6400 E. Chelsea St., 33610 5699. Tel: 813-626-6191; Fax: 813-621-5251. Email: maryhelptampa@juno.com. Web: maryhelptampa.org. Revs. William A. Ferruzzi, S.D.B. (CDL), Dir.; Michael Mendl, S.D.B., Treas.; Lawrence Urban, S.D.B., Youth Min.; Mr. Stuart Miller, Prin.; Revs. Donald Zarkoski, S.D.B.; Bernard Justen, S.D.B.; Bernard Lee, S.D.B., Korean Min.; Kenneth Shaw, S.D.B.; Gerard Pellegrino, S.D.B.; Bros. Joseph Ackroyd, S.D.B.; George Marquis, S.B.D.; John Versaggi, S.D.B.; David Iovacchini, S.D.B.
Legal Title: *Salesian Society, Inc.* Salesians of St. John Bosco, (Day School) Priests 4; Brothers 1; Lay Teachers 8; Students 116.

Villa Madonna School, 315 W. Columbus Dr., 33602. Tel: 813-229-1322; Fax: 813-223-4812. Email: fmavilla@aol.com. Web: www.villamadonna.org. Sr. Kim Keraitis, F.M.A., Prin.
Legal Title: *Salesian Sisters of Tampa, Inc.* Daughters of Mary Help of Christians 5; Lay Teachers 24; Students 419.

[F] PRESCHOOLS AND DAY CARE CENTERS

ST. PETERSBURG. *Immaculate Conception Early Childhood Center* Ages 2-5, Extended Care. , Lower Pinellas Deanery, 2100 26th Ave. S., 33712. Tel: 727-822-2156; Fax: 727-553-9133. Email: icrita@tampabay.rr.com. Mrs. Rita A. Jackson, Dir.; Mrs. Mary Calloway, Asst. Dir.; Rev. Timothy H. Sherwood. Lay Teachers 17; Children 143; Total Staff 25.

CLEARWATER. *Light of Christ Preschool* Ages 2-5, Extended Care. , Upper Pinellas Deanery, 2176 Marilyn St., 33765. Tel: 727-442-4797; Fax: 727-441-8777. Email: locecc@ij.net. Ms. Rebecca Daschbach, Preschool Dir. Lay Teachers 13; Students 80.

Little Nazareth Early Childhood Center Ages 3-4. , Upper Pinellas Deanery, 820 Jasmine Way, 33756. Tel: 727-447-3494; Fax: 727-442-4810. Email: sawb30@aol.com. Web: www.stceceliachurch.org. Mrs. Sandra A. Barbeau, Dir.; Rev. Msgr. Aiden Foynes. Lay Teachers 1; Children 36.

DADE CITY. *Sacred Heart Child Care Center* Infant-PreK, Extended Care. , Pasco Deanery, 32245 Saint Joe Rd., 33525. Tel: 352-588-4060; Fax: 352-588-4871. Email: sheccstjoe@3oaks.com. Mrs. Toni Watkins, Dir. Lay Teachers 30; Children 190.

LARGO. *St. Jerome Early Childhood Center* Ages 3-4. , 10895 Hamlin Blvd., 33774. Tel: 727-596-9491; Fax: 727-596-8953. Email: sjecc@tampabay.rr.com. Denise Roach, Dir.; Rev. Msgr. Brendan Muldoon, V.G. Lay Teachers 8; Total Staff 12; Children 82.

NEW PORT RICHEY. *St. Thomas Aquinas Early Childhood Center*, 8320 Old CR 54 34653. Tel: 727-376-2330; Fax: 727-376-2330. Email: staecc@aol.com. Mrs. Cindy McKallip, Dir.; Rev. Michael Lydon; Pamela Bruno, Sec. Lay Teachers 6; Assistants 6; Children 104.

PALM HARBOR. *St. Luke Early Childhood Center* Ages 2-4, Extended Care. , 2757 Alderman Rd., 34684. Tel: 727-787-2914; Fax: 727-786-8648. Email: stlecc@gte.net. Ms. Carol Hussin, Dir.; Rev. Ronald Poirier. Full-time Lay Teachers 1; Children 160; Total Staff 26.

TAMPA. *St. Paul Preschool* Ages 3-4. , 12708 N. Dale Mabry Hwy., 33618-2802. Tel: 813-961-3023, Ext. 3314; Fax: 813-962-8780. Email: jruddy@stpaulchurch.com. Mrs. Joanne Ruddy, Dir.; Rev. Leonard Piotrowski. Lay Teachers 16; Children 165.

St. Timothy Catholic Early Childhood Learning Center, 17512 Lakeshore Rd., Lutz, 33558. Tel: 813-960-4857; Fax: 813-961-9429. Email: daisy.cintron@sainttims.org. Web: www.sainttims.org. Ms. Daisy Cintron, Dir.; Rev. Paddy Kennedy. Lay Teachers 5; Students 95.

TARPON SPRINGS. *St. Ignatius Early Childhood Center* Ages 2-5. , 725 E. Orange St., 34689-1306. Tel: 727-937-5427; Fax: 727-942-3331. Email: ecenter123@aol.com. Mrs. Nancy Gorby, Dir.; Rev. Joseph A. Pellegrino. Full-time Lay Teacher 1; Children 88.

[G] SCHOOLS FOR EXCEPTIONAL CHILDREN

PINELLAS PARK. *Morning Star School*, 4661 80th Ave. N., 33781. Tel: 813-544-6036; Fax: 813-546-9058. Email: mschool2@tampabay.rrcom. Web: morningstarschool.com. Ms. Mary Lou Giacobbe, Prin. Lay Teachers 7; Students 55.

TAMPA. *Morning Star School*, 210 E. Linebaugh Ave., 33612. Tel: 813-935-0232; 813-932-2321; Fax: 813-932-2321. Email: jfriedheim@tampa-morningstar.org. Web: www.tampa-morningstar.org. Miss Jeanette Friedheim, Prin. Lay Teachers 10; Students 80.

[H] SCHOOLS FOR THEOLOGICAL AND SPIRITUAL TRAINING

ST. PETERSBURG. *St. Petersburg Diocesan Library*, 6533 Ninth Ave. N., 33710. Tel: 727-345-3338; Fax: 727-374-0210. Email: cmb@dosp.org. P.O. Box 43022, 33743-3022. Tel: 727-345-3338. Rev. Alan Weber, Exec. Dir.; Ms. Clara Blowers, Dir. Diocesan Library

CLEARWATER. *The Cenacle of Our Lady of Divine Providence* School of Spirituality. , 702 S. Bayview Ave., 33759. Tel: 727-724-9505; Fax: 727-724-9421. Email: cenacleofourlady@aol.com. Web: www.divineprovidence.org. Ronald W. Novotny, S.T.L., Ph.D., Dir. Lay Teachers 3; Total Staff 9; Total Enrollment 500.

[I] DAY CARE CENTERS

TAMPA. *Peter Claver Day Care Center, Inc.*, 1431 Tampa Park Plaza, 33605-4821. Tel: 813-229-7632; Fax: 813-259-9082. Email: vwithers@tampabay.rr.com. Total Staff 9; Total Assisted Annually 61.

[J] CATHOLIC CHARITIES

ST. PETERSBURG. *Catholic Charities, Diocese of St. Petersburg, Inc.* Tel: 727-893-1314; Fax: 727-893-1307. Email: catholic.charities@ccdosp.org. Web: www.ccdosp.org. Arnold Andrews, Exec. Dir.; Sheila Lopez, Dir. of Admin. & Contact Person. Sisters 95.

Jeff Forbes Center - Administrative Offices, 1213 16th St. N., 33705. Tel: 727-893-1313; Fax: 727-893-1307. Email: catholic.charities@ccdosp.org. Web: www.ccdosp.org.

Services Provided - Elder Services: Respite Programs for Caregivers of Memory Loss Clients; Parish based Volunteer Support ; - Family Services: Farm Worker Affordable Housing Counseling; Adoption; Homebuyer Education & Housing Counseling; Support during pregnancy and Parenting; Family Support and Case Management; Life Skills Education; Full-service center for migrant farm workers; Resettlement and Immigration Assistance ; - HIV services: Supportive Housing and Independent Living; Emergency Rent and Utilities Assistance; Support to Residence for Women and Children with HIV ; - Medical Services: Mobile Medical Unit for Farmworkers

Catholic Charities Community Development Corp., 1213 16th St. N., 33705. Tel: 727-893-1314, Ext. 202; Fax: 727-893-1307. Email: housing@ccdosp.org. Web: www.ccdosp.org.

[K] GENERAL HOSPITALS

ST. PETERSBURG. *St. Anthony's Hospital, Inc.*, 1200 7th Ave. N., 33705. Tel: 727-825-1103; Fax: 727-825-1223. Email: terryfleming@baycare.org. Web: www.bsahealth.org. Revs. Terence K. Fleming, Dir.; Jim Jones, O.F.M., Chap.; Rev. Al Hall, Chap. (Baptist); Sisters Susan McGillicudy, O.S.F., Chap.; Mary Ellen Keady, O.S.F., Chap.
Legal Title: *St. Anthony's Hospital, Inc.*
Legal Title: *St. Anthony's Ancillary Services, Inc.*
Legal Title: *St. Anthony's Professional Buildings and Services, Inc.*
Legal Title: *St. Anthony's Health Care Foundation, Inc.* Franciscan Sisters of Allegany

TAMPA. *St. Joseph's Hospital, Inc.*, 3001 W. Martin Luther King Blvd., 33607. Tel: 813-870-4258; Fax: 813-554-8191. Email: terry.fleming@baycare.org. Web: www.bsahealth.org. P.O. Box 4227, 33677. Tel: 813-870-4000. Revs. Terence K. Fleming, Dir.; Kenneth Gerth, M.C.C.J., Chap.; Peter Bwayo, A.J., Chap.; Marilyn Cummings, Chap.; Elle Wolf-Muhleck, Chap.; Sr. Anne Dougherty, O.S.F., Chap.; Ms. Annette Castello, Chap., Mgr.; Tina Imperato, Chap.; Gail Radu, Chap.
Legal Title: *St. Joseph's Hospital, Inc.*

Legal Title: *St. Joseph's Ancillary Services, Inc.*
Legal Title: *St. Joseph's Community Care, Inc.*
Legal Title: *St. Joseph's Enterprises, Inc.*
Legal Title: *St. Joseph's Health Care Center, Inc.*
Legal Title: *St. Joseph's Hospital of Tampa Foundation, Inc.*
Legal Title: *St. Joseph's Specialty Services, Inc.*
Legal Title: *John Knox Village of Tampa Bay, Inc.*
Legal Title: *Franciscan Properties, Inc.*
Legal Title: *San Damiano Enterprises, Inc.* Franciscan Sisters of Allegany Inpatient Admissions 38,656; Emergency Room Visits 104,432; Outpatient Visits 278,549.

[L] RETIREMENT AND HEALTH CARE CENTERS

ST. PETERSBURG. **Bon Secours-Maria Manor Nursing Care Center, Inc.*, 10300 Fourth St. N., 33716. Tel: 727-576-1025; Fax: 727-576-1447. Email: (See Web Site). Web: www.bonsecours.org/stpete. Mr. Michael Ward, Admin. Sisters of Bon Secours Bed Capacity 274; Total Assisted Annually 420; Total Staff 400.

CLEARWATER. *The Tepeyac Corporation* dba La Clinica Guadalupana , 1215 Drew St., Ste. 7B, 33755. Tel: 727-461-7730; Fax: 727-462-8117. Email: laclinica@compuserve.com. Dr. Jay E. Carpenter, M.D., Pres. Annually Assisted 1,500; Staff 1.

[M] RETIREMENT HOUSING

ST. PETERSBURG. *Blessed Sacrament Housing, Inc.*, c/o Diocese of St. Petersburg, P.O. Box 40200, 33743-0200. Tel: 727-344-1611; Fax: 727-345-3086.

Blessed Trinity Housing, Inc., 5701 16th St. S., 33705. Tel: 727-865-7590; Fax: 727-867-1701. Email: trinity.house@verizon.net. Residents 76; Total Staff 2.

Holy Cross Housing dba Casa Santa Cruz , 7825 54th Ave. N., 33709. Tel: 727-541-2631; Fax: 727-547-6741. Email: casasantacruz@htnet.net. Mr. Joseph A. DiVito, Registered Agent. Total Staff 4; Total in Residence 77.

CLEARWATER. *St. Michael's Housing, Inc.* dba Casa Miguel , 2285 State Rd. #580, 33763. Tel: 727-797-8551. Mrs. JoAnn Lungaro, Admin. Independent Living. Total Staff 5; Residents 82.

HUDSON. *Bethlehem Housing, Inc.* dba Bethlehem House , 8010 State Road 52, 34667. Tel: 727-819-2861; Fax: 727-869-2781. Email: bethlehem.house@verizon.net. Virginia Seamster, Mgr. Residents 60; Total Staff 3.

TAMPA. *Christ the King Housing, Inc.* dba Kings Arms , 4125 N. Lincoln Ave., 33607. Tel: 813-873-0234; Fax: 813-871-2061. Email: k.arms@verizon.net. Mrs. Yari Lopez, Mgr. Total Staff 4; Total in Residence 90.

Christ the King Housing, Inc., Formerly Christ the King Housing II, Inc. dba Kings Manor dba Kings Manor , 2946 W. Columbus Dr., 33607. Tel: 813-875-0139; Fax: 813-875-6061. Email: kingsmanor.km@verizon.net. Betsy Rowen, Admin. Residents 108; Total Staff 5.

Epiphany Housing of Tampa, Inc. dba Epiphany Arms , 2508 E. Hanna Ave., 33610. Tel: 813-232-2693; Fax: 813-232-2984. Email: epiparms@aol.com. Total Staff 10; Residents 77.

St. Patrick's Housing Corporation dba Patrician Arms , 4516 S. Manhattan Ave., 33611. Tel: 813-835-8227; Fax: 813-835-7918. Email: p.arms@verizon.net. Total Staff 6; Total in Residence 85.

[N] SENIOR CENTERS

LARGO. *Bethlehem Centre, Inc.*, 10895 Hamlin Blvd., 34644. Tel: 727-596-9394; Fax: 727-596-6792. Senior Center offering programs in Fitness, Exercise, Social, Educational, Music, Art, Computers, and Religious Nature on Tuesday, Wednesday, and Friday. Hot luncheon is available on Tuesday and Friday. Total Staff 1; Total Assisted/Wk. 400.

[O] MONASTERIES AND RESIDENCES OF PRIESTS AND BROTHERS

ST. PETERSBURG. *St. Anthony Friary* Franciscan Residence and Retirement Community. , 357 Second St. N., 33701. Tel: 727-822-7917; Fax: 727-821-8067. Email: s.saf@verizon.net. Revs. Roy Gasnick, O.F.M., Vicar; Cornelius Conti, O.F.M.; Venard Murphy, O.F.M.; Bros. Christopher A. Coccia, O.F.M., Guardian; Richard James, O.F.M.; Michael Madden, O.F.M.; Valerian Vaverchack, O.F.M. Total in Residence 18; Total Staff 8.
Full-time Active Ministry: Revs. James Jones, O.F.M.; Thomas K. Murphy, O.F.M.
Retirement Community: Revs. Theodore A. Blackowski, O.F.M.; Francis A. Gorman, O.F.M.; Guy Morgan, O.F.M.; Alexis P. Morris, O.F.M.; James P. Mulhern, O.F.M.; Alexius J. Mulrnan, O.F.M.

Missionaries of Africa, 5757 Seventh Ave. N., 33710. Tel: 727-343-1001; Fax: 727-343-4395. Email: jolmet@gte.net. Revs. Joseph E. Hebert, M.Afr., Coord.; Jean C. Robitaille, M.Afr., Coord.; John J. Braun, M.Afr.; Paul J. Heon, M.Afr.; Joseph Kay, M.Afr.; Charles E. Lebel, M.Afr.; Matthew Pathilchirayil, M.Afr.; Joseph Sys, M.Afr.; Bro. Charles Feldmann, M.Afr. Total in Residence 9.

Notre Dame Residence, 1101 66th St. N., 33710.

St. Peter Nolasco Residence, 5650 Seventh Ave. N., 33710-7112. Tel: 727-345-4766; Fax: 727-347-5345. Revs. Anthony Fortunato, O.de.M.; Oscar Kozyra, O.de.M.; Jerome Laubacker, O.de.M., Local Supr.; Benedict Ptacek, O.de.M.; Michael E. Perry, O.de.M.; Bro. Richard Henry, O.de.M. Total Staff 6; Total in Residence 6.

BELLEAIR BLUFFS. *St. James Friary*, 2433 Indian Ave., 33770-2032. Tel: 727-585-2521; Fax: 727-585-2460. Web: franmow.org. Revs. Roch A. Coogan, O.F.M.; Edward Flanagan, O.F.M. Franciscan Friars Ministry of the Word (New York)

CLEARWATER BEACH. *St. Paul Friary*, 50 Somerset St., 33767. Tel: 727-443-7351; Fax: 727-462-0150. Rev. Edmund Ansaloni, O.F.M., Vicar; Bro. Thomas Hollowood, O.F.M., Guardian.

PINELLAS PARK. *Priests of the Sacred Heart*, 6701 82nd Ave. N., 34665. Tel: 727-541-2661; Fax: 727-547-0408. Email: dmurphy@ij.net. Bro. Timothy Murphy, S.C.J., Coord.; Most Rev. Joseph A. DePalma, S.C.J., Retired Bishop of DeAar, S. Africa (Retired); Revs. Joseph Doscher, S.C.J. (Retired); Vincent McDonald, S.C.J. (Retired); John Kevin McInnis, S.C.J. (Retired); Kenneth Mitchell, S.C.J. (Retired); Raymond Vega, S.C.J. (Retired); Bro. Gabriel Kersting, S.C.J., (Retired). Total Staff 1; Total in Residence 7.

ST. LEO. *St. Leo Abbey*, P.O. Box 2350, 33574. Tel: 352-588-8624; Fax: 352-588-5217. Email: jtingerchal@saintleo.edu. Web: www.saintleoabbey.org. Very Rev. James Tingertal, O.S.B., Admin.; Revs. Robert Velten, O.S.B.; Gregory Traeger, O.S.B.; Damian DuQuesnay, O.S.B.; Andrew Metzger, O.S.B.; Paul Romfh, O.S.B.; Jude Krogol, O.S.B.; Boniface Steinwachs, O.S.B., Prior; Isaac Camacho, O.S.B.; Joseph Paek, O.S.B. Priests 14; Brothers 13; Internal Oblates 1.
On Duty Outside the Monastery: Rt. Rev. Patrick Shelton, O.S.B., Retired Abbot (Retired); Revs. James Hoge, O.S.B.; David Draim, O.S.B.; Richard Hugli, O.S.B.

ST. PETE BEACH. *Franciscan Friary*, 555 - 68th Ave., 33706. Tel: 727-367-2408.

SEMINOLE. *Capuchin Franciscan Residence*, 7171 128th St. N., 33776. Tel: 727-397-0011; Fax: 727-392-7183. Email: floridacaps@juno.com. Revs. Joseph Testagrossa, O.F.M.Cap.; Anthony Donahue, O.F.M.Cap.; Richard Donaldson, O.F.M.Cap., Contact, Guardian.

[P] CONVENTS AND RESIDENCES FOR SISTERS

ST. PETERSBURG. *St. Anthony Hospital Convent*, 631 11th St. N., 33705. Tel: 727-825-1142; Fax: 727-825-1490. Email: fsa_sta@juno.com. Web: www.fsalleg.org. Sr. Susan McGillicuddy, Contact. Franciscan Sisters of Allegany (Allegany, NY) Total in Residence 7.

ST. LEO. *Holy Name Monastery*, 33201 State Highway 52, 33574-2450. Tel: 352-588-8320; Fax: 352-588-8319. Email: holyname@saintleo.edu. Web: www.floridabenedictines.com. P.O. Box 2450, 33574-2450. Sr. Mary Clare Neuhofer, O.S.B., Prioress.
Legal Title: *Holy Name Academy, Inc.*, Motherhouse and Novitiate of the Benedictine Sisters of Florida. Professed Sisters 25.

TAMPA. *St. Clare Convent*, 2924 W. Curtis St., 33614-7102. Tel: 813-870-4272; Fax: 813-414-9074. Email: fsasisters. Franciscan Sisters of Allegany (Allegany, NY)

St. Elizabeth Convent, 3000 Perry Ave., 33603-5345. Tel: 813-229-1978; Fax: 813-228-9066. Email: e3000@juno.com. Franciscan Sisters of Allegany Total Staff 3; Total in Residence 25.

Franciscan Convent, 3006 Perry Ave., 33603-5345. Tel: 813-229-2492; Fax: 813-228-0748. Email: foonvent@aol.com. Franciscan Sisters of Allegany. Total in Residence 4.

Franciscan Sisters of Allegany, NY, 1303 W. Braddock St., 33603. Tel: 813-221-8510. Email: jeanneosf@aol.com.

Villa Madonna Convent, 2611 N. Massachusetts Ave., 33602. Tel: 813-229-1322, Ext. 393; Fax: 813-223-4812. Email: fmavilla@aol.com. Web: www.villamadonna.org. Daughters of Mary Help of Christians (Haledon, NJ) Total Staff 4; Total in Residence 4.

TREASURE ISLAND. *Franciscan Sisters of Allegany, NY, Region III Office*, 631 11th St. N., 33705. Tel: 717-824-0857; Fax: 727-895-5718.

[Q] RETREAT CENTERS

CLEARWATER. *Retreat Ministry of the Marian Servants of Divine Providence*, 725 South Bayview Ave., 33759. Tel: 727-799-4003; Fax: 727-726-1631. Email: msretreats@aol.com. Web: www.divineprovidence.org. Mary Brady, Dir. & Contact Person.

ST. LEO. *St. Leo Abbey Retreat Center*, P.O. Box 2350, 33574. Tel: 352-588-8182; Fax: 352-588-5217. Email: donna.cooper@saintleo.edu. Web: www.saintleoabbey.org. Mrs. Donna Cooper, Dir. Total Staff 4.

TAMPA. *Franciscan Center, Retreat House*, 3010 N. Perry Ave., 33603-5345. Tel: 813-229-2695; Fax: 813-228-0748. Email: francntr@tampabay.rr.com. Web: www.alleganyfranciscans.org/franciscancenter/htm. Sisters Catherine Cahill, O.S.F., Dir.; Kay Aherne, O.S.F.; Regina Kane, O.S.F.; Christina Strain, Admin.; Rev. Sam Vaccarella, T.O.R. Franciscan Sisters of Allegany Total Staff 13.

[R] PRIVATE ASSOCIATIONS OF THE CHRISTIAN FAITHFUL

CLEARWATER. *Community of the Marian Servants of Divine Providence*, 702 S. Bayview Ave., 33759. Tel: 727-797-7412; Fax: 727-726-1631. Email: marianservants@juno.com. Web: www.divineprovidence.org. Diane F. Brown, Dir.

Our Lady of Divine Providence House of Prayer Tel: 727-797-7412; Fax: 727-726-1631.

[S] SUMMER CAMPS

ST. PETERSBURG. *Our Lady of Good Counsel Camp*, 8888 E. Gobbler Dr., Floral City, 34436. Tel: 352-726-2198; Fax: 352-726-3212. Email: goodcounselcamp@aol.com. Web: http://goodcounselcamp.catholicweb.com. Rev. James B. Johnson, Dir.
Our Lady of Fatima Church: 550 U.S. Hwy. 41 S., Inverness, 34450. Tel: 352-726-1910; Fax: 352-344-8384.

[T] CAMPUS MINISTRY

ST. PETERSBURG. *Eckerd College - Campus Ministry* c/o 5650 7th Ave. N., 33710-7112. Tel: 727-864-8470; Fax: 727-384-9073. Bro. Richard Henry, O.de.M., Chap. Total in Residence 1.

TAMPA. *Catholic Student Center, University of South Florida* 13005 N. 50th St., 33617-1022. Tel: 813-988-3727; Fax: 813-988-3727. Email: director@catholicusf.org. Web: www.catholicusf.org. Rev. Alan Weber, Dir.; Jennifer Moreda, Campus Min.

University of Tampa - Campus Ministry c/o Sacred Heart Catholic Church, P.O. Box 1524, 33601. Tel: 813-229-1595; Fax: 813-221-2350. Rev. Paul Osterle, S.J.

[U] MISCELLANEOUS

ST. PETERSBURG. *Catholic Charities Housing, Inc.*, 1213 16th St. N., 33705. Tel: 727-893-1314, Ext. 202; Fax: 727-893-1307. Email: housing@ccdosp.org. Web: www.ccdosp.org.

Magnificat Inc., Lower Pinellas Deanery Chapter of the Diocese of St. Petersburg, Florida, 1448 83rd Ave. N., 33702. Tel: 727-576-4988. Email: abdiaco@aol.com.

Marian Servants of the Holy Spirit, Inc., 6363 9th Ave. N., P.O. Box 40200, 33710. Tel: 727-344-1611; Fax: 727-345-3086. Email: macmacdon@aol.com. Rev. Donat Michael McDonagh, Pres.

Pastoral Center, Formerly Chancery Office6363 9th Ave N., 33710. For detailed information on the following listings contact the Chancery Office.
Allegany Community Out Reach Grant Fund, Inc.
Catholic Charities Housing, Inc.
Catholic Education Foundation, Inc.
Catholic Media Ministry, Inc.
Christopher Assurance, Inc.
The Congregation of the Sisters of St. Clare (Florida), Inc., 625 Court St. 2nd Floor, Clearwater, 33756.
Allegany Franciscan Ministries, Inc.
Regis Manor, Inc.
WBVM, 90.5 FM, Inc., Clearwater.
Catholic Charities Foundation of Tampa Bay, Inc.
The Greater Tampa Catholic Lawyers Guild, Inc., P.O. Box 1816, Tampa, 33601.

Franciscan Center of Tampa, FL, Inc., 3010 Perry Ave., Tampa, 33603. Tel: 813-229-2695; Fax: 813-228-0748.

Region III Office, Franciscan Sisters of Allegany, NY, 631-11th St., N., 33705. Tel: 727-824-0857; Fax: 727-895-5718. Email: ks1187@tampabay.rr.com. Web: www.fsalleg.org; www.franciscansister.com. Sr. Marie Kathleen Stagnaro, O.S.F., Region III Min.

The Salesian Society of St. Petersburg, Inc., 6470 13th Ave., N., 33710. Tel: 727-374-0224. Bro. William J. Hanna, S.D.B., Contact Person.

CLEARWATER. *Allegany Franciscan Foundation, Tampa*

Bay, Inc., 19329 U.S. Hwy. 19 N., Ste. 100, 33764. Tel: 727-507-9668; Fax: 727-507-8557. Email: jolighter@francescanfdn.org. Web: www.franciscanfdn.org.

Alleghany Franciscan Foundation, Dade County, Inc., 19329 US Hwy. 19 N., Ste. 100, 33764. Tel: 727-507-9668; Fax: 727-507-8557.

NEW PORT RICHEY. *Stepping Stones to Independence, Inc.*, c/o Our Lady Queen of Peace Church, 5340 High St., 34652. Tel: 727-849-3476; Fax: 727-849-4814. Email: stones@pascohelp.net. Web: www.pascohelp.net. Rev. Kenneth Slattery; Judy Boynton, Dir.; Alex Groppe, Dir.; Carol Passenti, Dir.; David Katcher, Dir.

OLDSMAR. **Living His Life Abundantly International, Inc.*, 325 Scarlet Blvd., 34677-3019. Tel: 813-854-1518; Fax: 813-891-1267. Email: info@lhla.org. Web: www.lhla.org. Johnnette S. Benkovic, Pres.

ST. LEO. *St. Leo Abbey Foundation, Inc.*, P.O. Box 2350, 33574. Tel: 352-588-8679; Fax: 352-588-5217. Email: frpaul@saintleo.edu. Web: saintleoabbey.org.

VALRICO. **Knanya Catholic Congress of Central Florida, Inc.*, 2620 Washington, 33594. Tel: 813-681-6189; Fax: 813-230-8031. Email: jillikal@aol.com.

RELIGIOUS INSTITUTES OF MEN REPRESENTED IN THE DIOCESE

For further details refer to the corresponding bracketed number in the Religious Institutes of Men or Women section.

[]—*Apostles of Jesus*—A.P.
[0130]—*Assumptionists* (Brighton, MA)—A.A.
[0140]—*The Augustinians* (Villanova, PA)—O.S.A.
[0190]—*Basilian Salvatorian Fathers* (Methuen, MA)—B.S.O.
[0900]—*Cannons Regular of Premontre*—O.Praem.
[0350]—*Cistercians Order of the Strict Observance (Trappists)* (Spencer, MA)—O.C.S.O.
[0380]—*Comboni Missionaries of the Sacred Heart* (Verona)—M.C.C.J.
[0310]—*Congregation of Christian Brothers* (New Rochelle, NY)—C.F.C.
[0220]—*Congregation of the Blessed Sacrament* (Cleveland, OH)—S.S.S.
[1330]—*Congregation of the Missions* (Madrid, Spain)—C.M.
[0520]—*Franciscan Friars* (New York, NY; Cicinnati, OH; Kennebunkport, ME; Dublin, Ireland)—O.F.M.
[0530]—*Franciscan Friars of the Atonement* (Garrison, NY)—S.A.
[0650]—*Holy Ghost Fathers* (Dublin, Ireland)—C.S.Sp.
[]—*Holy Spirit Fathers*—A.L.C.P.
[0300]—*Institute of Charity* (Peoria, IL)—I.C.
[0780]—*Marist Brothers* (New York, NY)—F.M.S.
[0780]—*Marist Fathers* (Washington, DC)—S.M.
[0800]—*Maryknoll Brothers*—M.M.
[0850]—*Missionaries of Africa* (Washington, DC)—M.Afr.
[0840]—*Missionary Servants of the Most Holy Trinity* (Arlington, VA)—S.T.M.
[]—*Missionary Society of St. Thomas the Apostle*—MST
[0870]—*Montford Missionaries*—SMM
[0350]—*Order of Cistercians of the Strict Observance* Spencer, MA—OCSO
[0470]—*Order of Friar Minor Capuchin* (White Plains, NY; Union City, NJ)—O.F.M.Cap.
[]—*Order of Friars Minor Conventual* (St. Bonaventure Prov., Chicago)—O.F.M.Conv
[0970]—*Order of Our Lady of Mercy* (Cleveland, OH)—O.deM.
[0430]—*Order of Preachers (Dominicans)* (Dublin, Ireland)—O.P.
[0200]—*Order of St. Benedict* (St. Leo, FL)—O.S.B.
[0610]—*Priests of the Congregation of the Holy Cross* (Bridgeport, CT)—C.S.C.
[1130]—*Sacred Heart Fathers and Brothers* (Hales Corner, WI)—S.C.J.
[1190]—*Salesians of St. John Bosco* (New Rochelle, NY)—S.D.B.
[]—*Scarboro Foreign Missions* (Scarboro, Ontario, Canada)—S.F.M.
[0690]—*Society of Jesus* (New Orleans, LA; Baltimore, MD; Chicago, IL; Boston, MA)—S.J.
[1060]—*Society of the Precious Blood* (Dayton, OH)—C.PP.S.
[0520]—*The Order of Friars Minor* (Cincinnati, OH; Imm. Conception Prov.; Ireland; New York, NY; Kennebunkport, ME)—OFM
[0560]—*Third Order Regular of Saint Francis* (Pittsburgh, PA; Etlers, PA)—T.O.R.

RELIGIOUS INSTITUTES OF WOMEN REPRESENTED IN THE DIOCESE

[0230]—*Benedictine Sisters of Pontifical Jurisdiction* (St. Leo, FL; Pittsburgh, PA; Beech Grove, IN)—O.S.B.
[0270]—*Congregation of Bon Secours* (Marriottsville, MD)—C.B.S.
[1010]—*Congregation of Divine Providence* (San Antonio, TX)—C.D.P.
[3110]—*Congregation of Our Lady of Retreat in the Cenacle* Lake Ronkonkoma, NY)—R.C.
[1930]—*Congregation of the Sisters of Holy Cross* (Montreal; Quebec)—C.S.C.
[0760]—*Daughters of Charity of St. Vincent de Paul* (Emmitsburg, MD)—D.C.
[0850]—*Daughters of Mary Help of Christians* (Haledon, NJ)—F.M.A.
[0870]—*Daughters of Mary Immaculate* (Vietnam)—F.M.I.
[0960]—*Daughters of Wisdom* (Islip, NY)—D.W.
[1070-02]—*Dominican Sister of Mary of the Springs* (Columbus,OH)—O.P.
[1070-13]—*Dominican Sisters* (Adrian, MI)—O.P.
[1070-17]—*Dominican Sisters* (Elkins Park, PA)—O.P.
[0840]—*Dominican Sisters of Hope* (Ossining, NY)—O.P.
[1070-11]—*Dominican Sisters of Our Lady of the Rosary* (Sparkill, NY)—O.P.
[]—*Dominican Sisters of the Immaculate Conception* (Ecuador)
[1180]—*Franciscan Sisters of Allegany, New York*—O.S.F.
[1310]—*Franciscan Sisters of Little Falls, Minnesota*—O.S.F.
[1370]—*Franciscan Sisters of Mary* (Bronx, NY)—F.M.M.
[1430]—*Franciscan Sisters of Our Lady of P.H.* (St. Louis, MO)
[1460]—*Franciscan Sisters of St. Elizabeth* (Parsippany, NJ)—F.S.S.E.
[1260]—*Handmaids of the Holy Child Jesus* (Nigeria)—H.H.C.J.
[]—*Hermit: Consecrated Virgin* (St. Petersburg, FL)—HER.C.V.
[2420]—*Marist Missionary Sisters (Missionary Sisters of the Society of Mary)*—S.M.S.M.
[2490]—*Medical Mission Sisters* (Philadelphia, PA)—S.C.M.M./M
[2480]—*Medical Missionary Sisters of Mary* (City Island, NY)—M.M.M.
[2720]—*Mission Helpers of the Sacred Heart* (Baltimore, MD)—M.H.S.H.
[2710]—*Missionaries of Charity Contempletive)* (Bronx, NY)—M.C.
[D]—*Our Lady of Kilimanjaro* (Tanzania, Africa)—CDNK
[3760P]—*Poor Clare Sisters* (Evansville, IN; Jamaica Plains, MA)—O.S.C.
[1830]—*Religious of the Good Shepherd* (St. Louis, MO)—R.S.G.
[4180]—*Religious Venerini Sisters* (Worcester,MA)—M.P.V.
[2970]—*School Sisters of Notre Dame* (Baltimore, MD; Wilton, CT)—S.S.N.D.
[1680]—*School Sisters of St. Francis* (Milwaukee, WI)—S.S.S.F.
[3590]—*Servants of Mary (Servite Sisters)* (Ladysmith, WI)—O.S.M.
[1070-03]—*Sinsinawa Dominicans* (Sinsinawa, WI)—O.P.
[0140]—*Sisters Auxillaries of the Apostolate* (Monongah, WV)—S.A.A.
[]—*Sisters for Christian Community*—S.F.C.C.
[0440]—*Sisters of Charity of Cincinnati, Ohio* (Mt. St. Joseph, OH)—S.C.
[0500]—*Sisters of Charity of Nazareth*—S.C.N.
[0590]—*Sisters of Charity of Saint Elizabeth, Convent Station*—S.C.
[0570]—*Sisters of Charity of Seton Hill* (Greensberg, PA)—S.C.
[]—*Sisters of Mary, Mother of God* (Tampa, FL)—S.M.M.G.
[2575]—*Sisters of Mercy of The Americas* (Chicago, IL; Dobbs Ferry, NY; Erie, PA; Windham, NH)—R.S.M.
[2990]—*Sisters of Notre Dame* (Chardon, OH)—S.N.D.
[2670]—*Sisters of Our Lady of Mercy* (Pine Hill, NJ)—S.O.L.M.
[3360]—*Sisters of Providence* (St. Mary of the Woods, IN.)—S.P.
[3893]—*Sisters of Saint Joseph of Chestnut Hill, Philadelphia*—S.S.J.
[]—*Sisters of St. Anne Bangalone*—S.A.B.
[3750]—*Sisters of St. Chretienne* (Wrentham, MA)—S.S.Ch.
[3770]—*Sisters of St. Clare* (Dublin, Ireland)—O.S.C.
[1070-15]—*Sisters of St. Dominic* (Blauvelt, NY)—O.P.
[1710]—*Sisters of St. Francis of Mary Immaculate* (Joliet, IL)—O.S.F.
[1630]—*Sisters of St. Francis of Penance and Christian Charity* (Stella Niagara, NY)—O.S.F.
[1570]—*Sisters of St. Francis of the Holy Family* (Dubuque, IA)—O.S.F.
[1510]—*Sisters of St. Francis of the Mission of the Immaculate Virgin* (Hastings, NY)—O.S.F.
[3830-11]—*Sisters of St. Joseph* (Nazareth)—S.S.J.
[3830-14]—*Sisters of St. Joseph*—S.S.J.
[3840]—*Sisters of St. Joseph of Carondelet* (St. Louis, MO)—C.S.J.
[3890]—*Sisters of St. Joseph of Peace* (Englewood Cliffs, NJ)—C.S.J.P.
[3900]—*Sisters of St. Joseph of St. Augustine, Florida* (Chestnut Hill, PA)—S.S.J.
[1990]—*Sisters of the Holy Names of Jesus and Mary* (Albany, NY)—S.N.J.M.
[3730]—*Sisters of the St. Basil the Great* (Uniontown, PA)—O.S.B.M.
[1490]—*Sisters of the Third Franciscan Order*—O.S.F.
[2150]—*Sisters, Servants of the Immaculate Heart of Mary* (Monroe, MI)—I.H.M.
[2160]—*Sisters, Servants of the Immaculate Heart of Mary* (Scranton, PA)—I.H.M.
[4190P]—*Visitation of Holy Mary* (St. Louis, MO; Washington, DC; Wheeling, WV; Brooklyn, NY)—V.H.M.

DIOCESAN CEMETERIES

CLEARWATER. *Calvary Catholic*, 11801 U.S. Hwy. 19 N., 33764-7407.

NECROLOGY

† Obert, Martin—Died April 29, 2003
† Rittmeyer, Robert, (Retired)—Died Nov. 29, 2003

Diocese of Salina

(Dioecesis Salinensis)

Most Reverend

GEORGE K. FITZSIMONS, D.D.

Bishop of Salina; ordained March 18, 1961; appointed Titular Bishop of Pertusa and Auxiliary Bishop of Kansas City-St. Joseph May 27, 1975; Episcopal ordination July 3, 1975; appointed Bishop of Salina March 22, 1984; installed May 29, 1984 *P.O. Box 980, Salina, KS 67402.*

Chancery Office: 103 N. Ninth, P.O. Box 980, Salina, KS 67402-0980. Tel: 785-827-8746; Fax: 785-827-6133.

Email: chancery@midusa.net

Square Miles 26,685.

Formerly Diocese of Concordia.

Established August 2, 1887.

See transferred to Salina December 23, 1944.

(New boundaries established by Apostolic Letters dated July 1, 1897).

Bounded on the west by Colorado, on the north by Nebraska, on the east by the east lines of Washington, Riley, Geary and Dickinson Counties, and on the south by the south lines of Dickinson, Saline, Ellsworth, Russell, Ellis, Trego, Gove, Logan and Wallace Counties in the State of Kansas.

For legal titles of parishes and diocesan institutions, consult the Chancery Office.

STATISTICAL OVERVIEW

Personnel	
Bishop	1
Retired Bishops	1
Priests: Diocesan Active in Diocese	44
Priests: Diocesan Active Outside Diocese	1
Priests: Retired, Sick or Absent	21
Number of Diocesan Priests	66
Religious Priests in Diocese	7
Total Priests in Diocese	73
Extern Priests in Diocese	3
Ordinations:	
Diocesan Priests	1
Total Brothers	1
Total Sisters	198
Parishes	
Parishes	88
With Resident Pastor:	
Resident Diocesan Priests	37
Resident Religious Priests	1
Without Resident Pastor:	
Administered by Priests	35
Administered by Religious Women	4
Administered by Lay People	11
Closed Parishes	3
Welfare	
Homes for the Aged	4
Total Assisted	249
Educational	
Diocesan Students in Other Seminaries	7
Total Seminarians	7
High Schools, Diocesan and Parish	5
Total Students	651
High Schools, Private	1
Total Students	259
Elementary Schools, Diocesan and Parish	12
Total Students	1,834
Catechesis/Religious Education:	
High School Students	1,922
Elementary Students	4,591
Total Students under Catholic Instruction	9,264
Teachers in the Diocese:	
Priests	4
Sisters	4
Lay Teachers	206
Vital Statistics	
Receptions into the Church:	
Infant Baptism Totals	951
Adult Baptism Totals	89
Received into Full Communion	173
First Communions	824
Confirmations	770
Marriages:	
Catholic	241
Interfaith	180
Total Marriages	421
Deaths	628
Total Catholic Population	46,737
Total Population	318,145

Former Bishops—Rt. Revs. RICHARD SCANNELL, D.D., consecrated in Nashville, Tenn., Nov. 30, 1887; transferred to Omaha, Jan. 30, 1891; died Jan. 8, 1916; JOHN J. HENNESSY, D.D. Apostolic Administrator, 1891-98, Bishop of Wichita; THADDEUS BUTLER, D.D., Bishop-elect; died July 17, 1897; JOHN F. CUNNINGHAM, D.D., consecrated Sept. 21, 1898; died June 23, 1919; Most Revs. FRANCIS J. TIEF, D.D. (Retired), consecrated March 30, 1921; retired and appointed Titular Bishop of Nisa, June 11, 1938; died Sept. 22, 1965; FRANK A. THILL, D.D., consecrated Oct. 28, 1938; transferred to Salina, Dec. 23, 1944; died May 21, 1957; FREDERICK W. FREKING, D.D., J.C.D. (Retired), consecrated Nov. 30, 1957; transferred to LaCrosse, Dec. 30, 1964; CYRIL J. VOGEL, D.D., ord. Bishop, June 17, 1965; died Oct. 4, 1979; DANIEL W. KUCERA, O.S.B., Ph.D., D.D. (Retired), ord. May 26, 1949; appt. Titular Bishop of Natchez and Auxiliary Bishop of Joliet, June 6, 1977; consecrated July 21, 1977; appt. Bishop of Salina, March 11, 1980; installed May 7, 1980; transferred to Archbishop of Archdiocese of Dubuque, Feb. 23, 1984; retired Oct. 16, 1995.

Chancery Office—103 N. Ninth, P.O. Box 980, Salina, 67402-0980. Tel: 785-827-8746; Fax: 785-827-6133.

Vicar General—Rev. Msgr. JAMES E. HAKE, J.C.L., Res.: Sacred Heart Cathedral, 118 N. 9th, Salina, 67401.

Chancellor—Rev. BARRY BRINKMAN, J.C.L., P.O. Box 980, Salina, 67402-0980.

Diocesan Finance Officer—Rev. JEROME L. MORGAN, Res.: St. Wenceslaus, P.O. Box 528, Wilson, 67490; Mr. GREG LUST, Asst. Finance Officer & Business Mgr., P.O. Box 980, Salina, 67402-0980.

Diocesan Office of Planning—VACANT, Dir.

Diocesan Tribunal—103 N. Ninth, P.O. Box 980, Salina, 67402-0980. Tel: 785-827-8746; Fax: 785-827-6133.

Judicial Vicar-Officialis—Rev. KENNETH LOHRMEYER, J.C.L.

Associate Judges—Revs. KENNETH P. LOHRMEYER, J.C.L.; BARRY BRINKMAN, J.C.L.

Defender of the Bond—Rev. Msgr. JAMES E. HAKE, J.C.L.

Auditor-Notary—SUSAN OTTLEY.

Promoter of Justice and Guardian—Rev. DANIEL SCHEETZ, J.C.L.

Procurator and Advocate—Rev. RALPH ASCHENBRENNER.

Diocesan Finance Council—Most Rev. GEORGE K. FITZSIMONS, D.D.; Rev. JEROME L. MORGAN; BILL BECKMEYER; DONALD P. DIEDERICH; Mr. JOHN GRAHAM; Mr. GREG LUST; ROBERT SCHMIDT; JAN MARKS.

College of Consultors—Most Rev. GEORGE K. FITZSIMONS, D.D.; Rev. Msgr. JAMES E. HAKE, J.C.L.; Revs. JOE POPELKA; JEROME L. MORGAN; DONALD D. ZIMMERMAN; FRANK COADY; JAMES HOOVER.

Episcopal Vicars—Revs. ROGER MEITL, Western District; JOSEPH POPELKA, West Central District; JEROME L. MORGAN, East Central District; MARK WESELY, Eastern District.

Council of Priests—Revs. JOSEPH POPELKA, Chm.; BARRY BRINKMAN, Member At Large; MARK WESELY, Sec.; KEITH WEBER, Member At Large; Rev. Msgr. JAMES E. HAKE, J.C.L.; Revs. RANDALL WEBER, Vice Chm.; FRANK COADY, Member At Large; GILMARY TALLMAN, O.F.M.Cap.; JEROME L. MORGAN; JAMES HOOVER; DAMIAN RICHARDS; STEVE HEINA.

Diocesan Pastoral Council—Most Rev. GEORGE K. FITZSIMONS, D.D.; TERRY CHAPUT, Moderator; Revs. JEROME L. MORGAN; NORBERT DLABAL; DAVID METZ; MARK WESELY; Sisters MARY CATHERINE GRIEF, C.S.A.; KENNETH STRUCKHOFF, C.S.A.; MARY JO THUMMEL, C.S.J.; BARBARA BERTHIAUME, C.S.J. Laity:: TERRY CHAPUT, Chm.; STANLEY KRIER; ROSANN FELDER; RANDY HUSER; MARLENE MONTGOMERY; PHYLLIS TEMAAT; RICHARD KRAMER; THELMA BERLAND; FRANCIS SWEAT; GINGER THULL, Sec.; BOB HOLLERICH; Mrs. JUDY FISHER; JOE FARRELL; FRANCIS L'ECUYER; DAVE LICKTEIG; JANE JOHNSON; BARNEY DICKMAN; SUSAN BECHARD; ELIZABETH SABATKA.

Personnel Board—Most Rev. GEORGE K. FITZSIMONS, D.D.; Revs. ROGER MEITL, Chm.; HENRY BAXA, Sec.; LARRY GRENNAN; MARK WESELY; Rev. Msgr. JAMES E. HAKE, J.C.L., Ex Officio; Rev. BARRY BRINKMAN, Chancellor.

Vocation Ministry Committee—Most Rev. GEORGE K. FITZSIMONS, D.D.; Revs. DAVID METZ, Dir.; RANDALL WEBER; KEITH WEBER; FRED GATSCHET; DANA CLARK; Rev. Msgr. JAMES HAKE, J.C.L.; Bro. AUGUSTINE RHODE, O.F.M.Cap.; Sr. BARBARA ELLEN APACELLER, C.S.J.

Diocesan Offices and Directors

Art and Architecture Commission—Rev. JEROME L. MORGAN, Chm.; Rev. Msgrs. JAMES E. HAKE, J.C.L., Vice Chm.; JOHN GEORGE WEBER (Retired); Revs. FRANK COADY; DONALD D. ZIMMERMAN; KEITH WEBER; CHARLES BOSTER; Mr. GREG LUST.

Priests' Continuing Formation Committee—Revs. KERRY NINEMIRE, Chm.; RANDALL WEBER; FRANK COADY; BARRY BRINKMAN. Ex Officio: Most Rev. GEORGE K. FITZSIMONS, D.D.; Rev. Msgr. JAMES HAKE, J.C.L.

Catholic Charities Board—Dr. KAREN S. HAUSER, Ed.D., CEO; STAN KRIER, Pres.; ROD BATES, Vice Pres.; TOM WHITEHAIR, Sec.; Rev. ALLEN SCHEER; STEVE BROWN, Treas.; Rev. NORBERT DLABAL; RAUL PICAZO; RAQUEL PICAZO; LARRY CURRAN; ROSIE RUNDELL; PAM KRIER; JANET WHITEHAIR; OREN WINDHOLZ; PAT WINDHOLZ; Most Rev. GEORGE K. FITZSIMONS, D.D., Ex Officio.

Catholic Charities of Salina, Inc.—Dr. KAREN S. HAUSER, Ed.D., CEO; LILLIAN ANDROES, L.B., S.W., Adoption; JOSEPHINE HERNANDEZ, L.S.C.S.W., Counseling; LINDA VAJGRT, L.S.C.S.W., Counseling; CARLISLE BERGQUIST, M.A., L.C.M.F.T.; J. DANA WOOD, M.S., L.C.P.C.; BONNIE OTEY, Office Mgr., 425 W. Iron, P.O. Box 1366, Salina, 67401. Tel: 785-825-0208; 888-468-6909; Fax: 785-826-9708. Email: ccharsal@salhelp.org. Web: www.catholiccharitiessalina.org.

Family Life—SHEILA MARCOTTE, Exec. Sec.

Immigration—BEATRIZ ZAPATA; MARIA TORRES; MARIBEL PANUCO; Sr. JUDY STEPHENS, C.S.J.

Catholic Charities Outreach Office - Hays—JOAN PERKINS, Office Mgr.; JANET RUSSELL, L.S.C.S.W., Adoption & Counseling; Rev. BILL SURMEIER, Counseling; BELINDA HARTMAN, L.P.C., 2707 Vine, #17, P.O. Box 811, Hays, 67601. Tel: 785-625-2644; 877-625-2644; Fax: 785-625-6497. Email: cchaysof@ruraltel.net.

Catholic Charities Outreach Office - Manhattan—IRIS CURLEY-ROARK, L.M.S.W., Adoption, 1115 Westport, Ste. D7, Manhattan, 66502. Tel: 785-323-0644. Email: ccm@flinthills.com.

Catholic Charities - Colby—BELINDA HARTMAN, L.P.C., Counseling, 350 S. Range, Ste. 2, Colby, 67701. Tel: 785-426-3426.

Catholic Community Annual Appeal—P.O. Box 980, Salina, 67402-0980. Fax: 785-827-6133.

Office of Catholic Formation—Sr. BARBARA ELLEN APACELLER, C.S.J., Dir., 103 N. Ninth, P.O. Box 825, Salina, 67402. Tel: 785-827-8746; Fax: 785-827-6133.

Coordinator of Office of Catholic Formation—Sr. BARBARA ELLEN APACELLER, C.S.J.

Director of Religious Education—Sr. BARBARA ELLEN APACELLER, C.S.J.. Email: barbcsj@salinadiocese.org.

Superintendent of Schools—Dr. NICK COMPAGNONE. Email: ministry@salinadiocese.org Web: www.salinadiocese.com.

Consultant for Religious Education & Media—(Grades K-8), PEGGY HERBERT. Email: avlibrary@salinadiocese.org.

Consultant for Religious Education— (Grades 9-12), Sr. BARBARA ELLEN APACELLER, C.S.J.

Director of Religious Studies/School of Pastoral Leadership—Rev. FRANK COADY. Email: relstudies@salinadiocese.org.

Valuing Your Sexuality—PEGGY HEBERT, Dir.

Audio-Visual—PEGGY HEBERT. Email: avlibrary@salinadiocese.org.

Catholic Youth Organization and Youth Ministry—Sr. BARBARA ELLEN APACELLER, C.S.J., P.O. Box 980, Salina, 67402.

Office of Communications—P.O. Box 980 Salina, 67402.

Diocesan Council of Education—MARTHA BEUNGARDT, Pres.; TOM SCHMITZ; JEAN ROSS; PAT LEGLEITER; VERNA FLAX; Revs. CHARLES STEIER; ROGER MEITL; KEITH WEBER; DOUG STEIN; PAM BECKER; KIM COY. Ex Officio: Most Rev. GEORGE K. FITZSIMONS, D.D.; Sr. BARBARA APACELLER, C.S.J.; Dr. NICK COMPAGNONE; PEGGY HEBERT.

Due Process Board—Rev. KENNETH P. LOHRMEYER, J.C.L., Chm.; Sr. BETH STOVER, C.S.J. Dr. NICK COMPAGNONE; MARY JO HEATH; Mr. LEROY HERRMAN Rev. Msgr. JAMES E. HAKE, J.C.L., Clerk.

Holy Childhood, Pontifical Association—Rev. Msgr. JAMES E. HAKE, J.C.L., Dir., P.O. Box 980, Salina, 67402.

Office of Liturgy—Rev. FRANK COADY, Dir., P.O. Box 980, Salina, 67402. Tel: 785-827-8746 Fax: 785-827-6133. Email: liturgy@salinadiocese.org.

Newspaper—Rev. Msgr. RAYMOND MENARD, Editor; Mr. GREG LUST, Business Mgr.. Email: newspaper@salinadiocese.org; P.O. Box 1038, Salina, 67402. "The Register, Northwestern Kansas Edition"

Propagation of the Faith—Rev. Msgr. JAMES E. HAKE, J.C.L., Dir., P.O. Box 980, Salina, 67402. Tel: 785-827-8746.

Rural Life Conference—Rev. ALLEN SCHEER, Dir., St. Theresa, P.O. Box 265, Mankato, 66956. Tel: 785-378-3939; Fax: 785-378-3913. Email: rurallifecommission@hotmail.com.

Salina Diocesan Clergy Health and Retirement Association, Inc.—Board of Trustees: Most Rev. GEORGE K. FITZSIMONS, D.D., Pres., 103 N. Ninth, P.O. Box 980, Salina, 67402-0980; Revs. DONALD MCCARTHY; ROGER HOUGH; LOREN WERTH (Retired); LOUIS MATTAS (Retired); ALBERT DESANCTIS; KEITH WEBER. Ex Officio: Rev. JEROME MORGAN; Mr. GREG LUST.

Salina Diocesan Council of Catholic Women (S.D.CC.W.)—ELIZABETH SABATKA, Pres., Rte. 2, Box 26, Atwood, 67730; Rev. KEITH WEBER, Moderator, Immaculate Heart of Mary, 1805 Vine, Hays, 67601.

Boy Scouts—Rev. DONALD P. MCCARTHY, 625 Freeman Ave., Oakley, 67748.

Girl Scouts—Sr. BARBARA ELLEN, C.S.J., Dir., P.O. Box 825, Salina, 67402-0825.

Vocations—

Diocesan Director of Vocations—Rev. DAVID METZ, Immaculate Heart of Mary, 1805 Vine, Hays, 67601. Email: salinavocations@hotmail.com.

Diocesan Committee Regarding Alleged Cases of Child Sexual Abuse—Most Rev. GEORGE FITZSIMONS; Rev. BILL SURMEIER; Rev. Msgr. JAMES E. HAKE, J.C.L., Ex Officio; Revs. FRANK COADY; JEROME MORGAN; BARRY BRINKMAN; Mr. GEORGE YARNEVICH; Dr. GEORGE JERKOVICH; Dr. KAREN HAUSER; Mrs. KAREN MIZE; Mrs. JOYCE RATCLIFF; BRUCE MOORE.

Victim Assistance Coordinator—ANNE KRESIN. Tel: 785-827-5024. Email: reportabuse@salinadiocese.org.

CLERGY, PARISHES, MISSIONS AND PAROCHIAL SCHOOLS

CITY OF SALINA
(SALINE COUNTY)

1—CATHEDRAL OF THE SACRED HEART (1876), [JC] Rev. Msgr. James E. Hake, J.C.L.; Revs. Galen Long, Rector; Carlos Ruiz-Santos; Henry Saw Lone; Sr. Julia Norton, R.S.M., Pastoral Assoc. In Res., Rev. Msgr. Raymond Menard.
Res.: 118 N. Ninth St., 67401. Tel: 785-823-7221; Fax: 785-820-8063.
School—(Grades PreK-6), 406 W. Iron Ave., 67401. Tel: 785-825-4798. Pat Breckunitch, Prin. Lay Teachers 12; Students 114.
Catechesis/Religious Program—Sherry Headlee, D.R.E. Students 110.

2—ST. ELIZABETH ANN SETON (1982), [JC] Rev. Frank Coady, Priest Supvr.; Sr. Rose Walters, C.S.A., Parish Dir. & Pastoral Admin.
Res.: 1000 Burr Oak Ln., 67401. Tel: 785-825-5282; Fax: 785-825-1140.
Catechesis/Religious Program—Melanie Melander, D.R.E.; Lucy Larson, D.R.E. Students 144.

3—ST. MARY'S (1959), [JC] Revs. Kerry Ninemire; Steven Heina.
Res.: 230 E. Cloud St., 67401. Tel: 785-827-5575; Fax: 785-827-8997.
School—(Grades PreK-6), 304 E. Cloud St., 67401. Tel: 785-827-4200; Fax: 785-827-7765. Mr. Nick Compagnone, Prin. Lay Teachers 33; Students 470.
Catechesis/Religious Program—Mrs. Nancy Main, D.R.E.; Nancy Sherffius, D.R.E. Students 288.

OUTSIDE THE CITY OF SALINA

ABILENE, DICKINSON CO., ST. ANDREW'S (1874), [CEM] Rev. Randall Weber.
Res.: 311 S. Buckeye Ave., P.O. Box 429, 67410. Tel: 785-263-1570; Fax: 785-263-3570.
School—(Grades PreK-5) Tel: 785-263-2453. Christina Bacon, Prin. Lay Teachers 7; Students 109.
Catechesis/Religious Program—Tel: 785-263-1570. Theresa Brierton, D.R.E. Students 200.

ANGELUS, SHERIDAN CO., ST. PAUL'S (1887), (German), [CEM] Attended by, St. Joseph's Church, Oakley. , Mailing Address: 625 Freeman Ave., Oakley, 67748. Tel: 785-672-3828.
Church: Tel: 785-824-3256.
Catechesis/Religious Program—Students 51.

ANTONINO, ELLIS CO., OUR LADY HELP OF CHRISTIANS (1905), Attended by, St. Joseph, Hays. Rev. Earl Befort, O.F.M.Cap.
Mailing Address: 215 W. 13th, Hays, 67601. Tel: 785-625-7356; Fax: 785-625-7394.

ATWOOD, RAWLINS CO., SACRED HEART (1879), [CEM] [JC 3] Rev. Damian Richards.
Sacred Heart: 508 N. Railroad Ave., 67730. Tel: 785-626-3335; Fax: 785-626-3431.
Catechesis/Religious Program—Loretta A. Studer, D.R.E. Students 95.

AURORA, CLOUD CO., ST. PETER'S (1884), [CEM] [JC] Attended by, St. John the Baptist, Clyde.
Catechesis/Religious Program—Tel: 785-464-3461. Students 19.

BEARDSLEY, RAWLINS CO., ST. JOHN'S (1910), (Slovak), [CEM] Rev. Damian Richards.
Mailing Address: 508 N. Railroad Ave., Atwood, 67730. Tel: 785-626-3335; Fax: 785-626-3431.
Church: Atwood, 67730.
Catechesis/Religious Program—Students 32.

BELLEVILLE, REPUBLIC CO., ST. EDWARD'S (1901), [CEM] Rev. Ralph Aschenbrenner.
Res.: 1827 Q St., P.O. Box 99, 66935. Tel: 785-527-5559.
Catechesis/Religious Program—Sacred Hearts Center, 1813 Q St., 66935. Tel: 785-527-5819. Bev Lapo, D.R.E. Students 91.

BELOIT, MITCHELL CO., ST. JOHN THE BAPTIST (1869), [CEM] Rev. Henry R. Baxa.
Office: 622 E. Main, 67420.
Res.: 701 E. Court St., 67420. Tel: 785-738-2851; Fax: 785-738-3410.
School—(Grades PreK-6) Tel: 785-738-3941. Leonard Konda, Prin. Lay Teachers 9; Students 85.
High School—(Grades 7-12) Tel: 785-738-2942; Fax: 785-738-4462. Jim Wessling, Prin. Priests 1; Lay Teachers 11; Students 87.
Catechesis/Religious Program—Students 141.

BIRD CITY, CHEYENNE CO., ST. JOSEPH'S (1911), Attended by, St. Francis, St. Francis. Rev. Beryl Gibson.
Mailing Address: 625 River St., P.O. Box 1170, St. Francis, 67756. Tel: 785-332-2680.
Church: 67731. Tel: 785-734-2287.
Catechesis/Religious Program—Students 33.

BROOKVILLE, SALINE CO., ST. JOSEPH'S (1884), [CEM] Attended by, St. Patrick's, Lincoln. Rev. Msgr. James E. Hake, J.C.L.
Mailing Address: 206 N. 5th, P.O. Box 327, Lincoln, 67455. Tel: 785-524-4823.
Church: 67425.

CATHARINE, ELLIS CO., ST. CATHERINE'S (1892), [CEM 2] Attended by, St. Joseph's, Hays. Rev. Earl Befort, O.F.M.Cap., Canonical Pastor/ Sacramental Min.; Mrs. Glenda Schuetz, Pastoral Admin.
Mailing Address: 1681 St. Joseph St., P.O. Box 18, 67627. Tel: 785-625-5091.

CAWKER CITY, MITCHELL CO., SS. PETER AND PAUL (1878), (German), [CEM] Attended by, St. Boniface, Tipton.
Church: Tel: 785-781-4319; 785-373-4455.
Catechesis/Religious Program—1202 Holly, 67430. Tel 785-781-4835. Students 42.

CHAPMAN, DICKINSON CO., ST. MICHAEL'S (1883), [CEM] Rev. Randall Weber, Sacramental Priest & Canonical Pastor; Marita Campbell, Pastoral Admin.
Res.: P.O. Box 217, 67431. Tel: 785-922-6509.
Catechesis/Religious Program—Tel: 785-922-6509. Laurie McLaughlin, D.R.E. Students 72.

CLAUDELL, SMITH CO.
1—ST. FRANCIS (1914), Closed., For inquiries for parish records please see SS. Philip & James, Phillipsburg.

CLAY CENTER, CLAY CO., SS. PETER AND PAUL (1879), [CEM] Rev. Merlin Kieffer.
Res.: 730 Court St., 67432. Tel: 785-632-5011; Fax: 785-632-3914.
Catechesis/Religious Program—Tel: 785-632-3204. Cyndy Schwensen, D.R.E. Students 93.

CLIFTON, WASHINGTON CO., ST. MARY'S, (French—German), [CEM] Attended by, St. John the Baptist, Clyde. , Mailing Address: 204 N. High, Clyde, 66938. Tel: 785-446-3474.
Catechesis/Religious Program—Tel: 913-455-2291. Mrs. Linda Kantack, D.R.E. Students 71.

CLYDE, CLOUD CO., ST. JOHN THE BAPTIST'S (1880), (French—German), [CEM] Rev. LeRoy Metro; Brenda Koch, D.R.E.
Res.: 204 N. High, 66938. Tel: 785-446-3474.
Catechesis/Religious Program—Students 98.

COLBY, THOMAS CO., SACRED HEART (1886), [CEM] Rev. Dana Clark.
Res.: 585 N. French Ave., 67701. Tel: 785-462-2179; Fax: 785-462-6613.
School—(Grades PreK-5) Tel: 785-462-2813; Fax: 785-462-9688. Mr. David Everet, Prin. Lay Teachers 10; Students 98.
Catechesis/Religious Program—Tel: 785-462-3890. Students 171.

COLLYER, TREGO CO., ST. MICHAEL'S (1893), (German), [CEM] [JC] Attended by, Christ the King, WaKeeney , Mailing Address: Ainsie Ave., Box 174, 67631. Tel: 785-769-5272.
Catechesis/Religious Program—Laura Walt, D.R.E. Students 37.

CONCORDIA, CLOUD CO., OUR LADY OF PERPETUAL HELP (1887), (French), [CEM 2] Rev. Barry Brinkman.
Office—307 E. Fifth, P.O. Box 608, 66901. Tel: 785-243-1099; Fax: 785-243-1939.
Res.: 420 Kansas, P.O. Box 608, 66901. Tel: 785-243-4658.
Catechesis/Religious Program—Tel: 785-243-1410. Laura Jo Meyer, D.R.E. Students 207.

CUBA, REPUBLIC CO., ST. ISIDORE'S (1873), (Czech), [CEM] Attended by, St. Edward, Belleville. Rev. Ralph Aschenbrenner.
Mailing Address: P.O. Box 99, Belleville, 66935.

DAMAR, ROOKS CO., ST. JOSEPH'S (1912), (French), [CEM] Attended by, Immaculate Heart of Mary, Hill City. , Mailing Address: P.O.Box 68, 67632. Tel: 785-839-4343. In Res., Rev. Bill Kilian (Retired).
Catechesis/Religious Program—Tel: 785-839-4360. Gil Berland, D.R.E. Students 65.

DELPHOS, OTTAWA CO., ST. PAUL'S, [CEM] Attended by, Immaculate Conception, Minneapolis. Rev. Kenneth Lohrmeyer.
Res.: 216 Cherry St., Box 167, Minneapolis, 67467. Tel: 785-392-2079.

DENSMORE, NORTON CO., ST. MARY'S, Closed. For inquiries for parish records contact the chancery.

DORRANCE, RUSSELL CO., ST. JOSEPH'S (1902), (German—Irish), [CEM] Attended by, St. Wenceslaus, Wilson. Rev. Jerome Morgan.
Mailing Address: P.O. Box 528, Wilson, 67490. Tel: 785-658-3361.
Catechesis/Religious Program—Students 9.

DOWNS, OSBORNE CO., ST. MARY'S (1903), Attended by, St. Aloysius, Osborne. , Mailing Address: P.O.

Box 267, Osborne, 67473.
Church: 1312 Prentice, 67437. Tel: 785-454-3551.
Catechesis/Religious Program—Students 38.

ELLIS, ELLIS CO., ST. MARY'S (1870), Rev. Larry Letourneau; Sr. Doris M. Flax, C.S.J., Pastoral Assoc.
Church: 703 Monroe, 67637. Tel: 785-726-4522.
School—(Grades PreK-6) Tel: 785-726-3185. Ty Poell, Prin. Sisters of St. Joseph 2; Lay Teachers 9; Students 80.
Catechesis/Religious Program—Sr. Donna Otter, C.S.J., D.R.E. Students 104.

ELLSWORTH, ELLSWORTH CO., ST. BERNARD'S (1909), Rev. Daniel L. Scheetz.
Res.: 911 Kansas St., 67439. Tel: 785-472-3136; Fax: 785-472-3593.
Catechesis/Religious Program—Students 106.

ELMO, DICKINSON CO., ST. COLUMBA'S, [CEM] Attended by, St. John the Evangelist, Herington. Rev. Mark Wesely.
712 N. Broadway, Herington, 67449. Tel: 785-258-2013. Total Enrollment 8.
School—Judy Zimmer, D.R.E. Total Enrollment 8.

ESBON, JEWELL CO., SACRED HEART (1887), [CEM] Attended by, St. Theresa's, Mankato. Rev. Daryl Olmstead.
Mailing Address: P.O. Box 265, Mankato, 66956. Fax: 785-378-3913.
Church: Tel: 785-378-3939.

FORT RILEY, RILEY CO., FORT RILEY CATHOLIC COMMUNITY, Attended by, Archdiocese for the Military Services.

GLASCO, CLOUD CO., ST. MARY'S (1878), [CEM] Attended by, St. Patrick, Lincoln Rev. Msgr. James E. Hake, J.C.L.
Mailing Address: P.O. Box 327, Lincoln, 67455. Tel: 785-524-4823.
Church: 301 E. First St., P.O. Box 554, 67445.

GOODLAND, SHERMAN CO., OUR LADY OF PERPETUAL HELP (1887), Rev. Norbert Dlabal.
Church: 307 W. 13th, 67735. Tel: 785-890-7205; Fax: 785-890-7205.
Catechesis/Religious Program—Mary Ann Weishapl, D.R.E. Students 156.

GORHAM, RUSSELL CO., ST. MARY'S (1984), [CEM] Rev. Charles Steier, Supvr.; Sr. Mary Jo Thummel, C.S.J., Admin.
Res.: Box 135, 67640. Tel: 785-637-5241.
Catechesis/Religious Program—Students 23.

GRAINFIELD, GOVE CO., ST. AGNES (1910), (German), [JC] Attended by, Sacred Heart, Park. Rev. Mark Berland.
Mailing Address: P.O. Box 78, Park, 67751-0078. Tel: 785-673-4684.
Catechesis/Religious Program—Tel: 785-673-5510. Janice Manhart, D.R.E. Students 56.

GREENLEAF, WASHINGTON CO., SACRED HEART (1890), [CEM] Attended by, St. John the Baptist, Hanover. Rev. James Hoover.
Mailing Address: P.O. Box 395, Hanover, 66945. Tel: 785-337-2207.
Church: Tel: 785-747-2862.

GRINNELL, GOVE CO., IMMACULATE CONCEPTION (1888), (German), [CEM] Attended by, St. Joseph's Oakley. Rev. Roger K. Meitl, Parish Dir. & Pastoral Admin.
Mailing Address: 625 Freeman Ave., Oakley, 67748. Tel: 785-672-3828.
Church: Tel: 785-824-3221.
Catechesis/Religious Program—Fax: 785-824-3388. Sr. Kenneth Struckhoff, C.S.A., D.R.E. Students 61.

GYPSUM, SALINE CO., ST. PATRICK'S, Attended by, Immaculate Conception, Solomon. Rev. John A. Wolesky; Daylene Tracy, Pastoral Admin.

HANOVER, WASHINGTON CO., ST. JOHN THE BAPTIST (1868), (Bohemian), [CEM] Rev. James Hoover.
Res.: Box 395, 66945. Tel: 785-337-2207; Fax: 785-337-8974.
School—(Grades 1-8) Tel: 785-337-2368. Mr. Timothy Rundle, Prin. Lay Teachers 7; Students 92.
Catechesis/Religious Program—Students 138.

HAYS, ELLIS CO.
1—IMMACULATE HEART OF MARY (1967), [JC] Revs. Kevin Weber; David Metz; Francisco Montoya.
Res.: 1805 Vine, 67601. Tel: 785-625-7339; Fax: 785-625-7643.
Catechesis/Religious Program—Joseph Unrein Jr., D.R.E.; Pat Legleiter, D.R.E. Students 326.
2—ST. JOSEPH'S (1876), [JC] Rev. Gilmary Tallman, O.F.M.Cap.; Jane Vanek, Pastoral Admin. In Res., Revs. Felix Petrovsky, O.F.M.Cap.; Earl Befort, O.F.M.Cap.; Bennett Collucci.
Res.: P.O. Drawer 1000, 67601. Tel: 785-625-7356; Fax: 785-625-7394.
School— See separate listing under Grade Schools, Inter-Parochial in the Institution section.
Catechesis/Religious Program—Martha A. Brungardt, D.R.E. Students 137.
3—ST. NICHOLAS OF MYRA (1983), Jeanie Munsch, Pastoral Admin.; Rev. William J. Surmeier; Jennifer Willems, Pastoral Assoc.
Office & Mailing Address: 2901 E. 13th, 67601. Tel: 785-628-1446; Fax: 785-628-6627.
Res.: 2405 A Henry Dr., 67601. Tel: 785-628-6658.
Catechesis/Religious Program—Tel: 785-628-2188. Deb Eller. Students 165.

HERINGTON, DICKINSON CO., ST. JOHN THE EVANGELIST, [CEM]
Rev. Mark Wesely.
Res.: 712 N. Broadway, 67449. Tel: 785-258-2013.
Catechesis/Religious Program—Judy Zimmer, D.R.E. Students 79.

HERNDON, RAWLINS CO., ASSUMPTION (1880), (German), [CEM] Attended by, Sacred Heart, Atwood. Rev. Damian Richards.
Mailing Address: 508 N. Railroad Ave., Atwood, 67730. Tel: 785-626-3335; Fax: 785-626-3431.
Church: P.O. Box 247, 67739. Tel: 785-322-5560.
Catechesis/Religious Program—Students 31.

HILL CITY, GRAHAM CO., IMMACULATE HEART OF MARY (1958), Rev. Donald P. McCarthy.
Res.: 110 N. 10th Ave., 67642. Tel: 785-421-2535.
Catechesis/Religious Program—Tel: 785-421-2665. Joyce Tauber, D.R.E. Students 94.

HOLYROOD, ELLSWORTH CO., ST. MARY'S (1886), Attended by, St. Bernard's, Ellsworth. Rev. Daniel L. Scheetz.
Mailing Address: 911 Kansas, Ellsworth, 67439. Tel: 785-472-3136.

HOPE, DICKINSON CO., ST. PHILLIP'S, Attended by, St. John's, Herington. Rev. Mark Wesely.
Mailing Address: 712 N. Broadway, Herington, 67449. Tel: 785-258-2013.
Church: 67451. Tel: 785-366-7353.
Catechesis/Religious Program—Judy Zimmer, D.R.E. Students 43.

HOXIE, SHERIDAN CO., ST. FRANCES XAVIER CABRINI (1948), [CEM] Rev. Benjamin Saw (Burma).
Res.: 924 N. 17th, Box 38, 67740. Tel: 785-675-3300; Fax: 785-675-2235.
Catechesis/Religious Program—Verlene Feldt, D.R.E. Twinned with St. Martin's, Seguin, Hoxie, KS. Students 131.

JAMESTOWN, CLOUD CO., ST. MARY'S (1873), Closed., For sacramental records contact Our Lady of Perpetual Help, Concordia.

JUNCTION CITY, GEARY CO., ST. FRANCIS XAVIER'S (1867), [CEM] Rev. Aloysius Brungardt.
Res.: 218 N. Washington, P.O. Box 399, 66441. Tel: 785-238-2998; Fax: 785-238-4731.
School—(Grades PreK-8), 280 N. Jefferson St., 66441. Tel: 785-238-3867. Mr. Bob Diepenbrock, Prin. (Principal of Elementary and High School).. Lay Teachers 8; Students 84.
High School—Lay Teachers 13; Students 80.
Catechesis/Religious Program—Tel: 785-238-2841; Fax: 785-238-5021. Students 118.

KANOPOLIS, ELLSWORTH CO., ST. IGNATIUS LOYOLA (1947), (Mexican), [JC] Attended by, St. Bernard's, Ellsworth. Rev. Daniel L. Scheetz.
Mailing Address: 911 Kansas, Ellsworth, 67439. Tel: 785-472-3136.
Church: Tel: 785-472-4628.
Catechesis/Religious Program—127 N. Missouri. Students 25.

KIMEO, WASHINGTON CO., ST. MICHAEL'S, Closed., For inquiries for parish records contact St. John's, Hanover.

LEOVILLE, DECATUR CO., IMMACULATE CONCEPTION (1885), [CEM] Attended by, Sacred Heart Parish, Oberlin. Rev. George Kochuvelikkakam, C.M.I., Sacramental Priest; Deacon Stan Chapin.
Mailing Address: P.O. Box 57, Selden, 67757. Tel: 785-386-4496; Fax: 785-386-4445.
Church: Tel: 785-386-4409.
Catechesis/Religious Program—Jill Reichert, D.R.E. Students 44.

LINCOLN, LINCOLN CO., ST. PATRICK'S (1870), [CEM 2] Rev. Msgr. James E. Hake, J.C.L.
Res.: 206 N. Fifth, Box 327, 67455. Tel: 785-524-4823.
Catechesis/Religious Program—Tel: 785-524-3043. Mary Byarlay, D.R.E. Students 62.

LOGAN, PHILLIPS CO., ST. JOHN'S (1878), [CEM] Attended by, SS Philip & James, Philipsburg. Rev. Allen Scheer.
Mailing Address: P.O. Box 128, 67646. Tel: 785-689-4299.
Catechesis/Religious Program—Tel: 785-689-4299. Mary Sparks, D.R.E. Students 40.

MANHATTAN, RILEY CO.
1—ST. ISIDORE (1963), Rev. Keith Weber.
Res.: 711 Denison Ave., 66502. Tel: 785-539-7496; Fax: 785-539-0220.
2—SEVEN DOLORS (1880), Revs. Lawrence E. Grennan; Michael Elanjimattathil, C.M.I. (India).
Res.: 731 Pierre St., Box 844, 66502. Tel: 785-565-5000; Fax: 785-565-5003.
School—(Grades PreK-8), 306 S. Juliette, 66502. Tel: 785-565-5050; Fax: 785-565-5055. Tom Schmitz, Prin. Lay Teachers 19; Students 269.
Catechesis/Religious Program—Rosie Rundell, D.R.E.; Maggie Haag, D.R.E.; Jolene Amtower, D.R.E.; Adele Morales, D.R.E. Students 165.
3—ST. THOMAS MORE PARISH (1981), Rev. Donald Zimmerman.
Church Office: 2900 Kimball Ave., 66502. Tel: 785-776-5151; Fax: 785-776-5219.
Catechesis/Religious Program—Tel: 785-776-1398. Students 337.

MANKATO, JEWELL CO., ST. THERESA OF INFANT JESUS (1949), [CEM] Rev. Daryl Olmstead.
Res.: 422 N. Commercial, Box 265, 66956. Tel: 785-378-3939; Fax: 785-378-3913.

MCDOWELL, GEARY CO., ST. JOSEPH, Closed. For inquiries for parish records contact the chancery.

MEREDITH, CLOUD CO., ST. PETER'S, Closed., Sacramental records are located at St. Peter.

MILTONVALE, CLOUD CO., ST. ANTHONY'S (1910), Attended by, SS. Peter and Paul, Clay Center. , Mailing Address: 730 Court St., Clay Center, 67432. Tel: 785-632-5011; Fax: 785-632-3914.
Church: Tel: 785-427-2263.

MINNEAPOLIS, OTTAWA CO., IMMACULATE CONCEPTION OF THE BLESSED VIRGIN MARY, Rev. Kenneth Lohrmeyer.
Res.: 216 Cherry St., Box 167, 67467. Tel: 785-392-2079; 785-392-2013 (Church Hall).
Catechesis/Religious Program—Students 80.

MORROWVILLE, WASHINGTON CO., SS. PETER AND PAUL (1887), [CEM] Attended by, St. Augustine's, Washington. Rev. James Hoover; Sr. Marilyn Wall, C.S.J., Pastoral Admin.
410 B St., Washington, 66968. Tel: 785-325-2346; Fax: 785-325-3147.

MUNDEN, REPUBLIC CO., ST. GEORGE'S (1887), (Czech), [CEM] Attended by, St. Edward's, Belleville. Rev. Ralph Aschenbrenner.
Mailing Address: P.O. Box 99, Belleville, 66935.

MUNJOR, ELLIS CO., ST. FRANCIS OF ASSISI (1876), [CEM] Rev. William J. Surmeier, Canonical Pastor/ Sacramental Min.; Mrs. Lilly Binder, Pastoral Admin.
Church: 883 Moscow, 67601. Tel: 785-625-5314.

NEW ALMELO, NORTON CO., ST. JOSEPH'S (1874), [CEM] Attended by, St. Francis of Assisi, Norton. Rev. Vincent Thu Laing; Deacon Stan Chapin.
Res. & Mailing Address: HCR 1, P.O. Box 175, 67645-9742. Tel: 785-567-4875; Fax: 785-567-4261.

NILES, OTTAWA CO., SACRED HEART, Closed., Sacramental records are located at Immaculate Conception.

NORTON, NORTON CO., ST. FRANCIS OF ASSISI (1878), Rev. Vincent Thu Laing.
Res.: 108 S. Wabash, Box 148, 67654. Tel: 785-877-2234.
Catechesis/Religious Program—Jennifer Terrell, D.R.E. Students 131.
Mission—St. Joseph's Church HC-1 Box 175, New Almelo, Norton Co. 67652. Tel: 785-567-4875.

OAKLEY, LOGAN CO., ST. JOSEPH'S (1890), [CEM] Rev. Roger K. Meitl.
Res.: 625 Freeman Ave., 67748. Tel: 785-672-3828.
School—(Grades K-5), 725 Freeman Ave., 67748. Tel: 785-672-4451; Fax: 785-672-3819. Kimberly Shirley, Prin. Priests 1; Lay Teachers 7; Students 56.
Catechesis/Religious Program—St. Joseph Parish Annex, 405 E. Seventh, 67748. Tel: 785-672-4443. Phyllis Temaat, D.R.E. Students 85.

OBERLIN, DECATUR CO., SACRED HEART (1888), [JC] Revs. George Kochuvelikkakam, C.M.I., Sacramental Priest; Roger Meitl, Canonical Pastor; Deacon Stan Chapin, Pastoral Admin.
Res.: 210 E. Washington, 67749. Tel: 785-475-3103.
Catechesis/Religious Program—Doris Pauls, D.R.E. Students 69.

OGDEN, RILEY CO., ST. PATRICK'S (1866), [CEM] Attended by, Seven Dolors, Manhattan.
Res.: P.O. Box A, 66517. Tel: 785-565-5090.

OSBORNE, OSBORNE CO., ST. ALOYSIUS (1881), [CEM] Rev. Roger W. Hough.
Res.: Box 267, 67437. Tel: 785-346-5582.
Catechesis/Religious Program—Brenda Henke, D.R.E. Students 118.
Mission—St. Mary's 1312 Prentice, Downs, Osborne Co. 67437. Tel: 785-454-3551.

PARK, GOVE CO., SACRED HEART (1898), (German), [CEM] Rev. Mark Berland.
Res.: P.O. Box 78, 67751. Tel: 785-673-4684.
Catechesis/Religious Program—Dena Goetz, D.R.E. Students 85.

PFEIFER, ELLIS CO., HOLY CROSS, Closed., For sacramental records contact St. Fidelis, Victoria.

PHILLIPSBURG, PHILLIPS CO., SS. PHILIP AND JAMES (1875), Rev. Allen Scheer.
Res.: 690 S. 7th, 67661. Tel: 785-543-5577; 785-543-5367.
Catechesis/Religious Program—Patricia Dusin, D.R.E. Students 95.
Mission—St. Francis Claudell, Smith Co.

PLAINVILLE, ROOKS CO., SACRED HEART (1890), [CEM] Rev. Joseph Popelka.
Res.: 206 N. Washington, P.O. Box 100, 67663. Tel:

785-434-4658; Fax: 785-434-2480.
School—Tel: 785-434-2157. Sisters 1; Lay Teachers 6; Students 101.
Catechesis/Religious Program—Students 134.

RUSSELL, RUSSELL CO., ST. MARY'S (1886), [CEM] Rev. Charles Steier.
Res.: 28 N. Kansas St., 67665. Tel: 785-483-2871; Fax: 785-483-2871.
Catechesis/Religious Program—Tel: 785-483-2871. Bonita Ney, D.R.E. Students 123.

ST. FRANCIS, CHEYENNE CO., ST. FRANCIS (1912), (German), Rev. Beryl Gibson.
Res.: 625 S. River St., P.O. Box 1170, 67756. Tel: 785-332-2680.
Catechesis/Religious Program—Myra Douthit, D.R.E. Students 32.
Mission—St. Joseph's 203 N. Bird, Bird City, Cheyenne Co. 67731. Tel: 785-734-2287.
Mission—St. John's [JC] Rte. 2, Beardsley, Rawlins Co. 67756. Tel: 785-626-3946.

ST. JOSEPH, CLOUD CO., ST. JOSEPH'S, Closed., For sacramental records contact St. John the Baptist, Clyde.

ST. PETER, GRAHAM CO., ST. ANTHONY'S (1894), (German), Closed., For inquiries for parish records contact Christ the King, WaKeeney.

SCHOENCHEN, ELLIS CO., ST. ANTHONY'S (1877), [CEM] Attended by, St. Joseph's, Hays. Rev. Earl Befort, O.F.M.Cap.
Res.: 215 W. 13th, Hays, 67601. Tel: 785-625-7356; Fax: 785-625-7394.

SEGUIN, SHERIDAN CO., ST. MARTIN'S (1910), [CEM] Attended by, St. Frances Xavier Cabrini, Hoxie. Religious education twinned with St. Francis Xavier Cabrini, Hoxie, KS. , Mailing Address: P.O. Box 38, Hoxie, 67740. Tel: 785-675-3300; Fax: 785-675-2235.

SELDEN, SHERIDAN CO., SACRED HEART (1906), [CEM] Revs. Roger Meitl, Canonical Pastor; George Kochuvelikkakam, C.M.I., Sacramental Priest; Deacon Stan Chapin, Pastoral Admin.
Res.: 205 South Mission, P.O. Box 57, 67757. Tel: 785-475-3103.
Catechesis/Religious Program—Students 52.

SHARON SPRINGS, WALLACE CO., HOLY GHOST (1907), (German), Rev. Norbert Dlabal.
Res.: 403 N. Main St., 67758. Tel: 785-852-4984.
Catechesis/Religious Program—Shirley Blaesi, D.R.E. Students 62.
Mission—St. Peter Wallace, Wallace Co.

SMITH CENTER, SMITH CO., ST. MARY'S (1959), Attended by, St. Theresa, Mankato. Rev. Daryl Olmstead.
403 W. Hwy. 6, Box 263, 66967. Tel: 785-282-6888.
Catechesis/Religious Program—Mrs. Stacey Rempe, D.R.E. Students 64.

SOLOMON, DICKINSON CO., IMMACULATE CONCEPTION (1886), [CEM] Daylene Tracy, Pastoral Admin. In Res., Rev. John Wolesky.
Res.: 3599 N. Field Rd., P.O. Box 337, 67480. Tel: 785-655-2221; Fax: 785-655-2221.
Catechesis/Religious Program—Marcia Ryan, D.R.E. Students 40.

STOCKTON, ROOKS CO., ST. THOMAS (1878), (German), [CEM] Attended by, Sacred Heart, Plainville. Rev. Joseph Popelka.
Res.: 206 N. Washington, P.O. Box 100, Plainville, 67663. Tel: 785-434-4658; Fax: 785-434-2480.
Catechesis/Religious Program—Joanie Bellerive, D.R.E. Students 72.

TIPTON, MITCHELL CO., ST. BONIFACE'S (1874), [CEM] Rev. Albert DeSanctis.
Res.: P.O. Box 87, 67485. Tel: 785-373-4455.
High School—Tel: 785-373-5635. Priests 1; Lay Teachers 5; Students 32.
Catechesis/Religious Program—Janell Streit, Coord. Students 93.

VICTORIA, ELLIS CO., ST. FIDELIS (1876), (German—Russian), [CEM] Rev. David Gottschalk, O.F.M.Cap.
Church Office: 601 10th St., 67671. Tel: 785-735-2777.
Res.: 900 Cathedral Ave., 67671. Tel: 785-735-2777; 785-735-9456; Fax: 785-735-9455.
Catechesis/Religious Program—Tel: 785-735-9244. Shirley Brungardt, D.R.E. Students 147.

VINCENT, ELLIS CO., ST. BONIFACE (1904), (German—Russian), [CEM] Attended by, St. Fidelis, Victoria. Rev. David Gottschalk, O.F.M.Cap.
601 10th St., Victoria, 67671. Tel: 785-735-2777; 785-735-9456; Fax: 785-735-2779.

WAKEENEY, TREGO CO., CHRIST THE KING (1933), [CEM] Rev. Donald F. Pfannenstiel.
Res.: 412 N. Ninth St., 67672. Tel: 785-743-2330.
Catechesis/Religious Program—Tel: 785-743-2339. Verna Flax, D.R.E. Students 168.

WALKER, ELLIS CO., ST. ANN'S (1904), (German—Russian), [CEM] Attended by, St. Fidelis, Victoria. , Mailing Address: 601 10th St., Victoria, 67671. Tel: 785-735-2777; Fax: 785-735-2779.
Catechesis/Religious Program— Twinned with St. Fidelis Victoria.

WALLACE, WALLACE CO., ST. PETER'S (1877), Closed., For sacramental records contact Our Lady of Perpetual Help, Goodland.

WASHINGTON, WASHINGTON CO., ST. AUGUSTINE'S (1946), [JC] Rev. James Hoover; Sr. Marilyn Wall, C.S.J., Pastoral Admin.
Res.: 410 B St., 66968. Tel: 785-325-2346; Fax: 785-325-3147.
Catechesis/Religious Program— Twinned with SS. Peter & Paul, Morrowville, Washington, KS., and Sacred Heart, Greenleaf, Hanover KS. Cindy Kongs, Contact Person. Students 99.

WILSON, ELLSWORTH CO., ST. WENCESLAUS (1882), (Slovak), [CEM] Rev. Jerome Morgan.
Res.: P.O. Box 528, 67490. Tel: 785-658-3361; Fax: 785-658-3364.
Catechesis/Religious Program—Tel: 785-658-3474. Michelle Staudinger, D.R.E. Students 58.
Mission—St. Joseph P.O. Box 528, Dorrance, Russell Co. 67490.

ZURICH, ROOKS CO., ST. ANN'S (1886), [CEM] Closed., For sacramental records contact Sacred Heart, Plainville.

On Duty Outside the Diocese:
Rev.—
Dallen, James, W. 818 21st Ave., Spokane, WA 99203.

Retired:
Rev. Msgrs.—
Girard, Armand, 2150 Westchester, #3, Manhattan, 66503.
Kruse, Clement, Priest Retirement Center, 6900 E 45th N Street, Apt. F1, Bel Aire, 67226.
Lemoine, Vincent P., 426 Main St., P.O. Box 224, Osborne, 67473.
Weber, John George, McCall Manor, 626 S 3rd, 67401.
Revs.—
Dion, Maurice B., 214 E. North St., Hanover, 66945.
Grennan, James, 403 Barton St., Kussell, 67665.
Kilian, William T., St. Joseph Church, P.O. Box 68, Damar, 67632.
Kramer, Carl, New Horizons, 2225 Canterbury Road - Apt. 213, Hays, 67601.
Lahey, John, McCall Manor, 626 S 3rd #306, 67401.
Long, Melvin, P.O. Box 4350, Palm Springs, CA 92263-4350.
Lutgen, Richard, 100 W. 6th, Apt. 2, P.O. Box 271, Solomon, 67480-0271.
Mattas, Louis, 410 Jefferson, Abilene, 67410.
Moeder, August L., P.O. Box 74, 217 Grant, Quinter, 67752.
Moeder, John, 1414 N. Kuney St., P,O, Box 265, Abilene, 67410.
Pierce, Larry E., P.O. Box 237, Oakley, 67748.
Scheetz, Joseph, 510 Easter Ave., WaKeeney, 67672.
Torrez, Basil, P.O. Box 214, Collyer, 67631.
Walsh, John E., Sheridan Estates, 2025 Sheridan Ave., Apt. 9, Hoxie, 67740.
Werth, Alvin, 501 W. 37th #11, Hays, 67601.
Werth, Loren, 1725 Winne Dr., Manhattan, 66502.

INSTITUTIONS LOCATED IN THE DIOCESE

[A] HIGH SCHOOLS, INTER-PAROCHIAL

SALINA. *Sacred Heart Junior-Senior High School*, 234 E. Cloud, 67401. Tel: 785-827-4422; Fax: 785-827-8648. Email: heart@sacredheartknights.org. Web: www.sacredheartknights.org. John Krajicek, Prin. Sisters 1; Lay Teachers 18; Total 254.

[B] HIGH SCHOOLS, PRIVATE

HAYS. *Thomas More Prep-Marian*, 1701 Hall, 67601. Tel: 785-625-6577; Fax: 785-625-3912. Email: rossj@tmp-m.org. Web: www.tmp-m.org. Jean Ross, Pres.
Legal Title: *Thomas More Prep-Marian High Inc.*, Four-year Catholic High School, with college preparatory programs conducted by the local Catholic parishes; residency programs for boys and girls; special program for candidates for Priesthood and Religious Life. Sisters 1; Priests 1; Lay Teachers 29; Students 259; Total Staff 32.
Endowment Foundation of Thomas More Prep-Marian, Inc. Robert Wolf, Pres.
Thomas More Prep-Marian Alumni Assoc., 1701 Hall, 67601. Rev. Earl Befort, O.F.M.Cap., Pres.

[C] GRADE SCHOOLS, INTER-PAROCHIAL

HAYS. *Holy Family Grade School*, (Grades K-6), 1800 Milner, 67601-3796. Tel: 785-625-3131; Fax: 785-625-2098. Email: holyfamily@eaglecom.net. Web: www.hfehays.org. Melanie Moeder, Prin. Lay Teachers 17; Students 266.

[D] HOMES FOR AGED

HAYS. *St. John's New Horizons*, 2225 Canterbury, 67601. Tel: 785-628-8742; Fax: 785-625-3973. Web: stjohnsresthome.com. Vicki Frohling, Operator; Sr. Vera Bittel. Residents 47; Independent Living Apartments 4; Assisted Living Units 39; Total Staff 29.
St. John's of Hays, 2401 Canterbury, 67601. Tel: 785-628-3241; Fax: 785-628-3310. Joe Hess, Chairperson; Duane Everding, Admin.; Rev. Earl Befort, O.F.M.Cap., Chap.; Sr. Mary Ann Schippers, C.S.A., Pastoral Care. Bed Capacity 60; Total Staff 70.

MANHATTAN. *St. Joseph Village, Inc.* Owned & operated by the Via Christi Health System of Wichita. , 2800 Willow Grove, 66502. Tel: 785-539-7671 Fax: 785-539-9125. Email: dfrihart@via.christi.org. Web: www.via-christi.org/stjosephvillage. Total Staff 105; Residents 60.

VICTORIA. *St. John's Rest Home*, 701 Seventh St., 67671. Tel: 785-735-2208. Residents 90.

[E] MONASTERIES AND RESIDENCES OF PRIESTS AND BROTHERS

HAYS. *St. Joseph's Friary*, P.O. Drawer 1000, 67601. Tel: 785-625-7356; Fax: 785-625-7394. Revs. Gilmary Tallman, O.F.M.Cap.; Bennett Collucci, O.F.M.Cap.; Earl Befort, O.F.M.Cap. In Res. Revs. Earl Befort, O.F.M.Cap.; Bennett Collucci, O.F.M.Cap.; Felix Petrovsky, O.F.M.Cap.

VICTORIA. *St. Fidelis Friary* 67671. Tel: 785-735-9456; Fax: 785-735-9455. Most Rev. Firmin Schmidt, O.F.M.Cap.; Revs. Maris Goetz, O.F.M.Cap.; Dave Gottschalk, O.F.M.Cap.; Berard Tomassetti, O.F.M.Cap.; Gregory Beyer, O.F.M.Cap. (DEN); Bro. Augustine Rohde, O.F.M.Cap. Total in Residence 6.

[F] CONVENTS AND RESIDENCES FOR SISTERS

SALINA. *Medaille Center*, 148 N. Oakdale St., 67401. Tel: 785-827-3685. Email: medaille@cox.net. Sr. Mary Jean Assell, Coord. & Contact Person. Sisters of St. Joseph Sisters 15.

CONCORDIA. *Nazareth Convent & Academy Corporation Sisters of St. Joseph of Concordia*, Administration Offices, 215 Court St., P.O. Box 279, 66901. Tel: 785-243-2149; Fax: 785-243-4741. Email: csjcenter@dustdevil.com. Web: www.csj.kansas.org. Sr. Patricia McLennon, C.S.J., Pres., Nazareth Motherhouse for the Sisters of St. Joseph; Rev. Curtis E. Van Del, S.J., Chap.; Sr. Lucille Herman, C.S.J., Contact Person. Professed Sisters 198; Novices 5; In Community 203.
Saint Joseph Foundation for Apostolic and Charitable Purposes Tel: 785-243-2149; Fax: 785-243-4741.

[G] RETREAT CENTERS

CONCORDIA. *Manna House of Prayer*, 323 E. Fifth St., Box 675, 66901. Tel: 785-243-4428; Fax: 785-243-4321. Email: mannahse@dustdevil.com. Web: www.mannahouse.org. Sr. Bette Suther, C.S.J., Admin. Total Staff 12; Total in Residence 7.

VICTORIA. *Capuchin Center for Spiritual Life*, 900 Cathedral Ave., 67671. Tel: 913-735-9393; Fax: 913-735-9455. Email: ccsl@ruraltel.net. Bro. Augustine Rohde, O.F.M.Cap.

[H] CAMPUS MINISTRY

HAYS. *Comeau Catholic Campus Center at Fort Hays State University* Office: 506 W. Sixth, 67601. Tel: 785-625-7396. Email: comeauccc@yahoo.com. Rev. Fred Gatschet, Chap. Total Staff 2.

MANHATTAN. *St. Isidore's Catholic Student Center* , Kansas State University. , 711 Denison Ave., 66502. Tel: 785-539-7496. Email: stisidor@flinthills.com. Web: www.flinthills.com/~st.isidor. Total Staff 4; Total in Residence 1. In Res. Rev. Keith Weber, Chap.

[I] MISCELLANEOUS

SALINA. *St. Joseph Annex, Inc.*, 401 W. Iron; P.O. Box 980, 67401. Tel: 785-827-8746; Fax: 785-827-6133. Rev. Jerome Morgan.
Marymount Memorial Educational Trust Fund, P.O. Box 980, 67402-0980. Tel: 785-827-8746; Fax: 785-827-6133. Email: chancery@salinadiocese.org. Most Rev. George K. Fitzsimons, D.D., Trustee.
Sacred Heart Junior-Senior School Endowment Fund, 234 E. Cloud, 67401-6436. Tel: 785-827-8648; Fax: 785-827-8442. Email: heart@

sacredheartknights.org. Web: www.sacredheartknights.org. Kim Cochran.

Salina Catholic Diocese Education Endowment, Inc., 103 N. Ninth St., P.O. Box 980, 67402-0980. Tel: 785-827-8746; Fax: 785-827-6133. Email: chancery@salinadiocese.org.

Salina Catholic Diocese Gift & Annuity Fund, Inc., 103 N. Ninth St., P.O. Box 980, 67402-0980. Tel: 785-827-8746; Fax: 785-827-6133. Email: chancery@salinadiocese.org.

Salina Catholic Diocese Seminary Burses, Inc., 103 N. Ninth St., P.O. Box 980, 67402-0980. Tel: 785-827-8746; Fax: 785-827-6133. Email: chancery@salinadiocese.org.

Salina Diocesan Clergy Health and Retirement Association, Inc., Diocese of Salina, P.O. Box 980, 67402-0980. Tel: 785-827-8746; Fax: 785-827-6133. Most Rev. George K. Fitzsimons, D.D., Pres.

RELIGIOUS INSTITUTES OF MEN REPRESENTED IN THE DIOCESE

For further details refer to the corresponding bracketed number in the Religious Institutes of Men or Women section.

[0470]—*The Capuchin Friars* (Province of Mid-America)—O.F.M.Cap.

[0275]—*Carmelites of Mary Immaculate* (Provincial House - Kerala, India)—C.M.I.

[]—*Jesuits* (Missouri Prov. of Jesuits. St. Louis, MO)—S.J.

[0200]—*Monks of St. Benedict* (Conception, MO)—O.S.B.

[]—*Vincentian Congregation* (St. Joseph Prov. of the Vincentian Congregation - Kerala, India)—V.C.

RELIGIOUS INSTITUTES OF WOMEN REPRESENTED IN THE DIOCESE

[3710]—*Congregation of the Sisters of Saint Agnes*—C.S.A.

[1070-24]—*Dominican Sisters*—O.P.

[]—*Missionary Sisters of the Holy Spirit & the Holy Family*

[3830-15]—*Sisters of St. Joseph*—C.S.J.

NECROLOGY

† Sinner, Rev. Msgr. Emil E., (Retired)—Died Sept. 12, 2003

† Sterrett, Bradley, Manhattan, KS St. Isidore—Died April 16, 2003

Diocese of Salt Lake City

(Dioecesis Civitatis Lacus Salsi)

Most Reverend

GEORGE H. NIEDERAUER, D.D., PH.D.

Bishop of Salt Lake City; ordained April 30, 1962; appointed Bishop of Salt Lake City November 3, 1994; ordained January 25, 1995. *Office: 27 C St., Salt Lake City, UT 84103-2397.* Tel: 801-328-8641, Ext. 304; Fax: 801-328-0324.

Diocesan Offices and Organizations: 27 C St., Salt Lake City, UT 84103-2397. Tel: 801-328-8641; Fax: 801-328-9680.

Web: www.dioslc.org

ESTABLISHED AS A VICARIATE-APOSTOLIC ON NOV. 23, 1886.

Square Miles 84,990.

Erected a Diocese on January 27, 1891.

Originally comprised all Utah and the Counties of Eureka, Lander, Lincoln, White Pine, Nye, Elko and Clark in the State of Nevada. By Apostolic Constitution dated March 27, 1931, the Nevada section was separated from the Salt Lake Diocese and incorporated in the Reno Diocese. The name was changed to Diocese of Salt Lake City on March 31, 1951.

Comprises the State of Utah.

Patron of the Diocese of Salt Lake City: St. Mary Magdalene.

Legal Title: For legal titles of parishes and diocesan institutions, consult the Chancery Office.

STATISTICAL OVERVIEW

Personnel	
Bishop	1
Abbots	1
Retired Abbots	1
Priests: Diocesan Active in Diocese	40
Priests: Diocesan Active Outside Diocese	2
Priests: Diocesan in Foreign Missions	1
Priests: Retired, Sick or Absent	13
Number of Diocesan Priests	56
Religious Priests in Diocese	30
Total Priests in Diocese	86
Extern Priests in Diocese	8
Ordinations:	
Diocesan Priests	1
Transitional Deacons	1
Permanent Deacons in Diocese	43
Total Brothers	11
Total Sisters	50
Parishes	
Parishes	47
With Resident Pastor:	
Resident Diocesan Priests	30
Resident Religious Priests	9
Without Resident Pastor:	
Administered by Priests	3
Administered by Deacons	2
Administered by Religious Women	1
Administered by Lay People	2
Missions	16
Professional Ministry Personnel:	
Brothers	1
Sisters	6
Lay Ministers	27
Welfare	
Homes for the Aged	1
Total Assisted	1,084
Day Care Centers	12
Total Assisted	385
Special Centers for Social Services	3
Total Assisted	205,227
Educational	
Diocesan Students in Other Seminaries	10
Total Seminarians	10
High Schools, Diocesan and Parish	3
Total Students	1,709
Elementary Schools, Diocesan and Parish	11
Total Students	3,806
Catechesis/Religious Education:	
High School Students	1,477
Elementary Students	6,575
Total Students under Catholic Instruction	13,577
Teachers in the Diocese:	
Priests	5
Lay Teachers	390
Vital Statistics	
Receptions into the Church:	
Infant Baptism Totals	3,894
Adult Baptism Totals	403
Received into Full Communion	243
First Communions	2,614
Confirmations	1,436
Marriages:	
Catholic	420
Interfaith	194
Total Marriages	614
Deaths	569
Total Catholic Population	150,000
Total Population	2,316,256

Former Bishops—Rt. Revs. LAWRENCE SCANLAN, D.D., ord. June 24, 1868; appt. Vicar-Apostolic of Utah, Jan. 25, 1887; consecrated Titular Bishop of Larandum, June 29, 1887; named first Bishop of Salt Lake, Jan. 30, 1891; died May 10, 1915; JOSEPH S. GLASS, C.M., D.D., LL.D., ord. Aug. 15, 1897; consecrated Aug. 24, 1915; died Jan. 26, 1926; Most Revs. JOHN J. MITTY, D.D., ord. Dec. 22, 1906; consecrated Sept. 8, 1926; made Coadjutor Archbishop of San Francisco, cum jure successionis, Feb. 4, 1932; Titular Archbishop of Egina; succeeded to the See, March 5, 1935; died Oct. 15, 1961; JAMES E. KEARNEY, D.D., ord. Sept. 19, 1908; appt. July 4, 1932; consecrated Oct. 28, 1932; appt. Bishop of Rochester, July 31, 1937; installed Nov. 11, 1937; died Jan. 12, 1977; LEO J. STECK, D.D., ord. June 8, 1924; appt. Auxiliary Bishop of Salt Lake, March 3, 1948; consecrated Titular Bishop of Ilium, May 20, 1948; died June 19, 1950; DUANE G. HUNT, D.D., LL.D., ord. June 27, 1920; appt. Aug. 6, 1937; consecrated Oct. 28, 1937; appt. assistant at the Pontifical Throne; appt. May 25, 1946; died March 31, 1960; JOSEPH LENNOX FEDERAL, D.D. (Retired), ord. Dec. 8, 1934; appt. Auxiliary Bishop of Salt Lake City, Feb. 5, 1951; consecrated April 11, 1951; made Coadjutor Bishop of Salt Lake City, May 8, 1958; succeeded to the See, March 31, 1960; retired April 1980; died Aug. 31, 2000; WILLIAM KEITH WEIGAND, D.D., ord. May 25, 1963; appt. Sept. 3, 1980; ord. Bishop, Nov. 17, 1980; transferred to the See of Sacramento; installed Jan. 27, 1994.

Diocesan Pastoral Center—27 C St., Salt Lake City, 84103-2397. Tel: 801-328-8641; Fax: 801-328-9680.

Office of the Bishop—SHIRLEY MARES, Exec. Asst. Tel: 801-328-8641, Ext. 304; Fax: 801-328-0324.

Vicar General and Moderator of the Curia—Rev. Msgr. J. TERRENCE FITZGERALD. Tel: 801-328-8641, Ext. 305.

Chancellor—Deacon SILVIO MAYO. Tel: 801-328-8641, Ext. 315.

Vice Chancellor—Rev. LANGES J. SILVA. Tel: 801-328-8641, Ext. 312.

Diocesan Offices

Apostleship of Prayer—Rev. MATTHEW O. WIXTED, Dir., 15 S. 7th St., Tooele, 84074. Tel: 435-882-3860.

Archives—GARY TOPPING, Dir. Tel: 801-328-8641, Ext. 343.

Campus Ministry—Sr. MARYLIN MARK, O.S.B.

Catholic Community Services—NILE W. EATMON, Bd. Pres.; MAGGIE ST. CLAIRE, Exec. Dir., 2570 W. 1700 S., Salt Lake City, 84104. Tel: 801-977-9119; Fax: 801-977-8227.

Catholic Foundation of Utah—PETER SCHOLTE, Pres.; KURT SIMPSON, Exec. Dir. Tel: 801-328-8641, Ext. 306.

Catholic Relief Services—Deacon SILVIO MAYO. Tel: 801-328-8641, Ext. 315.

Catholic Schools Offices—Sr. CATHERINE KAMPHAUS, C.S.C., Supt. Tel: 801-328-8641, Ext. 330; MARY MONTANO, Sec. Tel: 801-328-8641, Ext. 329.

Cemetery--Mount Calvary—CURT ROSENTRETER, Dir. Tel: 801-355-2476; Fax: 801-328-3294; Deacon RICARDO ARIAS, Sec.

Chancery—KRISTINE MULHOLLAND, Sec. Tel: 801-328-8641, Ext. 317.

College of Consultors—Rev. Msgrs. ROBERT J. BUSSEN; J. TERRENCE FITZGERALD; ROBERT R. SERVATIUS; Revs. COLIN F. BIRCUMSHAW; HERNANDO DIAZ; Very Rev. JOSEPH M. MAYO.

Communications Media Office—MONICA HOWA-JOHNSON. Tel: 801-328-8641, Ext. 344.

Deans—Revs. JAMES E. BLAINE, Wasatch Deanery; JOSEPH W. MORRIS, S.J., Eastern Deanery; MARTIN ROCK, S.J., Northern Deanery; Rev. Msgr. RUDOLPH DAZ, Salt Lake Deanery; Rev. MICHAEL I. WINTERER, Southwestern Deanery.

Development Office—KURT SIMPSON, Dir. Tel: 801-328-8641, Ext. 306.

Continuing Diaconate Formation—Sr. JEREMIA JANUSCHKA, O.S.B., Coord. Tel: 801-328-8641, Ext. 327.

Ministry for Health Care—Sr. M. GEORGITA CUNNINGHAM, R.S.M., Dir. Tel: 801-328-8641, Ext. 345.

Diocesan Development Drive—SHANNON MASHER, Dir. Tel: 801-328-8641, Ext. 328.

Diocesan Office for Persons with Disabilities—DANIEL JOHN. Tel: 801-328-8641, Ext. 326.

Diocesan Pastoral Council—MADALYN SEAMAN, Pres.

Ecumenical Commission—Rev. Msgr. VICTOR G. BONNELL; Rev. LANGES J. SILVA; Very Rev. JOSEPH M. MAYO.

Engaged Encounter—NATHAN PAINTER; CHRYSTAL PAINTER. Tel: 801-273-8557.

Family Life-Natural Family Planning—VEOLA MARTINEZ-BURCHETT. Tel: 801-328-8641, Ext. 324.

Finance Council—Most Rev. GEORGE H. NIEDERAUER, Ex Officio; Rev. Msgr. J. TERRENCE FITZGERALD; Rev. COLIN F. BIRCUMSHAW; MARY KAY GRIFFIN; O. YOGI GILLILAND; MICHAEL JOSEPH; Rev. MICHAEL LEE; JILL MORBY; JOAN LOFFREDO, C.P.A.; GEORGE BEATON.

Finance Office—JOAN LOFFREDO, C.P.A., Dir. Tel: 801-328-8641, Ext. 309; DEBRA CANDELARIA, Sec. Tel: 801-328-8641, Ext. 310.

Government Liaison—DEE ROWLAND. Tel: 801-328-8641, Ext. 336.

Hispanic Ministry—MARIA-CRUZ GRAY, Dir. Tel: 801-328-8641, Ext. 361; MARYLIN ACOSTA, Sec. Tel: 801-328-8641, Ext. 338.

Holy Childhood Association—Deacon SILVIO MAYO, Dir. Tel: 801-328-8641, Ext. 315.

Liturgy Office—MAXINE KAISER. Tel: 801-328-8641, Ext. 321; DEBRA ALIRES, Sec. Tel: 801-328-8641, Ext. 322.

Liturgical Commission—Rev. COLIN F. BIRCUMSHAW, Chm. Tel: 801-399-5627.

Correctional Institution Ministry— (State Prison) Rev. JAMES E. BLAINE, Dir., P.O. Box 142, American Fork, 84003. Tel: 801-756-7771; ILLA WRIGHT, Coord. Ministry Foe Salt Lake Valley Detention Center, Decker Lake, Wasatch Youth Center and Adult Detention Complex 3357 Enterada Ave., West Valley City, 84119. Tel: 801-969-5617; Rev. PATRICK H. ELLIOTT State Prison, Gunnison, ut.Tel: 801-328-8641.

Ministry to Priests Team— Clergy Continuing Education, Rev. WILLIAM FLEGGE, Dir., 1085 E. 700 S., Salt Lake City, 84102. Tel: 801-322-2330. Team: Revs. DANA PELOTTE, S.S.S.; DAVID J. BITTMENN; ANDRZEJ SKRZYPIEC.

Native American Ministry—Sr. M. GEORGITA CUNNINGHAM, R.S.M.

Newspaper—BARBARA S. LEE, Editor. Tel: 801-328-8641, Ext. 340. "Intermountain Catholic" Staff Writers: CHRIS YOUNG. Tel: 801-328-8641, Ext. 341; KASE JOHNSTUN. Tel: 801-328-8641, Ext. 378; CRIS PAULSEN, Mktg. Dir. & Circulation Mgr. Tel: 801-328-8641, Ext. 356; DON SCHAEFFER, Layout & Ad Sales Rep. Tel: 801-328-8641, Ext. 339; RICK PLAUTZ. Tel: 801-328-8641, Ext. 342; CHRISTOPHER GRAY.

Peace and Justice Commission—DEE ROWLAND, Dir. Tel: 801-328-8641, Ext. 336.

Presbyteral Council—Very Rev. JOSEPH M. MAYO, Pres.; Revs. MICHAEL R. SCIUMBATO, Vice Pres.; ROBERT T. MORIARTY, Sec.

Priests' Mutual Benefit Society (Retirement)—Most Rev. GEORGE H. NIEDERAUER, Chm. Ex Officio. Board of Directors: Rev. Msgrs. J. TERRENCE FITZGERALD, Vice Chm.; VICTOR G. BONNELL; JOHN J. SULLIVAN (Retired); Very Rev. JOSEPH M. MAYO; Revs. DONALD E. HOPE; COLIN F. BIRCUMSHAW.

Priests' Personnel Board—Most Rev. GEORGE H. NIEDERAUER; Rev. Msgr. J. TERRENCE FITZGERALD; Very Rev. JOSEPH M. MAYO; Revs. MICHAEL R. SCIUMBATO; COLIN F. BIRCUMSHAW; LANGES J. SILVA; KENNETH L. VIALPANDO.

Real Estate Office—RICHARD SALVITTI, Dir. Tel: 801-328-8641, Ext. 360.

Religious Education—DANIEL JOHN, Dir. Tel: 801-328-8641, Ext. 326.

Retreat House—Sr. DANILE KNIGHT, O.S.B., Dir., 1794 Lake St., Ogden, 84401. Tel: 801-392-9231; Fax: 801-612-9619.

Sisters' Council—Executive Team: Sisters STELLA MARIE ZAHNER, D.C.; M. GEORGITA CUNNINGHAM, R.S.M.; MIRIAM JOANNE FRANKENFIELD, C.S.C.; MARTHA ANN NORWOOD, C.S.C.; MARY LOUISE DEROIN, C.S.C.

Society for the Propagation of the Faith—Deacon SILVIO MAYO, Dir. Tel: 801-328-8641, Ext. 315.

Pastoral Operations—Rev. MICHAEL LEE, Dir. Tel: 801-328-8641, Ext. 364.

Special Needs Program Scholarship Assistance—Sisters STELLA MARIE ZAHNER, D.C. Tel: 801-328-8641, Ext. 334; CHARLOTTE CLARK, D.C. Tel: 801-328-8641, Ext. 357.

Spirituality Center—Sr. BRIDGET CLARE MCKEEVER, S.S.L., Ph.D., Dir. Tel: 801-328-8641, Ext. 362.

Tribunal—

Judicial Vicar—Rev. LANGES J. SILVA. Tel: 801-328-8641, Ext. 318.

Secretary & Notary—VIOLA SMITH. Tel: 801-328-8641, Ext. 316.

Adjutant Judicial Vicar—Rev. ROBERT T. MORIARTY. Tel: 801-984-7630.

Promoter of Justice—Rev. COLIN F. BIRCUMSHAW.

Defenders of the Bond—Rev. Msgrs. ROBERT R. SERVATIUS; J. TERRENCE FITZGERALD; JOHN J. SULLIVAN (Retired); Very Rev. JOSEPH M. MAYO.

Judges—Rev. Msgr. JOHN J. HEDDERMAN (Retired); Revs. ROBERT T. MORIARTY; LANGES J. SILVA.

Victim Assistance Coordinator—MONICA HOWA-JOHNSON. Tel: 801-328-8641, Ext. 344. Email: monica.howa-johnson@dioslc.org.

Vocation Office—Rev. COLIN F. BIRCUMSHAW. Tel: 801-328-8641, Ext. 358.

Youth and Young Adult Ministry—MARY FASIG, Dir. Tel: 801-328-8641, Ext. 313.

CLERGY, PARISHES, MISSIONS AND PAROCHIAL SCHOOLS

SALT LAKE CITY
(SALT LAKE COUNTY)

1—CATHEDRAL OF THE MADELEINE (1866), Very Rev. Joseph M. Mayo, Rector; Rev. Patrick H. Elliott; Deacons Lynn R. Johnson; Silvio Mayo. In Res., Rev. Langes J. Silva.
Res.: 331 E. S. Temple St., 84111. Tel: 801-328-8941; Fax: 801-364-6504.
School—Madeleine Choir School, Tel: 801-323-9850; Fax: 801-323-0581. Robin Giovacchini, Prin. Lay Teachers 18; Students 211.
Catechesis/Religious Program—Tel: 801-328-1241; Fax: 801-364-6504. Students 31.

2—ST. AMBROSE (1948), Rev. William F. Wheaton. In Res., Revs. Stanislaw Herba; James Semple.
Res.: 2315 Redondo Ave., 84108. Tel: 801-485-5610; Fax: 801-484-3642.
School—J. E. Cosgriff Memorial School, 2335 Redondo Ave., 84108. Tel: 801-486-3197; Fax: 801-484-8270. Mrs. Mary Lane Grisley, Prin. Lay Teachers 21; Students 298.
Catechesis/Religious Program—Tel: 801-485-9324; Fax: 801-484-1065. Students 273.

3—ST. ANN (1917), Rev. Colin F. Bircumshaw; Deacon Mansueto Flaim.
Res.: 2119 S. 400 E., 84115-2872. Tel: 801-487-1000; Fax: 801-487-1416.
School—430 E. 2100 S., 84105. Tel: 801-486-0741; Fax: 801-486-0742. Kathleen Hood, Prin. Lay Teachers 18; Students 350.
Catechesis/Religious Program—Tel: 801-261-5943. Students 175.

4—ST. CATHERINE OF SIENA (1981), Revs. Denis Reilly, O.P.; James D. Thompson, O.P.
Res.: 170 S. University, 84102. Tel: 801-359-6066; Fax: 801-359-4547.
Catechesis/Religious Program—Students 70.

5—OUR LADY OF GUADALUPE (1944), (Hispanic), Rev. Kenneth L. Vialpando; Deacons Hector Mota; Mario A. Rodriguez.
Res.: 715 W. 300 N., 84116. Tel: 801-364-2019; Fax: 801-359-2678.
Catechesis/Religious Program—Students 349.

6—OUR LADY OF LOURDES (1913), [CEM] Rev. William Flegge; Deacon Lowell Palm.
Res.: 1085 E. 700 S. St., 84102. Tel: 801-322-3330; Fax: 801-363-6007.
School—1065 E. 700 S. St., 84102. Tel: 801-364-5624; Fax: 801-364-0925. Cathy Moore, Prin. Lay Teachers 13; Students 237.
Catechesis/Religious Program—Tel: 801-322-3330; Fax: 801-363-6007. Students 17.

7—OUR LADY OF PERPETUAL HELP (1994), (Vietnamese),, (Vietnamese Parish) Rev. Thuy Dang Ha.
Mailing Address: P.O. Box 18306, 84118-0306. Tel: 801-968-8981.
Church and Res.: 5415 S. 4360 W., Kearns, 84118. Tel: 801-968-8981.
Catechesis/Religious Program—Students 139.

8—ST. PATRICK'S (1892), (Hispanic—Korean), Rev. David J. Bittmenn; Bro. Anthony Ornelas, S.S.S., Pastoral Assoc.; Deacons Otto Johansson; Sefo A. Manu; Dan Herron.
Res.: 1058 W. 400 S., 84104-1261. Tel: 801-596-7233; Fax: 801-363-3743.
Catechesis/Religious Program—Tel: 801-596-7255. Bro. Anthony Ornelas, S.S.S., D.R.E. Students 79.

9—SACRED HEART (1917), (Hispanic), Rev. Eugenio Yarce; Deacon Fernando L. Godina.
Res.: 948 S. 2nd East St., 84111. Tel: 801-363-8632; Fax: 801-363-1539.
Catechesis/Religious Program—174 E. 900 S., 84111. Students 250.

10—ST. THOMAS MORE (1981), Revs. David L. Van Massenhove; Paul J. McCarthy, S.J.; Deacon Steven W. Kirts.
Res. & Parish Center: 3015 E. Creek Rd., Sandy, 84093-6575. Tel: 801-942-5285 (Office); 801-942-7678 (Rectory); Fax: 801-942-5287.
Catechesis/Religious Program—Tel: 801-942-5285. Students 82.

11—ST. VINCENT DE PAUL (1925), Rev. Msgr. Francis Mannion, Admin. In Res., Rev. Thomas J. Kaiser (Retired).
Res.: 1375 E. Spring Ln., 84117. Tel: 801-272-9216; Fax: 801-273-1156.
School—(Grades PreK-8), 1385 E. Spring Ln., 84117. Tel: 801-277-6702; Fax: 801-424-0450. Mark Longe, Prin. Lay Teachers 26; Students 319.
Catechesis/Religious Program—Tel: 801-527-2037. Students 165.

SUBURBAN SALT LAKE CITY

1—BLESSED SACRAMENT (1972), Rev. Msgr. Robert R. Servatius; Rev. James A. Janda; Deacon Russell Langner.
Res.: 9757 S. 1700 E., Sandy, 84092. Tel: 801-571-5517 (Office); 801-576-1644 (Rectory); Fax: 801-571-2071.
School—1745 E. 9800 S., Sandy, 84092. Tel: 801-572-5311; Fax: 801-572-0251. Mrs. Judy Julian, Prin. Lay Teachers 16; Students 284.
Catechesis/Religious Program—1745 E. 9800 S., Sandy, 84092. Tel: 801-571-2071. Students 187.
Station—Our Lady of the Snows Alta.

2—ST. FRANCIS XAVIER (1955), Rev. Wayne F. Epperely, C.S.Sp. In Res., Rev. James Burnie, C.S.Sp.
Res.: P.O. Box 18631, Kearns, 84118. Tel: 801-968-2123; Fax: 801-966-1639.
School—Tel: 801-966-1571; Fax: 801-966-1369. See separate listing under Elementary Schools, Regional in the Diocese.
Catechesis/Religious Program—Tel: 801-968-2123, Ext. 413. Students 585.

3—IMMACULATE CONCEPTION (1890), Rev. Mark J. Krylowicz.
Res.: P.O. Box 151, Copperton, Bingham Canyon, 84006. Tel: 801-569-2706.
Catechesis/Religious Program—Students 78.

4—ST. JOSEPH THE WORKER (1969), Rev. Patrick F. Carley, Sacramental Min.; Sr. Fabian Uriot, S.A., Parochial Admin.; Deacon Mel J. Sanchez.
Res.: P.O. Box 98, West Jordan, 84084. Tel: 801-255-8902; Fax: 801-255-5003.
Catechesis/Religious Program—Tel: 801-561-4062. Students 251.

5—ST. JUDE (1975), (Maronite), [CEM] Rev. Gebran Bou-Merhi.
Res.: 4893 Wasatch St., Murray, 84107. Tel: 801-268-2820; Fax: 801-268-2820.
Catechesis/Religious Program—Fax: 801-268-4404. Students 20.

6—ST. MARTIN DE PORRES (1982), Rev. Jan Bednarz.
Mailing Address: 4976 Valois Cir., Taylorsville, 84118. Tel: 801-969-8857; Fax: 801-966-9675.
Church: 4914 S. 2200 W., Taylorsville, 84118. Tel: 801-968-2369.
Catechesis/Religious Program—Students 65.

7—OUR LADY OF LOURDES (1916), (English), [CEM] Rev. Andrzej Skrzypiec (Poland).
Res.: P.O. Box 38, Magna, 84044. Tel: 801-250-6349; Fax: 801-250-3860.
Catechesis/Religious Program—8585 W. 3010 S., Magna, 84044. Tel: 801-250-6052. Students 145.

8—SS. PETER AND PAUL (1972), Rev. Javier G. Virgen; Deacon Rick C. Huffman.
Mailing Address: P.O. Box 70308, West Valley City, 84170.
Res.: 3560 W. 3650 S. Lancer Way, West Valley City, 84170. Tel: 801-966-5111; 801-966-5119.
Catechesis/Religious Program—Tel: 801-969-7116; Fax: 801-966-2114. Students 99.

9—ST. THERESE OF THE CHILD JESUS (1925), (Spanish), Revs. Francisco Pires; Samuel Dinsdale; Deacon Stanley L. Stott.
Office—7832 S. Allen St., Midvale, 84047. Tel: 801-255-3721; Fax: 801-255-4516.
Res.: 7860 S. Allen St., Midvale, 84047. Tel: 801-561-6015.
Catechesis/Religious Program—Tel: 801-561-2495. Students 465.

OUTSIDE SALT LAKE CITY

AMERICAN FORK, UTAH CO., ST. PETER'S (1969), Rev. James E. Blaine.
Res.: 622 N. 600 East, 84003. Tel: 801-756-7771; Fax: 801-756-7768.
Catechesis/Religious Program—Tel: 801-756-2747. Students 113.

BOUNTIFUL, DAVIS CO., ST. OLAF (1944), Rev. Rudolph A. Daz; Deacon Reyhaldo Mhrind.
Res.: 276 E. 1700 South, 84010. Tel: 801-295-3621; Fax: 801-295-8261.
School—1793 S. Orchard Dr., 84010. Tel: 801-295-5341; Fax: 801-295-5915. Lay Teachers 14; Students 218.
Catechesis/Religious Program—Students 104.

BRIGHAM CITY, BOX ELDER CO., ST. HENRY (1950), Rev. F. Warren Schoeppe, S.J.; Deacons Robert W. Bambrick; Dick Werling.
Res.: P.O. Box 872, 84302. Tel: 435-723-2941; Fax: 435-723-1215.
Catechesis/Religious Program—Tel: 435-723-1215. Students 200.
Mission—Santa Ana 760 W. 600 N., Tremonton, Box Elder Co. 84337.

CEDAR CITY, IRON CO., CHRIST THE KING (1934), [JC] Rev. Michael J. Winterer.
Res.: 680 Cove Dr., P.O. Box 626, 84721. Tel: 435-586-8298; Fax: 435-865-5960.
Catechesis/Religious Program—Students 140.
Mission—St. Gertrude Panguitch Lake Rd., Panguitch, Garfield Co. 84759.
Mission—St. Sylvester Escalalute, Wayne Co.
Station—Bryce Canyon St. Dominic.
Station— Beryl Junction.
Station— Brian Head. (Winter)

DRAPER, SALT LAKE CO., ST. JOHN THE BAPTIST (1999), Rev. Terence M. Moore.
300 E. 11800 S., 84020. Tel: 801-984-7101; Fax: 801-984-7114.
School—Tel: 801-984-7115; Fax: 801-984-7122. Sr. Karla McKinnie, C.S.C., Elementary Prin.; Mrs. Nicole Ward, Middle School Prin. Priests 1; Sisters

2; Lay Teachers 42; Students 980.
Catechesis/Religious Program—Students 450.
EAST CARBON, CARBON CO., GOOD SHEPHERD (1947), Rev. Donald E. Hope, Pastoral Admin.
Res.: P.O. Box 99, 84520. Tel: 435-888-3306.
Catechesis/Religious Program—Students 11.
Mission—St. Michael 140 N. Long St., Green River, Emery Co. 84525. Tel: 801-564-3320.
EUREKA, JUAB CO., ST. PATRICK'S (1885), (Irish), Rev. Robert T. Moriarty; Deacon Noel W. Spencer.
Res.: P.O. Box 387, Payson, 84651. Tel: 801-465-4782.
Catechesis/Religious Program—Students 2.
HELPER, CARBON CO., ST. ANTHONY'S (1944), [JC] Rev. Edward Metzger, O.F.M.
Res.: 5 S. Main, 84526. Tel: 435-472-5661; Fax: 435-472-3235.
Catechesis/Religious Program—Tel: 435-472-8367; Fax: 435-472-8367. Students 74.
HUNTSVILLE, WEBER CO., ST. FLORENCE CATHOLIC COMMUNITY (1990), Rev. Charles T. Cummins, Admin.
Mailing Address: 514-24th St., Ogden, 84401-1594. Tel: 801-399-9531.
Church: Tel: 801-745-5673.
Catechesis/Religious Program—Students 52.
KANAB, KANE CO., ST. CHRISTOPHER'S (1953), Rev. John Hart.
Res.: 39 W. 200 S., 84741. Tel: 435-644-5652; 435-644-3414 (Office).
Catechesis/Religious Program—Students 15.
Station—Grand Canyon North Rim. Tel: 435-644-3414.
LAYTON, DAVIS CO., ST. ROSE OF LIMA (1948), Rev. Msgr. Victor G. Bonnell; Rev. Oscar Ramirez Ruiz; Deacons Robert J. Quintana, (Retired); John C. Weis.
Mailing Address: 210 South Chapel St., P.O. Box 557, 84041. Tel: 801-544-4269; Fax: 801-593-0808.
Res.: 321 Whitesides St., 84041. Tel: 801-546-2541.
Catechesis/Religious Program—448 N. Constitution Cir., 84041. Tel: 801-544-5425. Students 297.
LOGAN, CACHE CO., ST. THOMAS AQUINAS (1941), Rev. Clarence J. Sandoval.
Res.: 795 N. 800 E., 84321. Tel: 435-752-1478; Fax: 435-792-3792.
Catechesis/Religious Program—Students 173.
MILFORD, BEAVER CO., ST. BRIDGET (1948), Revs. Michael Lee, Pastoral Admin.; Richard Sherman, Sacramental Min.
Res.: 210 S. 1st West, P.O. Box 785, 84751. Tel: 435-387-2732.
Catechesis/Religious Program—Students 20.
Mission—St. John Bosco P.O. Box 924, Delta, Millard Co. 84624. Tel: 435-864-3710.
Mission—Holy Family 390 N. Main St., Fillmore, Millard Co. 84631.
MOAB, GRAND CO., ST. PIUS X (1955), Rev. Joseph S. Rooney, S.J.
Res.: 122 W. 400 North, P.O. Box 357, 84532. Tel: 435-259-5211; Fax: 435-259-3984.
Catechesis/Religious Program—Students 41.
Mission—Sacred Heart Hwy. 46/Main, LaSal, San Juan Co. 84530. Tel: 435-686-2255.
MONROE, SEVIER CO., ST. ELIZABETH'S (1947), Revs. Michael Lee, Pastoral Admin.; Patrick H. Elliott, Sacramental Min.
Mailing Address: 810 N. Hwy. 228, 84754.
Res.: 840 Sunset Dr., Richfield, 84701. Tel: 435-896-5539; Fax: 435-896-5539.
Catechesis/Religious Program—Students 20.
Mission—St. Anthony of the Desert North on Sandcreek Rd., Torrey, Wayne Co. 84775. Tel: 435-425-3319.
Mission—St. Jude 160 E. Center St., Ephraim, Sanpete Co. 84627. Tel: 435-283-6242.
Station—Central Utah Correctional Facility [JC] Gunnison. Tel: 801-528-6000; Fax: 801-528-6259.
MONTICELLO, SAN JUAN CO., ST. JOSEPH (1935), (Spanish), [JC] Rev. Joseph S. Rooney, S.J.
Res.: P.O. Box 518, 84535. Tel: 435-587-2322.
Catechesis/Religious Program—Students 24.
Station— Blanding.
OGDEN, WEBER CO.
1—HOLY FAMILY (1979), Rev. Msgr. Lawrence P. Sweeney.
Res.: P.O. Box 3070, 84409. Tel: 801-479-1112; Fax: 801-479-1126.
Catechesis/Religious Program—Students 150.
2—ST. JAMES (1966), Rev. Erik J. Richtsteig; Deacon Bud J. Wardle.
Res.: 495 N. Harrison Blvd., 84404. Tel: 801-782-5393; Fax: 801-782-9559.
Catechesis/Religious Program—Tel: 801-782-7372; Fax: 801-479-4909. Students 184.
3—ST. JOSEPH'S (1875), Revs. Hernando Diaz; Jesus Montoya; Charles E. Cummins; Deacons John Conniff; Michael E. Bulson; Tony Lopez.
Res.: 514 24th St., 84401. Tel: 801-399-5627; Fax: 801-399-5918.
School—Tel: 801-393-6051; Fax: 801-393-6086. R. Louise Price, Prin. See separate listing under Elementary Schools, Regional located in the Diocese.
Catechesis/Religious Program—Tel: 801-621-3602. Students 505.
Mission—St. Florence 6481 E. Hwy. 39, Huntsville, Weber Co. 84317. Tel: 801-745-5673.
4—ST. MARY'S (1957), (Italian—Hispanic), Revs. Martin Rock, S.J.; John Ferguson, S.J.; Patrick Reuse, S.J.; Neale Herrlich, S.J.
Res.: P.O. Box 9196, 84409. Tel: 801-621-7961; Fax: 801-394-1244.
Catechesis/Religious Program—Tel: 801-621-2274. Students 378.
PARK CITY, SUMMIT CO., ST. MARY OF THE ASSUMPTION (1881), Revs. Robert J. Bussen; Richard Sherman.
Res.: P.O. Box 669, 84060. Tel: 435-649-9676; Fax: 435-658-0067.
Catechesis/Religious Program—Students 636.
Mission—St. Lawrence 1st West Center, Heber City, Wasatch Co. 84032. Tel: 435-654-4035; Fax: 435-654-4035.
PAYSON, UTAH CO., SAN ANDRES (1986), Rev. Robert T. Moriarty; Deacon Noel W. Spencer.
Mailing Address: P.O. Box 387, 84651. Tel: 801-465-4782.
Church: 315 E. 100 N., 84651.
Catechesis/Religious Program—Students 110.
Mission—Our Lady of Victory Mission c/o San Andres, Nephi, Utah Co. 84651.
PRICE, CARBON CO., NOTRE DAME DE LOURDES (1918), Rev. Donald E. Hope.
Res.: 160 N. Carbon Ave., 84501. Tel: 435-637-1846; Fax: 435-637-6338.
Catechesis/Religious Program—Tel: 435-637-1207. Students 170.
Mission—San Rafael 1716 S. Hwy. 10, Huntington, Emery Co. 84528. Tel: 435-687-2116; Fax: 435-384-3215.
PROVO, UTAH CO., ST. FRANCIS OF ASSISI (1892), Revs. Michael R. Sciumbato; Francisco Pires; Javier Pudota.
Res.: 65 E. 500 N., Orem, 84057-4030.
Catechesis/Religious Program—Tel: 801-221-0750, Ext. 16; Fax: 801-221-0759. Students 670.
Mission—San Isidro 12537 W. Hwy. 6, Elberta, Utah Co. 84626.
ROOSEVELT, DUCHESNE CO., ST. HELEN'S (1940), (Native American), [CEM] Rev. Albert Kileo.
Res.: 433 E. 200 North, P.O. Box 415, 84066. Tel: 435-722-2975; Fax: 435-722-0525.
Catechesis/Religious Program—Tel: 435-722-0525. Students 31.
Mission—Holy Spirit Duchesne, Duchesne Co.
Mission—Blessed Kateri Tekakwitha Fort Duchesne, Uintah Co. Tel: 435-722-4734.
ST. GEORGE, WASHINGTON CO., ST. GEORGE'S (1955), Revs. Gustavo Adolfo Vidal; James Burnie, C.S.Sp.; Deacons Jack Gorman; Rogaciano Tellez; John O'Brien; Joe Regan; Mark A. Bourget Sr.
Mailing Address: P.O. Box 188, 84771. Tel: 435-673-2604; Fax: 435-688-2704.
Res.: 289 W. 200 N., 84770. Tel: 435-673-7354.
Catechesis/Religious Program—Tel: 435-229-8041. Students 124.
Station—Zion National Park, Tel: 435-772-3256. (Lodge)
TOOELE, TOOELE CO., ST. MARGUERITE'S (1910), Rev. Matthew O. Wixted; Deacons Joseph Cormier; James D. Garcia; Robert Carranza; Sr. Patricia Riley, C.S.C., Pastoral Assoc.
Res.: 15 S. 7th St., 84074. Tel: 435-882-3860; Fax: 435-882-3866.
Pre-School—Tel: 435-882-0081. Mrs Janet Barbiero, Coord.
Catechesis/Religious Program—Tel: 435-882-3171. Students 280.
VERNAL, UINTAH CO., ST. JAMES THE GREATER (1923), [JC] Rev. Protas Swai, A.L.C.P. (Tanzania).
Res.: 138 N. 100 West St., 84078. Tel: 435-789-3016; Fax: 435-789-3016.
Catechesis/Religious Program—Tel: 435-789-3034. Students 60.
WENDOVER, TOOELE CO., SAN FELIPE (2000), (Hispanic), Rev. Fawaz Ayoub.
Res.: 606 E. Aria Blvd., P.O. Box 1270, 84083. Tel: 435-665-2339; Fax: 435-665-0368.
Catechesis/Religious Program—Tel: 801-665-2339; Fax: 801-665-2339. Students 115

Chaplains of Public Institutions

SALT LAKE CITY. *Adult Detention Complex*, Tel: 801-969-5617.
County Youth Detention Center.
Decker Lake Youth Detention Center, Tel: 801-969-5617. Rev. Thomas J. Kaiser (Retired).
Salt Lake County Jail.
Veterans Administration Hospital, 500 Foothill Dr., 84113. Tel: 801-582-1565. Rev. Gebran Bog-Merhi, Sr Julie Maher.
Wasatch Youth Center, Tel: 801-969-5617.
DRAPER. *Utah State Prison*, P.O. Box 142, American Fork, 84003. Rev. James E. Blaine.
GUNNISON. *Central Utah Correctional Facility*, Tel: 801-328-8941. Rev. Gustavo Adolfo Vidal.

On Duty Outside the Diocese:
Revs.—
Bauer, Rick, Mary Knoll Fathers & Brothers, P.O. Box 1125, Windhoek, Namibia.
Curran, Patrick J., 872 Farmington Ave., Hartford, CT 0611.
Gaeta, David R., 1225 E. Bennington St. E., Boston, MA 02128.

Retired:
Rev. Msgrs.—
Dauich, George
Hedderman, John J.
Kenny, James T.
Pelligrino, Francis B
Pollock, Robert C.
Sullivan, John J.
Revs.—
Curnutte, William G.
Fischer, Louis A.
Fogarty, James
Gouorchin, Vincent
Kaiser, Thomas J.
Rodriguez, Reyes G.

Permanent Deacons:
Aquirae, Rigeberto, Cedar City
Arias, Ricardo
Armendariz, Aniceto
Bambrick, Robert W., St. Henry's, Brigham City
Bash, John
Bassett, Willie
Bourget, Mark A., Sr., St. George
Bulson, Michael E., St. Joseph's, Ogden
Carranza, Robert, St. Marguerita, Tooele
Chisholm, Scott
Clark, Jack
Conniff, John, St. Joseph's, Ogden
Cormier, Joe H., St. Marguerite, Tooele
Davies, Dennis, Christ the King, Cedar City
Dodge, Scott
Essary, Dan
Farrell, Gene
Flaim, Mansueto, St. Ann's, Salt Lake City
Folkes, Willie
Garcia, James D., St. Marguerite's, Tooele
Glodowski, Robert J., (On Duty Outside the Diocese)
Godina, Fernando L., Sacred Heart, Salt Lake City
Gorman, Jack, St.George
Graham, Paul
Gray, Forrest
Herron, Dan, St. Patrick, Salt Lake City
Hester, Herschel
Huber, Roger
Huffman, Rick C., St. Peter & Paul, West Valley City
Januszewski, William A., (On Duty Outside the Diocese)
Johansson, Otto, St. Patrick, Salt Lake City
Johnson, Lynn R., Cathedral of the Madeleine
Keyser, John
Kirts, Steven W., St. Thomas More, Sandy
Kranz, John
Langner, Russell, Blessed Sacrament, Sandy
Lopez, Anthony J., St. Joseph, Ogden
Manu, Sefo A., St. Patrick, Salt Lake City
Martin, Billy
Mayo, Silvio, Cathedral of the Madeleine, Salt Lake
McElfresh, James L., (Retired)
Merino, Reynaldo Q., Bountiful, UT
Mota, Hector, Our Lady of Guadalupe, Salt Lake City
Neveraski, Steve
O'Brien, John P., St. George, St. George
Osman, Dave
Palm, Lowell, Our Lady of Lourdes, Salt Lake City
Quintana, Robert J., (Retired)
Reade, George
Reed, Joseph W., (On Duty Outside the Diocese)
Regan, Joe, St Christopher, Kauab
Rodriguez, Mario A., Our Lady of Guadalupe, Salt Lake City
Salaz, Rubel J., St. Francis Xavier
Sanchez, Mel J., St. Joseph the Worker, West Jordan
Shea, Gerald
Sliger, Douglas R., Hill Air Force Base, Ogden
Soklaski, Marcel
Spencer, Noel W., San Andres, Payson
Stewart, Thomas J., (On Duty Outside the Diocese)
Stott, Stanley L., St. Therese, Midvale
Tellez, Roqagimno, St. George
Toro, German A., (On Duty Outside the Diocese)
Tosti, Tom
Trujillo, Manuel
Velez, Manuel

Wardle, Bud J., St. James, Ogden

Weis, John C., St. Rose of Lima, Layton

Werling, Richard E., St. Henry, Brigham City

INSTITUTIONS LOCATED IN THE DIOCESE

[A] SEMINARIES, RELIGIOUS, OR SCHOLASTICATES

HUNTSVILLE. *Abbey of Our Lady of the Holy Trinity*, 1250 S. 9500 E., 84317. Tel: 801-745-3784; Fax: 801-745-6430. Email: hta@xmission.com. Web: www.xmission.com/~hta. Revs. Alan Hohl, O.C.S.O., Dir. of Studies; Charles J. Cummings, O.C.S.O., Novice Master. Priests 12; Brothers 9; Oblates 1.

[B] HIGH SCHOOLS, DIOCESAN

SALT LAKE CITY. *Judge Memorial Catholic High School*, 650 S. 11th E., 84102. Tel: 801-363-8895; Fax: 801-521-3920. Email: jmchs5@softsolutions.com. Web: www.judgememorial.com. Rev. John Norman, Pres.; James F. Hamburge, Prin.; Rev. James P. McHugh, O.S.F.S. Day School. (Coed) Priests 2; Lay Teachers 56; Students 880; Total Staff 115.

DRAPER. *Juan Diego Catholic High School*, 300 E. 11800 S., 84020. Tel: 801-984-7600; Fax: 801-984-7601. Email: Dr_Galey_Colosimo@SkaggsCatholicCenter.org. Web: www.skaggscatholiccenter.org. Dr. Galey Colosimo, Prin. Priests 3; Lay Teachers 49; Total Staff 63; Total Enrollment 660.

OGDEN. *St. Joseph Catholic High School*, 1790 Lake St., 84401. Tel: 801-394-1515; Fax: 801-394-6428. Email: formoreinformation@stjosephcatholichs.com. Web: www.stjosephcatholichs.com. Claudia Mavie Raab, Admin. & Prin. Priests 2; Brothers 2; Sisters 5; Lay Teachers 23; Students 185; Total Staff 30.

[C] ELEMENTARY SCHOOLS, REGIONAL

KEARNS. *St. Francis Xavier Regional School*, (Grades K-8), 4501 W. 5215 S., 84118. Tel: 801-966-1571; Fax: 801-966-1639. Email: slcxavier35@ihotmail.com. Rev. William F. Wheaton; Nancy Essary, Prin. Lay Teachers 15; Students 273.

OGDEN. *St. Joseph Regional School*, (Grades PreK-8), 2980 Quincy Ave., 84403. Tel: 801-393-6051; Fax: 801-393-6086. Email: dhanebrink@stjosephutah.com. Web: stjosephutah.com. Rev. Hernando Diaz; R. Louise Price, Prin. Lay Teachers 32; Total Staff 57; Students 551.

[D] FOUNDATIONS

SALT LAKE CITY. *Catholic Foundation of Utah*, 27 C St., 84103. Tel: 801-328-8641, Ext. 306; Fax: 801-355-5904. Email: kurt.simpson@dioslc.org. Web: www.dioslc.org. Kurt Simpson, Exec. Dir.; Peter Scholte, Pres.

OGDEN. *St. Benedict's Foundation*, 6000 S., 1075 E., Ste. 100, 84405-4945. Tel: 801-479-1800; Fax: 801-479-4997. Email: estelle@aol.com. Estelle G. Dahlkemper, Exec. Dir.; Steve Beierlein, Foundation Bd. Chm.

[E] HOMES FOR AGED

SALT LAKE CITY. CHRISTUS St. Joseph Villa: 451 Bishop Federal Ln., 84115-2295. Tel: 801-487-7557; Fax: 801-487-1112. Email: stjosephvilla@christussjv.org. Web: www.stjosephvilla.com. Galen K. Ewer, Pres. & CEO. Operated by CHRISTUS Health. Residents 300; Total in Residence 287; Total Assisted 1,080; Total Staff 375.

Christus Health Utah dba Christus St. Joseph Villa , 451 Bishop Federal Ave., 84115. Tel: 801-487-7557; Fax: 801-487-1112. Web: www.stjosephvilla.com. Galen K. Ewer, Pres. & Admin. Total Assisted 1,084; Total Staff 375.

[F] MONASTERIES AND RESIDENCES OF PRIESTS AND BROTHERS

SALT LAKE CITY. *Oblate House*, 554 E St., 84103. Tel: 801-359-8201. Email: jmosfs@softsolutions.com. Rev. James P. McHugh, O.S.F.S., Contact Person. Oblates of St. Francis de Sales Total in Residence 3.

HUNTSVILLE. *Abbey of Our Lady of the Holy Trinity of the Order of Cistercians*, 1250 S. 9500 E., 84317. Tel: 801-745-3784; Fax: 801-745-6430. Email: hta@xmission.com. Web: www.xmission.com/~hta. Revs. Casimir Bernas, O.C.S.O., Abbot; Alan Hohl, O.C.S.O.; David Altman, O.C.S.O.; Patrick Boyle, O.C.S.O.; Charles J. Cummings, O.C.S.O., Novice Master; Leander Dosch, O.C.S.O.; Malachy Flaherty, O.C.S.O.; Bartholomew Gottemoller, O.C.S.O.; Brendan Hanratty, O.C.S.O.; Joseph Schroer, O.C.S.O.; Baldwin Shea, O.C.S.O.; Emmanuel Spillane, O.C.S.O.

Legal Title: *Abbey of Our Lady of the Holy Trinity of the Order of Cistercians of the Strict Observance* Priests 12; Brothers 9; Oblates 1; Total in Community 22.

Residing Elsewhere: Rev. Gregory Santos, O.C.S.O.

[G] CONVENTS, MONASTERIES AND RESIDENCES FOR SISTERS

SALT LAKE CITY. **Carmel of the Immaculate Heart of Mary Monastery*, 5714 Holladay Blvd., 84121. Tel: 801-277-6075; Fax: 801-277-4263. Email: carmelslc@worldnet.att.net. Web: www.carmelslc.org. Sr. Margaret Mary Miller, O.C.D., Prioress. Professed Cloistered Sisters 7; Professed Out-Sisters 1.

St. Joseph Villa Convent, 451 Bishop Federal Ln., 84115-2295. Tel: 801-487-7557, Ext. 3064; Fax: 801-468-6851. Email: ccui@net-utah.net. Congregation of Sisters of Charity of the Incarnate Word 4.

Our Lady of Lourdes Convent, 675 S. 1100 E., 84102. Tel: 801-583-1204. Sisters of the Holy Cross 4.

St. Vincent de Paul Convent, 1385 E. Spring Ln., 84117-6797. Tel: 801-277-7890; Fax: 801-273-1156. Email: mlderoin@hotmail.com. Sisters of the Holy Family 1; Sisters of the Holy Cross 1.

DRAPER. *Sisters of the Holy Cross, Vivian Skaggs Armstrong Convent*, 554 E. 11800 S., 84020. Tel: 801-501-8349; Fax: 801-984-7122. Email: sr_karla_mckinnie@skaggscatholiccenter.org. Sisters 3.

MURRAY. *Sisters of the Holy Cross Convent*, 1238 W. Bullion St., 84123. Tel: 801-313-9611.

Legal Title: *Sisters of the Holy Cross, Inc.* Sisters 4.

OGDEN. *Mount Benedict Monastery*, 6000 S. 1075 E., 84405-4945. Tel: 801-479-6030; Fax: 801-479-4997. Email: mbmutah@hotmail.com. Web: www.mbmutah.org. Sisters of St. Benedict 9.

St. Benedict's Convent, 665 S. 1100 E., 84102. Tel: 801-582-1042; Fax: 801-328-9680.

WEST JORDAN. *St. Joseph the Worker Convent*, 7405 S. Redwood Rd., 84084. Tel: 801-561-4090.

[H] NEWMAN CENTERS

SALT LAKE CITY. *University of Utah, Newman Center* , (St. Catherine of Siena University Parish) , 170 S. University, 84102. Tel: 801-359-6066; Fax: 801-359-4547. Web: www.newman.utah.edu. Revs. Denis Reilly, O.P.; James D. Thompson, O.P. Total Students in Residence 5; Total Staff 3.

EPHRAIM. *St. Jude Catholic Center* 160 E. Center, 84627. Tel: 435-283-6242. Rev. Michael Lee, Pastoral Admin.

LOGAN. *St. Thomas Aquinas, Newman Center* , (Utah State University) , 795 N. 800 E., 84321. Tel: 435-752-1478; Fax: 435-792-3792. Web: http://st-thomasweb.org. Rev. Clarence J. Sandoval. Total in Residence 1; Total Staff 1.

OGDEN. *Weber State University, Newman Center* 3738 Custer Ave., 84403. Tel: 801-399-9531. Rev. Charles T. Cummins, Dir. Total in Residence 1; Total Staff 1.

PRICE. *College of Eastern Utah, Newman Club* 454 E. 400 North, 84501. Tel: 435-637-6785. Email: dremom@hotmail.com. 160 N. Carlon Ave., 84501. Rev. Donald E. Hope. Total Staff 1.

ST. GEORGE. *Dixie College, Newman Center* Tel: 435-673-2604; Fax: 435-688-2704. St. George Church, P.O. Box 188, 84771. Rev. Gustavo Adolfo Vidal. 289 W. 200 N., 84770. Tel: 435-673-7354.

[I] RETREAT HOUSES

OGDEN. *Our Lady of the Mountains*, 1794 Lake St., 84401. Tel: 801-392-9231; Fax: 801-612-9619. Email: olmrh@konnections.net. Sr. Danile Knight, O.S.B., Dir. Total Staff 5.

[J] CATHOLIC SOCIAL SERVICES

SALT LAKE CITY. *Catholic Community Services*, 2570 W. 1700 S., 84104. Tel: 801-977-9119; Fax: 801-977-8227; 801-977-9224. Email: mstclaire@ccsutah.org. Web: www.ccsutah.org. Nile W. Eatmon, Board Pres.; Maggie St.Claire, Exec. Dir. Total Assisted 185,227; Meals served at the St. Vincent de Paul Center 221,254; Total Staff 83.

Northern Utah Office, 2504 F. Ave., Ogden, 84401. Tel: 801-394-5944; Fax: 801-394-5948. Mailing Address: P.O. Box 869, Ogden, 84402.

Marillac House / Transitional Housing, 2570 W. 1700 S., 84104. Tel: 801-977-9119; 801-977-8227; Fax: 801-359-0830.

St. Mary's Home For Men, 1206 W. 200 S., 84104. Tel: 801-328-1894; Fax: 801-328-1895. Residential Substance Abuse Treatment for Adult Males

St. Vincent de Paul Center, 437 W. 200 S., 84101. Tel: 801-363-7710; Fax: 801-363-7647.

Weigand Homeless Day Center, 235 Rio Grande St., 84101. Tel: 801-363-7710; Fax: 801-363-7647. Home for Single Pregnant Women

Shelter Plus Housing, 622 23rd St., Ogden, 84401. Tel: 801-359-5944; Fax: 801-394-5948. Housing for people with AIDS/HIV.

Additional Programs:

Migration and Refugee Resettlement, 2570 W. 1700 S., 84104. Tel: 801-977-9119; Fax: 801-977-9224.

Community Services, 2570 W. 1700 S., 84104. Tel: 801-977-9119; Fax: 801-977-8227.

Adoption Services, 2570 W. 1700 S., 84104. Tel: 801-977-9119; Fax: 801-977-8227.

Holy Cross Ministries, 2570 W. 1700 S., 84102. Tel: 801-908-0293; Fax: 801-908-8854. Email: sbrennan@hcmutah.org. Web: www.holycrossministries.org. Sr. Suzanne Brennan, C.S.C. Outreach Program, English as a Second Language (ESL), Seniors, Children, Women, Legal Assistance for Immigration, School Health & Counseling, Parish Health, Afterschool Programs. Total Staff 25; Total Annually Assisted 19,500.

[K] MISCELLANEOUS

SALT LAKE CITY. *Mercy Housing Utah, Inc.*, 67 N. B St., 84103. Tel: 801-521-3183; Fax: 801-521-3093. Email: arowland@mercyhousing.org. Web: www.mercyhousing.org. Amy Rowland, Rgnl. Housing Dir.

RELIGIOUS INSTITUTES OF MEN REPRESENTED IN THE DIOCESE

For further details refer to the corresponding bracketed number in the Religious Institutes of Men or Women section.

[]—*Apostolic Life Community Priests in the Opus Spiritos Sanctu*—A.L.C.P.

[]—*Apostolic Life Community Priests in the Opus Spiritu Sancti*—A.L.C.P.

[0220]—*Congregation of the Blessed Sacrament*—S.S.S.

[0650]—*Holy Ghost Fathers*—C.S.Sp

[0690]—*Jesuit Fathers* (California Prov.)—S.J.

[0920]—*Oblates of St. Francis de Sales*—O.S.F.S.

[0350]—*Order of Cistercians of the Strict Observance (Trappists)*—O.C.S.O.

[0430]—*Order of Preachers (Dominicans)* (Western Province)—O.P.

RELIGIOUS INSTITUTES OF WOMEN REPRESENTED IN THE DIOCESE

[0230]—*Benedictine Sisters of Pontifical Jurisdiction*—O.S.B.

[0470]—*Congregation of the Sisters of Charity of the Incarnate Word, Houston, Texas*—C.C.V.I.

[3935]—*The Congregation of the Sisters of St. Louis, Juilly-Monaghan* (California Region)—S.S.L.

[1920]—*Congregation of the Sisters of the Holy Cross*—C.S.C.

[0760]—*Daughters of Charity of St. Vincent de Paul* (Province of the West)—D.C.

[0760]—*Daughters of Charity of St. Vincent De Paul*—D.C.

[0420]—*Discalced Carmelite Nuns*—O.C.D.

[1190]—*Franciscan Sisters of the Atonement*—S.A.

[2575]—*Institute of the Sisters of Mercy of the Americas*—R.S.M.

[3130]—*Our Lady of Victory Missionary Sisters*—O.L.V.M.

[]—*Sisters for Christian Community*—S.F.C.C.

[2575]—*Sisters of Mercy of the America's*—R.S.M.

[2990]—*Sisters of Notre Dame*—S.N.D.

[1960]—*Sisters of the Holy Family*—S.H.F.

DIOCESAN CEMETERIES

SALT LAKE CITY. *Mount Calvary Catholic*, Office, 275 U St., 84103. Tel: 801-355-2476. Mr. Cory Rosontretec, Dir.; Deacon Ricardo Arias, Sec.

NECROLOGY

† Spellen, Lawrence M.—Died Jan. 18, 2003
† Tkach, Norman A.—Died Feb. 20, 2003

Diocese of San Angelo

(Dioecesis Angeliana)

Most Reverend

MICHAEL D. PFEIFER, O.M.I.

Bishop of San Angelo; ordained December 21, 1964; consecrated and installed Bishop of San Angelo July 26, 1985. *Res.: P.O. Box 1829, San Angelo, TX 76902.*

The Chancery: P.O. Box 1829, San Angelo, TX 76902. Tel: 325-651-7500; Fax: 325-651-6688.

Web: www.san-angelo-diocese.org

Email: mdpomi@aol.com

ESTABLISHED OCTOBER 16, 1961.

Square Miles 37,433.

Comprises 29 Counties in the State of Texas as follows: Andrews, Brown, Callahan, Coke, Coleman, Concho, Crane, Crockett, Ector, Glasscock, Howard, Irion, Kimble, McCulloch, Martin, Menard, Midland, Mitchell, Nolan, Pecos, Reagan, Runnels, Schleicher, Sterling, Sutton, Taylor, Terrell, Tom Green and Upton.

Legal Title: For legal title of parishes and diocesan institutions, consult the Chancery Office.

STATISTICAL OVERVIEW

Personnel	
Bishop	1
Priests: Diocesan Active in Diocese	24
Priests: Diocesan Active Outside Diocese	2
Priests: Retired, Sick or Absent	8
Number of Diocesan Priests	34
Religious Priests in Diocese	17
Total Priests in Diocese	51
Extern Priests in Diocese	12
Ordinations:	
Diocesan Priests	2
Permanent Deacons	3
Permanent Deacons in Diocese	35
Total Brothers	1
Total Sisters	23
Parishes	
Parishes	49
With Resident Pastor:	
Resident Diocesan Priests	29
Resident Religious Priests	8
Without Resident Pastor:	
Administered by Priests	10
Administered by Deacons	1
Administered by Religious Women	1
Missions	24
Professional Ministry Personnel:	
Sisters	6
Lay Ministers	2
Educational	
Diocesan Students in Other Seminaries	6
Total Seminarians	6
Elementary Schools, Diocesan and Parish	3
Total Students	701
Catechesis/Religious Education:	
High School Students	4,531
Elementary Students	7,989
Total Students under Catholic Instruction	13,227
Teachers in the Diocese:	
Sisters	2
Lay Teachers	66
Vital Statistics	
Receptions into the Church:	
Infant Baptism Totals	1,834
Adult Baptism Totals	173
Received into Full Communion	244
First Communions	1,925
Confirmations	1,532
Marriages:	
Catholic	369
Interfaith	94
Total Marriages	463
Deaths	712
Total Catholic Population	82,734
Total Population	673,801

Former Bishops—Most Revs. THOMAS J. DRURY, D.D., LL.D., ord. June 2, 1935; appt. Oct. 16, 1961; consecrated and installed Jan. 24, 1962; transferred to Corpus Christi, July 19, 1965; died July 22, 1992; THOMAS TSCHOEPE, D.D., ord. May 30, 1943; appt. Bishop Jan. 12, 1966; consecrated March 9, 1966; transferred to Dallas, Aug. 27, 1969; STEPHEN A. LEVEN, D.D. (Retired), ord. June 10, 1928; consecrated Feb. 8, 1956, Auxiliary of San Antonio; appt. to San Angelo Oct. 22, 1969; retired April 16, 1979; died June 28, 1983; JOSEPH A. FIORENZA, ord. May 29, 1954; appt. Sept. 4, 1979; ord. and installed October 25, 1979; transferred to Galveston-Houston, Dec. 18, 1984.

Vicar General—Rev. Msgr. LARRY J. DROLL, J.C.L.

Chancery Office—804 Ford, San Angelo, 76905. Tel: 325-651-7500; Fax: 325-651-6688. *Mailing Address, Box 1829, San Angelo, 76902.* Office Hours: Mon.-Fri. 9-5

Chancellor—Mr. LES MAIMAN.

Diocesan Tribunal—P.O. Box 1829, San Angelo, 76902.

Judicial Vicar—Rev. WILLIAM DU BUISSON, O.M.I., P.O. Box 1829, San Angelo, 76902.

Judges—Revs. WILLIAM DUBUISSON, O.M.I., J.C.L., Adjutant Judicial Vicar; TOM BARLEY, J.C.L.; Very Rev. MAURICE VOITY, S.T.L.

Promoter Justitiae—Rev. JAMES PLAGENS.

Defensores Vinculi—Rev. Msgr. LARRY J. DROLL, J.C.L.; Revs. CHARLES GREENWELL; MARK WOODRUFF.

Diocesan Consultors—Rev. Msgr. LARRY J. DROLL, J.C.L. Revs. HUBERT WADE; MARK WOODRUFF; WILLIAM DU BUISSON, O.M.I.; TOM BARLEY.

Priests' Personnel Committee—Mr. LES MAIMAN, Ex Officio.

Presbyteral Council—Rev. TOM BARLEY, J.C.L., Chm.; Mr. LES MAIMAN; Revs. QUIRINO CORNEJO; HUBERT WADE, Chm.; Very Rev. MAURICE VOITY, S.T.L.; Revs. BERNARD GULLY; GEORGE VARAKUKALA, H.G.N.; BARRY MCLEAN; WILLIAM DU BUISSON, O.M.I.

Vicar for Women Religious—Sr. MALACHY GRIFFIN, O.P.

Diocesan Offices and Directors

Diocesan Finance Officer—Mr. LES MAIMAN.

Director of Seminarians—Rev. TOM BARLEY.

Campaign for Human Development—Mr. LES MAIMAN.

Catholic Relief Services—Rev. Msgr. LARRY J. DROLL, J.C.L.

Catholic University, Friends of—VACANT.

Communications Office—Mr. PETE MICALE.

Continuing Education of the Clergy—Rev. BARRY MCLEAN.

Cursillos de Cristiandad—Rev. BERNARD GULLY.

Deans—Revs. HUBERT WADE, San Angelo Deanery; BERNARD GULLY, Midland-Odessa Deanery; FRED NAWARSKAS, Abilene Deanery.

Diocesan Liturgical Commission—Mrs. JUDY PHAREF.

Holy Childhood, Pontifical Association—Miss MARY SUE BREWER.

Pastor Review Board—Rev. Msgr. FRED NAWARSKAS.

Newspaper—Mr. PETE MICALE, Editor. "West Texas Angelus"

Office of Education and Formation—Sr. HILDA MAROTTA, O.S.F.

Permanent Deacon Director—Deacon ALAN NEFF.

Prison Ministry Coordinator—Mrs. LINDA HILL.

Permanent Deacon Formation—Deacon TIM GRAHAM.

Pro-Life—Mr. PETE MICALE.

Priests' Pension Plan— Board of Directors: Rev. Msgr. LARRY J. DROLL, J.C.L.; Rev. CHARLES GREENWELL; Rev. Msgr. FRED NAWARSKAS; Rev. BENEDICT ZIENTEK.

Propagation of the Faith—VACANT.

Rural Life—BECK KNOX, Dir.

Schools—Sr. ELIZABETH ANN SWARTZ, S.S.N.D., Supt.

Victim Assistance Coordinator—Mr. MICHAEL WYSE. Tel: 325-651-7500.

Vocations—Rev. RODNEY WHITE, Dir.

CLERGY, PARISHES, MISSIONS AND PAROCHIAL SCHOOLS

CITY OF SAN ANGELO
(TOM GREEN COUNTY)

1—CATHEDRAL OF THE SACRED HEART (1884), Very Rev. Maurice Voity, S.T.L., Rector; Deacon Jerry Trevino, Pastoral Assoc.

Office: 19 S. Oakes St., 76903. Tel: 915-658-6567; Fax: 915-659-0588.

School—Angelo Catholic School, Sacred Heart Campus, (Grades 2-6) Tel: 915-655-3325; Fax: 915-655-1286. Mr. Charles Guenat, Prin. Lay Teachers 13; Students 110.

Catechesis/Religious Program—Mr. Charles Guenat, D.R.E. Students 165.

Sacred Heart Cathedral-Parish Educational Endowment Fund, Inc.—Tel: 915-658-6567.

2—HOLY ANGELS (1961), Rev. Charles C. Greenwell; Mr. Ed Bendinelli, Business Mgr.

Parish Office: 2202 Rutgers Ave., 76904. Tel: 915-949-3308; 915-944-8967; Fax: 915-944-3633.

School—Angelo Catholic School, (Grades PreK-1), 2315 A & M Ave.. Tel: 915-949-1747; Fax: 915-942-1547. Mr. Charles Guenat, Prin. Holy Angels Campus Lay Teachers 7; Students 61.

Catechesis/Religious Program—Tel: 915-942-8192; Fax: 915-944-3633. Mrs. Lori Hines, D.R.E., (Grades PreK-12). Students 411.

3—ST. JOSEPH (1942), (Hispanic), Rev. Quirino H. Cornejo; Deacon John Munoz. In Res., Rev. Miguel Dinio, O.P. Tel: 325-482-8438.

Res.: 301 W. 17th, 76903. Tel: 325-653-5006; Fax: 325-659-2795.

Catechesis/Religious Program—Tel: 325-658-8759. Michael R. Wyse, D.R.E. Students 388.

4—ST. MARGARET (1967), Rev. Joseph Choutapalli (India); Deacon Ray Smith, Pastoral Coord.
Office: 2619 Era St., 76905. Tel: 915-651-4633; Fax: 915-651-4366.
Catechesis/Religious Program—Muriel Emerson, D.R.E., (Grades PreK-6); Andy Gonzalez, D.R.E., (Grades 7-12). Students 27.

5—ST. MARY'S (1930), (Hispanic), Revs. Terence Brenon; Joey Faylona; Deacons Lazaro Sevier; Roy Ibarra.
Res.: 7 West Ave. N., 76903. Tel: 325-655-6278; Fax: 325-655-1524.
Catechesis/Religious Program—Tel: 325-665-9397; Fax: 325-665-1524. Minnie Ibarra, D.R.E. Students 245.

OUTSIDE THE CITY OF SAN ANGELO

ABILENE, TAYLOR CO.

1—ST. FRANCIS OF ASSISI (1906), (Hispanic), Revs. Joseph H. Uecker, C.PP.S.; Thomas Manimala; Deacon Jose Sanchez.
Office—826 Cottonwood St., 79601. Tel: 325-672-6695; Fax: 325-670-0129.
Catechesis/Religious Program—Donna C. Moreno, D.R.E. Students 175.

2—HOLY FAMILY (1976), Rev. Msgr. Frederick Nawarskas; Sr. Regina Decker, C.D.P., Pastoral Assoc.; Deacons Paul Klein; Gerald Schwalb.
Res.: 5410 Buffalo Gap Rd., P.O. Box 5970, 79606. Tel: 915-692-1820; Fax: 915-698-5131.
Catechesis/Religious Program—Sr. Helen Louise Rivas, C.D.P., D.R.E. Students 416.

3—SACRED HEART (1891), Rev. Robert Bush; Deacon Arturo Casarez.
Res.: 837 Jeanette St., 79602. Tel: 325-677-7951; Fax: 325-677-7710.
Catechesis/Religious Program—Tel: 325-673-0697. Gina Martinez, D.R.E. Students 217.
Mission—Sts. Joachim and Ann [CEM] N. 1st St. & Cherry St., Clyde, Callahan Co. 79510. Deacon Peter Ballaro.

4—ST. VINCENT PALLOTTI (1963), (Mexican-American), Rev. Joseph H. Uecker, C.PP.S. Tel: 325-673-7048; Sr. Rebecca Otter, O.P., Pastoral Assoc. Tel: 325-672-5933.
Res.: 2525 Westview, 79603. Tel: 325-672-1794 (Office); Fax: 325-672-8780.
Catechesis/Religious Program—Minerva Garcia, D.R.E. Students 243.

ANDREWS, ANDREWS CO., OUR LADY OF LOURDES (1958), (Hispanic), Rev. Bernard L. Gully.
Res.: 201 N.E. Ave. K, 79714. Tel: 432-523-4215; Fax: 432-523-5070.
Catechesis/Religious Program—Tel: 915-524-2789. Carol Garcia, D.R.E. Students 379.

BALLINGER, RUNNELS CO., ST. MARY STAR OF THE SEA (1885), [JC] Rev. Hubert Wade Jr.; Deacon Henry Martinez.
Res.: 608 Sixth St., 76821. Tel: 325-365-2687; Fax: 325-365-9986.
Catechesis/Religious Program—Caroline Toliver, D.R.E. Students 277.
Mission—St. James 215 N. Washington, Bronte, Coke Co. 76933.
Mission—Our Lady of Guadalupe 601 W. 10th, Robert Lee, Coke Co. 76945.

BIG LAKE, REAGAN CO., ST. MARGARET OF CORTONA (1949), (Hispanic), [JC] Rev. Hilary A. Thedioha.
107 First St., 76932. Tel: 325-884-2645; Fax: 325-884-3221.
Res.: P.O. Box 1320, McCamey, 79752.
Catechesis/Religious Program—Tel: 325-884-3321. Casaw Flores, D.R.E. Students 152.
Mission—St. Thomas Rankin, Upton Co.
Mission—St. Francis Iraan, Pecos Co.

BIG SPRING, HOWARD CO.

1—IMMACULATE HEART OF MARY (1961), Rev. Richard J. Regan; Deacons Wayne Rock; David King, (Retired).
Res.: 1009 Hearn St., 79720. Tel: 432-267-4124; Fax: 432-267-7844.
Catechesis/Religious Program— Mrs. Isabel Villarreal, D.R.E. Students 138.
Mission—St. Joseph P.O. Box 805, Howard Co. 79711. Tel: 915-394-4751.

2—SACRED HEART (1948), (Hispanic), Revs. James A. Plagens; Felix Cubelo.
Mailing Address: P.O. Box 2101, 79721-2101.
Res.: 508 N. Aylford, 79720. Tel: 915-263-7884; Fax: 915-263-3621.
Catechesis/Religious Program—Tel: 915-263-0648. Elaine Martinez, D.R.E. Students 317.

3—ST. THOMAS (1887), (Hispanic), Revs. Felix Cubelo; James A. Plagens.
Res.: 605 N. Main St., P.O. Box 627, 79721. Tel: 915-263-2864; Fax: 915-263-3621.
Catechesis/Religious Program—Sacred Heart/St. Thomas combined, Tel: 432-263-2864; Fax: 432-263-3621. Miss Mary Chavez, D.R.E. Students 317.

BRADY, MCCULLOCH CO., ST. PATRICK'S (1876), Rev. Colm Merlligan, M.S.C.
Res.: 406 Bridge, P.O. Box 1188, 76825. Tel: 325-597-2324; Fax: 325-597-2991.
Catechesis/Religious Program—Blanca Lafuente-Martinez, D.R.E. Students 121.
Mission—St. Francis Xavier Melvin, McCullogh Co.

BROWNWOOD, BROWN CO., ST. MARY'S (1896), (Hispanic), [JC] Rev. Msgr. Benedict Zientek (Retired); Rev. Barry L. McLean; Deacon John Specht.
Office: 1101 Booker, 76801.
Res.: 1105 Main Ave., 76801. Tel: 325-646-7455; Fax: 325-646-6643.
Catechesis/Religious Program—Tel: 325-646-9630. Leslie Redfern, D.R.E. Students 317.

CARLSBAD, TOM GREEN CO., ST. THERESE OF THE CHILD JESUS (1957), Revs. Joey Faylona, Sacramental Min.; Terry Brenon, Canonical Pastor; Sr. Mary Kay Bailey, O.P., Pastoral Coord.
Mailing Address: P.O. Box 416, 76934-0416. Tel: 915-465-8062; Fax: 915-465-4472.
Catechesis/Religious Program—Students 45.
Mission—St. Paschal Baylon P.O. Box 271, Sterling City, Sterling Co. 76951-0271.
Station—San Angelo State School for the Mentally Retarded, Tel: 915-465-4391.

COLEMAN, COLEMAN CO., SACRED HEART (1892), (Anglo—Hispanic), Rev. Lawrence S. Cyr, C.PP.S.; Sr. Esperanza Razura, A.S.C., Pastoral Assoc. & D.R.E.
Mailing Address: 303 E. College, 76834. Tel: 915-625-5773; Fax: 325-625-3320.
Rectory—303 E. Elm, 76834. Tel: 915-625-1348.
Catechesis/Religious Program—201 San Saba, 76834. Tel: 915-625-3893. Students 110.

COLORADO CITY, MITCHELL CO., ST. ANN'S (1943), (Hispanic), Rev. George Varakukala.
Res.: 2005 Walnut, 79512. Tel: 915-728-3252; Fax: 915-728-3266.
Catechesis/Religious Program—Tel: 915-728-5865. Students 249.
Mission—San Jose (1924), 403 S. Hinson, Loraine, Mitchell Co. 79532. Tel: 915-737-1022.

CRANE, CRANE CO., GOOD SHEPHERD, (Spanish), Rev. Nilo Nalugon; Deacons Julio Carrasco; Apolonio Gutierrez.
Mailing Address: P.O. Box 1294, 79731. Tel: 915-652-8216; Fax: 915-652-3219.
Res.: 1109 S. Virginia St., 79731. Tel: 915-558-2718. Church: 9th & S. Virginia St., 79731. Tel: 432-558-3024.
Catechesis/Religious Program—Minerva Garza, D.R.E.; Theresa Figuora, D.R.E. Students 184.
Mission—St. Isidore Coyanosa, Pecos Co.
Mission—Our Lady of Lourdes Imperial, Pecos Co.

EDEN, CONCHO CO., ST. CHARLES (1927), (Mexican—German), Rev. Romanus A. Akamike (Nigeria); Deacons Leroy Beach; Joe Lopez.
Res.: P.O. Box 575, 76837. Tel: 915-869-8311; Fax: 915-869-8311.
Catechesis/Religious Program—Tel: 915-869-5283; Fax: 915-869-5283. Students 21.
Mission—Our Lady of Guadalupe P.O. Box 123, Millersview, Concho C. 76862. Tel: 915-483-5426.

ELDORADO, SCHLEICHER CO., OUR LADY OF GUADALUPE (1924), (Hispanic), [CEM] [JC] Rev. Joseph Choutapalli (India).
Res.: P.O. Box 211, 76936. Tel: 325-853-2663; Fax: 915-853-2663.
Catechesis/Religious Program—Tel: 325-853-3366; Fax: 325-853-1288. Albert Torres, D.R.E.; Martha Acosta, D.R.E.; Muriel Emerson, D.R.E. Students 55.
Mission—Immaculate Conception P.O. Box 36, Knickerbocker, Tom Green Co. 76939. Tel: 325-944-2820.
Mission—St. Peter's 324 N. Commerce, P.O. Box 772, Mertzon, Irion Co. 76941. Tel: 325-835-2000.

FORT STOCKTON, PECOS CO.

1—ST. AGNES (1953), (Hispanic), [CEM] [JC] Rev. David Herrera; Deacon Simon Franco.
Mailing Address: P.O. Box 1487, 79735. Tel: 915-336-2724; Fax: 915-336-6950.
Catechesis/Religious Program—Tel: 915-336-5131; Fax: 915-336-6950. Lillian Subia, D.R.E.; Arabella Granado, D.R.E. Students 297.
Mission—St. Isidore Coyanosa, Pecos Co.
Mission—Our Lady of Lourdes Imperial, Pecos Co.

2—ST. JOSEPH'S (1875), (Hispanic), [CEM] [JC] Rev. David Herrera; Deacon Cosme Ureta Jr.
Res.: 403 S. Main, 79735. Tel: 432-336-5027; Fax: 432-336-6668.
Catechesis/Religious Program—Tel: 432-336-5037. Elva Valadez, D.R.E. Students 214.

JUNCTION, KIMBLE CO., ST. THERESA OF THE CHILD JESUS (1959), Rev. Floro Hinacay; Deacon James T. Graham.
Res.: P.O. Box 486, 76849. Tel: 325-446-3393.
Catechesis/Religious Program—Students 75.

MCCAMEY, UPTON CO., SACRED HEART (1935), (Hispanic), Rev. Nilo Nalugon.
Res.: Box 1320, 79752. Tel: 915-652-8216; Fax: 915-652-3219.
Catechesis/Religious Program—Tel: 915-652-8810. Students 97.

MENARD, MENARD CO., SACRED HEART (1873), Rev. Floro A. Hinacay.
Res.: P.O. Box 788, 76859. Tel: 915-396-4906; Fax: 915-396-2076.
Catechesis/Religious Program—Tel: 325-396-4906; Fax: 325-396-2076. Students 54.

MIDLAND, MIDLAND CO.

1—ST. ANN'S (1896), Rev. Msgr. Larry J. Droll, J.C.L.; Rev. Rodney White; Sr. Denise DuPlessis, D.C., Pastoral Assoc.
Mailing Address: P.O. Box 1231, 79702-1231. Tel: 432-682-6303; Fax: 432-684-4528.
Res.: 1908 W. Texas Ave., 79701. Tel: 915-682-6304; 915-682-6694; 915-682-8905; Fax: 915-684-4528.
School—(Grades PreK-8), 2000 W. Texas Ave.. Tel: 915-684-4563; Fax: 915-687-2468. Mrs. Audrey L. Curry, Prin. Lay Teachers 35; Students 361.
Catechesis/Religious Program—Tel: 915-687-0941; Fax: 915-683-2254. Carol Ann Hunt, D.R.E. Students 559.

2—OUR LADY OF GUADALUPE (1960), (Hispanic), Rev. Ray Wilhelm, O.M.I.; Deacon Jesse Guajardo, Pastoral Assoc.
Res.: 1401 E. Garden Ln., P.O. Box 7, 79702. Tel: 432-682-2581; Fax: 432-682-9364.
Catechesis/Religious Program—Tel: 915-683-8908. Sisters Rita Marie Cuevas, O.N.D., D.R.E.; Jeanine B. Dillera, D.R.E. Students 752.

3—OUR LADY OF SAN JUAN DE LOS LAGOS (1984), (Hispanic), Rev. Thomas Kelley.
Res.: 1008 W. New Jersey, 79701. Tel: 915-570-0952.
Catechesis/Religious Program—Tel: 915-570-0349; Fax: 915-687-5082. Elidia Padilla, D.R.E. Students 572.

4—ST. STEPHEN'S (1982), Rev. James P. Bridges.
Res. & Mailing Address: 4601 Neely Ave., 79707. Tel: 915-520-7394; Fax: 432-520-7395.
Catechesis/Religious Program—Tel: 432-520-3065. Clara Brummert, D.R.E. Students 475.

MILES, RUNNELS CO., ST. THOMAS (1962), [JC] Revs. Stephen Kennelly (Ireland); Prasad Gallela.
Res.: P.O. Box 306, 76861. Tel: 915-468-3171.
Catechesis/Religious Program—Tel: 915-442-4021. Students 121.

ODESSA, ECTOR CO.

1—ST. ANTHONY (1948), (Hispanic), Rev. Gilbert Rodriguez; Deacon Barney Rodriguez.
Office—1321 W. Monahans St., 79763. Tel: 915-337-6314; Fax: 915-333-3631.
Catechesis/Religious Program—Tel: 915-337-0241. Sr. Regina C. Javier, O.N.D., D.R.E. Students 333.

2—ST. ELIZABETH ANN SETON (1982), Rev. Mark Woodruff; Deacon Alan Neff, Pastoral Assoc. & Business Mgr.; Tom Burke, Pastoral Assoc.
Office—7601 N. Grandview, 79765. Tel: 915-367-4657; Fax: 915-367-0700. Victoria Detiveaux.
Catechesis/Religious Program—Tel: 915-367-4668. Barbara Nay, D.R.E.; Maria Isela Carrasco, D.R.E.; Dorothy Pepper. Students 459.

3—HOLY REDEEMER (1961), (Hispanic), Rev. Frank Chavez; Deacons Ignacio Cisneros; Antonio Gonzales. In Res., Rev. Michael Udegbumam (Nigeria).
Res.: 2633 Conover, 79763. Tel: 915-580-4295; Fax: 915-332-6631.
Catechesis/Religious Program—Tel: 915-332-9231. Anita Diaz, D.R.E.; Steven D. Rojo, D.R.E. (Elementary & RCIA). Students 996.

4—ST. JOSEPH (1948), (Hispanic), Rev. Gilbert Rodriguez; Deacon Jesus Mercado.
Res.: 907 S. Dixie St., 79761. Tel: 915-337-2213; Fax: 915-333-3631.
Catechesis/Religious Program—Tel: 915-337-4734. Sr. Regina C. Javier, O.N.D., D.R.E. Students 403.
Mission—St. Martin de Porres 2821 E. Hammett, Ector Co. 79766.

5—ST. MARY'S (1938), Revs. Francis Frey; Thomas Wempala (India).
Res.: 612 E. 18th St., 79761. Tel: 915-332-5334; Fax: 915-332-1844.
School—(Grades PreK-6), 1703 N. Adams, 79761. Tel: 915-337-6052; Fax: 915-337-6052. Mary Jaramillo, Prin. Sisters 2; Lay Teachers 11; Students 169.
Catechesis/Religious Program—Nan Goodwin, D.R.E. Students 340.
Mission—Our Lady of San Juan 905 Edgeport, Ector Co. 79765.

OLFEN, RUNNELS CO., ST. BONIFACE (1901), [CEM] Rev. Prasad Gallela.
Res.: P.O. Box 96, Rowena, 76875-0096. Tel: 325-442-2893; Fax: 325-442-4602.
Church: 1118 County Rd. 234, Rowena, 76875. Tel: 325-442-2893; Fax: 325-442-2893.
Catechesis/Religious Program—Students 20.

OZONA, CROCKETT CO., OUR LADY OF PERPETUAL HELP (1929), (Hispanic), Unassigned.
Res.: P.O. Box 1069, 76943. Tel: 915-392-3063; Fax: 915-392-3353.

Catechesis/Religious Program—Fannie Sanchez, D.R.E. Students 284.
Mission—Good Shepherd Sheffield, Pecos Co.

ROWENA, RUNNELS CO., ST. JOSEPH'S (1906), (German—Czech), [CEM] Rev. Prasad Gallela.
Res.: P.O. Box 96, 76875. Tel: 325-442-3521; Fax: 325-442-4602.
Catechesis/Religious Program—Charles Frerich, D.R.E. Students 145.

ST. LAWRENCE, GLASSCOCK CO., ST. LAWRENCE (1948), (German), [CEM] Rev. Bernardito Getigan.
Res.: 2400 FM 2401, Garden City, 79739. Tel: 915-397-2300; Fax: 915-397-2300.
Catechesis/Religious Program—Tel: 915-397-2777. Kay Donna Machicek, D.R.E. Students 161.
Mission—St. Thomas Midkiff, Upton Co. Tel: 915-535-2266.

SANDERSON, TERRELL CO., ST. JAMES (1916), (Hispanic), Rev. David Herrera.
Res.: 209 E. Hackberry, P.O. Box 520, 79848. Tel: 915-345-2354; Fax: 915-345-2354.
Catechesis/Religious Program—Tel: 915-345-2354. Dianna Escamilla, D.R.E. Students 43.

SONORA, SUTTON CO., ST. ANN'S (1927), (Hispanic), Very Rev. William Du Buisson, O.M.I.
Office—311 W. Plum St., P.O. Box 1397, 76950-1397. Tel: 325-387-2278; Fax: 915-387-2278.
Res.: 105 Oakwood, Box 1397, 76950. Tel: 325-387-5966.
Catechesis/Religious Program—Students 290.

STANTON, MARTIN CO., ST. JOSEPH'S (1881), (Mexican-American), Rev. George Thirumangalam, C.M.I. (India); Deacon Ernie Sanchez.
Res.: P.O. Box 846, 405 N. Convent St., 79782-0846. Tel: 432-756-3743; Fax: 432-756-3756.
Catechesis/Religious Program—Tel: 432-756-3743. Students 155.
Mission—St. Isidore [CEM] P.O. Box 846, Lenorah, Martin Co. 79782.

SWEETWATER, NOLAN CO.
1—HOLY FAMILY (1885), (Hispanic), Revs. Michael Rodriguez; Sam Homsey, C.PP.S.
Mailing Address: P.O. Box 847, 79556. Tel: 325-235-2694; Fax: 325-235-3483.
Res.: 507 Crane St., 79556. Tel: 915-235-2694; Fax: 915-235-3483.
Catechesis/Religious Program—Tel: 915-235-3529. Rhonda Moses, D.R.E. Students 34.
Mission—Our Mother of Mercy P.O. Box 206, Merkel, Taylor Co. 79536. Tel: 915-928-5239; Fax: 915-928-3739.
2—IMMACULATE HEART OF MARY (1962), (Hispanic), Revs. Michael Rodriguez; Sam Homsey, C.PP.S.
Res.: 511 W. Alabama, 79556. Tel: 915-235-3318 (Office); Fax: 915-235-0258.
Catechesis/Religious Program—Students 204.
Mission—St. Albert the Great 511 W. Alabama Ave., Roscoe, Nolan Co. 79556.

WALL, TOM GREEN CO., ST. AMBROSE (1941), [CEM] Rev. Msgr. Larry J. Droll, J.C.L.; Rev. Tom Barley.
Res.: P.O. Box 228, 76957. Tel: 915-651-7551; Fax: 915-651-6605.
Catechesis/Religious Program—Dolores Gully, D.R.E.; Jackie Droll, D.R.E.; Kathy Braden, D.R.E.; Sylvia Chappa, D.R.E. Students 311.
Mission—Holy Family P.O. Box 228, Mereta, Tom Green Co. 76957. Tel: 915-468-3101.

WINTERS, RUNNELS CO., OUR LADY OF MT. CARMEL (1962), (Hispanic), Rev. Obioma Desmond Obi.
Res.: 119 W. College, 79567. Tel: 325-754-4626; Fax: 325-754-4626.
Catechesis/Religious Program—Tel: 325-754-4893. Yolanda Bridgeman, D.R.E. Students 72.

On Special or Other Diocesan Assignment:
Rev.—
Barley, Tom, Box 1829, 76902.

Military Chaplains:
Revs.—
Diab, Thomas P., 2 BW/HC, 275 Barksdale Blvd. E., Barksdale AFB, LA 71710-2121.
Hicks, Steven, USNR, LCDR, 211A Lighthouse Ave., Kodiak, AK 99615.

Retired:
Rev. Msgr.—
Zientek, Benedict
Revs.—
Colaciccc, Frank L., St. Isidore Church, 445 LaGanda, Danville, CA 94526.
Droll, Louis J., 132 Retama Dr., Georgetown, 78626.
Gallagher, Raymond, 1352 Ford Rd., Lyndhurst, OH 44124.
Larue, Charles, Padua Place, 80 Peter Baque Rd., San Antonio, 78209.
Schultz, Russell, 209 S. 3rd St., Kenedy, 78119-0359.

Permanent Deacons:
Ballero, Peter, Sts. Joachim & Ann Mission, Clyde
Beach, Leroy, Our Lady of Guadalupe, Millersview
Camacho, Isaac, Holy Family, Abilene
Carrasco, Julio, Good Shepherd, Crane
Casarez, Art, Sacred Heart, Abillene
Cisneros, Ignacio, Holy Redeemer, Odessa
Crochet, Larry, Austin
Esparza, Jose, Our Lady Of Lourdes, Imperial
Franco, Simon, St. Agnes, Ft. Stockton
Giovannitti, Thomas, On Duty Outside the Diocese
Gonzales, Antonio, Holy Redeemer, Odessa
Graham, Tim, St. Theresa, Junction
Guajardo, Jesse, Our Lady of Guadalupe, Midland
Gutierrez, Apolonio, Good Shepherd, Crane
Hernandez, Andres, St. Agnes, Ft. Stockton
Ibarra, Roy, St. Mary, San Angelo
Kahlig, Michael, St. Peter, Mertzon
King, David, Immaculate Heart of Mary, Big Spring
Klein, Paul, Holy Family, Abilene
LaMonica, Michael, Our Lady of San Juan, Midland
Lopez, Joseph, St. Philip's, Eola
Luevano, Manuel, St. Elizabeth, Odessa
Martinez, Enrique, St. James, Bronte
Mercado, Jesus, St. Joseph, Odessa
Munoz, John, St. Joseph, San Angelo
Neff, Alan, St. Elizabeth Ann Seton, Odessa
Pena, Daniel, On Duty Outside the Diocese
Rock, Wayne, Immaculate Heart of Mary, Big Spring
Rodriguez, Bonfacio (Barney), St. Anthony's, Odessa
Samaniego, Enemencio, St. Ann, Sonora
Sanchez, Ernie, St. Joseph, Stanton
Sanchez, Pedro, St. Francis, Abilene
Santoya, Pedro, St. Elizabeth, Odessa
Schwalb, Gerald, Holy Family, Abilene
Sevier, Lazaro, St. Mary, San Angelo
Smith, Raymond, St. Margaret, San Angelo
Specht, John, St. Mary, Brownwood
Torres, Mario, St. Mary, San Angelo
Trevino, Jerry, Sacred Heart, San Angelo
Ureta, Cosme, St. Joseph, Fort Stockton
Yanez, Horacio, St. Thomas, Big Spring

INSTITUTIONS LOCATED IN THE DIOCESE

[A] MONASTERIES AND RESIDENCES OF PRIESTS & BROTHERS

CHRISTOVAL. *Hermits of the Blessed Virgin Mary of Mount Carmel*, Formerly Mount Carmel Hermitage, P.O. Box 337, 76935-0337. Tel: 325-896-2249; Fax: 325-896-2249. Email: fatherfabian@carmelitehermits.org. Web: www.CarmeliteHermits.org. Rev. Fabian Maria Rosette, O.Carm., Prior. Mt. Carmel Hermitage Hermits 5.

[B] CONVENTS AND RESIDENCES FOR SISTERS

SAN ANGELO. *School Sisters of Notre Dame*, 2627 Era St., 76905. Tel: 915-651-7500; Fax: 915-651-9532. Email: dosaoef@aol.com.

CHRISTOVAL. *Carmelite Nuns of the Ancient Observance*, Monastery of Our Lady of Grace, 6202 CR 339 Via Maria, 76935. Tel: 325-853-1722; Fax: 325-853-1722. Email: desertcarmel@carmelnet.org. Web: http://carmelnet.org/christoval/christoval.htm. Sr. Mary Grace Erl, O.Carm., Vicar Prioress.

MIDLAND. *Oblates of Notre Dame*, 1400 Garden Ln., 79701. Tel: 432-684-8318; Fax: 432-682-9364. Email: rcjavierond@prodigy.net.
1321 W. Monahans, Odessa, 79763. Tel: 432-580-8872; Fax: 432-333-3631.

[C] ST. VINCENT DE PAUL SOCIETY

SAN ANGELO. *Catholic Outreach Services*, 400 N. Chadbourne, 76903. Tel: 915-658-4124; Fax: 915-481-0315. Email: cos@wcc.net. Thrift Store Social Services

ABILENE. *St. Vincent De Paul Society*, 1241 Walnut, 79601. Tel: 915-677-6871. Total Assisted 12,000; Total Staff 4.
St. Vincent De Paul Thrift Store.

BIG SPRING. *St. Vincent De Paul Society* Food Distribution. , 1009 Hearn, 79720. Tel: 432-267-4124; Fax: 432-267-7844. Email: ihmch@crcom.net. Families 1,280; People 2,296.

MIDLAND. *St. Vincent De Paul Society*, P.O. Box 711, 79702-0711. Total Staff 2.

ODESSA. *Catholic Charities Community Services Odessa, Inc.*, 606 W. 10th, 79761. Tel: 915-332-1387.

STANTON. *St. Vincent De Paul Society*, P.O. Box 846, 79782. Tel: 432-756-3743; Fax: 432-756-3756.

[D] CAMPUS MINISTRY

SAN ANGELO. *Catholic Newman Center* 2431 Dena Dr., 76904. Tel: 325-949-8033. Email newman@wcc.net. Sr. Marie Malachy Griffin, O.P., Campus Min. Total Staff 1.

[E] MISCELLANEOUS

SAN ANGELO. *Christ the King Retreat Center*, 802 Ford, 76905. Tel: 325-651-5352; 325-651-5358; Fax: 325-651-5667. Email: ckrc@wcc.net. Rev. John Castro, O.M.I., Dir. Total in Residence 1; Total Staff 15.

RELIGIOUS INSTITUTES OF MEN REPRESENTED IN THE DIOCESE

For further details refer to the corresponding bracketed number in the Religious Institutes of Men or Women section.

[1110]—*Missionaries of the Sacred Heart* (Cork Ireland Prov.)—M.S.C.

[0910]—*Oblates of Mary Immaculate* (Southern American Prov.)—O.M.I.

[]—*Order of Preachers (Dominicans)* (Philippines)—O.P.

[1060]—*Society of the Precious Blood* (Kansas City Prov.)—C.PP.S.

RELIGIOUS INSTITUTES OF WOMEN REPRESENTED IN THE DIOCESE

[0320]—*Carmelite Nuns of the Ancient Observance*—O.Carm.

[1010]—*Congregation of Divine Providence of San Antonio, Texas*—C.D.P.

[0460]—*Congregation of Sisters of Charity of the Incarnate Word*—C.C.V.I.

[0760]—*Daughters of Charity of St. Vincent De Paul*—D.C.

[1070-24]—*Dominican Sisters of Great Bend, Kansas*—O.P.

[1070-19]—*Dominican Sisters, Houston*—O.P.

[1070-03]—*Dominican Sisters, Sinsinawa*—O.P.

[2960]—*Oblates of Notre Dame*—O.N.D.

[]—*Oblates of Notre Dame* (Midland, TX)

[]—*Oblates of Notre Dame, Philippines*

[1680]—*School Sisters of St. Francis*—S.S.S.F.

[0990]—*Sisters of Divine Providence*—C.D.P.

[1570]—*Sisters of St. Francis of the Holy Family*—O.S.F.

NECROLOGY

† Murphy, Rev. Msgr. Timothy J., Midland, TX St. Ann's—Died 2004
† Coleman, James, (Retired)—Died Nov. 10, 2002
† Espitia, David, Colorado City, TX St. Ann Church—Died June 13, 2003
† Vergauwen, Peter, (Retired)—Died Sept. 15, 2003

Archdiocese of San Antonio

(Archidioecesis Sancti Antonii)

Most Reverend

PATRICK F. FLORES, D.D.

Archbishop of San Antonio; ordained May 26, 1956; appointed Titular Bishop of Italica and Auxiliary of San Antonio March 18, 1970; consecrated May 5, 1970; appointed Bishop of El Paso April 4, 1978; installed May 29, 1978; promoted Archiepiscopal See of San Antonio August 28, 1979; installed October 13, 1979. *Res.: 2600 W. Woodlawn Ave., San Antonio, TX 78228. Chancery Office: P.O. Box 28410, San Antonio, TX 78228-0410.* Tel: 210-734-2620.

Chancery Office: 2718 W. Woodlawn Ave., P.O. Box 28410, San Antonio, TX 78228-0410. Tel: 210-734-2620; Fax: 210-734-0231.

Web: www.archdiosa.org

Email: administrator@archdiosa.org

Most Reverend

BERNARD F. POPP, D.D.

Retired Auxiliary Bishop of San Antonio; ordained February 24, 1943; appointed Titular Bishop of Capsus and Auxiliary Bishop of San Antonio June 7, 1983; consecrated July 25, 1983; retired March 23, 1993. *Res.: Casa de Padres*, 8520 Mountain Trail #1001, San Antonio, TX 78255. *Mailing Address: P.O. Box 28410, San Antonio, TX 78228-0410.* Tel: 210-698-5524.

Most Reverend

THOMAS J. FLANAGAN, D.D.

Auxiliary Bishop of San Antonio; ordained June 10, 1956; appointed Auxiliary Bishop of San Antonio and Titular Bishop of Bavagaliana January 15, 1998; consecrated February 16, 1998. *Res.: Oblate Madonna House*, 5722 Blanco Rd., San Antonio, TX 78216-6615. *Mailing Address: P.O. Box 28410, San Antonio, TX 78228-0410.* Tel: 210-734-2620.

Most Reverend

PATRICK J. ZUREK, D.D.

Auxiliary Bishop of San Antonio; ordained June 29, 1975; appointed Auxiliary Bishop of San Antonio and Titular Bishop of Tamugadi January 5, 1998; consecrated February 16, 1998. *Res.: 5015 Bayonne, San Antonio, TX 78228. Mailing Address: P.O. Box 28410, San Antonio, TX 78228-0410.* Tel: 210-734-2620.

ESTABLISHED AUGUST 28, 1874.

Square Miles 23,180.

Created an Archbishopric, August 3, 1926.

The San Antonio Archdiocese comprises Atascosa, Bandera, Bexar, Comal, Edwards, Frio, Gillespie, Gonzales, Guadalupe, Karnes, Kendall, Kerr, Kinney, McMullen (that part of McMullen County north of the Nueces River), Medina, Real, Uvalde, Val Verde and Wilson.

For legal titles of parishes and archdiocesan institutions, consult the Chancery Office.

STATISTICAL OVERVIEW

Personnel	
Archbishops	1
Auxiliary Bishops	2
Retired Bishops	1
Priests: Diocesan Active in Diocese	98
Priests: Diocesan Active Outside Diocese	13
Priests: Retired, Sick or Absent	41
Number of Diocesan Priests	152
Religious Priests in Diocese	198
Total Priests in Diocese	350
Extern Priests in Diocese	48
Ordinations:	
Diocesan Priests	2
Religious Priests	2
Transitional Deacons	1
Permanent Deacons	9
Permanent Deacons in Diocese	313
Total Brothers	78
Total Sisters	822
Parishes	
Parishes	139
With Resident Pastor:	
Resident Diocesan Priests	90
Resident Religious Priests	42
Without Resident Pastor:	
Administered by Priests	7
Missions	34
Pastoral Centers	2
Professional Ministry Personnel:	
Brothers	7
Sisters	36
Lay Ministers	289
Welfare	
Catholic Hospitals	3
Total Assisted	249,359
Health Care Centers	3
Homes for the Aged	8
Total Assisted	720
Residential Care of Children	3
Total Assisted	314
Day Care Centers	9
Total Assisted	847
Specialized Homes	5
Total Assisted	3,315
Special Centers for Social Services	10
Other Institutions	1
Total Assisted	139
Educational	
Seminaries, Diocesan	1
Students from This Diocese	14
Students from Other Diocese	45
Diocesan Students in Other Seminaries	2
Seminaries, Religious	11
Students Religious	36
Total Seminarians	52
Colleges and Universities	4
Total Students	13,020
High Schools, Diocesan and Parish	2
Total Students	815
High Schools, Private	6
Total Students	2,328
Elementary Schools, Diocesan and Parish	35
Total Students	9,386
Elementary Schools, Private	5
Total Students	1,900
Catechesis/Religious Education:	
High School Students	10,258
Elementary Students	34,106
Total Students under Catholic Instruction	71,865
Teachers in the Diocese:	
Priests	32
Scholastics	4
Brothers	14
Sisters	74
Lay Teachers	1,341
Vital Statistics	
Receptions into the Church:	
Infant Baptism Totals	11,896
Adult Baptism Totals	537
Received into Full Communion	597
First Communions	9,153
Confirmations	5,604
Marriages:	
Catholic	1,993
Interfaith	423
Total Marriages	2,416
Deaths	4,821
Total Catholic Population	667,667
Total Population	1,979,732

Former Bishops—Rt. Revs. ANTHONY DOMINIC PELLICER, D.D., consecrated Dec. 8, 1874; died April 14, 1880; JOHN C. NERAZ, D.D., consecrated May 8, 1881; died Nov. 15, 1894; JOHN ANTHONY FOREST, D.D., consecrated Oct. 28, 1895; died March 11, 1911; Most Revs. JOHN W. SHAW, D.D., Coadjutor Bishop of San Antonio; appt. Feb. 7, 1910; consecrated Titular Bishop of Castabala, April 14, 1910; succeeded to the See of San Antonio, March 11, 1911; made assistant at the Pontifical Throne, Sept., 1916; promoted to the See of New Orleans, Jan. 25, 1918; died Nov. 2, 1934; ARTHUR JEROME DROSSAERTS, D.D., LL.D., Bishop of San Antonio; appt. July 18, 1918; consecrated Dec. 8, 1918; named Archbishop, Aug. 3, 1926; assistant at the Pontifical Throne, Aug. 19, 1934; died Sept. 8, 1940; ROBERT E. LUCEY, S.T.D., Bishop of Amarillo; appt. Feb. 10, 1934; consecrated May 1, 1934; promoted to the Archiepiscopal See of San Antonio, Jan. 23, 1941; died Aug. 1, 1977; FRANCIS J. FUREY, Titular Bishop of Temnus and Auxiliary of Philadelphia; appt. Aug. 24, 1960; consecrated Dec. 22, 1960; promoted to Coadjutor and Apostolic Administrator "sede plena" of San Diego, July 25, 1963; promoted to Archiepiscopal See of San Antonio, June 4, 1969; Pallium conferred, Dec. 15, 1969; died April 23, 1979.

Vicar General and Moderator of the Curia—Rev. Msgr. LAWRENCE STUEBBEN, V.G.

Chancery Office—2718 W. Woodlawn Ave., P.O. Box 28410, San Antonio, 78228-0410. Tel: 210-734-2620; Fax: 210-734-0231. Office Hours: Mon.-Fri. 8:30-5:00

Chancellor—Rev. Msgr. TERENCE NOLAN.

Archives—Bro. EDWARD J. LOCH, S.M., Archivist.

Administrative Asst. to the Archbishop—Rev. Msgr. LAWRENCE J. STUEBBEN, V.G.

Office of the Archbishop—Secretaries to the Archbishop: MYRTLE G. SANCHEZ; CARMEN IRUEGAS, 2718 W. Woodlawn Ave., P.O. Box 28410, San Antonio, 78228-0410.

Office of Communications—Deacon PAT ROGERS, P.O. Box 28410, San Antonio, 78228-0410. Tel: 210-734-2620; Fax: 210-734-2774. Email: progers@archdiosa.org.

Office of the Synod—Sr. JANET MARIE ABBACCHI, S.S.N.D., Coord., P.O. Box 28410, San Antonio, 78228-0410. Tel: 210-734-2620; 800-796-6398 (Texas).

College of Consultors—Most Revs. BERNARD F. POPP, D.D., V.G.; THOMAS FLANAGAN, D.D., V.G.; PATRICK ZUREK, D.D., V.G.; Rev. Msgrs. LAWRENCE STUEBBEN, V.G.; TERENCE NOLAN; BALTHASAR JANACEK, V.U.; MICHAEL YARBROUGH, V.U.; Very Rev. MICHAEL BOULETTE, V.F.; Revs. DAVID GARCIA; WILLIAM MCNAMARA.

Deans—In Metropolitan Area: Rev. Msgrs. MICHAEL YARBROUGH, V.U., North; BALTHASAR JANACEK, V.U., Central; Very Revs. WALTER D'HEEDENE, C.I.C.M., V.U., Northwest; SAMUEL HEITKAMP, V.U., Northeast; CARLOS VELASQUEZ, V.U., Western; AMANDO TRUJILLO-CANO, T.O.R., V.U., Southwest; LAWRENCE BRUMMER, O.F.M., V.U., Southeast. In Rural Area: Very Revs. WILLIAM MCNAMARA, V.F., Floresville; MICHAEL BOULETTE, V.F., Fredericksburg; Rev. WALLIS STILES, Hondo; Very Rev. Msgr. EDWARD BILY, V.F., New Braunfels; Rev. CARLOS DAVALOS, V.F., Pleasanton; Very Rev. GERALD HUBERTUS, V.F., Seguin; Rev. JAMES FISCHLER, C.I.C.M., Uvalde; VACANT, North Urban.

Vicars for Religious—Rev. Msgr. THOMAS FRENCH, Incarnate Word Residence, 4707 Broadway, San Antonio, 78209. Tel: 210-822-0385; Sr. CHARLENE WEDELICH, C.D.P., P.O. Box 28410, San Antonio, 78228-0410. Tel: 210-734-2620.

Vicar for Priests—VACANT.

Vicar for Retired Priests—VACANT.

Archdiocesan Presbyteral Council—Most Revs. PATRICK F. FLORES, D.D.; BERNARD POPP, D.D., V.G. (Retired); THOMAS FLANAGAN, D.D., V.G.; PATRICK ZUREK, D.D., V.G.; Rev. Msgrs. TERENCE NOLAN; LAWRENCE STUEBBEN, V.G.; MICHAEL YARBROUGH, V.U., Chm.; BALTHASAR JANACEK, V.U.; Very Revs. WALTER D'HEEDENE, C.I.C.M., V.U.; SAMUEL HEITKAMP, V.U.; LAWRENCE BRUMMER, O.F.M., V.U.; CARLOS VELASQUEZ, V.U.; AMANDO TRUJILLO, T.O.R., V.U.; WILLIAM MCNAMARA, V.F.; MICHAEL BOULETTE, V.F.; Rev. WALLIS STILES; Very Revs. GERALD HUBERTUS, V.F.; CARLOS DAVALOS, V.F.; EDWARD BILY, V.F.; Revs. JAMES FISCHLER, C.I.C.M.; DAVID GARCIA, At Large.

Women's Commission—Mrs. CHRIS ALDERETE, Chm., 1602 Hillcrest Dr., E., San Antonio, 78228.

Archdiocesan Tribunal—P.O. Box 28410, San Antonio, 78228-0410. Tel: 210-734-2620, Ext. 135.

Judicial Vicar—Rev. Msgr. TERENCE NOLAN.

Assistant Director—Ms. MARGARITA M. PARRA.

Judges—Rev. Msgrs. TERENCE NOLAN; JAMES HENKE; JAMES JANISH; Revs. EMMET CAROLAN; JOSEPH LOPEZ.

Defenders of the Bond—Revs. KEVIN RYAN; PAUL CLEARY; Rev. Msgr. THOMAS MURPHY.

Promoter Justitiae—Rev. JOHN MAKOTHAKAT, J.C.D.

Approved Advocates—Mrs. ADRIANA FERRARO SEAWRIGHT; Mrs. EDNA BONO, M.S.W.; Mrs. JACQUIE NACEWSKI; Sr. MARY DOLORES DOYLE, C.C.V.I.

Notaries—Ms. MARGARITA M. PARRA; Ms. SYLVIA FALCON; Mrs. SUE FORBRICH; Ms. THERESA VALLEJO; Mrs. ANNA FOLLIS; Mr. DEREK LE BRANCH; Mrs. LORETTA REYES; Mrs. JANENE TIJERINA; Mrs. ROSE MCGUIRE.

Interdiocesan Appellate Court—P.O. Box 28410, San Antonio, 78228-0410. Tel: 210-736-9444; 210-736-2620, Ext. 145,.

Moderator—Most Rev. PATRICK F. FLORES, D.D.

Judicial Vicar—Rev. FREDERICK SACKETT, O.M.I., J.C.D.

Judges—Revs. LESLIE A. VANCE, J.C.L.; ALBERT HUBERTUS; TIMOTHY A. GOLLOB; DAVID-MARIE A. JAEGER, O.F.M., J.C.D.; JOHN M. MAKOTHAKAT; WARREN A. BROWN, O.M.I., J.C.D.; ALBERT E. VERBRUGGE, J.C.D. (Retired).

Defenders of the Bond—Revs. RAY WILHELM, O.M.I., J.C.L.; EMANUEL AFUNUGO, J.C.L.; ANH Q. TRAN, J.C.L.; JAMES A. KOTARA; EDWARD RODEN-LUCERO, J.C.L.; MICHAEL P. COLDWELL, J.C.L.; Sr. MARGARET A. RAMSDEN, S.F.C.C., J.C.L.; Ms. DENISE J. DOYLE, J.C.D., Ph.D.; Ms. LAURA L. LEFAVE, J.C.L.

Notaries—Mrs. LUANN HARTNETT; Mrs. DONNA MILLS.

Due Process: Councils of Conciliation and Arbitration—Chancery Office, 2718 W. Woodlawn Ave., San Antonio, 78228-5195. Tel: 210-734-2620.

Diocesan Administration

Administrative Services Department—Rev. Msgr. LAWRENCE J. STUEBBEN, V.G., Dir., P.O. Box 28410, San Antonio, 78228-0410. Tel: 210-734-2620.

Archives—Bro. EDWARD J. LOCH, S.M., P.O. Box 28410, San Antonio, 78228-0410. Tel: 210-734-2620.

Archdiocesan Finance Officer—Mr. DAVID CASTILLEJA, 2718 W. Woodlawn, San Antonio, 78228. Tel: 210-734-2620; Fax: 210-734-2774.

Archdiocesan Business Manager—Mr. MICHAEL WULCZYN, 2718 W. Woodlawn, San Antonio, 78228. Tel: 210-734-2620; Fax: 210-734-2774.

Archdiocesan Office of Stewardship and Development—Mr. CHRISTOPHER A. GRASSO, Dir., P.O. Box 28410, San Antonio, 78228-0410. Tel: 210-734-2620; Fax: 210-734-0231.

Archdiocesan Finance Council—Ms. VELIA GUERRA; Mr. THOMAS TARRILLION; Mr. GERARDO GONZALES; Mr. PABLO GUTIERREZ; Ms. SUSAN METARDUS; Deacon ROBERT KUSENBERGER SR.; Mr. ALAN CROSBY; Mr. ALTON PETSCH; Mr. DARRELL GRECO; Mrs. ELVIRA O. NANEZ; Mr. MARC HENRIQUEZ; Ms. PEGGY WILSON; Mr. EUGENE TSCHOEPE.

Archdiocesan Debt Review Committee—Mr. DAVID CASTILLEJA, Sec.; Mr. ALEX HINOJOSA; Mr. LOUIS SANCHEZ; Mr. ROBERT P. DUGAS; Mr. ALEX STEWART; Mr. JOHN D. SPECIA; Mr. S. E. DANYSH; Mrs. JENNITA POSTON; Mrs. DORA ANN VERDE; Mr. JOHN F. KRAMER.

Building Board—Mr. ROBERT ZEPEDA; Mr. COSMO F. GUIDO; Mr. JIM RODRIGUEZ; Mr. DAN CERNA; Mr. STEVE PERSYN.

Lay Pension Plan—Mr. RENE WILKES, Mgr., P.O. Box 28410, San Antonio, 78228-0410. Tel 210-734-2620.

Archdiocesan Cemeteries Office—Most Rev. THOMAS J. FLANAGAN, D.D., V.G., Dir.; Mr. ALBERT J. SANCHEZ, Supt., 746 Castroville Rd., San Antonio, 78207. Tel: 210-432-2303.

Computer Center—VACANT, P.O. Box 28410, San Antonio, 78228-0410. Tel: 210-734-2620

Director of Accounting—CARMELA MARTINEZ, 2718 W. Woodlawn, San Antonio, 78228. Tel: 210-734-2620.

Parish Accounting System—Mr. JESSE GARCIA. Tel: 210-734-2420.

Print/Mail Room—MARIA HINJOSA. Tel: 210-734-2620; Fax: 210-734-0231.

Department of Educational Services—Sr. THERESE SAN MIGUEL, O.S.F., Dir., P.O. Box 28410, San Antonio, 78228-0410. Tel: 210-734-2620.

Archdiocesan Schools Office—Mr. DALE HOYT, Supt., P.O. Box 28410, San Antonio, 78228-0410. Tel: 210-734-2620.

Archdiocesan Catechetical-Religious Education Center—BONNIE LE MELLE ABADIE, Dir., P.O. Box 28410, San Antonio, 78228-0410. Tel: 210-734-2620.

Adult Faith Formation—Mrs. MERSI ESPARZA-SCHORRAN, Asst. Dir., P.O. Box 28410, San Antonio, 78228-0410. Tel: 210-734-2620.

Office of Catholic Youth Ministry—Mr. PAT PERILLO, Dir., P.O. Box 28410, San Antonio, 78228-0410. Tel: 210-734-2620.

Catholic Committee on Scouting (Boys)—Sr. ANN CASSIDY, F.M.A., Chm., 2718 W. Woodlawn, San Antonio, 78228. Tel: 210-734-2620, Ext. 157.

Catholic Committee on Girl Scouting—Sr. ANN CASSIDY, F.M.A., Chm., 2718 W. Woodlawn, San Antonio, 78228. Tel: 210-734-2620, Ext. 157.

Catholic Campus Ministry (Newman Apostolate)—Mrs. CAROL WHITE, Dir., Catholic Student Center, 312 W. Courtland, San Antonio, 78212 Tel: 210-736-3752; Fax: 210-736-5365. St. Anthony Catholic Student Center at U.T.S.A., 14523 Roadrunner Way, San Antonio, 78249. Tel: 210-699-9594 SAC, St. Philip's, UTSA, UTSA Downtown, Texas A&M Extension, Palo Alto, Northwest Vista, Texas Lutheran, Schreiner University, Kerrville, Trinity, UT Health Science Center, S.W. Texas Junior College-Uvalde.

Catholic Campus Ministry Center—Palo Alto College, 1405 W. Villaret Blvd., San Antonio, 78224. Tel: 210-921-9380.

Family Life Office—STEVE GENGENBACHER, Dir., P.O. Box 28140, San Antonio, 78228-0410. Tel: 210-734-2620.

Natural Family Planning Office—Mrs. HENRIETTA O'CONNOR, Dir., P.O. Box 28410 San Antonio, 78228. Tel: 210-734-2620.

Office of Worship—Rev. Msgr. JAMES HENKE, Chm., Liturgy Commission; DOLORES MARTINEZ, Dir., P.O. Box 28410, San Antonio, 78228-0410. Tel: 210-734-2620.

Mission Awareness Office— (Holy Childhood Pontifical Assn.; Propagation of the Faith). MARY WISNIEWSKI, Dir., P.O. Box 28410, San Antonio, 78228-0410. Tel: 210-734-2620.

Young Adult Ministry—STEVE GENGENBACHER, Contact, Family Life Office, P.O. Box 28140, San Antonio, 78228-0410.

Department of Personnel Services—Most Rev. THOMAS J. FLANAGAN, D.D., V.G.

Priests Personnel Board—Most Rev. THOMAS FLANAGAN, D.D., Dir.; Rev. JIMMY DRENNAN, Chm.; Very Rev. CARLOS VELASQUEZ, V.U., Vice Chm.; Revs. LAWRENCE CHRISTIAN, Sec.; PABLO SICILIA; Rev. Msgrs. DOUGLAS EATER; BALTHASAR JANACEK, V.U.; Revs. CONOR MCGRATH; ANTHONY VILANO; ANTHONY CUMMINS; STUART JULEEN.

Office for Priests—Most Rev. THOMAS J. FLANAGAN, D.D., V.G.

Assumption-St. John's Seminary—Rev. GERALD L. BROWN, S.S., Rector, 2600 W. Woodlawn, San Antonio, 78228-5196. Tel: 210-734-5137.

Permanent Diaconate Program—Rev. JOHN O'DONOGHUE, Dir., 114 Shannon Lee, San Antonio, 78216-7316. Tel: 210-930-8118; Fax: 210-930-8377.

Vocation Office—Rev. ARTURO CEPEDA, Dir.; Sr. MARY FAGAN, S.H.S.P., Assoc. Dir., 2600 W. Woodlawn Ave., San Antonio, 78228-5196. Tel: 210-735-0553.

Communications Department—Most Rev. PATRICK ZUREK, D.D., V.G., Liaison; Deacon PAT ROGERS, Communications Dir., 2718 W. Woodlawn, San Antonio, 78228. Tel: 210-734-2620; Fax: 210-477-8910.

Catholic Television of San Antonio (CTSA), Channel 15—Deacon PAT ROGERS, Gen. Mgr., 2718 W. Woodlawn, San Antonio, 78228. Tel: 210-734-2620; Fax: 210-734-2939.

Today's Catholic Newspaper—Mr. JORDAN MC MORROUGH, Editor, 2718 W. Woodlawn, San Antonio, 78228. Tel: 210-734-2620; Fax: 210-734-2939.

Department of Social and Community Services—Mr. STEVE SALDANA, Dir., 1405 N. Main, Ste. 221, San Antonio, 78212. Tel: 210-222-1294; Fax: 210-227-0217.

Catholic Counseling and Consultation Center—Rev. JAMES RUTKOWSKI, S.T.L., Clinical Dir., Northside Center, 1840 Lockhill Selma, Ste. 102, San Antonio, 78216. Tel: 210-377-1133; Fax: 210-377-1230.

Office of Social Concerns—Mr. PETER MONOD DE FROIDEVILLE.

Campaign for Human Development—Mr. PETER MONOD DE FROIDEVILLE.

Ministry to Hearing Impaired—Rev. GUY BLAIR, S.C.J., San Francesco De Paola, 205 Piazza Italia, San Antonio, 78207. Tel: 210-227-0548.

Ministry to Persons with Disabilities—Mr. STEVE SALDANA, 1405 N. Main, Ste. 221, San Antonio, 78212. Tel: 210-222-1294.

Bexar County Detention Ministries—Sr. TERESA CARTER, C.S.B. Tel: 210-270-6329; Rev. CARL SCHINDLER, C.SS.R.; Deacons AUGUSTINE ARISMENDEZ. Tel: 210-270-6320. 200 N. Comal, San Antonio, 78207; HUGO SALINAS, Juvenile Detention, 600 Mission Rd., San Antonio, 78210. Tel: 210-531-1040.

St. Peter and Joseph's Home— (See Protective Institutions)

Seton Home— (See Protective Institutions)

Health Ministry Committee—Mrs. PAT SAMMIS. Tel: 210-302-2266.

Catholic Charities, Archdiocese of San Antonio—Mr. STEVEN SALDANA, Pres., 1405 N. Main Ave., Ste. 221, San Antonio, 78212-4315. Tel: 210-222-1294; Fax: 210-227-0217.

Refugee Resettlement Services—PAULA WALKER, 2903 W. Salinas, San Antonio, 78207. Tel: 210-433-3256; Fax: 210-433-0851.

Director Immigration Services—TERESA COLES-DAVILA, 2903 W. Salinas St., San Antonio, 78207. Tel: 210-433-3256; Fax: 210-433-0851.

Victim Assistance Coordinator and Safe Environment—JUDY ANDERSON PERILLO, M.A., S.W.A., St. Paul Community Center, 1202 Donaldson, San Antonio, 78228. Tel: 210-734-7786. Email: jperillo@archdiosa.org.

Diocesan Offices And Directors

Apostleship of Prayer—VACANT.

Archdiocesan Council of Catholic Women—Mrs. SYLVIA GARCIA, 2603 Whispering Dove, San Antonio, 78230. Tel: 210-492-9607; Rev. WILLIAM MCNAMARA, Spiritual Moderator, P.O. Box 248, Elmendorf, 78112-0248. Tel: 210-635-8539.

Catholic Center for Charismatic Renewal—Most Rev. THOMAS J. FLANAGAN, D.D., Dir., Liaison, 1707 S. Flores, San Antonio, 78204. Tel: 210-226-7545; Fax: 210-212-9330.

Catholic Lawyers Guild—Rev. Msgr. TERENCE NOLAN, Spiritual Moderator, P.O. Box 28410, San Antonio, 78228-0410. Tel: 210-734-2620.

Catholic Physicians Guild—Rev. JOHN A. LEIES, S.M., S.T.D.; MIGUEL BEDOLLA, M.D., Ph.D., Pres., 520 Fordham Ln., San Antonio, 78228. Tel: 210-436-3227.

Censores Librorum—Rev. FREDERICK SACKETT, O.M.I., J.C.D.

Movimiento de Apostolado Familiar & Marriage Encounter (Rural)—Rev. ABRAHAM LA TORRE (Retired) (Colombia) 6051 Monterey St., San Antonio, 78237. Tel: 210-732-6295.

Movimiento Familiar Cristano (Urban)—Presidents: MANUEL MORENO; JULIA MORENO, 1310 Clamp St., San Antonio, 78221. Tel: 210-923-1626.

Christian Life Communities—VACANT.

Black Catholic Apostolate—Deacon THOMAS WHITE, Dir., 1819 Nevada, San Antonio, 78203. Tel: 210-532-5358.

Cursillo Movement (Spanish)—Rev. ABRAHAM LA TORRE, 602 Urban Loop, San Antonio, 78207. Tel: 210-224-2796.

Cursillo Movement (English)—

Cursillos of Christianity of the Archdiocese of San Antonio—VERONICA TREVINO, Treas., P.O. Box

5152, San Antonio, 78201. Tel: 210-492-8788.
Ecumenical Affairs—VACANT.
Holy Childhood, Pontifical Association—MARY WISNIEWSKI, P.O. Box 28410, San Antonio, 78228-0410. Tel: 210-734-2620.
Holy Name Society—HENRY ALMAGUER JR., 306 Beryl Dr., San Antonio, 78213. Tel: 210-340-2914.
Pre-Seminary Program—Rev. ARTURO CEPEDA, Dir., Assumption Seminary, 2600 W. Woodlawn, San Antonio, 78228-5196. Tel: 210-735-0553.
Priests Eucharistic League—Most Rev. THOMAS J. FLANAGAN, D.D., V.G., Dir., P.O. Box 28410, San Antonio, 78228-0410. Tel: 210-734-2620.
Propagation of the Faith—MARY WISNIEWSKI, P.O. Box 28410, San Antonio, 78228-0410.
Public Relations Council—Col. JOSEPH B. MCSHANE, 1410 Treasure Way, San Antonio, 78209. Tel: 210-826-3361.
Retreats, Men—Bro. PATRICK MCGEE, O.M.I., M.A., Dir., Oblate Renewal Center, 127 Oblate Dr., San Antonio, 78216. Tel: 210-349-4173.
Respect Life Program—Rev. Msgr. SHERRILL SMITH, Moderator (Retired), 8520 Cross Mountain Tr., #201, San Antonio, 78255. Tel: 210-698-8819.
Rural Life Conference—VACANT.
St. Vincent de Paul Society—Mr. HOMER CADENA, Pres., Mailing Address, 928 W. Commerce, San Antonio, 78207. Tel: 210-225-7837.

CLERGY, PARISHES, MISSIONS AND PAROCHIAL SCHOOLS

CITY OF SAN ANTONIO

1—CATHEDRAL OF SAN FERNANDO (1731), (Hispanic), Revs. David Garcia; James L. Emperur, S.J.; Lenin Naffate; Deacons Albert Garza; Doroteo E. Pedroza; Enrique Barrera; Pedro Garza.
Res.: 115 Main Plaza, 78205. Tel: 210-227-1297; Fax: 210-271-0149.
Catechesis/Religious Program—Students 271.
Mission—San Francesco di Paola (Italian) 205 Piazza Italia, Bexar Co. 78207. Tel: 210-227-0548; Fax: 210-226-5086. Rev. Guy Blair, S.C.J.

2—ST. AGNES (1923), (Hispanic), Rev. Einer Ochoa. In Res., Very Rev. Lawrence Stuebben, V.G.
Office—814 Ruiz St., 78207. Fax: 210-212-7757.
Res.: 804 Ruiz St., 78207. Tel: 210-227-8258.
Catechesis/Religious Program—Sr. Margaret Mary Barrett, D.R.E. Students 363.

3—ST. ALPHONSUS (1925), (Hispanic), Rev. Arturo M. Ocampo, O.F.M.; Deacon Trinidad Gutierrez; Sr. Adele Massaro, Pastoral Assoc. In Res., Rev. Francisco Munoz, O.F.M.Conv.
Res.: 2004 Chihuahua St., 78207. Tel: 210-433-9365; Fax: 210-433-9365.
Catechesis/Religious Program—Tel: 210-432-3176. Students 125.

4—ST. ANN (1912), (Hispanic), Revs. Andrew K. Kolzow, O.P.; Cayet Mangiaracina, O.P.; Vincente M. Pena, O.P.; Wilmo A. Candanedo, O.P.; Bruce B. Schultz, O.P.; John E. Keefer, O.P.; Bros. Ramon Gonzalez, O.P.; Omomaro Okekaro, O.P.
Res.: 210 St. Ann St., 78201. Tel: 210-734-6687; Fax: 210-738-1755.
Catechesis/Religious Program—Tel: 210-733-9681. Students 371.

5—ST. ANTHONY MARY CLARET (1988), Rev. Jan Klak.
Res.: 6150 Roft Rd., 78253. Tel: 210-688-9033; Fax: 210-688-3575.
Catechesis/Religious Program—Sr. Marian Sturm, I.W.B.S., D.R.E. Students 542.

6—ST. ANTHONY OF PADUA (1957), Rev. Patrick O'Shea, M.S.C.; Deacon Gilbert Wiessler.
Res.: 102 Lorenz Rd., 78209. Tel: 210-824-1743; Fax: 210-824-3283.
Catechesis/Religious Program—Tel: 210-824-6740. Students 225.

7—BASILICA OF THE NATIONAL SHRINE OF OUR LADY OF MT. CARMEL AND ST. THERESE, DISCALCED CARMELITE FATHE (1926), (Hispanic), Revs. John M. Suenram, O.C.D.; Marion Bui, O.C.D.; Mary Philip Wurth, O.C.D.; Sam Anthony Morello, O.C.D.
Office—824 Kentucky Ave., 78201. Tel: 210-735-9126; Fax: 210-735-1389.
Res.: 906 Kentucky Ave., 78201-6097. Tel: 210-735-9127; Fax: 210-738-0818.
School—905 Kentucky Ave., 78201. Tel: 210-732-9207; Fax: 210-732-3214. Rita Graves, Prin. Sisters of the Holy Spirit 3; Notre Dame Sisters 1; Lay Teachers 13; Students 264.
Catechesis/Religious Program—Tel: 210-734-4893. Sr. Eileen Mannion, S.H.Sp., D.R.E. Students 240.

8—ST. BENEDICT (1958), (Polish—Hispanic), Revs. Edward Bernal; Yohanes Taosan, C.I.C.M. (Indonesia); Deacons Charles Lammons; James Raso.
Res.: 4535 Lord Rd., 78220. Tel: 210-648-0123; Fax: 210-648-1722.
School—Tel: 210-648-1611. Mrs. Frances Grams, Prin. Lay Teachers 14; Students 113.
Catechesis/Religious Program—Tel: 210-648-4632. Students 175.

9—BLESSED SACRAMENT (1956), Rev. John O'Donoghue; Deacons Joe Fertitta; Joseph Jorgensen; Bruce Bellg; Edward Lopez.
Office—600 Oblate Dr., 78216. Tel: 210-824-7231; Fax: 210-824-4293.
School—Tel: 210-824-3381; Fax: 210-826-6147. Mrs. Lucy Williams, Prin. Lay Teachers 20; Students 270; Day Care 114.
Catechesis/Religious Program—Students 380.

10—ST. BONAVENTURE (1959), (Hispanic), Rev. Raymond Schuster; Sr. Mary T. Phelan, Pastoral Assoc.; Deacons Fidel Hinojosa; Amador Gonzalez.
Res.: 1918 Palo Alto Rd., 78211. Tel: 210-922-1685; Fax: 210-922-7821.
Catechesis/Religious Program—Tel: 210-922-1882. Mrs. Diane Guerra, D.R.E. Students 516.

11—ST. BRIGID (1972), Rev. Leslie A. Vance, J.C.L.; Deacons Thomas Billimek; Pasquale M. Benigno; Patrick F. Frisina; Paul Heye; Juan Espinosa.
Res.: 6907 Kitchener Rd., 78240. Tel: 210-696-0896; Fax: 210-696-7319.
Catechesis/Religious Program—Charlene Staedtler, D.R.E. Students 449.

12—ST. CECILIA (1919), (Hispanic), Rev. Francis M. Landwermeyer, S.J.
Res.: 125 W. Whittier St., 78210-2897. Tel: 210-533-7109; Fax: 210-532-2599.
School—Tel: 210-534-2711; Fax: 210-533-8284. Mrs. Mary I. Crow, Prin. Sisters 5; Lay Teachers 14; Students 181.
Catechesis/Religious Program—Tel: 210-532-1994. Mrs. Limba Reyes, D.R.E. Students 213.
Mission—Purisima Concepcion 807 Mission Rd., Bexar Co. 78210.

13—CHRIST THE KING (1928), (Hispanic), Rev. Richard Pena; Esther Rodriguez, Admin.
Res.: 2623 Perez St., 78207. Tel: 210-433-6301; Fax: 210-435-2736.
Catechesis/Religious Program—Tel: 210-433-3640. Sr. Adelina Esquivel, M.C.M., D.R.E. Students 133.

14—ST. CLARE (1959), (Hispanic), Rev. Msgr. Lambert Bily.
Res.: 7701 Somerset Rd., 78211. Tel: 210-924-5252.
Catechesis/Religious Program—Tel: 210-922-6458. Maria Delores M. Marek, D.R.E. Students 205.

15—DIVINE PROVIDENCE (1981), (Hispanic), Rev. Phillip D. Henning; Deacons Jose Suniga; Juan G. Martinez.
Church: 5667 Old Pearsall Rd., 78242-2335. Tel: 210-623-3970; Fax: 210-623-3978.
Catechesis/Religious Program—Tel: 210-623-3971. Diane Garza-Valdez, D.R.E. Students 613.

16—ST. DOMINIC (1971), Rev. Paul Cleary; Deacons Lionel Garza; Alan Fitzpatrick; Jimmie Trevino; Bert Stewart; Sue Graves, Pastoral Assoc.
Res.: 5919 Ingram Rd., 78228. Tel: 210-435-6211; Fax: 210-435-1732.
Catechesis/Religious Program—Tel: 210-435-9267. Sue Graves, D.R.E. Students 654.

17—ST. FRANCIS OF ASSISI (1980), Rev. Msgr. James Henke; Sr. Frances Briseno, O.S.B., Pastoral Assoc.; Deacons Tom Franklin; Brian Clayton.
Residence and Education Office: 4201 De Zavala Rd., 78249-2000. Tel: 210-492-4600; Fax: 210-492-8128.
Catechesis/Religious Program—Gloria Clayton, D.R.E. Students 450.

18—ST. GABRIEL (1958), (Hispanic), Rev. Louis Jaspers, C.I.C.M. (Belgium); Deacon Frank Castellano. In Res., Rev. Edward Gonzalez-Martinez (Spain).
Res.: 747 S.W. 39th St., 78237. Tel: 210-433-3689; Fax: 210-433-0546.
Catechesis/Religious Program—Tel: 210-433-3354. Virginia Ibarra, D.R.E.; Nickie Cantu, D.R.E. Students 99.

19—ST. GERARD MAJELLA (1911), Revs. Alton Carr, C.SS.R.; John Farnik, C.SS.R. In Res., Revs. Francis Pham, C.SS.R.; Monroe Perrier, C.SS.R.
Res.: 1523 Iowa St., 78203. Tel: 210-533-0161 (Church Office); Fax: 210-533-0558.
High School—Archdiocesan Regional, 521 S. New Braunfels Ave., 78203. Tel: 210-533-8061; Fax: 210-533-3697. Maurice Abadie, Pres. Sisters 2; Brothers 1; Lay Teachers 14; Students 150.
Catechesis/Religious Program—Students 151.

20—ST. GREGORY'S (1955), Rev. Msgr. Michael B. O'Gorman (Ireland); Sisters M. Carmel O'Callaghan, P.B.V.M., Pastoral Assoc.; Luz Valdez, M.C.M.; Clare Conway, P.B.V.M.; Deacons Fred Campos Jr.; Donald A. Novian.
Res.: 700 Dewhurst, 78213. Tel: 210-342-5271; Fax: 210-342-0542.
School—Tel: 210-342-0281; Fax: 210-308-7177. Martha Gomez, Prin. Lay Teachers 35; Students 650.
Catechesis/Religious Program—Tel: 210-342-3826. Gloria Silva, D.R.E. Students 425.

21—ST. HELENA (1974), Rev. Msgr. Leo M. Dolan; Deacons Leonard Standcombe; Paul Gustowski; Rose Marden, Pastoral Assoc.
Office—14714 Edgemont, 78247. Tel: 210-653-3316; Fax: 210-653-3163.
Res.: 14527 Angora, 78247. Tel: 210-653-3850.
Catechesis/Religious Program—Tel: 210-653-3316; Fax: 210-653-2702. Corrie Solis, D.R.E.; Joan Martinez, D.R.E. Students 780.

22—ST. HENRY (1904), (Hispanic), Rev. Msgr. Emil J. Wesselsky.
Res.: 1619 S. Flores St., 78204. Tel: 210-225-6877; Fax: 210-225-6878.
Catechesis/Religious Program—Tel: 210-227-1585. Sr. Virginia Clara Ruiz, H.C.G., D.R.E. Students 397.

23—HOLY FAMILY (1963), (Hispanic), Rev. James Kotara; Deacons Manuel Carranza; Javier Tamez; Roman Soto; Pedro Castillo.
Res.: 152 Florencia, 78228-5899. Tel: 210-433-8216; Fax: 210-435-0090.
Catechesis/Religious Program—Tel: 210-433-3006. Ester Mango, D.R.E. Students 201.

24—HOLY NAME (1961), (Polish—Hispanic), Rev. Msgr. Franciszek Kurzaj; Deacons David L. Herbert; Reynaldo Hinojosa Sr.
Res.: 3814 Nash Blvd., 78223.
School—Tel: 210-333-7356; Fax: 210-333-7642. Mr. Chad Mills, Prin. Lay Teachers 11; Students 205.
Catechesis/Religious Program—Tel: 210-333-5020; Fax: 210-333-5021. Margaret Miksch, D.R.E. Students 262.

25—HOLY REDEEMER (1901), (African American), [CEM] Rev. Bruce B. Schultz, O.P.; Deacon Thomas White.
Res.: 1819 Nevada, 78203. Tel: 210-532-5358; Fax: 210-532-3699.
Catechesis/Religious Program—Students 80.

26—HOLY ROSARY (1948), (Hispanic), Revs. John J. Manahan, S.M.; Bernard Meyer, S.M.; Bros. Richard Schrader, S.M., Pastoral Assoc.; Robert Hatesohl, S.M., Pastoral Assoc.; Deacons Felipe Barajas, Pastoral Assoc.; Earl Colley, Pastoral Assoc.
Res.: 159 Camino Santa Maria, 78228. Tel: 210-433-3241; Fax: 210-433-2133.
School—155 Camino Santa Maria, 78228. Tel: 210-433-4312; Fax: 210-433-7055. Sr. Grechen Trautman, F.M.I., D.R.E. Sisters 2; Lay Teachers 11; Students 140.
Catechesis/Religious Program—Linda Chavez, D.R.E. Students 279.

27—HOLY SPIRIT (1964), Revs. Anthony Pesek; Daniel Cisneros; Deacons Sonny Staudt; Jesse Greer; Patrick Cunningham; William Peche.
Res.: 758 W. Ramsey Rd., 78216. Tel: 210-341-1395; Fax: 210-341-8438.
School—770 W. Ramsey Rd., 78216. Tel: 210-349-1169; Fax: 210-349-1247. Mrs. Joann Gawlik, Prin. Lay Teachers 51; Students 497.
Catechesis/Religious Program—Tel: 210-341-1397; Fax: 210-341-2287. Pat Keene, D.R.E. Students 837.

28—HOLY TRINITY (1987), Rev. Msgr. Douglas Fater; Deacons Jerry Micek; Chris Laskowski.
Res.: 20523 Huebner Rd., 78258. Tel: 210-497-4200; Fax: 210-497-4285.
Catechesis/Religious Program—Tel: 210-497-4145. Veronica Benson, D.R.E. Students 1,160.

29—IMMACULATE CONCEPTION (1933), (Hispanic), Rev. William Collins, M.S.C..; Deacons Jose Hernandez; Marcos Criado.
Res.: 314 Merida St., 78207. Tel: 210-225-2986; Fax: 210-225-2987.
Catechesis/Religious Program—Mercy Cortez, D.R.E. Students 152.

30—IMMACULATE HEART OF MARY (1912), (Hispanic), Revs. Ignacio Blanco, C.M.F.; Jose Sanchez, C.M.F.; Deacon Jorge Bonilla-Valentin. In Res., Revs. Roberto Alvarado, C.M.F.; Steven Sherwood, C.M.F.; George Sturm, C.M.F.
Res.: 617 S. Santa Rosa Blvd., 78204. Tel: 210-226-8268; 210-226-8269; Fax: 210-226-2412.
Catechesis/Religious Program—Tel: 210-224-8829. Alfonso Cervantes, D.R.E. Students 90.

31—ST. JAMES THE APOSTLE (1954), (Hispanic), Revs. Emmet Carolan; Michael McManus; Deacons Jesse P. Alcala; Ernest Huizar; Charlie Von Allmen; Onofre Toscano, Pastoral Assoc.
Res.: 907 W. Theo Ave., 78225. Tel: 210-922-2136; Fax: 210-923-0940.
School—Tel: 210-924-1201; Fax: 210-924-0201. Sr. Cecilia Henry, F.M.A., Prin. Daughters of Mary Help of Christians 3; Lay Teachers 21; Students 357.
Catechesis/Religious Program—Tel: 210-922-4061. Mary Toscano, D.R.E. Students 366.

32—ST. JOHN BERCHMANS (1910), (Hispanic), Rev. Carlos B. Velazquez; Deacon Jose G. Diaz.
Res.: 1147 Cupples Rd., 78226. Tel: 210-434-3247;

Fax: 210-432-0431.
School—Tel: 210-433-0411; Fax: 210-433-2335. Mrs. Beverly Abbott, Prin. Lay Teachers 27; Students 426.
Catechesis/Religious Program—Tel: 210-433-2121. Marta Lucia Garcia, D.R.E. Students 303.

33—ST. JOHN NEUMANN (1977), Rev. Msgr. Robert Silverman; Deacons William Bowlin; George Valenta. Mailing Address: 6680 Crestway Dr., 78239. Tel: 210-654-1643; Fax: 210-654-8031.
Catechesis/Religious Program—Tel: 210-654-3707. Students 225.

34—ST. JOHN, THE EVANGELIST (1956), Rev. Stuart Juleen; Deacons Rosendo Urrabazo; Evan Wittig; Hugo Chavez; Robert Schonhoff.
Office—4603 St. John's Way, 78212. Tel: 210-738-2201; Fax: 210-738-0599.
School—128 S. Audubon Dr., 78212. Tel: 210-735-3526; Fax: 210-735-3526. Mr. Warren Carter, Prin. Lay Teachers 11; Students 195.
Catechesis/Religious Program—Sr. Luz, D.R.E. Students 125.

35—ST. JOSEPH (Downtown) (1868), [CEM] Rev. Thomas J. Fitzgerald, S.S.S. In Res., Rev. Roger C. Prefontaine, S.S.S.; Bro. David Phelan, S.S.S.
Res.: 623 E. Commerce St., 78205. Tel: 210-227-0126; Fax: 210-227-7690.
Catechesis/Religious Program—618 Live Oak, 78202. Tel: 210-223-2944; Fax: 210-224-1033. Students 44.

36—ST. JOSEPH (South San) (1935), (Hispanic), Revs. Joe Aviles; Alejandro de La Torre; Deacon Genaro Herrera.
Res.: 535 New Laredo Hwy., 78211-1900. Tel: 210-924-4383; Fax: 210-928-9020.
School—Tel: 210-922-0193; Fax: 210-922-2002. Mrs. Margaret Schlueter, Prin. Lay Teachers 12; Students 165.
Catechesis/Religious Program—Tel: 210-924-4383. Carmen Sanchez, D.R.E.; Mary Alice Klein, D.R.E. Students 400.

37—ST. JUDE (1954), (Hispanic), Rev. Jose A. Giganto, O.S.A. In Res., Rev. Leonidas Fresno, O.S.A.
Res.: 130 S. San Augustine Ave., 78237. Tel: 210-432-8044; Fax: 210-432-1760.
Catechesis/Religious Program—Tel: 210-432-5786. Rosalinda F. Rodriguez, D.R.E. Students 566.
Mission—Santa Maria Goretti, Bexar Co.

38—ST. LAWRENCE (1959), (Hispanic), Rev. Florencio Rodriguez, T.O.R.; Deacons Alois Keller; Ernesto Leal; Arturo Garcia.
Res.: 236 E. Petaluma, 78221. Tel: 210-924-4401; Fax: 210-924-4075.
Catechesis/Religious Program—Tel: 210-924-6470. Students 590.

39—ST. LEO (1919), (Hispanic), Rev. Msgr. Enda McKenna; Rev. Eric Ritter; Deacons John Landez, Pastoral Assoc.; Alvino Pacheco, Pastoral Assoc.; Lupe Sielski, Pastoral Assoc.
Res.: 4401 S. Flores, 78214. Tel: 210-533-9108; Fax: 210-533-0643.
School—119 Octavia Pl., 78214. Tel: 210-532-3166; Fax: 210-532-5997. Carol Johnson, Prin. Lay Teachers 12; Students 149.
Catechesis/Religious Program—Tommy Winborne, D.R.E. Students 335.

40—ST. LEONARD'S (1966), (Hispanic), Revs. Amando Trujillo-Cano, T.O.R. (Mexico); Mauricio Alarcon-Martinez, T.O.R. (Mexico); Deacons Carlos Salinas, (Retired); Rey Ybarra.
Res.: 8510 S. Zarzamora, 78224-2099. Tel: 210-924-6000; Fax: 210-924-5552.
Catechesis/Religious Program—Tel: 210-924-6000, Ext. 19. Students 394.

41—ST. LUKE (1959), Revs. Michael Horan; Jose Francisco Puente. In Res., Rev. Michael Biewend, C.J.
Office—4603 Manitou, 78228-1889. Tel: 210-433-2777; Fax: 210-433-2778.
Res.: 6014 Horizon, 78228. Tel: 210-436-9777.
School—Tel: 210-434-2011; Fax: 210-432-2419. Marcella Salazar, Prin. Lay Teachers 44; Students 569.
Catechesis/Religious Program—Linda Johnson, D.R.E. Students 589.

42—ST. MARGARET MARY (1955), (Hispanic), Rev. Norman Ermis; Deacons Gerardo Mechler; Zeke Moczygemba; Jose Almanza; Wilfred Lamm.
Res.: 1314 Fair Ave., 78223. Tel: 210-532-6309; Fax: 210-532-6333. Email: maryannusmm@yahoo.com.
School—Tel: 210-534-6137; Fax: 210-534-2225. Mrs. Virginia Gegenbacher, Prin. Felician Sisters 1; Lay Teachers 10; Students 165.
Catechesis/Religious Program— Lucia Reyes, D.R.E. Students 170.
Mission—St. Catherine 2202 Hicks, Bexar Co. 78210.

43—ST. MARK THE EVANGELIST (1976), Revs. Kevin E. Ryan; Effendy LIwang, M.S.C.; Dorothea G. Hamlin, Pastoral Admin.; Deacons Steven Marques; Larry Stallings; Kevin Kanter.
Res.: 1602 Thousand Oaks Dr., 78232-2398. Tel: 210-494-1606; 210-494-1607; Fax: 210-494-4957.
Catechesis/Religious Program—Tel: 210-494-7434. Students 1,300.

44—ST. MARTIN DE PORRES (1964), (Hispanic), Rev. Gilbert Olbin, C.I.C.M.; Deacons Jose Menchaca; Anthony Patlan; Benito Resendiz; Jesus Lucio.
Res.: 1730 Dahlgreen St., 78237. Tel: 210-432-5203; Fax: 210-436-1187.
Catechesis/Religious Program—Tel: 210-436-2071. Students 259.

45—ST. MARY (1852), [CEM] Rev. Michael Levy, O.M.I.
Res.: 202 N. St. Mary's St., 78205. Tel: 210-226-8381; Fax: 210-226-8440.
School—207 N. St. Mary's St., 78205. Tel 210-223-8581; Fax: 210-223-5672. Mr. Randy Wilhelm, Prin. Lay Teachers 6; Students 105.

46—ST. MARY MAGDALEN (1940), (Hispanic), Revs. Robert E. Hogan, S.M.; Joseph Mary Marshall, S.M.; Deacons Gerald Campa; Ismael Casanova.
Res.: 1710 Clower St., 78201. Tel: 210-735-5269; Fax: 210-738-0698.
School—Tel: 210-735-1381; Fax: 210-735-2406. Mrs. Betty Keller, Prin. Sisters 2; Lay Teachers 10; Students 157.
Catechesis/Religious Program—Tel: 210-735-5284. Linda Froboese, D.R.E. Students 720.

47—ST. MATTHEW'S (1968), Rev. Msgr. Michael H. Yarbrough; Revs. Jerzy F. Sieczynski; Thomas Kavanaugh, C.M.; Deacons Tom Foz; Wilbur Hoelschler; Norman Kutschenreuter; Horacio Tudon; Keith Werner; Ernesto Garza; William Ziske, (Retired); Albert Hollstein, (Retired); Anton Svatek, (Retired).
Res.: 10703 Wurzbach Rd., 78230. Tel: 210-478-5000; Fax 210-696-8858.
School—Tel: 210-478-5099; Fax: 210-696-7624. Judith Priest, Prin. Sisters 1; Lay Teachers 42; Students 715.
Catechesis/Religious Program—Fax: 210-696-8858. Sr. Therese Gleitz, D.R.E. Students 1,132.

48—ST. MICHAEL (1866), (Hispanic), [CEM] Rev. Jesus Murugarren, O.S.A. (Spain); Lillie P. Ramirez, Admin.; Juan Garcia, Pastoral Assoc; Nicholas Farley, Pastoral Assoc.
Res.: 418 Indiana, 78210. Tel: 210-532-3707; Fax: 210-532-2707.
Catechesis/Religious Program—Students 125.

49—OUR LADY OF GOOD COUNSEL (1952), (Hispanic), Revs. Dennis Darilek; Fidele Dikete.
Res.: 1204 Castroville Rd., 78237. Tel: 210-432-0873; Fax: 210-432-7576.
Catechesis/Religious Program—Tel: 210-432-6430; Fax: 210-432-7571. Students 145.

50—OUR LADY OF GRACE (1938), Rev. Msgr. Lawrence Walsh; Deacon Robert Schonhoff.
Res.: 223 E. Summit Ave., 78212. Tel: 210-734-7285; Fax: 210-734-8334.
Catechesis/Religious Program—Students 91.

51—OUR LADY OF GUADALUPE (1911), (Hispanic), Revs. Martin L. Elsner, S.J.; James L. Lambert, S.J.; Samuel Rosales, S.J.; Bro. Alexander Gussio, S.J.; Deacons Joe Camero; Robert Galvan; John Huttinger; Carlos Sandoval.
Res.: 1321 El Paso St., 78207. Tel: 210-226-4064; Fax: 210-226-4973.
Catechesis/Religious Program—R. Lee Thielen, D.R.E. Students 90.

52—OUR LADY OF PERPETUAL HELP (1913), (Hispanic), Rev. Gilbert A. Enderle, C.SS.R.
Res.: 613 S. Grimes St., 78203. Tel: 210-532-7031; Fax: 210-534-1280.
Catechesis/Religious Program—Tel: 210-534-7193. Students 256.

53—OUR LADY OF SORROWS (1915), (Hispanic), Revs. Thaddeus Tabak, S.D.S.; Raphael E. Eke (Nigeria); Deacon Jesse Fraga. In Res., Rev. Marian A. Piekarczyk, S.D.S. (Poland), Dir. Polish Catholic Mission & Army Chap.
Res.: 3107 N. St. Mary's St., 78212. Tel: 210-732-6295; 210-736-6719 (Polish); Fax: 210-732-9249.
Catechesis/Religious Program—Tel: 210-732-9249. Donna Salas, D.R.E. Students 100.

54—OUR LADY OF THE ANGELS (1947), (Hispanic), Revs. James Hynes (Peru); Guillermo Ordenes, O.F.M. (Mexico) (ELP); Deacons Albert Ramirez; Jose F. Moreno.
Res.: 1214 Stonewall St., 78211. Tel: 210-924-6591; Fax: 210-924-6593.
Catechesis/Religious Program—Tel: 210-924-8046. Alicia Q. Gutierrez, D.R.E. Students 251.

55—OUR LADY OF THE ATONEMENT CATHOLIC (1983),, (A Personal Parish for the Anglican Use). Rev. Christopher G. Phillips; Deacons James P. Orr; Michael D'Agostino.
Res.: 8015 Shady Hollow Ln., 78255. Tel: 210-695-3332.
Church: 15415 Red Robin Rd., 78255. Tel: 210-695-2944; Fax: 210-695-9679.
School—Atonement Academy, Tel: 210-695-2240. Religious 1; Lay Teachers 9; Students 228.
Catechesis/Religious Program—Students 119.

56—SAINT PADRE PIO OF PIETRELCINA, Rev. Patrick Ragsdale; Deacons Everett Gorton; Ed Bozek.
Church & Mailing Address: PMB 611 Hwy 281 N., Ste. 108, 78258. Tel: 210-481-2576; Fax: 210-481-5107; Cell: 210-317-1729.
Catechesis/Religious Program—Students 110.

57—ST. PATRICK (1895), (Hispanic), Rev. Walter E. Ebarb (SHP). In Res., Rev. Thomas McSwiggan.
Res.: 1114 Willow St., 78208. Tel: 210-226-5223; Fax: 210-227-8616.
Catechesis/Religious Program—Tel: 210-227-5478. Mary Grace Rodriguez, D.R.E. Students 200.

58—ST. PAUL (1954), (Hispanic), Rev. Jimmy D. Drennan; Deacons Clayton Mangold; Daniel Muriada; Agustin Arismendez; Pedro Patlan.
Res.: 350 Sutton Dr., 78228-3199. Tel: 210-733-7152; Fax: 210-733-0929.
School—307 John Adams, 78228. Tel: 210-732-2741; Fax: 210-732-7702. Mrs. Sandra Sanchez, Interim Prin. Religious Sisters 1; Lay Teachers 25; Students 421.
Ministry & Service Office—1201 Donaldson, 78228. Tel: 210-732-8735; Fax: 210-732-6279. Deacon Pedro Patlan, Coord.
Community Center—Tel: 210-736-0055; Fax: 210-738-9600. Mrs. Cynthia Trevino, Dir.
Learning Center—Tel: 210-738-8715; Fax: 210-738-8403. (Daycare) Children 77.
Catechesis/Religious Program—Veronica Segundo, D.R.E. Students 287.

59—ST. PETER PRINCE OF THE APOSTLES (1923), Rev. Msgr. Thomas Murphy; Teresa Berg, Admin.; Deacons John Dunn, (Retired); John L. Spitzer, (Retired); Richard De Hoyos.
Res.: 111 Barilla Pl., 78209. Tel: 210-822-3367; Fax: 210-828-5826.
School—112 Marcia Pl., 78209. Tel: 210-824-3171; Fax: 210-822-4504. Ann Lander, Prin. Lay Teachers 29; Students 333.
Catechesis/Religious Program—Tel: 210-822-1605. Alma Small, D.R.E. Students 225.

60—ST. PHILIP OF JESUS (1914), (Hispanic), Rev. Michael DeGerolami; Deacons G. T. Zapata; Jose Sanchez.
Res.: 131 Bank St., 78204. Tel: 210-226-5024; Fax: 210-226-9005.
School—134 E. Lambert St., 78204. Tel: 210-222-2872; Fax: 210-229-1829. Sr. Celly Ann Amparano, S.S.N.D., Prin. Sisters 1; Lay Teachers 14; Aides 6; Students 268.
Catechesis/Religious Program—Tel: 210-225-6622. Sr. Arlene Vasquez, M.C.D.P., D.R.E. Students 265.

61—ST. PIUS X (1957), Rev. Msgr. Liam P. Brosnan; Deacons Thomas Crowley; Eugene Townsend; John Michel.
Office—3303 Urban Crest, 78209. Tel: 210-824-0139; Fax: 210-829-5125.
School—(Grades PreK-8), 7734 Robin Rest Dr., 78209. Tel: 210-824-6431; Fax: 210-824-7454. Kathy Schaub, Prin. Lay Teachers 26; Students 328.
Catechesis/Religious Program—Tel: 210-824-4533. Chris Henderson, D.R.E. Students 255.

62—PRINCE OF PEACE (1980), Rev. Msgr. Patrick Cronin; Deacons Scott Imburgia; Pino Sanabria; Tom Neal; William Thornberry; Art Marin.
Res.: 7893 N. Grissom Rd., 78251. Tel: 210-681-8330; Fax: 210-681-2286.
Catechesis/Religious Program—Tel: 210-681-5063. Students 1,169.

63—RESURRECTION OF THE LORD (1981), Rev. Paul A. Raaz; Deacon Thomas Swift.
Office & Mailing Address: 7990 W. Military Dr., 78227. Tel: 210-675-1470; Fax: 210-675-8203.
Res.: 7151 Cypress Grove, 78227.
Catechesis/Religious Program—Tel: 210-675-8360. Students 569.

64—ST. ROSE OF LIMA (1981), Revs. Juan Alfaro; Virgil Elizondo; Angelo Caparros; Deacons Rey Jasso; Antonio Lira; Chester Ostaszewski; Robert Espinosa.
Res.: 9883 Marbach Rd., 78245. Tel: 210-675-1920; Fax: 210-675-6067.
Catechesis/Religious Program—Students 1,056.

65—SACRED HEART (1899), (Hispanic), Rev. Walter O. D'heedene, C.I.C.M. (Belgium); Deacons Valentin Gallegos; Rudy Rodriguez; Bro. Randy Gonzales, C.I.C.M.
Res.: 2114 W. Houston St., 78207-3496. Tel: 210-227-5059; Fax: 210-227-6209. Email: sacredhearts@hotmail.com.
Catechesis/Religious Program—Tel: 210-227-9763; 210-227-3940 (Youth Office). Sisters Juanita Ramirez, D.R.E.; Maria Lasema, D.R.E. Students 318.

66—SAN FRANCISCO DE LA ESPADA (1731), (Hispanic), Rev. Lawrence Brummer, O.F.M.
Res.: 10040 Espada Rd., 78214. Tel: 210-627-2064; Fax: 210-627-2064.
Catechesis/Religious Program—Tel: 210-627-2962. Students 148.

Mission—St. Frances Cabrini 1606 San Casimiro, Bexar Co. 78214. Tel: 210-627-9263.

67—SAN JOSE Y SAN MIGUEL (1720), (Hispanic), Revs. Herbert Jones, O.F.M.; John Abts, O.F.M.; Sr. Immaculata Kelly, P.B.V.M., Pastoral Assoc.; Deacons Santiago Rodriguez; Tomas Torres. In Res., Revs. Maury Smith, O.F.M.; Michael Hill, O.F.M., M.S., M.Div.; Juan Jose Villa, O.F.M. (Mexico); Charles Gunti, O.F.M.; Edward Boren, O.F.M. (JOL); Bro. Thomas Eisenmenger, O.F.M.
Res.: 701 E. Pyron Ave., 78214. Tel: 210-922-0543; Fax: 210-932-2271.
Catechesis/Religious Program—Tel: 210-923-8681. Sr. Immaculata Kelly, P.B.V.M., D.R.E.; Kathleen Rollow, D.R.E. Students 292.

68—SAN JUAN CAPISTRANO (1731), (Hispanic), Rev. James G. Galvin (Ireland).
Mailing Address: P.O. Box 14308, 78214-0308.
Res.: 9101 Graf Rd., 78214.
Church: 78214. Tel: 210-534-3161; Fax: 210-534-2426.
Catechesis/Religious Program—Students 58.
Mission—St. Ann Southton, Bexar Co.

69—SAN JUAN DE LOS LAGOS (1952), (Hispanic), Revs. Tom Ovalle, O.M.I.; Arthur Flores; Deacons Albert Salinas; Eleodoro Vasquez. In Res., Rev. Stanley Zowada, O.M.I. (Poland) (STP).
Res.: 3231 El Paso St., 78207. Tel: 210-433-9722; Fax: 210-433-9526.
Catechesis/Religious Program—Tel: 210-433-2411. Students 320.

70—SANTO NINO DE CEBU (1993), (Filipino), Revs. Martin Parayno, O.S.B. (Philippines); Marcelino Ugaddan (Philippines); Dr. Salvador Baylan, Parish Council Chair. Tel: 210-731-4105.
Mailing Address: 5655 Rigsby Ave., 78222. Tel: 210-648-1705; Fax: 210-648-5365.
Catechesis/Religious Program—Students 65.

71—ST. STEPHEN (1965), (Hispanic), Rev. Luis Ruiz.
Res.: 2127 S. Zarzamora St., 78207. Tel: 210-224-8474; Fax: 210-224-8474.
Catechesis/Religious Program—Tel: 210-224-7116. Students 75.

72—ST. THOMAS MORE (1964), Rev. John M. Makothakat; Deacons Jerome Ciarrocchi; Paul Charron; Roberto Rosas.
Res.: 4411 Moana, 78218. Tel: 210-655-5070; Fax: 210-655-8446.
School—4427 Moana, 78218. Tel: 210-655-2882; Fax: 210-655-9603. Mrs. Mary Jane Regel, Prin. Lay Teachers 12; Students 170.
Catechesis/Religious Program—Tel: 210-654-6824. Students 215.

73—ST. TIMOTHY'S (1953), (Hispanic), Rev. Oscar Hernandez; Deacons Rudy Medrano; Antonio Caballero; Tomas Alvarado.
Res.: 1515 Saltillo St., 78207. Tel: 210-434-2391; Fax: 210-434-4828.
Catechesis/Religious Program—Students 124.

74—VIETNAMESE MARTYRS CATHOLIC CENTER (1976), Rev. Francis Pham, C.SS.R.
Center—1240 Holbrook, 78218. Tel: 210-646-0726; Fax: 210-646-0726.

75—ST. VINCENT DE PAUL (1961), Revs. Jose Luis De La Rosa; Alejandro DeJesus, O.S.B. (Philippines); Sr. Katrina Ruane, S.H.Sp., Pastoral Assoc.; Deacon Leobardo Longoria.
Res.: 4222 S.W. Loop 410, 78227-4495. Tel: 210-674-1200; Fax: 210-674-1640.
Catechesis/Religious Program—Tel: 210-674-4291. Maricella Salazar, D.R.E. Students 323.

OUTSIDE THE CITY OF SAN ANTONIO

BANDERA, BANDERA CO., ST. STANISLAUS (1855), (Polish), [CEM] [JC] Rev. Stanislaw Oleksy, S.D.S.
Res.: Box 757, 78003-0757. Tel: 830-460-4712; Fax: 830-796-7641.
Catechesis/Religious Program—Tel: 210-796-3573. Elouise Mangold, D.R.E. Students 190.
Mission—St. Victor's Chapel 10514 Park Rd. 37, Lakehills, Bandera Co. 78063. Tel: 830-612-3012.

BOERNE, KENDALL CO., ST. PETER THE APOSTLE (1866), (German), Rev. Anthony O. Cummins; Deacon Paul Rayburg; Mary Ann Chandler, Pastoral Assoc.
Mailing Address: 202 W. Kronkosky St., 78006. Tel: 830-816-2233; Fax: 830-249-6175.
Catechesis/Religious Program—Valerie Vogel, D.R.E.; Rick Zapf, D.R.E.; Jeanette Belter, D.R.E.; Michelle Pechacek, D.R.E. Students 857.

BRACKETTVILLE, KINNEY CO., ST. MARY MAGDALEN (1875), [CEM] Rev. Cornelius J. Scanlan, O.M.I.; Deacon James Bader.
Res.: Box 95, 78832. Tel: 830-563-2487; Fax: 830-563-3600.
Catechesis/Religious Program—Students 166.
Mission—St. Blaise Spofford Junction, Kinney Co.

CANYON LAKE, COMAL CO., ST. THOMAS THE APOSTLE (1967), Rev. Msgr. Marvin G. Doerfler.
Res.: 180 St. Thomas Dr., 78133-4131. Tel: 830-964-3497; Fax: 830-964-2574.
Catechesis/Religious Program—Students 190.

CASTROVILLE, MEDINA CO., ST. LOUIS (1844), (Alsatian), [CEM] Rev. James Conway; Deacon Gene Ebner.
Res.: 610 Madrid, 78009. Tel: 830-931-2826; Fax: 830-931-9016.
School—Tel: 830-931-3544. Sr. Marie Elise VanDijik, C.D.P., Prin. Lay Teachers 13; Students 228.
Catechesis/Religious Program—Tel: 830-931-2556; Fax: 830-931-2826. Deborah Ruiz, D.R.E. Students 427.
Mission—St. Francis of Assisi (Medina Lake Chapel) Mico, Medina Co.

CESTOHOWA, KARNES CO., NATIVITY OF THE BLESSED VIRGIN MARY (1873), (Polish), [CEM] Rev. Wojciech Pelczarski, S.D.S. (Poland).
Res.: 300 FM 3191 Cestohowa, Falls City, 78113. Tel: 830-745-2633.
Catechesis/Religious Program—Students 57.

CHARLOTTE, ATASCOSA CO., ST. ROSE OF LIMA (1909), (Hispanic), Rev. Mario Cardenas-Suarez (Colombia), Admin.
Mailing Address: P.O. Box 69, 78011. Tel: 830-277-1242; Fax: 830-277-1700.
Catechesis/Religious Program—Students 85.
Mission—St. Joseph 703 Congress St., P.O. Box 297, Tilden, McMullen Co. 78072. Tel: 361-274-3374.

COMFORT, KENDALL CO., SACRED HEART (1949), Rev. James Cashin.
Mailing Address: P.O. Box 599, 78013-0599. Tel: 830-995-3708.
Church: 510 Broadway, 78013. Tel: 830-995-3708; Fax: 830-995-2952.
Res.: 104 Daniel St., 78013. Tel: 830-995-3501.
Catechesis/Religious Program—Students 231.

CONVERSE, BEXAR CO., ST. MONICA (1959), Rev. Dennis Arechiga.
Res.: 501 North St., P.O. Box 429, 78109. Tel: 210-658-3816; Fax: 210-566-3821.
School—Tel: 210-658-6701; Fax: 210-658-6945. James Mollicone, Prin. Lay Teachers 26; Students 275; Day Care 265.
Catechesis/Religious Program—Tel: 210-658-7920. Janice Van Slambrouck, D.R.E. Students 438.

D'HANIS, MEDINA CO., HOLY CROSS (1847), (Hispanic), [CEM] Rev. Wallis Stiles.
Res.: P.O. Box 426, 78850. Tel: 830-363-7268; Fax: 830-363-7268.
Catechesis/Religious Program—Students 157.
Mission—Immaculate Heart of Mary Yancey, Medina Co.

DEL RIO, VAL VERDE CO.

1—ST. JOSEPH'S (1927), (Hispanic), [CEM] Revs. Ramiro Cortez, O.M.I.; William E. Zapalac, O.M.I.; Deacons Filomeno Salazar; Efrain Santana; Raymundo Mendoza; Ronnie Van Dyke.
Res.: 510 Wernett St., P.O. Box 1429, 78840. Tel: 830-775-4753; Fax: 830-774-7128.
Catechesis/Religious Program—Tel: 830-775-5200. Esther G. Cardenas, D.R.E.; Mr. Evaristo Patino, D.R.E.; Mrs. Blanca Patino, D.R.E. Students 823.

2—OUR LADY OF GUADALUPE (1906), (Hispanic), Rev. Jose de la Cruz Longoria Gomez, M.N.M. (Mexico); Deacons Elieser Hernandez; Adrian Falcon; Juan Padilla.
Res.: 509 Garza St., 78840. Tel: 830-775-3713; Fax: 830-775-9161.
Catechesis/Religious Program—Tel: 830-775-2178. Students 475.
Mission—San Juan Diego Chapel 523 Jeffery Dr., V V Park Estates, Valverde Co. 78840.

3—SACRED HEART (1895), [CEM] Revs. James Fischler, C.I.C.M.; Carl Sadsoeitoeboen, C.I.C.M. (Indonesia); Deacons John C. Graf; Robert C. Kusenberger; David B. Scarbo; Roger Rodriguez.
Mailing Address: P.O. Box 1503, 78841.
Office—307 E. Losoya, 78840. Tel: 830-775-2143; Fax: 830-775-9902.
Res.: 411 Spring St., 78840. Tel: 830-775-4240.
School—209 E. Greenwood, 78840. Tel: 830-775-3274; Fax: 830-774-2800. Mrs. Aurora Guerra, Prin. Lay Teachers 13; Students 258.
Catechesis/Religious Program—Sr. Luisita Iglesias, O.N.D., D.R.E. Students 260.
Mission—Mary, Queen of the Universe Comstock, Valverde Co.

DEVINE, MEDINA CO., ST. JOSEPH'S (1897), [CEM] Rev. Msgr. Adolfo Valdivia, Admin.
Res.: 108 S. Washington Dr., 78016. Tel: 830-663-2244; Fax: 830-665-3321.
Catechesis/Religious Program—Students 360.

DILLEY, FRIO CO., ST. JOSEPH'S (1899), (Hispanic), Rev. Msgr. Pablo Sicilia; Deacons Bernard Carroll; Salvador Tijerina.
Res.: 114 E. Frio, P.O. Box N, 78017. Tel: 830-965-1926; 830-965-2080 (Office); Fax: 830-965-2125.
Catechesis/Religious Program—Diana Carpenter, D.R.E. Students 170.
Mission—St. Mary, Frio Co.

ELMENDORF, BEXAR CO., ST. ANTHONY (1896), (Hispanic), [CEM] Rev. William McNamara; Deacons Allen K. Miller; Armando J. Scott; Robert Thayer.
Res.: P.O. Box 248, 78112. Tel: 210-635-8539; Fax: 210-635-8644.
Catechesis/Religious Program—Tel: 210-635-8570. Anita Casillas, D.R.E.; Catherine Halbardier, D.R.E. Students 160.
Mission—Our Lady of Perpetual Help [CEM] Saspamco, Bexar Co.

FALLS CITY, KARNES CO., HOLY TRINITY (1902), (Polish), [CEM] Rev. Gregory Sawicki, S.D.S. (Poland); Deacon Stanley Kolodzie.
Res.: Box 158, 78113. Tel: 830-254-3539; Fax: 830-254-3530.
Catechesis/Religious Program—Rose Lee Moczygemba, D.R.E. Students 158.

FLORESVILLE, WILSON CO., SACRED HEART (1882), [CEM] Rev. Stefan Wiera; Deacons Scott Donaho; Mike Perez.
Res.: 1009 Trail St., 78114. Tel: 830-393-6117; 830-216-7706 (Metro); Fax: 830-393-9071.
School—Tel: 830-393-2117; Fax: 830-393-6968. Ms. Lilia Holt, Prin. Lay Teachers 12; Students 73.
Catechesis/Religious Program—Lila Holt, D.R.E.; Ofelia Sanchez, D.R.E. Students 313.

FREDERICKSBURG, GILLESPIE CO., ST. MARY'S (1846), (German), [CEM] Revs. Tony Vilano; Gilberto Vallejo-Rodriguez; Deacons Gregorio Martinez Jr.; Francisco De La Torre; Louis Loth; James Bacon; Ken Knopp.
Res.: 306 W. San Antonio St., 78624. Tel: 830-997-9523; Fax: 830-997-1037.
School—Tel: 830-997-3914; Fax: 830-997-2382. Billy Pahl, Prin. Lay Teachers 19; Students 257.
Catechesis/Religious Program—Tel: 830-997-7487. Sr. Lucille Ann Fritsch, C.D.P., D.R.E. Students 300.
Mission—Our Lady of Guadalupe, Gillespie Co.

GONZALES, GONZALES CO., ST. JAMES (1885), [CEM] Rev. Martin Leopold; Deacons Alfonso Moreno; Terrance Brennan.
Res.: 417 N. College St., 78629. Tel: 830-672-2945; Fax: 830-672-1058.
Catechesis/Religious Program—Tel: 830-672-6291. Students 380.
Mission—Sacred Heart 426 St. John, Gonzales Co. 78629.
Mission—St. Patrick U.S. Hwy. 90 A, Waelder, Gonzales Co. 78959.
Station—Care Inn of Gonzales, Tel: 830-672-2867.
Station—Cartwheel Lodge, Tel: 830-672-2887.

HARPER, GILLESPIE CO., ST. ANTHONY'S (1908), [CEM] Rev. George Carlin, S.O.L.T.; Deacon Curtis Klein.
Res.: Box 318, 78631. Tel: 830-864-4026.
Catechesis/Religious Program—Students 30.

HELOTES, BEXAR CO., OUR LADY OF GUADALUPE (1942), [CEM] Revs. Gerald Hammel, S.M.; Gerald Pleva, S.M.; Charles Oyabu, S.M. (HON); Deacon Timothy Houlihan.
Res.: P.O. Box 639, 78023. Tel: 210-695-8791; Fax: 210-695-9957.
Catechesis/Religious Program—Nancy Drymala, D.R.E.; Sara Weir, D.R.E.; Cindy Adcock, D.R.E.; Nancy Baize, D.R.E.; Laura Garcia Brill, D.R.E. Students 2,270.

HOBSON, KARNES CO., ST. BONIFACE (1901), (German—Polish), [CEM] Rev. Gregory Sawicki, S.D.S. (Poland).
Res.: US Hwy. 181 S., 78117. Tel: 830-780-3559.
Catechesis/Religious Program—Students 44.

HONDO, MEDINA CO., ST. JOHN THE EVANGELIST (1892), [CEM] Rev. Jeffrey Pehl; Vangie Pimentel, Admin.
Res.: 2102 Avenue J, 78861. Tel: 830-741-2236; Fax: 830-426-3339.
Catechesis/Religious Program—Tel: 830-741-2513. Sylvia Fernandez, D.R.E.; John Miller, D.R.E. Students 429.

JOURDANTON, ATASCOSA CO., ST. MATTHEW'S (1912), (Hispanic), [CEM] Rev. Francis McHugh (Ireland); Deacons Eusebio Guevara; Welton Fiedler Jr.
Mailing Address: Box 670, 78026.
Res.: 1700 Campbell, 78026. Tel: 830-769-3687; Fax: 830-769-2861.
Catechesis/Religious Program—Sr. Karen Schwane, D.R.E. Students 160.
Mission—St. Ignatius 101 W. Ave. F, Christine, Atascosa Co. 78012.

KARNES CITY, KARNES CO., ST. CORNELIUS (1917), Rev. Adrian Adamik.
Res.: 605 E. Calvert St., 78118. Tel: 830-780-3947; Fax: 830-780-3948.
Catechesis/Religious Program—Tel: 830-780-3949. Geri Leonard, D.R.E.; Maggie Ybarra, D.R.E. Students 300.
Mission—St. Elizabeth Fashing, Atascosa Co.

KENEDY, KARNES CO., OUR LADY OF PEACE (1959), [CEM] Rev. Mauricio Lopez.
Mailing Address: P.O. Box 89, 78119.
Res.: One Notre Dame Pl., 78119. Tel: 830-583-2417; Fax: 830-583-2410.
Catechesis/Religious Program—Tel: 830-583-2247. Diana Lopez, D.R.E. Students 255.

KERRVILLE, KERR CO., NOTRE DAME (1889), Revs. Michael J. Boulette; Gregory Nevlud; Deacons Daniel Arriaga; Charles Domingues; Juan A. Martinez; Denis Link.
Res.: 959 Main St., 78028. Tel: 830-257-5961; Fax: 830-895-9771.
School—907 Main St., 78028. Tel: 830-257-6707; Fax: 830-792-4370. Dr. Joan Wagner, Prin. Lay Teachers 19; Students 173.
Catechesis/Religious Program—Tel: 830-896-4233. Students 358.

KIRBY, BEXAR CO., ST. JOAN OF ARC (1971), Very Rev. Samuel Heitkamp, V.U.; Deacons John Buchanan; Robert Galan Jr.; Gilbert P. Rivera.
Res.: 2829 Ackermann Rd., 78219-2100. Tel: 210-661-5277; Fax: 210-661-5735.
Catechesis/Religious Program—Tel: 210-661-2220. Mrs. Paulette Petron, D.R.E. Students 377.

KOSCIUSZKO, WILSON CO., ST. ANN'S (1898), (Polish), [CEM] Rev. Wojciech Pelczarski, S.D.S. (Poland).
Res.: 8161 FM 541-E, Stockdale, 78160-6554. Tel: 830-745-2541; Fax: 830-745-2434.
Catechesis/Religious Program—Students 75.

LA VERNIA, WILSON CO., ST. ANN (1917), [CEM] Rev. Victor M. Carillo.
Res.: 14151 U.S. Hwy. 87 W., LaVernia, 78121. Tel: 830-779-3131; Fax: 830-779-1749.
Catechesis/Religious Program—Tel: 830-303-5321. Marie Gerlich, D.R.E. Students 180.

LACOSTE, MEDINA CO., OUR LADY OF GRACE (1911), [CEM] Rev. John Mannion.
Res.: P.O. Box 39, 78039. Tel: 830-985-3357 (Office); 830-985-3346 (Rectory); Fax: 830-985-3357.
Catechesis/Religious Program—Tel: 830-985-3355. Mrs. Guadalupe Vega, D.R.E. Students 264.
Mission—St. John Vianney 12703 Cinco de Mayo, Meadow Wood Acres, Bexar Co. 78251. Tel: 210-677-0954.

LEON SPRINGS, BEXAR CO., ST. ELIZABETH ANN SETON (1961), Rev. Patrick L. Marron.
Res.: 8500 Cross Mountain Tr., 78255. Tel: 210-698-1941; Fax: 210-698-1983.
Catechesis/Religious Program—Students 243.

LOSOYA, BEXAR CO., EL CARMEN CATHOLIC CHURCH (1898), (Hispanic), [CEM], (Our Lady of Mt. Carmel) Rev. Carl Maurer.
Res.: 18555 Leal Rd. (Losoya), 78221. Tel: 210-626-2333; Fax: 210-626-1874.
Catechesis/Religious Program—Tel: 210-626-1063. Kathy Vargas, D.R.E. Students 235.

LYTLE, ATASCOSA CO., ST. ANDREW (1904), [CEM] Rev. Romeo D. Olivares, C.I.C.M.
Res.: P.O. Box 326, 78052. Tel: 830-709-4287; Fax: 830-772-3028.
Catechesis/Religious Program—Tel: 830-709-0069. Students 235.
Mission—St. John Bosco Natalia, Medina Co.
Mission—Immaculate Conception P.O. Box 326, Coal Mine, Atascosa Co. 78052.

MACDONA, BEXAR CO., OUR LADY QUEEN OF HEAVEN (1994), (Hispanic), Rev. Rudolph T. Carrola Jr.
Mailing Address: P.O. Box 94, 78054-0094. Tel: 210-622-3282; Fax: 210-622-3282.
Res.: 9961 Aliann, 78054.
Catechesis/Religious Program—Antonia Garcia, D.R.E. Students 62.

MARTINEZ, BEXAR CO., ST. JEROME (1925), [CEM] Rev. John J. Flanagan.
Res.: 7955 Real Rd., 78263. Tel: 210-648-2694; Fax: 210-648-3690.
Catechesis/Religious Program—Tel: 210-648-0336. Shirley Bordovsky, D.R.E. Students 295.

NEW BRAUNFELS, COMAL CO.

1—HOLY FAMILY (1964), (Hispanic), Rev. James Wasser, M.S.F.; Deacon Hugo Salinas; Bro. Robert DeLong, M.S.F.; Amelia Lankford, Pastoral Assoc.
Res.: 245 S. Hidalgo, 78130. Tel: 830-609-5320; Fax: 830-609-5322.
Catechesis/Religious Program—Tel: 210-608-9615. Angie Gomez, D.R.E. Students 375.

2—OUR LADY OF PERPETUAL HELP (1926), Rev. Eugene Ronan, M.S.F.; Deacons Cayetano Morales; Ramond Ybarra; Ralph Brock.
Res.: 138 W. Austin St., 78130. Tel: 830-625-3534; Fax: 830-625-3566.
Catechesis/Religious Program—Tel: 830-629-4506. Barbara Carrera, D.R.E. Students 268.

3—SS. PETER AND PAUL (1845), [CEM 2] Rev. Msgrs. Eugene O'Callaghan, V.F.; Edward Bily; Deacons Fred Fey; Ray Kaufman; Ben Wehman; Frank Fikac; William Schroeder; Michael Peinemann; Robert Gorman.
Res.: 386 N. Castell St., 78130. Tel: 830-625-4531; Fax: 830-606-5461.
School—Tel: 830-625-4531, Ext. 3; Fax: 830-606-6916. Suzette Anderson, Prin. Lay Teachers 17; Students 248.
Catechesis/Religious Program—386 N. Castell, 78130. Tel: 830-625-4531, Ext. 201. Bill Smith, D.R.E. Students 850.
Mission—St. Joseph Comal, Comal Co.

NIXON, GONZALES CO., ST. JOSEPH'S (1915), [CEM] Rev. David Tarlizzo, O.M.I.; Deacon Daniel Medina Sr.
Res.: 207 S. Washington Ave., 78140-2920. Tel: 830-582-1127.
Catechesis/Religious Program—Students 125.

PANNA MARIA, KARNES CO., IMMACULATE CONCEPTION OF THE BLESSED VIRGIN MARY (1854), (Polish), [CEM] Rev. Wojciech Reisch (Poland).
Res.: P.O. Box 9, 78144. Tel: 830-780-2748; Fax: 830-780-4564.
Catechesis/Religious Program—Tel: 830-789-4283. Students 50.
Mission—St. Helena Helena, Karnes Co.

PEARSALL, FRIO CO., IMMACULATE HEART OF MARY (1891), [CEM] [JC] Rev. Andrew Kafara (Poland).
Res.: 422 W. Brazos, P.O. Box AK, 78061. Tel: 830-334-2382.
Catechesis/Religious Program—Tel: 210-334-4879. Marcus Salazar, D.R.E. Students 408.

PLEASANTON, ATASCOSA CO.

1—ST. ANDREW (1913), (Hispanic), [CEM] [JC 3] Rev. Carlos Davalos; Deacons Norman Phillips; Jose Valenzuela; Bennie Garcia Jr.
Res.: 626 Market St., 78064-2747. Tel: 830-569-3356; 830-281-4902 (Metro).
Catechesis/Religious Program—Sr. Dorothy Moczygemba, C.S.S.F., D.R.E. Students 130.
Mission—Sacred Heart Campbell and St. Francis St., Campbellton, Atascosa Co. 78008.

2—ST. LUKE-LOIRE (1859), Rev. James Hoelscher; Deacons Jose Guadalupe Trevino; Richard Gonzalez.
Res.: 3930 FM 536, 78064. Tel: 830-393-6021; Fax: 830-216-4286.
Catechesis/Religious Program—Students 141.
Mission—Our Lady of Guadalupe [CEM] [JC 2] 170 Hackberry St., P. O. Box 110, Leming, Atascosa Co. 78050.

POTEET, ATASCOSA CO., ST. PHILIP BENIZI (1897), (Hispanic), [CEM] Rev. Jaime Diaz.
Res.: P.O. Box 348, 78065. Tel: 830-742-3796.
Catechesis/Religious Program—Rudy Gonzales, D.R.E. Students 200.

POTH, WILSON CO., BLESSED SACRAMENT (1910), [CEM] Rev. Grzegorz Szewczyk, S.D.S. (Poland) (BRK); Deacon Alan Crosby.
Res.: P.O. Box 339, 78147. Tel: 830-484-3302; Fax: 830-484-2903.
Catechesis/Religious Program—Tel: 830-484-3303. Students 185.

ROCKSPRINGS, EDWARDS CO., SACRED HEART OF MARY (1900), (Hispanic), [JC] Rev. Jose A. Villanueva.
Res.: P.O. Box 887, 78880. Tel: 830-683-2165; Fax: 830-683-3165.
Catechesis/Religious Program—Students 49.
Mission—St. Mary Magdalen P.O. Box 610, Camp Wood, Real Co. 78833. Tel: 830-597-5165.
Mission—St. Raymond of Pennafort P.O. Box 989, Leakey, Real Co. 78873. Tel: 830-232-5852. Deacons Reuben Navarro; Warren Seymour.

RUNGE, KARNES CO., ST. ANTHONY'S (1901), (Polish), [CEM 2] Rev. Paschal Bergin.
Mailing Address: P.O. Box 188, 78151.
Res.: 112 W. Arenosa St., 78151. Tel: 830-239-4146; Fax: 830-239-4146.
Catechesis/Religious Program—Students 114.

ST. HEDWIG, BEXAR CO., ANNUNCIATION OF THE BLESSED VIRGIN MARY (1857), (Polish), [CEM] Revs. Damien Tomiczek, S.D.S.; Boleslaw Zadora, S.D.S.
Res.: P.O. Box 100, 78152. Tel: 210-667-1232; Fax: 210-667-9088.
Catechesis/Religious Program—Students 315.

SABINAL, UVALDE CO., ST. PATRICK'S (1884), (Hispanic), [CEM] Rev. Pedro Molina (Mexico).
Res.: Box 117, 78881. Tel: 830-988-2255.
Catechesis/Religious Program—Fax: 830-988-2255. Students 85.
Mission—St. Joseph Knippa, Uvalde Co.
Mission—St. Mary Vanderpool, Bandera Co.

SCHERTZ, GUADALUPE CO., CHURCH OF THE GOOD SHEPHERD (1972), Rev. Msgr. Roger P. Robbins; Mrs. Micki Christy, Admin.; Deacons John J. Gorman; Paul La Combe; George Vick Jr.
Res.: P.O. Box 929, 78154. Tel: 210-658-4350; Fax: 210-658-7051.
Catechesis/Religious Program—Tel: 210-658-6188. Mrs. Gerry Stift, D.R.E.; Mrs. Jean Smith, D.R.E. Students 460.
Mission—Immaculate Conception Santa Clara and Klein, Marion, Guadalupe Co. 78124. Tel: 210-420-8122.

SEGUIN, GUADALUPE CO.

1—ST. JAMES (1873), [CEM] Very Rev. Gerald Hubertus, V.F.
Res.: 510 S. Camp St., 78155. Tel: 830-379-1796; Fax: 830-379-1797.
School—507 S. Camp St., 78155. Tel: 830-379-2878; Fax: 830-379-2878. Janice Jessen, Prin. Sisters 1; Lay Teachers 12; Students 185.
Catechesis/Religious Program—Tel: 830-379-7684. Sr. Pat Crehan, S.H.Sp., D.R.E. Students 280.

2—OUR LADY OF GUADALUPE (1908), (Hispanic), [CEM] Revs. David Tonary, M.S.F.; Jack Kilburg, M.S.F.; Deacon Nick Carillo; Bro. Rolland Kapsner, M.S.F.
Res.: 409 W. Krezdorn, 78155-4429. Tel: 830-379-4338; Fax: 830-303-1002.
Catechesis/Religious Program—Tel: 830-379-2818. Sr. Mary Louise Hernandez, M.C.D.P., D.R.E. Students 693.
Mission—St. Joseph San Marcos. 2858 Redwood Rd., Redwood, Guadalupe Co. 78666.
Mission—St. John 210 House St., New Braunfels, Comal Co. 78130.

SELMA, BEXAR CO., OUR LADY OF PERPETUAL HELP (1897), (German), [CEM] Rev. Conor McGrath; Deacons Clifford Friesenhahn; James Telfer; Robert Cnota; Paul Miller.
Res.: 16075 N. Evans Rd., 78154-3824. Tel: 210-651-6913; Fax: 210-651-5272.
School—Tel: 210-651-6811; Fax: 210-651-5516. Sr. Terry Taubert, Prin. Sisters of Incarnate Word and Blessed Sacrament 2; Lay Teachers 26; Students 414.
Catechesis/Religious Program—Vilma Vasquez De Torres, D.R.E.; Suzy Krisak, D.R.E. Students 850.

SMILEY, GONZALES CO., ST. PHILIP BENIZI (1963), (Hispanic), Rev. David Tarlizzo, O.M.I.; Deacons Frank Rojas, Pastoral Admin.; John J. Moreno.
Res.: P.O. Box 32, 78159-0032. Tel: 830-587-6258.
Catechesis/Religious Program—Students 88.

SOMERSET, BEXAR CO., ST. MARY'S (1920), (Hispanic), [CEM] Rev. Edward Pavlicek; Deacon Robert Cruz.
Mailing Address: Box 295, 78069.
Res.: 19711 N. Dixon St., 78069. Tel: 830-701-3123.
Catechesis/Religious Program—Mrs. Sylvia Cruz, D.R.E. Students 180.

SPRING BRANCH, COMAL CO. (HONEY CREEK), ST. JOSEPH (1876), [CEM] Rev. James Janish; Sandy Strange, Pastoral Assoc.; Deacons Johnny Gass; James Legendre.
Res.: 25781 Hwy. 46 W., 78070-3613. Tel: 830-980-2268; Fax: 830-980-3184.
Catechesis/Religious Program—Sandy Strange, D.R.E. Students 347.

STOCKDALE, WILSON CO., ST. MARY (1895), (Polish), [CEM] Rev. Wieslaw Iwaniec; Deacons Jack Karam; Benjamin Gimenez.
Res.: Box 535, 78160. Tel: 830-996-3415; Fax: 830-996-3415.
Catechesis/Religious Program—Students 128.

STONEWALL, GILLESPIE CO., ST. FRANCIS XAVIER (1945), (German—Hispanic), [CEM] Revs. Anthony Vilano; Gilberto Vallejo-Rodriguez.
Res.: 404 St. Francis St., P.O. Box 209, 78671-3717. Tel: 830-644-2368; Fax: 830-644-2068.
Catechesis/Religious Program—Students 40.

UVALDE, UVALDE CO., SACRED HEART (1883), (Hispanic), [CEM] Rev. Kenneth M. Dakin; Deacons Hector V. Garcia; Antonio Hinojosa; Fortunato Hinojosa; Gonzalo Uriegas; Ramon Castro; Gilbert Salazar; Daniel A. Ibarra; Federico Flores; Kenneth Dirksen.
Res.: 408 Fort Clark St., 78801. Tel: 830-278-3448; Fax: 830-278-2835.
School—Tel: 830-278-2661; Fax: 830-278-2833. Ms. Irma Menchaca, Prin. Teresian Sisters 2; Lay Teachers 10; Students 147.
Catechesis/Religious Program—Tel: 830-278-3060. Linda Milam, D.R.E. Students 980.

VON ORMY, BEXAR CO.

1—ST. PETER THE FISHERMAN (1990), (Hispanic), Rev. Miguel Arango (Colombia); Deacons Richard Wells; Ernesto Bravo.
Office—17534 N. State Hwy. 16, 78073. Tel: 830-276-8778; 830-276-4985 (Res.); Fax: 830-276-8778.
Catechesis/Religious Program—Students 120.

2—SACRED HEART (1935), (Hispanic), Rev. Rudolph T. Carrola Jr.; Deacon Carlos Rodriguez.
13466 IH 35 S., 78073-3302. Tel: 210-622-3457; 210-622-3282; Fax: 210-622-3282.
Res.: P.O. Box 94, Macdona, 78054-0094. Tel: 210-622-3282; Fax: 210-622-3282.
Catechesis/Religious Program—Florell Guerra, D.R.E. Students 62.

KOREAN APOSTOLATE

BOERNE, KENDALL CO., KOREAN MARTYRS CATHOLIC CHURCH (1982), (Korean), Rev. Augustine Doo Wan Kim (Korea, South); Deacon Philip C. Kim.
Res.: 7655 Curres Cir., 78015. Tel: 210-698-3877; Fax: 210-655-1838.

OLD SPANISH MISSIONS

SAN ANTONIO, BEXAR CO., OLD SPANISH MISSIONS, aka Las Misiones Rev. Msgr. Balthasar J. Janacek, Dir.
Mailing Address: *c/o Catholic Chancery*, P.O. Box 28410, 78228.
Purisima Concepcion—807 Mission Rd., 78210.
San Francisco de la Espada—10040 Espada Rd., 78214.
San Juan Capistrano—9101 Graf Rd., 78214.
San Jose—701 E. Pyron Rd., 78214.

Chaplains of Public Institutions

SAN ANTONIO. *Audie Murphy VA Hospital*, 7400 Merton Minter Blvd., 78229. Tel: 210-617-5308. Rev. Robert Chukwu, C.L.V.

Baptist Memorial Hospital, 111 Dallas St., 78205. Tel: 210-222-8431. Mrs. Pat Sammis, Bro. Omomaro Okekaro, O.P.

Brooke Army Medical Center, Tel: 210-916-1105; 210-916-2172; Fax: 210-916-1169. Rev. James Schellenberg, D.Min. Tel: 210-916-4141 (After 4:30 pm & Weekends).

Res.: Bldg. 3600, 3851 Roger Brooke Blvd., Fort Sam Houston, 78234. Tel: 210-916-4141 (After 4:30pm & Weekends).

St. Luke's Baptist Hospital; University Hospital, 4502 Medical Dr., 78229. Tel: 210-680-2635 (Residence). Rev. Nicholas Brown, S.C.J.

Methodist Hospital, 7700 Floyd Curl, 78229. Tel: 210-692-4030. Revs. Marian Piekarczyk, Joseph Determan, O.P.

San Antonio State Hospital, 6711 S. New Braunfels, 78223. Tel: 210-532-8811. Rev. Augustine Amanzeh.

Santa Rosa Hospital System, 519 W. Houston, 78207. Tel: 210-704-2021. Revs. Mark Scheffler, C.Ss.R., Michael Norton, C.PP.S., Palmer Maxwell, Akalawu Ambrose, C.S.Sp., Mr. Richard Woodley.

Southwest General Hospital, Tel: 210-921-2000. Deacon Leon Mueller.

Texas Center for Infectious Disease, 2303 S.E. Military Dr., 78233. Rev. Paul Anewka.

KERRVILLE. *Veterans' Administration Hospital*, Tel: 830-896-2020. Sr. Jane McKenzie, O.S.F.

Special Assignment:
Revs.—
Cepeda, Jose Arturo, Rome
Condon, Thomas M., O.P. (MEM)
Foster, John Mary, F.J., 150 W. Zink, New Braunfels, 78130.
Lamberty, Philip J., O.P. (STL)
LaRoche, Victor, O.P. (MIA)
Markey, John J., O.P. (OAK)
Martinez, Charles, O.F.M., 318 Oblate Dr., 78216-6632.
Spencer, Robert, L.C., Jail Ministry: Tilden, Charlotte
Williams, Richard B., O.P. (NO)

On Duty Outside the Archdiocese:
Revs.—
Dillane, Maurice, Ireland
Garret, Sean, 300 Miracle Strip Pkwy. S.W. 2G, Fort Walton Beach, FL 32548. Tel: 850-244-5952
Kelly, John Edward, 2204 N. Liberty, Victoria, 77901. Tel: 381-573-2446
Kownacki, Robert, 7224 Balmoral, Chicago, IL 60656. Tel: 312-775-7315
Martinez, Manuel, S.S., Providence Memorial Hospital, Dept. Spiritual Care, 2001 N. Oregon St., El Paso, 79902.
Pogorelc, Anthony, S.S., Washington, DC.
Rubaj, Leon, Incarnate Word Sister's Convent, 1101 N.E. Water St., Victoria, 77901.

Military Chaplains:
Revs.—
Barlow, James P., A.F.B., Chap. Major, P.O. Box 65285, Hampton, VA 23665. Tel: 203-241-2742
Gonzalez, George G., Chap. Major, 4707 Winged Foot Way, Columbus, GA 31909.
Hernandez, Alfred Ricardo, Col. Catholic Chap., 16289 Eagle Rock Rd., Middletown, CA 95461.
Nee, Eugene O., PFE 50, Box RET 667, APO, AE 09494.
Tellez, Jairo A., Major, U.S.A.F., Air Police CMR 480, Box 3029, APO, AE 09128.

On Leave:
Revs.—
Currie, Donald
Davila, Johnny
De La Rosa, Vincent
Dietz, Xavier Ortiz
Duran, Jorge
Hernandez, Antonio
Jarzombek, Dennis
Kammerer, James
Kenny, Michael
Martin, Harry
Morales, Edward D.
Ruiz, Enrique
Sandoval, Luis

Retired:
Most Rev.—
Popp, Bernard, D.D., V.G., 8520 Cross Mountain Tr. #1001, 78255. Tel: 210-698-5524
Rev. Msgrs.—
Brosnan, Dermot, 2006 Steves Ave., 78210. Tel: 210-534-7426
Costantino, Anthony J., 80 Peter Baque Rd., 78209. Tel: 210-826-7721
Fecher, Vincent, 8520 Cross Mountain Trail, #302, 78255. Tel: 210-698-3923
Flanagan, Patrick J., 3843 Barrington #204A, 78217. Tel: 210-599-4900
Garcia, Raymond, 80 Peter Baque Rd., 78209. Tel: 210-826-7721
Goertz, Alois J., 8520 Cross Mountain Tr., #100, 78255. Tel: 210-698-9067
Hubertus, Albert, 8520 Cross Mountain Tr. #4, 78255. Tel: 210-698-8682
Janacek, Balty, 2613 W. French, 78228.
Manning, J. Leroy, 80 Peter Baque Rd., 78209. Tel: 210-826-7721
Martinez, Leo, 8520 Cross Mountain Tr. #1101, 78255. Tel: 210-698-9875
Matocha, John L., Box 158B, Mathis, 78368. Tel: 512-547-9859
Mushala, Walter A., P.O. Box 467, Somerset, 78069. Tel: 830-429-3220
O'Callaghan, Peter, St. Francis Nursing Home, 630 W. Woodlawn Ave., 78202. Tel: 210-736-3177
Palmer, Patrick, Padua Place, 80 Peter Baque Rd., 78209. Tel: 210-826-7721
Palmer, Thomas, 2717 N. Flores, #26, 78202.
Palmer, Thomas, 2717 N. Flores #26, 78202. Tel: 210-736-3177
Petsch, Joseph, Casa de Padres, 8520 Cross Mountain Tr., #702, 78255. Tel: 210-698-7055
Pugh, Charles, Padua Place.
Rihn, Roy, 8520 Cross Mountain Tr., #301, 78255. Tel: 210-698-0287
Smith, Sherrill, 8520 Cross Mountain Tr., #201, 78255. Tel: 210-698-8819
Stuebben, George, 314 Cave Ln., 78209. Tel: 210-829-0238
Wagner, John A., No.202, 8520 Cross Mountain Rd., 78255. Tel: 210-698-1332
Revs.—
Baistra, Jorge, 442 Ceralvo St., 78207.
Benonis, Richard (PH), HC33, Box 850, Barksdale, 77828-9706.
De La Garza, Joseph, 1138 Plateau Ridge, New Braunfels, 78132-2114. Tel: 210-690-4987
Johnston, Robert F., 601 Van Ness Ave., #1052, San Francisco, CA 94102. Tel: 415-674-3572
La Torre, Abraham, 6051 Monterey, 78237.
McKenna, Peter, 123 Trillium, 78213. Tel: 210-366-2188
O'Callaghan, Patrick, 630 W. Woodlawn Ave., 78202. Tel: 210-736-3177
Paniagua, Pablo, 8520 Cross Mountain Tr., #401, 78255. Tel: 210-698-8036
Verbrugge, Albert E., J.C.D., Air Force Village One, 4917 N. Ravenswood Dr., Apt 1616, 78227-4344. Tel: 210-645-6986
Zumaya, David, Mexico

Permanent Deacons:
Torres, Thomas, San Jose Mission, San Antonio
Alcala, Jesse, St.James, San Antonio
Almanza, Jose M., St. Margaret Mary, San Antonio
Alvarado, Thomas, St. Timothy's, San Antonio
Amo, Ernest Roy, Christus Santa Rosa Hospice, San Antonio
Arismendez, Agustin, St. Paul, San Antonio
Arriaga, Dan, Notre Dame, Kerrville
Bacon, James, St. Mary's, Fredericksburg
Bader, James W., St. Mary Magdalen, Brackettville, 78832.
Baker, Robert L., Colonial Beach, VA
Barajas, Felipe, Holy Rosary, San Antonio
Barrera, Enrique, San Fernando, San Antonio
Bautista, Teofilo, Jr., Archdiocese of Oklahoma City; Tinker AFB, OK
Behling, James, Ss. Peter and Paul, New Braunfels
Bellg, Bruce J., Blessed Sacrament, San Antonio
Bemrich, Richard, (Retired)
Benigno, Pasquale, St. Brigid, San Antonio
Billimek, Thomas E., St. Brigid, San Antonio
Bonilla-Valentin, Jorge, Immaculate Heart of Mary, San Antonio
Bowlin, William, St. John Neumann, San Antonio
Bozek, Edwin J., Jr., St. Padre Pio, San Antonio
Bravo, Ernesto G., St. Peter the Fisherman, Von Ormy
Brennan, Terrance, St. James, Gonzales
Brock, Ralph, Our Lady of Perpetual Help, New Braunfels
Buchanan, John, (Retired)
Caballero, Antonio, St. Timothy, San Antonio
Caldwell, Robert M., Jr., Deaf Ministry, San Antonio
Callaway, George, Jr., St. Anthony Mary Claret, San Antonio
Camero, A. C., Our Lady of Guadalupe & Jail Ministry, San Antonio
Campa, Gerard, St. Mary Magdalen, San Antonio
Campos, Fred, Jr., St. Gregory the Great, San Antonio
Carranza, Manuel G., Jr., Holy Family, San Antonio
Carrillo, Nick L., Our Lady of Guadalupe, Seguin
Carrizales, Manuel, Our Lady of Mt. Carmel, Big Foot
Carroll, Bernard, St. Joseph, Dilley
Casanova, Ismael G., St. Mary Magdalen, San Antonio
Castellano, Frank V., St. Gabriel, San Antonio
Castillo, Pedro C., Holy Family, San Antonio
Cena, Librado, (Retired)
Champagne, Joseph, (Retired)
Charron, Paul, St. Thomas More, San Antonio
Chavez, Hugo V., St. John the Evangelist, San Antonio
Ciarrochi, Jerome, (Retired)
Clancey, Patrick, The Patrician Movement, San Antonio
Clayton, Brian J., St. Francis of Assisi, San Antonio
Cnota, Robert, Our Lady of Perpetual Help, Selma
Colley, Earl M., Holy Rosary, San Antonio
Criado, Marcos, Immaculate Conception, San Antonio
Crosby, Alan, Blessed Sacrament, Poth
Crowley, Thomas, St. Pius X, San Antonio
Cruz, Robert, Our Lady of Good Counsel, San Antonio
Cruz, Roberto, St. Mary's, Somerset
Cunningham, W. Patrick, Holy Spirit, San Antonio
D'Agostino, Michael, Our Lady of the Atonement, San Antonio
De Hoyos, Richard, St. Peter Prince, San Antonio
De la Torre, Francisco, St. Mary's, Fredericksburg
DeCuir, Harold, St. Brigid, San Antonio
DeLaGarza, Gustavo, (On Leave)
DeLaGarza, Ricardo, Diocese of St. Cloud, MN
DeLauter, Paul, (Retired)
DeLeon, Joseph L., Diocese of San Bernardino
Diaz, Jose G., St. John Berchman, San Antonio
Dillard, Henry, (On Leave)
Dirksen, Kenneth, Sacred Heart, Uvalde
Domingues, Charles, Notre Dame, Kerrville
Donaho, Scott, Jr., Sacred Heart, Floresville
Donias, Justo, Jr., Catholic Charities, Fort Wayne, IN
Dunn, John N., (Retired)
Ebner, Eugene, St. Louis, Castroville
Edminson, Richard, St. John Evangelist, Hondo
Elliot, Robert R., (Retired)
Enriquez, Marcos, (On Leave)
Espinosa, Jose R., (On Leave)
Espinosa, Juan, St. Brigid, San Antonio
Espinosa, Robert, St. Rose of Lima, San Antonio
Estrada, Melchor, (On Leave)
Exparza, James, St. Elizabeth Ann Seton, San Antonio
Falcon, Adrian, Our Lady of Guadalupe, Del Rio
Felan, Ruben, Our Lady of Guadalupe, San Antonio
Fertitta, J. V., Sr., Blessed Sacrament, San Antonio
Fey, Fred, Sts. Peter & Paul, New Braunfels
Fiedler, Welton J., St. Matthew, Jourdanton, TX
Fikac, Frank J., Sts. Peter & Paul, New Braunfels
Fitzpatrick, Alan, St. Dominic, San Antonio
Flores, Federico, Sacred Heart, Uvalde
Fox, Thomas J., St. Matthew's, San Antonio
Fraga, Jesse, Our Lady of Sorrows, San Antonio
Franklin, Thomas M., St. Francis of Assisi, San Antonio
Friesenhahn, Clifford, Our Lady of Perpetual Help, Selma
Frisina, Patrick, St. Brigid, San Antonio
Galan, Roberto L., Jr., St. Joan of Arc, Kirby
Gallegos, Valentine, Sacred Heart, San Antonio
Galvan, Jesse C., St. Anthony Mary Claret, San Antonio
Galvan, Robert, Our Lady of Guadalupe, San Antonio
Garcia, Arturo, St. Lawrence, San Antonio
Garcia, Bennie, St. Andrew, Pleasanton
Garcia, Hector, Sacred Heart, Uvalde
Garza, Albert G., (Retired)
Garza, Ernesto, St. Matthew, San Antonio
Garza, Juan, Our Lady of Guadalupe, Seguin
Garza, Lionel, Jr., St. Dominic, San Antonio
Garza, Pedro F., San Fernando Cathedral, San Antonio
Garza, Robert M., St. Luke, San Antonio
Gass, Johnny J., (Retired)
Gimenez, Benjamin, St. Mary's, Stockdale
Goebel, Joseph E., St. Mary Magdalen, Brackettville
Gonzalez, Amador, St. Bonaventure, San Antonio
Gonzalez, Gerald, St. Ann's, San Antonio
Gonzalez, Richard, St. Luke-Loire, Pleasanton
Gorman, John J., Good Shepherd, Schertz
Gorman, Robert, SS. Peter & Paul, New Braunfels
Gorton, Everett D., Bulverde, Encino Park
Graf, John E., Sacred Heart, Del Rio
Greer, Jesse R., Church of the Holy Spirit, San Antonio
Guerrero, Leon, (Retired)

Guevara, Eusebio, St. Matthew's, Jourdanton
Gustowski, Paul, St. Helena's, San Antonio
Gutierrez, Pedro, Diocese of Las Vegas, NV
Gutierrez, Ramon, (On Leave)
Gutierrez, Trinidad, St. Alphonsus, San Antonio
Hansbauer, Eugene, St. Luke, San Antonio
Henson, Archibald, St. Louis, Castroville
Herbert, David L., Holy Name, San Antonio
Hernandez, Elieser, Our Lady of Guadalupe, Del Rio
Hernandez, Jose D., Immaculate Concepcion, San Antonio
Herrera, Genaro M., St. Joseph's (South San), San Antonio
Herrera, Ramon, (Retired)
Heye, Paul F., St. Brigid, San Antonio
Hinojosa, Antonio, Sacred Heart, Uvalde
Hinojosa, Fidel, St. Bonaventure, San Antonio
Hinojosa, Fortunado, Sacred Heart, Uvalde
Hinojosa, Reynaldo G., Sr., Holy Name, San Antonio
Hobbs, John R., San Francisco di Paola, San Antonio
Hoelscher, Wilbur L., St. Matthew's, San Antonio
Hollstein, Albert, (Retired)
Holmstrom, Joseph, (On Leave)
Houle, Thomas W., St. Matthews, San Antonio
Houlihan, Timothy, Our Lady of Guadalupe, Helotes, TX
Huizar, Ernest, St. James, San Antonio
Hunsucker, Paul, St. Thomas the Apostle, Canyon Lake
Huttinger, John X., Our Lady of Guadalupe, San Antonio
Ibarra, Daniel A., Sacred Heart, Uvalde
Imburgia, Scott, Permanent Diaconate Office, San Antonio
Jasso, Reynaldo, St. Rose of Lima, San Antonio
Jorgensen, J. D., Blessed Sacrament, San Antonio
Kanter, Kevin, St. Mark's, San Antonio
Karam, Jack, St. Mary's, Stockdale
Kasavage, Richard, (Retired)
Kattengell, Leon E., (On Leave)
Kaufman, Raymond, (Retired)
Kearns, W. Daniel, Santo Nino de Cebu, San Antonio
Keller, Alois, Jr., (Retired)
Kim, Philip C., Korean Community, San Antonio; Sacred Heart Seminary, Hales Corners, WI
Klein, Curtis, St. Anthony, Harper
Knopp, Kenneth P., (Retired)
Kolodzie, Stanley, (Retired)
Krupa, Joseph, (On Leave)
Kusenberger, Robert, Sacred Heart, Del Rio
Kutschenreuter, Norman, St. Matthew's, San Antonio
La Combe, Paul B., (Retired)
Lamm, Wilfred, (Retired)
Lammons, Charles, St. Benedict, San Antonio
Landez, John, St. Leo & Permanent Diaconate Office, San Antonio
Laskowski, Norbert C., Holy Trinity, San Antonio
Lauer, Donald E., St. Monica, Converse
Leal, Ernesto T., St. Lawrence, San Antonio
Legendre, James F., St. Joseph, Honey Creek, Spring Branch
Link, John Dennis, Notre Dame, Kerrville
Lira, Antonio, St. Rose of Lima, San Antonio
Lira, Rodolfo, Toledo, OH
Longoria, Leobardo, (Retired)
Lopez, Edward V., Blessed Sacrament, San Antonio
Loth, Louis E., (Retired)
Lucio, Jesus, St. Martin de Porres, San Antonio
Ludolph, Anthony, Diocese of Little Rock
Mangold, Clayton, St. Paul, San Antonio
Marin, Arturo, Prince of Peace, San Antonio
Marques, Steven J., St. Mark the Evangelist, San Antonio
Martinez, Gregorio, Jr., St. Mary, Fredricksburg
Martinez, Juan G., Divine Providence, San Antonio
Martinez, Juan A., Notre Dame, Kerrville
McDonald, John, St. James, San Antonio
Mechler, Gerardo A., St. Margaret Mary, San Antonio
Medina, Damacio, St. Joseph, Nixon
Medina, Henry, (Retired)
Medina, Ricardo, III, Diocese of Fort Wayne
Medrano, Rudy C., St. Timothy, San Antonio
Menchaca, Jose, St. Martin De Porres, San Antonio
Mendoza, Raymundo V., St. Joseph, Del Rio
Meyers, Joseph L., (Retired)
Micek, Jerome, Holy Trinity, San Antonio
Michel, John A., St. Pius X, San Antonio
Miller, Allen K., St. Anthony, Elmendorf
Miller, Mark C., Indianapolis, IN
Miller, Myles, Diocese of Fort Worth
Miller, Paul, Our Lady of Perpetual Help, Selma
Miller, Robert, St. Thomas, Canyon Lake
Moczygemba, Zafirin, St. Margaret Mary, San Antonio
Morales, Cayetano, Our Lady of Perpetual Help, New Braunfels
Moreno, Alfonso, Sacred Heart, Gonzales
Moreno, Florencio, Jr., Diocese of El Paso, TX
Moreno, John J., St. Philip's, Smiley
Moreno, Jose F., Our Lady of Angels, San Antonio
Mueller, Leon, (Retired)
Munoz, Antonio, Immaculate Conception, San Antonio
Muraida, Daniel, St. Paul's, San Antonio
Navarro, Ruben W., St. Raymond Pennafort, Leakey
Neal, Thomas R., Prince of Peace, San Antonio
Nelson, Robert W., St. Mary Magdalen, Brackettville, TX
Neville, Richard F., Jr., Randolph, A.F.B., San Antonio
Novian, Donald, St. Gregory, San Antonio
Olivares Jesse, (On Leave)
Olivares Peter, St. Henry, San Antonio
Orr, James, Our Lady of Atonement, San Antonio
Ortega, Sylvester, St. Jude, San Antonio
Ostaszewski, Chester R., St. Rose of Lima, San Antonio
Pacheco Alvino, St. Leo, San Antonio
Padilla, Juan R., O.L., Guadalupe, Del Rio
Patlan, Antonio, St. Martin de Porres, San Antonio
Patlan, Pedro, St. Paul, San Antonio
Peche, William, Holy Spirit, San Antonio
Pedroza, Doroteo E., San Fernando, San Antonio
Peinemann, Michael E., Seminary: Hales Corners, WI
Perez, Julio T., Diocese of Arlington, VA
Perez, Miguel, Jr., Sacred Heart, Floresville
Perez, Oscar, Mission San Francisco de la Espada, San Antonio
Phillips, Norman D., (Retired)
Ponce, Cesar, Our Lady Queen of Peace, Kenedy
Pope, Charles F., Sr., St. Clare, San Antonio
Pratt, Gilbert, (Retired)
Prevott, Raymond, (Retired)
Quarles, Fred J., (On Leave)
Ramirez, Albert, Our Lady of Angels, San Antonio
Ramirez, Victor, (Retired)
Ramos, Bartolo, St. Jude, San Antonio
Raso, James, St. Benedict, San Antonio
Rayburg, Paul M., St. Peter, Boerne, TX
Resendiz, Benito, St. Martin de Porres, San Antonio
Richard, Joseph N., (On Leave)
Riojas, Francisco, St. Philip, Smiley
Rivera, Gilbert, St. Joan of Arc, Kirby
Rodriguez, Carlos, Sacred Heart, Von Ormy
Rodriguez, Jesus, St. Jude, San Antonio
Rodriguez, Roger, Sacred Heart, Del Rio, TX
Rodriguez, Rudolph, Sacred Heart, San Antonio
Rodriguez, Santiago, San Jose Mission, San Antonio
Rondon-Martinez, Angel
Rosas, Roberto, St. Thomas More, San Antonio
Ruiz, Roberto R., Espada Mission, San Antonio
Salazar, Filomeno, St. Joseph, Del Rio
Salazar, Gilberto, Sacred Heart, Uvalde
Salinas, Alberto, San Juan DeLos Lagos, San Antonio
Salinas, Carlos, (Retired)
Salinas, Hugo, Holy Family, New Braunfels
Sanabria, Agripino, Prince of Peace, San Antonio
Sanchez, Jose H., St. Philip of Jesus, San Antonio
Sandoval, Carlos, Our Lady of Guadalupe, San Antonio
Santana, Efrain, St. Joseph, Del Rio
Scarbo, David B., Sacred Heart, Del Rio
Schonhoff, Robert L., Our Lady of Grace, San Antonio
Schroeder, William, Sts. Peter and Paul, New Braunfels
Scott, Armando, St. Anthony, Elmendorf
Sekinger, Eugene E., Military Parochial, Brooks Air Force Base
Seymour, Warren V., (Retired)
Shockley, Gordon F. (Unassigned)
Shoemake, William, Diocese of Austin
Soto, Roman, Holy Family, San Antonio
Spitzer, John L., (Retired)
Stallings, Larry, St. Mark, San Antonio
Stancombe, Leonard, St. Helena, San Antonio
Staudt, Milton N., Church of the Holy Spirit, San Antonio
Stewart, Wilbert, St. Dominic, San Antonio
Stockton, Ree, St. Dominic, San Antonio
Stokes, Leslie, Diocese of Phoenix
Suniga, Jose A., Divine Providence, San Antonio
Svatek, Anton, (Retired)
Swift, Thomas N., Resurrection of the Lord, San Antonio
Tamez, Javier, Holy Family, San Antonio
Telfer, James, Our Lady of Perpetual Help, Selma
Terry, Frank, (Retired)
Thayer, Robert, St. Anthony, Elmendorf
Thornberry, William, Prince of Peace, San Antonio
Tijerina, Salvador, St. Joseph, Dilley
Townsend, Eugene, St. Pius X, San Antonio
Trevino, Jimmie, St. Dominic, San Antonio
Trevino, Jose S., St. Luke Loire, Pleasanton
Trujillo, Jose M., Diocese of Austin
Tudon, Horacio R., St. Matthew's, San Antonio
Uriegas, Gonzalo, (Retired)
Urrabazo, Rosendo, St. John the Evangelist, San Antonio
Valenta, George, St. John Neumann, San Antonio
Valenzuela, Jose J., (On Leave)
Van Dyke, Ronnie, St. Joseph, Del Rio
Vasquez, Eleodoro, San Juan de Los Lagos, San Antonio
Vick, George, Jr., Good Shepherd, Schertz
Villareal, Ricardo, St. Cecilia, San Antonio
Von Allmen, Charles, St. James, San Antonio
Wasniewski, Michael, (On Leave)
Wehman, Ben, Sts. Peter and Paul, New Braunfels
Weissler, Gilbert, St. Anthony of Padua, San Antonio
Wells, Richard, St. Peter The Fisherman, Von Ormy
Werner, Keith N., St. Matthew's, San Antonio
White, George, (Retired)
White, Thomas, St. Clair, Holy Redeemer, San Antonio
Wittig, Evan, St. John Evangelist, San Antonio
Wright, Michael, O.F.M.Conv., Diocese of Savanah
Ybarra, Hermengildo Rey, St. Leonard, San Antonio
Ybarra, Raymond, (On Leave)
Zamora, David, Our Lady of Guadalupe, San Antonio
Zapata, Gumercindo, St. Philip of Jesus, San Antonio
Zapata, Thomas, (On Leave)
Zizke, William, St. Matthew's, San Antonio

INSTITUTIONS LOCATED IN THE ARCHDIOCESE

[A] SEMINARIES, ARCHDIOCESAN

SAN ANTONIO. *Assumption Seminary aka Assumption-St. John's Seminary*, 2600 W. Woodlawn Ave., P.O. Box 28240, 78228. Tel: 210-734-5137; Fax: 210-734-2324. Email: jbrown07@ix.netcom.com. Web: www.AssumptionSeminary.org. Revs. Gerald L. Brown, S.S., Rector, Admissions & Devel. & Admin.; Lawrence Christian, Vice Rector & Assoc. Dir. Internship, Admissions & Community Life; Frank Macias, Dir. of Worship; James P. Oberle, S.S., S.T.L., Ph.D. (BAL), Dir. of Spirituality; Sisters Patricia E. Casey, O.P., Dir. Pastoral Formation & Coord. Cultural Prog.; Carmen Terese Lazo, M.C.D.P., Dir. Multicultural Formation; Rev. Jose A. Lopez, Formation Faculty Advisor.

Legal Title: *The Seminary of the Assumption of the Blessed Virgin Mary-St. John of San Antonio, TX* Priests 5; Sisters 2; Seminarians 62; Domestic Dept.: Josephine Sisters (Mexico City, Mexico) 14.

Diaconate Program, 114 Shannon Lee St., 78216-7316. Tel: 210-930-8118; Fax: 210-930-8377. Email: diacprog@swbell.net. Rev. John O'Donoghue, Dir.; Deacons John Landez, Asst. Dir.; George White, Asst. Dir.; Joe Fertitta, Asst. Dir.

[B] SEMINARIES, RELIGIOUS OR SCHOLASTICATES

SAN ANTONIO. *Congregation of Holy Cross - Formation Community*, Bro. Charles Andersen Residence, 320 Brahan Blvd., 78215-1020. Tel: 210-223-9117; Fax: 210-223-2081. Bro. Donald Blauvelt, C.S.C., Co-Dir.; Rev. Lawrence A. LeVasseur, C.S.C., Co-Dir. Brothers 2.

Dominican Priory of San Juan Macias and Novitiate, 210 St. Ann St., 78201-6393. Tel: 210-734-6688; Fax: 210-738-1755. Email: st-ann@juno.com. Revs. Wilmo A. Candanedo, O.P.; Joseph Determan, O.P.; John E. Keefer, O.P.; Andrew K. Kolzow, O.P.; Cayet Mangiaracina, O.P.; Vincente M. Pena, O.P.; Bruce B. Schutz, O.P.; Bros. Ramon Gonzalez, O.P.; Omomaro Okekaro, O.P. Novices 7.

Franciscan Formation Program in San Jose Friary (Casa Juan Diego), 701 E. Pyron Ave., 78214. Tel: 210-922-4976; Fax: 210-932-2271. Rev. Herbert Jones, O.F.M., Dir.; Bro. John Abts, O.F.M., Asst. Dir. Seminarians 3.

George Sexton House of Studies (Theology) , 314 E. King's Hwy., 78212. Tel: 210-735-7318; Fax: 210-734-3150. Revs. Mark Dean, O.M.I.; Joseph T. La Belle, O.M.I. Missionary Oblates of Mary Immaculate, United States Province Scholastics 9.

Missionaries of the Sacred Heart Formation House, 237 W. Magnolia, 78212-2916. Tel: 210-737-6394; Fax: 210-737-0327. Email: mobmsc@aol.com. Rev. Michael O'Brien, M.S.C., Dir.

Missionhurst Formation Community, 1147-A Cupples Rd., 78226. Tel: 210-434-5347; 210-432-2651 (Office); Fax: 210-432-2621. Email: MCICM49085@aol.com malonda@aol.com. Revs. Anselme Malonda, C.I.C.M., Dir. Formation; Roy Milton Quioque, C.I.C.M. Students 1.

MSF Formation Community, 104 Cas-Hills Dr., 78213-3322. Tel: 210-344-9145; Fax: 210-344-9146. Web: www.catholic-forum.com/msf. Bro. Camillo Botello, M.S.F. Seminarians 1.

Redemptorist Formation Program - Liguori House, 1523 Iowa, 78203-1817. Tel: 210-533-0442; 210-533-0443; Fax: 210-533-0558. Email: monper@satx.rr.com. Web: www.redemptorists-denver.org. Revs. Monroe Perrier, C.SS.R., Dir.; Francis Pham, C.SS.R., Assoc. Dir. & Vice Prov. of New Orleans. Students 5.

San Damiano Friary, Prenovitiate House of Formation, 1104 Kentucky Ave., 78201. Tel: 210-734-4962; Fax: 210-734-6322. Revs. Gerard Herman, O.F.M.Conv.; James Oberhausen, O.F.M.Conv., Guardian & Dir. House of Formation; Bro. Paul Clark, O.F.M.Conv. Conventual Franciscan Friars Seminarians 4.

[C] COLLEGES AND UNIVERSITIES

SAN ANTONIO. *St. Mary's University of San Antonio, Texas* (1852), One Camino Santa Maria, 78228-8572. Tel: 210-436-3011; Fax: 210-436-3500. Email: ccotrell@stmarytx.edu. Web: www.stmarytx.edu. Dr. Charles Cotrell, Pres.; Dr. David Manuel, Vice Pres. Academic Affairs; Ms. Katherine Sisoian, Vice Pres. Student Devel.; Dr. Janet Dizinno, Dean School of Humanities & Social Sciences; Dr. Suzanne Cory, Interim Dean School of Business; Dr. Anthony J. Kaufmann, Dean School of Science, Engineering and Technology; Dr. Ronald Merrell, Dean Graduate School; Mr. R. William Piatt, Dean School of Law; Ms. Louisa Avitua-Trevino, Registrar; Mr. Richard Castillo, Dir. Admissions; Dr. H. Palmer Hall, Dir. Academic Library; Mr. Robert Summers, Interim Dir. Law Library; Revs. Terrence Weik, S.M., Acting Dir. University Min.; Norbert C. Brockman, S.M.; Chris Janson, S.M.; Conrad J. Kaczkowski, S.M.; John A. Leies, S.M., S.T.D.; Bernard Lee, S.M.; Charles H. Miller, S.M.; George Montague, S.M.; W. Franz Schorp, S.M.; Rudy Vela, S.M. Conducted by the Society of Mary, (Coed) Priests 10; Brothers 4; Sisters 4; Lay Teachers 175; Students 4,118.

Oblate School of Theology (1903), (Coed) (Graduate Theology) , 285 Oblate Dr., 78216-6693. Tel: 210-341-1366; Fax: 210-341-4519. Email: info@ost.edu. Web: www.ost.edu. Rev. J. William Morell, O.M.I., M.Div., Pres.; Dr. Elaine Brothers, Ph.D., Vice Pres. Academic Affairs & Dean; Mr. Scott Woodward, M.A., Assoc. Academic Dean; Mrs. Christiane B. Scheel, Dir. Admissions, Registrar; Mr. Hector Rodriguez, Dir. of Personnel & Physical Plant; Rev. Michael Hill, O.F.M., M.S., M.Div., Dir. of Fin. & Personnel; Ms. Elva Ruiz, Admin. Asst. Pres. Conducted by the Missionary Oblates of Mary Immaculate Priests 25; Sisters 5; Brothers 1; Lay Professors 11; Students 384.

Faculty: Revs. Gerald Brown, S.S.; Warren Brown, O.M.I., J.C.D.; Ken Hannon, O.M.I., Ph.D.; Jan Heemrood, O.M.I., S.S.L.; Donald J. Joyce, O.M.I., M.Div., Dir. Library; John Kemper, S.S., D.Min., Vice Pres. Admin. Affairs; Jan Piotr Klak, Ph.L., S.T.L.; Joseph T. La Belle, O.M.I.; Jose A. Lopez; John M. Makothakat; Ray John Marek, O.M.I., D.Min.; John Markey, O.P., Ph.D. (MIA); William J. Meyer, S.M., Dir. Ministry to Ministers. Tel: 210-349-9928; Francis Kelly Nemeck, O.M.I., S.S.D.; James P. Oberle, S.S., S.T.L., Ph.D. (BAL); Leopoldo G. Perez, O.M.I., S.T.D., M.Div., Co-Dir. M. Div. Prog.; Frederick Sackett, O.M.I., J.C.D.; Stephen K. Sherwood, C.M.F., S.T.D.; Robert E. Wright, O.M.I., Ph.D., Co-Dir. M. Div. Prog.; Ronald W. Young, O.M.I., S.T.D.; Bro. Patrick McGee, O.M.I., M.A., Vice Pres. Spiritual Renewal Min.; Sisters Maria Cimperman, O.S.U., Ph.D.; Marcella Hoesl, M.M., S.T.D.; Mary Christine Morkovsky, C.D.P., Ph.D.; Sarah Ann Sharkey, O.P., Ph.D.; Ms. Margaret Escobedo, M.T.S., Dir. Lay Ministry; Mrs. Sally T. Gomez-Kelly, M.T.S., Dir. T.F.E.; Mrs. Rose A. Marden, M.T.S.; Dr. Ronald Quillo, Th.D., Dir. M.A.(TH) Prog.; Mr. Frank Spinner, Vice Pres. Devel.; Dr. Steven Spirey, Ph.D., Asst. Dir. D. Min. Prog.

**Our Lady of the Lake University*, 411 S.W. 24th, 78207-4689. Tel: 210-434-6711; Fax: 210-436-0824. Email: pollt@lake.ollusa.edu. Web: www.ollusa.edu. Dr. Tessa Martinez Pollack, Ph.D., Pres.; Dr. Maria Shelton, Provost; Dr. Howard Dean Sanchez, Ph.D., Information Svcs. Vice Provost; Allen R. Klaus, B.B.A., Vice Pres. Finance & Facilities; Mary Ellen Smith, M.S., Vice Pres. & Dean of Student Life; Mr. Jim Eskin, Vice Pres. Institutional Advancement; Dr. Fred Anyanwu, Chief Planning Office; Dr. Cora Le-Doux, Ph.D., Dean Worden School of Social Svcs.; Richard Slocum, Dean College of Arts & Sciences; Dr. Lois Graff, Ph.D., Dean School of Business; Dr. Robert Devillar, Ph.D., Dean School of Education & Clinical Studies; Mrs. Susan Schleicher, Chief Comm. Officer. Sponsored by Sisters of Divine Providence Sisters 8; Full-Time Faculty 128; Lay Teachers 120; Students 4,084.

Campus Ministry Team: Wayne Romo, M.T.S., Dir.

The United Colleges of San Antonio (A Consortium of Catholic Colleges in San Antonio) , 285 Oblate Dr., 78216. Tel: 210-341-1366; Fax: 210-341-4519. Rev. J. William Morell, O.M.I., M.Div.; Charles L. Cotrell, Ph.D.; Dr. Louis Agnese Jr., Ph.D.; Dr. Tessa Martinez Pollack, Ph.D.

University of the Incarnate Word, 4301 Broadway, 78209. Tel: 210-829-6000; Fax: 210-829-3901. Email: douge@universe.uiwtx.edu. Web: www.uiw.edu. Dr. Louis J. Agnese Jr., Ph.D., Pres.; Dr. Terry Dicianna, Ph.D., Provost; Sr. Kathleen Coughlin, C.C.V.I., Vice Pres. Institutional Advancement; Douglas B. Endsley, M.B.A., C.P.A., Vice Pres. Business & Fin.; David Jurenovich, Ph.D., Vice Pres. Admin.; Gilberto Hinojosa, Ph.D., Dean Graduate Studies & Research; Patricia Watkins, Ed.D., Dean Education; Denise Doyle, Ph.D., Vice Pres. Academic & Student Affairs; Renee Moore, Dean Campus Life; Andrea Cyterski, Dir. Admissions; Ms. Katherine Ruiz, Dir. Campus Min.; Sr. Eilish Ryan, Th.D., Dir. Pastoral Institute; Bobbye Fry, Ed.D., Registrar; Donna Aronson, Dean Humanities, Arts & Social Sciences; Patricia Burr, Ph.D., Vice Pres. Int'l Programs; Robert Connelly, Ph.D., Dean Math, Science & Engineering; Kathleen Light, Ph.D., Dean Nursing & Health Professionals; Mendell Morgan, Dean Library Svcs.; Edith Cogdell, C.P.A., Comptroller. Sisters of the Incarnate Word 13; Lay Faculty 138; Students 4,434.

[D] HIGH SCHOOLS, ARCHDIOCESAN

SAN ANTONIO. *Antonian College Preparatory High School*, 6425 West Ave., 78213. Tel: 210-344-9265; Fax: 210-344-9267. Email: gsaenz@Antonian.org. Web: Antonian.org. Dr. Gilbert L. Saenz, Prin.; Rev. Simon M. Zayas, Camero, TOR Chap. (Coed) Priests 1; Deacons 1; Lay Teachers 37; Students 665.

[E] HIGH SCHOOLS, REGIONAL

SAN ANTONIO. *St. Gerard Catholic High School*, 521 S. New Braunfels Ave., 78203. Tel: 210-533-8061; Fax: 210-533-3697. Email: KStanbridge@archdiosa.org. Web: www.stgerardhigh.org. Maurice Abadie, Pres.; Kathy Stanbridge, Prin. Sisters 3; Brothers 1; Lay Teachers 14; Students 151.

KERRVILLE. *Our Lady of the Hills Regional Catholic High School*, 575 Peterson Farm Rd., 78028. Tel: 830-895-0501; Fax: 830-895-0604. Email: olh@ktc.com. Web: OurLadyoftheHills.org. Mr. Barry J. Neuburger, Prin. Total Enrollment 29.

[F] HIGH SCHOOLS, PRIVATE

SAN ANTONIO. *St. Anthony Catholic High School*, 3200 McCullough Ave., 78212-3099. Tel: 210-832-5600; 210-829-6004; Fax: 210-832-5615. Email: ochoad@universe.uiw.edu. Web: www.sachs.org. Daniel Ochoa, Prin.; Rev. Leo Perez, O.M.I.; Douglas B. Endsley, M.B.A., C.P.A., Vice Pres. Business & Fin. Boys boarding department. Priests 1; Sisters 2; Lay Teachers 24; Students 315.

Blessed Sacrament Academy, 1135 Mission Rd., 78210. Tel: 210-532-4731; Fax: 210-534-2882. Email: odilia@sbcglobal.net. Web: sticky-wickets.org. Sr. M. Odilia Korenek, I.W.B.S., Dir. & Supr.

Child Development Center Tel: 210-532-5363; Fax: 210-532-2149. Sisters of the Incarnate Word and Blessed Sacrament 3; Lay Teachers 14; Students 150; Support Staff 11.

Parents Academy Tel: 210-534-0894; Fax: 210-532-6698. Sisters 1; Lay Teachers 2; Support Staff 5; Students 350.

Central Catholic High School, 1403 N. St. Mary's St., 78215-1785. Tel: 210-225-6794; Fax: 210-227-9353. Email: admissions@cchs-satx.org. Web: www.cchs-satx.org. Rev. Joseph A. Tarrillion, S.M., Pres.; Deacon W. Patrick Cunningham, Prin.; Revs. Donald Cowie, S.M.; Gerald Haby, S.M. Priests 3; Brothers 4; Deacons 2; Lay Teachers 33; Students 488.

Healy-Murphy Center, Inc., 618 Live Oak St., 78202. Tel: 210-223-2944; Fax: 210-224-1033. Email: dwatson@healymurphy.com. Douglas J. Watson, Exec. Dir. Day School for High School Students. Provides an alternative to the Regular School System. Sisters 2; Lay Teachers 17; Counselors 2; Nurses 1; Students 300; Child Development Department: Ages 6 wks. - 5 yrs 110; On Campus Clinic: Nurse 1.

Holy Cross of San Antonio, 426 N. San Felipe, 78228. Tel: 210-433-9395; Fax: 210-433-1666. Email: SAHCMAN@hotmail.com. Web: www.holycross-sa.org. Bro. Stanley Culotta, C.S.C., Pres.; Mr. Angel Cedillo, Prin. Brothers of the Holy Cross. Brothers 3; Lay Teachers 29; Students 476.

Incarnate Word High School, 727 E. Hildebrand Ave., 78212-2598. Tel: 210-829-3100; Fax: 210-829-3120. Email: SalinasC@universe.uiwtx.edu. Web: www.incarnatewordhs.org. Cindy Salinas, Prin. Sisters 1; Brothers 1; Lay Teachers 43; Students 600.

Providence High School, 1215 N. St. Mary's St., 78215-1787. Tel: 210-224-6651; Fax: 210-224-6214. Email: abristol@providencehs.net. Web: www.providencehs.net. Anne Bristol, Prin. Sisters 2; Lay Teachers 33; Students 418.

[G] ELEMENTARY SCHOOLS, PRIVATE

SAN ANTONIO. *St. Anthony's School*, 205 W. Huisache St., 78212. Tel: 210-732-8801; Fax: 210-732-5968. Email: jkennedy@archdiosa.org. Web: www.stanthonysa.org. John P. Kennedy, Ed.D., Prin.; Rev. Msgr. Vincent Fecher (Retired). Priests 2; Sisters 2; Lay Teachers 28; Students 390.

St. John Bosco School, (Grades K-8), 5630 W. Commerce St., 78237. Tel: 210-432-8011; Fax: 210-432-5168. Email: fmasuojbc@aol.com. Sisters Teresita Delgado, F.M.A., Supr.; Rosann Ruiz, F.M.A., Supr. Institute of the Daughters of Mary Help of Christians (Salesian Sisters of St. John Bosco), Day School. Sisters 16; Lay Teachers 25; Students 490.

St. Martin Hall, Our Lady of the Lake University of San Antonio, 411 S.W. 24th St., 78207-4617. Tel: 210-434-6711, Ext. 308; Fax: 210-432-8526. Email: peree@lake.ollusa.edu. Web: education.ollusa.edu/stmartinhall/. Dr. Ernest Perez, Prin. Campus Laboratory School, Preschool Kindergarten through Eighth Grade. Sisters 2; Lay Teachers 20; Students 365.

Mount Sacred Heart School, Inc., (Grades PreK-8), 619 Mount Sacred Heart Rd., 78216. Tel: 210-342-6711; Fax: 210-342-4032. Email: sherrera@archdiosa.org. Web: www.msheagles.com. Mrs. Sylvia D. Herrera, Prin. Sisters 6; Lay Teachers 28; Students 485.

Our Lady of Peace Catholic School, aka Westside Catholic Interparish School, (Grades K-8), 314 Merida St., 78207. Tel: 210-224-2450; Fax: 210-224-1101. Email: salval@aol.com. Mrs. Marianne Mongiello. Sisters 1; Lay Teachers 7; Students 88.

**Rolling Hills Academy, Inc.*, 21240 Gathering Oak, 78258. Tel: 210-497-0323; Fax: 210-497-1440. Email: shawn@rhacademy.org.

[H] GENERAL HOSPITALS

SAN ANTONIO. *Christus Santa Rosa Children's Hospital*, 333 N. Santa Rosa Blvd., 78207. Tel: 210-704-2011; Fax: 210-704-3632. Email: Richard.Wayne@ChristusHealth.org. Web: www.christussantarosa.org. Dr. Richard Wayne, Vice Pres. & Admin. Owned and operated by Christus Health, Santa Rosa Health Care Corp. Licensed Beds 262; Staff 472; Patients Assisted Annually 105,000.

Christus Santa Rosa Health Care Corporation, 333 N. Santa Rosa Blvd., 78207. Tel: 210-704-2011; Fax: 210-704-3632. Web: www.ChristusSantaRosaHealth.org. Don A. Beeler, Pres. & CEO; Rich Woodley, Dir. Pastoral Ministry; Revs. Michael Norton, C.PP.S.; Palmer Maxwell; Akalawu Ambrose, C.S.Sp. Health related activities. Sisters 10; Nurses 958; Bed Capacity 849; Patients Assisted Annually 200,241.

Christus Santa Rosa Hospital, 333 N. Santa Rosa Blvd., 78207. Tel: 210-704-2011; Fax: 210-704-3632. Email: Cary.Fox@ChristusHealth.org. Web: www.ChristusHealth.org. Cary A. Fox, Vice Pres. & Admin. Owned and operated by Christus Health, Santa Rosa Health Care Corp. Licensed Beds 587; Patients Assisted Annually 95,000; Total Staff 2,152.

Christus Santa Rosa Medical Center, 2827 Babcock Rd., 78229. Tel: 210-705-6300; Fax: 210-705-6094. Email: Michael.McBride@ChristusHealth.org. Web: www.christussantarosa.org. Michael McBride, Vice Pres. & Admin. Licensed Beds 178; Patients Assisted Annually 49,154.

Christus Santa Rosa Rehabilitation Hospital, 2827 Babcock, 78229. Tel: 210-705-6100; Fax: 210-705-6028. Owned and operated by Christus Health, Santa Rosa Health Care Corp. Bed Capacity 38; Staff 637.

Incarnate Word Health System, 4503 Broadway, 78209. Tel: 210-828-2224; Fax: 210-828-9741. Sr. Yolanda Tarango, C.C.V.I., Pres.

[I] PROTECTIVE INSTITUTIONS

SAN ANTONIO. *Father Flanagan's Boys' and Girls' Town of San Antonio*, 503 Urban Loop, 78204. Tel: 210-271-1010; Fax: 210-271-3333. Email: rascoe@boystown.org. Web: www.boystown.org. Mr. Wade Rascoe, Shelter Dir. Staff 61; Bed Capacity 50; Children Under Care 359.

Residential Center, 8400, 8401, 8402, 8405, 8406 Flanagan St., 78249. Tel: 210-271-1010; Fax: 210-271-3333. (For Children under 18) Staff 23; Bed Capacity 30; Children Served 61.

Youth Shelter, 503 Urban Loop, 78204. Tel: 210-271-3131; Fax: 210-271-9407. Staff 26; Bed Capacity 20; Total Assisted 298.

Family Preservation Services, 503 Urban Loop, 78204. Tel: 210-271-1010; Fax: 210-271-3333. Staff 13; Families Assisted 106.

St. Peter & Joseph Childrens Home, 919 Mission Rd., 78210. Tel: 210-533-1203; Fax: 210-533-6199. Email: sbomalaski@stpjhome.org. Web: www.stpjhome.org. Susan H. Bomalaski, Ph.D., L.P.C., Exec. Dir. House Parent Staff 27; Administrative & Support Staff 16; Bed Capacity 90; Children Under Care (ages 2-18) 78; Total Assisted 246.

Seton Home for Homeless, Pregnant Adolescents, 1115 Mission Rd., 78210. Tel: 210-533-3504; Fax: 210-533-3467. Email: ms-seton@swbell.net. Margaret Starkey, Dir. Bed Capacity 24; Total Assisted 100; Staff 28.

Visitation House Ministries, 945 W. Huisache, 78201. Tel: 210-735-6910; Fax: 210-738-8794. Web: www.visitationhouseministries.org. Sr. Yolanda Tarango, C.C.V.I., Dir. Operated by the Sisters of Charity of the Incarnate Word of San Antonio, TX, A non-profit corporation chartered under the laws of the State of Texas.; Provides a transitional housing program for homeless women and children on a temporary basis. Total Assisted 38.

Interconnections Tel: 210-653-7492; Fax: 210-653-7559. An Educational and Research Project.

BOERNE. *Childrens' Inn*, 216 W. Highland Dr., 78006. Tel: 830-249-9456; Fax: 830-249-3327. Email: childrensinn@netscape.net. Sr. Kathleen Kean, S.S.J., Co-Dir.; Marilyn Haider, Co-Dir. Provides foster care for children with special needs in a holistic setting. Total Assisted 7.

[J] DAY CARE CENTERS AND KINDERGARTENS

SAN ANTONIO. *St. Anthony Day Care Learning Center; Infant and Toddler Center*, 1707 Centennial Blvd., 78211. Tel: 210-924-4443; Fax: 210-924-4469. Email: salc@aol.com. Sisters Mary Ann Domagalski, M.S.S.A., Admin.; Lucelia Sanchez, M.S.S.A., Dir. Sisters 2; Lay Staff 25; Children 140.

Blessed Sacrament Learning Center, 222 W. Cevallos St., 78204. Tel: 210-223-5013; Fax: 210-444-0779. Email: MDoloresMunoz@aol.com. Sr. Rita Pinedo, H.M.S.S., Dir. Mercedarian Sisters of the Blessed Sacrament Sisters 3; Children 20.

St. Brigid's Kindergarten, 5118 Loma Linda Dr., 78201. Tel: 210-733-0037; Fax: 210-785-2820. Email: SDeegan@hotmail.com. Sr. Stephenie Deegan, C.S.B., Dir. Children 30.

Carmelite Learning Center, 2006 Martin Luther King Dr., 78203. Tel: 210-533-0651; Fax: 210-533-3910. Email: smf3964@yahoo.com. Sr. Maria Faustina, D.C.J., Dir. Attended from St. Patrick's Church. Carmelite Sisters of the Divine Heart of Jesus 14; Lay Staff 11; In Day Care 80.

Immaculate Conception Kindergarten and Nursery, 2407 W. Travis St., 78207. Tel: 210-226-3934; Fax: 210-226-3934. Sr. Maria Del Carmen Sanchez, A.P.G., Dir. Sisters 3; Lay Staff 12; Kindergarten & Nursery Children 58.

BOERNE. *St. Albert Hall dba St. Albert Early Learning Center - Head Start*, 216 W. Highland Dr., 78006. Tel: 830-816-2059; 830-249-3579; Fax: 830-249-1979. Email: benstrs@boernenet.com. Web: www.BoerneBenedictines.com. Janie Hernandez, Dir. Children 93; Staff 18.

[K] HOMES FOR AGED

SAN ANTONIO. *Casa De Padres*, 8520 Cross Mountain Tr., P.O. Box 100, 78255. Tel: 830-698-0175; Fax: 830-698-0175. Email: jengberg@gvtc.com. Mrs. Jeannine Engberg, Dir. Tel: 210-698-0175; 830-981-9192; Most Rev. Bernard Popp, D.D., V.G. (Retired). Tel: 210-698-5524; Rev. Msgr. Alois J. Goertz (Retired). Tel: 210-698-9067 No. 402; Rev. Pablo Paniagua. Tel: 210-698-8036 No. 401; Rev. Msgrs. Roy Rihn (Retired). Tel: 210-698-0287 No. 301; Sherrill Smith (Retired). Tel: 210-698-8819 No. 201; Vincent Fecher (Retired). Tel: 210-698-3923 No. 302; Albert Hubertus (Retired). Tel: 210-698-3183 No. 1002; Joseph Petsch (Retired). Tel: 210-698-7055 No. 702; Leo Martinez (Retired). Tel: 210-698-9875 No. 1002; John Wagner. Tel: 210-698-1332 No. 202. Home for retired Priests of San Antonio. In Res. Rev. Msgr. Terence Nolan. Tel: 201-698-0349 No. 701.

St. Francis Nursing Home, 630 W. Woodlawn, 78212. Tel: 210-736-3177; Fax: 210-783-2221. Sisters Alfonsa Bobek, S.O.L.S., Pres. of Corp.; Agnes Bochenek, S.O.L.S., Admin. Seraphic Sisters of Our Lady of Sorrows, Home for the Aged and Convalescents. Sisters 9; Bed Capacity 143; Total Staff 149.

Incarnate Word Retirement Community, 4707 Broadway, 78209. Tel: 210-829-7561; Fax: 210-828-0020. Email: sftxnc@aol.com Web: www.IwRetire.org. Mr. Steven E. Fuller, Exec. Dir.; Rev. Msgr. Thomas A. French, Chap. For lay persons also. Total in Residence 240.

Marianist Residence: Skilled Nursing, 520 Fordham Ln., 78228-4821. Tel: 210-436-3771 (Nurses' Station); Fax: 210-431-4240. Email: jjaeckle@stmarytx.edu. Bros. Joseph Grieshaber, S.M., Dir.; James Jaeckle, S.M., Sub Dir., Health Care Oper.; Revs. Lawrence Jordan, S.M.; Norbert Moellering, S.M. Tel: 210-436-3150; Paul Ryan, S.M. Tel: 210-436-3766; Thomas M. Schelble, S.M.; Herbert Pieper, S.M. (STL). Tel: 210-436-3773. Home for Infirm Marianist Brothers and Priests. Infirm Brothers 17; Infirm Priests 5; Total Assisted 28; Staff 43.

McCullough Hall Nursing Center, 603 S.W. 24th St., 78207-4696. Tel: 210-434-1866, Ext. 1150. Sr. Antoinette Kaiser, C.D.P., Treas.

Oblate Madonna Residence, 5722 Blanco Rd., 78216. Tel: 210-341-2350; Fax: 210-340-3732. Email: roblatemadonna@satx.rr.com. Revs. Patrick Guidon, O.M.I., Dir.; Jose Azpiazu, O.M.I.; Clifford Blackburn, O.M.I.; Charles Borgers, O.M.I.; James F. Delaney, O.M.I.; Laurent Dupuis, O.M.I.; Leo Gauvin, O.M.I.; Richard A. Houlahan, O.M.I.; Alfred Lavoie, O.M.I.; Joseph Lyons, O.M.I.; John McGrath, O.M.I., Supr.; Robert McGrath, O.M.I.; James Miller, O.M.I.; Sebastian Mozos, O.M.I.; Joseph O'Brien, O.M.I.; William L. O'Connor, O.M.I.; Raymond Pomaville, O.M.I.; Norman Racette O.M.I.; John Schwider, O.M.I.; John Sokolski, O.M.I.; Jose Velasco, O.M.I.; Robert Vreteau, O.M.I.; Andrew Wueste, O.M.I. Missionary Oblates of Mary Immaculate, Home for retired Priests and Brothers. Priests 27. In Res. Most Rev. Thomas Flanagan, D.D.

Padua Place, 80 Peter Baque Rd., 78209. Tel: 210-826-7721; Fax: 210-824-4554. Email: paduaplace@aol.com. Sr. Rose Mary Martinez, M.S.S.A., Admin. Home for infirm and retired Priests and Brothers. Priests 15. In Res. Rev. Msgrs. Gino Bernasconi (VIC); Anthony J. Costantino (Retired); Ramon V. Garcia; Leroy Manning; Patrick Palmer (Retired); Charles Pugh (Retired); Victor Schmidtzinsky (VIC); Revs. Eugene Janson (VIC); Charles Larue (SAN); Francis Nelan, M.S.C.; Daniel O'Brien (VIC); Martin Philip Wurth, O.C.D.; Edward Zaborowski, M.S.F.; Charles Zeyen, M.S.F.

The South Texas Catholic Retirement Center, Inc., 11931 Radium Dr., 78216. Tel: 210-341-8884; Fax: 210-341-0271. Sr. Bernadine Reyes O.S.B., Chm. Purpose: A collaborative effort of 16 Religious Congregations, men and women, to provide a facility for elderly religious and lay men and women who are economically disadvantaged.

KENEDY. *John Paul II Nursing Home*, 209 S. 3rd St., P.O. Box 359, 78119. Tel: 830-583-9841; Fax: 830-583-9458. Sr. Elizabeth Dubicka, S.O.L.S., Admin. Seraphic Sisters of Our Lady of Sorrows 5; Residents 64; Independent Living 13.

[L] BOARDING HOMES

SAN ANTONIO. *Seraphic Sisters Boarding Home for the Aged*, 619 W. Craig Pl., 78212. Tel: 210-736-3177; Fax: 210-738-2221. *c/o St. Francis Nursing Home*, 630 W. Woodlawn, 78212. Sr. Agnes Bochenek, S.O.L.S., Dir. Guests 2.

[M] MONASTERIES AND RESIDENCES OF PRIESTS AND BROTHERS

SAN ANTONIO. *Casa Maria Marianist Community*, St. Mary's University, One Camino Santa Maria, #18, 78228-8518. Tel: 210-436-3066; Fax: 210-431-4216. Revs. Chris Janson, S.M. Tel: 210-436-3273; Charles Stander, S.M. (CIN). Tel: 210-431-2269; Bros. Joseph Barrett, S.M. Tel: 210-436-3228; Edward Longbottom, S.M. Tel: 210-436-3239; Timothy Pieprzyca, S.M. Tel: 210-436-3513; Michael Sullivan, S.M., Dir. Tel: 210-436-3258. Aspirants 3.

Casa Pasionista Guadalupe, 700 Waverly, 78201-6138. Tel: 210-736-5228; Fax: 210-737-6549. Email: clementecp@cs.com. Web: www.passionist.org. Rev. Clemente Barron, C.P.; Deacon James Griffith, C.P.. Email: JGriffCP@aol.com.

Casa San Juan Marianist Community, 1701 Alametos, 78201. Tel: 210-734-6727; Fax: 210-431-6884. Email: GMontague@stmarytx.edu. Revs. George T. Montague, S.M., Dir.; Robert E. Hogan, S.M.; Joseph Mary Marshall, S.M. Deacons 1.

Central Catholic Marianist Community, 1403 N. St. Mary's St., 78215-1785. Tel: 210-225-1112; Fax: 210-227-9353. Email: hbcorn@cchs-satx.org. Revs. Donald Cowie, S.M.; Joseph G. Rasky, S.M.; Gerald Haby, S.M.; Bro. Harry Cornell, S.M., Dir. Brothers 7.

Chaminade Community House, 2818 Peppermill Run, 78231. Tel: 210-764-8626. Email: ckaczkowski@stmarytx.edu. Revs. Conrad J. Kaczkowski, S.M.; Joseph A. Tarrillion, S.M., Supr.; Charles H. Miller, S.M. Marianists

De Mazenod House (Faculty Residence) , 7707 Madonna Dr., 78216. Tel: 210-349-8572; Fax: 210-349-8572. Revs. Warren A. Brown, O.M.I., J.C.D.; Ken Hannon, O.M.I., Ph.D., Supr.; Jan Heemrood, O.M.I., S.S.L.; Ray John Marek, O.M.I., D.Min.; Frederick Sackett, O.M.I., J.C.D.; Ronald W. Young, O.M.I., S.T.D. Missionary Oblates of Mary Immaculate Priests 6.

Discalced Carmelites (Prov. of St. Therese), 906 Kentucky Ave., 78201-6097. Tel: 210-735-9126; Fax: 210-735-1389. Email: satfriar@aol.com. Web: www.2.dcci.com/ocdokla/. Revs. John Suenram, O.C.D., Supr. & Pastor; Marion Joseph Bui, O.C.D.; Sam Anthony Morello, O.C.D.; Christopher Timoney, O.C.D. (LR); Mary Philip Wurth, O.C.D.; Bro. Joseph Le. Priests 6; Scholastics 1. In Res. Rev. Ralph Reyes, O.C.D.

Holy Cross Community, 426 N. San Felipe St., 78228. Tel: 210-434-9100; Fax: 210-433-1666. Email: SAHCMAN@hotmail.com. Web: www.holycross-sa.org. Bro. Stanley Culotta, C.S.C., Dir.; Rev. Akalawu Ambrose, C.S.Sp. Priests 1; Brothers 5.

Bro. Charles Andersen Residence, 320 Brahan Blvd., 78215. Tel: 210-223-9117; Fax: 210-223-2081. Rev. Lawrence A. LeVasseur, C.S.C., Dir.; Bro. Donald Blauvelt, C.S.C., Co-Dir. Priests 1; Brothers 4.

Holy Rosary Marianist Community, 159 Camino Santa Maria, 78228-4997. Tel: 210-433-6137; Fax: 210-433-2133. Email: Jmanahan1@aol.com. Rev. John J. Manahan, S.M.; Bro. Richard Schrader, S.M.

Hospital Ministry House, 6111 Walking Gait, 78240. Tel: 210-680-3685. Rev. Nicholas Brown, S.C.J.

Joseph Gerard House, 302 Oblate Dr., 78216. Tel: 210-377-3462. Revs. Robert Wright, O.M.I. Tel: 210-348-0545; Edward DeLeon, O.M.I. Tel: 210-269-2395.

Marianist Residence, St. Mary's University, 520 Fordham Ave., 78228-4821. Tel: 210-436-3744; Fax: 210-436-3747. Email: JGrieshaber@stmarytx.edu. Bro. Joseph Grieshaber, S.M., Dir. Tel: 210-436-3745; Revs. John A. Leies, S.M., S.T.D. Tel: 210-436-3227; Bernard Meyer, S.M. Tel: 210-436-3761; W. Franz Schorp, S.M. Tel: 210-431-2259. Priests 3; Brothers 17.

Marianist Vocation Ministry, One Camino Santa Maria, 78228-8556. Tel: 210-431-2193; Fax: 210-436-3724. Email: mumike@stmarytx.edu. Web: www.buildingcommunity.org. Bro. Michael Sullivan, S.M., Dir.

Missionaries of the Sacred Heart Sectional Headquarters of the Irish Province for California and Southern States. , 123 W. Laurel St., 78212-2916. Tel: 210-737-5514; Fax: 210-226-5725. Email: magnoliamsc@sbcglobal.net. Rev. James Dudley, M.S.C., Supr.

Religious Activities Office, 3700 N. Capitol St. N.W., Washington, DC 20317. Tel: 202-882-1888.

Missionary Oblates of Mary Immaculate, Southwest Area Office, 327 Oblate Dr., 78216-6602. Tel: 210-349-1475; Fax: 210-349-7411. Email: swarea@omiusa.org. Web: www.omiusa.org. Revs. Thomas Singer, O.M.I., Regl. Councillor. Tel: 210-342-3492; Salvatore DeGeorge, O.M.I., Southwest Area Supr. Tel: 210-349-1475.

Oblate Vocation Office, 327 Oblate Dr., 78216-6602. Tel: 210-349-1475; 800-358-4394; Fax: 210-349-7411. Email: vocations@omiusa.org. Revs. Salvatore DeGeorge, O.M.I., Province Vicar for Vocations; Alejandro Roque, O.M.I., Vocations Dir.

214 Oblate Dr., 78216. Revs. Charles Breault, O.M.I. Tel: 210-348-9045; Galeb Mokarzel, O.M.I. Tel: 210-342-1951.

218 Oblate Dr., 78216. Revs. J. William Morell, O.M.I., M.Div. Tel: 210-377-3462; Thomas Singer, O.M.I. Tel: 210-342-3492.

302 Oblate Dr., 78216. Revs. Robert E. Wright, O.M.I., Ph.D. Tel: 210-348-0545; Edward DeLeon, O.M.I. Tel: 210-269-2395.

Missionhurst Community Residence, 1746 Donaldson, 78228. Revs. Francis Loos, C.I.C.M. Tel: 210-432-6062; Paul Newhouse, C.I.C.M.

(Retired). Tel: 210-435-4210; Paul Van Coillie, C.I.C.M. Tel: 210-432-1034; Felix A. Avau, C.I.C.M.
Other Addresses:
7600 Blanco Rd., Apt. 1605, 78216. Tel: 210-344-3813. Rev. Ralph Nuytten, C.I.C.M.

Oblate Benson Residence (Southwest Area), 334 W. Kings Hwy., 78212. Tel: 210-732-5162; Fax: 210-732-6143. Revs. Gerard Weber, O.M.I. Tel: 210-732-8024; Salvatore DeGeorge, O.M.I. Tel: 210-732-8771; Leo Perez, O.M.I. Tel: 210-735-5906. Missionary Oblates of Mary Immaculate - Southwest Area Priests 3.

Redemptorists of Texas-San Antonio #1, 1617 Iowa St., 78203. Tel: 210-534-4351; Fax: 210-534-1280. Email: RRUHNKE@sbcglobal.net. Web: www.marriagepreparation.com. Revs. Robert A. Ruhnke, C.SS.R., Supr.; Jose Chavez, C.SS.R.; Gilbert A. Enderle, C.SS.R.; Carl Schindler, C.SS.R.; Mark Scheffler, C.Ss.R.; Bro. Charles Fucik, C.SS.R. (Vice Province of New Orleans)

San Damiano Friary, 1104 Kentucky Ave., 78201. Tel: 210-734-4962; Fax: 210-734-6322. Revs. James Oberhausen, O.F.M.Conv.; Gerald Herman, O.F.M.Conv.; Bro. Paul Clark, O.F.M.Conv. Conventual Franciscan Friars

Woodlawn Marianist Community, 3303 W. Woodlawn Ave., 78228. Tel: 210-436-0182; Fax: 210-436-0188. Email: TWeik@StMaryTx.edu. Revs. Norbert Brockman, S.M.; Terrence Weik, S.M., Dir.; Bernard Lee, S.M.; Rudy Vela, S.M.; John Klobuka, S.M., Dir. Priests 5; Brothers 5.

NEW BRAUNFELS. *Congregation of the Holy Ghost*, 19440 IH 35 N., 78132-4839. Tel: 830-609-1200; Fax: 830-609-4738. Revs. Albert J. McKnight, C.S.Sp.; Christopher Chukwu, C.S.Sp. (ARE).

[N] CONVENTS AND RESIDENCES FOR SISTERS

SAN ANTONIO. *St. Anthony Convent*, 100 Peter Baque Rd., 78209. Tel: 210-824-4553; Fax: 210-824-4554. Email: mssa@aol.com. Sr. Mary Ann Domagalski, M.S.S.A., Supr. Motherhouse and Novitiate of the Missionary Servants of St. Anthony Sisters 4.

Blessed Sacrament Convent, 222 W. Cevallos St., 78204. Tel: 210-223-5013; Fax: 210-444-0779. Email: MDoloresMunoz@aol.com. Sr. Dolores Munoz, H.M.S.S., Supr. Mercedarian Sisters of the Blessed Sacrament Sisters 14.

Blessed Sacrament and Incarnate Word Convent, Formerly Incarnate Word and Blessed Sacrament Convent, 1135 Mission Rd., 78210. Tel: 210-534-8005; Fax: 210-534-2882. Email: odilia@sbcglobal.net. Web: sticky-wickets.org. Sr. M. Odilia Korenek, I.W.B.S., Supr. Sisters of the Incarnate Word and Blessed Sacrament Sisters 10.

Blessed Sacrament Parish Convent, 118 Melba, 78216. Tel: 210-828-0155. Sr. Mary Theresa Fritz, I.W.B.S., Supr. Sisters of the Incarnate Word and Blessed Sacrament Sisters 2.

St. Brigid's Convent, 5118 Loma Linda Dr., 78201. Tel: 210-733-0701; 210-738-1472; Fax: 210-785-2820. Email: Brigidines@aol.com. Web: www.brigidine.org. Sr. Mary Teresa Cullen, C.S.B., Regl. Coord. Regional House.; Address matters connected with congregation to the Regional Coord. Sisters 16.

Carmelite Convent, 2006 Martin Luther King Dr., 78203. Tel: 210-533-0651; Fax: 210-533-3910. Sr. M. Clare Guerra, D.C.J., Supr. Carmelite Sisters of the Divine Heart of Jesus Sisters 4.

Cordi-Marian Missionary Sisters, Cordi-Marian Villa, 11624 FM 471, 78253. Tel: 210-688-3099; 210-688-3103; Fax: 210-688-9268. Email: mcmsally@aol.com. Sisters Catalina Marquez, M.C.M., Prov. Supr.; Celina Martin, M.C.M., Supr.; Rev. Pedro Molina (Mexico), Chap. Convent, Provincial House and Retreat Center. Sisters 30.

Cordi-Marian Missionary Sisters Convent, 2902 Morales St., 78207. Tel: 210-433-5064; Fax: 210-433-5064. Email: mcmeliaj@aol.com. Sr. Mary Elia Jaime, M.C.M., Supr. Sisters 4.

Daughters of Charity Convent, 7603 Somerset Rd., 78211. Tel: 210-927-2795; Fax: 210-922-0332. Email: sanglim@dcssa.org. Sr. Suzanne Anglim, D.C., Supr. Daughters of Charity of St. Vincent de Paul Sisters 4.

The Daughters of St. Paul Convent (Pontifical F.S.P.) , 114 Main Plaza, 78205. Tel: 210-224-8101; Fax: 210-224-0938. Email: sanantonio@pauline.org. Web: www.pauline.org. Sr. Kathleen Thomas Lang, F.S.P., Supr. Sisters 4.

El Carmen Sister's Residence, 1835-1 Martinez-Losoya Rd., 78221. Tel: 210-626-2024; Fax: 210-626-1849; 210-627-9600. Email: dcelcarmen@attglobal.net. Web: www.famvin.org. Sr. Constance Hummel, D.C., Supr. Daughters of Charity of St. Vincent de Paul Sisters 4.

Eucharistic Franciscan Missionary Sisters, 558 Cumberland, 78204. Tel: 210-224-7993. Sr. Flora Ramirez, M.E.F., Supr. Sisters 4.

Generalate of the Congregation of Divine Providence, 515 S.W. 24th St., 78207. Tel: 210-434-1866; Fax: 210-695-6033. Email: generalate@cdptexas.org. Web: www.cdptexas.org. Sr. Antoinette Billeaud, C.D.P., Supr. Gen. Sisters 5.

Hermanas Catequistas Guadalupanas Convent, 4110 S. Flores St., 78214. Tel: 210-532-9344; Fax: 210-532-9344. Sr. Margarita Vasquez, H.C.G., Supr. Sisters 7.

Holy Spirit Motherhouse, 301 Yucca St., 78203. Tel: 210-533-5149; Fax: 210-533-3434. Email: holyspirit@shsp.org. Web: www.shsp.org. Sr. Veronica Cahill, S.H.Sp., Gen. Supr. Motherhouse of the Sisters of the Holy Spirit and Mary Immaculate Sisters 39.

Incarnate Word Generalate (1869), 4503 Broadway, 78209-6297. Tel: 210-828-2224; Fax: 210-828-9741. Email: iwg009@ccvisanantonio.org. Web: www.ccvisanantonio.org. Sr. Helena Monahan, C.C.V.I., Gen. Supr. General Administration of the Congregation of Sisters of Charity of the Incarnate Word. Total in Congregation 464; Total in U.S. Province 262.

U.S. Province, P.O. Box 15378, 78212-8578. Tel: 210-734-8310; Fax: 210-734-8369. Email: babluhm@universe.uiwtx.edu. Sr. Bette Ann Bluhm, C.C.V.I., Prov. Coord.

Incarnate Word Retirement Community, U.S. Province, 4707 Broadway, 78209-6200. Tel: 210-829-7561 (Retirement Center); Fax: 210-828-0020. Email: sftxnc@aol.com. Web: www.iwretire.org. Mr. Steven Fuller, CEO; Janete Eisenmenger, Admin. Extended Care; Sisters Marinela Flores, Coord. for Sisters; Ann Geever, Asst. Coord. Extended Care; Jill Trevino, Dir. Admissions & Mktg.; Rev. Msgr. Thomas A. French, Chap. Sisters in Extended Care 33; Sisters in Special Care 3; Sisters Independent Living 60; Sisters in Assisted Living 11; Lay Independent Living 55; Lay Assisted Living 36; Lay Extended Care 27; Lay in Special Care 19.

Institute of the Daughters of Mary Help of Christians, Province of Mary Immaculate, 6019 Buena Vista St., 78237. Tel: 210-432-0089; 210-432-0090; Fax: 210-432-4016. Email: fmasuopr@aol.com. Web: www.SalesianSistersWest.org. Sr. Phyllis Neves, F.M.A., Prov. Supr. Salesian Sisters of St. John Bosco

St. James Convent, 402 Nunes, 78225. Tel: 210-533-9659; Fax: 210-924-0201. Email: fmasuosj@stic.net. Sr. Cecilia Henry, F.M.A., Supr. Daughters of Mary Help of Christians (Salesian Sisters of St. John Bosco) Sisters 4.

St. John Bosco Convent, 5630 W. Commerce St., 78237. Tel: 210-432-8011; Fax: 210-434-8559. Email: fmasuojb@stic.net. Sr. Teresita Delgado, F.M.A., Supr. Daughters of Mary Help of Christians Sisters 16.

St. Joseph's Convent - S.S.N.D. House of Formation, 2372 W. Southcross, 78211-1898. Tel: 210-923-2364; Fax: 210-922-2611. Email: sjsassnd@aol.com. Sr. Dolores Marie Siebenmonger, Coord. Sisters 5.

McCullough Hall Nursing Center and Regan Hall, 603 S.W. 24th St., 78207-4696. Tel: 210-433-6011. Sisters 65.

Missionary Catechists of Divine Providence Central House and Admin. Offices , St. Andrew's Convent, 2318 Castroville Rd., 78237. Tel: 210-432-0113; Fax: 210-432-1709. Email: StAndrewsConvent@sbcglobal.net. Sr. Mary Lou Barba, M.C.D.P., Supr. Sisters 11.

Casa Benitia - House of Initial Formation, 2318 Castroville Rd., 78237. Tel: 210-431-0915. Sisters 2.

Monastery of the Discalced Carmelite Nuns, 6301 Culebra & St. Joseph Way, 78238-4909. Tel: 210-680-1834; Fax: 210-680-3106. Email: saocdnun@dcci.com. Web: www.carmelsanantonio.org. Sr. Therese Leonard, O.C.D., Prioress. Sisters 10.

North American Union, Sisters of Our Lady of Charity, 1900 Montana, 78210. Tel: 210-475-9390; Fax: 210-475-9373. P.O. Box 10443, 78210. Sr. Agnes O'Mahoney, O.L.C., Supr. Sisters 8.

Our Lady of the Lake Convent Center, 515 S.W. 24th St., 78207. Tel: 210-434-1866; Fax: 210-431-9965. Sr. Ramona Bezner, C.D.P., Coord. Sisters of Divine Providence, Home for retired Sisters of Divine Providence. Professed Sisters 45.
O.L.L. Convent Home for retired Sisters of Divine Prodivence Sisters Frances Lorene Lange, C.D.P., Coord.; Ramona Bezner, C.D.P., Coord.; Marion Morua, C.D.P., Coord.; Roberta Haby, C.D.P., Co-ord.

Our Lady of the Pillar Convent, 251 W. Ligustrum Dr., 78228. Tel: 210-433-5501; Fax: 210-431-9611. Email: escobarFMI@aol.com. Web: www.marianistsisters.org. Sisters Evangeline Escobar, F.M.I., Prov.; Eileen Cehyra, F.M.I., Dir. of Sisters. Centralhouse of the Congregation of the Daughters of Mary Immaculate.Marianist Sisters. Sisters 19.

Our Lady of Victory Missionary Sisters Convent, 1114 San Carlos, 78207-6727. Tel: 210-433-3296. Sr. M. Adele Massaro, O.L.V.M.

Presentation Convent, 8931 Callaghan Rd., 78230-4570. Tel: 210-342-2503; Fax: 210-349-4772. Email: pbvmsat@juno.com. Sr. Mary Carmel Callaghan, P.B.V.M., Supr. Residence of the Community of the Union of the Sisters of the Presentation of the B.V.M. Sisters 13.

Provincial Offices of the Sisters of the Sacred Heart of Jesus of St. Jacut, 11931 Radium St., 78216-2714. Tel: 210-344-7203; Fax: 210-341-0721. Email: jnlv@juno.com. Sr. Juana O. Villescas, S.S.C.J., Prov. Sisters 59.
1014 Spent Wing, 78216. Tel: 210-374-2914. Sisters 5.
818 Firefly, 78216. Tel: 210-349-6689. Sisters 4.
7112 Hagy Cir., 78216. Tel: 210-340-0249. Sisters 5.
10803 Silhouette Dr., 78213. Tel: 210-340-1872. Sisters 7.

Sacred Heart Sisters' Convent, 10802 Silhouette Dr, 78216. Tel: 210-344-4777; 210-344-7050. Sisters 9.

Novitiate, 1203 Viewridge, 78213. Sisters 4.

Religious of Mary Immaculate Convent, 719 Augusta St., 78215. Tel: 210-226-0025; Fax: 210-226-3305. Email: villamarmi@yahoo.com. Web: www.ReligiosasDeMariaInmaculada.org. Sr. Ada Mabel Mier, R.M.I., Local Supr. Religious of Mary Immaculate Sisters 12.

School Sisters of Notre Dame, Convents: Caroline House, 3415 W. Woodlawn, 78228. Tel: 210-435-3234; Fax: 210-434-6635. Sr. Ann Semel, S.S.N.D., Correspondent. Sisters 3.

Seraphic Sisters of Our Lady of Sorrows Convent, 621 W. Woodlawn Ave., 78212. Tel: 210-734-3364. Sr. Sancja Panek, S.O.L., Supr. Sisters 6.

The Sisters of Perpetual Adoration Convent, 2403 W. Travis St., 78207. Tel: 210-227-5546; Fax: 210-226-3934. Sr. Maria Del Carmen Sanchez, A.P.G., Supr. Sisters 8.

Stella Maris Convent, 2702 Castroville Rd., 78237-3341. Tel: 210-434-1314. Congregation of Divine Providence, Inc. Sisters 5.

St. Teresa's Convent, 138 Fair Ave., 78223-1014. Tel: 210-533-5330; Fax: 210-533-2532. Email: carmestj@aol.com. Web: www.teresians.org. Sr. Carmelina Guzman, S.T.J., Coord. Society of St. Teresa of Jesus 13.

Ursuline Residence, 3810 Portsmouth Dr., 78223. Tel: 210-333-2907; Fax: 210-333-4213. Email: ursuline.sisters@sbcglobal.net. Sr. Marianne Mullen, O.S.U., Prioress. Sisters 7.

BOERNE. *St. Scholastica Monastery*, 416 W. Highland, 78006. Tel: 830-249-2645; 830-816-8504; Fax: 830-249-1365. Email: benstrs@boernebenedictines.com. Web: www.boernebenedictines.com. Sr. Bernadine Reyes, O.S.B., Prioress. Congregation of Benedictine Sisters, Monastery, and Novitiate. Sisters 20.

UVALDE. *Society of St. Teresa of Jesus* (Teresian Sisters) , 343 N. Crisp St., 78801. Tel: 830-278-6724; Fax: 830-278-5170. Email: teresians@aol.com. Web: teresians.org. Sr. Maria Luisa Aldape, S.T.J., Coord. Sisters 2.

[O] RETREAT HOUSES

SAN ANTONIO. *Oblate Renewal Center*, Mailing Address: 5700 Blanco Rd., 78216-6615. Tel: 210-349-4173; Fax: 210-349-4281. Email: orc@ost.edu. Web: www.ost.edu/oblate_renewal_center.htm. Bro. Patrick McGee, O.M.I., M.A., Dir.; Rev. Thomas Horan, O.M.I.; Sr. Theresa O'Toole, S.H.Sp.; Ms. Shirley Russell, Hospitality Dir.

BOERNE. *Omega Retreat Center*, 216 W. Highland Dr., 78006. Tel: 830-816-8471 (San Antonio); 830-249-3894 (Boerne); Fax: 830-249-3327. Email: omegactr@boernenet.com. Web: www.boernebenedictines.com. Mr. Andrew Anderson, Dir.

CASTROVILLE. *Moye Center*, 600 London, 78009. Tel: 830-931-2233; Fax: 830-931-2227. Email: moyecenter@aol.com. Web: www.moyecenter.org. Linda Follis, Dir. Under the direction of the Sisters of Divine Providence, Center for Retreats, Renewal, and Conferences. Sisters 3.

[P] CATHOLIC CHARITABLE ORGANIZATIONS AND CLINICS

SAN ANTONIO. *Catholic Charities, Archdiocese of San Antonio* Adolescent Pregnancy Prog., Adoption, Counseling, Childrens' Health Insurance Programs.; Refugee Resettlement, Family Support Immigration Services; Senior community services, Foster Grandparents, RSVP, Older Worker Program

Administration, 1405 N. Main Ave., Ste. 222, 78212-4351. Tel: 210-222-1294; Fax: 210-227-0217.

Email: ccaosa@flash.net saldana@flash.net. Mr. Steve Saldana, Admin.

Office, 1405 N. Main Ave., Ste. 222, 78212-4351. Tel: 210-475-9011; Fax: 210-475-0436.

2903 W. Salinas St., 78207. Tel: 210-433-3256; Fax: 210-433-0851.

1405 N. Main Ave., Ste. 222, 78212-4351. Tel: 210-222-1294; Fax: 210-222-9326.

Guadalupe Home for Homeless Pregnant Women, 1223 S. Trinity St., 78207. Tel: 210-476-0707; Fax: 210-227-0217.

Catholic Counseling, Consultation Center, 1840 Lockhill-Selma, #102, 78213. Tel: 210-377-1133; Fax: 210-377-1230. Rev. James Rutkowski (STL), Clinical Dir. See Curia Section - Department of Social & Community Services.

Daughters of Charity Services of San Antonio, 7607 Somerset Rd., 78211-3752. Tel: 210-921-0071; Fax: 210-922-0332. Email: lmejia@dcssa.org. Web: www.dcssa.org. Mr. Larry Mejia, Pres., Daughters of Charity Svcs.

This corporation operates centers at three locations:

De Paul Family Center, 7603 Somerset, 78211. Tel: 210-924-5903; Fax: 210-922-0332. Sisters 3.

El Carmen Center, 18555-1 Leal Rd., 78221. Tel: 210-626-2121; Fax: 210-626-1848. Sisters 3.

La Mission Family Health Care, 19780 U.S. Hwy. 281 S., 78221. Tel: 210-626-3854; Fax: 210-626-1174.

Society of St. Vincent de Paul, 928 W. Commerce, 78207. Tel: 210-225-7837; Fax: 210-225-8878. Email: svdpsa@aol.com. Web: www.svdpsa.org. Homer Cadena, Pres.; Mary M. Armstrong, Exec. Dir.

[Q] NEWMAN CENTERS

SAN ANTONIO. *Catholic Campus Ministry* Catholic Student Center, 312 W. Courtland Pl., 78212-3923. Tel: 210-736-3752; Fax: 210-736-5365. Email: CWhite@archdiosa.org. Carol F. White, Dir. Archdiocesan Campus Ministry.

Campus Ministers: Joseph A. Leidecke Jr., San Antonio College; Imelda Morales, Palo Alto College & UTSA Downtown Campus; Gloria M. Keller. Tel: 210-533-9819 St. Philip's College; Rev. John E. Keefer, O.P., Trinity University; Veronica Martinez, Northwest Vista College.

St. Anthony Catholic Student Center at U.T.S.A. 1604 Campus, 14523 Roadrunner Way, 78249. Tel: 210-699-9594; Fax: 210-699-9572. Sr. Imelda Phelan, C.S.B.

Campus Ministry Center, Palo Alto College, 1405 W. Villarrett Blvd., 78224. Tel: 210-921-9380. Imelda Morales, Campus Min.

Southwest Texas Junior College, 2401 Garner Field Rd., Uvalde, 78801-6297. Tel: 830-278-4401; Fax: 830-951-7354.

Texas Lutheran University, 1000 W. Court St., Seguin, 78155-5999. Tel: 830-372-6047; Fax: 830-372-8188. Email: llewis@tlu.edu.

Schreiner University, Formerly Schreiner College 2100 Memorial Blvd., Kerrville, 78028-5697. Tel: 830-792-7443. Email: csullivan@shreiner.edu.

[R] PERSONAL PRELATURES

SAN ANTONIO. *Opus Dei Prelature of the Holy Cross and Opus Dei*, 345 E. Summit, 78212. Tel: 210-732-3065; Fax: 210-732-8613. Email: info@opusdei.org. Web: www.opusdei.org. Rev. Thomas J. Lamb (PRO).

[S] FOUNDATIONS, ENDOWMENTS AND TRUSTS

SAN ANTONIO. *The Archbishop Charity Fund*, P.O. Box 28410, 78228. Tel: 210-734-2620; Fax: 210-734-0708.

Archbishop Flores Charity Fund, P.O. Box 28410, 78228. Tel: 210-734-2620; Fax: 210-734-0708.

Archdiocesan Endowment Fund, P.O. Box 28410, 78228-0410. Tel: 210-734-2620; Fax: 210-734-0708. Most Rev. Patrick Flores.

Assumption Seminary Endowment Fund, P.O. Box 28410, 78228-0410. Tel: 210-734-2620; Fax: 210-734-0708. Most Rev. Patrick Flores.

Casa de Padres Endowment Fund, P.O. Box 28410, 78228-0410. Tel: 210-734-2620; Fax: 210-734-0708. Most Rev. Patrick Flores.

Foundation for Christian Education, STJ, 138 Fair Ave., 78223-1014. Tel: 210-533-3547; Fax: 210-533-2532. Email: RiccastjFce@aol.com. Sisters Hortense Ricca, S.T.J., Contact Person; Isabel Ordono, S.T.J., Pres.

Historical Centre Foundation, P.O. Box 831-078, 78283-1078. Tel: 210-576-1365; Fax: 210-576-1367. Email: bspinner@sfcathedral.org. Web: www.sfcathedral.org. Rev. David Garcia.

Holy Spirit Sisters' Trust, 301 Yucca St., 78203. Tel: 210-533-8142; Fax: 210-533-3434. Email: holyspirit@shsp.org. Sr. Veronica Cahill, S.H.Sp., Pres. Sisters of the Holy Spirit

National Foundation for Mexican-American Vocations, P.O. Box 7367, 78207-0367. Tel: 210-227-0548; Fax: 210-226-5086. A nonprofit organization to financially help Mexican American Seminarians.

Sts. Peter and Joseph Childrens' Home Endowment Fund, P.O Box 28410, 78228-0410. Tel 210-734-2620; Fax: 210-734-0708. Most Rev Patrick Flores.

Providence Trust, 515 S.W. 24th St., 78207. Tel: 210-434-1866; Fax: 210-431-9965. Sisters Imelda Gonzalez, C.D.P., Trustee; Ann Petrus, C.D.P., Trustee; Madonna Sangalli, C.D.P., Trustee. Congregation of Divine Providence, Inc. Charitable Trust.

Seton Home Endowment Fund, P.O. Box 28410, 78228-0410. Tel: 210-734-2620; Fax: 210-734-0708. Most Rev. Patrick Flores.

BOERNE. *Benedictine Sisters Charitable Trust One*, 416 W. Highland Dr., 78006. Tel: 210-735-4988; Fax: 210-735-2615. Email: srmika@texas.net Sr. Susan Mika, O.S.B., Contact Person.

Benedictine Sisters Charitable Trust Two, 416 W. Highland, 78006. Tel: 830-816-8504; Fax: 830-249-1365. Sr. Sylvia Ahr, O.S.B., Trustee.

[T] SHRINES

SAN ANTONIO. *Basilica of the National Shrine of the Little Flower* 906 Kentucky, 78201. Tel: 210-735-9127; Fax: 210-738-0818. Email: lfbasilica@msn.com. Web: www2.dcci.com/ocdokla. Rev. John M, Suenram, O.C.D., Supr. of Discalced Carmelites of San Antonio.

Oblate Lourdes Grotto Shrine of the Southwest, Tepeyac de San Antonio P.O. Box 659432, 78291-0096. 5722 Blanco Rd., 78265-9432. Tel: 210-342-9864; Fax: 210-342-7142. Email: omsa@oblatemissions.org. Web: www.oblatemissions.org. Revs. Richard A. Houlahan, O.M.I., Grotto Dir.; Gerard Weber, O.M.I., Ministries Dir.; Saturino Lajo, O.M.I., Spanish Liturgies, Spanish Services.

Our Lady of Czestochowa Grotto Shrine and Convent, 138 Beethoven St., 78210. Tel: 210-333-4582; 210-337-8193 (Convent). Sr. Helen Haladyna, S.O.L.S., Supr.; Rev. Louis V. LeDoux (LAF), Chap. Seraphic Franciscan Sisters of Our Lady of Sorrows Sisters 7.

[U] MISCELLANEOUS

SAN ANTONIO. *Acts Missions, c/o Oblate School of Theology*, 285 Oblate Dr., 78216. Tel: 210-342-1077. Email: acts@ost.edu. Web: www.actsmissions.org. Mr. Tom Peterson, Exec. Dir.

Archdiocesan Designated Catholic Schools Endowment Fund, 2718 W. Woodlawn, 78228. Tel: 210-734-2620.

Archdiocesan Union of Holy Name Societies, 2610 Perez St., 78207. Tel: 210-433-6301; Fax: 210-432-2271. Rev. Richard Pena, Spiritual Mod. & Dir.

Archdiocese of San Antonio Endowment Fund for Parishes, School and Ministries, 2718 W. Woodlawn, 78228. Tel: 210-734-2620. Rev. Msgr. Lawrence J. Stuebben, V.G.

Benitia Family Center, 4650 Eldridge Ave., 78237-2600. Tel: 210-433-9300; Fax 210-432-6739. Email: benitia@benitia.org. Web: www.benitia.org. Sr. Carmen M. Sanchez, M.C.D.P., Dir. Sisters 2.

The Blue Army, 6680 Crestway, 78239. Tel: 210-654-1643 Fax: 210-654-8031. Email: ljrs@global.net. Rev. Robert Silverman, Archdiocesan Chap.

Brothers of the Beloved Disciple A private association of the faithful. , 1701 Alametos, 78201. Tel: 210-734-6727; Fax: 210-431-6884. Email: GMontague@stmarytx.edu. Web: www.brothersofthebeloveddisciple.org. Revs. George Montague, S.M.; Robert E. Hogan, S.M.; Joseph Mary Marshall, S.M.; Bro. William H. Combs. Candidates 2.

Catholic Cemeteries of the Archdioces of San Antonio, 2718 W. Woodlawn, 78228. Tel: 210-734-2620. Mr. Albert Sanchez, General Mgr.

Catholic Television of San Antonio, P.O. Box 28410, 78228-0410. Tel: 210-734-2620; Fax: 210-734-2939. Email: vperez@archdiosa.org. 2718 W. Woodlawn, 78228. Deacon Pat Rogers, Gen. Mgr.

Christus Santa Rosa Family Health Center, 333 N. Santa Rosa, 78207. Tel: 210-704-2535; Fax: 210-704-2545. Email: ray.afaisen@christushealth.org. Web: www.christussantarosa.org. Dr. James Martin, M.D., Dir.

Christus Santa Rosa Homecare, 4415 Centerview Dr., 78228. Tel: 210-581-5200; Fax: 210-581-5291. Email: Pamela.Steding@ChristusHealth.org. Pamela Steding, Pres.

Cordi-Marian Education Center, 2910 Morales St., 78207. Tel: 210-391-6233. Email: MCMMatilda@aol.com. Sr. Matilda Jaime, M.C.M., Proj. Coord.

Daughters of Mary Help Development Office, 6019 Buena Vista St., 78237-1700. Tel: 210-436-1424; Fax: 210-436-1424. Email: sswdev@aol.com. Maryanne Oehler, Dir. Promotes the apostolic works of both the Daughters of Mary Help of Christians (Salesian Sisters) and VIDES-USA (Volunteers Internationally Dedicated to Education and Service, especially socially at-risk youth and women).

Deaf Ministries of San Antonio, 205 Piazza Italia, 78207. Tel: 210-227-0548. Rev. Guy Blair, S.C.J.

Eucharistic Adoration of San Antonio, Inc., P.O. Box 691006, 78269-1006. Tel: 210-558-8802; Fax: 210-522-9692. Email: adore24@aol.com. Web: www.adore24.org. Mary Therese Corcoran, Pres.

Federation of Catholic Parent Teacher Clubs of the Archdiocese of San Antonio, c/o Catholic Schools Office, 2718 W. Woodlawn, 78228. Tel: 210-734-2620; 210-734-5829 (Home). Web: www.archdiosa.org. Mr. Manuel Garcia, Pres.

Focolare Movement, Mailing Address: P.O. Box 15726, 78212. Tel: 210-341-8445; Fax: 210-341-4160. Email: czftx@sbcglobal.net. Web: www.focolare.org. (Work of Mary) (Men and Women), Founded in Trent, Italy, in 1943. International Headquarters is in Rome.

Women's Branch, Texas, 10714 Mt. Tipton, 78213. Tel: 210-341-8445; Fax: 210-341-4160. Sr. Graciela Martinez, O.S.F., Dir.

Men's Branch, Texas, 9315 Overton Rd., 78217. Tel: 210-590-8812; Fax: 210-590-8921. Mr. Claudio Amato, Dir.

Friends of Santa Rosa Foundation dba Friends of Christus Santa Rosa Foundation, 333 N. Santa Rosa Blvd., 78207. Tel: 210-704-2541; Fax: 210-704-2384. Web: www.ChristusSantaRosa.org. Stuart Turgel, CEO.

Friends of the Patrician Movement, 222 E. Mitchell St., 78210. Tel: 210-532-3126; Fax: 210-534-3779. Email: pclancey@thepm-sa.org. Patrick Clancey, Ed.D., Exec. Dir.

Hispanic Telecommunications Network, Inc., 7711 Madonna Dr., 78216. Tel: 210-227-5959; Fax: 210-979-7880. Email: jalamia@htn.org. Web: www.htn.org. Ms. Janice Alamia, Pres. Principal Activity is the production of Nuestra Familia, the National Catholic evangelization television series for U.S. Hispanics.

Ladies of Charity of El Carmen, 18555 Leal Rd., 78221. Tel: 210-626-1432. Beatrice Martinez, Pres.

Madonna Neighborhood Center, 1906 Castroville Rd., 78237. Tel: 210-432-2374; Fax: 210-432-2389. Email: normafunari@flash.net. Norma J. Funari, Dir. Casework, Day Care, After School Care, Social Services, Adult & Youth Socialization Programs. Emergency Food Pantry, Clothing, Furniture, Counseling, Evening Meal, Summer Recreation, Case Management, Sports.

Marian Center of San Antonio, P.O. Box 831001, 78283-1001. Tel: 210-225-6279; Fax: 210-225-0044. Email: mariancenterofsa@hotmail.com. Ms. Therese H. Palacios, Pres.

Mary Help Network (ADMA), 6019 Buena Vista St., 78234-1700. Tel: 210-432-0089; 210-432-0090; Fax: 210-432-4016. Sr. Mary Gloria Mar, F.M.A., Dir.

Mary Jane Ihle Clark Endowment Fund for Ministry to Persons with Disabilities, 2718 W. Woodlawn, 78228. Tel: 210-734-2620. Rev. Msgr. Lawrence J. Stuebben, V.G.

Merced Housing Texas, 212 W. Laurel St., 78212. Tel: 210-281-0234; Fax: 210-281-0238. Email: merced@mercedhousingtexas.org. Web: www.mercedhousingtexas.org. Susan R. Sheeran, Pres. Founded by a consortium of religious orders to provide quality, affordable, service enriched housing for the economically poor, to strengthen families and promote healthy communities.

St. Monica's Guild (1929), 6515 Broadway, 78209. Tel: 210-828-9266; Fax: 210-824-6110. Email: mcbarron@worldnet.att.net. Mrs. Celeste Barron, Contact Person. A social, civic, and charitable group.

Oblate Missions, 323 Oblate Dr., 78216-6629. Tel: 210-736-1685; Fax: 210-736-1314. Email: omsa@oblatemissions.org. Web: www.oblatemissions.org. P.O. Box 96, 78291-0096. Tel: 210-736-1685; Fax: 210-736-1314. P.O. Box 2904, 78299-2904. Most Rev. Philip F. Smith, O.M.I., D.D. (Philippines); Revs. Richard A. Houlahan, O.M.I., Dir.; Saturnino Lajo, O.M.I., Spanish Consultant; Edward DeLeon, O.M.I., Website Design & Services.

Office of Catholic Youth Ministry, P.O. Box 28036, 78228. Tel: 210-734-2620, Ext. 116; Fax: 210-735-2695. Email: pperillo@archdiosa.org. Pasquale A. Perillo, Exec. Dir.

The Patrician Movement, 222 E. Mitchell St., 78210. Tel: 210-532-3126; Fax: 210-534-3779. Email: pclancey@thepm-sa.org.

Field Offices:

1249 S. St. Mary St., 78210. Tel: 210-534-4029; Fax: 210-534-4835.

278 E. Mitchell, 78210. Tel: 210-533-2507.

215 Claudia, 78210. Tel: 210-533-0226; Fax: 210-533-8847. Deacon Patrick M. Clancey, Ed.D., Exec. Dir. & Contact Person.
222 E. Mitchell, 78210. Tel: 210-532-3161; Fax: 210-534-3779. Total Assisted 2,732.

Pauline Book and Media Center, 114 Main Plaza, 78205. Tel: 210-224-8101; Fax: 210-224-0938. Email: sanantonio@pauline.org. Web: www.pauline.org. Sr. Kathleen Thomas Lang, F.S.P., Supr. Daughters of St. Paul 4.

Pilgrim Center of Hope - Evangelization Center, 7680 Joe Newton, 78251. Tel: 210-521-3377; Fax: 210-521-0288. Email: DTMJFOX@netxpress.com. Web: www.pilgrimcenter.catholicweb.com. Deacon Tom Fox, Dir.; Mrs. Mary Jane Fox, Dir.

Polish American Priest Association (P.A.P.A.), 5035 Bernadine, 78220. Tel: 210-648-1991; Fax: 210-648-8252. Email: sanantoniopapa@juno.com. Rev. Thomas Machalski Jr., M.S.Ed., J.C.L. (BRK), Pres.

Project Rachel of San Antonio, 9862 Lorene Ln., Ste. 108, 78216. Tel: 210-342-4673. Email: prsa@sbcglobal.net. Web: www.4ProjectRachel.com. Mary Ann Parks, Dir.

Religious of Mary Immaculate (Pontifical) , Villa Maria, 719 Augusta St., 78215. Tel: 210-226-0025; Fax: 210-226-3305. Email: VillaMarmi@yahoo.com. Web: www.ReligiosasDeMariaInmaculada.org. Sr. Ada Mabel Meir, R.M.I., Local Supr. Apostolic Work: Counseling & guidance of young women of good moral conduct of any race or religion. Sisters 12; Girls 139.

San Antonio Community Law Center, 322 W. Woodlawn Ave., 78212. Tel: 210-271-9595; Fax: 210-734-4410. Email: SACommunityLawCenter@netzero.net. Bro. William Dooling, C.S.C., Attorney; Jaclyn Y. Roberson, Attorney; Charles E. Montemayor, Attorney. Provides legal assistance to the working poor, children, and underserved.

San Antonio Inter-Community Finance Office, 11931 Radium Dr., 78216. Tel: 210-341-8884; Fax: 210-341-0721. Email: saifo@juno.com. Sr. Susan Welsby, A.S.C., Dir.

Serra Club of San Antonio, Inc., 14301 Circle A Trail, Helotes, 78023-4965. Tel: 210-695-8973. Email: rpedrazine@satx.rr.com. Web: www.serraus.org. Mr. Ray Pedrazine, Pres.

Socially Responsible Investment Coalition, P.O. Box 90238, 78209. Tel: 210-344-6778; Fax: 210-344-6805. Email: sric@flashnet.net. Web: www.flash.net/~sric. James W. Donovan, Exec. Dir.

The Southside Consortium of Catholic Schools, Inc., 125 W. Whittier, 78210. Tel: 210-445-3379. Email: jesuitfrank@yahoo.com. Rev. Francis M. Landwermeyer, S.J., Chm.

Teleton Navideno, 1405 N. Main, Ste. 222, 78212. Tel: 210-222-1294; Fax: 210-222-9326. Mr. Olegario G. Tijerina, Volunteer Admin. Coord. Christmas Telethon-Branch of Catholic Charities of San Antonio, Inc.

Today's Catholic Newspaper, Mailing Address: P.O. Box 28410, 78228-0410. 2718 W. Woodlawn Ave., 78228. Tel: 210-734-2620; Fax: 210-734-2939. Email: tcpaper@archdiosa.org. Most Rev. Patrick F. Flores, D.D., Publisher; Mr. Jordan B. McMorrough, Editor. Official Catholic newspaper of the Archdiocese of San Antonio. Owned and operated by the San Antonio Archdiocesan Publishing Society.

VIDES Volunteers International Dedicated to Educational Service, 6019 Buena Vista, 78237-1313. Tel: 210-435-1919; Fax: 210-436-1919. Email: VIDESWUSA@prodigy.net. Web: www.vides.org. Sr. Mary Gloria Mar, F.M.A., Prog. Dir.

BOERNE. *Benedictine Ministries Corporation*, 416 Highland Dr., 78006. Tel: 830-816-8470; Fax: 830-249-7064. Email: smbbmc@boerne.net. Web: www.boernebenedictines.com. Sr. Michael Brandt, O.S.B., Contact Person.

MOUNTAIN HOME. *Tecaboca - A Marianist Center For Spiritual Renewal*, Formerly Tecaboca - A Center for Spiritual RenewalP.O. Box 69, 78058. Tel: 830-866-3425; Fax: 830-866-3781. Email: tecaboca@maverickbbs.com. Web: www.tecaboca.org. Deacon Denis Link, Exec. Dir. Operated by the Society of Mary, Province of the U.S.A., Texas Catholic Boy's Camp (mid-June to mid-August)

RELIGIOUS INSTITUTES OF MEN REPRESENTED IN THE ARCHDIOCESE

For further details refer to the corresponding bracketed number in the Religious Institutes of Men or Women section.

[0140]—*The Augustinians* (Prov. of Castile)—O.S.A.
[0200]—*Benedictine Monks*—O.S.B.
[0600]—*Brothers of the Congregation of Holy Cross*—C.S.C.
[0360]—*Claretian Missionaries* (Western Prov.)—C.M.F.
[0220]—*Congregation of the Blessed Sacrament*—S.S.S.
[1330]—*Congregation of the Mission* (Southern Prov.)—C.M.
[0630]—*Congregation of the Missionaries of the Holy Family*—M.S.F.
[1000]—*Congregation of the Passion*—C.P.
[1130]—*Congregation of the Priests of the Sacred Heart*—S.C.J.
[0480]—*Conventual Franciscans*—O.F.M.Conv
[0260]—*Discalced Carmelite Fathers*—O.C.D.
[0520]—*Franciscan Friars* (Sacred Heart Prov.)—O.F.M.
[0650]—*Holy Ghost Fathers* (Western Prov.)—C.S.Sp.
[0690]—*Jesuit Fathers and Brothers* (New Orleans Prov.)—S.J.
[0730]—*Legionaries of Christ*—L.C.
[]—*Missionaries of the Nativity of Mary* (Mexico)—M.N.M.
[1110]—*Missionaries of the Sacred Heart*—M.S.C.
[0860]—*Missionhurst Congregation of the Immaculate Heart of Mary*—C.I.C.M.
[0910]—*Oblates of Mary Immaculate*—O.M.I.
[0430]—*Order of Preachers (Dominican)* (New Orleans Prov.)—O.P.
[0610]—*Priests of the Congregation of Holy Cross*—C.S.C.
[1070]—*Redemptorist Fathers*—C.SS.R.
[0760]—*Society of Mary (Marianists)*—S.M.
[0975]—*Society of Our Lady of the Most Holy Trinity*—S.O.L.T.
[1200]—*Society of the Divine Savior*—S.D.S.
[1060]—*Society of the Precious Blood*—C.PP.S.
[0560]—*Third Order Regular of St. Francis*—T.O.R.

RELIGIOUS INSTITUTES OF WOMEN REPRESENTED IN THE ARCHDIOCESE

[0100]—*Adorers of the Blood of Christ*—A.S.C.
[0230]—*Benedictine Sisters of the Pontifical Jurisdiction*—O.S.B.
[1810]—*Bernardine Sisters of the Third Order of St. Francis*—O.S.F.
[]—*Carmelitas del Sagrado Corazon*—O.C.D.
[0360]—*Carmelite Sisters of the Divine Heart of Jesus*—Carmel.D.C
[0460]—*Congregation of Sisters of Charity of the Incarnate Word*—C.C.V.I.
[3735]—*Congregation of St. Brigid*—C.S.B.
[0870]—*Congregation of the Daughters of Mary Immaculate (Marianist Sisters)*—F.M.I.
[2200]—*Congregation of the Incarnate Word and Blessed Sacrament*—I.W.B.S.
[0725]—*Cordi-Marian Sisters*—M.C.M.
[0760]—*Daughters of Charity of St. Vincent de Paul*—D.C.
[0850]—*Daughters of Mary Help of Christians*—F.M.A.
[0420]—*Discalced Carmelite Nuns*—O.C.D.
[1070-13]—*Dominican Sisters*—O.P.
[1070-19]—*Dominican Sisters*—O.P.
[1150]—*Eucharistic Franciscan Missionary Sisters*—E.F.M.S.
[1170]—*Felician Sisters*—C.S.S.F.
[1310]—*Franciscan Sisters of Little Falls, MN*
[1430]—*Franciscan Sisters of Our Lady of Perpetual Help*—O.S.F.
[1900]—*Hermanas Catequistas Guadalupanas*—H.C.G.
[1910]—*Hermanas Josefinas*—H.J.
[2590]—*Hermanas Mercedarias Del Santisimo Sacramento*—H.M.S.S.
[2720]—*Mission Helpers of the Sacred Heart*—M.H.S.H.
[2770]—*Missionaries of Jesus, Mary and Joseph*—M.J.M.J.
[2690]—*Missionary Catechists of Divine Providence, San Antonio, Texas*—M.C.D.P.
[2890]—*Missionary Servants of St. Anthony*—M.S.S.A.
[]—*Missionary Sisters of Our Lady of Perpetual Help*—M.P.S.
[2760]—*Missionary Sisters of the Immaculate Conception of the Mother of God*—S.M.I.C.
[3070]—*North American Union of the Sisters of Our Lady of Charity*—O.L.C.
[]—*Oblate Missionaries of Mary Immaculate*—O.M.M.I.
[]—*Oblates of Notre Dame* (Phillipines)
[3130]—*Our Lady of Victory Missionary Sisters*—O.L.V.M.
[0950]—*Pious Society Daughters of St. Paul*—F.S.P.
[3460]—*Religious of Mary Immaculate*—R.M.I.
[2970]—*School Sisters of Notre Dame*—S.S.N.D.
[1680]—*School Sisters of St. Francis* WI—S.S.S.F.
[1690]—*School Sisters of the Third Order of St. Francis*—O.S.F.
[]—*Seraphic Franciscan Sisters of Our Lady of Sorrows* (Poland)—O.L.S.
[0480]—*Sisters of Charity of Leavenworth, KS*—S.C.L.
[1010]—*Sisters of Divine Providence of San Antonio, Texas*—C.D.P.
[3195]—*Sisters of Perpetual Adoration*—A.P.G.
[3460]—*Sisters of Providence of Saint Mary-of-the-Woods, Indiana*—S.P.
[1570]—*Sisters of St. Francis of the Holy Family*—O.S.F.
[3840]—*Sisters of St. Joseph of Carondolet*—C.S.J.
[1930]—*Sisters of the Holy Cross*—C.S.C.
[1960]—*Sisters of the Holy Family*—S.H.F.
[2050]—*Sisters of the Holy Spirit and Mary Immaculate*—S.H.Sp.
[2110]—*Sisters of the Humility of Mary*—H.M.
[3320]—*Sisters of the Presentation of the B.V.M.*—P.B.V.M.
[3670]—*Sisters of the Sacred Heart of Jesus*—S.S.C.J.
[2150]—*Sisters, Servants of the Immaculate Heart of Mary*—I.H.M.
[4020]—*Society of St. Theresa of Jesus*—S.T.J.
[4110]—*Ursuline Nuns (Roman Union)*—O.S.U.

ARCHDIOCESAN CEMETERIES

SAN ANTONIO. *Holy Cross*, 17501 Nacogdoches, 78218. Tel: 210-651-6011.
San Fernando No. 1, 1100 S. Colorado, 78207. Tel: 210-432-2303.
San Fernando No. 2, 746 Castroville Rd., 78237. Tel: 210-432-2303.
San Fernando No. 3 (Roselawn), 2500 Frio City Rd., 78226. Tel: 210-432-2364.

NECROLOGY

† Wangler, Rev. Msgr. Alexander C., (Retired)—Died March 4, 2003

Diocese of San Bernardino

ESTABLISHED NOVEMBER 6, 1978.

Square Miles 27,293.

Comprises the Counties of San Bernardino and Riverside.

Legal Titles:
The Roman Catholic Bishop of San Bernardino, a Corporation Sole (Churches, Rectories, Halls, Catechetical Centers, etc.).
Diocese of San Bernardino Education and Welfare Corporation (Schools, Convents, Newman Facilities, etc.).
Catholic Charities of San Bernardino / Riverside.
St. Bernardine Plaza.
La Paz Dev. Corp. (Senior Citizens Housing).
San Gorgonio Villa.
Caritas Telecommunications.
A California Non-profit Corporation.

Most Reverend

GERALD R. BARNES

Bishop of San Bernardino; ordained December 20, 1975; appointed Titular Bishop of Montefiascone and Auxiliary of San Bernardino January 27, 1992; succeeded to the See, December 28, 1995; installed as Second Bishop of San Bernadino March 12, 1996. *Office: 1201 E. Highland Av, San Bernardino, CA 92404-4641.*

Diocesan Pastoral Center: 1201 E. Highland Ave., San Bernardino, CA 92404-4641. Tel: 909-475-5300; Fax: 909-475-5155.

Web: www.sbdiocese.org

Email: sbdiocese@sbdiocese.org

STATISTICAL OVERVIEW

Personnel	
Bishop	1
Priests: Diocesan Active in Diocese	79
Priests: Diocesan Active Outside Diocese	3
Priests: Retired, Sick or Absent	54
Number of Diocesan Priests	136
Religious Priests in Diocese	98
Total Priests in Diocese	234
Extern Priests in Diocese	24
Permanent Deacons in Diocese	69
Total Brothers	19
Total Sisters	162
Parishes	
Parishes	97
With Resident Pastor:	
Resident Diocesan Priests	59
Resident Religious Priests	25
Without Resident Pastor:	
Administered by Priests	13
Administered by Deacons	1
Administered by Religious Women	5
Administered by Lay People	7
Missions	13
Professional Ministry Personnel:	
Sisters	17
Lay Ministers	159
Welfare	
Catholic Hospitals	2
Total Assisted	201,443
Homes for the Aged	2
Total Assisted	175
Day Care Centers	1
Total Assisted	400
Specialized Homes	3
Total Assisted	819
Special Centers for Social Services	19
Total Assisted	58,985
Educational	
Diocesan Students in Other Seminaries	16
Total Seminarians	16
High Schools, Diocesan and Parish	2
Total Students	925
Elementary Schools, Diocesan and Parish	30
Total Students	6,911
Elementary Schools, Private	1
Total Students	428
Catechesis/Religious Education:	
High School Students	7,639
Elementary Students	31,267
Total Students under Catholic Instruction	47,186
Teachers in the Diocese:	
Priests	3
Brothers	1
Sisters	373
Vital Statistics	
Receptions into the Church:	
Infant Baptism Totals	10,768
Adult Baptism Totals	889
Received into Full Communion	1,452
First Communions	12,602
Confirmations	4,823
Marriages:	
Catholic	1,848
Interfaith	214
Total Marriages	2,062
Deaths	2,732
Total Catholic Population	1,074,196
Total Population	3,556,631

Former Bishop—Most Rev. PHILLIP F. STRALING, D.D., ord. March 19, 1959; appt. Bishop of San Bernardino July 18, 1978; consecrated Nov. 16, 1978; transferred to See of Reno, June 29, 1995.

Diocesan Pastoral Center—1201 E. Highland Ave., San Bernardino, 92404-4641. Tel: 909-475-5300; Fax: 909-475-5155. Office Hours: Mon.-Fri. 8:30-4:30

Office of the Bishop—Email: bishopsoffice@sbdiocese.org.

Vicar General, Moderator of the Curia and Director of Priest Personnel—Very Rev. GERARD M. LOPEZ, S.T.L., V.G. Tel: 909-475-5120; Fax: 909-475-5109. Email: glopez@sbdiocese.org.

Chancellor—Sr. MARY FRANCES COLEMAN, R.S.M. Tel: 909-475-5100; Fax: 909-475-5109. Email: chancellor@sbdiocese.org.

Administrative Assistant to the Bishop, Priest Secretary & Director of Catholic Communications—Rev. PAUL C. GRANILLO, J.C.L. Tel: 909-475-5344; Fax: 909-475-5109. Email: pgranillo@sbdiocese.org.

Special Assistant to the Bishop—DOUGLAS RODRIGUES. Tel: 909-475-5105; Fax: 909-475-5109. Email: drodrigues@sbdiocese.org.

Senior Office Administrator to the Bishop—MARIA ECHEVERRIA. Tel: 909-475-5113; Fax: 909-475-5109. Email: mecheverria@sbdiocese.org.

Office Administrator to the Vicar General—YOLANDA LEAR. Tel: 909-475-5123; Fax: 909-475-5109. Email: ylear@sbdiocese.org.

Office Administrator to the Chancellor—MARTHA DE JIMENEZ. Tel: 909-475-5117; Fax: 909-475-5109. Email: mdejimenez@sbdiocese.org.

Office Administrator to the Assistant to the Bishop—ESTELA SANDOVAL. Tel: 909-475-5104; Fax: 909-475-5109. Email: esandoval@sbdiocese.org.

Coordinator of Diocesan Charter Initiatives—Deacon F. MICHAEL JELLEY. Tel: 909-475-5119; Fax: 909-475-5109.

Coordinator of Victim Assistance Ministry—Sr. ROSALINE O'CONNOR, R.S.M. Tel: 909-855-2296; Fax: 909-475-5109. Email: roconnor@sbdiocese.org.

Office of Pastoral Planning—1201 E. Highland Ave., San Bernardino, 92404-4641. Tel: 909-475-5146; Fax: 909-475-5109. Email: pastoralplanning@sbdiocese.org. THEODORE FURLOW, Dir. Tel: 909-475-5147. Email: tfurlow@sbdiocese.org.

Archives—JOHN DEGANO, Archivist (Volunteer). Tel: 909-475-5389. Email: jdegano@sbdiocese.org.

Office of Canonical Services (Tribunal)—1201 E. Highland Ave., San Bernardino, 92404-4641. Tel: 909-475-5320; Fax: 909-475-5330. Email: canonicalservices@sbdiocese.org.

Judicial Vicar—Rev. Msgr. DONALD S. WEBBER, J.C.L. Email: dwebber@sbdiocese.org.

Adjutant Judicial Vicar—Very Rev. Msgr. ANTHONY T. FERRERO, J.C.L., V.F. Email: tferrero@sbdiocese.org.

Director—Mr. STEPHEN H. OSBORN, J.D., J.C.L. Email: sosborn@sbdiocese.org.

Defender of the Bond—Rev. Msgr. ROBERT E. LAWRENCE, J.C.L.

Judges—Rev. Msgr. DONALD S. WEBBER, J.C.L.; Very Rev. Msgr. ANTHONY T. FERRERO, J.C.L., V.F.; Rev. DAVID ANDEL, J.C.L.; Mr. STEPHEN H. OSBORN, J.D., J.C.L.

Pre-Synodal Judges—Revs. ADRIAN BRINN; ROBERT ERICKSON; GEORGE GONZALEZ; Rev. Msgr. CORNELIUS O'LEARY, Col./Chap. (Retired).

Canonical Auditor and Consultant—Mrs. BETTY MAYNE, L.C.S.W.

Canonical Auditor—Deacon SCOTT HUNSICKER.

Assessors—Deacon GEORGE SCHMIT; BETTY SCHMIT.

Diocesan Notaries—GWENDOLYN GIFFORD. Email: ggifford@sbdiocese.org; GINA GRADIAS. Email: ggradias@sbdiocese.org; IRENE MARTINEZ. Email: imartinez@sbdiocese.org.

Secretaries—GINA GRADIAS; IRENE MARTINEZ.

Presbyteral Council—Most Rev. GERALD R. BARNES, D.D., Pres. Ex Officio Member: Very Rev. Msgr. GERALD M. LOPEZ, S.T.L., V.G., Moderator of the Curia & Vicar General. Appointed Members: Very Revs. STEVE C. PORTER, S.T.L., Chm.; ANTHONY FERRERO, V.F., J.C.L., Vice Chm.; Rev. PAUL GRANILLO, J.C.L., Sec.; Rev. Msgr. THOMAS WALLACE; Very Revs. MICHAEL LAMA, V.F.; JAMES MCLAUGHLIN, V.F.; JOHN FARAO, O.F.M.Conv., V.F.; Very Rev. Msgr. TOM M. WALLACE, V.F. Elected Members: Rev. DAVID ANDEL, J.C.L.; Rev. Msgr. DONALD WEBBER, J.C.L.; Rev. KENNETH JENKINS.

Presbyteral Council Committees—

Pastoral Practices Committee—Rev. GEORGE GONZALES, St. Edward Church, 610 Msgr. Thompson Cir., Corona, 92882. Tel: 909-549-6000; 909-549-6009.

Parish Status and Pastoral Relations Committee—Rev. PATRICK KIRSCH, St. Peter & St. Paul, P.O. Box 248, Alta Loma, 91701. Tel: 909-987-9312; 909-980-9404.

Education Committee—Rev. DAVID GEIB, O.P., St. Andrew Newman Center, 105 W. Big Springs Rd., Riverside, 92507. Tel: 909-682-8751; 909-682-3513.

Liturgy Committee—Rev. JOSE MARTELLI, C.S.C., Our Lady of Soledad, 52-525 Oasis Palm Ave., Coachella, 92236. Tel: 760-398-5577; 760-398-1783.

Priestly Life and Ministry Committee—Rev. RONALD

LARKIN, M.S.C., Diocesan Pastoral Center, 1201 E. Highland Ave., San Bernardino, 92404. Tel: 909-475-5458; 909-475-5343.

Peace and Justice Committee—Rev. EDMUND GOMEZ, Immaculate Conception, 1106 N. La Cadena Dr., Colton, 92324. Tel: 909-825-5110; 909-825-0925.

Finance Committee—Rev. HOWARD LINCOLN, Sacred Heart Church, 43775 Deep Canyon Rd., Palm Desert, 92260. Tel: 760-346-6502; 760-773-4873.

Vicars Forane—Very Revs. ANTHONY FERRERO, V.F., J.C.L., Hemet Vicariate. Tel: 909-657-2380; MICHAEL LAMA, V.F., High Desert Vicariate; Very Rev. Msgr. TOM WALLACE, V.F., Lower Desert Vicariate. Tel: 760-564-1255; Very Revs. JOHN FARAO, O.F.M.Conv., V.F., Riverside Vicariate. Tel: 909-689-3674; JAMES MCLAUGHLIN, V.F., San Bernardino Vicariate. Tel: 909-882-2931; Rev. PAT O'HAGAN, SS.CC., West End Vicariate. Tel: 909-465-5503.

Diocesan Curia—Most Rev. GERALD R. BARNES, D.D.; Sr. MARY FRANCES COLEMAN, R.S.M.; Very Rev. Msgr. GERARD M. LOPEZ, S.T.L., V.G.; Rev. Msgr. DONALD S. WEBBER, J.C.L.; MARY ROSE WALLACE; PETER BRADLEY; Sr. CARMEL CRIMMINS, R.S.M.; Rev. RONALD LARKIN, M.S.C.; Sisters ALICE MOLINA, R.S.H.M.; THERESA PHAN, L.H.C.; Rev. PAUL GRANILLO, J.C.L.; DOUGLAS RODRIGUES; Deacon JOHN SKORA.

College of Consultors—Most Rev. GERALD R. BARNES, D.D.; Rev. Msgrs. THOMAS WALLACE; DONALD S. WEBBER, J.C.L.; Rev. HOWARD LINCOLN; Very Rev. ROBERT MILLER, V.F.; Rev. PAUL GRANILLO, J.C.L.; Very Rev. Msgr. GERARD M. LOPEZ, S.T.L., V.G.; Very Rev. ANTHONY FERRERO, V.F., J.C.L.; Rev. MICHAEL MAHER, SS.CC.

Council of Religious—Most Rev. GERALD R. BARNES, D.D., Ex Officio. Council Members: Rev. RENO AIARDI, I.M.C.; Sr. LOUISE BOND, S.N.J.M.; Rev. WILLIAM CAFFREY, S.V.D.; Sisters MARILU COVANNI, S.P.; CHRISTINE DOMAN, C.S.J.; Bro. RICHARD GAULE, O.H.; Rev. EARL HENLEY, M.S.C.; Sisters EILEEN RAFFERTY, R.S.M.; SARAH SHREWSBURY, O.S.C.; MARY ANN SCHEPERS, O.S.B.

Finance Council—MARY ROSE WALLACE, Chm., 1201 E. Highland Ave., San Bernardino, 92404-4641. Tel: 909-475-5150.

Finance Council Members—Most Rev. GERALD R. BARNES, D.D., Ex Officio; Very Rev. Msgr. GERARD R. LOPEZ, S.T.L., V.G.; Sr. MARY FRANCES COLEMAN, R.S.M.; WILFRID C. LEMANN, Diocesan Attorney; STEPHEN H. OSBORN, J.C.L., Canonical Counsel; MARY ROSE WALLACE; PHILLIP BURBACK, Chm.; Revs. THOMAS BURDICK; CHARLES PATRON; JOSEPH BORBA; DON CAVAZOS; RICHARD GRANILLO; MICHAEL V. MCINTIRE; EDWARD J. TALEN; BRUCE SATZGER; WILLIAM KAFFER; Mrs. ELOISE REYES; ED BIEBRICH JR.; BURRELL HANDY; CHARLES N. JOHNSON.

Staff and Consultants—PEGGY KOSTER; SCOTT GARRETT.

Diocsan Commissions and Committees—

Ministerial Personnel and Placement Board—1201 E. Highland Ave., San Bernardino, 92404-4641. Tel: 909-475-5120. Personnel Board Members: Most Rev. GERALD R. BARNES, D.D., Ex Officio; Very Rev. Msgr. GERARD M. LOPEZ, S.T.L., V.G Elected Members: Sr. MAUREEN CHICOINE, R.S.C.J.; Deacon EDWIN CHAMBERLAYNE; Revs. JOHN VIEIRA; MARK E. KOTLARCZYK; Very Rev. Msgr. THOMAS WALLACE, V.F.; Very Rev. ROBERT MILLER, V.F. Appointed: MARIA COVARRUBIAS.

Diocesan Building Committee—1201 E. Highland Ave., San Bernardino, 92404-4641. Tel: 909-475-5310. Email: building@sbdiocese.org. Staff: Deacon JOHN SKORA, Dir.; ROSI MILLS, Sec.; JUDY JUREZ-FLORES; MARY ROSE WALLACE; VICTOR MENDEZ. Committee Members: KRISTI HANSON CLEARY, Chm.; Rev. Msgr. DONALD WEBBER, J.C.L., Vice Chm.; DAVID BENO; RAY KENZ; ANTON R. MEIER; Very Rev. Msgr. TOM WALLACE, V.F.; RAUL MONTOYA; JOHN EGAN.

Pastoral Coordinator Staffing Committee—Rev. EDWARD MOLUMBY, S.T.; Sr. LOUISE BOND, S.N.J.M., Chm.; PETER BRADLEY; KATHY JEFFRIES; PAT WOODS; HORACIO CORTEZ; Sr. LUCILLE MARTINEZ, O.L.V.M.; Deacon ED CHAMBERLYNE.

Committee for the Continuing Education of Priests—Very Rev. RON LARKIN, M.S.C., Vicar for Clergy. Tel: 909-475-5458; Fax: 909-475-5343. Email: rlarkin@sbdiocese.org.

Diocesan Ministries—

The Ministry of Administrative Services—1201 E. Highland Ave., San Bernardino, 92404-4641. Tel: 909-475-5310; Fax: 909-475-5319. Email: jskora@sbdiocese.org.

Director—Deacon JOHN SKORA. Tel: 909-475-5305. Email: jskora@sbdiocese.org.

Office of Human Resources (Personnel/Payroll)—Tel: 909-475-5170; Fax: 909-475-5189. Email: humanresources@sbdiocese.org. LYDIA MENDOZA, Dir. Tel: 909-475-5177. Email: lmendoza@sbdiocese.org; GEORGE ARGUELLO, Admin. Tel: 909-475-5172. Email: garguello@sbdiocese.org; CHRISTINE GLASS, Safety Coord. Tel: 909-475-5175. Email: cglass@sbdiocese.org.

Office of Construction and Real Estate—1201 E. Highland Ave., San Bernardino, 92404-4641. Tel: 909-475-5310; Fax: 909-475-5319. Email: ocre@sbdiocese.org. Deacon JOHN SKORA, Dir. Tel: 909-475-5305. Email: jskora@sbdiocese.org; JUDY A. JUAREZ-FLORES, Oper. Mgr. Tel: 909-475-5313. Email: jjuarezflores@sbdiocese.org.

The Ministry of Communications—1201 E. Highland Ave., San Bernardino, 92404-4641. Tel: 909-475-5350; Fax: 909-475-5357. Rev. PAUL GRANILLO, J.C.L., Dir. Tel: 909-475-5350; Fax: 909-475-5357. Communications Ministry: Rev. HOWARD LINCOLN, Dir. Media Rels. & Diocesan Spokesperson. Tel: 760-346-6502 (Parish); 909-316-5913 (Diocesan).

Caritas Telecommunications—1201 E. Highland Ave., San Bernardino, 92404-4641. Tel: 909-475-5350; Fax: 909-475-5357. Email: caritas@sbdiocese.org. Rev. PAUL GRANILLO, J.C.L., Dir. Tel: 909-475-5350. Email: pgranillo@sbdiocese.org.

Information Services—1201 E. Highland Ave., San Bernardino, 92404-4641. Tel: 909-475-5400; Fax: 909-475-5155. Email: informationservices@sbdiocese.org. DALE JONASSON, M.S., Dir. Tel: 909-475-5401. Email: djonasson@sbdiocese.org; ALFRED VELASQUEZ, Operations Mgr. Tel: 909-475-5405. Email: avelasquez@sbdiocese.org.

*The Ministry of Ecclesial Services—1201 E. Highland Ave., San Bernardino, 92404-4641*Email: vicar-for-clergy@sbdiocese.org.

Office of the Vicar for Clergy—Very Rev. RON LARKIN, M.S.C., Vicar for Clergy. Tel: 909-475-5458; Fax: 909-475-5343. Email: rlarkin@sbdiocese.org; JUNE MCDONALD, Priest Retirement Coord. Tel: 909-475-5190. Email: jmcdonald@sbdiocese.org.

Office for Consecrated Life—Tel: 909-475-5345; Fax: 909-475-5343. Email: religious@sbdiocese.org. Sr. LOUISE BOND, S.N.J.M., Dir. Tel: 909-475-5342; Fax: 909-475-5343. Email: lbond@sbdiocese.org.

Office of Seminarains—Rev. JOSE SANZ, D.L.P., Dir. Tel: 909-788-9931; Fax: 909-781-9031.

Office of Permanent Diaconate Formation—Tel: 909-475-5160; Fax: 909-475-5343. Email: diaconate@sbdiocese.org. Rev. KENNETH J. NOETZEL, S.J., Dir. Tel: 909-475-5162; 909-648-1562 (mobile); Fax: 909-475-5343. Email: rnogosek@sbdiocese.org.

Office of Vocations—Tel: 909-475-5470; Fax: 909-475-5343. Email: vocations@sbdiocese.org. Sr. SARAH SHREWSBURY, O.S.C., Dir. Tel: 909-475-5471. Email: vocations@sbdiocese.org.

Serra International, District 157, San Bernardino—BOB COYNE, Governor, 69558 Cimarron Ct., Cathedral City, 92234. Tel: 760-324-8498.

Palm Springs Chapter—GEORGE MURPHY, Pres., 47-845 Rosemary St., La Quinta, 92253. Tel: 760-777-7510.

Hemet Chapter—MARGIE HILLARD, Pres., 21130 Hansen Ave., Nuevo, 92567. Tel: 909-928-4404.

Riverside Chapter—JERRY KELLY, Pres., 725 Via Conception, Riverside, 92506. Tel: 909-682-2647.

San Bernardino Chapter—DENISE WERNER, Pres., 2375 N. Sycamore St., Rialto, 92377. Tel: 909-820-2377.

Blessed Junipero Serra House of Formation—3325 13th St., Riverside, 92501. Tel: 909-788-9931; Fax: 909-781-9031. Revs. JOSE SANZ, D.L.P., Rector; JUAN GARCIA, Spiritual Dir.

The Ministry of Educational Services—Tel: 909-475-5450; Fax: 909-475-5457. Email: educational-services@sbdiocese.org. Sr. ALICE MOLINA, R.S.H.M., Dir. Tel: 909-475-5454. Email: amolina@sbdiocese.org.

The Office of Catholic Schools—Tel: 909-475-5437; Fax: 909-475-5477. Email: catholicschools@sbdiocese.org. Dr. JIM BRENNAN, Supt. Tel: 909-475-5430. Email: jbrennan@sbdiocese.org. Assistant Superintendents:: Sr. SARA KANE, C.S.J. Tel: 909-475-5433. Email: skane@sbdiocese.org; STEPHEN KRUP, M.B.A. Tel: 909-475-5432. Email: skrup@diocese.org.

Diocesan Media Center—1201 E. Highland Ave., San Bernardino, 92404-4641. Tel: 909-475-5392; Fax: 909-475-5398. Email: mediacenter@sbdiocese.org. ROBERT MELEVIN, Dir. Tel: 909-475-5387; ROSE MARIE MOYLAN, Admin. Sec. Tel: 909-475-5392. Email: rmoylan@sbdiocese.org.

Ministry Formation Institute—Tel: 909-475-5370; Fax: 909-475-5379. Email: mfi@sbdiocese.org. Sr. NADINE MCGUINNESS, C.S.J., Dir. Tel: 909-475-5385. Email: nmcguinness@sbdiocese.org.

Mission Office of the Diocese of San Bernardino—1201 E. Highland Ave., San Bernardino, 92404-4641. Tel: 909-475-5130; Fax: 909-475-5135. Email: mission@sbdiocese.org. *Mailing Address, P.O. Box 1416, San Bernardino, 92402-1416.* Rev. RENO AIARDI, I.M.C., Dir. Tel: 909-475-5131. Email: mission@sbdiocese.org; Sr. ROSALINE O'CONNOR, R.S.M., Assoc. Dir. Tel: 909-475-5132. Email: mission@sbdiocese.org.

The Office of Religious Education and Formation—Tel: 909-475-5450; Fax: 909-475-5457. ROBERT MELEVIN, Dir.

Vicariate Pastoral Centers—

Center A: San Bernardino/High Desert—San Bernardino: TERESA ROCHA, Vicariate Consultant, 1201 E. Highland Ave., San Bernardino, 92404-4641. Tel: 909-475-5386; Cell: 909-533-8255; Fax: 909-475-5457. Email: trocha@sbdiocese.org. High Desert: MARIA COVARRUBIAS, Vicariate Consultant, 15437 Anacapa Rd., Ste. 28, Victorville, 92392. Tel: 760-843-0597; 909-475-5354 (Pastoral Center); Fax: 760-843-0796; Pager: 760-228-7261. Email: mcovarrubias@sbdiocese.org.

Center B: Hemet/Low Desert—LAURA LOPEZ, Vicariate Consultant. Tel: 909-475-5384. Email: llopez@sbdiocese.org.

Center C: Riverside/West End—ROLANDO ROSALES. Tel: 909-475-5388; Fax: 909-475-5457. Email: rrosoles@sbdiocese.org.

Ministry With Youth Office—Tel: 909-475-5165. EVELIA CENTENO-AGUILAR, Vicariate Field Consultant. Tel: 909-475-5380; Pager: 760-270-7579. Email: ecenteno@sbdiocese.orgFax: 909-475-5457; HUMBERTO "BERT" RIOS, Field Consultant and Program Coord. Tel: 909-475-5168; Cell: 909-855-8738. Email: brios@sbdiocese.org.

The Ministry of Ethnic Affairs—

Diocesan Commission and Assembly for Catholics of African Descent—1201 E. Highland Ave., San Bernardino, 92404-4641. Tel: 909-475-5194; Fax: 909-475-5155. LOIS J. CARSON, Chm. Tel: 909-885-1708; MAUDRY OWINGS, Coord. Tel: 909-475-5194. Email: mowings@sbdiocese.org; Rev. RICHARD MCGEE, C.R., Vicar for Catholics of African Descent, St. Catherine of Alexandria, 7050 Brockton Ave., Riverside, 92506. Tel: 909-781-9855; 909-421-7030 (Rialto). Mailing Address, Box 367, Rialto, 92377.

Arab-American Ministry—Rev. HISHAM DABAEN, St. Joseph Church, 1150 W. Holt Ave., Pomona, 91768. Tel: 909-865-6895; Fax: 909-623-0263.

Asian-Pacific Islander Ministry—Sr. THERESA PHAN, L.H.C., Dir., 1201 E. Highland Ave., San Bernardino, 92404-4641. Tel: 909-475-5348; Fax: 909-475-5457. Email: tphan@sbdiocese.org.

Filipino Ministry—Rev. Msgr. CESAR ENCINARES, Diocesan Dir., Immaculate Conception Church, 1106 N. la Cadena Dr., Colton, 92324. Tel: 909-825-5110. Email: msgching@sbcglobal.net; WILLIE BUGAOAN, Diocesan Liaison, 3224 Ashgate Way, Ontario, 91761. Tel: 909-923-9632. Email: wbugoan@aol.com.

Indonesian Ministry—JACK YOSY, Pres., 11759 Mt. Gunnison Court, Rancho Cucamonga, 91737. Tel: 909-989-8441. Email: jyosy@aol.com.

Korean Ministry—Rev. PETER IL SEONG KWON, St. Andrew Kim Korean Catholic Community, 4110 Corona Ave., Norco, 91760. Tel: 909-372-9932; PETER CHUNG, Diocesan Liaison, 5405 Via Cervantes, Yorba Linda, 92887. Tel: 909-787-3906. Email: peter.chung@ucr.edu.

Vietnamese Ministry—Mr. THIEU MINH TRAN, Pres., 2882 Priscilla St., Riverside, 92506. Tel: 909-788-4637; Revs. LUC TRAN, S.V.D., Parochial Vicar, St. Ann Vietnamese Community, 6885 Del Rosa Ave., San Bernardino, 92404. Tel: 909-884-6375; JOHN TINH TRAN, C.M.C., Chap., Our Lady of Perpetual Help Vietnamese Community, 5251 Central Ave., Riverside, 92504-1898; ALOYSIUS THOAI TRAN, C.M.C., Chap., St. George Vietnamese Community, 325 W. "E" St., Ontario, 91762.

Tongan Ministry—Leaders: ROY POMEE; NITA POMEE, Upland Community, 7752 Trey Ave., Riverside, 92503. Tel: 909-351-8140; ATU VAIPULU, Riverside Community, 8269 Verbena Dr., Riverside, 92504. Tel: 909-689-8841.

Native American Ministry—Rev. EARL HENLEY, M.S.C., 23600 Soboba Rd., P.O. Box 1027, San Jacinto, 92581. Tel: 909-654-2086; Fax: 909-654-2086 (call first).

Kateri Tekakwitha Fund—Sr. MARIANNA TORRANO, R.S.C.J., Sec. & CFO, P.O. Box 302, San Jacinto, 92581-0302. Tel: 909-654-2086; Fax: 909-654-2086.

The Ministry of Hispanic Affairs—1201 E. Highland Ave., San Bernardino, 92404-4641. Tel: 909-475-5451; Fax: 909-475-5422. Email: hispanicaffairs@sbdiocese.org. PETRA ALEXANDER, Coord. Tel: 909-475-5451. Email: palexander@sbdiocese.org.

The Ministry of Financial Affairs—Tel: 909-475-5150; Fax: 909-475-5489; 909-475-5155. Email:

financialaffairs@sbdiocese.org. MARY ROSE WALLACE, C.F.O. & Office Dir. Tel: 909-475-5150. Email: mrwallace@sbdiocese.org; URSULA HINKSON, Assoc. Dir. Finance. Tel: 909-475-5153. Email: uhinkson@sbdiocese.org.

Accounting Services—1201 E. Highland Ave., San Bernardino, 92404-4641. Tel: 909-475-5480; Fax: 909-475-5489. Email: accounting@sbdiocese.org. PEGGY KOSTER, Dir. Tel: 909-475-5482. Email: pkoster@sbdiocese.org.

Payroll Services Office—1201 E. Highland Ave., San Bernardino, 92404-4641. Tel: 909-475-5188; Fax: 909-475-5183. Email: payroll@sbdiocese.org. TRANG PHAM, Dir. Tel: 909-475-5182; Fax: 909-475-5183. Email: tpham@sbdiocese.org.

Parish Assistance Office—1201 E. Highland Ave., San Bernardino, 92404-4641. Tel: 909-475-5490; Fax: 909-475-5307. Email: parishassistance@sbdiocese.org. Web: www.sbdiocese.org/parish-assistance.htm. BARB LOGGINS, Dir. & Internal Auditor. Tel: 909-475-5490. Email: bloggins@sbdiocese.org.

Development Office—1201 E. Highland Ave., San Bernardino, 92404-4641. Tel: 909-475-5460; Fax: 909-475-5155. Email: development@sbdiocese.org. PETER ROELL, Dir. Tel: 909-475-5461. Email: proell@sbdiocese.org.

Catholic Mutual Insurance Group—1201 E. Highland Ave., San Bernardino, 92404-4641. Tel: 909-475-5140; Fax: 909-475-5144. Email: wnchales@sbdiocese.org. TAMAR BRINKERHOFF, Claims & Risk Mgr. Tel: 909-475-5140. Email: stbrinkerhoff@sbdiocese.org.

The Ministry of Pastoral Services—Tel: 909-475-5340; Fax: 909-475-5155. Email: pastoralservices@sbdiocese.org. PETER BRADLEY, Dept. Dir. Tel: 909-475-5340. Email: pbradley@sbdiocese.org.

Office of Pastoral Services—1201 E. Highland Ave., San Bernardino, 92404-4641. Tel: 909-475-5340; Fax: 909-475-5155. Email: pastoralservices@sbdiocese.org. PETER BRADLEY, Dir. Tel: 909-475-5340. Email: pbradley@sbdiocese.org; Sr. LOUISE BOND, S.N.J.M., Assoc. Dir. Tel: 909-475-5345. Email: lbond@sbdiocese.org.

Office of Worship—1201 E. Highland Ave., San Bernardino, 92404-4641. Tel: 909-475-5335; Fax: 909-475-5334. Email: worship@sbdiocese.org. Sr. MARILU COVANI, S.P., Dir. Tel: 909-475-5336. Email: mcovani@sbdiocese.org.

Office of Small Faith Communities/RENEW—1201 E. Highland Ave., San Bernardino, 92404-4641. Tel: 909-475-5195; Fax: 909-475-5155. Email: renew2000@sbdiocese.org. Sr. SUSAN DE GUIDE, R.S.M., Dir. Tel: 909-475-5193. Email: sdeguide@sbdiocese.org; STEVE VALENZUELA, Prog. Coord. Tel: 909-475-5197. Email: svalenzuela@sbdiocese.org.

Charismatic Renewal Center Prayer Communities—1201 E. Highland Ave., San Bernardino, 92404-4641. Tel: 909-475-5365; Fax: 909-475-5369. Email: crc@sbdiocese.org. MARINA CARRION, Dir. Tel: 909-475-5365. Email: mcarrion@sbdiocese.org.

Valley Missionary Program, Shrine of Our Lady of Guadalupe—Rev. JOSE MARTELLI, C.S.C., Dir., 52-565 Oasis Palm, Coachella, 92236. Tel: 909-398-9277; Fax: 760-398-9281.

The Ministry of Community Services—Sr. CARMEL CRIMMINS, R.S.M., Dir., 1201 E. Highland Ave., San Bernardino, 92404-4641. Tel: 909-475-5475; Fax: 909-475-5330. Email: ccrimmins@sbdiocese.org.

Office of Social Concerns—1450 N D St., San Bernardino, 92405. Tel: 909-885-7101; Fax: 909-885-6621. JEANETTE ARNQUIST, Dir.. Email: jarnquist@sbdiocese.org.

Catholic Campaign for Human Development—JEANETTE ARNQUIST, Dir., 1450 N D St., San Bernardino, 92405. Tel: 909-885-7101; Fax: 909-885-6621. Email: jarnquist@sbdiocese.org.

Natural Family Planning & Respect for Life Ministries—MARIE WIDMANN, Dir., 2879 Burnt Oak Dr., Chino Hills, 91709. Tel: 909-393-9498; Fax: 909-393-3165. Email: prolifecathmins@sbdiocese.org.

Catholic Charities San Bernardino/Riverside—Administrative Offices, 1450 N. D St., San Bernardino, 92405. Tel: 909-388-1239; Fax: 909-384-1130. Email: info@ccsbriv.org. KEN SAWA, M.S.W., A.C.S.W., L.C.S.W., CEO; Sr. IMELDA GONZALEZ, C.D.P., Assoc. Dir., Operations.

Caritas Counseling—Administration Office, 1265 LaCadena Dr., Ste. 4, Colton, 92324. Tel: 909-370-1293; Fax: 909-370-4679. SHARI LOWDER, M.S., M.F.T., Clinical Dir.

Refugee and Immigration Services—1450 N D St., San Bernardino, 92405. Tel: 909-388-1243; Fax: 909-383-0448. MY HANH LUU, Program Dir.

Senior Employment Services—

Senior AIDE Project—12540 Heacock St., Ste. 5, Moreno Valley, 92556. Tel: 909-485-2185; Fax: 909-485-2188. BELINDA MARQUEZ, Project Dir.

Emergency Services—

San Bernardino County

High Desert Regional Center—St. Mary's Regional Medical Center, 16051 Kasota Rd., Ste. 700, Apple Valley, 92307. Tel: 760-242 2311, Ext. 8454; Fax: 760-242-1801. MARTA MELENDEZ, Regl. Dir.

Adelanto Outreach Site—11424 Crippen Rd., Ste. 6, Adelanto, 92301. Tel: 760-246-8414; Fax: 760-246-8417. DOUGLAS RILEY, Program Coord.

San Bernardino Regional Center—1800 Medical Center Dr., Ste. 107, San Bernardino, 92411. Tel: 909-880-3625; Fax: 909-880-9847. BEVERLY EARL, Regl. Dir.

Needles Service Site—St. Anne's Parish. Tel: 909-880-3625; Fax: 909-880-9847.

West End Regional Center—635 Taylor St., Ontario, 91761. Tel: 909-391-1617; Fax: 909-391-1364. LORRAINE MEDINA, Regl. Mgr.

Riverside County

Coachella Valley Regional Center—35-325 E. Date Palm Dr., Ste. 153-A, Cathedral City, 92234. Tel: 760-202-1222; Fax: 760-202-1230. LINDA SALAS, Regl. Dir. formerly Cathedral City Regional Center

Emmanuel Outreach Services—73441 Fred Waring Dr., Palm Desert, 92260. Tel: 760-568-5101; Fax: 760-568-6568. Rev. DEREK SMYTH, Program Dir.

Indio Regional Center—81-557 Dr. Carreon Blvd., Ste B-2, Indio, 92201. Tel: 760-347-1188; Fax: 760-347-8388. SUSIE DEL TORO, Regl. Dir.

Blythe Outreach Center—c/o Family Service Center, 187 N. Seventh St., Blythe, 92225. Tel: 760-921-7739.

Farmworkers' Resource Center—91250 Avenue 66, Mecca, 92254. Tel: 760-396-6313; Fax: 760-396-0063. CRISTINA GARCIA, Case Mgr.

Inland Valleys Regional Center—12540 Heacock St., Ste. 5, P.O. Box 119, Moreno Valley, 92556-0119. Tel: 909-485-2185; Fax: 909-485-2188. BELINDA MARQUEZ, Regl. Mgr.

Perris Valley Resource Center—371 Wilkerson Ave., Perris, 92370. Tel: 909-441-1158. ROMELIA ZARAGOZA, Case Mgr.

Rubidoux Service Center—5473 Mission Blvd., Riverside, 92509. Tel: 909-328-1575. MARIA ISABELLE VALLE, Case Mgr.

Catholic Organizations in the Diocese—

Catholic Committee on Scouting—PHILIP COLELLA, 4862 Pershing Ave., San Bernardino, 92407. Tel: 909-882-6372.

Catholic Daughters of America—SUSAN KILLIAN, 9389 Tangelo Ave., Fontana, 92335. Tel: 909-822-6302.

Cursillo—

English Movement—JOHN CASAREZ. Tel: 909-888-0416.

Filipino Movement—MAR TIGNO. Tel: 562-940-2458.

Korean Movement—DANIEL HONG. Tel: 909-676-6711.

Spanish Movement—HECTOR J. LERMA JR. Tel: 909-796-8281.

Vietnamese Movement—TAM VINCE DO. Tel: 909-688-9073.

Council of Catholic Women—Sr. LOUISE BOND, S.N.J.M., 1201 E. Highland Ave., San Bernardino, 92404. Tel: 909-475-5342.

Equestrian Order of Holy Sepulchre of Jerusalem—MARY HUMANN, 1605 N. Laurel Ave., Upland, 91784. Tel: 909-982-7206.

Escuela de Evangelizacion Nazareth (E.D.E.N.)—VICENTE PRADO, 24743 Pace Dr., Moreno Valley, 92557. Tel: 909-805-4243.

Fellowship for Catholic Christian Women (FCCW)—PATRICIA SCLEPPI-KREVANICH, 5812 Perthshire Pl., Riverside, 92507. Tel: 909-788-4640.

Italian Catholic Federation—JAMES BUCKNER, 38-750 Elna Way, Cathedral City, 92316. Tel: 760-770-7235.

Knights of Columbus—DIETRICH RUBELIUS, 36204 Golden Gate Dr., Yucaipa, 92399. Tel: 909-797-3428.

Serra International Governor District 157—ROBERT COYNE, 69558 Cimarron Ct., Cathedral City, 92234. Tel: 760-324-8498.

World Apostolate of Fatima (Blue Army)-San Bernardino Division—FRED CARLONE, 3610 N. Morning Glory Dr., Rialto, 92377. Tel: 909-822-7056.

Ministry for Special Needs—

Desert Refuge for Peace Officer—Rev. MICHAEL MCCOLLOGH, 2525 W. Martin Luther King Jr. Blvd., Los Angeles, 90008-2728. Tel: 323-298-7174.

El Shaddai—Mrs. NAIDA CASTRO, 7099 Vettuno Ct., Rancho Cucamonga, 91701. Tel: 909-466-9706.

Engaged Encounter (English)—CHRIS STEVENSON; CHERYL STEVENSON. Tel: 909-463-4175.

Engaged Encounter (Spanish)—ALBERTO SANTANA; MONICA SANTANA. Tel: 909-872-0738.

Marriage Encounter (English)—DAN HITZMAN; MARIE HITZMAN, 323371 Corte San Vincente, Temecula, 92592. Tel: 909-699-0900.

Marriage Encounter (Spanish)—GUILLERMO MENDEZ; SOCORRO MENDEZ, 5686 Deodar St., Montclair, 91763. Tel: 909-986-9838.

Marriage Enrichment—CLAYTON TREJO; CECILIA TREJO, 1473 E. 13th St., Upland, 91786. Tel: 909-985-7864.

Couples for Christ—JIM KINCAID; MERLY KINCAID, 35640 Country Park Dr., Wildomar, 92595. Tel: 909-698-4920.

Retrouvaille Coordinators—BOB STEIGHNER; CATHY STEIGHNER, 1946 Wheaton Ave., Claremont, 91711. Tel: 909-624-3848.

CLERGY, PARISHES, MISSIONS AND PAROCHIAL SCHOOLS

CITY OF SAN BERNARDINO
(SAN BERNARDINO COUNTY)

1—OUR LADY OF THE ROSARY CATHEDRAL (1927), Very Rev. Robert Miller, V.F.; Rev. Joseph Kuehner. In Res., Rev. Msgr. Gerard Lopez; Rev. Robert J. Nogosek, C.S.C.; Deacon Michael Jelley.
Office: 265 W. 25th St., 92405. Tel: 909-883-8991; Fax: 909-882-2061.
Res.: 2525 Arrowhead Ave., 92405. Tel: 909-881-1588; Fax: 909-882-2061.
School—2620 Arrowhead Ave., 92405. Tel: 909-886-1088; Fax: 909-475-5263. Lay Teachers 9; Students 195.
Catechesis/Religious Program—Tel: 909-883-8991. Monica Havis, D.R.E. Students 349.

2—ST. ANNE (1938), Rev. Luc N. Tran.
Office: 6885 Del Rosa Ave., 92404. Tel: 909-884-6375; Fax: 909-884-8976.
Catechesis/Religious Program—Tel: 909-885-7472. Students 537.

3—ST. ANTHONY (1948), Revs. Michael Manning, S.V.D.; Anthony Hayon, S.V.D.; Deacon Joseph Key.
Res.: 1640 Western Ave., 92411. Tel: 909-887-3810; Fax: 909-880-0982.
School—1510 W. 16th St., 92411. Tel: 909-887-5413 Fax: 909-887-5413. Sisters of Mercy 3; Lay Teachers 6; Students 255.
Catechesis/Religious Program—Tel 909-887-3210. Students 325.

4—ST. BERNARDINE (1862), Sr. Marita Beumer, C.PP.S., Pastoral Coord.; Rev. Edward Molumby, S.T.
Office: 531 North F St., 92410. Tel: 909-884-0104; Fax: 909-885-4634.
Church: 584 W. 5th St., 92410.
Catechesis/Religious Program—Tel: 909-884-5463. Students 258.

5—CHRIST THE KING (1934), Deacon Carlos Morales, Interim Admin.
Office: 272 E. Rialto Ave., 92408. Tel: 909-885-1476; Fax: 909-885-3926.

6—OUR LADY OF FATIMA (1952), Sr. Lucille Martinez, O.L.V.M., Pastoral Coord.; Rev. Edward J. Molumby, S.T.
Office: 1000 N. Valencia Ave., 92410. Tel: 909-885-0948; Fax: 909-384-0576.
Catechesis/Religious Program—Students 333.

7—OUR LADY OF GUADALUPE (1925) (Hispanic), Revs. Eliseo Hernandez, O.R.C.; Ariel Munoz Sanchez, O.R.C.
Office: 1430 W. Fifth St., 92411. Tel: 909-888-0044; 909-884-8010; Fax: 909-888-4428.
Catechesis/Religious Program—1475 W. 7th St., 92411. Tel: 909-381-1628. Students 621.

8—OUR LADY OF THE ASSUMPTION (1954), Rev. James McLaughlin.
Office: 796 W. 48th St., 92407. Tel: 909-882-2931; Fax: 909-883-4851.
School—Tel: 909-881-2416. Religious 2; Lay Teachers 9; Students 278.
Catechesis/Religious Program—Students 241.

9—ST. PHILLIP THE APOSTLE (1989),, (Melkite-Greek Catholic Mission) Rev. Justin Rose; Deacon Steven Ghandou.
Res.: 923 W. Congress, 92410. Tel: 909-889-3579; Fax: 909-889-5461.
Catechesis/Religious Program—Students 65.

10—ST. THERESA, Closed. For inquiries for parish records contact the chancery.

OUTSIDE THE CITY OF SAN BERNARDINO

ADELANTO, SAN BERNARDINO CO., CHRIST THE GOOD SHEPHERD (1962), Rev. Michael Lama; Deacon Marcial Ampuero.
Office: P.O. Box 577, 92301. Tel: 760-246-7083; Fax: 760-246-4603.
Catechesis/Religious Program—Students 135.

ALTA LOMA, SAN BERNARDINO CO., ST. PETER & ST. PAUL (1970), Revs. Patrick V. Kirsch; Benny Justiniano; Deacons Mark Hodnick; Chris Carroll.
Office: 9135 Banyan St., 91737.
School—Lay Teachers 8; Students 118.
Catechesis/Religious Program—Tel: 909-980-9423. Sr. Mary Mackessy, S.N.J.M., D.R.E. Students 780.
Youth Ministry—Tel: 909-944-8483. Olivia Obregon. Students 300.

ANZA, RIVERSIDE CO., SACRED HEART (1979), Unassigned.
Office: P.O. Box 39118, 92539. Tel: 909-763-5636; Fax: 909-763-0236.
Church: 56032 Hwy. 371, 92539-0118.
Catechesis/Religious Program—William Torres, D.R.E. Students 78.
Mission—Our Lady of the Snows Cahuilla Indian Reservation, Riverside Co. 92539. Tel: 909-763-5549.
Mission—Cahuilla Indian Reservation Hwy. 371, Riverside Co. 92539.
Mission—Santa Rosa Indian Mission Santa Rosa Reservation, Riverside Co. Tel: 909-659-2708.
Mission—Santa Rosa Reservation Hwy. 74, Riverside Co. 92539.

APPLE VALLEY, SAN BERNARDINO CO., OUR LADY OF THE DESERT (1974), Rev. Bernard Taylor, M.S.; Deacons Robert Rittman; Carlos Reyes.
Office: 18386 Corwin Rd., 92307. Tel: 760-242-4427; Fax: 760-242-1195.
Catechesis/Religious Program—Tel: 760-242-5819. Sr. Leora Linnenkrugel, O.L.V.M., D.R.E. Students 393.

BANNING, RIVERSIDE CO., PRECIOUS BLOOD (1890), Rev. Frank E. Lowe.
Office: 157 W. Nicolet St., 92220. Tel: 909-849-2434; Fax: 909-849-8698.
School—117 W.Nicolet, 92220. Tel: 909-849-2433. Lay Teachers 9; Students 146.
Chapel—Morongo, St. Mary Morongo Indian Res., Morongo, 92220. Tel: 909-849-6170.
Catechesis/Religious Program—Tel: 909-849-1897. Jacqueline Macias, D.R.E.

BARSTOW, SAN BERNARDINO CO.
1—ST. JOSEPH (1914), Revs. Charles Anthony Patron; Joseph Quattropane, O.F.M.Cap.; Deacons Margarito Saenz; Donald Burgett; Francis Roman.
Office: 505 E. Mountain View Ave., 92311. Tel: 760-256-6818; Fax: 760-256-8307.
School—555 E. Mountain View Ave., 92311. Tel: 760-256-2397; Fax: 760-256-5328. Lay Teachers 5; Students 27.
Mission—Our Lady of the Desert Baker, San Bernardino Co. 92311.
Catechesis/Religious Program—Tel: 760-256-1801. John Salazar, D.R.E. Students 480.
2—ST. PHILIP NERI CHURCH (1979), [JC] Rev. Charles A. Patron; Deacon Donald Burgett.
Office: 909 Armory Rd., P.O. Box 409, 92311.
Church: 25333 Third St., 92311.
Catechesis/Religious Program—Students 36.

BEAUMONT, RIVERSIDE CO., SAN GORGONIO (1908), Lynn S. Zupan, Pastoral Coord.; Deacons Ralph Sepulveda; Roy Murvin.
Office: P.O. Box 155, 92223. Tel: 909-845-2849; Fax: 909-845-9259.
Church: 1234 Palm Ave., 92223-0155.
Catechesis/Religious Program—Vivian Roppelt, D.R.E. Students 188.

BIG BEAR LAKE, SAN BERNARDINO CO., ST. JOSEPH (1931), [JC] Deacon Ralph Partida Jr.
Office: P.O. Box 1709, 92315. Tel: 909-866-3030; Fax: 909-866-5087.
Church: 42242 N. Shore Dr., 92315-1709.
Catechesis/Religious Program—Tel: 909-866-4581; Fax: 909-866-4581. Students 100.

BLOOMINGTON, SAN BERNARDINO CO., ST. CHARLES BORROMEO (1939), (Hispanic), Rev. Richard Humphrys.
Office: P.O. Box 248, 92316-0248. Tel: 909-877-0792; Fax: 909-877-4304.
Res.: 11342 Spruce Ave., 92316-3400.
Catechesis/Religious Program—Tel: 909-421-1494. Socorro Olivas, D.R.E. Students 482.

BLYTHE, RIVERSIDE CO., ST. JOAN OF ARC (1920), Rev. George Gonzales.
Office and Church Address: 875 E. Chanslorway, 92225-1262. Tel: 760-922-3261; Fax: 760-922-5279.
Catechesis/Religious Program—Tel: 760-922-8934. Susan Tibbetts, D.R.E. Students 196.
Mission—Nuestra Senora de Guadalupe, Formerly Our Lady of Guadalupe 14040 W. Warmington, Ripley, Riverside Co. 92225.

CATHEDRAL CITY, RIVERSIDE CO., ST. LOUIS (1948), Deacons Pablo Benavides; Arcadio Salinas; John Bettencourt.
Office: 68633 C St., 92234. Tel: 760-328-2398; Fax: 760-770-4598.
Catechesis/Religious Program—Guadalupe Sifuentes, D.R.E. Students 450.

CHINO HILLS, SAN BERNARDINO CO., ST. PAUL THE APOSTLE (1986), Revs. Pat J. O'Hagan, SS.CC.; Kenneth McCabe, SS.CC.; Deacon Manuel Patrocineo Martinez.
Office: 14085 Peyton Dr., 91709. Tel: 909-465-5503; Fax: 909-465-1683.
Catechesis/Religious Program—Tel: 909-465-5503, Ext. 16. Lori Muniz, D.R.E. Students 2,511.

CHINO, SAN BERNARDINO CO.
1—ST. MARGARET MARY (1947), [JC] Rev. Adalberto Garcia, O.R.C.
Office: 12686 Central Ave., 91710. Tel: 909-627-8466; Fax: 909-627-8049.
School—Sisters of St. Francis 1; Lay Teachers 15; Students 348.
Catechesis/Religious Program—Tel: 909-591-7408; Fax: 909-591-0799. Nancy Keegan, D.R.E. Students 636.
2—OUR LADY OF GUADALUPE (1902), (Hispanic), [JC] Rev. Ramon Rosales.
Office: 5048 D St., 91710. Tel: 909-591-9402; Fax: 909-591-9404.
Catechesis/Religious Program—Tel: 909-628-3615. Martha Watters, D.R.E. Students 401.

COACHELLA, RIVERSIDE CO., OUR LADY OF SOLEDAD (1923), (Hispanic), Revs. Bruce Cecil, C.S.C.; John S. Connor, C.S.C.; Steven Sedlock, C.S.C. In Res., Rev. Jose M. Martelli, C.S.C.; Deacons Sergio Vazquez; Wayne Hoy; Jose Garcia; Victor Gonzalea.
Office: 52-525 Oasis Palm, 92236. Tel: 760-398-5577; Fax: 760-398-1783.
Catechesis/Religious Program—Tel: 760-398-1790. Judy Hoy, D.R.E. Students 70.
Mission—El Senor de la Misericordia Kokell St., Thermal, Riverside Co. 92274.
Mission—San Felipe de Jesus Thermal. Hwy. 86, One Hundred Palms, Riverside Co. 92274.
Chapel—Torres-Martinez Reservation, Sacred Heart

COLTON, SAN BERNARDINO CO.
1—OUR LADY OF THE IMMACULATE CONCEPTION, Formerly Immaculate Conception (1943), (Spanish), [CEM 2] [JC] Rev. Edmund Gomez, Admin.; Rev. Msgr. Cesar Encinares. In Res., Revs. Dennis Legaspi; A. Kris White; Deacon Wayne Joslin.
Office: 1106 N. La Cadena Dr., 92324. Tel: 909-825-5110; Fax: 909-825-0912.
Catechesis/Religious Program—Jessie Gomez, D.R.E. Students 710.
2—SAN SALVADOR (1893), (Hispanic), Rev. Msgr. Cesar Encinares; Deacon Robert Amador.
Office: 178 W. K St., 92324. Tel: 909-825-3481; Fax: 909-825-4473.
Church: Seventh St. & L St., 92324.
Catechesis/Religious Program—Lorenzo Rangel, D.R.E. Students 250.

CORONA, RIVERSIDE CO.
1—CORPUS CHRISTI CHURCH (1994), Rev. Gerald C. Deluney.
Office—3760 McKinley, 92879. Tel: 909-272-9043; Fax: 909-272-6821.
Catechesis/Religious Program—Maria Sell, D.R.E. Students 1,345.
2—ST. EDWARD (1896), Revs. Jose Varela, O.R.C.; Martin Rodriguez, O.R.C.; Eloy Trujillo, O.R.C.
Mailing Address: 417 W. Grand Blvd., 92882-2199.
Office: 610 Msgr. Thompson Cir., 92882-2155. Tel: 909-549-6000; Fax: 909-549-6009.
School—500 S. Merrill St., 91720. Tel: 909-737-2530. Lay Teachers 23; Students 569; Sisters 1.
Catechesis/Religious Program—Fax: 909-737-1074. Irinea Arrizon, D.R.E. Students 866.
3—ST. MARY MAGDALENE (1989), Sr. Maureen Chicoine, R.S.C.J., Pastoral Coord.; Rev. John Hindman, Min.; Deacon Martin Filipek.
Office: 8540 Weirick Rd., 92883. Tel: 909-277-1801; Fax: 909-277-2513.
Catechesis/Religious Program—Tel: 909-277-3038. Cathy Townsend, D.R.E. Students 156.
4—ST. MATTHEW (1973), Sandra Boyd, Pastoral Coord.; Rev. Vincent Connor, Min.
Office: 2140 W. Ontario, 92882. Tel: 909-737-1621; Fax: 909-737-9715.
Catechesis/Religious Program—Students 1,030.

CRESTLINE, SAN BERNARDINO CO., ST. FRANCES XAVIER CABRINI (1946), Unassigned.
Church: 23079 Crest Forest Dr., 92325-3817.
Office: P.O. Box 3817, 92325. Tel: 909-338-2303; Fax: 909-338-2383.
Catechesis/Religious Program—Tel: 909-338-4381. Laurie Elliott, D.R.E. Students 58.

DESERT HOT SPRINGS, RIVERSIDE CO., ST. ELIZABETH OF HUNGARY (1946), Rev. Edward McGuiness; Deacon Gerald Campbell.
Office: 66-700 E. Pierson Blvd., 92240. Tel: 760-329-8794; Fax: 760-329-6760.
Catechesis/Religious Program—Tel: 760-251-9268. Students 205.

FONTANA, SAN BERNARDINO CO.
1—CHURCH OF THE RESURRECTION (1953), Revs. Leonard Krzywda, C.R.; Henry Licznerski, C.R. In Res., Rev. Humphrey Ruszel, C.R.; Deacon Abel Zamora.
Office: 7650 Tamarind, 92336. Tel: 909-822-4732; Fax: 909-822-0620.
School—17434 Miller Ave., 92335. Tel: 909-822-4431; Fax: 909-822-0617. Lay Teachers 12; Students 315.
Catechesis/Religious Program—Tel: 909-822-2502. Students 1,130.
2—ST. GEORGE (1954), Rev. Gerardo Mendoza.
Office: 17895 San Bernardino Ave., 92335. Tel: 909-877-1531; Fax: 909-877-6531.
Catechesis/Religious Program—Tel: 909-877-3935.
3—ST. JOSEPH (1930), Rev. Henry Ruszel, C.R.; Deacon Michael Juback. In Res., Rev. Casmir Tadia, C.R.
Office: 17080 Arrow Blvd., 92335. Tel: 909-822-0566; Fax: 909-829-1739.
Catechesis/Religious Program—Tel: 909-822-3411. Students 560.
4—ST. MARY (1939), Rev. Robert Clark, S.S.C.
Mailing Address: 16550 Jurupa Ave., 92337. In Res., Rev. Bernard E. Toal, S.S.C.; Deacon Mario Gutierrez.
Office: 16548 Jurupa Ave., 92337-7452. Tel: 909-822-5670 (English); Fax: 909-357-4688.
Catechesis/Religious Program—Tel: 909-357-4683 (English).

GRAND TERRACE, SAN BERNARDINO CO., CHRIST THE REDEEMER (1980), Sr. Deanna M. O'Neill, O.S.B., Pastoral Coord.
Office: 12745 Oriole, 92313. Tel: 909-783-3811; Fax: 909-783-4689.
Catechesis/Religious Program—Tel: 909-783-3800. Students 126.

GUASTI, SAN BERNARDINO CO., SAN SECONDO D'ASTI (1926), (Italian), Rev. Louis Marx.
Mailing Address: 250 N. Turner Ave., 91743.
Res.: P.O. Box 1056, 91743. Tel: 909-390-0011; Fax: 909-390-9919.
Catechesis/Religious Program—Ilene Ramirez, D.R.E. Students 186.

HEMET, RIVERSIDE CO.
1—HOLY SPIRIT PARISH (1991), Joyce Frichtel, Pastoral Coord.; Rev. Patrick Vincent Aherne, C.M.
Mailing Address: 26340 Soboba Ave., 92544.
Office: Box 5268, 92544. Tel: 909-927-8544; Fax: 909-927-8546.
Catechesis/Religious Program—Lilia Hernandez, D.R.E. Students 270.
2—OUR LADY OF THE VALLEY (1946), Revs. Pierre L. Deglaire, C.S.Sp.; Joseph L. Deniger, C.S.Sp.; George Healy, C.S.Sp. In Res., Revs. Clement Lachowsky, C.S.Sp. (Retired); Joseph Maria Huy Quang Dihn, C.S.Sp.
Office: 780 S. State St., 92543. Tel: 909-929-6131; Fax: 909-929-8009.
Catechesis/Religious Program—Tel: 909-658-7436. Dolores Cannady, D.R.E. Students 501.

HESPERIA, SAN BERNARDINO CO., HOLY FAMILY, Revs. Charles E. Miller; John Fahnestock, M.S.C.; Deacons Santos Aguilera; Scott Hunsicker.
Office: 9974 I Ave., 92345. Tel: 760-244-9180; Fax: 760-244-1959.
Catechesis/Religious Program—Tel: 760-244-5423; Fax: 760-244-1959. Students 780.

HIGHLAND, SAN BERNARDINO CO., ST. ADELAIDE (1956), Sr. Maura Feeley, Admin. Coord.; Deacons Joe Acosta; Dan Taylor.
Office: 27457 E. Baseline, 92346. Tel: 909-862-8669; Fax: 909-862-1603.
Catechesis/Religious Program—Tel: 909-862-8184. Students 473.
Mission—St. John Bosco 28991 Merris St., East Highlands, San Bernardino Co. 92346. Tel: 909-425-0931. Rev. John Ryan.

IDYLLWILD, RIVERSIDE CO., QUEEN OF ANGELS (1942), Rev. Charles Devine.
Office: P.O. Box 1106, 92549-1106. Tel: 909-659-2708; Fax: 909-659-0208.
Church: 54525 N. Circle Dr., 92549-1106.
Catechesis/Religious Program—Students 62.

INDIO, RIVERSIDE CO., OUR LADY OF PERPETUAL HELP (1937), Revs. John S. Vieira, Admin.; Ramon Orozco; Abel Eduardo Balbi; Deacon Brijido Rodriguez.
Office: 82-450 Bliss St., 92201. Tel: 760-347-3507; Fax: 760-347-8367.
School—82-470 Bliss St., 92201. Tel: 760-347-3786; Fax: 760-347-7207. Sisters 1; Lay Teachers 10; Students 204.
Catechesis/Religious Program—Tel: 760-347-0594. Yolanda Nieves, D.R.E. Students 459.

JOSHUA TREE, SAN BERNARDINO CO., ST. CHRISTOPHER OF THE DESERT (1960), [JC] Rev. Gilbert Ignatius Rasquinha; Deacon Glen Miller.
Mailing Address: 61261 Sunburst Dr., 92252-2768.
Office: 61350 Wahl Terr., 92252-2768. Tel: 760-366-8710; Fax: 760-366-2690.

LA QUINTA, RIVERSIDE CO., ST. FRANCIS OF ASSISI (1974), Rev. Msgr. Thomas Wallace; Rev. Mark C. Lander. In Res., Rev. Tom Burns, M.S.C.
Office: 47-225 Washington St., 92253. Tel: 760-564-1255; Fax: 760-564-0763.

LAKE ARROWHEAD, SAN BERNARDINO CO., OUR LADY OF THE LAKE (1938), [CEM] Rev. Timothy F. Keppel, C.R., V.F.
Office: P.O. Box 7, Crest Park, 92326. Tel: 909-337-2333; Fax: 909-337-5041.
Church: 27627 Rim of the World Dr., 92352.
Catechesis/Religious Program—Tel: 909-336-1605. Julieta Avitia, D.R.E. Students 204.

LAKE TAMARISK, RIVERSIDE CO., ST. AUGUSTINE, Unassigned., Mailing Address: P.O. Box 768, Desert Center, 92239. Tel: 619-227-3191; Fax: 619-328-8392.

LOMA LINDA, SAN BERNARDINO CO., ST. JOSEPH THE WORKER (1944), Rev. Ignatius Rodrigues; Deacon William Shalhoub.
Office: 10816 Mt. View Ave., 92354. Tel: 909-796-2605; Fax: 909-796-0755.
Catechesis/Religious Program—Tel: 909-796-4308. Caridad Santiago, D.R.E. Students 200.

LUCERNE VALLEY, SAN BERNARDINO CO., ST. PAUL (1963), Unassigned. In Res., Rev. Enrique LaPuebla Jr., M.S.
Office: P.O. Box 588, 92356. Tel: 760-248-7410; Fax: 760-248-2559.
Church: 8973 Mesa Rd., 92356.
Catechesis/Religious Program—Students 6.

MECCA, RIVERSIDE CO., OUR LADY OF GUADALUPE SHRINE (1927), (Hispanic), Revs. John S. Vieira, Admin.; Abel Eduardo Balbi.
Church: 65-100 Dale Killer Rd., 92254.
Office: P.O. Box 218, 92254. Tel: 760-396-2717; Fax: 760-396-0047.
Catechesis/Religious Program—Fax: 909-684-0390. Conrada Valenzuela, D.R.E.

MONTCLAIR, SAN BERNARDINO CO., OUR LADY OF LOURDES (1956), Rev. Robert J. Donat.
Office: 10191 Central Ave., 91763. Tel: 909-626-7278; Fax: 909-626-0562.
School—5303 Orchard St., 91763. Tel: 909-621-4418. Sisters of the Presentation 1; Lay Teachers 9; Students 240.
Catechesis/Religious Program—Tel: 909-626-0318. Sr. Angela Callanan, D.R.E. Students 1,000.

MORENO VALLEY, RIVERSIDE CO., ST. CHRISTOPHER (1959), Revs. Romeo Seleccion, M.S.; Edison Pamintuan, M.S.; Deacon Samual Sanchez.
Office: 25075 Cottonwood Ave., 92553. Tel: 909-924-1968; Fax: 909-247-6477.
School—Lay Teachers 4; Students 30.
Catechesis/Religious Program—Cathy Wegner, D.R.E. Students 1,965.

MURRIETA, RIVERSIDE CO., ST. MARTHA (1992), Very Rev. Jack D. Barker, V.F.; Rev. Eliseo Lucas; Deacons Richard Ward; Harold Melton; George Paulicivic; Fred Von Voigt.
Office: 37200 Whitewood Rd., 92563. Tel: 909-698-8180; Fax: 909-698-7353.
Catechesis/Religious Program—Tel: 909-698-8180, Ext. 14. Annett Wester, D.R.E. Students 1,436.

NEEDLES, SAN BERNARDINO CO., ST. ANN (1888), [JC 2] Rev. Rafael A. Partida.
Office: P.O. Box 175, 92363. Tel: 760-326-2721; Fax: 760-326-3068.
Church: 218 D St., 92363.
Catechesis/Religious Program—Elaine Blake, D.R.E. Students 100.

NORCO, RIVERSIDE CO., ST. MEL (1959), Revs. Peter Il Seong Kwon; Patrick Crilly, O.S.A.; Deacons Joseph Vela; John Kim.
Mailing Address: 4140 Corona Ave., 92860.
Office: Box 700, 92860. Tel: 909-737-7144; Fax: 909-735-8332.
Catechesis/Religious Program—Tel: 909-737-8140. Emily Guilherme, D.R.E. Students 886.

ONTARIO, SAN BERNARDINO CO.

1—ST. ELIZABETH ANN SETON (1980), Revs. Charles F. Schultz, S.T.D.; Stanley Onwuegbule. In Res., Rev. Antonio Medeiros.
Office: 2713 S. Grove Ave., 91761. Tel: 909-947-2956; Fax: 909-947-2946.
Catechesis/Religious Program—Tel: 909-923-4097. Students 639.

2—ST. GEORGE (1905), [CEM] [JC] Rev. Arturo Balagat. In Res., Rev. Msgr. Timothy Lawlor; Rev. Aloysuis Tran, C.M.C.
Office: 505 N. Palm, 91762. Tel: 909-983-2637; Fax: 909-395-9707.
School—322 W. D St., 91762. Tel: 909-984-9123; Fax: 909-984-0921. Lay Teachers 10; Students 216.
Catechesis/Religious Program—Tel: 909-460-1578. Andres Verzosa, D.R.E. Students 703.

3—OUR LADY OF GUADALUPE (1948), (Hispanic), Rev. Victor Vargas.
Office: 710 S. Sultana St., 91761. Tel: 909-986-6154; Fax: 909-984-1541.
Catechesis/Religious Program—Tel: 909-983-2904. Marjorie Mares, D.R.E. Students 697.

PALM DESERT, RIVERSIDE CO.

1—CHRIST OF THE DESERT (1986),, (Newman Center) Rev. Howard A. Lincoln.
Office: 73441 Fred Waring Dr., 92260. Tel: 760-346-0089; Fax: 760-340-2245.

2—SACRED HEART (1956), Revs. Howard A. Lincoln; Edward McGuinness; Deacon Fernando Heredia.
Office: 43-775 N. Deep Canyon Rd., 92260. Tel: 760-346-6502; Fax: 760-773-4873.
School—Tel: 760-346-3513; Fax: 760-773-0673. Sr. Joan Griffin, O.S.F., Prin. Sisters 2; Lay Teachers 29; Students 412.
Catechesis/Religious Program—Tel: 760-340-0143; Fax: 760-773-0673. Jane Bannan, D.R.E. Students 257.

PALM SPRINGS, RIVERSIDE CO.

1—OUR LADY OF GUADALUPE (1912), (Cahuilla Indian), Rev. Adrian Brinn.
204 S. Calle El Segundo, 92263.
Office: P.O. Box 1947, 92263. Tel: 760-325-5809; Fax: 760-327-2049.

2—OUR LADY OF SOLITUDE (1929), (Hispanic), [JC] Rev. Miguel Ceja; Deacon John Skora.
Office: 151 W. Alejo Rd., 92262. Tel: 760-325-3816; Fax: 760-325-5316.
Catechesis/Religious Program—Lucia Rodriguez, D.R.E. Students 305.

3—ST. THERESA (1948), Rev. Msgr. Philip A. Behan; Deacon John Fausto.
Office: 2800 E. Ramon Rd., 92264. Tel: 760-323-2669; Fax: 760-322-8581.
School—455 S. Compadre, 92262. Tel: 760-327-4919. Lay Teachers 19; Students 327.
Catechesis/Religious Program—Tel: 760-323-4351 (English). Catherine Knox, D.R.E. Students 579.

PERRIS, RIVERSIDE CO., ST. JAMES (1907), Very Rev. Anthony Ferrero, V.F., J.C.L. In Res., Rev. John Niessen, S.V.D.
Office: 269 W. Third St., 92570. Tel: 909-657-2380; Fax: 909-943-7290.
School—250 W. Third St., 92570. Tel: 909-657-5226. Irish Sisters of Mercy 1; Lay Teachers 16; Students 276.
Catechesis/Religious Program—Tel: 909-657-8809. Sr. Noreen O'Connor, D.R.E. Students 1,189.

PHELAN, SAN BERNARDINO CO., BLESSED JUNIPERO SERRA CHURCH (1989), Rev. Frank T. Dicristina.
Mailing Address: 8820 Sheep Creek Rd., 92371. Fax: 760-868-2171.
Office: P.O. Box 292570, 92329-2570. Tel: 760-868-4342; Fax: 760-249-3438.
Catechesis/Religious Program—Students 114.

RANCHO CUCAMONGA, SAN BERNARDINO CO.

1—OUR LADY OF MOUNT CARMEL (1905), Josefina Herrera, Interim. Admin.
Office: 10079 Eighth St., 91729-0303. Tel: 909-987-2717; Fax: 909-987-3818.
Catechesis/Religious Program—Esthela Garcia, D.R.E.

2—SACRED HEART (1953), Peter Newburn, Pastoral Coord.; Rev. Peter Balili; Deacons Ed Clark; Robert Cardenas.
Office: 12704 Foothill Blvd., 91739. Tel: 909-899-1049; Fax: 909-899-3229.
School—12676 Foothill Blvd., 91739. Lay Teachers 10; Students 238.
Catechesis/Religious Program—Tel: 909-899-1049, Ext. 17; Fax: 909-899-3229. Mary Andel, D.R.E. Students 562.

REDLANDS, SAN BERNARDINO CO.

1—ST. MARY (1941), (Latino), [JC] Rev. Miguel A. Urrea.
Office: 1214 Columbia St., 92374 Tel: 909-792-3695 Fax: 909-798-2665.
Catechesis/Religious Program—Tel 909-335-0096. Students 295.

2—SACRED HEART (1894), [JC] Revs. Thomas Burdick; Jerome Ochetti; Deacons Richard Cover; William Keough, (Retired).
Office: 115 W. Olive Ave., 92373. Tel: 909-793-2469; Fax: 909-335-1719.
School—215 S. Eureka St., 92373. Tel: 909-792-3958. Lay Teachers 13; Students 236.
Catechesis/Religious Program—Tel: 909-798-4167. Christie McPeck, D.R.E. Students 442.

RIALTO, SAN BERNARDINO CO.

1—ST. CATHERINE OF SIENA (1949), Very Rev. Steve C. Porter, S.T.L.; Rev. David Fitzgerald, S.P.; Deacons Edwin Chamberlayne; Gonzalo Sotello; Victor Ramirez.
Office: 339 N. Sycamore, 92376-3517. Tel: 909-875-1360; Fax: 909-875-2822.
School—347 N. Sycamore Ave., 92376. Lay Teachers 10; Students 284.
Catechesis/Religious Program—Students 947.

2—ST. THOMAS MORE (1961), Rev. Timothy L. Jemejcic; Deacon Tom Brannick.
Office: P.O. Box 367, 92377. Tel: 909-421-7030; Fax: 909-421-1374.
Church: 222 E. Easton, 92376.
Catechesis/Religious Program—Tel: 909-421-7031. Carol Dugan, D.R.E. Students 294.

RIVERSIDE, RIVERSIDE CO.

1—ST. ANDREW, Formerly St. Andrew's Newman Center (1971),, Serving Riverside Community College & UCR. Rev. David Geib, O.P. In. Res., Revs. Vincent Benoit, O.P.; David Seid, O.P.
Office: 105 W. Big Springs Rd., 92507-4737. Tel: 909-682-8751; Fax: 909-682-3513.
Catechesis/Religious Program—Frances Hodgkinson, D.R.E. Students 202.

2—ST. ANTHONY OF PADUA, Formerly Anthony (1923), Rev. Sacramento Perez, O.deM.
Office: 3074 Madison St., 92504. Tel: 909-352-8393; Fax: 909-352-8816.
Catechesis/Religious Program—Tel: 909-785-4908. Guillermina Coria, D.R.E. Students 307.

3—ST. CATHERINE OF ALEXANDRIA (1946), Michael Norrie, Pastoral Coord.; Revs. David Andel; Richard McGee, C.R. In Res., Revs. Ted Wicki, C.R.; Paul Granillo, J.C.L.; Deacon Donald Tillitson.
Office: 7050 Brockton Ave., 92506. Tel: 909-683-0800; Fax: 909-683-4114.
School—3728 Arlington Ave., 92506. Tel: 909-684-1091. Sisters 1; Lay Teachers 10; Students 356.
Catechesis/Religious Program—Tel: 909-781-9855. Kathleen Serra, D.R.E. Students 63.

4—ST. FRANCIS DE SALES (1886), [JC] Rev. Louis Abdoo, I.M.C.; Deacon James Dale.
Office: 4268 Lime St., 92501. Tel: 909-686-4004; Fax: 909-686-3948.
School—4205 Mulberry St., 92501. Tel: 909-683-5083; Fax: 909-683-0249. Religious 1; Lay Teachers 11; Students 328.
Catechesis/Religious Program—Tel: 909-784-0987. Toni Bastian, D.R.E. Students 189.

5—ST. JOHN THE EVANGELIST (1956), Revs. Genaro Zavala, M.S.P.; Benito Rojas Barron, M.S.P.
Res.: 3980 Opal St., 92519. Tel: 909-684-6864; Fax: 909-684-3115.
Catechesis/Religious Program—Tel: 909-686-5181. Lori Pittman, D.R.E. Students 557.
Mission—Our Lady of Guadalupe 2518 Hall Ave., Riverside Co. 92509.

6—OUR LADY OF GUADALUPE SHRINE (1929), (Hispanic), Revs. Sacramento Perez, O.deM.; Adrian Ochoa, O.deM.; Deacons Rudy Ybarra; Joe Ortiz.
Office: 2858 Ninth St., 92507. Tel: 909-684-0279; Fax: 909-684-0390.
Catechesis/Religious Program—Tel: 909-683-1123. Students 325.

7—OUR LADY OF PERPETUAL HELP (1955), Revs. Rutilio J. del Riego, D.L.P.; Juan L. Garcia, D.L.P.; John Tinh Tran, C.M.C.; Deacons Joseph Gomeck; Larry Quilliam; Ysidro Gurrola.
Office: 5250 Central Ave., 92504. Tel: 909-689-8921; Fax: 909-689-3619.
School—6686 Streeter Ave., 92504. Tel: 909-689-2125; Fax: 909-689-9354. Lay Teachers 12; Students 271.
Catechesis/Religious Program—Students 647.

8—ST. PATRICK (1989), Kristen Thorstad, Pastoral Coord.; Rev. Paul Granillo, J.C.L. In Res., Rev. John Schweikert, M.S.C.; Deacons Austin Kilbourn; Edgar Borne.
Office: 10915 Pigeon Pass Rd., Moreno Valley, 92557. Tel: 909-485-6673; Fax: 909-485-3834.
Catechesis/Religious Program—Students 744.

9—QUEEN OF ANGELS (1949), Revs. John Farao, O.F.M.Conv.; Thomas Hamilton, O.F.M.Conv. In Res., Bro. Dario Garcia, O.F.M.Conv.; Deacon James Neufell.
Office: 4824 Jones Ave., 92505. Tel: 909-689-3674; Fax: 909-687-6146.
School—Tel: 909-689-1992. Sisters 2; Lay Teachers 6; Students 137.
Catechesis/Religious Program—Tel: 909-687-5407. Robert Caires, D.R.E. Students 581.

10—SACRED HEART (1945), [JC] Rev. Edward J. Connolly.
Office: 9935 Mission Blvd., 92509. Tel: 909-685-5058; Fax: 909-685-1056.
Catechesis/Religious Program—Tel: 909-685-8510. Patricia Raubold, D.R.E. Students 790.

11—ST. THOMAS THE APOSTLE (1903), Rev. Joseph Felker; Deacon Paul Myers.
Office: 3774 Jackson St., 92503. Tel: 909-689-1131; Fax: 909-354-7402.
School—9136 Magnolia Ave., 92503. Tel: 909-689-1981; Fax: 909-689-1985. Lay Teachers 11; Students 302.
Catechesis/Religious Program—Tel: 909-689-7180. Deacon Paul Myers, D.R.E. Students 397.
Mission—Our Lady of Guadalupe 9398 Indiana Ave., Riverside Co. 92503. Rev. Robert M. Herbst, O.F.M.Conv.

RUNNING SPRINGS, SAN BERNARDINO CO., ST. ANNE IN THE MOUNTAINS (1963), Rev. Timothy F. Keppel, C.R., V.F.
Office: P.O. Box 2400, 92382. Tel: 909-867-2832; Fax: 909-867-2832.
Church: 30480 Fredalba Rd., 92382.
Catechesis/Religious Program—Julieta Avitia, D.R.E.

SAN JACINTO, RIVERSIDE CO., ST. ANTHONY (1890), Rev. Ciro Libanati.

Office: 630 S. Santa Fe Ave., 92583. Tel: 909-654-7911; Fax: 909-654-2309.
School—St. Hyacinth Academy, 275 S. Victoria Ave., 92583. Tel: 909-654-2013. Lay Teachers 10; Students 249.
Catechesis/Religious Program—Tel: 909-654-3311; Fax: 909-654-5644. Students 436.

SOBOBA INDIAN RESERVATION, RIVERSIDE CO., ST. JOSEPH (1888), (Native American), [CEM] Rev. Earl Joseph Henley, M.S.C.
Mailing Address: P.O. Box 1027, San Jacinto, 92581. Tel: 909-654-2086; Fax: 909-654-2086.
Catechesis/Religious Program—Students 29.

SUN CITY, RIVERSIDE CO., ST. VINCENT FERRER (1965), [JC] Rev. Antonio C. Das Neves; Deacon Ronald Rehaume.
Office: 27931 Murrieta Rd., 92586-2320. Tel: 909-679-4531; Fax: 909-679-7521.
Catechesis/Religious Program—Tel: 909-672-4019. Mary Wedeking, D.R.E. Students 475.

TEMECULA, RIVERSIDE CO., ST. CATHERINE OF ALEXANDRIA, Formerly Catherine (1979), Rev. John Wagner; Deacons Robert Phillips; John Barth.
Office: 41875 C St., 92592. Tel: 909-676-4403; Fax: 909-695-6659.
Catechesis/Religious Program—Tel: 909-695-6656. Monique Jacobs, D.R.E. Students 919.

THOUSAND PALMS, SAN BERNARDINO, ST. PHILIP THE APOSTLE (1991), Rev. Joseph Mawicke.
Office: P.O. Box 405, 92276. Tel: 760-343-1911; Fax: 760-343-3211.
Church: 31525 Via Pared, 92276-3352.
Catechesis/Religious Program—Cecilia Hill, D.R.E. Students 44.

TRONA, SAN BERNARDINO CO., ST. MADELEINE SOPHIE BARAT, Rev. William J. Kiefer (Retired).
Office: 83395 Trona Rd., 93562. Tel: 760-372-4717.

TWENTYNINE PALMS, SAN BERNARDINO CO., BLESSED SACRAMENT, Rev. James Moore; Deacon John Stanley.
Office: 6785 Sage Ave., 92277. Tel: 760-367-3343; Fax: 760-367-0543.
School—6755 Sage Ave., 92277. Tel: 760-367-3341. Lay Teachers 7; Students 63.
Catechesis/Religious Program—Tel: 760-367-3347. Students 60.

UPLAND, SAN BERNARDINO CO.
1—ST. ANTHONY (1974), Deacons Eugene Bello; Jack Clinton.
Office: P.O. Box 608, 91785. Tel: 909-985-2803; Fax: 909-982-8643.
Church: 2110 N. San Antonio Ave., 91785.
Catechesis/Religious Program—Tel: 909-981-7080. Elizabeth Neapolitan, D.R.E.
2—ST. JOSEPH (1922), [JC] Revs. John Roche, SS.CC.; Tom Burns, M.S.C.; Michael Brooks, SS.CC. In Res, Rev. George Wuest, S.J.; Deacons George Schmit; Charles Pobjoy, (Retired); Frank Simoni; Greg Moore.
Office: 877 N. Campus Ave., 91786. Tel: 909-981-8110; Fax: 909-949-8090.
School—905 Campus Ave., 91786. Tel: 909-920-5185. Sisters of the Presentation 2; Lay Teachers 7; Students 350.
Catechesis/Religious Program—Tel: 909-982-9518. Sr. Maria Carlos, E.I.N., D.R.E. Students 548.

VICTORVILLE, SAN BERNARDINO CO.
1—HOLY INNOCENTS (1992), Rev. Mark E. Kotlarczyk; Deacons Frank Alaniz-Duncan; William Shellem.
Office: 13230 El Evado Rd., 92392. Tel: 760-955-6010; Fax: 760-955-2100.
Catechesis/Religious Program—Tel: 760-955-6262. Eileen Dutch, D.R.E. Students 920.
2—ST. JOAN OF ARC (1922), Rev. Lorenzo Paz; Deacon Manual Gomez.
Office: 15512 Sixth St., 92392. Tel: 760-245-7674; Fax: 760-245-7077.

WILDOMAR, RIVERSIDE CO., ST. FRANCES OF ROME (1887), [JC] Rev. Martin Tharakan, O.I.C.; Deacon Fred Von Voight.
Office: 21591 Lemon St., 92595. Tel: 909-674-6881; Fax: 909-674-6443.
School—Tel: 909-471-5144. Lay Teachers 6; Students 50.
Catechesis/Religious Program—Tel: 909-471-3703. Students 750.

WRIGHTWOOD, SAN BERNARDINO CO., OUR LADY OF THE SNOWS (1946), Rev. Frank T. Dicristina.
Mailing Address: 975 Lark, 92397. Tel: 760-868-4342; Fax: 760-868-2171.
Office: P.O. Box 29270, Phelan, 92329-2570. Tel: 760-868-4342; Fax: 760-868-2171.
Catechesis/Religious Program—Students 61.

YUCAIPA, SAN BERNARDINO CO., ST. FRANCES XAVIER CABRINI (1953), Rev. Kenneth Jenkins; Deacon Dan Taylor.
Office: 12687 California St., 92399. Tel: 909-797-2533; Fax: 909-790-5803.
Catechesis/Religious Program—Sr. Doris Market, O.S.B., D.R.E. Students 464.

YUCCA VALLEY, SAN BERNARDINO CO., ST. MARY OF THE VALLEY (1953), Unassigned.
Office: 7495 Church St., 92284-3247. Tel: 760-365-2287; Fax: 760-369-0622.
Catechesis/Religious Program—Students 160.

Chaplains of Public Institutions

SAN BERNARDINO. *Arrowhead Regional Medical Center*, 805 Medical Center Dr., 92404. Tel: 909-387-8111. Rev. Robert Marzullo, O.P.
San Bernardino City and County Jails. Vacant.
San Bernardino Juvenile Hall & Verdemont Boys Ranch. Vacant
Catholic Charities. 1450 N. D St., 92405. Tel: 909-388-1239.
San Bernardino Medical Center, 2101 N. Waterman Ave., 92404. Tel: 909-883-8711. Rev. Barnabas Laubach, O.S.B.

APPLE VALLEY. *St. Mary of the Desert Valley Hospital*, 18300 Highway 18, 92307-0404. Tel: 760-242-2311. Rev. Santiago Ner, M.S.

BLYTHE. *Ironwood State Prison*, 19005 Wileys Well Rd., P.O. Box 1968, 92226. Tel: 760-921-3000. Rev. Ron Rusk.

CHINO. *California Institute for Men*, P.O. Box 128, 91710. Tel: 909-681-6497; 909-597-1821. Rev. Michael Bucaro.
California Youth Authority. Vacant
Camp Prado. Vacant.
Southern Conservation Center, P.O. Box 128, 91710. Tel: 909-597-1821, Ext. 2289. Rev. Michael Bucaro.

COLTON. *Arrowhead Regional Medical Center*. Rev. Dennis Legaspi.

FONTANA. *Kaiser Permanente Hospital*, 9961 Sierra Ave., 92335. Tel: 909-829-5850; 909-829-5000 (Emergency). Rev. Peter Balili.
Kaiser Permanente Medical Center. Rev. Matthew Vanissery.

FRONTERA. *California Institute for Women*, 16756 Chino-Corona Rd., 91720. Tel: 909-597-1771. Rev. Neil D. Fuller, S.V.D., Chap.

LOMA LINDA. *Jerry Pettis Memorial Hospital*, 11201 Benton St., 92354. Tel: 909-825-7084. Rev. Leonard Mestos.
Loma Linda Community Hospital, 2533 Barton Rd., 92354. Tel: 909-796-7311, Ext. 4367. Rev. Msgr. Antonio Sudario.
Loma Linda University Medical Center, Barton Rd. and Anderson St., 92354. Tel: 909-824-0800. Rev. Msgr. Antonio Sudario.

MORENA VALLEY. *Riverside County Regional Medical Center*, 56520 Cactus Ave., 92555. Tel: 909-486-4000; 909-486-4334. Rev. Enrique LaPuebla, M.S.

NORCO. *California Rehabilitation Center*, Western & Fifth Sts., P.O. Box 1841, 91760. Tel: 909-737-2683, Ext. 4305. Rev. Msgr. Cosimo Corciulo.

PATTON. *Patton State Hospital*. Rev. Bernard Donaghey.

PILOT ROCK. *Crestline*, Tel: 909-338-2303. Vacant.

RIVERSIDE. *Riverside General Hospital*, 9851 Magnolia Ave., 92503. Tel: 909-358-7100; 909-689-3674. Bro. Dario Garcia, O.F.M.Conv.
Riverside Juvenile Hall. Vacant.

Special or Other Diocesan Assignment:
Rev. Msgrs.—
Lawrence, Robert E., J.C.L., Defender of the Bond
Webber, Donald S., J.C.L., Judicial Vicar, Canonical Svcs.
Very Rev.—
Aiardi, Reno, I.M.C., Dir. Missions Office
Rev.—
Andel, David, Judge, Canonical Svcs.
Very Rev.—
Ferrero, Anthony, V.F., J.C.L., Adjutant Judicial Vicar
Revs.—
Granillo, Paul, J.C.L., Admin. Asst. & Priest Secretary
Henley, Earl, M.S.C., Chap., St. Joseph Indian Mission
Jaramillo, Jose G., M.G., Diocesan Pastoral Center
Larkin, Ronald, M.S.C., Vicar for Clergy
Very Rev.—
Lopez, Gerard M., S.T.L., V.G., Moderator of the Curia, Dir. Priest Personnel, & Vicar Gen.
Revs.—
Martelli, Jose M., C.S.C., Valley Missionary Program
Noetzel, Kenneth J., S.J. (DET), Dir. Diaconate Formation
Sanz, Jose, D.L.P., Rector, Blessed Jnipero Serra House

On Duty Outside the Diocese:
Revs.—
Buchanan, Robert E., Our Lady of Snows, 1138 Wright St., Las Vegas, NV 89509.
Frankovich, Frank, Companions of the Cross, 100 Young St., Ottawa ON KIY 3P7 Canada.
Kurilec, Robert, 3908 Roebling Ln., Virginia Beach, VA 23452. USN
Lowe, Frank, Capt., Chap., PSC 80, Box 20531, Apo, AP 96367.

Military Chaplains:
Rev.—
Serban, Ron, Capt., National Training Center, Center Chapel, P.O. Box 105053, Fort Irwin, 92310. Tel: 760-380-4211; 760-380-4212

On Sabbatical:
Rev.—
Barker, Jack

On Leave of Absence:
Rev.—
Paz, Lorenzo

Retired:
Rev. Msgrs.—
Andreatta, Tullio, 2245 Fort Stockton Rd., San Diego, 92103.
Battle, Lawrence, 73450 Country Club Dr. #190, Palm Desert, 92260.
Lawlor, Timothy, St. George, 325 W. E St., Ontario, 91762.
Meagher, Thomas, 1011 St. Andrews #15, Upland, 91786.
O'Keeffe, Patrick, 1201 E. Highland Ave., 92404.
O'Leary, Cornelius, 25098 Jaclyn Ave., Moreno Valley, 92543.
Revs.—
Baseford, Paul, 485 Foxenwood Dr., Santa Maria, 92355.
Benjamin, Jonh, 19184 Palo Verde Drl., Apple Valley, 92308.
Bonacum, Thomas, 124 Box Garner Valley Rd., Mountain Center, 92561.
Cardoza, Edward, 21267 George Brown, 92518.
Casey, Donald A., 546 Reliance Ave., Henderson, NV 89015-9690.
Cerezo, Alfonso, 865 E. Yale, Ontario, 91764.
Chavez, Adolphus, 1201 E. Highland Ave., 92404.
Chavez, Arturo, 56520 Cactus Ave., Morevo Valley, 92555.
Cima, Jose, 23505 Evening Snow, Moreno Valley, 92557.
Coslowsky, Marion, 733 Belinda Ave., Barstow, 92311.
Covas, Peter, 1201 E. Highland Ave., 92404.
DePasquale, Dominic, Plymouth Tower, 3401 Lemon St., Apt.705, 92501.
Devine, Charles
DiLeo, Anthony, 43981 Northgate, Temecula, 92592.
Domas, John, 800 Pennslyvania Ave. #15, Beaumont, 92223.
Erickson, Robert, P.O. Box 460, Rim Forest, 92378.
Erstad, William, 8205 Mondavi Place, Rancho Cucamonga, 91730.
Fitzwilliam, Ivan, 1499 Old Mountain Ave., #29, San Jacinto, 92583.
Gaglia, Fred, 3250 W. 46th Ave., Denver, CO 80211.
Ganahl, James, 15767 Tuscola Rd., Apt. 1, Apple Valley, 92307.
Gill, Paul, 39335 Vineland, Sp. 66, Cherry Valley, 92223.
Gillespie, Thomas, 1201 E. Highland, 92404.
Gorman, John, Nazareth House, 6333 Rancho Mission Rd., San Diego, 92108.
Grajek, Lawrence, P.O. Box 2077, Big Bear City, 92314.
Greiner, Lawrence, 197 Via Lola, Apt. 10, Palm Springs, 92262.
Guillen, Patricio, 2002 S. Magnolia Ave., Ontario, 91762.
Kiefer, William J., 83395 Trona Rd., Trona, 93562.
Leahy, Anthony, P.O. Box 4027, Oceanside, 92051.
Lenoir, Jean, 79-925 Camelback Dr., Bermuda Dunes, 92201.
Lucking, Alousius, 61960 Sunburst Cr., Joshua Tree, 92252.
Marcotte, William, 2699 Maryknoll Dr., Colfon, 92324.
Marcotte, William
McNally, Michael R., P.O. Box 3802, 92413.
Morquillas, Fructuoso, 23883 Copper Hill Pl., Moreno Valley, 92557.
O'Day, Michael, 28710 Olympia Way, Sun City, 92586.
O'Donovan, Daniel, Goleen Skibberee, Co Cork Ireland.
O'Sullivan, Brendan, 1001 Encinitas Blvd., San Diego, 92024.
Roach, Joseph, 9466 Navajo Tr., Morongo Valley, 92256.
Rogan, Brian, 819 Sherwood St., Redlands, 92373.
Ryan, John, 934 N. Dearborn, Redlands, 92374.
Schilly, Joseph, Nazareth House, 6333 Rancho Mission Rd., San Diego, 92108.
Soupos, Christopher
Speno, Eugene, 1201 E. Highland, 92404.

Stauber, James, 4967 Chicago Ave., 92507.
Timlin, Anthony, 39-701 Palm Greens Pkwy., Palm Desert, 92260.
Trong, Joseph, 12772 Louise Cir., Garden Grove, 92643.
Valdes, Luis, 1201 E. Highland, 92404.
Vehovec, Valentine, 6333 Rancho Mission Rd., #104, San Diego, 92108.
Wadell, John, Cl. Fra. Pere Fornes, 13, Muro, Mallorca 07440 Spain.
Walters, Vincent, 4647 Braemer Pl. #26, 92501-3040.
Waterfall, Richard A., P.O. Box 409, Palm Springs, 92263.
White, Kris, Plymouth Tower, 3401 Lemon St., Stockton, 95201.

Permanent Deacons:
Acosta, Joseph, Highland
Aguilera, Santos, Hesperia
Alaniz, Frank, Victorville
Amador, Robert, Colton
Ampuero, Marcial, Adelanto
Barna, John, Alta Loma
Barth, John, Temecula
Bello, Eugene, Upland
Benavides, Pablo, Cathedral City
Borne, Edward, Moreno Valley
Brannick, Thomas, Rialto
Brenes-Rios, Anthony, Chino
Burgett, Donald, Barstow
Burris, Bud, Lake Elsinore
Campbell, Gerald, Desert Hot Springs
Cardenas, Roberto, Rancho Cucamonga
Carroll, Christopher, Alta Loma
Chamberlayne, Edwin, Rialto
Clark, Edward, Rancho Cucamonga
Clinton, Jack, Upland
Cover, Richard, Redlands
Dale, James R., Riverside
Fausto, John Joseph, Palm Springs
Filipek, Marlin, Corona
Garcia, Jose, Coachella
Garcia, Joseph, Riverside
Gomeck, Joseph, Riverside
Gomez, Manuel, Victorville
Gonzalez, Victor, Coachell
Gurrola, Ysidro, Riverside
Gutierrez, Mario, Fontana
Henke, Jack, Hemet
Heredia, Fernando, Palm Desert
Hodnick, Mark, Alta Loma
Hoy, Wayne, Coachella
Hunsicker, Scott, Hesperia
Hunt, Sam, La Qunita
Jelley, Michael, San Bernardino
Joslin, Wayne, Colton
Juback, Michael, Fontana
Kafka, Gene, San Bernardino
Keough, William, Redlands
Key, Joseph, San Bernardino
Kilbourn, Austin, Moreno Valley
Kim, John, Norco
Martinez, M. Pat, Chino Hills
Melton, Harold, Murrieta
Miller, Glenn, Joshua Tree
Mirci, Philip, Redlands
Moore, Greg, Upland
Murvin, Royal, Beaumont
Myers, Paul, Riverside
Neufell, James, Riverside
Olivas, Manuel, San Bernardino
Ortiz, Joseph, Riverside
Partida, Ralph, Jr., Big Bear
Paulicivic, George, Sr., Murrieta
Phillips, Robert, Temecula
Pimental, Simon, Victorville
Pobjoy, Charles, Upland
Quilliam, Larry, Riverside
Ramirez, Victor, Rialto
Rehaume, Ronald J., Sun City
Reyes, Carlos, Apple Valley
Rios, Joseph, Redlands
Rittman, Robert, Apple Valley
Rodriguez, Brijido, Indio
Roman, Francis, Barstow
Saenz, Margo, Barstow
Salinas, Arcadio, Jr., Cathedral City
Sanchez, Samuel, Moreno Valley
Schmit, George, Upland
Sepulveda, Ralph, Beaumont
Shalhoub, William J., Loma Linda
Simoni, Frank, Upland
Skora, John, Palm Springs
Sotelo, Gonzalo, Rialto
Taylor, Daniel, East Highland
Vasquez, Sergio, Coachella
Vela, Joe, Norco
Von Ins, Paul, Alta Loma
Von Voight, Fred, Wildomar
Ward, Richard, Murrieta
Ybarra, Rudy, Riverside
Zambrano, Jose, Corona

INSTITUTIONS LOCATED IN THE DIOCESE

[A] SEMINARIES, RELIGIOUS OR SCHOLASTICATES

RIVERSIDE. *Blessed Junipero Serra House of Formation*, 3325 13th St., 92501. Tel: 909-788-9931; Fax: 909-781-9031. Revs. Jose Sanz, D.L.P., Rector; Juan Garcia, D.L.P., Spiritual Dir. Priests 2; Seminarians 4.

Society of the Divine Word Missionaries, Formerly Divine Word Seminary, 11316 Cypress Ave., 92505. Tel: 909-689-4858; Fax: 909-785-0327. Email: wjcaffrey@aol.com. Revs. William Caffrey, S.V.D., Rector; John McHenry, S.V.D.; Henry Noga, S.V.D.; Donald O'Connor, S.V.D.; Joseph Scott, S.V.D.; John Neissen, S.V.D.; John Tran, S.V.D.; Paul Schmidt, S.V.D.; Ponciano Ramos, S.V.D.; Sony Sebastian; Bros. Bernard Dorade, S.V.D.; Daniel Yunck, S.V.D.; Steve Kerekes, S.V.D.; Andrew Hockiss, S.V.D.

[B] HIGH SCHOOLS, DIOCESAN

SAN BERNARDINO. *Aquinas High School* (Coed) , 2772 N. Sterling Ave., 92404. Tel: 909-886-4659; Fax: 909-886-7717. Email: Aquinas@Aquinashs.net. Web: www.aquinashs.net. Mr. Randall Adams, Prin. Priests 1; Brothers 1; Sisters 2; Lay Teachers 22; Students 344.

RIVERSIDE. *Notre Dame High School* (Coed) , 7085 Brockton Ave., 92506. Tel: 909-275-5896; Fax: 909-781-9020. Web: www.ndtitans.com. Dr. Jo Dean Salley, Prin. Priests 2; Sisters 1; Lay Teachers 43; Students 581.

[C] HOMES FOR SENIOR CITIZENS

SAN BERNARDINO. *St. Bernardine Plaza*, 550 W. Fifth St., 92401. Tel: 909-888-0153; Fax: 909-381-1589. Email: stbern2@adelphia.net. Staff 4; Units 148.

PALM DESERT. *La Paz Villas*, P.O. Box 1962, 92261. Tel: 760-346-6033; Fax: 760-773-5667. Email: brallo@dc.rr.com. Units 24.

[D] GENERAL HOSPITALS AND CLINICS

SAN BERNARDINO. *St. Bernardine Medical Center*, 2101 N. Waterman Ave., 92404. Tel: 909-883-8711; Fax: 909-881-4546. Web: www.stbernardinemedctr.org. Steven Barron, Pres.; Rev. Barnabas Laubach, O.S.B., Head Chap. Sponsored by Congregation of The Sisters of Charity of The Incarnate Word, Houston, Texas Sisters 4; Bed Capacity 463; Patients Assisted Annually 131,000; Total Staff 1,509.

APPLE VALLEY. *St. Mary Medical Center*, 18300 Hwy. 18, 92307. Tel: 760-946-8195; Fax: 760-242-2994. Sr. Marian Schubert, C.S.J., Vice Pres., Sponsorship.

St. Joseph Health System Tel: 714-347-7500. Sisters 4; Brothers 1; Bed Capacity 186.

St. Mary Medical Center Auxiliary Tel: 760-242-2311; Fax: 760-242-9750.

St. Mary Hospital Foundation Tel: 760-242-2311; Fax: 760-242-9750. Bed Capacity 186; Patients Assisted Annually 70,443.

[E] MONASTERIES AND RESIDENCES OF PRIESTS AND BROTHERS

APPLE VALLEY. *Hospitaller Brothers of St. John of God*, P.O. Box 1664, 92307. Tel: 760-242-6560; Fax: 760-242-6570. Bros. Edward Francis, O.H., Prior; Richard Gaule, O.H.; Eric Hoffer; Andre Azehuletta; Geara Kearns; Edward Francis McEnroe. Brothers 5.

Missionaries of Our Lady of La Salette, MS, 18368 Corwin Rd., 92367. Tel: 760-242-4427. Rev. Bernard Taylor, M.S.

CHINO HILLS. *Congregation of the Sacred Hearts, SS.CC.*, Western U.S. Province, St. Paul the Apostle Rectory, 14860 Cherry Dr. 91709. Tel: 909-465-5503; Fax: 909-465-1683. Revs. Ken McCabe, SS.CC.; Pat O'Hagan, SS.CC.

COACHELLA. *Congregation of the Holy Cross*, 52-525 Oasis Palm Dr., 92236. Tel: 760-398-5577; Fax: 760-398-1783. Revs. Jose Martelli, C.S.C.; Steven Sedlock, C.S.C.; Bruce Cecil, C.S.C.; John S. Connor, C.S.C.

CORONA. *Congregation of the Mother Co-Redemptrix*, 1775 S. Main St., 91720-4961. Tel: 909-737-4125; 909-340-9880; Fax: 909-479-0002. Email: corona@dongcong.net. Web: corona/dongcong.net. Revs. Pius M. Nguyen Dan, C.M.C., Dir.; Aloysius M. Tran Ngoc Thoai, C.M.C.; Luke M. Do Binh Dinh, C.M.C.; Matthias M. Nguyen Huy Chuong, C.M.C.; John Tran Dinh Diem, C.M.C. Shrine of Presentation (Den Thanh Duc Me Dang Con).

FONTANA. *Congregation of the Resurrection, CR*, 7650 Tamarind St., 92336. Tel: 909-822-0566; Fax: 909-822-0620. Revs. Leonard Krzywda, C.R.; Humphrey Ruszel, C.R.; Henry Licznerski, C.R.

St. Joseph, 17080 Arrow Blvd., 92336. Tel: 909-822-4732; Fax: 909-822-0620. Revs. Henry Ruszel, C.R.; Casimir Tadla, C.R.; Andrzej Lewandowski, C.R.

HEMET. *Holy Ghost Fathers*, Casa Laval, 309 E. Whitter Ave., 92546-3509. Tel: 909-658-6851; Fax: 909-765-3137. Email: spiritan@pc.net. Web: www.spiritan.org. Revs. George Healy, C.S.Sp., Supr. Tel: 909-929-2838; Edward Bernacki, C.S.Sp.; James Burke, C.S.Sp.; Charles Coffey, C.S.Sp.; Silvio D'Ostilio, C.S.Sp.; Norbert Rosso, C.S.Sp.

Holy Spirit, P.O. Box 5268, 92544-0268. Tel: 909-927-4478; Fax: 909-927-8546. Rev. Silvio D'Ostilio, C.S.Sp.

Our Lady of the Valley, P.O. Box 2446, 92546-0414. Tel: 909-929-6131. Revs. Clement Lachowsky, C.S.Sp. (Retired); Pierre L. Deglaire, C.S.Sp.; George Healy, C.S.Sp., Parochial Vicar; Joseph Maria Huy Q. Dinh, C.S.Sp.; Joseph L. Deniger, C.S.Sp.

MORENO VALLEY. *Missionaries of Our Lady of La Salette, MS*, 25075 Cottonwood Ave., 92553. Tel: 909-924-1968; Fax: 909-247-6477. Email: romy@pe.net. Revs. Antonio Abuan-Gaona, M.S.; Romeo N. Seleccion, M.S.; Pamintuan Edison, M.S.

NEWBERRY SPRINGS. *Holy Resurrection Community*, 45704 Valley Center Rd., 92365. Tel: 760-257-4008; Fax: 760-257-3362. Revs. Father Moses, C.R.; Father Maximilio, C.R.; Father Basil, C.R.; Abbot Nicholas Hegumen.

REDLANDS. *Discalced Carmelites, OCD*, P.O. Box 446, 92373. Tel: 909-792-1047; Fax: 909-798-3497. Email: elcarmelo@juno.com. Revs. Fernando Pinto, O.C.D., Superior; Gerald Werner, O.C.D. (SJ), Provincial; Dominic O'Callaghan, O.C.D.; Thomas Koller, O.C.D.; Bros. Michael Villagomez, O.C.D.; Boniface Scheerer, O.C.D.

RIVERSIDE. *Conventual Franciscans, OFM Conv.*, 4824 Jones Ave., 92505. Tel: 909-689-3674; Fax: 909-687-6146. Revs. Thomas Hamilton, O.F.M.Conv.; John Farao, O.F.M.Conv.

Diocesan Labor Priests, DLP, 5250 Central Ave., 92504. Tel: 909-689-8921; Fax: 909-689-3619. Revs. Juan Garcia, D.L.P.; Jose Sanz, D.L.P.; Rutilio Del Riego, D.L.P.

Operarios Del Reino De Cristo, O.R.C., c/o St. Edward, 417 W. Grand Blvd., Corona, 92882. Tel: 909-549-6000; Fax: 909-549-6009. Revs. Jose Varela, O.R.C., Local Contact; Edwardo Carmona (Mexico), Regl. Dir.; Eliseo Hernandez, O.R.C.; Martin S. Rodriguez, O.R.C.; Eloy Trujillo Contreras.

St. Vincent Ferrer House Dominican Priests and Brothers, Western Province, OP , 872 Spruce St., 92507. Tel: 909-784-0160; Fax: 909-682-3513. Email: catholicucr@earthlink.net. Revs. David Geib, O.P.; Lawrence Farrell, O.P.; Martin Diaz, O.P.; Cassian T. Lewinski, O.P. (PHX). Dominicans

UPLAND. *Congregation of the Sacred Hearts*, Formerly Missionaries of the Sacred Heart, MSC, 877 N. Campus Ave., 91786. Tel: 909-981-8110; Fax: 909-949-8090. Revs. John Roche, SS.CC.; Michael Brooks, SS.CC. In Res. Rev. Michael W. Barry, SS.CC. (LA).

[F] CONVENTS AND RESIDENCES FOR SISTERS

SAN BERNARDINO. *Daughters of St. Joseph of California, F.S.J.*, 6677 Del Rosa Ave., 02404. Tel: 909-888-4877; Fax: 909-888-4387. Email: daughtersjoseph@aol.com. Sr. Rosario Rodriguez, F.S.J., Major Supr. Sisters 4.

CALIMESA. *Missionary Sisters of the Immaculate Conception*, 1271 Nugget Ct., 92320. Fax: 909-795-8128. Email: judinefran@aol.com. Madonna of Desert Community 2.

GRAND TERRACE. *Sisters of St. Benedict, Holy Spirit Monastery*, 22791 Pico St., 92313-5750. Tel: 909-783-4446; Fax: 909-783-3525. Email: hsmonastery@prodigy.net. Web: www.re.net/sanbernardino.hsmonastery. Sr. Mary Ann Schepers, O.S.B., Prioress. Sisters 9.

REDLANDS. *Congregation of the Sisters of Mercy*, Provincial House, 1075 Bermuda Dr., 92374. Tel: 909-798-4747; Fax: 909-798-5300. Email: mbane-sm@sbdiocese.org. Web: www.sistersofmercy.ie. Total in Residence 4.

Sisters of Mercy, U.S. Province, 1075 Bermuda Dr., 92374. Tel: 909-798-4747; Fax: 909-798-5300. Email: tess1075@aol.com. Sr. Maura Bane, Prov. Total in Residence 4.

TEMECULA. *Congregation of Kkottongnae Sisters of Jesus*, 37885 Hwy. 79 S., 92592. Tel: 909-302-3400; Fax: 909-302-3400. Email: tmclkkot@hotmail.com.

TUSTIN. *Sisters of the Company of Mary (O.D.N.)*, 16791 E. Main St., 92780. Tel: 714-541-3125; Fax: 714-835-0648. Email: srdorisodn@sbcglobal.net. Web: www.lestonnac.org. Sr. Mary of Jesus Rodriguez, O.D.N., Major Supr. Total in Residence 12; Total Staff 4.

Vina de Lestonnac Ministry Center-Convent, 39300 De Portola Rd., Temecula, 92592. Tel: 909-302-2800; Fax: 909-302-2830. Total in Residence 9.

Vina de Lestonnac Ministry Center-Retreat, 39300 De Portola Rd., Temecula, 92592. Tel: 909-302-5571; Fax: 909-302-2830. Total Staff 8.

Lestonnac Chalet, 24719 San Moritz Dr., Colton, 92324. Tel: 909-338-1525; Fax: 714-835-0648.

St. Jeanne de Lestonnac School, 32650 Avenida Lestonnac, Temecula, 92592. Tel: 909-587-2505; Fax: 909-587-2515. Email: sjdltem@earthlink.com.

[G] CAMPS & RETREATS

BIG BEAR LAKE. *Sacred Heart Retreat Camp*, 896 Cienega Rd., P.O. Box 1795, 92315. Tel: 909-866-5696; Fax: 909-866-5650. Total in Residence 6; Total Staff 12.

REDLANDS. *El Carmelo Retreat House*, 926 E. Highland Ave., P.O. Box 446, 92373. Tel: 909-792-1047; Fax: 909-798-3479. Email: elcarmelo@juno.com. Revs. Fernando Pinto, O.C.D., Supr.; Dominic O'Callaghan, O.C.D.; Bros. Boniface Scheerer, O.C.D.; Michael Villagomez. Priests 3; Brothers 2; Sisters 4; Total in Residence 9; Total Staff 9.

RIVERSIDE. *Divine Word - Seminary*, Formerly Divine Word Retreat Center, 11316 Cypress Ave., 92505. Tel: 909-689-4858; Fax: 909-785-0327. Email: wjcaffrey@aol.com.

RUNNING SPRINGS. *St. Joachin & St. Anne Retreat Center*, P.O. Box 1760, 92382. Tel: 909-867-2832; Fax: 909-867-2830. Web: mountaincatholic.org.

[H] NEWMAN CENTERS

SAN BERNARDINO. *California State University at San Bernardino* 1201 E. Highland Ave., 92494. Tel: 909-880-7337; Cell: 909-475-5457. Email: wvaldez@sbdiocese.orgFax: 909-816-6393. Wendy Valdez.

REDLANDS. *University of Redlands Newman Community* 1200 E. Colton Ave., P.O. Box 3080, 92373-0999. Fax: 909-475-5457. Sr. Alice Molina, R.S.H.M.

RIVERSIDE. *St. Andrews Newman Center* 105 W. Big Springs Rd., 92507. Tel: 909-682-8751; Fax: 909-682-3513. Email: catholictucr@earthlink.net. Web: home.earthlink.net/~catholicucr/. Rev. David Geib, O.P., Dir. Serving Riverside Community College and University of California at Riverside.

[I] MISCELLANEOUS

SAN BERNARDINO. *Blessed Junipero Serra House of Formation, Inc.*, 1201 E. Highland Ave., 92404. Tel: 909-475-5150; Fax: 909-475-5489. Email: mrwallace@sbdiocese.org. Ms. MaryRose Wallace, CFO.

**Caritas Telecommunications*, 1201 E. Highland Ave., 92404. Tel: 909-475-5350; Fax: 909-475-5357. Email: caritas@sbdiocese.org. Web: www.caritastelecommunications.org. Rev. Paul Granillo, J.C.L., Dir.

The Catholic Foundation, 1201 E. Highland Ave., 92404. Tel: 909-475-5150; Fax: 909-475-5489. Email: mrwallace@sbdiocese.org. Ms. MaryRose Wallace, CFO.

Diocesan Development Fund, Inc., 1201 E. Highland Ave., 92404. Tel: 909-475-5150; Fax: 909-475-5489. Email: mrwallace@sbdiocese.org. Ms. MaryRose Wallace, CFO.

Diocese of San Bernardino Land Development Corporation, 1201 E. Highland Ave., 92404. Tel: 909-475-5150; Fax: 909-475-5489. Email: mrwallace@sbdiocese.org. Ms. MaryRose Wallace, CFO.

**Mary's Mercy Center, Inc.*, 641 Roberds Ave., P.O. Box 7563, 92411. Tel: 909-889-2558; Fax: 909-386-7704. Email: mmcinc@earthlink.net. Web: marysmercycenter.org. Adrienne Schubert, Contact Person.

INDIO. **Martha's Kitchen, Inc.*, 83-791 Date Ave., 92201. Tel: 760-347-4741; Fax: 760-347-9551. Email: gloriagomez@neighbor.org. Web: www.marthasvillage.org. Gloria Gomez, Contact Person.

RIVERSIDE. **Wordnet, Inc.*, 11316 Cypress Ave., 92505. Tel: 909-689-4885; Fax: 909-785-7041. Email: exdir@wordnetproductions.com. Web: wordnetproductions.com. Rev. Michael Manning, S.V.D., Pres.; Jeanne Harris, O.P., Contact Person.

SAN JACINTO. *Kateri Tekakwitha Fund*, P.O. Box 302, 92581-0302. Tel: 909-654-2086; Fax: 909-654-2086. Sr. Marianna Torrano, R.S.C.J., Sec. & CFO.

VICTORVILLE. *Casa Venegas*, 16694 Allen St., 92392-3511. Tel: 760-241-6607. Bro. Gerard Cole, O.H., Contact Person. Home for homeless.

St. John of God Health Care Services, 13333 Palmdale Rd., P.O. Box 2457, 92393. Tel: 760-241-4917; Fax: 760-241-8911. Email: sjghcs@aol.com. Sponsored by the Brothers of St. John of God., Alcohol & Drug Rehabilitation Program. Brothers 1; Staff 48; Bed Capacity 93; Patients Assisted Annually 760.

Board of Trustees: Bro. Richard Gaule, O.H., Pres. & CEO; Sr. Claudette Des Foyes, C.S.J., Chm.; Rev. Ignatius Sudol, O.H. (LA); Bros. Stephen De La Rosa, O.H.; Gabriel Stine, D.C.; Jean Trost, Sec.; Debbie Proper, Recording Sec.; Jim McManus, Treas.

Advisory Council: Rev. David Mousehild; Pete Worse, Chm.; Wayne Rutledge; Cheryl Norton; Barbara Bellflower; Richard Janzer.

RELIGIOUS INSTITUTUES OF MEN REPRESENTED IN THE DIOCESE

For further details refer to the corresponding bracketed number in the Religious Institutes of Men or Women section.

[0140]—*Augustinians*—O.S.A.
[0140]—*The Augustinians* (Phillippines)—O.S.A.
[0140]—*The Augustinians* (Mexico)—O.S.A.
[]—*Byzantine Brothers of St. Francis*—B.B.S.F.
[0470]—*Capuchin Friars*—O.F.M.Cap.
[0360]—*Claretian Missionaries*—C.M.F.
[0610]—*Congregation of Holy Cross*—C.S.C.
[]—*Congregation of Mother Coredemptrix*—C.M.C.
[1330]—*Congregation of the Mission*—C.M.
[1080]—*Congregation of the Resurrection*—C.R.
[1140]—*Congregation of the Sacred Hearts of Jesus and Mary* (Western Prov.)—SS.CC.
[0390]—*Consolata Missionaries*—I.M.C.
[]—*Diocesan Laborer Priests*—D.L.P.
[0260]—*Discalced Carmelite Friars* (Western Prov.)—O.C.D.
[0650]—*Holy Ghost Fathers*—C.S.Sp.
[0670]—*Hospitaller Brothers of St. John of God*—O.H.
[]—*Misioneros Servidores de la Palabra*—M.S.P.
[0720]—*Missionaries of Our Lady of La Salette*—M.S.
[1110]—*Missionaries of the Sacred Heart*—M.S.C.
[0840]—*Missionary Servants of the Most Holy Trinity*—S.T.
[]—*Missioneros de Guadalupe* (MG)
[]—*Operarios del Reino de Cristo*—O.R.C.
[0200]—*Order of Benedict* (MN)—O.S.B.
[0970]—*Order of Our Lady of Mercy*—O.de.M.
[]—*Order of Preachers*—O.P.
[0430]—*Order of Preachers (Dominicans)* (Western Province)—O.P.
[0480]—*Order of the Friars Minor, Conventual*—O.F.M.Conv
[]—*Order of the Imitation of Christ*—O.I.C.
[0690]—*Society of Jesus*—S.J.
[0760]—*Society of Mary*—S.M.
[0370]—*Society of St. Columbian*—S.S.C.
[0420]—*Society of the Divine Word* (Western Prov.)—S.V.D.

RELIGIOUS INSTITUTES OF WOMEN REPRESENTED IN THE DIOCESE

[]—*Adrian Dominican Sisters*—O.P.
[0230]—*Benedictine Sisters of Pontifical Jurisdiction* (Grand Terrace, CA)—O.S.B.
[2930]—*The California Institute of the Sisters of the Most Holy and Immaculate Heart of The Blessed Virgin*—I.H.M.
[3260]—*Congregation of Sisters of the Precious Blood*—C.PP.S.
[2549]—*Congregation of the Sisters of Mary* (U.S. Prov.)—R.S.M.
[3935]—*Congregation of the Sisters of St. Louis, Juilly-Monaghan*—S.S.L.
[0790]—*Daughters of Divine Charity*—F.D.C.
[0790]—*Daughters of Divine Charity* (Akron, OH)—F.D.C.
[0880]—*Daughters of Mary and Joseph*—D.M.J.
[1070-13]—*Dominican Sisters* (Adrian)—O.P.
[1070-20]—*Dominican Sisters* (Tacoma)—O.P.
[1070-19]—*Dominican Sisters* (Houston)—O.P.
[1070-15]—*Dominican Sisters* (Baurelt)—O.P.
[]—*Esclaveras de la Inmaculata Nina* Mexico—E.I.N.
[1170]—*Felician Sisters of the Southwest*—C.S.S.F.
[1230]—*Franciscan Sisters of Christian Charity*—O.S.F.
[]—*Franciscan Sisters of the Heart of Jesus* Pakistan—C.J.H.
[]—*Immaculate Heart Community*—I.H.M.
[2370]—*Institute of the Blessed Virgin Mary (Loretto Sisters)*—I.B.V.M.
[2390]—*Lovers of the Holy Cross Sisters*—L.H.C.
[]—*Misioneras Servidoras de la Palabra* Mexico—M.S.P.
[2800]—*Missionaries of the Sacred Heart of Jesus of Hiltrup*—M.S.C.
[2760]—*Missionary Sisters of the Immaculate Conception of the Mother of God*—S.M.I.C.
[1070]—*Oakford Dominicans*—O.P.
[]—*Oblates of Santa Marta*—O.S.M.
[3130]—*Our Lady of Victory Missionary Sisters*—O.L.V.M.
[3465]—*Religious of the Good Shepherd*—R.G.S.
[3465]—*Religious of the Sacred Heart of Mary*—R.S.H.M.
[1680]—*School Sisters of St. Francis*—O.S.F.
[]—*Servants of Holiness*—S.O.H.
[]—*Sisters for Christian Community*—S.F.C.C.
[0430]—*Sisters of Charity of the Blessed Virgin Mary*—B.V.M.
[]—*Sisters of Charity of the Incarnate Word*—C.C.V.I.
[1010]—*Sisters of Divine Providence of San Antonio, TX*—C.D.P.
[2360]—*Sisters of Loretto at the Foot of the Cross*—S.L.
[2549]—*Sisters of Mercy* (Sligo, Ireland)—R.S.M.
[2590]—*Sisters of Mercy of the Blessed Sacrament*—H.M.S.S.
[3360]—*Sisters of Providence of St. Mary of-the-Woods*—S.P.
[1540]—*Sisters of Saint Francis* Clinton, Iowa—O.S.F.
[4080]—*Sisters of Social Service*—S.S.S.
[]—*Sisters of St. Benedict*—O.S.B.
[3770]—*Sisters of St. Clare*—O.S.C.
[1070-12]—*Sisters of St. Dominic* (San Jose)—O.P.
[1720]—*Sisters of St. Francis*—O.S.F.
[1650]—*The Sisters of St. Francis of Philadelphia*—O.S.F.
[1550]—*Sisters of St. Francis of the Holy Cross*—O.S.F.
[3830-03]—*Sisters of St. Joseph*—C.S.J.
[3830-15]—*Sisters of St. Joseph* (Concordia, KS)—C.S.J.
[3840]—*Sisters of St. Joseph of Carondolet*—C.S.J.
[3890]—*Sisters of St. Joseph of Peace*—C.S.J.P.
[3830-03]—*Sisters of St. Joseph,Orange*—C.S.J.
[0700]—*Sisters of the Company of Mary Our Lady*—O.D.N.
[1990]—*Sisters of the Holy Names of Jesus and Mary*—S.N.J.M.
[4050]—*Sisters of the Society Devoted to the Sacred Heart*—S.D.S.H.
[1720]—*Sisters of the Third Order Regular of St. Francis of the Congregation of Our Lady of Lourdes* (Rochester)—O.S.F.
[2150]—*Sisters, Servants of the Immaculate Heart of Mary*—I.H.M.
[4070]—*Society of the Sacred Heart*—R.S.C.J.
[3320]—*Union of Sisters of the Presentation of the B.V.M.*—P.B.V.M.

NECROLOGY

✠ O'Neil, Most Rev. Dennis Patrick, Auxiliary Bishop of San Bernardino—Died Oct. 17, 2003
† Guillen, Manuel R., (Retired)—Died Dec. 1, 2003
† Jalbert, Marcel P., (Retired)—Died Aug. 23, 2003

Diocese of San Diego

(Dioecesis Sancti Didaci)

Most Reverend

ROBERT H. BROM, D.D.

Bishop of San Diego; ordained December 18, 1963; appointed Bishop of Duluth March 25, 1983; consecrated and installed May 23, 1983; appointed Coadjutor Bishop of San Diego April 22, 1989; appointed Bishop of San Diego July 10, 1990 *Office: P.O. Box 85728, San Diego, CA 92186-5728.* Tel: 858-490-8200.

Most Reverend

GILBERT E. CHAVEZ

Auxiliary Bishop of San Diego; ordained March 19, 1960; appointed Auxiliary Bishop of San Diego and Titular Bishop of Magarmel April 19, 1974; Episcopal ordination June 21, 1974. *Res.: 1535 Third Ave., San Diego, CA 92101.*

Pastoral Center: P.O. Box 85728, San Diego, CA 92186-5728. Tel: 858-490-8200; Fax: 858-490-8272.

Web: www.diocese-sdiego.org

Email: scallaha@diocese-sdiego.org

Most Reverend

SALVATORE J. CORDILEONE

Auxiliary Bishop of San Diego; ordained July 9, 1982; appointed Auxiliary Bishop of San Diego and Titular Bishop of Natchez July 5, 2002; Episcopal ordination August 21, 2002 *Office: P.O. Box 85728, San Diego, CA 92186-5728.*

ESTABLISHED JULY 11, 1936.

Square Miles 8,852.

Comprises the Counties of Imperial and San Diego in the State of California.

Legal Title: The Roman Catholic Bishop of San Diego, a Corporation Sole--(Churches, Rectories, Halls, Catechetical Centers, etc.) Diocese of San Diego.

Legal Title: *For legal titles of parishes and diocesan institutions, consult the Diocesan Office.*

STATISTICAL OVERVIEW

Personnel	
Bishop	1
Auxiliary Bishops	2
Abbots	1
Retired Abbots	1
Priests: Diocesan Active in Diocese	109
Priests: Diocesan Active Outside Diocese	7
Priests: Retired, Sick or Absent	80
Number of Diocesan Priests	196
Religious Priests in Diocese	98
Total Priests in Diocese	294
Extern Priests in Diocese	82
Ordinations:	
Transitional Deacons	1
Permanent Deacons	3
Permanent Deacons in Diocese	104
Total Brothers	20
Total Sisters	328
Parishes	
Parishes	98
With Resident Pastor:	
Resident Diocesan Priests	85
Resident Religious Priests	11
Without Resident Pastor:	
Administered by Priests	1
Administered by Lay People	1
Missions	17
Pastoral Centers	1
Welfare	
Catholic Hospitals	1
Total Assisted	20,974
Health Care Centers	1
Total Assisted	17,843
Homes for the Aged	5
Total Assisted	648
Residential Care of Children	1
Total Assisted	65
Day Care Centers	1
Total Assisted	632
Specialized Homes	16
Total Assisted	84,953
Special Centers for Social Services	9
Total Assisted	84,685
Residential Care of Disabled	1
Total Assisted	65
Other Institutions	3
Total Assisted	456
Educational	
Diocesan Students in Other Seminaries	11
Total Seminarians	11
Colleges and Universities	1
Total Students	7,262
High Schools, Diocesan and Parish	3
Total Students	2,321
High Schools, Private	2
Total Students	1,476
Elementary Schools, Diocesan and Parish	43
Total Students	13,366
Elementary Schools, Private	1
Total Students	238
Non-residential Schools for the Disabled	1
Total Students	217
Catechesis/Religious Education:	
High School Students	8,120
Elementary Students	38,500
Total Students under Catholic Instruction	71,511
Teachers in the Diocese:	
Priests	4
Sisters	36
Lay Teachers	1,055
Vital Statistics	
Receptions into the Church:	
Infant Baptism Totals	11,908
Adult Baptism Totals	1,845
Received into Full Communion	1,145
First Communions	8,994
Confirmations	4,255
Marriages:	
Catholic	1,430
Interfaith	443
Total Marriages	1,873
Deaths	2,345
Total Catholic Population	930,379
Total Population	3,041,195

Former Bishops—Most Revs. CHARLES F. BUDDY, D.D., S.T.D., Ph.D., ord. Sept. 19, 1914; appt. First Bishop of San Diego, Oct. 31, 1936; consecrated Dec. 21, 1936; named Asst. at Pontifical Throne, Jan. 12, 1964; died March 6, 1966; FRANCIS J. FUREY, D.D., Ph.D., LL.D., ord. March 15, 1930; appt. Auxiliary Bishop of Philadelphia, Aug. 24, 1960; consecrated Dec. 22, 1960; succeeded to the See of San Diego, March 6, 1966; translated to Archbishop of San Antonio, June 4, 1969; died April 23, 1979; LEO T. MAHER, D.D. (Retired), Bishop of San Diego; ord. Dec. 18, 1943; First Bishop of Santa Rosa; appt. Feb. 21, 1962; consecrated April 5, 1962; translated to San Diego, Aug. 27, 1969; retired July 10, 1990; died Feb. 23, 1991.

Pastoral Center—3888 Paducah Dr., San Diego, 92117. Mailing Address, P.O. Box 85728, San Diego, 92186-5728. Tel: 858-490-8200; Fax: 858-490-8272. Office Hours: Mon.-Fri. 8:30-4:30

Auxiliary Bishops—Most Revs. GILBERT E. CHAVEZ, D.D., 1535 Third Ave., San Diego, 92101-3192. Tel: 619-239-0229; SALVATORE J. CORDILEONE, J.C.D., P.O. Box 85728, San Diego, 92186-5728.

Vicar General—Very Rev. Msgr. STEVEN CALLAHAN, J.C.L. Tel: 858-490-8310.

Chancellor—RODRIGO VALDIVIA, J.C.L. Tel: 858-490-8310.

Assistant to Bishop Robert H. Brom—Rev. EARL EGGLESTON. Tel: 858-490-8315.

Judicial Vicar—Very Rev. Msgr. STEVEN CALLAHAN, J.C.L.

Diocesan Tribunal

Adjutant Judicial Vicar—Rev. EDWARD P. MCNULTY, J.C.L.

Promoter of Justice—Rev. Msgr. DANIEL DILLABOUGH, S.T.D., J.C.L.

Defenders of the Bond—Rev. Msgr. DANIEL DILLABOUGH; Rev. ANTHONY ODOZI JR., J.C.L.; MARY JO GRETZINGER, S.T.L., J.C.L.

Diocesan Judges—Revs. DAVID CROISETIERE, J.C.L., M.C.L.; BRIAN HAYES, J.C.L.; ROBERT IRWIN; RODRIGO VALDIVIA, J.C.L.

Tribunal Auditors—Deacons RAYMOND ARNOLD; ROBERT FITZMORRIS.

Notaries—CONNIE NOEL; LETICIA MENDOZA.

Diocesan Offices and Directors

Archivist—Contact: Chancellor's Office. Tel: 858-490-8208.

Catholic Charities—Sr. RAYMONDA DUVALL, C.H.S., Exec. Dir., 349 Cedar St., San Diego, 92101. Tel: 619-231-2828.

Cemetery Committee—Rev. Msgr. W. FRANCIS PATTISON, Dir., Holy Cross Cemetery, 4470 Hilltop Dr., San Diego, 92102. Tel: 619-264-3127.

Censores Librorum—Rev. Msgr. RICHARD DUNCANSON, S.T.D.; Revs. DENNIS KROUSE, S.T.D.; NORBERT RIGALI, S.J.; BERNADEANE CARR, S.T.L.; TERENCE MCGOLDRICK, S.T.D.

Civil Affairs—ALEXANDRA KELLY, Esq., Dir. Tel: 858-490-8277; JAMES MULLEN, Esq., Counsel.

Clergy Counseling and Spiritual Direction—Rev. JOHN FLANNERY, O.P., Dir. Tel: 619-291-5042.

Communications—BERNADEANE CARR, S.T.L., Dir. Tel: 858-490-8370.

Computer Services—Deacon JOHN ELLIS, Information Systems Admin. Tel: 858-490-8329; RAJESH BALAKRISHMAN, Senior Systems Analyst. Tel: 858-490-8222.

Construction Services—JOEL KING, Dir. Tel: 858-490-8215.

Ecumenical and Interreligious Affairs—Rev. Msgr. DENNIS MIKULANIS, S.T.D., Vicar, 17252 Bernardo Center Dr., Rancho Bernardo, 92128-2086. Tel: 858-487-4314.

Education—

Evangelization & Catechetical Ministry—GINGER INFANTINO, Dir. Tel: 858-490-8232; MARYJO WAGGONER, Assoc. Dir. for Hispanic Catechesis. Tel: 858-490-8233.

Hispanic Evangelization—Sr. GLORIA GALVAN, S.F.C.C., Assoc. Dir. for Hispanic Evangelization. Tel: 858-490-8214.

Institute for Adult Education and Formation for Ministry—TERENCE MCGOLDRICK, S.T.D., Dir. Tel: 858-490-8212.

Schools—THOMAS BEECHER, Dir. Tel: 858-490-8240; Sr. BREEGE BOYLE, S.S.L., Assoc. Dir. Tel: 858-490-8240; PATRICIA BANNON, Assoc. Dir. Tel: 858-490-8244.

Media Center—JOAN KOEHMSTEDT, Asst. Dir. Tel: 858-490-8237.

Youth and Young Adult Ministry—MARISSA ESPARZA, Dir. Tel: 619-490-8260. Assistant Directors:: SANTIAGO ROBLES; MARISSA ESPARAZA. Tel: 619-490-8260.

Facilities and Related Services—RODRIGO VALDIVIA, J.C.L., Dir. Tel: 858-490-8301.

Finance—H.L. "HAL" GARDNER, Finance Officer. Tel: 858-490-8284; KAREN JASSOY, Dir., Accounting. Tel: 858-490-8207.

Hispanic Affairs—ENRIQUE MENDEZ, Dir. Tel: 858-490-8249.

Human Resources—MICHAEL CROLL, Dir. Tel: 858-490-8282.

Liturgy and Spirituality—MARY ANN FALLON, Dir. Tel: 858-490-8290; JENSINE NOLAN, Asst. Dir. Liturgical Music. Tel: 858-490-8294.

Marriage and Family Life—Directors: JANICE KEITH; DON KEITH. Tel: 858-490-8295.

Missions—Rev. PETER RUGGERE, M.M., Dir.; Sr. MARY DIETZ, S.S.N.D., Assoc. Dir. Tel: 858-490-8250.

Multicultural Affairs—RODRIGO VALDIVIA, J.C.L., Dir. Tel: 858-490-8301.

Permanent Diaconate—Sr. CARLOTTA DI LORENZO, C.S.J., Dir.; JOSE ERNESTO GONZALEZ, Assoc. Tel: 858-490-8239.

Priests—Rev. MICHAEL MURPHY, Dir., 655 C Ave., Coronado, 92118-3167. Tel: 619-291-9539.

Priestly Formation -- St. Francis de Sales Center—Rev. MATTHEW SPAHR, Dir.

Social Ministry—KENT PETERS, Dir.; JIM WALSH, Asst. Dir.; LINDA ARREOLA, Asst. Dir. Tel: 858-490-8323.

"Southern Cross"--(Diocesan Newspaper)—CYRIL JONES-KELLETT, Editor. Tel: 858-490-8268; ANN BURKE, Advertising. Tel: 858-490-8366.

Special Events—JO-ELLEN LARUE, Dir. Tel: 858-490-8334.

Stewardship and Development—JAMES RICHARDS, Dir. Tel: 858-490-8280.

Vocations—Deacon RAY ARNOLD, Dir. Tel: 858-490-8351.

Women Religious—Tel: 858-490-8289.

Advisory Bodies

Clergy Personnel Board—Very Rev. Msgr. STEVEN CALLAHAN, J.C.L., Chm. Tel: 858-490-8310.

College of Consultors—Most Revs. GILBERT E. CHAVEZ, D.D.; SALVATORE J. CORDILEONE, J.C.D.; Rev. Msgrs. DANIEL J. DILLABOUGH; JOHN A. DICKIE; W. FRANCIS PATTISON; Very Rev. Msgrs. LAWRENCE PURCELL; STEVEN CALLAHAN, J.C.L.; Revs. EDWARD MCNULTY; MATTHEW SPAHR; CAVANA WALLACE.

Diocesan Pastoral Council—Most Rev. ROBERT H. BROM, Ex Officio.

Finance Council—Most Rev. ROBERT H. BROM, Chm.; Mr. THOMAS BLAKE; Very Rev. Msgr. STEVEN CALLAHAN, J.C.L.; Dr. CONSTANCE CARROLL; Mrs. SUSAN CARTER; Mr. DEAN DWYER; Mr. MICHAEL EYER; Mr. DAVID GARDNER; Mr. MICHAEL MAHER; Mr. TIMOTHY MEISSNER; Deacon FRANK MERCARDANTE; Mr. RICHARD MIRANDO; Mr. RALPH RUBIO; Rev. Msgr. DONAL SHEAHAN; Mr. RICHARD VANDERHOFF.

Presbyteral Council—Most Revs. ROBERT H. BROM, D.D.; GILBERT E. CHAVEZ, D.D.; SALVATORE J. CORDILEONE, J.C.D.; Rev. Msgr. W. FRANCIS PATTISON; Rev. EARL EGGLESTON, Exec. Sec.; Rev. Msgrs. JOHN DICKIE; ROGER LECHNER; Very Rev. Msgr. STEVEN CALLAHAN, J.C.L.; Rev. Msgr. EDWARD BROCKHAUS; Revs. BRIAN M. CORCORAN; CECILIO T. MORAGA; Very Rev. BRUCE ORSBORN; Revs. BRIAN HAYES, J.C.L.; GARY HOLTEY; MICHAEL MURPHY; CHARLES FULD; JOHN DOLAN; JAMES POULSEN; MATTHEW SPAHR; CAVANA WALLACE; FRANCIS P. FOLEY.

Vicars Forane—Very Revs. MICHAEL BAUMGARDNER, Cathedral; RAYMOND O'DONNELL, El Cajon; JAMES RAFFERTY, Escondido; RAMON MARRUFO, Oceanside; JAIME ESCOBEDO, El Centro; BRUCE ORSBORN, South Bay; Very Rev. Msgr. LAWRENCE PURCELL, Mission Deanery.

Miscellaneous

Apostleship of the Sea—Deacon JAIME AQUINO, Chap. Tel: 858-271-9386; Rev. JAMES BOYD, Chap.

Charismatic Renewal—SHAWN QUINN, Admin., 2725 55th St., San Diego, 92105-5094. Tel: 619-263-1700.

Hispanic Charismatic Renewal Center—PEDRO LUNA, Coord. Tel: 619-640-2474.

Christ Child Society—Rev. ANTON KOLLAR, O.Carm., Spiritual Advisor. Tel: 619-291-4529.

Cursillo—Rev. LOUIS LEVESQUE, C.J.M., Spiritual Advisor; JIM KOED, Lay Dir. Tel: 760-740-9324.

Filipino—REMY JIMENEZ, Lay Dir.; Rev. MANUEL EDIZA, Spiritual Advisor; Deacon JAIME AQUINO, Assoc. Spiritual Advisor. Tel: 619-424-6349.

Hispanic—MARGARITA SANDOVAL, Pres. Secretariat; Rev. ANDRES RIVERO, O.F.M., Spiritual Advisor. Tel: 619-232-6681.

Vietnamese—Rev. BIEN QUANG DO, Spiritual Advisor; NGHI VU, Lay Dir. Tel: 858-272-9356.

Holy Childhood Association—Rev. PETER RUGGERE, M.M., Dir., P.O. Box 82386, San Diego, 92138-2386. Tel: 858-490-8250.

Propagation of the Faith—Rev. PETER RUGGERE, M.M., Dir.; Sr. MARY DIETZ, S.S.N.D., Assoc. Dir., P.O. Box 82386, San Diego, 92186-2386. Tel: 858-490-8250.

Victim Assistance Coordinator—ADLIN DE CARDI. Tel: 858-571-8317. Email: adecardi@yahoo.com.

CLERGY, PARISHES, MISSIONS AND PAROCHIAL SCHOOLS

CITY OF SAN DIEGO
(SAN DIEGO COUNTY)

1—ST. JOSEPH CATHEDRAL (1874), Most Rev. Gilbert E. Chavez, D.D. In Res., Revs. Paul Balio; William Ortmann.
Res.: 1535 Third Ave., 92101-3192. Tel: 619-239-0229; Fax: 619-239-3788.
Catechesis/Religious Program—Students 305.

2—ST. AGNES (Pt. Loma) (1908), Rev. Joseph Mel Collier.
Res.: 1140 Evergreen St., 92106. Tel: 619-223-2200; Fax: 619-223-7568.
Catechesis/Religious Program—Tel: 619-223-9748; Fax: 619-223-4725. Mrs. Elise Spondike, D.R.E. Students 164.

3—ST. ANNE (1921), Rev. Robert D. Nikliborc, Admin.
Res.: 621 Sicard St., 92113-2334. Tel: 619-239-8253; Fax: 619-239-8253.
Catechesis/Religious Program—Tel: 619-263-5913. Students 300.

4—ASCENSION (1980), Rev. Charles L. Fuld (Retired); Deacon Jim Scull.
Res.: 11292 Clairemont Mesa Blvd., 92124-1524. Tel: 858-279-2735; Fax: 858-279-1023.
Catechesis/Religious Program—Tel: 858-279-2752. Students 185.

5—BLESSED SACRAMENT (1938), Revs. William F. Rowland, C.J.M.; Louis Levesque, C.J.M.; James Burson, C.J.M.; Deacons Alfred Albers; Frank Reilly. In Res., Rev. Jerry Hamperzonian.
Res.: 4540 El Cerrito Dr., 92115. Tel: 619-582-5722; Fax: 619-582-2505.
School—Tel: 619-582-3862; Fax: 619-265-9310. Ms. Theodora Furtado, Prin. Lay Teachers 19; Students 354.
Catechesis/Religious Program—Tel: 619-582-4633; Fax: 619-582-2525. Students 156.
Mission—SDSU Newman Center 5855 Hardy Ave., San Diego Co. 92115. Tel: 619-583-9181; Fax: 619-583-8925.

6—ST. BRIGID (Pacific Beach) (1940), Very Rev. Msgr. Steven Callahan; Rev. Msgr. Sean Murray, Pastor Emeritus; Rev. Anthony Odozi Jr., J.C.L.
Church & Res.: 4735 Cass St., 92109-2698. Tel: 858-483-3030; Fax: 858-483-7131.
Catechesis/Religious Program—Tel: 858-483-3032. Sisters Hilda McDonagh, R.S.M., D.R.E.; Josephine Breen, D.R.E. Students 195.

7—ST. CATHERINE LABOURE (1964), Rev. Joseph Brady.
Mailing Address: 4124 Mt. Abraham Ave., 92111.
Res.: 4026 Mt. Abraham Ave., 92111. Tel: 858-277-3133; Fax: 858-277-9181.
Catechesis/Religious Program—Tel: 619-279-0587. Sandra Welch, D.R.E. Students 320.

8—ST. CHARLES (1946), Revs. Fernando Ramirez; Remberto Selga; Deacons Seodello Martinez; Mick Dennison.
Res.: 990 Saturn Blvd., 92154. Tel: 619-423-0242; Fax: 619-423-1966.
School—Tel: 619-423-3701; Fax: 619-423-5331. Sisters of Mercy 1; Lay Teachers 13; Students 290.
Catechesis/Religious Program—Tel: 619-575-2240. Students 536.

9—ST. CHARLES BORROMEO (1946), Rev. Gary Holtey.
Res.: 2802 Cadiz St., 92110-4813. Tel: 619-225-8157; Fax: 619-225-2288.
School—Tel: 619-223-8271; Fax: 619-223-2695. Sisters 2; Lay Teachers 12; Students 244.
Catechesis/Religious Program—Students 21.

10—CHRIST THE KING (1938), Rev. Joseph Spieler, S.J.; Deacon Harry Guess Jr.
Res.: 29 N. 32nd St., 92102. Tel: 619-231-8906; Fax: 619-238-7060.
Catechesis/Religious Program—Students 250.

11—ST. COLUMBA (1955), Rev. Msgr. Patrick J. Mullarkey; Deacon Nick Santiago. In Res., Rev. Frank Mannion, S.S.C.
Res.: 3327 Glencolum Dr., 92123. Tel: 858-277-3863; Fax: 858-279-9053.
School—(Grades PreK-8) Tel: 858-279-1882; Fax: 858-279-1653. Lay Teachers 16; Students 318.
Catechesis/Religious Program—Tel: 858-277-3861. Students 132.

12—ST. DIDACUS (1926), Rev. Michael Baumgardner.
Res.: 4772 Felton St., 92116. Tel: 619-284-3472; Fax: 619-284-3484.
School—4630 34th St., 92116. Tel: 619-284-8730; Fax: 619-284-1764. Lay Teachers 15; Students 280.
Catechesis/Religious Program—Tel: 619-284-7050. Michael Molino, D.R.E. Students 68.

13—GOOD SHEPHERD (1970), Revs. Michael Robinson; Richard Huston; Jose Luis Muro; Deacons Magno Carpizo; Alberto Paras; Jaime Aquino.
Res.: 8200 Gold Coast Dr., 92126-3699. Tel: 858-271-0207; Fax: 858-271-0748.
School—8180 Gold Coast Dr., 92126. Tel: 858-693-1522; Fax: 858-271-3439. Mrs. Chris Corpora, Prin. Lay Teachers 14; Students 297.
Catechesis/Religious Program—Tel: 858-271-8769; Fax: 858-271-0207. Mrs. Emily Aquino, D.R.E. Lay Teachers 73; Students 1,050.

14—ST. GREGORY THE GREAT (1985), Rev. James N. Poulsen; Deacons L. Ferris Bell; Ronald H. Diem.
Mailing Address: 11451 Blue Cypress Dr., 92131. Tel: 858-653-3540; Fax: 858-653-3550.
Catechesis/Religious Program—Tel: 858-653-3594. Students 1,005.

15—HOLY FAMILY (Linda Vista) (1942), Revs. Jovencio Ricafort; Michael Pham, Co-Pastor; Gerardo Fernandez; Deacons Thomas Dougherty; Paul Davidson; John A. Ellis.
Res.: 1957 Coolidge St., 92111-7098. Tel: 858-277-0404; Fax: 858-279-6414.
School—Tel: 858-277-0222; Fax: 858-277-0224. Lay Teachers 14; Students 207.
Catechesis/Religious Program—Tel: 619-268-0557. Students 600.

16—HOLY SPIRIT (1952), Rev. Msgr. Roger A. Lechner; Rev. Doan Van Lai; Deacon Marvin Threatt.
Res.: 2725-55th St., 92105-5094. Tel: 619-262-2435; Fax: 619-262-8718.
Catechesis/Religious Program—Tel: 619-263-9307. Students 280.

17—IMMACULATA (1958), Rev. Matthew Spahr.
University of San Diego Campus: 5998 Alcala Park, 92110-2492. Tel: 619-574-5700; Fax: 619-574-5707.
Catechesis/Religious Program—Tel: 619-574-5702; 619-574-5703. Students 130.

18—IMMACULATE CONCEPTION (1849), [CEM] Rev. Msgr. Mark Campbell.
Res.: 2540 San Diego Ave., 92110-2840. Tel: 619-295-4148; Fax: 619-297-6916.

19—ST. JEROME (1985), Very Rev. Bruce J. Orsborn; Deacon Raul Hernandez.
Office—2515 Beyer Blvd., 92154-1502. Tel: 619-423-0405; Fax: 619-423-9363.
Catechesis/Religious Program—Tel: 619-423-5302. Veronica Arce, D.R.E. Students 356.

20—ST. JOHN THE EVANGELIST (1913), Rev. William Dillard. In Res., Rev. Manuel Ediza.
Res.: 1638 Polk Ave., 92103. Tel: 619-291-1660; Fax: 619-291-4597.
Catechesis/Religious Program—Students 31.

21—ST. JUDE (1946), (Hispanic), [CEM] Revs. Henry Rodriguez; Carlos Torres; Deacon Manuel Nunez.
Res.: 1129 S. 38th St., 92113-3210. Tel: 619-264-2195; Fax: 619-264-8528.
School—1228 S. 38th St., 92113. Tel: 619-264-3154; Fax: 619-264-8050. Lay Teachers 13; Students 305.
School—St. Jude's Child Care and Development Center, 1129 S. 38th St., 92113. Tel: 619-264-8256; Fax: 619-264-8256.
St. Jude's Senior Nutrition Program—Tel: 619-264-4771; Fax: 619-264-9175.
Catechesis/Religious Program—Tel: 619-264-4795. Enedina Sauceda, D.R.E. (Spanish); Eddie Johnson,

D.R.E. (English). Students 711.

22—ST. MARY MAGDALENE (Clairemont) (1953), Rev. Msgr. John A. Dickie; Rev. Anthony C. May; Deacons Robert H. Fitzmorris; James Keeley.
Res.: 1945 Illion St., 92110. Tel: 619-276-1041; Fax: 619-276-0144.
School—Tel: 619-276-6545; Fax: 619-276-5359. Lay Teachers 33; Students 596.
Catechesis/Religious Program—Tel: 619-276-1248. Mrs. Margaret Mansur, D.R.E. Students 135.

23—ST. MAXIMILIAN KOLBE MISSION (1971), (Polish),, (Quasi Parish) Rev. Edward Traczyk, S.Ch.
Res.: 1735 Grand Ave., 92109. Tel: 858-272-7655; Fax: 858-668-0485.
Catechesis/Religious Program—Tel: 619-668-0485. Students 50.

24—ST. MICHAEL (1957), (Filipino), Revs. Ronald Cochran; Bernard Ranoa.
Res.: 2643 Homedale St., 92139. Tel: 619-470-1977; Fax: 619-470-6357.
School—Preschool, 6285 Seascape Dr.. Tel: 619-472-5437; Fax: 619-470-5231.
School—2637 Homedale St., 92139. Tel: 619-470-4880; Fax: 619-470-1050. Lay Teachers 14; Students 385.
Catechesis/Religious Program—Tel: 619-470-2291; Fax: 619-267-9397. Mr. Louis Costa, D.R.E. Students 934.

25—MISSION BASILICA SAN DIEGO DE ALCALA (1769),, (California's First Mission) Rev. Msgr. Thomas Prendergast; Revs. Earl E. Eggleston; William A. Springer; Deacons Bill Vasquez; Ernest Grosso.
Res.: 10818 San Diego Mission Rd., 92108-2429. Tel: 619-283-7319; Fax: 619-283-7762.
Catechesis/Religious Program—Tel: 619-624-0900; Fax: 619-624-0019. Students 255.

26—OUR LADY OF ANGELS (1906), (Hispanic), Rev. Higinio Garcia. In Res., Most Rev. Salvatore J. Cordileone, J.C.D.
Res.: 656 24th St., 92102-2911. Tel: 619-239-1231; Fax: 619-234-5520.
School—Our Lady's School-North Campus, 650 24th St., 92102. Tel: 619-233-8888; Fax: 619-501-2951. Sisters 1; Lay Teachers 11; Students 271.
Catechesis/Religious Program—Alicia Gutierrez, D.R.E. Students 426.

27—OUR LADY OF GUADALUPE (1919), (Mexican), Revs. Richard H. Brown, S.J.; James I. Rasura, S.J.; Augusto Berrio, S.J.; John P. Auther, S.J.; Gilbert Chacon, S.J.
Res.: 1770 Kearny Ave., 92113-1128. Tel: 619-233-3838; Fax: 619-233-3252.
School—Our Lady's School-South Campus, 744 Beardsley, 92113. Tel: 619-233-8888; Fax: 619-233-0982. Lay Teachers 4; Students 97.
Catechesis/Religious Program—Tel: 619-233-3838; Fax: 619-233-3252. Students 420.

28—OUR LADY OF MT. CARMEL (Rancho Penasquitos) (1976), Rev. Msgr. Henry F. Fawcett; Rev. Andre Ramos; Deacons Bernard Yeatts; H. Thomas Jones; Manuel Porciuncula; John Phelps.
Res.: 13541 Stoney Creek Rd., 92129. Tel: 858-566-3550; 858-484-1070; Fax: 858-484-6157.
Catechesis/Religious Program—Students 1,600.

29—OUR LADY OF REFUGE (Pacific Beach) (1977), Rev. David N. Croisetiere.
Res.: 4226 Jewell St., 92109. Tel: 858-274-9670; Fax: 858-274-7486.
Catechesis/Religious Program—Tel: 858-274-2959. Jose Ferrer, D.R.E. Students 59.

30—OUR LADY OF THE ROSARY (1925), (Italian), Revs. Steven M. Grancini, C.R.S.P.; Louis M. Solcia, C.R.S.P.
Res.: 1659 Columbia St., 92101-2584. Tel: 619-234-4820; Fax: 619-234-3559.
Catechesis/Religious Program—Tel: 619-234-4820; Fax: 619-234-3445. Esther Leuzzi, D.R.E. Students 196.

31—OUR LADY OF THE SACRED HEART (1911), Revs. Edmundo Zarate-Suarez; Joseph Phien Van Pham.
Res.: 4177 Marlborough Ave., 92105-1412. Tel: 619-280-0515; Fax: 619-280-0517.
School—Tel: 619-284-1715; Fax: 619-284-8332. Sr. Linda Lutz, Prin. Lay Teachers 14; Students 220.
Catechesis/Religious Program—Tel: 619-283-9262; Fax: 619-283-0159. Ms. Ada Padilla, D.R.E. Students 660.

32—OUR MOTHER OF CONFIDENCE (University City) (1964), Rev. Msgr. Donal C. Sheahan; Deacons William Klopchin; Arnold Hess.
Res.: 3131 Governor Dr., 92122. Tel: 858-453-0222; Fax: 858-453-2547.
Catechesis/Religious Program—Tel: 858-453-3554. Pat Baker, D.R.E. Students 303.

33—ST. PATRICK (1921), Rev. Thomas G. Verber, O.S.A.; Deacon Carl Shelton. In Res., Rev. Anthony J. Wasko, O.S.A.
Res.: 3585 30th St., 92104. Tel: 619-295-2157; Fax: 619-688-1225.
School—Tel: 619-297-1314; Fax: 619-297-3346. Lay Teachers 10; Students 205.
Catechesis/Religious Program—Students 110.
Chapel—St. Augustine 3266 Nutmeg St., 92104. Tel: 619-282-2028; Fax: 619-282-1203.

34—ST. RITA (1941), Rev. Msgr. Francis Pattison; Rev. Elmer Mandac.
Res.: 5124 Churchward St., 92114-3797 Tel: 619-264-3165; Fax: 619-264-2907.
School—Tel: 619-264-0109. Lay Teachers 13; Students 259.
Catechesis/Religious Program—Tel: 619-264-4399. Sr. Margaret Castro, D.R.E. Students 483.

35—SACRED HEART (Ocean Beach) (1911), Rev. Ronald Hebert; Deacon Giles Schmitt.
Res.: 4776 Saratoga, 92107-9990. Tel: 619-224-2746; Fax: 619-224-0459.
School—Tel: 619-222-7252; Fax: 619-222-2836. Mr. Robert Hamm, Prin. Lay Teachers 12; Students 245.
Catechesis/Religious Program—Tel: 619-223-4594. Cathleen Hornsby, D.R.E. Students 77.

36—SAN RAFAEL (Rancho Bernardo) (1974), Rev. Msgrs. Dennis Mikulanis; Lloyd Bourgeois, Pastor Emeritus; Deacon Leonard Vaillancourt, Pastoral Assoc.
Res.: 17252 Bernardo Center, 92128. Tel: 858-487-4314; Fax: 858-487-1498.
Catechesis/Religious Program—Tel: 858-487-0491. Sisters Laura Abat, O.S.F., D.R.E.; Ann Gertrude Vierra, O.S.F., D.R.E. Students 711.

37—ST. THERESE (1956), Rev. Msgr. Frederick J. Florek; Rev. John Cuddigan, S.J.; Deacons Leo Dube; Robert Ekhaml.
Res.: 6016 Camino Rico, 92120-3099. Tel: 619-582-3716; Fax: 619-582-2535.
School—St. Therese Academy, Tel: 619-583-6270; Fax: 619-583-5721. Sisters 4; Lay Teachers 16; Students 324.
Catechesis/Religious Program—Tel: 619-582-2585. Sr. Damien Peters, F.D.C., D.R.E. Students 242.

38—ST. VINCENT DE PAUL (1910), Rev. Nicholas P. Clavin.
Res.: 4077 Ibis St., 92103-1899. Tel: 619-299-3881; Fax: 619-299-9509.
School—Tel: 619-296-2222; Fax: 619-296-2763. Sisters of Mercy 2; Lay Teachers 16; Students 244.
Catechesis/Religious Program—Tel: 619-295-9672. Students 107.

OUTSIDE THE CITY OF SAN DIEGO

ALPINE, SAN DIEGO CO., QUEEN OF ANGELS (1950), Revs. Edward McNulty; Matthew D. Spahr.
Res.: 2569 Victoria Dr., 91901-3662. Tel: 619-445-2145; Fax: 619-445-9682.
Catechesis/Religious Program—Students 360.

BONITA, SAN DIEGO CO., CORPUS CHRISTI (1984), Rev. John G. Proctor Jr.; Deacon James H. Hitch.
Mailing Address: P.O. Box 1349, 91908-1349.
Res.: 2934 Degen Dr., 91902. Tel: 619-482-3954; Fax: 619-482-7236.
Church: 450 Corral Canyon Rd., 91902-4072.
Catechesis/Religious Program—Tel: 619-482-3953; Fax: 619-482-7236. Michael Wickham, D.R.E. Students 600.

BORREGO SPRINGS, SAN DIEGO CO., ST. RICHARD (1954), [CEM] Rev. Brian C. Hayes.
Res.: P.O. Box 1128, 92004-1128. Tel: 760-767-5701; Fax: 760-767-5701.
Catechesis/Religious Program—Students 124.
Mission— P.O. Box 5660, Salton City, Imperial Co. 92275.

BRAWLEY, IMPERIAL CO.

1—ST. MARGARET MARY (1934), (Hispanic), Rev. Roque P. Vano.
Res.: 620 S. Cesar Chavez St., 92227. Tel: 760-344-3571; Fax: 760-344-3598.
Catechesis/Religious Program—Tel: 760-344-6515; Fax: 760-344-7598. Students 451.

2—OUR LADY OF PERPETUAL HELP (1956), (Hispanic), Rev. Jorge Moreno.
Res.: 1250 B St., P.O. Box 1283, 92227. Tel: 760-344-2226; Fax: 760-344-1557.
Catechesis/Religious Program—Tel: 760-344-5787. Maria Elena Estrada, D.R.E. Students 263.

3—SACRED HEART (1908), Rev. Ben Davison; Deacon Donald L. Spinney.
Res.: 402 S. Imperial St., 92227 Tel: 760-344-3171; Fax: 760-344-3174.
School—(Grades PreK-8) Tel: 760-344-2662; Fax: 760-344-1910. Lay Teachers 7; Students 95.
Catechesis/Religious Program—Eugenia Martinez, D.R.E. Students 115.

CALEXICO, IMPERIAL CO., OUR LADY OF GUADALUPE (1907), Revs. James Bahash; David Sereno; Deacon Refugio Gonzalez.
Res.: 124 E. Fifth St., 92231 Tel: 760-357-1822; Fax: 760-357-0115.
School—Our Lady of Guadalupe Academy, Tel: 760-357-1986; Fax: 760-357-3282. Lay Teachers 25; Students 608.
Catechesis/Religious Program—Tel: 760-357-2532. Sr. Maria Teresa Bandera, C.V.I., D.R.E. Students 655.

CALIPATRIA, IMPERIAL CO., ST. PATRICK (1919), Revs. Amador Lopez, O.M.I.; James Kernan, O.M.I.; Jose Moreno.
Res.: 133 E. Church St., P.O. Box 238, 92233. Tel: 760-348-2733; Fax: 760-348-7070.
Catechesis/Religious Program—Tel: 760-348-2454. Students 219.
Mission—Immaculate Heart of Mary P.O. Box 238, 92233. 19 Sixth St., Niland, 92257.

CARLSBAD, SAN DIEGO CO.

1—ST. ELIZABETH SETON (1977), Rev. Donald E. Coleman; Deacon Henry Chia.
Res.: 6628 Santa Isabel St., 92009-5148. Tel: 760-438-3393; Fax: 760-438-7739.
Catechesis/Religious Program—Tel: 760-438-3438. Larry Broding, D.R.E. Students 650.

2—ST. PATRICK (1943), (Spanish), Revs. Stephen P. McCall; Joseph E. Mullen, S.J. (BO); Silvester Sarihaddula; Deacons Michael Frazee; Richard Mather; Gerald McClellan Jr.; Miguel Enriquez.
Res.: 3821 Adams St., 92008-0249. Tel: 760-729-2866; Fax: 760-434-3325.
School—3820 Pio Pico, 92008. Tel: 760-729-1333; Fax: 760-729-4643. Mary Beth Lents, Prin.; Denise Coates, Prin. Lay Teachers 23; Students 419.
Catechesis/Religious Program—Tel: 760-729-8442. Students 795.

CARMEL VALLEY, SAN DIEGO CO., ST. WILLIAM OF YORK (1985), Rev. Nicholas Dempsey.
Res.: 4343 Del Mar Trails Rd., 92130. Tel: 858-481-3232; Fax: 858-481-3289.
Catechesis/Religious Program—Tel: 858-481-4061. Ann Marie Moznett, D.R.E.; Laura Perkins, D.R.E. Students 743.

CHULA VISTA, SAN DIEGO CO.

1—MOST PRECIOUS BLOOD (1957), Rev. Frank Wagner, O.M.I.; Deacon Daniel Parra.
Res.: 1245 4th Ave., 91911-3012. Tel: 619-422-2100; Fax: 619-422-1375.
Catechesis/Religious Program—Tel: 619-422-2159. Sr. Camille Crabbe, C.V.I., D.R.E. Students 447.

2—OUR LADY OF GUADALUPE (1945), (Hispanic), Rev. Mario Vesga; Deacon Margarito Lozoya.
Res.: 345 Anita St., 91911-4198. Tel: 619-422-3977; Fax: 619-422-1056.
Catechesis/Religious Program—Tel: 619-427-2774. Students 530.

3—ST. PIUS X (1955), Revs. Joseph G. Masar; Patrick Ryan (PAT); Donald R. Kulleck, Pastor Emeritus; Deacons Dan De Pozo; Glenn Vecchitto.
Res.: 1120 Cuyamaca Ave., 91911-3506. Tel: 619-420-9193; Fax: 619-420-9353.
School—37 E. Emerson, 91911. Tel: 619-422-2015; Fax: 619-422-0048. Eileen Hanson, Prin. Lay Teachers 12; Students 314.
Catechesis/Religious Program—Tel: 619-426-2263; Fax: 619-427-0015. Lois Richards, D.R.E. Students 595.

4—ST. ROSE OF LIMA (1913), Revs. John Dolan; Joseph Lal; Deacons Gerardo Marquez; Gregory Smyth.
Res.: 293 H St., 91910-4703. Tel: 619-427-0230; Fax: 619-427-5786.
School—473 Third Ave., 91910. Tel: 619-422-1121; Fax: 619-422-8007. Religious 1; Lay Teachers 12; Students 350.
Catechesis/Religious Program—Tel: 619-426-6717. Sr. Patricia Weldon, D.R.E. Students 1,080.

CORONADO, SAN DIEGO CO., SACRED HEART (1897), Rev. Michael F. Murphy; Deacon Robert E. Griffin Jr. In Res., Rev. Msgr. Jeremiah O'Sullivan, Pastor Emeritus.
Res.: 655 C Ave., 92118-2299. Tel: 619-435-3167; Fax: 619-437-1572.
School—Tel: 619-437-4431; Fax: 619-437-1559. Lay Teachers 9; Students 230.
Catechesis/Religious Program—Tel: 619-435-3167, Ext. 306. Students 325.

DESCANSO, SAN DIEGO CO., OUR LADY OF LIGHT (1935), Rev. Gerald F. Palcheck.
Res.: 9136 Riverside Dr., P.O. Box 219, 91916. Tel: 619-445-3620; Fax: 619-445-3620.
Catechesis/Religious Program—Eleanor Denton, D.R.E. Students 38.

EL CAJON, SAN DIEGO CO.

1—HOLY TRINITY (1903), Revs. Brian M. Corcoran; Eddie Ruiz, Pastoral Assoc.; Deacon Louis Rocha.
Res.: 405 Ballard St., 92019. Tel: 619-444-9425; Fax: 619-444-9426. Web: www.holytrinityelcajon.org.
School—Tel: 619-444-7529; Fax: 619-444-3721. Web: www.holytrinityschool.mswin.net. Lay Teachers 19; Students 351.
Catechesis/Religious Program—Tel: 619-444-9402. Students 674.

2—ST. KIERAN (1958), Rev. Francis G. Penko.
Mailing Address: P.O. Box 2428, 92021-0428.
Office—1510 Greenfield Dr., 92021-0428. Tel: 619-588-6881; Fax: 619-588-5274.
School—1347 Camillo Way. Tel: 619-588-6398; Fax: 619-588-6382. Ms. Michaele Durant, Prin. Lay Teachers 15; Students 335.

Catechesis/Religious Program—Tel: 619-447-2424. Students 157.
3—ST. LOUISE DE MARILLAC (1944), Rev. Robert Irwin.
Res.: 2005 Crest Dr., 92021-4309. Tel: 619-444-3076; Fax: 619-440-1325.
Catechesis/Religious Program—Students 15.
4—ST. LUKE (1985), Very Rev. Raymond G. O'Donnell; Deacon Dennie C. Nickell.
Res.: 1980 Hillsdale Rd., 92019. Tel: 619-442-1697; Fax: 619-442-2293.
Catechesis/Religious Program—Tel: 619-442-2515. Maureen Sterk, D.R.E. (K-5); Jane Alfano, D.R.E. (6-12). Students 447.
5—OUR LADY OF GRACE (1954), Rev. Msgr. Michael J. Gallagher; Revs. Ralph Poirier, C.S.Sp.; Joseph Bien Quang Do; Omer LeBlanc, C.J.M.; Deacons George Shea; Ray Arnold; Bill Korty; Sr. Carmel Lohan, S.M., Pastoral Asst.
Res.: 2766 Navajo Rd., 92020-2183. Tel: 619-469-0133; Fax: 619-469-0575.
School—Tel: 619-466-0055; Fax: 619-466-8994. Lay Teachers 17; Students 292.
Catechesis/Religious Program—Tel: 619-466-5656. Students 539.
Mission—St. Mary Magdalene P.O. Box 406, Jacumba, San Diego Co. 91934-0406.
Mission—St. Adelaide at Cameron Corners Campo, San Diego Co.

EL CENTRO, IMPERIAL CO.
1—ST. MARY (1907), [JC] Rev. Michael Sinor; Deacon Luciano Arias.
Res.: 795 LaBrucherie, P.O. Box 3425, 92244. Tel: 760-352-4211; Fax: 760-352-7397.
School—Tel: 760-352-7285; Fax: 760-352-9727. Sister Servants of the Blessed Sacrament 6; Lay Teachers 13; Students 310.
Catechesis/Religious Program—Tel: 760-353-8260. Students 203.
2—OUR LADY OF GUADALUPE (1946), Very Rev. Jaime Escobedo; Rev. Gil Espuelas; Deacon Domingo Enriquez.
Res.: 153 E. Brighton Ave., 92243. Tel: 760-352-5535; Fax: 760-352-8003.
Catechesis/Religious Program—Tel: 760-352-5554. Sr. Martha Aldana, C.V.I., D.R.E.; Maria Diaz, D.R.E. Students 772.
Mission—Sacred Heart 40 E. Main, Heber, Imperial Co. 92249.

ENCINITAS, SAN DIEGO CO., ST. JOHN THE EVANGELIST (1946), Rev. Msgr. Timothy Harnett; Rev. Burt Boudoin.
Res.: 1001 Encinitas Blvd., 92024-0457. Tel: 760-753-6254; Fax: 760-753-7118.
School—Tel: 760-944-8227; Fax: 760-944-8939. Lay Teachers 40; Students 502.
Catechesis/Religious Program—Tel: 760-436-0664. Students 1,163.

ESCONDIDO, SAN DIEGO CO.
1—CHURCH OF ST. TIMOTHY (1985), Rev. James E. Rafferty; Deacon Mike Early.
Church and Administration Center: 2960 Canyon Rd., 92025-7402. Tel: 760-489-1200; Fax: 760-489-2731.
Catechesis/Religious Program—Tel: 760-489-0482. Christopher O'Donnell, D.R.E. Students 380.
2—CHURCH OF THE RESURRECTION (1970), [JC] Revs. Kenneth Del Priore; Eduardo Bernardino; Deacons James Kostick; Mitch Rennix.
Res.: 1445 Conway Dr., 92027. Tel: 760-747-2322; Fax: 760-747-7079.
Catechesis/Religious Program—Tel: 760-747-4550. Georgiana Partida, D.R.E. Students 1,550.
Comunidad Hispana—
3—ST. MARY (1890), Revs. Peter Navarra; Gustavo Benitez.
Res.: 1160 S. Broadway Ave., 92025-5815. Tel: 760-745-1611; Fax: 760-745-1238.
School—Tel: 760-743-3431; Fax: 760-743-6808. Lay Teachers 17; Students 342.
Catechesis/Religious Program—130 E. 13th Ave., 92025. Tel: 760-745-8255. Sharon Twilliger, D.R.E. Students 740.

FALLBROOK, SAN DIEGO CO., ST. PETER (1946), Revs. Edward Kaicher; Bernard A. Rapp; Deacons James Cooper; Manuel Villarreal.
Res.: 450 S. Stage Coach Ln., 92028. Tel: 760-728-7034; Fax: 760-723-4050.
School—St. Peter's Catholic School, Tel: 760-728-6961; Fax: 760-723-4050. Lay Teachers 9; Students 206.
Catechesis/Religious Program—Tel: 760-728-3412. Students 650.

HOLTVILLE, IMPERIAL CO., ST. JOSEPH (1911), Rev. Cecilio T. Moraga; Deacon Rube Valenzuela.
Res.: 560 Maple Ave., 92250. Tel: 760-356-2147; Fax: 760-356-1985.
Catechesis/Religious Program—Tel: 760-356-5738. Melissa Guadi, D.R.E. Students 288.

IMPERIAL, IMPERIAL CO., ST. ANTHONY OF PADUA (1948), Revs. Gianantonio Baggio, C.S. (Italy); Jesus Olivares, C.S.
Res.: 210 W. Seventh St., 92251. Tel: 760-355-1347; Fax: 760-355-1226.
Catechesis/Religious Program—Tel: 760-355-1304. Maria Fugett, D.R.E. Students 350.
Mission—Holy Spirit 1798 Rio Vista, Seeley, Imperial Co. 92273. Tel: 760-352-3811.

JACUMBA, SAN DIEGO CO., ST. MARY MAGDALENE (1947),, A mission of Our Lady of Grace, El Cajon.

JAMUL, SAN DIEGO CO., ST. PIUS X (1956), Rev. Scott A. Burnia; Deacon John Trumble.
Res.: 14107 Lyons Valley Rd., P.O. Box 369, 91935-0369. Tel: 619-669-0085; Fax: 619-669-0087.
Catechesis/Religious Program—Tel: 619-669-0086. Students 87.

JULIAN, SAN DIEGO CO., ST. ELIZABETH (1949), Rev. William Stevenson.
Res.: P.O. Box 366, 92036-0366. Tel: 760-765-0613; Fax: 760-765-0552.
Catechesis/Religious Program—Students 38.

LA JOLLA, SAN DIEGO CO.
1—ALL HALLOWS (1959), Very Rev. Msgr. Lawrence M. Purcell.
Res.: 6602 La Jolla Scenic Dr. S., 92037-5799. Tel: 858-459-2975; Fax: 858-459-9712.
School—2390 Nautilus, 92037. Tel: 858-459-6074; Fax: 858-459-4602. Lay Teachers 19; Students 273.
Catechesis/Religious Program—Karen Downs, D.R.E. Students 150.
2—MARY, STAR OF THE SEA (1906), Rev. Msgrs. Eamonn F. Lyng; James M. Gilfillan, Pastor Emeritus (Retired); Rev. Reynaldo Manahan; Deacon William Dalzell.
Res.: 7727 Girard Ave., 92037-4480. Tel: 858-454-2631; Fax: 858-454-5968.
Office: 7669 Girard Ave., 92037.
School—Stella Maris Academy, 7654 Herschel Ave., 92037. Tel: 858-454-2461; Fax: 858-454-4913. Lay Teachers 15; Students 241.
Catechesis/Religious Program—Tel: 858-551-8359. Donna Widmer, D.R.E.; Martin Magana, D.R.E. Students 119.

LA MESA, SAN DIEGO CO., ST. MARTIN OF TOURS (1921), Revs. John M. Sproul; Scott McColl. In Res., Rev. Msgr. Patrick O'Neill; Deacon Timothy Treadwell.
Res.: 7710 El Cajon Blvd., 91941. Tel: 619-465-5334; Fax: 619-465-7297.
School—Tel: 619-466-3241; Fax: 619-466-0285. Lay Teachers 15; Students 303.
Catechesis/Religious Program—Tel: 619-698-8434. Christine Davis, D.R.E. Students 284.

LAKESIDE, SAN DIEGO CO.
1—BLESSED KATERI TEKAKWITHA (1982), (Native American), [CEM] [JC 3] Rev. Michael Tran; Deacon Bill Clarke.
Res.: 1054 Barona Rd., 92040-1502. Tel: 619-443-3412; Fax: 619-443-3018.
Catechesis/Religious Program—Tel: 619-445-8333. Edward Nolan, D.R.E. Students 80.
Mission—Assumption of BVM 1054 Barona Rd., San Diego Co. 92040-1502. Tel: 619-443-3412.
Mission—Nativity of BVM Alpine, San Diego Co.
Mission—Immaculate Conception of BVM El Cajon, San Diego Co.
2—OUR LADY OF PERPETUAL HELP (1947), Revs. Ronald J. Buchmiller; Joseph Khuyen Van Lai.
Res.: 13208 Lakeshore Dr., 92040. Tel: 619-443-1412; Fax: 619-443-1733.
School—Tel: 619-443-1440. Ms. Jeanne Nickoli, Prin. St. Joseph of Carondelet Sisters 1; Lay Teachers 12; Students 210.
Catechesis/Religious Program—Tel: 619-443-5018. Joan Lopez, D.R.E. (Preschool & Elementary); Matt Conley, D.R.E. (Jr. High & High School); Carol Lane, D.R.E. (Adult Ed.). Students 379.

LEMON GROVE, SAN DIEGO CO., ST. JOHN OF THE CROSS (1939), Rev. Msgr. Edward Brockhaus; Revs. Alexander Aquino; Ruben Fuentes, O.F.M.; Deacons Juan Santoyo; Martin Villafana.
Res.: 8086 Broadway, 91945-2598. Tel: 619-466-3209; Fax: 619-466-9276.
School—8175 Lemon Grove Way, 91945. Tel: 619-466-8624; Fax: 619-466-3732. Sr. Marilupe Mier Y Teran, H.M.S.S., Prin. Sisters 3; Lay Teachers 20; Students 451.
Catechesis/Religious Program—Tel: 619-461-2681. Karen Dey, D.R.E. Students 720.
Convent—8171 Lemon Grove Way, 91945. Tel: 619-460-4271. Sisters of Mercy of the Blessed Sacrament 5.

NATIONAL CITY, SAN DIEGO CO.
1—ST. ANTHONY OF PADUA (1910), (Hispanic), Rev. Emmet L. Farrell; Deacon Joe Arismendez.
410 W. 18th St., 91950.
Res.: 1816 Harding Ave., 91950. Tel: 619-477-4520; Fax: 619-477-8708.
Catechesis/Religious Program—Angelina Sampo, D.R.E. Students 80.
2—ST. MARY (1926), Revs. Dionisio Macalintal (PH); Mario Elias; Deacon Daniel Prado.
Mailing Address: 426 E. Seventh St., 91950-2322.
In Res., Rev. Romeo Ramos.
Res.: 1310 L Ave., 91950-4811. Tel: 619-474-1501; Fax: 619-474-1502.
Catechesis/Religious Program—Tel: 619-474-5777; Fax: 619-474-5777. Students 350.

NILAND, IMPERIAL CO., IMMACULATE HEART OF MARY, , No longer a parish; now a mission of St. Patrick, Calipatria.

OCEANSIDE, SAN DIEGO CO.
1—ST. MARGARET (1977), Rev. Cavana Wallace; Deacon Lewis Beatty.
Res.: 4300 Oceanside Blvd., 92056-2999. Tel: 760-941-5560; Fax: 760-941-1857.
Catechesis/Religious Program—Pam Talbot, D.R.E. Students 200.
2—ST. MARY, STAR OF THE SEA (1937), (Hispanic), Revs. Patrick J. Mulcahy; Joseph Viet Hoang.
Res.: 609 Pier View Way, 92054-2861. Tel: 760-722-1688; Fax: 760-722-2653.
School—Tel: 760-722-7259; Fax: 760-722-0862. Lay Teachers 20; Students 360.
Catechesis/Religious Program—Tel: 760-722-1000. Students 540.
3—MISSION SAN LUIS REY (1798), Revs. Peter Kirwin, O.F.M.; Jorge Hernandez, O.F.M.; Garrett Edmunds, O.F.M.; Deacon Jesse Pagliaro.
Res.: 4070 Mission Ave., 92057-6497. Tel: 760-757-3250; Fax: 760-757-3299.
Catechesis/Religious Program—Tel: 760-757-3250, Ext. 334. Students 697.
Mission—San Luis Rey de Francia (1798), [CEM] 4050 Mission Ave., San Luis Rey, San Diego Co. 92057. Tel: 760-757-3651; Fax: 760-757-4613.
4—ST. THOMAS MORE (1985), Rev. Michael Ratajczak; Deacons Thomas A. Goeltz; Frank Mercardante.
Church & Mailing Address: 1450 S. Melrose Dr., 92056. Tel: 760-758-4100; Fax: 760-758-4165.
Res.: 1145 Countrywood Ln., Vista, 92083.
Catechesis/Religious Program—Students 300.

PALA, SAN DIEGO CO., MISSION SAN ANTONIO DE PALA (1816), (Native American), Revs. Paul Marconi, C.R.S.P.; Luciano Visconti, C.R.S.P.
Res.: P.O. Box 70, 92059-0070. Tel: 760-742-3317; Fax: 760-742-3040.
Catechesis/Religious Program—Tel: 760-742-1600. Students 160.
Convent—Tel: 760-742-1714. Franciscan Sisters of Philadelphia 2.
Chapel—Rincon Indian Reservation, St. Bartholomew
Chapel—La Jolla Indian Reservation, Our Lady of Refuge
Chapel—Pauma Indian Reservation, St. James

POWAY, SAN DIEGO CO.
1—ST. GABRIEL (1973), Rev. Michael Froidurot.
Res.: 13734 Twin Peaks Rd., P.O. Box 867, 92074-0867. Tel: 858-748-5348; Fax: 858-748-5764.
Catechesis/Religious Program—Tel: 858-748-7475. Martha Lyles, D.R.E. Students 758.
2—ST. MICHAEL (1959), Rev. Msgrs. Neal Dolan; Joseph L. Finnerty, Pastor Emeritus; Rev. William Mooney.
Res.: 15546 Pomerado Rd., 92064-2404. Tel: 858-487-4755; Fax: 858-487-5937.
School—15542 Pomerado Rd., 92064. Tel: 858-485-1303; Fax: 858-485-5059. Sisters of Mercy of Sligo 1; Lay Teachers 24; Students 476.
Catechesis/Religious Program—Tel: 858-485-1392; 858-487-0473. M.J. Heggeness, D.R.E. Students 1,060.

RAMONA, SAN DIEGO CO., IMMACULATE HEART OF MARY (1947), Rev. Patrick J. Murphy; Deacon Gustavo Magana.
Res.: 537 E St., 92065. Tel: 760-789-0583; Fax: 760-789-3875.
Catechesis/Religious Program—Tel: 760-789-6151. Charlie McGuire, D.R.E. Students 666.

RANCHO SANTA FE, SAN DIEGO CO., CHURCH OF THE NATIVITY (1985), Rev. Msgr. Dennis R. Clark.
Mailing Address: P.O. Box 8770, 92067-8770.
Res.: 6309 El Apajo Rd., 92067. Tel: 858-756-1911; Fax: 858-756-9562.
School—(Grades K-8), P.O. Box 9180, 92067. Tel: 858-756-6763; Fax: 858-756-9128. Students 178.
Catechesis/Religious Program—Tel: 858-756-0937. Mrs. Patti Smiley, D.R.E. Students 322.

SAN MARCOS, SAN DIEGO CO., ST. MARK (1963), [CEM] Revs. George Dunkley; Armando Escurel, S.V.D.; Deacons Dick Jansing; Frank Mercardante.
Res.: 1147 Discovery, 92069. Tel: 760-744-1540; Fax: 760-744-3828.
Catechesis/Religious Program—Tel: 760-744-1130. Students 1,800.
Mission— 568 Deer Springs Rd., San Diego Co. 92069.

SAN YSIDRO, SAN DIEGO CO., OUR LADY OF MT. CARMEL (1927), (Hispanic), Rev. Jose Castillo; Deacon Jose Luis Medina. In Res., Rev. Peter Ruggere, M.M.

Res.: 2020 Alaquinas Dr., 92173-2107. Tel: 619-428-1415; Fax: 619-428-5626.
School—Tel: 619-428-2091; Fax: 619-428-8324. Sr. Ana Rosa Aceves, Prin. Sisters of the Most Blessed Sacrament 9; Lay Teachers 18; Students 450.
Catechesis/Religious Program—109 Seaward Ave., 92173. Tel: 619-428-3686. Students 260.

SANTA YSABEL, SAN DIEGO CO., SANTA YSABEL INDIAN MISSION (1818), (Native American), [CEM] Rev. Dennis O'Connor.
Res.: 23013 Hwy. 79, P.O. Box 129, 92070-1010. Tel: 760-765-0810; Fax: 760-765-3494.
Mission—St. Francis Hwy. 79, Warner Springs, San Diego Co. 92086.
Catechesis/Religious Program—Tel: 760-782-0578. Students 14.

SANTEE, SAN DIEGO CO., GUARDIAN ANGELS (1962), Revs. Michael A. Cunnane; Kevin P. Casey, S.J.; Deacon Louis Principe.
Res.: 9310 Dalehurst Rd., 92071-1010. Tel: 619-448-1213; Fax: 619-448-2980.
Catechesis/Religious Program—9310 Dalehurst, 92071. Tel: 619-448-1213, Ext. 312. Sr. Mary Potter, R.S.M., D.R.E. Students 458.

SOLANA BEACH, SAN DIEGO CO., ST. JAMES (Del Mar) (1911), Rev. Msgr. Richard F. Duncanson; Deacons John Brice; Jack Gallagher; Joseph R. Santen; Al Graff; Luis Aguilar. In Res., Rev. John Howard, C.J.M.
Office:—625 S. Nardo Ave., 92075-2398. Tel: 858-755-2545; Fax: 858-755-3845.
School—Tel: 858-755-1777; Fax: 858-755-3124. Donna Kruszona, Prin. (St. James Academy). Lay Teachers 13; Students 266.
Catechesis/Religious Program—Tel: 858-755-2545. Robert Kidd, D.R.E. Students 439.
Mission—St. Leo 936 Genevieve, San Diego Co. 92075. Tel: 858-481-6788; Fax: 858-481-5832.

SPRING VALLEY, SAN DIEGO CO., SANTA SOPHIA (1956), Rev. Peter Escalante; Deacon Michael Maria. In Res., Rev. Masilamony Devadhason.
Res.: 9800 San Juan St., 91977. Tel: 619-463-6629; Fax: 619-463-8101.
School—Tel: 619-463-0488; Fax: 619-668-5469. Lay Teachers 15; Aides 8; Students 325.
Catechesis/Religious Program—Tel: 619-463-6011; Fax: 619-668-5458. Sr. Alyce Waters, D.R.E. Students 439.

VALLEY CENTER, SAN DIEGO CO., ST. STEPHEN (1981), Rev. William A. Kernan.
Res.: 31020 Cole Grade Rd., P.O. Box 1015, 92082. Tel: 760-749-3324; Fax: 760-749-6684.
Catechesis/Religious Program—Tel: 760-749-3352; Fax: 760-749-6608. Ellen MacPhee, D.R.E. Students 280.

VISTA, SAN DIEGO CO., ST. FRANCIS OF ASSISI (1941), Revs. Ramon R. Marrufo; Brendan McKeever, C.P. (Ireland); Deacons Michael Collins; Frank Mercardante; Ronald Arnold; Pedro Enciso.
Res.: 525 W. Vista Way, 92083-5974. Tel: 760-945-8000; Fax: 760-945-8036.
School—Tel: 760-630-7960; Fax: 760-726-2910. Linda McCotter, Prin. Lay Teachers 22; Students 361.
Catechesis/Religious Program—Tel: 760-945-8010. Susan Ferraris, D.R.E. Students 1,075.

WESTMORLAND, IMPERIAL CO., ST. JOSEPH (1939), (Mexican-American),, Administered by St. Patrick, Calipatria.
Res.: 300 N. Center St., 92281. Tel: 760-348-2733.
Catechesis/Religious Program—Students 95.

WINTERHAVEN, IMPERIAL CO., ST. THOMAS (1780),, (Native American Mission) Rev. Duncan W. Monohan.
Res.: P.O. Box 1176, 92283-1176. Tel: 760-572-0283; Fax: 760-572-0283.
Catechesis/Religious Program—Students 28.
Mission—St. Mary, Imperial Co. 92283.

Eastern Churches

EL CAJON, SAN DIEGO CO., ST. PETER CATHEDRAL (1973),, (Chaldean Eastern Catholic) Rev. Michael J. Bazzi.
Res.: 1627 Jamacha Way, 92019. Tel: 619-579-7913; 619-588-9921; Fax: 619-588-8281.
Catechesis/Religious Program—Khelood Allos, D.R.E. Students 710.
Convent—Chaldean Sisters, 1591 Jamacha Way, 92019. Tel: 619-447-4842.

SAN DIEGO, SAN DIEGO CO., OUR LADY OF PERPETUAL HELP (1960),, (Ukrainian Catholic) Rev. John Hritzko (STN).
Res.: 4061 Winona Ave., 92105. Tel: 619-269-7999; Fax: 619-269-2303.

Chaplains of Public Institutions
Hospitals

SAN DIEGO. *Alvarado, Grossmont and Kaiser Hospitals.*
Children's Hospital, Tel: 858-541-3475. Rev. Manuel Ediza.
Scripps Hospital. Rev. Thomas Thompson. Tel: 858-457-4123.
Scripps Mercy Hospital. Revs. James P. Retzner, O.S.A., Frank Hoffmann. Tel: 619-260-7020.
Sharp Memorial Hospital. Revs. Manuel Ediza. Tel: 858-541-3475, James V. Corrigan, O.S.A. (CHI), Clinical Pastoral Ed.
UCSD Medical Center. 619-543-6737

CHULA VISTA. *Scripps Memorial Hospital*, 435 H St., 91910. Tel: 619-691-7000. Rev. Romeo Ramos, Chap.
Sharp Rees-Stealy Medical Center, East 752 Medical Center Ct., 91910. Tel: 858-499-2777. Rev. Romeo Ramos, Chap.

LA JOLLA. *Thornton Hospital*. Rev. Thomas Thompson. Tel: 858-657-7000.
Veterans Administration Hospital, Tel: 858-552-8585. Rev. Jerry Hamperzonian. Tel: 858-552-8585, Ext. 421.

OCEANSIDE. *Tri City Hospital*, 4002 Vista Way. Tel: 760-724-8411. Revs. Victor Maristela, Eduardo Gudino, Chap.

Retirement Homes

SAN DIEGO. *Nazareth House*. (Vacant)

LA MESA. *Little Flower Haven*. Rev. Philip Bronk, S.T. Tel: 619-466-3163.

Detention Ministries

SAN DIEGO. *Central Detention Facility and San Diego City Jail*. Rev. James I. Rasura, S.J. Tel: 619-236-3011.
East Mesa Detention Facility, Tel: 619-233-1048. Rev. John E. Arthur, S.J.
George F. Bailey Maximum Security Facility, Tel: 619-233-1048. Rev. John P. Auther, S.J.
Juvenile Hall, Office for Social Ministry. Tel: 858-490-8323. (Vacant)
Metropolitan Correction Center, Tel: 619-232-4311, Ext. 336. Rev. Msgr. Fernando Gutierrez.
R.J. Donovan Correctional Facility Rev. Romeo Supnet, O.S.A. Tel: 619-661-6500, Ext. 6632.
San Diego Detention Center. Deacon Peter Nguyen.
Wackenhut Detention Facility, Office for Social Ministry. Tel: 858-490-8323. (Vacant)

BRAWLEY. *Calipatria State Prison*, Tel: 760-348-7000. Deacon Michael Heidenreich. Tel: 769-348-7000, Ext. 5339. (Vacant)

CHULA VISTA. *South Bay Detention Facility*. Rev. James V. Caldwell (Retired). Tel: 619-423-7360.

EL CENTRO. *El Centro Juvenile Hall*. Rev. Refugio Hernandez. Tel: 760-352-2895.
Imperial County Jail. Rev. Refugio Hernandez. Tel: 760-339-6367.

IMPERIAL. *Centinela State Prison*. Rev. Luis Valenciano. Tel: 760-337-7900, Ext. 6372.

SANTEE. *Las Colinas Women's Detention Facility*. *Office for Social Ministry*, Tel: 858-490-8323.

VISTA. *Vista Detention Facility*. Rev. Cliff Sumrall. Tel: 760-451-5095.

State Conservation Camps

SAN DIEGO. *Rainbow Work Camp*. Rev. Bud Kaicher. Tel: 760-728-7034.

Ports

SAN DIEGO. *Port of San Diego*. Deacon Jaime Aquino, Chap., Rev. James Boyd.
San Diego Airport, 2802 Cadiz St., 92110-4813. Tel: 619-225-8157. Rev. Gary Holtey, Chap.

On Special Assignment:
Rev.—
McGuine, Peter M., North American College, Rome, Italy.

On Duty Outside the Diocese:
Revs.—
Conwill, Giles
Parrales, Napoleon J.
Perozich, Richard L.
Stanonik, Anthony
White, Robert

Military Chaplains:
Revs.—
Diaz, Michael, CHC, USN
Jennings, Tommie, CHC, USNR
Merris, Christopher

Unassigned:
Revs.—
Dunn, Stephen
Foley, Patrick
Gomes-Kelly, John R.
Langille, Justin
Mejia, Ricardo

Retired:
Rev. Msgrs.—
Aldasoro, Francisco
Bolger, William
Bourgeois, Lloyd
Brennan, Joseph F.
Briody, Thomas
Chylewski, Anthony
Coughlan, Michael J.
Creighton, Edward
Cuddihy, William
Elliott, William
Finnerty, Joseph
Fox, Patrick
Giesing, Anthony
Gilfillan, James M.
Hanley, Andrew W.
Kearney, Patrick J.
Kulleck, Donald
McDermott, Thomas J.
Moloney, Alphonsus
Moore, J. Raymond
Murray, Sean
O'Donoghue, James P.
O'Neill, Patrick J.
O'Sullivan, Jeremiah
Portman, John R.
Shipley, William
Vidra, Thomas
Revs.—
Borda, Peter Paul
Buchanan, Donald
Byrne, George
Caldwell, James V.
Chase, Maurice
Crisologo, Aurelio
Fischer, Eugene
Flynn, Edward R.
Fuld, Charles L.
Holland, Kilian
Keenan, John J.
Lorenz, Vincent E.
Lucev, John
Nesbitt, John B.
Nguyen, Peter
Nikliborc, Robert
Ortiz, Michael
Ortmann, William
Palmitessa, Paul
Quinn, John T.
Rankin, James
Roll, David H.
Russell, Richard J.
Ryland, Raymond
Salada, Urbano
Salca, Louis
Sheslo, Charles
Sierra, Francis A.
Smith, Aquinas
Sostrich, John L.
Thompson, J. Noel
Tindall, Harold
Twarog, Theodore S.
Walsh, Donal
Wheeler, John

Permanent Deacons:
Aguilar, Adolfo L., St. James, Solana Beach
Aguilar, Adolfo L.
Albers, Tony, Blessed Sacrament, San Diego
Aquino, Jaime, Good Shepherd, San Diego
Arias, Luciano, St. Mary, El Centro
Arismendez, Joe, St. Anthony, National City
Arnold, Ray, Our Lady of Grace, El Cajon
Arnold, Ron, St. Francis, Vista
Beatty, Lewis, St. Margaret, Oceanside
Bell, L. Ferris, (Retired)
Brice, John, St. James, Solona Beach
Carpizo, Manuel, Corpus Christi, San Diego
Chia, Henry, St. Elizabeth Seton, Carlsbad
Clarke, William G., Blessed Kateri Tekakwitha, Jamul
Collins, Michael, St. Francis, Vista
Cooper, Jim, St. Peter, Fallbrook
Corrao, Jack P., (Retired)
Costello, John M., (Retired)
Dalzell, William, Mary, Star of the Sea, San Diego, La Jolla
Davidson, Paul, Holy Family, San Diego
Dean, Ben, (On Leave)
Delano, Joe, (On Leave)
Dennison, Mick, St. Charles, San Diego
DePozo, Daniel, St. Pius X, Chula Vista
Diem, Ronald H., St. Gregory the Great, San Diego
Dougherty, Thomas P., Holy Family, San Diego
Dube, Leo, St. Therese, San Diego
Early, John M., St. Timothy, Escondido
Ekhaml, Robert T., St. Therese, San Diego
Ellis, John A., Holy Family, San Diego
Enciso, Pedro, St. Francis, Vista
Enriquez, Domingo, Our Lady of Guadalupe, El Centro
Enriquez, Miguel, St. Patrick, Oceanside
Finn, Kenneth, (Retired)
Fitzmorris, Robert H., St. Mary Magdalene, San Diego

Frazee, Mike, St. Patrick, Carlsbad
Gallagher, John V., St. James, Solana Beach
Gasparovic, Anthony L., Our Lady of Perpetual Help, Lakeside
Goeltz, Thomas A., St. Thomas More, Vista
Gonzalez, Refugio, Our Lady of Guadalupe, Calexico
Graff, Albert P., St. James, Solana Beach
Griffin, Robert E., Jr., Sacred Heart, Coronado
Grosso, Ernest, Mission San Diego de Alcala, San Diego
Guess, Harry, Jr., Christ the King, San Diego
Guess, Harry, Jr.
Gullotta, Daniel, Lakeside, MT
Hernandez, Raul, St. Jerome, San Diego
Hess, Arnie, Our Mother of Confidence, San Diego
Hitch, James, Corpus Christi, Bonita
Hunt, Sam, Seal Beach, CA
Jansing, Dick, (Retired)
Jones, Thom, Our Lady of Mt. Carmel, San Diego
Keeley, James, Santa Sophia, Spring Valley
Klopchin, Bill, Our Mother of Confidence, San Diego
Korty, Bill, Our Lady of Grace, El Cajon
Kostick, Jim, Resurrection, Escondido
Kutler, Harold, (Retired)
Leach, Dave, San Luis Obispo
Lozoya, Margarito, Our Lady of Guadalupe, Chula Vista
Mackey, Bob, (Retired)
Magana, Gustavo, Immaculate Heart of Mary, Ramona
Maria, Michael, Santa Sophia, La Mesa
Marquez, Gerardo, St. Rose of Lima, Chula Vista
Martinez, Seodello A., St. Charles, San Diego
Mather, Dick, St. Patrick, Carlsbad
McClellan, Gerald, Jr., St. Patrick, Carlsbad
McDaniel, Al, Arlington, VA
Medina, Jose, Our Lady of Mt. Carmel, San Ysidro
Mercardante, F., St. Francis, Vista
Michaels, Larry, (Unassigned)
Montoya, Ken, (Unassigned)
Mueller, Robert, St. Francis, Vista
Nevins, William J., (Retired)
Nguyen, Peter Can, St. Didacus, San Diego
Nickell, Dennie, St. Luke, El Cajon
Nunez, Manuel, St. Jude, San Diego
Osgood, Franklin B., (Retired)
Pagliaro, Jesse, Mission San Luis Rey, Oceanside
Parra, Daniel, Most Precious Blood, Chula Vista
Paulicivic, George, Sr., Murrieta, CA
Perez, Modesto, St. Mary
Phelps, John, Our Lady of Mt. Carmel
Pollock, William, (Retired)
Porciuncula, Manny, Our Lady of Mt. Carmel, San Diego
Prado, Daniel, St. Mary, National City
Principe, Louis, Our Lady of Perpetual Help, Lakeside
Reilly, Douglas Frank
Reilly, Frank, Blessed Sacrament
Rennix, Mitchell, Resurrection, Escondido
Robbins, Ralph, (Retired)
Robles, Manny, Holy Spirit, San Diego
Rocha, Louis, Holy Trinity, El Cajon
Roy, James, Klamath Falls, OR
Santen, Joseph R., St. James, Solana Beach
Santiago, Nicholas M., St. Columba, San Diego
Santoyo, Juan, St. John of the Cross, Lemon Grove
Schmitt, Giles V., Sacred Heart, San Diego
Schmitz, Ron, Guardian Angels, Santee
Scull, James, Ascension, San Diego
Shea, George, (Retired)
Shelton, Carl, St. Patrick, San Diego
Shockley, Gordon E., San Antonio, TX
Skupnik, Ray, Long Beach, CA
Smyth, Greg, St. Rose of Lima, Chula Vista
Snyder, John A., Queen of Angels, Alpine
Threatt, Marvin, Holy Spirit, San Diego
Treadwell, Timothy, St. Martin of Tours, La Mesa
Trumble, John, St. Kieran, El Cajon
Vaillancourt, Leonard
Valenzuela, Ruben, St. Joseph, Imperial
Vasquez, Bill, Mission San Diego de Alcala, San Diego
Vecchitto, Glenn, St. Pius X, Chula Vista
Villafana, Martin, St. John of the Cross, Lemon Grove
Villarreal, Manuel, St. Peter, Fallbrook
Vivio, Bill, Phoenix, AZ
Walling, Robert, Bend, OR
Wisocky, Joe, St. Mark, San Marcos
Wood, Joseph, All Hallows, La Jolla
Woznicki, Walt, Boise, ID
Yeatts, Bernard, Our Lady of Mt. Carmel, San Diego

INSTITUTIONS LOCATED IN THE DIOCESE

[A] SEMINARIES, DIOCESAN

SAN DIEGO. *St. Francis De Sales Center*, 1667 Santa Paula Dr., 92111. Tel: 619-291-7446; Fax: 619-291-7011. Email: eceliceo@diocese-sdiego.org. Web: www.diocese-sdiego.org. Revs. Matthew D. Spahr, Dir.; Earl E. Eggleston, Asst. Dir. For priests and priestly formation. Priests 2; Students 6.

[B] COLLEGES AND UNIVERSITIES

SAN DIEGO. *Austin House*, 1605 28th St., 92102-1417. Tel: 619-233-9141. Email: friars@cts.com. Revs. Jerome Bevilacqua, O.S.A.; Gary C. Rye, O.S.A.; Deacon Richard Hardick, O.S.A. Total in Residence 3.

Office of the Provincial Tel: 619-235-0247; Fax: 619-231-2814. Email: osa-west@k-online.com. Web: www.osa-west.org. Very Rev. Steven M. Ochoa, O.S.A., Prior Prov. Tel: 619-235-0247; Fax: 619-231-2814.

University of San Diego, 5998 Alcala Park, 92110-2492. Tel: 619-260-4600. Web: www.sandiego.edu. Dr. Mary E. Lyons, Pres.; Dr. Francis M. Lazarus, Vice Pres. & Provost; Rev. Msgr. Daniel Dillabough, Vice Pres. Mission & Univ. Relations; Mr. Paul Bissonnette, Vice Pres. Finance & Admin.; Dr. Robert Pastoor, Acting Vice Pres. Student Affairs; Mr. Thomas Burke, Interim Vice Pres. Univ. Rels.; Dr. Patrick Drinan, Dean College of Arts & Sciences; Dr. Curtis Cook, Dean School of Business Admin.; Dr. Paula Cordeiro, Dean School of Education; Dr. Daniel Rodriguez, Dean School of Law; Dr. Sally B. Hardin, Dean Hahn School of Nursing & Health Science. Students 1,350; School of Law: Lay Teachers 95; Students 1,109; University: Priests 8; Sisters 9; Lay Teachers 661; Total Staff 1,222; Students 7,262.

University Ministers: Mike McIntyre, Dir. Univ. Ministry; Victor Cruz, Asst.; Scott Drain, Assoc.; Lisa Diefecto, Assoc.; Amy Gualtieri, Sacristan; Mary Kruer, Assoc.; Paula Chapman, Asst.; Katie Foley, Asst.; Cara McMahon, Assoc.; Chris Nichols, Asst.; Revs. J. J. O'Leary, S.J., Asst. to Vice Pres.; Mark Peters, Assoc.; Sr. Virginia Rodee, R.S.C.J., Dir. Mission; Hilary Andaya, Eccles Asst.; Mark Maxwell, Asst.; Annette Walsh, Assoc.; Rev. Michael White, C.S.Sp., Chap.

Faculty: Revs. Stephen Dunn; Dennis Krouse; James McGray; Norbert Rigali, S.J.; Ron Pachence; Berard L. Marthaler, O.F.M. (Retired).

Msgr. John Portman Chair of Roman Catholic Systematic Theology Tel: 619-260-7824; Fax: 619-260-2260.

Center for the Study of Latino/Latina Catholicism Tel: 619-260-4049; Fax: 619-260-2260. Dr. Orlando Espin, Dir.

Center for Christian Spirituality Tel: 619-260-4784; Fax: 619-260-7905. Sr. Barbara Quinn, R.S.C.J., Dir.

Pratical Theology Program Tel: 619-260-4784; Fax: 619-260-7905. Rev. Ron Pachence, Dir.

Pastoral Care and Counseling Program Tel: 619-260-4784; Fax: 619-260-7905. Rev. Ron Pachence (SAV).

Values Institute Tel: 619-260-7732; Fax: 619-260-5950. Dr. Larry Hinman, Dir.

School of Law: Daniel Rodriguez, Dean.

[C] HIGH SCHOOLS, DIOCESAN

SAN DIEGO. *Academy of Our Lady of Peace*, (Grades 9-12), 4860 Oregon St., 92116. Tel: 619-297-2266; Fax: 619-297-2473. Email: aolpadmin@excite.com. Web: www.aolp.org. Sr. Dolores Anchondo, C.S.J., Prin. (Girls) Sisters of St. Joseph of Carondelet 4; Lay Teachers 40; Students 750.

St. Augustine High School, 3266 Nutmeg St., 92104-5199. Tel: 619-282-2184; Fax: 619-282-1203. Email: ksteven@sahs.org. Web: www.sahs.org. James Horne, Prin.; Revs. John D. Keller, O.S.A., Pres.; Harry Neely, O.S.A., Campus Min.; Bro. Stephen McKenna, O.S.A.; Deacon Richard Hardick, O.S.A. Conducted by The Augustinians, (Boys); (For information concerning the monastery see separate listing under Monasteries). Priests 2; Brothers 1; Deacons 1; Lay Teachers 42; Students 707.

Marian Catholic High School, 1002 18th St., 92154. Tel: 619-423-2121; Fax: 619-423-6910. Email: mchs@cox.net. Web: www.mariancatholic.org. Dr. Estelle Kassebaum, Prin. (Coed) Lay Teachers 33; Students 600.

University of San Diego High School (Coed) , 5961 Linda Vista Rd., 92110-1947. Tel: 619-298-8277; Fax: 619-293-7535. Email: rkelly@usdhs.org. Web: usdhs.org. Richard E. Kelly, Ph.D., Pres.; Timothy Derenthal, Prin. Lay Teachers 92; Students 1,480.

CALEXICO. *Vincent Memorial High*, (Grades 9-12), 525 W. Sheridan, 92231. Tel: 760-357-3461; Fax: 760-357-0902. Email: vmchs@aol.com. Web: vmhs.com. (Coed). Conducted by Sisters Servants of the Blessed Sacrament Sisters 2; Lay Teachers 14; Students 238.

[D] SPECIAL SCHOOLS

EL CAJON. *St. Madeleine Sophie's Center for Developmentally Disabled Adults*, 2119 E. Madison Ave., 92019-1111. Tel: 619-442-5129; Fax: 619-442-2590. Email: dturnerc@stmsc.org. Web: www.stmsc.org. Debra Turner, Exec. Dir. Lay Teachers 56; Enrollment 225.

[E] PROTECTIVE INSTITUTIONS

SPRING VALLEY. *Noah Homes*, 12526 Campo Rd., 91978. Tel: 619-660-6200; Fax: 619-660-1481. Email: NoahSKJ@aol.com. Kathryn Jennings, Exec. Dir. Total Assisted Annually 65; Total Staff 42.

[F] HOSPITALS

SAN DIEGO. *Scripps Mercy Hospital*, 4077 Fifth Ave., 92103. Tel: 619-294-8111; Fax: 619-686-3530. Web: www.scrippshealth.org. Tom Gammiere, Admin.; Sr. JoCeal Young, R.S.M., Dir. Mission Svcs.; Revs. Frank Hoffmann; James Retzner, O.S.A.; Sr. Barbara Checkhart, R.S.M., Chap.; Michael Harkay, Chap.; Rev. Loran Long, Chap. (Baptist); Sr. Mary Gallagher, R.S.M., Chap. Bed Capacity 517; Total Staff 2,056; Patients Assisted Annually 20,974.

[G] HOMES FOR SENIOR CITIZENS

SAN DIEGO. *Cathedral Plaza*, 1551 Third Ave., 92101. Tel: 619-234-0093; Fax: 619-234-5168. Email: cathplaza@aol.com. Bobbi Pentchev, Resident Mgr.; Jack Pentchev, Resident Mgr.

Legal Title: *Cathedral Plaza Development Corp., A California Nonprofit Corporation* Apartments 222; In Residence 256; Total Staff 7; Total Staff 5; Total Assisted 172.

Guadalupe Plaza, 4142 42nd St., 92105. Tel: 619-584-2414; Fax: 619-584-2886. Email: guad126@pacbell.net. Marie Creveling, Resident Mgr.

Legal Title: *Guadalupe Plaza Development Corp., A California Nonprofit Corporation* Apartments 126; In Residence 142.

St. John's Plaza Tel: 619-466-5354; Fax: 619-466-6643.

Legal Title: *Calexico Plaza Development Corp., A California Nonprofit Corporation* Residences 99; Total In Residence 106; Total Staff 6.

8150 Broadway, Lemon Grove, 91945. Tel: 619-466-5354; Fax: 619-466-6643. Email: STJPlaza@aol.com. Betty Johnson, Resident Mgr.; Milton Johnson, Resident Mgr.

Nazareth House Retirement Home, 6333 Rancho Mission Rd., 92108. Tel: 619-563-0480; Fax: 619-624-9215. Email: fmack@cts.com. Sr. Ellen O'Dwyer, C.S.N., Admin. Retired Priests Residential and Nursing Capacity 139; Priests 20; Poor Sisters of Nazareth of San Diego 8.

LA MESA. *Little Flower Haven*, 8585 La Mesa Blvd., 91941. Tel: 619-466-3163; Fax: 619-466-9642. Email: littleflwrhaven@yahoo.com. Sr. M. Carmela Lovato, D.C.J., Admin.; Rev. Philip Bronk, S.T., Chap. Total Staff 25; Aged Residents 85.

[H] MONASTERIES AND RESIDENCES OF PRIESTS AND BROTHERS

SAN DIEGO. *Augustinian Community*, 3266 Nutmeg St., 92104. Tel: 619-282-2028; Fax: 619-282-2233. Email: mtbube@earthink.net. Revs. Thomas P. Garrett, O.S.A.; James E. Hannan, O.S.A.; John D. Keller, O.S.A., Prior & Pres.; James Mott, O.S.A.; Harry M. Neely, O.S.A.; James P. Retzner, O.S.A.; Bro. Michael Bube, O.S.A., Procurator.

Augustinian Community, St. Patrick's Parish, 3585 30th St., 92104-4196. Tel: 619-295-2157; Fax: 619-688-1225. Revs. Anthony J. Wasko, O.S.A., Procurator; Thomas G. Verber, O.S.A., Pastor, Supr.

1605 28th St., 92102. Tel: 619-233-9141. Revs. Stephen Ochoa, O.S.A., Prov.; Jerome Bevilacqua, O.S.A.; Gary C. Rye, O.S.A.; Bro. J. Stephen McKenna, O.S.A.; Deacon Richard Hardick, O.S.A.

Monica House - Augustinian Community, 1621 28th St., 92102-1417. Tel: 619-338-9268. Email: osa-west@k-online.com. 1605 28th St., 92102-1417. Very Rev. Steven M. Ochoa, O.S.A.; Bro. J. Stephen McKenna, O.S.A. Total in Residence 2.

BOULEVARD. *Holy Trinity Hermitage-Augustinian Community*, 1371 Tierra del Sol Rd., 91905-4694. Tel: 619-766-4101. Email: eleos@wwdb.org. *Provincial Office*, 1605 28th St., 92102-1417. A contemplative retreat setting that only accommodates 8 people.

OCEANSIDE. *Mission San Luis Rey*, 4050 Mission Ave., 92057-6402. Tel: 760-757-3651; Fax: 760-757-4613. Email: ben@sanluisrey.org. Web: www.sanluisrey.org. Rev. Ben R. Innes, O.F.M., Guardian; Bros. Maurice Peltier, O.F.M.; Ed

Dunn, O.F.M.; Martin Soto, O.F.M.; Tom Thing, O.F.M.; Mark Schroeder, O.F.M.; Revs. Mel Bucher, O.F.M.; Michael Gagnon, O.F.M.; Garrett Edmunds, O.F.M.; Jorge Hernandez, O.F.M.; Peter Kirwin, O.F.M.; Unbert Zanett, O.F.M. Franciscan Friars Priests 7; Brothers 5.

Prince of Peace Abbey, Benet Hill 92054. Tel: 760-430-1305; 760-430-1306; Fax: 760-967-8711. Email: princeabby@aol.com. Rev. Charles Wright, O.S.B., Abbot; Rt. Rev. Claude Ehringer, O.S.B., Abbot (Retired); Revs. Sharbel Ewen, O.S.B.; Anselm Fister, O.S.B. (Oregon); Alexis Foyo, O.S.B.; Basil Mattingly, O.S.B.; Aquinas Nichols, O.S.B. (DM); Herbert Palmer, O.S.B.; Stephanos Pedrano, O.S.B.; Bros. Peter Aslin, O.S.B.; Timothy Balk, O.S.B., Bro. Oblate; Joseph Black, O.S.B.; Anselm Clark, O.S.B.; Blaise Heuke, O.S.B.; Clement Kennedy, O.S.B.; Benedict Menezes, O.S.B.; Raphael Meyer, O.S.B.; Michel Pham, O.S.B.; Mario Quizon, O.S.B.; Daniel Sokol, O.S.B.; Meinrad Taylor, O.S.B. Benedictine Fathers Priests 9; Brothers 12.

[I] CONVENTS AND RESIDENCES FOR SISTERS

SAN DIEGO. *Carmelite Monastery of San Diego, California* (Discalced) , 5158 Hawley Blvd., 92116-1934. Tel: 619-280-5425; Fax: 619-283-2121. Email: carmelsd@sbcglobal.net. Web: www.carmelsandiego.com. Sr. Ancilla Murray, O.C.D., Prioress. Sisters 13.

Community of the Holy Spirit, 6151 Rancho Mission Rd., #205, 92108. Tel: 619-584-0809. Email: chsanderson@att.net. Sr. Mary Jo Anderson, C.H.S., Gen. Coord. Sisters 17.

Congregation of the Sisters of Nazareth, 6330 Rancho Mission Rd., 92108. Tel: 619-563-0480; Fax: 619-624-9215. Email: fmack@cts.com. Sisters 10.

Daughters of Divine Charity, 6036 Camino Rico, 92120. Tel: 619-287-1320. Sisters 4.

Daughters of St. Paul, 5945 Balboa Ave., 92111. Tel: 858-565-9181. Sr. Frances Obravac, Contact Person.

Maryknoll Sisters, 4070 Kansas St. #312, 92104. Tel: 619-283-5678. Sisters 4.

Missionaries of Charity, 3877 Boston Ave., 92113. Tel: 619-263-9566. Sisters 7.

Religious of Jesus and Mary, 1510 Third Ave., 92101. Tel: 619-234-0556; Fax: 619-234-0202. Email: rosienrjm@aol.com. Sisters 8.

Religious of the Sacred Heart Tel: 619-299-3639; Fax: 619-291-4207. Email: shaffer@sandiego.edu.

Casa Maria Community, Univ. of San Diego, 5998 Alcala Park, F.H. 115, 92110-2492. Tel: 619-299-3639; Fax: 619-291-4207.

School Sisters of Notre Dame, 1997 Magdalene Way, 92110. Tel: 619-276-5830. Email: jweisma1@san.rr.com. Sisters 5.

Sisters of Loretto, 440 San Antonio Ave. #6, 92106. Tel: 619-224-2341. Sisters 2.

Sisters of Mercy (Ireland & South Africa), 10726 Caminito Cascara, 92108. Tel: 619-284-1027; Fax: 619-284-1027.

Sisters of Mercy of the Americas (Burlingame), 4216 Albatross Dr., 92103. Tel: 619-260-8047. Sisters 2.

Sisters of Social Service, 3525 Third Ave., 92103-4908. Tel: 619-295-1896. Sisters 3.

Sisters of St. Joseph Brentwood, NY, 4158 Utah St., 92104. Tel: 619-528-1531.

Sisters of St. Joseph of Carondelet, 4860 Oregon St., 92116. Tel: 619-295-2887; Fax: 619-297-2473. Email: aolpadmin@excite.com. Sisters 4.

Sisters of St. Joseph of Peace, 2880 Caulfield Dr., 92154. Tel: 619-423-7360. Sisters 4.

Sisters of St. Louis, 5824 Kantor Ct., 92122. Tel: 858-490-8240. Email: bboyle@diocese-sdiego.org. Web: www.st-louis-sisters.org.

Sisters of the Holy Family, 6333 College Grove Way, B9, 92115. Tel: 619-286-3371.

Sisters of the Precious Blood, 4202 58th St., 92115. Tel: 619-229-1817. Email: kelliecpps@juno.com. Sisters 2.

Society of the Holy Child Jesus, 6243 Caminito Telmo, 92111. Tel: 858-277-0309. Email: corneliasd@aol.com. Sisters 2.

BONITA. *Sisters Servants of the Blessed Sacrament*, 3173 Winnetka Dr., 91902. Tel: 619-267-0721; Fax: 619-267-0902. Email: sup@sjs-vicep.org. Sr. Maria Paz Uribe, S.J.S., Viceprovincial Supr.

CALEXICO. *Sister Servants of the Blessed Sacrament*, 536 Rockwood, 92231. Tel: 760-357-1046; Fax: 760-357-3282. Email: sjsclx@aol.com. Sisters 8.

CARLSBAD. *Sisters of Charity of the Blessed Virgin Mary*, 7238 Santa Barbara, 92009. Tel: 760-804-0841. Sr. Mary Kay Dum, Regl. Supr. Sisters 4.

CHULA VISTA. *Benedictine Sisters of Glendora*, 236 Alvarado, 91910-3610. Tel: 619-422-3610; Fax: 619-427-5786. Email: jokingestrosecv.com. Sisters 2.

Franciscan Missionaries of Our Lady of Peace, 575 E. St., #20, 91910. Tel: 619-691-9008; Fax: 619-425-7514. Email: marumFP@hotmail.com.

Religious of Jesus and Mary, 1354 Hilltop Dr., 91911. Tel: 619-427-5834; Fax: 619-427-6803. Email: rosienrjm@aol.com. Sr. Rosemary Nicholson, R.J.M., Regl. Supr. Sisters 3.

Religious of the Incarnate Word, 153 Rainier Ct., 91911. Tel: 619-420-0231; Fax: 619-691-5939. Email: iwsisters@aol.com. Sisters (Chula Vista) 3; (El Centro) 3.

Sisters of the Third Franciscan Order, 130 Jefferson Ave., #C, 91910. Tel: 619-425-3964.

EL CAJON. *Sisters of Mercy (Ireland & South Africa)*, 2766 Navajo Rd., 92020. Tel: 619-465-2233; Fax: 619-463-4421.

EL CENTRO. *Our Lady of Victory Convent*, 229 W. Rose Ave. #170, 92243. Tel: 760-353-0963. Sisters 2.

Religious of the Incarnate Word, 102 W. Holt, 92243-2730. Tel: 760-353-4146; Fax: 760-353-1261. Sisters 4.

FALLBROOK. *Hermanas del Corazon de Jesus Sacramentado*, 133 Alvarado Ct., 92028. Tel: 760-723-2271; Fax: 760-723-2271. Email hcjsfbrk@aol.com. Sisters 3.

LA JOLLA. *Dominican Sisters of Adrian*, 6570 La Jolla Scenic Dr., 92037. Tel: 619-459-3681; Fax: 619-459-4602. Email: kathleen@allhallows.com. Web: www.allhallows.com. Sisters 2.

LA MESA. *Carmelite Sisters of the Divine Heart of Jesus*, 8585 La Mesa Blvd., 91941. Tel: 619-466-3163; Fax: 619-462-8261. Sr. M. Angela Therese Lovato, D.C.J., Prov. Supr. Sisters 12; Novices 1; Postulants 1.

Franciscan Sisters of Little Falls, MN, 8681 Lemon Ave., #1, 91941. Tel: 619-698-5301. Email: 43835swald@aol.com.

Medical Mission Sisters (Western Office) , 5949 Severin Dr., 91942. Tel: 619-589-7000; Fax: 619-698-2815. Email: mmscalsd@juno.com. Web: www.medicalmissionsisters.org. Sr. Myrtle Keller, M.M.S., Western Coord. Sec. N. Amer.

Legal Title: *Society of Catholic Medical Missionaries, Inc.*

3270 Holly Way, Chula Vista, 91910-3217. Tel: 619-422-4374. Sisters 2.

2250 Tampa Ave., #1, El Cajon, 92020. Tel: 619-466-7100.

8585 La Mesa Blvd., 91941.

369 E St., #49, Chula Vista, 91911 Tel: 619-425-3829. Sisters 2.

8150 Broadway, Lemon Grove, 91945. Tel: 619-462-3888. Sisters 3.

LAKE SAN MARCOS. *Daughters of Mary and Joseph*, 1545 Via Brisa del Lago, 92069. Tel: 760-744-6578; Fax: 760-744-3828. Email: kallygoughlan@aol.com.

LEMON GROVE. *Mercedarian Sisters of the Blessed Sacrament*, 8171 Lemon Grove Way, 91945. Tel: 619-460-4271; Fax: 619-460-1060. Email: smarlup@stjohncross.org. Sisters 5.

PALA. *Sisters of St. Francis (Philadelphia)*, P.O. Box M, 92059. Tel: 760-742-1714. Sisters 2.

SAN YSIDRO. *Dominican Sisters, Tacoma WA*, 1879 Via Las Tonadas, 92173. Tel: 619-428-1529.

Medical Missionaries of Mary, 438 Blackshaw Ln., 92173. Tel: 619-690-9237; Fax: 619-428-9551. Email: mmmsy@aol.com. Web: www.mmmusa.org. Sisters 4.

Sisters Servants of the Blessed Sacrament, 333 W. Park Ave., 92173. Tel: 619-428-1314; Fax: 619-428-1314. Email: sjsolmc@cox.net. Sisters 11.

SPRING VALLEY. *Sisters of St. Joseph of Orange*, 10771 Del Rio Rd., 91978. Tel: 619-670-9663. Email: sjdelrio@pacbell.net. Sisters 3.

VISTA. *Religious of the Sacred Heart of Mary*, 820 Brooktree Ln., 92083. Tel: 760-727-3561.

Sisters of St. Clare, Santa Clara, 1974 Cherrywood St., 92081. Tel: 760-597-0981; Fax: 760-597-0986.

[J] SOCIAL SERVICES

SAN DIEGO. *Catholic Charities*, 349 Cedar St., 92101. Tel: 619-231-2828; Fax: 619-234-2272. Email: srmduvall@ccdsd.org. Web: www.ccdsd.org. Sr. RayMonda DuVall, C.H.S., Exec. Dir.; Dr. Robert Moser, Deputy Dir. Counseling Services.; Homeless Women's Services.

Emergency Services (Main Office) Tel: 619-231-2828; Fax: 619-234-2272. Michele Durne, Dir.

St. Francis Center--Vista Tel: 760-631-2819; Fax: 760-631-8238. Joan Landguth, L.C.S.W. Tel: 619-231-2828; Fax: 619-234-2272.

Pregnancy, Parenting, and Adoption Tel: 619-231-2828; Fax: 619-234-2272. Mollie McCormick, Dir.

Refugee & Immigrant Services--San Diego Tel: 619-287-9454; Fax: 619-234-2272. Michael McKay, Dir.

La Posada de Guadalupe de Carlsbad Tel: 619-929-2322; Fax: 760-929-8712. Eduardo Presiado, Dir.

El Centro--Imperial Valley Services, 250 W. Orange, El Centro, 92243. Tel: 760-353-6822; Fax: 760-353-0120.

House of Hope--Imperial Valley Tel: 760-352-1182; Fax: 760-352-5492.

Our Lady of Guadalupe Shelter Tel: 760-357-2894; Fax: 760-357-0895.

Rachel's Women's Center--San Diego, 92101. Tel: 619-696-0873; Fax: 619-696-9042. Martha Ranson, Dir.

The Tomarrow Project Tel: 619-230-1151; Fax: 619-234-9316. Barbara Sage, Dir.

Joan of Arc Residence, 1510 Third Ave., 92101. Tel: 619-239-2663; Fax: 619-234-0202. Email: agnes1050@juno.com. Sr. Agnes Bell, R.J.M., Admin. Residence for Employed Young Women and College Students 18-60 Years. Religious 9; Permanent Residents 60; Capacity 71.

**Mexican American Neighbor Organization*, P.O. Box 81635, 92138. Tel: 858-272-5285; Fax: 888-221-7609. Email: rroy@san.rr.com.

S.V.D.P. Management Inc., 3350 E St., 92102. Tel: 619-687-1000; Fax: 619-687-1010. Web: fatherjoesvillages.org. Rev. Msgr. Joseph A. Carroll, Pres. Owns and manages the property for St. Vincent de Paul Village, Inc.; Fr. Joe's Villages; Martha's Village & Kitchen in Indio, CA, and Toussaint Youth Villages in San Diego. Total Staff 85.

**St. Vincent de Paul Village*, 3350 E St., 92102-3332. Tel: 619-687-1000; Fax: 619-687-1010. Rev. Msgr. Joseph A. Carroll, Pres. Total Staff 400; Total Assisted Annually 162,540.

Joan Kroc Homeless Center, 1501 Imperial Ave., 92101. Tel: 619-687-1000; Fax: 619-687-1010. Mary Case, Vice Pres.

Bishop Maher Men's Center, 1501 Imperial Ave., 92101. Tel: 619-687-1000; Fax: 619-687-1010.

Josue Homes dba National Aids Foundation , 3350 E St., 92102. Tel: 619-466-4827; Fax: 619-687-1010.

Paul Mirabile Center--Mirabile Housing Inc., 1501 Imperial Ave., 92101. Tel: 619-233-8500; Fax: 619-687-1010.

Toussaint Teen Centers, 1404-5th St., 92101. Tel: 619-687-1080, Ext. 3399; Fax: 619-687-1010. 54 unit low to moderate apartments.

Village Place, 32-17th St., 92102. Tel: 619-687-1000; Fax: 619-687-1010.

Thrift Stores, 815 33rd St., 92102. Tel: 619-687-1021; Fax: 619-687-1010. Keith MacKay, Vice Pres.

Promiseland Ranch, Campo. Tel: 619-687-1000; Fax: 619-687-1010. Rev. Msgr. Joseph A. Carroll, Devel. Dir.

3350 E St., 92102. Tel: 619-687-1315; Fax: 619-687-1010.

[K] RETREATS

SAN DIEGO. *Spiritual Ministry Center*, 4822 Del Mar Ave., 92107-3407. Tel: 619-224-9444; Fax: 619-224-1082. Email: spiritmin@aol.com.

Whispering Winds Catholic Conference Center, 8186 Commercial St., La Mesa, 91942-2926. Tel: 619-464-1479; Fax: 619-464-4491. Email: wwccc@aol.com. Don Kojis, Exec. Dir.

ALPINE. *La Providencia Spiritual Renewal Center*, 1510 Peutz Valley Rd., 91901-1223. Tel: 619-445-4570; Fax: 619-445-8289. Email: laprovda@adnc.com. Web: www.geocities.com/laprov. Sr. Patricia Hanson, C.S.J.O.

DESCANSO. *Camp Oliver*, P.O. Box 712525, 92171. Tel: 858-492-9171; Fax: 858-874-2939. Email: camp_oliver@yahoo.com. Web: www.campoliver.com. David L. Kaplan, Exec. Dir. Summer Resident Camp for Girls & Boys, ages 6-16. Directed by Sisters of Social Service. (June-Aug.; Available Sept.-June for rental groups).

OCEANSIDE. *Mission San Luis Rey Retreat*, 4050 Mission Ave., 92057-6402. Tel: 760-757-3659; Fax: 760-757-8025. Email: slretreat@sanluisrey.org. Web: www.sanluisrey.org. Revs. Ben R. Innes, O.F.M., Retreat Dir.; Michel Gagnon, O.F.M., Retreat Assoc.; Mel Bucher, O.F.M., Retreat Office Mgr.

Prince of Peace Retreat Center, 650 Benet Hill Rd., 92054-1208. Tel: 760-430-1305; 760-430-1306; Fax: 760-967-8711. Email: princeabby@aol.com. Web: hometown.aol.com/princeabby/princeofpeaceabbey.html. Bro. Benedict Menezes, O.S.B., Guest Master. Benedictine Fathers-Benet Hill

PALA. *Pala Rey Youth Camp & Retreat Center*, 10779 Pala Rd., 92059. Tel: 760-742-8767. Mr. Roy Alvarado, Contact Person.

[L] NEWMAN CENTERS

SAN DIEGO. *Newman Center - SDSU* 5855 Hardy Ave., 92115. Tel: 619-583-9181; Fax: 619-583-8925. Email: newmancentersdsu@aol.com. Revs. Andres Arango, C.J.M.; Ricardo Chinchilla, C.J.M., Dir.

University of California at San Diego (Campus Ministry) 4321 Eastgate Mall, 92121-2102. Tel:

858-452-1957 (Office); Fax: 858-452-1985. Email: cathcom@ucsd.edu. Web: www.orpheus.ucsd.edu/CSA. Rev. John Forte, O.P., Dir.

[M] MISCELLANEOUS

SAN DIEGO. *Catholic Committee on Scouting*, 3350 E St., 92102. Tel: 619-687-1000; Fax: 619-687-1010. Rev. Msgr. Joseph A. Carroll, Scout Chap.; Mike McNelly, Chm.; Jim Freed, Coord. Tel: 619-687-1024.

Catholic Secondary Education - Diocese of San Diego, Incorporated, P.O. Box 85728, 92186. Tel: 858-490-8277; Fax: 858-490-8272.

Central San Diego Magnificat, 5592 Gala Ave., 92120. Tel: 619-583-3389. Barbara Faucher, Coord.

Mercy Hospital Foundation, San Diego, 4077 Fifth Ave., 92103. Tel: 619-686-3836; Fax: 619-293-0095. Email: stone.karen@scrippshealth.org. Web: www.scrippsfoundation.org. Karen Stone, Exec. Vice Pres.

Pauline Book and Media Center, 5945 Balboa Ave., 92111. Tel: 858-565-9181; Fax: 858-565-9295. Email: sandiego@pauline.org. Web: www.pauline.org. Sr. Armanda Santos, F.S.P., Supvr. Daughters of St. Paul Sisters 2.

**SVDP Management, Inc.*, c/o Msgr. Joseph Carroll, 3350 E. St., 92102-1332. Tel: 619-687-1000; Fax: 619-687-1010.

EL CAJON. **Catholic Answers, Inc.*, 2020 Gillespie Way, 92020. Tel: 619-387-7200; Fax: 619-387-0042. Email: publications@catholic.com. Web: www.catholic.com. Karl Keating, Pres.

Kraemer Endowment Foundation, Inc., 2119 E. Madison Ave., 92019-1111. Tel: 619-462-9034; Fax: 619-462-9034. Email: mercedes@kraemerendowment.org. Web: www.kraemerendowment.org.

ENCINITAS. **Catholic Exchange*, P.O. Box 231820, 92023. Tel: 760-635-1122; Fax: 760-635-1132.

ESCONDIDO. **Benedictus*, 8975-76 Lawrence Welk Dr., 92026. Tel: 760-751-8541; Fax: 760-751-8505. Email: bendictus1@aol.com. Web: www.stdismas.org. Deacon Kenneth J. Finn, Contact Person.

RELIGIOUS INSTITUTES OF MEN REPRESENTED IN THE DIOCESE

For further details refer to the corresponding bracketed number in the Religious Institutes of Men or Women section.

[0140]—*The Augustinians*—O.S.A.
[0200]—*Benedictine Monks*—O.S.B.
[0270]—*Carmelite Fathers*—O.Carm.
[1320]—*Clerics of St. Viator*—C.S.V.
[0160]—*Clerics Regular of St. Paul*—C.R.S.P.
[0450]—*Congregation of Jesus and Mary*—C.J.M.
[1330]—*Congregation of the Mission*—C.M.
[1000]—*Congregation of the Passion*—C.P.
[0520]—*Franciscan Friars*—O.F.M.
[0650]—*Holy Ghost Fathers*—C.S.Sp.
[]—*Holy Ghost Fathers of Ireland*—C.S.Sp.
[0690]—*Jesuit Fathers and Brothers*—S.J.
[0800]—*Maryknoll Fathers*—M.M.
[1210]—*Missionaries of St. Charles (Scalabrinians)*—C.S.
[1110]—*Missionaries of the Sacred Heart*—M.S.C.
[0840]—*Missionary Servants of the Most Holy Trinity*—S.T.
[0910]—*Oblates of Mary Immaculate*—O.M.I.
[0430]—*Order of Preachers (Dominicans)*—O.P.
[1030]—*Paulist Fathers*—C.S.P.
[1260]—*Society of Christ*—S.Ch.
[0370]—*Society of St. Columban*—S.S.C.
[0420]—*Society of the Divine Word*

RELIGIOUS INSTITUTES OF WOMEN REPRESENTED IN THE DIOCESE

[0230]—*Benedictine Sisters of Pontifical Jurisdiction* (Glendora, CA; St. Joseph, MN)—O.S.B.
[0360]—*Carmelite Sisters of the Divine Heart of Jesus*—Carmel.D.C
[2020]—*Community of the Holy Spirit*—C.H.S.
[3242]—*Congregation of the Sisters of Nazareth*—C.S.N.
[1920]—*Congregation of the Sisters of the Holy Cross*—C.S.C.
[1710]—*Congregation of the Third Order of St. Francis of Mary Immaculate, Joliet, IL*—O.S.F.
[0790]—*Daughters of Divine Charity*—F.D.C.
[0880]—*Daughters of Mary and Joseph*—D.M.J.
[0420]—*Discalced Carmelite Nuns*—O.C.D.
[1070-03]—*Dominican Sisters*—O.P.
[1070-13]—*Dominican Sisters*—O.P.
[1070-21]—*Dominican Sisters*—O.P.
[1070-20]—*Dominican Sisters*—O.P.
[1070-11]—*Dominican Sisters*—O.P.
[]—*Franciscan Missionaries of Our Lady of Peace*—M.F.P.
[1310]—*Franciscan Sisters of Little Falls, MN*—O.S.F.
[1845]—*Guadalupan Missionaries of the Holy Spirit*—M.G.Sp.S.
[]—*Hermanas del Corazon de Jesus Sacramentado*—H.C.J.S.
[2470]—*Maryknoll Sisters of St. Dominic*—M.M.
[2490]—*Medical Mission Sisters*—M.M.S.
[2480]—*Medical Missionaries of Mary*—M.M.M.
[2590]—*Mercedarian Sisters of the Blessed Sacrament*—H.M.S.S.
[2710]—*Missionaries of Charity*—M.C.
[3070]—*North American Unions of Sisters of Our Lady of Charity*—N.A.U.-O.L.C.
[3130]—*Our Lady of Victory Missionary Sisters*—O.L.V.M.
[0950]—*Pious Society Daughters of St. Paul*—F.S.P.
[3450]—*Religious of Jesus and Mary*—R.J.M.
[3449]—*Religious of the Incarnate Word*—C.V.I.
[3465]—*Religious of the Sacred Heart of Mary*—R.S.H.M.
[2970]—*School Sisters of Notre Dame*—S.S.N.D.
[1680]—*School Sisters of St. Francis*—O.S.F.
[0480]—*Sisters of Charity of Leavenworth, KS*
[0520]—*Sisters of Charity of Our Lady, Mother of Mercy*—S.C.M.M.
[0430]—*Sisters of Charity of the Blessed Virgin Mary*—B.V.M.
[2360]—*Sisters of Loretto At the Foot of the Cross*—S.L.
[2549]—*Sisters of Mercy of Ireland & U.S. Province*—R.S.M.
[2575]—*Sisters of Mercy of The Americas* (Burlingame, CA; Omaha, NE)—R.S.M.
[1540]—*Sisters of Saint Francis, Clinton, Iowa*—O.S.F.
[4080]—*Sisters of Social Service of Los Angeles, Inc.*—S.S.S.
[3770]—*Sisters of St. Clare*—O.S.C.
[1705]—*The Sisters of St. Francis of Assisi*—O.S.F.
[1630]—*Sisters of St. Francis of Penance and Christian Charity*—O.S.F.
[1650]—*Sisters of St. Francis of Philadelphia*—O.S.F.
[3830-03]—*Sisters of St. Joseph* (Orange)—C.S.J.
[3830-05]—*Sisters of St. Joseph* (Brentwood, NY)—C.S.J.
[3840]—*Sisters of St. Joseph of Carondelet* (Los Angeles, CA; St. Louis, MO)—C.S.J.
[3890]—*Sisters of St. Joseph of Peace* (Bellevue, WA)—C.S.J.P.
[3935]—*Sisters of St. Louis*—S.S.L.
[1960]—*Sisters of the Holy Family*—S.H.F.
[1990]—*Sisters of the Holy Names of Jesus and Mary*—S.N.J.M.
[3260]—*Sisters of the Precious Blood (Dayton, Ohio)*—C.PP.S.
[1720]—*Sisters of the Third Order Regular of St. Francis of The Congregation of Our Lady of Lourdes*—O.S.F.
[1490]—*Sisters of Third Franciscan Order*—O.S.F.
[3499]—*Sisters Servants of the Blessed Sacrament*—S.J.S.
[4060]—*Society of the Holy Child Jesus*—S.H.C.J.
[4070]—*Society of the Sacred Heart*—R.S.C.J.

DIOCESAN CEMETERIES

SAN DIEGO. *Holy Cross, El Campo, Mission San Diego de Alcala*
DEL MAR. *Calvary*
JACUMBA. 3 Indian Reservation cemeteries.
PALA INDIAN MISSIONS. 6 separate Indian burial grounds.
SAN LUIS REY. *Mission San Luis Rey*
SANTA YSABEL INDIAN MISSIONS. 15 separate Indian burial grounds.

NECROLOGY

† Gudino, Eduardo, Oceanside, CA St. Mary Star of the Sea—Died April 30, 2003
† Keith, John C., (Retired)—Died May 1, 2003
† McDonnell, Francis, (Retired)—Died Nov. 19, 2003
† Polizzi, Daniel, (Unassigned)—Died July 12, 2003

Archdiocese of San Francisco

(Archidioecesis Sancti Francisci)

Most Reverend

WILLIAM J. LEVADA, S.T.D.

Archbishop of San Francisco; ordained December 20, 1961; appointed Titular Bishop of Capri and Auxiliary Bishop of Los Angeles March 29, 1983; Episcopal ordination May 12, 1983; appointed Archbishop of Portland in Oregon July 1, 1986; installed as Archbishop of Portland in Oregon September 21, 1986; appointed Coadjutor Archbishop of San Francisco August 17, 1995; succeeded to See December 27, 1995 *Office: One Peter Yorke Way, San Francisco, CA 94109-6602.*

Most Reverend

JOHN C. WESTER, D.D.

Auxiliary Bishop of San Francisco; ordained May 15, 1976; appointed Auxiliary Bishop of San Francisco and Titular Bishop of Lamiggiga June 30, 1998; Episcopal ordination September 18, 1998 *Office: One Peter Yorke Way, San Francisco, CA 94109-6602.*

Most Reverend

IGNATIUS WANG

Auxiliary Bishop of San Francisco; ordained July 4, 1959; appointed Titular Bishop of Sitipa and Auxiliary Bishop of San Francisco December 13, 2002; installed January 30, 2003 *Office: One Peter Yorke Way, San Francisco, CA 94109-6602.*

The Chancery Office: One Peter Yorke Way, San Francisco, CA 94109-6602. Tel: 415-614-5500; Fax: 415-614-5555.

Web: www.sfarchdiocese.org

Email: info@sfarchdiocese.org

Most Reverend

JOHN R. QUINN

Archbishop Emeritus of San Francisco; ordained July 19, 1953; appointed Auxiliary Bishop of San Diego and Titular Bishop of Thisiduo October 21, 1967; Episcopal ordination December 12, 1967; Transferred to Oklahoma City and Tulsa November 18, 1971; appointed as Archbishop of the Archdiocese of Oklahoma City on February 6, 1973; appointed Archbishop of San Francisco February 22, 1977; installed as Archbishop of San Francisco April 26, 1977; resigned December 27, 1995 *Res.: 322 Middlefield Rd., Menlo Park, CA 94025-3509.* Tel: 650-325-2674; Fax: 650-326-6870.

ESTABLISHED JULY 29, 1853.

Square Miles 1,012.

Code Address: Roman, San Francisco.

Comprises the Counties of San Francisco, San Mateo and Marin in the State of California.

Patrons of the Archdiocese of San Francisco: St. Francis of Assisi, October 4; St. Patrick, March 17.

Legal Title: The Roman Catholic Archbishop of San Francisco, a Corporation Sole.

For legal titles of parishes and archdiocesan institutions, consult the Chancery Office.

STATISTICAL OVERVIEW

Personnel	
Archbishops	1
Retired Archbishops	1
Auxiliary Bishops	2
Priests: Diocesan Active in Diocese	138
Priests: Diocesan Active Outside Diocese	10
Priests: Diocesan in Foreign Missions	1
Priests: Retired, Sick or Absent	70
Number of Diocesan Priests	219
Religious Priests in Diocese	153
Total Priests in Diocese	372
Extern Priests in Diocese	65
Ordinations:	
Diocesan Priests	2
Religious Priests	3
Transitional Deacons	3
Permanent Deacons in Diocese	66
Total Brothers	55
Total Sisters	800
Parishes	
Parishes	93
With Resident Pastor:	
Resident Diocesan Priests	79
Resident Religious Priests	14
Missions	11
Pastoral Centers	5
Professional Ministry Personnel:	
Brothers	6
Sisters	66
Lay Ministers	2,522
Welfare	
Catholic Hospitals	3
Total Assisted	417,335
Health Care Centers	20
Total Assisted	211,500
Homes for the Aged	18
Total Assisted	2,859
Residential Care of Children	16
Total Assisted	16,500
Day Care Centers	5
Total Assisted	500
Specialized Homes	8
Total Assisted	55,000
Special Centers for Social Services	8
Total Assisted	16,750
Residential Care of Disabled	8
Total Assisted	400
Other Institutions	38
Total Assisted	802,000
Educational	
Seminaries, Diocesan	1
Students from This Diocese	14
Students from Other Diocese	74
Diocesan Students in Other Seminaries	4
Seminaries, Religious	1
Total Seminarians	18
Colleges and Universities	3
Total Students	11,499
High Schools, Diocesan and Parish	4
Total Students	3,713
High Schools, Private	10
Total Students	4,802
Elementary Schools, Diocesan and Parish	66
Total Students	17,942
Elementary Schools, Private	7
Total Students	1,850
Catechesis/Religious Education:	
High School Students	8,262
Elementary Students	20,004
Total Students under Catholic Instruction	68,090
Teachers in the Diocese:	
Priests	15
Brothers	15
Sisters	117
Lay Teachers	1,934
Vital Statistics	
Receptions into the Church:	
Infant Baptism Totals	7,670
Adult Baptism Totals	487
Received into Full Communion	493
First Communions	5,386
Confirmations	3,417
Marriages:	
Catholic	1,143
Interfaith	442
Total Marriages	1,585
Deaths	3,278
Total Catholic Population	422,500
Total Population	1,720,450

Former Bishops—Rt. Rev. FRANCIS GARCIA DIEGO Y MORENO, O.F.M., D.D., consecrated Bishop of both Californias, Oct. 4, 1840; died in Santa Barbara, April 30, 1846; Most Revs. JOSEPH SADOC ALEMANY, O.P., D.D., consecrated Bishop of Monterey, June 30, 1850; appt. first Archbishop of San Francisco, July 29, 1853; resigned and appt. Titular Archbishop of Pelusio, Dec. 28, 1884; died in Valencia, Spain, April 14, 1888; PATRICK WILLIAM RIORDAN, D.D., consecrated Titular Archbishop of Cabasa and appt. Coadjutor Archbishop of San Francisco cum jure successionis Sept. 16, 1883; succeeded to Dec. 28, 1884; died in San Francisco, Dec. 27, 1914; GEORGE MONTGOMERY, D.D., consecrated Titular Bishop of Tmui and appt. Coadjutor Bishop of Monterey and Los Angeles cum jure successionis April 8, 1894; succeeded to May 6, 1896; appt. Titular Archbishop of Osimo and Coadjutor Archbishop of San Francisco cum jure successionis March 27, 1903; died in San Francisco, Jan. 10, 1907; EDWARD J. HANNA, D.D., consecrated Titular Bishop of Titopolis and appt. Auxiliary Bishop of San Francisco Dec. 4, 1912; appt. Archbishop of San Francisco, June 1, 1915; resigned and appt. Titular Archbishop of Gortyna, March 2, 1935; died July 10, 1944; JOHN JOSEPH MITTY, D.D., consecrated Bishop of Salt Lake City, June 21, 1926; appt. Coadjutor Archbishop of San Francisco cum jure successionis, Jan. 29, 1932; succeeded to March 2, 1935; died Oct. 15, 1961; JOSEPH T. MCGUCKEN, S.T.D. (Retired), appt. Auxiliary of Los Angeles, Feb. 4, 1941; consecrated Titular Bishop of Sanavo March 19, 1941; appt. Coadjutor Bishop of Sacramento cum jure successionis, Oct. 26, 1955; succeeded to Jan. 14, 1957; appt. Archbishop of San Francisco, Feb. 21, 1962; appt. Assistant at the Pontifical Throne, March 19, 1966; retired Feb. 22, 1977; died Oct. 26, 1983; JOHN R. QUINN, appt. Auxiliary Bishop of San Diego, Oct. 21, 1967; consecrated Titular Bishop of Thisiduo, Dec. 12, 1967; transferred to Oklahoma City and Tulsa, Nov. 18, 1971; appt. Archbishop of the Archdiocese of Oklahoma City, Feb. 6, 1973; appt. Archbishop of San Francisco, April 26, 1977; resigned Dec. 27, 1995.

Chancery and Pastoral Center—One Peter Yorke Way, San Francisco, 94109-6602. Tel: 415-614-5500; Fax: 415-614-5555. Open Mon.-Fri. All applications for dispensations, faculties, etc., and all correspondence should be addressed: Chancery and Pastoral Center.

Office of the Archbishop—

Archbishop—Most Rev. WILLIAM J. LEVADA, S.T.D.

Secretary to the Archbishop—Rev. Msgr. THOMAS S. MERSON.
Executive Assistant to the Archbishop—LAURIE M. HAWKINS.
Office of the Auxiliary Bishop, Vicar General and Vicar for Clergy—Most Rev. JOHN C. WESTER, V.G., Auxiliary Bishop.
Administrative Assistant—ANNABELLE GROH.
Secretary to the Priests' Personnel Board—Rev. DAVID M. PETTINGILL.
Office of the Permanent Diaconate—Deacon LEON KORTENKAMP. Tel: 415-614-5530; Fax: 415-614-5555.
Office of Diaconate Formation—Rev. DAVID M. PETTINGILL.
Office of Clergy Formation—VACANT.
Office of Vocations—Rev. THOMAS A. DALY, Dir. Tel: 415-614-5683.
Office of the Vicar for Religious—Rev. ANDREW F. MAGINNIS, S.J. Tel: 415-614-5535.
Retired Priests—Rev. CLIFFORD MARTIN, Liaison.
Auxiliary Bishop & Episcopal Vicar for Promotion of Spiritual & Apostolic Life, & Ethnic Ministries—Most Rev. IGNATIUS C. WANG. Administrative Assistants: PEGGY MORRIS; POSIM YUEN.
Episcopal Vicar for the Spanish Speaking—Rev. Msgr. JOSE RODRIGUEZ.
College of Consultors—Most Revs. WILLIAM J. LEVADA; JOHN C. WESTER, V.G.; IGNATIUS C. WANG; Revs. RANDOLPH R. CALVO, J.C.D.; THOMAS A. DALY; Rev. Msgrs. MICHAEL D. HARRIMAN; ROBERT W. MCELROY; JOSE A. RODRIGUEZ; HARRY G. SCHLITT; Revs. JAMES T. TARANTINO; EUGENE D. TUNGOL.
Deans—Rev. Msgr. FRED A. BITANGA; Rev. DONALD S. D'ANGELO; Rev. Msgr. BRUCE A. DREIER; Revs. MARIO P. FARANA; XAVIER LAVAGETTO, O.P.; MICHAEL J. KEANE; JAMES H. MACDONALD; DOMINGO ORIMACO; MICHAEL C. PADAZINSKI, J.C.D.; ANTONIO PETILLA; JAMES T. TARANTINO.
Council of Priests—Rev. THOMAS A. DALY, Chm.; MARY ELLEN HOFFMAN, Sec.
Archdiocesan Pastoral Council—Deacon BERNARD O'HALLORAN, Chm.; MARY ELLEN HOFFMAN, Sec.
Censores Librorum—Rev. Msgr. WARREN HOLLERAN, S.T.D.; Rev. GERALD D. COLEMAN, S.S., S.T.L., Ph.D.
Moderator of the Curia and Vicar for Administration—Rev. Msgr. HARRY G. SCHLITT.
Administrative Assistant—DOROTHY YIP. Tel: 415-614-5615.
Director of Finance / Chief Finance Officer—RICHARD P. HANNON.
Office of Development—Deacon JOHN NORRIS.
Archdiocesan Legal Office—Mr. JACK M. HAMMEL, Esq.; Mr. LARRY JANNUZZI, Esq.
Office of the Propagation of the Faith—Most Rev. IGNATIUS C. WANG, Dir.
Office of Real Estate—Mr. LES MCDONALD.
Real Estate Committee—Mr. BILL HALEY; Mr. JOHN A. CATTALINI; Mr. TERRENCE E. O'BRIEN.
Office of Human Resources—Mr. CARL FEIL.
Catholic Cemeteries—KATHERINE ATKINSON, P.O. Box 1577, Colma, 94014. Tel: 650-756-2060; Fax: 650-994-8147. Email: sfcathcems@aol.com.
Chancellor—Rev. STEPHEN A. MERIWETHER, J.C.L. Tel: 415-614-5677; Fax: 415-614-5555.
Vice Chancellor—Rev. C. MICHAEL PADAZINSKI.
Archdiocesan Archives—JEFFREY BURNS, Ph.D.
Office of Ecumenism and Interreligious Affairs—Rev. STEPHEN A. MERIWETHER, J.C.L.
Metropolitan Tribunal—
San Francisco Metropolitan Tribunal—One Peter Yorke Way, San Francisco, 94109-6602. Tel: 415-614-5500; Fax: 415-614-5555.
Judicial Vicar and Director—Rev. C. MICHAEL PADAZINSKI.
Adjutant Judicial Vicar—Rev. JOSE CHAVARIN, J.C.L.
Promoter of Justice—Rev. Msgr. RICHARD S. KNAPP.
Defenders of the Bond—Rev. THUAN V. HOANG, J.C.L.; DIANE L. BARR, J.C.L.
Judges—ROBERT J.B. FLUMMERFELT, J.C.L.; Revs. ROBERT M. HERBST, O.F.M.Conv., J.C.L.; STEPHEN MERIWETHER, J.C.L.; KRYSTYNA AMBORSKI, J.C.L.; Rev. WILLIAM E. DUGGAN, J.C.L. (Retired).
Tribunal Auditors—Sr. BERNADETTE HESLIN, R.S.M.; BRETT WILLIAMS; REINA PARADA.
Notaries and Secretaries to the Tribunal—FRANCINE SPOLTORE; JOSEPH MURPHY; REINA A. PARADA.
Archbishop's Cabinet—Most Revs. WILLIAM J. LEVADA, S.T.D.; JOHN C. WESTER, V.G.; IGNATIUS C. WANG; Rev. Msgrs. HARRY G. SCHLITT; JOHN A. RODRIGUEZ; THOMAS S. MERSON; Rev. STEPHEN A. MERIWETHER, J.C.L.; Sr. ANTONIO HEAPHY, P.B.V.M.; MAUREEN HUNTINGTON; MAURY HEALY.
Department of Pastoral Ministry—Sr. ANTONIO HEAPHY, P.B.V.M., Dir. Tel: 415-614-5504; Fax: 415-614-5658. Email: heaphya@sfarchdiocese.org; ROSA GOMEZ, Admin. Asst.
Office of Evangelization—Sr. ANTONIO HEAPHY, P.B.V.M. Tel: 415-614-5504; Fax: 415-614-5658. Email: heaphya@sfarchdiocese.org.
Office of Ethnic Ministries—Ms. NOEMI CASTILLO, Dir.
Hispanic Coordinator—CECILIA ARIAS-RIVAS.
Chinese Ministry—Sr. MARIA HSU, Fd.CC.
Japanese Mission—Mr. HIROKO SAKAMAKI, Liaison, St. Francis Xavier Church, 1801 Octavia St., San Francisco, 94109. Tel: 415-346-7309.
Arab-American Catholic Ministry—Rev. LABIB KOBTI, St. Thomas More Church, 1300 Junipero Serra Blvd., San Francisco, 94132. Tel: 415-452-9634.
Polish, Croatian, Slovenian Mission—Rev. JERZY FRYDRYCH, S.Ch., Nativity Church, 245 Linden St., San Francisco, 94102. Tel: 415-252-5799.
Korean Catholic Ministry—Rev. BENEDICT JEONG BAY PAK, 32 Broad St., San Francisco, 94112. Tel: 415-333-1194; Fax: 415-333-1196.
Tongan Ministry—Rev. SAIMONE MOALA, St. Timothy Church, 1515 Dolan Ave., San Mateo, 94401. Tel: 650-342-2470; Fax: 650-342-8156.
Vietnamese Catholic Ministry—Rev. TE VAN NGUYEN, Holy Name of Jesus Church, 3240 Lawton St., San Francisco, 94122. Tel: 415-759-4293; Fax: 415-664-9775.
Brazilian Ministry—JOSEPH FREITAS, 1500 Elm, El Cerrito, 94530.
Burmese Ministry—ELIZABETH LAW, Coord., 2900 19th Ave., San Francisco, 94132. Tel: 415-584-2487.
Congolese Ministry—Rev. JEAN PIERRE BONGILA, Contact, 1075 Ellis St., San Francisco, 94109. Tel: 415-775-3727.
Filipino Ministry—NOEMI CASTILLO, Coord.
Haitian Ministry—PIERRE LABOSSIERE, Coord., P.O. Box 13381, Berkeley, 94712. Tel: 510-533-0633.
Irish Ministry—Rev. BRENDAN MCBRIDE, Coord., St. Philip the Apostle Parish, 725 Diamond St., San Francisco, 94114. Tel: 415-282-0104.
Italian Ministry—Sts. Peter and Paul Parish, San Francisco, 94133.
Native American—SACHEEN LITTLEFEATHER, Coord.
Nigerian Ministry—Rev. CHARLES ONUBUGO, 3261 16th St., San Francisco, 94114. Tel: 415-621-8203.
Samoan Ministry—JOANNA LEFAO, Contact, 1715 Oakdale Ave., San Francisco, 94124. Tel: 650-758-5812.
Office of Marriage and Family Life—CHRISTOPHER LYFORD, Dir. Tel: 415-614-5680; Fax: 415-614-5658. Email: Chris@CatholicFamilyLife2000.com.
Office of Religious Education and Youth Ministry—Sisters CELESTE ARBUCKLE, S.S.S., Dir. Tel: 415-614-5655; MAUREEN ROE, R.S.M., Assoc. Dir. Special Needs. Tel: 415-614-5655; MARC GONZALEZ, Assoc. Dir. Hispanic Ministry. Tel: 415-614-5653; ELAINE RACHKO, Assoc. Dir. Youth Ministry. Tel: 415-614-5651; NOELE KOSTELIC, Coord. Catechetical Ministries. Tel: 415-614-5654.
Victim Assistance Coordinator—BARBARA ELORDI. Tel: 415-614-5506; Fax: 415-614-5658. Email: belordi@ccasf.org.
Office of Young Adult Ministry—Sr. CHRISTINE WILCOX, O.P., Dir. Tel: 415-614-5595; Fax: 415-614-5658. Email: wilcoxc@sfarchdiocese.org; MARY JANSEN, Assoc. Dir. Tel: 415-614-5596; Fax: 415-614-5658. Email: jansenm@sfarchdiocese.org.
School of Pastoral Leadership—Mr. DAVID MCCUTCHEN, Dir. Tel: 415-614-5547; Fax: 415-614-5543.
Office of Worship—Rev. JOHN TALESFORE, Dir.; PATRICK VALLEZ-KELLY, Asst. Dir.
Department of Catholic Schools—MAUREEN HUNTINGTON, Supt.; PAUL BERGEZ, Assoc. Supt. Devel. & Finance; MARILYN LYNCH, Assoc. Supt. for Personnel & Staff Devel.; Sr. MARIANNE VIANI, S.N.J.M., Assoc. Supt. Curriculum/School Improvement; ROBERT MEANEY, Asst. Supt. Faith Formation & Rel. Instruction; JEFF BRAID, Technology Specialist, Government Programs & Public Policy. Tel: 415-614-5660; Fax: 415-614-5664.
Archdiocesan Board of Education—Most Rev. WILLIAM J. LEVADA; THOMAS VOCKER, Chm.; Dr. ROBERT GROSS, Vice Chm.; Sr. DIANE ARUDA, O.P.; Rev. WILLIAM BRADY; MICHAEL SMYLLIE; RUSSELL JACKSON; JOHN SEBASTINELLI; ANDREINA GROSS; LORRAINE WELCH PAUL; ANTHONY RAMIREZ; JOSEPH TOBONI.
The Roman Catholic Welfare Corporation of San Francisco—Board of Directors: Most Revs. WILLIAM J. LEVADA, S.T.D., Pres.; JOHN C. WESTER, V.G.; IGNATIUS C. WANG; Rev. Msgrs. HARRY G. SCHLITT; STEVEN D. OTELLINI; JOSE A. RODRIGUEZ; Revs. JAMES H. MACDONALD; RANDOLPH R. CALVO, J.C.D.; STEPHEN A. MERIWETHER, J.C.L.; Sisters ANTONIO HEAPHY, P.B.V.M.; LEONARDA MONTEALTO, O.P.; MARIANNE VIANI, S.N.J.M.; MAUREEN HUNTINGTON; PAUL BERGEZ; RICHARD P. HANNON; NOREEN MURPHY.
Department of Communications and Outreach—MAURICE E. HEALY, Dir.
Archdiocesan Publication: "Catholic San Francisco"—Most Rev. WILLIAM J. LEVADA, S.T.D., Publisher; MAURICE E. HEALY, Editor; JACK SMITH, Asst. Editor.
Office of Public Policy and Social Concerns—GEORGE WESOLEK, Dir. Tel: 415-614-5571; Fax: 415-614-5568. Email: wesolekg@sfarchdiocese.org.
Detention Ministry—RAY MCKEON. Tel: 415-614-5569. Email: mckeonr@sfarchdiocese.org.
Justice and Peace—
Respect Life—
Hospitals / Healthcare—
CCHD—MELANIE PIENDAK.

CLERGY, PARISHES, MISSIONS AND PAROCHIAL SCHOOLS

CITY OF SAN FRANCISCO
(SAN FRANCISCO COUNTY)

1—CATHEDRAL OF ST. MARY (ASSUMPTION) (1891), Revs. John J. Talesfore, Admin.; Jean Pierre Bongila; Lawrence J. Finegan; Deacon Peter Boulware. In Res., Rev. James Atkins (Retired).
Cathedral Office—1111 Gough St., 94109. Tel: 415-567-2020; Fax: 415-567-2040.
Catechesis / Religious Program—Students 90.

2—ST. AGNES (1893), Rev. J. Cameron Ayers, S.J. In Res., Revs. Michael M. Turnacliff, S.J.; Donald Sharp, S.J., S.T.D.
Res.: 1025 Masonic Ave., 94117. Tel: 415-487-8560; Fax: 415-487-8575.

3—ALL HALLOWS CHAPEL OF OUR LADY OF LOURDES (1886), Closed., For sacramental records please contact Our Lady of Lourdes, San Francisco.
Chapel—Our Lady of Lourdes

4—ST. ANNE (1904), Revs. Eduardo Dura; William Myers; Deacon John Dupre. In Res., Rev. Msgr. Thomas S. Merson.
Res.: 850 Judah St., 94122. Tel: 415-665-1600; Fax: 415-665-1603.
School—1320 14th Ave., 94122. Tel: 415-664-7977; Fax: 415-661-6904. Sisters 2; Lay Teachers 23; Students 585.
Catechesis / Religious Program—Tel: 415-665-1600, Ext. 25. Students 70.

5—ST. ANTHONY OF PADUA (1893), Revs. Oscar A. Mendez, O.F.M.; Guglielmo Lauriola, O.F.M.; Javier Rayes, O.F.M. In Res., Revs. Robert Pfisterer, O.F.M.; Floyd A. Lotito, O.F.M., Guardian; Anthony Baumann, O.F.M.; Finian McGinn, O.F.M.; Francisco Reyes, O.F.M.; Francisco Akso, O.F.M.; Bros. David Cobian, O.F.M.; Alberto Villafon, O.F.M.
Res.: 3215 Cesar Chavez St., 94110. Tel: 415-647-2704; Fax: 415-647-7282.
Chapel—Immaculate Conception Chapel 3255 Folsom St., 94110. Tel: 415-824-1762; Fax: 415-824-0129.
School—St. Anthony-Immaculate Conception, 299 Precita Ave., 94110. Tel: 415-648-2008; Fax: 415-648-1825. Sr. Carolin Marie Monahan, O.P., Prin. Sisters 4; Lay Teachers 23; Students 320.
Catechesis / Religious Program—Tel: 415-641-2704. Students 320.

6—ST. BENEDICT PARISH AT ST. FRANCIS XAVIER CHURCH (1913), (Japanese),, (Founded 1962 for Deaf and Hearing Impaired). Rev. Thomas Coughlin, H.N.L., Admin.
Res.: 1801 Octavia, 94109. Tel: 415-567-9855; 415-567-0438 (TDD); Fax: 415-567-0916.
Catechesis / Religious Program—Students 5.

7—ST. BONIFACE (1860), (German), Revs. Louis Vitale, O.F.M.; Sergio Santos; John Vaughn, O.F.M.; Hoang Trinh, O.F.M. (ORG). In Res., Revs. Stephen Tan Nguyen, O.F.M.; Richard Purcell, O.F.M.; Bros. Robert Brady, O.F.M.; Kelly Cullen, O.F.M.; Dennis Duffy, O.F.M.; Stephen Gillis, O.F.M.
Res.: 133 Golden Gate Ave., 94102. Tel: 415-863-0111; Fax: 415-863-7602.
Catechesis / Religious Program—Students 225.

8—ST. BRENDAN (1929), Revs. Thomas M. Parenti; Balaswamy Govindu. In Res., Rev. John J. Talesfore; Deacon Andrew Johnson; Kathy Lorentz, Pastoral Assoc.
Res.: 29 Rockaway Ave., 94127. Tel: 415-681-4225; Fax: 415-681-3976.
School—234 Ulloa St., 94127. Tel: 415-731-2665; Fax: 415-731-7207. Sisters of St. Dominic, Adrian, MI 2; Lay Teachers 21; Students 346.

Catechesis/Religious Program—Tel: 415-664-8481. Students 16.

9—St. Brigid (1863), Closed., For sacramental records please contact St. Vincent de Paul, San Francisco.

10—St. Cecilia (1917), Rev. Msgr. Michael D. Harriman; Revs. Lodovico Joseph Landi; Vito J. Perrone. In Res., Rev. Msgr. John T. Foudy (Retired).
Res.: 2555 17th Ave., 94116. Tel: 415-664-8481; Fax: 415-661-2957.
School—660 Vicente St., 94116. Tel: 415-731-8400; Fax: 415-731-5686. Sisters of the Holy Names 4; Lay Teachers 17; Students 580.
Catechesis/Religious Program—Students 123.

11—St. Charles Borromeo (1887), Revs. Moises Agudo, Admin.; Nestor Aterado.
Res.: 713 S. Van Ness Ave., 94110. Tel: 415-824-1700; Fax: 415-824-0844.
School—3250 18th St., 94110. Tel: 415-861-7652; Fax: 415-861-0221. Dominican Sisters of the Most Holy Rosary (Philippines) 6; Lay Teachers 10; Students 315.
Catechesis/Religious Program—Tel: 415-282-8956. Students 100.

12—Church of the Epiphany (1914), Rev. Msgr. Bruce A. Dreier; Revs. Charito Suan; Julio Recio, O.P.; Deacons Manuel Ocon; Ding Viray.
Res.: 827 Vienna St., 94112. Tel: 415-333-7630; Fax: 415-333-1803.
School—600 Italy Ave., 94112. Tel: 415-337-4030; Fax: 415-337-8583. Sisters 1; Lay Teachers 23; Students 601.
Catechesis/Religious Program—Tel: 415-333-5051. Students 330.

13—Corpus Christi (1898), Revs. John M. O'Brien, S.D.B.; Ubaldo A. Chueca, S.D.B. (LA); Aloysius J. Pestun, S.D.B.; Marvin P. Felipe, S.D.B.
Res.: 62 Santa Rosa Ave., 94112. Tel: 415-585-2291; Fax: 415-585-0773.
School—75 Francis St., 94112. Tel: 415-587-7014; Fax: 415-587-1575. Salesian Sisters of St. John Bosco (Daughters of Mary Help of Christians) 5; Lay Teachers 10; Students 295.
Catechesis/Religious Program—Tel: 415-585-3240. Students 200.

14—St. Dominic (1873), Very Rev. Emmerich W. Vogt, O.P. (P), Dir., Shrine of St. Jude; Revs. Xavier M. Lavagetto, O.P.; Francis Goode, O.P.; Peter Rogers, O.P.; Bro. Mark Gorski, O.P.; Deacons Fred Swanson; Charles McNeil. In Res., Revs. Felix F. Cassidy, O.P.; Gregory T. Tatum, O.P.; Joseph M. Sergott, O.P., Prior; Anthony Rosevear, O.P., Novice Master.
Res.: 2390 Bush St., 94115. Tel: 415-567-7824; Fax: 415-567-1608.
School—2445 Pine St., 94115. Tel: 415-346-9500; Fax: 415-346-8001. Sisters of the Third Order of St. Dominic, Congregation of the Most Holy Name 4; Sisters of the Holy Names of Jesus and Mary 1; Lay Teachers 8; Students 237.
Catechesis/Religious Program—Students 80.

15—St. Edward (1916), Closed., For sacramental records please contact St. Dominic, San Francisco.

16—St. Elizabeth (1912), Revs. Edwin W. Farrugia; Toan X. Nguyen.
Res.: 449 Holyoke Ave., 94134. Tel: 415-468-0820; Fax: 415-468-1457.
School—450 Somerset St., 94134. Tel: 415-468-3247; Fax: 415-468-1804. Lay Teachers 10; Students 239.
Catechesis/Religious Program—Tel: 415-468-0423. Students 100.

17—St. Emydius (1913), Revs. William J. Brady; David M. Pettingill.
Res.: 286 Ashton Ave., 94112. Tel: 415-587-7066; Fax: 415-587-6690.
School—301 DeMontfort Ave., 94112. Tel: 415-333-4877; Fax: 415-333-3040. Mrs. Judith Borelli, Prin. Lay Teachers 11; Students 151.
Catechesis/Religious Program—Students 21.

18—St. Finn Barr (1926), Revs. Jose Corral, Admin.; Dominic Savio Lee; Deacons Romeo Ayalin; Thomas Ilao.
Res.: 415 Edna St., 94112. Tel: 415-333-3627; Fax: 415-333-4090. Email: stfinnbarrparish@aol.com.
School—419 Hearst Ave., 94112. Tel: 415-333-1800; Fax: 415-452-0177. Dominican Sisters of the Holy Rosary (Philippines) 5; Adrian Dominican Sisters 1; Lay Teachers 14; Students 179.
Catechesis/Religious Program—Students 30.

19—St. Francis of Assisi, National Shrine, Closed. Rev. Allen Ramirez, O.F.M.Conv., Rector; Bro. Robert Ouellette, O.F.M.Conv., Prog. Dir.
610 Vallejo St., 94133. Tel: 415-983-0405; Fax: 415-983-0407. Email: shrinesf@flash.net.

20—St. Gabriel (1941), Revs. John A. Ryan; Mark G. Mazza (GRY). In Res., Rev. P. Gerard O'Rourke.
Res.: 2559 40th Ave., 94116. Tel: 415-731-6161; Fax: 415-731-1270.
School—2550 41st Ave., 94116. Tel: 415-566-0314; Fax: 415-566-3223. Lay Teachers 20; Students 471.
Catechesis/Religious Program—Students 126.

21—Holy Cross (1887), (Korean), Closed. For inquiries for parish records contact the chancery.

22—Holy Family Chinese Mission (1921), (Chinese), Rev. Daniel E. McCotter, C.S.P.; Sr. Paulette Yueng, M.M., Pastoral Assoc., Teahouse Ministry; Ms. Lisa Tom French, Exec. Dir. (aka St. Mary's Chinese Catholic Center--1903)
Res.: 660 California St., 94108. Tel: 415-421-5636; Fax: 415-929-4698.
School—St. Mary Chinese Day School, 910 Broadway 94133. Tel: 415-929-4690; Fax: 415-929-4699. Dr. Jerry DiNoto, Prin. Sisters 4; Lay Teachers 15; Students 240.
School—Chinese Language School, Tel: 415-929-4694. Stephen Woon Wah Tang, Prin. Chinese Teachers 14; Elementary Students 500; High School Students 100; Total Students 600.
Holy Family Association—Fax: 415-929-4698. Lance Hall, Pres.; Frances Hall, Pres.
Catechesis/Religious Program—Students 9.

23—Holy Name of Jesus (1925), Revs. Donald S. D'Angelo; Charles I. Puthota, S.J. In Res., Most Rev. Ignatius Wang; Revs. Te Van Nuyen; Edward S. Inyanwach; Deacon Dennis Rivera.
Res.: 3240 Lawton St., 94122. Tel: 415-664-8590; Fax: 415-664-9775.
School—1560 40th Ave., 94122. Tel: 415-731-4077; Fax: 415-731-3328. Sisters 1; Lay Teachers 31; Students 474.
Catechesis/Religious Program—Students 100.

24—St. Ignatius (1855), Revs. Charles R. Gagan, S.J.; Albert A. Grosskopf, S.J.; James Blaettler, S.J.
Res.: 2170 Hayes St., 94117. Tel: 415-422-2188; Fax: 415-387-1867.
Catechesis/Religious Program—Students 262.

25—St. James (1888), Rev. James P. Foley. In Res., Rev. Jose Chavarin.
Res.: 1086 Guerrero St., 94110. Tel: 415-824-4232; Fax: 415-824-0605.
School—321 Fair Oaks St., 94110. Tel: 415-647-8972; Fax: 415-647-0166. Lay Teachers 9; Students 206.
Catechesis/Religious Program—Tel: 415-824-4233. Students 130.

26—St. John of God (1967), Rev. Thomas L. Seagrave; Deacon John Hutzler.
Res.: 1290 Fifth Ave., 94122. Tel: 415-566-5610; Fax: 415-566-5073.
Catechesis/Religious Program—Tel: 415-334-5655. Anne Donjacour, D.R.E. Students 40.

27—St. John the Evangelist (1893), Rev. Msgr. Jose A. Rodriguez; Rev. Jose Shaji; Sr. Louise O'Reilly, S.N.D., Pastoral Assoc.
Res.: 19 St. Mary's Ave., 94112-1098. Tel: 415-334-4646; Fax: 415-334-0891.
Parish Center—98 Bosworth St., 94112. Tel: 415-334-4646; Fax: 415-334-0891.
School—925 Chenery St., 94131. Tel: 415-584-8383; Fax: 415-584-8359. Kenneth Willers, Prin. Lay Teachers 8; Students 245.
Catechesis/Religious Program—Tel: 415-334-4646, Ext. 15. Ms. Anelita Reyes, D.R.E. Students 105.

28—St. Joseph (1861), Closed., For sacramental records please contact St. Patrick, San Francisco.

29—St. Kevin (1922), Rev. Craig Forner.
Res.: 704 Cortland Ave., 94110. Tel: 415-648-5751; Fax: 415-648-4441.
Catechesis/Religious Program—Tel: 415-282-0277. Students 85.

30—St. Michael Church, Formerly St. Michael Korean Church (1898), (Korean), Rev. Benedict Jeong-Hay-Pak.
Res.: 32 Broad St., 94112. Tel: 415-333-1194; Fax: 415-333-1196.
Catechesis/Religious Program—Students 75.

31—Mission Dolores Basilica (1776), [CEM], (San Francisco de Asis), Revs. William J. Justice; Gabriel Flores. In Res., Rev. Msgr. Maurice M. McCormick, (Retired); Rev. Charles Onubogu; Deacon Vicente Cervantes.
Res.: 3321 16th St., 94114. Tel: 415-621-8203; Fax: 415-621-2294.
School—3371 16th St., 94114. Tel: 415-861-7673; Fax: 415-861-7620. Andreina Gualco, Prin. Sisters 2; Lay Teachers 10; Students 215.
Catechesis/Religious Program—Roberto Vilalta, D.R.E. Students 94.

32—St. Monica (1911), Rev. John L. Greene. In Res., Rev. Didacus W. Ma (Retired); Deacon John Carpenter.
Res.: 470 24th Ave., 94121. Tel: 415-751-5275; Fax: 415-751-0440.
School—5950 Geary Blvd., 94121. Tel: 415-751-9564; Fax: 415-751-0781. Lay Teachers 12; Students 220.
Catechesis/Religious Program—Students 120.

33—Most Holy Redeemer (1900), Rev. Edward Phelan, Admin. In Res., Rev. William W. Young.
Res.: 100 Diamond St., 94114-2414. Tel: 415-863-6259; Fax: 415-552-8786.

34—Nativity (1902), (Polish—Croatian), Rev. Jerzy Frydrych, S.Ch. (GAL).
Res.: 245 Linden St., 94102. Tel: 415-252-5799; Fax: 415-252-5799.
Catechesis/Religious Program—Students 10.

35—Notre Dame des Victoires (1856), (French), Revs. Etienne Siffert, S.M.; Rene Iturbe, S.M.; Bruce Lery, S.M. (HON); Bro. Joseph Grima, S.M., Pastoral Assoc.
Res.: 566 Bush St., 94108. Tel: 415-397-0113; Fax: 415-397-3217.
School—659 Pine St., 94108. Tel: 415-421-0069; Fax: 415-421-1440. Mary K. Ghisolfo, Prin. Lay Teachers 18; Students 250.
Catechesis/Religious Program—Tel: 415-397-0113; Fax: 415-397-3217. Students 42.

36—Old St. Mary's Cathedral (1854), Revs. Charles R. Kullmann; Peter G. Shea, C.S.P.; Thomas F. Foley. In Res., Revs. Philip Cunningham, C.S.P. (Retired); Charles A. Donovan, C.S.P. (NY) (Retired); Thomas J. Dove, C.S.P. (Retired); Daniel E. McCotter, C.S.P.; Joseph M. Hanly, C.S.P. (Retired); Edward A. Maher, C.S.P. (Retired); Vincent P. Manalo, C.S.P.
Res.: 660 California St., 94108. Tel: 415-288-3800; Fax: 415-288-3838.

37—Our Lady of Fatima Byzantine Catholic Church (1954), Rev. Mark Ciccone, S.J.; Deacon Cyrill Bruce Pagacz.
Res.: 101 20th Ave., 94121-1398. Tel: 415-752-2052; Fax: 415-752-6073.

38—Our Lady of Guadalupe, Closed., For sacramental records please contact Church of the Visitation, San Francisco.

39—Our Lady of Lourdes (1942), Rev. Kirk Ullery.
Res.: 1715 Oakdale Ave., 94124. Tel: 415-285-3377; Fax: 415-285-2191.
Catechesis/Religious Program— Joint program with St. Paul of the Shipwreck. Students 37.
Mission—All Hallows Chapel 1400 Newhall St., San Francisco Co. 94124.

40—St. Patrick (1851), Rev. Msgr. Fred A. Bitanga; Revs. Elmer Magat; Samuel Licanda; John A. Balleza.
Res.: 756 Mission St., 94103. Tel: 415-421-3730; Fax: 415-512-9730.
Catechesis/Religious Program—Students 90.

41—St. Paul (1880), Revs. Mario P. Farana; Mamerto Sigaran; Mary Tan, Pastoral Assoc. In Res., Rev. Msgr. Daniel R. Cahill (Retired).
Res.: 221 Valley St., 94131. Tel: 415-648-7538; Fax: 415-648-4740.
School—St. Paul Littlest Angel Pre-School, Tel: 415-824-5437; Fax: 415-824-5430. Ms. Peg Kayser, Prin. Students 40.
School—St. Paul, 1690 Church St., 94131. Tel: 415-648-2055; Fax: 415-648-1920. Bruce Colville, Prin. Lay Teachers 12; Students 269.
Catechesis/Religious Program—Tel: 415-826-4484. Dorothy Vigna, D.R.E. Students 158.
Convent—Novitiate of the Missionaries of Charity, 312 29th St., 94131. Tel: 415-647-1889.

42—St. Paul of the Shipwreck (1915), Revs. John Heinz, O.F.M.Conv.; Robert Herb; Paul Gawlowski, O.F.M.Conv.; Bros. Anthony Sciberras, O.F.M-.Conv.; George Cherrie, O.F.M.Conv.
Res.: 3350 Jennings St., 94124. Tel: 415-468-3434; Fax: 415-468-1400.
Catechesis/Religious Program—Students 25.

43—St. Peter (1867), Revs. Fabio E. Medina; Jose Eduardo Mendoza; Jorge Ramon del Real; Deacons Roger Hernandez; David Gamarra; Nate Bacon. In Res., Revs. Edmund N. Shipp; Michael Brilliantes.
Res.: 1200 Florida St., 94110. Tel: 415-282-1652; Fax: 415-282-6097.
School—1266 Florida St., 94110. Tel: 415-647-8662; Fax: 415-647-4618. Vicki Butler, Prin. Sisters 5; Lay Teachers 17; Students 500.
Catechesis/Religious Program—Tel: 415-643-9885. Students 320.

44—SS. Peter and Paul (1884), (Italian), Revs. John J. Malloy, S.D.B.; Salvatore Giacomini, S.D.B.; John Lam, S.D.B.; Steve Whelan, S.D.B.; Harold Danielson, S.D.B. (LAR). In Res., Revs. Austin Conterno, S.D.B.; Paul Maniscalco, S.D.B.; Michael Ribotta, S.D.B.
Res.: 666 Filbert St., 94133. Tel: 415-421-0809; Fax: 415-421-0217.
School—632 Filbert St., 94133. Tel: 415-421-5219; Fax: 415-421-1831. Lisa Haris, Prin. Salesian Sisters 5; Lay Teachers 10; Students 298.
Catechesis/Religious Program—Students 60.

45—St. Philip the Apostle (1910), Revs. Michael J. Healy; Thuan V. Hoang, J.C.L., (Part-time). In Res., Rev. Brendan McBride.
Res.: 725 Diamond St., 94114. Tel: 415-282-0141; Fax: 415-282-8962.
School—665 Elizabeth St., 94114. Tel: 415-824-8467; Fax: 415-282-5746. Sr. Ann Cronin, Prin. Lay Teachers 14; Students 216.
Catechesis/Religious Program—Students 44.

46—Sacred Heart (1885), Rev. Paulinus M.

Mangesho, A.L.C.P.
Res.: 546 Fillmore St., 94117. Tel: 415-861-5460; Fax: 415-861-7839.
School—735 Fell St., 94117. Tel: 415-621-8035; Fax: 415-861-7039. Mrs. Reese Fernandes, Prin. Religious 2; Lay Teachers 4; Students 118.
Catechesis/Religious Program—Students 2.

47—STAR OF THE SEA (1894), Rev. Msgrs. Flors B. Arcams; John R. Pernia; Revs. Benedict Chang; Greg Aherne, S.J.
Res.: 4420 Geary Blvd., 94118. Tel: 415-751-0450; Fax: 415-386-5651.
School—360 Ninth Ave., 94118. Tel: 415-221-8558; Fax: 415-221-7118. Mrs. Carol Grewal, Prin. Sisters 2; Lay Teachers 15; Students 241.
Catechesis/Religious Program—Tel: 415-831-6047. Students 60.
Convent—Sisters of St. Joseph of Carondelet, 4350 Geary Blvd., 94118. Tel: 415-752-6050.

48—ST. STEPHEN (1950), Revs. Joseph R. Walsh; John Schwartz; Jevino Pereira; Deacon Gary West. In Res., Rev. Joseph P. O'Reilly (Retired).
Res.: 601 Eucalyptus Dr., 94132. Tel: 415-681-2707.
Office:—451 Eucalyptus Dr., 94132. Tel: 415-681-2444; Fax: 415-681-7843.
School—401 Eucalyptus Dr., 94132. Tel: 415-664-8331; Fax: 415-242-5608. Mrs. Sharon McCarthy Allen, Prin. Lay Teachers 14; Students 310.
Catechesis/Religious Program—Cathy Collins, D.R.E. Students 75.

49—ST. TERESA (1880), Rev. Edward K. Murray; Deacon Charles Allen Jr.; Sisters Kathleen Healy, P.B.V.M., Pastoral Assoc.; Lucia Lodolo, P.B.V.M., Pastoral Assoc. In Res., Rev. Stephen A. Meriwether, J.C.L.
Res.: 390 Missouri St., 94107. Tel: 415-285-5272; Fax: 415-285-8510.
Catechesis/Religious Program—Students 52.

50—ST. THOMAS MORE (1950), Revs. Labib Kobti; Canon Francis Tiso, Chap. Newman Club, San Francisco State Univ.
Res.: 1300 Junipero Serra Blvd., 94132. Tel: 415-452-9634; Fax: 415-452-9653.
Catechesis/Religious Program—Students 20.

51—ST. THOMAS THE APOSTLE (1922), Rev. Daniel J. Maguire. In Res., Revs. Stanley Wu (Retired); Francis Filice (Retired).
Res.: 3835 Balboa St., 94121. Tel: 415-387-5545; Fax: 415-221-0868.
School—3801 Balboa St., 94121. Tel: 415-221-2711; Fax: 415-221-8611. Lay Teachers 10; Students 320.
Catechesis/Religious Program—Students 8.

52—ST. VINCENT DE PAUL (1901), Revs. John K. Ring; Benjamin A. Nombrado.
Res.: 2320 Green St., 94123. Tel: 415-922-1010; Fax: 415-922-7203.
School—2350 Green St., 94123. Tel: 415-346-0970; Fax: 415-346-0970. Ms. Barbara Harvey, Prin. Lay Teachers 22; Students 258.

53—VISITACION, CHURCH OF THE (1907), Revs. Zachary Shore; John T. Jimenez; Sr. Maureen O'Brien, B.V.M., Pastoral Assoc.
Res.: 655 Sunnydale Ave., 94134. Tel: 415-239-5950; Fax: 415-239-0538.
School—Our Lady of the Visitacion, 785 Sunnydale Ave., 94134. Tel: 415-239-7840; Fax: 415-239-2559. Sr. Lois Lapeyre, D.C., Prin. Daughters of Charity of St. Vincent de Paul 4; Lay Teachers 8; Students 259.
Catechesis/Religious Program—Tel: 415-239-6723. Sulema Ochoa, D.R.E. Students 200.
Mission—Our Lady of Guadalupe 285 Alvarado St., Brisbane, San Mateo Co. 94005. Tel: 415-467-9727.

OUTSIDE THE CITY OF SAN FRANCISCO

BELMONT, SAN MATEO CO.

1—IMMACULATE HEART OF MARY (1947), Revs. Stephen H. Howell, Admin.; Joseph Healy; Roberto Andrey. In Res., Deacons Steven Hackett; Henry Jacquemet; Robert Kahn.
Res.: 1040 Alameda de las Pulgas, 94002. Tel: 650-593-6157; Fax: 650-593-1665.
School—1000 Alameda de las Pulgas, 94002. Tel: 650-593-4265; Fax: 650-593-4342. Dr. Margaret Purcell, Prin. Lay Teachers 12; Students 307.
Catechesis/Religious Program—Mrs. Genny Pereira, D.R.E. Students 310.

2—ST. MARK (1965), Rev. Al Furtado, C.S.Sp. In Res., Rev. William J. Flanagan (Retired).
Res.: 325 Marine View Ave., 94002. Tel: 650-591-5937; Fax: 650-591-7645.
Catechesis/Religious Program—Tel: 650-591-7072. Students 136.

BURLINGAME, SAN MATEO CO.

1—ST. CATHERINE OF SIENA (1908), Revs. Albert P. Vucinovich; Augusto E. Villote; Deacon Roy Twitty. In Res., Revs. Frank Murray (Retired); Joseph Bradley; James Livingstone.
Res.: 1310 Bayswater Ave., 94010. Tel: 650-344-6884; Fax: 650-344-1022.
School—1300 Bayswater Ave., 94010. Tel: 650-344-7176; Fax: 650-344-7426. Ms. Penny Donovan, Prin. Missionary Sisters of the "Sacro Costato" 2; Lay Teachers 11; Students 301.
Catechesis/Religious Program—Students 113.

2—OUR LADY OF ANGELS (1926), Revs. Harold Snider, O.F.M.Cap.; Flavian Welstead, O.F.M.Cap.; John De La Riva, O.F.M.Cap. In Res., Rev. Eugene Ludwig, O.F.M.Cap.
Res.: 1721 Hillside Dr., 94010. Tel: 650-347-7768; Fax: 650-347-3550.
School—1328 Cabrillo Ave., 94010. Tel: 650-343-9200; Fax: 650-343-5260. Carol Meshinsky, Prin. Lay Teachers 21; Students 312.
School—Preschool, 1341 Cortez Ave., 94010. Tel: 650-343-3115. Theresa DeBarbrie, Co-Dir.; Sandy Sterling, Co-Dir. Lay Teachers 9; Students 76.
Catechesis/Religious Program—Tel: 650-347-3671. Mrs. Kathryn Jones, D.R.E. Students 420.

COLMA, SAN MATEO CO., HOLY ANGELS (1914), Revs. Manuel Curso; Victorio Balagapo; Joseph Bravo; Deacons John Ruiz; Lernito Prudenciado.
Res.: 107 San Pedro Rd., 94014. Tel: 650-755-0478; Fax: 650-755-7653.
School—20 Reiner St., 94014. Tel: 650-755-0220. Sisters 4; Lay Teachers 9; Students 311.
Catechesis/Religious Program—Tel: 650-992-5539. Sr. Anita Torres, P.B.V.M., D.R.E. Students 430.

DALY CITY, SAN MATEO CO.

1—ST. ANDREW (1968), (Filipino), Revs. Alex L. Legaspi; Rolando de la Rosa; Deacons Tom Buenavista, Pastoral Assoc.; Noel Santillan.
Church: 1571 Southgate Ave., 94015. Tel: 650-756-3223; Fax: 650-756-0251.
Rectory—One Ridgefield Ave., 94015. Tel: 650-756-3222; Fax: 650-756-0251.
Catechesis/Religious Program—Tel: 650-991-2937. Michele Bussey, D.R.E. Students 305.

2—OUR LADY OF MERCY (Westlake) (1954), Revs. William E. Brown; Angel N. Quitalig, S.S.P. (Philippines). In Res., Rev. Joseph Palathingal.
Res.: One Elmwood Dr., 94015. Tel: 650-755-2727; Fax: 650-755-6704.
School—7 Elmwood Dr., 94015. Tel: 650-756-3395; Fax: 650-756-5872. Arlene Fife, Prin.; Sr. Virginia Barcelona, R.S.M., Pastoral Assoc. Sisters 1; Lay Teachers 27; Students 567.
Catechesis/Religious Program—Tel: 650-992-5769; Fax: 650-756-3457. Sr. Margie Aguilar, R.V.M., D.R.E. Students 153.
Convent—Religious of the Virgin Mary, Our Lady of Mercy, 15 Elmwood Dr., 94015.

3—OUR LADY OF PERPETUAL HELP (1925), Revs. Antonio Petilla; Aquino D. Padilla; Deacon William Bruening.
Res.: 60 Wellington Ave., 94014. Tel: 650-755-9786; Fax: 650-756-2268.
School—80 Wellington Ave., 94014. Tel: 650-755-4438; Fax: 650-755-7366. James Costello, Prin. Religious 1; Lay Teachers 9; Students 281.
Catechesis/Religious Program—Tel: 650-755-4010. Students 230.

EAST PALO ALTO, SAN MATEO CO., ST. FRANCIS OF ASSISI (1951), Rev. Lawrence C. Goode; Deacon Louis Dixon. In Res., Rev. Msgrs. Edgar P. McCarren (RVC) (Retired); John Weeney (Retired).
Res.: 1425 Bay Rd., 94303. Tel: 650-322-2152; Fax: 650-322-7319.
Catechesis/Religious Program—Tel: 650-325-6236. Students 500.

FAIRFAX, MARIN CO., ST. RITA (1930), Rev. Robert P. Cipriano; Deacons Peter Kehrlein; William Turrentine.
Res.: 100 Marinda Dr., 94930. Tel: 415-456-4815; Fax: 415-456-3677.
School—102 Marinda Dr., 94930. Tel: 415-456-1003; Fax: 415-456-7946. Jan Lovette, Prin. Lay Teachers 12; Students 208.
Catechesis/Religious Program—Tel: 415-456-1489. Students 75.

FOSTER CITY, SAN MATEO CO., ST. LUKE (1970), Revs. John P. Penebsky; Jonathan Paala; Deacons Mar Tano; Paul Lucia.
Res.: 1111 Beach Park Blvd., 94404. Tel: 650-345-6660; Fax: 650-345-8167.
Catechesis/Religious Program—Tel: 650-574-9191; 650-573-7409. Students 380.

GREENBRAE, MARIN CO., ST. SEBASTIAN (1951), Revs. Kenneth M. Westray; Paul E. Perry.
Res.: 373 Bon Air Rd., 94904. Tel: 415-461-0704; Fax: 415-461-2018.
Catechesis/Religious Program—Students 94.

HALF MOON BAY, SAN MATEO CO., OUR LADY OF THE PILLAR (1868), [CEM] Revs. Domingo Orimaco; Rafael de Avila; Deacons John McGhee; Virgil Capati.
Res.: 400 Church St., 94019. Tel: 650-726-4674; Fax: 650-726-0980.
Catechesis/Religious Program—Tel: 650-726-5587; 650-726-0900. Sr. Angelina Moctezuma, C.F.P., D.R.E. Students 491.
Mission—St. Anthony [CEM] 696 North St., Pescadero, San Mateo Co. 94060.
Mission—Our Lady of Refuge 146 Sears Ranch Rd., La Honda, San Mateo Co. 94060. Tel: 650-747-9555; Fax: 650-747-0419.

LAGUNITAS, MARIN CO., ST. CECILIA (1937), Rev. Joseph E. Richard.
Box 289, 94938.
Rectory—450 West Cintura Ave., 94938. Tel: 415-488-9799; Fax: 415-488-1963.
Catechesis/Religious Program—Students 20.
Mission—St. Mary (1867), Town Square, Nicasio, Marin Co. 94946.

LARKSPUR, MARIN CO., ST. PATRICK (1915), Rev. John D. Shanahan. In Res., Rev. Joseph Eagan, S.J. (Retired).
Res.: 114 King St., 94939. Tel: 415-924-0600; Fax: 415-924-3617.
School—120 King St., 94939. Tel: 415-924-0501; Fax: 415-924-3554. Ann Kalayjian, Prin. Lay Teachers 9; Students 270.
Catechesis/Religious Program—Tel: 415-924-3719. Students 150.

MENLO PARK, SAN MATEO CO.

1—ST. ANTHONY (1951), Revs. James L. Garcia; Eric Arauz (Panama).
Res.: 3500 Middlefield Rd., 94025. Tel: 650-366-4692; Fax: 650-366-4135.
Catechesis/Religious Program—Tel: 650-365-6071. Gladys Fields, D.R.E. Students 879.
Mission—San Jose Obrero 400 Heller St., Redwood City, San Mateo Co. 94063.

2—THE CHURCH OF THE NATIVITY (1877), Rev. Msgr. Steven D. Otellini; Rev. William C. Nicholas Jr.; Deacon Dominick Peloso. In Res., Rev. Peter Correa.
Res.: 210 Oak Grove Ave., 94025. Tel: 650-323-7914; Fax: 650-323-3231.
School—1250 Laurel St., 94025. Tel: 650-325-7304; Fax: 650-325-3841. Sisters 3; Lay Teachers 12; Students 300.
Catechesis/Religious Program—Tel: 650-327-2319. Sr. Merlynn Martin, C.S.J., D.R.E. Students 206.

3—ST. DENIS (1853; Restored 1961), Rev. Msgr. John F. Rodriguez.
Res.: 2250 Avy Ave., 94025. Tel: 650-854-5976; Fax: 650-854-3754.
Mission—Our Lady of the Wayside (1902), 930 Portola Rd., Portola Valley, San Mateo Co. 94028. Tel: 650-851-5085; Fax: 650-851-1019. Rev. George L. Thomas, Pastor Emeritus (Retired).
Catechesis/Religious Program—Tel: 650-854-3754; Fax: 650-854-3734. Students 452.

4—ST. RAYMOND (1950), Revs. Patrick T. Michaels; James Morris.
Office—1100 Santa Cruz Ave., 94025. Tel: 650-323-1755; Fax: 650-323-3206.
Res.: 1231 Arbor Rd., 94025. Tel: 650-321-1339.
School—1211 Arbor Rd., 94025. Tel: 650-322-2312; Fax: 650-322-2910. Sr. Ann Bernard O'Shea, C.S.J., Prin. Sisters 2; Lay Teachers 19; Students 259.
Catechesis/Religious Program—Tel: 650-323-6353; Fax: 650-323-3206. Michele Otto, D.R.E. Students 155.

MILL VALLEY, MARIN CO., OUR LADY OF MT. CARMEL (1910), Rev. John J. Clonerty; Deacon Bruce Hall. In Res., Revs. Feliciano T. Mofan; Richard C. Bain.
Res.: 3 Oakdale Ave., 94941. Tel: 415-388-4190; Fax: 415-388-4197.
Catechesis/Religious Program—17 Buena Vista, 94941. Tel: 415-388-1008; Fax: 415-388-4297.

MILLBRAE, SAN MATEO CO., ST. DUNSTAN (1940), Revs. Kevin Corrigan, C.S.Sp. (Ireland) (SJ); Francis Mulloy, C.S.Sp.; Joseph Glynn, C.S.Sp.
Res.: 1133 Broadway, 94030. Tel: 650-697-4730; 650-697-4736; Fax: 650-697-5203.
School—1150 Magnolia Ave., 94030. Tel: 650-697-8119; Fax: 650-697-9295. Mr. Thomas Dooher, Prin. Lay Teachers 14; Students 287.
Catechesis/Religious Program—Tel: 650-697-7451. Sherre Leone, D.R.E. Students 229.

NOVATO, MARIN CO.

1—ST. ANTHONY OF PADUA (1968), Rev. Brian L. Costello, Admin.; Deacon Joseph Brumbaugh. In Res., Rev. James E. O'Malley (Retired).
Res.: 1000 Cambridge St., 94947. Tel: 415-883-2177; Fax: 415-883-4049.
Catechesis/Religious Program—Tel: 415-883-9000. Judith Ann Ross, D.R.E.; Marianne Iacobucci, D.R.E. Students 450.

2—OUR LADY OF LORETTO (1892), Revs. William H. McCain; Francis Mark Maria Garbo; Deacon William Mitchell; Sr. Jeanette Lombardi, O.S.U., Pastoral Assoc. In Res., Rev. Msgr. Richard Knapp (Retired).
Res.: 1806 Novato Blvd., 94947. Tel: 415-897-2171; Fax: 415-897-8251.
School—1811 Virginia Ave., 94945. Tel: 415-892-8621; Fax: 415-892-9631. Ms. Susan Maino, Prin. Lay Teachers 15; Students 248.
Catechesis/Religious Program—Tel: 415-897-6714. Mary Furnanz, D.R.E.; Victoria Birnberg, D.R.E. Students 488.

OLEMA, MARIN CO., SACRED HEART (1867), [CEM] Rev. John O'Neill.
Mailing Address: P.O. Box 70, 94950. Tel: 415-663-1139; Fax: 415-663-9660.
Res.: 10189 State Route # 1, 94950.
Catechesis/Religious Program—Students 52.
Mission—St. Mary Magdalen 17 Horseshoe Hill, Bolinas, Marin Co. 94924.

PACIFICA, SAN MATEO CO.
1—GOOD SHEPHERD (1951), Rev. Piers M. Lahey; Sr. Carol Fleitz, S.N.J.M., Pastoral Assoc. In Res., Rev. Steven E. Davis (Retired).
Res.: 901 Oceana Blvd., 94044. Tel: 650-355-2593; Fax: 650-355-1832.
School—909 Oceana Blvd., 94044. Tel: 650-359-4544. Patricia Volan, Prin. Lay Teachers 31; Students 310.
Catechesis/Religious Program—Tel: 650-355-4214. Mr. Kenneth Schwind, D.R.E. Students 179.
2—ST. PETER (1956), Rev. Leonard J. Calegari; Deacon Peter Solan. In Res., Most Rev. John C. Wester, V.G.
Res.: 700 Oddstad Blvd., 94044. Tel: 650-359-6313; Fax: 650-359-2262.
Catechesis/Religious Program—Tel: 650-359-5000. Mrs. Barbara Malone, D.R.E. Students 463.

PORTOLA VALLEY, SAN MATEO CO., OUR LADY OF THE WAYSIDE (1941),, See St. Denis, Menlo Park.

REDWOOD CITY, SAN MATEO CO.
1—ST. MATTHIAS (1961), Rev. John Glogowski; Deacon George Salinger.
Res.: 1685 Cordilleras Rd., 94062. Tel: 650-366-9544; Fax: 650-366-4817.
School—St. Matthias Preschool, 533 Canyon Rd., 94062. Tel: 650-367-1320; Fax: 650-366-1049. Students 89.
Catechesis/Religious Program—Tel: 650-366-7085. Students 159.
2—OUR LADY OF MOUNT CARMEL (1887), Revs. Randolph Calvo; David Ghiorso; Deacon Thomas Boyle. In Res., Rev. Msgr. Dominic DesJardins (Retired).
Res.: 347 Grand St., 94062.
Parish Center—300 Fulton St., 94062. Tel: 650-366-3802; Fax: 650-366-1421.
School—301 Grand St., 94062. Tel: 650-366-6127; Fax: 650-366-0902. Lay Teachers 12; Students 294.
Catechesis/Religious Program—Tel: 650-368-8237. Students 475.
3—ST. PIUS (1951), Revs. James H. MacDonald; Ireneo Ramoso. In Res., Rev. Kevin Kennedy; Deacon Steve Michaelson.
Res.: 1100 Woodside Rd., 94061. Tel: 650-361-1411; Fax: 650-369-3641.
School—Tel: 650-368-8327; Fax: 650-368-7031. Rita Carroll, Prin. Lay Teachers 14; Students 304.
Catechesis/Religious Program—Tel: 650-368-0429. Sr. Mary Keefe, D.R.E. Students 207.

SAN ANSELMO, MARIN CO., ST. ANSELM (1907), Rev. Neil Healy; Deacons Bernard O'Halloran; Edward Cunningham; Dennis Gooch.
Mailing Address: P.O. Box 1061, Ross, 94957. In Res., Rev. Peter McDonald.
Res.: Shady Ln. & Bolinas Ave., P.O. Box 1061, Ross, 94947. Tel: 415-453-2342; Fax: 415-453-8713.
School—40 Belle Ave., 94960. Tel: 415-454-8667; Fax: 415-454-4730. Odile Steel, Prin. Lay Teachers 21; Students 260.
Catechesis/Religious Program—Tel: 415-453-2342. Tom Kavanaugh, D.R.E. Students 188.

SAN BRUNO, SAN MATEO CO.
1—ST. BRUNO (1912), Rev. Rene J. Gomez; Deacons Ramon De La Rosa; Joseph Lavulo.
Res.: 555 San Bruno Ave. W., 94066. Tel: 650-588-2121; Fax: 650-588-6087.
Catechesis/Religious Program—Tel: 650-588-4509. Mrs. Beverly Kious, D.R.E.; Raquel Comacho, D.R.E. (Spanish). Tel: 650-588-6621. Students 316.
2—ST. ROBERT (1958), Revs. Vincent D. Ring; Thomas M. Hamilton, S.M.; Deacon Rusty Duffey. In Res., Rev. Joseph J. Marini (Retired).
Res.: 1380 Crystal Springs Rd., 94066. Tel: 650-589-2800; Fax: 650-588-3628.
School—345 Oak Ave., 94066. Tel: 650-583-5065; Fax: 650-583-1418. Lay Teachers 13; Students 306.
Catechesis/Religious Program—Tel: 650-588-0477. Students 378.

SAN CARLOS, SAN MATEO CO., ST. CHARLES (1928), Revs. Kieran D. McCormick; Tony LaTorre.
Res.: 880 Tamarack Ave., 94070. Tel: 650-591-7349; Fax: 650-637-1968.
School—850 Tamarack Ave., 94070. Tel: 650-593-1629; Fax: 650-593-9723. Arlene B. Weidner, Prin. Lay Teachers 17; Students 305.
Catechesis/Religious Program—Terri Mooney, D.R.E.; Tami Palladino, D.R.E. Students 600.

SAN MATEO, SAN MATEO CO.
1—ST. BARTHOLOMEW (1955), Revs. Daniel T. Keohane; Tom Moran; Deacon John Sequeira.
Res.: 600 Columbia Dr., 94402. Tel: 650-347-0701; Fax: 650-347-2429.
Catechesis/Religious Program—Barbara Regan, D.R.E. Students 360.
2—ST. GREGORY (1941), Rev. Msgr. Robert W. McElroy; Revs. Joseph Pham Hung; Paul Warren; Deacon Fred Iskander.
Res.: 2715 Hacienda St., 94403. Tel: 650-345-8506; Fax: 650-345-9329.
School—2701 Hacienda St., 94403. Tel: 650-573-0111; Fax: 650-573-6548. Linda Grund, Prin. Lay Teachers 15; Students 322.
Catechesis/Religious Program—Tel: 650-574-8716. Students 473.
3—ST. MATTHEW (1863), Rev. Msgr. James McKay (Retired); Revs. William J. Ahlbach; Paul Arnoult; Francisco J. Gamez. In Res., Rev. Clement A. Davenport (Retired).
Res.: One Notre Dame Ave., 94402. Tel 650-344-7622; Fax: 650-344-4830.
School—910 S. El Camino Real, 94402. Tel: 650-343-1373; Fax: 650-343-2046. Mr. Kenneth F. Boegel, Prin. Lay Teachers 26; Students 594.
Catechesis/Religious Program—Students 451.
4—ST. TIMOTHY (1954), Revs. Arturo L. Albano; Olivete Rojas; Deacons Angel Aguilar; Nicolas Rodriguez; Faiva Po'oi; Sr. Mary Mark Berdin, Pastoral Assoc. In Res., Rev. Saimone Moala.
Res.: 1515 Dolan Ave., 94401. Tel: 650-342-2468; Fax: 650-342-8156.
School—Tel: 650-342-6567; Fax: 650-342-5913. Mrs. Evelyn Nordberg, Prin. Lay Teachers 10; Students 280.
Catechesis/Religious Program—Tel: 650-579-0901. Mrs. Irl Bolin, D.R.E. Students 275.

SAN RAFAEL, MARIN CO.
1—BLESSED SACRAMENT (1951), Closed., For sacramental records please contact St. Isabella, San Rafael.
2—ST. ISABELLA (Terra Linda) (1961), Revs. Michael J. Keane; Cyril O'Sullivan; Raymund Reyes; Deacons Jerry Friedman, (Retired); James Myers.
Mailing Address: P.O. Box 6166, 94903. In Res., Rev. William L. Knapp (Retired).
Res.: One Trinity Way, 94903. Tel: 415-479-1560; Fax: 415-479-8303.
School—P.O. Box 6188, 94903. Tel: 415-479-3727; Fax: 415-479-9961. Cynthia Bergez, Prin. Sisters 1; Lay Teachers 17; Students 257.
Catechesis/Religious Program—Tel: 415-479-1222. Monica Hinman, D.R.E. Students 429.
3—ST. RAPHAEL (1817), Revs. Paul J. Rossi; Honesto DeGuzman Gile Jr.; Manuel Estrada. In Res., Rev. Denis McManus, C.S.Sp.
Res.: 1104 Fifth Ave., 94901. Tel: 415-454-8141; Fax: 415-454-8193.
School—1100 Fifth Ave., 94901. Tel: 415-454-4455; Fax: 415-454-5927. Mrs. Maureen Albritton, Prin. Lay Teachers 18; Students 182.
Catechesis/Religious Program—Tel: 415-459-7331; Fax: 415-454-8193. Students 650.
Mission—St. Sylvester 1115 Point San Pedro Rd., Marin Co. 94901.
Station—San Quentin State Prison San Quentin, NM. Tel: 415-456-8161.
4—ST. SYLVESTER (1961), Closed., For sacramental records please contact St. Raphael, San Rafael.

SAUSALITO, MARIN CO., ST. MARY STAR OF THE SEA (1881), Rev. Richard S. Deitch. In Res., Rev. Eugene F. Duggan (Retired).
Res.: 180 Harrison Ave., 94965. Tel: 415-332-1765; Fax: 415-332-4962.
Catechesis/Religious Program—Students 17.

SOUTH SAN FRANCISCO, SAN MATEO CO.
1—ALL SOULS (1913), Revs. Agnel De Heredia; Santos Rodriguez; Kenneth M. Weare; Deacon Alex Aragon.
Res.: 315 Walnut Ave., 94080. Tel: 650-871-8944; Fax: 650-871-5806.
School—479 Miller Ave., 94080. Tel: 650-583-3562; Fax: 650-952-1167. Eileen Gorman, Prin. Lay Teachers 14; Students 300.
Catechesis/Religious Program—Tel: 650-873-5356. Dr. Alex Aragon, D.R.E. Students 261.
2—ST. AUGUSTINE (1970), Revs. Eugene D. Tungol; Antonio C. Claudio; Deacons Robert Bertolani; Frank Almeida.
Res.: 3700 Callan Blvd., 94080. Tel: 650-873-2282; Fax: 650-873-1356.
Catechesis/Religious Program—Tel: 650-873-2878. Sr. Nona Barairo, D.R.E. Students 544.
3—MATER DOLOROSA (1961), Revs. Hugh O'Donnell; Rolando A. Caverte. In Res., Rev. C. Michael Padazinski.
Res. 307 Willow Ave., 94080. Tel: 650-583-4131; Fax: 650-761-2232.
School—1040 Miller Ave., 94080. Tel: 650-588-8175; Fax: 650-588-0426. Jeanette Swain, Prin. Sisters 2; Lay Teachers 8; Students 214.
Catechesis/Religious Program—Tel: 650-589-4448; Fax 650-589-4448. Sr. Bernard Joseph, P.B.V.M., D.R.E. Students 150.
4—ST. VERONICA (1951), Revs. Edward A. Bohnert; Mark Taheny; Deacons Roger Beaudry; Joseph LeBlanc.
Res.: 434 Alida Way, 94080. Tel: 650-588-1455; Fax: 650-588-1481.
School—Tel: 650-589-3909; Fax: 650-589-2826. Teri Palitto, Prin. Lay Teachers 17; Students 324.
Catechesis/Religious Program—Tel: 650-871-5607. Sr. M. Julie O'Neill, B.V.M., D.R.E. Students 324.

TIBURON, MARIN CO., ST. HILARY (1951), Revs. James Tarantino; William Paul O'Dell. In Res., Rev. Msgr. Francis A. Lacey, P.A., Pastor Emeritus (Retired).
Res.: 761 Hilary Dr., 94920-1498. Tel: 415-435-1122; Fax: 415-435-1862.
School—765 Hilary Dr., 94920. Tel: 415-435-2224; Fax: 415-435-5895. Mrs. Theresa Canizzaro, Prin. Lay Teachers 22; Students 240.
Catechesis/Religious Program—Tel: 415-435-1639; Fax: 415-435-1639. Maureen Buscher, D.R.E. Students 110.

TOMALES, MARIN CO., CHURCH OF THE ASSUMPTION (1860), Rev. Robert K. White.
Mailing Address: P.O. Box 82, 94971-0082.
Res.: 26825 Shoreline Hwy., 94971-0082. Tel: 707-878-2208; Fax: 707-878-9422.
Catechesis/Religious Program—Students 38.
Mission—St. Helen (1902), Marshall. P.O. Box 82, Marin Co. 94971-0082.

WOODSIDE, SAN MATEO CO., ST. MARCELLA MISSION, Closed., For sacramental records please contact St. Denis, Menlo Park.

Chaplains of Public Institutions

SAN FRANCISCO. *St. Anne's Home*. Rev. Terence J. Horan, Chap.
Catholic Healthcare West/Bay Area Region. Rev. Edgar Brennickmeyer, S.J.
St. Francis Hospital. Rev. Louis Vitale, O.F.M.
Kaiser Hospital San Francisco. Rev. Michael Greenwell, O.Carm.
Knights of Malta. The Sovereign Military Order of Malta (Western U.S.A. Association of the Sovereign Military Hospitaller Order of St. John of Jerusalem of Rhodes and of Malta--a Nonprofit Corporation). Rev. Msgr. Steven D. Otellini, Revs. Egon J. Javor, O.S.B., John P. Kavanaugh (Retired).
Laguna Honda Home. Rev. Balaswamy Govindu.
St. Mary's Medical Center. Revs. Michael Greenwell, O.Carm., Contact, Edward K. Murray.
San Francisco Fire Department. Revs. John L. Greene, George M. Twigg-Porter, S.J.
San Francisco General Hospital. Revs. Edmund M. Shipp, Michael Brilliantes.
San Francisco Police Department. Revs. Thomas A. Daly, Michael J. Healy.
San Francisco State Univ., Newman Center. Rev. Francis Tiso.
Serra Club of San Francisco (Downtown). Rev. Thomas A. Daly.
Serra Club of San Francisco (Golden Gate). Rev. Msgr. Edward P. McTaggart (Retired).
St. Thomas More Society. (Legal). Rev. Jose Chavarin.
Veterans' Hospital. Rev. Richard A. Bain.
Young Ladies' Institute. Rev. Msgr. Edward P. McTaggart, Moderator-ACCW (Retired), Rev. Richard S. Deitch, Grand Chap.
Youth Guidance Center. (Vacant)

DALY CITY. *Seton Hospital*. Rev. Quoc Nguyen, O.F.M.Cap.

MARIN. *Serra Club of Marin*. Rev. Paul J. Rossi.

REDWOOD CITY. *Sequoia Hospital*. Rev. Paul E. Perry, Chap.

SAN MATEO. *Serra Club of San Mateo*. Rev. Msgr. James McKay (Retired).
Seton Medical Center. Rev. Rory Murphy (SJ).
Sheriff's Honor Camp and Medium Security Facility. Served by Archdiocese and St. Vincent de Paul volunteers, San Mateo District Council.

SAN QUENTIN. *California State Prison*, Tel: 415-456-8161. Rev. Stephen A. Barber, S.J. (LA), Chap., Deacon George Salinger, Asst. Chap.

On Special Assignment:
Revs.—
Brennan, Bernard, Chap. Ft. Mason (Retired)
Daly, Thomas A., Dir. Vocations, Marin Catholic High School, Kentfield & St. Vincent School for Boys, San Rafael
Lopes, Steven, S.T.L., North American College, Rome, Italy

On Duty Outside the Archdiocese:
Revs.—
Coleman, John, VA Hospital, Palo Alto, Diocese of San Jose
Duggan, William, Diocese of Santa Rosa
Escalante, Augustin, Laredo, TX
Fredericks, James L., Faculty, Loyola-Marymount Univ., Los Angeles
Hagan, James, Mexico
McElligott, Thomas J., St. Mary College, Moraga, Diocese of Oakland

McGuire, Anthony, USCCB
Ochylski, Ronald S., Archdiocese of Madrid, Spain
Smith, Raymond K., Silver Penny Farm, Petaluma, Diocese of Santa Rosa

Absent on Leave:
Rev. Msgr.—
O'Connor, John, V.F. (R)
Revs.—
Aylward, James W.
Ervin, Thomas
Ingels, Gregory G., J.C.D.
Kaylor, Lee
Leach, Jerome
Trainor, Henry J.
Walsh, Milton T.

Retired:
Most Rev.—
Quinn, John R., D.D.
Rev. Msgrs.—
Armstrong, Peter G.
Cahill, Daniel R.
Durkin, Charles J.
Foudy, John T.
Heaney, John P.
Keane, James P.
Knapp, Richard
Lacey, Francis A., P.A.
McCormick, Maurice
McKay, James
McTaggart, Edward P.
Sullivan, Joseph P.
Revs.—
Atkins, James
Avila, Martin C.
Bitangjol, Albert P.
Brennan, Bernard
Burke, Ronald A.
Burns, Thomas J.
Chung, Anthony
Cleary, Edward M.
Davenport, Clement A.
Decker, Raymond G.
Duggan, Eugene F.
Duggan, Paul E.
Duggan, William E., J.C.L.
Flanagan, William J.
Gaffey, Kevin
Greenlaw, Martin
Hanson, Kirby C.
Jocson, Salvador, Portugal
Kavanaugh, John P.
Keane, Patrick J., O.S.A. (LA)
Knapp, William L.
Lee, Anthony
Ma, Didacus W.
Madden, Thomas
Marini, Joseph J.
McCarthy, Patrick P.
McDonald, Peter
McDonnell, Donald C.
Mihovilovich, John B., Croatia
Murray, Francis
O'Connell, Joseph A.
O'Connell, William A.
O'Malley, James E.
O'Reilly, Joseph P.
O'Rourke, Gerald
Ojeda, Filemon G.
Piro, Frank R.
Quinn, William P.
Raimondi, Michele
Riley, Miles O'Brien
Robello, Louis J.
Rodriguez, Guillermo
Schipper, Carl A.
Smith, Wilton
Thomas, George L.
Ward, John J.
Woods, Warren L.
Worner, William H.
Wu, Stanley
Zohlen, Ray J.

Permanent Deacons:
Aguilar, Angel, St. Timothy, San Mateo
Allen, Charles, St. Teresa, San Francisco
Almeida, Frank, St. Augustine, South San Francisco
Aragon, Alex, All Souls, South San Francisco
Ayalin, Romeo, St. Finn Barr, San Francisco
Bacon, Nate, St. Peter, San Francisco
Beaudry, Roger, St. Veronica, South San Francisco
Bertolani, Robert, St. Augustine, San Francisco
Borg, Joseph, St. Hilary Church, Tiburon
Boulware, Peter, St. Mary's Cathedral, San Francisco
Boyle, Thomas J., Our Lady of Mount Carmel, Redwood City
Bruening, William, Our Lady of Perpetual Help, Daly City
Brumbaugh, Joseph, St. Anthony of Padua, Novato
Capati, Virgil
Carpenter, John, St. Monica, San Francisco
Cervantes, Vicente, Mission Dolores, San Francisco
Cunningham, Ed, St. Anselm, San Anselmo
DeLaRosa, Ramon, St. Bruno, San Bruno
Dixon, Louis, St. Francis of Assisi, East Palo Alto
Duffey, Rusty, St. Robert, San Bruno
Dupre, John, St. Anne, San Francisco
Friedman, Jerome, Nazareth House
Gamarra, David, St. Peter, San Francisco
Hackett, Steven, Immaculate Heart of Mary, Belmont
Hall, J. Bruce, Our Lady of Mt. Carmel, Mill Valley
Hernandez, Roger, St. Peter, San Francisco
Holm, Russell, (Retired)
Hutzler, John, St. John of God, San Francisco
Ilao, Thomas, St. Finn Barr, San Francisco
Iskander, Fred, St. Gregory, San Mateo
Jacquemet, Henry, Immaculate Heart of Mary, Belmont
Kehrlein, Peter, St. Rita, Fairfax
Kortenkamp, Leon, Dir., Permanent Diaconate Office
Lavulo, Joseph, St. Bruno, San Bruno
LeBlanc, Joseph, St. Veronica, South San Francisco
Lucia, Paul, St. Luke, Foster City
McGhee, John, Our Lady of Pillar, Half Moon Bay; Our Lady of Refuge, La Honda; St. Anthony Mission, Pescadero
McNeil, Chuck, St. Dominic's, San Francisco
Michaelson, Steven, St. Pius, Redwood City
Mitchell, William, Our Lady of Loretto, Novato
Myers, Jim, St. Isabella, San Rafael
O'Halloran, Bernard, St. Anselm, San Anselmo
Ocon, Manuel, Epiphany, San Francisco
Paulino, Tony, Holy Angels, Colma
Pelimiano, Pete, St. Augustine, South San Francisco
Peloso, Dominick, Church of the Nativity, Menlo Park
Po'oi, Faiva, St. Timothy, San Mateo
Prudenciado, Lernito, Holy Angels, Colma
Rivera, Dennis, Holy Name of Jesus, San Francisco
Rodriguez, Nicolas, St. Timothy, San Mateo
Rosen, Dan, St. Vincent de Paul Society, San Francisco
Ruiz, Juan, Holy Angels, Colma
Salinger, George, St. Matthias, Redwood City
Santillan, Noel, St. Andrews, Daly City
Sequeira, John, St. Bartholomew, San Mateo
Solan, Peter, St. Peter, Pacifica
Solano, Jose, St. John the Evangelist, San Francisco
Swanson, Fred, St. Dominic, San Francisco
Tano, Mar, St. Luke, Foster City
Turrentine, William, St. Rita, Fairfax
Twitty, Roy, St. Catherine, Burlingame
Viray, Ricardo, Epiphany, San Francisco
West, Gary, St. Stephen, San Francisco

INSTITUTIONS LOCATED IN THE ARCHDIOCESE

[A] SEMINARIES, ARCHDIOCESAN

MENLO PARK. *St. Patrick Seminary and University* (1898), Major Seminary of the Archdiocese of San Francisco, under the direction of the Society of St. Sulpice. , 320 Middlefield Rd., 94025. Tel: 650-325-5621; 650-321-5655 (Library); Fax: 650-322-0997. Email: info@stpatricksseminary.org. Web: www.stpatricksseminary.org. Most Rev. William J. Levada, Chancellor.
Legal Title: *(1891, 1944): The Roman Catholic Seminary of San Francisco* Priests 14; Religious 2; Lay Teachers 4; Students 80.
Officers of the Administration: Revs. Gerald D. Coleman, S.S., S.T.L., Ph.D., Pres., Rector & Vice Chancellor; Frederick J. Cwiekowski, S.S., S.T.D., On Sabbatical; Melvin C. Blanchette, S.S., Ph.D., Vice Rector, Vice Pres. Admin.; Dr. Charles W. James, S.T.D., Dir. of Pre-Theology Program; Dr. Dorothy A. Tully, Academic Dean.
Resident Faculty: Rev. Msgr. J. Warren Holleran; Revs. Michael C. Barber, S.J.; Vincent D. Bui, S.S., J.C.L., Dean of Students; Melvin C. Blanchette, S.S., Ph.D., Vice Rector, Vice Pres. Admin.; Gerald D. Coleman, S.S., S.T.L., Ph.D., Pres. Rectory, Vice Chancellor; Timothy J. Cusick, S.S., S.T.B.; Frederick J. Cwiekowski, S.S., S.T.D.; Thomas K. Diaz, M.A., Dir. of the Pastoral Year; Eugene J. Konkel, S.S., S.T.L.; Paul A. Maillet, S.S., M.Div. (BAL); Gerardo Menchaca, M.Div. (SJ).
Non-Resident Faculty and Staff: Dr. Charles W. James, S.T.D.; Sisters Lynn Jarrell, O.S.U., J.C.D.; Mary Lange, S.H.F., M.A., Dir. of Field Education; Sharon McMillan, S.N.D.; Dr. Michael Neri, Ph.D.; Rev. Donald Sharp, S.J., S.T.D.; Dr. Dorothy Tully, D.A., Registrar; Dr. Margaret M. Turek, S.T.D.; Dr. Cecil White, Ph.D., Librarian.

Vatican II Institute for Clergy Formation, 320 Middlefield Rd., 94025. Tel: 650-325-9122; Fax: 650-325-6765. Web: www.stpatrickseminary.org. Rev. Melvin C. Blanchette, S.S., Ph.D., Dir.

St. Joseph's-St. Patrick's College Alumni Association, St. Patrick's Seminary, 320 Middlefield Rd., 94025. Tel: 650-591-3492; Fax: 650-654-3503. Email: murpur@aol.com. Web: www.saintjosephscollege.us. Mr. James P. Murphy, Contact.

[B] SEMINARIES, RELIGIOUS OR SCHOLASTICATES

SAN FRANCISCO. *Capuchin House of Studies*, San Buenavista Friary, 750 Anza St., 94118. Tel: 415-387-7005. Revs. Julian Gonzalez-Montenegro, O.F.M.Cap., Guardian Instructor; James M. Stump, O.F.M.Cap.; Bros. Francis Driscoll, O.F.M.Cap., Hospital Chap.; Mark Ortega, Instructor. Priests 4; Brothers 2.

[C] COLLEGES AND UNIVERSITIES

SAN FRANCISCO. **University of San Francisco* Established 1855; Chartered by State, 1859. , 2130 Fulton St., 94117-1080. Tel: 415-422-5555; Fax: 415-422-2303. Web: www.usfca.edu. Rev. Stephen A. Privett, S.J., Pres.; Dr. James L. Wiser, Provost & Academic Vice Pres.; Rev. John Lo Schiavo, S.J., Chancellor; Mr. David F. Macmillan, Vice Pres., Univ. Advancement; Mr. Charles E. Cross, Vice Pres., Business & Finance; Dr. Margaret M. Higgins, Vice Pres., Student Affairs; Mr. Jeffrey S. Brand, Dean, School of Law; Dr. Lawrence G. Brewster, Dean, College of Professional Studies; Mr. Tyrone H. Cannon, Dean, University Library; Dr. Elizabeth J. Johnson, Dean, Academic Services; Dr. John Lantz, Dean, School of Nursing; Dr. Jennifer E. Turpin, Dean, College of Arts & Sciences; Dr. Lawrence G. Brewster, Acting Dean, School of Education. Jesuit Fathers Priests 9; Sisters 5; Lay Faculty 312; Students 7,951.

BELMONT. *Notre Dame de Namur University*, 1500 Ralston Ave., 94002. Tel: 650-508-3500; Fax: 650-508-3660. Email: gwhite@ndnu.edu. Web: www.ndnu.edu. Dr. John B. Oblak, Pres.; Lucille H. Sansing, Ph.D., Provost; Mr. Robert Mallon, Dir. Campus Ministry; Revs. Xavier J. Harris, O.F.M. (OAK); Eric Freed (SJ). Sisters of Notre Dame de Namur Priests 2; Sisters 4; Lay Faculty 62; Students 1,799.

SAN RAFAEL. *Dominican University of California*, 50 Acacia Ave., 94901-2298. Tel: 415-457-4440; Fax: 415-485-3205. Email: enroll@dominican.edu. Web: www.dominican.edu. Dr. Joseph R. Fink, Pres.; Dr. Kenneth Porada, Provost; Rev. Robert Haberman, Campus Ministry. Resident and non-resident students. Priests 1; Sisters 3; Lay Teachers 225; Students 1,749.

[D] HIGH SCHOOLS, ARCHDIOCESAN

SAN FRANCISCO. *Archbishop Riordan High School (Boys)*, 175 Phelan Ave., 94112. Tel: 415-586-8200; Fax: 415-587-1310. Email: jimdods2001@yahoo.com. Web: www.riordanhs.org. Bro. James A. Dods, S.M., Co-Prin.; Rev. Thomas French, S.M., Co-Prin. Priests 3; Sisters 1; Brothers 4; Lay Teachers 55; Students 788.

Sacred Heart Cathedral Preparatory (Coed), 1055 Ellis St., 94109. Tel: 415-775-6626; Fax: 415-931-6941. Email: margbapt@shep.edu. Web: shcp.edu. John Scudder, Prin. Brothers 2; Sisters 2; Lay Teachers 85; Students 1,218.

KENTFIELD. *Marin Catholic College Preparatory (Coed)*, 675 Sir Francis Drake Blvd., 94904. Tel: 415-464-3800; Fax: 415-461-7161. Web: www.marincatholic.marin.k12.ca.us. Rev. Thomas A. Daly, Pres.; Peter Imperial, Pres. Priests 2; Lay Teachers 52; Students 720. In Res. Revs. Thomas A. Daly, Chap.; John J. Ward (Retired).

SAN MATEO. *Junipero Serra High School (Boys)*, 451 W. 20th Ave., 94403-1385. Tel: 650-345-8207; Fax: 650-573-6638. Email: PADRES@SERRAHS.COM. Web: www.serrahs.com. Rev. Joseph Bradley, Pres.; Mr. Lars Lund, Prin. Priests 1; Lay Teachers 65; Students 987.

[E] HIGH SCHOOLS, PRIVATE

SAN FRANCISCO. *St. Ignatius College Preparatory (Coed)*, 2001 37th Ave., 94116. Tel: 415-731-7500; Fax: 415-731-9704. Email: postmaster@sicp.org. Web: www.siprep.org. Revs. Gregory M. Goethals, S.J., Supr.; Anthony P. Sauer, S.J., Pres.; Paul F. Capitolo, S.J.; Harry V. Carlin, S.J., Exec. Vice Pres.; Gerald F. Hudson, S.J.; Michael J. Kotlanger, S.J.; Andrew F. Maginnis, S.J.; Michel Marcil, S.J.; David S. Robinson, S.J.; A. Francis

Stiegeler, S.J.; Theodore T. Taheny, S.J.; Gerardo Valenzuela; Warren J. Wright, S.J. Priests 11; Brothers 4; Lay Teachers 96; Students 1,415.

Immaculate Conception Academy, (Girls), 3625 24th St., 94110. Tel: 415-824-2052; Fax: 415-821-4677. Email: ICA@ICACADEMY.ORG. Web: www.icacademy.org. Sr. Janice Therese Willington, O.P., Prin. Sisters 4; Lay Teachers 22; Students 258.

Mercy High School (Girls), 3250 19th Ave., 94132. Tel: 415-334-0525; Fax: 415-334-9726. Email: DMcCrea138@aol.com. Web: www.mercyhs.org. Ms. Dorothy McCrea, Prin. Sisters 1; Lay Teachers 43; Students 580.

Schools of the Sacred Heart, Convent of the Sacred Heart High School (Girls), 2222 Broadway, 94115. Tel: 415-563-2900; Fax: 415-929-0553. Email: heart@sacred.sf.ca.us. Web: www.sacred.sf.ca.us. Pamela Hayes, Dir.; Mr. Douglas Grant, Head. Lay Teachers 29; Students 204.

Schools of the Sacred Heart, Stuart Hall High School (Boys) , 1715 Octavia St., 94109. Tel: 415-345-5811; Fax: 415-931-9161. Email: heart@sacred.sf.ca.us. Web: www.sacred.sf.ca.us. Pamela Hayes, Dir.; Mr. Gordon Sharafinski, Head. Lay Teachers 22; Students 164.

ATHERTON. *Sacred Heart Schools, Atherton (Co-Ed)* (Sacred Heart Preparatory) , 150 Valparaiso, 94027. Tel: 650-322-1866; Fax: 650-322-7151. Web: www.shschools.org. Dr. Joseph J. Ciancaglini, Ed.D., Dir. Schools; Mr. Richard Dioli, Prin. Religious of the Sacred Heart Religious 1; Lay Teachers 55; Students 450.

BELMONT. *Notre Dame High School (Girls)*, 1540 Ralston Ave., 94002. Tel: 650-595-1913; Fax: 650-595-2116. Email: rgleason@ndhsb.org. Web: www.ndhsb.org. Ms. Rita Gleason, Prin.; Rev. Stephen H. Howell. Priests 1; Lay Teachers 60; Students 730.

BURLINGAME. *Mercy High School (Girls)*, 2750 Adeline Dr., 94010-5597. Tel: 650-343-3631; Fax: 650-343-2316. Email: mercyhsb@aol.com. Web: www.mercyhsb.com. Laura M. Held, Prin. Sisters 1; Lay Teachers 33; Students 461.

PORTOLA VALLEY. *Woodside Priory School* (Coed, Boarding). , 302 Portola Rd., 94028. Tel: 650-851-8221; Fax: 650-851-2839. Email: mmager@woodsidepriory.com. Web: www.woodsidepriory.com. Mr. Tim Molak, Headmaster.

Legal Title: *Benedictine Fathers of the Priory, Inc.* Priests 1; Lay Teachers 34; Students 340.

SAN ANSELMO. *San Domenico School* (Grades PreK-8, Coed; Grades 9-12, Girls. Boarding and Day Students.); See separate listing under Elementary Schools, Private in the Institution section.

[F] ELEMENTARY SCHOOLS, ARCHDIOCESAN

SAN FRANCISCO. *St. Brigid Elementary School*, (Grades K-8), 2250 Franklin St., 94109. Tel: 415-673-4523; Fax: 415-674-4187. Email: sbschool@saint-brigid.net. Web: www.saint-brigid.net. Sr. Carmen Santluste, Prin. Sisters 4; Lay Teachers 14; Students 300.

St. Thomas More School, (Grades K-8), 50 St. Thomas More Way, 94132. Tel: 415-337-0100. Email: stthomasmoreschoolsf@hotmail.com. Web: www.stthomasmoreschool.org. Joseph T. Elsbernd, Prin. Lay Teachers 10; Students 312.

[G] ELEMENTARY SCHOOLS, PRIVATE

SAN FRANCISCO. *DeMarillac Middle School of San Francisco*, 175 Golden Gate Ave., 94102. Tel: 415-552-5220; Fax: 415-621-5632. Email: Catherine_Karrels@demarillac.org. Web: www.demarillac.org. Catherine Karrels, Prin. Sisters 1; Brothers 2; Lay Teachers 6; Students 59.

Schools of the Sacred Heart, Convent of the Sacred Heart Elementary School, (Grades K-8) , (Girls) , 2222 Broadway, 94115. Tel: 415-563-2900; Fax: 415-563-0438. Email: heart@sacred.sf.ca.us. Web: www.sacred.sf.ca.us. Pamela Hayes, Dir.; Sr. Anne Wachter, R.S.C.J., Head. Lay Teachers 37; Students 334.

Schools of the Sacred Heart, Stuart Hall For Boys, (Grades K-8) , (Boys) , 2222 Broadway, 94115. Tel: 415-563-2900; Fax: 415-292-3165. Email: heart@sacred.sf.ca.us. Web: www.sacred.sf.ca.us. Pamela Hayes, Dir.; Mr. Gerald Grossman, Head. Schools of the Sacred Heart Sisters 1; Lay Teachers 43; Students 317.

ATHERTON. *Sacred Heart Schools, Atherton (Co-Ed)*, (Grades PreK-8) , (St. Joseph's School) , 50 Emilie Ave., 94027. Tel: 650-322-9931; Fax: 650-322-7656. Web: www.shschools.org. Dr. Joseph J. Ciancaglini, Ed.D., Dir. Schools. Sisters 1; Lay Teachers 62; Students 529.

Interim Heads: Mrs. Cee Salberg, Prin., (Grades PreK-K); Ms. Karen Eshoo, Prin., (Grades 1-8).

BELMONT. *Notre Dame Elementary School*, 1200 Notre Dame Ave., 94002. Tel: 650-591-2209; Fax: 650-591-4798. Email: SDQuigg@NDE.org. Web: NDE.org. Sr. Dolores Quigg, S.N.D.deN., Prin. Sisters 5; Lay Teachers 19; Students 255.

SAN ANSELMO. *San Domenico School* (Grades PreK-8, Coed; Grades 9-12, Girls; Boarding & Day Students) , 1500 Butterfield Rd., 94960-1099. Tel: 415-258-1900; Fax: 415-258-1901. Email: mheersche@sandomenico.org. Web: www.sandomenico.org. Matt Heersche, Ed.D., Head of School; John Bowermaster, Upper School Prin. (Grades 9-12); Andre Demian, Middle School Prin. (Grades 6-8); Carole Chase, Primary School Prin. (Grades PreK-5). Chaplains 1; Lay Teachers 86; Students 556.

[H] ST. VINCENT DE PAUL SOCIETY

SAN FRANCISCO. *St. Vincent de Paul Society*, 425 Fourth St., 94107. Tel: 415-977-1270; Fax: 415-977-1271. Email: svdp@pac.bell.net. Web: www.svdp-sf.org. Ben Vaissade, Exec. Dir.

S.F. District Council, 425 Fourth St., 94107. Tel: 415-977-1270; Fax: 415-977-1271. Tony Peligrino, Pres.; Louis Alessandria Jr., Exec. Dir.

Pickups of Household Items Tel: 415-908 3656.

Vehicle Donations Tel: 1-8-0-9-7-78.

Vehicle Donor Program Tel: 415-977-1270; 415-977-1270. Jim Vlantis, Gift Admin.

Vincentian Villa, 1825 Mission St., 94103. Tel: 415-621-5305. Housing project for fixed income seniors and handicapped Capacity 124.

Arlington Residence, 480 Ellis St., 94102. Tel: 415-673-9600; Fax: 415-673-8452. A safe and sober residential, low cost hotel for men and women in recovery Rooms 172.

Ozanam Center, 1175 Howard St., 94103. Tel: 415-864-3057; Fax: 415-864-3163. Substance abuse detoxification and recovery facility

Riley Center, 3543 18th St., #4, 94110. Tel: 415-552-2943; Fax: 415-552-0337. Services for former residents of battered women's shelters. Provides domestic violence prevention, education and referral services for the public as well as volunteer training. Bed Capacity 20.

San Francisco Vincentian Life, 425 Fourth St., 94107. Tel: 415-977-1270, Ext. 3003; Fax: 415-977-1271. Steve Maraccini, Dir. Vincentian Life. Supports and develops membership of the Society through parish conferences and involvement in the programs

South of Market Multi-Service Center, 525 Fifth St., 94107. Tel: 415-597-7970; Fax: 415-597-7946. A 24-hour shelter for homeless men, offering social, physical and counseling services Bed Capacity 345.

Brennan House Tel: 415-255-2894; 415-255-0165 (Crisis Hotline); Fax: 415-255-2895. Transitional housing program for the survivors of domestic violence. Program provides in-depth counseling, job rehabilitation, education, children's programs, and support groups Bed Capacity 30.

Rosalie House Tel: 415-503-4101; Fax: 415-503-4105. Emergency shelter for victims of domestic violence Bed Capacity 25.

San Francisco Vincentian Desk, 411 Fourth St., 94107. Tel: 415-202-9955, Ext. 3005; Fax: 415-202-9956 Distribution of men's clothing and non-perishable food for the poor.

SAN MATEO. *San Mateo County District Council* Main Office, St. Vincent de Paul Society , 50 N. B St., 94401. Tel: 650-343-4405; Fax: 650-343-9495. Email: svdpLM@yahoo.com. Web: www.svdp.org/sanmateo. Edward Watson, Pres.; Lorraine Moriarty, Exec. Dir.; Loretta Pehanich, Dir. of Development & Pub. Rels.

Thrift Stores:

40 North B St., 94401. Tel: 650-347-5101; Fax: 650-244-0543.

344 Grand Ave., South San Francisco, 94080. Tel: 650-589-8445; Fax: 650-244-0543.

6293 Mission St., Daly City, 94014. Tel: 650-992-9271; Fax: 650-244-0543.

2406 El Camino Real, Redwood City, 94063. Tel: 650-366-6367; Fax: 650-244-0543.

Thrift Store Pickups:

South San Francisco, 94080. Tel: 650-871-6844; Fax: 650-244-0543.

94497. Tel: 650-342-1860; Fax: 650-244-0543.

Redwood City, 94063. Tel: 650-369-2837; Fax: 650-244-0543.

Catherine's Center, 50 N. "B" St., 94401. Tel: 650-246-1520. Safe, supportive housing program for women previously incarcerated.

Vehicle Donation & Sales Tel: 650-871-6844; Fax: 650-598-9150.

St. Vincent de Paul Dining Room at St. Francis of Assisi Church, 1425 Bay Rd. East Palo Alto, 94303. Tel: 650-322-2152; Fax: 650-322-7319. Monday evenings 5-6:30pm

Services for the Incarcerated - Hope in Action Ministry, 50 N. B St., 94401. Tel: 650-366-9847; Fax: 650-343-9495.

Homeless Help Centers: Tel: 650-343-4403; Fax: 650-343-9495.

Central County, 50 N. B St., 94401. Tel: 650-343-4403; 650-343-9251; Fax: 650-343-9495. M-F, 10am-12noon

North County, 344 Grand Ave., South San Francisco, 94080. Tel: 650-589-9039; Fax: 650-244-0543. M-F, 10am-12noon

South County, 2600 Middlefield Rd., Redwood City, 94063. Tel: 650-343-4403. M-F, 1:00pm-2:00pm

Youth-Service Learning Opportunities Tel: 650-589-9039; Fax: 650-244-0543.

SAN RAFAEL. *St. Vincent de Paul Society Marin County District Council*, 820 B St., P.O. Box 150527, 94915. Tel: 415-454-3303; Fax: 415-454-3406. Email: svdpmarin@vinnies.org. Web: vinnies.org. John R. Maurer, Pres.; Steven R. Boyer, Exec. Dir.

Affordable Housing, 822 B St., 94901. Tel: 415-454-3303; Fax: 415-454-3406.

Free Dining Room, 820 B St., 94901. Tel: 415-454-0366; Fax: 415-454-3406.

Emergency Help Desk, 822 B. St., 94915. Tel: 415-454-3303; Fax: 415-454-3406.

Thrift Store Pickups Tel: 800-584-1579.

Vehicle Donations Tel: 800-YES-SVDP.

Vehicle Sales & Distribution Tel: 415-258-5226.

[I] DAY NURSERIES

SAN FRANCISCO. *Holy Family Day Home*, 299 Dolores St., 94103. Tel: 415-861-5361; Fax: 415-703-0125. Email: ADMIN@holyfamilydayhome.org. Web: www.holyfamilydayhome.org. Donna M. Cahill, Exec. Dir.

Legal Title: *Holy Family Day Homes of San Francisco* Religious 1; Lay Staff 37; Capacity 125.

[J] GENERAL HOSPITALS

SAN FRANCISCO. *St. Mary's Medical Center* dba Catholic Healthcare West , 450 Stanyan St., 94117. Tel: 415-668-1000; Fax: 415-668-4531. Web: www.stmarysmedicalcenter.org. Ken Steele, Pres.; Rev. Edward K. Murray, Chap. Sponsored by Burlingame Regional Community of the Sisters of Mercy Sisters 6; Bed Capacity 531; Patients Assisted Annually 86,836; Total Staff 1,182.

DALY CITY. *Seton Medical Center*, 1900 Sullivan Ave., 94015-2229. Tel: 650-992-4000; Fax: 650-991-6024. Email: srwilliameileendunne@dochs.org. Web: www.setonmedicalcenter.org. Bernadette M. Smith, Pres. & CEO; Rev. Rory Murphy (SJ), Dir. Spiritual Care. Daughters of Charity of St. Vincent de Paul Province of the West, Member of Daughters of Charity Health System. Daughters of Charity 5; Patients Assisted Annually 318,999.

Seton Health Services Foundation Tel: 650-991-6464; Fax: 650-991-6098.

San Francisco Heart Institute Tel: 650-991-6712; Fax: 650-755-7315.

MOSS BEACH. *Seton Medical Center Coastside*, 600 Marine Blvd., 94038. Tel: 650-563-7100; Fax: 650-728-5314. Email: sflinn@dochs.org. Web: www.setonmedicalcenter.com. Bernadette M. Smith, Pres. & CEO; Susie Flinn, R.N., Dir. Daughters of Charity of St. Vincent de Paul, Province of the West, Member of Daughters of Charity Health System Religious 1; Patients assisted annually 11,500.

[K] SENIOR CITIZEN RESIDENCES

SAN FRANCISCO. *Alexis Apartments of St. Patrick's Parish*, 390 Clementina St., 94103-4138. Tel: 415-495-3690; Fax: 415-495-3629. Email: alexisapts@aol.com.

756 Mission St., 94103. Tel: 415-421-3730; Fax: 415-512-9730. Brenda Thomas, Exec. Dir. Residents 246.

Home for the Aged of the Little Sisters of the Poor, St. Anne's Home, 300 Lake St., 94118. Tel: 415-751-6510; Fax: 415-751-0650. Email: mslspsf@hotmail.com. Sr. Patricia Mary Metzgar, L.S.P., Supr. Religious 12; Residents 87. In Res. Revs. Heribert Duquet, M.E.P.; Terrence Horan, Chap.; Anthony Lee; Mario Mich, S.D.B.; George M. Twigg-Porter, S.J.

Madonna Senior Center and Residence, 350 Golden Gate Ave., 94102. Tel: 415-592-2864; Fax: 415-928-5867. Email: ckoger@stanthonysf.org. Web: www.stanthonysf.org. Cathy Koger, Mgr. Nonprofit social services and senior drop-in center; residence for women over 60 on SSI. Total in Residence 51.

Mercy Terrace Corporation Apartments, 333 Baker St., 94117. Tel: 415-931-2325; Fax: 415-931-7206. Email: vagostino@mercyhousing.org. Web: www.mercyhousing.org. The purpose of this corporation is to develop, construct, own, and operate housing for low and moderate income persons and families. Units 158.

SAN RAFAEL. *Nazareth House*, 245 Nova Albion Way, 94903. Tel: 415-479-8282; Fax: 415-479-8824. Email: sisroseh@nazarethhousesr.com. Web: www.nazarethhouse.org. Sr. Rose Hoye, C.S.N., Supr.; Rev. Warren Woods, Chap. Sisters of Nazareth 6; Residents 135. In Res. Rev. Msgrs. George Monaghan (Retired); Andre Tourneir (Retired); Revs. Martin Avia (Retired); Edward Cleary (Retired); Donald W. Eagleson (SR) (Retired); George Meyers (Retired); Joseph O'Looney, C.S.P. (Retired); Charles Tracy (Retired).

[L] RESIDENTIAL GROUP HOMES

SAN FRANCISCO. *The Good Shepherd Gracenter*, 1310 Bacon St., 94134. Tel: 415-337-1938; Fax: 415-586-0355. Email: smmunday@aol.com. Web: www.gsgracecenter.org. Residential treatment program for women recovering from drug and alcohol addiction. Sisters 5; Lay Staff 13; Residence capacity 13; Total Assisted 45.

Mount St. Joseph-St. Elizabeth (1976), 100 Masonic Ave., 94118. Tel: 415-567-8370; Fax: 415-351-5531. Email: jschindler@msjse.org. Web: www.msjse.org. Sr. Eileen Kenny, D.C., Exec. Dir. Successor Corporation to Mount St. Joseph Home for Girls and St. Elizabeth Infant Hospital. Sisters 3; Lay Staff 126; Total Assisted 275.

Mount St. Joseph-St. Elizabeth Adolescent Program Tel: 415-567-8370, Ext. 4223. Residential care for abused and neglected girls who may be pregnant or parenting, ages 13-17 Number Assisted: Girls 43; Infants 21.

Simpatico School Tel: 415-351-4056; Fax: 415-440-5033. On-site non-public and San Francisco Unified School District junior-senior high school offering basic education and vocational training to school-age residents of our programs. Students 40.

Epiphany Center for Families in Recovery Tel: 415-351-4052; Fax: 415-346-2356. 1. Comprehensive drug treatment with parenting, life skills, and health education groups.; 2. Epiphany In-Home Services for Families at Risk.; 4. Epiphany House -Transitional living for women and children. Families Served 60; Families Served by In-Home Services 85; Individuals Assisted 26.

[M] RETREAT HOUSES

BURLINGAME. *Mercy Center, Spirituality and Conference Center*, 2300 Adeline Dr., 94010. Tel: 650-340-7474; Fax: 650-340-1299. Email: mc@mercyburl.org. Web: mercy-center.org. H. William Goehring, Exec. Dir.; Diarmuid Rooney, Prog. Mgr.; Sue Thourson, Supvr., Guest Svcs. Staff 21; Overnight capacity 90; Daytime use 300.

MENLO PARK. *Vallombrosa Center* (1946), 250 Oak Grove Ave., 94025. Tel: 650-325-5614; Fax: 650-325-0908. Email: host@vallombrosa.org. Web: www.vallombrosa.org. Rev. Kevin P. Gaffey, Acting Dir.
Legal Title: *Vallombrosa Center, Conference and Retreat Center of the Archdiocese of San Francisco*

PETALUMA. *Silver Penny Farm Retreat Center*, 5215 Old Lakeville Rd., No. 1, 94954. Tel: 707-762-1498. Rev. Raymond K. Smith, Dir.

SAN RAFAEL. *Santa Sabina Center*, 25 Magnolia, 94901. Tel: 415-457-7727; Fax: 415-457-2310. Email: sntasabina@aol.com. Sr. Susannah Malarkey, O.P., Dir. Dominican Sisters Retreat and Conference Center.

[N] MONASTERIES AND RESIDENCES OF PRIESTS AND BROTHERS

SAN FRANCISCO. *St. Dominic Priory*, 2390 Bush St., 94115-3124. Tel: 415-567-7824; Fax: 415-567-3360; 415-567-1608 (Parish). Email: jmoopes@dominics.org. Web: www.stdominics.org. Very Revs. Joseph Sergott, O.P., Prior; Emmerich W. Vogt, O.P. (P); Revs. Xavier Lavagetto, O.P., Pastor & Sub-Prior; Anthony Rosevear, O.P., Novice Master & Vicar; Felix F. Cassidy, O.P.; Francis Goode, O.P.; Gregory T. Tatum, O.P.; Peter Rogers, O.P.; Bro. Mark A. Gorski, O.P. Priests 8; Brothers 1; Novices 8.

Jesuit Community at St. Ignatius College Preparatory, 2001 37th Ave., 94116-1165. Tel: 415-731-7500; Fax: 415-731-9408. Email: postmaster@siprep.org. Web: www.siprep.org. Revs. Paul F. Capitolo, S.J.; Harry V. Carlin, S.J.; Gregory M. Goethals, S.J., Rector; Gerald F. Hudson, S.J.; Michael J. Kotlanger; Most Rev. Andrew Maginnis, S.J.; Revs. Michel Marcil, S.J.; David S. Robinson, S.J.; Anthony P. Sauer, S.J.; A. Francis Stiegeler, S.J.; Theodore T. Tahney, S.J.; Gerardo Valenzuela; Warren J. Wright, S.J.; Bros. Douglas E. Draper; Charles J. Jackson, S.J.; Thomas J. Koller; Arthur W. Lee; John E. Maloney; Fred Kabwe, Scholastic. Priests 11; Brothers 4.

Jesuit Community at University of San Francisco (Corporate Title: Jesuit Community at University of San Francisco) , 2600 Turk Blvd., 94118-4347. Tel: 415-422-4200; Fax: 415-422-5651. Email: treacyj@usfca.edu. Web: www.usfca.edu/jesuit. Revs. John R. Treacy, S.J., Rector; Edward V. Stackpoole, S.J.; Joseph T. Angilella, S.J., Min.; Stephen A. Barber, S.J. (LA); James R. Blaettler, S.J.; James T. Bretzke, S.J. (OAK); Francis J. Buckley, S.J.; Denis E. Collins, S.J.; Stephen J. Corder, S.J. (OAK); Geoffrey R. Dillon, S.J. (NOR); Charles R. Gagan, S.J.; Albert A. Grosskopf, S.J.; R. Daniel Kendall, S.J.; John P. Koeplin, S.J.; Jeffrey T. LaBelle, S.J.; John J. Lo Schiavo, S.J.; Thomas M. Lucas, S.J.; David P. Marcotte, S.J. (BGP); Bernard Muhigirwa, S.J. (Congo); Robert L. Niehoff, S.J. (ORE); Christopher T. Nguyen, S.J.; Thomas H. O'Neill, S.J.; Anthony C. Pabayo, S.J. (PH); Stephen A. Privett, S.J., Pres. Univ. of San Francisco; Jean de Dieu Randrianaivo, S.J. (Madagascar) (OAK); David C. Robinson, S.J.; Vernon J. Ruland, S.J.; John D. Savard, S.J.; George E. Schultze, S.J.; Peter J. Togni, S.J.; Eric G. Velandria, S.J. (PH); Bro. John Keck, S.J. Priests 31; Brothers 1; Scholastic 1.

Marianist Community, 175 Phelan Ave., 94112. Tel: 415-586-8082. Revs. Thomas French, S.M., Supr.; Timothy M. Kenney, S.M.; Joseph Hartzler, S.M.; Bros. Thomas Deasy, S.M.; James Dods, S.M.; Paul Fennelly, S.M.; John Haster, S.M.; Thomas Jalbert, S.M.; James Leahy, S.M.; Patrick McMahon, S.M.; Richard Olsen, S.M. Priests 3; Brothers 8.

Marist Center of the West Atlanta Province of the Society of Mary (Marist) , 625 Pine St., 94108-3210. Tel: 415-398-3543; Fax: 415-781-4937. Revs. James L. Pratt, S.M.; Francis Springer, S.M.; Nicholas Kutulas, S.M.; Edward C. Blee, S.M.; Juan Carranco, S.M.; Patrick J. Coyle, S.M.; Phillip d'Auby, S.M.; Bros. Patrick Souza, S.M., Admin.; John J. O'Brien, S.M. Priests 7; Brothers 2.

Paris Foreign Mission Society Residence, 930 Ashbury St., 94117. Tel: 415-664-6747; Fax: 415-564-5335. Revs. Jacques R. Didier, M.E.P., Dir.; Heribert Duquet, M.E.P. Priests 2.

Salesian Provincial Residence, 1100 Franklin St., 94109. Tel: 415-441-7144; Fax: 415-441-7155. Email: suosec@aol.com. Revs. David Purdy, S.D.B. (MRY), Prov.; Richard Presenti, S.D.B., Prov. Treas.; Ralph Murphy, S.D.B. Priests 9. In Res. Revs. Bernard Dabbene, S.D.B.; Larry Lorenzoni, S.D.B.; Roger Luna, S.D.B.; Mario Mich, S.D.B.; Joseph Scanagatta, S.D.B.; Gabriel Zavattaro, S.D.B.
Military Chaplain:
2172 S. Coast Hwy, Oceanside, 92054. Tel: 760-725-3534. Rev. Robert Delis, S.D.B.

BURLINGAME. *Capuchin Provincial House*, 1345 Cortez Ave., 94010. Tel: 650-342-1489; Fax: 650-342-5664. Email: ofmcap@aol.com. Web: www.beafriar.com. Revs. Antonio E. Marti, O.F.M.Cap., Prov.; Julian Gonzalez-Montenegro, O.F.M.Cap.; Richard Lopes, O.F.M.Cap.; Bertram Mulligan, O.F.M.Cap.; Miguel Angel Ortiz, O.F.M.Cap.; Camillus MacRory, O.F.M.Cap.

DALY CITY. *Verbum Dei Missionary Fraternity*, 59 Risel St., 94014. Tel: 415-585-8804. Web: fratvdei@pacbell.net. Rev. Gerardo Flores, V.D.M.F. Priests 1.

PORTOLA VALLEY. *Woodside Priory*, 302 Portola Rd., 94028. Tel: 650-851-8220; Fax: 650-851-2839. Email: mmager@woodsidepriory.com. Web: www.woodsidepriory.com. Very Rev. Martin J. Mager, O.S.B., Supr.; Revs. Pius L. Horvath, O.S.B.; Egon J. Javor, O.S.B.; Maurus B. Nemeth, O.S.B.; Bro. Edward Englund.
Legal Title: *Benedictine Fathers of the Priory, Inc.* Priests 4; Brothers 1.

[O] CONVENTS AND RESIDENCES FOR SISTERS

SAN FRANCISCO. *Carmelite Monastery of Cristo Rey, Discalced Carmelite Nuns*, 721 Parker Ave., 94118-4227. Tel: 415-387-2640; Fax: 415-751-5330. Sr. Elizabeth Ramirez, O.C.D., Prioress. Professed Nuns 15.

Daughters of St. Paul, 46 Geary St., 94108. Tel: 415-781-5180; Fax: 415-781-1905. Email: fspsanfran@aol.com. Web: www.pauline.org. Sr. Mary Bernardine Sattler, F.S.P., Supr. Sisters 5.

St. Francis Convent of Mercy (Sisters of Mercy-Burlingame), 826 30th Ave., 94121-3522. Tel: 415-221-8874. Sisters 2.

Franciscan Missionaries of Our Lady of Peace
Our Lady of Guadalupe Convent, 46 Harrington St., 94112. Tel: 415-587-3729; Fax: 415-824-0605. Sr. Hilda Sandoval, M.F.P., Supr.

Monastery of Perpetual Adoration, Nuns of Perpetual Adoration, 771 Ashbury St., 94117. Tel: 415-566-2743; Fax: 415-564-4469. Sr. Rosalba Vargas, A.P., Supr. Cloistered Nuns 18.

Presentation Convent, Motherhouse of the Sisters of the Presentation of B.V.M., 281 Masonic Ave., 94118. Tel: 415-422-5001; Fax: 415-422-5026. Email: pelower@pbvmsf.org. Web: www.presentationsisterssf.org. Sr. Ann Therese Lynch, P.B.V.M., Pres. Sisters in Archdiocese 69; Total in congregation 118.

Sisters of Social Service, 1850 Ulloa St., 94116. Tel: 415-681-9219. Email: SSSSF@earthlink.net. Web: www.socialservicesisters.org. Sisters 2.

Sisters of St. Joseph of Orange, 544 Bush St., 94108. Tel: 415-398-7383; Fax: 415-421-2572. Email: ndvsf@earthlink.net. Sisters 3.

Sisters of St. Joseph of Orange, 1737 Silliman St., 94134. Tel: 415-585-0159. Email: csjsf@earthlink.net. Sisters 3.

Sisters of the Good Shepherd, 1310 Bacon St., 94134. Tel: 415-586-2822; Fax: 415-586-0355. Email: smmunday@aol.com. Sisters 6.

Sisters of the Holy Family, 174 Stanyan St. Upper, 94118. Tel: 415-221-7704. Sisters 4.

Sisters of the Precious Blood, 326 Ewing Ter., 94118.

Society of Helpers (Helpers of the Holy Souls), 855 Lincoln Way, 94122. Tel: 415-661-6316; Fax: 415-661-6346. Email: vdonlon@aol.com. Sr. Veronica Donlon, Local Supr. Sisters 6.

Verbum Dei Missionary Fraternity (Apostolic Institute: Instituto Apostolico Verbum Dei, Rome, Italy) , 3373 19th St., 94110. Tel: 415-282-4979; Fax: 415-282-0252. Email: sfverbumdei@aol.com. Web: www.fmverbumdei.com. Sr. Ellen Hess, V.D.M.F., Supr. Prayer and ministry of the Word, working with youth, young adults & adults.

ATHERTON. *Religious of the Sacred Heart Oakwood*, 140 Valparaiso Ave., 94027. Tel: 650-323-8343; Fax: 650-326-2251. Sr. Nancy Salisbury, R.S.C.J., Dir. Infirmary for elderly Religious of the Sacred Heart. Sisters 45.

BURLINGAME. *Regional Community of the Sisters of Mercy of the Americas*, 2300 Adeline Dr., 94010-5599. Tel: 650-340-7410; Fax: 650-347-2550. Email: sombur@mercyburl.org. Web: www.mercyburl.org. Sisters 50; Total in congregation 184; Total in Archdiocese 114; Retreat Centers 1; Total In Residence 4; Total Staff 17.

DALY CITY. *Daughters of Charity of St. Vincent de Paul*, 2000 Sullivan Ave., 94015-2202. Tel: 650-991-6715. Email: DOCSMC@aol.com. Sr. William Eileen Dunn, Supr.

Quinhon Missionary Sisters of the Holy Cross, 298 Southgate Ave., 94015. Tel: 650-992-1560. Email: hocviendaly@hotmail.com. Sisters Josephine Dao Vu; Marie Gorett Pham Lam; Cecilia Luyen Nguyen; Rosina Mai Pham; Conceptua Huang Thuy Nguyen. Sisters 5.

Religious of the Virgin Mary, Our Lady of Mercy Convent, 15 Elmwood Dr., 94015. Tel: 650-992-5769; Fax: 650-756-3457. Email: sismargie@yahoo.com. Sr. M. Virginia Bardilona, R.S.M., Contact Person.

MENLO PARK. *Corpus Christi Monastery*, 215 Oak Grove Ave., 94025-3272. Tel: 650-322-1801; Fax: 650-322-6816. Email: nunsmenlo@aol.com. Web: www.op.org/nunsmenlo. Sr. Mary of the Holy Family, Prioress. Nuns of the Order of Preachers Cloistered Religious 17; Extern Sisters 1.

PACIFICA. *Missionaries of Charity* (India) , 164 Milagra Dr., 94044. Tel: 650-355-3091. Sisters 8.
Noviciate, 312 29th St., 94131. Tel: 415-647-1889. Sisters 4; Novices 31.
55 Sadowa St., 94117. Tel: 415-586-3449. Sisters 5.

REDWOOD CITY. *Casa Chiara Community*, 3910 Bret Harte Dr., Box 685, 94064-0685. Tel: 650-366-3968; Fax: 650-780-9182. Email: casachiara@juno.com. P.O. Box 685, 94064-0685. Franciscan Sisters Sisters 3.

SAN RAFAEL. *Carmelite Monastery of the Mother of God, Discalced Carmelite Nuns*, 530 Blackstone Dr., 94093. Tel: 415-479-6872; Fax: 415-491-4964. Sr. Anna Marie Vanni, O.C.D., Prioress. Sisters 6.

Dominican Sisters of San Rafael Generalate & Convent, 1520 Grand Ave., 94901-2236. Tel: 415-453-8303; Fax: 415-453-8367. Email: patsimpsonop@juno.com. Web: sanrafaelop.org. Sr. Patricia Simpson, O.P., Prioress Gen. Total in Community 140; Total in Archdiocese 90.

Dominican Convent, 1540 Grand Ave., 94901. Tel: 415-454-9221. Sisters 23.

Our Lady of Lourdes Convent (Infirmary), 77 Locust Ave., 94901. Tel: 415-457-3171. Sisters 27.

Our Lady of Mt. Carmel Convent, 34 Buena Vista Ave., Mill Valley, 94941. Tel: 415-389-0328. Sisters 7.

San Domenico Convent, 1500 Butterfield Rd., San Anselmo, 94960. Tel: 415-453-9172. Sisters 6.

St. Margaret Convent, 40 Locust Ave., 94901. Tel: 415-458-2952. Sisters 8.

St. Dominic Convent, 2517 Pine St., 94115. Tel: 415-567-8282; Fax: 415-776-7384. Sisters 7.

St. Rose Convent, 2515 Pine St., 94115. Tel: 415-441-2685. Sisters 10.

SOUTH SAN FRANCISCO. *Holy Family Convent*, 381 Avalon Dr., 94080. Tel: 650-588-3471. Email: shfavalon@juno.com. Web: holyfamilysisters.com. Sisters 2.

[P] CATHOLIC CHARITIES & THE CATHOLIC YOUTH ORGANIZATION

SAN FRANCISCO. *Catholic Charities & The Catholic Youth Organization (CYO) of the Archdiocese of San Francisco*

Administrative Office, 2255 Hayes St., 4th Floor, 94117. Tel: 415-592-9200; Fax: 415-592-9201. Web: cccyo.org. Brian F. Cahill, Exec. Dir.; Timothy O'Keefe, Assoc. Exec. Dir.; Kimberly Watts, Dir. Finance; Tony Michelini, Controller; Steve Grant, Dir. Facilities; Kathy Scollin, Dir. Devel.; Ashley Clay, Dir. Human Resources; Marty Rea, Dir. CYO Programs; Glenn Motola, Dir., HIV Svcs.; Mary Male Schembri, Dir. Aging & Behavioral Healthcare Svcs.; Tere Brown, Dir. Children & Family Svcs.; Kent Eagleson, Dir. St. Vincent's Svcs.; Mary Redington, Dir., Comm. & Mktg.

Board of Directors: Most Rev. William J. Levada, Chm.; Clinton Reilly, Pres.; Kathryn Parish-Reese, Sec.; Jack Fitzpatrick, Treas.; Steve Borden; Mark Cleary; Rev. Thomas A. Daly; Deborah Dasovich; Felicito Desuasido; Rev. Eduardo Dura; Jeffrey Fenton; Patricia Garbarino; Lawrence Gray; Bernard Hagan; Mrs. Cecilia Herbert; Rev. Msgr. Robert W. McElroy; Robert McLalan; Nanette Lee Miller; Alison Morey; Christopher Needham; Michael Nevin; Tim Rea; William Ring; Rita Semel; Brian Swift; Jenny Theleen; Burl Toler Jr.; Rev. Kenneth M. Westray; Jacqueline Woodford.

Behavioral Health Care and Senior Services:

Behavioral Health Care:

Grief Care & General Counseling, 2559 40th Ave., 94116. Tel: 415-564-7882; Fax: 415-731-1270. Barbara Elordi, Admin.

Marin Behavioral Healthcare Services, 179 Los Ranchitos, San Rafael, 94903. Tel: 415-499-1470; Fax: 415-479-2667. Betty Wheelwright, Admin.

Information and Referral, 179 Los Ranchitos, San Rafael, 94903. Tel: 415-499-1470; Fax: 415-479-2667. Stephanie Earle, Admin.

San Mateo Behavioral Healthcare Services, 36 37th Ave., San Mateo, 94403. Tel: 650-295-2192; Fax: 650-286-1325. Dave Ross, Admin.

Information and Referral, 36 37th Ave., San Mateo, 94403. Tel: 650-295-2160; Fax: 650-286-1140. Madeline Velasco, Admin.

Senior Services:

Marin Senior Case Management, 179 Los Ranchitos, San Rafael, 94903. Tel: 415-499-1470; Fax: 415-479-2667. Barbara Gluck, Admin.

Meals on Wheels, 36 37th Ave., San Mateo, 94403. Tel: 650-295-2172; Fax: 650-286-1141. Barbara Murray, Admin.

OMI Senior Center, 1948 Ocean Ave., 94127. Tel: 415-587-1443; Fax: 415-586-7960. Brian Clement, Admin.

San Carlos Adult Day Support, 787 Walnut St., San Carlos, 94070. Tel: 650-592-9325; Fax: 650-592-2316. Nancy Knific, Admin.

San Francisco Adult Day Support, 55 Faraliones, 94112. Tel: 415-452-3500; Fax: 415-452-3505. Patty Clement, Admin.

Marin Family Support Services:

Marin Transitional Housing, 179 Los Ranchitos, San Rafael, 94903. Tel: 415-499-1470; Fax: 415-479-2667. Jemar Faulis, Admin.

Children & Family Services:

Adoptions, Foster Care & Pregnancy Counseling

Adoption Network, 98 Bosworth St., 94112. Tel: 415-406-2387; Fax: 415-406-2386. Terry Watters, Admin.

Pregnancy Counseling Hotline Tel: 800-CAR--002.

Child Care Services:

Canal Family Support Program, Pickelweed Community Center, 50 Canal St., San Rafael, 94901. Tel: 415-454-8596; Fax: 415-485-3185. Carlos Garcia, Admin.

Children's Village Child Development Center, 250 10th St., 94103. Tel: 415-865-2610; Fax: 415-503-0750. Gonsalo Toscano, Admin.

Mission Day Care, 180 Fair Oaks St., 94110. Tel: 415-826-6880; Fax: 415-920-2743. Lilliana Rossi, Admin.

Family Services:

Refugee & Immigrant Services, Formerly Family & Immigrant Services 98 Bosworth St., 94112. Tel: 415-486-2360; Fax: 415-406-2363. Christopher Martinez, Admin.

Information and Referral, 240 Golden Gate Ave., #100, 94102. Tel: 415-345-1290; Fax: 415-345-1280. Elaine Simmons, Admin.

Guerrero, 899 Guerrero St., 94110. Tel: 415-550-4478; Fax: 415-550-4481. Chris Callandrillo, Admin.

Richmond Hills Family Center, 6324 Geary Blvd., 94121. Tel: 415-750-5080; Fax: 415-750-5085. Jeanne Foulis, Admin.

St. Joseph's Family Center, 220 10th St., 94103. Tel: 415-575-4920; Fax: 415-575-4925. Chris Callandrillo, Admin.

Treasure Island Housing, P.O. Box 78037, 94107. Tel: 415-981-3038; Fax: 415-981-3039. Nella Goncalves, Admin.

Group Homes:

St. Vincent's School for Boys, One St. Vincent Dr., San Rafael, 94903. Tel: 415-507-2000; 415-507-4264 (Intake); Fax: 415-491-0842. Dan Gallagher, Admin.

San Francisco Boys' and Girls' Home, One St. Vincent Dr., San Rafael, 94903. Tel: 415-221-3443; Fax: 415-387-1627. Denise Mayfield, Admin.

HIV Services

Derek Silva Community, 1594 Market St., 94102. Tel: 415-575-3725; Fax: 415-575-3729. Brenda Goldhammer, Admin.

HIV Housing & Health Programs, Formerly HIV Direct Services 240 Golden Gate Ave., 3rd Floor, 94102. Tel: 415-345-9112, Ext. 130; Fax: 415-345-1269. George Simmons, Admin.

Leland House, 141 Leland Ave., 94134. Tel: 415-405-2056; Fax: 415-337-1137. Kevin Cuny, Admin.

Peter Claver Community, 1340 Golden Gate, 94115. Tel: 415-749-3800; Fax: 415-563-3153. Rodney Murphy, Admin.

Rita da Cascia, 3268 Sacramento, 94115. Tel: 415-202-0235; Fax: 415-202-0930. George Simmons, Admin.

Catholic Youth Organization Programs:

CYO Athletics

Marin, One St. Vincent Dr., San Rafael, 94903. Tel: 415-507-4237; Fax: 415-491-0842. Steve Farbstein, Admin.

San Francisco, 2255 Hayes St., 4th Floor, 94117. Tel: 415-406-2373; Fax: 415-592-9201. Joann Dillon, Admin.

CYO Outdoor Programs

CYO Camp, P.O. Box 188, Occidental, 95465. Tel: 707-874-0200; Fax: 707-874-0230. Paul Raia, Admin.

CYO Caritas Creek, P.O. Box 188, Occidental, 95465. Tel: 707-874-0200; Fax: 707-874-0230. Paul Raia, Admin.

CYO Transportation Services

699 Serramonte Blvd., Ste. 210, Daly City, 94015. Tel: 650-757-2110; Fax: 650-758-1425. Bill Avalos, Admin.

McGucken Center:

Facility Manager, 2136 Bohemian Hwy., Occidental, 95465. Tel: 707-874-0225; Fax: 707-874-0230. Bruce Blagsvedt, Admin.

Reservations, 2136 Bohemian Hwy., Occidental, 95465. Tel: 707-874-0210; Fax: 707-874-0230. Lynn Schenck, Admin.

St. Vincent's Services:

St. Vincent's Foster Family and Adoption Agency, One St. Vincent Dr., San Rafael, 94903. Tel: 415-507-4289; Fax: 415-491-0842. Megan Chesnet, Admin.

[Q] NEWMAN CENTERS

SAN FRANCISCO. *Newman Center, San Francisco State University* St. Thomas More Church, 1300 Junipero Serra Blvd., 94132-2913. Tel: 415-452-9634; Fax: 415-452-9653. Email: stmchurch2002@aol.com. Web: www.STMChurch.com. Revs. Labib Kobti, Admin.; Francis Tiso, Campus Min.; Martha Blandon, Admin. Office Mgr.

Newman Center, University of California Medical Center 1290 Fifth Ave., 94122. Tel: 415-566-5610; Fax: 415-566-5073. Email: labibkobti@aol.com. Web: www.sjog.org.

[R] PERSONAL PRELATURES

SAN FRANCISCO. *Prelature of the Holy Cross and Opus Dei*, 765 14th Ave., 94118. Tel: 415-386-0431; Fax: 415-752-7177. Web: www.opusdei.org. Very Rev. John R. Meyer, Vicar for California; Rev. Msgr. James A. Kelly; Rev. Jerome L. Jung (CHI).

Other Priests in the Archdiocese: Revs. Torlach C. Delargy; William G. Shaughanessy.

Menlough Study Center, 1160 Santa Cruz Ave., Menlo Park, 94025. Tel: 650-327-1675.

Westwood Study Center, 108 Kipling Dr., Mill Valley, 94941. Tel: 415-388-4531.

[S] MISCELLANEOUS LISTINGS

Rev. Msgr. Maurice M. McCormick, Chap., Gen. Secretariat, Cursillo, 3321 16th St., 94114. Tel: 415-621-8203; Fax: 415-621-2294. Email: mdolores@earthlink.net.

SAN FRANCISCO. *St. Anthony Foundation*, 121 Golden Gate Ave., 94102. Tel: 415-241-2600; Fax: 415-252-1635. Email: info@stanthonysf.org. Web: www.stanthonysf.org. Revs. John Hardin, O.F.M., Exec. Dir.; Dan Lackie, O.F.M., Chap.; Floyd A. Lotito, O.F.M., Consultant. A nonprofit, charitable corporation assisting the homeless and low-income.

Apostleship of Prayer, 300 Lake St., 94118-1357. Tel: 415-831-0941; Fax: 415-751-1423; Pager: 415-540-3179. Rev. George M. Twigg-Porter, S.J., Dir.

Archdiocesan Council of Catholic Women, One Peter Yorke Way, 94109-6602. Tel: 415-614-5500; Fax: 415-353-5555. Hildegarde Thums, Pres.

St. Benedict Center for Deaf and Hearing Impaired at St. Francis Xavier Church, 1801 Octavia, 94109. Tel: 415-567-9855; Teletype: 415-567-0438; Fax: 415-567-0916.

Masses for the Hearing Impaired. Tel: 415-567-0438 (TDD); Fax: 415-567-0916. Rev. Thomas Coughlin, Admin.

St. Anthony, 3500 Middlefield Rd., Menlo Park, 94025. Tel: 650-366-4692.

California Handicapables, Inc. (1965), 1311 Montgomery St., 94133-3521. Tel: 415-781-1311; Fax: 415-576-1826. Email: saltooley@aol.com. Miss Nadine Calligiuri, Founder; Sally Tooley, Treas. To give shut-ins and handicapped people of all faiths an opportunity for monthly Mass, lunch and general fellowship. We generally meet the third Saturday of every month at St. Mary's Cathedral, San Francisco. Please call for more information.

Catholic Healthcare West, 185 Berry St., Ste. 300, 94107. Tel: 415-438-5500; Fax: 415-438-5726. Email: Rsahagi@chw.edu. Web: www.chwHEALTH.com. Lloyd H. Dean, Pres. & CEO. A nonprofit public benefit corporation. CHW is a multi-congregational Health System co-sponsored by the Auburn Regional Community of the Sisters of Mercy; the Burlingame Regional Community of the Sisters of Mercy; the Sisters of St. Dominic of the Congregation of the Most Holy Rosary, Adrian, MI; the Sisters of the Third Order of St. Dominic, Congregation of the Most Holy Name, San Rafael, CA; the Congregation of the Sisters of St. Catherine of Siena of Kenosha, WI; the Franciscan Sisters of the Sacred Heart of Frankfurt, IL; the Sisters of St. Francis of Penance and Christian Charity, St. Francis Province; the Congregation of the Sisters of Charity of the Incarnate Word, Houston, Texas. CHW includes several affiliated hospitals, retirement homes, long-term facilities, and related corporations located in California, Arizona and Nevada.; The Corporate Office staff provides centralized management and support functions for the following affiliated nonprofit organizations in the Archdiocese of San Francisco (other affiliates are listed in their respective dioceses): St. Mary's Medical Center; St. Mary's Medical Center Foundation; MSC Psychiatric Services Corporation. Sisters 2.

St. Mary's Medical Center Foundation, 450 Stanyan St., 94117-1079. Tel: 415-750-5790; Fax: 415-750-8132.

MSC Psychiatric Services Corporation, 450 Stanyan St., 94117-1079. Tel: 415-668-1000; Fax: 415-750-4531.

Catholic Kolping Society, 440 Taraval St., 94116. Tel: 415-661-8305. Patrick Biesty, Pres.; Catherine Vennemeyer, Treas.

Catholic Scouting Boy and Girl Scouts.

Catholics for Truth & Justice, P.O. Box 26756, 94126-0756. Tel: 415-693-2TRU. Rev. Msgr. Harry Schlitt.

Charismatic Movement, Advisory Board, 2555 - 17th Ave., 94116. Tel: 415-664-8481; Fax: 415-661-2957. Email: sfccr@sfspirit.com. Web: sfspirit.com. Revs. L. Joseph Landi, Liason; Jose Corral, Liaison to Spanish Speaking.

Equestrian Order of the Holy Sepulchre of Jerusalem - Northwest Lieutenancy, Two Ashbury Ter., 94117-4502. Tel: 415-566-9639; Fax: 415-765-2945. Albert E. Maggio, Honorary Lieutenant; Robert F. Begley, Honorary Lieutenant.

Father Raphael Piperni Charitable Trust, 1100 Franklin St., 94109. Tel: 415-441-7144; Fax: 415-441-8151. Email: svoecon@aol.com. (The FRPC (R) Trust)

Franciscan Friars of California, Provincial Office of Communications Consultant, 121 Golden Gate Ave., 94102-3809. Tel: 415-592-2740; Fax: 415-863-8240. Email: falfonso@aol.com. Rev. Floyd A. Lotito, O.F.M., Dir.

Jesuit Volunteer Corps: Southwest, 474 Valencia St., #230, 94103. P.O. Box 40039, 94140. Tel: 415-522-1599; Fax: 415-522-1633. Email: jvcsw@JesuitVolunteers.org. Web: www.JesuitVolunteers.org. Yvonne Prowse, Exec. Dir.

Legion of Mary, 1425 Bay Rd., Palo Alto, 94303. Tel: 650-322-2152; Fax: 650-322-1219. Rev. Lawrence C. Goode, Spiritual Dir., San Francisco Comitium.

Mercy Housing California, 1360 Mission St., Suite 300, 94103. Tel: 415-355-7100; Fax: 415-355-7101. Email: VAgostino@mercyhousing.org. Web: www.mercyhousing.org. Housing development for low-income families, elderly, and singles.

Mercy Family Plaza, c/o Mercy Housing California, 1360 Mission St., Suite 300, 94103. Tel: 415-355-7100; Fax: 415-355-7101. Thirty-six affordable units for families.

**The Ordinary Mutual, RRG*, P.O. Box 191867, 94119-4002. Tel: 415-536-8440; Fax: 415-536-4002. Email: dennis_o'hara@ajg.com. Dennis O'Hara, Underwriting Mgr.; Randolph E. Steiner, Pres. A Risk Retention Group Corporation, incorporated in Vermont, serving the Dioceses of Boise, Tucson, Fresno, Monterey, Oakland, Orange, Sacramento, San Jose, Santa Rosa, and Stockton, and the Archdioceses of Los Angeles and San Francisco.

Pauline Books & Media, 46 Geary St., 94108. Tel: 415-781-5180; Fax: 415-781-1905. Email: fspsanfran@aol.com. Web: www.pauline.org. Sr. Mary Bernardine Sattler, F.S.P., Supr. Daughters of St. Paul Sisters 5.

Philip Rinaldi Charitable Trust, 1100 Franklin St., 94109. Tel: 415-441-7144; Fax: 415-441-8151. Email: suoecon@aol.com. For the care of needy youth and for the formation needs of Salesians of St. John Bosco.

Religious Trust (RETA), Box 7443, 94120. Tel: 415-536-9300; Fax: 415-536-4002. Email: david_wiesner@asg.com. A nonprofit religious employer health plan

The Ricci Institute for Chinese-Western Cultural History at the Center for the Pacific Rim, University of San Francisco, 2130 Fulton St., 94117-1080. Tel: 415-422-6401; Fax: 415-422-2291. Email: ricci@usfca.edu. Web: www.usfca.edu/ricci. Xiaoxin Wu, Ed.D., Dir.; Rev. Albert Chan, S.J., Ph.D., Senior Research Fellow; Monica Chang, Asst. Dir.; Mark Mir, Research Fellow & Chinese Library Cataloguer; May Lee, Prog. Asst.

St. Rose Corporation, 2501 Pine St., 94115. Tel: 415-440-9568; Fax: 415-440-9568. Email: patsimpsonop@juno.com.
Officers of the Board: Sr. Patricia Simpson, O.P., Pres.; Thomas Bertelsen Jr., CFO & Sec.; Sisters Patricia Simpson, O.P., Dir.; Ann Bertain, O.P., Dir.; Kristin Wombacher, O.P., Dir.; Sandy Mori, Dir.; Valerie Street, Dir.; Thomas Bertelsen Jr., Dir.; Kathleen Connolly, Dir.

Shrine of St. Jude Thaddeus, 2390 Bush St., 94115. Tel: 415-931-5919. Email: info@stjude-shrine.org. Web: www.stjude-shrine.org.

Sisters of the Presentation Community Support Trust Fund, 2340 Turk Blvd., 94118. Tel: 415-564-9455; Fax: 415-731-3071. Email: SRRT12@aol.com. 1409 12th Ave., 94122. Sisters Pamela Chiesa, P.B.V.M., Trustee; Patricia Anne Cloherty, P.B.V.M., Trustee; Roberta Green, P.B.V.M., Trustee; Patricia Marie Mulpeters, P.B.V.M., Trustee; Rose Therese Sousa, P.B.V.M., Trustee; Judith Cunningham, Trustee. Trust used for the religious and charitable needs of the Sisters of the Presentation of the Blessed Virgin Mary.

Together in the Mission of Education (T.I.M.E.), 301 DeMontfort Ave., 94112. Tel: 415-334-4334; Fax: 415-333-3040. Email: TIME2000@juno.com. Brett E. Allen, Exec. Dir.; Steve Farren, Treas.; Caitlin Jeffrey, Devel. Dir.

BURLINGAME. *Italian Catholic Federation, St. Catherine of Siena Church*, 1310 Bayswater Ave., 94010. Tel: 415-751-0450. Rev. Francis Murray, Chap. (Retired).

Music at Kohl Mansion, Inc., 2750 Adeline Dr., 94010. Tel: 650-762-1130; Fax: 650-343-2316. Email: musicatkohl@earthlink.net. Web: www.musicatkohl.org. To develop and promote public knowledge and appreciation of musical arts by sponsoring chamber music concerts and other public performances of music, as well as music education activities.

DALY CITY. *Association of Catholic Student Councils*, 86 Cityview Dr., 94014-3400. Tel: 415-584-9877; 650-270-9259; Fax: 415-584-9877. Email: tacsc@tacsc.org. Web: www.tacsc.org. Marilyn Thickett, Exec. Dir.

Vincentian Service Corps West, Seton Medical Center, 1900 Sullivan Ave., 94015. Tel: 650-991-6465; Fax: 650-991-6878. Email: vscwesi@edochs.org. Web: www.vscorps.org. Sisters Judith Schomisch, D.C., Exec. Dir.; Eileen Kenny, D.C., Chairperson; Kitty Mullooly, Vice Chairperson; Steve Dells, Sec. & Treas.

REDWOOD CITY. *The Catholic Worker Community*, 545 Cassia St., 94063. Tel: 650-366-4415. Lawrence P. Purcell, Dir. A foster home for teenagers.

**St. Francis Center of Redwood City*, 101 Buckingham Ave., 94064. Tel: 650-365-7829; Fax: 650-365-7829. Email: SChristina@aol.com. Web: www.stfrancisrwc.org. P.O. Box 7134, 94064. Sr. Christina Heltsley, O.P., Exec. Dir.

SAN RAFAEL. **Center Interfaith Housing*, 164 N. San Pedro Rd., 94903. Fax: 415-453-8367.

Mission Holding Corporation, 1520 Grand Ave., 94901. Tel: 415-453-8303; Fax: 415-453-8367. Email: patsimpsonop@juno.com. Web: sanrafaelop.org.
Governing Board: Sisters Patricia Simpson, O.P.; Margaret Diener, O.P.; Raya Hanlon, O.P.; Maureen McInerney, O.P.; Lois Silvo, O.P.

Sisters of the Third Order of St. Dominic Support Charitable Trust Fund, 1520 Grand Ave., 94901. Tel: 415-453-8303; Fax: 415-453-8367. Email: patsimpsonop@juno.com. Web: sanrafaelop.org. Sisters Patricia Boss, O.P., Staff; Patricia Simpson, O.P., Trustee; Lois Silvo, O.P.; Cathryn deBack, O.P.; Rev. Msgr. Richard Knapp, Trustee; Dr. Dennis Burke, Trustee; Mr. Thomas Bertelsen, Staff.
Legal Title: *Sisters of the Third Order of St. Dominic, Congregation of the Most Holy Name, Support Charitable Trust Fund*, Trust used for the religious and charitable needs of the Sisters of the Third Order of St. Dominic, Congregation of the Most Holy Name.

[T] CLOSED INSTITUTIONS

SAN FRANCISCO. *All Hallows Church* For sacramental records please contact Our Lady of Lourdes, 1715 Oakdale Ave., San Francisco 94124. Tel: 415-285-3377; Fax: 415-285-2191

St. Brigid Church For sacramental records please contact St. Vincent de Paul, 2320 Green St., San Francisco 94123. Tel: 415-992-1010; Fax: 415-922-7203

St. Edward the Confessor Church For sacramental records please contact St. Dominic, 2390 Bush St., San Francisco, 94115. Tel: 415-567-7854; Fax: 415-567-1608

St. Francis of Assisi Church For sacramental records please contact SS. Peter and Paul, 666 Filbert St., San Francisco, 94133. Tel: 415-421-0809; Fax: 415-421-0217

Holy Cross Korean Church For sacramental records please contact Chancery Office, One Peter Yorke Way, San Francisco, 94109. Tel: 415-614-5500; Fax: 415-614-5555

Immaculate Conception Church For sacramental records please contact St. Anthony of Padua, 3215 Cesar Chavez St., San Francisco, 94110. Tel: 415-647-2704; Fax: 415-647-7282

St. Joseph Church For sacramental records please contact St. Patrick, 756 Mission St., San Francisco, 94103. Tel: 415-421-0547; 512-9730 For sacramental records please contact St. Patrick, 756 Mission St., San Francisco, 94103. Tel: 415-421-0547; 512-9730

Our Lady of Guadalupe Church For sacramental records please contact SS. Peter and Paul, 666 Filbert St., San Francisco, 94133. Tel: 415-421-0809; Fax: 415-421-0217

SAN RAFAEL. *Blessed Sacrament Church* For sacramental records please contact St. Isabella, One Trinity Way, San Rafael, 94901. Tel: 415-479-1560; Fax: 415-479-8303

St. Sylvester Church For sacramental records please contact St. Raphael, 1104 Fifth Ave., San Rafael, 94901. Tel: 415-453-2314; Fax: 415-453-5402

WOODSIDE. *St. Marcella Mission* For sacramental records please contact St. Denis, 2250 Avy Ave., Menlo Park, 94025. Tel: 650-854-5976; Fax: 650-854-3754

RELIGIOUS INSTITUTES OF MEN REPRESENTED IN THE ARCHDIOCESE

For further details refer to the corresponding bracketed number in the Religious Institutes of Men or Women section.

[]—*Apostolic Life Community of Priests* Moshe, Tanzania
[0140]—*The Augustinians*—O.S.A
[0200]—*Benedictine Monks* (Hungary)—O.S.B.
[0330]—*Brothers of the Christian Schools* (Prov. of San Francisco)—F.S.C.
[0470]—*The Capuchin Franciscans* (Irish Prov.)—O.F.M.Cap.
[0310]—*Congregation of Christian Brothers*—C.F.C.
[0480]—*Conventual Franciscans*—O.F.M.Conv
[0520]—*Franciscan Friars* (Santa Barbara Prov.)—O.F.M.
[0650]—*Holy Ghost Fathers*—C.S.Sp.
[0690]—*Jesuit Fathers and Brothers* (California Prov.)—S.J.
[0780]—*Marist Fathers* (American Prov.)—S.M.
[0800]—*Maryknoll*—M.M.
[]—*Order of Carmelites*—O.Carm.
[0430]—*Order of Preachers (Dominicans)* (Western Prov.)—O.P.
[0897]—*Paris Foreign Mission Society*—M.E.P.
[1030]—*Paulist Fathers*—C.S.P.
[]—*Pilgrim Brothers*—P.B.S.F.
[1190]—*Salesian Don Bosco*—S.D.B.
[1260]—*Society of Christ* (Chicago Prov.)—S.Ch.
[0760]—*Society of Mary (Marianists)* (Prov. of the Pacific)—S.M.
[1200]—*Society of the Divine Savior*—S.D.S.
[1290]—*Society of the Priests of Saint Sulpice* (American Prov.)—S.S.
[]—*Verbum Dei Missionary Fraternity*—V.D.M.F.

RELIGIOUS INSTITUTES OF WOMEN REPRESENTED IN THE ARCHDIOCESE

[]—*Apostolic Society, Society of the Divine Will*—D.D.W.
[]—*Congregation of Divine Providence*—C.D.P.
[]—*Congregation of the Holy Family of the Holy Family of Kerala, India*
[3242]—*Congregation of the Sisters of Nazareth*—C.S.N.
[1920]—*Congregation of the Sisters of the Holy Cross* (Notre Dame, IN)—C.S.C.
[1940]—*Congregation of the Sisters of the Holy Faith*—C.H.F.
[1710]—*Congregation of the Third Order of St. Francis of Mary Immaculate, Joliet, IL*—O.S.F.
[0730]—*Daughters of Charity of Canossa*—F.D.C.C.
[0760]—*Daughters of Charity of St. Vincent de Paul* (Prov. of the West)—D.C.
[0880]—*Daughters of Mary and Joseph*—D.M.J
[0850]—*Daughters of Mary Help of Christians*—F.M.A.
[0420]—*Discalced Carmelite Nuns*—O.C.D.
[]—*Domincan Sisters of the Philippines*
[1050]—*Dominican Contemplative Nuns*—O.P.
[1070-03]—*Dominican Sisters*—O.P.
[1070-13]—*Dominican Sisters*—O.P.
[1070-19]—*Dominican Sisters of Houston*—O.S.F.
[1070-04]—*Dominican Sisters of San Rafael*—O.P.
[]—*Franciscan Missionaries of Mary*—F.M.M.
[]—*Franciscan Missionaries, Our Lady of Peace*—M.F.P.
[]—*Las Hermanas Misioneras*—M.S.C.Gpe.
[2340]—*Little Sisters of the Poor*—L.S.P.
[2390]—*Lovers of the Holy Cross Sisters*—L.H.C.
[2420]—*Marist Missionary Sisters, Society of Mary*—S.M.S.M.
[2470]—*Maryknoll Sisters of St. Dominc*—M.M.
[2720]—*Mission Helpers of the Sacred Heart*—M.H.S.H.
[2710]—*Missionary Sisters of Charity*—M.C.
[]—*Missionary Sisters of the Sacred Side*—M.C.S.
[3190]—*Nuns of the Perpetual Adoration of the Blessed Sacrament*—A.P.
[]—*Oblates Sisters of Jesus the Priest*—O.S.J.
[]—*Order of Preachers (Dominican Nuns)*—O.P.
[0950]—*Pious Society Daughters of St. Paul*—F.S.P.
[]—*Religious of the Sacred Heart of Jesus*—R.S.C.J.
[3465]—*Religious of the Sacred Heart of Mary*—R.S.H.M.
[]—*Religious of the Virgin Mary*—R.V.M.
[0440]—*Sisters of Charity of Cincinnati, Ohio*—S.C.
[0430]—*Sisters of Charity of the Blessed Virgin Mary*—B.V.M.
[2575]—*Sisters of Mercy of the Americas* (Burlingame, CA)—R.S.M.
[2580]—*Sisters of Mercy of the United States of America*—R.S.M.
[3000]—*Sisters of Notre Dame de Namur* (Prov. of CA)—S.N.D.deN.
[3360]—*Sisters of Providence of Saint Mary-of-the-Woods, Indiana*—S.P.
[4080]—*Sisters of Social Service of Los Angeles, Inc.*—S.S.S.
[]—*Sisters of St. Dominic of Mission San Jose*—O.P.
[1570]—*Sisters of St. Francis of Holy Family*—O.S.F.
[1630]—*Sisters of St. Francis of Penance and Christian Charity*—O.S.F.
[]—*Sisters of St. Joseph* Nazareth, MI
[3840]—*Sisters of St. Joseph of Carondelet* (Los Angeles Prov.)—C.S.J.
[3930-03]—*Sisters of St. Joseph of Orange*—C.S.J.O.
[3890]—*Sisters of St. Joseph of Peace*—C.S.J.P.
[1830]—*The Sisters of the Good Shepherd*—R.G.S.
[1960]—*Sisters of the Holy Family* (San Francisco, CA)—S.H.F.
[1990]—*Sisters of the Holy Names of Jesus and Mary* (Provs. of CA; Oregon; Washington)—S.N.J.M.
[2130]—*Sisters of the Immaculate Conception* (Prov. of Madrid)—R.C.M.
[3260]—*Sisters of the Precious Blood (Dayton, Ohio)*—C.PP.S.
[3320]—*Sisters of the Presentation of the B.V.M.*—P.B.V.M.
[1720]—*Sisters of the Third Order Regular of St. Francis of the Congregation of Our Lady of Lourdes*—O.S.F.

[1890]—*Society of Helpers*—H.H.S.
[3330]—*Union Sisters of the Presentation of the Blessed Virgin Mary*—P.B.V.M.
[4110]—*Ursuline Nuns (Roman Union)*—O.S.U.
[]—*Ursuline Sisters of the Immaculate Conception* (Louisville, KY)—O.S.U.
[]—*Verbum Dei Missionary Fraternity*

ARCHDIOCESAN CEMETERIES AND MAUSOLEUMS

SAN FRANCISCO. *Holy Cross Cemetery and Mausoleum*, P.O. Box 1577, Colma, 94014. Tel: 650-756-2060; Fax: 650-994-8147. Email: suemhcc@aol.com.

MENLO PARK. *Holy Cross*, P.O. Box 1577, Colma, 94014. Tel: 650-756-2060; Fax: 650-994-8147. Email: suemhcc@aol.com.

SAN RAFAEL. *Mount Olivet*, P.O. Box 4368, 94903. Email: suemhcc@aol.com.

NECROLOGY

† Kennedy, Rev. Msgr. Thomas I., Novato, CA Our Lady of Loretto.—Died Feb. 5, 2003
† Chang, Simeon, (Retired)—Died Nov. 1, 2002
† Pyne, Donald E., (Retired)—Died July 17, 2003
† Zoph, John L., (Retired)—Died Dec. 6, 2002

Diocese of San Jose in California

(Dioecesis Sancti Josephi in California)

Most Reverend

PATRICK J. McGRATH, D.D., J.C.D.

Bishop of San Jose; ordained June 7, 1970; appointed Auxiliary Bishop of San Francisco and Titular Bishop of Allegheny December 6, 1988; Episcopal ordination January 25, 1989; appointed Coadjutor Bishop of San Jose June 29, 1998; succeeded to See November 27, 1999

Most Reverend

PIERRE DUMAINE, D.D., PH.D.

Bishop Emeritus of San Jose; ordained June 15, 1957; appointed Auxiliary Bishop of San Francisco and Titular Bishop of Sarda April 28, 1978; Episcopal ordination June 29, 1978; appointed Bishop of San Jose January 27, 1981; installed as Bishop of San Jose March 18, 1981; retired November 27, 1999 *Office: Diocese of San Jose*, 900 Lafayette St., Ste. 301, Santa Clara, CA 95050-4966.

ESTABLISHED JANUARY 27, 1981.

Square Miles 1,300.

The Diocese of San Jose comprises the County of Santa Clara in the State of California.

Patrons of the Diocese of San Jose: St. Joseph, Husband of Mary, March 19; St. Clare of Assisi, August 11.

Legal Title: The Roman Catholic Bishop of San Jose, a Corporation Sole.

For legal titles of parishes and diocesan institutions, consult the Chancery Office.

Diocese of San Jose: 900 Lafayette St., Ste. 301, Santa Clara, CA 95050-4966. Tel: 408-983-0100; Fax: 408-983-0295.

Web: www.dsj.org

Email: chancellor@dsj.org

STATISTICAL OVERVIEW

Personnel	
Bishop	1
Retired Bishops	1
Priests: Diocesan Active in Diocese	79
Priests: Diocesan Active Outside Diocese	4
Priests: Retired, Sick or Absent	48
Number of Diocesan Priests	131
Religious Priests in Diocese	194
Total Priests in Diocese	325
Extern Priests in Diocese	11
Ordinations:	
Diocesan Priests	3
Transitional Deacons	3
Permanent Deacons in Diocese	7
Total Brothers	60
Total Sisters	375
Parishes	
Parishes	48
With Resident Pastor:	
Resident Diocesan Priests	39
Resident Religious Priests	8
Without Resident Pastor:	
Administered by Priests	1
Missions	3
Pastoral Centers	1
Professional Ministry Personnel:	
Brothers	5
Sisters	36
Lay Ministers	107
Welfare	
Catholic Hospitals	2
Total Assisted	173,736
Health Care Centers	1
Homes for the Aged	1
Day Care Centers	1
Total Assisted	150
Special Centers for Social Services	1
Total Assisted	50,000
Educational	
Diocesan Students in Other Seminaries	27
Total Seminarians	27
Colleges and Universities	1
Total Students	8,047
High Schools, Diocesan and Parish	2
Total Students	1,961
High Schools, Private	4
Total Students	4,294
Elementary Schools, Diocesan and Parish	29
Total Students	9,862
Elementary Schools, Private	1
Total Students	54
Catechesis/Religious Education:	
High School Students	2,388
Elementary Students	14,856
Total Students under Catholic Instruction	41,489
Teachers in the Diocese:	
Priests	1
Sisters	27
Lay Teachers	516
Vital Statistics	
Receptions into the Church:	
Infant Baptism Totals	8,674
Adult Baptism Totals	551
Received into Full Communion	383
First Communions	5,793
Confirmations	2,733
Marriages:	
Catholic	1,144
Interfaith	274
Total Marriages	1,418
Deaths	1,661
Total Catholic Population	630,000
Total Population	1,825,000

Former Bishop—Most Rev. PIERRE DUMAINE, D.D., Ph.D. (Retired), ord. June 15, 1957; appt. Auxiliary Bishop of San Francisco and Titular Bishop of Sarda, April 28, 1978; Episcopal ordination June 29, 1978;; appt. Bishop of San Jose January 27, 1981; installed as Bishop of San Jose March 18, 1981; retired November 27, 1999.

Diocese of San Jose—900 Lafayette St., Ste. 301, Santa Clara, 95050-4966. Tel: 408-983-0100; Fax: 408-983-0295. Web: www.dsj.org.

Vicar General and Moderator of the Curia—Rev. FRANCIS V. CILIA, V.G. Tel: 408-983-0154; Fax: 408-983-0242.

Chancellor—LINDA BEARIE. Tel: 408-983-0160.

Vicar for Clergy—Rev. WILFREDO S. MANRIQUE, J.C.D. Tel: 408-983-0253.

Judicial Vicar—Rev. HIEN MINH NGUYEN, J.C.D. Tel: 408-983-0215.

Delegate to Religious—Sr. MARIE GERTRUDE ROLDAN, C.S.J., J.C.L. Tel: 408-983-0216.

Episcopal Director for Pastoral Ministry—TERRIE IACINO. Tel: 408-983-0122.

Director, Office of Stewardship & Development—MARIE BERNARD. Tel: 408-983-0245.

Director, Office of Parish & Planning—Sr. PATRICIA MITCHELL, S.F.C.C.

Bishop's Executive Committee—Most Rev. PATRICK J. MCGRATH, D.D., J.C.D.; Revs. WILFREDO MANRIQUE, Episcopal Vicar for Clergy; FRANCIS V. CILIA, V.G., Vicar General & Moderator of the Curia; Sr. PATRICIA MITCHELL, S.F.C.C., Dir., Office of Parish & Planning; MARIE BERNARD, Dir. Stewardship & Devel.; MARIAN STUCKEY, Supt., Educ.; TERRIE IACINO, Episcopal Dir., Pastoral Ministry; LINDA BEARIE, Chancellor; DIANE PELOSI SAIGN, CEO, Catholic Charities; ROBERTA WARD, Dir. Media Rels.; Mr. RICK WESNER, Interim Dir. Cemeteries; ROBERT SERVENTI, CFO.

College of Consultors—Rev. Msgr. MICHAEL J. MITCHELL (Retired); Rev. FRANCIS V. CILIA, V.G.; Rev. Msgr. J. PATRICK BROWNE; Revs. V. WARWICK JAMES; EUGENE P. O'DONNELL; LAWRENCE HENDEL; Rev. Msgr. ALEXANDER C. LARKIN.

Council of Priests—Most Rev. PATRICK J. MCGRATH, D.D., J.C.D.; Rev. Msgr. ALEXANDER C. LARKIN, Chm.; Revs. FRANCIS V. CILIA, V.G.; MARK CATALANA; GARY THOMAS; WILFREDO S. MANRIQUE, J.C.D.; LOI HUYNH; JON PEDIGO; EUGENE P. O'DONNELL; FRANCISCO RIOS, I.V.E.

Council of Religious—Sr. MARIE GERTRUDE ROLDAN, C.S.J., J.C.L., Liaison; Revs. PETER FILICE, S.J., Chm.; RAYMOND ALLENDER, S.J.; CHRISTOPHER LA ROCCA, O.C.D.; FRANCISCO RIOS, I.V.E.; Sisters DORIS CAVANAUGH, P.B.V.M.; AILEEN DONOHUE, S.N.D.deN.; ROSINA CONROTTO, P.B.V.M.; MARY PETER MCCUSKER, R.S.M.; ETHEL DIGNAN, B.V.M.; INGRID HONORE-LALLANDE, C.S.J.; Bro. THOMAS FREY, C.S.C.

Deans—Revs. ANTHONY J. MANCUSO, Northern Deanery; JUSTIN ZAWADSKI, Northwestern Deanery; V. WARWICK JAMES, Northeastern Deanery; EUGENE P. O'DONNELL, Southwestern Deanery; Rev. Msgr. J. PATRICK BROWNE, Central Deanery; Rev. KEVIN P. JOYCE, Southeastern Deanery.

Ecumenical and Interreligious Affairs—Rev. JOSE ANTONIO RUBIO, Dir. & Delegate to Eastern Rite Churches.

Chinese Catholic Community—Rev. MATTHEW KOO, Chap.; KATHERINE NIE, Sec., 900 Lafayette St., Ste. 301, Santa Clara, 95050. Tel: 408-983-0211; Fax: 408-983-0212.

Catholic Charities— Catholic Charities of Santa Clara County DIANE PELOSI SAIGN, CEO, 2625 Zanker Rd., Ste. 200, San Jose, 95134. Tel: 408-468-0100;

Fax: 408-944-0275.

Catholic Telemedia Network—Ron Loiacano, Gen. Mgr., 324 Middlefield Rd., Menlo Park, 94025. Tel: 650-326-7850; Fax: 650-326-4605.

Propagation of the Faith-Holy Childhood Association-Catholic Relief Service—Linda Batton, Dir. Tel: 408-983-0158.

Roman Catholic Welfare Corporation—Most Rev. Patrick J. McGrath, D.D., J.C.D., Pres.; Linda Bearie, Sec.; Robert Serventi, Treas.; Rev. Msgr. Joseph Milani; Priscilla Murphy; Marian Stuckey; Rev. Msgr. Terrence J. Sullivan.

"The Valley Catholic" (Diocesan Newspaper)—Roberta Ward, Editor; Michael Hawkins, Business Mgr., Diocese of San Jose, 900 Lafayette St., Ste. 301, Santa Clara, 95050-4966. Tel: 408-983-0260.

Diocesan Tribunal—Diocese of San Jose, 900 Lafayette St., Ste. 301, Santa Clara, 95050-4966. Tel: 408-983-0219.

Judicial Vicar—Rev. Hien Minh Nguyen, J.C.D.

Judges—Revs. Wilfredo Manrique; Andres "Andy" Ligot, J.C.D.; Abel Lopez, J.C.L.; Hien Minh Nguyen, J.C.D.; Sr. Marie Gertrude Roldan, C.S.J., J.C.L.

Defenders of the Bond—Revs. Francis V. Cilia, V.G.; Robert Hayes, J.C.L.

Case Instructors—Sisters Sofia Berrones, M.C.D.P. Tel: 408-983-0221; Michele Mangan, O.S.F. Tel: 408-983-0224.

Promoter of Justice—Rev. Andres "Andy" Ligot, J.C.D.

Administrative Assistant—Mrs. Belva M. DiCarolis. Tel: 408-983-0219.

Finance Office—Robert Serventi, CFO; Vacant, Controller & Assoc. Dir.

Finance Council—Most Rev. Patrick J. McGrath, D.D., J.C.D.; George A. Dies, Chm.; Robert McAdams; Michael Blach; William Del Biaggio; Michael Hope; Eugene Toomey; Donald Waite; Diane S. Giannini.

Building Committee—Rev. Msgr. Michael J. Mitchell, Chm. (Retired); Revs. Francis V. Cilia, V.G.; Mark Catalana; Daniel Derry; Hao Dinh; Stephen E. Perata; Enrico Hernandez; Mr. Robert Serventi; Mr. Charles F. Buckley, Consultant.

Stewardship & Development Office—Marie Bernard, Dir. Tel: 408-983-0245.

Department of Cemeteries—Rick Wesner, Interim Dir. Tel: 650-428-3730.

Office of the Vicar for Clergy—Rev. Wilfredo S. Manrique, J.C.D., Episcopal Vicar for Clergy. Tel: 408-983-0253.

Diocesan Clergy Personnel Board—Most Rev. Patrick J. McGrath, D.D., J.C.D., Ex Officio; Revs. Wilfredo S. Manrique, J.C.D., Ex Officio & Chm.; Mark Catalana; Robert Moran; Justin Zawadski; Enrico Hernandez; Rev. Msgr. Joseph Milani; Linda Bearie; Dorothy Carlson.

Ongoing Formation of Clergy Committee—Revs. Nathan Mamo, Chm.; Cuong Paul Phan; Michael Hendrickson; Rev. Msgr. John Sandersfeld; Revs. Joseph Thannickal, S.D.B.; David Mercer; Rick Rodoni; Robert Hayes, J.C.L.; Enrico Hernandez; Anthony Mancuso.

Priests' Retirement Board—Rev. Msgr. Terrence J. Sullivan, Chm.; Robert Serventi, Ex Officio; Revs. Francis V. Cilia, V.G., Ex Officio; Wilfredo S. Manrique, J.C.D., Ex Officio; Rev. Msgr. James Walsh; Revs. Stephen Perata; Thomas Ahern; Brian Blach; Robert Kiefer; Ronald Pelzel.

Vocation Office—Rev. Mark Catalana, Dir. Tel: 408-983-0255.

Deacon Formation—Rev. Joseph Benedict, Dir. Tel: 408-983-0256.

Department of the Chancellor—Linda Bearie, Chancellor. Tel: 408-983-0160.

Diocesan Archives and Records Management—Bayne Bentley, 396 Martin Ave., Santa Clara, 95050. Tel: 408-970-9417.

Personnel Office—Linda Bearie, Dir.; Ms. Patricia Weis, Assoc. for Personnel. Tel: 408-983-0149.

Education Department—Marian Stuckey, Supt. of Schools; Priscilla Murphy, Asst. Supt. of Schools; Charlene Lemann, Curriculum Consultant; Sr. Claude Power, P.B.V.M., Consultant to the Dept. of Educ., Diocese of San Jose, 900 Lafayette St., Ste. 301, Santa Clara, 95050-4966. Tel: 408-983-0185.

Office of Pastoral Ministry—

Episcopal Director of Pastoral Ministry—Terrie Iacino. Tel: 408-983-0122.

Associate for Catechetics—Jeannine Leichner. Tel: 408-983-0138.

Associate for Hispanic Catechetics—Lupita Vital. Tel: 408-983-0133.

Associate for Hispanic Youth and Young Adults—Antonio Ojeda. Tel: 408-983-0134.

Associate for Youth and Young Adults—Sandy Scott. Tel: 408-983-0135.

Missions Office—Linda Batton, Dir. Tel: 408-983-0158.

Associate for Liturgy—Diana Macalintal. Tel: 408-983-0136.

Associate for Evangelization for Justice and Peace—Linda Batton. Tel: 408-983-0158.

Detention Ministry—Marilu Eder, Dir. Tel: 408-983-0180.

Human Concerns Commission—Linda Batton, Liaison. Tel: 408-983-0158.

Liturgical Commission—Diana Macalintal, Liaison. Tel: 408-983-0136.

Pastoral Care Advisory Committee—Terrie Iacino, Liaison. Tel: 408-983-0122.

Pastoral Resource Committee for Ministry to Gay and Lesbian Catholics—Terrie Iacino, Liaison. Tel: 408-983-0122.

Respect Life Program—Linda Batton, Liaison. Tel: 408-983-0158.

Office of Women—Terrie Iacino, Dir. Tel: 408-983-0122.

Office for Evangelization—Linda Batton, Dir. Tel: 408-983-0158.

Institute for Leadership in Ministry—Anne Grycz, Dir. Tel: 408-983-0111; Sandra Torres, Asst. Dir. Tel: 408-983-0112.

Office for Parish & Planning—Sr. Patricia Mitchell, S.F.C.C., Dir. Tel: 408-983-0143.

Victim Assistance Coordinator—Bernard Nojadera. Tel: 408-983-0113. Email: nojadera@dsj.org.

CLERGY, PARISHES, MISSIONS AND PAROCHIAL SCHOOLS

CITY OF SAN JOSE

1—Cathedral Basilica of St. Joseph (1849), (Hispanic—Latino), Rev. Msgr. J. Patrick Browne; Revs. Walter Suarez, I.V.E.; Ritche Bueza.
Res. and Church: 80 S. Market St., San Jose, 95113. Tel: 408-283-8100; Fax: 408-283-8110.
Catechesis/Religious Program—Susan Olsen, D.R.E. Students 203.

2—St. Anthony (1982), Rev. George Mancha.
Mailing Address: 20101 McKean Rd., San Jose, 95120. Tel: 408-997-4800. In Res., Rev. Antonio Medina.
Catechesis/Religious Program—Tel: 408-997-4808; Fax: 408-997-4801. Joann Maier, D.R.E. Students 188.

3—St. Brother Albert Chmielowski Polish Catholic Pastoral Mission (1986), (Polish), Rev. Jan Karpowicz, S.Chr. (Poland).
Res.: 10250 Clayton Rd., San Jose, 95127-4336. Tel: 408-251-8490; Fax: 408-251-8960.
Catechesis/Religious Program—Students 61.

4—Christ the King (1997), Rev. Robert Brocato.
Res.: 5284 Monterey Rd., San Jose, 95111. Tel: 408-362-9958; Fax: 408-362-9695.
Catechesis/Religious Program—Students 275.

5—St. Christopher (1951), Rev. Msgr. James Walsh; Revs. Gregory McGivern (Ireland); William Pegnam (Ireland).
Office—2278 Booksin Ave., San Jose, 95125. Tel: 408-269-2226; Fax: 408-269-2784.
School—Tel: 408-723-7223; Fax: 408-978-5458. Catherine Parent, Prin. Sisters of the Presentation 2; Lay Teachers 36; Students 620.
Catechesis/Religious Program—Tel: 408-264-8764; Fax: 408-978-5458. Sr. Felicia Gross, O.S.F., D.R.E. Students 411.

6—Church of the Transfiguration (1965), Rev. Walter M. McMahon.
Mailing Address: 4325 Jarvis Ave., San Jose, 95118. Tel: 408-264-3600; Fax: 408-266-2745.
Catechesis/Religious Program—Tel: 408-266-2743. Paula Ramos, D.R.E. Students 152.

7—Five Wounds Portuguese National Church (1914), (Portuguese), Rev. Jose Antonio Rubio. In Res., Revs. Francisco Xavier Bettencourt (Portugal); Anthony Chacko (Brazil).
Res.: 1375 E. Santa Clara St., San Jose, 95116. Tel: 408-292-2123; Fax: 408-292-0201.
School—1390 Five Wounds Ln., San Jose, 95116. Tel: 408-293-0425; Fax: 408-971-7607. Sandra Jewett-Silva, Prin. Lay Teachers 11; Students 280.
Catechesis/Religious Program—Tel: 408-293-3938; Fax: 408-293-0431. Joanne Dobrzynski, D.R.E. Students 220.

8—St. Frances Cabrini (1955), Revs. Robert Kiefer; Dominic Joseph (India). In Res., Rev. Don D. Flickinger (FRS).
Res.: 15333 Woodard Rd., San Jose, 95124. Tel: 408-879-1120; Fax: 408-377-3587.
School—15325 Woodard Rd., San Jose, 95124. Tel: 408-377-6545; Fax: 408-377-8491. Yvonne Gomez, Prin. Sisters 1; Lay Teachers 29; Students 632.
Catechesis/Religious Program—Tel: 408-377-2111. Students 157.

9—St. Francis of Assisi (1997), Rev. Msgr. John Sandersfeld; Revs. Arthur Yabes, S.V.D.; Joseph Benedict.
Res.: 5111 San Felipe Rd., San Jose, 95135. Tel: 408-223-1562; Fax: 408-223-1759.
Catechesis/Religious Program—Ginny Hinkle, D.R.E. Students 252.

10—Holy Cross (1911), (Italian), Revs. Antonio DeAngelis, C.S.; Fernando Cuevas, C.S.
Res.: 580 E. Jackson St., San Jose, 95112. Tel: 408-294-2440; Fax: 408-294-8609.
Catechesis/Religious Program—Tel: 408-294-1310; Fax: 408-294-8609. Bro. Charles Muscat, C.S., D.R.E. Students 500.

11—Holy Family (1905), Revs. Matthew D. Stanley; Hao Dinh.
Res.: 4848 Pearl Ave., San Jose, 95136. Tel: 408-265-4040; Fax: 408-978-9979.
School—4850 Pearl Ave., San Jose. Tel: 408-978-0290; Fax: 408-978-0290. Gail Harrell, Prin. Lay Teachers 23; Students 536.
Catechesis/Religious Program—Tel: 408-265-6201. Virginia Silvers, D.R.E. Students 259.

12—Holy Spirit (1963), Rev. Brendan McGuire.
Res.: 1200 Redmond Ave., San Jose, 95120. Tel: 408-997-5101; Fax: 408-997-5102.
School—1198 Redmond Ave., San Jose, 95120. Tel: 408-268-0794; Fax: 408-268-5281. Eileen Beck, Prin. Lay Teachers 24; Students 340.
Catechesis/Religious Program—Tel: 408-997-5115. Joy Hill, D.R.E. Students 306.

13—St. John Vianney (1952), Revs. Lawrence Hendel; Paul Mensah (Ghana); Andres "Andy" Ligot, J.C.D.; Deacon Joseph Alvarez. In Res., Rev. James E. Graham (NTN).
Church: 4600 Hyland Ave., San Jose, 95127. Tel: 408-258-7832 (Office); Fax: 408-258-6152 (Office).
School—4601 Hyland Ave., San Jose, 95127. Tel: 408-258-7677; Fax: 408-258-5997. Sr. Michele Anne Murphy, P.B.V.M., Prin. Sisters of the Presentation B.V.M. 2; Lay Teachers 28; Students 621.
Catechesis/Religious Program—Julie Moody, D.R.E. Students 354.

14—St. Julie Billiart (1974), Revs. Jon Pedigo; Saju Joseph (India).
Res.: 366 St. Julie Dr., San Jose, 95119. Tel: 408-629-3030; Fax: 408-629-3343.
Catechesis/Religious Program—Tel: 408-226-3595. Sheila Baldi, D.R.E. Students 378.

15—St. Leo the Great (1923), Revs. Pablo Bonello, I.V.E. (Argentina); Juan Esteban Furlan (Argentina). In Res., Rev. Matthew Koo.
Res.: 88 Race St., San Jose, 95126. Tel: 408-293-3503; Fax: 408-293-3516.
School—Tel: 408-293-4846. Phyllis Taurosa, Prin. Lay Teachers 12; Students 270.
Catechesis/Religious Program—Tel: 408-293-1662. Gayle Morrissette, D.R.E. Students 280.

16—St. Maria Goretti (1961), Rev. Msgr. Dominic Dinh Do; Revs. Kevin Joyce; Francisco Rios, I.V.E. (Argentina); Joseph Pacquing (Philippines).
Res.: 2980 Senter Rd., San Jose, 95111. Tel: 408-363-2300; Fax: 408-363-2305.
Catechesis/Religious Program—Tel: 408-363-2300, Ext. 23. Jeanne Gaffney, D.R.E. Students 1,250.

17—St. Martin of Tours (1914), Revs. Jack Bonsor; Raymond G. Kenny.
Res.: 200 O'Connor Dr., San Jose, 95128. Tel: 408-294-8953; Fax: 408-294-2624.
School—300 O'Connor Dr., San Jose, 95128. Tel: 408-287-3630; Fax: 408-287-4313. Karen DeMonner, Prin. Lay Teachers 17; Students 351.
Catechesis/Religious Program—Tel: 408-289-9608. Paula Liu-Smith, D.C.M., D.R.E. Students 137.

18—St. Mary of the Assumption (1975), (Croatian),, (Croatian Mission) Revs. Dujo Boban, O.F.M.; Ante Juric, O.F.M.
Res.: 901 Lincoln Ave., San Jose, 95126. Tel: 408-279-0279; Fax: 408-292-5868.
Catechesis/Religious Program—Students 47.
Croatian Franciscan Fathers Corporation—Tel: 408-279-0279; Fax: 408-292-5868.
Franciscan Fathers—Tel: 408-276-0279; Fax: 408-292-5868.

19—Most Holy Trinity (1961), Revs. Eduardo Samaniego, S.J.; Kevin Ballard, S.J.; Gilbert Sunghera, S.J.; Duc Vu, S.J.
Res.: 2040 Nassau Dr., San Jose, 95122. Tel: 408-729-0101; Fax: 408-258-4131.
School—Tel: 408-729-3431; Fax: 408-729-3432. Susan Barry, O.S.U., Prin. Sisters 2; Lay Teachers 8; Students 300.
Catechesis/Religious Program—Clara R. Morales, D.R.E. Students 270.

20—Our Lady of Guadalupe (1962), (Hispanic), Revs. Rene Juarez, O.F.M.; Javier Alvarez, O.F.M. (LA); Deacon Eloy Chavez. In Res., Rev. Miguel Obregon, O.F.M.

Office—2020 E. San Antonio St., San Jose, 95116. Tel: 408-258-7057; Fax: 408-258-8249.
Catechesis/Religious Program—Tel: 408-258-0544. Connie Torres, D.R.E. Students 618.

21—ST. PATRICK (1871), (Vietnamese), Revs. Peter Luc The Phan; Leonard Traverso, Parochial Vicar; Jose Antonio Medina, M.G. (Mexico), Parochial Vicar; Cuong Paul Phan, Parochial Vicar; Anthony Tuong Nguyen, Parochial Vicar.
Res.: 389 E. Santa Clara St., San Jose, 95113. Tel: 408-294-8120; Fax: 408-291-6277.
Vietnamese Ministry—Tel: 408-291-6280; Fax: 408-291-6289.
School—51 N. 9th St., San Jose, 95112. Tel: 408-283-5858; Fax: 408-283-5852. Sr. Rosemarie Carroll, C.S.J., Prin. Lay Teachers 11; Students 256.
Catechesis/Religious Program—Tel: 408-291-6279 (English/Spanish); 408-283-4978 (Vietnamese); Fax: 408-291-6277 (Eng./Sp.); 408-291-6289 (Viet.). Bro. Fortunat Tran Trong An Phong, F.S.C., D.R.E. (Vietnamese); Sr. Rita Claire Dorner, O.P., D.R.E. (English & Spanish). Students 1,889.

22—QUEEN OF APOSTLES (1960), Rev. James J. Mifsud, S.M.; Bro. T. William Bolts, S.M.
Res.: 4911 Moorpark Ave., San Jose, 95129. Tel: 408-253-7560; Fax: 408-253-9530.
School—Tel: 408-252-3659; Fax: 408-873-2645. Marianna Willis, Prin. Sisters 1; Lay Teachers 14; Students 301.
Catechesis/Religious Program—Tel: 408-225-9950. Patricia Sarria, D.R.E. Students 413.

23—SACRED HEART OF JESUS (1920), Revs. Jeronimo Gutierrez; Luis Vargas.
Res.: 325 Willow St., San Jose, 95110. Tel: 408-292-0146; Fax: 408-292-0172.
Catechesis/Religious Program—Tel: 408-292-0146, Ext. 202; Fax: 408-292-0172. Students 175.

24—SANTA TERESA (1967), Rev. Christoper Bennett.
Res.: 794 Calero Ave., San Jose, 95123. Tel: 408-629-7777; Fax: 408-629-5260.
Catechesis/Religious Program—Tel: 408-227-5915; Fax: 408-629-5260. Students 112.

25—ST. THOMAS OF CANTERBURY (1967), Rev. Gregory C. Kimm; Yvonne Chow, Pastoral Assoc.
Res.: 1522 McCoy Ave., San Jose, 95130. Tel: 408-378-1595; Fax: 408-378-1215.
Catechesis/Religious Program—Students 109.

26—ST. VICTOR (1961), Revs. Stephen F. Perata; Robert R. Taheny, S.J.; Candido O. Lim, S.J.
Res.: 3108 Sierra Rd., San Jose, 95132. Tel: 408-251-7055; Fax: 408-251-5528.
School—Tel: 408-251-1740; Fax: 408-251-1492. Sr. Sharon Breden, C.S.J., Prin. Sisters of St. Joseph of Carondelet 1; Lay Teachers 15; Students 314.
Catechesis/Religious Program—Tel: 408-251-0154; Fax: 408-251-5528. Angela Giampaoli, D.R.E. Students 420.

OUTSIDE THE CITY OF SAN JOSE

ALVISO, SANTA CLARA CO., OUR LADY, STAR OF THE SEA (1984), Rev. Steven P. Brown.
Mailing Address: P.O. Box 426, 95002-0426.
Res.: 1385 Michigan Ave., 95002. Tel: 408-263-2121; Fax: 408-263-1182.
Catechesis/Religious Program—Tel: 408-262-7539. Sr. Josefina Montalvo, R.S.C.J. Students 217.

CAMPBELL, SANTA CLARA CO., ST. LUCY (1947), Rev. Msgr. Terrence J. Sullivan; Rev. Michael Carson. In Res., Revs. Robert Passalacqua; Felix Ethapemi (Nigeria).
Res.: 2350 Winchester Blvd., 95008. Tel: 408-378-2464; Fax: 408-378-5548.
School—76 Kennedy Ave., 95008. Tel: 408-871-8023; Fax: 408-378-4945. Sr. Jolene Schmitz, C.H.S., Prin. Sisters 1; Lay Teachers 19; Students 319.
Catechesis/Religious Program—Tel: 408-379-5900; Fax: 408-378-5548. Sr. Fidelma Heeran, R.S.M., D.R.E. Students 296.

CUPERTINO, SANTA CLARA CO., ST. JOSEPH OF CUPERTINO (1913), Revs. Robert Hayes; Nathan Mamo; Jack Greer. In Res., Rev. Msgr. Joseph J. Milani, Pastor Emeritus (Retired).
Res.: 10110 N. DeAnza Blvd., 95014. Tel: 408-252-7653; Fax: 408-252-5263.
School—10120 N. DeAnza Blvd., 95014. Tel: 408-252-6441. Mary Lyons, Prin. Lay Teachers 25; Students 306.
Catechesis/Religious Program—Tel: 408-253-0660. Donna Brock, D.R.E. Students 315.

GILROY, SANTA CLARA CO., ST. MARY (1865), [CEM] Revs. Daniel Derry; Peter Seimas; Francisco Miramontes (Mexico). In Res., Rev. Msgr. John Coleman.
Res.: 11 First St., 95020. Tel: 408-847-5151; Fax: 408-847-4851.
School—7900 Church St., 95020-4499. Tel: 408-842-2827; Fax: 408-847-7679. Christa Hanson, Prin. Sisters 1; Lay Teachers 12; Students 314.
Catechesis/Religious Program—7950 Church St., 95020. Tel: 408-847-2652; Fax: 408-847-4851. Barbara Zarka, D.R.E.; Hilda Porcella, D.R.E. Students 1,455.

LOS ALTOS, SANTA CLARA CO.

1—ST. NICHOLAS (1947), Revs. Gary R. Thomas; Lawrence Percell.
Res.: 473 Lincoln Ave., 94022. Tel: 650-948-2158; Fax: 408-948-2056.
School—12816 S. El Monte Ave., Los Altos Hills, 94022. Tel: 650-941-4056. Matt Komar, Prin. Lay Teachers 19; Students 270.
Catechesis/Religious Program—Tel: 650-941-7672; Fax: 650-917-9872. Jan Cicoletti, D.R.E. Students 332.
Station—Bridgepoint at Los Altos Senior Living, Formerly Seven Oaks Residential Park for the Aged 1174 Los Altos Ave., 94022. Tel: 650-948-7337; Fax: 650-948-7779.

2—ST. SIMON (1955), Revs. Anthony J. Mancuso; Alexander Affonso; Joseph Thannickal, S.D.B. (India). In Res., Rev. Maurice Shortall, C.S.Sp. (Ireland).
Res.: 1860 Grant Rd., 94024. Tel: 650-967-8311; Fax: 650-967-8876.
School—1840 Grant Rd., 94024. Tel: 650-968-9952; Fax: 650-988-9308. Mrs. Mary Johnson, Prin. Lay Teachers 24; Students 607.
Catechesis/Religious Program—Tel: 650-968-9552, Ext. 38. Danielle Sigrist, D.R.E. Students 200.

3—ST. WILLIAM (1959), Rev. Paul Weisbeck. In Res., Rev. Robert McKay (South Africa).
Res.: 611 S. El Monte Ave., 94022-4058. Tel: 650-559-2080; Fax: 650-968-8508.
Catechesis/Religious Program—Tel: 650-941-7672. Jan Cicoletti, D.R.E. Students 105.

LOS GATOS, SANTA CLARA CO., ST. MARY OF THE IMMACULATE CONCEPTION (1912), Revs. Justin Zawadzki; Christopher Bransfield.
Res.: 219 Bean Ave., 95030. Tel: 408-354-3726; Fax: 408-354-9302.
School—30 Lyndon Ave., 95030. Tel: 408-354-3944; Fax: 408-395-9151. Sr. Nicki Thomas, S.N.J.M., Prin. Sisters of the Holy Names of Jesus and Mary 3; Lay Teachers 20; Students 311.
Catechesis/Religious Program—Tel: 408-354-4061; Fax: 408-354-9302. Terri Trotter, D.R.E. Students 520.

MILPITAS, SANTA CLARA CO.

1—ST. ELIZABETH (1968), Revs. Edward Samy; Lieu Vu. In Res., Rev. John Halloran.
Res.: 750 Sequoia Dr., 95035. Tel: 408-262-8100; Fax: 408-946-8703.
Catechesis/Religious Program—Tel: 408-263-1995. Jeff Fernandez, D.R.E. Students 200.

2—ST. JOHN THE BAPTIST (1877), Revs. Norman Segovia; Peter Loi Huynh. In Res., Rev. Wilfredo S. Manrique, J.C.D.
Res.: 279 S. Main St., 95035. Tel: 408-262-2546; Fax: 408-263-2564.
School—360 S. Abel St., 95035. Tel: 408-262-8110; Fax: 408-262-0814. Judy Perkowski, Prin. Augustinian Recollect Sisters 2; Lay Teachers 9; Students 300.
Catechesis/Religious Program—Tel: 408-262-3955; Fax: 408-262-7726. Cory Mollat, D.R.E. Students 100.

MORGAN HILL, SANTA CLARA CO., ST. CATHERINE OF ALEXANDRIA (1909), Revs. Eugene P. O'Donnell; Oscar Morales (Mexico); Truyen Nguyen.
Res.: 17400 Peak Ave., 95037. Tel: 408-779-3959; Fax: 408-779-0289.
School—Tel: 408-779-9950; Fax: 408-779-9928. Suzanne Rich, Prin.; Judy Cory, Vice Prin. Lay Teachers 13; Students 296.
Catechesis/Religious Program—Tel: 408-779-0542. Mrs. Wendy Scherbart, D.R.E. Students 754.

MOUNTAIN VIEW, SANTA CLARA CO.

1—ST. ATHANASIUS (1959), Revs. Diarmuid Casey, C.S.Sp. (Ireland); John Fitzpatrick, C.S.Sp. (Ireland).
Res.: 160 N. Rengstorff Ave., 94043. Tel: 650-961-8600; Fax: 650-968-5633.
Catechesis/Religious Program—Tel: 650-967-7900; Fax: 650-968-5633. Margery Ryan, D.R.E. Students 248.

2—ST. JOSEPH (1901), Revs. Oscar D. Tabujara; Robert B. Moran.
Res.: 582 Hope St., 94041. Tel: 650-967-3831; Fax: 650-691-1522.
School—1120 Miramonte Ave., 94040. Tel: 650-967-1839; Fax: 650-691-1530. Stephanie Mirenda-Knight, Prin. Lay Teachers 16; Students 263.
Catechesis/Religious Program—Tel: 650-691-1525. Sr. Elizabeth Daly, O.P., D.R.E. Students 108.

PALO ALTO, SANTA CLARA CO.

1—ST. ALBERT THE GREAT (1961), Merged, with St. Thomas Aquinas Parish.

2—OUR LADY OF THE ROSARY (1959), Merged, with St. Thomas Aquinas Parish.

3—ST. THOMAS AQUINAS (1901), Revs. George Aranha; Eduardo Obero; Deacon Carl Bunje. In Res., Rev. John Hester; Rev. Msgr. William Lenane; Revs. James Woolever; Charles Macedo.
Office—3290 Middlefield Rd., 94306. Tel: 650-494-2496; Fax: 650-494-3780.
School—St. Elizabeth Seton Catholic Community School, 1095 Channing Ave., 94306. Tel: 650-326-9004; Fax: 650-326-2949. Sr. Theresa Marie McDermott, Prin. Priests 1; Sisters 7; Lay Teachers 11; Students 265.
Catechesis/Religious Program—Tel: 650-494-3097; Fax: 650-494-3780. Students 295.

SANTA CLARA, SANTA CLARA CO.

1—CHINESE CATHOLIC COMMUNITY (1983), (Chinese), Rev. Matthew Koo.
Res.: 900 Layfayette St., Ste. 301, 95050-4966. Tel: 408-983-0211; Fax: 408-983-0212.
Catechesis/Religious Program—Students 153.

2—ST. CLARE (1777), Revs. Rick G. Rodoni; Daniel Urcia.
Mailing Address: 725 Washington St., 95050-4935. Tel: 408-248-7786; Fax: 408-248-8150. In Res., Rev. Richard Fry.
Church: 941 Lexington St., 95050.
School—Tel: 408-246-6797; Fax: 408-246-6726. Kathy Almazol, Prin. Sisters 1; Lay Teachers 14; Students 310.
Catechesis/Religious Program—Tel: 408-248-7786; Fax: 408-248-8150. Mrs. Diane Madruga, D.R.E. Lay Teachers 25; Aides 8; Students 200.

3—ST. JUSTIN (1951), Revs. Jose Galang; Michael O'Connor; Joseph Prendergast.
Res.: 2655 Homestead Rd., 95051. Tel: 408-296-1193; Fax: 408-244-9437.
School—Tel: 408-248-1094. Jeannie Mahan Visger, Prin. Lay Teachers 17; Students 306.
Catechesis/Religious Program—Tel: 408-983-0361. Dorothy Carlson, D.R.E. Students 321.

4—ST. LAWRENCE THE MARTYR (1959), Rev. V. Warwick James (South Africa). In Res., Rev. Victor L. Wilkiemeyer, Pastor Emeritus (Retired).
Res.: 1971 St. Lawrence Dr., 95051. Tel: 408-296-3000; Fax: 408-296-3100.
School—(Grades PreK-5), 1977 St. Lawrence Dr., 95051. Tel: 408-296-2260; Fax: 408-296-1068. Lay Teachers 7; Students 183.
School—(Grades 6-8) Tel: 408-296-2260. Sr. Kathleen Hanley, R.S.M., Prin. Sisters 1; Lay Teachers 7; Students 134.
School—(Grades 9-12), 2000 Lawrence Ct., 95051. Tel: 408-296-3013; Fax: 408-296-3794. Christie Filios, Prin. Sisters 1; Lay Teachers 28; Students 338.
Catechesis/Religious Program—Tel: 408-296-0208; Fax: 408-296-3100. Sr. Kathleen Hanley, R.S.M., D.R.E. Students 95.

5—OUR LADY OF PEACE (1961), Revs. Walter Mallo, I.V.E. (Argentina); Rolando Santoianni, I.V.E. (Argentina); Paul Coleman, I.V.E.
Res.: 2800 Mission College Blvd., 95054. Tel: 408-988-4585; Fax: 408-988-0679.
School—Tel: 408-988-4160. Sisters 1; Students 35.
Catechesis/Religious Program—Tel: 408-988-7543; Fax: 408-980-9436. Students 609.

SARATOGA, SANTA CLARA CO.

1—CHURCH OF THE ASCENSION (1964), Revs. Paul Duong; Charles Dougherty. In Res., Rev. Raymund Field, C.S.V.
Res.: 12033 Miller Ave., 95070. Tel: 408-725-3939.
Catechesis/Religious Program—Tel: 408-725-3930; Fax: 408-725-3932. Ann Liebmann, D.R.E. Students 166.

2—SACRED HEART (1951), Rev. Msgr. Alexander C. Larkin; Rev. Rolando T. Benas.
Res.: 13724 Saratoga Ave., 95070. Tel: 408-867-3634; Fax: 408-867-5339.
School—13718 Saratoga Ave., 95070. Tel: 408-867-9241; Fax: 408-867-9242. Jane Daigle, Prin. Lay Teachers 15; Students 303.
School—Pre-School Lay Teachers 5; Students 48.
Catechesis/Religious Program—Tel: 408-867-1530. Maureen Wright, D.R.E. Students 377.

STANFORD, SANTA CLARA CO., CATHOLIC COMMUNITY AT STANFORD (1977), Revs. Patrick LaBelle, O.P.; Carl Schlichte, O.P.
Mailing Address: P.O. Box 20301, 94309. Tel: 650-725-0080; Fax: 650-723-6797.
Catechesis/Religious Program—Tel: 650-857-9023; Fax: 650-857-9067. Students 21.

SUNNYVALE, SANTA CLARA CO.

1—STS. ANDREW AND PAUL KOREAN CATHOLIC MISSION OF SAN JOSE (1981), (Korean), Rev. Paul Hyeong-Kwon Yang.
Res.: 531 E. Weddell Dr., 94089-2162. Tel: 408-734-9721; Fax: 408-734-9723.
Catechesis/Religious Program—John Choi, D.R.E. Students 346.

2—CHURCH OF THE RESURRECTION (1963), Revs. G. Robert Leger; Joseph N. Vanthu, Parochial Vicar.
Res.: 725 Cascade Dr., 94087. Tel: 408-245-5554; Fax: 408-245-5589.
Church: 1399 Hollenbeck Ave., 94087.
School—1395 Hollenbeck Ave., 94087. Tel: 408-245-4571; Fax: 408-733-7301. Sr. Georgianna Coonis, S.N.D., Prin. Lay Teachers 14; Students 275.

Catechesis/Religious Program—Tel: 908-746-0172. Students 168.

3—ST. CYPRIAN (1961), Rev. Timothy Kidney.
Res.: 1133 W. Washington, 94086. Tel: 408-739-8506; Fax: 408-739-2815.
School—195 Leota Ave., 94086. Tel: 408-738-3444; Fax: 408-733-3730. Kay Ingalls, Prin. Lay Teachers 9; Students 237.
Catechesis/Religious Program—Tel: 408-739-1669. Loretta Martinez Fennell, D.R.E. Students 81.

4—ST. MARTIN (1916), Revs. Benito O. Manding; Luat Hoang.
Res.: 590 Central Ave., 94086. Tel: 408-736-3725; Fax: 408-736-4968.
School—597 Central Ave., 94086. Tel: 408-736-5534. Eugenie Florczyk, Prin. Lay Teachers 14; Students 243.
Catechesis/Religious Program—Tel: 408-736-3725. Judy Kelch, D.R.E. Students 410.

Chaplains of Public Institutions

SAN JOSE. *Archbishop Mitty High School*. Rev. Enrico Hernandez.
Catholic Scouting. Rev. Paul A. Soukup, S.J. Tel: 408-554-4124.
Columbia Regional Hospital. Rev. Arturo Mateo, M.S.C. Tel: 408-259-5000.
Detention Ministry for Juveniles. Rev. Anthony Chacko (Brazil). Tel: 408-280-7744.
St. Francis High School. Rev. Eric Freed.
Notra Dame Club of San Jose/Silicon Valley. Rev. Brendan McGuire.
O'Connor Hospital. Revs. Basil Royston, Robert McKay (South Africa), Capetown, South Africa.
Presentation High School. Rev. George Aranha.
San Jose State University Catholic Campus. Rev. Joseph Kamugisha (Tanzania).
Santa Clara County Jail. Rev. Miguel Obregon, O.F.M.
Santa Clara County Sherriffs Dept.. Rev. Paul Weisbeck.
Santa Clara County Women's Facility. Ms. Marilu Eder.
Santa Clara Valley Medical Center. Revs. Eugene Corbett, S.J., Leo Prengaman, S.J.
Villa Siena. Rev. Salvatore M. DiNardo, O.P.

LOS GATOS. *Presentation Center*. Rev. Kevin Joyce. Tel: 408-354-2346.

MILPITAS. *Stanford Medical Center*. Rev. John Hester. Tel: 650-723-4000.

Special Assignment:
Rev. Msgr.—
Mitchell, Michael J., Vicar Gen. (Retired)
Revs.—
Catalana, Mark, Dir. Vocations
Cilia, Francis V., V.G., Vicar Gen.
Manrique, Wilfredo, Vicar for Clergy
Menchaca, Luis Gerardo, Vicar Hispanic Min.
Nguyen, Hien Minh, J.C.D., Judicial Vicar, Vicar for Vietnamese Ministry
Rubio, Jose Antonio, Dir. Ecumenical & Interreligious Affairs & Delegate Eastern Rite Churches
Segovia, Norman, Vicar for Filipino Ministry

On Duty Outside the Diocese:
Revs.—
Menchaca, Gerardo, M.Div., Menlo Park, CA
Rich, Joseph, Newport Beach, CA
Saso, Michael, Carmel, CA

Military Chaplains:
Revs.—
Hendel, Lawrence. Tel: 408-252-7653 Army National Guard
Hendrickson, Michael D., U.S. Navy

On Leave of Absence:
Revs.—
Arnone, A.
Browne, Dennis
Delgado, Joseph
Gray, Robert
Hilliard, Richard
Keulman, Kenneth P.
Lagututta, Nunzio J.
Marx, Robert
Nabbefeld, Grant
Pereira, Anthony
Smith, Brian
Sullivan, Mervyn

On Sabbatical:
Revs.—
Dinh, Hao
Galang, Jose

Absent on Sick Leave:
Rev.—
Neary, Mark

Retired:
Rev. Msgrs.—
Andre, Ludwig
Boyle, Eugene
Coleman, John
Lenane, William
Milani, Joseph J.
Mitchell, Michael J.
Suarez, Jose V. (Philippines)
Sweeny, John J.
Revs.—
Ahern, Thomas
Balthazar, Ayala
Burns, Michael J.
Davis, Terrence
Field, Raymund, C.S.V.
Freyne, Bernard
Fry, Richard C.
Harrison, Arthur
Hlebs, Milan
Kilcoyne, Patrick
Largente, Laurent
Leininger, William
Lopez, Abel
Macedo, Charles
Maher, Raymond
McCrillis, Philip
Noia, Leonel
O'Connor, William
Passalacqua, Robert
Re, Angelo
Shea, Thomas
Tinh, Joseph Nguyen
Wilkiemeyer, Victor L.

Permanent Deacons:
Alvarez, Jose, St. John Vianney
Alvarez, Salvador, St. Francis of Assisi
Bunje, Carl, St. Thomas Aquinas
Chavez, Eloy, Our Lady of Guadalupe
Combellick, Thomas, Holy Spirit
Huynh, Joseph N., St. Patrick
Perez, Vicente, Most Holy Trinity

INSTITUTIONS LOCATED IN THE DIOCESE

[A] SHRINES

SANTA CLARA. *Shrine of Our Lady of Peace* 2800 Mission College Blvd., 95054. Tel: 408-988-4585; Fax: 408-988-0679. Rev. Walter Mallo, I.V.E. (Argentina), Dir.; Mary Jean Kula, Staff.
Our Lady of Peace Gift Shop Tel: 408-980-9825; Fax: 408-988-2488.

[B] COLLEGES AND UNIVERSITIES

SANTA CLARA. *Santa Clara University*, 500 El Camino Real, 95053-0001. Tel: 408-554-4000; Fax: 408-554-2700. Email: username@scu.edu. Web: www.scu.edu. Society of Jesus, Mission Santa Clara. Founded in 1777. University established in 1851 and chartered by the State in 1855. Priest Teachers 30; Brothers 2; Sisters 2; Lay Teachers 390; Students 8,060.
Administrators: Revs. Paul L. Locatelli, S.J., Pres.; Mario J. Prietto, S.J., Dir. Campus Ministry; Dr. Denise Carmody, Provost; Dr. Daniel A.. Pitt, Dean School of Engineering; Dr. Donald J. Polden, Dean School of Law; Dr. Barry Posner, Dean Leavey School of Business Admin.; Mr. James M. Purcell, Vice Pres. Univ. Rels.; Mr. Robert Warren, Vice Pres. Finance Admin.; Dr. W. Atom Yee, Acting Dean College of Arts & Sciences.
Jesuit Community, 500 El Camino Real, 95053-1600. Tel: 408-554-4124; Fax: 408-554-4795. Revs. Dennis R. Parnell, S.J., Rector; Peter F. Filice, S.J., Min. & Contact; Luis F. Calero, S.J.; Matthew E. Carnes, S.J.; Paul G. Crowley, S.J.; William F. Donnelly, S.J.; James W. Felt, S.J.; Paul J. Fitzgerald, S.J.; Paul J. Goda, S.J.; Carl H. Hayn, S.J.; Arthur F. Liebscher, S.J.; Paul L. Locatelli, S.J.; Michael C. McCarthy, S.J.; Gerald L. McKevitt, S.J.; Gerdenio M. Manuel, S.J.; Norman F. Martin, S.J.; Alfred E. Naucke, S.J.; Charles T. Phipps, S.J.; Mario J. Prietto, S.J.; Mark A. Ravizza, S.J.; James W. Reites, S.J.; Theodore J. Rynes, S.J.; Joseph C. Sands, S.J.; Thomas J.E. Schwarz, S.J.; Francis R. Smith, S.J.; Dennis C. Smolarski, S.J.; Paul A. Soukup, S.J.; Robert L. St. Clair, S.J.; Gerald P. Sullivan, S.J.; Salvatore A. Tassone, S.J.; Frederick P. Tollini, S.J.; Edward V. Warren, S.J.; Tennant C. Wright, S.J.; Michael A. Zampelli, S.J.; Bros. Thomas C. Bracco, S.J.; James C. Siwicki, S.J.; Russell A. Powell, S.J., Scholastic.
Legal Title: *Jesuit Community at Santa Clara University, Inc.* Priests 34; Brothers 2; Scholastics 1.

[C] HIGH SCHOOLS, DIOCESAN

SAN JOSE. *Archbishop Mitty High School* (Coed) , 5000 Mitty Ave., 95129. Tel: 408-252-6610; Fax: 408-252-6967. Email: brosnan@mitty.com. Web: www.mitty.com. Mr. Timothy Brosnan, Prin.; Rev. Enrico Hernandez, Campus Chap. Priests 1; Sisters 1; Lay Teachers 96; Students 1,624; Total Staff 145.

SANTA CLARA. *Saint Lawrence Academy*, 2000 Lawrence Ct., 95051. Tel: 408-296-3013; Fax: 408-296-3794. Email: cfilios@saintlawrence.org. Web: www.saintlawrence.org. Christie Filios, Prin.; Anne Eubanks, Asst. Prin. College Prep Coed. Sisters 1; Lay Teachers 25; Students 337; Total Staff 38.

[D] HIGH SCHOOLS, PRIVATE

SAN JOSE. *Bellarmine College Preparatory*, 850 Elm St., 95126-1899. Tel: 408-294-9224; Fax: 408-294-1894. Web: www.bcp.org. Society of Jesus Priests 14; Lay Teachers 100; Students 1,483.
Non-Resident Students: Revs. Raymond P. Allender, S.J., Supr. & Contact; Mario L. Capitolo, S.J.; Ronald M. Clemo, S.J.; Richard E. Cobb, S.J.; Eugene J. Corbett, S.J.; Carlo A. Farina, S.J.; John L. Flynn, S.J.; Edwin B. Harris, S.J.; Gerald J. Lentz, S.J.; Robert B. Mathewson, S.J.; Leo P. Prengaman, S.J.; Robert J. Shinney, S.J.; Gerald T. Wade, S.J., Interim Pres./Chancellor; Carlton E. Whitten, S.J. (S.J.); Bro. Charles E. Jackson, S.J.; Mark Pierroti, Prin.
Notre Dame High School, 596 S. Second St., 95112. Tel: 408-294-1113; Fax: 408-293-9779. Web: www.ndsj.org. Sisters of Notre Dame de Namur Lay Teachers 39; Total Staff 61; Students 590.
Non-Resident Students: Mary Lou Schoone, Prin.
Presentation High School, 2281 Plummer Ave., 95125. Tel: 408-264-1664; Fax: 408-266-3028. Web: www.Pres-Net.com. Mary Miller, Prin.; Rev. George Aranha, Chap. Sisters of the Presentation Priests 1; Sisters 1; Lay Teachers 63; Students 740; Total Staff 73.

MOUNTAIN VIEW. *St. Francis High School*, 1885 Miramonte Ave., 94040. Tel: 650-968-1213; Fax: 650-968-3241. Email: kemakley@sfhs.com. Web: www.sfhs.com. Mr. Kevin Makley, Pres.; Mr. Simon Raines, Dir. Activities; Mrs. Patricia Tennant, Prin.; Angelo Aguiar, Exec. Dir. Devel.; Rev. Eric Freed, Chap. Brothers of Holy Cross Brothers 1; Sisters 1; Lay Teachers 85; Students 1,511; Total Staff 139.

[E] MIDDLE SCHOOLS, PRIVATE

SAN JOSE. *Sacred Heart Nativity School*, 310 Edwards, 95110. Tel: 408-993-1293; Fax: 408-993-0675. Email: shnativity@shnativity.org. Web: www.shnativity.org. Rev. Peter Pabst, S.J., Pres.; Kevin Eagleson, Prin. Students 54; Lay Teachers 7; Total Staff 15.

[F] THE CATHOLIC CHARITIES OF THE DIOCESE OF SAN JOSE

SAN JOSE. *Catholic Charities of Santa Clara County*, 2625 Zanker Rd., 95134. Tel: 408-468-0100; Fax: 408-944-0275. Web: www.ccsj.org. Diane Pelosi Saign, CEO; Michael Veuve, CFO; Victoria Contreras, Parish Liaison; Marilou Cristina, Div. Dir. Older Adult Svcs.; Jennifer Xuan, Grants & Database Mgr.; Ellen Dumesnil, Div. Dir. Economic Dev. Svcs.; Claudia Sandoval, Div. Dir. Youth Svcs.; Kitty Mason, Div. Dir., Behavioral Health Svcs.; Betsy Renner, Human Resources Mgr.; Magi Young, Chief Devel. Officer.
Immigration, Refugee & Employment Services:
Older Adult Services, 2625 Zanker Rd., Ste. 200, 95134-2107.
Foster Grandparent Program, 2625 Zanker Rd., Ste. 200. Tel: 408-325-5206 Foster Grandparent Program.
Long Term Care Ombudsman Program, 2625 Zanker Rd., Ste. 200, 95134-2107. Tel: 408-944-0567.
Grandparent Caregiver Resource Center (GCRC), 2625 Zanker Rd., Ste. 200, 95134. Tel: 408-325-5164.
Handicapables, 2625 Zanker Rd., 95134. Tel: 408-325-5123.
Daybreak I Respite and Caregiver Support Programs, 5111 San Felipe Rd., 95135. Tel: 408-270-4900; Fax: 408-238-7257.
Day Break II Asian Respite and Support Programs, John XXIII Multi-Service Ctr., 195 E. San Fernando St., 95112. Tel: 408-280-8665; Fax: 408-280-0126.

Senior Immigration Services

Eastside Neighborhood Center, 2150 Alum Rock Ave., 95112. Tel: 408-251-0215; Fax: 408-251-0218.
John XXIII Multi-Service Center, 195 E. San Fernando St., 95112. Tel: 408-282-8600; 408-282-8607; Fax: 408-280-1026.
Eastside Neighborhood Center, 2150 Alum Rock Ave., 95112. Tel: 408-937-3924.

Economic Development Services, 2625 Zanker Rd., Ste. 200, 95134-2107.
Immigration Legal Services Tel: 408-944-0691; Fax: 408-944-0347. Email: immigration@ccsj.org.

Employment and Financial Education Services

The Job Market Tel: 408-325-5150.
Vocational Training Courses Tel: 408-325-5173.
Asset Building/IDA Tel: 408-325-5107.
Refugee Services Tel: 408-325-3155. Refugee Resettlement, Parish Partnerships, Initial Employment

Housing Services

Shared Housing Program Tel: 408-325-5277. Case Management and Relocation
Behavioral Health Services, 2625 Zanker Rd., Ste. 200, 95134-2107.
Dual Diagnosis/Substance Abuse, 2625 Zanker Rd., Ste. 200, 95134-2107. Tel: 408-325-5180; Fax: 408-468-0147.
Family, Youth, and Children's Services, 2625 Zanker Rd., Ste. 200, 95134-2107. Tel: 408-944-0146; Fax: 408-468-0147.
Community Counseling & Educational Services, 2625 Zanker Rd., Ste. 200, 95134-2107. Tel: 408-944-0469; Fax: 408-468-0147.

Employment Services

Focus for Work Tel: 408-944-0591.
Supportive Housing Initiative Tel: 408-955-9170 Older Adult Srvs. (Oasis); 408-325-5230 CalWorks Health Alliance.

Youth Services

Youth Empowered for Success (YES), 645 Wool Creek Dr., Ste. A, 95112. Tel: 408-938-6731; Fax: 408-283-6152.
Washington United Youth Center (WUYC), 921 First St., 95110. Tel: 408-938-6731; Fax: 408-947-1107.
CORAL, 645 Wool Creek Dr., 95112. Tel: 408-283-6150; Fax: 408-283-6152.
Charities Housing Development Corporation, 465 S. First St., 95113. Tel: 408-282-1125. Chris Block, Exec. Dir.
Palo Alto/Los Altos Auxiliary, 26932 Beatrice Ln., Los Altos, 94022. Tel: 650-948-3425.

GILROY. *Gilroy Senior Nutrition Center*, 7371 Hanna St., 95020. Tel: 408-842-4200.

MORGAN HILL. *Morgan Hill Senior Nutrition Center*, 17666 Crest Ave., 95037. Tel: 408-776-1413.

[G] DAY CARE CENTERS

SAN JOSE. *St. Elizabeth's Day Home*, 950 St. Elizabeth Dr., 95126. Tel: 408-295-3456; Fax: 408-295-5917. Email: info@stelizabethdayhom.org. Web: www.stelizabethsdayhome.org. Robert Freiri, Dir. Lay Staff 35; Children 150.

[H] GENERAL HOSPITALS

SAN JOSE. *O'Connor Hospital*, 2105 Forest Ave., 95218. Tel: 408-947-2500; Fax: 408-995-0117. Web: www.oconnorhospital.org. Robert H. Curry, CEO; Revs. Robert McKay (South Africa), Capetown, South Africa; Basil Royston; Ms. Elsamma James, Chap.; Mr. Raymond Dougherty, Chap.
Legal Title: *O'Connor Hospital*, Sponsored by Daughters of Charity Health System Total Staff 1,372; Bed Capacity 358; Patients Assisted Annually 121,896.
O'Connor Foundation, 2105 Forest Ave., 95128. Tel: 408-947-2717; Fax: 408-947-2649. Tina Ahn, Exec. Dir.

GILROY. *St. Louise Regional Hospital*, Admin. Office, 9400 No Name Uno, 95020. Tel: 408-848-2000; Fax: 408-842-2155. Email: tedfox@dochs.org. Web: www.dochs.org. Sr. Paula Baker, P.B.V.M., Contact Person; Theodore P. Fox, Regl. Vice Pres. & CEO. Sponsored by Daughters of Charity Health System Sisters 3; Staff 445; Bed Capacity 93; Patients Assisted Annually 54,180.

[I] SPECIAL SANATORIUM AND HOSPITALS

SARATOGA. *Our Lady of Fatima Villa*, 20400 Saratoga-Los Gatos Rd., 95070. Tel: 408-741-2950; Fax: 408-741-4930. Email: ourlady@earthlink.com. Web: www.fatimavilla.org. Preston Wisner, Ph.D., Pres. & CEO; Sisters Susan Snyder, O.P., Prioress; Andrea Mendoza, S.N.D.deN., Pastoral Care; Gertrude Boracca, S.N.D.deN. Sponsored by Dominican Sisters of St. Catherine of Siena of Kenosha, Inc., Provides skilled nursing care for aged women and men and Special Alzheimer's Unit. Sisters 3; Residents 65; Total Staff 94.

[J] HOTEL, SENIOR CITIZENS RESIDENCE

SAN JOSE. *Giovanni Center, Inc.*, 85 S. Fifth St., 95112. Tel: 408-288-7436; Fax: 408-288-7264. Email: alaujdm@aol.com. Web: hometown.aol.com/alaujdm/myhomepage/business.html. Alvin Lau, Admin. A California nonprofit charitable, public-benefit, housing project for low-income elderly. Sponsored by the Roman Catholic Bishop of San Jose, a corporation sole. Lay Staff 3; Residents 33.
Jeanne d'Arc Manor, 85 S. Fifth St., 95112. Tel: 408-288-7421; Fax: 408-288-7264. Email: alaujdm@aol.com. Web: members.aol.com/_ht_a/alaujdm/myhomepage/business.html. Alvin Lau, Admin. Housing project for low-income elderly and handicapped. Sponsored by the Roman Catholic Bishop of San Jose, A Corporation Sole. Lay Staff 12; Residents 105; Units 87.

[K] HOMES FOR THE AGED

MOUNTAIN VIEW. *Villa Siena*, 1855 Miramonte Ave., 94040. Tel: 650-961-6484; Fax: 650-961-6254. Email: vsiena@pacbell.net. Mrs. Corine Bernard, Exec. Dir.; Sr. Christina Papavaro, D.C., Pres. & Bd. Chm.; Rev. Salvatore M. DiNardo, D.C., Chap. Daughters of Charity of St. Vincent de Paul., Residential Care and Skilled Nursing Facility. Professed Sisters 3; Residents 66; In Nursing Care 20; Nursing Staff 27; Total Staff 56.

[L] RETREATS

LOS ALTOS. *Jesuit Retreat House*, 300 Manresa Way, 94022. Tel: 650-948-4491; Fax: 650-948-0640. Email: retreat@elretiro.org. Web: www.elretiro.org. Revs. William J. Rewak, S.J., Supr. & Contact; Gerald P. McCourt, S.J.; Bernard J. Bush, S.J.; Robert J. Fabing, S.J.; Joseph J. Fice, S.J.; Dare J. Morgan, S.J.; James R. Hanley, S.J. Priests 7.

LOS GATOS. *Presentation Center*, 19480 Bear Creek Rd., 95033-9519. Tel: 408-354-2346; Fax: 408-354-5226. Web: www.prescenter.org. Sr. Patricia Marie Mulpeters, P.B.V.M., Exec. Dir. & Contact. Retreat and Conference Center Capacity 200; Staff 17; In Residence: Religious 6; Lay People 1.
Villa Holy Names, 82 Prospect Ave., 95032. Tel: 408-354-2312; Fax: 408-354-8305. Email: jmvillalg@yahoo.com. Sr. Dorothy Clare Klingler, S.N.J.M. Total Staff 1.

[M] MONASTERIES AND RESIDENCES OF PRIESTS AND BROTHERS

SAN JOSE. *Carmelite Monastery, Novitiate*, P.O. Box 3420, 95156-3420. Tel: 408-251-1361; Fax: 408-251-1854. Revs. Christopher La Rocca, O.C.D., Prior & Contact; Ailbe Doolan, O.C.D.; Patrick Sugrue, O.C.D.; Jan Lundberg, O.C.D.; Richard Mandoli, O.C.D.; Pascal Pierini, O.C.D.; Bros. Mark Silva, O.C.D.; Mark Kissner, O.C.D.; Juan Medina, O.C.D.; Mark Moran, O.C.D.
Marianist Community, 10381 Singleton Rd., 95111. Tel: 408-972-2716. Email: wmjoseph@subglobal.net. Bro. William Farrell, S.M., Contact. Brothers 1.

CUPERTINO. *Villa Saint Joseph*, 22840 Mercedes Rd., 95014-3920. Tel: 408-257-4427; Fax: 408-255-9006. Revs. Joseph Stefanelli, S.M.; James Imhoff, S.M. Marianist Retirement Home. Priests 2; Brothers 10; Total in Residence 12. In Res. Bros. Charles Boglitz, S.M.; Thomas Deasy, S.M.; Raymond Dotzler, S.M.; Charles Ehrenfeld, S.M.; Edward Fick, S.M.; Eugene Frank, S.M.; Stanley Murakami, S.M., Sub-Dir.; John Samaha, S.M.; Robert Wade, S.M.; Joseph Wasy, S.M.
Alcalde Residence, 22683 Alcalde Rd., 95014-3903. Tel: 408-253-6209. Rev. David Schuyler, S.M.; Bro. John Haster, S.M., Sub-Dir. Priests 1; Brothers 1; Total in Residence 2.
San Juan Residence, 22825 San Juan Rd., 95014. P.O. Box 1775, 95015-1775. Tel: 408-253-4841; Fax: 408-253-5280. Revs. John McEnhill, S.M.; John Reilly, S.M.; Bros. Joseph Nuuanu, S.M., Sub-Dir.; Paul Fennelly, S.M.; James Riley, S.M.; Vincent Wayer, S.M. Priests 2; Brothers 4; Total in Residence 6.

LOS ALTOS. *Maryknoll*, 23000 Cristo Rey Dr., 94024. Tel: 650-967-3822; Fax: 650-965-3473. Retirement House for Priests and Brothers. Priests 22; Brothers 6. In Res. Revs. Richard A. Bell, M.M.; John M. Breen, M.M.; James V. Buttino, M.M.; Bernard P. Byrne, M.M.; Clyde F. Davis, M.M.; Gilbert J. DeRitis, M.M.; Patrick J. Donovan, M.M.; Arthur J. Dwyer, M.M. (NY); Francis J. Garvey, M.M.; Donald J. Haren, M.M.; Daniel P. Jensen, M.M.; Walter W. Johnson; Joseph A. Klecha, M.M.; Joseph W. Kowalczyk, M.M.; Joseph J. O'Neill, M.M.; Francis Rebol, M.M.; Michael J. Ruck, M.M.; Philip F. Sheerin, M.M.; Richard P. Smith, M.M. (NY), Admin.; Norbert M. Verhagen, M.M.; John J. Vinsko, M.M.; James R. Whitmore, M.M.; Bros. Luke R. Baldwin, M.M.; John Brown, M.M.; Gordon M. Burns, M.M.; Duane S. Crockett, M.M.; Conrad Fleisch, M.M.; Thomas A. Hickey, Asst. Admin.

LOS GATOS. *California Province of the Society of Jesus, Jesuit Provincial Office*, P.O. Box 519, 95031. Tel: 408-884-1600; Fax: 408-884-1601. Email: calprovsj@aol.com. Web: www.calprov.org. Revs. Thomas H. Smolich, S.J., Regl. Prov.; Alfred E. Naucke, S.J., Exec. Asst. & Contact; Anthony E. Sholander, S.J.; Thomas H. Smolich, S.J.; Robert L. St. Clair, S.J.
Sacred Heart Jesuit Center, Box 128, 95031. Tel: 408-884-1700; Fax: 408-884-1701. Revs. John M. Martin, S.J., Supr. & Contact; Joseph G Azadian, S.J.; Bro. Joseph Avila; Revs. Philip C. Blake, S.J (PHX); Philip L. Bourret, S.J. (China); John L. Boyle, S.J.; Edward T. Burke, S.J.; J. Ripley Caldwell; Joseph P. Carroll, S.J.; William Carroll, S.J.; Albert Chan, S.J. (SFR); Paul D. Devot, S.J.; Charles W. Dullea, S.J.; James N. Chevedden, S.J.; Eugene J. Colosimo; Lenox C. Day, S.J.; Raymond A. Devlin, S.J.; Paul D. Devot, S.J.; Patrick D. Doherty, S.J.; Bros. Charles L. Connor, S.J.; Howard C. Ellis, S.J.; Revs. Thomas P. Finsterbach, S.J.; David Fitch, S.J.; Thomas W. Foster, S.J.; Francis A. Frugoli, S.J.; Francis J. Gallagher, S.J.; Reynold J. Gatto, S.J. (SAC); John C. Geary, S.J.; Daniel V. Germann, S.J.; Hugh Gray, S.J.; Bros. William C. Farrington, S.J.; Robert H. Griffin, S.J.; John F. Graham, S.J.; Revs. Leo J. Hombach, S.J. (LA); Jerold W. Lindner, S.J.; Edwin J. McDermott, S.J.; James E. Morse, S.J.; George J. Koch, S.J.; Terrence E. Koch, S.J.; Bro. Norbert J. Korte, S.J.; Revs. George E. Krivanek, S.J.; William F. Lester, S.J.; Robert L. Maloney, S.J.; Thomas Maloney, S.J.; William J. Maring, S.J.; Bro. Thomas A. Marshall, S.J.; Revs. Roger D. McAuliffe, S.J.; Robert McDevitt, S.J.; James R. Menard, S.J.; Everett J. Mibach, S.J.; Cornelius J. Monacell, S.J.; James Monaghan, S.J.; Stephen G. Olivo, S.J.; Bros. Daniel J. Peterson, S.J.; Charles J. Onorato, S.J.; Revs. John J. Perlite, S.J.; Gerald J. Phelan; Alfred G. Playoust, S.J.; Camille J. Pratt, S.J.; Bro. Theodore C. Rohrer, S.J.; Revs. Arthur F. Rutledge, S.J.; Ronald J. Sanfilippo, S.J.; Arthur J. Schenk, S.J.; Francis J. Silva, S.J.; Alden F. Stevenson, S.J.; Bros. Lawrence Thoo Fook, S.J.; William E. Sessing, S.J.; Leonard J. Sullivan, S.J.; Revs. Silvano P. Votto, S.J.; Francis X. Wang, S.J. (China); Ronald D. Wolf, S.J.; Gregg D. Wood, S.J (FBK); Eugene R. Zimmers, S.J.; Michael J. Zimmers, S.J.
Legal Title: *California Province of the Society of Jesus dba Sacred Heart Jesuit Center* Priests 70; Brothers 15.
Priests of the Province residing elsewhere: Revs. Thomas G. Allender, S.J., San Francisco; Ernesto Arbelaez, S.J. (COL); George K. Aziz, S.J.; Patrick T. Brannan, S.J.; Robert F. Curran, S.J.; Joseph D. Fessio, S.J.; Thomas G. Hand, S.J.; Candido O. Lim, S.J. (PHI); James P. McCauley, S.J., (Nevada); Charles C. Murphy, S.J.; Robert R. Taheny, S.J.; Bro. John Moniz, S.J., Dittmer, MO.

SARATOGA. *St. Patrick's Missionary Society* (St. Patrick Fathers) , 19536 Eric Dr., 95070. Tel: 408-253-3135; Fax: 408-253-5433. Email: spsca@spms.org. Web: www.stpatrickfathers.org. Revs. Michael Moore, S.P.S.; Steven Donohue, S.P.S., Supr. Priests 2.

[N] CONVENTS AND RESIDENCES FOR SISTERS

SAN JOSE. *Community of the Holy Spirit*, 1275 Naglee Ave., 95126. Tel: 408-275-1710. Sr. Jolene M. Schmitz, C.H.S., Contact.
Daughters of Charity of St. Vincent de Paul, O'Connor Sisters Home, 350 O'Connor Dr., 95128. Tel: 408-289-9215; Fax: 408-298-8779. Email: dococon@sbcglobal.net. Sr. Rachela Silvestri, D.C., Contact. Sisters 7.
Dominican Sisters, Congregation of the Sacred Heart, Houston, 1092 W. San Fernando St., 95126. Tel: 408-294-7151. Email: srclar@juno.com. Sr. Clarice Sparkman, O.P., Contact.
Eucharistic Missionaries of the Most Holy Trinity, 815 S. Daniel Way, 95128. Tel: 408-243-3157; Fax: 408-244-1178. Email: sjosemesst@aol.com. Sr. Maria Luisa Chapa, M.E.S.S.T., Supr. Sisters 5.
La Salle Sisters, 3867 Silver Creek Rd., 95121-1969. Tel: 408-238-9351; Fax: 408-258-4870. Email: lasankirk@aol.com. Web: saigon.com/-vietedu. Sr. Therese Claire Nguyen, Treas. Sisters 20.
Pious Disciples of the Divine Master, 2076 Lincoln Ave., 95125. Tel: 408-265-8105; Fax: 408-265-9051. Email: sddmsjca@aol.com. Web: www.pddm.us. Sr. Michelle Hernandez, P.D.D.M., Local Contact. Sisters 3.
Quinhon Missionary Sisters of the Holy Cross, 368 Neilson Ct., 95111. Tel: 408-362-9719. Sr. Josefa Ngoc Nguyen, L.H.C., Local Contact. Sisters 7.
Sinsinawa Dominican Congregation of the Most Holy Rosary, 6345 Whaley Dr., 95135. Tel: 408-270-5200. Email: rdorner@infionline.net. Sr. Rita Dorner, O.P., Local Contact. Sisters 5.
Sisters of Charity of Nazareth, 3208 Neal Ave., 95117. Tel: 408-244-4206. Email: rmmaguire@juno.com. Sr. Rose Mary Maguire, S.C.N., Contact. Sisters 2.
Sisters of St. Joseph of Carondelet, 3383 Whitman Way, 95132. Tel: 408-347-8407; Fax: 408-347-8407.

Email: fhansencsj@juno.com. Web: www.csjla.org/membersonly. Sisters Margaret Gregg, Contact Person (St. Louis); Francis Marie Hansen, Contact Person (Los Angeles). Sisters 9.

Sisters of the Holy Family, 1825 Via El Capitan, 95124. Tel: 408-445-1810; Fax: 408-445-1810. Sisters 6.

St. Elizabeth's Day Home Day Care Center Children 147.

Society of the Sacred Heart, 2520 Lagoon Way, 95132. Tel: 408-325-5211. Email: rstatt@rscj.org. Web: www.sofie.org/rscj/. Sr. Rosemary Statt, R.S.C.J., Contact. Sisters 3.

CUPERTINO. *Blessed Virgin Missionaries of Carmel (B.V.M.C.)*, 10130 N. Deanza Blvd., 95014. Tel: 408-257-1022. Sr. Adelpha Luminate, B.V.M.C., Supr. Sisters 3.

Intercommunity Convent, 10351 S. Blaney Ave., 95014-3122. Tel: 408-725-0898; Fax: 408-252-4848. Email: J96write@aol.com. Web: www.insytegraphology.com. Sisters 1.

LOS ALTOS HILLS. *Daughters of Charity of St. Vincent de Paul, Seton Provincialate*, 26000 Altamont Rd., 94022. Tel: 650-941-4490; Fax: 650-949-3874. Email: docpsec@aol.com. Web: www.daughtersofcharity.com. Sr. Margaret Keaveney, D.C., Prov.; Rev. Andrew E. Bellisario, C.M. (LA), Dir. Sisters 45; Total in Province 142; Total in Diocese 59.

Immaculate Heart Monastery of the Poor Clares, 28210 Natoma Rd., 94022. Tel: 650-948-2947. Sr. Maura Heinen, P.C.C., Abbess. Sisters 16.

LOS GATOS. *Sisters of the Holy Names of Jesus & Mary*, Provincial Administration, P.O. Box 907, 95031. Tel: 408-395-5150; Fax: 408-354-8305. Email: snjmcaasm@yahoo.com. Web: www.holynames.net. Sisters Margaret Spiller, S.N.J.M., Prov. Supr. & Contact; Sally Gunn, S.N.J.M., Northern Regl.; Barbara Boundreau, S.N.J.M., Southern Regl.; Mary Ondreyco, S.N.J.M., Leadership Team; Marguerite Kirk, S.N.J.M., Leadership Team. Other sisters reside in communities in Santa Clara, Los Gatos, San Jose, Cupertino, and Sunnyvale. Total in Province 231; Total in Diocese 85.

Convent of the Holy Names, P.O. Box 1906, 95031. Tel: 408-354-1730; Fax: 408-395-6447. Ms. Julie Harrigan, Admin.; Sr. Joan Doyle, S.N.J.M., Community Life Coord. Total in Convent 63.

MILPITAS. *Sisters of Mercy of Americas (Burlingame)*, 186 Beresford Ct. #F303, 95035. Tel: 408-946-5946. Email: mjvanbommel@att.net. Sr. Maria Juanita Van Bommel, R.S.M., Local Contact. Sisters 9.

REDWOOD CITY. *Sisters of St. Francis of Penance and of Christian Charity*, P.O. Box 685, 94064. Tel: 650-366-3968. Sr. Felicia Gross, O.S.F., Contact Person. Sisters 3.

SANTA CLARA. *Carmelite Monastery of the Infant Jesus, Discalced Carmelite Nuns*, 1000 Lincoln St., 95050. Tel: 408-296-8412; Fax: 408-248-4846. Email: santaclaracarmel@aol.com. Web: www.members.aol.com/santaclaracarmel. Sr. Roseanne Scofield, O.C.D., Prioress. Sisters 15.

Dominican Sisters of San Rafael Congregation of the Most Holy Name , 1156 Santa Clara St., #11, 95050. Tel: 408-554-6431. Sr. Francine McCarthy, O.P., Contact Person. Sisters 2.

Sisters of Charity of the Blessed Virgin Mary, 1220 Tasman Dr. #303, Sunnyvale, 94089. Tel: 408-744-9143. Sr. Bette Gambonini, B.V.M., Contact. Email: bgambonini@aol.com. Sisters 5.

[O] NEWMAN CENTERS

SAN JOSE. *The Newman Community/Catholic Campus Ministry* San Jose State University, 300 S. 10th St., 95112-3645. Tel: 408-938-1610; Fax: 408-938-1612. Email: sjsuccm@earthlink.net. Web: director@sjsuccm.org. *Catholic Campus Ministry/SJSU*, The Newman Community, 300 S. 10th St., 95112-3645. Sr. Marcia Krause, O.P., Dir.; Rev. Joseph Kamugisha (Tanzania), Chap.

[P] MISCELLANEOUS LISTINGS

SAN JOSE. *Caritas Housing Corporation*, 465 S. 1st St., 95113. Tel: 408-282-1125; Fax: 408-280-1311. Email: cblock@charitieshousing.org. Web: www.charitieshousing.org. Chris Block, Exec. Dir.

Charities Housing Development Corporation of Santa Clara County, 465 S. 1st St., 95113. Tel: 408-282-1125; Fax: 408-280-1311. Email: cblock@charitieshousing.org. Web: www.charitieshousing.org. Chris Block, Exec. Dir. Units 54; Total in Residence 92; Total Staff 2.

Hand of Help Christian Service Program, 300 S. 10th St., 95112-3645. Tel: 408-983-0166. Email: serve@theriver.com. Web: www.handofhelp.info. Bro. Fred Buerman, Exec. Dir.

Hope Charities Housing Corporation, 465 S. 1st St., 95113. Tel: 408-282-1125; Fax: 408-280-1311. Email: cblock@charitieshousing.org. Web: www.charitieshousing.org. Chris Block, Contact Person.

San Jose Cathedral Foundation (A nonprofit, charitable, public-benefit California corporation.) , 80 S. Market St., 95113. Tel: 408-283-8100, Ext. 2208; Fax: 408-280-0752. Email: ntranchina@stjosephcathedral.org. Web: www.stjosephcathedral.org. Mr. Theodore Biagini, Pres.

San Jose English Cursillo, P.O. Box 6648, 95150. Tel: 408-253-1880. Email: daverobert@abac.com. Web: www.sanjosecursillo.com. Mr. Dave Roberts, Lay Dir.

San Tomas Charities Housing Corporation, 465 S. 1st St., 95113. Tel: 408-282-1125; Fax 408-280-1311. Email: cblock@charitieshousing.org. Web: www.charitieshousing.org. Chris Block, Exec. Dir. Units 100 In Residence 300; Total Staff 3.

Sierra Vista I/Charities Housing Corporation, 465 S. 1st St., 95113. Tel: 408-282-1125; Fax: 408-280-1311. Email: cblock@charitieshousing.org. Web: www.charitieshousing.org. Chris Block, Contact Person.

Society of Christ for Polonia, 10250 Clayton Rd., 95127. Tel: 408-251-8490. Rev. Jan Karpowicz, S.Chr. (Poland), Contact Person; Sr. Elizabeth, Contact Person.

Stoney Pine Charities Housing Corporation, 465 S. 1st St., 95113. Tel: 408-282-1125; Fax: 408-280-1311. Email: cblock@charitieshousing.org. Web: www.charitieshousing.org. Chris Block, Contact Person.

Sunset Charities Housing Corporation, 465 S. 1st St., 95113. Tel: 408-282-1131; Fax: 408-280-1311. Email: cblock@charitieshousing.org. Web: www.charitieshousing.org. Mr. Chris Block, Dir.

Vietnamese Catholic Center, Our Lady Queen of Martyrs, Formerly Vietnamese Cultural Center2849 S. White Rd., 95148. Tel: 408-983-0215. Email: nguyen@dsj.org. Web: www.dsj.org. Rev. Hien Minh Nguyen, J.C.D., Vicar for Vietnamese Ministry.

Vietnamese Youth and Culture Association, La Salle Vietnam House, 1103 Maxey Ct., 95132. Tel: 408-926-4665; Fax: 408-254-3379. Email: lasanvnsj@aol.com. Web: www.lasan.org. Bro. Valery Nguyen Van An F.S.C., Dir. Brothers of the Christian Schools San Francisco Prov.)

St. Vincent de Paul Society, District Council of Santa Clara County, 749 Story Rd., 95122. Tel: 408-298 7290; Fax: 408-993-0885. Email: help@svdp.org. Web: www.svdp.org. Mr. Stephen J. Pehanich, Exec. Dir. Total Assisted 70,000; Total Staff 38.

CUPERTINO. *St. Joseph Cupertino Retirement Residence*, 10130 N. DeAnza Blvd., 95014. Tel: 408-257-1022; Fax: 408-257-3272. Rev. Msgr. Joseph J. Milani, Dir. (Retired).

GILROY. *St. Louise Regional Hospital Foundation*, 9400 No Name Uno, 95020. Tel: 408-848-2000. Email: jamesroosevelt@doch.org. Web: www.saintlouisehospital.org. Mr. James Roosevelt, Dir.

LOS ALTOS. *Daughters of Charity Health System*, 26000 Altamont Rd., 94022. Tel: 650-917-4500; Fax: 650-917-4534. Email: robertissai@dochs.org. Web: www.dochs.org. Mr. Robert Issai, EVP & CFO; Brian Connolly, Pres. & CEO.

Jesuit Institute for Family Life, 300 Manresa Way, 94022. Tel: 650-948-4854; Fax: 650-948-0640. Web: www.elretiro.org. Rev. Robert J. Fabing, S.J., Dir.

Voluntas Dei Institute, 615 Palm Ave., 94022. Tel: 650-917-4500; Fax: 650-941-6309. Web: www.voluntasdeiusa.org. Rev. George F. Hazler, Regl. Dir.

LOS GATOS. *California Jesuit Missions*, P.O. Box 68, 95031-0068. Tel: 408-884-1600; Fax: 408-884-1631. Rev. Theodore Gabrielli, Dir.

Jesuit Seminary Association, P.O. Box 68, 95031-0068. Tel: 408-884-1600; Fax: 408-884-1631. Mr. William F. Masterson, Dir.

MENLO PARK. *Roman Catholic Communications Corp.* The Catholic Telemedia Network. , 324 Middlefield Rd., 94025. Tel: 650-326-7850; Fax: 650-326-4605. Email: ron@ctnba.org. Web: www.ctnba.org. Most Revs. John S. Cummins, D.D. (SAC), Chm.; Patrick J. McGrath, Vice Chm.; Ronald J. Loiacono, Gen. Mgr.
Legal Title: *Roman Catholic Communications Corporation of the Bay Area.*

MOUNTAIN VIEW. *Day Worker Center at Calvary Church*, Formerly St. Joseph the Worker Center1880 California St., 94041. Tel: 650-938-1298; Fax: 650-938-1915. Email: sjwcmv@sbcglobal.net.
Additional Center:
747 Story Rd., San Jose, 95122. Tel: 408-993-0837; Fax: 408-993-0885.

Villa Siena Foundation, 1855 Miramonte Ave., 94040. Tel: 650-961-6484; Fax: 650-961-6254. Email: vsiena@pacbell.net. Corine Bernard, Exec. Dir.

SANTA CLARA. *Catholic Professional and Business Club of the San Jose Diocese*, 900 Lafayette St., Ste. 301, 95050. Tel: 408-371-2825; Fax: 408-371-5494. Rev. Jon Pedigo, Chap.; Philip Gregory, Pres.

Roman Catholic Seminary Corporation of San Jose, 900 Lafayette St., Ste. 301, 95050-4966. Tel: 408-983-0154; Fax: 408-983-0242. Email: cilia@dsj.org. Rev. Francis V. Cilia, V.G., Contact Person.

The Roman Catholic Welfare Corporation of San Jose, 900 Lafayette St., Ste. 301, 95050-4966. Tel: 408-983-0168; Fax: 408-983-0296. Email: serventi@dsj.org. Mr. Robert Serventi, Contact Person.

Serra International Region 11, District 31, 1892 Miramonte Ave., Mountain View, 94040. Tel: 650-961-8878; Fax: 650-961-8878. Robert Thompson, Dist. 31 Gov.

SARATOGA. *Our Lady of Fatima Villa Foundation*, 20400 Saratoga-Los Gatos Rd., 95070. Tel: 408-741-2968; Fax: 408-741-4930. Email: drakkar@earthlink.net. Web: www.fatimavilla.org. Preston Wisner, Contact Person.

RELIGIOUS INSTITUTES OF MEN REPRESENTED IN THE DIOCESE

For further details refer to the corresponding bracketed number in the Religious Institutes of Men or Women section.

[0330]—*Brothers of the Christian Schools*—F.S.C.
[0600]—*Brothers of the Congregation of the Holy Cross (Southwest Province)*—C.S.C.
[1320]—*Clerics of St. Viator*—C.S.V.
[0260]—*Discalced Carmelite Friars*—O.C.D.
[]—*Franciscan Friars* (Croatia)—O.F.M.
[]—*Guadalupe Missionaries* (Mexico)—M.G.
[0650]—*Holy Ghost Fathers*—C.S.Sp.
[]—*Institute of Incarnate Word* (Argentina)—I.V.E.
[0690]—*Jesuit Fathers and Brothers (Society of Jesus)* (California Prov.)—S.J.
[0760]—*Marianists (Society of Mary)*—S.M.
[0800]—*Maryknoll (Catholic Foreign Mission Society of America, Inc.)*—M.M.
[1210]—*Missionaries of St. Charles - Scalabrinians (Province of St. John Baptist)*—C.S.
[1110]—*Missionaries of the Sacred Heart*—M.S.C.
[0520]—*Order of Friars Minor (Province of St. Barbara)*—O.F.M.
[0430]—*Order of Preachers (Province of the Most Holy Name of Jesus-Western Dominican Province)*—O.P.
[1190]—*Salesians of Don Bosco*—S.D.B.
[1260]—*Society of Christ*—S.Ch.
[0420]—*Society of the Divine Word*—S.V.D.
[1290]—*Society of the Priests of St. Sulpice*—S.S.
[1170]—*St. Patrick's Missionary Society*—S.P.S.

RELIGIOUS INSTITUTES OF WOMEN REPRESENTED IN THE DIOCESE

[]—*Blessed Virgin Missionaries of Carmel*—B.V.M.C.
[]—*Caritas Sisters of Miyazaki*—C.S.M.
[2020]—*Community of the Holy Spirit*—C.H.S.
[]—*Congregation of the Augustinian Recollects*—A.R.
[1070-25]—*Congregation of the Dominican Sisters of Saint Catherine of Siena of Kenosha*—O.P.
[2100]—*Congregation of the Humility of Mary*—C.H.M.
[]—*Congregation of the Most Holy Name*
[1070-13]—*Congregation of the Most Holy Rosary (Dominican Sisters)*—O.P.
[1070-12]—*Congregation of the Queen of the Holy Rosary (Dominican Sisters)*—O.P.
[0760]—*Daughters of Charity of St. Vincent De Paul*—D.C.
[0420]—*Discalced Carmelite Nuns*—O.C.D.
[1070-19]—*Dominican Sisters of Houston, Texas (Congregation of the Sacred Heart)*—O.P.
[1070-30]—*Dominican Sisters of Oakford*—O.P.
[]—*Dominican Sisters of San Rafael*
[]—*Eucharistic Missionaries of the Most Holy Trinity* (Mexico)—M.E.S.S.T.
[]—*LaSallian Sisters* (Vietnam)—L.S.
[2470]—*Maryknoll Sisters of St. Dominic*—M.M.
[2490]—*Medical Mission Sisters*—M.M.S.
[]—*Missionary Sisters Oblates of the Holy Family* (Taiwan)—O.H.F.
[2715]—*Missionary Sisters of Christ the King*—M.S.C.K.
[3760]—*Order of St. Clare (Immaculate Heart Monastery of Poor Clares)*—M.Chr.
[0980]—*Pious Disciples of the Divine Master*—P.D.D.M.
[]—*Quinhon Missionary Sisters of the Holy Cross*

(Vietnam)—Q.M.H.C.

[1070-03]—*Sinsinawa Dominican Congregation of the Most Holy Rosary*—O.P.

[0500]—*Sisters of Charity of Nazareth (Southern Region)*—S.C.N.

[0430]—*Sisters of Charity of the Blessed Virgin Mary*—B.V.M.

[2516]—*Sisters of Mercy (Ireland)*—R.S.M.

[2570]—*Sisters of Mercy of the Americas (Regional Community of Burlingame)*—R.S.M.

[3840]—*Sisters of St. Joseph of Carondelet (Province of Los Angeles)*—C.S.J.

[3840]—*Sisters of St. Joseph of Carondelet (Province of St. Louis)*—C.S.J.

[1960]—*Sisters of the Holy Family*—S.H.F.

[1990]—*Sisters of the Holy Names of Jesus and Mary (California Province)*—S.N.J.M.

[3320]—*Sisters of the Presentation of the Blessed Virgin Mary*—P.B.V.M.

[1630]—*Sisters of the Third Order of Saint Francis of Penance and Christian Charity*—O.S.F.

[2170]—*Sisters, Servants of the Immaculate Heart of Mary*—I.H.M.

[2150]—*Sisters, Servants of the Immaculate Heart of Mary, Monroe, Michigan*—I.H.M.

[]—*Society of Christ for Polonia* (San Jose, CA)

[1890]—*Society of Helpers (American Province)*—H.H.S.

[4070]—*Society of the Sacred Heart*—R.S.C.J.

DIOCESAN CEMETERIES AND MAUSOLEUMS

SAN JOSE. *Calvary*, 2655A Madden Ave., 95126. Tel: 408-258-2940; Fax: 408-258-5614. Mr. Rick Wesner, Interim Dir. (Santa Clara Co.)

LOS ALTOS. *Gate of Heaven*, 22555 Cristo Rey Dr., 94024. Tel: 415-428-3730; Fax: 415-428-3733. Mr. Rick Wesner, Interim Dir.

NECROLOGY

† Maher, Rev. Msgr. James, (Retired)—Died Dec. 8, 2002

† Lopez, Fausto, (Retired)—Died Sept. 20, 2003

Archdiocese of Santa Fe

(Archidioecesis Sanctae Fidei)

Most Reverend

MICHAEL J. SHEEHAN, S.T.L., J.C.D.

Archbishop of Santa Fe; ordained July 12, 1964; consecrated and installed as First Bishop of Lubbock June 17, 1983; appointed Apostolic Administrator of Santa Fe April 6, 1993; installed as Eleventh Archbishop of Santa Fe September 21, 1993. *Res.: Catholic Center*, 4000 St. Joseph Pl., N.W., Albuquerque, NM 87120.

Archdiocese of Santa Fe Catholic Center: 4000 St. Joseph Pl., N.W., Albuquerque, NM 87120. Tel: 505-831-8100.

ESTABLISHED IN 1850.

Square Miles 61,142.

Created an Archbishopric in 1875.

Solemnly consecrated to the Immaculate Heart of Mary on October 7, 1945.

Comprises the Counties of Colfax, Curry, DeBaca, Guadalupe, Harding, Los Alamos, Mora, Quay, Roosevelt, San Miguel, Santa Fe, Socorro, Taos, Torrance and Union with a part of Bernalillo, Sandoval, Rio Arriba and Valencia Counties.

Patron of the Archdiocese: St. Francis of Assisi.

For legal titles of parishes and archdiocesan institutions, consult the Chancery Office.

STATISTICAL OVERVIEW

Personnel	
Archbishops	1
Retired Archbishops	1
Priests: Diocesan Active in Diocese	81
Priests: Diocesan Active Outside Diocese	2
Priests: Retired, Sick or Absent	35
Number of Diocesan Priests	118
Religious Priests in Diocese	86
Total Priests in Diocese	204
Extern Priests in Diocese	4
Ordinations:	
Diocesan Priests	5
Religious Priests	1
Transitional Deacons	4
Permanent Deacons	61
Permanent Deacons in Diocese	199
Total Brothers	75
Total Sisters	245
Parishes	
Parishes	93
With Resident Pastor:	
Resident Diocesan Priests	65
Resident Religious Priests	23
Without Resident Pastor:	
Administered by Deacons	2
Administered by Religious Women	3
Missions	216

Pastoral Centers	4
Professional Ministry Personnel:	
Brothers	2
Sisters	29
Lay Ministers	163
Welfare	
Health Care Centers	1
Total Assisted	6,500
Homes for the Aged	2
Total Assisted	35
Day Care Centers	1
Total Assisted	149
Specialized Homes	4
Total Assisted	1,810
Special Centers for Social Services	5
Total Assisted	301,396
Residential Care of Disabled	1
Total Assisted	16
Educational	
Diocesan Students in Other Seminaries	21
Seminaries, Religious	5
Students Religious	12
Total Seminarians	33
Colleges and Universities	1
Total Students	1,829
High Schools, Diocesan and Parish	1

Total Students	1,050
High Schools, Private	1
Total Students	781
Elementary Schools, Diocesan and Parish	17
Total Students	4,043
Catechesis/Religious Education:	
High School Students	5,824
Elementary Students	17,589
Total Students under Catholic Instruction	31,149
Teachers in the Diocese:	
Brothers	4
Sisters	17
Lay Teachers	406
Vital Statistics	
Receptions into the Church:	
Infant Baptism Totals	5,821
Adult Baptism Totals	274
Received into Full Communion	548
First Communions	5,372
Confirmations	3,032
Marriages:	
Catholic	1,045
Interfaith	168
Total Marriages	1,213
Deaths	2,959
Total Catholic Population	254,110
Total Population	1,260,385

Former Archbishops—Most Revs. J. B. LAMY, consecrated Nov. 24, 1850; created first Archbishop, 1875; resigned July 18, 1885; died Feb. 13, 1888; J. B. SALPOINTE, D.D., consecrated Bishop of Doryla and Vicar Apostolic of Arizona, June 20, 1869; appt. Coadjutor of Santa Fe "cum jure successionis", April, 22, 1884; promoted to the Titular Archiepiscopal See of Anazarba, Oct. 11 of same year; succeeded to the See of Santa Fe, July 18, 1885; resigned Jan. 7, 1894 Titular Archbishop of Tomi; died July 15, 1898; P. L. CHAPELLE, consecrated Nov. 1, 1891; Archbishop of Santa Fe, Jan. 7, 1894; transferred to New Orleans, Dec. 1, 1897; died Aug. 9, 1905; PETER BOURGADE, D.D., consecrated May 1, 1885 Bishop of Thaumacum and Vic. Ap. of Arizona; Bishop of Tucson, May 8, 1897; transferred to Santa Fe, Jan. 7, 1899; died May 17, 1908; J. B. PITAVAL, D.D., consecrated Titular Bishop of Sora and Auxiliary of Santa Fe, July 25, 1902; promoted to the See of Santa Fe, Jan. 3, 1909; resigned Feb., 1918; appt. Titular Archbishop of Amida, July 29, 1918; died May 23, 1928; ALBERT T. DAEGER, O.F.M., D.D., consecrated May 7, 1919; died Dec. 2, 1932; RUDOLPH ALOYSIUS GERKEN, D.D., consecrated Bishop of Amarillo, April 26, 1927; appt. Archbishop of Santa Fe, June 2, 1933; installed as Archbishop of Santa Fe, Aug. 23, 1933; died March 2, 1943; EDWIN V. BYRNE, D.D., consecrated Bishop of Ponce, P.R.; transferred to Diocese of San Juan, P.R.; promoted to Archbishop of Santa Fe, June 15, 1943; died July 25, 1963; JAMES P. DAVIS, D.D. (Retired), consecrated Bishop of San Juan, P.R., Oct. 6, 1943; promoted to Archbishop, April 30, 1960; transferred to Archdiocese of Santa Fe, Jan. 3, 1964; retired Oct. 1974; died March 4, 1988; ROBERT F. SANCHEZ, consecrated 10th Archbishop of Santa Fe, July 25, 1974; resigned April 6, 1993.

All offices are located at the Archdiocese of Santa Fe Catholic Center, 4000 Saint Joseph Pl., N.W., Albuquerque, NM 87120. Tel. 505-831-8100, unless otherwise indicated.

Office of the Archbishop

Vicar-General—Very Rev. RICHARD OLONA, V.G., 7701 Wyoming Blvd., N.E., Albuquerque, 87109.

Secretary to the Archbishop—Ms. DOLORES CORDOVA. Tel: 505-831-8120.

Office of the Chancellor

Chancellor—Rev. BENNETT J. VOORHIES. Tel: 505-831-8158. Vice Chancellors:: Sr. NANCY KAZIK, O.S.F. Tel: 505-831-8188; Rev. DONALD STARKEY. Tel: 505-831-8348.

Archivist and Artistic Patrimony—Mrs. MARINA OCHOA, 213 Cathedral Pl., Santa Fe, 87501. Tel: 505-983-3811.

Attorney for the Archdiocese—Mr. CHARLES P. REYNOLDS, 718 Central Ave., S.W., Albuquerque, 87102. Tel: 505-842-8188.

Communications-Media—Mrs. CELINE RADIGAN, Dir. Tel: 505-831-8180.

Ecumenical Commission and Inter-Religious Affairs—Rev. MICHAEL T. DEMKOVICH, O.P., Dir., Aquinas Newman Center, 1815 Las Lomas Rd., N.E., Albuquerque, 87106. Tel: 505-243-0525.

Madonna Retreat and Conference Center—Ms. MARIE VILLANUEVA, Dir., 4040 St. Joseph Pl., N.W., Albuquerque, 87120. Tel: 505-831-8196.

Newspaper, Archdiocesan "People of God"—Most Rev. MICHAEL J. SHEEHAN, S.T.L., J.C.D., Publisher; Sr. NANCY KAZIK, O.S.F., Editor, 4000 St. Joseph Pl., N.W., Albuquerque, 87120. Tel: 505-831-8188.

Parish Bulletin Service, "The Catholic Communicator"—JENNY CHILSON, P.O. Box 93244, Albuquerque, 87199-3244. Tel: 505-856-0333; Fax: 505-822-5589.

Human Resources—Mr. WALTER DUGUAY, Dir. Tel: 505-831-8130.

Immaculate Heart of Mary Retreat and Conference Center—BEN ARMIJO, Dir. Tel: 505-988-1975.

Canonical Services Division

Judicial Vicar—Rev. JEROME PLOTKOWSKI, J.C.L. Tel: 505-831-8177.

College of Consultors—Very Rev. RICHARD OLONA, V.G.; Revs. LARRY DUNHAM, O.F.M.; JEROME PLOTKOWSKI, J.C.L.; BENNETT J. VOORHIES; FRANCIS EGGERT; MIKE SHEA; LAMBERT LUNA.

Council of Men and Women Religious—VACANT.

Holy Childhood Association— See Mission Office Svcs.

Mission Office—Rev. ARKAD BICZAK Dir. Propagation of the Faith; Holy Childhood; Catholic Relief Svcs. John XXIII Catholic Community, 4831 Tramway Ridge Dr., N.E., Albuquerque, 87111. Tel: 505-293-0088.

Office of Religious—Sr. NANCY KAZIK, O.S.F., Dir. Tel: 505-831-8188.

Permanent Diaconate Program—Deacon DONATO LUCERO, Dir., Immaculate Heart of Mary, 3700 Canyon Rd., Los Alamos, 87544. Tel: 505-662-6193.

Pilgrimage for Vocations—Rev. EDMOND SAVILLA, Dir., Ascension Parish, 2150 Raymac Rd., S.W., Albuquerque, 87105. Tel: 505-877-8550.

Presbyteral Council of the Archdiocese of Santa Fe—Most Rev. MICHAEL J. SHEEHAN, S.T.L., J.C.D., Pres.; Revs. BENNETT J. VOORHIES, Ex Officio; RON CARRILLO, S.F., Chm.; CLARENCE MAES, Vice Chm.; GARY ORTIZ, Sec. Exec. Committee. Exec. Board Members:: Revs. DENNIS GARCIA; EDWARD DOMME.

Propagation of the Faith— See Mission Office.

Vicars Forane (Deans)—Rev. JEROME MARTINEZ Y

ALIRE, J.C.L., Santa Fe Deanery; Rev. Msgr. DOUGLAS A. RAUN, Albuquerque-Deanery A; Revs. RONALD BRUCKNER, Albuquerque-Deanery B; EDMOND SAVILLA, Albuquerque-Deanery C; JOHN DANIEL, Southwest Deanery; TIMOTHY MARTINEZ, Northwest Deanery; FRANCIS MALLEY, Northeast Deanery; LEO L. PADGET, Southeast Deanery.

Tribunal—Tel: 505-831-8177.

Judicial Vicar—Rev. JEROME PLOTKOWSKI, J.C.L.

Adjutant Judicial Vicar—Rev. KEVIN NIEHOFF, O.P.

Promoter of Justice—Rev. JEROME MARTINEZ Y ALIRE, J.C.L.

Defenders of the Bond—Revs. SOTERO SENA; ADAM ORTEGA Y ORTIZ; Deacons HARRY BEARE; GEORGE SANDOVAL.

Associate Judges—Revs. C. JOHN BRASHER; CRISPIN C. BUTZ, O.F.M.; JOHN R. CONWAY; NORMAN R. FALARDEAU, S.S.S.

Notaries—Mrs. LEDIA APODACA; Ms. JULIANA JARAMILLO; Ms. HELEN WILLS.

Delegate for Matrimonial Dispensations—Revs. JEROME PLOTKOWSKI, J.C.L.; DONALD J. STARKEY.

Appeal Court—Tel: 505-831-8177.

Vocations—Revs. SCOTT MANSFIELD, Dir. Tel: 505-831-8143; DENNIS GARCIA, Assoc. Dir.; Mr. ROBERT MARTINEZ, Asst. Dir.

Finance Division

Executive Director of Finance—Mr. TONY SALGADO, C.P.A. Tel: 505-831-8132.

Annual Catholic Appeal Foundation— Archdiocesan Annual Appeal Program, LINDA J. GARCIA, C.F.R.E., C.F.R.E., Exec. Dir. & Dir.of Devel. Tel: 505-831-8155.

Archdiocese of Santa Fe Catholic Foundation—MARY P. DUNN, Exec. Dir., 2201 San Pedro, N.E., Bldg. 2, Ste. 211, Albuquerque, 87110. Tel: 505-872-2901 Nonprofit corporation for financial support of Archdiocese of Santa Fe.

Finance Council—Most Rev. MICHAEL J. SHEEHAN, S.T.L., J.C.D., Pres.; Mr. WILLIAM GRADY, Chm.; Very Rev. LARRY DUNHAM, O.F.M.; Revs. BENNETT J. VOORHIES; JOHN CONWAY; Mr. GIG BRUMMEL; Mr. TONY SALGADO, C.P.A.; Mr. TIM SHEEHAN; Ms. JENNIFER CANTRELL; Sr. NANCY KAZIK, O.S.F.

Property Managers and Construction Contract Coord.—Mr. JOHN HUCHMALA. Tel: 505-831-8136.

Pastoral Ministries

Executive Director—Ms. FRANCES VOGEL-MONTANO, 4000 St. Joseph Pl., N.W., Albuquerque, 87120. Tel: 505-831-8151.

AIDS/HIV Ministry of the Archdiocese of Santa Fe—Mr. STEVE HAY, 4000 St. Joseph Pl., N.W., Albuquerque, 87120. Tel: 505-831-8174.

Campaign for Human Development—Mrs. JOAN LEAHIGH, Coord., 4000 St. Joseph Pl., N.W., Albuquerque, 87120. Tel: 505-831-8167.

Catholic Committee on Scouting— (Boy Scouts and Girl Scouts) Deacon DONALD BRUCKNER, Dir. Scouting.

Catholic Schools Office—Sr. MICHELLE MICEK, O.S.F., Supt. Tel: 505-831-8173.

Catholic Charities of Albuquerque—GREGORY R. KEPFERLE, M.A., M.Div., Exec. Dir., 2010 Bridge, S.W., Albuquerque, 87105. Mailing Address, P.O. Box 25405, Albuquerque, 87125. Tel: 505-247-9521.

Catholic Charities of Santa Fe, Inc.—GREGORY R. KEPFERLE, M.A., M.Div., Exec. Dir., 138 Park Ave., Santa Fe, 87501. Mailing Address, P.O. Box 443, Santa Fe, 87504. Tel: 505-982-0441.

Cursillo Movement—Rev. CHRYSOSTOM PARTEE, O.F.M., Coord., San Diego Friary, P.O. Box 79, Jemez Pueblo, 87024. Tel: 505-834-7300.

Ministry to the Disabled—Directors: Mr. STEVE HAY; PALMIRA HAY.

Ministry to the Deaf—Mrs. ARDITH MONTANO, Coord. Tel: 505-831-8174.

Evangelization—Deacon JUAN BARAJAS. Tel: 505-831-8152.

Formation for Christian Service—FRANCES VOGEL-MONTANO, Dir. Tel: 505-831-8151.

Hospital Ministry—PALMIRA HAY, Coord. Tel: 505-831-8174.

Prison & Detention Ministry—Mr. STEVE HAY, Dir. Tel: 505-831-8174.

Archdiocesan Network for Catholic Legislative Advocacy—Mrs. JOAN LEAHIGH. Tel: 505-831-8167.

Liturgical Commission—Most Rev. MICHAEL J. SHEEHAN, Pres.; BARBARA GUENTHER, Chm., 4000 St. Joseph Pl., N.W., Albuquerque, 87120. Tel: 505-831-8194.

Marriage and Family Life Office—Mrs. REMEDIOS (HEDDY) LONG, Dir. Tel: 505-831-8117.

Ministry to Spanish Speaking—Deacon JUAN BARAJAS. Tel: 505-831-8152.

African American Ministry—Ms. BRENDA DABNEY. Tel: 505-831-8167.

Native American Ministry—Mr. MIKE VALDO. Tel: 505-831-8243.

Newman Centers—

ALBQ: Aquinas Newman Center—Rev. ROBERT J. KELLER, O.P., Dir., Univ. of New Mexico, 1815 Las Lomas Rd., N.E., Albuquerque, 87106. Tel: 505-247-1095.

LAS VEGAS: Newman Center—Rev. VINCENT CHAVEZ, Coord., Highlands University, 811 Sixth St., Las Vegas, 87701. Tel: 505-425-9295.

PORTALES: St. Thomas Moore Newman Center—Rev. TOBIN HITT, Chap., Eastern New Mexico University, P.O. Box 2253, Portales, 88130. Tel: 505-356-5615.

SANTE FE: College of Santa Fe—Rev. JOSEPH LAVOIE, Dir., St. Michael's Dr., Santa Fe, 87501. Tel: 505-473-6011.

Santa Fe Community College—Bro. JAMES BROWN, Campus Min. Tel: 505-473-6587.

Office of Worship—Mrs. DOLORES SOKOL. Tel: 505-831-8194.

Peace Pilgrimage—Mrs. JOAN LEAHIGH, Coord. Tel: 505-255-4171.

Pro Life Commission—ANNE AVELLONE, Dir., 4000 St. Joseph Pl., N.W., Albuquerque, 87120. Tel: 505-831-8167.

RCIA—Mrs. DOLORES SOKOL. Tel: 505-831-8194.

Religious Education—MARY ANN HOLLAND, Dir. Religious Educ. & Catechetical Support. Tel: 505-831-8127. 4000 St. Joseph Pl., N.W., Albuquerque, 87120. Tel: 505-831-8128.

Schools of Lay Ministry Formation—

Albuquerque Deanery A,B,C, "Emmaus Journey"—FRANCES VOGEL-MONTANO, Coord., 4000 St. Joseph Pl., N.W., Albuquerque, 87120. Tel: 505-831-8151.

Northwest Deanery—JOANNE DUPONT-SANDOVAL, Coord., P.O. Box 429, Truchas, 87578. Tel: 505-689-2404.

Santa Fe Deanery— (Jornada de Fe) JUANITA MONTOYA, Coord., 2727 Calle Cedro, Santa Fe, 87505. Tel: 505-471-6489.

Spanish School of Ministry—Deacon JUAN BARAJAS. Tel: 505-831-8152.

Liturgical Institute of the Southwest—DOLLY SOLCOL.

St. Vincent de Paul Council—Deacon SANTOS ABEYTA, Spiritual Dir., Holy Family Parish, P.O. Box 12127, Albuquerque, 87195. Tel: 505-842-5426.

Social Justice—ANNE AVELLONE. Tel: 505-831-8167.

Stewardship—Deacon JUAN BARAJAS, Dir. Tel: 505-831-8152.

Youth and Young Adult Ministry—Mrs. BERNADETTE JARAMILLO, Dir. Tel: 505-831-8145.

Ministry Resource Center—Mrs. PATRICIA MCINTIRE, Dir. Tel: 505-831-8187.

Victim Assistance Coordinator—Sr. NANCY KAZIK, O.S.F. Tel: 505-831-8188. Email: nk@archdiocesesantafe.org.

CLERGY, PARISHES, MISSIONS AND PAROCHIAL SCHOOLS

CITY OF SANTA FE
(SANTA FE COUNTY)

1—THE CATHEDRAL OF SAN FRANCISCO DE ASIS (1610), [CEM] Revs. Jerome Martinez y Alire, J.C.L., Rector; Mark Schultz, M.Div.; Vidal Martinez; Deacons William Kollasch; Juan Martinez; Jeffrey T. Toliver. In Res., Rev. Robert Lussier, O.S.B.
Res.: P.O. Box 2127, Santa Fe, 87504. Tel: 505-982-5619; Fax: 505-989-1952.
School—Tel: 505-982-0331; Fax: 505-982-0667. Sisters Josephine Macias, C.D.P., Admin.; Phyllis Stowell, S.C.L., Prin. Sisters 2; Lay Teachers 22; Students 255.
Catechesis/Religious Program—Tel: 505-982-3625; 505-820-3429; Fax: 505-989-3760. Juanita Montoya, D.R.E. Students 240.

2—ST. ANNE'S (1942), (Spanish), [JC] Rev. Clarence Maes.
Res.: 511 Alicia, Santa Fe, 87501. Tel: 505-983-4430; Fax: 505-983-7483.
Catechesis/Religious Program—Students 195.

3—CRISTO REY (1940), [JC] Rev. Lambert Joseph Luna; Deacons Randy Rodriguez; Martin Gallegos Jr.
Office—1120 Canyon Rd., Santa Fe, 87501. Tel: 505-983-8528; Fax: 505-992-6836.
School—Tel: 505-983-8411; Fax: 505-983-8411 (Call first). Terry Lopez, Prin. Lay Teachers 6; Students 103.
Mission—Our Lady of Guadalupe La Canada de los Alamos, Santa Fe, Santa Fe Co. 87501.
Catechesis/Religious Program—Students 56.

4—ST. JOHN THE BAPTIST (1953), (Hispanic), Rev. Nathan Libaire, O.S.B.; Deacons Andres Carrillo; Tony Rodriguez; Andres Dimas.
Res.: 1301 Osage Ave., Santa Fe, 87505. Tel: 505-983-5034; Fax: 505-983-1861.
Catechesis/Religious Program—Connie C. Smith, D.R.E. Students 228.

5—OUR LADY OF GUADALUPE (1882), (Hispanic), [CEM] [JC] Rev. Tien-Tri Nguyen; Deacons Anthony Trujillo; Carlos F. Pacheco, (Retired).
Res.: 417 Agua Fria St., Santa Fe, 87501. Tel: 505-983-8868; Fax: 505-983-4304.
Catechesis/Religious Program—Tel: 505-988-3336. Students 536.
Mission—San Ysidro P.O. Box 65, Tesuque, Santa Fe Co. 87574. Tel: 505-984-2930.
Mission—Our Lady of Sorrows Rio en Medio, Sante Fe Co. Tel: 505-982-5588.

6—SAN ISIDRO (1835), (Hispanic), [CEM 2] Rev. Franklin D. Pretto.
Res.: 3552 Agua Fria St., Santa Fe, 87507. Tel: 505-471-0710.
Catechesis/Religious Program—Alfreda Fielek, D.R.E. Tel: 505-471-6385 (Home). Students 214.
Mission— La Cienega, Santa Fe Co.

7—SANTA MARIA DE LA PAZ CATHOLIC COMMUNITY (1990), Rev. Adam Lee Ortega y Ortiz; Paul H. Lujan, Business Mgr.; Sisters Paula Gallagher, I.H.M., Liturgy Dir.; Colleen Shanahan, O.S.F., Family Life Dir.; Deacons Juan M. Rodriguez; Tom Van Valkenburgh; Diana Hall, Youth Dir.
Res.: 11 College Ave., Santa Fe, 87508-9225. Tel: 505-473-4200 (Office); Fax: 505-473-1602.
Catechesis/Religious Program—Mrs. Patricia Lopez, D.R.E. Students 519.

OUTSIDE THE CITY OF SANTA FE

ABIQUIU, RIO ARRIBA CO., ST. THOMAS APOSTLE (1745), (Hispanic), [CEM 5] Rev. Mark E. Granito.
Res.: P.O. Box 117, 87510. Tel: 505-685-4462; Fax: 505-685-4462.
Catechesis/Religious Program—Tel: 505-685-4462 (All Missions). Students 205.
Mission— Canones, Rio Arriba Co.
Mission— Medanales, Rio Arriba Co.
Mission— Youngsville, Rio Arriba Co.
Mission— Coyote, Rio Arriba Co.
Mission— Mesa de Poleo, Rio Arriba Co.
Mission— Capulin, Rio Arriba Co.
Mission— Gallina, Rio Arriba Co.

ALBUQUERQUE, BERNALILLO CO.

1—ST. ANNE (1929), Revs. Daniel M. Balizan; Robert Lancaster; Deacons Tibo Chavez; Edgar Torres; Paul LeFebre.
Res.: 1400 Arenal Rd., S.W., 87105. Tel: 505-877-3121; Fax: 505-877-0084.
Catechesis/Religious Program—Tel: 505-877-0581. Sisters Abigail Lopez, H.N., D.R.E.; Guadalupe Valdovinos, D.R.E. Students 490.
Mission—Morada de San Jose 2100 La Vega Rd., S.W., Bernalillo Co. 87105.

2—ANNUNCIATION (1959), Revs. Ronald L. Bruckner; Clement Niggel; Deacons Harry Gogan; Victor J. Bachechi; Kevin Maloney; Robert Morrow.
Res.: 2600 Vermont, N.E., 87110. Tel: 505-293-5462; 505-298-7553.
Office—2532 Vermont, N.E., 87110. Tel: 505-298-7553; Fax: 505-294-7418.
School—2610 Utah N.E., 87110. Tel: 505-299-6783; Fax: 505-299-2182. Sr. Rose Therese Wich, S.C., Prin. Lay Teachers 26; Students 384.
Catechesis/Religious Program—Tel: 505-296-0411. Sr. Grace De Paole, Fd.C.C., D.R.E. Students 198.

3—ASCENSION (1962), [CEM 2] Rev. Edmund Savilla; Deacon Bill Hoefler.
Res.: 2150 Raymac Rd., S.W., 87105. Tel: 505-877-8550; Fax: 508-877-8508.
Catechesis/Religious Program—Tel: 505-877-8144. Pam Pitchford, D.R.E. Students 266.

4—ST. CHARLES BORROMEO (1934), [JC] Revs. John Thomas Lane, S.S.S. (GAL); Normand R. Falardeau, S.S.S.; Robert Lussier, S.S.S. (GB); Robert Stark, S.S.S.; Joseph Thai Minh Tran, S.S.S.; Bro. Peter Mahady, S.S.S.; Deacons Lorenzo Castillo; William "Bill" Barry; Ron Schultz; Paul Dung Van Nguyen.
Res.: 1818 Coal Pl., S.E., 87106. Tel: 505-242-3462; Fax: 505-247-1292.
School—Tel: 505-243-5788; Fax: 505-764-8842. Ms. Barbara Rossow, Prin. Sisters 1; Lay Teachers 24; Students 386.
Catechesis/Religious Program—Tel: 505-242-3462, Ext. 42. Sr. Conchita Carrillo, D.R.E. Students 144.

5—COMMUNITY OF THE RISEN SAVIOR (1979), Very Rev. Richard Olona, V.G.; Rev. Edward Rivera; Sr. Marie Luisa Vasquez, O.P., Pastoral Assoc.; Deacons Mark Bussemeier; Kenn Sinatra; Ricardo Chavez; Manuel Garcia.

Church: 7701 Wyoming, N.E., 87109. Tel: 505-821-1571; Fax: 505-857-0065.
Catechesis/Religious Program—Gerry Wood, D.R.E.; Jennifer Murphy-Dye, D.R.E.; Janet Estepp, D.R.E. Students 800.

6—St. Edwin (1965), (Hispanic), Rev. William E. Sanchez; Deacons Nestor Garcia; Patrick Santistevan.
Res.: 2105 Barcelona, S.W., 87105. Tel: 505-877-2967; Fax: 505-877-6810.
Catechesis/Religious Program—Tel: 505-877-3727. Students 81.

7—St. Francis Xavier (1928), (Hispanic), [JC] Rev. Dennis Garcia; Sr. Bernice Garcia, Parish Life Coord. Tel: 505-268-0158.
Mailing Address: 820 Broadway, S.E., 87110.
Res.: 901 Adams, N.E., 87110.
Catechesis/Religious Program—Tel: 505-243-5201; Fax: 505-243-1179. Students 140.

8—Holy Family (1953), (Hispanic), Rev. Gino Correa, O.F.M.; Deacons Santos Abeyta; Eddie Blea; Enrique Padilla. In Res., Rev. Richard Rohr, O.F.M.; Bros. Duane A. Torisky, O.F.M.; Andres Gallegos, O.F.M.
Res.: 562 Atrisco Dr., S.W., P.O. Box 12127, 87105. Tel: 505-842-5426; Fax: 505-842-9767.
Catechesis/Religious Program—Karen Mitchell, D.R.E.; Agatha Herrera, D.R.E.; Juliane Jaramillo, D.R.E.; Maria Padilla, D.R.E. Students 500.

9—Holy Ghost (1953), Rev. Thomas J. Mayefske; Deacons Pat Kneafsey; Ubaldo Chavez; Jose Ayala.
Res.: 833 Arizona Ave., S.E., 87108. Tel: 505-265-5957; Fax: 505-265-5958.
School—Tel: 505-256-1563; Fax: 505-262-9635. Dr. Noreen Copeland, Ph.D., Prin. Sisters 2; Lay Teachers 19; Students 225.
Catechesis/Religious Program—Tel: 505-265-1975. Sr. Connie Martinez, Fd.CC., D.R.E. Spanish Program; Theresa Montoya, D.R.E. English Program. Students 312.

10—Immaculate Conception (1883), (Hispanic), Revs. Edmundo Rodriguez, S.J.; Richard W. McGowan, S.J.; Louis J. Lambert, S.J.; Thomas J. Steele, S.J.; William M. King, S.J.; Joseph Vanderholt, S.J.; Ronald D. Gonzales; Deacons Gilbert Valverde; George Sandoval.
Res.: 619 Copper Ave., N.W., 87102. Tel: 505-247-4272; Fax: 505-243-0402.
School—St. Mary, 227 Seventh St., 87102. Tel: 505-242-6271; Fax: 505-242-4837. Sr. Marianella Domenici, S.C., Prin. Sisters 2; Lay Teachers 35; Students 597.
Catechesis/Religious Program—Tel: 505-247-2555; Fax: 505-247-2555. Students 155.

11—St. John the Apostle (1984),, (John XXIII Catholic Community) Rev. Arkad Biczak; Deacons John Russo; Alex Trujillo; Peter Broussard; Clara Maestas, Business Mgr.
Res.: 4831 Tramway Ridge Dr., N.E., 87111. Tel: 505-293-0088; Fax: 505-293-7276.
Catechesis/Religious Program—Tel: 505-293-7756. Kyle Kemp, D.R.E. Students 338.

12—Saint Joseph on the Rio Grande (1986), Rev. Frank Prieto; Deacons Don Bruckner; Frank Lucero; Jerry Hietpas; Rene Greivel; Bert Dohle.
Office—5901 St. Joseph's Dr., N.W., 87120. Tel: 505-839-7952; Fax: 505-839-7955.
Catechesis/Religious Program—Tel: 505-831-8346; Fax: 505-831-8264. Harv Weakland, D.R.E.; Linda Weakland, D.R.E. Students 673.

13—St. Jude Thaddeus (Paradise Hills) (1968), Rev. John R. Conway; Deacons Robert Aragon; Stephen Rangel.
Mailing Address: P.O. Box 67710, 87193. Tel: 505-898-0826 (Church); 505-897-0391 (Res.); Fax: 505-792-9810.
Catechesis/Religious Program—Tel: 505-897-4006. Students 420.

14—Nativity of the Blessed Virgin Mary (1936), [CEM] [JC 2] Rev. Juan Mendez; Deacon Leonard Martinez.
Res.: 9502 Fourth St., N.W., 87114. Tel: 505-898-5253; Fax: 505-898-0496.
Catechesis/Religious Program—Tel: 505-898-1441. Mary Duneman, D.R.E. Students 495.
Mission—Our Lady of Mount Carmel 7807 Edith, Bernalillo Co. 87114.

15—Our Lady of Fatima (1949), [JC] Revs. Francis X. Eggert; David Phillipson; Deacons Thomas Jones; Frank See; Hugh Hackett; Sandy Hall. In Res., Rev. Stephen A. Sanchez.
Res.: 4020 Lomas, N.E., 87110. Tel: 505-265-5868; Fax: 505-268-0680.
School—Tel: 505-255-6391; Fax: 505-268-3279. Linda Honeyfield, Prin. Lay Teachers 25; Students (K-5) 197; Students (6-8) 81.
Catechesis/Religious Program—Students 158.

16—Our Lady of Guadalupe (1954), (Hispanic), Rev. Joe Vigil; Deacons Manuel Facio, Pastoral Assoc. & Business Mgr.; George Valverde; Manuel Cabrera. In Res., Rev. Ramon Aragon.
Res.: 1860 Griegos, N.W., 87107. Tel: 505-345-4596; Fax: 505-342-2984.
Catechesis/Religious Program—Tel: 505-344-7153. Molly C. De Baca, D.R.E. Students 242.

17—Our Lady of Lavang (1986), (Vietnamese), [JC] Rev. Tin Mahn Bui.
Mailing Address: 2115 Inez, N.E., 87110. Tel: 505-275-3079.
Church: 8500 Gonzales Rd., S.W., 87105. Tel: 505-839-4738.

18—Our Lady of Most Holy Rosary (1950), (Hispanic), Revs. Joel P. Garner, O.Praem.; Eugene Gries, O.Praem.; Deacons Juan Barajas; Harry Beare; Charles Johnson; Frank Perez; Gene Tuma; Tino Cevallos; Joe Herrara.
Office:—5415 Fortuna, N.W., 87105. Tel 505-836-5011; Fax: 505-836-7562.
Santa Maria de la Vid Priory: 5825 Coors S.W., 87121. Tel: 505-873-4399; Fax: 505-873-4667.
Catechesis/Religious Program—Tel: 505-831-2525. Christina Spahn, D.R.E.; Sr. Evangeline Salazar, O.S.B., D.R.E. Students 569.

19—Our Lady of the Assumption (1954), Revs. Edward C. Domme; Michael Cimino; Deacons Jim Delgado; Jack Granato.
Office & Mailing Address: 811 Guaymas, N.E., 87108-2398. Tel: 505-256-9818; 505-256-9877; Fax: 505-256-3131.
Res.: 8030 Fruit, N.E., 87108. Tel: 505-255-5727.
School—317 Guaymas, N.E., 87108. Tel: 505-256-3167; Fax: 505-256-3167 (Call first). Robert M. Kaiser, Prin. Lay Teachers 20; Students 191.
Catechesis/Religious Program—Lora Lee Ortiz, D.R.E. Students 166.

20—Prince of Peace Catholic Community (2000), *Office*:—12500 Carmel, N.E., 87122. Tel: 505-856-7657; Fax: 505-856-2560. Rev. Michael J. Shea.
Catechesis/Religious Program—Tel: 505-797-5115. Students 343.

21—Queen of Angels Native American Center and Archdiocesan Shrine to Kateri Tekakwitha (1952), (Native American), Rev. Emeric Nordmeyer, O.F.M.
Res.: I 40 & 12 St., N.W., P.O. Box 6881, 87197. Tel: 505-243-0835.
Catechesis/Religious Program—Tel: 505-836-0529.

22—Queen of Heaven (1952), Rev. Johnny Lee Chavez; Deacons Ruben Barela; Larry Cleveland; Pilar Garcia; Dan Lopez; Julian Padilla. In Res., Rev. Fernando Rubio-Boitel.
Office—5311 Phoenix, N.E., 87110. Tel: 505-881-1772; Fax: 505-883-5222.
School—Tel: 505-881-2484; Fax: 505-837-1123. Mary Cunning, Prin. Lay Teachers 24; Students 358.
Catechesis/Religious Program—Tel: 505-881-0715. Donna Duran, D.R.E. Students 490.

23—Sacred Heart (1903), [JC] Rev. James Moore; Deacon Thomas Perez.
Res.: 412 Stover Ave., S.W., 87102. Tel: 505-242-0561; Fax: 505-243-7857.
Catechesis/Religious Program—Students 115.

24—San Felipe de Neri (1706), (Hispanic), Rev. Msgr. Leo Lucero; Deacons Jose Lucero; James Robert (Bob) Lewis; Maurice Menke. In Res., Very Rev. Jerome A. Plotkowski.
Res.: P.O. Box 7007, 87194. Tel: 505-243-4628; Fax: 505-224-9495.
School—2000 Lomas Blvd., N.W., 87104. Tel: 505-242-2411; Fax: 505-242-7355. Nancy A. Suedkamp, Prin. Sisters 1; Lay Teachers 15; Students 232.
Catechesis/Religious Program—Tel: 505-247-2041. Sr. Rosina Sandoval, D.R.E. Students 122.
Mission—San Jose de los Duranes 2110 Los Luceros Rd., N.W., Bernalillo Co. 87104.

25—San Ignacio (1916), (Hispanic), Deacon Merce Villareal, Admin.
Res.: 1300 Walter, N.E., 87102. Tel: 505-243-4287; Fax: 505-243-7346.
Catechesis/Religious Program—Students 23.

26—San Jose (1938), [CEM] Revs. Dennis Garcia; Gabriel Paredes; Deacon Gregario Henderson.
Res.: 2401 Broadway, S.E., 87102-5009. Tel: 505-242-3658; Fax: 505-248-0810.
Catechesis/Religious Program—Tel: 505-243-7130. Sr Marlene Torres, Fd.C.C., D.R.E. Students 570.

27—Sangre de Cristo (1972), Rev Albert J. Podvin; Deacons Lloyd Martinez; Paul Ortwerth.
Res.: 8901 Candelaria, N.E., 87112. Tel: 505-293-2327; Fax: 505-292-0590.
Catechesis/Religious Program—Tel: 505-293-2328. Students 181.

28—Santuario San Martin de Porres (1979), Rev. James Vance; Deacon James Beaudette.
Res.: 8321 Camino San Martin, S.W., 87121. Tel: 505-836-4676; Fax: 505-836-3253.
Catechesis/Religious Program—Sr. Marcella Campos, D.R.E. Students 300.

29—Shrine of St. Bernadette (1959), Rev. Thomas A. Zotter; Deacons Alfred McLane; Byron Wicker, Pastoral Assoc.; J. Robert Martinez; Joe Santana; Terry Palmer.
Res.: 1800 Martha, N.E., 87112. Tel: 505-298-7557; Fax: 505-271-8099.
Catechesis/Religious Program—Tel: 505-293-7779; Fax: 505-298-2412. Students 429.

30—St. Therese of the Infant Jesus of the Little Flower (1947), Revs. Jim Suntum, S.F.; Charles L Stoeber, S.F. (Retired); Deacons Esequiel Torres, (Retired); Manuel Montoya.
Res.: 300 Mildred, N.W., 87107. Tel: 505-344-8050.
School—Tel: 505-344-4479; Fax: 505-344-3349. Antoinette Crump, Prin. Lay Teachers 16; Students 248.
Catechesis/Religious Program—Tel: 505-344-7643. Students 245.

31—St. Thomas Aquinas University Parish (1950),, (Serving the University of New Mexico) Rev. Robert J. Keller, O.P.; Sr. Mary Ann Barrett, O.P., Campus Min.; Meg Ashcroft, Liturgy Dir.; Deacons Bruce Eklund; Donald Contreras. In Res., Revs. Michael T. Demkovich, O.P.; Kevin W. Niehoff, O.P.; Wilfrid Hoff, O.P.
Res.: 1815 Las Lomas Rd., N.E., 87106-3803. Tel: 505-247-1094; Fax: 505-247-2933.
Catechesis/Religious Program—Tel: 505-247-1094, Ext. 15. Carole A. Everton, D.R.E. Students 224.

Anton Chico, Guadalupe Co., San Jose (1857), (Hispanic), [CEM] [JC 5] Rev. Patrick S. Duffy.
Res.: 1 Plaza Real, Box 99, 87711. Tel: 505-427-1164.
Catechesis/Religious Program—Tel: 505-427-4114. Students 30.
Mission— Dilia, Guadalupe Co.
Mission— Dahlia, Guadalupe Co.
Mission— Tecolotito, San Miguel Co.
Mission—Sangro de Christo (1834), Plaza de.

Arroyo Seco, Taos Co., La Santisima Trinidad (1834), (Spanish), [CEM] [JC 4] Rev. Ron G. Stone; Deacons Michael L. Kittredge; Romolo Arellano.
Res.: Box 189, 87514. Tel: 505-776-2273; Fax: 505-776-1543.
Catechesis/Religious Program—Michael L.K. Hredge, D.R.E. Students 140.
Mission—Nuestra Senora de Dolores Upper Plaza, Arroyo Hondo, Taos Co. 87513.
Mission—San Antonio de Padua Valdez Plaza, Valdez, Taos Co. 87580.
Mission—Santo Nino de Atocha Santo Nino Rd., Las Colonias, Taos Co. 87529.
Mission—San Cristobal San Cristobal, Taos Co.

Belen, Valencia Co., Our Lady of Belen (1793), [CEM] [JC] Rev. Stephen Schultz; Deacons Felix Barela; Manuel Gallegos; Norbert C. Sanchez; Robert Sanchez; Rudy Zamora. In Res., Rev. Mark Honhart.
Res.: 101-A N. 10th St., 87002. Tel: 505-864-8043; Fax: 505-861-0969.
School—Tel: 505-864-0484. Viola Martinez, Prin. Sisters 1; Lay Teachers 7; Students 207.
Catechesis/Religious Program—Tel: 505-864-7869. Judith Quintana, D.R.E. Students 700.
Mission— Los Chavez, Valencia Co.
Mission— Jarales, Valencia Co.
Mission— Pueblitos, Valencia Co.
Mission— Bosque, Valencia Co.

Bernalillo, Sandoval Co., Our Lady of Sorrows (1699), (Indian—Hispanic), [CEM 3] Rev. Virgil Furfaro; Deacons Pete Santistevan; Jose de Jesus Cervantes.
Office—P.O. Box 607, 87004. Tel: 505-867-5252; Fax: 505-867-0267.
Res.: 301 Camino del Pueblo, P.O. Box 607, 87004. Tel: 505-867-0585.
Catechesis/Religious Program—Ursulita Perez, D.R.E. Students 455.
Mission— 43 San Antonio, Placitas, Sandoval Co. 87043.
Mission— 1416 Hwy. 313, Algodones, Sandoval Co. 87001.
Mission— 300 Parrot Blvd., Sandia Indian Pueblo, Sandoval Co. 87004.

Cerrillos, Santa Fe Co., St. Joseph (1850), [CEM 4] Deacon Tomas A. Baca.
Res.: Box 98, 87010. Tel: 505-471-1562; Fax: 505-471-1562.
Catechesis/Religious Program—Tel: 505-471-8759. Students 46.
Mission— Golden, Santa Fe Co.
Mission— Galisteo, Santa Fe Co.

Chama, Rio Arriba Co., St. Patrick (1963), (Hispanic—Anglo), [JC] Rev. John T. McKenna.
Res.: 352 Pine Ave., Hwy. 29, P.O. Box 36, 87520-0036. Tel: 505-756-2926; Fax: 505-756-2926.
Catechesis/Religious Program—Students 82.
Mission—Santo Nino Hwy. 84 & State Rd. 310, P.O. Box 36, Cebolla, Rio Arriba Co. 87518.
Mission—San Juan Nepumoceno County Rd. 295, Canjilon, Rio Arriba Co. 87515.

Chimayo, Rio Arriba Co., Holy Family (1955), (Hispanic), [CEM] [JC 2] Revs. Casimiro Roca, S.F.; Julio Gonzalez, S.F.; Deacon Jose Lopez.
Res.: P.O. Box 235, 87522. Tel: 505-351-4360; Fax: 505-351-4698.

Catechesis/Religious Program—Students 146.
Mission—Holy Rosary Truchas, Rio Arriba Co.
Mission—San Jose de Gracia Trampas, Taos Co.
Mission—Santo Domingo Cundiyo, Rio Arriba Co.
Mission—San Antonio Cordova, Rio Arriba Co.
Mission—Sagrado Corazon Rio Chiquito, Rio Arriba Co.
Mission—Santo Tomas Ojo Sarco, Rio Arriba Co.
Mission—San Miguel Archangel El Valle, Taos Co.
Mission—El Santuario Shrine El Santuario, Santa Fe Co. Tel: 505-351-4889.

CIMARRON, COLFAX CO., IMMACULATE CONCEPTION CHURCH (1864), (Hispanic—Mexican), [JC] Rev. John Dear, S.J. (NY); Sr. Hildegard Smith, S.C.C., Pastoral Assoc.
Res.: Rte. 1, Box 11, 87714. Tel: 505-376-2553; Fax: 505-376-2553.
Catechesis/Religious Program—Sr. Hildegarde Smith, S.C.C., D.R.E.; Mrs. Linda Pavletich, D.R.E.; Maria Sedillo, D.R.E. Students 51.
Convent—Sisters of Christian Charity, Tel: 505-376-2553; Fax: 505-376-2553.
Mission—St. Mel 200 Willow Creek, Eagle Nest, Colfax Co. 87718. Tel: 505-376-2553.
Mission—St. Anthony Black Lake, Colfax Co.

CLAYTON, UNION CO., ST. FRANCIS XAVIER (1937), [JC] Rev. James McGowan; Deacon P. Louis Montoya.
Res.: 115 N. First St., 88415. Tel: 505-374-9500; Fax: 505-374-8897.
Catechesis/Religious Program—Students 55.
Mission—Our Lady of Guadalupe Des Moines, Union Co.
Mission—St. Joseph Folsom, Union Co.
Mission—Sacred Heart Moses, Union Co.
Mission—Holy Trinity Hayden, Quay Co.

CLOVIS, CURRY CO.
1—OUR LADY OF GUADALUPE (1945), [CEM 2] [JC 2] Rev. Sotero A. Sena; Sr. Rose Urban, Pastoral Assoc.; Deacons Bob Pullings; Daniel Chavez.
Res.: 108 Davis St., 88101. Tel: 505-763-4445; Fax: 505-763-0261.
Catechesis/Religious Program—Tel: 505-762-7343. Sally Romero, D.R.E. (Grades K-6); Deacon Bob Pullings, D.R.E. (RCIA Prog.); Manuela Torres, D.R.E. (Grade K-6); Elena Vigil, D.R.E. (Grades 7-12). Students 550.
Mission— Box 122, Texico, Curry Co. 88135.
2—SACRED HEART (1908), Rev. Carlos Chavez; Deacons Juan A. Rodriguez; Michael A. Rowley.
Res.: 921 Merriwether St., 88101. Tel: 505-763-6947; Fax: 505-762-5557.
Catechesis/Religious Program—Students 306.
Mission— Melrose, Curry Co. 88124.

CORRALES, SANDOVAL CO., SAN YSIDRO (1966), [CEM] Rev. Clarence F. Galli; Deacon Faustin Archuleta.
Res.: 5005 Corrales Rd., Box 182, 87048. Tel: 505-898-1779; Fax: 505-897-6967.
Catechesis/Religious Program—Tel: 505-899-0276. Mary Kendzterski, D.R.E. Students 185.

DIXON, RIO ARRIBA CO., ST. ANTHONY (1929), [CEM 3] Rev. Christopher J. Pieroni.
Res.: 1114 Private Dr. #5, P.O. Box 39, 87527-0039. Tel: 505-579-4389; Fax: 505-579-4389.
Catechesis/Religious Program—Students 38.
Mission—Nuestra Senora de Guadalupe Velarde, Rio Arriba Co.
Mission—Nuestra Senora de los Dolores Pilar, Taos Co.
Mission—San Jose Lyden, Rio Arriba Co.

EL RITO, RIO ARRIBA CO., SAN JUAN NEPOMUCENO (1832), (Spanish), [CEM] [JC 9] Rev. Patrick J. Chavez; Deacon Fabian Garcia, (Retired).
Res.: P.O. Box 7, 87530. Tel: 505-581-4714.
Catechesis/Religious Program—Students 58.
Mission— Gen. Del., La Madera, Rio Arriba Co. 87539.
Mission— Gen. Del., Las Tablas, Taos Co. 87539.
Mission— Gen. Del., Ojo Caliente, Rio Arriba Co. 87549.
Mission— Gen. Del., Petaca, Taos Co. 87539.
Mission— Gen. Del., Servilleta, Taos Co. 87539.
Mission— Gen. Del., Vallecitos, Rio Arriba Co. 87581.
Mission— Gen. Del., Canon de Vallecitos, Rio Arriba Co. 87581.
Mission— Gen. Del., Tres Piedras, Taos Co. 87579.
Mission— P.O. Box 7, Placitas, Rio Arriba Co. 87530.

ESPANOLA, RIO ARRIBA CO.
1—FRANCISCAN TEWA MISSIONS, Rev. Dale Jamison, O.F.M.
Mailing Address: P. O. Box 1040, 87532. Tel: 505-747-9443.
2—SACRED HEART (1950), (Hispanic), [CEM 2] Rev. Augustine J. Moore, Ph.D.; Sr. Bernardita Abeyta, O.P.; Deacons Diego Herrera; Benjie Lopez.
Res.: P.O. Box 69, 87532. Tel: 505-753-4225; Fax: 505-753-1282.
Catechesis/Religious Program—Tel: 505-753-9413; 505-753-1695. Teresa Sandoval Espanola, D.R.E.; Dixie Garcia Hernandez, D.R.E. Students 250.
Mission— Hernandez, Rio Arriba Co.
Mission— El Guache, Rio Arriba Co.
Mission— Guachupanque, Rio Arriba Co.
Mission— El Duende, Rio Arriba Co.

FORT SUMNER, DE BACA CO., ST. ANTHONY (1958), (Hispanic), [CEM] Attended by, St. Rose of Lima, Santa Rosa. Rev. Irby "Nick" Nichols, M.Div.; Sr. Teresita Garcia, O.P., Parish Life Coord.
Church & Mailing Address: 114 W. Richard Ave., P.O. Box 370, 88119. Tel: 505-355-2320; Fax: 505-355-2320.
Catechesis/Religious Program—Students 60.

ISLETA, PUEBLO BERNALILLO CO., ST. AUGUSTINE (1613), (Native American), [CEM] Rev. Hilaire Valiquette, O.F.M.
Res.: P.O. Box 463, 87022. Tel: 505-869-3398; 505-565-0574; Fax: 505-565-0582.
Catechesis/Religious Program—Students 160.

JEMEZ PUEBLO, SANDOVAL CO., SAN DIEGO INDIAN MISSIONS (1608), (Native American—Spanish), [CEM] [JC 4] Revs. Chrysostom Partee, O.F.M.; Don Billiard, O.F.M.
Res.: P.O. Box 79, 87024. Tel: 505-834-7300; Fax: 505-834-7060.
School—Sisters 2; Lay Teachers 7; Students 85.
Catechesis/Religious Program—Verna Tosa, D.R.E. Students 45.
Mission— Canyon, Sandoval Co.
Mission— Ponderosa, Sandoval Co.
Mission— San Ysidro, Sandoval Co.
Mission— Santa Ana, Sandoval Co.
Mission— Zia, Sandoval Co.

JEMEZ SPRINGS, SANDOVAL CO., OUR LADY OF THE ASSUMPTION (1947), [CEM] Rev. James Sampson, s.P.
Res.: Tel: 505-829-3586; Fax: 505-829-3592.

LA JOYA, SOCORRO CO., OUR LADY OF SORROWS (1830), (Spanish), [CEM 6] Rev. Dennis R. Dolter, S.O.L.T.; Deacon Alfred Edwin Esquibel.
Mailing Address: 19 Calle de la Iglesia, P.O. Box 32, 87028. Tel: 505-864-4461; Fax: 505-861-3552.
Res.: 1249 Hwy. 304, Veguita, 87062. Tel: 505-864-0745.
Catechesis/Religious Program—Students 120.
Mission—San Antonio Abeytas, Socorro Co.
Mission—San Jose Contreras, Socorro Co.
Mission—San Isidro Las Nutrias, Socorro Co.
Mission—San Juan Veguita, Socorro Co.
Mission—San Antonio Sabinal, Socorro Co.

LAS VEGAS, SAN MIGUEL CO.
1—IMMACULATE CONCEPTION (1885), [CEM] Rev. Vincent P. Chavez.
Res.: 811 Sixth St., 87701. Tel: 505-425-7791; Fax: 505-425-6991.
Catechesis/Religious Program—Tel: 505-454-0685. Velma Salazar, D.R.E. Students 130.
Mission—Los Vigiles (Our Lady of Refuge) 811 6th, San Antonio, San Miguel Co. 87701.
2—OUR LADY OF SORROWS CHURCH (1851), (Hispanic), [CEM] [JC 2] Rev. C. John Brasher; Deacons Jose Leroy Martinez; Macedon Montoya Jr.
Res.: 403 Valencia St., 87701. Tel: 505-454-1469; Fax: 505-425-0949.
Catechesis/Religious Program—Tel: 505-425-6823. Mrs. Velma Salazar, D.R.E. Students 268.
Mission—Our Lady of Guadalupe HC 68, Box 11, Sapello, San Miguel Co. 87745. Tel: 505-425-8084.
Mission—San Isidro HC 32 Box 26, Trujillo, San Miguel Co. 87701. Tel: 505-641-5367.
Mission—Holy Family Garita. Box 1020, Variadero, San Miguel Co. 88421. Tel: 505-641-5339.
Mission—Santo Nino HC 69 Box 4, Rociada Abajo, San Miguel Co. 87742. Tel: 505-425-8251.
Mission—Santo Nino Montezuma. Box 63 El Porvenir Rte., Gallinas, San Miguel Co. 87731. Tel: 505-425-6015.
Chapel—Christ the King 2609 Encino St., 87701. Tel: 505-425-6894.
Chapel—San Jose Hot Springs.
Chapel—San Antonio Rte. Box 90, El Porvenir, 87731. Tel: 505-425-8010.
Chapel—San Ignacio HC 68 Box 15, Sapello, 87745. Tel: 505-425-3092; 505-454-1139.
Chapel—Our Lady of Sorrows Box 39 Anton Chico Rte., 87701. Tel: 505-421-5599.
Chapel—San Geronimo Box 310 Mineral Hill Rte., 87701. Tel: 505-425-3011.
Chapel—San Antonio P.O. Box 85, 87701. Tel: 505-425-3405.
Chapel—Lourdes
Chapel—San Jose HC 69 Box 12A, Rociada, 87742. Tel: 505-425-2809.
Chapel—San Rafael c/o Al Sanchez Jr., General Delivery, Trementina, 88439. Tel: 505-641-5384.
Chapel—Santo Nino de Atocha Anton Chico Rte., Box 20, 87701. Tel: 505-425-8014.
Chapel—Ojitos Frios
Chapel—Manuelitas
Chapel—Santo Nino, Tel: 505-454-0409.

LOS ALAMOS, LOS ALAMOS CO., IMMACULATE HEART OF MARY (1946), Rev. John F. Carney; Deacons Gerald Langner; Don Lucero; Ray Alcouffe; Roberto Villarreal; Rochelle Sparks, Business Mgr.; Terry Coggeshall, Liturgy Dir.; Robin Roach, Youth Dir.
Mailing Address: 3700 Canyon Rd., 87544. Tel: 505-662-6193.
Res.: 3694 Canyon Rd., 87544. Tel: 505-662-6921; Fax: 505-662-5191.
Catechesis/Religious Program—Tel: 505-662-7773. Helen Juzaitis, D.R.E. Students 515.
Mission—St. Joseph 196 Meadow, White Rock, Los Alamos Co. 87544. Tel: 505-672-1270.

LOS LUNAS, VALENCIA CO., SAN CLEMENTE (1961), [CEM 2] [JC] Rev. Rick Zerwas; Deacons Edward Espinosa; Jim Snell; Robert Burkhard; Juan Ortiz.
Res.: P.O. Box 147, 87031. Tel: 505-865-7385; Fax: 505-865-8323.
Catechesis/Religious Program—Tel: 505-865-9370. Mary Margaret Baca, D.R.E. Students 410.
Mission—San Antonio Los Lentes, Valencia Co.

LOS OJOS, RIO ARRIBA CO., SAN JOSE (1883), (Spanish), [CEM] [JC 2] Rev. Salvador Aragon, O.F.M.
Res.: Box 6, 87551. Tel: 505-588-7473; Fax: 505-588-7239.
Catechesis/Religious Program— Twinned with Santo Nino, Tierra Amarilla. Students 64.
Mission— Ensenada, Rio Arriba Co.
Mission— La Puente, Rio Arriba Co.
Mission— Plaza Blanca, Rio Arriba Co.

MORA, MORA CO., ST. GERTRUDE (1851), (Hispanic), [CEM] [JC 9] Rev. Michael Jordan, S.O.L.T.; Deacons Reynaldo Cordova; Cristobal Eloy Roybal; Gilbert Valdez.
Res.: P.O. Box 599, 87732. Tel: 505-387-2336; Fax: 505-387-5786.
Catechesis/Religious Program—Annette Chavez, D.R.E. Students 200.
Mission— Le Doux, Mora Co.
Mission— El Carmen, Mora Co.
Mission— Lucero, Mora Co.
Mission— Santiago-Talco, Mora Co.
Mission— Ojo Feliz, Mora Co.
Mission— Buenavista, Mora Co.
Mission— Golondrinas, Mora Co.
Mission— Rainsville, Mora Co.
Mission— Chacon, Mora Co.
Mission— Holman, Mora Co.
Mission— Cleveland, Mora Co.
Mission— Guadalupita, Mora Co.
Mission— Monte Aplanado, Mora Co.
Mission— Turquillo, Mora Co.
Mission— La Cueva, Mora Co.
Mission— Canoncito, Mora Co.

MORIARTY, TORRANCE CO., ESTANCIA VALLEY CATHOLIC PARISH (1972), [CEM 3] Rev. Anthony L. Martinez; Deacons Juan S. Lucero; Stephen R. Moffett.
Res.: P.O. Box 129, 87035. Tel: 505-832-6655; Fax: 505-832-6057.
Catechesis/Religious Program—Corrine Lucero, D.R.E. Students 415.
Mission—Sts. Peter & Paul St. Joseph St. & Third St., Estancia, Torrance Co. 87016. Tel: 505-384-5333.
Mission— Hwy. 55, Tajique, Torrance Co. 87047.
Mission—St. Elizabeth Ann Seton Hwy. 344, Edgewood, Santa Fe Co. 87015. Tel: 505-286-5456.

MOUNTAINAIR, TORRANCE CO., ST. ALICE (1946), (Hispanic), [CEM 5] [JC] Rev. Floria Renaud.
Res.: P.O. Box 206, 87036. Tel: 505-847-2264.
Catechesis/Religious Program—Tel: 505-847-0803. Prescilla Quintana, D.R.E. Students 131.
Mission— Abo, Torrance Co.
Mission— Punta de Agua, Torrance Co.
Mission— Manzano, Torrance Co.
Mission— Torreon, Torrance Co.
Mission— Willard, Torrance Co.

PECOS, SAN MIGUEL CO., ST. ANTHONY (1862), [CEM 5] Rev. Leo W. Ortiz.
Res.: HC 70, Box 23, 87552. Tel: 505-757-6345; Fax: 505-757-6377.
Catechesis/Religious Program—Tel: 505-757-6305. Students 257.
Mission— Canoncito, Santa Fe Co.
Mission— Las Colonias, San Miguel Co.
Mission— Glorieta, Santa Fe Co.
Mission— Rowe, San Miguel Co.
Mission— El Macho, San Miguel Co.

PENA BLANCA, SANDOVAL CO., NUESTRA SENORA DE GUADALUPE (1877), (Hispanic—Native American), [CEM 3] Revs. Wayne Gibbeaut, O.F.M.; Manuel Viera, O.F.M.; Deacons Albert Arquero; Joe Segura. In Res., Rev. Donnan Herbe, O.F.M.
Res.: P.O. Box 1270, 87041. Tel: 505-465-2226; Fax: 505-465-1336.
Catechesis/Religious Program—Tel: 505-465-0962. Maura Nieto, D.R.E. Students 121.
Mission—Indian Pueblo Cochiti, Sandoval Co.
Mission—Indian Pueblo San Felipe, Sandoval Co.
Mission—Indian Pueblo Santo Domingo, Sandoval Co.
Mission— Sile, Sandoval Co.
Mission— La Bajada, Sandoval Co.

PENASCO, TAOS CO., SAN ANTONIO DE PADUA (1866),

[CEM] Rev. Christopher J. Pieroni; Deacon Alberto Sandoval. Tel: 505-587-0447.
Res.: 14079 N. Hwy. 75, P.O. Box 460, 87553-0460. Tel: 505-587-2111 (Res); 505-587-0399 (Office); Fax: 505-587-2188.
Catechesis/Religious Program—Tel: 505-587-2216. Joyce Kilgore, D.R.E. Students 169.
Mission—Santa Cruz Mission Chamisal, Taos Co.
Mission—San Acacio Mission Llano Largo, Taos Co.
Mission—Sagrado Corazon Mission Rio Lucio, Taos Co.
Mission—Nuestra Senora de los Dolores Mission Vadito, Taos Co.
Mission—San Lorenzo Mission Picuris Indian Pueblo, Taos Co.
Mission—San Juan Nepomuceno Mission Llano San Juan, Taos Co.
Mission—Nuestra Senora de la Asuncion Mission Placita, Taos Co.
Mission—Santa Barbara Mission Rodarte, Taos Co.

PERALTA, VALENCIA CO., OUR LADY OF GUADALUPE (1970), (Hispanic), [CEM] Rev. Albert Gallegos, O.S.M.; Deacon Joe Trujillo, (Retired).
Res.: P.O. Box 288, 87042. Tel: 505-869-2189; Fax: 505-869-5850.
Catechesis/Religious Program—Tel: 505-869-6993. Betty Mascarena, D.R.E. Students 356.
Mission—Juan Diego Meadow Lake, Valencia Co.
Mission—Sangre de Cristo Valencia, Valencia Co.
Station—Valencia

POJOAQUE, SANTA FE CO., N.S. DE GUADALUPE DEL VALLE DE POJOAQUE (1959), (Spanish—Native American), [CEM 2] Rev. Jose Flavio Santillanes; Deacons John Archuleta; Pedro Garcia; Daniel Valdez; Reuben Roybal.
Res.: 9 Grazing Elk, Santa Fe, 87506-7140. Tel: 505-455-2472; Fax: 505-455-3849.
Catechesis/Religious Program—Tel: 505-455-2267. Donna Martinez, D.R.E. Students 228.
Mission— Nambe, Santa Fe Co.
Mission— El Rancho, Santa Fe Co.
Mission— Nambe Indian Pueblo, Santa Fe Co.

PORTALES, ROOSEVELT CO., ST. HELEN (1952), Rev. Tobin E. Hitt.
Office—Tel: 505-356-4241; Fax: 505-359-1721.
Res.: 1600 S. Avenue O, 88130.
Catechesis/Religious Program—Tel: 505-356-4241. Tom Sullivan, D.R.E.; Cathy Sullivan, D.R.E. Students 335.
Mission—University Catholic Center P.O. Box 2253, Roosevelt Co. 88130. Tel: 505-356-5615.

QUESTA, TAOS CO., ST. ANTHONY (1841), [CEM 6] Rev. Douglas J. Mitchell; Deacons Marcus J. Rael; Jose Leroy Lucero.
Res.: Box 200, 87556. Tel: 505-586-0470; 505-586-0471; Fax: 505-586-1755.
Catechesis/Religious Program—Tel: 505-586-0388. Students 175.
Mission— Cerro, Taos Co.
Mission— Red River, Taos Co.
Mission— Costilla, Taos Co.
Mission— Amalia, Taos Co.

RANCHOS DE TAOS, TAOS CO., SAN FRANCISCO DE ASIS (1936), (Hispanic), [CEM] Rev. Tim Martinez; Deacon Pat Delozier.
Res.: P.O. Box 72, 87557-0072. Tel: 505-758-2754; Fax: 505-751-3923.
School—(Grades K-6), P.O. Box 463, 87557. Tel: 505-758-1236; Fax: 505-751-4875. Deborah Anglada, Prin. Lay Teachers 6; Students 86.
Catechesis/Religious Program—Students 190.
Mission—N.S. de San Juan de Los Lagos Talpa, Taos Co.
Mission—N.S. del Carmel Llano Quemado, Taos Co.
Mission—San Isidro Los Cordovas, Taos Co.

RATON, COLFAX CO., ST. PATRICK/ST. JOSEPH (1891), [CEM] [JC] Rev. George Silva; Deacon Thomas Alderette.
Res.: 105 Buena Vista St., Box 278, 87740. Tel: 505-445-9763; Fax: 505-445-8621.
School—401 S. Fourth St., 87740. Tel: 505-445-3862; Fax: 505-445-3862. Sisters 2; Lay Teachers 5; Students 60.
Catechesis/Religious Program—104 Buena Vista St., 87740. Tel: 505-445-9563. Deacon Thomas Alderette, D.R.E. Students 120.

RIBERA, SAN MIGUEL CO., SAN MIGUEL DEL VADO (1804), (Hispanic—Native American), [CEM] [JC 7] Rev. Francis Malley.
Res.: P.O. Box 507, 87560. Tel: 505-421-2405; 505-421-2780 (Office); Fax: 505-421-2779.
Catechesis/Religious Program—Students 91.
Mission— [CEM] [JC] San Isidro Norte, San Miguel Co.
Mission— [CEM] [JC] San Jose, San Miguel Co.
Mission— [CEM] [JC] San Juan, San Miguel Co.
Mission— [CEM] [JC] Santa Rita, San Miguel Co.
Mission—San Antonio de Padua [CEM] [JC] El Pueblo, San Miguel Co.
Mission— [CEM] [JC] La Lagunita, San Miguel Co.
Mission— [CEM] [JC] San Isidro Sur, San Miguel Co.

RIO RANCHO, SANDOVAL CO.

1—CHURCH OF THE INCARNATION, Rev. Guy R. Roberts.
Mailing Address: 2309 Monterey Rd., NE, 87144. Tel: 505-771-8331.

2—ST. THOMAS AQUINAS (1974), Rev. Msgr. Douglas A. Raun; Rev. Michael DePalma; Deacons James Baca; Aston Bailey; Kenneth Hill; Rodger Ayers; David Little; Leroy Sanchez; Frank Smith. In Res., Rev. Scott Mansfield.
Res.: 1502 Sara Rd., S.E., 87124. Tel: 505-892-1511; Fax: 505-891-3044.
School—1100 Hood Rd., S.E., 87124. Tel: 505-892-3221; Fax: 505-892-3350. Sr. Mary Klessy, M.P.F., Prin. Religious 3; Lay Teachers 23; Students 392.
Catechesis/Religious Program—Tel: 505 892-1497. Students 1,300.
Mission—St. John Vianney 1100 Hood Rd., S.E., Sandoval Co. 87124.

ROY, HARDING CO., HOLY FAMILY-ST. JOSEPH (1918), (Hispanic), [CEM 4] Rev. Larry Brito.
Res.: P.O. Box 37, 87743. Tel: 505-485-9633; Fax: 505-485-9633.
Catechesis/Religious Program—Students 40.
Mission— Bueyeros, Harding Co.
Mission— Gallegos, Harding Co.
Mission— Sabinoso, San Miguel Co.
Mission— Mosquero, Harding Co.

SAN JUAN PUEBLO, RIO ARRIBA CO. (INDIAN PUEBLO), ST. JOHN THE BAPTIST (1598), Rev. Terrence P. Brennan; Deacons Eloy E. Martinez; Michael Salazar.
Res.: P.O. Box 1075, 87566. Tel: 505-852-4179; Fax: 505-852-9719.
Catechesis/Religious Program—Tel: 505-852-2270; Fax: 505-852-9719. Melany Gallegos, D.R.E. Students 250.
Mission— Alcalde, Rio Arriba Co.
Mission— Chamita, Rio Arriba Co.
Mission— El Guique, Rio Arriba Co.
Mission— Ranchitos, Rio Arriba Co.
Mission— [CEM] Estaca, Rio Arriba Co.
Shrine—Our Lady of Lourdes, Pilgrimage shrine.

SANTA CRUZ, SANTA FE CO., HOLY CROSS (1695), (Hispanic), [CEM] Revs. Ron Carrillo, S.F.; Jose Maria Blanch, S.F.
Res.: P.O. Box 1228, 87567. Tel: 505-753-3345.
School—Tel: 505-753-4644; Fax: 505-753-7401. Mrs. Cordelia Garcia, Prin. Sisters 2; Lay Teachers 10; Students 187.
Catechesis/Religious Program—Tel: 505-753-4567; Fax: 505-753-7401. Sr. Angelina Gonzales, O.P., D.R.E. (Elementary); Mrs. Lynda Martinez, D.R.E. (Junior & Senior High). Students 1,072.
Convent—Box 1137, 87567. Tel: 505-753-3340.

SANTA ROSA, GUADALUPE CO., ST. ROSE OF LIMA (1907), (Hispanic), [CEM] Rev. Irby "Nick" Nichols, M.Div.; Deacon Arsenio C. Sanchez
Res.: 439 Third St., 88435. Tel: 505-472-3724.
Catechesis/Religious Program—Tel: 505-472-3992. Sisters Helen Halligan, D.R.E.; Ann Kaufmann, D.R.E. Students 357.
Mission— Puerto de Luna, Guadalupe Co.
Mission— San Ignacio, Guadalupe Co.
Mission— Borica, Guadalupe Co.
Mission— Cuervo, Guadalupe Co.
Mission— Colonias, Guadalupe Co.
Mission— Pintada, Guadalupe Co.
Mission— Milagro, Guadalupe Co.

SOCORRO, SOCORRO CO., SAN MIGUEL (1615), (Native American—Hispanic), [CEM 8] [JC] Rev. John Daniel; Deacons Alfred Gilbert; Miguel Ybarra; Robert Jiron.
Res.: 403 El Camino Real, N.W., 87801. Tel: 505-835-2891; Fax: 505-835-1620
Catechesis/Religious Program—Joyce Aguilar, D.R.E. Students 239.
Mission— Lemitar, Socorro Co.
Mission— Polvadera, Socorro Co.
Mission— Luis Lopez, Socorro Co.
Mission— San Antonio, Socorro Co.
Mission— Alamillo, Socorro Co.
Mission— Magdalena, Socorro Co.
Mission— Kelly, Socorro Co.
Mission— Riley, Socorro Co.

SPRINGER, COLFAX CO., ST. JOSEPH (1882), (Hispanic), [JC] Rev. John Dear, S.J. (NY); Deacon Edward Clona.
Res.: 605 Fifth St., P.O. Box 516, 87747. Tel: 505-483-2775; Fax: 505-483-2518.
Catechesis/Religious Program—Elaine Valdez, D.R.E. Students 33.
Mission— Palo Blanco, Colfax Co.
Mission— Maxwell, Colfax Co.
Mission— Tinaja, Colfax Co.
Station—New Mexico Boys' School, Tel: 505-483-2775. Rev. Jacob McLeroy, Chap. (Detention Facility)

TAOS, TAOS CO., NUESTRA SENORA DE GUADALUPE (1801), (Spanish), [CEM] Rev. George Salazar; Deacons Donald Martinez; Jerry Quintana.
Res.: 205 Don Fernando St., 87571. Tel: 505-758-2095; Fax: 505-758-2745.
Catechesis/Religious Program—Tel: 505-758-9208. Students 224.
Mission—St. Jerome Taos Pueblo, Taos Co. 87571.
Mission— Taos Pueblo, Taos Co.
Chapel—El Prado, St. Theresa
Chapel—Canon, Our Lady of Sorrows
Chapel—Ranchitos, Immaculate Conception
Chapel—La Loma, San Antonio

TIERRA AMARILLA, RIO ARRIBA CO., SANTO NINO (1966), (Spanish), [JC] Rev. Salvador Aragon, O.F.M.
Mailing Address: Box 193, 87575. Tel: 505-588-7463.
Catechesis/Religious Program—Tel: 505-588-7473. Twinned with San Jose, Los Ojos.

TIJERAS, BERNALILLO CO., HOLY CHILD (1962), [CEM 9] [JC 2] Rev. Mark E. Granito; Deacons Jose Escandon, Pastoral Assoc.; John Rasinski; Larry Carmony.
Res.: Box 130, 87059. Tel: 505-281-1502; 505-281-2297 (Office); Fax: 505-281-0355.
Catechesis/Religious Program—Students 350.
Mission—Holy Child Carnuel, Bernalillo Co.
Mission—San Juan de Nepumoceno Chilili, Bernalillo Co.
Mission—San Isidro Escobosa, Bernalillo Co.
Mission— San Antonio, Bernalillo Co.
Mission—San Isidro Sedillo, Bernalillo Co.
Mission— Canoncito, Bernalillo Co.
Mission—, Bernalillo Co.

TOME, VALENCIA CO., IMMACULATE CONCEPTION (1739), (Spanish), [CEM] Rev. Jose A. Hernandez.
Res.: P.O. Box 100, 87060-0100. Tel: 505-865-7497; Fax: 505-865-7497.
Catechesis/Religious Program—7 Church Loop, Juan Diego Hall. Tel: 505-865-2958. Students 312.
Mission— State Hwy. 304 S., Casa Colorada, Valencia Co. 87002.

TUCUMCARI, QUAY CO., ST. ANNE (1910), [JC] Rev. Leo L. Padget; Deacon Robert Welch.
Res.: 306 W. High St., 88401. Tel: 505-461-2515; Fax: 505-461-3058.
Catechesis/Religious Program—Tel: 505-461-3568. Nancy Arias, D.R.E. Students 341.
Mission—San Antonio Logan, Quay Co.
Mission—Sacred Heart Nara Visa, Quay Co.
Mission—Our Lady of Guadalupe San Jon, Quay Co.

VAUGHN, GUADALUPE CO., ST. MARY (1936), (Hispanic), [JC] Rev. Hoi Tran.
Res.: P.O. Box 276, 88353. Tel: 505-584-2954.
Catechesis/Religious Program—Students 27.
Mission— Encino, Torrance Co.
Mission— Duran, Torrance Co.
Mission— Pastura, Guadalupe Co.
Mission— Pinos Wells, Torrance Co.

VILLANUEVA, OUR LADY OF GUADALUPE (1830), (Hispanic), [CEM 6] Rev. Francis Malley, Sacramental Min.
Mailing Address: P.O. Box 39, 87583. Tel: 505-421-2548; Fax: 505-421-2548. In Res., Sr. Helen L. Carney, O.L.V.M., Parish Life Coord.
Catechesis/Religious Program—Students 78.
Mission— Sena, San Miguel Co.
Mission— Cerrito, San Miguel Co.
Mission— Gonzales Ranch, San Miguel Co.
Mission— Leyba, San Miguel Co.
Mission— Aurora, San Miguel Co.

WAGON MOUND, MORA CO., SANTA CLARA (1882), (Hispanic), [CEM] Rev. Larry R. Brito; Deacon Charlie Duran.
Res.: P.O. Box 186, 87752. Tel: 505-666-2478; Fax: 505-666-2478.
Catechesis/Religious Program—Students 18.
Mission— Ocate, Mora Co.
Mission— Los Hueros, Mora Co.
Mission— Los Le Febres, Mora Co.
Mission— Watrous, Mora Co.

PILGRIMAGE SHRINES

ALBUQUERQUE
SHRINE—SHRINE OF ST. BERNADETTE, Formerly St. Bernadette 1800 Martha, N.E., 87112-3161.

CHIMAYO, SANTUARIO DE CHIMAYO, , Attended by Holy Family, Chimayo. , 87522.

SAN JUAN, OUR LADY OF LOURDES, , P.O. Box 1075, 87566.

Priests Serving Private and Public Institutions

SANTA FE. *Hospital & Prison Ministry*. Rev. John Shedlock.
New Mexico State Penitentiary. Rev. Ricardo Russo, O.F.M.
St. Vincent's Hospital. Rev. Arthur Jakobiak, Chap.

ALBUQUERQUE. *St. Joseph Medical Center*. Revs.

Christian T. O'Brien, O.Praem., James P. Huth, O.Praem.
Lovelace Hospital. (Vacant)
Presbyterian Hospital. Rev. Stephen A. Sanchez.
Prison Ministry. Revs. Millan Garcia, John Shedlock.
University Hospital. Rev. Pio O'Connor, O.F.M.
Veterans Administration Medical Center. Rev. David Klein, C.S.B.

LAS VEGAS. *State Hospital*. Attended by Immaculate Conception Parish.

LOS LUNAS. *Correctional Facility (State)*. Deacon Lorenzo Castillo.

SPRINGER. *New Mexico Boys School*. Attended by St. Joseph Parish, Springer.

On Duty Outside the Archdiocese:
Rev.—
Berg, Timothy

Absent on Leave:
Rev.—
Ortega, Eduardo

Retired:
Rev. Msgrs.—
McNiff, James
Salas, Sipio
Stadtmueller, Fred
Revs.—
Amiro, Raymond M.
Aragon, Ramon
Auman, Robert
Bayer, Leonard
Bolman, Anthony P.
Bortolotti, Serafino
Brand, Fred
Brown, Charles
Coughlan, Robert
Cuesta, Benedicto
Cushing, Alan
Debaenst, Emmanuel
DeFazio, Vincent
Falbo, Samuel
Flaska, John A., Jr.
Galli, Clarence
Hendren, Lucien
Jakobiak, Arthur
Jaramillo, Luis
Kapitz, Donald
LaVoie, Joseph
Rebold, John
Rivera, Guadalupe
Runnebaum, Conrad
Savard, Wilfred

Permanent Deacons:
Abeyta, Santos, Holy Family, Albuquerque
Adams, Alton, St. Alice, Mountainair
Aguilar, Gregory, Santa Clara, Pueblo
Alcouffe, Raymond, Immaculate Heart of Mary, Los Alamos
Alderette, Thomas, St. Joseph-St. Patrick, Raton
Allen, Charles, John XXIII, Albuquerque
Aragon, Raphael, Cannon A.F.B.
Aragon, Robert, St. Jude Thaddeus, Paradise Hills
Archuleta, Faustin, Our Lady of Fatima, Albuquerque
Archuleta, John, Our Lady of Guadalupe, Pojoaque
Archunde, Gregory, St. Francis Xavier, Albuquerque
Arellano, Romolo, La Santisima Trinidad, Arroyo Seco
Arquero, Albert, Nuestra Senora de Guadalupe, Pene Blanca
Avalos-Sanchez, Constantino, Holy Rosary, Albuquerque
Ayala, Jose, Our Lady of Guadalupe, Albuquerque
Ayers, Roger, St. Tomas, Rio Rancho
Baca, James, (Retired)
Baca, Rudolph, Our Lady of Fatima, Albuquerque
Baca, Tomas, St. Michael's School
Bachechi, Victor, Annunciation, Albuquerque
Bailey, Aston, St. Thomas Aquinas, Rio Rancho
Ballard, Alphonse L., (Retired)
Barajas, Juan, Holy Rosary, Albuquerque, Stewardship, Evangelization
Barela, Felix, Our Lady of Belen, Belen
Barela, Ruben, Queen of Heaven, Albuquerque
Barry, William, St. Charles, Albuquerque
Beare, Harry, Holy Rosary, Albuquerque
Beaudette, James, San Martin, Albuquerque
Blea, Edward, Holy Family, Albuquerque
Broussard, Peter, John XXIII, Albuquerque
Bruckner, Donald G., St. Joseph on the Rio Grande, Albuquerque
Burkhard, Robert, San Clemente, Los Lunas
Bussemeier, Mark, Risen Savior, Albuquerque
Cabrera, Juan, Our Lady of Guadalupe, Albuquerque
Carmony, Larry, Holy Child, Tijeras
Carrillo, Andres, St. John the Baptist, Santa Fe
Casaus, Luis, Immaculate Conception, Las Vegas
Castillo, Lorenzo, St. Charles, Albuquerque
Cervantes, Jose de Jesus, Our Lady of Sorrows, Bernalillo
Chavez, Andrew, St. Francis Xavier, Albuquerque
Chavez, Daniel, Our Lady of Guadalupe, Clovis
Chavez, Ricardo, Risen Savior, Albuquerque
Chavez, Tiburci, St. Anne, Albuquerque
Chavez, Ubaldo, Holy Ghost, Albuquerque
Cleveland, Larry, Queen of Heaven, Albuquerque; Ministry to Deaf, Santa Fe
Contreras, Donald, Newman Center, Albuquerque
Contreras, Robert, Nativity of Blessed Virgin Mary, Alameda
Cooney, Patrick, Newman Center, Albuquerque
Cordova, Raynaldo A., Our Lady of Sorrows, Las Vegas
Cullen, Charles, Prince of Peace, Albuquerque
Delgado, James P., Our Lady of the Assumption, Albuquerque
Delozier, Patrick, Holy Trinity, Arroyo Seco
Dimas, Juan (Andy), St. John's, Santa Fe
Dohle, Albert, St. Joseph, Albuquerque
Duran, Charles, Santa Clara, Wagon Mound
Eklund, Bruce, St. Thomas Aquinas Newman Center, Albuquerque
Elsberg, Alexander, San Miguel, Socorro
Escandon, Jose, St. Bernadette, Albuquerque
Espinosa, Edward, San Clemente, Los Lunas
Esquibel, A. Edwin, Our Lady of Sorrows, La Joya
Facio, Manuel, Our Lady of Guadalupe, Albuquerque
Fraker, Steven, Prince of Peace, Albuquerque
Gagnon, Fabian, Lovelace Medical Center, Albuquerque
Gallegos, Eloy, Santa Maria, Santa Fe
Gallegos, Manuel A., Our Lady of Belen, Belen
Gallegos, Martin, Jr., Cristo Rey, Santa Fe
Garcia, David, Holy Trinity, Arroyo Seco
Garcia, Fabian A., San Juan Nepomuceno, El Rito
Garcia, Manuel, Risen Savior, Albuquerque
Garcia, Nestor, St. Edwin, Albuquerque
Garcia, Pedro, Our Lady of Guadalupe, Pojoaque
Garcia, Pilar, Queen of Heaven, Albuquerque
Gilbert, Alfred, San Miguel, Socorro
Gogan, Harry L., Annunciation, Albuquerque
Granato, John, Assumption, Albuquerque
Greivel, Rene, St. Anne, Albuquerque
Grossman, William L., St. Edwin, Albuquerque
Hackett, Hugh, Our Lady of Fatima, Albuquerque
Hall, Sandy, Our Lady of Fatima, Albuquerque
Henderson, Gregorio, San Jose, Albuquerque
Herrera, Diego A., Sacred Heart, Espanola
Herrera, Joseph, Holy Rosary, Albuquerque
Hietpas, Gerald M., San Felipe de Neri, Albuquerque
Hill, Kenneth, St. Thomas, Rio Rancho
Hoefler, William C., Ascension, Albuquerque
Jiron, Robert, San Miguel, Socorro
Johnson, Charles V., Holy Rosary, Albuquerque
Jones, Thomas E., Our Lady of Fatima, Albuquerque
Kazek, Chester, (Retired)
Kittredge, Michael, Holy Trinity, Arroyo Seco
Kneafsey, John, Holy Ghost, Albuquerque
Kollasch, William, St. Francis Cathedral, Santa Fe
Langner, Gerald, Immaculate Heart of Mary, Los Alamos
LeFebre, Pablo, St. Anne, Albuquerque
Lewis, Bob, San Felipe de Neri, Albuquerque
Little, David, St. Thomas, Rio Rancho
Lopez, Benjamin, Sacred Heart, Espanola
Lopez, Demetrio, Queen of Heaven, Albuquerque
Lopez, Jose O., Holy Family, Chimayo
Lovato, Frank, (Retired)
Lucero, Charles, San Jose, Albuquerque
Lucero, Donato, Dir. of Deacons; Immaculate Heart of Mary, Los Alamos
Lucero, Frank, St. Joseph on the Rio Grande, Albuquerque
Lucero, Jose E., San Felipe de Neri, Albuquerque
Lucero, Juan S., Estancia Valley Parish, Estancia
Lucoro, Leroy, St. Anthony, Questa
Luna, Desiderio, St. Edwin, Albuquerque
Maloney, Kevin, Annunciation, Albuquerque
Martinez, Donald J., Our Lady of Guadalupe, Taos
Martinez, Eloy, San Juan, San Juan Pueblo
Martinez, J. Robert, St. Bernadette, Albuquerque
Martinez, Jose Leroy, Our Lady of Sorrows, Las Vegas
Martinez, Juan K., St. Francis Cathedral, Santa Fe
Martinez, Leonard, Nativity, Albuquerque
Martinez, Lloyd, Sangre de Cristo, Albuquerque
Martinez, Robert, St. Bernadette, Albuquerque
McLane, Alfred, St. Bernadette, Albuquerque
Medina, Jesus, San Jose, Albuquerque
Menke, Maurice, San Felipe, Albuquerque
Meyerson, George, Incarnation, Rio Rancho
Meyrick, Earl, John XXIII, Albuquerque
Mishler, Richard
Moffett, Stephen, Estancia Valley Parish, Estancia
Montoya, Enrique, St. Anne, Santa Fe
Montoya, Filberto, Santa Maria, Santa Fe
Montoya, Macedon, Jr., Our Lady of Sorrows, Las Vegas
Montoya, Manuel, St. Therese, Albuquerque
Montoya, P. Louis, St. Francis Xavier, Clayton
Morrow, Robert, Annunciation, Albuquerque
Nguyen, Dung (Paul), San Jose, Albuquerque
O'Hare, John J., Our Lady of Belen, Belen
Olona, Edward, St. Joseph, Springer
Ortiz, Juan, San Clemente, Los Lunas
Ortwerth, Paul, Sangre de Cristo, Albuquerque
Pacheco, Carlos Felix, Our Lady of Guadalupe, Santa Fe
Pacheco, Charles, Immaculate Heart of Mary, Los Alamos
Padilla, Enrique, Our Lady of Sorrows, Bernalillo
Padilla, Julian, Queen of Heaven, Albuquerque
Palmer, Terry, St. Bernadette, Albuquerque
Perez, Frank, Holy Rosary, Albuquerque
Perez, Tomas, Sacred Heart, Albuquerque
Porto, Tony, (Retired)
Pullings, Harold, Our Lady of Guadalupe, Clovis
Quintana, Jerry, Our Lady of Guadalupe, Taos
Rael, Marcus, St. Anthony, Questa
Rangel, Stephen, St. Jude, Albuquerque
Rasinski, John, Holy Child, Tijeras
Rodriguez, Antonio, St. John the Baptist, Santa Fe
Rodriguez, Juan, Santa Maria de la Paz, Santa Fe
Rodriguez, Juan A., Sacred Heart, Clovis
Rodriguez, Randall, Cristo Rey, Santa Fe
Rowley, Michael, Sacred Heart, Clovis
Roybal, Christobel, St. Gertrude, Mora
Roybal, Reuben, Our Lady of Guadalupe, Santa Fe
Roybal, Richard, St. Anthony, Pecos
Russo, John L., John XXIII Catholic Community, Albuquerque
Salazar, Miguel, St. John, Santa Fe
Salazar, Phillip, Incarnation, Rio Rancho
Salazar, Samuel, San Miguel, Ribera
Sanchez, Arsenio, St. Rose of Lima, Santa Rosa
Sanchez, Leroy, St. Thomas, Rio Rancho
Sanchez, Norbert C., Our Lady of Belen, Belen
Sanchez, Robert, Our Lady of Belen, Belen
Sandoval, Alberto, San Antonio de Padua, Penasco
Sandoval, George, Immaculate Conception, Albuquerque
Santana, Joe, St. Bernadette, Albuquerque
Santistevan, Patrick, San Martin de Porres, Albuquerque
Santistevan, Peter, Our Lady of Sorrows, Bernalillo
Schultz, Ronald, St. Charles, Albuquerque
Schwenn, Charles E., St. Joseph, Cerrillos
See, Frank C., Our Lady of Fatima, Albuquerque
Segura, Jose, Our Lady of Guadalupe, Pena Blanca
Siegel, Michael, San Isidro/San Jose, Santa Fe
Sinatra, Kenneth, Risen Savior, Albuquerque
Smith, Frank, St. Thomas, Rio Rancho
Snell, Jimmie, San Clemente, Los Lunas
Toliver, Jeffrey, St. Francis Cathedral, Santa Fe
Toquinto, Jesus, Ascension, Albuquerque
Torres, Edgar, St. Anne, Albuquerque
Torres, H. Esequiel, St. Therese, Albuquerque
Tourville, John, St. Edwin, Albuquerque
Trujillo, Alex, John XXIII, Albuquerque
Trujillo, Anthony, Our Lady of Guadalupe, Santa Fe
Trujillo, Joseph, Our Lady of Guadalupe, Peralta
Tuma, Eugene, St. Jude Thaddeus, Albuquerque
Valdez, Gilbert, St. Gertrude, Mora
Valdez, Jose, Our Lady of Guadalupe, Pojoaque
Valkenburgh, Thomas Van, Santa Maria de Paz, Santa Fe
Valverde, George, Our Lady of Guadalupe, Albuquerque
Valverde, Gilbert, Immaculate Conception, Albuquerque
Vigil, Ralph, Sacred Heart, Espanola
Villareal, Merce A., Admin., Sacred Heart, Espanola
Villarreal, Robert, Immaculate Heart of Mary, Los Alamos
Welch, Robert, St. Anne, Tucumcari
Wertz, John, John XXIII Catholic Community, Albuquerque
Wesley, Michael, Our Lady of Guadalupe, Albuquerque
White, Rue, Our Lady of the Assumption, Albuquerque
Wicker, Byron, St. Bernadette, Albuquerque
Ybarra, Miguel, San Miguel, Socorro
Zamora, Rudy R., Our Lady of Belen, Belen

INSTITUTIONS LOCATED IN THE ARCHDIOCESE

[A] SEMINARIES, RELIGIOUS OR SCHOLASTICATES

SANTA FE. *Sangre de Cristo Center*, 410 State Rd. 592, 87506-0070. Tel: 505-983-7291; Fax: 505-983-6963. Email: SANGRE@newmexico.com. Web: www.sangredecristo.org. Bros. William Clarey, F.S.C., Dir.; Joseph Schmidt, F.S.C., Assoc. Dir.; Sisters Helen Collier, C.C.V.I., Assoc. Dir.; Susan Kuse, S.N.D., Assoc. Dir.; Janet Schumacher, P.B.V.M., Assoc. Dir.; Cynthia Gray, Admissions Coord. Program of refoundation for religious and priests, under the administration of the Christian Brothers. Participants 68 annually. Brothers 2; Sisters 3; Total Staff 6; Layperson 1.

[B] COLLEGES AND UNIVERSITIES

SANTA FE. *College of Santa Fe* (1874), (Coed Four Year Liberal Arts College) , 1600 St. Michaels Dr., 87505. Tel: 505-473-6011; Fax: 505-473-6129. Email: admissions@csf.edu. Web: www.csf.edu. Dr. Linda Hanson, Pres.; Dr. Mark Lombardi, Vice Pres. Academic & Student Affairs; Dr. Tammy Gocial, Dean of Students; Rev. Wanda Kile, Dir. Campus Ministry; Rev. Joseph LaVoie. Brothers of the Christian Schools Brothers 8; Lay Teachers 268; Students 1,829.

[C] HIGH SCHOOLS, ARCHDIOCESAN AND PAROCHIAL

ALBUQUERQUE. *St. Pius X High School*, 5301 St. Joseph Dr., N.W., 87120. Tel: 505-831-8400. Lay Teachers 69; Students 1,050.

[D] HIGH SCHOOLS, PRIVATE

SANTA FE. *St. Michael's High School*, (Grades 7-12) , (Coed Day School) , 100 Siringo Rd., 87505. Tel: 505-983-7353; Fax: 505-982-8722. Email: mainoffice@stmikes.k12.nm.us. Web: www.stmichaelshs.org. Bro. Richard Kovatch, F.S.C., Prin. Brothers of the Christian Schools 4; Deacons 1; Lay Teachers 41; Students 781.

[E] GENERAL HOSPITALS

ALBUQUERQUE. *St. Joseph Healthcare Foundation*, 500 Walter, N.E., 87102. Tel: 505-727-2709; Fax: 505-727-7034. Email: conem@sjhs.org. P.O. Box 25555, 87125-0555. Affiliate of Catholic Health Initiatives. Total Staff 4.

St. Joseph Healthcare System, 1999 Broadway, Ste. 2600, Denver, CO 80202. Tel: 303-383-2746; Fax: 303-298-9690. Email: peggymartin@catholichealth.net. Jim Kaskie, Pres.; Sr. Peggy Martin, Senior Vice Pres., Sponsorship & Governance. Affiliate of Catholic Health Initiatives.

[F] SPECIAL HOSPITALS AND SANATORIA FOR INVALIDS

SANTA FE. *Villa Therese Catholic Clinic*, 219 Cathedral Pl., 87501. Tel: 505-983-8561; Fax: 505-983-8561. Email: vtcc@juno.com. Sr. Patrick Marie Bernard, S.C., Dir. Sisters of Charity of Cincinnati, Ohio 1; Total Staff 3; Patients Assisted Annually 6,500.

[G] SHELTER CARE HOMES

ALBUQUERQUE. *Good Shepherd Center, Inc.*, 218 Iron St., S.W., P.O. Box 749, 87103. Tel: 505-243-2527; Fax: 505-247-2207. Barbara Ischay, Pres. Direct Service Agency for the Homeless. Total Assisted 192,000; Total Staff 7.

Good Shepherd Manor, 10127 Guadalupe Tr., N.W., P.O. Box 10248, 87184. Tel: 505-898-0177; Fax: 505-898-9756. Bro. Gerard Sullivan, B.G.S., Admin. Sponsored by Bro. Mathias Barrett, Inc. of New Mexico. Shelter Care Facility for aged adults. Residents 40; Staff 21.

Marie Amadea Shelter for Unwed Mothers (Alternative to Abortion) , P.O. Box 708, 87103. Tel: 505-242-1516; Fax: 505-243-0402. Mrs. Dorothy Wickens, Dir. Home for unwed expectant women. Total Assisted 23; Total Staff 6.

[H] CARE HOMES FOR PHYSICALLY AND MENTALLY HANDICAPPED

ALBUQUERQUE. *Casa Angelica*, 5629 Isleta Blvd., S.W., 87105. Tel: 505-877-5763; Fax: 505-873-2786. Email: lturner@casaangelica.org. The Daughters of Charity of Canossa, Home for developmentally disabled children. Sisters 1; Residents 16; Lay Staff 47; Total Assisted 16; Total Staff 48.

[I] MONASTERIES AND RESIDENCES OF PRIESTS AND BROTHERS

ABIQUIU. *Monastery of Christ in the Desert* 87510. Tel: 801-545-8567; Fax: 419-831-9113. Email: porter@christdesert.org. Web: www.christdesert.org. Rt. Rev. Philip Lawrence, O.S.B., Abbot; Revs. Christian Leisy, O.S.B.; Bernard Cranor, O.S.B.; Ezequiel Bas Luna, O.S.B.; Luis Regalado, O.S.B., Prior; Fernando Hool, O.S.B.; Tomas Mitchell, O.S.B.; Odon Nguyen, O.S.B.; Francisco Alanis Rios Gabriel Cusimano, O.S.B.; Miguel Laguna Ochoa, O.S.B. Subiaco Congregation Monks 50.

ALBUQUERQUE. *Curia Juan Diego*, 1350 Lakeview Rd., SW, 87105-6178. Tel: 505-877-5425; Fax 505-877-1440. Email: ofmprovsec@aol.com. Web: www.olgofm.org. Very Rev. Larry C. Dunham, O.F.M., Min. Prov.; Revs. Gino Correa, O.F.M., Vicar Prov.; Don Billiard, O.F.M., Treas of Prov.; Charlie Martinez, O.F.M., Vocation Dir.; Nils F. Thompson, O.F.M. (VNN), Ministry of Word; Bros. Duane Torisky, O.F.M., Sec. of Prov.; Bruce Michalek O.F.M., Dir. of Devel.; George Ward, O.F.M., Guardian.

Legal Title: *Franciscan Indian Missions*

Legal Title: *Franciscan Mission Center*

Legal Title: *The Province of Our Lady of Guadalupe of the Order of Friars Minor, Inc.* Priests 48; Brothers 18; Postulants 4; Novices 3.

Little Brothers of the Good Shepherd, Villa Mathias-Foundation House, 901 Bro. Mathias Pl., N.W., P.O. Box 389, 87103. Tel: 505-243-4233; Fax: 505-764-9721. Brothers 9; Total Staff 2.

Santa Maria de la Vid Priory, 5825 Coors Rd., S.W., 87121-6700. Tel: 505-873-4399; Fax: 505-873-4667. Email: norbertines@norbertinecommunity.org. Web: www.norbertine~community.org Revs. Joel P. Garner, O.Praem., Prior & Vocation Dir.; Vincent J. DeLeers, O.Praem.; Eugene Gries, O.Praem.; James P. Huth, O.Praem.; Nicholas E. Nirschl, O.Praem.; Francis W. Dorff, O.Praem.; Christian T. O'Brien, O.Praem.; Rod Fenzl, O.Praem.; Bro. Dennis Butler. Canons Regular of Premontre (Norbertine Community), Sponsor of "Center for Spiritual Life" and Hermitage Retreat Priests 8.

JEMEZ SPRINGS. *Our Lady of Lourdes*, Formerly Our Lady of Lourdes Novitiate, P.O. Box 10, 87025-0010. Tel: 505-829-3586; Fax: 505-829-3706. Email servants@theservants.org. Web: www.theservants.org. Revs. Gregory McCormick, s.P., Servant Gen.; Paul Valley, s.P., Vicar General. Priests 2.

Formation House Tel: 505-829-3720; Fax: 505-829-3706

PECOS. *Our Lady of Guadalupe Abbey*, P.O. Box 1080, 87552-1080. Tel: 505-757-6415; Fax 505-757-2285. Email: guestmaster@juno.com. Web: www.pecosabbey.org. Revs. Christopher Zielenski, O.S.B., Temporary Admin.; Paul Meaden, O.S.B., Claustral Prior; Sam Dennis, O.S.B.; Colman Heffern, O.S.B.; Bernard Lebiedz, O.S.B.; Michael Leek, O.S.B.; Robert Lussier, O.S.B.; Andrew Miles, O.S.B.; Wilfrid Tunink, O.S.B. (Olivetan Benedictine Monks) Priests 9; Brothers 3.

[J] CONVENTS AND RESIDENCES FOR SISTERS

SANTA FE. *Discalced Carmelite Monastery*, 49 Mount Carmel Rd., 87505-0352. Tel: 505-983-7232. Sr. Rose Teresa, O.C.D., Prioress; Revs. Crispin Bietz, O.F.M., Chap.; Ricardo Russo, O.F.M., Chap. Solemn Professed Nuns 7; Extern Sisters 2.

ABIQUIU. *Monastery of Our Lady of the Desert*, P.O. Box 1040, 87510. Tel: 505-470-3407. Email: soeurjulie@aol.com. Very Sr. Julianne Allen, Prioress; Sr. Benedicta Serna, Sub. Prioress. Benedictine Nuns Subiaco Congregation Sisters 9.

ALBUQUERQUE. *Cristo Rey Provincial House*, 5625 Isleta Blvd., S.W., 87105. Tel: 505-873-2854; Fax: 505-873-0678. Email: fdccalb@aol.com. Web: www.fdcc.org. Sr. Anne Bosio, Prov. Supr. Canossian Daughters of Charity Sisters 40.

JEMEZ SPRINGS. *Cor Jesu Monastery* Motherhouse and Novitiate of the Handmaids of the Precious Blood. , 87025. Tel: 505-829-3906; Fax: 505-829-3423. Sr. John Paul, H.P.B., Mother Prioress. Perpetually Professed Sisters 23.

RIO RANCHO. *Felician Sisters*, Provincial House & Novitiate, 4210 Meadowlark Ln., S.E., 87124-1021. Tel: 505-892-8862; Fax: 505-891-3893. Email: cssfrrnm@nm.net. Sr. Mary Seraphine Moynier, C.S.S.F., Prov. Min. Assumption of the Blessed Virgin Mary Residents 40; Professed Sisters of Province 68; Total Assisted per Month 100; Total Staff 19. In Res Rev. Cecil Kleber, O.F.M., Chap.

[K] RETREAT HOUSES

ALBUQUERQUE. *Madonna Retreat and Conference Center*, 4040 St. Joseph Pl., N.W., 87120. Tel: 505-831-8196; Fax: 505-831-8103. Email: madonnacenter@archdiocesesantafe.org. Web: www.archdiocesesantafe.org. Marie Villahuevc, Dir. Total in Residence 2; Total Staff 4.

The Spiritual Renewal Center, Inc., 6400 Coors Blvd., N.W., 87120. Tel: 505-877-4211; Fax: 505-890-4110. Email: domreths@juno.com. Web: www.christdesert.org/dominican. Dominican Sisters (Elkins Park, PA), Center for Retreats. Sisters 2; Total Staff 3.

PECOS. *Our Lady of Guadalupe Olivetan Benedictine Abbey*, P.O. Box 1080, 87552. Tel: 505-757-6415; Fax: 505-757-2285. Email: guestmaster@juno.com. Web: www.pecosabbey.org. Rt. Rev. James Liprie, O.S.B., Abbot; Revs. Paul Meaden, O.S.B., Claustral Prior; Samuel Dennis, O.S.B.; Robert Lussier, O.S.B.; Bernard Lebiedz, O.S.B.; Andrew Miles, O.S.B.; Colman Heffern, O.S.B.; Michael Leek, O.S.B.; Wilfrid Tunink, O.S.B. Monastery. Priests 9; Brothers 4; Monastic Oblate Sisters 7; Total in Residence 17.

SANTE FE. *Immaculate Heart of Mary Retreat and Conference Center*, Mt. Carmel Rd., 87505. Tel: 505-988-1975; Fax: 505-988-3963. Email: barmijo@archdiocesesantafe.org. Ben Armijo, Dir.

[L] NEWMAN CENTERS

ALBUQUERQUE. *St. Thomas Aquinas (Newman Center) University Parish* 1815 Las Lomas Rd., N.E., 87106. Tel: 505-247-1094; Fax: 505-247-2933. Email: aquinasnew@aol.com. Web: www.swcp.com/newmancenter. Revs. Robert J. Keller, O.P.; Matthew T. Strabala, O.P. Total in Residence 4; Total Staff 9.

LAS VEGAS. *Highlands University Newman Center* 909 Eighth St., 87701. Tel: 505-454-6050. Email: s_lopez_c@hotmail.com. Attended by Immaculate Conception Parish, Las Vegas.

PORTALES. *University Catholic Center - St. Thomas More Chapel* P.O. Box 2253, E.N.M.U., 88130. Tel: 505-356-5615; Fax: 505-359-1721. Rev. Tobin Hitt, Chap. Total Staff 1.

[M] MISCELLANEOUS LISTINGS

SANTA FE. *Medjugorje Group*, 1010 A Calle Hermosa, 87505. Tel: 505-471-2229; Fax: 505-471-1920. Rosie Sweeney, Pres.

St. Michael's High School Foundation, 100 Siringo Rd., 87505. Tel: 505-988-2264; Fax: 505-988-2264. Mrs. Clarice Pick, Pres.

ALBUQUERQUE. *Annual Catholic Appeal Foundation of the Archdiocese of Santa Fe*, 4000 St. Joseph Pl., N.W., 87120. Tel: 505-831-8155; Fax: 505-831-8111. Email: lgarcia@archdiocesesantafe.org. Web: www.archdiocesesantafe.org. Linda J. Garcia, C.F.R.E., Exec. Dir.

Archbishop's School Fund, 4000 St. Joseph Pl., N.W., 87120. Tel: 505-831-8173; Fax: 505-831-8107. Email: cso@archdiocesesantafe.org. Web: www.nm.org/catholicschools. Carol Zonski, Pres.

Archdiocese of Santa Fe Catholic Foundation, 2201 San Pedro, N.E., Bldg. 2, Ste. 211, 87110. Tel: 505-872-2901; Fax: 505-872-2905. Email: cathfdn@aol.com. Mary P. Dunn, Contact Person. Total Staff 4.

**St. Bernadette Institute of Sacred Art*, P.O. Box 8249, 87198. Tel: 505-265-9126; Fax: 505-266-4678. Email: paulos@nmia.com. Web: www.stbernadette-abq.org/. Dan Paulos, Contact Person. Sponsors and supports Catholic art and artists.

Brother Mathias Barrett, Inc., dba Good Shepherd Manor, P.O. Box 10248, 87184. Tel: 505-898-0177; Fax: 505-898-9756. Email: brgsullivan@aol.com. Rita Adkins, Pres. Total Assisted 40; Total Staff 20.

Brothers of the Good Shepherd Inc. of New Mexico, 901 Brother Mathias Pl., N.W., P.O. Box 389, 87102-7103. Tel: 505-243-4238; Fax: 505-764-9721. Email: Chasschreiner@aol.com. Web: www.LittleBrothersoftheGoodShepherd. Total in Residence 9; Total Staff 2.

Caritas Deus Inc., P.O. Box 749, 87103. Tel: 505-243-2527; Fax: 505-247-2207. Property management nonprofit corporation.

Catholic Charismatic Center, 1412 Fifth St., N.W., 87102. Tel: 505-247-0398; Fax: 505-843-9147. Email: mcgarrysmjccc@aol.com. Web: www.asfccc.web.com. Sr. Martha Jean McGarry, I.H.M., Dir. Total in Residence 1; Total Staff 5.

Center for Action and Contemplation, P.O. Box 12464, 87195. Tel: 505-242-9588; Fax: 505-242-9518. Email: info@cacradicalgrace.org. Web: cacradicalgrace.org. Rev. Richard Rohr, O.F.M., Founder & Animator; Stephen Picha, Exec. Dir. Total in Residence 1; Total Staff 11.

Charity Unlimited, Inc., P.O. Box 389, 87103. Tel: 505-243-4238; Fax: 505-764-9721. Property management nonprofit corporation.

Dominican Ecclesial Institute, 1815 Las Lomas, N.E., 87106. Tel: 505-243-0525; Fax: 505-243-0005. Email: lumen@sprynet.com. Web:

www.op.org/dei. Rev. Michael T. Demkovich, O.P. Total in Residence 1; Total Staff 1.

Fraternidad Piadosa de Nuestro Padre Jesus Nazareno (Vacant) , 4000 St. Joseph Pl., N.W., 87120. Tel: 505-243-1811; Fax: 505-224-9495.

Good Shepherd Center, Inc. of New Mexico, 218 Iron St., S.W., P.O. Box 749, 87103. Tel: 505-243-2527; Fax: 505-247-2207. Total Staff 8; Total Assisted 190,000.

Good Shepherd Formation Center, Inc. of New Mexico, dba St. Joseph House Property Management Corporation for St. Joseph House, Novice Formation Centre for Little Brothers of Good Shepherd. , 1323 Espanola, N.E., 87110. Tel: 505-232-4546. Bro. Raphael Mieszala, B.G.S.

**The Marriage Enrichment Weekend Program, Inc.*, P.O. Box 94026, 87199-4026. Tel: 505-821-1571; Fax: 505-857-0065. Web: www.tmewpi.org. Ralph Johnson, Pres.

Norbertine Community of New Mexico, Inc., 5825 Coors Rd., N.W., 87121-6700. Tel: 505-873-4399; Fax: 505-873-4667. Email: santamariadelavid@hotmail.com norbertines@norbertinecommunity.org. Web: www.norbertinecommunity.org. Rev. Joel P. Garner, O.Praem. Total in Residence 11; Total Staff 4.

St. Pius X High School Foundation, Inc., 5301 St. Joseph Dr., N.W., 87120. Tel: 505-831-8423; Fax: 505-831-8413. Email: jlucero@spx.k12.nm.us. Web: www.saintpiusx.com. Dr. Mary McLeod, Prin. Nonprofit corporation for the financial support of St. Pius X High School.

St. Joseph Fertility Care Center, 4000 St. Joseph Pl., N.W., Lourdes Hall, #130, 87120. Tel: 505-831-8122. Email: angelgarcia@comcast.net. Angelique N. Garcia, Pres.

SPX Towers, 5301 St. Joseph's Pl., N.W., 87120. Tel: 505-884-1309; Fax: 505-889-2720. Allen Jackson, Contact Person. To generate funds for use as financial aid for economically disadvantaged children to attend St. Puis X High School.

Villa Mathias Inc., P.O. Box 389, 87103. Tel: 505-243-4238; Fax: 505-764-9721.

JEMEZ SPRINGS. *EDSA Charitable Trust*, Tel: 505-829-3586. Email: jcostner@primary.net. 4000 St. Joseph's Pl., N.W., 87120. Jackie Costner, Contact Person.

Fitzgerald Charitable Trust, P.O. Box 10, 87025. Tel: 505-829-3586; Fax: 505-829-3706. Email: manilasp@aol.com. Web: www.theservants.org. Very Rev. Peter Lechner, s.P.

RIO RANCHO. *St. Felix Pantry, Inc.*, 4020 Barbara Loop, 87124-1023. Tel: 505-891-8075. Sr. Seraphine Moynier, Contact Person. Total Assisted per Month 8,000; Total Staff 65.

RELIGIOUS INSTITUTES OF MEN REPRESENTED IN THE ARCHDIOCESE

For further details refer to the corresponding bracketed number in the Religious Institutes of Men or Women section.

[0170]—*Basilian Fathers* (Houston, TX)—C.S.B.
[0200]—*Benedictine Monks* (Our Lady of Guadalupe Abbey, Pecos; Abbey of Christ in the Desert, Abiquiu; St. John Abbey, College—O.S.B.
[1350]—*Brothers of St. Francis Xavier* (Baltimore, MD)—C.F.X.
[0330]—*Brothers of the Christian Schools* (Baltimore, Midwest & De La Salle Provinces)—F.S.C.
[0580]—*Brothers of the Good Shepherd* (Albuquerque, NM)—B.G.S.
[0900]—*Canons Regular of Premontre* (Norbertine Fathers and Brothers of De Pere, Wisconsin)—O.Praem.
[0220]—*Congregation of the Blessed Sacrament* (Province of St. Anne - Cleveland, OH)—S.S.S.
[0520]—*Franciscan Friars* (Our Lady of Guadalupe, St. John the Baptist & St. Barbara Provinces)—O.F.M.
[0535]—*Franciscan Friars of the Renewal* (Bronx, NY)—C.F.R.
[1240]—*Order of Friar Servants of Mary* (U.S.A. Prov. Chicago, IL)
[0430]—*Order of Preachers-Dominicans* (St. Albert the Great Province)—O.P.
[1230]—*Servants of the Paraclete* (Jemez Springs, NM)—s.P.
[0690]—*Society of Jesus* (New Orleans Prov., Missouri Prov., Baltimore, MD)—S.J.
[0975]—*Society of Our Lady of the Most Holy Trinity* (Robstown, TX)—S.O.L.T.
[1200]—*Society of the Divine Savior* (Merrillville, IN)—S.D.S.
[0640]—*Sons of the Holy Family* (Silver Spring, MD)—S.F.

RELIGIOUS INSTITUTES OF WOMEN REPRESENTED IN THE ARCHDIOCESE

[0200]—*Benedictine Sisters* (Pecos and Abiquiu, NM)—O.S.B.
[0230]—*Benedictine Sisters* (Colorado Springs, CO)—O.S.B.
[0730]—*Canossian Daughters of Charity* (Albuquerque, NM)—Fd.C.C.
[1780]—*Congregation of the Sisters of the Third Order of St. Francis of Perpetual Adoration* (La Crosse, WI)—F.S.P.A.
[0420]—*Discalced Carmelite Nuns* (Santa Fe, NM)—O.C.D.
[1070-02]—*Dominican Sisters* (Columbus, OH)—O.P.
[1070-03]—*Dominican Sisters* (Sinsinawa, WI)—O.P.
[1070-13]—*Dominican Sisters* (Adrian, MI)—O.P.
[1070-17]—*Dominican Sisters* (Elkins Park, PA)—O.P.
[1070-14]—*Dominican Sisters* (Grand Rapids, MI)—O.P.
[1070-09]—*Dominican Sisters* (Racine, WI)—O.P.
[1170]—*Felician Sisters* (Congregation of Sisters of St. Felix of Cantalice)—C.S.S.F.
[1310]—*Franciscan Sisters* (Little Falls, MN)—O.S.F.
[1500]—*Franciscan Sisters of Mary Immaculate of the Third Order of St. Francis of Assisi* (Amarillo, TX)—F.M.I.
[1430]—*Franciscan Sisters of Our Lady of Perpetual Help* (St. Louis, MO)—O.S.F.
[1860]—*Handmaids of the Precious Blood* (Jemez Springs, NM)—H.P.B.
[2470]—*Maryknoll Sisters of St. Dominic* (Maryknoll, NY)—M.M.
[2690]—*Missionary Catechists of Divine Providence* (San Antonio, TX)—M.C.D.P.
[2760]—*Missionary Sisters of the Immaculate Conception of the Mother of God* (Paterson, NJ)—S.M.I.C.
[3130]—*Our Lady of Victory Missionary Sisters* (Huntington, IN)—O.L.V.M.
[3430]—*Religious Teahers Filippine* (St. Lucy Filippine Province, Morristown, NJ)—M.P.F.
[]—*Sisters for Christian Community*—S.F.C.C.
[0430]—*Sisters of Charity of Blessed Virgin Mary* (Dubuque, IA)—B.V.M.
[0440]—*Sisters of Charity of Cincinnati, Ohio* (Mt. St. Joseph, OH)—S.C.
[0480]—*Sisters of Charity of Leavenworth, Kansas*—S.C.L.
[0460]—*Sisters of Charity of the Incarnate Word* (San Antonio, TX)—C.C.V.I.
[0660]—*Sisters of Christian Charity* (Wilmette, IL)—S.C.C.
[0990]—*Sisters of Divine Providence* (Allison Park, PA)—C.D.P.
[2360]—*Sisters of Loretto at the Foot of the Cross* (Denver, CO)—S.L.
[2575]—*Sisters of Mercy of the Americas* (Omaha, NE)—R.S.M.
[2990]—*Sisters of Notre Dame* (Toledo, OH)—S.N.D.
[]—*Sisters of Our Lady of Guadalupe & St. Joseph*—H.N.S.G.
[0230]—*Sisters of Pontifical Jurisdiction* (Colorado Springs, CO)—O.S.B.
[1705]—*The Sisters of St. Francis of Assisi* (Milwaukee, WI)—O.S.F.
[1620]—*Sisters of St. Francis of Millvale, PA*—O.S.F.
[1630]—*Sisters of St. Francis of Penance and Christian Charity* (Sacred Heart & Holy Name Provinces)—O.S.F.
[1640]—*Sisters of St. Francis of Perpetual Adoration* (St. Joseph Province, Colorado Springs, CO)—O.S.F.
[1530]—*Sisters of St. Francis of the Congregation of Our Lady of Lourdes, Sylvania, Ohio*—O.S.F.
[3830-01]—*Sisters of St. Joseph* (Boston, MA)—C.S.J.
[3830-11]—*Sisters of St. Joseph of Nazareth* (Nazareth, MI)—S.S.J.
[0260]—*Sisters of the Blessed Sacrament for Indians and Colored People* (Bensalem, PA)—S.B.S
[3320]—*Sisters of the Presentation of B.V.M.* (Aberdeen, SD)—P.B.V.M.
[3670]—*Sisters of the Sacred Heart of Jesus* (San Antonio, TX)—S.S.C.J.
[1760]—*Sisters of the Third Order of St. Francis of Penance and Charity* (Tiffin, OH)—O.S.F.
[1720]—*Sisters of the Third Order Regular of St. Francis of the Congregation of Our Lady of Lourdes* (Rochester, MN)—O.S.F.
[2150-60]—*Sisters, Servants of the Immaculate Heart of Mary* (Monroe, MI; Scranton, PA)—I.H.M.
[3105]—*Society of Our Lady of the Most Holy Trinity* (Skidmore, TX)—S.O.L.T.
[4120]—*Ursuline Nuns, of the Congregation of Paris* (Maple Mount, KY)—O.S.U.

ARCHDIOCESAN CEMETERIES

ALBUQUERQUE. *Archdiocesan Cemetery Association*, 4000 St. Joseph Pl., N.W., 87120. Tel: 505-831-8100. Operates Rosario Cemetery, Santa Fe; Mount Calvary & Gate of Heaven, Albuquerque.

Catholic Cemetery Association, 4000 St. Joseph Pl., N.W., 87120. Tel: 505-831-8100.

NECROLOGY

† Hill, Rev. Msgr. Peter J., (Retired)—Died July 26, 2003
† Anstiss, Arthur, (Retired)—Died Nov. 17, 2003
† Fitzgerald, John W., (Retired)—Died March 23, 2003
† Hendriks, Boniface, (Retired)—Died Nov. 9, 2003

Diocese of Santa Rosa in California

(Dioecesis Sanctae Rosae in California)

Most Reverend

DANIEL F. WALSH, D.D.

Bishop of Santa Rosa in California; ordained March 30, 1963; appointed Titular Bishop of Tigia and Auxiliary of San Francisco September 24, 1981; appointed Bishop of Reno-Las Vegas June 9, 1987; installed August 6, 1987; appointed Bishop of Las Vegas March 21, 1995; installed July 28, 1995; appointed Bishop of Santa Rosa in California on April 4, 2000; installed May 22, 2000 *Res.: 320 Tenth St., Santa Rosa, CA 95401.*

Most Reverend

G. PATRICK ZIEMANN, D.D.

Retired Bishop of Santa Rosa; ordained April 29, 1967; appointed Titular Bishop of Obba and Auxiliary of Los Angeles on December 29, 1986; ordained Bishop on February 23, 1987; appointed Bishop of Santa Rosa July 14, 1992; resigned July 22, 1999

Chancery Office: 320 Tenth St., P.O. Box 1297, Santa Rosa, CA 95402-1297. Tel: 707-545-7610; Fax: 707-542-9702.

Web: www.santarosacatholic.org

ESTABLISHED FEBRUARY 21, 1962.

Square Miles 11,711.

Comprises six Counties in the State of California-viz., Del Norte, Humboldt, Lake, Mendocino, Napa and Sonoma.

Legal Title: "The Roman Catholic Bishop of Santa Rosa, a Corporation Sole" and "The Roman Catholic Welfare Corporation of Santa Rosa."

For legal titles of parishes and diocesan institutions, consult the Chancery Office.

STATISTICAL OVERVIEW

Personnel	
Bishop	1
Retired Bishops	1
Priests: Diocesan Active in Diocese	63
Priests: Diocesan Active Outside Diocese	7
Priests: Retired, Sick or Absent	19
Number of Diocesan Priests	89
Religious Priests in Diocese	10
Total Priests in Diocese	99
Extern Priests in Diocese	10
Permanent Deacons in Diocese	35
Total Brothers	38
Total Sisters	50
Parishes	
Parishes	42
With Resident Pastor:	
Resident Diocesan Priests	40
Without Resident Pastor:	
Administered by Priests	1
Administered by Religious Women	1
Missions	20
Pastoral Centers	13
Professional Ministry Personnel:	
Brothers	1
Sisters	4
Lay Ministers	35
Welfare	
Catholic Hospitals	5
Total Assisted	540,967
Homes for the Aged	1
Total Assisted	53
Residential Care of Children	1
Total Assisted	119
Day Care Centers	1
Total Assisted	75
Special Centers for Social Services	39
Total Assisted	60,751
Educational	
High Schools, Diocesan and Parish	2
Total Students	777
High Schools, Private	4
Total Students	1,149
Elementary Schools, Diocesan and Parish	11
Total Students	2,618
Elementary Schools, Private	2
Total Students	175
Catechesis/Religious Education:	
High School Students	1,682
Elementary Students	5,556
Total Students under Catholic Instruction	11,957
Teachers in the Diocese:	
Priests	1
Brothers	2
Sisters	2
Lay Teachers	329
Vital Statistics	
Receptions into the Church:	
Infant Baptism Totals	3,577
Adult Baptism Totals	122
Received into Full Communion	114
First Communions	2,488
Confirmations	956
Marriages:	
Catholic	508
Interfaith	173
Total Marriages	681
Deaths	971
Total Catholic Population	154,060
Total Population	753,893

Former Bishops—Most Revs. LEO T. MAHER, D.D., ord. Dec. 18, 1943; appt. First Bishop of Santa Rosa, Feb. 21, 1962; consecrated April 5, 1962; translated San Diego, Aug. 27, 1969; died Feb. 23, 1991; MARK J. HURLEY, D.D., Ph.D., J.C.B., LL.D., ord. Sept. 23, 1944; appt. Titular Bishop of Thunusuda and Auxiliary of San Francisco, Oct. 12, 1967; consecrated Jan. 4, 1968; translated Santa Rosa, Nov. 9, 1969; appt. member of the Vatican Secretariat for Non-Believers, consultor to the Congregation for Catholic Education; resigned as Bishop of Santa Rosa, April 15, 1986; died Feb. 5, 2001; JOHN T. STEINBOCK, D.D., ord. May 1, 1963; Titular Bishop of Midila and Auxiliary Bishop of Orange; appt. May 29, 1984; translated Santa Rosa, March 31, 1987; translated Fresno, Nov. 25, 1991; G. PATRICK ZIEMANN, D.D., ord. April 29, 1967; appt. Titular Bishop of Obba and Auxiliary Bishop of Los Angeles, Dec. 29, 1986; ord. Bishop, Feb. 23, 1987; appt. Bishop of Santa Rosa, July 14, 1992; resigned as Bishop of Santa Rosa, July 21, 1999.

Chancery Office—320 Tenth St., P.O. Box 1297, Santa Rosa, 95402-1297. Tel: 707-545-7610; Fax: 707-542-9702. Office Hours: Mon.-Fri. 8:30-4:30; All applications for dispensations, faculties, etc., and all correspondence should be addressed to the Chancery Office.

Vicar General—Rev. Msgr. JAMES E. PULSKAMP, V.G.

Members of the Curia—Rev. Msgrs. JOHN J. BRENKLE, J.C.D.; JAMES E. PULSKAMP, V.G.; Revs. DANIEL P. WHELTON, J.C.L.; GEORGE RISDEN; GARY LOMBARDI; TED OSWALD; DAVID SHAW; PATRICK STEPHENSON; LOREN ALLEN.

Deans—Revs. DAVID SHAW, Sonoma-North; PATRICK STEPHENSON, Napa; GARY LOMBARDI, Sonoma-South; TED OSWALD, Mendocino-Lake; GEORGE RISDEN, Humboldt-Del Norte.

Chancellor—Rev. Msgr. JAMES E. PULSKAMP, V.G.

Director of Clergy Personnel—Rev. Msgr. JAMES E. PULSKAMP, V.G.

Vicar for Priests—Rev. DANIEL P. WHELTON, J.C.L.

Diocesan Finance Officer—Deacon MICHAEL URICK.

Secretary to the Bishop—PAM HAWKINS. Tel: 707-566-3325; Fax: 707-566-3310.

Diocesan Tribunal—P.O. Box 1297, Santa Rosa, 95402-1297. Tel: 707-566-3370; Fax: 707-566-3385.

Judicial Vicar—Rev. DANIEL P. WHELTON, J.C.L.

Adjutant Judicial Vicars—Rev. Msgr. JOHN J. BRENKLE, J.C.D.; Rev. FERGAL MCGUINNESS.

Promoter of Justice—Rev. STEPHEN J. CANNY.

Defender of the Bond—Rev. DAVID SHAW.

Diocesan Judges—Rev. Msgrs. JOHN J. BRENKLE, J.C.D.; JAMES P. GAFFEY; Revs. JOHN CREWS; WILLIAM E. DUGGAN, J.C.L. (Retired); FERGAL MCGUINNESS; DANIEL P. WHELTON, J.C.L.

Advocates—Revs. MICHAEL M. KELLY; RAMON PONS; WALTER ROGINA; Sr. MAURA MURPHY, O.S.U.

Auditor—Sr. ROSE MARY KUKLOK, O.S.B.

Notaries—Rev. Msgr. JAMES E. PULSKAMP, V.G.; PAM HAWKINS.

Board of Consultors—Rev. Msgrs. JOHN J. BRENKLE, J.C.D.; JAMES E. PULSKAMP, V.G.; Revs. LOREN ALLEN; GEORGE RISDEN; GARY LOMBARDI; TED OSWALD; DAVID SHAW; PATRICK STEPHENSON; DANIEL P. WHELTON, J.C.L.

Priests' Council—Rev. Msgrs. JAMES E. PULSKAMP, V.G.; JOHN J. BRENKLE, J.C.D.; Revs. LOREN ALLEN; GARY LOMBARDI; DAVID SHAW; PATRICK STEPHENSON; TED OSWALD; GEORGE RISDEN; DANIEL P. WHELTON, J.C.L.; FRANK EPPERSON; ANDREW METCALF; LOUIS NICHOLS; Rev. Msgr. JOHN J. O'HARE (Retired); Rev. OSCAR DIAZ.

Finance Committee—Rev. Msgrs. JOHN J. BRENKLE, J.C.D.; JAMES P. GAFFEY; JAMES E. PULSKAMP, V.G.; Rev. GARY LOMBARDI; Deacon JIM HERCHER; Sr. KAREN CLOCK, C.S.J.; JUDY BARRETT; CLEM CARINALLI; WILLIAM CORNELISON; JAMES DILLON; PEGGY FURTH; BARBARA HILL; PAUL LESAGE; MARY LEITTEM-THOMAS; JOHN MOYNIER; MARY O'BRIEN;

VALARIE PRESTON; RICK ROSA; JOSEPH SCHUNK.

Diocesan Building Committee—WILLIAM CORNELISON, Chm.; Rev. Msgrs. JAMES E. PULSKAMP, V.G.; JOHN J. BRENKLE, J.C.D.; ANTHONY BATTAGLIA; LOWELL ALLEN; TOM FELLENZ; ED RONCHELLI.

Diocesan Communications Committee—DEIRDRE FRONTCZAK, Chm.; JUDY BARRETT; MIKE CARTER; JAMES DILLON; SANDY HIMEL; BILL PEATMAN; VALERIE PRESTON.

Review Board—Rev. Msgrs. JAMES E. PULSKAMP, V.G.; JOHN J. BRENKLE, J.C.D.; LEONARD SCHWARTZBURD, Ph.D.; Hon. JOSEPH MURPHY; MARGARET FOCHA; FRANK M. HEFFERNAN JR.; CATHY HUGHES, M.F.T.; BOB MCKEEVER. Consultants: DAN GALVIN II, Esq.; JULIE SPARACIO, Asst. Coord.

Education and Prevention of Sexual Misconduct Committee—Rev. DANIEL WHELTON; Sr. OLIVE MURPHY, R.S.M.; JOHN COLLINS, Ph.D.; FRANK SIROKY; STANLEY CORDERO; JULIE SPARACIO; DAVID STEFFEN; JOANN CONSIGLIERI, M.A., M.F.T., 320 Tenth St., P.O. Box 1297, Santa Rosa, 95402-1297. Tel: 707-545-7610.

Diocesan Offices and Directors

AIDS Ministry Outreach—Rev. RODNEY DEMARTINI, P.O. Box 960, Occidental, 95465. Tel: 707-874-1344.

Archivist—Rev. Msgr. JAMES E. PULSKAMP, V.G., 320 Tenth St., P.O. Box 1297, Santa Rosa, 95402-1297. Tel: 707-566-3312.

Assistance Coordinator—JULIE SPARACIO, 320 Tenth St., P.O. Box 1297, Santa Rosa, 95402-1297. Tel: 707-566-3308.

Attorney for the Diocese—DANIEL J. GALVIN III, Shapiro, Galvin, Shapiro, Piasta & Moran, 640 Third St., Santa Rosa, 95401. Tel: 707-544-5858; Fax: 707-544-6702.

Boy Scouts—Rev. ALVIN VILLARUEL, 2323 Montgomery Dr., Santa Rosa, 95405. Tel: 707-542-6984; Fax: 707-542-1621.

Catholic Charities, Central Admin. Office—MAUREEN E. SHAW, A.C.S.W, Diocesan Dir., 2325 Montgomery Dr., P.O. Box 4900, Santa Rosa, 95402-4900. Tel: 707-528-8712; Fax: 707-575-4910.

Catholic Community Foundation—JAMES DILLON, Acting Exec. Dir., 320 Tenth St., P.O. Box 1297, Santa Rosa, 95402-1297. Tel: 707-545-2311; 707-566-3357; Fax: 707-566-3310.

Catholic Youth Organization—KATHY DONLEY, Liaison, Office, 320 Tenth St., P.O. Box 1297, Santa Rosa, 95402-1297. Tel: 707-566-3349.

Cemeteries—Rev. Msgr. GERARD FAHEY, Dir., Office, P.O. Box 2098, 2930 Bennett Valley Rd., Santa Rosa, 95404. Tel: 707-546-6290; Fax: 707-546-2773.

Clergy Formation—Rev. RAY RIOUX, Dir., 1690 Janes Rd., Arcata, 95521. Tel: 707-822-7696; Fax: 707-822-6931.

Clergy Personnel Committee—Rev. Msgr. JAMES E. PULSKAMP, V.G.; Revs. LOREN ALLEN; MANUEL CHAVEZ; GORDON KALIL; MICHAEL M. KELLY; DAVID SHAW; Deacon JIM HERCHER.

Communications—DEIRDRE FRONTCZAK, Dir., 320 Tenth St., P.O. Box 1297, Santa Rosa, 95402. Tel: 707-566-3395; Fax: 707-542-9702.

Custodian of Records—Rev. Msgr. JAMES E. PULSKAMP, V.G., 320 Tenth St., P.O. Box 1297, Santa Rosa, 95402-1297. Tel: 707-566-3312.

Detention Ministry, Adult & Juvenile—24A Ursuline Rd., Santa Rosa, 95403. Tel: 707-544-9080; Fax: 707-544-9081.

Development—JAMES DILLON, Dir., 320 Tenth St., P.O. Box 1297, Santa Rosa, 95402. Tel: 707-545-7610.

Disabled—Chancery Office, 320 Tenth St., P.O. Box 1297, Santa Rosa, 95402. Tel: 707-545-7610.

Ecumenical and Interreligious Affairs—Rev. THOMAS W. DEVEREAUX, Dir., 208 Matheson St., Healdsburg, 95448. Tel: 707-433-5536; Fax: 707-433-1813.

Engaged Encounter—Coordinators:: BRAD PETERSEN; LORI PETERSEN, 30580 Gilmore Rd., Cloverdale, 95425. Tel: 707-566-3347.

Hispanic Ministry - South—Rev. OSCAR DIAZ, Dir., P.O. Box 178, Napa, 94559. Tel: 707-226-9379; Fax: 707-254-9262.

Hispanic Ministry - North—Rev. RAMON PONS, Dir., P.O. Box 430, Fortuna, 95540. Tel: 707-725-1148; Fax: 707-725-1149.

Cursillos De Cristiandad—Rev. RAUL LEMUS, Spiritual Dir., 208 Matheson St., Healdsburg, 95448. Tel: 707-433-5536.

Movimiento Familiar Cristiano—Deacon RODRIGO AGUDELO, Spiritual Dir., 3727 View Ct., Santa Rosa, 95403. Tel: 707-526-4892.

Renovacion Carismatica Catolica—Rev. JOSE GONZALEZ, Dir., 303 Stony Point Rd., Santa Rosa, 95401. Tel: 707-544-7272.

National Council of Catholic Women—Sr. ANTONIA KILLIAN, S.M., Spiritual Dir., 320 Tenth St., P.O. Box 1297, Santa Rosa, 95402-1297. Tel: 707-545-7610; Fax: 707-542-9702.

Newspaper—DEIRDRE FRONTCZAK, Editor, 320 Tenth St., P.O. Box 1297, Santa Rosa, 95402-1297. Tel: 707-566-3395; Fax: 707-542-9702. "North Coast Catholic".

Parish Priest Consultors—Rev. Msgr. GERARD BRADY; Revs. STEPHEN CANNY; MICHAELRAJ PHILOMINSAMY; MICHAEL M. KELLY.

Permanent Diaconate—Directors: Deacon JIM HERCHER; BETTY HERCHER, 320 Tenth St., P.O. Box 1297, Santa Rosa, 95402-1297. Tel: 707-566-3371.

Pontifical Association of Holy Childhood—Deacon KENNETH BEGIN, P.O. Box 1297, Santa Rosa, 95402-1297. Tel: 707-762-2367.

Propagation of the Faith—Deacon KENNETH BEGIN, P.O. Box 1297, Santa Rosa, 95402-1297. Tel: 707-762-2367.

Religious Education—Sr. OLIVE MURPHY, R.S.M., Dir., 320 Tenth St., P.O. Box 11574, Santa Rosa, 95406. Tel: 707-566-3366; Fax: 707-566-3320.

Respect Life—JUDY BARRETT, P.O. Box 618, Calistoga, 94515. Tel: 707-942-6143.

Schools—Dr. JOHN COLLINS, Supt. of Schools, Office, 320 Tenth St., P.O. Box 6654, Santa Rosa, 95406. Tel: 707-566-3311.

Vocations—Revs. THOMAS DIAZ, Dir., P.O. Box 1297, Santa Rosa, 95402. Tel: 707-545-7610; Fax: 707-542-9702; BRUCE LAMB, Dir. Seminarians, 61 W. San Francisco Ave., Willits, 95490. Tel: 707-459-2252; Fax: 707-459-0715.

CLERGY, PARISHES, MISSIONS AND PAROCHIAL SCHOOLS

CITY OF SANTA ROSA
(SONOMA COUNTY)

1—CATHEDRAL OF ST. EUGENE (1950), [CEM] Rev. Msgr. James P. Gaffey; Deacons W. Everett Woodruff; Michael Heinzelman. In Res., Rev. Alvin M. Villaruel.
Res.: 2323 Montgomery Dr., 95405. Tel: 707-542-6984; Fax: 707-542-1621.
School—300 Farmers Ln., 95405. Tel: 707-545-7252; Fax: 707-545-2594. Mrs. Barbara Gasparini, Prin. Lay Teachers 13; Students 350.
Catechesis/Religious Program—Tel: 707-542-1525; Fax: 707-542-1621. Diane Drew, D.R.E. Students 330.

2—HOLY SPIRIT (1964), Rev. Msgr. James E. Pulskamp, V.G.; Rev. Roger Lamoureux; Deacon Jim Hercher.
Res.: 1244 St. Francis Rd., 95409. Tel: 707-539-4495; Fax: 707-539-3343.
Catechesis/Religious Program—Bernard Ciernick, D.R.E. Students 175.

3—RESURRECTION (1967), Revs. David Shaw; Jose Gonzalez; Deacons Rodrigo Agudelo; Stephen Ellis. In Res., Rev. Fergal McGuinness.
Res.: 303 Stony Point Rd., 95401. Tel: 707-544-7272; Fax: 707-544-2901.
Catechesis/Religious Program—Tel: 707-544-0708. Betty Kovanis, D.R.E. Students 400.

4—ST. ROSE OF LIMA (1877), Revs. Denis A. O'Sullivan; Gerard Gormley; David Villalobos.
Res.: 398 10th St., 95401. Tel: 707-542-6448; Fax: 707-542-3359.
School—4300 Old Redwood Hwy., 95403. Tel: 707-545-0379; Fax: 707-545-7150. Kathy Ryan, Prin. Lay Teachers 14; Students 351.
Catechesis/Religious Program—Tel: 707-542-3080; Fax: 707-542-3359. Sr. Shelia Coffey, S.M., D.R.E. Students 280.

5—STAR OF THE VALLEY (1981), Rev. Msgrs. Thomas J. Keys; Gerard Fahey, Pastor Emeritus. In Res., Rev. Patrick J. Leslie, S.A.C.
Parish Center—545 White Oak Dr., 95409. Tel: 707-539-6262; Fax: 707-539-8620.

OUTSIDE CITY OF SANTA ROSA

AMERICAN CANYON, NAPA CO., HOLY FAMILY, Rev. Patrick Stephenson; Deacon Michael Simmons.
Res.: 402 Donaldson Way, 94589. Tel: 707-645-9331; Fax: 707-645-0424.
Catechesis/Religious Program—Tel: 707-554-1183. Lia Estupin, D.R.E. Students 121.

ARCATA, HUMBOLDT CO., ST. MARY'S (1883), [CEM] Rev. Ray Rioux; Deacon John Gai.
Res.: 1690 Janes Rd., 95521. Tel: 707-822-7696; Fax: 707-822-6931.
School—1730 Janes Rd., 95521. Tel: 707-822-3877; Fax: 707-822-6931. Susan Buchanan, Prin. Lay Teachers 5; Students 66.
Catechesis/Religious Program—Tel: 707-822-7696. Patricia Heavilin, D.R.E. Students 93.
Mission—St. Joseph Blue Lake.

BOYES HOT SPRINGS, SONOMA CO., ST. LEO (1966), Revs. J. Lawrence Carolan; Aurelio Villa, O.F.M.
Res.: 601 Agua Caliente Rd., Sonoma, 95476. Tel: 707-996-8422; Fax: 707-996-3984.
Church: P.O. Box 666, 95416.
Catechesis/Religious Program—Tel: 707-996-7503; Fax: 707-996-3984. Gloria Fetta, D.R.E. Students 220.

CALISTOGA, NAPA CO., OUR LADY OF PERPETUAL HELP (1915), Rev. Andrew Metcalf.
Res.: 901 Washington St., 94515. Tel: 707-942-6894; Fax: 707-942-1091.
Catechesis/Religious Program—Tel: 707-942-4769; Fax: 707-942-4681. Esperanza Pacheco, D.R.E. Students 87.

CLEARLAKE, LAKE CO., OUR LADY, QUEEN OF PEACE (1967), Rev. Louis J. Nichols (SY), Admin.; Deacon Ruben De Los Santos.
Res.: P.O. Box 460, 95422. Tel: 707-994-6618; Fax: 707-994-2223.
Catechesis/Religious Program—Helen Layne, D.R.E.; Carol Combs, D.R.E. Students 115.
Mission—Queen of the Rosary Lucerne, 95458.

CLOVERDALE, SONOMA CO., ST. PETER'S (1917), Rev. Robert Blake; Deacon Harry Martin.
Res.: 491 S. Franklin St., 95425. Tel: 707-894-2535; Fax: 707-894-9603.
Catechesis/Religious Program—Fax: 707-894-9603. Jeannie Barnes, D.R.E. Students 50.
Mission—Our Lady of Mt. Carmel Asti.

COTATI, SONOMA CO., ST. JOSEPH (1913), Rev. Stephen J. Canny. In Res., Rev. Daniel P. Whelton, J.C.L.
Res.: 150 St. Joseph Way, 94931-4117. Tel: 707-795-4807; Fax: 707-795-7851.
Catechesis/Religious Program—Tel: 707-795-7678; Fax: 707-795-7851. Georgette Parry, Parish Min. Dir.; Beverly Casella, D.R.E. Students 368.

CRESCENT CITY, DEL NORTE CO., ST. JOSEPH (1869), [CEM] Rev. George Risden.
Res.: 319 E St., 95531. Tel: 707-465-1762; Fax: 707-465-1763.
School—330 E St., 95531. Tel: 707-464-3477. Becky Wood, Prin. Lay Teachers 4; Students 60.
Catechesis/Religious Program—Students 30.
Mission—St. Robert and Ann Klamath.

EUREKA, HUMBOLDT CO.

1—ST. BERNARD (1864), [CEM] Revs. Loren Allen; Daniel F. Kassis; Ron Serban; Deacon Frank Weber.
Res.: P.O. Box 169, 95502. Tel: 707-442-6466; Fax: 707-443-0914.
Catechesis/Religious Program—Tel: 707-442-6466; Fax: 707-476-9286. Students 193.
Mission—St. Joseph

2—SACRED HEART (1963), Rev. Luis M. Penaloza; Ann Lynch, Pastoral Assoc.; Deacons Steven Justus; Anthony Viegas.
Res.: 2085 Myrtle Ave., 95501. Tel: 707-443-8429; Fax: 707-443-8420.
Catechesis/Religious Program—Larry McNeil, D.R.E. Students 100.

FERNDALE, HUMBOLDT CO., CHURCH OF THE ASSUMPTION (1878), [CEM] Rev. Robert L. Benjamin.
Res.: 546 Berding St., P.O. Box 1097, 95536. Tel: 707-786-9551; Fax: 707-786-9502.
Catechesis/Religious Program—Maura Eastman, D.R.E. Students 70.
Mission—St. Patrick Petrolia.

FORT BRAGG, MENDOCINO CO., OUR LADY OF GOOD COUNSEL (1890), Rev. Michaelraj Philominsamy.
Res.: 255 S. Harold St., 95437. Tel: 707-964-0229; Fax: 707-964-0728.
Catechesis/Religious Program—Tel: 707-964-5727. Kate Dougherty, D.R.E. Students 125.

FORTUNA, HUMBOLDT CO., ST. JOSEPH (1909), [CEM] Revs. James Trent (DET); Ramon Pons; Deacons Thomas Silva; Francisco Nunez; Jeffery Jacobs.
Res.: P.O. Box 430, 95540. Tel: 707-725-1148; Fax: 707-725-1149.
Catechesis/Religious Program—2292 Newburg Rd., 95540. Tel: 707-725-1216. Students 150.
Mission—St. Patrick Loleta.

GARBERVILLE, HUMBOLDT CO., OUR LADY OF THE REDWOODS (1950), Rev. Thomas Gowing, Admin.
Mailing Address: P.O. Box 115, 95542.
Res.: 515 Maple Ln., 95542. Tel: 707-923-7864; Fax: 707-723-7864.
Catechesis/Religious Program—Students 11.
Mission—St. Cecilia (1954), Leggett.

GUERNEVILLE, SONOMA CO., ST. ELIZABETH (1916), Rev. Gary Logan.
Res.: 14095 Woodland Dr., 95446-9553. Tel: 707-869-2107.
Catechesis/Religious Program—Tel: 707-923-7864. Students 11.
Mission—St. Catherine Monte Rio.
Mission—St. Colman Cazadero.

HEALDSBURG, SONOMA CO., ST. JOHN THE BAPTIST (1884), Revs. Thomas W. Devereaux; Raul Lemus;

Deacon Juventino Vera; Jon Jones, Pastoral Assoc.; Aimee Jones, Pastoral Assoc.
Res.: 208 Matheson St., 95448. Tel: 707-433-5536; Fax: 707-433-1813.
School—217 Fitch St., 95448. Tel: 707-433-2758; Fax: 707-433-0353. Sandra Passalacqua, Prin. Lay Teachers 14; Students 264.
Catechesis/Religious Program—Tel: 707-433-5112. Students 219.

HOOPA, HUMBOLDT CO., BLESSED KATERI TEKAKWITHA MISSION, Formerly Mission of Blessed Kateri Tekakwitha (1986), Unassigned.
Res.: P.O. Box 429, 95546. Tel: 530-625-4415; Fax: 530-625-4530.
Catechesis/Religious Program—Students 8.
Tekakwitha Center—P.O. Box 845, 95546. Tel: 530-625-4739. Sr. Patricia Carson, R.S.M., Dir.

LAKEPORT, LAKE CO., ST. MARY (1871), [CEM] Rev. Ted Oswald.
Res.: 801 N. Main St., 95453. Tel: 707-263-4401; Fax: 707-263-6325.
Catechesis/Religious Program—Tel: 707-263-0606. Lisa Lambert, D.R.E. Students 56.
Mission—St. Peter [CEM] Kelseyville.

MCKINLEYVILLE, HUMBOLDT COUNTY, CHRIST THE KING (1967), Rev. Stephen E.C. MacPherson; Deacon Robert Shell.
Res.: P.O. Box 2367, 95519. Tel: 707-839-2911; Fax: 707-839-9823.
Catechesis/Religious Program—Eva Adams, D.R.E. Students 65.
Mission—Holy Trinity Trinidad.

MENDOCINO, MENDOCINO CO., ST. ANTHONY (1864), [CEM] Rev. John J. Martin, Admin.
Res.: P.O. Box 665, 95460. Tel: 707-937-5808; Fax: 707-937-2476.

MIDDLETOWN, LAKE CO., ST. JOSEPH (1894), Rev. James McSweeney.
Res.: P.O. Box 1350, 95461. Tel: 707-987-3676; Fax: 707-987-2792.
Catechesis/Religious Program—Students 37.
Mission—Our Lady of the Lake Loch Lomond.
Station—Our Lady of the Pines Forest Lake.

NAPA, NAPA CO.
1—ST. APOLLINARIS (1957), Rev. Msgr. Joseph Alzugaray; Rev. Robert Castro; Deacons Francis Dahl; Joel Momsen.
Res.: 3700 Lassen St., 94558. Tel: 707-257-2555; Fax: 707-224-5400.
School—Tel: 707-224-6525. Patricia Granucci, Prin. Sisters 1; Lay Teachers 18; Students 320.
Catechesis/Religious Program—Tel: 707-255-7200. Sr. Peggy Cruise, S.M., D.R.E. Students 386.
2—ST. JOHN THE BAPTIST (1859), Revs. Gordon Kalil; Oscar Diaz; Rodolfo Gramajo.
Res.: Box 178, 94559. Tel: 707-226-9379; Fax: 707-254-9262.
School—983 Napa St., 94559. Tel: 707-224-8388; Fax: 707-224-0236. Ruth A. Matz, Prin. Sisters 1; Lay Teachers 18; Students 240.
Catechesis/Religious Program—Tel: 707-255-3533. Darlene Hirtz, D.R.E.; Eleanor Valenzuela, D.R.E.; Eustolia Valasquez, D.R.E.; Teresa Alguin, D.R.E. Students 425.
Station—State Hospital, St. Luke's Chapel Imola.
3—ST. THOMAS AQUINAS (1964), Rev. Msgr. Gerard J. Brady. In Res., Rev. Chinh Nguyen.
Res.: 2725 Elm St., 94558. Tel: 707-255-2949; Fax: 707-255-2439.
Catechesis/Religious Program—Students 113.

OCCIDENTAL, SONOMA CO., ST. PHILIP (1964), Rev. Walter Rogina.
Res.: P.O. Box 339, 95465. Tel: 707-874-3812; Fax: 707-874-9201.
Catechesis/Religious Program—Stephanie Larson, D.R.E. Students 35.
Mission—St. Teresa [CEM] Bodega.

PETALUMA, SONOMA CO.
1—ST. JAMES (1964), Rev. Michael A. Culligan; Deacons Ray Noll; Ken Manz; Kenneth Begin.
Res.: 125 Sonoma Mt. Pkwy., 94954. Tel: 707-762-4256; Fax: 707-762-4044.
Catechesis/Religious Program—Tel: 707-762-9063. Students 719.
2—ST. VINCENT DE PAUL (1857), Revs. Gary Lombardi; Abel Mena; Deacons James Carr; Armando Lemos; John Norris.
Res.: 35 Liberty St., 94952. Tel: 707-762-4278; Fax: 707-763-8188.
School—Howard & Union Sts., 94952. Tel: 707-762-6426; Fax: 707-762-6791. Susan Roffmann, Prin. Lay Teachers 15; Students 305.
High School—849 Keokuk, P.O. Box 517, 94953. Tel: 707-763-1032; Fax: 707-763-9448. Mr. Edward Kavanaugh, Prin. Lay Teachers 28; Students 378.
Catechesis/Religious Program—Rose Marie Woodruff, D.R.E.; Abraham Solar, D.R.E. Students 601.

POINT ARENA, MENDOCINO CO., ST. ALOYSIUS (1950), [CEM] Rev. Thomas P. O'Sullivan (SAC), Admin.
Res.: P.O. Box 66, 95468. Tel: 707-884-4920; Fax: 707-884-4920.
Catechesis/Religious Program—Students 17.
Mission—Mary, Star of the Sea Gualala.

ROHNERT PARK, SONOMA CO., ST. ELIZABETH SETON (1981), Rev. John Griffin; Deacon Joseph Olsen Jr.
Res.: 4595 Snyder Ln., 94928. Tel: 707-585-3708; Fax: 707-585-1201.
Catechesis/Religious Program—Tel: 707-585-8821; Fax: 707-585-1202. Alicia Slaugh, D.R.E. Students 121.

SAINT HELENA, NAPA CO., ST. HELENA (1857), [CEM] Rev. Msgr. John J. Brenkle, J.C.D.; Rev. Carlos Ortega; Deacon Robert Little.
Res.: 1340 Tainter St., St. Helena, 94574. Tel: 707-963-1228; Fax: 707-963-2894.
School—1255 Oak Ave., St. Helena, 94574. Tel: 707-963-4677; Fax: 707-963-4677. Jim Ritchie, Prin. Lay Teachers 6; Students 132.
Catechesis/Religious Program—Tel: 707-963-8290. Mary McKeever, D.R.E.; Maria Pena, D.R.E. Students 237.

SCOTIA, HUMBOLDT CO., ST. PATRICK (1930), Rev. Thomas Gowing, Admin.
Res.: P.O. Box 98, 95565. Tel: 707-764-5446.
Catechesis/Religious Program—Students 15.

SEBASTOPOL, SONOMA CO., ST. SEBASTIAN, Rev. Msgr. William Hynes; Rev. Perfecto Nacional (Philippines).
Res.: 7983 Covert Ln., 95472. Tel: 707-823-2208; Fax: 707-823-1098.
Catechesis/Religious Program—Julie Poirier, D.R.E. Students 126.

SONOMA, SONOMA CO., ST. FRANCIS SOLANO (1878), [CEM] Revs. Michael M. Kelly; Xavier Ochoa; Frank Epperson.
Res.: 469 Third St., W., 95476. Tel: 707-996-6759; Fax: 707-939-8128.
School—342 W. Napa St., 95476. Tel: 707-996-4994; Fax: 707-996-2662. Dr. Lydia Treadwell-Blecksmith, Prin. Lay Teachers 25; Students 340.
Catechesis/Religious Program—Tel: 707-996-6994; Fax: 707-996-2662. Leticia Perez, D.R.E. Students 199.

UKIAH, MENDOCINO CO., ST. MARY OF THE ANGELS (1887), Revs. Michael Cloney; Ismael Mora; Mary Leittem-Thomas, Pastoral Assoc.
Res.: 900 S. Oak St., 95482. Tel: 707-462-1431; Fax: 707-462-2879.
School—991 S. Dora St., 95482. Tel: 707-462-3888; Fax: 707-462-6014. Ms. Debra Cabral, Prin. Lay Teachers 12; Students 190.
Catechesis/Religious Program—Tel: 707-462-1131. Leslie Loopstra, D.R.E. Students 320.
Mission—St. Francis Rancheria Hopland.
Mission—St. Elizabeth Seton Boonville, Mendocino Co. 95415.

WILLITS, MENDOCINO CO., ST. ANTHONY (1923), Rev. Bruce Lamb.
Res.: 61 W. San Francisco Ave., 95490. Tel: 707-459-2252; Fax: 707-459-0715.
Catechesis/Religious Program—Students 49.
Mission—Our Lady, Queen of Peace [CEM] Covelo, Mendocino Co.

WINDSOR, SONOMA CO., OUR LADY OF GUADALUPE (1969), Revs. Angelito Peries, C.Ss.R.; Manuel Chavez; Deacon Paul Bromham.
Mailing Address: 8460 Alden Ln., 95492. Tel: 707-837-8962; Fax: 707-837-9157.
Catechesis/Religious Program—Dawn Graverson, D.R.E. Students 650.

YOUNTVILLE, NAPA CO., ST. JOAN OF ARC (1920), Rev. Mathew Ittiyappara.
Res.: Box 2009, 94599. Tel: 707-944-2461; Fax: 707-944-2202.
Catechesis/Religious Program—Students 89.
Mission—Holy Family Rutherford.

Chaplains Of Public Institutions

ELDRIDGE. *Sonoma Developmental Center*. Rev. Patrick J. Leslie, S.A.C., Chap.
IMOLA. *Napa State Hospital* 94558. Rev. James Lantsberger, O.M.I., Chap.
PETALUMA. *U.S. Coast Guard Training Center*. Rev. Donald R. Steed, M.M.
YOUNTVILLE. *Veterans Administration Home*. Rev. Paul F. Ledermann (OG), Chap.

Special Assignment:
Revs.—
Diaz De Leon, Juan Ramon
Kilianski, Edward, S.J.C.

Unassigned:
Revs.—
Donahue, William P.
McCormick, John
Talcott, Peter

On Duty Outside the Diocese:
Revs.—
Baptista, Diego
Boettcher, John
Diaz, Thomas K., M.A. (SFR)
Freed, Eric
Ruygt, Hans
Sumpter, Gary

On Leave:
Revs.—
Hernandez, Apolinar
Martinez, Luis
McAllister, Alex

Retired:
Rev. Msgrs.—
Fleming, Vincent A.
Monaghan, George D.
O'Hare, John J.
Serado, William
Tournier, Andre
Revs.—
Bernard, Andre
Bohner, Allan G.
Eagleson, Donald W.
Healy, John
Keffer, Thomas
Keogh, Thomas
McIntyre, Justin
Ryan, Philip
Sheehy, Wilfred
Thomas, Jerald
Tracy, Charles
Vallooran, Joseph

Permanent Deacons:
Agudelo, Rodrigo, Santa Rosa
Andrews, Bradley, (On Leave)
Begin, Kenneth, Petaluma
Bond, Ken, Arcata
Bromham, Paul, Windsor
Carr, James, Petaluma
Dahl, Francis, Napa
De Los Santos, Ruben, Clearlake
Duncan, Steve, (On Leave)
Ellis, Stephen, Santa Rosa
Fernandez, Jesus, Santa Rosa
Gai, John, Aracata
Heinzelman, Michael, Santa Rosa
Hercher, James, Santa Rosa
Jacobs, Jeff, Fortuna
Justus, Steven, Eureka
Lemos, Armando, Petaluma
Little, Robert, St. Helena
Manz, Kenneth, Petaluma
Martin, Harry, Cloverdale
Momsen, Joel, Napa
Moody, William, Palm Court, FL
Naumann, Richard, Mission Viejo
Noll, Ray, Petaluma
Norris, John, Petaluma
Nunez, Francisco, Fortuna
Olsen, Joseph, Rohnert Park
Ramirez, Arturo, Chehalis, WA
Robinson, David, Turlock
Shell, Robert, McKinleyville
Silva, Thomas, Fortuna
Simmons, Michael, American Canyon
Stanton, Charles, Mission Viejo
Vera, Juventino, Healdsburg
Viegas, Anthony, Eureka
Weber, Frank
Woodruff, W. Everett, Santa Rosa

INSTITUTIONS LOCATED IN THE DIOCESE

[A] SEMINARIES, RELIGIOUS, OR SCHOLASTICATES

NAPA. *Mont La Salle Novitiate*, 4405 Redwood Dr., 94558. Tel: 707-252-3821; Fax: 707-252-3731. Email: novitiate@dlsi.org. Web: www.delasalle.org. Bro. Richard Moratto, F.S.C., Dir. Brothers of the Christian Schools Brothers 1.

[B] HIGH SCHOOLS, DIOCESAN

SANTA ROSA. *Cardinal Newman High School*, 50 Ursuline Rd., 95403. Tel: 707-546-6470; Fax: 707-544-8502. Email: cnhsinfo@yahoo.com. Web: cardinalnewman.org. Dennis Crandall, Prin.; Rev. Alvin M. Villaruel. Priests 1; Lay Teachers 27; Students 399.

EUREKA. *St. Bernard's Catholic School*, 222 Dollison St., 95501. Tel: 707-443-2735; Fax: 707-443-4723. Email: pwdaly1964@yahoo.com. Patrick W. Daly, Prin.; Craig Brown, Campus Min. Lay Teachers

23; Students 262.
High School Campus Tel: 707-443-2735; Fax: 707-443-4723.
Elementary School Campus Tel: 707-443-2226; Fax: 707-443-2227.

[C] HIGH SCHOOLS, PRIVATE

SANTA ROSA. **Ursuline High School*, 90 Ursuline Rd., 95403. Tel: 707-524-1130; Fax: 707-542-0131. Email: cellis@ursulinehs.org. Web: www.ursulinehs.org. Carole Ellis, Prin.
Legal Title: *Santa Rosa Ursuline Corporation* Ursuline Sisters of the Roman Union Lay Teachers 36; Students 367.
**Ursuline Parent Association of Santa Rosa* Tel: 707-524-1128; Fax: 707-542-0131.
**Ursuline Memorial Scholarship Fund* Tel: 707-524-1128; Fax: 707-542-0131.

NAPA. *Justin-Siena High School*, 4026 Maher St., 94558. Tel: 707-255-0950; Fax: 707-255-0334. Email: schmitzg@justin-siena.com. Web: Justin-siena.com. Joseph W. Bracco, Pres. & CEO; Gregory J. Schmitz, Prin.; James Day, Vice Pres. Dean of Studies; Robert Bailey, Vice Pres. Dean of Student Affairs. Sisters 1; Brothers 2; Lay Teachers 51; Students 655.
**Justin-Siena High School Corporation, Inc.*
**Justin-Siena High School Foundation, Inc.*
**Kolbe Academy for Boys and Girls*, 1600 F St., 94559. Tel: 707-256-4306; Fax: 707-255-1581. Email: KOLBEACAD@EARTHLINK.NET. Web: www.KOLBE.ORG. Dianne Muth, Prin. Lay Teachers 2; Students 10.

[D] ELEMENTARY SCHOOLS, PRIVATE

NAPA. **Kolbe Academy for Boys and Girls*, 1600 F St., 94559. Tel: 707-256-4306; Fax: 707-256-4313. Email: dayinfo@kolbe.org. Web: www.KOLBE.ORG. Dianne Muth, Prin. Lay Teachers 3; Students 30.

[E] CATHOLIC CHARITIES

SANTA ROSA. **Diocese of Santa Rosa, Catholic Charities* Tel: 707-528-8712; Fax: 707-575-4910. Email: ccharity@sonic.net. Web: srcharities.org. P.O. Box 4900, 95402. Tel: 707-528-8712; Fax: 707-575-4910.
CENTRAL ADMINISTRATIVE OFFICES:, 2325 Montgomery Dr., 95405. Tel: 707-528-8712; Fax: 707-575-4910. Maureen E. Shaw, A.C.S.W, Regl. Dir.; Mary Ann McGee, R.N., Sonoma, Mendocino & Lake Counties; Sharon McCarty, Dir. Admin. Svcs. & Human Resources; Robert Mullin, Dir. Accounting Svcs. & Finance; Patsy Vincent, Dir. Devel. & Communication.
REGIONAL OFFICES:, 3295 Claremont Way, Ste. 1, Napa, 94558. Tel: 707-224-4403; Fax: 707-224-2889. Danda Winford, Regl. Dir., Napa.
2936 J St., Eureka, 95501. Tel: 707-444-9611; Fax: 707-444-9613. Charles Herbelin, Regl. Dir., Humboldt & Del Norte.
Humboldt/Del Norte Counties:
Professional Counseling Services of Humboldt/Del Norte, 2936 J St., Eureka, 95501. Tel: 707-444-9611; Fax: 707-444-9313. Charles Herbelin, Regl. Dir., Humboldt & Del Norte.
Pyramid, 2936 J St., Eureka, 95501. Tel: 707-444-9611; Fax: 707-444-9613.
Lake County:
Lake County Programs, Formerly Interfaith Volunteer Caregiver Programs 18713 Spyglass Rd., Middletown, 95461. Tel: 707-987-8139; Fax: 707-987-8139. Hedy Montoya, Prog. Dir.
Napa County:
Drug and Alcohol Prevention Services, 3295 Claremont Way, Ste. 1, Napa, 94558. Tel: 707-224-4403; Fax: 707-224-2889.
HomeBase, 3295 Claremont Way, Ste. 1, Napa, 94558. Tel: 707-224-4403; Fax: 707-224-2889. Kealoha Keliikoa, Dir.
Housing Options, 3295 Claremont Way, Ste. 1, Napa, 94558. Tel: 707-224-4403; Fax: 707-224-2889. Kealoha Keliikoa, Dir.
Rainbow House, 1209 Jefferson St., Napa, 94559. Tel: 707-258-0260; Fax: 707-258-0442. Judy Harrison, Prog. Mgr.
Teen Mom Program, 3295 Claremont Way, Ste. 1, Napa, 94558. Tel: 707-224-4403; Fax: 707-224-2889.
Sonoma County:
Alzheimer's Respite/Resource Center, 320 Tenth St., 95401. Tel: 707-528-8712; Fax: 707-575-4910. P.O. Box 4900, 95402.
1000 N. Gravenstein Hwy., Sebastopol, 95472. Tel: 707-528-8712; Fax: 707-575-4910. Ann McGee, Prog. Dir.
DeMeo House, 310 Ridgeway Ave., 95401. Tel: 707-542-5426; Fax: 707-542-3148. P.O. Box 4900, 95402.
Family Support Center, 465 A St., 95401. Tel: 707-542-5426; Fax: 707-542-3148. P.O. Box 4900, 95402. Sr. Kathleen McGrath, BVM, Prog. Dir.
Free-to-Be, 576 B St., Ste. B, 95401. Tel: 707-526-3819; Fax: 707-526-3851. P.O. Box 4900, 95402. Sue Bisbee, Prog. Dir.
Homeless Services Center/Brookwood Center, 600 Morgan St., 95401. Tel: 707-525-0226; Fax: 707-545-1920. P.O. Box 4900, 95402. Nick Baker, Prog. Dir.
Housing Counseling, 465 A St., 95401. Tel: 707-542-5426; Fax: 707-542-3148. P.O. Box 4900, 95402.
Immigration and Resettlement Services, 2325 Montgomery Dr., 95405. Tel: 707-578-6000; Fax: 707-575-4910. P.O. Box 4900, 95401. Vicki Mayster, Prog. Dir.
Parish/Community Services, 2325 Montgomery Dr., 95405. Tel: 707-528-8712; Fax: 707-575-4910. P.O. Box 4900, 95402. Michele Osmon, Prog. Dir.
Phase Two - Supportive Services, 465 A St., 95401. Tel: 707-542-5426; Fax: 707-542-3148. P.O. Box 4900, 95402.
Rural Food Program, 465 A St., 95401. Tel: 707-542-5426; Fax: 707-542-3148. Sr. Kathleen McGrath, BVM, B.V.M., Prog. Dir.

[F] VOLUNTEER SERVICES

EUREKA. *Society of St. Vincent de Paul, District Council of the Redwood Region*, 528 Second St., P.O. Box 1386, 95502. Tel: 707-443-8676; Fax: 707-443-6321. Email: dj-heinen@yahoo.com. Web: www.humstvincentdepaul.org. Gerald Bronder, Pres.; Dan Heinen, Exec Dir.

NAPA. *Society of St. Vincent de Paul, District Council of Napa County*, 386 Minihen St., 94559. Tel: 707-224-1384. Email: fitchpj@aol.com. Bob Cavagnaro, Pres.

ROHNERT PARK. *Society of St. Vincent de Paul, District Council of Sonoma County*, P.O. Box 1095, 94957. Tel: 800-584-1579; Fax: 707-586-8128. Email: SVPAUL@PACBEL.NET. Mr. Bob Solak, Pres.

[G] GENERAL HOSPITALS

SANTA ROSA. *Santa Rosa Memorial Hospital*, 1165 Montgomery Dr., 95405. Tel: 707-546-3210; Fax: 707-547-4685. Email: rwelling@srm.stjoe.org. Web: www.stjosephhealth.org. Mr. David Ameen, Pres. & CEO. Sisters of St. Joseph of Orange Corporation Sisters 3; Employees 1,883; Bed Capacity 346; Patients Assisted Annually 80,198.

EUREKA. *St. Joseph Hospital of Eureka*, 2700 Dolbeer St., 95501. Tel: 707-445-8121; Fax: 707-269-3897. Web: www.sjhshumboldtcounty.org. Mike Purvis, Pres. & CEO; Ken Meece, Area Dir. of Pastoral Care. Sisters of St. Joseph of Orange Bed Capacity 214; Sisters 3; Employees 1,250; Patients Assisted Annually 151,644.

FORTUNA. *Redwood Memorial Hospital*, 3300 Renner Dr., 95540. Tel: 707-725-3361; Fax: 707-725-7212. Web: www.sjhhumboldtcounty.org. Mike Purvis, Pres. & CEO. Sisters of St. Joseph of Orange Sisters 2; Total Staff 237; Bed Capacity 46; Patients Assisted Annually 46,422.

NAPA. *Queen of the Valley Hospital of Napa*, 1000 Trancas St., 94558. Tel: 707-252-4411; Fax: 707-257-4173. Email: PHaley@qvh.stjoe.org. Web: www.thequeen.org. Dennis Sisto, Pres. & CEO; Rev. Gerard Heintzelman (HBG), Chap.; Rev. Jim Warnock, Chap. (Lutheran Min.); Rev. Michael Angula (Nigeria). Sisters of St. Joseph of Orange, California Priests 2; Sisters 4; Lay Staff 1,343; Bed Capacity 179; Patients Assisted Annually 239,143.

PETALUMA. *Petaluma Valley Hospital*, 400 N. McDowell Blvd., 94954. Tel: 707-778-1111; Fax: 707-778-9117. Web: www.stjosephhealth.org. Sisters of St. Joseph of Orange Lay Staff 500; Bed Capacity 80; Patients Assisted Annually 23,550.

[H] RESIDENTIAL TREATMENT CENTERS

SONOMA. *Hanna Boys Center*, P.O. Box 100, 95476. Tel: 707-996-6767; Fax: 707-996-4742. Web: www.hannacenter.org. Revs. John S. Crews, Ed.D., Exec. Dir.; Gregory Klaas.
Legal Title: *Hanna Boys Center*, For underprivileged, emotionally disturbed and pre-delinquent boys, ages 9 to 18 years. Priests 2; Total Staff 136; Students 119.

[I] HOMES FOR SENIOR CITIZENS

SANTA ROSA. **Vigil Light Apartments (The Vigil Light, Inc.)*, 1945 Long Dr., 95405. Tel: 707-544-2810; Fax: 707-544-1219. Email: vigillight@worldnet.att.net. Sr. Teresita Poulin, BVM, Mgr. Sisters 1; Residents 53.

[J] CAMPS AND COMMUNITY CENTERS

DUNCAN MILLS. *St. Joseph Camp*, P.O. Box 198, 95430-0198. Tel: 707-865-2135; Fax: 707-865-1025. Bro. Raphael-Philip, F.S.C., Dir. Tel: 707-865-9304. Brothers of the Christian Schools

LEGGETT. *Camp St. Michael* (Boys - Girls) , P.O. Box 9447, 95405. Tel: 707-984-6877; Fax: 707-566-4665. Email: office@camp-st-michael.org. Web: www.camp-st-michael.org.

MIDDLETOWN. *Camp Salesian* 95461. Tel: 707-987-9700. *Office, Salesian Provincial Office*, 1100 Franklin St., San Francisco, 94109. Tel: 415-441-7144; Fax: 415-441-8151. Conducted by the Salesians of St. John Bosco.

[K] NEWMAN CENTERS

ARCATA. *Newman Community, Humboldt State University* 700 Union St., 95521. Tel: 707-822-6057; Fax: 707-822-6057. Email: Newman@ave.humboldT.edu. Web: www.humboldT.edu/newman. Rev. Louis Coddaire; Deacon Kenneth M. Bond.

PENNGROVE. *Newman Hall, Sonoma State University, Intercollegiate Catholic Ministries* 1798 E. Cotati Ave., 94951. Tel: 707-794-7957. Rev. Chinh Nguyen.

[L] HOUSES OF PRAYER AND RETREAT HOUSES

SANTA ROSA. *Angela Center*, 535 Angela Dr., 95403. Tel: 707-528-8578; Fax: 707-528-0144. Email: ANGELACENTER@juno.com. Web: www.ANGELACENTER.com. Sr. Christine Van Swearingen, O.S.U., Dir.
Cardinal Newman Retreat Center, 24 A Ursuline Rd., 95403. Tel: 707-568-6822; Fax: 707-566-3360. Richard Boyer, Mgr.

NAPA. *Christian Brothers Retreat and Conference Center*, 4401 Redwood Rd., P.O. Box 3720, 94558. Tel: 707-252-3810; 707-252-3811; Fax: 707-252-3818. Email: confctr@dlsi.org. Web: www.christianbrosretreat.com. Steve Taylor, CFO.

OAKVILLE. *Carmelite House of Prayer*, P.O. Box 347, 94562. Tel: 707-944-2454; Fax: 707-944-8533. Email: CARMELOAKVILLE@aol.com. Rev. John Reginald McSweeney, O.C.D., Dir.

[M] MONASTERIES AND RESIDENCES FOR PRIESTS AND BROTHERS

MONTE RIO. *St. Benilde Community*, 22410 Moscow Rd., 95462-0367. Tel: 707-865-9304; Fax: 707-865-3064. P.O. Box 367, 95462-0367. Bro. Raphael-Philip, F.S.C., Dir. Brothers of the Christian Schools Brothers 2.

NAPA. *De La Salle Institute/Provincial Office*, 4401 Redwood Rd., 94558-9708. Tel: 707-252-0222; Fax: 707-252-0407. Email: bsokol@dlsi.org. Web: www.delasalle.org. P.O. Box 3720, 94558-0372. Bro. Stanislaus Campbell, F.S.C., Pres. Brothers of the Christian Schools
Lasallian Education Corporation Tel: 707-252-0222; Fax: 707-252-0407.
District of San Francisco Christian Brothers Charitable Trust Tel: 707-252-0222; Fax: 707-252-7046.
Lasallian Education Fund, 465 California St., Ste. 640, San Francisco, 94104. Tel: 415-835-5969; Fax: 415-835-5943.
Holy Family Community, 4405 Redwood Rd., 94558-9708. Tel: 707-252-3887; Fax: 707-252-3842. Email: rroggenb@dlsi.org. Web: www.delasalle.org. Bro. Ronald Roggenback, F.S.C., Dir. Brothers of the Christian Schools Brothers 19.
Provincialate Community, 4403 Redwood Rd., 94558. Tel: 707-252-0802; Fax: 707-252-7046. Email: twestberg@dlsi.org. Bros. Stanislaus Campbell, F.S.C., Prov.; Thomas Jones, F.S.C., Asst. Prov.; Thomas Westberg, F.S.C., Dir.; Arnold Stewart, F.S.C., Sub Dir.; Rev. David L. Deibel, Chap. Brothers of the Christian Schools Brothers 8.

OAKVILLE. *Carmelite House of Prayer*, P.O. Box 347, 94562. Tel: 707-944-2454; 707-944-2460; Fax: 707-944-8533. Email: CARMELOAKVILLE@aol.com. Revs. John R. McSweeney, O.C.D., Supr.; Mark Kristy, O.C.D.; Michael Buckley, O.C.D.; John Melka, O.C.D.; Xavier Pappalliyil, O.C.D.; Bro. Roger Larre, O.C.D. Discalced Carmelite Friars Priests 5; Brothers 1.

SEBASTOPOL. *Franciscan Hermitage of St. Clare*, 6501 Orchard Station Rd., 95472. Tel: 707-792-5033. Brothers 1.

[N] CONVENTS AND RESIDENCES FOR SISTERS

SANTA ROSA. *Memorial Hospital Convent*, 271 Doyle Park Dr., 95405. Tel: 707-525-5235; Fax: 707-522-1558. Email: srmconvent@srm.stejoe.org. Sister St. Joseph of Orange Sisters 4.
Provincialate of Ursuline Nuns, 639 Angela Dr., 95403. Tel: 707-545-6811; Fax: 707-579-8571. Email: stister2@aol.com. Web: www.ursulinewest.com. Sisters Margaret Johnson, O.S.U., Co-Prin. Tel: 208-301-0293; Shirley Ann Garibaldi, O.S.U., Co-Prin. Tel: 650-346-9897. Ursulines of the Roman Union - Western Province

FORTUNA. *Redwood Memorial Hospital Convent*, 3300

Renner Dr., 95540. Tel: 707-725-3361; Fax: 707-725-7212. Email: glaroche@sje.stjoe.org. Web: www.sjhshumboldtcounty.org. Sisters St. Joseph of Orange Sisters 2.

NAPA. *St. Apollinaris Convent*, 3700 Lassen St., P.O. Box 3012, 94558. Tel: 707-255-2185; Fax: 707-251-0621. Congregation of the Sisters of Mercy - The United States Province Sisters 3.

Queen of the Valley Convent, 1000 Trancas St., 94558. Tel: 707-255-6169; Fax: 707-257-4192. Email: sisters@qvh.stjoe.org. Web: www.sistersofstjosephoforange.org. Sisters St. Joseph of Orange Sisters 4.

Siena Convent, 4038 Maher St., 94558. Tel: 707-255-6110. Dominican Sisters of San Rafael; Franciscan Sisters Sisters 5.

ROHNERT PARK. *Sisters of Christ the King*, 300 Enterprise Dr., #138, 94928. Tel: 707-584-8555. Sr. Michael Bird, S.C.K., Supr. Sisters of Christ the King Sisters 2; Associate Sisters 3.

WHITETHORN. *Our Lady of the Redwoods Abbey*, 18104 Briceland-Thorn Rd., 95589. Tel: 707-986-7419; Fax: 707-986-1176. Web: www.redwoodsabbey.org. Sr. Kathy De Vico, O.C.S.O., Abbess; Rev. Maurice Flood, O.C.S.O., Chap. Cistercian Nuns of the Strict Observance Priests 1; Sisters 9.

WINDSOR. *Ursuline Residence*, 9248 Lakewood Dr., 95492. Tel: 707-838-4973. Email: fxporter@juno.com. Web: www.ursulinewest.com. Ursuline Nuns Sisters 1.

[O] MISCELLANEOUS

SANTA ROSA. **Catholic Community Foundation*, 320 Tenth St., P.O. Box 1297, 95402. Tel: 707-545-2311; 707-566-3397; Fax: 707-566-3310. James Dillon, Acting Exec. Dir.

Loyola Counseling Institute, 24 A Ursuline Rd., 95403. Tel: 707-526-1167; Fax: 707-526-1287. Robert Dalzell, Dir.

NAPA. **Life Legal Defense Foundation*, P.O. Box 2105, 94558. Tel: 707-224-6675; Fax: 707-224-6676. Email: lifelegaldefense@cs.com. Web: lldf.org. Mary Riley, Dir.

RELIGIOUS INSTITUTES OF MEN REPRESENTED IN THE DIOCESE

For further details refer to the corresponding bracketed number in the Religious Institutes of Men or Women section.

[0330]—*Brothers of the Christian Schools* (San Francisco Prov.)—F.S.C.

[0350]—*Cistercian Order of the Strict Observance*—O.C.S.O.

[1130]—*Congregation of the Priests of the Sacred Heart*—S.C.J.

[0260]—*Discalced Carmelite Friars* (Anglo-Irish Prov.)—C.C.D.

[0520]—*Franciscan Friars*—O.F.M.

[0910]—*Oblates of Mary Immaculate*—O.M.I.

[0430]—*Oblates of the Virgin Mary*—O.M.V.

RELIGIOUS INSTITUTES OF WOMEN REPRESENTED IN THE DIOCESE

[0670]—*Cistercian Nuns of the Strict Observance*—O.C.S.O

[3110]—*Congregation of Our Lady of Retreat in the Cenacle*—R.C.

[1070-04]—*Dominican Sisters*—O.P.

[2575]—*Institute of the Sisters of Mercy of the Americas*—R.S.M.

[0430]—*Sisters of Charity of the Blessed Virgin Mary* (Dubuque, IA)—B.V.M.

[]—*Sisters of Christ the King*—S.C.K.

[2516]—*Sisters of Mercy*—S.M.

[4090]—*Sisters of Social Service*—S.S.S.

[0230]—*Sisters of St. Benedict*—O.S.B.

[3740]—*Sisters of St. Casimir*—S.S.C.

[3830-03]—*Sisters of St. Joseph*—C.S.J.

[3840]—*Sisters of St. Joseph of Carondelet*—C.S.J.

[3320]—*Sisters of the Presentation of the B.V.M.*—P.B.V.M.

[4110]—*Ursuline Nuns* (Western Prov.)—O.S.U.

DIOCESAN CEMETERIES

SANTA ROSA. *Calvary Catholic*

EUREKA. *St. Bernard*

PETALUMA. *Calvary Catholic*

ST. HELENA. *Holy Cross*

SONOMA. *St. Francis Solano*

NECROLOGY

† Faucher, Henry L., (Retired)—Died April 16, 2003

† Munari, Mario, (Retired)—Died March 11, 2003

Diocese of Savannah

(Dioecesis Savannensis)

Most Reverend

J. KEVIN BOLAND, D.D.

Bishop of Savannah; ordained June 14, 1959; appointed Bishop of Savannah February 7, 1995; ordained and installed April 18, 1995.

Chancery: Catholic Pastoral Center, 601 E. Liberty St., Savannah, GA 31401-5196. Tel: 912-201-4100; Fax: 912-201-4101.

Web: www.dioceseofsavannah.org

Email: Diosav@msn.com

Most Reverend

RAYMOND W. LESSARD, D.D.

Retired Bishop of Savannah; ordained December 16, 1956; appointed March 5, 1973; consecrated and installed April 27, 1973; retired February 7, 1995. *Catholic Pastoral Center*, 601 E. Liberty St., Savannah, GA 31401-5196. Tel: 912-201-4100.

Square Miles 37,038.

Established as Diocese of Savannah July 19, 1850. Name changed to Diocese of Savannah-Atlanta Jan. 5, 1937; Redesignated Nov. 8, 1956.

Comprises 90 Counties in the southern part of the State of Georgia.

Patrons of the Diocese: I. St. John the Baptist; II. Our Lady of Perpetual Help. This diocese was solemnly consecrated to the Sacred Heart of Jesus, May 7, 1872, and on Dec. 8, 1943, it was solemnly consecrated to the Immaculate Heart of Mary.

For legal titles of parishes and diocesan institutions, consult the Chancery.

STATISTICAL OVERVIEW

Personnel	
Bishop	1
Retired Bishops	1
Priests: Diocesan Active in Diocese	47
Priests: Diocesan Active Outside Diocese	7
Priests: Retired, Sick or Absent	15
Number of Diocesan Priests	69
Religious Priests in Diocese	24
Total Priests in Diocese	93
Extern Priests in Diocese	15
Ordinations:	
Diocesan Priests	2
Transitional Deacons	4
Permanent Deacons in Diocese	43
Total Brothers	8
Total Sisters	107
Parishes	
Parishes	52
With Resident Pastor:	
Resident Diocesan Priests	40
Resident Religious Priests	12
Missions	26
Professional Ministry Personnel:	
Brothers	1
Sisters	25
Lay Ministers	20
Welfare	
Catholic Hospitals	3
Total Assisted	350,000
Residential Care of Children	1
Total Assisted	51
Specialized Homes	1
Total Assisted	35
Special Centers for Social Services	20
Total Assisted	145,000
Educational	
Diocesan Students in Other Seminaries	22
Total Seminarians	22
High Schools, Diocesan and Parish	2
Total Students	800
High Schools, Private	3
Total Students	796
Elementary Schools, Diocesan and Parish	16
Total Students	4,407
Catechesis/Religious Education:	
High School Students	822
Elementary Students	4,212
Total Students under Catholic Instruction	11,059
Teachers in the Diocese:	
Priests	1
Brothers	4
Sisters	18
Lay Teachers	422
Vital Statistics	
Receptions into the Church:	
Infant Baptism Totals	1,754
Adult Baptism Totals	215
Received into Full Communion	403
First Communions	1,440
Confirmations	1,301
Marriages:	
Catholic	219
Interfaith	164
Total Marriages	383
Deaths	621
Total Catholic Population	75,987
Total Population	2,630,026

Former Bishops—Rt. Revs. FRANCIS X. GARTLAND, D.D., first bishop; consecrated Nov. 10, 1850; died Sept. 20, 1854; JOHN BARRY, D.D., second bishop; consecrated Aug. 2, 1857; died Nov. 21, 1859; AUGUSTIN VEROT, S.S., D.D., consecrated April 25, 1858; Vic. Ap. of Florida; transferred to Savannah, July 14, 1861; returned to Florida as first Bishop of St. Augustine, 1870; died June 10, 1876; His Eminence IGNATIUS CARDINAL PERSICO, D.D., transferred to this See March 11, 1870; resigned 1872; created Cardinal Jan. 16, 1893; died Dec. 7, 1895; Rt. Revs. W. H. GROSS, C.SS.R., D.D., consecrated April 27, 1873; promoted to Oregon 1885; died Nov. 14, 1898; THOMAS A. BECKER, D.D., consecrated Bishop of Wilmington, Aug. 16, 1868; transferred to Savannah, March 26, 1886; died July 29, 1899; BENJAMIN J. KEILEY, D.D., consecrated June 3, 1900; resigned Feb. 13, 1922; appt. Titular Bishop of Scillium, March 24, 1922; died June 17, 1925; Most Revs. MICHAEL J. KEYES, S.M., D.D., appt. July 8, 1922; consecrated Oct. 18, 1922; resigned Sept. 23, 1935; appt. Titular Bishop of Areopolis and Assistant at the Pontifical Throne; died July 31, 1959; GERALD P. O'HARA, D.D., J.U.D., appt. Titular Bishop of Heliopolis and Auxiliary Bishop of Philadelphia, April 26, 1929; consecrated May 20, 1929; transferred to See of Savannah, Nov. 16, 1935; received personal title of Archbishop July 12, 1950; appt. Apostolic Nuncio to Ireland, 1951; appt. Apostolic Delegate to Great Britain, 1954; resigned Nov. 11, 1959; died July 16, 1963; THOMAS J. MCDONOUGH, D.D., J.C.D., appt. Titular Bishop of Thaenae and Auxiliary Bishop of St. Augustine, March 10, 1947; consecrated April 30, 1947; transferred to Savannah, Jan. 2, 1957; succeeded to See, March 2, 1960; promoted to Archbishop of Louisville, March 1, 1967; resigned Sept. 29, 1981; died Aug. 4, 1998; GERARD L. FREY, D.D., appt. May 31, 1967; consecrated Aug. 8, 1967; transferred to Bishop of Lafayette, Nov. 7, 1972; retired May 13, 1989; RAYMOND W. LESSARD, D.D., appt. March 5, 1973; consecrated April 27, 1973; resigned Feb. 7, 1995.

Chancellor—Rev. Msgr. FRANCIS J. NELSON, J.C.L., V.G., Catholic Pastoral Center, 601 E. Liberty St., Savannah, 31401-5196. Tel: 912-201-4126.

Vicars General—Rev. Msgr. FRANCIS J. NELSON, J.C.L., V.G.; Rev. JOHN A. KENNEALLY, V.G., Catholic Pastoral Center, 601 E. Liberty St., Savannah, 31401-5196. Tel: 912-201-4126.

Chancery—Catholic Pastoral Center, 601 E. Liberty St., Savannah, 31401-5196. Tel: 912-201-4100; Fax: 912-201-4101.

Director of Pastoral Services—Mr. STEPHEN B. WILLIAMS. Tel: 912-201-4110.

Business Manager—Mr. LAWRENCE P. SAUNDERS, Catholic Pastoral Center, 601 E. Liberty St., Savannah, 31401-5196. Tel: 912-201-4123; Fax: 912-201-4101.

Diocesan Tribunal—Catholic Pastoral Center, 601 E. Liberty St., Savannah, 31401-5196. Tel: 912-201-4134; Fax: 912-201-4099.

Officialis—Rev. JEREMIAH J. MCCARTHY, J.C.L.

Director of the Tribunal—Ms. CATHERINE A. GILLIGAN, J.C.L.

Tribunal Judges—Rev. JEREMIAH J. MCCARTHY, J.C.L.; Rev. Msgr. FRANCIS J. NELSON, J.C.L., V.G.; Ms. CATHERINE A. GILLIGAN, J.C.L.

Defender of the Bond—Rev. J. GERARD SCHRECK, J.C.D., V.F.

Case Assessors & Notaries—CAROLE BARRAS; KATHLEEN TRAHAN.

Promoter of Justice—Rev. HERBERT J. WELLMEIER (Retired).

Censor Librorum—Rev. DOUGLAS K. CLARK, S.T.L.

Archivist—Ms. GILLIAN BROWN, Catholic Pastoral Center, 601 E. Liberty St., Savannah, 31401-5196. Tel: 912-201-4070.

Legal Counsel—Mr. JOSEPH P. BRENNAN, Catholic Pastoral Center, 601 E. Liberty St., Savannah, 31401-5196. Tel: 912-201-4100.

Finance Council—Mr. S. SCOTT VOYNICH, Chm.; Most Rev. J. KEVIN BOLAND, D.D.; Revs. JOHN A. KENNEALLY, V.G.; DOUGLAS K. CLARK, S.T.L.; Mr. E. J. MADDOCKS; Mr. JESSIE CLARK; Mr. ROBERT W. SCHIVERA; Mr. EDWARD C. MIZELLE; Mrs. JULIE FORTUNATO; Mr. JAMES M. PIETTE SR.; Dr. KENNETH L. STANLEY; Mr. STEPHEN B. WILLIAMS; Mr. LAWRENCE P. SAUNDERS; Dr. MARY F. HAZELDINE; Mr. JOSEPH P. BRENNAN. Staff:: Ms. PATRICIA SIGNS; Mr. DONALD FREW; Mrs. MARIE G. BRYANT; Mrs. CHARISSE ROUSE.

Investment Committee—Most Rev. J. KEVIN BOLAND, D.D.; Mr. EDWARD C. MIZELLE, Chm.; Mr. JAMES M. PIETTE SR.; Dr. MARY F. HAZELDINE; Dr. KENNETH L. STANLEY; Mr. LAWRENCE P. SAUNDERS.

Clergy Personnel—VACANT.

Deans—

Savannah Deanery—Rev. Msgr. WILLIAM O. O'NEILL, V.F., Cathedral of St. John the Baptist, 222 E. Harris St., Savannah, 31401-4699. Tel: 912-233-4709.

Augusta Deanery—Rev. JOHN J. LYONS, V.F., 2607 Lumpkin Rd., Augusta, 30906-3222. Tel: 706-798-1920.

Albany Deanery—Rev. FINBARR P. STANTON, V.F., 421 Edgewood Ln., Albany, 31707-3910. Tel: 229-439-2302.

Columbus Deanery—Rev. J. GERARD SCHRECK, J.C.D., V.F., 2000 Kay Circle, Columbus, 31907-3229. Tel: 706-561-8678.

Macon Deanery—Rev. FRED J. NIJEM, V.F., P.O. Box 5052, Warner Robins, 31099-5052. Tel: 478-923-0124.

Statesboro Deanery—Rev. DAVID STACHURSKI, O.F.M.Conv., V.F., 221 John Paul Ave., Statesboro, 30458-5016. Tel: 912-681-2445.

Valdosta-Brunswick Deanery—Rev. JOHN O'BRIEN, 800 Gornto Rd., Valdosta, 31602-1699. Tel: 229-244-2430.

College of Consultors—Revs. JOHN J. FITZPATRICK (Retired); BRETT A. BRANNEN; DOUGLAS K. CLARK, S.T.L.; JEREMIAH MCCARTHY; Rev. Msgr. FRANCIS J. NELSON, J.C.L., V.G.; Revs. DANIEL P. O'CONNELL; J. GERARD SCHRECK, J.C.D., V.F.

Council of Priests—Revs. BRETT A. BRANNEN; ROBERT GIRARDEAU; DOUGLAS K. CLARK, S.T.L.; RICHARD HART; LORENZO GARCIA; JEREMIAH MCCARTHY; Rev. Msgr. FRANCIS J. NELSON, J.C.L., V.G.; Revs. TIMOTHY C. DONAHUE; THOMAS J. PEYTON; FRANK PATTERSON.

Diocesan Offices and Directors

Newspaper—Rev. DOUGLAS K. CLARK, S.T.L., Editor, Catholic Pastoral Center, 601 E. Liberty St., Savannah, 31401-5196. Tel: 912-201-4054; Fax: 912-201-4101. Email: editor@diosav.org; Printing Office, 601 E. 6th St., Waynesboro, 30830. Tel: 706-554-7888. "The Southern Cross"

Director of Communications—Mrs. BARBARA KING, Catholic Pastoral Center, 601 E. Liberty St., Savannah, 31401-5196. Tel: 912-201-4052; Fax: 912-201-4101. Email: communications@diosav.org.

Superintendent of Schools—Sr. ROSE MARY COLLINS, S.S.J., Catholic Pastoral Center, 601 E. Liberty St., Savannah, 31401-5196. Tel: 912-201-4100; Fax: 912-201-4101. Email: rmcollins@diosav.org.

Director of African American Ministry—Rev. ROBERT E. CHANEY, Catholic Pastoral Center, 601 E. Liberty St., Savannah, 31401-5196. Tel: 912-201-4100; Fax: 912-201-4101.

Director of Campus Ministry—Ms. JANE HALL, 221 John Paul Ave., Statesboro, 30458-5016. Tel: 912-681-6726. Email: jchallgsa@yahoo.com.

Director of Catholic Social Services—Sr. JACQUELINE GRIFFITH, S.S.J., 601 E. Liberty St., Savannah, 31401-5196. Tel: 912-201-4068; Fax: 912-201-4101. Email: jagriffith@diosav.org.

Director of Family Life—Sr. PATRICIA BROWN, S.S.M.N., Catholic Pastoral Center, 601 E. Liberty St., Savannah, 31401-5196. Tel: 912-201-4058. Email: familylife@diosav.org.

Director of Hispanic/Migrant Ministry—Rev. MICHAEL H. SMITH, 1135 Second St., S.E., Moultrie, 31768-5970. Tel: 229-985-6550; Fax: 229-217-4970.

Director of Permanent Diaconate—Deacon GEORGE H. FOSTER, 4568 Betty's Branch Way, Evans, 30809. Tel: 706-651-8989; Fax: 706-651-0370.

Director of Religious Education—Ms. ANN PINCKNEY, Catholic Pastoral Center, 601 E. Liberty St., Savannah, 31401-5196. Tel: 912-201-4041; Fax: 912-201-4101. Email: apinckney@diosav.org.

Director of Stewardship and Development—Ms. PATRICIA SIGNS, Catholic Pastoral Center, 601 E. Liberty St., Savannah, 31401-5196. Tel: 912-201-4050. Email: psigns@diosav.org.

Director of Vocations—Rev. BRETT A. BRANNEN, 131 Ward St., Macon, 31204-3193. Tel: 478-743-1454; Fax: 478-743-9868. Email: FrBrett@savannahpriest.com.

Director of Vocations— Irish Seminarians Rev. JOHN O'BRIEN, 800 Gornto Rd., Valdosta, 31602-1699. Tel: 229-244-2430; Fax: 912-244-5352. Email: jobrien@johnevang.org.

Director of Youth Ministry—Mr. CHARLES R. FROST, Catholic Pastoral Center, 601 E. Liberty St., Savannah, 31401-5196. Tel: 912-201-4056; Fax: 912-201-4101. Email: youthsav@bellsouth.net.

Apostleship of the Sea—Rev. RICHARD YOUNG, 912 E. 35th St., Savannah, 31401. Tel: 912-236-4547; Deacon MICHAEL WRIGHT, O.F.M.Conv., 729 Union St., Brunswick, 31520-8018. Tel: 912-265-3249.

Campaign for Human Development—Sr. JACQUELINE GRIFFITH, S.S.J., Catholic Pastoral Center, 601 E. Liberty St., Savannah, 31401-5196. Tel: 912-201-4067; Fax: 912-201-4101. Email: csssav246@aol.com.

Catholic Cemetery Advisory Board—Board Members: FRANK A. RIZZA, M.D.; JOHN E. JAUGSTETTER, Ph.D.; Mr. JOE COUNIHAN, 601 E. Liberty St., Savannah, 31401-5196. Tel: 912-201-4100; Mr. LAWRENCE P. SAUNDERS. Staff: Mrs. MARIE G. BRYANT; Mr. M. SCOTT CLARK, 601 E. Liberty St., Savannah, 31401-5196. Tel: 912-201-4100.

Catholic Relief Services—Mr. STEPHEN B. WILLIAMS, Dir., Catholic Pastoral Center, 601 E. Liberty St., Savannah, 31401-5196. Tel: 912-201-4110.

Council of Catholic Women—Rev. ALLAN J. MCDONALD, Chap., P.O. Box 2446, Augusta, 30903-2446. Tel: 706-722-4944; Mrs. CARMEN PULLIAM, Pres., 516 Hedge Row Dr., Byron, 31008. Tel: 912-956-1780.

Diocesan Worship Commission—VACANT, Chm.

Diocesan Scout Chairman—Mr. CHARLES R. FROST; Mrs. BETTY G. PURDY, Catholic Pastoral Center, 601 E. Liberty St., Savannah, 31401-5196. Tel: 912-201-4057.

Ecumenism and Interreligious Affairs—Rev. MICHAEL J. KAVANAUGH, Dir., P.O. Box 4056, Port Wentworth, 31407-4056. Tel: 912-964-0219; Fax: 912-966-5468. Email: mjkavanaug@aol.com.

Georgia Catholic Conference—FRANCIS J. MULCAHY, Esq., Exec. Sec., Ste. 440, 100 N. Point Center E., Alpharetta, 30022-8261. Tel: 770-521-8799; Fax: 770-521-6337.

Holy Childhood Association—Sr. ROSE MARY COLLINS, S.S.J., Dir., Catholic Pastoral Center, 601 E. Liberty St., Savannah, 31406-5196. Tel: 912-201-4121.

Home Missions—Rev. LAWRENCE A. LUCREE, V.F., Dir., St. Teresa Church, 807 Third St., S., Cordele, 31015-1722. Tel: 229-273-3446. Email: llucree@yahoo.com.

Natural Family Planning—Mrs. RENEE LOFTON, Coord., 601 E. Liberty St., Savannah, 31401-5196. Tel: 912-201-4059. Email: savannahofl@aol.com.

Mission Cooperative Appeal—Mr. STEPHEN B. WILLIAMS, Catholic Pastoral Center, 601 E. Liberty St., Savannah, 31401-5196. Tel: 912-201-4110; Fax: 912-201-4081.

Propagation of the Faith—Ms. ANN PINCKNEY, Catholic Pastoral Center, 601 E. Liberty St., Savannah, 31401-5196. Tel: 912-201-4041; Fax: 912-201-4101.

Victim Assistance Coordinator—ROSEMARY DOWNING. Tel: 912-356-2112; 912-921-6121.

CLERGY, PARISHES, MISSIONS AND PAROCHIAL SCHOOLS

CITY OF SAVANNAH
(CHATHAM COUNTY)

1—CATHEDRAL OF ST. JOHN THE BAPTIST (1873), Rev. Msgr. William O. O'Neill, V.F.; Rev. Douglas K. Clark, S.T.L.; Bro. Robert Sokolowski, S.M., Pastoral Assoc.; Deacon Dewain Smith. In Res., Rev. Herbert J. Wellmeier (Retired).
Res.: 222 E. Harris St., 31401-4699. Tel: 912-233-4709; Fax: 912-233-8229.

2—ST. ANTHONY OF PADUA (1909), Closed. For inquiries for parish records contact the chancery.

3—ST. BENEDICT THE MOOR (1874), (African American), Rev. Desmond Ohankwere, M.S.P.
Res.: 556 E. Gordon St., 31401-5000. Tel: 912-232-7147; Fax: 912-238-0184.
School—Notre Dame Academy, Tel: 912-232-5473; Fax: 912-232-3352. Ms. Kim Chappell-Stevens, Prin. Lay Teachers 9; Sisters 1; Students 131.

4—ST. FRANCES XAVIER CABRINI (1968), Rev. Msgr. Francis J. Nelson, J.C.L., V.G.; Rev. Joseph F. Ware.
Res.: 11500 Middleground Rd., 31419-1227. Tel: 912-925-4725; Fax: 912-925-1379.
School—Tel: 912-925-6249. Ms. Nina Delk, Prin. Lay Teachers 6; Students 102.

5—ST. JAMES (1956), Revs. Mark J. Ross; Adam J. Kasela; Gaspar Hegedus; Sr. Ann Lyons, F.S.S.J., Pastoral Assoc.
Res.: 8412 Whitfield Ave., 31406-6198. Tel: 912-355-1523; Fax: 912-353-7226.
School—Tel: 912-355-3132; Fax: 912-355-1996. Sr. Cecilia DiDonato, I.H.M., Prin. Sisters 2; Lay Teachers 24; Students 517.
Mission—Our Lady of Good Hope Isle of Hope, Chatham Co.

6—MOST BLESSED SACRAMENT (1920), Revs. Jeremiah J. McCarthy; Timothy P. McKeown; John C. Markham; Deacon Michael F. Daly; Sr. Anna Gaffney, S.S.M.N., Pastoral Assoc.
Res.: 1003 E. Victory Dr., 31405-2499. Tel: 912-356-6980; Fax: 912-692-0010.
School—Tel: 912-356-6987; Fax: 912-356-6988. Mrs. Lynn Brown, Prin. Lay Teachers 25; Students 370.

7—MOST PURE HEART OF MARY (1907), Closed.

8—STS. PETER AND PAUL (1980), (Vietnamese), Rev. Kim Son Nguyen.
Res.: 3115 Victory Dr., 31404-4598. Tel: 912-354-4014.

9—ST. PETER THE APOSTLE CHURCH (1993), Revs. Patrick O'Brien; Robert T. Hand.
Mailing Address: 7020 Concord Rd., P.O. Box 30859, 31410.
Res.: 302 Bryson Dr., 31410. Tel: 912-897-5156; Fax: 912-897-7924.
School—Tel: 912-897-5224; Fax: 912-897-0801. Dr. James Gibson, Prin. Lay Teachers 19; Sisters 2; Students 362.

10—RESURRECTION OF OUR LORD, Rev. Robert E. Chaney.
112 Fell St., 31415-1828. Tel: 912-232-5258.

11—SACRED HEART OF JESUS (1880), Rev. Francis C. Higgins; Sisters Josephine Quinlan, M.F.I.C., Pastoral Assoc.; Isabella Lohan, M.F.I.C., Pastoral Assoc.
Res.: 1707 Bull St., 31401-7422. Tel: 912-232-0792; Fax: 912-236-0065.

OUTSIDE THE CITY OF SAVANNAH

ALBANY, DOUGHERTY CO., ST. TERESA (1875), Revs. Finbarr P. Stanton, V.F.; Jacek Szuster.
Res.: 421 Edgewood Ln., 31707. Tel: 229-432-0891; 229-439-2302 (Office); Fax: 229-439-0516.
School—417 Edgewood Ln., 31707-3991. Tel: 912-436-0134; Fax: 912-436-0135. Mrs. Grace Ledwitch, Prin. Lay Teachers 24; Students 277.

AMERICUS, SUMTER CO., ST. MARY (1891), Rev. Clif Marquis, S.T. (ORG).
Res.: 332 S. Lee St., 31709-3916. Tel: 229-924-3495; Fax: 229-924-7124.
Mission—St. Michael N. Dooly St., Montezuma, Macon Co. 31063-1507. Tel: 478-472-5124; Fax: 478-924-7124.

AUGUSTA, RICHMOND CO.

1—CHURCH OF THE MOST HOLY TRINITY (1810), Revs. Allan J. McDonald; Michael Lubinsky; Andrew T. Doris (Retired); Daniel M. Munn; Deacons Donald R. McArdle; Ephraim J. Williams; Rev. Elmore J. Butler; Sr. Bernadette Quinlan, M.F.I.C., Pastoral Assoc.; Dr. Kent M. Plowman, Pastoral Assoc.
Mailing Address: P.O. Box 2446, 30903-2446. Tel: 706-722-4944; Fax: 706-722-7774. Missionary Franciscan Sisters of the Immaculate Conception
Res.: 303 Broad St., 30901. Tel: 706-724-4367.
School—Immaculate Conception School, Tel: 706-722-9964; Fax: 706-722-9994. Sr. Margaret Mary Mohr, M.F.I.C., Prin. Lay Teachers 9; Students 141.
Convent & Chapel—Immaculate Conception, 1018 Laney Walker Blvd., 30901. Tel: 706-722-2380.

2—ST. JOSEPH (1954), Rev. John Lyons, V.F.; Deacon Gregory L. Bernard.
Res.: 2607 Lumpkin Rd., 30906-3222. Tel: 706-798-1920; Fax: 706-798-8594.

3—ST. MARY ON THE HILL (1917), Revs. Gerald Ragan; Ifeanyi Ethelbert Iwu; Edward R. Frank (Retired); Benjamin Dallas; Deacons George Foster; Brian Goodman.
Res.: 1420 Monte Sano Ave., 30904-5394. Tel: 706-733-6627; Fax: 706-733-4887.
School—1220 Monte Sano Ave., 30904-5394. Tel: 706-733-6193; Fax: 706-737-7985. Mr. Charles McCormack, Prin. Lay Teachers 19; Students 328.
Chapel—St. Joseph Hospital, Tel: 706-481-7000; Fax: 706-481-7850.
Chapel—Aquinas High School, Tel: 706-736-5516; Fax: 706-736-2678.

4—ST. TERESA OF AVILA (1968), Revs. Thomas J. Peyton; Robert A. Cushing; Michael Roverse; Deacon William L. Johnson; Sr. Laura Ann Grady, C.S.J., Pastoral Assoc.
Res.: 117 Pleasant Home Rd., 30907-3517. Tel: 706-863-4956; Fax: 706-863-5001.
Catechesis/Religious Program—Tel: 706-863-0252.

BAINBRIDGE, DECATUR CO., ST. JOSEPH'S (1887), Rev. Joel S. Bladt, S.T.
Res.: 822 Ramsey St., P.O. Box 192, 31717-0151. Tel: 229-248-0030.
Mission—Church of the Incarnation 5541 Hwy. 91, Donalsonville, Seminole Co. 31745.

BLAKELY, EARLY CO., HOLY FAMILY (1965), Rev. Walter O'Donnell, S.T.
Mailing Address: Box 425, 31723-0425.
Res.: 109 Arlington St., P.O. Box 425, 31723-0425. Tel: 229-723-3339; Fax: 229-723-6358.
Mission—St. Luke P.O. Box 491, Cuthbert, Randolph Co. 31740.

BRUNSWICK, GLYNN CO., ST. FRANCIS XAVIER (1884), Revs. Wilfrid Logsdon, O.F.M.Conv.; Cletus Pifher, O.F.M.Conv.; Bro. Michael Wright, O.F.M.Conv.; Deacon Ntungwa Maasha.

Res.: 729 Union St., 31520-8018. Tel: 912-265-3249; 912-466-0235 (Hispanic Min.); Fax: 912-265-6797.
School—Tel: 912-265-9470; Fax: 912-265-9950. Ms. Erin Mary Finn, Prin. Sisters 1; Lay Teachers 15; Students 238.
Catechesis/Religious Program—Christian Formation Center, 116 Richmond St., 31520. Tel: 912-264-6805; Fax: 912-264-6885.
Mission—Nativity of Our Lady 1000 N. Way St., Darien, McIntosh Co. 31305.

CLAXTON, EVANS CO., ST. CHRISTOPHER (1958), Rev. Brian LaBurt, G.H.M.; Sr. Janet Fischer, F.S.P.A., Pastoral Assoc.
Res.: 400 S. River St., 30417-2150. Tel: 912-739-3913.
Convent—Franciscan Sisters of Perpetual Adoration, 402 S. River St., 30417-2150. Tel: 912-739-2275.
Mission—St. Jude Glennville, Tattnall Co. 30427-0772. Tel: 912-654-1908. Deacon Louis Andruzzi.
Mission—Holy Cross Pembroke, Bryan Co. 30417.

COLUMBUS, MUSCOGEE CO.

1—ST. ANNE (1961), Revs. J. Gerard Schreck, J.C.D., V.F.; John R. Madden; Walter Mike Ingram; Mrs. Margo Truett, Pastoral Assoc.
Mailing Address: 2000 Kay Circle, 31907-3229. Tel: 706-561-8678; Fax: 706-568-0179.
Res.: 3544 Trinity Dr., 31907-3229. Tel: 706-561-8678; Fax: 706-568-0179.
School—2020 Kay Cir., 31907. Tel: 706-561-8232; Fax: 706-563-0211. Mrs. Patricia Nobes, Prin. Lay Teachers 25; Students 420.
High School—Pacelli High School, Tel: 706-561-8243; Fax: 706-561-3243. Students 172.
Mission—Christ the King Hamilton. P.O. Box 32, Pine Mountain, Harris Co. 31811-0066. Tel: 706-628-5158. Sr. Philomena Fogarty, F.M.M., Pastoral Assoc.
Chapel—St. Francis Hospital
Chapel—Pacelli High School

2—ST. BENEDICT THE MOOR (1958), (African American), Rev. Paul T. Brick, S.D.S.
Church: 2935 Ninth St., P.O. Box 5705, 31906-0714. Tel: 706-323-1749; Fax: 706-324-2641.
Res.: 2939 Ninth St., 31906. Tel: 706-323-8300; Fax: 706-324-7099.

3—HOLY FAMILY (1835), Rev. Frank Patterson.
Res.: 320 12th St., 31901-2454. Tel: 706-323-6908; Fax: 706-323-2043.

4—OUR LADY OF LOURDES (1958), Rev. Robert A. Girardeau; Deacon Francis P. Benyo.
Res.: 1953 Torch Hill Rd., 31903-2745. Tel: 706-689-5720; Fax: 706-687-9579.
School—1973 Torch Hill Rd., 31903. Tel: 706-689-5644; Fax: 706-689-5646. Mrs. Maureen Orr, Prin. Lay Teachers 10; Students 149.
Mission—St. Mary Magdalen S. Hwy. 41, Buena Vista, Marion Co. 31803-2745.

CORDELE, CRISP CO., ST. THERESA (1993), Rev. Lawrence A. Lucree, V.F.
Res.: 807 Third St. S., 31015-1705. Tel: 229-273-3446.

DOUGLAS, COFFEE CO., ST. PAUL'S (1938), Rev. Daniel O'Connell; Sr. Bertha Capetillo, C.S.S., Pastoral Assoc.
Res.: 523 E. Ward St., 31533-3912. Tel: 912-384-3560; Fax: 912-383-0779.
Mission—St. William 807 S. Merrimac, Fitzgerald, Ben Hill Co. 31750-0801. Tel: 229-423-5076.
Mission—Holy Family Willacoochee, Atkinson Co. Tel: 912-384-3560.

DUBLIN, LAURENS CO., IMMACULATE CONCEPTION (1911), Rev. Richard Hart.
Res.: 204 N. Church St., 31021-6152. Tel: 478-272-0266; Fax: 478-275-8806.
Chapel—Dublin, VA Hospital, Tel: 912-272-1210.
Mission—St. William 301 S. Smith St., Sandersville, Washington Co. 31082. Tel: 478-552-3352.

EASTMAN, DODGE CO., ST. MARK, Rev. William Leahy; Bro. Tom Sheehy, G.H.M., Pastoral Asst.
Mailing Address: P.O. Box 4304, 31023-4241. Tel: 478-374-0238; Fax: 478-374-4454.

HAZLEHURST, JEFF DAVIS CO., GOOD SHEPHERD (1967), Rev. Lorenzo Garcia.
Mailing Address: P.O. Box 1468, 31539-1381. Tel: 912-375-5948.
Mission—St. Rose of Lima N. City Circle Rd., Baxley, Appling Co. 31513.
Mission—St. Raymond P.O. Box 431, Alma, Bacon Co. 31510.

HINESVILLE, LIBERTY CO., ST. STEPHEN, FIRST MARTYR (1980), Rev. James M. Mayo.
Res.: 399 Woodland Ave., 31313-2719. Tel: 912-876-4364; 912-876-4368 (Rectory); Fax: 912-876-3150.

JESUP, WAYNE CO., ST. JOSEPH, Rev. Keith O'Neill, O.F.M.Conv., Admin.
Res.: 1048 E. Cherry St.,, 31546-4012. Tel: 912-427-9239; Fax: 912-427-9238.

LAKELAND, LANIER CO., QUEEN OF PEACE (1940), Rev. Carlos Santiago Granados, Admin.; Joseph T. Henkels Jr., Pastoral Assoc.; Rita T. Henkels, Pastoral Assoc.
Res.: 1332 S. Mill St., P.O. Box 26, 31635-0087. Tel: 229-482-3555.
Mission—St. Mary Nashville, Berrien Co. Tel: 229-686-2752.
Mission—St. Margaret Mary Adel, Cook Co. Tel: 229-896-4555.
Mission—St. Jose Twin Lakes, Lowndes Co.

MACON, BIBB CO.

1—HOLY SPIRIT (1968), Rev. Timothy C. Donahue.
Res.: 4074 Chambers Rd., 31206-4702. Tel: 478-788-6386; Fax: 478-788-2837.
Parish Center—4074 Chambers Rd., 31206-4702. Tel: 478-788-6386.

2—ST. JOSEPH (1841), Revs. John Cuddy; Steven Schraufnagel.
Res.: 830 Poplar St., 31201-2093. Tel: 478-745-1631; Fax: 478-745-2254.
School—Tel: 478-742-0636; Fax: 478-746-7685. Mrs. Nan Gillespie, Prin. Lay Teachers 19; Students 328.

3—ST. PETER CLAVER (1915), Rev. Brett A. Brannen.
Res.: 131 Ward St., 31204-3193. Tel: 478-743-1454, Ext. 478; Fax: 478-743-9868.
School—133 Ward St., 31204-3193. Tel: 478-743-3985. Sr. Ellen Marie Hagar, D.C., Prin. Sisters 1; Lay Teachers 12; Students 255.

MCRAE, TELFAIR CO., HOLY REDEEMER (1968), Rev. William J. Leahy.
201 Telfair, 31055-1625. Tel: 478-868-2002; Fax: 478-868-2939.

MOULTRIE, COLQUITT CO., IMMACULATE CONCEPTION (1978), Rev. Michael H. Smith; Deacons Philip J. Walsh; Richard F. Fetterman.
Res.: 202 Hillcrest Ave., S.E., 31768-5932. Tel: 229-985-6550; Fax: 229-217-4970.
Mission—St. John Vianney P.O. Box 391, Camilla, Mitchell Co. 31730-0394. Tel: 229-336-8685.

PERRY, HOUSTON CO., ST. PATRICK (1969), Rev. Charles Roland, Admin.; Deacons Ralph H. McAtee; Ken Hutnick.
Res.: 1241 St. Patrick Dr., 31069-0611. Tel: 478-987-4213; Fax: 478-988-3759.
Mission—St. Juliana Hwy. 341 S., Fort Valley, Peach Co. 31030. Tel: 478-825-7127.

PORT WENTWORTH, CHATHAM CO., OUR LADY OF LOURDES (1940), Rev. Michael J. Kavanaugh; Sr. Georgette Cunniff, M.F.I.C., Pastoral Assoc.
Res.: 501 S. Coastal Hwy., (GA Hwy. 25), P.O. Box 4056, 31407-4056. Tel: 912-964-0219; Fax: 912-966-5468.
Mission—St. Boniface P.O. Box 941, Springfield, 31329-5207. Tel: 912-754-7473; Fax: 912-754-1201. Sr. Nuala Mulleady, M.F.I.C., Pastoral Assoc.

RICHMOND HILL, BRYAN CO., ST. ANNE (1951), Rev. Joseph A. Smith.
Res.: P.O. Box 648, 31324-0601. Tel: 912-756-3338.

ST. MARYS, CAMDEN CO., OUR LADY STAR OF THE SEA (1969), Rev. Gabriel Cummings; Deacon William H. Wilson.
Res.: P.O. Box 290, 31558-0221. Tel: 912-882-4718; Fax: 912-882-5845.
Mission—St. Francis of Assisi P.O. Box 487, Folkston, Charlton Co. 31537-0151. Tel: 912-496-3219.

ST. SIMONS ISLAND, GLYNN CO., ST. WILLIAMS (1968), Rev. John A. Kenneally, V.G.; Deacon Lawrence A. Guyer.
Res. & Mailing Address: 2300 Frederica, 31522-1965. Tel: 912-638-2647; Fax: 912-638-7577.

STATESBORO, BULLOCH CO., ST. MATTHEW (1944), Rev. David Stachurski, O.F.M.Conv., V.F.
Res.: 221 John Paul Ave., 30458-5016. Tel: 912-681-6726; Fax: 912-681-6727.

SWAINSBORO, EMANUEL CO., HOLY TRINITY (1957), Rev. Victor Subb, G.H.M.
Res.: 928 W. Main St., 30401-5502. Tel: 478-237-8722.
Mission—Holy Family P.O. Box 231, Metter, Candler Co. 30439-0231. Tel: 912-685-5811. Sr. Paul Marie Westlake, R.S.M., Pastoral Assoc.

SYLVANIA, SCREVEN CO., OUR LADY OF THE ASSUMPTION (1957), Rev. Charles Hughes, G.H.M.; Sr. Mary Ellen Barrette, G.H.M., Pastoral Assoc.
Res.: 121 Ridgecrest Dr., 30467-1840. Tel: 912-564-2312.
Mission—St. Bernadette P.O. Box 616, Millen, Jenkins Co. 30442-0501. Tel: 478-982-1445.
Chapel—Bay Branch, St. Joseph

THOMASVILLE, THOMAS CO., ST. AUGUSTINE (1936), Rev. Thomas J. Murphy; Deacon Howard G. Halladay.
Res.: 211 N. Pinetree Blvd., 31792-3973. Tel: 229-226-3624; Fax: 229-226-8808.
Mission—St. Elizabeth Ann Seton 11th Ave. N.W., Cairo, Grady Co. 31728-4007. Tel: 229-377-6996.

THUNDERBOLT, CHATHAM CO., NATIVITY OF OUR LORD, Closed. For inquiries for parish records contact the chancery.

TIFTON, TIFT CO., OUR DIVINE SAVIOUR (1953), Rev. Alfonso Gutierrez.
Res.: P.O. Box 212, 31793-0201. Tel: 229-382-4600; Fax: 229-382-7611.
Mission—St. Ann Hwy. 82 E., Alapaha, Berrien Co. 31622. Tel: 229-532-2216.

TYBEE ISLAND, CHATHAM CO., ST. MICHAEL, Rev. P. James Costigan; Deacons Charles J. Hosti; Fretwell G. Crider.
Res.: 802 Lovell Ave., P.O. Box 38, 31328-0001. Tel: 912-786-4505; Fax: 912-786-6653.
School—808 Lovell Ave., P.O. Box 740, 31328-0001. Tel: 912-786-4507; Fax: 912-786-4551. Mr. Peter J. Iten, Prin. Lay Teachers 9; Students 95.

VALDOSTA, LOWNDES CO., ST. JOHN THE EVANGELIST, Rev. John O'Brien; Deacon David Lasseter. In Res., Rev. Msgr. Marvin LeFrois.
Church Office: 800 Gornto Rd., 31602-1699. Tel: 229-244-2430; Fax: 229-244-5352.
Res.: 2402 Berkley Dr., 31602-1699. Tel: 229-244-9920.
Newman Center—412 Baytree Rd., 31602. Tel: 229-247-6707. Dr. Doug Farwell, Campus Min.
School—Sisters of St. Joseph, Tel: 229-244-2556; 229-244-0050 (Convent); Fax: 229-244-0865. Sr. Pauline Oetgen, C.S.J., Prin. Sisters 2; Lay Teachers 18; Students 281.

VIDALIA, TOOMBS CO., SACRED HEART (1979), Rev. Raul Perez; Deacon Joseph P. Claroni.
Mailing Address: P.O. Box 1086, 30474-1086. Tel: 912-537-7709; Fax: 912-537-4691.
Res.: 3119 E. North St., 30474. Tel: 912-537-7709.
Mission—St. Andrew the Apostle 138 Industrial Blvd., P.O. Box 955, Reidsville, Tattnall Co. 30453. Tel: 912-557-6570. In Res., Rev. Robert Healy, G.H.M. (Retired).

WARNER ROBINS, HOUSTON CO., SACRED HEART (1945), Revs. Fred J. Nijem, V.F.; Paul O'Connell; Sr. Teresa Baugh, P.B.V.M., Pastoral Assoc.; Deacons Harold P. Kimball; James A. Hunt.
Mailing Address: P.O. Box 5052, 31099-5052. Tel: 478-923-0124; Fax: 478-328-3078.
School—Sisters of Presentation, Tel: 912-923-9668; Fax: 912-923-5822. Mrs. Sylvia Villarreal, Prin. Sisters 19; Students 253.

WAYCROSS, WARE CO., ST. JOSEPH'S (1960), Rev. Kirk Mansell, S.J. (BR).
Res.: 2011 Darling Ave., 31501-1846. Tel: 912-283-7700; Fax: 912-283-1944.

WAYNESBORO, BURKE CO., SACRED HEART (1961), Rev. Laurence Goulding, G.H.M.
Res.: 115 S. Liberty St., 30830-4548. Tel: 706-554-2535; Fax: 706-554-1448.
Mission—St. Joan of Arc Louisville, Jefferson Co. Tel: 478-625-3433.

Special Assignment:
Revs.—
Canty, Richard J. (Retired), Memorial Medical Center & Candler General Hospital
Cushing, Robert A., St. Teresa of Avila Church, 117 Pleasant Home Rd., Augusta, 30907-3517. Tel: 706-854-7653
Ryan, Timothy K., 1310 Primrose Dr., Roswell, 30076. Tel: 404-667-1313; Fax: 404-667-6305

On Duty Outside the Diocese:
Revs.—
Healy, Thomas, St. Thomas More Catholic Community, Kennedyallee 150, Bonn 53175 Germany. Tel: 011-49-288-3775749
Keohane, Donal
Pachence, Ronald A., University of San Diego, 5998 Alcala Park, San Diego, CA 92110. Tel: 619-260-4784
Schreck, Christopher J., S.T.B., S.S.L., Ph.D., S.T.D., St. Charles Borromeo Seminary, 1000 E. Wynnewood Rd., Wynnewood, PA 19096-3099. Tel: 610-667-3394

Military Chaplains:
Revs.—
Cerrone, Michael J., U.S.A.
Minch, Richard, U.S.A.
Quang, John, U.S.N.

Retired:
Rev. Msgr.—
LeFrois, Marvin J., 800 Gornto Rd., Valdosta, 31602-1699. Tel: 912-253-0041
Revs.—
Barry, Francis, St. Brendan's Village, Mulrany, County Mayo Ireland.
Canty, Richard J., 309 E. 53rd St., 31405. Tel: 912-233-6142
Doris, Andrew T., 2346 McDowell St., Augusta, 30904. Tel: 706-736-0593
Dowling, William P., 322 E. Taylor St., #317, Savanah, 31401. Tel: 912-231-9227
Fitzpatrick, John J., 4648 Mossburg Ct., Marietta, 30066. Tel: 770-591-4296
Frank, Edward R., 1420 Monte Sano Ave., Augusta,

30904. Tel: 706-738-5623
Healy, Robert, G.H.M., P.O. Box 874, Reidsville, 30453. Tel: 912-557-6570
Keohane, Donal, St. Martin of Tours, 11967 Sunset Boulevard, Los Angeles, CA 90049. Tel: 310-476-7403
Kumbalaprampil, Xavier, Ponel, P.O. Elamakkara, DT. Ernakulam 682026 India. Tel: 91-484-234-9268
O'Keeffe, Michael, Blessed Trinity Church, 5 S.E. 17th St., Ocala, FL 34471.
Payne, Thomas H., P.O. Box 24683, St. Simons Island, 31522. Tel: 912-634-9189
Ryan, Timothy, 1310 Primrose Dr., Roswell, 30076-4221. Tel: 770-667-1313
Wellmeier, Herbert J., Cathedral of St. John the Baptist, 222 E. Harris St., 31401. Tel: 912-233-4709

Permanent Deacons:
Andruzzi, Louis J., St. Jude Church, Glennville
Arcand, Dennis A., St Juliana Church, Perry
Barbour, Antonio, St. Jude, Glennville
Benyo, Francis P., Our Lady of Lourdes, Columbus
Bernard, Gregory L., St. Joseph's, Augusta
Butler, Elmore J., Holy Trinity, Augusta
Claroni, Joseph B., Sacred Heart, Vidalia
Crider, Freewell G., St. Michael's, Tybee Island
Dallas, John C., St. Teresa, Albany
Daly, Michael F., Blessed Sacrament, Savannah
Ensley, Edgar L., Jr., St. Anne, Columbus
Fetterman Richard F., Immaculate Conception, Moultrie
Foster, George H., St. Michael, Fort Gordon
Goodman, Brian, St. Mary on the Hill, Augusta
Gutting, Paul, St. Peter the Apostle, Savannah
Guyer, Lawrence A., St. William, St. Simons Island
Halladay, Howard G., St. Augustine, Thomasville
Herrmann, Robert, St. Anne, Columbus
Hosti, Charles J., St. Michael, Tybee Island
Houghton Arthur A., Good Shepherd, Hazlehurst
Hunt, James A., Sacred Heart, Warner Robins
Hutnick, Kenneth P., St. Patrick Church, Perry
Jackson, Prince A., Jr., 1215 E. Duffy St., 31404.
Johnson, William L., St. Teresa of Avila, Augusta
Joiner, Ronnie F., St. Mark, Eastman
Kimball, Harold P., Sacred Heart, Warner Robins
Lasseter, R. David, St. John the Evangelist, Valdosta
Leslie, Cedric T., St. Peter Claver, Macon
Maasha, Ntungwa, St. Francis Xavier, Brunswick
Marchek, Michael V., St. Michael's, Fort Gordon
McArdle, Donald R., St. Mary on the Hill, Augusta
McAtee, Ralph H., St. Patrick, Perry
O'Neill, Robert, (Retired)
Pierce, Raymond G., (Retired)
Quillen, John R., Christ the King, Pine Mountain
Ruehling, George F., III, 702 Cedar St., St. Simons Island, 31522-1259.
Sanchez, Aurelio, Holy Trinity Church, Swainsboro
Smith, Dewain E., Cathedral of St. John the Baptist, Savannah
Walsh, Philip J., Immaculate Conception, Moultrie
White, George H., 4 Dolan Dr., 31406.
Williams, Ephraim J., Holy Trinity, Augusta
Wilson, William H., St. Francis of Assisi, Folkston
Wright, Michael, St. Francis Xavier, Brunswick

INSTITUTIONS LOCATED IN THE DIOCESE

[A] HIGH SCHOOLS, DIOCESAN

AUGUSTA. *Aquinas High School*, 1920 Highland Ave., 30904-5305. Tel: 706-736-5516; Fax: 706-736-2678. Web: www.aquinashigh.org. Robert Larcher, Prin.; Mr. Kelley Culver, Asst. Prin. Sisters 1; Lay Teachers 21; Students 279.

COLUMBUS. *Pacelli Catholic High School*, 3556 Trinity Dr., 31907. Tel: 706-561-8243; Fax: 706-561-3243. Email: Pacelli@fiac.net. Web: www.pacelli.net. Mr. John Albert, Prin.; Rev. J. Gerard Schreck, J.C.D., V.F., Diocesan Moderator. Lay Teachers 16; Students 183.

[B] HIGH SCHOOLS, PRIVATE

SAVANNAH. *Benedictine Military School*, (Grades 9-12), 6502 Seawright Dr., P.O. Drawer 13577, 31416-3577. Tel: 912-644-7000; Fax: 912-356-3527. Email: fr_jude.brady@besav.net. Web: bccadets.org. Very Rev. Jude W. Brady, O.S.B., Pres.; Ms. Kelly Burke, Prin.; Revs. Wilfred M. Dumm, O.S.B.; Ronald P. Gatman, O.S.B.; Anthony P. Wesolowski, O.S.B.; Jeffrey S. Nyardy, O.S.B.; Bros. Gerard J. Klaric, O.S.B.; Timothy J. Brown, O.S.B.; Francis G. Ehnat, O.S.B.; Mark Floreanini, O.S.B.; Lee Yokum, O.S.B. Secondary school conducted by the Dependent Priory of Benedictine Monks of St. Vincent Archabbey, Latrobe, PA. Priests 4; Brothers 3; Lay Teachers 31; Boys 371.

Convent and Academy of St. Vincent de Paul, 207 E. Liberty St., 31401-3577. Tel: 912-236-9541; Fax: 912-236-7877. Email: srhelenmarie@stvincentacademy.com. Web: www.asd.com/#114491. Sr. Helen Marie Buttimer, R.S.M., Prin. Sisters of Mercy of the Americas Sisters 6; Lay Teachers 25; Girls 357.

MACON. *Mount de Sales Academy*, (Grades 7-12), 851 Orange St., 31201-6136. Tel: 478-751-3240; Fax: 478-751-3241. Email: srosina@mds.macon.ga.us. Web: www.mds.macon.ga.us. Mrs. Katy Prebble, Prin. Sisters of Mercy of the Americas Lay Teachers 50; Students 606.

[C] CHILD CARE HOMES

SAVANNAH. *St. Mary's Home*, 2170 E. Victory Dr., P.O. Box 3627-B, 31414. Tel: 912-236-7164; Fax: 912-236-9699. Email: STMARYHOME@aol.com. Sr. Mary Alvin Seubott, R.S.M., Admin. Sisters of Mercy of the Americas Sisters 3; Lay Staff 24; Residents 27; Total Assisted 35.

Summer Program Total Assisted 51; Total Staff 24.

[D] RESIDENCES FOR SINGLE PREGNANT WOMEN

MACON. *Nazareth Home, Residence for Single Pregnant Women*, 538 Orange St., P.O. Box 204, 31202-0204. Tel: 478-746-9803; Fax: 478-746-9803. Email: Nazareth@hom.net. Web: www.hom.net/~nazareth. Janet Manley, Dir.

[E] GENERAL HOSPITALS

SAVANNAH. *St. Joseph's Hospital*, 11705 Mercy Blvd., P.O. Box 60129, 31419-1791. Tel: 912-925-4100. Mr. Paul P. Hinchey, Pres. & CEO. Tel: 912-927-5404.

AUGUSTA. *St. Joseph Hospital, Augusta, GA, Inc.*, 2260 Wrightsboro Rd., 30904-4726. Tel: 706-481-7400; Fax: 706-481-7599. Web: www.stjosephhospital.org. Dr. Andrew A. Lasser, Pres. & CEO; Rev. Miquel Grave de Peralta, Dir. Pastoral Care.

COLUMBUS. *St. Francis Hospital*, 2122 Manchester Expwy., P.O. Box 7000, 31908-7000. Tel: 706-596-4000. Michael E. Garrigan, FACHE Pres.; John B. Hartman, D.Min., Dir. Pastoral Svcs. Bed Capacity 376; Patients Assisted Annually 93,500.

[F] MONASTERIES AND RESIDENCES OF PRIESTS

SAVANNAH. *The Benedictine Priory*, 6502 Seawright Dr., P.O. Drawer 13577, 31416-3577. Tel: 912-356-3520; Fax: 912-356-3527. Web: bccadets.org. Very Rev. Jude W. Brady, O.S.B., Prior; Revs. Wilfred M. Dumm, O.S.B.; Anthony P. Wesolowski, O.S.B.; Ronald P. Gatman, O.S.B.; Jeffrey S. Nyardy, O.S.B.; Bros. Gerard J. Klaric, O.S.B.; Timothy Brown, O.S.B.; Francis Ehnat, O.S.B.; Mark Floreanini, O.S.B.; Lee Yokum, O.S.B. Dependent Priory of St. Vincent Archabbey, Latrobe, PA.

[G] CONVENTS AND RESIDENCES FOR SISTERS

SAVANNAH. *Carmelite Monastery*, 11 W. Back St., 31419-2219. Tel: 912-925-8505; Fax: 912-925-0797. Email: carmelite@csam.net. Sr. Carmela Marolda, O.C.D., Prioress. Professed Nuns 4.

Mercy Convent, 11801 McAuley Dr., 31419-1709. Tel: 912-925-3800; Fax: 912-925-3823. Email: mercyconv@aol.com. Ms. Mary Frew Hussey, Dir. Retired Sisters of Mercy Sisters 7.

[H] NEWMAN CENTERS

SAVANNAH *Savannah State University Newman Group* 4 Indigo Ct., 31406. Tel: 912-925-5477. Mrs. Ann Lipsey, Campus Min.

MACON. *Mercer University, Wesleyan College Newman Center* c/o St. Joseph Church, 830 Poplar St., 31201-2093. Tel: 478-745-1631. Email: newman@st-joseph.cc. John Kiehl, Campus Min.; Teresa Kiehl, Campus Min.

STATESBORO. *St. Matthew Newman Center at Georgia Southern University* 221 John Paul Ave., 30458-5016. Tel: 912-681-6726; Fax 912-681-6727. Email: jcgallgsa@yahoo.com. Ms Jane Hall, Campus Min.

VALDOSTA. *Valdosta State College Newman Center* 800 Gornto Rd., 31602. 412 Baytree Rd., 31602. Tel: 229-247-6707. Dr. Doug Farwell, Campus Min.

[I] RETREAT HOUSES

SAVANNAH. *Dominican Friars*, 108 Palmetto Dr., Wilmington Island, 31410. Email HGrooverOP@aol.com.

[J] MISCELLANEOUS

SAVANNAH. *Catholic Social Services*, 601 E. Liberty St., 31401-5196. Tel: 912-201-4063; Fax: 912-201-4101. Email: csssav246@aol.com Sr. Jacqueline Griffith, S.S.J., Dir.

Mercy Properties Georgia, Inc., 11705 Mercy Blvd., 31419. Tel: 912-920-6495; Fax: 912-920-6463. Email: haddockr@sjchs.org. Web: www.mercyhousing.org. Robin Haddock, Project Devel.; Kathleen Brownlee, Pres.

Social Apostolate of Savannah, 502 E. Liberty St., P.O. Box 8703, 31412. Tel: 912-233-1877; Fax: 912-651-3638. Email: socapsa@aol.com. Sr. Pauline O'Brien, M.F.I.C., Dir.

ALBANY. *St. Clare's Evangelization-Community Center*, 2005 Martin Luther King Dr. P.O. Box 4123, 31706-4194. Tel: 912-883-2566; Fax: 912-883-9116. Email: srnoelle@aol.com. Sisters Noelle Hart, Co-Dir.; Maura Molloy, M.F.I.C., Co-Dir.

Neighbors in Need, 2005 Martin Luther King Dr., P.O. Box 3032, 31706-3001. Tel: 229-883-2872; Fax: 229-883-9116. Email: nin3032@juno.com. Mrs. Rosemary Baughman, Dir.

AUGUSTA. *Alleluia Catholic Fellowship*, 2110 Richards St., P.O. Box 6805, 30916-6805. Tel: 706-798-1882; Fax: 706-560-2759. Mr. Dennis McBride, Moderator.

Catholic Social Services, 811 12th St., 30901-2749. Tel: 706-722-4390; Fax: 706-722-4758. Web: www.cssaugusta.com. Mr. Richard Tuchscherer, Dir.

BRUNSWICK. *Society of St. Vincent de Paul*, 1217 Newcastle St., 31520-7534. Tel: 912-262-6027; Fax: 912-265-6797. Marilee Williamson, Pres.

CLAXTON. *Clothesbasket*, 402 S. River St., 30417-2150. Tel: 912-739-2275. Email: JFischer@G-Net.net. Sr. Janet Fischer, F.S.P.A., Dir.

COLUMBUS. *St. Benedict Social Concerns*, 2935 Ninth St., 31906-6354. Tel: 706-323-8300. Mrs. Helen Linton, Dir.

Holy Family Soup Kitchen, 320 12th St., 31901-2454. Tel: 706-322-0098; Fax: 706-327-8191. Mrs. Frances Cummings, Dir.

Our Lady of Lourdes, 1953 Torch Hill Rd., 31903-2754. Tel: 706-689-5720; Fax: 706-687-9579. Mrs. Judie Huff, Dir.

St. Vincent de Paul, St. Anne Conference, 3502 Kay Cir., 31907-3254. Tel: 706-568-1592. Mrs. Donna Bushaw, Dir.

HAMILTON. *Christ the King (FOCUS)*, Hwy. 27, Box 32, 31811-0066. Tel: 706-628-5158; Fax: 706-628-5158. Lynda Frerichs, Pres.

MACON. *Mother & Child Ministries, Inc.*, 570 High Pl., 31201-2073. Tel: 478-745-7165; Fax: 478-745-9662. Email: mother_childm@bellsouth.net. Sr. Marian Hamwey, D.C., Dir.

MILLEN. *Catholic Thrift Shop*, 130-B Gray St., 30442. Tel: 478-982-8361. Sr. Mary Ellen Barrette, G.H.M., Dir.

VALDOSTA. *St. Francis Center*, P.O. Box 1331, 31601-1321. Tel: 229-242-8656; Fax: 229-244-5352. Email: jcarver@datasys.net. Mr. Dwight Carver, Dir.

WARNER ROBINS. *Sacred Heart Christian Service Center*, P.O. Box 5052, 31099-5052. Tel: 478-929-3897; Fax: 478-328-3078. Email: sheart@hom.net. Web: www.hom.net/~sheart. Mr. Ermal Sirmans, Dir.

RELIGIOUS INSTITUTES OF MEN REPRESENTED IN THE DIOCESE

For further details refer to the corresponding bracketed number in the Religious Institutes of Men or Women section.

[0200]—*Benedictine Monks* (St. Vincent Archabbey)—O.S.B.
[0480]—*Conventual Franciscans* (Provs. of Our Lady of Consolation & St. Anthony of Padua)—O.F.M.Conv
[0570]—*Glenmary Home Missioners* (Glendale, OH)—G.H.M
[0840]—*Missionary Servants of Most Holy Trinity* (Dublin)—S.T.
[1310]—*Order of the Most Holy Trinity*—O.SS.T.
[0760]—*Society of Mary*—S.M.
[1200]—*Society of the Divine Savior* (American Prov.)—S.D.S.

RELIGIOUS INSTITUTES OF WOMEN REPRESENTED IN THE DIOCESE

[1780]—*Congregation of the Sisters of the Third Order of St. Francis of Perpetual Adoration*—F.S.P.A.
[0760]—*Daughters of Charity of St. Vincent De Paul* (Emmitsburg, MD)—D.C.
[0420]—*Discalced Carmelite Nuns*—O.C.D.
[1370]—*Franciscan Missionaries of Mary*—F.M.M.
[1470]—*Franciscan Sisters of St. Joseph*—F.S.S.J.
[1845]—*Guadalupan Missionaries of the Holy Spirit*—M.G.Sp.S.

[2080]—*Home Mission Sisters of America*
[61]—*Missionary Cathechrists of Divine Providence*—M.C.D.P.
[1360]—*Missionary Franciscan Sisters of the Immaculate Conception*—M.F.I.C.
[3230]—*Poor Handmaids of Jesus Christ* (Indiana)—P.H.J.C.
[0440]—*Sisters of Charity of Cincinnati*—S.C.
[2575]—*Sisters of Mercy of the Americas* (Baltimore, Burlingame, Erie)—R.S.M.
[3950]—*Sisters of Saint Mary of Namur*—S.S.M.N.
[1070-18]—*Sisters of St. Dominic of the American Congregation of the Sacred Heart of Jesus*—O.P.
[3893]—*Sisters of St. Joseph* (Chestnut Hill, PA)—S.S.J.
[3840]—*Sisters of St. Joseph of Carondelet* (St. Louis, MO)—C.S.J.
[2170]—*Sisters, Servants of the Immaculate Heart of Mary*—I.H.M.
[3330]—*Union of the Sisters of the Presentation of the Blessed Virgin Mary*—P.B.V.M.

DIOCESAN CEMETERIES

SAVANNAH. *Catholic Cemetery and Properties, Catholic Pastoral Center*, 601 E. Liberty St., 31401-5196. Tel: 912-238-2320. Mr. Lawrence P. Saunders, Dir.

AUGUSTA. *Catholic Cemetery*
Holy Trinity: 720 Telfair St., P.O. Box 2446, 30903. Tel: 706-722-4944. Rev. Allan J. McDonald.

DOUGLAS. *St. Paul's*, c/o 523 Ward St., 31533. Tel: 912-384-3560.

SYLVANIA. *Catholic Cemetery*
Our Lady of the Assumption: 121 Ridgecrest Dr., 30467. Tel: 912-564-2312.

WILLACOOCHEE. *Catholic Cemetery* Rev. Daniel P. O'Connell.

NECROLOGY

† Campbell, Thomas E., (Retired)—Died June 1, 2003

Diocese of Scranton

(Dioecesis Scrantonensis)

Most Reverend

JOSEPH F. MARTINO

Bishop of Scranton; ordained December 18, 1970; appointed Titular Bishop of Cellae in Mauretania and Auxiliary Bishop of Philadelphia January 24, 1996; consecrated March 11, 1996; appointed Bishop of Scranton July 25, 2003 *Office: 300 Wyoming Ave., Scranton, PA 18503.* Tel: 570-207-2216.

Chancery Office: 300 Wyoming Ave., Scranton, PA 18503. Tel: 570-207-2216; Fax: 570-207-2236.

Web: www.dioceseofscranton.org

Most Reverend

JAMES C. TIMLIN, D.D.

Bishop Emeritus of Scranton; ordained July 16, 1951; appointed Titular Bishop of Gunugo and Auxiliary Bishop of Scranton August 3, 1976; consecrated September 21, 1976; succeeded to See of Scranton April 24, 1984; installed June 7, 1984; resigned July 25, 2003

Most Reverend

JOHN M. DOUGHERTY, D.D., V.G.

Auxiliary Bishop of Scranton; ordained June 15, 1957; appointed Titular Bishop of Sufetula and Auxiliary Bishop of Scranton February 7, 1995; Episcopal ordination received March 7, 1995 *Office: 300 Wyoming Ave., Scranton, PA 18503.* Tel: 570-207-2216.

ESTABLISHED MARCH 3, 1868.

Square Miles 8,847.

Comprises the Counties of Luzerne, Lackawanna, Bradford, Susquehanna, Wayne, Tioga, Sullivan, Wyoming, Lycoming, Pike and Monroe in Pennsylvania.

For legal titles of parishes and diocesan institutions, consult the Chancery Office.

STATISTICAL OVERVIEW

Personnel	
Bishop	1
Auxiliary Bishops	1
Retired Bishops	1
Priests: Diocesan Active in Diocese	242
Priests: Diocesan Active Outside Diocese	17
Priests: Retired, Sick or Absent	64
Number of Diocesan Priests	323
Religious Priests in Diocese	70
Total Priests in Diocese	393
Extern Priests in Diocese	13
Ordinations:	
Diocesan Priests	5
Transitional Deacons	3
Permanent Deacons in Diocese	52
Total Brothers	12
Total Sisters	673
Parishes	
Parishes	193
With Resident Pastor:	
Resident Diocesan Priests	187
Resident Religious Priests	6
Without Resident Pastor:	
Administered by Priests	5
Missions	85
Pastoral Centers	25
Closed Parishes	2
Professional Ministry Personnel:	
Sisters	30
Lay Ministers	25
Welfare	
Catholic Hospitals	7
Total Assisted	737,035
Health Care Centers	2
Total Assisted	89,215
Homes for the Aged	4
Total Assisted	743
Residential Care of Children	5
Total Assisted	973
Day Care Centers	9
Total Assisted	389
Specialized Homes	9
Total Assisted	1,815
Special Centers for Social Services	13
Total Assisted	199,294
Residential Care of Disabled	1
Total Assisted	155
Educational	
Seminaries, Diocesan	1
Students from This Diocese	5
Students from Other Diocese	7
Diocesan Students in Other Seminaries	18
Seminaries, Religious	1
Total Seminarians	23
Colleges and Universities	4
Total Students	12,280
High Schools, Diocesan and Parish	9
Total Students	3,034
High Schools, Private	2
Total Students	810
Elementary Schools, Diocesan and Parish	45
Total Students	10,032
Non-residential Schools for the Disabled	1
Total Students	20
Catechesis/Religious Education:	
High School Students	15,099
Elementary Students	30,461
Total Students under Catholic Instruction	71,759
Teachers in the Diocese:	
Priests	4
Sisters	87
Lay Teachers	848
Vital Statistics	
Receptions into the Church:	
Infant Baptism Totals	3,695
Adult Baptism Totals	526
Received into Full Communion	280
First Communions	5,032
Confirmations	7,441
Marriages:	
Catholic	1,213
Interfaith	454
Total Marriages	1,667
Deaths	5,580
Total Catholic Population	348,542
Total Population	1,072,813

Former Bishops—Rt. Revs. WILLIAM O'HARA, D.D., First Bishop; consecrated July 12, 1868; died Feb. 3, 1899; MICHAEL J. HOBAN, D.D., Second Bishop; consecrated Coadjutor, March 22, 1896; succeeded to See, Feb. 3, 1899; died Nov. 13, 1926; Most Revs. THOMAS C. O'REILLY, D.D., Third Bishop; ord. June 4, 1898; elected Dec. 19, 1927,; consecrated Feb. 16, 1928; installed March 8, 1928; died March 25, 1938; WILLIAM J. HAFEY, D.D., Fourth Bishop; ord. June 16, 1914; appt. First Bishop of Raleigh, April 6, 1925; consecrated June 24, 1925; transferred to Scranton as Coadjutor cum jure successionis and Apostolic Administrator, Oct. 2, 1937; succeeded to See, March 25, 1938; died May 12, 1954; JEROME D. HANNAN, D.D., Fifth Bishop; ord. May 22, 1921; appt. August 17, 1954; consecrated Sept. 21, 1954; died Dec. 15, 1965; J. CARROLL M. MCCORMICK, D.D. (Retired), Sixth Bishop; ord. July 10, 1932; appt. Titular Bishop of Ruspae and Auxiliary of Philadelphia, Jan. 11, 1947; consecrated April 23, 1947; appt. Bishop of Altoona-Johnstown, June 25, 1960; transferred to the See of Scranton, March 4, 1966; installed May 25, 1966; retired Feb. 15, 1983; died Nov. 2, 1996; JOHN J. O'CONNOR, D.D., Seventh Bishop; ord. Dec. 15, 1945; appt. Titular Bishop of Cuzola and Auxiliary Bishop to the Military Vicar April 24, 1979; consecrated May 27, 1979; appt. Bishop of Scranton, May 10, 1983; installed June 29, 1983; transferred to the See of New York, Jan. 31, 1984; died May 3, 2000; JAMES C. TIMLIN, D.D. (Retired), Eigth Bishop; ordained July 16, 1951; appointed Titular Bishop of Gunugo and Auxiliary Bishop of Scranton August 3, 1976; consecrated September 21, 1976; succeeded to See of Scranton April 24, 1984; installed June 7, 1984; resigned July 25, 2003.

Vicar General—Most Rev. JOHN M. DOUGHERTY, D.D., V.G., 300 Wyoming Ave., Scranton, 18503-1279. Tel: 570-207-2216.

Chancery Office—300 Wyoming Ave., Scranton, 18503-1279. Tel: 570-207-2216; Fax: 570-207-2236.

Moderator of the Curia—Most Rev. JOHN M. DOUGHERTY, D.D., V.G. Tel: 570-207-2216.

Chancellor—JAMES B. EARLEY. Tel: 570-207-2216; Fax: 570-207-2236.

Secretary to Bishop Timlin—Rev. CHRISTOPHER S. SAHD. Tel: 570-207-2216; 570-344-7231 (After 5 P.M.).

Diocesan Financial Office—JAMES M. QUINN, Dir. Tel: 570-207-2237.

Diocesan Tribunal—300 Wyoming Ave., Scranton, 18503-1279. Tel: 570-207-2246; Fax: 570-207-2274. Direct all inquiries concerning marriage nullity, dispensations and permissions to this office.

Judicial Vicar—Rev. Msgr. PATRICK J. PRATICO, J.C.D.

Coordinator—JOSEPH V. FOX.

Judges—Rev. Msgr. JOSEPH C. BAMBERA, J.C.L.; CHARLES J. REID, J.D., J.C.L.; Rev. Msgr. PATRICK J. PRATICO, J.C.D.; LINDA E. PRICE, J.C.L.; Rev. JOHN L. SULLIVAN, J.C.L.

Defenders of the Bond—Rev. Msgrs. JOSEPH G. QUINN, J.D., J.C.L.; JOHN A. BERGAMO, J.C.L.; Very Rev. JAMES J. WALSH, V.F., J.C.L.

Promoter of Justice—Rev. Msgr. JOHN A. BERGAMO, J.C.L.

Auditors—JOSEPH A. BARRETT, Ph.D.; JOSEPH V. FOX; Rev. Msgr. JOHN A. BERGAMO, J.C.L.

Procurator/Advocates—JOSEPH V. FOX; Very Rev. PHILIP A. ALTAVILLA, V.F.

Psychological Expert—JOSEPH A. BARRETT, Ph.D.

Notaries—ANN WALSH; PATRICIA WALTON; JOSETTE JORDAN; PATRICIA VANCOSKY.

Diocesan Finance Council—Most Rev. JOHN M. DOUGHERTY, D.D., V.G.; Rev. Msgrs. DONALD A.

McAndrews; William P. Ward; Very Rev. John A. Doris, V.F.; Mrs. Ellen Dermody; John W. Eck; James E. O'Brien Jr., Esq.; Melinda Ghilardi, Esq.; Thomas L. Kennedy, Esq.; James M. Quinn; James B. Earley; Ernest G. Pappa.

Diocesan Consultors—Most Rev. John M. Dougherty, D.D., V.G.; Rev. Msgrs. Joseph C. Bambera, J.C.L.; Vincent J. Grimalia, V.F.; Stephen D. McGough; Very Rev. Richard J. Loch, V.F.; Revs. John J. Kilpatrick; Joseph R. Kopacz; Albert M. Liberatore; Richard J. Polmounter; Charles W. Rokosz; Edward R. Scott; Phillip J. Sladicka; John J. Turi.

Ex Officio—Rev. Christopher S. Sahd, Sec.

Diocesan Pastoral Council— Contact: Ellen C. Dermody, Diocesan Dir., Pastoral Planning, 300 Wyoming Ave., Scranton, 18503-1279. Tel: 570-207-2267.

Deans—Very Rev. Richard J. Loch, V.F., Scranton-Central; Rev. Msgr. Philip A. Gray, V.F., Scranton-South; Very Revs. Edward J. Shoback, V.F., Scranton-West; William J. Flynn, S.S., V.F., Abingtons; John S. Terry, V.F., Ashley; Ronald J. Hughes, V.F., Bradford and Sullivan; James J. Walsh, V.F., J.C.L., Carbondale; John A. Doris, V.F., Dunmore; Gerard F. Safko, V.F., Freeland; Patrick J. McLaughlin, V.F., Hazleton; Rev. Msgr. Neil J. Van Loon, V.F., Kingston; Very Revs. Charles J. Cummings, V.F., Lycoming; Santino J. Fanucci, V.F., Mid-Valley; Thomas D. McLaughlin, V.F., Monroe; James E. McGahagan, V.F., Nanticoke; Philip A. Altavilla, V.F., Old Forge; Gerald F. Mullally, V.F., Pike; James J. Paisley, V.F., Pittston; Rev. Msgr. Vincent J. Grimalia, V.F., Plymouth; Very Revs. W. Jeffrey Paulish, V.F., Susquehanna; Albert P. Leonard, V.F., Tioga; Martin M. Boylan, V.F., Wayne; Michael J. Piccola, V.F., West Pittston; James B. Shimsky, V.F., Wilkes-Barre/Central South; E. Francis Kelly, V.F., Wilkes-Barre/Plains.

Presbyteral Council—Most Rev. Joseph F. Martino, D.D., H.E.D., Pres.; Rev. Msgr. Joseph C. Bambera, J.C.L., Chm.; Rev. Paul M. Mullen, Vice Chm.; Very Rev. Philip A. Altavilla, V.F., Sec.; Rev. Msgrs. John A. Bergamo, J.C.L.; William L. Donovan (Retired); Vincent J. Grimalia, V.F.; John H. Louis; Donald A. McAndrews; James J. McGarry; Stephen D. McGough; Joseph G. Rauscher; Neil J. Van Loon, V.F.; Bernard E. Yarrish, S.T.L.; Very Rev. Richard J. Loch, V.F.; Revs. Cyril D. Edwards; Richard E. Fox; Michael B. Harris; John J. Kilpatrick; Andrew Kurovsky; Albert M. Liberatore; John K. Manno; Richard J. Polmounter; Charles W. Rokosz; Daniel L. Schwebs, O.S.J.; Edward R. Scott; Thomas P. Shoback; Thomas G. Sinnott; Phillip J. Sladicka; John J. Turi; Jeffrey J. Walsh; Joseph O. Weber; Cassian J. Yuhaus, C.P. Ex Officio: Most Rev. John M. Dougherty, D.D., V.G.; Revs. Christopher S. Sahd; Joseph R. Kopacz.

Diocesan Building Commission— All plans for building should be sent to Chancery Office, *300 Wyoming Ave., Scranton, 18503-1279.* Rev. Msgr. Philip A. Gray, V.F.; Revs. Joseph A. Greskiewicz; John M. Lapera; Al Brocavich; James Devers; John Pocius; Paul Talerico. Ex Officio: Most Rev. John M. Dougherty, D.D., V.G.; James B. Earley; James M. Quinn.

Vicar for Canonical Services—Rev. Msgr. Patrick J. Pratico, J.C.D., 300 Wyoming Ave., Scranton, 18503-1279. Tel: 570-207-2246.

Vicar for Priests—Rev. Joseph R. Kopacz, 300 Wyoming Ave., Scranton, 18503-1279. Tel: 570-207-2269.

Vicars for Religious—Most Rev. John M. Dougherty, D.D., V.G., 300 Wyoming Ave., Scranton, 18503-1279. Tel: 570-207-2216; Sr. M. Gabriel Kane, I.H.M., 300 Wyoming Ave., Scranton, 18503-1279. Tel: 570-207-2243.

Diocesan Offices and Directors

Blue Army of Our Lady of Fatima—Deacon Florian J. Gyza, Diocesan Spiritual Dir., 357 Blackman St., Wilkes-Barre, 18702. Tel: 570-829-0921. St. Stanislaus Church, Nanticoke, 18634.

Catholic Campaign for Human Development—Rev. William B. Pickard, Interim Dir., 2010 Adams Ave., Scranton, 18509. Tel: 570-207-8713; Fax: 570-207-6875.

Campus Ministry—Sr. Catherine Ann Gilvary, I.H.M., Dir., Lycoming College, 700 College Pl., Box 149, Williamsport, 17701. Tel: 570-321-4111; Fax: 570-321-4337.

Catholic Charismatic Renewal—Very Rev. Richard J. Loch, V.F., Spiritual Advisor; Robert Valiante, Coord., P.O. Box 3306, Scranton, 18505. Tel: 570-344-2214.

Catholic Health Care Facilities Dir. and Representative to Catholic Institutions of Higher Learning—Rev. Andrew J. McGowan, Mercy Hospital, Scranton, 18501. Tel: 570-348-7010.

Catholic Relief Services—James B. Earley, Chancellor, 300 Wyoming Ave., Scranton, 18503-1279. Tel: 570-207-2216.

Catholic Social Services—Mr. Ned Delaney, M.A., Diocesan Dir., 33 E. Northampton St., Wilkes-Barre, 18701. Tel: 570-822-7118; Fax: 570-829-7781.

Lackawanna County—

Scranton Office—Mr. Stephen R. Nocilla, M.A., Exec. Dir., 400 Wyoming Ave., Scranton, 18503-1272. Tel: 570-207-2283; Fax: 570-207-2206.

Carbondale Office—39 S. Main St., Carbondale, 18407. Tel: 570-282-0460.

Luzerne County—

Wyoming Valley Office—Mr. Ned Delaney, M.A., Exec. Dir., 33 E. Northampton St., Wilkes-Barre, 18701. Tel: 570-822-7118; Fax: 570-829-7781.

Hazleton Office—Mr. Neil Oberto, M.A., Exec. Dir., 81 S. Church St., Hazleton, 18201. Tel: 570-455-1521; Fax: 570-455-2707.

Lycoming County—

Williamsport Office—Mr. Robert Makos, L.S.W., Exec. Dir., 1201 Grampian Blvd., Ste. 2G, Williamsport, 17701. Tel: 570-322-4220; Fax: 570-322-4276.

Monroe County—

Stroudsburg Office—Mrs. Mary Lou Malloy, L.S.W., Exec. Dir., 411 Main St., Stroudsburg, 18360. Tel: 570-476-6460; Fax: 570-476-6466.

Pike County—

Milford Office—Ms. Erin Bustelos, Rte. 6, P.O. Box 1195, Milford, 18337. Tel: 800-916-1913; 570-296-1054; Fax: 570-296-9227.

Tioga County—

Wellsboro Office—Mr. Bern Makos, L.S.W., 109 East Ave., Wellsboro, 16901. Tel: 570-724-2734; Fax: 570-724-7760.

Wyoming County—

Tunkhannock Office—Ms. Joanne Donato, L.S.W., 102 Warren St., Tunkhannock, 18657-0704. Tel: 570-836-1101; Fax: 570-836-3765.

Natural Family Planning Coordinator—Mary Ann Paulukonis, Diocesan Coord., 300 Wyoming Ave., Scranton, 18503-1279. Tel: 570-207-2213.

Diocesan Board of Education—Rev. Msgr. Vincent J. Grimalia, V.F., Pres.; James Redington, Vice Pres.; Sr. Mary Alice Kane, I.H.M., Sec.

Cemeteries—Mr. Walter Bennett, Dir., 1708 Oram St., Scranton, 18504. Tel: 570-207-2209.

Censor Librorum—Rev. Msgr. David A. Bohr, S.T.D., St. Pius X Seminary, Dalton, 18414. Tel: 570-563-1131.

Continuing Education of Priests—Rev. Msgr. Bernard E. Yarrish, S.T.L., Dir., St. Pius X Seminary, 1000 Seminary Rd., Dalton, 18414. Tel: 570-563-8507.

Cursillo Movement—Rev. Phillip J. Sladicka, Spiritual Moderator, 200 Delaware Ave., Olyphant, 18447. Tel: 570-489-0752.

Diocesan Commission on Ethics for Catholic Health Care Facilities—Rev. Msgr. David A. Bohr, S.T.D., Chm.; Lynn Marie Busch, O.C.V.; Joseph Casciano; Deacon Thomas M. Cesarini; Sr. Kathryn Clauss, I.H.M.; James McKenna, M.D.; Joanne Orloski, M.D.; Rev. James A. Rafferty, S.T.L.; William P. Smedley, M.D.; Glen Yanik, Esq.

Diocesan Commission on Ecumenism and Inter-Faith Matters—Very Rev. Philip A. Altavilla, V.F., Diocesan Dir., St. John the Baptist Rectory, 408 N. Main St., Taylor, 18517-1108. Tel: 570-562-1341.

Diocesan Director of Public Relations—Vacant, Dir.

Diocesan Safety Inspector—Mr. Terry K. Stephens, 300 Wyoming Ave., Scranton, 18503-1279. Tel: 570-207-2232; 570-207-2240; Fax: 570-207-2273.

Diocesan Historian—Rev. Charles P. Connor, Ph.D., St. Rose of Lima Rectory, 6 N. Church St., Carbondale, 18407. Tel: 570-282-2991.

Diocesan Office for Communications—Mrs. Maria Orzel, Exec. Dir., 400 Wyoming Ave., Scranton, 18503-1272. Tel: 570-207-2219; 800-246-0288; Fax: 570-207-2281.

Diocesan Office of Development—Ernest Pappa, Dir., 300 Wyoming Ave., Scranton, 18503-1279. Tel: 570-207-2250; Fax: 570-207-1835. Email: ernest-pappa@dioceseofscranton.org.

Diocesan Appeal Office—Ernest Pappa, Dir., 300 Wyoming Ave., Scranton, 18503-1279. Tel: 570-207-2250; Fax: 570-207-1835. Email: ernest-pappa@dioceseofscranton.org.

Diocese of Scranton Catholic Community Foundation—Ernest Pappa, Dir., 300 Wyoming Ave., Scranton, 18503-1279. Tel: 570-207-2250; Fax: 570-207-1835. Email: ernest-pappa@dioceseofscranton.org.

Diocese of Scranton Scholarship Foundation—Ernest G. Pappa, Dir., 300 Wyoming Ave., Scranton, 18503-1279. Tel: 570-207-2250; Fax: 570-207-1835. Email: ernest-pappa@dioceseofscranton.org.

Diocesan Office of Ecumenism—Very Rev. Philip A. Altavilla, V.F., Dir., St. John the Baptist Rectory, 408 N. Main St., Taylor, 18517-1108. Tel: 570-562-1341.

Diocesan Office of Parish Ministries—Joseph Casciano, Exec. Dir.; Vacant, Worship Dir.; Sarah Mountain, Youth & Young Adult Ministry Dir.; Christopher Tigue, Dir, C.Y.O.; Mary Ann Paulukonis, Family Life Dir.; David Clarke, Social Concerns Dir., 300 Wyoming Ave., Scranton, 18503-1279. Tel: 570-207-2213.

Ministry for Persons with Disabilities—Sr. Mary Beth Makuch, SS.C.M., Dir., 400 Wyoming Ave., Scranton, 18503-1272. Tel: 570-207-2213.

Ministry with Deaf and Hard of Hearing—Sr. Mary Beth Makuch, SS.C.M., Dir., 400 Wyoming Ave., Scranton, 18503-1272. Tel: 570-207-2213. Audio-Visual Resource Center. Tel: 570-207-2284.

Diocesan Pro-Life Office—Joseph Casciano, Diocesan Dir., 300 Wyoming Ave., Scranton, 18503-1279. Tel: 570-207-2213.

Religious Education—Janet Benestad, Dir., 400 Wyoming Ave., Scranton, 18503-1272. Tel: 570-207-2213.

RENEW—Sr. Teresa Marie Skierkowski, S.C.C., Dir., 400 Wyoming Ave., Scranton, 18503-1272. Tel: 570-207-2213.

Holy Childhood Association—Rev. Michael J. Kloton, Dir.; Miriam Heverline, Mission Educ. Coord., 300 Wyoming Ave., Scranton, 18503-1279. Tel: 570-207-2259; Fax: 570-207-2268. Email: spofhcadiodirector@yahoo.com.

Holy Name Society—Rev. Scott P. Sterowski, Spiritual Moderator, St. Patrick's Rectory, 200 Delaware Ave., Olyphant, 18447-1535. Tel: 570-489-0752.

Legion of Mary—Rev. Patrick D. Healey, Spiritual Dir. (Retired), St. Mary of the Assumption Rectory, 430 Pittston Ave., Scranton, 18505. Tel: 570-961-2297.

Liturgical Commission—Revs. Albert M. Liberatore, Chm.; Doreen Ignatovich, Vice Chm.

Marriage Encounter—Very Rev. Richard J. Loch, V.F., Spiritual Advisor, Immaculate Conception Rectory, 801 Taylor Ave., Scranton, 18510. Tel: 570-961-5211; Fax: 570-961-5212.

D.C.C.M.—Rev. Scott P. Sterowski, Spiritual Moderator, St. Patrick's Rectory, 200 Delaware Ave., Olyphant, 18447. Tel: 570-489-0752; Fax: 570-489-0225.

D.C.C.W.—Rev. Msgr. Constantine V. Siconolfi, Spiritual Moderator, Holy Family Rectory, 510 E. Gibson St., Scranton, 18509. Tel: 570-342-8548.

Newspaper—Mr. William R. Genello, Editor, 300 Wyoming Ave., Scranton, 18503-1279. Tel: 570-207-2229; 570-207-2272; Fax: 570-207-2271. "The Catholic Light"

Office of Pastoral Planning—Ellen C. Dermody, Exec. Dir., 300 Wyoming Ave., Scranton, 18503-1279. Tel: 570-207-2267.

Diocesan Television Station-CTV—Mrs. Maria Orzel, Exec. Dir.; James Brennan, Mgr., 400 Wyoming Ave., Scranton, 18503-1272. Tel: 570-207-2219; Fax: 570-207-2281.

Permanent Diaconate Office—Rev. Msgr. David A. Bohr, S.T.D., Dir., St. Pius X Seminary, 1000 Seminary Rd., Dalton, 18414. Tel: 570-563-1131.

Pilgrimages—Rev. Andrew S. Hvozdovic, Diocesan Dir., 118 Kendall Ave., Jersey Shore, 18705. Tel: 570-398-2557.

Priests' Purgatorial Society—Rev. Joseph R. Kopacz, Sec., 300 Wyoming Ave., Scranton, 18503-1279. Tel: 570-207-2269.

Priests' Retirement Advisory Board—Most Rev. John M. Dougherty, D.D., V.G.; Rev. Msgr. William J. Pakutka (Retired); Very Rev. Richard J. Loch, V.F.; Revs. John J. Kilpatrick; John C. Lambert; Joseph R. Kopacz; James B. Earley; James M. Quinn.

Propagation of the Faith—Rev. Michael J. Kloton, Dir.; Miriam Heverline, Mission Educ. Coord., 300 Wyoming Ave., Scranton, 18503-1279. Tel: 570-207-2259; Fax: 570-207-2268. Email: spofhcadiodirector@yahoo.com.

Pastoral Formation Institute—Rev. Msgr. David A. Bohr, S.T.D., Dir.; Lynn Marie Busch, O.C.V., Coord., St. Pius X Seminary, 1000 Seminary Rd., Dalton, 18414. Tel: 570-563-8501.

Renewal--Fatima Center—Rev. Msgr. David A. Bohr, S.T.D., Exec. Dir., 1000 Seminary Rd., Dalton, 18414. Tel: 570-563-8500; Fax: 570-563-1857.

Retirement Fund for Religious—Sr. M. Gabriel Kane, I.H.M., Dir. Tel: 570-207-1452; 570-207-2243.

Schools—Ruth A. Connolly, Ed.D., Supt., 300 Wyoming Ave., Scranton, 18503-1279. Tel: 570-207-2253; Janet Donovan, Ed.D., Asst. Supt. Curriculum & Staff Devel. Tel: 570-207-2254;

DANIEL F. DONOVAN, Asst. Supt., Personnel. Tel: 570-207-2252; LOUIS H. CARDONI JR., Fiscal Mgr.

Scouts of America—Rev. BRYAN B. WRIGHT, Diocesan Chap., St. Joachim's Rectory, Box 67, Meshoppen, 18630. Tel: 570-833-2114.

Council of Women Religious— Contact: Sr. M. GABRIEL KANE, I.H.M., Vicar for Religious, 300 Wyoming Ave., Scranton, 18503-1279. Tel: 570-207-2243.

Victim Assistance Coordinator—JOAN L. HOLMES. Tel: 570-344-5216. Email: jloueliz@aol.com.

Vocations—Rev. THOMAS G. SINNOTT, 300 Wyoming Ave., Scranton, 18503. Tel: 570-207-1452; Fax: 570-207-1833.

CLERGY, PARISHES, MISSIONS AND PAROCHIAL SCHOOLS

CITY OF SCRANTON
(LACKAWANNA COUNTY)

1—ST. PETER'S CATHEDRAL (1853), Rev. Msgr. Joseph G. Quinn, J.D., J.C.L.; Revs. Christopher S. Sahd; Thomas G. Sinnott. In Res., Most Revs. Joseph F. Martino, D.D., H.E.D., V.G. (PH); James C. Timlin, D.D. (Retired).
Res.: 315 Wyoming Ave., 18503. Tel: 570-344-7231; Fax: 570-344-4749.

2—ST. ANN'S BASILICA PARISH (1901), Revs. Roger Elliott, C.P.; Kenneth Walsh, C.P.; William Maguire, C.P.
Res.: 1250 St. Ann St., 18504. Tel: 570-342-5166; Fax: 570-348-3750.
School—All Saints AcademySt. Ann's Campus, 1228 St Ann St., 18504. Tel: 570-348-3753; Fax: 570-348-3758. Lay Teachers 11; Students 111.
Catechesis/Religious Program—Tel: 570-344-8408. Katherine Stocki, D.R.E. Students 160.

3—ST. ANTHONY OF PADUA (1913), (Italian), Rev. Michael A. Penn. In Res., Rev. Robert J. Barone.
Res.: 1402 Short Ave., 18508. Tel: 570-342-4190.
Catechesis/Religious Program—Karen Forsette, D.R.E. Students 62.

4—ST. CLARE (1967), Rev. Msgr. William J. Feldcamp. In Res., Rev. Msgr. Joseph A. Fadden (Retired).
Res.: 2301 N. Washington Ave., 18509. Tel: 570-344-9884; Fax: 570-344-9885.
School—2215 N. Washington Ave., 18509. Tel: 570-343-2790; Fax: 570-343-4905. Sisters of the I.H.M. 6; Lay Teachers 8; Students 270.
Catechesis/Religious Program—Sr. Margaret Mary Kane, D.R.E. Students 150.

5—ST. DAVID'S (1946),, (Merged with St. Stanislaus, Old Forge, Tel.: 570-457-5103; Fax.: 570-344-4176) Rev. Thomas G. Sarnecki.
Res.: 2523 Jackson St., 18504. Tel: 570-344-9745; Fax: 570-344-4176.
Catechesis/Religious Program—Robin Lipik, D.R.E. Students 151.

6—ST. FRANCIS (1920), (Italian), Rev. Msgr. Philip A. Gray, V.F.
Res.: 630 Genet St., 18505. Tel: 570-346-0797; Fax: 570-346-7187.
Catechesis/Religious Program—Mary Ann Lucchi, D.R.E. Students 83.

7—HOLY CROSS (1897), Merged, with St. Patrick's, Scranton.

8—HOLY FAMILY (1891), [CEM] Rev. Msgr. Constantine V. Siconolfi.
Res.: 510 Gibson St., 18509. Tel: 570-342-8548; Fax: 570-342-2581.
Catechesis/Religious Program—Mary Jule Kapacs, D.R.E. Students 28.

9—HOLY NAME (1938), Rev. Michael H. Marchetti.
Res.: 1414 E. Elm St., 18505. Tel: 570-346-3859; Fax: 570-346-4971.
Catechesis/Religious Program—Lin Williams, D.R.E. Students 32.

10—HOLY ROSARY (1871),, (Merged with St. Stanislaus and its mission, St. Stephen's Church, Scranton) Rev. Cyril D. Edwards; Deacon Edward Protzman.
Res.: 316 William St., 18508. Tel: 570-342-4881; Fax: 570-344-2130.
School—312 William St., 18508. Tel: 570-344-7565. Priests 1; Sisters of the I.H.M. 4; Lay Teachers 11; Students 220.
Catechesis/Religious Program—Marie Purcell, D.R.E. Students 324.

11—IMMACULATE CONCEPTION (1967), Very Rev. Richard J. Loch, V.F.; Revs. Edward F. Barrett; Thomas J. Sokolowski.
Res.: 801 Taylor Ave., 18510. Tel: 570-961-5211; Fax: 570-961-5212.
Catechesis/Religious Program—Michele Donovan, D.R.E. Students 361.

12—ST. JOHN THE BAPTIST (1885), (German), Merged, with St. Patrick's, Scranton.

13—ST. JOHN THE EVANGELIST (1886), Rev. Eugene L. Gunning.
Res.: 516 Fig St., 18505. Tel: 570-343-6026; Fax: 570-344-8101.
Catechesis/Religious Program—Students 48.

14—ST. JOSEPH'S (1894), (Lithuanian), [CEM] Rev. Msgr. Peter P. Madus.
Res.: 116 Theodore St., 18508. Tel: 570-342-4339; Fax: 570-342-4245.
Catechesis/Religious Program—Donna Shotwell, D.R.E. Students 51.

15—ST. JOSEPH'S (1875), [CEM] Rev. John M. Lapera.
Res.: 312 Davis St., 18505. Tel: 570-344-1724; Fax: 570-344-1787.
Catechesis/Religious Program—Nancy Mott, D.R.E. Students 226.

16—ST. LUCY'S (1901), (Italian), Revs. John J. Chmil; Thomas Yuen.
Res.: 949 Scranton St., 18504. Tel: 570 347-9421; Fax: 570-541-8252.
Catechesis/Religious Program—Students 80.

17—ST. MARY OF THE ASSUMPTION (1854), (German), [CEM 2] Rev. Msgr. Dale R. Rupert. In Res., Rev. Patrick D Healey (Retired).
Res.: 430 Pittston Ave., 18505. Tel: 570-961-2297; Fax: 570-961-1468.
School— Please see Marian Catholic Interparochial School in the Institutions section located under Inter-Parochial Elementary Schools
Catechesis/Religious Program—Marie Merkel, D.R.E. Students 127.

18—ST. MARY'S (1904), (Polish), [CEM] Rev. Albert E. Oldfield.
Res.: 3325 Greenwood Ave., Moosic, 18507. Tel: 570-343-4024; Fax: 570-343-8323.
School— Please see Marian Catholic Interparochial School in the Institutions section located under Inter-Parochial Elementary Schools
Catechesis/Religious Program—Students 56.

19—ST. MICHAEL'S (1914), (Lithuanian), Rev. Carl Gismondi, F.S.S.P. In Res., Rev. Joseph R. Howard, F.S.S.P.
Res.: 1703 Jackson St., 18504. Tel: 570-961-1205; Fax: 570-961-2284.

20—NATIVITY OF OUR LORD (1903), Rev. Msgr. Joseph P. Kelly. In Res., Rev. John C. Ruth.
Res.: 633 Orchard St., 18505. Tel: 570-344-6159; Fax: 570-207-4932.
School— Please see Marian Catholic Interparochial School in the Institutions section located under Inter-Parochial Elementary Schools
Catechesis/Religious Program—Sr. Joan Marie Thompson, I.H.M., D.R.E. Students 149.

21—ST. PATRICK'S (1870),, (Merged with Holy Cross and St. John the Baptist, Scranton) Rev. Msgr. David L. Tressler; Revs. James P. Dougher; Philip S. Rayappan.
Res.: 1403 Jackson St., 18504. Tel: 570-344-2679; 570-343-4353; Fax: 570-343-2835.
School—All Saints AcademySt. Patrick's Campus, 120 S. Lincoln Ave., 18504. Tel: 570-343-8114. Sisters of the I.H.M. 1; Lay Teachers 13; Students 220.
Catechesis/Religious Program—Linda Sepkowski, D.R.E. Students 1,246.
Chapel—Scranton, Immaculate Heart of Mary

22—ST. PAUL'S (1887), Rev. Michael B. Harris.
Res.: 1510 Penn Ave., 18509. Tel: 570-961-1549; Fax: 570-961-0335.
School—1527 Penn Ave., 18509. Tel: 570-343-7880; Fax: 570-343-0069. Lay Teachers 14 Students 222.
Catechesis/Religious Program—Jean Evans, D.R.E. Students 140.

23—SS. PETER AND PAUL (1910), (Polish), [CEM] Very Rev. Edward J. Shoback, V.F.
Res.: 1309 W. Locust St., 18504. Tel 570-343-7015; Fax: 570-343-7023.
Catechesis/Religious Program—Christine Loyek, D.R.E. Students 32.

24—SACRED HEARTS OF JESUS AND MARY (1885), (Polish), [CEM] Rev. Joseph R. Kopacz; Deacon Joseph Levine. In Res., Rev. Walter L. Ferrett.
Res.: 1217 Prospect Ave., 18505. Tel: 570-343-6420; Fax: 570-343-3664.
Catechesis/Religious Program—Students 107.

25—ST. STANISLAUS (1915), (Polish), Merged, with Holy Rosary, Scranton and its mission, St. Stephen's Church, Scranton.

26—ST. VINCENT DE PAUL (1925), Rev. Msgr. Peter P. Madus.
Res.: 116 Theodore St.. Tel: 570-342-4339; Fax: 570-342-4245.
Catechesis/Religious Program—Students 85.

OUTSIDE THE CITY OF SCRANTON

ARCHBALD, LACKAWANNA CO., ST. THOMAS AQUINAS (1858), [CEM] Revs. Gerard M. Gannon; Edward P. Lyman.
Res.: 411 Church St., 18403. Tel: 570-876-1701; Fax: 570-876-3617.
Catechesis/Religious Program—Tel: 570-876-1411. Rosanne Cherney, D.R.E.; Teresa Mattise, D.R.E. Students 387.

ASHLEY, LUZERNE CO.
1—HOLY ROSARY (1900), (Slovak), Rev. John F. Samson.
Res.: 60 Charles St., 18706. Tel: 570-822-7543.
Catechesis/Religious Program—Students 45.
2—ST. LEO'S (1887), Rev. Thomas J. O'Malley.
Res.: 33 Manhattan St., 18706. Tel: 570-825-6669; Fax: 570-823-3714.
Catechesis/Religious Program—Michele Casey, D.R.E. Students 196.

ATHENS, BRADFORD CO., ST. JOSEPH (1852), Merged, with St. John the Evangelist, South Waverly.

AVOCA, LUZERNE CO.
1—ST. MARY'S (1871), [CEM] Rev. Joseph Elston.
Res.: 715 Hawthorne St., 18641. Tel: 570-457-3412; Fax: 570-655-8218.
School—742 Spring St., 18641. Tel: 570-457-9700; 570-457-9600; Fax: 570-457-3677. Lay Teachers 10; Students 152.
Catechesis/Religious Program—Debbie Callahan, D.R.E. Students 343.
2—SS. PETER AND PAUL (1909), (Polish), [CEM] Rev. Mark J. Bochinski.
Res.: 912 Vine St., 18641. Tel: 570-457-2483; 570-457-9806; Fax: 570-451-2993.
Catechesis/Religious Program—Debby Yuschovitz, D.R.E. Students 193.

BASTRESS, LYCOMING CO., IMMACULATE CONCEPTION (1838), (German), [CEM] Rev. Robert T. Busteed.
Res.: 5973 Jacks Hollow Rd., Williamsport, 17702. Tel: 570-745-3301.
School—6101 Jacks Hollow Rd., Williamsport, 17702. Tel: 570-745-3320; Fax: 570-745-3723. Sisters of Christian Charity 2; Lay Teachers 5; Students 74.
Catechesis/Religious Program—Tel: 570-745-3316. Students 127.

BEAR CREEK TOWNSHIP, LUZERNE CO.
1—ST. CHRISTOPHER (1962), Merged, with Holy Saviour, Wilkes-Barre.
2—ST. ELIZABETH (1938), Rev. Anthony M. Urban.
5700 Bear Creek Blvd., P.O. Box 25, 18602. Tel: 570-472-3061.
Catechesis/Religious Program—Elsie DeLuca, D.R.E. Students 114.
Mission—St. Mark Thornhurst, Luzerne Co.

BENTLEY CREEK, BRADFORD CO., ST. ANN'S (1843), [CEM] Rev. Thomas J. Major.
Res.: R.R. No. 3, Box 138A, Gillett, 16925. Tel: 570-596-2109; Fax: 570-596-2107.
Catechesis/Religious Program—Students 17.
Mission—Our Lady of Perpetual Help Ridgebury, Bradford Co.

BLAKESLEE, MONROE CO., CHRIST THE KING (1976), Rev. Raymond L. Deviney.
Res.: P.O. Box 171, 18610. Tel: 570-646-8990.
Catechesis/Religious Program—Tel: 570-646-7456. Adele Lewis, D.R.E. Students 175.

BLOSSBURG, TIOGA CO.
1—ST. ANDREW'S, Merged, with St. Mary, Blossburg.
2—ST. MARY'S (1874), (Polish), [CEM 3], (Merged with St. Andrew, Blossburg) Rev. Brian J.W. Clarke, Admin.
Res.: 138 St. Mary's St., 16912. Tel: 570-638-3241; Fax: 570-638-2952.
Catechesis/Religious Program—Students 48.
Mission—St. Stanislaus Kostka Arnot, Tioga Co.
Mission—St. Joseph Morris Run, Tioga Co.

BRODHEADSVILLE, MONROE CO., OUR LADY QUEEN OF PEACE (1968), Rev. William J. McCawley.
Res.: P.O. Box 38, 18322. Tel: 610-681-6137; Fax: 610-681-6139.
Catechesis/Religious Program—Mary Beth Stevens, D.R.E. Students 1,161.

BUTTONWOOD, LUZERNE CO., EXALTATION OF THE HOLY CROSS (1917), (Polish), [CEM] Very Rev. James E. McGahagan, V.F.
Res.: 420 Main Rd., Hanover Township, 18706-6094. Tel: 570-823-6242; Fax: 570-829-4732.
Catechesis/Religious Program—Students 90.

CANADENSIS, MONROE CO., ST. BERNADETTE (1967), Rev. Alfred J. Vito; Deacon Ronald P. Verkon.
Res.: P.O. Box 14, 18325. Tel: 570-595-2139; 570-595-7622 (Maloney Hall); 570-595-6277 (Worship Line); 570-595-9249 (Youth); Fax: 570-595-6235.
Catechesis/Religious Program—Dorothy Lewis, D.R.E. Students 49.
Mission—Our Lady of Fatima Promised Land, Monroe Co.

CANTON, BRADFORD CO., ST. MICHAEL (1853), [CEM] Rev. Peter J. O'Rourke; Deacon William H. Graham.
Res.: 24 N. Washington St., 17724. Tel: 570-673-5253; Fax: 570-673-5630.
Catechesis/Religious Program—Deacon William H. Graham, D.R.E. Students 67.
Mission—St. John Nepomucene [CEM] Troy, Bradford Co. Tel: 570-297-4405.
Mission—St. Aloysius Ralston, Lycoming Co.

CARBONDALE, LACKAWANNA CO.
1—OUR LADY OF MT. CARMEL (1882), (Italian), [CEM] Rev. Russell E. Motsay.
Res.: 15 Fallbrook St., 18407. Tel: 570-282-5172.
Catechesis/Religious Program—Students 94.
2—ST. ROSE OF LIMA (1832), [CEM 2] Revs. Charles P. Connor, Ph.D.; William D. Campbell.
Res.: 6 N. Church St., 18407. Tel: 570-282-2991; Fax: 570-282-7580.
Catechesis/Religious Program—Patricia Dragwa, D.R.E. Students 477.
CARVERTON, LUZERNE CO., ST. FRANCES CABRINI (1947), Rev. Joseph O. Weber.
Res.: 585 Mt. Olivet Rd., Kingston Twp., Wyoming, 18644-9333. Tel: 570-696-3737; Fax: 570-696-9767.
Catechesis/Religious Program—Regina Ference, D.R.E. Students 139.
Mission—Blessed Sacrament Centermoreland, Luzerne Co.
CLARKS GREEN, LACKAWANNA CO., ST. GREGORY (1974), Rev. Msgr. John H. Louis.
Res.: 330 N. Abington Rd., 18411. Tel: 570-587-4808; Fax: 570-586-4515.
Catechesis/Religious Program—Joanne Judge, D.R.E. Students 600.
CLARKS SUMMIT, LACKAWANNA CO., OUR LADY OF THE SNOWS (1911), Rev. Msgr. James J. McGarry; Rev. Thomas M. Muldowney.
Res.: 301 S. State St., 18411. Tel: 570-586-1741; Fax: 570-586-2504.
Catechesis/Religious Program—Michele O'Brien, D.R.E. Students 1,125.
Mission—St. Benedict Newton, Lackawanna Co.
CONYNGHAM, LUZERNE CO., ST. JOHN BOSCO (1964), Revs. Joseph J. Evanko; Thomas George.
Res.: 2 Charles Ave. P.O. Box 919, 18219. Tel: 570-788-1997; Fax: 570-788-6667.
Catechesis/Religious Program—Gerry Olenick, D.R.E. Students 420.
DALLAS, LUZERNE CO., GATE OF HEAVEN (1951), Rev. Kevin P. Mulhern; Deacon Thomas M. Cesarini.
Res.: Machell Ave., 18612. Tel: 570-675-2121; Fax: 570-675-7143.
Catechesis/Religious Program—Tel: 570-675-6488. Sonya Cesarini, D.R.E. Students 310.
DALTON, LACKAWANNA CO., OUR LADY OF THE ABINGTONS (1967), Very Rev. David W. Cramer, V.F.; Deacon James F. Graham.
Res.: 700 W. Main St., 18414. Tel: 570-563-1622; Fax: 570-563-0988.
Catechesis/Religious Program—Barbara Foley, D.R.E. Students 126.
DICKSON CITY, LACKAWANNA CO.
1—ST. THOMAS THE APOSTLE, Closed., For inquiries for parish records please see Visitaton of the Blessed Virgin Mary
2—VISITATION OF THE BLESSED VIRGIN MARY (1890), (Polish), [CEM], Merged with St. Thomas the Apostle, Dickson City. Rev. Msgr. Joseph C. Bambera, J.C.L.; Rev. Joseph F. Orloski.
Res.: 1090 Carmalt St., 18519. Tel: 570-489-2091; Fax: 570-489-0349.
School—Tel: 570-489-0061; Fax: 570-489-0157. Bernardine Sisters of St. Francis 3; Lay Teachers 10; Students 210.
Catechesis/Religious Program—Sr. Carmencita Pozarzecki, D.R.E. Students 350.
DORRANCE, LUZERNE CO., OUR LADY HELP OF CHRISTIANS (1948), (Polish), [CEM] Rev. Mark G. Balczeniuk.
Res.: 3529 St. Mary's Rd. (Dorrance), Wapwallopen, 18660-9765. Tel: 570-868-5855; Fax: 570-868-5876.
Catechesis/Religious Program—Mrs. Patricia Heller, D.R.E. Students 133.
DRUMS, LUZERNE CO., CHURCH OF THE GOOD SHEPHERD (1940),, Merged with St. Nazarius, Pardeesville. Very Rev. Gerard F. Safko, V.F.; Revs. Augustine Poonelil, O.C.D.; Michael P. Litcheck.
Res.: 87 South Hunter Hwy., 18222. Tel: 570-788-3141; Fax: 570-788-2916.
Catechesis/Religious Program—Jean Kunger, D.R.E.; Carol Matz, D.R.E.; Marguerita Benderavich, D.R.E. Students 140.
DUNMORE, LACKAWANNA CO.
1—ALL SAINTS (1905), (Slovak), Merged, with St. Mary of Mount Carmel, Dunmore.
2—ST. ANTHONY OF PADUA (1894), (Italian), Rev. Msgr. Anthony C. Marra; Deacon Carmine Mendicino.
Res.: 303 Smith St., 18512. Tel: 570-344-1209; Fax: 570-344-1200.
School—208 Smith St., 18512. Tel: 570-342-1182; Fax: 570-342-1182. Sisters 2; Lay Teachers 9; Students 162.
Catechesis/Religious Program—Sr. Donna Cerminaro, D.R.E. Students 122.
Convent—Religious Teachers Filippini, 215 Franklin St., 18512. Tel: 570-343-1422; Fax: 570-346-3099.
3—ST. CASIMIR, (Polish), Merged, with St. Mary of Mount Carmel, Dunmore.
4—CHRIST THE KING (1949), Very Rev. Richard J. Loch, V.F.
Res.: 1214 Quincy Ave., 18510. Tel: 570-343-2777; Fax: 570-341-7274.
Catechesis/Religious Program—Ursula Ann Yerus, D.R.E. Students 47.
5—ST. MARY OF MOUNT CARMEL (1856), [CEM 2], (Merged with All Saints and St. Casimir, Dunmore.) Very Rev. John A. Doris, V.F.; Rev. Thomas Augustine Desam (India); Roy E. Brahm, Pastoral Assoc. In Res., Rev. Albert M. Liberatore.
Res.: 322 Chestnut St., 18512. Tel: 570-346-7429; Fax: 570-346-0523.
School—325 Chestnut St., 18512. Tel: 570-346-4429; Fax: 570-346-3016. Lay Teachers 15; Students 185.
Catechesis/Religious Program—Lisa Murphy, D.R.E.; Dorothy Smith, D.R.E.; Ang Dempsey, D.R.E. Students 797.
6—ST. ROCCO'S (1905), (Italian), Rev. Anthony R. Tombasco.
Res.: 118 Kurtz St., 18510-1539. Tel: 570-344-1239.
Catechesis/Religious Program—Tel: 570-343-1476. Nancy Gillette, D.R.E. Students 16.
DUPONT, LUZERNE CO., SACRED HEART OF JESUS (1902), (Polish), [CEM] Rev. Joseph D. Verespy.
Res.: 215 Lackawanna Ave., 18641. Tel: 570-654-3713; Fax: 570-654-7952.
School—217 Lackawanna Ave., 18641. Tel: 570-654-8822; Fax: 570-654-8827. Lay Teachers 10; Students 166.
Catechesis/Religious Program—Elaine Starinski, D.R.E. Students 80.
DURYEA, LUZERNE CO.
1—HOLY ROSARY (1893), (Polish), [CEM] Revs. Charles W. Rokosz; Edward J. Williams; Deacon Santo Agolino.
Res.: 127 Stephenson St., 18642. Tel: 570-457-3502; Fax: 570-457-3341.
School—110 1/2 Stephenson St., 18642. Tel: 570-457-2553; Fax: 570-457-3537. Lay Teachers 11; Students 242.
Catechesis/Religious Program—Joseph Szewczk, D.R.E.; Judy Lambert, D.R.E. Students 162.
2—ST. JOSEPH'S (1909), (Lithuanian), [CEM], Merged with Sacred Heart of Jesus, Duryea.
3—SACRED HEART OF JESUS (1889), (German),
DUSHORE, SULLIVAN CO., ST. BASIL'S (1838), [CEM] Rev. David R. Betts.
Res.: 101 Churchill St., P.O. Box 307, 18614-0307. Tel: 570-928-8865; Fax: 570-928-7972.
Catechesis/Religious Program—Carol Roinick, D.R.E. Students 148.
Mission—St. Francis Xavier Overton, Sullivan Co.
Mission—Sacred Heart Laporte, Sullivan Co.
Mission—St. Francis of Assisi Eagles Mere, Sullivan Co.
Mission—St. Frances of Assisi Mildred, Sullivan Co.
Shrine—S. Philip and James Church-St. John Neumann Shrine Sugar Ridge.
EAST STROUDSBURG, MONROE CO.
1—ST. JOHN (1986), Rev. John C. Lambert; Deacon Al Schito.
Mailing Address: 5171 Milford Rd., 18301. Tel: 570-223-9144; Fax: 570-223-9146.
Catechesis/Religious Program—Tel: 570-223-0888. Marie Mead, D.R.E. Students 431.
2—ST. MATTHEW'S (1902), Rev. Msgr. John A. Bergamo, J.C.L.; Revs. Albert Bellantonio; Daniel A. Toomey; Deacon Svetko Jurjevic.
Res.: 200 Brodhead Ave., 18301. Tel: 570-421-2342; Fax: 570-421-8414.
Catechesis/Religious Program—Tel: 570-421-0113. Nancy Lavelle, D.R.E. Students 739.
EDWARDSVILLE, LUZERNE CO., SS. CYRIL AND METHODIUS (1900), (Slovak), Merged, with St. Anthony of Padua, Larksville.
ELKLAND, TIOGA CO., ST. THOMAS THE APOSTLE (1907), Rev. Wieslaw M. Ziebacz.
Res.: 111 First St., 16920. Tel: 814-258-5121; Fax: 814-258-5122.
Catechesis/Religious Program—Patrick Kennedy, D.R.E. Students 42.
Mission—St. Catherine Lincoln St., Westfield, Tioga Co. 16950.
ELMHURST, LACKAWANNA CO., ST. EULALIA (1950), Rev. Msgr. F. Allan Conlan, Ph.D. In Res., Rev. Gerard F. Lupa.
Res.: P.O. Box 143, 18416. Tel: 570-842-7656; Fax: 570-842-7193.
Catechesis/Religious Program—Elizabeth Strasburger, D.R.E. Students 330.
EXETER, LUZERNE CO.
1—ST. ANTHONY OF PADUA (1928), (Italian), Revs. Daniel L. Schwebs, O.S.J.; Raymond Tabon, O.S.J.
Res.: 28 Memorial Ave., Exeter Boro, Pittston, 18643. Tel: 570-654-2103; Fax: 570-655-3313.
Catechesis/Religious Program—Denise Adams, D.R.E. Students 190.
2—ST. CECILIA (1900), [CEM], Merged with St. John the Baptist, Exeter. Rev. Daniel D. Hitchko; Deacon William A. Dervinis.
Res.: 1700 Wyoming Ave., 18643. Tel: 570-654-2133; Fax: 570-654-3449.
Catechesis/Religious Program—Students 142.
Convent—1690 Wyoming Ave., 18643. Tel: 570-655-8119.
3—ST. JOHN THE BAPTIST (1898), (Polish), Merged, with St. Cecilia, Exeter.
EYNON, LACKAWANNA CO.
1—ST. MARY OF VILNA, (Lithuanian), Merged, with St. Mary's Czestochowa, Eynon.
2—ST. MARY'S CZESTOCHOWA (1915), (Polish),, Merged with St. Mary of Vilna, Eynon. Rev. Msgr. Patrick J. Pratico, J.C.D.
Res.: 417 Main St., 18403. Tel: 570-876-2223; Fax: 570-876-3081.
Catechesis/Religious Program—Students 78.
FAIRMOUNT SPRINGS, LUZERNE CO., ST. MARTHA'S (1966), Rev. Joseph R. Kakareka.
Res.: 260 Bonnieville Rd., Stillwater, 17878. Tel: 570-864-8588; Fax: 570-864-0689.
FOREST CITY, SUSQUEHANNA CO.
1—ST. JOSEPH'S (1904), (Slovenian), Merged, with Sacred Heart of Jesus, Forest City.
2—SACRED HEART OF JESUS (1904), (Polish),, Merged with St. Agnes, Forest City. Rev. Patrick L. Albert.
Res.: 612 Hudson St., 18421. Tel: 570-785-3838; Fax: 570-785-3713.
Catechesis/Religious Program—
FREELAND, LUZERNE CO.
1—ST. ANN'S (1862), [CEM] Revs. John E. Melnick; Joseph J. Mattey; Deacon Cyril J. Kowalchick.
Office—898 Centre St., 18224. Tel: 570-636-3035; Fax: 570-636-1743.
Res.: 420 Vine St., 18224.
Catechesis/Religious Program—Safko Centre, Chestnut St., 18224. Tel: 570-636-3698. Students 520.
2—ST. ANTHONY'S, Merged, with St. Ann's, Freeland.
3—ST. CASIMIR'S, Merged, with St. Ann's, Freeland.
4—ST. JOHN NEPOMUCENE, Merged, with St. Ann's, Freeland.
FRIENDSVILLE, SUSQUEHANNA CO.
1—ST. FRANCIS XAVIER, Formerly St. Francis Xavier's (1831), [CEM 3], Merged with St. Thomas the Apostle, Little Meadows. Very Rev. W. Jeffrey Paulish, V.F.
Res.: P.O. Box 50, 18818. Tel: 570-553-2288; Fax: 570-553-2975.
Catechesis/Religious Program—Jane Conboy, D.R.E.; Janet Brown, D.R.E. Students 45.
Mission—St. Patrick Middletown, Susquehanna Co.
2—ST. JOSEPH'S (1829), [CEM 2] [JC] Rev. Richard G. Ghezzi.
Res.: Quinn Rd., R.R. #1, Box 1402, 18818. Tel: 570-553-2300; Fax: 570-553-2958.
Catechesis/Religious Program—Margaret Flaherty, D.R.E. Students 95.
Mission—St. Augustine Silver Lake, Susquehanna Co.
GLEN LYON, LUZERNE CO.
1—ST. ADALBERT'S, Merged, with Corpus Christi, Glen Lyon
2—CORPUS CHRISTI (2001),, (Merging of St. Adalbert, St. Denis & St. Michael's, Glen Lyon & St. Mary's, Wanamie. For inquires for parish records, contact Corpus Christi.) Rev. Jacek Bialkowski.
Res.: 43 W. Main St., 18617. Tel: 570-736-6372; Fax: 570-736-6232.
Catechesis/Religious Program—Ann Marie O'Donnell, D.R.E. Students 90.
3—ST. DENIS, Merged, with Corpus Christi, Glen Lyon.
4—ST. MARY'S (Wanamie) (1906), (Lithuanian), Merged, with Corpus Christi, Glen Lyon.
5—ST. MICHAEL'S, Merged, with Corpus Christi, Glen Lyon.
GOULDSBORO, WAYNE CO., ST. RITA (1975), Rev. Robert P. Arnold.
Res.: P.O. Box 537, 18424. Tel: 570-842-4995; Fax: 570-842-5429.
Catechesis/Religious Program—Kathy Napolitano, D.R.E. Students 259.
Mission—St. Mary Magdalene South Sterling, Wayne Co.
Mission—St. Anthony of Padua Newfoundland, Wayne Co.
GREAT BEND, SUSQUEHANNA CO., ST. LAWRENCE'S (1872), [CEM] Rev. Louis T. Kaminski.
Res.: 506 Franklin St., 18821. Tel: 570-879-2392; Fax: 570-879-0126.
Catechesis/Religious Program—Sheila Guinan, D.R.E. Students 95.
Mission—St. John [CEM] New Milford, Susquehanna Co.
HARDING, LUZERNE CO., CHURCH OF THE HOLY REDEEMER (1952), Rev. Thomas P. Shoback.
Res.: RR 1, Box 247-B, Pittston, 18643. Tel: 570-388-6300; Fax: 570-388-2034.

Catechesis/Religious Program—Students 120.
HARLEIGH, LUZERNE CO., SACRED HEART OF JESUS (1903), Rev. Peter D. Menghini.
Res.: One Church Pl., 18225. Tel: 570-455-1162; Fax: 570-455-0306.
Catechesis/Religious Program—Students 51.
Shrine—National Shrine of the Sacred Heart (1975),
Shrine—Men of the Sacred Heart, National Office (1977),Tel: 570-455-1162.
HARVEYS LAKE, LUZERNE CO., OUR LADY OF VICTORY (1969), Rev. Joseph P. Rafferty.
Res.: R.D. #1, Box 309, 18618. Tel: 570-639-1535; Fax: 570-639-1294.
Catechesis/Religious Program—Maureen Devine, D.R.E. Students 260.
HAWLEY, WAYNE CO., BLESSED VIRGIN MARY, QUEEN OF PEACE (1852), [CEM] Rev. William B. Healey.
Res.: 314 Chestnut Ave., 18428. Tel: 570-226-3183; Fax: 570-226-2126.
Catechesis/Religious Program—Tel: 570-226-2955. Marie Ribeiro, D.R.E. Students 294.
Mission—St. Veronica Lake Wallenpaupack, Pike Co.
HAZLETON, LUZERNE CO.
1—CHURCH OF THE MOST PRECIOUS BLOOD (1885), (Italian), Revs. Maurice L. Raymond; Samuel T. Perrins.
Res.: 131 E. Fourth St., 18201. Tel: 570-454-8714; Fax: 570-454-8754.
Catechesis/Religious Program—Tel: 570-454-5916. Sr. Mary Pauline Posedly, D.R.E. Students 486.
2—ST. GABRIEL'S (1855), [CEM] Rev. Msgr. Michael J. Delaney; Rev. Paul Ines, S.D.B. (Philippines); Deacon Bernardino Velez.
Res.: 122 S. Wyoming St., 18201. Tel: 570-454-0212; Fax: 570-459-5187.
Catechesis/Religious Program—Students 160.
3—HOLY ROSARY (1916), (Italian), Rev. Patrick J. Genello.
Res.: 240 S. Poplar St., 18201. Tel: 570-454-6693.
Catechesis/Religious Program—Christine LaMonica, D.R.E. Students 140.
4—HOLY TRINITY (1887), (German), [CEM 2], Merged with Our Lady of Mount Carmel, Tyrolese. Very Rev. Patrick J. McLaughlin, V.F.
Res.: 123 W. Oak St., 18201. Tel: 570-454-5394; Fax: 570-454-0767.
School—35 N. Church St., 18201. Tel: 570-455-9645; Fax: 570-459-9776. Lay Teachers 10; Students 143.
Catechesis/Religious Program—Students 12.
5—HOLY TRINITY (1907), (Slovak), [CEM] Rev. Leonard M. Butcavage; Deacon Louis Smolinsky.
Res.: 178 N. Wyoming St., 18201. Tel: 570-454-3233; Fax: 570-454-0237.
Catechesis/Religious Program—Tel: 570-788-7308. Joe Zola, D.R.E. Students 34.
6—ST. JOSEPH'S (1882), (Slovak), [CEM] Rev. Msgr. Francis J. Beeda; Rev. Stephen A. Krawontka; Deacon Leonard G. Kassick.
Res.: 604 N. Laurel St., 18201. Tel: 570-454-0881; Fax: 570-454-1285.
School—600 N. Laurel St., 18201. Tel: 570-454-4411; Fax: 570-454-4411. Sisters of SS. Cyril and Methodius 2; Lay Teachers 8; Students 145.
Catechesis/Religious Program—Patricia Kibbler, D.R.E. Students 62.
Mission—St. Ladislaus, Luzerne Co.
7—OUR LADY OF GRACE (1910), (Italian), [CEM] Rev. Thomas A. Cappelloni; Deacon Robert A. Roman.
Res.: 750 N. Vine St., 18201. Tel: 570-454-8797; Fax: 570-454-1922.
Catechesis/Religious Program—Students 97.
8—OUR LADY OF MOUNT CARMEL (1905), (Tyrolese), Merged, with Holy Trinity (German), Hazleton.
9—SS. PETER AND PAUL (1887), (Lithuanian), Merged, with Transfiguration, West Hazleton.
10—ST. STANISLAUS (1893), (Polish), [CEM] Rev. Louis S. Garbacik.
Res.: 652 Carson St., 18201-4423. Tel: 570-454-0662; Fax: 570-454-0662.
Catechesis/Religious Program—Carol Baran, D.R.E. Students 82.
HONESDALE, WAYNE CO., ST. JOHN THE EVANGELIST (1842), [CEM 3] Very Rev. Martin M. Boylan, V.F.; Rev. Joji Reddy Allam (India); Deacon Mark S. Jennings.
Res.: 414 Church St., 18431. Tel: 570-253-4561; Fax: 570-253-1058.
Catechesis/Religious Program—Angie Swendsen, D.R.E. Students 651.
Mission—St. Joseph Rileyville, Wayne Co.
Chapel—Honesdale, St. Mary Magdalene (1853),
HUDSON, LUZERNE CO., ST. JOSEPH'S (1889), (Polish), [CEM], Merged with Sacred Heart, Plains. Rev. Casimir M. Stanis, Admin.
Res.: 25 Oak St., (Hudson), Wilkes-Barre, 18705. Tel: 570-823-0238; Fax: 570-822-0394.
Catechesis/Religious Program—Mr. & Mrs. John Woloski, D.R.E. Students 75.
HUGHESTOWN, LUZERNE CO., BLESSED SACRAMENT (1945), Rev. Thomas J. Maloney.
Res.: 65 Rock St., 18640. Tel: 570-654-6553; Fax: 570-654-0466.
Catechesis/Religious Program—Kathy Masulis, D.R.E. Students 116.
INKERMAN, LUZERNE CO., ST. MARK'S (1900), Rev. Edward M. Masakowski.
Res.: 1 St. Mark Ln., 18640. Tel: 570-654-0033.
Catechesis/Religious Program—Bernice Podrasky, D.R.E. Students 102.
JACKSON, SUSQUEHANNA CO., ST. MARTIN OF TOURS (1940), Rev. John C. O'Bell.
Res.: RR 1, Box 396, 18825. Tel: 570-756-2541; Fax: 570-756-2105.
Catechesis/Religious Program—Patricia Stewart, D.R.E. Students 76.
Mission—St. Paul Starrucca, Wayne Co.
JERMYN, LACKAWANNA CO., SACRED HEART OF MARY (1889), [CEM] Very Rev. James J. Walsh, V.F., J.C.L.
Res.: 624 Madison Ave., 18433-1697. Tel 570-876-1061; Fax: 570-876-2493.
Catechesis/Religious Program—Margaret Pidgeon, D.R.E. Students 151.
JERSEY SHORE, LYCOMING CO., ST. LUKE'S (1902), Rev. Andrew S. Hvozdovic.
Res.: 118 Kendall Ave., 17740. Tel: 570-398-2557; Fax: 570-398-0126.
Catechesis/Religious Program—Barb Fedele, D.R.E. Students 138.
JESSUP, LACKAWANNA CO.
1—ST. JAMES (1899), [CEM], Merged with St. Michael, Jessup. Rev. William B. Blake. In Res., Rev. Joseph A. Matz; Deacon John Hatala.
Res.: 605 Church St., 18434. Tel: 570-489-2252; Fax: 570-489-2527.
Catechesis/Religious Program—Mary Kay McHale, D.R.E. Students 224.
Mission—St. Stanislaus, Lackawanna Co.
2—ST. MARY'S ASSUMPTION (1904), (Italian), [CEM] Rev. Andrew R. Gallia.
Res.: 516 Third Ave., 18434. Tel: 570-489-4726.
Catechesis/Religious Program—Michele Daley, D.R.E. Students 167.
KINGSTON, LUZERNE CO.
1—ST. HEDWIG'S (1901), (Polish), [CEM] Rev. Richard A. Zavachi.
Res.: 207 Zerbey Ave., 18704. Tel: 570-287-5634; Fax: 570-287-8566.
Catechesis/Religious Program—Paulette Rapach, D.R.E. Students 40.
2—ST. IGNATIUS (1885), [CEM] Rev. Msgr. Neil J. VanLoon V.F.; Rev. Vara Prasad (India); Deacon John E. O'Connor.
Res.: 339 N. Maple Ave., 18704. Tel: 570-288-6446; Fax: 570-288-0463.
Catechesis/Religious Program—Carmella Faust, D.R.E. Students 289.
Chapel—St. Ann's, Tel: 570-288-5919.
3—ST. MARY'S ANNUNCIATION (1902), (Lithuanian), Rev. Daniel J. Yenkevich; Rev. Msgr. Joseph J. Lasky (Retired).
Res.: 258 Zerbey Ave., 18704. Tel: 570-287-5096; Fax: 570-283-0162.
Catechesis/Religious Program—Carol Cardoni, D.R.E. Students 55.
LAFLIN, LUZERNE CO., ST. MARIA GORETTI (1967), Very Rev. James J. Paisley, V.F.
Res.: 42 Redwood Dr., 18702. Tel: 570-655-8956; Fax: 570-655-1746.
Catechesis/Religious Program—Mary Anne Susek, D.R.E. Students 120.
LAKE ARIEL, WAYNE CO., ST. THOMAS MORE (1941), [CEM] Rev. Edward R. Scott.
Mailing Address: Box 188, 18436. Tel: 570-698-5584; Fax: 570-698-8468.
Catechesis/Religious Program—Tel: 570-698-7150. Marie Barbagallo, D.R.E. Students 290.
Mission—St. Mary Ledgedale, Wayne Co.
LAKE SILKWORTH, LUZERNE CO., OUR LADY OF MOUNT CARMEL (1923), [CEM], Merged with St. Martha's, Fairmount Springs. Rev. Joseph J. Pisaneschi.
Res.: 2011 State Rd. 29, Hunlock Creek, 18621. Tel: 570-477-5040; Fax: 570-477-5030.
Catechesis/Religious Program—Maggie Fishel, D.R.E. Students 112.
LAKE WINOLA, WYOMING CO., ST. MARY OF THE LAKE (1986), Rev. Jeffrey J. Walsh; Deacon Raymond A. Pieretti.
Res.: P.O. Box 1, Fairview Rd., 18625. Tel: 570-378-2181; Fax: 570-378-3948.
Catechesis/Religious Program—Glenda Evans, D.R.E. Students 104.
LARKSVILLE, LUZERNE CO., ST. ANTHONY OF PADUA (1908), (Slovak), [CEM], Merged with St. John the Baptist, Plymouth and SS. Cyril and Methodius, Edwardsville. Rev. Gerald J. Gurka.
Catechesis/Religious Program—Patricia Cresho, D.R.E. Students 10.
LATTIMER MINES, LUZERNE CO., ST. MARY'S (1903), (Italian), Merged, with St. Nazarius, Pardeesville and Good Shepherd, Drums.
LITTLE MEADOWS, SUSQUEHANNA CO., ST. THOMAS THE APOSTLE (1887), Merged, with St. Francis Xavier, Friendsville.
LORDS VALLEY, PIKE CO., ST. JOHN NEUMANN (1976), Rev. Gerard L. Hawley; Deacons John Nash; Philip Bouwmann; Robert Rettino.
Res.: Lords Valley, HC8, Box 8390, Hawley, 18428. Tel: 570-775-6791; Fax: 570-775-1527.
Catechesis/Religious Program—Lenore Rogan, D.R.E. Students 100.
Mission—Good Shepherd Blooming Grove.
LUZERNE, LUZERNE CO.
1—ST. ANN'S (1924), (Lithuanian), Merged, with Holy Family, Luzerne.
2—HOLY FAMILY (1999), Rev. David P. Cappelloni; Deacon John B. Ziegler.
Res.: Rear 574 Bennett St. , P.O. Box 125, 18709. Tel: 570-287-6600; Fax: 570-283-0706.
School—469 Miller St., 18709. Tel: 570-287-3431; Fax: 570-283-2986. Sisters of Christian Charity 1; Lay Teachers 8; Students 133.
Catechesis/Religious Program—Diane Janoski, D.R.E. Students 313.
3—ST. JOHN NEPOMUCENE (1907), (Slovak), Merged, with Holy Family, Luzerne.
4—SACRED HEART CHURCH (1893), (German), Closed., For inquiries for parish records contact Holy Family, Luzerne.
MANSFIELD, TIOGA CO., HOLY CHILD (1953), Very Rev. Albert P. Leonard, V.F.
Res.: 237 S. Main St., 16933. Tel: 570-662-3568; Fax: 570-662-2113.
Catechesis/Religious Program—Students 120.
Mission—St. Mary Center St., Tioga, Tioga Co. 16946. Tel: 570-835-5266.
MATAMORAS, PIKE CO., ST. JOSEPH'S (1892), Rev. John J. Turi.
Res.: 309 Ave. F, 18336. Tel: 570-491-2618; Fax: 570-491-4404.
Catechesis/Religious Program—Christine Marcial, D.R.E.; Cristin Cavallaro, D.R.E. Students 369.
Mission—Holy Family Cemetery Rd., Mill Rift, Pike Co. 18340.
MAYFIELD, LACKAWANNA CO., SACRED HEART OF JESUS (1904), (Polish), [CEM] Rev. John J. Kulavich.
Res.: 420 Hudson St., 18433. Tel: 570-876-1950; Fax: 570-876-1950.
Catechesis/Religious Program—Students 56.
MESHOPPEN, WYOMING CO., ST. JOACHIM'S (1873), [CEM] Rev. Joseph J. Manarchuck.
Res.: P.O. Box 67, 18630. Tel: 570-833-2114; Fax: 570-833-2115.
Catechesis/Religious Program—Valerie Trowbridge, D.R.E. Students 87.
Mission—St. Bonaventure [CEM] Auburn, Susquehanna Co.
MILDRED, SULLIVAN CO., ST. FRANCIS OF ASSISI (1894), Merged, with St. Basil, Dushore.
Catechesis/Religious Program—Students 82.
Mission—St. Francis of Assisi Eagles Mere, Sullivan Co.
Mission—Sacred Heart Laporte, Sullivan Co.
MILFORD, PIKE CO.
1—ST. PATRICK'S (1946), Very Rev. Gerald F. Mullally, V.F.
Res.: 111 E. High St., P.O. Box W, 18337. Tel: 570-296-7451; Fax: 570-296-3070.
Catechesis/Religious Program—Cliff Jorgenson, D.R.E. Students 214.
2—ST. VINCENT DE PAUL (1976), Rev. Msgr. William P. Ward; Deacons Albert W. Perreault; Joseph A. LaCorte; Donald F. O'Brien.
Res.: 101 St. Vincent Dr., 18337-9672. Tel: 570-686-4545; Fax: 800-565-1762.
Catechesis/Religious Program—Tel: 570-686-3493. Students 652.
MOCANAQUA, LUZERNE CO., ST. MARY, OUR LADY OF PERPETUAL HELP (1904), (Polish), [CEM] Rev. Anthony J. Generose.
Res.: 150 Main St., 18655. Tel: 570-542-4157; Fax: 570-542-4158.
Catechesis/Religious Program—Tel: 570-542-4878. Kathleen Czeck, D.R.E. Students 90.
MONTDALE, LACKAWANNA CO., CORPUS CHRISTI (1942), Very Rev. William J. Flynn, S.S., V.F.
Res.: R.R. 1, Box 389, Olyphant, 18447. Tel: 570-254-9502; Fax: 570-254-6233.
Catechesis/Religious Program—Students 212.
MONTOURSVILLE, LYCOMING CO., OUR LADY OF LOURDES (1942), Rev. Leo J. McKernan, Admin.
Res.: 800 Mulberry St., 17754. Tel: 570-368-8598; Fax: 570-368-2912.
Catechesis/Religious Program—Barbara Burchanowski, D.R.E. Students 162.
MONTROSE, SUSQUEHANNA CO., HOLY NAME OF MARY (1898), [CEM] Rev. James R. Nash; Rev. Msgr. Bernard A. Toloczko.
Res.: 60 S. Main St., 18801. Tel: 570-278-1504; Fax: 570-278-1504.
Catechesis/Religious Program—Jackie Kane, D.R.E.

Students 163.

MOSCOW, LACKAWANNA CO., ST. CATHERINE OF SIENA (1861), Rev. Michael E. Finn; Deacon John J. Franceschelli.
Res.: 220 Church St., P.O. Box 250, 18444. Tel: 570-842-4561; Fax: 570-842-6648.
Catechesis/Religious Program—Tel: 570-848-2158. Students 475.

MOUNT POCONO, MONROE CO., ST. MARY OF THE MOUNT (1909), Rev. Msgr. Arthur J. Kaschenbach; Deacon Paul A. Liotard.
Res.: 27 Fairview Ave., 18344. Tel: 570-839-7138; Fax: 570-839-2537.
Catechesis/Religious Program—Mary Lou Dumas, D.R.E. Students 757.
Mission—St. Joan of Arc Pocono Summit, Monroe Co.

MOUNTAINTOP, LUZERNE CO., ST. JUDE, Formerly St. Jude's (1953), Rev. Michael F. Quinnan; Deacon Eugene J. Kovatch.
Res.: 420 S. Mountain Blvd., 18707. Tel: 570-474-6315; Fax: 570-474-0775.
School—Tel: 570-474-5803; Fax: 570-403-6159. Lay Teachers 25; Students 371.
Catechesis/Religious Program—Amy Hoegen, D.R.E.; Pamela Urbanski, D.R.E. Students 500.

MUNCY, LYCOMING CO., RESURRECTION (1941), Rev. Glenn E. McCreary.
Res.: 526 S. Main St., 17756. Tel: 570-546-3900; Fax: 570-546-5272.
Catechesis/Religious Program—Doreen Klimek, D.R.E. Students 200.

NANTICOKE, LUZERNE CO.
1—ST. FRANCIS OF ASSISI (1872), [CEM], Merged with St. Joseph's, Nanticoke. Rev. William J.P. Langan.
Res.: 173 E. Green St., 18634. Tel: 570-735-6903; Fax: 570-735-2366.
Catechesis/Religious Program—Susan Saunders, D.R.E. Students 97.
2—HOLY CHILD (1942), (Polish), Merged, with Holy Trinity (Polish), Nanticoke.
3—HOLY TRINITY (1894), (Polish), [CEM] Revs. Richard E. Fox, Admin.; Joseph F. Orloski. In Res., Rev. Carl T. Prushinski.
Res.: 520 S. Hanover St., 18634-2799. Tel: 570-735-4833; Fax: 570-735-2281.
Catechesis/Religious Program—Students 204.
4—ST. JOSEPH'S (1888), [CEM], Merged with St. Francis of Asissi, Nanticoke. Rev. William J.P. Langan.
Res.: 107 E. Noble St., 18634. Tel: 570-735-0331.
Catechesis/Religious Program—Mrs. Gerald Hudak, D.R.E. Twinned with St. Francis of Assisi, Nanticoke. Students 61.
5—ST. MARY OF CZESTOCHOWA (1901), (Polish), [CEM] Rev. John S. Krafchak.
Res.: 1030 S. Hanover St., 18634. Tel: 570-735-6911; Fax: 570-735-6913.
Catechesis/Religious Program—Tel: 570-735-0313; Fax: 570-735-2123. Sr. Ursula Yerns, D.R.E. Students 68.
6—ST. STANISLAUS (1875), (Polish), [CEM] Rev. John F. Poplawski.
Res.: 38 W. Church St., 18634. Tel: 570-735-0313; Fax: 570-735-2123.
Catechesis/Religious Program—Ann Morgas, D.R.E. Students 92.

NICHOLSON, WYOMING CO., ST. PATRICK'S (1888), [CEM] Rev. John V. Polednak; Deacon Paul J. Brojack.
Res.: 100 Main St., 18446. Tel: 570-942-6602.
Catechesis/Religious Program—Karen Magnotta, D.R.E. Students 157.

OLD FORGE, LACKAWANNA CO.
1—ST. LAWRENCE O'TOOLE (1895), Rev. Michael J. Kirwin.
Res.: 620 S. Main St., 18518. Tel: 570-457-2032.
Catechesis/Religious Program—JoAnn Wilbur, D.R.E. Students 109.
2—ST. MARY'S (1897), (Italian), Revs. Joseph F. Cipriano; Stanley J. Kurash.
Res.: 123 W. Grace St., 18518. Tel: 570-457-5900.
School—216 W. Grace St., 18518. Tel: 570-457-6750. Sisters 2; Lay Teachers 10; Students 180.
Catechesis/Religious Program—Sr. Gertrude, D.R.E. Students 365.
3—ST. MICHAEL'S (1905), (Polish), Rev. Joseph M. Brozena.
Res.: 236 Vine St., 18518. Tel: 570-457-3353.
Catechesis/Religious Program—Students 26.
4—ST. STANISLAUS, Merged, Merged with St. David's, Scranton.
Catechesis/Religious Program—Students 17.

OLYPHANT, LACKAWANNA CO.
1—HOLY GHOST (1888), (Slovak), Merged, with St. Patrick's Church, Olyphant.
Catechesis/Religious Program—Tel: 570-489-2023. Students 95.
Convent—Sisters of SS. Cyril and Methodius, 126 Willow Ave., 18447. Tel: 570-489-0792.
2—ST. MICHAEL THE ARCHANGEL (1909), (Polish), [CEM], Merged with St. Patrick and Holy Ghost, Olyphant. Rev. Phillip J. Sladicka.
Res.: 132 Lincoln St., 18447. Tel: 570-489-0623; Fax: 570-383-4918.
Catechesis/Religious Program—Students 46.
3—ST. PATRICK'S (1875), [CEM], Merged with Holy Ghost (Slovak), Olyphant. Revs. Phillip J. Sladicka; Scott P. Sterowski.
Res.: 200 Delaware Ave., 18447. Tel: 570-489-0752; Fax: 570-489-0225.
Catechesis/Religious Program—Tel: 570-489-2023. Sr. Gabriella LaGanga, D.R.E. Students 204.

PARDEESVILLE, LUZERNE CO., ST. NAZARIUS (1966), (Italian),, (Merged with St. Mary, Lattimer Mines and Good Shepherd, Drums. For inquries for parish records, contact Good Shepherd, Drums.) Very Rev. Gerard F. Safko, V.F.; Rev. Augustine Poonelil, O.C.D. In Res., Rev. Michael P. Litcheck.
Res.: R.D. 2, P3D3, Hazleton, 18201. Tel: 570-788-3141; Fax: 570-788-2916.
Catechesis/Religious Program—Marguerita Benderavich, D.R.E.; Jean Kunger, D.R.E.; Carol Matz, D.R.E. Students 140.

PECKVILLE, LACKAWANNA CO., SACRED HEART OF JESUS (1946), Very Rev. Santino J. Fanucci, V.F.
Res.: 1101 Willow St., 18452. Tel: 570-383-3244; Fax: 570-383-8697.
Catechesis/Religious Program—Tel: 570-383-2777. Janet Conte, D.R.E. Students 328.

PITTSTON, LUZERNE CO.
1—ST. CASIMIR'S (1890), (Lithuanian), Merged, with St. John the Evangelist, Pittston.
2—ST. JOHN THE BAPTIST (1892), (Slovak), [CEM 2] Rev. Andrew F. Strish.
Res.: 16 William St., 18640. Tel: 570-654-2112; Fax: 570-654-4210.
School—12 William St., 18640. Tel: 570-654-0845; Fax: 570-883-1817. Robert Kaluzavich, Prin. Lay Teachers 9; Students 225.
Catechesis/Religious Program—Students 96.
3—ST. JOHN THE EVANGELIST (1854), [CEM], Merged with St. Casimir and St. Joseph, Pittston. Rev. Msgr. John J. Bendik; Rev. Arbogaste Satoun. In Res., Rev. Hugh H. McGroarty; Deacon James G. Cortegerone.
Res.: 35 William St., 18640. Tel: 570-654-0053; Fax: 570-654-3751.
Catechesis/Religious Program—Lorraine Cortegerone, D.R.E.; Jim Cortegerone, D.R.E. Students 97.
4—ST. JOSEPH'S (1909), (Polish), Merged, with St. John the Evangelist, Pittston.
5—ST. MARY'S ASSUMPTION (1863), (German), Merged, with St. Mary, Help of Christians, Pittson.
School—41 Carroll St., 18640. Tel: 570-654-8313; Fax: 570-654-7052. Sisters of Christian Charity 3; Lay Teachers 10; Students 236.
Catechesis/Religious Program—Karen Ann Reilly, D.R.E. Students 71.
6—ST. MARY, HELP OF CHRISTIANS (1851), [CEM] Rev. Richard J. Polmounter.
Res.: 535 N. Main St., 18640. Tel: 570-654-0263; Fax: 570-654-0195.
Catechesis/Religious Program—Students 71.
7—OUR LADY OF MT. CARMEL (1904), (Italian), Very Rev. Paul A. McDonnell, O.S.J.
Res.: 237 William St., 18640. Tel: 570-654-6902; Fax: 570-655-5448.
Catechesis/Religious Program—Ann Hrobak, D.R.E. Students 181.
8—ST. ROCCO (1919), (Italian), [CEM] Rev. Joseph D. Sibilano, O.S.J.
Res.: 62 W. Oak St., 18640. Tel: 570-654-2914; Fax: 570-654-1614.
Catechesis/Religious Program—Students 165.

PLAINS, LUZERNE CO.
1—SS. PETER AND PAUL (1898), (Polish), [CEM] Rev. Joseph A. Greskiewicz.
Res.: 13 Hudson Rd., 18705. Tel: 570-825-6663; Fax: 570-823-4556.
School—15 Hudson St., 18705. Tel: 570-824-9433. Lay Teachers 10; Students 221.
Catechesis/Religious Program—Sanrda Holena, D.R.E. Students 230.
2—SACRED HEART (1883),, Merged with St. Joseph's, Hudson. Rev. Casimir M. Stanis, Admin.
Res.: 25 Oak St., Hudson, 18705-3499. Tel: 570-823-0238; Fax: 570-822-0394.
Catechesis/Religious Program—David Lepore, D.R.E. Students 121.

PLEASANT MOUNT, WAYNE CO., ST. JAMES (1887), Rev. Richard W. Beck.
Res.: P.O. Box 53, 18453. Tel: 570-448-2211.
Catechesis/Religious Program—Students 145.
Mission—St. Cecilia Hill Top, Wayne Co.
Mission—Assumption of the B.V.M. Lake Como, Wayne Co.

PLYMOUTH, LUZERNE CO.
1—ST. JOHN THE BAPTIST (1899), (Polish), Merged, with St. Anthony of Padua, Larksville and SS. Cyril and Methodius, Edwardsville.
2—NATIVITY OF THE BLESSED VIRGIN MARY (1885), (Polish), [CEM 2] Rev. Msgr. Vincent J. Grimalia, V.F.; Deacons Leo R. Thompson; Peter Smith; James Lane.
Res.: 66 Willow St., 18651. Tel: 570-779-5324; Fax: 570-779-4921.
Catechesis/Religious Program—Helen Cebula, D.R.E. Students 91.
3—ST. STEPHEN'S (1886), (Slovak), Merged, with Nativity of the Blessed Virgin Mary, Plymouth.
4—ST. VINCENT DE PAUL (1872), [CEM] Rev. Donald J. Williams; Deacon Peter G. Smith.
Res.: 101 Church St., 18651. Tel: 570-779-9508; Fax: 570-779-2332.
Catechesis/Religious Program—Barbara Hogan, D.R.E. Students 424.

POCONO PINES, MONROE CO., OUR LADY OF THE LAKE (1985), Revs. John B. Boyle; John B. DeMayo (PH) (Retired).
Res.: P.O. Box 0, 18350. Tel: 570-646-6424; Fax: 570-646-1047.
Catechesis/Religious Program—Lynnette Smith, D.R.E. Students 222.

ROCK LAKE, WAYNE CO., ST. JULIANA'S (1838), Merged, with St. James, Pleasant Mount.

ROYAL, SUSQUEHANNA CO., ST. PIUS X (1967), Rev. Joseph S. Sitko.
Res.: Box 64, Clifford, 18413. Tel: 570-222-4209.
Catechesis/Religious Program—Students 78.

SAYRE, BRADFORD CO., CHURCH OF THE EPIPHANY (1888), Revs. William J. Karle; Joseph Michael Tarigopula (India).
Res.: 304 S. Elmer Ave., 18840. Tel: 570-888-9641; Fax: 570-888-2608.
School—627 Stevenson St., 18840. Tel: 570-888-5802. Sisters of I.H.M. 2; Lay Teachers 12; Students 160.
Catechesis/Religious Program—Students 106.

SHAVERTOWN, LUZERNE CO., ST. THERESE (1926), Rev. Msgr. J. Peter Crynes.
Res.: 64 Davis St., 18708. Tel: 570-696-1144; Fax: 570-696-1210.
Catechesis/Religious Program—Denise Murphy, D.R.E. Students 553.

SHOHOLA, PIKE CO., ST. ANN'S (1928), [CEM] Rev. Thomas J. Petro.
Res.: 123 Richardson Ave., P.O. Box 86, 18458. Tel: 570-559-7642; Fax: 570-559-7499.
Catechesis/Religious Program—Tel: 570-559-7422. Christine Barnansky, D.R.E. Students 200.
Mission—St. Mary of the Assumption Lackawaxen, Pike Co.
Mission—Sacred Heart of Jesus Greeley, Pike Co.

SIMPSON, LACKAWANNA CO., ST. MICHAEL'S (1903), [CEM] Rev. Hilary L. Malinowski.
Res.: 46 Midland St., 18407. Tel: 570-282-2161.
Catechesis/Religious Program—Kathryn Yaklic, D.R.E. Students 110.

SOUTH WAVERLY, BRADFORD CO., ST. JOHN THE EVANGELIST (1902),, (Merged with St. Joseph, Athens, Tel.: 570-888-2129) Rev. Vincent F. Langan.
Res.: 85 Division St., 18840-2847. Tel: 570-888-2123.
Catechesis/Religious Program—Elizabeth Hill, D.R.E.; LeAnn Stevens, D.R.E. Students 75.

SOUTH WILLIAMSPORT, LYCOMING CO., ST. LAWRENCE'S (1931), Rev. Francis L. Pauselli.
Res.: 344 Winthrop St., 17701. Tel: 570-322-0403; Fax: 570-322-4335.
Catechesis/Religious Program—Students 264.

STROUDSBURG, MONROE CO., ST. LUKE'S (1968), Very Rev. Thomas D. McLaughlin, V.F.; Rev. Carmen J. Perry.
Office—818 Main St., 18360. Tel: 570-421-9097; 421-986-; Fax: 570-421-6015.
Res.: 906 Main St., 18360. Tel: 570-421-8460; Fax: 570-421-6015.
Catechesis/Religious Program—Scott Fabian, D.R.E. Students 1,418.

SUGAR NOTCH, LUZERNE CO.
1—HOLY FAMILY (1901), (Polish), [CEM], Merged with St. Charles, Borromeo. Very Rev. John S. Terry, V.F.; Deacon Philip Harris.
Office—828 Main St., 18706. Tel: 570-822-8983; Fax: 570-822-6016.
Catechesis/Religious Program—Sylvia Zula, D.R.E. Students 133.
2—SS. PETER AND PAUL (1847), (Lithuanian), Merged, with Holy Family, Sugar Notch.

SUSQUEHANNA, SUSQUEHANNA CO., ST. JOHN THE EVANGELIST (1847), [CEM] Rev. Robert J. Simon.
Res.: 101 Jackson Ave., 18847. Tel: 570-853-4634; Fax: 570-853-3356.
Catechesis/Religious Program—Victoria Mulligan, D.R.E. Students 163.

SWOYERSVILLE, LUZERNE CO.
1—HOLY NAME OF JESUS (1905), Merged, with St. Mary of Czestochowa, Swoyersville.
2—HOLY NAME/ST. MARY'S, [CEM] Rev. Louis A. Grippe; Deacon George Mochin Jr.
Res.: 283 Shoemaker St. (P.O. Kingston), 18704. Tel: 570-287-2139; Fax: 570-287-6474.

Catechesis/Religious Program—Students 160.
3—HOLY TRINITY (1895), (Slovak), [CEM] Rev. Richard J. Cirba.
Res.: 116 Hughes St. (P.O. Kingston), 18704. Tel: 570-287-6624; Fax: 570-287-4704.
Catechesis/Religious Program—Margaret Semanek, D.R.E. Students 220.
4—ST. MARY OF CZESTOCHOWA (1909), Merged, with Holy Name of Jesus, Swoyersville.
TANNERSVILLE, MONROE CO., OUR LADY OF VICTORY (1968), Rev. Richard E. Czachor; Deacon Ralph Weichand.
Res.: Cherry Lane Rd., P.O. Box 195, 18372. Tel: 570-629-4572; Fax: 570-629-5325.
Catechesis/Religious Program—Students 779.
TAYLOR, LACKAWANNA CO.
1—IMMACULATE CONCEPTION (1898), Very Rev. Philip A. Altavilla, V.F.
408 N. Main St., 18517. Tel: 570-562-2390; 570-562-1341; Fax: 570-562-2807.
Catechesis/Religious Program—Students 35.
2—ST. JOHN THE BAPTIST (1904), (Slovak), Merged, with Immaculate Conception, Taylor.
THROOP, LACKAWANNA CO.
1—ST. ANTHONY'S (1911), (Polish), [CEM], Merged with St. Bridget's and St. John the Baptist, Throop. Rev. August A. Ricciardi.
Office—215 Rebecca St., 18519. Tel: 570-489-1963; Fax: 570-489-3291.
Res.: 520 Charles St., 18512. Tel: 570-489-1682.
Catechesis/Religious Program—Students 90.
2—ST. BRIDGET'S (1916),, Merged with St. John the Baptist & St. Anthony's, Throop. Rev. August A. Ricciardi.
Office—520 Sanderson St., 18512. Tel: 570-489-1822; Fax: 570-489-3291.
Res.: 520 Charles St., 18512. Tel: 570-489-1682.
Catechesis/Religious Program—Students 43.
3—ST. JOHN THE BAPTIST (1905), (Slovak), [CEM], Merged with St. Bridget's and St. Anthony's, Throop. Rev. August A. Ricciardi.
Office—520 Sanderson St., 18512. Tel: 570-489-1822; Fax: 570-489-3291.
Res.: 520 Charles St., 18512. Tel: 570-489-1682.
TOBYHANNA, MONROE CO., ST. ANN (1923), [CEM 2] Revs. Michael J. Kloton; Albert Bellantonio; Wilfredo T. Comellas.
Res.: Main St., P.O. Box 188, 18466-0188. Tel: 570-894-8018; Fax: 570-894-9619.
Catechesis/Religious Program—Students 674.
TOWANDA, BRADFORD CO., SS. PETER AND PAUL (1841), [CEM 3] Very Rev. Ronald J. Hughes, V.F.
Res.: 106 Third St., 18848. Tel: 570-265-2113; Fax: 570-265-2114.
School—St. Agnes, 102 Third St., 18848. Tel: 570-265-6803; Fax: 570-265-3065. Lay Teachers 10; Students 140.
Catechesis/Religious Program—Maria VanHaute, D.R.E.; Edward VanHaute, D.R.E. Students 236.
Mission—Immaculate Conception Ulster, Bradford Co. Tel: 570-358-3558.
TUNKHANNOCK, WYOMING CO., NATIVITY OF BLESSED VIRGIN MARY (1884), [CEM 2] Rev. J. Duane Gavitt.
Res.: 99 E. Tioga St., 18657. Tel: 570-836-3275; Fax: 570-836-4268.
Catechesis/Religious Program—Students 727.
WAYMART, WAYNE CO., ST. MARY'S (1915), [CEM] Rev. John T. Albosta.
Res.: 242 Carbondale Rd., P.O. Box 160, 18472. Tel: 570-488-6440; Fax: 570-488-7440.
Catechesis/Religious Program—Marion Menapace, D.R.E. Students 123.
Mission—St. Patrick Canaan, Wayne Co.
WELLSBORO, TIOGA CO., ST. PETER'S (1879), [CEM 2] Rev. Joseph J. Manarchuck.
Res.: 38 Central Ave., 16901. Tel: 570-724-3371; Fax: 570-724-6322.
Catechesis/Religious Program—Linda Henneman, D.R.E. Students 154.
Mission—Sacred Heart Morris, Tioga Co.
WEST HAZLETON, LUZERNE CO.
1—ST. FRANCIS OF ASSISI (1940), Rev. Connell A. McHugh.
Res.: 544 N. Broad St., 18201. Tel: 570-454-3072; Fax: 570-454-2729.
Catechesis/Religious Program—Joanne Karchner, D.R.E. Students 96.
Mission—St. Michael Harwood, Luzerne Co.
2—TRANSFIGURATION (1907), (Polish), [CEM] Rev. Robert M. Timchak.
Res.: 213 W. Green St., Hazleton, 18202. Tel: 570-454-3933; Fax: 570-454-8326.
School—217 W. Green St., Hazleton, 18202. Tel: 570-454-6131. Lay Teachers 9; Students 175.
Catechesis/Religious Program—Peggy Popalis, D.R.E. Students 140.
WEST PITTSTON, LUZERNE CO., IMMACULATE CONCEPTION (1910), Very Rev. Michael J. Piccola, V.F.
Res.: 605 Luzerne Ave., 18643. Tel: 570-654-2753; Fax: 570-654-9244.
Catechesis/Religious Program—Cathy Hagadorn, D.R.E.; Annette Falzone, D.R.E. Students 92.
WEST WYOMING, LUZERNE CO., OUR LADY OF SORROWS (1953), Rev. Michael J. Rafferty.
Res.: 363 W. 8th St., 18644. Tel: 570-693-1991; Fax: 570-693-1339.
Catechesis/Religious Program—Students 148.
WESTON, LUZERNE CO., SACRED HEART (1885), [CEM] Rev. Patrick D. McDowell.
Res.: P.O. Box A, 18256. Tel: 570-384-4121; Fax: 570-384-3976.
Catechesis/Religious Program—Students 97.
Mission—St. Joseph Nuremberg, Luzerne Co.
WHITE HAVEN, LUZERNE CO., ST. PATRICK'S (1874), [CEM] Rev. Stephen J. Stavoy.
Res.: 580 Elmira St., 18661. Tel: 570-443-9944; Fax: 570-443-9777.
Catechesis/Religious Program—Linda Kistler, D.R.E. Students 155.
Station—White Haven Center, Tel: 570-453-9564.
WHITE MILLS, WAYNE CO., ST. JOSEPH'S (1958), Rev. Joseph P. Kutch.
Mailing Address: Box 153, 18473. Tel: 570-253-0307; Fax: 570-253-0314.
Catechesis/Religious Program—Carol Davis, D.R.E. Students 106.
Mission—St. Bernard Beach Lake, Wayne Co. Tel: 570-729-7247.
WILKES-BARRE, LUZERNE CO.
1—ST. ALOYSIUS (1899), Rev. Msgr. Donald A. McAndrews; Rev. Joseph F. Sica; Deacon James Calderone.
Res.: 143 W. Division St., 18706. Tel: 570-323-3791; Fax: 570-826-0233.
School—321 Barney St., 18702. Tel: 570-324-6131; Fax: 570-824-1643. Lay Teachers 16; Students 237.
Catechesis/Religious Program—Sr. James Margaret Purcell D.R.E. Students 128.
2—BLESSED SACRAMENT (1917), [CEM], Merged with St. Francis of Assisi and St. John the Baptist. Rev. Joseph A. Kearney.
Res.: 213 E. Main St., 18705. Tel: 570-322-9561; Fax: 570-822-4347.
Catechesis/Religious Program—Cathy Riccetti, D.R.E. Students 120.
Station—Geisinger Wyoming Valley Hospital, Tel: 570-826-7300.
3—ST. BONIFACE (1896), (German), Rev. Andrew R. Sinnott; Deacon Francis J. Bradigan.
Res.: 225 Blackman St., 18702. Tel: 570-822-8330; Fax: 570-819-4125.
Catechesis/Religious Program—Students 55.
4—ST. CASIMIR'S (1889), (Lithuanian), [CEM] Rev. James F. Hoyle, C.S.C. In Res., Bro. Richard Kyle, C.S.C.
Res.: 301 Delaney St., 18706. Tel: 570-825-2598; Fax: 570-825-6525.
5—ST. DOMINIC (1882), Rev. William R. Cunnane.
Res.: 155 Austin Ave., 18705. Tel: 570-822-8871.
Catechesis/Religious Program—Janice Horn, D.R.E. Students 89.
6—ST. FRANCIS OF ASSISI (1913), (Lithuanian), Merged, with St. John the Baptist and Blessed Sacrament, Wilkes-Barre.
7—HOLY ROSARY (1906), (Italian), Very Rev. James B. Shimsky, V.F.
Res.: 363 Park Ave., 18702. Tel: 570-822-1183; Fax: 570-822-2755.
Catechesis/Religious Program—Maria Malf, D.R.E. Students 82.
8—HOLY SAVIOUR (1895),, Merged With St. Christopher, Bear Creek. Very Rev. E. Francis Kelly, V.F.; Deacon Carl J. Orbon.
Res.: 54 Hillard St., 18702. Tel: 570-822-1186; Fax: 570-822-1074.
Catechesis/Religious Program—Students 80.
9—HOLY TRINITY (1893), (Lithuanian), [CEM 2] Rev. Theodore L. Obaza.
Res.: 416 E. South St., 18702. Tel: 570-823-1081.
Catechesis/Religious Program—Students 73.
10—ST. JOHN THE BAPTIST (1924), (Slovak), Merged, with Blessed Sacrament and St. Francis of Assisi, Wilkes-Barre.
11—ST. JOHN THE EVANGELIST (1927), Merged, with Sacred Heart of Jesus, Wilkes-Barre.
12—ST. JOSEPH (Georgetown) (1898), Rev. James J. Alco.
Res.: 783 E. Northampton St., 18702. Tel: 570-822-8023; Fax 570-822-2891.
13—ST. JOSEPH'S (1927), (Slovak), Merged, with St. Mary's Church of the Immaculate Conception, Wilkes-Barre.
14—ST. MARY'S CHURCH OF THE IMMACULATE CONCEPTION (1845), [CEM] Rev. Msgr. Thomas V. Banick; Rev. Vincent Dang.
Res.: P.O. Box 348, 134 S. Washington St., 18703-0348. Tel: 570-823-4168; Fax: 570-822-3477.
Catechesis/Religious Program—Sr. Dolores M. Banick, I.H.M., D.R.E. Students 100.
15—MATERNITY OF THE BLESSED VIRGIN MARY (1885), (Polish), [CEM 2] Rev. Msgr. Alexander T. Kulik; Deacon Andrew F. Stoshak.
Res.: 40 Park Ave., 18702. Tel: 570-824-7832.
Catechesis/Religious Program—Frances Jacobs, D.R.E. Students 148.
16—ST. NICHOLAS (1856), (German), [CEM 2] Rev. Msgr. Joseph G. Rauscher; Rev. Lawrence Emmareddy. In Res., Rev. Francis P. Skitzki.
Res.: 226 S. Washington St., 18701-2897. Tel: 570-823-7736; 823-584-; Fax: 570-823-0256.
Catechesis/Religious Program—Mr. James McDermott, D.R.E. Students 563.
17—ST. PATRICK'S (1920), Revs. John J. Kilpatrick; Paul C. Fontanella.
Res.: 316 Parrish St., 18702. Tel: 570-823-1948; Fax: 570-823-3177.
Catechesis/Religious Program—Kathleen Smith, D.R.E. Students 111.
18—SACRED HEART-ST. JOHN (1896), (Slovak), [CEM], Merged with St. John the Evangelist, Wilkes-Barre. Rev. Msgr. John J. Sempa; Rev. Joseph T. Gilbert; Sr. Carol, Pastoral Assoc.; Deacons Joseph F. DeVizia; Pete Hoegen.
Res.: 601 N. Main St., 18705-1794. Tel: 570-823-4988; Fax: 570-823-5932.
School—607 N. Main St., 18705. Tel: 570-824-0818; Fax: 570-824-4824. Lay Teachers 14; Students 230.
Catechesis/Religious Program—Students 170.
19—ST. STANISLAUS KOSTKA (1908), (Polish), [CEM] Rev. Joseph M. Horanzy.
Res.: 666 N. Main St., 18705. Tel: 570-822-8026.
Catechesis/Religious Program—Ann Bozinski, D.R.E. Students 25.
20—ST. THERESE'S (1929), Rev. Msgr. Francis J. Callahan. In Res., Rev. George A. Jeffrey.
Res.: 25 Old River Rd., 18702. Tel: 570-822-1075; 570-824-3052; Fax: 570-829-4147.
Catechesis/Religious Program—Mark Kalaus, D.R.E. Students 101.
WILLIAMSPORT, LYCOMING CO.
1—ST. ANN'S (1959), Rev. Andrew Kurovsky.
Res.: 1220 Northway Rd., 17701. Tel: 570-322-5935; Fax: 570-322-2451.
School—1225 Northway Rd., 17701. Tel: 570-323-0500; Fax: 570-323-3315. Sisters of Christian Charity 1; Lay Teachers 8; Students 165.
Catechesis/Religious Program—Sr. Daria Bisulca, D.R.E. Students 279.
Mission—Assumption of the B.V.M. Cascade, Lycoming Co.
2—ANNUNCIATION (1865), [CEM] Revs. John K. Manno; Gregory T. Villaescusa; Deacon J. Morris Smith.
Res.: 410 Walnut St., 17701. Tel: 570-323-9456; Fax: 570-323-3728.
School—711 W. Edwin St., 17701. Tel: 570-322-6036; Fax: 570-322-1479. Sisters of I.H.M. 1; Lay Teachers 8; Students 120.
Catechesis/Religious Program—Tel: 570-323-3799. James Foran, D.R.E. Students 215.
3—ASCENSION (1907), Very Rev. Charles J. Cummings, V.F.
Office & Res.: 2111 Linn St., 17701. Tel: 570-326-4922; Fax: 570-327-1196.
4—ST. BONIFACE (1853), (German), Rev. Msgr. Stephen D. McGough; Rev. Michael J. Zipay; Deacon Clair J. Raisch.
Res.: 326 Washington Blvd., 17701. Tel: 570-326-1544; Fax: 570-326-6746.
School—710 Franklin St., 17701. Tel: 570-326-3738; Fax: 570-326-7385. Sisters of Christian Charity 1; Lay Teachers 11; Students 187.
5—HOLY ROSARY (1915), (Polish), Rev. Andrew J. Krusinski.
Res.: 313 Arch St., 17701. Tel: 570-323-6316.
Catechesis/Religious Program—Students 2.
6—MATER DOLOROSA (1908), (Italian), Rev. Msgr. Francis J. Castellano.
Res.: 635 Hepburn St., 17701. Tel: 570-326-9769; Fax: 570-327-8141.
Catechesis/Religious Program—Students 146.
WYALUSING, BRADFORD CO., ST. MARY'S ASSUMPTION (1950), Rev. Kenneth M. Seegar.
Parish Office & Mailing Address—R.R. 4, Box 4003, 18853. Tel: 570-746-1006; Fax: 570-746-0389.
Res.: 200 Front St., 18853. Tel: 570-746-2162.
Catechesis/Religious Program—Cathy Hagadon, D.R.E. Students 79.
Mission—St. Anthony Stowell, Wyoming Co.
WYOMING, LUZERNE CO., ST. JOSEPH'S (1914), (Polish), [CEM] Rev. Walter F. Skiba.
Res.: 97 E. Sixth St., 18644. Tel: 570-693-0510.
Catechesis/Religious Program—Anne Zendian, D.R.E. Students 146.

Chaplains of Public Institutions

CLARKS SUMMIT. *Clarks Summit State Hospital* 18411. Attended by Our Lady of the Snows, Clarks Summit. Tel: 570-586-1741.

DALLAS. *State Correctional Institution* 18612. Tel: 570-675-1101. Deacon John Munoz.

EAST STROUDSBURG. *East Stroudsburg State*

University, 200 Prospect St., 18301. Tel: 570-422-3525; Fax: 570-422-3777. Joan Fabian, Campus Min.

LA PLUME. *Keystone Junior College*. Rev. Thomas M. Muldowney.
Clarks Summit. Tel: 570-586-1741.

MUNCY. *Muncy Prison*, Tel: 570-546-3900. Rev. Glenn E. McCreary, Chap.
Resurrection Rectory: 526 S. Main St., 17756.

WILKES-BARRE. *Geisinger Wyoming Valley Hospital*, Tel: 570-822-9561. Rev. Joseph A. Kearney.
Blessed Sacrament Rectory: 213 E. Main St., 18705.
Veteran's Administration Hospital. Rev. Joseph J. Long, C.S.C., Chap. Tel: 570-208-5815.
King's College: 133 N. River St., 18711.

WILLIAMSPORT. *Lycoming College*, 700 College Pl., Box 149, 17701. Tel: 570-321-4111. Sr. Catherine Ann Gilvary, I.H.M., Campus Min.

On Special or Other Diocesan Assignment:
Rev. Msgr.—
McGowan, Andrew J., Mercy Hospital, 18501. Tel: 570-348-7010 Dir., Catholic Health Care Facilities & Rep., Catholic Institutions of Higher Learning
Revs.—
Finn, Edward S., Chap., R.D. #1, Box 310A, Equinunk, 18417. Tel: 717-224-4380
Yaszcz, Thomas A., 52 W. Grove St., Nanticoke, 18634. Tel: 570-735-8754, Ext. 315

On Duty Outside the Diocese:
Rev. Msgr.—
Jordan, John J., Save Our Schools, Inc., NCEA, 1077 30th St., N.W., Washington, DC 20007-3852. Tel: 202-378-5767
Revs.—
Doherty, Daniel J., S.S. (BAL), Society of St. Sulpice, Theological College, The Catholic Univ. of America, 401 Michigan Ave., N.E., Washington, DC 20017-1578. Tel: 202-756-5469
Evanko, Joseph J., St. Bernard's Church, 248 S. Harbor Dr., Holmes Beach, FL 34217. Tel: 941-778-4769
Evanofski, Bernard P. (VEN), Church of San Marco, 851 San Marco Rd., Marco Island, FL 34145. Tel: 239-394-5181
Fives, Carl J., Mt. St. Mary's College, Emmitsburg, MD 21727. Tel: 301-447-6122
Gabuzda, Richard J. (OM), Dir., Institute for Priestly Formation, Kenefick #1208, 320 N. 20th St., Omaha, NE 68178. Tel: 402-546-6384
Gregoris, Nicholas L., Newman House, 5401 S. 33rd St., Omaha, NE 68107. Tel: 402-733-2423
Rable, Cyril J., Chap., Maria Hall, Maria Hall Dr., Danville, 17821. Tel: 570-275-5566 (private); 570-275-1120 (Maria Hall Number)
Rossi, Walter R., Assoc. Rector & Dir., Pilgrimages, Basilica of the National Shrine of the Immaculate Conception, 400 Michigan Ave., N.E., Washington, DC 20017. Tel: 202-526-8300
Walsh, John A., 14710 County Rd. 561A, Clermont, FL 34711-8789.
Waznak, Robert J., S.S.
Wysocki, Joseph A., Immaculate Conception, 1315 8th St., N.W., Washington, DC 20001. Tel: 301-654-9155; 301-332-8888

Military Chaplains:
Revs.—
Dormer, David J., Chap. Major, U.S. Army, P.O. Box 35522, Fort Wainwright, AK 99703.
Ferretti, Samuel J., Chap., U.S. Navy, USCG TRACEN Chapel, 1 Munro Ave., Cape May, NJ 08204.
Hochreiter, Robert S., Chap., Col., U.S.A.F., HQ ACC/HC, 216 Sweeney Blvd., Ste. 114, Langley AFB, VA 23665. Tel: 757-764-7801
Kelly, Brian F., Chap., Capt., U.S.N., 7183 Willet Cir., Carlsbad, CA 92009. Tel: 360-649-8047
Kozen, Bert S., U.S. Army, 463 Wilson St., 17701.
Motsay, Joseph R., Chap. Lt. Col., 134-A Crescent Dr., Columbus AFB, MS 39705. U.S.A.F.
Petruska, William M., Cap., U.S.N., 4421 Collwood Ln., San Diego, CA 92115-2015. Tel: 619-795-8485

Unassigned or Leave of Absence:
Rev. Msgrs.—
Leonard, Paul F.
O'Neill, Kevin P.
Revs.—
Clay, Christopher R.
Ensey, Eric S.
Gibson, Robert J.
Hudak, Thomas R.
Kilpatrick, Andrew W.
Kita, John M.
Kringe, Charles J., 708 N. Broad St. W., West Hazleton, 18202. Tel: 717-454-1380
Kulik, Francis J.
McGee, James J., S.S.
Munkelt, Richard A., 142 Market St., Greely, 18425.
Pilon, Jean-Pierre G.
Rossetti, Mark T.
Sullivan, Michael J.
Tetherow, Gabriel Francis, S.M.F.
Urrutigoity, Carlos
Young, Vincent J.

Retired:
Rev. Msgrs.—
Casey, George T., P.O. Box 1578, Hollywood, FL 33022. Tel: 954-920-0681
Clarke, James T., Villa St. Joseph, Dunmore, 18509. Tel: 570-969-1235
Cottone, Paul P., Villa St. Joseph, Dunmore, 18509. Tel: 570-343-0782
Demuth, George R., Holy Family Pavilion, 2510 Adams Ave., Apt. 303, 18509-1597. Tel: 570-344-3719
Donovan, William L., Villa St. Joseph, Dunmore, 18509. Tel: 570-963-9383
Esseff, John A., St. Pius X Seminary, 1000 Seminary Rd., Clarks Summit, 18411. Tel: 570-563-8525
Fadden, Joseph A., 2301 N. Washington Ave., 18509. Tel: 570-344-9884
Gajewski, Chester A., Villa St. Joseph, Dunmore, 18509. Tel: 570-347-1851
Gallagher, John P., Ph.D., 1026 Wheeler Ave., 18510. Tel: 570-342-1991
Lasky, Joseph J., 258 Zerbey Ave., Kingston, 18704. Tel: 570-287-5096
Law, Joseph A., Villa St. Joseph, Dunmore, 18509. Tel: 570-343-2388
Masakowski, John C., 157 W. Church St., Nanticoke, 18634.
Norkunas, Anthony J., 253 S. Meade St., Wilkes-Barre, 18702. Tel: 570-824-6490
O'Brien, John J., Villa St. Joseph, Dunmore, 18509. Tel: 570-961-1865
Pakutka, William J., Villa St. Joseph, Dunmore, 18509. Tel: 570-341-9168
Penkala, Edmund S., Villa St. Joseph, Dunmore, 18509. Tel: 570-344-6288
Piorkowski, Stanley W., Villa St. Joseph, Dunmore, 18509. Tel: 570-343-1184
Revs.—
Adonizio, Joseph J., 154 Rock St., Pittston, 18640. Tel: 570-654-8032
Alisauskas, Peter J., 366 Indian Lake Tr., White Haven, 18661. Tel: 570-472-3360
Angelo, Girard F., Two W. 21st St., Hazleton, 18201. Tel: 570-455-0177
Boles, Joseph M., Villa St. Joseph, Dunmore, 18509. Tel: 570-343-0394
Brogus, Albert G., 43 James St., Plains, 18705.
Burnett, Robert E., 158 Wyoming St., Carbondale, 18407. Tel: 570-282-1600
Carr, Eugene R., P.O.Box 1063, Killington, VT 05751. Tel: 802-422-3589
Casey, John W., P.O. Box 1578, Hollywood, FL 33022. Tel: 954-920-0681
Conboy, Joseph T., St. Therese Residence, 200 S. Meade St., Wilkes-Barre, 18702. Tel: 570-823-6131
Cortese, Patrick S., 1007 Crossroad Ln., Hazleton, 18201. Tel: 570-459-5929
Delaney, T. Timothy, 180 Madison St., Wilkes-Barre, 18702. Tel: 570-824-5552
Everling, Robert M., Villa St. Joseph, Dunmore, 18509. Tel: 570-343-4925
Fabian, John L., Villa St. Joseph, Dunmore, 18509. Tel: 570-348-0728
Flannery, Joseph D., Villa St. Joseph, Dunmore, 18509. Tel: 570-347-8019
Flynn, Thomas A., Villa St. Joseph, Dunmore, 18509. Tel: 570-348-0589
Fox, Joseph F., 1706 Delaware St., Dunmore, 18509. Tel: 570-343-5522
Gaiardo, Martin J., Mulberry Tower, 499 Mulberry St., Apt. 1216, 18503. Tel: 570-347-4826
Gardzalla, Leo M., 259 Carver St., Plymouth, 18651. Tel: 570-779-3044
Hazzouri, Alex J., Villa St. Joseph, Dunmore, 18509. Tel: 570-343-2859
Healey, Patrick D., St. Mary of the Assumption Rectory, 430 Pittston Ave., 18505. Tel: 570-961-2297
Herhenrerder, Peter V., 86 Washington St., Carbondale, 18407. Tel: 570-282-0304
Hines, William F., 2461 S.W. 82nd Ave., Bldg. 2-Apt. 105, Fort Lauderdale, FL 33324. Tel: 305-423-9301
Hlopko, John J., Lake Rd., P.O. Box 67, Bear Creek, 18602. Tel: 570-472-3483
Kalinowski, Stainslaus J., 3020 Cedar Ave., 18505.
Kizis, Kenneth G., Holy Family Pavilion, 2510 Adams Ave., Apt. 304, 18509. Tel: 570-342-7406
Langan, James J., 2420 S.W. 81st Ave., Arrowhead Condominium, Bldg. 7, Apt. 402, Davie, FL 33324.
Lewis, Harry J., Villa St. Joseph, Dunmore, 18509. Tel: 570-343-5499
Marinko, John S., St. Therese Residence, 260 S. Meade St., Wilkes - Barre, 18702. Tel: 570-823-6131
McCann, Thomas E., Pollock Dr., Pittston, 18640.
Mulrooney, F. Harold, Villa St. Joseph, 1600 Green Ridge St., 18509. Tel: 570-343-8704
Noviello, Anthony A., 301 Tallman Ave., South Williamsport, 17702. Tel: 570-323-6552
Olszewski, Daniel D., 74 Pinewood Dr., Laflin, 18702. Tel: 570-655-2165
Ostrowski, Joseph C., Villa St. Joseph, Dunmore, 18509. Tel: 570-342-7396
Pace, William J., Villa St. Joseph, Dunmore, 18509. Tel: 570-961-5856
Plevyak, Valentine R., Villa St. Joseph, Dunmore, 18509. Tel: 570-969-9109
Rusin, Joseph C., R.R.I., Box 34, Carbondale, 18407. Tel: 570-282-4767
Sokolowski, Edward V., 3 Regina Dr., Mountaintop, 18707. Tel: 570-474-2269
Zapotocki, Henry E., P.O. Box 847, Tannersville, 18372. Tel: 570-629-1235
Zawadzki, Victor C., 5 O'Donnell St., Wilkes-Barre, 18702. Tel: 570-819-1629
Zawodniak, Edward J., 25 Hickory Tree Rd., Loyalville, Dallas, 18612. Tel: 570-477-2086

INSTITUTIONS LOCATED IN THE DIOCESE

[A] SEMINARIES, DIOCESAN

DALTON. *Saint Pius X Seminary* (Collaborative College/Pre-Theology Seminary) , 1000 Seminary Rd., 18414. Tel: 570-563-1131; Fax: 570-563-8520. Email: spxedu@ptdprolog.net. Web: www.dioceseofscranton.org/stpius. Rev. Msgrs. David A. Bohr, S.T.D., Rector; Bernard E. Yarrish, S.T.L., Vice Rector; John A. Esseff, Dir., Apostolic Formation (Retired); Revs. James A. Rafferty, S.T.L., Academic Dean; Jeffrey J. Walsh, Spiritual Dir. & Dir., Liturgical Formation. Seminarians 11.

[B] SEMINARIES, RELIGIOUS

PITTSTON. *St. Joseph's Oblate Seminary*, 1880 Hwy. 315, 18640. Tel: 570-654-7542; Fax: 570-654-8621. Email: finnosj@adelphia.net. Very Rev. Gregory T. Finn, O.S.J., Prov., Seminary Dir., Rector; Rev. Salvatore Bentivegna, O.S.J. In Res. Revs. Mario Buttini, O.S.J.; Paul J. Pavese, O.S.J., Rector.

[C] COLLEGES AND UNIVERSITIES

SCRANTON. *Marywood University* 18509. Tel: 570-348-6211; Fax: 570-340-6014. Email: mreap@marywood.edu. Web: www.marywood.edu. Sisters Mary Reap, I.H.M., Ph.D., Pres.; Patricia Ann Matthews, I.H.M., Ph.D., Vice Pres. Academic Affairs; Mr. Leo J. Danylak, M.B.A., Vice Pres. Business Affairs; Dr. Clayton N. Pheasant, Vice Pres. Univ. Advancement; Dr. Raymond P. Heath, Vice Pres. Student Life; Dr. Louis S. Farmanski, Dean College of Liberal Arts & Sciences; Dr. Lois K. Draina, Dean College of Education & Human Devel.; Dr. Lloyd L. Lyter, Dir., School of Social Work; Dr. Ronald Bulbulian, Dean College of Health and Human Svcs.; Dr. Devorah Namm, Dean College of Creative Arts & Mgmt.; Dr. Bernadette M. Russell, Dean School of Continuing Education; Ann Boland-Chase, M.A., Registrar; Dr. Mary Anne Fedrick, Asst. Vice Pres., Academic Affairs; Dr. Barbara R. Sadowski, Asst. to Pres. for Planning & Inst. Research. Sisters, Servants of the Immaculate Heart of Mary Faculty: Sisters 15; Lay Teachers 125; Students 3,136.

The University of Scranton (Society of Jesus) , 18510. Tel: 570-941-7400; Fax: 570-941-4097. Email: info@scranton.edu. Web: www.scranton.edu. Rev. Scott R. Pilarz, S.J. (WDC), Pres.; Dr. Beth E. Barnett, Provost & Academic Vice Pres.; Rev. George A. Aschenbrenner, S.J. (ALN), Rector of the Jesuit Community; Mr. David E. Christiansen, Vice Pres. Finance & Treas.; Mr. Paul J. Strunk, Vice Pres. Institutional Advancement; Mr. Jerome P. DeSanto, Interim Vice Pres. Planning and Assoc. Provost Info. Resources; Rev. John J. Shea, S.J., Vice Pres. Univ. Ministries; Dr. Joseph H. Dreisbach, Dean of the College of Arts & Sciences; Dr. Ronald D. Johnson, Dean of the Kania School of Mgmt.; Dr. Kathleen V. Davis, Dean of Dexter

Hanley College; Dr. Duncan Perry, Dean of the Graduate School; Ms. Helen Stager, Registrar; Dr. James J. Pallante, Dean Panuska College of Professional Studies; Dr. Thomas Smith, Dean Student Devel. & Dir. Counseling Center; Dr. Vincent Carilli, Vice Pres. Student Affairs; Dr. Reuban Rodriguez, Dean of Student Life; Mr. Martin L. Langan, Assoc. Vice Pres. Admin. Svcs.; Mr. Charles E. Kratz, Dean Library; Ms. Abigail Byman, Sec. of the Univ. & Gen. Counsel; Revs. John J. Begley, S.J.; Paul R. Beining, S.J.; Louis A. Bonacci, S.J. (WH); Timothy J. Cadigan, S.J.; Vincent G. Conti, S.J. (WDC); Henry C. Coster, S.J.; John H. Duggan, S.J.; Philip A. Florio, S.J.; Joseph M. Kakalec, S.J. (PH); Herbert B. Keller, S.J., Pres., Scranton Prep; Francis J. Kownacki, S.J.; John W. Lange, S.J.; John J. Levko, S.J.; Francis J. MacEntee, S.J.; Leonard A. Martin, S.J.; Thomas D. Masterson, S.J.; William J. McGrath, S.J.; Bernard R. McIlhenny, S.J., Min. Jesuit Community; Ronald H. McKinney, S.J.; Neil P. McLaughlin, S.J.; J. Patrick Mohr, S.J.; Joseph A. Newell, S.J. (ALN); G. Donald Pantle, S.J.; John J. Quinn, S.J.; Joseph L. Quinn, S.J.; Richard W. Rousseau, S.J.; Thomas F. Sable, S.J.; Joseph N. Tylenda, S.J. (WDC), Chap., Marian Convent; Bros. Darrell J. Burns, S.J.; James C. Lemon, S.J. Priests 33; Students 4,728.

Center for Eastern Christian Studies, University of Scranton, 18510. Tel: 570-941-6116; Fax: 570-941-4030. Revs. John J. Shea, S.J., Dir.; Thomas F. Sable, S.J., Editor Diakonia.

DALLAS. *College Misericordia* 18612. Tel: 570-674-6400; Fax: 570-675-2441. Web: www.misericordia.edu. Religious Sisters of Mercy of the Americas. Priests 1; Sisters Teaching 3; Students 2,122.

Administration: Michael A. MacDowell, Ed.D., Pres.; Mr. John Risboskin, Vice Pres. of Finance & Admin.; Rev. Michael M. Bryant, M.Th., Chap.; Mr. Michael McGovern, Ed.D., Vice Pres. of Academic Affairs; Ms. Susan Helwig, Vice Pres. Institutional Advancement; Sr. Jean Messaros, R.S.M., Dean of Students; Mrs. Jane Dessoye, M.S., Exec. Dir., Admissions & Financial Aid; Mr. Edward Lahart, M.S., Registrar; Mr. Chrstopher Sutzko, Dir., Career Svcs.; Ms. Jacqueline Ghormoz, M.S., Dir. Counseling Svcs.; Mr. Joseph Mack, M.B.A., Dir. Mgmt. Information Svcs.; Dr. John Sumansky, Chief Information & Planning Officer; Mrs. Sharon Wiggins, Dir., Library Svcs.; Ms. Kathleen A. Foley, B.S., M.S., Asst. Dean of Students; Mr. Ronald Hromisin, C.P.A., Comptroller; Mr. James Roberts, Dir. of Public Communication.

WILKES-BARRE. **Kings College* 18711. Tel: 570-208-5900; Fax: 570-825-9046. Web: www.kings.edu. Priests 13; Brothers 5; Lay Teachers 113; Students 2,294.

Officers of the College: Revs. Thomas J. O'Hara, C.S.C., Ph.D., Pres.; Donald J. Grimes, C.S.C., Ph.D., Vice Pres. Academic Affairs; Mr. Steven H. Seitchik, Vice Pres. Business Affairs & Treas.; Ms. Janet Mercincavage, Vice Pres. Student Affairs; Mr. Frank J. Pasquini, Vice Pres. Institutional Advancement; Rev. Richard C. Hockman, C.S.C., College Chap. & Dir. Campus Ministry; Dr. David G. Martin, Dir. William J. McGowan School of Business; Mr. Paul J. Moran, Exec. Dir. Information and Instructional Technology Svcs.; Ms. Michelle Lawrence-Schmude, Dir. Admissions; Mr. Daniel T. Cebrick, Registrar; Rev. Anthony R. Grasso, C.S.C., Rel. Supr. Holy Cross Community Revs. Francis Cafareilli, C.S.C.; Thomas F. Carten, C.S.C.; John R. Geraci, C.S.C.; Anthony R. Grasso, C.S.C.; Donald J. Grimes, C.S.C., Ph.D.; Richard C. Hockman, C.S.C.; Charles J. Kociolek, C.S.C.; Thomas P. Looney, C.S.C.; Thomas J. O'Hara, C.S.C., Ph.D.; William R. Ribando, C.S.C.; John J. Ryan, C.S.C.; Patrick J. Sullivan, C.S.C.; Bros. Richard F. Kyle, C.S.C.; James H. Miller, C.S.C.; Thomas Sawyer, C.S.C.; Mr. John P. Reardon, C.S.C. In Res. Rev. Joseph J. Long, C.S.C.; Bros. Jerome Matthews, C.S.C.; Harold J. Rogan, C.S.C.

[D] HIGH SCHOOLS, DIOCESAN

SCRANTON. *Bishop Hannan High School*, 330 Wyoming Ave., 18503. Tel: 570-346-4643; Fax: 570-346-0048. Mr. James P. Marcks, Prin.; Rev. James P. Dougher, Dir., Religious Formation; Mr. Timothy Ferguson, Dean Students. Priests 3; Sisters Servants of the Immaculate Heart of Mary 3; Lay Teachers 25; Students 326.

CARBONDALE. *Sacred Heart Junior/Senior High School*, 44 S. Church St., 18407. Tel: 570-282-2790; Fax: 570-282-2380. Email: croosader@msn.com. Web: shhrs.s5.com. Mr. Charles Barlow, Prin.; Sr. Patricia Scalese, I.H.M., Dir. Religious Formation; Mr. James Allan, Dean of Students; Rev. Patrick L. Albert, Chap. Priests 1; Sisters 3; Lay Teachers 14; Students 160.

DUNMORE. *Bishop O'Hara High School*, 501 E. Drinker St., 18512. Tel: 570-346-7541; Fax: 570-348-1070. Email: bishopohara@adelphia.net. Mrs. Anita M. Strak, Prin.; Mr. Charles J. Buzad, Vice Prin.; Rev. Scott P. Sterowski, Dir., Religious Formation. Sisters, Servants of the Immaculate Heart of Mary Priests 1; Sisters 1; Lay Teachers 25; Students 349.

EAST STROUDSBURG. *Notre Dame Junior/Senior High School*, 60 Spangenburg Ave., 18301. Tel: 570-421-0466; Fax 570-476-0629. Email: notredame@usnetway.com. Web: notredamehigh.com. Jeffrey N. Lyons, Prin.; Rev. Msgr. John A. Bergamo, J.C.L., Dir., Religious Formation; John D. Gormley, Dean of Students. Priests 2; Sisters, Servants of the Immaculate Heart of Mary 1; Lay Teachers 26; Students 351.

HAZLETON. *Bishop Hafey Junior/Senior High School*, 1700 W. 22nd St., 18202. Tel: 570-455-9431; Fax: 570-455-2847. Email: hafeymainoffice@choiceonemail.com. Web: www.bishophafey.20m.com. Mr. P.J. Melvin, Prin.; Rev. Joseph J. Evanko, Chap.; Mr. Michael Stofko, Academic Dean of Students; Mr. Richard Smith, Athletic Dir.; Mr. Thomas A. Kostic, Dir., Religious Formation; Mrs. Miriam Jamelli, Dir., Guidance; Mr. Cameo Zola, Business Mgr. Priests 1; Lay Teachers 31; Students 430.

KINGSTON. *Bishop O'Reilly High School*, 316 N. Maple Ave., P.O. Box 1346, 18704. Tel: 570-288-1404; Fax: 570-288-6634. Email: borhsbor@epix.net. Web: www.bishoporeillyhighschool.pvt.k12.pa.us. Miss Susan Dennen, Prin.; Mr. Robert Beviglia, Asst. Prin.; Rev. Paul C. Fontanella, Dir. Rel. Formation; Mr. Robert Musso, Dir., Guidance; Mr. Ralph Mancuso, Business Mgr. Priests 1; Sisters 1; Lay Teachers 27; Students 303.

PITTSTON. *Seton Catholic High School*, 37 William St., 18640. Tel: 570-654-4831; 570-655-0208; Fax: 570-654-2599. Email: redingtonjj@hotmail.com. James J. Redington, Prin.; Deacon Robert A. Roman, Dir., Religious Formation & Chap.; John Zongilla, Dean of Students; Sr. Mary Ann Cody, I.H.M., Dir. of Devel. Sisters 2; Lay Teachers 18; Students 224.

WILKES-BARRE *Bishop Hoban High School*, 159 S. Penna Blvd., 18701-3394. Tel: 570-829-2424; Fax: 570-829-4412. Email: libhoban@ptd.net. Web: www.bishophoban.com. Rev. Msgr. David L. Tressler, Prin.; Sisters Leonita Duhoski, R.S.M., Dir. of Devel.; Catherine Ann Morris, SS.C.M., Dir. of Guidance; Ellen Maroney, I.H.M., Dean of Students; Mr. James McDermott, Acting Dir. of Religious Formation; Mrs. Anne Thomas, Dean of Academic Studies. Priests 1; Sisters 6; Lay Teachers 40; Students 715.

WILLIAMSPORT *Bishop Neumann Junior/Senior High School*, 901 Penn St., 17701. Tel: 570 323-9953; Fax: 570-321-7146. Mr. Paul Ward, Prin.; Ms. Judith Folmar, Asst. Prin.; Patricia Dougherty, Dir., Religious Formation; Rev. Michael J. Zipay, Chap. Priests 1; Sisters 1; Lay Teachers 19; Students 194.

[E] HIGH SCHOOLS, PRIVATE

SCRANTON. **Scranton Preparatory School*, 1000 Wyoming Ave., 18509. Tel: 570-941-7737; Fax: 570-941-6118. Email: pmarx@scrantonprep.com. Web: www.scrantonprep.com. Rev. Herbert B. Keller, S.J., Pres. Society of Jesus Priests 5; Brothers 2; Lay Teachers 56; Students 749.

Faculty: Revs. Vincent G. Conti, S.J. (WDC); Leonard A. Martin, S.J.; William J. McGrath, S.J.; Joseph A. Newell, S.J. (ALN); Bros. James C. Lemon, S.J.; Darrell Burns, S.J., Chap.

MOSCOW. *St. Gregory's Academy*, R.R. 8, Box 8214, 18444. Tel: 570-842-8112; Fax: 570-842-4513. Email: stgregory@epix.net. Rev. Bruno Stemler, F.S.S.P., Chap.; E. Howard Clark, Headmaster. Priestly Fraternity of St. Peter Lay Teachers 10; Students 61.

[F] INTER-PAROCHIAL ELEMENTARY SCHOOLS

SCRANTON. *Marian Catholic Interparochial School*, 430 River St., 18505-1157. Tel: 570-342 9700; Fax: 570-341-7664. Email: mcips@epix.net.

Upper Campus (Grades 4-8), 638 Hemlock St., 18505. Tel: 570-346-9922; Fax: 570-207-2652. Email: mcips@epix.net. Karen DeSandis, Prin. Sisters of the I.H.M. 1; Sisters of Christian Charity 1; Lay Teachers 17; Students 347.

Primary Campus (Grades PreK-3), 430 River St., 18505-1157. Tel: 570-342-9700; Fax: 570-341-7664. Email: mcips@epix.net. Mrs. Jean M. Rossi, Prin. Lay Teachers 12; Students 207.

CARBONDALE. *Sacred Heart Elementary School Primary Center*, 27-33 Fairview St., 18407. Tel: 570-282-0340; Fax: 570-281-3677. Email: emm.59@aol.com. Web: www.edline.net/page/scared-heart-Jr-Sr-HS. Mrs. Ellen M. Murphy, Prin. Sisters 2; Lay Teachers 13; Students 236.

Sacred Heart Intermediate Center, 7th Ave. & Church St., 18407. Tel: 570-282-7930; Fax: 570-282-2380. Email: skms116@aol.com. Sr. Karen Steinberg, I.H.M., Prin. Sisters 2; Lay Teachers 4; Students 70.

CLARKS GREEN. *Saint Gregory Early Childhood Center*, 330 N. Abington Rd., 18411. Tel: 570-587-4808; Fax: 570-586-4515. Email: jlouis3662@aol. Web: www.NVDS.com.STGREGORY.html. Rev. Msgr. John H. Louis, Acting Prin. Lay Teachers 3; Students 53.

Our Lady of Peace Elementary School, 410 N. Abington Rd., 18411. Tel: 570-587-4152; Fax: 570-586-5393. Email: OLP@epix.net. Web: www.olpeace.com. Mrs. Jane Quinn, Prin. Lay Teachers 21; Students 405.

CRESCO. *Monsignor McHugh Elementary School*, R.R. 1, Box 1780, 18326. Tel: 570-595-7463; Fax: 570-595-9639. Email: msgrmchugh@enter.net. Web: www.msgrmchugh.com. Kathleen A. Serafin, Prin. Sisters, Servants of the Immaculate Heart of Mary 1; Lay Teachers 20; Students 489.

Immaculate Heart of Mary Convent, R.R. 1, Box 568, 18326. Tel: 570-595-7548.

DALLAS. *Gate of Heaven Elementary School*, 40 Machell Ave., 18612. Tel: 570-675-6566; Fax: 570-674-0198. Email: gohtiguem@hotmail.com. Web: www.gateofheaven.dalla.pa.us. Mrs. Mary Tigue, Prin. Lay Teachers 25; Students 383.

EAST STROUDSBURG. *Notre Dame Elementary School*, 78 Ridgeway St., 18301. Tel: 570-421-3651; Fax: 570-422-6935. Email: ndelem@usnetway.com. Sr. Mary Alice Kane, I.H.M., Prin. I.H.M. Sisters 4; Lay Teachers 20; Students 430.

EXETER. *Wyoming Area Catholic Elementary School*, 1690 Wyoming Ave., 18643. Tel: 570-654-7982; Fax: 570-654-0605. Email: wacs@adelphia.net. Web: www.wacsh.com. Mr. Thomas Killino, Prin. Lay Teachers 13; Students 188.

FORTY FORT. *Regis Elementary School*, 1133 Wyoming Ave., 18704. Tel: 570-288-5558; Fax: 570-288-5560. Email: regiselementary@adelphia.net. Web: www.regiselementary.com. Mr. Russell P. Bigus, Prin. Lay Teachers 12; Students 200.

HAZLETON. *Holy Spirit Academy*, 225 E. Fourth St., 18201. Tel: 570-459-0054; Fax: 570-459-2567. Email: holysprt@intergrafix.net. Mrs. Alice Flynn, Prin. Priests 5; Sisters 2; Lay Teachers 10; Students 204.

HONESDALE. *Saint Vincent Elementary School*, 329 Cliff St., 18431. Tel: 570-253-1074; Fax: 570-253-2014. Web: www.myschoolonline.com/PA/stvincentsschool. Mr. Carl Klach, Prin. Lay Teachers 10; Students 230.

JESSUP. *La Salle Academy*, 309 First Ave., 18434. Tel: 570-489-2010; Fax: 570-489-3887. Email: tarrity@lasallejessup.com. Web: Lasallejessup.com. Dr. James Tarity Jr., Prin. Sisters 2; Lay Teachers 21; Students 365.

KINGSTON. *Bishop O'Reilly Junior High School*, 316 N. Maple Ave., P.O. Box 1346, 18704. Tel: 570-288-1404; Fax: 570-288-6634. Email: bor@epix.net. Web: www.bishoporeillyhighschool.pvt.k12.pa.us. Susan Dennen, Prin. Lay Teachers 8; Students 77.

NANTICOKE. *Pope John Paul II Elementary School*, 518 S. Hanover St., 18634. Tel: 570-735-7935; Fax: 570-735-2281. Email: pjp@adelphia.net. Anthony Prushinski, Prin. Lay Teachers 13; Students 325.

WILKES-BARRE. *Saint Boniface Interparochial School*, 221 Blackman St., 18702-4576. Tel: 570-823-0939; Fax: 570-823-2856. Email: stbon@epix.net. Mary Ann Olszewski, Prin. S.C.C. Sisters 1; Lay Teachers 8; Students 215.

Saint Nicholas-Saint Mary Elementary School, 242 S. Washington St., 18701. Tel: 570-823-8089; Fax: 570-823-1402. Email: snsm46@hotmail.com. Sr. Mary Catherine Slattery, S.C.C., Prin. S.C.C. Sisters 3; Lay Teachers 16; Students 492.

[G] PRESCHOOLS AND CHILD CARE CENTERS

SCRANTON. *Immaculate Care Preschool*, 800 Taylor Ave., 18510. Tel: 570-344-4380; Fax: 570-961-5212. Ann Marie McDonald, Dir. Head Teacher.

Marywood-Tony Domiano Early Childhood Center Marywood University , 2300 Adams Ave., 18509. Tel: 570-340-6085; Fax: 570-961-4739. Email: muro@ac.marywood.edu. Web: marywood.edu. Sr. Marilyn Muro, I.H.M., Dir.

MILFORD. *St. Patrick Preschool*, 111 E. High St., P.O. Box W, 18337-9672. Tel: 570-296-4721; Fax: 570-296-7451. Email: ritastraka@nac.net. Rita Straka, Teacher.

St. Vincent de Paul Preschool, 101 St. Vincent Dr., 18337-9672. Tel: 570-686-1867; Fax: 800-565-1762. Email: stvincentdepaul@pikeonline.net. Web: members.xoom.com/saintvincent. Susan Plaxe, Teacher.

MOSCOW. *St. Catherine Preschool*, Church St., P.O.

Box 250, 18444. Tel: 570-848-1258; Fax: 570-842-6648. Email: nedda02@yahoo.com. Kathy LoRusso, Dir.

MUNCY. *Resurrection Early Childhood Center*, 526 S. Main St., 17756. Tel: 570-546-5272; Fax: 570-546-5272. Web: resurrectiononline.net. Jennifer Richards, Co-Dir.; Cynthia Murphy, Co-Dir.

PITTSTON. *St. Mary's Early Childhood Learning Center*, 535 N. Main Ave., 18640-2244. Tel: 570-654-8188; Fax: 570-654-7052. Email: srestherfalzone@aol.com. Web: www.sma-pittston.org. Sr. Esther Falzone, S.C.C., Prin.

[H] RENEWAL CENTERS

CRESCO. *The Immaculate Heart of Mary Spiritual Renewal Center*, R.R. 1, Box 1781, 18326. Tel: 570-595-7548; 570-595-7549; Fax: 570-595-9698. Email: ihmcresco@yahoo.com. Web: ihm.marywood.edu. Sr. Anne Mary Boslett, I.H.M., Dir.

DALTON. *Fatima Renewal Center*, 1000 Seminary Rd., 18414. Tel: 570-563-8500; Fax: 570-563-1857. Email: fatima@ptdprolog.net. Web: www.dioceseofscranton.org/fatima. Mr. Paul R. Tomczyk, Retreat & Program Coord.

NANTICOKE. *Holy Family Spiritual Renewal Center*, 151 Old Newport St., 18634-1300. Tel; 570-735-2599; Fax: 570-735-2679. Email: marhudak@voicenet.com.
Co-Directors: Martin J. Hudak; Louise V. Hudak.

[I] GENERAL HOSPITALS

SCRANTON. *Mercy Hospital* Mercy Health Partners , 746 Jefferson Ave., 18501. Tel: 570-348-7100; Fax: 570-348-7639. Email: jmay@health-partners.org curlamb@health-partners.org. Web: mercyhealthpartners.com. James E. May, Pres. & CEO, Mercy Health Partners; C.J. Urlab, Chief Admin. Officer; Rev. John C. Ruth, Chap. Sisters of Mercy 9; Bed Capacity 274; Bassinets 18; Total Capacity 292; Patients Assisted Annually 251,887.
Mercy Foundation, 746 Jefferson Ave., 18501. Tel: 570-340-5902; Fax: 570-348-7685. Sr. Mary Ellen Fuhrman, R.S.M., Pres.
Mercy Med-Care, Inc., 746 Jefferson Ave., 18501. Tel: 570-348-7074; Fax: 570-348-7021. Email: sfrank@health-partners.org. Web: health-partners.org. Patients Assisted Annually 2,500.

CARBONDALE. *Marian Community Hospital*, 100 Lincoln Ave., 18407. Tel: 570-281-1000; Fax: 570-282-7177. Email: Prdept@marian.hcrn.com. Web: www.mariancommunityhospital.org. Sr. Jean Coughlin, I.H.M., Pres. & CEO; Rev. Leo P. Cummings, Chap. Sisters, Servants of the Immaculate Heart of Mary Bed Capacity 104; Patients Assisted Annually 65,773; Sisters 8.
Maxis Foundation, 100 Lincoln Ave., 18407. Tel: 570-281-1000; Fax: 570-282-7177. Web: www.mariancommunityhospital.org. Sr. Jean Coughlin, I.H.M., Pres.
Maxis Medical Services, 100 Lincoln Ave., 18407. Tel: 570-281-1000; Fax: 570-282-7177. Web: www.mariancommunityhospital.org. Sr. Jean Coughlin, I.H.M., Pres. Patients Assisted Annually 13,225.

HAZLETON. *Hazleton-Saint Joseph Medical Center*, 687 N. Church St., 18201. Tel: 570-501-6000; Fax: 570-501-6203. Email: brudegeair@ghha.org. Web: www.ghha.org. Sisters Bernard C. Rudegeair, Pres.; M. Lorentia Kocun, O.S.F., Supr. Bernardine Sisters of the Third Order of St. Francis 9; Bed Capacity 122; Patients Assisted Annually 133,934.

MUNCY. *Muncy Valley Hospital*, 215 E. Water St., 17756. Tel: 570-546-8282; Fax: 570-546-4150. Email: Lcioffi@shscares.org. Web: www.shscares.org. Kirby O. Smith, Pres.; Sr. Sharon Hartman, S.C.C., Dir., Pastoral Care. Capacity 184; Patients Assisted Annually 99,332.

NANTICOKE. *Mercy Special Care Hospital*, 128 W. Washington St., 18634. Tel: 570-740-5204; Fax: 570-740-5220. Email: rwilliams@health-partners.org. Web: www.mercyhealthpartners.com. Robert D. Williams, Admin. Bed Capacity 69; Patients Assisted Annually 20,000.

WILKES-BARRE. *Mercy Hospital*, 25 Church St., 18765. Tel: 570-826-3100; Fax: 570-831-8989. Web: mercyhealthpartners.com. James E. May, Pres. & CEO; Eugene Bassett, Chief Admin. Officer; Sr. Mary Ellen Fuhrman, R.S.M., Sisters Liaison; Rev. Joseph R. Kakareka, Chap. Mercy Health Partners Sisters of Mercy 5; Bed Capacity 191; Bassinets 15; Patients Assisted Annually 106,043.

WILLIAMSPORT. *Divine Providence Hospital of the Sisters of Christian Charity*, 1100 Grampian Blvd., 17701. Tel: 570-326-8000; Fax: 570-326-8902; 570-326-8181. Email: Lcioffi@shscares.org. Web: shscares.org. Kirby O. Smith, Pres.; Sr. Marlene Weitzel, S.C.C., Supr. Bed Capacity 167; Patients Assisted Annually 116,170.
Providence Health System Foundation, Inc., 1100 Grampian Blvd., 17701. Tel: 570-320-7010; 570-320-7610; Fax: 570-326-8902. Email: jbednar@shscares.org. Web: www.shscares.org. Sr. Joanne Bednar, S.C.C., Pres.
Sisters of Christian Charity Healthcare Corporation, 1100 Grampian Blvd., 17701. Tel: 570-320-7610; Fax: 570-326-8902. Email: jbednar@shscares.org. Web: www.shscares.org.
**Susquehanna Regional Home Health Services*, 1100 Grampian Blvd., 17701. Tel: 570-320-7690; Fax: 570-323-0716. Email: lcioffi@shscares.org. Web: www.shscares.org. Patients Assisted Annually 2,292.

[J] SPECIAL HOSPITALS

SCRANTON. *St. Joseph's Center*, 2010 Adams Ave., 18509. Tel: 570-342-8379; Fax: 570-342-6080. Email: wecare@stjosephscenter.org. Web: www.stjosephscenter.org. Sr. Therese O'Rourke, I.H.M., Pres. & CEO; Rev. William B. Pickard, Chap. Sisters, Servants of the Immaculate Heart of Mary 9; Bed Capacity 147; Patients Assisted Annually 155.

[K] SPECIAL EDUCATION SCHOOLS

CLARKS GREEN. *Lourdesmont*, 537 Venard Rd., 18411. Tel: 570-587-4741; Fax: 570-586-0030. Email: mlesho@lourdesmont.com. Web: www.lourdesmont.com. Sr. Mary Pauline Bilbrough, R.G.S., Coord.; Barry Rogers, Prin.; John A. Antognoli, Ed.D., CEO.
Legal Title: *Good Shepherd Corporation of Clarks Summit, PA* Sisters of the Good Shepherd 3; Staff 108; Total Assisted 508.

PINE GROVE. *St. Michael's Group Home*, 25 Oak Grove Rd., 17963. Tel: 570-345-1160; Fax: 570-345-6307. Email: pggirls1995@yahoo.com. Web: www.dioceseofscranton.org. Total Assisted 10; Total Staff 7.

TUNKHANNOCK. *St. Michael's Group Home-Tunkhannock*, 28 Putnam St., 18657. Tel: 570-836-6932; Fax: 570-836-6979. Email: stmikes@epix.net. Web: www.dioceseofscranton.org. Andrew Varzaly, Contact Person.
St. Michael's School, Box 370, 18657. Tel: 570-388-6155; Fax: 570-388-6979. Email: stmikes@epix.net. Web: www.dioceseofscranton.org. Mr. Andrew M. Varzaly, M.S.W., L.S.W., Exec. Dir. Students Assisted 315; Total Staff 170.

WEST PITTSTON. *St. Michael's Group Home-West Pittston*, 225-227 Damon St., 18643. Tel: 570-602-6579; Fax: 570-602-6979. Andrew Varzaly, Contact Person.

WILLIAMSPORT. *St. Michael's Group Home*, 119 E. Fourth St., 17701. Tel: 570-322-0561; Fax: 570-322-8901. Email: stmichaels@chilitech.net. Web: www.dioceseofscranton.org. Total Assisted 8; Total Staff 7.

[L] HOMES FOR AGED

SCRANTON. *Home for Aged of the Little Sisters of the Poor, Holy Family Residence*, 2500 Adams Ave., 18509. Tel: 570-343-4065; 570-346-5788; Fax: 570-346-1196. Email: scmslsp@attglobal.net. Sr. Alice Marie Jones, P.S.D.P., Supr.; Rev. Joseph Fanti, Chap. Little Sisters of the Poor 11; Aged Residents 52; Residents in Independent Living Apartments 21.

DALLAS. *Mercy Center Nursing Unit, Inc.*, Lake St., Box 370, 18612. Tel: 570-675-2131; Fax: 570-674-7606. Email: jwhite@mcnu.org. Web: www.mcnu.org. Sr. Sara Sweeney, R.S.M., Admin.; Sheila Heck, Dir. of Nursing.

MOSCOW. *St. Mary's Villa Nursing Home*, 675 St. Mary's Villa Rd., 18444. Tel: 570-842-7621; Fax: 570-842-2953. Email: smvcadmin@adelphia.net. J. Gregory Cauterucci Sr., Campus CEO; Sr. Sebastian, C.J.C., Convent Supr. Tel: 570-842-7466; Rev. Gerard F. Lupa, Chap. Poor Sisters of Jesus Crucified and the Sorrowful Mother 6; Residents 112; Total Staff 165.
St. Mary's Villa Residence, One Pioneer Pl., 18444. Tel: 570-842-5274; Fax: 570-842-3472. Lisa Trygar, L.P.N., Personal Care Home Admin.; Rev. Gerard F. Lupa, Chap. Residents 64; Total Staff 45.

WILKES-BARRE. *Little Flower Manor of the Diocese of Scranton*, 200 S. Meade St., 18702. Tel: 570-823-6131; Fax: 570-823-5171. Email: sjd@lfmstr.com. Sr. M. Jeanette Lindsay, O.Carm., Supr. & Admin.; Rev. Gerard M. McGlone, Chap. Conducted by the Carmelite Sisters for the Aged and Infirm. Sisters 4; Aged Residents 133; Total Staff 260.
St. Therese Residence, 260 S. Meade St., 18702. Tel: 570-823-6131; Fax: 570-208-0143. Mark Williams, Admin.; Rev. Gerard M. McGlone, Chap. Conducted by the Carmelite Sisters for the Aged and Infirm. Residents 60; Total Staff 43.

[M] MONASTERIES AND RESIDENCES OF PRIESTS AND BROTHERS

SCRANTON. *Saint Ann's Passionist Monastery*, 1233 St. Ann St., 18504. Tel: 570-347-5691; Fax: 570-347-9387. Email: rburke@cpprov.org. Congregation of the Passion
Chaplaincies:
St. Gabriel's Convent, Clarks Summit, 18411. Tel: 570-586-9099; Fax: 570-586-9203. Very Rev. Richard Burke, C.P. Tel: 570-586-9099; 570-586-9203 Rector, Monastery & Shrine-Basilica; Revs. Jack Connor, C.P., Vice Rector; Berard Tierney, C.P.; Kenneth Walsh, C.P.; Benedict Berlo, C.P.; Vincent Boney, C.P.; Alphonsus Coen, C.P.; Conan Conaboy, C.P.; Cassian Yuhaus, C.P.; Roger Elliott, C.P.; Edward Buchheit, C.P.; Earl Keating, C.P.; William Maguire, C.P.; Bro. Daniel Turner, C.P. Priests 13.

BRODHEADSVILLE. *Salesian Monastery*, HC 1, Frantz Rd., Box 455, 18322-9630. Tel: 570-992-0230 (Monastery); 570-992-3448 (Abbot's Office); Fax: 570-992-3448 (Monastery); 570-992-3448. Email: monk@epix.net. Web: gentlestrength.org. Bro. Bernard Seif, S.M.C., Abbot.

ELMHURST. *Priestly Fraternity of St. Peter (F.S.S.P.), North American District Headquarters*, St. Peter's House, Griffin Rd., P.O. Box 196, 18416. Tel: 570-842-4000; Fax: 570-842-4001. Email: info@fssp.com. Web: www.fssp.com. Revs. George G. Gabet, F.S.S.P., Dist. Supr.; Neal A. Nichols, F.S.S.P., Dir. of Devel.; Carl Gismondi, F.S.S.P. Tel: 570-961-1205; Bruno Stemler, F.S.S.P. Tel: 570-842-8112; Thomas Longua, F.S.S.P. Tel: 570-842-8112; Joseph R. Howard, F.S.S.P., Dist. Bursar; Nicholas Zolnerowicz, F.S.S.P. Priests 47; Seminarians 63.
On Duty Outside the Diocese: Revs. Anwar Amar Mubarak, F.S.S.P.; Hubert Bizard, F.S.S.P.; Christopher Blust, F.S.S.P.; Denis Bouchard, F.S.S.P.; James B. Buckley, F.S.S.P.; Domenic Gentile, F.S.S.P.; Calvin R. Goodwin, F.S.S.P.; Michael T. Irwin, F.S.S.P.; James Jackson, F.S.S.P.; Robert Novokowsky, F.S.S.P.; Joseph Portzer, F.S.S.P.; Chad Ripperger, F.S.S.P.; Charles Ryan, F.S.S.P.; Joseph Terra, F.S.S.P.; Charles Van Vliet, F.S.S.P.
Priests Working Elsewhere: Rev. Paul Roman, F.S.S.P., Chap.
St. Michael the Archangel Latin Mass Community: 3146 Saratoga Blvd., Box 44, Corpus Christi, TX 78415. Tel: 361-855-8244. Revs. William Define, F.S.S.P., Chap.; Joseph Hearty, F.S.S.P. (LR), Asst.
Community of St. John the Baptist: 919 W. 47th St., North Little Rock, AR 72118. Tel: 501-812-9155; Fax: 501-812-9225. Rev. Joseph Valentine, F.S.S.P.
Queen of the Holy Rosary Parish: 291 Scoville Dr., Vienna, OH 44473. Tel: 330-856-4204; Fax: 330-856-9587. Revs. Robert Fromageot, F.S.S.P.; Laurent Demets, F.S.S.P. (ATL), Asst.
St. Francis de Sales Catholic Church: 587 Landers Dr., Mableton, GA 30126. Tel: 770-948-6888; Fax: 770-948-6888. Rev. Valentine Young, O.F.M., Asst. Pastor.
St. Michael the Archangel Latin Mass Community: 522 Columbus St., Rapid City, SD 57701. Tel: 605-341-1578; Fax: 605-341-8751. Rev. Robert Ferguson, F.S.S.P., Chap.
Community of St. Peter: 1720 E. Apache, Tulsa, OK 74148. Tel: 918-425-0486; Fax: 918-425-2077. Rev. Philip Wolfe, F.S.S.P., Chap. (St. Augustine Church) Community of St. Philippine Duchesne: 5412 Bluejacket St., Shawnee, KS 66203. Tel: 913-248-7703; Fax: 913-248-0648. Rev. Dennis M. Duvelius, F.S.S.P. (IND), Assoc. Pastor.
Holy Rosary Church, 520 Stevens St., Indianapolis, IN 46203. Tel: 317-636-4478; Fax: 317-636-2522. Revs. John Berg, F.S.S.P., Chap.; Stephane Dupre, F.S.S.P. (SAC), Asst.
P.O. Box 5382, Sacramento, CA 95817. Tel: 916-446-5908; Fax: 916-446-5702. Revs. Jose Salgado, F.S.S.P. (DEN), Chap.; Peter Byrne, F.S.S.P., Asst.
Our Lady of Mount Carmel Community, 5620 S. Hickory Cir., Littleton, CO 80120. Tel: 303-703-8538; Fax: 303-795-5411. Revs. Mark Fischer, F.S.S.P. (ATL), Admin.; Arnaud de Boisse, F.S.S.P., Asst.
Our Lady of Fatima Chapel 32 W. Franklin Ave., Pequannock, NJ 07440. Tel: 973-694-6727; Fax: 973-694-7629. Rev. Christopher Hathaway, F.S.S.P., Chap.
Mater Dei Community, 6228 Winton St., Dallas, TX 75214. Tel: 214-887-8696; Fax: 214-887-8717. Rev. Howard Remski, F.S.S.P., Asst. Pastor, St. Patrick.
St. Patrick Church, 1404 Castelar St., Omaha, NE 68180. Tel: 402-341-1305; Fax: 402-342-5510. Rev. Eric Flood, F.S.S.P., Chap. In Res. Rev. Ulrich Theuerer, F.S.S.P.
St. John-Mary Vianney Latin Mass Community: 14631 Waterman Crossing Rd., Maple Hill, KS 66507. Tel: 785-256-4727; Fax: 785-256-4115. Rev. Thomas Fritschen, F.S.S.P.
Immaculate Conception Latin Mass Mission, P.O. Box 145, Fountain, CO 80817. Tel: 719-635-2379.

Rev. Karl Pikus, F.S.S.P. (LIN), Chap.
St. Francis of Assisi Church, 3400 S. 17th St., Lincoln, NE 68502. Tel: 402-477-5145; Fax: 402-477-5159. Rev. Joseph Poisson, F.S.S.P., Rector.
Oklahoma City Latin Mass Community, 4701 N. McMillian, Bethany, OK 73008. Tel: 405-440-9168; Fax: 405-782-0767.
St. George's Church, P.O. Box 10, Post Falls, ID 83877-0010. Tel: 208-773-4715; Fax: 208-777-1549. Rev. John V. Rizzo, F.S.S.P. (B).
St. Joseph the Worker Mission, 310 Gateridge Dr., Tyler, TX 75703. Tel: 903-939-3221. Rev. Carlos S. Casavantes, F.S.S.P., Chap.

LACEYVILLE. *Franciscan Missionary Hermits of St. Joseph*, R.R. 1, Box 1590, 18623. Tel: 570-869-2918. Web: www.franciscanhermits.org. Rev. Pio Mandato, F.M.H.J.

PITTSTON. *Eastern Province of the Oblates of St. Joseph*, 1880 Hwy. 315, 18640. Tel: 570-654-7542; Fax: 717-654-8621. Very Revs. Paul A. McDonnell, O.S.J., Prov.; Gregory T. Finn, O.S.J., 1st Councilor; Rev. Daniel L. Schwebs, O.S.J., 2nd Councilor. Priests 8.

SHOHOLA. *Society of Saint John*, 702 Rte. 434, 18458-9979. Tel: 570-685-5151; Fax: 570-685-5152. Email: info@ssjohn.org. Web: www.ssjohn.org. Revs. Dominic E. O'Connor, Supr. Gen.; Carlos Urrutigoity; Dominic A. Carey; Eric S. Ensey; Daniel J. Fullerton; Marshall M. Roberts; Basel R. Sarweh.

WILKES-BARRE. *Moreau House* (House of Formation for the Congregation of Holy Cross - C.S.C.) , 847 Scott St., 18705. Tel: 570-824-2622. Revs. Charles Kociolek, C.S.C.; Thomas P. Looney, C.S.C.

[N] DIOCESAN RESIDENCE FOR RETIRED PRIESTS

DUNMORE. *Villa St. Joseph*, 1600 Green Ridge St., 18509. Tel: 570-343-4791. Most Rev. John M. Dougherty, D.D., V.G., Rector. Tel: 570-344-3272 In Res. Rev. Msgrs. James T. Clarke (Retired). Tel: 570-969-1235; Paul P. Cottone (Retired). Tel: 570-343-3706; William L. Donovan (Retired). Tel: 570-963-9383; Chester A. Gajewski (Retired). Tel: 570-347-1851; Joseph A. Law (Retired). Tel: 570-343-2388; John J. O'Brien (Retired). Tel: 570-961-1865; Kevin P. O'Neill. Tel: 570-343-4786; William J. Pakutka (Retired). Tel: 570-341-9168; Edmund S. Penkala (Retired). Tel: 570-344-6288; Stanley W. Piorkowski (Retired). Tel: 570-343-1184; Paul J. Purcell, V.F. Tel: 570-963-9453; Revs. Joseph M. Boles (Retired). Tel: 570-343-0394; Robert M. Everling (Retired). Tel: 570-343-4925; John L. Fabian (Retired). Tel: 570-348-0728; Joseph D. Flannery (Retired). Tel: 570-347-8019; Thomas A. Flynn (Retired). Tel: 570-348-0589; Alex J. Hazzouri (Retired). Tel: 570-343-2859; Harry J. Lewis (Retired). Tel: 570-343-5499; F. Harold Mulrooney (Retired). Tel: 570-343-8704; Joseph C. Ostrowski (Retired). Tel: 570-342-7396; William J. Pace (Retired). Tel: 570-961-5856; Valentine R. Plevyak (Retired). Tel: 570-969-9109.

[O] CONVENTS AND RESIDENCES FOR SISTERS

SCRANTON. *Immaculate Heart of Mary Center, Marywood*, 2300 Adams Ave., 18509. Tel: 570-342-6850; Fax: 570-346-5439. Email: communications@sistersofihm.org. Web: ihm.marywood.edu. Sr. Mary Persico, I.H.M., Pres. Tel: 570-346-5425; Rev. Robert J. Barone, Chap.; Sisters Mary Jo Gallagher, I.H.M., Vice Pres., Councilor Spiritual Devel. Tel: 570-346-5402; Barbara Jablonski, I.H.M., Councilor, Temporal Resources. Tel: 570-346-5405; Deborah Worlinsky, I.H.M., Business Mgr. Tel: 570-346-5406; Sisters Francine Fasolka, I.H.M., Dir. Communications. Tel: 570-346-5404, Ext. 508; Maria del Rey Shevlin, I.H.M., Dir. Office of Missioning Resources. Tel: 570-346-5401; Rosemarie Mozzachio, I.H.M., Dir. Novices & Candidates. Tel: 570-346-5414; Ruth Harkins, I.H.M., Dir. Vocations. Tel: 570-346-5413; Kathleen Mary Lunsman, I.H.M., Dir. Devel. Tel: 570-346-5431, Ext. 599. Sisters, Servants of the Immaculate Heart of Mary Professed Sisters 573. Councilors, Missioning & Community Life: Sisters Eleanor Mary Marconi, I.H.M. Tel: 570-346-5407; Kathryn Clauss. Tel: 570-346-5409; Susan Hadzima, I.H.M. Tel: 570-346-5410; Mary Mark Lowery, I.M.H., I.H.M. Center Administrator. Tel: 570-346-5408; Eileen Coleman, I.H.M., Dir. Volunteers. Tel: 570-963-2480; Joan Coyne, I.H.M., Dir. Assoc. Tel: 570-346-5411.
Marian Convent, Marywood, 2300 Adams Ave., 18509. Tel: 570-346-5423; Fax: 570-346-5418. Sisters St. Mel Wright, I.H.M., Coord. Tel: 570-346-5422; Rosemary Goulet, I.H.M., Admin. Tel: 570-346-5423; Rev. Joseph N. Tylenda, S.J. (WDC), Chap. Sisters, Servants of the Immaculate Heart of Mary 140.
Parish Visitors of Mary Immaculate, 410 S. Main Ave., 18504 Tel: 570-343-7841; Fax: 570-343-7841. Sr. Jean Marie Furr, P.V.M.I., Supr. Sisters 4.

CLARKS SUMMIT. *St. Gabriel's Monastery*, 631 Griffin Pond Rd., 18411. Tel: 570-586-2791; Fax: 570-586-8210. Email: cpnuns@intiques.com. Web: www.intiques.con/cpnuns/. Sisters Mary Regina, C.P., Pres.; Paul Colette, C.P., Councilor; Teresita, C.P., Vicar Religious of the Passion of Jesus Christ; Passionist Nuns (Contemplative) Professed Sisters 8.

DALLAS. *Sisters of Mercy of the Americas, Regional Community of Dallas, PA*, P.O. Box 369, 18612-0369 Tel: 570-675-2048; Fax: 570-675-9051. Email: srcatherinem@somdallasreg.org Web: www.somdallasreg.org. Sisters Catherine McGroarty, R.S.M., Pres.; Marie Parker R.S.M., Vice Pres. Tel: 570-675-2048. Sisters 277.

STARRUCCA. *Oblates of Mary, Queen of Apostles*, Priory of Our Lady of Ephesus, 1 Starrucca Creek Rd., 18462-0058. Tel: 570-727-3341; Fax: 570-727-3941. Professed Oblates of Mary, Queen of Apostles 5; Novices 2; Postulants 1.

TUNKHANNOCK. *Capuchin Sisters of Nazareth*, Mother of God Convent, 215 Wellwood Dr., 18657. Tel: 570-836-2737. Sr. Theresa May, Supr.

[P] RETREAT HOUSES

CLARKS SUMMIT. *St. Gabriel's Retreat Center*, 631 Griffin Pond Rd., 18411. Tel: 570-586-4957; Fax: 570-587-3314. Email: steresita@intiques kporter@intiques.com. Web: www.intiques.com/cpnuns/. Religious of the Passion of Jesus Christ; Passionist Nuns (Contemplative)

MOUNT POCONO. *Villa Our Lady Retreat House*, HCR 1, Box 41 18344-9714. Tel: 570-839-7217; Fax: 570-839-7553. Email: sbona@earthlink.net. Web: www.villaourlady.com. Sr. M. Bonaventa, O.S.F., Supr. & Dir. Retreat. Bernadine Sisters 7.

[Q] CAMPS AND COMMUNITY CENTERS

TUNKHANNOCK. *Camp St. Andrew*, P.O. Box 679, 18657. Tel: 570-836-2975. Email: jjpkel@aol.com. *Off-Season Mailing Address:*, 633 Orchard St., 18505. Tel: 570-344-6159. Rev. Msgr. Joseph P. Kelly, Exec. Dir. Regular Camp, Basketball Clinics 1,000.

WILKES-BARRE. *Catholic Youth Center*, 36 S. Washington St., 18701. Tel: 570-823-6121; Fax: 570-823-0175. Email: wvcyc@epix.net. Very Rev. John S. Terry, V.F., Dir.; Mr. Anthony L. English Jr., Exec. Dir.; Mr. Mark Soprano, Assoc. Dir.

[R] MISCELLANEOUS LISTINGS

SCRANTON. **Aid to the Church in Russia*, 300 Wyoming Ave., 18503-1279. Tel: 570-207-2216; Fax: 570-207-2236. James B. Earley, Dir., Scranton Office.
St. Ann's Foundation, 1239 St. Ann's St., 18504. Tel: 570-347-7710; Fax: 570-347-4382. Rev. Berard Tierney, C.P., Exec. Dir.
Saint Ann's Media, Inc., Box 111, 1230 St. Ann St., 18504-0111. Tel: 570-941-0100; Fax: 570 941-0185. Email: webmaster@themass.com. Web: www.theMass.org; www.prayerline.org; www.theMass.com. Rev. Michael Salvagna, C.P. (PIT), Dir.; Mr. Walter Tigue Jr., Bus. Admin.; Mrs. Vera Kowal Krewsun, Mktg. & Devel. Dir.; Mr. Rich Shelp, Webmaster. Sponsored by the Passionist Community
St. Anthony's Haven, 409 Olive St., 18509. Tel: 570-342-1295, Ext. 204; Fax: 570-341-6623. Email: cssrp@epix.net.
St. James Manor, 600 Wyoming Ave., 18509. Tel: 570-342-1295, Ext. 202; Fax: 570-341-6623.
The Catherine McAuley Center, c/o 709 Madison Ave., 18510. Tel: 570-342-1342; Fax: 570-341-8108. Email: cathmc709@aol.com. Sr. Therese Marie Marques, R.S.M., Exec. Dir.
The Catherine McAuley Center - Bridge Program, 709 Madison Ave., 18510. Tel: 570-342-1342; Fax: 570-341-8108. Email: cathmc709@aol.com. Sr. Therese Marie Marques, R.S.M., Exec. Dir.
The Catherine McAuley Center - Maple Street House, c/o 709 Madison Ave., 18510. Tel: 570-342-1342; Fax: 570-341-8108. Email: cathmc709@aol.com. Sr. Therese Marie Marques, R.S.M., Exec. Dir.
The Catherine McAuley Center - Program House, 747 Madison Ave., 18510. Tel: 570-342-3944; Fax: 570-341-8108. Sr. Therese Marie Marques, R.S.M., Exec. Dir
The Catherine McAuley Center - Swetland Street House, 709 Madison Ave., 18510. Tel: 570-342-1342; Fax: 570-341-8108. Email: cathmc709@aol.com. Sr. Therese Marie Marques, R.S.M., Exec. Dir.
The Catherine McAuley House Annex, 115 Ferdinand St., 18508. Tel: 570-342-1342; Fax: 570-341-8108. Email: cathmc709@aol.com. Sr. Therese Marie Marques, R.S.M., Exec. Dir.
Cross Apartments, 507 Broadway, 18505. Tel: 570-342-1342; Fax: 570-341-8108. Email: cathmc709@aol.com. Sisters Therese Marie Marques, R.S.M., Exec. Dir.; Marise Fabie, R.S.M., Dir. Housing.
Frances Warde House, 1646 Capouse Ave., 18509. Tel: 570-342-6962; Fax: 570-341-8108. Email: cathmc709@aol.com. Sisters Therese Marie Marques, R.S.M., Exec. Dir.; Marise Fabie, R.S.M., Dir. Housing.
St. Francis of Assisi Kitchen, 500 Penn Ave., 18509. Tel: 570-342-5556; Fax: 570-963-8832. Email: cvsiconolfi@aol.com. Web: www.stfranciskitchen.com. Rev. Msgr. Constantine V. Siconolfi, Dir.
Friends of the Poor, 400 Adams Ave., 18510. Tel: 570-348-4428; Fax: 570-344-9582. Sr. Adrian Barrett, I.H.M., CEO.
The Guild Studios, 400 Wyoming Ave., 18503. Tel: 800-367-6610; 570-342-8246; Fax: 570-342-5940. Email: guild01@aol.com. Trish Morrow, Gen. Mgr.
Religious Store, 400 Wyoming Ave., 18503. Tel: 800-367-6610; 570-342-8246; Fax: 570-342-5940. Email: guild01@aol.com. Joseph McGuire, Store Mgr.
I.H.M. Congregation Charitable Trust, 2300 Adams Ave., 18509. Tel: 570-342-6850; Fax: 570-346-5439. Email: jablon@sistersofihm.org. Web: ihm.marywood.edu. Congregation of the Sisters, Servants of the Immaculate Heart of Mary
Ministry for Religious Research and Consultancy, 1233 St. Ann St., 18504. Tel: 570-586-9099; Fax: 570-586-9203. Email: cyuhaus@aol.com. Rev. Cassian J. Yuhaus, C.P., Exec. Dir.
VMR Charitable Trust (Vehicle Management for Religious) Tel: 570-586-9099; Fax: 570-586-9203.

DALLAS. *Studio I*, Mercy Center, Box 370, 18612. Tel: 570-675-1865; 570-674-3281; 570-675-2131; Fax: 570-674-5658. Email: srkiel@aol.com. Web: www.sister-regina-jewelry.com. Sr. Regina Kiel, R.S.M., Designer & Artist. Designing and handcrafting fine original jewelry and sculpture. Workshops in jewelry making using the lost wax casting technique: A. Couples - make their own wedding bands/engagement rings. B. All ages interested in learning the art of jewelry making.

HARLEIGH. *National Shrine of the Sacred Heart*, 1 Church Pl., 18225. Tel: 570-455-1162; Fax: 570-455-0306.
National Office: Men of the Sacred Heart, P.O. Box 500, 18225. Tel: 570-455-1162; Fax: 570-455-0306.

NANTICOKE. *People of God Community of Northeastern PA*, 151 Old Newport St., 18634-1300. Tel: 570-735-2599; Fax: 570-735-2679. Email: marhudak@voicenet.com. Martin J. Hudak, Pres.

PITTSTON. *The Gabriel House*, 13 William St., 18640. Tel: 570-654-7157. Email: ghpit@aol.com. Anne Marie McCawley, Project Dir. Transitional housing facility for women and women with young children

PLYMOUTH. *The Catherine McAuley House*, 121 Church St., 18651. Tel: 570-779-2801; Fax: 570-779-5240. Email: cathmc709@aol.com. Sr. Therese Marie Marques, R.S.M., Exec. Dir.

WILKES-BARRE. *Project REMAIN* Service for the elderly and the needy residents in the High Rises. , Valley View Terrace, 215 High St., Apt. 100, 18702. Tel: 570-829-5373. Email: glcm@epix.net. Sr. Mary Glennon, R.S.M., Dir.
McGlynn Learning Center, 72 Midland Ct., 18701. Tel: 570-824-8891. Sr. Miriam Francis Stadulis, R.S.M., Dir. Outreach to low income families in the housing projects.
St. Vincent De Paul Kitchen, 39 E. Jackson St., 18701. Tel: 570-829-7796; Fax: 570-208-9182. Email: kitchenwb@aol.com. Ned Delaney, M.A., Exec. Dir.; Anne Marie McCawley, Project Dir.

RELIGIOUS INSTITUTES OF MEN REPRESENTED IN THE DIOCESE

For further details refer to the corresponding bracketed number in the Religious Institutes of Men or Women section.

[1000]—*Congregation of the Passion* (Union City, NJ)—C.P.
[0690]—*Jesuit Fathers and Brothers* (Maryland Prov.)—S.J.
[0930]—*Oblates of St. Joseph* (Asti, Italy)—O.S.J.
[1065]—*Priestly Fraternity of St. Peter*—F.S.S.P.
[0610]—*Priests of the Congregation of Holy Cross* (Wilkes-Barre, PA)—C.S.C.
[]—*Society of St. John*—S.S.J.
[1290]—*Society of the Priests of St. Sulpice*—S.S.

RELIGIOUS INSTITUTES OF WOMEN REPRESENTED IN THE DIOCESE

[1810]—*Bernardine Sisters of the Third Order of St. Francis*—O.S.F.
[0330]—*Carmelite Sisters of the Aged and Infirm*—O.Carm.

[2980]—*Congregation of Notre Dame*—C.N.D.
[3830-05]—*Congregation of the Sisters of St. Joseph*—C.S.J.
[0890]—*Daughters of Our Lady of Mercy*—D.M.
[]—*Domincan Sisters of Sparkhill*
[1180]—*Franciscan Sisters of Allegany, N.Y.*—O.S.F.
[1310]—*Franciscan Sisters of Little Falls, Minnesota*—O.S.F.
[2575]—*Institute of the Sisters of Mercy of the Americas*—R.S.M.
[2340]—*Little Sisters of the Poor*—P.S.D.P.
[]—*Oblates of Mary, Queen of Apostles*
[3160]—*Parish Visitors of Mary Immaculate*—P.V.M.I.
[3240]—*Poor Sisters of Jesus Crucified and the Sorrowful Mother*—C.J.C.
[3170]—*Religious of the Passion of Jesus Christ*—C.P.
[3430]—*Religious Teachers Filippini*—M.P.F.
[1700]—*School Sisters of the Third Order of St. Francis* (Bethlehem, PA)—O.S.F.
[0660]—*Sisters of Christian Charity*—S.C.C.
[2990]—*Sisters of Notre Dame* (Ohio)—S.N.D.
[3780]—*Sisters of Saints Cyril and Methodius*—SS.C.M.
[3840]—*Sisters of St. Joseph of Carondelet*—C.S.J.
[3893]—*Sisters of St. Joseph of Chestnut Hill*—S.S.J.
[1830]—*Sisters of the Good Shepherd*—R.G.S.
[2160]—*Sisters, Servants of the Immaculate Heart of Mary*—I.H.M.
[]—*Union sisters of the Presentation of the Blessed Virgin Mary* (Ireland)—P.V.B.M.

DIOCESAN CEMETERIES

SCRANTON. *Cathedral*, 1708 Oram St., 18504. Tel: 570-347-9251; Fax: 570-347-4354.

Diocesan Cemeteries Office, 1708 Oram St., 18504. Tel: 570-207-2209; Fax: 570-347-4354. Walter Bennett, Dir.

CARVERTON. *Mount Olivet*, P.O. Box 257, 18644. Tel: 570-696-3636; Fax: 570-696-4705.

DRUMS. *Calvary*, P.O. Box 485, 18222. Tel: 570-788-2150; Fax: 570-708-2938.

MOSCOW. *St. Catherine's*, Main St., P.O. Box 114, 18444. Tel: 570-842-8411; Fax: 570-842-8406.

OLD FORGE. *Holy Cross* 18518. Tel: 570-347-9251; Fax: 570-347-4354.

WILLIAMSPORT. *Resurrection*, P.O. Box 12, 17754. Tel: 570-368-2727; Fax: 570-368-2727.

NECROLOGY

† Meier, Rev. Msgr. Joseph F., Wilkes-Barre, PA Church of St. Nicholas—Died Jan. 21, 2003
† Kelley, John J., (Retired)—Died Feb. 20, 2003
† Markowski, Clement A., St. John the Baptist, Exeter—Died Nov. 19, 2002
† McDermott, Thomas J., (Retired)—Died Oct. 10, 2003
† Miller, Paul E., Scranton, PA St. Patrick's—Died Nov. 5, 2003
† O'Haire, John A., (Retired)—Died April 22, 2003

Archdiocese of Seattle

Archidioecesis Seattlensis

Most Reverend

ALEXANDER J. BRUNETT, PH.D.

Archbishop of Seattle; ordained July 13, 1958; appointed Bishop of Helena April 19, 1994; consecrated and installed July 6, 1994; appointed Archbishop of Seattle October 28, 1997; installed December 18, 1997 *Res.: Connolly House*, 1104 Spring St., Seattle, WA 98104. Tel: 206-623-2625; Fax: 206-682-9661.

Most Reverend

RAYMOND G. HUNTHAUSEN

Retired Archbishop of Seattle; ordained June 1, 1946; appointed Bishop of Helena, Montana July 8, 1962; consecrated August 30, 1962; appointed Archbishop of Seattle February 25, 1975; installed May 22, 1975; retired August 21, 1991 *Office: 910 Marion St., Seattle, WA 98104*. Tel: 206-382-4884; Fax: 206-382-3495.

Chancery Office: 910 Marion St., Seattle, WA 98104. Tel: 206-382-4886; Fax: 206-382-3495.

Web: www.seattlearch.org

Email: kathyj@seattlearch.org

Square Miles 24,834.

Established May 31, 1850. Name Changed to Seattle, September 11, 1907.

Created Archdiocese, June 23, 1951.

Comprises the Counties of Clallam, Clark, Cowlitz, Grays Harbor, Island, Jefferson, King, Kitsap, Lewis, Mason, Pacific, Pierce, San Juan, Skagit, Skamania, Snohomish, Thurston, Wahkiakum and Whatcom in the State of Washington.

Legal Title: "Corporation of the Catholic Archbishop of Seattle."

For legal titles of parishes and archdiocesan institutions, consult The Chancery.

STATISTICAL OVERVIEW

Personnel	
Archbishops	1
Retired Archbishops	1
Auxiliary Bishops	1
Abbots	1
Retired Abbots	1
Priests: Diocesan Active in Diocese	120
Priests: Diocesan Active Outside Diocese	2
Priests: Diocesan in Foreign Missions	1
Priests: Retired, Sick or Absent	64
Number of Diocesan Priests	187
Religious Priests in Diocese	108
Total Priests in Diocese	295
Extern Priests in Diocese	27
Ordinations:	
Diocesan Priests	5
Transitional Deacons	2
Permanent Deacons in Diocese	69
Total Brothers	25
Total Sisters	459
Parishes	
Parishes	139
With Resident Pastor:	
Resident Diocesan Priests	104
Resident Religious Priests	11
Without Resident Pastor:	
Administered by Priests	13
Administered by Religious Women	1
Administered by Lay People	10
Missions	30
Pastoral Centers	9
Welfare	
Catholic Hospitals	9
Total Assisted	1,366,172
Health Care Centers	16
Total Assisted	15,332
Homes for the Aged	19
Total Assisted	2,236
Day Care Centers	8
Total Assisted	529
Specialized Homes	4
Total Assisted	107
Special Centers for Social Services	43
Total Assisted	79,095
Residential Care of Disabled	10
Educational	
Diocesan Students in Other Seminaries	31
Total Seminarians	31
Colleges and Universities	2
Total Students	7,900
High Schools, Diocesan and Parish	3
Total Students	2,407
High Schools, Private	6
Total Students	3,248
Elementary Schools, Diocesan and Parish	53
Total Students	15,870
Elementary Schools, Private	4
Total Students	810
Catechesis/Religious Education:	
High School Students	6,260
Elementary Students	32,800
Total Students under Catholic Instruction	69,326
Teachers in the Diocese:	
Priests	8
Brothers	8
Sisters	30
Lay Teachers	1,716
Vital Statistics	
Receptions into the Church:	
Infant Baptism Totals	6,811
Adult Baptism Totals	1,086
Received into Full Communion	574
First Communions	6,422
Confirmations	3,363
Marriages:	
Catholic	920
Interfaith	693
Total Marriages	1,613
Deaths	2,884
Total Catholic Population	550,450
Total Population	4,755,500

Former Bishops—Rt. Revs. A. M. A. BLANCHET, consecrated Bishop of Walla Walla, Sept. 27, 1846; transferred to Nesqually, May 31, 1850; resigned 1879; made Bishop of Ibora; died Feb. 25, 1887; AEGIDIUS JUNGER, D.D., consecrated Oct. 28, 1879; died Dec. 26, 1895; Most Revs. EDWARD JOHN O'DEA, D.D., consecrated Bishop of Nesqually, Sept. 8, 1896; See transferred to Seattle, Sept. 11, 1907; died Dec. 25, 1932; GERALD SHAUGHNESSY, S.M., S.T.D., appt. Bishop of Seattle July 1, 1933; consecrated Sept. 19, 1933; died May 18, 1950; THOMAS A. CONNOLLY, D.D. (Retired), consecrated Aug. 24, 1939; succeeded, May 18, 1950; retired Feb. 25, 1975; died April 18, 1991; RAYMOND G. HUNTHAUSEN, D.D. (Retired), ord. June 1, 1946; appt. Bishop of Helena, Montana, July 8, 1962; consecrated Aug. 30, 1962; appt. Archbishop of Seattle, Feb. 25, 1975; installed May 22, 1975; retired Aug. 21, 1991; THOMAS J. MURPHY, D.D., S.T.D., ord. April 12, 1958; appt. Bishop of Great Falls, July 5, 1978; appt. Coadjutor Archbishop of Seattle, May 26, 1987; succeeded to See Aug. 21, 1991; died June 26, 1997.

Chancery Office—Office of the Archbishop, 910 Marion St., Seattle, 98104. Tel: 206-382-4886 Fax: 206-382-3495.

Auxiliary Bishop and Vicar General—Most Rev. GEORGE L. THOMAS, D.D., Ph.D., V.G., 910 Marion St., Seattle, 98104. Tel: 204-382-4888.

Chancellor—CHRISTINE M. TAYLOR, 910 Marion St., Seattle, 98104. Tel: 206-382-4857.

Executive Assistant to the Archbishop—Ms. ANGELA KISON. Tel: 206-382-4525.

Presbyteral Council—Most Rev. GEORGE L. THOMAS, D.D., Ph.D., V.G.; Very Revs. JAMES D. PICTON, J.D.; PAUL A. MAGNANO, Ph.D.; JOSEPH DEFOLCO; STEPHEN C. ROWAN, Ph.D.; RICHARD MCCALLISTER; JOHN WALMESLEY; OLIVER DUGGAN; LAWRENCE MINDER; KEVIN MORAN; Rev. MICHAEL J. MCDERMOTT; Very Revs. PATRICK FREITAG; JAMES LEE; Revs. TUAN V. NGUYEN; JAMES NORTHROP; HANS OLSON; JAMES JOHNSON JR.; PATRICK RITTER; TIMOTHY SAUER; Very Rev. J. PATRICK MCDERMOTT; Revs. STEPHEN J. SZEMAN (Retired); MICHAEL TYRRELL, S.J.; TERENCE WAGER, O.S.B.; Very Rev. MICHAEL H. WRIGHT.

College of Consultors—Most Rev. GEORGE L. THOMAS, D.D., Ph.D., V.G.; Very Revs. JAMES D. PICTON, J.D.; LAWRENCE H. MINDER; PAUL A. MAGNANO, Ph.D.; STEPHEN C. ROWAN, Ph.D.; Revs. TUAN V. NGUYEN; MICHAEL J. MCDERMOTT; HANS M. OLSON; PATRICK RITTER; TIMOTHY SAUER; STEPHEN J. SZEMAN (Retired).

Deans—Very Revs. J. PATRICK MCDERMOTT, Northern; JOSEPH DEFOLCO, Snohomish; PATRICK FREITAG, Olympic; OLIVER DUGGAN, North Seattle; LAWRENCE H. MINDER, Eastside; JOHN WALMESLEY, South Seattle; KEVIN MORAN, South King; RICHARD MCCALLISTER, Pierce; JAMES LEE, South Sound; MICHAEL H. WRIGHT, Southern.

Metropolitan Tribunal

Judicial Vicar—Very Rev. ANTHONY E. BAWYN, J.C.D., 910 Marion St., Seattle, 98104. Tel: 206-382-4830; Fax: 206-382-2071.

Adjunct Judicial Vicar—Rev. JOSEPH H. DOOGAN, J.C.L. (Retired).

Judges—Rev. ANTHONY BAWYN, J.C.D.; JAMES L. BROOKS, M.Ed.; Revs. JOSEPH H. DOOGAN, J.C.L. (Retired); JAMES EBLEN, S.T.L., Ph.D.; DONALD R. ESPEN, J.C.D.; Deacon JOHN LARUSSA; Rev. PHILIP LUCID, S.J., J.D.; Deacon LAWRENCE J. SULLIVAN; Ms. LYNDA ROBITAILLE, J.C.D.; Revs. PAUL PLUTH;

JAMES A. WILLIAMS, J.C.L.

Defenders of the Bond—KAREN GIFFIN; Sisters ANNE HERKENRATH, S.N.J.M.; GAIL MILHOLLAND, S.N.J.M.; Very Rev. JAMES D. PICTON, J.D.; CHARLENE CRAM, J.C.L.

Notaries—VALERIE BLESENER; MARK DEMRY.

Archdiocesan Offices and Directors

Accounting Services—NAN SEVERNS, Controller, 910 Marion St., Seattle, 98104. Tel: 206-382-4599; Fax: 206-903-4624. Asst. Controllers: TOM GRECHIS. Tel: 206-382-4287; DOUG HITSMAN. Tel: 206-382-4849.

Administration and Finance, Office of—Mr. PATRICK SURSELY, Archbishop's Delegate, 910 Marion St., Seattle, 98104. Tel: 206-382-4529; Fax: 206-274-3199.

African American/Black Ministry Resources—SHARON PITRE-WILLIAMS, Dir., 910 Marion St., Seattle, 98104. Tel: 206-382-4059, Ext. 2061; Fax: 206-382-2069.

Archdiocesan Finance Council—Mr. PATRICK SURSELY, Staff; Mr. TOM HOOVER, Chm., 910 Marion St., Seattle, 98104. Tel: 206-382-4529; Fax: 206-382-4266.

Archdiocesan Housing Authority—Mr. MICHAEL REICHERT, Pres., 100 23rd Ave. S., Seattle, 98144. Tel: 206-448-3360; Fax: 206-328-5692.

Archdiocesan Liturgical Commission—Ms. CAROLYN LASSEK, 910 Marion St., Seattle, 98104. Tel: 206-382-4838; Fax: 206-903-4612.

Archdiocesan Pastoral Council—Mr. DENNIS O'LEARY, Exec. Sec., 910 Marion St., Seattle, 98104. Tel: 206-382-4289; Fax: 206-382-4840.

Archdiocesan Women's Commission—Ms. CARLA CALDWELL, Liaison, 910 Marion St., Seattle, 98104. Tel: 206-382-4268.

Archives and Records—Ms. CHRISTINE TAYLOR, 910 Marion St., Seattle, 98104. Tel: 206-382-4857; Fax: 206-382-4840.

Asian/Pacific American Ministry Resources—PHILIP TRAN, Dir., 910 Marion St., Seattle, 98104. Tel: 206-382-4509, Ext. 3828.

Associated Catholic Cemeteries—Mr. RICHARD PETERSON, Dir., 910 Marion St., Seattle, 98104. Tel: 206-522-0996; 253-838-2240.

Benefits Services—GERALYN MIRANTE-MARLEY, Admin., 910 Marion St., Seattle, 98104. Tel: 206-382-4566; Fax: 206-382-3493.

Campaign for Human Development—Mr. J. L. DROUHARD, Dir., 910 Marion St., Seattle, 98104. Tel: 206-382-4869; Fax: 206-382-3487.

Campus Ministry—CARLA CALDWELL, Liaison, 910 Marion St., Seattle, 98104. Tel: 206-382-4268.

Canonical Services—Very Rev. ANTHONY E. BAWYN, J.C.D., Judicial Vicar, 910 Marion St., Seattle, 98104. Tel: 206-382-4565.

Catholic Community Services of Western Washington—Mr. MICHAEL REICHERT, Pres., 100 23rd Ave. S., Seattle, 98144-2302. Tel: 206-328-5696; Fax: 206-328-5699.

Catholic Faith Formation, Office of—Dr. MARY CROSS, Archbishop's Delegate, 910 Marion St., Seattle, 98104. Tel: 206-382-4835.

Catholic Relief Services—J.L. DROUHARD, Dir., 910 Marion St., Seattle, 98104. Tel: 206-382-4869.

Catholic Schools Department—Rev. STEPHEN ROWAN, Vicar for Educ. & Supt. Schools, 910 Marion St., Seattle, 98104. Tel: 206-382-4855.

Catholic Youth Organization—VACANT, Dir., 814 N.E. 85th St., Seattle, 98115. Tel: 206-382-4260; Fax: 206-903-4627.

Censores Librorum—Revs. WILLIAM TREACY (Retired); MICHAEL RASCHKO, Ph.D.

Chancery Operations—Mr. DENNIS J. O'LEARY, Dir., 910 Marion St., Seattle, 98104. Tel: 206-382-4289.

Chinese, Ministry to—Rev. JAMES K. ELLIOTT, Chap., 1531 Bradner Pl., S., Seattle, 98144. Tel: 206-324-8521.

Communications, Office of—Mr. GREG MAGNONI, Archbishop's Delegate, 910 Marion St., Seattle, 98104. Tel: 206-382-4862; Fax: 206-382-3487.

Broadcast Division—Ms. TERRY MURPHY, Exec. Producer.

Web Division—Ms. KATHRYN L. JOHNSON, Mgr.

Newspaper "The Catholic Northwest Progress"—Mr. STEPHEN M. KENT, Exec. Editor. Tel: 206-382-4850.

Criminal Justice Ministry Resources—ERICA COHEN MOORE, Coord., 910 Marion St., Seattle, 98104. Tel: 206-382-4509, Ext. 3477.

Cultural and Ethnic Faith Formation Department—Mr. JOSE RAMIREZ-LOMELI, Dir., 910 Marion St., Seattle, 98104. Tel: 206-654-4644.

Deacon Services—DAVID REYNOLDS, Assoc. Dir., Office of Vicar for Clergy, 910 Marion St., Seattle, 98104. Tel: 206-903-4611; Fax: 206-654-4654.

Disability Ministry Resources—Ms. FRANCES FARRELL, Dir., 910 Marion St., Seattle, 98104. Tel: 206-382-4509, Ext. 2014.

Due Process—Sr. JOYCE COX, B.V.M., 910 Marion St., Seattle, 98104. Tel: 206-382-4592.

Ecumenical and Interfaith Commission—Sr. JOYCE COX, B.V.M., Archbishop's Delegate for Rel. Communities & Ecumenism, 910 Marion St., Seattle, 98104. Tel: 206-382-4829; Fax: 206-382-4840.

Events Planning—Ms. KATHLEEN NELSON, Dir., 910 Marion St., Seattle, 98104. Tel: 206-382-4879; Fax: 206-264-2081.

Hispanic/Latino Ministry Resources—ISAAC GOVEA, Dir., 910 Marion St., Seattle, 98104. Tel: 206-382-4825.

Holy Childhood, Pontifical Association of the—J.L. DROUHARD, Dir., 910 Marion St., Seattle, 98104. Tel: 206-382-4583.

Human Resources—Ms. MARY SANTI, Archbishop's Delegate, 910 Marion St., Seattle, 98104. Tel: 206-264-2089; Fax: 206-382-4267.

Information Technology & Services—Mr. HOWARD CHANG, 910 Marion St., Seattle, 98104. Tel: 206-382-4282; Fax: 206-382-4840.

Justice and Peace Ministry Resources—GARY LAZZERONI, Dir., 910 Marion St., Seattle, 98104. Tel: 206-382-4509, Ext. 3236; Fax: 206-382-2069.

Koreans, Ministry to—Rev. STEPHANO INSOO KIM, St. Andrew Kim Korean Community, 11700 1st Ave., N.E., Seattle, 98125. Tel: 206-362-2492; 206-362-2278.

Lay Ecclesial Ministry Deptartment—Ms. CARLA CALDWELL, Dir., 910 Marion St., Seattle, 98104. Tel: 206-382-4268; Fax: 206-264-2084.

Leadership and Transition Ministry Resources—LEIGH STRINGFELLOW, Dir., 910 Marion St., Seattle, 98104. Tel: 206-382-4852.

Library Media Center—Ms. SARAH SWANER, Librarian, 910 Marion St., Seattle, 98104. Tel: 206-382-4883; Fax: 206-382-3487.

Liturgy—Ms. CAROLYN LASSEK, 910 Marion St., Seattle, 98104. Tel: 206-382-4838; Fax: 206-903-4612.

Missions—Mr. J. L. DROUHARD, Dir., 910 Marion St., Seattle, 98104. Tel: 206-382-4580; Fax: 206-382-3487.

Native American Ministry Resources/Native American Advisory Circle—Ms. FRANCES FARRELL, Dir., 910 Marion St., Seattle, 98104. Tel: 206-264-2082.

Parishes and Faith Communities, Office of—Mr. STEPHEN HUEFFED, Archbishop's Delegate, 910 Marion St., Seattle, 98104. Tel: 206-382-2016.

Parish and School Faith Formation Department—Dr. JUDITH E. FORD, Dir., 910 Marion St., Seattle, 98104. Tel: 206-382-4614; TRACY ANDERSON, Assoc. Dir. Youth Formation. Tel: 206-382-3491.

Parish Financial Services—Mr. ED WILLIAMS, Dir., 910 Marion St., Seattle, 98104. Tel: 206-382-7316; Fax: 206-382-4279.

Parish Stewardship—Mr. SCOTT BADER, Dir., 910 Marion St., Seattle, 98104. Tel: 206-903-4620; Fax: 206-903-4610.

Pastoral Care of the Sick & Dying Ministry Resources—Ms. FRANCES FARRELL, Dir., 910 Marion St., Seattle, 98104. Tel: 206-382-4509, Ext. 2014.

Pastoral Outreach Coordinator—Ms. JESSIE C. DYE, J.D., 910 Marion St., Seattle, 98104. Tel: 206-382-4592.

Pastoral Planning and Research—DENNIS O'LEARY, Dir. Tel: 206-382-4832; MARY BETH CELIO, Dir. Research, 910 Marion St., Seattle, 98104. Tel: 206-382-4272.

Planned Giving—VACANT, Dir., 910 Marion St., Seattle, 98104. Tel: 206-382-4865.

Polish Speaking, Ministry to—Revs. PIOTR DZIKOWSKI, S.Ch., 3422 Portland Ave., Tacoma, 98404. Tel: 206-272-5232; JOZEF CALIK, S.Ch., 3221 14th Ave., W., Seattle, 98119. Tel: 206-282-1804.

Priests' Health Plan—Most Rev. ALEXANDER J. BRUNETT, D.D., Ph.D., Pres.; Rev. SEAN FOX, Chm.; GERALYN MIRANTE-MARLEY, Admin. Tel: 206-382-4286.

Priests' Pension Plan—Most Rev. ALEXANDER J. BRUNETT, D.D., Ph.D.; Rev. SEAN FOX, Chm.; GERALYN MIRANTE-MARLEY, Admin. Tel: 206-382-4286.

Propagation of the Faith, Society for the—J.L. DROUHARD, Dir., 910 Marion St., Seattle, Wa 98104. Tel: 206-382-4869.

Property and Construction Services—Mr. EDWARD FOSTER, Dir., 910 Marion St., Seattle, 98104. Tel: 206-382-4851; Fax: 206-382-4266.

Religious Communities/Ecumenism, Office of—Sr. JOYCE COX, B.V.M., Archbishop's Delegate, 910 Marion St., Seattle, 98104. Tel: 206-382-4829; Fax: 206-382-4840.

Seminarian Services—RICHARD SHIVELY, Assoc. Dir., Office of Vicar for Clergy, 910 Marion St., Seattle, 98104. Tel: 206-382-4839; Fax: 206-654-4654; Rev. TIMOTHY SAUER, Asst. Dir. Tel: 206-382-4880.

Sisters' Council—Sr. SHARON PARK, O.P., 508 2nd Ave. W., Seattle, 98119-3928. Tel: 206-301-0556; Fax: 206-301-0558.

Stewardship and Devleopment Department—Mr. RICK FERSCH, 910 Marion St., Seattle, 98104. Tel: 206-903-4621.

Theological Resources—Revs. JAMES EBLEN, S.T.L., Ph.D., 131 Bellevue Ave. E., #203, Seattle, 98102-5566. Tel: 206-329-5692; MICHAEL RASCHKO, Ph.D., 1614 Summit Ave., #502, Seattle, 98122. Tel: 206-296-5311.

Vicar for Clergy, Office of—Very Rev. PAUL A. MAGNANO, Ph.D., 910 Marion St., Seattle, 98104. Tel: 206-382-7317; Fax: 206-654-4654.

Vicar for Education, Office of—Very Rev. STEPHEN C. ROWAN, Ph.D., 910 Marion St., Seattle, 98104. Tel: 206-382-4861; Fax: 206-654-4651.

Vicar to Faith Communities—Very Rev. JAMES D. PICTON, J.D., 910 Marion St., Seattle, 98104. Tel: 206-382-4509.

Victim Assistance Coordinator—JESSIE CLAYTON DYE, J.D. Tel: 800-446-7762. Email: hotline@seattlearch.org.

Vietnamese, Ministry to—Rev. ANTHONY TON, Chap. Assistant Chaplains: Revs. FRANCES MIEN; ANTHONY LAN TRAN, Church of the Vietnamese Martyrs, 1230 E. Fir St., Seattle, 98122. Tel: 206-325-5626.

Vocations—Rev. TIMOTHY SAUER, Asst. Dir., 910 Marion St., Seattle, 98104. Tel: 206-382-4595.

CLERGY, PARISHES, MISSIONS AND PAROCHIAL SCHOOLS

CITY OF SEATTLE
(KING COUNTY)

1—ST. JAMES CATHEDRAL (1904), Very Rev. Michael G. Ryan. In Res., Revs. David A. Brant (Retired); John Kilisara Thomas, A.J.
Res.: 804 Ninth Ave., 98104. Tel: 206-622-3559; Fax: 206-622-5303.
Convent—907 Columbia St., 98104. Tel: 206-682-1308. Sisters 4.

2—ST. ALPHONSUS (1901), Revs. Ramon Santa Cruz, S.O.L.T.; Steven Sallis; Karen Lasko, Pastoral Admin.
Res.: 5816 15th Ave., N.W., 98107. Tel: 206-784-6464; Fax: 206-789-5709.
School—Tel: 206-782-4363. Dr. Robert Scripko, Prin. Lay Teachers 16; Students 181.
Catechesis/Religious Program—Students 27.

3—ST. ANNE (1908), Rev. Robert Camuso.
Res.: 1411 1st Ave. W., 98119. Tel: 206-282-0223; Fax: 206-217-9541.
School—101 W. Lee St., 98119. Tel: 206-282-3538; Fax: 206-284-4191. Mrs. Pat Durand, Prin. Lay Teachers 10; Students 237.

4—ASSUMPTION (1924), Very Rev. Oliver Duggan.
Office—3214 N.E. 62nd St., 98115. Tel: 206-522-7674; Fax: 206-522-6308.
School—6220 32nd Ave., N.E., 98115-7233. Tel: 206-524-7452; Fax: 206-524-6757. Michael Foy, Prin. Lay Teachers 28; Students 540.
Catechesis/Religious Program—Students 30.

5—ST. BENEDICT (1906), Rev. Steven Sallis.
Res.: 1805 N. 49th St., 98103. Tel: 206-632-0843; Fax: 206-632-2167.
School—4811 Wallingford N., 98103. Tel: 206-633-3375; Fax: 206-632-3236. Dr. Fred McCarthy, Prin. Lay Teachers 16; Students 155.
Catechesis/Religious Program—Tel: 206-632-0843. Students 40.

6—ST. BERNADETTE (1958), Rev. James A. Williams, J.C.L.; Deacon Joseph Krempl.
Res.: 861 S.W. 126th St., 98146. Tel: 206-242-7370; Fax: 206-242-7371.
School—1028 S.W. 128th St., 98146. Tel: 206-244-4934; Fax: 206-244-4943. Carol Homanics, Prin. Lay Teachers 16; Students 240.
Catechesis/Religious Program—Students 155.

7—BLESSED SACRAMENT (1908), Revs. Daniel Syverstad, O.P. (OAK); John Adams, O.P. In Res., Revs. Michael Sweeney, O.P.; James Jenner, O.P.; Augustine Hartman, O.P.; Steven Maekawa, O.P.
Res.: 5041 Ninth Ave., N.E., 98105. Tel: 206-547-3020; Fax: 206-547-6371.
Catechesis/Religious Program—Students 61.

8—ST. BRIDGET (1968), [CEM] Rev. Marlin Connole; Deacon Dennis Duffell.
Res.: 4900 N.E. 50th St., 98105. Tel: 206-523-8787; Fax: 206-528-7511.
Catechesis/Religious Program—Tel: 206-523-9760. Students 119.

9—ST. CATHERINE (1929), Very Revs. Anthony Bawyn;

Paul Magnano, Moderator; Victoria Ries, Pastoral Life Dir.
Res.: 8610 8th Ave., N.E., 98115. Tel: 206-524-8800; Fax: 206-527-6339.
School—8524 8th Ave., N.E., 98115. Tel: 206-525-0581. Steve Mezich, Prin. Lay Teachers 14; Students 198.
Catechesis/Religious Program—Students 72.

10—CHRIST THE KING (1930), Rev. Ward Oakshott; Very Rev. Paul Magnano, Moderator; Rev. Arturo Araujo, S.J.; Ms. Patricia Repikoff, Pastoral Life Dir.
Res.: 405 N. 117th St., 98133. Tel: 206-362-1545; Fax: 206-364-8325.
School—415 N. 117th St., 98133. Tel: 206-364-6890. Terry Maguire, Prin. Lay Teachers 16; Students 175.
Catechesis/Religious Program—Students 195.

11—ST. EDWARD (1906), Revs. Joseph J. Tyson; Felino Paulino; Fausto Kaverenge.
Res.: 4250 S. Mead St., 98118. Tel: 206-722-7888; Fax: 206-722-7895.
School—Tel: 206-725-1774; Fax: 206-725-4569. Mary Lundeen, Prin. Sisters 4; Lay Teachers 5; Students 123.
Catechesis/Religious Program—Students 15.

12—ST. GEORGE (1903), Revs. Joseph J. Tyson; Felino Paulino; Fausto Kaverenge; Deacon Sagoto Pele.
Res.: 5306 13th Ave. S., 98108. Tel: 206-762-7744; Fax: 206-762-4207.
School—5117 13th Ave. S., 98108. Tel: 206-762-0656; Fax: 206-763-3220. Bernadette O'Leary, Prin. Lay Teachers 15; Students 214.
Catechesis/Religious Program—Students 81.

13—HOLY FAMILY (1921), Revs. Phillip Bloom; Ramon Velasco; Deacons Ted Wiese; Abel Magana.
Res.: 9622 20th Ave., S.W., 98106. Tel: 206-767-6220; Fax: 206-767-0374.
School—Tel: 206-767-6640; Fax: 206-767-9466. Stephen Morissette, Prin. Sisters 1; Lay Teachers 15; Students 244.
Catechesis/Religious Program—Students 420.

14—HOLY ROSARY (1907), Rev. Jeffery L. Sarkies.
Res.: 4139 42nd Ave., S.W., 98116. Tel: 206-935-8353; Fax: 206-935-4303.
School—Tel: 206-937-7255; Fax: 206-937-2610. Kristi Brown, Prin. Lay Teachers 32; Students 476.
Catechesis/Religious Program—Tel: 206-937-1488, Ext. 203. Students 208.

15—IMMACULATE CONCEPTION (1891), Rev. Fabian MacDonald, Parochial Vicar; Very Rev. James Picton, Moderator; Deacons Joseph Connor; Frederic Cordova; Mrs. Joan McGuire, Pastoral Coord. In Res., Rev. Jaime Tolang.
Res.: 820 18th Ave., 98122. Tel: 206-322-5970; Fax: 206-322-9417.
Catechesis/Religious Program—Students 43.

16—ST. JOHN (1917), Rev. William A. McKee.
Office—121 N. 80th St., 98103. Tel: 206-782-2810; Fax: 206-782-0242.
School—(Grades PreK-8) Tel: 206-783-0337; Fax: 206-706-2704. Agnes Jacobson, Prin. Lay Teachers 32; Students 420.
Catechesis/Religious Program—Students 129.

17—ST. JOSEPH (1907), Revs. Craig Boly, S.J.; Lee Kapfer, S.J.; Joseph O. McGowan, S.J.; Deacon Stephen Wodzanowski.
Res.: 732 18th Ave. E., 98112. Tel: 206-324-2522; Fax: 206-329-5698.
School—700 18th Ave. E., 98112. Tel: 206-329-3260; Fax: 206-324-7773. George Hofbauer, Prin. Sisters 1; Lay Teachers 42; Students 625.
Catechesis/Religious Program—Students 350.

18—ST. MARGARET OF SCOTLAND (1910), Rev. Robert Camuso. In Res., Rev. Joseph Calik, S.Ch., Polish Ministry.
Res.: 3221 14th Ave. W., 98119. Tel: 206-282-1804; Fax: 206-282-6461.

19—ST. MARY (1899), Rev. Anthony J. Haycock. Religious of the Sacred Heart of Jesus
Res.: 611 20th Ave. S., 98144. Tel: 206-324-7100; Fax: 206-329-4596.
Catechesis/Religious Program—Students 45.
Convent—2021 S. Weller St., 98144. Tel: 206-324-1535.

20—ST. MATTHEW (1954), Rev. Peter Karam.
Res.: 1240 N.E. 127th St., 98125. Tel: 206-363-6767; Fax: 206-362-4863.
School—1230 N.E. 127th St., 98125. Tel: 206-362-2785; Fax: 206-440-9476. Maureen Reid, Prin. Lay Teachers 13; Students 226.
Catechesis/Religious Program—Students 120.

21—OUR LADY OF FATIMA (1952), Rev. James Johnson Jr.; Deacon Walter Shields. In Res., Rev. Joseph H. Doogan, J.C.L. (Retired).
Res.: 3218 W. Barrett, 98199. Tel: 206-283-1456; Fax: 206-283-5788.
School—3301 W. Dravus St., 98199. Tel: 206-283-7031; Fax: 206-283-7696. Susan Burdett, Prin. Sisters 1; Lay Teachers 24; Students 296.
Catechesis/Religious Program—Tel: 206-352-4571. Students 185.

22—OUR LADY OF GUADALUPE (1960), Very Rev. John Walmesley.
Res.: 7000-35th Ave., S.W., 98126. Tel: 206-935-0358; Fax: 206-935-1230.
School—3401 S.W. Myrtle, 98126. Tel: 206-935-0651; Fax: 206-938-3695. Kristin Dixon, Prin. Lay Teachers 17. Students 225.
Catechesis/Religious Program—Students 38.

23—OUR LADY OF LOURDES (1892), Rev. Gerald L. Mayovsky.
Res.: 10240 12th Ave. S., 98168-1525. Tel: 206-762-3343; Fax: 206-768-1507.

24—OUR LADY OF MOUNT VIRGIN (1911), Very Rev. James Picton, Moderator; Rev. Roger Blanchette, S.J.; Deacon Joua Pao Yang, Pastoral Admin.; Charlene P. Collora, Pastoral Admin.
Res.: 1531 Bradner Pl. S., 98144. Tel: 206-324-8521; Fax: 206-322-6406.
Catechesis/Religious Program—Students 32.

25—OUR LADY OF THE LAKE (1929), Rev. Paul Pluth, Admin.; Sr. Kate Bazard, S.N.J.M., Pastoral Life Dir.
Res.: 8900 35th Ave., N.E., 98115. Tel: 206-523-6776; Fax: 206-524-0848.
School—3520 N.E. 89th St., 98115. Tel: 206-525-9980; Fax: 206-523-2858. Mrs. Maureen Blum, Prin. Lay Teachers 14; Students 204.
Catechesis/Religious Program—Tel: 206-522-2840. Students 160.

26—ST. PATRICK (1918), Rev. Patrick S. Clark.
Res.: 2702 Broadway E., 98102. Tel: 206-329-2960; Fax: 206-329-2961.
Catechesis/Religious Program—Students 40.

27—ST. PAUL (1953), Revs. Joseph J. Tyson; Felino Paulino; Fausto Kaverenge.
Parish Office—5600 S. Ryan St., 98178. Tel: 206-725-2050; Fax: 206-725-7476.
School—10001 57th Ave. S., 98178. Tel: 206-725-0780; Fax: 206-722-5732. Wayne Melonson, Prin. Lay Teachers 15; Students 215.
Catechesis/Religious Program—Students 40.

28—ST. PETER (1931), Rev. Peter Duggan.
Res.: 2807 15th Ave. S., 98144. Tel: 206-324-2290; Fax: 206-324-4020.
Catechesis/Religious Program—Tel: 206-329-1946. Students 34.

29—SACRED HEART OF JESUS (1889), Revs. Richard Quinn, C.SS.R.; Joseph J. Morin, C.SS.R.; The Pham, C.SS.R. In Res., Revs. Joseph Nuttman, C.SS.R.; Lyle Konen, C.SS.R.
Res.: 205 2nd Ave. N., 98109. Tel: 206-284-4680; Fax: 206-284-3161.
Catechesis/Religious Program—Students 3.

30—ST. THERESE (1926), Rev. James Harbaugh, S.J., Admin.
Res.: 3416 E. Marion St., 98122. Tel: 206-325-2711; Fax: 206-329-8373.
School—900-35th Ave., 98122. Tel: 206-324-0460; Fax: 206-324-8464. Mrs. Eileen Gray, Prin. Sisters 1; Lay Teachers 17; Students 210.
Catechesis/Religious Program—Students 61.

OUTSIDE THE CITY OF SEATTLE

ABERDEEN, GRAYS HARBOR CO.

1—ST. MARY (1885), Revs. Martin Bourke; Stephen Roman.
Res.: 306 E. Third St., 98520. Tel: 360-532-8300; Fax: 360-538-9987.
School—518 N. H St., 98520. Tel: 360-532-1230; Fax: 360-532-1209. Deona Behrens, Prin. Lay Teachers 11; Students 143.
Catechesis/Religious Program—Students 33.
Mission—*St. Paul* P.O. Box 332, Westport, Grays Harbor Co. 98585. Tel: 206-268-9625; Fax: 206-268-9625.

2—SS. PETER AND PAUL (1907), (Polish), Revs. Martin Bourke; Stephen Roman.
Res.: 306 E. Third St., 98520. Tel: 360-532-8300; Fax: 360-538-9987.

ANACORTES, SKAGIT CO., ST. MARY (1910), Rev. William E. Harris.
Res.: 4001 St. Mary's Dr., 98221. Tel: 360-293-2101; Fax: 360-293-6396.
Catechesis/Religious Program—Tel: 360-293-6882; Fax: 360-293-2102. Students 108.

ARLINGTON, SNOHOMISH CO., IMMACULATE CONCEPTION (1890), Rev. L. John Topel, S.J.
Res.: 1200 E. Fifth, P.O. Box 69, 98223. Tel: 360-435-3565; Fax: 360-435-9732.
Catechesis/Religious Program—Tel: 360-435-8519. Students 197.
Mission—*St. John Mary Vianney* 1150 Riddle St., Darrington, Snohomish Co. 98241.

AUBURN, KING CO., HOLY FAMILY (1904), Rev. Phuong Hoang.
Res.: 505 17th St., S.E., P.O. Box 290, 98071. Tel: 253-833-5130; Fax: 253-833-3421.
School—(Grades K-8), 505 17th St., S.E., 98002. Tel: 253-833-8688; Fax: 253-833-931_. Kathleen Cowin, Prin. Lay Teachers 18; Students 200.
Catechesis/Religious Program—Tel: 253-833-5730; Fax: 253-833-5130. Students 382.

BAINBRIDGE ISLAND, KITSAP CO., ST. CECILIA (1950), Rev. Sean O'Loughlin.
Res.: 1310 Madison Ave. N., 98110. Tel: 206-842-3594; Fax: 206-842-6988.
Catechesis/Religious Program—Tel: 206-842-6031. Students 258.

BATTLE GROUND, CLARK CO., SACRED HEART (1877), [CEM] Rev. David Rogerson; Deacons Carl Anderson; Jack Roscoe.
Mailing Address: 1603 N. Parkway Ave., P.O. Box 38, 98604. Tel: 360-687-4515; Fax: 360-687-3322.
Catechesis/Religious Program—Tel: 360-687-4515; Fax: 360-687-3322. Students 180.
Mission—*St. Joseph the Workman* 200 Jones St., Yacolt, Clark Co. 98675.
Mission—*St. Mary of Guadalupe* (1888), 28309 N.W. 11th, Ridgefield, Clark Co. 98642. Deacon Carl Anderson.

BELLEVUE, KING CO.

1—ST. LOUISE (1960), Revs. Thomas Belleque; Philip Wallace; Deacon Carlos Naranjo.
Res.: 141 156th Ave., S.E., 98007. Tel: 425-747-4450; Fax: 425-644-3678.
School—133 156th Ave., S.E., 98007. Tel: 425-746-4220; Fax: 425-644-3294. Dan Fitzpatrick, Prin. Lay Teachers 28; Students 460.
Catechesis/Religious Program—Students 255.

2—ST. MADELEINE SOPHIE (1968), Very Rev. James D. Picton, J.D.; Rev. Emmanuel Iweh; Deacon Eugene R. Vanderzanden.
Res.: 4400 130th Pl., S.E., 98006-2014. Tel: 425-747-6770; Fax: 425-747-6349.
Catechesis/Religious Program—Tel: 425-747-6771; Fax: 425-747-1825. Students 392.

3—SACRED HEART (1946), Rev. Patrick Ritter.
Res.: 9460 N.E. 14th St., 98004. Tel: 425-454-9536; Fax: 425-450-3909.
School—9450 N.E. 14th St., 98004. Tel: 425-451-1773; Fax: 425-454-9538. Dr. Carola Wittman, Prin. Lay Teachers 26; Students 460.
Catechesis/Religious Program—Tel: 425-451-1775. Students 627.

BELLINGHAM, WHATCOM CO.

1—ASSUMPTION B.V.M. (1889), Rev. Frank Schuster; Deacon Lawrence Kheriaty.
Res.: 2116 Cornwall Ave., 98225. Tel: 360-733-1380; Fax: 360-733-5644.
School—Tel: 360-733-6133; Fax: 360-733-3601. Ms. Anne Brand, Prin. Lay Teachers 22; Students 384.
Catechesis/Religious Program—Students 228.

2—SACRED HEART (1905), [JC] Rev. David Mulholland, Admin.; Deacon Lawrence Gorman.
Res.: 1110 14th St., 98225. Tel: 360-734-2850; 360-733-3400 (Campus Min.); Fax: 360-734-0947.
Catechesis/Religious Program—Students 63.

BLACK DIAMOND, KING CO., ST. BARBARA (1912), Rev. M. Charles Palluck.
Res.: Sixth Ave. near Baker, P.O. Box 189, 98010. Tel: 360-886-2229.
Catechesis/Religious Program—Students 471.

BOTHELL, KING CO., ST. BRENDAN (1949), Very Rev. Lawrence Minder; Deacon Eamon Parsons.
Res.: 10051 N.E. 195th, 98011-2931. Tel: 425-483-9400; Fax: 425-486-9735.
School—Tel: 425-483-8300; Fax: 425-483-2839. Arlene Sullivan, Prin. Lay Teachers 14; Students 264.
Catechesis/Religious Program—Students 386.

BOTHELL, SNOHOMISH CO., ST. ELIZABETH ANN SETON (1983), Revs. Eusebio Elizondo, M.Sp.S.; Jorge Gomez del Valle, M.Sp.S.; Deacon Robert Dolan.
Res.: P.O. Box 12429, Mill Creek, 98082-0429. Tel: 425-481-0303; Fax: 425-485-8510.
Catechesis/Religious Program—Tel: 425-481-9358. Mavis Kalbrener, D.R.E. Students 639.

BREMERTON, KITSAP CO.

1—HOLY TRINITY (1964), Rev. Jack Buckalew.
Mailing Address: P.O. Box 910, Tracyton, 98393.
Res.: 4215 Pine Rd., 98310. Tel: 360-377-7674; Fax: 360-377-6181.
Catechesis/Religious Program—Tel: 360-479-9525. Students 307.

2—OUR LADY, STAR OF THE SEA (1902), Very Rev. Patrick W. Freitag; Deacon James Bemis.
Office—1513-6th St., 98337. Tel: 360-479-3777; Fax: 360-479-1468.
School—1516-5th St., 98337. Tel: 360-373-5162. Glen Lutz, Prin. Lay Teachers 11; Students 189.
Catechesis/Religious Program—Students 206.

BUCKLEY, PIERCE CO., ST. ALOYSIUS (1892), Revs. James Northrop, Admin.; George Limbani.
Res.: 211 W. Mason St., P.O. Box 2120, 98321. Tel: 253-862-6014; Fax: 360-829-5190.
Catechesis/Religious Program—Tel: 360-829-9958. Students 62.
Mission—*Our Lady of Lourdes* (1894), [CEM] Wilkeson, Pierce Co.

BURLINGTON, SKAGIT CO., ST. CHARLES (1885), Very Rev. J. Patrick McDermott; Revs. Gilberto Mora Tapia; John Nwanze, O.P.; Daniel Chiezey, O.P.
Res.: 935 Peterson Rd., 98233. Tel: 360-757-0128;

Fax: 360-757-0418.
CAMAS, CLARK CO., ST. THOMAS AQUINAS (1870), [CEM] Rev. Derek Lappe.
Res.: 324 N.E. Oak, 98607. Tel: 360-834-2126; Fax: 360-834-5106.
Catechesis/Religious Program—Tel: 360-834-2126, Ext. 2. Students 193.
Mission—Star of the Sea P.O. Box 901, Stevenson, Skamania Co. 98648. Tel: 509-427-8478; Fax: 509-427-8478. Deacon William Townsend.
CASTLE ROCK, COWLITZ CO., ST. MARY (1976), Very Rev. Michael H. Wright.
Mailing Address: P.O. Box 960, 98611-0960.
Rectory: 635 Buland Dr., 98611-0960. Tel: 360-274-7404; Fax: 360-274-7328.
Church: 120 Powell Rd., 98611-0960.
Catechesis/Religious Program—Students 43.
CENTRALIA, LEWIS CO., ST. MARY (1910), Revs. Tuan Nguyen; Timothy W. Ilgen; Deacon Loren Lane.
Res.: 225 N. Washington Ave., 98531. Tel: 360-736-4356; Fax: 360-807-0758.
Catechesis/Religious Program—Tel: 360-736-3470. Students 72.
CHEHALIS, LEWIS CO., ST. JOSEPH (1888), Revs. Tuan Nguyen; Timothy W. Ilgen; Deacon Loren Lane.
Mailing Address: 157 S.W. 6th St., 98532.
Res.: 682 S.W. Cascade Ave., 98532. Tel: 360-748-4953; Fax: 360-748-3149.
School—123 S.W. 6th St., 98532. Tel: 360-748-0961; Fax: 360-748-8502. Kendra Meek, Prin. Lay Teachers 10; Students 172.
Catechesis/Religious Program—Tel: 360-748-4161. Students 73.
COVINGTON, KING CO., ST. JOHN THE BAPTIST (1990), Rev. James Coyne; Deacon Ted Childs.
Church: 25810 156th Ave., S.E., 98042. Tel: 253-630-0701; Fax: 253-630-3174.
Catechesis/Religious Program—Sr. Carol Ann McMullen, S.N.J.M., D.R.E. Students 803.
DES MOINES, KING CO., ST. PHILOMENA (1927), Revs. Bryan Hersey; Adrian Luevano Carillo.
Res.: 1790 S. 222nd St., 98198. Tel: 206-878-8709; Fax: 206-824-3480.
School—1815 S. 220th, 98198. Tel: 206-824-4051. Sandra Barton Smith, Prin. Tel: 206-878-8646. Lay Teachers 18; Students 252.
Catechesis/Religious Program—Tel: 206-878-1761. Monesa Grant, D.R.E. Students 144.
EDMONDS, SNOHOMISH CO., HOLY ROSARY (1940), Revs. Kenneth Haydock; Donald Perea.
Res.: 630 7th Ave. N., P.O. Box 206, 98020. Tel: 425-778-3122; Fax: 425-672-4909.
School—770 Aloha St. P.O. Box 206, 98020. Tel: 425-778-3197; Fax: 425-771-8144. Kathy Carr, Prin. Sisters 1; Lay Teachers 19; Students 259.
Catechesis/Religious Program—Students 325.
ELMA, GRAYS HARBOR CO., ST. JOSEPH (1890), [CEM] Rev. David Gese; Deacon Frank Hawkins.
Res.: 510 W. Waldrip St., P.O. Box AA, 98541. Tel: 360-482-3190; Fax: 360-482-6490.
Catechesis/Religious Program—Tel: 360-495-3415. Students 86.
Mission—St. John Broadway and Church St., Montesano, Grays Harbor Co. 98563. Tel: 360-249-5766.
ENUMCLAW, KING CO., SACRED HEART OF JESUS (1888), [CEM] Rev. James Northrop.
Res.: 1614 Farrelly St., 98022. Tel: 360-825-3759; Fax: 360-825-6832.
Catechesis/Religious Program—Tel: 360-825-2333. Students 303.
Station—Crystal Mountain Chapel Crystal Mountain.
EVERETT, SNOHOMISH CO.
1—IMMACULATE CONCEPTION (1904), Rev. Dennis E. Robb; Deacon Matt Zuanich.
Mailing Address: 2619 Cedar St., 98201. In Res., Rev. Boniface Kasulo.
Res.: 2509 Hoyt Ave., 98201. Tel: 425-349-7014; Fax: 425-349-7015.
Church: 2501 Hoyt Ave., 98201.
School—2508 Hoyt Ave., 98201. Tel: 425-349-7777; Fax: 425-349-7048. Pat Green, Prin. Lay Teachers 26; Students 411.
Catechesis/Religious Program—Students 183.
2—ST. MARY MAGDALEN (1957), Revs. Joseph M. Marquart; Armando Guzman; Deacon David P. Alcorta.
Res.: 8717 7th Ave., S.E., 98208. Tel: 425-353-1211; Fax: 425-348-0458.
School—8615 7th Ave., S.E., 98208. Tel: 425-353-7559; Fax: 425-356-2687. Sr. Joanne McCauley, O.P., Prin. Sisters 2; Lay Teachers 22; Students 428.
Catechesis/Religious Program—Tel: 425-355-3133. Students 365.
Mission—St. John Mukilteo, Snohomish Co.
3—OUR LADY OF PERPETUAL HELP (1891), [CEM] Rev. Dennis E. Robb; Deacon Matt Zuanich. In Res., Rev. Boniface Kasulo.
Res.: 2619 Cedar St., 98201. Tel: 425-349-7014; Fax: 425-349-7015.
Catechesis/Religious Program—Students 115.
FEDERAL WAY, KING & PIERCE COS., ST. THERESA (1924), Very Rev. Kevin Moran.
Res.: 3939 S.W. 331st, 98023. Tel: 253-838-5924; Fax: 253-838-0300.
Catechesis/Religious Program—Students 487.
FEDERAL WAY, KING CO., ST. VINCENT DE PAUL (1961), Revs. Thomas L. Vandenberg; Clarence Jones, C.O.; Deacons Delbert Hoover; Juan Lezcano.
Res.: 30525 8th Ave. S., 98003. Tel: 253-839-2320; Fax: 253-839-1819.
School—30527 8th Ave. S., 98003. Tel: 253-839-3532; Fax: 253-839-1819. Wanda Stewart, Prin. Lay Teachers 19; Students 288.
Catechesis/Religious Program—Tel: 253-839-4333. Students 439.
FERNDALE, WHATCOM CO., ST. JOSEPH (1893), Revs. Timothy J. Sauer; Matthew L. O'Leary; Deacon George Ficken.
Res.: 5781 Hendrickson Ave., 98248. Tel: 360-384-3651; Fax: 360-384-1879.
Catechesis/Religious Program—Tel: 360-384-8818. Students 236.
Mission—St. Anne 604 H St., Blaine, Whatcom Co. 98230. Tel: 360-332-3651.
Mission—St. Joachim (Indian Reservation) Bellingham. Kwina & Lummi Shore Rds., Lummi, Whatcom Co. 98226. Tel: 360-734-3651.
FIFE, LAKEWOOD CO., ST. MARTIN OF TOURS (1947), Revs. Richard Ward; Thomas L. Vandenberg; Kathi Thornhill, Pastoral Admin.
Res.: 2303-54th Ave. E., 98424. Tel: 253-922-7882; Fax: 253-922-2068.
School—All Saints, 2323 54th Ave. E., 98424. Tel: 253-922-5360; Fax: 253-922-6746.
Catechesis/Religious Program—Tel: 253-922-6858. Students 85.
FORKS, CLALLAM CO., ST. ANNE PARISH (1930), Revs. Kurt Nagel; Reynaldo Yu.
Res.: 511-5th Ave., P.O. Box 2359, 98331. Tel: 360-374-9184.
Catechesis/Religious Program—Tel: 360-374-6405. Students 34.
Mission—St. Thomas the Apostle Clallam Bay, Clallam Co.
FRIDAY HARBOR, SAN JUAN CO., ST. FRANCIS (1860), [CEM] Rev. Raymond Heffernan (Retired).
Res.: 425 Price St., P.O. Box 1489, 98250. Tel: 360-378-2910 (Office); Fax: 360-378-2910.
Catechesis/Religious Program—Students 69.
Station—St. Francis 956 N. Beach Rd., Eastsound, 98245.
Station—St. Francis: Lopez Island Community, Center Church Lopez Island.
Station—Our Lady of Good Voyage Chapel Roche Harbor, San Juan Island. Lay Ministers 2.
GIG HARBOR, PIERCE CO., ST. NICHOLAS (1931), Rev. Gary Weisenberger; Deacons John Ricciardi; Patrick Kelley.
Res.: 3510 Rosedale St., 98335. Tel: 253-851-8850; Fax: 253-851-8823.
School—3555 Edwards St., 98335. Tel: 253-858-7632; Fax: 253-858-1597. Joanne Lott, Prin. Lay Teachers 13; Students 190.
Catechesis/Religious Program—Tel: 253-851-9040. Students 195.
HOQUIAM, GRAYS HARBOR CO., OUR LADY OF GOOD HELP (1906), Rev. Martin Bourke.
Mailing Address: 611 2nd St., 98550. In Res., Rev. Stephen Roman.
Res.: 200 L St., 98550. Tel: 360-532-6103; Fax: 360-533-9012.
Catechesis/Religious Program—Students 10.
Mission—Our Lady of the Olympics Lake Quinault. Box 45, Quinault, Grays Harbor & Jefferson Cos. 98526. Tel: 360-288-2802.
ISSAQUAH, KING CO., ST. JOSEPH (1962), Very Rev. James Picton; Rev. Robert L. Evenson; Deacon Patrick Moynihan; Judy Sender, Pastoral Admin.
Res.: 220 Mt. Park Blvd., S.W., P.O. Box 200, 98027. Tel: 425-392-5516; Fax: 425-392-2722.
School—(Grades PreK-8) Tel: 425-313-9129. Jackie Olund, Prin. Lay Teachers 9; Students 224.
KELSO, COWLITZ CO., IMMACULATE HEART OF MARY (1910), Very Rev. Michael H. Wright.
Res.: 2200 Allen St., 98626. Tel: 360-423-3650; Fax: 360-423-4165.
Catechesis/Religious Program—Tel: 360-423-3653. Students 129.
KENT, KING CO., HOLY SPIRIT PARISH (1890), [CEM] Revs. Michael J. Ryan; Michael A. Tyrrell, S.J.; Steven Sallis; Cathy Peters, Pastoral Admin.
Res.: 310 3rd Ave. S., 98032. Tel: 253-859-0444; Fax: 253-859-5974.
Catechesis/Religious Program—Students 349.
KIRKLAND, KING CO.
1—HOLY FAMILY (1915), Rev. Gary Morelli.
Res.: 7355 120th Ave., N.E., 98033. Tel: 425-822-0295; Fax: 425-827-0648.
School—Tel: 425-827-0444; Fax: 425-827-0150. Doug Arthur, Prin. Lay Teachers 17; Students 262.
Catechesis/Religious Program—Students 410.
2—ST. JOHN MARY VIANNEY (1971), Rev. Kevin F.X. Duggan; Deacon David Warmuth.
Res.: 12600 84th Ave., N.E., 98034. Tel: 425-823-0787; Fax: 425-814-2115.
Catechesis/Religious Program—Students 385.
LACONNER, SKAGIT CO.
1—ST. PAUL (Swinomish) (1867), (Native American), Very Rev. J. Patrick McDermott; Rev. Patrick Twohy, S.J., Parochial Vicar.
Mailing Address: P.O. Box 2100, 98257. Tel: 360-466-4680; Fax: 360-466-4039.
Church: 17456 Pioneer Pkwy. Rd., Swinomish, 98257. Tel: 360-466-5737.
2—SACRED HEART (1875), Very Rev. J. Patrick McDermott; Revs. John Nwanze, O.P.; Daniel Chiezey, O.P.; Gilberto Mora Tapia; Deacon George Peterson.
Res.: P.O. Box 757, 98257-0757. Tel: 360-466-3967; Fax: 360-466-3942.
Catechesis/Religious Program—410 Douglas St., 98257. Students 42.
LACEY, THURSTON CO., SACRED HEART OF JESUS (1923), Very Rev. James Picton; Rev. Richard Parle; Ms. Ferrell Gilson, Pastoral Coord. In Res., Rev. Gorgonio Silagan Jr.
Res.: P.O. Box 3805, 98509-3805. Tel: 360-491-0890; Fax: 360-456-1028.
Catechesis/Religious Program—Students 542.
LAKEWOOD, PIERCE CO.
1—ST. FRANCES CABRINI (1952), Rev. Timothy McKenna; Deacon George Mounce III.
Res.: 5505 108th St., S.W., 98499. Tel: 253-588-2141; Fax: 253-582-5351.
School—Tel: 253-584-3850; Fax: 253-582-5351. Stephanie Van Leuven, Prin. Sisters 1; Lay Teachers 13; Students 243.
Catechesis/Religious Program—Students 181.
2—ST. JOHN BOSCO (1968), Rev. Oliver Lee Hightower; Deacons Daniel Allen; Jeffrey Greer.
Res.: 10508 112 St., S.W., 98498. Tel: 253-582-1028; Fax: 253-584-0633.
Catechesis/Religious Program—Students 229.
Mission—Immaculate Conception Nisqually & Main, Steilacoom, Pierce Co. 98388.
LANGLEY, ISLAND CO., ST. HUBERT (1938), Rev. Richard J. Spicer.
Mailing Address: P.O. Box 388, 98260-0388.
Res.: 815 Saratoga Ave., 98260. Tel: 360-221-5383; Fax: 360-221-2011.
Catechesis/Religious Program—Tel: 360-221-7453. Students 130.
LONGVIEW, COWLITZ CO., ST. ROSE DE VITERBO (1928), Rev. K. Scott Connolly.
Mailing Address: 701-26th, 98632.
Res.: 2571 Nichols Blvd., 98632. Tel: 360-425-4660; Fax: 360-577-5820.
School—727 25th Ave., 98632. Tel: 360-577-6760; Fax: 360-577-3689. Kay Purcell, Prin. Lay Teachers 16; Students 206.
Catechesis/Religious Program—Tel: 360-577-7346. Students 190.
Mission—St. Catherine Cathlamet. 400 Columbia St., Cathlamet, Wahkiakum Co. 98612. Tel: 360-795-8725.
LYNDEN, WHATCOM CO., ST. JOSEPH (1897), Rev. Emilio Gonzalez.
Res.: 205 Twelfth St., 98264. Tel: 360-354-2334; Fax: 360-354-5889.
Catechesis/Religious Program—Students 223.
Mission—St. Peter [CEM 3] 6210 Mt. Baker Hwy., Deming, Whatcom Co. 98244.
LYNNWOOD, SNOHOMISH CO., ST. THOMAS MORE (1962), Rev. James Dalton.
Res.: 6511-176th, S.W., 98037. Tel: 425-743-2929; Fax: 425-743-3652.
School—Tel: 425-743-4242; Fax: 425-745-8367. Patrick White, Prin. Sisters 1; Lay Teachers 15; Students 247.
Catechesis/Religious Program—Tel: 425-743-5780. Students 305.
MARYSVILLE, SNOHOMISH CO., ST. MARY (1888), [CEM] Rev. Horacio Yanez.
Res.: 4200 88th St., N.E., 98270. Tel: 360-653-9400; Fax: 360-658-7439.
Catechesis/Religious Program—Students 299.
Mission—Tulalip Indian Reservation, St. Anne 7213 Totem Beach Rd., Tulalip, Snohomish Co. 98271. Rev. Patrick Twohy, S.J.
MERCER ISLAND, KING CO., ST. MONICA (1958), Rev. Dennis Kemp; Deacon Jack Warfield.
Res.: 4301 88th, S.E., P.O. Box 730, 98040. Tel: 206-232-2900; Fax: 206-232-7875. In Res., Rev. James Elliott.
School—4320 87th, S.E., 98040. Tel: 206-232-5432; Fax: 206-275-2874. Mrs. Pamela Dellino, Prin. Lay Teachers 19; Students 245.
Catechesis/Religious Program—Tel: 206-232-9829; Fax: 206-232-3321. Students 275.
MONROE, SNOHOMISH CO., ST. MARY OF THE VALLEY (1902), Rev. Michael C. OBrien.

Res.: 601 W. Columbia, P.O. Box 279, 98272. Tel: 360-794-8945; Fax: 360-805-0201.
Catechesis/Religious Program—Students 234.

MORTON, LEWIS CO., SACRED HEART (1922), Rev. Roger J. Smith.
Res.: 277 7th St., P.O. Box 880, 98356. Tel: 360-496-5456; Fax: 360-496-5616.
Catechesis/Religious Program—Students 12.
Mission—St. Yves [CEM] Harmony, Lewis Co.
Station— Packwood.

MOUNT VERNON, SKAGIT CO., IMMACULATE CONCEPTION (1899), Very Rev. J. Patrick McDermott; Revs. John Nwanze, O.P.; Daniel Chiezey, O.P.; Gilberto Mora Tapia.
Office—215 N. 15th St., 98273. Tel: 360-336-6622; Fax: 360-336-5203.
School—Immaculate Conception Regional School, 1321 E. Division St., 98273. Tel: 360-428-3912; Fax: 360-424-8838. Kathleen Cartee, Prin. Lay Teachers 19; Students 290.

MOUNTLAKE TERRACE, SNOHOMISH CO., ST. PIUS X (1955), Revs. Sean P. Fox; Ronald Knudsen.
Res.: 22301 58th Ave. W., 98043. Tel: 425-775-7545; Fax: 425-775-8744.
School—22105 58th W., 98043. Tel: 425-778-9861; Fax: 425-776-2663. Mrs. Terri McDermott, Prin. Lay Teachers 14; Students 160.
Catechesis/Religious Program—Students 116.

OAK HARBOR, ISLAND CO., ST. AUGUSTINE (1957), Rev. Ronald Belisle.
Res.: 185 N. Oak Harbor St., 98277. Tel: 360-675-2303; Fax: 360-675-9490.
Catechesis/Religious Program—Tel: 360-675-2303, Ext. 25. Students 191.
Mission—St. Mary 207 N. Main, P.O. Box 1443, Coupeville, Island Co. 98239. Tel: 360-678-6536.

OCEAN SHORES, GRAYS HARBOR CO., ST. JEROME (1969), Revs. Martin Bourke; Stephen Roman.
Res.: P.O. Box 190, 98569. Tel: 360-289-2838; Fax: 360-289-0163.

OLYMPIA, THURSTON CO., ST. MICHAEL (1848), [CEM] Very Rev. James Lee; Rev. Robert J. Kenny; Deacon William Shawver.
Res.: 1021 Boundary St., S.E., P.O. Box 766, 98507. Tel: 360-754-4667; Fax: 360-754-0628.
School—1203 E. 10th, 98501. Tel: 360-754-5131; Fax: 360-753-6090. Sally Merriwether, Prin. Lay Teachers 18; Students 261.
Catechesis/Religious Program—P.O. Box 766, 98507. Students 614.

PE ELL, LEWIS CO., ST. JOSEPH (1894), [CEM 2] Revs. Tuan Nguyen; Timothy W. Ilgen.
Res.: 417 N. Main, P.O. Box 235, 98572. Tel: 360-291-3434; Fax: 360-291-3434.
Catechesis/Religious Program—Students 9.
Mission—Holy Family State Hwy. 6, Frances, Pacific Co. 98572. Rev. Timothy W. Ilgen.

PORT ANGELES, CLALLAM CO., QUEEN OF ANGELS (1891), Revs. Kurt Nagel; Reynaldo Yu.
Res.: 209 W. 11th St., 98362. Tel: 360-452-2351; Fax: 360-452-1447.
School—1107 S. Oak, 98362. Tel: 360-457-6903; Fax: 360-457-6866. Debra Brines, Prin. Lay Teachers 18; Students 135.
Catechesis/Religious Program—Tel: 360-457-4171. Students 155.

PORT ORCHARD, KITSAP CO., ST. GABRIEL (1942), Revs. Clyde Vincent Peterson; Jeffery L. Sarkies; Sr. Deanna Carr, B.V.M., Pastoral Life Dir.
Res.: 1150 Mitchell Ave., 98366-4416. Tel: 360-876-2762; Fax: 360-876-6085.
Catechesis/Religious Program—Tel: 360-876-2834. Students 320.
Mission—Prince of Peace (1970), N.E. 1171 Sand Hill Rd., P.O. Box 517, Belfair, Mason Co. 98528. Tel: 360-275-8760; Fax: 360-275-4418.
Catechesis/Religious Program—Students 37.

PORT TOWNSEND, JEFFERSON CO., ST. MARY STAR OF THE SEA (1859), [CEM] Revs. Kurt Nagel, Admin.; Gary Sumpter.
Res.: 1335 Blaine St., 98368. Tel: 360-385-3700; Fax: 360-379-1989.
Catechesis/Religious Program—Tel: 360-385-1662. Students 90.

POULSBO, KITSAP CO., ST. OLAF (1968), Revs. David L. Mayovsky; Adrian Luevano Carillo; Deacon Carl Moyer.
Res.: 18943 Caldart Ave., N.E., 98370. Tel: 360-779-4291; Fax: 360-779-1240.
Catechesis/Religious Program—Tel: 360-779-6558. Students 390.
Mission—St. Peter 910 South St., Suquamish, Kitsap Co. 98392.

PUYALLUP, PIERCE CO.
1—ALL SAINTS (1899), Very Rev. Richard McCallister; Deacon Michael McGillicuddy.
Office—204 6th, S.W., 98371. Tel: 253-845-7521; Fax: 253-845-3105.
School—504 2nd, S.W., 98371. Tel: 253-845-5025; Fax: 253-435-9841. Lay Teachers 24; Students 379.
School—St. Martin of Tours School (Satellite School), (Grades PreK-2), 2303 54th Ave., E., Fife, 98424. Tel: 253-922-5360. Jack Nelson, Prin.
Catechesis/Religious Program—Students 397.
2—HOLY DISCIPLES (1996), Revs. James Eblen; John Renggli; Rosemary Busby, Pastoral Admin.
Res.: 10425 187th St. E., 98374. Tel: 253-875-6630; Fax: 253-846-9535.
Catechesis/Religious Program—Students 394.
Mission—Our Lady of Good Counsel 229 Antonie Ave. N., Eatonville, Pierce Co. 98328. Tel: 360-832-6363; Fax: 360-832-6363. Deacon Rodney McGuire.

RAYMOND, PACIFIC CO., ST. LAWRENCE (1904), Rev. Victor A. Olvida.
1112 Blake St., P.O. Box 31, 98577. Tel: 360-942-3000; Fax: 360-942-3000.
Catechesis/Religious Program—Fax: 360-942-3028. Students 17.

REDMOND, KING CO., ST. JUDE (1978), [CEM] Revs. Timothy Clark, Admin.; Joseph Stocking, S.J.
Res.: 10526 166th, N.E., 98052. Tel: 425-883-7685; Fax: 425-881-2207.
Catechesis/Religious Program—Tel: 425-883-1456. Students 774.

RENTON, KING CO.
1—ST. ANTHONY (1901), Revs. Gary Zender; Thanh X. Dao; Deacons Richard Combs; Teodoro Rodriguez.
Res.: 314 S. 4th St., 98055. Tel: 425-255-3132; Fax: 425-271-4729.
School—336 Shattuck Ave. S., 98055. Tel: 425-255-0059; Fax: 425-235-6555. Gary Teale, Prin. Sisters 1; Lay Teachers 30; Students 519.
Catechesis/Religious Program—Students 293.
2—ST. STEPHEN THE MARTYR (1966), Revs. John C. Madigan; Brian Snyder; Deacons Marshall Denby; William Eckert; Anselmo Pardo.
Res.: 13055 S.E. 192nd St., 98058. Tel: 253-631-1940; Fax: 425-255-2943.
Catechesis/Religious Program—Tel: 253-631-6175. Students 622.

SAMMAMISH, KING CO., MARY, QUEEN OF PEACE (1987), Revs. J. Paul Dalton; Michael Raschko; Deacons William Taube; William Haines Jr.
Res.: 1121 228th Ave., S.E., 98075. Tel: 425-391-1178; Fax: 425-391-3797.
Catechesis/Religious Program—Students 1,014.

SEAHURST, KING CO., ST. FRANCIS OF ASSISI (1929), Revs. Richard K. Hayatsu; Michael Angelovic.
Res.: 15226 21st Ave., S.W., P.O. Box 929, 98062. Tel: 206-242-4575; Fax: 206-242-1957.
School—P.O. Box 870, 98062. Tel: 206-243-5690; Fax: 206-433-8593. Sheila Keaton, Prin. Lay Teachers 26; Students 484.
Catechesis/Religious Program—Students 130.

SEAVIEW, PACIFIC CO., ST. MARY (1965), Rev. Victor A. Olvida; Deacon Glenn Cliffton.
Res.: P.O. Box 274, 98644. Tel: 360-642-2002; Fax: 360-642-7100.
Catechesis/Religious Program—Students 17.
Station— McGowan.

SEDRO-WOOLLEY, SKAGIT CO., IMMACULATE HEART OF MARY (1890), Very Rev. J. Patrick McDermott; Revs. John Nwanze, O.P.; Daniel Chiezey, O.P.; Gilberto Mora Tapia.
Office:—719 Ferry St., Sedro Woolley, 98284. Tel: 360-855-0077; Fax: 360-855-2282.
Catechesis/Religious Program—Students 54.
Mission—St. Catherine 239 Limestone, Concrete, Skagit Co. 98237.

SEQUIM, CLALLAM CO., ST. JOSEPH (1916), Rev. Thomas Beattie.
Res.: 121 E. Maple, P.O. Box 1209, 98382. Tel: 360-683-6076; Fax: 360-683-4674.
Catechesis/Religious Program—Tel: 360-683-1640. Students 110.

SHELTON, MASON CO., ST. EDWARD (1892), [JC] Rev. Dominic D. Hahn; Deacon William Batstone.
Res.: 321 N. 3rd St., P.O. Box 758, 98584. Tel: 360-426-6134; Fax: 360-426-6231.
Catechesis/Religious Program—Students 125.

SHORELINE, KING CO.
1—ST. LUKE (1955), Rev. John Bowman.
Res.: 322 N. 175th St., 98133. Tel 206-546-2451; Fax: 206-546-0328.
School—17533 St. Luke Pl. N., 98133. Tel: 206-542-1133 Fax: 206-546-8693. Mr. John Allen, Prin. Sisters of St. Dominic 2; Lay Teachers 20; Students 404.
Catechesis/Religious Program—Students 329.
2—ST. MARK (1954), Rev. Otto Koltzenburg. In Res., Very Rev. Anthony Bawyn.
Res.: 18033 15th Pl., N.E., 98155. Tel: 206-364-7900; Fax: 206-367-3919.
School—Tel: 206-364-1633. Kathryn Palmquist-Keck, Prin. Lay Teachers 12; Students 200
Catechesis/Religious Program—Students 180.

SNOHOMISH, SNOHOMISH CO., ST. MICHAEL (1886), Very Rev. Joseph A. De Folco; Deacon Ed White.
Res.: 1512 Pine Ave., 98290. Tel: 360-568-0821; Fax: 360-568-6426.
Catechesis/Religious Program—Tel: 360-568-9660. Students 366.
Mission—Holy Cross 412 W. Wallace St., Granite Falls, Snohomish Co. 98252.

SNOQUALMIE, KING CO., OUR LADY OF SORROWS (1929), Rev. Jan Larson; Deacon Carl Smith.
Res.: 39025 S.E. Alpha St., P.O. Box 909, 98065. Tel: 425-888-2974; Fax: 425-888-7098.
Catechesis/Religious Program—Students 673.
Mission—St. Anthony P.O. Box 175, Carnation, King Co. 98014. Tel: 425-333-4930; Fax: 425-333-5001.
Mission—Holy Innocents P.O. Box 850, Duvall, King Co. 98019. Tel: 425-788-1400; Fax: 425-844-2384. Rev. William Heric.
Station—St. Bernard's Chapel Snoqualmie Summit. Tel: 206-454-6161.

STANWOOD, SNOHOMISH CO., ST. CECILIA (1908), Rev. Paul Koenig, O.C.D. In Res., Rev. Charles Garrity, O.C.D.
Res.: 26900 78th Ave., N.W., P.O. Box 1002, 98292. Tel: 360-629-3737; Fax: 360-629-6127.
Catechesis/Religious Program—Tel: 360-629-4425. Students 197.

SUMNER, PIERCE CO., ST. ANDREW (1921), Rev. David H. Young.
Res.: 704 Kincaid Ave., 98390. Tel: 253-863-2253; Fax: 253-863-3567.
Catechesis/Religious Program—Tel: 253-863-4394. Students 500.
Mission—SS. Cosmas and Damian 213 W. Leber St., Orting, Pierce Co. 98360. Tel: 360-893-3154.

TACOMA, PIERCE CO.
1—ST. ANN (1924), Revs. Vincent Pastro; Dominic Nguyen, S.J.; Poao Saena.
Res.: 7001 S. Park Ave., 98408. Tel: 253-472-1360, Ext. 13; Fax: 253-475-6335.
Catechesis/Religious Program—Tel: 253-472-1360, Ext. 16. Students 77.
2—ST. CHARLES BORROMEO (1956), Revs. Michael J. McDermott; Marc L. Powell.
Res.: 7112 S. 12th St., 98465. Tel: 253-564-5185; Fax: 253-565-0936.
School—Patrick Feist, Prin. Lay Teachers 31; Students 509.
Catechesis/Religious Program—Tel: 253-564-5185, Ext. 3036. Students 310.
3—HOLY CROSS (1915), Rev. Robert Rekofke, S.J.
Res.: 5510 N. 44th St., 98407. Tel: 253-759-3368; Fax: 253-759-6126.
Catechesis/Religious Program—Tel: 253-759-3491. Students 40.
4—HOLY ROSARY (1891), Rev. John J. Wilkie; Deacon Michael Teskey.
Res.: 424 S. 30th St., 98402. Tel: 253-383-4549; Fax: 253-779-0622.
School—504 S. 30th, 98402. Tel: 253-272-7012. Michael Hart, Prin. Lay Teachers 16; Students 197.
5—ST. JOHN OF THE WOODS (1924), Revs. Vincent Pastro; Dominic Nguyen, S.J.; Poao Saena.
Res.: 9903 24th Ave., E., 98445. Tel: 253-537-8551; Fax: 253-537-0459.
Catechesis/Religious Program—Tel: 253-531-7110. Students 97.
6—ST. JOSEPH (1911), (Slovak), Rev. John J. Wilkie; Deacon Michael Teskey.
Res.: 608 S. 34th St., 98418. Tel: 253-472-2489.
7—ST. LEO THE GREAT (1879), Revs. Stephen C. Lantry, S.J. (P); John O'Leary, S.J.; Deacon Michael Riggio.
Res.: 710 S. 13th St., 98405. Tel: 253-272-5136; Fax: 253-272-6285.
Catechesis/Religious Program—Students 141.
8—OUR LADY, QUEEN OF HEAVEN (1893), Rev. John Renggli.
Parish Office—14601 A St. S., 98444. Tel: 253-537-3252; Fax: 253-536-2662.
Catechesis/Religious Program—Students 257.
9—ST. PATRICK (1891), Rev. Seamus Laverty.
Res.: 1001 N. J St., 98403. Tel: 253-383-2783; Fax: 253-627-5396.
School—1112 N. G St., 98403. Tel: 253-272-2297; Fax: 253-383-2003. Mrs. Francie Jordan, Prin. Sisters 1; Lay Teachers 26; Students 440.
Catechesis/Religious Program—Students 175.
10—SS. PETER & PAUL (1892), (Polish), Rev. Piotr Dzikowski, S.Ch.
Res.: 3422 Portland Ave., 98404. Tel: 253-272-5232; Fax: 253-627-7848.
11—ST. RITA (1922), (Italian), Rev. Carmine J. Sacco, S.J.
Res.: 1403 S. Ainsworth, 98405. Tel: 253-627-4851; Fax: 253-274-0436.
Catechesis/Religious Program—Students 51.
12—SACRED HEART (1912), Revs. Vincent Pastro; Dominic Nguyen, S.J.; Poao Saena; Deacon Mauricio Anaya.
Res.: 4520 McKinley Ave., 98404. Tel: 253-472-7738; Fax: 253-475-0071.
Catechesis/Religious Program—Students 147.
13—VISITATION (1892), Rev. Thomas Williams, S.J.
Res.: 3314 S. 58th St., 98409. Tel: 253-473-4960;

Fax: 253-474-8378.
School—3306 S. 58th St., 98409. Tel: 253-474-6424; Fax: 253-474-6718. Constance Gray, Prin. Lay Teachers 10; Students 152.
Catechesis/Religious Program—Students 186.

TOLEDO, LEWIS CO., ST. FRANCIS XAVIER (1838), [CEM] Revs. Tuan V. Nguyen; Timothy W. Ilgen.
Res.: 139 Spencer Rd., 98591. Tel: 360-864-4126; Fax: 360-864-4130.
Catechesis/Religious Program—Students 18.

TUKWILA, KING CO., ST. THOMAS (1912), Rev. Gerald L. Mayovsky.
Res.: 4415 S. 140th St., 98168. Tel: 206-242-5501; Fax: 206-244-9387.
Catechesis/Religious Program—Tel: 206-242-8189. Students 116.

VANCOUVER, CLARK CO.
1—HOLY REDEEMER (2000), Rev. Joseph P. Mitchell. Mailing Address: P.O. Box 871417, 98687-1417. Tel: 360-885-7780; Fax: 360-885-0472.
Church: Mill Plain Center, Ste. A-100, 705 S.E. Parkcrest Ave., 98683.
Catechesis/Religious Program—Students 229.
2—ST. JAMES (1836), [CEM] Revs. Paul Weckert, O.S.B.; Phuong Duc Tran.
Res.: 218 W. 12th St., 98660. Tel: 360-693-3052; Fax: 360-693-3077.
Catechesis/Religious Program—Students 144.
3—ST. JOHN (1868), [CEM] Rev. Armando S. Perez.
Res.: 8701 N.E. 119 St., 98662. Tel: 360-573-3325; Fax: 360-573-3344.
Catechesis/Religious Program—Students 217.
4—ST. JOSEPH (1952), Revs. Hans Olson; Peter Gillette; Robert Hagan.
Res.: 6600 Highland Dr., 98661. Tel: 360-696-4407; Fax: 360-696-3959.
School—6500 Highland Dr., 98661. Tel: 360-696-2586; Fax: 360-696-3959. Lesley Harrison, Prin. Lay Teachers 24; Students 385.
Catechesis/Religious Program—Students 596.
5—OUR LADY OF LOURDES (1958), Rev. John J. Ludvik, Admin.; Deacon Robert Tomich.
Res.: 4723 N.W. Franklin St., 98663. Tel: 360-695-1366; Fax: 360-695-7966.
School—Tel: 360-696-2301; Fax: 360-696-6700. Mrs. Leigh Ann Scherer, Prin. Lay Teachers 22; Students 351.
Catechesis/Religious Program—Students 491.

VASHON, KING CO., ST. JOHN VIANNEY (1964), Rev. Richard R. Roach, S.J.
Res.: P.O. Box 308, 98070. Tel: 206-567-4149; Fax: 206-567-4198.
Mission—St. Patrick 26100 99th Ave., S.W., Dockton, King Co. 98070.

WINLOCK, LEWIS CO., SACRED HEART (1909), [CEM] Revs. Tuan Nguyen; Timothy W. Ilgen.
Res.: 216 N.W. Arden, P.O. Box 69, 98596. Tel: 360-864-4126; Fax: 360-864-4130.
Station— St. Urban.

WOODLAND, COWLITZ CO., ST. PHILIP (1950), [CEM] Rev. Gerald Woodman.
Res.: 430 Bozarth, Box 2169, 98674. Tel: 360-225-8308; Fax: 360-225-8866.
Catechesis/Religious Program—Students 90.
Mission—St. Joseph 4th & Elm, Kalama, Cowlitz Co. 98625. Tel: 360-673-4682 (Hall).

YELM, THURSTON CO., ST. COLUMBAN (1960), Rev. Terence J. Wager, O.S.B.
Res.: 506 1st St. S., 98597. Tel: 360-458-3031; Fax: 360-458-4094.
Mission—St. Peter P.O. Box 744, Sussex & Keithan St., Tenino, Thurston Co. 98589. Tel: 360-264-2124; Fax: 360-264-2666.
Catechesis/Religious Program—Tel: 360-458-2360. Students 132.

Chaplains of Public Institutions

SEATTLE. *Callum Bay Correction Center*. Revs. Kurt Nagel, Reynaldo Yu.
Federal Detention Center SEA-TAC. Deacon Anselmo Pardo, Pastoral Care Min.
Immigration & Naturalization Services. Deacon Anselmo Pardo, Pastoral Care Min.
King County Jail. Sr. Patricia Eilers, O.P., Pastoral Care Min.
U.S. Public Health Hospital. Attended by St. Peter Church, Seattle.
Veterans Administration Medical Center. Rev. Thomas R. Park, O.S.B.

ABERDEEN. *Stafford Creek Correction Center*. Joseph Pelligrino, Pastoral Care Min.

BUCKLEY. *Rainier School*. Rev. James Boyle.
Western State Custodial School. Attended from St. Aloysius Church, Buckley.

CHEHALIS. *Green Hill School*. Rev. Tuan Nguyen.

EVERETT. *Snohomish County Jail*. (Vacant)

FORKS. *Clearwater / Olympic Correction Center*. Revs. Kurt Nagel, Reynaldo Yu.

GIG HARBOR. *Washington Corrections Center for Women*. Mary Rutter, Pastoral Care Min.

KENT. *Regional Justice Center*. Mary Rutter, Pastoral Care Min.

LITTLE ROCK. *Cedar Creek Correction Center*. Joenne Harrhy, Pastoral Care Min.

MCNEIL ISLAND. *McNeil Island Correction Center*. Rev. Thomas Suss.

MONROE. *Monroe Correctional Complex*.
Minimum Security Unit. Sr. Renee Kittleson, M.S.C., Pastoral Min.
Special Offenders Center. Sr. Renee Kittleson, M.S.C., Pastoral Min.
Twin Rivers Correction Center. Rev. Lyle Konen, C.SS.R., Chap.
Monroe Washington State Reformatory. Rev. Lyle Konen, C.Ss.R., Chap., Linda Haptonstall, Pastoral Care Min.

ORTING. *U.S. Soldiers' Home*. Attended by St. Andrew Church, Sumner.

PORT ORCHARD. *Washington Veterans Home Hospital*. Attended by St. Gabriel Church, Port Orchard.

SHELTON. *Washington Corrections Center*, P.O. Box 900, 98584. Shannon O'Donnell, Pastoral Care Min.

SNOQUALMIE. *Echo Glen Children's Center*. Betsy Staal, Pastoral Care Min., Rev. Jan Larson.

STEILACOOM. *Western State Hospital*. Rev. Robert Tino.

TACOMA. *Remann Hall*. Sr. Mary Reitz, S.F.C.C., Pastoral Min.
Veterans Admin. Medical Center. Rev. Leo R. Rimmele, O.S.B.

VANCOUVER. *Veterans Administration Hospital*. Attended from Archdiocese of Portland in Oregon.
Washington State School for the Blind. Attended from St. James Church, Vancouver.
Washington State School for the Deaf. Attended from St. John Church, Vancouver.

YACOLT. *Larch Mountain Correction Center*. Attended by Sacred Heart Church, Battle Ground.

Special Assignment:
Very Revs.—
Magnano, Paul, Vicar for Clergy, 910 Marion St., 98104.
Picton, James, Vicar for Parishes & Faith Communities, 910 Marion St., 98104.
Revs.—
Bawyn, Anthony, Judicial Vicar, 910 Marion St., 98104.
Doogan, Joseph H., J.C.L., Adjunct Judicial Vicar (Retired), 910 Marion St., 98104.
Eblen, James, Theologian, 910 Marion St., 98104.
Raschko, Michael, Theologian, 1614 Summit, #602, 98122.
Rowan, Stephen, Vicar for Education, 910 Marion St., 98104.
Sauer, Timothy J., Dir. Seminarians, 910 Marion St., 98104.
Sevilla, Dennis, Chap., St. Joseph Medical Center, Tacoma, % 910 Marion St., 98104.
Silagan, Gorgonio, Jr., Chap., St. Peter Hospital, Olympia, %Sacred Heart, P.O. Box 3805, Lacey, 98509.
Stehly, Mark, Hospital Ministry, South Seattle, Deanery, 910 Marion St., 98104. Tel: 201-382-3492

On Duty Outside the Archdiocese:
Revs.—
Larrivee, Leo J., S.S., 4210 N. Charles St., #3, Baltimore, MD 21218.
Nguyen, Hung, c/o 910 Marion St., 98104.

Military Chaplains:
Rev.—
Bailey, J. Lawrence, 4648 Clint Ct., Montgomery, AL 36106-3551.

Unassigned:
Revs.—
Hart, Brian, 910 Marion St., 98104.
Southerton, Gary, 910 Marion St., 98104.

Retired:
Revs.—
Aspiras, Jose, Station Rita East, Agoo, La Union Philippines.
Basso, Richard, 6909 Weedin Pl., N.E. #B202, 98115.
Brant, David A., 804 9th Ave., 98104.
Bulger, John, 54 Mitchell St., Pittson, PA 18640.
Chirico, Peter, S.S., 603 Maiden Choice Ln., Baltimore, MD 21228.
Cloquet, Victor, P.O. Box 1232, Allyn, 98524-1232.
Crosse, Charles, 8539 Zircon Dr., S.W. #74, Tacoma, 98498.
Delahunty, Thomas, 4700 S.W. Dash Point Rd. #G-2, Federal Way, 98023.
Domandich, Anthony, 4457 S.E. Oatfield Hill Rd. #1B, Milwaukie, OR 97267.
Doogan, Joseph H., J.C.L., 3307 Dravus, 98199.
Gallagher, Richard, 5809 S. 234th Pl., Kent, 98032.
Gallagher, William E., 6108 N. Park, Tacoma, 98407.
Gandrau, James, 910 Marion St., 98104.
Godley, Patrick, 15892 West Arrowhead Dr., Surprise, AR 85374.
Heffernan, Raymond, P.O. Box 1489, Friday Harbor, 98250.
Heneghan, Jarlath, Knock, Claremorris, County Mayo, Ireland.
Horan, John, 4700 Dash Point Rd., #E4, Federal Way, 98023.
Jennings, John A., 4700 Dash Point Rd., #E2, Federal Way, 98023.
Jonientz, Bernard, 12028 71st Ave. S., #F-294, 98178.
Koehler, John, Harborview Apartments #14, 2902 N. Carr St., Tacoma, 98403.
Kramis, Joseph, 2009 Walker Park Rd., Shelton, 98584.
Lane, William, 4700 S.W. Dash Point Rd. #E1, Federal Way, 98023.
Lovett, Gerald F., 4700 S.W. Dash Point Rd. #G3, Federal Way, 98023.
Lynch, Ibar, 1964 26th Ave. W. #201, 98199.
Mallahan, James, 949 N. 35th St., #103, 98103.
McCloskey, Lester, 502 43rd Ave. S.E. 14B, Puyallup, 98374.
McEnnis, Thomas, 10343 W. Cameo Dr., Sun City, AZ 85351.
McLaughlin, John, 1930 S.E. Oakview Dr., Chehalis, 98532.
McMullan, John, Mary Queen of Universe Shrine, 8300 Vineland Ave., Orlando, FL 32821.
Meyer, Clayton, 721 S.E. Fairwinds Loop, Vancouver, 98661.
Moore, Gerald T., c/o 910 Marion St., 98104.
Naumes, Matthew, 8818 East G. St., Tacoma, 98445.
O'Brien, Patrick, 2303 54th Ave. E., Fife, 98424.
O'Brien, Roger, 7328 196th St., S.W., #203, Lynnwood, 98036.
O'Callaghan, Thomas, P.O. Box 346, Suquamish, 98392.
O'Neil, Michael, 8700 E. University Dr. #1712, Mesa, AZ 85207.
O'Shea, Joseph, P.O. Box 675, Woodland, 98674.
Petosa, Joseph, 17117 40th Ave. W., Lynnwood, 98037.
Phelan, Thomas, 512 S.E. 169th Ave., Vancouver, 98684-8413.
Quigg, Harold, 910 Marion St., 98104.
Quinn, Thomas, Aclare P.O., Cligo, Ireland.
Rice, John A., 1208-6455 Willingdon Ave., Burnaby BC V5H 4E4 Canada.
Rink, George, 1828 S.W. 318th Pl., Unit D, Federal Way, 98023.
Slate, William, P.O. Box 4258, Kent, 98032.
Sondergeld, Theodore, 2627 S. 310th, Federal Way, 98003.
Szeman, Stephen J., 4814 N.E. 5th Ct., Renton, 98059.
Tolang, Jaime, 820 18th Ave., 98122.
Treacy, William, 6511 176th St. S.W., Lynnwood, 98037.
White, David, 10501 8th Ave. N., 98125.

Permanent Deacons:
Alcorta, David P.
Alexander, Richard
Allen, Daniel
Anaya, Mauricio
Anderson, Carl
Anderson, David
Batstone, William
Bell, Robert
Bemis, James
Benedict, Nathan
Bentley, Ernest
Cavanaugh, Robert
Childs, Ted
Cliffton, Glenn
Combs, Richard
Connor, Joseph
Cordova, Frederick
Crandall, Charles
Cummins, Donald
Curtis, Joseph
Dardis, Robert
Denby, Marshall
Dolan, Robert
Duffell, Dennis
Dunne, Joseph
Eckert, William
Edtl, Leland
Ellis, Rolland
Erskine, Thomas
Ficken, George
Fraczek, Henry
Gorman, Lawrence
Greer, Jeffrey

Haines, William, Jr.
Hanika, Donald
Hartzell, Clay
Hawkins, F. Thomas
Hoover, Delbert
Huelett, William
Kelley, Patrick
Khieraty, Lawrence
Kim, Duk
Kreilkamp, Ben
Krempl, Joseph
La Russa, John
Lane, Loren
Lezcano, Juan
MacPherson, Bruce
Magana, Abel
Magnuson, John
Maher, Dean
Marcell, Terrance
McGillicuddy, Michael
McGuire, Rodney
Miller, Gene
Monuteaux, Lawrence
Mounce, George, III
Moyer, Carlton
Moynihan, Patrick
Murdy, Don
Myer, Philip
Naranjo, Carlos
O'Loane, Philip
Olsen, Richard
Pardo, Anselmo
Parsons, Eamon D.
Pele, Sagato
Pellegrino, Joseph
Peterson, George
Read, Edward
Ricciardi, John
Riggio, Michael
Rodriguez, Theodoro
Roscoe, John
Rupno, Robert
Scupp, John
Shawver, William
Shields, Walter J.
Smith, Carl
Snider, Lloyd
Stenson, Mark
Sullivan, Lawrence
Tanasse, William
Taube, William
Teskey, Michael
Tomich, Robert
Townsend, William
Vanderzanden, Gene
Warfield, T. Jackson
Warmuth, David
White, Edward, Sr.
Wiese, Theodore
Wilson, Howard
Wodzanowski, Stephen
Yang, Joua Pao
Yuen, Joseph
Zellmer, Gary
Zuanich, Matthew

INSTITUTIONS LOCATED IN THE ARCHDIOCESE

[A] COLLEGES AND UNIVERSITIES

SEATTLE. *Seattle University*, 900 Broadway, 98122. Tel: 206-296-6000; Fax: 206-296-6200. Web: www.seattleu.edu. Revs. Stephen V. Sundborg, S.J., Pres.; Michael S. Bayard, S.J.; Arturo Araujo, S.J.; Gerald T. Cobb, S.J.; Peter B. Ely, S.J., Rector; Joseph C. Fortier, S.J.; John F. Foster, S.J.; Ronald R. Funke, S.J.; Roger S. Gillis, S.J.; Anton T. Harris, S.J.; Patrick J. Howell, S.J.; Paul A. Janowiak, S.J.; Michael M. Kelliher, S.J.; William F. LeRoux, S.J.; David J. Leigh, S.J.; Joseph O. McGowan, S.J.; Thomas R.E. Murphy, S.J.; Patrick B. O'Leary, S.J.; Lammert B. Otten, S.J.; James B. Reichmann, S.J.; Richard R. Roach, S.J.; Joseph Stocking, S.J.; William J. Sullivan, S.J.; Michael J. Taylor, S.J.; L. John Topel, S.J.; Josef V. Venker, S.J.; Theodore E. Zembal, S.J. Priests 28; Lay Teachers 426; Students 6,337.

LACEY. *Saint Martin's College*, 5300 Pacific Ave., S.E., 98503. Tel: 360-491-4700; Fax: 360-459-4124. Email: admissions@stmartin.edu. Web: www.stmartin.edu. Dr. David R. Spangler, Pres.; Mr. Robert Miller, Interim Vice Pres. Academic Affairs. Order of St. Benedict Master's Comprehesive College., Resident and non-resident students. Main Campus & Extension Campuses 1,502.

[B] HIGH SCHOOLS, ARCHDIOCESAN

SEATTLE. *Bishop Blanchet High School* (Coed) , 8200 Wallingford Ave. N., 98103. Tel: 206-527-7711; Fax: 206-527-7712. Email: info@blanchet.k12.wa.us. Web: www.blanchet.k12.wa.us. Mr. Kent P. Hickey, Prin.; Rev. Gordon Douglas. Sisters 1; Lay Teachers 75; Students 1,070.

John F. Kennedy Memorial High School (Coed) , 140 S. 140th, 98168. Tel: 206-246-0500; Fax: 206-242-0831. Email: info@kennedyhs.org. Web: www.kennedyhs.org. Mr. John Schuster, Prin.; Rev. Michael J. Batterberry. Priests 1; Lay Teachers 67; Students 860.

O'Dea High School (Boys) , 802 Terry Ave., 98104. Tel: 206-622-6596; Fax: 206-340-4110. Email: dmuray@odea.org. Web: www.odea.org. Bro. Dominic Murray, C.F.C., Prin. Conducted by the Congregation of Christian Brothers. Brothers 7; Lay Teachers 30; Students 485.

[C] HIGH SCHOOLS, PRIVATE

SEATTLE. *Holy Names Academy* (Girls) , 728 21st Ave. E., 98112. Tel: 206-323-4272; Fax: 206-323-5254. Email: eswift@holynames-sea.org. Web: www.holynames-sea.org. Ms. Elizabeth Swift, Prin. Congregation of the Sisters of the Holy Names of Jesus and Mary Sisters 4; Lay Teachers 38; Students 610.

Seattle Preparatory School, 2400-11th Ave. E., 98102. Tel: 206-324-0400; Fax: 206-323-6509. Email: tfields@seaprep.org. Web: www.seaprep.org. Rev. Robert D. Vance, S.J., Pres.; Dr. Matt Barmore, Prin. Priests 2; Lay Teachers 43; Students 657.

BELLEVUE. *Eastside Catholic High School* (Coed) , 11650 S.E. 60th, 98006. Tel: 425-644-7737; Fax: 425-644-8127. Web: www.echs.bellevue.wa.us. Jim Kubacki, Pres.; Greg Marsh, Prin. Priests 1; Lay Teachers 42; Students 460.

Forest Ridge School of the Sacred Heart, (Grades 5-12) , (Girls) , 4800 139th Ave., S.E., 98006. Tel: 425-641-0700; Fax: 425-643-3881. Email: msmith@forestridge.org. Web: www.forestridge.org. Dr. Mary M. Smith, Head of School. Religious of the Sacred Heart 1; Lay Teachers 44; Students 352.

EVERETT. *Archbishop Thomas J. Murphy High School* (Coed) , 12911 39th Ave., S.E., 98208-6159. Tel: 425-379-6363; Fax: 425-385-2875. Web: www.archbishopmurphyhs.org. Dr. Kristine Brynildsen-Smith, Prin. Students 331; Lay Teachers 29.

TACOMA. *Bellarmine Preparatory School* (Coed) , 2300 S. Washington, 98405. Tel: 253-752-7701; Fax: 253-756-3887. Web: www.bellarmineprep.org. Rev. Michael A. Tyrrell, S.J., Rector; Mr. Jack Peterson, Pres. Owned by the Jesuit Fathers. Board of Directors: 4 members of the Jesuit order and 16 others. Priests 10; Brothers 2; Sisters 1; Scholastics 1; Lay Teachers 77; Students 1,015. In Res. Revs. Gerard E. Chapdelaine, S.J.; Robert A. Goebel, S.J. (SRA); Frederick P. Mayovsky, S.J.; Dominic Nguyen, S.J.; Thomas Sexton, S.J.; Francis Walsh, S.J.; Michael B. Walsh, S.J.; Daniel C. Weber, S.J.; Thomas G. Williams, S.J.; Bros. Patrick Flannigan, S.J.; Michael Richards, S.J.; Mr. Stephen J. Kieta.

[D] ELEMENTARY SCHOOLS, PRIVATE

SEATTLE. *Villa Academy*, (Grades PreK-8) , (Coed) , 5001 N.E. 50th St., 98105. Tel: 206-524-8885; Fax: 206-523-7131. Email: pskinner@thevilla.org. Web: www.thevilla.org. Pauline Skinner Head of School. Lay Teachers 39; Students 399.

CAMAS. *Pacific Crest Academy*, (Grades PreK-8), 324 N.E. Oak St., P.O. Box 1031, 98607-1031. Tel: 360-834-9913; Fax: 360-834-9926. Email: paccrest@familink.com. Web: www.pacificcrestacademy.org. Mrs. Carolyn Simms, Prin. Lay Teachers 8; Students 70.

LACEY. *Holy Family School*, (Grades PreK-8), 2606 Carpenter Rd., S.E., P.O. Box 3700, 98503. Tel: 360-491-7060; Fax: 360-456-3725. Email: holyfamilyschool@comcast.net. Web: hfslacey.com. Linda Farrimond, Prin. Lay Teachers 15; Students 153.

[E] CATHOLIC COMMUNITY SERVICES OF THE ARCHDIOCESE OF SEATTLE

SEATTLE. *Catholic Charities Foundation*, 100 23rd Ave., S., 98144-2302. Tel: 206-328-5696; Fax: 206-328-5699. Michael Reichert, Pres.

Catholic Community Services of Western Washington, 100 23rd Ave. S., 98144-2302. Tel: 206-328-5696; 206-328-5646 (TTY); Fax: 206-328-5699. Web: www.catholiccharitiesseattlearch.org. Michael L. Reichert, Pres.

Catholic Community Services Northwest, 1918 Everett Ave., Everett, 98201. Tel: 425-257-2111; Fax: 425-257-2120. Thomas MacIntyre, Agency Dir.

Whatcom Family Center, 1133 Railroad Ave., Ste. 100, Bellingham, 98225-5054. Tel: 360-676-2164; Fax: 360-676-2144. Kathy McNaughton, Dir.

Skagit Family Center, 320 Pacific Pl. P.O. Box 2909, Mt. Vernon, 98273-7909. Tel: 360-416-7546; Fax: 360-416-7541. Janet Simpson, Dir.

Snohomish Family Center, 1918 Everett Ave., Everett, 98201. Tel: 425-257-2111; Fax: 425 257-2120.

Catholic Community Services of King County, 100-23rd Ave. S., 98144-2302. Tel: 206-323-6336; 206-328-5646 (TDD); Fax: 206-324-4835. Josephine Tamayo Murray, Agency Dir. Tel: 206-328-5701.

Randolph Carter Family Learning Center, 100 23rd Ave S., 98144-2302. Tel: 206-328 5774; Fax: 206-324-4835. Evelyn Thomas Allen, Dir.

East King County Family Center, 14044 N.E. 8th, Bellevue, 98007. Tel: 425-643-1937; Fax: 425-562-6871. Michelle Robertson, Dir.

South King County Family Center, 1229 W. Smith St., P.O. Box 398, Kent, 98035. Tel: 253-854-0077; Fax: 253-850-2503. Cameryn Flynn, Dir.

Catholic Community Services Southwest, 1323 S. Yakima St., Tacoma, 98405. Tel: 253-383-3697; Fax: 253-572-3193. Denny Hunthausen, Agency Dir.

Grays Harbor Family Center, 306 E. 3rd St., Aberdeen, 98520. Tel: 360-533-9470; Fax: 360-533-9473. Web: www.ccsww.org. Mike Curry, Dir.

Clark / Skamania Family Center, 902 Esther, Vancouver, 98660. Tel: 360-750-6918; Fax: 360-750-6921. Patricia deVargas Walker, Dir.

Cowlitz / Wahkiakum Family Center, 2200 Alllen St., Kelso, 98626. Tel: 360-577-2200; Fax: 360-577-2205. Patricia deVargas Walker, Dir.

Tahoma Family Center, 1323 S. Yakima, Tacoma, 98405-4457. Tel: 253-383-3697; Fax: 253-572-3193. Susie Hofstedt, Dir.

Northend Family Center, 5410 N. 44th St., Tacoma, 98407. Tel: 253-759-9544; Fax: 253-759-9512. Mary Stone Smith.

Max Hale Family Center, 285 Fifth St., Ste. 2, Bremerton, 98337. Tel: 360-792-2020; Fax: 360-478-6993.

Thurston County Family Center, 2940 Limited Ln., N.W., P.O. Box 11399, Olympia, 98508. Tel: 360-586-2960; Fax: 360-586-2930. Gary Sandwick, Dir.

Archdiocesan Housing Authority (AHA), 1902 Second Ave., 98101. Tel: 206-328-5660; Fax: 206-328-5692. Michael L. Reichert, Pres.

Redmond Elderly Housing Association, 7960-169th Ave, N.E., Redmond, 98053. Tel: 425-869-2424. Michael L. Reichert, Pres.

AHA-Pierce County Association, 112 S. 127th, Tacoma, 98444. Tel: 253-845-3557. Michael L. Reichert, Pres.

St. Martin's Housing Institute, 2008 Westlake Ave., 98121. Tel: 206-340-0410. Michael L. Reichert, Pres.

Halcyon Foundation, 1200 134th Ave., N.E., Bellevue, 98005. Tel: 425-643-7806.

Catholic Community Services of Western Washington Long Term Care System Tel: 253-383-3697; Fax: 253-272-6356. Peter Nazzal, Dir.

Seattle & North King Co. Office, 100 23rd Ave. S., 98144-2302. Tel: 800-310-5654. Lynn Joebgen, Contact Person.

Aberdeen Office, P.O. Box 1734, 3rd St. & H St., Aderdeen, 98520-4003. Tel: 877-870-1582. Dawn Clark, Contact Person.

Bellingham Office, 1133 Railroad Ave., Bellingham, 98225. Tel: 888-300-2493. Lynn Joebgen, Contact Person.

Bremerton Office, 285 5th St.. Ste. 3, Bremerton, 98337. Tel: 800-642-8019.

Chehalis Office, P.O. Box 1152, Chehalis, 98532. Tel: 800-642-8021. Dawn Clark, Contact Person.

Everett Office, 1918 Everett Ave., Everett, 98201. Tel: 800-562-4663. Lynn Joebgen, Contact Person.

Kent Office, P.O. Box 398, Kent, 98035. Tel: 800-722-3479. Lynn Joebgen, Contact Person.

Port Angeles Office Tel: 877-870-1582. Carol Krula, Contact Person.

Shelton Office, P.O. Box 1228, Shelton, 98584-0947. Tel: 800-642-8026. Dawn Clark.

Tacoma Office, 1323 S. Yakima St., Tacoma, 98405. Tel: 253-502-2716; Fax: 253-272-6356. Carol Krula, Dir.

Olympia Office, P.O. Box 11399, Olympia, 98508-1399. Tel: 360-586-2960; Fax: 360-586-2930.

[F] CHILD CARE SERVICES

SEATTLE. *Martin Luther King. Jr., Day Home Center*, 1855 S. Ln., 98144. Tel: 206-328-5670; Fax: 206-325-5922. Email: michaelk@ccsww.org. Mr. Michael L. Koetje, Dir. Total Staff 9; Total Assisted 75.

Our Place Day Care, 1307 E. Spring St., 98122. Tel: 206-328-5724; Fax: 206-720-0337. Email: debrab@

ccsww.org. Debra Brown, Dir.

Providence Mt. St. Vincent Child Care, 4831 35th Ave., S.W., 98126-2799. Tel: 206-938-6784; Fax: 206-938-8999.

EVERETT. *Tree of Life Program*, 10110 19th Ave., S.E., #R100, 98208. Tel: 425-337-7817; Fax: 425-337-6586.

OLYMPIA. *St. Mike's Tikes*, 1010 Eastside St., S.E., 98501. Tel: 360-586-1585; Fax: 360-586-1584.

POULSBO. *St. Olaf's Daycare*, 18943 Caldart Ave., N.E., 98370. Tel: 360-779-5791; Fax: 360-598-5888.

TACOMA. *Kids' Place Child Care Center*, P.O. Box 1637, 98405. Tel: 253-305-0836; Fax: 253-383-5273. Email: deborahh@ccsww.org. Web: www.ccsww.org.

System Child Care Director, 1323 S. Yakima St., 98405. Tel: 253-502-2686; Fax: 253-502-2750. Email: dawnl@ccsww.org. Dawn Larsen, Coord.

[G] HOSPITALS

SEATTLE. *Providence Health System*, 506 2nd Ave., Ste.1200, 98104-2329. Tel: 206-464-3355; Fax: 206-464-3038. Email: hankwalker@providence.org. Sr. Barbara Schamber, S.P., Team Leader/Prov. Supr.; Hank Walker, Pres. & CEO.

BELLINGHAM. *St. Joseph Hospital*, 2901 Squalicum Pkwy., 98225. Tel: 360-734-5400; Fax: 360-738-6393. Web: www.peacehealth.org. Nancy Bitting, Admin.; Chris Phillips, Dir. Mission and Community Outreach. Sisters of St. Joseph of Peace and PeaceHealth Sisters 4; Bed Capacity 253; Patients Assisted Annually 25,426; Total Staff 1,950.

The Martin Center (A children's mental health hospital) , 2806 Douglas Ave., 98225. Tel: 306-676-2187. Total Staff 50; Children 14.

CENTRALIA. *Providence Centralia Hospital*, 914 S. Scheuber Rd., 98531. Tel: 360-736-2803; Fax: 360-330-8614. Email: steveburdick@providence.org. Web: providence.org. Steven Burdick, Admin.

Legal Title: *Providence Health Sytem dba Providence Centralia Hospital* Bed Capacity 191; Patients Assisted Annually 140,000; Total Staff 690.

EVERETT. *Providence Everett Medical Center - Colby Campus*, 1321 Colby Ave., P.O. Box 1147, 98206. Tel: 425-261-2000; Fax: 425-261-4051. Web: www.providence.org/everett/. Gail C. Larson, CEO; Sr. Dorothy Klingele, S.P., Sister Representative. Sisters 3; Bed Capacity 369; Patients Assisted Annually 181,474; Total Staff 3,227.

FEDERAL WAY. *St. Francis Hospital of Federal Way*, 34515 9th Ave. S., 98003-6761. Tel: 253-927-9700; 253-838-9700; Fax: 253-952-7988. Email: sydbersaute@chiwest.com. Web: fhshealth.org. Sisters of St. Francis of Philadelphia Bed Capacity 110; Patients Assisted Annually 87,675; Total Staff 810.

LAKEWOOD. *St. Clare Hospital*, 11315 Bridgeport Way, S.W., 98499. Tel: 253-588-1711; Fax: 253-512-2833. Email: bettyumemoto@chiwest.com. Web: www.fhshealth.org. Brooks Sutton, COO; Dianna Kielian, Vice Pres., Mission & Ministry. Sisters of St. Francis of Philadelphia Bed Capacity 106; Patients Assisted Annually 70,247; Total Staff 623.

LONGVIEW. *PeaceHealth, St. John Medical Center*, 1615 Delaware St., P.O. Box 3002, 98632. Tel: 360-414-2000; Fax: 360-414-7550. Web: www.peacehealth.org. Sisters of St. Joseph of Peace and PeaceHealth Sisters of St. Joseph of Peace 3; Bed Capacity 346; Patients Assisted Annually 173,838; Total Staff 1,570.

OLYMPIA. *Providence St. Peter Hospital*, 413 Lilly Rd., N.E., 98506. Tel: 360-491-9480; Fax: 360-493-7268. Mr. Scott Bond, Admin.

Legal Title: *Sisters of Providence - Mother Joseph Province* Bed Capacity 390; Patients Assisted Annually 313,569; Total Staff 1,422.

TACOMA. *St. Joseph Medical Center*, 1717 S. J St., P.O. Box 2197, 98405-2197. Tel: 253-627-4101; Fax: 253-591-6880. Email: annemcnamara@chiwest.com. Web: www.fhshealth.org. Joseph Wilczek, CEO; Rev. Urban Feucht, O.S.B. Sisters of St. Francis of Philadelphia Sisters 3; Bed Capacity 320; Patients Assisted Annually 373,929; Total Staff 3,131.

[H] NURSING HOMES

SEATTLE. *Providence Mount St. Vincent*, 4831 35th Ave., S.W., 98126. Tel: 206-937-3700; Fax: 206-938-8999. Email: charleneboyd@providence.org. Web: www.providence.org/themount. Ms. Charlene Boyd, Admin.; Rev. Brian J. McGovern, Chap.

Legal Title: *Sisters of Providence - Mother Joseph Province* Sisters 3; Bed Capacity 215; Apartments 112; Total Assisted Annually 575; Total Staff 500.

ISSAQUAH. *Providence Marianwood*, 3725 Providence Point Dr., S.E., 98029. Tel: 425-391-2800; Fax: 425-391-5440. Email: ahughes@providence.org. Web: www.providencemarianwood.org. Ms. Ann E. Hughes, Admin.; Deanna Murray, Pastoral Care Svcs. Sisters of Providence Health System Bed Capacity 120; Total Assisted Annually 450; Total Staff 200.

[I] HOSPICES

EVERETT. *Providence Home Care and Hospice of Snohomish County*, 2731 Wetmore Ave., #520, 98201. Tel: 425-261-4805; Fax: 425-261-4868. Web: www.providence.org/phhc. Served 3,964; Total Staff 160.

OLYMPIA. *Providence Mother Joseph Care Center*, 3333 Ensign Rd., N.E., 98506. Tel: 360-493-4900; Fax: 360-493-4000. Vivian Currie, Admin.; Beverly Jenden, Pastoral Care. Total Staff 235; Patients Assisted Annually 837.

Providence Sound HomeCare and Hospice, 3432 South Bay Rd., P.O. Box 5008, 98501. Tel: 800-869-7062; 360-459-8311; Fax: 360-493-4657. Web: www.providence.org. Doug Jena, Exec. Dir. Staff 208; Patients Assisted Annually 6,800.

[J] RESIDENCES FOR ELDERLY, DISABLED, OR LOW INCOME

SEATTLE. *Broadway House*, 2609 Broadway Ave. E., 98102. Tel: 206-860-4272; Fax: 206-860-5155. Email: shelleyd@ccsww.org. Total Assisted 7; Total Staff 2.

Chancery Place, 910 Marion St., # 1307, 98104. Tel: 206-343-9415; Fax: 206-343-0680. Barbara Lindahl, Mgr. Total Apartments 84; Total Staff 4.

The Franciscan, 15237 21st Ave., S.W., 98166. Tel: 206-431-8001; Fax: 206-431-1254. Total Units 38; Total Staff 4.

Heritage House at The Market, 1533 Western Ave., 98101. Tel: 206-382-4119; Fax: 206-382-0201. Email: heritagehouse@providence.org. Total Assisted 75; Total Staff 40.

Providence Mount St. Vincent, 4831 35th Ave. S., 98126. Tel: 206-937-3700; Fax: 206-938-8999. Email: charlene.boyd@providence.org. Web: www.providence.org/themount. Rev. Brian J. McGovern, Chap.; Sr. Mary Rose Deloria, Dir. of Spiritual Care. Total Assisted 500; Residents 319; Total Staff 500.

Providence Peter Claver House, Formerly Providence Peter Claver, 7101 38th Ave. S., 98118. Tel: 206-721-6265; Fax: 206-721-1327. Email: chauneyboyle@providence.org. Sr. Chauney Boyle, S.P., Housing Dir. Units 80; Total Assisted Annually 96; Total Staff 4.

Providence Vincent House, 1423 First Ave., 98101. Tel: 206-682-9307; Fax: 206-682-0548. Sponsored by the Sisters of Providence. Staff 3; Residents 60.

Spruce Park Apartments, 155 21st Ave., 98122. Tel: 206-322-0450; Fax: 206-328-6637. Email: brendag@ccsww.org. Staff 3; Assisted 119.

The Westlake, 2008 Westlake Ave., 98121. Tel: 206-340-0410; Fax: 206-682-8843. Email: west1@drizzle.com. Total Staff 10; Total in Residence 63.

BELLEVUE. *Champion House*, 1800 145th Pl., S.E., 98007-6209. Tel: 425-644-4477; Fax: 425-746-0438. Email: championhse@aol.com. Web: www.hhftd.org. Total Staff 13; Total Assisted 8.

Elbert House, 16000 N.E. 8th St., 98008. Tel: 206-747-5111; Fax: 425-641-3141. Total Assisted Annually 49; Total Staff 2.

Halcyon, 1200 134th Ave., N.E., 98005. Tel: 206-643-7806; Fax: 206-746-0438. Email: bblhelpinghands@comcast.net. Web: www.hhftd.org. Total Assisted Annually 8; Total Staff 13.

CHEHALIS. *Providence Place*, 350 S.E. Washington Ave., 98532. Tel: 360-740-8389; Fax: 360-740-6504. Sponsored by The Sisters of Providence. Residents 60.

REDMOND. *Emma McRedmond Manor*, 7960 169th, N.E., 98052. Tel: 206-869-2424; Fax: 425-558-5526. Apartments 31; Total Staff 2.

SPANAWAY. *Norm Fournier Court*, 112 S. 127th, 98444. Tel: 253-531-5087. Units 20; Total Staff 2.

TACOMA. *Franciscan Health System, Care Center at Tacoma*, 6220 S. Alaska, 98408. Tel: 253-473-2273; Fax: 253-475-2921. Linda Larson, Admin. CHI-Catholic Health Initiatives. Total Staff 150; Licensed skilled beds 123.

TUMWATER. *Tumwater Apartments*, 5701 6th Ave., S.W., G - 1, 98501-8517. Tel: 360-352-4321; Fax: 360-352-3557. Email: jerryb@ccsww.org. Units 53; Total Staff 1.

[K] SOCIAL SERVICES

SEATTLE. *Association for Catholic Childhood*, 100 23rd Ave. S., 98144. Tel: 206-328-5973; Fax: 206-328-5699. Email: acc@ccsww.org. Mary Lou Wickwire, Pres.

Catholic Seamen's Club, 2330 1st Ave., 98121. Tel: 206-441-4773; Fax: 206-441-8059. Email: aosseattle@aol.com. Rev. Anthony J. Haycock, Chap. Total Assisted 21,450.

Sea-Tac Airport Tel: 206-324-7100, Ext. 14. Deacon Joseph Dunne. Tel: 206-324-7100, Ext. 14.

St. Mary Church: 611 20th Ave. S., 98144. Tel: 206-324-7100, Ext. 14.

St. Francis House, 169 12th Ave., 98122. Tel: 206-621-0945. Stephanie Ragland, Dir. Third Order of St. Francis, Sponsor

Providence ElderPlace, 5900 Martin Luther King Jr. Way S., 98118. Tel: 206-320-5325; Fax: 206-320-5326. Email: ellengarcia@providence.org. Ellen Garcia, Exec. Dir.

Providence Regina House, 8201 10th Ave. S. #6, 98108. Tel: 206-763-9204. Lisa McAlister, Mgr.

Sojourner Place, 5071 8th Ave., N.E., 98105. Tel: 206-545-4200; Fax: 206-633-3525. Email: sojourner@faxinternet.net. Sisters of Providence - Mother Joseph Province Staff 1; Residents 8.

AUBURN. *Society of St. Vincent de Paul - Mother Joseph Council Store*, 926 Auburn Way N. & 717 Auburn Way N., P.O. Box 604, 98002. Tel: 253-833-0400. P.O. Box 604, 98071. Total Staff 21; Total Assisted 2,375.

BREMERTON. *St. Vincent de Paul Assistance Office*, 1137 N. Callow, 98312. Tel: 360-479-7017; Fax: 360-479-2182. Email: stupbrem@douobi.net. Total Staff 3; Total Assisted Annually 13,820.

Thrift Store, 1117 N. Callow, 98312. Tel: 360-377-2929; Fax: 360-479-2182.

CENTRALIA. *Upper Room Ministry*, 115 S. Oak, 98531-4241. Tel: 360-807-1618; Fax: 360-802-9490. Email: elizjoyce@localaccess.com. Sisters Elizabeth Joyce, S.P., Dir.; Virinia Miller, S.P., Dir.

EVERETT. *Society of St. Vincent de Paul* Council of Snohomish County , 6424 Broadway, P.O. Box 2269, 98213. Tel: 425-513-6052; Fax: 425-513-6051. Email: davealcorta_svdp@hotmail.com. Web: www.svdpsnoh.org. Deacon David P. Alcorta, Exec. Dir.

KENMORE. *Society of St. Vincent de Paul - Archdiocesan Council of Seattle/Western Washington*, Formerly Society of St. Vincent de Paul - Archdiocesan Council7304 N.E. Bothell Way, 98028. Tel: 425-483-5038. Email: elleprin@aol.com. Ellen Pringle, Pres.

Society of St. Vincent de Paul District - Archdiocesan Council of Seattle/Western Washington, 5950 4th Ave. S., 98108-3208. Tel: 206-767-9975. Mr. Joseph Roberts, Pres.- District Council of Seattle/King Co.

Society of St. Vincent de Paul - Stores - District Council of Seattle/King Co.

No. 1, 13555 Aurora Ave. N., 98133. Tel: 206-364-8495.

No. 2, 9835 16th Ave., S.W., 98106. Tel: 206-763-2130.

No. 3, 13445 1st Ave. S., 98166. Tel: 206-243-6370.

No. 4, 2825 Sunset Blvd., N.E., Renton, 98056. Tel: 425-226-9426.

No. 5 Reunion Store, 5950 4th Ave. S., 98108-3208. Tel: 206-763-8729.

No. 6, 4503 Tolt Ave. S., Carnation, 98014. Tel: 425-333-6944.

OLYMPIA. *Sunshine House/Providence of St. Peter Hospital*, Formerly Sunshine House413 N. Lilly Rd., 98506. Tel: 360-493-7900; Fax: 360-493-5569. Email: kristina.trebil@providence.org. Web: www.providence.org/swsa/patient_resouces/sunshine.htm.

Legal Title: *Providence Health System, WA* Total Staff 8; Total Assisted 5,000.

SEQUIM. *Society of St. Vincent de Paul and Related Stores* District Council of Olympic Peninsula , 1884 Cays Rd., 98382. Tel: 360-681-5342. Email: bjmuir@tenforward.com. Mr. James B. Muir, Pres.

TACOMA. *Society of St. Vincent de Paul - Particular Council of Tacoma*, 4009 S. 56th, 98409. Tel: 253-474-0519; Fax: 253-473-2176. Email: supptacoma@aol.com. Thomas Erskine, Exec. Dir.

Society of St. Vincent de Paul Stores- District Council of Tacoma Stores and Workshop, Tel: 253-474-0519. Email: suppTacoma@aol.com.

No. 1, 4009 S. 56th St., 98409. Tel: 253-474-0519; Fax: 253-473-2176.

No. 2, 3805-07 S. Yakima Ave., 98408. Tel: 253-472-7334.

No. 3, 113 Meeker W., 98371. Tel: 253-848-5637. Total Assisted 3,882.

[L] MONASTERIES AND RESIDENCES OF PRIESTS AND BROTHERS

SEATTLE. *Congregation of Christian Brothers* (Irish Christian Brothers) , 1021 Columbia St., 98104-2018. Tel: 206-622-2639; Fax: 206-340-4110. Bros. John Austin Pettit, C.F.C., Community Leader; William A. Dogan, C.F.C.; J. Hugh Greenan, C.F.C.; Jerome A. Heustis, C.F.C., Deputy Community Leader; Robert A. Koppes, C.F.C.; G. Gregory Lindeman, C.F.C.; James R.

McDonald, C.F.C.; D. Dominic Murray, C.F.C., Prin.; E. E. St. Martin, C.F.C. Brothers 9.

Jesuit Community, 2838 Broadway E., 98102. Tel: 206-324-0329. Email: ecarroll@nwjesuits.org. Revs. Emmett H. Carroll, S.J., Supr.; L. Paul Fitterer, S.J.; James M. Harbaugh, S.J.; Philip J. Lucid, S.J.; John T. Rashford, S.J.; Gregory D. Vance, S.J.; Mr. David L. Thomas.

Jesuit House, Seattle, 621 17th Ave. E., 98112. Tel: 206-324-7496. Revs. Robert J. Egan, S.J.; Joseph Stocking, S.J.; Roger E. Blanchette, S.J.

Maryknoll Fathers & Brothers, 958-16th Ave. E., 98112. Tel: 206-322-8831; Fax: 206-324-6909. Email: mklseatl@aol.com. Web: www.maryknoll.org. Bro. W. Timothy Raible, M.M., Regl. Dir.

The Redemptionist Society of Washington, 205 2nd Ave. N., 98109. Tel: 206-284-4680; Fax: 203-284-4681. Email: grace@speakeasy.com info@sacredheartseattle.com. Revs. Richard Quinn, C.SS.R., Contact Person; Lyle Konen, C.SS.R.; Joseph J. Morin, C.SS.R.; The Pham, C.SS.R.; Joseph Nuttman, C.SS.R.

Seattle Oratory, 1210 S.W. 157th St., 98166. Tel: 206-268-0043. Email: seattleoratory@aol.com. Revs. Robert Dell, C.O.; Clarence Edward Jones, C.O.

LACEY. *St. Martin's Abbey* Order of St. Benedict, College, and Novitiate. , 5300 Pacific Ave, S.E., 98503-1297. Tel: 360-491-4700; 360-438-4440 (Abbot); Fax: 360-438-4441. Email: thabbot@stmartin.edu. Web: www.stmartin.edu. Rt. Revs. Neal G. Roth, O.S.B., Abbot; Vocation Team; Conrad R. Rausch, O.S.B., Resigned Abbot; Adrian J. Parcher, O.S.B., Resigned Abbot; Very Revs. Alfred J. Hulscher, O.S.B., Prior, Treas. & Dir. Fiscal Affairs; Kieran P. Cunningham, O.S.B., Subprior; Revs. Bede Classik, O.S.B, Novice Master; Junior Master; Vocation Team; Thaddaeus R. Arledge, O.S.B.; Benedict L. Auer, O.S.B., Postulant Dir.; Socius; Vocation Team; Richard S. Cebula, O.S.B.; Edward R. Receconi, O.S.B.; Urban C. Feucht; Gerard D. Kirsch, O.S.B.; Timothy J. Lamm, O.S.B.; William A. Maat, O.S.B.; Killian Malvey, O.S.B.; Sean R. Malvey, O.S.B.; Justin D. McCreedy, O.S.B.; Clement H. Pangratz, O.S.B.; Thomas R. Park, O.S.B.; David W. Prebula, O.S.B.; George J. Seidel, O.S.B.; John Scott, O.S.B.; Terence J. Wager, O.S.B.; Harvey J. Wingfield, O.S.B.; Paul M. Weckert, O.S.B. Priests 25; Brothers 12.

[M] CONVENTS AND RESIDENCES FOR SISTERS

SEATTLE. *St. Joseph's Carmelite Monastery*, 2215 N.E. 147th, Shoreline, 98155. Tel: 206-363-7150; Fax: 206-365-7335. Email: seattlecarmel@att.net. Sr. Michael Marie, O.C.D., Prioress. Discalced Carmelites 9; In Formation 3.

St. Joseph's Residence, 4800 37th Ave., S.W., 98126. Tel: 206-937-4600; Fax: 206-923-4001 (8:30am-8:30pm). Email: anita.butler@providence.org. Sr. Anita Butler, S.P., Supr. & Admin.; Rev. John A. Jennings, Chap. (Retired). Sisters of Providence 37; Dominican Sisters of Tacoma 9; Daughters of Mary 2; Carmelites 1; Sisters of St. Joseph of Peace 2; Dominican Sisters of Adrian 4.

Sisters of St. Joseph of Peace, 1104 21st Ave. E., 98112. Tel: 206-324-1529. Web: csjp.org. Sisters 4.

BELLEVUE. *St. Mary's Provincialate*, 1663 Killarney Way, Box 248, 98009-0248. Tel: 425-451-1770; Fax: 425-462-9760. Email: mchristenson@csjp-olp.org. Web: www.csjp-olp.org. Sr. Audrea Nenzel, C.S.J.P., Prov. Leader. Sisters of St. Joseph of Peace, Our Lady Province

St. Mary's Residence and Novitiate, 1663 Killarney Way, P.O. Box 1763, 98009. Tel: 425-451-1833; Fax: 425-462-9760. Email: eabrennan@csjp-olp.org. Web: www.csjp-olp.org. Sr. Judy Johnson, C.S.J.P., Admin. Our Lady Province. Sisters of St. Joseph of Peace 30.

EDMONDS. *Rosary Heights* (Dominican Sisters Congregation of the Most Holy Rosary, Adrian MI) , 23120 Woodway Park Rd., P.O. Box 280, 98020-0280. Tel: 206-542-7511; Fax: 206-546-9490.

Holy Angels Alumnae Assoc., 942 N.W. 60th, 98107. Tel: 206-782-1181.

LACEY. *St. Placid Priory*, 500 College St., N.E., 98516. Tel: 360-438-1771; Fax: 360-438-9236. Email: stplacid@stplacid.org. Web: www.stplacid.org. Sr. Laura Swan, O.S.B., Prioress. Includes The Priory Spirituality Center and The Priory Store. Sisters of St. Benedict 21.

SHAW ISLAND. *Franciscan Sisters of the Eucharist*, P.O. Box 455, 98286. Tel: 360-468-2288; Fax: 360-468-3766. Email: fse@rockisland.com. Sr. Helen Jean Brinkman, F.S.E., Supr. Sisters 4.

Our Lady of the Rock Priory (Cloistered) , P.O. Box 425, 98286. Tel: 360-468-2321; Fax: 360-468-2319. Web: www.rockisland.com/~mhildegard. Sr. Therese Critchley, O.S.B., Supr. Benedictine Nuns Professed Nuns 7; Novices 1.

TACOMA. *III Order of St. Dominic*, Tacoma Dominican Center, 935 Fawcett Ave. S., 98402. Tel: 253-272-9688; Fax: 253-272-8790. Email: dominicans@tacoma-op.org. Web: www.tacoma-op.org. Sr. Patricia Morrisset, O.P., Pres. (Congregation of St. Thomas Aquinas), Sisters of Saint Dominic of Tacoma Charitable Trust - Tacoma Dominican Center.

Sister of St. Francis of Philadelphia, St. Ann Retirement Convent, 6602 S. Alaska St., 98408. Tel: 253-474-8319; 253-475-0791; Fax 253-474-0734. Email: saintann@worldnet.att.net.

Serra House, 6602 S. Alaska St., 98408. Tel: 253-474-8026.

Evergreen House, 6602 S. Alaska St., 98408. Tel: 253-474-9803.

Olympus House, 6602 S. Alaska St., 98408. Tel: 253-474-8573.

Marian House, 6802 47th St. W., 98466. Tel: 253-564-1816.

St. Marguerite Convent, 4019 S. Thompson, 98408. Tel: 253-472-9702.

[N] RETREAT HOUSES, CONFERENCE CENTERS AND CAMPS

SEATTLE. *Camp Don Bosco*, Contact C.Y.O., 814 N.E. 85th St., 98115. Tel: 206-382-4350; Fax: 206-903-4627. Email: cyo@seattlearch.org. Web: www.seattlearch.org/cyo.

EDMONDS. *Dominican Reflection Center*, 23120 Woodway Park Rd., P.O. Box 280, 98020. Tel: 206-542-3740 206-546-6561; Fax: 206-546-9490. Email: drc@netos.com. Web: www.sophiasystems.com/drc/. Sr. Mary White, O.P., Dir.

FEDERAL WAY. *The Palisades Archdiocesan Retreat & Faith Formation Center*, 4700 S.W. Dash Point Rd., #100, 98023. Tel: 253-927-9621 (Tacoma); 206-748-7991 (Seattle); Fax: 206-382-3482. Email: palisades@seattlearch.org. Web: www.seattlearch.org/formationandeducation/palisades+retreat+center. David Jones, Dir.

ISSAQUAH. *WomanSpirit Center*, 18528 S.E. 58th St., 98027-8511. Tel: 425-641-1527; Fax: 425-653-2419. Email: womanspiritoncm@hotmail.com. Web: www.womanspiritcenter.org. Sr. Dona Taylor, S.P., Coord.

MONROE. *Camp Hamilton*, 25405 Lake Fontal Rd., 98272. Email: cyo@seattlearch.org. Web: www.seattlecvch.org/cyo. *Contact C.Y.O.*, 814 N.E. 85th St., 98115. Tel: 206-903-4625; Fax: 206-903-4627.

[O] NEWMAN CENTERS

SEATTLE. *Seattle University Campus Ministry* 900 Broadway, 98122. Tel: 206-296-6075; Fax: 206-296-6097. Ms. Mary Romer Cline, Dir.

University of Washington, Catholic Newman Center 4502 20th Ave., N.E., 98105. Tel: 206-527-5072. Rev. Steven Maekawa, O.P., Dir. & Chap.

Western Washington University (Bellingham), 102 Highland Dr., Bellingham, 98225. Tel: 206-733-3400. Rev. Frank Schuster, Chap. Catholic Campus Ministry.

Saint Martin's College (Lacey), 5300 Pacific Ave., S.E., Lacey, 98503. Tel: 360-438-4381. Susan Leyster, Dir. Campus Ministry.

[P] MISCELLANEOUS

SEATTLE. *Cursillo Movement*, P.O. Box 68803, 98168-0803. Tel: 206-780-5813. Pete Jancola, Lay Dir.. Email: pjjancala@worldnet.att.net.

The Food Bank at St. Mary's, 611 20th Ave. S., 98144. Tel: 206-324-7100, Ext. 21; Fax: 206-329-4596. Email: stmaryfb@teleport.com. Ms. Sue Smith, Dir.

Fulcrum Foundation, Formerly Catholic Schools Foundation/Archdiocese of Seattle910 Marion St., 98104. Tel: 206-748-7988; Fax: 206-654-4651. Email: colleenoglesby@fulcrumfoundation.org. Web: www.fulcrumfoundation.org. Rev. Stephen Rowan, Chm.

Intercommunity Housing Ferndale, 2505 3rd Ave., Ste. 325, 98121. Tel: 206-838-5700; Fax: 206-838-5705. Email: intercommunity@mercyhousing.org. Web: www.mercyhousing.org. Jane Graf, Regl. Pres.

Intercommunity Housing/Mercy Housing System, Formerly Intercommunity Housing2505 3rd Ave., Ste. 325, 98121. Tel: 206-838-5700; Fax: 206-838-5705. Email: intercommunity@mercyhousing.org. Web: www.mercyhousing.org. Jane Graf, Regl. Pres.

Intercommunity Ministry Volunteer Program, 1216 N.E. 65th St., Ste. 200, 98115. Tel: 206-442-4268; Fax: 206-621-7046. Email: volunteer@imvp.org. Web: www.imvp.org. Sr. Mary Mecved, S.N.J.M., Dir.

**Intercommunity Peace & Justice Center*, 1216 N.E. 65th St., 98115. Tel: 206-223-1138; Fax: 206-621-7046. Email: ipjc@ipjc.org. Web: www.ipjc.org. Sr. Linda Haydock, S.N.J.M., Exec. Dir.

**L'Arche Noah Sealth of Seattle*, P.O. Box 22023, 98122-0023. Tel: 206-325-9434; Fax: 206-568-0367. Email: info@larcheseattle.org. Web: www.larcheseattle.org.

Palisades Retreat Association, c/o Sacred Heart Church, 205 2nd Ave. N., 98109. A school of Christian learning.

Sisters of Providence, Mother Joseph Province, 506 2nd Ave., Ste. 1200, 98104. Tel: 206-464-3394; Fax: 206-464-3984. Email: barbaraschamber@providence.org. Web: For Seattle Health Systems Only: www.providence.org. Sr. Barbara Schamber, S.P., Prov. Supr.

For detailed information on corporate holdings for the Sisters of Providence, Mother Joseph Province, please refer to Religious Institutes of Women in the back of the directory.

Providence Health System-Oregon Tel: 503-215-4700; Fax: 503-215-4703.

Providence Health System-Washington Tel: 206-464-2698; Fax: 206-464-4686.

Providence Health System-California Tel: 818-843-5111; Fax: 818-843-0641.

Providence Pariseau Corporation, 506 2nd Ave., Ste. 1200, 98104-2329. Tel: 206-464-3394. Sisters Lynn Chappell, S.P., Team Member; Barbara Schamber, S.P., Pres.

Sisters of Providence Retirement Trust Fund, 506 2nd Ave., Ste. 1200, 98104-2329. Tel: 206-464-3386. Email: lynn.chappell@providence.org. Sr. Lynn Chappell, S.J., Chair & Contact Person.

Providence Everett Medical Center - Pacific Campus, 916 Pacific Ave., P.O. Box 1067, Everett, 98206. Tel: 425-258-7992. Sr. Lynn Chappell, S.P., Team Member.

Providence St. Peter Foundation, 413 Lilly Rd., N.E., Olympia, 98506-5116. Tel: 360-493-7980; Fax: 360-493-4631. Sr. Lynn Chappell, S.P., Team Member; Nancy Riordan, Regl. Dir.

Providence General Foundation, 916 Pacific Ave., P.O. Box 1067, Everett, 98206. Tel: 425-258-7992; Fax: 425-258-7142. Sr. Lynn Chappell, S.P., Team Member; Dottie Piasecki, Exec. Dir.

Providence Mt. St. Vincent Foundation, 4831 35th Ave., S.W., 98126. Tel: 206-938-8994; Fax: 206-938-8999. Email: cscollins@providence.org. Sr. Lynn Chappell, S.P., Team Member; Carol Collins, Exec. Dir.

Providence Hospice & Home Care of Snohomish Co. Foundation, 2731 Wetmore Ave., Everett, 98201. Tel: 425-261-4805. Email: cwittern@providence.org. Connie Wittern, Devel. Dir.

Providence Marianwood Foundation, 3725 Providence Point Dr., S.E., Issaquah, 98029. Tel: 425-391-2895. Sr. Lynn Chappell, S.P., Team Member; Cindy Sharek, Foundation Dir.

Providence of St. Francis, 3415 12th Ave., Olympia, 98506. Tel: 360-493-5700; Fax: 360-493-5801.

Providence Blanchet, 1700 Providence Pl., Centralia, 98531. Tel: 360-330-8748; Fax: 360-330-8795.

Providence Rossi, 1700 Providence Pl., Centralia, 98531. Tel: 360-330-8748; Fax: 360-330-8795.

Sterling Senior Housing, 2505 Third Ave., Ste. 325, 98121. Tel: 206-838-5700. Heidi Rathmann, Contact.

Vietnamese Catholic Center, 1230 E. Fir St., 98122-5425. Tel: 206-325-5626; Fax: 206-324-5849. Email: niemtin_sea@hotmail.com. Web: niemtinseattle.org. Rev. Anthony Ton.

Washington State Catholic Conference, 508-2nd Ave. W., 98119-3928. Tel: 206-301-0556; Fax: 206-301-0558. Email: wscc@thewscc.org. Sr. Sharon Park, O.P., Exec. Dir.

BELLEVUE. *Sisters of St. Joseph of Peace, Our Lady Province, Charitable Trust*, 1663 Killarney Way, P.O. Box 248, 98009-0248. Tel: 425-451-1770; Fax: 425-462-9760. Email: sdewitt@csjp-olp.org. Web: www.csjp.org/olp. Sr. Audrea Nenzel, C.S.J.P., Prov. Leader.

Sisters of St. Joseph of Peace, PeaceHealth, Corporate Center, 15325 S.E. 30th Pl., Ste. 300, 98007. Tel: 425-747-1711; Fax: 425-649-3825. John Hayward, Pres. & CEO.

EDMONDS. *Edmonds Dominicans, Holy Angels Alumnae Assoc.*, Tel: 206-546-6561. 942 N.W. 60th, 98107. Tel: 206-782-1181; Fax: 206-789-2498.

LA CONNER. *Archdiocesan Council of Catholic Women, Northern Deanery*, P.O. Box 906, 98257. Tel: 360-466-4158. Shirlee Dessert, Pres.

MONTESANO. *Archdiocesan Council of Catholic Women-Southern Deanery*, P.O. Box 88, 98563. Tel: 360-249-2633. Email: eehig@lightstream.net. Edith Higginbothaan, Pres.

MOUNT VERNON. *Skagit Valley Regional Ministry*, 215 N. 15th St., 98273. Tel: 360-336-6622; Fax: 360-336-5203. Email: admin@svcc.us. Web: www.svcc.us. Very Rev. J. Patrick McDermott.

PORT ANGELES. *Archdiocesan Council for Catholic Women-Western Deanery*, P.O. Box 535, 98362. Tel: 360-461-0642. Barbara Townsend, Pres.

RENTON. *Archdiocesan Council for Catholic Women-Central Deanery*, Formerly Archdiocesan Council for Catholic Women17016 129th Ave., S.E., 98058. Tel: 253-631-4654. Rochelle Heye, Pres.

TACOMA. *Catholic Pastoral Care-Hospital Tacoma Ministry*, 1001 N. "J" St., 98403. Tel: 253-591-9474; Fax: 253-627-5396. Email: pcdeauery@juno.com. Rev. Michael E. Walsh, S.J., Dir.

Pierce County Association for Catholic Education (PACE), 1001 N. "J" St., 98403. Tel: 253-756-7830; Fax: 253-627-5396. Email: pace4schools@juno.com.

Pierce County Deanery, 1001 N. J St., 98403. Tel: 253-383-3496; Fax: 253-627-5396. Email: pcdeanery@juno.com. Mary DeForrest, Admin.

UNIVERSITY PLACE. *Archdiocesan Council of Catholic Women*, 4408 Merry Ln., 98466. Tel: 253-564-1497; Fax: 253-564-7447. Email: kjrmcent@mindspring.com. Katherine J. McEntee, Pres.

RELIGIOUS INSTITUTES OF MEN REPRESENTED IN THE ARCHDIOCESE

For further details refer to the corresponding bracketed number in the Religious Institutes of Men or Women section.

[0200]—*Benedictine Monks* (Olympia, WA)—O.S.B.
[0310]—*Congregation of Christian Brothers* (Western U.S.)—C.F.C.
[0260]—*Discalced Carmelites Friars* (California Prov.)—O.C.D.
[0690]—*Jesuit Fathers and Brothers* (Oregon Province)—S.J.
[0800]—*Maryknoll*—M.M.
[]—*Oratorian Community*
[0430]—*Order of Preachers (Dominicans)* (San Francisco, CA)—O.P.
[1070]—*Redemptorist Fathers* (Denver Province)—C.SS.R.
[1250]—*Society of Christ* (American-Canadian Prov.)—S.Ch.
[1290]—*Society of the Priests of Saint Sulpice*—S.S.

RELIGIOUS INSTITUTES OF WOMEN REPRESENTED IN THE ARCHDIOCESE

[0180]—*Benedictine Nuns of the Primitive Observance*—O.S.B.
[0230]—*Benedictine Sisters of Pontifical Jurisdiction* (Lacey, WA; Duluth, MN)—O.S.B.
[]—*Carmelite*—O.L.
[2100]—*Congregation of the Humility of Mary*—C.H.M.
[1920]—*Congregation of the Sisters of the Holy Cross*—C.S.C.
[1780]—*Congregation of the Sisters of the Third Order of St. Francis of Perpetual Adoration* (Western Region)—F.S.P.A.
[0420]—*Discalced Carmelite Nuns*—O.C.D.
[1070-03]—*Dominican Sisters* (Adrian, MI)—O.P.
[1070-19]—*Dominican Sisters* (Sinsinawa)—O.P.
[1070-21]—*Dominican Sisters* (Houston)—O.P.
[1070-04]—*Dominican Sisters* (Tacoma)—O.P.
[]—*Eucharistic Heart of Jesus*
[]—*Franciscan Sisters of Rochester*—O.S.F.
[1250]—*The Institute of the Franciscan Sisters of the Eucharist*—F.S.E.
[]—*Missionary Sisters of the Rosary of Fatima*—M.R.F.
[2860]—*Missionary Sisters of the Sacred Heart*—M.S.C.
[]—*Our Lady of Perpetual Help (Korean)*
[4070]—*Religious of the Sacred Heart*—R.S.C.J.
[]—*Religious Sisters of Mercy*—R.S.M.
[2970]—*School Sisters of Notre Dame*—S.S.N.D.
[]—*Sisters for Christian Community*—S.F.C.C.
[0430]—*Sisters of Charity of the Blessed Virgin Mary*—B.V.M.
[3000]—*Sisters of Notre Dame De Namur*—S.N.D.deN.
[3350]—*Sisters of Providence*—S.P.
[1650]—*The Sisters of St. Francis of Philadelphia*—O.S.F.
[3840]—*Sisters of St. Joseph of Carondelet* (California Prov.)—C.S.J.
[3890]—*Sisters of St. Joseph of Peace*—C.S.J.P.
[1990]—*Sisters of the Holy Names of Jesus and Mary*—S.N.J.M.
[]—*Sisters of the Holy Names of Jesus and Mary* (Oregon Prov.)—S.N.J.M.
[]—*Sisters of the Holy Names of Jesus and Mary* (California Prov.)—S.N.J.M.

ARCHDIOCESAN CEMETERIES

Central Office: 910 Marion, 98104. Tel: 206-382-9281

SEATTLE

Calvary, 5041 35th Ave., N.E., 98105. Tel: 206-522-0996.

Holyrood, 205 N.E. 205th, 98155. Tel: 206-363-8404.

FEDERAL WAY

Gethsemane, 37600 Pacific Hwy. S., 98003. Tel: 206-838-2240.

KENT

St. Patrick, 20400 Orillia Rd., 98032. Tel: 206-838-2240.

NECROLOGY

† Doogan, Rev. Msgr. John P., Mercer Island, WA St. Monica—Died July 22, 2003

Diocese of Shreveport

(Dioecesis Sreveportuensis in Louisiana)

Most Reverend

WILLIAM R. FRIEND, D.D.

Bishop of Shreveport; ordained May 7, 1959; appointed Titular Bishop of Pomaria and Auxiliary Bishop of Alexandria-Shreveport August 31, 1979; ordained Bishop October 30, 1979; appointed Bishop of Alexandria-Shreveport November 23, 1982; installed January 11, 1983; appointed Bishop of Shreveport June 16, 1986 *Catholic Center: 3500 Fairfield Ave., Shreveport, LA 71104.* Tel: 318-868-4441; Fax: 318-868-4605.

Chancery Office: 3500 Fairfield Ave., Shreveport, LA 71104. Tel: 318-868-4441; Fax: 318-868-4605.

Web: www.dioshpt.org

ESTABLISHED AND CREATED A DIOCESE JUNE 16, 1986.

Comprises the Counties (parishes) of Bienville, Bossier, Caddo, Claiborne, DeSoto, East Carroll, Jackson, Lincoln, Morehouse, Ouachita, Red River, Richland, Sabine, Union, Webster and West Carroll.

Legal Title: For legal titles of parishes and diocesan institutions, consult the Chancery Office.

STATISTICAL OVERVIEW

Personnel	
Bishop	1
Priests: Diocesan Active in Diocese	28
Priests: Diocesan Active Outside Diocese	2
Priests: Retired, Sick or Absent	11
Number of Diocesan Priests	41
Religious Priests in Diocese	15
Total Priests in Diocese	56
Extern Priests in Diocese	6
Permanent Deacons in Diocese	6
Total Brothers	10
Total Sisters	58
Parishes	
Parishes	32
With Resident Pastor:	
Resident Diocesan Priests	22
Resident Religious Priests	9
Without Resident Pastor:	
Administered by Priests	1
Missions	13
Pastoral Centers	2
Professional Ministry Personnel:	
Brothers	2
Sisters	1
Lay Ministers	37
Welfare	
Catholic Hospitals	2
Total Assisted	1,097
Health Care Centers	3
Total Assisted	322,235
Homes for the Aged	1
Total Assisted	190
Day Care Centers	2
Total Assisted	195
Specialized Homes	2
Total Assisted	350
Special Centers for Social Services	20
Total Assisted	27,469
Residential Care of Disabled	1
Total Assisted	184
Other Institutions	4
Total Assisted	2,335
Educational	
Diocesan Students in Other Seminaries	2
Total Seminarians	2
High Schools, Diocesan and Parish	2
Total Students	735
Elementary Schools, Diocesan and Parish	6
Total Students	1,543
Catechesis/Religious Education:	
High School Students	635
Elementary Students	2,489
Total Students under Catholic Instruction	5,404
Teachers in the Diocese:	
Sisters	7
Lay Teachers	163
Vital Statistics	
Receptions into the Church:	
Infant Baptism Totals	532
Adult Baptism Totals	87
Received into Full Communion	144
First Communions	538
Confirmations	443
Marriages:	
Catholic	83
Interfaith	105
Total Marriages	188
Deaths	383
Total Catholic Population	39,436
Total Population	784,665

Vicar General and Moderator of the Curia—Very Rev. DAVID T. RICHTER, V.G.

Vicars Forane—Rev. Msgr. EARL V. PROVENZA, V.F., Western Deanery; Very Revs. JOSEPH PUTHUPPALLY, V.F., Eastern Deanery; PHILIP MICHIELS, V.F., Southern Deanery.

Chancery Office—Catholic Center, 3500 Fairfield Ave., Shreveport, 71104. Tel: 318-868-4441; Fax: 318-868-4605.

Chancellor—Mrs. CHRISTINE RIVERS.

Treasurer and Director of Mission Effectiveness—Sr. MARGARET DAUES, C.S.J., Ph.D.

Diocesan Tribunal—3500 Fairfield Ave., Shreveport, 71104. Tel: 318-868-4441; Fax: 318-868-4605.

Judicial Vicar—Rev. PETER B. MANGUM, J.C.L., J.V.. Email: pmangum@dioshpt.org.

Associate Judge—Rev. ROTHELL PRICE. Email: rprice@dioshpt.org.

Director of the Tribunal—Sr. MARILYN R. VASSALLO, C.S.J., J.C.L.. Email: mvassallo@dioshpt.org.

Assessor-Auditor—RICOLE WILLIAMS. Email: rwilliam@dioshpt.org.

Secretary—SUSAN R. MCQUEEN. Email: smcqueen@dioshpt.org.

Judges—Rev. PETER B. MANGUM, J.C.L., J.V.; Rev. Msgr. FRANZ GRAEF, S.T.D.; Revs. EDMUND A. NIEHOFF; ROTHELL PRICE; Sr. MARILYN R. VASSALLO, C.S.J., J.C.L.; Rev. CURTIS WOODS; Rev. Msgr. EDMUND J. MOORE (Retired).

Defenders of the Bond—Very Rev. PHILIP F. MICHIELS, V.F.; Rev. WILLIAM H. CAREY, Ph.D. (Retired).

Promoter of Justice—Rev. WILLIAM H. CAREY, Ph.D. (Retired).

Advocates—Revs. KARL DAIGLE; RICHARD J. LOMBARD; Very Rev. DAVID T. RICHTER, V.G.; Rev. MARK WATSON.

Notaries—RICOLE WILLIAMS. Email: rwilliam@dioshpt.org; DEBBY SMITH. Email: dsmith@dioshpt.org; SUE MCQUEEN. Email: smcqueen@dioshpt.org.

Corporate Council—Most Rev. WILLIAM B. FRIEND, D.D.; Very Rev. DAVID T. RICHTER, V.G.; Sr. MARGARET DAUES, C.S.J., Ph.D. CHRISTINE RIVERS.

College of Consultors—Revs. WILLIAM H. CAREY, Ph.D. (Retired); KARL J. DAIGLE; CHARLES GLORIOSO; TIMOTHY C. HURD; JAMES MCLELLAND; PATRICK J. MADDEN, Ph.D.; PETER B. MANGUM, J.C.L., J.V.; EDMUND A. (LARRY) NIEHOFF; ANDRE MCGRATH, O.F.M. LAVERNE (PIKE) THOMAS; Very Revs. PHILIP F. MICHIELS, V.F.; JOSEPH PUTHUPPALLY, V.F.; DAVID T. RICHTER, V.G.; Rev. MARK A. WATSON; Rev. Msgrs. EARL V. PROVENZA, V.F.; FRANZ GRAEF, S.T.D.

Finance Council—Most Rev. WILLIAM B. FRIEND, D.D.; Very Rev. DAVID T. RICHTER, V.G., Ex Officio; Sr. MARGARET DAUES, C.S.J., Ex Officio; CHRISTINE RIVERS, Ex Officio; Rev. RICHARD J. LOMBARD; REGINALD W. ABRAMS; MARY A. BROWN; DAVID CATTAR; NONA DAILEY; JOAN FISHER; MARGARET GREEN; GLENN KINSEY; Dr. JAMES ROBERT MICHAEL; PHYLLIS MURDOCK; NICHOLAS ROPPOLO; LAWRENCE H. RUSSO III.

Presbyteral Council—Most Rev. WILLIAM B. FRIEND, D.D.; Very Rev. DAVID T. RICHTER, V.G., Chm.; Rev. Msgr. EARL V. PROVENZA, V.F.; Revs. WILLIAM H. CAREY, Ph.D. (Retired); CHARLES GLORIOSO, Vice Chm.; JAMES MCLELLAND, Sec.; KARL J. DAIGLE; TIMOTHY C. HURD; PATRICK J. MADDEN, Ph.D. PETER B. MANGUM, J.C.L., J.V.; EDMUND A. (LARRY) NIEHOFF; ANDRE MCGRATH, O.F.M.; Very Revs. PHILIP F. MICHIELS, V.F.; JOSEPH PUTHUPPALLY, V.F.; Rev. Msgr. FRANZ GRAEF, S.T.D.; Revs. LAVERNE (PIKE) THOMAS; MARK A. WATSON.

Diocesan Pastoral Council—Mr. RICHARD K. BRADFORD, West Monroe; Mrs. MARY ELLEN BRIEHN, Bossier City; Mr. A. J. CANALES, Minden; Mrs. YVETTE COLEMAN-SMITH, Shreveport; MARY ELLEN FOLEY, Shreveport; Mr. CHARLES HARPER, West Monroe; Mrs. DEBBIE KETHLEY, Bossier City; Mrs. ANGEL M. KLEINPETER, Mansfield; Mrs. LUCY A. RIVERO, Chm., Shreveport; Mr. CHARLES SCOTT, Monroe; Mr. RANDY G. TILLER, Shreveport; Mr. ANTHONY TUMINELLO, Shreveport; Mrs. LAURI B. WALLACE, Shreveport; Sr. MARGARET DAUES, C.S.J., Shreveport.

Priests' Retirement Board—Rev. Msgr. J. CARSON LACAZE, Chm.; Revs. J. ROBERT INZINA; EDMUND A. (LARRY) NIEHOFF; NICHOLAS ROPPOLO; Rev. Msgr. EARL V. PROVENZA, V.F.; Rev. JAMES MCLELLAND.

The Catholic Foundation of North-Central Louisiana, Inc.—Contact the Catholic Center for information: . Tel: 318-868-4441; Fax: 318-868-4605.

Diocesan Offices and Directors

Black Catholic Commission—Rev. ROTHELL PRICE, Chap., St. Jude Church, 3800 Viking Dr. E., Bossier City, 71111-7403. Tel: 318-746-2508.

Business Affairs—JILL BRANIFF, C.P.A., Catholic Center, 3500 Fairfield Ave., Shreveport, 71104. Tel: 318-868-4441; Fax: 318-868-4605.

Campaign for Human Development—Very Rev. DAVID T. RICHTER, V.G., Address Communications to: Catholic Center, 3500 Fairfield Ave., Shreveport, 71104. Tel: 318-868-4441; Fax: 318-868-4605.

Campus Ministry—Mrs. TAMMY YATCKO, Coord., Catholic Center, 3500 Fairfield Ave., Shreveport, 71104. Tel: 318-868-4441; Fax: 318-868-4605.

Catechetics and Worship—Mrs. MARY MCGILL, M.A., Catholic Center, 3500 Fairfield Ave., Shreveport, 71104. Tel: 318-868-4441; Fax: 318-868-4605.

Catholic Charities— Address Communications to: Office of Mission Effectiveness *Catholic Center, 3500 Fairfield Ave., Shreveport, 71104.* Tel: 318-868-4441; Fax: 318-868-4605.

Catholic Relief Services—Very Rev. DAVID T. RICHTER, V.G., Catholic Center, 3500 Fairfield Ave., Shreveport, 71104. Tel: 318-868-4441; Fax: 318-868-4605.

Cemeteries—JILL BRANIFF, C.P.A., Catholic Center, 3500 Fairfield Ave., Shreveport, 71104. Tel: 318-868-4441; Fax: 318-868-4605.

Censor of Books—Rev. Msgr. FRANZ GRAEF, S.T.D.

Charismatic Movement—Mr. THOMAS HARLAN, 9536 Pitch Pine, Shreveport, 71118-4527.

Church Vocations—Rev. JOSEPH MARTINA JR., Dir., 3500 Fairfield Ave., Shreveport, 71104. Tel: 318-868-4441; Fax: 318-868-4605.

Church Vocations Board—Rev. JOSEPH MARTINA JR., Dir.; Mr. RICHARD BRADFORD; Mr. DAVID GARCIE; Dr. J. MICHAEL COOK; Mrs. SUSAN LANIER; KAREN DILL, L.P.C., Chm.; Sr. LAUREEN PAINTER, O.S.F.; Rev. Msgr. FRANZ GRAEF, S.T.D.; Rev. ROTHELL PRICE; Mrs. CHRISTIE WEEKS; Mr. BRIAN D. LANDRY; Deacon CLARY NASH; Sr. SANDRA NORSWORTHY, O.L.S.; Rev. MARK WATSON. Ex Officio Members: Most Rev. WILLIAM B. FRIEND, D.D.; Very Rev. DAVID T. RICHTER, V.G.

Continuing Education for the Clergy—Rev. CHARLES GLORIOSO, Dir., St. Pius X Church, 4300 N. Market St., Shreveport, 71107. Tel: 318-222-2165.

Development and Public Relations—Mr. JOHN MARK WILLCOX, Dir.; KATIE SMITH, Coord., Catholic Center, 3500 Fairfield Ave., Shreveport, 71104. Tel: 318-868-4441; Fax: 318-868-4605.

Diocesan Publications—SHERRY SWANEY HEFLIN, Editor, Catholic Center, 3500 Fairfield Ave., Shreveport, 71104. Tel: 318-868-4441; Fax: 318-868-4605.

Ecumenism and Interreligious Affairs—Rev. Msgr. CARSON J. LACAZE, Our Lady of the Holy Rosary Church, 1755 Corbitt St., Shreveport, 71108-3098. Tel: 318-636-3530.

Facility Director, Catholic Center—ROBERT MORGAN, Catholic Center, 3500 Fairfield Ave., Shreveport, 71104. Tel: 318-868-4441; Fax: 318-868-4605.

Fairview House (Residence for Clergy)—1000 Fairview, Shreveport, 71104. Tel: 318-868-4441; Fax: 318-868-4605.

Greco Institute—Rev. PATRICK J. MADDEN, Ph.D., Dir., Catholic Center, 3500 Fairfield Ave., Shreveport, 71104. Tel: 318-868-4441; Fax: 318-868-4605.

Health Ministry—Rev. WILLIAM H. CAREY, Ph.D., Coord. (Retired), 1603 West St., Monroe, 71201.

Hispanic Ministry—Sr. DOLORES SANCHEZ, O.S.F., Dir., Catholic Center, 3500 Fairfield Ave., Shreveport, 71104. Tel: 318-868-4441; Fax: 318-868-4605; Rev. RIGOBERTO BETANCURT, Chap. & Assoc. Dir.

Holy Childhood—Sr. CAROL SHIVELY, O.S.U., Contact Person, Catholic Center, 3500 Fairfield Ave., Shreveport, 71104. Tel: 318-868-4441; Fax: 318-868-4605.

Human Resources—Mrs. CHRISTIE WEEKS, Dir., Catholic Center, 3500 Fairfield Ave., Shreveport, 71104. Tel: 318-868-4441; Fax: 318-868-4605.

Information Systems Management—Ms. PATRICIA PILLORS, Dir., Catholic Center, 3500 Fairfield Ave., Shreveport, 71104. Tel: 318-868-4441; Fax: 318-868-4605.

Jail-Prison Ministry—Rev. RICHARD PUSCH, Chap., Forcht Wade Correctional Center, P.O. Box 53043, Shreveport, 71135-3043.

Diocesan Liturgy Commission—MICHAEL KENNEY, Chm.; Rev. MICHAEL HANEY, O.F.M.; MARY CUNNINGHAM; GINA HAMPTON; Very Rev. PHILIP F. MICHIELS, V.F.; Rev. LAVERNE (PIKE) THOMAS; Deacon CLARY NASH; CAROLE MOON; VONNY JAUBERT; KIM KOHLMAN; MARY MCGILL, Ex Officio.

Mission Director—Very Rev. DAVID T. RICHTER, V.G., Catholic Center, 3500 Fairfield Ave., Shreveport, 71104. Tel: 318-868-4441; Fax: 318-868-4605.

Permanent Deacon Formation Program—Mr. CLARY NASH, Dir., Catholic Center, 3500 Fairfield Ave., Shreveport, 71104. Tel: 318-868-4441; Fax: 318-868-4605.

Propagation of the Faith—Very Rev. DAVID T. RICHTER, V.G., Catholic Center, 3500 Fairfield Ave., Shreveport, 71104. Tel: 318-868-4441; Fax: 318-868-4605.

Religious Education—Mrs. MARY MCGILL, M.A., Dir., Catholic Center, 3500 Fairfield Ave., Shreveport, 71104. Tel: 318-868-4441; Fax: 318-868-4605.

Resource Center (Library)—Sr. EILEEN MCGRORY, Dir., Catholic Center, 3500 Fairfield Ave., Shreveport, 71104. Tel: 318-868-4441; Fax: 318-868-4605.

Schools—Sisters CAROL SHIVELY, O.S.U., Supt.; ANN MIDDLEBROOKS, S.E.C., Assoc. Supt., Catholic Center, 3500 Fairfield Ave., Shreveport, 71104. Tel: 318-868-4441; Fax: 318-868-4605. Web: www.nlacs.org.

Child Nutrition Program—3500 Fairfield Ave., Shreveport, 71104. Tel: 318-868-4441; Fax: 318-868-5057.

Scouting—Rev. MARK FRANKLIN, Chap., St. Jude Church, 3800 Viking Dr., E., Bossier City, 71111. Tel: 318-746-2508.

St. Catherine Community Center—Mr. GUS GRASSI, Dir., 331 E. 71st St., Shreveport, 71106-4305. Tel: 318-865-9817.

St. Vincent de Paul Society—DOTYE STANFORD, Contact Person, P.O. Box 3911, Shreveport, 71133-3911. Tel: 318-865-7807.

Victim Assistance Coordinator—Ms. ANN INABNET. Tel: 318-221-6121.

Youth and Young Adult Ministry—Mrs. TAMMY YATCKO, Dir., Catholic Center, 3500 Fairfield Ave., Shreveport, 71104. Tel: 318-868-4441; Fax: 318-868-4605.

CLERGY, PARISHES, MISSIONS AND PAROCHIAL SCHOOLS

CITY OF SHREVEPORT
(CADDO PARISH)

1—ST. JOHN BERCHMANS CATHEDRAL (1902), Revs. Curtis W. Woods, Rector; Joseph Ampatt Chacko, C.M.I. (India); Deacons Clary Nash; Ronald Morris.
Office—939 Jordan St., 71101-4391. Tel: 318-221-5296; Fax: 318-221-8076.
School—Tel: 318-221-6005; Fax: 318-425-0648. Mr. Jerry Fowler, Prin. Lay Teachers 15; Students 250.
Catechesis/Religious Program—Students 65.

2—ST. CATHERINE OF SIENA (1938), Rev. James R. McLelland.
Res.: 331 E. 71st St., 71106-4305. Tel: 318-868-6506; Fax: 318-861-6177.
Catechesis/Religious Program—Students 28.

3—ST. ELIZABETH ANN SETON (1984), Rev. LaVerne Thomas III; Deacon William Long.
Res.: 522 E. Flournoy-Lucas Rd., 71115-2073. Tel: 318-798-1887; Fax: 318-797-7302.
Catechesis/Religious Program—Students 350.

4—HOLY TRINITY (1856), Rev. Msgr. Franz Graef.
Res.: 315 Marshall St., P.O. Box 144, 71161-0144. Tel: 318-221-5990; Fax: 318-221-3545.

5—ST. JOSEPH (1949), Revs. Peter B. Mangum, J.C.L., J.V.; Richard J. Lombard; Douglas S. Sweet, (PRO).
Res.: 211 Atlantic Ave., 71105. Tel: 318-865-3581; Fax: 318-865-5125.
School—1210 Anniston Ave., 71105. Tel: 318-865-3585; Fax: 318-868-1859. Mrs. Susan J. Belanger, Prin.; Ms. Mary Whelan, Asst. Prin. Lay Teachers 40; Students 499.
Catechesis/Religious Program—Students 275.

6—ST. MARY OF THE PINES (1973), Rev. Edmund A. Niehoff.
Res.: 1050 Bert Kouns Industrial Loop, 71118-3499. Tel: 318-687-5121; Fax: 318-687-5124.
Catechesis/Religious Program—Students 157.

7—OUR LADY OF THE BLESSED SACRAMENT (1923), (African American), Rev. Andre McGrath, O.F.M.
Res.: 1558 Buena Vista St., 71101-2448. Tel: 318-222-3790; Fax: 318-222-3793.
School—2932 Murphy St., 71103-2241. Tel: 318-222-5051; Fax: 318-222-5840. Winnie Vance-Antoine, Prin. Lay Teachers 14; Students 200.
Catechesis/Religious Program—Bro. John Basi-imwa Rwakiviiga, F.M.H., D.R.E. Students 21.

8—OUR LADY OF THE HOLY ROSARY (1952), Rev. Msgr. J. Carson LaCaze.
Res.: 1755 Corbitt St., 71108-3098. Tel: 318-636-3530; Fax: 318-632-5586.
Catechesis/Religious Program—Tel: 318-525-9339. Students 16.

9—ST. PIUS X (1955), Rev. Charles Glorioso; Susan R. Lanier, Pastoral Assoc.
Res.: 4300 N. Market St., 71107-2953. Tel: 318-222-2165; Fax: 318-222-9160.
Child Development Center—Tel: 318-425-2192. Students 68.
Catechesis/Religious Program—Students 127.

10—SACRED HEART OF JESUS (1966), Rev. Msgr. C. Murray Clayton.
Res.: 4736 Lyba St., P.O. Box 19467, 71149-0467. Tel: 318-635-2121; Fax: 318-635-5226.
Catechesis/Religious Program—Tel: 318-635-5446; Fax: 318-635-5227. Students 59.

11—ST. THERESA, Consolidated, with St. John Berchmans Cathedral.

OUTSIDE THE CITY OF SHREVEPORT

BASTROP, MOREHOUSE PARISH

1—ST. JOSEPH (1943), [CEM] Rev. Joseph Robert Inzina.
Res.: 217 Harrington Ave., 71220-3025. Tel: 318-281-4327; Fax: 318-281-0982.
School—Tel: 318-281-5894; Fax: 318-281-5890. Frank Zametto, Prin. Lay Teachers 11; Students 110.
Catechesis/Religious Program—Students 20.

2—OUR LADY HELP OF CHRISTIANS, Consolidated, with St. Joseph, Bastrop.

BOSSIER CITY, BOSSIER PARISH

1—CHRIST THE KING (1939), Revs. Rigoberto Betancurt; Dariusz Pawlowski (Poland).
Res.: 425 McCormick St., 71111-4692. Tel: 318-221-0238; Fax: 318-425-0011.
Catechesis/Religious Program—Students 79.
Mission—Mary, Queen of the Most Holy Rosary Chapel Fuller Rd., Doyline, Webster Parish 71023.

2—ST. JUDE (1964), Revs. Rothell Price; Mark E. Franklin.
Res.: 3800 Viking Dr., E., 71111-7403. Tel: 318-746-2508; Fax: 318-742-4526.
Catechesis/Religious Program—Students 455.
Mission—Mary, Queen of Heaven 1659 Palmetto Rd., Benton, Bossier Parish 71006.

3—MARY, QUEEN OF PEACE (1999), Rev. Msgr. Earl V. Provenza, V.F.
Res.: 2101 Hope St., 71112. Tel: 318-752-5971; Fax: 318-752-5973.
Catechesis/Religious Program—Students 89.
Mission—St. George P.O. Box 937, Coushatta, Red River Parish 71019-0937. Tel: 318-932-3733.

GRAMBLING, LINCOLN PARISH, ST. BENEDICT THE BLACK (1966), (African American), Rev. Nicholas Owino Onyach, F.M.H. (Kenya).
Res.: 471 Main St., 71245-3088. Tel: 318-247-6734; Fax: 318-247-6288.

HODGE, JACKSON PARISH, ST. LUCY (1935), [CEM] Rev. Robert A. Leonhardt, O.F.M.
Res.: 1104 S. 2nd St., P.O. Drawer 100, 71247-0100. Tel: 318-259-2326; Fax: 318-259-2326 (Call first.).
Catechesis/Religious Program—Students 24.

LAKE PROVIDENCE, EAST CARROLL PARISH, ST. PATRICK (1870), [CEM] Rev. Zacharias Prakuzhy, C.M.I. (India).
Res.: 207 Scarborough St., P.O. Box 351, 71254-0351. Tel: 318-559-1276; Fax: 318-559-7733.
Catechesis/Religious Program—Students 18.

MANSFIELD, DESOTO PARISH, ST. JOSEPH (1907), [CEM 4] Very Rev. Philip F. Michiels, V.F.
Res.: 305 Jefferson St., 71052-0760. Tel: 318-872-1158.
Catechesis/Religious Program—Tel: 318-872-0905; Fax: 318-872-1161. Students 71.
Mission—St. Ann's Chapel 2260 Hwy. 171, P.O. Box 271, Stonewall, DeSoto Parish 71078. Tel: 318-858-3976.

MANY, SABINE PARISH, ST. JOHN THE BAPTIST (1871), [CEM] Rev. John Pardue.
Res.: 1130 E. San Antonio Ave., 71449-3226. Tel: 318-256-5680; 318-256-5689; Fax: 318-256-9177.
Catechesis/Religious Program—Students 97.
Mission—St. Terence Hwys. 191 & 476, 1130 E. San Antonio Ave., Sabine Parish 71449. Tel: 318-586-7444.

MINDEN, WEBSTER PARISH, ST. PAUL (1942), Rev. Karl J. Daigle.
P.O. Box 799, 71058-0799. Tel: 318-377-5364; Fax: 318-377-5394.
Catechesis/Religious Program—Students 76.
Mission—Blessed Sacrament Hwy. 7 at Hwy. 4, Ringgold, Bienville Parish 71068. Tel: 318-894-5785.
Mission—St. Margaret 600 E. 2nd St., Homer, Claiborne Parish 71040. Tel: 318-927-2865.
Mission—Sacred Heart 304 Gaisser St., Springhill, Webster Parish 71075. Tel: 318-539-4919.

MONROE, OUACHITA PARISH

1—JESUS THE GOOD SHEPHERD (1958), Rev. Mark Watson. In Res., Rev. Msgr. Edmund J. Moore (Retired).
Office—2510 Emerson St., 71201-2699. Tel: 318-325-7549; Fax: 318-322-6969.
Priest's Residence—800 Marquette St., 71201. Tel: 318-325-6956.
School—900 Good Shepherd Ln., 71201. Tel: 318-325-8569; Fax: 318-325-9730. Lay Teachers 16; Students 306.
Catechesis/Religious Program—Students 85.

2—ST. JOSEPH (1956), Rev. Boby Mannamplackal Alex (India).
Res.: 506 Benton Ave., P.O. Box 1203, 71210-1203. Tel: 318-325-4527; Fax: 318-325-4599.
Catechesis/Religious Program—Students 5.

3—LITTLE FLOWER OF JESUS (1940), (African American), Rev. Frank Probst, O.F.M.; Bro. Roch Pfeifer, O.F.M.
Res.: 616 S. 16th St., 71201. Tel: 318-324-9706.
Church Office: 600 S. 16th St., 71201. Tel: 318-322-1224; Fax: 318-322-1261.
School—610 S. 16th St., 71201. Tel: 318-322-7379. Mrs. Emma Williams, Dir. Preschool. Lay Teachers 5; Students 60.
Catechesis/Religious Program—Students 50.

4—ST. MATTHEW (1851), [CEM] Rev. Joseph Puthuppally.
Res.: 121 Jackson St., 71201. Tel: 318-323-8878; 318-323-8879; Fax: 318-323-2537.

Catechesis/Religious Program—Students 46.
5—OUR LADY OF FATIMA (1952), [JC] Revs. Sebastian Kallarackal, C.M.I. (India); Job Edathinatt, C.M.I.
Res.: 3205 Concordia, P.O. Box 4136, 71211-4136. Tel: 318-325-7595; Fax: 318-325-8544.
School—3202 Franklin St., 71211. Tel: 318-387-1851; Fax: 318-387-7593. Sherry Fontana, Prin. Lay Teachers 12; Students 178.
Catechesis/Religious Program—Tel: 318-325-7596. Students 180.
Mission—St. Lawrence 357 Swartz School Rd., Swartz, Ouachita Parish 71281. Tel: 318-343-1618.
NOBLE, SABINE PARISH, ST. ANN (1955), (Native American), [CEM] Rev. Kenneth Williams.
Res.: 5272 Hwy. 482, 71462. Tel: 318-645-9419; Fax: 318-645-7033.
Catechesis/Religious Program—Students 76.
Mission—St. Catherine [CEM] 5272 Hwy. 482, Sabine Parish 71462.
OAK GROVE, WEST CARROLL PARISH, SACRED HEART (1947), Rev. Zacharias Prakuzhy, C.M.I. (India).
Church: 203 Purvis St., P.O. Box 419, 71263-0419. Tel: 318-428-2683.
Catechesis/Religious Program—Students 27.
RAMBIN, DESOTO PARISH, ST. MARY, Consolidated, with St. Joseph, Mansfield.
RAYVILLE, RICHLAND PARISH, SACRED HEART (1920), Rev. Philip Pazhayakari, C.M.I., Ph.D.
Res.: 716 Francis St., 71269. Tel: 318-728-0009; Fax: 318-728-2806.
Catechesis/Religious Program—Tel: 318-728-2445. Students 14.
Mission—St. Theresa 420 Main St., P.O. Box 363, Delhi, Richland Parish 71232-0363. Tel: 318-878-3484.
RUSTON, LINCOLN PARISH, ST. THOMAS AQUINAS (1941), Revs. Jeffrey Salwach, O.F.M.; Jose Antonio Posadas, O.F.M.; John Ostdiek, O.F.M.; Deacon John J. Serio.
Res.: 810 Carey Ave., 71270-4915. Tel: 318-255-2870; Fax: 318-254-8319.
Catechesis/Religious Program—Tel: 318-251-2142. Students 130.
VIVIAN, CADDO PARISH, ST. CLEMENT (1945), [CEM] [JC] Rev. Patrick A. Scully.
Office—819 N. Pine, 71082-3354. Tel: 318-375-2789; Fax: 318-375-3571.
Catechesis/Religious Program—Students 20.
WEST MONROE, OUACHITA PARISH, ST. PASCHAL (1940), [CEM] Rev. Michael Haney, O.F.M. In Res., Rev. Donatus Grunloh, O.F.M.; Bros. Claver Boerner, O.F.M.; Jose Martinez Valenzula, O.F.M.
Res.: 711 N. Seventh St., 71291-4211. Tel: 318-323-1631; Fax: 318-361-0527.
Catechesis/Religious Program—Debi Book, D.R.E. Students 135.
Mission—St. Francis of Assisi Calhoun, Ouachita Parish. Tel: 318-322-1487.
Mission—Our Lady of Perpetual Help Farmerville, Union Parish. Tel: 318-368-9239. Revs. Nicholas Owino Onyach, F.M.H. (Kenya); Glenn Phillips, O.F.M., Admin.
Res.: 471 Main St., Grambling, 71245-3088. Tel: 318-247-6734.
ZWOLLE, SABINE PARISH, ST. JOSEPH (1881), [CEM 2] Rev. Timothy C. Hurd.
Res.: P.O. Box 8, 71486-0008. Tel: 318-645-6155; Fax: 318-645-9852.
Catechesis/Religious Program—Students 372.

Chaplains of Public Institutions

SHREVEPORT. *Forcht Wade Correctional Center*. Rev. Richard Pusch, Chap.
Res.: P.O. Box 53043, 71135-3043.
Overton Brooks Veteran's Administration Medical Center, 510 E. Stoner Ave., 71101. Very Rev. Philip F. Michiels, V.F., Chap. Emergencies.
St. Joseph Church: P.O. Box 760, Mansfield, 71052-0730. Tel: 318-872-1158.
MONROE. *Swanson Correctional Center for Youth*, 4701 S. Grand, 71202-6499. (Formerly Louisiana Training Institute). Vacant.

Unassigned:
Rev.—
Garcia, Juan

On Duty Outside the Diocese:
Revs.—
Ebarb, Walter E.
Howard, Joseph, Jr.

Absent on Sick Leave:
Rev.—
Kennedy, John D.

Retired:
Rev. Msgrs.—
Buvens, Norman C.
Moore, Edmund J.
Revs.—
Beaulieu, Earl G.
Binh, John Phan Cong
Carey, William H., Ph.D.
Flynn, Thomas J., C.S.Sp.
Germain, Jean M.
McMullen, Roger
Moraus, Govie

Permanent Deacons:
Finnorn, John J., Jr.
Long, William R.
Morris, Ronald J.
Nash, Clary
Serio, John J.
Wisdom, Clarence, Inactive

INSTITUTIONS LOCATED IN THE DIOCESE

[A] HIGH SCHOOLS, DIOCESAN

SHREVEPORT. *Loyola College Prep*, 921 Jordan St., 71101-4390. Tel: 318-221-2675; Fax: 318-226-6334. Email: flyers@loyolaprep.org. Web: www.loyolaprep.org. Mr. Frank Israel, Prin. Lay Teachers 37; Students 403.
MONROE. *St. Frederick High School*, 3300 Westminster, 71201-3299. Tel: 318-323-9636; Fax: 318-323-7456. Email: apowers@stfredrickhigh.org. Web: www.stfrederickhigh.org. Rev. Msgr. Edmund J. Moore, Chap. (Retired); Alan Powers, Prin. Franciscan Sisters of Our Lady of Perpetual Help Sisters 2; Lay Teachers 30; Students 377.

[B] GENERAL HOSPITALS

SHREVEPORT. *Christus Health Northern Louisiana* (1907), dba Christus Schumpert Health System , One St. Mary Pl., P.O. Box 21976, 71120-1976. Tel: 318-681-4500; Fax: 318-681-4177 (Administration). Web: christusschumpert.org. Sr. Rose Marie McDermott, Vice Pres., Mission Effectiveness; Betsy Williams, Chap., Dir. Spiritual Care; Revs. Thomas John Vadakemuriyil, C.M.I. (India), Chap.; Richard Norsworthy, Asst. Chap.; Sr. Ernestine Mulvey, C.C.V.I., Chap. Operated by Christus Health Sisters 6; Bed Capacity 756; Patients Assisted Annually 161,652; Total Staff 1,885.
Christus Schumpert Bossier, 2105 Airline Dr., Bossier City, 71111. Tel: 318-848-8000; Fax: 318-848-8440. Carolyn Moore, Admin.; Betsy Williams, Dir. Spiritual Care; Sr. Antonius Martin, C.C.V.I., Chap. (Sub. of Christus Schumpert Health System)
Christus Schumpert Highland, 1453 E. Bert Kouns Industrial Loop, 71105. Tel: 318-681-5000; Fax: 318-681-5475. Mr. Mark Kerlin, Admin.; Betsy Williams, Dir. Spiritual Care; Rev. Dariusz Pawlowski (Poland), Chap. (Sub. of Christus Schumpert Health System)
COUSHATTA. *Christus Coushatta Health Care Center*, 1635 Marvel St., 71019. Tel: 318-932-2000; Fax: 318-932-2198. Email: laureen.painter@christushealth.org. Sr. Laureen Marie Painter, O.S.F., Pres. & CEO. Christus Health West Central Louisiana. Bed Capacity 40.
MONROE. *St. Francis Medical Center*, P.O. Box 1901, 71210-1901. Tel: 318-327-4000; Fax: 318-327-4142. Email: hoganr@stfran.com. Web: www.stfran.com. Mr. H. Gerald Smith, Pres. & CEO; Revs. Joseph Puthuppally, Chap.; Philip Chacko Theempalangattu (India), Chap.; James Dominic Thekkemury (India), Chap.; Ana Anzelmo, M.P.S., B.S.R.N., Dir. Mission, Pastoral Care. Franciscan Missionaries of Our Lady 3; Bed Capacity 372; Patients Assisted Annually 101,071; Total Staff 1,764; Hospice & Ancillary Care 104,560; Total Staff 196.
Non-Catholic Chaplains: Rev. Randy Farmer; Rev. Eddy Shoemaker; Rev. Everett Slack.
**St. Francis Specialty Hospital* (1995), 309 Jackson St., P.O. Box 1532, 71210. Tel: 318-327-4600; Fax: 318-327-4082. Email: hightob@stfran.com. Web: www.specialtyhospital.com. Mr. Bill Hightower, Pres. & CEO. Licensed Beds 50; Physicians 159; Employees 180; Patient admissions 472.
**St. Patrick Psychiatric Hospital, Inc.*, 309 Jackson St., P.O. Box 1901, 71210-1901. Tel: 318-327-4686; Fax: 318-327-4951. Email: rogersc@stfran.com. Web: www.stpatrickshospital.net. Cindy J. Rogers, CEO. Franciscan Missionaries of Our Lady Health System. Bed Capacity 28; Patients assisted annually: Inpatients 500; Outpatients 130; Total Staff 55.

[C] PROTECTIVE INSTITUTIONS

SHREVEPORT. *Holy Angels Residential Facility*, 10450 Ellerbe Rd., 71106-7712. Tel: 318-797-8500; 318-797-9070; Fax: 318-798-0159. Email: sherry@laholyangels.org. Sisters Concetta Scipione, O.L.S., Admin.; Gemma Forlani, O.L.S., Assoc. Admin.; Pasquina Tonwgnimi, O.L.S., Dorm Supvr.; Most Rev. William B. Friend, D.D., Pres. Sisters of Our Lady of Sorrows Sisters 3; Lay Personnel 265; Residents 184.

[D] HOMES FOR AGED

MONROE. *Christus St. Joseph Home*, 2301 Sterlington Rd., P.O. Box 6057, 71211-6057. Tel: 318-323-3426; Fax: 318-387-7157. Rev. Msgr. Patrick Murphy (ALX), Chap.; Mrs. Joy Huff, Admin. Operated by Christus Health Monroe. Licensed capacity nursing care 130; Assisted living 60; Sisters 2; Total Staff 150.

[E] SPECIAL CENTERS FOR SOCIAL SERVICES & ASSISTANCE

SHREVEPORT. *St. Catherine Community Center*, 331 E. 71st St., 71106-4305. Tel: 318-865-9817; Fax: 318-861-6177. Email: sccc@sport.rr.com. Web: www.rc.net/shreveport/stcatherine. Mr. Gus Grassi, Dir. Afterschool Enrichment, Summer Day Camp, Parenting, Arts, GED, Anger Management, Computers Total Assisted 1,125; Total Staff 24.

[F] CONVENTS AND RESIDENCES FOR SISTERS

SHREVEPORT. *Motherhouse of the Daughters of the Cross in America*, 411 E. Flournoy-Lucas Rd., 71115-3901. Tel: 318-797-0887; Fax: 318-797-7102. Email: dcsrs@bayou.com. Sr. Mary Louise Parisy, D.C., Supr. Sisters 6.
Religious House of Formation and Retirement-Our Lady of Sorrows, 9894 Norris Ferry Rd., 71106-7724. Tel: 318-797-0213; Fax: 318-797-7003. Email olsmotherhouse@aol.com. Web: www.ols.org. Sr. Seraphine Ricci, O.L.S., Supr. Sisters 11; Novices 2.

[G] NEWMAN CENTERS

GRAMBLING. *Student Center* 471 S. Main St., 71245-3088. Tel: 318-247-6734 (Office); Fax: 318-247-6288. Rev. Nicholas Owino Onyach, F.M.H. (Kenya), Dir.
MONROE. *Catholic Campus Ministry at the University of Louisiana at Monroe* , (formerly Northeast Louisiana University) , 911 University Ave., P.O. Box 7250, 71211-7250. Tel: 318-343-4897; Fax: 318-325-8544. Email: fatimachurch@msn.com. Revs. Sebastian Kallarackal, C.M.I. (India); Job Edathinatt, C.M.I., Campus Min.
RUSTON. *E. Donn Piatt Catholic Student Center at Louisiana Tech University* 600 S. Thornton St., 71270-4946. Tel: 318-231-0793; Fax: 318-254-8319. Email: specialred@cox-internet.com. Ethel Papillion, Campus Min.

[H] MISCELLANEOUS

BOSSIER CITY. *Magnificat-Nowela Chapter*, 3634 Greenacres Pl., No. 243, 71111. Tel: 318-742-7311. June Finnorn, Dir. & Contact Person.

RELIGIOUS INSTITUTES OF MEN REPRESENTED IN THE DIOCESE

For further details refer to the corresponding bracketed number in the Religious Institutes of Men or Women section.
[0275]—*Carmelites of Mary Immaculate (India)*—C.M.I.
[0520]—*Franciscan Friars* (Sacred Heart Prov.)—O.F.M.
[0520]—*Franciscan Friars* (Prov. of St. John the Baptist)—O.F.M.
[]—*Franciscan Missionaries of Hope* (Nairobi, Kenya)—F.M.H.
[0650]—*Holy Ghost Fathers of Ireland* (Louisiana Prov.)—C.S.Sp.

RELIGIOUS INSTITUTES OF WOMEN REPRESENTED IN THE DIOCESE

[]—*Congregation of the Mother of Carmel* (India)—C.M.C.
[0470]—*Congregation of the Sisters of Charity of the Incarnate Word, Houston, Texas*—C.C.V.I.
[1950]—*Congregation of the Sisters of the Holy Family*—S.S.F.
[0760]—*Daughters of Charity of St. Vincent de Paul*—D.C.
[0770]—*Daughters of the Cross*—D.C.
[1380]—*Franciscan Missionaries of Our Lady*—O.S.F.
[1430]—*Franciscan Sisters of Our Lady of Perpetual Help*—O.S.F.
[1530]—*Franciscan Sisters of Sylvania* Ohio—O.S.F.

[2970]—*School Sisters of Notre Dame* (St. Louis Prov.)—S.S.N.D.

[2970]—*School Sisters of Notre Dame* (Milwaukee Prov.)—S.S.N.D.

[0650]—*Sisters of Charity of St. Vincent de Paul of New York*—S.C.

[3120]—*Sisters of Our Lady of Sorrows*—O.L.S.

[3840]—*Sisters of St. Joseph of Carondelet*—C.S.J.

[]—*Sisters of the Eucharistic Covenant*—S.E.C.

[2050]—*Sisters of the Holy Spirit and Mary Immaculate*—S.H.Sp.

[4120-03]—*Ursuline Nuns of the Congregation of Paris*—O.S.U.

DIOCESAN CEMETERIES

SHREVEPORT. *St. Joseph*, Catholic Center, 3500 Fairfield Ave., 71104. Tel: 318-868-4441; Fax: 318-868-4605. Jill Braniff, Contact Person.

NECROLOGY

† Fuoco, Armando, (Retired)—Died Aug. 27, 2003

Diocese of Sioux City

(Dioecesis Siopolitana)

Most Reverend

LAWRENCE D. SOENS, D.D.

Retired Bishop of Sioux City; ordained May 6, 1950; appointed Bishop of Sioux City June 15, 1983; consecrated and installed August 17, 1983; retired November 28, 1998 *P.O. Box 3379, Sioux City, IA 51102-3379*. Fax: 712-233-7598.

(VACANT SEE)

Chancery: Administrative Offices, 1821 Jackson St., P.O. Box 3379, Sioux City, IA 51102-3379. Tel: 712-255-7933; Fax: 712-2?3-7598.

Web: www.scdiocese.org

Email: sernett@scdiocese.org

ESTABLISHED JANUARY 15, 1902.

Square Miles 14,518.

Corporate Title: "The Diocese of Sioux City."

Comprises 24 Counties in the northwest part of Iowa, west of Winnebago, Hancock, Wright, Hamilton and Story Counties, and north of Harrison, Shelby, Audubon, Guthrie and Dallas Counties.

Legal Title: For legal titles of parishes and diocesan institutions, consult the Chancery.

STATISTICAL OVERVIEW

Personnel	
Bishop	1
Retired Bishops	1
Priests: Diocesan Active in Diocese	90
Priests: Diocesan Active Outside Diocese	11
Priests: Retired, Sick or Absent	54
Number of Diocesan Priests	155
Religious Priests in Diocese	3
Total Priests in Diocese	158
Ordinations:	
Diocesan Priests	1
Transitional Deacons	1
Permanent Deacons in Diocese	36
Total Sisters	83
Parishes	
Parishes	124
With Resident Pastor:	
Resident Diocesan Priests	74
Resident Religious Priests	1
Without Resident Pastor:	
Administered by Priests	46
Administered by Professed Religious Men	3
Pastoral Centers	1
Professional Ministry Personnel:	
Sisters	3
Lay Ministers	65
Welfare	
Catholic Hospitals	3
Total Assisted	429,610
Homes for the Aged	3
Total Assisted	301
Special Centers for Social Services	5
Total Assisted	6,400
Educational	
Diocesan Students in Other Seminaries	9
Total Seminarians	9
Colleges and Universities	1
Total Students	1,168
High Schools, Diocesan and Parish	8
Total Students	2,203
Elementary Schools, Diocesan and Parish	23
Total Students	4,628
Catechesis/Religious Education:	
High School Students	3,223
Elementary Students	7,262
Total Students under Catholic Instruction	18,493
Teachers in the Diocese:	
Priests	2
Sisters	24
Lay Teachers	509
Vital Statistics	
Receptions into the Church:	
Infant Baptism Totals	1,626
Adult Baptism Totals	96
Received into Full Communion	233
First Communions	1,785
Confirmations	1,904
Marriages:	
Catholic	331
Interfaith	276
Total Marriages	607
Deaths	1,095
Total Catholic Population	94,186
Total Population	468,549

Former Bishops—Most Revs. PHILIP J. GARRIGAN, D.D., ord. June 11, 1870; appt. March 21, 1902; consecrated May 25, 1902; died Oct. 14, 1919.; EDMOND HEELAN, D.D., ord. June 24, 1890; consecrated April 8, 1919; died Sept. 20, 1948; JOSEPH M. MUELLER, D.D., ord. June 14, 1919; consecrated Oct. 16, 1947; died Aug. 9, 1981; FRANK H. GRETEMAN, D.D. (Retired), ord. Dec. 8, 1932; appt. Titular Bishop of Vissalsa April 14, 1965; consecrated May 26, 1965; appt. Bishop of Sioux City Oct. 20, 1970; installed Dec. 9, 1970; retired Aug. 17, 1983; died March 21, 1987; LAWRENCE D. SOENS, D.D. (Retired), ord. May 6, 1950; appt. Bishop of Sioux City June 15, 1983; installed Aug. 17, 1983; retired Nov. 28, 1998.

Vicars General—Rev. Msgrs. ROGER J. AUGUSTINE, V.G., Immaculate Conception Church, 419 Jones St., P.O. Box C, Moville, 51039-0802. Tel: 712-873-3745; MICHAEL D. SERNETT, V.G., J.C.D., 1821 Jackson St., P.O. Box 3379, Sioux City, 51102-3379.

Episcopal Vicar for Canonical Affairs—Rev. Msgr. R. MARK DUCHAINE, J.C.L., P.O. Box 3379, Sioux City, 51102. Tel: 712-255-7933.

Chancery—Administrative Offices, 1821 Jackson St., P.O. Box 3379, Sioux City, 51102-3379. Tel: 712-255-7933; Fax: 712-233-7598.

Chancellor—Rev. Msgr. MICHAEL D. SERNETT, V.G., J.C.D., Res.: 1821 Jackson St., P.O. Box 3379, Sioux City, 51104. Tel: 712-277-1606.

Vice Chancellors—Rev. MARK J. STOLL, J.C.L., St. Joseph Church, 28172 Nature Ave., Hinton, 51024. Tel: 712-233-7537; Mrs. KAY MORRISSEY, P.O. Box 3379, Sioux City, 51102. Tel: 712-233-7532.

Diocesan Tribunal—Address all marriage related materials to, P.O. Box 3379, Sioux City, 51102-3379. Tel: 712-233-7533; Fax: 712-233-7588.

Judicial Vicar—Rev. Msgr. R. MARK DUCHAINE, J.C.L., 1821 Jackson St., P.O. Box 3379, Sioux City 51102-3379. Res.: St. Mary Church, 703 Heisler, Mapleton, 51034-1222. Tel: 712-882-1780.

Promoter of Justice—Rev. Msgr. RICHARD E. ZENK, J.C.D.

Defenders of the Bond—Rev. ROBERT P. BROWN, S.T.L.; Rev. Msgr. RICHARD E. ZENK, J.C.D.

Judges—Rev. Msgrs. R. MARK DUCHAINE, J.C.L.; MICHAEL D. SERNETT, V.G., J.C.D.; ROGER AUGUSTINE, V.G.; Revs. PAUL-LOUIS ARTS; JEROME COSGROVE; MARK J. STOLL, J.C.L.; DONALD J. SLAVEN, J.C.L.

Notary—JUDY E. PUETZ.

Diocesan Corporate Board—Most Rev. DANIEL N. DINARDO, Pres.; Rev. Msgrs. ROGER J. AUGUSTINE, V.G., Vice Pres.; MICHAEL D. SERNETT, V.G., J.C.D., Sec. Directors:: Most Rev. LAWRENCE D. SOENS, D.D. (Retired); Revs. THOMAS E. GEELAN; ROGER J. LINNAN; Mr. DENNIS BERTE; Mr. JEFFREY R. MOHRHAUSER; Mr. RICHARD MONTGOMERY; Mrs. SUSAN H. PIERCE; Ms. SANDRA MUELLER; Dr. DANIEL J. SHEY; Mr. JAMES COSGROVE; Mr. JACK KAMMERER.

Diocesan Legal Counsel—Mr. MAURICE NIELAND, (Rawlings, Nieland, Probasco, Killinger, Ellenwanger, Jacobs, Mohrhauser, Law Firm, Sioux City). Refer all legal matters to The Chancery.

Presbyteral Council—Most Rev. DANIEL N. DINARDO; Rev. Msgrs. ROGER J. AUGUSTINE, V.G.; KENNETH A. SEIFRIED, V.F.; MERVIN J. HOOD (Retired); Revs. PAUL D. BORMANN; GERALD F. FEIERFEIL; DOUGLAS KLEIN; LAWRENCE L. MCCARTY; STEVEN J. MCLOUD; CLEMENT W. CURRANS; JEROME A. DEGEN (Retired); DALE E. REIFF; KEVIN M. RICHTER; RICHARD S. RIES; Very Rev. ROBERT J. SCHIMMER, V.F.; Rev. MERLIN J. SCHRAD; Rev. Msgr. MICHAEL D. SERNETT, V.G., J.C.D.

Diocesan Consultors—Rev. Msgrs. ROGER J. AUGUSTINE, V.G.; MICHAEL D. SERNETT, V.G., J.C.D.; MERVIN J. HOOD (Retired); Revs. PAUL-LOUIS ARTS; TIMOTHY J. HOGAN; VICTOR F. RAMAEKER; A. E. MCCOY; Very Rev. ROBERT J. SCHIMMER, V.F.; Rev. JOHN M. THOMAS.

Deans—Revs. GARY B. SNYDER, V.F., Southwestern Deanery; LAWRENCE L. MCCARTY, Central Deanery; JAMES C. MCALPIN, V.F., South Central Deanery; LAURENCE J. BURNS, V.F., Southeastern Deanery; Very Rev. DANIEL C. GUENTHER, V.F., Northeastern Deanery; Rev. Msgr. KENNETH A. SEIFRIED, V.F., Northwestern Deanery.

Diocesan Offices and Directors

Board of Education—Most Rev. DANIEL DINARDO, Ex Officio Chm.; Revs. PATRICK WALSH; TERRY RODER; GERALD FEIERFEIL; Mr. DALE HANSEN; Mrs. LINDA ANDERSON; Mr. JIM REISER; Sisters MARY LOUISE SCIESZINSKI; RUTH SCHOCK, O.S.F.; JOAN STOFFEL, O.S.F.; Mr. KEN HAJEK; Mrs. MAUREEN ELBERT; Mr. JAMES SCHALL; Mr. KEVIN VICKERY; Mrs. KATHEE FROEHLICH; Mrs. LORI GOETZINGER; Dr.

STEPHAN DAVIS.

Building Commission—Most Rev. DANIEL N. DINARDO, Chm.; Revs. BRIAN HUGHES; TIMOTHY FITZGERALD; PAUL-LOUIS ARTS; TIMOTHY SCHOTT; Ms. ROBIN BARBER; Mr. MICHAEL WILLIS; Mr. BRAD MOLLET; Mr. THOMAS VOGT.

Catholic School Foundation of the Diocese of Sioux City—Most Rev. DANIEL N. DINARDO, Pres., 1821 Jackson St., P.O. Box 3379, Sioux City, 51102.

Archives—DANIEL P. BURNS, 1821 Jackson St., P.O. Box 3379, Sioux City, 51102-3379. Tel: 712-233-7525.

Catholic Youth Organization—Rev. RANDY L. SCHON, St. Joseph Church, 1023 Hwy. 169, Bode, 50519-7031. Tel: 515-379-1470.

Office of Religious Education and Youth Ministry—Dr. STEPHAN DAVIS, Dir., 1821 Jackson St., P.O. Box 3379, Sioux City, 51102-3379.

Censor Librorum—Rev. Msgr. JAMES K. LAFFERTY, Ph.D. (Retired), St. John's Church, P.O. Box J, Ogden, 50212-0810. Tel: 515-275-2580.

Catholic Charities—Mr. JERRY EATON, Dir., 1601 Military Rd., Sioux City, 51103. Tel: 712-252-4547. Fort Dodge Office: 3 N. 16th, Fort Dodge, 50501. Tel: 515-576-4156. Carroll Office: 409 1/2 W. 7th St., P.O. Box 13, Carroll, 51401. Tel: 712-792-9597. Storm Lake Office: 1709 Richland St., Storm Lake, 50588.

Office of Hispanic Ministry—Sr. MARIA DE JESUS YBARRA, O.P., Dir., 1821 Jackson St., P.O. Box 3379, Sioux City, 51102-3379. Tel: 712-233-7581.

Continuing Education for Priests—Very Rev. DANIEL C. GUENTHER, V.F., Dir., Holy Family Church, P.O. Box 322, Emmetsburg, 50536-3187.

Council of Catholic Women—Rev. JAMES TIGGES, Moderator, St. James Church, 109 6th Ave., S.W., LeMars, 51031-3434. Tel: 712-546-5201.

Ecumenical Commission—VACANT, Chm.; Revs. ROBERT W. GRALAPP; JAMES C. MCALPIN, V.F.; ALFRED E. MCCOY (Retired).

Episcopal Representative for Religious—Sr. ROSALIE ERDMANN, S.L.W., 3636 Glen Oaks Blvd., Apt. 16, Sioux City, 51104-1564. Tel: 712-258-2579.

Episcopal Representative for Hospitals and Health Care—Rev. GERALD F. FEIERFEIL, Nativity Parish, 4242 Natalia Way, Sioux City, 51106-4099.

Office of Faith Formation—Mrs. KAY MORRISSEY, Dir.; Mrs. BEV HURNI, Adult & Family Ministries Programs; Ms. LINDA ANDERSON, Catechesis; Dr. STEPHAN DAVIS, Youth & InterGenerational Ministry, 1821 Jackson St., P.O. Box 3379, Sioux City, 51102-3379. Tel: 712-233-7530.

Holy Childhood Association—Rev. Msgr. RICHARD E. ZENK, J.C.D., Dir., P.O. Box 3379, Sioux City, 51102-3379.

Liturgy Commission—Rev. TIM FITZGERALD; Mrs. MONICA PEARSON; Revs. BRIAN DANNER, Chm.; BRUCE LAWLER; Sisters MARGE STAUDT, O.S.F.; JANICE HOFFMAN, O.S.F.; M. ARNOLD STAUDT, O.S.F.; Mrs. MARLENE FITZPATRICK; Rev. DAVE HEMANN; Mr. MATTHEW GEERLINGS; Mr. TIM PICK; Mr. MICHAEL WILLIS.

Office Of "The Globe"—Ms. RENEE WEBB, Editor, 1825 Jackson St., P.O. Box 5079, Sioux City, 51102-5079. Tel: 712-255-2550 Editorial Office; Circulation.

Office of Catholic Education—Mr. KEVIN VICKERY, Supt., 1821 Jackson, P.O. Box 3379, Sioux City, 51102-3379. Tel: 712-233-7589.

Permanent Diaconate—Co-Directors:: Rev. ARMAND J. BERTRAND, Res.: Immaculate Conception Church, P.O. Box 658, Cherokee, 51012-0658. Tel: 712-225-4606; Deacon RONALD M. FORREST, 1821 Jackson St., P.O. Box 3379, Sioux City, 51102-3379.

Priests' Personnel Board—Rev. Msgr. ROGER J. AUGUSTINE, V.G., Bishop's Liaison; Revs. KEVIN M. RICHTER; EDWARD M. GIRRES; PATRICK O'KANE; PAUL J. KELLY.

Priests' Pension Plan - Board of Trustees—Most Rev. DANIEL N. DINARDO; Rev. Msgr. MICHAEL SERNETT; Revs. GARY B. SNYDER, V.F.; ROGER LINNAN; DANIEL LYNCH; BRUCE A. LAWLER; Mr. RICHARD L. BILLINGS, Chm.; Mr. THOMAS P. GRIMSLEY; Mr. PATRICK D. KUEHL; Mr. MICHAEL J. MOELLER; Mr. JEFFREY R. MOHRHAUSER; Mr. ROBERT V. WILLIAMS.

Propagation of the Faith, Association of the Holy Childhood, Catholic Students' Mission Crusade—Rev. Msgr. RICHARD E. ZENK, J.C.D., Dir., 1821 Jackson St., P.O. Box 3379, Sioux City, 51102-3379.

Office of Communications—Mr. JAMES WHARTON, Dir., P.O. Box 3379, Sioux City, 51102-3379.

Rural Life Conference—Mrs. MARILYN MURPHY, Dir., 1601 Military Rd., Sioux City, 51103. Tel: 712-252-4547.

St. Joseph Education Society— (Diocesan Seminarian Board). Very Rev. PAUL-LOUIS ARTS, Exec. Sec., Res.: 1000 Douglas St., Sioux City, 51105-1333. Tel: 712-255-1637.

Victim Assistance Coordinator—ANGIE MACK, Mercy Child Advocacy Center. Tel: 712-279-5610; 866-435-4397 (Toll Free). Email: macka@mercyhealth.com.

Vocations—Rev. BRIAN C. HUGHES, 5000 Military Rd., Sioux City, 51103-1564. Tel: 712-233-7523; 712-233-1652.

CLERGY, PARISHES, MISSIONS AND PAROCHIAL SCHOOLS

CITY OF SIOUX CITY
(WOODBURY COUNTY)

1—CATHEDRAL OF THE EPIPHANY (1867), Very Rev. Paul-Louis Arts; Revs. Paul J. Kelly; Hieu Nguyen (Vietnam).
Res.: 1011 Douglas St., 51105-1399. Tel: 712-255-1637; Fax: 712-255-4194.
School—Tel: 712-252-3181; Fax: 712-252-3181. Please refer to Catholic Schools of Sioux City under Inter-Parochial Schools in the Institution section.
Catechesis/Religious Program—Tel: 712-258-4962; Fax: 712-258-4962. Students 358.

2—BLESSED SACRAMENT (1922), Revs. Nickolas Becker; Merlin J. Shrad; Deacons John Hefferman; Fred Karpuk; Ronald C. Pietz, Business Mgr.
Res.: 3012 Jackson St., 51104-2799. Tel: 712-277-2949; Fax: 712-277-2963.
School— Please refer to the listing under Inter-Parochial Schools in the Institution section.
Catechesis/Religious Program—Tel: 712-277-4155; Fax: 712-258-3698. Patricia Walsh, D.R.E. Students 169.

3—ST. BONIFACE (1887), (German), [JC] Rev. Kevin M. Richter; Deacon James Sands. In Res., Rev. Richard A. Sitzmann.
Res.: 703 W. Fifth St., 51103-3799. Tel: 712-255-3577; Fax: 712-279-0751.
School— Please refer to the listing under Inter-Parochial Schools in the Institution section.
Catechesis/Religious Program—Tel: 712-258-4962; Fax: 712-258-7101. Students 92.

4—ST. CASIMIR (1915), (Lithuanian), Closed. For inquiries for parish records contact the chancery.

5—ST. FRANCIS OF ASSISI (1907), (Polish), Closed. For inquiries for parish records contact the chancery.

6—IMMACULATE CONCEPTION (1905), [JC] Rev. Steven W. Brodersen.
Res.: P.O. Box 2817, 51106-2817. Tel: 712-276-4821; Fax: 712-276-1321.
School— Please refer to the listing under Inter-Parochial Schools in the Institution section.
Catechesis/Religious Program—Tel: 712-276-4571; Fax: 712-276-1321. Students 178.

7—ST. JOSEPH (1887), [JC] Rev. Gary B. Snyder, V.F.; Deacons Jerome Reicks; Ronald Pietz.
Res.: 1112 Eighth St., 51105-1899. Tel: 712-258-3813; Fax: 712-255-4018.
School— Please refer to the listing under Inter-Parochial Schools in the Institution section.
Catechesis/Religious Program—Tel: 712-258-4962. Students 39.

8—ST. MICHAEL (1907), [JC] Rev. Timothy J. Hogan; Sr. Jean Ann Rausch, F.S.P.A., Pastoral Min.; Deacons Larry Sitzman; William Berger, (Retired). Office and Res. Address: 2223 Indian Hills Dr., 51104-1605. Tel: 712-239-2411; Fax: 712-239-4710.
School— Please refer to the listing under Inter-Parochial Schools in the Institution section.
Catechesis/Religious Program—Tel: 712-239-2411. Students 153.

9—NATIVITY OF OUR LORD JESUS CHRIST (1966), Rev. Gerald Feierfeil.
Res.: 4242 Natalia Way, 51106-4099. Tel: 712-276-3022; Fax: 712-274-2703.
School— Please refer to the listing under Inter-Parochial Schools in the Institution section.
Catechesis/Religious Program—Tel: 712-274-0497. Students 412.

10—SACRED HEART (1907), [JC] Rev. Craig A. Collison. In Res., Rev. Brian Hughes.
Res.: 5000 Military Rd., 51103-1564. Tel: 712-233-1652; Fax: 712-255-3056.
School— Please refer to the listing under Inter-Parochial Schools in the Institution section.
Catechesis/Religious Program—Students 123.

OUTSIDE SIOUX CITY

AKRON, PLYMOUTH CO., ST. PATRICK (1888), [CEM] Rev. Msgr. Richard E. Zenk, J.C.D.
Res.: 650 Dakota St., P.O. Box 317, 51001-0317. Tel: 712-568-3292.
Catechesis/Religious Program—Students 60.

ALGONA, KOSSUTH CO., ST. CECELIA (1892), [CEM] Rev. Paul Eisele; Deacon Bob Larsen.
Res.: P.O. Box 633, 50511-0633. Tel: 515-295-3435; Fax: 515-295-9290.
School—Seton Elementary, Tel: 515-295-3509; Fax: 515-295-7739. Consolidation of St. Cecelia, Algona, St. Benedict, St. Joseph, Wesley, St. Joseph, Bode Presentation Sisters 1; Lay Teachers 25; Students 225.
Catechesis/Religious Program—Students 296.

ALTON, SIOUX CO., ST. MARY'S (1870), (German), [CEM] Rev. John A. Vakulskas Jr.
Res.: 609 10th St., 51003. Tel: 712-756-4224; Fax: 712-756-4431.
School—Spalding Catholic, (Grades 4-6) Tel: 712-756-4532; Fax: 712-756-4532. Consolidation of Alton, Hospers and Granville. Lay Teachers 3; Students 57.
Catechesis/Religious Program— Cluster of St. Mary, St. Anthony's, and St. Joseph's. Students 95.

ANTHON, WOODBURY CO., ST. JOSEPH'S (1890), [CEM] Rev. Terry A. Roder.
Res.: P.O. Box 285, 51004-0285. Tel: 712-373-5573.
Catechesis/Religious Program—Tel: 712-373-5573. Students 60.

ARCADIA, CARROLL CO., ST. JOHN THE BAPTIST (1875), (German), [CEM] Rev. John M. Thomas.
Res.: P.O. Box 23, 51430-0023. Tel: 712-689-2595; Fax: 712-689-2282.
Catechesis/Religious Program—Students 32.

ARMSTRONG, EMMET CO., ST. MARY'S (1892), [CEM] [JC] Rev. Jerome P. Cosgrove.
Office—404 Fifth Ave., P.O. Box 437, 50514-9301. Tel: 712-864-3160.
Catechesis/Religious Program—Tel: 712-362-4172. Students 47.

ASHTON, OSCEOLA CO., ST. MARY'S CATHOLIC CHURCH (1880), [CEM] Rev. Clair L. Boes.
Res.: P.O. Box 157, 51232-0157. Tel: 712-724-6411.
Catechesis/Religious Program—2191 Nettle Ave., 51232. Tel: 712-724-6297. Mrs. Nancy Marnach, D.R.E. Students 38.

AUBURN, SAC CO., ST. MARY'S (1893), (German), [JC] Rev. Lawrence L. McCarty.
Res.: P.O. Box H, 51433. Tel: 712-688-2845.
Catechesis/Religious Program—Students 40.

BANCROFT, KOSSUTH CO., ST. JOHN THE BAPTIST'S (1891), [CEM] [JC] Rev. Paul D. Bormann; Deacon Philip Doocy.
Res.: P.O. Box 195, 50517-0195. Tel: 515-885-2462; Fax: 515-885-2424.
School—St. John's Elementary School, Tel: 515-885-2580; Fax: 515-885-2402. Lay Teachers 5; Students 46.
Catechesis/Religious Program—Tel: 515-885-2580. Lori Geitzenauer, D.R.E. Students 166.

BARNUM, WEBSTER CO., ST. JOSEPH'S (1891), [CEM] Unassigned.
Catholic Team Office—P.O. Box 994, Fort Dodge, 50501. Tel: 515-573-3616; Fax: 515-573-4556. Church: 326 West St., 50518.
Catechesis/Religious Program—Students 207.

BODE, KOSSUTH CO., ST. JOSEPH'S (1876), [CEM] Rev. Randy L. Schon.
Res.: 1023 Hwy. 169, 50519. Tel: 515-379-1470.
Catechesis/Religious Program—Tel: 515-295-3435. Students 11.

BOONE, BOONE CO., SACRED HEART (1868), [CEM] Rev. Clem W. Currans.
Res.: 921 12th St., 50036-2295. Tel: 515-432-1975.
Catechesis/Religious Program—Tel: 515-432-2884; Fax: 515-432-1975. Students 202.

BREDA, CARROLL CO., ST. BERNARD'S (1880), [CEM] Rev. James R. Smith.
Res.: P.O. Box 39, 51436-0031. Tel: 712-673-2351; Fax: 712-673-2351.
School— Parish is a member of newly consolidated K-12 Kuemper Catholic School System, Carroll, IA. Please refer to Keumper Catholic School System under Inter-Parochial Schools in the Insititution section.
Catechesis/Religious Program—Tel: 712-792-0513. Students 27.

CARROLL, CARROLL CO.

1—HOLY SPIRIT (1964), [JC], SS Peter / Paul, and St. Joseph, Carroll merged to form Holy Spirit, Carroll. Revs. James D. McCormick; Sunny Domininc (India); Siby Punnoose; Deacon William Schroeder.
Res.: 421 E. Bluff St., 51401-3099. Tel: 712-792-4386; Fax: 712-792-8038.
School— Parish is a member of newly consolidated K-12 Kuemper Catholic School System, Carroll, IA. Please refer to Keumper Catholic School System under Inter-Parochial Schools in the Insititution section.
Catechesis/Religious Program—Tel: 712-792-0513; Fax: 712-792-9245. Deacon Timothy Murphy, D.R.E. Shared with St. Lawrence & surrounding parishes. Students 357.

2—ST. LAWRENCE (1914), [JC] Rev. Timothy R. Schott; Deacons Robert Bruner; Louis Westendorf;

Tim Murphy.
Res.: 1607 N. West St., 51401-4198. Tel: 712-792-9244; Fax: 712-792-9245.
School— Parish is a member of newly consolidated K-12 Kuemper Catholic School System, Carroll, IA. Please refer to Keumper Catholic School System under Inter-Parochial Schools in the Insititution section.
Catechesis/Religious Program—Tel: 712-792-0513. Shared with Holy Spirit and surrounding parishes. Students 357.

CHARTER OAK, CRAWFORD CO., ST. BONIFACE (1883), (German—Irish), [CEM] Rev. Richard D. Ball.
Res.: P.O. Box 317, Dow City, 51528. Tel: 712-678-3449.
Mission—St. Mary's [CEM] c/o Box 317, Ute, Monona Co. 51528. Tel: 712-674-3329.
Catechesis/Religious Program—Students 62.

CHEROKEE, CHEROKEE CO.
1—ST. DYMPHNA CHAPEL (1960),, (Chapel for Patients) Rev. Eugene E. Sitzmann.
Mailing Address: 1251 W. Cedar Loop, 51012. Tel: 712-225-2429; Fax: 712-225-6925.
Res.: 975 540th St., 51012. Tel: 712-225-2131; Fax: 712-225-2742.
2—IMMACULATE CONCEPTION (1870), [CEM] Rev. Armand J. Bertrand; Deacon Leroy Rupp.
Res.: 709 W. Cedar St., P.O. Box 658, 51012-0658. Tel: 712-225-4606.
Catechesis/Religious Program—7th & Willow, 51012. Tel: 712-225-4466. Students 225.

CHURDAN, GREENE CO., ST. COLUMBKILLE'S (1886), (German—Irish), [CEM] Rev. Steven J. McLoud; Deacon Donald Kunecke.
Res.: 807 Head St., P.O. Box 128, 50050-0128. Tel: 515-389-3625; Fax: 515-389-3795.
Catechesis/Religious Program—Tel: 515-386-4010; Fax: 515-386-3672. Students 58.

CLARE, WEBSTER CO., ST. MATTHEW'S (1886), [CEM] Rev. Laurence J. Burns, V.F.
Catholic Team Office—P.O. Box 994, Fort Dodge, 50501. Tel: 515-573-3616; Fax: 515-573-4556.
Church: 420 Front St., 50524-0105. Tel: 515-546-4505.

COON RAPIDS, CARROLL CO., ANNUNCIATION (1891), [CEM] Rev. Anthony Pick.
Res.: P.O. Box 76, 50058-0076. Tel: 712-999-2823; Fax: 712-999-2823.
Catechesis/Religious Program—Tel: 712-999-5235. Students 134.

DANBURY, WOODBURY CO., ST. MARY'S (1897), (German), [CEM] Rev. Terry A. Roder.
Res.: P.O. Box 318, 51019-0318. Tel: 712-883-2406; Fax: 712-883-2458.
School—Danbury Elementary, Tel: 712-883-2244. Priests 1; Sisters 2; Lay Teachers 4; Students 47.
Catechesis/Religious Program—Students 70.

DAYTON, WEBSTER CO., CHRIST THE KING (1950), [CEM] Sr. Mary Lois Lehmann, P.B.V.M., Pastoral Min.
Catholic Team Office—P.O, Box 994, Fort Dodge, 50501. Tel: 515-573-3616; Fax: 515-573-4556.
Catechesis/Religious Program—Tel: 515-547-2743.

DEDHAM, CARROLL CO., ST. JOSEPH'S (1892), [CEM] Rev. Anthony Pick.
Res.: P.O. Box 47, 51440-0047. Tel: 712-683-5744.
School—Kuemper Catholic Grade Schools, Tel: 712-792-3610; Fax: 712-792-3365. Consolidation of Dedham, Willey Elementary, Holy Spirit and St. Lawrence.
Catechesis/Religious Program—Students 47.

DENISON, CRAWFORD CO., ST. ROSE OF LIMA (1872), [CEM] Rev. Edward G. Murray.
Res.: 1008 2nd Ave. S., P.O. Box 280, 51442-0280. Tel: 712-263-2152; Fax: 712-263-2153.
School—Tel: 712-263-5408; Fax: 712-263-2153. Lay Teachers 10; Students 91.
Catechesis/Religious Program—Tel: 712-263-5408. Students 270.

DOW CITY, CRAWFORD CO., ST. MARYS (1947), (German—Irish), Rev. Richard D. Ball.
Res.: 215 Clark St., P.O. Box 317, 51528-0317. Tel: 712-674-3329.
Catechesis/Religious Program—Students 20.

DUNCOMBE, WEBSTER CO., ST. JOSEPH'S (1880), [CEM] Rev. Timothy J. Boekelman.
Catholic Team Office—P.O. Box 994, Fort Dodge, 50501. Tel: 515-573-3616; Fax: 515-573-4556.

EARLY, SAC CO., SACRED HEART (1882), [CEM] Rev. Patrick J. O'Kane.
Res.: 501 Church St., P.O. Box 378, 50535-0378. Tel: 712-273-5482; Fax: 712-273-5798.
Catechesis/Religious Program—Tel: 712-273-5577. Students 93.

EMMETSBURG, PALO ALTO CO.
1—HOLY FAMILY (1870), (Irish), [CEM] Very Rev. Daniel C. Guenther, V.F.
Res.: 2001 S. Broadway, P.O. Box 322, 50536-0322. Tel: 712-852-3187; Fax: 712-852-4406.
School—Emmetsburg Catholic School, (Grades K-8) Tel: 712-852-3464; Fax: 712-852-3464. Mrs. Jean Hyslop, O.S.F., Prin. Lay Teachers 10; Students 89.
Catechesis/Religious Program—Tel: 712-852-3187. Angie Strohman, D.R.E. Students 100.
2—ST. THOMAS, Closed., For sacramental records contact Holy Family, Emmetsburg.

ESTHERVILLE, EMMET CO., ST. PATRICK'S (1891), [CEM] Rev. Jerome P. Cosgrove.
Res.: P.O. Box 383, 51334-0383. Tel: 712 362-5851; Fax: 712-362-5852.
Catechesis/Religious Program—Duhigg Center, 902 Central Ave., 51334. Tel: 712-362-4172. Students 187.

FONDA, POCAHONTAS CO., OUR LADY OF GOOD COUNSEL (1884), [CEM] Rev. Thomas J. Hart; Deacons J. R. Hogan; Eldon Sullivan.
Res.: P.O. Box 339, 50540-0339. Tel: 712-288-6480; Fax: 712-288-4465.
School—Tel: 712-288-4465. Lay Teachers 5; Students 48.
Catechesis/Religious Program—Students 73.

FORT DODGE, WEBSTER CO.
1—CORPUS CHRISTI (1856), [JC] Revs. Christian J. Van Oosbree; Bradley C. Pelzel.
Catholic Team Office—P.O. Box 994, 50501-0994. Tel: 515-573-3616; Fax: 515-573-4556.
Church: 416 N. 8th St., 50501.
School— Please refer to Fort Dodge Catholic Schools Inc. under the Inter-Parochial Schools in the Institution section.
Catechesis/Religious Program—Students 207.
2—HOLY ROSARY (1946), [JC] Rev. Lynn Bruch.
Catholic Team Office—P.O. Box 994, 50501. Tel: 515-573-3616; Fax: 515-573-4556.
Res.: 2401 9th Ave. S., 50501-6246. Tel: 515-573-3162 (Res.).
School— See separate listing under Inter-Parochial Schools in Institution Section.
Catechesis/Religious Program—Students 207.
3—SACRED HEART (1897), [JC] Rev. Edward M. Girres.
Catholic Team Office—P.O. Box 994, 50501. Tel: 515-573-3616; Fax: 515-573-4556.
Res.: 1329 Second Ave. S., 50501-4925. Tel: 515-573-7669.
Catechesis/Religious Program—Students 207.

GILMORE CITY, POCAHONTAS CO., ST. JOHN'S (1889), [CEM] Rev. William A. Schreiber.
Res.: 311 4th St. N., Humboldt, 50548. Tel: 515-373-6016.
Catechesis/Religious Program—Tel: 515-332-2784. Students 11.

GRAETTINGER, PALO ALTO CO., IMMACULATE CONCEPTION (1891), [CEM] Rev. Thomas E. Geelan.
Res.: 305 N. Cumeron, P.O. Box 448, 51342. Tel: 712-859-3327; Fax: 712-859-3327.
Catechesis/Religious Program—503 W. Olive St., 51342. Tel: 712-859-3990. Students 92.

GRAND JUNCTION, GREENE CO., ST. BRIGID'S (1873), (Irish), [CEM] Rev. Donald C. Ries.
Res.: Jefferson, 50129. Tel: 515-738-2684; Fax: 515-386-3672.
Catechesis/Religious Program—St. Brigid Parish Center 602 Hager St. E., 50107. Tel: 515-738-2254. Students 29.

GRANVILLE, SIOUX CO., ST. JOSEPH (1886), [CEM] Rev. Msgr. Kenneth A. Seifried, V.F.
Res.: P.O. Box 127, 51022-0127. Tel: 712-727-3551.
School—Spalding Catholic School, (Grades 7-8) Tel: 712-727-3451; Fax: 712-727-3455. Consolidation of Alton, Hospers and Granville. Lay Teachers 2; Students 49.
High School—Spalding Catholic High School Priests 1; Lay Teachers 18; Students 84.
Catechesis/Religious Program— Pilgrim cluster held at St. Mary's, Alton.

HALBUR CARROLL CO., ST. AUGUSTINE'S (1904), [CEM] Rev. Dale E. Reiff.
Res.: P.O. Box 13, 51444-0013. Tel: 712-658-2464.
School— Parish is a member of newly consolidated K-12 Kuemper Catholic School System, Carroll, IA. Please refer to Keumper Catholic School System under Inter-Parochial Schools in the Institution section.
Catechesis/Religious Program—Tel: 712-792-0513 (Carroll); 712-653-2131 (Mannina). Students 17.

HAWARDEN, SIOUX CO., ST. MARY'S (1887), [JC] Rev. LeRoy L. Seuntjens.
Res.: 1125 Avenue L., P.O. Box 271, 51023-0271. Tel: 712-551-1501.
Catechesis/Religious Program—Students 132.

HOLSTEIN, IDA CO., OUR LADY OF GOOD COUNSEL (1884), [CEM] Rev. David Hemann
Mailing Address: 513 Mueller St., 51025-9802.
Office: 800 N. Main, Ida Grove, 51445. Tel: 712-368-4755.
Catechesis/Religious Program—Tel: 712-368-2504. Students 95.

HORNICK, WOODBURY CO., ST. PHILIP'S (1900), Closed. For inquiries for parish records contact the chancery

HOSPERS, SIOUX CO., ST. ANTHONY'S (1877), [CEM] Rev. John A. Vakulskas Jr.
Res.: 506 Elm, P.O. Box 86, 51238-0086. Tel: 712-752-8784.
School—Spalding Elementary, (Grades K-2) Tel: 712-752-8286. Consolidation of Alton, Hospers and Granville. Lay Teachers 4; Students 64.
Catechesis/Religious Program— Clustered with St. Mary, Alton, and St. Joseph, Granville. Students 95.

HUMBOLDT, HUMBOLDT CO., ST. MARY'S (1878), [CEM] Rev. William A. Schreiber.
Res.: 311 Fourth St. N., 50548-1647. Tel: 515-332-2856; Fax: 515-332-1487.
School—Tel: 515-332-2134. Sisters 3; Lay Teachers 10; Students 115.
Catechesis/Religious Program—Tel: 515-332-2784. Students 160.

IDA GROVE, IDA CO., SACRED HEART (1878), [CEM] Rev. David Hemann.
Res.: 800 N. Main, P.O. Box 244, 51445-1297. Tel: 712-364-2718.
Catechesis/Religious Program—Tel: 712-364-3628. Students 158.

JEFFERSON, GREENE CO., ST. JOSEPH'S (1875), Rev. Donald C. Ries.
Res.: 503 N. Chestnut St., 50129-1507. Tel: 515-386-2638; Fax: 515-386-3672.
Catechesis/Religious Program—501 N. Locust, 50129. Tel: 515-386-4010. Students 186.
Mission—St. Brigid [CEM] 602 Hager, Grand Junction, Greene Co. 50107. Tel: 515-738-2254.

KINGSLEY, PLYMOUTH CO., ST. MICHAEL'S (1888), [CEM] Rev. Thomas J. Topf.
Res.: P.O. Box 99, 51028-0099. Tel: 712-378-2722.
Catechesis/Religious Program—Tel: 712-378-2021. Students 146.

LAKE CITY, CALHOUN CO., ST. MARY'S (1894), [CEM] [JC] Rev. Timothy J. Boekelman; Deacon Don Kunecke.
Res.: P.O. Box 131, 51449-0131. Tel: 712-464-3395; Fax: 712-464-7669.
Catechesis/Religious Program—Students 138.

LARCHWOOD, LYON CO., ST. MARY (1898), (German—Dutch), [JC] Rev. Jeffrey Schleisman; Deacon Jeff Gallagher.
Res.: P.O. Box 37, 51241-0037. Tel: 712-477-2273; Fax: 712-477-2162.
Catechesis/Religious Program—Tel: 712-477-2803; Fax: 712-477-2403. Students 118.

LAURENS, POCAHONTAS CO., SACRED HEART (1893), [CEM] Rev. Verne P. Stapenhorst.
Res.: P.O. Box 171, 50554-0171. Tel: 712-845-4596.
Catechesis/Religious Program—Tel: 712-289-6481. Students 85.

LE MARS, PLYMOUTH CO.
1—ST. JAMES (1883), [JC] Rev. James T. Tigges; Deacon Donald Kunkel.
Res.: 109 Sixth Ave., S.W., 51031-3434. Tel: 712-546-5201; Fax: 712-546-8696.
School—Gehlen Catholic Elementary, Tel: 712-546-5126. Lay Teachers 21; Students 254.
High School—Gehlen Catholic High School, Tel: 712-546-4181. Lay Teachers 23; Students 273.
Catechesis/Religious Program—20 Sixth Ave., N.E., 51031. Tel: 712-546-6038. Students 260.
2—ST. JOSEPH'S (1875), (German), [CEM] [JC] Rev. Andrew W. Hoffmann.
Res.: 20 Sixth Ave., N.E., 51031-3714. Tel: 712-546-5223; Fax: 712-546-8346.
School—Gehlen Catholic School, Plymouth St., S.E., 51031. Tel: 712-546-4181; Fax: 712-546-9384.
Catechesis/Religious Program—Tel: 712-546-6038. Mr. Ronald Rene, D.R.E. Students 205.

LEDYARD, KOSSUTH CO., SACRED HEART (1887), [CEM] [JC] Rev. Paul D. Bormann.
Mailing Address: P.O. Box 126, 50556-0067. Tel: 515-646-2525.
Res.: 204 S. Summit Ave., P.O. Box 195, Bancroft, 50517. Tel: 515-885-2462; Fax: 515-885-2424.
Catechesis/Religious Program— Twinned with St. John's, Bancroft. Students 24.

LIDDERDALE, CARROLL CO., HOLY FAMILY (1914), (German), [CEM] Rev. Joseph A. Dillinger.
Res.: P.O. Box 160, 51452-0160. Tel: 712-822-5522.
School— Parish is a member of newly consolidated K-12 Kuemper Catholic School System, Carroll, IA. Please refer to Keumper Catholic School System under Inter-Parochial Schools in the Institution section.
Catechesis/Religious Program—Tel: 712-792-0513. Students 30.
Mission—St. Elizabeth Seton Church Glidden, Carroll Co. Tel: 712-659-3051.

LIVERMORE, HUMBOLDT CO., SACRED HEART (1881), [CEM] Rev. Dan Greving.
Res.: 403 East St. S., P.O. Box 38, Wesley, 50483-0038. Tel: 515-679-4279.
Catechesis/Religious Program—Tel: 515-379-2508. Students 66.

LOHRVILLE, CALHOUN CO., ST. JOSEPH'S (1885), (Irish), [CEM] Rev. Timothy J. Boekelman.

Res.: N. Lloyd St., P.O. Box 131, Lake City, 51449. Tel: 712-464-3395; Fax: 712-464-7669.
Catechesis/Religious Program—Students 44.

MADRID, BOONE CO., ST. MALACHY'S (1923), [JC] Rev. Brian J. Danner; Deacon Frank Milani.
Res.: 207 Gerald St., 50156-1464. Tel: 515-795-2731; Fax: 515-795-2731.
Church: 405 Gerald St., 50156. Tel: 515-795-2613.
Catechesis/Religious Program—Tel: 515-795-3928. Students 263.
Mission—St. John of God Woodward, 50276.

MALLARD, PALO ALTO CO., ST. MARY'S (1889), [CEM] Rev. Edmund H. Tiedeman.
Res.: P.O. Box 207, 50562-0236. Tel: 712-425-3359.
Catechesis/Religious Program—Tel: 515-887-3333; Fax: 515-887-3334. Students 7.

MANILLA, CRAWFORD CO., SACRED HEART (1887), [CEM] Rev. Robert W. Gralapp.
Res.: 269 6th St., P.O. Box 339, 51454-0339. Tel: 712-654-9511.
Catechesis/Religious Program—Students 108.

MANNING, CARROLL CO., SACRED HEART (1916), (German), [CEM] Rev. James C. McAlpin, V.F.
Res.: 203 Sue St., 51455-1399. Tel: 712-655-3804. Email: sacredheart@ionet.net.
Catechesis/Religious Program—Tel: 712-655-2933. Students 211.

MANSON, CALHOUN CO., ST. THOMAS (1885), [CEM 2] Rev. Richard S. Ries.
Res.: P.O. Box 99, 50563-0099. Tel: 712-469-3743; Fax: 712-469-3066.
Catechesis/Religious Program—Tel: 712-469-3334. Students 128.

MAPLE RIVER, CARROLL CO., ST. FRANCIS OF ASSISI (1904), (German), [CEM] Rev. Robert Brown.
Res.: 19481 140th St., Carroll, 51401-9499. Tel: 712-792-3934; Fax: 712-792-3977.
School— Parish is a member of newly consolidated K-12 Kuemper Catholic School System, Carroll, IA. Please refer to Keumper Catholic School System under Inter-Parochial Schools in the Institution section.
Catechesis/Religious Program—Tel: 712-792-9422. Students 6.

MAPLETON, MONONA CO., ST. MARY'S (1894), [CEM 2] Rev. Msgr. R. Mark Duchaine, J.C.L. In Res., Rev. Gerald Zensen.
Res.: 703 Heisler St., 51034. Tel: 712-882-1780. Email: sacredhe@ionet.net.
Catechesis/Religious Program—Tel: 712-882-1780. Students 108.
Mission—St. Mary's Oto. 620 State St., Box 67, Oto, Woodbury Co. 51044-6007. Tel: 712-827-4467.

MARCUS, CHEROKEE CO., HOLY NAME (1877), [CEM] Revs. Eugene L. Murray; Jerry Bertrand.
Res.: 102 N. Elm St., P.O. Box 366, 51035-0366. Tel: 712-376-2628.
Catechesis/Religious Program—Tel: 712-376-2625. Students 161.

MARYHILL, CHEROKEE CO., VISITATION OF THE B.V.M. (1895), [CEM] Rev. Eugene E. Sitzmann.
Res.: 975-540th St., Cherokee, 51012-7151. Tel: 712-225-2131; Fax: 712-225-2742.
Catechesis/Religious Program—Tel: 712-225-2131. Students 38.
Mission—St. John the Baptist Church Quimby, Cherokee Co.

MERRILL, PLYMOUTH CO., ASSUMPTION CHURCH (1890), [CEM 2] Rev. Robert J. Waters.
Mailing Address: 28172 Nature Ave., Hinton, 51024-8553. Tel: 712-546-8228. Email: sacredhe@ionet.net.
Church: 615 5th St., 51038.
Catechesis/Religious Program—Tel: 712-938-2596. Students 90.
Catechesis/Religious Program—Students 53.
Mission—St. Joseph at Ellendale, Plymouth Co. Tel: 712-546-8228.

MILFORD, DICKINSON CO., ST. JOSEPH'S (1884), [CEM] Rev. James A. Bruch.
1413 Okoboji Ave., 51351-1232. Tel: 712-338-2172.
Res.: 1014 13th St., 51351. Tel: 712-338-2274; Fax: 712-338-2191.
Catechesis/Religious Program—Students 203.

MOORLAND, WEBSTER CO., OUR LADY OF GOOD COUNSEL (1902), [CEM] Unassigned.
Catholic Team Office—P.O. Box 994, Fort Dodge, 50501. Tel: 515-573-3616; Fax: 515-573-4556.
Catechesis/Religious Program—Tel: 515-549-3443. (Value for entire 8 parish team) 207.

MOUNT CARMEL, CARROLL CO., OUR LADY OF MT. CARMEL (1869), (German), [CEM] Rev. Robert Brown.
Res.: 19481 140th St., Carroll, 51401-9499. Tel: 712-792-3934; Fax: 712-792-3977.
School— Parish is a member of newly consolidated K-12 Kuemper Catholic School System, Carroll, IA. Please refer to Keumper Catholic School System under Inter-Parochial Schools in the Institution section.
Catechesis/Religious Program—Tel: 712-792-9244. Students 21.

MOVILLE, WOODBURY CO., IMMACULATE CONCEPTION (1892), Rev. Msgr. Roger J. Augustine, V.G.
Res.: 419 Jones St., P.O. Box C, 51039-0802. Tel: 712-873-3745.
Catechesis/Religious Program—Tel: 712-873-3644. Students 211.

NEPTUNE, PLYMOUTH CO., ST. JOSEPH (Hinton) (1884), (German), [CEM] Rev. Mark J. Stoll, J.C.L.
Res.: 28172 Nature Ave., Hinton, 51024-8553. Tel: 712-546-8228.
Catechesis/Religious Program—LeMars Religious Education Program, 815 Plymouth St., N.E., P.O. Box 1103, LeMars, 51031. Tel: 712-546-6038. Students 40.

ODEBOLT, SAC CO., ST. MARTIN'S (1877), [CEM] Rev. John J. McGuirk.
Res.: P.O. Box 500, 51458-0500. Tel: 712-668-2690.
Catechesis/Religious Program—Students 102.

OGDEN, BOONE CO., ST. JOHN'S (1896), [CEM] Rev. Brian J. Danner.
Res.: 801 West Division St., 50212-0810. Tel: 515-275-2580; Fax: 515-275-3245.
Catechesis/Religious Program—Tel: 515-275-4095. Students 97.

ONAWA, MONONA CO., ST. JOHN (1900), Rev. Harry D. McAlpine; Deacons Thomas Morgan; Joseph Scurlock.
Res.: 1009 13th St., 51040-1508. Tel: 712-423-2656.
Catechesis/Religious Program—Tel: 712-423-1004. Students 116.
Mission—St. Bernard Blencoe, Monona Co.

OYENS, PLYMOUTH CO., ST. CATHERINE'S (1900), [CEM] Rev. Randy L. Schon.
Res.: P.O. Box 538, 51045-0538. Tel: 712-546-4588.
School—St. Catherine-St. Mary's Elementary, Tel: 712-786-2764. Email: sacredhe@ionet.net. (Oyens-Remsen) Lay Teachers 11; Students 23.
Catechesis/Religious Program—321 Fulton St., Remsen, 51050. Tel: 712-786-1160. Students 17.

POCAHONTAS, POCAHONTAS CO., CHURCH OF THE RESURRECTION (1973), [CEM] Rev. Merle F. Kollasch.
Res.: 21 3rd St., S.W., 50574-0157. Tel: 712-335-3242; Fax: 712-335-3919.
School—Pocahontas Catholic Elementary, Tel: 712-335-3603; Fax: 712-335-3603. Email: sacredhe@ionet.net. Lay Teachers 7; Students 76.
Catechesis/Religious Program—Students 103.

POMEROY, CALHOUN CO., ST. MARY'S (1881), [CEM] Rev. Richard Ries; Deacon Robert Lenz.
Mailing Address: P.O. Box 99, Manson, 50563-0099.
Res.: 1076 8th St., Manson, 50563. Tel: 712-469-3743; Fax: 712-469-3066.
Catechesis/Religious Program—Tel: 712-468-2248. Students 34.

REMSEN, PLYMOUTH CO., ST. MARY'S (1889), [CEM] Rev. Tim A. Johnson; Deacon Allan Wieler.
Res.: Box #509, 51050. Tel: 712-786-1437; 712-786-1444.
School—St. Catherine-St. Mary's Elementary, Tel: 712-786-1160; Fax: 712-786-1167. Email: sacredhe@ionet.net. (Oyens-Remsen) Sisters 1; Lay Teachers 15; Students 185.
High School— See full listing in the (B) Inter-Parochial Schools section under Institutions Located in the Diocese.
Catechesis/Religious Program—Tel: 712-786-2376; Fax: 712-786-1167. Students 266.

ROCK RAPIDS, LYON CO., HOLY NAME (1871), (Irish), [CEM] Rev. Jeffrey Schleisman.
Res.: 1108 S. Carroll St., 51246-9529. Tel: 712-472-3248; Fax: 712-472-3189.
Catechesis/Religious Program—Students 78.

ROCK VALLEY, SIOUX CO., ST. MARY'S (1895), [CEM] Rev. Douglas M. Klein.
Res.: 1821 14th St., 51247-0098. Tel: 712-476-2060; Fax: 712-476-9074.
Catechesis/Religious Program— Totals include Sacred Heart and Christ the King, Sioux Center. Students 156.
Mission—Sacred Heart [CEM] 301 Seefield St., Alvord, Lyon Co. 51230. Tel: 712-473-2215.

ROCKWELL CITY, CALHOUN CO., ST. FRANCIS OF ASSISI (1899), (German), [CEM] Rev. Dennis L. Sefcik.
Res.: 744 Main St., 50579-1399. Tel: 712-297-8263; Fax: 712-297-8330.
Catechesis/Religious Program—Tel: 712-297-7183. Students 93.

ROLFE, POCAHONTAS CO., ST. MARGARET'S (1895), [CEM] Rev. Merle Kollasch.
Res.: 21 S.W. 3, Pocahontas, 50574. Tel: 712-335-3242.
Catechesis/Religious Program—Tel: 712-848-3301. Lori Pedersen, D.R.E. Students 27.

ROSELLE, CARROLL CO., HOLY ANGELS (1874), [CEM] Rev. Dale E. Reiff.
Res.: Box 13, Halbur, 51444-0013. Tel: 712-658-2464; Fax: 712-658-2464.
School— Parish is a member of newly consolidated K-12 Kuemper Catholic School System, Carroll, IA. Please refer to Keumper Catholic School System under Inter-Parochial Schools in the Institution section.
Catechesis/Religious Program—Tel: 712-792-0513 (Carroll); 712-653-2131 (Mennina). Students 12.

ROYAL, CLAY CO., ST. LOUIS (1923), (French—German), Rev. Timothy J. Fitzgerald.
Res.: P.O. Box 49, 300 1st Ave., 51357. Tel: 712-933-2667.
Catechesis/Religious Program—Fax: 712-933-2356. Students 68.
Mission—St. Mary's P.O. Box 49, Everly, Clay Co. 51357. Tel: 712-834-2681.

RUTHVEN, PALO ALTO CO., SACRED HEART (1888), (German—Irish), [CEM] Rev. Peter Duc Hung Nguyen.
Church: P.O. Box 400, 51358-0400. Tel: 712-837-5240.
Catechesis/Religious Program—Students 57.
Mission—Sacred Heart P.O. Box 207, Ayrshire, Palo Alto Co. 50515. Tel: 515-426-3260.

ST. BENEDICT, KOSSUTH CO., ST. BENEDICT'S (1877), [CEM] Rev. Daniel M. Greving.
Res.: P.O. Box 38, Wesley, 50483. Tel: 515-679-4279.
School—Seton Elementary, Tel: 515-295-3509; Fax: 515-295-7739. Email: sacredhe@ionet.net. Consolidation of St. Cecelia, Algona, St. Benedict and St. Joseph, Wesley. Students 21.
High School—Bishop Garrigan, Tel: 515-295-3521. Email: sacredhe@ionet.net. Students 12.
Catechesis/Religious Program—St. Cecelia, 715 E. North St., Algona, 50511. Students 10.

SAC CITY, SAC CO., ST. MARY'S (1892), (German—Irish), [CEM] Rev. Lawrence L. McCarty.
Res.: P.O. Box 324, 50583-0324. Tel: 712-662-7240; Fax: 712-662-4371.
Catechesis/Religious Program—Fax: 712-662-7240. Students 121.

SALIX, WOODBURY CO., ST. JOSEPH'S (1869), [CEM] [JC] Rev. Donald J. Slaven, J.C.L.
Res.: P.O. Box 270, 51052-0270. Tel: 712-946-5635.
Catechesis/Religious Program—Students 129.

SCHALLER, SAC CO., ST. JOSEPH'S (1891), [CEM] Rev. Patrick J. O'Kane.
Res.: P.O. Box 457, 51053-0457. Tel: 712-275-4238.
Catechesis/Religious Program—Students 48.

SCRANTON, GREENE CO., ST. PAUL'S (1926), (German—Irish), Rev. Steven J. McLoud.
Res.: 807 Head St., Churdan, 50050. Tel: 515-389-3625 (Church); Fax: 515-389-3795.
Catechesis/Religious Program—Tel: 515-386-4010; Fax: 515-386-3672. Students 34.

SHELDON, O'BRIEN CO., ST. PATRICK'S (1873), (Irish), [CEM] Rev. Robert Schimmer.
Res.: 310 10th St., 51201-1530. Tel: 712-324-3220; Fax: 712-324-3559.
School—Tel: 712-324-3181. Sisters 1; Lay Teachers 11; Students 102.
Catechesis/Religious Program—Tel: 712-324-4588. Students 165.

SIBLEY, OSCEOLA CO., ST. ANDREW'S (1896), [CEM] Rev. Clair L. Boes.
Res.: 716 Eighth St., 51249-0130. Tel: 712-754-3311.
Catechesis/Religious Program—Tel: 712-754-2739. Students 147.

SIOUX RAPIDS, BUENA VISTA CO., ST. JOSEPH (1886), [CEM] Rev. John F. Cain (Retired).
Res.: 708 Thomas St., P.O. Box 450, 50585-0450. Tel: 712-283-2765; Fax: 712-283-2332.
Catechesis/Religious Program—Tel: 712-843-2052. Students 90.

SPENCER, CLAY CO., SACRED HEART (1883), Rev. Roger Linnan; Deacon Jack Easter, (Retired).
Res.: 1111 4th Ave. W., P.O. Box 817, 51301-0817. Tel: 712-262-3047; Fax: 712-262-4067.
School—Tel: 712-262-6428. Lay Teachers 14; Students 172.
Catechesis/Religious Program—Tel: 712-262-4486. Students 222.

SPIRIT LAKE, DICKINSON CO., ST. MARY'S (1914), [CEM] Rev. Albert O. Grendler.
Res.: P.O. Box 354, 51360-0354. Tel: 712-336-1742; Fax: 712-336-0546.
Catechesis/Religious Program—Tel: 712-336-1742. Students 208.

STORM LAKE, BUENA VISTA CO., ST. MARY'S (1872), [CEM] Revs. Bruce A. Lawler; Eriberto DaCosta.
Res.: Third & Seneca Sts., P.O. Box 1106, 50588-1106. Tel: 712-732-3110; Fax: 712-732-8173.
School—Elementary & High School, Tel: 712-732-1856 (Elementary); 712-732-4166 (High School); Fax: 712-732-4590. Sisters of the Presentation 2; Lay Teachers 31; Students 252; Preschool 30.
Catechesis/Religious Program—Tel: 712-732-4585. Students 161.

STRUBLE, PLYMOUTH CO., ST. JOSEPH'S (1903), [CEM 2] Rev. William A. McCarthy.
Res.: *c/o St. Joseph Church LeMars*, 20 Sixth Ave. N.E, Le Mars, 51031. Tel: 712-546-1522.

Catechesis/Religious Program—Tel: 712-546-6038. Students 42.

SUTHERLAND, O'BRIEN CO.

1—ST. CECILIA'S (1882), [CEM] Rev. William Paul McKane, O.S.B.

Res.: P.O. Box 70, 51058. Tel: 712-729-3423; Fax: 712-446-2149.

Catechesis/Religious Program—Tel: 712-728-2626. Nancy Williams, D.R.E. (Grades K-8). Students 93.

Mission—St. Joseph's 260 N. 4th Ave. W. Hartley, O'Brien Co. 51346. Tel: 712-728-2626.

2—SACRED HEART (1883), [CEM] Rev. William Paul McKane, O.S.B.

Res.: P.O. Box 70, 51058-0070. Tel: 712-446-3742; Fax: 712-446-2149.

Catechesis/Religious Program—Tel: 712-448-2119. Students 17.

Mission—St. Anthony of Padua [CEM] Primghar. 375 S. Green St., Primghar, O'Brien Co. 51245. Tel: 712-757-3735.

TEMPLETON, CARROLL CO., SACRED HEART (1882), [CEM] Rev. Dale C. Reiff.

Res.: Box 13, Halbur, 51444. Tel: 712-658-2464; Fax: 712-658-2464.

School— Parish is a member of newly consolidated K-12 Keumper Catholic School System, Carroll, IA. Please refer to Keumper Catholic School System under Inter-Parochial Schools in the Institution section.

Catechesis/Religious Program—Tel: 712-792-0513 (Carroll); 712-653-2131 (Mannina). Students 23.

VAIL, CRAWFORD CO., ST. ANN'S (1878), [CEM] Rev. John M. Thomas. Sisters of St. Francis of Clinton

Res.: P.O. Box 158, 51465-0158. Tel: 712-677-5556.

School— Please refer to Keumper Catholic School System under Inter-Parochial Schools in the Institution section.

Catechesis/Religious Program—Tel: 712-677-5556. Students 73.

VARINA, POCAHONTAS CO., ST. COLUMBKILLE'S (1882), [CEM] Rev. Thomas J. Hart.

Res.: Box 339, Fonda, 50540-0339. Tel: 712-288-6480; Fax: 712-288-4465.

Catechesis/Religious Program—Students 5.

WALL LAKE, SAC CO., ST. JOSEPH'S (1878), (German), Rev. John J. McGuirk.

Res.: P.O. Box 130, 51466-0130. Tel: 712-664-2915.

Catechesis/Religious Program—Tel: 712-664-2910. Students 134.

WESLEY, KOSSUTH CO., ST. JOSEPH'S (1891), [CEM] Rev. Daniel M. Greving.

Res.: P.O. Box 38, 50483-0038. Tel: 515-679-4279; 515-679-4135.

School—Seton Elementary, Tel: 515-295-3509. Consolidation of St. Cecelia, Algona, St. Benedict, St. Joseph, Wesley, St. Michael's, Whittemore, and St. Joseph, Bode. Students 49.

High School—Bishop Garrigan High School, Tel: 515-295-3521. Students 32.

Catechesis/Religious Program—Students 18.

WEST BEND, PALO ALTO CO., SS. PETER AND PAUL (1888), [CEM] Revs. Edmund H. Tiedeman; Verne P. Stapenhorst; Deacon Gerald Streit.

Res.: P.O. Box 316, 50597-0316. Tel: 515-887-3333; Fax: 515-887-3334.

School—Tel: 515-887-4542; Fax: 515-887-3334. Lay Teachers 8; Students 37.

Catechesis/Religious Program—Tel: 515-887-4586. Students 114.

WHITTEMORE, KOSSUTH CO., ST. MICHAEL'S (1889), [CEM] Rev. Victor F. Ramaeker; Deacon Joseph Straub.

Res.: P.O. Box 337, 50598-0337. Tel: 515-884-2669; Fax: 515-884-2618.

Catechesis/Religious Program— See separate listing at St. Cecelia, Algona Students 23.

WILLEY, CARROLL CO., ST. MARY'S (1882), [CEM] Rev. Craig A. Collison.

Res.: 201 Olympic Ave., Carroll, 51401-9726. Tel: 712-792-4516; Fax: 712-792-2549.

School—Tel: 712-792-3610. Consolidation of Holy Spirit, Dedham, Willey and St. Lawrence Elementary. Students 34.

High School—Kuemper Catholic High School, Tel: 712-792-3596; Fax: 712-792-8070. Students 30.

Catechesis/Religious Program—Tel: 712-792-4386. Students 63.

WOODWARD, BOONE CO., ST. JOHN OF GOD (1965),, (State Hospital and School) Rev. Brian J. Danner; Deacon Frank Milani.

Res.: 207 Gerald St., Madrid, 50156-1464. Tel: 515-795-2731; Fax: 515-795-2731.

Chaplains of Public Institutions

SIOUX CITY. *Mercy Medical Center*. Rev. Richard A. Sitzmann.

CARROLL. *St. Anthony Regional Hospital*. Rev. Jim McCormick, Most Rev. Sunny Dominic, Rev. Siby Punnoose.

CHEROKEE. *State Mental Health Institute*. Rev. Eugene E. Sitzmann.

FORT DODGE. *Marian Village*. Rev. Eugene F. Walding. *Trinity Regional Hospital*. Rev. P. Joseph Nooney.

ROCKWELL CITY. *Calhoun County State Reformatory, Minimum Security for Men*. Rev. Dennis L. Sefcik.

WOODWARD. *Woodward State Hospital and School*. Deacon Frank Milani.

Special Assignment:

Revs.—

Larkin, Michael T., Sioux City Nursing Homes, 1122 Grandview Blvd., Apt. 7, 51103-4398. Tel: 712-258-5202

Meinen, Dennis W., Ministry to People with Disabilities, 1701 W. 25th St., 51103-1799. Tel: 712-258-9120

On Duty Outside the Diocese:

Rev. Msgr.—

McCoy, Kevin C., North American College 00120 Vatican City State.

Revs.—

Adam, Richard A., St Mary's Rectory, P.O. Box C, Riverside, 52327.

Barrett, Miles J., 1 Perry Circle Apt. B Annapolis, MD 21402.

Dandurand, Douglas E., Ph.D. (STP), Archdiocese of St. Paul and Minneapolis, MN

Farrell, Emmet L. (SD), 410 W. 18th St., National City, CA.

Flanagan, Thomas J., Friedrichsstr.41 55124, Mainz, Germany.

Friedrichsen, Timothy A., 10690 Weymouth St. #102, Bethesda, MD 20814-4245.

Harrington, Mark E., 11625 111th Ave., Sun City, AZ 85351. Tel: 623-972-1179

Higgins, Francis E., 154 Savage Loop Canon City, CO 81212. Tel: 719-276-1504

Kurzak, John F., 966 Marion St., Denver, CO 80218. Tel: 303-832-3658 USAF

Graduate Studies:

Rev.—

Erpelding, Michael J., Ediface Deschatelets, 175 Rue Main, Ottawa ON KIS 1C3 Canada. Graduate Student

---

Retired:

Rev. Msgrs.—

Hood, Mervin J., 458 N. 26th Pl. Portside, Apt. 9, Fort Dodge. Tel: 515-576-3268

Lafferty, James K., Ph.D., St. Anthony Nursing Home, 406 E. Anthony St., Carroll, 51401.

Lyon, Gerald F., Marian Hall, 1122 Grandview Blvd., 51105. Tel: 712-258-3022

Quinn, Robert J., P.O. Box 1346, Imperial Beach, CA 91933-1346. Tel: 619-437-0180

Ruba, Nicholas J., 403 Cleveland Ct., Remsen, 51050. Tel: 712-786-2719

Ziegmann, Leonard M., 2300 Indian Hills Dr. #3-328, Fort Dodge, 50501. Tel: 712-239-1538

Revs.—

Adams, Edmond F., 2661 3rd. Ave. N., Fort Dodge, 50501. Tel: 515-955-4859

Alvey, J. Paul, 8241 Orange Blossom Lane, Scottsdale, AZ 85258-7315.

Beacom, Vincent L., 1701 W. 25th St., 51103.

Boes, Marvin, 55 W. Clifton Ave., Apt. 303, 51104. Tel: 712-277-2046

Cain, John F., St. Joseph Church, P.O. Box 450, Sioux Rapids, 50585-0450. Tel: 712-283-2765

Calkins, Raymond J., 326 Green Chase Cir., Montgomery, AL 36117. Tel: 334-215-1813

Ceperley, Eugene F., Marian Village, 2320 6th Ave. N., Apt. 102, Fort Dodge, 50501.

Condon, Robert M., 2300 Indian Hills Dr., Apt. 2-201, 51104.

Cooper, Harold V., 1701 W. 25th St., 51105.

Degen, Jerome A., 509 E. Oak St., Algona. Tel: 515-295-3329

Devine, William B., 1703 W. 25th St., Apt. 212, 51103. Tel: 712-234-0857

Donahoe, Thomas, 916 3 Williams Dr., Fort Dodge, 50501. Tel: 515-573-8612

Fangman, James E., P.O. Box J, Ogden, 50212-0810. Tel: 515-275-4799

Fangman, Robert M., 904 Amy Circle, Carroll, 51401.

Fisch, Gerald M., 122 Grandview Blvd., Apt. 6, 51103. Tel: 712-258-3892

Fransco, Peter J., 1803 Bruce St., Ruthven, 51358. Tel: 712-837-4323

Friedman, Cecil H., 1703 E. Lucas St., Algona, 50511. Tel: 515-295-5403

George, Dale J., 5013 E. Smokehouse Trail, Cave Creek, AZ 85331. Tel: 480-437-1026

Hartz, Gerald A., 3800 Littlefalls Ct., Bakersfield, CA 93305. Tel: 661-327-2744

Hogan, David J., 1701 W. 25th St., 51103. Tel: 712-255-3032

Kielbasa, Richard, Marian Village, 2320 6th Ave. N. Apt. F3, Fort Dodge, 50501. Tel: 515-955-8990

Kollasch, Louis, Marian Village, 2320 6th Ave. N., Apt. A2, Fort Dodge, 50501. Tel: 515-573-8500

Koster, Dale F., P.O. Box 264 W. St., Apt. 8, Auburn, 51433.

Leiting, Robert L., 240 S. Clark St., Carroll, 51401. Tel: 712-792-3122

Lynch, Daniel C., 407 S. 13th St., Sac City, 50583.

Macke, Richard J., 100 Circle Dr., Lake City, 51449.

McCoy, Alfred E., P.O. Box 114, 51102. Tel: 712-279-5461

Nemmers, Francis J., P.O. Box 244, Bancroft, 50517-0244. Tel: 515-885-0212

Nooney, Patrick J., 2638 4th Ave. N., Apt. H, Fort Dodge, 50501-5795. Tel: 515-576-5567

Remmes, Richard R., P.O. Box 20, Arcadia, 51430. Tel: 712-689-2744

Riesberg, Leo L., Steffes Apts., 304 S. Clark St., Apt. 2, Carroll, 51401-3067. Tel: 712-792-8560

Schumacher, Eugene T., 303 S. Portland St., Bancroft. Tel: 515-885-2231

Smith, Donald R., 3929 Winona Way, Apt. 4, 51104-4447. Tel: 712-239-5865

Thiele, Robert A., 101 N. Earl, Lake City, 51449. Tel: 712-464-8024

Thom, Elmer D., 1122 Grandview Blvd., Apt. 9, 51105. Tel: 712-277-3954

Waite, Patrick J., 5682 Tulane St., San Diego, CA 92122-3244.

Waters, Robert J. (CHR), 5021 Defiance Way, San Diego, CA 92115. Tel: 619-255-5952

White, Lloyd W., 130 Peeble Ln., Apt. 6, Carroll, 51401-3020. Tel: 712-792-5633

Wieling, Raymond P., 3015 Chicago Ave., 51106-1259. Tel: 712-276-7065

Wingert, D. William, 110 W. Maple Dr., Hartley, 51346-7606. Tel: 712-728-9911

Wingert, Gerald R., 216 W. Nebraska, Algona, 50511-2608. Tel: 515-295-3123

Zeman, Gerald L., 2400 6th Ave. N., Fort Dodge, 50501-3541.

Zensen, Gerald F., P.O. Box 65, Oto, 51044-0067.

Permanent Deacons:

Berger, William J., St. Michael's, Sioux City

Bertrand, Gerald L., Holy Name, Marcus

Bruner, Robert S., St. Lawrence, Carroll

Doocy, Philip F., St. John the Baptist, Bancroft

Easter, Jack L., Sacred Heart, Spencer

Forrest, Ronald M., Co-Dir., Permanent Diaconate; Cathedral, Sioux City

Gallagher, Jeffrey F., Holy Name, Rock Rapids

Hand, Michael J., Church of the Nativity, Sioux City

Hart, M. Peter, St. Joseph, Milford

Heffernan, John J., Blessed Sacrament Church, Sioux City

Hogan, Joseph R., Our Lady of Good Counsel Church, Fonda

Karpuk, Fred P., Blessed Sacrament Church, Sioux City

Kunecke, Donald L., St. Columbkille, Churdan

Kunkel, Donald M., St. Joseph Church, LeMars

Larson, Robert, St. Cecelia, Algona

Lenz, Robert D., St. Mary's Church, Pomeroy

Lester, Jary, Cathedral, Sioux City

MacDonald, W. B., St. Cecelia Church, Algona

Milani, Frank J., St. Malachy's Church, Madrid

Morgan, Tom, St. John's, Onawa

Murphy, Tim, St. Lawrence, Carroll

Pietz, Ronald C., St. Joseph Church, Sioux City

Portz, Ray, St. Patrick, Sheldon

Reicks, Jerome A., St. Joseph Church, Sioux City

Reuter, Anthony C., Bella Vista, AR 72715

Rupp, J. LeRoy, Immaculate Conception Church, Cherokee

Sands, James H., St. Boniface, Sioux City

Sitzman, Larry K., St. Michael's Church, Sioux City

Straub, Joseph J., St. Michael's Church, Whittmore

Streit, Gerald B., Sts. Peter & Paul Church, West Bend

Sullivan, Eldon, Our Lady of Good Counsel, Fonda

Westendorf, Louis B., M.D., St. Lawrence Church, Carroll

Wiskus, Robert A., Sacred Heart Church, Sioux City

INSTITUTIONS LOCATED IN THE DIOCESE

[A] COLLEGES AND UNIVERSITIES

SIOUX CITY. *Briar Cliff University*, 3303 Rebecca St., P.O. Box 2100, 51104-2100. Tel: 712-279-5200; Fax: 712-279-5410. Web: www.briarcliff.edu. Bev Wharton, Pres.; Deidre Engel, Registrar; Sharisue Wilcoxon, Vice Pres. of Enrollment Mgmt.; Deidre Engel, Registrar; Revs. Alfred E. McCoy (Retired); Robert M. Condon (Retired). Sisters of St. Francis of the Holy Family of Dubuque, Iowa, Liberal Arts University. Sisters 11; Lay Teachers 46; Lay Administrators & Staff 89; Students 1,063.

[B] INTER-PAROCHIAL SCHOOLS

SIOUX CITY. *Catholic Schools of Sioux City*, 1018 Grandview Blvd., 51102. Tel: 712-252-1350; Fax: 712-252-9086. Email: rbancke@heelan.pvt.k12.ia.us. Web: www.siouxlan.com/heelan. Rev. Patrick Walsh, Supt. Serving the parishes of Nativity, Immaculate Conception, Cathedral, St. Boniface, St. Joseph, Blessed Sacrament, Sacred Heart, St. Michael. Sisters 4; Lay Teachers 131; Students 1,866; Total Staff 135.

Bishop Heelan High School, 1021 Douglas St., 51104. Tel: 712-252-0573; Fax: 712-252-4897. Web: www.siouxlan.com/heelan. Priests 1; Lay Teachers 45; Students 588.

Holy Family St. Boniface Center (Grades K-2), 700 W. Sixth St., 51103. Tel: 712-258-9464; Fax: 712-258-9464. Email: hfs-ec@cableone.net. Web: www.sccatholicschools.org. Lay Teachers 6; Students 93; Total Staff 12.

Holy Family St. Joseph Center (Grades 3-5), 709 Iowa St., 51105. Tel: 712-258-7101; Fax: 712-258-7101. Email: gbsnyder74@aol.com. Web: www.sccatholicschools.org. Consolidated with Cathedral of the Epiphany and St. Boniface. Lay Teachers 3; Students 81.

Holy Cross School-Blessed Sacrament Center, 3030 Jackson St., 51104. Tel: 712-277-4739; Fax: 712-258-3698. Email: babrahamson@blessedsac.put.k12.ia.us. Lay Teachers 24; Students 373.

St. Michael, 4105 Harrison, 51108. Tel: 712-239-1090; Fax: 712-239-8546. Web: www.sccatholicschools.org. Priests 1; Lay Teachers 8; Students 128.

Sacred Heart, 5010 Military Rd., 51103. Tel: 712-233-1624; Fax: 712-233-1469. Email: blumm@sacredheart.pvt.k12.ia.us. Web: www.sccatholicschools.org. Priests 1; Lay Teachers 18; Students 284; Total Staff 18.

Mater Dei School Immaculate Conception Center, 3719 Ridge Ave., 51106. Tel: 712-276-6216; Fax: 712-274-1221. Web: www.sccatholicschools.org. Priests 1; Lay Teachers 17; Students 215.

Mater Dei School Nativity Center (Grades 6-8), 4242 Natalia Way, 51106-4099. Tel: 712-276-3022; Fax: 712-274-2703. Email: sweeneym@cssc.pvt.k12.ia.us. Web: www.sccatholicschools.org. Consolidated with Immaculate Conception Parish. Priests 1; Lay Teachers 9; Total Enrollment 112.

ALGONA. *Bishop Garrigan Catholic High School*, 1224 N. McCoy St., 50511. Tel: 515-295-3521; Fax: 515-295-7739. Email: stencem@garrigan.pvt.k12.ia.us. Web: www.garrigan.unlimitedweb.net. Mr. Eugene Meister, Pres. Serving the parishes at Algona, St. Benedict, Bode, Wesley, and Whittemore. Priests 1; Sisters 1; Deacons 1; Lay Teachers 21; Students 218.

CARROLL. *Kuemper Catholic School System*, 116 S. East St., 51401. Tel: 712-792-3313; Fax: 712-792-8073. Email: tstacheny@kuemper.pvt.k12.ia.us. Web: www.kuemper.pvt.k12.ia.us. Dr. Thomas Tacheny, Supt. Grades K-12 Lay Teachers 96; Students 1,188.

Holy Spirit Center (Grades K-3), 201 S. Clark St., 51401. Tel: 712-792-3610.

St. Angela Center (Grades 4-5), 116 N. East St., 51401. Tel: 710-792-8071.

St. Lawrence Center (Grades 6-8), 1519 N. West St., 51401. Tel: 712-792-2123.

Kuemper Catholic High School (Grades 9-12), 109 S. Clark St., 51401. Tel: 712-792-3596.

FORT DODGE. *Fort Dodge Catholic Schools, Inc.*, (Grades K-12), 501 N. 22nd St., 50501. Tel: 515-955-5850; Fax: 515-955-3569. Web: hannond@st.-edmod.put.k12.ia.us. Sr. Delores Hannon, Pres.; Mr. Chuck Elbert, Prin.; Mr. Thomas Miklo, Dir. Devel.; Ms. Mary Ricke, D.R.E. Sisters 2; Lay Teachers 59; Students 820.

GRANVILLE. *Spalding Catholic Schools, Inc.* 51022. Tel: 712-727-3451; Fax: 712-727-3455. Email: tulses@spalding-catholic.pvt.k12.ia.us. Web: spalding-catholic.pvt.k12.ia.us. Rev. Msgr. Kenneth A. Seifried, V.F., Pres. Serving the parishes of Granville; Alton and Hospers. Priests 2; Lay Teachers 9; Students 85.

LE MARS. *Gehlen Catholic School*, 709 Plymouth St. N.E., 51031. Tel: 712-546-4181; Fax: 712-546-9384. Email: gehlen@pionet.net. Web: www.gehlencatholic.com. Rev. Andrew Hoffman, Pres.; Steve Shanks, Prin. (7-12); Lorie A. Nussbaum, Prin. (K-6). Lay Teachers 39; Students 460.

REMSEN. *St. Mary's High School*, 523 Madison, 51050. Tel: 712-786-1433; Fax: 712-786-2499. Web: www.remsenstmarys.org. Mr. Ken Hajek, Prin. Priests 1; Lay Teachers 11; Students 102.

STORM LAKE. *St. Mary's High School* 50588. Tel: 712-732-4166; Fax: 712-732-4590. Email: rdavis@main.stmarys-storm.pvt.k12.ia.us. Serving St. Mary's. Sisters 1; Lay Teachers 12; Students 71.

[C] GENERAL HOSPITALS

SIOUX CITY. *Mercy Medical Center - Sioux City*, 801 Fifth St., 51101. Tel: 712-279-2010; Fax: 712-279-2494. Email: brehanyj@mercyhealth.com. Web: www.mercy-siouxcity.com. Peter Makowski, Pres. & CEO; John F. Brehany, Ph.D., S.T.L., Dir. of Mission Svcs. & Ethics; Rev. Richard A. Sitzmann, Chap.; Sr. Marlys Becker, O.S.F., Chap.; Rev. Dennis Grohn, Lutheran Chap.; Rev. B. J. Van Kalsbeek, Reformed Presbyterian Chap. Trinity Health, Catholic Health Ministries Sisters 1; Total Staff 1,500; Bed Capacity 484; Patients Assisted Annually 326,000.

CARROLL. *St. Anthony Regional Hospital* 51401. Tel: 712-792-3581; Fax: 712-792-2124. Email: esmith@stanthonyhospital.org. Web: www.StAnthonyHospital.org. Gary P. Riedmann, Pres.; Revs. Jim McCormick; Sunny Dominic; Siby Punnoose. Bed Capacity 99; Patients Assisted Annually 99,000; Total Staff 450.

St. Anthony Regional Nursing Home Tel: 712-792-3581; Fax: 712-792-2124.

Orchard View, Inc., S. Clark St., 51401. Tel: 712-792-3581; Fax: 712-792-2124.

ESTHERVILLE. *Avera Holy Family Health*, 826 N. Eighth St., 51334. Tel: 712-362-2631; Fax: 712-362-2636. Email: info@avera-holyfamily.org. Web: www.avera-holyfamily.org. Sisters of the Presentation of the B.V.M. (Aberdeen, SD) Bed Capacity 58; Patients Assisted Annually 22,861; Total Staff 127.

Holy Family Hospital Foundation. Tel: 712-362-2631; Fax: 712-362-2636.

[D] HOMES FOR THE AGED

SIOUX CITY. *Holy Spirit Retirement Home*, 1701 W. 25th St., 51103. Tel: 712-252-2726. Patrick J. Tomscha, Admin.; Rev. Dennis W. Meinen. Total in Residence 125; Total Assisted 150; Total Staff 120.

CARROLL. *St. Anthony Nursing Home*, 406 E. Anthony St., 51401. Tel: 712-792-3581; Fax: 712-792-8288. Email: stanthony@netins.net. Web: www.netins.net/showcase/sarh/. Gary Riedmann, Admin.; Peg Scheidt, Dir. Pastoral Care. Total Staff 60; Residents 79.

FORT DODGE. *The Marian Home*, 2400 Sixth Ave. N., 50501. Tel: 515-576-1138; Fax: 515-576-5099. Email: marianhome1@dodgenet.com. Mr. Gerald Bruening, Admin.; Rev. Eugene F. Walding. Guests 97; Total in Residence 29; Total Staff 110.

[E] CONVENTS AND RESIDENCES FOR SISTERS

SIOUX CITY. *Monastery of the Discalced Carmelite Nuns*, 2901 S. Cecelia St., 51106-3299. Tel: 712-276-1680; Fax: 712-276-5966. Email: carmelitesiouxc@aol.com. Web: www.siouxcitycarmel.com. Sr. Kateri Marie of the Eucharist, O.C.D., Prioress. Solemn Professed 10.

[F] SECULAR INSTITUTES

CARROLL. *Opus Spiritus Sancti*, .421 E. Bluff St., 51401. Tel: 712-792-4386; Fax: 712-792-8038. Email: frjim@pionet.net. Rev. James Daniel McCormick, Regl. Coord. Community Activities & Member Secular Institute of Priests.

[G] MISCELLANEOUS

SIOUX CITY. *Cathedral Arts Guild*, 1000 Douglas St., 51105. Tel: 712-255-1637; Fax: 712-255-4194. Email: placath@aol.com.

The Catholic Schools Foundation of the Diocese of Sioux City, 1821 Jackson St., 51105. Tel: 712-255-7933; Fax: 712-233-7598. Email: kevinv@scdiocese.org. Web: www.scdiocese.org.

Holy Spirit Retirement Home Foundation, Inc., 1701 W. 25th St., 51103. Tel: 712-252-2726. Daniel DiNardo, Pres.; Roger J. Augustine, Dir.; Patrick J. Tomscha, Dir.

ALGONA. *Friends of Garrigan High School, Inc.*, Garrigan High School, 1224 N. McCoy, 50511. Tel: 515-295-3521. Mr. Eugene Meister, Contact Person.

CARROLL. *St. Anthony Foundation*, S. Clark St., 51401. Tel: 712-792-3581; Fax: 712-792-2124. Email: esmith@stanthonyhospital.org. Web: www.StAnthonyHospital.org. Mr. Gary P. Rildmann.

Kuemper Catholic Schools Foundation, Inc., 1st St. & Clark St., 50511. Tel: 712-792-3596; Fax: 712-792-8070. Email: jsteffes@kuemper.pvt.k12.ia.us. Web: www.kuemper.pvt.k12.ia.us. Dr. Thomas Tacheny, Supt.

Orchard View, Inc., 421 S. Clark St., 51401. Tel: 712-792-2042; Fax: 712-792-2124. Email: esmith@stanthonyhospital.org. Web: www.StAnthonyHospital.org. Gary P. Riedmann, Admin. Franciscan Sisters of Perpetual Adoration Total in Residence 53.

FORT DODGE. *Corpus Christi Parish Foundation of Fort Dodge*, P.O. Box 994, 50501. Tel: 515-573-3616; Fax: 515-573-4556. Email: fdcatholic@fdcatholic.org. Rev. Lynn Bruch, Contact.

St. Edmond High School Foundation, 2220 4th Ave., N., 50501. Tel: 515-955-5850; Fax: 515-955-8473. Email: walshp@st-edmond.pvt.k12.ia.us. Web: www.st-edmond.pvt.k12.ia.us. Rev. Patrick Walsh, Pres.

Fort Dodge Catholic Grade School Foundation, 2220 4th Ave., N., 50501. Tel: 515-955-5850; Fax: 515-955-8473. Email: walshp@st-edmond.pvt.k12.ia.us. Web: www.st-edmond.pvt.k12.ia.us. Rev. Patrick Walsh, Pres.

Fort Dodge Catholic Grade School Foundation, 2220 4th Ave., N., 50501. Tel: 515-955-5850; Fax: 515-955-8473. Email: walshp@st-edmond.pvt.k12.ia.us. Web: www.st-edmond.pvt.k12.ia.us. Rev. Patrick Walsh, Pres.

Holy Rosary Parish Foundation of Fort Dodge, P.O. Box 994, 50501. Tel: 515-573-3616; Fax: 515-573-4556. Email: fdcatholic@fdcatholic.org. Rev. Edward M. Girres, Contact.

The Marion Home Foundation, 2400 6th Ave. N., 50501. Tel: 515-576-1138; Fax: 515-576-5099. Email: marianhome1@dodgenet.com. Gerald Bruening, Contact Person.

Sacred Heart Parish Foundation of Fort Dodge, P.O. Box 994, 50501. Tel: 515-573-3616; Fax: 515-573-4556. Email: fdcatholic@fdcatholic.org. Rev. Edward M. Girres, Contact.

STORM LAKE. *St. Mary's Foundation of Storm Lake, Iowa*, 320 Seneca St., 50588. Tel: 712-732-3110; Fax: 712-732-8173. Email: parishstm@iw.net. Web: www.saintman/salumni.org. Rev. Bruce A. Lawler.

WEST BEND. *Grotto of the Redemption*, Tel: 515-887-2371. Email: info@westbendgrotto.com. Web: www.westbendgrotto.com. P.O. Box 376, 50597. Tel: 515-887-2371; Fax: 515-887-2372.

RELIGIOUS INSTITUTES OF WOMEN REPRESENTED IN THE DIOCESE

For further details refer to the corresponding bracketed number in the Religious Institutes of Men or Women section.

[0230]—*Benedictine Sisters of the Pontifical Jurisdiction*—O.S.B.

[1780]—*Congregation of the Sisters of the Third Order of St. Francis of Perpetual Adoration* (Central Prov.)—F.S.P.A.

[0420]—*Discalced Carmelite Nuns*—O.C.D.

[1070-20]—*Dominican Sisters Order of Preachers* Tacoma, WA

[]—*Opus Spiritus Sancti*—O.S.S.

[]—*Sisters For Christian Community*—S.F.C.C.

[0430]—*Sisters of Charity of the Blessed Virgin Mary*—B.V.M.

[2575]—*Sisters of Mercy of the Americas* (Cedar Rapids Regional Community)—R.S.M.

[2575]—*Sisters of Mercy of the Union in USA Comm.* Cedar Rapids—O.S.F.

[1705]—*Sisters of St. Francis of Assisi*—O.S.F.

[1570]—*Sisters of St. Francis of the Holy Family*—O.S.F.

[1540]—*Sisters of St. Francis, Clinton, IA*—O.S.F.

[2350]—*Sisters of the Living Word*—S.L.W.

[3320]—*Sisters of the Presentation of the B.V.M.* Dubuque, IA & Aberdeen, SD—P.B.V.M.

[1720]—*Sisters of the Third Order Regular of St. Francis of the Congregation of Our Lady of Lourdes*—O.S.F.

DIOCESAN CEMETERIES

SIOUX CITY. *Calvary*, Office, 1821 Jackson St., P.O. Box 3379, 51102-3379. Tel: 712-233-7511.

FORT DODGE. *Catholic Cemetery Improvement Society*, Tel: 515-573-3616. Rev. Lynn Bruch, Contact Person.

LEMARS. *Calvary Cemetery*, c/o Joan Thommes, 18031 Lake Ave., 51031. Tel: 712-233-7510. Joan Thommes, Contact Person.

NECROLOGY

† Lilly, Rev. Msgr. Edward C., (Retired)—Died Oct. 30, 2003

† Becker, Nicholas J., (Retired)—Died Aug. 20, 2003

Diocese of Sioux Falls

(Dioecesis Siouxormensis)

Most Reverend

ROBERT J. CARLSON

Bishop of Sioux Falls; ordained May 22, 1970; appointed Titular Bishop of Aviocala and Auxiliary Bishop of Saint Paul and Minneapolis November 22, 1983; consecrated January 11, 1984; appointed Coadjutor Bishop of Sioux Falls, 1994; succeeded to the See, March 21, 1995

Most Reverend

PAUL V. DUDLEY

Retired Bishop of Sioux Falls; ordained June 2, 1951; appointed Titular Bishop of Ursona and Auxiliary Bishop of St. Paul and Minneapolis November 16, 1976; Episcopal ordination January 25, 1977; appointed Bishop of Sioux Falls September 26, 1978; installed December 13, 1978; retired March 21, 1995 *Res.: 2500 W. 320th St., Northfield, MN 55057.* Tel: 507-663-1145; Fax: 507-645-0558.

"Jesus is Lord"

Chancery Office: 523 N. Duluth Ave., Sioux Falls, SD 57104. Tel: 605-334-9861; Fax: 605-334-2092.

Web: sfcatholic.org

Email: jklein@sfcatholic.org

ESTABLISHED NOVEMBER 12, 1889.

Square Miles 35,091.

Comprises that part of the State of South Dakota East of the Missouri River.

For legal titles of parishes and diocesan institutions, consult the Chancery Office.

STATISTICAL OVERVIEW

Personnel	
Bishop	1
Retired Bishops	1
Abbots	1
Retired Abbots	1
Priests: Diocesan Active in Diocese	82
Priests: Diocesan Active Outside Diocese	4
Priests: Retired, Sick or Absent	35
Number of Diocesan Priests	121
Religious Priests in Diocese	32
Total Priests in Diocese	153
Extern Priests in Diocese	5
Ordinations:	
Diocesan Priests	2
Transitional Deacons	2
Permanent Deacons	1
Permanent Deacons in Diocese	30
Total Brothers	13
Total Sisters	364
Parishes	
Parishes	151
With Resident Pastor:	
Resident Diocesan Priests	64
Resident Religious Priests	10
Without Resident Pastor:	
Administered by Priests	72
Administered by Deacons	4
Administered by Professed Religious Men	1
Professional Ministry Personnel:	
Brothers	3
Sisters	23
Lay Ministers	46
Welfare	
Catholic Hospitals	11
Total Assisted	550,000
Homes for the Aged	9
Total Assisted	1,500
Day Care Centers	1
Total Assisted	71
Specialized Homes	1
Total Assisted	60
Special Centers for Social Services	4
Total Assisted	170,000
Residential Care of Disabled	1
Total Assisted	20
Educational	
Diocesan Students in Other Seminaries	25
Total Seminarians	25
Colleges and Universities	2
Total Students	1,800
High Schools, Diocesan and Parish	3
Total Students	899
Elementary Schools, Diocesan and Parish	25
Total Students	4,293
Catechesis/Religious Education:	
High School Students	7,542
Elementary Students	10,348
Total Students under Catholic Instruction	24,917
Teachers in the Diocese:	
Priests	2
Sisters	8
Lay Teachers	316
Vital Statistics	
Receptions into the Church:	
Infant Baptism Totals	1,727
Adult Baptism Totals	80
Received into Full Communion	265
First Communions	1,845
Confirmations	1,817
Marriages:	
Catholic	343
Interfaith	327
Total Marriages	670
Deaths	1,033
Total Catholic Population	125,332
Total Population	524,153

Former Bishops—Rt. Revs. MARTIN MARTY, O.S.B., D.D., appt. Bishop of Tiberias, Aug. 8, 1879; appt. Vicar Apostolic of Dakota, Aug. 12, 1879; consecrated Feb. 1, 1880; Bishop of Sioux Falls, 1889; transferred to St. Cloud, MN, 1894; died Sept. 19, 1896; THOMAS O'GORMAN, D.D., appt. Jan. 24, 1896; consecrated April 19, 1896; died Sept. 18, 1921; Most Revs. BERNARD J. MAHONEY, D.D., appt. May 22, 1922; consecrated June 29, 1922; died March 20, 1939; WILLIAM O. BRADY, S.T.D., D.D., appt. Bishop of Sioux Falls, June 10, 1939; consecrated Aug. 24, 1939; appt. Coadjutor of St. Paul, June 21, 1956; succeeded to the See, Oct. 11, 1956; died Oct. 1, 1961; LAMBERT A. HOCH, D.D. (Retired), ord. May 30, 1928; Bishop of Bismarck; appt. Jan. 23, 1952; consecrated March 25, 1952; transferred to Sioux Falls, Nov. 27, 1956; retired June 13, 1978; died June 27, 1990; PAUL V. DUDLEY, D.D. (Retired), ord. June 2, 1951; ord. Auxiliary Bishop of Archdiocese of St. Paul/Minneapolis, Jan. 25, 1977; appt. Bishop of Sioux Falls Sept. 26, 1978; installed Dec. 13, 1978; retired March 21, 1995.

Vicar General—Rev. Msgr. MARVIN MCPHEE, V.G., 523 N. Duluth Ave., Sioux Falls, 57104.

Episcopal Vicar for Clergy—Rev. Msgr. MARVIN MCPHEE (Retired).

Chancery Office—523 N. Duluth Ave., Sioux Falls, 57104. Tel: 605-334-9861; Fax: 605-334-2092. Refer all official business to this address.

Chancellor—Mr. JEROME KLEIN, 523 N. Duluth Ave., Sioux Falls, 57104. Tel: 605-988-3745.

Vice Chancellors—Ms. NANCY WERNER. Tel: 605-988-3798; Rev. JAMES MASON. Tel: 605-988-3749. 523 N. Duluth Ave., Sioux Falls, 57104.

Diocesan Tribunal—523 N. Duluth Ave., Sioux Falls, 57104. Tel: 605-988-3757. (Address all marriage papers and rogatory commissions to this address).

Judicial Vicar—Rev. GREGORY TSCHAKERT, J.C.L.

Promoter of Justice—Rev. SYMPHORIEN LOPOKE-OHAMAMBOYA, J.C.L.

Tribunal Judges—Revs. AL KRZYZOPOLSKI; RODNEY FARKE; KEN KOSTER; JOHN LANTSBERGER; CHARLES CIMPL; GARY TERNES; JORDAN HITE, T.O.R.; Deacon WILLIAM FRANKMAN; Rev. SCOTT TRAYNOR; CHARLES MANGAN, J.C.L.; Rev. SYMPHORIEN LOPOKE-OHAMAMBOYA, J.C.L.

Defender of the Matrimonial Bond—Rev. GREGORY TSCHAKERT, J.C.L.; Sr. LYNN MARIE WELBIG, J.C.L., Ph.D.; Rev. JAMES FRIEDRICH.

Director of Matrimonial Tribunal—Sr. LYNN MARIE WELBIG, J.C.L., Ph.D.

Auditors—Deacon WILLIAM FRANKMAN; Sr. PHYLLIS GILL; HEIDI EVERS.

Notary of Matrimonial Tribunal—Ms. VICKIE BEACH, Ecclesiastical Notary.

Diocesan Consultors—Rev. Msgrs. MARVIN MCPHEE, V.G.; STEVEN BARNETT; Revs. ROBERT KRANTZ; KEN LULF; RODNEY FARKE; DAVID JANES; HAL BARBER; DAVID KROGMAN; MICHAEL WENSING.

Consilium Administrationis— Most Rev. Bishop, Vicar General, Chancellor

Deans—Rev. Msgr. STEVEN BARNETT; Revs. HAL BARBER; RODNEY FARKE; DAVID JANES; MICHAEL WENSING; KEN LULF; ROBERT KRANTZ; DAVID KROGMAN.

Presbyteral Council—Most Rev. ROBERT J. CARLSON; Rev. Msgrs. MARVIN MCPHEE, V.G.; STEVEN BARNETT; Revs. HAL BARBER; RODNEY FARKE; DAVID JANES; THOMAS HILLENBRAND, O.S.B.; KEN LULF; ROBERT KRANTZ; DAVID KROGMAN; JAMES P. MORGAN; MICHAEL WENSING.

Diocesan Offices and Directors

Apostleship of Prayer—523 N. Duluth Ave., Sioux Falls, 57105.

Bishop's Bulletin—Rev. MICHAEL GRIFFIN, Exec. Editor; Mr. GENE YOUNG, Mgr. Editor, 523 N. Duluth Ave., Sioux Falls, 57104. Tel: 605-988-3789.

Building Commission—Mr. JEROME KLEIN, Chancellor, Catholic Chancery Office, 523 N. Duluth Ave., Sioux Falls, 57104.

Catholic Charities—TRAVIS BENSON, J.D., Dir., 523 N. Duluth Ave., Sioux Falls, 57104. Tel: 605-988-3748.

Catholic Foundation for Eastern South Dakota—MARK CONZEMIUS, Exec. Dir.; ELIZABETH THEOBALD, Dir., Planned Giving, 523 N. Duluth Ave., Sioux Falls, 57104. Tel: 605-988-3788.

Catholic Relief Services—Mr. JEROME KLEIN, Chancellor, 523 N. Duluth Ave., Sioux Falls, 57104.

Catholic Family Services—Sr. MARY CAROLE CURRAN, O.S.B., Ph.D., Exec. Dir., 523 N. Duluth Ave., Sioux Falls, 57104. Tel: 605-988-3775.

Catholic Family Sharing Appeal and Stewardship—Mr. KEVIN MILES, Dir., 523 N. Duluth Ave., Sioux Falls, 57104. Tel: 605-988-3788.

Censor Librorum—CHRISTOPHER BURGWALD, S.T.L., 523 N. Duluth Ave., Sioux Falls, 57104.

Communications Office—Mr. JEROME KLEIN, Chancellor, 523 N. Duluth Ave., Sioux Falls, 57104. Tel: 605-988-3789.

Cursillo—Rev. RODNEY FARKE, P.O. Box 689, Yankton, 57078. Tel: 605-664-6214.

Development Office—MARK CONZEMIUS, Dir., 523 N. Duluth Ave., Sioux Falls, 57104. Tel: 605-988-3788.

Diocesan Archivist—Mr. JEROME KLEIN, Chancellor, 523 N. Duluth Ave., Sioux Falls, 57104. Tel: 605-334-9861.

Diocesan Office of Education—Sr. NATHALIE MEYER, O.P., Ph.D., Supt. of Schools; CHRIS BURGWALD, S.T.L., Dir. Adult Faith Formation and Evangelization Inc. RCIA, 523 N. Duluth Ave., Sioux Falls, 57104. Tel: 605-988-3766.

Ecumenical Commission—Rev. ANTHONY OPEM, 995 Sioux Point Rd., Dakota Dunes, 57049. Tel: 605-235-1942.

Family and Children Faith Formation—JEAN LORANG, 523 N. Duluth Ave., Sioux Falls, 57104. Tel: 605-988-3767.

Finance Officer—MICHAEL BANNWARTH, 523 N. Duluth Ave., Sioux Falls, 57104. Tel: 605-988-3759; Fax: 605-988-3746.

Good Shepherd Center—MARIA RAE, Dir., 300 N. Main Ave., Sioux Falls, 57104. Tel: 605-335-3321.

Worldwide Marriage Encounter—Rev. JAMES M. JOYCE, 900 E. 14th St., Apt. 112, Sioux Falls, 57104. Tel: 605-978-1592.

Newman Apostolate—Rev. JOSEPH FORCELLE, St. Thomas More Newman Center, 320 E. Cherry St., Vermillion, 57069. Tel: 605-624-2697.

Office of Worship—Rev. MICHAEL D. KELLY, 523 N. Duluth Ave., Sioux Falls, 57104. Tel: 605-988-3751.

Permanent Diaconate Formation—CHRIS BURGWALD, S.T.L., 523 N. Duluth Ave., Sioux Falls, 57104. Tel: 605-334-9861.

Permanent Diaconate Council—Deacon LEON CANTIN, 305 E. 26th St., Yankton, 57078. Tel: 605-664-2363.

Personnel Board—Most Rev. ROBERT J. CARLSON, Chm.

Propagation of the Faith—Rev. JEROME RANEK, Dir., St. Margaret Church, P.O. Box 137, Kimball, 57355.

Respect Life Office—Directors: TRAVIS BENSON; KELLY BENSON, 523 N. Duluth Ave., Sioux Falls, 57104. Tel: 605-988-3755.

Search—523 N. Duluth Ave., Sioux Falls, 57104. Tel: 605-334-9861.

Spanish-Speaking Apostolate—Rev. LUIS MESA, 1220 E. 8th St., Sioux Falls, 57103. Tel: 605-338-8126.

Teens Encounter Christ—523 N. Duluth Ave., Sioux Falls, 57104. Tel: 605-334-9861.

Victim Assistance Coordinator—Sr. MARY CAROLE CURRAN, O.S.B., Ph.D. Tel: 605-988-3775. Email: mcurran@sfcatholic.org.

Vocations—Rev. JAMES MASON, Dir., 523 N. Duluth Ave., Sioux Falls, 57104. Tel: 605-988-3772.

Adolescent Faith Formation—ROBERT SIEMENS, 523 N. Duluth Ave., Sioux Falls, 57104. Tel: 605-988-3785.

CLERGY, PARISHES, MISSIONS AND PAROCHIAL SCHOOLS

CITY OF SIOUX FALLS
(MINNEHAHA COUNTY)

1—ST. JOSEPH CATHEDRAL, [JC] Most Rev. Robert J. Carlson; Revs. Martin E. Lawrence; David A. Desmond.
Res.: 521 Duluth Ave., 57104. Tel: 605-336-7390; Fax: 605-330-0416.
School—Tel: 605-338-3159; Fax: 605-338-2647. See separate listing under Inter-Parochial Schools in the Institution section.
Catechesis/Religious Program—Students 397.

2—CHRIST THE KING (1949), Revs. Michael Griffin; Mark Axtmann; Deacon James J. Walden.
Res.: 1501 W. 26th St., 57105. Tel: 605-332-5477; Fax: 605-332-0552.
School—Tel: 605-338-5103; Fax: 605-335-1231. See separate listing under Inter-Parochial Schools in the Institution section.
Catechesis/Religious Program—Students 232.

3—HOLY SPIRIT (1988), Rev. Msgr. James F. Andraschko.
Res.: 3601 E. Dudley Ln., 57103. Tel: 605-371-2320; Fax: 605-371-1957.
Catechesis/Religious Program—Students 587.

4—ST. LAMBERT (1957), Revs. Mark Lichter; Symphorien Lopoke-Ohamamboya, J.C.L. (Congo); Deacons Ralph C. Counter; Jerome F. Wathen.
Res.: 1000 S. Bahnson Ave., 57103. Tel: 605-336-8808; Fax: 605-339-4389.
School—Tel: 605-338-7042; Fax: 605-336-8727. See separate listing under Inter-Parochial Schools in the Institution section.
Catechesis/Religious Program—Tel: 605-338-4728. Students 398.

5—ST. MARY (1947), Rev. David Krogman; Deacon Henry Knapp. In Res., Rev. Jim Friedrich.
Res.: 2109 S. Fifth Ave., 57105. Tel: 605-332-6391; Fax: 605-338-2953.
School—Tel: 605-334-9881; Fax: 605-334-9224. See separate listing under Inter-Parochial Schools in the Institution section.
Catechesis/Religious Program—Tel: 605-334-1912. Students 334.

6—ST. MICHAEL (1979), [JC] Revs. Joseph Vogel; Todd Reitmeyer. In Res., Rev. Antonio Ramos.
Res.: 1600 S. Marion Rd., 57106. Tel: 605-361-1600; Fax: 605-361-4350.
School—Tel: 605-361-0021; Fax: 605-361-0094. See separate listing under Inter-Parochial Schools in the Institution section.
Catechesis/Religious Program—Tel: 605-361-1317. Students 1,257.

7—OUR LADY OF GUADALUPE (1996), [JC] Rev. Luis Mesa.
Res.: 1220 E. 8th St., 57103-1702. Tel: 605-338-8126; Fax: 605-338-0419.
Catechesis/Religious Program—Students 69.

8—ST. THERESE (1917), Rev. Charles L. Cimpl; Deacon Michael Conrads. In Res., Rev. Gary Ternes.
Res.: 901 Tahoe Tr., 57110-5779. Tel: 605-338-2433; Fax: 605-339-2203.
Catechesis/Religious Program—Students 337.

OUTSIDE THE CITY OF SIOUX FALLS

ABERDEEN, BROWN CO.

1—ST. MARY, [CEM] Revs. Gregory Tschakert; Paul A. Rutten.
Res.: 215 N. Arch St., 57401. Tel: 605-229-4422; Fax: 605-226-4908.
School— See separate listing under Inter-Parochial Schools in the Institution section.
Catechesis/Religious Program—Students 275.

2—SACRED HEART (1882), [CEM] Revs. Terry Anderson; James P. Morgan; Deacon Peter Mehlhaff.
Res.: 409 3rd Ave., S.E., 57401. Tel: 605-225-7065; Fax: 605-226-5992.
School— See separate listing under Inter-Parochial Schools in the Institution section.
Catechesis/Religious Program—Tel: 605-229-4100. Students 329.

ALEXANDRIA, HANSON CO., ST. MARY OF MERCY (1880), [CEM] Rev. Edward J. Pierce.
Res.: P.O. Box 158, 57331. Tel: 605-239-4833; Fax: 605-239-9833.
Catechesis/Religious Program—Students 103.

ANDOVER, DAY CO., ALL SAINTS (1880), Closed. For inquiries for parish records contact the chancery.

ARLINGTON, KINGSBURY CO., ST. JOHN THE EVANGELIST (1907),, Served from Ramona. Rev. Darrell Lamberty.
Mailing Address: P.O. Box 128, Ramona, 57054. Tel: 605-482-8214; Fax: 605-482-8214.
Catechesis/Religious Program—Tel: 605-983-4704. Students 49.

ARMOUR, DOUGLAS CO., ST. PAUL THE APOSTLE (1886), Rev. Albert Cizewski.
Res.: Box 400, 57313. Tel: 605-724-2191; Fax: 605-724-2121.
Catechesis/Religious Program—Tel: 605-724-2121. Students 68.

ARTESIAN, SANBORN CO., ST. CHARLES (1908), [JC] Attended by, St. Wilfrid, Woonsocket. , Mailing Address: Box 266, Woonsocket, 57385. Tel: 605-796-4666; Fax: 605-796-4666.
Catechesis/Religious Program—Students 40.

ATHOL, SPINK CO., ST. MARY (1885), Closed., For inquiries for parish records contact All Saints, Mellette.

AURORA, BROOKINGS CO., ST. WILLIAM (1881), [CEM] Deacon Edwin Gruhot, Admin.
Mailing Address: 47483 215th St., 57002-6535. Tel: 605-693-3910.
Catechesis/Religious Program—Students 13.

BERESFORD, UNION CO., ST. TERESA OF AVILA (1885), [CEM] Rev. Denis Meier.
Res.: 903 S. Third, P.O. Box 472, 57004. Tel: 605-763-2028 (Church); 605-763-5159 (Rectory).
Catechesis/Religious Program—Students 121.

BIG BEND, HUGHES CO., ST. CATHERINE (1950), [CEM] Attended by, Fort Thompson. , Mailing Address: Box 47, Fort Thompson, 57339. Tel: 605-245-2350; Fax: 605-245-2450.
Catechesis/Religious Program—Students 35.

BIG STONE CITY, GRANT CO., ST. CHARLES (1882), [CEM] Unassigned.
Res.: P.O. Box 68, 57216. Tel: 605-862-8319; Fax: 605-862-8319.
Catechesis/Religious Program—Students 48.

BLUNT, HUGHES CO., HOLY SPIRIT, Closed. For inquiries for parish records contact the chancery.

BOWDLE, EDMUNDS CO., ST. AUGUSTINE (1894), [CEM] Rev. John Rader.
Mailing Address: Box 310, 57428. Tel: 605-285-6466; Fax: 605-285-6160.
Catechesis/Religious Program—Students 37.

BRANDON, MINNEHAHA CO., RISEN SAVIOR (1979), [JC] Rev. Jerome Kopel.
Res.: 301 N. Splitrock Blvd., P.O. Box 80, 57005-0080. Tel: 605-582-8535 (Rectory); 605-582-6902 (Church); Fax: 605-582-3993.
Catechesis/Religious Program—Tel: 605-582-2292. Students 413.

BRIDGEWATER, MCCOOK CO., ST. STEPHEN (1883), [CEM] Rev. Paul Offerman.
Res.: Box 49, 57319. Tel: 605-729-2505; Fax: 605-729-2505.
Catechesis/Religious Program—Students 77.

BRISTOL, DAY CO., ST. ANTHONY (1885), [CEM], Served from Groton Rev. David Janes.
Res.: Box 336, 57219. Tel: 605-492-3135.
Catechesis/Religious Program—Students 22.

BRITTON, MARSHALL CO., ST. JOHN DE BRITTO (1888), [JC] Rev. DeWayne Kayser.
Res.: Box 108, 57430. Tel: 605-448-5379; Fax: 605-448-5388.
Catechesis/Religious Program—Students 60.

BROOKINGS, BROOKINGS CO., ST. THOMAS MORE (1904), [CEM] Rev. Michael Wensing.
Res.: 1700 8th St. S., 57006. Tel: 605-692-4361; Fax: 605-692-6176.
Catechesis/Religious Program—Tel: 605-692-6941. Students 509.

BRYANT, HAMLIN CO., ST. MARY (1881), [CEM] Attended by, St. Thomas, De Smet.
Res.: Box 15, De Smet, 57231. Tel: 605-854-3564; Fax: 605-854-3564.
Catechesis/Religious Program—Students 28.

CANTON, LINCOLN CO., ST. DOMINIC, Rev. Terry Weber; Deacon Edward B. Oliver.
Res.: 809 E. Walnut, 57013. Tel: 605-764-5640; Fax: 605-764-3085.
Catechesis/Religious Program—Students 133.

CASTLEWOOD, HAMLIN CO., ST. JOHN (1885), [JC] Attended by, Kranzburg. , Mailing Address: Box 166, Kranzburg, 57245. Tel: 605-886-9166; Fax: 605-886-2715.
Catechesis/Religious Program—Students 49.

CAVOUR, BEADLE CO., ST. PATRICK (1883), Closed., For inquiries for parish records contact Holy Trinity, Huron.

CENTERVILLE, TURNER CO., GOOD SHEPHERD (1888), [JC] Attended by, Beresford. , Mailing Address: P.O. Box 98, 57014. Tel: 605-563-2220.
Catechesis/Religious Program—Students 67.

CHAMBERLAIN, BRULE CO., ST. JAMES (1891), [JC] Rev. William Pitcavage, S.C.J.; Deacon Alfred Bud Jetty.
Res.: 400 S. Main, 57325. Tel: 605-734-6122; Fax: 605-734-6729.
Catechesis/Religious Program—Tel: 605-734-6122; Fax: 605-734-6729. Students 195.

CHELSEA, FAULK CO., SACRED HEART (1910), Attended by, Mellette. , Mailing Address: P.O. Box 46, Mellette, 57461. Tel: 605-887-3414.
Catechesis/Religious Program—Students 14.

CLARK, CLARK CO., ST. MICHAEL (1887), [CEM] Rev. Ken Bain.
Res.: 110 N. Idaho St., 57225. Tel: 605-532-3855; Fax: 605-532-3866.
Catechesis/Religious Program—112 N. Idaho St., 57225. Tel: 605-532-3776. Students 91.

CLEAR LAKE, DEUEL CO., ST. MARY (1900), Rev. Msgr.

Steven Barnett.
Res.: 408 Third St. W., Box 589, 57226. Tel: 605-874-2080; Fax: 605-874-1333.
Catechesis/Religious Program—Students 112.

Colman, Moody Co., St. Peter (1905), [CEM] Rev. Richard Fox; Deacon Michael Huntington.
Res.: Box J, 57017. Tel: 605-534-3612; Fax: 605-534-3612.
Catechesis/Religious Program—Students 106.

Conde, Spink Co., St. John the Baptist (1906), [CEM] Rev. Daniel Wolfgram.
Res.: P.O. Box 228, 57434. Tel: 605-382-5902; Fax: 605-382-5257.
Catechesis/Religious Program—Students 33.

Dakota Dunes, Union Co., Mother Teresa Catholic Community (1999), Rev. Anthony Opem.
Church: 995 Sioux Point, 57049. Tel: 605-235-1942.
Catechesis/Religious Program—Students 42.

Dante, Charles Mix Co., Assumption B.V.M. (1909), [CEM] Rev. Jordan Hite, T.O.R.
Mailing Address: P.O. Box 36, 57329-0036. Tel: 605-384-5155.
Catechesis/Religious Program—Students 100.

De Smet, Kingsbury Co., St. Thomas Aquinas (1901), [CEM] Rev. Cathal Gallagher.
Res.: Box 15, 57231. Tel: 605-854-3564; Fax: 605-854-3564.
Catechesis/Religious Program—Students 81.

Dell Rapids, Minnehaha Co., St. Mary's (1898), [CEM] [JC] Rev. Chester Murtha.
Res.: 608 E. 8th St., 57022. Tel: 605-428-3390; Fax: 605-428-5304.
School—Preschool Lay Teachers 1; Students 14.
School—Tel: 605-428-3459. Lay Teachers 8; Students 109.
School—Middle School Lay Teachers 4; Students 64.
High School—Tel: 605-428-5591; Fax: 605-428-5377. Lay Teachers 7; Students 72.
Catechesis/Religious Program—Tel: 605-428-3597. Students 225.

Dimock, Hutchinson Co., SS. Peter and Paul (1885), [CEM] Rev. Joseph Glancy, T.O.R.
Res.: 146 W. 1st St., 57331. Tel: 605-928-3883; Fax: 605-928-3498.
Catechesis/Religious Program—Students 76.

Doland, Spink Co., St. Joseph of Doland (1909), Attended by, Conde. , Mailing Address: P.O. Box 393, 57436-0393. Tel: 605-635-6301; Fax: 605-635-6411.
Catechesis/Religious Program—Students 47.

Duncan, Buffalo Co., St. Placidus (1887), [CEM] Attended by, Wessington Springs. , 510 N. Wallace, P.O. Box N, Wessington Springs, 57382-0348. Tel: 605-293-3484.
Church: HCR 3, Box 17, Gann Valley, 57341.
Catechesis/Religious Program—Students 9.

Eden, Marshall Co., Sacred Heart (1917), [CEM] Rev. Jesudas Thaliyan, C.M.I. (India).
Res.: Box 15, 57232. Tel: 605-486-4702; Fax: 605-486-4772.
Catechesis/Religious Program—Students 62.

Elk Point, Union Co., St. Joseph (1901), [CEM] Rev. David Roehrich.
Box 340, 605 E. Main St., 57025. Tel: 605-356-2693; Fax: 605-356-3284.
Catechesis/Religious Program—Students 238.

Elkton, Brookings Co., Our Lady of Good Counsel (1879), [CEM] Attended by, Flandreau. , Mailing Address: 105 S. Bates, Flandreau, 57028. Tel: 605-997-2610; Fax: 605-573-2080.
Res.: Box E, 57026. Tel: 605-542-8221; Fax: 605-542-8221.
Catechesis/Religious Program—Students 101.

Emery, Hanson Co., St. Martin (1884), [CEM] Rev. Edward J. Pierce.
Res.: Box 312, 57332. Tel: 605-449-4374.
Catechesis/Religious Program—Students 73.

Epiphany, Hanson Co., Church of the Epiphany (1896), [CEM] Attended by, Howard. , Mailing Address: Box 100, Howard, 57349. In Res., Rev. Arnold Petrosky, T.O.R. (Retired).
Catechesis/Religious Program—Students 54.

Estelline, Hamlin Co., St. Francis de Sales (1884), [CEM] Attended by, Clear Lake.
Res.: P.O. Box 589, Clear Lake, 57226. Tel: 605-873-2254; Fax: 605-874-1333.
Catechesis/Religious Program—Tel: 605-874-2080. Students 52.

Ethan, Davison Co., Holy Trinity (1889), [CEM] Attended by, Dimock. , 146 W. 1st St., Dimock, 57331. Tel: 605-928-3883.
Catechesis/Religious Program—Tel: 605-227-4666. Patty Scheich, D.R.E. Students 62.

Eureka, McPherson Co., St. Joseph (1896), Attended by, Herreid. , Mailing Address: P.O. Box 37, Herreid, 57632. Tel: 605-437-2614; Fax: 605-437-2505.
Catechesis/Religious Program—Tel: 605-284-2043. Students 34.

Farmer, Hanson Co., St. Peter (1889), Closed. For inquiries for parish records contact the chancery.

Faulkton, Faulk Co., St. Thomas the Apostle (1903), [CEM] Rev. Randy Phillips; Deacon Arvid Holsing.
Res.: P.O. Box 394, 57438. Tel: 605-598-6590; Fax: 605-598-6745.
Catechesis/Religious Program—Deb Clement, D.R.E. Students 75.

Flandreau, Moody Co., SS. Simon and Jude (1882), [CEM] Rev. Richard Fox.
Res.: 105 S. Bates, 57028. Tel: 605-997-2610; Fax: 605-573-2080.
Catechesis/Religious Program—Students 150.

Florence, Codington Co., Blessed Sacrament (1889), [CEM] Rev. Douglas Binsfeld.
Res.: Box 6, 57235. Tel: 605-758-2271; Fax: 605-758-2113.
Catechesis/Religious Program—Students 58.

Fort Thompson, Buffalo Co., St. Joseph (1889), [CEM] Revs. Stephen Huffstetter, S.C.J. (RC), Moderator; Charles Wonch, S.C.J.
Mailing Address: Box 47, 57339. Tel: 605-245-2350.
Catechesis/Religious Program—Students 145.

Frankfort Spink Co., St. Ann (1884), Attended by, Mellette. , Mailing Address: Box 46, Mellette, 57461. Tel: 605-887-3414.
Catechesis/Religious Program—Students 21.

Garretson, Minnehaha Co., St. Rose of Lima (1898), [CEM] Rev. James E. Mason.
Res.: Drawer O, 57030. Tel: 605-594-3750.
Catechesis/Religious Program—Students 103.

Garryowen, Union Co., St. Mary, Closed. For inquiries for parish records contact the chancery.

Gary, Deuel Co., St. Peter (1900), Attended by, Clear Lake. , 408 3rd St. W., Box 589, Clear Lake, 57226. Tel: 605-874-2080; Fax: 605-874-1333.
Catechesis/Religious Program—Students 32.

Geddes, Charles Mix Co., St. Ann (1902), [CEM] [JC] Attended by, Platte. , Mailing Address: P.O. Box 335, Platte, 57369-0335. Tel: 605-337-2465; 605-337-3710; Fax: 605-337-9717.
Catechesis/Religious Program—Students 41.

Gettysburg, Potter Co., Sacred Heart (1905), [CEM] Rev. Ken Lulf.
Res.: Box 285, 57442. Tel: 605-765-2161.
Catechesis/Religious Program—Tel: 605-765-2359. Students 83.

Grenville, Day Co., St. Joseph (1885), [CEM] Attended by, Eden.
Res.: Box 191, 57239. Tel: 605-486-4655; 605-486-4702 (Eden).
Catechesis/Religious Program—Students 36.

Groton, Brown Co., St. Elizabeth Ann Seton (1883), [CEM], (formerly St. John the Baptist). Rev. David Janes.
Res.: 803 1st St. North, P.O. Box 407, 57445. Tel: 605-397-8448; Fax: 605-397-8632.
Catechesis/Religious Program—Students 107.

Grover, Codington Co., St. Peter (1901), Attended by, Blessed Sacrament, Florence. , Mailing Address: P.O. Box 6, Florence, 57235. Tel: 605-758-2271; Fax: 605-758-2113.
Catechesis/Religious Program—Students 20.

Harrold, Hughes Co., St. John the Evangelist, [CEM] Attended by, Highmore. , Mailing Address: Box 457, Highmore, 57345. Tel: 605-852-2733; Fax: 605-852-2076.
Catechesis/Religious Program—Students 45.

Hartford, Minnehaha Co., St. George (1882), [CEM] Rev. Michael D. Kelly; Sr. Muriel Spartz, O.S.B., Pastoral Assoc.
100 N. Mundt, Box 577, 57033. Tel: 605-528-3902; Fax: 605-528-3902.
Res.: 300 W. Mickelson, 57033.
Catechesis/Religious Program—St. George Center, 408 S. Western Ave., 57033. Students 247.

Hecla, Brown Co., St. Anthony of Padua (1904), [JC] Attended by, St. John, Britton. , Mailing Address: Box 108, Britton, 57430. Tel: 605-448-5379 Fax: 605-528-3902.
Catechesis/Religious Program—Students 7.

Henry Codington Co., St. Henry, Rev. Douglas Binsfeld.
Mailing Address: P.O. Box 78, 57243. Tel: 605-758-2271.
Catechesis/Religious Program—Students 38.

Herreid, Campbell Co., St. Michael (1895), [CEM] Unassigned.
Res.: Box 37, 57632. Tel: 605-437-2614; Fax: 605-437-2505.
Catechesis/Religious Program—Students 71.

Highmore, Hyde Co., St. Mary (1906), [CEM] Rev. John Short.
Res.: Box 457, 57345. Tel: 605-852-2733.
Catechesis/Religious Program—Students 59.

Hosmer, Edmunds Co., Holy Trinity (1912), [CEM] Attended by, Bowdle.
Res.: P.O. Box 46, 57448. Tel: 605-283-2275.
Catechesis/Religious Program—Students 27.

Hoven, Potter Co., St. Anthony of Padua (1887), [CEM] Rev. Lance Oser.
Res.: Box 98, 57450. Tel: 605-948-2451; Fax: 605-948-2245.
Catechesis/Religious Program—Students 142.

Howard, Miner Co., St. Agatha (1882), [CEM] Rev. Michael Schneider.
Res.: Box 100, 57349. Tel: 605-772-5564.
Catechesis/Religious Program—Students 100.

Humboldt, Minnehaha Co., St. Ann (1912), [CEM] Rev. John Riedman; Sr. Jane Schoenfelder, O.S.B.
Res.: 204 S. Jefferson, 57035. Tel: 605-363-3330; Fax: 605-363-3856.
Catechesis/Religious Program—Students 92.

Huntimer, Minnehaha Co., St. Joseph the Workman (1889), [CEM] Rev. Anthony Imberi.
Mailing Address: 25216 481st Ave., Garretson, 57030. Tel: 605-594-2353.
Catechesis/Religious Program—Students 119.

Huron, Beadle Co., Holy Trinity (1999), [CEM] Revs. J. Joseph Holzhauser; James Zimmer.
Mailing Address: 133 5th St., S.E., 57350.
Res.: 425 20th St., S.W., 57350. Tel: 605-352-2203; Fax: 605-353-0889.
School—Tel: 605-352-9344; Fax: 605-352-0988. Lay Teachers 9; Students 85.
Catechesis/Religious Program—Tel: 605-352-2237. Students 385.

Idylwilde, Turner Co., St. Boniface (1885), [CEM] Attended by, St. Nicholas, P.O. Box 116, Tea, SD 57064-0116.
Res.: P.O. Box 116, Tea, 57064-0116. Tel: 605-498-5449; Fax: 605-498-2110.
Catechesis/Religious Program—Students 63.

Ipswich, Edmunds Co., Holy Cross (1886), [CEM] Rev. Thomas Clement.
Res.: Box 67, 57451. Tel: 605-426-6967; Fax: 605-426-6588.
School—Tel: 605-426-6222. Lay Teachers 5; Students 52.
Catechesis/Religious Program—Students 110.

Iroquois, Kingsbury Co., St. Paul (1914), [CEM] Attended by, St. Thomas Aquinas, De Smet. , Mailing Address: Box 15, De Smet, 57231. Tel: 605-854-3564; Fax: 605-854-3564.
Catechesis/Religious Program—Students 44.

Jefferson, Union Co., St. Peter (1867), [CEM] Rev. David Roehrich.
Res.: 105 Dakota Rd., P.O. Box 188, 57038-0188. Tel: 605-966-5716; Fax: 605-966-5716.
School—Preschool, P.O. Box 98, 57038-0098. Tel: 605-966-5756. Students 30.
Catechesis/Religious Program— (Combined with St. Joseph, Elk Point) Students 88.

Kimball, Brule Co., St. Margaret (1884), [CEM] Rev. Jerome Ranek.
Res.: Box 137, 57355. Tel: 605-778-6420; Fax: 605-778-6487.
Catechesis/Religious Program—Tel: 605-778-6487. Students 149.

Kranzburg, Codington Co., Holy Rosary (1879), [CEM] Rev. Gregory Frankman.
Res.: Box 166, 57245. Tel: 605-886-9166; Fax: 605-886-2715.
School—(Grades K-6) Tel: 605-886-8114; Fax: 605-886-9166. Lay Teachers 4; Students 41.
Catechesis/Religious Program—Students 101.

Lake Andes, Charles Mix Co., St. Mark (1904), [CEM] Bro. Martin Zatsick, T.O.R., Admin.
Res.: Box 250, 57356. Tel: 605-487-7300.
Catechesis/Religious Program—Tel: 605-487-7056. Students 40.

Lake City, Marshall Co., St. Joseph (1919), [CEM] Attended by, Eden. , Mailing Address: Box 15, Eden, 57232. Tel: 605-486-4702; Fax: 605-486-4772.

Lennox, Lincoln Co., St. Magdalen, [CEM] Attended by, St. Dominic, Canton. , Mailing Address: Box 136, 57039. Tel: 605-647-2187.
Catechesis/Religious Program—Students 108.

Leola, McPherson Co., Our Lady of Perpetual Help (1891), [CEM] Rev. Thomas Clement.
Res.: P.O. Box 67, Ipswich, 57451. Tel: 605-426-6967; Fax: 605-426-6588.
Catechesis/Religious Program—Students 51.

Lesterville, Yankton Co., St. John the Baptist (1904), [CEM] Attended by, St. Wenceslaus, Tabor. , Mailing Address: 205 N. Lidice, Tabor, 57063. Tel: 605-463-2336; Fax: 605-463-2518.
Catechesis/Religious Program—Students 40.

Letcher, Sanborn Co., St. Scholastica, Closed. For inquiries for parish records contact the chancery.

Lily, Day Co., St. Joseph, Closed., For sacramental records contact St. Anthony, Bristol.

Madison, Lake Co., St. Thomas Aquinas (1881), [CEM] Rev. Robert B. Vinslauski.
Res.: 217 N.W. Fourth St., 57042. Tel: 605-256-2304; Fax: 605-256-3953.
School—Tel: 605-256-4419. Lay Teachers 11; Students 110.
Catechesis/Religious Program—Students 210.

Marion, Turner Co., Our Lady of Perpetual Help (1880), [CEM] Attended by, St. Mary, P.O. Box 308, Salem, SD 57058.

Res.: Box 237, 57043. Tel: 605-648-3928.
Catechesis/Religious Program—Students 50.

MARTY, CHARLES MIX CO., ST. PAUL'S CHURCH (1913), (Native American), [CEM] Rev. David Tickerhoof, T.O.R.; Sr. Miriam Shindelar, O.S.B.S., Admin.; Deacon Edward P. Zephier.
Res.: P.O. Box 266, 57361. Tel: 605-384-3234; Fax: 605-384-3575.
Catechesis/Religious Program—Students 41.

MAYFIELD, YANKTON CO., ST. COLUMBA (1902), [CEM] Rev. John Rasmussen.
900 E. 14th St., Apt. 212, 57104-5258. Tel: 605-331-1121.
Catechesis/Religious Program—Students 38.

MELLETTE, SPINK CO., ALL SAINTS (1944), [CEM] Rev. Christopher Hughes.
Mailing Address: Box 46, 57461. Tel: 605-887-3414.
Catechesis/Religious Program—Students 56.

MILBANK, GRANT CO., ST. LAWRENCE (1882), [CEM] Rev. Wilfred Lambertz, O.S.B.
Res.: 101 6th St. S., 57252. Tel: 605-432-5353.
School—Tel: 605-432-5673. Lay Teachers 9; Students 135.
Catechesis/Religious Program—Tel: 605-432-5353. Students 322.

MILLER, HAND CO., ST. ANN (1884), [CEM] Rev. Terry Weber.
Res.: 709 E. 4th, P.O. Box 198, 57362. Tel: 605-853-2207; Fax: 605-853-3037.
Catechesis/Religious Program—Tel: 605-853-2735. Students 150.

MITCHELL, DAVISON CO.
1—HOLY FAMILY (1880), [JC] Rev. Larry Regynski; Deacon Joseph Graves.
Res.: 321 E. 3rd Ave., 57301. Tel: 605-996-3639; Fax: 605-996-3937.
School—John Paul II Elementary, Tel: 605-996-2365; Fax: 605-995-0378. Lay Teachers 15; Students 277.
Catechesis/Religious Program—1510 W. Elm, 57301. Tel: 605-996-3842. Students 485.
2—HOLY SPIRIT (1962), Rev. Andrew Swietochowski.
Res.: 1412 W. Cedar Ave., 57301. Tel: 605-996-7424; Fax: 605-996-6964.
School—John Paul II Elementary, Tel: 605-996-2365; Fax: 605-995-0378. See Holy Family for details
Catechesis/Religious Program—Tel: 605-996-3842. Students 325.

MOBRIDGE, WALWORTH CO., ST. JOSEPH (1912), [JC] Rev. Brian Simon.
Res.: 514 2nd Ave. W., 57601. Tel: 605-845-2100.
School—Preschool Lay Teachers 1; Students 30.
Catechesis/Religious Program—614 W. Second Ave., 57601. Tel: 605-845-2646. Students 157.

MONTROSE, MCCOOK CO., ST. PATRICK (1904), [CEM] Rev. John Reidman.
211 S. Church, P.O. Box 158, 57048. Tel: 605-363-5068; Fax: 605-363-3856.
Catechesis/Religious Program—Students 125.

MOUNT VERNON, DAVISON CO., ST. MICHAEL (1900), Attended by, Plankinton. , Mailing Address: Box 430, Plankinton, 57368. Tel: 605-942-7125.
Catechesis/Religious Program—Students 71.

NEW EFFINGTON, ROBERTS CO., SACRED HEART (1913), Attended by, Rosholt. , Mailing Address: P.O. Box 45, Rosholt, 57260. Tel: 605-537-4583.
Catechesis/Religious Program—Students 10.

OLDHAM, KINGSBURY CO., ST. CATHERINE OF SIENNA (1899), Attended by, St. William, Ramona. , Mailing Address: P.O. Box 128, Ramona, 57054-0128. Tel: 605-482-8214; Fax: 605-482-8243.
Catechesis/Religious Program—Students 16.

ONAKA, FAULK CO., ST. JOHN THE BAPTIST (1906), [CEM] Attended by, St. Anthony of Padua, Hoven. , Mailing Address: P.O. Box 98, Hoven, 57450. Tel: 605-948-2451; Fax: 605-948-2245.
Catechesis/Religious Program—Students 10.

ONIDA, SULLY CO., ST. PIUS X (1959), [CEM] Attended by, Sacred Heart, Gettysburg. Sr. Veronica Haag, O.S.B., Pastoral Assoc.
Mailing Address: P.O. Box 13, 57564. Tel: 605-258-2336.
Catechesis/Religious Program—Students 49.

ORIENT, FAULK CO., ST. JOSEPH (1884), Deacon James Boorman.
17985 354th Ave., 57467. Tel: 605-392-2440.
Catechesis/Religious Program—Students 40.

PARKER, TURNER CO., ST. CHRISTINA (1887), [CEM] Rev. Ken Koster.
Res.: Maple St., Box 116, Tea, 57064. Tel: 605-498-5449; Fax: 605-498-2110.
Catechesis/Religious Program—Students 68.

PARKSTON, HUTCHINSON CO., SACRED HEART (1887), [CEM 2] Rev. Robert V. Krantz; Deacon Barry Wagner.
Res.: Box 460, 57366. Tel: 605-928-3676; Fax: 605-928-3862.
Catechesis/Religious Program—Students 201.

PIERRE, HUGHES CO., SS. PETER AND PAUL (1882), [CEM] Revs. Hal Barber; Thomas L. Cool; Deacon Roger Heidt.
Res.: 304 N. Euclid, 57501. Tel: 605-224-2483; Fax: 605-224-1483.
School—Tel: 605-224-7185; Fax: 605-224-1014. Benedictine Sisters 3; Lay Teachers 8; Students 157.
Catechesis/Religious Program—Students 386.

PLANKINTON, AURORA CO., ST. JOHN, Rev. Alex Bombera, T.O.R.
Res.: Box 430, 57368. Tel: 605-942-7125.
Catechesis/Religious Program—Students 120.

PLATTE, CHARLES MIX CO., ST. PETER THE APOSTLE (1904), [CEM] Rev. Paul Josten.
Res.: Box 335, 57369. Tel: 605-337-3710; 605-337-2465; Fax: 605-337-9717.
Catechesis/Religious Program—Students 67.

POLO, HAND CO., ST. LIBORIUS (1904), [CEM] Rev. John J. Helmueller; Deacon James Boorman, Pastoral Admin.
Res.: 17985 354th Ave., Orient, 57467. Tel: 605-392-2440.
Catechesis/Religious Program—Students 24.

PUKWANA, BRULE CO., ST. ANTHONY (1891), Attended by, Chamberlain. , 400 S. Main, Chamberlain, 57325. Tel: 605-734-6122; Fax: 605-734-6729.
Catechesis/Religious Program—Students 9.

RAMONA, LAKE CO., ST. WILLIAM OF VERCELLI (1899), Rev. Darrell Lamberty.
Mailing Address: P.O. Box 128, 57054-0128. Tel: 605-482-8214; Fax: 605-482-8243.
Catechesis/Religious Program—Students 14.

REDFIELD, SPINK CO., ST. BERNARD (1884), [CEM] Rev. William Osborn.
Res.: 213 E. 6th Ave., 57469-1249. Tel: 605-472-2500; Fax: 605-472-3397.
Catechesis/Religious Program—Tel: 605-472-1482. Students 203.

REVILLO, GRANT CO., ANNUNCIATION (1889), [CEM] Unassigned.
Res.: 901 E. Virgil, Milbank, 57252-0432. Tel: 605-432-4623; Fax: 605-432-5412.
Catechesis/Religious Program—Students 43.

ROSCOE, EDMUNDS CO., ST. THOMAS APOSTLE (1906), [JC] Attended by, Bowdle.
Res.: P.O. Box 213, 57471. Tel: 605-285-6466.
Catechesis/Religious Program—Students 39.

ROSHOLT, ROBERTS CO., ST. JOHN THE BAPTIST (1911), [CEM] Rev. Dennis Deis, O.M.I.
Res.: Box 45, 57260. Tel: 605-537-4583.
Catechesis/Religious Program—Students 83.

SALEM, MCCOOK CO., ST. MARY (1885), [CEM] Rev. Kevin O'Dell. In Res., Rev. Charles J. Duman (Retired).
Res.: Box 264, 330 N. Idaho, 57058. Tel: 605-425-3220; Fax: 605-425-2600.
School—Tel: 605-425-2607. Lay Teachers 9; Students 83.
Catechesis/Religious Program—Students 75.

SCOTLAND, BON HOMME CO., ST. GEORGE (1906), [CEM] Rev. David E. Stevens.
Res.: Box 449, 57059. Tel: 605-583-4318; Fax: 605-583-4318.
Catechesis/Religious Program—Tel: 605-583-4696. Students 48.

SELBY, WALWORTH CO., ST. ANTHONY (1900), Attended by, Herreid. , Mailing Address: P.O. Box 37, Herreid, 57632-0037. Tel: 605-437-2614; Fax: 605-437-2505.
Catechesis/Religious Program—Students 32.

SENECA, FAULK CO., ST. BONIFACE (1903), Attended by, St. Thomas the Apostle, Faulkton. , Mailing Address: P.O. Box 394, Faulkton, 57438-0094. Tel: 605-598-6590.
Catechesis/Religious Program—Students 9.

SIGEL, YANKTON CO., ST. AGNES (1885), [CEM] Rev. John Rasmussen.
900 E. 14th, Apt. 212, 57108. Tel: 605-331-1121.
Catechesis/Religious Program—Students 9.

SISSETON, ROBERTS CO.
1—ST. CATHERINE (1962), [CEM 2] Revs. Norman Volk, O.M.I.; Walter Butor, O.M.I.
Office—120 E. Chestnut, 57262. Tel: 605-698-7414; Fax: 605-698-7236.
Catechesis/Religious Program— (Combined with St. Peter, Sisseton.)
2—ST. PETER (1899), [CEM] Revs. Norman Volk, O.M.I.; Walter Butor, O.M.I.
Office—120 E. Chestnut, 57262. Tel: 605-698-7414; Fax: 605-698-7236.
Catechesis/Religious Program—Students 126.

SPENCER, MCCOOK CO., ST. MARY (1906), Merged, with St. Peter, Farmer to form St. John Neumann, Spencer-Farmer.

SPENCER-FARMER, MCCOOK CO., ST. JOHN NEUMANN, Attended by, Bridgewater. , Mailing Address: P.O. Box 49, Bridgewater, 57319. Tel: 615-729-2505.
Catechesis/Religious Program—Parish Center, 620 Cordo St., 57374. Tel: 605-246-2391. Students 16.

SPRINGFIELD, BON HOMME CO., ST. VINCENT, Attended by, Tyndall. , Mailing Address: P.O. Box 130, 57062-0130. Tel: 605-589-3504.
Catechesis/Religious Program—Students 29.

STEPHAN, HYDE CO., IMMACULATE CONCEPTION (1886), [CEM] [JC] Revs. Stephen Huffstetter, S.C.J. (RC), Moderator; Charles Wonch, S.C.J.
Mailing Address: P.O. Box 185, Lower Brule, 57548. Tel: 605-852-2216.
Catechesis/Religious Program—Students 33.

STICKNEY, AURORA CO., ST. MARY (1908), [CEM] Attended by, Armour. , Mailing Address: Box 400, Armour, 57313. Tel: 605-724-2191; Fax: 605-724-2121.
Catechesis/Religious Program—Students 28.

TABOR, BON HOMME CO., ST. WENCESLAUS (1872), [CEM] Rev. Joseph Puthenkulathil (India); Deacon David Kostel.
Res.: 205 N. Lidice St., 57063-2005. Tel: 605-463-2336; Fax: 605-463-2518.
Catechesis/Religious Program—Students 66.

TEA, LINCOLN CO., ST. NICHOLAS (1905), [JC] Rev. Kenneth J. Koster.
Res.: 510 W. Maple, P.O. Box 116, 57064. Tel: 605-498-5449; Fax: 605-498-2110.
Church: 140 W. Brian St., 57064. Tel: 605-498-5449.
Catechesis/Religious Program—Students 150.

TRIPP, HUTCHINSON CO., HOLY ROSARY, Attended by, Parkston. , Mailing Address: P.O. Box 358, 57376-0358. Tel: 605-935-7225.
Catechesis/Religious Program—Students 30.

TURTON, SPINK CO., ST. JOSEPH (1888), [CEM] [JC] Attended by, Conde. , Mailing Address: P.O. Box 127, 57477. Tel: 605-382-5902.
Catechesis/Religious Program—Students 8.

TYNDALL, BON HOMME CO., ST. LEO (1890), [CEM] Rev. Gerald Thury.
Res.: Box 47, 57066. Tel: 605-589-3504; Fax: 605-589-3392.
Catechesis/Religious Program—Students 140.
Station—Springfield Correctional Facility Springfield. Tel: 605-369-2201.

VEBLEN, MARSHALL CO., ST. JOHN NEPOMUCENE (1907), [CEM] Attended by, Catholic Community, Sisseton. , 120 Chestnut St. E., Sisseton, 57262-1428. Tel: 605-698-7414; Fax: 605-698-7236.
Catechesis/Religious Program—Students 10.

VERMILLION, CLAY CO., ST. AGNES (1860), [CEM 2] [JC] Rev. Donald Imming.
Res.: 416 Walker St., 57069. Tel: 605-624-4478 (Church); 605-624-4479 (Rec.); Fax: 605-624-4418.
School—909 E. Lewis St., 57069. Tel: 605-624-4144. Lay Teachers 7; Students 84.
Catechesis/Religious Program—Tel: 605-624-5161. Students 202.

VODNANY, BON HOMME CO., SS. CYRIL AND METHODIUS (1886), [CEM] Attended by, Scotland. , P.O. Box 449, Scotland, 57059.
Catechesis/Religious Program—Students 6.

WAGNER, CHARLES MIX CO., ST. JOHN THE BAPTIST (1903), [CEM] Rev. Jordan Hite, T.O.R.; Deacon Albert J. Kocer.
Res.: Box 637, 57380. Tel: 605-384-5518; Fax: 605-384-5518.
Catechesis/Religious Program—Tel: 605-384-5157. Students 176.

WAKONDA, CLAY CO., ST. PATRICK (1904), [CEM 2] Attended by, Newman Center, Vermillion. Rev. Joseph Forcelle, Admin.; Deacon Thomas Vogel.
320 Cherry St., Vermillion, 57069. Tel: 605-624-2697.
Catechesis/Religious Program—Tel: 605-267-2676; Fax: 605-624-4145. Students 40.

WATERTOWN, CODINGTON CO.
1—HOLY NAME (1955), [JC] Rev. John Lantsberger.
Res.: 1009 Skyline Dr., 57201. Tel: 605-886-2628; Fax: 605-886-2142.
Catechesis/Religious Program—Tel: 605-886-3368; Fax: 605-886-2141. Students 388.
2—IMMACULATE CONCEPTION (1887), [CEM] Rev. James Bream.
Res.: 309 Second Ave., S.E., 57201. Tel: 605-886-4049; Fax: 605-882-2911.
School—Tel: 605-886-3883; Fax: 605-886-0199. Lay Teachers 12; Students 185.
Catechesis/Religious Program—103 Third St., S.E., 57201. Tel: 605-886-2772; Fax: 605-886-2772. Students 390.

WAUBAY, DAY CO., IMMACULATE CONCEPTION (1894), [CEM] Attended by, Webster. , Mailing Address: 1101 E. 1st St., Webster, 57274. Tel: 605-345-3447; Fax: 605-345-4871.
Catechesis/Religious Program—Students 81.

WAVERLY, CODINGTON CO., ST. JOSEPH (1889), [CEM] Attended by, Kranzburg. , Mailing Address: Box 166, Kranzburg, 57245. Tel: 605-886-9166; Fax: 605-886-2715.
Catechesis/Religious Program—Students 47.

WEBSTER, DAY CO., CHRIST THE KING (1884), [CEM] Rev. William Hamak.
Res.: 1101 E. 1st St., 57274. Tel: 605-345-3447; Fax: 605-345-4871.
Catechesis/Religious Program—Students 173.

WELLINGTON, MINNEHAHA CO., ST. JOSEPH, Closed.,

For sacramental records contact St. Ann, Humboldt.

WESSINGTON SPRINGS, JERAULD CO., ST. JOSEPH (1906), [JC] Rev. Msgr. Edward Burian.
Mailing Address: P.O. Box N, 510 N. Wallace, 57382. Tel: 605-539-9569; Fax: 605-539-9569.
Catechesis/Religious Program—Students 58.

WESSINGTON, BEADLE CO., ST. JOSEPH, Attended by, Miller. , Mailing Address: P.O. Box 198, Miller, 57362-0198. Tel: 605-853-2207; Fax: 605-853-3037.
Catechesis/Religious Program—Students 30.

WESTPORT, BROWN CO., SACRED HEART OF WESTPORT (1889), [CEM] Attended by, St. Mary, Aberdeen. , 215 N. Arch, Aberdeen, 57401. Tel: 605-229-4422; Fax: 605-226-3274.
Catechesis/Religious Program—Tel: 605-226-3713. Students 59.

WHITE LAKE, AURORA CO., ST. PETER (1883), [CEM] Attended by, Kimball
Res.: Box 277, 57383. Tel: 605-249-2700; Fax: 605-249-2700.
Catechesis/Religious Program—Students 106.

WHITE, BROOKINGS CO., ST. PAUL (1898), [JC] Rev. Scott Traynor.
Mailing Address: Box 7019, University Sta., Brookings, 57007. Tel: 605-692-9461.
Catechesis/Religious Program—Students 68.

WILLOW LAKE, CLARK CO., ST. JAMES (1895), Attended by, St. Michael, Clark. , 110 N. Idaho St., Clark, 57225. Tel: 605-532-3855; Fax: 605-532-3866.
Catechesis/Religious Program—Students 14.

WILMOT, ROBERTS CO., ST. MARY (1886), [CEM] Rev. John McMullen, O.S.B.
Res.: Box 204, 57279. Tel: 605-938-4289; Fax: 605-398-9201.
Catechesis/Religious Program—Students 44.

WOONSOCKET, SANBORN CO., ST. WILFRID (1884), [CEM] Rev. John Maliyekal, V.C. (India).
Res.: Box 266, 57385. Tel: 605-796-4666; Fax: 605-796-4666.
Catechesis/Religious Program—Students 64.

WORTHING, LINCOLN CO., ST. EDWARD (1908), [CEM] Attended by, St. Dominic, Canton. , 800 E. Walnut, Canton, 57013. Tel: 605-764-5640; Fax: 605-764-3085.

YANKTON, YANKTON CO.
1—ST. BENEDICT (1993), [JC] Rev. Rodney Farke; Deacons Leon Cantin; Ronald Kachena.
Res.: 1500 St. Benedict Dr., 57078. Tel: 605-664-6214; Fax: 605-664-2305.
Catechesis/Religious Program—1500 St. Benedict Dr., 57078. Tel: 605-665-6214. Students 301.
2—SACRED HEART (1871), [CEM] Revs. John Fischer; Richard Baumberger.
Res.: 509 Capitol St., 57078. Tel: 605-665-3655; Fax: 605-665-6768.
School—Tel: 605-665-5841; Fax: 605-668-9787. Sisters 1; Lay Teachers 15; Students 313.
Catechesis/Religious Program—Students 332.

ZELL, HAND CO., ST. MARY (1883), Attended by, Redfield. , 213 E. 6th Ave., Redfield, 57469. Tel: 605-472-2500; Fax: 605-472-2500.
Catechesis/Religious Program—Students 3.

Chaplains of Public Institutions

SIOUX FALLS. *South Dakota State Penitentiary & Minnehaha County Jail*. Revs. Gary Ternes, Antonio Ramos.
State School for the Deaf, 523 N. Duluth Ave., 57104. (Vacant)
Veteran's Hospital. Rev. Kenneth J. Koster.

FLANDREAU. *Government Indian School*. Attended by SS. Simon & Jude, Flandreau

REDFIELD. *State Hospital and State School, SD*. Attended by St. Bernard Church, Redfield

SPRINGFIELD. *State Prison*. Attended by St. Leo, Tyndall

YANKTON. *Federal Prison Camp*. Rev. Lawrence Marbach.
Michelson Center for the Neurosciences. Rev. Leonard Kayser (Retired).

On Duty Outside the Diocese:
Rev. Msgrs.—
Gullickson, Thomas E., Apostolic Nunciature, Postfach 610218, 10923, Berlin, Germany.
Mahowald, Richard J., P.A., Casa Santa Maria, Via del 'Umilta '30, 00187, Rome, Italy.
Rev.—
Mangan, Charles M., Congregation for Institutes of Consecrated Life and Societies of Apostolic Life, Villa Stritch, Via della Nocetta, 63, Roma 00164 Italy.

Retired:
Rev. Msgrs.—
Doyle, James Michael, 2913 Ridgeview Way, 57105.
Duraczynski, Jerome A., 1041 Singer Ln., Norristown, PA 19403.
Hermann, Carlton P., 505 Burgess Rd., 57078-1819.
McEneaney, John P. A., 423 N. Duluth Ave., 57104.
McPhee, Marvin, 609 W. 5th St., 57104
Wagner, Joseph, 11119 Quail Pass, San Antonio, TX 78249.
Zwinger, Leonard, Avera Brady, 500 S. Ohlman St., Rm. A-31, Mitchell, 57301.
Revs.—
Ashfeld, Bernard, 4510 S. Prince of Peace Pl., #205, 57103.
Brady, John, 509 Broadway, 57078.
Cashel, Richard, 811 W. Norway, Mitchell, 57301.
Connolly, Thomas, 3109 Corona Dr., Holiday, FL 34690.
Duman, Charles J., 330 N. Idaho, Salem, 57058.
Fox, Leo, P.O. Box 1441, Watertown, 57201.
Fox, Leonard, P.O. Box 264, Vermillion, 57069.
Friedrich, Lawrence, 4510 S. Prince of Peace Pl., Apt. #213, 57103. Tel: 605-371-4537
Garvey, John, 1105 W. 8th St., 57078.
Geditz, Roger, P.O. Box 136, Geddes, 57342. Tel: 605-337-2465
Holtzman, Jerome, 77 Paradise Dr., Watertown, 57201.
Joyce, James, 900 E. 14th St., #112, 57104.
Kayser, Leonard, 304 Greenview Dr., #11, 57078-1445.
Keating, David, c/o Ann Lemon, P.O. Box 177, 57078.
Krzyzopolski, Al, 4700 S. Cliff Ave., #210, 57103.
Marbach, Lawrence J., 617 Maple St., 57078-3823.
Mardian, Pius, 4510 Prince of Peace Pl., #120, 57103.
Martini, Ivo, St. Benedict Center, 1810 Minnesota Blvd., S.E., Apt. 222, St. Cloud, MN 56304.
McPhillips, Thomas J., Bishop Hoch Villa, 500 S. Ohlman, Mitchell, 57301.
Molumby, Donald, Laurel Oaks, 4510 S. Prince of Peace Pl., #210, 57103.
Murphy, Joseph, St. Catharine's, 5617-A Hibernia Dr., Columbus, OH 43232.
Ortmeier, Richard J., Mother of God Monastery, Benet Place, 100 28th Ave., S.E., #311, Watertown, 57201.
Petrucci, Dominic, c/o Gloria Cunningham, 102 Christine Ct., Fairmont, WV 26554.
Wolf, James, St. Charles Rectory, P.O. Box 68, Big Stone City, 57216.

Permanent Deacons:
Bierer, Richard B., (Retired), Sioux Falls
Boorman, James, St. Liborius, Polo; St. Joseph, Orient
Cantin, Leon, St. Benedict, Yankton
Cheskie, Pete, (Out of Diocese)
Cole, John M., (Retired), Holy Spirit, Sioux Falls
Conrads, Michael, St. Therese, Sioux Falls
Counter, Ralph, St. Lambert, Sioux Falls
Frankman, William, Marriage Tribunal
Graff, Francis, (Retired)
Graves, Joseph, Holy Family, Mitchell
Gruhot, Edward, St. William, Aurora
Healy, Thomas, (Retired), Yankton
Heidt, Roger, SS. Peter and Paul, Pierre
Holsing, Arvid, St. Thomas the Apostle, Faulkton
Huntington, Michael, Admin., St. Peter, Colman
Jetty, Alfred "Bud", Native American Ministry
Kachena, Ronald, St. Benedict, Yankton
Knapp, Henry J., St. Mary's, Sioux Falls
Kocer, Albert, St. John the Baptist, Wagner
Kostel, David, (Retired)
Mehlhaff, Peter, Sacred Heart, Aberdeen
Nagel, David, St. Joseph Indian School
Oliver, Edward B., St. Dominic, Canton
Pardew, Harold, Hospital Chap.
Vogel, Thomas, St. Patrick, Wakonda
Wagner, Barry, Sacred Heart, Parkston
Wagner, Donald, St. Rose of Lima, Garretson
Walden, James I., Christ the King Parish, Sioux Falls
Wathen, Jerome F., St. Lambert, Sioux Falls
Zephier, Edward P., St. Paul Parish, Marty

INSTITUTIONS LOCATED IN THE DIOCESE

[A] COLLEGES AND UNIVERSITIES

ABERDEEN. *Presentation College*, 1500 N. Main St., 57401. Tel: 605-225-1634; Fax: 605-229-8430. Email: lorhale@presentation.edu. Web: www.presentation.edu. Dr. Lorraine M. Hale, P.B.V.M., Pres.; Rev. Joseph Sheehan, O.Carm., Chap. Sisters of the Presentation of the B.V.M. Priests 1; Sisters 3; Lay Teachers 23; Students 615.

YANKTON. *Mount Marty College*, 1105 W. 8th St., 57078. Tel: 800-658-4552; Fax: 605-668-1357. Email: bzhang@mtmc.edu. Web: www.mtmc.edu. Dr. James Barry. Benedictine Sisters Sisters 7; Lay Teachers 37; Students 1,185.
Mount Marty College - Watertown Campus, 1225 Arrow Ave., P.O. Box 1385, Watertown, 57201. Tel: 605-886-6777; Fax: 605-882-6347. Email: mmcwatwn@dailypost.com. Linda Schurmann, Dir. Conducted by Benedictine Sisters

[B] EDUCATION CENTERS, PRIVATE

CHAMBERLAIN. *St. Joseph Indian School*, P.O. Box 89, 57325. Tel: 605-734-3300; Fax: 605-734-3480. Web: www.stjo.org. Deacon David Nagel, Exec. Dir. Priests 1; Brothers 1; Lay Teachers 24; Students 220.

[C] INTER-PAROCHIAL SCHOOLS

SIOUX FALLS. *Sioux Falls Catholic School System*, 3100 W. 41st St., 57105. Tel: 605-336-6241; Fax: 605-373-1035. Email: tlorang@sfcss.org. Web: sfcss.org. Dr. Thomas Lorang, Supt.
O'Gorman High School (Grades 9-12), 3201 S. Kiwanis Ave., 57105. Tel: 605-336-3644; Fax: 605-373-1035. Kyle Groos, Prin.; Rev. David A. Desmond, Chap. Priests 1; Sisters 3; Lay Teachers 42; Students 626.
St. Joseph Cathedral Elementary (Grades PreK-6), 601 W. 4th St., 57104. Tel: 605-333-3159; Fax: 605-338-2647. John Bradbury, Prin. Lay Teachers 6; Students 113.
O'Gorman Catholic Junior High (Grades 7-8), 3100 W. 41st St., 57105. Tel: 605-988-0546; Fax: 605-336-9839. Colley Broveliet, Prin. Lay Teachers 20; Students 339.
SMHS - St. Mary, Formerly St. Mary - Holy Spirit Elementary (Grades K-6), 2001 S. 5th Ave., 57105. Tel: 605-334-9881; Fax: 605-334-9224. Courtney Tielke, Prin. Lay Teachers 23; Students 345.
SMHS - Holy Spirit (Grades PreK-4), 4309 S. Bahnson, 57103. Tel: 605-371-1481; Fax: 605-371-1483. Laurie Murray, Prin. Lay Teachers 7; Students 182.
Christ the King Elementary School (Grades PreK-6), 1801 S. Lake Ave., 57105. Tel: 605-338-5103; Fax: 605-335-1231. Nancy Clarey, Prin. Benedictine Sisters 1; Lay Teachers 7; Students 182.
St. Lambert Elementary School (Grades K-6), 1000 S. Bahnson Ave., 57103. Tel: 605-338-7042; Fax: 605-336-8727. Barbara Lockwood, Prin. Lay Teachers 18; Students 306.
St. Michael Elementary School (Grades PreK-6), 1600 S. Marion Rd., 57106. Tel: 605-361-0021; Fax: 605-361-0094. Lisa Huemoeller, Prin. Lay Teachers 18; Students 395.

ABERDEEN. *Aberdeen Catholic Schools Education Office* 1400 N. Dakota St., S.E., 57401. Tel: 605-226-2100; Fax: 605-226-0616. Email: drahm@midco.net.
Roncalli Elementary School (Grades PreK-2), 815 N. 2nd St., 57401. Tel: 605-225-3460. Email: schwabm@midco.net. Mary Schwab, Prin. Sisters 1; Lay Teachers 19; Students 332.
Roncalli Elementary School (Grades 3-6), 815 N. 2nd St., 57401. Tel: 605-229-4100; Fax: 605-229-4101. Email: schwabm@midco.net. Mary Schwab, Prin. (Elementary) Lay Teachers 12; Students 179.
Roncalli High School (Grades 7-12), 1400 N. Dakota St., 57401. Tel: 605-225-7440; Fax: 605-226-0616. Email: drahm@midco.net. Sandra Levsen, Dean. Priests 3; Lay Teachers 21; Students 309.

YANKTON. *Sacred Heart School*, 1500 St. Benedict Dr., Ste. 200, 57078-6305. Tel: 605-665-5841; Fax: 605-260-9787. Email: tbuck_shs@yahoo.com. Barb Rezac, Devel. Dir. Sisters 1; Lay Teachers 16; Total Enrollment 314.

[D] GENERAL HOSPITALS

SIOUX FALLS. *Avera McKennan* 57110-5045. Tel: 605-322-8000; Fax: 605-322-7822. Web: www.averamckennan.org. Mr. Fredrick W. Slunecka, Regl. Pres. & CEO; Rev. James Friedrich, Chap. Sponsored by Sisters of the Presentation of the B.V.M. of Aberdeen, S.D., and Benedictine Sisters of Sacred Heart Monastery, Yankton, S.D. Sisters of the Presentation of the B.V.M. (Aberdeen, SD) 4; Bed Capacity 429; Total Staff 3,964; Patients Assisted Annually 178,306.
Avera McKennan dba Avera Prince of Peace Retirement Community , 4500 S. Prince of Peace Pl., 57103. Tel: 605-322-5600; Fax: 605-322-5622. Presentation Sisters of B.V.M. 1; Nursing Home Beds 90; Congregate Apartments 74; Assisted Living Apartments 32; Total Assisted 199; Total Staff 126.

ABERDEEN. *Avera St. Luke's*, 305 S. State St., 57401. Tel: 605-622-5000; Fax: 605-622-5127. Web: www.averastlukes.org. Ron Jacobson, Interim Pres. & CEO; Rev. Charles Emezie (Nigeria), Chap.; Elaine Van Dover, Dir. Pastoral Care; Mike Sandsmark, Vice Pres. Mission. Sponsored by

Sisters of the Presentation of the B.V.M. of Aberdeen, SD, and Benedictine Sisters of Sacred Heart Monastery, Yankton, SD. Presentation Sisters of the B.V.M.(Aberdeen, SD) 16; Bed Capacity 137; Bassinets 20; Annually Assisted 208,467; Total Staff 892.

Avera St. Luke's dba Avera Mother Joseph Manor Retirement Community , 1002 N. Jay St., 57401. Tel: 605-622-5850; Fax: 605-622-5851. Email: tom.snyder@averastlukes.org. Tom Snyder, Admin.; Rev. Charles Emezie (Nigeria). Adult Day Care, Community Outreach, Respite Care, Health Screening Clinics, and Family Support Council. Presentation Sisters of the B.V.M. (Aberdeen, SD) 4; Residents 81; Units for Apartment Living 58; Assisted Living Beds 34; Total Staff 130.

DELL RAPIDS. *Dells Area Health Center/Avera Health*, 909 N. Iowa St., 57022. Tel: 605-428-5431. Jim Faulwell, Admin. Acute Care Beds 23; Staff 55.

GETTYSBURG. *Gettysburg Medical Center*, 606 E. Garfield, 57442. Tel: 605-765-2488. Mark C. Schmidt, Exec. Dir. Bed Capacity 55; Assisted Living Units 16; Residential Living Units 12.

MILBANK. *Milbank Area Hospital/Avera Health*, 901 E. Virgil Ave., 57252. Tel: 605-432-4538; Fax: 605-432-5412. Rev. Ray Otto, O.S.B., Chap.; Jeff Lang, Admin. Bed Capacity 35; Staff 73.

MITCHELL. *Avera Queen of Peace*, 525 N. Foster, 57301. Tel: 605-995-2000; Fax: 605-995-2441. Email: tom.rasmusson@averaqueenofpeace.org. Web: www.averaqueenofpeace.org. Tom Rasmusson, Pres. & CEO. Sponsored by Sisters of the Presentation of the B.V.M., Aberdeen, SD, and Benedictine Sisters of Sacred Heart Monastery, Yankton, SD. Sisters 2; Bed Capacity 120; Staff 585; Patients Assisted Annually 69,300.

Avera Queen of Peace dba Avera Brady Health & Rehabilitation, Avera Brady Assisted Living , 500 S. Ohlman, 57301. Tel: 605-996-7701; Fax: 605-995-6134. Mrs. Veronica Smith, Admin.; Rev. Thomas J. McPhillips, Chap. (Retired). Sponsored by Sisters of the Presentation of the B.V.M., Aberdeen, SD, and Benedictine Sisters of Sacred Heart Monastery, Yankton, SD. Skilled Nursing Care Units 84; Assisted Living 30; Total Staff 133.

Bishop Hoch Villa Units for Congregate Living 6; Additional Senior Units 3.

PARKSTON. *St. Benedict Health Care Center* dba Avera St. Benedict Health Center 57366. Tel: 605-928-3311; Fax: 605-928-7368. Email: gale.walker@averastbenedict.org. Web: www.averastbenedict.org. Gale N. Walker, Admin. Benedictine Sisters (Yankton, SD) 2; Bed Capacity 105; Annually Assisted 26,896; Total Staff 210.

PIERRE. *St. Mary's Foundation*, 800 E. Dakota, 57501. Tel: 605-224-3451; Fax: 605-224-3459. Email: ellenlee@catholichealth.net. Web: www.St_Marys.com. Ellen J. Lee, Exec. Dir.

St. Mary's Healthcare Center of Pierre, South Dakota, 800 E. Sioux Ave., 57501. Tel: 605-224-3100; Fax: 605-224-3439. Email: jimrussell@catholichealth.net. Web: www.St_Mary's.com. James D.M. Russell, CEO. Includes: Maryhouse Residential Nursing Facility and Parkwood Retirement Apartments. Sisters 1; Bed Capacity 91; Annually Assisted 27,758; Staff 435.

TYNDALL. *St. Michael's Hospital*, P.O. Box 27, 57066. Tel: 605-589-3341; Fax: 605-589-3288. Email: smhceo@byelectric.com. Carol Deurmier, CEO. Bed Capacity 25; Nursing Home Beds 9; Annually Assisted 6,000; Total Staff 80.

YANKTON. *Sacred Heart Health Services* dba Avera Sacred Heart Hospital , 501 Summit, 57078. Tel: 605-668-8000; Fax: 605-665-0170. Pamela Rezac, Pres. & CEO. Sisters 5; Bed Capacity 144.

Sacred Heart Health Services dba Avera Sister James Nursing Homes , 501 Summit, 57078. Tel: 605-668-8000; Fax: 605-665-0170. Bed Capacity 187.

[E] HOMES FOR AGED

MILBANK. *St. William Home Care Center*, 100 S. 9th St., 57252. Tel: 605-432-4538; Fax: 605-432-5412. Rev. Ray Otto, O.S.B. Conducted by Daughters of St. Mary of Providence, Milbank Guests 60.

Angela Hall Tel: 605-432-3171; Fax: 605-432-3187. Assisted Living Center Guests 15; Sisters 4.

SISSETON. *Tekakwitha Nursing Center, Inc.* (sub. of Benedictine Health System) , 6 E. Chestnut, 57262. Tel: 698-698-7693; Fax: 605-698-3091. Email: tncceo@hotmail.com. James P. Cornelius, Admin.; Lois Bates, Dir. Pastoral Care. (Owned and operated by: Benedictine Health System) Bed Capacity 81; Total Staff 105.

Rainbow Daycare Center Tel: 605-698-3257; Fax: 605-698-3091.

[F] MONASTERIES AND RESIDENCES OF PRIESTS AND BROTHERS

EMERY. *Vincentian Congregation* North American Headquarters , Vincentian House, P.O. Box 93, Woonsocket, 57385-0093. Tel: 605-796-4666. Email: vincentians@yahoo.com. Rev. John Maliyekal, V.C. (India), Regl. Coord.

MARVIN. *Blue Cloud Abbey*, 46561 147th St., P.O. Box 98, 57251-0098. Tel: 605-398-9200; Fax: 605-398-9201. Email: abbey@bluecloud.org. Web: www.bluecloud.org. Rt. Revs. Thomas Hillenbrand, O.S.B.; Alan Berndt, O.S.B., Retired Abbot (Retired); Denis Quinkert, O.S.B., Retired Abbot (Retired); Revs. George Lyon, O.S.B., Prior; Stanislaus Maudlin, O.S.B.; Julius Armbruster, O.S.B.; Thomas Roznowski, O.S.B.; Guy Gau, O.S.B.; John McMullen, O.S.B.; Basil Dilger, O.S.B.; Cletus Miller, O.S.B.; Odilo Burkhardt, O.S.B.; Bernardine Ness, O.S.B.; Theophane Gonnelly, O.S.B.; Larry Barnett, O.S.B.; Christopher Uehlein, O.S.B.; Wilfrid Lambertz, O.S.B.; Pedro Choc, O.S.B.; Francisco Arrivillaga Lemus, O.S.B.; Matthew Kowalski; Carlos Antonio Pop, O.S.B.; Elias Juan Tello Aburto, O.S.B. Priests 23; Brothers 17.

[G] CONVENTS AND RESIDENCES FOR SISTERS

SIOUX FALLS. *Adoration Sisters of the Blessed Sacrament*, 521 N. Duluth Ave., 57104. Tel: 605-336-2374; Fax: 605-336-2374. Email: adoratrices@msn.com. Sr. Caridad Morales Olarte, A.P., Supr. Sisters 6; Novices 3.

ABERDEEN. *Presentation Convent*, 1500 N. 24th St., 57401. Tel: 605-225-0420; Fax: 605-229-8412. Email: psertoss@presentationsisters.org. Web: www.presentationsisters.org. Sr. Virginia McCall, P.B.V.M., Pres. Motherhouse and Novitiate of the Sisters of the Presentation of the B.V.M. Final Professed Sisters 122.

ALEXANDRIA. *Monastery of Our Mother of Mercy, Discalced Carmelite Nuns*, 221 5th St. W., P.O. Box 67, 57311-0067. Tel: 605-239-4382; Fax: 605-239-4676. Sr. Marie Therese of the Child Jesus, O.C.D., Prioress.
Legal Title: *Discalced Carmelite Nuns of Alexandria, South Dakota, Inc.* Solemnly Professed Sisters 5; First Professed 3.

MARTY. *Motherhouse Oblate Sisters of the Blessed Sacrament*

St. Sylvester's Convent, Box 217, 57361-0217. Tel: 605-384-3305; Fax: 605-384-3305. Email: osbs@cme.com. Professed Sisters 7.

MITCHELL. *Sisters of St. Francis of Our Lady of Guadulupe*, 1417 W. Ash, 57301. Tel: 605-996-1410. Email: sistersofstfrancis@mit.midco.net. Sr. M. Loretta Von Rueden, Sister Leader. Private Association of the Faithful Professed Sisters 5.

WATERTOWN. *Mother of God Monastery*, 110 28th Ave., S.E., 57201-8419. Tel: 605-882-6600; Fax: 605-882-6658. Email: monastery@dailypost.com. Web: watertownbenedictines.org. Sr. Judith Fischer, O.S.B., Prioress. Motherhouse and Novitiate of Benedictine Sisters Sisters 65; Novices 1.

YANKTON. *Sacred Heart Monastery*, 1005 W. Eighth St., 57078-3389. Tel: 605-668-6000; Fax: 605-668-6153. Email: jernster@mtmc.edu. Web: yanktonbenedictines.org. Sr. Jacquelyn Ernster, O.S.B., Prioress; Rev. Mel Patton, O.S.B., Chap. Motherhouse and Novitiate of the Benedictine Sisters Sisters 144.

[H] NEWMAN CENTERS

ABERDEEN. *Aquinas Student Center* Email: nsunewman@dtgnet.com.

Northern State University, 310 15th Ave., S.E., 57401. Tel: 605-229-1011; Fax: 605-226-3274. Email: nsunewman@iw.net. Rev. James P. Morgan, Chap.; Michala Heller, Campus Min.

BROOKINGS. *Pius XII Student Center* Box 7019 University Station, 57007. Tel: 605-692-9461; Fax: 605-692-9461. Email: ccpoffice@brookings.net. Rev. Scott Traynor.

MADISON. *Dakota State University Newman Club Office* , Attended by St. Thomas Parish, Madison. , 217 N.W. 4th St., 57042. Tel: 606-256-4135. Email: schaefbt@pluto.dsu.edu.

VERMILLION. *St. Thomas More Catholic Newman Center* Email: newmanpc@usd.edu.

University of South Dakota, 320 E. Cherry St., 57069. Tel: 605-624-2697; Fax: 605-624-4145. Rev. Joseph Forcelle; Sr. Rosemarie Maly, O.S.B., Assoc. Dir.

[I] MISCELLANEOUS LISTINGS

SIOUX FALLS. *Avera Health*, 3900 W. Avera Dr., 57108-5721. Tel: 605-322-4700; Fax: 605-322-4799. Email: joanne.herman@avera.org. Web: www.avera.org. Sponsored by the Sisters of the Presentation of the B.V.M., Aberdeen, SD, and the Benedictine Sisters of Sacred Heart Monastery, Yankton, SD.

Avera Health Foundation, 3900 W. Avera Dr., Ste. 301, 57108-5721. Tel: 605-322-4750; Fax: 605-322-4798. Email: jerry.soholt@avera.org. Web: www.avera.org.

The Banquet, 300 N. Main Ave., 57104. Tel: 605-335-7066; Fax: 605-335-1091. Email: bthe@qwest.net. Carolyn Downs, Exec. Dir. Total Staff 7; Total Assisted 114,290.

The Berakhah House, 400 Western Ave. N., 57104. Tel: 605-332-4017; Fax: 605-332-3869. Email: Berakhahho@aol.com. Sr. Mary Anthony Menting, S.C.S.C., Dir. Total Assisted 8.

The Catholic Foundation for Eastern South Dakota, 523 N. Duluth Ave., 57104. Tel: 605-988-3788; Fax: 605-988-3746. Email: mconzemi@sfcatholic.org. Web: www.sfcatholic.org. Mark Conzemius, Exec. Dir.

Community Outreach, 431 N. Cliff Ave., 57103. Tel: 605-331-3935; Fax: 605-336-8924. Email: com.out@iw.net. Jerry Bohnhoff, Dir. Total Staff 2; Total Families Assisted Annually 1,005.

St. Francis House, 1301 E. Austin St., 57103. Tel: 605-334-3879; Fax: 605-575-3999. Email: stfranhse@netzero.net. Dennis Lepkowski, Dir. Bed Capacity 39.

Good Shepherd Center, 300 N. Main Ave., 57104. Tel: 605-332-3176; Fax: 605-977-4807. Maria Rae, Dir. Total Staff 5; Patients Assisted Annually 20,000.

Holy Family Child Care Center, 217 N. Sherman, 57103. Tel: 605-357-9227; Fax: 605-357-0273. Elsa Johnson, Dir.

St. Joseph Catholic Housing, Inc., Catholic Chancery Office, 523 N. Duluth Ave., 57104. Tel: 605-334-9861; Fax: 605-988-3746. Email: kbenson@SFCatholic.org.

Kateri Indian Center, 300 N. Main Ave., 57104. Tel: 605-335-3321; Fax: 605-332-3041. Total Staff 2; Patients Assisted Annually 31,611.

Little Flower of Jesus School Foundation, Inc., 901 N. Tahoe Tr., 57110-5779. Tel: 605-338-2433; Fax: 605-339-2203.

St. Mary/Holy Spirit School Endowment Trust, 3601 E. Dudley Ln., 57103. Tel: 605-371-2320; Fax: 605-371-1957. Email: hspirit@sfcss.org. Rev. Msgr. James Andraschko, Trustee.

Pension Plan for Priests of the Diocese of Sioux Falls, 523 N. Duluth Ave., 57104. Tel: 605-334-9861; Fax: 605-334-2092. Web: www.sfcatholic.org. Most Rev. Robert Carlson, Pres.

Sioux Falls Catholic School Corporation, 3100 W. 41st St., 57105. Tel: 605-336-6241; Fax: 605-373-1035. Email: sgross@sfcss.org. Web: sfcss.org. Total Staff 13.

St. Vincent DePaul Ministries of Sioux Falls, 431 N. Cliff Ave., 57103. Tel: 605-335-5823; Fax: 605-977-0669. Email: vdpsf@aol.com. Mary Beth Piatt, Mgr. Staff 7.

ABERDEEN. *The Presentation Sisters Heritage Trust*, 1500 North Second, 57401. Tel: 605-229-8419; Fax: 605-229-8412. Email: vmccall@presentationsisters.org. Web: www.presentationsisters.org. Sr. Virginia McCall, Contact Person. Sponsored by: Sisters of the Presentation of the Blessed Virgin Mary of Aberdeen, South Dakota.

IRENE. *Catholic Retreat Ministries*, Mailing Address:: 523 N. Duluth, 57104. Broom Tree Farm, 29827 446th St., 57039. Tel: 605-334-9861; Fax: 605-334-2092.

MARVIN. *Blue Cloud Abbey Retirement Trust*, P.O. Box 98, 57251-0098. Tel: 605-398-9200; Fax: 605-398-9201. Email: mcmullen@tnics.com. Rev. John McMullen, O.S.B., Treas.

RENNER. *St. Margaret's Fellowship*, 47311 Rogness Pl., 57055. Tel: 605-543-6384. Email: nmg8860@aol.com. Mark Gerdes, Leader; Nancy Gerdes, Leader.

SISSETON. *Tekakwitha Housing Corp.*, Mailing Address:: 6 E. Chestnut, 57262. 711 Veteran's Ave., 57262. Tel: 605-698-7414; Fax: 605-698-7236.

Tekakwitha Indian Mission, Inc., 120 E. Chestnut, 57262. Tel: 605-698-7414; Fax: 605-698-7236.

WATERTOWN. *St. Ann's Corporation*, Mother of God Monastery, 110 28th Ave., S.E., 57201. Tel: 605-882-6600; Fax: 605-882-6658. Email: monastery@dailypost.com. Web: watertownbenedictines.org.

Benet Place, 100 28th Ave., S.E., 57201. Tel: 605-886-9177; Fax: 605-882-3193. Independent Living. Units 39; Staff 11.

Evergreen Assisted Living, 90 28th Ave., S.E., 57201. Tel: 605-882-8555; Fax: 605-882-8556. Units 16; Staff 11.

The Benedictine Sisters Foundation of Watertown, 110 28th Ave., S.E., #219, 57201. Tel: 605-886-4188; Fax: 605-882-6658. Email: leonagauer@hotmail.com. Web: watertownbenedictines.org. Sr. Leona Gauer, Dir.

Holy Name Foundation, Inc., 1009 Skyline Dr., 57201. Tel: 605-886-5885; Fax: 605-886-2142.

Immaculate Conception School Foundation, Inc.,

309 2nd Ave., S.E., 57201. Tel: 605-886-3883; Fax: 605-886-0199.

Retirement Trust, Mother of God Monastery, 110 28th Ave., S.E., 57201. Tel: 605-882-6654; Fax: 605-882-6658. Email: monastery@dailypost.com. Web: watertownbenedictines.org.

YANKTON. *Benedictine Center, Inc.*, 1005 W. 8th, 57078. Tel: 605-668-6000; Fax: 605-668-6153.

Benedictine Health Foundation, Inc., 1000 W. 4th, 57078. Tel: 605-668-8310; Fax: 605-665-0170. Email: BHF@SHHServices.com. Kelly Kathol, Exec. Dir.

The House of Mary Shrine, Inc., Box 455, Lewis & Clark Lake, 57078-0455. Tel: 605-668-0121. Matt Hanson, Pres. Bd. of Directors; Rev. Rodney Farke, Spiritual Dir.

Yankton Catholic Community Development Office, 1500 St. Benedict Dr., Ste. 103, 57078. Tel: 605-665-4585; Fax: 605-665-4585. Email: yccdo@iw.net. Barb Rezac, Devel. Dir.

RELIGIOUS INSTITUTES OF MEN REPRESENTED IN THE DIOCESE

For further details refer to the corresponding bracketed number in the Religious Institutes of Men or Women section.

[0200]—*Benedictine Monks* (Aurora, IL; Marvin, SD)—O.S.B.

[]—*Carmelite* (India)

[1130]—*Congregation of the Priests of the Sacred Heart* (Hales Corners, WI)—S.C.J.

[0690]—*Jesuit Fathers and Brothers* (Wisconsin Prov.)—S.J.

[0910]—*Oblates of Mary Immaculate* (Central Prov.)—O.M.I.

[0560]—*Third Order Regular of Saint Francis* (Loretto, PA)—T.O.R.

[1335]—*Vincentian Congregation* (India)—V.C

RELIGIOUS INSTITUTES OF WOMEN REPRESENTED IN THE DIOCESE

[0230]—*Benedictine Sisters of Pontifical Jurisdiction* (Yankton, Watertown, SD)—O.S.B.

[0940]—*Daughters of St. Mary of Providence*—D.S.M.P.

[0420]—*Discalced Carmelite Nuns of the Monastery of Our Mother of Mercy* (Alexandria, SD)—O.C.D.

[1070-14]—*Dominican Sisters* Grand Rapids—O.P.

[1310]—*Franciscan Sisters of Little Falls, MN*—O.S.F.

[3010]—*Oblate Sisters of the Blessed Sacrament*—O.S.B.S.

[3130]—*Our Lady of Victory Missionary Sisters*—O.L.V.M.

[2970]—*School Sisters of Notre Dame* (Mankato Prov.)—S.S.N.D.

[2630]—*Sisters of Mercy of the Holy Cross*—S.C.S.C.

[3000]—*Sisters of Notre Dame de Namur*—S.N.D.deN.

[1030]—*Sisters of the Divine Savior*—S.D.S.

[3320]—*Sisters of the Presentation of the B.V.M.*—P.B.V.M.

[1720]—*Sisters of the Third Order Regular of St. Francis of the Congregation of Our Lady of Lourdes*—O.S.F.

INTER-PAROCHIAL CEMETERIES

SIOUX FALLS. *St. Michael*, 3001 N. Cliff, 57104. Tel: 605-338-3376.

NECROLOGY

† Mociun, Casimir T., (Retired)—Died June 30, 2003
† Morgen, Paul H., (Retired)—Died March 6, 2003
† Ripp, Joseph L., (Retired)—Died Dec. 21, 2002

Diocese of Spokane

(Dioecesis Spokanensis)

Most Reverend

WILLIAM S. SKYLSTAD, D.D.

Bishop of Spokane; ordained May 21, 1960; appointed Bishop of Yakima February 22, 1977; consecrated and installed May 12, 1977; Transferred to Spokane April 17, 1990; succeeded to the See April 27, 1990 *Office: W. 1023 Riverside Ave., P.O. Box 1453, Spokane, WA 99210-1453. Res.: W. 1025 Cleveland, Spokane, WA 99205-3320.*

Catholic Pastoral Center: W. 1023 Riverside Ave., P.O. Box 1453, Spokane, WA 99210-1453. Tel: 509-358-7300.

Web: www.dioceseofspokane.org

Email: chancellor@dioceseofspokane.org

ESTABLISHED DECEMBER 17, 1913.

Square Miles 24,356.

Solemnly consecrated to the Immaculate Heart of Mary on December 8, 1948.

Corporate Title: "The Catholic Bishop of Spokane, a Corporation Sole."

Comprises the following Counties in the State of Washington: Okanogan, Ferry, Stevens, Pend Oreille, Lincoln, Spokane, Adams, Whitman, Franklin, Walla Walla, Columbia, Garfield and Asotin.

For legal titles of parishes and diocesan institutions, consult the Catholic Pastoral Center.

STATISTICAL OVERVIEW

Personnel	
Bishop	1
Retired Abbots	1
Priests: Diocesan Active in Diocese	43
Priests: Diocesan Active Outside Diocese	8
Priests: Diocesan in Foreign Missions	1
Priests: Retired, Sick or Absent	31
Number of Diocesan Priests	83
Religious Priests in Diocese	89
Total Priests in Diocese	172
Extern Priests in Diocese	4
Ordinations:	
Diocesan Priests	1
Transitional Deacons	1
Permanent Deacons in Diocese	47
Total Brothers	11
Total Sisters	247
Parishes	
Parishes	83
With Resident Pastor:	
Resident Diocesan Priests	39
Resident Religious Priests	5
Without Resident Pastor:	
Administered by Priests	34
Administered by Religious Women	1
Administered by Lay People	4
Missions	2
Pastoral Centers	1
New Parishes Created	1
Closed Parishes	1
Professional Ministry Personnel:	
Brothers	1
Sisters	8
Lay Ministers	28
Welfare	
Catholic Hospitals	7
Total Assisted	506,987
Residential Care of Children	1
Total Assisted	35
Specialized Homes	2
Total Assisted	260
Special Centers for Social Services	15
Total Assisted	162,665
Residential Care of Disabled	1
Total Assisted	12
Educational	
Seminaries, Diocesan	1
Students from This Diocese	10
Students from Other Diocese	4
Diocesan Students in Other Seminaries	9
Total Seminarians	19
Colleges and Universities	1
Total Students	4,515
High Schools, Diocesan and Parish	2
Total Students	330
High Schools, Private	1
Total Students	880
Elementary Schools, Diocesan and Parish	16
Total Students	3,575
Catechesis/Religious Education:	
High School Students	789
Elementary Students	1,540
Total Students under Catholic Instruction	11,648
Teachers in the Diocese:	
Brothers	1
Lay Teachers	231
Vital Statistics	
Receptions into the Church:	
Infant Baptism Totals	1,311
Adult Baptism Totals	256
First Communions	1,478
Confirmations	1,704
Marriages:	
Catholic	188
Interfaith	144
Total Marriages	332
Deaths	631
Total Catholic Population	86,721
Total Population	722,677

Former Bishops—Most Revs. A. F. SCHINNER, D.D., consecrated Bishop of Superior, July 25, 1905; resigned from that See, Jan. 15, 1913; appt. first Bishop of Spokane, March 18, 1914; resigned Dec. 17, 1925, and made Titular Bishop of Sala; died Feb. 7, 1937; CHARLES D. WHITE, D.D., ord. Sept. 24, 1910; appt. Dec. 20, 1926; consecrated Feb. 24, 1927; died Sept. 25, 1955; BERNARD J. TOPEL, D.D., Ph.D. (Retired), appt. Coadjutor Bishop Aug. 9, 1955; consecrated Sept. 21, 1955; succeeded to the See Sept. 25, 1955; retired April 11, 1978; died Oct. 22, 1986; LAWRENCE H. WELSH, D.D., ord. May 26, 1962; appt. Bishop of Spokane Nov. 7, 1978; consecrated and installed Dec. 14, 1978; resigned April 17, 1990; appt. Auxiliary of St. Paul-Minneapolis, Nov. 5, 1991; died Jan. 13, 1999.

Vicars General—Rev. STEVE DUBLINSKI, P.O. Box 1453, Spokane, 99210-1453. Tel: 509-358-7303. Email: sdublinski@dioceseofspokane.org; Rev. Msgr. JOHN M. STEINER, St. Mary's Parish, 304 S. Adams Rd., Spokane, 99216-2195. Tel: 509-928-3210. Email: jsteiner@dioceseofspokane.org.

Special Assistant to the Vicar General—MARY BUTLER, Asst. Coord., P.O. Box 1453, Spokane, 99210-1453. Tel: 509-353-0442. Email: mbutler@dioceseofspokane.org.

Catholic Pastoral Center—W. 1023 Riverside Ave., P.O. Box 1453, Spokane, 99210-1453. Tel: 509-358-7300; Fax: 509-358-7302. Email: chancellor@dioceseofspokane.org. Office Hours: Mon.-Fri. 9-5

Moderator of the Curia—Rev. STEVEN DUBLINSKI, P.O. Box 1453, Spokane, 99210-1453. Tel: 509-358-7303. Email: sdublinski@dioceseofspokane.org.

Chancellor—Rev. MARK PAUTLER, P.O. Box 1453, Spokane, 99210-1453. Tel: 509-358-7339. Email: mpautler@dioceseofspokane.org.

Archivist—VACANT, P.O. Box 1453, Spokane, 99210-1453. Tel: 509-358-7300.

Diocesan Tribunal—W. 1023 Riverside Ave., P.O. Box 1453, Spokane, 99210-1453. Tel: 509-358-7336. Email: tribunal@dioceseofspokane.org.

Judicial Vicar—Rev. MARK PAUTLER.

Defensor Vinculi—Rev. Msgr. JOHN M. STEINER; Rev. JOSE LUIS MILLAN.

Secretary—JUDY ELLIFRITT.

Diocesan Consultors/Presbyteral Council—Revs. JOSE LUIS MILLAN, Chm.; DANIEL BARNETT, Vice Chm. Members: Revs. RORY PITSTICK; ROBERT MCNEESE; TIM HAYS; LEN FORSMANN; TY SCHAFF; JAMES KUHNS; STEVE WERNER; MIKE SAVELESKY; MICHAEL MOYNAHAN, S.J.; ROBERT LYONS, S.J.; STEVEN DUBLINSKI; MARK PAUTLER.

Diocesan Pastoral Council—Most Rev. WILLIAM S. SKYLSTAD, D.D.; Rev. STEVEN DUBLINSKI, Ex Officio; MARGARET ALBO; HECTOR ANDRADE; JOE BUSCH; LIDWYNA DALLA; RON DALLA; ERNIE FULLMER; CAROL FULLMER; Sr. MARY GARVIN, S.N.J.M.; DONNA GIVEN; DONNA JO GOOLEY; KATIE GRANT; Mrs. LESTER GUSKE; Mrs. LESTER GUSKE; KATHRYN HILL; JANICE HOUSE; KATHY JOHNSON; JANICE LATHROP; TESSA LEACH; ROB LOHMEYER; ELIZABETH MARSHALL; RICHARD OLBERDING; CHRIS PANAS; DICK PELKIE; TRACEY RICE; MAGGIE SANCHEZ; ANNIE SMART; ROGER SMART; Rev. Msgr. WILLIAM VAN OMMEREN.

Diocesan Offices and Directors

Administrative Division: Diocesan Business Affairs—MICHAEL D. MILLER, P.O. Box 1453, Spokane, 99210-1453. Email: mmiller@dioceseofspokane.org; 1023 W. Riverside Ave., Spokane, 99201. Tel: 509-358-7333; Fax: 509-358-7302.

Director of Fiscal Services—MERRILIN FULTON, P.O. Box 1453, Spokane, 99210-1453. Tel: 509-358-7320. Email: mfulton@dioceseofspokane.org.

Catholic Foundation-Development Office—STEVEN C. KOCHARHOOK, Ph.D., P.O. Box 1453, Spokane, 99210-1453. Tel: 509-358-4280. Email: skocharhook@dioceseofspokane.org.

Computer Department—MARY GREEN, P.O. Box 1453, Spokane, 99210-1453. Tel: 509-358-7346. Email: magreen@dioceseofspokane.org.

Administrative Division: Catholic Schools—Mr. DUANE SCHAFER, Supt., Office of Education, P.O. Box 1453, Spokane, 99210-1453. Tel: 509-358-7330. Email: dschafer@dioceseofspokane.org.

Administrative Division: Evangelization and Ministries Formation—BETTY NEWSTROM, P.O. Box 1453, Spokane, 99210-1453. Tel: 509-358-7311. Email: bnewstrom@dioceseofspokane.org.

Parish Services Office—BETTY NEWSTROM, Dir., P.O. Box 1453, Spokane, 99210-1453. Tel: 409-358-7311. Email: pso@dioceseofspokane.org.

Communications Office—Deacon ERIC MEISFJORD, Dir. & Editor, P.O. Box 1453, Spokane, 99210-1453. Tel: 509-358-7340. Email: emeisfjord@dioceseofspokane.org; NANCY LOBERG, Advertising Mgr. Tel: 509-358-7343. Email: nloberg@dioceseofspokane.org.

Charismatic Renewal—Rev. DANIEL WETZLER (Retired), 11517 Pebble Beach Dr., Harrison, ID 83833. Email: dwetzler@dioceseofspokane.org.

Ecumenical Relations—Rev. THOMAS CASWELL, St.

Rose of Lima Parish, 460 N. 5th St., Cheney, 99004-2210. Tel: 509-235-6229. Email: tcaswell@dioceseofspokane.org.

Spanish Speaking Apostolates—VACANT.

Vietnamese Apostolate— Vietnamese Catholic Community of the Diocese of Spokane, Rev. JOACHIM L. HIEN, St. Anthony's Parish, 2320 N. Cedar, Spokane, 99205. Tel: 509-327-1162; Fax: 509-328-8728. Email: jhien@dioceseofspokane.org.

Vocation Director—Rev. DARRIN CONNALL, Bishop White Seminary, 429 E. Sharp Ave., Spokane, 99202. Tel: 509-326-3761. Email: bws@gonzaga.edu. Web: bishopwhiteseminary.org.

Diocesan Liturgical Commission—Rev. STEVE DUBLINSKI, P.O. Box 1453, Spokane, 99210-1453. Tel: 509-358-7303. Email: sdublinski@dioceseofspokane.org.

Director of Deacon Formation—Rev. MICHAEL KWIATKOWSKI, St. Joseph's Parish, 3720 E. Colbert Rd., Colbert, 99005-9661. Tel: 509-466-4991. Email: mkwiatkowski@dioceseofspokane.org.

Director of Deacons—Deacon JOHN SICILIA, St. Charles Parish, 4515 N. Alberta St., Spokane, 99205-1598. Tel: 509-327-9573.

Deacon Council—Deacon JOHN RUSCHEINSKY, 6910 S. Ben Burr Rd., Spokane, 99223. Tel: 509-448-1224.

Catholic Committee on Scouting—Deacon STEVE PRAWDZIK, Chap., 11828 S. Player Dr., Spokane, 99223-9524. Tel: 509-448-8934.

Bishop White Seminary—Rev. DARRIN CONNALL, Dir. Seminarians & Rector, 429 E. Sharp Ave., Spokane, 99202. Tel: 509-326-3255. Email: bws@gonzaga.edu. Web: bishopwhiteseminary.org.

Administrative Division: Social Ministries/Catholic Charities Diocesan Director—Mrs. DONNA HANSON, W. 1023 Riverside, P.O. Box 1453, Spokane, 99210-1453. Tel: 509-358-4250 Email: dhanson@dioceseofspokane.org.

Catholic Charities Associate Director—ROB MCCANN, W. 1023 Riverside, P.O. Box 1453, Spokane, 99210-1453. Tel: 509-358-4260. Email: rmccann@dioceseofspokane.org.

St. Vincent de Paul Society—E. 2901 Trent Ave., Spokane, 99202. Tel: 509-535-2491.

Censor Librorum—Rev. MICHAEL SAVELESKY, Ph.D., Assumption of the Blessed Virgin Parish 3624 W. Indian Trail Rd., Spokane, 99208-4794. Tel: 509-326-0144; Fax: 509-326-0538. Email: msavelesky@dioceseofspokane.org.

Continuing Education of Priests—Rev. Msgr. ROBERT A. PEARSON, St. Augustine Parish, 428 W. 19th, Spokane, 99203-2098. Tel: 509-747-4421; Fax: 509-747-9086. Email: rpearson@dioceseofspokane.org.

Detention Ministry—Sr. MYRTA ITURRIAGA, S.P., P.O. Box 1453, Spokane, 99210-1453. Tel: 509-358-7315. Email: miturriaga@dioceseofspokane.org.

Director of Cemeteries—DENNIS FAIRBANK, P.O. Box 18006, Spokane, 99208-0006. Tel: 509-467-5496. Email: dfairbank@dioceseofspokane.org. Web: catholicdioceseofspokane.org.

Immaculate Heart Retreat Center—Deacon JOHN RUSCHEINSKY, Dir., 6910 S. Ben Burr Rd., Spokane, 99223. Tel: 509-448-1224. Web: www.ihrc.net. Email: ihrc@ihrc.net.

Priests' Personnel Board—Rev. Msgr. FRANK BACH; Revs. DARRIN CONNALL; JOSEPH BELL; PATRICK KERST; Rev. Msgr. PEDRO RAMIREZ; Rev. MARK PAUTLER, Sec., P.O. Box 1453, Spokane, 99210-1453. Tel: 509-358-7336.

Society for the Propagation of the Faith—STEVEN C. KOCHARHOOK, Ph.D., W. 1023 Riverside Ave., P.O. Box 1453, Spokane, 99210. Tel: 509-358-4280. Email: skocharhook@dioceseofspokane.org.

Victim Assistance Coordinator—Mrs. MARY BUTLER. Tel: 509-353-0442. Email: mbutler@dioceseofspokane.org.

CLERGY, PARISHES, MISSIONS AND PAROCHIAL SCHOOLS

CITY OF SPOKANE
(SPOKANE COUNTY)

1—CATHEDRAL OF OUR LADY OF LOURDES (1881), Rev. Msgr. James M. Ribble, Ph.D.; Deacon Gonzalo Martinez.
Res.: 1115 W. Riverside Ave., 99201. Tel: 509-358-4290; Fax: 509-358-4277.
Catechesis/Religious Program—Tel: 509-358-4293. Carol R. Pelo, D.R.E. Students 47.

2—ST. ALOYSIUS (1890), Revs. Ignatius F. Ohno, S.J. (P); Robert L. Fitts, S.J.; Deacon Jack Back; Mr. Donald Weber, Pastoral Admin.
Res.: 330 E. Boone Ave., 99202. Tel: 509-323-5896; Fax: 509-323-5892.
School—611 E. Mission Ave., 99202. Tel: 509-323-5876; Fax: 509-323-5892. Kerry Rowland, Prin.
School—Montessori Education Center, Tel: 509-489-7825. Marta Schollenberger, Dir. Lay Teachers 13; Students 300.

3—ST. ANN (1902), Rev. John Rompa; Craig Bartmess, Parish Life Coord.
Church: 2120 E. First Ave., 99202. Tel: 509-535-3031.

4—ST. ANTHONY (1909), Rev. Joachim Hien.
Res.: 2320 N. Cedar St., 99205. Tel: 509-327-1162; Fax: 509-328-8728.
School—Trinity Interparochial School, Tel: 509-327-9369; Fax: 509-328-4128. Mike Trudeau, Prin. Serving St. Anthony and St. Joseph. Lay Teachers 7; Students 145.
Educare Center— Lay Teachers 7; Students 56.

5—ASSUMPTION OF THE BLESSED VIRGIN MARY (1958), Rev. Michael T. Savelesky; Deacons John Crow; Kelly Stewart.
Office—3624 W. Indian Trail Rd., 99208. Tel: 509-326-0144; Fax: 509-326-0538.
School—Tel: 509-328-1115; Fax: 509-328-7872. Sonia Flores-Davis, Prin. Lay Teachers 17; Students 258.
Station—Our Lady of the Lake Tum Tum. Tel: 509-276-7532.

6—ST. AUGUSTINE (1914), Rev. Msgr. Robert A. Pearson; Deacons Kenneth Dunlap; Gary Cooper, Pastoral Assoc.
Res.: 428 W. 19th Ave., 99203. Tel: 509-747-4421; Fax: 509-747-9086.
School—Cataldo Catholic Interparochial, Tel: 509-624-8759; Fax: 509-624-8763. Lay Teachers 23; Students 321.
Catechesis/Religious Program—Tel: 509-747-7972. Susan C. Harmon, D.R.E. Students 117.

7—ST. CHARLES (1950), Rev. Eugene Tracy; Deacon John F. Sicilia.
Res.: 4515 N. Alberta St., 99205. Tel: 509-327-9573; Fax: 509-327-9574.
School—Tel: 509-327-9575; Fax: 509-325-9353. Tom Feldhausen, Prin. Lay Teachers 14; Students 211.
Catechesis/Religious Program—Students 68.

8—ST. FRANCIS OF ASSISI (1915), Rev. Brian V. Flynn, O.F.M.
Res.: 1104 W. Heroy Ave., 99205. Tel: 509-325-1321; Fax: 509-482-2490.

9—ST. FRANCIS XAVIER (1906), Rev. Daniel Barnett; Deacon Roy Dahl.
Office:—3715 N. Standard St., 99207. Tel: 509-487-6363, Ext. 200; Fax: 509-487-6363.

10—ST. JOHN VIANNEY (1949), Revs. Tyrone J. Schaff; Charles Skok (Retired); Deacons Derwood Braungardt; David Dudinsky.
P.O. Box 141125, 99214-1125.
Office—503 N. Walnut Rd., 99206. Tel: 509-926-5428; Fax: 509-922-5282.
School—(Grades PreK-8), N. 501 Walnut Rd., 99206. Tel: 509-926-7987; Fax: 509-891-9030. Dr. Judith Morbeck, Prin. Lay Teachers 12; Students 206.
Catechesis/Religious Program—Tel: 509-926-5553. Janet R. Meyer, D.R.E. Students 56.

11—ST. JOSEPH (1890), Sr. Irene Knopes, S.N.J.M., Parish Admin.
Res.: 1503 W. Dean Ave., 99201. Tel: 509-328-4841; Fax: 509-328-4841.
School—Trinity Interparochial School See listing under St. Anthony)
Catechesis/Religious Program—Tel: 509-326-4742. Barbara LaCombe, D.R.E. Students 45

12—ST. MARY (1913), Rev. Msgr. John Steiner; Deacons Cary Heth; Donald Bentley.
Res.: 304 S. Adams Rd., 99216. Tel: 509-928-3210; Fax: 509-928-3215.
School—14601 E. 4th Ave., 99216. Tel: 509-924-4300. Mrs. Jeanne Brown, Prin. Lay Teachers 18; Students 236.
Catechesis/Religious Program—Tel: 509-926-9559; Fax: 509-926-9550. Dona Mohr, D.R.E. Students 255.

13—MARY QUEEN (1957), Rt. Rev. Paul Vevik; Deacon Donald Whitney.
Res.: 3423 E. Carlisle Ave., 99217-7208. Tel: 509-483-4384.

14—OUR LADY OF FATIMA (1956), Rev. James Kuhns; Deacons John Byrne; Walter Weid.
Office:—1517 E. 33rd Ave., 99203. Tel: 509-747-7213; Fax: 509-747-7217.
School—All Saints Interparochial, (Grades 5-8) Tel: 509-624-5712; Fax: 509-624-7752. Ms Kathy Hicks, Prin. Lay Teachers 8; Students 67.
Catechesis/Religious Program—Jean Leeds, D.R.E. Students 92.

15—ST. PASCHAL (1916), Rev. Patrick Hartin; Deacon John Crandall; Donald McKenzie, Pastoral Admin. P.O. Box 11128, 99212-1128. Tel: 509-924-4871; Fax: 509-924-8731.
School—N. 2521 Park Rd., 99212. Tel: 509-924-5090; Fax: 509-924-6106. Mr. Richard Pelkie Jr., Prin. Lay Teachers 12; Students 115.
Educare Center—Tel: 509-922-7616 Dawn Davis, Dir. & Prog. Supvr. Lay Teachers 12 Students 115.

16—ST. PATRICK (1893), Rev. Daniel Barnett; Deacon John Gress.
Res.: 5021 N. Nelson St., 99217-6161. Tel: 509-487-1325 Fax: 509-484-3101.
School—Tel: 509-487-2830. Randy Wallace, Ph.D., Prin. Lay Teachers 13; Students 105.
Catechesis/Religious Program—Sheila Kries, D.R.E. Students 191.
Convent—5008 N. Lacey St., 99207.

17—ST. PETER (1956), Rev. Joseph W. Bell.
Res. 3520 E. 18th Ave., 99223-3814. Tel: 509-534-2227; Fax: 509-534-5522.
School—All Saints Interparochial, (Grades K-4) Tel: 509-534-1098; Fax: 509-534-1529. Ms. Kathy Hicks, Prin. Lay Teachers 15; Students 231.

18—SACRED HEART (1911), Rev. Mark Pautler; Deacon Jim Blaine, Pastoral Assoc.
Res.: 219 E. Rockwood Blvd., 99202. Tel: 509-747-5810; Fax: 509-747-5033.

19—ST. THOMAS MORE (1957), Rt. Rev. Adrian Parcher, O.S.B.
Res.: N. 8112 Howard Dr., 99208. Tel: 509-466-0220; Fax: 509-466-0220.
School—Doug Banks, Prin. Lay Teachers 12; Students 271.

OUTSIDE THE CITY OF SPOKANE

BREWSTER, OKANOGAN CO., SACRED HEART (1958), Rev. Jose Luis Hernandez.
Res.: P.O. Box 548, 98812. Tel: 509-689-2931; Fax: 509-689-2931.

CHENEY, SPOKANE CO., ST. ROSE OF LIMA (1881), Rev. Thomas C. Caswell; Deacon Eric Meisfjord.
Res.: 460 N. Fifth St., 99004. Tel: 509-235-6229.
Catechesis/Religious Program—Tel: 509-235-9330; Fax: 509-559-5188. Barbara Wodynski, D.R.E. Students 75.

CHEWELAH, STEVENS CO., ST. MARY OF THE ROSARY (1885), [CEM] Rev. Jose Luis Millan.
Res.: P.O. Box 188, Valley, 99181. Tel: 509-937-2452.
Church: 502 E. Main St., P.O. Box 26, 99109. Tel: 509-935-8028; Fax: 509-935-8028.
Catechesis/Religious Program—Tel: 509-935-6367. Sr. Judith Nilles, O.P., D.R.E. Students 78.

CLARKSTON, ASOTIN CO., HOLY FAMILY (1914), [CEM] Rev. Leonard Forsmann.
Res.: 917 Chestnut St., 99403. Tel: 509-758-6102; Fax: 509-751-9281.
School—(Grades PreK-6) Tel: 509-758-6621; Fax: 509-758-7025. Mrs. Sharon Clizer, Prin. Lay Teachers 7; Students 126.
School—Educare Preschool, Tel: 509-758-2737. Students 48.

CLAYTON, STEVENS CO., ST. JOSEPH, Closed. For inquiries for parish records contact the chancery.

COLBERT, SPOKANE CO., ST. JOSEPH (1970), Rev. Michael Kwiatkowski.
Res.: 3720 E. Colbert Rd., 99005. Tel: 509-466-4991; Fax: 509-466-4992.
Catechesis/Religious Program—Sr. Kathleen Reynolds, D.R.E. Students 315.

COLFAX, WHITMAN CO., ST. PATRICK (1878), Rev. Felix P. Lorge.
Res.: 1108 S. Main St., 99111. Tel: 509-397-3921.

COLTON, WHITMAN CO., ST. GALL (1893), [CEM] Rev. Victor M. Blazovich.
Res.: P.O. Box 108, 99113. Tel: 509-229-3548.
School—Guardian Angel-St. Boniface Interparochial, Tel: 509-299-3579. Guy Pitzer, Prin. Lay Teachers 4; Students 46.

COLVILLE, STEVENS CO., IMMACULATE CONCEPTION (1861), Rev. Robert J. McNeese.
Res.: 320 N. Maple St., 99114. Tel: 509-684-6223; Fax: 509-684-8084.

CONNELL, FRANKLIN CO., ST. VINCENT (1964), Rev. Richard Poole.
Res.: P.O. Box 1030, 99326. Tel: 509-234-2262; Fax: 509-234-0295.

COULEE DAM, OKANOGAN CO., ST. BENEDICT, Closed., For sacramental records, contact St. Henry's, Grand Coulee (Diocese of Yakima).

CURLEW, FERRY CO., ST. PATRICK, Rev. George H. Morbeck (Retired).
Res.: P.O. Box 333, Republic, 99166. Tel: 509-775-3935.

CUSICK, KALISPEL INDIAN RESERVATION, OUR LADY OF SORROWS, Rev. Edward Marier.
Res.: 612 W. First St., Box C, Newport, 99156. Tel: 509-447-4231.

DAVENPORT, LINCOLN CO., IMMACULATE CONCEPTION

(1893), [CEM] Rev. Patrick MacMahon.
Res.: 1310 Adams, P.O. Box 910, 99122. Tel: 509-725-1761.

DAYTON, COLUMBIA CO., ST. JOSEPH (1890), Rev. Thomas Connolly; Deacon Mike Breier.
Church: 112 S. First St., 99328-1307. Tel: 509-382-2311.

DEER PARK, SPOKANE CO., ST. MARY'S PRESENTATION (1912), [CEM] Rev. Al Grasher.
Res.: 316 N. Main St., P.O. Box 749, 99006. Tel: 509-276-2948.

ELTOPIA, FRANKLIN CO., ST. PAUL (1964), Rev. Richard Poole.
Res.: 14181 Glade North Rd., 99330. Tel: 509-297-4371.

FORD, STEVENS CO., ST. PHILIP BENIZI (1912), Rev. Robert L. Fitts, S.J.
Indian-Spokane Reservation: P.O. Box 214, Wellpinit, 99040. Tel: 509-258-7233.

HARRINGTON, LINCOLN CO., ST. FRANCIS OF ASSISI (1906), Rev. Patrick MacMahon.
Res.: P.O. Box 166, 99134. Tel: 509-253-4310.

INCHELIUM, FERRY CO., ST. MICHAEL'S MISSION, Rev. Robert L. Fitts, S.J.; Jenny-Ann Edgen, Admin.; Deacon Alvin Toulou.
Res.: P.O. Box 122, 99138. Tel: 509-722-4592.

IONE, PEND OREILLE CO., ST. BERNARD, Rev. Edward Marier.
Mailing Address: Box 731, 99139. Tel: 509-447-4231.
Res.: 612 W. First St., P.O. Box C, Newport, 99156. Tel: 509-447-4231.

KELLER, FERRY CO., ST. ROSE OF LIMA, Rev. Jake Morton, S.J.
Res.: P.O. Box 70, Nespelem, 99155. Tel: 509-634-4249.

KETTLE FALLS, STEVENS CO., SACRED HEART OF JESUS (1906), Rev. Robert McNeese.
Mailing Address: P.O. Box 303, 99141. Tel: 509-738-2356; Fax: 509-684-8084.

LACROSSE, WHITMAN CO., ST. JOSEPH (1906), Rev. Felix P. Lorge.
St. Patrick Parish: 1018 S. Main St., Colfax, 99111. Tel: 509-397-3921.

LIND, ADAMS CO., ST. AMBROSE (1920), Rev. Bonaventure Obisike.
Res.: 404 E. Fifth Ave., Ritzville, 99169. Tel: 509-659-0437.

MEDICAL LAKE, SPOKANE CO., ST. ANNE (1889), Rev. John P. Krier (GF); Deacon Robert King.
Res.: 708 E. Lake St., P.O. Box 125, 99022. Tel: 509-299-3585; Fax: 509-351-3217.

METALINE FALLS, PEND OREILLE CO., ST. JOSEPH (1950), Rev. Edward Marier.
Mailing Address: P.O. Box 417, 99153. Tel: 509-446-2651.
Res.: 612 W. First St., P.O. Box C, Newport, 99156. Tel: 509-447-4231; Fax: 509-299-9250.

NESPELEM, OKANOGAN CO., SACRED HEART MISSION (1915), [CEM] Rev. Jake Morton, S.J.
Res.: P.O. Box 70, 99155. Tel: 509-634-4249; Fax: 509-634-4249.

NEWPORT, PEND OREILLE CO., ST. ANTHONY (1908), Rev. Edward Marier.
Res.: 612 W. First St., P.O. Box C, 99156. Tel: 509-447-4231.

NORTHPORT, STEVENS CO., PURE HEART OF MARY (1898), Rev. Robert McNeese.
Mailing Address: 320 N. Maple, Colville, 99114.
Res.: P.O. Box 29, 99157. Tel: 509-684-6223; Fax: 509-684-6223.

OAKESDALE, WHITMAN CO., ST. CATHERINE OF ALEXANDRIA, Rev. Steven L. Dublinski.
Res.: P.O. Box 8, Rosalia, 99170. Tel: 509-523-4011.

ODESSA, LINCOLN CO., ST. JOSEPH (1905), Rev. W. Roy Floch.
Res. & Mailing Address: P.O. Box 106, Wilbur, 99185. Tel: 509-647-2380.
Catechesis/Religious Program—Students 7.

OKANOGAN-OMAK, OKANOGAN CO., OUR LADY OF THE VALLEY (1976), Rev. Rory Pittstick.
Res.: Rte. 2, 2511 N. Elmway, 98840. Tel: 509-422-5049.

OMAK, OKANOGAN CO.
1—ST. JOSEPH (1945), Rev. Charles Peterson, S.J.
Mailing Address: 6th & Jackson, Rte. 2, P.O. Box 12, 98841.
Res.: 323 Edmonds, 98841. Tel: 509-826-6401.
2—ST. MARY MISSION, [CEM] Rev. Charles Peterson, S.J.; Bettejo Passalaqua, Pastoral Assoc.
Res.: Rte. 2, P.O. Box 66A, 98841. Tel: 509-826-6401.

OROVILLE, OKANOGAN CO., IMMACULATE CONCEPTION (1898), Rev. Fernando Maldonado.
Res.: 1715 Main St., P.O. Box 2270, 98844. Tel: 509-476-2110; Fax: 509-476-2110.

OTHELLO, ADAMS CO., SACRED HEART (1956), Rev. Miguel Mejia; Deacons Antonio Beraza; Joel Pruneda.
Res.: 616 E. Juniper St., 99344. Tel: 509-488-5653; Fax: 509-488-5654.

OTIS ORCHARDS, SPOKANE CO., ST. JOSEPH (1892), Rev. James Mangan; Deacon Tom Heafey.
Res.: 4521 N. Arden Rd., 99027-9358. Tel: 509-926-7133; Fax: 509-926-9454.
Catechesis/Religious Program—Teresa McCann, D.R.E. Students 159.

PASCO, FRANKLIN CO., ST. PATRICK (1909), (Mexican), Rev. Msgr. Pedro Ramirez-Alejos; Revs. John G. Birk; Jose Jamie Maldonado; Deacons Robert Kalinowski; Gary Franz, Pastoral Assoc.; Juanita Contreras, Pastoral Assoc.
Res.: 1320 W. Henry, 99301. Tel: 509-547-8841; Fax: 509-547-3604.
School—1016 N. 14th Ave., 99301. Tel: 509-547-7261; Fax: 509-547-2604. Rev. Thomas Burnell, S.J., Prin. Lay Teachers 11; Students 125.
Catechesis/Religious Program—Peggy DeBord, D.R.E.; Maria Aguirre, D.R.E. Students 1,050.

POMEROY, GARFIELD CO., HOLY ROSARY (1878), [CEM] Rev. Thomas Connolly.
Mailing Address: R.R.1, P.O. Box 4, 99347-9702.
Res.: 634 High St., 99347. Tel: 509-843-3801; Fax: 509-843-3684.

PULLMAN, WHITMAN CO., SACRED HEART (1913), Rev. Edgar Borchardt.
Office—440 N.E. Ash St., 99163. Tel: 509-332-5312; Fax: 509-334-0575.
Catechesis/Religious Program—Tel: 509-332-4402. Theresa Paul, D.R.E. Students 175.

REARDAN, LINCOLN CO., ST. MICHAEL (1907), Rev. Patrick MacMahon.
Mailing Address: P.O. Box 451, Rearden, 99029. Tel: 509-725-1761.

REPUBLIC, FERRY CO., IMMACULATE CONCEPTION (1898), Rev. George H. Morbeck (Retired).
Res.: 756 S. Portland, 99166. Tel: 509-775-3935.

RITZVILLE, ADAMS CO., ST. AGNES (1915), Rev. Bonaventure Obisike.
Res.: 404 E. Fifth Ave., 99169. Tel: 509-659-0437.

ROCKFORD, SPOKANE CO., ST. JOSEPH (1901), Rev. Eric Zuckerman, S.J.
Res.: P.O. Box 54, 99030. Tel: 509-291-3481.

ROSALIA, WHITMAN CO., HOLY ROSARY (1892), Rev. Steven L. Dublinski.
Res.: 600 N. Whitman Ave., P.O. Box 8, 99170. Tel: 509-523-4011.

ST. JOHN, WHITMAN CO., OUR LADY OF PERPETUAL HELP (1960), Rev. Steven L. Dublinski.
Mailing Address: P.O. Box 325, 99171.
Res.: P.O. Box 8, Rosalia, 99170. Tel: 509-523-4011.

SPRAGUE, LINCOLN CO., MARY QUEEN OF HEAVEN (1885), [CEM] Rev. Bonaventure Obisike.
Res.: 404 E. Fifth Ave., Ritzville, 99160. Tel: 509-659-0437; Fax: 509-935-8028.

SPRINGDALE, STEVENS CO., SACRED HEART (1911), Rev. Jose Luis Millan.
Res.: P.O. Box 188, Valley, 99181. Tel: 509-937-2452; Fax: 509-935-8028.
Catechesis/Religious Program—Tel: 509-935-6367. Sr. Judith Nilles, D.R.E. Students 8.

TEKOA, WHITMAN CO., SACRED HEART (1893), [CEM] Rev. Steven L. Dublinski.
Res.: P.O. Box 8, Rosalia, 99170. Tel: 509-523-4011.

TONASKET, OKANOGAN CO., HOLY ROSARY, Rev. Fernando Maldonado.
Res. & Mailing Address: 1715 Main St., P.O. Box 2270, Oroville, 98844. Tel: 509-476-2110; Fax: 509-476-2110.

TWISP, OKANOGAN CO., ST. GENEVIEVE (1907), Rev. Jose Luis Hernandez.
Res.: P.O. Box 6, 98856. Tel: 509-997-4201.

UNIONTOWN, WHITMAN CO., ST. BONIFACE (1882), [CEM] Rev. Victor M. Blazovich.
Res.: P.O. Box 108, Colton, 99113. Tel: 509-229-3548.
School—Guardian Angel-St. Boniface Interparochial See St. Gall, Colton.

USK, PEND OREILLE CO., ST. JUDE (1941), Rev. Edward Marier.
Res.: 612 W. First St., P.O. Box C, Newport, 99156. Tel: 509-447-4231.

VALLEY, STEVENS CO., HOLY GHOST (1914), Rev. Jose Luis Millan.
Res.: P.O. Box 188, 9918. Tel: 509-937-2452; Fax: 509-935-8028.
Catechesis/Religious Program—Tel: 509-935-6367. Sr. Judith Nilles, O.P., D.R.E. Students 13.
Station—St. Joseph Jump-off Joe, Stevens Co., St. Joseph.

WAITSBURG, WALLA WALLA CO., ST. MARK (1888), Rev. Thomas Connolly; Deacon Mike Breier.
Office—112 S. 1st St., Dayton, 99328-1307. Tel: 509-382-2311.

WALLA WALLA, WALLA WALLA CO.
1—ASSUMPTION OF THE BLESSED VIRGIN MARY (1953), Rev. Timothy Hays; Sr. Helen Mason, S.P., Pastoral Assoc.
Res.: 2098 E. Alder St., 99362. Tel: 509-525-8163.
School—Assumption Interparochial, Tel: 509-525-9283. Mrs. Michele Acock, Prin. Lay Teachers 13; Students 191.
2—ST. FRANCIS OF ASSISI (1915), Revs. Patrick Kerst; Joseph Sullivan; Sr. Sharon Bongiorno, F.S.P.A., Pastoral Min.
Res.: 722 W. Alder St., 99362. Tel: 509-525-1663; Fax: 509-529-7849. Sisters 3.
3—ST. PATRICK (1859), Revs. Patrick Kerst; Joseph Sullivan; Deacon Olegario Reyes, Pastoral Assoc.
Office and Res.: 408 W. Poplar St., 99362. Tel: 509-525-1602; Fax: 509-529-7849.
Catechesis/Religious Program—Susan Logsdon. Tel: 509-529-5141; Patricia Garanzuary. Tel: 509-525-1602. Students 140.

WASHTUNCA, ADAMS CO., HOLY TRINITY (1967), Rev. Bonaventure Obisike.
Res.: 404 E. Fifth St., Ritzville, 99169. Tel: 509-659-0437.

WELLPINIT, STEVENS CO., SACRED HEART (1943), [CEM] Rev. Robert L. Fitts, S.J.
Indian-Spokane Reservation: P.O. Box 214, 99040. Tel: 509-258-7233.

WESTEND, STEVENS CO., OUR LADY OF LOURDES (1938), Rev. Robert L. Fitts, S.J.
Indian-Spokane Reservation: P.O. Box 214, Wellpinit, 99040. Tel: 509-258-7233.

WILBUR, LINCOLN CO., SACRED HEART (1900), Rev. W. Roy Floch.
Res.: P.O. Box 106, 99185. Tel: 509-647-2380.

Chaplains of Public Institutions

WALLA WALLA. *Washington State Penitentiary*. Served by priests of Walla Walla.

Special Ministry:
Revs.—
Birk, John, Our Lady of Lourdes Health Center, Pasco
Venneri, Michael D., Sacred Heart Medical Center, Spokane

On Duty Outside the Diocese:
Revs.—
Baronti, David, Guatemala
Codd, Kevin
Koltzenburg, Otto
Lucatero, Heliodoro
McGrann, John E., St. Rose of Lima, Eugene, OR.
Turner, Robert D., Carroll College, Helena, MT.

Absent on Leave:
Revs.—
Root, Richard
Semple, Richard

Retired:
Rev. Msgrs.—
Bach, Frank J., 1306 N. Blake Rd., Unit B, 99216-1149.
Donnelly, John, 221 E. Rockwood Blvd., Apt. 208, 99202-1270.
Rosage, David E., 221 E. Rockwood Blvd., No. 222, 99202.
Van Ommeren, William, Immaculate Heart Retreat, 6910 S. Ben Burr Rd., 99203-1899.
Revs.—
Brennan, William J., 2030 Delaware, 99362.
Caffrey, Edward, 1105 S.W. Alver St., Pullman, 99163-2006.
Donnelly, Sean, 1 Parkview, Freshford Rd., Kilkenny, Ireland.
Dugan, William M., 272 Kennedy St., No. 48, Chula Vista, CA 92011.
Eis, Charles R., 9202 Irvington Ave., San Diego, CA 92123-3129.
Grant, James, 217 W. Spokane Falls, No. 1802, 99201.
Hanley, William, Killula, Newmarket-on-Fergus, Claire Co. Ireland.
Haspedis, George, 3916 Salder Cir., 99228-7300.
Hullings, Clifford, 3110 E. Chattaroy Rd., No. 43, Chattaroy, 99003.
Morbeck, George H., P.O. Box 333, Republic, 99166-0333.
O'Brien, John P., P.O. Box 1808, Santa Rosa, CA 95402.
Pash, Joseph, 221 E. Rockwood Blvd., No. 204, 99202.
Sand, John, 1344 Mishaw Ave., Clarkston, 99403-2977.
Schoffelmeer, Arnold L., N. Findlay Rd., Box 36123, Deer Park, 99006.
Schwemin, Ralph H., 3915 N. Washington St., 99205.
Westbrook, J. Severyn, 221 E. Rockwood Blvd., No. 318, 99202.
Wetzler, Daniel, 11517 Pebble Beach Dr., Harrison, ID 83833.
Wietensteiner, Joseph M., P.O. Box 8087, 99203.

Permanent Deacons:
Back, Jack, St. Aloysius, Spokane; Prison Ministry
Barnufsky, Stephen, Retirement Residences
Bentley, Donald, St. Joseph, Rockfort

Beraza, Antonio, Sacred Heart, Othello
Blaine, Jim, St. Mary, Spokane
Braungardt, Derwood, St. John Vianney, Spokane
Breier, Michael, St. Joseph, Dayton; St. Mark, Waitsburg
Buckman, Thomas, Kateri Institute
Byrne, John, Our Lady of Fatima, Spokane
Cooper, Gary, St. Augustine, Spokane
Crandall, John, St. Paschal, Spokane
Crow, John, Assumption Parish, Spokane
Dahl, Roy, St. Peter, Spokane
Dalecki, Robert, On Duty Outside the Diocese
Dudinsky, David, St. John Vianney, Spokane
Dunlap, Kenneth, St. Augustine, Spokane
Farrell, Daniel, St. Henry, Grand Coulee
Franz, Gary, St. Patrick, Pasco
Gerber, Vincent, (Retired)
Gress, John, St. Patrick's Parish, Spokane
Heafy, Thomas, St. Joseph, Ottis Orchards
Heth, Cary, St. Mary, Spokane
Kalinowski, Robert, St. Patrick, Pasco
King, Robert, St. Anne, Medical Lake
Lukach, George, Our Lady of the Lake, Tum Tum
Mackin, Francis, Sitka, AK
Malone, Richard, St. Mary, Spokane
Martinez, Gonzalo, St. Mary's, Spokane
Meisfjord, Eric, St. Rose of Lima, Cheney
Murphy, James E., Sacred Heart Medical Center, Spokane
Polensky, Hugh, Sacred Heart Medical Center, Spokane
Prawdzik, Steve, Fairchild AFB; Holy Family, Clarkston
Pruneda, Joel, Sacred Heart, Othello
Reyes, Olegario, St. Patrick, Walla Walla
Riherd, John, St. Joseph, Colbert
Ritchie, Dan, Sacred Heart, Spokane
Ruscheinsky, John, St. Peter, Spokane
Sando, William, (Retired)
Sicilia, John F., St. Charles, Spokane
Stewart, Kelly, Assumption, Spokane
Toulou, Alvin, St. Michael, Inchelium
Weid, Walter, Our Lady of Fatima, Spokane
Whitney, Donald, Mary Queen, Spokane
Wilson, Charles, Archdiocese of Seattle

INSTITUTIONS LOCATED IN THE DIOCESE

[A] SEMINARIES, DIOCESAN

SPOKANE. *Bishop White Seminary*, E. 429 Sharp Ave., 99202. Tel: 509-326-3255; Fax: 509-326-3761. Email: bws@gonzaga.edu. Web: www.bishopwhiteseminary.org. Revs. Darrin Connall, Rector; Matthew Gamber, S.J., Dir. of Spiritual Formation. Students 15.

[B] COLLEGES AND UNIVERSITIES

SPOKANE. *Gonzaga University* 99258. Tel: 509-328-4220; Fax: 509-323-5819. Email: renouard@gonzaga.edu. Revs. Robert J. Araujo, S.J.; Donald R. Cadden, S.J.; J. Alfred Carroll, S.J.; Timothy R. Clancy, S.J.; Joseph C. Fortier, S.J. (SEA); Scott W. Coble, S.J.; Michael J. Connolly, S.J. (BO); Michael L. Cook, S.J.; Frank B. Costello, S.J.; Bernard J. Coughlin, S.J. (Missouri); Robert R. Dorin, S.J. (BO); Robert J. Egan, S.J.; Matthew Gamber, S.J.; Gerald R. Gordon, S.J.; Kenneth R. Krall, S.J.; Stephen R. Kuder, S.J.; Stephen Lantry, S.J.; Walter F. Leedale, S.J.; Robert Lyons, S.J.; James M. McDonough, S.J.; Alfred Morisette, S.J.; George O. Morris, S.J.; John P. Mossi, S.J. (California); Michael Moyahan, S.J.; James G. Powers, S.J.; Louis Renner, S.J.; William F. Ryan, S.J.; Fredric Schlatter, S.J.; Leonard F. Sitter, S.J.; M. Delmar Skillingstad, S.J.; Robert J. Spitzer, S.J., Pres.; Michael Treleaven, S.J.; Bernard J. Tyrrell, S.J.; Gary D. Uhlenkott, S.J.; Anthony P. Via, S.J.; J. Kevin Waters, S.J.; William M. Watson, S.J.; John H. Wright, S.J. (OAK); Bros. Edward S. Jennings, S.J.; Joseph Nguyen, S.J.; Stephen J. Souza, S.J.; Adam C. Weisgerber, S.J. College of Arts and Sciences, and Schools of Law, Engineering, Education, Business Administration, Graduate School. Professional Studies Education conducted by the Fathers of the Society of Jesus. Priests 38; Brothers 4; Sisters 4; Lay Teachers 282; Students 4,515.

The Ministry Institute (at Gonzaga University) , E. 405 Sinto Ave., 99202-1849. Tel: 509-328-8332; Fax: 509-325-4011. Email: troman@gonzaga.edu. Web: gonzaga.edu/materdei. Robert Troman, Ph.D.; Donna Crow, Formation Dir.; Diane Imes, Business Mgr.; Mary Lee Gaston, Sabbatical Coord. Full Time Enrollment 14.

[C] HIGH SCHOOLS, INTERPAROCHIAL

WALLA WALLA. *Walla Walla Catholic School System*, (Grades N-12), E. 919 Sumach, 99362. Tel: 509-525-3030; Fax: 509-527-0361. Email: wa2cs.org. Web: desales-irish.org. Mrs. Michele Acock, Prin. (Grades K-5); John Lesko, Admin. & Prin. (Grades 6-12). Lay Teachers 30; Students: Elementary 191; High School 255.

[D] HIGH SCHOOLS, PRIVATE

SPOKANE. *Gonzaga Preparatory School*, E. 1224 Euclid Ave., 99207. Tel: 509-483-8511; Fax: 509-483-3124. Email: jtraynor@gprep.com. Web: gprep.com. Dr. John Traynor, Pres.; Mr. Al Falkner, Prin.; Revs. Ignatius F. Ohno, S.J. (P); Robert L. Fitts, S.J.; Richard R. Mercy, S.J.; Joseph Showalter, S.J.; Joseph Small, S.J.; Joseph Conwell, S.J.; Mr. Paul Grubb, Scholastic. Priests 6; Scholastics 1; Lay Teachers 60; Students 880.

PASCO. *Tri Cities Prep, A Catholic High School*, (Grades 9-12), 9612 St. Thomas Dr., P.O. Box 4744, 99302-4744. Tel: 509-546-2465; Fax: 509-546-2490. Email: tcprep@tcprep.org. Rev. Thomas Bunnell, S.J., Prin. & Pres. Priests 1; Lay Teachers 7; Students 75.

[E] INTERPAROCHIAL GRADE SCHOOLS

SPOKANE. *All Saints School*, (Grades 5-8), E. 1428 33rd Ave., 99203. Tel: 509-624-5712; Fax: 509-624-7752. Email: khicks@dioceseofspokane.org. Web: web3.foxinternet.net/asmiddle. Ms. Kathy Hicks, Prin.

All Saints Primary (Grades PreK-4), E. 3510 18th Ave., 99223. Tel: 509-534-1098; Fax: 509-534-1529. Email: khicks@dioceaseofspokane.org. Ms. Kathy Hicks, Prin. Serving St. Peter, St. Ann and Our Lady of Fatima Parishes. Lay Teachers 25; Students 454.

Cataldo Catholic School, (Grades K-8), 455 W. 18th Ave., 99203. Tel: 509-624-8759; Fax: 509-624-8763. Email: office@cataldo.org. Mr. Richard Pelkie Jr., Prin. Serving St. Augustine, Sacred Heart, and Our Lady of Lourdes Parishes. Lay Teachers 21; Students 342.

Trinity School, (Grades PreK-8), W. 1306 Montgomery Ave., 99205. Tel: 509-327-9369; Fax: 509-328-4128. Email: trinitycathschool@dioceseofspokane.org. Mr. Michael S. Trudeau, Prin. Serving St. Anthony and St. Joseph Parishes Lay Teachers 7; Students 173.

COLTON. *Guardian Angel-St. Boniface School*, P.O. Box 48, 99113. Tel: 509-229-3579. Email: gasbsch@inlandnet.com. Web: inlandnet.com/gasbsch. Guy Pitzer, Prin. Serving St. Gall and St. Boniface Parishes. Lay Teachers 4; Students 46.

WALLA WALLA. *Assumption Elementary School*, (Grades PreK-5), E. 2066 Alder St., 99362. Tel: 509-525-9283; Fax: 509-527-0848. Email: macock@dioceseofspokane.org. Mrs. Michele Acock, Prin. & Bldg. Admin. Serving Assumption, St. Francis of Assisi, and St. Patrick Parishes. Lay Teachers 11; Students 184.

Walla Walla Catholic School System See listing under High Schools, Interparochial.

[F] GENERAL HOSPITALS

SPOKANE. *Holy Family Adult Day Health*, 6018 N. Astor, 99207. Tel: 509-482-2475; Fax: 509-482-2490. Web: www.hfadc.org. Mrs. Marie Raschko, Pres. Purpose: to perform and provide adult day health care services, including rehab & nursing, to the elderly and disadvantaged.

Holy Family Hospital, N. 5633 Lidgerwood St., 99207. Tel: 509-482-0111; Fax: 509-482-2456. Web: www.holy-family.org. Mr. Thomas Corley, Pres.; Mr. Richard Spinal, Dir. Pastoral Care. Chaplains 8; Sisters 2; Bed Capacity 272.

School of Radiology Tel: 509-482-2189; Fax: 509-482-2441. Students 18.

Sacred Heart Medical Center, W. 101 Eighth Ave., TAF-C9, 99220. Tel: 509-474-3131; Fax: 509-474-3153. Mr. Ryland P. Davis, Pres.; Revs. Bob Dorin, S.J., Chap.; Gerald R. Gordon, S.J., Chap.; Michael D. Venneri, Chap. Chaplains 20; Total Staff 4,000; Bed Capacity 623; Patients Assisted Annually 195,000.

CHEWELAH. *St. Joseph's Hospital*, E 500 Webster, 99109. Tel: 509-935-8211; Fax: 509-935-5257. Gary V. Peck, Pres.; Sisters Mary Agnes Koenit, O.P., Pastoral Care; Humilitas Lamber O.P., Pastoral Care; Alberta Nett, O.P., Pastoral Care; Mary Toeckes, O.P., Pastoral Care; David Verwolf, Pastoral Care. Sisters 4; Bed Capacity 65; Patients Assisted Annually 21,721

COLVILLE. *Mount Carmel Hospital*, 982 E. Columbia, 99114. Tel: 509-684-2561; Fax 509-685-2492. Email: michaed@mtcarmelhospital.org. Web: www.mtcarmelhospital.org. Gordon McLean, Admin. Total Staff 236; Bed Capacity 33; Patients Assisted Annually 33,819.

DEER PARK. *Deer Park Health Center and Hospital*, 1015 E. "D" St., 99006. Tel: 509-276-3500; Fax: 509-276-2777. Email: Olsong@mhs.org. Garvin Olson, COO. Total Staff 75; Bed Capacity 25; Patients Assisted Annually 14,200.

PASCO. *Lourdes Medical Center*, 520 N. Fourth Ave., P.O. Box 2568, 99302. Tel: 509-547-7704; Fax: 509-546-2291. James F. Dover Fache Pres. & CEO. Sisters of St. Joseph of Carondelet 4; Total Staff 725; Bed Capacity 132; Patients Assisted Annually 147,893. In Res. Rev. John Birk.

WALLA WALLA. *St. Mary Medical Center*, 401 W. Poplar St., 99362. Tel: 509-525-3320; Fax: 509-522-5950. Web: www.smmc.com. Mr. John A. Isely, Pres. Sisters of Providence Total Staff 825; Bed Capacity 141; Patients Assisted Annually 94,354.

[G] PROTECTIVE INSTITUTIONS

(Catholic Social Service)

SPOKANE

St. Anne's Children's Home & Family Center, N. 707 Cedar St., 99201-1999. Tel: 509-325-7672. Bonnie Diebler, Dir. Therapeutic child care for abused/neglected children and assistance to their parents through parent education and counseling.

Catholic Charities, Inc., W. 1023 Riverside Ave., P.O. Box 1453, 99210-1453. Tel: 509-358-4250; Fax: 509-358-4259. Web: www.catholiccharitiesspokane-.org. Mrs. Donna Hanson, Bishop's Sec. for Social Ministries & Catholic Charities Diocesan Dir.

Guse Summit View Tel: 509-327-9524. P.O. Box 1453, 99210-1453. 820 N. Summit Blvd., 99210. Email: trothrock@dioceseofspokane.org. 27 units of housing for single parents with children.

House of Charity, 32 W. Pacific, P.O. Box 1453, 99210-1453. Tel: 509-624-7821; Fax: 509-742-3463. Web: catholiccharitiesspokane.org. Email: emccarron@dioceseofspokane.org. Ed McCarron, Dir. Housing for homeless men. Total Assisted 69,456.

St. Joseph's Counseling Center, N. 1016 Superior St., 99202. Tel: 509-483-6495; Fax: 509-483-1541. Email: sjfc@stjosephfamilycenter.org. Web: www.st-josephfamilycenter.net. Sr. Elaine Theden, O.S.F., M.A., Dir., St. Joseph Family Center. Sisters of St. Francis of Philadelphia 3.

St. Margaret's Shelter, P.O. Box 1453, 99210-9788. Tel: 509-624-9288; Fax: 509-624-1461. Email: nvanstone@dioceseofspokane.org. Nadine Van Stone, Dir. Emergency and transitional shelter for single women & children. Total Staff 8; Total Assisted Annually 170.

Miryam's House, 1805 W. 9th St., 99204. Tel: 509-747-9222; Fax: 509-747-7261. Email: miryamshouse@aol.com. Web: www.help4women.com. 3102 W. Fort George Wright Dr., 99224. A long-term residence for women in transition. Total Staff 5; Total Assisted 70.

Morning Star Boys' Ranch, P.O. Box 8087, 99203. Tel: 509-448-1411; Fax: 509-448-1413. Email: msbr@morningstarboysranch.org. Web: morning-starboysranch.org. Rev. Joseph M. Weitensteiner, Dir. Total Staff 32; Children in residence 19; Total Assisted 45.

Transitional Living Center, 3128 N. Hemlock, 92205. Tel: 509-325-2959; Fax: 509-325-8319. Email: tlcenter@aol.com. 3102 W. Fort George Wright Dr., 99224. Tel: 509-328-6702. Housing for homeless women & children.

St. Vincent de Paul Social Service Office, E. 2901 Trent Ave., 99202. Tel: 509-534-2824 (Social Svc.); 509-535-2491 (Main Store & Office); Fax: 509-535-2559. George Vasil, Pres.; James Springer, Operations Mgr.

Legal Title: *St. Vincent de Paul Social Service Office and Main Store St. Business Office* Total Assisted 67,000.

St. Vincent de Paul Society, E. 2901 Trent Ave., 99202. Tel: 509-534-2824; Fax: 509-535-2559. Dick Bennett, Pres. Spokane District Council

Women's Drop In Center, 218 S. Howard, 99201. Tel: 509-455-4249; Fax: 509-455-3544. Web: www.help4women.com. Sr. Mary Rathert, O.P., Prog. Dir. A safe place for women at risk.

CHEWELAH

DominiCare, 303 E. King St., P.O. Box 1070, 99109. Tel: 509-935-4925; Fax: 509-935-4082. Email: dominicare@plix.com. Sr. Sharon Stangler, O.P., Pres. A home care/chore service in Stevens County.

CLARKSTON

Lewis and Clark District Council of St. Vincent de Paul, Office, 604 Second St., 99403. Tel: 509-758-7061; Fax: 509-758-9545. Email: svdp@rmci.net.

Stores:

609 Third St., 99403. Tel: 509-758-7061; Fax: 509-758-9545.

3138 5th St., Lewiston, ID 83501. Tel: 208-746-7860.

COLVILLE
The Rhodena, A Washington Nonprofit Organization, P.O. Box 1453, 99210-1453. Tel: 509-358-4264. Email: trothrock@dioceseofspokane.org. A six unit affordable housing complex for families living in Colville, WA.

DAYTON
St. Vincent de Paul Store, 247 E. Main St., 99328. Tel: 509-382-4146. Rev. Theresa Overfield, Pres.

PASCO
St. Vincent de Paul Store, 1120 W. Sylvester, 99301. Tel: 509-547-2341; Fax: 509-547-7804.

WALLA WALLA
Catholic Children and Family Service, 5 W. Alder St., Ste. 333, 99362. Tel: 509-525-0572; Fax: 509-525-0576. Email: cchildww@bmi.net. Web: cchildww@bmi.net. Richard A. Garcia, M.S.W., Dir.
St. Vincent de Paul Store, 308 W. Main St., 99362. Tel: 509-525-3903 (Store); 509-529-6778 (Office); Fax: 509-525-3903. Dale Peck, Society Pres.

[H] SENIOR CITIZEN HOUSING

SPOKANE. *Cathedral Plaza Apartments*, W. 1120 Sprague Ave., 99204. Tel: 509-747-6777. Email: trothrock@dioceseofspokane.org. Capacity 150.
The Delaney, W. 242 Riverside Ave., 99201. Tel: 509-747-5081. Email: trothrock@dioceseofspokane.org. Capacity 83.
Fahy Garden Apartments, W. 1403 Dean Ave., 99201. Tel: 509-326-6759. Email: trothrock@dioceseofspokane.org. Capacity 31.
Fahy West Apartments, W. 1523 Dean Ave., 99201. Tel: 509-326-6759. Email: trothrock@dioceseofspokane.org. Capacity 54.
The O'Malley, E. 707 Mission Ave., 99202. Tel: 509-326-6759. Email: trothrock@dioceseofspokane.org. Capacity 99.
Rockwood Lane/Court, E. 221 Rockwood Blvd., 99202. Tel: 509-838-3200. Email: trothrock@dioceseofspokane.org. Capacity 106.
Senior Service - Senior Nutrition, W. 242 Riverside Ave., 99201. Tel: 509-624-6060.

CLARKSTON. *Austen Manor*, 1222 Chestnut St., 99403. Tel: 509-751-9640. Email: trothrock@dioceseofspokane.org. Charles Grasseschi, Mgr. Capacity 30.

PULLMAN. *Pioneer Square*, S.E. 220 Kamiaken, 99163. Tel: 509-332-1106; Fax: 509-332-2516. Email: trothrock@dioceseofspokane.org. Capacity 45.

WALLA WALLA. *Garden Court Apartments*, Sixth & Alder Sts., 99362. Tel: 509-529-4706. Email: trothrock@dioceseofspokane.org. Capacity 20.
Mike Foye Apartments Tel: 509-529-9062. Email: trothrock@dioceseofspokane.org. P.O. Box 1453, 99210. Sixth & Alder Sts., 99362. Capacity 25.

[I] HOMES FOR AGED

SPOKANE. *St. Joseph Care Center* (A Non-profit Corporation) , E. 17 Eighth Ave., 99202. Tel: 509-474-5678; Fax: 509-455-4020. Sally Denton, Admin. Sisters of Providence Bed Capacity 145.

[J] MONASTERIES AND RESIDENCES OF PRIESTS AND BROTHERS

SPOKANE. *Regis Community*, N. 1107 Astor St., 99202. Tel: 509-328-4220; Fax: 509-484-2818. Revs. Robert L. Fitts, S.J., Supr.; William C. Dibb, S.J.; James P. Goodwin, S.J.; Robert Lyons, S.J.; Anton P. Jahner, S.J.; John S. Harrington, S.J.; Patrick J. Hurley, S.J.; Pasquale M. Spoletini, S.J.; Francis E. Mueller, S.J. (P); Charles A. Wollsen, S.J.; Lawrence P. Gooley, S.J.; Michael McHugh, S.J.; Paul P. Luger, S.J.; James E. Poole, S.J. (SEA); Edmund J. Robinson, S.J.; Robert J. Schlim, S.J.; Gordon L. Keys, S.J.; John D. McCluskey, S.J.; John Schwarz, S.J.; John R. Thatcher, S.J.; Arnold R. Beezer, S.J.; L. Donald Davis, S.J.; Thomas R. Garvin, S.J.; Francis A. Logan, S.J.; William J. Loyens, S.J.; Alexander F. McDonald, S.J.; Joseph L. Obersinner, S.J.; William M. O'Malley, S.J.; Bros. Michael J. Bennett, S.J.; James J. Lee, S.J.; Fenton J. Melia, S.J.

[K] CONVENTS AND RESIDENCES FOR SISTERS

SPOKANE. *Convent of the Holy Names*, 2911 W. Fort George Wright Dr., 99224. Tel: 509-328-4310; Fax: 509-328-9824. Email: snjmchni@aol.com. Web: www.snjm.org. Sr. Ann Pizelo, S.N.J.M., Prov. Dir. Sisters of the Holy Names of Jesus and Mary Professed Sisters 165.
Dominican Center, Sinsinawa Dominican Sisters, 3102 W. Fort George Wright Dr., 99224-5203. Tel: 509-328-8033; Fax: 509-325-9877. Email: dcenters@aol.com. Sisters 18.
Holy Names Foundation, 2911 W. Fort George Wright Dr., 99224. Tel: 509-328-7470; Fax: 509-328-9824. Sr. Ann Pizelo, S.N.J.M., Prov. Dir. Support for educational activities of Sisters of the Holy Names of Jesus and Mary.
Holy Spirit Community, 2416 E. 46th Ave., 99223-6412. Tel: 509-448-6224. Email: Roy2428@msn.com. Sr. Margaret Beilenbach, Pres.
Monastery of St. Clare, 4419 N. Hawthorne St., 99205-1399. Tel: 509-327-4479; Fax: 509-327-5171. Sr. Mary Rita Dolan, O.S.C., Abbess. Papal Enclosure Novitiate. Professed Cloistered Nuns 8; Poor Claire Nuns, Solem Vows 8.
Mount St. Joseph Retirement residence and community. , 12 W. Ninth Ave., 99204-2394. Tel: 509-474-2300; Fax: 509-474-2302. Laurie Crane, Gen. Mgr.; Sr. Mary K. Cummings, Supr. Sisters of Providence, Mother Joseph, Province Sisters 31.
Sisters of Providence, Mother Joseph Province, 9 E. 9th Ave., 99202. Tel: 509-474-2307; Fax: 509-474-2302. Email: barbara.schamber@providene.org. Web: www.sistersofprovidence.net. Sr. Barbara Schamber, S.P., Team Leader & Prov. Supr. Sisters of Providence, Mother Joseph Province (a Washington nonprofit corporation). Members of Providence Services (a Washington nonprofit corporation). Sisters 6.

NEWPORT. *Carmelite Sisters of Mary*, 2892 State Rte. 211, 99156. Tel: 509-292-0978. Sr. Leslie L. Lund, Prioress. Sisters 2; Hermitages 5.

PULLMAN. *Sisters of the Humility of Mary*, 233 N.W. Ann St, 99163-3543. Tel: 509-332-8388.
3410 S. Regal St., Apt. 22, 99223-4669. Tel: 509-328-4220.

[L] RETREAT HOUSES

SPOKANE. *Clare Center, Franciscan Spirituality Center*, P.O. Box 30250, 99223-3004. Tel: 509-448-4887; Fax: 509-448-1553. Email: director@clarecenter.org. Sr. Betty Bradley, F.S.P.A., Dir. Sisters 3.
Immaculate Heart Retreat Center, 6910 S. Ben Burr Rd., 99223. Tel: 509-448-1224; Fax: 509-448-1623. Email: ihrc@ihrc.net. Web: www.ihrc.net. Deacon John Ruscheinsky, Exec. Dir.; Rev. Msgr. William Van Ommeren.
KAIROS House of Prayer, 1714 W. Stearns Rd., 99208. Tel: 509-466-2187. Sr. M. Florence Leone Poch, O.S.F., Coord. Provides a place called to a prayerful, reflective environment for people of all faiths. Spiritual accompaniment is available.
Spiritual Exercise in Everyday Life (SEEL), 330 E. Boone, 99202. Tel: 509-323-5898; Fax: 509-323-5892. Email: mcevoy@gonzaga.edu. Sr. Sheila McEvoy, S.N.J.M., Dir.

TUM TUM. *House of the Lord Retreat Center, Inc.*, P.O. Box 1034, 99034. Tel: 509-276-2219. Web: www.houseofthelordministries.com. Ramona Salvatore, Dir.

[M] NEWMAN CENTERS

CHENEY. *Catholic Newman Center at Eastern Washington University* 837 Elm St., 99004. Tel: 509-235-8402. Rev. Thomas C. Caswell, Chap.; Tara Young-Brown, Campus Min.

PULLMAN. *Washington State University - St. Thomas More Catholic Newman Center* 820 N.E. B St., P.O. Box 2070, College Station, 99165-2070. Tel: 509-332-6311; Fax: 509-332-2089. Email: stthomaswsu@earthlink.net. Web: cub.wsu.edu/sthomore/index.htm. Rev. Steven Warner, Dir.

[N] MISCELLANEOUS

SPOKANE. *Bernadette Place*, P.O. Box 1453, 99210-1453. Tel: 509-326-2023. This complex houses twelve developmentally delayed women 6 units of affordable housing for persons with disabilities and special needs.
Office:, 1023 W. Riverside Ave, P.O. Box 1453, 99210-1453.
2819 W. Mallon Ave., 99201.
2925 W. Mallon Ave., 99201.
The Catholic Foundation of the Spokane Diocese, W. 1023 Riverside Ave., P.O. Box 1453, 99210-1453. Tel: 509-358-4280; Fax: 509-358-7302. Email: skocharhook@dioceseofspokane.org. Web: www.spokanecatholicfoundation.com. Steven C. Kocharhook, Ph.D., Exec. Dir.
Dominican Health Services, N. 5633 Lidgerwood, 99207. Tel: 509-482-2576. Mr. Ryland P. Davis, Pres.
Dominican Outreach Foundation, c/o Dominican Center, W. 3102 Fort George Wright Dr., 99224. Tel: 509-328-8033; Fax: 509-328-0597. Email: falknersr@hotmail.com. James G. Falkner, Pres. Supports the Sisters educational, religious, and charitable ministries.
Emilie Court Assisted Living, 34 E. 8th Ave., 99202-1202. Tel: 509-474-2550; Fax: 509-474-2618. Email: schlick@shmc.org. Kathleen Schlicht, Dir.; Charlene Steindort, Asst. Dir.
Holy Names Music Center, 3910 W. Custer Dr., 99224. Tel: 509-326-9516; Fax: 509-326-7155. Email: music@hnmc.org. Web: www.hnmc.org. John A. Morgan, Exec. Dir. Sponsored by Sisters of the Holy Names, Washington Province. Sisters 2; Lay Teachers 35; Students 500.
Immaculate Heart Retreat Center Foundation, S. 6910 Ben Burr Rd., 99223-1819. Tel: 509-448-1224; Fax: 509-448-1623.
Kateri Northwest Ministry Institute, 330 E. Boone, 99202-1778. Tel: 509-324-6305; Fax: 509-324-6305. Email: rmercy@gntech.net. Revs. Richard R. Mercy, S.J., Dir.; Thomas A. Colgan, Dir. Purpose: Evangelization and training of Native Americans in the four Northwestern states for all ministries in the Catholic Church and service in the native community, with attention to ongoing social analysis and to recovery ministries from Alcoholism and Dysfunctional Families. Goal: The development of fully indigenous Catholic churches in Urban centers and on Reservations.
Providence Services, 9 E. Ninth Ave., 99202-1295. Tel: 509-474-7337; Fax: 509-474-4882. Web: www.providenceservices.org. Richard Umbdenstock, Pres. & CEO.
Providence Services Health Care, 101 W. 8th Ave., 99220. Tel: 509-482-3335; Fax: 509-474-4925. Ryland (Skip) P. Davis, Pres. Providence Services Health Care is an integrated healthcare delivery network made up of: Sacred Heart Medical Center, Spokane Visiting Nurse Association, St. Joseph Care Center, Emilie Court, Pathology Associates Medical Laboratories, DominiCare, Holy Family Adult Day Centers, Deer Park Hospital health center and Holy Family Hospital, St. Joseph Hospital of Chewelah and Mount Carmel Hospital.
Serra Club of Spokane, P.O. Box 9169, 99209-9169. Tel: 509-327-4344.
Spokane Catholic Investment Trust, P.O. Box 1453, 99210-1453. Tel: 509-358-7300; Fax: 509-358-7302. Most Rev. William S. Skylstad, Pres. A Washington Nonprofit Corporation established to invest funds on behalf of the charitable organizations organized within the Catholic Diocese of Spokane.
Transitional Programs for Women, W. 3102 Fort George Wright Dr., 99224. Tel: 509-328-6702; Fax: 509-325-9877. Email: transprog@aol.com. Web: www.help4women.com.

DAYTON. *Project Timothy: Christian Service Center*, 238 E. Main St., 99328. Tel: 509-382-2943. Sponsored by St. Joseph's & St. Mark's Churches Total Assisted 4,550.

RELIGIOUS INSTITUTES OF MEN REPRESENTED IN THE DIOCESE

For further details refer to the corresponding bracketed number in the Religious Institutes of Men or Women section.

[0520]—*Franciscan Friars* (Santa Barbara Prov.)—O.F.M.

[0690]—*Jesuit Fathers and Brothers*—S.J.

RELIGIOUS INSTITUTES OF WOMEN REPRESENTED IN THE DIOCESE

[1780]—*Congregation of the Sisters of the Third Order of St. Francis of Perpetual Adoration*—F.S.P.A.

[1070-03]—*Dominican Sisters*—O.P.

[3760]—*Order of St. Clare*—O.S.C.

[3350]—*Sisters of Providence*—S.P.

[1650]—*The Sisters of St. Francis of Philadelphia*—O.S.F.

[3840]—*Sisters of St. Joseph of Carondelet*—C.S.J.

[1990]—*Sisters of the Holy Names of Jesus and Mary*—S.N.J.M.

[2110]—*Sisters of the Humility of Mary*—H.M.

DIOCESAN CEMETERIES

SPOKANE. *Catholic Cemeteries of Spokane*, 7200 N. Wall St., 99208. Dennis Fairbank, Dir.
Holy Cross, 7200 N. Wall St., 99208. Tel: 509-328-1070.
St. Joseph, 17825 Trent, 99216. Tel: 509-891-6240.

NECROLOGY

† Kelley, John P., (Retired)—Died Oct. 28, 2003
† Tully, Terence, (Retired)—Died Nov. 17, 2002
† Wenning, Paul A., (Retired)—Died Sept. 5, 2003

Diocese of Springfield-Cape Girardeau

(Dioecesis Campifontis-Capitis Girardeauensis)

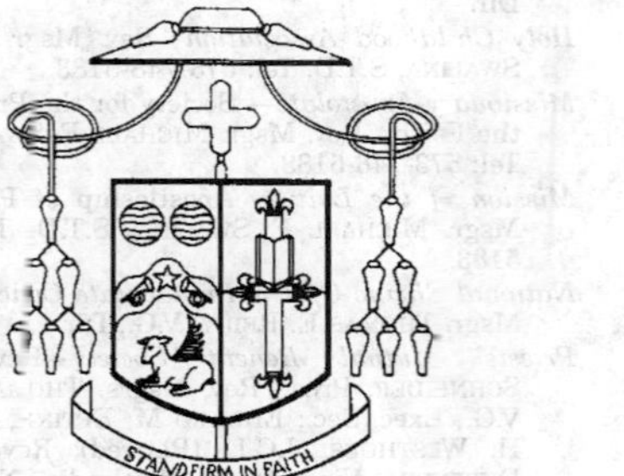

Most Reverend

JOHN J. LEIBRECHT, D.D., PH.D.

Bishop of Springfield-Cape Girardeau; ordained March 17, 1956; appointed Bishop of Springfield-Cape Girardeau October 23, 1984; consecrated December 12, 1984. *Office: The Catholic Center,* 601 S. Jefferson Ave., Springfield, MO 65806-3143.

Chancery Office: The Catholic Center, 601 S. Jefferson Ave., Springfield, MO 65806-3143. Tel: 417-866-0841; Fax: 417-866-1140.

Web: www.diocspfdcape.org

Email: treidy@diocspfdcape.org

ESTABLISHED AUGUST 24, 1956.

Square Miles 25,719.

Comprises the following Counties in the State of Missouri: Barry, Barton, Bollinger, Butler, Cape Girardeau, Carter, Cedar, Christian, Dade, Dallas, Dent, Douglas, Dunklin, Greene, Howell, Iron, Jasper, Laclede, Lawrence, McDonald, Madison, Mississippi, New Madrid, Newton, Oregon, Ozark, Pemiscot, Polk, Reynolds, Ripley, Scott, Shannon, Stoddard, Stone, Taney, Texas, Wayne, Webster and Wright.

For legal titles of parishes and diocesan institutions, consult The Catholic Center.

STATISTICAL OVERVIEW

Personnel	
Bishop	1
Abbots	1
Retired Abbots	2
Priests: Diocesan Active in Diocese	50
Priests: Diocesan Active Outside Diocese	1
Priests: Retired, Sick or Absent	17
Number of Diocesan Priests	68
Religious Priests in Diocese	55
Total Priests in Diocese	123
Extern Priests in Diocese	11
Ordinations:	
Diocesan Priests	1
Religious Priests	3
Transitional Deacons	1
Permanent Deacons in Diocese	8
Total Brothers	64
Total Sisters	98
Parishes	
Parishes	65
With Resident Pastor:	
Resident Diocesan Priests	47
Resident Religious Priests	7
Without Resident Pastor:	
Administered by Priests	8
Administered by Deacons	1
Administered by Religious Women	2
Missions	19
Pastoral Centers	4
Professional Ministry Personnel:	
Sisters	18
Lay Ministers	25
Welfare	
Catholic Hospitals	6
Total Assisted	843,936
Homes for the Aged	2
Total Assisted	351
Day Care Centers	1
Total Assisted	45
Special Centers for Social Services	2
Total Assisted	1,350
Other Institutions	1
Total Assisted	47,231
Educational	
Diocesan Students in Other Seminaries	7
Seminaries, Religious	2
Students Religious	16
Total Seminarians	23
High Schools, Diocesan and Parish	3
Total Students	953
Elementary Schools, Diocesan and Parish	22
Total Students	3,720
Catechesis/Religious Education:	
High School Students	1,525
Elementary Students	4,279
Total Students under Catholic Instruction	10,500
Teachers in the Diocese:	
Priests	1
Brothers	1
Sisters	1
Lay Teachers	275
Vital Statistics	
Receptions into the Church:	
Infant Baptism Totals	810
Adult Baptism Totals	517
Received into Full Communion	264
First Communions	1,292
Confirmations	969
Marriages:	
Catholic	174
Interfaith	245
Total Marriages	419
Deaths	630
Total Catholic Population	63,162
Total Population	1,226,079

Former Bishops—Most Revs. CHARLES H. HELMSING, D.D., consecrated as Titular Bishop of Axomis and Auxiliary Bishop of Archdiocese of St. Louis, April 19, 1949; appt. Bishop of Springfield-Cape Girardeau, Aug. 24, 1956; transferred to Diocese of Kansas City-St. Joseph, Jan. 27, 1962; died Dec. 20, 1993; IGNATIUS J. STRECKER, D.D., appt. April 7, 1962; consecrated June 20, 1962; transferred to Archdiocese of Kansas City in Kansas, Sept. 10, 1969; retired Sept. 8, 1993; died Oct. 16, 2003; His Eminence WILLIAM CARDINAL BAUM, S.T.D. (Retired), appt. Feb. 18, 1970; consecrated April 6, 1970; transferred to Archdiocese of Washington, May 8, 1973; elevated to Cardinal, May 24, 1976; appointed Prefect, Congregation for Catholic Education in the Vatican, Jan. 15, 1980; Major Penitentiary, appointed April 6, 1990.; retired Nov. 22, 2001; BERNARD CARDINAL LAW, D.D., ord. May 21, 1961; appt. Bishop of Springfield-Cape Girardeau, Oct. 22, 1973; consecrated Dec. 5, 1973; appt. Archbishop of Boston, Jan. 23, 1984; elevated to Cardinal, May 25, 1985; retired Dec. 13, 2002.

Vicars General—Rev. Msgrs. PHILIP A. BUCHER, V.G.; THOMAS E. REIDY, V.G.; RICHARD C. ROLWING, V.G. (Retired).

Chancery Office—The Catholic Center, 601 S. Jefferson Ave., Springfield, 65806-3143. Tel: 417-866-0841; Fax: 417-866-1140.

Chancellor—Rev. Msgr. THOMAS E. REIDY, V.G.

Vice Chancellor—Rev. THOMAS P. KIEFER, J.C.L.

Regional Priest Moderators—Region I: Rev. JUSTIN D. MONAGHAN. Region II: Rev. PETER J. MORCINIEC. Region III: Rev. J. PATRICK WISSMAN. Region IV: Rev. J. FERGUS MONAGHAN. Region V: Rev. DANIEL J. HIRTZ. Region VI: Rev. JAMES J. UNTERREINER. Region VII (A): Rev. J. FRIEDEL. Region VII (B): Rev. JOHN M. HARTH. Region VIII: Rev. STEPHEN A. SCHNEIDER. Region IX: Rev. DAVID J. DOHOGNE.

Office of Administration

Catholic Foundation Of The Diocese Of Springfield-Cape Girardeau—Most Rev. JOHN J. LEIBRECHT, D.D., Ph.D., Pres.; Rev. Msgr. THOMAS E. REIDY, V.G., Vice Pres.; Ms. JANET L. SMITH, Sec. Treas.

Development and Properties—Mr. THOMAS B. WALMSLEY, Dir.

Diocesan Development Fund—Mr. THOMAS B. WALMSLEY, Dir. Devel. & Properties; Rev. GLENN A EFTINK; Mr. LEE E. LARSCHEID; Mr. ROSE M. POBST.

Finance—Ms. JANET L. SMITH, Dir.

Financial Council—Ms. JANET L. SMITH, Dir. Finance; Mr. THOMAS B. WALMSLEY, Diocesan Dir., Devel. & Properties; Mrs. MAUREEN M. JERSAK, Diocesan Dir., Planned Giving; Mr. LARRY G. GRINSTEAD; Mrs. PATRICIA HOPKINS; Mr. GEORGE MARINO; JAMES MOORE, Ph.D.; Mr. JAMES P. REINAGEL; Mr. KEVIN FITZGERALD; Mrs. KAY A. VAN PELT; Mr. CHRIS CHURCHWELL.

Planned Giving—Mrs. MAUREEN M. JERSAK, Dir.

Office Of Education

Catholic Schools—Mr. LEON WITT, Supt. of Schools.

Communications (Public Relations)—Mrs. RECY MOORE, Dir.

Ecumenism—Rev. JOHN F. GAGNEPAIN, C.M.

Media Library—Mrs. RECY MOORE, Supvr.

Newspaper, Diocese of Springfield-Cape Girardeau—LESLIE A. EIDSON, Editor; Ms. JOAN WARD, Sec. "The Mirror"

Religious Education—Sr. ROSALIE DIGENAN, D.C., M.Ed., Dir.

Office Of Ministry

Campus Ministries—Revs. EDDIE DELEON, C.M.F., Southwest Missouri State Univ. Campus Min. Tel: 417-865-0802; JOHN (J.) F. FRIEDEL, M.A., M.Div., Southeast Missouri State Univ. Campus Min. Tel: 573-335-3899.

Diaconate (Permanent)—Deacon WILLIAM MCNAMEE. Tel: 417-724-9705.

Diocesan Director of Continuing Formation of Clergy—Rev. JOHN F. GAGNEPAIN, C.M. Tel: 573-547-7276.

Family Ministries—Mr. TROY CASTEEL, M.S., L.P.C., Dir.

Diocesan Council on Family Ministry—Region I: JIM NEWTON; MARGE NEWTON. Region II: DIANE WHITNEY. Region III: Rev. J. PATRICK WISSMAN. Region IV: Rev. MICHAEL V. MCDEVITT, M.A.; ROSIE SAN PAOLO; MARGARET SCHATZ; SHARON WEIDELMAN; PATTI STRAUS. Region V; Rev. ERNEST J. MARQUART. Region VI: Rev. JAMES J. UNTERREINER. Region VII: GREG ILLERS; LINDA ILLERS. Region VIII: JACK JACKOVIC; PAT JACKOVIC. Region IX: SHERRY LAMPE.

Natural Family Planning—Mr. TROY CASTEEL, M.S., L.P.C., Dir.

Rite Of Christian Initiation Of Adults—Rev. ROBERT F. MANSO, Co-Dir.; Sr. ROSALIE DIGENAN, D.C., Co-Dir.

Hispanic Ministries—Mrs. MILAGROS CALVETTI, Dir.

Social Ministry-Resettlement—Dr. DONALD R. EMGE, Ph.D., Dir.

Regional Catholic Planning— Regional Priest

Moderators serve as Conveners
Victim Assistance Coordinator—KATHLEEN GRIESEMER, Psy.D. Tel: 417-848-4601. Email: kpoirotg@aol.com.
Tribunal—
Judicial Vicar—Rev. Msgr. THOMAS E. REIDY, V.G.
Adjutant Judicial Vicars—Revs. VINCENT E. BERTRAND, J.C.L.; THOMAS P. KIEFER, J.C.L.
Judges—Rev. Msgrs. MICHAEL F. SWALINA, S.T.D.; JOHN H. WESTHUES, J.C.L. (Retired).
Auditor—Sr. INEZ HALLINAN, C.S.J., M.A.
Promoter of Justice—Rev. Msgr. PHILIP A. BUCHER, V.G.
Advocate—Rev. Msgr. EDWARD M. EFTINK, Ph.D.; Rev. DAVID F. HULSHOF.
Defenders of the Bond—Rev. Msgr. PHILIP A. BUCHER, V.G.; Rev. MICHAEL V. MCDEVITT, M.A.
Notaries—Mrs. LINDA MURPHY; Mrs. MARIE MEYER.
Vicar For The Religious—Rev. Msgr. THOMAS E. REIDY, V.G.
Vocations-Seminarians—Rev. DAVID F. HULSHOF, Dir.
Associate Director of Vocations/Seminarians—Rev. THOMAS P. KIEFER, J.C.L.
Youth Ministry—Ms. LEIGH STERTEN, Dir.
Catholic Scouting—Rev. SCOTT M. SUNNENBERG, Diocesan Chap. Tel: 573-335-9347; Mrs. JEAN WEISSLER, Assoc. Diocesan Chap. Tel: 417-887-0979.
Camp Re-NEW-All—Ms. VIRGINIA SANDER, Camp Dir.; Ms. KATHY MILOSHEWSKI, Camp Dir.

Office Of Worship

Office of Worship—Revs. ROBERT MANSO, Dir.; ROBERT F. MANSO, Assoc. Dir.
Liturgical Commission—Rev. ROBERT F. MANSO, Dir. Worship.
Priests' Eucharistic League Confraternity Of The Most Blessed Sacrament—Rev. MICHAEL V. MCDEVITT, M.A., Dir.

Officials And Committees

Catholic Relief Services—Rev. Msgr. THOMAS E. REIDY, V.G.
Cemeteries—Rev. Msgr. THOMAS E. REIDY, V.G.
Censor Of Books—Rev. MARK C. ERNSTMANN, S.T.L., M.Ed. Tel: 417-546-5208.
Health Affairs—Mr. TROY S. CASTEEL, M.S., L.P.C., Dir.
Holy Childhood Association—Rev. Msgr. MICHAEL F. SWALINA, S.T.D. Tel: 573-748-5183.
Missionary Apostolate— Society for the Propagation of the Faith, Rev. Msgr. MICHAEL F. SWALINA, S.T.D. Tel: 573-748-5183.
Mission of the Laity— Apostleship of Prayer, Rev. Msgr. MICHAEL F. SWALINA, S.T.D. Tel: 573-748-5183.
National Shrine Of The Immaculate Conception—Rev. Msgr. THOMAS E. REIDY, V.G., Dir.
Priests' Mutual Benefit Society—Rev. STEPHEN SCHNEIDER, Pres.; Rev. Msgrs. THOMAS E. REIDY, V.G., Exec. Sec.; EDWARD M. EFTINK, Ph.D.; JOHN H. WESTHUES, J.C.L. (Retired); Revs. RALPH J. DUFFNER, Vice Pres. (Retired); NORMAND G. VARONE; JOHN M. HARTH; Rev. Msgr. PHILIP A. BUCHER, V.G.
Priests' Purgatorial Society—Revs. MARK C. ERNSTMANN, S.T.L., M.Ed., Dir. Tel: 417-546-5208; BENEDICT W. HARTER, Sec. (Retired).
Pro-Life Director—Dr. DONALD R. EMGE, Ph.D., Dir.
Rural Life Movement—Rev. SYLVESTER W. BAUER. Tel: 573-744-5913.

Diocesan Consultative Groups

Diocesan Consultors—Rev. JOHN (J) F. FRIEDEL, M.A., M.Div.; Rev. Msgrs. PHILIP A. BUCHER, V.G.; RICHARD C. ROLWING, V.G. (Retired); MICHAEL F. SWALINA, S.T.D.; Rev. THOMAS P. KIEFER, J.C.L.; Rev. Msgr. THOMAS E. REIDY, V.G.; Rev. JAMES J. UNTERREINER.
Presbyteral Council—Rev. Msgr. MICHAEL F. SWALINA, S.T.D., Chm.; Revs. LEWIS E. HEJNA, Vice Chm.; JAMES J. UNTERREINER, Sec.; MARK J. BINDER; DENIS DOUGHERTY, O.S.B.; MICHAEL V. MCDEVITT, M.A.; MATTHEW J. REHRAUER; SCOTT M. SUNNENBERG; PAUL WIGHTMAN, O.M.I.; J. PATRICK WISSMAN. Appointed Members: Rev. Msgrs. PHILIP A. BUCHER, V.G.; RICHARD C. ROLWING, V.G. (Retired); THOMAS E. REIDY, V.G.
Diocesan Pastoral Council—Rev. DAVID J. DOHOGNE, Exec. Sec.
Diocesan School Board—Mr. LEON WITT, Supt.
Diocesan Lay Endowment Board—Rev. DAVID F. HULSHOF, Chm.

Catholic Organizations And Movements

Cursillo Movement—
Secretariat for Cursillo—Rev. WILLIAM M. HODGSON, Diocesan Chap.
St. Francis de Sales Association—Rev. JOHN P. KENNEHAN, Chap.; Rev. Msgr. WILLIAM J. STANTON, Chap. (Retired).
Diocesan Council Of Catholic Women (DCCW)—Revs. JAMES J. UNTERREINER, Diocesan Spiritual Moderator; DAVID F. HULSHOF, Assoc. Spiritual Moderator; VIRGINIA BINGLE, Pres. Tel: 417-338-2088.
St. Vincent De Paul Society—Rev. Msgr. THOMAS E. REIDY, V.G., Diocesan Chap.

Apostolates And Commissions

Apostolate to the Deaf—Rev. DAVID L. MILLER, Dir. Tel: 417-847-4948; 417-858-2518.
Diocesan Peace and Justice Commission—Rev. SYLVESTER BAUER. Tel: 573-744-5913.

State Office

Diocesan Delegates To The Missouri Catholic Conference—
Public Policy Committee—Dr. DONALD R. EMGE, Ph.D.; Dr. RICHARD J. CRAWFORD JR., Vice Chm.

CLERGY, PARISHES, MISSIONS AND PAROCHIAL SCHOOLS

CITY OF SPRINGFIELD
(GREENE COUNTY)

1—CATHEDRAL OF ST. AGNES (1908), [CEM] [JC] Rev. Michael V. McDevitt, M.A.; Rev. Msgr. John H. Westhues, J.C.L. (Retired); Rev. David F. Hulshof; Sr. Barbara Dingman, D.C., Min. of Care. In Res., Rev. John P. Kennehan (OG).
Res.: 533 S. Jefferson Ave., 65806. Tel: 417-831-3565; Fax: 417-865-0367.
School—531 S. Jefferson Ave., 65806. Tel: 417-866-5038; Fax: 417-866-2906. Mrs. Jeanne Skahan, Prin. Sisters 1; Lay Teachers 15; Students 266.
Catechesis/Religious Program—Ken Pesek, D.R.E.; Karen Pesek, D.R.E. Students 282.

2—ST. ELIZABETH ANN SETON (1981), [CEM] Revs. J. Fergus Monaghan; Patrick I. Nwokoye; Sr. Barbara Geers, S.S.N.D., Parish Min.
Church: 2200 W. Republic Rd., 65807. Tel: 417-887-6472; Fax: 417-887-7027.
Catechesis/Religious Program—Debbie Randell, D.R.E. Students 419.

3—HOLY TRINITY (1966), [JC] Rev. Msgr. Thomas E. Reidy, V.G. In Res., Rev. Frank C. Palermo (Retired).
Res.: 2818 E. Bennett, 65804. Tel: 417-883-3440; Fax: 417-883-0072.
Catechesis/Religious Program—Students 215.

4—IMMACULATE CONCEPTION (1868), [JC] Rev. Lewis E. Hejna; Deacon William McNamee; Margaret Ellen Buscher, S.S.N.D., Dir. In Res., Rev. Msgr. Raymond V. Orf (Retired).
Res.: 3535 S. Fremont, 65804. Tel: 417-799-0062.
Church: 3555 S. Fremont, 65804. Tel: 417-887-0600; Fax: 417-887-0027.
School—3555A S. Fremont, 65804. Tel: 417-881-7000; Fax: 417-881-7087. Mrs. Paula Baird, Prin. Lay Teachers 29; Students 578.
Catechesis/Religious Program—Mrs. Sharon Weidekman, D.R.E. Students 139.

5—ST. JOSEPH'S (1892), [JC] Rev. Denis Dougherty, O.S.B.
Res.: 1115 N. Campbell Ave., 65802. Tel: 417-865-1112; Fax: 417-865-7488.
School—515 W. Scott, 65802. Tel: 417-866-0667; Fax: 417-866-2862. Mrs. Marilyn Batson, Prin. Lay Teachers 16; Students 149.
Catechesis/Religious Program—Students 86.

6—SACRED HEART (1882), [JC] Revs. Joseph Peplansky, C.M.F.; Richard Farrell, C.M.F.; Deacon Edward Ellman.
Mailing Address: 1609 N. Summit Ave., 65803. Tel: 417-869-3646; Fax: 417-869-2218.
Villa Claret: 1530 N. Summit, 65803. Tel: 417-869-0075.
Catechesis/Religious Program—Students 144.

CITY OF CAPE GIRARDEAU
(CAPE GIRARDEAU COUNTY)

1—CATHEDRAL OF ST. MARY (1868), [CEM] [JC] Revs. Thomas P. Kiefer, J.C.L.; Scott M. Sunnenberg.
Res.: 629 William St., 63703. Tel: 573-335-9347; Fax: 573-335-0649.
School—210 S. Sprigg, 63703. Tel: 573-335-3840. Mrs. Carol Strattman, Prin. Lay Teachers 16; Students 237.
Catechesis/Religious Program—Mrs. Ellen Shuck, D.R.E. Students 18.
Old St. Vincent's— (Chapel of Ease).

2—ST. VINCENT DE PAUL (1838), Revs. Charles Prost, C.M.; Derek Swanson, C.M.; Kathy Hotop-Raines, Dir.
Res.: 741 N. Forest, 63701. Tel: 573-335-7667; Fax: 573-335-0034.
Office: 1913 Ritter Dr., 63701.
School—1919 Ritter Dr., 63701. Tel: 573-334-9594. Mrs. Nancy Heberlie, Prin. Lay Teachers 22; Students 361.
Catechesis/Religious Program—Students 134.

OUTSIDE THE CITIES OF SPRINGFIELD AND CAPE GIRARDEAU

ADVANCE, STODDARD CO., ST. JOSEPH (1905), [CEM] Rev. David J. Dohogne.
Res.: P.O. Box 640, 63730. Tel: 573-722-3504.
Catechesis/Religious Program—Students 42.

AURORA, LAWRENCE CO., HOLY TRINITY (1906), [CEM] Rev. David F. Hulshof; Sr. Jean Schmid, S.S.N.D., Parish Life Coord.
Res.: Hwy. 60 & Carnation Rd., P.O. Box 533, 65605. Tel: 417-678-2403; Fax: 417-678-3714.
Catechesis/Religious Program—Mrs. Agnes Elsey, D.R.E. Students 114.

BENTON, SCOTT CO., ST. DENIS (1840), [CEM] Rev. Normand G. Varone.
Res.: P.O. Box 127, 63736. Tel: 573-545-3864.
School—Tel: 573-545-3017; Fax: 573-545-9185. Mrs. Deborah McCann, Prin. Lay Teachers 6; Students 83.
Catechesis/Religious Program—Students 46.

BILLINGS, CHRISTIAN CO., ST. JOSEPH (1879), [CEM] Rev. Gary M. Carr.
Res.: P.O. Box 100, 65610. Tel: 417-744-2490; Fax: 417-744-2528.
Catechesis/Religious Program—Students 190.

BOLIVAR, POLK CO., SACRED HEART (1946), [CEM] Rev. J. Patrick Wissman.
Res.: 1405 W. Fair Play St., 65613. Tel: 417-326-5596; Fax: 417-326-5596.
Catechesis/Religious Program—Students 97.
Mission—St. Catherine P.O. Box 42, Humansville, Polk Co. 65674. Tel: 417-754-8825.

BRANSON, TANEY CO., OUR LADY OF THE LAKE (1951), Rev. Msgr. Philip A. Bucher, V.G.
Res.: 203 Vaughn Dr., 65616. Tel: 417-334-2928; Fax: 417-334-6883.
Catechesis/Religious Program—Mrs. Pat Hutcheson, D.R.E. Students 193.

BUFFALO, DALLAS CO., ST. WILLIAM (1946), Rev. Patrick A. Teter.
Res.: P.O. Box 518, 65622. Tel: 417-345-2744.
Catechesis/Religious Program—Students 34.

CARTHAGE, JASPER CO., ST. ANN (1872), Rev. William M. Hodgson.
Res.: 908 S. Clinton St., 64836. Tel: 417-358-1841; Fax: 417-358-1841.
School—1156 Grand, 64836. Tel: 417-358-2674; Fax: 417-358-8976. Mr. Dan Chapman, Prin. Lay Teachers 7; Students 76.
Catechesis/Religious Program—Mrs. Janet Williams, D.R.E. Students 94.

CARUTHERSVILLE, PEMISCOT CO., SACRED HEART (1900), Rev. Joseph Campbell.
Res.: 605 Ward Ave., 63830. Tel: 573-333-4301.
Catechesis/Religious Program—Students 49.

CASSVILLE, BARRY CO., ST. EDWARD, Rev. David L. Miller; Sr. Jilana Soto, M.C.M., Pastoral Assoc.
Mailing Address: 107 W. 17th St., P.O. Box 492, 65625. Tel: 417-847-4948; Fax: 417-847-4947.
Res.: 1802 Y Hwy., P.O. Box 492, 65625. Tel: 417-847-8526.
Catechesis/Religious Program—Students 54.

CHAFFEE, SCOTT CO., ST. AMBROSE (1907), [CEM] Rev. Ralph J. Duffner (Retired).
Res.: 418 S. Third St., 63740. Tel: 573-887-3953.
School—419 S. Third St., 63740. Tel: 573-887-6711; Fax: 573-887-6711. Mrs. Barbara Tyler, Prin. Lay Teachers 8; Students 106.
Catechesis/Religious Program—Students 44.

CHARLESTON, MISSISSIPPI CO., ST. HENRY (1874), Rev. Stephen A. Schneider.
Res.: 304 Court St., 63834. Tel: 573-683-2114.
School—306 Court St., 63834. Tel: 573-683-6218; Fax: 573-683-2969. Mrs. Kay Glastetter, Prin. Lay Teachers 7; Students 92.
Catechesis/Religious Program—Students 1.

CONWAY, LACLEDE CO., SACRED HEART (1908), [CEM] Rev. Patrick A. Teter.
Res.: P.O. Box 8, 65632. Tel: 417-589-6782.
Catechesis/Religious Program—Students 34.

DEXTER, STODDARD CO., SACRED HEART (1889), Rev. David J. Dohogne.
Res.: 103 E. Market St., 63841. Tel: 573-624-8888; 800-735-2466.
Church: 102 E. Castor, 63841. Tel: 573-624-7333; Fax: 578-624-4076.
Catechesis/Religious Program—Students 110.

DONIPHAN, RIPLEY CO., ST. BENEDICT (1859), [CEM] Rev. Frederick J. Lutz.
Res.: 306 Kegler, 63935. Tel: 573-996-3301.
Catechesis/Religious Program—Students 23.
Mission—St. Anne Grandin, Carter Co.

EL DORADO SPRINGS, CEDAR CO., ST. ELIZABETH (1946), [CEM] Rev. William C. Krudwig.
Res.: 609 S. Main, 64744. Tel: 417-876-3216; Fax: 417-876-6448.

Catechesis/Religious Program—Students 40.
Mission—St. Peter the Apostle 308 E. Oak St., P.O. Box 583, Stockton, Cedar Co. 65785. Tel: 417-276-5588.

FORSYTH, TANEY CO., OUR LADY OF THE OZARKS (1980), Rev. Mark C. Ernstmann, S.T.L., M.Ed.
Res.: 355 Shadowrock Dr., P.O. Box 639, 65653. Tel: 417-546-5208; Fax: 417-546-6615.

FREDERICKTOWN, MADISON CO., ST. MICHAEL (1827), [CEM] Rev. Msgr. William J. Stanton (Retired).
Res.: 304 W. Main St., 63645. Tel: 573-783-2182; Fax: 573-783-5230.
Catechesis/Religious Program—Mrs. Cynthia Belken, D.R.E. Students 82.

GLENNONVILLE, DUNKLIN CO., ST. TERESA (1905), [CEM] Rev. Glenn A. Eftink; Deacon Fred Hirtz.
Res.: 824 State Hwy. JJ, Campbell, 63933. Tel: 573-328-4544; Fax: 578-328-4544.
School—748 State Hwy. JJ, Campbell, 63933. Tel: 573-328-4197; Fax: 573-328-4197. Mrs. Janet Kuper, Prin. Lay Teachers 7; Students 79.
Catechesis/Religious Program—Students 34.

HOUSTON, TEXAS CO., ST. MARK (1975), Rev. Joseph A. Orthel, Parochial Admin.
Res.: 117 E. South Oak Crest, 65483. Tel: 417-967-3589; Fax: 417-967-3747.
Catechesis/Religious Program—Students 22.
Mission—St. Vincent de Paul Roby, Texas Co.
Mission—St. John The Baptist Licking, Texas Co.

IRONTON, IRON CO., STE. MARIE DU LAC (1878), [CEM] Revs. James J. Unterreiner; Anthony M. Gaydos, O.S.M. (CHI), Senior Priest.
Res.: 350 S. Main St., 63650. Tel: 573-546-2611; Fax: 573-546-3711.
Catechesis/Religious Program—Students 27.
Mission—Our Lady of Sorrows Lesterville, Reynolds Co.
Mission—St. Philip Benizi Viburnum, Iron Co.

JACKSON, CAPE GIRARDEAU CO., IMMACULATE CONCEPTION (1874), [CEM] Rev. Msgr. Edward M. Eftink, Ph.D.
Res.: 208 S. Hope St., Ste. 101, 63755. Tel: 573-243-3182; Fax: 573-243-6833.
School—300 S. Hope St., 63755. Tel: 573-243-5013. Mrs. Tamara Nenninger, Prin. Lay Teachers 14; Students 263.
Catechesis/Religious Program—Students 247.

JOPLIN, JASPER CO.
1—ST. MARY (1938), [JC] Rev. Justin D. Monaghan.
Res.: 2415 Moffet Ave., 64804. Tel: 417-623-3333; Fax: 417-623-4015.
School—505 W. 25th St., 64804. Tel: 417-623-1465; Fax: 417-623-4749. Mrs. Tracey Welch, Prin. Lay Teachers 18; Students 314.
Catechesis/Religious Program—Students 77.
2—ST. PETER (1877), [JC] Rev. Raymond E. O'Connor, C.M.F.
Res.: 812 S. Pearl Ave., 64801-4396. Tel: 417-623-8643; Fax: 417-623-0866.
School—802 Byers, 64801-4396. Tel: 417-624-5605; Fax: 417-624-6254. Mr. Greg Emory, Prin. Lay Teachers 12; Students 91.
Catechesis/Religious Program—Students 51.

KELSO, SCOTT CO., ST. AUGUSTINE (1878), Rev. M. Oliver Clavin.
Res.: 201 S. Messmer, Box 26, 63758. Tel: 573-264-4724; Fax: 573-264-4106.
School—230 S. Messmer, P.O. Box 97, 63758-0097. Tel: 573-264-4644; Fax: 573-264-1475. Ron Greenlee, Prin. Lay Teachers 8; Students 122.
Catechesis/Religious Program—Students 115.

KENNETT, DUNKLIN CO., ST. CECILIA (1923), Rev. Allan L. Saunders; Sisters Carol Prenger, S.S.N.D., Pastoral Assoc.; Mary Frances Reis, B.V.M., Pastoral Assoc.
Res.: College & North Bypass, P.O. Box 306, 63857. Tel: 573-888-2412; Fax: 573-888-0613.
Catechesis/Religious Program—Students 104.

KIMBERLING CITY, STONE CO., OUR LADY OF THE COVE (1979), Rev. Mark J. Binder.
Res.: 20 Kimberling Blvd., P.O. Box 548, 65686. Tel: 417-739-4700; Fax: 417-739-5279.
Catechesis/Religious Program—Marge Halbert, D.R.E. Students 138.

LAMAR, BARTON CO., ST. MARY (1904), [CEM] Rev. James L. Reynolds.
Res.: 200 E. 17th St., 64759. Tel: 417-682-2492.
Catechesis/Religious Program—Students 56.

LEBANON, LACLEDE CO., ST. FRANCIS DE SALES (1870), [CEM] Rev. Robert F. Manso.
Res.: 345 Grand St., 65536. Tel: 417-532-4811; Fax: 417-532-8847.
Catechesis/Religious Program—Students 155.
Chapel—Bennett Springs, Sportman's Chapel

LEOPOLD, BOLLINGER CO., ST. JOHN (1856), [CEM] Rev. William A. Huggins.
Res.: 103 Main St., P.O. Box 83, 63760. Tel: 573-238-3300; Fax: 573-238-2450.
Catechesis/Religious Program—Students 223.
Mission—St. Anthony [CEM] Glennon, Bollinger Co.

MALDEN, DUNKLIN CO., ST. ANN (1890), Rev. Glenn A. Eftink; Deacon Fred Hirtz.
Mailing Address: *c/o St. Teresa Parish*, 824 State Hwy. JJ, Campbell, 63933.
Church: 304 N. Douglas St., 63863.
Catechesis/Religious Program—Students 4.

MANSFIELD, WRIGHT CO., IMMACULATE HEART OF MARY (1943), Rev. Paul Wightman, O.M.I.
Res.: Rte. 6, Box 6700, Ava, 65608. Tel: 417-924-3779; 417-683-5249.
Catechesis/Religious Program—Students 31.
Mission—St. Leo the Great Rte. 6, Box 6700, Ava, Douglas Co. 65608. Tel: 417-683-5249.
Mission—St. William P.O. Box 367, Gainesville, Ozark Co. 65655. Tel: 417-679-4804; Fax: 417-679-2037. Rev. Eugene Prendeville, O.M.I. (CHI).

MARSHFIELD, WEBSTER CO., HOLY TRINITY (1892), Rev. Michael J. Casteel.
515 E. Washington, 65706-1865. Tel: 417-859-2228.
Catechesis/Religious Program—Students 113.

MONETT, BARRY CO., ST. LAWRENCE (189[illegible]), [CEM] Rev. Daniel Robles.
Res.: 405 Seventh St., 65708. Tel: 417-235-3286; Fax: 417-235-3721.
School—407 Seventh St., 65708. Tel: 417-235-3721. Rev. Gary M. Carr, Prin. Priests 1; Lay Teachers 5; Students 36.
Catechesis/Religious Program—Students 119.

MOUNT VERNON, LAWRENCE CO., ST. SUSANNE (1939), Rev. Robert A. Landewe.
Res.: P.O. Box 126, 65712. Tel: 417-466-4190.
Catechesis/Religious Program—Students 41.
Mission—St. Patrick Greenfield, Dade Co.

MOUNTAIN GROVE, WRIGHT CO., SACRED HEART (1893), Rev. Mark G. Boyer; Deacon Joseph Eurtenbach, Parish Life Coord.
Res.: 302 E. State St., 65711. Tel: 417-926-3803.
Catechesis/Religious Program—Students 18.
Mission—St. Michael Cabool, Texas Co.

MOUNTAIN VIEW, HOWELL CO., ST. JOHN VIANNEY (1951), Rev. Ernest J. Marquart.
Res.: 808 State Rd. Y, P.O. Box 38, 65548. Tel: 417-934-2649.
Catechesis/Religious Program—Students 18.
Mission—St. Sylvester Eminence, Shannon Co.

NEOSHO, NEWTON CO., ST. CANERA (1871), [JC] Revs. John S. Braun; Marek B. Bozek; Sisters Guadelupe Carillo, M.R.F., Pastoral Assoc.; Anabell Carmona, M.R.F., Pastoral Assoc.
Res.: 504 S. Washington St., 64850. Tel: 417-451-3411; 417-451-3432.
Catechesis/Religious Program—Students 84.
Mission—Nativity of Our Lord P.O. Box 555, Noel, McDonald Co. 64854.

NEW HAMBURG, SCOTT CO., ST. LAWRENCE (1847), [CEM] Rev. Normand G. Varone.
Res.: 1017 State Hwy. A, Benton, 63736. Tel: 573-545-3317; Fax: 573-545-9185.
Catechesis/Religious Program—Students 115.

NEW MADRID, NEW MADRID CO., IMMACULATE CONCEPTION (1789), Rev. Randolph G. Tochtrop.
Res.: 605 Davis St., 63869. Tel: 573-748-5183.
School—560 Powell, 63869. Tel: 573-748-5123; Fax: 573-748-5123. Mrs. Sara Ramsey, Prin. Lay Teachers 5; Students 48.
Catechesis/Religious Program—Students 12.

ORAN, SCOTT CO., GUARDIAN ANGEL (1892), [CEM 2] Rev. John M. Harth.
Res.: 604 Church St., P.O. Box 158, 63771. Tel: 573-262-3210; Fax: 573-262-3583.
School—514 Church St., 63771. Tel: 573-262-3583. Mrs. Michelle Huffman, Prin. Lay Teachers 7; Students 107.
Catechesis/Religious Program—Students 34.

OZARK, CHRISTIAN CO., ST. JOSEPH THE WORKER (1961), Rev. Paul J. McLoughlin; Deacon Mike Steele.
Res.: 1796 N. State Hwy. NN, 65721. Tel: 417-581-6323; Fax: 417-581-4957.
Catechesis/Religious Program—Students 233.

PIEDMONT, WAYNE CO., ST. CATHERINE OF SIENA (1873), Rev. Matthew J. Rehrauer; Sr. Mary Sheila Higdon, O.S.U., Pastoral Assoc.
Res.: 109 Piedmont Ave., 63957. Tel: 573-223-4924.
Catechesis/Religious Program—Students 62.
Mission—St. George Van Buren Carter Co. Tel: 573-323-8576.
Mission—Our Lady of Sorrows Williamsville, Wayne Co.

PIERCE CITY, LAWRENCE CO., ST. MARY (1883), [CEM 2] Rev. Peter J. Morciniec.
Res.: 200 Front St., 65723. Tel: 417-476-2827; Fax: 417-476-2824.
School—202 Front St., 65723. Tel: 417-476-2824. Mrs. Catherine Birkenbach, Prin. Lay Teachers 5; Students 54.
Catechesis/Religious Program—Mellanie Carter, D.R.E. Students 67.

POPLAR BLUFF, BUTLER CO., SACRED HEART (1891), [CEM] Rev. Msgr. Michael F. Svalina, S.T.D.; Rev. Gefford C. Lamprea.
Res.: 123 N. Eighth St., 63901. Tel: 573-785-9635; Fax: 573-785-2069.
School—Tel: 573-785-5836; Fax: 573-785-3908. Ms. Gloria Wilson, Prin. Sisters 1; Lay Teachers 10; Students 211.
Catechesis/Religious Program—Students 78.
Station—V.A. Hospital

PORTAGEVILLE, NEW MADRID CO., ST. EUSTACHIUS (1902), Rev. Allan L. Saunders.
Res.: 200 W. Fourth St., 63873. Tel: 573-379-3401.
School—214 W. Fourth St., 63873. Tel: 573-379-3525; Fax: 573-379-3843. Mrs. Sue Ellen Flynn, Prin. Sisters 2; Lay Teachers 5; Students 74.
Catechesis/Religious Program—Students 13.

PULASKIFIELD, BARRY CO., SS. PETER AND PAUL (1892), [CEM] Rev. Daniel Robles.
Res.: P.O. Drawer L, Pierce City, 65723. Tel: 417-476-2463.
Catechesis/Religious Program—Students 24.

SALEM, DENT CO., SACRED HEART (1880), Rev. Daniel J. Hirtz.
Res.: 602 W. Butler, 65560. Tel: 573-729-4291; Fax: 573-729-3811.
Catechesis/Religious Program—Students 73.
Mission—Christ the King P.O. Box 177, Bunker, Reynolds Co. 63629.
Chapel—Montauk, St. Jude

SARCOXIE, NEWTON CO., ST. AGNES (1870), [CEM] Rev. Peter J. Morciniec.
Res.: P.O. Box 218, Pierce City, 65723-0218. Tel: 417-548-3540.
Catechesis/Religious Program—Jane Kutz, D.R.E. Students 22.

SCOTT CITY, SCOTT CO., ST. JOSEPH (1911), [CEM] Rev. David N. Coon.
Res.: 604 Sycamore, 63780. Tel: 573-264-4500; Fax: 573-264-1506.
School—606 Sycamore, 63780. Tel: 573-264-2600; Fax: 573-264-1325. Mrs. Elaine Blair, Prin. Lay Teachers 5; Students 74.
Catechesis/Religious Program—Students 33.

SENECA, NEWTON CO., ST. MARY (1884), [CEM] Revs. John S. Braun; Marek B Bozek.
Res.: P.O. Box 1169, 64865. Tel: 417-776-3786.
Catechesis/Religious Program—Students 32.

SHELL KNOB, BARRY CO., HOLY FAMILY (1978), Rev. David L. Miller.
Res.: Lake Rd. 39-30, P.O. Box 229, 65747. Tel: 417-858-2518; Fax: 417-847-4947.
Catechesis/Religious Program—Students 15.

SIKESTON, SCOTT CO., ST. FRANCIS XAVIER'S (1893), Rev. Stephen A. Schneider; Rev. Msgr. Richard C. Rolwing, V.G. (Retired).
Res.: 217 W. Center St., 63801. Tel: 573-471-2447; Fax: 573-471-9820.
School—106 N. Stoddard, 63801. Tel: 573-471-0841. Mr. Michael Eftink, Prin. Lay Teachers 11; Students 165.
Catechesis/Religious Program—Mrs. Toni Grojean, D.R.E. Students 52.

VERONA, LAWRENCE CO., SACRED HEART (1874), [CEM] Rev. David F. Hulshof; Sr. Jean Schmid, S.S.N.D., Parish Life Coord.
Mailing Address: P.O. Box 533, Aurora, 65605.
Church: Adams & Second St., Aurora, 65605. Tel: 417-678-2403; Fax: 417-678-3714.
Catechesis/Religious Program—Sr. Francis Rose Rivers, S.S.N.D., D.R.E. Students 63.

WEBB CITY, JASPER CO., SACRED HEART (1908), Revs. Joseph Than Van Liem, C.M.C.; Timothy Mai Vinh Loc, C.M.C.
Res.: 909 N. Madison, 64870. Tel: 417-673-2044; Fax: 417-673-1944.
Catechesis/Religious Program—Students 143.

WEST PLAINS, HOWELL CO., ST. MARY (1902), Rev. John A. Brath.
Res.: 965 S. Thayer Ave., 65775. Tel: 417-256-2556; Fax: 417-256-9251.
Catechesis/Religious Program—Students 76.
Mission—Sacred Heart Thayer, Oregon Co.

WILLOW SPRINGS, HOWELL CO., SACRED HEART (1897), [CEM] Rev. Sherman B. Wall, O.M.I.
Church: 1050 W. Bus Hwy. 60-63, 65793. Tel: 417-469-2447.
Catechesis/Religious Program—Students 29.
Mission—St. Joseph White Church, Howell Co.

Chaplains of Public Institutions

SPRINGFIELD. *Diocesan Hospital Ministry*, Tel: 417-866-0841.
St. John's Regional Health Center, Tel: 417-820-2735. Rev. John P. Kennehan.
U.S. Medical Center, 1900 W. Sunshine, 65802. Tel: 417-862-7041, Ext. 255.

CHARLESTON. *Southeast Correctional Center*, Tel: 573-748-5183. Rev. Randolph G. Tochtrop, Pastoral Min.

FORDLAND. *Ozark Correctional Center*, Tel: 417-589-6782. Rev. Patrick A. Teter.

JOPLIN. *Joplin Hospital Ministry*, Tel: 417-781-2727. (Vacant)

LICKING. *South Central Correctional Center*, Tel: 573-729-4291. Rev. Daniel J. Hirtz. Tel: 417-967-3589.

POPLAR BLUFF. *Poplar Bluff Hospital Ministry*. Rev. Msgr. Michael F. Swalina, S.T.D. Tel: 573-785-9635.

Special Assignment:
Revs.—
Bertrand, Vincent E., J.C.L., Tribunal Office, 601 S. Jefferson Ave., 65806. Tel: 417-866-0841
Boyer, Mark G., 1140 E. Stanford, 65807. Tel: 417-887-4811
Hulshof, David F., Vocation Dir., 601 S. Jefferson Ave., 65806. Tel: 417-866-0841 (Office)

Military Chaplains:
Rev.—
Wilk, Mitchell S., Major, U.S. Army Chap., Office of the Chaplain, CMR 414, Box 0999, Apo, AE 09173. Tel: 011-49-1702634341

Leave of Absence:
Revs.—
Jones, Rick L., 700 Eubank Blvd. SE Apt. 1025, Albuquerque, NM 87123. Tel: 505-292-0872
Sheley, John, 1624 Hough Park Rd., Jefferson City, 65101. Tel: 800-735-2466 ask calling assistant for VCO call to 573-635-2679
Zatina, Gregory E.J., 686 Tam O'Shanter Dr., Las Vegas, NV 89119. Tel: 702-734-0949

Retired:
Rev. Msgrs.—
Gosche, Joseph E., Saxon Manor L.H. R.C.E. Rm. 12A 2825 Bloomfield Rd., 63701. Tel: 573-335-0158
Orf, Raymond V., 3535 S. Fremont, 65804. Tel: 417-887-0600; 417-799-0062
Rolwing, Richard C., V.G., 217 W. Center St., Sikeston, 63801-4111. Tel: 573-471-5018
Stanton, William J., 358 Etherton Dr., 36703-7576. Tel: 573-651-6465
Westhues, John H., J.C.L., 533 S. Jefferson Ave., 65806-3198. Tel: 417-831-3565; 417-863-7287
Revs.—
Bauer, Sylvester W., Rte. 1, P.O. Box 24B, Freeburg, 65035. Tel: 573-744-5913
Biernacki, Jacob S., 620 W. Scott St., 65802. Tel: 417-869-5417
Duffner, Ralph J., 383 Etherton Dr., 63703. Tel: 573-332-8951
Edwards, Byron H., 35 Air Rd., P.O. Box 422, Higden, AR 72067. Tel: 501-825-8085
Harter, Benedict W., St. John's Medical Center, 2032 Zora Ave., Apt. 118, Joplin, 64801. Tel: 417-624-1594
Palermo, Frank C., 2818 E. Bennett, 65804-1943. Tel: 417-883-3440
Schumacher, Robert A., 2825 Bloomfield Road Room 309, 63703. Tel: 573-335-0158
Seyer, James A., 150 S. Silver Springs Rd., #4, 63703. Tel: 573-651-3939

Permanent Deacons:
Brewer, Thomas, 1850 E. Canterbury, 65804. Tel: 417-881-4450
Costello, Charles R., 3660 S. Cox Road #201, 65807-5920. Tel: 417-889-9497
Ellman, Edward V., 398 N. Harmon Ave., Republic, 65738. Tel: 417-732-5511
Hirtz, Fred, 2208 CR 207, Campbell, 63933-9706. Tel: 573-328-1388
Kurtenbach, Joseph, Rte. 6, Box 6754, Ava, 65608. Tel: 417-683-6298
McNamee, William, 780 Brook Forest, Nixa, 65714. Tel: 417-724-9705
Steele, Mike, 3325 S. Winton Pl., 65804-6415. Tel: 417-890-4629
Vrooman, David, 1006 S. Jackson St., Kennett, 63857. Tel: 573-888-5607

INSTITUTIONS LOCATED IN THE DIOCESE

[A] SEMINARIES, RELIGIOUS, OR SCHOLASTICATES

AVA. *Assumption Novitiate (Trappists)*, Mailing Address: Rte. 5, Box 1056, 65608. Tel: 417-683-5110; Fax: 417-683-5658. Email: assumptionabbey@usa.net. Revs. Mark A. Scott, O.C.S.O., Abbot; Robert Matter, O.C.S.O., Abbot Emeritus; Cyprian Harrison, O.C.S.O., Abbot Emeritus.

CARTHAGE. *Congregation of the Mother Co-Redemptrix*, 1900 Grand Ave., 64836. Tel: 417-358-7787; Fax: 417-358-9508. Email: cmc@dongcong.net. Web: www.dongcong.net. Very Rev. Francis Xavier M. Do Cao Tung, C.M.C., Prov. Supr.

[B] HIGH SCHOOLS, DIOCESAN

SPRINGFIELD. *Springfield Catholic High School* (Coed), 2340 S. Eastgate, 65809-2832. Tel: 417-887-8817; Fax: 417-885-1165. Email: derayton@springfieldcatholicschools.org. Web: www.springfieldcatholicschools.org. Mr. Dean O. Crayton, Prin. Lay Teachers 30; Students 326.

Springfield Catholic School System, 3520 S. Culpepper Cir., Ste C, 65804-4206. Tel: 417-865-5567; Fax: 417-865-5278. Email: scscentraloffice@springfieldcatholicschools.org. Web: www.springfieldcatholicschools.org.

CAPE GIRARDEAU. *Notre Dame Regional High School*, 265 Notre Dame Dr., 63701-8517. Tel: 573-335-6772; Fax: 573-335-3458. Email: principal@notredamehighschool.org. Web: www.notredamehighschool.org. Bro. David Anthony Migliorino, O.S.F., Prin. Co-Instructional Regional High School Brothers 1; Lay Teachers 35; Students 476.

JOPLIN. *St. Mary*, (Grades PreK-5), 505 W. 25th St., 64804. Tel: 417-623-1465; Fax: 417-623-4749. Email: stmarys505@sbcglobal.net. Web: http://users.joplin.com/jacs. Mrs. Tracey Welch, Prin. Lay Teachers 18; Students 314.

McAuley Regional High School, 930 Pearl Ave., 64801. Tel: 417-624-9320; Fax: 417-626-8334. Email: gkoester@jacss.org. Web: http://users.joplin.com/jacs. Mr. Gene Koster, Prin. Lay Teachers 15; Students 155.

St. Peter's Junior High School, (Grades 6-8), 802 Byers, 64801. Tel: 417-624-5605; Fax: 417-624-6254. Email: gregemory@sbcglobal.net. Web: http://users.joplin.com/jacs. Mr. Greg Emory, Prin. Lay Teachers 12; Students 91.

[C] GENERAL HOSPITALS

SPRINGFIELD. *St. John's Regional Health Center*, 1235 E. Cherokee, 65804. Tel: 417-820-2000; Fax: 417-820-6960. Web: www.stjohns.com. Mr. Jay W. Eckersley, Pres. & CEO. Sisters of Mercy Health System (St. Louis), Member of St. John's Health System, Inc. Sisters 3; Bed Capacity 866; Inpatients 32,369; Outpatients 409,654.

CAPE GIRARDEAU. **Saint Francis Medical Center*, 211 St. Francis Dr., 63703-8399. Tel: 573-331-5128. Email: sfmc@showme.net. Web: www.sfmc.net. Mr. Steven C. Bjelich, FACHE, Pres. & CEO; Rev. John Cantore, C.M., Chap. Owned and operated by a lay board with Diocesan sponsorship. Sisters 2; Bed Capacity 249; Inpatients 9,511; Outpatients 156,970.

Saint Francis Foundation, 211 St. Francis Dr., 63703.

Saint Francis Healthcare System (formerly known as St. Francis Hospital of Franciscan Sisters), 211 St. Francis Dr., 63703.

AURORA. *St. John's Aurora, Inc.*, Formerly St. John's Aurora, 500 Porter Ave., 65605. Tel: 417-678-2122; Fax: 417-678-7877. Email: fourdbs@aol.com. Don Buchanan, Admin. Bed Capacity 53.

CASSVILLE. *St. John's Cassville, Inc.*, 94 S. Main St., 65625. Tel: 417-847-6000; Fax: 417-847-6047. Email: sbcd@mo-net.com. Web: www.southbarrycountyhospital.com. Debbie Stubbs, Pres. Bed Capacity 18; Inpatients 442; Outpatients 28,961.

JOPLIN. *St. John's Regional Medical Center; Mercy Lifecare Systems, Inc.* Affiliates of Catholic Health Initiatives. , 2727 McClelland Blvd., 64804-1694. Tel: 417-781-2727; Fax: 417-625-2910. Email: growe@stj.com. Web: www.stj.com. Mr. Gary L. Rowe, Pres.; Rev. Benedict W. Harter, Chap. (Retired). Sisters of Mercy (Omaha) Sisters 6; Bed Capacity 367; Inpatients 15,816; Outpatients 167,394.

Mercy Regional Health Foundation, Inc., 2727 McClelland Blvd., 64804.

MOUNTAIN VIEW. *St. Francis Hospital*, P.O. Box 82, 65548. Tel: 417-934-7000; Fax: 417-934-7089. Email: gjordan@sprg.mercy.net. Web: http://members.socket.net/~stfran. Gary W. Jordan, Pres. Daughters of St. Francis of Assisi and Sisters of Mercy (Managed by St. John's Health System) Sisters 6; Bed Capacity 42; Inpatients 562; Outpatients 22,257.

The Sister Cornelia Blasko Foundation, Inc., 100 W. Hwy. 60, P.O. Box 82, 65548. Tel: 417-934-7090.

[D] SPECIAL HOSPITALS

SPRINGFIELD. *St. John's Mercy Villa*, 1100 E. Montclair, 65807. Tel: 417-820-8500; Fax: 417-820-8532. Mr. Don Swafford, Admin. Sisters of Mercy Healthcare System (St. Louis), Skilled Care of Long Term Nursing Home, for the Aged and Chronically Ill. Bed Capacity 150.

[E] MONASTERIES AND RESIDENCES OF PRIESTS AND BROTHERS

SPRINGFIELD. *Claretians Missionaries' Residence-Villa Claret*, 1530 N. Summit, 65803. Tel: 417-869-0075. Revs. Anselm Amendikwa, C.M.F.; Eddie DeLeon, C.M.F.; Joseph Peplansky, C.M.F.; Richard Farrell, C.M.

Congregation of Mother Coredemptrix, Our Lady of the Rosary House, 418 S. Kimbrough, 65806. Tel: 417-869-3822. Email: cmcspringfield@hotmail.com. Rev. Francis M. Luong Minh Tuat, C.M.C., Min.; Bros. Justin M. Nguyen Tri Ky, C.M.C.; John M. Nguyen Hung Dao, C.M.C.; Dominic M. Vu Van Hao, C.M.C.; Josaphat M. Tran Tuan Trinh, C.M.C.; John Vu Manh Thong, C.M.C. Priests 1; Brothers 5.

AVA. *Assumption Abbey (Trappist)*, Rte. 5, Box 1056, 65608. Tel: 417-683-5110; Fax: 417-683-5658. Email: assumptionabbey@usa.net. Web: www.assumptionabbey.org. Rev. Mark A. Scott, O.C.S.O., Abbot; Rt. Rev. Robert Matter, O.C.S.O., Abbot Emeritus; Revs. Cyprian Harrison, O.C.S.O., Abbot Emeritus; Leon Brockman, O.C.S.O.; Richard Fox, O.C.S.O.; Donald Joseph Hamilton, O.C.S.O.; Alberic Maisog, O.C.S.O.; Anthony Menz, O.C.S.O., (Manhattan, KS); Anthony Sloan, O.C.S.O.; Bros. Boniface Domas, O.C.S.O.; Thomas Imhoff, O.C.S.O.; Dominic Pitagora, O.C.S.O.; Fidel Manuel, O.C.S.O.; Tobias Shanahan, O.C.S.O.; Simin Preap, O.C.S.O. Priests 6; Brothers 6.

CARTHAGE. *Congregation of the Mother Coredemptrix, United States Assumption Province*, 1900 Grand Ave., 64836. Tel: 417-358-7787; Fax: 417-358-9508. Email: cmc@dongcong.net. Web: www.dongcong.com. Very Rev. Francis Xavier M. Do Cao Tung, C.M.C., Prov.; Revs. Felix M. Dinh Viet Luan, C.M.C., Asst. I; Anselm M. Dinh Vuong Can, C.M.C., Asst. II; John D.M. Ngo Duc Vuong, C.M.C., Treas.; John Eudes M. Cao Tien Vu, C.M.C., Sec.; Paul M. Nguyen Mang Cach, C.M.C.; Raymond M. Nguyen Chau Dien, C.M.C.; Bartholomew M. Pham An Su, C.M.C.; Vincent de Paul M. Au Quoc Thanh, C.M.C.; Francis M. Vu Van Vinh, C.M.C.; Athanasius M. Bui Anh Tuan, C.M.C.; Joseph M. Tran Ngoc Diep, C.M.C.; Raymond M. Nguyen Manh Thu, C.M.C.; Bartholomew Pham Minh Van, C.M.C.; Mark M. Doan Quang Bau, C.M.C.; Isidore M. Dinh Thanh Bac, C.M.C., Asst. III; Michael Do Quang Chinh, C.M.C. (BO); James M. Vu Dai Luong, C.M.C.; Camillus M. Nguyen Duc Tuan, C.M.C.; Bernadine M. Dang Minh Tan, C.M.C.; Vincent de Paul M. Au Quoc Thanh, C.M.C.; Philip M. Tran Binh, C.M.C.; Simon M. Le Phuc Diem, C.M.C.; Albert M. Pham Kim Ban, C.M.C.; Ephrem M. Vu Khiem Cung, C.M.C.; Peter M. Ngo Chau Minh, C.M.C.; Bros. John Vianney M. Do Thanh Nhan, C.M.C.; Henry M. Nguyen Minh Han, C.M.C.; Anthony M. Nguyen Gia Huu, C.M.C.; Pius V M. Nguyen Trung Thu, C.M.C.; Thomas More M. Nguyen Long Truong, C.M.C.; Bede M. Nguyen Quang Tuyen, C.M.C.; Mathew M. Pham Ngoc Thach, C.M.C.; Joseph C.M. Pham Cong Tho, C.M.C.; Stephen Tran Minh Giac, C.M.C.; Bernardine M. Tran Hien Si, C.M.C.; John Tran Trung Thanh, C.M.C.; Thomas M. Trinh Van Chi, C.M.C.; Anthony M. Vu Dinh Huan, C.M.C.; Matthew Vu Duc Kim, C.M.C.; Alphonsus M. Vu Toan Tri, C.M.C.; Cyprian M. Nguyen Van Hien, C.M.C.; Joachim M. Nguyen Khoa Cu, C.M.C.; John B.M. Nguyen Duc Hien, C.M.C.; Anthony M. Le Dat Chuan, C.M.C.; John M. Pham Lan Ai, C.M.C.; John M. Do Hoan Anh, C.M.C.; Michael M. Dao Trung Dan, C.M.C.; Thomas M. Nguyen Juan Binh, C.M.C.; Mark M. Letien Hoa, C.M.C.; Peter Chrysologus M. Dinh Tuyen Vien, C.M.C.; Phillip M. Do Thanh Cao, C.M.C.; Bonaventure M. Nguyen Tuan Bao, C.M.C.; Raphael M. Pham Vu Tuan Tu, C.M.C.; Dominic M. Nguyen Trung Chanh, C.M.C.; Simon M. Nguyen Hieu Tu, C.M.C.; Hilary M. Tran Ha Nhuan, C.M.C.; Deacons Andrew M. Nguyen Tuan Nha, C.M.C.; Dominic M. Nguyen Hoan Luong, C.M.C.; Luke M. Vu Thien My, C.M.C.; Bros. Pius M. Nguyen Hoa Dong, C.M.C.; Stephen M. Lam Tuan Vu, C.M.C.; John M. Bui Quang Trieu, C.M.C.; Titus M. Nguyen Si Hanh, C.M.C.; Ignatius Loyola M. Tran Thanh Tien, C.M.C.; Ambrose M. Nguyen Tam Niem, C.M.C.; Patrick M. Nguyen Ngoc Quang, C.M.C.; Maximilian M. Vu Ngoc Ba, C.M.C.; Paul M. Tran An Dinh, C.M.C.; Aloysius M. Nguyen An Khang, C.M.C.; Lawrence M. Nguyen Chau Hy, C.M.C.; Timothy M. Tran Viet Thang, C.M.C.; Boniface M. Ngo Ang Triet, C.M.C.; Norbert M. Truong Thinh Dat, C.M.C.; Leo M. Do Quy Hien, C.M.C.; Alphonse M. Do Van Kiet, C.M.C.; Irenaeus M. Vu Hai Nam,

C.M.C.; Francis M. Pham Thuan Tu, C.M.C.; Barnabus M. Pham Hieu Tam, C.M.C. Priests 27; Brothers 53; Novices 1; Postulants 12; Candidates 29.

Mater Dei Building, 1900 Grand Ave., 64836. Tel: 417-358-7787; Fax: 417-358-9508. (Home for retired priests) In Res. Revs. Joseph Cao Phuong Ky, S.S.; Joseph Dinh Tuan Ngan; James Do Ba Cong; Dominic Mai Minh Luan; Joseph To Ngoc Lien; John M. Phan Cong Binh; Peter Tran Dien; James Thuc Van Truong, O.S.B.

MARIONVILLE. *The Society of Our Mother of Peace, Sons of Our Mother of Peace*, Queen of Heaven Solitude, 12494 Hwy. T, 65705. Tel: 417-744-2011. Rev. Placid Guste, S.M.P., Supr.

Legal Title: *The Society of Our Mother of Peace, Sons of Our Mother of Peace - Queen of Heaven Solitude*

[F] CONVENTS AND RESIDENCES FOR SISTERS

SPRINGFIELD. *St. Anne Monastery*, 424 E. Monastery St., 65807-6099. Tel: 417-881-2115; Fax: 417-881-2115. Email: ozarkcarmel@juno.com. Sr. Mary Gemma Guanci, O.C.D., Prioress. Discalced Carmelite Nuns 4.

Congregation of Mary Queen, 625 S. Jefferson Ave., 65806. Tel: 417-869-9842; Fax: 417-832-0852. Email: trinhvuong2@yahoo.com. Web: www.trinhvuong.org. Sr. Irene Dinh, C.M.R., Regl. Supr. Sisters 7.

Sisters of Mercy of the Americas (St. Louis) , 1330 E. Cherokee, 65804. Tel: 417-882-1297; Fax: 417-885-6960. Sisters 3.

AVA. *Nazareth Hermitage*, Rte. 5, Box 1122, 65608. Sisters 4.

MARIONVILLE. *The Society of Our Mother of Peace, Daughters of Our Mother of Peace*, 12494 Hwy. T, 65705. Tel: 417-744-2011.

Legal Title: *The Society of Our Mother of Peace, Daughters of Our Mother of Peace, Queen of Heaven Solitude* Sisters 7.

PILOT KNOB. *Our Lady of the Valley Community*, 320 S. McCune St. Box 545, 63663-0545. Tel: 573-546-7229. Franciscan Sisters of Mary Sisters 2.

REPUBLIC. *Little Portion Franciscans*, 645 Assisi Way, 65738. Tel: 417-732-6684. Email: lportion@juno.com. Sisters 3.

[G] RETREAT HOUSES

AVA. *Assumption Abbey* (Trappist) , Rte. 5, Box 1056, 65608. Tel: 417-683-5110; Fax: 417-683-5658. Email: assumptionabbey@usa.net. Web: www.assumptionabbey.org. Rev. Mark A. Scott, O.C.S.O.

MARIONVILLE. *The Society of Our Mother of Peace, Daughters of Our Mother of Peace*, 12494 Hwy. T, 65705. Tel: 417-744-2011. Sr. Mary Emmanuel GrenFell, S.M.P., Dir.

Legal Title: *The Society of Our Mother of Peace, Daughters of Our Mother of Peace, Queen of Heaven Solitude*

REPUBLIC. *Little Portion Retreat Center*, 645 S. Assisi Way, 65738. Tel: 417-732-6684. Email: lportion@juno.com. Web: www.littleportionretreat.org. Sr. Lorraine Biebel, O.S.F., Coord.

[H] SHRINES

CARTHAGE. *Shrine of Immaculate Heart of Mary* 1900 Grand Ave., 64836. Tel: 417-358-8580; Fax: 417-358-3954. Email: khiettam@cox-internet.com. Very Rt. Rev. Francis Xavier M. Do Cao Tuna, C.M.C., Prov.

[I] NEWMAN CENTERS

SPRINGFIELD. *O'Reilly Catholic Student Center, Southwest MO State University, Drury College, Ozarks Technical Com* Catholic Campus Ministry, 847 S. Holland, 65806-3513. Tel: 417-865-0802; Fax: 417-865-0895. Web: www.ccm847.org. Revs. Eddie DeLeon, C.M.F., Dir.; Anselm Amandikwa, C.M.F., Chap.

CAPE GIRARDEAU. *Southeast Missouri State University, Newman Center* 512 N. Pacific, 63701-4712. Tel: 573-335-3899; Fax: 573-334-0088. Email: catholic@semo.edu. Web: www5.semo.edu/ccm. Rev. John J. Freidel, Chap. & Dir.

BRANSON. *Catholic Christian Newman Association* , (College of the Ozarks) , 203 Vaughn Dr., 65616. Tel: 417-334-2928; Fax: 417-334-6882. Email: LadyLakebr@aol.com. Web: www.LadyoftheLakeparish.org. Lynn Melendez, Campus Min.

JOPLIN. *Newman Club, Missouri Southern State College* 812 S. Pearl Ave., 64801-4336. Tel: 417-623-8643. Rev. Raymond O'Connor, C.M.F., Chap.

[J] MISCELLANEOUS

SPRINGFIELD. *St. John's Health System, Inc.*, 1235 E. Cherokee 65804. Tel: 417-885-2845.

**St. John's Physicians & Clinics, Inc.*, 1965 S. Fremont St., Ste. 2950, 65804. Tel: 417-820-2849.

St. John's Regional Health Center (subsidiary of St. John's Health System, Inc.) , 1235 East Cherokee, 65804. Tel: 417-820-2000; Fax: 417-820 6960. Web: www.stjohns.com. Mr. Jay W. Eckersley, Pres. & CEO. Sisters of Mercy Health System (St. Louis) Sisters 5; Bed Capacity 866; Inpatients 32,369; Outpatients 409,654.

St. John's Regional Medicine of the Ozarks, Inc., 1965 S. Fremont St., Ste. 2900, 65804. Tel: 417-885-2211.

The Kitchen, 1630 N. Jefferson, 65803. Tel: 417-837-1500; Fax: 417-831-6709. Email: info@kitcheninc.org. Web: www.thekitcherinc.org. Mr. Tobias Meeker, CEO.

The Kitchen Foundation, 1630 N. Jefferson, 65803.

**McAuley Counseling Services, Inc.*, 2200 E. Sunshine, Ste. 334, 65804. Tel: 417-823-0498. Sr. Ann Crouse, R.S.M., M.A., Dir.

Queen of Angels Day Care Center, 625 S. Jefferson, 65806. Tel: 417-869-9842; Fax: 417-832-0852. Email: cmrangels@hotmail.com. Web: www.trinhvuong.org.

CARTHAGE. *Office of the Immaculate Heart of Mary Shrine*, 1749 Grand Ave., 64836. Tel: 417-358-8580; Fax: 417-358-3954.

ELLINGTON. **Whole Health Outreach*, Rte. 4, Box 4398, 63638-9302. Tel: 573-663-7757; Fax: 573-663-2915. Email: who@semo.net. Sr. Rita Marie Schorhoff, Coord.

**Whole Kids Outreach, Inc.*, Rte. 2, Box 301-X, 63638. Tel: 573-663-3257; Fax: 573-663-2933. Email: wko@mcmo.net. Sr. Anne Francioni, S.S.N.D., Exec. Dir.

JOPLIN. *Mercy Village Joplin, Inc.*, c/o St. John's Administration Office, 2727 McClelland Blvd., 64804-1694. Tel: 417-625-2209.

RELIGIOUS INSTITUTES OF MEN REPRESENTED IN THE DIOCESE

For further details refer to the corresponding bracketed number in the Religious Institutes of Men or Women section.

[1330]—*Congregation of the Missions (Vincentians)*—C.M.

[0865]—*Congregation of the Mother Coredemptrix*—C.M.C.

[0360]—*Missionary Sons of the Immaculate Heart of Mary (Claretians)*—C.M.F.

[0910]—*Oblates of Mary Immaculate (Oblates)* (Central Prov.)—O.M.I.

[0350]—*Order of Cistercians of the Strict Observance (Trappist)*—O.C.S.O.

[0200]—*Order of St. Benedict (Benedictines)*—O.S.B.

[1240]—*Order of the Servants of Mary (Servites)* (Chicago Prov.)—O.S.M.

[0515]—*Religious Brothers of the Third Order Regular of St. Francis (Generalate, St. Francis Monastery, Bro*—O.S.F.

[]—*The Society of Our Mother of Peace*—S.M.P.

[1290]—*Society of the Priests of Saint Sulpice*—S.S.

RELIGIOUS INSTITUTES OF WOMEN REPRESENTED IN THE DIOCESE

[0100]—*Adorers of the Blood of Christ* (Ruma)—A.S.C.

[0230]—*Benedictine Sisters of the Pontifical Jurisdiction* (Columbia)—O.S.B.

[0230]—*Benedictine Sisters of the Pontifical Jurisdiction* (Eau Claire, WI)—O.S.B.

[0397]—*Congregation of Mary, Queen*—C.M.R.

[0460]—*Congregation of the Sisters of Charity of the Incarnate Word* (San Antonio)—C.C.V.I.

[0725]—*Cordi-Marian Missionary Sisters Congregation*—M.C.M.

[0760]—*Daughters of Charity of St. Vincent de Paul* (St. Louis)—D.C.

[0920]—*Daughters of St. Francis of Assisi* (Lacon, Illinois)—D.S.F.

[0420]—*Discalced Carmelite Nuns*—O.C.D.

[1415]—*Franciscan Sisters of Mary*—F.S.M.

[1240]—*Franciscan Sisters, Daughters of the Sacred Hearts of Jesus and Mary* (Wheaton)—O.S.F.

[]—*Little Portion Franciscans*—O.S.F.

[]—*Missionary Sisters of the Rosary of Fatima*—M.R.F.

[]—*Nazareth Hermitage*

[2970]—*School Sisters of Notre Dame* (St. Louis)—S.S.N.D.

[0430]—*Sisters of Charity of the Blessed Virgin Mary* (Dubuque)—B.V.M.

[2360]—*Sisters of Loretto at the Foot of the Cross*—S.L.

[2575]—*Sisters of Mercy of the Americas* (Dallas, PA Region)—R.S.M.

[2575]—*Sisters of Mercy of the Americas* (Omaha, NE Region)—R.S.M.

[2575]—*Sisters of Mercy of the Americas* (St. Louis, MO Region)—R.S.M.

[1570]—*Sisters of St. Francis of the Holy Family* (Dubuque)—O.S.F.

[3840]—*Sisters of St. Joseph of Carondelet* (St. Louis)—C.S.J.

[3830]—*Sisters of St. Joseph of LaGrange, IL*—C.S.J.

[3320]—*Sisters of the Presentation of the B.V.M.* (Fargo)—P.B.V.M.

[1720]—*Sisters of the Third Order Regular of St. Francis of Our Lady of Lourdes* (Rochester, MN)—O.S.F.

[]—*The Society of Our Mother of Peace*—S.M.P.

[4120]—*Ursuline Nuns of the Congregation of Paris* (Owensboro, Kentucky)—O.S.U.

[4110]—*Ursuline Nuns (Roman Union)* (Crystal City, MO)—O.S.U.

[4160]—*Vincentian Sisters of Charity* (Pittsburgh, PA)—V.S.C.

NECROLOGY

† Boeding, Damian G., (Retired)—Died Sept. 29, 2003

† Eschbacher, Jerome J.—Died April 3, 2003

† Leveillee, Rev. Roger L., Neosho, MO St. Canera—Died May 6, 2003

Diocese of Springfield in Illinois

(Dioecesis Campifontis in Illinois)

Most Reverend

GEORGE J. LUCAS, D.D.

Bishop of Springfield in Illinois; ordained May 24, 1975; appointed Bishop of Springfield in Illinois October 19, 1999; ordained and installed December 14, 1999 *Res.: P.O. Box 1667, Springfield, IL 62705-1667. Office: Catholic Pastoral Center,* 1615 W. Washington St., P.O. Box 3187, Springfield, IL 62708-3187. Tel: 217-698-8500; Fax: 217-698-0802.

Most Reverend

DANIEL L. RYAN

Retired Bishop of Springfield in Illinois; ordained May 3, 1956; ordained Titular Bishop of Surista in Mauritania and auxiliary to the Bishop of Joliet in Illinois September 30, 1981; appointed Bishop of Springfield in Illinois November 22, 1983; installed January 18, 1984; retired October 19, 1999 *Res.: 1625 W. Washington St., Springfield, IL 62702. Office: Catholic Pastoral Center,* 1615 W. Washington St., P.O. Box 3187, Springfield, IL 62708-3187. Tel: 217-698-8500; Fax: 217-698-0802.

Catholic Pastoral Center: 1615 W. Washington St., P.O. Box 3187, Springfield, IL 62708-3187. Tel: 217-698-8500; Fax: 217-698-0802.

ERECTED JULY 29, 1853.

Square Miles 15,139.

Formerly Diocese of Quincy.

See Transferred to Alton, January 9, 1857. To Springfield, October 26, 1923.

Comprises the following Counties of Illinois: Adams, Bond, Brown, Calhoun, Cass, Christian, Clark, Coles, Crawford, Cumberland, Douglas, Edgar, Effingham, Fayette, Greene, Jasper, Jersey, Macon, Macoupin, Madison, Menard, Montgomery, Morgan, Moultrie, Pike, Sangamon, Scott and Shelby.

For legal titles of parishes and diocesan institutions, consult the Chancery Office.

STATISTICAL OVERVIEW

Personnel	
Bishop	1
Retired Bishops	1
Priests: Diocesan Active in Diocese	94
Priests: Diocesan Active Outside Diocese	7
Priests: Diocesan in Foreign Missions	1
Priests: Retired, Sick or Absent	26
Number of Diocesan Priests	128
Religious Priests in Diocese	59
Total Priests in Diocese	187
Extern Priests in Diocese	8
Permanent Deacons in Diocese	5
Total Brothers	31
Total Sisters	563
Parishes	
Parishes	156
With Resident Pastor:	
Resident Diocesan Priests	64
Resident Religious Priests	7
Without Resident Pastor:	
Administered by Priests	77
Administered by Religious Women	7
Administered by Lay People	1
Closed Parishes	6
Welfare	
Catholic Hospitals	7
Total Assisted	717,457
Homes for the Aged	2
Total Assisted	235
Residential Care of Children	1
Total Assisted	314
Day Care Centers	1
Total Assisted	120
Residential Care of Disabled	1
Total Assisted	93
Educational	
Diocesan Students in Other Seminaries	13
Total Seminarians	13
Colleges and Universities	2
Total Students	1,694
High Schools, Diocesan and Parish	2
Total Students	547
High Schools, Private	5
Total Students	1,960
Elementary Schools, Diocesan and Parish	49
Total Students	11,316
Catechesis/Religious Education:	
High School Students	2,811
Elementary Students	9,444
Total Students under Catholic Instruction	27,785
Teachers in the Diocese:	
Priests	1
Brothers	4
Sisters	44
Lay Teachers	611
Vital Statistics	
Receptions into the Church:	
Infant Baptism Totals	2,131
Adult Baptism Totals	333
Received into Full Communion	486
First Communions	2,506
Confirmations	2,933
Marriages:	
Catholic	470
Interfaith	423
Total Marriages	893
Deaths	1,690
Total Catholic Population	161,325
Total Population	1,106,124

Former Bishops—Rt. Revs. HENRY DAMIAN JUNCKER, D.D., consecrated April 28, 1857; died Oct. 2, 1868; PETER JOSEPH BALTES, D.D., consecrated Jan. 23, 1870; died Feb. 15, 1886; JAMES RYAN, D.D., consecrated May 1, 1888; died July 2, 1923; Most Revs. JAMES A. GRIFFIN, D.D., consecrated Feb. 25, 1924; died Aug. 5, 1948; WILLIAM A. O'CONNOR, D.D. (Retired), consecrated March 7, 1949; installed March 17, 1949; retired July 22, 1975; died Nov. 14, 1983; JOSEPH A. MCNICHOLAS, D.D., consecrated March 25, 1969; installed Sept. 3, 1975; died April 17, 1983; DANIEL L. RYAN, D.D., J.C.L. (Retired), ord. May 3, 1956; ord. Titular Bishop of Surista in Mauritania and Auxiliary to the Bishop of Joliet in Illinois, Sept. 30, 1981; appt. Bishop of Springfield in Illinois, Nov. 22, 1983; installed Jan. 18, 1984; retired Oct. 19, 1999.

Vicars General—Rev. Msgrs. CARL KEMME, V.G., Moderator of the Curia; JOHN A. RENKEN, S.T.D., J.C.D., M.A. (Civil Law), V.G., Moderator for Canonical and Civil Affairs.

Vicar for Priests—Rev. Msgr. KEVIN W. VANN, J.C.D.

Chancellor—Rev. Msgr. EUGENE E. COSTA, S.T.L.

Tribunal Officers—Rev. Msgrs. JOHN A. RENKEN, S.T.D., J.C.D., M.A. (Civil Law), V.G., Judicial Vicar; KENNETH C. STEFFEN, J.C.L., M.A., M.Div., D.Min., Adjutant Judicial Vicar; Mr. PATRICK FITZGERALD, J.D., J.C.L. (Cand.), Defender of the Bond.

Finance Officer—Mr. JOHN J. MAXWELL, C.P.A.

Vicars Forane—

Alton Deanery—Rev. Msgr. VIRGIL W. MANK, V.F.

Decatur Deanery—Very Rev. JAMES D. O'SHEA, V.F.

Effingham Deanery—Rev. Msgr. LEO J. ENLOW, V.F.

Jacksonville Deanery—Very Rev. KENNETH J. VENVERTLOH, V.F.

Litchfield Deanery—Rev. Msgr. LAWRENCE AUDA, V.F.

Quincy Deanery—Very Rev. ROBERT J. JALLAS, V.F.

Springfield Deanery—Rev. Msgr. PATRICK J. WRIGHT, V.F.

Diocesan Curia—

All diocesan agencies and councils are located at the Catholic Pastoral Center, unless otherwise indicated. *Catholic Pastoral Center, 1615 W. Washington St., P.O. Box 3187, Springfield, 62708-3187.* Tel: 217-698-8500; Fax: 217-698-0802.

Office of the Bishop—Most Rev. GEORGE LUCAS, D.D.; CHERYL KANNALL, Exec. Asst.

Office for Campus Ministry—ROY LANHAM, Dir., 500 Roosevelt Ave., Charleston, 61920. Tel: 217-348-0188. Email: roylanham@eiu.newman.org.

Office for Catholic Charities— (Central Administration) STEVEN E. ROACH, Exec. Dir. Associate Directors: ELAINE PERINE; MICHAEL SAKOLSKY, 800 S. Fifth St., Springfield, 62703. Tel: 217-523-9201; Fax: 217-523-5624.

Corporate Board Members—Most Rev. GEORGE J. LUCAS, D.D., Pres.; Rev. Msgrs. CARL KEMME, V.G.; JOHN A. RENKEN, S.T.D., J.C.D., M.A. (Civil Law), V.G.; EUGENE E. COSTA, S.T.L.; Mr. JOHN J. MAXWELL, C.P.A.

Corporate Board Directors—ROBERT BUDNIK, Chm.; REGINALD COLEMAN, Vice Chm.; DOUG DELANEY; Sen. VINCENT DEMUZIO; THEODORE L. EILERMAN; JAMES M. GRAHAM; MICHAEL HOFFMANN; WILLIAM KESSLER; AMY MAHER; Sr. ANN PITSENBERGER, O.S.F.; Rev. JOSEPH RING; ROBERT SCHULTZ; JOHN C. WEBSTER; ROBERT D. WESSELINK; Sr. JOAN WINKLER, O.S.F.

Office for Catholic Education—ROSE MERSINGER, Dir.; CHRIS MALMEVICK, Assoc. Dir., Adult Education/Catechist Formation; BARB BURRIS, Assoc. Dir., School Planning; JEAN JOHNSON, Assoc. Dir., Elementary Educ.; SHERYL SPEARS, Exec. Sec.; BERNADINE SMITH, Sec. for Assoc. Directors; SUSAN DONNELLY, Statistics & Data Specialist. Fax: 217-698-8620; 618-654-5775 (Home Office).

Board of Catholic Education—GIL WEYHAUPT, Pres.; Rev. GERALD BUNSE; THOMAS CANTWELL, 1st Vice Pres.; BARBARA COLLINS, 2nd Vice Pres.; PATRICIA EMMERICH; Rev. Msgr. CARL KEMME, V.G., Ex-Officio; MARTHA RILEY; Bro. JOHN FRANCIS TYRRELL, F.F.S.C.; Sr. MARY MORIN, O.S.F.; Bro. DAVID SCHACHTSIEK, Ph.D.; Rev. DELIX MICHEL, S.S.L.; SHERRY DANIELS; BRIAN SULLIVAN; JOAN RYAN; Sisters JOAN SCHNORBUS, C.P.P.S.; JOANN VOLK, S.S.N.D.

Office for Chancellor/Planning Coordinator—Rev. Msgr. EUGENE E. COSTA, S.T.L., Dir.; TONI COLCLASURE, Sec.

Office for Communications—KATHIE SASS, Dir.; TAMMY WOLTERS, Sec. Tel: 217-467-5535 (Pager); Fax: 217-698-0619.

"Catholic Times" Newspaper—KATHIE SASS, Editor; LAURIE WEAKLEY, Office Mgr.; Mr. WILLIAM CALLAN, Layout & Design Coord.; CATHERINE LOCHER, Reporter; PAULA RUOT, Advertising.

Office for the Diaconate—Rev. Msgr. JOHN A. RENKEN, S.T.D., J.C.D., M.A. (Civil Law), V.G., Dir.; JOAN REED, Sec.

Office for Family and Youth Ministry—DONNA DAUSMAN, Dir.; JANA DOTY, Assoc. Dir.; JOAN ANDERSON, Sec.

Office for Finances—Mr. JOHN J. MAXWELL, C.P.A., Dir.; Mr. TOM REISER, Assoc. Dir. Property, Buildings and Cemeteries; Mr. DAN JAMES, Assoc. Dir. Insurance-Fire, Extended Coverage, Vandalism, Multi-Peril Liability, Workers Compensation, Boiler, Unemployment, Lay Employee Pension Plan, Priests' Personal Property, Seminarians' Medical Care and Coordinator for Lay Employee Health Insurance; DAN GAUWITZ, Programmer & Analyst; Ms. JANET WESTENBERGER, Accounting Mgr. Accountants: ROBYN DOOLEY; BARBARA SCOGGINS; BOBBI OZANIC, Coord., Annual Catholic Svcs. Appeal and Sec. Clerks, Annual Catholic Svcs. Appeal: KAREN REGAN, Clerks, Annual Catholic Svcs. Appeal; HEATHER CLEVENGER, Clerks, Annual Catholic Svcs. Appeal; DOROTHY BROWN, Insurance Asst.

Diocesan Health Insurance Program Committee—PATRICE ARSENEAULT; Mrs. EDNA MAE BROWN; Rev. GERALD BUNSE; BARB BURRIS; Mr. DAN JAMES; Rev. Msgr. CARL A. KEMME, V.G.; Ms. PATRICIA KORNFELD; LEO LENN; Rev. Msgr. VIRGIL MANK, V.F.; JOHN MAXWELL, Chairperson; JOAN MCKINNEY; THOMAS REISER; Rev. Msgr. JOHN RENKEN, V.G.; JULIE YOST.

Lay Employees' Pension Plan Administrative Committee—LEO LENN, Chm.; JOHN MAXWELL, Treas.; Mr. JERALD T. BARKMEIER, Consultant; Mrs. EDNA MAE BROWN; BETH DALTON; Mr. PATRICK FITZGERALD, Esq., J.D., J.C.L. (Cand.); THOMAS FRIER; ROSE MERSINGER; Mr. DAN JAMES, Sec.; Rev. Msgr. CARL A. KEMME, V.G.; Ms. PATRICIA KORNFELD; THOMAS REISER; Rev. Msgr. PAUL SHERIDAN; Very Rev. KENNETH VENVERTLOH, V.F.

Commission for Buildings and Property—Rev. DANIEL BERGBOWER; ROBERT BUDNIK, Chm.; ANN CARR; GERALD L. CLAUS SR.; Rev. Msgrs. CARL KEMME, V.G.; VIRGIL MANK, V.F.; JOHN MAXWELL; THOMAS C. PAVLIK JR.; Rev. Msgr. JOHN RENKEN, V.G.; THOMAS REISER, Consultant.

Office for Human Resources—PATRICIA J. KORNFELD, Dir.

Office for Ministry Formation—Rev. DAVID LANTZ, Dir.; JOAN REED, Sec.

Advisory Board—Sr. JANE BOOS, S.S.N.D.; DONNA DAUSMAN; JANA DOTY; MARY HANDLEY; ELIOT KAPITAN; CHRIS MALMEVICK; ROSE MERSINGER; Rev. Msgrs. JOHN A. RENKEN, S.T.D., J.C.D., M.A. (Civil Law), V.G.; KENNETH STEFFEN.

Area Specialization Coordinators—Catechetical Leadership Ministry:: CHRIS MALMEVICK. Catholic School Leadership Ministry:: ROSE MERSINGER. Clinical Pastoral Care Ministry:: MARY HANDLEY. Family Life Ministry:: Rev. Msgr. KENNETH STEFFEN; DONNA DAUSMAN. Liturgical Ministry: Christian Initiation of Adult Leadership,: ELIOT KAPITAN. Liturgical Ministry: Liturgical Leadership:: ELIOT KAPITAN. Parish Life Ministry:: Rev. Msgr. JOHN A. RENKEN, S.T.D., J.C.D., M.A. (Civil Law), V.G Social Concerns Ministry:: Sr. JANE BOOS, S.S.N.D. Tribunal Advocacy Ministry:: Rev. Msgrs. JOHN A. RENKEN, S.T.D., J.C.D., M.A. (Civil Law), V.G.; KENNETH STEFFEN, Youth Ministry:. Youth Ministry:: DONNA DAUSMAN; JANA DOTY.

Office for the Missions—VICKY COMPTON, Dir.; TERESA BETTIS, Sec., P.O. Box 7025, Springfield, 62791-7025.

Office for Social Concerns—Sr. JANE BOOS, S.S.N.D., Dir.; JOSEPH KAUFMANN, Assoc. Dir.; ELAINE VONDERHEIDE, Part-time Assoc. Dir., Special Needs; MARTHA MAYFIELD, Assoc. Dir., Operations. Associate Directors for Rural Life: JAMES SCHUMACHER; KAREN SCHUMACHER; CHRISTINE LANSAW, Part-time Coord. Catholic Religious Education at Illinois School for the Deaf; LEROY JORDAN, Part-time Coord., Black Catholic Ministry.

Black Catholic Advisory Board—LEROY JORDAN, Chm.; Dr. LENORA BROWN, Alton Deanery; Rev. FELIX MICHAEL, S.S.L., Alton Deanery; Mrs. FREDDIE MCEWEN-RANDLE, Decatur Deanery; RENEE SAUNCHES, Decatur Deanery; REGINALD COLEMAN, Quincy Deanery; HUGH HARRIS, Springfield Deanery; Sr. JUDI ROBBINS, O.P., Alton Deanery; FRED ROBINSON, Springfield Deanery; Sr. JANE BOOS, S.S.N.D., Ex Officio; Rev. Msgrs. CARL KEMME, V.G., Ex Officio; JOHN A. RENKEN, S.T.D., J.C.D., M.A. (Civil Law), V.G., Ex Officio.

Campaign for Human Development Advisory Board and Allocation Committee—Sr. JANE BOOS, S.S.N.D., Dir. Deanery Representatives: WALT UNGER, Alton Deanery; KEN HANDLEY, Decatur Deanery; MARY MULCAHY, Decatur/Springfield Deaneries; BECKY LOEHR, Effingham Deanery; KATHLEEN ROGERS, Jacksonville Deanery; SAM ELIZONDO, Litchfield Deanery; MARGUERITE SCHNEIDER, Quincy Deanery; BRENDA HEATON, Springfield Deanery; KEN STEINER, Member At Large. Ex Officio: Rev. Msgrs. CARL KEMME, V.G.; JOHN A. RENKEN, S.T.D., J.C.D., M.A. (Civil Law), V.G.

Hispanic Minsitry—Rev. Msgr. KEVIN W. VANN, J.C.D., Episcopal Contact; Sr. JANE BOOS, S.S.N.D., Coord.

Pastoral Ministers—Sisters RENE LAWLESS, O.P. Tel: 217-243-2815; DELFINA MARAVILLA MORALES, M.A.G.; LUCIA MOROLES, M.A.G.; ELIZABETH ROMERO MARTINEZ, M.A.G.; MARIA DE LOURDES ORTIZ VENTURA, M.A.G. Tel: 217-726-8159.

Comite Diocesano de Ministerio Hispano - Diocesan Committee for Hispanic Ministry—Revs. CARLOS M. BOHORQUEZ; CHRIS BREY; ALLEN KEMME; Sisters RENE LAWLESS, O.P.; DELFINA MARAVILLA MORALES, M.A.G.; ELIZABETH ROMERO MARTINEZ, M.A.G.; Rev. THOMAS MEYER; Sisters LUCIA MOROLES, M.A.G.; ANN PITSENBERGER, O.S.F.; Rev. ROBERT REBERT (Retired); Rev. Msgr. JOHN A. RENKEN, S.T.D., J.C.D., M.A. (Civil Law), V.G.; Sr. MARIA DE LOURDES ORTIZ VENTURA, M.A.G.; Rev. ANGEL SIERRA; Rev. Msgrs. KENNETH STEFFEN; KEVIN W. VANN, J.C.D.; Sr. JANE BOOS, S.S.N.D. Rev. RICHARD W WELTIN; Rev. Msgr. CARL A. KEMME, V.G., Ex Officio.

Task Force For Racial Justice—JAMES FORSTALL, Chm.; Rev. JOSEPH ZIMMERMAN, O.F.M., Vice Chm.; Sr. JANE BOOS, S.S.N.D. Ex Officios: Rev. Msgrs. CARL A. KEMME, V.G.; JOHN A. RENKEN, S.T.D., J.C.D., M.A. (Civil Law) V.G.

Office for Stewardship and Development—MARLENE MULFORD, Dir.; CATHY FURKIN, Administrative Asst.

Office for the Tribunal—Rev. Msgrs. JOHN A. RENKEN, S.T.D., J.C.D., M.A. (Civil Law), V.G., Dir., Judicial Vicar; KENNETH STEFFEN, J.C.L., M.A., D.Min., Assoc. Dir., Adjutant Judicial Vicar; Mr. PATRICK FITZGERALD, Esq., J.D., J.C.L. (Cand.), Defender of the Bond; BECKY DONALDSON, Office Mgr., Notary & Sec.; Bro. JOEL MARK ROUSSEAU, F.F.S.C., Sec. & Notary.

Office of the Vicars General—

Moderator of the Curia—Rev. Msgr. CARL KEMME, V.G.

Moderator of the Canonical and Civil Affairs—Rev. Msgr. JOHN A. RENKEN, S.T.D., J.C.D., M.A. (Civil Law), V.G. Tel: 217-629-9109 (evenings & weekends); Cell: (217) 629-9109.

Staff—PATRICK W. FITZGERALD, Esq., J.D., J.C.L. (Cand.), Assoc. Exec. Asst. to Vicar Gen. & Assoc. Legal Counsel; JOAN REED, Exec. Sec., Special Projects & Notary; CAROL MULLER, Assoc. to Vicar Gen., Records Mgmt. Office Mgr. & Notary; Bro. ANTHONY JOSEPH MCCOY, F.F.S.C., Sec. & Notary; PATRICIA POLONUS, Receptionist for Catholic Pastoral Center; HEATHER MCMILLEN, Central Purchasing.

Archives—Sr. SUSAN KARINA DICKEY, O.P., Ph.D., Dir. Tel: 217-522-3986.

CPC Media Resource Center—VACANT, Dir.

Diocesan Historian—Sr. SUSAN KARINA DICKEY, O.P., Ph.D.

Pilgrimage Director—Rev. Msgr KENNETH STEFFEN, J.C.L., M.A., D.Min.

Training and Human Resources—Ms. PATRICIA KORNFELD, Dir.

Office of the Vicar for Priests—Rev. Msgr. KEVIN W. VANN, J.C.D.

Commission for the Care of Infirm and Retired Priests—Rev. GERALD BUNSE, Chm.; Rev. Msgr. THOMAS P. HOLINGA; Revs. DENNIS D. KOLLROSS; DONALD J. MEEHLING; JAMES NEUMAN; DAVID PETERS; Rev. Msgrs. JOHN RENKEN, V.G., Sec.; JOHN SPREEN, V.F. (Retired); KEVIN W. VANN, J.C.D.

Priests' Personnel Board—Revs. GERALD BUNSE; PAUL SKELTON; ROBERT DEGRAND; THOMAS HAGSTROM; R. DEAN PROBST; J. MICHAEL JENKINS; Rev. Msgrs. KENNETH STEFFEN; KEVIN W. VANN, J.C.D., Chm. Consultants: Rev. Msgrs. CARL KEMME, V.G.; JOHN A. RENKEN, S.T.D., J.C.D., M.A. (Civil Law), V.G.; EUGENE E. COSTA, S.T.L.

Office for Vocations—Rev. JOHN M. TITUS, Dir.

Office of Worship—ELIOT KAPITAN, Dir.; JAN GRIGGS, Sec.

Commission for the Liturgy—ANNA F. HAINE; Rev. PETER HARMAN; ELIOT KAPITAN; ANGELA J. PRZYBILLA; CAROL SEIFERT.

Victim Assistance Coordinator—Ms. PATRICIA KORNFELD. Tel: 217-698-8500. Email: pkornfeld@dio.org.

Councils

Diocesan Finance Council—Mrs. BARBARA BORDERS; Mr. JAMES DAVIS; WILLIAM KESSLER; LEO LENN, Chm.; Mr. LEE MARTEN; Mr. MICHAEL MAURER; Mr. DAN MCGUIRE; Rev. JAMES NEUMAN; Mr. JOHN STAUDT; Ms. JANET WESTENBERGER, Accounting Mgr.; JOAN WOLF. Consultants: Most Rev. GEORGE J. LUCAS; Rev. Msgrs. CARL KEMME, V.G.; JOHN RENKEN, V.G.; JOHN MAXWELL; MARLENE MULFORD; THOMAS REISER.

Presbyteral Council—Most Rev. GEORGE LUCAS; Rev. GERALD BUNSE; Rev. Msgr. EUGENE COSTA; Revs. JEFFREY GOECKNER; PETER HARMAN; BARRY J. HARMON; KURT HARTRICH, O.F.M.; CHRISTOPHER A. HOUSE; PAT G. JAKEL; ALLEN KEMME, Vice Chm.; Rev. Msgr. CARL KEMME, V.G.; Rev. DONALD KNUFFMAN; Rev. Msgr. MICHAEL KUSE, Chm.; Revs. THOMAS MEYER; JAMES NEUMAN; Rev. Msgrs. JOHN A. RENKEN, S.T.D., J.C.D., M.A. (Civil Law), V.G., Sec. & Treas.; KENNETH STEFFEN; Rev. JOHN M. TITUS; Rev. Msgr. KEVIN W. VANN, J.C.D.; Revs. EUGENE WEITZEL, C.S.V.; RICHARD WELTIN; DAVID ZIMMERMAN.

Catholic Charities Institutions

Administrative Office—

Springfield. Catholic Charities—STEVEN E. ROACH, Exec. Dir., 800 S. Fifth St., Springfield, 62703. Tel: 217-523-9201; Fax: 217-523-5624.

Area Offices—

Alton. Catholic Charities of Alton and Wood River—THERESA SCHULTE, Area Dir., 735 Park Dr., Alton, 62002. Tel: 618-462-0634; Fax: 618-462-3209.

Carlinville. Catholic Charities—PATRICIA A. POPE, Area Dir., 525 W. Second South St., P.O. Box 618, Carlinville, 62626-0618. Tel: 217-854-4511; Fax: 217-854-8049.

Decatur. Catholic Charities—MARIE RADEMACHER, Area Dir., 247 W. Prairie, Decatur, 62523. Tel: 217-428-3458; Fax: 217-428-4415.

Effingham. Catholic Charities—Sr. BRENDA FRITZ, D.C., Area Dir., 601 W. Fayette, Effingham, 62401. Tel: 217-342-9800; Fax: 217-342-3873.

Granite City. Catholic Charities—MARY PHILLIPS, Area Dir., 2105 State St., Granite City, 62040. Tel: 618-877-1184; Fax: 618-798-4287.

Mattoon. Catholic Charities of Coles, Douglas and Edgar Counties—MICHAEL WOOLWORTH, Area Dir., 4217 DeWitt Ave., Mattoon, 61938. Tel: 217-235-0420; Fax: 217-235-0425.

Quincy. Catholic Charities of Quincy—KURT STUCKMAN, Area Dir., 620 Maine St., Quincy, 62301. Tel: 217-222-0958; Fax: 217-222-8737.

Springfield. Catholic Charities—DANIELLE K. KELLERS, Area Dir., 120 S. 11th St., Springfield, 62703. Tel: 217-525-0500; Fax: 217-525-0554.

Institutions—

Alton, Catholic Children's Home—STEVEN E. ROACH, Exec. Dir.; CANDACE HOVEY, Admin., 1400 State St., Alton, 62002. Tel: 618-465-3594; Fax: 618-465-4023. Email: cch1400@ezl.com.

Beardstown. St. Francis Community Clinic—KILLIE STOCKER, Clinic Dir., 111 S. State St., Beardstown, 62618. Tel: 217-323-5264; Fax: 217-323-4680.

Springfield. St. John's Breadline—JOHN R. LYERLA, Supvr., 430 N. Fifth St., Springfield, 62701. Tel: 217-528-6098; Fax: 217-528-3605.

Springfield. St. Clare's Health Clinic—CONNIE MARZINZIK, Clinic Supvr., 700 N. Seventh St., Ste. A, Springfield, 62702. Tel: 217-523-1474; Fax: 217-523-0194.

CLERGY, PARISHES, MISSIONS AND PAROCHIAL SCHOOLS

CITY OF SPRINGFIELD
(SANGAMON COUNTY)

1—CATHEDRAL OF THE IMMACULATE CONCEPTION (1928), [JC] Rev. Msgr. John R. Ossola. In Res., Revs. John M. Titus; Samuel Kothapalli (India).
Res.: 524 E. Lawrence Ave., P.O. Box 1667, 62705. Tel: 217-522-3342; Fax: 217-522-1151.
School—Tel: 217-523-2652; Fax: 217-523-2750. Springfield Dominican Sisters 3; Lay Teachers 15; Students 236.
Catechesis/Religious Program—Students 60.

2—ST. AGNES (1889), Rev. Msgr. Patrick J. Wright, V.F.; Revs. Robert T. Becker; Peter C. Harman.
Res.: 245 N. Amos Ave., 62702. Tel: 217-793-1330; Fax: 217-793-3212.
School—Tel: 217-793-1370; Fax: 217-793-1238. Lay Teachers 25; Students 450.
Catechesis/Religious Program—Students 200.

3—ST. ALOYSIUS (1928), [JC] Revs. Thomas R. Liebler; Donald J. Meehling.
Res.: 2119 N. 20th St., 62702. Tel: 217-544-4554; Fax: 217-544-4963.
School—Tel: 217-544-4553; Fax: 217-544-1680. Lay Teachers 26; Students 397.
Catechesis/Religious Program—Students 78.

4—BLESSED SACRAMENT (1924), Rev. Msgr. Kevin W. Vann, J.C.D.; Rev. David J. Hoefler.
Res.: 1725 S. Walnut Ave., 62704. Tel: 217-528-7521; Fax: 217-528-3137.
School—Tel: 217-522-7534; Fax: 217-522-7542. Lay Teachers 39; Students 398.
Catechesis/Religious Program—Students 585.

5—CHRIST THE KING (1963), Rev. Msgr. David S. Lantz.
Res.: 1930 Barberry Dr., 62704. Tel: 217-546-3527; Fax: 217-793-6393.
School—Tel: 217-546-2159; Fax: 217-546-0291. Lay Teachers 23; Students 490.
Catechesis/Religious Program—Elementary, 1920 Barberry Dr., 62704. Tel: 217-546-2159. Students 68.

6—ST. FRANCES CABRINI (1948), Rev. Rodney A. Schwartz, Admin.
Res.: 1020 N. Milton Ave., 62702. Tel: 217-522-8555; Fax: 217-522-3585.

7—ST. JOSEPH (1875), Rev. Msgr. Thomas P. Holinga.
Res.: 1345 N. Sixth St., 62702. Tel: 217-544-7426; Fax: 217-544-7467.
School—Tel: 217-523-6597; Fax: 217-523-6434. Ursuline Sisters 1; Lay Teachers 15; Students 211.
Catechesis/Religious Program—Students 68.

8—ST. KATHARINE DREXEL (2001), Rev. Msgrs. John A. Renken, S.T.D., J.C.D., M.A. (Civil Law), V.G., Co-Pastor; Kenneth Steffen, Co-Pastor.
Office—700 S. 12th St., P.O. Box 4302, 62708-4302. Tel: 217-744-0578; Fax: 217-698-0802.
Res.: P.O. Box 4302, 62708-4302.
Catechesis/Religious Program—Students 9.

9—LITTLE FLOWER (1947), [JC] Rev. Charles Edwards.
800 Stevenson Dr., 62703. Tel: 217-529-1606; Fax: 217-529-1649.
School—Tel: 217-529-4511; Fax: 217-529-0405. Sisters 3; Lay Teachers 26; Students 387.
Catechesis/Religious Program—Students 65.

10—ST. PATRICK, Merged, with Sacred Heart of Jesus, Springfield to form St. Katharine Drexel, Springfield.

11—SS. PETER AND PAUL (1859), (German), Closed., For inquiries for parish records, contact the Cathedral of the Immaculate Conception, Springfield.

12—SACRED HEART OF JESUS (1884), (German), Merged, with St. Patrick, Springfield to form St. Katharine Drexel.

OUTSIDE THE CITY OF SPRINGFIELD

ALEXANDER, MORGAN CO., VISITATION B.V.M. (1909), [CEM] Rev. Joseph P. Kerber.
Mailing Address: P.O. Box 20, New Berlin, 62670. Tel: 217-488-2410; Fax: 217-488-2410.
Church: Old U.S. 36, 62601.
Catechesis/Religious Program—Tel: 217-488-3545; Fax: 217-488-3545. Students 1.

ALTAMONT, EFFINGHAM CO., ST. CLARE (1874), (German), [CEM] Rev. John M. Savoree, Admin.
Res.: 216 N. Ninth St., 62411. Tel: 618-483-5346.
Catechesis/Religious Program—Students 40.
Mission—St. Mary St. Elmo, Fayette Co.

ALTON, MADISON CO.

1—ST. MARY'S (1858), [CEM] Revs. James Walther, O.M.V.; John Wykes, O.M.V.; Fernando Augusto Cuenca, O.M.V.; Christopher Uhl, O.M.V.; Bros. David Guza; Frank Dolan.
Mailing Address: 519 E. 4th St., 62002. Tel: 618-465-4284; Fax: 618-463-4637.
Res.: 525 E. Fourth St., 62002. Tel: 618-465-4284.
School—Tel: 618-465-8523. Sisters of St. Francis of the Martyr of St. George 3; Lay Teachers 11; Students 287; Preschool 45.
Catechesis/Religious Program—Students 75.

2—ST. MATTHEW (1947), Rev. David Schmidt.
Res.: 1015 Milton Rd., 62002-3197. Tel: 618-465-8582; Fax: 618-465-5994.
Catechesis/Religious Program—Students 26.

3—ST. PATRICK (1883), Closed., For inquiries for parish records, contact St. Mary's, Alton.

4—SS. PETER AND PAUL (1855), [JC] Rev. Roger Schoenhofen, O.M.I.
Res.: 717 State St., 62002. Tel: 618-465-4221; Fax: 618-465-0346.
School—Tel: 618-465-8711; Fax: 618-465-6405. Lay Teachers 9; Students 199.
Catechesis/Religious Program—Students 40.

ARCOLA, DOUGLAS CO., ST. JOHN THE BAPTIST (1865), [JC] Rev. Allen Kemme.
Res.: 205 S. Locust St., Box 133, 61910. Tel: 217-268-3766; Fax: 217-268-3545.
Catechesis/Religious Program—210 S. Pine St., 61910. Students 85.

ARENZVILLE, CASS CO., ST. FIDELIS (1853), (German—Irish), Rev. Eugene J. Weitzel, C.S.V., Admin.
Res.: 215 W. Fifth St., Beardstown, 62618. Tel: 217-323-4345; Fax: 217-323-5464.
Catechesis/Religious Program—Students 11.

ASHLAND, CASS CO., ST. AUGUSTINE (1875), [CEM] Rev. Richard L. Chiola, Admin.
Res.: 320 N. Saratoga, P.O. Box 438, 62612. Tel: 217-476-8856.
Catechesis/Religious Program—Students 47.

ASSUMPTION, CHRISTIAN CO., ASSUMPTION B.V.M. (1870), [CEM] Rev. Angel Sierra.
Res.: 301 St. Peter St., 62510. Tel: 217-226-3536; Fax: 217-226-3538.
Catechesis/Religious Program—Tel: 217-226-3205. Students 50.

ATHENS, MENARD CO., HOLY FAMILY (1903), [CEM] Rev. Msgr. Eugene E. Costa, S.T.L.
Mailing Address: P.O. Box 229, Sherman, 62684.
Res.: 129 Stardust Dr., Sherman, 62684. Tel: 217-523-3816; Fax: 217-523-3954.
Church: Springfield Rd., 62613. Tel: 217-636-8238.
Catechesis/Religious Program—Students 41.

AUBURN, SANGAMON CO., ST. BENEDICT (1903), [JC] Rev. Kevin Michael Laughery.
125 E. Washington St., P.O. Box 168, 62615. Tel: 217-438-6222; Fax: 217-438-6732.
Catechesis/Religious Program—Students 107.

BARRY, PIKE CO., HOLY REDEEMER (1954), [JC] Rev. J. Michael Jenkins; Very Rev. Robert J. Jallas, V.F., Admin.
Res.: 226 E. Adams, Pittsfield, 62363. Tel: 217-285-4321; Fax: 217-285-9400.
Catechesis/Religious Program—Tel: 217-285-4774. Students 16.

BATCHTOWN, CALHOUN CO., ST. BARBARA (1910), (German), [CEM] Rev. Thomas Hagstrom.
Office—P.O. Box 38, Brussels, 62013. Tel: 618-883-2400; Fax: 618-883-2511.
Res.: Meppen Ln., Meppen, 62013. Tel: 618-883-2309.
Catechesis/Religious Program—Students 12.

BEARDSTOWN, CASS CO., ST. ALEXIUS (1838), [CEM] Rev. Eugene J. Weitzel, C.S.V., Admin.
Res.: 215 W. 5th St., 62618. Tel: 217-323-4345; Fax: 217-323-5464.
Catechesis/Religious Program—Tel: 217-323-1888; Fax: 217-323-5464. Students 138.

BELLEVIEW, CALHOUN CO., ST. AGNES (1900), (German), [CEM] Rev. Thomas Hagstrom, Admin.
Res.: 404 Main St., P.O. Box C, Hardin, 62047. Tel: 618-576-2628; Fax: 618-576-9448.

BELTREES, JERSEY CO., ST. MICHAEL (1877), [CEM] Rev. Robert L. Meyer.
Res.: 11 N. Evans St., P.O. Box 218, Grafton, 62037. Tel: 618-786-3512; Fax: 618-786-2027.
Church: Beltrees Rd., 62022.
Catechesis/Religious Program—Students 12.

BENLD, MACOUPIN CO., ST. JOSEPH (1915), Rev. Msgr. Lawrence Auda.
Res.: 304 N. Macoupin, Gillespie, 62033. Tel: 217-839-3456.
Church: 310 W. Central Ave., 62009. Tel: 217-835-4701.
Catechesis/Religious Program—Students 25.

BETHALTO, MADISON CO., OUR LADY QUEEN OF PEACE (1945), Rev. Donald Blickhan.
Res.: 132 Butcher St., P.O. Box 100, 62010. Tel: 618-377-6519; Fax: 618-377-9550. Email: olqpchurch@ezl.com frblickhan@ezl.com.
School—Tel: 618-377-6401; Fax: 618-377-6146. Lay Teachers 13; Students 222.
Catechesis/Religious Program—Students 75.

BETHANY, MOULTRIE CO., ST. ISIDORE (1864), [CEM] Very Rev. James D. O'Shea, V.F.
Res.: 400 Woodland Ln., Mount Zion, 62549. Tel: 217-864-3467; Fax: 217-864-3091.
Catechesis/Religious Program—Tel: 217-873-8667. Students 18.

BISHOP CREEK, EFFINGHAM CO., ST. ALOYSIUS (1865), [CEM] Rev. Edwin O. Albers, O.F.M.
Res.: 19812 E. 1000th Ave., Dieterich, 62424. Tel: 217-925-5579; Fax: 217-925-5578.
Catechesis/Religious Program—Students 248.

BLACK JACK, MADISON CO., ST. JOHN THE BAPTIST, Closed. For inquiries for parish records contact the chancery.

BLUFFS, SCOTT CO., ST. PATRICK (1871), Rev. Charles T. Nelson.
Res.: 108 Pearl St., Winchester, 62694. Tel: 217-742-5224.
Catechesis/Religious Program—Students 4.

BRIGHTON, MACOUPIN CO., ST. ALPHONSUS (1868), (German), Rev. Raphael Paul.
Res.: 918 N. Main St., 62012. Tel: 618-372-3352; Fax: 618-372-8133.
Catechesis/Religious Program—Students 5.

BROCTON, EDGAR CO., ST. THOMAS AQUINAS (1899), Closed. For inquiries for parish records contact the chancery.

BRUSSELS, CALHOUN CO., ST. MARY (1851), (German), [CEM] Rev. Thomas Hagstrom.
Office—P.O. Box 38, 62013. Tel: 618-883-2400; Fax: 618-883-2511.
Res.: Meppen Ln., Meppen, 62013. Tel: 618-883-2309.
School—Tel: 618-883-2124. Mrs. Brenda Paynic, Prin. Lay Teachers 3; Students 54.
Catechesis/Religious Program—Students 20.

BUFFALO, SANGAMON CO., ST. JOSEPH (1882), Sr. Lois Kikkert, O.P., Parish Life Coord.
Mailing Address: P.O. Box 47, Illiopolis, 62539. Tel: 217-486-3851; Fax: 217-486-3851.
Church: 302 W.S. St.. Tel: 217-364-4696.
Catechesis/Religious Program—Students 12.

BUNKER HILL, MACOUPIN CO., ST. MARY (1854), [CEM] Rev. Robert N. Porter.
Res.: 300 S. Putnam, P.O. Box A-H, 62014-9512. Tel: 618-585-4700; Fax: 618-585-3449.
Catechesis/Religious Program—Students 38.

CAMP POINT, ADAMS CO., ST. THOMAS (1860), Rev. Rayappa Repudi, Admin.
Res.: P.O. Box 228, Liberty, 62347-0228. Tel: 217-645-3444; Fax: 217-645-3546.
Church: 109 E. Spring St., 62320.
Parish Hall:—103 E. Spring St., 62320.
Catechesis/Religious Program—Sr. Joan Schnorbus, C.PP.S., D.R.E. Students 59.

CARLINVILLE, MACOUPIN CO.

1—SS. MARY & JOSEPH (1996), [JC], SS. Mary & Joseph was formed by the merger of St. Mary's of the Immaculate Conception & St. Joseph. Rev. R. Dean Probst.
Res.: 1011 Ravine, P.O. Box 647, 62626. Tel: 217-854-8034; Fax: 217-854-9228.
Office & Mailing Address: 2010 E. First S. St., P.O. Box 647, 62626-0647. Tel: 217-854-7151.
Catechesis/Religious Program—Students 223.

2—ST. MARY'S OF THE IMMACULATE CONCEPTION, Closed., For inquiries for parish records contact St. Joseph.

CARROLLTON, GREENE CO., ST. JOHN THE EVANGELIST (1858), [CEM] Rev. Henry Schmidt.
Res.: 414 Third St., 62016-1319. Tel: 217-942-3551; Fax: 217-942-6767.
School—426 Third St., 62016-1319. Tel: 217-942-6814. Mr. Gary E. Miller, Prin. Lay Teachers 9; Students 126.
Catechesis/Religious Program—426 Third St., 62016. Students 218.

CASEY, CLARK CO., ST. CHARLES BORROMEO (1878), Rev. Christopher Brey.
Church: 300 E. Jefferson, P.O. Box 72, 62420.
Res.: 110 Lincoln Dr., P.O. Box 156, Greenup, 62428. Tel: 217-923-3523; Fax: 217-923-3523.

CHANDLERVILLE, CASS CO., ST. BASIL, Merged, with St. Luke, Virginia.

CHARLESTON, COLES CO., ST. CHARLES BORROMEO (1873), Rev. Joseph G. Ring.
Res.: 921 E. Madison St., 61920. Tel: 217-345-3332; Fax: 217-348-8449.
Catechesis/Religious Program—Students 168.

CHATHAM, SANGAMON CO., ST. JOSEPH (1920), Rev. Robert B. Franzen.
Res.: 700 E. Spruce, 62629. Tel: 217-483-3772; Fax: 217-483-4581.
Catechesis/Religious Program— 62629. Tel: 217-483-4514. Students 551.

COFFEEN, MONTGOMERY CO., ST. JOHN THE BAPTIST (1898), [CEM] [JC] Rev. Carl Schmidt, Admin.
Res.: 400 Jefferson, P.O. Box 278, 62017. Tel: 217-534-2220.
Catechesis/Religious Program—Students 18.

COLLINSVILLE, MADISON CO., SS. PETER AND PAUL (1855), (Italian), [CEM] Revs. John P. Beveridge; Christopher A. House; Deacon James J. Ghiglione, Youth Minister.
Res.: 207 Vandalia St., 62234. Tel: 618-345-4343; Fax: 618-345-1145.
School—Tel: 618-344-5450; Fax: 618-344-5536. Lay Teachers 25; Students 330.

Catechesis/Religious Program—Students 86.
DALTON CITY, MOULTRIE CO., SACRED HEART (1891), Closed. For inquiries for parish records contact the chancery.
DECATUR, MACON CO.
1—HOLY FAMILY (1959), [JC] Rev. Joseph Molloy; Sr. Marianne Nolan, O.P., Pastoral Assoc.
Res.: 2400 S. Franklin St., 62521. Tel: 217-423-6223; Fax: 217-423-6237.
School—Tel: 217-423-7049; Fax: 217-423-7098. Springfield Dominican Sisters 2; Lay Teachers 16; Students 243; Preschool 17.
Catechesis/Religious Program—Students 64.
2—ST. JAMES (1877), [JC] Very Rev. James D. O'Shea, V.F.; Revs. Jeffery A. Grant; Dennis D. Kollross; Sr. Glenda Bourgeois, O.S.U., Parish Life Coord.
Res.: 742 E. Clay St., 62521. Tel: 217-428-7733; Fax: 217-428-7426.
School—Tel: 217-422-7031; Fax: 217-422-2121. Religious 1; Lay Teachers 12; Students 93.
Catechesis/Religious Program—Students 88.
3—OUR LADY OF LOURDES (1958), [JC] Revs. Richard W. Weltin; Carlos M. Bohorquez.
Res.: 3850 Lourdes Dr., 62526. Tel: 217-877-4404; Fax: 217-877-5257.
School—3950 Lourdes Dr., 62526-1799. Tel: 217-877-4408; Fax: 217-872-3655. Lay Teachers 20; Students 327.
Catechesis/Religious Program—Students 154.
4—ST. PATRICK (1853), [JC] Rev. Jeffery A. Grant.
Res.: 407 E. Eldorado St., 62523. Tel: 217-429-5363; Fax: 217-429-8206.
School—Tel: 217-423-4351; Fax: 217-423-7288. Lay Teachers 12; Students 193.
Catechesis/Religious Program—Students 26.
5—ST. THOMAS THE APOSTLE (1925), Rev. Dennis D. Kollross.
Res.: 2160 N. Edward St., P.O. Box 2697, 62524-2697. Tel: 217-877-4146; Fax: 217-877-4147.
Catechesis/Religious Program— 62524-2697. Students 32.
DIETERICH, EFFINGHAM CO., IMMACULATE CONCEPTION (1905), [CEM] Rev. Edwin O. Albers, O.F.M.
Res.: 19812 E. 1000th Ave., 62424. Tel: 217-925-5579; Fax: 217-925-5578.
Catechesis/Religious Program—Students 99.
DIVERNON, SANGAMON CO., SACRED HEART (1905), [CEM] Rev. Kevin Michael Laughery.
Office & Res.: 125 E. Washington St., P.O. Box 168, Auburn, 62515. Tel: 217-438-6222; Fax: 217-438-6732.
Church: 224 S. Lincoln, 62530.
Catechesis/Religious Program—Students 9.
EAST ALTON, MADISON CO., ST. KEVIN (1959), Rev. Delix Michel, S.S.L., Admin.
Res.: 108 Airwood Dr., E., 62024. Tel: 618-259-3363; Fax: 618-259-2276.
School—Tel: 618-259-6040. Lay Teachers 9; Aides 2; Students 178.
Catechesis/Religious Program—Students 62.
EDGEWOOD, EFFINGHAM CO., ST. ANNE (1865), (German), [CEM] Rev. John M. Savoree, Admin.
Res.: 216 N. Ninth, Altamont, 62411. Tel: 618-483-5346.
Catechesis/Religious Program—Tel: 614-238-4513. Students 23.
EDWARDSVILLE, MADISON CO.
1—ST. BONIFACE (1869), (German), [CEM] Rev. John Corredato, C.S.V.
Res.: 110 N. Buchanan St., P.O. Box 423, 62025. Tel: 618-656-6450; Fax: 618-656-7669.
School—Preschool, Tel: 618-692-9315. Students 74.
School—Tel: 618-656-6917. Lay Teachers 12; Students 229; Preschool 74.
Catechesis/Religious Program—Students 216.
2—ST. MARY (1842), [CEM] [JC] Rev. Gerald L. Bunse.
Res.: 1802 Madison, 62025. Tel: 618-656-4857; Fax: 618-656-1715.
School—Tel: 618-656-1230; Fax: 618-656-1230. Priests 1; Lay Teachers 16; Students 254.
Catechesis/Religious Program—Tel: 618-656-4230. Students 90.
EFFINGHAM, EFFINGHAM CO.
1—ST. ANTHONY OF PADUA (1858), [CEM] Rev. Msgr. Leo J. Enlow, V.F.; Rev. William Kessler.
Res.: 417 N. Third, P.O. Box 764, 62401. Tel: 217-347-7129; Fax: 217-342-6980.
School—Tel: 217-347-0419; Fax: 217-347-2749. Sisters 1; Lay Teachers 31; Students 405.
High School—Tel: 217-342-6969; Fax: 217-342-6997. Priests 2; Lay Teachers 18; Students 217.
Catechesis/Religious Program—Tel: 217-347-7129; Fax: 217-347-6980. Students 100.
2—SACRED HEART (1892), [JC] Rev. Daniel J. Bergbower.
Res.: 405 S. Henrietta, P.O. Box 870, 62401. Tel: 217-347-7177; Fax: 217-347-0728.
School—Tel: 217-342-4060; Fax: 217-342-9251. Lay Teachers 14; Students 205.
Catechesis/Religious Program—Students 145.
FARMERSVILLE, MONTGOMERY CO., ST. MARY (1876), [CEM] [JC] Rev. David Zimmerman.
Res.: 310 Nobbe St., P.O. Box 80, 62533-0080. Tel: 217-227-3349; Fax: 217-227-3324.
School—St. Isidore, Tel: 217-227-3359. Lay Teachers 6; Students 50.
Catechesis/Religious Program—Students 10.
FIELDON, JERSEY CO., ST. MARY, [CEM] Rev William Hembrow.
Res.: 306 N. Washington, Jerseyville, 62052. Tel: 618-498-3416; Fax: 618-498-3414.
Catechesis/Religious Program— Clustered with Holy Ghost, Jerseyville. Students 26.
FRANKLIN, MORGAN CO., SACRED HEART OF JESUS (1886), [CEM] Rev. Joseph P. Kerber.
Mailing Address: P.O. Box 20, New Berlin, 62670. Tel: 217-488-2410; Fax: 217-488-2410.
Office & Res.: P.O. Box 20, New Berlin, 62670.
Church: 62638. Tel: 217-675-2631.
Parish Center—Tel: 217-675-2631.
Catechesis/Religious Program—Students 46.
GILLESPIE, MACOUPIN CO., SS. SIMON AND JUDE (1879), [CEM] Rev. Msgr. Lawrence Auda.
Res.: 304 N. Macoupin St., 62033. Tel: 217-839-3456.
Catechesis/Religious Program—Students 57.
GIRARD, MACOUPIN CO., ST. PATRICK (1887), Rev. David Zimmerman.
Mailing and Res.: 310 Nobbe St., P.O. Box 80, Farmersville, 62533-0080. Tel: 217-227-3349; Fax: 217-227-3324 (Call First).
Church: 745 W. Center, 62640.
Catechesis/Religious Program—Tel: 217-627-3575. Students 81.
GLEN CARBON, MADISON CO., ST. CECILIA (1928), Rev. Stephen J. Pohlman.
Res.: 155 N. Main St., 62034. Tel: 618-288-3200; Fax: 618-288-3292.
Catechesis/Religious Program—St. Cecilia Family Life Center, Tel: 618-288-5523. Students 245.
GODFREY, MADISON CO., ST. AMBROSE (1947), [JC] Rev. Msgr. Virgil Mank, V.F.
Church: 820 W. Homer Adams Pkwy., 62035. Tel: 618-466-2921; Fax: 618-466-2959.
Res.: 3307 Morkel Dr., 62035. Tel: 618-466-6408.
School—Tel: 618-466-4216; Fax: 618-466-4575. Mary Jo Jacobs, Prin. Lay Teachers 20; Students 295.
Catechesis/Religious Program—Students 90.
GRAFTON, JERSEY CO., ST. PATRICK (1871), Rev. Robert L. Meyer.
Res.: 11 N. Evans, P.O. Box 218, 62037. Tel: 618-786-3512; Fax: 618-786-2027.
Catechesis/Religious Program—Students 19.
GRANITE CITY, MADISON CO.
1—ST. ELIZABETH (1871), [CEM] [JC] Rev. Pat G. Jakel.
Office: 2300 Pontoon Rd., 62040. Tel: 618-877-3300; Fax: 618-877-9800.
Res.: 3235 Edgewood, 62040. Tel: 618-877-0776.
School—Tel: 618-877-3348. Lay Teachers 12; Students 186.
School—St. Elizabeth Preschool, Tel: 618-877-3350.
Catechesis/Religious Program—Students 125.
2—HOLY FAMILY (1988), [JC] Rev. Larry H. Brunette.
Res.: 2606 Washington Ave., 62040-4810. Tel: 618-877-7158; Fax: 618-877-7105.
School—Tel: 618-877-5500; Fax: 618-877-5502. Lay Teachers 18; Students 298.
Catechesis/Religious Program—Tel: 618-452-8244. Students 78.
GRANTFORK, MADISON CO., ST. GERTRUDE (1872), [CEM] Rev. James A. Flach.
Res.: 120 N. Windmill, P.O. Box 457, Marine, 62061. Tel: 618-887-4535.
Catechesis/Religious Program—Tel: 618-654-4095. Amanda Raynor, D.R.E. Students 54.
GREEN CREEK, EFFINGHAM CO., ST. MARY HELP OF CHRISTIANS (1860), (German), [CEM] Rev. Sylvano J. Pera, O.F.M.
Res.: 20057 N. 1525th St., Effingham, 62401. Tel: 217-844-2062; Fax: 217-844-2062.
Catechesis/Religious Program—Tel: 217-844-2673. Students 111.
GREENFIELD, GREENE CO., ST. MICHAEL (1880), [CEM] Rev. Henry Schmidt.
Res.: 411 Sheffield, 62044. Tel: 217-368-2176.
Catechesis/Religious Program—Students 32.
GREENUP, CUMBERLAND CO., CHRIST THE KING (1937), Rev. Christopher Brey.
Res.: 110 Lincoln Dr., P.O. Box 156, 62428. Tel: 217-923-3523; Fax: 217-923-3523.
GREENVILLE, BOND CO., ST. LAWRENCE (1868), [CEM] Rev. Victor J. Kaltenbach.
Res.: 512 S. Prairie St., 62246. Tel: 618-664-3169; 618-664-9149. Email: stlawgranl@papadocs.com.
Catechesis/Religious Program—Students 156.
GRIGGSVILLE, PIKE CO., HOLY FAMILY, Closed., For details for parish records see St. Mary, Pittsfield.
HAGAMAN, MACOUPIN CO., ST CATHERINE (1905), Closed. For inquiries for parish records contact the chancery.
HARDIN, CALHOUN CO., ST. NORBERT (1872), (German), [CEM] Rev. Thomas Hagstrom.
Office:—404 Main St., P.O. Box C, 62047. Tel: 618-576-2517; Fax: 618-576-9448.
Res.: Meppen Ln., Meppen, 62013. Tel: 618-883-2309; Fax: 618-883-2108.
School—(Grades 1-7) Tel: 618-576-2514. Lay Teachers 4; Aides 2; Students 93.
Catechesis/Religious Program—Tel: 618-576-2628. Students 93.
HIGHLAND, MADISON CO., ST. PAUL (1844), [CEM] Revs. David L. Peters; Robert W. Spriggs.
Res.: 1412 Ninth St., 62249. Tel: 618-654-2339; Fax: 618-654-9980.
School—(Grades PreK-8) Tel: 618-654-7525; Fax: 618-654-8795. Sisters 1; Lay Teachers 25; Students 364.
Catechesis/Religious Program—1420 Ninth St., 62249. Tel: 618-654-4313. Students 349.
HILLSBORO, MONTGOMERY CO., ST. AGNES (1840), [CEM] Rev. James L. Neuman.
Res.: 216 E. Tremont St., 62049. Tel: 217-532-5288; Fax: 217-532-2631.
Catechesis/Religious Program—Tel: 217-532-2631. Students 139.
HUME, EDGAR CO., ST. MICHAEL (1876), Rev. Paul H. Skelton.
Res.: 208 N. Pine, Box 17, Villa Grove, 61956. Tel: 217-832-8352; Fax: 217-832-8352.
Catechesis/Religious Program—Students 13.
ILLIOPOLIS, SANGAMON CO., VISITATION B.V.M. (1866), [CEM] [JC] Sr. Lois Kikkert, O.P., Parish Life Coord.
Res.: 410 Anne St., P.O. Box 47, 62539. Tel: 217-486-3851; Fax: 217-486-3851.
Catechesis/Religious Program—Students 22.
ISLAND GROVE, JASPER CO., ST. JOSEPH (1874), [CEM] Rev. Edwin O. Albers, O.F.M.
Res.: 19812 E. 1000th Ave., Dieterich, 62424. Tel: 217-925-5579; Fax: 217-925-5578.
Catechesis/Religious Program—Students 83.
JACKSONVILLE, MORGAN CO., OUR SAVIOUR (1851), [CEM] Revs. Ken J. Venvertloh; Thomas C. Meyer.
Mailing Address: 453 E. State St., 62650. Tel: 217-245-6184; Fax: 217-245-6185.
School— 62650. Tel: 217-243-8621. Mrs. Peggy Goodwin, Prin. Lay Teachers 22; Students 294.
Catechesis/Religious Program—Tel: 217-245-7633. Students 115.
JERSEYVILLE, JERSEY CO.
1—ST. FRANCIS XAVIER (1857), (Irish—German), [CEM] [JC] Rev. Donald Patrick Gibbons.
Res.: 506 S. State St., P.O. Box 260, 62052-0260. Tel: 618-498-3518.
School—St. Francis/Holy Ghost School, Tel: 618-498-4823.
School—St. Francis, 412 S. State St., 62052. Tel: 618-498-4823; Fax: 618-498-4823. (Grades 5-8)
Holy Ghost—309 N. Washington St., 62052. Tel: 618-498-4910. Mrs. Janet Goben, Prin. (Grades K-4) Lay Teachers 21; Students 430.
Catechesis/Religious Program—Tel: 618-498-5497. Students 77.
2—HOLY GHOST, (German), [JC] Rev. William Hembrow.
Res.: 306 N. Washington St., 62052. Tel: 618-498-3416; Fax: 618-498-3414.
School—St. Francis/Holy Ghost School, Tel: 618-498-4823. See St. Francis.
Catechesis/Religious Program—Students 243.
KAMPSVILLE, CALHOUN CO., ST. ANSELM (1877), (German), [CEM] Rev. Thomas Hagstrom.
Office:—404 Main St., P.O. Box C, Hardin, 62047. Tel: 618-576-2517; Fax: 618-576-9448.
Res.: Meppen Ln., Meppen, 62013. Tel: 618-883-2309.
Catechesis/Religious Program—Tel: 618-576-2628. Clustered with St. Norbert, Hardin.
KINCAID, CHRISTIAN CO., ST. RITA (1920), Rev. Charles G. Dahlby.
Res.: 30 St. Rita Ct., P.O. Box 439, 62540. Tel: 217-237-4339; Fax: 217-237-2477.
Catechesis/Religious Program—Students 62.
LIBERTY, ADAMS CO., ST. BRIGID (1860), [CEM] Rev. Rayappa Repudi, Admin.
Mailing Address: P.O. Box 228, 62347.
Church: 706 N. Main St., 62347. Tel: 217-645-3444; Fax: 217-645-3546.
Rectory: 806 N. Main St., 62347-0228.
Catechesis/Religious Program—Sr. Joan Schnorbus, C.PP.S., D.R.E. Students 107.
LILLYVILLE, CUMBERLAND CO., SACRED HEART (1877), (German), [CEM] Rev. Sylvano Pera, O.F.M.
Mailing Address: 127 County Rd. 100 E., Sigel, 62462.
Res.: 20057 N. 1525 St., Effingham, 62401. Tel: 217-844-2062.
Catechesis/Religious Program—Tel: 217-844-3603. Students 50.
LITCHFIELD, MONTGOMERY CO., HOLY FAMILY (1988), [CEM], Former St. Mary, founded in 1857 Rev. James L. Neuman.
Res.: 216 E. Tremont St., Hillsboro, 62049. Tel:

217-532-5288; Fax: 217-532-2631.
Church: 410 S. State St., P.O. Box 8, 62056. Tel: 217-324-2776; Fax: 217-324-2868.
Catechesis/Religious Program—211 E. Columbia St., 62056. Tel: 217-324-5834. Students 102.

LIVINGSTON, MADISON CO., SACRED HEART (1913), [CEM] Rev. George Radosevich. Tel: 618-635-8490.
Res.: 188 Livingston Ave., P.O. Box 458, 62058. Tel: 618-637-2211.
Catechesis/Religious Program— Combined with St. Michael Parish, Staunton. Students 21.

LOVINGTON, MOULTRIE CO., ST. MARY, Closed., Sacramental records are located at Our Lady of the Holy Spirit.

MACON, MACON CO., ST. STANISLAUS (1866), Closed. For inquiries for parish records contact the chancery.

MADISON, MADISON CO., ST. MARY AND ST. MARK (2002), [JC] In Res., Rev. Francis Tebangura, Sacramental Min.; Sharon Brinker, Pastoral Assoc.; Sr. Judith Robbins, Pastoral Assoc.
Res.: 1621 10th St., 62060. Tel: 618-452-5180; Fax: 618-877-4255.

MARINE, MADISON CO., ST. ELIZABETH (1856), [CEM] Rev. James A. Flach.
Res.: 120 N. Windmill St., P.O. Box 457, 62061. Tel: 618-887-4535.
Catechesis/Religious Program—P.O. Box 169, 62061. Tel: 618-887-4262. Mary Dykes, D.R.E. Students 30.

MARSHALL, CLARK CO., ST. MARY (1847), [CEM] Rev. Christopher Brey.
Mailing Address: 414 S. Sixth St., 62441. Tel: 217-826-2845; Fax: 217-826-1137.
Res.: 110 Lincoln Dr., P.O. Box 156, Greenup, 62428. Tel: 217-923-3523; 217-826-2845.
Catechesis/Religious Program—Students 99.

MARYVILLE, MADISON CO., MOTHER OF PERPETUAL HELP (1938), Rev. W. Jeffrey Holtman, S.F.O.
Res.: 200 N. Lange, 62062. Tel: 618-344-6464; Fax: 618-344-6493.
School—St. John Neumann School, Tel: 618-345-7230; Fax: 618-345-4350. Lay Teachers 19; Students 343.
Catechesis/Religious Program—Students 105.

MATTOON, COLES CO., IMMACULATE CONCEPTION (1856), [CEM] Rev. Herman J. Niebrugge.
Res.: 320 N. 21st St., P.O. Box 468, 61938-0468. Tel: 217-235-0539; Fax: 217-235-0593.
School—Tel: 217-235-0431; Fax: 217-235-5447. Lay Teachers 8; Students 122.
Catechesis/Religious Program—Tel: 217-234-6648. Students 151.

MEDORA, MACOUPIN CO., ST. JOHN THE EVANGELIST (1914), (German), Rev. Raphael Paul, Admin.
Res.: *c/o St. Alphonsus Church*, 918 N. Main St., Brighton, 62012. Tel: 618-372-3352; Fax: 618-372-8133.
Catechesis/Religious Program— Clustered with St. Alphonsus, Brighton. Students 10.

MENDON, ADAMS CO., ST. EDWARD (1891), [CEM] Rev. Louis Schlangen.
Res.: 214 S. State Rd., 62351. Tel: 217-936-2289.
Catechesis/Religious Program—Students 64.

MEPPEN, CALHOUN CO., ST. JOSEPH (1864), (German), [CEM] Rev. Thomas Hagstrom.
Office—P.O. Box 38, Brussels, 62013. Tel: 618-883-2400; Fax: 618-883-2511.
Res.: Meppen Ln., 62013. Tel: 618-883-2309; Fax: 618-883-2108.
Catechesis/Religious Program—Students 10.

MICHAEL, CALHOUN CO., ST. MICHAEL (1864), (Irish), [CEM] Rev. Thomas Hagstrom.
Office:—404 Main St., P.O. Box C, Hardin, 62047. Tel: 618-576-2517; Fax: 618-576-9448.
Res.: Meppen Ln., Meppen, 62013. Tel: 618-883-2309; Fax: 618-883-2108.
Catechesis/Religious Program— Clustered with St. Norbert, Hardin.

MONTROSE, EFFINGHAM CO., ST. ROSE OF LIMA (1879), [CEM] Revs. Austin Albers, O.F.M.; Ken Rosswog, O.F.M.; Vernon Olmer, O.F.M.
Mailing Address: P.O. Box 68, 62445. Tel: 217-924-4337; Fax: 217-924-4312.
Catechesis/Religious Program—Tel: 217-924-4465. Students 94.

MORRISONVILLE, CHRISTIAN CO., ST. MAURICE (1870), [CEM] Rev. John T. Hannigan (CHI), Admin.
Res.: 706 E. Fourth St., P.O. Box 45, 62546-0045. Tel: 217-526-3363; Fax: 217-526-3110.
School—(Grades 1-8) Tel: 217-526-3534. Lay Teachers 4; Students 40.
Catechesis/Religious Program—Students 57.

MOUNT OLIVE, MACOUPIN CO.

1—ASCENSION (1886), (Croatian), [CEM] Rev. Larry Anschutz, Admin.
Res.: 705 E. Main St., 62069. Tel: 217-999-4981; Fax: 217-999-4036.
Catechesis/Religious Program—Students 50.

2—HOLY TRINITY (1912), (Slovak), [CEM] Rev. Larry Anschutz, Admin.
Res.: 705 E. Main St., 62069. Tel: 217-999-4981; Fax: 217-999-4036.
Church: 410 Garfield, 62069.
Catechesis/Religious Program—Students 29.

MOUNT STERLING, BROWN CO., HOLY FAMILY (1864), [CEM] Rev. Thomas Henseler.
Res.: 401 W. North St., P.O. Box 252, 62353. Tel: 217-773-3233.
School—Tel: 217-773-2825; Fax: 217-773-2825. Lay Teachers 8; Students 97.
Catechesis/Religious Program—Students 110.

MOWEAQUA, SHELBY CO., ST. FRANCES DE SALES (1895), [JC] Rev. Angel Sierra.
Res.: 301 St. Peter St., Assumption, 62510. Tel: 217-226-3536; Fax: 217-226-3538.
Catechesis/Religious Program—Tel: 217-226-3205. Students 51.

MT. ZION, MACON CO., OUR LADY OF THE HOLY SPIRIT (1974), Very Rev. James D. O'Shea, V.F.
Res.: 400 Woodland, 62549. Tel: 217-864-3467; Fax: 217-864-3091.
Catechesis/Religious Program—Tel: 217-864-4941. Students 105.

MURRAYVILLE, MORGAN CO., ST. BARTHOLOMEW (1884), [CEM] Rev. Charles T. Nelson.
Res.: P.O. Box 47, 62668. Tel: 217-882-3781; 217-742-5224.
Catechesis/Religious Program—Students 6.

NEOGA, CUMBERLAND CO., ST. MARY OF THE ASSUMPTION (1897), (German), [CEM] Rev. Robert L. DeGrand, Admin.
Res.: Church St., P.O. Box 68, Sigel, 62462. Tel: 217-844-3371; Fax: 217-844-2309.
Church: 690 N. Walnut St., 62447. Tel: 217-895-2166.
Catechesis/Religious Program—Students 90.

NEW BERLIN, SANGAMON CO., SACRED HEART OF MARY (1858), [CEM] Rev. Joseph P. Kerber.
Res.: 404 E. Birch, P.O. Box 20, 62670. Tel: 217-488-2410; Fax: 217-488-2410.
Catechesis/Religious Program—Tel: 217-488-3545; Fax: 217-488-3545. Students 40.

NEW DOUGLAS, MADISON CO., ST. UBALDUS (1872), [CEM] Rev. George Radosevich. Tel: 618-635-8490.
Res.: 322 E. Main St., Staunton, 62088. Tel: 618-635-8490.
Catechesis/Religious Program—Students 7.

NEWTON, JASPER CO., ST. THOMAS THE APOSTLE (1873), [CEM 3] Rev. Barry J. Harmon.
Res.: 402 W. Jourdan St., P.O. Box 225, 62448. Tel: 618-783-8741; Fax: 618-783-8742.
School—Tel: 618-783-3517; Fax: 618-783-2224. Lay Teachers 9; Students 164.
Catechesis/Religious Program—Students 115.

NIANTIC, MACON CO., ST. ANN (1889), [JC] Sr. Lois Kikkert, O.P., Parish Life Coord.
Mailing Address: P.O. Box 47, Illiopolis, 62539.
Res.: 410 Anne St., Illiopolis, 62539. Tel: 217-486-3851; Fax: 217-486-3851.
Church: North St. & Pritchett St., 62551.
Catechesis/Religious Program—Students 9.

NOKOMIS, MONTGOMERY CO., ST. LOUIS (1870), [CEM] Rev. Christopher J. Comerford.
Res.: 311 S. Elm St., 62075-1310. Tel: 217-563-7146; 217-563-7808 (Personal); Fax: 217-563-8671.
School—509 E. Union, 62075. Tel: 217-563-7445; Fax: 217-563-7450. Lay Teachers 6; Students 104.
Catechesis/Religious Program—Students 58.

NORTH ARM, EDGAR CO., ST. ALOYSIUS (1817), [CEM] Rev. William J. Overmann.
Res.: P.O. Box 577, Paris, 61944. Tel: 217-466-3355; Fax: 217-463-3005.
Catechesis/Religious Program— Clustered with St. Mary's, Paris.

OBLONG, CRAWFORD CO., OUR LADY OF LOURDES (1954), Rev. Jeffrey Goeckner.
Res.: 207 E. Walnut St., Robinson, 62454. Tel: 618-544-7526; Fax: 618-546-5693.
Catechesis/Religious Program—Tel: 618-544-9327. Students 8.

OCONEE, SHELBY CO., SACRED HEART (1872), (German), [CEM] Rev. Don J. Roberts, Admin.
Res.: P.O. Box 45, 62553. Tel: 217-539-4325.
Catechesis/Religious Program—Students 20.

PALMYRA, MACOUPIN CO., HOLY ROSARY (1954), Closed. For inquiries for parish records contact the chancery.

PANA, CHRISTIAN CO., ST. PATRICK (1858), [CEM] Rev. Don Roberts.
Res.: 6 E. Fifth St., P.O. Box 440, 62557. Tel: 217-562-5396; Fax: 217-562-2308.
School—Sacred Heart, Tel: 217-562-2425. Mr. John Pastor, Prin. Lay Teachers 9; Students 139; Pre-K 18.
Catechesis/Religious Program—Tel: 217-824-6120. Students 67.

PANAMA, BOND CO., SACRED HEART (1916), [JC] Rev. Carl Schmidt.
Res.: 400 Jefferson, P.O. Box 278, Coffeen, 62017. Tel: 217-534-2220.
Catechesis/Religious Program—Students 17.

PARIS, EDGAR CO., ST. MARY (1849), [CEM] Rev. William J. Overmann.
Res.: 528 N. Main St., P.O. Box 577, 61944. Tel: 217-466-3355; Fax: 217-466-5215.
School—Tel: 217-463-3005; Fax: 217-463-3005. Lay Teachers 6; Students 54.
Catechesis/Religious Program—Students 91.

PAWNEE, SANGAMON CO., ST. MARY (1899), (German), [CEM] Rev. Charles G. Dahlby.
Res.: P.O. Box 439, Kincaid, 62540. Tel: 217-237-4339.
Catechesis/Religious Program—Tel: 217-625-7540. Students 94.

PETERSBURG, MENARD CO., ST. PETER (1868), [CEM] Rev. Msgr. Carl A. Kemme, V.G.
Res.: 711 S. Sixth St., 62675. Tel: 217-632-2561; Fax: 217-632-7118.
Catechesis/Religious Program—Tel: 217-632-7118. Students 108.

PIERRON, MADISON AND BOND COS., IMMACULATE CONCEPTION (1892), [CEM] Rev. Msgr. Paul W. Sheridan.
Res.: P.O. Box 410, 62273. Tel: 618-654-3604; Fax: 618-654-8764.
Catechesis/Religious Program—Students 85.

PITTSFIELD, PIKE CO., ST. MARY (1870), [CEM] [JC] Rev. J. Michael Jenkins; Very Rev. Robert J. Jallas, V.F., Admin.
Res.: 226 E. Adams, 62363. Tel: 217-285-4321; Fax: 217-285-9400.
Catechesis/Religious Program—Tel: 217-285-4774. Students 46.

POCAHONTAS, BOND CO., ST. NICHOLAS (1871), Rev. Msgr. Paul W. Sheridan.
Res.: P.O. Box 410, Pierron, 62273. Tel: 618-654-3604; Fax: 618-654-8764.
Catechesis/Religious Program—Students 19.

QUINCY, ADAMS CO.

1—ALL SAINTS (1999), [JC] Very Rev. Robert J. Jallas, V.F.
1019 Cedar St., 62301-2027. Tel: 217-222-4622; Fax: 217-222-5554.
School—Preschool Noah's Ark Lay Teachers 2; Aides 2; Students 65.
School—(Grades K-8), 1236 N. 10th, 62301. Tel: 217-228-1477. Sisters of Notre Dame 1; Lay Teachers 8; Students 132.
Catechesis/Religious Program—Students 38.

2—ST. ANTHONY OF PADUA (1859), [CEM] Very Rev. Robert J. Jallas, V.F.; Sr. Mary Shaw, A.S.C., Parish Life Coord.
Res. & Church address: 2223 St. Anthony Rd., 62305. Tel: 217-222-5996; Fax: 217-222-5996.
School—Tel: 217-224-6477. Lay Teachers 5; Students 68.
Catechesis/Religious Program—Students 81.

3—ST. BONIFACE (1837), (German), [JC] Rev. John Carberry.
Res.: 117 N. Seventh St., 62301. Tel: 217-222-3000; Fax: 217-223-6999.
School—Tel: 217-223-6999. Lay Teachers 6; Students 70.
Catechesis/Religious Program—Students 21.

4—ST. DOMINIC (1977), [JC] Rev. Donald Knuffman.
Res.: 3800 Columbus Rd., P.O. Box 3364, 62301. Tel: 217-224-9102; Fax: 217-224-0042.
Church: 4100 Columbus Rd., 62301.
School—Tel: 217-224-0041. Lay Teachers 12; Students 189.
Catechesis/Religious Program—Students 35.

5—ST. FRANCIS SOLANUS (1860), [JC] Revs. Kurt Hartrich, O.F.M.; Eugene Middendorf, O.F.M.; James Wheeler, O.F.M.; James F. Finn, O.F.M.
Res.: 1721 College Ave., 62301. Tel: 217-222-2898; Fax: 217-222-3020.
School—Tel: 217-222-4077; Fax: 217-222-5049. Lay Teachers 12; Students 261.
Catechesis/Religious Program—1721 College Ave., 62301. Students 95.

6—ST. JOHN THE BAPTIST (1880), (German), Merged, with St. Rose of Lima, Quincy to form All Saints, Quincy.

7—ST. JOSEPH (1868), [CEM] Very Rev. Robert J. Jallas, V.F.; Sr. Mary Shaw, A.S.C., Parish Life Coord.
Church and Mailing: 1435 E. 1500 St., 62305. Tel: 217-434-8442; Fax: 217-434-8058.
Catechesis/Religious Program—Students 95.

8—ST. MARY (1867), [JC], (Immaculate Conception) Rev. Msgr. Michael Kuse.
Res.: 1119 S. Seventh St., 62301. Tel: 217-222-2759; Fax: 217-222-6463.
School—Tel: 217-223-3388. Lay Teachers 9; Students 147.
Catechesis/Religious Program—Students 113.

9—ST. PETER (1839), (Irish), [JC] Rev. Roy R. Bauer.
Res.: 2600 Maine St., 62301. Tel: 217-222-3155; Fax: 217-222-3584.
School—Tel: 217-223-1120; Fax: 217-223-1173. Lay Teachers 22; Students 487.
Catechesis/Religious Program—Students 86.

10—ST. ROSE OF LIMA (1892), (Irish), Merged, with

St. John the Baptist, Quincy to form All Saints, Quincy.

RAMSEY, FAYETTE CO., ST. JOSEPH (1870), (German—Irish), [CEM] Rev. Steven Sotiroff.
Res.: 118 E. Main, P.O. Box 455, 62080. Tel: 618-423-2424.
Catechesis/Religious Program—Students 26.

RAYMOND, MONTGOMERY CO., ST RAYMOND (1874), [CEM] Rev. John T. Hannigan (CHI), Admin.
Res.: 306 S. McElroy, P.O. Box 349, 62560. Tel: 217-229-4435.
Catechesis/Religious Program—Tel: 217-229-3655. Students 80.

RIVERTON, SANGAMON CO., ST. JAMES (1871), Very Rev. John A. Renken, V.G., Co-Pastor; Rev. Msgr. Kenneth C. Steffen, J.C.L., M.A., M.Div., D.Min., Co-Pastor.
Res.: 112 N. Sixth St., P.O. Box 590, 62561-0590. Tel: 217-629-9109 (Rectory); 217-629-7717 (Office).
Catechesis/Religious Program—Tel: 217-629-7717. Bro. Anthony Joseph McCoy, F.F.S.C., D.R.E. Students 78.

ROBINSON, CRAWFORD CO., ST. ELIZABETH (1908), Rev. Jeffrey Goeckner.
Res.: 207 E. Walnut St., 62454. Tel: 618-544-7526; Fax: 618-546-5693.
Catechesis/Religious Program—Tel: 618-544-9327. Students 160.

ROCHESTER, SANGAMON CO., ST. JUDE (1976), Rev. William Carpenter, C.S.V.
Res.: 633 S. Walnut St., 62563. Tel: 217-498-7133; Fax: 217-498-7180.
Parish Center—635 S. Walnut St., 62563. Tel: 217-498-9524.
Catechesis/Religious Program—Tel: 217-498-9197. Students 300.

ST. ELMO, FAYETTE CO.
1—ST. BONAVENTURE (1843), (Irish—German), [CEM] Rev. John M. Savoree, Admin.
Res.: 216 N. Ninth, Altamont, 62411. Tel: 618-483-5346.
2—ST. MARY (1904), (German), Rev. John M. Savoree, Admin.
Res.: 216 N. Ninth, Altamont, 62411. Tel: 618-483-5341.
Catechesis/Religious Program—Students 18.

ST. JACOB, MADISON CO., ST. JAMES (1894), Rev. James A. Flach.
Res.: 120 N. Windmill St., Box 457, Marine, 62061. Tel: 618-887-4535.
Catechesis/Religious Program—Students 26.

SHELBYVILLE, SHELBY CO., IMMACULATE CONCEPTION (1879), Rev. Donald L. Wolford.
Res.: N. Rte. 128, P.O. Box 233, 62565. Tel: 217-774-3434; Fax: 217-774-3516.
Catechesis/Religious Program—Students 66.

SHERMAN, SANGAMON CO., ST. JOHN VIANNEY (1931), [CEM] Rev. Msgr. Eugene E. Costa, S.T.L.
Res.: 129 Stardust Dr., P.O. Box 229, 62684. Tel: 217-523-3816; Fax: 217-523-3954.
Catechesis/Religious Program—Students 174.

SHIPMAN, MACOUPIN CO., ST. DENIS (1876), [CEM] Rev. Robert N. Porter.
Res.: P.O. Box A H, Bunker Hill, 62014-9512. Tel: 618-585-4700; Fax: 618-585-3449.
Catechesis/Religious Program—Students 17.

SHUMWAY, EFFINGHAM CO., ANNUNCIATION (1879), [CEM] Very Rev. Leo Enlow, V.F.
Res.: P.O. Box 96, 62461. Tel: 217-857-6404.
Catechesis/Religious Program—Tel: 618-487-5503. Students 93.

SIGEL, SHELBY CO., ST. MICHAEL THE ARCHANGEL (1867), (German), [CEM] Rev. Robert L. DeGrand, Admin.
Res.: Box 68, 62462. Tel: 217-844-3371; Fax: 217-844-2309.
School—Tel: 217-844-2231. Lay Teachers 10; Students 112.
Catechesis/Religious Program—Students 78.

STAUNTON, MACOUPIN CO., ST. MICHAEL THE ARCHANGEL (1875), [JC 2] Rev. George Radosevich.
Office—P.O. Box 240, 62088. Tel: 618-635-3140; Fax: 618-635-3140.
Res.: 322 E. Main, 62088. Tel: 618-635-8490.
School—419 E. Main, 62088. Tel: 618-635-3210; Fax: 618-635-3210. Religious 1; Lay Teachers 6; Students 74.
Catechesis/Religious Program—Students 121.

STE. MARIE, JASPER CO., ST. MARY (1837), (French—German), [CEM] [JC] Rev. Barry J. Harmon.
Res.: P.O. Box 68, 62459. Tel: 618-455-3155; Fax: 618-455-3665.
Catechesis/Religious Program—112 W. Embarras St., P.O. Box 68, 62459. Students 71.

STONINGTON, CHRISTIAN CO., HOLY TRINITY (1879), (Irish—German), Rev. Martin O'Hara.
Mailing Address: P.O. Box 257, 62567. Tel: 217-325-3697.
Res. & Church: 108 N. Elm, P.O. Box 257, 62567. Tel: 217-325-3691.
Catechesis/Religious Program—Students 55.

SULLIVAN, MOULTRIE CO., ST. COLUMCILLE (1905), Rev. John E. Sohm.
Res.: 516 W. Jackson, P.O. Box 464, 61951. Tel: 217-728-4040.
Catechesis Religious Program—Students 65.

TAYLORVILLE, CHRISTIAN CO., ST. MARY (1845), Rev. Alan Hunter.
Res.: 116 W. Adams St., P.O. Box 470, 62568. Tel: 217-824-8178; Fax: 217-824-8225.
School—(Grades PreK-6) Tel: 217-824-6501; Fax: 217-824-2303. Lay Teachers 17; Students 159.
Catechesis/Religious Program—Students 153.

TEUTOPOLIS, EFFINGHAM CO., ST. FRANCIS OF ASSISI (1839), [CEM] Revs. Austin Albers, O.F.M.; Kenneth Rosswog, O.F.M.; Bro. Paulinus Johnson, O.F.M.; Rev. Vernon Olmer, O.F.M.
Res.: 203 E. Main St., 62467. Tel: 217-857-6404; Fax: 217-857-1031.
Catechesis/Religious Program—Tel: 217-857-6477. Sr. Ann Siemer, S.S.N.D., D.R.E.; Lisa Siemer, D.R.E.; Sr. Ann Pierre Wilken, O.S.F., D.R.E. Students 733.

TROY, MADISON CO., ST. JEROME (1870), [CEM 2] Rev. Steven A. Janoski.
Res.: P.O. Box 94, 62294. Tel: 618-667-6571; Fax: 618-667-2697.
School—St. John Neumann, 511 S. Main St., Maryville. Tel: 618-345-7230; Fax: 618-345-4350.
Catechesis/Religious Program—107 Wayland, 62294. Fax: 618-667-2697. Students 278.

TUSCOLA, DOUGLAS CO., FORTY MARTYRS (1865), Rev. Allen Kemme.
Res.: 201 E. Van Allen St., P.O. Box 352, 61953. Tel: 217-253-4412; Fax: 217-253-5010.
Catechesis/Religious Program—Students 199.

VANDALIA, FAYETTE CO., MOTHER OF DOLORS (1850), [CEM] Rev. Stephen T. Sotiroff.
Res.: 222 N. Seventh St., P.O. Box 377, 62471. Tel: 618-283-0214; Fax: 618-283-0278.
Catechesis/Religious Program—Students 93.

VENICE, MADISON CO., ST. MARK (1871), Closed. For inquiries for parish records contact the chancery.

VILLA GROVE, DOUGLAS CO., SACRED HEART (1906), Rev. Paul H. Skelton.
Res.: 208 N. Pine, Box 17, 61956 Tel: 217-832-8352; Fax: 217-832-8352.
Catechesis/Religious Program—Students 47.
Mission—St. Michael's Center St. Hume, Edgar Co. 61932. Tel: 217-887-2482.

VIRDEN, MACOUPIN CO., SACRED HEART (1914), (Slovak),, St. Catherine's (1866) Merged in 1978 Rev. August J. Sperl.
Res.: 721 N. Springfield, 62690. Tel: 217-965-4545; Fax: 217-965-3889.
Catechesis/Religious Program—Tel: 217-965-5370. Students 84.

VIRGINIA, CASS CO., ST. LUKE (1849), Revs. Ken J. Venvertloh; Thomas Meyer.
Church: 240 E. Myrtle St., 62691. Tel: 217-245-6184.
Catechesis/Religious Program—Students 22.

WAVERLY, MORGAN CO., ST. SEBASTIAN (1856), [CEM] Rev. Kevin Michael Laughery.
Office and Res.: 125 E. Washington St., P.O. Box 168, Auburn, 62615. Tel: 217-438-6222; Fax: 217-438-6732.
Church: 265 E. Elm St., 62692.
Catechesis/Religious Program— Clustered with St. Benedict's, Auburn. Students 21.

WHITE HALL, GREENE CO., ALL SAINTS (1883), Rev. Henry Schmidt.
Res.: 414 Third St., Carrollton, 62016. Tel: 217-942-3551; Fax: 217-942-6767.
Church: S. Main St., 62092.
Catechesis/Religious Program—Students 58.

WILSONVILLE, MACOUPIN CO., HOLY CROSS (1926), Rev. Robert N. Porter.
Res.: 300 S. Putnam, P.O. Box A-H, Bunker Hill, 62014-9512. Tel: 618-585-4700; Fax: 618-585-3449.

WINCHESTER, SCOTT CO., ST. MARK (1860), [CEM] Rev. Charles T. Nelson.
Res.: 108 Pearl St., 62694. Tel: 217-742-5224.
Catechesis/Religious Program—Students 37.

WITT, MONTGOMERY CO., ST. BARBARA (1905), [CEM] Rev. Christopher J. Comerford.
Res.: 311 S. Elm St., Nokomis, 62075-1310. Tel: 217-563-7146; 217-563-7808 Personal); Fax: 217-563-8671.

WOOD RIVER, MADISON CO., ST. BERNARD (1919), Rev. Mark A. Schulte.
Res.: 345 Acton Ave., 62095. Tel: 618-254-0679 (Office); Fax: 618-254-2690.
Catechesis/Religious Program—Students 25.

Chaplains of Public Institutions

ALTON. *Alton State Hospital*, St. Matthew Parish, 1015 Milton Rd., 62002. Tel: 618-465-8582. Vacant.

HILLSBORO. *Graham Correctional Center*.
11132 Catatoga Dr., Plainview, 62685. Tel: 618-836-7447. Rev. George L. Morelock, Chap.

JACKSONVILLE. *Illinois State Hospital*, 462 E. State St., 62650. Tel: 217-245-6184. Attended by Our Savior Parish.
School for the Blind, 462 E. State St., 62650. Tel: 217-245-6184. Attended by Our Savior Parish.
School for the Deaf, 462 E. State St., 62650. Tel: 217-245-6184. Attended by Our Savior Parish.

MOUNT STERLING. *Western Illinois Correctional Center*, 401 W. North St., 62353. Tel: 217-773-3233. Attended by Holy Family Parish.

QUINCY. *Illinois Veterans' Home*, 1901 N. 18th, 62301. Tel: 217-224-0591. Rev. Richard M. Jeske, O.F.M.

TAYLORVILLE. *Taylorville Correctional Center*, 116 W. Adams St., P.O. Box 248, 62658. Tel: 217-824-8178. Attended by St. Mary Parish.

VANDALIA. *Vandalia Correctional Center*, 322 N. Seventh, 62471. Tel: 618-283-0214. Attended by Mother of Dolors Parish.

On Duty Outside the Diocese:
Revs.—
Gallenbach, Thomas, 7075 Del Ray, Las Vegas, NV 89117. Tel: 540-254-5488 (Home); 540-363-1902 (Office)
Habing, Paul, Prelatura, Apt. 102, Ayaviri-Puno, Peru.
Kromenaker, Joseph, St. Ferdinand Church, 5900 Barry Ave., Chicago, 60634. Tel: 773-622-5900; ; Fax: 773-622-5903
Simburger, Joseph, Magdalen College, 511 Kearsarge Mountain Rd., Warner, NH 03278-4012. Tel: 603-456-2656

Graduate Studies:
Rev.—
Dennis, Thomas J., Loyola Univ., Chicago.

Military Chaplains:
Revs.—
Burnett, John, Chap., U.S. Navy
Nolan, John, Chap., U.S. Air Force

Special or Other Diocesan Assignment:
Revs.—
Kraft, Philip, 929 Rickard Rd. Ct., P.O. Box 7492, 62791. Tel: 217-793-3218
Morelock, George, 11132 Catatoga Dr., Plainview, 62685. Tel: 618-836-7447
Rebert, Robert (Retired), Capital Plaza Apartments, 1210 E. Washington St., 62703. Tel: 217-553-6775
Thieman, Anthony, 2651 W. Lawrence, Bldg. 2-F, 62704. Tel: 217-698-8134
Titus, John M., Office for Vocations Catholic Pastoral Center, P.O. Box 3187, 62708-3187. Tel: 217-698-8500, Ext. 182
Trojcak, Ronald, 1717 Madison St., Quincy, 62301. Tel: 217-228-5404

Absent on Leave:
Revs.—
La Count, Daniel
Sullivan, Kevin B.

Retired:
Rev. Msgrs.—
Mulcrone, Charles P., St. Joseph Home, 3306 S. 6th St. Rd., 62703.
Spreen, John, V.F., St. Joseph Home, 3306 S. 6th St. Rd., 62703.
Revs.—
Corrigan, F. J., Villa Health Care West, 100 Stardust Dr., Sherman, 62684. Tel: 217-522-2596
Davenport, Thomas J., St. Joseph Home, 3306 S. 6th St. Rd., 62703. Tel: 217-529-5596
Donohoe, Peter, 714 Douglas Pl., Alton, 62002. Tel: 618-463-0521
Gierut, Casimir, 410 W. Burlington Ave., LaGrange, 60525. Tel: 708-588-8237
Heintz, Robert L., 422 Foulds Ave., Alton, 62002. Tel: 618-462-9767
Houran, J. William, 3233 N.E. 32nd Ave., Apt. 902, Fort Lauderdale, FL 33308. Tel: 954-566-9802
Keane, Brendan, Addolorata Villa, 555 McHenry Rd., Wheeling, 60090. Tel: 847-808-6888
Kekeisen, William, 934 Capris Isles Blvd., Apt. 208, Venice, FL 34292-4408. Tel: 941-484-1261
Kennedy, John, 411 Spring Lake Dr., Quincy, 62301. Tel: 217-224-5288
Maul, William R., 211 Pinewood Dr., Godfrey, 62035. Tel: 618-466-2515
McCarthy, Joseph F., 130 Curtis Ave., Burlington, VT 05401. Tel: 802-862-3138
Meyer, Bernard A., 2425 Sage Rd., Apt. 45, Houston, TX 77056. Tel: 713-629-4822
Morris, Robert, St. Joseph Home, 3306 S. 6th St. Rd., 62703. Tel: 217-529-5596
O'Hara, Frank, Brighton Gardens, 16051 S. LaGrange Rd., Orland Park, 60467. Tel: 708-403-2001

O'Reilly, Joseph, 1319 Tendick St., #3, Jacksonville, 62650-3120. Tel: 217-243-5483

Quilligan, Maurice, 905 Andra Dr., Maryville, 62062. Tel: 618-344-5164

Rebert, Robert, Capitol Plaza Apts., 1210 E. Washington, 62703. Tel: 217-553-6775

Schmidt, Anthony, 520 S. Second St., #906, Lincoln Tower Suites, 62701. Tel: 217-528-6315

Sheahan, John F., St. Clare's Villa, 915 E. 5th St., Apt. 401, P.O. Box 340, Alton, 62002. Tel: 618-462-7964; Fax: 618-463-0995

Simpson, Roger, 271 E. Myrtle St., Virginia, 62691. Tel: 217-452-3168

Sullivan, James, 1270 Village Dr., Apt. 114, Lemont, 60439. Tel: 630-243-9057

Westhoff, Frank, 3930 Brandonshire Dr., 62704-6710. Tel: 217-726-8837

INSTITUTIONS LOCATED IN THE DIOCESE

[A] SEMINARIES, RELIGIOUS OR SCHOLASTICATES

GODFREY. *Immaculate Heart of Mary Novitiate*, 4563 Levis Ln., 62035. Tel: 618-466-2233; Fax: 618-466-2430. Email: ominov@aol.com. Web: www.ominov.itgo.com/ominov.htm. Revs. Sylvester Lewans, O.M.I.; Louis Lougen, O.M.I.; Maurice Lange, O.M.I.; Lawrence Rosebaugh, O.M.I. Priests 4; Clerical Novices 3.

[B] COLLEGES AND UNIVERSITIES

QUINCY. *Quincy University* (1860), 1800 College Ave., 62301. Tel: 217-222-8020; 217-228-5318. Web: www.quincy.edu. Revs. Mario DiCicco, O.F.M. (CHI); Ralph Parthie, O.F.M., Chap.; William Burton, O.F.M.; Philibert Hoebing, O.F.M.; Richard M. Jeske, O.F.M., Chap., Illinois Veteran's Home; Irenaeus Kimminau, O.F.M.; John J. Lakers, O.F.M.; George Windolph, O.F.M.; Joseph Zimmerman, O.F.M.; Bros. Jack Hardesty, O.F.M.; Edward Arambasich, O.F.M. Franciscan Friars, Sacred Heart Province Priests 9; Brothers 2; Lay Faculty - Administrators 101; Students 1,263.

[C] JUNIOR COLLEGES

SPRINGFIELD. *Springfield College in Illinois*, 1500 N. Fifth St., 62702. Tel: 217-525-1420; Fax: 217-789-1698. Email: rappe@sci.edu. Web: www.sci.edu. William J. Carroll, Pres.; Rev. Msgr. David S. Lantz, Dir. Ursuline Sisters 1; Lay Teachers 42; Students 431.

[D] HIGH SCHOOLS, PRIVATE

SPRINGFIELD. *Sacred Heart-Griffin*, 1200 W. Washington St., 62702. Tel: 217-787-1595; Fax: 217-787-9856. Email: smjrunkel@shg.org. Web: www.shg.org. Sisters Marilyn Jean Runkel, O.P., Pres.; Margaret Joanne Grueter, O.P., Prin.; Mr. Robert Brenneisen, Asst. Prin.; Mrs. Beverly Neisler, Vice Pres. for Institutional Advancement; Mr. Thomas Fiaush, Business Mgr.; Dr. William Moredock, Dir. Student & Family Svcs. Springfield Dominican Sisters Priests 2; Sisters 11; Lay Teachers 53; Additional Support Staff 29; Executive Team 6; Students 785.

Ursuline Academy, 1400 N. Fifth St., 62702. Tel: 217-523-5169; Fax: 217-523-2131. Email: bbernardi@ursuline-il.org. Web: www.ursulin-il.org. Barbara A. Bernardi, Prin. Priests 1; Brothers 2; Lay Teachers 17; Students 203.

DECATUR. *St. Teresa High School*, 2710 N. Water St., 62526. Tel: 217-875-2431; Fax: 217-875-2436. Email: stadmin@st-teresahs.org. Web: www.st-teresahs.org. Mr. Joseph A. McDaniel, Prin. Ursuline Sisters 1; Lay Teachers 28; Students 342.

JACKSONVILLE. *Routt Catholic High School*, 500 E. College, 62650. Tel: 217-243-8563; Fax: 217-243-3138. Email: rverticchio@routtcatholic.com. Web: www.routtcatholic.com. Lay Teachers 14; Students 124.

QUINCY. *Quincy Notre Dame High School*, 1400 S. 11th, 62301-7299. Tel: 217-223-2479; Fax: 217-223-0023. Email: rheilmann@quincynotredame.org. Web: www.quincynotredame.org. Ray E. Heilmann, Prin.; Lori Shepard, Vice Prin.; Rev. Charles A. Edwards, Dir. Christian Formation. Priests 1; Lay Teachers 33; School Sisters of Notre Dame 1; Students 506.

[E] HIGH SCHOOLS, DIOCESAN AND PAROCHIAL

ALTON. *Marquette Catholic High School*, 219 E. Fourth St., 62002. Tel: 618-463-0580; Fax: 618-463-0582. Email: marquettH.hs@home.com. Web: alton-marquette.com. Vincent Schmidt, Prin. Sisters 1; Lay Teachers 28; Students 330.

EFFINGHAM. *St. Anthony High School*, 304 E. Roadway Ave., P.O. Box 545, 62401. Tel: 217-342-6969; Fax: 217-342-6997. Email: sahs@stanthony.com. Web: www.stanthony.com. Tom Theiss, Prin. Priests 3; Lay Teachers 20; Students 217.

[F] ELEMENTARY SCHOOLS, PRIVATE

SPRINGFIELD. *Saint Patrick Catholic Grade School*, (Grades K-4), 1800 S. Grand Ave. E., 62703. Tel: 217-523-7670; Fax: 217-523-0760. Joan McKinney, Prin.; Rose Mersinger, Pres. Lay Teachers 4; Students 38.

[G] THE CATHOLIC CHARITIES OF THE DIOCESE OF SPRINGFIELD IN ILLINOIS

SPRINGFIELD. *Catholic Charities of Springfield*, 120 S. 11th St., 62703. Tel: 217-525-0500; Fax: 217-525-0554. Web: www.cc.dio.org. Danielle K. Zellers, Area Dir. Total Assisted 9,306; Total Staff 46.

Catholic Charities Administrative Office, 800 South Fifth St., 62703. Tel: 217-523-9201; Fax: 217-523-5624. Mr. Steven E. Roach, M.S., Exec. Dir. Total Staff 35.

Crisis Assistance, 1023 E. Washington, 62703. Tel: 217-523-4551; Fax: 217-523-8425.

St. Clare's Health Clinic, 700 N. 7th St., Ste. A, 62702. Tel: 217-523-1474; Fax: 217-523-0194.

St. John's Breadline, 430 N. Fifth St., 62702. Tel: 217-528-6098; Fax: 217-528-3605. Email: stjohnsbreadline@mcleod.net. Meals Served Annually 207,000; Total Staff 9.

ALTON. *Alton Catholic Charities*, 735 Park Dr., 62002. Tel: 618-462-0634; Fax: 618-462-3209. Theresa Schulte, Area Dir. Total Assisted 581; Total Staff 15.

BEARDSTOWN. *St. Francis Community Clinic*, 111 S. State St., 62618. Tel: 217-323-5264; Fax: 217-323-4680. Web: www.cc.dio.org. Mr. Steven E. Roach, M.S., Exec. Dir. Total Staff 8; Total Assisted Annually 1,234.

CARLINVILLE. *Carlinville Catholic Charities*, 525 W. Second South, Box 618, 62626. Tel: 217-854-4511; Fax: 217-854-8049. Web: www.cc.dio.org. Ms. Patricia Pope, Area Dir. Total Assisted 1,164; Total Staff 8.

DECATUR. *Catholic Charities Community Services*, 401 N. Martin Luther King, Jr. Dr., 62523. Tel: 217-428-5724; Fax: 217-428-5729. Judy Rogers, On Site Supvr.; Marie Rademacher, Area Dir. Total Assisted 12,949; Total Staff 7.

Decatur Catholic Charities, 247 W. Prairie Ave., 62523. Tel: 217-428-3458; Fax: 217-428-4415. Mrs. Marie Rademacher, Area Dir. Total Assisted 16,000; Total Staff 36.

EFFINGHAM. *Catholic Charities of Effingham*, 601 W. Fayette, 62401. Tel: 217-342-9800; Fax: 217-342-3873. Web: www.cc.dio.org. Sr. Brenda Fritz, D.C., Area Dir. Total Assisted 4,431; Total Staff 22.

GRANITE CITY. *Granite City Catholic Charities*, 2105 State St., 62040. Tel: 618-877-1184; Fax: 618-798-4287. Email: ccdaly@peaknet.net. Web: www.cc.dio.org. Mary Phillips, Area Dir. Total Assisted 11,500; Total Staff 6.

MATTOON. *Catholic Charities of Coles, Douglas, and Edgar Counties*, 4217 Dewitt Ave., 61938-6620. Tel: 217-235-0420; Fax: 217-235-0425. Email: catholicchar@consolidated.net. Web: www.cc.dio.org. Mr. Michael Woolworth, Area Dir.

QUINCY. *Quincy Catholic Charities*, 620 Maine St., 62301. Tel: 217-222-0958; Fax: 217-222-8737. Web: www.cc.dio.org. Kurt Stuckman, Area Dir. Total Assisted 2,200; Total Staff 10.

WOOD RIVER. *Society of St. Vincent de Paul (Diocesan Central Council)*, 1026 Poplar St., 62095-1364. Tel: 618-254-3215. Email: mlesicko@juno.com.

[H] CHILDREN'S HOMES

ALTON. *Catholic Children's Home*, 1400 State St., 62002. Tel: 618-465-3594; Fax: 618-465-4023. Email: cch1400@ezl.com. Mr. Steven Roach, Exec. Dir.; Candace Hovey, Admin. Day Care 112; Total Staff 120; Special Education 202.

[I] GENERAL HOSPITALS

SPRINGFIELD. *St. John's Hospital*, 800 E. Carpenter St., 62769. Tel: 217-544-6464; Fax: 217-535-3989. Email: rcarlson@st-johns.org. Web: www.st_johns.org. Richard J. Carlson, Exec. Vice Pres.; Mary-Jo Gardiner, Dir. Pastoral Care. Patients Assisted Annually 263,296; Bed Capacity 560; Staff 3,434.

St. John's College, Department of Nursing Tel: 217-544-6464, Ext. 45165; Fax: 217-757-6870. Jane Schachtsiek, R.N., Ph.D., Chancellor. Students 65.

ALTON. *Saint Anthony's Health Center*, Saint Anthony's Way, P.O. Box 340, 62002-0340. Tel: 618-465-2571; Fax: 618-465-4569. Web: www.sahc.org. William E. Kessler, Pres. & CEO; Rev. John Wykes, O.M.V., Chap. Three Campuses: Saint Anthony's Hospital, Saint Clare's Hospital and Saint Anthony's Medical Mall. Sisters of St. Francis of the Martyr St. George 13; Bed Capacity 243; Patients Assisted Annually 142,317; Staff 854.

DECATUR. *St. Mary's Hospital*, 1800 E. Lake Shore Dr., 62521. Tel: 217-464-2473; Fax: 217-464-1616. Email: tpfitzer@smd.hshs.org. Web: www.stmarys-hospital.com. Anthony D. Pfitzer, Exec. Vice Pres. Hospital Sisters of the Third Order of St. Francis 5; Patients Assisted Annually 102,500; Bed Capacity 224; Staff 1,083.

EFFINGHAM. *St. Anthony's Memorial Hospital*, 503 N. Maple St., 62401. Tel: 217-342-2121; Fax: 217-347-1563. Email: hospital@effingham.net. Web: www.stanthonyshospital.org. Daniel J. Woods, Admin.; Rev. Ralph Zetzl, O.F.M., Chap. Bed Capacity 146; Patients Assisted Annually 72,662; Staff 608.

HIGHLAND. *St. Joseph's Hospital*, 1515 Main St., 62249. Tel: 618-654-7421; Fax: 618-654-2012. Email: dherzig@sjh.hshs.org. Web: www.stjosephs-highland.org. Dennis Herzig, Chief Financial Officer. Hospital Sisters of the Third Order of St. Francis 2; Patients Assisted Annually 42,682; Bed Capacity 106; Staff 300.

LITCHFIELD. *St. Francis Hospital*, 1215 Franciscan Dr., P.O. Box 1215, 62056. Tel: 217-324-2191. Web: www.stfrancis-litchfield.org. Michael Sipkoski, Admin.; Rev. Theodosius A. Schelich, O.F.M., Chap.; Sr. Mary Flynn, O.S.F., Religious Coord. Hospital Sisters of the Third Order of St. Francis 1; Patients Assisted Annually 65,000; Bed Capacity 138; Staff 380.

TAYLORVILLE. *St. Vincent Memorial Hospital*, 201 E. Pleasant St., 62568. Tel: 217-824-3331; Fax: 217-824-2099. Email: walsh.virginia@mhsil.com. Adorers of the Blood of Christ 4; Patients Assisted Annually 29,000; Bed Capacity 129; Bassinets 8; Extended care facility 50; Staff 440.

[J] SPECIAL CARE INSTITUTIONS

SPRINGFIELD. *Brother James Court*, 2508 St. James Rd., 62707. Tel: 217-544-4876; Fax: 217-747-5971. Email: bjcicfdd@aol.com. Web: www.ffsc.net. Bro. David Sarnecki, F.F.S.C., Admin. Franciscan Brothers of the Holy Cross, Residence for Mentally Retarded Male Adults. Franciscan Brothers of the Holy Cross 4; Bed Capacity 93; Residents 93; Total Staff 86.

[K] HOMES FOR AGED

SPRINGFIELD. *St. Joseph's Home*, 3306 S. Sixth St. Rd., 62703. Tel: 217-529-5596; Fax: 217-529-8590. Sisters Judith Morris, O.S.F., Co-Admin.; Mary Barbara Buckley, O.S.F., Co-Admin. Residence for the Elderly & Nursing Home. Sisters of St. Francis of the Immaculate Conception 7; Residents 142; Staff 97.

[L] MONASTERIES AND RESIDENCES OF PRIESTS AND BROTHERS

SPRINGFIELD. *Franciscan Brothers of the Holy Cross*, St. James Monastery, 2500 Saint James Rd., 62707-9736. Tel: 217-747-5947; Fax: 217-747-5950. Email: brojohnfrancis@aol.com. Web: www.springfieldfranciscanbrothers.org. Bros. John Francis Tyrrell, F.F.S.C., Supr.; Stephen Bissler, F.F.S.C., Vicar; Joel Mark Rousseau, F.F.S.C., Councilor. Total in Residence 10.

Our Lady of Angels Friary, P.O. Box 2153, 62705. Tel: 217-522-9822; Fax: 217-522-5004. Email: seniorfriars@aol.com kleni70138@aol.com. Web: www.quincy.edu/shp-friar/senior-friars/. Bros. Kevin Lenihan, Guardian; Earl Benz, O.F.M., Vicar; Barnabas Diekemper, O.F.M., Vicar; Revs. Wilbert Hegener, O.F.M.; Roger Niemeyer, O.F.M.; John Sullivan, O.F.M.; Victorian Haladus, O.F.M.; Floribert Veverka, O.F.M.; Mathias Kiemen, O.F.M; Elias Koppert, O.F.M.; Leonard Paskert, O.F.M.; Melchior Toczek, O.F.M.; Eugene Katoski, O.F.M.; Method Wilson, O.F.M.; James Kelly, O.F.M.; Michael Ewert, O.F.M.; Joseph Tan Nguyen, O.F.M.; Benet Fonck, O.F.M.; David Eckelkamp, O.F.M.; Fred Schneider, O.F.M. (STL); Elstan Coghill, O.F.M. (GAY); Raymar Bobber, O.F.M. (FWT); Victor Kingery, O.F.M.; Bros. Jack Sweeney, O.F.M.; Kevin O'Connell, O.F.M.; Joseph Sandlin, O.F.M.; Denis Snelling, O.F.M.; Joseph Weithman, O.F.M.; Crispin Koeppl, O.F.M.; Dan Piasecki, O.F.M.; James Finnegan, O.F.M.; Allan Haiar, O.F.M.; Terence Santiapillai, O.F.M.; Rev. Anthony McKillip, O.F.M. Retirement Community of Our Lady of Friars Minor (Sacred Heart Province).

QUINCY. *St. Francis Solanus Friary*, 1721 College Ave., 62301. Tel: 217-222-2898; Fax: 217-222-3020.

Email: church@stfrancissolanus.com. Web: www.stfrancissolanus.com. Revs. Kurt Hartrich, O.F.M.; James Wheeler, O.F.M.; James F. Finn, O.F.M. Priests 4.

TEUTOPOLIS. *St. Francis Assisi Friary*, 203 E. Main St., P.O. Box 730, 62467-0730. Tel: 217-857-6404; Fax: 217-857-1031. Email: parish@advancenet.net. Revs. Austin Albers, O.F.M.; Ralph Zetzl, O.F.M.; Theodore Bracco, O.F.M.; Edwin O. Albers, O.F.M.; Kenneth Rosswog, O.F.M.; Vernon Olmer, O.F.M.; Sylvano J. Pera, O.F.M.; Bros. Paulinus Johnson, O.F.M.; James Lammers, O.F.M. Priests 7.

[M] CONVENTS AND RESIDENCES FOR SISTERS

SPRINGFIELD. *Congregation of Our Lady of Charity of the Good Shepherd*, 725 S. 12th St., 62703. Tel: 217-544-4613; Fax: 217-544-5356. Email: csgshepherd@aol.com. Sr. Mary Caroline McQuaid, R.G.S., Contact Person. Sisters 5.

Convent of Our Lady of the Sacred Heart, 1237 W. Monroe St., 62704. Tel: 217-787-0481; Fax: 217-787-8169. Email: smjtraeger@spdom.org. Web: www.springfieldop.org. Sisters Mary Jean Traeger, O.P., Prioress Gen.; Rose Marie Riley, O.P., Vicaress Gen.; M. Noel Plummer, O.P., Prioress; Rev. Peter Witchousky, O.P., Chap.

Legal Title: *Dominican Sisters of Springfield in Illinois* Motherhouse of the Springfield Dominican SistersMotherhouse and Novitiate of the Dominican Sisters of Springfield, Illinois. Sisters in the Congregation 287; In Motherhouse 113.

Daughters of Divine Love Congregation, 2523 St. James Rd., 62707. Tel: 217-528-0262. Email: chieze93@yahoo.com. Sisters 4.

St. Francis Convent, 4849 LaVerna Rd., P.O. Box 19431, 62794-9431. Tel: 217-522-3386; Fax: 217-522-2483. Web: www.springfieldfranciscans.org. Sisters Joan Winkler, O.S.F., Prov. Supr.; Mary Kelly, O.S.F., Religious Coord.; Revs. Barnabas Diekemper, Chap.; David Eckelkamp, O.F.M., Chap. Motherhouse of the Hospital Sisters of the Third Order of St. Francis Sisters 112.

Other Locations:

2101 Shabbona, 62702. Tel: 217-789-4936. Sisters 3.

4145 Sunderland Dr., Decatur, 62526. Tel: 217-877-2278. Sisters 2.

52 Fairview, 62704. Tel: 217-529-3050.

75 Sunflower Dr., Highland, 62249. Tel: 618-654-9759. Sisters 2.

Missionary Sisters of the Sacred Heart of Jesus "Ad Gentes", 260 N. Amos Ave., 62702. Tel: 217-726-8159. Sr. Delfina Maravillla, M.A.G., Local Supr. Sisters 5.

Ursuline Convent, 1400 N. Fifth St., 62702. Tel: 217-789-7910; Fax: 217-789-7913. Email: dfulgenzi@juno.com. Sr. Darlene Fulgenzi, O.S.U., Prioress. Ursuline Nuns of the Roman Union in Community 12.

ALTON. *St. Clare's Villa*, 915 E. 5th St., 62002. Tel: 618-465-2617. Sr. Mary Thomas, Contact Person.

St. Francis Convent, 2120 Central Ave., P.O. Box 9020, 62002-9020. Tel: 618-463-2750; Fax: 618-465-5064. Email: franciscansisters@piasanet.com. Web: www.sahc.org/sisters. Sr. M. Regina Pacis Coury, F.S.G.M., Prov. Supr. Final Professed 84; Junior Professed 24; Novices 11; Postulants 6.

Ursuline Convent of the Holy Family of the Ursuline Nuns of the Roman Union, 845 Danforth St., 62002. Tel: 618-465-9112; Fax: 618-465-0358. Email: paulineosu@juno.com. Sr. Pauline Lorch, O.S.U., Prioress. Sisters 13.

Ursuline Infirmary, 845 Danforth St., 62002. Tel: 618-465-0791; Fax: 618-465-0792. Sisters 35.

[N] NEWMAN CENTERS

CARLINVILLE. *Blackburn College Newman Club*, Formerly Blackburn College 2010 E. 1st South St., P.O. Box 647, 62626. Tel: 217-854-7151; Fax: 217-854-9228. Email: ssmary-joseph@accunet.net. Web: www.accunet.net/ssmary+joseph. Chaplains 1; Students 200.

CHARLESTON. *Eastern Illinois University Newman Catholic Center* 500 Roosevelt Ave., 61920. Tel: 217-348-0188; Fax: 217-348-8964. Email: newman@eiu-newman.org. Web: www.eiu-newman.org. Rev. Joseph G. Ring, Chap.; Mr. Roy Lanham, Dir.; Ms. Edrianna Ezell, Campus Min.

DECATUR. *Millikin University Newman Catholic Community* P.O. Box 2697, 62524-2697. Tel: 217-877-4146; 217-424-6211 College; Fax: 217-877-4147. Rev. Dennis D. Kollross, Chap.

EDWARDSVILLE. *Southern Illinois University Catholic Campus Ministry* The Religious Center, P.O. Box 1059, 62026. Tel: 618-650-3205; Fax: 618-650-3264. Email: ccalzet@siue.edu. Web: www.siue.edu/religion/catholic. Sr. Claudia Calzetta, SL, Dir. Total Staff 1.

JACKSONVILLE. *Illinois College Newman Center* 453 E. State St., 62650. Tel: 217-245-6184; Fax: 217-245-6185. Email: tomeyer@irtc.net. Web: www2.ic.edu/religiouslife/newman/index.htm. Rev. Tom Meyer, Chap.

MacMurray College Newman Center c/o 453 E. State St., 62650. Tel: 217-245-6184; Fax: 217 245-6185. Email: tomeyer@irtc.net. Rev. Tom Meyer, Chap.

[O] MISCELLANEOUS LISTINGS

SPRINGFIELD. *Benincasa Ministries*, 6760 Old Jacksonville Rd., New Berlin, 62670. Tel: 217-787-6927; Fax: 217-793-5470. Email: sienahall@spdom.org. Sr. Sharon Zayac, O.P., Dir. Total in Residence 2; Total Staff 5.

Catholic Care Center, Inc., Catholic Pastoral Center, P.O. Box 3187, 62708. Tel: 217-698-8500, Ext. 148; Fax: 217-698-0802. Email: treiser@dio.org. Web: www.dio.org. Mr. Leo A. Lenn, Pres.; Most Rev. George J. Lucas, Dir.; John Maxwell, Treas. & Dir.; James Forstall, Sec. & Dir.; Bob Budnik, Dir.; Hugh Graham III, Dir.; Thomas Reiser, Exec. Sec. & Dir.; Sr. Joan Winkler, D.S.F., Dir.; Mrs. Eugena Costa, Dir.

Diocesan Care Management, Inc., Catholic Pastoral Center, P.O. Box 3187, 62708. Tel: 217-698-8500, Ext. 148; Fax: 217-698-0802. Email: treiser@dio.org. Web: www.dio.org. Most Rev. George J. Lucas, Pres. & Dir.; Mr. John J. Maxwell, C.P.A., Sec., Treas. & Dir.; Mr. Thomas E. Reiser, Exec. Vice Pres. & Dir.

Dominican Sisters of Springfield in Illinois Charitable Trust, Sacred Heart Convent, 1237 W. Monroe, 62704. Tel: 217-787-0481; Fax: 217-787-8169. Email: smjtraeger@spdom.org.

Foundation for the People of the Diocese of Springfield in Illinois, Catholic Pastoral Center, 1615 W. Washington, 62702. Tel: 217-698-8500, Ext. 108; Fax: 217-698-0802. Email: mmulford@dio.org. Web: dio.org.

Legal Title: *The Foundation for the People of the Roman Catholic Diocese of Springfield in Illinois*

Saint Francis Catholic Care of Beardstown, NFP, 800 E. Fifth St., 62703. Tel: 217-523-9201; Fax: 217-523-5624. Email: roach_ccadmin@hansoninfosys.com. Web: www.cc.dio.org. Mr. Steven E. Roach, M.S., Registered Agent.

Hospital Sisters Haiti, St. Francis Convent-La Verna Rd., P.O. Box 19431, 62794-9431. Tel: 217-522-3386; Fax: 217-522-2483. Email: MOC@hsosfusa.org. Sisters Joan Winkler, O.S.F., Pres. & Prov. Supr; Maureen O'Connor, O.S.F., Prov. Sec. & Treas.

Hospital Sisters Health System, 4936 LaVerna Rd., P.O. Box 19456, 62794-9456. Tel: 217-523-4747. Sr. Jomary Trstensky, O.S.F., Pres

Hospital Sisters of St. Francis Foundation, Inc., 4936 LaVerna Rd., P.O. Box 19456, 62794-9456. Tel: 217-523-4747. Sr. Jomary Trstensky, O.S.F., Contact Person.

Hospital Sisters Services, Inc., 4936 LaVerna Rd., P.O. Box 19456, 62794-9456. Tel: 217-523-4747. Sr. Jomary Trstensky, O.S.F., Pres.

Hospital Sisters Tanzania, St. Francis Convent-La Verna Rd., P.O. Box 19431, 62794-9431. Tel: 217-522-3386; Fax: 217-522-2483. Email: MOC@hsosfusa.org. Sisters Joan Winkler, O.S.F., Pres. & Prov. Supr.; Maureen O'Connor, O.S.F., Prov. Sec. & Treas.

Leadership Conference of Women Religious, 1237 W. Monroe, 62704. Tel: 217-787-0481; Fax: 217-787-8169. Sisters Jeanne Bessette, O.S.F., Chm.; Joetta Huelsmann, P.H.J.C., Vice Chm.; Andrea Chudzik, C.S.S.F., Sec.; Marcelline Koch, O.P., Treas.. Email: projectirene@aol.com.

Sponsored Activity: Projfect IRENE Sr. Rose Mary Meyer, B.V.M., Project Dir.

Legion of Mary, 4030 Thornbrock Dr., 62707. Tel: 217-546-4922. Jean Heroux, Comitium Pres.

Priests' Purgatorial Society Catholic Pastoral Center , 1615 W. Washington, P.O. Box 3187, 62708-3187. Tel: 217-698-8500; Fax: 217-698-0802. Email: jrenken@dio.org.

**Springfield Developmental Center Ltd.*, 4595 Laverna Rd., 62707. Tel: 217-525-8271; Fax: 217-525-5801. Email: sdcstjames@aol.com. Web: www.ffsc.net. Cathy S. Barnett, Dir. Developmental Training Program for Developmentally Disabled Adults. Lay Staff 26; Clients 89.

Theresians of the United States, Inc. Theresian World Ministry , 1237 W. Monroe St., 62704. Tel: 217-726-5484; Fax: 217-726-5531. Email: tustwm@cityscape.net. Web: www.theresians.org. Victoria S. Schmidt, Exec. Dir. Sacred Heart Convent

Villa Maria - Catholic Life Center, 1903 E. Lake Dr., 62707. Tel: 217-529-2213; Fax: 217-529-2215. Email: mkocher@dio.org. Mrs. Martina Kocher, Dir.

Weber House - Weber Care Corporation, 2520 St. James Rd., 62707. Tel: 217-522-8406. Email: weber1@famvid.com. Bro. John Francis Tyrrell, F.F.S.C., Admin.; Laura Rape, Dir. Bed capacity 8; Residence capacity 8.

ALTON. *Saint Anthony's Foundation*, Saint Anthony's Way, P.O. Box 340, 62002-0340. Tel: 618-465-2571; Fax: 618-465-4569. Email: foundation@sahc.org. Web: www.sahc.org.

Affiliates: Saint Anthony's Health System and Saint Anthony's Health Center. William E. Kessler, Pres.

Saint Anthony's Health System, St. Anthony's Way, P.O. Box 340, 62002-0340. Tel: 618-465-2571; Fax: 618-465-4569. Web: www.sahc.org. William E. Kessler, Pres.; Rev. John Wykes, O.M.V., Chap. Affiliates: Saint Anthony's Health Center and Saint Anthony's Foundation. Sisters of St. Francis of the Martyr St. George 1.

Saint Clare's Hospital, 915 E. Fifth St., 62002. Tel: 618-463-5150; Fax: 618-463-5641. Web: www.sahc.org. William E. Kessler, Pres. & CEO; Rev. John Wykes, O.M.V., Chap. A Division of Saint Anthony's Health Center.

St. Francis Day Care Center, 710 College Ave., P.O. Box 9020, 62002-9020. Tel: 618-463-2766; Fax: 618-465-5064. Day Care Center Sisters of St. Francis of the Martyr St. George 4; Assisted Daily 120; Total Staff 33.

BRIDGETON. *Sisters of Divine Providence*, 3415 Bridgeland Dr., MO 63044. Tel: 314-209-9181; Fax: 314-209-9207. Email: mjcoultas@yahoo.com. Web: www.divineprovidence-cdpmo.org. Sr. Zita Telcamp, C.D.P., Contact Person.

RELIGIOUS INSTITUTES OF MEN REPRESENTED IN THE DIOCESE

For further details refer to the corresponding bracketed number in the Religious Institutes of Men or Women section.

[1320]—*Clerics of St. Viator* (Chicago Prov.)—C.S.V.

[0510]—*Franciscan Brothers of the Holy Cross*—F.F.S.C.

[0520]—*Franciscan Friars* (Sacred Heart Province)—O.F.M.

[0690]—*Jesuit Fathers and Brothers* (Missouri Province)—S.J.

[0910]—*Oblates of Mary Immaculate* (Central Province)—O.M.I.

[0940]—*Oblates of the Virgin Mary*—O.M.V.

[0430]—*Order of Preachers (Dominicans)*—O.P.

[]—*Society of Jesus* (Missouri Prov.)—S.J.

RELIGIOUS INSTITUTES OF WOMEN REPRESENTED IN THE DIOCESE

[0100]—*Adorers of the Blood of Christ* (Ruma, IL; Wichita, KS)—A.S.C.

[0230]—*Benedictine Sisters of Pontifical Jurisdiction* (Nauvoo, IL)—O.S.B.

[]—*Congregation of Daughters of Divine Love*—D.D.L.

[2100]—*Congregation of the Humility of Mary*—C.H.M.

[1710]—*Congregation of the Third Order of St. Francis of Mary Immaculate, Joliet, IL*—O.S.F.

[1830]—*Contemplative Sisters of the Good Shepherd*—C.G.S.

[0760]—*Daughters of Charity of St. Vincent De Paul* (East Central Prov.)—D.C.

[1070-10]—*Dominican Sisters*—O.P.

[1070-13]—*Dominican Sisters*—O.P.

[1440]—*Franciscan Sisters of the Poor*—S.F.P.

[1770]—*Hospital Sisters of Third Order of St. Francis*—O.S.F.

[2575]—*Institute of the Sisters of Mercy of the Union of the Americas* (Chicago, IL)—R.S.M.

[]—*Missionary Sisters of the Sacred Heart of Jesus "Ad Gentes"*—M.A.G.

[3230]—*Poor Handmaids of Jesus Christ*—P.H.J.C.

[2970]—*School Sisters of Notre Dame* (St. Louis, MO)—S.S.N.D.

[1680]—*School Sisters of St. Francis*—O.S.F.

[3520]—*Servants of the Holy Heart of Mary*—S.S.C.M.

[0430]—*Sisters of Charity of the Blessed Virgin Mary*—B.V.M.

[0990]—*Sisters of Divine Providence* (St. Louis Prov.)—C.D.P.

[3360]—*Sisters of Providence of Saint Mary-of-the-Woods, Indiana*—S.P.

[1570]—*Sisters of St. Francis of the Holy Family*—O.S.F.

[1580]—*Sisters of St. Francis of the Immaculate Conception*—O.S.F.

[1600]—*Sisters of St. Francis of the Martyr St. George*—S.F.G.M.

[]—*Sisters of St. Joseph* (India)

[3270]—*Sisters of the Most Precious Blood (O'Fallon, MO)*—C.PP.S.

[4110]—*Ursuline Nuns (Roman Union)* (Central Prov.)—O.S.U.

DIOCESAN CEMETERIES

SPRINGFIELD. *Calvary Cemetery Association*
CARLINVILLE. *Calvary Cemetery Association*
DECATUR. *Calvary Cemetery Association*
EDWARDSVILLE. *Calvary Cemetery Association*
LITCHFIELD. *Holy Cross Cemetery Association*
MOUNT STERLING. *Catholic Cemetery Association*
QUINCY. *Catholic Cemetery Association*

NECROLOGY

† Groesch, Edward, (Retired)—Died Sept. 2, 2003

Diocese of Springfield in Massachusetts

(Dioecesis Campifontis)

Most Reverend

TIMOTHY A. McDONNELL

Bishop of Springfield in Massachusetts; ordained June 1, 1963; appointed Titular Bishop of Semina and Auxiliary Bishop of New York October 30, 2001; consecrated December 12, 2001; appointed Bishop of Springfield in Massachusetts March 9, 2004; installed April 1, 2004 *Mailing Address: P.O. Box 1730, Springfield, MA 01101.*

Most Reverend

THOMAS LUDGER DUPRE

Retired Bishop of Springfield; ordained May 23, 1959; appointed Auxiliary Bishop of Springfield and Titular Bishop of Hodelm April 19, 1990; consecrated May 31, 1990; appointed Bishop of Springfield March 14, 1995; installed May 8, 1995; retired February 11, 2004 *Mailing Address: P.O. Box 1730, Springfield, MA 01101.*

Most Reverend

JOSEPH F. MAGUIRE, D.D.

Retired Bishop of Springfield; ordained June 29, 1945; appointed Auxiliary Bishop of Boston and Titular Bishop of Mactaris December 1, 1971; consecrated February 2, 1972; appointed Coadjutor Bishop of Springfield with right of succession April 3, 1976; officially installed as Bishop of Springfield on November 4, 1977; resigned December 27, 1991 *Res.: 76 Elliot St., P.O. Box 1730, Springfield, MA 01101.*

ESTABLISHED JUNE 14, 1870.

Square Miles 2,822.

Comprises the Counties of Berkshire, Franklin, Hampden and Hampshire in the State of Massachusetts.

For legal titles of parishes and diocesan institutions, consult the Chancery Office.

Chancery Office: P.O. Box 1730, Springfield, MA 01101. Tel: 413-732-3175; Fax: 413-737-2337.

Web: www.diospringfield.org

Email: mail@diospringfield.org

STATISTICAL OVERVIEW

Personnel	
Bishop	1
Retired Bishops	1
Priests: Diocesan Active in Diocese	118
Priests: Diocesan Active Outside Diocese	5
Priests: Diocesan in Foreign Missions	1
Priests: Retired, Sick or Absent	42
Number of Diocesan Priests	166
Religious Priests in Diocese	35
Total Priests in Diocese	201
Extern Priests in Diocese	1
Ordinations:	
Diocesan Priests	2
Transitional Deacons	2
Permanent Deacons in Diocese	57
Total Brothers	9
Total Sisters	575
Parishes	
Parishes	124
With Resident Pastor:	
Resident Diocesan Priests	115
Resident Religious Priests	9
Missions	14
Pastoral Centers	1
New Parishes Created	1
Closed Parishes	1
Professional Ministry Personnel:	
Brothers	1
Sisters	31
Lay Ministers	54
Welfare	
Catholic Hospitals	1
Total Assisted	218,314
Health Care Centers	3
Total Assisted	6,800
Homes for the Aged	11
Total Assisted	1,300
Residential Care of Children	1
Total Assisted	139
Day Care Centers	1
Total Assisted	125
Specialized Homes	1
Total Assisted	4,900
Special Centers for Social Services	3
Total Assisted	62,909
Residential Care of Disabled	1
Total Assisted	1,200
Educational	
Diocesan Students in Other Seminaries	8
Total Seminarians	8
Colleges and Universities	1
Total Students	1,002
High Schools, Diocesan and Parish	4
Total Students	1,620
Elementary Schools, Diocesan and Parish	23
Total Students	6,088
Catechesis/Religious Education:	
High School Students	8,119
Elementary Students	20,544
Total Students under Catholic Instruction	37,381
Teachers in the Diocese:	
Priests	1
Sisters	29
Lay Teachers	360
Vital Statistics	
Receptions into the Church:	
Infant Baptism Totals	3,503
Adult Baptism Totals	126
Received into Full Communion	111
First Communions	3,380
Confirmations	2,673
Marriages:	
Catholic	825
Interfaith	234
Total Marriages	1,059
Deaths	4,168
Total Catholic Population	240,730
Total Population	800,000

Former Bishops—Most Revs. PATRICK THOMAS O'REILLY, D.D., consecrated Sept. 25, 1870; died May 28, 1892; THOMAS DANIEL BEAVEN, consecrated Oct. 18, 1892; died Oct. 5, 1920; THOMAS M. O'LEARY, D.D., consecrated Sept. 8, 1921; died Oct. 10, 1949; CHRISTOPHER J. WELDON, D.D. (Retired), consecrated March 24, 1950; retired Oct. 15, 1977; died March 19, 1982; JOHN A. MARSHALL, D.D., consecrated Bishop of Burlington, Jan. 25, 1972; installed Bishop of Springfield, Feb. 18, 1992; died July 3, 1994; JOSEPH F. MAGUIRE, D.D. (Retired), consecrated Auxiliary Bishop of Boston, Feb. 2, 1972; installed Bishop of Springfield, Nov. 4, 1977; retired Dec. 27, 1991; THOMAS LUDGER DUPRE, D.D., J.C.D. (Retired), ordained May 23, 1959; appointed Auxiliary Bishop of Springfield and Titular Bishop of Hodelm April 19, 1990; consecrated May 31, 1990; appointed Bishop of Springfield March 14, 1995; installed May 8, 1995; retired February 11, 2004.

Diocesan Administrator—Diocese of Springfield, P.O. Box 1730, Springfield, 01105.

Vicar General—Rev. Msgrs. RICHARD S. SNIEZYK, V.G., Vicar General and Moderator of the Curia, 65 Elliot St., P.O. Box 1730, Springfield, 01101; LEO A. LECLERC, V.G., St. Rose de Lima Rectory, 600 Grattan St., Chicopee, 01020.

Episcopal Vicars—Vicars for the Clergy: Revs. DAVID JOYCE; GEORGE FARLAND; Sr. JUDITH O'CONNELL, S.S.J., Vicar for Religious, 65 Elliot St., P.O. Box 1730, Springfield, 01101; Revs. JOHN J. VARLEY, Berkshire Vicariate; RONALD G. YARGEAU, Franklin-Hampshire Vicariate; VERNON P. DECOTEAU, Hampden East Vicariate; DANIEL R. FOLEY, V.F., Hampden Central and Hampden West Vicariate.

Chancery Office—76 Elliot St., Springfield, 01105. Mailing Address, P.O. Box 1730, Springfield, 01101. Tel: 413-732-3175; Fax: 413-737-2337.

Chancellor—Rev. DANIEL P. LISTON, J.C.L.

Vice-Chancellors—Revs. ROBERT W. THRASHER, J.C.D.; CHRISTOPHER D. CONNELLY; Sr. CAROL CIFATTE, C.S.J., J.C.L.

Vicar for Canonical Affairs—Rev. DANIEL P. LISTON, J.C.L.

Secretary to the Bishop—Rev. CHRISTOPHER D. CONNELLY.

Judicial Vicar—Rev. JOHN L. SULLIVAN, J.C.L.

Adjutant Judicial Vicar—Rev. JOHN J. BONZAGNI, J.C.L.

Judges—Revs. DANIEL R. FOLEY, V.F.; DANIEL P. LISTON, J.C.L.; JOHN J. SHEA, J.C.D. (Retired); ROBERT W. THRASHER, J.C.D.; Sr. CAROL CIFATTE, C.S.J., J.C.L.; Mrs. CAROL MENDREK.

Promoter of Justice—Rev. Msgr. JOHN F. HARRINGTON, P.A., J.C.L. (Retired).

Defender of the Bond—Sr. CLAIRE LAPOINTE, S.A.S.V., J.C.L.

Procurators-Advocate—Revs. JEDDIE P. BROOKS; JUAN GARCIA, C.R.I.C.; DANIEL B. BRUNTON (Retired); RONALD E. WAMSHER, Mailing Address, 65 Elliot St., P.O. Box 1730, Springfield, 01101-1730.

Psychotherapeutic Counselor—Rev. J. DONALD R. LAPOINTE, L.I.C.S.W.

Psychological Experts—MARTIN J. MARKEY, Ph.D.; ROBERT SAISI, Ph.D., Ed.D.; DAVID ARMSTRONG, L.I.C.S.W.

Notaries—Mrs. CAROL MENDREK; MARGARET COLLINS; Mrs. ELLEN RIVERS.

Diocesan Tribunal—Mrs. CAROL MENDREK, Dir., 65 Elliot St., P.O. Box 1730, Springfield, 01101. Tel: 413-452-0664; Fax: 413-747-8482.

Bishop's Commission for Clergy—Rev. Msgrs. RICHARD S. SNIEZYK, V.G., Chm.; LEO A. LECLERC, V.G.; Revs. HUGH F. CREAN; GARY M. DAILEY; GEORGE A. FARLAND; DAVID J. JOYCE; DANIEL P. LISTON, J.C.L.; CHRISTOPHER A. MALATESTA; HOWARD W. MCCORMICK (Retired); BRIAN F. MCGRATH; DANIEL S. PACHOLEC; THOMAS M. SHEA; RONALD G. YARGEAU.

Bishop's Cabinet—Rev. Msgr. RICHARD S. SNIEZYK, V.G.; Rev. DANIEL P. LISTON, J.C.L.; LAURA REILLY; Sisters JUDITH O'CONNELL, S.S.J.; BETTE GOULD, S.S.J.; Mr. MARK DUPONT; Mr. JOHN SHUMAN.

Diocesan Commission for Ecumenism—VACANT, 76 Elliot St., P.O. Box 1730, Springfield, 01101. Tel: 413-732-3175.

Diocesan Charismatic Renewal—Rev. GERALD BRADY, Dir.

Diocesan Commission for the Liturgy—Rev. WILLIAM J. HAMILTON, Chm., Christian Education Center, 625 Carew St., Springfield, 01104. Tel: 413-732-3175.

Diocesan Director of Ceremonies—Rev. CHRISTOPHER D. CONNELLY, 76 Elliot St., P.O. Box 1730, Springfield, 01101. Tel: 413-732-3175; Fax: 413-737-2337.

Diocesan Consultors—Rev. Msgrs. JOHN F. HARRINGTON, P.A., J.C.L. (Retired); RICHARD S. SNIEZYK, V.G.; LEO A. LECLERC, V.G.; Revs. HUGH F. CREAN; GEORGE A. FARLAND; DANIEL FOLEY; DAVID J. JOYCE; GERARD A. LAFLEUR, V.F.; DANIEL P. LISTON, J.C.L.

Deans—Revs. TIMOTHY J. CAMPOLI, V.F., Franklin Deanery; ROLAND J. GALIPEAU, Greater Holyoke Deanery; JOSEPH SORANNO, Greater Springfield I Deanery; GEORGE A. FARLAND, Greater Springfield II Deanery; GERARD A. LAFLEUR, V.F., Hampden Central Deanery; JEDDIE P. BROOKS, Hampden East Deanery; HUGH F. CREAN, Hampden West Deanery; ROBERT J. COONAN, Hampshire Deanery; DANIEL J. BOYLE, Northern Berkshire Deanery; MICHAEL SHERSHANOVICH, Southern Berkshire Deanery.

Presbyteral Council—Rev. Msgrs. JOHN F. HARRINGTON, P.A., J.C.L. (Retired); RICHARD SNIEZYK; LEO LECLERC; Revs. HUGH F. CREAN; VERNON P. DECOTEAU; GEORGE FARLAND; DAVID J. JOYCE; DANIEL P. LISTON, J.C.L.; DANIEL R. FOLEY, V.F.; CHRISTOPHER D. CONNELLY; MICHAEL ZIELKE, O.F.M.Conv.; GERARD LAFLEUR; JOHN CONNORS; CHRISTOPHER MALATESTA; JAMES J. SCAHILL; THOMAS M. SHEA; CHRISTOPHER J. WAITEKUS; DANIEL S. PACHOLEC.

Co-Vicars For Clergy—Revs. GEORGE A. FARLAND; DAVID J. JOYCE, 65 Elliot St., P.O. Box 1730, Springfield, 01101. Tel: 413-732-3175.

Secretary for Financial Affairs—Mr. JOHN SHUMAN, 65 Elliot St., P.O. Box 1730, Springfield, 01101. Tel: 413-732-3175.

Vicar for Religious—Sr. JUDITH O'CONNELL, S.S.J., Vicar, 65 Elliot St., P.O. Box 1730, Springfield, 01101. Tel: 413-452-0609.

Diocesan Offices and Directors

Apostolate to the Handicapped—Rev. ROBERT F. WAGNER, Chap.; Sr. JOAN MAGNANI, S.S.J., Dir., Bureau for Exceptional Children and Adults, 537 Northampton St., P.O. Box 1039, Holyoke, 01041. Tel: 413-538-7450 (Voice and TTY); Fax: 413-536-5691.

Apostolate of the Suffering—ROBERT J. LETASZ, Dir., P.O. Box 535, Chicopee, 01021; Rev. ALBERT BRETON, Chap., Mont Marie, Holyoke, 01040.

Blue Army—Rev. ALBERT E. BRETON, Mont Marie, Holyoke, 01040.

Building Commission—Rev. ADRIAN BENOIT, Chm., Immaculate Heart of Mary Parish, 356 State St., Granby, 01033.

Building Consultant—Mr. FREDERICK R. PIQUETTE, 65 Elliot St., P.O. Box 1730, Springfield, 01101. Tel: 413-452-0672; Fax: 413-785-5449.

Campaign for Human Development—LAURA REILLY, Dir., 65 Elliot St., P.O. Box 1730, Springfield, 01101. Tel: 413-452-0697; Fax: 413-746-3421.

Office for the Protection of Children and Youth—LAURA REILLY, Dir., 65 Elliot St., P.O. Box 1730, Springfield, 01101-1730. Tel: 413-452-0624.

The Catholic Charismatic Renewal of Springfield, Inc.—Rev. GERALD BRADY, St. Patrick Parish, 80 Main St., Northfield, 01362; Sr. MARGARET WALSH, S.S.J., Coord., P.O. Box 4668, Springfield, 01101-4668. Tel: 413-247-9001; Fax: 413-247-5605.

Catholic Charities—LAURA REILLY, 65 Elliot St., P.O. Box 1730, Springfield, 01103. Tel: 413-452-0613.

Annual Catholic Appeal—Mr. JOHN SHUMAN, Exec. Dir.; VIRGINIA WEBB, Dir. & Coord. of Admin., 65 Elliot St., Springfield, 01101. Mailing Address, P.O. Box 1730, Springfield, 01101. Tel: 413-452-0629; Fax: 413-732-4297.

Catholic Nurses Council—VACANT.

Catholic Relief Services—LAURA REILLY, 65 Elliot St., P.O. Box 1730, Springfield, 01101. Tel: 413-732-3175.

Cemeteries—Mr. JOSEPH KOSTEK, Diocesan Dir. of Cemeteries, 65 Elliot St., Springfield, 01101-1730. Tel: 413-452-0692; Fax: 413-785-5449. Saint Michael's Cemetery, 1601 State St., Springfield, 01109. Tel: 413-733-0659. Gate of Heaven Cemetery, 421 Tinkham Rd., Springfield, 01129. Tel: 413-782-4731. St. Aloysius Cemetery, 1601 State St., Springfield, 01109. Tel: 413-733-0695. St. Benedict Cemetery, Liberty St., Springfield, 01104. Tel: 413-782-4731. St. Matthew Cemetery, 366 Springfield St., Springfield, 01109. Tel: 413-733-0659. Calvary Cemetery, Northampton St., Springfield, 01040. Tel: 413-733-8140.

Censor of Books—Rev. MARK S. STELZER.

Clergy Counseling Service—Rev. GEORGE A. FARLAND, Sacred Heart Rectory, 395 Chestnut St., Springfield, 01104. Tel: 413-732-3721.

Commission on Church Music—Rev. WILLIAM J. HAMILTON, Chm., Christian Education Center, 625 Carew St., Springfield, 01104. Tel: 413-732-3175; Fax: 413-732-1944.

Communications Committee—Mr. MICHAEL GRAZIANO, Chm., 65 Elliot St., P.O. Box 1730, Springfield, 01101. Tel: 413-732-4546; Fax: 413-747-0273.

Communications and Public Relations—

Catholic Communications Corporation—Mr. MICHAEL GRAZIANO, Chm., 65 Elliot St., P.O. Box 1730, Springfield, 01101. Tel: 413-737-4744; Fax: 413-747-0273.

Open Window Book and Gift Shop—12-14 Center St., Chicopee, 01013. Tel: 413-594-5111; Fax: 413-594-2862.

Services—

Chalice of Salvation (Televised Mass)—Bro. TERRENCE A. SCANLON, C.P., Exec. Dir., 65 Elliot St., P.O. Box 1730, Springfield, 01101. Tel: 413-452-0642.

Real to Reel (Television News Magazine)—MARK DUPONT, Exec. Producer, 65 Elliot St., P.O. Box 1730, Springfield, 01101. Tel: 413-452-0648.

The Catholic Observer (Newspaper)—REBECCA DRAKE, Editor, 65 Elliot St., P.O. Box 1730, Springfield, 01101. Tel: 413-452-0636.

Continuing Education for Priests—Rev. JOHN T. SMEGAL, St. Brigid Rectory, 122 N. Pleasant St., Amherst, 01004. Tel: 413-256-6181.

Office of Religious Education-CCD—Sisters PAULA ROBILLARD, S.S.J., Dir.; CAROL DATZ, S.S.N.D., Evangelization & Consultant for R.C.I.A. & Adult Education; JAYNE DOUGHTERTY, Consultant for School Age Catechesis, 625 Carew St., Springfield, 01104. Tel: 413-452-0807; Fax: 413-452-0817; CHARLES CONAGHAN, Berkshire Consultant, 100 Briggs Ave., Pittsfield, 01201. Tel: 413-443-3187.

Cursillo Movement—Deacon JOHN BLEDSOE, Dir. English-Speaking Cursillo Movement, 84 Bardwell St., South Hadley, 01075. Tel: 413-532-6671; VACANT, Dir. Spanish-Speaking Cursillo Movement, 445 Plainfield St., Springfield, 01107. Tel: 413-736-0076.

Diocesan Board of Christian Education—Mr. TIMOTHY J. MURPHY, Chm., 625 Carew St., Springfield, 01104. Tel: 413-732-3175.

Diocesan Office of Black Catholic Ministry—Rev. PAUL E. MANSHIP, Dir., All Souls Rectory, 445 Plainfield St., Springfield, 01107.

Diocesan Office for Communications—Mr. MICHAEL A. GRAZIANO, Coord., 65 Elliot St., P.O. Box 1730, Springfield, 01101. Tel: 413-732-4546; Fax: 413-747-0273.

Personnel—DOROTHY ORR, Dir. Human Resources, Office, 65 Elliot St., P.O. Box 1730, Springfield, 01101-1730. Tel: 413-452-0691.

Education—Sr. BETTE GOULD, S.S.J., Supt. of Schools; ELAINE BERTHIAUME, Coord. Student Svcs.; Sr. MAUREEN TOOMEY, S.N.D., Dir. Personnel, Christian Education Center, 625 Carew St., Springfield, 01104. Tel: 413-452-0830; Fax: 413-452-0817.

Director of Pittsfield Catholic Schools—Priests Committee: Revs. JAMES JOYCE, Chm.; GARY DAILEY; MICHAEL SHERSHANOVICH; JOHN VARLEY, 22 Maplewood Ave., Pittsfield, 01201. Tel: 413-443-9686.

Family Life Bureau—625 Carew St., Springfield, 01104. Tel: 413-732-3175.

Fiscal Affairs—WILLIAM F. LABROAD JR., Controller; Miss JEANNE M. DESROSIERS, Treas., 65 Elliot St., P.O. Box 1730, Springfield, 01101. Tel: 413-452-0696; Fax: 413-785-5449.

Holy Childhood Association—Rev. Msgr. JOHN F. HARRINGTON, P.A., J.C.L., Dir. (Retired), 65 Elliot St., P.O. Box 1730, Springfield, 01101. Tel: 413-732-3175.

Holy Family League of Charity—c/o Office of Catholic Charities, P.O. Box 1730, Springfield, 01101. Tel: 413-732-3175.

Counseling Office—LAURA REILLY, Dir. Counselors:: Dr. ALFRED A. D'AMATO, Ed.D., L.M.F.T.; Mrs. ROSEMARY CASTONGUAY, 65 Elliot St., P.O. Box 1730, Springfield, 01101. Tel: 413-452-0621; Fax: 413-747-0273.

Massachusetts Catholic Conference—Rev. Msgrs. LEO A. LECLERC, V.G.; RICHARD S. SNIEZYK, V.G., 65 Elliot St., P.O. Box 1730, Springfield, 01101. Tel: 413-732-3175.

Ministry to the Deaf—Sr. CAROL LAREAU, S.S.J., 34 Nye St., Springfield, 01104. Tel: 413-736-0020.

Ministry to the Divorced and Separated—Pastoral Ministry Office, 65 Elliot St., P.O. Box 1730, Springfield, 01101-1730. Tel: 413-732-3175.

Ministry to Priests—Rev. JOHN T. SMEGAL, St. Brigid Rectory, 122 N. Pleasant St., Amherst, 01004. Tel: 413-256-6181.

Newman Apostolate and Campus Ministry—Rev. JOHN P. MCDONAGH, Newman Center, 472 N. Pleasant St., Amherst, 01002. Tel: 413-549-0300.

Office of Social Concerns—LAURA REILLY, 65 Elliot St., P.O. Box 1730, Springfield, 01101-1730. Tel: 413-452-0615.

Parish Councils—

Pastoral Ministry—65 Elliot St., P.O. Box 1730, Springfield, 01101-1730. Tel: 413-732-3175.

Permanent Diaconate—Rev. TIMOTHY J. MURPHY, Dir.; Deacon LEO COUGHLIN, Co-Dir., 65 Elliot St., P.O. Box 1730, Springfield, 01101. Tel: 413-452-0674; Fax: 413-747-0273.

Priests' Retirement Program—Rev. Msgr. RICHARD S. SNIEZYK, V.G., Chm., 65 Elliot St., P.O. Box 1730, Springfield, 01101.

Pro-Life Commission—Rev. JOHN L. SULLIVAN, J.C.L., 65 Elliot St., P.O. Box 1730, Springfield, 01101-1730. Tel: 413-732-3175.

Propagation of the Faith—Rev. Msgr. JOHN F. HARRINGTON, P.A., J.C.L. (Retired), 65 Elliot St., P.O. Box 1730, Springfield, 01101. Tel: 413-452-0675.

Refugee Resettlement Program/Immigration Services—65 Elliot St., P.O. Box 1730, Springfield, 01101-1730. Tel: 413-732-3175.

Office of Social Concerns—65 Elliot St., P.O. Box 1730, Springfield, 01101. Tel: 413-732-3175.

Representative of the Bishop at—Mercy Hospital, Springfield: Dr. KEVIN SCHMIDT. Mont Marie Health Care Center: Rev. DANIEL P. LISTON, J.C.L. Sisters of Providence Care Centers, Inc.: Rev. JOHN L. SULLIVAN, J.C.L. Our Lady of Providence Children's Center, West Springfield: Rev. J. DONALD R. LAPOINTE. Sisters of Providence Health System: WILLIAM COLLINS.

Retired Priests' Service—Rev. FRANCIS MANNING.

Southeast Asian Apostolate—Rev. QUYNH DINH TRAN, Dir., Holy Name Rectory, 323 Dickinson St., Springfield, 01108. Tel: 413-733-5823.

Spanish Apostolate—

Catholic Latino Ministry—Rev. PAUL E. MANSHIP, Dir.; LUCY RAMOS, Exec. Sec., 65 Elliot St., P.O. Box 1730, Springfield, 01101-1730. Tel: 413-452-0631; Fax: 413-747-0273. Email: hispanicmin@diospringfield.org.

The Saint Thomas More Society—

Bishop Marshall Center—JAMES H. TOURTELOTTE, Esq., Dir., St. Michael's Cathedral, 260 State St., Springfield, 01105. Tel: 413-732-2301.

Springfield Diocesan Council of Catholic Women—Mrs. KATHERINE KUBERA, Pres., 11 Orchard Rd., East Longmeadow, 01028.

Victim Assistance Coordinator—LAURA F. REILLY. Tel: 413-452-0624. Email: l.reilly@diospringfield.org.

Vigilance, Council of— The Deans.

Vocations—Rev. DANIEL S. PACHOLEC, Christian Education Center, 625 Carew St., Springfield, 01104. Tel: 413-452-0816; Fax: 413-452-0817.

Office of Youth Ministry—Mr. DONALD BOUCHER, Dir. Youth Min., Christian Education Center, 625 Carew St., Springfield, 01104. Tel: 413-732-3175; Fax: 413-732-1944.

Western Massachusetts Funding and Resource Center—65 Elliot St., P.O. Box 1730, Springfield, 01101. Tel: 413-452-0615.

CLERGY, PARISHES, MISSIONS AND PAROCHIAL SCHOOLS

CITY OF SPRINGFIELD
(HAMPDEN COUNTY)

1—ST. MICHAEL'S CATHEDRAL (1847), Rev. Msgr. Richard S. Sniezyk, V.G., Rector; Sisters Margaret McNaughton, S.S.J., Pastoral Assoc.; Eileen Sullivan, S.S.J., Outreach Min. In Res., Rev. John L. Sullivan, J.C.L.
Res.: 260 State St., 01103. Tel: 413-781-3656; Fax: 413-788-7752.
Catechesis/Religious Program—Students 48.
Mission—St. Joseph 01105. Tel: 413-733-3527. In Res., Revs. Damien Ilokaba; Donatus Ironuma.

2—ALL SOULS (1908), (Spanish), Revs. Juan F. Garcia (Peru); Diomedes Calle (Peru). In Res., Revs. Paul E. Manship; Hector Rojas (Colombia); Deacon Jose Rivera.
Office—35 Harriet St., 01107. Tel: 413-736-8208; 413-736-2167.
Res.: 445 Plainfield St., 01107. Tel: 413-736-0076; Fax: 413-731-0962.
Catechesis/Religious Program—Students 58.

3—ST. ALOYSIUS (1873), (French), Merged, with St. Matthew, Springfield, to form St. Jude, Indian Orchard.

4—BLESSED SACRAMENT (1953), (Hispanic), Revs. Juan F. Garcia (Peru); Diomedes Calle (Peru); Deacons Genaro Medina; Osvaldo Ramos.
Pastoral Center—35 Harriet St., 01107. Tel: 413-736-8208; 413-736-2167; Fax: 413-731-0962.
Res.: 445 Plainfield St., 01107. Tel: 413-736-0076.
Catechesis/Religious Program—Tel: 413-736-8208. Maria Ramos, D.R.E. Students 290.

5—ST. CATHERINE OF SIENA (1961), Rev. William F. Cyr; Deacon Joseph M. Garde.
Res.: 1023 Parker St., 01129. Tel: 413-783-8619; Fax: 413-783-2344.
Catechesis/Religious Program—Students 373.

6—HOLY CROSS (1949), Revs. J. Victor Carrier; Jeffrey A. Ballou; Deacon William Toller. In Res., Rev. Jack Sheaffer.
Res.: 221 Plumtree Rd., 01118. Tel: 413-783-4111; Fax: 413-783-4112.
School—153 Eddywood St., 01118. Tel: 413-782-5246; Fax: 413-782-8137. Lay Teachers 25; Students 414.
Catechesis/Religious Program—175 Eddywood St., 01118. Tel: 413-782-8284. Students 217.

7—HOLY FAMILY (1901), (African American—Hispanic), Rev. Msgr. Richard S. Sniezyk, V.G.; Deacon Raphael Velazquez. In Res., Rev. John Tibahinirwa.
Res.: 235 Eastern Ave., 01109. Tel: 413-732-1422.
Catechesis/Religious Program—Students 90.

8—HOLY NAME (1909), Revs. John E. Connors, Pastor; Quynh Tran, Vietnamese Apostolate; Anne Marie Ferraro, Pastoral Min.; Gerri Kacoyannakis, Business Mgr.
Res.: 323 Dickinson St., 01108. Tel: 413-733-5823; Fax: 413-788-6481.
Center—57 Alderman St., 01108. Tel: 413-734-7113.
School—37 Alderman St., 01108. Tel: 413-736-4235; Fax: 413-747-8237. Nelly DeCarvalho, Prin. Lay Teachers 16; Students 270.
Catechesis/Religious Program—Tel: 413-736-4145. Jan Dipetro, D.R.E.; Sherry Armstrong, D.R.E. Students 213.

9—IMMACULATE CONCEPTION (1905), (Polish), Rev. Stanley Sokol, Admin.; Deacon Rodney Szymczyk.
Res.: 25 Parker St. (Indian Orchard), 01151. Tel: 413-543-3627; Fax: 413-543-4301.
Catechesis/Religious Program—Mrs. Mary Arabik, D.R.E. Students 123.

10—ST. JOSEPH'S (1873), (French), See Separate Listing, Now a Mission of Saint Michael Cathedral, Springfield

11—ST. MARY'S (1948), Rev. Kenneth J. Tatro.
Res.: 840 Page Blvd., 01104. Tel: 413-739-0456; Fax: 413-733-6155.
Catechesis/Religious Program—Tel: 413-736-1622. Students 405.

12—OUR LADY OF HOPE (1906), Rev. David J. Joyce. In Res., Rev. Andrew Dodo.
Res.: 577 Carew St., 01104. Tel: 413-739-7369; Fax: 413-788-9313.
School—474 Armory St., 01104. Tel: 413-734-4125; Fax: 413-734-4998. Lay Teachers 27; Students 438.
Catechesis/Religious Program—Students 137.

13—OUR LADY OF MT. CARMEL (1907), (Italian), Revs. Robert S. White, C.S.S.; Paul D. Burns, C.S.S.; Sr. Elizabeth A. Matuszek, S.S.J., Pastoral Assoc. In Res., Rev. Anthony M. Corigliano, C.S.S.
Res.: 123 William St., 01105. Tel: 413-734-5433; Fax: 413-731-0680.
School—Preschool, 56 Margaret St., 01105. Tel: 413-733-7410.
School—36 Margaret St., 01105. Tel: 413-739-3616; Fax: 413-730-6131. Lay Teachers 12; Students 138.
Catechesis/Religious Program—Tel: 413-782-9318. Students 180.
Mission—St. Ann 576 Memorial Ave, West Springfield, Hampden Co. 01089. Tel: 413-736-3101; Fax: 413-732-4614. Rev. Joseph Massaro, C.S.S. In Res., Rev. Donald Higgins, C.S.S.

14—OUR LADY OF THE ROSARY (1917), (Polish), [JC] Rev. Stanley Sokol.
Res.: 28 Underwood St., 01104. Tel: 413-733-0508; Fax: 413-733-7512.
Catechesis/Religious Program—Tel: 413-739-2210. Students 35.

15—OUR LADY OF THE SACRED HEART (1929), Rev. William Tourigny.
Office—51 Rosewell Ave., 01109. Tel: 413-782-8041; Fax: 413-783-9150.
Res.: 417 Boston Rd., 01109. Tel: 413-782-8041; Fax: 413-783-9150.
School—52 Rosewell Ave., 01109. Tel 413-782-8021. Lay Teachers 17; Students 376.
Catechesis/Religious Program—Cindee Gagnon, D.R.E. Students 150.

16—ST. PATRICK'S (1961), Rev. Francis E. Crombie; Deacon George Kozach. Tel: 413-783-2455.
Res.: 1900 Allen St., 01118-1820. Tel: 413-783-6201; Fax: 413-783-7787.
Catechesis/Religious Program—Alan E. O'Dell, D.R.E. Students 188.

17—ST. PAUL (1960), Rev. C. Lee Gilbertson.
Res.: 51 Fenimore Blvd., 01108. Tel: 413-737-4422 (Rectory); 413-736-1539 (Church); Fax: 413-736-8378.
Catechesis/Religious Program—Students 124.
Mission—St. Joseph's 146 Vineland Ave., East Longmeadow, Hampden Co. 01028. Tel: 413-737-8650.

18—SACRED HEART (1872), Rev. George A. Farland. In Res., Revs. Mark S. Stelzer; Christopher D. Connelly.
Res.: 395 Chestnut St., 01104. Tel: 413-732-3721; Fax: 413-733-5731.
Catechesis/Religious Program—Students 163.

19—ST THOMAS AQUINAS (1908), (French—Vietnamese), Closed., For inquiries for sacramental records contact Blessed Sacrament, Springfield.

OUTSIDE THE CITY OF SPRINGFIELD

ADAMS BERKSHIRE CO.

1—NOTRE DAME DES SEPT DOULEURS (1882), (French), Merged, with St. Thomas Aquinas, Adams, to form Notre Dame des Sept Douleurs and St. Thomas Aquinas, Adams.

2—NOTRE DAME DES SEPT DOULEURS AND ST. THOMAS AQUINAS (1998), Rev. Daniel J. Boyle; Deacon Robert R. Moulton.
Res.: P.O. Box 231, 01220-0231. Tel: 413-743-0577; Fax: 413-743-4665.
Catechesis/Religious Program—Students 607.

3—ST. STANISLAUS KOSTKA (1902), (Polish), [CEM] Rev. Daniel J. Boyle.
Res.: 25 Hoosac St., 01220. Tel: 413-743-0041.
School—108 Summer St., 01220. Tel: 413-743-1091. Felician Sisters 1; Lay Teachers 10; Students 173.
Catechesis/Religious Program—Students 100.
Convent—23 Hoosac St., 01220. Tel: 413-743-1221.

4—ST. THOMAS AQUINAS (1875), Merged, with Notre Dame des Sept Douleurs, Adams, to form Notre Dame des Sept Douleurs and St. Thomas Aquinas, Adams.

AGAWAM, HAMDEN CO., ST. THERESA OF THE CHILD JESUS (1883), Merged, with Saint Anthony Mission to form All Saints, Agawam.

AGAWAM, HAMPDEN CO.

1—ALL SAINTS (2001), Rev. Steven C. Amo.
Res.: 74 Bridge St., 01220-023_. Tel: 413-786-4451; Fax: 413-786-6441.
Catechesis/Religious Program—Students 179.

2—ST. JOHN THE EVANGELIST (1946), Rev. John J. Brennan.
Res.: 833 Main St., 01001. Tel: 413-786-8105; Fax: 413-789-6266.
Catechesis/Religious Program—Tel: 413-789-2484. Students 482.

AMHERST, HAMPSHIRE CO., ST. BRIGID'S (1872), [CEM] Rev. John T. Smegal. Tel: 413-253-1828.
Res.: 122 N. Pleasant St., P.O. Box 424, 01004-0424. Tel: 413-253-2829; Fax: 413-253-7935.
Catechesis/Religious Program—Jane Bacon, D.R.E.; Susan Nagy, D.R.E.; Patty Bonsigneur, D.R.E. Students 227.

BELCHERTOWN, HAMPSHIRE CO., ST. FRANCIS OF ASSISI (1926), Revs. Vernon Decoteau; John K. Sheaffer.
Res.: 10 Park St., 01007. Tel: 413-323-6272; Fax: 413-323-6272.
Catechesis/Religious Program—Mrs. Judy Trickey, D.R.E.; Mrs. Nadra McKenzie, D.R.E. Students 763.

BONDSVILLE, HAMPDEN CO.

1—ST. ADALBERT'S (1910), Rev. Normand F. Mailloux, M.S.
Res.: 18 Depot St., P.O. Box 1083, 01009. Tel: 413-283-3000.
Catechesis/Religious Program—Students 16.

2—ST. BARTHOLOMEW'S (1878), [JC] Rev. Eugene J. Plasse.
Res.: 76 Thorndike St., Palmer, 01069. Tel: 413-283-5091; 413-283-8841 (Church).
Catechesis/Religious Program—Students 36.

BRIMFIELD, HAMPDEN CO., ST. CHRISTOPHER'S (1953), Revs. Walter A. Swift; Jeddie P. Brooks.
Church: 20 Sturbridge Rd., Rte. 20, P.O. Box 387, 01010. Tel: 413-245-7274; Fax: 413-245-8376.
Rectory—16 Sturbridge Rd., Rte. 20, 01010.
Catechesis/Religious Program—Students 188.
Mission—St. Monica Wales, Hampden Co.
Station—Holland, St. Bernadette's

CHESHIRE, BERKSHIRE CO., ST. MARY OF THE ASSUMPTION (1926), [JC] Rev. David R. Raymond; Deacon Robert Hitter.
Res.: 159 Church St., 01225. Tel: 413-743-2110.
Catechesis/Religious Program—Students 265.

CHICOPEE, HAMPDEN CO.

1—ST. ANNE'S (1912), Rev. William C. Rousseau; Deacon Edward J. Finnie, (Retired).
Res.: 30 College St., 01020. Tel: 413-532-7503; Fax: 413-542-5970.
Catechesis/Religious Program—Tel: 413-533-8038. Students 264.

2—ST. ANTHONY'S (1926), (Polish), Rev. Benedict Fagone, O.F.M.Conv.
Res.: 56 St. Anthony St., 01013. Tel: 413-538-9475; Fax: 413-538-9859.
Catechesis/Religious Program—Students 55.

3—ASSUMPTION (1885), (French), Rev. Gerard A. LaFleur, V.F. In Res., Rev. Michael H. Devlin.
Res.: 104 Springfield St., 01013. Tel: 413-592-1597; Fax: 413-592-1597.
Catechesis/Religious Program—Tel: 413-592-9344. Students 150.

4—ST. GEORGE'S (1893), (French), Rev. Robert H. Riel; Deacon Leo Bergeron.
Res.: 202 E. Main St., 01020. Tel: 413-598-8622; Fax: 413-592-8353. Web: www.stgeorgechicopee.org.
School—587 Grattan St., 01020. Tel: 413-533-1475; Fax: 413-533-1418. Consolidated to form St. Joan of Arc/St. George School.
Catechesis/Religious Program—Tel: 413-592-4456. Students 185.

5—HOLY NAME OF JESUS (1838), [CEM] Rev. Mark S. Stelzer.
Office: 33 South St., 01013. Tel: 413-594-8700; Fax: 413-592-3871. Email: holynamechicopee@aol.com.
School—63 South St., 01013. Tel: 413-592-6857. Sisters of Notre Dame 3; Lay Teachers 11; Students 230.
Catechesis/Religious Program—Tel: 413-592-7813. Students 53.

6—ST. MARY'S (1939), Rev. Francis M. Kennedy; Deacon Joseph A. Smith.
Res.: 840 Chicopee St., 01013. Tel: 413-532-1854.
Catechesis/Religious Program—Students 90.

7—NATIVITY OF THE BLESSED VIRGIN MARY (1897), (French), [JC] Rev. Francis M. Kennedy.
Res.: 780 Chicopee St., 01013-2747. Tel: 413-532-9421; Fax: 413-532-1410.
Catechesis/Religious Program—Tel: 413-536-3310. Students 60.

8—ST. PATRICK'S (1872), (Irish), [CEM] Rev. Richard M. Turner; Deacon Francis D. Rogers.
Res.: 319 Broadway, 01020. Tel: 413-592-4178; Fax: 413-592-4170.
School—125 Montgomery St., 01020. Tel: 413-594-8166; Fax: 413-594-8167. Sisters of Saint Joseph 1; Lay Teachers 12; Students 208.
Catechesis/Religious Program—Tel: 413-592-4344. Students 149.

9—ST. ROSE DE LIMA (1909), (French), [CEM] Rev. Msgr. Leo A. Leclerc, V.G.; Rev. Michael F. Bernier; Deacon Leon Mireault. In Res., Rev. Daniel S. Pacholec.
Res.: 600 Grattan St., 01020. Tel: 413-536-4558; Fax: 413-536-4559.
School—St. Joan of Arc/St. George School, 587 Grattan St., 01020. Tel: 413-533-1475; Fax: 413-533-1418. Sisters of the Presentation of Mary 2; Sisters of the Assumption 1; Lay Teachers 15; Students 339.
Catechesis/Religious Program—Students 365.

10—ST. STANISLAUS BASILICA (1891), (Polish), [CEM] Revs. Michael Zielke, O.F.M.Conv.; Mieczyslaw Wit, O.F.M.Conv.; Jeremy Chodacki, O.F.M.Conv.; Gary Johnson, O.F.M.Conv.; Timothy Dore, O.F.M-.Conv.; Bro. William Surdyka, O.F.M.Conv. In Res., Bro. Frank Grimaldi, O.F.M.Conv.
Res.: 566 Front St., 01013. Tel: 413-594-6669; Fax: 413-594-5259.
School—Tel: 413-592-5135; Fax: 413-598-0187. Sr. Cecelia Haier, F.S.S.J., Prin. Franciscan Sisters of St. Joseph 2; Lay Teachers 26; Students 417.

Catechesis/Religious Program—Tel: 413-592-7955. Students 143.

DALTON, BERKSHIRE CO., ST. AGNES (1907), Rev. Christopher A. Malatesta; Deacon Pasqual Baldasaro.
Res.: 489 Main St., 01226. Tel: 413-684-0125.
School—30 Carson St., 01226. Tel: 413-684-3143. Sisters of St. Joseph 1; Lay Teachers 16; Students 202.
Catechesis/Religious Program—35 Deming St., 01226. Tel: 413-684-3879. Students 495.
Chapel—St. Patrick Chapel 43 Church St., Hinsdale, 01235.
Chapel—St. Matthew Chapel, Formerly St. Matthew Mission, Hinsdale 78 Washington St., Becket, 01223.

EAST LONGMEADOW, HAMPDEN CO., ST. MICHAEL'S (1894), Rev. James J. Scahill; Sisters Mary McGeer, S.S.J., Pastoral Assoc.; Betty Broughan, S.S.J., Pastoral Assoc.
Res. & Mailing Address: 128 Maple St., 01028. Tel: 413-525-4253; Fax: 413-525-4254.
Catechesis/Religious Program—Tel: 413-525-0371. Mrs. Shirley Skiffington, D.R.E. Students 1,037.

EASTHAMPTON, HAMPSHIRE CO.

1—IMMACULATE CONCEPTION (1871), [CEM] Rev. William J. Hamilton, K.H.S.
Res.: 33 Adams St., 01027. Tel: 413-527-9778; Fax: 413-527-9353.
School—Notre Dame-Immaculate Conception School, Tel: 413-527-6133; Fax: 413-527-6625. Mrs. Sharon Sarrasin, Prin. Lay Teachers 14; Students 201.
Catechesis/Religious Program—11 Clifford St., 01027. Tel: 413-527-7222. Students 298.

2—OUR LADY OF GOOD COUNSEL (1906), (French), Rev. Thomas R. Champigny.
Res.: 35 Pleasant St., 01027. Tel: 413-527-9588; Fax: 413-529-0517.
School—Notre Dame-Immaculate Conception, Tel: 413-527-6133; Fax: 413-527-6625. Lay Teachers 11; Students 201.
Catechesis/Religious Program—Students 208.

3—SACRED HEART (1909), (Polish), [CEM] Rev. James A. Sipitkowski.
Res.: 33 Knipfer Ave., 01027. Tel: 413-527-9036; Fax: 413-529-0936.
Catechesis/Religious Program—Students 168.

FEEDING HILLS, HAMPDEN CO., SACRED HEART (1946), Rev. Ronald F. Sadlowski; Deacon L. Joseph Kaiser.
Res.: 1103 Springfield St., 01030. Tel: 413-786-8200; Fax: 413-786-7802.
Catechesis/Religious Program— Rev. Ronald F. Sadlowski, D.R.E. Students 1,198.

GRANBY, HAMPSHIRE CO., IMMACULATE HEART OF MARY (1951), Rev. Adrian J. Benoit.
Res.: 256 State St., 01033. Tel: 413-467-9821; Fax: 413-467-2988.
Catechesis/Religious Program—Tel: 413-467-3566. Students 477.

GREAT BARRINGTON, BERKSHIRE CO., ST. PETER'S (1864), [CEM] Revs. Daniel R. Papineau, M.I.C.; Shawn O'Connor, M.I.C.; Bro. Kenneth Galisa, M.I.C.
Res.: 16 Russell St., 01230. Tel: 413-528-1157; Fax: 413-644-8916.
Catechesis/Religious Program—Tel: 413-528-2037. Students 195.

GREENFIELD, FRANKLIN CO.

1—BLESSED SACRAMENT (1960), [CEM] Rev. Timothy J. Campoli, V.F.
Res.: 182 High St., 01301. Tel: 413-773-3311; Fax: 413-773-5785.
School—Holy Trinity School, 10 Beacon St., 01301. Tel: 413-773-3831; Fax: 413-774-3852. Arlene Ashby, Prin. Lay Teachers 9; Students 134.
Catechesis/Religious Program—Tel: 413-774-2918. Students 97.

2—HOLY TRINITY (1868), Rev. Ronald G. Yargeau.
Res.: 133 Main St., 01301-3209. Tel: 413-774-2884; Fax: 413-774-3852.
Catechesis/Religious Program—Students 166.

3—SACRED HEART (1912), (Polish), [CEM] Rev. Stanley J. Aksamit; Deacon Albert Routhier.
Res.: St. Mary's, 90 Seventh St., Turners Falls, 01376. Tel: 413-863-2585; 413-772-6377; Fax: 413-863-8978.
Catechesis/Religious Program—Students 54.

HADLEY, HAMPSHIRE CO.

1—HOLY ROSARY (1916), (Polish), Merged, with St. John, Hadley, to form Most Holy Redeemer, Hadley.

2—ST. JOHN'S (1915), Merged, with Holy Rosary, Hadley, to form Most Holy Redeemer, Hadley.

3—MOST HOLY REDEEMER (1998), [CEM] Rev. William P. Murphy.
Res.: 120 Russell St., P.O. Box 375, 01035-0375. Tel: 413-584-1326; Fax: 413-587-0224.
Catechesis/Religious Program—Tel: 413-586-6209. Students 251.

HAMPDEN, HAMPDEN CO., ST. MARY'S (1951), [CEM] Rev. Timothy J. Murphy.
Res.: 27 Somers Rd., 01036. Tel: 413-566-8843; Fax: 413-566-5845.
Catechesis/Religious Program—Students 375.

HATFIELD, HAMPSHIRE CO.

1—HOLY TRINITY (1916), (Polish), [CEM] Rev. Robert J. Coonan.
73 Main St., P.O. Box 110, 01038. Tel: 413-247-3133; Fax: 413-247-5605.
Catechesis/Religious Program—Tel: 413-247-9079. Students 31.

2—ST. JOSEPH'S (1899), Rev. Robert J. Coonan.
Mailing Address: P.O. Box 34, 01038.
Res.: 11 School St., 01038. Tel: 413-247-9079.
Catechesis/Religious Program—Students 188.

HAYDENVILLE, HAMPSHIRE CO., ST. MARY'S (1889), [CEM] Rev. J. Donald R. Lapointe.
Mailing Address: P.O. Box 277, 01039-0277. Tel: 413-268-7212; Fax: 413-268-8264.
Church: 173 Main St., P.O. Box 277, 01039-0277. Tel: 413-268-7212; Fax: 413-268-8264.
Catechesis/Religious Program—Students 127.

HINSDALE, BERKSHIRE CO., ST. PATRICK'S (1868), See Separate Listing, Now a chapel under St. Agnes, Dalton.

HOLYOKE, HAMPDEN CO.

1—BLESSED SACRAMENT (1913), Revs. Norman B. Bolton; Richard A. Riendeau.
Res.: 1945 Northampton St., 01040. Tel: 413-532-0713.
School—21 Westfield Rd., 01040. Tel: 413-536-2236; Fax: 413-534-0795. Sisters of St. Joseph 1; Lay Teachers 26; Students 348.
Catechesis/Religious Program—15 Westfield Rd., 01040. Tel: 413-532-8647. Students 159.
Mission—Holyoke Soldier's Home Chapel 110 Cherry St., Hampden Co. 01040. Tel: 413-532-9475.

2—HOLY CROSS (1905), Rev. Roland J. Galipeau.
Res.: 23 Sycamore St., 01040. Tel: 413-532-5661; Fax: 413-535-1759.
Catechesis/Religious Program—Tel: 413-536-8832. Maureen P. Callahan, D.R.E. Students 321.

3—HOLY FAMILY (1949), Rev. Robert W. Thrasher, J.C.D.; Deacon Joseph A. Badame.
Res.: 15 Holy Family Rd., 01040. Tel: 413-536-6777.
Catechesis/Religious Program—Tel: 413-536-1665. Students 76.

4—IMMACULATE CONCEPTION (1905), [JC] Rev. James Aherne, M.S.; Deacon Frederick Pelletier. In Res., Rev. William J. Doherty, M.S.
Res.: 54 N. Summer St., 01040. Tel: 413-532-5784; Fax: 413-532-8852.
Catechesis/Religious Program—Tel: 413-532-0468. Students 200.

5—ST. JEROME'S (1854), [CEM] Rev. Daniel R. Foley, V.F.
Res.: 169 Hampden St., 01040. Tel: 413-532-6381; Fax: 413-540-9831.

6—MATER DOLOROSA (1896), (Polish), [CEM] Revs. Alexander B. Cymerman, O.F.M.Conv.; Anthony Francis Spilka, O.F.M.Conv.; Bro. Stephen Murphy, O.F.M.Conv., Pastoral Assoc.
Offices—Tel: 413-532-7889; Fax: 413-538-6754.
Res.: 71 Maple St., 01040. Tel: 413-532-8272.
School—25 Maple St., 01040. Tel: 413-532-2831. Venerini Sisters 1; Franciscan Sisters of St. Joseph 1; Lay Teachers 18; Students 306.
Catechesis/Religious Program—Tel: 413-532-8272. Students 136.

7—OUR LADY OF GUADALUPE (2001), [CEM 3] [JC] Revs. John G. Lessard-Thibodeau; Jose A. Bermudez.
Res.: 435 Maple St., 01040. Tel: 413-532-4282; Fax: 413-532-2182.
Catechesis/Religious Program—Students 257.

8—OUR LADY OF PERPETUAL HELP (1890), (French), Merged, with Sacred Heart to form Our Lady of Guadalupe, Holyoke.

9—OUR LADY OF THE ROSARY (1886), Closed. For inquiries for parish records contact the chancery.

10—PRECIOUS BLOOD (1869), Closed., For inquiries for parish records contact Our Lady of Guadalupe, Holyoke.

11—SACRED HEART (1876), Merged, with Our Lady of Perpetual Help to form Our Lady of Guadalupe, Holyoke.

HOUSATONIC, BERKSHIRE CO.

1—ALL SAINTS (1913), (Polish), Rev. Anthony J. Jutt.
Res.: 204 High St., 01236. Tel: 413-274-3443.
Catechesis/Religious Program—Students 31.

2—CORPUS CHRISTI (1899), [CEM] Rev. Anthony J. Jutt.
Res.: 1085 Main St., Box 569, 01236. Tel: 413-274-3443.
Catechesis/Religious Program—Students 62.

HUNTINGTON, HAMPSHIRE CO., ST. THOMAS (1886), [CEM] Rev. Donald A. Noiseux.
Res.: 8 E. Main St., P.O. Box 547, 01050. Tel: 413-667-3350.
Catechesis/Religious Program—Students 108.
Mission—St. John Middlefield St., Chester, Hampden Co. 01011.

INDIAN ORCHARD, HAMPDEN CO., ST. JUDE (1998), Rev. William A. Pomerleau.
Res.: 1326 Worcester St., 01151. Tel: 413-543-3739; Fax: 413-543-5573.
Church: 221 Main St..
Catechesis/Religious Program—Students 36.

LANESBORO, BERKSHIRE CO., NORTH AMERICAN MARTYRS (1969), Rev. David R. Raymond, Admin.
Res.: 17 Juleann Dr., 01237. Tel: 413-442-2063.
Catechesis/Religious Program—Students 110.

LEE, BERKSHIRE CO., ST. MARY'S (1857), [CEM] Revs. Gary M. Dailey; Paul C. LaFlamme.
Res.: 40 Academy St., 01238. Tel: 413-243-0275; Fax: 413-243-1926.
School—115 Orchard St., 01238. Tel: 413-243-1079; Fax: 413-243-1022. Sisters of St. Joseph 1; Lay Teachers 10; Students 175.
Catechesis/Religious Program—Tel: 413-243-4476. Students 225.
Mission—St. Mary of the Lakes Otis, Berkshire Co. Tel: 413-269-4200.
Mission—St. Francis of Assisi South Lee, Berkshire Co. Fax: 413-292-1926.

LEEDS, HAMPSHIRE CO., ST. CATHERINE'S (1911), [JC] Rev. J. Donald R. Lapointe.
Res.: 195 Main St., 01053. Tel: 413-268-7290; Fax: 413-268-8264.
Catechesis/Religious Program—Students 85.

LENOX DALE, BERKSHIRE CO., ST. VINCENT DE PAUL'S (1904), Rev. Christopher J. Waitekus.
Mailing Address: P.O. Box 259, 01242-0259. In Res., Rev. John J. Bonzagni, J.C.L. Tel: 413-637-1085.
Church & Res.: 29 Crystal St., 01242. Tel: 413-637-3525.
Catechesis/Religious Program—Tel: 413-637-0519. Students 46.

LENOX, BERKSHIRE CO., ST. ANN'S (1891), [CEM] Rev. Christopher J. Waitekus; Deacon George Keator.
Res.: 134 Main St., 01240. Tel: 413-637-0157; Fax: 413-637-2945.
Catechesis/Religious Program—Tel: 413-637-4027; Fax: 413-637-2945. Students 260.

LONGMEADOW, HAMPDEN CO., ST. MARY'S (1936), Rev. Francis E. Reilly; Deacon Donald J. Higby.
Res.: 519 Longmeadow St., 01106. Tel: 413-567-3124; Fax: 413-567-4640. Email: parishoffice@stmarylong.org.
School—56 Hopkins Pl., 01106. Tel: 413-567-0907; Fax: 413-567-7695. Sisters of St. Joseph 1; Lay Teachers 13; Students 210.
Catechesis/Religious Program—Tel: 413-567-3420; Fax: 413-567-0264. Students 1,200.

LUDLOW, HAMPDEN CO.

1—CHRIST THE KING (1948), (Polish), Rev. Raymond A. Soltys.
Res.: 41 Warsaw Ave., 01056. Tel: 413-583-2630; Fax: 413-583-2630.
Catechesis/Religious Program—Students 310.

2—ST. JOHN THE BAPTIST (1904), (French), Rev. Homer P. Gosselin; Deacon Edward Meyer. In Res., Rev. Lionel E. Bonneville.
Res.: 181 Hubbard St., 01056. Tel: 413-583-3467; Fax: 413-583-2036.
School—217 Hubbard St., 01056. Tel: 413-583-8550; Fax: 413-589-0544. Sisters of St. Ann 1; Lay Teachers 14; Students 307.
Catechesis/Religious Program—Tel: 413-529-9551. Students 378.

3—ST. MARY (1968), Rev. David M. Darcy; Deacon Robert L. Duval, Admin.
Res.: 12 Cedar St., 01056. Tel: 413-583-2691; Fax: 413-589-1868.
Catechesis/Religious Program—Tel: 413-583-2153. Students 350.

4—OUR LADY OF FATIMA (1948), (Portuguese), Rev. Vitor Oliveira, Admin.
Res.: 438 Winsor St., 01056. Tel: 413-583-2312; Fax: 413-547-0207.
Catechesis/Religious Program—Students 409.

MILLERS FALLS, FRANKLIN CO., ST. JOHN'S (1898), Rev. Dennis P. Bombardier.
Res.: 5 Church St., 01349. Tel: 413-659-3435.
Catechesis/Religious Program—Students 13.
Mission—St. Blanche Erving, Franklin Co. Closed. For sacramental records, please contact St. John Church, Millers Falls.

MONSON, HAMPDEN CO., ST. PATRICK'S (1878), [CEM] Rev. Jeddie P. Brooks; Deacon Bernard Pellissier; Wilfred Fredette, Pastoral Assoc.
Res.: 22 Green St., P.O. Box 473, 01057. Tel: 413-267-3622; Fax: 413-267-0272.
Catechesis/Religious Program—Students 277.

NORTH ADAMS, BERKSHIRE CO.

1—ST. ANTHONY OF PADUA (1903), (Italian), Rev. Daniel J. O'Hear; Deacon Francis Ryan.
Res.: 70 Marshall St., 01247. Tel: 413-663-3112.
Catechesis/Religious Program—Tel: 413-663-7331. Students 129.

2—ST. FRANCIS (1863), [CEM] Rev. Michael W.T. Twardzik.
Res.: 12 Union St., 01247. Tel: 413-663-5316; Fax: 413-663-3938.

Catechesis/Religious Program—Tel: 413-664-6173; Fax: 413-664-6174. Students 168.

3—HOLY FAMILY (1997), Merged, with Our Lady of Incarnation, North Adams, to form Our Lady of Mercy, North Adams.

4—NOTRE DAME (1875), (French-Canadian), Rev. Michael W.T. Twardzik.
Res.: 12 Union St., 01247. Tel: 413-663-7131; Fax: 413-663-3938.
Catechesis/Religious Program—Tel: 413-664-6173; Fax: 413-664-6174. Students 35.

5—OUR LADY OF MERCY (1997), Rev. Michael W.T. Twardzik.
Church: 635 State Rd., 01247. Tel: 413-663-3976; Fax: 413-663-3938.
Catechesis/Religious Program—Tel: 413-664-6173; Fax: 413-664-6174. Students 60.
Shrine— 1288 Massachusetts Ave., 01247.

6—OUR LADY OF MERCY SHRINE (1997),, Consolidation of Holy Family, North Adams, and Our Lady of the Incarnation, North Adams. Rev. Michael W.T. Twardzik.
1288 Massachusetts Ave., 01247. Tel: 413-663-7131; Fax: 413-664-4940.

7—OUR LADY OF THE INCARNATION (1955), Merged, with Holy Family, North Adams, to form Our Lady of Mercy, North Adams.

NORTHAMPTON, HAMPSHIRE CO.

1—ANNUNCIATION (1878), Revs. Roy H. Duquette; John Gawienawski.
Res.: 87 Beacon St., P.O. Box 60055, Florence, 01062-0055. Tel: 413-584-1520; Fax: 413-586-7530.
Catechesis/Religious Program—87 Beacon St., Florence, 01062-0055. Tel: 413-584-2041. Students 145.

2—BLESSED SACRAMENT (1899), Rev. Daniel P. Liston, J.C.L.; Deacon Francis McCarthy; Susan C. McVeigh, Pastoral Assoc.
Res.: 336 Elm St., 01060. Tel: 413-584-1280.
Catechesis/Religious Program—Tel: 413-586-1111. Students 178.

3—ST. JOHN CANTIUS (1904), (Polish), Rev. Merle L. Lavoie.
Res.: 10 Hawley St., 01060. Tel: 413-584-1510; Fax: 413-586-5776.
Catechesis/Religious Program—101 King St., 01060. Tel: 413-584-7422. Students 27.

4—ST. MARY OF THE ASSUMPTION (1866), (Irish), [CEM] Rev. Eugene D. Honan. In Res., Rev. Leo James Hoar.
Res.: 3 Elm St., P.O. Box 180, 01061. Tel: 413-584-7310; Fax: 413-584-4788.
Catechesis/Religious Program—Tel: 413-586-1111. Students 137.

5—SACRED HEART (1886), (French), Rev. Merle L. Lavoie.
Res.: 101 King St., 01060. Tel: 413-584-7422.
Catechesis/Religious Program—Tel: 413-584-4339. Students 90.

NORTHFIELD, FRANKLIN CO., ST. PATRICK (1973), [CEM] Rev. Gerald Brady; Deacon Arthur E. Ratte.
Res.: 80 Main St., 01360-1022. Tel: 413-498-2728.
Catechesis/Religious Program—Tel: 413-498-5039. Students 140.

ORANGE, FRANKLIN CO., ST. MARY (1903), Rev. William Lunney; Deacon Joseph S. Bucci Jr.
Res.: 19 Congress St., 01364. Tel: 978-544-2900; Fax: 978-544-8105.
Catechesis/Religious Program—Students 175.

PALMER, HAMPDEN CO., ST. THOMAS THE APOSTLE (1864), [CEM] Rev. Eugene J. Plasse; Deacon Edward J. Tenczar.
Res.: 76 Thorndike St., 01069. Tel: 413-283-5091.
Catechesis/Religious Program—Tel: 413-283-5651. Students 338.

PITTSFIELD, BERKSHIRE CO.

1—ST. CHARLES (1893), Rev. Peter A. Gregory; Sr. Barbara A. Faille, S.S.J., Pastoral Assoc.; Deacon William G. Moesley.
Res.: 89 Briggs Ave., 01201. Tel: 413-442-7470; Fax: 413-445-5267.
Catechesis/Religious Program—100 Briggs Ave., 01201. Tel: 413-442-0591. Students 279.

2—ST. FRANCIS (1960), Rev. Paul A. Bombardier.
Res.: 80 Morningview Dr., 01201. Tel: 413-499-1955.
Catechesis/Religious Program—Tel: 413-448-2987. Donna Quallen, D.R.E. Students 66.

3—HOLY FAMILY (1912), (Polish), Rev. Michael Shershanovich.
Res.: 133 Seymour St., 01201. Tel: 413-442-2036; Fax: 413-442-2036.
Catechesis/Religious Program—133 Seymout St., 01201. Tel: 413-442-4065. John Arasimowicz, D.R.E. Students 30.

4—ST. JOSEPH'S (1849), [CEM] Revs. Michael Shershanovich; Venace Max Kishe; Deacon Eugene C. Momnie.
Res.: 414 North St., 01201. Tel: 413-445-5789; Fax: 413-443-5466.
Catechesis/Religious Program—Students 212.

5—ST. MARK'S (1913), Rev. John C. Salatino.
Res.: 27 Onota St., 01201. Tel: 413-447-7510; Fax: 413-448-2164.
Catechesis/Religious Program—400 Columbus Ave. Ext., 01201. Tel: 413-442-8444; Fax: 413-448-2164. Students 271.

6—ST. MARY THE MORNING STAR (1915), Rev. Paul A. Bombardier.
Res.: 665 Tyler St., 01201. Tel: 413-445-5008; Fax: 413-447-9999.
Catechesis/Religious Program—Donna Quallen, D.R.E. Students 120.
Parish Center—75 Plunkett St., 01201. Tel: 413-447-7533.

7—NOTRE DAME (1868), (French), Rev. Michael Shershanovich; Deacon Ralph R. Cyr.
Res.: 50 Melville St., 01201. Tel: 413-499-2736; Fax: 413-499-2736.
Catechesis/Religious Program—41 Melville St., 01021. Tel: 413-499-9554; Fax: 413-499-9514. Students 43.

8—OUR LADY OF MT. CARMEL (1903), (Italian), Rev. Geoffrey J. Deeker, C.S.S.
Res.: 359 Fenn St., 01201. Tel: 413-442-4458; Fax: 413-499-9607.
Catechesis/Religious Program—Tel: 413-445-4856. Students 169.
Mission—All Souls 51 Pembroke Ave., Berkshire Co. 01201. Tel: 413-442-5090.

9—SACRED HEART (1919), Rev. James K. Joyce; Sr. Kathryn Flanagan, Pastoral Min.; Deacon James A. Hager, Pastoral Min.
Res.: 191 Elm St., 01201. Tel: 413-443-6960; Fax: 413-442-9649.
School—Regional School, (Grades K-5), One Meadow Lane, 01201. Tel: 413-443-6379. Lay Teachers 16; Students 224.
Catechesis/Religious Program—Tel: 413-442-5564. Mr. Robert Esposito, D.R.E.; Mrs Kim Joseph, Administrative Asst. Students 567.

10—ST TERESA (1926), Rev. John J. Varley; Deacon Sean T. Mulholland. In Res., Rev. Royal J. Gardner (Retired).
Res.: 290 South St., 01201. Tel: 413-442-2202; Fax: 413-443-9876.
Catechesis/Religious Program—Tel: 413-443-5366. Sr. Shirleyanne Greene, S.S.J., D.R.E. Students 148

RUSSELL, HAMPDEN CO., OUR LADY OF THE ROSARY (1969), [JC] Rev. Armando C. Russo.
Res.: 5 Main St., P.O. Box 16, 01071-0016. Tel: 413-862-4418.
Catechesis/Religious Program—Students 93.

SHEFFIELD, BERKSHIRE CO., OUR LADY OF THE VALLEY (1901), [CEM] Rev. John Lis; Deacon Herbert L. Cary.
Res. & Mailing Address: 99 Maple Ave., P.O. Box 515, 01257. Tel: 413-229-3028.
Catechesis/Religious Program—Students 126.
Mission—Immaculate Conception Main St., Mill River, Berkshire Co. 01244.
Mission—Our Lady of the Hills Beartown Rd., Monterey, Berkshire Co. 01245.

SHELBURNE FALLS, FRANKLIN CO., ST. JOSEPH'S (1883), Rev. John A. Roach.
Res.: 34 Monroe Ave., 01370. Tel: 413-625-6405; Fax: 413-625-6405.
Catechesis/Religious Program—Students 88.
Mission—St. John the Baptist Church St., Colrain, Franklin Co. 01346.
Mission—St. Christopher Rte. 2, Charlemont, Franklin Co. 01339.

SOUTH DEERFIELD, FRANKLIN CO.

1—ST. JAMES (1895), Rev. Philippe D. Roux.
Res.: 85 Main St., 01373. Tel: 413-665-4535.
Catechesis/Religious Program—Students 266.
Mission—St. Mark Delabarre Ave., Conway, Franklin Co. 01341.

2—ST. STANISLAUS B. AND M. (1908), (Polish), [CEM] Rev. Philippe D. Roux; Deacon Theodore J. Tudryn.
Mailing Address: 29 Sugarloaf St., 01373. Tel: 413-665-3254.
Res.: 27 Sugarloaf St., 01373. Tel: 413-665-2417.
Catechesis/Religious Program—33 Sugarloaf St., 01373. Tel: 413-665-4656. Students 321.

SOUTH HADLEY, HAMPSHIRE CO.

1—ST. PATRICK'S (1878), Rev. Thomas M. Shea; Deacon John Bledsoe.
Res.: 30 Main St., 01075. Tel: 413-532-2850; Fax: 413-552-0241.
Catechesis/Religious Program—Tel: 413-534-7080. Students 743.

2—ST. THERESA OF THE INFANT JESUS (1946), Rev. Richard A. Bondi.
Res.: 9 East Parkview Dr., 01075. Tel: 413-532-3228; Fax: 413-540-0964.
Catechesis/Religious Program—Fax: 413-540-0944. Linda Duggin, D.R.E. Students 236.

SOUTHWICK, HAMPDEN CO., OUR LADY OF THE LAKE (1951), Rev. Henry L. Dorsch.
Res.: 224 Sheep Pasture Rd., P.O. Box 1150, 01077. Tel: 413-569-0161.
Catechesis/Religious Program—Rose Salzer, D.R.E. Students 286.

STOCKBRIDGE, BERKSHIRE CO., ST. JOSEPH'S (1922), [CEM] Rev. Steven F.C. McGuigan. Tel: 413-298-3748.
Res. and Mailing Address: 11 Elm St., P.O. Box 863, 01262-0863. Tel: 413-298-3748; Fax: 413-298-3748 (call first).
Catechesis/Religious Program—Students 6.

THORNDIKE, HAMPDEN CO., ST. MARY'S (1876), Closed. For inquiries for parish records contact the chancery., for parish records please see St. Thomas Parish, Palmer, MA.

THREE RIVERS, HAMPDEN CO.

1—ST. ANNE'S (1882), (French), [CEM] Rev. Sylvio E. Levesque.
Res.: 2230 Main St., 01080. Tel: 413-283-5041; Fax: 413-283-5041.
Catechesis/Religious Program—Tel: 413-283-7286. Students 190.

2—SS. PETER AND PAUL (1903), (Polish), [CEM] Rev. Stefan J. Niemczyk.
Res.: 2267 Main St., 01080. Tel: 413-283-6030.
Catechesis/Religious Program—Tel: 413-283-8814. Students 238.
Convent—358 Main St., 01080. Tel: 413-283-7402.

TURNERS FALLS, FRANKLIN CO.

1—ST. ANNE (1884), (French), [CEM] Rev. Stanley J. Aksamit; Deacon Albert Routhier.
Mailing Address: 90 Seventh St., 01376. Tel: 413-863-2585; Fax: 413-863-8978.
Church: J St., 01376.
Catechesis/Religious Program—Students 9.

2—ST. MARY'S (1872), [CEM] Rev. Stanley J. Aksamit; Deacon Albert Routhier.
Res.: 90 Seventh St., 01376. Tel: 413-863-2585; Fax: 413-863-8978.
Catechesis/Religious Program—Students 146.

3—OUR LADY OF CZESTOCHOWA (1909), (Polish), [CEM] Rev. Charles J. DiMascola.
Res.: 84 K St., 01376. Tel: 413-863-4748; Fax: 413-863-9263.
Catechesis/Religious Program—Students 106.

WARE, HAMPSHIRE CO.

1—ALL SAINTS (1860), [CEM] [JC 2] Rev. Edward T. Fitzgerald.
Res.: 17 North St., 01082. Tel: 413-967-4963.
Catechesis/Religious Program—Students 145.

2—ST. MARY'S (1905), (Polish), [CEM] Rev. Charles H. Kuzmeski.
Res.: 60 South St., 01082. Tel: 413-967-5913; Fax: 413-967-4679.
School—59 South St., 01082. Tel: 413-967-9936; Fax: 413-967-8217. Sisters of Immaculate Conception 6; Lay Teachers 9; Students 199.
Catechesis/Religious Program—Tel: 413-967-0449. Students 253.

3—OUR LADY OF MT. CARMEL (1871), (French), Closed., For inquiries for sacramental records contact All Saints, Ware.

WEST SPRINGFIELD, HAMPDEN CO.

1—IMMACULATE CONCEPTION (1877), Rev. Michael J. Twohig.
Res.: 475 Main St., 01089-3998. Tel: 413-736-4071; Fax: 413-734-5484.
Catechesis/Religious Program—Students 92.

2—ST. LOUIS DE FRANCE (1895), (French), Rev. Michael J. Twohig, Admin.
Mailing Address: 475 Main St., 01089. Tel: 413-736-4071; Fax: 413-734-5484.

3—ST. THOMAS THE APOSTLE (1900), [CEM] Revs. Richard M. Runte; Douglas McGonagle; Robert A. Gentile.
Res.: 47 Pine St., 01089. Tel: 413-739-4779; Fax: 413-739-1608.
School—75 Pine St., 01089. Tel: 413-739-4131. Sisters of St. Joseph 4; Lay Teachers 24; Students 451.
Catechesis/Religious Program—89 Pine St., 01089. Tel: 413-737-8267; Fax: 413-731-8768. Students 567.

WEST STOCKBRIDGE, BERKSHIRE CO., ST. PATRICK'S (1871), [CEM] Rev. Steven F.C. McGuigan, Admin.
Res.: 30 Albany Rd., 01266. Tel: 413-232-4427.
Catechesis/Religious Program—Students 65.

WESTFIELD, HAMPDEN CO.

1—ST. CASIMIR'S (1915), Merged, with St. Peter's, Westfield to form St. Peter and St. Casimir, Westfield.

2—HOLY TRINITY (1903), (Polish), Revs. Gerard R. Boulanger, M.S.; Lukasz Krzanowski, M.S.
Res.: 335 Elm St., 01085. Tel: 413-568-1506; Fax: 413-572-2533.
School—(Grades K-8), 331 Elm St., 01085. Tel: 413-568-4352. Mrs. Janet Snow, Prin. Lay Teachers 11; Students 77.
Catechesis/Religious Program—Students 231.

3—ST. MARY'S (1862), Revs. Brian F. McGrath; John C. Salatino, Pastoral Assoc.; Hector Rojas (Colombia), Pastoral Assoc. In Res., Rev. William H. Wallis.

Res.: 30 Bartlett St., 01085. Tel: 413-562-5477; Fax: 413-562-5478.
School—Tel: 413-568-2388; Fax: 413-568-2388. Sr. Christine Lavoie, Prin. Sisters 3; Lay Teachers 15; Students 237.
High School—Tel: 413-568-5692; Fax: 413-562-3501. Mr. Paul E. Romani Jr., Prin. Sisters 2; Lay Teachers 15; Students 155.
Catechesis/Religious Program—Tel: 413-568-1127. Mrs. Kay Mowatt, D.R.E. (Elementary); Mrs. Dona Kane, D.R.E. (Elementary); Mrs. Barbara Queenin, D.R.E. (High School). Students 777.
Convent—86 Mechanic St., 01085. Tel: 413-568-8077. Sisters of St. Joseph 3.

4—OUR LADY OF THE BLESSED SACRAMENT (1910), Rev. Hugh F. Crean. In Res., Rev. Anthony J. Creane.
Res.: 6 Union St., 01085. Tel: 413-562-3450; Fax: 413-562-0399.
Catechesis/Religious Program—Tel: 413-562-6978. Sr. M. Barbara Ebbe, D.R.E.; Mrs. Deborah Lanoue, D.R.E. Students 532.

5—ST. PETER AND ST. CASIMIR, Formerly St. Peter, Westfield (2003), Rev. Dariusz P. Wudarski. In Res., Rev. John T. Dean.
Res.: 22 State St., 01085. Tel: 413-568-5421; Fax: 413-562-3879.
Catechesis/Religious Program—32 State St., 01085. Tel: 413-568-6261. Sr. Marcella Meluch, O.S.F., D.R.E. Students 231.

6—ST. PETER'S (1913), Merged, with St. Casimir, Westfield to form St. Peter and St. Casimir, Westfield.

WILBRAHAM, HAMPDEN CO., ST. CECILIA'S (1951), Revs. Joseph M. Soranno; Douglas McGonagle. Tel: 413-596-8304; Sr. Mary McCue, S.N.D., Pastoral Min. Tel: 413-599-1833.
Res.: Tel: 413-596-4232; Fax: 413-596-6272.
Catechesis/Religious Program—42 Main St., 01095. Tel: 413-596-9937. Sr. Mary Patrice Mahoney, S.N.D., D.R.E. Students 1,300.

WILLIAMSTOWN, BERKSHIRE CO.

1—SS. PATRICK AND RAPHAEL (1997), Rev. Mark J. Burke, S.J.
Res. & Mailing Address: 54 Southworth St., 01267-2414. Tel: 413-458-4946; Fax: 413-458-4954.
Catechesis/Religious Program—53 Southworth St., 01267. Tel: 413-458-5443. Students 172.

2—ST. PATRICK'S (1887), Merged, with St. Raphael, Williamstown, to form SS. Patrick and Raphael, Williamstown.

3—ST. RAPHAEL (1891), Merged, with St. Patrick, Williamstown, to form SS. Patrick and Raphael, Williamstown.

Chaplains of Public Institutions

SPRINGFIELD. *Baystate Medical Center*, Office of Pastoral Ministry at Baystate.
Olympus Specialty Hospital, Sacred Heart Rectory, 395 Chestnut St., 01104. Tel: 413-732-3721.

HOLYOKE. *Soldiers' Home*, Tel: 413-532-0713. Served by Blessed Sacrament Parish.

MONSON. *State Hospital*. Bureau for Exceptional Children and Adults.
537 Northampton St., Box 1039, Holyoke, 01041. Tel: 413-538-7450. Rev. Robert F. Wagner, Deacon Rodney Szymczk.

NORTHAMPTON. *Veterans Administration Hospital*, 421 N. Main St., 01060. Tel: 413-584-4040. Rev. Lionel E. Bonneville.

PITTSFIELD. *Berkshire Medical Center*, Tel: 413-447-2000. Rev. Leroy Smith.
One County Rte. 13, Chatham Center, NY 12184-9639. Tel: 413-392-4516.

WESTFIELD. *Western Massachusetts Hospital*, Tel: 413-562-3450. Served by Our Lady of the Blessed Sacrament Parish.

Sabbatical:
Rev.—
Giroux, Regis J.

On Duty Outside the Diocese:
Revs.—
Courneyer, Alfred, A.P. 207, C.P. 21105 San Pedro, Sula, Honduras.
Marchese, Joseph P., Boston College, Chestnut Hill, 02167. Chap.
Pham, Pierre
Potvin, Raymond H., Ph.D., Prof. Emeritus (Retired), Catholic University, Box 1264, Washington, DC 20064.
Schmitt, Thomas F., Pope John XXII National Seminary, 558 S. St., Weston, 02493.
Tuohey, John F., Providence St. Vincent Medical Center, 9205 S.W. Barnes Rd.., Portland, OR 97225.

Military Chaplains:
Rev.—
Walsh, Francis E., Office of the Chap., PSC 476, Box 61, FPO, AP 96322-1102.

Absent on Leave:
Revs.—
LaFlamme, Paul C.
Lavelle, Francis P.
Savage, Warren J.

Retired:
Rev. Msgr.—
Harrington, John F., P.A., J.C.L., 65 Elliot St., P.O. Box 1730, 01101-1730.
Revs.—
Anoia, John
Ayers, John J., 32 Sylvester St., 01109.
Begley, Thomas B., P.O. Box 517, Hinsdale, 01235.
Bernier, Lawrence J., 123 Tatham Hill Rd., West Springfield, 01089.
Boudreau, Paul, 3020 N.E. 16 Ave. E101, Fort Lauderdale, FL 33334.
Breton, Albert, Nativity Rectory, 780 Chicopee St., Chicopee, 01013.
Brunton, Daniel B., 66 Harding St., Pittsfield, 01201.
Callahan, Edward M., Sacred Heart Parish, 395 Chestnut St., 01104.
Chwalek, John, 420 Old Cheshire Rd., P.O. Box 56, Windsor, 01270.
Courtney, Thomas M., Saint Michael Residence, 86 Wendover Rd., 01118.
Creane, Anthony, Blessed Sacrament Rectory, 6 Union St., 01085-2494.
Darling, Franklin, 10 D Elm Terrace, Greenfield, 01301. Tel: 413-772-6187
Delehanty, Thomas F., 2C Stonypoint Dr., P.O. Box 425, Ware, 01082.
Diemand, James E., P.O. Box 141, Turners Falls, 01376.
Forand, Clarence W., #293, 281 Chauncey Walker St., Belchertown, 01007.
Fournier, W. Donald, 474 Grattan St., Chicopee, 01020.
Gallerini, Philip G., 102 Hermit Dr., Warwick, RI 02889.
Gardner, Royal J., Saint Teresa Parish, 290 South St., Pittsfield, 01201.
Gonet, Charles F., Saint Michael Residence, 86 Wendover Rd., 01118.
Greene, Thomas S., St. Michael's Residence, 86 Wendover Rd., 01118.
Greenway, George G., 29 Orchard Rd., East Longmeadow, 01028.
Hallahan, Timothy J., P.O. Box 150112, Cape Coral, FL 33915.
Heberle, Frederick L., 109 Westfield St., Holyoke, 01040.
Hebert, Earl, 581 Chauncey Walker St. #350, Belchertown, 01007.
LeVay, R. Joseph, 45 Fort Hill Terr., Northampton, 01060.
Loughran, Peter G., 34 Lower Westfield Rd., Ste. 1, Holyoke, 01040.
Manning, Francis J., 29 Oakhurst St., P.O. Box 3122, 01101-3122.
McCormick, Howard W., Saint Michael Residence, 86 Wendover Rd., 01118.
Menge, James P., Landmark at Monastery Heights, Monastery Ave., West Springfield, 01089.
O'Connor, Matthew J., 69 Beacon St., Holyoke, 01040.
O'Connor, Vincent, P.O. Box 346, Leeds, 01053.
Ozimek, Eugene F., Mount St. Vincent Nursing Home, 35 Holy Family Rd., Holyoke, 01040.
Pagano, Peter E., 1215 Massachusetts Ave., North Adams, 01247.
Perreault, Leonard J., P.O. Box 144, Spencertown, NY 12165.
Quigley, J. Joseph, Newman Center, 472 N. Pleasant St., Amherst, 1002.
Remy, Adrien T., Mont Marie Motherhouse, Holyoke, 01040.
Sgueglia, Charles J.M., Mary Immaculate Nursing-Restorative Center, 172 Lawrence St., Lawrence, 01841.
Shea, John J., J.C.D., Providence Place, 5 Gamelin St., Holyoke, 01040.
Sullivan, Francis J., St. Michael's Residence, 86 Wendover Rd., 01118.
Sullivan, Francis X., 102 Allyn St., Holyoke, 01040.
Tokarz, John, Loomis House, 298 Jarvis Ave., Holyoke, 01040.

Permanent Deacons:
Picard, Adrien, St. Patrick, Monson
Antaya, John
Badame, Joseph, Holy Family, Holyoke
Baldasaro, Pasqual, St. Agnes, Dalton
Bergeron, Leo, St. George, Chicopee
Bledsoe, John, St. Patrick, South Hadley
Bucci, Joseph, St. Mary's, Orange
Callahan, Thomas A., Holy Cross, Holyoke
Cary, Herbert L., Our Lady of the Valley, Sheffield
Chapdelaine, Roland G., Parkview Specialty Hospital, Springfield
Coughlin, Leo, St. Mary, Hampden
Cyr, Ralph R., Notre Dame, Pittsfield
Diaz, Celso B., On Duty Outside the Diocese
Duval, Robert L., St. Mary of the Assumption, Ludlow
Finnie, Edward J., (Retired)
Garde, Joseph, St. Catherine, Springfield
Hager, James A., Sacred Heart, Pittsfield
Herrick, Eugene, Burlington, VT
Higby, Donald, St. Mary, Longmeadow
Hitter, Robert, St. Mary, Cheshire
Kaiser, L. Joseph, St. Michael, East Longmeadow
Keator, George, St. Ann, Lenox
Kozach, George, St. Patrick Church, Springfield
Martone, James A., Immaculate Conception, West Springfield
McCarthy, Francis J., (Retired)
Medina, Genaro, Sr., All Souls, Latino Ministry, Springfield
Meyer, Edward, St. John the Baptist, Ludlow
Miller, Lucien M., Campus Ministry, University of Massachusetts, Amherst
Mireault, Leon, St. Rose de Lima, Chicopee
Moesley, William C., St. Charles, Pittsfield
Momnie, Eugene C., St. Joseph, Pittsfield
Monat, Noe, 240 Skycrest Loop, Davenport, FL 33837.
Moore, Donald E., (Retired)
Morrisey, Robert
Moulton, Robert R., Notre Dame/St. Thomas, Adams
Mulholland, Sean, St. Teresa, Pittsfield
O'Brien, John P., On Duty Outside the Diocese
Pelletier, Frederick J., Immaculate Conception, Holyoke
Pellissier, Bernard, St. Patrick, Monson
Przybylowski, David, Our Lady of the Lake, Southwick
Rabbitt, Thomas, St. Joseph, Shelburne Falls
Ramos, Oswaldo, Blessed Sacrament, Springfield
Ratte, Arthur E., St. Patrick, Northfield
Rivera, Jose, All Souls, Springfield
Rogers, Francis D., St. Patrick, Chicopee
Routhier, Albert, St. Anne & St. Mary's, Turners Falls
Ryan, Francis, Saint Anthony, North Adams
Smith, Joseph, St. Mary's, Chicopee
Szymzyk, Rodney J., Immaculate Conception, Indian Orchard
Talbot, Richard, Newman Center, Amherst
Tenczar, Edward J., St. Thomas the Apostle, Palmer & St. Mary, Thorndyke
Toller, William, Holy Cross, Springfield
Tudryn, Theodore, St. Stanislaus, South Deerfield
Velazquez, Raphael, Holy Family, Springfield
Wallen, Paul, (Retired), Springfield, MA
Williams, Walter

INSTITUTIONS LOCATED IN THE DIOCESE

[A] COLLEGES AND UNIVERSITIES

CHICOPEE. *College of Our Lady of the Elms* 01013. Tel: 413-594-2761; Fax: 413-592-4871. Email: froehlichj@elms.edu. Web: www.elms.edu. Most Rev. Thomas L. Dupre, Bishop of Springfield; Joachim W. Froehlich, Ph.D., Pres.; Dr. Anne Harrison, Academic Dean. Sisters of St. Joseph Sisters 4; Professors 43; Lay Teachers 43; Total Staff 116; Students 1,002.

[B] HIGH SCHOOLS, DIOCESAN

SPRINGFIELD. *Cathedral High School*, 260 Surrey Rd., 01118. Tel: 413-782-5285; Fax: 413-782-5065. Email: info@cathedralhigh.org. Web: www.cathedralhigh.org. Roy F. Dado, Pres.; Sr. Denise Granger, S.S.J., Prin. Sisters 7; Lay Teachers 58; Students 785.

GRANBY. *Holyoke Catholic High School*, 66 School St., 01033. Tel: 413-467-2477; Fax: 413-467-2012. Email: gaels_hchs@yahoo.com. Web: www.gaels.org. Sr. Cornelia Roy, S.S.J., Prin. Sisters of St. Joseph Sisters of St. Joseph 6; Lay Teachers 32; Students 434.

PITTSFIELD. *St. Joseph Central High School*, 22 Maplewood Ave., 01201. Tel: 413-447-9121; Fax: 413-443-7020. Web: bewan.net/~stjoe. Margaret Downing, Prin. Sisters of St. Joseph Sisters 1; Lay Teachers 24; Students 241; Total Staff 25.

[C] ELEMENTARY SCHOOLS, DIOCESAN

INDIAN ORCHARD. *St. Matthew* (1902), (Grades PreK-8), 90 Berkshire St., 01151. Tel: 413-543-1066; Fax: 413-543-2330. Email: stmattschool@aol.com. Web: www.11school.masslive.com/school/stmatthew. Ann Dougal, Prin. Lay Teachers 12; Students 180; Total Staff 12.

PITTSFIELD. *Saint Mark Middle School*, (Grades 5-8), 400 Columbus Ave. Ext., 01201. Tel: 413-442-6040; Fax: 413-448-5645. Ms. Beth Gannon, Prin. Tel: 413-442-6040. Staff 16; Enrollment 243.

[D] PRIVATE SCHOOLS

GREENFIELD. **Mariamante Academy*, 64 North St., 01301. Tel: 413-773-1781; Fax: 413-773-1782. Email: markpfusco@yahoo.com. Web: mariamante.org. Mark P. Fusco, Headmaster. Lay Teachers 19; Students 45; Total Staff 23.

[E] ORPHANAGES

WEST SPRINGFIELD. *Brightside, Inc.* Private, Nonprofit Agency. , 2112 Riverdale St., 01089. Tel: 413-788-7366; Fax: 413-747-0182. Email: brightside.intake@sphs.com. Web: www.mercycares.com. *Sisters of Providence Health System*, P.O. Box 9012, 01102-9012. Tel: 413-827-4244; Fax: 413-827-4250. Mr. Vincent J. McCorkle, Pres.; Mr. Robert Simpson Jr., D.S.W., C.O.O., Behavioral Health Network. Sisters of Providence Children in Residence 139; Children in Day Treatment Program 34; Placement Services: Children in Foster Homes 10; Adoption Services 85; Pregnant Parenting Youth Services 13; Outpatient Mental Health Clinic 4,900; Family Stabilization Team 181; Total Staff 492.

[F] GENERAL HOSPITALS

SPRINGFIELD. *CHE - The Mercy Hospital, Inc.*, 271 Carew St., Box 9012, 01102-9012. Tel: 413-748-9000; Fax: 413-781-7217. Web: www.mercycares.com. Mr. Vincent J. McCorkle, Pres.; Sr. Margaret M. McCarthy, S.N.D., Dir. Dept. of Spiritual Care; Rev. Damien Ilokaba, Chap.; Sr. Madeline Joy, S.P., Chap.; Rev. Donatus Ironomo, Chap.; Katherine Mastorakis, Chap.; Beverly Kiley Matakaetis, Chap. For both Mercy and Providence Campuses: Sisters of Providence 2; Bed Capacity 230; Patients Assisted Annually 218,314; Total Staff (Mercy Hospital) 1,537; Nurses: RNs 338; LPNs 8.

Providence Behavioral Health Hospital, 1233 Main St., Holyoke, 01040. Tel: 413-536-5111; Fax: 413-539-2992. Sr. Therese Dube, S.A.S.V. Spiritual Care Dept. 1; Bed Capacity 120; Total Staff 508.

TURNERS FALLS. *Farren Care Center, Inc.*, 340 Montague City Rd., 01376. Tel: 413-774-3111; Fax: 413-774-7049. Web: www.mercycares.com. *Sisters of Providence Health Systems*, P.O. Box 9012, 01102. Email: jim.clifford@sphs.com. James Clifford, Admin. Bed Capacity 122; Total Staff 237; Total Assisted Annually 145.

[G] FAMILY SERVICES

SPRINGFIELD. *Diocesan Office for Counseling Services*, 65 Elliot St., P.O. Box 1730, 01101-1730. Tel: 413-732-3175; 413-452-0621; Fax: 413-452-0618. Web: www.diospringfield.org/MC.html. Laura Failla Riley, Dir.; Sr. Dorothy Santarpia, S.S.J., Counselor; Dr. Alfred A. D'Amato, Ed.D., L.M.F.T., Counselor; Mrs. Rosemary Castonguay, M.Ed., L.M.H.C., Counselor; Ms. Janet O'Brien, LCSW, Counselor. Total Staff 5; Total Assisted Annually 257.

HOLYOKE. *Mont Marie Child Care Center, Inc.*, Mont Marie, 01040. Tel: 413-536-2964; Fax: 413-536-5557. Email: eharrington@ssjspringfield.com. Sr. Eleanor T. Harrington, S.S.J., Dir. Sisters of St. Joseph 2; Total Staff 21; Children 126.

Providence Ministries for the Needy, Inc., 51 Hamilton St., P.O. Box 6269, 01041. Tel: 413-536-9109; Fax: 413-536-1137. Email: PMN3@hotmail.com. Web: www.providenceministries.freeservers.com. Mr. Robin L. Goshea, Admin. Sponsored by the Sisters of Providence of Holyoke, MA Total Staff 28; Total Assisted Annually 62,909.

Broderick House, 56 Cabot St., P.O. Box 6269, 01041. Tel: 413-534-7610; Fax: 413-536-8536. An around-the-clock family shelter. Capacity 56.

Margaret's Pantry Tel: 413-538-8026; Fax: 413-536-8536. Provides emergency food to families and individuals.

St. Jude's Center Tel: 413-534-7610; Fax: 413-536-8536. Distributes clothing and household items to the poor.

St. Jude's Furniture & Furnishing Store, 51 Hamilton St., 01040. Tel: 413-536-9109; Fax: 413-536-1137. Provides new and pre-owned furniture and furnishings to the community.

Loreto House, 51 Hamilton St., 01041. Tel: 413-533-5909; Fax: 413-536-1137. An around-the-clock shelter for homeless men. Capacity 20.

Kate's Kitchen, 51 Hamilton St., 01040. Tel: 413-532-0233; Fax: 413-536-1137. A community kitchen which provides one meal daily to anyone in need - no questions asked. Capacity 99.

PITTSFIELD. *Catholic Charities Counseling Office*, 467 North St., Rm. 15, P.O. Box 1372, 01202. Tel: 413-443-3169; Fax: 413-443-3169. Total Staff 3; Total Assisted 720.

41 Mahaiwe St., Great Barrington, 01230. Tel: 413-528-9006. Thomas A. Duane, L.I.C.S.W., Supr.; Robert T. Sykes, M.A., Counselor; Janet M. O'Brien, M.A., Counselor.

TURNERS FALLS. *Montague Catholic Social Ministries, Inc.*, 41 Third St., 01376. Tel: 413-863-4805; Fax: 413-863-8593. Email: mcsm@shaysnet.com. Maria Tarajano Rodma, Exec. Dir. Purpose: To be a resource to children and families in the areas of parent education, family literacy, positive conflict resolution, communication skills, and community building to assist in providing information and referral, the formation of community partnerships and neighborhood development and to facilitate parish concerns and social justice efforts. Total Staff 4; Total Assisted 550.

[H] HOMES FOR AGED

SPRINGFIELD. *St. Michael's Residence*, 86 Wendover Rd., 01118. Tel: 413-783-6773. Total Staff 2; Total in Residence 8. In Res. Revs. Edward M. Callahan (Retired); Thomas M. Courtney (Retired); James J. Flahive; Charles F. Gonet (Retired); Thomas S. Greene (Retired); Howard W. McCormick (Retired); Francis J. Sullivan (Retired).

Sisters of Providence Care Centers, Inc., 271 Carew St., 01104. Tel: 413-748-9000; Fax: 413-781-7217. Web: www.mercycares.com. *Sisters of Providence Health Systems*, P.O. Box 9012, 01102-9012. Total Staff 443; Total Assisted Annually 465.

Beaven Kelly Home, 25 Brightside Dr., Holyoke, 01040. Tel: 413-532-4892; Fax: 413-535-2355. Sr. Sheila McGuirk, S.S.J., Spiritual Care Coord.; Mrs Cynthia Brown, Admin. Residents 55; Staff 30.

Mount St. Vincent Nursing Home, 35 Holy Family Rd. Holyoke, 01040-2758. Tel: 413-532-3246; Fax: 413-532-0309. Persons under care 125; Total Staff 150. In Res. Rev. Eugene F. Ozimek (Retired); Sisters Rose Webber (Dominican Republic); Ramona Williams, S.P., Spiritual Care Dir.; Eriko Umana, Admin.

St. Luke's Home, 85 Spring St., 01105. Tel: 413-736-5494; Fax: 413-746-5075. Albert Blanchard, Spiritual Care Coord.; Sr. Geraldine Noonan, S.P., Admin. Residents 89; Staff 42. In Res. Sr. Grace Lane, O.P.

Providence Care Center of Lenox, 320 Pittsfield Rd., Lenox, 01240. Tel: 413-627-2650; Fax: 413-637-3085. Elizabeth Stroshine, Admin.; Rev. Daniel B. Brunton, Spiritual Care Coord. (Retired). Residents 69; Staff 96.

Mercy Care Center of Springfield, 370 Pine St., 01105. Tel: 413-731-5318; Fax 413-731-5384. Sr. Sheila McGuirk, S.S.J., Spiritual Care Coord. Residents 127; Staff 125.

HOLYOKE. *Mont Marie Health Care Center, Inc.*, 34 Lower Westfield Rd., 01040. Tel: 413-536-0853; Fax: 413-533-4505. Email: bsullivan@ssjspringfield.com. Sr. Elizabeth Sullivan, S.S.J., Admin. Total Staff 115; Total Resident Days 29,565; Total Census 81. In Res. Revs. John Bambol, O.F.M.Conv.; Augustine Paul Hennessy, C.P.; Adrien T. Remy (Retired); Michel St. Pierre (BR VT).

Providence Place, Inc., 5 Gamelin St., 01040. Tel: 413-534-9700; Fax: 413-534-9782. Web: providenceplace.org. Richard Pelland, Exec. Dir.; Rev. Michael H. Devlin Chap. Sisters of Providence Total in Residence 160; Total Staff 46.

[I] MONASTERIES AND RESIDENCES OF PRIESTS AND BROTHERS

STOCKBRIDGE. *Congregation of Marians of The Immaculate Conception of the Most Blessed Virgin Mary*, Eden Hill, 2 Prospect Hill Rd., 01262. Tel: 413-298-3691; Fax: 413-298-1211. Email: wadziordz@aol.com. Web: www.marian.org.

Provincial Office Tel: 413-298-1101; Fax: 413-298-0207. Revs. Walter Dziordz, M.I.C., Prov. Supr.; Kazimierz Chwalek, M.I.C., Prov. Econome; Bro. Kenneth Galisa, M.I.C., Prov. Sec.

The National Shrine of The Divine Mercy Tel: 413-298-3931; Fax: 413-298-3910. Email: dmshrine@marian.org. Rev. David Lord, M.I.C.

Association of Marian Helpers, Marian Helpers Center Tel: 413-298-3691; Fax: 413-298-3583. Email: info@marian.org. Rev. Shaun P. O'Connor, M.I.C., Dir., Marian Helpers Center; Mr. Francis Bourdon, Exec. Dir.

John Paul II Institute of Divine Mercy Tel: 413-298-1184; Fax: 413-298-4559. Email: divinemerc@aol.com. Mr. Robert Stackpole, Dir.

Lay Outreach Ministry of the Province:

Eucharistic Apostles of The Divine Mercy Tel: 813-681-3699; Fax: 813-681-3009. Email: tampa@thedivinemercy.org. Web: www.thedivinemercy.org. Priests 12; Brothers 5. In Res. Most Rev. Elliott G. Thomas, D.D. (STV), Assoc. Member (Retired); Revs. Bernard Backiel, M.I.C.; Michael Callea, M.I.C.; Donald Calloway, M.I.C.; Kazimierz Chwalek, M.I.C.; Richard Drabik, M.I.C.; Walter Dziordz, M.I.C.; Walter Gurgul, M.I.C.; David Lord, M.I.C.; Shaun P. O'Connor, M.I.C.; Daniel Papineau, M.I.C.; Martin Rzeszutek, M.I.C.; Bros. John Bryda, M.I.C.; Ken Galisa, M.I.C.; Andrew Maczynski, M.I.C., House Supr.; Ronald McBride; Albin Milewski, M.I.C.; Fred Wells, M.I.C.

On Duty Outside of House: Revs. Ireneusz Chodakowski, M.I.C. (PRT); Donald J. Van Alstyne, M.I.C. (MO).

On Duty Outside the U.S.A.: Revs. Mark Garrow, M.I.C., Supr. Gen., Rome; Casimir Krzyzanowski, M.I.C., Rome.

[J] CONVENTS AND RESIDENCES FOR SISTERS

HOLYOKE. *Daughters of the Heart of Mary Provincial Residence*, 1339 Northampton St., 01040-1958. Tel: 413-532-7406; Fax: 413-533-4217. Email: Ncfell@aol.com. Web: www.SDHM.net. Sr. Nancy Fell, D.H.M., Prov. Total in Residence 27; Total Staff 3.

Marian Center, Inc., 1365 Northampton St., 01040. Tel: 413-534-4502; Fax: 413-534-7353. Sr. Agnes E. Murphy, D.H.M., Supr. Daughters of the Heart of Mary 28.

Mont Marie, 34 Lower Westfield Rd., Ste. 1, 01040. Tel: 413-536-0853; Fax: 413-533-3275. Email: mail@ssjspringfield.com. Sisters Jane F. Morrissey, S.S.J., Pres.; Maureen Broughan, S.S.J., Vice Pres. Motherhouse of the Sisters of St. Joseph of Springfield Sisters 365; Total Staff 56.

Mont Marie Child Care, Inc. Tel: 413-536-2964; Fax: 413-533-3275. Total Assisted Annually 125; Total Staff 20.

Mont Marie Health Care Center, Inc. Tel: 413-536-0853; Fax: 413-533-4505. Total Assisted Annually 81; Total Staff 110.

Mont Marie Conference Center Tel: 413-536-0853; Fax: 413-532-0285. Total Staff 8.

Sisters of Providence, Providence Place, 5 Gamelin St., 01040. Tel: 413-536-7511; Fax: 413-536-7917. Email: sisters@sisofprov.org. Web: www.sisofprov.org. Motherhouse of the Sisters of Providence Sisters 90.

Sisters of Providence Infirmary, 1233 Main St., 3rd Floor, 01040-5394. Tel: 413-493-2750; Fax: 413-493-2759.

Providence Ministries for the Needy, Inc., P.O. Box 6269, 01041-6269. Tel: 413-536-9109; Fax: 413-536-1137.

Genesis Spiritual Life Center, 53 Mill St., Westfield, 01085-4253. Tel: 413-562-3627; Fax: 413-572-1060.

Vice-Provincial House and Formation House, 1039 Northampton St., 01040-1320. Tel: 413-532-8156; Fax: 413-534-7741. Email: sistersofassisi@aol.com. Sr. Mary D'Angelo, S.F.M.A., Vice Prov.

Legal Title: *Franciscan Missionary Sisters of Assisi* Sisters 6.

TYRINGHAM. *Order of the Visitation of Holy Mary*, Monastery of the Visitation, P.O. Box 432, 01264. Tel: 413-243-3995; Fax: 413-243-3543. Email: vistyr@aol.com. Sr. Mary Ruth Dolch, Supr. Order of the Visitation of Holy Mary 19.

WEST SPRINGFIELD. *Monastery of the Mother of God, Dominican Nuns (Contemplative)*, 1430 Riverdale St., 01089-4698. Tel: 413-736-3639; Fax: 413-736-0850. Email: monasteryws@aol. Sr. Mary of the Immaculate Concept, O.P., Prioress; Rev. Jacob Restrick, O.P., Chap. Adoration to the Blessed Sacrament Chapel Solemnly Professed Nuns 22; Temporarily Professed 1.

[K] RETREAT HOUSES AND CHRISTIAN LIFE CENTERS

SPRINGFIELD. *Center for Spiritual Direction*, 1365 Northampton St., Holyoke, 01040. Tel: 413-538-9197; Fax: 413-533-3955. Sisters 3; Total Staff 5; Lay Staff 2.

WESTFIELD. *Genesis Spiritual Life Center*, 53 Mill St., 01085. Tel: 413-562-3627; Fax: 413-572-1060. Email: genesis@genesiscenter.us. Web: www.genesiscenter.us. Sisters Catherine Walsh, R.S.M., Admin., Program Coord.; Ann Horgan, S.P., Asst. Admin./Sabbatical Coord.; Ms. Trisha Riga, Registrar; Mrs. Christine Morrissey, Asst. Program Coord. Retreats, workshops and spiritual guidance designed to promote health of body, mind and spirit. Also, host day and overnight conferences.. Total Staff 15; Total in Residence 3.

[L] INFORMATION CENTERS

CHICOPEE. *Open Window Book and Gift Shop of the*

Diocese of Springfield, Inc., 12-14 Center St., 01013. Tel: 413-594-5111; Fax: 413-594-2862. Email: openwindow@diospringfield.org. Barbara Y. McMahon, Mgr.; Barbara B. Moran, Mgr.

[M] SPANISH APOSTOLATES

SPRINGFIELD. *Catholic Latino Ministry*, 65 Elliott St., P.O. Box 1730, 01101-1730. Tel: 413-452-0631; Fax: 413-747-0273. Email: hispanicmin@diospringfield.org. Rev. Paul E. Manship, Dir.; Lucy Ramos, Exec. Sec.

[N] BUREAU FOR EXCEPTIONAL CHILDREN AND ADULTS

HOLYOKE. *Bureau for Exceptional Children and Adults Inc.*, 537 Northampton St., Box 1039, 01041. Tel: 413-538-7450; Fax: 413-536-5691. Email: jerichobeca@aol.com. Rev. Robert F. Wagner, Chap.; Sr. Joan Magnani, S.S.J., Dir.; Deacon Rodney Szymczyk, Assoc. Director. Sisters 2; Deacons 1; Lay Staff 4.

[O] YOUTH SERVICES

GOSHEN. *Holy Cross Camp Grounds*, Cape St., P.O. Box 501, 01032-0501. Tel: 413-268-7819. Email: camp.holycross@diospringfield.org. Web: www.campholycross.org. Rev. Christopher A. Malatesta. Total Staff 3.

PITTSFIELD. *Catholic Youth Center*, 26 Melville St., 01201. Tel: 413-445-5496; Fax: 413-445-5248. Email: vinnycyc@aol.com. Mr. Vincent P. Marinaro, Exec. Dir. Total Assisted 1,200; Total Staff 25.

[P] NEWMAN APOSTOLATES AND CAMPUS MINISTRIES

SPRINGFIELD. *Newman Apostolates and Campus Ministries* Tel: 413-549-0300; Fax: 413-548-9182. Email: info@ncc-umass.org. Web: www.umass.edu/catholic/.

The Newman Center 472 N. Pleasant, Amherst, 01002-1739. Tel: 413-549-0300; Fax: 413-548-9182. Rev. John P. McDonagh.

Amherst, MA:

Amherst College, 122 N. Pleasant St., Amherst, 01004. Tel: 413-253-1828; Fax: 413-253-7935. Rev. Bruce N. Teague, Chap.

Center for Religious Life Box 5000, Amherst, 01002-5000. Email: padre@cesmail.net.

University of Massachusetts, Newman Center, 472 N. Pleasant St., Amherst, 01002-1739. Tel: 413-549-0300; Fax: 413-548-9182. Web: www.umass.edu/catholic. Revs. John P. McDonagh, Dir. & Chap.; Richard Cleary, S.J., Chap.; Lynn Campbell, Campus Min.; Chris Clark, Campus Min.; Mary Ellen Foley, Campus Min.; Deacons Lucian Miller, Campus Min.; Richard Talbot, Campus Min. In Res. Rev. J. Joseph Quigley, Emeritus Dir. (Retired).

Chicopee, MA:

College of Our Lady of the Elms College, 291 Springfield St., Chicopee, 01013. Tel: 413-594-2761, Ext. 289; Fax: 413-592-4871.

Longmeadow, MA:

Bay Path College, 519 Longmeadow St., Longmeadow, 01106-2299. Tel: 413-567-3124. Rev. Francis E. Reilly, Chap. Served by St. Mary's.

161 Wenonah Rd., Longmeadow, 01106. Tel: 413-567-1322. Email: alyac@aol.com. Ms. Sheila Hanifan, Campus Min.

North Adams, MA:

Massachusetts College of the Liberal Arts, 70 Marshall St., North Adams, 01247-3593. Tel: 413-664-1041; Fax: 413-663-6385. Email: ryansofflorida@aol.com. Deacon Francis Ryan, Campus Min. Served by St. Anthony of Padua

Northampton, MA:

Smith College, Helen Hills, Hills Chapel, Northampton, 01063. Tel: 413-585-2750; 413-585-2752; Fax: 413-585-2794. Email: ecarr@smith.edu. Elizabeth E. Carr, Ph.D., Chap.

Pittsfield, MA:

Berkshire Community College, 27 Onota St., Pittsfield, 01201-3194. Tel: 413-447-7510. Rev. Henry L. Dorsch, Chap. Served by St. Mark's

South Hadley, MA:

Mount Holyoke College, 9 E. Parkview Dr., South Hadley, 01075-2103. Tel: 413-538-2054. Email: amagovern@mtholyoke.edu. Rev. Richard A. Bondi, Chap. Served by St. Theresa.

Res.: Office of the Chaplain, Eliot House, South Hadley, 01075. Tel: 413-538-2054; Fax: 413-538-2687. Sr. Anita Magovern, M.M., Religious Advisor. Tel: 413-538-2787.

Springfield, MA:

American International College; Springfield College; Springfield Tech. Comm. College Rev. Leo James Hoar, Chap.

St. Mary Rectory: 3 Elm St., P.O. Box 180, Northampton, 01061-0180. Tel: 413-748-3210; Fax: 413-584-4788.

Springfield College Campus Ministry Center Beveridge Center, 263 Alden St., 01109-3797. Tel: 413-748-3210; Fax: 413-748-3764. Email: leohoar@spfldcol.edu.

Western New England College, 1215 Wilbraham Rd., 01119-2684. Tel: 413-782-1628. Rev. Norman B. Bolton, Chap.

Blessed Sacrament Rectory: 1945 Northampton St., Holyoke, 01040-3498. Tel: 413-493-6550. Email: nbolton@aol.com.

Westfield, MA:

Westfield State College, Interfaith Center, Westfield, 01085. Tel: 413-572-5567; Fax: 413-562-3613. Rev. John T. Dean, Chap.

St. Peter's Rectory: 22 State St., Westfield, 01085-3814. Tel: 413-568-5421.

Williamstown, MA:

Williams College, 54 Southwoth St., P.O. Box 616, Williamstown, 01267-0616. Tel: 413-458-4946; Fax: 413-458-4954. Dr. Peter Feudo, Campus Min. Served by St. Patrick's.

Res.: Baxter Hall, 39 Chapin Hall Dr., Williamstown, 01267-2569. Tel: 413-597-2483; Fax: 413-597-3955. Email: peter.feudo@williams.edu.

[Q] MISCELLANEOUS

SPRINGFIELD. *The Foundation of the Roman Catholic Diocese of Springfield, Massachusetts, Inc.*, 65 Elliot St., P.O. Box 1730, 01101-1730. Tel: 413-732-3175; Fax: 413-732-4297. Email: v.webb@diospringfield.org. Web: www.diospringfield.org.

Sisters of Providence Health Systems, Inc., 271 Carew St., 01104. Tel: 413-748-9000; Fax: 413-781-7217. Web: www.mercycares.com. *Sisters of Providence Health Systems*, P.O. Box 9012, 01102-9012. Mr. Vincent J. McCorkle, Pres. & CEO.

HOLYOKE. *Mont Marie Conference Center*, 34 Lower Westfield Rd., 01040-2739. Tel: 413-536-0853; Fax: 413-532-0285. Email: montconf@ssjspringfield.com. Agnes Fleming, Dir.

RELIGIOUS INSTITUTES OF MEN REPRESENTED IN THE DIOCESE

For further details refer to the corresponding bracketed number in the Religious Institutes of Men or Women section.

[]—*The Association of Marian Helpers of Stockbridge, MA*
[0470]—*The Capuchin Fathers* (St. Mary's Prov.)—O.F.M.Cap.
[0270]—*Carmelite Fathers and Brothers* (St. Elias Prov.)—O.Carm.
[0740]—*Congregation of Marians of the Immaculate Conception*—M.I.C.
[1000]—*Congregation of the Passion* (West Hoboken, NJ)—C.P.
[0480]—*Conventual Franciscans*—O.F.M.Conv
[0720]—*The Missionaries of Our Lady of La Salette*—M.S.
[1280]—*Stigmatine Fathers and Brothers*—C.S.S.

RELIGIOUS INSTITUTES OF WOMEN REPRESENTED IN THE DIOCESE

[1830]—*Contemplative Sisters of the Good Shepherd*—C.G.S.
[0860]—*Daughters of Mary of the Immaculate Conception*—D.M.
[0890]—*Daughters of Our Lady of Mercy*—D.M.
[0810]—*Daughters of the Heart of Mary*—D.H.M.
[0820]—*Daughters of the Holy Spirit*—D.H.S.
[1050]—*Dominican Contemplative Nuns*—O.P.
[1170]—*Felician Sisters*—C.S.S.F.
[1330]—*Franciscan Missionary Sisters of Assisi*—S.F.M.A.
[1470]—*Franciscan Sisters of St. Joseph*—F.S.S.J.
[1180]—*Franciscan Sisters of the Allegany, New York*—O.S.F.
[]—*Schonestatt Sisters of Mary*
[1700]—*School Sisters of St. Francis*—O.S.F.
[]—*Sister of the Most Holy Soul of Christ*—S.S.Ch.
[]—*Sisters Minor of Mary Immaculate*—S.M.M.I.
[3000]—*Sisters of Notre Dame de Namur*—S.N.D.deN.
[3340]—*Sisters of Providence*—S.P.
[3718]—*Sisters of St. Ann*—S.S.A.
[3750]—*Sisters of St. Chretienne*—S.S.Ch.
[3830-16]—*Sisters of St. Joseph*—S.S.J.
[3850]—*Sisters of St. Joseph of Chambery*—C.S.J.
[0150]—*Sisters of the Assumption*—S.A.S.V.
[3310]—*Sisters of the Presentation of Mary*—P.M.
[3320]—*Sisters of the Presentation of the B.V.M.*—P.B.V.M.
[4190]—*Visitation Nuns*—V.H.M.

DIOCESAN CEMETERIES

SPRINGFIELD. *St. Benedict Cemetery*, Liberty St., 01104. Tel: 413-782-0341.

Gate of Heaven, 421 Tinkham Rd., 01129. Tel: 413-782-0341. Mr. Joseph Kostek, Diocesan Dir. of Cemeteries. Tel: 413-452-0692.

St. Matthew Cemetery, 366 Springfield St., 01109. Tel: 413-782-0341.

St. Michael's, 1601 State St., 01109. Tel: 413-782-0341.

HOLYOKE. *Calvary*, Northampton St., 01040. *Office*, 1601 State St., 01109. Tel: 413-782-0341.

INDIAN ORCHARD. *St. Aloysius Cemetary*, Berkshire Ave., 01151. *Office*, 1601 State St., 01109. Tel: 413-782-0341.

NECROLOGY

† Ford, John—Died 2003
† Jutt, Julius A., South Deerfield, MA St. James—Died April 10, 2003
† Lapan, Robert—Died 2003
† Lucey, John P., (Retired)—Died July 15, 2003
† McCarthy, Thomas J., (Retired)—Died June 9, 2003

Diocese of Steubenville

(Dioecesis Steubenvicensis)

Most Reverend

R. DANIEL CONLON, D.D., J.C.D., PH.D.

Bishop of Steubenville; ordained January 15, 1977; appointed Bishop of Steubenville May 22, 2002; consecrated and installed August 6, 2002 *P.O. Box 969, Steubenville, OH 43952-5969.*

Most Reverend

ALBERT H. OTTENWELLER, D.D., S.T.L.

Bishop Emeritus of Steubenville; ordained June 19, 1943; appointed Titular Bishop of Perdices and Auxiliary of Toledo April 17, 1974; consecrated May 29, 1974; appointed to Steubenville October 11, 1977; installed November 22, 1977; retired April 2, 1992 *Res.: 2544 Parkwood Ave., Toledo, OH 43610-1317.*

TAKE COURAGE

Chancery Office: 422 Washington St., P.O. Box 969, Steubenville, OH 43952-5969. Tel: 740-282-3631; Fax: 740-282-3327.

Web: www.diosteub.org

Email: lnichols@diosteub.org

Most Reverend

GILBERT I. SHELDON, D.D., D.MIN.

Bishop Emeritus of Steubenville; ordained February 28, 1953; appointed Auxiliary and Titular Bishop of Taparura April 20, 1976; consecrated June 11, 1976; appointed to Steubenville January 28, 1992; installed April 2, 1992; retired August 6, 2002

ESTABLISHED 1944.

Square Miles 5,913.

Comprises these thirteen Counties in the State of Ohio: Athens, Belmont, Carroll, Gallia, Guernsey, Harrison, Jefferson, Lawrence, Meigs, Morgan, Monroe, Noble and Washington.

For legal titles of parishes and diocesan institutions, consult the Chancery Office.

STATISTICAL OVERVIEW

Personnel	
Bishop	1
Retired Bishops	2
Priests: Diocesan Active in Diocese	54
Priests: Diocesan Active Outside Diocese	12
Priests: Retired, Sick or Absent	32
Number of Diocesan Priests	98
Religious Priests in Diocese	24
Total Priests in Diocese	122
Extern Priests in Diocese	18
Ordinations:	
Diocesan Priests	1
Transitional Deacons	3
Permanent Deacons in Diocese	6
Total Brothers	9
Total Sisters	79
Parishes	
Parishes	70
With Resident Pastor:	
Resident Diocesan Priests	70
Resident Religious Priests	1
Missions	3
Closed Parishes	3
Welfare	
Catholic Hospitals	1
Total Assisted	273,924
Special Centers for Social Services	1
Total Assisted	18,338
Residential Care of Disabled	1
Total Assisted	165
Educational	
Diocesan Students in Other Seminaries	9
Students Religious	2
Total Seminarians	11
Colleges and Universities	1
Total Students	2,253
High Schools, Diocesan and Parish	3
Total Students	717
Elementary Schools, Diocesan and Parish	14
Total Students	2,409
Catechesis/Religious Education:	
High School Students	618
Elementary Students	2,323
Total Students under Catholic Instruction	8,331
Teachers in the Diocese:	
Sisters	8
Lay Teachers	203
Vital Statistics	
Receptions into the Church:	
Infant Baptism Totals	502
Adult Baptism Totals	206
Received into Full Communion	111
First Communions	660
Confirmations	724
Marriages:	
Catholic	142
Interfaith	147
Total Marriages	289
Deaths	718
Total Catholic Population	40,411
Total Population	513,734

Former Bishops—Most Revs. JOHN KING MUSSIO, D.D., J.C.D. (Retired), named First Bishop of Steubenville.; ord. for Diocese of Cincinnati Aug. 15, 1935; appt. First Bishop of Steubenville March 16, 1945; consecrated May 1, 1945; retired Oct. 11, 1977; died April 15, 1978; ALBERT H. OTTENWELLER, D.D., S.T.L. (Retired), named Second Bishop of Steubenville.; ord. June 19, 1943; appt. Titular Bishop of Perdices and Auxiliary of Toledo April 17, 1974; consecrated May 29, 1974; appt. Second Bishop of Steubenville Oct. 11, 1977; installed Nov. 22, 1977; retired April 2, 1992; GILBERT I. SHELDON, D.D., D.Min. (Retired), named Third Bishop of Steubenville.; ord. Feb. 28, 1953; appt. Auxiliary and Titular Bishop of Taparura April 20, 1976; consecrated June 11, 1976; appt. Third Bishop of Steubenville Jan. 28, 1992; installed April 2, 1992; retired Aug. 6, 2002.

Vicar General—Rev. Msgr. KURT H. KEMO, J.C.L., V.G., 422 Washington St., P.O. Box 969, Steubenville, 43952-5969. Tel: 740-282-3631.

Moderator of the Curia—Rev. Msgr. KURT H. KEMO, J.C.L., V.G., 422 Washington St., P.O. Box 969, Steubenville, 43952-5969. Tel: 740-282-3631.

Episcopal Vicar for Pastoral Planning & Personnel—Rev. THOMAS A. CHILLOG, M.Div., 422 Washington St., P.O. Box 969, Steubenville, 43952-5969. Tel: 740-282-3631.

Chancellor—Mrs. LINDA A. NICHOLS.

Chancery Office—422 Washington St., P.O. Box 969, Steubenville, 43952-5969. Tel: 740-282-3631; Fax: 740-282-3327.

Diocesan Finance Office—Rev. Msgr. KURT H. KEMO, J.C.L., V.G., Finance Officer; Mr. DAVID FRANKLIN, Comptroller, P.O. Box 969, Steubenville, 43952-5969. Tel: 740-282-3631.

Diocesan/Parish Share Campaign—Rev. Msgr. KURT H. KEMO, J.C.L., V.G., Dir.; Mr. MARTIN B. THOMPSON, Assoc. Dir. Tel: 740-282-3631.

Diocesan Tribunal—422 Washington St., P.O. Box 969, Steubenville, 43952-5969. Tel: 740-282-3631.

Judicial Vicar—Rev. Msgr. KURT H. KEMO, J.C.L., V.G.

Auditors—Revs. THOMAS A. CHILLOG, M.Div.; WILLIAM D. CROSS; DANIEL HEUSEL.

Notary—Rev. DANIEL HEUSEL, M.Div.

Defenders of the Bond—Rev. Msgr. GERALD E. CALOVINI, V.F.; Revs. THOMAS A. CHILLOG, M.Div.; WILLIAM D. CROSS.

Secretary to the Tribunal & Notary—COLLEEN BAHEN.

Judges—Most Rev. GILBERT I SHELDON, D.D., D.Min. (Retired); Rev. Msgr. MARK J. FROEHLICH; Rev. JAMES M. DUNFEE; Rev. Msgr. GENE W. MULLETT; Rev. VINCENT J. HUBER, M.Ed.

Information & Technology—Mr. MARTIN B. THOMPSON, Dir.; Mr. ANTHONY TARGOSS, Mgr., 422 Washington St., P.O. Box 969, Steubenville, 43952-5969. Tel: 740-282-3631.

Diocesan Deaneries and Deans

Deans—Rev. Msgrs. GEORGE W. YONTZ, V.F., Annunciation Deanery; GERALD E. CALOVINI, V.F., Coronation Deanery; PATRICK GAUGHAN, V.F., Nativity of Mary Deanery; JOHN C. KOLESAR, V.F., Presentation Deanery; ROBERT KAWA, V.F., Visitation Deanery.

Child Protection Review Board—Rev. Msgr. KURT H. KEMO, J.C.L., V.G., Contact Person, P.O. Box 969, Steubenville, 43952-5969. Tel: 740-282-3631; Fax: 740-282-3327. Email: kkemo@diosteub.org.

Pastoral Staff—Most Rev. R. DANIEL CONLON, D.D., J.C.D., Ph.D.; Rev. Msgr. KURT H. KEMO, J.C.L., V.G.; Mrs. PAT DEFRANCIS; Mrs. LINDA A. NICHOLS; Rev. THOMAS A. CHILLOG, M.Div.; Rev. Msgrs. GERALD E. CALOVINI, V.F.; THOMAS C. PETRONEK; Sr. MARY ANN CORR, S.C., Ed.D.; Dr. PETER CHILA; Rev. WILLIAM D. CROSS; Mr. BRIAN HARVEY.

Presbyteral Council—Most Rev. R. DANIEL CONLON, D.D., J.C.D., Ph.D., Pres.; Rev. Msgrs. GERALD E. CALOVINI, V.F.; WILLIAM R. CORNELIUS (Retired); GEORGE R. COYNE; J. MICHAEL CAMPBELL; Revs. NORBERT T. CONNELLY; VICTOR CINSON; WAYNE MORRIS; Rev. Msgr. KURT H. KEMO, J.C.L., V.G., Vice Chm.; Revs. TIM MCGUIRE; THOMAS A. CHILLOG, M.Div., Chm.; JAMES MORMAN; Mrs. LINDA A. NICHOLS, Recording Sec.

College of Consultors—Rev. Msgrs. GERALD D. CALOVINI, V.F.; WILLIAM R. CORNELIUS (Retired); Rev. WAYNE MORRIS; Rev. Msgr. J. MICHAEL CAMPBELL; Revs. THOMAS A. CHILLOG, M.Div.; WILLIAM D. CROSS; VICTOR CINSON; Rev. Msgr. GEORGE R. COYNE.

Priests Personnel Board—Rev. VICTOR CINSON, Southern Area; Rev. Msgrs. GEORGE R. COYNE,

Senior Clergy; PATRICK GAUGHAN, V.F., Middle Age Clergy; J. MICHAEL CAMPBELL, Northern Area; Revs. JOHN MUCHA, Younger Clergy; DALE TORNES, Central Area; Rev. Msgr. KURT H. KEMO, J.C.L., V.G.; Rev. THOMAS A. CHILLOG, M.Div., Ex Officio.

Diocesan Offices and Directors

Building Commission—Mr. BRIAN HARVEY, Chm., P.O. Box 969, Steubenville, 43952-5969. Tel: 740-282-3631; Fax: 740-282-3327.

Building & Property Director—Mr. BRIAN HARVEY, P.O. Box 969, Steubenville, 43952-5969. Tel: 740-282-3631; Fax: 740-282-3327.

Campus Ministry—Rev. MARTIN J. HOLLER, 75 Stewart St., Athens, 45701. Tel: 740-592-2711.

Office of Christian Formation—Sr. MARY ANN CORR, S.C., Ed.D., Dir., P.O. Box 969, Steubenville, 43952-5969. Tel: 740-282-3631; Fax: 740-282-3327.

Diocesan Communications—Rev. Msgr. GERALD E. CALOVINI, V.F., P.O. Box 969, Steubenville, 43952-5969. Tel: 740-282-3631; Fax: 740-282-3327.

Continuing Education of Priests—Rev. Msgr. KURT H. KEMO, J.C.L., V.G., Dir., P.O. Box 969, Steubenville, 43952-5969. Tel: 740-282-3631; Fax: 740-282-3327.

Diocesan Finance Council—Most Rev. R. DANIEL CONLON, D.D., J.C.D., Ph.D., Pres.; Rev. Msgr. KURT H. KEMO, J.C.L., V.G., Chm. Council Members: Rev. Msgr. FREDERICK A. PASQUINELLI (Retired); GREGORY J. AGRESTA; RICHARD DOLAN; PAMELA DUNLAP; ROBERT DYER; DAVID A. FRANKLIN; THOMAS H. HISRICH, 422 Washington St., P.O. Box 969, Steubenville, 43952-5969. Tel: 740-282-3631; Fax: 740-282-3327.

Diocesan Director of Cemeteries—Rev. Msgr. JOHN C. KOLESAR, V.F., 221 Hanna Ave., Adena, 43901. Tel: 740-546-3463.

Diocesan Director of Ecumenism—Rev. Msgr. DONAL O'CARROLL, P.O. Box 65, Beverly, 45715. Tel: 740-984-4204.

Diocesan Office of Worship—Rev. Msgr. THOMAS C. PETRONEK, Dir., P.O. Box 969, Steubenville, 43952-5969. Tel: 740-282-3631; Fax: 740-282-3327.

Health Panel of the Clergy—Rev. THOMAS A. CHILLOG, M.Div., Contact Person, P.O. Box 969, Steubenville, 43952-5969. Tel: 740-282-3631.

Hospitals— Trinity Health System: *Trinity Medical Center, West, 4000 Johnson Rd., Steubenville, 43952*. Tel: 740-264-8000; Fax: 740-283-7104. *Trinity Medical Center, East, 380 Summit Ave., Steubenville, 43952*. Tel: 740-283-7000; Fax: 740-283-7104. FRED B. BROWER, Pres. Tel: 740-283-7390; 740-264-8303; Rev. JOHN MCCOY, Chap. Tel: 740-264-8000.

National Catholic Rural Life Conference—VACANT.

Central Office of Catholic Charities—Rev. Msgr. GERALD E. CALOVINI, V.F., Dir., P.O. Box 969, Steubenville, 43952-5969. Tel: 740-282-3631; 800-339-7890; Fax: 740-282-3327. Services: Campaign for Human Devel.; Respect Life; Information & Referral, Jefferson County RSVP. Tel: 740-282-9232. Ft. Steuben, Housing for Elderly. Tel: 740-282-9232. Samaritan House. Tel: 740-282-0563.

Priests' Retirement Board—Rev. Msgr. GEORGE R. COYNE, Chm.

Propagation of the Faith—Rev. PAUL HREZO, St. Benedict Church, 714 Gomber Ave., Cambridge, 43725. Tel: 740-432-7609.

Publication, "Steubenville Register"—Most Rev. R. DANIEL CONLON, D.D., J.C.D., Ph.D., Pres. & Publisher; Mrs. PAT DEFRANCIS, Editor, 422 Washington St., P.O. Box 160, Steubenville, 43952-5969. Tel: 740-282-3631; Fax: 740-282-3238.

RCIA—Rev. Msgr. THOMAS PETRONEK, Dir., P.O. Box 969, Steubenville, 43952-5969. Tel: 740-282-3631; Fax: 740-282-3327.

St. Vincent de Paul Society—Rev. Msgr. GERALD E. CALOVINI, V.F., Dir., 422 Washington St., P.O. Box 969, Steubenville, 43952-5969. Tel: 740-282-3631.

Schools—Dr. PETER CHILA, Ed.D., Supt., P.O. Box 969, Steubenville, 43952-5969. Tel: 740-282-3631; Fax: 740-282-3327.

Vicar for Priests—Rev. THOMAS A. CHILLOG, M.Div., P.O. Box 969, Steubenville, 43952-5969. Tel: 740-282-3631.

Vicar for Religious—Rev. Msgr. J. MICHAEL CAMPBELL, St. Gabriel, P.O. Box 275, Minerva, 44657. Tel: 330-868-4498.

Vicar for Retired Priests—Rev. VINCENT J. HUBER, M.Ed., 1225 N. River Ave., Toronto, 43964. Tel: 740-537-4433.

Victim Assistance Coordinators—Carroll County Area: Dr. THERESA PEACH, Ph.D., 407 Tonawanda Trail, Hartville, 44632. Tel: 330-877-2766. Steubenville/ Carroll/Harrison County Area: DAN OBERTANCE, 500 Market St., Steubenville, 43952. Tel: 740-282-1300; ROSEANN BRANIFF, 827 N. Fourth St., Steubenville, 43952. Tel: 740-282-3631. Belmont/ Monroe County Area: CHAD SOKOLOWSKI, 102 Park Dr., St. Clairsville, 43950. Tel: 740-695-3500. Athens/Meigs/Washington County Area:: Dr. SUZANNE APPLE, Ph.D., 3 W. Stimson Ave., Athens, 45701. Tel: 740-592-2103; Dr. JIM HAYES, Ph.D., 90 Hospital Dr., Athens, 45701. Tel: 740-592-3091. Guernsey/Noble County Area: ELIZABETH BRISLEN, 1041 Gomber Ave., Cambridge, 43725. Tel: 740-282-3631; JANE ENGOTT, 575 Harding Rd., Zanesville, 43701. Tel: 740-432-2611; PATTY JOHNSON, 111 N. 7th St., Cambridge, 43725. Tel: 740-439-4532. Noble/Morgan/Monroe/Washington County Area: ANGELA MIRACLE, 108 Riley Dr., Apt. 5, Marietta, 45750. Tel: 740-376-6882. Lawrence/ Gallia County Area: Dr. ELIZABETH EVANS, Ph.D., 160 TWP Rd. 1273, Chesapeake, 45619-8565. Tel: 740-867-6123; VICTORIA NEIGHBORGALL, 912 S. Sixth St., Ironton, 45638. Tel: 740-532-1485.

Vocations—Rev. Msgr. KURT H. KEMO, J.C.L., V.G., Dir.; Revs. DANIEL HEUSEL, M.Div., Asst. Dir., P.O. Box 969, Steubenville, 43952-5969. Tel: 740-282-3631; Fax: 740-282-3327. Email: kkemo@ diosteub.org; JASON PRATI, Asst. Dir., 330 S. Main St., Woodsfield, 43793. Tel: 740-472-0187.

Woman's Club—Rev. Msgr. KURT H. KEMO, J.C.L., V.G.; Mrs. BARBARA JEAN APPLEGARTH, Pres., 73911 Pleasant Grove, Adena, 43901. Tel: 740-546-3913.

CLERGY, PARISHES, MISSIONS AND PAROCHIAL SCHOOLS

CITY OF STEUBENVILLE
(JEFFERSON COUNTY)

1—HOLY NAME CATHEDRAL, [JC] Very Rev. Timothy Shannon, Rector.
Rectory—411 S. Fifth St., 43952. Tel: 740-282-7322; Fax: 740-284-7195.

2—ST. ANTHONY OF PADUA, [JC] Very Rev. Timothy Shannon.
Res.: 411 S. 5th St., 43952. Tel: 740-282-0832; Fax: 740-284-7195.
School—All Saints, Tel: 740-282-4201; Fax: 740-282-7195.

3—HOLY FAMILY, [JC] Rev. Richard Tuttle; Deacon Dominic Cerrato, Pastoral Assoc.
Res.: 2608 Hollywood Blvd., 43952. Tel: 740-264-2825; Fax: 740-264-9348.

4—HOLY ROSARY, [JC] Revs. Timothy P. McGuire, Admin.; John McCoy; Deacon Randall Redington.
Res.: 200 Rosemont Ave., 43952. Tel: 740-264-4880; Fax: 740-266-2843.
School—Central Grade School, Tel: 740-264-2550; Fax: 740-266-2844. Lay Teachers 24; Students 341.

5—IMMACULATE HEART OF MARY CHAPEL, Closed. For inquiries for parish records contact the chancery.

6—OUR LADY OF NORTH AMERICA MARTYRS, Closed., For inquires for parish records please see St. Peter's, Steubenville.

7—ST. PETER'S, [JC] Rev. Msgr. George W. Yontz, V.F.; Bro. Patrick Geary, I.H.M., Pastoral Assoc.
Res.: 425 N. Fourth St., 43952. Tel: 740-282-7612; 740-282-9263.
School—All Saints Central School, Tel: 740-282-4201; Fax: 740-282-4991. Lay Teachers 11; Students 106.

8—ST. PIUS X, [JC] Rev. Leonard T. Cencula.
Res.: 700 Lovers Ln., 43953. Tel: 740-264-7681; Fax: 740-264-6113.
School—Aquinas Central, 625 Lovers Ln., 43953. Tel: 740-264-3651; Fax: 740-264-4277. Lay Teachers 13; Students 222.

9—SERVANTS OF CHRIST THE KING, Rev. Timothy P. McGuire.
Res.: 320 W. View, 43964. Tel: 740-264-5538; Fax: 740-264-5443.

10—ST. STANISLAUS, [JC] Rev. Msgr. George W. Yontz, V.F.
Mailing Address: 425 N. 4th St., 43952. Tel: 740-282-7612; Fax: 740-282-9263.

OUTSIDE THE CITY OF STEUBENVILLE

ADENA, JEFFERSON CO., ST. CASIMIR'S, [CEM] Rev. Msgr. John C. Kolesar, V.F.
Res.: 221 Hanna Ave., 43901. Tel: 740-546-3463; Fax: 740-546-3763.
Catechesis/Religious Program—Students 54.

AMSTERDAM, JEFFERSON CO., ST. JOSEPH, [CEM] Rev. WillRoger Malave.
Res.: P.O. Box 35, 43903. Tel: 740-543-3652.

ATHENS, ATHENS CO.

1—CHRIST THE KING UNIVERSITY PARISH, Rev. Martin J. Holler, Dir. Campus Ministry; Rev. Msgr. Donald E. Horak (Retired).
Res.: 75 Stewart St., 45701. Tel: 740-592-2711; Fax: 740-593-8908.
Catechesis/Religious Program—Tel: 740-594-8718. Nancy Denhart, D.R.E. Students 250.

2—ST. PAUL'S, [CEM] Rev. Msgr. Patrick E. Gaughan, V.F. In Res., Rev. Msgr. Donald E. Horak (Retired).
Res.: 38 N. College St., 45701. Tel: 740-593-7822; Fax: 740-593-8602.
Catechesis/Religious Program—Tel: 740-594-8718. Mrs. Nancy Denhart, D.R.E. Students 76.
Chapel—Guysville, St. John

BARNESVILLE, BELMONT CO., ASSUMPTION, [CEM] Rev. Virgil Reischman.
Res.: 306 W. Main St., 43713. Tel: 740-425-2181.
Catechesis/Religious Program—Students 111.

BARTON, BELMONT CO., OUR LADY OF ANGELS, Closed., For inquiries for parish records see St. Joseph, Bridgeport.

BELLAIRE, BELMONT CO.

1—ST. JOHN, [JC] Rev. Msgr. Gene W. Mullett.
Res.: 3745 Tallman Ave., 43906. Tel: 740-676-0051.
School—Central Grade School, Tel: 740-676-2620; Fax: 740-676-8502. Lay Teachers 17; Students 251.

2—ST. MICHAEL'S, [CEM] [JC] Rev. Msgr. Gene W. Mullett.
c/o St. John Church: 415 37th St., 43906. Tel: 740-676-0051.

BELLE VALLEY, NOBLE CO., CORPUS CHRISTI, [CEM] Rev. Dale F. Tornes.
c/o St. Stephen Church: P.O. Box 186, Caldwell, 43724. Tel: 740-732-4129.
Church: Main St., 43717. Tel: 614-732-7202.

BEVERLY, WASHINGTON CO., ST. BERNARD, [CEM] Rev. Msgr. Robert J. Kawa.
Res.: 307 Seventh St., P.O. Box 98, 45715. Tel: 740-984-2555; Fax: 740-984-2555.
Catechesis/Religious Program—Tel: 740-984-2387. Yvonne Huck, D.R.E. Tel: 740-984-0298. Students 186.

BLAINE, BELMONT CO., ALL SAINTS, Closed., For inquiries for parish records please see St. Joseph, Bridgeport.

BRIDGEPORT, BELMONT CO.

1—ST. ANTHONY OF PADUA, [JC] Rev. Msgr. Thomas C. Petronek.
Res.: 630 Main St., 43912. Tel: 740-635-0283.

2—ST. JOSEPH, [JC] Rev. Msgr. Mark J. Froehlich.
Res.: 68210 Neola Ave., 43912. Tel: 740-635-0408; Fax: 740-635-1166.
School—Tel: 740-635-3313. Lay Teachers 13; Students 180.

BRILLIANT, JEFFERSON CO., OUR LADY OF FATIMA, Closed., Sacramental records are located at St. Agnes, Mingo Junction.

BUCHTEL, ATHENS CO., ST. PATRICK, Consolidated, with St. Andrew to form St. Mary of the Hills, Nelsonville.

BURKHART, MONROE CO., ST. JOSEPH'S, Revs. David L. Gaydosik; Jason Prati.
Mailing Address: *c/o St. Sylvester Church*, 334 S. Main St., Woodsfield, 43793. Tel: 740-472-0187; Fax: 740-472-0182.

BYESVILLE, GUERNSEY CO., HOLY TRINITY, [CEM] Rev. Msgr. William C. Yontz.
Res.: 222 S. Fifth St., Box 26, 43723. Tel: 740-685-2184.

CADIZ, HARRISON CO., ST. TERESA, Rev. Thomas A. Vennitti.
Res.: 143 E. South St., 43907. Tel: 740-942-2211.

CALDWELL, NOBLE CO., ST. STEPHEN, [CEM] Rev. Dale F. Tornes.
Res.: 1036 Belford St., Box 186, 43724. Tel: 740-732-4129; Fax: 740-732-1520.

CAMBRIDGE, GUERNSEY CO., ST. BENEDICT, Rev. Robert D. Borer.
Res.: 714 Gomber Ave., 43725. Tel: 740-432-7609; Fax: 740-439-0800.
School—Tel: 740-432-6751; Fax: 740-432-4961. Franciscan Sisters of Christian Charity 4; Lay Teachers 8; Students 159.
Catechesis/Religious Program—Patricia Farley, D.R.E. Students 143.

CARLISLE, NOBLE CO., ST. MICHAEL, [CEM] Rev. Samuel Saprano.
Res.: 43700 Fulda Rd., Caldwell, 43724. Tel: 740-838-4842.

CARROLLTON, CARROLL CO., OUR LADY OF MERCY, Rev. Thomas Marut.
Res.: 616 Roswell Rd., N.W., P.O. Box 155, 44615. Tel: 330-627-4664; Fax: 330-627-4664.
Catechesis/Religious Program—Sr. Rita Murphy, D.R.E. Students 64.

CHESAPEAKE, LAWRENCE CO., ST. ANN, Rev. Charles Moran.
310 Third Ave., Box 428, 45619-0428. Tel: 740-867-4434; Fax: 740-867-5829.
Catechesis/Religious Program—Tel: 740-867-4434, Ext. 11. Mrs. Marion Hutton, D.R.E. Students 66.

CHURCHTOWN, WASHINGTON CO., ST. JOHN THE BAPTIST, [CEM] Rev. Frederick C. Kihm.

Res.: 17784 State Rte. 676, Marietta, 45750. Tel: 740-896-2060; Fax: 740-896-3700.
School—Central Grade School, Tel: 740-896-2697; Fax: 740-896-2555. Lay Teachers 10; Students 125.

COLERAIN, BELMONT CO., ST. FRANCES CABRINI, Rev. Msgr. David E. Reasbeck.
Res.: Rte. 250, Box 38, 43916. Tel: 740-635-9933.

DILLONVALE, JEFFERSON CO., ST. ADALBERT, [CEM] Rev. Msgr. John C. Kolesar, V.F.
Res.: c/o 221 Hanna Ave., Adena, 43901. Tel: 740-546-3463; Fax: 740-546-3763.
Catechesis/Religious Program—Tel: 740-769-7858. Rosemary Zelek, D.R.E. Students 54.

FAIRPOINT, BELMONT CO., ST. JOSEPH, Rev. Thomas J. Graven.
Mailing Address: 71793 Church St., P.O. Box 308, Maynard, 43937. Tel: 740-695-2618; Fax: 740-695-2618.
Church: 46982 Columbia St., Box 98, 43927. Tel: 740-695-0840.

FLUSHING, BELMONT CO., ST. PAUL'S, [CEM] Rev. Msgr. John A. Cymbor.
Res.: 115 Morristown Rd., Box 45, 43977. Tel: 740-968-4159.
Catechesis/Religious Program—Tel: 740-782-1223. Marianne Fraley, D.R.E. Students 13.

FULDA, NOBLE CO., IMMACULATE CONCEPTION, [CEM] Rev. Samuel Saprano.
Res.: 43700 Fulda Rd., Caldwell, 43724. Tel: 740-732-4576.

GALLIPOLIS, GALLIA CO., ST. LOUIS, [CEM] Rev. Msgr. William R. Myers, V.F.
Res.: 85 State St., 45631. Tel: 740-446-0669; Fax: 740-446-9858.

GLOUSTER, ATHENS CO., HOLY CROSS, [CEM] Rev. John Mucha.
Mailing Address: 110 E. Washington St., Nelsonville, 45764. Tel: 740-753-1770; Fax: 740-753-4480.
Rectory—31 Republic Ave., 45732. Tel: 740-767-3068.
Church: Corner of Madison & Republic Avenues, 45732.

HARRIETTSVILLE, NOBLE CO., ST. HENRY, [CEM] Rev. Victor Cinson Jr., Admin.
Mailing Address: 5001 Lowell Hill Rd., Lowell, 45744. Tel: 740-896-2207; Fax: 740-896-2207.
Church: Rte. 1, 36575 Church St., CR 47, Lower Salem, 45745. Tel: 740-585-2383.

HOPEDALE, HARRISON CO., SACRED HEART, [JC] Rev. Thomas A. Vennitti.
Mailing Address: 143 E. South St., Cadiz, 43907. Tel: 740-942-2211.
Res.: 205 Cross St., 43976.

IRONTON, LAWRENCE CO.
1—ST. JOSEPH, [JC] Revs. Thomas R. Nau; Wayne E. Morris.
Res.: 905 S. Fifth St., P.O. Box 499, 45638. Tel: 740-532-0561; 740-532-0712; Fax: 740-534-0557.
Catechesis/Religious Program—Jane Rudmann, D.R.E. Students 63.
2—ST. LAWRENCE, [JC] Revs. Thomas R. Nau; Wayne E. Morris.
Res.: 905 S. Fifth St., P.O. Box 499, 45638-0499. Tel: 740-532-0561; Fax: 740-534-0557.
School—St. Lawrence Central Grade School, (Grades K-6) Tel: 740-532-5052; Fax: 740-532-5082. Lay Teachers 11; Students 99.
High School—St. Joseph Central High School, (Grades 7-12) Tel: 740-532-0485; Fax: 740-532-3699. Lay Teachers 13; Students 79.

LAFFERTY, BELMONT CO., ST. MARY, [CEM] Rev. Chester J. Pabin.
Res.: P.O. Box 188, 43951. Tel: 740-968-3200.
Catechesis/Religious Program—Tel: 740-782-1487. Jill A. Clift, D.R.E. Students 19.

LITTLE HOCKING, WASHINGTON CO., ST. AMBROSE, [CEM] Rev. David L. Huffman.
Res.: 5080 School House Rd., 45742. Tel: 740-423-7422; Fax: 740-423-7422.
Catechesis/Religious Program—Tel: 740-374-0848. Mrs. Joan Smith, D.R.E. Students 195.

LORE CITY, GUERNSEY CO., SS. PETER AND PAUL, [CEM] Rev. Robert D. Borer.
Res.: P.O. Box 175, 43755. Tel: 740-685-5582; 740-432-7609; Fax: 740-685-6336.

LOWELL, WASHINGTON CO., OUR LADY OF MERCY, [CEM] Rev. Victor Cinson Jr.
Res.: 5001 Lowell Hill Rd., 45744. Tel: 740-896-2207; Fax: 740-896-2207.

MALVERN, CARROLL CO., ST. FRANCIS XAVIER, [CEM] Rev. Msgr. J. Michael Campbell.
Res.: P.O. Box 275, Minerva, 44657. Tel: 330-868-4498.
Catechesis/Religious Program—Tel: 330-863-2634. Leslie Moushey, D.R.E. Students 83.

MARIETTA, WASHINGTON CO., ST. MARY'S, [CEM 2] Rev. Msgr. Edward Kakascik; Revs. Paul Hrezo; Mark J. Moore.
Res.: 506 Fourth St., 45750. Tel: 740-373-3643; Fax: 740-376-2956.
School—320 Marion St., 45750. Tel: 740-374-8181; Fax: 740-374-8602. Lay Teachers 22; Students 226.
Catechesis/Religious Program—Students 275.

MARTINS FERRY, BELMONT CO., ST. MARY, [CEM] Rev. Thomas A. Magary. In Res., Rev. Richard L. Battocletti (Retired).
Res.: 20 N. Fourth St., 43935. Tel: 740-633-1416; Fax: 740-633-1490.
School—St. Mary Central, 24 N. Fourth St., 43935. Tel: 740-633-5424; Fax: 740-633-5462. Sr. Benita DeMatteis, Prin. Sisters 3; Lay Teachers 10; Students 140.
Catechesis/Religious Program—Tel: 740-633-5898. Judy Kacsmar, D.R.E. Students 16.

MAYNARD, BELMONT CO., ST. STANISLAUS, Rev. Thomas J. Graven.
Res.: 71793 Church St., P.O. Box 308, 43937. Tel: 740-695-2618; Fax: 740-695-2618.

MCCONNELSVILLE, MORGAN CO., ST. JAMES, Rev. Paul Walker.
Res.: 257 Bell Ave., P.O. Box 539, 43756. Tel: 740-962-2856.

MILTONSBURG, MONROE CO., ST. JOHN THE BAPTIST, [CEM 2] Revs. David L. Gaydosik; Jason M. Prati.
Church: 35560 Miltonsburg-Calais Rd., Woodsfield, 43793. Tel 740-472-0187; Fax: 740-472-0182.
Res.: 334 S. Main St., Woodsfield, 43793.

MINERVA, STARK CO., ST. GABRIEL THE ARCHANGEL, Rev. Msgr. John Michael Campbell.
Res.: 400 West High, P.O. Box 275, 44657. Tel: 330-868-4498; Fax: 330-868-2188.
Catechesis/Religious Program—Students 188.

MINGO JUNCTION, JEFFERSON CO.
1—ST. AGNES, [JC] Rev. James M. Dunfee; Sr. June Smith, O.S.F., Pastoral Assoc.
Mailing Address: 204 St. Clair Ave., 43938. Tel: 740-535-1491.
School—Central Grade School, Tel: 740-535-1012. Franciscan Sisters of Christian Charity 3; Lay Teachers 12; Students 85.
Catechesis/Religious Program—Students 14.
2—ANNUNCIATION, Closed., Parish records can be found at St. Agnes Church, Mingo Junction.
3—ST. BERNADETTE, Closed., Sacramental records are located at St. Agnes, Mingo Junction.

MORGES, CARROLL CO., ST. MARY, [CEM] Rev. Thomas Marut.
Res.: P.O. Box 690, Waynesburg, 44688. Tel: 330-866-2023.
Catechesis/Religious Program—Bobbi Niemeyer, D.R.E. Students 25.

NEFFS, BELMONT CO., SACRED HEART, Rev. Gary Zalenski.
Res.: 54038 St. Mary Ave., P.O. Box 425, 43940-0425. Tel: 740-676-3277; Fax: 740-676-3400.
Catechesis/Religious Program—Students 44.

NELSONVILLE, ATHENS CO., ST. MARY OF THE HILLS, Consolidated, St. Andrew, Nelsonville with St. Patrick, Buchtel to form St. Mary of the Hills. Rev. John Mucha.
Res.: 110 E. Washington St., 45764. Tel: 740-753-1770; Fax: 740-753-4480.

PINE GROVE, LAWRENCE CO., ST. MARY, [CEM] Rev. Francis L. Kinney, C.PP.S.
Res.: Box 639, Ironton, 45638. Tel: 740-532-2420.

PINEY FORK, JEFFERSON CO., ST. THERESE, Rev. A. Donald Mantica, Admin.
Res.: Box 25, 43941. Tel: 740-733-7820; 740-733-7595.

POMEROY, MEIGS CO., SACRED HEART, [CEM] Rev. Walter F. Heinz.
Res.: 161 Mulberry Ave., 45769. Tel: 740-992-5898; Fax: 740-992-6771.
Catechesis/Religious Program—Cindy Nau, D.R.E. Students 49.

POWHATAN POINT, BELMONT CO., ST. JOHN VIANNEY, Rev. Frank C. Cronin.
Mailing Address: St. Mary Church, P.O. Box 68, Shadyside, 43947. Tel: 740-676-3282.
Church: 295 Hwy. 7 N., 43942.

RICHMOND, JEFFERSON CO., ST. JOHN FISHER, Rev. Msgr. Kenneth Uram.
Res.: 7457 St. Hwy. 152, 43944. Tel: 740-765-4142.

ST. CLAIRSVILLE, BELMONT CO., ST. MARY'S, Rev. Thomas A. Chillog, M.Div.
Office—212 W. Main St., 43950. Tel: 740-695-9993.
Res.: 220 W. Main St., 43950. Tel: 740-695-2076.
School—Central Grade School, 226 W. Main St., 43950. Tel: 740-695-3189; Fax: 740-695-3851. Lay Teachers 10; Students 211.
Catechesis/Religious Program—Tel: 740-695-6855; Fax: 740-695-6503. Jean Clark, D.R.E. Students 116.

SHADYSIDE, BELMONT CO., ST. MARY'S, Rev. Frank C. Cronin
350 E. 40th St., P.O. Box 68, 43947. Tel: 740-676-3282; Fax: 740-676-1424.

SMITHFIELD, JEFFERSON CO., OUR LADY, QUEEN OF PEACE, [JC] Rev. A. Donald Mantica.
Res.: P.O. Box 453, 43948. Tel: 740-733-7595.

TEMPERANCEVILLE, BELMONT CO., ST. MARY'S, [CEM] Rev. Virgil Reischman.
Res.: 306 W. Main St., Barnesville, 43713. Tel: 740-425-2181.

TILTONSVILLE, JEFFERSON CO., ST. JOSEPH, Rev. Msgr. George R. Coyne.
Res.: 204 Mound St., 43963. Tel: 740-859-4018; Fax: 740-859-6041.

TORONTO, JEFFERSON CO.
1—ST. FRANCIS OF ASSISI, [JC] Rev. Msgr. Kurt H. Kemo, J.C.L., V.G.; Revs. Daniel Heusel, M.Div.; Vincent J. Huber, M.Ed.; Bro. Anthony Motto, I.H.M., Pastoral Assoc.
Res.: 1225 N. River Ave., 43964. Tel: 740-537-4433; Fax: 740-537-9305.
School—Tel: 740-537-2151. Sisters of Charity 1; Lay Teachers 6; Students 62.
2—ST. JOSEPH'S, [JC] Rev. Msgr. Kurt H. Kemo, J.C.L., V.G.; Revs. Daniel Heusel, M.Div.; Vincent J. Huber, M.Ed.; Bro. Anthony Motto, I.H.M., Pastoral Assoc.
Res.: 1225 N. River Ave., 43964. Tel: 740-537-4433; Fax: 740-537-9305.

VINCENT, WASHINGTON CO., ST. AMBROSE, Consolidated, with St. Ambrose, Belpre.

WINTERSVILLE, JEFFERSON CO.
1—BLESSED SACRAMENT, [JC] Rev. Msgr. Gerald E. Calovini, V.F.; Rev. Thomas F. Hamm.
Res.: 852 Main St., 43953-3870. Tel: 740-264-0868; Fax: 740-264-5449.
School—Aquinas Elementary, (Grades K-8), 625 Lovers Ln., 43953. Tel: 740-264-3651; Fax: 740-264-4277.
2—OUR LADY OF LOURDES, [JC] Rev. Msgr. Gerald E. Calovini, V.F.; Rev. Thomas F. Hamm.
Res.: 1521 Bantam Ridge Rd., P.O. Box 2612, 43953. Tel: 740-264-2798; 740-282-3631 (Office); Fax: 740-264-5449.

WOODSFIELD, MONROE CO., ST. SYLVESTER, [CEM] Revs. David Gaydosik; Jason M. Prati.
Res.: 334 S. Main St., 43793. Tel: 740-472-0187; Fax: 740-472-0182.
School—Central Grade School, Tel: 740-472-0321; Fax: 740-472-1994. Lay Teachers 14; Students 106.

YORKVILLE, JEFFERSON CO., ST. LUCY'S, Rev. Msgr. George R. Coyne.
Mailing Address: 204 Mound St., Tiltonsville, 43963. Tel: 740-859-4018; Fax: 740-859-6041.

DIOCESAN MISSIONS

BLOOMINGDALE, JEFFERSON CO., ST. THOMAS MORE MISSION, Closed., Sacramental records are located at St. John Fisher, Richmond.

CHAUNCEY, ATHENS CO., ST. JUDE MISSION, Closed., Sacramental records are located at St. Paul Church, Athens.

CRESCENT, BELMONT CO., ST. ELIZABETH MISSION, Closed., Sacramental records are located at St. Stanislaus Church, Maynard.

FREEPORT, HARRISON CO., ST. MATTHIAS MISSION, Rev. Thomas A. Vennitti.
Res.: 143 E. South St., Cadiz, 43907. Tel: 740-942-2211.
Church: Main St., Box 195, 43973. Tel: 740-658-3300.

HAMMONDSVILLE, JEFFERSON CO., NATIVITY OF OUR LORD MISSION, Closed., Sacramental records are located at St. Joseph Church, Toronto.

JEWETT, HARRISON CO., OUR LADY OF PERPETUAL HELP MISSION, Rev. John M. Galea (Retired).
Mailing Address & Res.: 1685 Twp. Rd. 378, 43952-6959. Tel: 740-946-2400; Fax: 740-283-2107.

SARDIS, MONROE CO., ST. JOHN BOSCO MISSION, [CEM] Revs. David L. Gaydosik; Jason Prati.
c/o St. Sylvester Church: 334 S. Main St., Woodsfield, 43793. Tel: 740-472-0187; Fax: 740-472-1994.

TAPPAN LAKE, HARRISON CO., CHRIST THE KING SUMMER MISSION, Closed., Sacramental records are located at: 143 E. South St., Cadiz 43907. Tel: 740-942-2211.

TUPPER PLAINS, MEIGS CO., OUR LADY OF LORETTO CHURCH, Closed., Sacramental records are located at Sacred Heart Church, Pomeroy.

On Duty Outside the Diocese:
Rev. Msgr.—
Wippel, John, Ph.D., 10105 Portland Pl., Silver Springs, MD 20901. Tel: 301-593-9345; 816-942-8400
Revs.—
Calabrese, Charles L., TCU, Box 297310, Fort Worth, TX 76129-0001. Tel: 817-923-2176; 817-921-7830
DiRenzo, Michael J. (LA), U.S.A.F. Chap. (Lt. Col.), 2731 Englewood Dr., Melbourne, FL 32940. Tel: 321-253-3303
Gaetano, Lewis F., 423 Pebblebrook S.W., Canton, 44709.
Gallagher, Robert A., U.S.A.F. Chap., PSC 76 Box 3163, Apo, AP 96319. Email: robert.gallagher@misawa.af.mil
Massucci, Joseph D. (CIN), University of Dayton, 324 Chaminade Hall, Dayton, 45469-0534. Tel:

937-229-3737; 513-299-3730. Email: josephmassucci@notes.udayton.edu
McCarthy, Francis X. (MIA) (Retired), 2533 S.W. Ninth Ave., Fort Lauderdale, FL 33315.
McCarthy, John R., St. Philomena Church, 13824 Euclid Ave., Cleveland, 44114. Tel: 216-541-3540
Pliauplis, Christopher, St. James the Apostle, 14 Gleneida Ave., Carmel, NY 10512. Tel: 914-225-2079
Safraniec, Joseph, Chap., Chaplain's Office, 3601A St. Francis Way, Eagan, MN 55123-1167.
Smith, Martin D., 4 Golfside Cir., Canandaigua, NY 14424. Tel: 585-394-0264

Graduate Studies:
Rev.—
Cross, William D., c/o Front Desk, 341 Maclaren St., Ohawa ON K2P 2E2 Canada. Tel: 613-594-5757

Absent on Leave:
Revs.—
Bielanski, Joseph J., 246 Dorland, #4, San Francisco, CA 94114.
Greenwood, Kevin L., The Americana Apts., 380 S. 5th St., Apt. 314, Columbus, 43215.
McGough, Thomas V., Jr.

Retired:
Most Revs.—
Ottenweller, Albert H., D.D., S.T.L.
Sheldon, Gilbert I., D.D., D.Min.
Rev. Msgrs.—
Adams, George J., 785 Broad St., Brockway, PA 15824. Tel: 814-265-8371
Boehm, James A., 124 N. Main St., Hendersonville, NC 28792-5876. Tel: 828-697-8269
Cappelli, Angelo J., DeSeranno, 17255 Common Rd., Unit A148, Roseville, MI 48066. Tel: 586-447-4747
Cornelius, William R., 4333 Steuben Woods Dr., 43953. Tel: 740-264-0741
Giannamore, Anthony J., 380 E. Alex Bell Rd., #1, Dayton, 45459-1741. Tel: 973-435-3626; 973-433-7224
Horak, Donald E., 75 Stewart St., Athens, 45701. Tel: 740-592-5745
Manieri, Frank P., Heritage Pines, 11529 Baronwood Ct., Hudson, FL 34667. Tel: 727-861-3831
Metzger, Paul E., 428 Cambridge Dr., Middleton, 45042. Tel: 513-424-4576
Nealon, Joseph A., P.O. Box 158, Carrollton, 44615-0158. Tel: 330-627-7083
Nugent, James B., 3440 Olentangy River Rd., Apt. 4D, Columbus, 43202. Tel: 614-262-0629
O'Carroll, Donal A., P.O. Box 65, Beverly, 45715. Tel: 740-984-4204
Pasquinelli, Frederick A., 4337 Steuben Woods Dr., 43953. Tel: 740-264-0970
Wadowicz, Joseph M., 106 Via Estrada, #A, Laguna Hills, CA 92653-4077. Tel: 714-770-6691
Zekas, Stanley, 4335 Steuben Woods Dr., 43953. Tel: 740-266-6947
Revs.—
Battocletti, Richard L., St. Mary Church, 20 N. 4th St., Martins Ferry, 43935. Tel: 740-633-1416
Belfield, John, P.O. Box 119, Avon Park, FL 33825. Tel: 941-386-0631
Borosh, Carl A., Box 587, Barton, 43905. Tel: 740-695-0827
Connelly, Norbert, 4339 Steuben Woods Dr., 43953. Tel: 740-264-0699
Deasio, August J., M.A., 935 Yellow Mills Rd., Shortsville, NY 14548. Tel: 716-289-3074
Galea, John M., 206 Grant St., Mingo Jct., 43938. Tel: 740-535-1578
Gallagher, Cornelius F., 10520 Oakmont Ave., Sun City, AZ 85351. Tel: 623-974-5902
Krajcovic, Bernard, 107 St. Lucy Ave., Yorkville, 43971. Tel: 740-859-0262
Lyden, Dennis P., St. Joseph Church, P.O. Box 98, Fairpoint, 43927. Tel: 740-695-0840
Martinosky, Joseph A., 603 Franklin Ave., Apt. #1, Columbus, 43215. Tel: 614-224-4498
Mascolino, Charles E., 4338 Steuben Woods Dr., Wintersville, 43953. Tel: 740-266-9032
Mascolino, Robert A., P.O. Box 4032, 43952-8032. Tel: 740-282-7675
Nadzam, John B., Lancia Country Club Manor, 575 Lovers Ln., 43952. Tel: 740-264-2585
Stabene, Edmondo, 2063 Bantam Ridge Rd., P.O. Box 2373, Wintersville, 43953. Tel: 740-264-9761
Stromski, Adam F.X., 17530 S.W. 90th Ave., Miami, FL 33157-5800. Tel: 305-251-9948

Permanent Deacons:
Cerrato, Dominic, 162 Twp. Hwy. 202, Bloomingdale, 43910. Tel: 740-944-1846
Hickey, Gerald, 1803 Williams Pl., 43952. Tel: 740-283-1585
Meagher, Lawrence, 4620 Lexington Dr., 43952. Tel: 740-264-3122
Miravalle, Mark, P.O. Box 338, Hopedale, 43976. Tel: 740-283-6433; Fax: 740-937-2555
Pettie, Paul, 1591 San Carlos St., St. Augustine, FL 32080-5480. Tel: 904-471-4541
Piasecki, Stanley T., 44906 Kacsmar Estates Dr., St. Clairsville, 43950. Tel: 740-695-2825
Redington, Randall, 401 Rosemont Ave., 43952. Tel: 740-266-7255

INSTITUTIONS LOCATED IN THE DIOCESE

[A] COLLEGES AND UNIVERSITIES

STEUBENVILLE. *Franciscan University of Steubenville*, 1235 University Blvd., 43952. Tel: 740-283-3771; Fax: 740-283-6472. Email: admissions@franciscan.edu. Web: www.franciscan.edu. Revs. Terence Henry, T.O.R., Pres.; Michael Scanlan, T.O.R., Chancellor; Mr. David Skiviat, Vice Pres. Finance & Admin.; Dr. Stephen Miletic, Dean of Faculty; Mr. Frank Glazer, Vice Pres. Advancement; Mr. Thomas Kneier, Dean of Students; Dr. Robert Filby, Vice Pres. Community Rels. & Acting Vice Pres.; Mr. Joel Recznik, Dean, Enrollment Mgmt.; Mrs. Liz Loizzo, Sec. of the Pres.; Revs. Brian Cavanaugh, T.O.R., Coord. of Prog. Devel. & Tech. Initiatives; Augustine Donegan, T.O.R.; Dennis Gang, T.O.R., Chap., Austrian Prog.; Conrad Harkins, O.F.M., Assoc. Prof. Theology; Stan Holland, T.O.R., Dir. of Works of Mercy; James Morman, Religious Admin.; Daniel Pattee, T.O.R, Asst. Prof. of Theology; David Pivonka, T.O.R., Vice Pres. Mission Effectiveness; Dominic Scotto, T.O.R., Univ. Chap. & Lecturer in Theology; Joseph Yelenc, T.O.R., Biology Prof.; David Morrier, T.O.R., Asst. Univ. Chap.; Bros. John Paul McMahon, T.O.R., Sec. of the Univ.; Francis Haworth, T.O.R., Dir. of Community Rels. Priests 13; Brothers 2; Lay Teachers 100; Students 2,253.

[B] HIGH SCHOOLS, CENTRAL

STEUBENVILLE. *Catholic Central High School*, 320 West View, 43952. Tel: 740-264-5538; Fax: 740-264-5443. Email: cchs_frank@omereso.net. Web: cchs.sbd.pvt.k12.oh.us. Mr. Frank Rose, Prin. Lay Teachers 28; Students 391.

BELLAIRE. *St. John Central High School*, 3625 Guernsey St., 43906. Tel: 740-676-4932; Fax: 740-676-4934. Email: BSJH_gh@omeresa.ohio.gov. Web: www.bellairestjohn.sbd.pvt.k12.oh.us. Mr. C. Gary Hill, Prin. Sisters 1; Lay Teachers 20; Students 250.

[C] JUNIOR-SENIOR CENTRAL HIGH SCHOOLS

IRONTON. *St. Joseph Central*, (Grades 7-12), 912 S. Sixth St., 45638. Tel: 740-532-0485; Fax: 740-532-3699. Email: jmains@Scoca-k12.org. James J. Mains III, Prin. Total Staff 16; Students 76.

[D] PRIVATE SCHOOLS

CARROLLTON. *St. John Villa*, P.O. Box 457, 44615. Tel: 330-627-9789; Fax: 330-627-4826. Email: sjvinc@raex.com. Sr. Elaine Weber, O.S.F., Exec. Dir. Residential facility for persons with developmental disabilities. Faculty Staff 100; Child Care Services 120; Adult Day Care 10; Residents 55.

[E] GENERAL HOSPITALS

STEUBENVILLE. *Trinity Health System*, 380 Summit Ave., 43952. Tel: 740-283-7212; Fax: 740-283-7104. Web: www.trinityhealth.com. Patients Assisted Annually: Admissions 13,525; Outpatients 206,581; Emergency Room 53,818; Births 436.
Trinity Medical Center, West, 4000 Johnson Rd., 43952. Tel: 740-264-8000; Fax: 740-283-7104. Web: www.trinityhealth.com. Rev. John McCoy, Chap.
Trinity Medical Center, East, 380 Summit Ave., 43952. Tel: 740-283-7000; Fax: 740-283-7104. Sisters Maria Consuelo, O.S.F., Chap.; Mary Patrick Gillen, O.S.F., Chap.; Rev. John McCoy, Chap.
Trinity Health System Foundation, 380 Summit Ave., 43952. Tel: 740-283-7128; Fax: 740-283-7104. Bed Capacity 488; Sisters 5; RNs 425; LPNs 38; Nurse Anesthetists 17.

[F] MONASTERIES AND RESIDENCES OF PRIESTS AND BROTHERS

STEUBENVILLE. *Diocesan Brotherhood of Immaculate Heart of Mary* Villa Maria Motherhouse. , Villa Maria Motherhouse, 609 N. Seventh St., 43952. Tel: 740-283-2462. Bro. Dominic Carroll, I.H.M., Supr. Gen. Professed Brothers 4.
Holy Spirit Friary, 1235 University Blvd., 43952. Tel: 740-283-3771; Fax: 740-283-6348. Email: hsfriar@ibm.net. Web: www.franuniv.edu. Revs. Brian Cavanaugh, T.O.R.; Augustine Donegan, T.O.R.; Donald S. Frinsko, T.O.R.; Dennis Gang, T.O.R.; Terence Henry, T.O.R.; Stanley Holland, T.O.R.; Ronald J. Mohnickey, T.O.R. (ARL); James Morman; David Morrier, T.O.R.; Daniel Pattee, T.O.R; David Pivonka, T.O.R.; Michael Scanlan, T.O.R.; Dominic Scotto, T.O.R.; Joseph Yelenc, T.O.R.; Bros. Seraphim Beshoner, T.O.R.; James Boyle, T.O.R.; Timothy Harris, T.O.R.; Francis Haworth, T.O.R.; John Paul McMahon, T.O.R. Priests 12; Brothers 3. In Res. Revs. John Cody, C.SS.R.; John Gordon (NEW); Conrad Harkins, O.F.M.

BLOOMINGDALE. *Holy Family Hermitage*, 1501 Fairplay Rd., 43910-7971. Tel: 740-765-4511; Fax: 740-765-4511. Revs. Basil Corriere, E.C., Prior; Paul Vankeirsbilck, E.C. Hermits 2.

[G] CONVENTS AND RESIDENCES FOR SISTERS

STEUBENVILLE. *Sacred Heart Villa*, 36 Villa Dr., 43953-7129. Tel: 740-282-3801; Fax: 740-282-3801. Sr. Ernestine Vitello, Supr. Handmaids of Reparation of the Sacred Heart of Jesus, Motherhouse of America Foundation. Engaged in Kindergarten, Pre-Kindergarten and Parish work.

CARROLLTON. *North American Union Sisters of Our Lady of Charity*, P.O. Box 158, 620 Roswell Rd., N.W., 44615-0158. Tel: 330-627-7647; Fax: 330-627-4415. Sr. Carol Pregno, Local Supr. Professed Sisters 29.

[H] ASSOCIATIONS OF THE FAITHFUL

BLOOMINGDALE. *Carmelite Sisters-Mount Carmel Hermitage*, 388 Fairplay Rd., 43910-7914. Tel: 740-944-1048. Sisters 2.

STEUBENVILLE. *Sisters of Reparation to the Most Sacred Heart of Jesus*, P.O. Box 3, 354 Rinker Rd., 43952. Tel: 740-282-2144; Fax: 740-282-7919. Email: srmwendy@sisters-of-reparation.org. Web: sisters-of-reparation.org. Sr. Wendy McMenamy, S.R., Local Supr. Sisters 3.

TORONTO. *Franciscan Sisters Third Order Regular of Penance of the Sorrowful Mother*, 170 Little Church Rd., 43964. Tel: 740-544-5542; Fax: 740-544-5543. Email: torsisters@juno.com. Web: www.torsisters.com. Sr. Catherine Caldwell, T.O.R., Supr. Sisters 20; Novices 3; Postulants 3.

[I] SHRINES

FRANKLIN FURNACE, LAWRENCE CO.. *Our Lady of Fatima Shrine* Old Rte. 52, 45629. P.O. Box 499, Ironton, 45638-0499. Rev. Thomas Nau. Tel: 740-532-7780.

[J] NEWMAN CENTERS

ATHENS. *Christ the King University Parish - Ohio University* 75 Stewart St., 45701. Tel: 740-592-2711; Fax: 740-593-8908. Email: ctkinfo@ctkathens.org. Web: www.ctkathens.org. Rev. Msgr. Donald E. Horak (Retired); Rev. Martin J. Holler, Dir. Campus Ministry.

MARIETTA. *Marietta College* c/o St. Mary Church, 506 Fourth St., 45750. Tel: 740-373-3643. Rev. Msgr. Edward Kakascik, Dir.

NELSONVILLE. *Hocking Technical College* 45764. Rev. John Mucha, Dir.
Res.: 110 E. Washington St., 45764. Tel: 740-753-1770.

RIO GRANDE. *Rio Grande University* 91 State St., 45674. Tel: 740-446-0669. Rev. Msgr. William R. Myers, V.F., Contact Person.

ST. CLAIRSVILLE. *Ohio University - Eastern* c/o St. Mary's Church, 212 W. Main St., 43950. Tel: 740-695-9993; Fax: 740-695-6503. Web: www.stmarystc.com. Rev. Thomas A. Chillog, M.Div., Contact Person.

[K] MISCELLANEOUS LISTINGS

STEUBENVILLE. *Campaign for Human Development*, c/o Catholic Charities, P.O. Box 969, 43952. Tel: 740-282-3631; Fax: 740-282-3327. Email: gcalovini@diosteub.org. Web: www.diosteub.org. Rev. Msgr. Gerald E. Calovini, V.F., Diocesan Dir.
Catholic Community Center, P.O. Box 521, 148 S. Fourth St., 43952. Tel: 740-282-7566. Mr. Brian Harvey, Board Chm.; Mr. Michael J. Barber, Exec. Dir.; Mr. Raymond Saccoccia, Business Mgr.
**Catholics United for the Faith, Inc.*, 827 N. Fourth St., 43952. Tel: 740-283-2484; Fax: 740-283-4011. Email: info@cuf.org. Web: www.cuf.org. Leon J. Suprenant Jr., Pres.
F.I.R.E., Franciscan University, 1235 University Blvd., 43952. Tel: 412-951-0306; Fax: 740-282-4300. Email: jrook@fireministry.org. Web:

fireministry.org. Mr. Jack Rook, Admin. A Catholic Alliance for Faith, Intercession, Repentance, and Evangelism.

**Fraternity of Priests, Inc.*, 100 Belleview Blvd., 43952. Tel: 740-283-4400; Fax: 740-283-3622. Email: contact@fraternityofpriests.org. Web: www.fraternityofpriests.org.

Information & Referral, c/o Catholic Charities, P.O. Box 969, 43952. Tel: 740-282-6880; 800-339-7890; Fax: 740-282-3327. Email: djackson@diosteub.org. Web: www.diosteub.org. Ms. Diana Jackson, Dir.

Lay Employees Pension Plan, P.O. Box 969, 43952. Tel: 740-282-3631; Fax: 740-282-3327.

Marian Manor, Inc., 180 N. Fourth St., 43952. Tel: 740-282-9232; Fax: 740-282-4517. Email: ftsteuben@stratuswave.net. Shirley Miller, Mgr.

**St. Paul Center for Biblical Theology*, 5A Hawthorne Ct., 43952. Tel: 740-284-1778; Fax: 740-284-1825. Dr. Scott Hahn, Pres.

RCIA, P.O. Box 969, 43952. Tel: 740-282-3631; Fax: 740-282-3327. Email: kkemo@diosteub.org. Web: www.diosteub.org. Rev. Msgr. Kurt H. Kemo, J.C.L., V.G., Dir.

**Trinity Time, Inc.*, Prime Time, One Ross Park, 43952-2671. Tel: 740-283-7841; Fax: 740-283-7838.

BEVERLY. *Marriage Encounter, St. Bernard Church*, 307 Seventh St., 45715. Tel: 740-984-2555; Fax: 740-984-2555. Email: kawa4@juno.com. Rev. Msgr. Robert J. Kawa, Dir.

BLOOMINGDALE. *Apostolate for Family Consecration*, John Paul II Holy Family Center, 3375 County Rd. 36, 43910-7903. Tel: 740-765-5500; Fax: 740-765-4941. Email: info@familyland.org. Web: www.familyland.org.

CARROLLTON. *Our Lady of Charity Center Caritas House, Inc.*, 620 Roswell Rd., N.W., 44615. Tel: 330-627-5765; Fax: 304-627-4415. Sr. Mary Annunciata Mason, O.L.C., Prog. Dir.

LITTLE HOCKING. *Boy Scouts*, 5080 School House Rd., 45742. Tel: 740-423-7422; Fax: 740-423-7422. Email: fatherhuffman@netassoc.net. Web: www.stambroseparishohio.org. Rev. David L. Huffman, Dir.

RELIGIOUS INSTITUTES OF MEN REPRESENTED IN THE DIOCESE

For further details refer to the corresponding bracketed number in the Religious Institutes of Men or Women section.

[0680]—*Brothers of the Immaculate Heart of Mary*—I.H.M.

[0230]—*Camaldolese Hermits of the Congregation of Monte Corona*

[]—*Carmelite Missionaries of Mary Immaculate*—C.M.M.I.

[0740]—*Marians of the Immaculate Conception (St. Stanislaus Kostka Province)*—M.I.C.

[]—*The Order of the Sacred & Immaculate Hearts of Jesus & Mary*—O.S.B.

[0560]—*Third Order of Saint Francis. (Sacred Heart Prov.)*—T.O.R.

RELIGIOUS INSTITUTES OF WOMEN REPRESENTED IN THE DIOCESE

[0230]—*Benedictine Sisters of Pontifical Jurisdiction*—O.S.B.

[0370]—*Carmelite Sisters of the Most Sacred Heart of Los Angeles*—O.C.D.

[1070-02]—*Dominican Sisters, Columbus*—O.P.

[1230]—*Franciscan Sisters of Christian Charity, Manitowac, WI*—O.S.F.

[1880]—*Handmaids of the Sacred Heart of Jesus for Reparation*—A.R.

[3073]—*North American Union Sisters of Our Lady of Charity*—O.L.C.

[]—

[2970]—*School Sisters of Notre Dame*—S.S.N.D.

[0500]—*Sisters of Charity of Nazareth*—S.C.N.

[0570]—*Sisters of Charity of Seton Hill, Greensburg, PA*—S.C.

[]—*Sisters of Holy Family of Nazareth*—C.S.F.N.

[]—*Sisters of Holy Nazareth*—H.N.

[]—*Sisters of St. Francis*

[]—*Sisters of St. Francis of Assisi, Milwaukee, WI*

[]—*Sisters of St. Francis of the Martyr St. George*—F.S.G.M.

[1690]—*Sisters of St. Francis, Pittsburgh, PA* (Mt. Alvernia)—O.S.F.

[3840]—*Sisters of St. Joseph of Carondelet*—C.S.J.

[1720]—*Sisters of the Third Order Regular of St. Francis of the Congregation of Our Lady of Lourdes*—O.S.F.

[4160]—*Vincentian Sisters of Charity*—V.S.C.

NECROLOGY

† Pandolfo, Anthony, (Retired)—Died Nov. 6, 2003

Diocese of Stockton

(Dioecesis Stocktoniensis)

Most Reverend

STEPHEN E. BLAIRE, D.D.

Bishop of Stockton; ordained April 29, 1967; appointed Titular Bishop of Lamzella on March 20, 1990; ordained Auxiliary Bishop of Los Angeles May 31, 1990; appointed Bishop of Stockton January 18, 1999. *Office: 1105 N. Lincoln St., Stockton, CA 95203.* Tel: 209-466-0636.

Chancery Office: 1105 N. Lincoln St., Stockton, CA 95203. Tel: 209-466-0636; Fax: 209-941-9722.

Most Reverend

DONALD W. MONTROSE, D.D.

Retired Bishop of Stockton; ordained May 7, 1949; appointed Titular Bishop of Vescovio and Auxiliary of Los Angeles on March 25, 1983; consecrated May 12, 1983; Bishop of Stockton December 19, 1985; installed February 20, 1986; retired January 18, 1999.

ESTABLISHED JANUARY 13, 1962

Square Miles 10,023.

Comprises six Counties in the State of California-viz., Alpine, Calaveras, Mono, San Joaquin, Stanislaus and Tuolumne.

Legal Title: The Roman Catholic Bishop of Stockton, a Corporation Sole.

For legal titles of parishes and diocesan institutions, consult the Chancery Office.

STATISTICAL OVERVIEW

Personnel	
Bishop	1
Retired Bishops	1
Priests: Diocesan Active in Diocese	46
Priests: Diocesan Active Outside Diocese	5
Priests: Retired, Sick or Absent	15
Number of Diocesan Priests	66
Religious Priests in Diocese	15
Total Priests in Diocese	81
Extern Priests in Diocese	15
Permanent Deacons in Diocese	41
Total Brothers	4
Total Sisters	66
Parishes	
Parishes	33
With Resident Pastor:	
Resident Diocesan Priests	29
Resident Religious Priests	4
Missions	10
New Parishes Created	1
Professional Ministry Personnel:	
Brothers	1
Sisters	15
Lay Ministers	47
Welfare	
Catholic Hospitals	3
Total Assisted	332,115
Health Care Centers	1
Total Assisted	2,259
Homes for the Aged	1
Total Assisted	470
Special Centers for Social Services	1
Total Assisted	24,934
Educational	
Diocesan Students in Other Seminaries	9
Total Seminarians	9
High Schools, Diocesan and Parish	2
Total Students	1,574
Elementary Schools, Diocesan and Parish	12
Total Students	3,134
Catechesis/Religious Education:	
High School Students	2,016
Elementary Students	15,529
Total Students under Catholic Instruction	22,262
Teachers in the Diocese:	
Priests	2
Brothers	2
Sisters	3
Lay Teachers	233
Vital Statistics	
Receptions into the Church:	
Infant Baptism Totals	5,879
Adult Baptism Totals	332
Received into Full Communion	1,110
First Communions	3,938
Confirmations	2,946
Marriages:	
Catholic	726
Interfaith	182
Total Marriages	908
Deaths	1,554
Total Catholic Population	194,945
Total Population	1,234,010

Former Bishops—Most Revs. HUGH A. DONOHOE, D.D., Ph.D., ord. June 14, 1930; appt. Titular Bishop of Taium and Auxiliary of San Francisco Aug. 2, 1947; consecrated Oct. 7, 1947; appt. to Stockton Feb. 21, 1962; transferred to Fresno Aug. 27, 1969; died Oct. 26, 1987; MERLIN J. GUILFOYLE, D.D., J.C.D. (Retired), ord. June 10, 1933; appt. Titular Bishop of Bulla and Auxiliary of San Francisco Aug. 15, 1950; consecrated Sept. 21, 1950; translated to Bishop of Stockton Nov. 19, 1969; retired Feb. 26, 1980; died Nov. 20, 1981; ROGER M. MAHONY, D.D., ord. May 1, 1962; appt. Titular Bishop of Tamascani and Auxiliary of Fresno, Jan. 7, 1975; consecrated March 19, 1975; translated Bishop of Stockton Feb. 26, 1980; elevated to Archbishop of Los Angeles July 16, 1985; elevated to Cardinal, June 28, 1991; DONALD W. MONTROSE, D.D. (Retired), ord. May 7, 1949; appt. Titular Bishop of Vescovio and Auxiliary of Los Angeles March 25, 1983; consecrated May 12, 1983; translated Bishop of Stockton Dec. 19, 1985; installed Feb. 20, 1986; retired Jan. 18, 1999.

Chancery Office—1105 N. Lincoln St., Stockton, 95203. Tel: 209-466-0636; Fax: 209-941-9722. Web: www.stocktondiocese.org.

Vicar General—Rev. Msgr. RICHARD J. RYAN, J.C.D., V.G.

Chancellor—Sr. BARBARA THIELLA, S.N.D.deN.

Chief Financial Officer—Mr. DOUG ADEL.

Director of Human Resources—Mrs. COLLEEN BRANAGAN.

Social Action Director—VACANT.

Diocesan Tribunal—1105 N. Lincoln St., Stockton, 95203. Tel: 209-466-0636; Fax: 209-941-9722. Web: stocktondiocese.org.

Judicial Vicar—Very Rev. JOHN J.M. FOSTER, J.C.L.

Vice-Officialis—Rev. Msgr. RICHARD J. RYAN, J.C.D., V.G.

Judges—Rev. DAVID DEIBEL, J.C.L.; Mrs. DEBORAH A. BARTON, J.C.L.; Sr. BEVERLY DUNN, S.P., J.C.D.

Tribunal Personnel—Notaries:: MARY BARTON; DIANE LEWIS; DIANE TARICCO; DEBORAH DEEM.

Defenders of the Bond—Revs. HARMON SKILLIN, J.C.D.; GARY M. LUIZ, C.PP.S., J.C.L.; JOVITO ROLDAN, J.C.L.

College of Consultors/Presbyteral Council—Rev. JOHN P. FALLON, O.S.F.S., Chm.; Rev. Msgr. JOHN ARMISTEAD, Vice Chm.; Revs. LAWRENCE MCGOVERN, S.T.L., Sec. & Treas.; PETER CAROTA; EDITHO MASCARDO; MATTHEW O'DONNELL; KHOI PHAM; IVO ROCHA; Rev. Msgr. RICHARD RYAN, J.C.D., V.G.; Revs. HARMON SKILLIN, J.C.D.; FRANCISCO CAMPECHANO; Most Rev. STEPHEN E. BLAIRE, D.D.

Deans—Revs. WILLIAM C. MOORE, Deanery 1; ALVARO U. ARAQUE, Deanery 2; THOMAS P. HAYES, Deanery 3; RICHARD MORSE, O.S.F.S., Deanery 4; THOMAS MAHENDRAN, Deanery 5; RAMON BEJARANO, Deanery 6; JOSEPH ILLO, Deanery 7; JOHN FITZGERALD, Deanery 8.

The Roman Catholic Welfare Corporation of Stockton—1105 N. Lincoln St., Stockton, 95203. Tel: 209-466-0636; Fax: 209-941-9722.

Diocesan Building Committee—Rev. Msgr. RICHARD J. RYAN, J.C.D., V.G., Chm.; Mr. DOUG ADEL; Very Rev. JOHN J.M. FOSTER, J.C.L.; Mr. HARRY MOORE; Revs. WILLIAM MOORE; RICHARD MORSE, O.S.F.S.; IVO ROCHA.

Diocesan Finance Council—Mr. PAUL SCHAEFER, Chm.; Mr. JOSEPH ARIAS; Mr. DOUG ADEL, Staff; Mr. KEVIN DOUGHERTY; Mr. TOM DRISCOLL; Rev. JOHN P. FALLON, O.S.F.S.; Mr. JOSE LOUIS SOLORIO; Mrs. MARIA STOKMAN; Rev. Msgr. RICHARD RYAN, J.C.D., V.G., Staff.

Personnel Board—Revs. JOSEPH ILLO; JOHN PRUETT, Chm.; HARMON SKILLIN, J.C.D.; LEO SUAREZ; ARMANDO VERGARA; MARK WAGNER; MATTHEW O'DONNELL; Rev. Msgr. RICHARD RYAN.

Diocesan Offices and Directors

Apostleship of the Sea—VACANT. Tel: 209-466-0636.

Catholic Charities—RICHARD FOWLER, 1106 N. El Dorado, Stockton, 95202. Tel: 209-948-1501; Fax: 209-948-2559.

Catholic Youth Organization—Mr. TOM O'NEILL, Sports Dir., 1105 N. Lincoln St., Stockton, 95203. Tel: 209-466-0636.

Cemeteries—Rev. Msgr. JAMES E. CAIN, Dir. (Retired), 1105 N. Lincoln St., Stockton, 95203. Tel: 209-466-0636; Mr. AL VIGIL, Supt. Cemeteries, P.O. Box 1137, Stockton, 95201.

Censor Librorum—VACANT.

Apostolado Hispano—Mrs. DIGNA RAMIREZ-LOPEZ, Dir., 1105 N. Lincoln St., Stockton, 95203. Tel: 209-466-0636.

Development—Mrs. SHARON CAPORUSSO, Dir.

Continuing Education of Clergy—Sr. EMILIE SHENONE, O.P., 1105 N. Lincoln St., Stockton, 95203. Tel: 209-466-0636; Fax: 209-941-9722.

Cursillo Movement-English and Spanish—Rev. ARMANDO VERGARA, Dir.

Ecumenism—Mr. ARTHUR VALDEZ; Deacons RAYMOND FLANDERS; JOHN RYAN.

Office of Religious Education—Sr. GLORIA DEJESUS SANCHEZ, E.F.M.S., Dir., 1105 N. Lincoln St., Stockton, 95203. Tel: 209-466-0636 Contact this office for various CCD Centers.

Office of Special Education—Mrs. YVONNE HARROLD, Dir., 1105 N. Lincoln St., Stockton, 95203. Tel: 209-466-0636 Programs for physically & mentally impaired.

Engaged Encounter—PAT BIVENS; CONNIE BIVENS.

School of Ministry—Sisters DIANE SMITH, Dir., 1105 N. Lincoln St., Stockton, 95203. Tel: 209-466-0636; GRACIELLA MARTINEZ, O.S.F., Hispanic Dir.

Episcopal Liaison of Catholic Charismatic Renewal—WILLIAM BRENNAN, Ph.D., 13 Pardee Ln., Stockton, 95207. Tel: 209-474-0571.

Liturgical Commission—Mr. DAVID SPRINGER, Chm., 1105 N. Lincoln St., Stockton, 95203. Tel: 209-466-0636; Fax: 209-941-9722.

Newman Apostolate— The Newman House at University of the Pacific Revs. ANTHONY SMITH, C.SS.R., Dir., Res.: 4101 N. Manchester, Stockton, 95207. Tel: 209-951-0881; LONACHAN W. AROUJE, All Saints Newman Community at Stanislaus State University, 4040 McKenna Dr., Turlock, 95382. Tel: 209-669-0473.

Office of Catechumenate—Mrs. LINDA HENKEL, Dir., 1105 North Lincoln St., Stockton, 95203. Tel: 209-466-0636.

Permanent Diaconate Program—Deacon JOHN RYAN, Chm., 163 W. Eaton Ave., Tracy, 95376. Tel: 209-835-4560.

Diaconate Formation—Sr. EMILIE SCHENONE, O.P., Dir., 1105 N. Lincoln St., Stockton, 95203. Tel: 209-466-0636.

Pontifical Association of Holy Childhood—VACANT, 1105 N. Lincoln St., Stockton, 95203. Tel: 209-466-0636.

Propagation of the Faith—VACANT, 1105 N. Lincoln St., Stockton, 95203. Tel: 209-466-0636.

Respect Life Office--Community of Caring Program & Natural Family Planning Program—Mrs. NANCY BONNET, Dir., 1105 N. Lincoln St., Stockton, 95203. Tel: 209-466-0636.

Vicar for Religious Women—Sr. ANN VENITA BRITTO, F.C., St. Joseph Convent, 1168 S. Country Club Dr., Stockon, 95204. Tel: 209-466-0636.

Catholic School Office—Sr. MARIAN CLARE VALENTEEN, R.S.M., Supt.; Mr. CHRISTOPHER MARICLE, M.A., Asst. Supt., 1105 N. Lincoln St., Stockton, 95203. Tel: 209-466-0636; Fax: 209-941-9722.

Vocations Director—Sr. WANDA BILLION, 1105 N. Lincoln St., Stockton, 95203. Tel: 209-466-0636.

Office for Worship—Very Rev. JOHN J.M. FOSTER, J.C.L., Dir., 1105 N. Lincoln St., Stockton, 95203. Tel: 209-466-0636.

Office of Youth Ministry—CHRISTIANE ROCELI, English Coord.; JOSE LOPEZ CEJA, Spanish Coord., 1105 N. Lincoln St., Stockton, 95203. Tel: 209-466-0636.

Catholic Committee on Scouting—Ms. JAMIE BURNS, Chm.; Very Rev. JOHN J.M. FOSTER, J.C.L., Chap., 1105 N. Lincoln St., Stockton, 95203. Tel: 209-466-0636.

Migrant Ministry Team—Mr. JOSE LOPEZ-CEJA, Leader; Sisters MARIA J. GARCIA, M.G.Sp.S.; ANTONITA ZAPATA, M.G.Sp.S.; JULIA MORENO, M.G.Sp.S.

Victim Assistance Coordinator—Sr. BARBARA THIELLA, S.N.D.deN. Tel: 209-466-0636. Email: bthiella@stocktondiocese.org.

CLERGY, PARISHES, MISSIONS AND PAROCHIAL SCHOOLS

CITY OF STOCKTON
(SAN JOAQUIN COUNTY)

1—CATHEDRAL OF THE ANNUNCIATION (PASTOR OF) (1944), Rev. Msgr. John M. Armistead. In Res., Very Rev. John J.M. Foster, J.C.L.
Res.: 425 W. Magnolia St., 95203-2412. Tel: 209-463-1305; Fax: 209-463-0807.
School—1110 N. Lincoln St., 95203. Tel: 209-444-4000; Fax: 209-444-4013. Mrs. Carla Donaldson, Prin. Lay Teachers 12; Students 293.
Catechesis/Religious Program—Tel: 209-462-1194. Students 550.

2—ST. BERNADETTE CHURCH (PASTOR OF) (1955), Rev. William C. Moore.
Res.: 2544 Plymouth Rd., 95204. Tel: 209-465-3081; Fax: 209-547-1327.
Catechesis/Religious Program—Students 150.

3—ST. EDWARD CHURCH (PASTOR OF) (1967), (Hispanic), Rev. Leo Suarez, Admin.
Res.: 731 S. Cardinal Ave., 95215. Tel: 209-466-3020; Fax: 209-466-0719.
Catechesis/Religious Program—Students 336.

4—ST. GEORGE CHURCH (PASTOR OF) (1951), Revs. Khoi D. Pham; Rolando Petronio; Jorge W. Arboleda; Deacons Jim Janukites; Don Rodgers; Jesus Aguilar; Kevin Amen; Joe Orzal.
Res.: 120 W. Fifth St., 95206-2695. Tel: 209-463-3413; Fax: 209-463-0167.
School—144 W. Fifth St., 95206. Tel: 209-463-1540; Fax: 209-463-2707. Mr. Alan Cook, Prin. Lay Teachers 10; Students 206.
St. George REALMS Foundation—
Catechesis/Religious Program—Tel: 209-463-3564. Students 588.
Mission—Good Shepherd P.O. Box 354, French Camp, San Joaquin Co. 95231. Tel: 209-982-0578; Fax: 209-858-4836.

5—ST. GERTRUDE CHURCH (PASTOR OF) (1913), (Mexican-American), [CEM] Revs. Alvaro U. Araque; Jose Salvador Ledesma (Spain); Deacons Hector Garza; Louis Juarez.
Res.: 1663 E. Main St., 95205. Tel: 209-466-0278; Fax: 209-466-1927.
School—1701 E. Main St., 95205. Tel: 209-941-0301; Fax: 209-941-4515. Mrs. Olga Rodriguez, Prin. Lay Teachers 8; Students 199.
Catechesis/Religious Program—Tel: 209-941-0501. Students 251.

6—ST. LINUS CHURCH (PASTOR OF) (1965), (Hispanic—Asian), Rev. Gustavo Quintero V. In Res., Rev. Jose Domingo Ruiz.
Res.: 2620 S. B St., 95206. Tel: 209-465-1430; Fax: 209-465-0299.
Catechesis/Religious Program—Students 350.

7—ST. LUKE CHURCH OF STOCKTON (PASTOR OF) (1951), (Vietnamese), Revs. Harmon D. Skillin, J.C.D.; Tuan Nguyen, S.D.B. (Vietnam); Titian A. Miani (Retired); Deacons Joseph Artesi; Haet Tansaeng; Glenn Sell; Ms. Victoria Kimball, Parish Admin.
Res.: 3847 N. Sutter St., 95204. Tel: 209-948-3450; Fax: 209-948-2841.
School—4005 N. Sutter St., 95204. Tel: 209-464-0801; Fax: 209-466-1150. Ms. Pat Simon, Prin. Lay Teachers 14; Students 315.
Catechesis/Religious Program—Tel: 209-462-0410. Students 230.
Convent—230 E. Atlee St., 95204. Tel: 209-463-6533.

8—ST. MARY OF THE ASSUMPTION CHURCH (PASTOR OF) (1851), Revs. Editho Mascardo, Admin.; Misael Aeila; Deacon Julian Sepulveda. In Res., Rev. Jovy Roldan.
Res.: 203 E. Washington St., 95202. Tel: 209-948-0661; Fax: 209-948-0673.
Catechesis/Religious Program—Tel: 209-948-0665. Students 327.

9—ST. MICHAEL CHURCH OF STOCKTON (PASTOR OF) (1921), (Italian), Rev. J. Patrick Walker. In Res., Rev. Msgr. Richard Ryan; Deacon Allen Moznett.
Res.: 5882 N. Ashley Ln., 95215-9308. Tel: 209-931-0639; Fax: 209-931-3621.
Catechesis/Religious Program—Tel: 209-931-2696. Students 296.

10—PRESENTATION CHURCH (PASTOR OF) (1952), Revs. Lawrence McGovern, S.T.L.; Juan Serna, S.T.L.
Res.: 6715 Leesburg Pl., 95207. Tel: 209-472-2150; Fax: 209-472-0541.
School—1635 W. Benjamin Holt Dr., 95207. Tel: 209-472-2140. Diane Rothschild, Prin. Lay Teachers 13; Students 300.
Catechesis/Religious Program—Tel: 209-320-5714. Students 754.

OUTSIDE CITY OF STOCKTON

ANGELS CAMP, CALAVERAS CO., ST. PATRICK CHURCH OF ANGELS CAMP (PASTOR OF) (1856), (Italian), [CEM] [JC] Rev. Eugene D. Trainer; Deacon Adam Pietras.
Res.: P.O. Box 576, 95222. Tel: 209-736-4575; Fax: 209-736-2217.
Catechesis/Religious Program—820 S. Main, 95222. Tel: 209-736-4458. Students 127.
Mission—St. Patrick 619 Sheepranch Rd., Murphys, Murphys Co. 95247. Tel: 209-728-2854.
Mission—Our Lady of the Sierra 1301 Linebaugh Rd., Arnold, Arnold Co. 95223. Tel: 209-795-7625.

CERES, STANISLAUS CO., ST. JUDE CHURCH (PASTOR OF) (1962), (Hispanic), [CEM] Revs. Jose Reyes (Mexico); Jose Trinidad Rodriguez (Mexico); Gilberto Moya (Mexico); Deacon Kenneth Ocninero.
Res.: 3824 Mitchell Rd., 95307-9422. Tel: 209-537-0516; Fax: 209-537-3412.
Catechesis/Religious Program—Tel: 209-537-7439. Students 1,900.

HUGHSON, STANISLAUS CO., ST. ANTHONY CHURCH OF HUGHSON (PASTOR OF) (1921), (Hispanic), [CEM] Revs. Ernesto Arbelaez, S.J., Admin.; Nathan R. White; Deacon Raymond Flanders.
Mailing Address: P.O. Box 909, 95326. Tel: 209-883-4310; Fax: 209-883-2531.
Res.: 2020 Euclid Rd..
Catechesis/Religious Program—Tel: 209-883-2280. Students 378.
Mission—St. Louis [CEM] Floto St., La Grange, Stanislaus Co. 95329. Tel: 209-852-0144; Fax: 209-852-0818. Doris Quinones, Contact Person.

LATHROP, SAN JOAQUIN CO., OUR LADY OF GUADALUPE CHURCH (PASTOR OF), Rev. Dean McFalls; Deacons Art Sanchez; Jeff Vierra; Jim Kottinger.
16019 Cambridge Dr., 95330. Tel: 209-858-9391.

LINDEN, SAN JOAQUIN CO., HOLY CROSS CHURCH (PASTOR OF) (1963), (Italian—Hispanic), Rev. Armando Vergara (Colombia).
Res.: 18633 E. Front St., P.O. Box 52, 95236. Tel: 209-887-3341; Fax: 209-887-2973.
Catechesis/Religious Program—Tel: 209-887-2263. Students 192.

LOCKEFORD, SAN JOAQUIN CO., ST. JOACHIM CHURCH OF LOCKEFORD (PASTOR OF) (1882), (Hispanic), [CEM] Revs. Enda J. Maguire; Jose Domingo Ruiz, Spanish Min.; Deacon Bill Warren.
Mailing Address: P.O. Box 232, 95237. Tel: 209-727-3912; Fax: 209-727-0403.
Catechesis/Religious Program—Tel: 209-334-0743. Students 56.

LODI, SAN JOAQUIN CO., ST. ANNE CHURCH (PASTOR OF) (1904), [CEM] Revs. Thomas P. Hayes; Alfred Alexander, S.S.S.; Jairo H. Ramirez (Colombia); Deacons Juan Mendez; Porfirio Cisneros; Don Bo; Karl Welsbacher.
Mailing Address: P.O. Box 480, 95241. Tel: 209-369-1907; Fax: 209-369-1971.
Office—215 W. Walnut St., 95240.
Res.: 150 S. Pleasant St., 95241.
School—200 S. Pleasant St., 95241. Tel: 209-333-7580. Mr. Dennis Taricco, Prin. Lay Teachers 14; Students 264.
Catechesis/Religious Program—Sisters Catherine Marie Diaz, E.F.M.S., D.R.E.; Isabel de la Eucaristia Abril, E.F.M.S., D.R.E.; Guadalupe Romualdo, E.F.M.S. Students 697.
Mission—Mater Ecclesiae 26500 Sacramento Blvd., Thornton, San Joaquin Co. 95241.

MAMMOTH LAKES, MONO CO., ST. JOSEPH CHURCH OF MAMMOTH LAKES (2002), Rev. Andrew C. Dachauer, S.J.; Bro. Daniel C. Corona, S.J.
Res.: P.O. Box 372, 93546. Tel: 760-934-6276; Fax: 760-934-4047.
Mission—Infant of Prague Mission Church Hwy. 395, Bridgeport, Mono Co. 93517.
Mission—Our Savior of the Mountains 2nd & Mono, Lee Vining, Mono Co. 93541.
Catechesis/Religious Program—Students 135.

MANTECA, SAN JOAQUIN CO., ST. ANTHONY CHURCH OF MANTECA (PASTOR OF) (1917), Revs. Richard E. Morse, O.S.F.S.; Gilberto Arango; Deacon Harvey Parolari.
Res.: 525 E. North St., 95336. Tel: 209-823-7197; Fax: 209-823-5238.
School—Tel: 209-823-4513; Fax: 209-825-7447. Dr. John Black, Prin.; Judy Rosendin, Prin. Sisters 2; Lay Teachers 11; Students 269.
Catechesis/Religious Program—Tel: 209-239-7848. Students 1,384.
St. Vincent de Paul Society—Tel: 209-823-8099.
St. Anthony School Educational Foundation—Tel: 209-239-4513.

MODESTO, STANISLAUS CO.

1—ST. JOSEPH CHURCH OF MODESTO (PASTOR OF) (1967), Revs. Joseph Illo; Francis A. Joseph, O.C.D. (India); Dante U. Dammay (Philippines). In Res., Rev. Theodore Lambert (Sri Lanka).
Res.: 1813 Oakdale Rd., 95355. Tel: 209-551-4973; Fax: 209-551-3213.
Catechesis/Religious Program—Tel: 209-551-0593; Fax: 209-551-2987. Students 935.

2—OUR LADY OF FATIMA CHURCH (PASTOR OF) (1951), Revs. John M. Pruett, V.F.; Hung Nguyen; Alvaro H. Delgado.
Res.: 505 W. Granger Ave., 95350. Tel: 209-524-7421; Fax: 209-524-7713.
School—501 W. Granger Ave., 95350. Tel: 209-524-4170; Fax: 209-524-3960. Linda Partlow, Prin. Lay Teachers 14; Students 250; Extended Day Care 100.
Catechesis/Religious Program—Tel: 209-491-3462. Students 653.
The Monsignor William P. Kennedy Education Foundation:—

3—ST. STANISLAUS CHURCH (PASTOR OF) (2002), Revs. Bill McDonald; Eduardo Perez (Colombia); Jose M. Maghinay; Hector Villegas.
Mailing Address: P.O. Box 292, 95353.
Res.: 709 J St., 95353. Tel: 209-524-4381; Fax: 209-524-1910.
School—1416 Maze Blvd., 95351. Tel: 209-524-9036; Fax: 209-524-4344. Lay Teachers 13; Students 287.
Catechesis/Religious Program—Tel: 209-522-6534;

Fax: 209-523-9128. Students 1,400.

NEWMAN, STANISLAUS CO., ST. JOACHIM CHURCH OF NEWMAN (PASTOR OF) (1909), (Spanish—English), Rev. Lawrence M. Guerrero.
Res.: 1121 Main St., 95360. Tel: 209-862-3528; Fax: 209-862-3512.
Catechesis/Religious Program—Tel: 209-862-2878. Students 430.

OAKDALE, STANISLAUS CO., ST. MARY OF THE ANNUNCIATION CHURCH (PASTOR OF) (1902), Rev. Aloys Conrad Gruber, V.F., Pastor; Deacon Roberto Magdaleno.
Res.: 1225 Olive St., 95361. Tel: 209-847-2715; Fax: 209-847-7348.
Catechesis/Religious Program—Tel: 209-847-3498. Students 280.

PATTERSON, STANISLAUS CO., SACRED HEART CHURCH OF PATTERSON (PASTOR OF) (1917), Rev. Luis Ariel Ramirez, C.M.; Bro. Tom Juneman, C.M.
Res.: 529 I St., 95363. Tel: 209-892-9321; Fax: 209-892-2102.
School—505 M St., 95363. Tel: 209-892-3544; Fax: 209-892-3544. Jason Oliveira, Prin. Lay Teachers 11; Students 212.
Catechesis/Religious Program—Tel: 209-892-6381. Students 426.
Mission—Immaculate Heart of Mary H St., Crows Landing, Stanislaus Co. 95313.

RIPON, SAN JOAQUIN CO., ST. PATRICK CHURCH OF RIPON (PASTOR OF) (1878), Rev. Peter Carota.
Res.: 19399 E St., Rte. 120 Hwy., 95366. Tel: 209-838-2133; Fax: 209-838-1077.
Catechesis/Religious Program—Tel: 209-838-3101. Students 420.

RIVERBANK, STANISLAUS CO., ST. FRANCES OF ROME CHURCH (PASTOR OF) (1953), Revs. Thomas M. Rajanayagam (Sri Lanka); Camilo Garcia (Mexico); Deacon Felipe Vallejo.
Res.: 2827 Topeka St., 95367. Tel: 209-869-2996; Fax: 209-863-1004.
Catechesis/Religious Program—Tel: 209-869-5830. Students 560.

SAN ANDREAS, CALAVERAS CO., ST. ANDREW CHURCH OF SAN ANDREAS (PASTOR OF) (1963), [CEM] Rev. Matthew O'Donnell; Deacon Greg Yeager.
Res.: 162 Church Hill Rd., P.O. Box 550, 95249. Tel: 209-754-3815.
Catechesis/Religious Program—Fax: 209-754-5116. Students 138.
Mission—St. Thomas Aquinas 8398 Lafayette St., Mokelumne Hill, Calaveras Co. 95245.
Mission—Our Lady of Fatima 22581 Hwy. 26, West Point, Calaveras Co. 95255.

SONORA, TUOLUMNE CO., ST. PATRICK CHURCH OF SONORA (PASTOR OF) (1851), [CEM 5] [JC] Revs. William Kraft; Alex Panakal, O.C.D.
Res.: 116 W. Bradford Ave., 95370. Tel: 209-532-7139; Fax: 209-532-4389.
Catechesis/Religious Program—Tel: 209-532-7139, Ext. 105. Students 40.
Mission—Our Lady of Mt. Carmel Cemetery Rd., Big Oak Flat, Tuolumne Co. 95321. Tel: 209-962-2156.
Mission—St. Anne 22518 Church Ln., Columbia, Tuolumne Co. 95310.

TRACY, SAN JOAQUIN CO., ST. BERNARD CHURCH (PASTOR OF) (1908), Revs. Ivo D. Rocha (Portugal); Francisco Campechano (Mexico); Michael Brady; Edwin Musico (Philippines); Deacons John Ryan; Ray Whitlock; Peter Ryza.
Res.: 163 W. Eaton Ave., 95376. Tel: 209-835-4560, Ext. 110; Fax: 209-835-4588.
School—165 W. Eaton Ave., 95376. Tel: 209-835-4560, Ext. 130; Fax: 209-835-2496. Gary Abate, Prin.; Francesca Preston, Curriculum Admin. Lay Teachers 9; Students 267.
Catechesis/Religious Program—Tel: 209-835-4560, Ext. 117. Students 181.
Convent—Daughters of the Cross, 165 W. Eaton Ave., 95376. Tel: 209-835-7391; Fax: 209-830-6137.

TURLOCK, STANISLAUS CO.
1—OUR LADY OF THE ASSUMPTION OF THE PORTUGUESE CHURCH (PASTOR OF) (1973), (Portuguese), Rev. Manuel F. Sousa.
Mailing Address: P.O. Box 2030, 95381. Fax: 209-634-2360.
Res.: 1343 W. Greenway, 95380. Tel: 209-634-2222; 209-634-3140; Fax: 209-634-2366.
Catechesis/Religious Program—Connie Madruga, D.R.E. Students 395.
2—SACRED HEART CHURCH OF TURLOCK (PASTOR OF) (1910), Revs. Mark Wagner; Ramon Bejarano; Patrick Curran.
Res.: 1301 Cooper Ave., 95380. Tel: 209-634-8578; 209-634-8579; Fax: 209-634-7124.
School—1225 Cooper Ave., 95380. Tel: 209-634-7787; Fax: 209-634-0156. Mrs. Donna Noceti, Prin. Lay Teachers 15; Students 272.
School—Preschool, Tel: 209-667-5512; Fax: 209-664-9428. Debra Cannella, Prin. Lay Teachers 12; Students 102.
Catechesis/Religious Program—Sacred Heart Religious Education, 1250 Cooper #1, 95380. Tel: 209-634-5111. Students 1,610.
Convent—674 Oak, 95380. Tel: 209-634-7708.

TWAIN HARTE, TUOLUMNE CO., ALL SAINTS CHURCH (PASTOR OF) (1962), [JC] Rev. John Fitzgerald; Deacon Edward Zoma.
Res.: 18674 Cherokee Dr., P.O. Box 642, 95383. Tel: 209-586-3161; Fax: 209-586-3161.
Catechesis/Religious Program—Students 99.
Mission—St. Joseph Gardner St., Tuolumne, Tuolumne Co. 95379.
Station— Pinecrest. (Summer)
Station— Strawberry. (Winter)

Chaplains of Public Institutions

STOCKTON. *DeWitt Nelson Training Center*, 7650 Newcastle Rd., P.O. Box 213003, 95213-9003. Tel: 209-944-6187. Rev. Randall Rainwater, Chap.
O.H. Close School, 7650 Newcastle Rd., P.O. Box 213002, 95213-9001. Tel: 209-944-6364. Rev. Theodore Lambert, Chap.

FRENCH CAMP. *San Joaquin County Jail*, 999 W. Matthews Rd., 95231. Tel: 209-468-4562. Vacant.
San Joaquin General Hospital, 500 W. Hospital Rd., 95231. Tel: 209-468-6000. St. George Church

JAMESTOWN. *Sierra Conservation Center*, P.O. Box 497, 95327-1213. Tel: 209-984-5291, Ext. 5281. Rev. Ray Abella, O.S.F.S., Chap.

TRACY. *Deuel Vocational Institution*, P.O. Box 400, 95376-3593. Tel: 209-835-4141, Ext. 5076. Sr. Elizabeth O'Keefe, R.S.H.M.

On Duty Outside the Diocese:
Revs.—
Castenada, Mario
Myers, William
O'Neill, Robert
Pintacura, Michael
Silva, Robert J.

Absent on Leave:
Revs.—
Palez, Oscar
Ryan, William

Retired:
Rev. Msgrs.—
Cain, James E., Vicar Gen. Emeritus, 1105 N. Lincoln St., 95203.
Doyle, Walter H., Pastor Emeritus
Hughes, William C., Casa Manana, 3700 N. Sutter St., #272, 95204.
Revs.—
Coghlan, John A., Pastor Emeritus, 1152 De Haro, San Francisco, 94107.
Donohoe, Edward, 5835 Cherokee Rd., #69, 95215.
Ford, William A., St. Mary Star of the Sea, 888 Blvd. of the Arts, #1508, Sarasota, FL 34236.
Johnson, Henry, P.O. Box 2147, Arnold, 95223.
McCaffrey, James Leo, 27 Miramonte Dr., Moraga, 94556.
Miani, Titian A., Casa Manana, 3700 N. Sutter St., #207, 95204.
O'Dwyer, James, Pastor Emeritus, Casa Santa Fe, 24 Dillon St., Clonmel, Ireland.
Pereira, Robert J., P.O. Box 78072, 95267.
Wang, John, 3700 N. Sutter St. #352, 95204.

Permanent Deacons:
Tansaeng, Haet, St. Luke, Stockton
Aguilar, Jesus, St. George, Stockton
Amen, Kevin, St. George, Stockton
Artesi, Joseph, (Retired), St. Luke's, Stockton
Bo, Donald, St. Anne, Lodi
Brennan, William, Newman UOP, Stockton
Broderick, Thomas, School of Ministry, Stockton
Cisneros, Porfirio, St. Anne, Lodi
Flanders, Raymond, St. Anthony, Hughson
Garza, Hector, St. Edward, Stockton
Griego, Nick, St. Patrick, Sonora
Gumerlock, Francis, (Retired), Our Lady of Fatima, Modesto
Janukites, James, St. George, Stockton
Juarez, Louis, St. Gertrude's, Stockton
Kottinger, Jim, St. Anthony, Manteca
Lopez, Isreal, St. Edward's, Stockton
Magdaleno, Roberto, St. Mary, Oakdale
Mendez, Juan, St. Anne, Lodi
Moznett, Al, St. Michael, Stockton
Ochinero, Kenneth, St. Jude's, Ceres
Orzal, Joe, St. George, Stockton
Parolari, Harvey, St. Anthony, Manteca
Pietras, Adam, St. Patrick, Angel's Camp
Reyes, Jose, St. Stanislaus, Modesto
Rodgers, Donald, Good Shepherd, French Camp
Ryan, John G., St. Bernard, Tracy
Ryza, Peter, St. Bernard's, Tracy
Sanchez, Arturo, Our Lady of Guadalupe, Lathrop
Santiago, Edwin, Our Lady of the Assumption, Turlock
Sell, William (Glenn), St. Luke's, Stockton
Sepulveda, Julian R., St. Mary of the Assumption, Stockton
Torres, Jorge, St. Edward, Stockton
Vallejo, Felipe, St. Frances of Rome, Riverbank
Vierra, Jeffrey, St. Anthony, Manteca
Warren, William E., St. Joachim, Lockeford
Welsbacher, Karl, St. Anne, Lodi
Whitlock, Ray, St. Bernard, Tracy
Wofford, Michael, Cathedral of Annunciation, Stockton
Yeager, Gregory, St. Andrews, San Andreas
Zoma, Edward T., All Saints, Twain Harte

INSTITUTIONS LOCATED IN THE DIOCESE

[A] HIGH SCHOOLS, DIOCESAN

STOCKTON. *St. Mary's High School*, 5648 N. El Dorado St., P.O. Box 7247, 95267-0247. Tel: 209-957-3340; Fax: 209-957-0861. Email: jfallon@saintmaryshighshool.org. Web: www.saintmaryshighschool.org. Rev. John P. Fallon, O.S.F.S., Pres.; Mr. Peter Morelli, Prin.; Rev. Clark T. Kelley, O.S.F.S.; Bros. James Dorazio, O.S.F.S.; Neil McMenamin, O.S.F.S. Nonresident students. Priests 2; Brothers 2; Sisters 1; Lay Teachers 60; Students 1,125.
St. Mary's High School Foundation Tel: 209-957-3340; Fax: 209-957-0861.

MODESTO. *Central Catholic High School*, 200 S. Carpenter Rd., 95351. Tel: 209-524-9611; Fax: 209-524-5646. Email: jehardee@cchsca.org. Web: www.cchsca.org. Mr. Jim Pecchenino, Pres. Nonresident students. Lay Teachers 29; Administrators 5; Students 449.
Central Catholic High School Foundation Tel: 209-524-6822; Fax: 209-524-5646.

[B] CATHOLIC CHARITIES

STOCKTON. *The Catholic Charities of the Diocese of Stockton*, 1106 N. El Dorado St., 95202. Tel: 209-948-1501; 209-444-5900; Fax: 209-948-2559; 209-444-5933. Email: rfowler@catholiccharitiesstk.org. Oscar Anzaldo, Chm. Corp. Bd.
San Joaquin County Senior Services, 1106 N. El Dorado St., 95202. Juliana Homan, Prog. Dir. Friendly Visiting, Homemaker (Housekeeping), Personal Care, Respite Care Program, Home Security & Fall Prevention. Clients 350.
Basic Needs Services Clients 18,730.
1106 N. El Dorado St., 95202. Tel: 209-444-5900.
Making the Right Decision, 1106 N. El Dorado St., 95202. Tel: 209-858-4834. Sr. Gladys Guenther, S.H.F., Prog. Dir. (Youth Services/Gang Prevention Program.); Summer enrichment programs involve: working with children on social, cultural, academic, and recreational activities; weekly field trips presentations by local community groups and leaders. Clients 800.
Immigration & Refugee Services Program, 1106 N. Eldorado St., 95202. Tel: 209-444-5910; Fax: 209-460-1624. Madalene Kirkconnell, Co-Dir.; Sr. Judith McDonnell, Co-Dir. Naturalization/Citizenship, Green Card Renewal/Replacement, Special Case Waivers, Adjustment of Status, Family Immigration and Affidavit of Support Clients 1,371.
Emergency Food Distribution, 1106 N. El Dorado, 95202. Tel: 209-466-4210; Fax: 209-948-2559. Allen Nesset, Coord.
Stanislaus County Senior Services, 400 12th St., Ste. 4, Modesto, 95354. Tel: 209-529-3784; Fax: 209-529-6083. Jane Weinheimer, Prog. Dir. Homemaker Program, Long Term Care Ombudsman Program, Senior Transportation, Elder Abuse Program, Elder Care Management, Home Repair, Social Security Representative Payee Program, Stanislaus Elder Abuse Prevention Alliance, Senior Network Advocacy Program Clients 3,843.
Mother Lode - Long Term Care Ombudsman Program, 14855 Mono Way, Ste. 105, Sonora, 95370. Tel: 209-532-7632; Fax: 209-532-8448. Clients 2,362.

[C] GENERAL HOSPITALS

STOCKTON. *St. Joseph's Behavioral Health Center* dba Catholic Healthcare West , 2510 N. California St., 95204. Tel: 209-948-2100; Fax: 209-464-2270. Web: www.stjosephscares.org. Jim Sondecker, Pres. Sponsored by the Sisters of the Third Order of St. Dominic, Congregation of the Most Holy Name, San Rafael, CA. Bed Capacity 35; Total Assisted Annually 2,259; Total Staff 93.
St. Joseph's Medical Center of Stockton dba Catholic Healthcare West , 1800 N. California St.,

95204-9008. Tel: 209-943-2000; Fax: 209-461-3299. Web: www.stjosephscares.org. Donald J. Wiley, Pres. Sisters 2; Bed Capacity 323; Total Assisted Annually 295,703; Total Staff 2,366.

MANTECA. *St. Dominic's Hospital* dba Catholic Healthcare West , 1777 W. Yosemite Ave., 95337. Tel: 209-825-3500; Fax: 209-825-3524. Web: www.stdominicscares.org. Margaret Hepburn, Pres. Bed Capacity 83; Total Assisted Annually 34,153; Total Staff 314.

[D] HOMES FOR AGED

STOCKTON. *Casa Manana Inn*, 3700 N. Sutter St., 95204. Tel: 209-466-4046; Fax: 209-466-3450. Chris Burnett, Mgr. Total in Residence 162; Total Staff 3.

St. Joseph's Regional Housing Corp., 3400 Wagner Heights Rd., 95209. Tel: 209-956-3400; Fax: 209-952-6201. Email: info@oconnorwoods.org. Web: www.oconnorwoods.org.

O'Connor Woods Housing Corp., 3400 Wagner Heights Rd., 95209. Tel: 209-956-3400; Fax: 209-952-6201.

O'Connor Woods, A Calif. Corp., 3400 Wagner Heights Rd., 95209. Tel: 209-956-3400; Fax: 209-952-6201. E. G. Schroeder, Pres. and CEO; R. Scot Sinclair, Exec. Dir. St. Joseph's Regional Housing Corp., sponsored by the Sisters of the Third Order of St. Dominic, Congregation of the Most Holy Name, provides a residential community for seniors offering a variety of living arrangements from active to assisted, skilled and rehabilitation services. This non-profit Corporation operates O'Connor Woods, Garden Oaks, Oak Creek and Meadowood Health and Rehabilitation Center. St. Joseph's Medical Center provides management and support functions for this Corporation. Total Assisted Annually 470; Total Staff 290.

[E] CONVENTS AND RESIDENCES FOR SISTERS

STOCKTON. *Daughters of the Holy Spirit*, St. Gertrude Convent, 1655 E. Main St., 95205. Tel: 209-941-4515. Email: sfriedicg@aol.com. Sisters 3.

Eucharistic Franciscan Missionary Sisters, 1205 N. San Joaquin St., 95202. Tel: 209-462-3906; Fax: 209-469-3759. Sisters 4.

Holy Cross Sisters, Casita Esperanza, P.O. Box 9, 95201. Tel: 209-467-8042.

Maryknoll Sisters, 25 S. Commerce St., No. 237, 95202. Tel: 209-462-9394.

Sacro Costato Missionary Sisters, St. Luke's Convent, 230 E. Atlee St., 95204. Tel: 209-462-6533; Fax: 209-464-5342. Email: mscstockton@aol.com. Sisters 4.

Sisters of Notre Dame de Namur, 1105 N. Lincoln, 95203. Tel: 209-466-0636; Fax: 209-941-9722. Email: BThiella@stocktondiocese.org.

Sisters of St. Joseph of Carondelet, 411 E. Walnut St., 95204. Tel: 209-462-8486.

MODESTO. *Sisters of the Cross of the Sacred Heart of Jesus* Cloistered Convent. , 1320 Maze Blvd., 95351. Tel: 209-526-3525; Fax: 209-526-3525. Email: rcscjmodesto@hotmail.com. Web: www.sistersofthecross.org. Sisters 12.

PATTERSON. *Daughters of the Holy Spirit* Sacred Heart Convent. , 503 M St., 95363. Tel: 209-892-3410. Email: samdhs@juno.com. Sisters 3.

TRACY. *The Daughters of the Cross*, St. Bernard Convent, 165 W. Eaton Ave., 95376. Tel 209-835-7391; Fax: 209-830-6137. Email: fc1833@inreach.com. Sisters 6.

TURLOCK. *Sisters of the Sacred Hearts of Jesus and Mary* Sacred Heart Convent , 674 Oak St., 95380. Tel: 209-634-7708; Fax: 209-634-7124.

[F] RETREAT CENTERS

COPPEROPOLIS. *Madonna of Peace Renewal Center* (Youth Facility) , 2010 Hunt Rd., P.O. Box 71, 95228. Tel: 209-785-2157 (Office); Fax: 209-785-2157; 209-785-2157. Total in Residence 2; Total Staff 2.

[G] MISCELLANEOUS

STOCKTON. *The Bishop's Educational Foundation, Diocese of Stockton*, 1105 N. Lincoln St., 95203. Tel: 209-466-0636; Fax: 209-941-9722.

Instituto Fe y Vida, 1737 W. Benjamin Holt Dr., 95207. Tel: 209-951-3483; Fax: 209-478-5357. Email: info@feyvida.org. Web: www.feyvida.org. Total Staff 6.

St. Mary's High School Foundation, Box 7247, 95267-0247. Tel: 209-957-3340; Fax: 209-957-0861. Email: jfallon@saintmaryshighschool.org. Web: www.saintmaryshighschool.org.

The O'Connor Foundation of San Joaquin Co., 1800 N. California St., 95204. Tel: 209-943-2000; Fax: 209-461-3299. Email: dwiley@chw.edu.

San Lorenzo Ruiz De Manila (1988), Filipino Plaza, 6 West Main St., Ste. 1, 95202. Tel: 209-464-8572; Fax: 209-546-0191. Email: rubanusa@aol.com. Web: www.rubanusa.com.

LODI. *St. Anne's Endowment*, 215 W. Walnut St., 95240. Tel: 209-369-1907; Fax: 209-369-1971.

MANTECA. *St. Vincent de Paul Society*, 525 E. North St., 95336. Tel: 209-823-8099. P.O. Box 1644, 95336. Total Staff 25; Total Assisted 13,000.

MODESTO. *The Catholic Social Service Guild*, 2805 Schiphol Ln., 95356. Tel: 209-577-5017. Liz Cottrell, Pres.

Central Catholic High School Foundation, 200 Carpenter Rd., 95351. Tel: 209-524-6822; Fax: 209-524-5846. Volunteer Board Members 25.

Father John C. Silva Education Foundation, P.O. Box 292, 95353. Tel: 209-524-4381; Fax: 209-524-1910.

The Monsignor William P. Kennedy Education Foundation, 501 W. Granger Ave., 95350. Tel: 209-524-4170; Fax: 209-524-7713.

TURLOCK. *The McElligott Sacred Heart School Foundation*, 1225 Cooper St., 95380-4113. Tel: 209-634-7787; Fax: 209-634-0156. Email: dnocetishs@hotmail.com. Rev. Mark Wagner, Dir. Total Students 271; Total Staff 28.

RELIGIOUS INSTITUTES OF MEN REPRESENTED IN THE DIOCESE

For further details refer to the corresponding bracketed number in the Religious Institutes of Men or Women section.

[0260]—*Discalced Carmelite Friars*—O.C.D

[0690]—*Jesuit Fathers and Brothers* California, Columbia Prov.)—S.J.

[0910]—*Oblates of Mary Immaculate*—O.M.I.

[0920]—*Oblates of St. Francis De Sales* (Toledo-Detroit Prov.)—O.S.F.S.

[1070]—*Redemptorist Fathers*—C.SS.R.

[1190]—*Salesians of St. John Bosco*—S.D.B.

[0975]—*Society of Our Lady of the Most Holy Trinity*—S.O.L.T.

[]—*Vincentian Fathers*

RELIGIOUS INSTITUTES OF WOMEN REPRESENTED IN THE DIOCESE

[1920]—*Congregation of the Sisters of the Holy Cross* (Notre Dame, IN)—C.S.C.

[0770]—*Daughters of the Cross*

[0780]—*Daughters of the Cross of Liege*—F.C.

[0820]—*Daughters of the Holy Spirit* (Putnam, CT)—D.H.S.

[1070-04]—*Dominican Sisters* (San Rafael)—O.P.

[1150]—*Eucharistic Franciscan Missionary Sisters*—E.F.M.S.

[1845]—*Guadalupan Missionaries of the Holy Spirit*—M.G.Sp.S.

[]—*Holy Family Sisters*

[2470]—*Maryknoll Sisters of St. Dominic*—M.M.

[]—*Missionary Sisters of the Sacred Side of Jesus and the Sorrowful Mother* (Italy)—M.S.C.

[3465]—*Religious of the Sacred Heart of Mary*—R.S.H.M.

[]—*Sisters for Christian Community*—S.F.C.C.

[2575]—*Sisters of Mercy of the Americas*—R.S.M.

[3000]—*Sisters of Notre Dame de Namur*—S.N.D.deN.

[3340]—*Sisters of Providence*—S.P.

[]—*Sisters of St. Francis of Mary Immaculate*—O.S.F.

[3840]—*Sisters of St. Joseph of Carondelet*—C.S.J.

[3830-03]—*Sisters of St. Joseph of Orange*—C.S.J.O.

[]—*Sisters of the Cross of the Sacred Heart of Jesus* (Tijuana, Mexico)—R.C.S.C.J.

[1960]—*Sisters of the Holy Family* (San Francisco)—S.H.F.

[3680]—*Sisters of the Sacred Hearts of Jesus and Mary*—S.H.J.M.

[]—*Sisters of the Third Order of St. Francis of Perpetual Adoration*

[4070]—*Society of the Sacred Heart*—R.S.C.J.

[]—*St. Francis Province*—O.S.F.

DIOCESAN CEMETERIES AND MAUSOLEUMS

STOCKTON. *San Joaquin Cemetery and Mausoleum* Mr. Al Vigil, Supt.

ESCALON. *St. John Cemetery* Cynthia A. Rodriguez, Office Mgr.

MODESTO. *St. Stanislaus Cemetery and Chapel Crypts* Gretchen Storm, Office Mgr.

NECROLOGY

† Escobar, Octavio, Ceres, CA St. Jude's Church—Died March 12, 2003

† Mannion, B. Joseph, (Retired)—Died Jan. 22, 2003

† Prendergast, Francis, Turlock, CA Sacred Heart Church—Died Feb. 4, 2003

Diocese of Superior

(Dioecesis Superiorensis)

Most Reverend

RAPHAEL M FLISS, D.D.

Bishop of Superior; ordained May 26, 1956; appointed Coadjutor Bishop of Superior with right of succession November 6, 1979; ordained December 20, 1979; succeeded to See, June 27, 1985. *Res.: 1 Gitchinadji Dr., Superior, WI 54880. Office: 1201 Hughitt Ave., Superior, WI 54880. Box 969, Superior, WI 54880.*

Chancery Office: 1201 Hughitt Ave., Box 969, Superior, WI 54880. Tel: 715-392-2937; Fax: 715-395-3149.

ESTABLISHED MAY 3, 1905

Square Miles 15,715.

Comprises the Counties of Ashland, Barron, Bayfield, Burnett, Douglas, Iron, Lincoln, Oneida, Polk, Price, Rusk, Sawyer, St. Croix, Taylor, Vilas and Washburn in the State of Wisconsin.

Incorporated under the laws of the State of Wisconsin as the Diocese of Superior.

For legal titles of parishes and diocesan institutions, consult the Chancery.

STATISTICAL OVERVIEW

Personnel	
Bishop	1
Priests: Diocesan Active in Diocese	42
Priests: Diocesan Active Outside Diocese	1
Priests: Retired, Sick or Absent	30
Number of Diocesan Priests	73
Religious Priests in Diocese	12
Total Priests in Diocese	85
Extern Priests in Diocese	3
Ordinations:	
Diocesan Priests	1
Permanent Deacons	5
Permanent Deacons in Diocese	56
Total Brothers	1
Total Sisters	102
Parishes	
Parishes	112
With Resident Pastor:	
Resident Diocesan Priests	40
Resident Religious Priests	5
Without Resident Pastor:	
Administered by Priests	62
Administered by Religious Women	1
Administered by Lay People	4
Professional Ministry Personnel:	
Sisters	8
Lay Ministers	33
Welfare	
Catholic Hospitals	7
Total Assisted	286,756
Health Care Centers	1
Homes for the Aged	22
Total Assisted	214
Day Care Centers	2
Total Assisted	162
Special Centers for Social Services	6
Total Assisted	530
Residential Care of Disabled	19
Total Assisted	194
Other Institutions	16
Total Assisted	890
Educational	
Diocesan Students in Other Seminaries	7
Total Seminarians	7
Elementary Schools, Diocesan and Parish	17
Total Students	2,715
Catechesis/Religious Education:	
High School Students	3,329
Elementary Students	7,343
Total Students under Catholic Instruction	13,394
Teachers in the Diocese:	
Brothers	1
Sisters	8
Lay Teachers	156
Vital Statistics	
Receptions into the Church:	
Infant Baptism Totals	959
Adult Baptism Totals	245
Received into Full Communion	143
First Communions	1,265
Confirmations	1,106
Marriages:	
Catholic	254
Interfaith	194
Total Marriages	448
Deaths	1,231
Total Catholic Population	83,622
Total Population	431,544

Former Bishops—Rt. Revs. AUGUSTIN FRANCIS SCHINNER, D.D., ord. March 7, 1886; consecrated July 25, 1905; resigned Jan. 15, 1913; appt. Bishop of Spokane, WA, March 18, 1914; died Feb. 7, 1937; JOSEPH M. KOUDELKA, D.D., ord. Oct. 8, 1875; consecrated Auxiliary Bishop of Cleveland and Titular Bishop of Germanicopolis, Feb. 25, 1908; transferred to Milwaukee as Auxiliary Bishop, Sept. 4, 1911; appt. to the See of Superior, Aug. 6, 1913; died June 24, 1921; JOSEPH G. PINTEN, D.D. (Retired), ord. Nov. 1, 1890; elected Dec. 3, 1921; consecrated May 3, 1922; transferred to the See of Grand Rapids, June 25, 1926; retired Nov. 1, 1940; died Nov. 6, 1945; Most Revs. THEODORE H. REVERMAN, D.D., ord. July 26, 1901; consecrated Nov. 30, 1926; died July 18, 1941; WILLIAM PATRICK O'CONNOR, D.D., Ph.D., ord. March 10, 1912; consecrated March 7, 1942; transferred to the See of Madison, Jan. 15, 1946; ALBERT GREGORY MEYER, S.S.L., D.D., ord. July 11, 1926; appt. Feb. 18, 1946; consecrated April 11, 1946; promoted to Archbishop of Milwaukee, July 21, 1953; transferred to Archbishop of Chicago, Sept. 19, 1958; created Cardinal, Dec. 14, 1959; died April 9, 1965; JOSEPH JOHN ANNABRING, D.D., ord. May 3, 1927; appt. Jan. 27, 1954; consecrated March 25, 1954; died Aug. 27, 1959; GEORGE A. HAMMES, D.D. (Retired), Bishop Emeritus of Superior; appt. March 28, 1960; consecrated May 24, 1960; retired June 27, 1985; died April 11, 1993.

Chancery—1201 Hughitt Ave., Box 969, Superior, 54880. Tel: 715-392-2937; Fax: 715-392-2015.

Vicar General—Very Rev. DANIEL J. DAHLBERG, V.G., Office, 1410 Baxter Ave., Superior, 54880. Tel: 715-392-8511; Fax: 715-392-3457.

Moderator of the Curia—Very Rev. PHILIP J. HESLIN.

Chancellor—Sr. EILEEN LANG, F.S.P.A., D.Min.

Secretary to Bishop—Mrs. PATRICIA WILDENBERG.

Diocesan Tribunal—

Judicial Vicar—Very Rev. JAMES F. TOBOLSKI, J.C.L.

Adjutant Judicial Vicar—Rev. JAMES P. POWERS, J.C.L.

Promoter of Justice— Appointed by case

Defender of the Bond—Rev. WILLIAM G. HORATH.

Procurator and Advocate—Sr. RITA M. SCHNEIDER, S.S.N.D.

Notary and Secretary—Mrs. PATTI J. HOLT.

Vicar for Canonical Affairs—Very Rev. JAMES F. TOBOLSKI, J.C.L.

Vicar for Religious—Sr. EILEEN LANG, F.S.P.A.

Diocesan Pastoral Council—Most Rev. RAPHAEL M. FLISS, D.D., Pres. South Central Deanery:: MICHAEL DOWNEY; GLENN HARDER; NANCY KUKSTIS. Eastern Deanery:: RUTH ANN JOHNSON; RANDY SAMUELSON, Chm.; CAROL PLUTA; JAMES ROBINSON. Northwest Deanery:: JEAN CALCAGNO; MARY LU GALLAGHER; LYNN KRAUSE, Vice Chm. North Central Deanery:: CECILIA GEORGE; THOMAS HENKE; CHERYL ROCKENBACH. Southwest Deanery:: KENNETH SCHAEFER; TIMOTHY HEFFERNAN; BETTY LISKA; Deacon PHILIP L. MARTINEAU, Bishop's Appointee. Ex Officio Members:: Very Revs. DANIEL J. DAHLBERG, V.G.; PHILIP J. HESLIN; Sisters PAT CORMACK, S.C.S.C.; THERESA SANDOK, O.S.M.; EILEEN LANG, F.S.P.A., Liaison.

Deaneries and Deans—Northwest Deanery: Very Rev. DEAN T. BUTTRICK. Southwest Deanery: Very Rev. JOHN A. DRUMMY. North Central Deanery: Very Rev. ROBERT E. O'CONNELL. South Central Deanery: Very Rev. JAMES J. JACKSON. East Deanery: Very Rev. JAMES A. HOFFMAN.

Pastoral Consultors—Very Rev. JOHN A. DRUMMY; Revs. WILLIAM H. GREEN; GERALD P. HARRIS; DAVID P. OBERTS.

Presbyteral Council & Diocesan Consultors—Most Rev. RAPHAEL M. FLISS, D.D., Pres.; Very Revs. PHILIP J. HESLIN; DANIEL J. DAHLBERG, V.G., Vice Chm.; Rev. PETER F. SZLESZINSKI, Treas.; Very Rev. DEAN T. BUTTRICK; Rev. MICHAEL L. CRISP; Very Rev. JOHN A. DRUMMY; Revs. JOHN EATON, O.F.M.; JOHN R. GERRITTS; KEVIN M. GORDON; MICHAEL T. HAYDEN; ROBERT J. KOSZAREK.

Personnel Placement Board—Revs. DAVID P. OBERTS, Chm.; JOHN C. ANDERSON; KEVIN M. GORDON; GERALD P. HARRIS; GREGORY J. HOPEFL; Very Rev. JAMES F. TOBOLSKI, J.C.L.

Conciliation and Arbitration Board—THOMAS DUFFY, Chm.; REBECCA JEAN ECK; Rev. DAVID P. OBERTS; RAYMOND RYNDA; Sr. RITA M. SCHNEIDER, S.S.N.D., Sec.

Diocesan Offices and Directors

Bureau of Information—JULIE GODFREY MILLER, Dir., 1512 N. 12th St., P.O. Box 969, Superior, 54880. Tel: 715-392-8268.

Catholic Charities Bureau—Mr. BRIAN SOLAND, M.A., Exec. Dir., Office, 1416 Cummings Ave., Superior, 54880. Tel: 715-394-6617; Fax: 715-394-5951.

Catholic Boy and Girl Scout—Rev. THOMAS E. THOMPSON, P.O. Box 399, Osceola, 54020. Tel: 715-294-2243; Fax: 715-294-2495.

Catholic Mutual Group—PAUL ALTMANN, Claims/Risk Mgr., 1201 Hughitt Ave., P.O. Box 969, Superior, 54880. Tel: 715-392-2937, Ext. 122.

Catholic Women, Council of—Rev. PHILIP J. JUZA, Moderator, Office, 315 E. Davlin St., Gilman, 54433. Tel: 715-452-5374; DIANA MAKI, Pres., P.O. Box 191, Woodruff, 54568. Tel: 715-356-2645.

Charismatic Renewal Liaison—Deacon MICHAEL D. CULLEN, 513 State Rd., Rib Lake, 54470. Tel: 715-427-5259; Sr. CASIMIRA BENBENEK, O.S.M., Assoc. Liaison, 1002 N. Bridget St., Tomahawk, 54487. Tel: 715-453-8090.

Christian Formation—RICHARD W. LYONS, Dir., 1201 Hughitt Ave., P.O. Box 969, Superior, 54880. Tel: 715-392-2937, Ext. 103.

Diocesan Coordinator of Health Affairs—Rev. KEVIN GORDON, 1201 Hughitt Ave., P.O. Box 969, Superior, 54880. Tel: 715-392-2937, Ext. 134.

Diocesan Sisters Council—Sr. MARY BERNICE VANDERLOOP, O.S.M., Pres., 1000 College Ave., W., Ladysmith, 54848. Tel: 715-532-3364.

Ecumenical Commission—Very Rev. JAMES F. TOBOLSKI, J.C.L., P.O. Box 969, Superior, 54880. Tel: 715-392-2937, Ext. 107.

Evangelization, Office of—Sr. EILEEN LANG, F.S.P.A.,

Dir., P.O. Box 969, Superior, 54880. Tel: 715-392-2937, Ext. 104.

Finance, Department of—VIRGIL S. VAVRA, Dir., 1201 Hughitt Ave., P.O. Box 969, Superior, 54880. Tel: 715-392-7571, Ext. 121.

Holy Childhood Association—Rev. GREGORY J. HOPEFL, Dir., 13891 Mission Rd, Stone Lake, 54876. Tel: 715-865-3669.

Insurance/Employee Benefits and Payroll, Office of—CINDY GRONSKI, Dir., 1201 Hughitt Ave., P.O. Box 969, Superior, 54880. Tel: 715-392-7571, Ext. 130.

Newman Apostolate— Superior: Newman and Young Adult Ministry Center, University of Wisconsin Mr. PAUL BIRCH, Coord. of Ministry, 823 N. 16th Ave., Superior, 54880. Tel: 715-394-7710. St. Thomas More Newman Center,: THOMAS J. WEISS, Coord., Newman Ministry, 423 E. Cascade Ave., River Falls, 54022. Tel: 715-425-7234; Fax: 715-425-6959. Email: thomasjweiss@uwrf.edu.

Catholic Herald, Superior Edition—JULIE GODFREY MILLER, Editor, 1512 N. 12th St., P.O. Box 969, Superior, 54880. Tel: 715-392-8268. Res.: 1714 E. 8th St., Duluth, MN 55812. Tel: 218-724-4486.

Parish Accounting, Office of—CINDY GRONSKI, Contact, 1201 Hughitt Ave., P.O. Box 969, Superior, 54880. Tel: 715-392-7571, Ext. 130.

Pastoral Services, Department of—RICHARD W. LYONS, Dir., 1201 Hughitt Ave., P.O. Box 969, Superior, 54880. Tel 715-392-2937, Ext. 103.

Planning, Office of—RICHARD W. LYONS, Dir., 1201 Hughitt Ave., P.O. Box 969, Superior, 54880. Tel: 715-392-2937, Ext. 103.

Permanent Diaconate—Deacon TIMOTHY J. KUEHN, Dir., P.O. Box 969, 1201 Hughitt Ave., Superior, 54880. Tel: 715-392-2937, Ext. 117.

Respect Life Office—RUTH SCHIMKE, Dir. W13066 South St., Lublin, 54447. Tel: 715-669-7353.

Propagation of the Faith—Rev. GREGORY J. HOPEFL, 13891 Mission Rd., Stone Lake, 54876 Tel: 715-865-3669.

Radio and Television—JULIE GODFREY MILLER, Dir., 1512 N. 12th St., P.O. Box 969, Superior, 54880. Tel: 715-392-8268.

The Bishop George A. Hammes Center for Religious Education and Youth Ministry—Deacon ROGER CADOTTE, Dir., 315 W. Fifth St., P.O. Box 280, Haugen, 54841. Tel: 715-234-5044; Fax: 715-234-5241.

St. Pius Priest Fund— Bd. of Dirs.: Most Rev. RAPHAEL M. FLISS, D.D., Pres.; Revs. DENNIS MULLEN, Vice Pres.; PETER F. SZLESZINSKI, Treas.; JAMES P. POWERS, J.C.L., Sec.; JOHN C. ANDERSON; JAMES J. BRINKMAN; WILLIAM H. GREEN; DENNIS T. MEULEMANS (Retired); DAVID P. OBERTS; WILLIAM J. MURPHY; JOHN J. SPANJERS (Retired).

Stewardship and Development, Department of—Mr. STEVEN P. TARNOWSKI, Dir., 1201 Hughitt Ave., P.O. Box 969, Superior, 54880. Tel: 715-392-2937, Ext. 123; Fax: 715-392-2015.

Superintendent of Schools—PHYLLIS SCHLAGEL, Office, 1201 Hughitt Ave., P.O. Box 969, Superior, 54880. Tel: 715-392-1042, Ext. 115.

Victim Assistance Coordinator—BARBARA DICKENSON, M.S.W. Tel: 715-398-7765. Email: tgd56@aol.com.

Vocations, Office of—Rev. ANDREW P. RICCI, Dir., 409 Summit St., Spooner, 54801. Tel: 715-635-3105.

Office of Worship—Rev. GABRIEL BALTES, O.S.B., Dir., 1201 Hughitt Ave., P.O. Box 969, Superior, 54880. Tel: 715-392-2937, Ext. 145.

CLERGY, PARISHES, MISSIONS AND PAROCHIAL SCHOOLS

CITY OF SUPERIOR
(DOUGLAS COUNTY)

1—CATHEDRAL OF CHRIST THE KING (1886), [CEM] Very Rev. Daniel J. Dahlberg, V.G., Rector; Rev. Leon Flaherty, C.P.P.S.; Deacon Arthur Gil de Lamadrid.
Mailing Address: 1410 Baxter Ave., 54880.
Church: Belknap Ave. & Grand, 54880. Tel: 715-392-8511; Fax: 715-392-3457.
School—Cathedral School, 1419 Baxter Ave., 54880. Tel: 715-392-2976; Fax: 715-392-2977. Timothy Johnson, Prin. Lay Teachers 16; Students 290.
Catechesis/Religious Program—Janette Gil de Lamadrid, D.R.E. Students 233.

2—ST. ANTHONY (1870),, Also serves St. Anthony, Lake Nebagamon. Very Rev. Dean T. Buttrick; Deacon Timothy J. Kuehn.
Church & Mailing Address: 4315 E. 3rd St., 54880. Tel: 715-398-3261; Fax: 715-398-3257.
Catechesis/Religious Program—Annette Minter, D.R.E. Students 76.

3—SS. CYRIL AND METHODIUS, (Slovak), Closed., For inquiries for sacramental records contact Cathedral of Christ the King.

4—ST. FRANCIS XAVIER (1853), [CEM] Very Rev. James F. Tobolski, J.C.L.; Deacon Philip Martineau.
Church and Mailing Address: 2316 E. 4th St., 54880. Tel: 715-398-7174; Fax: 715-398-3074.
Catechesis/Religious Program—Ernest Swartz, D.R.E. Students 198.

5—HOLY ASSUMPTION OF THE B.V.M. (1891),, (Also serves St. William, Superior). Rev. Ronald Olson, O.F.M.Conv.; Deacon Robert J. Chammings.
Church & Mailing Address: 5601 Tower Ave., 54880. Tel: 715-394-7919; Fax: 715-394-4883.
Catechesis/Religious Program—Tel: 715-394-4883. Kathy Drinkwine, D.R.E. Students 106.

6—ST. LOUIS, Closed., For inquiries for sacramental records contact Cathedral of Christ the King.

7—ST. PATRICK, Closed., For inquiries for sacramental records contact Cathedral of Christ the King.

8—ST. STANISLAUS, (Polish), Closed., For inquiries for sacramental records contact Cathedral of Christ the King.

9—ST. WILLIAM (1908), [CEM] Rev. Ronald Olson, O.F.M.Conv.; Deacon Jack McKenna.
Mailing Address: 5601 Tower Ave., 54880.
Church: 3095 E. County Rd. B. Tel: 715-394-7919.
Catechesis/Religious Program—Carol Weeks, D.R.E. Students 47.

OUTSIDE THE CITY OF SUPERIOR

ALMENA, BARRON CO., SACRED HEART OF JESUS CHURCH (1890), [CEM] Revs. Eugene H. Hornung; Dennis M. Mullen.
Mailing Address: 900 St. Anthony St., Cumberland, 54829. Tel: 715-822-2948; Fax: 715-822-3588.
Church: 114 Soo Ave., 54805.
Catechesis/Religious Program—Mary Hickok, D.R.E. Students 70.

AMERY, POLK CO., ST. JOSEPH (1890), [CEM] Very Rev. John A. Drummy; Deacons Larry K. Bauer; Florian Heiser.
Church and Mailing Address: 1050 Keller Ave. N., 54001. Tel: 715-268-7717; Fax: 715-268-9986.
Catechesis/Religious Program—Mary Modjeski, D.R.E.; Lisa Cerney, D.R.E.; Marita Beaudette, D.R.E. Students 213.

ASHLAND, ASHLAND CO.

1—HOLY FAMILY, (Polish), Closed., For inquiries for sacramental records contact Our Lady of the Lake Catholic Community, Ashland.

2—OUR LADY OF THE LAKE CATHOLIC COMMUNITY (1872), [CEM] Revs. William Rooney, O.F.M.; Michael J. Jennrich, O.F.M.
Mailing Address: 106 N. 2nd Ave. E., 54806.
Church: 201 Lake Shore Dr. E., 54806. Tel: 715-682-7620; Fax: 715-682-7626.
School—215 Lake Shore Dr. E., 54806. Tel: 715-682-7622. Mr. David Eaton, Prin. Brothers 1; Lay Teachers 17; Students 158.
Catechesis/Religious Program—Students 353.

BALSAM LAKE, POLK CO., OUR LADY OF THE LAKES (1875), [CEM 2] Rev. Thomas E. Thompson.
Mailing Address: P.O. Box 399, 54810.
Church: 507 W. Main, 58410. Tel: 715-405-2253; Fax: 715-405-2743.
Catechesis/Religious Program—Tel: 715-294-2243. Gwen Nies, D.R.E. Tel: 715-405-2258. Students 108.

BARRON, BARRON CO., ST. JOSEPH (1907),, Also serves St. Peter, Cameron and St. Boniface, Chetek. Rev. Gerard I. Willger.
Church and Mailing Address: 827 E. LaSalle Ave., 54812. Tel: 715-637-3255; Fax: 715-637-3252.
Catechesis/Religious Program—Anne Stephens, D.R.E. Students 143.

BAYFIELD, BAYFIELD CO., HOLY FAMILY (1878), [CEM] Revs. John Eaton, O.F.M.; Gary Bernhardt, O.F.M.; Joseph B. Hagen, O.F.M.; Sr. Phyllis Wilhelm, O.S.F., Pastoral Assoc.; Deacon Roger L. Cadotte.
Mailing Address: P.O. Box 1290, 54814.
Church: 232 N. 1st. St., 54814. Tel: 715-779-3316; Fax: 715 779-9804.
Catechesis/Religious Program—Sr. Phyllis Wilhelm, O.S.F., D.R.E. Students 23.

BIRCHWOOD, WASHBURN CO., ST. JOHN EVANGELIST (1908), Rev. David P. Oberts.
Mailing Address: 2411 23rd St., Rice Lake, 54868.
Church: 408 S. Main, 54868. Tel: 715-234-2917; Fax: 715-236-7865.
Catechesis/Religious Program—Laurie Smith, D.R.E. Students 55.

BLOOMVILLE, LINCOLN CO., ST. JOHN THE BAPTIST (1908), [CEM] Rev. John R. Scheer, S.A.C.; Michele Rein, Parish Dir.
Mailing Address: N10090 County B., Tomahawk, 54487.
Church: Hwy. 17 & County J, Gleason 54435. Tel: 715-453-2561; Fax: 715-453-4813.
Catechesis/Religious Program—Students 74.

BOULDER JUNCTION, VILAS CO., ST. ANNE (1938), [CEM], Also serves St. Mary, Sayner, and St. Rita, Presque Isle. Rev. John R. Long.
Mailing Address: P.O. Box 110, 54512.
Church: 10315 Main St., 54512. Tel: 715-385-2390; Fax: 715-385-2282.
Catechesis/Religious Program—Chris Sprister, D.R.E. Students 11.

BRUCE, RUSK CO., ST. MARY (1893), [CEM 2] Rev. Lewis E. Burden.
Mailing Address: P.O. Box 207, Weyerhaeuser, 54895.
Church: 727 N. 2nd St., 58419. Tel: 715-353-2400; Fax: 715-353-2400.
Catechesis/Religious Program—Lenore Krajewski, D.R.E.; Matie Dedenbach, D.R.E. Students 99.

BUTTERNUT, ASHLAND CO., IMMACULATE CONCEPTION (1880), [CEM] Very Rev. James J. Jackson.
Mailing Address: 276 S. 5th Ave., Park Falls, 54552.
Church: Hwy. F, 54514. Tel: 715-769-3644.
Catechesis/Religious Program—Bette Hirtreiter, D.R.E. Students 94.

CABLE, BAYFIELD CO., ST. ANN (1902), Rev. William H. Green; Sr. Virginia Schwartz, O.S.M., Parish Dir.
Mailing Address: P.O. Box 37, 54821-0037.
Church: 13645 County Hwy. M, 54821 Tel: 715-798-3855; Fax: 715-798-3850.
Catechesis/Religious Program—Cheryl Rockenbach, D.R.E. Students 20.

CAMERON, BARRON CO., ST. PETER (1908), Rev. Gerard I. Willger.
Mailing Address: 827 E. LaSalle Ave., Barron, 54812.
Church: Creamery Rd. & Hwy. 8, 54822. Tel: 715-637-3255.
Catechesis/Religious Program—Bev Kramer, D.R.E. Students 131.

CATAWBA, PRICE CO., ST. PAUL THE APOSTLE (1907), [CEM] Rev. Gerald A. Hagen.
Mailing Address: 125 Argyle Ave., Phillips, 54555.
Church: W9485 Hwy. 8, 54515. Tel: 715-339-2222; Fax: 715-339-2216.
Catechesis/Religious Program—Jennifer Krell, D.R.E. Students 45.

CENTURIA, POLK CO., ST. PATRICK (1856), Closed., For inquiries for sacramental records, please contact Our Lady of the Lakes, Balsam Lake

CHELSEA, TAYLOR CO., ASSUMPTION OF THE BLESSED VIRGIN MARY (1887), Rev. Ronald C. Kowalski; Deacon Michael D. Cullen, Parish Life Dir.
Mailing Address: 513 State Rd., Rib Lake, 54470.
Church: 100 Hemlock Ave., 54451. Tel: 715-427-5259; Fax: 715-427-5266.
Catechesis/Religious Program—Chris Wille, D.R.E. Students 28.

CHETEK, BARRON CO., ST. BONIFACE (1880), [CEM] Rev. Gerard I. Willger; Deacon James Dennis.
Mailing Address: 419 S. 3rd St., 54728.
Church: 425 S. 3rd St., 54812. Tel: 715-924-3514; Fax: 715-637-3252.
Catechesis/Religious Program—Dawn Langman, D.R.E.; Gayle Walgrave, D.R.E. Students 115.

CLAM LAKE, ASHLAND CO., ST. GEORGE (1890), Rev. Jozef A. Barszcz.
Mailing Address: P.O. Box 17, Mellen, 54546.
Church: Hwy. 77 W., 54546. Tel: 715-274-3701.

CLEAR LAKE, POLK CO., ST. JOHN (1890), Rev. Joseph C. Trinka.
Mailing Address: P.O. Box 337, 54005.
Church: 811 Fourth St., 54005. Tel: 715-263-2032; Fax: 715-263-2032.
Catechesis/Religious Program—Rosemary Koenig, D.R.E. Students 64.

CORNUCOPIA, BAYFIELD CO., ST. ANN (1914), [CEM] Revs. John Eaton, O.F.M.; Gary Bernhardt, O.F.M.; Joseph B. Hagen, O.F.M.
Mailing Address: P.O. Box 070, Washburn, 54891.
Church: Superior Ave. & Ash St., 54827. Tel: 715-373-2676; Fax: 715-373-0365.
Catechesis/Religious Program—Colleen Greene, D.R.E.; Tiffany Fruehe, D.R.E. Students 9.

CRESCENT LAKE, BURNETT CO., SACRED HEARTS OF JESUS AND MARY (1857), [CEM] Rev. Michael J. Tupa.
Mailing Address: P.O. Box 7, Webster, 54893.
Church: County Rd. A & H. Tel: 715-866-7321; Fax: 715-866-7305.
Catechesis/Religious Program—Mary Pabst, D.R.E.; Julie Gibb, D.R.E. Students 6.

CUMBERLAND, BARRON CO., ST. ANTHONY ABBOT (1883), [CEM 2], Also serves Sacred Heart of Jesus, Almena and St. Ann, Turtle Lake. Revs. Dennis M. Mullen; Eugene H. Hornung; Deacon Gregory J. Ricci.
Church and Mailing Address: 900 St. Anthony St., 54829. Tel: 715-822-2948; Fax: 715-822-3588.
Catechesis/Religious Program—Gina Simon, D.R.E.; Mary Modjeski, D.R.E. Students 164.

DANBURY, BURNETT CO., OUR LADY OF PERPETUAL HELP (1920), Rev. Michael J. Tupa.
Mailing Address: P.O. Box 7, Webster, 54893.
Church and Mailing: 7586 Main St., 54830. Tel: 715-866-7321.

Catechesis/Religious Program—Mary Pabst, D.R.E.; Julie Gibb, D.R.E. Students 7.

DAUBY, BAYFIELD CO., ST. PETER (1918), [CEM] Rev. Michael L. Crisp.
Mailing Address: P.O. Box 97, Iron River, 54847.
Church: Hwy. 2 & County Rd. F. Tel: 715-372-4756.
Catechesis/Religious Program—Linda Sandor, D.R.E. Students 41.

DOBIE, BARRON CO., OUR LADY OF LOURDES (1875), [CEM], Also serves Holy Trinity, Haugen, and St. John the Evangelist, Birchwood. Rev. David P. Oberts.
Church and Mailing Address: 2411 23rd St., Rice Lake, 54868. Tel: 715-234-2917; Fax: 715-236-7865.
Catechesis/Religious Program—Mary Jane Wahl, D.R.E. Students 135.

EAGLE RIVER, VILAS CO., ST. PETER THE FISHERMAN (1890), [CEM], Also serves St. Albert, Land O' Lakes, and St. Mary, Phelps. Rev. Robert J. Koszarek; Sr. Jeanne Wiest, O.P., Pastoral Assoc.
Church and Mailing Address: 5001 County Rd. G, 54521. Tel: 715-479-8704; Fax: 715-477-2017.
School—115 S. 3rd St., P.O. Box 729, 54521. Tel: 715-479-4332. Marie Hafer, Prin. Lay Teachers 8; Students 67.
Catechesis/Religious Program—Christine Gall, D.R.E. Students 147.

ERIN, ST. CROIX CO., ST. PATRICK (1857), [CEM 2] Rev. Allan P. Bradley.
Mailing Address: 151 S. Washington Ave., New Richmond, 54017.
Church: 1880 County Rd. G, 54017. Tel: 715-246-4652.
Catechesis/Religious Program—Kim Palmer, D.R.E. Students 27.

FARMINGTON, ST. CROIX CO., ASSUMPTION OF THE BLESSED VIRGIN MARY (1869), [CEM] Rev. James J. Brinkman.
Mailing Address: P.O. Box 9, Somerset, 54025.
Church: 255 State Hwy. 35, 54025. Tel: 715-247-3310; Fax: 715-247-3174.
Catechesis/Religious Program—Barbara Ziegler, D.R.E. Students 55.

FIFIELD, PRICE CO., ST. FRANCIS OF ASSISI (1888), Very Rev. James J. Jackson.
Mailing Address: 276 S. 5th Ave., Park Falls, 54552.
Church: Balsam St., 54524. Tel: 715-762-4494.

FLAMBEAU, RUSK CO., ST. FRANCIS OF ASSISI (1866), [CEM] Rev. Lewis E. Burden.
Mailing Address: P.O. Box 207, Weyerhaeuser, 54895.
Church: W10193 Lehman Rd., Holcombe, 54745. Tel: 715-353-2400; Fax: 715-353-2400.
Catechesis/Religious Program—Sue Zoromski, D.R.E. Students 25.

FREDERIC, POLK CO., ST. DOMINIC (1904), [CEM], (Also serves Immaculate Conception, Grantsburg). Rev. David R. Lusson, Parochial Admin.; Deacon Stanley J. Marczak.
Mailing Address: P.O. Box 606, 54837.
Rectory/Parish Office—107 W. Birch St., 54837.
Church: 103 W. Birch St., 54837. Tel: 715-327-8119; Fax: 715-327-8125.
Catechesis/Religious Program—Sue Wallin, D.R.E. Students 105.

GEORGETOWN, POLK CO., OUR LADY OF THE HOLY ROSARY, Closed., For inquiries for sacramental records contact Our Lady of the Lakes Balsam Lake.

GILMAN, TAYLOR CO., SS. PETER AND PAUL (1910), [CEM], (Also serves St. Michael, Jump River; St. John, Sheldon and St. Stanislaus, Lublin). Rev. Philip J. Juza.
Church and Mailing: 315 E. Davlin St., 54433. Tel: 715-447-8510; Fax: 715-447-8615.
Catechesis/Religious Program—Students 121.

GLENWOOD CITY, ST. CROIX CO., ST. JOHN THE BAPTIST (1886), [CEM] Rev. William J. Murphy; Deacon Wesley G. Tuttle.
Mailing Address: P.O. Box 18, Hammond, 54015.
Church: 753 1st St., 54013. Tel: 715-265-7133; Fax: 715-265-7339.
Catechesis/Religious Program—Wes Tuttle, D.R.E. Students 183.

GLIDDEN, ASHLAND CO., MOST PRECIOUS BLOOD (1884), [CEM] Rev. Jozef A. Barszcz.
Mailing Address: P.O. Box 17, Mellen, 54546. Tel: 715-264-3471; 715-274-3701.
Church: 256 E. 2nd St., 54527.
Catechesis/Religious Program—Kathy Witt, D.R.E. Students 63.

GORDON, DOUGLAS CO., ST. ANTHONY OF PADUA (1878), Rev. James J. Kinney.
Mailing Address: P.O. Box 303, Solon Springs, 54873.
Church: 9718 E. County Rd. Y, 54838. Tel: 715-378-4431.
Catechesis/Religious Program—Pat Denhartog, D.R.E. Students 8.

GRANTSBURG, BURNETT CO., IMMACULATE CONCEPTION (1909), Rev. David R. Lusson, Parochial Admin.
Mailing Address: P.O. Box 606, Frederic, 54837.
Church: 411 State Rd. 70, 54840. Tel: 715-327-8119.
Catechesis/Religious Program—Joan Lauer, D.R.E. Students 61.

HAMMOND, ST. CROIX CO., IMMACULATE CONCEPTION (1877), [CEM], Also serves St. John the Baptist, Glenwood City and St. Bridget, Wilson. Rev. William J. Murphy; Deacon Joseph F. Paron.
Mailing Address: P.O. Box 18, 54015-0018.
Church: 1265 Ridgeway, 54015. Tel: 715-796-2244; Fax: 715-796-2599.
Catechesis/Religious Program—Barb Lyons, D.R.E. Students 234.

HARRISON, LINCOLN CO., ST. AUGUSTINE (1905), [CEM] Rev. John R. Scheer, S.A.C.; Deacon Clarence D. Towle; Michele Rein, Parish Dir.
Mailing Address: Tomahawk N10090 Cty. B, Tomahawk, 54487. Tel: 715-453-2561; Fax: 715-453-4813.
Church: Highways B & D, 54435.
Catechesis/Religious Program—Students 38.

HAUGEN, BARRON CO., HOLY TRINITY (1896), [CEM] Rev. David P. Oberts; Deacon Harvey G. Drost.
Mailing Address: 2411 23rd St., Rice Lake, 54868.
Church: 317 W. 5th St., 54841. Tel: 715-234-2917; Fax: 715-236-7865.
Catechesis/Religious Program—Kris Deering, D.R.E. Students 60.

HAWKINS, RUSK CO., ST. MARY OF CZESTOWCHOWA (1913), [CEM] Revs. John C. Anderson; Ryan G. Erickson.
Mailing Address: 611 1st St. S., Ladysmith, 54848.
Church: N7386 CTY M, 54530. Tel: 715-532-3051.
Catechesis/Religious Program—Gayle Spencer, D.R.E. Students 26.

HAYWARD, SAWYER CO., ST. JOSEPH'S (1882),, Also serves St. Ann, Cable. Rev. William H. Green.
Mailing Address: P.O. Box 877, 54843.
Church: 10586 N. Dakota Ave., 54843. Tel: 715-634-2867; Fax: 715-634-9037.
Catechesis/Religious Program—Students 216.

HIGHBRIDGE, ASHLAND CO., ST. ANTHONY (1880), Rev. Jozef Barszcz.
Mailing Address: P.O. Box 17, Mellen, 54546.
Church: Hwy. 13, 54846. Tel: 715-274-3701.
Catechesis/Religious Program—Debbie Schutte, D.R.E. Students 5.

HUDSON, ST. CROIX CO., ST. PATRICK (1840), [CEM] Revs. Peter F. Szleszinski; John L. Parr (LC); Deacons Peter R. Braum; Bernard M. Drevnick.
Church and Mailing Address: 1500 Vine St., 54016. Tel: 715-381-5120; Fax: 715-381-5125.
School—403 St. Croix St., 54016. Tel: 715-386-3941. Mary Piasecki, Prin. Sisters 1; Lay Teachers 24; Students 395.
Catechesis/Religious Program—Tel: 715-386-9209. Mary Ann Kapler, D.R.E.; Tim O'Brien, D.R.E. Students 685.

HURLEY, IRON CO., ST. MARY OF THE SEVEN DOLORS (1885), [CEM], (Also serves Sacred Heart, Montreal; Holy Redeemer, Pence; and St. Ann, Saxon). Very Rev. Robert E. O'Connell; Deacon Russell J. Lundgren.
Mailing Address: 404 Iron St., 54534.
Church: Iron Street & 5th Ave., 54534. Tel: 715-561-2606; Fax: 715-561-3739.
Catechesis/Religious Program—Faye Lundgren, D.R.E. Students 158.

INO, BAYFIELD CO., ST. FLORIAN (1913), [CEM] Rev. Michael L. Crisp.
Mailing Address: P.O. Box 97, Iron River, 54847.
Church: 19315 Keystone Rd.. Tel: 715-746-2549.
Catechesis/Religious Program—Loretta Skaj, D.R.E. Students 7.

IRON RIVER, BAYFIELD CO., ST. MICHAEL (1892), [CEM], Also serves St. Peter, Dauby. Rev. Barry Schneider, O.F.M.
Mailing Address: P.O. Box 97, 54847.
Church: 22 George St., 54847. Tel: 715-372-4756; Fax: 715-372-4753.
Catechesis/Religious Program—Micky Mullozzi, D.R.E. Students 65.

JUMP RIVER, TAYLOR CO., ST. MICHAEL (1915), Rev. Philip J. Juza.
Mailing Address: 315 E. Davlin St., Gilman, 54433. Tel: 715-452-5374.
Church: Hwy. 73, 54434.
Catechesis/Religious Program—Students 8.

LAPOINTE, BAYFIELD CO., ST. JOSEPH (1669), [CEM] Revs. John Eaton, O.F.M.; Gary Bernhardt, O.F.M.; Joseph B. Hagen, O.F.M.
Mailing Address: P.O. Box 1290, Bayfield, 54814.
Church: 266 Airport Rd., 54850. Tel: 715-779-3316; Fax: 715-779-9804.

LAC DU FLAMBEAU, VILAS CO., ST. ANTHONY OF PADUA (1862),, Also serves St. Mary, Odanah. Rev. James P. Bartelme; Sr. Marianna Ableidinger, F.S.P.A., Pastoral Admin.; Deacon John J. Bardos.
Mailing Address: P.O. Box 38, 54538.
Church: 650 Old Abe Rd., 54538. Tel: 715-588-3148; Fax: 715-588-2278.
Catechesis/Religious Program—Tel: 715-588-7439. Sr. Marianna Ableidinger, F.S.P.A., D.R.E. Students 31.

LADYSMITH, RUSK CO., OUR LADY OF SORROWS (1906),, (Also serves St. Mary, Hawkins, and St. Anthony, Tony). Revs. John C. Anderson; Ryan G. Erickson; Sr. Jovita Winkel, C.S.A., Pastoral Assoc.; Deacons Richard J. Brockbank; Jerome J. Drahos; Richard D. Leonhard; Craig J. Voldberg.
Church and Mailing Address: 611 1st St. S., 54848. Tel: 715-532-3051; Fax: 715-532-7368.
School—105 E. Washington Ave., 54848. Tel: 715-532-3232. Tami Stewart, Prin. Lay Teachers 10; Students 105.
Catechesis/Religious Program—Tel: 715-532-3703. Gayle Spencer, D.R.E. Students 175.

LAKE NEBAGAMON, DOUGLAS CO., ST. ANTHONY (1899), [CEM] Very Rev. Dean T. Buttrick.
Mailing Address: 4315 E. 3rd St., 54880.
Church: 11648 E. County Rd. B, 54849. Tel: 715-398-3261.
Catechesis/Religious Program—Tina Markon, D.R.E. Students 56.

LAKE TOMAHAWK, ONEIDA CO., ST. JOHN VIANNEY (1859), Very Rev. James A. Hoffman; Joan Laut, Pastoral Assoc.
Mailing Address: P.O. Box 30, Woodruff, 54568.
Church: 7997 Choate Blvd., 54539. Tel: 715-356-6284.
Catechesis/Religious Program—Sue Marciniak, D.R.E. Students 12.

LAND-O'-LAKES, VILAS CO., ST. ALBERT (1894),, Also serves St. Mary, Phelps. Rev. Robert J. Koszarek; Patricia Pintens, Parish Dir.
Mailing Address: P.O. Box 237, Land O'Lakes, 54540.
Church: 4351 Hwy. B, Land O'Lakes, 54550. Tel: 715-547-3558; Fax: 715-547-3614.
Catechesis/Religious Program—Nancy Dittmer, D.R.E. Students 35.

LUBLIN, TAYLOR CO., ST. STANISLAUS (1907), (Polish), [CEM] Rev. Philip J. Juza.
Mailing Address: 315 E. Davlin St., Gilman, 54433.
Church: W13381 South St., 54447. Tel: 715-447-8510.
Catechesis/Religious Program—Students 43.

MANITOWISH WATERS, VILAS CO., OUR LADY QUEEN OF PEACE (1858), Rev. Ephrem Pottamplackal, M.C.B.S.
Mailing Address: 5214N Lakeview Ave., P.O. Box 575, Mercer, 54547.
Church: Hwy. 51, 54545. Tel: 715-476-2697.
Catechesis/Religious Program—Nancy Chapes, D.R.E. Students 5.

MEDFORD, TAYLOR CO., OUR LADY OF THE HOLY ROSARY (1870), [CEM] Rev. Michael T. Hayden; Deacon Joseph Stefancin, Pastoral Assoc.
Mailing Address: P.O. Box 503, 54451.
Church: Washington & Cedar Streets, 54451. Tel: 715-748-3288; Fax: 715-748-6643.
School—215 S. Washington Ave., P.O. Box 503, 54451. Tel: 715-748-3336. Barbara Bugar, Prin. Servants of Mary 1; Lay Teachers 11; Students 137.
Catechesis/Religious Program—Tel: 715-748-4733. Jeff Armbrust, D.R.E.; Audrey Stefancin, D.R.E. Students 494.

MELLEN, ASHLAND CO., HOLY ROSARY (1886),, (Also serves St. George, Clam Lake; Most Precious Blood, Glidden, St. Anthony, Highbridge, and St. Anne, Sanborn). Rev. Jozef A. Barszcz.
Mailing Address: P.O. Box 17, 54546.
Church: 203 N. Main St., 54546. Tel: 715-274-3701; Fax: 715-274-3701.
Catechesis/Religious Program—Sara Schultz, D.R.E. Students 73.

MERCER, IRON CO., ST. ISAAC JOGUES AND COMPANIONS (1912),, (Also serves Our Lady Queen of Peace, Manitowish Waters). Rev. Ephrem Pottamplackal, M.C.B.S.; Deacon Norbert G. Brossmer.
Mailing Address: P.O. Box 575, 54547.
Church: 2611 W. Garnet St., 54547. Tel: 715-476-2697; Fax: 715-476-2697.
Catechesis/Religious Program—Colleen Roeder, D.R.E. Students 57.

MERRILL, LINCOLN CO.

1—ST. FRANCIS XAVIER (1875), [CEM] Rev. James R. Horath; Deacon Richard G. Heckman.
Church and Mailing Address: 1708 E. 10th St., 54452. Tel: 715-536-2803; Fax: 715-536-7536.
School—St. Francis, (Grades PreK-8) Tel: 715-536-6083. R. Ira Rebella, Prin. Lay Teachers 18; Students 153.
Catechesis/Religious Program—Sr. Kathleen Walli, O.P., D.R.E.; Judy Warren, D.R.E. Students 440.

2—ST. ROBERT BELLARMINE (1886), Closed., For inquiries for sacramental records contact St. Francis Xavier, Merrill.

MINOCQUA, ONEIDA CO., ST. PATRICK (1894), [CEM] Very Rev. James A. Hoffman; Rev. James P. Bartelme.
Mailing Address: P.O. Box 30, Woodruff, 54568.

Church: 131 Milwaukee St., 54548. Tel: 715-356-6284; Fax: 715-358-2940.
Parish Office: 1106 4th Ave., Woodruff, 54568.
Catechesis/Religious Program—Theresa Strasburg, D.R.E. Students 18.

MINONG, WASHBURN CO., ST. MARY (1904), Rev. James J. Kinney; Deacon Peter R. Huntowski.
Mailing Address: P.O. Box 303, Solon Springs, 54873.
Church: 506 Main St., 54859. Tel: 715-378-4431; Fax: 715-378-2480.
Catechesis/Religious Program—Pat Denhartog, D.R.E. Students 16.

MONTREAL, IRON CO., SACRED HEART OF JESUS (1904), Very Rev. Robert E. O'Connell.
Mailing Address: 404 Iron St., Hurley, 54534.
Church: Michigan Ave. & Saxon Rd., 54550. Tel: 715-561-2606.
Catechesis/Religious Program—Faye Lundgren, D.R.E. Students 9.

MOQUAH, BAYFIELD CO., SS. PETER AND PAUL (1912), [CEM 2], (Also serves St. Florian, Ino). Rev. Michael L. Crisp.
Mailing Address: 23515 Cty. Rd. G., Ashland, 54806.
Church: 23505 County Rd. G, 54806. Tel: 715-746-2549.
Catechesis/Religious Program—Kathy Huybrecht, D.R.E. Students 28.

NEW POST, SAWYER CO., ST. IGNATIUS (1884), Rev. Gregory J. Hopefl.
Mailing Address: 13891 W. Mission Rd., Stone Lake, 54876. Tel: 715-865-3669; Fax: 715-865-3669.
Catechesis/Religious Program—Students 3.

NEW RICHMOND, ST. CROIX CO., IMMACULATE CONCEPTION (1883), [CEM], (Also serves St. Patrick, Erin). Rev. Allan P. Bradley; Deacons Hugh C. Mayer; Michael J. Germain.
Church and Office Address: 151 S. Washington Ave., 54017-1523. Tel: 715-246-4652; 715-246-2294; Fax: 715-246-2526.
School—257 S. Washington Ave., 54017. Tel: 715-246-2469; Fax: 715-246-6195. Mari Zarcone-Patterson, Prin. Lay Teachers 15; Students 149.
Catechesis/Religious Program—Kim Palmer, D.R.E. Students 524.

ODANAH, ASHLAND CO., ST. MARY (1855), Rev. James P. Bartelme.
Mailing Address: P.O. Box 38, Lac du Flambeau, 54538. Tel: 715-588-3148.
Catechesis/Religious Program—

OSCEOLA, POLK CO., ST. JOSEPH (1915),, (Also serves Our Lady of the Lakes, Balsam Lake). Rev. Thomas E. Thompson; Deacon Fred E. Johnson.
Mailing Address: P.O. Box 399, 54020-0399.
Church: 255 10th Ave., 54020. Tel: 715-294-2243; Fax: 715-294-2495.
Catechesis/Religious Program—Tel: 715-405-2258. Gwen Nies, D.R.E. Students 190.

PARK FALLS, PRICE CO., ST. ANTHONY (1881),, (Also serves Immaculate Conception, Butternut and St. Francis of Assisi, Fifield). Very Rev. James J. Jackson; Deacon Chester E. Ball.
Church and Mailing Address: 276 S. 5th Ave., 54552. Tel: 715-762-4494; Fax: 715-762-0079.
School—200 S. 5th Ave., 54552. Tel: 715-762-4494. Brent Balsavich, Prin. Lay Teachers 13; Students 138.
Catechesis/Religious Program—Tel: 715-762-4476. Gayle Hilgart, D.R.E.; Dennis Kronberger, D.R.E. Students 178.

PELICAN LAKE, ONEIDA CO., ST. JOHN (1905), [CEM] Rev. John R. Gerritts, Parochial Admin.
Mailing Address: 110 S. Conro St., Rhinelander, 54501.
Church: Appleton St. Cty. & Hwy. B, 54463. Tel: 715-362-4012.
Catechesis/Religious Program—Jean Porten, D.R.E. Students 22.

PENCE, IRON CO., HOLY REDEEMER (1908), Very Rev. Robert E. O'Connell.
Mailing Address: 404 Iron St., Hurley, 54534.
Church: Hibbert & Birch Streets, 54550. Tel: 715-561-2606.

PHELPS, VILAS CO., ST. MARY (1908), Rev. Robert J. Koszarek; Deacon Norman Meson Jr.; Patricia Pintens, Parish Dir.
Mailing Address: P.O. Box 237, Land O'Lakes, 54540.
Church: 4494 Town Hall Rd., 54554. Tel: 715-547-3558.
Catechesis/Religious Program—Students 23.

PHILLIPS, PRICE CO., OUR LADY OF THE NORTH (1876), [CEM] Rev. Gerald A. Hagen; Deacon James J. Celba.
Church and Mailing Address: 125 N. Argyle Ave., 54555. Tel: 715-339-2222; Fax: 715-339-2216.
Catechesis/Religious Program—Sherrie Kandutsch, D.R.E. Students 182.

PIER-WILLOW, ONEIDA CO., ST. FRANCIS OF ASSISI (1887), [CEM] Rev. John R. Scheer, S.A.C.
Mailing Address: 320 E. Washington Ave., Tomahawk, 54487.
Church: N. Willow Rd., 54487. Tel: 715-453-2878.

PRENTICE, PRICE CO., ST. JOHN THE BAPTIST (1886), Rev. Gerald A. Hagen.
Mailing Address: 125 N. Argyle Ave., Phillips, 54555.
Church: 935 Town St., 54556. Tel: 715-339-2222; Fax: 715-339-2216.
Catechesis/Religious Program—Celine Lofland, D.R.E. Students 34.

PRESQUE ISLE, VILAS CO., ST. RITA (1950), Rev. John R. Long.
Mailing Address: P.O. Box 110, Boulder Junction, 54512.
Church: Lake St., 54557. Tel: 715-385-2390.
Catechesis/Religious Program—Chris Sprister, D.R.E. Students 12.

RADISSON, SAWYER CO., SACRED HEART (1919), Rev. Vincent M. Bromley.
Mailing Address: P.O. Box 216, Winter, 54896.
Church: Hwy. 27, 54867. Tel: 715-266-3441.

RED CLIFF, BAYFIELD CO., ST. FRANCIS (1861), [CEM] Revs. John Eaton, O.F.M.; Gary Bernhardt, O.F.M.; Joseph B. Hagen, O.F.M.; Sr. Phyllis Wilhelm, O.S.F., Pastoral Assoc.
Mailing Address: P.O. Box 1290, Bayfield, 54814.
Church: Church Rd., 54814. Tel: 715-779-3316.
Catechesis/Religious Program—Students 14.

RESERVE, SAWYER CO., ST. FRANCIS OF SOLANUS (1885), (Indian), [CEM], (Also serves St. Ignatius, New Post, and St. Philip, Stone Lake). Rev. Gregory J Hopefl.
Church and Mailing Address: 13891 Mission Rd., Stone Lake, 54876. Tel: 715-865-3669; Fax: 715-865-3669.
School—*St. Francis Solanus*, 13885 Mission Rd., Stone Lake, 54876. Tel: 715-865-3662. Sr. Felissa Zander, S.S.S.F., Prin. Sisters of St. Francis 2; Lay Teachers 1; Students 30.
Catechesis/Religious Program—Students 4.

RHINELANDER, ONEIDA CO.

1—IMMACULATE CONCEPTION (1883), [CEM], (Also serves St. John, Pelican Lake; St. Joseph, Rhinelander). Rev. John R. Gerritts; Deacons Michael O. Harvey; Mathew C. Porten.
Mailing Address: 110 S. Conro St., 54501.
Church: 125 E. King St., 54501. Tel: 715-362-4012; Fax: 715-362-2385.
Catechesis/Religious Program—Julianne Donlin, D.R.E. Students 157.

2—ST. JOSEPH'S (1909), [CEM], (Also serves St. John, Pelican Lake; Immaculate Conception, Rhinelander). Rev. John R. Gerritts; Deacons Ronald J. Bosi; Richard J. Meier.
Mailing Address: 1350 N. Stevens St., 54501. Tel: 715-362-3169; Fax: 715-362-1811.
Church: 1360 N. Stevens St., 54501.
School—*Rhinelander Catholic Central* Shirley Heise, Prin.
St. Joseph—1340 N. Stevens St., 54501. Tel: 715-362-3366.
St. Mary—103 E. King, 54501. Tel: 715-362-5588; Fax: 715-362-0952. Franciscan Sisters of Christian Charity 3; Lay Teachers 19; Students 295.
Catechesis/Religious Program—Lori Novak, D.R.E.; Patti Shepherd, D.R.E. Students 266.

RIB LAKE, TAYLOR CO., ST. JOHN THE BAPTIST (1896),, (Also serves Assumption of the B. V. M., Chelsea; St. Theresa, Westboro and Our Lady of Perpetual Help, Whittlesey). Revs. Ronald C. Kowalski; John A. Regh. Deacons Paul M. Ochodnicky; Michael D. Cullen, Parish Life Dir.
Church and Mailing Address: 513 State Rd., 54470. Tel: 715-427-5259; Fax: 715-427-5266.
Catechesis/Religious Program—Joseph A. Hebda, D.R.E. Students 116.

RICE LAKE, BARRON CO., ST. JOSEPH (1878), [CEM] Rev. James P. Powers, J.C.L.; Sr. Bonnie Alho, O.S.M., Pastoral Assoc.; Deacon Kenneth J. Schaefer.
Church and Mailing Address: 111 W. Marshall St., 54868. Tel: 715-234-2032; Fax: 715-234-7757.
School—*St. Joseph School*, 128 Humbird St., 54868. Tel: 715-234-7721; Fax: 715-234-5062. Sr. Claudine Balio, S.S.J.T.O.S.F., Prin. Lay Teachers 11; Students 164.
Catechesis/Religious Program—Rose Schullo, D.R.E. Students 224.

RIVER FALLS, ST. CROIX CO., ST. BRIDGET (1854), [CEM] Rev. Gerald P. Harris; Deacons Lawrence Murphy, Pastoral Assoc.; Lawrence P. Hennemann; Thomas J. Weiss.
Mailing Address: P.O. Box 86, 54022. Tel: 715-425-1870; Fax: 715-425-1871.
Church: 211 E. Division St., 54022.
School—135 E. Division St., 54022. Tel: 715-425-1872; Fax: 715-425-1873. Sheila Warren, Prin. Sisters 1; Lay Teachers 21; Students 164.
Catechesis/Religious Program—Tel: 715-425-1874. Doris Murphy, D.R.E. Students 356.

SANBORN, ASHLAND CO., ST. ANNE (1895), Rev. Jozef A. Barszcz.
Mailing Address: P.O. Box 17, Mellen, 54546.
Church: County Hwy. E, 54806. Tel: 715-274-3701.
Catechesis/Religious Program—Zora Eid, D.R.E. Students 25.

SARONA, WASHBURN CO., ST. CATHERINE (1917), Rev. Andrew P. Ricci, Parochial Admin.
Mailing Address: 409 Summit St., Spooner, 54801.
Church: W5262 County Hwy. D, 54870. Tel: 715-635-3105.
Catechesis/Religious Program—Susan Hughes, D.R.E. Students 11.

SAXON, IRON CO., ST. ANN'S (1886), Very Rev. Robert E. O'Connell; Sr. Caroline Pfeiffer, C.S.J., Pastoral Assoc.
Mailing Address: 404 Iron St., Hurley, 54534.
Church: 200 Church St., 54559. Tel: 715-561-2606.

SAYNER, VILAS CO., ST. MARY (1912), Rev. John R. Long.
Mailing Address: P.O. Box 110, Boulder Junction, 54512.
Church: 2820 Hwy N, 54560. Tel: 715-542-3480.
Catechesis/Religious Program—Monica Fath, D.R.E. Students 36.

SHELDON, RUSK CO., ST. JOHN THE APOSTLE (1955), Rev. Philip J. Juza.
Mailing Address: 315 E. Davlin St., Gilman, 54433.
Church: N657 County Rd. VV, 54766. Tel: 715-452-5374.
Catechesis/Religious Program—Students 69.

SHELL LAKE, WASHBURN CO., ST. JOSEPH (1880), [CEM] Rev. Andrew P. Ricci.
Mailing Address: 409 Summit St., Spooner, 54801.
Church: 502 N. 2nd St., 54871. Tel: 715-635-3105.
Catechesis/Religious Program—Susan Hughes, D.R.E. Students 39.

SOLON SPRINGS, DOUGLAS CO., ST. PIUS X (1878), [CEM], (Also serves St. Anthony of Padua, Gordon; St. Mary, Minong). Rev. James J. Kinney.
Mailing Address: Box 303, 54873.
Church: 11651 Business 53, 54873. Tel: 715-378-4431; Fax: 715-378-2064.
Catechesis/Religious Program—Patricia DenHartog, D.R.E. Students 23.

SOMERSET, ST. CROIX CO., ST. ANNE (1851), [CEM], (Also serves Assumption of the Blessed Virgin Mary, Farmington). Rev. James J. Brinkman; Deacon A. Maurice Baillargeon.
Mailing Address: P.O. Box 9, 54025.
Church: 141 Church Hill Rd., 54025. Tel: 715-247-3310; Fax: 715-247-3174.
School—140 Church Hill Rd., 54025. Tel: 715-247-3762; Fax: 715-247-4335. Ann Mitchell, Prin. Lay Teachers 15; Students 176.
Catechesis/Religious Program—Ann Mitchell, D.R.E. Students 218.

SPOONER, WASHBURN CO., ST. FRANCIS DE SALES (1886), [CEM 2], (Also serves St. Joseph, Shell Lake & St. Catherine, Sarona). Rev. Andrew P. Ricci; Deacon Robert T. Jetto.
Church and Mailing Address: 409 Summit St., 54801. Tel: 715-635-3105; Fax: 715-635-7341.
School—300 Oak St., 54801. Tel: 715-635-2774. Linda L. Havlicek, Prin. Lay Teachers 13; Students 104.
Catechesis/Religious Program—Betty Gabriel, D.R.E.; Amy Tyler, D.R.E. Students 155.

STANTON, ST. CROIX CO., ST. BRIDGET (1875), Closed., For inquiries for parish records please see St. Joseph, Amery.

STETSONVILLE, TAYLOR CO., SACRED HEART OF JESUS (1884), [CEM] Rev. Frederick Brost; Deacon Joseph F. Roe.
Church and Mailing Address: 322 W. CTH A, 54480. Tel: 715-678-2395; Fax: 715-678-2395.
Catechesis/Religious Program—Karleen Sperl, D.R.E. Students 77.

STONE LAKE, SAWYER CO., ST. PHILIP (1905), Rev. Gregory J. Hopefl.
Mailing Address: 13891 Mission Rd., 54876.
Church: 5750 Frost Ave., 54876. Tel: 715-865-3669; Fax: 715-865-3669.

STRICKLAND, RUSK CO., ASSUMPTION OF THE BLESSED VIRGIN MARY (1897), [CEM] Rev. Lewis E. Burden; Deacon James E. Roberge.
Mailing Address: N3739 1st St., P.O. Box 207, Weyerhaeuser, 54895.
Church: Old Hwy. 14. Tel: 715-353-2400.
Catechesis/Religious Program—James E. Roberge, D.R.E.

SUGAR CAMP, ONEIDA CO., ST. KUNEGUNDA (1892), [CEM] Rev. William G. Horath; Deacon Albert A. Goodrich.
Mailing Address: P.O. Box 8, Three Lakes, 54562.
Church: 6895 Hwy. 17 N., Rhinelander. Tel: 715-272-1191.
Catechesis/Religious Program—Patricia Sand, D.R.E. Students 103.

THREE LAKES, ONEIDA CO., ST. THERESA (1892),, Also serves St. Kunegunda of Poland, Sugar Camp. Rev.

William G. Horath; Deacon John McCaughn.
Church and Mailing Address: 1701 Superior St., P.O. Box 8, 54562. Tel: 715-546-2159; Fax: 715-546-2159.
Catechesis/Religious Program—Students 90.

TOMAHAWK, LINCOLN CO., ST. MARY (1887), [CEM], (Also serves St. Francis of Assisi, Pier-Willow, St. Augustine, Harrison and St. John the Baptist, Bloomville). Rev. John R. Scheer, S.A.C.; Deacons David C. Bablick; Bernard J. Lyngdal; Darrell P. Smerz; John E. Ramassini; Clifford F. Eggett.
Church and Mailing Address: 320 E. Washington Ave., 54487. Tel: 715-453-2878; Fax: 715-453-6678.
School—110 N. 7th St., 54487. Tel: 715-453-3542. Mary A. Cherf, Prin. Lay Teachers 8; Students 115.
Catechesis/Religious Program—Kay Jarvensivu, D.R.E. Students 199.

TONY, RUSK CO., ST. ANTHONY DE PADUA (1901), [CEM] Revs. John C. Anderson; Ryan G. Erickson; Sr. Jovita Winkel, C.S.A., Pastoral Assoc.
Mailing Address: 611 1st St. S., Ladysmith, 54848.
Church: N5333 Maple St., 54563. Tel: 715-532-3051.
Catechesis/Religious Program—Linda Applebee, D.R.E. Students 53.

TURTLE LAKE, BARRON CO., ST. ANN (1882), [CEM 4] Revs. Dennis M. Mullen; Eugene H. Hornung.
Mailing Address: 900 St. Anthony St., Cumberland, 54829.
Church: 300 Pine St. S., 54889. Tel: 715-822-2948; Fax: 715-822-3588.
Catechesis/Religious Program—Amy Corbett, D.R.E. Students 93.

WASHBURN, BAYFIELD CO., ST. LOUIS (1882), [CEM], Also serves Holy Family, Bayfield; St. Anne, Cornucopia; St. Joseph, La Pointe; St. Francis, Red Cliff. Revs. John Eaton, O.F.M.; Gary Bernhardt, O.F.M.; Joseph B. Hagen, O.F.M.
Mailing Address: Box 070, 54891. Tel: 715-373-2676; Fax: 715-373-0365.
Church: 217 W. 7th St., 54891.
School—713 Washington Ave., P.O. Box 70, 54891. Tel: 715-373-5322. Betty Swiston, Prin. Lay Teachers 6; Students 75.
Catechesis/Religious Program—Colleen Greene, D.R.E.; Tiffany Fruehe, D.R.E. Students 61.

WEBSTER, BURNETT CO., ST. JOHN THE BAPTIST (1880), [CEM], (Also serves Sacred Hearts of Jesus and Mary, Crescent Lake, and Our Lady of Perpetual Help, Danbury). Rev. Michael J. Tupa.
Mailing Address: P.O. Box 7, 54893.
Church: 26455 S. Muskey Ave., 54893. Tel: 715-866-7321; Fax: 715-866-7305.
Catechesis/Religious Program—Julie Gibb, D.R.E.; Mary Pabst, D.R.E. Students 52.

WESTBORO, TAYLOR CO., ST. THERESA (1904), Rev. Ronald C. Kowalski.
Mailing Address: 513 State Rd., Rib Lake, 54490. Tel: 715-427-5259; Fax: 715-427-5266.
Church: N8855 2nd St.,, 54490.
Catechesis/Religious Program—Karen Firnstahl, D.R.E. Students 16.

WEYERHAEUSER, RUSK CO., SS. PETER AND PAUL (1897), [CEM], (Also serves Assumption B.V.M., Strickland; St. Mary, Bruce and St. Francis of Assisi, Flambeau). Rev. Lewis E. Burden; Deacon James E. Roberge.
Mailing Address: P.O. Box 207, 54895.
Church: 251 First St., 54895. Tel: 715-353-2400; Fax: 715-353-2400.
Catechesis/Religious Program—Lenore Krajewski; Judy Bullard, D.R.E. Students 100.

WHITTLESEY, TAYLOR CO., OUR LADY OF PERPETUAL HELP (1891), [CEM] Rev. Ronald C. Kowalski; Deacons Paul M. Ochodnicky; Michael D. Cullen, Parish Life Dir.
Mailing Address: 513 State Rd., Rib Lake, 54470.
Church: W5409 Whittlesey Ave., 54451. Tel: 715-427-5259; Fax: 715-427-5266.
Catechesis/Religious Program—Ron Mahner, D.R.E. Students 64.

WILSON, ST. CROIX CO., ST. BRIDGET (1886), [CEM] Rev. William J. Murphy.
Mailing Address: P.O. Box 18, Hammond, 54015-0018.
Church: 120 Depot St., 54027. Tel: 715-265-7133.
Catechesis/Religious Program—Martha Erickson, D.R.E. Students 14.

WINTER, SAWYER CO., ST. PETER (1908), [CEM], (Also serves Sacred Heart, Radisson). Rev. Vincent M. Bromley.
Mailing Address: P.O. Box 216, 54896.
Church: 5106 N. Main St., 54896. Tel: 715-266-3441.
Catechesis/Religious Program—Marie Martin, D.R.E.; Warren Wagner, D.R.E. Students 55.

WOODRUFF, ONEIDA CO., OUR LADY QUEEN OF THE UNIVERSE (1955),, (Also serves St. Patrick, Minocqua, St. John Vianney, Lake Tomahawk). Very Rev. James A. Hoffman; Rev. James P. Bartelme; Joan Laut, Pastoral Assoc.; Ric Johnson, Business Mgr.
Mailing Address: Box 30, 54568.
Church: 1025 Margaret St., 54568. Tel: 715-356-6284; Fax: 715-356-2940.
Catechesis/Religious Program—Diana Maki, D.R.E.; Cheryl Vos, D.R.E.; Brett Gustafson, D.R.E. Students 357.

Chaplains of Public Institutions

On Special or Other Diocesan Assignment:
Very Rev.—
Heslin, Philip J., Moderator of the Curia, Chancery, Box 969, 54880.

Military Chaplains:
Rev.—
Gonia, Raymond L., 801 Red Maple Dr., Wright Patterson Airforce Base, OH 45433-1142.

On Leave:
Revs.—
Beutner, Edward F.
Krajewski, Robert L.

Retired:
Revs.—
Anctil, Leo, 645 Knotty Oak Rd., Coventry, RI 02816-8227. Tel: 401-821-8199
Briody, Hugh J., Woodmount, Ballinasloe, Co. Galway Ireland. Tel: 353-905-44439
Cary, William J., 3750 Summerset Way, Apt. #2, Oshkosh, 54901. Tel: 920-426-1883
Cyz, Edward T., P.O. Box 1544, 54880. Tel: 715-392-6713
Dabruzzi, James S., 1348 B Carriage Dr., Hudson, 54016. Tel: 715-381-2815
Fraher, Leonard W., 804 Woodland Ln., New Richmond, 54017. Tel: 715-246-7855
Heinen, Virgil O., 1336 A Carriaoe Dr., Hudson, 54016. Tel: 715-381-9778
Kelchak, Joseph M., 4156 Oakmont Ct., Crown Point, IN 46307. Tel: 219-663-6726
Kleinheinz, Joseph L., 1012 Elm St., Merrill, 54452. Tel: 715-536-0065
Kowalski, Wladyslaw J., St. John the Baptist Parish (Peplin), 3308 Hwy. 153, Mosinee, 54455. Tel: 715-693-3604
Krynski, Leo J., c/o Patricia M. Burgess, 10225 60th Ave.,, Merrill, 54452. Tel: 715-848-5545
Kunda, Brendan J., 4090 Mill Lake Rd., Rhinelander, 54501. Tel: 715-272-1464
Meulemans, Dennis T., 718 Hulden Rd., Rib Lake, 54470.
Meulemans, Edward G., Reflections, 2601 E. McKellips Rd , Apt. 2020, Mesa, AZ 85213. Tel: 480-969-3180
Meyett, Irving C., 2528 E. 3rd St., 54880. Tel: 715-398-7196
Pakosta, Francis J., 3055 N. Fratney St., Milwaukee, 53212. Tel: 414-264-2563
Powell, Edward F., W6771 Branch Rd., Tomahawk, 54487-9230. Tel: 715-453-1357
Regh, John, W4598 Emery/Hackett Rd., Phillips, 54555-8574. Tel: 715-428-2268
Schoone, Raymond L., c/o Mary Van Ryen, N10050 Hwy. D, Tomahawke, 54487. Tel: 715-539-1477
Slowey, John P., 184 N. Eyder Ave., Phillips, 54555-1244. Tel: 715-339-4068
Spanjers, John J., P.O. Box 118,, Turtle Lake, 54889.
Speerstra, William F., 9896 Morgan Oaks Dr., Minocqua, 54548-8713. Tel: 715-358-3424
Stremski, John P., 1820 Estates Ln., Apt. 2, Shawano, 54166. Tel: 715-526-1812
Urban, Robert M., 1715 Oakes Ave., #4, 54880. Tel: 715-394-3479
Verdegan, Albert L., 403 E. Corbett Ave., Apt. #3, Ladysmith, 54848-1954. Tel: 715-532-0861
Votruba, George L., 132 W. Marshall St., Rice Lake, 54868. Tel: 715-236-7091
West, Norbert R., House of Loreto, 2812 Harvard Ave., N.W., Canton, OH 44709. Tel: 216-492-1240
Zepczyk, Gabriel C., 23515 County Rd. G, Ashland, 54806. Tel: 715-746-2549

Permanent Deacons:
Bablick, David C., St. Mary, Tomahawk
Baillargeon, Maurice A., St. Anne, Somerset
Ball, Chester E., St. Anthony, Park Falls
Bardos, John J., St. Anthony of Padua, Lac Du Flambeau
Bauer, Larry K., St. Joseph, Amery
Bosi, Ronald J., St. Joseph, Rhinelander
Braam, Peter R., St. Patrick, Hudson
Brockbank, Richard J., Our Lady of Sorrows, Ladysmith
Brossmer, Norbert G., St. Isaac Joques and Companions, Mercer
Byrnes, Timothy J., St. Ann, Beaver Dam
Cadotte, Roger, Holy Family, Bayfield
Celba, James J., Our Lady of the North, Phillips
Chammings, Robert J., Holy Assumption, Superior
Cullen, Michael D., St. John the Baptist, Rib Lake
Dennis, James, St. Boniface Parish, Chetek
Drahos, Jerome J., Our Lady of Sorrows, Ladysmith
Drevnick, Bernard M., St. Patrick, Hudson
Drost, Harvey G., Holy Trinity, Haugen
Eggett, Clifford, St. Mary, Tomahawk
Germain, Michael J., Immaculate Conception, New Richmond
Gil de Lamadrid, Arthur, Cathedral of Christ the King, Superior
Goodrich, Albert A., St. Kunegunda of Poland, Sugar Camp
Harvey, Michael O., Immaculate Conception, Rhinelander
Heckman, Richard G., St. Francis Xavier, Merrill
Heffner, Ralph W., St. John the Baptist, Webster
Heiser, Florian H., St. Joseph, Amery
Hennemann, Lawrence P., St. Bridget, River Falls
Huntowski, Peter R., St. Mary, Minong
Jetto, Robert T., St. Francis de Sales Parish, Spooner
Johnson, Fred E., St. Joseph, Osceola
Kuehn, Timothy J., St. Anthony, Superior
Leonhard, Richard D., Our Lady of Sorrows, Ladysmith
Lundgren, Russell J., St. Mary, Hurley
Lyngdal, Bernard J., St. Mary, Tomahawk
Marczak, Stanley J., St. Dominic, Frederic
Martineau, Philip L., St. Francis Xavier, Superior
Mayer, Hugh C., Immaculate Conception, New Richmond
McCaughn, John, St. Theresa, Three Lakes
McKenna, Jack, St. William, Pattison Park
Meier, Richard J., St. Joseph, Rhinelander
Mercier, Stanley J., St. Vincent de Paul Society, Rice Lake
Mesun, Norman J., Jr., St. Mary, Phelps
Ochodnicky, Paul M., St. John the Baptist, Rib Lake
Paron, Joseph F., Immaculate Conception, Hammond
Porten, Matthew C., Immaculate Conception, Rhinelander
Ramassini, John E., St. Mary Parish, Tomahawk
Reuter, Joseph E., St. Joseph, Hayward
Ricci, Gregory J., St. Anthony Abbot, Cumberland
Roberge, James E., SS. Peter & Paul, Weyerhaeuser
Roe, Joseph F., Sacred Heart of Jesus, Stetsonville
Schaefer, Kenneth J., St. Joseph, Rice Lake
Smerz, Darrell P., St. Mary, Tomahawk
Stefancin, Joseph, Our Lady of the Holy Rosary, Medford
Towle, C. Dan, St. Augustine, Harrison
Tuttle, Wesley G., St. John the Baptist, Glenwood City
Voldberg, Craig J., Our Lady of Sorrows, Ladysmith
Weiss, Thomas J., St. Bridget Parish, River Falls

INSTITUTIONS LOCATED IN THE DIOCESE

[A] GENERAL HOSPITALS

SUPERIOR. *St. Mary's Hospital of Superior*, 3500 Tower Ave., 54880. Tel: 715-392-8281; Fax: 715-392-8395. Email: tjacobson@smdl.org. Web: www.smdc.org. Mr. Terry R. Jacobson, CEO. Bed Capacity 31; Patients Assisted Annually 35,811; Total Staff 160.

EAGLE RIVER. **Eagle River Memorial Hospital, Inc.*, 201 Hospital Rd., 54521. Tel: 715-479-7411; Fax: 715-479-0395. Email: vanpat@hyhc.com. Web: www.ministryhealth.org. Brian Kief, CEO. Sponsored by the Sisters of the Sorrowful Mother, Corporate Sponsor: Ministry Health Care, Inc. (Milwaukee, WI) Bed Capacity 25; Patients Assisted Annually 45,000; Total Staff 105.

MERRILL. *Good Samaritan Health Center of Merrill, Wisconsin, Inc.*, 601 S. Center Ave., 54452. Tel: 715-536-5511; Fax: 715-539-2170. Michael Hammer, Pres. & CEO. Bed Capacity 73; Patients Assisted Annually 42,000; Total Staff 220.

NEW RICHMOND. *Holy Family Hospital*, 535 Hospital Rd., 54017. Tel: 715-246-2101; Fax: 715-243-7203. Email: jneedham@holyfamilyhospital.org. Web: www.holyfamilyhospital.org. Jean Needham, Pres. Bed Capacity 40; Patients Assisted Annually 17,500; Total Staff 210.

RHINELANDER. *Sacred Heart-St. Mary's Hospital*, 1044 Kabel Ave., 54501. Tel: 715-369-6600; Fax: 715-369-6441. Kevin O'Donnell, Pres. & CEO. Sisters of the Sorrowful MotherCorporate Sponsor:

Ministry Health Care., Inc. (Milwaukee, WI) Bed Capacity 73; Patients Assisted Annually 48,332.

TOMAHAWK. *Sacred Heart-St. Mary's Hospitals, Inc.*, 216 N. 7th St., 54487. Tel: 715-453-7700; Fax: 715-453-7716. Mr. Kevin O'Donnell, Pres. & CEO. Corporate Sponsor: Ministry Health Care, Inc. (Milwaukee, WI) Bed Capacity 14; Patients Assisted Annually 11,718.

WOODRUFF. **The Howard Young Medical Center, Inc.* Corporate Sponsor: Ministry Health Care, Inc. (Milwaukee, WI) , 240 Maple St., P.O. Box 470, 54868. Tel: 715-356-8000; Fax: 715-356-6097. Email: kiebrlehyhc.com. Web: www.ministryhealth.org. Brian J. Kief, CEO. Sponsored by the Sisters of the Sorrowful Mother Bed Capacity 99; (Includes inpatient admissions) 86,395; Staff 494.

[B] HOMES FOR AGED

SUPERIOR. *St. Francis Home, Inc.*, 1416 Cumming Ave., 54880. Tel: 715-394-6617; Fax: 715-394-5951. Brian Soland, Acting CEO.

MERRILL. *Bell Tower Residence, Inc.*, 1500 O'Day St., 54452. Tel: 715-536-5575; Fax: 715-536-1765. Email: dives@belltowerresidence.org. Web: www.belltowerresidence.org. Sr. Peggy Jackelen, S.C.S.C., Dir. Residence for the elderly. Sisters 11; Lay Residents 63; Total Residents 74; Total Staff 71.

WOODRUFF. **Dr. Kate Newcomb Convalescent Center, Inc.*, 301 Elm St., P.O. Box 829, 54568. Tel: 715-356-8888; Fax: 715-356-8861. Brian Kief, CEO; Rhonda Sherwood, Admin. Asst. Sponsored by the Sisters of the Sorrowful Mother. Corporate Sponsor: Ministry Health Care, Inc. (Milwaukee, WI). Bed Capacity 65; Total Staff 60.

[C] CONVENTS AND RESIDENCES FOR SISTERS

HUDSON. *Carmel of the Sacred Heart*, 430 Laurel Ave., 54016. Tel: 715-386-2156; Fax: 715-386-6446. Email: carmelit@pressenter.com. Web: www.pressenter.com/~carmelit/. Sr. Mary O'Neill, O.Carm., Prioress. Sisters 6.

LADYSMITH. *Servants of Mary*, 1000 College Ave. W., 54848-2199. Tel: 715-532-3364; 715-532-3365; Fax: 715-532-9611. Email: sistersosm@centurytel.net. Web: www.servitesisters.org/index.htm. Sr. Theresa Sandok, O.S.M., Pres. Sisters 71.

MERRILL. *Sisters of Mercy of the Holy Cross*, 501 S. Center Ave., 54452-3402. Tel: 715-539-5000; Fax: 715-539-5012. Email: provincialoffices@holycrosssisters.org. Web: www.holycrosssisters.org. Sr. Pat Cormack, S.C.S.C., Prov.

[D] CATHOLIC CHARITIES BUREAU

SUPERIOR. *Catholic Charities Bureau, Inc.*, 1416 Cummings Ave., 54880. Tel: 715-394-6617; Fax: 715-394-5951. Web: www.ccbsuperior.org. Brian Soland, Exec. Dir.; William Anderson, CFO; Beth Carlson, Assoc. Dir.; Terry Hendrick, Dir. Devel. Svcs.; Marilyn Christopherson, Coord. Diocesan Rels.; Brenda Osterlund, Admin. Coord.

Catholic Community Services, Inc., 1416 Cumming Ave., 54880. Tel: 715-394-6617; Fax: 715-394-5951. Gary Valley, Dir.

Housing Counseling Program, 1416 Cumming Ave., 54880. Tel: 715-394-6617; Fax: 715-394-5951. Gary Valley, Dir.

Superior Affordable Housing and Health Care Alliance, 1416 Cumming Ave., 54880. Tel: 715-394-6617; Fax: 715-394-5951. Gary Valley, Dir.

United Day Care, Inc., dba Hudson Community Day Care, 816 Fourth St., Hudson, 54016. Tel: 715-386-5912; Fax: 715-386-1467. Paula Hyde, Dir. Home Health Service.

Dove Agency, Inc. (Douglas Co.), 1416 Cumming Ave., 54880. Tel: 715-392-3133; Fax: 715-392-3190. Beth Carlson, Dir.

Dove, Inc. (Douglas Co.), 1416 Cumming Ave., 54880. Tel: 715-392-3133; Fax: 715-392-3190. Beth Carlson, Dir. Housing-Disabled.

Acorn Apartments (Wisconsin Rapids), 2721 Tenth St. S., Wisconsin Rapids, 54494. Tel: 715-369-2550; Fax: 715-369-5857. Carol Pederson, Mgr.

Apple River, Inc. (Amery), 401 Minneapolis Ave., Amery, 54001. Tel: 715-236-2366; Fax: 715-236-3161. Robert Heinze, Mgr.

Challenge Center A, Inc. (Superior), 3105 Cumming Ave., 54880. Tel: 715-394-2771; Fax: 715-394-2100. Eugene Chuzles, Dir.

Blue Valley, Inc., 1310 N. Wisconsin Ave., Rice Lake, 54868. Tel: 715-236-2366; Fax: 715-236-3161. Robert Heinze, Mgr.

Cypress Group Home, 1415 Cypress, 54880. Tel: 715-394-2771; Fax: 715-394-2100. Eugene Chuzles, Dir.

Eastwood Apartments, Inc. (Medford), Del Rae Ct., Medford, 54451. Tel: 715-369-2550; Fax: 715-369-5857. Carol Pederson, Mgr.

Elmwood Apartments, 1020 Weeks Ave., 54880. Tel: 715-392-3447; Fax: 715-395-2470. Bruce Todd, Mgr.

Evergreen Apartments, Inc.. (Timberlane), 880 E. Timber Dr., Rhinelander, 54501. Tel: 715-369-2550; Fax: 715-369-5857. Carol Pederson, Mgr.

Evergreen Apartments, 24121 Fourth St., Siren, 54872. Tel: 715-236-2366; Fax: 715-236-3161. Robert Heinze Mgr.

Harborview Group Home, 910 E. 5th St., 54880. Tel: 715-394-2771; Fax: 715-394-2100. Eugene Chuzles, Dir.

Maywood Apartments, (Medford), 521 Lemke Ave.., Medford, 54451. Tel: 715-369-2550; Fax: 715-369-5857. Carol Pederson, Mgr.

McKenzie Manor, 3317 N. 21st St., 54880. Tel: 715-394-2771; Fax: 715-394-2100. Eugene Chuzles, Dir.

Northfield Apartments, Inc., 2713 W. Superior St., Winter, 54896. Robert Heinze, Mgr.

Phoenix Villa of Superior Inc. (Oakwood), Formerly Oakwood Apartments (Superior) 1112 John Ave., 54880. Tel: 715-392-3447; Fax: 715-395-2470. Bruce Todd, Mgr.

Phoenix Villa North, Inc. (Cumberland) 1490 Arcade, Cumberland, 54829. Tel: 715-236-2366; Fax: 715-236-3161. Robert Heinze, Mgr.

Phoenix Villa of Hayward, Inc. (Hayward), Rt. 10, 430 Murel St., Hayward, 54843. Tel: 715-236-2366; Fax: 715-236-3161. Robert Heinze, Mgr.

Phoenix Villa North, Inc., 1305 N. Wisconsin St., Rice Lake, 54868. Tel: 715-236-2366; Fax: 715-236-3161. Robert Heinze, Mgr.

Sumac Trail Apartments, Inc., Sumac Tr. and Philip St., Rhinelander, 54501. Tel: 715-369-2550; Fax: 715-369-5857. Carol Pederson, Mgr.

Timberlane Apartments, 880 E. Timber Dr., Rhinelander, 54501. Tel: 715-369-2550; Fax: 715-369-5857. Carol Pederson, Mgr.

Westbay, Inc., 1104 John Ave., 54880. Tel: 715-392-3447; Fax: 715-395-2470. Bruce Todd, Mgr.

Winterhaven Apartments, Inc., 5038 N. Ellen St., Winter, 54896. Tel: 715-236-2366; Fax: 715-236-3161. Robert Heinze, Mgr.

Woodview Group Home, 6001 E. Third St., 54880. Tel: 715-394-2771; Fax: 715-394-2100. Eugene Chuzles. Dir. Housing - Seniors.

Acorn Apartments, Inc. (Crandon), 508 W. Washington, Crandon, 54520. Tel: 715-369-2550; Fax: 715-369-5857. Carol Pederson, Mgr.

Acorn Apartments, Inc. (Minong), P.O. Box 438, Minong, 54859. Tel: 715-236-2366; Fax: 715-236-3161. Robert Heinze, Mgr.

Evergreen Apartments, Inc. (Chetek), 707 Tainter Ave., Chetek, 54728. Tel: 715-236-2366; Fax: 715-236-3161. Robert Heinze, Mgr.

Evergreen Apartments, Inc. (Shell Lake), 801 N. Lake Dr., Shell Lake, 54871. Tel: 715-236-2366; Fax: 715-236-3161. Robert Heinze, Mgr.

Maywood Apartments, Inc. (Plover), 2501 Madison Ave., Plover, 54467. Tel: 715-369-2550; Fax: 715-369-5857. Carol Pederson, Mgr.

Phoenix Villa, Inc., 1100 Weeks Ave., 54880. Tel: 715-392-3447; Fax: 715-395-2470. Bruce Todd, Mgr.

Phoenix Villa of Iron River (Iron River), Hwy. H, Iron River, 54847. Tel: 715-392-3447; Fax: 715-395-2470. Bruce Todd, Mgr.

Phoenix Villa, Inc. (Lake Nebagamon), Formerly Phoenix Villa of Lake Nebagamon (Lake Nebagamon) 6250 S. Fitch Ave., Lake Nebagamon, 54849. Tel: 715-392-3447; Fax: 715-395-2470. Bruce Todd, Mgr.

Phoenix Villa of Rhinelander (Rhinelander), 1011 Mason St., Rhinelander, 54501. Tel: 715-369-2550; Fax: 715-369-5857. Carol Pederson, Mgr. Rehabilitation Centers.

Black River Industries, Inc. (Medford), 650 Jensen Dr., Medford, 54451. Tel: 715-748-2950; Fax: 715-748-6363. John Prindle, Dir.

Cedarwood Apartments, Inc., 1416 Cumming Ave., 54880. Tel: 715-394-6617; Fax: 715-394-5951. Beth Carlson, Mgr.

Challenge Center, Inc., 39 N. 25th St E., 54880. Tel: 715-394-2771; Fax: 715-394-2100. Eugene Chuzles, Dir.

Diversified Services, Inc., (Siren), P.O. Box 501, Siren, 54872. Tel: 715-349-5724; Fax: 715-349-5505. Joe Wacek, Dir.

Headwaters. Inc. (Rhinelander), 1441 E. Timber Dr., Box 618, Rhinelander, 54501. Tel: 715-369-1337; Fax: 715-369-1793. Mary Hardtke, Dir. Senior Programs.

Foster Grandparent Program (NW WI, NE MN), 1509 Tower Ave., 54880. Tel: 715-394-5384; Fax: 715-394-9724. Margaret Hogg, Dir.

Retired Senior Volunteer Program (Douglas Co.), 1509 Tower Ave., 54880. Tel: 715-394-4425; Fax: 715-394-5775. Kendra-Sue Rohde, Dir.

Retired Senior Volunteer Program, 1835 N. Stevens St., Ste. 22, Rhinelander, 54501. Tel: 715-369-1919; Fax: 715-369-3686. Lori Bushong, Dir.

Servants of Mary Continuing Care Trust, 1000 College Ave. W., Ladysmith, 54848. Tel: 414-744-1160. Email: scott@lakeosfs.org. Rev. Scott Wallenfelsz, S.D.S. (SFD), OSM Fin. Dir.

[E] RETREAT HOUSES

AMERY. *Mount Carmel Hermitage*, 897 U.S. Hwy. 8, 54001-2541. Tel: 715-268-9313; Fax: 715-268-7495. Sr. Kristine Haugen, O.C.D.H, Coord.

ARBOR VITAE. *Marywood Franciscan Spirituality Center (FSPA)*, 3560 Hwy. 51 N., 54568-9538. Tel: 715-385-3750; Fax: 715-385-9118. Email: marywood@newnorth.net. Web: www.fspa.org. Sr. Jolynn Brehm, F.S.P.A., Dir.

[F] NEWMAN CENTERS

SUPERIOR. *Superior-UW* , Newman Center Ministry to Young Adults. , 823 N. 16th St., 54880. Tel: 715-394-7710. Paul Birch, Coord. Ministry.

RIVER FALLS. *St. Thomas More Newman Center* 423 E. Cascade, 54022. Tel: 715-425-7234; Fax: 715-425-6959. Email: thomasjweiss@uwrf.edu. Web: www.uwrf.edu. Thomas J. Weiss, Coord. for Newman Min.

[G] ASSOCIATION OF THE FAITHFUL

AMERY. *Hermits of Mt. Carmel*, 897 Hwy. 8, 54001. Tel: 715-268-9313; Fax: 715-268-7495. Sr. Kristine Haugen, O.C.D.H, Coord.

[H] MISCELLANEOUS

SUPERIOR. *Society of St. Vincent de Paul Sacred Heart of Jesus Conference of Superior, WI*, P.O. Box 372, 54880. Tel: 715-394-6617. Sr. Rita M. Schneider, S.S.N.D., Pres.

LADYSMITH. *Mary Bradley Corporation*, 1000 College Ave. W., 54848-2199. Tel: 715-532-3364; Fax: 715-532-6153. Sr. Theresa Sandok, O.S.M., Pres.

MERRILL. *Good Samaritan Health Center Foundation of Merrill, Wisconsin, Inc.* A not for profit corporation for the purpose of soliciting and receiving contributions for the benefit of Good Samaritan Health Center of Merrill, WI, Inc. , 601 S. Center Ave., 54452. Tel: 715-536-5511; Fax: 715-539-2170. Michael Hammer, Pres.

Sisters of Mercy of the Holy Cross Community Support Charitable Trust, 501 S. Center Ave., 54452-3402. Tel: 715-539-5000; Fax: 715-539-5012. Sisters Anita Wolf, S.C.S.C., Trustee; Anita Hirt, S.C.S.C., Trustee; John Tortolani, Trustee.

Society of St. Vincent dePaul-St. Francis Xavier Conference, 1708 E. 10th St., 54452. Tel: 715-539-8811; Fax: 715-536-4484. Email: jmccarthy816@aol.com. Denis McCarthy, Contact Person.

NEW RICHMOND. *Holy Family Hospital Foundation, Inc.*, 535 Hospital Rd., 54017. Tel: 715-246-2101; Fax: 715-243-7203. Email: jneedham@holyfamilyhospital.org. Web: www.holyfamilyhospital.org. Jean Needham, Pres.

RHINELANDER. **Ministry Medical Group, Inc.*, 1020 Kabel Ave., 54501. Tel: 715-361-4700; 715-361-4780; 800-866-8673. Email: mijones@shsmh.org. Web: www.ministrymedicalgroup.org. Michael J. Kryda, M.D., Pres.; Michael Jones, Admin. Corporate Sponsor: Ministry Health Care, Inc., Milwaukee, WI

Saints, Inc., 1044 Kabel Ave., 54501. Tel: 715-369-6400; Fax: 715-369-6441. Jack Sutliff, Pres.

WEBSTER. *Thomas More Center for Preaching and Prayer, Inc.*, 27781 Leef Rd., 54893. Tel: 715-866-7436; Fax: 715-866-4277. Email: tmcmike@attglobal.net. Web: www.thomasmorecenter.org. Revs. Michael A. Champlin, O.P., Pres.; Nicholas W. Punch, O.P., Treas.; Sr. Joan Bukrey, O.S.F., Vice Pres.

WINTER. *Camp We-Ha-Kee* (Girls) , 8104 N. Barker Lake Rd., 54896. Tel: 715-266-3263; Fax: 715-266-2267. Email: wehakee@pctcnet.net. Web: www.campwehakee.com. Sr. Arturo Cranston, O.P., Dir.

WOODRUFF. **Howard Young Clinics, Inc.*, 240 Maple St., 54568. Tel: 715-356-8000; Fax: 715-356-6097. Web: www.ministryhealth.org. Brian J. Kief, CEO. Sponsored by the Sisters of the Sorrowful Mother, Corporate Sponsor: Ministry Health Care, Inc. (Milwaukee, WI) Patients Assisted Annually 20,361; Total Staff 46.

**Howard Young Health Care, Inc.*, 240 Maple St., 54568. Tel: 715-356-8000; Fax: 715-356-6097. Email: kiebrl@hyhc.com. Web: www.ministryhealth.org. Brian J. Kief, CEO. Sponsored by the Sisters of the Sorrowful Mother, Corporate Sponsor: Ministry Health Care, Inc. (Milwaukee, WI) Total Staff 48.

RELIGIOUS INSTITUTES OF MEN REPRESENTED IN THE DIOCESE

For further details refer to the corresponding bracketed number in the Religious Institutes of Men or Women section.

[0200]—*Benedictine Monks* (Lisle, IL).—O.S.B.

[0480]—*Conventual Franciscans* (Arroyo Grande, CA)—O.F.M.Conv

[0520]—*Franciscan Friars* (St. Louis, MO)—O.F.M.

[0825]—*Missionary Congregation of the Blessed Sacrament*—M.C.B.S.

[0430]—*Order of Preachers-Province of St. Albert the Great* Chicago—O.P.

[1990]—*Society of the Catholic Apostolate* (Milwaukee, WI)—S.A.C.

[1060]—*Society of the Precious Blood* (Prov. of Cincinnati - Dayton, OH)—C.P.P.S.

RELIGIOUS INSTITUTES OF WOMEN REPRESENTED IN THE DIOCESE

[0320]—*Carmelite Nuns of the Ancient Observance*—O.Carm.

[1070-13]—*Congregation of the Most Holy Rosary*—O.P.

[3710]—*Congregation of the Sisters of Saint Agnes*—C.S.A.

[1780]—*Congregation of the Sisters of the Third Order of St. Francis of Perpetual Adoration (Franciscan Sis*—F.S.P.A.

[1710]—*Congregation of the Third Order of St. Francis of Mary Immaculate* (Joilet, IL)—O.S.F.

[1230]—*Franciscan Sisters of Christian Charity*—O.S.F.

[2970]—*School Sisters of Notre Dame* (Mankato/ Milwaukee)—S.S.N.D.

[1680]—*School Sisters of St. Francis*—S.S.S.F.

[3590]—*Servants of Mary (Servite Sisters)*—O.S.M.

[1070-03]—*Sinsinawa Dominican Congregation of the Most Holy Rosary*—O.P.

[2630]—*Sisters of Mercy of the Holy Cross*—S.C.S.C.

[1705]—*Sisters of St. Francis of Assisi, Milwaukee*—O.S.F.

[3840]—*Sisters of St. Joseph of Carondelet* (Prov. of St. Paul)—C.S.J.

[3880]—*Sisters of St. Joseph of Medaille*—C.S.J.

[3930]—*Sisters of St. Joseph of the Third Order of St. Francis* (Prov. of Immaculate Conception; St. Joseph Prov.)—S.S.J.-T.O.S.F.

[4100]—*Sisters of the Sorrowful Mother* (Third Order of St. Francis)—S.S.M.

[1720]—*Sisters of the Third Order Regular of St. Francis of the Congregation of Our Lady of Lourdes*—O.S.F.

NECROLOGY

(No Deaths)

Diocese of Syracuse

(Dioecesis Syracusensis)

Most Reverend

JAMES M. MOYNIHAN, D.D.

Bishop of Syracuse; ordained December 15, 1957; appointed Bishop of Syracuse April 4, 1995; consecrated and installed in See of Syracuse May 29, 1995 *Office: 240 E. Onondaga St., P.O. Box 511, Syracuse, NY 13201-0511. Res.: Cathedral of the Immaculate Conception*, 259 E. Onondaga St., Syracuse, NY 13202.

Most Reverend

THOMAS J. COSTELLO, D.D., V.G.

Retired Auxiliary Bishop of Syracuse; ordained June 5, 1954; appointed Auxiliary Bishop of Syracuse and Titular Bishop of Perdices January 10, 1978; consecrated March 13, 1978; retired March 23, 2004 *Res.: 1515 Midland Ave., Syracuse, NY 13205.*

Chancery Office: P.O. Box 511, Syracuse, NY 13201. Tel: 315-422-7203; Fax: 315-478-4619.

ESTABLISHED NOVEMBER 26, 1886

Square Miles 5,749.

Corporate Title: The Roman Catholic Diocese of Syracuse NY.

Comprises the Counties of Broome, Chenango, Cortland, Madison, Oneida, Onondaga and Oswego.

For legal titles of parishes and diocesan institutions, consult the Chancery Office.

STATISTICAL OVERVIEW

Statistical report was not submitted for 2004.

Personnel	
Bishop	1
Auxiliary Bishops	1
Retired Bishops	1
Priests: Diocesan Active in Diocese	196
Priests: Diocesan Active Outside Diocese	14
Priests: Retired, Sick or Absent	61
Number of Diocesan Priests	271
Religious Priests in Diocese	68
Total Priests in Diocese	339
Extern Priests in Diocese	8
Ordinations:	
Diocesan Priests	1
Transitional Deacons	1
Permanent Deacons	5
Permanent Deacons in Diocese	77
Total Brothers	16
Total Sisters	405
Parishes	
Parishes	169
With Resident Pastor:	
Resident Diocesan Priests	153
Resident Religious Priests	4
Without Resident Pastor:	
Administered by Priests	12
Completely Vacant	3
Missions	15
Pastoral Centers	20
Professional Ministry Personnel:	
Brothers	18
Sisters	472
Welfare	
Catholic Hospitals	3
Total Assisted	1,466,340
Health Care Centers	1
Total Assisted	300
Homes for the Aged	54
Residential Care of Children	10
Total Assisted	150
Specialized Homes	3
Total Assisted	60
Special Centers for Social Services	86
Total Assisted	62,800
Residential Care of Disabled	13
Total Assisted	125
Educational	
Diocesan Students in Other Seminaries	20
Seminaries, Religious	1
Students Religious	11
Total Seminarians	31
Colleges and Universities	1
Total Students	3,129
High Schools, Diocesan and Parish	5
Total Students	2,627
High Schools, Private	1
Total Students	750
Elementary Schools, Diocesan and Parish	29
Total Students	6,096
Catechesis/Religious Education:	
High School Students	7,777
Elementary Students	31,003
Total Students under Catholic Instruction	51,413
Teachers in the Diocese:	
Priests	4
Brothers	1
Sisters	43
Lay Teachers	689
Vital Statistics	
Receptions into the Church:	
Infant Baptism Totals	4,919
Adult Baptism Totals	256
Received into Full Communion	400
First Communions	5,242
Confirmations	4,260
Marriages:	
Catholic	1,289
Interfaith	507
Total Marriages	1,796
Deaths	4,711
Total Catholic Population	345,736
Total Population	1,174,887

Former Bishops—Rt. Revs. PATRICK ANTHONY LUDDEN, D.D., ord. June 21, 1864; consecrated May 1, 1887; died Aug. 6, 1912; JOHN GRIMES, D.D., ord. Feb. 19, 1882; consecrated May 16, 1909; Coadjutor Bishop, 1909-1912; succeeded to the See, Aug. 6, 1912; died July 26, 1922; Most Revs. DANIEL JOSEPH CURLEY, D.D., ord. May 19, 1894; consecrated May 1, 1923; died Aug. 3, 1932; JOHN ALOYSIUS DUFFY, D.D., ord. June 13, 1908; consecrated June 29, 1933; installed July 11, 1933; appt. Bishop of Buffalo, Jan. 9, 1937; installed in See of Buffalo, April 14, 1937; died Sept. 27, 1944; WALTER A. FOERY, D.D., Ph.D. (Retired), ord. June 10, 1916; appt. May 26, 1937; consecrated Aug. 18, 1937; appt. assistant at the Pontifical Throne, Dec. 11, 1961; retired and named Titular Bishop of Miseno-Cape, Aug. 4, 1970; died May 10, 1978; DAVID F. CUNNINGHAM, D.D., ord. June 12, 1926; appt. Titular Bishop of Lampsacus and Auxiliary Bishop of Syracuse, April 5, 1950; consecrated June 8, 1950; appt. Coadjutor Bishop "Cum jure successiones," June 19, 1967; succeeded to the See, Aug. 4, 1970; died Feb. 22, 1979; FRANK J. HARRISON, D.D. (Retired), ord. June 4, 1937; appt. Titular Bishop of Aquae and Auxiliary Bishop of Syracuse, March 1, 1971; consecrated April 22, 1971; appt. Bishop of Syracuse, Nov. 16, 1976; retired June 16, 1987; died May 1, 2004; JOSEPH T. O'KEEFE, D.D. (Retired), ord. April 17, 1948; appt. Titular Bishop of Tre Taverne and Auxiliary Bishop of New York, July 3, 1982; consecrated Sept. 8, 1982; appt. Bishop of Syracuse, June 16, 1987; installed in See of Syracuse, Aug. 3, 1987; retired April 4, 1995; died Sept. 2, 1997.

Vicar General/Vicar for Priests—Most Rev. THOMAS J. COSTELLO, D.D., Res.: 1515 Midland Ave., Syracuse, 13205.

Vicars Forane—Northern Area Vicar: VACANT. Southern Area Vicar: Rev. THOMAS J. RYAN, 155 Main St., Johnson City, 13790. Eastern Area Vicars: Revs. PHILIP A. HEARN, 105 E. Liberty St., Rome, 13440; JOHN A. BUEHLER, 240 Bleecker St., Utica, 13501. Western Area Vicars: Revs. RICHARD M. KOPP, 47 Syracuse St., Baldwinsville, 13027; GEORGE F. SHEEHAN, 6651 Kirkville Rd., East Syracuse, 13057.

Chancery Office—240 E. Onondaga St., Syracuse, 13202. Mailing Address, P.O. Box 511, Syracuse, 13201. Tel: 315-422-7203; Fax: 315-478-4619. Office Hours: Mon.-Fri. 8:30-4:30; Send official mail, including marriage dispensations, to Chancery.

Chancellor—Rev. MICHAEL P. MINEHAN, J.C.L., 240 E. Onondaga St., Syracuse, 13202.

Assistant Chancellor/Secretary to Bishop Moynihan—Rev. ANDREW E. BARANSKI, 240 E. Onondaga St., Syracuse, 13202.

Board of Diocesan Consultors—Most Rev. THOMAS J. COSTELLO, D.D.; Revs. PHILIP A. HEARN; DONALD H. KARLEN; RICHARD M. KOPP; JAMES P. LANG; THOMAS J. MCGRATH; THOMAS J. RYAN; GEORGE F. SHEEHAN.

Management Team—Most Revs. JAMES M. MOYNIHAN, D.D.; THOMAS J. COSTELLO, D.D.; Revs. JAMES P. LANG; TIMOTHY S. ELMER, J.C.L.; MICHAEL P. MINEHAN, J.C.L.; JOSEPH H. PHILLIPS; ANDREW E. BARANSKI; Sr. KATIE EIFFE, C.S.J.; RALPH JONES; Mr. JOHN CATALDO; Mr. CHRISTOPHER PARKER; Sr. EILEEN MCCANN, C.S.J.; Mr. DENNIS J. MANNING, A.C.S.W.; Ms. DANIELLE CUMMINGS.

Pastoral Council—Most Rev. JAMES M. MOYNIHAN, D.D., Pres.; Ms. KATHLEEN M. DYER, Exec. Sec., Res.: 101 Ridge Rd., Fulton, 13069. Tel: 315-592-5566.

Pastoral Examiners—Revs. JOHN P. FENLON; MORITZ FUCHS; THOMAS KEATING; JAMES KENNEDY; RICHARD V. O'NEILL; DANIEL G. MURPHY (Retired); JOHN F. ROSE; JOSEPH SALERNO; JOSEPH S. ZARESKI.

Presbyteral Council—Most Revs. JAMES M. MOYNIHAN, D.D., Pres.; THOMAS J. COSTELLO, D.D. Ex Officio: Revs. MICHAEL P. MINEHAN, J.C.L.; JAMES P. LANG; THOMAS J. RYAN; RICHARD M. KOPP; GEORGE F. SHEEHAN; PHILIP A. HEARN; JOHN A. BUEHLER. Elected: Revs. THOMAS F. HOBBES; GREGORY C. LESTRANGE; TIMOTHY S. ELMER,

J.C.L.; PETER A. WILLIAMS; MARK A. PASIK; PAUL J. DROBIN; RONALD C. BILL; Rev. Msgr. CHARLES H. ECKERMANN (Retired); Revs. JAMES F. SMITH, S.J.; JUSTIN A. BIASE, O.F.M.Conv.

Diocesan Tribunal—

*Judicial Vicar—*Rev. TIMOTHY S. ELMER, J.C.L. Tel: 315-470-1480; Fax: 315-474-6893.

*Judges—*Revs. JOHN P. DONOVAN, J.C.L.; ROBERT P. HYDE, J.C.L.

*Defender of the Bond—*Rev. MICHAEL P. MINEHAN, J.C.L.

*Promoter of Justice—*Rev. Msgr. JAMES A. MCCLOSKEY (Retired); Rev. PAUL CARMAN, J.C.L.

*Notary of the Tribunal—*BARBARA REITER.

*Advocates—*Sr. ANNA WALTER MOSSDORF, O.S.F.; MARGARET EDGECOMB.

*Case Coordinators/Staff—*BARBARA REITER.

*Vicar for Administration—*Rev. MICHAEL P. MINEHAN, J.C.L., 240 E. Onondaga St., P.O. Box 511, Syracuse, 13201. Tel: 315-422-7203.

*Director for Community Services—*Mr. DENNIS J. MANNING, A.C.S.W., 240 E. Onondaga St., P.O. Box 511, Syracuse, 13201. Tel: 315-424-1830.

*Vicar for Parishes—*Rev. JAMES P. LANG, 240 E. Onondaga St., P.O. Box 511, Syracuse, 13201. Tel: 315-470-1437.

*Vicar for Priests—*Most Rev. THOMAS J. COSTELLO, D.D., 240 E. Onondaga St., P.O. Box 511, Syracuse, 13201. Tel: 315-470-1460.

*Vicar for Religious—*VACANT, 240 E. Onondaga St., P.O. Box 511, Syracuse, 13201. Tel: 315-422-7203; 315-470-1424.

Diocesan Offices

*Accounting—*Ms. DEBRA SOCHAN, CFO, P.O. Box 511, Syracuse, 13201. Tel: 315-422-9045; Fax: 315-422-9139.

*Administration—*Rev. MICHAEL P. MINEHAN, J.C.L., Vicar, P.O. Box 511, Syracuse, 13201. Tel: 315-422-7203.

*Archives—*Mr. CARL ROESCH, Archivist, P.O. Box 511, Syracuse, 13201. Tel: 315-470-1493.

*Asian Apostolate—*Rev. MARTIN TRAN VAN BAN, C.M.C.; Sr. JUDITH HOWLEY, C.S.J., 215 N. State St., Syracuse, 13203. Tel: 315-472-7043.

*Benefits—*Ms. CAROLYN CAIN, Dir., P.O. Box 511, Syracuse, 13201. Tel: 315-422-9091.

*Black Catholic Ministry—*Mr. RALPH JONES, P.O. Box 511, Syracuse, 13201. Tel: 315-470-1463.

*Boy Scouts/Girl Scouts—*Rev. JAMES P. LANG, Chap., 240 E. Onondaga St., P.O. Box 511, Syracuse, 13201-0511. Tel: 315-470-1437.

*Building Commission—*Most Revs. JAMES M. MOYNIHAN, D.D.; THOMAS J. COSTELLO, D.D.; Revs. MICHAEL P. MINEHAN, J.C.L.; JOSEPH E. SCARDELLA; Mr. THOMAS V. DADEY, Esq.; Mr. EDWARD T. KING; Mr. J. DOUGLAS ROSS; WILLIAM DORAN; JAMES A. MURPHY; EDWARD SAMOLIS; Ms. DEBRA J. SOCHAN.

*Catholic Cemeteries—*Rev. JAMES C. FRITZEN, Dir.; Mr. MARK LAZAROSKI, Exec. Dir., 2315 South Ave., Syracuse, 13207. Tel: 315-475-4639; Fax: 315-422-0363.

*Catholic Charities—*Mr. DENNIS J. MANNING, A.C.S.W., P.O. Box 511, Syracuse, 13201. Tel: 315-424-1830; Fax: 315-478-4619.

*Onondaga County Director—*Mr. BRIAN WALTON, 1654 W. Onondaga St., Syracuse, 13204. Tel: 315-424-1806.

*Broome County Director—*Mr. JOSEPH G. SLAVIK, 232 Main St., Binghamton, 13905. Tel: 607-729-9166.

*Chenango County Director—*JANE CODDINGTON, Dir., 3 O'Hara Dr., Norwich, 13815. Tel: 607-334-8244.

*Cortland County Director—*PAULA CURRIE, 33-35 Central Ave., Cortland, 13045. Tel: 607-756-5992.

*Oneida and Madison Counties Director—*KATHLEEN EICHENLAUB, 1408 Genesee St., Utica, 13502. Tel: 315-724-2150.

*Oswego County Director—*ANDREA MCCABE, 365 First St., Fulton, 13069. Tel: 315-598-3980.

*Catholic Deaf Community—*MARY MARGARET VAN DAMME, Dir., 1119 Elm St., Utica, 13501. Tel: 315-735-8184 (TTY/Voice).

*Catholic Relief Services—*Mr. DENNIS J. MANNING, A.C.S.W., Dir., P.O. Box 511, Syracuse, 13201. Tel: 315-424-1830.

*Catholic Schools—*Mr. JOHN CATALDO, Supt., P.O. Box 511, Syracuse, 13201. Tel: 315-470-1450; Fax: 315-470-1470; Rev. CHARLES S. VAVONESE, Asst. Supt.; Mrs. LESLEY HUGHES, Dir. Curriculum; Sr. PATRICIA GIBSON, Dir. Govt. Programs.

*Northern & Western Regions—*Sr. HELEN ANN CHARLEBOIS, I.H.M., Asst. Supt., P.O. Box 511, Syracuse, 13201. Tel: 315-470-1450; Fax: 315-470-1470.

*Southern Region—*Dr. PAUL KING, Asst. Supt., 19 Lincoln Ave., P.O. Box 90, Binghamton, 13905. Tel: 607-723-1547; Fax: 607-723-5697.

*"The Catholic Sun"—*CONNIE CISSELL, Editor in Chief & Gen. Mgr.; Rev. DONALD BOURGEOIS, Episcopal Liaison, 421 S. Warren St., Syracuse, 13202. Tel: 315-422-8153; 800-333-0571; Fax: 315-422-7549. Email: catholicsun@yahoo.com. Web: www.sydio.org.

*Catholic Television—*Mr. JAMES FUNSON, Dir., 1342 Lancaster Ave., Syracuse, 13210. Tel: 315-472-3584; Fax: 315-472-8409.

*Christopher Community—*Mr. PETER WHITE, Exec. Dir., 1654 W. Onondaga St., Syracuse, 13204. Tel: 315-414-1821.

*Clerical Fund Society of the Roman Catholic Diocese of Syracuse—*Most Revs. JAMES M. MOYNIHAN, D.D., Pres.; THOMAS J. COSTELLO, D.D., Vice Pres.; Rev. MICHAEL P. MINEHAN, J.C.L., Sec. & Treas.

*Office of Communications—*Ms. DANIELLE CUMMINGS, Dir., P.O. Box 511, Syracuse, 13201. Tel: 315-470-1476; Fax: 315-478-4619. Email: daniellecummings@worldnet.att.

*Council of Religious—*Sr. ROSE GARRAMONE, O.S.F., Pres., P.O. Box 511, Syracuse, 13201.

*Development Office—*Mr. CHRISTOPHER PARKER, 1342 Lancaster Ave., Syracuse, 13210. Tel: 315-472-0203; 315-472-7902; Fax: 315-472-8409.

*Ecumenical Commission—*Rev. Msgr. RONALD C. BILL, Dir. (Retired), 8229 S. Main St., Cicero, 13039. Tel: 315-699-2752.

*Family Life Education—*Rev. JOSEPH H. PHILLIPS, Dir., 1342 Lancaster Ave., Syracuse, 13210. Tel: 315-472-6754; Fax: 315-472-8409.

*Finance Committee—*Most Rev. JAMES M. MOYNIHAN, D.D.; Revs. MICHAEL P. MINEHAN, J.C.L.; J. ROBERT YEAZEL; Mr. JOSEPH MCGLYNN; Mr. JAMES MURPHY; Ms. CAROL PIEKLIK; Ms. DOREEN SIMMONS, Esq.; Ms. DEBRA SOCHAN; Mr. THOMAS PRINZING; Mr. KEVIN CONSIDINE; Mr. J. DANIEL PLUFF; Mr. JOHN VENSEL.

*Formation for Ministry—*Rev. JOSEPH SCARDELLA, Dir., P.O. Box 511, Syracuse, 13202. Tel: 315-470-1421; Fax: 315-478-4619.

*Health Care—*Mr. DENNIS J. MANNING, A.C.S.W., Coord., P.O. Box 511, Syracuse, 13201. Tel: 315-424-1830; Fax: 315-478-4619.

Heritage Campaign—c/o Development Office, 1342 Lancaster Ave., Syracuse, 13210. Tel: 315-472-0203.

*HOPE Appeal—*Mr. CHRISTOPHER PARKER, 1342 Lancaster Ave., Syracuse, 13210. Tel: 315-472-0203; Fax: 315-472-8409.

Ruth Ministry— Syracuse Diocese Response to Domestic Violence Mrs. CINDY FALISE, Dir., P.O. Box 511, Syracuse, 13201. Tel: 315-424-1830; Fax: 315-478-4619.

*Liturgy—*Rev. ANDREW E. BARANSKI, Dir., P.O. Box 511, Syracuse, 13201. Tel: 315-470-1434.

*Parish Services—*Mr. NICK CROSBY, P.O. Box 511, Syracuse, 13201. Tel: 315-470-9089.

*Permanent Diaconate—*Deacon LESLIE F. DISTIN, Dir., P.O. Box 511, Syracuse, 13201. Tel: 315-470-1466.

*Priest Personnel—*Most Rev. THOMAS J. COSTELLO, D.D., Dir., P.O. Box 511, Syracuse, 13201. Tel: 315-470-1460; Fax: 315-478-4619.

*Priests' Personnel Committee—*Most Revs. JAMES M. MOYNIHAN, D.D.; THOMAS J. COSTELLO, D.D.; Revs. STEPHEN WIRKES; JOHN A. BUEHLER; HENRY J. PEDZICH; JOSEPH SALERNO; MICHAEL T. MEAGHER; JOHN P. PUTANO; RICHARD PRIOR; MICHAEL P. MINEHAN, J.C.L.; WILLIAM R. JONES; JOHN P. CROGHAN; JAMES P. LANG; JOHN P. DONOVAN, J.C.L.

*Project Rachel—*Mrs. CINDY FALISE, Dir., P.O. Box 511, Syracuse, 13201. Tel: 315-424-3737.

*Personal Resource Center—*Rev. NEAL QUARTIER, Dir., 420 Montgomery St., Syracuse, 13202. Tel: 315-470-1462.

*Propagation of the Faith—*Rev. JOSEPH H. PHILLIPS, Dir.; Sr. JUDITH MARKERT, C.S.J., Coord., 1342 Lancaster Ave., Syracuse, 13210. Tel: 315-472-3442; Fax: 315-472-8409.

*Religious Education—*Sr. KATIE EIFFE, C.S.J., Dir., P.O. Box 511, Syracuse, 13202. Tel: 315-470-1431; Fax: 315-478-4619.

*Eastern Region—*CATHERINE CORNUE, Dir., One Sherman St., New Hartford, 13413. Tel: 315-797-4030.

*Northern Region—*Sr. GERMANE HILSTON, Dir., 108 E. 6th St., Oswego, 13126. Tel: 315-343-5557.

*Southern Region—*Sr. LOIS BARTON, C.S.J., Dir., 705 W. Main St., Endicott, 13760. Tel: 607-786-9650.

*South (Norwich)—*ANGIE DIAMOND, Resource Center, 30 Pleasant St., Norwich, 13815. Tel: 607-337-2201.

*Western Region—*THERESA MAY, Dir., 1342 Lancaster Ave., Syracuse, 13210. Tel: 315-472-6753.

*West (Cortland)—*ELANA MOSES, Resource Center, 44 N. Main St., Cortland, 13045. Tel: 607-756-2532.

*Respect for Life—*Mrs. CINDY FALISE, Dir., P.O. Box 511, Syracuse, 13201. Tel: 315-424-1859.

*Laymen & Laywomen Retreat Movements—*Rev. MICHAEL J. CARMOLA, Dir., Christ the King Retreat House, 500 Brookford Rd., Syracuse, 13224. Tel: 315-446-2680.

*Spanish Apostolate—*Rev. ROBERT D. CHRYST, Dir., 170 Seymour St., Syracuse, 13204. Tel: 315-442-9390.

*Syracuse Catholic Press Association, Inc.—*CONNIE CISSELL, Editor in Chief & Gen. Mgr.; Most Rev. JAMES M. MOYNIHAN, D.D., Pres., 421 S. Warren St., Syracuse, 13202. Tel: 315-422-8153; 800-333-0571; Fax: 315-422-7549. "The Catholic Sun"

*Victim Assistance Coordinator—*TERESA SECRETI, P.O. Box 511, Syracuse, 13201-0511. Tel: 315-470-1465; Fax: 315-478-4619. Email: tsecreti@broadviewnet.net.

*Vocation Formation—*Rev. NEAL E. QUARTIER, Dir., P.O. Box 511, Syracuse, 13201. Tel: 315-470-1452; Fax: 315-478-4619.

*Vocation Promotion—*Rev. JOHN P. DONOVAN, J.C.L., Dir., P.O. Box 511, Syracuse, 13201. Tel: 315-470-1468; Fax: 315-478-4619.

*Youth Ministry—*Sr. EILEEN MCCANN, C.S.J., Dir., P.O. Box 511, Syracuse, 13201. Tel: 315-470-1419; Fax: 315-478-4619. Email: oymsyr@dreamscape.com.

CLERGY, PARISHES, MISSIONS AND PAROCHIAL SCHOOLS

CITY OF SYRACUSE
(ONONDAGA COUNTY)

SYRACUSE

1—THE CATHEDRAL OF THE IMMACULATE CONCEPTION (1841), Rev. Msgr. Joseph M. Champlin, Rector; Most Rev. James M. Moynihan; Revs. John C. Schopfer; Neal E. Quartier; Amedeo Guida; Peter Ben Opara; Sr. Maureen D'Onofrio, C.S.J., Pastoral Assoc.; Deacon Pio Peter Carranti.

Res.: 259 E. Onondaga St., 13202. Tel: 315-422-4177; Fax: 315-478-4619.

*School—*420 Montgomery St., 13202. Tel: 315-422-7217. Sr. Donna Smith, D.C., Prin. Daughters of Charity of St. Vincent de Paul 1; Lay Teachers 14; Students 85.

Station—Vivian Teal Howard, Tel: 315-478-1641.

Station—Clinton Plaza Oneonta. Tel: 315-475-2141.

Station—McCarthy Manor, Tel: 315-475-6390.

Station—Rosewood Heights, Tel: 315-474-4431.

2—ST. ANDREW THE APOSTLE (1953), Rev. James D. Mathews, Admin.; Sr. Patricia Bergan, O.S.F., Pastoral Assoc.

Res.: 124 Alden St., 13210. Tel: 315-476-8656.

*Catechesis/Religious Program—*Students 37.

3—ST. ANN (1955), In Res., Revs. Joseph H. Phillips; John Roark (Retired).

Res.: 4461 Onondaga Blvd., 13219. Tel: 315-468-1803; Fax: 315-487-6312.

*School—*Tel: 315-468-6441. Mrs. Nancy Tario, Prin. Sisters 1; Lay Teachers 7; Students 157.

*Catechesis/Religious Program—*Tel: 315-487-6201. Students 160.

4—ST. ANTHONY OF PADUA (1901), Rev. Robert D. Chryst. In Res., Most Rev. Thomas J. Costello, D.D.

Res.: 1515 Midland Ave., 13205. Tel: 315-475-4114.

*Catechesis/Religious Program—*Students 22.

5—ASSUMPTION B.V.M. (1844), (German), [CEM] Revs. Justin A. Biase, O.F.M.Conv., Rector; Robert Amrhein, O.F.M.Conv., Pastoral Assoc.; Bartholomew Gaske, O.F.M.Conv.; Jeffrey Keefe, O.F.M.Conv., Ph.D., Prov. Psychologist, Franciscan Counseling; Regis Rodda, O.F.M.Conv.; Herman Seibert, O.F.M.Conv.; Conrad Sommerville, O.F.M.Conv.; Michael Taylor, O.F.M.Conv.; Bro. Phillip Kelly, O.F.M.Conv.

St. Francis Friary: 812 N. Salina St., 13208. Tel: 315-422-4833; Fax: 315-422-4363.

*Assumption Cemetery Corporation—*2401 Court St., 13208. Tel: 315-454-3841; Fax: 315-454-4931.

6—BLESSED SACRAMENT (1921), Rev. James T. O'Brien. In Res., Rev. Msgr. Charles H. Eckermann (Retired); Rev. Clifford H. Auth.

Res.: 3127 James St., 13206. Tel: 315-437-3394; Fax: 315-432-9198.

School—(Grades PreK-6), 3129 James St., 13206. Tel: 315-437-1261; Fax: 315-463-1628. Mrs. Andrea Polcaro, Prin. Sisters of St. Joseph of Carondelet 1; Lay Teachers 16; Students 365.

*Catechesis/Religious Program—*Students 346.

7—ST. BRIGID AND ST. JOSEPH (1926 and 1869), Rev. Laurence W. Kennedy; Deacon Leonard S. Monnat.

Res.: 318 Herkimer St., 13204. Tel: 315-488-7122; Fax: 315-484-9723.

Catechesis/Religious Program—Students 60.
8—St. Charles (1929), Rev. Louis F. Aiello; Sr. Jean A. Burns, Parish Min.; Deacon Peter Vanelli.
In Res:—Rev. Philip S. Keane, S.S., (Weekend: In Res).
Res.: 417 S. Orchard Rd., 13219. Tel: 315-468-4122; Fax: 315-468-4122.
School—200 W. High Ter., 13219. Tel: 315-488-7631; Fax: 315-488-0617. Sr. Donna Driscoll, Prin. Sisters 2; Lay Teachers 15; Students 209.
Catechesis/Religious Program—Tel: 315-488-7645. Students 260.
Convent—Missionary Franciscan Sisters of the Immaculate Conception, 401 E. Corey Rd., 13219. Tel: 315-468-6041.
9—St. Daniel (1932), Rev. Msgr. Eugene M. Yennock.
Res.: 3004 Court St., 13208. Tel: 315-454-4946; Fax: 315-454-0978.
School—Tel: 315-455-7021. Deacon Joseph Caldentano Sr., Prin. Sisters of the Third Franciscan Order 1; Lay Teachers 9; Students (Grades K-6) 169; Students (Grades PreK-K) 30.
Catechesis/Religious Program—621 Roxford Rd., S., 13208. Tel: 315-454-4946. Students 250.
10—Holy Trinity (1891), (German), Rev. Charles S. Vavonese, Admin.; Sr. Frances Ann Thom, O.S.F., Pastoral Assoc.
Res.: 501 Park St., 13203. Tel: 315-474-8681; Fax: 315-474-3154.
Catechesis/Religious Program—Students 48.
11—St. James (1925), Rev. Daniel J. O'Hara. In Res., Rev. James P. Lang; Sr. Carolyn Chmielewski, C.S.J., Pastoral Assoc.; Deacon Donald M. McCabe, Pastoral Assoc.
Res.: 4845 S. Salina St., 13205. Tel: 315-469-7789; Fax: 315-492-2707.
School—(Grades PreK-6), 4837 S. Salina St., 13205. Tel: 315-492-1054; Fax: 315-492-9274. Mrs. Helen Chajka, Prin. Lay Teachers 12; Students 106.
Catechesis/Religious Program—Tel: 315-469-7873. Students 140.
Station—Brighton Towers
12—St. John the Baptist (1827), Rev. John R. DeLorenzo. In Res., Rev. Daniel C. Muscalino.
Res.: 406 Court St., 13208. Tel: 315-478-0916; Fax: 315-423-8096.
Catechesis/Religious Program—Students 89.
13—St. John the Evangelist (1851), Revs. Neal E. Quartier, Admin.; Martin Tran Van Ban, C.M.C.; Deacon John H. Collins.
Mailing Address: 215 N. State St., P.O. Box 6482, 13217-6482. Tel: 315-474-2363; 315-474-7322; Fax: 315-474-1045.
Catechesis/Religious Program—Tel: 315-474-7322. Students 140.
14—St. Lucy (1872), Rev. James D. Mathews. In Res., Rev. Msgr. Charles J. Fahey.
Res.: 432 Gifford St., 13204. Tel: 315-475-7273; Fax: 315-423-0128.
Catechesis/Religious Program—Tel: 315-478-6312. Students 83.
15—Most Holy Rosary (1913), Rev. Frederick R. Mannara.
Res.: 111 Roberts Ave., 13207-1397. Tel: 315-478-5749; Fax: 315-478-8629.
School—(Grades PreK-6), 1031 Bellevue Ave., 13207. Tel: 315-476-6035; Fax: 315-476-0219. Sisters 2; Lay Teachers 14; Students 147.
Catechesis/Religious Program—Tel: 315-474-0052. Students 177.
16—Our Lady of Lourdes (1947), Rev. Thomas P. Fitzpatrick; Deacon Leo Needham.
Res.: 300 Valley Dr., 13207. Tel: 315-476-9576.
Catechesis/Religious Program—Tel: 315-478-6383. Students 75.
17—Our Lady of Pompei (1924), (Italian), Rev. Paul F. Angelicchio. In Res., Revs. Frederick A. Pompei; Martin Tran Van Ban, C.M.C.; Rev. Msgr. John McGraw (Retired).
Res.: 301 Ash St., 13208. Tel: 315-422-7163; Fax: 315-422-7164.
School—915-917 N. McBride St., 13208. Tel: 315-422-8548; Fax: 315-472-0754. Lay Teachers 14; Students 123.
Catechesis/Religious Program—Tel: 315-472-2260. Students 85.
Convent—Franciscan Missionary Sisters of the Immaculate Conception, 920 N. McBride St., 13208. Tel: 315-422-7922.
18—Our Lady of Solace (1926), Rev. William R. Jones. In Res., Rev. Alfred J. Bebel.
Res.: 516 Salt Springs Rd., 13224. Tel: 315-446-2060; Fax: 315-446-2061.
Catechesis/Religious Program—Students 80.
19—St. Patrick (1870), Rev. E. Peter Reddick.
Res.: 216 N. Lowell Ave., 13204. Tel: 315-475-2185; Fax: 315-476-1565.
School—(Grades PreK-6), 210 Schuyler St., 13204. Tel: 315-476-4076; Fax: 315-476-4052. Cheryl Canfield, Prin. Sisters of St. Joseph of Carondelet 2; Lay Teachers 10; Students 116.
Catechesis/Religious Program—Students 35.
20—St. Peter (1890), (Italian), Rev. Paul F. Angelicchio. In Res., Rev. Msgr. Paul Brigandi (Retired); Rev. Robert J. Birchmeyer.
Res.: 709 James St., 13203. Tel: 315-472-4451; Fax: 315-422-3441.
Catechesis/Religious Program—Tel: 315-472-2260. Students 23.
21—Sacred Heart Basilica (1892), (Polish), [CEM 2] Revs. Peter W. Gleba; Stanley Dudkiewicz (Poland); Stanley Matula (Poland); Deacons James L. Morse; Joseph Daniszewski.
Res.: 927 Park Ave., 13204. Tel: 315-422-2343; Fax: 315-422-2344.
Catechesis/Religious Program—Tel: 315 422-8883; Fax: 315-422-7372. Students 122.
22—St. Stephen (1915), (Slovak), Rev. Peter W. Gleba.
Res.: 305 N. Geddes St., 13204. Tel: 315 422-5224.
23—St. Therese the Little Flower of Jesus (1926), Rev. William R. Jones.
Res.: 112 Lancaster Pl., 13210. Tel: 315-472-9934; Fax: 315-472-9941 (call first).
Catechesis/Religious Program—Students 84.
24—Transfiguration (1911), (Polish), Rev. Thomas P. Kobuszewski. In Res., Rev. Leo J. Heizman.
Res.: 740 Teall Ave., 13206. Tel: 315-479-6129; Fax: 315-426-0684. Email: ctransfi@twcnyrr.com.
25—St. Vincent de Paul (1893), Rev. Alfred E. Nortz. In Res., Revs. Wilbur J. Votraw (Retired); Theodore C. Sizing (Retired).
Res.: 342 Vine St., 13203. Tel: 315-479-6689; Fax: 315-479-6689.
Catechesis/Religious Program—Tel: 315-479-6301. Students 56.
Convent—Sisters of St. Joseph of Carondelet, 1101 Burnet Ave., 13203. Tel: 315-479-8012

OUTSIDE THE CITY OF SYRACUSE

Bainbridge, Chenango Co., St. John the Evangelist (1914), Rev. Robert D. Dwyer.
Res.: 34 S. Main St., 13733. Tel: 607-967-4481.
Catechesis/Religious Program—Students 69.
Mission—St. Agnes Spring St., Afton, Chenango Co. 13730. Tel: 607-639-1200.
Baldwinsville, Onondaga Co.
1—St. Augustine (1966), Rev. Paul Alcuati.
Res.: 7333 O'Brien Rd., 13027. Tel: 315-638-0585.
Catechesis/Religious Program—Tel: 315-638-0864. Students 378.
2—St. Elizabeth Ann Seton (1985), Rev. John P. Wagner.
Res.: 2494 NY State Rte. 31, 13027. Tel: 315-652-4300; Fax: 315-622-1761.
Catechesis/Religious Program—Tel: 315-652-3900. Students 1,009.
3—St. Mary (1852), [CEM] Rev. Richard M. Kopp.
Res.: 47 Syracuse St., 13027. Tel: 315-635-5762; Fax: 315-635-8137.
School—49 Syracuse St., 13027. Tel: 315-635-3977. Mrs. Debra Brillante, D.C., Prin. Sisters of the Third Franciscan Order M.C. 1; Lay Teachers 8; Students 158.
Catechesis/Religious Program—Tel: 315-635-5454. Students 430.
Binghamton, Broome Co.
1—St. Andrew (1955), Rev. Michael T. Meagher.
Res. & Parish Center: 356 Conklin Ave., 13903. Tel: 607-722-4049; Fax: 607-651-9140.
Catechesis/Religious Program—Tel: 607-722-9474. Students 178.
2—St. Ann (1925), (Slovak), Merged, with St. Joseph, Binghamton and St. Stanislaus Kostka, Binghamton to form Holy Trinity, Binghamton.
3—St. Catherine of Siena (1929), Rev. Brian E. Lang; Sr. Karen Gaube, C.S.J., Pastoral Assoc.; Deacon Raymond Goskowski.
Res.: 1031 Chenango St., 13901. Tel: 607-722-4388; Fax: 607-722-1336.
Catechesis/Religious Program—1031 Chenango St., 13901. Tel: 607-722-4177. Students 514.
4—St. Christopher (1940), Rev. Donald C. VanAmburgh.
Res.: 103 Castle Creek Rd., 13901. Tel: 607-723-0677; Fax: 607-773-0268.
Catechesis/Religious Program—Tel: 607-723-7010. Students 235.
5—SS. Cyril and Method (1904), (Slovak), Rev. George Sandor, O.F.M.Conv. In Res., Revs. Kenan McGowan, O.F.M.Conv.; Simeon Rukstalis, O.F.M.Conv.; James Fukes; Bro. Edward Falsey, O.F.M.Conv.
Res.: 148 Clinton St., 13905. Tel: 607-724-1372; Fax: 607-724-1468.
Catechesis/Religious Program—Tel: 607-723-2183. Students 73.
6—Holy Trinity (2003), Rev. George Sandor, O.F.M.Conv.; Bro. Edward Falsey, O.F.M.Conv., Admin.
Res.: 346 Prospect St., 13905. Tel: 607-797-1856; Fax: 607-797-8452.
Catechesis/Religious Program—Students 36.
7—St. John the Evangelist (1907), Rev. John E. Mikalajunas. In Res., Revs. Christopher Boretto; Artur Krawczenko (Poland).
Res.: 1263 Vestal Ave., 13903. Tel: 607-722-0493; Fax: 607-723-5171.
Catechesis/Religious Program—Students 360.
8—St. Joseph (1914), (Lithuanian), Merged, with St. Ann, Binghamton and St. Stanislaus Kostka, Binghamton to form Holy Trinity, Binghamton.
9—St. Mary of the Assumption (1887; 1913), Revs. Daniel Caruso; Clarence J. Cerwonka (Retired); Sr. Caritas Barajingitiva.
Res.: 37 Fayette St., 13901. Tel: 607-723-5383.
Catechesis/Religious Program—Students 180.
10—St. Patrick (1838), (Irish), Rev. Laurence J. Lord. In Res., Rev. Robert A. Ours.
Res.: 9 Leroy St., 13905. Tel: 607-722-1060.
Catechesis/Religious Program—Students 173.
Convent—Sisters of St. Joseph of Carondelet, 46 Oak St., 13905. Tel: 607-722-4745.
11—St. Paul (1896), Rev. Corey S. Van Kuren.
Res.: 15 Doubleday St., 13901. Tel: 607-722-6492.
Catechesis/Religious Program—Tel: 607-724-5449. Students 157.
12—St. Stanislaus Kostka (1914), (Polish), Merged, with St. Ann, Binghamton and St. Joseph, Binghamton to form Holy Trinity, Binghamton.
13—St. Thomas Aquinas (1927), Rev. James D. Tormey.
Res.: One Aquinas St., 13905. Tel: 607-797-4015; Fax: 607-729-9727.
Catechesis/Religious Program—4 Aquinas St., 13905. Tel: 607-797-3304. Students 163.
Boonville, Oneida Co., St. Joseph (1875), [CEM] Rev. Donald H. Karlen.
Res.: 110 Charles St., 13309. Tel: 315-942-4618.
Catechesis/Religious Program—Tel: 315-942-5955; Fax: 315-942-4618. Students 104.
Brewerton, Onondaga Co., St. Agnes (1958), Rev. William T. Guckert.
Res.: 5472 Miller Rd., 13029. Tel: 315-676-7050; Fax: 315-676-7050.
Catechesis/Religious Program—Tel: 315-676-5662. Students 95.
Bridgeport, Onondaga Co., St. Francis of Assisi (1951), Rev. Ralph White, O.F.M.Conv.
Res.: P.O. Box 550, 13030-0550. Tel: 315-633-2561; Fax: 315-633-0672.
Parish Center— 13030-0550. Tel: 315-633-9682; Fax: 315-633-2743.
Catechesis/Religious Program—Tel: 315-633-5661. Students 341.
Camden, Oneida Co., St. John (1852), [CEM] Rev. Joseph E. Moskal.
Res.: 22 Church St., 13316. Tel: 315-245-1603.
Catechesis/Religious Program—Students 123.
Camillus, Onondaga Co., St. Joseph (1852), Revs. Jerome A. Katz; Paul Carman.
Res.: 5600 W. Genesee St., 13031. Tel: 315-488-8490; Fax: 315-488-4214.
Catechesis/Religious Program—Students 1,100.
Canastota, Madison Co., St. Agatha (1883), [CEM] Rev. Kevin Corcoran.
Res.: 329 N. Peterboro St., 13032. Tel: 315-697-7104; Fax: 315-697-7108.
Catechesis/Religious Program—Tel: 315-697-7827. Students 259.
Cazenovia, Madison Co., St. James (1847), [CEM] Rev. G. Peter Worn.
Res.: 6 Green St., 13035. Tel: 315-655-3441; Fax: 315-655-3442.
Catechesis/Religious Program—Tel: 315-655-4871. Students 520.
Central Square, Oswego Co., St. Michael (1928), Rev. John J. Smegelsky.
Res.: 598 S. Main St., P.O. Box 514, 13036. Tel: 315-676-2898; Fax: 315-676-3103.
Catechesis/Religious Program—Tel: 315-676-4210. Students 270.
Chadwicks, Oneida Co., St. Anthony of Padua (1907), Rev. Edward J. Hayes.
Res.: 3364 Oneida St., P.O. Box 310, 13319. Tel: 315-737-8066.
Catechesis/Religious Program—Tel: 315-737-8692. Students 258.
Chenango Forks, Broome Co., St. Rita (1946), Rev. Stanley J. Gerlock; Deacon Paul Powers.
Res.: 2530 NY State Rte. 12, 13746. Tel: 607-648-8816.
Catechesis/Religious Program—Students 90.
Chittenango, Madison Co., St. Patrick (1853), [CEM] Rev. Edward J. Reimer.
Res.: 1341 Murray Dr., 13037. Tel: 315-687-6105; Fax: 315-687-0046.
Catechesis/Religious Program—Tel: 315-687-6561. Students 329.
Cicero, Onondaga Co., Sacred Heart (1888), Revs. James E. Gehl; Simon Mugo.
Res.: 8229 S. Main St., 13039. Tel: 315-699-2752; Fax: 315-699-3775.
Catechesis/Religious Program—Tel: 315-699-7678. Students 1,041.

CLARK MILLS, ONEIDA CO., CHURCH OF THE ANNUNCIATION (1908), Rev. Robert Bogan, Admin.
Mailing Address: 7616 E. South St., Clinton, 13323.
Res.: 25 South St., 13321. Tel: 315-853-6138.
Catechesis/Religious Program—Tel: 315-853-6139. Students 194.

CLAYVILLE, ONEIDA CO., ST. PATRICK (1864), [CEM] Rev. William S. Baker.
Res.: 8 Church St., Box 285, 13322. Tel: 315-839-5483; Fax: 315-839-5446.
Catechesis/Religious Program—Students 265.

CLEVELAND, OSWEGO CO., ST. MARY OF THE ASSUMPTION (1854), [CEM] Rev. R. Paul Mathis.
Res.: 148 State Rte. 49, 13042. Tel: 315-675-3542.
Catechesis/Religious Program—Tel: 315-675-3165. Students 153.
Mission—St. Bernadette State Rte. 49, Constantia, Oswego Co. 13044. Tel: 315-623-9803.

CLINTON, ONEIDA CO., ST. MARY (1850), [CEM] Rev. John P. Croghan.
Res.: 13 Marvin St., 13323. Tel: 315-853-2935; Fax: 315-859-1097.
School—(Grades K-6), Prospect St., 13323. Tel: 315-853-6196; Fax: 315-853-1440. Mrs. Linda DePhillips, Prin. Lay Teachers 12; Students 201.
Catechesis/Religious Program—Tel: 315-853-2492. Students 424.

CORTLAND, CORTLAND CO.
1—ST. ANTHONY (1917), (Italian), Rev. Mark P. Kaminski, Ph.D.
Res.: 45 Crandall St., 13045. Tel: 607-756-7533; Fax: 607-756-7697.
Catechesis/Religious Program—Students 73.
2—ST. MARY (1855), Rev. John P. Fenlon; Deacons Laurence Brickner; Joseph Caminiti; Stephen Smith.
Res.: 44 N. Main St., 13045. Tel: 607-756-9967; Fax: 607-756-9968.
School—61 N. Main St., 13045. Tel: 607-756-5614. Sr. Harriet Hamilton, O.S.F., Prin. Franciscan Sisters of Allegany 1; Lay Teachers 22; Students 384.
Catechesis/Religious Program—Tel: 607-753-6489; Fax: 607-753-1039. Students 210.

DEPOSIT, BROOME CO., ST. JOSEPH (1851), [CEM] Rev. John A. Booth.
Res.: 98 Second St., 13754. Tel: 607-467-2291; Fax: 607-467-2288.
Parish Center—74 Second St., 13754. Tel: 607-467-2226.
Catechesis/Religious Program—Students 75.

DEWITT, ONONDAGA CO., HOLY CROSS (1943), Revs. J. Robert Yeazel; John Canarro.
Res.: 4112 E. Genesee St., 13214. Tel: 315-446-0473; Fax: 315-446-7608.
School—Tel: 315-446-4890; Fax: 315-446-4799. David Wheeler, Prin. Lay Teachers 13; Students 197.
Catechesis/Religious Program—Students 583.

DURHAMVILLE, ONEIDA CO., ST. FRANCIS (1860), (German), [CEM] Rev. Joseph F. Kehoe.
Res.: 5334 Foster St., 13054. Tel: 315-363-1572.
Chapel—St. Mary [CEM] Irish Ridge.
Catechesis/Religious Program—Students 28.

EAST SYRACUSE, ONONDAGA CO., ST. MATTHEW (1880), Rev. Joseph J. Clemente. In Res., Rev. Msgr. Francis L. Sammons (Retired); Rev. Timothy S. Elmer, J.C.L.
Res.: 229 W. Yates St., 13057. Tel: 315-437-8318; Fax: 315-463-6399.
School—214 Kinne St., 13057. Tel: 315-437-1339; Fax: 315-463-1339. Sr. Marianne Baehr, C.S.J., Prin. Sisters of the Third Franciscan Order M.C. 2; Lay Teachers 20; Students 303.
Catechesis/Religious Program—Tel: 315-437-3685. Students 470.

ENDICOTT, BROOME CO.
1—ST. AMBROSE (1908), Rev. Charles Opondo-Owora (Africa). In Res., Revs. James J. O'Hanlon (Retired); Joseph Mattath, C.M.I. (India).
Res.: 203 Washington Ave., 13760. Tel: 607-754-2330; Fax: 607-785-6947.
2—ST. ANTHONY OF PADUA (1917), (Italian), Revs. Clarence F. Rumble; Cletus M.K. Forson (BRK); Deacon Frank Longo.
Res.: 306 Odell Ave., 13760. Tel: 607-754-4333; Fax: 607-757-3221.
School—St. Anthony's Learning Center, Tel: 607-748-5184; Fax: 607-786-3965. (Pre-School)
Convent—Little Sisters of St. Francis, 304 Oak Hill Ave., 13760.
Catechesis/Religious Program—1000 Jenkins St., 13760. Tel: 607-748-5184. Students 507.
3—ST. CASIMIR (1928), (Polish), Rev. Matthew S. Wieczorek.
Res.: 212 N. McKinley Ave., 13760. Tel: 607-785-3262; Fax: 607-785-4772.
Catechesis/Religious Program—Students 50.
4—ST. JOSEPH (1923), (Slovak), Rev. James P. Serowik; Gabriel Berko, Pastoral Assoc.; Deacon Dominic L. Rossi (Ghana).
Res.: 207 Hayes Ave., 13760. Tel: 607-748-0442; Fax: 607-748-7725.
School—210 N. Jackson Ave., 13760. Tel: 607-748-8631; Fax: 607-748-7745. Sr. Denise Marie, S.S.C.M., Prin. Sisters 4; Lay Teachers 12; Students 220.
Catechesis/Religious Program—Students 245.
5—OUR LADY OF GOOD COUNSEL (1941), Revs. Edward J. Zandy; Edward Owusu-Ansah; Deacon Thomas M. Harley.
Res.: 701 W. Main St., 13760. Tel: 607-748-7417; Fax: 607-785-6454.
Catechesis/Religious Program—Tel: 607-754-2213; Fax: 607-754-2213. Students 470.

ENDWELL, BROOME CO.
1—CHRIST THE KING (1949), Rev. Thomas F. Hobbes; Deacon George Phillips.
Res.: 1501 Davis Ave., 13760. Tel: 607-785-3180.
Catechesis/Religious Program—Tel: 607-785-5016. Students 47.
2—OUR LADY OF ANGELS (1964), Rev. John D. Roock.
Res.: 3600 Phyllis St., 13760. Tel: 607-754-1266; Fax: 607-754-1325 (Call First).
Catechesis/Religious Program—Tel: 607-785-4581. Students 280.

FAIRMOUNT, ONONDAGA CO., HOLY FAMILY (1935), Revs. Richard Prior; Philip J. Brockmyre; Deacon Nick Alvaro.
Res.: 127 Chapel Dr., 13219. Tel: 315-488-3139; Fax: 315-487-1112.
School—130 Chapel Dr., 13219. Tel: 315-487-8515; Fax: 315-487-8515. Linda Shulkin, Prin.
Catechesis/Religious Program—Tel: 315-488-5884. Students 1,010.

FAYETTEVILLE, ONONDAGA CO., IMMACULATE CONCEPTION (1869), [CEM] Rev. Gregory C. LeStrange; Sr. Monica Zmolek, O.S.F., Pastoral Min. In Res., Rev. Msgrs. James A. McCloskey (Retired); Ronald C. Bill (Retired).
Res.: 400 Salt Springs St., 13066. Tel: 315-637-9846; Fax: 315-637-9846.
School—Tel: 315-637-3961; Fax: 315-637-2672. Mrs. Sally Lisi, Prin. Sisters of the Third Franciscan Order M.C. 1; Lay Teachers 28; Students 347.
Catechesis/Religious Program—Tel: 315-637-9840. Students 714.

FLORENCE, ONEIDA CO., ST. MARY (1845), [CEM] Rev. Joseph E. Moskal.
Res.: 22 Church St., Camden, 13316. Tel: 315-245-1603.

FORESTPORT, ONEIDA CO., ST. PATRICK (1848), [CEM] Rev. Donald H. Karlen.
Mailing Address: P.O. Box 1, 13338. Tel: 315-392-2341; Fax: 315-392-5651.
Mission—St. Mary of the Snows Otter Lake, Oneida Co.
Catechesis/Religious Program—Students 140.

FULTON, OSWEGO CO.
1—HOLY FAMILY-ST. MICHAEL'S, Formerly Holy Family (1930), Rev. Peter A. Williams. In Res., Rev. John J. Daley (Retired).
Res.: 45 W. Fourth St., 13069. Tel: 315-592-4159.
Catechesis/Religious Program—300 Hart St., 13069. Tel: 315-592-4156; Fax: 315-598-3128. Students 163.
2—IMMACULATE CONCEPTION (1854), Rev. Stephen P. Wirkes.
Office—309 Buffalo St., 13069. Tel: 315-598-2118.
Res.: Tel: 315-598-9094; Fax: 315-598-3355.
Catechesis/Religious Program—Students 107.
3—ST. MICHAEL (1924), (Polish), Merged, with Holy Family, Fulton to form Holy Family-St. Michael's, Fulton.

GREENE, CHENANGO CO., IMMACULATE CONCEPTION (1889), Rev. Thomas I. Ward.
Res.: 1180 NY Hwy. 206, 13778. Tel: 607-656-9546; Fax: 607-656-7667.
Catechesis/Religious Program—Tel: 607-656-7667. Students 147.

HAMILTON, MADISON CO., ST. MARY (1869), [CEM] Rev. Msgr. John R. Madden.
Res.: 16 Wylie St., 13346. Tel: 315-824-2164.
Catechesis/Religious Program—Tel: 315-824-5024. Students 133.

HANNIBAL, OSWEGO CO., OUR LADY OF THE ROSARY (1954), Rev. Edmund A. Wolak.
Office—923 Cayuga St., P.O. Box 185, 13074-3138. Tel: 315-564-5201.
Catechesis/Religious Program—Students 246.
Mission—St. Joseph Southwest Oswego, Oswego Co.

HINCKLEY, ONEIDA CO., ST. ANN (1895), [CEM] Rev. Vincent P. Long.
Res.: 13352. Tel: 315-896-2540.

HOLLAND PATENT, ONEIDA CO., ST. LEO (1882), Rev. Vincent P. Long; Sally Millick, Pastoral Assoc. In Res., Rev. Robert C. Weber.
Res.: 7937 Elm St., P.O. Box 185, 13354. Tel: 315-865-5371; Fax: 315-865-5868.
Catechesis/Religious Program—Students 407.

HOMER, CORTLAND CO., ST. MARGARET (1908), Rev. R. Daniel DeLorme.
Res.: 14 Copeland Ave., P.O. Box 356, 13077. Tel: 607-749-2542; Fax: 607-749-4623.
Catechesis/Religious Program—Tel: 607-749-2080; Fax: 607-749-4623. Students 179.

JAMESVILLE, ONONDAGA CO., ST. MARY (1899), Rev. Raymond B. Wood.
Res.: 6437 E. Seneca Tpke., P.O. Box 368, 13078-0368. Tel: 315-469-6949; Fax: 315-469-5093.
Catechesis/Religious Program—Students 215.

JOHNSON CITY, BROOME CO.
1—BLESSED SACRAMENT (1945), Rev. Donald E. Bourgeois.
Res.: Cenacle Plaza, 13790. Tel: 607-797-5151; Fax: 607-797-8603.
Catechesis/Religious Program—Tel: 607-797-8603. Students 170.
2—ST. JAMES (1900), Revs. Thomas J. Ryan; Thomas Servatius; Sisters Rose Margaret Noonan, C.S.J., Pastoral Assoc.; Catherine Joseph McDonough, D.C., Pastoral Assoc.; Mr. William P. Gallagher, Pastoral Assoc. In Res., Rev. James J. Fallon (Retired).
Res.: 155 Main St., 13790. Tel: 607-729-6147; Fax: 607-797-5966.
Catechesis/Religious Program—Tel: 607-729-4083. Students 601.
Convent—147 Main St., 13790.

JORDAN, ONONDAGA CO., ST. PATRICK (1858), [CEM] Rev. John E. Phelan.
Res.: 28 N. Main St., 13080. Tel: 315-689-9051.
Catechesis/Religious Program—Tel: 315-689-1695; Fax: 315-689-6240. Students 133.

KIRKWOOD, BROOME CO., ST. MARY (1888), Rev. Thomas F. Catucci.
Res.: 975 NY Rte. 11, 13795. Tel: 607-775-0086.
Catechesis/Religious Program—Students 175.

LACONA, OSWEGO CO., ST. FRANCES XAVIER CABRINI (1946), Rev. Sean Patrick O'Brien.
Mailing Address: 23 Niagara St., Pulaski, 13142. Tel: 315-387-3016; Fax: 315-298-3749.
Catechesis/Religious Program—Tel: 315-298-5350. Students 44.

LAFAYETTE, ONONDAGA CO., ST. JOSEPH (1866), Rev. Michael P. Minehan, J.C.L.
Res.: 6104 Cherry Valley Rd., Box 169, 13084. Tel: 315-677-3439.
Catechesis/Religious Program—Tel: 315-677-7735; Fax: 315-677-3858. Students 175.

LAKELAND, ONONDAGA CO., OUR LADY OF PEACE (1935), Rev. John E. Fetcho.
Res.: 203 Halcomb St., 13209. Tel: 315-487-6832; Fax: 315-487-9722.
Catechesis/Religious Program—Students 160.

LEE CENTER, ONEIDA CO., ST. JOSEPH (1923), Rev. Paul V. Carey; Sr. Dorothy Root, Pastoral Assoc.
Res.: 13363. Tel: 315-336-2661; Fax: 315-336-8418.
Parish Center—Tel: 315-339-1890.
Catechesis/Religious Program—Tel: 315-339-3080. Students 278.

LIVERPOOL, ONONDAGA CO.
1—CHRIST THE KING (1964), Rev. Jon K. Werner.
Res.: 21 Cherry Tree Cir., 13090. Tel: 315-652-3233; 315-652-9266 (Parish Center); Fax: 315-652-5680.
Catechesis/Religious Program—Tel: 315-652-5782. Students 425.
2—IMMACULATE HEART OF MARY (1950), Revs. John V. Ahern; Innocent Onyenagubo (Nigeria); Sisters Mary Ann Fetcho, Pastoral Assoc.; Rose Marie Caravaglio, Pastoral Assoc.; Deacon John Woloszyn.
Res.: 425 Beechwood Ave., 13088. Tel: 315-457-8060; Fax: 315-457-6078.
Catechesis/Religious Program—427 Beechwood Ave., 13088. Tel: 315-457-5367. Students 453.
3—ST. JOHN (1971), Rev. Gaetano T. Baccaro.
Res.: 8290 Soule Rd., 13090. Tel: 315-652-6591; Fax: 315-652-6631.
Catechesis/Religious Program—Tel: 315-652-1094. Students 705.
4—ST. JOSEPH THE WORKER (1890), Rev. Charles M. Major.
Res.: 1001 Tulip St., 13088. Tel: 315-457-6060; Fax: 315-457-4119.
Catechesis/Religious Program—Students 585.

MAINE, BROOME CO., MOST HOLY ROSARY (1944), Rev. Thomas F. Keating.
Res.: 2596 Main St., Box 248, 13802. Tel: 607-862-3216; Fax: 607-862-0096.
Catechesis/Religious Program—Tel: 607-862-4758. Students 200.

MANLIUS, ONONDAGA CO., ST. ANN (1920), Rev. Kevin Hannon; Deacon Gerard T. Pittman. In Res., Rev. James F. Quinn.
Res.: 104 Academy St., 13104. Tel: 315-682-5181; Fax: 315-682-5248.
Catechesis/Religious Program—Tel: 315-682-9443. Students 412.

MARATHON, CORTLAND CO., ST. STEPHEN (1870), Rev. Tadeusz Rudnik (Poland).
Res.: 12 Academy St., P.O. Box 475, 13803. Tel: 607-849-3480; Fax: 607-849-4078.
Catechesis/Religious Program—Students 106.
Mission—Our Lady of Perpetual Help Cincinnatus, Cortland Co.

MARCELLUS, ONONDAGA CO., ST. FRANCIS XAVIER (1873), [CEM] Rev. J. Michael Donovan.
Res.: P.O. Box 177, 1 W. Main St., 13108. Tel: 315-673-2531; Fax: 315-673-9305.
Catechesis/Religious Program—53 North St., Marellus. Tel: 315-673-4107.

MATTYDALE, ONONDAGA CO., ST. MARGARET (1926), Revs. David Baehr; Joachim Mahugu Kinuthia; Deacons Donald R. Whiting; Fred Cholette.
Res.: 203 Roxboro Rd., 13211. Tel: 315-455-5534; Fax: 315-454-4102.
School—Tel: 315-455-5791; Fax: 315-455-1250. Sr. Miriam Anthony, Prin. Sisters of the Third Franciscan Order M.C. 2; Lay Teachers 21; Students 362.
Catechesis/Religious Program—200 Roxboro Rd., 13211. Tel: 315-455-2203. Students 645.

MEXICO, OSWEGO CO., ST. MARY, STAR OF THE SEA (1914), Unassigned.
Res.: 3352 Main St., P.O. Box 487, 13114. Tel: 315-963-7182; Fax: 315-963-7204.
Catechesis/Religious Program—Fax: 315-963-4032. Students 163.

MINETTO, OSWEGO CO., OUR LADY OF PERPETUAL HELP (1932), Rev. Joseph M. Larkin.
Res.: West River Rd., P.O. Box 236, 13115. Tel: 315-343-7922.

MINOA, ONONDAGA CO., ST. MARY (1834), [CEM] Rev. Dominic E. McGee, O.F.M.Conv.
Res.: 401 N. Main St., 13116. Tel: 315-633-0712; Fax: 315-633-0672.
Office—Tel: 315-656-3441.
Catechesis/Religious Program—Tel: 315-656-4220. Students 415.

MORRISVILLE, MADISON CO., ST. JOAN OF ARC (1931), Rev. Msgr. John R. Madden.
Parish Office—P.O. Box 1087, 13408. Tel: 315-684-9551.
St. Mary: 16 Wylie St., Hamilton, 13346. Tel: 315-824-2164.
Catechesis/Religious Program—Tel: 315-684-9527. Students 153.

MUNNSVILLE, MADISON CO., ST. THERESE OF THE INFANT JESUS (1926), Rev. Joseph F. Kehoe.
Res.: 5334 Foster St., Durhamville, 13054. Tel: 315-363-1572.
Catechesis/Religious Program—Students 7.

NEW BERLIN, CHENANGO CO., ST. THERESA OF THE INFANT JESUS (1955), Rev. Francis J. Case, Admin. Mailing Address: P.O. Box 780, 13411-0780.
Res.: 24 N. Main St., 13411. Tel: 607-846-6851.
Catechesis/Religious Program—Tel: 607-847-8732. Students 68.

NEW HARTFORD, ONEIDA CO.

1—ST. JOHN THE EVANGELIST (1883), Revs. Joseph Zareski; Bogdan Siewiera (Poland).
Res.: 66 Oxford Rd., 13413. Tel: 315-732-8521; Fax: 315-735-1569.
Catechesis/Religious Program—One Sherman St., 13413. Tel: 315-724-4347. Sr. Martha Vincent Larkin, C.S.J., D.R.E. Students 800.

2—OUR LADY OF THE ROSARY (1949), Rev. Felix R. Colosimo.
Res.: 1736 Burrstone Rd., 13413. Tel: 315-724-0402.
Catechesis/Religious Program—Students 205.

3—ST. THOMAS (1957), Rev. G. David Sears, M.S., C.S.W. In Res., Rev. John M. Quinn.
Res.: 150 Clinton Rd., 13413. Tel: 315-735-8381.
Catechesis/Religious Program—Students 212.

NEW LONDON, ONEIDA CO., HOLY CROSS (1968), Closed., For inquiries for parish records please see St. Francis, Durhamville.

NEW YORK MILLS, ONEIDA CO., ST. MARY (1909), [CEM] Rev. Valentine C. Krul.
Res.: 201 Main St., 13417. Tel: 315-736-4432; Fax: 315-736-8079.
School— Consolidated. See separate listing under Institutions Located in the Diocese.
Catechesis/Religious Program—Tel: 315-736-9132. Students 155.

NORTH BAY, ONEIDA CO., ST. JOHN (1843), [CEM] Rev. Leo J. Wimett.
Res.: P.O. Box 289, 13123. Tel: 315-245-0853; Fax: 315-675-3213.
Mission—St. Mary Verona Beach, Oneida Co. 13162.

NORTH SYRACUSE, ONONDAGA CO., ST. ROSE OF LIMA (1926), Revs. James M. Kennedy; Daniel Heintz (Retired); Jerome Amaechi; Sr. Corinne Mullen, O.S.F., Pastoral Min.
Parish Office—409 S. Main St., 13212. Tel: 315-458-0283; Fax: 315-458-1290.
Res.: 407 S. Main St., 13212. Tel: 315-458-0283.
School—Preschool, Tel: 315-458-6036. Students 71.
School—(Grades K-6), 411 S. Main St., 13212. Tel: 315-458-6036; Fax: 315-458-6038. Sr. Catherine Laboure, Prin. Sisters of the Third Franciscan Order of Syracuse 4; Lay Teachers 27; Students 550.
Catechesis/Religious Program—Tel: 315-458-6592; Fax: 315-458-1290. Students 1,000.

NORWICH, CHENANGO CO.

1—ST. BARTHOLOMEW THE APOSTLE (1919), (Italian), Merged, with St. Paul, Norwich to form Church of the Holy Apostles, St. Paul Roman Catholic Community of Norwich, NY.

2—CHURCH OF THE HOLY APOSTLES, ST. PAUL ROMAN CATHOLIC COMMUNITY OF NORWICH, NY, Rev. Douglas Cunningham; Sr. Julie Eigo, C.S.J. Pastoral Min.; Mary Ann Bodiot, Pastoral Min.
Office—8 Silver St., 13815. Tel: 607-336-2222; Fax: 607-334-2229.
Res.: 30 Pleasant St., 13815. Tel: 607-334-4931; Fax: 607-334-6521.
Catechesis/Religious Program—Tel: 607-337-2001. Students 190.
Convent—79 E. Main St., 13815. Tel: 607-337-2219.

3—ST. PAUL (1851), Merged, with St. Bartholomew the Apostle, Norwich to form Church of the Holy Apostles, St. Paul Roman Catholic Community of Norwich, NY.

ONEIDA, MADISON CO.

1—ST. JOSEPH (1893), Rev. Edmund A. Castronovo; Rev. Msgr. Matthew C. Luczycki (Retired).
Res.: 121 St. Joseph Pl., 13421. Tel: 315-363-3280.
Parish Center—111 St. Joseph Pl., 13421. Tel: 315-363-5061.
Catechesis/Religious Program—Students 113.

2—ST. PATRICK (1843), [CEM] Rev. David J. Orzel. In Res., Rev. John J. Mulranen (Retired).
Res.: 347 Main St., 13421. Tel: 315-363-7570.
School—354 Elizabeth St., 13421. Tel: 315-363-3620. Peg Brown, Prin. Lay Teachers 10; Students 112.
Catechesis/Religious Program—Tel: 315-361-1378. Students 233.

ONONDAGA HILL, ONONDAGA CO., ST. MICHAEL (1874), Rev. Henry J. Pedzich; Deacon Jack Mulvey, Pastoral Assoc.
Res.: 4782 W. Seneca Tpke., 13215. Tel: 315-469-6995; Fax: 315-469-6996.
Catechesis/Religious Program—Tel: 315-469-6600. Students 632.
Mission—St. Peter Split Rock Rd., Split Rock, Onondaga Co. 13031.

ORISKANY FALLS, ONEIDA CO., ST. JOSEPH (1870), [CEM] Rev. Vincent J. Kelly.
Res.: 229 Main St., 13425. Tel: 315-821-6122.
Catechesis/Religious Program—Students 43.

ORISKANY, ONEIDA CO., ST. STEPHEN, PROTOMARTYR (1929) Rev. Walter F. Cannan.
Res.: 106 Dexter Ave., P.O. Box 780, 13424. Tel: 315-736-9033.
Catechesis/Religious Program—Students 143.

OSWEGO, OSWEGO CO.

1—ST. JOHN THE EVANGELIST (1869), Closed., For inquiries for parish records please see St. Mary, Oswego.

2—ST. JOSEPH (1915), (Italian), Rev. James M. Cesta; Deacon Joseph Chillemi.
Res.: 178 W. Second St., 13126. Tel: 315-343-2160; Fax: 315-343-2164 (call first).
Catechesis/Religious Program—Tel: 315-343-5462. Students 170.

3—ST. LOUIS (1870), (French), Closed., For inquiries for parish records, please contact St. Peter, Oswego.

4—ST. MARY (1850), Rev. Robert Stephenson.
Res.: 103 W. Seventh St., P.O. Box 118, 13126. Tel: 315-343-3953; Fax: 315-342-5538.
School—Trinity Catholic School, (Grades PreK-PreK) *St. Paul's Campus*, 76 W. 6th St., 13126. Tel: 315-343-0700; Fax: 315-342-9471. Regional Catholic School System Lay Teachers 23; Students 322.
Catechesis/Religious Program—Tel: 315-343-7210. Students 240.

5—ST. PAUL (1840), (Irish), Rev. Eric K. Harer; Deacon Frank Warren.
Res.: 50 E. Mohawk St., 13126. Tel: 315-343-2333; Fax: 315-343-2334.
Church: 134 E. Fifth St., 13126. Tel: 315-343-9764.
School—Trinity Catholic School 115 E. 5th St., 13126. Tel: 315-343-6700; Fax: 315-343-7210. Mr. David Friedlander, Prin. Lay Teachers 13; Students 141.
Catechesis/Religious Program—Students 220.

6—ST. PETER (1862), (German), Rev. George E. Wurz, Admin.
Res.: 83 E. Albany St., 13126. Tel: 315-343-1352.
Mission—Sacred Heart Scriba, Oswego Co. Tel: 315-342-5705.

7—ST. STEPHEN THE KING (1908), (Polish), Revs. Edmund Wolak; Andrzej (Andrew) Szczesnowicz (Poland), Pastoral Assoc.
Res.: 138 Niagara St., Box 417, 13126. Tel: 315-343-6350; Fax: 315-343-8850.
Catechesis/Religious Program—Tel: 315-343-9350. Students 123.

OXFORD, CHENANGO CO., ST. JOSEPH (1849), [CEM] Rev. Thomas I. Ward.
Res.: 1180 NY Hwy. 206, Greene, 13778. Tel: 607-843-7021; Fax: 607-843-7021.
Catechesis/Religious Program—Students 109.
Station—New York State Veterans' Home 13830. Tel: 607-843-3100.

PARISH, OSWEGO CO., ST. ANNE, Formerly St. Ann (1950), [CEM] Unassigned.
Res. and Mailing Address: P.O. Box 487, Mexico, 13114. Tel: 315-625-7093.
Catechesis/Religious Program—Students 51.
Mission—St. Patrick Williamstown, Oswego Co. Tel: 315-964-2400.

PHOENIX, OSWEGO CO., ST. STEPHEN (1880), Rev. Darr F. Schoenhofen; Deacon Frank Forish.
Res.: 469 Main St., 13135. Tel: 315-695-4531; 315-695-4608.
Catechesis/Religious Program—Tel: 315-695-4608. Students 289.

POMPEY, ONONDAGA CO., IMMACULATE CONCEPTION (1850), [CEM] Rev. David J. James.
Res.: 7386 Academy St., 13138. Tel: 315-677-3061; Fax: 315-677-2873.
Catechesis/Religious Program—Tel: 315-677-5126. Students 89.
Mission—St. Paul Fabius, Onondaga Co. 13063.

PULASKI, OSWEGO CO., CHRIST OUR LIGHT, Formerly St. John the Evangelist (1888), Rev. Sean O'Brien. 23 Niagara St., 13142-4425. Tel: 315-298-5350; 315-298-3863 (Res.); Fax: 315-298-3749.
Catechesis/Religious Program—Students 156.

ROME, ONEIDA CO.

1—ST. JOHN THE BAPTIST (1909), (Italian), [CEM] Revs. John F. Hogan Jr.; John M. Wood; Grzegorz Golyzniak (Poland).
Res.: 210 E. Dominick St., 13440. Tel: 315-337-0990; Fax: 315-336-3841.
Catechesis/Religious Program—Students 386.

2—ST. MARY OF THE ASSUMPTION (1848), [CEM] Rev. Philip A. Hearn. In Res., Rev. Msgr. Francis J. Culkin (Retired).
Res.: 210 W. Liberty St., 13440. Tel: 315-336-4832; Fax: 315-339-2744.
Catechesis/Religious Program—Students 95.
Station—Betsy Ross HRF

3—ST. PAUL (1954), Rev. James T. Queen; Deacon Edgar Doyle Jr. In Res., Rev. Msgr. William M. Kelly.
Res.: 1807 Bedford St., 13440-2199. Tel: 315-336-3082; Fax: 315-336-3083.
Catechesis/Religious Program—Tel: 315-334-9570. Students 187.

4—ST. PETER (1837), [CEM] Rev. Philip A. Hearn; Sisters Elizabeth Colby, C.S.J., Pastoral Assoc.; Phyllis Wulforst, C.S.J., Pastoral Assoc. In Res., Rev. James A. Culver (Retired).
Res.: 105 E. Liberty St., 13440. Tel: 315-336-5072; 315-337-8307.
Catechesis/Religious Program—Tel: 315-336-5066; Fax: 315-336-0855. Students 315.

5—TRANSFIGURATION (1909), (Polish), Rev. Mark A. Pasik. In Res., Rev. William C. Cahill.
Res.: 111 Ridge St., 13440. Tel: 315-336-1152; Fax: 315-339-5931.

SANITARIA SPRINGS, BROOME CO., ST. JOSEPH (1914), Rev. Kevin J. Bunger, Admin.
Res.: 659 New York Rte. 7, P.O. Box 429, Port Crane, 13833. Tel: 607-648-5209; Fax: 607-648-3570.

SHERBURNE, CHENANGO CO., ST. MALACHY OF ARMAGH (1858), [CEM] Rev. John W. Broderick, Admin. Mailing Address: P.O. Box 722, 13460-0722. Tel: 607-674-9625.
Catechesis/Religious Program—Tel: 315-674-4628. Students 110.

SHERRILL, ONEIDA CO., ST. HELENA (1917), [CEM] Rev. William A. Mesmer.
Res.: 210 Primo Ave., 13461. Tel: 315-363-3882.
Catechesis/Religious Program—Tel: 315-361-1566. Students 250.

SKANEATELES, ONONDAGA CO., ST. MARY OF THE LAKE (1855), [CEM] Rev. Thomas J. McGrath; Deacon Robert Borchert.
Res.: 81 Jordan St., 13152. Tel: 315-685-5083; Fax: 315-685-8327.
Catechesis/Religious Program—Tel: 315-685-6377. Students 452.

SOLVAY, ONONDAGA CO., ST. CECILIA (1903), (Italian), Revs. George F. Hartnett; Paul Machira (Africa); Deacon Julius Kulak.
Res.: 1001 Woods Rd., 13209. Tel: 315-488-3221; Fax: 315-488-3222.
Catechesis/Religious Program—Students 191.

SOUTH ONONDAGA, ONONDAGA CO., CORPUS CHRISTI (1938), Rev. Dennis J. Hayes.
Res.: P.O. Box 288, Marietta, 13110. Tel: 315-492-0814.
Church: 3126 Cedarvale Rd., R.D. 1, Nedrow, 13120. Tel: 315-492-0814.

TABERG, ONEIDA CO., ST. PATRICK (1876), [CEM] Rev. Francis A. Wapen.
Res.: 9168 Main St., 13471. Tel: 315-336-4079.
Catechesis/Religious Program—Students 78.

Mission—St. Anne (1846), Glenmore, Oneida Co.
TRUXTON, CORTLAND CO., ST. PATRICK (1854), [CEM] Rev. Daniel C. Muscalino, Admin.
Res.: 3656 Rte. 13, Box 15, 13158. Tel: 607-842-6326.
Mission—St. Lawrence De Ruyter, Madison Co.
TULLY, ONONDAGA CO., ST. LEO (1891), Rev. James H. Carey.
Res.: 10 Onondaga St., 13159. Tel: 315-696-5092; Fax: 315-696-8721.
Catechesis/Religious Program—Students 313.
Mission—St. Patrick [CEM] P.O. Box 574, Otisco, Onondaga Co. 13159. Tel: 315-696-8601.
UTICA, ONEIDA CO.
1—ST. AGNES (1887), Rev. Msgr. Francis J. Willenburg.
Res.: 700 Kossuth Ave., 13501. Tel: 315-735-5273.
Catechesis/Religious Program—Students 190.
Convent—783 Blandina St., 13501. Tel: 315-732-1078.
2—ST. ANTHONY OF PADUA (1911), (Italian), Rev. Anthony LaFache; Deacon William Dischiavo, Sec.
Res.: 422 Tilden Ave., 13501. Tel: 315-732-1177.
Catechesis/Religious Program—1521 Bleeker St., 13501. Tel: 315-724-3324. Students 430.
3—BLESSED SACRAMENT (1924), Rev. Robert L. Kelly. In Res., Rev. Msgr. Thomas M. Doran (Retired).
Res.: 1603 St. Agnes Ave., 13501. Tel: 315-724-8131; Fax: 315-724-5024.
School— Consolidated. See separate listing under Institutions Located in the Diocese.
Catechesis/Religious Program—1627 St. Agnes Ave., 13501. Tel: 315-733-3946. Students 75.
4—ST. FRANCIS DE SALES (1876), Rev. Frederick D. Daley.
Res.: 1119 Elm St., 13501. Tel: 315-732-6171; Fax: 315-735-3503.
5—ST. GEORGE (1911), (Lithuanian), [CEM] Rev. Richard E. Dellos.
Res.: 702 Columbia St., 13502. Tel: 315-735-4429; Fax: 315-735-1691.
6—HOLY TRINITY (1896), (Polish), [CEM] Revs. Arthur R. Hapanowicz; Richard J. Wilczynski (Poland).
Res.: 1206 Lincoln Ave., 13502. Tel: 315-724-7238; Fax: 315-732-5448.
Catechesis/Religious Program—Tel: 315-733-5492. Students 60.
Convent—1218 Lincoln Ave., 13502. Fax: 315-733-5492.
7—ST. JOHN (1819), Revs. John A. Buehler; Luis Olguin, Spanish Apostolate. Tel: 315-724-0389; Sisters Mary Theresa Kobosinski, D.C., Pastoral Assoc.; Sharon Whellahan, C.S.J., Pastoral Assoc.; Deacon William R. Dischiavo, Pastoral Assoc.
Res.: 240 Bleecker St., 13501. Tel: 315-724-6159.
Parish Center—520 John St., 13501. Tel: 315-732-2417. Sr. Linda Abdelhour, C.S.J.
Catechesis/Religious Program—Tel: 315-732-1334. Students 222.
8—ST. JOSEPH AND ST. PATRICK (1841 and 1849), Rev. Richard E. Dellos. In Res., Rev. John S. Drozdzal.
Res.: 702 Columbia St., 13502. Tel: 315-735-4429; Fax: 315-735-1691.
Catechesis/Religious Program—530 Varick St., 13502. Students 104.
9—ST. MARK (1963), Rev. Lucian Urbaniak.
Res.: 440 Keyes Rd., 13502. Tel: 315-724-1645.
Catechesis/Religious Program—Students 324.
10—ST. MARY (1870), (German), Rev. Richard V. O'Neill.
Res.: 421 South St., 13501. Tel: 315-724-0083; Fax: 315-724-0083.
Catechesis/Religious Program—Students 25.
11—ST. MARY OF MT. CARMEL (1896), (Italian), Rev. John F. Rose; Sisters Lois Paciello, C.S.J., Pastoral Assoc.; Elizabeth Paciello, C.S.J., Pastoral Assoc.; Linda Love, O.S.F., Pastoral Assoc.; Deacon Robert Riggalls, Pastoral Assoc. In Res., Rev. Luis Olguin.
Res.: 648 Jay St., 13501. Tel: 315-735-1482; Fax: 315-735-9806.
Catechesis/Religious Program—Tel: 315-724-3950. Sr. Linda Love, O.S.F., D.R.E. Students 200.
12—OUR LADY OF LOURDES (1919), Revs. Joseph Salerno; John Manno; Deacon William P. Hotaling; Sisters Julia Coyle, S.A.; Elizabeth Mary Paciello; Lois Mary Paciello, C.S.J.
Res.: 2 Barton Ave., 13502. Tel: 315-724-3155; Fax: 315-732-3770.
School—Tel: 315-732-4374; Fax: 315-738-9720. Consolidated. See separate listing under Institutions Located in the Diocese.
Catechesis/Religious Program—Students 418.
13—ST. PETER (1872), [CEM] Rev. Thomas M. Durant. In Res., Rev. James A. Quinn.
Res.: 422 Coventry Ave., 13502. Tel: 315-724-6310; Fax: 315-724-4942.
School—(Grades PreK-6), 19 Herkimer Rd., 13502. Tel: 315-724-4708. Ms. Judy Hauck, Prin. Lay Teachers 9; Students 178.
Catechesis/Religious Program—Tel: 315-735-7077. Students 375.
14—SACRED HEART (1926), Rev. John Flanagan. In Res., Rev. Hyacinth Seremet; Deacon John Lee.
Res.: 2115 Caroline St., 13502. Tel: 315-735-6105; Fax: 315-735-0216.
Catechesis/Religious Program—Tel: 315-735-3611. Students 96.
15—ST. STANISLAUS (1911), (Polish), [CEM] Rev. Casimir J. Krzysiak.
Res.: 607 Nichols St., 13501. Tel: 315-732-5919.
VERNON, ONEIDA CO., HOLY FAMILY (1926; 1976), Rev. Richard P. Morisette.
Res.: 4343 Peterboro St., P.O. Box 988, 13476. Tel: 315-829-3295.
Catechesis/Religious Program—Tel: 315-829-2820. Students 170.
VERONA, ONEIDA CO., OUR LADY OF GOOD COUNSEL (1913), Rev. Edmund J. Morelle.
Res.: 5259 Beacon Rd., P.O. Box 135, 13478. Tel: 315-363-7696.
Catechesis/Religious Program—Students 91.
VESTAL, BROOME CO.
1—OUR LADY OF SORROWS (1941), Rev. John P. Putano; Deacon Dale Crotsley. In Res., Rev. Matthew F. Brown.
Res.: 157 Clark St., 13850. Tel: 607-748-8287; Fax: 607-748-8016.
Catechesis/Religious Program—Tel: 607-748-4766. Students 600.
2—ST. VINCENT DE PAUL (1965), Rev. Richard J. Giblin; Deacon James P. Crowley.
Res.: 165 Clifton Blvd., 13850. Tel: 607-722-3988; Fax: 607-722-8787.
Catechesis/Religious Program—465 Clubhouse Rd., 13850. Tel: 607-722-8372. Students 357.
WARNERS, ONONDAGA CO., OUR LADY OF GOOD COUNSEL (1913), In Res., Rev. Vincent J. Kilpatrick.
Res.: Newport Rd., Box 67, 13164. Tel: 315-672-3725.
Catechesis/Religious Program—Students 80.
WATERVILLE, ONEIDA CO., ST. BERNARD (1850), [CEM] Rev. Richard J. Kapral.
Res.: 199 Stafford Ave., 13480. Tel: 315-841-4481.
Catechesis/Religious Program—Students 165.
Mission—St. Mary North Brookfield, Madison Co.
WHITESBORO, ONEIDA CO.
1—ST. ANNE (1965), Rev. Walter F. Cannan, Admin.
Res.: 8539 Clark Mills Rd., 13492-2754. Tel: 315-736-7672.
Catechesis/Religious Program—Students 350.
2—ST. PAUL (1883), Rev. Abraham L. Esper.
Res.: 16 Park Ave., 13492. Tel: 315-736-1124; Fax: 315-768-7915.
Catechesis/Religious Program—Tel: 315-736-4807. Students 499.
WHITNEY POINT, BROOME CO., ST. PATRICK (1869), [CEM] Rev. Robert P. Hyde, J.C.L.
Res.: Box 711, 13862. Fax: 607-692-7171.
Catechesis/Religious Program—Students 101.
WINDSOR, BROOME CO., OUR LADY OF LOURDES (1947), Rev. John Booth Jr.
Res.: P.O. Box 361, 13865. Fax: 607-655-8118.
Catechesis/Religious Program—Tel: 607-655-8118. Students 106.

Chaplains of Public Institutions

Hospitals

SYRACUSE. *St. Camillus Health & Rehab Center*, 813 Fay Rd., 13219. Tel: 315-488-2951. Ms. Kathy Falso, Pastoral Care Coord.
Community General Hospital, 4900 Broad Rd., 13215. Tel: 315-492-5011. Sr. Winifred Guinan, O.S.F.
Crouse Irving Memorial Hospital, 736 Irving Ave., 13210. Tel: 315-470-7615. Rev. Les Heizman, Sr. Monica Czechowicz.
James Square Nursing Home. Attended from Blessed Sacrament Parish.
St. Joseph's Hospital Health Center, 301 Prospect Ave., 13203. Tel: 315-448-5116. Rev. Michael Taylor, O.F.M.Conv., Sisters Marie Therese Nicholson, O.S.F., Patrice Ward, O.S.F., Mary Louise Williams, O.S.F., Jacqueline Spiridlozzi, Dir., Frances Agnes Ryan, Mary Daniel Golmbieski, Patricia Scofield, Jane Patrick.
Loretto Geriatric Center, 700 E. Brighton Ave., 13205. Tel: 315-469-5570. Deacon Charles O'Connor.
Rosewood Heights Nursing Home, Formerly Plaza Extended Care FacilityTel: 315-474-4431. Sr. Frances Ann Thom, O.S.F.
University Hospital, 750 E. Adams St., 13210. Tel: 315-464-5540. Rev. Alfred J. Bebel, Kathy Ball.
Van Duyn Home & Hospital, 5060 W. Seneca Tpke., 13215. Tel: 315-469-5511. Susan Marcoccia.
Veterans Administration Hospital, Res: 800 Irving Ave., 13210. Tel: 315-476-7461. Rev. Msgr. Wilfred F. Evans.
BINGHAMTON. *Binghamton General Hospital*, Tel: 607-762-2200. Rev. John Mikalajunas, Sr. Annellen Kelly.
Binghamton Psychiatric Hospital. Revs. John Booth, Gerald J. Buckley (Retired).
Our Lady of Lourdes Memorial Hospital, 179 Riverside Dr., 13905. Tel: 607-798-5111. Sr. Ann Molesevick, D.C., Dir., Rev. Christopher Boretto, Bro. James Bagana, Sr. Kathleen Haley, Laura Allen.
JOHNSON CITY. *Wilson Memorial Hospital*, 33 Harrison St., 13790. Tel: 607-763-6000.
LIVERPOOL. *Developmental Center*, 36 Grampian Rd. #5, 13090. Rev. Charles A. Aho.
UTICA. *St. Elizabeth Hospital*, 2209 Genesee St., 13501. Tel: 315-798-8100. Rev. John H. Comeskey (Retired), Sisters Irene Zegarelli, O.S.F., Anthony Marie Eddo.
Faxton Hospital, 1676 Sunset Ave., 13502. Tel: 315-738-6545. Sr. Maureen Denn, C.S.J.
St. Luke, 1656 Champlin Ave., 13503. Tel: 315-798-6000. Sr. Genevieve Ciscek, C.S.J.
VESTAL. *Binghamton Nursing Homes*, Our Lady of Sorrows, 157 Clark St., 13850. Tel: 607-748-8287. Rev. Matthew F. Brown, Pastoral Care Chap.

Psychiatric Facilities

BINGHAMTON. *Binghamton Psychiatric Hospital*, Tel: 607-724-1391. Revs. John Booth, Gerald J. Buckley (Retired).
MARCY. *Central New York Psychiatric Center*, Old River Rd., Box 330, 13403. Tel: 315-736-8271. Rev. Richard V. O'Neill.
UTICA. *Mohawk Valley Psychiatric Center*, 1400 Noyes at York, 13502. Rev. Frederick D. Daley.

Jails

SYRACUSE. *Elmcrest Children's Center*, Salt Springs Rd., 13224. Vacant.
Hillbrook Detention Center, 4949 Velasko Rd., 13215. Tel: 315-492-1721. Sr. Judith Falk.
Jail Ministry Office, 208 Slocum Ave., 13204. Tel: 315-424-1877. Mary Czelusniak.
Public Safety Building, 259 E. Onondaga St., 13202. Rev. John Schopfer.
BINGHAMTON. *Broome County Jail*. Rev. Stanley J. Gerlock.
CORTLAND. *Cortland County Jail*. Vacant.
GEORGETOWN. *Camp Georgetown*, 31 E. State St., Sheburne, 13346. Tel: 315-837-4446. Rev. Edmund A. Castronovo.
JAMESVILLE. *Jamesville Penitentiary*, P.O. Box 143, 13078. Tel: 315-469-5581. Rev. Edward J. Reimer, Sr. Maura Rhode.
MARCY. *Mid-State Correctional Facility*, 210 W. Liberty St., 13403. Tel: 315-768-8581. Rev. Robert C. Weber.
MOHAWK. *Oneida Correctional Facility I.*, P.O. Box 8450, Rome, 13440. Tel: 315-339-6880. Rev. William C. Cahill.
Oneida Correctional Facility II, 578 Main St., P.O. Box 8450, Oneida, 13421. Deacon James Chappell.
NORWICH. *Norwich County Jail*. Vacant.
ORISKANY. *Oneida County Jail*, 120 Dexter Ave., 13424. Tel: 315-736-9033. Rev. Richard J. Stuczko (Retired).
OSWEGO. *Oswego County Jail*, 178 W. Second St., 13126. Tel: 315-343-2160. Rev. James M. Cesta.
ROME. *Walsh Facility*, Tel: 315-339-5232. Rev. Luis Olguin.
SOUTH PLYMOUTH. *Camp Pharsalia*. Rev. Edmund A. Castronovo.
UTICA. *Marcy Correctional Facility*, 15-8 Rox Pl., 13502. Tel: 315-768-1400. Deacon William Hotaling.

Special Assignment:
Most Revs.—
Costello, Thomas J., D.D.
Moynihan, James M., D.D.
Rev. Msgr.—
Evans, Wilfred F.
Revs.—
Aho, Charles A.
Baranski, Andrew E.
Bebel, Alfred J.
Cahill, William C.
Carmola, Michael J.
Chryst, Robert D. Tel: 315-422-9390
Donovan, John P., J.C.L.
Jones, Robert S.
Lang, James Paul
Mattice, George F.
Minehan, Michael P., J.C.L.
Muscalino, Daniel C.
Olguin, Luis
Ours, Robert A.
Phillips, Joseph H.
Pompei, Frederick A.
Quartier, Neal E.
Sambor, David R.
Schopfer, John C.
Sullivan, Robert J.
Vavonese, Charles S.
Weber, Robert C.

On Duty Outside the Diocese:
Rev. Msgr.—
Fahey, Charles J., Fordham University, New York.

Revs.—
Bassano, Michael, Mary Knoll (Incardinated)
Cincotta, Anthony
Creed, Peter, Cathedral of the Sacred Heart, 811 B Cathedral Pl., Richmond, VA 23220-1801.
Keane, Philip S., S.S.
Nichols, Louis J.
Rossetti, Stephen
Wallace, Harry C.
Woolever, James

Military Chaplains:
Revs.—
Dunn, Richard B., PSC 2 Box 953, APO, AP 96264.
Fukes, Gary M., 1st Lt. & Chap., 1420 Waterford Place #7, Manhattan, KS 66502.
Gryga, Theodore, U.S. Navy
Madej, Paul D., Office of the Installation Chaplain, U.S. Army Infantry Center, Fort Benning, GA 31905. U.S. Navy

On Sabbatical:
Rev. Msgr.—
Elkin, Frederic F., 3942 Roebling Ln., Virginia Beach, VA 23452.
Revs.—
Smith, Lester E.
Taugher, Timothy J.
Tosti, Anthony F., P.O. Box 201, Canastota, 13032-0201.

Absent on Leave:
Rev.—
Quinn, James F.

Study Leave:
Rev.—
Auth, Clifford H., Catholic University of America

Retired:
Rev. Msgrs.—
Bill, Ronald C., Immaculate Conception Rectory, 400 Salt Springs St., Fayetteville, 13060.
Borgognoni, Charles L.
Brigandi, Paul A.
Culkin, Francis J.
Davern, Robert
Denti, Carl J.
Donovan, William
Doran, Thomas M.
Eckermann, Charles H.
Giblin, Lawrence E.
Kane, James D.
Kantor, Adolph A.
Kelly, William M.
Kiernan, Thomas
Luczycki, Matthew C.
Lutz, James M.
McCloskey, James A.
McGraw, John T.
Sammons, Francis L.
Revs.—
Bauer, Donald J., St. Joseph's Nursing Home.
Brown, William J., St. Luke's Nursing Home, Oswego.
Buckley, Gerald J.
Comeskey, Edwin T.
Comeskey, John H.
Culver, James A.
Daley, John J.
Dwyer, William M.
Esposito, William C., 104 David Dr., North Syracuse, 13212.
Fallon, James J.
Florczyk, Walker
Fuchs, Moritz A.
Gleba, William P.
Guyder, Thomas F., c/o Helen Gingell 1700 W. Oondaga St., Apt. 201, 13204.
Heagerty, John J.
Jutton, David J.
Kane, Joseph F.
Keeffe, Anthony J., 1124 Oak St., 13203.
Kilpatrick, Vincent
Lauducci James V.
Libera, Angelo
Majdanik, Albin J.
Manning, Thomas J.
McKay, Robert J.
Morbito, Angelo L.
Mulranen, John J.
Murphy, Daniel G.
Nold, Joseph K.
O'Hanlon, James J.
Pilat, Edmund S.
Pilla, P. Carl
Regan, William P.
Roark, John D.
Sizing, Theodore C.
Slater, Dennis
Stuczko, Richard J.
Thompson, Richard R., St. Joseph's Rectory, 110 Charles St., Boonville, 13309.
Tucker Richard
Votraw, Wilbur J.
Walsh, Bernard

Permanent Deacons:
Altmeier, Robert, Norwich
Alvaro, Nick A., Syracuse
Ashe, Wayne, Kirkville
Ashley, John, Binghamton
Benz, Peter F., Baldwinsville
Blaine, Edward, Endicott
Borchert, Robert, Skaneateles
Brickner, Lawrence, Marathon
Brody, John P., Camillus
Brush, Wesley J., Madison, WI, (On Leave)
Caminiti, Joseph, Cortland
Carranti, Pio Peter, Syracuse
Castro, Joseph, North Syracuse
Celentano, Joseph, Sr., Syracuse
Chappell, James C., Oneida
Chiesa, Richard J., Camillus
Chillemi, Joseph, Oswego
Chouette, Frederick, Liverpool
Collins, John H., Pennellville
Cretaro, John T., Oswego
Crosby, James P., Syracuse (On Leave)
Crossett, Thomas F., Johnson City (On Leave)
Crotsley, Dale, Vestal
Crowley, James, Vestal
Daniszewski, Joseph, Syracuse
Dischiavo, William R., Utica
Distin, Leslie, Johnson City
Dotterer, William A., Liverpool
Doyle, Edgar A., Rome, NY
Droz, John J., Sr., (Retired), New Hartford
Dwyer, Richard J., Cortland
Forish, Frank M., Baldwinsville
Gallagher, James T., Binghamton (On Leave)
Goskowski, Raymond, Binghamton
Graff, Stephen, Baldwinsville
Hachey, Thomas, North Syracuse
Hammond, Charles, Cazenovia
Harley, Thomas, Endicott
Hart, Guy W., Bridgeport
Hazard, Wilbur, Utica
Heizman, Bernard, La Fayette
Hotaling, William P., Utica
Joslin, Donald E., Holland Patent
Klockowski, Daniel A., Utica; Eastern Rite
Kopec, John, NY Mills
Kotch, Myron, (Eastern Rite), Syracuse
Kulak, Jules F., Solvay
Lalande, John, Oswego
Lee, John, Utica
Manzene, Stephen, Liverpool
Maynard, George E., Clay
McCabe, Donald, Syracuse
McGrath, Michael B., Syracuse
Money, Kenneth, Liverpool
Monnat, Leonard S., Syracuse (On Sick Leave)
Morse, James L., Syracuse
Mullin, Paul, New Hartford
Mulvey, John, Syracuse
Murray, John, Manlius
Needham, Leo I., Syracuse
Niles, Elbert, Oneida
O'Connor, Charles, Syracuse
Page, Warren C., (Retired), Syracuse
Phillips, George, Endwell
Pittman, Gerard, Fayetteville
Powers, Paul F., Afton
Riggalls, Robert, Sr., Waterville
Rosher, Nicholas (Vatican City State), Rome, NY
Rossi, Dominic L. (Ghana), Endicott
Sims, John E., Endwell (On Leave from Diocese)
Smith, Stephen, Cortland
Stella, John, Binghamton
Sweenie, David, Oswego
Trepa, John, Greene
Vanelli, Peter P., Syracuse
Whiting, Donald R., North Syracuse
Wilbur, Richard, Chesire, CT, (On Leave)
Winslow, Frank L., Utica
Woeste, James, Syracuse
Woloszyn, John, Liverpool
Young, Stephen, Cazenovia

INSTITUTIONS LOCATED IN THE DIOCESE

[A] SEMINARIES, RELIGIOUS, OR SCHOLASTICATES

SYRACUSE. *Saint Andrew Hall*, 420 Demong Dr., 13214-1499. Tel: 315-445-3500; Fax: 315-446-9472. Revs. Joseph Lingan, S.J. (BAL), Rector & Dir. Novices; Frederick J. Pellegrini, Asst. Dir. Novices; James P. Carr, S.J., Asst. Dir. Novices. Novitiate for the Maryland , New England, and New York Provinces, Society of Jesus. Priests 3; Novices 24.

[B] COLLEGES AND UNIVERSITIES

SYRACUSE. *Le Moyne College*, 1419 Salt Springs Rd., 13214-1399. Tel: 315-445-4100; Fax: 315-445-4540. Dr. John R. Smarrelli Jr., Academic Vice Pres.; Dr. Shawn L. Ward, Vice Pres. Student Dev.; Mr. Michael M. Crough, Esq., Vice Pres. & Asst. to the Pres.; Mr. Daniel T. Konstalid, Vice Pres. Fin. & Admin.; Mrs. Barbara M. Karper, Asst. Vice Pres. Campus Prog. Affairs; Mr. Mark G. Godelski, Dir. Residence Life & Coord. Judicial Affairs; Dr. Linda M. LeMura, Dean, Arts & Sciences; Dr. Marcia Ruwe, Dir. Continuing Educ.; Mrs. Mary M. Chandler, Registrar; Mr. Dennis R. DePerro, Vice Pres.,Enrollment Mgmt. Jesuits 16; Brothers 1; Lay Teachers 147; Total Enrollment 3,403.

[C] HIGH SCHOOLS, DIOCESAN

SYRACUSE. *Bishop Ludden Junior/Senior High School*, 815 Fay Rd., 13219. Tel: 315-468-2591; Fax: 315-468-0097. Email: blhs@syrdiocese.org. Mr. Dennis J. Meehan, Prin. Priests 1; Sisters 4; Lay Teachers 65; Students 830.

BINGHAMTON. *Seton Catholic Central High School of Broome County*, 70 Seminary Ave., 13905. Tel: 607-723-5307; Fax: 607-723-4811. Ms. Kathleen M. Dwyer, Prin.; Ms. Dawn A. Hover, Asst. Prin.; Rev. Robert A. Ours. Priests 1 Sisters 7; Lay Teachers 31; Students 409.

EAST SYRACUSE. *Bishop Grimes Jr./Sr. High School*, 6653 Kirkville Rd., 13057. Tel: 315-437-0356; Fax: 315-437-0358. Email: bghs@syrdiocese.org/exchange. Rev. George F. Sheehan, Prin. Priests 2; Friar 1; Sisters 4; Lay Teachers 41; Students 607.

ROME. *Rome Catholic Junior-Senior High School*, 800 Cypress St., 13440. Tel: 315-336-6190; Fax: 315-336-6194. Email: romecath@syndiocese.org. Priests 1; Lay Teachers 17; Students 136.

UTICA. *Notre Dame Jr./Sr. High School*, 2 Notre Dame Lane, 13502. Tel: 315-724-5118; Fax: 315-724-9460. Email: ndlibrar@borg.com. Miss Kathleen Donovan. Sisters 4; Lay Teachers 47; Students 562.

[D] HIGH SCHOOLS, PRIVATE

SYRACUSE. *Christian Brothers Academy*, (Grades 7-12), 6245 Randall Rd., 13214. Tel: 315-446-5960; Fax: 315-446-3393. Web: www.cbasyracuse.org. Bro. Thomas Zoppo, F.S.C., Prin. Brothers of the Christian Schools 6; Lay Teachers 54; Students 750; Sisters of Third Order of St. Francis 3.

[E] CONSOLIDATED SCHOOLS

BINGHAMTON, BROOME CO.. *St. John the Evangelist*, (Grades K-8), 9 Livingston St., 13903. Tel: 607-723-0703; Fax: 607-772-6210. Email: mekelley@syndiocese.org. Mary Ellen Kelley, Prin. Religious 4; Lay Teachers 23; Students 289.

St. Thomas Aquinas, (Grades PreK-3), 3 Aquinas St., 13905. Tel: 607-797-6528; Fax: 607-797-6541. Email: stthomas@stny.rr.com. Sr. Patricia Coyle, O.S.F., Prin. Religious 1; Lay Teachers 11; Students 170.

ENDICOTT, BROOME CO.. *Seton Catholic Middle School*, (Grades 5-8), 1112 Broad St., 13760. Tel: 607-748-7423. Email: syrsetonmend@connectinc.com. Marguerite DiFulvio, Prin. Lay Teachers 16; Students 227.

JOHNSON CITY, BROOME CO.. *St. James Middle School*, 143 Main St., 13790. Tel: 607-797-5444; Fax: 607-797-6794. Email: ePrincipal@aol.com. George Clancy, Prin. Sisters 2; Lay Teachers 13; Students 165.

NORWICH. *Holy Family School*, (Grades PreK-8), 17 Prospect St., 13815. Tel: 607-337-2207; Fax: 607-337-2210. Email: hfamilyn@syndiocese.org. Sr. Joseph Gutosky, Prin. Lay Teachers 14; Students 150.

OSWEGO. *Trinity Catholic School*, 115 E. 5th St., 13126. Tel: 315-343-6700; Fax: 315-342-9471. Mr. David Friedlander, Admin.

St. Mary's Campus Students 66; Lay Teachers 19.

St. Paul's Campus Tel: 315-343-6700; Fax: 315-342-9471. Students 141.

ROME. *St. Peter*, (Grades K-6), 400 Floyd Ave., 13440. Tel: 315-336-2360. Sr. Cheryl Canfield, C.S.S.F., Prin. Religious 1; Lay Teachers 12; Students 166.

UTICA. *Our Lady of Lourdes*, (Grades PreK-6), 11 Barton Ave., 13502. Tel: 315-732-4374; Fax: 315-738-9720. Email: lourdesu@syrdiocese.org. Web: www.lourdes-school.com. Sr. Carol Polito, Prin. Sisters 1; Lay Teachers 24; Students 362.

VESTAL, BROOME CO.. *Our Lady of Sorrows - Seton*

Middle, (Grades PreK-4), 1112 Broad St., 13850. Tel: 607-748-7423. Email: syrolsves@connect.net. Margaret Di Fulvio, Prin. Lay Teachers 22; Students 199.

[F] CATHOLIC CHARITIES OF SYRACUSE

SYRACUSE. *Bishop Joseph T. O'Keefe, Inc.*, c/o 240 E. Onondaga St., 13202. Tel: 315-424-1830; Fax: 315-478-4619. Most Rev. James M. Moynihan; Rev. Michael P. Minehan, J.C.L., Chancellor; Most Rev. Thomas J. Costello, D.D., Vicar Gen.

Catholic Charities of the Roman Catholic Diocese of Syracuse, 240 E. Onondaga St., 13202. Tel: 315-424-1830; Fax: 315-478-4619. Email: dmanning@syracusediocese.org. Web: www.syrdio.org. Mr. Dennis J. Manning, A.C.S.W., Pres. & CEO. Catholic Charities Onondaga County: Mr. Brian Walton, Area Dir.

1654 W. Onondaga St., 13204. Tel: 315-424-1800; Fax: 315-424-6045. Email: bwalton@ccoc.us.

Jail Ministry, Slocum House, 208 Slocum Ave., 13204. Tel: 315-424-1877. Mary Czelusniak, Coord.

Keener Seniors, 1654 W. Onondaga St., 13204. Tel: 315-424-1804. Mr. Michael Gannon, Dir. Nutrition Program for the Elderly.

BINGHAMTON. *Associated Catholic Charities*, 232 Main St., 13905. Tel: 607-729-9166; Fax: 607-729-2062. Email: jslavik@ccbc.net. Web: www.catholiccharities.bc.org. Mr. Joseph G. Slavik, Exec. Admin.

Catholic Charities Adolescent Group Home, 57 Chestnut St., 13905. Tel: 607-723-6355; Fax: 607-231-2755. Email: kcerasaro@ccbc.net. Ms. Karen Cerasaro, Dir.

The Catholic Foundation of Broome County, 232 Main St., 13905. Tel: 607-729-9166; Fax: 607-729-2062. Mr. Robert W. Aber, Pres.

Legal Title: *The Bishops Catholic Education and Charities Foundation, Inc.*

Catholic Social Services of Broome County, 232 Main St., 13905. Tel: 607-729-9166; Fax: 607-729-2062. Email: dyeager@ccbc.net. Web: www.catholiccharitiesbc.org. Mr. Daniel L. Yeager, M.A., Exec. Dir.; Grazia Tonelli, C.S.W., Supvr. of Clinical Svcs.; Kathy Ford, C.S.W., Supvr. Pregnancy, Parenting & Adopting Program.

CORTLAND. *Catholic Charities of Cortland County*, 33-35 Central Ave., 13045. Tel: 607-756-5992; Fax: 607-756-5999. Email: pcurrie56@ccocc.org. Paula Currie, Exec. Dir.

Case Management Services for Teens Tel: 607-756-5992; Fax: 607-756-5999. Ann Marie Phelps, Assoc. Dir.

Case Management Services for Psychiatrically Disabled Tel: 607-756-5992; Fax: 607-756-5999. Marie Walsh, Assoc. Dir.

Residential Services Tel: 607-753-3550; 607-753-7780 (Lawrence House); Fax: 607-756-4697. Mike Pisa, Assoc. Dir. Lawrence House Community Residence: Supported Housing; Supportive Apartments; Alcohol Halfway House & Recovery Apartments, Independent Housing Option for Long-Term Mentally Ill (Lawrence House).

"Essentials" Tel: 607-299-0029; Fax: 607-756-5999. Ann Marie Phelps, Assoc. Dir. Emergency & Basic Needs Assistance (Food Pantry, Clothing, Medication, Advocacy Referral & Support).; Summer Lunch Program for Children.

Catholic Charities-STEPS-TASA, 33-35 Central Ave., 13045. Tel: 607-756-5992; Fax: 607-756-5999. (Supportive Teen Education-Parents Services), TASA; Case Management; Men's Support Group.

FULTON. *Catholic Charities of Oswego County*, 365 W. First St., 13069. Tel: 315-598-3980.

108 E. Sixth St., Oswego, 13126. Tel: 315-343-9540. Andrea McCabe, Area Dir.

NORWICH. *Chenango County Catholic Charities*, 3 O'Hara Dr., 13815. Tel: 607-334-8244.

The Counseling Program See separate listing.

Chenango House, 49 Fair St., 13815. Tel: 607-336-8939. Supervised by Community Residence Program.

Intensive Supportive Apartment Program
49 Fair St., 13815. Tel: 607-336-4359.

Supported Housing Program
49 Fair St., 13815. Tel: 607-336-4492.

Crossbridge Adolescent Home
Granville Hill Rd., 13460. Tel: 607-674-9422.

Community Residence Program Provides housing for mentally ill adults and adolescent boys.

Catholic Charities of Chenango County, 3 O'Hara Dr., 13815. Tel: 607-334-8244; Fax: 607-336-5779. Email: ccccharity@adelphia.net.

The Counseling Program Provides comprehensive counseling for children and adults, also specialized counseling for abused children.

Catholic Charities of Chenango County, 3 O'Hara Dr., 13815. Tel: 607-334-8244; Fax: 607-336-5779. Jane Coddington, Dir.

Crime Victims-Witness Assistance Program Tel: 607-334-3532; Fax: 607-336-5779. Provides 24 hour Hotline at 607-336-1101, Crisis Intervention, Safe Dwelling, Safe Housing; Court accompaniment; filing affidavits and claims with Crime Victims Board; advocacy with law enforcement agencies; information and referrals.

Catholic Charities of Chenango County, 3 O'Hara Dr., 13815. Tel: 607-336-1528; Fax: 607-336-5779.

ONEIDA. *Madison County Catholic Charities*, 119 E. Walnut St., 13421. Tel: 315-363-5274. Dennis Manning, Exec. Dir.; Sue Panetta, Assoc. Dir.

ROME. *Catholic Charities of Oneida - Madison Counties*, Formerly Catholic Charities of Rome, 212 W. Liberty St., 13440. Tel: 315-337-8600; Fax: 315-337-2433. Kathleen C. Eichenlaub, Area Dir.

UTICA. *Catholic Charities of Oneida - Madison Counties*, Formerly Catholic Charities, Eastern Region, 1408 Genesee St., 13502. Tel: 315-724-2158; Fax: 315-724-5318. Kathleen C. Eichenlaub, Area Dir.; Jan Stasaitis, Dir. Admin.; Anthony J. Conestabile, Dir. Finance; Nanette Conney, Dir. Residential Support.

Catholic Social Services of Utica, 1408 Genesee St., 13502. Tel: 315-724-3167; Fax: 315-724-5318. Email: ddimeo@ccharityyom.org. Kathleen C. Eichenlaub, Area Dir.; Dianne DiMeo, Dir. Family & Community Support Srvs. Div.

[G] OFFICES OF HUMAN DEVELOPMENT

SYRACUSE. *Bishop Foery Foundation*, 416 W. Onondaga St., 13202. Tel: 315-475-8316. Socio-Educational instruction center for racial minorities.

Caseworkers Larry King, Dir. Elementary program for children ages 6-12.

BINGHAMTON. *Broome County Catholic Charities Office of Social Concerns*, 232 Main St., 13905. Tel: 607-729-9166; Fax: 607-729-2062. Email: jslavik@ccbc.net. Web: www.catholiccharitiesbc.org. Joseph Slavik, Contact Person.

[H] ST. VINCENT DE PAUL SOCIETY

SYRACUSE. *St. Vincent de Paul Furniture and Clothing, a Catholic Charities Program* Thrift Shop , 500 Seymour St., 13204. Tel: 315-476-4797. Web: www.ccoc.us.

Thrift Shop, Distribution & Processing Center, 755 N. Salina, 13208. Tel: 315-475-4659.

Lakeshore Heights Plaza Thrift Shop, 6195 Rte. 31, Cicero, 13039. Tel: 315-699-5365. Mr. Richard Wagoner, Dir.; Kris Craven, Warehouse & Store Mgr.

St. Vincent de Paul Society, 500 Seymour St., 13204. Tel: 315-476-4797. Web: www.ccoc.us.

FULTON. *St. Vincent de Paul Thrift Shop*, 365 W. First St., 13069. Tel: 315-598-3980; Fax: 315-593-8440. Email: jme52@powerfcu.net.

[I] CATHOLIC YOUTH ORGANIZATIONS

SYRACUSE. *Alliance Division, Catholic Charities*, 1654 W. Onondaga St., 13204. Tel: 315-424-1880; Fax: 315-424-6045. Mark Clary, Assoc. Dir.

Brighton Family Center, 100 Edmund Ave., 13205. Tel: 315-424-9378. Ms. Patricia Campany, Dir.

Catholic Charities, 1654 W. Onondaga St., 13204. Tel: 315-424-1800; Fax: 315-424-8388. Brian Walton, Area Dir.

Family Division, Catholic Charities, 1654 W. Onondaga St., 13204. Tel: 315-424-1840; Fax: 315-424-6079. Web: www.ccoc.us.

Hawley Youth Organization, 716 Hawley Ave., 13203. Tel: 315-472-6343. Dotti Barraco Hetnar, Dir.

Near East Side Adventures Program, 1085 E. Genesee St., 13210. Tel: 315-472-6362. Richard Kline, Dir.

Neighborhood Division, Catholic Charities, 1654 W. Onondaga St., 13204. Tel: 315-424-8133; Fax: 315-424-8262. Email: PWalton@ccoc.us.

Northside CYO, 527 N. Salina St., 13208. Tel: 315-474-7428.

Salina Civic Center, 2826 Lemoyne Ave., Mattydale, 13211. Tel: 315-455-7096; Fax: 315-455-2352. Email: saccscc@msn.com. Beth Scanlon, Dir.

Toomey Residential and Community Services Corp., 1654 W. Onondaga St., 13204. Tel: 315-424-1845; Fax: 315-424-7567. Email: 4460xx@dfa.state.ny.us. Judith D'Amore, Exec. Dir.

Vincent House, 514 Seymour St., 13204. Tel: 315-475-9844; Fax: 315-474-3939. Mr. John Graham, Branch Dir.

BINGHAMTON. *Broome County CYO*, 232 Main St., 13905. Tel: 607-729-5190. Email: kmcgoff@stny.rr.com. Kevin McGoff, Exec. Dir.

FULTON. *CYO Fulton*, 365 W. First St., 13069. Tel: 315-598-3980. Mr. James Smiley, Dir.

UTICA. *Catholic Charities, Youth Services Division*, 1408 Genesee St., 13502. Tel: 315-724-6118; Fax: 315-724-5318. Dianne DiMeo, Dir.

[J] CHILDREN'S INSTITUTIONS AND DAY CARE CENTERS

SYRACUSE. *DePaul Day Care Corporation*, 1654 W. Onondaga St., 13204. Tel: 315-424-8129; Fax: 315-424-7654. Mrs. Sharon Coulter, Dir.

House of Providence, 1654 W. Onondaga St., 13204. Tel: 315-424-1800; Fax: 315-424-6045. Email: BWalton@ccoc.us. Web: www.ccoc.us. Mr. Brian Walton. Records only.

Sister Patricia Ann's Preschool dba Gingerbread House Preschool, 2500 Grant Blvd., 13208. Tel: 315-471-4198; Fax: 315-471-4198. Email: missjoanie@att.net.

Dorn Day Care Center dba Gingerbread House Day Care Center , 2500 Grant Blvd., 13208. Tel: 315-471-4198. Joan Raven, Dir.

[K] DIOCESAN SUMMER CAMPS

SYRACUSE. *Lourdes Camp*, Office: 1654 W. Onondaga St., 13204. Tel: 315-424-1812; 315-673-2888 (Summer).

Camp Address:, 10 Mile Point, Skaneateles, 13152. Michael Preston, Dir.

UTICA. *Camp Nazareth*, Office: 1408 Genesee St., 13502. Tel: 315-724-6118.

112 Long Lake Rd., Woodgate, 13494. Tel: 315-392-3791; Fax: 315-392-6545. Dianne DiMeo, Dir.

[L] FAMILY LIFE BUREAUS

SYRACUSE. *Family Life Education*, 1342 Lancaster Ave., 13210. Tel: 315-472-6754; Fax: 315-472-8409. Email: famlifed.broadviewnet.net. Web: www.familylifeeducation.catholicweb.com. Rev. Joseph H. Phillips, Dir.; Margaret Dupee, Coord., Family & Marriage Enrichment; Karen Bandoblu, Coord., Marriage Prep. & Speakers Bureau & Natural Family Planning; Patricia Ennis, Coord., Separated/Divorced, The Third Option, and Parenting; Sue & Ronald Kielar, Coordinators Eastern Region; Kathy Colligan, Coord. Southern Region.

Northern Region Religious Education Office & Special Education for Catechetics, 108 E. Sixth St., Oswego, 13126. Tel: 315-343-5557; Fax: 315-343-5557. Email: germcsj@aol.com. Sr. Germaine Hilston, C.S.J., Dir.; Deanne Hall, Resource Center Admin.

Western Region Religious Education Office, c/o 1342 Lancaster Ave., 13210. Tel: 315-472-6751; Fax: 315-472-8409. Email: tmay@syracusediocese.org. Theresa May, Dir.

Resource Center Bishop Harrison Diocesan Center, 1342 Lancaster Ave., 13210. Tel: 315-472-6752; Fax: 315-472-8409. Email: resctr@syracusediocese.org. Marge Babcock, Admin.

ENDWELL. *Southern Region Family Life Education*, 400 Corey Ave., 13760. Tel: 607-786-0828. Email: JColligan@stny.rr.com. John Colligan, Dir.; Kathleen Colligan, Dir.

Cortland Resource Center, 44 N. Main St., Cortland, 13045. Tel: 607-756-2532; Fax: 607-756-2532. Elena Moses.

[M] GENERAL HOSPITALS

SYRACUSE. *St. Joseph's Hospital Health Center*, 301 Prospect Ave., 13203. Tel: 315-448-5111; Fax: 315-448-6161. Email: teresalavalle@sjhsyr.org. Web: www.sjhsyr.org. Mr. Theodore M. Pasinski, Pres. & CEO; Rev. Michael Taylor, Chap. School for Nurses. Sisters of the Third Franciscan Order 18; Bed Capacity 431; Patients Assisted Annually 400,000; Total Staff 3,300; Students 295.

BINGHAMTON. *Our Lady of Lourdes Memorial Hospital*, 169 Riverside Dr., 13905. Tel: 607-798-5111; Fax: 607-798-7681. Web: lourdes.com. Mr. John D. O'Neil, Pres. Daughters of Charity of St. Vincent de Paul 9; Bed Capacity 267; Patients assisted annually 400,000; Total Staff 1,300.

UTICA. *St. Elizabeth Hospital*, 2209 Genesee St., 13501. Tel: 315-798-8100; Fax: 315-734-3092. Email: svincent@STEMC.org. Web: www.stemc.org. Sisters Rose Vincent Gleason, CEO; M. Johanna Delelys, COO; Rev. John H. Comeskey (Retired). College of Nursing. Sisters of the Third Franciscan Order 16; Bed Capacity 201; Total Staff 1,758; Patients assisted annually 400,155; Students 194.

[N] FACILITIES FOR THE AGED

SYRACUSE. *Bernardine Apartments, Inc.*, 417 Churchill Ave., 13205. Tel: 315-469-7786. Mr. James Introne, Pres.; Howard Jenkins, Admin.

St. Camillus Health & Rehabilitation Center, 813 Fay Rd., 13219. Tel: 315-488-2951; Fax: 315-488-3255. Web: www.st-camillus.org. Mrs. Aileen M. Balitz, Pres.; Ms. Caroline Rouer-Dixon, Dir. Social Svcs. Total Staff 590.

St. Camillus Foundation, 813 Fay Rd., 13219. Tel: 315-488-2951, Ext. 404. Mr. Richard Storto, Foundation Chm.; Thomas Honan, Exec. Dir.

Loretto, 700 E. Brighton Ave., 13205. Tel: 315-469-5561; Fax: 315-469-6558. Mr. Mitchell Marsh, Admin. Cunningham Bldg.; Deacon Charles O'Connor, Chap.
Legal Title: *Loretto Rest Nursing Home Company, Inc.*

Loretto Geriatric Community Residences, Inc., 5018 S. Salina St., 13205. Tel: 315-492-0896.
4810 S. Salina St., 13205. Tel: 315-469-8562.
50 Syracuse St., Baldwinsville, 13027. Tel: 315-635-1647.
8659 Carpenter Rd., Baldwinsville, 13027. Tel: 315-635-1763.

Loretto Rest, Inc., 750 E. Brighton Ave., 13205. Tel: 315-469-5061. Mr. Patrick Deptula, Exec. Vice Pres.; Deacon Charles O'Connor, Chap.; Mr. Mitchell Marsh, Admin. Adult Home.

OSWEGO. *Saint Luke's Health Care Services*, 299 E. First St., 13126. Tel: 315-342-3166; Fax: 315-343-6531. Email: stluke@global2000.net. Web: www.stlukehs.com. Mr. Terrence Gorman, Admin. Total Staff 270.

UTICA. *St. Joseph Nursing Home*, 2535 Genesee St., 13501. Tel: 315-797-1230; Fax: 315-797-5171. Email: frank@stjosephnh.org. Web: www.stjosephnh.org. Sr. Barbara Connolly, O.Carm., Admin. Total Staff 196.

[O] SPECIALTY HOUSING

SYRACUSE. *Christopher Community, Inc.* Professional management and consultants of housing programs for the elderly, families and special populations. , 1654 W. Onondaga St., 13204. Tel: 315-424-1821; Fax: 315-424-6048. Mr. Peter White, Exec. Dir.; Fred Zolna, Housing Devel. Specialist.

Churchill Manor, Inc., 750 E. Brighton Ave., 13205. Tel: 315-492-1329; Fax: 315-492-6076. Email: cahika@lorettosystem.org. A non-profit corporation founded to provide housing for low and moderate income families and individuals.

Harbor View Housing Development Fund Co., Inc., c/o 1654 W. Onondaga St., 13204. Tel: 315-424-1822.

Hawley Winton Housing Development Fund, Inc., Walter Ludovico Apts., 340 Winton St., 13203. Tel: 315-422-0475; Fax: 315-471-1554. 32 one bedroom units occupied. Christopher Community, (Managing Agent).

Ludden Housing Development Fund Company, Inc., 1654 W. Onondaga St., 13204. Tel: 315-424-1821. Fifty one bedroom apartments for the elderly and handicapped. Christopher Community Inc., (Managing Agent).

Marcellus Apartments Housing Development Fund Company, Inc., 1654 W. Onondaga St., 13204. Tel: 315-424-1821. Christopher Community, Inc., (Managing Agent).

Miller Road Housing Development Co., Inc. (Brewerton) , 1654 W. Onondaga St., 13204. Tel: 315-424-1821. Housing for well elderly.

Mother Marianne Cope Housing Development Fund Co., Inc., 1047 E. Fayette St., 13210. Tel: 315-422-5611; Fax: 315-478-6972. 24 Units for HIV+ patients.

Mount St. James Corporation, 1654 W. Onondaga St., 13204. Tel: 315-424-1821. Engaged in the operation of a non-profit housing facility known as Mount St. James Apartments, at 338 Jamesville Ave., for persons of low to moderate income. Christopher Community, Inc., (Managing Agents).

St. Peter's Italian Church Housing Development Fund Co., Inc. Villa Scalabrini Apts., 709 James St., 13203. Raymond A. Banach, Vice Pres. & Treas.; Mario Rossi, Sec. Operation of a non-profit housing facility for aged, well persons of low income at the 800 Block of E. Willow St. in Syracuse. 120 units, one-bedroom apartments. Christopher Community, Inc., (Managing Agent).

Pompei Housing Development Fund Company, Inc. 50 one bedroom apartments for the elderly and handicapped. Christopher Community, Inc., (Managing Agent).
c/o Christopher Community, Inc., 1654 W. Onondaga St., 13204. Tel: 315-424-1821.

Pond St. Housing Development Fund Co., Inc., Bishop Harrison Apartments, 300 Pond St., 13208. Tel: 315-476-8630; Fax: 315-474-0806. Email: kalibrandi@christopher-community.org. Operation of 47 units, one bedroom apartments for the elderly and handicapped. Christopher Community Inc., (Managing Agent).

Providence House Apartments, 1700 W. Onondaga St., 13204. Tel: 315-471-8427; Fax: 315-474-1224. Email: slucas@christopher-community.org. Senior citizen housing, 100 units. Christopher Community, (Managing Agent).

Stoneleigh Housing Development Fund Co., Inc., Stoneleigh Apartments, 400 Lamb Ave., Canastota, 13032. Engaged in the construction and operation of a non-profit housing facility for elderly and handicapped persons of low income. 100 units, one bedroom apartments. Christopher Community, Inc., (Managing Agent).

Tyson Place Housing Development Fund Company, Inc. (40 apartments for the elderly) , *St. Joseph Manor*, 1654 W. Onondaga St., 13204. Tel: 315-424-1821. Christopher Community, Inc., (Managing Agent).

AUBURN. *Mercy Housing Development Fund Co., Inc., Mercy Apartments*, 1 Thornton Ave., 13021. Tel: 315-253-2015; Fax: 315-258-8516. Email: dmechowski@christopher-community.org. 1654 W. Onondaga St., 13204. 40 one bedroom units for the elderly and handicapped. Christopher Community, Inc., (Managing Agent).

BALDWINSVILLE. *Smokey Hollow Housing Development Fund Company, Inc., St. Mary's Apartments c/o Christopher Community*, 1654 W. Onondaga St., 13204. Tel: 315-424-1821. Christopher Community, Inc., (Managing Agent).

BREWERTON. *Bartell Road Housing Development Fund Co., Inc. - dba Long Manor Apts.*, 5500 Miller Rd., 13029. Tel: 315-668-9871; Fax: 315-676-2544. Email: longmanor@christophercommunity.org. 20 units, one bedroom apartments. Christopher Community, Inc., (Managing Agent).

CICERO. *Cicero Housing Development Fund Company Inc.*, 1654 W. Onondaga St., 13204. Tel: 315-424-1821.
Sacred Heart Apartments, 13039. Christopher Community, Inc., (Managing Agent).

FAYETTEVILLE *Redfield South Housing Development Fund Co. Inc.*, Redfield Village Apartments, 380 Salt Springs Rd., 13066. Tel: 315-637-3280; Fax: 315-637-2376. 50 one bedroom units. Christopher Community, Inc., (Managing Agent). Total Assisted 50; Total Staff 2.

NORTH SYRACUSE. *Pitcher Hill-Christopher Housing Development Fund Co., Inc.*, 1654 W. Onondaga St., 13204. Tel: 315-454-0697; Fax: 315-454-0053. Email: pitcherhill@christophercommunity.org. Engaged in the construction and operation of non-profit housing facilities for elderly and handicapped persons of low income. 100 units, one bedroom apartments. Christopher Community, Inc., (Managing Agent). Total Assisted 98; Total Staff 4.

OSWEGO. *St. Luke's Housing Development Fund Co., Inc.*, St. Luke's Apartments, W. First St., 13126. Tel: 315-343-0821; Fax: 315-343-0619. Engaged in the construction and operation of a non-profit housing facility for elderly and handicapped persons of low income. 100 units, one bedroom apartments. Christopher Community, Inc., (Managing Agent).

ROME. *C.N.C. Inc.*, W. Thomas St., 13440. Tel: 315-735-7545; Fax: 315-724-5318. Utica Catholic Charities, 1408 Genese St., Utica, 13502. Facility for ten deinstitutionalized chronically mentally ill individuals living in a group home.
Rome Mall Housing Development Fund Company, Inc., 1654 W. Onondaga St., 13204. Tel: 315-424-1821. 40 one bedroom units for the elderly. Christopher Community, Inc., (Managing Agent).
Rome Mall Apts., 13440.

TOWN OF GATES. *Steger Housing Development Fund Co., Inc.*, 4100 Lyell Rd.. 56 apartments for well elderly.
1654 W. Onondaga St., 13204. Tel: 315-424-1821.

UTICA. *Catherine St. Housing Development Fund Company, Inc., Mt. Carmel Apartments*, 1654 W. Onondaga St., 13201-0511. Tel: 315-424-1821. Christopher Community, Inc., (Managing Agent).

[P] PROGRAMS FOR THE HANDICAPPED

SYRACUSE. *L'Arche*, 1232 Teall Ave., 13206. Tel: 315-479-8088; Fax: 315-479-8118. Email: larchesyracuse@aol.com. Web: www.larchesyracuse.com. Francis H. Woolever, Community Leader. A Christian Community concerned with life sharing between persons with a developmental disability and persons who assist them. Homes at 1701 James St., 1226 Butternut St., 1240-42 Teall Ave., Syracuse, 140 Highland Ave., Syracuse.

UTICA. *St. John and St. Joseph Home, Inc.*, 1408 Genesee St., 13502. Tel: 315-724-2158; Fax: 315-724-5318. Kathleen C. Eichenlaub, Contact Person.

YORKVILLE. *The Heenan Spiritual Program for the Handicapped, Inc.*, 17 Sixth St., 13495. Tel: 315-736-4858. Mr. Stanley Zima, Dir.

[Q] MONASTERIES AND RESIDENCES OF PRIESTS AND BROTHERS

SYRACUSE. *Friary of Francis, Brother of Peace Conventual Franciscan Friars*, 702 Danforth St., 13208. Tel: 315-424-8641; Fax: 315-424-0048. Revs. Justin A. Biase, O.F.M.Conv., Guardian; Odoric Foley, O.F.M.Conv.; Adam Keltos, O.F.M.Conv.; Michael McCaffrey, O.F.M.Conv.; Timothy Mulligan, O.F.M.Conv.; Bros. Thomas Purcell, O.F.M.Conv.; James Doyle, O.F.M.Conv.; Joseph Freitag, O.F.M.Conv.

Jesuits at LeMoyne, Inc., 1419 Salt Springs Rd., 13214. Tel: 315-445-4100; Fax: 315-445-4722. Email: jesuit@maple.lemoyne.edu. Web: www.web.lemoyne.edu/jesuit/index.html. Revs. Arthur R. Madigan, S.J., Rector; James F. Smith, S.J., Treas.; Charles J. Beirne, S.J., Pres.; William J. Bosch, S.J.; Paul B. Campbell, S.J.; Theodore J. Clarkson, S.J.; James H. Dahlinger, S.J.; William S. Dolan, S.J.; Vincent W. Hevern, S.J.; Donald J. Kirby, S.J.; Donald C. Maldari, S.J.; Thomas R. Marciniak, S.J.; Gerald J. McIntyre, S.J.; Daniel J. Mulhauser, S.J.; Paul S. Naumann, S.J.; Joseph B. Neville, S.J.; Vincent B. Ryan, S.J.; Thomas J. Kent, S.J.; Robert E. Scully, S.J.; Michael T. Siconolfi, S.J.; Andrew L. Szebenyi, S.J. (Hungary); M. Donald Zewe, S.J. Priests 22.

Tommy Coyne Residence @ Dillon Hall, Formerly St. Pius X Home, Inc., 714 E. Brighton Ave., 13205. Tel: 315-469-0078. Diocesan home for priests. In Res. Rev. Msgr. Robert B. Davern; Revs. Charles A. Aho; John Fallon (OG); Joseph F. Kane (Retired); Robert J. McKay (Retired); Joseph M. McNamara (ROC) (Retired); Angelo L. Morbito (Retired); Joseph Nold; P. Carl Pilla (Retired); William Regan; Francis Young.

BINGHAMTON. *McDevitt Residence for Retired Priests*, 68 Seminary Ave., 13905. Tel: 607-771-6207. Rev. Msgrs. Lawrence E. Giblin (Retired); James D. Kane (Retired); Revs. Gerald J. Buckley (Retired); Daniel G. Murphy (Retired).

EAST SYRACUSE. *Vianney House*, 6651 Kirkville Rd., 13057. Tel: 315-463-2619. Revs. Andrew E. Baranski; George F. Sheehan.

UTICA. *Mother Marianne Cope Residence for Retired Priests*, 14 Foery Dr., 13502. Tel: 315-724-2539.

[R] CONVENTS AND RESIDENCES FOR SISTERS

SYRACUSE. *Convent of St. Anthony and Motherhouse Sisters of the Third Franciscan Order*, 1024 Court St., 13208. Tel: 315-422-8652. Email: sisters@osf.org. Web: www.osfsyr.org. Sr. Catherine Hoefer, O.S.F., Local Min.

Generalate Offices, 2500 Grant Blvd., 13208. Tel: 315-634-7000; Fax: 315-634-7023. Sr. Grace Ann Dillenschneider, Gen. Min. Total Sisters in Diocese 205; Total in Community 317.

Dominican Monastery of the Perpetual Rosary, 802 Court St., 13208-1766. Tel: 315-471-6762. Sr. Bernadette Marie, O.P., Prioress. Cloistered Nuns 7; Extern Sisters 2; Novices 3.

Franciscan Formation House, 1001 Court St., 13208-1708. Tel: 315-471-7893. Email: sr_ann@yahoo.com. Sisters of the Third Franciscan Order Sisters 4.

WINDSOR. *Transfiguration Monastery*, 701 NY Rte. 79, 13865-2700. Tel: 607-655-2366; Fax: 607-655-4024. Email: bendon@dep.tds.net. Camaldolese Benedictine Nuns Sisters 4.

[S] RETREAT HOUSES

SYRACUSE. *Christ the King Retreat House*, 500 Brookford Rd., 13224. Tel: 315-446-2680; Fax: 315-446-2689. Email: retreats@christthekingretreat.com. Rev. Michael J. Carmola, Dir.; Charlene Oppedisano, Asst.; Marianne Carbone, Admin. Asst. General retreat house for priests, nuns, laity and youth of upstate New York. Priests 1.

SKANEATELES. *Stella Maris Retreat Center* 13152. Tel: 315-685-6836; Fax: 315-685-6836. Email: wwtkal@aol.com. Web: www.stellamarisretreat.org. Geraldine Kaluzny, Admin.; Sr. Rose Raymond, Prog. Dir. Sisters of the Third Franciscan Order, M.C., Franciscan oriented center for renewal.

UTICA. *The Good News Foundation of Central New York*, 10475 Cosby Manor Rd., 13502. Tel: 315-735-6210; Fax: 315-735-7090. Email: goodnews@borg.com. Web: www.goodnewsfoundation.org. Deacon John Droz, Co-Exec. Dir.; Elizabeth Scheidelman Droz, Co-Exec. Dir.

[T] NEWMAN CENTERS

SYRACUSE. *LeMoyne College Newman Center* 13214. Tel: 315-445-4110. Rev. Thomas R. Marciniak, S.J., Dir.

Onondaga Community College Newman Center c/o 204 Alton St., 13210. Tel: 315-476-5857. Deacon John Mulvey, Chap.

Syracuse University, St. Thomas More Foundation, Inc. Alibrandi Catholic Center, 110 Walnut Pl., P.O. Box 0038, 13210-0038. Tel: 315-478-5959; Fax: 315-443-4465. Email: stmfsu@aol.com. Rev. Timothy Mulligan, O.F.M.Conv.

BINGHAMTON. *Broome Community College Newman Center* P.O. Box 1017, 13902. Tel: 607-778-5033; Fax: 607-778-5330. Email: phillips_g@

sunybroome.edu.

CAZENOVIA. *Cazenovia College Newman Center* 10 Seminary St., 13035. Tel: 315-655-7375; Fax: 315-655-7536. Email: syoung@cazenovia.edu. Web: www.cazcollege.edu/zinterfaith.htm. Deacon Steven R. Young, Chap.

CLINTON. *Hamilton College Newman Center* 198 College Hill Rd., 13323. Tel: 315-859-4129; Fax: 315-859-4041. Email: jcroghan@hamilton.edu. Web: www.hamilton.edu/college/newman. Rev. John P. Croghan, Chap.

CORTLAND. *Newman Foundation of Cortland, Inc. at the State University College of New York* 8 Calvert St., 13045. Tel: 607-753-6737. Email: agenm@cortland.edu. Web: www.cortland.edu/ministry/catholic. Marie C. Agen, Ph.D., Campus Min.

MORRISVILLE. *Newman Association at SUNY Morrisville* Mathasis Health Bldg., 13408. Tel: 315-684-6201. Email: YoungSR@morrisville.edu. Web: www.morrisville.edu/pages/newman. Deacon Steven R. Young, Chap.

Legal Title: *St. Joan of Arc Newman Association at the State University of New York (SUNY) Morrisville Agricultural and Technical College*

OSWEGO. *Newman Foundation, Inc., State University of New York* Hall Newman Center, 36 New St., P.O. Box 207, 13126. Tel: 315-312-7222; Fax: 315-312-7561. Email: mcnally@oswego.edu. Rev. Edward F. McNally.

UTICA. *Mohawk Valley Community College Newman Center*, P.O. Box 8087, 13505-8087. Tel: 315-792-3284; Fax: 315-792-4401. Deacon William Hotaling.

SUNY Institute of Technology at Newman Center P.O. Box 8087, 13505-8087. Tel: 315-792-3284; Fax: 315-792-4401. Rev. Paul J. Drobin, Chap.

Legal Title: *State University of New York (SUNY) Institute of Technology at Utica/Rome Newman Center*

Utica College Newman Center, Formerly Utica College of Syracuse University Newman Center P.O. Box 8087, 13505-8087. Tel: 315-792-3284; Fax: 315-792-4401. Rev. Paul J. Drobin, Chap. Res.: P.O. Box 8087, 13505-8087. Tel: 315-792-3284.

VESTAL. *Binghamton University Newman Center* 400 Murray Hill Rd., 13850. Tel: 607-798-7202; Fax: 607-798-7202. Email: frbob@binghamton.edu. Web: www.sa.binghamton.edu/~newman/newman.htm. Rev. Robert J. Sullivan, Chap.

[U] MISCELLANEOUS LISTINGS

SYRACUSE. **Brady Faith Center, Inc.*, 404 South Ave., P.O. Box 993, 13201. Tel: 315-472-9077. Web: www.bradyfaithcenter.org. Rev. John C. Schopfer, Pres.

**David W. Barry Foundation*, 240 E. Onondaga St., P.O. Box 511, 13201-0511. Tel: 315-422-7203; Fax: 315-478-4619. Most Revs. James M. Moynihan, D.D., Pres.; Thomas J. Costello, D.D., Vice Pres.; Rev. Michael P. Minehan, J.C.L., Sec. & Treas.

St. Francis Social Adult Day Service, 1108 Court St., 13208. Tel: 315-424-1003; 315-424-1004; Fax: 315-472-9899. Email: sfadc@traknet.com. Web: www.sfadc.org. Sr. Christopher Dixon, O.S.F., Admin. Operated by the Sisters of the Third Franciscan Order, A non-residential adult day-service providing holistic care for the frail elderly.

Grimes Foundation (Incorporated by special act of the New York State Legislature, May 1, 1916), 240 E. Onondaga St., 13202. Most Rev. James M. Moynihan, Pres. Ex-Officio. Corporation created to establish and maintain charitable, religious and educational facilities within the Roman Catholic Diocese of Syracuse, New York.

Lasalle Syracuse, Inc., 6245 Randall Rd., 13214. Tel: 315-446-5960; Fax: 315-446-3393. Web: www.cbasyracuse.org.

Loretto Apartments Housing Development Fund Co., Inc., 700 E. Brighton Ave., 13205. Tel: 315-469-5570, Ext. 277; Fax: 315-498-9073. Email: collka@lorettosystem.com.

Onondaga County Catholic School Foundation (Western Region Catholic School Foundation), 240 E. Onondaga St., P.O. Box 511, 13201-0511. Tel: 315-470-1450; Fax: 315-478-4619. (Vacant)

Sisters of the Third Franciscan Order-Retirement Trust Fund, 2500 Grant Blvd., 13208. Tel: 315-634-7000; Fax: 315-634-7023. Email: sisters@osfsyr.org. Web: www.osfsyr.org.

Spiritual Renewal Center, 1118 Court St., 13208. Tel: 315-472-6546. Email: mail@spiritualrenewalcenter.com. Web: www.spiritualrenewalcenter.com.

Saint Thomas Preparatory Seminary Fund, P.O. Box 511, 13201. Incorporated under the Laws of the State of New York, 1963, as a Membership Corporation to solicit funds for the construction of a diocesan seminary.

BINGHAMTON. *Ladies of Charity*, 100 Main St., 13905. Tel: 607-723-0194.

Samaritan House, 11 Fayette St., 13901. Tel: 607-724-3969; Fax: 607-771-0356. Email: duncankath@aol.com. Sr. Kathleen Duncan, C.S.J., Dir.

CANASTOTA. *Catholic Diocese of Nakuru Mission Office, Inc.*, 406 Spencer St., 13032. Tel: 315-697-8795; Fax: 315-697-8959. Email: smugo65266@aol.com. Rev. Simon K. Mugo (Africa), Dir.

ENDICOTT. *Roman Catholic Diocese - Bishop Harrison Education Foundation*, Formerly Bishop Harrison Education FoundationP.O. Box 511, 13201-0511.

MAINE. *Mount St. Francis Hermitage, Inc.*, Tel: 607-754-0001; Fax: 607-754-0001. Email: ffimaine@marymediatrix.com. Web: www.marymediatrix.com. P.O. Box 236, 13802. Tel: 607-754-0001. Revs. Maximilian Dean, F.I.; John Joseph Cook, F.I.; Bros. Didacus Cortes, F.I.; Francis Duarte, F.I.

RICHLAND. *Rural & Migrant Ministry of Oswego Co. Inc.*, 15 Stewart St., P.O. Box 192, 13144-0192. Tel: 315-298-1154; Fax: 315-298-1154. Email: rmmoc@myoswego.com. Sr. Louise Macchia, D.C., Contact Person. Staffed by the Daughters of Charity of St. Vincent de Paul and the Sisters of the Third Franciscan Order.

UTICA. *Christ Child Society of Utica*, 140 Hawthorne Ave., 13502. Cindy Kelly, Treas.

RELIGIOUS INSTITUTES OF MEN REPRESENTED IN THE DIOCESE

For further details refer to the corresponding bracketed number in the Religious Institutes of Men or Women section.

[1350]—*Brothers of St. Francis Xavier* (St. Joseph Prov., Milton, MA)—C.F.X.

[0330]—*Brothers of the Christian Schools* (New York Prov.)—F.S.C.

[0480]—*Conventual Franciscans*—O.F.M.Conv

[0690]—*Jesuit Fathers and Brothers* (New York Prov.)—S.J.

RELIGIOUS INSTITUTES OF WOMEN REPRESENTED IN THE DIOCESE

[0230]—*Benedictine Sisters of Pontifical Jurisdiction* (Erie, PA)—O.S.B.

[]—*Camaldolese Benedictine Sisters*—O.S.B.Cam.

[0330]—*Carmelite Sisters for the Aged and Infirm*—O.Carm.

[]—*Congregation of the Sisters of the Cross of Chavanod* (India)

[0760]—*Daughters of Charity of St. Vincent de Paul*—D.C.

[1050]—*Dominican Contemplative Nuns*—O.P.

[1070-01]—*Dominican Sisters*—O.P.

[1170]—*Felician Sisters*—C.S.S.F.

[1180]—*Franciscan Sisters of Allegany, New York*—O.S.F.

[1410]—*Franciscan Sisters of St. Joseph (Mill Hill)*—F.M.S.J.

[2575]—*Institute of the Sisters of Mercy of the Americas* (New York, NY; Omaha, NE)—R.S.M.

[]—*Little Sisters of St. Francis*—L.S.O.S.F.

[1360]—*Missionary Franciscan Sisters of the Immaculate Conception*—O.S.F.

[3160]—*Parish Visitors of Mary Immaculate*—P.V.M.I.

[0590]—*Sisters of Charity of Saint Elizabeth, Convent Station*—S.C.

[3340]—*Sisters of Providence (Holyoke)*—S.P.

[3950]—*Sisters of Saint Mary of Namur*—S.S.M.N.

[3780]—*Sisters of Saints Cyril and Methodius*—SS.C.M.

[1800]—*Sisters of St. Francis of the Third Order Regular* (Williamsville, New York)—O.S.F.

[3830-14]—*Sisters of St. Joseph* (Rochester, NY)—S.S.J.

[3840]—*Sisters of St. Joseph of Carondelet*—C.S.J.

[1970]—*Sisters of the Holy Family of Nazareth*—C.S.F.N.

[]—*Sisters of the Immaculate Heart of Mary, Mother of Christ* (Africa)—I.H.M.

[1490]—*Sisters of the Third Franciscan Order*—O.S.F.

[2160]—*Sisters, Servants of the Immaculate Heart of Mary*—I.H.M.

[4110]—*Ursuline Nuns (Roman Union)*—O.S.U.

DIOCESAN CEMETERIES

SYRACUSE. *St. Mary-St. Agnes*, 2315 South Ave., 13207. Tel: 315-475-4639. Rev. James C. Fritzen, Dir.; Christopher Naley, Supt.; Daniel Moorhead, Asst. Supt.

BALDWINSVILLE. *Our Lady of Peace*, 8668 Oswego Rd., 13027. Tel: 315-652-0559. Jason Germaine, Supt.

CORTLAND. *St. Mary*, 4101 West Road, 13045. Tel: 607-756-8838. Andrew Cook, Supt.

JOHNSON CITY. *Calvary-St. Patrick*, 501 Fairview St., 13790. Tel: 607-797-2906. Daniel Vuille, Supt.; Sally Hinkel, Sec.

OSWEGO. *St. Peter & St. Paul*, R.R. 04 Box 4B, Rte. 481, E. River Rd., 13126. Tel: 315-343-5002. Rev. Eric K. Harer, Dir.; Jason Germaine, Supt.

UTICA. *St. Agnes*, 601 Arthur St., 13501. Tel: 315-732-8588. Vincent Gieroy, Coord.; John McCarthy, Supt.

Calvary, 2407 Oneida St., 13501. Tel: 315-735-2727. David Pritchard, Supt.

Holy Trinity, Chaplain Ave., 13502. Tel: 315-724-0616. Rev. Arthur R. Hapanowicz, Dir.; Daniel Williams, Supt.

St. Mary, Webster St., 13501. Tel: 315-735-2727. David Pritchard, Supt.

WHITESBORO. *Mount Olivet*, 70 Wood Rd., 13492. Tel: 315-736-4446. Thomas Stepanowicz, Supt.

NECROLOGY

✠ Harrison, Most Rev. Frank J., Retired Bishop of Syracuse—Died May 1, 2004

† Brennan, Robert E., (Retired)—Died March 26, 2003

† Prevost, Frederick J., Whitesboro, NY St. Anne—Died May 22, 2003

† Prozny, Leopold V.—Died 2003

Diocese of Toledo

(Dioecesis Toletana in America)

Most Reverend

LEONARD P. BLAIR

Bishop of Toledo; ordained June 16, 1976; appointed Titular Bishop of Voncariana and Auxiliary Bishop of Detroit July 8, 1999; consecrated August 24, 1999; appointed Bishop of Toledo October 7, 2003; installed December 4, 2003

Most Reverend

ROBERT W. DONNELLY, D.D.

Auxiliary Bishop of Toledo; ordained May 25, 1957; appointed Titular Bishop of Garba and Auxiliary Bishop of Toledo March 20, 1984; ordained Bishop May 3, 1984 *Res.: 2544 Parkwood Ave., Toledo, OH 43610.*

Chancery: P.O. Box 985, Toledo, OH 43697-0985. Tel: 419-244-6711 Fax: 419-244-4791.

Web: www.toledodiocese.org

Email: chancery@toledodiocese.org

ESTABLISHED APRIL 15, 1910.

Square Miles 8,222.

Comprises the following Counties of northwest Ohio: Williams, Fulton, Lucas, Ottawa, Defiance, Henry, Wood, Sandusky, Erie, Paulding, Putnam, Hancock, Seneca, Huron, Van Wert, Allen, Wyandot, Crawford and Richland.

For legal titles of parishes and diocesan institutions, consult the Chancery.

STATISTICAL OVERVIEW

Personnel	
Bishop	1
Auxiliary Bishops	1
Retired Bishops	1
Priests: Diocesan Active in Diocese	129
Priests: Diocesan Active Outside Diocese	7
Priests: Diocesan in Foreign Missions	1
Priests: Retired, Sick or Absent	57
Number of Diocesan Priests	194
Religious Priests in Diocese	54
Total Priests in Diocese	248
Extern Priests in Diocese	12
Ordinations:	
Diocesan Priests	2
Permanent Deacons	5
Permanent Deacons in Diocese	191
Total Brothers	5
Total Sisters	671
Parishes	
Parishes	159
With Resident Pastor:	
Resident Diocesan Priests	93
Resident Religious Priests	10
Without Resident Pastor:	
Administered by Priests	50
Administered by Deacons	1
Administered by Religious Women	5
Pastoral Centers	6
New Parishes Created	1
Closed Parishes	3
Welfare	
Catholic Hospitals	6
Total Assisted	941,685
Homes for the Aged	4
Total Assisted	1,811
Special Centers for Social Services	15
Total Assisted	19,486
Educational	
Diocesan Students in Other Seminaries	21
Total Seminarians	21
Colleges and Universities	2
Total Students	1,876
High Schools, Diocesan and Parish	10
Total Students	3,562
High Schools, Private	4
Total Students	2,682
Elementary Schools, Diocesan and Parish	79
Total Students	18,683
Elementary Schools, Private	3
Total Students	671
Non-residential Schools for the Disabled	1
Total Students	60
Catechesis/Religious Education:	
High School Students	2,100
Elementary Students	17,568
Total Students under Catholic Instruction	47,223
Teachers in the Diocese:	
Priests	30
Brothers	1
Sisters	59
Lay Teachers	348
Vital Statistics	
Receptions into the Church:	
Infant Baptism Totals	3,262
Adult Baptism Totals	630
Received into Full Communion	539
First Communions	4,690
Confirmations	4,918
Marriages:	
Catholic	921
Interfaith	743
Total Marriages	1,664
Deaths	3,589
Total Catholic Population	298,069
Total Population	1,489,769

Former Bishops—Most Rev. JOSEPH SCHREMBS, D.D., appt. auxiliary of Grand Rapids, MI Jan. 8, 1911; consecrated Feb. 22, 1911; transferred to Toledo, Aug. 11, 1911; transferred to Cleveland, OH, May 11, 1921; died Nov. 2, 1945; His Eminence SAMUEL CARDINAL STRITCH, D.D., consecrated Bishop of Toledo, Nov. 30, 1921; appt. Archbishop of Milwaukee, Aug. 30, 1930; appt. Archbishop of Chicago, Dec. 27, 1939; created Cardinal, Feb. 18, 1946; named Pro-Prefect of the Sacred Congregation of the Propagation of the Faith, March 1, 1958; died in Rome, May 27, 1958; Most Revs. KARL J. ALTER, D.D., LL.D. (Retired), appt. Bishop of Toledo, April 17, 1931; consecrated June 17, 1931; appt. Archbishop of Cincinnati, June 21, 1950; retired July 23, 1969; died Aug. 23, 1977; GEORGE REHRING, D.D. (Retired), consecrated Oct. 7, 1937; appt. Auxiliary Bishop of Cincinnati, Oct. 7, 1937; appt. Bishop of Toledo, July 18, 1950; retired Feb. 25, 1967; died Feb. 29, 1976; JOHN A. DONOVAN, D.D. (Retired), ord. Dec. 8, 1935; Titular Bishop of Rhasus and Auxiliary of Detroit, Michigan Sept. 6, 1954; ord. Bishop of Detroit, Michigan Oct. 26, 1954; appt. to Toledo, Feb. 25, 1967; retired July 29, 1980; died Sept. 18, 1991; JAMES R. HOFFMAN, D.D., J.C.L., ord. July 28, 1957; appt. Titular Bishop of Italica and Auxiliary Bishop of Toledo April 18, 1978; ord. June 23, 1978; appt. Bishop of Toledo Dec. 16, 1980; died Feb. 8, 2003.

Chancery—P.O. Box 985, Toledo, 43697-0985. 1933 Spielbusch Ave., Toledo, 43624-1371. Tel: 419-244-6711; Fax 419-244-4791. Office Hours: Mon.-Fri. 8:30-5

Vicar General—Very Rev. MICHAEL R. BILLIAN, V.G., 1933 Spielbusch Ave., Toledo, 43624-1371. Mailing Address, P.O. Box 985, Toledo, 43697-0985. Tel: 419-244-6711.

Chancellor—Very Rev. MICHAEL R. BILLIAN, V.G., 1933 Spielbusch Ave., Toledo, 43624. Tel: 419-244-6711. Mailing Address, P.O. Box 985, Toledo, 43697-0985.

Cabinet—Most Rev. ROBERT W. DONNELLY, D.D., Sec. Personnel & Admin. Svcs.; Very Rev. MICHAEL R. BILLIAN, V.G., Chancellor; MICHAEL L. WASSERMAN, Secretariat for Pastoral Leadership; Mr. JACK J. ALTENBURGER, Sec. of Catholic Youth & School Svcs.; Mr. LOUIS A. COCCHIARELLA, J.T., M.T.S., Sec. Catholic Charities; SALLY A. OBERSKI, Dir. Communications, 1933 Spielbusch Ave., Toledo, 43624. Tel: 419-244-6711; Fax: 419-244-4791.

Advisory To Bishop

Unless otherwise indicated all Diocesan Offices and Secretaries are located at The Catholic Center, 1933 Spielbusch Ave., Toledo, OH 43624-1371. Address all mail to: P.O. Box 985, Toldedo, OH 43697-0985. Tel: 419-244-6711

Bishop's Education Council—Mr. MICHAEL BEAZLEY, Pres.; Mr. THOMAS YOUNG, Vice Pres.; Rev. ALBERT B. CERANOWSKI; Very Rev. HERBERT F. WEBER, V.F.; Mr. MICHAEL ANDERSON; Mrs. MICHELLE HILLS; Mr. DENNIS JOHNSON; Mrs. RITA KISSNER; Judge JUDITH LANZINGER; Mr. RICHARD LAVALLEY; Mrs. GERILYN LEIBFARTH; Mr. TIMOTHY MAHONEY; Mrs. SYLVIA MUNIZ-MUTCHLER; Mr. RAYMOND OLCZAK; Mrs. SUE RILEY; Mrs. ODESSA ROWAN; Mrs. DIANE SACCONE; Mrs. MARY WERNER; Mrs. MARY K. WILLIAMS; Mr. GENE ZMUDA.

Building Commission—Dr. GEORGE MURNEN, Chm.; Rev. GERALD J. CHMIEL; Very Rev. FRANK K. ECKART; Mr. DAVID BAGGETT; Mr. JAMES CIHAK; Dr. MARK PICKETT; Mr. JOHN BURGAN.

Consultors—Revs. DAVID M. ROSS, S.T.L., J.C.D.; MARVIN G. BORGER, J.C.L.; F. ANTHONY GALLAGHER; THOMAS J. LANDGRAFF, O.S.F.S.; HENRY SATTLER, C.SS.R.; RONALD R. WARNIMONT, J.C.L.

Deans—Defiance Deanery: Very Rev. G. ALLAN FILLMAN, V.F., Defiance, Henry and Paulding Counties. Fremont Deanery: Very Rev. RAYMOND E. ENSMAN, V.F., Ottawa and Sandusky Counties.

Lima Deanery: Very Rev. CHRISTOPHER P. VASKO, J.C.L., Allen, Van Wert and Putnam Counties. Mansfield Deanery: Very Rev. HERBERT F. WEBER, V.F., Richland and Crawford Counties. Tiffin Deanery: Very Rev. MICHAEL G. HOHENBRINK, V.F., Seneca, Wyandot and Hancock Counties. Toledo Central: Very Rev. THOMAS J. EXTEJT, V.F. Toledo Northwest: Very Rev. ROBERT J. REINHART. Toledo Southwest: Very Rev. KENNETH G. MORMAN, V.F. To-Lu-Wo Deanery: Very Rev. JOHN R. BLASER, V.F., Dean for East Lucas and Wood Counties. Sandusky Deanery: Very Rev. FRANKLIN P. KEHRES, V.F., Erie and Huron Counties. Will-Ful-L Deanery: Very Rev. FREDERICK J. DUSCHL, V.F., Williams, Fulton and West Lucas Counties.

Diocesan Pastoral Advisory Council—Mr. STEVEN J. NOWAK, Pres., P.O. Box 985, Toledo, 43697-0985.

Finance Council—Most Revs. LEONARD P. BLAIR, S.T.D.; ROBERT W. DONNELLY, D.D.; Very Rev. MICHAEL R. BILLIAN, V.G.; Mr. RICHARD FAIST; Mr. ROBERT J. KIRK; Mr. THOMAS KRESS.

Priests' Council—Revs. DAVID M. ROSS, S.T.L., J.C.D., Chm. Tel: 419-693-1150; HENRY SATTLER, C.SS.R., Vice Chm., Sec. & Treas. Tel: 419-475-4348.

Secretariat Of Administrative Services

Secretary—Most Rev. ROBERT W. DONNELLY, D.D., P.O. Box 985, Toledo, 43697-0985. Tel: 419-244-6711.

Financial Services—Mr. JOHN HEINZE, Dir.

Internal Auditor—Ms. SARA G. MARTIN, C.P.A., (Inactive).

Associate Auditor—Ms. SUZANNE STAPLETON.

Cemeteries Office—Mr. JACK HOEFLINGER, Dir., 5725 Hill Ave., Toledo, 43615-5852. Tel: 419-531-5747; Fax: 419-531-0946. Web: cathcemtoledo.org. Email: info@cathcemtoledo.org.

Cemeteries—Calvary, 2424 Dorr St., Toledo, 43607. Tel: 419-536-3751. *Mount Carmel, 15 E. Manhattan Blvd., Toledo, 43608.* Tel: 419-536-3751. *Resurrection, 5725 Hill Ave., Toledo, 43615.* Tel: 419-531-5747.

Court of Equity—Mrs. JUDITH GAJDOSTIK, Clerk; FRANK LINK, Presiding Judge, 3250 Hazelton Dr., Oregon, 43616. Tel: 419-691-7436.

Judges—Rev. GREGORY R. HITE; FRANCIS LANDRY; Sr. EMILY LECHLAK, O.S.F.; COLIN MCQUADE; PAULA MINZING; Rev. DANIEL J. RING; Sr. DOROTHY THUM, R.S.M.; HARRY WELSH; BRUCE WINTERS.

Conciliators—JAMES CARUSO; RICHARD HANUSZ; Sr. THERESE MILNE, I.H.M.; REGINA SCHIMMOELLER; JUDE SUTTER; JOHN F. WETLI.

Intake Officers—JANET KLAUSING; ROBERT J. SUTTER; CLARA WESOLEK; ELIZABETH ZEPF.

Chancery—

Chancellor—Very Rev. MICHAEL R. BILLIAN, V.G., Catholic Center, P.O. Box 985, Toledo, 43697-0985. Tel: 419-244-6711.

Diocesan Archives—Mrs. SUSAN K. WIETNIK, P.O. Box 985, Toledo, 43697-0985. Tel: 419-244-6711; Fax: 419-244-4791.

Catholic Center—Ms. PATRICIA STEIN, Mgr.

Stewardship and Development Office—VACANT, Dir.

Faith in the Future Program—Rev. ROBERT J. YEAGER, Dir.

Director of Communications—SALLY A. OBERSKI, P.O. Box 985, Toledo, 43697-0985. Tel: 419-244-6711; Fax: 419-244-0468. Email: communications@toledodiocese.org.

Diocesan Directory—Mrs. RITA BAUR, Editor.

"Catholic Chronicle"—CHRISTINE ALEXANDER, Editor, P.O. Box 1866, Toledo, 43603. Tel: 419-244-6711; Fax: 419-244-0468. Email: ccnews@toledodiocese.org.

Information Technology—Mr. FRANK BEIER, Dir.; Ms. SHARON LANDIS, Assoc. Dir.

Parish/School Technical Support—Mr. THOMAS KURT.

Secretariat Of Personnel

Secretary—Most Rev. ROBERT W. DONNELLY, D.D., Catholic Center, 1933 Spielbusch Ave., Toledo, 43624-1371. Tel: 419-244-6711; Fax: 419-244-4791. P.O. Box 985, Toledo, 43697-0985.

Ministry to Priests Program—

Vicar for Priests—Rev. NICHOLAS WEIBL.

Associate Vicar for Priests—Rev. THOMAS RADLOFF, S.J.

Continuing Formation for Priests Program—Rev. NICHOLAS WEIBL, Dir.; Sr. MARGARET MCGUINESS, O.P., Assoc. Dir.

Vicar for Deacons—Rev. NICHOLAS WEIBL.

Vicar For Religious—Sr. NANCY MATHIAS, O.S.U.

Diocesan Case Manager—Mr. FRANK DILALLO.

Office of Vocations—Rev. DAVID W. NUSS, Dir.; Sr. MARILYN MARIE ELLERBROOK, S.N.D., Assoc. Dir.

Priests' Personnel Board—Rev. KENNETH J. LILL, Chm. Members: Very Revs. JOHN R. BLASER, V.F.; RAYMOND E. ENSMAN, V.F.; Revs. KEITH A. STRIPE; JOSEPH R. STEINBAUER; ROBERT J. WILHELM, P.O. Box 985, Toledo, 43697-0985. Tel: 419-244-6711; Fax: 419-244-4791.

Human Resources—Mr. MICHAEL CONNELL, Dir.; Mrs. BARBARA NAVARRO, Assoc. Dir.

Tribunal—Catholic Center, 1933 Spielbusch Ave., Toledo, 43624-1371. Tel: 419-244-6711. *Mailing Address, P.O. Box 985, Toledo, 43697-0985.*

Director—Sr. MARCIA MARIE DESTATTE, S.N.D., J.C.L.. Email: mdestatte@toledodiocese.org.

Judicial Vicar—Very Rev. JOHN A. MCCLURE, J.C.L. (Retired). Email: jmcclure@toledodiocese.org.

Judges—Revs. JAMES E. AUTH, J.C.L.; MARVIN G. BORGER, J.C.L.; JOSEPH P. JAROS (Retired); GEORGE P. MILLER, J.C.L.; WILLIAM C. PARKER; DAVID M. ROSS, S.T.L., J.C.D.; DENNIS A. SCHROEDER; Very Rev. CHRISTOPHER P. VASKO, J.C.L.; Rev. RICHARD T. WURZEL, S.T.D.

Defenders of the Bond—Sr. MARCELLA HERMAN, O.S.F., J.C.L.; Revs. JOSEPH L. VAMOS (Retired); RONALD R. WARNIMONT, J.C.L.

Auditor/Assessor—Sr. DIANE MARIE PFAHLER, S.N.D.

Notaries—Mrs. PAULA S. BUTLER; Mrs. MARIAN A. KRASNIEWSKI; Mrs. CHARLOTTE A. LAMMERS; Mrs. ANGELA D. WALKER.

Retirement Plan for Lay Employees—Mrs. LINDA MILLER, Admin.; Mrs. MARY P. BERNING, Asst.

Employee Benefit Fund—Mrs. LINDA MILLER, Admin.; Mrs. MARY P. BERNING, Asst.

Secretariat for Pastoral Leadership

Secretary—Mr. MICHAEL L. WASSERMAN, Catholic Center, 1933 Spielbusch Ave., Toledo, 43624-1371. Tel: 419-244-6711; Fax: 419-244-4791. Web: toledodiocese-spl.org; P.O. Box 985, Toledo, 43697-0985.

Assistant Secretary—Deacon ALFREDO DIAZ.

Adult Catholic Formation—Mr. MICHAEL YOUNGBLOOD, Lead Agent.

Deacon Formation—Deacon LEO T. BISTAK.

Equal Access Ministry—Ms. MARSHA RIVAS, Dir. Tel: 419-243-1475 (TTY).

Inner Vision Ministry—Ms. MARY ANN SMITH. Tel: 419-698-3224.

Evangelization—Deacon LEO T. BISTAK.

Office of Global Concerns—VACANT.

Mission of Accompaniment Pastoral Team—Revs. BERNARD J. BOFF, Stateside Dir. (Retired); CHRISTOPHER KARDZIS, All Souls Catholic Mission, Box 37, Binga, Zimbabwe, Africa. Associates: Rev. THOMAS J. MCQUILLEN; RUTH ANN LEIDORF.

Hispanic Pastoral Ministry—Mr. MISAEL MAYORA, Dir.

Migrant Ministry—Sr. MARY JO TOLL, S.N.D., Dir., 150 Perry St., P.O. Box 548, Fostoria, 44830. Tel: 419-436-1582.

Lay Ministry—Mrs. PATRICIA OEDY-MURRAY, Dir.

Pastoral Planning—Sr. JOYCE LEHMAN, C.PP.S.

Office of Worship—VACANT, Dir.

Toledo Diocesan Liturgical Commission—Sr. ANN CARMEN BARONE, O.S.F., Chm.

Ecumenical & Interreligious Affairs Commission—Rev. JAMES E. PEIFFER, Chm., 215 Church St., Oak Harbor, 43449. Tel: 419-898-1389; Fax: 419-898-2212.

DCCW (Diocesan Council of Catholic Women)—Mrs. AUDREY ENGLEHART, Pres., Catholic Center.

Secretariat of Catholic Youth & School Services

Superintendent—Mr. JACK ALTENBURGER. Tel: 419-244-6711; Fax: 419-255-8269. Web: www.cyss.org. Team Members: Mrs. CAROLYN SCHMIDBAUER; Ms. ANN SARDESON; Mr. FRANK DILALLO, M.Ed., L.P.C.

Religious Education—

Assistant Superintendent for Religious Education—Sr. MIRIAM EBLE, S.N.D.Web: religiousd@toledodiocese.org.

Religious Education Consultant—Ms. BARBARA HOLDCROFT; Mr. GARY LANDOLL.

Catholic Youth Organization (CYO)—Mr. JEFF MIELCAREK, Dir.; Ms. JULIE DUBIELAK, Assoc. Dir.Web: cyo@toledodiocese.org.

Northwest Ohio Scholarship Fund—VACANT, Coord.

Catholic Club—Mr. PAUL SZYMANSKI, Dir., 1601 Jefferson Ave., Toledo, 43604. Tel: 419-243-7255; Fax: 419-243-6337. Web: catholicclub.org.

Youth, Young Adult Ministry and Campus Ministry—Ms. DIANE VERHOFF, Dir.; Rev. DAVID A. REINHART, Youth Chap.

Campus Ministry—Sr. MARGARET SLOWICK, O.S.F. Youth - Area Coordinators: Mrs. PATTI TACKETT, Back to Earth, Mansfield Deanery. Tel: 419-347-3910; Mrs. LORI KAMELESKY, Beacon, Fremont Deanery. Tel: 419-862-3452; Ms. LORRIE SEIPLE, Crossroads, Defiance & Will-Ful-L Deaneries. Tel: 419-782-5329; Mrs. CONNIE CLEEMPUT, Hearthstone, Lima Deanery. Tel: 419-532-3038; Mrs. PATTI TACKETT, Heartland, Sandusky Deanery. Tel: 419-347-3910; Ms. JENNY BINE, Kaleidoscope, Toledo N & S Deaneries. Tel: 419-475-1951; Mrs. PATTI IRONS, Prism, East Toledo. Tel: 419-385-4832; VACANT, Two Rivers & Tiffin Deanery.

Secretariat of Catholic Charities

Catholic Charities—Mr. LOUIS A. COCCHIARELLA, J.T., M.T.S., Sec. & Exec. Dir.Web: www.catholiccharitieswo.org. Email: ccharities@toledodiocese.orgFax: 419-244-4860.

Regional Offices—

Erie, Crawford, Huron and Richland Counties—PATRICIA ULMER, Regl. Dir.. Email: pulmer@toledodiocese.org; Norwalk: 55 E. Main St., Norwalk, 44857-0288. Tel: 419-668-3073; 800-668-3110; Fax: 419-663-5070. Mansfield: 35 N. Park St., Mansfield, 44902. Tel: 419-524-0733; Fax: 419-524-2055.

Hancock, Ottawa, Sandusky, Seneca and Wyandot Counties—VACANT, Regl. Dir., Fremont: 925 Croghan St., Fremont, 43420. Tel: 419-334-5061; Fax: 419-334-9837. Fostoria: 304 N. Main St., Ste. 8, Fostoria, 44830. Tel: 419-435-1775; Fax: 419-435-0733.

Allen, Defiance, Fulton, Henry, Paulding, Putnam, Van Wert and Williams Counties—PATRICIA DEATRICK-DAILEY, Regl. Dir.. Email: pdailey@toledodiocese.org; Defiance: 511 Perry St., Defiance, 43512. Tel: 419-782-4933; Fax: 419-784-4760. Bryan: 202 S. Union St., Bryan, 43506. Tel: 419-636-6848. Lima: 222 N. West St., Lima, 45801. Tel: 419-222-8110; Fax: 419-222-7627. Napoleon: 219 E. Washington, Ste. 220, Napoleon, 43545-1698. Tel: 419-592-0634. Ottawa: 227 E. Main St., Ottawa, 45875. Tel: 419-523-3501.

Adoption & Pregnancy Services—Mr. RICHARD SEVIGNY, Dir.

Counseling Services—Mr. RICHARD SEVIGNY, Dir.

Family Life/Respect Life Office—Mrs. LUCY ABU-ABSI, Dir.

Healthy Beginnings—MARY LINDQUIST, Program Coord.

Housing Services—VACANT, Dir.

C.H.I.P (Charities Homeowners Initiative Program)—

S.A.F.A.H. (Supplemental Assistance for Families Accessing Housing)—LaPosade (Family Emergency Shelter), 435 Eastern Ave., Toledo, 43609. Tel: 419-244-5931; Fax: 419-244-4993. *Mirian House (Transitional Housing in Huron County), 249 W. Main St., Norwalk, 44857.* Tel: 419-668-3073; 800-668-3110.

Mediation Services—VACANT, Dir.

Parish Social Ministry—Sr. MARY THILL, O.S.F., Program Coord.

Rural Life Ministries—Sr. CHRISTINE PRATT, O.S.U., Dir., 1021 W. State St., Fremont, 43420. Tel: 419-334-1331; Fax: 419-335-0936. Email: rurallife@toledodiocese.org.

Social Action Office—Sr. JOAN MICHALIK, I.H.M., Dir.

Mareda, Inc. (Vistula Management Co.)—JOHN KIELY, Dir., P.O. Box 4719, Toledo, 43620. Tel: 419-242-2300; Fax: 419-246-4703.

Madonna Homes—DENISE LITTON, Mgr., 722 Huron St., Toledo, 43604.

Regina Manor—LORRIE RICHARDS, Mgr., 3731 N. Erie St., Toledo, 43611.

Delaware Acres—MARCELLA WHITE, Mgr., 725 Buchanan, Fremont, 43420.

Moody Manor—Ms. CRYSTAL MCFADDEN, Mgr., 2293-1/2 Kent St., Toledo, 43620.

Hope Manor—Ms. ORA MILTON, Mgr., 4702 Violet Rd., Toledo, 43623.

Michaelmas Manor—Ms. LOUVENIA MCQUEEN, Mgr., 3260 Schneider Rd., Toledo, 43614.

Other Organizations

St. Vincent De Paul Society—Mr. HAROLD HANLEY, Central Council Pres.; Ms. SANDRA BLOOMQUIST, Exec. Dir.; Mr. WILLIAM MAHONEY, Store Mgr., 1001 Washington St., Toledo, 43624. Tel: 419-243-6963.

Apostleship of the Sea—Deacon EDWARD H. GRYCZEWSKI, Port Chap., 4448 289th St., Toledo, 43611.

CCMT (Central City Ministries of Toledo)—Very Rev. THOMAS J. EXTEJT, V.F., Dean. Co-chairpersons: Rev. RICHARD E. NOTTER; Mr. THOMAS WILLIAM; SHARON RAPPAPORT, Exec. Dir.; DENNIS PAKULSKI, Business Mgr., 1119 W. Bancroft St., Toledo, 43606. Tel: 419-244-9516; Fax: 419-244-3676. Email: ccmt@glasscity.net.

Cursillo Movement—Spiritual Directors: Revs. EDWARD J. LITTELMANN, 3030 Tremainsville Rd., Toledo, 43613. Tel: 419-474-3679; JAMES E. BROWN, 802 Barclay St., Marblehead, 43440. Tel: 419-798-4177; Deacon ALFREDO DIAZ, 1008 Garfield, Fremont, 43420. Tel: 419-244-6711; Sr. EDNA MICHEL, O.S.F., P.O. Box 576, Wakeman, 44889-0576. Tel: 440-839-2023. Lay Directors: JUAN DURAN; MONA DURAN, 1847 Clinton St.,

Toledo, 43606. Tel: 419-531-2501.
Diocesan Attorneys—JOHN HAYWARD; TOM PLETZ, 1000 Jackson St., Toledo, 43624. Tel: 419-241-4201; Fax: 419-241-6894.
Diocesan Insurance Program—JOSEPH SPENTHOFF, Branch Mgr., Gallagher-Bassett Insurance Services, 5640 Southwyck Blvd., Toledo, 43614. Tel: 419-865-8821; Fax: 419-865-1494.
MCCR (Ministry To Catholic Charismatic Renewal)—Mr. ROY HANDY, 550 Clark St., Toledo, 43605-2296. Tel: 419-691-6686; Fax: 419-691-1755.
Philippine-American Catholic Council (P.A.C.C.)—Rev. PETER V. ZAFE, Coord., 3854 Berkeley Dr., Toledo, 43612. Email: pvz64@msn.com.
Serra International—Mr. DOUGLAS MCROY, District Governor, 1554 Walnut Ct., Lima, 45805.
Lima Serra Club—CLAUDE BERGFELD, Pres., 1009 Dickman, Delphos, 45833.
Mansfield Serra Club—MARGIE JOYCE, 785 S. Home Rd., Mansfield, 44906.
Tiffin Serra Club—LARRY KIRIAN, 3720 E.C.R. 38, Tiffin, 44883.
Toledo Serra Club—Ms. MUR BOOKMILLER, 6119 Deepwood Dr., Sylvania, 43560.
Defiance Serra Club—BELINDA WALKER, 07382 St. Rte. 15, Defiance, 43512.
Fremont Serra Club—ANN BRENNEN, 1006 Birdseye, Fremont, 43420.
Secular Order of Discalced Carmelites—KAREN MOMENEE, Contact Person, Our Lady of the Holy Rosary Fraternity, 2533 Thoman Place, Toledo, 43613.
Secular Franciscans—
St. Maximilian Kolbe Region, Ohio—DENNIS ROSS, Contact Person, 8933 Trailwood Ct., Mentor, 44060.
St. Anthony of Padua Fraternity, Carey—Ms. MARY LOU DEER, Contact, 8659 County Hwy. 95, Wharton, 43359.
St. Anthony of Padua Fraternity, Fostoria—Ms. JENNIFER GILLIG, Contact, 1435 N. Union St., Fostoria, 44830.
St. Maximilian Mary Kolbe Fraternity, Findlay—Mr. ROBERT HILDRETH, Contact, 1020 Hurd Ave., Findlay, 45840.
St. Joseph Fraternity, Green Springs—KATHY VAN WEY, S.F.O., Contact, 528 Glenwood Dr., Fremont, 43420.
Queen of the Angels Fraternity, Lima—Ms. SHERYL ODENWELLER, Contact, 340 W. 6th St., Delphos, 45833.
St. Paschal Fraternity—JERRY MAZUCHOWSKI, S.F.O., Contact Person, 2812 Chestnut St., Toledo, 43608.
Worldwide Marriage Encounter—JEFF COMPTON; CHERIE COMPTON, 7142 E. Lake St., Perrysburg, 43551.
Retrouvaille—Exec. Team Couple: GARY GLADIEUX; LAURIE GLADIEUX, 3606 Greenlawn St., Toledo, 43614.
Victim Assistance Coordinator—Mr. FRANK DILALLO, M.Ed., L.P.C. Tel: 419-243-2150. Email: fdilallo@toledodiocese.org.

CLERGY, PARISHES, MISSIONS AND PAROCHIAL SCHOOLS

CITY OF TOLEDO
(LUCAS COUNTY)

1—QUEEN OF THE MOST HOLY ROSARY CATHEDRAL (1915), [JC] Rev. Charles Singler, M.A., Rector; Deacons Lawrence Adams; Jesus Villagomez; Richard D. Mishler; William Keran. In Res., Most Revs. Leonard P. Blair, S.T.D.; Robert W. Donnelly, D.D.; Albert H. Ottenweller; Rev. Bernard J. Boff (Retired).
Office—2535 Collingwood Blvd., 43610. Tel: 419-244-9575; Fax: 419-242-1901.
Res.: 2544 Parkwood Ave., 43610-1300. Tel: 419-255-1890; Fax: 419-244-0471.
Church: 2561 Collingwood Blvd. and Islington St., 43610.
School—Tel: 419-243-4396. Lay Teachers 18; Students 166.
Catechesis/Religious Program—Students 15.

2—ST. ADALBERT (1907), (Polish), [JC] Rev. Marek Ciesla, S.Ch.
Res.: 3233 Lagrange St., 43608. Tel: 419-241-4179; Fax: 419-241-1136.
School—Tel: 419-243-5257; Fax: 419-243-6763. Felician Sisters 1; Lay Teachers 9; Students 136.

3—ST. AGNES (1910), [JC] Rev. Daniel J. Fraser; Deacons John C. Vogel; Clarence Fisher. In Res., Rev. Peter V. Zafe (Philippines).
Res.: 3854 Berkeley Dr., 43612. Tel: 419-478-2384; Fax: 419-478-6556.
School—Tel: 419-478-7778; Fax: 419-478-6776. Franciscan Sisters 2; Lay Teachers 13; Students 210.
Catechesis/Religious Program—Students 39.

4—ST. ANN, Consolidated, with St. Teresa to form St. Martin de Porres. See separate listing.

5—ST. ANTHONY (1882), (Polish), [JC] Rev. Gerald E. Knueven, Admin.
Res.: 1416 Nebraska Ave., 43607. Tel: 419-241-6465.

6—BLESSED SACRAMENT (1924), [JC] Very Rev. Robert J. Reinhart; Rev. Thomas S. Quinn; Deacons Robert Gillen; Zenon Selmek; Harold Welch. In Res., Rev. Joseph L. Vamos (Retired).
Res.: 4227 Bellevue Rd., 43613-3999. Tel: 419-472-2288; Fax: 419-472-0493.
School—2216 Castlewood Dr., 43613. Tel: 419-472-1121; Fax: 419-472-1679. Lay Teachers 26; Students 427.
Catechesis/Religious Program—Tel: 419-472-7526. Students 66.

7—ST. CATHERINE OF SIENA (1930), [JC] Rev. Gary R. Walters.
Res.: 4555 N. Haven Ave., 43612. Tel: 419-478-9558; Fax: 419-478-9434.
School—1155 Corbin Rd., 43612. Tel: 419-478-9900. Lay Teachers 23; Students 438.
Catechesis/Religious Program—Students 40.

8—ST. CHARLES BORROMEO (1903), [JC] Very Rev. Thomas J. Extejt, V.F.
Res.: 1842 Airport Hwy., 43609-2069. Tel: 419-385-7431; Fax: 419-385-9152.
School—Tel: 419-382-7271; Fax: 419-385-1083. Lay Teachers 11; Students 186.
Catechesis/Religious Program—Tel: 419-382-1643. Students 50.

9—CHRIST THE KING (1953), [JC 3] Revs. Michael O. Brown; David L. Ritchie; Deacons Gerald Sortman; Robert Beisser; Mrs. Suzanne Marciniak, Pastoral Assoc.
Office—4100 Harvest Ln., 43623-4399. Tel: 419-475-4348; Fax: 419-475-4050.
School—Tel: 419-475-0909. Lay Teachers 23; Students 601.
Catechesis/Religious Program—Tel: 419-475-1954. Students 190.

10—ST. CLEMENT (1947), [JC] Revs. Edward J. Littelmann; Stephen L. Schroeder; Deacons Wilbur Moore; Ronald Peeps; Ray Burzynski; LeRoy Houghton
Res.: 3030 Tremainsville Rd., 43613. Tel: 419-472-2111; Fax: 419-479-3215.
School—Tel: 419-474-9657. Lay Teachers 22; Students 283.
Catechesis/Religious Program—Tel: 419-472-1259. Students 285.

11—COMMUNITY OF THE RISEN CHRIST (1972), Closed. For inquiries for parish records contact the chancery.

12—CORPUS CHRISTI, UNIVERSITY OF TOLEDO (1970), [JC] Rev. James J. Bacik; Deacon James Moncher; Ms. Pam Meseroll, Admin.
Res.: 2955 Dorr St., 43607-3023. Tel: 419-531-4992 (Office); Fax: 419-531-1775.

13—ST. FRANCIS DE SALES (1841), Sr. Kathleen Scott, L.C.M., Pastoral Admin.; Rev. John E. Laudick, Chap.
Office—501 Cherry St., 43604. Tel: 419-243-4242; Fax: 419-243-4243.
Catechesis/Religious Program—Students 10.

14—GESU (1920), [JC] Revs. David E. Watson, S.J., Admin.; Edward A. Flint, S.J. (COL); Paul A. Woefl, S.J.; Deacons Larry Petersen; Ed Kelley; Richard Warren.
Res.: 2049 Parkside Blvd., 43607. Tel: 419-531-1421; Fax: 419-531-0270.
School—Tel: 419-536-5634; Fax: 419-531-8932. Sisters of Notre Dame 2; Lay Teachers 25; Students 407.
Catechesis/Religious Program—Students 95.

15—GOOD SHEPHERD (1873), [JC] Very Rev. John R. Blaser, V.F.; Rev. Jerome F. Nowakowski; Deacon Leon Holmer. In Res., Rev. Gerald E. Knueven.
Res.: 550 Clark St., 43605. Tel: 419-691-5815; Fax: 419-693-6612.
Catechesis/Religious Program—Tel: 419-698-1519; Fax: 419-698-2050. Students 24.

16—ST. HEDWIG (1875), (Polish), [JC] Rev. Joseph J. Przybysz.
Res.: 2916 Lagrange St., 43608. Tel: 419-729-3148; Fax: 419-729-0743.
School—Tel: 419-729-3658; Fax: 419-729-7001. Franciscan Sisters 1; Lay Teachers 14; Students 135.
Catechesis/Religious Program—Students 15.

17—HISTORIC CHURCH OF ST. PATRICK (1863), (Irish), [JC] Very Rev. Michael R. Billian, V.G. In Res., Revs. Michael A. Geiger; David W. Nuss; Deacon Thomas S. Carone.
Res.: 130 Avondale Ave., 43602. Tel: 419-243-6452; Fax: 419-243-7032.
Catechesis/Religious Program—Students 75.

18—HOLY ROSARY (1906), (Slovak), [JC] Revs. Frank E. Eckart; Ronald A. Schock; Deacon Richard Fazekas.
Res.: 821 N. Wheeling St., 43605. Tel: 419-693-2198; Fax: 419-693-2198.
School—Holy Rosary/St. Stephen United (For details, please refer to Consolidated Elementary Schools located in the Institution Section.)

19—ST. HYACINTH (1927), (Polish), [JC] Rev. James R. Sanford, O.S.F.S., Admin.
Res.: 719 Evesham Ave., 43607. Tel: 419-535-7077; Fax: 419-535-5915.
School—Tel: 419-535-7078. Sisters of Notre Dame 2; Lay Teachers 8; Students 182.

20—IMMACULATE CONCEPTION (1868), [JC] Rev. Paul M. Kwiatkowski; Deacon Leo T. Bistak.
Res.: 434 Western Ave., 43609. Tel: 419-243-1829; Fax: 419-243-0067.
School—Queen of Apostles Consolidated, 235 Courtland St., 43609. Tel: 419-241-7829; Fax: 419-241-4180. Sr. Brenda Haynes, S.N.D., Prin. Also serves St. James Parish and SS. Peter and Paul Parish. Lay Teachers 10; Students 131; Religious 4.
Catechesis/Religious Program—Students 90.

21—ST. JAMES (1913), [JC] Rev. Paul M. Kwiatkowski; Deacon Bernabe Romo.
Mailing Address: 434 Western Ave., 43609.
Church: 914 Colburn St., 43609. Tel: 419-243-1829; Fax: 419-243-0067.
School—Queen of Apostles, Tel: 419-241-7829; Fax: 419-241-4180. Consolidated. Immaculate Conception Parish, SS Peter and Paul Parish and St. James Parish. Religious 4; Lay Teachers 10; Students 131.
Catechesis/Religious Program—Queen of Apostles School, 235 Courtland Ave., 43609. Students 90.

22—ST. JOAN OF ARC (1978), [JC] Rev. Gerald L. Ceranowski; Deacons Stan Przybylek; Larry Lottier; Thomas Sheehan.
Res.: 5856 Heatherdowns Blvd., 43614. Tel: 419-866-6181; Fax: 419-866-6142.
School—5850 Heatherdowns Blvd., 43614. Tel: 419-866-6177; Fax: 419-866-4107. Lay Teachers 27; Students 581.
Catechesis/Religious Program—Tel: 419-866-6177. Students 165.

23—ST. JOHN THE BAPTIST (1918), [JC] Revs. Francis J. Speier; Douglas D. Taylor.
Res.: 5153 Summit St., 43611. Tel: 419-726-2034; Fax: 419-726-1447.
School—Tel: 419-726-7761; Fax: 419-726-1031. Sisters 1; Lay Teachers 21; Students 346.
Catechesis/Religious Program—Tel: 419-726-9141. Students 175.

24—ST. JOSEPH (1854), [JC] Rev. Stephen R. Majoros. Mailing Address: P.O. Box 790, 43697. Tel: 419-255-5556.
Res.: 626 Locust St., 43604.
Church: Erie & 628 Locust Sts., 43604.

25—ST. JUDE (1955), [JC] Rev. David J. Beck, Admin.
Res.: 3650 Victory Ave., 43607. Tel: 419-531-1294; Fax: 419-531-5812.

26—LITTLE FLOWER OF JESUS (1928), [JC] Rev. Joseph R. Steinbauer, Admin.
Res.: 5522 Dorr St., 43615. Tel: 419-537-6997; Fax: 419-537-1469.
School—Tel: 419-536-1194; Fax: 419-531-5140. Lay Teachers 14; Students 229.
Catechesis/Religious Program—Tel: 419-537-6655. Students 280.

27—ST. LOUIS (1872), (French), [JC] Very Rev. John R. Blaser, V.F.; Rev. Jerome F. Nowakowski; Sr. Joy Barker, O.S.F., Pastoral Assoc.
Res.: 459 6th St., 43605. Tel: 419-691-0422; Fax: 419-691-0422.
Outreach—Helping Hands Soup Kitchen. Tel: 419-691-0613; Fax: 419-697-4223. Linda Lupien, Prog. Dir.
Catechesis/Religious Program—Tel: 419-698-1519; Fax: 419-698-2050. Sr. Joy Barker, O.S.F., D.R.E. Students 115.

28—ST. MARTIN DE PORRES (1990), [JC] Rev. P. Martin Donnelly; Deacon John Algee.
Res.: 1119 W. Bancroft, 43606. Tel: 419-241-4544; Fax: 419-244-6214.

29—ST. MARY OF THE ASSUMPTION (1854), [JC] Rev. P. Martin Donnelly, Admin.; Deacon Stanley Gogol.
Res.: 219 Page St., 43620. Tel: 419-243-9213; Fax: 419-243-5405.
Catechesis/Religious Program—Students 160.

30—ST. MICHAEL THE ARCHANGEL (1900), [JC] Rev. John R. Laudick, Admin.
Res.: 420 Sandusky St., 43611. Tel: 419-726-1947; Fax: 419-726-2223.
School—St. Elizabeth Seton School, 1030 Clay St., 43608. Tel: 419-726-4471; Fax: 419-729-2481. Sisters 1; Lay Teachers 12; Students 172.

31—OUR LADY OF LOURDES (1926), [JC] Rev. Thomas

E. Wehinger; Deacons Clifford Kujawa; Robert Pacholski; Steve Veselka.
Res.: 6149 Hill Ave., 43615. Tel: 419-865-2345; Fax: 419-865-2545.
School—Tel: 419-866-0736; Fax: 419-866-1351. Lay Teachers 14; Students 223.
Catechesis/Religious Program—P.R.E.P., Tel: 419-531-1744. Students 76.

32—OUR LADY OF PERPETUAL HELP (1918), [JC] Rev. Robert J. Wilhelm; Deacons Daniel Quinn; Robert Lesinski; Michael Learned.
Mailing Address: 2255 Central Grove, 43614. Tel: 419-382-5511; Fax: 419-382-7360.
Res.: 3464 Glynn Dr., 43614. Tel: 419-382-4992.
School—(Grades PreK-8) Tel: 419-382-5696. Lay Teachers 26; Students 446.
Catechesis/Religious Program—Kathy Dusseau, D.R.E. Students 91.

33—ST. PATRICK OF HEATHERDOWNS (1956), [JC] Revs. William J. Kubacki; Walter R. Oxley; Deacons Joe Kest; Albert Righi; Ms. Germaine Kirk, Pastoral Assoc. In Res., Revs. Michael G. Madden (Retired); David A. Reinhart.
Res.: 4201 Heatherdowns Blvd., 43614. Tel: 419-381-1540; Fax: 419-381-2727.
School—Tel: 419-381-1775; Fax: 419-389-1161. Sisters 3; Lay Teachers 36; Students 734.
Catechesis/Religious Program—Tel: 419-381-0240. Ms. Christine Kramer, D.R.E.; Mrs. Marla Overholt, D.R.E. Students 148.

34—SS. PETER AND PAUL (1866), (Hispanic), [JC] Rev. Richard E. Notter.
Office—728 S. St. Clair St., 43609. Tel: 419-241-5822; Fax: 419-241-5822.
School—*Queen of Apostles*, 235 Courtland, 43609. Tel: 419-241-7829; Fax: 419-241-4140. (Consolidated with Immaculate Conception Parish and St. James Parish). Sisters 4; Lay Teachers 10; Students 131.
Catechesis/Religious Program—Tel: 419-243-1829; Fax: 419-536-0019. Students 110.

35—ST. PIUS X (1953), [JC] Rev. Thomas A. Landgraff, O.S.F.S.; Deacon Timothy Etue.
Res.: 2929 Ilger Ave., 43606. Tel: 419-535-7672; Fax: 419-535-7810.
School—Tel: 419-535-7688. Lay Teachers 16; Students 225.
Catechesis/Religious Program—Students 77.

36—REGINA COELI (1954), [JC] Rev. James E. Auth, J.C.L.; Deacons James Dudley; George Mitchell; John Wiciak.
Res.: 530 Regina Pkwy., 43612. Tel: 419-476-0922 (Office); 419-476-2281 (Home); Fax: 419-478-5846 (7:30 AM-4 PM).
School—Tel: 419-476-0920; Fax: 419-476-6792. Lay Teachers 22; Students 406; Religious 1.
Catechesis/Religious Program—Students 114.

37—SACRED HEART OF JESUS (1883), (German), [JC] Very Rev. Frank K. Eckart; Rev. Philip J. Suehr, O.S.C.; Mr. Royce Wicks, Pastoral Assoc.
Res.: 509 Oswald St., 43605. Tel: 419-698-1664; Fax: 419-698-9708.
School—Tel: 419-691-0869; Fax: 419-691-7720. Sisters of Notre Dame 2; Lay Teachers 11; Students 185.
Catechesis/Religious Program—Students 213.

38—ST. STANISLAUS (1908), (Polish), [JC] Rev. Gerald E. Knueven.
Mailing Address: 1416 Nebraska Ave., 43607. Tel: 419-241-6465.
Church: 421 N. Detroit Ave., 43607. Tel: 419-255-6245.

39—ST. STEPHEN (1898), (Hungarian), [JC] Very Rev. Frank K. Eckart; Rev. Philip J. Suehr, O.S.C.
Res.: 1880 Genesee St., 43605-1440. Tel: 419-691-1673.
School—*Holy Rosary/St. Stephen United School*, Tel: 419-691-8760. For more details, please see Consolidated Elementary Schools in the Institution section.

40—ST. TERESA, Consolidated, with St. Ann to form St. Martin de Porres. See separate listing.

41—ST. THOMAS AQUINAS (1915), [JC] Very Rev. John R. Blaser, V.F.; Rev. Jerome F. Nowakowski; Sr. Joy Barker, O.S.F., Pastoral Assoc.
Res.: 729 White St., 43605-2719. Tel: 419-698-1519; Fax: 419-698-2050.
School—Tel: 419-691-4328; Fax: 419-691-4365. Lay Teachers 12; Students 212.
Catechesis/Religious Program— Clustered with St. Louis & Good Shepherd. Students 140.

42—ST. VINCENT DE PAUL (1928), [JC] Rev. John R. Laudick; Deacon Jerry Ignatowski.
Res.: 1035 Woodward Ave., 43608. Tel: 419-726-1448; Fax: 419-726-1448.
School—*St. Elizabeth Seton School*, 1030 Clay St., 43608. Tel: 419-726-4471; Fax: 419-729-2481. Also serves St. Michael. Sisters 1; Lay Teachers 12; Students 172.
Catechesis/Religious Program—Students 15.

OUTSIDE THE CITY OF TOLEDO

ALVADA, SENECA CO., ST. PETER (1854), [CEM] Rev. Ronald A. Schock, Admin.; Deacon Lewis E. Reinhart.
Mailing Address: 41 N. Perry St., P.O. Box 89, New Riegel, 44853. Tel: 419-595-2567; Fax: 419-595-2303.
Catechesis/Religious Program—Students 87.

ANTWERP, PAULDING CO., ST. MARY (1868), [JC] Rev. Herman F. Scherger; Deacon Robert L. Nighswander, Admin.
Res.: 303 S. Monroe St., P.O. Box 1005, 45813. Tel: 419-258-8335.
Catechesis/Religious Program—Tel: 419-258-2651. Students 90.

ARCHBOLD, FULTON CO., ST. PETER (1846), [CEM] Rev. Gary M. Ferguson.
Res.: 614 N. Defiance St., 43502. Tel: 419-446-9288.
Catechesis/Religious Program—Tel: 419-446-2150; Fax: 419-446-0282. Students 126.

ASSUMPTION, FULTON CO.

1—HOLY TRINITY (2003), (German—Irish), [CEM] Rev. Dennis M. Metzger; Deacon Joseph Repka.
Res. & Mailing Address: 2649 U.S. 20, Swanton, 43558. Tel: 419-644-4014; Fax: 419-644-2159. Email: HTParish@thewavz.com.
School—2639 U.S. 20, Swanton, 43558. Tel: 419-644-3971; Fax: 419-644-5018. Email: HOLYTS@aol.com. Web: www.HTEagles.com. Christopher Knight, Prin. Lay Teachers 16; Students 196.
Catechesis/Religious Program—12829 Brint Rd., Berkey, 43504. Tel: 419-829-3717. Rosemary Ott, D.R.E. Students 69.

2—ST. MARY OF ASSUMPTION (1877), (German—Irish), Merged, with Immaculate Conception, Marygrove and Saint Elizabeth of Hungary, Richfield Center to form Holy Trinity Catholic Parish, Assumption.

ATTICA, SENECA CO., SS. PETER AND PAUL (1882), [CEM] Rev. Joseph P. Szybka.
Res.: P.O. Box 461, 44807. Tel: 419-426-3043; Fax: 419-426-3043.
Church: 14204 E. County Rd. 56, 44807.
Catechesis/Religious Program—(Grades K-8) Students 102.

BASCOM, SENECA CO., ST. PATRICK (1864), [CEM] Rev. Arthur J. Niewiadomski.
Res.: 6230 W. Tiffin, Box 226, 44809. Tel: 419-937-2715; Fax: 419-937-2751.
Catechesis/Religious Program—Students 145.

BELLEVUE, HURON CO., IMMACULATE CONCEPTION (1859), [CEM] Rev. Keith A. Stripe, Admin.; Deacon Robert Swartz.
Res.: 231 E. Center St., 44811. Tel: 419-483-3417; 419-483-0164 (Parish Center); Fax: 419-483-2585.
School—*Immaculate Conception School*, Tel: 419-483-6066; Fax: 419-483-2736. Sisters 1; Lay Teachers 19; Students 286.
Catechesis/Religious Program—Tel: 419-483-8374. Students 210.

BETHLEHEM, RICHLAND CO., SACRED HEART OF JESUS (1833), (German), [CEM] Rev. Nicholas J. Cunningham; Deacons Leo Hartings; Stephen R. Keller.
Office—5742 State Rte. 61 S., Shelby, 44875. Tel: 419-342-2797; Fax: 419-342-3638.
School—Tel: 419-683-1697. Krista L. Wilson, Prin. Lay Teachers 6; Students 73.
Catechesis/Religious Program—Students 25.

BISMARK, HURON CO., ST. SEBASTIAN (1846), (German), [CEM] Rev. John M. Nagele, C.PP.S.
Res.: 16209 E. C. Rd. #46, Bellevue, 44811. Tel: 419-483-2826; Fax: 419-483-4661.
Church: 5582 Bismark Rd., Bellevue, 44811.
Catechesis/Religious Program—Students 82.

BLAKESLEE, WILLIAMS CO., ST. JOSEPH (1865), (German), [CEM] Very Rev. Frederick J. Duschl, V.F.
Res.: P.O. Box 196, 43505. Tel: 419-272-2214.
School—Tel: 419-272-2914; Fax: 419-272-3400. Lay Teachers 6; Students 51.
Catechesis/Religious Program—Tel: 419-485-5914. Students 45.

BLUFFTON, ALLEN CO., ST. MARY (1865), Sr. Carol Inkrott, O.S.F., Pastoral Leader; Rev. Dennis P. Hartigan, Chap.
Mailing Address: 160 N. Spring,, 45817. Tel: 419-358-8631; Fax: 419-358-8602.
Catechesis/Religious Program—Students 135.

BONO, LUCAS CO., OUR LADY OF MT. CARMEL (1917), Sr. Jane Schimmoeller, O.S.F., Pastoral Leader; Rev. Charles J. Denny, Chap.
Res.: 1105 Elliston Rd., Martin, 43445. Tel: 419-836-7681; Fax: 419-836-7680.
Catechesis/Religious Program—Students 62.

BOWLING GREEN, WOOD CO.

1—ST. ALOYSIUS (1862), Rev. Edward J. Schleter; Deacon Ramon Llanas.
Res.: 150 S. Enterprise, P.O. Box 485, 43402. Tel: 419-352-4195; Fax: 419-352-4738.
School—Tel: 419-352-8614; Fax: 419-352-4738. Mrs. Mary K. Williams, Prin. Lay Teachers 15; Students 244.
Catechesis/Religious Program—Tel: 419-352-1139. Students 236.

2—ST. THOMAS MORE UNIVERSITY PARISH (1967), Sr. Mary Kuhlman, O.S.F., Pastoral Leader; Very Rev. Kenneth G. Morman, V.F., Chap. In Res., Rev. Richard J. Saelzler, Chap.
Res.: 425 Thurstin, 43402. Tel: 419-352-7555; 419-255-3609; Fax: 419-352-7557.
Catechesis/Religious Program—Students 121.

BRYAN, WILLIAMS CO., ST. PATRICK (1857), Rev. Charles F. Ritter; Deacons Dennis Jackson; Ignacio Garza; Tom Dominique.
Church: 610 S. Portland St., 43506.
Res.: 704 S. Portland, 43506. Tel: 419-636-1044; Fax: 419-636-5054.
School—Tel: 419-636-3592; Fax: 419-633-9112. Judy Davis, Prin. Lay Teachers 11; Students 156.
Catechesis/Religious Program—Tel: 419-636-1044. Students 173.

BUCYRUS, CRAWFORD CO., HOLY TRINITY (1865), (German), [CEM] Rev. Ronald J. LeJeune; Deacons Julius Fritz; Jerome Gubernath.
Res.: 760 Tiffin Rd., 44820. Tel: 419-562-1346; Fax: 419-562-2784.
School—(Grades PreK-8) Tel: 419-562-2741. Lay Teachers 11; Students 158.
Catechesis/Religious Program—Tel: 419-562-2645. Students 133.

CAREY, WYANDOT CO., OUR LADY OF CONSOLATION, BASILICA-NATIONAL SHRINE (1867), [CEM] Revs. Regis Schlagheck, O.F.M.Conv., Rector; Herbert Graf, O.F.M.Conv. (SAV); Ernest Waechter, O.F.M-.Conv.; George Schroeder, O.F.M.Conv.; Kieran Kay, O.F.M.Conv.; Leo Kennedy, O.F.M.Conv.; Bros. Donald Hart, O.F.M.Conv.; Bryan Hoban, O.F.M-.Conv.; Deacons Arden Harold Nye; Jim Kitzler.
Res.: 315 W. Clay St., 43316. Tel: 419-396-7107; Fax: 419-396-3355.
School—Tel: 419-396-6166. Jean Schott, Prin. Lay Teachers 12; Students 176.
Catechesis/Religious Program—Tel: 419-396-1523. Students 75.

CECIL, PAULDING CO., IMMACULATE CONCEPTION (1879), [CEM] Rev. Herman F. Scherger; Deacon David Laker. Tel: 419-899-2479.
Res.: 21706 State Rte. 114, Cloverdale, 45827. Tel: 419-488-3563.
Church: 202 S. Main St., 45821. Tel: 419-399-5644.
Catechesis/Religious Program—Students 15.

CLOVERDALE, PUTNAM CO., ST. BARBARA (1898), (German), [CEM] Rev. Robert J. Kill.
Res.: 160 Main St., P.O. Box 8, 45827. Tel: 419-488-2391; Fax: 419-488-2390.
Catechesis/Religious Program—Students 31.

CLYDE, SANDUSKY CO., ST. MARY (1890), [CEM] Rev. Dennis A. Schroeder.
Res.: 609 Vine St., 43410. Tel: 419-547-9610.
School—615 Vine St., 43410. Tel: 419-547-9687; Fax: 419-547-9687. Miss Kathy Holcomb, Prin. Sisters 1; Lay Teachers 9; Students 78.
Catechesis/Religious Program—Sr. Bonnie Smith, D.R.E. Students 130.

COLUMBUS GROVE, PUTNAM CO., ST. ANTHONY OF PADUA (1912), (German), [CEM] Rev. Ronald R. Warnimont, J.C.L., Admin.
Res.: 512 W. Sycamore St., 45830. Tel: 419-659-2263; Fax: 419-659-5202.
School—Tel: 419-659-2103; Fax: 419-659-2974. Lois Karhoff, Prin. Lay Teachers 11; Students 216.
Catechesis/Religious Program—Students 223.

CONTINENTAL, PUTNAM CO., ST. JOHN THE BAPTIST (1907), [JC] Rev. Robert J. Kill; Deacon Joseph Heeter.
Mailing Address: P.O. Box 8, Cloverdale, 45827-0008.
Church: 203 E. Elm St., P.O. Box 368, 45831. Tel: 419-488-2391; Fax: 419-488-2390.
Catechesis/Religious Program—Students 97.

CRESTLINE, CRAWFORD CO., ST. JOSEPH (1861), (German), [CEM] Rev. Michael E. Schelling; Deacons Joseph Burkhart; William Rall.
Res.: 331 N. Thoman St., 44827. Tel: 419-683-2015; Fax: 419-683-3415.
School—333 N. Thoman St., 44827. Tel: 419-683-1284; Fax: 419-683-1284. Lay Teachers 6; Students 71.
Catechesis/Religious Program—Students 20.

CUBA, PUTNAM CO., ST. ISIDORE (1917), [CEM], Shared with St. Michael, Kalida. Rev. Scott Kramer, C.PP.S.; Deacon Robert Klausing.
Res.: 312 N. Broad St., Kalida, 45853. Tel: 419-532-3431; Fax: 419-532-3470.

CUSTAR, WOOD CO., ST. LOUIS (1864), [CEM] [JC] Rev. Paul A. Fahrbach; Sr. Dionne Sartor, O.S.F., Pastoral Assoc. Tel: 419-669-3920.
Res.: 22792 Defiance Pike, 43511. Tel: 419-669-2845; Fax: 419-669-1864.
School—22676 Defiance Pike, 43511-9716. Tel: 419-669-2878. Sue Hammer, Prin. Sisters of St. Francis 1; Lay Teachers 4; Students 45.

CYGNET, WOOD CO., SACRED HEART (1890), Consolidated, with Our Lady of Miraculous Medal,

North Baltimore to form Holy Family, North Baltimore.

DEFIANCE, DEFIANCE CO.

1—ST. JOHN THE EVANGELIST (1850), [CEM] Rev. Dennis G. Walsh; Deacons Chris Mendez; Charles Baker; Donald Meyer.
Res.: 510 Jackson St., 43512. Tel: 419-782-7121; Fax: 419-782-7300.
School—Tel: 419-782-2136; Fax: 419-784-5410. Lay Teachers 10; Students 98.
Catechesis/Religious Program—Students 280.

2—ST. MARY (1873), Rev. Timothy M. Kummerer; Deacon George Newton.
Res.: 707 Jefferson Ave., 43512. Tel: 419-782-2776; Fax: 419-782-1958.
School—(Grades PreK-6) Tel: 419-782-2751; Fax: 419-782-8835. Lay Teachers 12; Students 134.
Catechesis/Religious Program—Students 268.

DELPHOS, ALLEN CO., ST. JOHN THE EVANGELIST (1844), (German), [CEM] Revs. Thomas J. Gorman; Randy P. Giesige; Charles Obinwa (Nigeria).
Res.: 331 E. Second St., 45833. Tel: 419-695-4050; Fax: 419-695-4060.
School—Tel: 419-692-8561; Fax: 419-692-8561. Sisters of Notre Dame 1; Lay Teachers 23; Students 637.
High School—Tel: 419-692-5371; Fax: 419-692-5371. Sisters 1; Lay Teachers 21; Students 359.
Catechesis/Religious Program—Tel: 419-692-1286. Students 207.

DESHLER, HENRY CO., IMMACULATE CONCEPTION (1871), Rev. Paul A. Fahrbach; Sr. Dionne Sartor, O.S.F., Pastoral Assoc. Tel: 419-669-3920.
Mailing Address: 230 Allendale Ave., 43516. Tel: 419-278-3686.
Res.: 22767 Defiance Pike, Custar, 43511. Tel: 419-669-3920.
Catechesis/Religious Program—Students 84.

EDGERTON, WILLIAMS CO., ST. MARY (1865), (German), [CEM] Rev. Thomas E. Oedy.
Res.: 133 Bement St., P.O. Box 355, 43517. Tel: 419-298-2932; Fax: 419-298-3123.
School—Tel: 419-298-2531. Sisters of St. Francis 1; Lay Teachers 6; Students 105.
Catechesis/Religious Program—Tel: 419-298-3350. Students 138.

FAYETTE, FULTON CO., OUR LADY OF MERCY (1943), Rev. James Steinle, Admin. (Retired); Deacon Guillermo Rodriguez.
Mailing Address: Box 429, 43521. Tel: 419-237-8042; Fax: 419-237-1042.
Church: 409 E. Main St., 43521.
Catechesis/Religious Program—14691 E. Camden Rd., Waldron, MI 49288. Tel: 517-286-6496. Linda Higgins, D.R.E. Students 77.

FINDLAY, HANCOCK CO., ST. MICHAEL THE ARCHANGEL (1834), [CEM] Very Rev. Michael G. Hohenbrink, V.F.; Rev. Adam L. Hertzfeld; Deacons Robert Billmaier; Dorsey Hazelton; David Sadler; Aggie Hempfling, Business Mgr.
Mailing Address: 422 Western Ave., 45840. Tel: 419-422-2646; Fax: 419-422-2602.
School—Tel: 419-422-2512; Fax: 419-422-2517. Lay Teachers 34; Students 546.
Catechesis/Religious Program—Tel: 419-423-2123. Geri Leibfarth, D.R.E. Students 570.

FORT JENNINGS, PUTNAM CO., ST. JOSEPH (1848), (German), [CEM] Rev. Anthony A. Borgia.
Church: Main & Second Sts., 45844.
Res.: 135 Water St., P.O. Box 68, 45844-0068. Tel: 419-286-2132.
Catechesis/Religious Program—Tel: 419-286-2019. Students 336.

FOSTORIA, SENECA CO., ST. WENDELIN (1850), [CEM] Revs. Daniel J. Ring; J. Douglas Garand.
Res.: 222 N. Wood St., P.O. Box 836, 44830. Tel: 419-435-1875; Fax: 419-435-7826.
School—Tel: 419-435-1809. Sisters of Notre Dame 1; Lay Teachers 22; Students 343; Preschool 39.
High School—Tel: 419-435-8144; Fax: 419-436-4042. Sisters 1; Lay Teachers 19; Students 182.
Catechesis/Religious Program—Tel: 419-435-6681. Sr. Elaine Marie Clement, S.N.D., D.R.E. Students 227.

FREMONT, SANDUSKY CO.

1—ST. ANN (1843), [JC] Rev. Gerald J. Chmiel; Deacon Alfredo Diaz.
Res.: 1021 W. State St., 43420. Tel: 419-332-7472; Fax: 419-332-3556.
School—Tel: 419-332-2461. Lay Teachers 10; Students 161.
Catechesis/Religious Program—Students 90.

2—ST. CASIMIR (1915), (Polish), [JC] Rev. Robert J. Weithman.
Res.: 537 Lime St., 43420. Tel: 419-332-1157.

3—ST. JOSEPH (1857), (German), [CEM] [JC] Rev. David R. Bruning; Deacons William Snyder; James Hammer; Norbert Wethington; Thomas Mosser, Business Mgr.
Res.: 709 Croghan St., 43420. Tel: 419-334-2638; Fax: 419-334-6929.
School—Tel: 419-332-5161; Fax: 419-332-7299. Sisters 2; Lay Teachers 16; Students Grades (K-8) 244; Preschool 21.
Catechesis/Religious Program—120 N. Clover St., 43420. Sr. Janice M. Peer, O.S.F., D.R.E. Students 48.

4—SACRED HEART (1956), [JC] Rev. Mark J Herzog; Sr. M. Dean Pfahler, S.N.D., Pastoral Assoc.; Deacons Jose Sanchez; Tom Ackerman.
Res.: 550 Smith Rd., 43420. Tel: 419-332-7339; Fax: 419-332-9808.
School—(Grades K-8) Tel: 419-332-7102; Fax: 419-332-1542. Sisters 1; Lay Teachers 16; Students 297.
Catechesis/Religious Program—Students 92.

FRENCHTOWN, SENECA CO., ST. NICHOLAS (1856), (German—French), [CEM] Rev. Ronald A. Schock, Admin.; Deacon Floyd Hohman.
Res.: 41 N. Perry St., New Riegel, 44853. Tel: 419-595-2567; Fax: 419-595-2303.
Church: 8981 W. County Rd., 43316.
Catechesis/Religious Program—Tel: 419-595-2455. Students 140.

GALION, CRAWFORD CO., ST. JOSEPH (1853), [CEM] Rev. Michael E. Schelling; Deacons Kevin Wintersteller; Alfred Sisson; Gregory Kirk; Raymond Lyons Jr.
Res.: 135 N. Liberty St., 44833. Tel: 419-468-2884; Fax: 419-468-9464.
School—(Grades PreK-8) Tel: 419-468-5436; Fax: 419-468-3611. Sisters 1; Lay Teachers 8; Students 178.
Catechesis/Religious Program—Students 145.

GENOA, OTTAWA CO., OUR LADY OF LOURDES (1856), Rev. James E. Peiffer; Deacons William Perez; Phillip Dazley; Sr. Gemma Fenbert, O.S.F., Pastoral Admin.
Church: 204 Main St., 43430. Tel: 419-855-8501; Fax: 419-855-8159.
Catechesis/Religious Program—Tel: 419-855-7181. Sr. Alice Marie Schmersal, C.D.P., D.R.E. Students 174.

GIBSONBURG, SANDUSKY CO., ST. MICHAEL CHURCH (1892), [CEM] Rev. Theodore J. Miller; Deacon Rene Gonzalez.
Res.: 317 E. Madison St., 43431. Tel: 419-637-2255; Fax: 419-637-2255.
Catechesis/Religious Program—Tel: 419-637-9929. Sr. M. Louisa Heinl, S.N.D., D.R.E. Students 228.

GLANDORF, PUTNAM CO., ST. JOHN THE BAPTIST (1834), (German), [CEM] [JC] Rev. Harold C. Brown, C.PP.S.; Sr. Carol Pothast, O.S.F., Pastoral Assoc.
Res.: 109 Main St., Box 48, 45848. Tel: 419-538-6928; Fax: 419-538-6147.
Catechesis/Religious Program—Tel: 419-538-6335. Students 680.

HAMLER, HENRY CO., ST. PAUL (1886), [CEM] Rev. Stephen L. Stanbery.
Res.: 316 Chicago Ave., Holgate, 43527. Tel: 419-264-3321.
Church: State Rte. 109 at Cowen St., 43527.
Catechesis/Religious Program—Tel: 419-274-7322. Students 65.

HICKSVILLE, DEFIANCE CO., ST. MICHAEL (1878), Attended by, Edgerton. Rev. Thomas E. Oedy; Deacon Walter Conkle.
Mailing Address: P.O. Box 52, 43526. Tel: 419-542-8202; Fax: 419-542-8202.
Res.: 133 W. Bement St., P.O. Box 355, Edgerton, 43517. Tel: 419-298-2932.
Catechesis/Religious Program—Students 173.

HOLGATE, HENRY CO., ST. MARY (1886), [CEM] Rev. Stephen L. Stanbery; Deacon LaVon Mack.
Res.: 316 Chicago Ave., P.O. Box 487, 43527. Tel: 419-264-3321.
Catechesis/Religious Program—Tel: 419-264-6596. Students 82.

HURON, ERIE CO., ST. PETER (1888), [JC] Rev. Jeffery P. Sikorski, Admin.; Deacons John Barrett; Jack Busam.
Res.: 430 Main St., 44839. Tel: 419-433-5725; Fax: 419-433-2118.
School—Tel: 419-433-4640; Fax: 419-433-2118. Lay Teachers 10; Students 160.
Catechesis/Religious Program—Students 384.

JUNCTION, PAULDING CO., ST. MARY (1846), Rev. Herman F. Scherger; Deacon Richard Carnahan.
Mailing Address: 21706 SR 114, Cloverdale, 45827. Tel: 419-393-2890.
Church: 18788 CTY Rte. 111, Junction, OH.
Catechesis/Religious Program—Tel: 419-594-2615. Students 61.

KALIDA, PUTNAM CO., ST. MICHAEL (1878), [CEM] Rev. Scott Kramer, C.PP.S.; Deacon Robert Klausing.
Office—312 N. Broad St., 45853. Tel: 419-532-3474; Fax 419-532-3470.
Church: Road H-13 @ State Rte. 115, Cuba, 45114.
Res.: 206 N. Broad St., 45853. Tel 419-532-3431.
Catechesis/Religious Program—Tel: 419-532-3494. Jan Kahle, D.R.E. Students 482.
Mission—St. Isidore [CEM] Cuba, Putnam Co.

KANSAS, SENECA CO., ST. JAMES (1890), [CEM] Rev. Theodore J. Miller.
Res.: c/o 875 State Rte. 635, Helena, 43435. Tel: 419-638-3042.
Parish Office—Tel: 419-638-3042; Fax: 419-638-3043.
Catechesis/Religious Program—Students 40.

KELLEY'S ISLAND, ERIE CO., ST. MICHAEL (1861), Rev. Jeffrey J. Nordhaus.
Mailing Address: P.O. Box 490, 43438-0490. Tel: 419-746-2481.

KIRBY, WYANDOT CO., ST. MARY (1861), [CEM] Rev. Kent R. Kaufman, Admin.
Mailing Address: 225 N. Eighth St., Upper Sandusky, 43351. Tel: 419-294-1268; Fax: 419-294-1555.
Church: Main St. at SR 639, 43351.
Catechesis/Religious Program—Students 130.

LANDECK, ALLEN CO., ST. JOHN BAPTIST (1866), [CEM] Rev. John W. Fleck.
Res.: 14755 Landeck Rd., Rte. 1, Delphos, 45833. Tel: 419-692-0636.
Catechesis/Religious Program—Tel: 419-695-2141. Students 181.
Mission—St. Patrick 500 S. Canal, Spencerville, Allen Co. 45887. Tel: 419-695-4138.

LEIPSIC, PUTNAM CO., ST. MARY (1873), [CEM] Rev. George E. Wenzinger, Admin.
Res.: 318 State St., 45856. Tel: 419-943-2952.
School—Tel: 419-943-2801. Sisters of Notre Dame 2; Lay Teachers 8; Students 202.
Catechesis/Religious Program—Tel: 419-943-3197. Students 243.

LEXINGTON, RICHLAND CO., RESURRECTION (1969), Rev. Stanley S. Szybka; Deacon Thomas Dubois.
Res.: 2600 Lexington Ave., 44904. Tel: 419-884-0060; Fax: 419-884-0261.
Catechesis/Religious Program—Students 320.

LIBERTY, SENECA CO., ST. ANDREW (1834), [CEM] Rev. Arthur J. Niewiadomski.
Church: 3761 State Rte. 635 N., P.O. Box 226, Bascom, 44809. Tel: 419-937-2613; Fax: 419-937-2751.
Res.: 6230 W. Tiffin St., Bascom, 44809. Tel: 419-937-2715.
Catechesis/Religious Program—Students 51.

LIMA, ALLEN CO.

1—ST. CHARLES BORROMEO (1953), [JC] Revs. Stephen J. Blum, Admin.; David M. Ross, S.T.L., J.C.D.; William J. Rose.
Res.: 2200 W. Elm, 45805. Tel: 419-228-7635; Fax: 419-229-2835.
School—Tel: 419-222-2536; Fax: 419-222-8720. Lay Teachers 29; Students 585.
Catechesis/Religious Program—Students 527.

2—ST. GERARD (1916), Very Rev. Henry E. Sattler, C.SS.R.; Revs. Thomas Lacey, C.SS.R.; George Blasick, C.SS.R.; Deacon Elias Pina. In Res., Rev. Thomas J. Barrett, C.Ss.R.
Res.: 240 W. Robb Ave., 45801. Tel: 419-224-3080; Fax: 419-225-2231.
School—(Grades PreK-8) Tel: 419-222-0431; Fax: 419-224-6580. Lay Teachers 18; Students 284.
Catechesis/Religious Program—Students 230.
Station—Plus Health Care, Tel: 419-221-1346; Fax: 419-221-1125.
Station—Lima Manor, Tel: 419-227-2611; Fax: 419-224-4755.
Station—Allen Correctional Institute, Tel: 419-224-8000.
Station—Lima Correctional Institute, Tel: 419-225-8060.
Station—Oakwood Correctional Institute, Tel: 419-225-8052.

3—ST. JOHN THE EVANGELIST (1901), [JC] Very Rev. Christopher P. Vasko, J.C.L.; Sr. Judy Leibengood, O.S.F., Pastoral Assoc.; Deacon Richard Gleason.
Mailing Address: 222 S. West St., 45801-4842. In Res., Rev. Dennis P. Hartigan.
Res.: 781 S. Main St., 45804. Tel: 419-223-4476; Fax: 419-228-1825.
Catechesis/Religious Program—Tel: 419-228-3870. Students 19.

4—ST. ROSE (1856), [JC] Very Rev. Christopher P. Vasko, J.C.L.
Mailing Address: 222 S. West St., 45801-4842.
Res.: 479 N. West St., 45801-4294. Tel: 419-222-5521; Fax: 419-228-8439.
School—Tel: 419-223-6361; Fax: 419-222-2032. Mr. Ronald Huysman, Prin. Sisters 1; Lay Teachers 12; Students 133.
Catechesis/Religious Program—Tel: 419-222-2087. Students 76.

LYONS, FULTON CO., OUR LADY OF FATIMA (1946), Rev. James Steinle, Admin. (Retired); Deacon Gene Betz.
Mailing Address & Church: P.O. Box 112, 43533. Tel: 419-923-8017; Fax: 419-237-1042.
Catechesis/Religious Program—236 Kennedy Dr., 43533. Tel: 419-923-7714. Sally Kovar, D.R.E. Students 130.

MANSFIELD, RICHLAND CO.

1—ST. MARY OF THE SNOW (1949), [JC] Rev. Keith J. McCormack; Deacons Allan D. Kopp; Russell Shoemaker.
Res.: 1630 Ashland Rd., 44905. Tel: 419-589-5464; Fax: 419-589-7085.
School—Tel: 419-589-2114; Fax: 419-589-7085. Lay Teachers 11; Students 145.
Catechesis/Religious Program—Students 79.

2—ST. PETER (1844), [CEM] Very Rev. Herbert F. Weber, V.F.; Revs. Michael J. Zacharias; Vicente Antonio Vera (Philippines).
Church: 54 S. Mulberry St., 44902. Tel: 419-524-2572; Fax: 419-522-2553.
School—63 S. Mulberry St., 44902. Tel: 419-524-3351; Fax: 419-524-3366. Sisters of St. Francis of Mary Immaculate (Joliet, IL) 1; Lay Teachers 34; Students 463.
High School—104 W. First St., 44903. Tel: 419-524-0979; Fax: 419-524-0979. Sisters of St. Francis of Mary Immaculate (Joliet, IL) 1; Lay Teachers 24; Students 207.
Catechesis/Religious Program—Students 144.

MARBLEHEAD, OTTAWA CO., ST. JOSEPH (1867), (Slovak), [CEM] [JC] Rev. James E. Brown.
Mailing Address: 113 James St., 43440-2118. Tel: 419-798-4177; Fax: 419-798-4260.
Res.: 802 Barclay, 43440-2101.
Catechesis/Religious Program—113 James St., 43440. Tel: 419-798-5543. Students 98.

MARYGROVE, LUCAS CO., IMMACULATE CONCEPTION (1840), Merged, with Saint Elizabeth of Hungary, Richfield Center, and St. Mary of Assumption, Assumption to form Holy Trinity Catholic Parish, Assumption.

MARYSDALE, DEFIANCE CO., IMMACULATE CONCEPTION (1873), [CEM] Rev. David D. Tscherne.
Mailing Address: 05480 Moser Rd., Defiance, 43512. Tel: 419-899-2549; Fax: 419-899-2549.
Church: State Rte. 15 at Glenburg Rd., Defiance, 43512.
Catechesis/Religious Program—Tel: 419-658-2512. Students 52.

MARYWOOD, SENECA CO., ST. MICHAEL'S (1839), (German), [CEM] Rev. John M. Nagele, C.PP.S.
Res.: 16209 E.County Rd. 46, Bellevue, 44811. Tel: 419-483-3231; Fax: 419-483-4661.
Catechesis/Religious Program—Students 61.

MAUMEE, LUCAS CO., ST. JOSEPH (1841), [CEM] Very Rev. Francis A. Murd, Admin.; Rev. Mark E. Davis; Deacons John Campbell; Kenneth Dickey; Richard Heban; Edward Irelan; Paul Morris; Eileen Williams, Pastoral Assoc.
Res.: 104 W. Broadway, 43537. Tel: 419-893-4848; Fax: 419-891-6968.
School—Tel: 419-893-3304; Fax: 419-891-6969. Lay Teachers 21; Students 315.
Catechesis/Religious Program—Tel: 419-893-7025; Fax: 419-891-6969. Students 420.

MILAN, ERIE CO., ST. ANTHONY (1862), [CEM] Rev. James A. Walsh.
Res.: 145 Center St., P.O. Box 1200, 44846-1200. Tel: 419-499-4274; Fax: 419-499-4274.
Catechesis/Religious Program—Tel: 419-499-4300. Linda Salmons, D.R.E. Students 170.

MILLER CITY, PUTNAM CO., ST. NICHOLAS (1888), [CEM] Rev. A. Robert DeSloover.
Mailing Address: Box 36, 45864. Tel: 419-876-3481; Fax: 419-876-3480.
Catechesis/Religious Program—Deborah Wehri, D.R.E. Students 370.
Sister Parish—Holy Family, New Cleveland.

MILLERSVILLE, SANDUSKY CO., ST. MARY (1859), [CEM] Rev. Theodore J. Miller; Deacon George P. Miller.
Res.: c/o 875 State Rte. 635, Helena, 43435. Tel: 419-638-3042.
Parish Office—Tel: 419-638-3042; Fax: 419-638-3043.
School—Tel: 419-638-3631. Lay Teachers 2; Students 44; Sisters 1.
Catechesis/Religious Program—Students 102.
Mission—St. James 875 SR635 Helena, Kansas, Seneca Co. 43435.

MONROEVILLE, HURON CO., ST. JOSEPH (1861), [CEM] Rev. Kenneth J. Lill.
Res.: 66 Chapel St., 44847. Tel: 419-465-4142; Fax: 419-465-2170.
School—Tel: 419-465-2625; Fax: 419-465-2319. Sisters of Notre Dame 2; Lay Teachers 11; Students 140.
Catechesis/Religious Program—Students 50.

MONTPELIER, WILLIAMS CO., SACRED HEART (1911), Very Rev. Frederick J. Duschl, V.F.; Deacon Ralph Dominique.
Mailing Address: P.O. Box 196, Blakeslee, 43505. Tel: 419-485-5914; Fax: 419-272-3400.
Res.: 210 S. East Ave., 43543.
Catechesis/Religious Program—Students 125.

NAPOLEON, HENRY CO., ST. AUGUSTINE (1856), [CEM] Rev. Daniel E. Borgelt; Deacons Louis Recker; Robert Bost; Bruce Buckmaster.
Office—210 E. Clinton St., 43545. Tel: 419-592-7656; Fax: 419-592-6316.
School—722 Monroe St., 43545. Tel: 419-592-3641. Lay Teachers 9; Students 95.
Catechesis/Religious Program—Students 221.

NEW BAVARIA, HENRY CO., SACRED HEART OF JESUS (1893), (German), [CEM] Rev. Stephen L. Stanbery; Deacon Kenneth Klear.
Res.: 13-779 Road Y, Rte. 1, 43548. Tel: 419-653-4157.
Catechesis/Religious Program—Tel: 419-635-4121. Students 115.

NEW CLEVELAND, PUTNAM CO., HOLY FAMILY (1862), [CEM] Rev. A. Robert DeSloover.
Res.: c/o Box 40, Miller City, 45864. Tel: 419-876-3481; Fax: 419-876-3480.
Sister Parish—St. Nicholas, Miller City.
Catechesis/Religious Program—Tel: 419-876-3480. Students 165.

NEW LONDON, HURON CO., OUR LADY OF LOURDES (1853), [CEM] Rev. Robert L. Haas.
Res.: 18 Park Ave., 44851. Tel: 419-929-4401.
Catechesis/Religious Program—Tel: 419-929-4402. Students 132.

NEW RIEGEL, SENECA CO., ST. BONIFACE (1834), [CEM] Revs. Harry M. Cavanaugh, C.PP.S. ((TOL)); Ronald A. Schock, Admin.; Deacon Lewis E. Reinhart.
Res.: 41 N. Perry St., P.O. Box 89, 44853. Tel: 419-595-2567; Fax: 419-595-2303.
Catechesis/Religious Program—Students 191.

NEW WASHINGTON, CRAWFORD CO., ST. BERNARD (1844), [CEM] Rev. Robert L. Dendinger.
Res.: 422 W. Mansfield, 44854-0337. Tel: 419-492-2295; Fax: 419-492-2604.
School—Tel: 419-492-2693. Lay Teachers 12; Students 161.
Catechesis/Religious Program—Tel: 419-492-2973. Students 55.

NORTH AUBURN, CRAWFORD CO., MOTHER OF SORROWS (1879), [CEM] Rev. Robert L. Dendinger.
Mailing Address: 422 W. Mansfield, New Washington, 44854-0337. Tel: 419-492-2295.
Church: 720 N. Auburn Rd..

NORTH BALTIMORE, WOOD CO.

1—HOLY FAMILY (2001), Rev. Stephen P. Cairns, Admin.
Res.: 115 E. Cherry St., 45872-1134. Tel: 419-257-2319.
Catechesis/Religious Program—Students 75.

2—OUR LADY OF THE MIRACULOUS MEDAL (1891), Consolidated, with Sacred Heart, New Baltimore to form Holy Family, New Baltimore.

NORTH CREEK, PUTNAM CO., ST. JOSEPH (1887), (German), [CEM] Rev. Robert J. Kill; Deacon Kenneth Klear.
Mailing Address: P.O. Box 8, Cloverdale, 45827.
Church: Putnam County Rd. B-13 at Rd. 18A, New Bavaria, 43548. Tel: 419-488-2391; Fax: 419-488-2390.
Catechesis/Religious Program—Students 9.

NORWALK, HURON CO.

1—ST. MARY, MOTHER OF THE REDEEMER (1860), (Irish), [CEM] Rev. Nelson G. Beaver; Deacon Jack Bleile.
Res.: 38 W. League St., 44857. Tel: 419-668-2005; Fax: 419-663-6234.
School—Tel: 419-668-8480; Fax: 419-668-3269. Sisters of Notre Dame 1; Lay Teachers 15; Students 156.
Catechesis/Religious Program—77 State St., 44857. Tel: 419-668-8480; Fax: 419-668-3269. Students 47.

2—ST. PAUL (1876), (German), [CEM] Very Rev. Franklin P. Kehres, V.F.; Rev. Douglas D. Taylor; Marian Bermudez, Pastoral Assoc. In Res., Rev. William A. Pifher, C.S.C.
Res.: 91 E. Main St., 44857. Tel: 419-668-6044; Fax: 419-663-5770.
School—Tel: 419-668-6091; Fax: 419-663-2420. Lay Teachers 26; Students 532.
High School—Tel: 419-668-3005; Fax: 419-668-6417. Lay Teachers 26; Students 263.
Catechesis/Religious Program—Julie Wise, D.R.E. Students 135.

OAK HARBOR, OTTAWA CO., ST. BONIFACE (1866), Rev. James E. Peiffer.
Res.: 215 Church St., 43449. Tel: 419-898-1389; Fax: 419-898-2212.
School—Tel: 419-898-1340; Fax: 419-898-4193. Sisters 1; Lay Teachers 6; Students 40.
Catechesis/Religious Program—Tel: 419-855-7181; Fax: 419-855-8159. Students 102.

OREGON, LUCAS CO., ST. IGNATIUS (1883), (Territorial), [CEM] Rev. Albert B. Ceranowski.
Res.: 212 N. Stadium Rd., 43616. Tel: 419-693-1150; Fax: 419-693-0063.
Catechesis/Religious Program—Tel: 419-693-7662. Students 315.

OTTAWA, PUTNAM CO., SS. PETER AND PAUL (1868), [CEM] Revs. Thomas Hemm, C.PP.S.; Bernard Meiring, C.PP.S.; Timothy P. Knepper, C.PP.S.; Deacon Jim Rump.
Res.: 307 N. Locust St., 45875. Tel: 419-523-5216; Fax: 419-523-4048.
School—Tel: 419-523-3697. Lay Teachers 17; Students 342.
Catechesis/Religious Program—320 N. Locust St.. Tel: 419-523-5078. Students 234.

OTTOVILLE, PUTNAM CO., IMMACULATE CONCEPTION (1848), [CEM] Rev. Anthony A. Borgia; Deacon Jose Flores.
Res.: 189 Church St., Box 296, 45876. Tel: 419-453-3513; Fax: 419-453-2513.
Catechesis/Religious Program—Tel: 419-453-3702. Students 525.

PAULDING, PAULDING CO., ST. JOSEPH (1894), Very Rev. G. Allan Fillman, V.F.; Deacons Francis Koenn; Rosalio Martinez; Heather Miller, Business Mgr.
Res.: 314 N. Main St., 45879. Tel: 419-399-2576; Fax: 419-399-2577.
Catechesis/Religious Program—Tel: 419-399-5668. Sr. Michaelynn Hempfling, S.N.D., D.R.E. Students 150.

PAYNE, PAULDING CO., ST. JOHN THE BAPTIST (1892), [CEM] Very Rev. G. Allan Fillman, V.F.; Deacons Donald Coughlin; David Jordan.
Res.: 203 W. Townline, P.O. Box 38, 45880. Tel: 419-263-2469; Fax: 419-263-2938.
School—Tel: 419-263-2114; Fax: 419-263-2114. Lay Teachers 6; Students 113.
Catechesis/Religious Program—Students 60.

PERRYSBURG, WOOD CO., ST. ROSE (1861), [CEM] Revs. Thomas J. Leyland; Michael G. Dandurand; Deacons Lawrence Tiefenbach; Ken Cappelletty; Ray Kemer; Victor DeFilippis. In Res., Rev. Nicholas Weibl.
Res.: 215 E. Front St., 43551-2254. Tel: 419-874-2217; Fax: 419-874-7462.
School—217 E. Front St., 43551-2254. Tel: 419-874-5631; Fax: 419-874-1002. Lay Teachers 26; Students 560.
Catechesis/Religious Program—Tel: 419-874-9474. Sr. Jeanne Marie Holtz, O.S.U, D.R.E. Students 482.

PERU, HURON CO., ST. ALPHONSUS LIGUORI (1828), (German), [CEM] Rev. Nelson G. Beaver; Deacon George Stepanic.
Res.: 38 W. League St., Norwalk, 44857. Tel: 419-668-2005; Fax: 419-663-6234.
Catechesis/Religious Program—1360 Settlement Dr., Norwalk, 44857. Tel: 419-668-5030; Fax: 419-663-6234. Students 61.

PLYMOUTH, HURON CO., ST. JOSEPH (1864), Rev. Melvin T. Verhoff.
Res.: 117 Sandusky St., 44865. Tel: 419-687-4611; Fax: 419-687-4611.
Catechesis/Religious Program—Students 72.

PORT CLINTON, OTTAWA CO., IMMACULATE CONCEPTION (1861), Very Rev. Raymond E. Ensman, V.F.; Sr. Mary Jane Fisher, R.S.M., Pastoral Assoc.
414 Madison St., 43452-1922. Tel: 419-734-4004; Fax: 419-734-3477.
School—109 W. Fourth St., 43452. Tel: 419-734-3315; Fax: 419-734-6172. Sisters of Notre Dame 1; Lay Teachers 9; Students 132.
Catechesis/Religious Program—Students 139.

PROVIDENCE, LUCAS CO., ST. PATRICK (1842), (Irish), [CEM] Rev. F. Anthony Gallagher.
Mailing Address: 14010 U.S. 24, Grand Rapids, 43522-9678. Tel: 419-832-5215; Fax: 419-832-4075.
Catechesis/Religious Program—Students 204.

PUT-IN-BAY, OTTAWA CO., MOTHER OF SORROWS (1866), Rev. Jeffrey J. Nordhaus, Admin.
Mailing Address: Box 179, 43456. Tel: 419-285-2741.

REED, SENECA CO., ASSUMPTION (1867), (German), [CEM] Rev. John M. Nagele, C.PP.S.
Res.: 16209 E. County Rd. 46, Bellevue, 44811. Tel: 419-483-3231; Fax: 419-483-4661.
Church: 15030 E. Township Rd. 126, Bellevue, 44811.
Catechesis/Religious Program—Students 43.

REPUBLIC, SENECA CO., ST. ALOYSIUS (1879), Rev. Joseph P. Szybka; Deacon Urban Arbogast.
Res.: 211 East St., Box 250, 44867. Tel: 419-585-4411; Fax: 419-585-4411.
Catechesis/Religious Program—Students 94.

RICHFIELD CENTER, LUCAS CO., ST. ELIZABETH OF HUNGARY (1914), Merged, with Immaculate Conception, Marygrove and St. Mary of Assumption, Assumption to form Holy Trinity Catholic Parish, Assumption.

ROSSFORD, WOOD CO., ALL SAINTS (1990), Consolidated Rev. Jonathan C. Wight, Admin.; Deacons Jerry Nellett; Rick Vascik; Susan VanHersett, Pastoral Assoc. of SS. Cyril and Methodius and St. Mary Magdalene.
Church: 628 Lime City Rd., 43460. Tel: 419-666-1393; Fax: 419-666-5764.
School—630 Lime City Rd., 43460. Tel: 419-661-2070; Fax: 419-661-2077. Sisters 4; Lay Teachers 9; Total Staff 40; Students 317.
Catechesis/Religious Program—Students 203.

ST. MICHAEL'S RIDGE, DEFIANCE CO., ST. MICHAEL (1861), [CEM] Rev. David D. Tscherne; Sr. Margie Verhoff, C.D.P., Pastoral Assoc. & D.R.E.
Res.: 05480 Moser Rd., Defiance, 43512. Tel: 419-497-2161; Fax: 419-497-2058.
Catechesis/Religious Program—Tel: 419-497-3122. Students 130.

ST. STEPHEN, SENECA CO., ST. STEPHEN (1844), [CEM] Rev. Joseph P. Szybka; Deacon Robert Felter.
Res.: 11658 E. Township Rd. 44, Attica, 44807. Tel: 419-426-1145; Fax: 419-426-1145.
Church: Seneca County Rd. 6 at Seneca County Rd. 23, Attica, 44807.
Catechesis/Religious Program—Students 27.

SALEM TWP., WYANDOT CO., ST. JOSEPH (1849), (English), [CEM] Rev. Kent R. Kaufman, Admin.; Deacon Floyd Derr.
Mailing Address: 225 N. 8th St., Upper Sandusky, 43351. Tel: 419-294-1268; Fax: 419-294-1555.
Church: 07975 Township Hwy. 103, Carey, 43316.
Catechesis/Religious Program— Clustered with St. Peter, Upper Sandusky and St. Mary, Kirby. Students 32.

SANDUSKY, ERIE CO.

1—HOLY ANGELS (1839), [JC] Rev. John C. Missler; Sr. Mary de Porres Westrick, S.N.D., Pastoral Assoc.
Res.: 1605 W. Jefferson Ave., 44870. Tel: 419-625-3698; Fax: 419-625-5183.
School— For details, please see Sandusky Central Catholic School under Consolidated Elementary Schools in the Institution section.
Catechesis/Religious Program—Mary A. Zang, D.R.E. Students 144.

2—ST. MARY (1855), (German), [CEM] [JC 3] Revs. Philip S. Feltman; Todd M. Dominique; Deacon Joseph A. Singler; Sr. Regina Marie Fisher, S.N.D., Pastoral Assoc.
Res.: 429 Central Ave., 44870. Tel: 419-625-7465; Fax: 419-626-2834.
School— For details, please see Sandusky Central Catholic School under Consolidated Elementary Schools in the Institution section.
Catechesis/Religious Program—Tel: 419-621-7456. Students 186.

3—SS. PETER AND PAUL (1866), [CEM] [JC] Revs. Martin B. Nassr; John E. Brennen; Deacons Milton Opper; John Downey; Sr. Martha Bertke, C.PP.S., Pastoral Assoc. In Res., Rev. Tommy Rodriguez (India).
Res.: 510 Columbus Ave., 44870. Tel: 419-625-6655; Fax: 419-625-6576.
School— For details, please see Sandusky Central Catholic School under Consolidated Elementary Schools in the Institution section.
Catechesis/Religious Program—Cheryl Pawlowski, D.R.E. Students 212.

SHELBY, RICHLAND CO., MOST PURE HEART OF MARY (1866), (German), [CEM] Rev. Nicholas J. Cunningham; Deacon Dennis Burkett.
Res.: 29 West St., 44875. Tel: 419-347-2381; Fax: 419-347-3934.
School—Tel: 419-342-2626; Fax: 419-347-2763. Sisters 1; Lay Teachers 7; Students 136.
Catechesis/Religious Program—Lois Steele, D.R.E. Students 174.

SPENCERVILLE, ALLEN CO., ST. PATRICK (1858), [JC] Rev. John W. Fleck.
Res.: 14755 Landeck Rd., Rte. 1, Delphos, 45833. Tel: 419-692-0636.
Catechesis/Religious Program—Tel: 419-647-6202. Students 135.

STRYKER, WILLIAM CO., ST. JOHN THE EVANGELIST (1861), (German—Hispanic), [JC] Rev. Gary M. Ferguson.
Res.: c/o 614 N. Defiance St., Archbold, 43502. Tel: 419-682-1372; 419-446-9288; Fax: 419-446-9288 (Call first).
Catechesis/Religious Program—Tel: 419-446-2150. Students 30.

SWANTON, FULTON CO., ST. RICHARD (1893), [CEM] Rev. Daniel J. Zak; Deacon Timothy Worline.
Res.: 333 Brookside Dr., 43558. Tel: 419-826-2791; Fax: 419-826-7256.
School—Tel: 419-826-5041. Kathleen Gallagher, Prin. Lay Teachers 11; Students 169; Religious 1.
Catechesis/Religious Program—Kathy Kpupitzer, D.R.E. Students 120.

SYCAMORE, WYANDOT CO., ST. PIUS X (1951), Revs. David M. Ross, S.T.L., J.C.D., Admin.; Stephen L. Schroeder; Deacon John Daniel.
Res.: P.O. Box 382, 44882. Tel: 419-447-2087; Fax: 419-927-6062.
Catechesis/Religious Program—P.O. Box 282, 44882. Tel: 419-927-6062. Students 57.

SYLVANIA, LUCAS CO., ST. JOSEPH (1873), [CEM] Revs. Richard T. Wurzel, S.T.D.; Gregory L. Peatee; Sr. Patricia Gist, C.PP.S., Pastoral Assoc.; Deacons Robert Bodette; William Ulmer; Timothy Krukowski; Paul White.
Res.: 5373 S. Main St., 43560. Tel: 419-885-5791; Fax: 419-882-5235.
School—5411 S. Main St., 43560. Tel: 419-882-6670; Fax: 419-885-1990. Sisters 1; Lay Teachers 36; Students 788.
Catechesis/Religious Program—Tel: 419-885-2181; Fax: 419-885-8251. Students 424.

THE BEND, DEFIANCE CO., ST. STEPHEN (1855), [CEM] Rev. David D. Tscherne.
Mailing Address: 05480 Moser Rd., Defiance, 43512-9150.
Church: 16166 Speaker Rd., Sherwood, 43556. Tel: 419-899-2549; Fax: 419-497-2058.
Catechesis/Religious Program—Students 54.
Mission—*Immaculate Conception* Marysdale, Defiance Co.

TIFFIN, SENECA CO.

1—ST. JOSEPH (1845), [CEM] Rev. James K. Say; Deacon Daniel Scherger. In Res., Rev. Msgr. Edward C. Dunn (Retired).
Res.: 36 Melmore St., 44883-3098. Tel: 419-447-5848; Fax: 419-447-7580.
School—357 S. Washington St., 44883. Tel: 419-447-5790. Sisters 1; Lay Teachers 17; Students 327.
Catechesis/Religious Program—Students 159.

2—ST. MARY (1831), [CEM] Revs. David M. Ross, S.T.L., J.C.D., Admin.; Timothy F. Ferris; Sr. Maryann Drians, O.S.F., Pastoral Assoc.; Deacons Walter Beat; Robert Hartzell.
Res.: 85 S Sandusky St., 44883. Tel: 419-447-2087; Fax: 419-447-9940.
School—75 S. Sandusky St., 44883. Tel: 419-447-5202; Fax: 419-447-0142. Lay Teachers 24; Students 272; Preschool 81.
Catechesis/Religious Program—Tel: 419-448-9341. Students 263.

UPPER SANDUSKY, WYANDOT CO., ST. PETER (1857), [CEM] [JC] Rev. Kent R. Kaufman, Admin.
Res.: 225 N. 8th St., 43351. Tel: 419-294-1268; Fax: 419-294-1555.
School—Tel: 419-294-1395; Fax: 419-294-1395. Sisters of Mercy 1; Lay Teachers 9; Students 168.
Catechesis/Religious Program—Fax: 419-294-1555. Students 184.

VAN WERT, VAN WERT CO., ST. MARY OF THE ASSUMPTION (1876), Deacons Andrew McMahon; Norbert Reinhart.
Res.: 601 Jennings Rd., 45891. Tel: 419-238-3979; Fax: 419-238-3957.
School—Tel: 419-238-5186. Lay Teachers 7; Students 115.
Catechesis/Religious Program—611 Jennings Rd., 45891. Tel: 419-238-3079. Mrs. Cherie Freewalt, D.R.E. Students 153.

VERMILION, ERIE CO., ST. MARY (1851), [JC] Rev. James J. Holmer, Admin.; Sr. Eve Marie Korzym, O.S.F., Pastoral Assoc.
Res.: 731 Exchange St., 44089. Tel: 440-967-8711; Fax: 440-967-8712.
School—5450 Ohio St., 44089. Tel: 440-967-7911. Lay Teachers 8; Students 145.
Catechesis/Religious Program—Students 324.

WAKEMAN, HURON CO., ST. MARY (1852), [CEM] Sr. Edna Michel, O.S.F., Pastoral Leader; Rev. Robert L. Haas, Chap.
Mailing Address: P.O. Box 576, 44889-0576. Tel: 440-839-2023; Fax: 440-839-2881.
Church: 46 E. Main St., 44889. Tel: 440-839-2023.
Catechesis/Religious Program—Students 61.

WALBRIDGE, WOOD CO., ST. JEROME (1962), Rev. William C. Parker.
Res.: 300 Warner St., 43465. Tel: 419-666-2857; Fax: 419-661-2281.
School—(Grades PreK-8) Tel: 419-666-2855; Fax: 419-661-2285. Sisters of St. Francis 1; Lay Teachers 10; Students 240.
Catechesis/Religious Program—Students 85.

WAUSEON, FULTON CO., ST. CASPAR (1850), [CEM] [JC] Rev. Robert A. Holden; Deacons Juan Rodriguez; James Dominique; James Schmidt.
Res.: 1205 N. Shoop Ave., 43567. Tel: 419-335-3656; Fax: 419-337-2413.
Catechesis/Religious Program—Tel: 419-337-2322. Students 70.

WILLARD, HURON CO., ST. FRANCIS XAVIER (1875), [CEM] Rev. Melvin T. Verhoff; Deacons Vincent Foos; Russell Niedermeier; Paul Jones.
Res.: 21 W. Perry St., 44890. Tel: 419-935-1149; Fax: 419-933-6000.
School—Tel: 419-935-4744. Lay Teachers 10; Students 152.
Catechesis/Religious Program—Students 151.

Chaplains of Public Institutions

TOLEDO. *Sisters of Notre Dame*, 3837 Secor Rd., 43623. Rev. Bruce L. Farmer.
St. Vincent Mercy Medical Center, 2213 Cherry St., 43608-2691. Tel: 419-321-3232. (Vacant)

LIMA. *St. Rita Hospital and Medical Center*, 730 W. Market St., 45801.

MANSFIELD. *Mercy Hospital*. Vacant.

OREGON. *St. Charles Mercy Hospital*, 2600 Navarre, 43616. Rev. Charles J. Denny.

SANDUSKY. *Soldiers and Sailors Home*. Rev. Tommy Rodrieguez (India).

Special Assignment:
Revs.—
Cardone, Joseph P., Admin. Dir. Pastoral Care, Mercy Health Partners.
Weigman, Joseph A., Assoc. Dir. Spiritual Formation, St. Meinrad School of Theology, St. Meinrad, IN.
Yeager, Robert J., Diocesan Finance Management Conference, Waterville.

On Duty Outside the Diocese:
Revs.—
Buchman, Joel R., M.A., S.T.B. (LA), Torrance, CA.
Corral, Jose, Menlo Park, CA.
Kardzis, Christopher, All Souls Catholic Mission, P.O. Box 37, Binga, Zimbabwe, Africa.
McQuillen, Thomas J., All Saints Catholic Mission, P.O. Box 37, Binga, Zimbabwe, Africa.

Graduate Studies:
Rev.—
Poggemeyer, Joseph T., Pontifical College Josephinum, Columbus.

Military Chaplains:
Revs.—
Borger, Marvin G., J.C.L., Chap., U.S. Navy
Kirk, David R., Chap. U.S. Army
Rohen, Patrick J., Chap., U.S. Army

Awaiting Assignment:
Revs.—
Kokocinski, Bernard A.
Lautermilch, David J.

Health Leave:
Revs.—
Bowers, Mark R.
Tucceri, Robert A.

Retired:
Rev. Msgr.—
Dunn, Edward C., 36 Melmore St., Tiffin, 44883.
Revs.—
Ankenbrandt, Thomas W., 182 Saint Francis #334 W., Tiffin, 44883-3456.
Badger, Arthur A., 3607 Naples Dr., 43615-1155.
Boff, Bernard J., 2544 Parkwood Ave., 43610-1317.
Bonifas, Roger D., 3651 US Hwy. 27S, Sebring, FL 33870.
Caballero, Francisco, P.O. Box 985, 43697-0985.
Curtis, Robert J., 1220 Tiffin Ave., Fremont, 43420-3562.
Dorley, Paul D., 4811 Estero Pl., 43623-3734.
Dunn, Richard C., 190 St. Francis Ave., #106, Tiffin, 44883-3455.
Etzel, Raymond A., 5679 Monroe St., #1015, Sylvania, 43560-2722.
Hiltz, John T., 19767 Yorba Linda Blvd., Yorba Linda, CA 92886.
Howe, J. Norbert, 165 N. Seriff Dr., Lima, 45807-2258.
Jaros, Joseph P., 29317 Bates Rd., Perrysburg, 43551.
Keller, Harvey M., 175 Shady Ln., Norwalk, 44857.
Kirtland, Robert B., P.O. Box 12407, 43606.
Koerber, George M., 5431 Cresthaven, 43614.
Kuhn, Thomas W., 182 St. Francis Ave. (Rm. 331W), Tiffin, 44883.
Lamantia, A. Robert, 247 Meadowwood, Perrysburg, 42551-1620.
Lehmkuhl, John J., 321 E. Madison St., Gibsonburg, 43431.
Lester, John E., 1001 N. Byrne Rd., Apt. 207, 43607.
Loeffler, Earl A., 2967 Dorr St., 43607-2023.
Lovisa, Eugene L., 930 S. Wynn Rd., Oregon, 43616.
Madden, Michael G., 4201 Heatherdowns Blvd., 43614-3019.
Martin, William J., 16166 Speaker Rd., Rte. 1, Sherwood, 43556-9766.
Very Rev.—
McClure, John A., J.C.L., P.O. Box 985, 43697.
Revs.—
McCullen, John L., Box 999, Deerfield Beach, FL 33441.
Miller, Richard G., 934 S. Wynn Rd., Oregon, 43616.
Miorin, Albert C., 3423 Blackstone Island, P.O. Box 414, Colon, MI 49040.
Mueller, Donald R., 321 E. Madison St., Gibsonburg, 43431.
Niedermier, Jerome G., 5341 Glendale Dr., Harrison, MI 48625-9631.

Nieset, Frank E., 1825 W. Emelita Ave. #149, Mesa, AZ 85202.
Nietfeld, Fred J., 3521 Environ Blvd. #301, Lauderhill, FL 33311.
O'Brien, Joseph L., 4125 King Rd., Sylvania, 43560.
Obergefell, Sylvan W., P.O. Box 173, Ottoville, 45876.
Ott, Carlton A., 4496 Whittlesey, Norwark, 44857-9244.
Radecki, Albin A., 4312 Holland-Sylvania Rd., #323, 43623-4703.
Reichert, Ralph J., 3230 Centennial Rd. #31, Sylvania, 43560-9744.
Rethinger, Omer, 1010 Brush, Apt. A, Fremont, 43420-1410.
Richter, William L., 5679 Monroe St. #809, Sylvania, 43560-2718.
Ricker, John Michael, 212 N. Stadium Rd., Oregon, 43616-1536.
Ringholz, Benedict E., 117 Leisure Ln., Norwalk, 44857-7032.
Rinkowski, George M., 3409 W. Alexis, #7D, 43623-1430.
Risacher, James E., 8820 Walther Blvd. #4215, Baltimore, MD 21234.
Schill, Frederick J., 586 Kaler, Bucyrus, 44820-2565.
Schmenk, Cleo S., 4337 Mt. Carmel Dr., Melbourne, FL 32901.
Shenk, Bertrand J., 59 Executive Dr., Norwalk, 44857-2471.
Sheperd, Raymond C., 11129 Dyke Rd., Curtice, 43412-9453.
Sherbno, John C., P.O. Box 26378, Fairview Park, 44126.
Snyder, Fred, 2645 U.S. Rt. 20, Swanton, 43558.
Steinle, James, 312 Greenfield St., Tiffin, 44883-2427.
Sutton, John, 5000 Providence Dr. #304, 44870-1413.
Vamos, Joseph L., 4227 Bellevue Rd., 43613-3936.
Varney, Lawrence F., 27484 Oregon Rd. Lot 105, Perrysburg, 43551.
Yeager, Robert J., P.O. Box 199, Waterville, 43566.

Permanent Deacons:
Ackerman, Thomas L.
Adams, Lawrence
Algee, John R.
Arbogast, Urban
Badenhop, Donald F.
Baker, Charles R.
Barrett, John
Beat, Walter
Beisser, Robert A.
Betz, Eugene N.
Billmaier, Robert C.
Bistak, Leo T.
Bleile, Jack
Bodette, Robert
Bost, Robert
Buckmaster, Bruce
Burch, William G.
Burkett, Dennis W.
Burkhart, Joseph L.
Burzynski, Raymond
Busam, John
Calvillo, Pedro
Campbell, John E.
Cappelletty, Ken
Carnahan, Richard
Carone, Thomas
Collard, Paul
Conkle, Walter H.
Coughlin, Donald J.
Daniel, John
Dazley, Phil
DeFilippis, Victor
Derr, Floyd
Diaz, Alfredo
Dickey, Kenneth G.
Dominique, Ivan James M.
Dominique, Ralph J.
Dominique, Thomas
Downey, John F.
Dubois, Thomas
Dudley, James M.
Dunn, James
Etue, Timothy W.
Fazekas, Richard S.
Felter, Robert
Fisher, Clarence
Flores, Jose
Foos, Vincent
Fox, Leonard
Fritz, Julius
Garza, Ignacio
Gillen, Robert
Gleason, Richard
Gogol, Stanley S.
Gonzalez, Rene S.
Gryczewski, Edward
Gubernath, Jerome
Hall, Maury
Hammer, James E.
Hartings, Leo J.
Hartzell, Robert J.
Hazelton, Dorsey A.
Heban, Richard D.
Heeter, Joseph M.
Hirn, Robert
Hohman, Floyd
Holmer, Leon
Horning, William L.
Hostutler, James E.
Houghton, LeRoy H.
Huffman, David A.
Hulderman, Joseph
Ignatowski, Gerald
Irelan, Edgar
Jackson, Dennis
Jones, Gary
Jones, Paul R.
Jordan, David
Karpanty, David J.
Keller, Stephen
Kelley, Edward L.
Kemer, Raymond
Keran, William
Kest, Joseph, Jr.
Kirk, Gregory
Kitzler, James F.
Klausing, Robert R.
Klear, Kenneth
Koenn, Francis
Kopp, Allan D.
Kozek, Richard
Krukowski, Timothy K.
Kujawa, Clifford
Lackney, Robert
Laker, David C.
Learned, Michael R., Sr.
Lesinski, Robert J.
Lester, Thomas
Lira, Rudy
Lisk, Fred
Llanos, Ramon
Lochotzki, William
Lopez, Valentin G.
Lottier, Larry F.
Lyons, Raymond E., Jr.
Mack, La Von L.
Marshall, James
Martinez, Rosalio
McCabe, Patrick
McCauley, Terry L.
McMahon, Andrew P.
Mendez, Chris
Meyer, Donald
Middaugh, Raymond D.
Miller, George
Mishler, Richard
Mitchell, George R.
Moncher, James
Moore, Wilbur
Morris, Paul J.
Nellett, Gerald L.
Newton, George E.
Niedermeier, Russell
Niese, Thomas B.
Nighswander, Robert L.
Nissen, John
Nye, Harold
Opper, Milton C.
Pacholski, Robert
Parmelee, Ray H.
Peeps, Ronald G.
Pence, Michael W.
Perez, Diego E.A.
Perez, William
Petersen, Laurence
Phillips, Eugene D.
Philpott, Terry B.
Pina, Elias
Plenzler, Ronald
Przybylek, Stanley
Quinn, Daniel P.
Rall, William
Recker, Louis E.
Reinhart, Lewis E.
Reinhart, Norbert
Repka, Joseph
Ricker, David J.
Righi, Albert
Rodriguez, Guillermo
Rodriguez, Juan
Romo, Bernabe
Romo, Jose
Rump, James A.
Sadler, David L.
Sanchez, Jose
Sanchez, Salvador
Schaupp, Lawrence
Scherger, Daniel
Schmidt, James
Selmek, Zenon J.
Sheehan, Thomas M.
Shoemaker, Russell M.
Sisson, Alfred N.
Snyder, William J.
Sortman, Jerome E.
Stepanic, George C.
Swartz, Robert L.
Tholl, James
Tiefenbach, Lawrence
Ulmer, William A.
Vascik, Richard J.
Veselka, Stephen J.
Villagomez, Jesus
Vogel, Curt
Warren, Richard
Welch, Harold
Westrick, Eugene
Wethington, Norbert A.
White, Paul
White, Richard
Wiciak, John
Willford, Stephen
Wilson, Larry J.
Winterstellar, Kevin
Worland, Donald W.
Worline, Timothy R.
Wurm, Eugene L.
Yakir, Michael D.
Young, James A.

INSTITUTIONS LOCATED IN THE DIOCESE

[A] COLLEGES AND UNIVERSITIES

TOLEDO. *Mercy College of Northwest Ohio,* 2221 Madison Ave., 43624-1132. Tel: 415-251-1279; Fax: 419-251-1570. Email: paul.kessler@mercycollege.edu. Web: www.mercycollege.edu. Dr. Paul Kessler, Pres.; Dr. Martha Shouldis, Vice Pres.; Mr. James Harter, Dean of Student Svcs.; Mrs. Joan Rutherford, Dir. of College Finances & Resource Planning; Mrs. Heather Hoppe, Registrar. Sisters of Mercy of the Americas, Mercy Sisters; Sister of Charity of Montreal, Grey Nuns Sisters of Mercy 1; Total Staff 81; Students 566.

SYLVANIA. *Lourdes College,* 6832 Convent Blvd., 43560. Tel: 419-885-3211; Fax: 419-882-3987. Email: jenderli@lourdes.edu. Web: www.lourdes.edu. Dr. Robert Helmer, Pres.; Dr. Robert Helmer, Vice Pres. Academic Affairs; Michael Killian, Vice Pres. Finance & Admin.; Dr. Robert Turek, Vice Pres. Student Svcs.; Sr. Ann Carmen Barone, O.S.F., Vice Pres. Mission & Ministry; Mary Arquette, Vice Pres. Institutional Advancement; Michelle Rable, Registrar. Sisters of St. Francis of the Congregation of Our Lady of Lourdes, (O.S.F.). Sisters 9; Full-time faculty 56; Lay instructors 50; Enrollment 1,310.

Franciscan Center, 6832 Convent Blvd., 43560. Tel: 419-824-3975. Email: pspitler@lourdes.edu. Web: www.franciscancenter.org. Barbara Barkan, Dir. Total Staff 10.

[B] HIGH SCHOOLS, DIOCESAN

TOLEDO. *Central Catholic High School,* 2550 Cherry St., 43608-2394. Tel: 419-255-2280; Fax: 419-259-2848. Email: fgrh@centralcatholic.org. Web: www.centralcatholic.org. Revs. Gregory R. Hite, Pastor & Pres.; Michael A. Geiger; Mr. Michael Kaucher, Prin.; Mr. William G. Axe, Asst. Prin.; Mr. Randal J. Euckert, Asst. Prin. Conducted by Diocesan Priests, Sisters and Laity Priests 1; Teaching Sisters 3; Lay Teachers 68; Students 1,156.

FREMONT. *St. Joseph Central Catholic High School* Consolidated from St. Joseph, Fremont, St. Ann, Fremont, Sacred Heart, Fremont, St. Casimir, Fremont, St. Mary, Clyde, St. Mary, Millersville, & Immaculate Conception, Bellevue. , 702 Croghan St., 43420-2480. Tel: 419-332-9947; Fax: 419-332-4945. Email: skusmer@fremontstjoe.org. Web: www.cdeducation.org/talkk/fjo. Michael Gabel, Prin.; Rev. Ronald J. Brickner, Chap. Priests 1; Lay Teachers 27; Students 280.

LIMA. *Central Catholic High School,* 720 S. Cable Rd., 45805. Tel: 419-222-4276; Fax: 419-222-6933. Email: frdenny@lcchs.edu. Web: www.lcchs.edu. Rev. Dennis P. Hartigan, Pres. Priests 1; Sisters 2; Lay Teachers 28; Students 393.

OREGON. *Cardinal Stritch High School,* 3225 Pickle Rd., 43616. Tel: 419-693-0465; Fax: 419-697-2816. Email: tmahoney@cardinalstritch.org. Web: www.cardinalstritch.org. Rev. John F. Stites, Pastor & Pres.; Mr. Timothy Mahoney, Prin.

Serves parishes in Greater Toledo, including Oregon, Rossford, Perrysburg, Bono, Walbridge and Genoa. Priests 1; Sisters 2; Lay Teachers 22; Students 368.

TIFFIN. *Calvert High School*, 152 Madison St., 44883. Tel: 419-447-3844; Fax: 419-447-2922. Email: calv_hs_prin@noeca.esu.k12.oh.us. Web: www.calvert.tld.pvt.k12.oh.us. Mr. Anthony J. Mass, Prin.; Rev. James E. Halleron, Chap. Priests 1; Sisters 1; Lay Teachers 12; Students 238.

[C] HIGH SCHOOLS, PRIVATE

TOLEDO. *St. Francis de Sales High School*, 2323 W. Bancroft St., 43607. Tel: 419-531-1618; Fax: 419-531-9740. Email: olsz@sfstoledo.edu. Web: www.sfstoledo.edu. Mr. James Mello; Revs. Ronald W. Olszewski, O.S.F.S., Pres.; John Lehner, O.S.F.S., Chap.; John I. Extejt, O.S.F.S., Treas. & Network Admin.; James H. Roth, O.S.F.S., Asst. Prin. (Academics); John O. Ebenhoeh, O.S.F.S.; Jonathan C. Wight. Oblates of St. Francis de Sales, School for boys Priests 6; Lay Teachers 42; Students 677; Total Staff 65. In Res. Revs. Daniel J. Earley, O.S.F.S. (Retired); Paul G. Gillespie, O.S.F.S. (Retired); John J. McMenamin, O.S.F.S. (Retired); John O'Neill, O.S.F.S. (Retired); Bro. Alfred D. Durant, O.S.F.S.

St. John's Jesuit High School, 5901 Airport Hwy., 43615. Tel: 419-865-5743; Fax: 419-861-5002. Email: tmalone@sjjtitans.org. Web: www.sjjtitans.org. Mr. Tim Malone, Prin.; Revs. Thomas J. Pipp, S.J., Rector; Charles J. Sweeney, S.J.; Francis E. Canfield, S.J.; Thomas H. Radloff, S.J.; Patrick Hussey, S.J.; Bro. John Sebian, S.J.; Rev. Donald Vettese, S.J., Pres. Jesuits of the Detroit Province, School for boys Priests 6; Brothers 1; Lay Teachers 49; Students 781; Total Staff 96.

Notre Dame Academy, 3535 Sylvania Ave., 43623. Tel: 419-475-9359; Fax: 419-724-2640. Email: toledonda@nda.org. Web: www.nda.org. Sisters Mary Carol Gregory, S.N.D., Pres.; Mary Ann Culpert, S.N.D., Prin. Sisters of Notre Dame, School for girls. Sisters 12; Lay Teachers 40; Lay Staff 32; Students 625.

St. Ursula Academy, 4025 Indian Rd., 43606. Tel: 419-531-1693; Fax: 419-534-5777. Email: toledosua@accesstoledo.com. Web: www.toledosua.org. Mrs. Jane Charette, Pres.; Mrs. Jane McGee, Prin. Sponsored by Ursuline Sisters of the Sacred Heart Lay Teachers 44; Students 599; Total Staff 92.

[D] CONSOLIDATED ELEMENTARY SCHOOLS

TOLEDO. *St. Elizabeth Seton Consolidated* Consolidated from St. Vincent de Paul and St. Michael , 1030 Clay St., 43608. Tel: 419-726-4471; Fax: 419-729-2481. Email: steseton_princ@nwoca.org. Sisters 1; Lay Teachers 9; Students 172.

Holy Rosary/St. Stephen United School Consolidated from Holy Rosary and St. Stephen. , 2018 Consaul, 43605. Tel: 419-691-8760. Email: hrssu_princ@nwoca.org. Lay Teachers 13; Students 177.

Queen of Apostles Consolidated from Immaculate Conception, St. James and SS. Peter & Paul. , 235 Courtland, 43609. Tel: 419-241-7829; Fax: 419-241-4180. Email: smbhaynes@yahoo.com. Sr. Mary Brenda Haynes, S.N.D., Prin. Sisters 4; Lay Teachers 8; Total Staff 12; Students 131.

SANDUSKY. *Sandusky Central Catholic School*, 410 W. Jefferson St., 44870. Tel: 419-626-1872; Fax: 419-621-2252. Email: sccs_supt@noeca.net. Web: www.sanduskycentralcatholicschool.com.

Holy Angels Campus, 1603 W. Jefferson St., 44870. Tel: 419-626-3075; Fax: 419-625-5183. Sally Dwight, Dir. (Early Childhood Center) Preschool 85; Day Care 34.

Ss. Peter and Paul Campus (Grades K-3), 514 Jackson St., 44870. Tel: 419-625-1017; Fax: 419-325-9741. Rita Dominick, Prin. (Primary-Elementary)

St. Mary Campus, 530 Decatur St., 44870. Tel: 419-626-1648; Fax: 419-621-0404. Sr. Christine Foos, Prin. (Elementary-Junior High) Students 350.

St. Mary Central Catholic High School, 410 W. Jefferson St., 44870. Tel: 419-626-1892; Fax: 419-621-2252. Mike Cole, Prin.

[E] ELEMENTARY SCHOOLS, PRIVATE

SYLVANIA. *Sylvania Franciscan Academy*, 5335 Silica Dr., 43560. Tel: 419-885-3273; Fax: 419-855-3062. Email: sfa_tallarico@nwoca.org. JoAnn Tallarico, Prin.

TOLEDO. *Ladyfield School*, 3837 Secor Rd., 43623. Tel: 419-475-5451; Fax: 419-479-3083. Email: ladyfieldscm@accesstoledo.com. Web: www.ladyfieldschool.org. Sr. Carolyn Marie Schaffer, S.N.D., Prin. Sisters of Notre Dame Sisters 6; Lay Teachers 12; Students 229.

WHITEHOUSE. *Lial Elementary School*, 5700 Davis Rd., 43571. Tel: 419-877-5167; Fax: 419-877-9385. Email: lial_school@nwoca.org. Web: www.lialschool.tld.pvt.k12.oh.us. Sr. Patricia M. McClain, S.N.D. Sisters of Notre Dame Sisters 3; Lay Teachers 16; Students 192.

[F] ELEMENTARY SCHOOLS

TOLEDO. *Mary Immaculate School*, 3837 Secor Rd., 43623. Tel: 419-474-1688; Fax: 419-479-3062. Email: maryim_miller@nwoca.org. Web: www.maryimmaculatetoledo.org. Sr. Mary Alan Miller, S.N.D., Prin. Day School for Children with Learning Disabilities, Attention Deficit Disorder and Other Health Impairments. Sisters of Notre Dame 15; Students 72; Lay Teachers 5; Total Staff 20.

SYLVANIA. *Sylvania Franciscan Academy*, 5335 Silica Dr., 43560. Tel: 419-885-3273; Fax: 419-882-5653. Email: sfa_sfa@nwoca.org. Web: www.sylvania-franciscan-academy.net. JoAnn Tallarico, Prin. Preschool & Elementary Extended Care Lay Teachers 30; Students 250.

[G] GENERAL HOSPITALS

TOLEDO. *St. Anne Mercy Hospital*, 3404 W. Sylvania Ave., 43623. Tel: 419-407-2663; Fax: 419-407-3888. Web: www.mhsnr.org. Deacon Michael Pence, Chap.; Karen H. Connors, Pres. & CEO. Total Staff 500 Beds 34,276; Bed Capacity 106.

St. Vincent Mercy Medical Center, 2213 Cherry St., 43608-2691. Tel: 419-251-2536; Fax: 419-251-3872. Email: elizabeth_geiger@mhsnr.org. Web: www.mercyweb.org. Mr. Jeffrey D. Peterson, Pres. & CEO; Elaine Ladd, Admin.; Sharon Belisle, Chap.; Sr. Michelle Gillespie, Chap. Grey Nuns, Affiliated with Mercy Health Partners Sisters 3; Total Staff 4,220; Patients Assisted Annually 325,000; Bed Capacity 576.

LIMA. *St. Rita's Medical Center*, 730 W. Market St., 45801. Tel: 419-227-3361; Fax: 419-226-9750. Web: www.stritas.org. Mr. James P. Reber, Pres.; Mr. Kenneth G. Payne, Vice Pres. Finance; Mr. Mark Skaja, Vice Pres. Mission Svcs.; Rev. Vincent Hoying, C.PP.S., Chap.; Sr. Noel Frey, R.S.M., Chap. Sisters 1; Bed Capacity 437; Patients Assisted Annually 325,000; Total Staff 2,702.

OREGON. *St. Charles Mercy Hospital*, 2600 Navarre Ave., 43616. Tel: 419-696-7200; Fax: 419-696-7328. Web: www.mercyweb.org. Cathleen K. Nelson, Pres. & CEO; Revs. Charles J. Denny, Chap.; Don Corbin, Pastoral Care Dir. & Chap. Mercy Health Partners. Sisters 4; Bed Capacity 250; Patients Assisted Annually 160,507; Total Staff 1,281.

TIFFIN. *Mercy Hospital*, 485 W. Market St., 44883. Tel: 419-447-3130; Fax: 419-448-3131. Email: jane_weber@mhsnr.org. Web: www.mercyweb.org. Sisters of Mercy of the Americas - Catholic Healthcare Partners Sisters 3; Bed Capacity 74; Patients Assisted Annually 96,902; Total Staff 511.

WILLARD. *Mercy Hospital of Willard*, 110 E. Howard St., 44890. Tel: 419-964-5000; Fax: 419-935-8966. Email paula_karr@mhsnr.org. Web: www.mercyweb.org. Mr. Dale E. Thornton, Pres. & CEO. Sisters of Mercy of the Americas Sisters 1; Bed Capacity 25; Total Staff 240; Patients Assisted Annually 58,648.

[H] SPECIAL HOSPITALS AND SANITORIA FOR INVALIDS

GREEN SPRINGS. *St. Francis Health Care Centre*, 401 N. Broadway St., 44836. Tel: 419-639-2626; Fax: 419-639-6225. Email: jsmith@sfhcc.org. Web: www.sfhcc.org. Daniel P. Schwanke, Exec. Dir.; John Yuhas, M.D., Medical Dir.; Rev. Raymond A. Fisher, Chap. Owned by Franciscan Sisters of Our Lady of Perpetual Help (St. Louis, MO), Operated by Franciscan Sisters of Our Lady of Perpetual Help of Ohio Corp. Sisters 1; Bed Capacity 184; Total Assisted 1,312; Total Staff 270.

[I] HOMES FOR AGED

OREGON *Sacred Heart Home*, 934 S. Wynn Rd., 43616. Tel: 419-698-4331; Fax: 419-698-1109. Sr. Judith Mary Meredith, L.S.P. Revs. Jovan Malanyaon (Philippines), Chap.; Richard G. Miller (Retired); Eugene L. Lovisa (Retired); Robert A. Tucceri. Little Sisters of the Poor Sisters 9; Aged Residents 70; Independent Living Apartments 20; Total Staff 90.

SANDUSKY. **The Commons of Providence*, 5000 Providence Dr.. Tel: 419-624-1171; Fax: 419-624-1175. Rick DiDomenico, Admin. Apartment assisted living facility. Bed Capacity 92; Residents 86; Total Staff 85.

Providence Care Center, 2025 Hayes Ave., 44870. Tel: 419-627-2273; Fax: 419-627-0092. Email: agotilik@providencecarecenters.org. Web: www.providencecarecenters.org. Amie Gohlike, Admin.; Rev. Benedict E. Ringholz, Chap. (Retired). Sisters 2; Bed Capacity 138; Patients Assisted Annually 236; Total Staff 170.

**Providence Residential Community Corp Apartment and Villa Home Independent Living*, 5000 Providence Dr., 44870. Tel: 419-624-1171; Fax: 419-624-1175. Rick DiDomenico, Admin. Residents 27.

TIFFIN. *St. Francis Home Inc.*, 182 St. Francis Ave., 44883. Tel: 419-447-2723; Fax: 419-448-1337. Email: ceo@stfrancishome.org. Web: www.stfrancishome.org. Sr. Doretta Meier, O.S.F., Pres. & CEO; Mr. Tim Sacksteder, Dir. Residents 173; Total Staff 250.

TOLEDO. *Oblate Residences*, 1225 Flaire Dr., 43620-1616. Tel: 419-536-3862; Fax: 419-536-6372. c/o 2056 Parkwood Ave., 43620-1616. Apartments 100.

[J] MONASTERIES AND RESIDENCES OF PRIESTS AND BROTHERS

TOLEDO. *Oblates of St. Francis de Sales* Tel: 419-243-5105; Fax: 419-243-8827. Web: www.desales.org.

Provincial Residence, 2056 Parkwood Ave., 43620-1616. Tel: 419-243-5105; Fax: 419-243-8827. Very Rev. David M. Whalen, O.S.F.S., Prov.; Revs. Martin C. Lukas, O.S.F.S., Vocation Dir.; James F. Cryan, O.S.F.S.; James H. Roth, O.S.F.S., Teacher, St. Francis de Sales High School; Bro. Thomas Kovar, O.S.F.S., Teacher Regina Coeli School.

Priests serving elsewhere:

Rev. Kenneth N. McKenna, O.S.F.S., Novice Dir.

152 Plymouth Ave., Buffalo, NY 14201. Tel: 716-886-6597. Rev. Thomas A. Ribits, O.S.F.S.

554 E. Second St., Salt Lake City, UT 84103. Tel: 801-359-8201. Revs. Anthony R. Ceresko, O.S.F.S., Foreign Missions; William G. Auth, O.S.F.S., Mexican Missions; Charles A. LaPenta, O.S.F.S. (Retired).

St. Francis de Sales High School Faculty House 2323 W. Bancroft, 43607. Tel: 419-531-1619; Fax: 419-531-9740. Revs. Ronald W. Olszewski, O.S.F.S., Pres.; John Lehner, O.S.F.S., Chap.; John J. McMenamin, O.S.F.S. (Retired); Paul G. Gillespie, O.S.F.S. (Retired); Daniel J. Earley, O.S.F.S. (Retired); John O. Ebenhoeh, O.S.F.S.; John I. Extejt, O.S.F.S.; Bros. Paul V. Spaeder, O.S.F.S., (Retired); Alfred D. Durant, O.S.F.S.

St. Mary's Home of Erie, 4855 W. Ridge Rd., Rm. 1113, Erie, PA 16506.

Annecy Hall, P.O. Box 43, Childs, MD 21916-0043. Rev. Joseph Baraniewicz, O.S.F.S. (Retired).

St. Francis de Sale High School Endowment Fund, Inc. Rev. Ronald W. Olszewski, O.S.F.S., Pres. Priests 18; Brothers 3.

BELLEVUE. **Mary Lay Center*, 4500 State Rte. 269, P.O. Box 319, 44811-0319. Tel: 419-483-0762; Fax: 419-483-6400. Total in Residence 8.

Residence for Staff of Sorrowful Mother Shrine. Revs. Emil Dinkel, C.PP.S., Prov.; William Eilerman, C.PP.S. (CIN), Admin.; Robert Kunisch, C.PP.S.; George W. Blasick, C.PP.S.; Donald Shea, C.PP.S.; Bro. Charles McCafferty, C.PP.S.

[K] CONVENTS AND RESIDENCES FOR SISTERS

TOLEDO. *Monastery of the Visitation* (Contemplative) Tel: 419-536-1343; Fax: 419-536-0685.

Legal Title: *The Contemplative Order of the Visitation of Toledo, Ohio*, Comtemplative Order of the Sisters of the Visitation of Toledo, Ohio.

1745 Parkside Blvd., 43607-1599. Tel: 419-536-1343; Fax: 419-536-0685. Sr. Sharon Elizabeth Gworek, V.H.M., Supr. Sisters 18; Perpetual Vows 15; In Formation 3.

Notre Dame Convent, 3535 Sylvania Ave., 43623. Tel: 419-475-4909; Fax: 419-724-2640. Email: chug@nda.org. Sr. Mary Charleen Hug, S.N.D. Sisters of Notre Dame Sisters 23.

Notre Dame Provincialate, 3837 Secor Rd., 43623-4484. Tel: 419-474-5485; Fax: 419-474-1336. Email: awillman@toledosnd.org. Web: www.toledosnd.org. Rev. Bruce L. Farmer, Chap.; Sisters Anne Mary Molyet, S.N.D., Prov.; Mary Rose Moser, S.N.D., Local Supr. Sisters of Notre Dame Sisters 253.

Ursuline Convent of the Sacred Heart Tel: 419-536-9587; Fax: 419-536-0019. Email: ursulines@accesstoledo.com. Web: www.toledoursulines.org. *Congregational Offices & Novitiate*, 4045 Indian Rd., 43606. Tel: 419-536-9587; Fax: 419-536-0019. Sr. Donna Frey, O.S.U., Gen. Supr.; Rev. Thomas S. Quinn, Chap. Professed Sisters 79; Associates 121.

FREMONT. *St. Bernardine Home*, 1220 Tiffin St., 43420. Tel: 419-332-8208; Fax: 419-332-4423. Email: mercyfre@ezworks.net. Sisters Joan Marie Warnement, R.S.M., Admin.; Rose Olivieri,

R.S.M., Dir.; Mrs. Carolyn Sue Hartenstein, Health Coord. Sisters of Mercy of the Americas, Cincinnati Regional Community Sisters 35.

SYLVANIA. *Sisters of St. Francis of the Congregation of Our Lady of Lourdes*, 6832 Convent Blvd., 43560-2897. Tel: 419-882-2016; Fax: 419-885-8643. Email: Premley@sistersosf.org. Web: www.sistersosf.org. Sr. Carolyn Giera, O.S.F., Min. Gen.; Very Rev. John A. McClure, J.C.L., Chap. (Retired).
Legal Title: *Sisters of St. Francis of the Congregation of Our Lady of Lourdes, Motherhouse and Novitiate* Professed Sisters 240.

TIFFIN. *St. Francis Convent*, 200 St. Francis Ave., 44883. Tel: 419-447-0435; Fax: 419-447-1612. Email: smagers@tiffinfranciscans.org. Web: www.tiffinfranciscans.org. Sr. Virginia Welsh, Community Min. Motherhouse and Novitiate, Sisters of St. Francis of Tiffin Sisters 132; Total Staff 46.

WHITEHOUSE. *Lial Residence, Sisters of Notre Dame*, 5900 Davis Rd., 43571. Tel: 419-877-0431. Email: mjuliesnd@hotmail.com. Sr. Marie Julie Reineke, S.N.D., Supr. Sisters 29.

[L] RETREAT HOUSES AND CENTERS OF SPIRITUALITY

BELLEVUE. *Sorrowful Mother Shrine*, 4106 State Rte. 269, P.O. Box 319, 44811-0319. Tel: 419-483-3435; Fax: 419-483-6400. Email: sorrowful@cros.net. Revs. William Eilerman, C.PP.S. (CIN), Admin.; George Blasick, C.PP.S.; Robert Kunisch, C.PP.S.; Donald Shea, C.PP.S.; Emil Dinkel, C.PP.S.; Bro. Charles McCafferty, C.PP.S.

CAREY. *Our Lady of Consolation Retreat House*, 321 Clay St., 43316. Tel: 419-396-7970; Fax: 419-396-3355. Email: olcretreathouse@aol.com. Web: www.olcshrine.com. Lucy Pahl, Admin. Diocese of Toledo, auspices of Shrine of Our Lady of Consolation, Carey, OH.

FREMONT. *Our Lady of the Pines Retreat Center*, 1250 Tiffin St., 43420. Tel: 419-332-6522. Email: olprc@ezworks.net. Web: www.pinesretreat.org. Judith Thompson, Exec. Dir. Sisters of Mercy Total in Residence 5; Total Staff 15.

SYLVANIA. *Sophia Counseling Center, Inc.*, 6832 Convent Blvd., 43560. Tel: 419-882-4529; Fax: 419-885-7612. Email: sophiacc@mindspring.com. Sisters Rachel Marie Nijakowski, O.S.F.S., Psychologist (Ohio 4699); Sharon Pollnow, C.S.A., M.Ed., M.S.W., L.I.S.W., Counselor; Ann Hovest, M.S.Ed., Counselor LPCC; Bonnie Schrock, M.A., L.S.W., Counselor; Joan Dvorak, B.Ed., Learning Disability Specialist; Mary Igoe Meyers, LPCC, CCDC III; Sr. Mary Ann Szydlowski, O.S.F.S., R.N., Massage/Polarity Therapy; Mary Goebel-Komala, Ph.D., Clinical Assistant, Counselor. Total Staff 8.

TIFFIN. *St. Francis Spirituality Center*, 36 Melmore St., 44883. Tel: 419-443-1485; Fax: 419-447-1478. Email: retreats@stfrancisspiritualitycenter.org. Web: www.stfrancisspiritualitycenter.org. Judith Thompson, Prog. Dir.; Carol Theis, Admin. Sisters of St. Francis, Tiffin

[M] CAMPUS MINISTRY

TOLEDO. *University of Toledo Campus Ministry* , Attended by Corpus Christi University Parish. , 2955 Dorr St., 43607. Tel: 419-531-4992; Fax: 419-531-1775. Web: www.ccup.org. Rev. James J. Bacik.

BLUFFTON. *Bluffton College Campus Ministry* 160 N. spring St., 45817. Tel: 419-358-8631. Sr. Carol Inkrott, O.S.F., Campus Min.

BOWLING GREEN. *Bowling Green State University Campus Ministry* , Attended by St. Thomas More University Parish. , 425 Thurstin Ave., 43402. Tel: 419-352-7555; Fax: 419-352-7557. Email: srmary@sttoms.com. Web: www.sttoms.com. Very Rev. Kenneth G. Morman, V.F.; Sr. Mary Kuhlman, O.S.F., Pastoral Leader. Total in Residence 27; Total Staff 15.

DEFIANCE. *Defiance College Newman Campus Ministry* 701 N. Clinton, 43512. Tel: 419-784-4010, Ext. 444.

FINDLAY. *University of Findlay Campus Ministry* 422 Western Ave., 45840. Tel: 419-423-2123; Fax: 419-422-2602. Email: dkarch@hotmail.com. Donna Brown, Campus Min.

TIFFIN. *Heidelberg College Campus Ministry* 310 E. Market St., 44883. Email: bbishop@heidelberg.edu. Web: www.heidelberg.edu/offices/student/affairs/religion.html. Bobbi Bishop, Campus Min.

[N] MISCELLANEOUS LISTINGS

TOLEDO. *Catholic Club, The*, 1601 Jefferson Ave., 43624. Tel: 419-243-7255; Fax: 419-243-6337. Email: info@catholicclub.org. Web: www.catholicclub.org. Mr. Paul Szymanski, Dir.

Catholic Foundation of the Diocese of Toledo, P.O. Box 985, 43697-0985. Tel: 419-244-6711; Fax: 419-244-4791. Email: jheinee@toledodiocese.org. Web: www.toledodiocese.org. Mr. John Heinze, Contact Person.

Christ Child Society of Toledo, 2238 Jefferson Ave., 43624. Tel: 419-882-2319; Fax: 419-824-8040. Web: www.ccsoftoledo.org. Carol Koury, Pres.; Gay Deiger, Pres.-Elect; Ellen Hoover, Treas.; Sheila Johnson, Sec.

Double ARC, 3837 Secor Rd., 43623-4484. Tel: 419-479-3060; Fax: 419-724-1372. Sr. Mary Dianne Rumschlag, S.N.D., Pres.

Family Health Plan, 2200 Jefferson Ave., Sixth Floor, 43624. Tel: 419-241-6501; Fax: 419-241-1482. Web: www.familyhealthplan.org. Samatha Platzke, Dir. Affiliated with Mercy Health Partners.

St. Francis de Sales High School Endowment Fund, Inc., 2323 W. Bancroft St., 43607. Tel: 419-531-1618; Fax: 419-531-9740. Email: rolszewski@sfstoledo.org. Web: sfstoledo.org.

Hope Manor, 4702 Violet Rd., 43623. Tel: 419-246-4733. Ms. Ora Milton, Mgr. Units 100.

Saint John's Jesuit High School Foundation, 5901 Airport Hwy., 43615. Tel: 419-865-5743; Fax: 419-861-5002. Email: dvettese@sjjtitans.org. Rev. Donald Vettese, S.J., Pres.

LifeStar Ambulance, Inc. Ambulance & medical transport company. , 732 Main St., 43605. Tel: 419-693-1611; Fax: 419-693-5931. Web: www.mercyweb.org. Cathleen Nelson, Pres.

Madonna Homes, Inc., P.O. Box 4719, 43620. 722 N. Huron St., 43604. Tel: 419-244-3758; Fax: 419-246-4738. Denise Litton, Mgr. Units 196.

Mareda, Inc., P.O. Box 4719, 43620. 1931 Scottwood Ave., Ste. 700, 43620. Tel: 419-242-2300; Fax: 419-246-4703. Email: jkiely@vmc.org. John Kiely, Dir. Housing Agency of the Diocese of Toledo.

St. Marguerite D'Youville Foundation, c/o Diocese of Toledo, P.O. Box 985, 43697-0985. Richard Hanley, Agent. Tel: 419-824-2145 6465 Monroe St. Suite M-8, Sylvania, OH 43560.

Mercy Health System-Northern Region, dba Mercy Health Partners, 2200 Jefferson Ave., 43624. Tel: 419-251-0700; Fax: 419-251-0711. Web: www.mercyweb.org. Mr. Steven L. Mickus, Pres. Total Staff 625.

Michaelmas Manor, Inc., P.O. Box 4719, 43620. 3250-3260 Schneider Rd., 46314. Tel: 419-389-4615; Fax: 419-389-4620. Email: jkiely@vmc.org. Stephanie Downey, Mgr. A corporation organized and operated for the purpose of providing housing facilities and services to elderly persons and handicapped persons. Units for the Elderly 70; Units for the Physically Handicapped 24.

Moody Manor, P.O. Box 4719, 43620. 2293 1/2 Kent St., 43620. Tel: 419-241-6985. Tracy Fails, Mgr. Family & Elderly Units 119.

Office of Global Concerns, P.O. Box 985, 43697-0985. 1933 Spielbusch Ave., 43624. Tel: 419-244-6711; Fax: 419-244-4791. Email: rmishler@toledodiocese.org. Web: www.toledodiocese.org/globalconcerns/index.html. Deacon Richard Mishler. Society for the Propagation of the Faith; Holy Childhood Association; Catholic Relief Services.

Regina Manor, Inc., 3739 N. Erie St., 1B, 43611. Tel: 419-726-6186; Fax: 419-726-6343. Email: jkiely@vmc.org jldowney@hotmail.com. P.O. Box 4719, 43620. Lorrie Richards, Mgr. Family & Elderly Units 180.

St. Vincent Mercy Medical Center Foundation, 2213 Cherry St., 43608. Tel: 419-251-2117. Tony Werner, Pres.

Toledo Catholic Charities Corporation, 1933 Spielbusch Ave., 43624. Tel: 419-244-6711; Fax: 419-244-4791. Web: www.catholiccharitiesnwo.org. John F. Heinze, Dir., Financial Svcs. The Catholic Charities Corporation is the Diocesan vehicle to collect and distribute endowment funds and bequests for charitable purposes.

U.T. Newman Foundation for Student Education and Development, 2955 Dorr St., 43607-3023. Tel: 419-531-4992; Fax: 419-531-1775. Rev. James J. Bacik.

**Women Blessing Women*, 223 Page St., 43620. Tel: 419-241-9789; Fax: 419-241-9791. Email: wbw@womenblessingwomen.org. Web: www.womenblessingwomen.org.

CAREY. *Franciscan Mission Association*, 322 West St., 43316. Tel: 419-396-6455. Email: CarlosBH@aol.com. Bro. Bryan Hoban, O.F.M.Conv., Dir.

DELPHOS. *St. John Parish Foundation, Inc.*, Tel: 419-695-4050; Fax: 419-695-4060.
St. John the Evangelist Church: 331 E. Second St., 45833.

FINDLAY. *St. Michael Schools Educational Foundation*, 422 Western Ave., 45840. Tel: 419-422-2646; Fax: 419-422-2602. Clifford Cook, Pres.

FREMONT. *Delaware Acres, Inc.*, P.O. Box 4719, 43620. 725 S. Buchanan St., 43420. Tel: 419-334-9558; Fax: 419-334-9555. Email: jkiely@vmc.org. Marcella White, Mgr. Family Units 68.

GREEN SPRINGS. *St. Francis Hospital Foundation*, 401 N. Broadway, 44836. Tel: 419-639-2626; Fax: 419-639-6225. Email: graubenolt@sfhcc.org. Web: www.sfhcc.org.

LIMA. *Lima Central Catholic Educational Foundation*, 720 S. Cable Rd., 45805. Tel: 419-222-4276; Fax: 419-222-6933. Email: frdenny@lcchs.edu. Lawrence S. Huffman, Chm.

S.R.H.C. Foundation, 730 W. Market St., 45801-4667. Tel: 419-226-9775; Fax: 419-226-9750. Mr. James P. Reber, Pres.; Mr. Kenneth G. Payne, Sec. & Treas.

OREGON. *St. Charles Mercy Health Foundation*, 2600 Navarre Ave., 43616. Tel: 419-676-7200; Fax: 419-676-7328. Donald Turner, Foundation Chm.

SANDUSKY. *The Providence Fund*, 2023 Hayes Ave., 44870. Tel: 419-627-8707; Fax: 419-627-9535. Email: ProvidenceFund@sbcglobal.net. Margaret Mahnami, Chm.; Angela M. Arreche, Dir. Healthcare Foundation.

SWANTON. *St. Richard's School Endowment Foundation*, 333 Brookside Dr., 43558-1097. Gary Harden, Chmn.

SYLVANIA. *Franciscan Properties, Inc.*, 6832 Convent Blvd., 43560. Tel: 419-882-8373; Fax: 419-882-7360. Email: rwangler@fscsylvania.org. Sr. Jeanne Stack, O.S.F., Pres. Total in Residence 109; Total Staff 3; Apartments 98.

Franciscan Services Corporation, 6832 Convent Blvd., 43560. Tel: 419-882-8373; Fax: 419-882-7360. Mr. John W. O'Connell, Pres.

Franciscan Shelters-Bethany House, 6832 Convent Blvd., 43560. Tel: 419-882-2016. Email: bethany_exdirector@yahoo.com. Kathleen Griffin, Contact Person.

Rosary Care Center, 6832 Convent Blvd., 43560. Tel: 419-824-3600; Fax: 419-824-3931. John W. O'Connell, Pres. & Chm. Bd. of Trustees.

TIFFIN. *St. Francis Home Memorial Foundation, Inc.*, 182 St. Francis Ave., 44883. Tel: 419-447-2723; Fax: 419-448-1337. Email: ceo@stfrancishome.org. Web: www.stfrancishome.org. Cliff Farmer, Chm. Bd. of Directors.

St. Francis Villas, Inc., 182 St. Francis Ave., 44883. Tel: 419-447-2723; Fax: 419-448-1337. Email: ceo@stfrancishome.inc. Web: www.stfrancishome.org. Sr. Judy Leibengood, O.S.F., Chm. & Bd. of Directors.

Mercy Tiffin Health Foundation, 485 W. Market St., P.O. Box 727, 44883. Tel: 419-447-3130; Fax: 419-448-3181. Email: bernie_steinmetz@mhsnr.org. Web: www.mercyweb.org. Dennis Eberly, Chm.

Tiffin Calvert Foundation, P.O. Box 45, 44883. Tel: 419-447-3844. James Ewald, Pres.

Vision Time, Inc., 200 St. Francis Ave., 44883. Tel: 419-243-6723; Fax: 419-243-6723. Email: nancyw@totalink.net. P.O. Box 4887, 43620. Sr. Nancy Westmeyer, O.S.F.

VERMILION. *St. Mary's Church Education Endowment Foundation*, 731 Exchange St., 44089-1330. Tel: 440-967-8711; Fax: 440-967-8712. Email: parish@stmaryvermilion.org. Web: www.stmaryvermilion.org. Mr. David Nocjar, Pres.

WATERVILLE. *Diocesan Fiscal Management Conference - National Office*, P.O. Box 199, 43566-0199. Tel: 419-878-3146; 877-709-3362; Fax: 419-878-7265. Email: 104227.110@compuserve.com. Web: www.dfmconf.org. Rev. Robert J. Yeager, Exec. Dir.

RELIGIOUS INSTITUTES OF MEN REPRESENTED IN THE DIOCESE

For further details refer to the corresponding bracketed number in the Religious Institutes of Men or Women section.

[0480]—*Conventual Franciscans* (Our Lady of Consolation Prov.)—O.F.M.Conv

[0400]—*Crusier Father and Brothers*—O.S.C.

[0690]—*Jesuit Fathers and Brothers*—S.J.

[0910]—*Oblates of St. Francis de Sales*—O.S.F.S.

[1070]—*Redemptorist Fathers* (Baltimore Prov.)—C.SS.R.

[1260]—*Society of Christ*—S.Ch.

[1060]—*Society of the Precious Blood* (Cincinnati Prov.)—C.PP.S.

RELIGIOUS INSTITUTES OF WOMEN REPRESENTED IN THE DIOCESE

[3710]—*Congregation of the Sisters of Saint Agnes*—C.S.A.

[1710]—*Congregation of the Third Order of St. Francis of Mary Immaculate, Joliet, IL*—O.S.F.

[4190]—*The Contemplative Order of the Sisters of the Visitation of Toledo, Ohio*—V.H.M.

[1070-13]—*Dominican Sisters* (Adrian, MI)—O.P.

[1070-09]—*Dominican Sisters* (Racine, WI)—O.P.
[1070-28]—*Dominican Sisters* (Akron, OH)—O.P.
[1170]—*Felician Sisters*—C.S.S.F.
[1310]—*Franciscan Sisters of Little Falls, Minnesota*—O.S.F.
[1430]—*Franciscan Sisters of Our Lady of Perpetual Help*—O.S.F.
[2575]—*Institute of the Sisters of Mercy of the Americas* (Cincinnati, OH)—R.S.M.
[2340]—*Little Sisters of the Poor* (Baltimore Prov.)—L.S.P.
[3130]—*Our Lady of Victory Missionary Sisters*—O.L.V.M.
[0440]—*Sisters of Charity of Cincinnati, Ohio*—S.C.
[0490]—*Sisters of Charity of Montreal (Grey Nuns)*—S.G.M.
[1000]—*Sisters of Divine Providence of Kentucky*—C.D.P.
[2990]—*Sisters of Notre Dame*—S.N.D.
[1530]—*Sisters of St. Francis of the Congregation of Our Lady of Lourdes, Sylvania, Ohio*—O.S.F.
[3930]—*Sisters of St. Joseph of the Third Order of St. Francis*—S.S.J.-T.O.S.F.
[]—*Sisters of the Assumption of the Blessed Virgin Mary of Nairobi*—A.S.N.
[2110]—*Sisters of the Humility of Mary*—H.M
[2270]—*Sisters of the Little Company of Mary*—L.C.M.
[3260]—*Sisters of the Precious Blood* (Dayton, OH)—C.PP.S.
[1760]—*Sisters of the Third Order of St. Francis of Penance and Charity*—O.S.F.
[2150]—*Sisters Servants of the Immaculate Heart of Mary*—I.H.M.
[4120-06]—*Ursuline Nuns of the Congregation of Paris*—O.S.U.
[4120]—*Ursuline Sisters of the Congregation of Paris*—O.S.U.-B.C

DIOCESAN CEMETERIES

TOLEDO. *Calvary*, 2224 Dorr St., 43607. Tel 419-536-3751. Mr. John O'Connell, Mgr.
Mount Carmel, 15 E. Manhattan Blvd., 43608. Tel: 419-241-2015.
Resurrection, 5725 Hill Ave., 43615. Tel: 419-531-5747; Fax: 419-531-0746.
FREMONT. *St. Joseph*, Tel: 419-332-9758.
LIMA. *Gethsemane*, Tel: 419-223-1651.
SANDUSKY. *Calvary*, 2020 Sanford St., 44870. Tel: 419-625-2673.

NECROLOGY

✠ Hoffman, Most Rev. James R., Bishop of the Diocese of Toledo—Died Feb. 8, 2003
† Smith, Rev. Msgr. Bernard E., (Retired)—Died March 29, 2003
† Downey, Timothy M., (Retired)—Died Jan. 21, 2003
† Miller, Gary R., Huron, OH St. Peter—Died April 7, 2003
† Ollivier, John J., (Retired)—Died Feb. 19, 2003

Diocese of Trenton

(Dioecesis Trentonensis)

Most Reverend

JOHN M. SMITH, J.C.D., D.D.

Bishop of Trenton; ordained May 27, 1961; appointed Titular Bishop of Tre Taverne and Auxiliary Bishop of Newark December 1, 1987; consecrated January 25, 1988; appointed Bishop of Pensacola-Tallahassee June 25, 1991; installed July 31, 1991; appointed Coadjutor Bishop of Trenton November 21, 1995; appointed Bishop of Trenton July 1, 1997 *Res.: 901 W. State St., Trenton, NJ 08618.*

Most Reverend

JOHN C. REISS, D.D., J.C.D.

Retired Bishop of Trenton; ordained May 31, 1947; appointed Titular Bishop of Simidicca and Auxiliary of Trenton October 21, 1967; consecrated December 12, 1967; appointed Bishop of Trenton March 4, 1980; installed April 22, 1980; resigned July 1, 1997 *Res.: Villa Vianney,* 2301 Lawrenceville Rd., Trenton, NJ 08648.

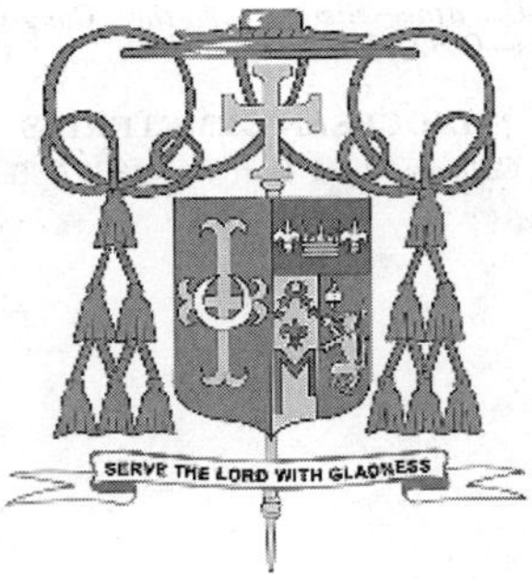

Chancery Office: 701 Lawrenceville Rd., P.O. Box 5147, Trenton, NJ 08638. Tel: 609-406-7400; Fax: 609-406-7412.

Established August 11, 1881.

Square Miles 2,156.

Legal Corporate Title: "The Diocese of Trenton."

Comprises four Counties in the State of New Jersey: Burlington, Mercer, Monmouth and Ocean.

For legal titles of parishes and diocesan institutions, consult the Chancery Office.

STATISTICAL OVERVIEW

Statistical report was not submitted for 2004.

Personnel	
Bishop	1
Retired Bishops	1
Priests: Diocesan Active in Diocese	160
Priests: Diocesan Active Outside Diocese	8
Priests: Retired, Sick or Absent	71
Number of Diocesan Priests	239
Religious Priests in Diocese	43
Total Priests in Diocese	282
Extern Priests in Diocese	40
Ordinations:	
Diocesan Priests	1
Transitional Deacons	6
Permanent Deacons	13
Permanent Deacons in Diocese	276
Total Brothers	72
Total Sisters	433
Parishes	
Parishes	126
With Resident Pastor:	
Resident Diocesan Priests	111
Resident Religious Priests	15
Without Resident Pastor:	
Administered by Priests	1
Missions	11
Professional Ministry Personnel:	
Brothers	4
Sisters	71
Lay Ministers	174
Welfare	
Catholic Hospitals	1
Total Assisted	139,000
Health Care Centers	1
Total Assisted	4,000
Homes for the Aged	1
Total Assisted	384
Residential Care of Children	1
Total Assisted	22
Day Care Centers	7
Total Assisted	650
Specialized Homes	11
Total Assisted	20,806
Special Centers for Social Services	15
Total Assisted	30,000
Residential Care of Disabled	1
Total Assisted	163
Other Institutions	1
Total Assisted	2,000
Educational	
Diocesan Students in Other Seminaries	27
Total Seminarians	27
Colleges and Universities	1
Total Students	2,420
High Schools, Diocesan and Parish	8
Total Students	6,480
High Schools, Private	3
Total Students	1,131
Elementary Schools, Diocesan and Parish	50
Total Students	27,491
Elementary Schools, Private	2
Total Students	594
Non-residential Schools for the Disabled	1
Total Students	18
Catechesis/Religious Education:	
High School Students	1,411
Elementary Students	63,021
Total Students under Catholic Instruction	102,593
Teachers in the Diocese:	
Priests	7
Brothers	14
Sisters	90
Lay Teachers	1,766
Vital Statistics	
Receptions into the Church:	
Infant Baptism Totals	10,446
Adult Baptism Totals	391
Received into Full Communion	445
First Communions	11,589
Confirmations	9,180
Marriages:	
Catholic	2,071
Interfaith	622
Total Marriages	2,693
Deaths	7,182
Total Catholic Population	740,357
Total Population	1,367,348

Former Bishops—Rt. Revs. Michael J. O'Farrell, D.D., consecrated Nov. 1, 1881; died April 2, 1894; James A. McFaul, D.D., LL.D., consecrated Oct. 18, 1894; died June 16, 1917; Most Revs. Thomas J. Walsh, S.T.D., J.C.D., consecrated July 25, 1918; transferred to Newark, NJ, March 2, 1928; John J. McMahon, D.D., consecrated April 26, 1928; died Dec. 31, 1932; Moses E. Kiley, S.T.D., consecrated March 17, 1934; appt. Archbishop of Milwaukee, Jan. 1, 1940; William A. Griffin, D.D., appt. Bishop of Trenton, May 22, 1940; consecrated May 1, 1938; died Jan 1, 1950; George W. Ahr, S.T.D. (Retired), appt. Bishop of Trenton, Jan. 28, 1950; consecrated March 20, 1950; retired June 23, 1979; died May 5, 1993; John C. Reiss, D.D., J.C.D. (Retired), appt. Bishop of Trenton, March 4, 1980; installed April 22, 1980; retired July 1, 1997.

Chancery Office—701 Lawrenceville Rd., P.O. Box 5147, Trenton, 08638-0147. Tel: 609-406-7400; Fax: 609-406-7412.

Vicar General and Moderator of the Curia—Rev. Msgr. Gregory D. Vaughan, V.G., 701 Lawrenceville Rd., Trenton, 08648.

Chancellor—Rev. Msgr. Richard C. Brietske, 701 Lawrenceville Rd., Trenton, 08648.

Episcopal Vicars—Burlington County and Ocean County: Rev. Msgr. Casimir H. Ladzinski. Monmouth and Mercer County: Rev. Msgr. Eugene M. Rebeck.

Vice Chancellors—Rev. Msgr. Edward J. Arnister, J.C.L.; Rev. Joseph N. Rosie, S.T.L.

Assistant Chancellors—Rev. Msgrs. John K. Dermond, J.C.L.; James G. Innocenzi.

Secretary to the Bishop—Rev. Joseph N. Rosie, S.T.L.

Records Manager and Archivist—Sr. Catherine Thibault, S.S.J.

Diocesan Tribunal—701 Lawrenceville Rd., Trenton, 08648. Tel: 609-406-7411; Fax: 609-406-7424.

Judicial Vicar—Rev. Msgr. John K. Dermond, J.C.L.

Associate Judicial Vicar—Rev. Msgr. James G. Innocenzi.

Defender of the Bond—Rev. Peter J. Alindogan, J.C.L.

Promoters of Justice—Rev. Peter J. Alindogan, J.C.L.; Rev. Msgr. Leonard R. Toomey (Retired).

Tribunal Judges—Rev. Msgrs. Edward J. Arnister, J.C.L.; Anthony L. Capitani, J.C.L. (Retired); Rev. Emmett J. Carroll, O.F.M.Conv.; Rev. Msgr. Samuel C. Constance (Retired); Deacon Joseph Hannawacker, J.C.L.; Rev. Louis W. Kralovich; Rev. Msgrs. William E. Maguire, S.T.D. (Retired); Walter E. Nolan; Armand A. Pedata, J.C.D.; Eugene M. Rebeck; Rev. John J. Scully; Rev. Msgr. Joseph C. Shenrock, P.A.; Rev. Ralph W. Stansley; Rev. Msgr. Leonard R. Toomey (Retired); Rev. Charles B. Weiser.

Secretary of the Tribunal and Notary—Ms. Patricia Adamo.

Diocesan Consultors—Rev. Msgr. William F. Fitzgerald (Retired); Revs. Edward J. Griswold; James J. McConnell (Retired); Thomas J. Mullelly, J.D.; Rev. Msgrs. Walter E. Nolan; Hugh F. Ronan; Revs. Joseph S. Tedesco; Kenard J. Tuzeneu; Rev. Msgrs. Gregory D. Vaughan, V.G.; Michael J. Walsh.

Diocesan Council of Priests—Most Rev. John M. Smith, J.C.D., D.D., Pres.; Revs. Michael D. Sullivan, Chm.; Ronald J. Bacovin, Vice Chm.; Stanislaus T. Polczyk, Sec. & Treas.; K. Michael Lambeth, At-Large; Daniel J. Ryan, At-Large.

Council of Deacons and Vicariate Representatives—Deacon JAMES CASA, Pres. Burlington Co.:: Deacons JAMES CASA; FRANK GIGLIO. Mercer Co.:: Deacons THOMAS LAVELLE; WILLIAM A. WILSON. Monmouth Co.:: Deacons JOHN KLINCEWICZ; RAYMOND RAINVILLE. Ocean Co.:: Deacons EDWARD FISCHER; DONALD MCCARRICK; EDUARDO TRANI, At Large.

Diocesan Pastoral Council—Most Rev. JOHN M. SMITH, J.C.D., D.D., Chm.; VACANT, Liaison; Mr. PAUL LAPLANTE, Pres.; Mr. JOSEPH MANZI, Vice Pres. & Sec.

Diocesan Finance Council—Most Rev. JOHN M. SMITH, J.C.D., D.D., Pres.; Mr. LAURENCE M. DOWNES, Chm.; Rev. Msgr. RICHARD C. BRIETSKE; Mr. HARRY W. DWYER; Mr. HARRY R. HILL, Esq.; Mr. BERNARD M. MCGLONE; Mr. ANTHONY J. MINGARINO, C.A.O.; Mr. EMIL SCHROTH JR.; Ms. SUSANNE SVIZENY; Mr. FRANK T. VANGROFSKI; Rev. Msgr. GREGORY D. VAUGHAN, V.G.

Censores Librorum—Rev. Msgr. WILLIAM E. MAGUIRE, S.T.D. (Retired); Rev. JOSEPH N. ROSIE, S.T.L.

Secretariat for Temporal Administration

Secretary—Mr. ANTHONY J. MINGARINO, C.A.O., Pastoral Center, 701 Lawrenceville Rd., Trenton, 08648. Tel: 609-406-7400; Fax: 609-406-7414.

Department of Finance & Resources

Office of Administrative Services—Mr. JOSEPH BIANCHI, Dir., Pastoral Center, 701 Lawrenceville Rd., Trenton, 08648. Tel: 609-406-7400; Fax: 609-406-7413.

Budget Committee—Rev. Msgr. GREGORY D. VAUGHAN, V.G., Chm. Tel: 609-406-7400; Fax: 609-406-7412.

Office of Computer Services—Ms. KATHLEEN MOORE, Dir., Pastoral Center, 701 Lawrenceville Rd., Trenton, 08648. Tel: 609-406-7400; Fax: 609-406-7414.

Office of Finance—Ms. DARYL ROWE, Dir., Pastoral Center, 701 Lawrenceville Rd., Trenton, 08648. Tel: 609-406-7400; Fax: 609-406-7414.

Department of Marketing & Development

Building Commission—Rev. Msgr. RICHARD C. BRIETSKE, Chm.; Deacon WILLIAM A. WILSON, Dir., Pastoral Center, 701 Lawrenceville Rd., Trenton, 08648. Tel: 609-406-7400; Fax: 609-406-7412.

Cemeteries—Rev. Msgr. JAMES H. DUBELL, Dir., St. Mary of the Lakes, 40 Jackson Rd., Medford, 08055. Tel: 609-654-8208; Fax: 609-654-1734.

Expansion Commission—Rev. JOSEPH A. TEDESCO, Chm., Pastoral Center, 701 Lawrenceville Rd., Trenton, 08648. Tel: 609-406-7400; Fax: 609-406-7443.

Office of Stewardship and Development—Mr. JOHN M. BRADY, Dir.; Mrs. BARBARA WARNER, Assoc. Dir., Pastoral Center, 701 Lawrenceville Rd., Trenton, 08648. Tel: 609-406-7400; Fax: 609-406-7443.

Office of Research and Planning—Rev. JOSEPH A. TEDESCO, Dir.; Mr. KENNETH J. NOWAK, Assoc. Dir., Pastoral Center, 701 Lawrenceville Rd., Trenton, 08648. Tel: 609-406-7400; Fax: 609-406-7443.

Secretariat for Catholic Education

Secretary—Dr. JUDITH CAVISTON, Pastoral Center, 701 Lawrenceville Rd., Trenton, 08648. Tel: 609-406-7400; Fax: 609-406-7416.

Office of Catholic Schools

Office of Catholic Schools—Dr. JUDITH CAVISTON, Supt. & Coord., 701 Lawrenceville Rd., Trenton, 08648. Tel: 609-406-7400; Fax: 609-406-7416; MARGARET BOLAND, Sr. Assoc. Supt., Pastoral Center, 701 Lawrenceville Rd., Trenton, 08648. Tel: 609-406-7400; Fax: 609-406-7416. Associate Directors: Sr. DOROTHY PAYNE, S.S.J., Pastoral Center, 701 Lawrenceville Rd., Trenton, 08648. Tel: 609-406-7400; Fax: 609-406-7416; Mrs. MARIANNE FINNEGAN, Pastoral Center, 701 Lawrenceville Rd., Trenton, 08648. Tel: 609-406-7400; Fax: 609-406-7416.

Office of Catechesis—Dr. JUDITH CAVISTON, Dir., Pastoral Center, 701 Lawrenceville Rd., Trenton, 08648. Tel: 609-406-7400; Fax: 609-406-7416; Mr. MARTIN J. ARSENAULT, Sr. Assoc. Dir., 701 Lawrenceville Rd., Trenton, 08648. Tel: 609-406-7400; Fax: 609-406-7418; Mrs. EILEEN HOEFLING, Assoc. Dir., Pastoral Center, 701 Lawrenceville Rd., Trenton, 08648. Tel: 609-406-7400; Fax: 609-406-7418; Ms. TERRY GINTHER, Assoc. Dir., Pastoral Center, 701 Lawrenceville Rd., Trenton, 08648. Tel: 609-406-7400; Fax: 609-406-7418.

Campus Ministry—Dr. JUDITH CAVISTON, Coord., Pastoral Center, 701 Lawrenceville Rd., Trenton, 08648. Tel: 609-406-7400; Fax: 609-406-7416.

CUSP Director—Mrs. JOANN TIER, Pastoral Center, 701 Lawrenceville Rd., Trenton, 08648. Tel: 609-406-7400; Fax: 609-406-7416.

Holy Innocents—Mr. ANGELO ROMANELLO, Pres., 5 Shelburne Dr., Trenton, 08638. Tel: 609-882-4567.

Secretariat for Community Relations

Secretary—Mr. JAMES A. CASSIDY, Pastoral Center, 701 Lawrenceville Rd., Trenton, 08648. Tel: 609-406-7400; Fax: 609-409-7423.

Department of Mission & Church Relations

Ecumenical/Interreligious Affairs—Rev. JEFFREY E. LEE, Dir., Pastoral Center, 701 Lawrenceville Rd., Trenton, 08648. Tel: 609-406-7400; Fax: 609-406-7403.

Pontifical Mission Aid Societies—Rev. Msgr RICHARD L. TOFANI, Dir., Pastoral Center, 701 Lawrenceville Rd., Trenton, 08648. Tel 609-406-7400; Fax 609-406-7421.

Department of Media Relations

Office of Public Relations—Ms. AUDRA MILLER, Diocesan Media Spokesperson, Pastoral Center, 701 Lawrenceville Rd., Trenton, 08648. Tel: 609-406-7400; Fax: 609-406-7412.

The Monitor—Mr. JAMES A. CASSIDY, Gen. Mgr.; Mr. JOSEPH DONADIEU, Editor, Pastoral Center, 701 Lawrenceville Rd., Trenton, 08648. Tel: 609-406-7400; Fax: 609-406-7423.

Office of Radio and TV—Mrs. MARIANNE HARTMAN, Sr. Producer of Communications, Pastoral Center, 701 Lawrenceville Rd., Trenton, 08648. Tel: 609-406-7400; Fax: 609-406-7423.

Secretariat for Ethnic Ministries

Secretary—Ms. ELLIEEN ANCRUM, Pastoral Center, 701 Lawrenceville Rd., Trenton, 08648. Tel: 609-406-7400; Fax: 609-406-7413.

The Black Apostolate—Ms. ELLIEEN ANCRUM, Dir., Pastoral Center, 701 Lawrenceville Rd., Trenton, 08648. Tel: 609-406-7400; Fax: 609-406-7413.

The Haitian Apostolate—Rev. Msgr. JOHN K. DERMOND, J.C.L., Dir. (Trenton Area) St. Francis of Assisi Church, 31 W. Front St., Trenton, 08608. Tel: 609-393-4851; Fax: 609-393-4555; Rev. WILLIAM J. MCLAUGHLIN, Dir. (Asbury Park Area), Holy Spirit Church, 705 Second Ave., P.O. Box 617, Asbury Park, 07712. Tel: 732-775-0030; Fax: 732-775-7358.

The Hispanic Apostolate—Rev. JAVIER DIAZ-MUNOZ, Dir., St. Joseph Church, 540 N. Olden Ave., Trenton, 08638. Tel: 609-394-5757; Fax: 609-599-4402.

The Korean Apostolate—Rev. GABRIEL YONG-HWAN OH, Dir., Immaculate Conception Church, 64 Broad St., Eatontown, 07724. Tel: 732-542-0148; Fax: 732-389-2705.

The Portuguese Apostolate—Rev. JAVIER DIAZ-MUNOZ, Dir., St. Joseph Church, 540 N. Olden Ave., Trenton, 08638. Tel: 609-394-5757; Fax 609-599-4402.

Secretariat for Pastoral Life

Secretary—Rev. RICHARD D. LAVERGHETTA, St. Gregory the Great Church, 4620 Nottingham Way, Trenton, 08690. Tel: 609-587-4877; Fax: 609-538-0192.

Department of Parish Life

Office of Family Life/Respect Life—Rev. JEFFREY E. LEE, Dir.; Mrs. LINDA G. RICHARDSON, Assoc. Dir., Pastoral Center, 701 Lawrenceville Rd., Trenton, 08648. Tel: 609-406-7400; Fax: 609-406-7403.

Office of Parish Services—Mr. JOHN BOUCHER, Dir.; Mrs. DEANNA V. SASS, M.A., Assoc. Dir., Pastoral Center, 701 Lawrenceville Rd., Trenton, 08648. Tel: 609-406-7400; Fax: 609-406-7415.

Scouting—Rev. MICHAEL A. SANTANGELO, Chap., St. Paul Church, 223 E. Union St., Burlington, 08016. Tel: 609-386-0152; Fax: 609-386-0190.

Office of Youth/Young Adult Ministry—Sr. DONNA D'ALIA, R.S.M., Dir.; Ms. MICHELLE HOUMIS, Assoc. Dir., Pastoral Center, 701 Lawrenceville Rd., Trenton, 08648. Tel: 609-406-7400; Fax: 609-406-7419.

Department of Spiritual Renewal

Charismatic Renewal—Rev. H. BRENDAN WILLIAMS, Liaison, St. Veronica Church, 4215 Hwy. 9 N., Howell, 08724. Tel: 732-363-4200; Fax: 732-370-3891. Email: willcron@world.net.att.net.

Cursillo—Rev. JOHN V. BOWDEN, Chap., Church of Epiphany, 615 Thiele Rd., Brick, 08724. Tel: 732-458-0220; Fax: 732-458-6921.

Francis House of Prayer—Sr. MARCELLA SPRINGER, S.S.J., Dir., P.O. Box 392, Rancocas, 08073. Tel: 609-877-0509; Fax: 609-877-5810. Web: www.francishouseofprayer.org. Email: fhop@pics.com.

Legion of Mary—Rev. MICHAEL J. BURNS, Chap., St. Mary Church, 45 Crosswicks St., Bordentown, 08505. Tel: 609-298-0261; Fax: 609-298-7178.

Upper Room—Co-Directors: Sisters MAUREEN CHRISTENSEN, R.S.M.; MAUREEN CONROY, R.S.M.; TRUDY AHERN, S.S.J., W. Bangs Ave. & Rte. 33, Neptune, 07754-1104. Tel: 732-922-0550; Fax: 732-922-3904. Web: www.theupper-room.org. Email: upperroom@bytheshore.com; P.O. Box 1104, Neptune, 07754.

Department of Worship—Rev. SAM A. SIRIANNI, Dir.; Sr. ELEANOR MCCANN, Assoc. Dir., Pastoral Center, 701 Lawrenceville Rd., Trenton, 08648. Tel: 609-406-7400; Fax: 609-406-7403.

Secretariat for Personnel in Ministry

Secretary—Rev. KENARD J. TUZENEU, St. Mary Church, 724 W. Bay Ave., P.O. Box 609, Barnegat, 08005. Tel: 609-698-5531; Fax: 609-698-6255.

Office of Continuing Formation for Priests—Rev. EDWARD J. GRISWOLD, Dir., St. Mary Church, Hwy. 34 & Phalanx Rd., Colts Neck, 07722. Tel: 732-780-2666; Fax: 732-780-0394. Web: www.stmaryscoltsneck.com.

Office of Permanent Deacons—Rev. RALPH W. STANSLEY, Dir. Assistant Directors: Deacons GERALD HENWOOD; NEIL PIRROZZI, Pastoral Center, 701 Lawrenceville Rd., Trenton, 08648. Tel: 609-406-7400; Fax: 609-406-7417.

Office of Priest Personnel—Rev. RONALD J. BACOVIN, Dir., Pastoral Center, 701 Lawrenceville Rd., Trenton, 08648. Tel: 609-406-7400; Fax: 609-406-7422.

Delegate for Religious—Sr. DONNA WATSON, I.H.M., Delegate, Pastoral Center, 701 Lawrenceville Rd., Trenton, 08648. Tel: 609-406-7400; Fax: 609-406-7413.

Office of Vocations—Rev. K. MICHAEL LAMBETH, Dir., Sacred Heart Church, 343 S. Broad St., Trenton, 08608. Tel: 609-393-2801; Fax: 609-989-8997. Web: www.godiscallingyou.com; Ms. NANCY MADDEN, Exec. Asst., Pastoral Center, 701 Lawrenceville Rd., Trenton, 08648. Tel: 609-406-7400; Fax: 609-406-7413.

Secretariat for Social Justice & Social Services

Secretary—Rev. THOMAS J. MULLELLY, J.D., Aquinas Institute, 65 Stockton St., Princeton, 08540. Tel: 609-924-1820; Fax: 609-219-9203.

Department of Social Justice

Migration & Refugee Services—Sr. JANET YURKANIN, I.H.M., Dir., 33 W. Front St., Trenton, 08608. Tel: 609-394-8299; Fax: 609-394-0240. Email: jyurkanin@aol.com.

Office of Pastoral Care—Sr. REGINA J. WHITE, M.S.C., Dir., Pastoral Center, 701 Lawrenceville Rd., Trenton, 08648. Tel: 609-406-7400; Fax: 609-406-7412.

Prison Ministry—Rev. ROBERT R. SCHULZE, Dir., Pastoral Center, 701 Lawrenceville Rd., Trenton, 08648. Tel: 609-406-7400; Fax: 609-406-7413.

Office of Social Concerns—Rev. RONALD CIOFFI, Dir., St. Joseph Church, 376 Maple Pl., Keyport, 07735. Tel: 732-264-0322; Fax: 732-888-3280. Email: stjoeskeyport@aol.com.

Victim Assistance Coordinator—Rev. Msgr. GREGORY D. VAUGHAN, V.G. Tel: 609-406-7400. Email: gvaugh@dioceseoftrenton.org.

Department of Social Services

Catholic Charities—Mr. FRANCIS E. DOLAN, Dir., 383 W. State St., P.O. Box 1423, Trenton, 08607-1423. Tel: 609-394-5181; Fax: 609-695-6978. Web: www.catholiccharitiestrenton.org.

Catholic Relief Services and Human Development—Rev. BRIAN T. BUTCH, Dir., Holy Innocents Church, 3455 W. Bangs Ave., P.O. Box 806, Neptune, 07753. Tel: 732-922-4242; Fax: 732-922-2848.

Martin House—Rev. BRIAN MCCORMICK, Dir., 802 E. State St., P.O. Box 1025, Trenton, 08606. Tel: 609-989-8143; Fax: 609-989-0933. Email: mhlcmaster@aol.com.

Mount Carmel Guild—Mr. RUSSELL J. HANSEL, Exec. Dir., 73 N. Clinton Ave., Trenton, 08609. Tel: 609-392-5159; Fax: 609-392-5903. Email: mtcarmelguild@aol.com.

St. Vincent DePaul Society—Mrs. MARGE MCGINLEY, Dir., Sacred Heart Church, 260 High St., Mount Holly, 08060. Tel: 609-267-0209; Fax: 609-267-9293.

CLERGY, PARISHES, MISSIONS AND PAROCHIAL SCHOOLS

CITY OF TRENTON
(MERCER COUNTY)

1—ST. MARY CATHEDRAL (1868), (Hispanic), [CEM] Rev. Msgr. John K. Dermond, J.C.L., Rector; Revs. Rodolfo Gonzalez; Pedro L. Bou, S.V.D.; Javier Diaz; Deacons Emiliano Vazquez; Jose Beauchamps; Luis Ramos; Juan A. Rivera Jr.
Res.: 151 N. Warren St., 08608. Tel: 609-396-8447; Fax: 609-396-5624.

Catechesis/Religious Program—Tel: 609-448-2872; Fax: 609-278-7526. Sr. Maria Lorando, D.R.E. & Dir.; Mrs. Marisol Rodriguez, D.R.E. Students 307.

2—St. Anthony (1921), (Irish—Italian), Rev. Msgr. Thomas N. Gervasio; Deacon Dennis Slavin.
Res.: 626 S. Olden Ave., 08629. Tel: 609-586-4181; Fax: 609-586-7206.
School—St. Anthony Elementary School, 177 Leonard Ave., 08610. Tel: 609-586-5888; Fax: 609-631-9295. Sr. Marie Angela Presenza, O.S.F., Prin. Sisters 1; Lay Teachers 23; Students 300.
High School—McCorristin High School, 175 Leonard Ave., 08610. Tel: 609-586-3705; Fax: 609-586-6584. Mr. Timothy M. Lynch, Prin. Sisters 3; Lay Teachers 23; Students 347.
Catechesis/Religious Program—530 South Olden Ave., 08629. Fax: 609-631-9295. Ms. Sharon Flynn, D.R.E. Students 180.
Convent—530 S. Olden Ave., 08629. Tel: 609-586-4355.

3—Blessed Sacrament (1912), Rev. Albert Ricciardelli, Admin.; Deacon Louis F. Slee.
Res.: 716 Bellevue Ave., 08618. Tel: 609-396-9231; Fax: 609-396-6432.
Catechesis/Religious Program—Ms. Sharon Flynn, Dir. Students 36.
Station—Mercer Hospital, Tel: 609-394-4000.

4—St. Francis of Assisium (1864), (German), [CEM 2] Rev. Msgr. John K. Dermond, J.C.L.
Res.: 31 W. Front St., 08608. Tel: 609-393-4851; Fax: 609-393-4555.
Catechesis/Religious Program—Tel: 609-394-5841. Sr. Frances Paglione, R.S.M., D.R.E. Students 42.

5—St. Gregory the Great (1953), Revs. Richard D. LaVerghetta; Damian McElroy; Sr. Jean Makovsky, O.S.F., Pastoral Assoc.; Mrs. Lori LaPlante, Pastoral Assoc.; Deacons Richard D'Angelo; John Groffie; Allan Parr; Neil Pirozzi; William A. Wilson; Ralph LaMachia; Andrew A. Sabados Sr.; Joseph E. Latini.
Res.: 4620 Nottingham Way, Hamilton Square, 08690. Tel: 609-587-4877; Fax: 609-588-0192.
School—4680 Nottingham Way, Hamilton Square, 08690. Tel: 609-587-1131; Fax: 609-587-0322. Regina McIntyre, Prin. Sisters 1; Lay Teachers 51; Students 529.
Catechesis/Religious Program—Fax: 609-587-0322. Sr. Alice Gallagher, S.S.J., D.R.E. Students 1,750.
Convent—13 Stanley Dr., Robbinsville, 08691. Tel: 609-259-3384.

6—St. Hedwig (1904), (Polish), [CEM 2] Revs. Henry F. Schabowski; Arcadius Klejnowski; Deacons Anthony Vogel; Barry Zadworny.
Res.: 872 Brunswick Ave., 08638. Tel: 609-396-9068; Fax: 609-396-3171.
Catechesis/Religious Program—Mrs. Marion Vogel, Dir. Students 200.

7—Holy Angels (1921), Revs. Sam A. Sirianni; Garrett J. Fitzgerald (MET); Deacons Daniel Chase; Manuel Iglesias; Thomas Lavelle; Salvatore Marcello; Robert Tharp; Sr. Sandra Kulick, Pastoral Ministry. Tel: 609-396-2220.
Res.: 1733 S. Broad St., 08610. Tel: 609-396-8316; Fax: 609-393-3747.
School—10 New Cedar Ln., 08610. Tel: 609-396-8916; Fax: 609-396-8903. Donna Tyburski, Prin. Lay Teachers 12; Students 250.
Catechesis/Religious Program—Tel: 609-695-1024. Sr. Jane Urban, R.S.M., D.R.E. Students 210.

8—Holy Cross (1891), (Polish), [CEM] Rev. Msgr. Edward J. Arnister, J.C.L.; Rev. Leslaw P. Tymoszuk; Deacon John R. Grussler.
Res.: 201 Adeline St., 08611. Tel: 609-393-4826; Fax: 609-278-1192.
School—22 Grand St., 08611. Tel: 609-393-8407; Fax: 609-393-5313. Patricia Palinczar, Prin. Lay Teachers 22; Students 250.
Catechesis/Religious Program—Tel: 609-393-3380. Mrs. Rosemarie Micharski, Dir. Students 80.

9—Immaculate Conception (1874), Revs. Raynald Yudin, O.F.M.Conv.; George Sabol; Christopher Balas, O.F.M.Conv.; Bro. Kenneth Lucas, O.F.M.Conv.; Sr. Kathleen Boland, S.S.N.D., Pastoral Assoc.
Res.: 540 Chestnut Ave., 08611. Tel: 609-392-5193; Fax: 609-989-1913.
School—520 Chestnut Ave., 08611. Tel: 609-396-8347; Fax: 609-396-0714. Anne Reap, Prin. Sisters of St. Francis of Philadelphia 1; Lay Teachers 20; Students 240.
Catechesis/Religious Program—Tel: 609-695-6541. Mr. Raymond Bucci, Dir. Students 100.
Convent—171 Division St., 08611. Tel: 609-396-9824.

10—Incarnation (1947), Rev. Msgr. Hugh F. Ronan; Rev. Leon Inverso. In Res., Rev. Msgr. Henry S. Bogdan (Retired); Deacon Thomas H. Rivella.
Res.: 1545 Pennington Rd., 08618. Tel: 609-882-2860; Fax: 609-637-0460.
School—1555 Pennington Rd., 08618. Tel: 609-882-3228; Fax: 609-671-1629. Sr. Margaret Fagan, Prin. Sisters, Servants of the Immaculate Heart of Mary (Immaculata, PA) 2; Lay Teachers 10; Students 232.
Catechesis/Religious Program—Tel: 609-882-5116. Sr. Mary Ellen Diehl, I.H.M., Dir. Students 210.
Convent—45 Harrop Pl., 08618.

11—St. James (1919), Revs. Boniface Ruzich, O.SS.T.; Philip Cordisco, O.SS.T.
Res.: 29 E. Paul Ave., 08638. Tel: 609-393-4403; Fax: 609-393-6078.
Catechesis/Religious Program—Students 8.
Convent—1016 Princeton Ave., 08638. Tel: 609-695-4088. Sr. Nancy DeAngelo, M.P.F.

12—St. Joachim (1901), (Italian), Rev. Jeffrey E. Lee; Deacon Guido Mattozzi.
Res.: 19 Bayard St., 08611. Tel: 609-695-6089; Fax: 609-695-4376.
Catechesis/Religious Program—Tel: 609-695-6089, Ext. 115. Mr. Edwin Sevilland, Coordinator, Faith Formation. Total Enrollment 22.

13—St. Joseph (1891), (Spanish), Revs. Javier A. Diaz-Munoz; Miguel D. Valle-Toro.
Res.: 540 N. Olden Ave., 08638. Tel: 609-394-5757; Fax: 609-599-4402.
Catechesis/Religious Program—Tel: 609-394-3580; Fax: 609-394-3418. Ms. Marlene Lao'-Collins, Dir. Students 182.
Station—Helene Fuld Hospital, Tel: 609-394-6000.

14—St. Michael (1921), (Slovak), Rev. Msgr. James G. Innocenzi; Rev. Henry Militante.
Res.: 1130 Brunswick Ave., 08638. Tel: 609-393-4050; Fax: 609-393-7335.
Catechesis/Religious Program—Tel: 609-393-4563; Fax: 609-393-3773. Students 70.

15—Our Lady of Good Counsel (1942), Rev. Ralph W. Stansley; Deacon Robert Brady.
Res.: 137 W. Upper Ferry Rd., West Trenton, 08628. Tel: 609-882-3277; Fax: 609-882-4375.
Catechesis/Religious Program—Tel: 609-883-9005. Sr. Marie Therese Staiger, Dir. Students 112.

16—Our Lady of Mount Carmel, Closed., For Sacramental records please contact St. Mary Cathedral, Trenton.

17—Our Lady of Sorrows (1939), Revs. Joseph Tedesco; Adam Midor; Deacons Joseph Malloy; Jeffery Pierfy; Tim Moore; Kevin J. O'Boyle.
Res.: 3816 E. State St. Ext., 08619. Tel: 609-587-4372; Fax: 609-587-7998.
School—3800 E. State St. Ext., 08619. Tel: 609-587-4140; Fax: 609-584-8853. Elizabeth Komar, Prin. Lay Teachers 26; Students 418.
Catechesis/Religious Program—3800 E. State St. Ext., 08619. Tel: 609-587-2555; Fax: 609-587-4213. Mrs. Rita Lynn Everist, D.R.E. Lay Teachers 55; Students 675.
Station—Mercer County Geriatric, Tel: 609-588-5859.

18—Our Lady of the Divine Shepherd (1941), (African American), Rev. Edward Tetteh, S.V.D. (CHI).
Res.: 72 Pennington Ave., 08618. Tel: 609-393-4493; Fax: 609-989-7510.
Catechesis/Religious Program—Patricia Vincent, Dir. Students 32.

19—SS. Peter and Paul (1899), (Slovak), [CEM] Revs. Francis Zalewski; George A. Medina; Deacon Benito Torres.
Res.: 480 Centre St., 08611. Tel: 609-346-2214.
Church: 480 Second St., 08611.
Catechesis/Religious Program—Students 71.

20—St. Raphael (1943), Rev. Msgr. Gregory D. Vaughan, V.G.; Revs. Peter James R. Alindogan; Michael B. Figler; Deacon Richard Arcari.
Res.: 3500 S. Broad St., Hamilton, 08610. Tel: 609-585-7049; Fax: 609-585-5876.
School—151 Gropp Ave., 08610. Tel: 609-585-7733; Fax: 609-581-8436. Diane M. Kowalewski, Prin. Sisters 2; Lay Teachers 16; Students 266.
Catechesis/Religious Program—151 Gropp Ave., 08610. Tel: 609-585-3848; Fax: 609-585-4925. Mr. John Margicin, D.R.E. Students 487.
Convent—3472 Broad St., 08610. Tel: 609-585-8203; Fax: 609-585-5536. Contemplative Sisters of the Good Shepherd 6.
Convent—68 Lakeview Ct., 08620. Tel: 609-585-7041. Sisters 2.
Station—Robert Wood Johnson University Hospital at Hamilton Hamilton. Tel: 609-585-7900.

21—Sacred Heart (1814), Rev. K. Michael Lambeth; Deacon Juan A. Valentin.
Res.: 343 S. Broad St., 08608. Tel: 609-393-2801; Fax: 609-989-8997.
Catechesis/Religious Program—Mrs. Donna Lee-Kuebler, Dir. Students 72.

22—St. Stanislaus (1890), (Polish), [CEM] Rev. Msgr. Edward J. Arnister, J.C.L.; Rev. Stanislaus T. Polczyk; Deacon Frank Sowa.
Res.: 60 Randall Ave., 08611. Tel: 609-396-9366; Fax: 609-396-3346.
Catechesis/Religious Program—Tel: 609-695-6424. Sr. Karen Crawford, F.SS.J., D.R.E. Students 20.
Convent—333 Home Ave., 08611.

23—St. Stephen (1903), (Hungarian), [CEM] Rev. Francis Zalewski.
Mailing Address: P.O. Box 4563, 08611. Tel: 609-394-5965.

24—St. Vincent de Paul (1954), Revs. Stanley Krzyston; Rogatus Mpeka.
Res.: 555 Allentown Rd., Yardville, 08620. Tel: 609-585-6470; Fax: 609-585-0137.
Catechesis/Religious Program—Tel: 609-585-5484. Johanna Kraemer, D.R.E. Students 259.

OUTSIDE THE CITY OF TRENTON

Allentown, Monmouth Co., St. John (1878), [CEM] Rev. Patrick J. Castles; Deacon Frank Prihoda.
Res.: 1282 Yardville-Allentown Rd., 08501-1830. Tel: 609-259-3391; Fax: 609-259-0313.
Catechesis/Religious Program—Tel: 609-259-3586; Fax: 609-259-0313. Mrs. Maureen Maglio, D.R.E. Students 443.

Asbury Park, Monmouth Co.

1—Holy Spirit (1879), [CEM] Rev. William J. McLaughlin; Deacons Joseph D. Carroll; Edner Andre.
Res.: 705 2nd Ave., P.O. Box 617, 07712. Tel: 732-775-0030; Fax: 732-775-7358.
Catechesis/Religious Program—Students 13.
Mt. Calvary Cemetery—Rte. 66 and Neptune Blvd., Box 2037, Ocean, 07712. Tel: 732-775-3320.

2—Our Lady of Mt. Carmel (1905), (Italian), Revs. Gerard F. Lynch, O.SS.T.; Kenneth G. Borgesen, O.SS.T.; Deacon Kenneth M. McKenna.
Res.: 805 Pine St., 07712. Tel: 732-775-1056; Fax: 732-775-8767.
School—First Ave. & Pine St., 07712. Tel: 732-775-8989; Fax: 732-775-0108. Linda Hurley, Prin. Sisters 2; Lay Teachers 15; Students 160.
Catechesis/Religious Program—Tel: 732-988-5060. Sr. Christina Aldarelli, I.H.M., D.R.E. Students 254.

3—St. Peter Claver (1943), (African American), Revs. Marek Pardon, S.V.D. (WH); Alfred Ayem, S.V.D.
Res.: 108 Ridge Ave., 07712. Tel: 732-775-4157; Fax: 732-774-4531.
Catechesis/Religious Program—Mrs. Helen Jackson, D.R.E. Students 40.

Atlantic Highlands, Monmouth Co., St. Agnes (1890), Rev. Robert M. Tynski; Deacon Raymond Rainville.
Res.: 103 Center Ave., 07716. Tel: 732-291-0272; Fax: 732-291-4982.
School—55 South Ave., 07716. Tel: 732-291-1050; Fax: 732-872-2293. Janet McGee, Prin. Lay Teachers 19; Students 250.
Catechesis/Religious Program—Tel: 732-291-2035. Mrs. Margaret Krasutsky, D.R.E. Students 420.
Convent—44 South Ave., 07716. Tel: 732-291-8246.

Avon, Monmouth Co., St. Elizabeth (1907), Rev. Joseph A. Radomski.
Res.: 424 Lincoln Ave., 07717. Tel: 732-774-4089; Fax: 732-774-5848.
Catechesis/Religious Program—Mrs. Beatrice Murday, D.R.E. Students 210.

Barnegat, Ocean Co., St. Mary (1942), [CEM] Revs. Kenard J. Tuzeneu; John T. Jakub; Deacons Robert Armstrong; Richard Hambleton; James Johnson; Earl Lombardo; Patrick Martin; Joseph A. Fiorillo; Ronald Haunss; Thomas C. Topoleski.
Res.: 747 West Bay Ave., P.O. Box 609, 08005-0609. Tel: 609-698-5531; Fax: 609-698-6255.
Catechesis/Religious Program—Tel: 609-597-7600; Fax: 609-597-7178. Mrs. Joan Haldenwang, D.R.E. Students 1,739.

Bay Head, Ocean Co., Sacred Heart (1913), Rev. Patrick F. Magee; Deacons John Czarnecki; Richard Tobin.
Res.: 751 Main Ave., 08742. Tel: 732-899-1398; Fax: 732-899-2233.
Catechesis/Religious Program—Students 89.

Bayville, Ocean Co., St. Barnabas (1966), Revs. Joseph P. McLaughlin; Kevin T. Keelen, Admin.; Sr. Patricia Lally, O.P., Pastoral Assoc.; Deacons Michael A. Taylor, Pastoral Assoc.; Peter M. Clausen; James H. Cummings; Jack Grimes; James McGrath; Michael Taylor.
Res.: 33 Woodland Rd., P.O. Box I, 08721. Tel: 732-269-2208; Fax: 732-269-2557.
Catechesis/Religious Program—Mary Britanak, D.R.E. Students 1,173.

Belmar, Monmouth Co., St. Rose (1888), Rev. Msgr. Casmir H. Ladzinski; Rev. William J. Lago; Deacons Normand C. Bailey; Eugene G. Malhame Jr.
Res.: 603 Seventh Ave., 07719. Tel: 732-681-0512; Fax: 732-280-3107.
School—605 Sixth Ave., 07719. Tel: 732-681-5555; Fax: 732-681-5890. Charlene Mokos Hoverter, Prin. Sisters 1; Lay Teachers 24; Students 472.
High School—607 Seventh Ave., 07719. Tel: 732-681-2858; Fax: 732-280-2745. Dr. Michelle Campbell, Prin. Sisters 6; Lay Teachers 47; Students 650.

Catechesis/Religious Program—Tel: 732-681-6266. Sr. Cecelia Leipert, S.S.J., D.R.E. Students 365.
Convent—610 Eighth Ave., 07719. Tel: 732-681-1039.

BEVERLY, BURLINGTON CO., ST. JOSEPH (1864), Rev. Michael J. Lynch; Deacons Herman J. Mosteller; Matthew J. Stap, (Retired); Ronald J. Ulmer; Charles A. Perkins; Michael P. Hagan.
Res.: 524 Warren St., 08010. Tel: 609-387-0172; Fax: 609-386-8535.
Catechesis/Religious Program—524 Warren St., 08010. Tel: 609-387-2928. JoAnn Di Noia, D.R.E. Students 102.

BORDENTOWN, BURLINGTON CO., ST. MARY (1837), [CEM] Rev. Michael J. Burns; Deacons David M. Harris Jr.; Harry A. Putnam; Gary T. Richardson; Thomas F. Shea.
Res.: 45 Crosswicks St., 08505. Tel: 609-298-0261; Fax: 609-298-7178.
School—30 Elizabeth St., 08505. Tel: 609-298-1448; Fax: 609-298-3803. Mary Ellen Moss, Prin. Lay Teachers 13; Students 171.
Catechesis/Religious Program—Tel: 609-291-8281; Fax: 609-298-7178. Mrs. Barbara Markowski, D.R.E. Students 463.

BRADLEY BEACH, MONMOUTH CO., ASCENSION (1907), Rev. Robert A. Connors, Admin.; Deacons John Gerard; James McNulty.
Res.: 501 Brinley Ave., 07720. Tel: 732-774-0456; Fax: 732-775-9335.
Catechesis/Religious Program—Joan Royere, Dir. Students 152.

BRANT BEACH, OCEAN CO., ST. FRANCIS OF ASSISI (1971), Revs. Andrew J. Reitz, O.F.M.; Kevin Daly, O.F.M.; Stephen Kluge, O.F.M.; John R. Ullrich, O.F.M. (BO); Bro. Kevin Kriso, O.F.M.; Deacons Albert J. Schwind; James Dougherty; George Walker; Richard Titmas; Robert Cunningham.
Office—4700 Long Beach Blvd., 08008-3926. Tel: 609-494-8813; Fax: 609-494-1466.
Catechesis/Religious Program—Sr. Sharon Desipio, S.F.O., D.R.E. Students 585.
Mission—St. Thomas Aquinas 2nd & Atlantic, Beach Haven, Ocean Co. 08008. Tel: 609-492-2633.
Mission—St. Clare 56th & Long Beach Blvd., Loveladies, Ocean Co. 08008. Tel: 609-494-6662.
Mission—St. Thomas of Villanova 13th & Long Beach Blvd., Surf City, Ocean Co. 08008. Tel: 609-494-2371.

BRICK TOWN, OCEAN CO.
1—ST. DOMINIC (1962), Revs. James J. Brady; Joseph Gnarackatt; Alejandro Gronifilo; Deacons Damian Ayers; Gerald Riedinger; Edward Buecker; Sr. Silvia Asselin, M.S.C., Pastoral Ministry.
Res.: 250 Old Squan Rd., 08724. Tel: 732-840-1410; Fax: 732-840-0522.
School—Tel: 732-840-1412; Fax: 732-840-6457. Carol Bathmann, Prin. Lay Teachers 31; Students 598.
Catechesis/Religious Program—Mrs. Ann M. Cramer, D.R.E. Students 850.
2—EPIPHANY (1973), Revs. John V. Bowden; Cesar R. Anson; Deacons Ron Nowak; Michael Mullarkey; William Heard; Thomas Dello Russo; Louis Commisso.
Res.: 615 Thiele Rd., 08724. Tel: 732-458-0220; Fax: 732-458-0855.
Catechesis/Religious Program—Tel: 732-785-0576; 732-785-0872; Fax: 732-458-0855. Mrs. Corey Viola, D.R.E. Students 633.
3—VISITATION (1942), Revs. William M. Dunlap; James J. Sauchelli; Velanmarukudiyil Christudasl, O.S.B.; Deacons Edward Fischer III; Salvatore Vicari; Leonard Kruk; Bradford A. Krupa; David S. Kohut.
Res.: 730 Lynnwood Ave., 08723-5397. Tel: 732-477-0028; Fax: 732-477-1274.
Catechesis/Religious Program—Tel: 732-477-5217. Mrs. Nancy Grodberg, D.R.E. Students 1,310.

BROWNS MILLS, BURLINGTON CO., ST. ANN (1906), Revs. Edwin J. Mathias; Thomas Kunnath; Deacons Daniel Earley; Walter Price; Frank Sherpensky; Michael O'Brien.
Church & Res.: 22 Trenton Rd., 08015. Tel: 609-893-3246; Fax: 609-893-8056.
Catechesis/Religious Program—Students 374.
Station—Burlington Co. Minimum Security Jail Pemberton Township.
Station—Burlington Co. Juvenile Detention Center Pemberton.
Station—Deborah Heart & Lung Center, Tel: 609-893-6611.
Station—Evergreen Park, Buttonwood Hall, Tel: 609-726-7000.

BURLINGTON, BURLINGTON CO.
1—ALL SAINTS (1910), (Polish), Rev. Jacek Labinski.
Res.: 502 High St., 08016. Tel: 609-386-0152; Fax: 609-386-0190.
School—510 High St., 08016. Tel: 609-387-9207; Fax: 609-387-1358. Mrs. Linda Weight, Prin. Lay Teachers 13; Students 185.
Catechesis/Religious Program—Mrs. Ellen A. Tiene, D.R.E. Students 74.
Convent—500 High St., 08016. Tel: 609-383-0951.
2—ST. PAUL (1864), Revs. Michael A. Santangelo; Clodorico V Bagabaldo; Deacons George Carlin; Francis A. Jones; Alfred Pennise.
Res.: 223 E. Union St., 08016. Tel: 609-386-0163; Fax: 609-383-0085.
School—6th & James Sts., 08016. Tel: 609-386-1645; Fax: 609-386-1345. Sr. Peter Damian, R.S.M., Prin. Sisters of Mercy 1; Lay Teachers 21; Students 415.
Catechesis/Religious Program—Miss Anna Jones, D.R.E. Students 314.
Convent—122 James St., 08016-3319. Tel: 609-386-4083.

CINNAMINSON, BURLINGTON CO., ST. CHARLES BORROMEO (1961), Rev. Thomas J. Triggs Deacons William S. Sepich; William Gallagher; Carl Sondeen; Gerald Doughty; John Hvizdos; Sr. Jeanne Belli, S.S.J., Pastoral Assoc.
Res.: 2226 Riverton Rd., P.O. Box 2220, 08077. Tel: 856-829-3322; Fax: 856-829-1852.
School—2500 Branch Pike, 08077. Tel: 856-829-2778; Fax: 856-829-3411. Mrs. Patricia Sacks, Prin. Sisters of Mercy 1; Lay Teachers 20; Students 333.
Catechesis/Religious Program—Tel: 856-829-9119. Kathy Kraemer, D.R.E. Students 820.
Convent—201 Wayne Dr., 08077. Tel: 856-829-8883.

COLTS NECK, MONMOUTH CO., ST. MARY (1887), Rev. Edward J. Griswold; Deacons Paul Daniele; Caleb Weller; Ralph Imholte.
Res.: Hwy. 34 & Phalanx Rd., P.O. Box H, 07722. Tel: 732-780-2666; Fax: 732-780-0394.
Catechesis/Religious Program—Tel: 732-294-8841. Mrs. Joan Celiano, D.R.E. Students 1,320.

DEAL, MONMOUTH CO., ST. MARY OF THE ASSUMPTION (1901), Revs. John G. DeSandre; Matthew Thelly; Deacon John McCabe.
Res.: 46 Richmond Ave., 07723. Tel: 732-531-1409; Fax: 732 531-3931.
School—73 Wickapecko Dr., Ocean, 07712. Tel: 732-531-4433; Fax: 732-531-4054. Marie Busch-Beebe, Prin. Lay Teachers 16; Students 210.
Catechesis/Religious Program—Tel: 732-531-1889. Mrs. Maureen Melofchik, D.R.E. Students 260.

DELRAN, BURLINGTON CO., HOLY NAME (1972), Revs. Michael J. O'Connor; Joy T. Chacko (India); Deacons Jim Mamaloris; Joseph Barbara.
Res.: 260 Conrow Rd., P.O. Box 1099 08075. Tel: 856-461-6555; Fax: 856-461-1293.
Catechesis/Religious Program—Patricia Higgins, D.R.E.; Kathy McHugh, D.R.E. Students 746.

EATONTOWN, MONMOUTH CO.
1—ST. DOROTHEA (1905), Revs. G. William Evans; Angelito Anarcon; Deacons Stephen W. Andrews; Edward R. Herr.
Res.: 240 Broad St., 07724. Tel: 732-542-0148; Fax: 732-542-1531.
Catechesis/Religious Program—Tel: 732-542-0303. Mrs. Jean Arnold, Dir. Students 560.
2—IMMACULATE CONCEPTION (1984), (Korean), Rev. Gabriel Yong-Hwan Oh.
Res.: 64 Broad St., 07724. Tel: 732-389-3830; Fax: 732-389-2705.
Catechesis/Religious Program—Mrs Gratia Min, Dir. Students 59.

ENGLISHTOWN, MONMOUTH CO., OUR LADY OF MERCY (1948), [CEM] Rev. Charles R. Valentine.
Res.: 58 Main St., 07726. Tel: 732-446-6324; Fax: 732-446-5179.
Catechesis/Religious Program—Tel: 732-786-1835. Mrs. Cathy Napolitano, D.R.E. Students 730.
Mission—St. Joseph [CEM] 58 Main St., Perrineville, Monmouth Co. 07726. Tel: 732-446-6324.

EVESHAM TOWNSHIP, BURLINGTON CO., ST. ISAAC JOGUES (1996), Rev. Phillip C. Pfleger; Deacons Edward Gwiazda; Frank E. Giglio; Armando Acosta.
3 Lord Pl., Marlton, 08053. Tel: 856 797-0999; Fax: 856-797-0463.
Catechesis/Religious Program—Tel: 856-797-1811. Ms. Martha Bachman, D.R.E. Students 610.

FAIR HAVEN, MONMOUTH CO., NATIVITY (1954), Revs. Jerome M. Nolan; Richard R. Sweeny; Deacon John A. Cole.
Res.: Ridge Rd. & Hance Rd., P.O. Box 66, 07704-0066. Tel: 732-741-1714; Fax: 732-741-6837.
Catechesis/Religious Program—Tel: 732-741-4543. Ms. Jane Shaheen, D.R.E. Students 941.

FARMINGDALE, MONMOUTH CO., ST. CATHERINE OF SIENA (1912), Rev. Michael S. Vona; Deacon Michael J. Principato.
Res.: 31 Asbury Rd., P.O. Box 667, 07727-0667. Tel: 732 938-5375; Fax: 732-938-3260.
Catechesis/Religious Program—Tel: 732-938-6229. Dr. Anthony Novembre, D.R.E. Students 612.

FLORENCE, BURLINGTON CO., ST. CLARE (1874), (Irish—Italian), [CEM] Rev. Felix F. Venza.
Res.: 232 E. Front St., 08518. Tel: 609-499-0122.
Catechesis/Religious Program—Duffy House, 306 E. Front St., 08518. Miss Mary Filipponi, D.R.E. Students 170.

FORKED RIVER, OCEAN CO., ST. PIUS X (1961), Rev. Richard Basznianin; Cynthia Craft, Pastoral Assoc.; Deacons James Heller; Robert Klein; Anthony Martucci.
Res.: 203 W. Lacey Rd., 08731-3598. Tel: 609-693-5107; Fax: 609-693-6829.
Catechesis/Religious Program—Tel: 609-693-0368. Mrs. Patricia Colando, D.R.E. Students 1,120.

FREEHOLD, MONMOUTH CO.
1—ST. ROBERT BELLARMINE (1971), Revs. Thomas J. O'Connor; Matthew Adackapara; Edward M. Jawidzik; Deacon Gerald Henwood.
61 Georgia Rd., 07728. Tel: 732-462-7429; Fax: 732-409-3496.
Catechesis/Religious Program—Tel: 732-431-3404. Students 1,492.
2—ST. ROSE OF LIMA (1871), [CEM] Revs. Richard R. Milewski; Roman Modino, Hispanic Ministry. Tel: 732-303-7800; Fax: 732-303-1228; Norman St. John, S.V.D.; Rocco A. Cuomo; Deacon John Wanat.
Res.: 16 McLean St., 07728. Tel: 732-462-0859; Fax: 732-462-8173.
School—51 Lincoln Pl., 07728. Tel: 732-462-2646; Fax: 732-462-0331. Sr. Patricia Doyle, Prin. Sisters 2; Lay Teachers 31; Students 506.
Catechesis/Religious Program—Tel: 732-308-0215. Mrs. Deborah Moroney, D.R.E. Students 1,085.
Convent—81 Randolph St., 07728. Tel: 732-462-0599.

HAINESPORT, BURLINGTON CO., OUR LADY QUEEN OF PEACE (1944), Rev. Msgr. Richard L. Tofani; Rev. Lex Lumine; Sr. Janis McQuade, S.S.J., Pastoral Assoc.; Deacon John J. O'Donnell.
Res.: 1603 Marne Hwy., P.O. Box 188, 08036. Tel: 609-267-0230; Fax: 609-267-0372.
Catechesis/Religious Program—Tel: 609-267-3641. Mrs. Ginny Fama, D.R.E. Students 417.

HIGHLANDS, MONMOUTH CO., OUR LADY OF PERPETUAL HELP (1883), Rev. Daniel F. Gowen; Deacons James Kelly; Edward J. Moresco; Richard A. Cheu.
Res.: 141 Navesink Ave., 07732. Tel: 732-872-1290; Fax: 732-872-2796.
School—121 Miller St., 07732. Tel: 732-872-0281; Fax: 732-291-7907. Mrs. Melissa Molloy, Prin. Franciscan Missionary Sisters of the Infant Jesus 2; Lay Teachers 10; Students 140.
Catechesis/Religious Program—Ms. Theresa E. Kelly, D.R.E. Students 66.

HIGHTSTOWN, MERCER CO., ST. ANTHONY OF PADUA (1885), Revs. Patrick J. McDonnell; Joseph L. Roldan; Deacons Thomas Garvey; Joseph Hepp; Patrick Kennedy.
Res.: 251 Franklin St., 08520. Tel: 609-448-0141; Fax: 609-448-8878.
Catechesis/Religious Program—Tel: 609-443-3318; Fax: 609-443-3390. Mrs. Veronica Martella, D.R.E.; Sr. Maria doCarmo Lorando, A.SS.E., D.R.E. Students 1,095.

HOLMDEL, MONMOUTH CO.
1—ST. BENEDICT (1959), Revs. Leon S. Buni; John Zec; Deacons Herbert J. Schwarz; Raymond R. Pelkowski; Mr. Joseph Bulla, Pastoral Assoc.; Joan Orlando, Business Admin.
Res.: 165 Bethany Rd., 07733-1699. Tel: 732-264-4712; Fax: 732-264-9080.
School—Tel: 732-264-5578; Fax: 732-264-8679. Mary Ellen Lilly, Prin.; Jo-Anne Bent, Vice Prin. Lay Teachers 25; Students 490.
Catechesis/Religious Program—Tel: 732-264-4714. Ms. Rae Cristino, D.R.E. Students 588.
2—ST. CATHARINE (1879), Rev. Msgr. Eugene M. Rebeck; Deacons John P. Flanagan; Peter Fullen; Anthony Mustillo; Barbara McGahan, Pastoral Assoc.
Res.: P.O. Box 655, 07733. Tel: 732-842-3963; Fax: 732-842-9283.
Catechesis/Religious Program—Tel: 732-758-8568. Sr. Patricia Schladebeck, M.S.C., D.R.E. Students 1,240.

HOPEWELL, MERCER CO., ST. ALPHONSUS (1877), [CEM] Rev. Dennis A. Apoldite; Deacons Robert Lafond; John Grant.
Res.: 54 E. Prospect St., 08525. Tel: 609-466-0332; Fax: 609-466-2023.
Catechesis/Religious Program—Tel: 609-466-2694. Sr. Rosemary Hendry, O.S.F., D.R.E. Students 184.

HOWELL TOWNSHIP, MONMOUTH CO.
1—ST. VERONICA (1962), Revs. H. Brendan Williams; Peter Kochery; Raymond E. Hughes; Jeffrey Kegley; Deacons Gene F. Moir Sr.; Theodore V. Gularek; James Littlefield; Eugene Genovese; Tomasz Cechulski; Uku Mannikus.
Res.: 4215 Hwy. 9 N., 07731. Tel: 732-363-4200; Fax: 732-370-3891.
School—4219 Hwy. 9 N., 07731. Tel: 732-364-4130; Fax: 732-363-4932. Sr. Cherree Ann Power, Prin. Sisters 5; Lay Teachers 36; Students 594.
Catechesis/Religious Program—Tel: 732-364-4137; Fax: 732-886-5064. Sr. Valerie Paccone, C.R., D.R.E.

Students 2,069.
Convent—4217 Hwy. 9 N., 07731. Tel: 732-364-2361.
2—St. William the Abbot (1985), Rev. Michael Manning, M.D.
Mailing Address & Church: 2740 Lakewood-Allenwood Rd., 07731. Tel: 732-840-3535; Fax: 732-840-3663.
Res.: 2400 Allenwood-Lakewood Rd., Allenwood, 08720. Tel: 732-840-3628.
Catechesis/Religious Program—Mrs. Mary Cleary, D.R.E. Students 535.
Station—Geraldine Thompson Nursing Home Allenwood. Tel: 732-938-5250.
Station—Brisbane Child Treatment Center Farmingdale.

Jackson, Ocean Co.
1—St. Aloysius Gonzaga (1964), Revs. G. Scott Shaffer; Robert Holtz; Deacons Rene Perez; Frank Jackson.
Res.: 935 Bennetts Mills Rd., P.O. Box 1285, 08527. Tel: 732-370-0500; Fax: 732-886-9336.
School—Saint Aloysius Grammar School, Tel: 732-370-1515; Fax: 732-370-3555. Ms. Elizabeth O'Connor, Prin. Lay Teachers 28; Students 511.
Catechesis/Religious Program—Tel: 732-370-1515. Ms. Rosemary V. Perry, D.R.E. Students 1,606.
2—Church of St. Monica, Revs. G. Scott Schaffer; Robert R. Schulze.
679 W. Veteran's Hwy., 08527. Tel: 732-928-0279; Fax: 732-928-1853.

Keansburg, Monmouth Co., St. Ann (1924), Revs. Daniel Cahill; Angelo Amaral; Chiu Abraham; Deacons Edwin Cook; Robert Vlcej; Robert Mintz.
Res.: 311 Carr Ave., 07734. Tel: 732-787-0315; Fax: 732-787-5254.
School—285 Carr Ave., 07734. Tel: 732-787-1027; Fax: 732-495-3338. Sr. Mary Dora McGrath, R.S.M., Prin. Sisters 2; Lay Teachers 12; Students 208.
Catechesis/Religious Program—Tel: 732-787-5744. Mrs. Mary Jane Cody, D.R.E. Students 555.
School—St. Ann Child Care Center, 121 Main St., 07734. Tel: 732-787-7220; Fax: 732-787-2136. Sisters 2; Students 80.
Bayshore Senior Day Center—100 Main St., 07734. Tel: 732-495-2454; Fax: 732-495-7897. Sisters 2; Seniors Serviced 13,500.
School—Hansel and Gretel Preschool, 267 Carr Ave., 07734. Tel: 732-787-9237; Fax: 732-787-9237. Sisters 1; Children 80.
Project Paul—211 Carr Ave., 07734. Tel: 732-787-4887; Fax: 732-495-7072.

Keyport, Monmouth Co.
1—Jesus the Lord (1978), (Hispanic), Rev. Kenneth W. Ekdahl.
Res.: 123 Broad St., 07735-0673. Tel: 732-739-0323; Fax: 732-264-8276.
Church: 120 Broad St., 07735.
Catechesis/Religious Program—Mrs. Rita Neff, D.R.E. Students 225.
2—St. Joseph (1854), [CEM] Rev. James A. Conover; Deacon Christopher O'Brien; Revs. Francis P. Tam; Ronald J. Cioffi.
Res.: 376 Maple Pl., 07735. Tel: 732-264-0322; Fax: 732-888-3280.
School—St. Joseph School, 376 Maple Pl., 07735. Tel: 732-264-2114; Fax: 732-264-8696. Ruth Mazzarela, Prin. Lay Teachers 28; Students 361.
Catechesis/Religious Program—Tel: 732-888-1274. Ms. Kay Hetherington, D.R.E. Students 400.

Lakehurst, Ocean Co., St. John (1969), Revs. Bernard Keigher; Castor Sanchez; Deacons Edward Holowienka; Ronald Kerr; Robert Gooden; Michael Pirylis.
Res.: 619 Chestnut St., 08733. Tel: 732-657-6347; Fax: 732-657-8690.
Catechesis/Religious Program—Tel: 732-657-2348. Mrs. Mary Ann Dempkowski, D.R.E. Students 457.

Lakewood, Ocean Co.
1—St. Anthony Claret (1977),, (Hispanic Parish for Ocean Co.) Revs. Walter Miller, S.V.D. (LA); Pelagio Calambia Peteno Jr., S.V.D.
Res.: 780 Ocean Ave., 08701-3644. Tel: 732-367-8486; Fax: 732-367-0460.
Catechesis/Religious Program—Mrs. Elizabeth Lee, D.R.E. Students 375.
2—St. Mary of the Lake (1889), [CEM] Revs. Michael P. Lang; James J. Selvaraj; Edward Kwoka; Bernadino Esguerra; Deacons James Lacey; Silverius Galvan; John Cullinane; Anthony Martucci, Pastoral Min.; Sisters Mary Franey, R.S.M., Pastoral Min.; Geraldine Contento, M.P.F., Pastoral Min.; Ms. Terry Ginther, Pastoral Min.
Res.: 43 Madison Ave., 08701. Tel: 732-363-0139; Fax: 732-905-1410.
School—Holy Family School, 1141 E. County Line Rd., 08701. Tel: 732-363-4771; Fax: 732-363-2914. Sisters Carolyn Houck, M.P.F., Prin.; Domenica Troiana, M.P.F., Asst. Prin. Sisters 2; Lay Teachers 28; Students 527.
Catechesis/Religious Program—Tel: 732-363-3043; Fax: 732-961-0382. Donna Marie Clancy, D.R.E. Students 557.
Mission—Holy Family Church, Ocean Co. Fax: 732-905-1410.

Lavallette, Ocean Co., St. Bonaventure (1921), Rev. Msgr. Leonard F. Troiano. In Res., Rev. Msgr. Alfred D. Smith (Retired).
Res.: 103 Washington Ave., 08735. Tel: 732-793-7291; Fax: 732-793-8204.
Catechesis/Religious Program—Tel: 732-793-3020. Ms. Theresa Petrik, D.R.E. Students 79.

Lawrenceville, Mercer Co.
1—St. Ann (1937), Revs. R. Vincent Gartland; Joseph N. Rosie, S.T.L., Parochial Vicar; Sr. Beth Dempsey, Pastoral Assoc.; Deacons Thomas J. Everist; Edward A. Hoag; Mr. Gary Maccaroni, Pastoral Assoc.
Res.: 1253 Lawrence Rd., 08648. Tel: 609-882-6491; Fax: 609-882-4366.
School—34 Rossa Ave., 08648. Tel: 609-882-8077; Fax: 609-882-0327. Mr. John McKenna, Prin. Lay Teachers 32; Students 392.
Catechesis/Religious Program—Tel: 609-882-1212. Sr. Carol Heffner, S.S.J., D.R.E. Students 650.
2—The Church of the Korean Martyrs (1994), (Korean), Rev. Seong K. Lee, Admin.
Res.: 3311 Town Ct. S., 08648. Tel: 609-716-9144; Fax: 609-897-9094.
Catechesis/Religious Program—Students 56.

Lincroft, Monmouth Co., St. Leo the Great (1958), Revs. Leonard P. Lang; Joseph M. Quinlan (NEW) (Retired); Sisters Joan Dreisbach, O.S.F., Pastoral Assoc.; Ann Barry, S.S.J., Pastoral Assoc.; Deacon Joseph DePaolis. In Res., Rev. Eugene B. Vavrick.
Res.: 50 Hurley's Ln., 07738. Tel: 732-747-5466; Fax: 732-219-5181.
School—550 Newman-Springs Rd., 07738. Tel: 732-741-3133; Fax: 732-741-2241. Elena Torregrossa, Prin. Lay Teachers 33; Students 650.
Catechesis/Religious Program—Tel: 732-530-0717. Mrs. Nancy Daluise, D.R.E. Students 1,012.

Long Branch, Monmouth Co.
1—Holy Trinity (1906), (Italian), Rev. Daniel F. Swift; Deacon Albert M. Pacitti.
Res.: 408 Prospect St., 07740. Tel: 732-222-3216; Fax: 732-222-4313.
School—375 Exchange Pl., 07740. Tel: 732-222-8878; Fax: 732-222-8854. Sr. Roseann Fernandez, M.P.F., Prin. Religious Teachers Filippini 4; Lay Teachers 13; Students 135.
Catechesis/Religious Program—Mrs. Larissa Strano, D.R.E. Students 200.
Convent—380 Division St., 07740. Tel: 732-222-8535. Religious Teachers Filippini 4.
2—St. John the Baptist (1984), (Spanish—Portuguese), Revs. George E. Berrios; Helio deSilva.
Res.: 272 Willow Ave., 07740. Tel: 732-229-8527; 732-229-8905; Fax: 732-571-0280.
Catechesis/Religious Program—Tel: 732-571-1003. Ms. Preciosa Vieira, D.R.E. Students 195.
3—St. Michael (1885), Rev. Charles B. Weiser; Deacon Eugene A. Somma.
Res.: 800 Ocean Ave., West End, 07740. Tel: 732-222-8080; Fax: 732-870-1174.
Catechesis/Religious Program—Tel: 732-483-0360; Fax: 732-483-0363. Students 400.
4—Our Lady Star of the Sea (1878), [CEM] Rev. M. Joseph Mokrzycki; Deacon Donald A. Young; Sr. Diane Matera, R.S.M., Hospital Pastoral Min.
Res.: 101 Chelsea Ave., 07740. Tel: 732-229-0526; Fax: 732-229-2886.
Catechesis/Religious Program—Tel: 732-229-0952. Mrs. Madeline Ottino, D.R.E. Students 138.

Manalapan, Monmouth Co., St. Thomas More (1970), Revs. John P. Bambrick; Gerald E. McBride; Deacons Keith J. Casey; James Davis; John J. Zebrowski; John J. Walsh.
Res.: 186 Gordons Corner Rd., 07726. Tel: 732-446-6661; Fax: 732-446-6507.
Catechesis/Religious Program—Tel: 732-446-3232. Deacon Keith Casey, D.R.E. Students 1,200.

Manasquan, Monmouth Co., St. Denis (1909), Revs. Stanley P. Lukaszewski; William J. Bausch (Retired); Rev. Msgr. Harrold Murray; Revs. Joseph J. Miele (Retired); Michael J. Waites; Deacons George R. Kelder Jr.; Donald L. Perusi; Sr. Josephine Wade, S.S.J., Pastoral Ministry.
Res.: 90 Union Ave., Box 340, 08736. Tel: 732-223-0287; Fax: 732-528-1901.
School—119 Virginia Ave., 08736. Tel: 732-223-4928; Fax: 732-223-1807. Trudy Bonavita, Prin. Lay Teachers 16; Students 273.
Catechesis/Religious Program—Tel: 732-223-1161. Sr. Mary Veasy, S.S.J., D.R.E. Students 964.
Chapel—Manasquan Beach, Our Lady Star of the Sea, (Summer)

Maple Shade, Burlington Co., Our Lady of Perpetual Help (1920), Revs. John F. Wake; Vicente Magdaraog; Deacons Joseph A. Card; Michael P. Boehm; Lawrence W. Finn Sr.; Ronald S. Meyers.
Res.: 236 E. Main St., 08052. Tel: 856-667-8850; Fax: 856-667-1046.
School—236 E. Main St.. Tel: 856-779-7526; Fax: 856-667-3083. Mary Ann Figura, Prin. Sisters 4; Lay Teachers 14; Students 285.
Catechesis/Religious Program—Tel: 856-779-7529. Ms. Cynthia Fisher, D.R.E. Students 500.

Marlboro, Monmouth Co., St. Gabriel (1885), Rev. Eugene J. Roberts; Deacons James C. Russo; Lester Owens; Stephen Sansevere.
Res.: 100 N. Main St., 07746. Tel: 732-946-4487; Fax: 732-946-7276.
Catechesis/Religious Program—Tel: 732-946-2696; Fax: 732-946-2080. Dr. James J. Bridges, D.R.E. Students 1,460.

Marlton, Burlington Co., St. Joan of Arc (1961), Rev. Msgr. Armand A. Pedata, J.C.D.; Revs. Charles M. Schwartz; Francis Ravi; Sr. Eleanor O'Connell, S.S.J., Pastoral Assoc.; Deacons Barry Tarzy; George Johnston.
Church & Res.: 100 Willow Bend Rd., 08053. Tel: 856-983-0077; Fax: 856-983-7716.
School—101 Evans Rd., 08053. Tel: 856-983-0774. Sr. Patricia Pycik, Prin. Sisters of St. Joseph 3; Lay Teachers 25; Students 496.
Catechesis/Religious Program—Tel: 856-983-7575; Fax: 856-983-3479. Mrs. Linda Mueller, D.R.E. Students 1,515.
Convent—99 Evans Rd., 08053. Tel: 856-983-0258.

Matawan, Monmouth Co., St. Clement (1965), Rev. John J. Scully.
Res.: 172 Freneau Ave., 07747. Tel: 732-566-3616; Fax: 732-566-9275.
Catechesis/Religious Program—Tel: 732-591-8090. Mrs. Carol Capasso, Dir. Students 997.

Medford, Burlington Co., St. Mary of the Lakes (1943), Rev. Msgr. James H. Dubell; Revs. Richard C. Vila; Charles Muorah; Deacons Joseph R. Patton; W. Norman Talbot; John Fanelle; Ronald Little; Joseph Tedeschi.
Res.: 40 Jackson Rd., 08055. Tel: 609-654-8208; Fax: 609-654-1734.
School—196 Rte. 70, 08055. Tel: 609-654-2546; Fax: 609-654-8125. Sr. Justina Marie Miller, Prin. Sisters of St. Francis of Philadelphia 2; Sisters of St. Joseph 4; Lay Teachers 23; Students 482.
Catechesis/Religious Program—196 Rte. 70, 08055. Tel: 609-654-8243; Fax: 609-953-8630. Mrs. Cathleen Sheridan, D.R.E. Students 1,388.
Convent—Sisters of St. Francis, 27 Schoolhouse Dr., 08055. Tel: 609-654-5896.
Convent—Sisters of St. Joseph, 24 Summerhill Lane, 08055. Tel: 609-654-1941.
St. Vincent DePaul Society-Medford—P.O. Box 1131, 08055. Tel: 609-953-0021; Fax: 609-953-2432. Mr. Paul V. Cannon, Treas.

Middletown, Monmouth Co., St. Catherine (1948), Rev. Daniel C. Hesko; Deacons Henry J. Ernst; Kenneth R. Sheehan; John C. Orlando; L. Jacqueline Callahan, Pastoral Ministry.
Res.: 5 Shore Acres Ave., 07748. Tel: 732-787-1318; Fax: 732-787-6139.
Catechesis/Religious Program—Tel: 732-495-7779; Fax: 732-495-7779. Mrs. L. Jackie Callahan, D.R.E. Students 660.

Monmouth Beach, Monmouth Co., Church of the Precious Blood (1947), Rev. John T. Kielb; Deacon William Murray.
Res.: 72 Riverdale Ave., 07750. Tel: 732-222-4756; Fax: 732-229-6448.
Catechesis/Religious Program—Tel: 732-870-1293. Mrs. Suzanne Goyette, D.R.E. Students 320.

Moorestown, Burlington Co., Our Lady of Good Counsel (1879), [CEM] Rev. Msgr. James J. McGovern; Rev. Joseph G. Hlubik; Deacons Peter DeLuca, (Retired); Francis P. McGann Jr., (Retired); Joseph A. Paul.
Res.: 42 W. Main St., 08057. Tel: 856-235-0181; Fax: 856-235-4987.
School—23 W. Prospect St., 08057. Tel: 856-235-7885; Fax: 856-235-2570. Jerome McGowan, Prin. Dominic Sisters of Hope 1; Lay Teachers 26; Students 534.
Catechesis/Religious Program—Tel: 856-235-7136. Dr. Linda M. Dix, D.Min., D.R.E. Students 1,140.

Mount Holly, Burlington Co.
1—Christ the Redeemer (1976), (Hispanic), Rev. Jamie Gonzalez, Temp. Admin.; Deacon Michael Adorno.
Res.: 35 South Ave., 08060. Tel: 609-261-0181; Fax: 609-702-0017.
Catechesis/Religious Program—426 Pine St., Mt. Holly, 08060. Students 59.
2—Sacred Heart (1848), [CEM] Revs. Robert J.W. Schecker; David A. Adams; Deacons Louis C. Restivo; James Casa; William Rowley; John F. Hoefling; Stanley Orkis; Michael Auleta.
Res.: 260 High St., 08060-1404. Tel: 609-267-0209; Fax: 609-267-9293.
School—250 High St., 08060. Tel: 609-267-1728; Fax: 609-267-4476. Ronald J. Maniglia, Prin. Lay Teachers 22; Students 280.

Catechesis/Religious Program—Tel: 609-267-6319; Fax: 609-518-9010. Mrs. Deborah Clardy, D.R.E. Students 800.
Mission—St. Andrew 2489 Monmouth Rd., Jobstown, Burlington Co. 08041. Tel: 609-702-1848.
Station—County Jail, Tel: 609-267-3300.
Station—Burlington County Hospital Extended Care Center, Tel: 609-367-0700.

MOUNT LAUREL, BURLINGTON CO., ST. JOHN NEUMANN (1978), Revs. Lino S. Parente, O.Cist. (Italy); Maurizio Nicoletti, O.Cist (Italy); Deacons Gene Hoch; James Cattanea.
Res.: 560 Walton Ave., 08054. Tel: 856-235-1330; Fax: 856-235-9632.
Catechesis/Religious Program—Tel: 856-235-6555; Fax: 856-235-6555. Mrs. Helen Graziano, D.R.E. Students 875.

NEPTUNE, MONMOUTH CO.

1—HOLY INNOCENTS (1959), Revs. Brian T. Butch; Lawrence Kunnel; Deacons James Walsh; John Klincewicz.
Res.: 3441 W. Bangs Ave., P.O. Box 806, 07753. Tel: 732-922-4242; Fax: 732-922-2848.
School—3455 W. Bangs Ave., 07753. Tel: 732-922-3141; Fax: 732-922-6531. Sr. Elizabeth Calello, Prin. Religious Teachers Filippini 1; Lay Teachers 14; Students 268.
Catechesis/Religious Program—Tel: 732-922-4242, Ext. 20; Fax: 732-922-3752. Sr. Elizabeth Arcangeli, M.P.F., D.R.E. Students 420.
Station—Convacenter Nursing Home, Tel: 732-774-3500.
Station—Imperial Nursing Home, Tel: 732-922-3400.
Station—Heritage Hall Nursing Home Norwood. Tel: 732-922-9330.
Station—Medicenter Nursing Home Lakewood. Tel: 732-774-8300.
Station—The Lodge, Kings Manor, Tel: 732-922-1900.

2—OUR LADY OF PROVIDENCE (1981), (Spanish), Rev. Miguel Virella, S.V.D.; Sr. Grace Forker, S.S.J., Pastoral Assoc.
Res.: 1228 Fifth Ave., 07753. Tel: 732-776-7164; Fax: 732-776-7164.
Catechesis/Religious Program—Sr. Grace Forker, S.S.J., D.R.E. Students 133.

NEW EGYPT, OCEAN CO., THE CHURCH OF THE ASSUMPTION (1853), [CEM] Rev. Joseph J. Farrell; Deacon Raymond W. Staub Jr.
Res.: 76 Evergreen Rd., 08533. Tel: 609-758-2153; Fax: 609-758-6240.
Catechesis/Religious Program—Mrs. Diane Gregorio, D.R.E. Students 542.

NEW MONMOUTH, MONMOUTH CO., ST. MARY (1878), Rev. Msgr. Michael J. Walsh; Revs. Mark A. Kreder; Pasquale Papalia; Mr. Glen Leo Mendonca, Pastoral Assoc.
Res.: 26 Leonardville Rd., 07748. Tel: 732-671-0071; Fax: 732-671-6125.
School—538 Church St., 07748. Tel: 732-671-0129; Fax: 732-671-2653. Dr. William V. Smith, Prin. Lay Teachers 38; Aides 7; Students 655.
High School—Mater Dei High School, Tel: 732-671-9100; Fax: 732-671-9214. Mr. Frank Poleski Jr., Prin.; Mrs. L. Jorgensen-Walsh, Asst. Prin. Lay Teachers 33; Students 355.
Catechesis/Religious Program—Tel: 732-671-0124; Fax: 732-671-6612. Sr. Sharon Santos, F.C.L.G., D.R.E. Students 1,065.

NORMANDY BEACH, OCEAN CO., OUR LADY OF PEACE (1979), Rev. Gerard J. McCarron.
Residence and Mailing: P.O. Box 728, 7th Ave. & Rte. 35 S., 08739. Tel: 732-793-7803; Fax: 732-793-1808.
Catechesis/Religious Program—Tel: 732-793-7291; Fax: 732-793-8204. Ms. Theresa Petrick, D.R.E. Students 22.

PENNINGTON, MERCER CO., ST. JAMES (1897), Rev. Ronald J. Bacovin; Deacons James W. Palsir; Samuel Sciarrotta; Richard Currie; Kevin Byrne; William Moore Hank.
Res.: 115 E. Delaware Ave., 08534. Tel: 609-737-0122; Fax: 609-737-6912.
Catechesis/Religious Program—Tel: 609-737-2717. Deacon James W. Palsir, D.R.E. Students 804.

POINT PLEASANT BEACH, OCEAN CO., ST. PETER'S (1882), Revs. Richard Rossell, O.F.M.Conv.; Edward Costello, O.F.M.Conv.; Crispin Fuino, O.F.M.Conv.; Julius Toth, O.F.M.Conv.; Deacon Thomas P. Porter.
Res.: 406 Forman Ave., P.O. Box 1006, 08742. Tel: 732-892-0049; Fax: 732-295-9782.
School—415 Atlantic Ave., 08742. Tel: 732-892-1260; Fax: 732-892-3488. Sr. Phyllis Tracy, Prin. Sisters 4; Lay Teachers 10; Students 241.
Catechesis/Religious Program—Tel: 732-899-4839. Mrs. Merrie Brambilla, D.R.E. Students 665.
Convent—401 Atlantic Ave., 08742. Tel: 732-899-2390.

POINT PLEASANT, OCEAN CO., ST. MARTHA (1972), Rev. Michael D. Sullivan; Deacons John Haney; Francis Groff.
Res. & Mailing Address: 3800 Herbertsville Rd., 08742. Tel: 732-295-3630; Fax: 732-295-9315.
Catechesis/Religious Program—Tel: 732-295-3630, Ext. 48; Fax: 732-295-9325. Mrs. Gerry Groff, D.R.E. Students 990.

PRINCETON, MERCER CO., ST. PAUL (1864), [CEM] Rev. Msgr. Walter E. Nolan; Rev. Michael Dunn; Deacons Maurice Benedetti; Paul LaChance; Joseph Lynch.
Res.: 214 Nassau St., 08542. Tel: 609-924-1743; Fax: 609-924-7510.
School—213 Nassau St., 08540. Tel: 609-921-7587; Fax: 609-921-0264. Elizabeth Barrella, Prin. Sisters 1; Lay Teachers 24; Students 399.
Catechesis/Religious Program—Tel: 609-924-1743, Ext. 118. Mrs. Anne-Marie Calderone, D.R.E. Students 430.
Convent—216 Nassau St., 08540. Tel: 609-924-4414.

RED BANK, MONMOUTH CO.

1—ST. ANTHONY (1920), (Italian), Rev. Anthony M. Carotenuto; Deacon Arthur Fama.
Res.: 121 Bridge Ave., 07701. Tel: 732 747-0813; Fax: 732-224-0059.
Catechesis/Religious Program—Mrs. Michele McCue, D.R.E. Students 318.

2—ST. JAMES (1864), [CEM] Rev. Msgr. Philip A. Lowery; Revs. Alex Enriquez; John O. Chang; Jose Atibagos.
Res.: 94 Broad St., 07701. Tel: 732-741-0500; Fax: 732-741-1489.
School—Preschool, Tel: 732-933-1041. Lay Teachers 4; Students 64.
School—St. James Grammar School, 30 Peters Pl., 07701. Tel: 732-741-3363; Fax: 732-933-4960. Janet Dolan, Prin. Lay Teachers 32; Students 535.
High School—Red Bank Catholic High School, 112 Broad St., 07701. Tel: 732-747-1774; Fax: 732-747-1936. Robert Abatemarco, Prin. Sisters 4; Lay Teachers 90; Students 1,101.
Catechesis/Religious Program—Tel: 732-747-6006. Ms. Joan M. Savarese, D.R.E. Students 694.
Convent—25 Drummond Pl., 07701. Tel: 732-741-0724.
Station—Riverview Hospital, Tel: 732-530-2231; Fax: 732-530-2394.

RIVERSIDE, BURLINGTON CO.

1—ST. CASIMIR (1913), (Polish), Revs. Dennis Mason, O.F.M.Conv.; Christian Wojciechowski, O.F.M.Conv. In Res. Revs. Jude Michael Krill, O.F.M.Conv.; George Maslar, O.F.M.Conv.; Deacon William E. Briggs.
Res.: 502 New Jersey Ave., 08075. Tel: 856-461-0532; Fax: 856-461-5781.
School—School & Preschool: 500 New Jersey Ave., 08075. Tel: 856-461-7410; Fax: 856-461-2619. Sr. Lydia Etter, O.S.F., Prin. Sisters 2; Lay Teachers 14; Students 153.
Catechesis/Religious Program—Sr. Mary Jude Stewart, O.S.F., D.R.E. Students 136
Convent—116 Huelings Ave., 08075. Tel: 856-461-0045.

2—ST. PETER (1878), Revs. Thomas R Rittenhouse; Jose Luis Magalhaes, O.F.M.Conv.; Deacon Joseph Fuoco.
Res.: 102 Middleton St., P.O. Box 248, 08075. Tel: 856-461-0100; Fax: 856-764-6133.
School—St. Peter, 101 Middleton St., 08075. Tel: 856-461-1087; Fax: 856-461-6983. Joseph Chinnici, Prin. Sisters 1; Lay Teachers 18; Students 267.
Catechesis/Religious Program—Tel: 856-461-9343. Mrs. Maria B. Gimello, D.R.E. Students 318.

RIVERTON, BURLINGTON CO., SACRED HEART (1878), Rev. John P. Czahur; Deacons Joseph Knipp; Joseph Donadieu.
Res.: 400 Thomas Ave., 08077. Tel: 856-829-0090; Fax: 856-829-2087.
Catechesis/Religious Program—Tel 609-829-1848; Fax: 609-829-7404. Mrs. Patricia Hutchinson, D.R.E. Students 503.

ROEBLING, BURLINGTON CO., HOLY ASSUMPTION (1913), Rev. Matthew Morreale, O.F.M. (NY); Deacon Robert D. Machion.
Res. 1290 Hornberger Ave., 08554. Tel: 609-499-0161; Fax: 609-499-3074.
School—1300 Hornberger Ave., 08554. Tel: 609-499-0045. Gerard Steffe, Prin. Lay Teachers 9; Students 153.
Catechesis/Religious Program—Mrs. Martha Wright, D.R.E. Students 200.
Convent—1238 Hornberger Ave., 08554.

RUMSON, MONMOUTH CO., HOLY CROSS (1884), Rev. Joseph W. Hughes; Eugena Kelly, Pastoral Assoc.; Deacon Jay C. Harbeck.
Res.: 30 Ward Ave., 07760. Tel: 732-842-0348; Fax: 732-842-3226.
School—(Grades PreK-8), 40 Rumson Rd., 07760. Tel 732-842-0348. Thomas Bugliaro, Prin. Lay Teachers 28; Students 478.
Catechesis/Religious Program—Mrs. Susan Vandeventer, D.R.E. Students 694.

SEA GIRT, MONMOUTH CO., ST. MARK (1953), Rev. Msgr. William J. Carton; Deacon Dennis Saake.
Res.: 215 Crescent Pkwy., 08750. Tel: 732-449-6364; Fax: 732-449-1646.
Catechesis/Religious Program—Tel: 732-449-8360. Mrs. Mary Ann Hirsch, D.R.E. Students 420.

SEASIDE HEIGHTS, OCEAN CO., OUR LADY OF PERPETUAL HELP (1942), Revs. Emmett Carroll, O.F.M.Conv.; Augustine Kapinus. In Res., Bro. Nicholas Lorson.
Res.: 100 Grant Ave., 08751. Tel: 732-793-6881; Fax: 732-793-7632.

SEASIDE PARK, OCEAN CO., ST. CATHARINE OF SIENA (1906), Revs. Brennan Joseph Farleo, O.F.M.Conv., Supr. & Pastor; Eric Fenner, O.F.M.Conv.; George Sullivan, O.F.M.Conv.; Bro. Robert Lynch, O.F.M.Conv.
Res.: 50 E. St., Box A, 08752. Tel: 732-793-0041; Fax: 732-793-5483.
Catechesis/Religious Program—Mrs. Mary Britanak, D.R.E. Students 258.

SPRING LAKE, MONMOUTH CO., ST. CATHARINE (1901), [CEM 2] Rev. Msgr. Thomas A. Luebking; Revs. Stephen M. Piga; Luis Lacson; Deacons John P. O'Connor; David Fursman; Edward Jennings; John L. Little.
Res.: 215 Essex Ave., 07762. Tel: 732-449-5765; Fax: 732-449-0916.
School—Second and Salem Ave.. Tel: 732-449-4424; Fax: 732-449-7876. Sr. Margo Kavanaugh, R.S.M., Prin. Sisters 3; Lay Teachers 29; Students 515.
Catechesis/Religious Program—Mrs. Diane Osieck, D.R.E. Students 690.
Convent—211 Essex Ave., 07762. Tel: 732-449-6199.
Mission—St. Margaret Ludlow Ave., Monmouth Co. 07762.

TABERNACLE, BURLINGTON CO., HOLY EUCHARIST (1982), Rev. Andrew Jamieson; Deacon Joseph De Luca; Carol Schulz, Pastoral Assoc.
Office—520 Medford Lakes Rd., 08088. Tel: 609-268-8383; Fax: 609-268-3294.
Catechesis/Religious Program—Tel: 609-268-7742. Dolores Wright, D.R.E. Students 860.
Station—New Lisbon Developmental Center New Lisbon. Tel: 609-726-1000.
Station—Leisuretown Senior Citizen Community Southampton.

TOMS RIVER, OCEAN CO.

1—ST. JOSEPH (Dover Township) (1883), [CEM] Rev. Msgr. Sean P. Flynn; Revs. William P. Gardner; Roberto Ignacio; Dean A. Gaudio; Deacons Francis J. Babuschak; Edwin L. Voll Jr.; Frank J. McKenna; Romeo D. Aquino; Myron J. Novitsky.
Mailing Address: 685 Hooper Ave., P.O. Box 387, 08753. Tel: 732-349-0018; Fax: 732-286-7064.
School—711 Hooper Ave., 08753. Tel: 732-349-2355; Fax: 732-349-1064. Mrs. Michele Williams, Prin. Sisters 2; Lay Teachers 47; Students 946.
High School—Monsignor Donovan High School, Tel: 732-349-8801; Fax: 732-349-8956. Dr. Edward Gere, Prin. Sisters 5; Lay Teachers 78; Students 960.
Catechesis/Religious Program—Tel: 732-914-2420. Sr. Celine Fowler, I.H.M., D.R.E. Students 1,450.
Convent—509 Hooper Ave., 08753. Tel: 732-349-2450.
Mission—St. Gertrude Ocean & Central Aves., Island Heights, Ocean Co. 08732. Tel: 732-288-0036.

2—ST. JUSTIN (Dover Township) (1972), Revs. William J. Nolan; Silvano Amora; Chrispin Obico; Deacons Richard Hauenstein; David L. Shapiro; Brent McNally; Michael Fullen.
Res.: 975 Fischer Blvd., 08753. Tel: 732-270-3980; Fax: 732-929-9411.
Catechesis/Religious Program—Tel: 732-270-3797. Ms. Rose Ciallella, D.R.E. Students 12.

3—ST. LUKE (Dover Township) (1982), Rev. Louis W. Kralovich; Deacons Donald G. MacCarrick; Ronald R. Wicks; Stephen F. Delligatti; Louis Cartnick; Gregory Wallack.
Res.: 1674 Old Freehold Rd., 08753. Tel: 732-286-2222; Fax: 732-914-1080.
Catechesis/Religious Program—Tel: 732-505-0108. Students 1,110.

4—ST. MAXIMILIAN KOLBE (Dover Township) (1985), Revs. Francis E. Santitoro; Nilo Apura. In Res., Rev. George M. Albano (Retired); Deacons Raymond Shea; Albert M. Pacitti; Robert Desnon.
Res. & Mailing Address: P.O. Box 4144, 08757. Tel: 732-914-0300; 732-914-8550 (Res.); Fax: 732-240-9517.

TUCKERTON, OCEAN CO., ST. THERESA (1944), Revs. Terence O. McAlinden; Mark Devlin, Assoc.; Deacons James Petrauskas; Charles Comito; Henry Palan; William Sulzmann; Joseph Vivona.
Res.: 128 Cedar St., 08087. Tel: 609-296-2504; Fax: 609-296-4530.
Catechesis/Religious Program—Tel: 609-296-1940; Fax: 609-296-3537. Mrs. Sheila D'Avino, D.R.E. Students 575.

UNION BEACH, MONMOUTH CO., HOLY FAMILY (1942), Revs. Patrick G. Fitzpatrick; Mar B. Ortiz; Francis Cheruparambil; Sisters Rose Mary Malague, R.S.M., Pastoral Min.; Gloria Jean Bateman, R.S.M., Pastoral Min.; Deacons John Clymore; James Hewitt.
Res.: 727 Hwy. 36 W., P.O. Box 56, Keyport, 07735. Tel: 732-264-1484; Fax: 732-264-8369.
School—910 Hwy. 36, Hazlet, 07730. Tel: 732-264-9549; Fax: 732-335-9605. Sr. Mary Nadine Boyle, Prin. Sisters 2; Lay Teachers 19; Students 336.
Catechesis/Religious Program—Tel: 732-264-7043. Patricia McCarthy, D.R.E. Students 890.
Convent—Mercy Convent, 440 Sullivan Pl., 07735. Tel: 732-739-3065. Sisters 2.
Convent—Holy Family Convent, 41 Hemlock St., Hazlet, 07730. Tel: 732-335-9605; Fax: 732-264-5353. Sisters 2.

WASHINGTON CROSSING, MERCER CO., ST. GEORGE (1924), Rev. Msgr. George A. Ardos; Sr. Dorothy Jancola, R.S.M., Pastoral Assoc.; Deacons James Toolan; Thomas Daily.
Res.: 1370 River Rd., P.O. Box 324, Titusville, 08560. Tel: 609-737-2015; Fax: 609-737-7863.
Catechesis/Religious Program—Tel: 609-730-1703. Mrs. Rose Gallagher, D.R.E.; Virginia Clawson, D.R.E.; Jo Hendrickson, D.R.E. Students 120.
Station—Mercer County Correction Center, Tel: 609-989-6901.

WAYSIDE, MONMOUTH CO., ST. ANSELM (1972), Rev. Robert F. Kaeding.
Res.: 1028 Wayside Rd., 07712. Tel: 732-493-4411; Fax: 732-493-4272.
Catechesis/Religious Program—Students 670.

WEST LONG BRANCH, MONMOUTH CO., ST. JEROME (1956), Rev. Michael G. Lankford.
Res.: 254 Wall St., 07764. Tel: 732-222-1424; Fax: 732-222-2291.
School—250 Wall St., 07764. Tel: 732-222-8686; Fax: 732-263-0343. Sr. Angelina Pelliccia, Prin. Sisters 3; Lay Teachers 16; Students 265.
Catechesis/Religious Program—250 Wall St., 07764. Sr. Elizabeth Toft, D.R.E. Students 159.
Convent—250A Wall St., 07764. Tel: 732-222-2016.

WEST WINDSOR, MERCER CO., CHURCH OF ST. DAVID THE KING (1988), Rev. Timothy J. Capewell; Deacons Thomas Baker; Roger Dinella.
Res.: 517 Village Rd. W., Princeton Jct., 08550.
Church: One New Village Rd., Princeton Jct., 08550-2003. Tel: 609-275-7111; Fax: 609-799-1984.
Catechesis/Religious Program—Deacon Roger Dinella, D.R.E. Students 875.

WHITING, OCEAN CO., ST. ELIZABETH ANN SETON (1976), Rev. Msgr. Joseph C. Shenrock, P.A.; Rev. Antony P. Poovakulam; Deacons Kyran J. Purcell; Joseph Rider; Robert Wolfe; Russell Alexander; Ralph Cordasco; Donald Miller; Thomas Cater; Edward J. Hoefling.
Res.: 30 Schoolhouse Rd., 08759. Tel: 732-350-5001; Fax: 732-350-0912.
Catechesis/Religious Program—Tel: 732-350-7391. Ms. Linda Quinn, D.R.E. Students 225.

WILLINGBORO, BURLINGTON CO., CORPUS CHRISTI (1959), Rev. Daniel J. Ryan; Deacons James E. Ayrer; Stanley R. Olshevski; John F. Vassallo Jr. In Res., Rev. Msgr. Richard C. Brietske.
Res.: 63 Sylvan Ln., 08046. Tel: 609-877-5322; Fax: 609-877-1695.
School—11 S. Sunset Rd., 08046. Tel: 609-877-2144; Fax: 609-877-3153. Mary O'Donnell, Prin. Lay Teachers 14; Students 168.
Catechesis/Religious Program—Charleston & Sunset Rds., 08046. Tel: 609-871-4680; Fax: 609-871-5213. Sr. Rosemary Bucchi, O.S.F., D.R.E. Students 201.
Convent—150 Charleston Rd., 08046. Tel: 609-871-4226.

Chaplains of Public Institutions

TRENTON. *Donnelly Memorial Hospital of City of Trenton*. Attended from Our Lady of Sorrows Church, Tel: 609-587-4372
St. Francis Medical Center. Rev. Joel F. Szydlowski, O.F.M.
Helene Fuld Hospital. Attended from St. Michael Church, Tel: 609-393-4050
Katzenbach School for the Deaf. (Vacant)
Mercer County Correction Center. Attended from St. George Church, Titusville, NJ 08560, Tel: 609-737-2015
New Jersey State Prison, CN 861, 08629. Sr. Elizabeth Gnaum.

BORDENTOWN. *Albert C. Wagner Youth Correction Facility*. Sr. Rose Huber, Chap.
Edward R. Johnstone Training and Research Center.

BURLINGTON. *Burlington County Hospital & Extended Care Center*. Attended from Sacred Heart Church 260 High St., Mount Holly, 08060. Tel: 609-702-1848.
Burlington County Jail. Attended from Sacred Heart Church
260 High St., Mount Holly, 08060. Tel: 609-702-1848.

NEPTUNE. *Jersey Shore Medical Center*. Rev. Anthony Luis Lacson. Attended by St. Catherine Church, 215 Essex Ave. Spring Lake, NJ 07762, Tel: 732-449-5765

NEW LISBON. *New Jersey State Colony*. Attended from Holy Eucharist Church, Tabernacle, NJ 08088, Tel: 609-726-1000
Ocean County Jail. Attended by St. Joseph, Toms River, Tel: 732-349-0018

WAYSIDE. *Monmouth County Jail*, 1028 Wayside Rd., 07712. Tel: 732-493-4411. Attended from St. Rose Church, Freehold NJ, Tel: 732-462-7429

YARDVILLE. *Garden State Correctional Center*, P.O. Box 11401, 08620. Deacon James A. Manaloris. Tel: 609-298-6300, Ext. 2251.

Military Installations

COLTS NECK. *Naval Weapons Station Earle*. Served by chaplains. Assigned by the Archdiocese for the Military Service.

FORT DIX. *Fort Dix*. Served by chaplains. Assigned by the Archdiocese for the Military Service.

LAKEHURST. *U.S. Naval Air Warfare Center*. Served by chaplains. Assigned by the Archdiocese for the Military Service.

LITTLE SILVER. *Fort Monmouth*. Served by chaplains. Assigned by the Archdiocese for the Military Service.

MCGUIRE AIR FORCE BASE. *McGuire Air Force Base*. Served by chaplains. Assigned by the Archdiocese for the Military Service.

On Duty Outside the Diocese:
Rev. Msgr.—
Punderson, Joseph R., Villa Stritch, Via Della Nocetta 63, Rome 00164 Italy.
Revs.—
Bicomong, Sergio, Federal Correctional Institution, Fairton.
Campoli, John F., His Love Ministry, P.O. Box 433, Allenhurst, 07711.
Gadenz, Pablo, Casa Santa Maria, Via dell'Umilta, 30, Rome 00187 Italy.
Krisak, Anthony F., S.S., 618 East St., N.E., #B, Washington, DC 20002.
Kselman, John J., S.S., Weston School of Theology, Three Phillips Pl., Cambridge, MA 02138.
McKeone, William, Voluntas Dei Society Canada.

Military Chaplains:
Revs.—
Inghilterra, Vincent J., 5904 Mt. Eagle Dr., Apt. 1012, Alexandria, VA 22302.
Liguori, Henry A., 14 Rising Sun Ct., Henderson, NV 89014-6127.

Leave of Absence:
Revs.—
Brown, Gerard J.
Christian, John S.
Dobrosky, John M.
Donadio, Vincent J.
Gallagher, Richard
Hillier, David A.
Jackiewicz, Frederick W.
Keenan, Eugene, 101-B Conestoga Dr., Manchester Township, 08759-1939.
Milewski, Casimir (Retired)
Pienciak, Daniel B.
Russo, John W.
Schneider, William T.
Siecinski, A. Edward
Sullivan, Daniel

Retired:
Most Rev.—
Reiss, John C., D.D., J.C.D., St. Lawrence Rehabilitation Center, 2381 Lawrenceville Rd., Lawrenceville, 08648.
Rev. Msgrs.—
Bogdan, Henry S., Incarnation Church, 1545 Pennington Rd., 08618.
Bradley, Paul F., 14 Mark Dr., Long Branch, 07740.
Capitani, Anthony L., J.C.L., 1305 Chambers St., 08610.
Coffey, Thomas A., Villa Vianney, 2301 Lawrenceville Rd., Lawrenceville, 08648.
Constance, Samuel C., Villa Vianney, 2301 Lawrenceville Rd., Lawrenceville, 08648.
Fitzgerald, William F., Villa Vianney, 2301 Lawrenceville Rd., Lawrenceville, 08648.
Gibbons, John, 114 Ivanhoe Path, Manasquan, 08736.
Kelty, Leo, P.O. Box 281, Allenwood, 08720.
Komosinski, Martin M., 362 6th St., South Amboy, 08879.
Maguire, William E., S.T.D., 9-C Lafayette Dr., Whiting, 08759.
O'Connor, Joseph A., Villa Vianney, 2301 Lawrenceville Rd., Lawrenceville, 08648.
Smith, Alfred D., Bonaventure Church, 103 Washington Ave., Lavallette, 08735.
Strano, Edward, 431 S.E. 3rd St, Apt. 403, Dania, FL 33004.
Toomey, Leonard R., Villa Vianney, 2301 Lawrenceville Rd., Lawrenceville, 08648.
Valentino, Frederick A., 509 Woodland Ave., Brielle, 08730.
Wilus, John M., 7311 Bellerive, Apt. F, Houston, TX 77036.
Wojciehowski, Thaddeus J., Villa Vianney, 2301 Lawrenceville Rd., Lawrenceville, 08648.
Revs.—
Albano, George M., St. Maximillian Kolbe Church, P.O. Box 4144, Toms River, 08756-4144.
Anderson, William C., 116 Crape Myrtle Dr., Holmdel, 07733.
Bausch, William J., Box 1068, Point Pleasant Beach, 08742.
Bianchi, Raymond S., Italy.
Brennan, Thomas, 1122 Skiff Way, Forked River, 08731.
Byrnes, John P., 73 Connell St., Quincy, MA 02169.
Cammisa, James N., 15 Hastings Pl., Monmouth Beach, 07750.
Cenefeldt, Harry E., Villa Vianney, 2301 Lawrenceville Rd., Lawrenceville, 08648.
Cervenak, Andrew, Janosikova 21, Presov 08001 Slovakia.
Coley, James E., 115 E. Delaware Ave., Pennington, 08530.
Conlon, Arthur F., 1015 Nottinghill Ln., 08619.
Cook, John B., 7777 46th Ave. N., Lot 12, St. Petersburg, FL 33709.
Delzell, David G., Tower of David, P.O. Box 292, Uniondale, PA 18470.
Deutsch, George E., Pastor Emeritus, 1229 Aquarius Ct., Forked River, 08731. Tel: 609-242-9456
Dougherty, Edward J., Villa Vianney, 2301 Lawrenceville Rd., Lawrenceville, 08648.
Eelman, William C., 17 Lakeshore Dr., Southampton, 08088.
Farre, Raymond P., Spain.
Flood, Peter J., 31336 High Ridge Dr., Bulverde, TX 78163.
Halpin, Joseph A., 72A Belhaven Ct., Whiting, 08759.
Horvath, Stephen G., P.O. Box 112, Bushkill, PA 18324.
Kearns, Adam, Villa Vianney, 2301 Lawrenceville Rd., Lawrenceville, 08648.
Matera, Philip T., 1047 Lyndale Ave., 08629.
McConnell, James J., Villa Vianney, 2301 Lawrenceville Rd., Lawrenceville, 08648.
Miele, Joseph J., 388 Cherry Quay Rd., Brick, 08723-6308.
Milewski, Casimir, Bren 57 "B", Gora, Poland.
O'Brien, Donald J., Villa Vianney, 2301 Lawrenceville Rd., Lawrenceville, 08648.
Pearson, Robert A., 16 Chestnut Pl., West Long Branch, 07764.
Petri, John C., 259 Squirrel Ridge Rd., Leasburg, NC 27291.
Porazzo, Francis J., 61 Foxglove Rd., Pleasant Plains, Toms River, 08753.
Rucinski, Joseph S., 181 N.E. 14th Ave., Hallandale, FL 33009.
Siska, Ernest J., St. Lawrence Rehabilitation Center, 2381 Lawrenceville Rd., Lawrenceville, 08648.
Sloyan, Gerard S., 6216 41st Ave., Hyattsville, MD 27082.
Thompson, James A., Leisure Village West, 49A Cambridge Cir., Manchester, 08759.

Permanent Deacons:
Garvey, Thomas J. (STP) (Retired), St. Anthony of Padua, Hightstown
Wolfe, Robert A., O.Carm. (NEW) (Retired), St. Elizabeth Ann Seton, Whiting
Acosta, Amado F., (Retired), St. Isaac Jogues, Marlton
Adorno, Miguel, Christ the Redeemer, Mt. Holly
Alexander, Russell, (Retired), St. Elizabeth Ann Seton, Whiting
Allen, John W., (Retired), St. George, Titusville
Andre, Edner, Holy Spirit, Asbury Park
Andrews, Stephen W., St. Dorothea, Eatontown
Aquino, Romeo D., St. Joseph's, Toms River
Arcari, Richard A., St. Raphael, Hamilton
Armstrong, Robert B., St. Mary, Barnegat
Auleta, Michael A., Holy Innocents, Neptune
Ayers, Damian, St. Dominic's, Brick
Ayrer, James E., Corpus Christi, Willingboro
Babuschak, Francis J., St. Joseph, Toms River
Bailey, Normand C., St. Rose, Belmar
Baker, Thomas, St. David the King, Princeton Junction
Barbara, Joseph F., Holy Name, Delran
Beauchamps, Jose, St. Mary Cathedral, Trenton
Benedetti, Maurice T., (Retired), St. Paul, Princeton

Billbrough, Joseph C., (Retired), Corpus Christi, Willingboro
Bittner, Robert W., (Outside Diocese)
Blackwell, M. Darrell, On Duty Outside the Diocese (Maine)
Boehm, Michael P., Our Lady of Perpetual Help, Maple Shade
Briggs, William E., St. Casimir, Riverside
Bueker, Edward J., St. Dominic, Brick
Byrne, Kevin M., St. James, Pennington
Caponigro, Alfred E., On Duty Outside the Diocese (Arizona)
Card, Joseph A., Our Lady of Perpetual Help, Maple Shade
Carlin, George M., St. Paul, Burlington
Carroll, Joseph D., (Retired), Holy Spirit, Asbury Park
Cartnick, Louis C., St. Luke, Toms River
Casa, James L., Sacred Heart, Mount Holly
Casey, Keith J., St. Thomas More, Manalapan
Cater, Thomas H., St. Elizabeth Ann Seton, Whiting
Cattanea, James F., St. John Neumann, Mt. Laurel
Cechulski, Thomas J., St. Veronica, Howell
Chase, Daniel A., (Retired), Holy Angels, Trenton
Cheu, Richard A., Our Lady of Perpetual Help, Highlands
Clausen, Peter M., St. Barnabas, Bayville
Clymore, John L., Holy Family, Union Beach
Coccia, Brother Christopher A., On Duty Outside the Diocese (Florida)
Cole, John A., (Retired), Nativity, Fair Haven
Comito, Charles J., St. Theresa, Tuckerton
Commisso, Louis V., Epiphany, Brick
Cook, Edwin, (Retired), St. Ann, Keansburg
Cook, James P., On Duty Outside the Diocese (Florida)
Cortright, William L., On Duty Outside the Diocese (N. Carolina)
Crowley, James, (Retired), St. Agnes Church, Atlantic Highlands
Cummings, James H., St. Barnabas, Bayville
Cunningham, Robert, St. Francis of Assisi, Brant Beach
Currie, Richard J., St. James, Pennington
Czarnecki, John W., Sacred Heart, Bay Head
D'Angelo, V. Richard, St. Gregory the Great, Trenton
Daily, Thomas P., St. George, Titusville
Davis, James R., St. Thomas More, Manalapan
Dello Russo, Thomas J., Epiphany, Brick
DeLuca, Joseph W., Holy Eucharist, Tabernacle
DeLuca, Peter J., On Duty Outside the Diocese (Florida)
DeMauro, Gerald, On Duty Outside the Diocese (New York)
DePaolis, Joseph, St. Leo the Great, Lincroft
Dinella, Roger P., St. David the King, Princeton Junction
Donadieu, Joseph M., Diocesan Office of Communications
Dougherty, James, (Retired), St. Francis of Assisi, Brant Beach
Doughty, Gerald A., St. Charles Borromeo, Cinnaminson
Doyle, Donald P., (Retired), St. Mary of the Lakes, Medford
Earley, Daniel C., St. Ann, Browns Mills
Ernst, Henry J., St. Catherine, Middletown
Ervin, Martin A., St. Aloysius, Jackson
Everist, Thomas J., St. Ann, Lawrenceville
Fanelle, John D., St. Mary of the Lakes, Medford
Fatovic, Andrew J., St. Vincent de Paul, Yardville
Finn, Lawrence W., Sr., Our Lady of Perpetual Help, Maple Shade
Fiorillo, Joseph A., St. Mary, Barnegat
Fischer, Edward, III, Visitation, Brick
Flanagan, John P., St. Catharine, Holmdel
Fullen, Michael P., Sr., St. Justin, Toms River
Fullen, Peter J., St. Catherine, Holmdel
Fuoco, Joseph R., (Retired), St. Peter, Riverside
Fursman, James David, St. Catharine, Spring Lake
Gallagher, Paul A., San Alfonso Retreat House, Long Branch
Gallagher, William J., St. Charles Borromeo, Cinnaminson
Galvan, Silverius F., St. Mary of the Lake, Lakewood
Genovese, Eugene, St. Veronica, Howell
Gerard, John J., (Retired), Ascension, Bradley Beach
Gettlefinger, Robert J., On Duty Outside the Diocese (North Carolina)
Giglio, Frank E., St. Isaac, Jogues, Marlton
Gomez, Victor L., Jesus the Lord, Keyport
Gooden, Robert, St. John, Lakehurst
Goodrow, Joseph H., On Duty Outside the Diocese (North Carolina)
Grant, John D., St. Alphonsus, Hopewell
Gray, William G., On Duty Outside the Diocese (Florida)
Gregory, Gabriel, On Duty Outside Diocese (Minnesota)
Gregory, Thomas J., (Retired) Arizona
Grimes, John D., St. Barnabas, Bayville
Groff, Francis W., St. Martha, Point Pleasant
Groffie, John F., St. Gregory the Great, Trenton
Grogan, Michael P., St. Mark, Sea Girt
Groh, Alfred, On Duty Outside the Diocese (Florida)
Grussler, John R., Holy Cross, Trenton
Gularek, Theodore V., St. Veronica, Howell
Gwiazda, Edward J., St. Isaac Jogues, Marlton
Hagan, Michael P., St. Joseph, Beverly
Hambleton, Richard N., St. Mary, Barnegat
Haney, John J., St. Martha, Point Pleasant
Hank, William Moore, St. James, Pennington
Hannawacker, Joseph A., Blessed Sacrament, Trenton
Harbeck, Jay C., On Duty Outside the Diocese (So. Carolina)
Harris, David M., St. Mary, Bordentown
Hauenstein, Richard A., St. Justin, Toms River
Haunes, Ronald J., St. Mary, Barnegat
Hayes, William K., On Duty Outside the Diocese (Virginia)
Heard, William R., Epiphany, Brick Town
Heller, James T., (Retired), St. Pius X, Forked River
Henwood, Gerald V., St. Robert Bellarmine, Freehold
Hepp, Joseph L., St. Anthony of Padua, Hightstown
Herr, Edward R., St. Dorothea, Eatontown
Hilerio, Pedro, Christ the Redeemer, Mount Holly
Hoag, Edward A., St. Ann, Lawrenceville
Hoch, Eugene, St. John Neumann, Mount Laurel
Hoefling, John F., Sacred Heart, Mount Holly
Hooker, George C., (Retired) South Carolina
Hughes John P., (Retired), St. John Neumann, Mount Laurel
Hvizdos, John F., St. Charles Borromeo, Cinnaminson
Iadanza, John M., On Duty Outside the Diocese (Florida)
Iglesias, Manuel F., Holy Angels, Trenton
Imholte, Ralph, St. Mary, Colts Neck
Jackson, Frank W., St, Aloysius, Jackson
Jennings, Edward F., St. Catharine, Spring Lake
Johnson, George A., St. Mary, Barnegat
Johnston, James G., St. Joan of Arc, Marlton
Jones, Francis A., St. Paul, Burlington
Kelder, George R., Jr., St. Denis, Manasquan
Kelly, James A., Our Lady of Perpetual Help, Highlands
Kennedy, Patrick W., St. Anthony of Padua, Hightstown
Kerr, Ronald J., Sr., St. John, Lakehurst
Klimaszewski, Norbert J., On Duty Outside the Diocese (Camden)
Klincewicz, John G., Holy Innocents, Neptune
Knipp, Joseph P., Sacred Heart, Riverton
Kohut, David S., Visitation, Brick
Krupa, Bradford A., Visitation, Brick
Lacey, James A., St. Mary of the Lake, Lakewood
Lachance, Paul A., St. Paul, Princeton
Lafond, Robert H., St. Alphonsus, Hopewell
LaMachia, Ralph A., St. Gregory the Great, Hamilton Square
Latini, Joseph E., St. Gregory the Great, Hamilton
Laurita, Daniel J., On Duty Outside the Diocese (Alabama)
Lavalle, Thomas J., Jr., Holy Angels, Trenton
Little, John L., St. Catherine, Spring Lake
Little, Ronald J., St. Mary of the Lake, Medford
Littlefield, James J., St. Veronica, Howell
Lombardo, Earl H., St. Mary, Barnegat
Lopez, Heriberto, On Duty Outside the Diocese (Florida)
Lydick, Donald E., On Duty Outside the Diocese (Delaware)
Lynch, Joseph A., St. Paul, Princeton
MacCarrick, Donald G., St. Luke, Toms River
MacDonald, Lawrence J., (Retired), St. Mary of the Lakes, Medford
Machion, Robert D., Holy Assumption, Roebling
Malhame, Eugene G., Jr., St. Rose, Belmar
Malloy, Joseph J., Our Lady of Sorrows, Trenton
Manaloris, James A., Holy Name, Delran
Mannikus, Uku R., St. Veronica, Howell
Marcello, Salvatore, Holy Angels, Trenton
Martin, Patrick J., St. Mary, Barnegat
Martucci, Anthony R., St. Pius X, Forked River
Mattozzi, Guido J., St. Joachim, Trenton
McCabe, John, St. Mary, Deal
McGahran, Andrew R., On Duty Outside the Diocese (North Carolina)
McGann, Francis P., Jr., On Duty Outside the Diocese (Canada)
McGrath, James, St. Barnabas, Bayville
McHugh, Joseph, On Duty Outside the Diocese (Camden)
McKenna, Francis A., St. Joseph, Toms River
McKenna, Kenneth M., Our Lady of Mt. Carmel, Asbury Park
McKeon, James, Our Lady of Mercy, Englishtown
McNally, Brent G., St. Justin, Toms River
McNerny, Daniel J., Jesus the Lord, Keyport
Meyer, Richard G., On Duty Outside the Diocese (Florida)
Meyers, Ronald S., Our Lady of Perpetual Help, Maple Shade
Micali, James Mark, St. Clement, Matawan
Miller, Donald C., (Retired), St. Elizabeth Ann Seton, Whiting
Mintz, Robert E., St. Ann, Keansburg
Moir, Gene F., Sr., St. Veronica, Howell
Moore, Timothy E., Our Lady of Sorrows, Trenton
Moresco, Edward J., Our Lady of Perpetual Help, Highlands
Mosteller, Herman J., St. Joseph, Beverly
Mullarkey, Michael F., Epiphany, Brick
Murray, William J., Precious Blood Church, Monmouth Beach
Mustillo, Anthony D., St. Catharine, Holmdel
Mylod, Philip J., (Retired), Jersey Shore Medical Center, Neptune
Nimon, Robert R., On Duty Outside the Diocese (Florida)
Novitsky, Myron J., St. Joseph, Toms River
Nowak, Ronald, Epiphany, Bricktown
O'Boyle, Kevin J., Our Lady of Sorrows, Mercerville
O'Brien, Christopher D., St. Joseph, Keyport
O'Connor, John P., (Retired), St. Catharine, Spring Lake
O'Donnell, John J., Our Lady Queen of Peace, Hainesport
Olshevski, Stanley R., Corpus Christi, Willingboro
Orkis, Stanley, Sacred Heart, Mt. Holly
Orlando, John C., St. Catherine, Middletown
Owens, Lester J., St. Gabriel's, Marlboro
Pacitti, Albert, St. Maximilian Kolbe, Toms River
Palan, Henry N., St. Theresa, Tuckerton
Palsir, James W., St. James, Pennington
Parr, Allan T., Sr., St. Gregory the Great, Trenton
Patton, Joseph R., (Retired), St. Mary of the Lakes, Medford
Paul, Joseph A., Our Lady of Good Counsel, Moorestown
Pelkowski, Raymond R., St. Benedict, Holmdel
Pennise, Alfred, St. Paul, Burlington
Perez, Rene P., St. Aloysius, Jackson
Perkins, Charles A., St. Joseph, Beverly
Perusi, Donald L., St. Denis, Manasquan
Petrauskas, James J., St. Theresa's, Tuckerton
Pierfy, Jeffrey, Our Lady of Sorrows, Mercerville
Pirozzi, Neil, St. Gregory the Great, Trenton
Policastro, Donald M., St. Joseph, Keyport
Porter, Thomas P., St. Peter, Point Pleasant Beach
Price, Walter L., St. Ann, Browns Mills
Prihoda, Frank J., St. John, Allentown
Principato, Michael, St. Catherine, Farmingdale
Provencher, Conrad J., On Duty Outside the Diocese (Pennsylvania)
Purcell, Kyran J., St. Elizabeth Ann Seton, Whiting
Putnam, Harry A., (Retired), St. Mary, Bordentown
Rainville, Raymond R., St. Agnes, Atlantic Highlands
Ramos, Luis A., St. Mary's Cathedral, Trenton
Richardson, Gary T., St. Mary, Bordentown
Rider, Joseph H., St. Elizabeth Ann Seton, Whiting
Riedinger, Gerald, St. Dominic, Brick
Rivella, Thomas H., Incarnation, Trenton
Rivera, Juan A., Jr., St. Mary Cathedral, Trenton
Rodriguez, Feliz, On Duty Outside the Diocese (Puerto Rico)
Ross, Michael D., On Duty Outside Diocese (Columbus, OH)
Rowley, William R., Sacred Heart, Mt. Holly
Russo, James C., St. Gabriel, Marlboro
Saake, Dennis J., St. Mark, Sea Girt
Sabados, Andrew A., Sr., St. Gregory the Great, Hamilton
Sansevere, Stephen A., St. Gabriel, Marlboro
Schwarz, Herbert, St. Benedict, Holmdel
Schwind, Albert, (Retired), St. Francis of Assisi, Brant Beach
Sciarrotta, Samuel P., St. James Church, Pennington
Seaton, George L., On Duty Outside the Diocese (Florida)
Sepich, William S., St. Charles Borromeo, Cinnaminson
Shapiro, David L., St. Justin, Toms River
Shea, Thomas F., St. Mary, Bordentown
Sheehan, Kenneth R., St. Catherine, Middletown
Sherpensky, Frank, St. Ann, Browns Mills
Slavin, Dennis E., Office of Family Life, Trenton
Slee, Louis, Blessed Sacrament, Trenton
Somma, Eugene A., St. Michael, West End
Sondeen, Carl R., St. Charles Borromeo, Cinnaminson

Sowa, Frank J., (Retired), St. Stanislaus, Trenton
Stap, Matthew J., (Retired), St. Joseph, Beverly
Staub, Raymond W., Jr., Assumption, New Egypt
Sulzmann, William P., St. Theresa, Tuckerton
Tarzy, Barry R., St. Joan of Arc, Marlton
Taylor, Michael A., St. Barnabas, Bayville
Tedeschi, Joseph R., St. Mary of the Lakes, Medford
Tharp, Robert, Holy Angels, Trenton
Tobin, James, Sacred Heart, Bay Head
Toca, Frederick M., Our Lady of the Divine Shepherd, Trenton
Toolan, James W., St. George, Titusville
Topoleski, Thomas C., St. Mary, Barnegat
Torres, Benito, S.S. Peter & Paul, Trenton
Trani, Eduardo, Christ the Redeemer, Mount Holly
Ulmer, Ronald J., St. Joseph, Beverly
Vagrin, Stephen R., St. Catherine, Seaside Park
Valentin, Juan E., Sacred Heart, Trenton
Vassallo, John F., Jr., Corpus Christi, Willingboro
Vazquez, Emiliano, St. Mary Cathedral, Trenton
Vicari, Salvatore J., Jr., Visitation, Brick Town
Vilches, Arnaldo, Christ the Redeemer, Mount Holly
Vlcej, Robert J., St. Ann's, Keansburg
Vogel, Anthony D., St. Hedwig, Trenton
Voll, Edwin L., Jr., (Retired), St. Joseph, Toms River
Wallack, Gregory B., St. Luke, Toms River
Walsh, James P., Holy Innocent, Neptune
Walsh, John J., (Retired), St. Thomas More, Manalapan
Wanat, John A., St. Rose of Lima, Freehold
Watkins, Thomas H., All Saints, Burlington
Weller, Caleb J., St. Mary, Colts Neck
White, Edward A., On Duty Outside the Diocese (Washington)
Whitfield, Robert J., On Duty Outside the Diocese (Maryland)
Wilson, William A., St. Gregory the Great, Hamilton Square
Yaccarine, John A., Holy Trinity, Long Branch
Young, Donald A., Our Lady Star of the Sea, Long Branch
Zadworny, Barry J., St. Hedwig, Trenton
Zebrowski, John J., St. Thomas More, Manalapan
Seaman, Joseph F., On Duty outside Diocese (Camden)

INSTITUTIONS LOCATED IN THE DIOCESE

[A] COLLEGES AND UNIVERSITIES

LAKEWOOD. *Georgian Court College*, 900 Lakewood Ave., 08701-2697. Tel: 732-364-2200; Fax: 732-901-9466. Email: briordy@georgian.edu. Web: www.georgian.edu. Sr. Rosemary E. Jeffries, R.S.M., Ph.D., Pres.; Dr. Eduardo S. Paderon, Provost; Rev. Norman Demeck, C.P. Sisters of Mercy Priests 4; Sisters 23; Lay Teachers 226; Students 3,656.

[B] HIGH SCHOOLS, DIOCESAN AND PARISH

TRENTON. *Notre Dame High School*, 601 Lawrence Rd., 08648. Tel: 609-882-7900; Fax: 609-882-5723. Email: mivins@notredame.k12.nj.us. Web: www.notredame.k12.nj.us. Ms. Mary Liz Ivins, Prin.; Miss Joan Pilkington, Asst. Prin.; Anton J. Witherspoon, Asst. Prin.; Rev. Dennis Apoldite, Chap. Sisters of Mercy 1; Lay Teachers 87; Students 1,272.

BELMAR. *Saint Rose High School*, 607 Seventh Ave., 07719. Tel: 732-681-2858; Fax: 732-280-2745. Email: mrc@strose.k12.nj.us. Web: www.strose.k12.nj.us. Dr. Michele R. Campbell, Ph.D. Students 650; Sisters 7; Lay Teachers 46.

DELRAN. *Holy Cross High School*, 5035 Rte. 130 S., 08075. Tel: 856-461-5400; Fax: 856-764-0806. Email: joseph.lemme@hclance.org. Web: www.hclance.org. Mr. Joseph R. Lemme, Prin. Sisters of I.H.M., Scranton, PA Priests 1; Sisters 4; Lay Teachers 55; Students 943.

HAMILTON. *McCorristin High School*, 175 Leonard Ave., 08610. Tel: 609-586-3705; Fax: 609-586-6584. Email: tlynch@mccorristin.com. Web: www.mccorristin.com. Mr. Timothy M. Lynch, Prin. Sisters 2; Brothers 1; Lay Teachers 32; Students 347.

HOLMDEL. *St. John Vianney High School*, 540 Line Rd., 07733. Tel: 732-739-0800; Fax: 732-739-0824. Email: deroba@sjvhs.com. Web: www.sjvhs.com. Mr. Joseph F. Deroba, Prin.; Rev. Eugene B. Vavrick, Chap. Sisters 2; Lay Teachers 63; Students 982.

NEW MONMOUTH. *Mater Dei High School*, 538 Church St., 07748. Tel: 732-671-9100; Fax: 732-671-9214. Email: materdeihighschool@nac.net. Web: www.materdeihs.org. Mr. Frank Poleski Jr., Prin. Students 380; Lay Teachers 28.

RED BANK. *Red Bank Catholic High School*, 112 Broad St., 07701. Tel: 732-747-1774; Fax: 732-747-1936. Email: alabat@redbankcatholic.com. Web: www.redbankcatholic.com. Mr. Robert Abatemarco, Prin. Sisters 4; Lay Teachers 90; Students 1,099.

TOMS RIVER. *Monsignor Donovan High School*, 711 Hooper Ave., 08753. Tel: 732-349-8801; Fax: 732-349-8956. Email: egere@mondonhs.com. Web: www.mondonhs.com. Dr. Edward Gere, Prin. Priests 2; Sisters 5; Lay Teachers 74; Students 957.

[C] HIGH SCHOOLS, PRIVATE

TRENTON. *Villa Victoria Academy*, 376 W. Upper Ferry Rd., 08628. Tel: 609-882-1700; Fax: 609-882-8421. Email: srlillian@villavictoria.org. Web: www.villavictoria.org. Sr. Mary Ann Gecina, M.P.F., Prin. Upper School, Grades 7-8 (Girls); Grades 9-12 (Girls). Sisters 3; Lay Teachers 17; Students 150.

LINCROFT. *Christian Brothers Academy*, 850 Newman Springs Rd., 07738. Tel: 732-747-1959; Fax: 732-747-1643. Email: adminoff@cbalincroftnj.org. Web: www.delasalle.org. Bros. Andrew O'Gara, F.S.C., Pres.; Ralph Montedoro, F.S.C., Prin. Priests 1; Brothers 11; Lay Teachers 57; Students 925.

PRINCETON. *Stuart Country Day School of the Sacred Heart*, (Grades 9-12), 1200 Stuart Rd., 08540. Tel: 609-921-2330; Fax: 609-497-0784. Email: asoos@sturat.k12.nj.us. Web: www.stuart.k12.nj.us. Sr. Frances de la Chapelle, Headmistress; Anne Soos, Prin. Lay Teachers 28; Students 138.

[D] INTER-PARISH ELEMENTARY SCHOOLS

MANAHAWKIN. *All Saints Regional Catholic School*, (Grades PreK-8), 400 Doc Cramer Blvd., 08050. Tel: 609-597-3800; Fax: 609-597-2223. Email: asrc@eticomm.net. Web: asrcs.org. Sr. Jeanette Daily, Prin. Lay Teachers 16; Total Enrollment 311.

[E] ELEMENTARY SCHOOLS, PRIVATE

TRENTON. *Villa Victoria Academy*, (Grades PreK-6) , (Coed) , 376 W. Upper Ferry Rd., 08628. Tel: 609-883-5760; Fax: 609-882-8421. Email: mahuges@villavictoria.org. Web: www.villavictoria.org. Mrs. Mary Ann Hughes, Prin. Lower School. Sisters 1; Lay Teachers 8; Students 120.

PRINCETON. *Stuart County Day School of the Sacred Heart*, (Grades PreK-8), 1200 Stuart Rd., 08540. Tel: 609-921-2330; Fax: 609-497-0784. Web: www.stuart.k12.nj.us. Email: stuart.k12.nj.us. Sr. Frances de la Chapelle, Headmistress; Mrs. Patricia Schorr, Prin. (PreK-5); Mrs. Tamara Skvir, Prin. (Grades 6-8). Sisters 1; Lay Teachers 53; Students 409.

[F] CATHOLIC CHARITIES, DIOCESE OF TRENTON

TRENTON. *Catholic Charities*, 383 W. State St., P.O. Box 1423, 08607-1423. Tel: 609-394-5181; Fax: 609-695-6978. Email: fdolan@cctrenton.org. Web: catholiccharitiestrenton.org. Mr. Francis E. Dolan, Exec. Dir.; George Bontcue, Assoc. Exec. Dir., Fiscal Affairs; Barry H. Cole, Ph.D., Assoc. Exec. Dir., Prog. Svcs.; Michael R. Allen, Assoc. Exec. Dir., Community Affairs; Kathryn Jean Turner, Assoc. Exec. Dir. Human Resources; Mark G. Siegel, Assoc. Exec. Dir. Development.

Burlington Behavioral Healthcare Division, 25 Ikea Dr., Westampton, 08060. Tel: 609-267-9339; Fax: 609-267-6655. Frank J. Helverson, Dir.

Mercer Behavioral Healthcare Division, 39 N. Clinton Ave., 08609. Tel: 609-394-9398; Fax: 609-396-8420. Harry Postel, Dir.

Monmouth/Ocean Behavioral Healthcare Division, 145 Maple Ave., Red Bank, 07701. Tel: 732-747-9660; Fax: 732-747-7590. Robert G. Hodnett, Dir.

Emergency Services Division, 801 Burlington Ave., Delanco, 08075. Tel: 856-764-6945; Fax: 856-764-6948. Joyce Campbell, Dir.

Family Development & Child Advocacy Division, 55 N. Clinton Ave., 08609. Tel: 609-394-7680; Fax: 609-278-1836. Ronald C. Gering, Dir. Services for victims and perpetuators of family violence.

Providence House Division, 950A Chester Ave., Delran, 08075. Tel: 856-824-0599; Fax: 856-824-9340. Jean Metz, Dir. Services to women and children in danger of physical abuse.

St. Michael Children's Home, c/o Diocese of Trenton, 701 Lawrenceville Rd., 08648.

[G] DAY CARE CENTERS

TRENTON. *Mount Carmel Guild Day Care Center*, 73 N. Clinton Ave., 08609. Tel: 609-392-5159. Email: mtcarmelguild@aol.com. Web: www.mcgtrenton.org. Mr. Russell J. Hansel, Exec. Dir.; Paula Maugans, Contact Person.

BRANT BEACH. *St. Francis of Assisi Day Care Center*, 4700 Long Beach Blvd., 08008. Tel: 609-494-8861; Fax: 609-494-0489. Joan Wickert, Contact Person.

HAMILTON. *Our Lady of Sorrows Day Care Center*, 3710 E. State St. Ext., 08619. Tel: 609-586-1422; Fax: 609-586-1214. Email: mbruder@olsparish.org.

KEANSBURG. *St. Ann Day Care*, 121 Main St., 07734. Tel: 732-787-7220; Fax: 732-787-2136. Sr. Mary Faith, Contact Person.

LONG BRANCH. *St. John the Baptist Family Center*, 272 Willow Ave., 07740. Tel: 732-229-8905; 732-229-8527; 732-571-1003; Fax: 732-571-0280. Email: daycarestjohnbaptist@comcast.net. Day Care and Child Development Center. Children 153.

[H] CARE INSTITUTIONS FOR CHILDREN

TRENTON. *Sister Georgine School*, 544 Chestnut Ave., 08611. Tel: 609-396-5444; Fax: 609-396-0989. Email: bfurst@srgeorgineschool.org. Web: www.srgeorgineschool.org. Sr. Barbara Furst, Prin. Sisters of St. Francis Students 18; Staff 13.

HOPEWELL. *St. Michael's Orphanage and Industrial School, c/o the Diocese of Trenton*, 701 Lawrenceville Rd., 08648.

[I] GENERAL HOSPITALS

TRENTON. *St. Francis Medical Center*, 601 Hamilton Ave., 08629. Tel: 609-599-5000; Fax: 609-695-2744. Email: bdraper@che-east.org. Web: www.stfrancismedical.com. Affiliate of Catholic Health East. Sisters of St. Francis of Philadelphia 8; Bed Capacity 240; Patients Assisted Annually 142,000.

Schools for Nurses Tel: 609-599-5192; Fax: 609-599-5799. Bonny Ross, Dir. School of Nursing; Rev. Joel F. Szydlowski, O.F.M., Dir. Pastoral Care. Student Nurses 50.

[J] SPECIAL HOSPITALS AND SANATORIA FOR INVALIDS

LAWRENCEVILLE. *Morris Hall/Saint Lawrence, Inc.*, 2381 Lawrenceville Rd., 08648. Tel: 609-896-9500; Fax: 609-895-0242. Email: clb950@aol.com. Web: www.slrc.org. Mr. Charles L. Brennan, Admin.; Rev. Justin J. Herbst, Chap.; Sr. Claire DeStefano, S.S.J., Dir. Pastoral Care. St. Lawrence Rehabilitation Center. Bed Capacity 139; Bed Licensure 139.

Morris Hall/Saint Lawrence, Inc. Morris Hall - St. Joseph's Nursing Center , 1 Bishops' Dr., 08648-2050. Tel: 609-896-0006; Fax: 609-896-8037. Email: info@morrishall.org. Web: www.morrishall.org. Mark Sorrento, L.N.H.A., C.A.L.A., COO. Skilled Nursing Care Facility for the Chronically Ill. Bed Capacity 120; Total in Residence 116.

Residences and Assisted Living for Senior Citizens Tel: 609-896-0006; Fax: 609-896-8037.

[K] SPECIALIZED CHILD CARE AGENCIES

RED BANK. *Collier Group Home*, 180 Spring St., 07701. Tel: 732-842-8337; Fax: 732-530-7096. Email: pauldesantis@earthlink.net. Mr. Paul DeSantis, Dir. 24 Hour Program-Therapy and Educational Services. Provided Under the Supervision of the Sisters of the Good Shepherd. Capacity 10.

WICKATUNK. *Collier Services*, Collier High School, 160 Conover Rd., 07765. Tel: 732-946-4771; Fax: 732-946-3519. Email: info@collierservices.com. Web: www.collierservices.com. Ms. Aideen Bugler, Prog. Dir.; Sr. Ellen Kelly, Exec. Dir. Adolescent Boys and Girls. Capacity 150.

Kateri Environmental Education Center Mr. Edward Margotti, Prog. Dir. of Kateri Center. Tel: 732-946-9694; Fax: 732-946-9785. Open to the public. Summer day camp serves children 5-12 years of age.; Six week extended school year program. Capacity 40.

[L] HOMES FOR AGED

TRENTON. *Cathedral Square Housing, Inc.*, 26 W. Hanover Pl., 08608. Tel: 609-392-1111; Fax: 609-683-7227. Email: cs@gershengroup.com. Most Rev. John M. Smith, Dir. Senior Citizen Housing Project.

LAWRENCEVILLE. *Morris Hall-Saint Lawrence, Inc.* Morris Hall - St. Mary's Residence & Assisted Living. , 1 Bishops' Dr., 08648-2050. Tel: 609-896-0006; Fax: 609-895-8037. Email: info@morrishall.org. Web: www.morrishall.org. Mr. Charles L. Brennan, CEO; Mark Sorrento, L.N.H.A., C.A.L.A., COO. Guests 65; Beds 78. In Res. Rev. Justin J. Herbst, Chap.

[M] MONASTERIES AND RESIDENCES FOR PRIESTS AND BROTHERS

TRENTON. *St. Lawrence Rehabilitation Center* (Lawrenceville) , 2381 Lawrenceville Rd., 08648. Tel: 609-896-9500; Fax: 609-895-0242. Email:

clb950@aol.com. Web: www.slrc.org. Charles Brennan, CEO. Assisted living for priests In Res. Most Rev. John C. Reiss, D.D., J.C.D. (Retired); Rev. Msgrs. George A. Ardos; Joseph A. O'Connor (Retired); Thaddeus J. Wojciehowski (Retired); Revs. James Coley; Ernest J. Siska (Retired).

Villa Vianney (Lawrenceville) , 2301 Lawrenceville Rd., 08648. Tel: 609-219-0177; Fax: 609-896-8037. In Res. Rev. Msgrs. Thomas A. Coffey (Retired); Samuel C. Constance (Retired); William F. Fitzgerald (Retired); Joseph A. O'Connor (Retired); Leonard R. Toomey (Retired); Thaddeus J. Wojciehowski (Retired); Revs. Harry E. Cenefeldt (Retired); Edward Dougherty; Adam Kearns (Retired); Rev. Msgr. William E. Maguire; Revs. James J. McConnell (Retired); Donald J. O'Brien (Retired).

BORDENTOWN. *Society of the Divine Word*, 101 Park St., 08505. Tel: 609-298-0549; Fax: 609-298-6014. Very Rev. Raymond T. Lennon, S.V.D., Rector; Revs. Patrick Connor, S.V.D.; Francis Mahon, S.V.D.; Norman R. St. John, S.V.D. (MET); Victor Butler, S.V.D.; James Artzer, S.V.D.; Vance Thorne, S.V.D.; Jefferson Pool, S.V.D.; Leo Dusheck, S.V.D.; Paul Connors, S.V.D.; Bros. Jochim Brignac, S.V.D.; Louis Gagnon, S.V.D.; Patrick Hegarty, S.V.D.; James Mullen, S.V.D.; Joseph Hornek, S.V.D.; Robert Zalikowski, S.V.D.

LINCROFT. *Christian Brothers, St. La Salle Auxiliary*, 850 Newman Springs Rd., P.O. Box 238, 07738. Tel: 732-842-4359; Fax: 732-219-1619. Email: cards@dlsaux.org. Web: dlsaux.org.

LaSalle Lincroft, Inc., 850 Newman Springs Rd., 07738. Tel: 732-842-7420; Fax: 732-530-3504. Bro. William Martin, F.S.C., Contact Person. Brothers 3.

De La Salle Hall, Inc., 810 Newman Springs Rd., 07738. Tel: 732-530-9470; Fax: 732-530-8072. Bro. Stephen Mc Cabe, F.S.C., Dir. Brothers Retirement Home. Brothers 3; Lay Staff 40; Patients 28.

La Salle Provincialate Inc., 800 Newman Springs Rd., 07738. Tel: 732-842-7420; Fax: 732-530-3504. Email: cbny@cbnewyork.org. Web: cbnewyork.org. Bro. Frank Byrne, F.S.C., Prov. Brothers of the Christian Schools

The Vaugirard Religious & Charitable Trust, 800 Newman Springs Rd., 07738. Tel: 732-842-4359; Fax: 732-219-1619.

MOUNT LAUREL. *Cistercian Monastery of Our Lady of Fatima*, 564 Walton Ave., 08054-9582. Tel: 856-235-1330; Fax: 856-235-9632. Revs. Lino S. Parente, O.Cist. (Italy), Prior, (Italy); Maurizio Nicoletti, O.Cist (Italy), (Italy); Teclezghi Ucbaghiorghis, O.Cist. Cistercian Fathers

[N] CONVENTS AND RESIDENCES FOR SISTERS

TRENTON. *Morning Star House of Prayer*, 312 Upper Ferry Rd., 08628. Tel: 609-882-2766; Fax: 609-882-2766. Email: sisterjo@morningstarprayerhouse.org. Web: www.morningstarprayerhouse.org. Religious Sisters Filippini

Notre Dame Diocesan Convent Lawrenceville ; Intercongregational Living , 681 Lawrence Rd., 08648. Tel: 609-406-7437; Fax: 609-406-7412. Web: dioceseoftrenton.org. Sisters 20.

Sisters of St. Francis of Philadelphia, St. Clare Convent, 917 Melrose Ave., 08629. Tel: 609-695-7805; Fax: 609-695-2308. Email: clarecon@bellatlantic.net.

Villa Victoria Academy Convent, 376 W. Upper Ferry Rd., 08628. Tel: 609-883-0064; Fax: 609-882-8066. Religious Sisters Filippini

ASBURY PARK. *Missionaries of Charity-St. Clare Convent*, 917 Melrose Ave., 07712. Tel: 609-695-7805.

COLUMBUS. *Monastery of Saint Clare*, 150 White Pine Rd., 08022. Tel: 609-324-2638; Fax: 609-324-2938. Email: clandreosc@aol.com. Web: www.poorclare.org/newjersey. Sr. Clare Andre Gagliardi, O.S.C., Abbess.

Sisters of Good Shepherd, Contemplative Monastery, 150 White Pine Rd., 08022. Tel: 609-324-2638.

DELRAN. *Holy Cross High School Convent*, Sisters of the Immaculate Heart of Mary, 5035 Rte. 130 S., 08075. Tel: 856-461-1792.

ELBERON. *Emmaus House*, 80 Norwood Ave., 07740. Tel: 732-229-6843; Fax: 732-870-2538.

HARVEY CEDARS. *Maris Stella Retreat and Vacation Center*, 7201 Long Beach Blvd., 08008. Tel: 609-361-8663. Email: stmsalerno@aol.com. Sr. Thomas Mary Salerno, S.C., Admin. Sisters of Charity of St. Elizabeth, Convent Station

HIGHTSTOWN. *Religiose Agostiniane*, Augustinae House, 200 Maxwell Ave., 08520. Tel: 609-448-2872.

LAKEWOOD. *Sisters of Mercy of the Americas, NJ*, Georgian Court College Convent, 900 Lakewood Ave., 08701. Tel: 732-364-2200; Fax: 732-364-5640.

LAWRENCEVILLE. *Religious of the Sacred Heart of Mary*, 43 Coral Ct., 08648. Tel: 609-896-2413.

NEW MONMOUTH. *Siena New Hope Home*, P.O. Box 518, 07748 Tel: 732-671-3622. Religious Sisters Filippini

OCEAN GROVE. *Memorare*, 20 Pitman Ave., 07756. Tel: 732-774-3158.

WICKATUNK. *Convent of the Sisters of Good Shepherd*, 160 Conover Rd., 07765. Tel: 732-946-7877; 732-946-7886; Fax: 732-332-1240. Email: srdebbie@optonline.net. Web: www.goodshepherdsisters.org. Sr. Deborah Drago, Coord. Sisters of Good Shepherd of New Jersey Sisters 9.

[O] CHAPELS

BURLINGTON. *Our Lady of Light Chapel* 115 W. Pearl St., 08016 Tel: 609-386-6221; Fax: 609-386-6993.

LAWRENCEVILLE. *Our Lady of the Rosary Chapel* 1 Bishops' Dr., 08648-2050. Tel: 609-896-0006; Fax: 609-895-0466. Email: info@morrishall.org. Web: www.morrishall.org. Rev. Justin J. Herbst, Chap. Located in Morris Hall.

[P] HOUSES OF PRAYER

TRENTON. *Morning Star House of Prayer*, 312 W. Upper Ferry Rd., 08628. Tel: 609-882-2766; Fax: 609-882-2766. Email: sisterjo@morningstarprayerhouse.org. Web: morningstarprayerhouse.org. Sr. Geraldine Calabrese, M.P.F. Religious Teachers Filippini 2.

MOUNT HOLLY. *Francis House of Prayer*, P.O. Box 392, Rancocas, 08073. Tel: 609-877-0509; Fax: 609-877-5810. 39 Springside Rd., Westampton, 08060. Email: fhop@pics.com. Web: www.francishouseofprayer.org. Sr. Marcella Springer, S.S.J.

NEPTUNE. *The Upper Room Spiritual Center*, P.O. Box 1104, 07754-1104. Tel: 732-922-0550; Fax: 732-922-3904. Email: upperroom@bytheshore.com. Web: www.theupper-room.org. Sisters Maureen Christensen, Co-Dir.; Maureen Conroy, Co-Dir.; Trudy Ahern, Co-Dir.

[Q] RETREAT HOUSES

ELBERON. *Stella Maris Retreat Center* 981 Ocean Ave., 07740. Tel: 732-229-0602; Fax: 732-229-8960. Email: smreservation@mycomcast.com. Web: www.stellamarisretreatcenter.org. Sr. Clare McNerney, C.S.J.P., Dir. Sisters of St. Joseph of Peace 2.

HARVEY CEDARS. *Maris Stella, Retreat and Vacation Center*, 7201 Long Beach Blvd., 08008. Tel: 609-361-8663; Fax: 609-361-8863. Email: stmsalerno@aol.com. Sisters Thomas Mary Salerno, S.C., Admin.; Maria Magdalena Studer, S.C., Asst. Admin. Sisters of Charity of St. Elizabeth, Convent Station

LONG BRANCH. *San Alfonso Retreat House*, 755 Ocean Ave., P.O. Box 3098, 07740. Tel: 732-222-2731; Fax: 732-870-8892. Email: sanalfonso755@aol.com. Web: www.sanalfonsoretreats.org. Revs. John McGowan, C.SS.R., Rector Dir.; William Collins, C.SS.R.; Dennis Foley, C.SS.R.; Andrew Skeabeck, C.SS.R.; John M. O'Connor, C.SS.R.; Timothy Keating, C.SS.R.; Bro. Bernard Colleran, C.SS.R.; Sr. Miriam Carmelita Romanelli, S.S.J. Priests 3; Brothers 1; Sisters 1.

SOUTH MANTOLOKING. *St. Joseph by the Sea Retreat House*, 400 Rte. 35 N., 08738. Tel: 732-892-8494; Fax: 732-892-9905. Email: falauretti@aol.com. Web: www.filippiniusa.org. Sr. Frances Lauretti, M.P.F., Dir. Sisters 2.

[R] PERSONAL PRELATURES

PRINCETON. *Opus Dei* Prelature of the Holy Cross and Opus Dei , 34 Mercer St., 08540. Tel: 609-497-9448; Fax: 609-497-0906. Email: jrvg98@yahoo.com. Web: www.opusdei.org. Rev. Juan R. Velez.

[S] NEWMAN CENTERS

PRINCETON. *Campus Ministry for the Diocese of Trenton* Aquinas Institute, Princeton University, 65 Stockton St., 08540. Tel: 609-924-1820; Fax: 609-924-8322. Email: mullelly@princeton.edu. Rev. Thomas J. Mullelly, J.D., Dir. & Chap.

Emmaus House, Rider University 2116 Lawrenceville Rd., 08648. Tel: 609-896-0394; Fax: 609-219-9203. Email: bugliano@rider.edu. Rev. Bruno A. Ugliano, O.S.B., Chap.

Mercer County Community College 1200 Old Trenton Rd., Hamilton Township, 08690. Tel: 609-896-0394; Fax: 609-219-9203. Rev. Bruno A. Ugliano, O.S.B., Chap.

Bede House, College of New Jersey 492 Ewingville Rd., 08638. Tel: 609-771-9091. Rev. Gabriel Zeis, T.O.R., Chap.

Georgian Court College 900 Lakewood Ave., Lakewood, 08701. Tel: 732-364-2200, Ext. 600; Fax: 732-901-7151. Sr. Mariann Mahon, R.S.M., Dir. Campus Ministry.

Catholic Center at Monmouth University 16 Beechwood Ave., West Long Branch, 07764. Tel: 732-229-9300; Fax: 732-229-1050. Web: mvcatholic.com. Rev. Michael Lankford, Chap.; Mary Jakub, Assoc. Dir.

[T] MISCELLANEOUS LISTINGS

TRENTON. *The Haitian Community Center*, 31 West Front St., 08608. Tel: 609-394-5693; Fax: 609-394-3276. Rev. Msgr. John K. Dermond, J.C.L., Admin.

Martin House, 802 E. State St., P.O. Box 1025, 08606. Tel: 609-989-0271; Fax: 609-989-0933. Rev. Brian McCormick.

Martin House Learning Center, 794 E. State St., P.O. Box 1025, 08606. Tel: 609-989-8143; Fax: 609-989-0933.

New Jersey Catholic Conference, 211 N. Warren St., 08618-4894. Tel: 609-599-2110; Fax: 609-392-3094. Email: info@njcathconf.com. Web: www.njcathconf.com. Most Rev. John J. Myers, D.D., J.C.D., Pres.; William F. Bolan Jr., J.D., Exec. Dir.

ASBURY PARK. *Mercy Center, Inc.*, 1106 Main St., 07712. Tel: 732-774-9397; Fax: 732-988-8709. Email: mcyctn@aol.com. Web: mercycenternj.org. Carol Ann Henry, R.S.M., Dir.

BRICK. *Mid-Life Directions*, 4 Palm Ave., 08723. Tel: 732-255-1239; Fax: 732-255-1239. Sr. Anne Brennan, C.S.J., Contact Person. Purpose: Ministry for personal and spiritual growth specifically for people in midlife and later years.

ELBERON. *Emmaus House*, 80 Norwood Ave., 07740. Tel: 732-229-5834; Fax: 732-870-2538. Email: dwisw1118@aol.com. Sr. Patricia Mary Walsh, O.P., Admin.

LAWRENCEVILLE. *The Foundation of Morris Hall/St. Lawrence, Inc.*, 2381 Lawrenceville Rd., 08648. Tel: 609-896-9500; Fax: 609-895-1602. Email: jmillnet@SLRC.org. Web: www.slrc.org. Mr. Thomas E. Boyle, CFO & Contact Person.

Morris Hall/St. Lawrence, Inc., 2381 Lawrenceville Rd., 08648-2050. Tel: 609-896-0006; Fax: 609-896-8037. Bed Capacity 220; Bed Licensure 220.

Morris Hall Home for the Aged Mr. Charles Brennan, CEO; Mark Sorrento, L.N.H.A., C.A.L.A., COO; Rev. Justin J. Herbst, Chap.; Sr. Claire DeStefano, S.S.J., Dir. of Pastoral Care.

LINCROFT. *The Bethlehem University Foundation, Inc.*, 800 Newman Springs Rd., 07738. Tel: 732-842-7420; Fax: 732-530-3504. Rev. Msgr. Robert L. Sterns, Bd. Chm.; Bro. David Carroll, F.S.C., Sec.; Victor York, Treas.

Christian Brothers of Lincroft, NJ, Inc., 850 Newman Springs Rd., 07738. Tel: 732-842-6712; Fax: 732-576-8057. Bro. Peter Mannion, F.S.C., Contact Person.

MIDDLETOWN. *The Gathering Place*, 130 Bray Ave., 07748. Tel: 732-495-7615; Fax: 732-495-6422. Email: mnoone3161@aol.com. Sr. Margaret Noone, R.S.M., Contact Person. Ministry which promotes systemic change through programs of human development and spiritual growth, with special emphasis on those who are poor.

POINT PLEASANT. *Trenton Diocesan Union of Holy Name Societies*, 650 Delaware Ave., 08742. Tel: 732-295-2111; Fax: 732-295-2333. Email: hudsoncorp@msn.com. Web: dioceseoftrenton.org. William R. Wosnitzer, Pres. Federation of Holy Name Societies: Burlington County: Kevin Rooney, 2503 Salem Dr., Cinnaminson, NJ 08077; Mercer County: Frank Jones, 23 Delaware Ave., Ewing, NJ 08638; Monmouth County: Theodore Ferraro, 92 Oakwood Ave., West Long Branch, NJ 07764; Ocean County: Robert A. Murawski, 831 Fay Ct., Point Pleasant, NJ 08742

SWAINTON. *Holy Redeemer Visiting Nurse Agency, Inc.*, 1801 Rte. 9 N., 08210. Tel: 609-465-2082; 800-745-4693; Fax: 609-463-6121; 609-463-6124. Web: www.holyredeemer.com. Toni Hague, Vice Pres. & Admin. Sponsor: Sisters of the Holy Redeemer, C.S.R., A subsidiary of Holy Redeemer Health System, Inc.; A Medicare Certified Home Health Agency serving patients in their own homes. A Medicare Certified Hospice Program providing services for terminally ill patients and their families.

Atlantic County Office, 6727 Delilah Rd., Egg Harbor Township, 08234. Tel: 609-625-2200; 800-788-3029; Fax: 609-625-2992.

Ocean County Office, 1228 Rte. 37 W., Toms River, 08755. Tel: 800-488-2669; 732-240-2449; Fax: 732-288-2669.

RELIGIOUS INSTITUTES OF MEN REPRESENTED IN THE DIOCESE

For further details refer to the corresponding bracketed number in the Religious Institutes of Men or Women section.

[0140]—*The Augustinians*—O.S.A.
[0200]—*Benedictine Monks* (St. Mary's Abbey, Morristown, NJ)—O.S.B.
[0030]—*Brothers of the Christian Schools*—F.S.C.
[0270]—*Carmelite Fathers and Brothers*—O.Carm.
[0340]—*Cistercian Fathers* (Cistercian Monastery of Our Lady of Fatima)—O.Cist.
[0480]—*Conventual Franciscans* (Provs. of the Immaculate Conception & St. Anthony of Padua)—O.F.M.Conv
[0520]—*Franciscan Friars* (Prov. of the Most Holy Name of Jesus)—O.F.M.
[1310]—*Order of the Holy Trinity*—O.SS.T.
[0610]—*Priests of the Congregation of Holy Cross*—C.S.C.
[1070]—*Redemptorist Fathers* (Baltimore Prov.)—C.SS.R.
[0420]—*Society of the Divine Word*—S.V.D.
[0560]—*Third Order Regular of Saint Francis* (Prov. of the Most Sacred Heart of Jesus)—T.O.R.
[]—*Vincentian Congregation*—V.C.

RELIGIOUS INSTITUTES OF WOMEN REPRESENTED IN THE DIOCESE

[1810]—*Bernardine Sisters of Third Order of St. Francis*—O.S.F.
[2410]—*Congregation of the Marianites of Holy Cross*—M.S.C.
[1830]—*Contemplative Sisters of the Good Shepherd*—R.G.S.
[1070-05]—*Dominican Sisters* (Amityville, NY)—O.P.
[1070-18]—*Dominican Sisters* (Caldwell, NJ)—O.P.
[1070]—*Dominican Sisters* Houston, TX—O.P.
[1070-11]—*Dominican Sisters* (Sparkhill, NY)—O.P.
[1070-15]—*Dominican Sisters* (Blauvelt, NY)—O.P.
[1105]—*Dominican Sisters of Hope* (Ossining, NY)—O.P.
[1180]—*Franciscan Sisters of Allegany, NY*—O.S.F.
[1470]—*Franciscan Sisters of St. Joseph* (Hamburg, NY)—F.S.S.J.
[1190]—*Franciscan Sisters of the Atonement (Graymoor)*—S.A.
[1840]—*Grey Nuns of the Sacred Heart*—G.N.S.H.
[2710]—*Missionaries of Charity*—M.C.
[3760]—*Order of St. Clare*—O.S.C.
[]—*Religiose Agostiniane Civitavecchia, Italy*—A.S.S.E.
[3465]—*Religious of the Sacred Heart of Mary*—R.S.H.M.
[3430]—*Religious Teachers Filippini*—M.P.F.
[2970]—*School Sisters of Notre Dame, Baltimore* (Province)—S.S.N.D.
[]—*School Sisters of the Third Order Regular of St. Francis* (Bethlehem, PA)—O.S.F.
[]—*Sisters for Christian Community*—S.F.C.C.
[0590]—*Sisters of Charity of Saint Elizabeth, Convent Station*—S.C.
[2575]—*Sisters of Mercy of the Americas* (Merion; New Jersey)—R.S.M.
[3730]—*Sisters of Order of St. Basil the Great*—O.S.B.M.
[3360]—*Sisters of Providence of Saint Mary of the Woods, IN*—S.P.
[3830]—*Sisters of Saint Joseph of Brentwood* (New York)—C.S.J.
[1630]—*Sisters of St. Francis of Penance and Christian Charity*—O.S.F.
[1650]—*The Sisters of St. Francis of Philadelphia*—O.S.F.
[3840]—*Sisters of St. Joseph of Carondelet*—C.S.J.
[3893]—*Sisters of St. Joseph of Chestnut Hill, Philadelphia*—S.S.J.
[3890]—*Sisters of St. Joseph of Peace*—C.S.J.P.
[1830]—*The Sisters of the Good Shepherd*—R.G.S.
[1970]—*Sisters of the Holy Family of Nazareth*—C.S.F.N.
[2000]—*Sisters of the Holy Redeemer*—C.S.R.
[2110]—*Sisters of the Humility of Mary*—H.M.
[3270]—*Sisters of the Most Precious Blood*—C.PP.S.
[3480]—*Sisters of the Resurrection*—C.R.
[1490]—*Sisters of the Third Franciscan Order* (Syracuse)—O.S.F.
[2170]—*Sisters, Servants of the Immaculate Heart of Mary* (Immaculata, PA)—I.H.M.
[2160]—*Sisters, Servants of the Immaculate Heart of Mary* (Scranton)—I.H.M.
[0810]—*Society of the Daughters of the Heart of Mary*—D.H.M.
[4060]—*Society of the Holy Child Jesus*—S.H.C.J.
[4070]—*Society of the Sacred Heart*—R.S.C.J.

NECROLOGY

† Clark, James M., Lincroft, NJ St. Leo the Great Church—Died Feb. 24, 2003
† Hendricks, John J., (Retired)—Died Feb. 7, 2003
† Miller, Joseph B., (Retired)—Died March 25, 2003
† Quinn, John J., (Retired)—Died June 15, 2003

Diocese of Tucson

(Dioecesis Tucsonensis)

Most Reverend

GERALD G. KICANAS, D.D.

Bishop of Tucson; ordained April 27, 1967; appointed Titular Bishop of Bela and Auxiliary Bishop of Chicago January 24, 1995; consecrated March 20, 1995; appointed Coadjutor Bishop of Tucson October 30, 2001; installed January 15, 2002; succeeded to See of Tucson March 7, 2003 *P.O. Box 31, Tucson, AZ 85702*. Tel: 520-792-3410; Fax: 520-792-0291.

Most Reverend

MANUEL D. MORENO, D.D.

Bishop Emeritus of Tucson; ordained April 25, 1961; appointed Titular Bishop of Tanagra and Auxiliary of Los Angeles December 20, 1976; consecrated February 19, 1977; appointed Bishop of Tucson January 12, 1982; retired March 7, 2003 *Mailing Address: P.O. Box 31, Tucson, AZ 85702*.

Chancery Office: 111 S. Church Ave., P.O. Box 31, Tucson, AZ 85702. Tel: 520-792-3410.

Web: www.diocesetucson.org

Email: diocese@diocesetucson.org

ESTABLISHED A VICARIATE-APOSTOLIC 1868.

Square Miles 42,707.

Erected by His Holiness Pope Leo XIII, May 8, 1897.

Comprises the Counties of Cochise, Gila, Greenlee, Graham, La Paz, Pima, Pinal, Santa Cruz and Yuma in the State of Arizona.

For legal titles of parishes and diocesan institutions, consult the Chancery Office.

STATISTICAL OVERVIEW

Personnel	
Bishop	1
Retired Bishops	1
Priests: Diocesan Active in Diocese	67
Priests: Diocesan Active Outside Diocese	8
Priests: Retired, Sick or Absent	42
Number of Diocesan Priests	117
Religious Priests in Diocese	72
Total Priests in Diocese	189
Extern Priests in Diocese	45
Ordinations:	
Diocesan Priests	5
Permanent Deacons in Diocese	143
Total Brothers	10
Total Sisters	238
Parishes	
Parishes	72
With Resident Pastor:	
Resident Diocesan Priests	49
Resident Religious Priests	19
Without Resident Pastor:	
Administered by Priests	2
Administered by Religious Women	2
Missions	40
Professional Ministry Personnel:	
Brothers	10
Sisters	73
Welfare	
Catholic Hospitals	3
Total Assisted	411,300
Health Care Centers	1
Total Assisted	26,457
Special Centers for Social Services	1
Total Assisted	405,300
Other Institutions	1
Total Assisted	2,500
Educational	
Diocesan Students in Other Seminaries	13
Total Seminarians	13
High Schools, Private	5
Total Students	1,903
Elementary Schools, Diocesan and Parish	22
Total Students	5,577
Elementary Schools, Private	2
Total Students	810
Catechesis/Religious Education:	
High School Students	4,629
Elementary Students	18,401
Total Students under Catholic Instruction	31,333
Teachers in the Diocese:	
Priests	3
Brothers	7
Sisters	26
Lay Teachers	447
Vital Statistics	
Receptions into the Church:	
Infant Baptism Totals	7,023
Adult Baptism Totals	335
Received into Full Communion	665
First Communions	6,143
Confirmations	3,183
Marriages:	
Catholic	773
Interfaith	180
Total Marriages	953
Deaths	2,409
Total Catholic Population	350,000
Total Population	1,517,428

Former Bishops—Most Revs. JOHN BAPTIST SALPOINTE, D.D., ord. December 21, 1851; appt. Vicar Apostolic of Arizona and Titular Bishop of Doryla Sept. 25, 1868; ord. June 20, 1869; appt. Coadjutor Archbishop of Santa Fe with right of succession April 12, 1884 and Titular Archbishop of Anazarba Oct. 3, 1884; succeeded to the See of Santa Fe July 18, 1885; resigned; appt. Titular Archbishop of Tomi Jan. 27, 1894; died Tucson, July 15, 1898; PETER BOURGADE, D.D., ord. Nov. 30, 1869; appt. Vicar Apostolic of Arizona Jan. 23, 1885 and Titular Bishop of Thaumacum Feb. 7, 1885 and ordained May 1, 1885; appt. first Bishop of Tucson May 10, 1897; appt. fourth Archbishop of Santa Fe Jan. 7, 1899; died Chicago, May 17, 1908; HENRY REGIS GRANJON, D.D., ord. Dec. 17, 1887; appt. second Bishop of Tucson April 19, 1900; ord. June 17, 1900; died Brignais, France, Nov. 9, 1922; DANIEL JAMES GERCKE, D.D., ord. June 1, 1901; appt. third Bishop of Tucson June 21, 1923; ord. Nov. 6, 1923; resigned; appt. Titular Archbishop of Cotyaeum Oct. 26, 1960; died Tucson, March 19, 1964; FRANCIS JOSEPH GREEN, D.D. (Retired), ord. May 15, 1932; appt. Titular Bishop of Serra in Proconsulari and Auxiliary Bishop of Tucson May 29, 1953; consecrated Sept. 17, 1953; appt. Coadjutor "cum jure successionis" May 11, 1960; succeeded to See to become fourth Bishop of Tucson Oct. 26, 1960; retired July 28, 1981; died May 11, 1995; MANUEL D. MORENO, D.D. (Retired), ord. April 25, 1961; appt. Titular Bishop of Tanagra and Auxiliary of Los Angeles Dec. 20, 1976; consecrated Feb. 19, 1977; appt. Bishop of Tucson Jan. 12, 1982; retired March 7, 2003.

Vicar General—Rev. Msgr. ARSENIO S. CARRILLO, V.G. (Retired).

Vicar General/Moderator of the Curia—Rev. VAN A. WAGNER, V.G.

Episcopal Vicar—Rev. Msgr. RICHARD W. O'KEEFFE, Yuma La Paz Vicariate.

Chancery Office—111 S. Church Ave., P.O. Box 31, Tucson, 85702. Tel: 520-792-3410.

Chancellor—Mrs. JUNE KELLEN, Office, 111 S. Church Ave., Tucson, 85701. Tel: 520-792-3410.

Fiscal Manager Office—Mrs. MARY HUERSTEL, CFO; DAVID KNIGHT, Senior Staff Acct., P.O. Box 31, Tucson, 85702. Tel: 520-792-3410.

Matrimonial Tribunal—Office, 111 S. Church Ave., P.O. Box 31, Tucson, 85702. Tel: 520-792-3410.

Judicial Vicar—Rev. JOHN P. LYONS, J.C.L.

Adjutant Judicial Vicar—VACANT.

Promoter of Justice - Penal Cases—Rev. PATRICK R. LAGGES, J.C.D.

Promoter of Justice—Rev. BRYAN SHERRY, J.C.L.

Judge—Rev. JOSEPH KRAUSE.

Defenders of the Bond—Revs. MICHAEL BUCCIARELLI; CHARLES KNAPP; MICHAEL STALLINGS.

Advocates and Auditors—Revs. CHARLES CLOUD; JAMES HOBERT; Deacon OSCAR MAGALLANES; Mr. KEVIN ARNOLD; CHARLES ASHLEY; RICHARD COSGROVE; JOHN HAAS; LUIS KAME; VINCENT LACSAMANA; THOMAS MCHUGH; Mr. MICHAEL MURRAY; Mr. PEDRO NAJERA; PETER RAPTIS; GERALD SWEENEY; MORTON SWEENEY.

Auditors, Notaries, Secretaries—MARTHA JORDAN; HELEN EVANS.

Professional Consultant—STEPHEN J. SCHILTZ, M.S.W.; IRENE GRAM, Ph.D.

Finance Council—Ex Officio: Most Revs. MANUEL D. MORENO, D.D. (Retired); GERALD F. KICANAS, D.D., Bishop of Tucson; Rev. VAN A. WAGNER, V.G., Moderator of the Curia; Mrs. MARY HUERSTEL, CFO. O.F.C. Members: TOM CLANCY; LUIS DABDOUB; HUMBERTO LOPEZ; LAWRENCE MCDONOUGH; GARY PASQUINELLI; Rev. AL SCHIFANO; LIRAIN URREIZTIETA.

Investment Sub-Committee—Mrs. MARY HUERSTEL; THOMAS FEENEY.

Catholic Foundation for the Diocese of Tucson—Most Rev. GERALD F. KICANAS, D.D., Chm. Bd.; GARY P. BROUSSARD, Exec. Dir.; Hon. JOSEPH HOWARD, Past Pres.; BRUNO DISPOTO, Pres.; ERNEST T. NEDDER, Vice Pres.; ANN S. DICKSON, Treas.; CHARLES MAHN, Sec.; CLARA I. MORENO, Admin. Asst.; MICHELE ANTLE, Bookkeeper. Ex Officio Members: Rev. VAN A. WAGNER, V.G.; Mrs. MARY HUERSTEL, C.F.O. Members: Rev. JOSEPH A. LOMBARDO; MARTIN CAMACHO; ANN CHARLES; GINNY CLEMENTS; BARBARA GURWITZ-HALL; ALONZO MORADO; JEFFRY NORDENSSON; Rev. TODD O'LEARY; DANIEL QUIGLEY; DAVE SITTON; WILLIAM STOUT; Sr. CAROLE RULAND, M.H.S.H.

Catholic Relief Services—ERICA DAHL-BREDINE, CRS/ Mexico Country Mgr., P.O. Box 928, Tucson, 85702-0928. Tel: 520-838-2534; LOURDES AGUILAR, Administrative Asst., CRS/Mexico.

Diocesan Consultors—Rev. Msgrs. ARSENIO S. CARRILLO, V.G. (Retired); RICHARD O'KEEFFE, E.V., Yuma La Paz; Revs. VAN A. WAGNER, V.G., Vicar Gen. and Moderator of the Curia; MICHAEL BUCCIARELLI; RAUL TREVIZO; JOHN P. LYONS, J.C.L.

Council of Priests—Most Rev. MANUEL D. MORENO, D.D. (Retired); Rev. Msgrs. ARSENIO S. CARRILLO, V.G. (Retired); THOMAS CAHALANE; Rev. JOHN P. LYONS, J.C.L.; Rev. Msgr. ROBERT D. FULLER; Revs. PATRICK M. CRINO; RAYMOND RATZENBERGER; RICHARD TROUTMAN; MARTIN MARTINEZ; RAUL TREVIZO, Vicar for Hispanic Affairs; DOMENICO C. PINTI; REMIGIO "MIGUEL" MARIANO, Dir. Vocations; MAXIMILIAN HOTTLE, O.F.M.; DALE A. BRANSON; GONZALO J. VILLEGAS; MARCOS VELASQUEZ; EDWARD RYLE; VAN A. WAGNER, V.G., Moderator of the Curia.

Vicar for Native Americans—Rev. MAXIMILIAN HOTTLE, O.F.M.

Clergy Health—Rev. EDWARD C. CARSCALLEN (Retired).

Ministry to Priests Program—Rev. EDWARD C. CARSCALLEN, Spiritual Dir. (Retired), 221 C. Paseo Tierra, Green Valley, 85614. Tel: 520-625-4330.

Vicar for Priests—Rev. JAMES M. HOBERT, St. Ambrose Parish, 300 S. Tucson Blvd., Tucson, 85702. Tel: 520-622-6749. Members: Revs. RICHARD TROUTMAN; DOMENICO C. PINTI.

Vicar for Women Religious—Sr. JEAN OLMSTEAD, P.O. Box 31, Tucson, 85702. Tel: 520-792-3410.

Vicars Forane—Revs. RAYMOND RATZENBERGER, Cochise Vicariate; DALE A. BRANSON, Gila-Pinal East Vicariate; DOMENICO C. PINTI, Graham-Greenlee Vicariate; Rev. Msgrs. ROBERT D. FULLER, Pima-Central Vicariate; THOMAS CAHALANE, Pima-East Vicariate; Revs. GONZALO J. VILLEGAS, Pima-South Vicariate; RICHARD E. TROUTMAN, Pima-North Vicariate; MAXIMILIAN HOTTLE, O.F.M., Pima West Vicariate; CHRISTOPHER M. ORNDORFF II, Pinal-West Vicariate; MARCOS VELASQUEZ, Santa Cruz Vicariate; PATRICK M. CRINO, Yuma-La Paz Vicariate.

Diocesan Offices and Directors

Archives—DAN BROSNAN, Archivist, 8800 E. 22nd St., Tucson, 85710. Tel: 520-886-5201; 520-886-5223.

Board of Education—Ex Officio Members: Most Rev. GERALD F. KICANAS, D.D.; Rev. VAN A. WAGNER, V.G., Vicar Gen.; Sr. ROSA MARIA RUIZ, C.F.M.M., Supt.; Ms. JO ANN SAYRE, Asst. Supt.; HENRY RILLOS, Pres. Members: Rev. JOHN P. ARNOLD; Dr. FRANK FELIX; Rev. JAMES HOBERT; LONI MANNINI; CLOTILDE PHILLIPS; Sr. BARBARA ANNE STOWASSER, C.S.J.; ROBERT TESO.

Diocesan Building Committee—Most Rev. GERALD F. KICANAS, D.D., Honorary Chm.; Rev. VAN A. WAGNER, V.G., Moderator of the Curia; JAMES RONSTADT, Chm.; BRIAN MCCARTHY, Vice Chm.; Mrs. MARY HUERSTEL, Fiscal; LIZ AGUALLO, Sec.; JOHN C. SHAHEEN, A.I.A., Property & Insurance Mgr.; Rev. TODD O'LEARY; HECTOR MARTINEZ; BOB SUAREZ; CAROL E. SCHRADER; ERNIE DUARTE; DANIEL RORBACH; Rev. DAVID REINDERS.

Cemeteries—Holy Hope Cemetery, 3555 N. Oracle Rd., P.O. Box 5158, Tucson, 85705. Tel: 520-888-0860; Fax: 520-888-7788.

Catholic Chaplain—Rev. EDWARD C. CARSCALLEN (Retired). Tel: 520-888-0860.

Our Lady of the Desert Cemetery—2151 S. Avenida Los Reyes, Tucson, 85748. Tel: 520-885-9173.

Desert Vista Cemetery—2151 S. Avenida Los Reyes, Tucson, 85748. Tel: 520-885-9173.

Censor Librorum—VACANT.

Catholic Social Mission Diocese of Tucson—JOANNE WELTER, Dir., P.O. Box 31, Tucson, 85702. Tel: 520-792-3410; Fax: 520-792-0291. Email: socialmission@diocesetucson.org.

Charismatic Renewal Movement—Deacon RICHARD ORNELAS, Liaison; Rev. FRANK G. CADY, Spiritual Dir. Centro de Renovacion Carismatica: SALVADOR GONZALES, Hispanic Speaking Contact, 1748 S. 4th Ave., Tucson, 85713. Tel: 520-628-1692.

Catholic Schools—Sr. ROSA MARIA RUIZ, C.F.M.M., Supt.; JO ANN SAYRE, Asst. Supt., P.O. Box 31, Tucson, 85702. Tel: 520-792-3410.

Community Relations—FRED ALLISON, Dir., P.O. Box 31, Tucson, 85702. Tel: 520-792-3410.

Employee Services—RICHARD M. SERRANO, Dir.; JOY MITCHELL, Employee Benefits Admin.; ADRIA WOUDSTRA, Employee Benefits Asst., 111 S. Church Ave., P.O. Box 31, Tucson, 85702. Tel: 520-792-3410; Fax: 520-838-2583.

Cursillo Movement—Deacon JOHN KEATING ACKERLEY, Spiritual Dir., St. Augustine Cathedral, P.O. Box 324, Cortaro, 85652. Tel: 520-624-6944.

Detention Ministry—Ms. BARBARA MATTUS, M.A., Coord., 111 S. Church Ave., P.O. Box 31, Tucson, 85702. Tel: 520-298-0021.

Stewardship and Development—THOMAS Q. SMITH, Dir., 111 S. Church Ave., P.O. Box 31, Tucson, 85702. Tel: 520-838-2509.

Ecumenical Commission—Rev. Msgr. THOMAS F. CAHALANE, 1800 S. Kolb Rd., Tucson, 85710. Tel: 520-747-1321.

Chief Financial Officer—Mrs. MARY HUERSTEL, P.O. Box 31, Tucson, 85702. Tel: 520-792-3410.

Holy Childhood Association—Rev. VAN A. WAGNER, V.G., Dir., P.O. Box 31, Tucson, 85702. Tel: 520-792-3410.

Interfaith Council—LAUVER EDIE. Tel: 520-745-9443.

Legion of Decency—Chancery Office, 111 S. Church Ave., Tucson, 85701.

Diocesan Liturgical Commission—Rev. REMIGIO "MIGUEL" MARIANO, 111 S. Church Ave., P.O. Box 31, Tucson, 85702. Tel: 520-792-3410.

Office of Catechesis for Children, Youth and Families—J. MICHAEL BERGER, Dir., 111 S. Church, P.O. Box 31, Tucson, 85702-0031. Tel: 520-792-3410; Fax: 520-838-2584. Email: mberg@diocesetucson.org; JANET TOWNER, Admin. Support.

Office of Evangelization and Hispanic Ministry—RUBEN C. DAVALOS, Dir.; MARIA DAVALOS, Admin. Support (Spanish); JANET TOWNER, Admin. Support (English), 111 S. Church Ave., P.O. Box 31, Tucson, 85702-0031. Tel: 520-792-3410; Fax: 520-838-2584. Email: rcdavalos@diocesetucson.org.

Office of Formation—VACANT, Dir., 111 S. Church, P.O. Box 31, Tucson, 85702-0031. Tel: 520-792-3410; Fax: 520-838-2584. Email: dirformation@diocesetucson.org.

Lay Ministry Leadership—MARGARET LORDON, Program Coord.. Email: livstones@diocesetucson.org.

Ministero Shalom—VIDAL HARO, Treas., P.O. Box 22378, Tucson, 85734. Tel: 520-889-0411.

Newspaper—MAGGIE BURNETT, Mng. Editor; CLAUDIA BORDERS, Advertising Rep., P.O. Box 31, Tucson, 85702. Tel: 520-792-3410; Fax: 520-838-2583. Email: vision@catholic-vision.org. Web: www.catholic-vision.org. "Catholic Vision"

Office for the Protection of Children, Adolescents & Adults—PAUL N. DUCKRO, Ph.D., P.O. Box 31, Tucson, 85702. Tel: 520-792-3410. Email: pauld@diocesetucson.org.

Office of Due Process—Chancery Office, P.O. Box 31, Tucson, 85702. Tel: 520-792-3410.

Office of Permanent Diaconate—Deacon JAMES BURNS, Dir., P.O. Box 31, Tucson, 85702. Tel: 520-792-3410.

Deacon Formation—VACANT, Dir., 111 S. Church Ave., Tucson, 85701. Tel: 520-792-3410.

Priests' Assurance Association—Most Rev. MANUEL D. MORENO, D.D., Pres. Ex Officio (Retired); Rev. VAN A. WAGNER, V.G., Sec. & Treas. Directors: Rev. Msgr. ROBERT D. FULLER; Revs. THOMAS MILLANE; DOMENICO C. PINTI; JOHN F. ALLT.

Priests' Placement Advisory Board—All Vicars Forane: Rev. Msgr. THOMAS CAHALANE; Revs. PATRICK M. CRINO; DOMENICO C. PINTI; MICHAEL R. BUCCIARELLI; RAYMOND RATZENBERGER; RAUL TREVIZO; REMIGIO "MIGUEL" MARIANO; MAXIMILIAN HOTTLE, O.F.M.; MARTIN MARTINEZ; MARCOS VELASQUEZ; JOHN P. LYONS, J.C.L.; RICHARD C. TROUTMAN.

Chancellor—Mrs. JUNE KELLEN.

Episcopal Vicar—YUMA LAPAZ, Vicariate; Rev. Msgr. RICHARD W. O'KEEFFE.

Moderator of the Curia—Rev. VAN A. WAGNER, V.G.

Propagation of the Faith—Rev. Msgr. ARSENIO CARRILLO, V.G., Dir. Pro Tem., P.O. Box 31, Tucson, 85702. Tel: 520-792-3410.

Property and Insurance Manager—JOHN C. SHAHEEN, A.I.A., Office, 111 S. Church Ave., Tucson, 85701. Tel: 520-792-3410; Fax: 520-792-3410.

Real Estate & Future Parish Sites Committee—CAROL SCHRADER, Chm.; DAN RORBACH; HECTOR MARTINEZ; Rev. TODD O'LEARY; Mrs. MARY HUERSTEL; LIZ AGUALLO, Sec.

Rural Life Bureau—Box 31, Tucson, 85702. Tel: 520-792-3410.

Council of Women Religious, Leadership Team & Office for Religious—Sr. JEAN OLMSTEAD, 111 S. Church Ave., P.O. Box 31, Tucson, 85702. Tel: 520-792-3410; Fax: 520-792-0291.

Victim Assistance Coordinator—PAUL N. DUCKRO, Ph.D. Tel: 520-792-3410. Email: pauld@diocesetucson.org.

Vocations—Rev. REMIGIO "MIGUEL" MARIANO, Dir.; Mrs. MARTY HAMMOND, Exec. Asst., 111 S. Church Ave., P.O. Box 31, Tucson, 85702. Tel: 520-792-3410; Fax: 520-792-0291. Email: vocations@diocesetucson.org.

**Catholic Commission*—JIM DOBRY, Pres., 231 W. Smoot Dr., Tucson, 85705.

Encuentros de Promocion Juvenile—Rev. FRANCISCO MALDONADO, P.O. Box 444, Tucson, 85702. Tel: 520-792-3410.

CLERGY, PARISHES, MISSIONS AND PAROCHIAL SCHOOLS

CITY OF TUCSON
(PIMA COUNTY)

1—ST. AUGUSTINE'S CATHEDRAL (1863), Rev. Msgr. Carlos Romero Moreno; Revs. Francisco Maldonado, Rector; Salvador A. Cazares; Gregory Okafor.
Res.: 192 S. Stone Ave., 85701. Tel: 520-623-6351; Fax: 520-623-0088.
Catechesis/Religious Program—Miss Barbara Valenzuela, D.R.E. Tel: 520-624-8627. Students 819.

2—ST. AMBROSE (1946), Revs. James Hobert; Bardo Fabian Antunez; Deacon Henry M. Gamboa. In Res., Rev. Vidal Robles.
Res.: 300 S. Tucson Blvd., 85716. Tel: 520-622-6749; Fax: 520-882-3057.
School—Tel: 520-882-8678; Fax: 520-624-6853. Jean-Marie Bushell, Prin. Lay Teachers 23; Students 356.
Catechesis/Religious Program—Tel: 520-623-2925.

3—BLESSED KATERI TEKAKWITHA (1984), (Native American), Revs. Francisco Nunez, S.T.; Daniel P. McLaughlin, S.T.; Abram E. Dono, S.T.
Res. & Office: 507 W. 29th St., 85713. Tel: 520-791-7774; 520-792-0230; Fax: 520-792-0230.
Catechesis/Religious Program—Tel: 520-622-5363. Students 400.
Mission—Blessed Kateri Tekakwitha Parish Center 507 W. 29th St., South Tucson, Pima Co. 85713. Tel: 520-622-1654.
Mission—San Martin 418 W. 39th St., Tuscon, Pima Co. 85713.
Mission—Santa Rosa 2015 N. Calle Central, Pima Co. 85705. Tel: 520-622-3514.
Mission—Cristo Rey 7500 S. Camino Benem, Pima Co. 85746. Tel: 520-578-0423.
Mission—El Senor de los Milagros 3410 S. 16th Ave., Pima Co. 85713.
Mission—San Ignacio 785 W. Sahuaro, Tuscon, Pima Co. 85705.
Mission—San Juan Bautista Yoem Pueblo 1322 Sandario Rd., Marana, Pima Co. 85238.

4—CORPUS CHRISTI (1999), Rev. Richard Kingsley.
Res.: 300 N.Tanque Verde Loop, 85748. Tel: 520-751-4235; Fax: 520-751-1304.
Catechesis/Religious Program—Joey Perdreauville, D.R.E. Students 210.

5—ST. CYRIL OF ALEXANDRIA (1948), Revs. James R. McCauley, C.S.P.; James Moran, C.S.P.; Gilbert S. Martinez, C.S.P.
Mailing Address: 4725 E. Pima St., Tuscon, 85712. Tel: 520-795-1633; Fax: 520-795-1639. In Res., Rev. Edward S. Pietrucha, C.S.P.
Res.: 1722 N. Mountain View Ave., 85712. Tel: 520-795-7640.
School—Tel: 520-881-4240; Fax: 520-795-0325. Mrs. Peggy Guerrero, Prin. Lay Teachers 26; Students 376.
Catechesis/Religious Program—Students 300.

6—ST. ELIZABETH ANN SETON (1980), Revs. Thomas J. Millane; Michael Martinez; Deacons James L. Burns; Leo Longoria; Alfred Caponigro; William Krueger; Jose Zapata; Robert P. Carlin; Jorge Munoz; Francis C. Sherlock; Anthony T. Underwood.
Res.: 8650 N. Shannon Rd., 85742. Tel: 520-297-7357; Fax: 520-797-8886.
School—(Grades PreK-PreK) Tel: 520-797-7327. Suzanne Shadonix, Prin.
Catechesis/Religious Program—Tel: 520-297-8150 (Elementary); 520-297-1150 (Middle and High School). Roseanne Skapura, D.R.E. Students 1,200.

7—ST. FRANCES CABRINI (1961), Rev. Msgr. Robert D. Fuller.

Res.: 3201 E. Presidio Rd., 85716. Tel: 520-326-7670; Fax: 520-881-8480.
Catechesis/Religious Program—Tel: 520-795-1110. Students 118.

8—St. Francis de Sales (1971), Revs. Robert G. Tamminga; Gerald Meyers; Deacon Frank J. Collura; Mr. Charles Girard, Esq.; Deacons Carlos Martinez; Keith Pavlik; Dennis Scalpone; Robert Nevins; William Vigil. In Res., Rev. Robert E. Carney; Deacons Donald Ferris; Thomas Morgan.
Res.: 1375 S. Camino Seco, 85710. Tel: 520-885-5908; Fax: 520-885-3109.
Catechesis/Religious Program—Marian Gilbert, D.R.E. Students 525.

9—Holy Family (1915), Rev. Joseph M. Baker; Deacons Carl Leinfelder; Michael "Danny" Hoerr.
Res.: 338 W. University Blvd., 85705. Tel: 520-623-6773; Fax: 520-623-3578.
Catechesis/Religious Program—Students 214.
Mission—Santa Rosa 2015 N. Calle, Pima Co. 85705. Tel: 520-622-3514.

10—St. John the Evangelist (1934), Revs. Raul P. Trevizo; Juan Carlos Aguirre; Adolfo Martinez Escobar; Deacons Jose Ojeda; Don Baker; Jose Duarte; Charles Gallegos Jr. In Res., Revs. Fred Henley, S.J.; Adolfo Martinez.
Res.: 602 W. Ajo Way, 85713. Tel: 520-624-7409; Fax: 520-740-1145.
School—Tel: 502-624-7409, Ext. 3008. Ms. Lourdes Amaro, Prin. Lay Teachers 9; Students 173.
Catechesis/Religious Program—Mrs. Gloria Figueroa, D.R.E. Students 950.

11—St. Joseph (1953), Revs. John F. Allt; Frederic F. Curry, Pastor Emeritus (Retired); Deacons George Herrick; Leon Mazza; John Broussard; Efren Medrano; Albert Callie. In Res., Revs. James A. Freeman; Isaac A. Fynn; William (Guillo) Kohler, C.SS.R.; Deacons Jim Espinosa; Philip Garcia.
Res.: 215 S. Craycroft Rd., 85711. Tel: 520-747-3100; Fax: 520-745-4606.
School—Tel: 520-747-3060. Mrs. Ellen S. Kwader, Prin.; Mrs. Joan McCormick, Vice Prin. Lay Teachers 28; Students 518.
Catechesis/Religious Program—Sharon Takerer, D.R.E. Students 350.

12—St. Margaret Mary (1951), [CEM] Rev. Bernard Perkins, O.C.D. In Res., Revs. Kevin McArdle, O.C.D.; Cyprian Killackey, O.C.D.; Deacons Carlos Gelabert; Miguel Lopez.
Res.: 801 N. Grande Ave., 85745. Tel: 520-622-0168; Fax: 520-882-8022.
Catechesis/Religious Program—Tel: 520-622-5982. Students 500.

13—St. Mark The Evangelist (1999), Rev. Liam Leahy; Deacon Anthony R. Miller.
P.O.Box 68650, 85737. Tel: 520-469-7835; Fax: 520-219-6003. Mailing Address: 2727 W. Tangerine Rd., 85737-0003.
Catechesis/Religious Program—Students 290.

14—Mission San Xavier del Bac (1692), (Native American), Revs. Stephen Barnufsky, O.F.M.; Edgar Mangana, O.F.M. In Res., Revs. Walter Holly, O.F.M.; Camillus Cavagnaro, O.F.M.
Res.: 1950 W. San Xavier Rd., 85746. Tel: 520-294-2624; Fax: 520-294-3438.
School—1980 W. San Xavier Rd., 85746. Tel: 520-294-0628; Fax: 520-294-3465. Sr. Jacqueline Koenig, O.F.M., Prin. Sisters 4; Students 180.
Catechesis/Religious Program—Tel: 520-294-0628. Students 162.
Convent—1996 W. San Xavier Rd., 85746. Tel: 520-746-4779.

15—St. Monica (1964), Revs. James Hobert; Raul Valencia Garcia; Deacons Don Fisher; Tomas Morales; Eugene Fernandez; John A. Garcia; Armando L. Valenzuela; Nicolas De La Torre.
Res.: 212 W. Medina, 85706. Tel: 520-294-2694; Fax: 520-295-0339.
Catechesis/Religious Program—Tel: 520-889-1944. Students 2,002.

16—Most Holy Trinity (1975), Rev. William Remmel.
Res.: 1300 N. Greasewood Rd., 85745. Tel: 520-620-0977; Fax: 520-620-0977.
Catechesis/Religious Program—Tel: 520-884-9021. Students 216.

17—Saint Odilia (1965), Revs. Richard E. Troutman; Delfin Perras; Deacon George Scherf.
Res. & Mailing Address: 7570 Paseo del Norte, 85704. Tel: 520-297-7271; 520-297-7272 (Office); Fax: 520-297-8247.
Catechesis/Religious Program—Students 500.
Mission—Santa Catalina 14380 N. Oracle, Pima Co. 85739-9599. Tel: 520-825-9611; Fax: 520-825-9866. Sr. Carole Ruland, M.H.S.H., Admin.

18—Our Lady of Fatima (1972), Rev. Peter M. McGloin; Deacons Frank S. Lundgren Jr.; Robert Negrette.
Res.: 5969 S. Sorrel Ln., 85746. Tel: 520-883-1717; Fax: 520-883-4669.
Catechesis/Religious Program—Tel: 520-883-1717. Students 380.
Mission—St. Mary of the Desert MSC 55 HC 137, P.O. Box 2000, Pima Co. 85735.

19—Our Lady of La Vang (1999), (Vietnamese), Rev. Hoa Francis Dang, C.SS.R.
Mailing Address: 800 S. Tuscon Blvd., 85716. Tel: 520-903-2895; Fax: 520-290-9679.
Res.: 8800 E. 22nd St., Tuscon, 85710. Tel: 520-751-2060.
Catechesis/Religious Program—Students 55.

20—Our Lady, Queen of All Saints (1987), (Hispanic), Rev. Gonzalo J. Villegas; Deacons Oscar Magallanes; James Stotler; Burt Nehmer.
Res.: 2915 E. 36th St., 85713-4041. Tel 520-622-8602; Fax: 520-622-4581.
Catechesis/Religious Program—Maria Rodriguez, D.R.E. Students 400.

21—Our Mother of Sorrows (1958), Rev. Msgr. Thomas P. Cahalane; Deacons Paul J. Welsh; Alfredo Silva; George Rodriguez.
Res.: 1800 S. Kolb Rd., 85710. Tel: 520-747-1321; Fax: 520-790-3308.
School—Tel: 520-747-1027; Fax: 520-747-0797. Jean McKenzie, Ed.S., Prin. Lay Teachers 37; Students 514.
Catechesis/Religious Program—Laura Stehle, D.R.E. Students 500.

22—St. Pius X (1969), Rev. Harry Ledwith; Deacons Michael Ammerman; Tom Wagner; Dennis Ranke.
Res.: 1800 N. Camino Pio Decimo, 85715. Tel: 520-885-3573; Fax: 520-885-0945.
Catechesis/Religious Program—Karen Horton, D.R.E. Students 803.

23—Sacred Heart (1942), Rev. Joseph F. McGowan, O.Carm.
Res.: 601 E. Fort Lowell Rd., 85705. Tel: 520-888-1530; Fax: 520-888-1227.
Catechesis/Religious Program—Tel: 520-888-3401. Students 320.

24—Saints Peter and Paul (1930), Revs. John P. Lyons, J.C.L.; Albert I. Schifano. In Res., Revs. Van A. Wagner, V.G.; Godfrey Oparaekwe.
Res.: 1946 E. Lee St., 85719-4337. Tel: 520-327-6015; Fax: 520-318-3918.
School—Tel: 520-325-2431; Fax: 520-881-4690. Sr. Ann Patrick Adams, S.C., Prin. Sisters of Charity from Seton Hill 3; Lay Teachers 22; Students 512.
Catechesis/Religious Program—Tel: 520-321-1892. Students 211.
Convent—1947 E. Adams St., 85719. Tel: 520-325-2234.

25—Santa Catalina, Sr. Carole Ruland, M.H.S.H., Admin.
14380 N. Oracle Rd., 85739. Tel: 520-825-9611; Fax: 520-825-9866. Email: scmission1@aol.com.

26—Santa Cruz (1919), Revs. Gilbert Lavario, O.C.D.; John Williamson, O.C.D.; Justin Kannamparambil Vakko, O.C.D. In Res., Bro. Mario Caungal, O.C.D.
Res.: P.O. Box 2830, 85702. Tel: 520-623-3833; Fax: 520-903-2742.
School—Tel: 520-624-2093; Fax: 520-624-2833. Donna Gary, Prin. Lay Teachers 10; Students 170.
Catechesis/Religious Program—Tel: 520-882-9687. Students 438.
Mission—Our Lady of Guadalupe 401 E. 31st St., Pima Co. 85713.
Mission—St. Anthony's Catholic Instruction Center and Capilla 225 W. 34th St., Pima Co. 85713.

27—St. Thomas More Chapel (1926), Revs. Michael S. Fones, O.P.; Daniel J. Rolland, O.P.; Bede Wilks, O.P. (LA).
1615 E. 2nd St., Tuscon, 85719. Tel: 520-327-6662; Fax: 520-327-6559. In Res., Rev. Robert A. Burns, O.P.
Catechesis/Religious Program—Tel: 520-327-6663. Students 40.

28—St. Thomas the Apostle (1984), Rev. Todd O'Leary (Ireland); Deacons Russell F. Kingery; Kenneth McNealy; Edward P. Sheffer.
Res.: 5150 N. Valley View Rd., 85718. Tel: 520-577-8780; Fax: 520-577-0441.
Catechesis/Religious Program—Tel: 520-577-8782; Fax: 520-577-0441. Leslie Schulz-Crist, D.R.E. Students 475.

OUTSIDE THE CITY OF TUCSON

Ajo, Pima Co., Immaculate Conception (1916), Rev. Richard J. Rego.
Office—101 Rocalla, P.O.Box 550 85321. Tel: 520-387-7049; Fax: 520-387-5817.
Catechesis/Religious Program—Students 60.

Apache Junction, Pinal Co., St. George (1968), Revs. Bernard A. Konda, M.B.A., J.C.D.; Stanley J. Nadolny; Ariel Lustan; Deacons Bill Hughes; Craig Hintze.
Res.: 300 E. 16th Ave., 85219. Tel: 480-982-2929; Fax: 480-982-0036.
Catechesis/Religious Program—Angie Sigler, D.R.E. (K-5); Sande Altug, D.R.E. (6-8). Students 368.

Benson, Cochise Co., Our Lady of Lourdes (1895), Rev. Raymond Ratzenberger; Deacons Thomas Adams; Ronald Desmarais.
Mailing Address: 244 S. Gila, P.O. Box 2198, 85602. Tel: 520-586-3394; Fax: 520-586-3919.
Res.: 210 Eighth St., 85602.
Catechesis/Religious Program—Students 117.

Bisbee, Cochise Co., St. Patrick (1902), Rev. Larry Kasper; Deacons Guillermo Lugo; Joseph L. Delgado.
Res.: P.O. Box 164, 85603. Tel: 520-456-5152.
Catechesis/Religious Program—Tel: 520-432-4012. Students 412.
Mission—St. Michael 2090 W. Martinez, Naco, Cochise Co. 85620. Tel: 520-432-3768.

Casa Grande, Pinal Co., St. Anthony of Padua (1932), Rev. Kevin O. Clinch; Deacons Bill Kinney; Barnabas Radke; Patrick L. Dugan; Ramon G. Garcia; Mario Ortega. In Res., Revs. Peter C. Nwachukwu; Marco Antonio Basulto-Pitol.
Res.: P.O. Drawer 12335, 85230-2335. Tel: 520-836-0601; Fax: 520-836-2985.
School—Tel: 520-836-7247; Fax: 520-836-7289. Mrs. Mary People, Prin. Lay Teachers 13; Students 200.
Catechesis/Religious Program—Students 355.
Mission—St. Mary 89 N. Yogui Way, Stanfield, Pinal Co. 85272.
Mission—St. Francis de Sales P.O. Box 368, Maricopa, Pinal Co. 85239-0368. Tel: 520-568-4605.

Clifton, Greenlee Co., Sacred Heart (1899), Revs. Raul H. Rosales, Admin.; Mark J. Stein; Deacon Richard A. Gonzalez.
Mailing Address: P.O. Box 938, 85533. Tel: 928-865-2285; Fax: 928-865-1228.
Res.: 329 Chase Creek, 85533. Tel: 928-865-2285; Fax: 928-865-1228.
Catechesis/Religious Program—North Cornado Boulevard Parish Center, Tel: 928-865-3497. Students 165.
Mission—St. Mary Third St., P.O. Box 938, Greenlee Co. 85533. Tel: 928-359-2343.

Coolidge, Pinal Co., St. James (1947), (Hispanic), Rev. Christopher M. Orndorff II; Deacons Florentino Tarango; Viviano Leon.
Parish Center—437 W. Wilson Ave., 85228. Tel: 520-723-3063; Fax: 520-723-5137.
Res.: 401 W. Wilson Ave., 85228. Tel: 520-723-7656; Fax: 520-723-5137.
Catechesis/Religious Program—Tel: 520-723-3063. Students 268.

Douglas, Cochise Co.

1—Immaculate Conception (1907), Rev. Gilbert Malu Musumbu.
Mailing Address: P.O. Box 1176, 85607. Tel: 520-364-8494; Fax: 520-364-8495.
Res.: 928 C Ave., 85607. Tel: 520-364-8494.
School—Lestonnac Kindergarten and Day Care Center, Tel: 520-364-3956; 520-364-3470; Fax: 520-364-3470. Sr. Jean Ramirez, O.D.N., Dir. Sisters of the Company of Mary 4; Lay Teachers 3; Students 40.
Catechesis/Religious Program—Students 261.
Convent—Sisters of the Company of Mary, Tel: 520-364-7658; Fax: 520-364-3645.

2—St. Luke (1950), Revs. Gilbert Malu Musumbu; Martin Atanga Baabuge; Francisco Salas Valle; Deacons Armando Moulinet; Gabe Saspe; Raul Cantua.
Res.: 1211 15th St., 85607. Tel: 520-364-4411; Fax: 520-364-2397.
School—Loretto Central Catholic, 1200 14th St., 85607. Tel: 520-364-5754; Fax: 520-364-7707. Sr. Caridad Sandoval, O.C.D., Prin. Sisters 6; Lay Teachers 13; Students 302.
Catechesis/Religious Program—Tel: 520-364-4852; Fax: 520-364-2397. Students 300.
Convent—Carmelite Sisters of the Most Sacred Heart of Los Angeles, Loretto Convent, Tel: 520-364-7571; Fax: 520-364-7844.

Eloy, Pinal Co., St. Helen (1952), (Hispanic), Rev. Martin S. Martinez.
Res.: 205 W. 8th St., 85231. Tel: 520-466-7258; Fax: 520-466-0486.
Catechesis/Religious Program—Tel: 520-466-9422. Sylvia Diaz, D.R.E. Students 480.

Florence, Pinal Co., Assumption of the Blessed Virgin Mary (1870), Rev. Charles W. Cloud.
Res.: P.O. Box 2550, 85232. Tel: 520-868-5940; Fax: 503-961-9145.
Catechesis/Religious Program—Tel: 520-868-3075. Students 249.

Globe, Gila Co., Holy Angels (1905), Rev. Michael W. Stallings; Deacons Frank Castillo; Richard Le Mieux.
Res.: 201 S. Broad St., 85501. Tel: 928-425-3137; Fax: 928-425-3136.
School—1300 E. Cedar St., 85501. Tel: 928-425-5703; Fax: 928-425-5704. Sr. Leonie Bracken, Prin. & Admin. Presentation Sisters 6; Lay Teachers 7; Students 230.
Catechesis/Religious Program—Students 230.
Convent—Tel: 928-425-2034.

Green Valley, Pima Co., Our Lady of the Valley (1970), Rev. Joseph A. Lombardo; Deacons Rudy Noriega; Charles Pennington.

Res.: 505 N. La Canada Dr., 85614. Tel: 520-625-4536; Fax: 520-625-1084.
Catechesis/Religious Program— 85614. Tel: 520-625-4536. Students 117.

HAYDEN, GILA CO., ST. JOSEPH'S (1913), Rev. Dale A. Branson.
Res.: P.O. Drawer C, 85235. Tel: 520-356-7223; Fax: 520-356-7376.
Catechesis/Religious Program—Tel: 520-356-7223. Students 24.

KEARNY, PINAL CO., INFANT JESUS OF PRAGUE (1961), Rev. William A. Taft, Admin.
Res.: 501 Victoria Cir., P.O. Box 459, 85237. Tel: 520-363-7205; Fax: 520-363-7025.
Catechesis/Religious Program—Tel: 520-363-7428. Students 68.

MAMMOTH, PINAL CO., BLESSED SACRAMENT (1970), (Hispanic), Sr. Maria Canez, O.P., Admin.
Res.: 122 W. Church Dr., P.O. Box 220, 85618-0220. Tel: 520-487-2451; Fax: 520-487-0340.
Catechesis/Religious Program—Students 165.
Convent—Blessed Sacrament Convent, Mammouth.

MARANA, PIMA CO., ST. CHRISTOPHER'S (1954), Rev. Abran R. Tadeo.
Res.: 12101 Moore Rd., P.O. Box 188, 85653. Tel: 520-682-3035; Fax: 520-682-4044.
Catechesis/Religious Program—Tel: 520-665-0127. Students 75.

MIAMI, GILA CO., OUR LADY OF THE BLESSED SACRAMENT (1915), Rev. Jay R. Luczak; Deacon Jesus Castillo.
Res.: 914 Sullivan St., 85539. Tel: 928-473-3568.
Catechesis/Religious Program—Students 151.
Mission—St. Joseph 5678 Pineway St., Claypool, Gila Co. 85532.
Mission—St. Theresa Roosevelt Lake, Gila Co.

MORENCI, GREENLEE CO., HOLY CROSS (1913), Revs. Raul H. Rosales; Mark J. Stein.
Res. & Mailing Address: 205 Fairbanks Rd., 85540. Tel: 928-865-3183.
Catechesis/Religious Program—Fax: 520-865-1228. Students 256.

NOGALES, SANTA CRUZ CO.
1—ST. HELEN'S, , Mailing Address: HCR 01 Box 2000, Oracle, 85623. Tel: 520-896-2708; Fax: 520-896-2631. Email: sthelens@worblinkisp.com. In Res., Rev. Joseph Neitlong.
2—SACRED HEART (1897), Revs. Marcos C. Velasquez; Eduardo Lopez-Romo; Dominic Kamilwa.
Res.: P.O. Box 968, 85628. Tel: 520-287-9221; Fax: 520-287-9224.
Catechesis/Religious Program—Tel: 520-397-0963; Fax: 520-397-0909. Students 620.
3—SAN FELIPE DE JESUS (1987), Revs. Fernando L. Manzo; Fernando Cosio.
Mailing Address: P.O. Box 6600, 85628.
Res.: 2901 N. Grande Ave., Sp. #132, 85628. Tel: 520-761-3100; Fax: 520-281-4380.
Church: 1901 N. Jose Gallego Dr., #1, 85628.
Catechesis/Religious Program—Students 1,270.

PARKER, LA PAZ CO., SACRED HEART (1950), Rev. Theodore Lobo.
Res.: 916 11th St., 85344. Tel: 928-669-2502.
Catechesis/Religious Program—Tel: 928-667-2150. Students 52.
Mission—Kateri Tekawitha Indian Mission Poston.
Mission—St. John the Baptist Wenden.
Mission—Queen of Peace Quartzsite.

PATAGONIA, SANTA CRUZ CO., ST. THERESA (1955), Rev. Marcos C. Velasquez, Canonical Pastor; Sr. Guadalupe Jurado, O.P., Pastoral Admin.
Res.: Box 435, 85624. Tel: 520-394-2954; Fax: 520-394-2831.
Catechesis/Religious Program—Tel: 520-394-0068. Students 81.
Mission—Our Lady of Angels Fire Station, Sonoita, Santa Cruz Co. 85637.

PAYSON, GILA CO., SAINT PHILIP THE APOSTLE (1957), Rev. Joseph A. Krause.
Res.: 511 S. St. Philip, 85541-5144. Tel: 928-474-2392; Fax: 928-474-9661.
Catechesis/Religious Program—Tel: 928-474-1269. Students 97.

PIRTLEVILLE, COCHISE CO., ST. BERNARD'S (1914), Revs. Gilbert Malu Musumbu; Martin Atanga Baabuge; Francisco Salas Valle.
Res.: P.O. Box 3101, 85626. Tel: 520-364-2762; Fax: 520-364-2520.
Catechesis/Religious Program—Tel: 520-364-5994. Students 115.
Chapel—Double Adobe, Our Lady of La Salette
Chapel—Douglas, Sacred Heart

RIO RICO, SANTA CRUZ CO., NATIVITY OF OUR LORD JESUS CHRIST (1987), Rev. Frank G. Cady.
Mailing Address: P.O. Box 4024, 85648.
Res.: 384 Cancun Corte, 85648. Tel: 520-281-8702; 520-281-7414.
Catechesis/Religious Program—Students 192.

SAFFORD, GRAHAM CO., ST. ROSE OF LIMA (1937), Rev. Domenico C. Pinti; Deacons Marcello Arbizo; Ralph Duran; John Terry; Carlos Vessels.
Res.: 311 Central Ave., 85546. Tel: 928-428-4920.
Catechesis/Religious Program—Tel: 928-428-4922. Students 521.
Mission—Pima Mission 28 S. Main, Pima, Graham Co. 85543.
Mission—Neuman Center 528 4th St., Thatcher, Graham Co. 85552.

SAHUARITA, PIMA CO., SAN MARTIN DE PORRES (2002), Rev. Michael Shay, S.D.S.
Mailing Address: P.O. Box 65, 85629. Tel: 520-625-1154. Email: michaelshay@att.net.

SAN CARLOS, GILA CO., SAN CARLOS CATHOLIC MISSION (1918), (Native American), Rev. Gino L. Piccoli, O.F.M.
Res.: P.O. Box 28, 85550. Tel: 928-475-2210; Fax: 928-475-8935.
School—Tel: 520-475-2449; Fax: 520-475-2449. Sisters 5; Students 140.
Catechesis/Religious Program—Students 40.
Convent—St. Charles, P.O. Box 338, 85550. Tel: 928-475-2460.
Mission—Blessed Kateri Tekakwitha Bylas, Graham Co. 85530.

SAN LUIS, YUMA CO., ST. JUDE THADDEUS, Rev. Gerardo De La Torre, Admin.; Deacon Jose Manuel Lopez.
984 N. Main St., P.O. Box 2888, 85349. Tel: 928-627-8011; Fax: 928-627-3916.
Catechesis/Religious Program—Students 424.

SAN MANUEL, PINAL CO., ST. BARTHOLOMEW (1954), Rev. Michael R. Bucciarelli; Deacon Flavio Sanchez.
Res.: 609 Park Pl., Box 607, 85631. Tel: 520-385-4156.
Catechesis/Religious Program—Students 165.
Mission—St. Helen HCR 1, Box 2000, Oracle, Pinal Co. 85623. Tel: 520-896-2708. Rev. Joseph Nietlong.

SIERRA VISTA, COCHISE CO.
1—ST. ANDREW (1959), Revs. Gregory P. Adolf; German Bartolome Vasquez Johnston, O.S.B.; Deacons Fernando Mezquita; George Gaun; Michael Milazzo; Joseph Kushner III.
Res.: 800 Taylor Dr., N.W., 85635. Tel: 520-458-2925; Fax: 520-452-0235.
Catechesis/Religious Program—Students 281.
Mission—Good Shepherd Whetstone, Cochise Co.
2—OUR LADY OF THE MOUNTAINS (1991), Rev. Robert R. Bryerton; Deacons William Merritt; James Schaff; Robert Sadorf; Robert J. Gonzales; Rodger Miller; Gene Tackett.
Res.: 1425 Yaqui St., 85650. Tel: 520-378-2720; Fax: 520-378-6825.
Catechesis/Religious Program—Tel: 520-378-7012. Students 250.

SOLOMON, GRAHAM CO., OUR LADY OF GUADALUPE (1891), Rev. John J. Ancharski.
Res.: P.O. Box 147, 85551. Tel: 920-428-0149.
Catechesis/Religious Program—Students 36.
Mission—San Jose San Jose, Graham Co.

SOMERTON, YUMA CO., IMMACULATE HEART OF MARY (1954), Revs. Javier H. Perez; Raphael Gutierrez.
Res.: 310 W. Spring St., P.O. Box 597, 85350. Tel: 920-627-2918; Fax: 920-627-2918.
Catechesis/Religious Program—Tel: 920-627-2244. Students 1,789.

SUNSITES, COCHISE CO., ST. JUDE THADDEUS (1983), Rev. Bob Brazaskas.
Res.: P.O. Box 328, Pearce, 85625. Tel: 520-826-3869; Fax: 520-826-1166.
Catechesis/Religious Program—Students 70.
Mission—St. Francis of Assisi Elfrida. c/o St. Jude, P.O. Box 328, Pearce, Cochise Co. 85625. Tel: 520-642-3879.

SUPERIOR, PINAL CO., ST. FRANCIS OF ASSISI PARISH (1930), Rev. Augustine Kattady; Deacon Jesus Yanez.
Res.: 11 Church Ave., 85273. Tel: 520-689-2250.
Catechesis/Religious Program—St. Mary's Center, 100 Sunset Dr., 85273. Tel: 520-689-2116. Students 110.

TOMBSTONE, COCHISE CO., SACRED HEART (1880), Rev. Sylvester N. Nwaogu.
Res.: P.O. Box 547, 594 E. Safford St., 85638. Tel: 520-457-3364; Fax: 520-457-0017.
Catechesis/Religious Program—Students 30.

TOPAWA, PIMA CO., SAN SOLANO MISSIONS - TOHONO O'ODHAM INDIAN RESERVATION (1908), (Native American),, (For office and sacramental records pertaining to Tohono O'odham Indians and mission churches on the reservation, please refer to San Solano Missions at the P.O. Box 210, Topawa, AZ, 85639 address). Revs. Maximilian Hottle, O.F.M.; Thomas Frost, O.F.M.
Mailing Address: P.O. Box 210, 85639. Tel: 520-383-2350; Fax: 520-383-3063.
Catechesis/Religious Program—San Solano Pastoral Center, P.O. Box 209, 85639. Tel: 520-383-2400. Students 100.

TUBAC, SANTA CRUZ CO., ST. ANN (1987), Rev. Alexander M. Mills, O.S.B.
Mailing Address: P.O. Box 2911, 85646-2911. Tel: 520-398-2646; Fax: 520-398-3036.
Catechesis/Religious Program—Students 35.
Mission—Assumption Chapel Amado, Santa Cruz Co.
Mission—St. Ferdinand P.O. Box 2911, Arivaca, Pima Co. 85646.

VAIL, PIMA CO., SHRINE OF ST. RITA IN THE DESERT (1937), Rev. Robert Wicht, S.D.S. In Res., Rev. Alan Wagner, S.D.S.
Res.: P.O. Box 400, 85641. Tel: 520-762-5363; Fax: 520-762-5967.
Catechesis/Religious Program—Tel: 520-762-9688. Students 115.

WELLTON, PIMA CO., ST. JOSEPH THE WORKER, Rev. Msgr. Richard W. O'Keeffe, Admin.; Rev. Tomas G. Munoz.
Mailing Address: P.O. Box 157, 85356. Tel: 928-785-4275; Fax: 928-785-8706.

WILLCOX, COCHISE CO., SACRED HEART (1936), Rev. John Emanuel.
Res.: 215 W. Maley St., 85643. Tel: 520-384-3432; Fax: 520-384-3573.
Catechesis/Religious Program—Tel: 520-384-2194. Students 70.
Mission—Our Lady of Perpetual Help San Simon, Cochise Co. 85605.
Mission—Our Lady of Guadalupe Bowie, Cochise Co. 85605.

YUMA, YUMA CO.
1—ST. FRANCIS OF ASSISI (1948), Revs. Patrick Crino; Francis Iber; Jose Manuel Padilla; Deacons Paul Muthart; Gary Pasquinelli; Rick Hernandez; Rafael Vidal; Arnulfo Carbajal; Florencio Moreno Jr.; Don Larson; Jose Valadez; George Fischbach.
Res.: 1815 S. 8th Ave., 85364. Tel: 928-782-1875; Fax: 928-329-9479.
School—700 18th St., 85364. Tel: 928-782-1539; Fax: 928-782-0430. Robert Anderson, Prin. Franciscan Sisters of Christian Charity 2; Lay Teachers 11; Students 220.
Catechesis/Religious Program—Tel: 520-783-7461. Sr. Nancy Perez, D.R.E. Students 130.
2—IMMACULATE CONCEPTION (1866), Rev. Msgr. Richard W. O'Keeffe; Rev. Bernardo Iniesta Avila; Deacons Mark Nixen; David Sampson; Daniel L. Mulloy. In Res., Rev. Matthew Asemagema.
Res.: 509 Ave. B, 85364. Tel: 928-782-7516; Fax: 928-343-0172.
School—501 Ave. B, 85364. Tel: 928-783-5225. Sr. Theresa Feldkamp, O.S.F., Prin. Franciscan Sisters of Christian Charity 5; Lay Teachers 11; Students 263.
Catechesis/Religious Program—Tel: 928-783-1324. Mark Nixen, D.R.E.; Maria Jones, D.R.E. Students 1,005.
Mission—Our Lady of Guadalupe 417 15th Ave., Yuma Co. 85364. Tel: 928-376-6707.
Mission—St. Joseph the Worker P.O. Box 157, Wellton, Yuma Co. 85356. Tel: 928-785-4275; Fax: 928-785-8706. Rev. Msgr. Richard W. O'Keeffe, Admin.; Rev. Tomas G. Munoz.
Convent—500 24th Ave., 85364. Tel: 928-783-5224. Franciscan Sisters of Christian Charity 9.
3—ST. JOHN NEUMANN (1987), Rev. John F. Fried.
Res.: 11750 S. Mesa Dr., 85367. Tel: 928-342-3544; Fax: 928-342-7513.
Catechesis/Religious Program—Students 147.

Chaplains of Public Institutions

TUCSON. *Arizona Correctional Training Center*. Sr. Joyce M. Blum, F.S.P.A., Chap.
Santa Rita Unit, 10000 S. Wilmot Rd., 85777.
Detention Ministry, P.O. Box 31, 85702. Tel: 520-792-3410, Ext. 131. Ms. Barbara Mattus, M.A., Dir.
Arizona Western College, 11750 S. Mesa Dr., 85365. Tel: 520-342-3544. Attended from St. John Newmann Parish, Yuma.
Christ the King Chapel, 355 WG/HC, Davis Monthan Air Force Base, 85707. Tel: 520-750-5411. Rev. Albert N. Sanchez (Philippines) (MO), Chap.
St. Joseph's Hospital, 350 N. Wilmot Rd., 85732. Tel: 520-296-3211. Rev. Isaac A. Fynn.
Kino Community Hospital, 1220 S. Sixth, 85707. Tel: 520-623-3833.
2800 E. Ajo Way, 85713. Rev. Ignacio Bach, O.C.D.
St. Mary's Hospital, 1601 W. St. Mary's Rd., 85745. Tel: 520-622-5883. Rev. Joseph Saba.
Metropolitan Correctional Complex, 8901 S. Wilmont Rd., 85706. Tel: 520-741-3118.
Detention Ministry, P.O. Box 31, 85702. Tel: 520-792-3410, Ext. 131. Ms. Barbara Mattus, M.A., Dir.
Tucson Medical Center, 5301 E. Grant Rd., 85712. Rev. William (Guillo) Kohler, C.S.S.R., Chap. Tel: 520-324-1290; Fax: 520-324-1702.
U.S. Veterans Hospital, S. Sixth Ave., 85713. Tel: 520-792-1450. Rev. David H. Reinders.
Villa Maria Chapel, 4310 E. Grant Rd., 85712. Tel: 520-323-9351. Rev. Alexander Mills, Chap., Sr. Dorothy Ann Lesher, Dir. Pastoral Care.

CATALINA. *Arizona Youth Center*, Santa Catalina Mission, Catalina Rural Branch, P.O. Box 8601, 85738. Tel: 520-825-9611. Attended from St.

Odilia Parish.

FLORENCE. *Arizona State Prison*, St. Dismas Chapel, P.O. Box 550, 85232. Tel: 520-868-5940. Vacant

FORT GRANT RURAL STATION. *Fort Grant Training Center* 85632. Revs. John Emanuel, John J. Ancharski.

FORT HUCHUCA. *Fort Huchuca Army Post* 85613. Rev. Anthony S. Kazarnowski, Chap.

SAFFORD. *Conservation Center*, Tel: 520-428-0149. Rev. John J. Ancharski.

SOLOMON. *Our Lady of Guadalupe*, P.O. Box 147, 85551. Tel: 520-428-1049. Rev. John J. Ancharski.

WILLCOX. *Federal Prison Camp* 85546. Tel: 520-428-6600. Rev. John Emanuel.

YUMA. *MCAS Chapel*, Marine Corps Air Station, 85369. Tel: 520-269-2371. Rev. James Gay, Chap.

Yuma Regional Medical Center, 1815 8th Ave., 85364. Tel: 520-782-1875. Attended from St. Francis of Assisi.

Special Assignment:

Rev. Msgr.—

Carrillo, Arsenio S., V.G., Vicar Gen. & Propagation of the Faith, Dir. Pro-Tem (Retired), P.O. Box 31, 85702. Tel: 520-792-3410

Revs.—

Carscallen, Edward C., Spiritual Dir. Ministry to Priests & Catholic Cemeteries Chap. (Retired). Tel: 520-625-4330

Lyons, John P., J.C.L., Adjutant Judicial Vicar

O'Keeffe, Richard W., Episcopal Vicar

Sherry, Bryan W., J.C.L., Canonical Consultant, 321 Washington Ave., Florence, 85232. Tel: 520-886-3371

Wagner, Van A., V.G., Vicar Gen. & Curia Moderator

On Duty Outside the Diocese:

Revs.—

Bell, Brian T., 56 FW/HC, 13968 W. Shooting Star St., Lake AFB, 85309-1932.

Gonzales, Robert A., Ph.D., Pontifical College Josephinum, 7625 N. High St., Columbus, OH 43085.

McCarthy, Jeremiah J., Rector, 10 Summit Park Dr., Pittsburg, PA 15275.

Ryle, Edward J., Exec. Dir., c/o Arizona Catholic Conference, 400 E. Monroe St., Phoenix, 85004.

Shuppert, William T.J., 16619 Larch Way, Apt. # A304, Lynnwood, WA 98037. U.S.N. Dept. of Religious Ministries

Underwood, Gary E., U.S.A.F., 100 ARW/HC, Unit 4905, Box 230, Apo, AE 09459-5230.

Administrative Leave of Absence:

Rev. Msgrs.—

Coleman, James G. (HRT)

Trupia, Robert C.

Revs.—

Cocio, Carlos

Garzon-Blanco, Armando

Guillen, Juan

Sanz, Julian

Stencil, Steven G.

Taylor, Daniel

Teta, Michael J.

On Medical Leave:

Revs.—

Gameros, Ignacio L.

Manzo, Fernando L.

Noriega, Arnoldo

Thuerauf, Jeffrey P.

Retired - Administrative Leave:

Rev. Msgrs.—

Oliver, John A.

Rosensweig, Walter F.

Revs.—

Costigan, Richard J.

Hyman, Robert A.

Schlueter, Clemens

Stromberg, Floyd G.

Retired:

Most Rev.—

Moreno, Manuel D., D.D., 192 S. Stone Ave., Box 31, 85702.

Rev. Msgrs.—

Brynda, Gerald J., 1724 Minnewawa #53, Clovis, CA 93612.

Carrillo, Arsenio S., V.G., 9281 E. Summer Trail, 85749.

Oliver, John A., 1020 W. 1st St., 85364.

Rosensweig, Walter F., 800 E. Baffert Dr., # 31, Nogales, 85621.

Revs.—

Carscallen, Edward C., 221 S. Pas Tera C., Green Valley, 85614.

Costigan, Richard J., 1307 W. Niagara St., 85745.

Cote, Gerald M., 5715 W. Box R St., 85713.

Curry, Frederic F., 870 Natachee, 85710.

Diehl, Michael C., 6333 Rancho Mission Rd., San Diego, CA 92109.

Fahey, John M., 94 Carrington Ave., Woonsocket, RI 02895.

Gagnon, Ronald P., 2727 W. Star Trails Dr., #1, 85742.

Graff, Robert L., 5464 E. Boston St., Mesa, 85205.

Hyman, Robert A., 2240 E. Monte Vista Dr., 85719.

Larocque, Paul M., 392 W. Camino del Sonador, Green Valley, 85614.

Moore, Clarke W., 2727 W. Star Trail Dr., #3, 85742-9607.

O'Flannigan, Thomas L., 409 W. Pontiac Dr. #6, Phoenix, 85027.

Padilla, Gilbert, 1948 E. 5th St., 85716.

Ruiz, Antonio A., 7727 E. Black Crest Pl., 85750.

Schlueter, Clements M., P.O. Box 5886, Phoenix, 85010.

Stromberg, Floyd G., 3003 N. Alvernon, # 112, 85712.

Whalen, Norman M., P.O. Box 911, San Marcos, TX 78666.

Permanent Deacons:

Ackerley, John K., St. Augustine Cathedral, Tucson

Adams, Thomas, Our Lady of Lourdes, Benson

Ammerman, Michael D., St. Pius X, Tucson

Arbizo, Marcello A., St. Rose of Lima, Safford

Baker, Don, St. John the Evangelist, Tuscon

Borquez Henry S., St. Augustine Cathedral, Tucson

Bracamonte, Gilbert, Most Holy Trinity, Tucson

Broussard, John O., St. Joseph, Tucson

Bueno, Oscar L., St. Augustine's, Tucson

Burns, James, St. Elizabeth Ann Seton, Tucson

Callie, Albert, Holy Trinity Monastery, St. David

Caponigro, Alfred E., St. Elizabeth Ann Seton

Carbajal, Arnulfo, St. Francis of Assisi, Yuma

Carlin, Robert P., St. Elizabeth Ann Seton, Tucson

Carmona, Salvador, St. Augustine Cathedral, Tuscon

Carrasco, Joaquin, Immaculate Conception, Douglas

Castillo, Frank R., Holy Angels, Globe

Castillo, Jesus, Our Lady of the Blessed Sacrament, Miami

Castillo, Mario V., St. Luke, Douglas

Collura, Frank J., St. Francis de Sales, Tucson

Converse, Paul E., (Retired), St. Joseph, Tucson

Crockette, Alvin, St. Francis de Sales, Tucson

De La Torre, Nicolas, St. Monica, Tucson

Delgado, Joseph, St. Patrick, Bisbee

Desmarais, Ronald, Our Lady of Lourdes, Benson

Doherty, James, Our Lady of the Valley, Green Valley

Duarte, Carlos V., St. Francis of Assisi, Yuma

Duarte, Jose, St. John the Evangelist, Tucson

Dugan, Patrick, St. Anthony of Padua, Casa Grande

Duran, Ralph, St. Rose of Lima, Safford

Espinosa, Jim, St. Joseph, Tucson

Fernandez, Eugene, St. Monica, Tucson

Fischbach, George, St. Francis of Assisi, Yuma

Fisher, Donald, St. Monica, Tucson

Flam, Richard (Retired)

Force, Richard C., Villa Maria de Guadalupe Geriatric Center, Tucson

Fullen, Samuel, Holy Cross, Morenci

Gallegos, Charles A., St. John the Evangelist, Tucson

Gamboa, Henry W., St. Ambrose, Tuscon

Garcia, John A., St. Monica, Tucson

Garcia, Marcario, Immaculate Heart of Mary, Somerton

Garcia, Philip, (Retired), St. Joseph, Tucson

Garcia, Ramon, St. Anthony of Padua, Casa Grande

Gaun, George, St. Andrew the Apostle, Sierra Vista

Gelabert, Carlos G., St. Margaret, Tucson

Gersitz, James M., Holy Angels, Globe

Girard, Charles, Esq., St. Francis de Sales, Tucson

Glowdowski, Robert

Gonzales, Alfred M., San Solano Missions, Sells

Gonzales, Luciano, Jr., Immaculate Conception, Douglas

Gonzales, Richard A., Sacred Heart, Clifton

Gonzales, Robert J., St. Patrick, Bisbee & St. Michael Mission, Naco

Grijalva, Richard, St. Ambrose, Tucson

Grimaldo, Pedro, Our Lady of the Valley, Green Valley

Hernandez, Nieves J., Office of Catholic Chaplain, Yuma

Hernandez, Richard R., St. Francis of Assisi, Yuma

Herrick, George R., St. Joseph's, Tucson

Hintze, Craig, St. George, Apache Junction

Hoerr, Michael "Danny", Holy Family, Tucson

Hughes, William G., St. George, Apache Junction

Jones, William E.

Kingery, Russell, St. Thomas the Apostle, Tucson

Kinney, William, St. Anthony of Padua, Casa Grande

Krueger, William, St. Elizabeth Ann Seton, Tucson

Kushner, Joseph, III, St. Andrew the Apostle, Tucson

Lambert, Frank, Dir. Diocesan Permanent Diaconate

Larson, Donald L., St. Francis of Assisi Parish, Yuma

LaSalle, James F., St. Thomas More Newman Center, Tucson

Leinfelder, Carl, Holy Family, Tucson

LeMieux, Richard, Holy Angels, Globe

Leon, Viviano, St. James, Coolidge

Longoria, Leopoldo "Leo", St. Elizabeth Ann Seton, Tucson

Lopez, Jose, St. Jude Thaddeus Mission, San Luis

Lopez, Miguel, St. Margaret Mary, Tucson

Lugo, Guillermo A. (Bill), St. Patrick's, Bisbee

Lundgren, Frank S., Jr., Our Lady of Fatima, Tucson

Magallanes, Oscar, Our Lady, Queen of All Saints, Tucson

Martinez, Carlos C., St. Augustine Cathedral, Tucson

Mazza, Leon S., St. Joseph, Tucson

McDonald, William, St. Francis of Assisi, Yuma

McNealy, Kenneth J., St. Thomas the Apostle, Tucson

Medrano, Efren, St. Joseph, Tucson

Merritt, William, Our Lady of the Mountains, Sierra Vista

Mezquita, Fernando, St. Andrew the Apostle, Sierra Vista

Milazzo, Mike, St. Andrew the Apostle, Sierra Vista

Miller, Anthony, St. Mark the Evangelist, Tuscon

Miller, Rodger, Our Lady of the Mountains, Sierra Vista

Minetti, Bernard, St. John the Evangelist, Tucson

Morales, Tomas, St. Monica, Tucson

Moreland, Kenneth, Most Holy Trinity, Tucson

Moreno, Florencio, Jr., St. Francis of Assisi, Yuma

Morgan, Thomas, St. Francis de Sales, Tucson

Moulinet, Armando A., St. Luke's, Douglas

Mulloy, Daniel L., Immaculate Conception, Yuma

Munoz, Jorge, St. Elizabeth Ann Seton, Tucson

Muthart, Paul, St. Francis of Assisi, Yuma

Negrette, Robert, Our Lady of Fatima, Tucson

Nehmer, David, Our Lady Queen of All Saints, Tucson

Nevins, Robert, St. Francis de Sales, Tucson

Nixen, Mark, Immaculate Conception, Yuma

Noriega, Rudy, Our Lady of the Valley, Green Valley

Ojeda, Jose, St. John the Evangelist, Tucson

Ornelas, Richard, Santa Cruz, Tucson

Ortega, Mario, St. Anthony of Padua, Casa Grande

Pasquinelli, Gary, St. Francis of Assisi, Yuma

Paulus, Raymond V., Sacred Heart, Tucson

Pavlik, Keith F., St. Francis de Sales, Tucson

Pawloski, Chester E., Saints Peter and Paul, Tucson

Pennington, Charles H., St. Cyril of Alexandria, Tucson

Radke, Robert, St. Francis de Sales Mission, Maricopa

Ramirez, Frank, Santa Cruz, Tucson

Ranke, Dennis, St. Pius X, Tucson

Roche, Ernest C., (Retired), St. John the Evangelist, Tucson

Rodriguez, George M., Our Lady Queen of All Saints, Tucson

Rombach, Lionel E., St. Joseph, Tucson

Sadorf, Robert G., Our Lady of the Mountains, Sierra Vista; Sacred Heart, Tombstone

Saladin, Jerry, St. John Newmann, Yuma

Sampson, David, Immaculate Conception, Yuma

Sanchez, Falvio, St. Bartholomew, San Manuel

Saspe, Gabriel, St. Luke, Douglas

Scalpone, Dennis R., St. Francis de Sales, Tucson

Schaff, James, Our Lady of the Mountains, Sierra Vista

Scherf, George, St. Odilia, Tucson

Schneider, Paul L., Our Mother of Sorrows, Tucson

Sheffer, Edward P., St. Thomas the Apostle, Tucson

Sherlock, Francis C., St. Elizabeth Ann Seton, Tucson

Silva, Alfredo A., Our Mother of Sorrows, Tucson

Stotler, Jim, Our Lady of the Valley, Green Valley

Tackett, Gene, Our Lady of the Mountains, Sierra Vista

Tarango, Florentino, St. James, Coolidge

Tellez, Frank J., St. Rose of Lima, Safford

Terry, John, St. Rose of Lima, Safford

Underwood, Anthony E., St. Elizabeth Ann Seton, Tucson

Valadez, Jose, St. Francis of Assisi, Yuma

Valenzuela, Armando L., St. Monica, Tucson

Valenzuela, Carlos, St. Augustine Cathedral, Tucson

Vessels, Carlos, St. Rose of Lima, Safford

Vidal, Rafael, St. Francis of Assisi, Yuma
Vigil, William, St. Francis de Sales, Tucson
Wagner, Thomas, St. Pius X, Tucson
Welsh, Paul J., Our Mother of Sorrows, Tucson
Yanez, Jesus L. "Chuy", St. Francis of Assisi, Superior
Zapata, Jose S., Immaculate Conception, Douglas

INSTITUTIONS LOCATED IN THE DIOCESE

[A] HIGH SCHOOLS, PRIVATE

TUCSON. *St. Augustine Catholic High School*, 8800 E. 22nd St., 85710. Tel: 520-751-8300; Fax: 520-751-8304. Email: catrejo@staugustinehigh.com. Web: www.staugustinehigh.com. Sr. Lauren Moss, O.S.F., Ed.D. Prin. Sisters of St. Francis of Assisi Students 150.

Immaculate Heart High School, 625 E. Magee Rd., 85704. Tel: 520-297-2851; Fax: 520-797-7374. Email: ihhsekholt@earthlink.net. Web: www.edline.net/pages/Immaculate_Heart. Sr. Miriam Claire Arnold, Prin. Sisters of the Immaculate Heart of Mary 4; Lay Teachers 10; Students 67.

Salpointe Catholic High School, 1545 E. Copper St., 85719. Tel: 520-327-6581; Fax: 520-327-8477. Email: president@salpointe.org. Web: www.salpointe.org. Mrs. Ruth Jenson, Prin. Carmelite Order Sisters 1; Lay Teachers 72; Students 1,315.

Priory, 1540 E. Glenn St., 85719. Tel: 520-325-1537. Email: www.salpointe.org. In Res. Revs. Thomas Butler, O.Carm.; Roy Conry, O.Carm.; Foster Hanley, O.Carm.; Brian Henden, O.Carm.; John Malley, O.Carm.; Vernon Malley, O.Carm.; Angelo Mastria, O.Carm.; Bradley Peterson, O.Carm.; Glenn Snow, O.Carm.; Frederick J. Tillolson, O.Carm., Pres.; Bro. Tom Conlon, O.Carm.

San Miguel of Tucson Corporation - San Miguel Catholic High School, P.O. Box 22199, 85734. 212 W. Medina Rd., 85706. Tel: 520-294-6403; Fax: 520-294-6417. Email: vanderzg@sanmiguelhigh.com. Web: www.sanmiguelhigh.com. Gregory R. VanderZanden, Pres.; Henry S. Rillos, Proj. Dir.

NOGALES. *Lourdes Catholic School*, (Grades PreK-12) , (High School) , 555 Patagonia Rd., P.O. Box 1865, 85628. Tel: 520-287-5659; Fax: 520-287-2910. Email: bmcfmm@yahoo.com. Web: www.lourdescatholicschool.org. Sr. Barbara Monsequr, C.F.F.M., Prin.; Rev. Frank Cady. Priests 1; Minim Daughters of Mary Immaculate 4; Lay Teachers 22; Students 435.

YUMA. *Yuma Catholic High School*, 2100 W. 28th St., 85364. Tel: 928-317-7900; Fax: 928-317-8558. Email: jfriel@yumaed.org. Web: yumacatholic.org. Mr. Tom Hurt, Interim Prin. Sisters 3; Lay Teachers 29; Students 371.

[B] ELEMENTARY SCHOOLS, PRIVATE

TUCSON. *Immaculate Heart Academy*, 410 E. Magee Rd., 85704. Tel: 520-297-6672; Fax: 520-297-9152. Email: IHABeth@aol.com. Web: www.azstarnet.com/~ihhs/. Mrs. Beth Piekarski, Prin. Sisters of the Immaculate Heart of Mary 2; Lay Teachers 27; Students 375.

[C] CATHOLIC COMMUNITY SERVICES

TUCSON. *Catholic Community Service of Southern Arizona, Inc.*, 140 W. Speedway, Ste. 230, 85705. Tel: 520-623-0344; Fax: 520-770-8514. Email: peghccs@ccs-soaz.org. Web: www.ccs-soaz.org. Celestino Fernandez, Corp. Board Pres.; Marguerite Harmon, M.S., CEO.

Social Service Agencies: Pima County (Including City of Tucson) , 140 W. Speedway, Ste. 230, 85705. Tel: 520-623-0344; Fax: 520-770-8514. Email: peghccs@ccs-soaz.org. Web: ccs-soaz.org.

Catholic Community Services of Southern Arizona, Inc. Marguerite Harmon, CEO of CCS; Ronald A. Dankowski, Ph.D., Exec. Dir., Catholic Social Svc. of CSS.

Counseling Services, 140 W. Speedway, Ste. 130, 85705. Tel: 520-623-0344; Fax: 520-770-8578. Mary LeBron, C.P.C., Admin.

Catholic Community Services of Southeastern Arizona, 19 Howell Ave., Bisbee, 85603. Tel: 520-432-2285; Fax: 520-432-2009. Chuck Fisher, Exec. Dir. of CCSSEAZ.

Forgasch House, P.O. Box 1961, Sierra Vista, 85636. Tel: 520-459-0595. Chuck Fisher, Exec. Dir.

House of Hope, P.O. Box 121, Douglas, 85608. Tel: 520-364-2465. Chuck Fisher, Exec. Dir.

Migration and Refugee Services, 140 W. Speedway, Ste. 130, 85705. Tel: 520-623-0344; Fax: 520-770-8556. Mahvash Yazdani, Admin.

Santa Cruz Project, 2020 S. Sixth Ave., 85713. Tel: 520-623-0344; Fax: 520-770-8578. Sr. M. Teresa Apalategui, O.P., M.S.W., Admin.

Senior Nutrition Services, 5009 E. 29th St., 85711. Tel: 520-624-1562; Fax: 520-519-1303. Ms. Linda Hutchings, M.S.R.D., Admin.

Merilac Lodge and Casa de Crianza, 140 W. Speedway, Ste. 130, 85705. Tel: 520-623-0344; Fax: 520-770-8578. Sr. Mary Ann Bogosoff, C.S.A., Dir.

Immigration Counseling Service, 140 W. Speedway, Ste. 130, 85705. Tel: 520-623-0344; Fax: 520-770-8578.
Field Offices: Rene Franco, Dir.

Gila County Case Management, 175 E. Cedar St., Globe, 85501. Tel: 520-425-5130; Fax: 520-425-2888. Sherlyn Harris, M.A., C.O.G.

Catholic Community Services in Western Arizona, 690 E. 32nd St., Yuma, 85365. Tel: 520-341-9400; Fax: 520-341-8428. Marjorie Coffaro, M.A., Exec. Dir.

Chaplaincy-Pastoral Ministry to Non-Denominational Nursing Homes, 140 W. Speedway, Ste. 230, 85705. Tel: 520-623-0344; Fax: 520-770-8514. Sr. Carolyn Nicolai, F.S.P., Coord.; Rev. Angelo Mastria, O.Carm., Chap.

Community Outreach Program for the Deaf, 268 W. Adams, 85705. Tel: 520-792-1906; Fax: 520-770-8544. Anne Levy, M.A., Exec. Dir.

Community Living Program, 268 W. Adams, 85705. Tel: 520-792-1906; Fax: 520-770-8544. Sue Henning-Mitchell, B.A., Dir.

Detention Ministry, 140 W. Speedway, Ste. 230, 85705. Tel: 520-623-0344; Fax: 520-770-8514. Ms. Barbara Mattus, M.A., Dir.

St. Elizabeth of Hungary Out-Patient Clinic, 140 W. Speedway, Ste. 100, 85705. Tel: 520-628-7871; Fax: 520-770-8528. Sr. Barbara Anne Stowasser, C.S.J., Exec. Dir.

Pio Decimo Neighborhood Center, 848 S. 7th Ave., 85701. Tel: 520-622-2801; Fax: 520-622-4704. Margaret Kish, M.S.W., Exec. Dir.

Valley Center for the Deaf, 3130 E. Roosevelt, Phoenix, 85008. Tel: 602-267-1921; Fax: 602-273-1872. Anne Levy, M.A., Executive Dir.

[D] GENERAL HOSPITALS

TUCSON. *Carondelet Health Network*, 2202 N. Forbes Blvd., 85745-2682. Tel: 520-872-7690; Fax: 520-872-7852. Email: sjeffcoat@carondelet.org. Sally E. Jeffcoat, Pres. & CEO.

St. Joseph Hospital, 350 N. Wilmot Rd., 85711. Tel: 520-873-3000; Fax: 520-872-3921. Wes Colvin, Senior Vice Pres. & CEO; Revs. James A. Freeman; Isaac A. Fynn; Alan Wagner, S.D.S.; Mrs. Beth Bebee, Dir. Chap. Svcs. Div. of Carondelet Health Network. Sisters of St. Joseph of Carondelet 4; Bed Capacity 301; Bassinets 43; Patients Assisted Annually 214,300.

St. Mary's Hospital, 1601 W. St. Mary's Rd., 85745-2682. Tel: 520-872-3000; Fax: 520-872-6641. Greg Angle, Senior Vice Pres. & CEO; Revs. Joseph Saba; James Modeen; Alan Wagner, S.D.S.; Alfred Greenwald. Div. of Carondelet Health Network. Sisters of St. Joseph 4; Bed Capacity 393; Patients Assisted Annually 197,000.

Carondelet Foundation, 120 N. Tuscon Blvd., 85716. Tel: 520-873-5000; Fax: 520-873-5030. Ms. Jannie Cox, Vice Pres., CEO.

St. Elizabeth of Hungary Out-Patient Clinic, 140 W. Speedway Blvd., Ste. 100, 85705. Tel: 520-628-7871; Fax: 520-205-8461. Email: mariaeste@ccs-soaz.org. Web: www.ccs-soaz.org. Sr. Barbara Anne Stowasser, C.S.J., Exec. Dir., Admin. Patients Assisted Annually 26,457.

NOGALES. *Holy Cross Hospital, Inc.* Div. of Carondelet Health Network , 1171 W. Target Range Rd., 85621. Tel: 520-285-3000; Fax: 520-285-8015. Email: rpolheber@carondelet.org. Web: carondelet.org. Sr. Claudia Rushlow, S.C., Hospital Chap.; Sally E. Jeffcoat, Pres. & CEO; Richard Polheber, Senior Vice Pres. & CEO, Holy Cross. Bed Capacity 31.

Holy Cross Geriatric Center, 1171 W. Target Range, 85621. Patients Assisted Annually 125; Total Geriatric Patients Days 16,167; Admissions 1,935.

[E] MONASTERIES AND RESIDENCES OF PRIESTS AND BROTHERS

TUCSON. *Carmelite Priory*, 1540 E. Glenn St., 85719. Tel: 520-325-1537; Fax: 520-318-4651. Revs. John Malley, O.Carm., Former Prior Gen.; Angelo Mastria, O.Carm.; Frederick Tillotson, O.Carm., Pres.; Roy Conry, O.Carm.; Foster Hanley, O.Carm.; Vernon Malley, O.Carm.; Brian Henden, O.Carm., Prior; Thomas Butler, O.Carm.; Bradley Peterson, O.Carm.; Glenn Snow, O.Carm.; Bro. Thomas Conlon, O.Carm. Fathers and Brothers at Salpointe Catholic High School. Priests 10; Brothers 1.

Discalced Carmelite Friars of St. Margaret Mary's, 801 N. Grande Ave., 85745. Tel: 520-622-0168; Fax: 520-882-8022. Revs. Cypprian Killackey, O.C.D.; Bernard Perkins, O.C.D.; Kevin McArdle, O.C.D.

Jesuit Community of the Vatican Observatory, 2017 E. Lee St., 85719. Tel: 520-795-9866; Fax: 520-326-0756. Revs. Richard J. Murphy, S.J., Supr.; Richard P. Boyle, S.J.; George V. Coyne, S.J., Dir. Vatican Observatory; Jose G. Funes, S.J.; William R. Stoeger, S.J.; Andrew P. Whitman, S.J.; Bro. Guy Consolmagno, S.J. Jesuit Residence.

**Vatican Observatory Foundation* Tel: 520-621-3225; Fax: 520-621-1532.

Offices of The Vatican Observatory, Steward Observatory, The University of Arizona, 85721. Tel: 520-621-3225; Fax: 520-621-1532.

Kino House-Jesuit Fathers of Southern Arizona, 2844 E. 1st St., 85716. Tel: 520-327-7130; Fax: 520-327-7573. Email: polzerc@qwest.net.

Regina Cleri Center, 8800 E. 22nd St, 85710. Sisters of the Oblates of St. Martha 3. In Res. Most Rev. Francis A. Quinn, D.D., Ed.D. (SAC), Bishop Emeritus of Sacramento (Retired).

Society of the Divine Word House, Eight Tucson Ter., 85745. Tel: 520-622-6545.

CORTARO. *Redemptorist Society of Arizona* dba Desert House of Prayer , 7350 W. Picture Rocks Rd., P.O. Box 570, 85652. Tel: 520-744-3825; Fax: 520-744-0774. Web: deserthouseofprayer.org. Rev. Paul Curtin, C.Ss.R., Dir.

ST. DAVID. *Holy Trinity Monastery*, P.O. Box 298, 85630. Tel: 520-720-4642; 520-720-4016; Fax: 520-720-4202. Email: frhenri@theriver.com. Web: www.holytrinitymonastery.org. Revs. Alexander M. Mills, O.S.B.; Lawrence M. Fedor, O.S.B.; Henri Capdeville, O.S.B., Prior. Benedictines Professed 7; Postulants 1; Perpetually Professed 1.

Hand of Help Christian Service Program Bro. Fred Buerman, Dir. A mission society in the Benedictine tradition is home based at Holy Trinity Monastery.

SONOITA. *The Benedictine Monastery of Erlac in Sonoita*, P.O. Box 534, 85637. Tel: 520-394-2961; Fax: 520-394-0163. Email: monksonoita@theriver.com. Rt. Rev. James R. Straif.

[F] CONVENTS AND RESIDENCES FOR SISTERS

TUCSON. *St. Ann Convent*, 3820 Sabino Canyon Rd., 85750-6503. Tel: 520-298-0064. Email: stanns@theriver.com. Sr. Luisa Sanchez, I.H.M., Supr. Sisters of the Immaculate Heart of Mary 10.

Benedictine Monastery, 800 N. Country Club Rd., 85716-4583. Tel: 520-325-6401; Fax: 520-321-4358. Email: osbtucson@benedictinesisters.org. Web: www.benedictinesisters.org. Sr. Lupita Barajas, O.S.B., Prioress. Sisters 23.

Carondelet Community, 6571 E. Carondelet Dr., 85710-2156. Tel: 520-721-3832. Sisters 3.

Convento Maria Nazareth - Minim Daughters of Mary, 2821 W. Calle Gardenias, 85745. Tel: 520-743-0414. Sr. Rosa Maria Ruiz, C.F.M.M., Rgnl. Supr. Sisters 4.

Guadalupe Community, 1833 W. St. Mary's Rd., 85745-2653. Tel: 520-620-4944. Email: conventg2@hotmail.com. Sisters 2.

Immaculate Heart Lodge Convent, 410 E. Magee Rd., 85704. Tel: 520-742-5896. Sr. Barbara Ann Gamboa, Supr. Sisters of the Immaculate Heart of Mary 6.

Masmitja Community, 634 E. Magee Rd., 85704. Tel: 520-575-6002. Sr. Blanche M. Felix, Supr. Sisters of the Immaculate Heart of Mary 3.

Immaculate Heart Novitiate, 3820 N. Sabino Canyon Rd., 85750-6503. Tel: 520-885-4981; Fax: 520-886-4273. Email: miriam.arnold@comcast.com. Sisters of the Immaculate Heart of Mary 4.

Immaculate Heart of Mary Provincial House, 3820 N. Sabino Canyon Rd., 85750-6503. Tel: 520-886-4273; Fax: 520-886-4273. Sisters Miriam Claire Arnold, IHM Prov. Supr.; Alicia Martinez, Sec. & Community Archivist. Sisters of the Immaculate Heart of Mary 5.

Immaculate Heart Religious Center, 4100 N. Sabino Canyon Rd., 85715. Tel: 520-886-4273; Fax: 520-886-4273. Sr. Miriam Claire Arnold, Provincial. Sisters of the Immaculate Heart of Mary 2.

St. Joseph Community, 6569 E. Carondelet Dr., 85710-2156. Tel: 520-873-3816. Email: stjoetucson@aol.com.

Maria Community, 1835 W. St. Mary's Rd., 85745-2653. Tel: 520-872-4940; Fax: 520-872-7840. Email: conventm@aol.com. Sisters 8.

Regina Cleri Convent, 8800 E. 22nd St., 85710. Tel: 520-296-9077. Sisters of the Oblates of St. Martha 4.

Saints Peter and Paul Convent, 1947 E. Adams St., 85719. Tel: 520-325-2234; Fax: 520-881-4690. Email: smug1@juno.com. Sisters of Charity of Seton Hill

San Xavier Mission, 1950 W. San Xavier Rd., 85746. Tel: 520-294-2624; Fax: 520-294-3438. Email: sanxaviermision@aol.com.

Sisters of the Holy Cross, 1947 E. Adams, 85719-4301. Tel: 520-325-2234.

SS. Peter and Paul Convent

Saint Charles Convent, 355 San Carlos Ave., San Carlos, 85550. Tel: 520-475-2460.

DOUGLAS. *Loretto Convent*, 1200 - 14th St., 85607. Tel: 520-364-7571; Fax: 520-364-7844. Email: lorettoc@digital.ody.com. Web: carmelitegeneralate.homestead.com.

FLORENCE. *Chapel of the Gila* (Historical Site) , 255 E. 8th St., 85232. P.O. Box 2550, 85232-0550.

GLOBE. *Holy Angels Convent*, 1300 E. Cedar, 85501. Tel: 928-425-2034; Fax: 928-425-5704. Email: presglobe@yahoo.com. Web: www.presglobe@yahoo.com. Union of the Sisters of the P.B.V.M. 5.

NOGALES. *St. Joseph Convent*, 405 N. Carondelet Dr., 85621-2454. Tel: 520-287-7139; Fax: 520-287-2982. Sr. Celia Ma. Ponce, C.F.M.M., Asst. Supr. Minim Daughters of Mary Immaculate C.F.M.M. 10.

Our Lady of Lourdes Convent, P.O. Box 1865, 85628-1865. Tel: 520-287-3377; Fax: 520-287-2910. Email: lourdescatholicschool.org. Minim Daughters of Mary Immaculate C.F.M.M. 10.

SOMERTON. *Immaculate Heart of Mary Convent*, P.O. Box 2888, 85340.

SONOITA. *Santa Rita Abbey*, HC 1, Box 929, 85637-9705. Tel: 520-455-5595; Fax: 520-455-5770. Email: mesamaria@aol.com. Web: www.santaritabbey.org. Sr. Miriam Pollard, O.C.S.O., Prioress. Cistercian Nuns of the Strict Observance, O.C.S.O. Solemn Professed 12.

YUMA. *Immaculate Conception Convent*, 500 - 24th Ave., 85364. Tel: 928-783-5224; Fax: 928-343-0172. Email: sbettinardi@hotmail.com. Sisters 10.

[G] RETREAT HOUSES

TUCSON. *Redemptorist Society of Arizona* dba Redemptorist Renewal Center , 7101 W. Picture Rocks Rd., 85743. Tel: 520-744-3400; Fax: 520-744-8021. Email: tmscssr.desertrenewal.org. Web: DesertRenewal.org. P.O. Box 569, Cortaro, 85652. Revs. Thomas Santa, C.SS.R.; John Steingraeber, C.SS.R.; Patrick Hawk, C.SS.R.; Theodore Lawson, C.SS.R.; Bro. John Matthys, C.SS.R.

CORTARO. *Redemptorist Society of Arizona* dba Desert House of Prayer , 7350 W. Picture Rocks Rd., P.O. Box 570, 85652. Tel: 520-744-3825; Fax: 520-744-0774. Web: deserthouseofprayer.org. In Res. Rev. Paul Curtin, C.SS.R., Dir.

DOUGLAS. *Joshua Retreat Center of the Saylah Corp.*, 1530 23rd St., 85607. Tel: 520-364-9460; Fax: 520-364-9460. Janet E. Fullen, Contact Person.

ST. DAVID. *Holy Trinity Monastery*, P.O. Box 298, 85630. Tel: 520-720-4642; Fax: 520-720-4016. Email: frhenri@theriver.com. Web: www.holytrinitymonastery.org.

SIERRA VISTA. *La Purisima Retreat Center, Inc.*, 800 Taylor Dr., N.W., 85635. Tel: 520-458-2925; Fax: 520-452-0235. Email: office@standrewapostlechurch.org. Web: lpretreat.org. Ann S. Dickson, Contact Person.

[H] NEWMAN CENTERS

TUCSON. *University of Arizona* , St. Thomas More Newman Center , 1615 E. 2nd St., 85719. Tel: 520-327-6662; Fax: 520-327-6559. Email: jhn1@mindspring.com. Web: w3.arizona.edu. Revs. Michael S. Fones, O.P., Dir. Supr.; Daniel J. Rolland, O.P.; Bede Wilks, O.P. (LA); Sisters Diane Bridenbecker, O.P.; Reinilde Cade, O.P. In Res. Rev. Robert A. Burns, O.P.

CASA GRANDE. *Central Arizona College, Holy Family Newman Center* P.O. Box 12335, 85230-2335. Tel: 520-836-0601; Fax: 520-836-2985. Email: stanthony@c2i2.com. Rev. Kevin D. Clinch.

DOUGLAS. *Cochise Community College* St. Luke, 1211 15th St., 85607. Tel: 520-364-4411; Fax: 520-364-2397. Revs. Gilbert Malu Musumbu; Marco Antonio Basulto-Pitol, Vicar; Marsha John, Office Mgr.

SAFFORD. *Eastern Arizona Junior College* P.O.Box 1375, 85546. Rev. Domenico C. Pinti.

St. Rose of Lima, 311 Central Ave.. Tel: 928-348-0232; Fax: 928-348-0232. Email: deacjbt@net.com. Mike De Leo, Pres., Newman Sustaining Council.

[I] MISCELLANEOUS LISTINGS

TUCSON. *Carondelet Foundation*, 120 N. Tucson Blvd., 85716-4740. Tel: 520-873-5000; Fax: 520-873-5030. Email: janniecox@aol.com. Web: www.carondelet.org. Jannie Cox, F.A.H.P., CEO.

Casa de los Ninos Crisis Center, 1101 N. 4th Ave., 85705. Tel: 520-624-5600; Fax: 520-623-2443. Email: info@casadelosninos.org. Web: www.casadelosninos.org. Jeanne Landdeck-Sisco, Exec. Dir.

Casa Maria, 401 E. 26th St., 85713. Tel: 520-624-0312. Mr. Brian Flagg, Coord.

Christ Child Society of Tucson, P.O. Box 36212, 85740-6212. Tel: 520-579-2596; Fax: 520-579-2597. Email: cplunsford@aol.com. Pat Lunsford, Pres.; Claire Lunsford, First Vice Pres.; Sarita McCann, Second Vice Pres.; Dodie Christensen, Treas.; Donna Spackeen, Sec.; Norma Greenbaum, Corresponding Sec.

Diocese of Tucson Catholic Cemeteries (Sole Corporation) , 3555 N. Oracle Rd., 85705. Tel: 520-888-0860; Fax: 520-887-7360. Email: stomchin@dotcc.org. Web: www.dotcc.org.

Diocese of Tucson Catholic Committee on Scouting, 3360 E. Ajo Way, 85713. Fax: 520-294-3333. Web: www.azstarnet.com/~rccdot/dotscts.html.

Diocese of Tucson Catholic Tuition Organization (CTSO), P.O. Box 31, 85702. Tel: 520-792-3410; Fax: 520-838-2589. Email: ctso@ctso-tucson.org. Web: www.ctso-tucson.org. Ms. JoAnn Sayre, Contact Person.

Integrated Auxiliaries The Friends of John Paul II Foundation

10121 Prairie Hills Cir., Sun City, 85352. Dr. S.F. Poray-Tucholski, Pres.

5611 E. Rochridge Dr., Phoenix, 85018. Dr. E.J. Bratkowsha-Kendall, Vice Pres. & Treas.

10347 Campana Dr., Sun City, 85351. Czeslaw A. Kozdroj, Esq.

10121 Prairie Hills Cir., Sun City, 85351. Mrs. Jacquelina M. Poray-Tucholski.

Knights of Columbus, 5515 E. Hawthorne St., 85711-1423. Tel: 520-748-0536. Mr. Pedro Najera, State Deputy.

Magnificat - Tucson Chapter, 3560 N. Via San Juanito, 85749. Tel: 520-749-0633; Fax: 520-207-6211. Email: carolyn3270@cox.net. Mrs. L. J. Elizabeth Celenza, Pres. A ministry to Catholic women.

Ministerio Shalom, P.O. Box 22378, 85734. Tel: 520-889-0411. Vidal Haro, Treas.

Redemptorist Community Support Charity Trust (Western Province) , 7101 W. Picture Rocks Rd., 85743. Tel: 520-744-3400; Fax: 520-744-8021. Revs. Patrick O'Brien, C.SS.R., Trustee. Tel: 510-562-9740; Raymond Maiser, C.SS.R., Trustee.

Retorno (Marriage Retorno), 4321 N. Ventana Dr., 85750. Tel: 520-722-2931; Fax: 520-722-2152. Email: stogskk@mindspring.com. Web: www.mindspring.com/~stogskk/marriageretorno.htm/. Rev. Patrick O'Brien, C.SS.R., Contact Person. Tel: 847-724-0425; Kathie & Kevin Stogsdill, Contact Person. Tel: 520-722-2931. Prayer Retreat for Couples

Society of St. Vincent de Paul, 829 S. 6th Ave., 85701. Tel: 520-628-7837; Fax: 520-624-9102.

The St. Thomas More Society of Southern Arizona, 459 N. Granada Ave., 85701. Tel: 520-838-2507; Fax: 520-882-9861. Gary P. Broussard, Contact Person.

HEREFORD. *Our Lady of the Sierras Foundation*, 10310 Twin Oaks Dr., P.O. Box 269, 85615. Tel: 520-378-2950; Fax: 520-378-2950. Email: ourladysierras@theriver.com. Web: www.ourladyofthesierras.org. Mr. Gerald A. Chouinard, Pres.

ST. DAVID. *San Pedro Valley Center for the Arts*, Holy Trinity Monastery, Box 160, 85630. Tel: 520-720-4009. Patricia J. Don, Contact Person.

SOUTH TUCSON. *Blessed Kateri Tekakwitha Parish Center*, 507 W. 29th St., 85713. Tel: 520-622-1654; Fax: 520-792-0230. Email: danielmclaughlin@colisp.com. Revs. Daniel P. McLaughlin, S.T.; Abram E. Dono, S.T.; Francisco Nunez, S.T.

[J] DIOCESAN CEMETERIES

TUCSON. *Holy Hope Cemetery and Mausoleum*, Office, 3555 N. Oracle Rd., P.O. Box 5158, 85703. Fax: 520-885-9173. Arnold Elias, Dir.; Rev. Edward C. Carscallen, Catholic Chap. (Retired).

Our Lady of the Desert Cemetery and Mausoleum, Office, 2151 S. Avenida Los Reyes, P.O. Box 5158, 85703. Tel: 520-885-9173.

RELIGIOUS INSTITUTES OF MEN REPRESENTED IN THE DIOCESE

For further details refer to the corresponding bracketed number in the Religious Institutes of Men or Women section.

[0200]—*Benedictine Monks*—O.S.B.

[0470]—*The Capuchin Friars* (Prov. of St. Joseph)—O.F.M.Cap.

[0270]—*Carmelite Fathers and Brothers* (Prov. of Most Pure Heart of Mary)—O.Carm.

[0350]—*The Cisterian Order of Strict Observance (Trappists)*—O.C.S.O.

[0360]—*Claretian Missionaries*—C.M.F.

[1320]—*Clerics of St. Viator*—C.S.V.

[1330]—*Congregation of the Mission*—C.M.

[0260]—*Discalced Carmelites* (Anglo-Irish Prov.)—O.C.D.

[0520]—*Franciscan Friars*—O.F.M.

[0650]—*Holy Ghost Fathers* (Western Prov.)—C.S.Sp.

[0300]—*Institute of Charity*—I.C.

[0690]—*Jesuit Fathers and Brothers* (Western Prov.)—S.J.

[0800]—*Maryknoll*—M.M.

[0720]—*The Missionaries of Our Lady La Salette* (Immaculate Heart of Mary Prov.)—M.S.

[0840]—*Missionary Servants of the Most Holy Trinity*—S.T.

[0910]—*Oblates of Mary Immaculate*—O.M.I.

[0430]—*Order of Preachers (Dominicans)*—O.P.

[1030]—*Paulist Fathers*—C.S.P.

[1070]—*Redemptorist Fathers* (Oakland Prov.)—C.SS.R.

[1200]—*Society of the Divine Savior*—S.D.S.

[0420]—*Society of the Divine Word*—S.V.D.

[1060]—*Society of the Precious Blood*—C.PP.S.

RELIGIOUS INSTITUTES OF WOMEN REPRESENTED IN THE DIOCESE

[0100]—*Adorers of the Blood of Christ*—A.S.C.

[0160]—*Augustine Nuns of Contemplative Life*—O.S.A.

[0233]—*Benedictine Nuns*—O.S.B.

[0230]—*Benedictine Sisters of Pontifical Jurisdiction*—O.S.B.

[0370]—*Carmelite Sisters of the Most Sacred Heart of Los Angeles*—O.C.D.

[0670]—*Cistercian Nuns of the Strict Observance*—O.C.S.O.

[0700]—*Company of Mary*—O.D.N.

[1010]—*Congregation of Divine Providence*—C.D.P.

[0220]—*Congregation of the Benedictine Sisters of Perpetual Adoration of Pontifical Jurisdiction*—O.S.B.

[0460]—*Congregation of the Sisters of Charity of the Incarnate Word*—C.C.V.I.

[3710]—*Congregation of the Sisters of St. Agnes*—C.S.A.

[1920]—*Congregation of the Sisters of the Holy Cross*—C.S.C.

[1780]—*Congregation of the Sisters of the Third Order of St. Francis of Perpetual Adoration*—F.S.P.A.

[1070-03]—*Dominican Sisters*—O.P.

[1070-09]—*Dominican Sisters*—O.P.

[1070-12]—*Dominican Sisters*—O.P.

[1070-13]—*Dominican Sisters*—O.P.

[1070-30]—*Dominican Sisters*—O.P.

[1140]—*Eucharistic Missionaries of St. Dominic*—O.P.

[1230]—*Franciscan Sisters of Christian Charity*—O.S.F.

[1310]—*Franciscan Sisters of Little Falls, Minnesota*—O.S.F.

[1415]—*Franciscan Sisters of Mary*—F.S.M.

[1425]—*Franciscan Sisters of Peace*—F.S.P.

[2575]—*Institute of the Sisters of Mercy of the Americas*—R.S.M.

[2675]—*Minim Daughters of Mary Immaculate*—C.F.M.M.

[2690]—*Mission Catechists of Divine Providence*—M.C.D.P.

[2720]—*Mission Helpers of the Sacred Heart*—M.H.S.H.

[]—*Oblates of St. Martha*—O.S.M.

[3130]—*Our Lady of Victory Missionary Sisters*—O.L.V.M.

[2970]—*School Sisters of Notre Dame*—S.S.N.D.

[1680]—*School Sisters of St. Francis*—S.S.S.F.-O.S.F.

[3580]—*Servants of Mary*—O.S.M.

[3590]—*Servants of Mary (Servite Sisters)*—O.S.M.

[0440]—*Sisters of Charity of Cincinnati, Ohio*—S.C.

[480]—*Sisters of Charity of Leavenworth, Kansas*—S.C.L.

[0570]—*Sisters of Charity of Seton Hill, Greensburg, Pennsylvania*—S.C.

[0660]—*Sisters of Christian Charity*—S.C.C.

[3720]—*Sisters of Notre Dame de Namur*—S.N.D.deN.

[1705]—*The Sisters of St. Francis of Assisi*—O.S.F.

[1800]—*Sisters of St. Francis of the Third Order Regular (Williamsville, New York)*—O.S.F.

[3830-13]—*Sisters of St. Joseph*—C.S.J.

[3840]—*Sisters of St. Joseph of Carondelet*—C.S.J.

[0260]—*The Sisters of the Blessed Sacrament for Indians and Colored People*—S.B.S.

[1030]—*Sisters of the Divine Savior*—S.D.S.

[2180]—*Sisters of the Immaculate Heart of Mary*—I.H.M.

[3270]—*Sisters of the Most Precious Blood*—C.PP.S.

[3260]—*Sisters of the Precious Blood* (Dayton, Ohio)—C.PP.S.

[3320]—*Sisters of the Presentation of the Blessed Virgin Mary*—P.B.V.M.

[1720]—*Sisters of the Third Order Regular of St. Francis of the Congregation of Our Lady of Lourdes*—O.S.F.

[2150]—*Sisters, Servants of the Immaculate Heart of Mary* (Monroe)—I.H.M.

NECROLOGY

† Connelly, George R., (Retired)—Died Aug. 27, 2003

† Parenteau, William, (Retired)—Died July 24, 2003

† Rook, Paul J., (Retired)—Died Feb. 2, 2003

† Wiesler, Willard P., (Retired)—Died Dec. 26, 2002

Diocese of Tulsa

(Dioecesis Tulsensis)

Most Reverend

EDWARD J. SLATTERY

Bishop of Tulsa; ordained April 26, 1966; appointed Bishop of Tulsa November 11, 1993; ordained January 6, 1994 in Rome; installed January 12, 1994

Chancery Office: 12300 E. 91st St., S., Broken Arrow, OK 74012P.O. Box 690240, Tulsa, OK 74169-0240. Tel: 918-294-1904; Fax: 918-294-0920.

Web: www.dioceseoftulsa.org

Email: bishop.office@dioceseoftulsa.org

ESTABLISHED FEBRUARY 7, 1973.

Square Miles 26,417.

The Diocese of Tulsa comprises the following 31 Counties: Adair, Atoka, Bryan, Cherokee, Choctaw, Coal, Craig, Creek, Delaware, Haskell, Hughes, Latimer, LeFlore, McCurtain, McIntosh, Mayes, Muskogee, Nowata, Okfuskee, Okmulgee, Osage, Ottawa, Pawnee, Payne, Pittsburg, Pushmataha, Rogers, Sequoyah, Tulsa, Wagoner and Washington.

For legal titles of parishes and institutions, consult the Chancery Office.

STATISTICAL OVERVIEW

Personnel	
Bishop	1
Priests: Diocesan Active in Diocese	46
Priests: Diocesan Active Outside Diocese	6
Priests: Retired, Sick or Absent	24
Number of Diocesan Priests	76
Religious Priests in Diocese	28
Total Priests in Diocese	104
Extern Priests in Diocese	11
Ordinations:	
Diocesan Priests	3
Permanent Deacons in Diocese	57
Total Brothers	10
Total Sisters	92
Parishes	
Parishes	80
With Resident Pastor:	
Resident Diocesan Priests	40
Resident Religious Priests	5
Without Resident Pastor:	
Administered by Priests	33
Administered by Deacons	1
Completely Vacant	1
Closed Parishes	1
Professional Ministry Personnel:	
Brothers	1
Sisters	13
Lay Ministers	63
Welfare	
Catholic Hospitals	5
Total Assisted	356,000
Homes for the Aged	4
Total Assisted	420
Specialized Homes	2
Total Assisted	80
Special Centers for Social Services	4
Total Assisted	90,000
Educational	
Diocesan Students in Other Seminaries	13
Total Seminarians	13
High Schools, Diocesan and Parish	1
Total Students	928
High Schools, Private	1
Total Students	587
Elementary Schools, Diocesan and Parish	10
Total Students	4,115
Elementary Schools, Private	1
Total Students	1,036
Catechesis/Religious Education:	
High School Students	1,624
Elementary Students	4,835
Total Students under Catholic Instruction	13,138
Teachers in the Diocese:	
Brothers	6
Sisters	5
Lay Teachers	346
Vital Statistics	
Receptions into the Church:	
Infant Baptism Totals	1,399
Adult Baptism Totals	190
Received into Full Communion	234
First Communions	1,096
Confirmations	749
Marriages:	
Catholic	195
Interfaith	163
Total Marriages	358
Deaths	493
Total Catholic Population	56,094
Total Population	1,527,376

Former Bishops—Most Revs. BERNARD J. GANTER, D.D., ord. May 22, 1952; appt. Bishop of Tulsa, Dec. 19, 1972; ord. Feb. 7, 1973; transferred to Beaumont, Oct. 18, 1977; EUSEBIUS J. BELTRAN, ord. May 14, 1960; appt. Bishop of Tulsa, Feb. 28, 1978; ord. April 20, 1978; transferred to Archdiocese of Oklahoma City, Nov. 24, 1992.

Vicar General—Rev. Msgr. DENNIS C. DORNEY, V.G.

Chancery Office—12300 E. 91st St. S., Broken Arrow, 74012. Mailing Address, P.O. Box 690240, Tulsa, 74169. Tel: 918-294-1904; Fax: 918-294-0920. Office Hours: Mon.-Fri. 9-5

Chancellor—HENRY L. HARDER, Ph.D.

Vice Chancellor—Rev. PATRICK J. GAALAAS.

Finance Office—Mr. PHILIP J. CREIDER, Assets Mgr.; Mr. THOMAS SCHADLE, Controller, P.O. Box 690240, Tulsa, 74169-0240. Tel: 918-294-1904.

Diocesan Senators—Most Rev. EDWARD J. SLATTERY; Rev. Msgr. DENNIS C. DORNEY, V.G.; Revs. PAUL E. EICHHOFF; TIMOTHY L. DAVISON; J. PAUL DONOVAN (Retired); GREGORY A. GIER; BERNARD C. JEWITT; AMALOR VIMA; PATRICK BRANKIN; DAVID MEDINA; JACK GLEASON.

Ex Officio—Rev. Msgr. DENNIS C. DORNEY, V.G.

Diocesan Consultors—Revs. JACK GLEASON; BERNARD C. SCIANNA, O.S.A.; PATRICK J. GAALAAS; Rev. Msgr. DENNIS C. DORNEY, V.G.; Revs. DANIEL H. MUEGGENBORG; TAM N. NGUYEN; JOHN J. WADE; PAUL EICHHOFF.

Diocesan Marriage Tribunal—

Judicial Vicar—Rev. MICHAEL J. KNIPE.

Defender of the Bond—Rev. MICHAEL A. DODD, J.C.L.

Judges—Revs. MICHAEL J. KNIPE; KENNETH J. HARDER, J.C.L.; Deacon KASPER E. WEIGANT.

Auditors—HENRY L. HARDER, Ph.D.; Mr. ROBERT GERMANY; Mrs. DONNA GERMANY.

Notary—Mrs. MARY JONES.

Promoter of Justice—Rev. MICHAEL A. DODD, J.C.L.

Priests' Personnel Committee—Rev. Msgr. DENNIS C. DORNEY, V.G.; Revs. TAM N. NGUYEN; BRYAN V. BROOKS.

Seminary Board—Rev. Msgr. DENNIS C. DORNEY, V.G.; Mr. ROBERT J. LAFORTUNE; Revs. JACK GLEASON; DANIEL H. MUEGGENBORG; JOE C. TOWNSEND; Ms. ANDREA HYATT.

Federation of Religious of the Diocese of Tulsa—Leadership Team: Sisters MARILYN NORWOOD, O.S.B.; EUGENIA BROWN, O.S.B., 2200 S. Lewis, Tulsa, 74114. Tel: 918-746-4211.

Diocesan Offices

Archivist—Rev. JAMES D. WHITE; Ms. DIANNE BILECK, Asst., P.O. Box 690240, Tulsa, 74169-0240. Tel: 918-294-1904.

Campaign for Human Development—HENRY L. HARDER, Ph.D., P.O. Box 690240, Tulsa, 74169. Tel: 918-294-1904.

Campus Ministry—Rev. STUART CREVCOURE, Chap.; Mrs. SUZIE CURTIN, Dir. Operations; Mr. STEVE NELSON, Campus Ministry, St. Philip Neri Newman Center at The University of Tulsa, 440 S. Florence, Tulsa, 74104. Tel: 918-599-0204; Fax: 918-587-0115; Rev. KENNETH J. HARDER, J.C.L., 201 N. Knoblock St., Stillwater, 74074. Tel: 405-372-6408. Oklahoma State University, 201 N. Knoblock St., Stillwater, 74075. Tel: 405-372-6408.

Catholic Charities of the Diocese of Tulsa—Deacon TIMOTHY SULLIVAN, Dir., 739 N. Denver, Tulsa, 74106. Tel: 918-585-8167; Fax: 918-582-2123. Mailing Address, P.O. Box 6429, Tulsa, 74148.

Adoption—Tel: 918-585-8167.

Hispanic Helping Center—2436 E. Admiral Blvd., Tulsa, 74110. Tel: 918-585-8199.

Madonna House—749 N. Denver, Tulsa, 74106. Tel: 918-585-5186.

Immigration Office—2444 E. Admiral Blvd., Tulsa, 74110. Tel: 918-582-0881.

Sallisaw Helping Center—Sallisaw.

St. Elizabeth Lodge—Tulsa. Tel: 918-585-5068.

St. Joseph Residence—Tulsa. Tel: 918-585-8167.

Xavier Medical Center—Tulsa. Tel: 918-583-7233.

Calvary Cemetery—9101 S. Harvard, Tulsa, 74137. Tel: 918-299-7348.

Clergy Education—Rev. DANIEL H. MUEGGENBORG, P.O. Box 690240, Tulsa, 74169. Tel: 918-294-1904.

Diocesan Catholic Committee on Scouting—Mr. GREGG SLIEF, Dir. Tel: 918-588-7379.

Diocesan Council of Catholic Women—KAREN PAINTER, 1006 23rd, S.W., Miami, 74354. Tel: 918-542-3747.

Ecumenism—Rev. PATRICK J. GAALAAS, Dir., 2200 W. Ithica, Broken Arrow, 74012.

Education—Ms. MONICA SKRZYPCZAK, Dir. Religious Formation, P.O. Box 690240, Tulsa, 74169. Tel: 918-294-1904.

Family Life Office—Deacon TIMOTHY J. SULLIVAN, Dir., P.O. Box 6429, Tulsa, 74148.

Parochial Schools—TODD GOLDSMITH, Supt. Catholic Schools, 820 S. Boulder, Tulsa, 74119. Tel: 918-582-9177; Fax: 918-582-1851.

Prison and Social Ministry—Deacon BILL DUNBAR, P.O. Box 690240, Tulsa, 74169.

Hispanic Ministry—Revs. PATRICK BRANKIN, Dir.; ROBERT M. DYE, Assoc. Dir., 1541 E. Newton Pl., Tulsa, 74106. Tel: 918-584-2424.

Historian—Rev. JAMES D. WHITE, P.O. Box 690240,

Tulsa, 74169.
Pastoral Studies Institute—Ms. MONICA SKRZYPCZAK, Coord., P.O. Box 690240, Tulsa, 74169-0240. Tel: 918-294-1904.
Office of Divine Worship—Rev. MATTHEW J. GERLACH, Dir., P.O. Box 690240, Tulsa, 74169-0240. Tel: 918-294-1904.
Newspaper "Eastern Oklahoma Catholic"—Mr. JAMES SELLARS, Editor, P.O. Box 690240, Tulsa, 74169. Tel: 918-294-1904.
Office of Permanent Diaconate—Rev. PATRICK M. BRANKIN, Vicar for Deacons, P.O. Box 690240, Tulsa, 74169. Tel: 918-294-1904.
Office for the Synod—Rev. DANIEL H. MUEGGENBORG, Dir., P.O. Box 690240, Tulsa, 74169. Tel: 918-294-1904.
Propagation of Faith—Rev. MATTHEW J. GERLACH, Coord., 4532 S. 25th West Ave., Tulsa, 74107. Tel: 918-446-8124.
Stewardship and Development—Mr. CHARLES R. GISLER, Dir., P.O. Box 690240, Tulsa, 74169. Tel: 918-294-1904.
Victim Assistance Coordinator—Mr. QUENTIN HENLEY. Tel: 918-585-8167.
Vocations—Rev. JACK GLEASON; Mrs. THERESA WITCHER, Seminarians; Mr. WAYNE RZIHA, Promotion & Recruitment, 3188 E. 22nd St., Tulsa, 74114. Tel: 918-744-0023.
Young Adult Ministry—Mr. CHARLES MICHIE, P.O. Box 690240, Tulsa, 74169-0240. Tel: 918-294-1904.
Youth Ministry—Mr. CHARLES MICHIE, P.O. Box 690240, Tulsa, 74169-0240. Tel: 918-294-1904.

CLERGY, PARISHES, MISSIONS AND PAROCHIAL SCHOOLS

CITY OF TULSA
(TULSA COUNTY)

1—HOLY FAMILY CATHEDRAL (1899), [JC] Rev. Gregory A. Gier, Rector; Rev. Msgr. James F. Halpine, Rector Emeritus; Rev. Michael A. Dodd, J.C.L.; Deacons Millard Kizzia; Jerry Mattox.
Res.: 122 W. 8th St., P.O. Box 3204, 74101. Tel: 918-582-6247; Fax: 918-599-8334.
School—820 S. Boulder St., 74119. Tel: 918-582-0422; Fax: 918-582-9705. Mrs. Holly Goodwin, Prin. Lay Teachers 18; Students 198.
Catechesis/Religious Program—Monica Skrzypczak, D.R.E. Students 160.

2—ST. AUGUSTINE'S (1955), (African American), Rev. Desmond Okpogba (Nigeria); Deacon Steve Litwack.
Church: 1728 E. Apache, 74110. Tel: 918-428-3280.
Catechesis/Religious Program—Students 33.

3—ST. BERNARD OF CLAIRVAUX (1978), Revs. Bernard C. Jewitt; Joshua E. Litwack; Deacons Richard Campbell; Alan Mikell; Robert Martin; David Johnson.
Res.: 4001 E. 101st St., 74137. Tel: 918-299-9406; Fax: 918-299-7796.
Catechesis/Religious Program—Sharon Lechtenberg, D.R.E. Students 632.

4—ST. CATHERINE (1925), [JC] Rev. Matthew J. Gerlach; Deacon Ned Doty.
Res.: 4532 S. 25th West Ave., 74107. Tel: 918-446-8124; Fax: 918-446-4506.
School—2515 W. 46th St., 74107. Tel: 918-446-9756. Sisters of St. Francis of the Martyr St. George 4; Lay Teachers 9; Students 115.
Catechesis/Religious Program—Students 33.
Mission—St. Joseph P.O. Box 603, Bristow, Creek Co. 74010. Deacon Tom Loney.

5—CHRIST THE KING (1917), [JC] Revs. Tam Nguyen; James A. Caldwell Jr.; Sr. Connie Lennartz, O.P.; Deacon Loren F. Luschen.
Office—1520 S. Rockford Ave., 74120. Tel: 918-584-4788; 918-584-4789; Fax: 918-584-0055.
Res.: 1530 S. Rockford Ave., 74120. Tel: 918-584-6693.
School—Marquette School, 1519 S. Quincy, 74120. Tel: 918-584-4631; Fax: 918-584-0055. John Kraus, Prin. Lay Teachers 26; Students 374.
Catechesis/Religious Program—Students 82.

6—CHURCH OF ST. MARY (1954), [JC] Rev. Msgr. Dennis C. Dorney, V.G.; Revs. Samuel Perez; William J. Swift; Deacon Richard Bender.
Office—1347 E. 49th Pl., 74105. Tel: 918-749-1423; Fax: 918-747-9532.
School—1365 E. 49th Pl., 74105. Tel: 918-749-9361; Fax: 918-712-9604. Suzanne Nelson, Prin. Lay Teachers 17; Students 263.
Catechesis/Religious Program—Linda Schoonover, D.R.E. Students 320.

7—CHURCH OF THE MADALENE (1946), [JC] Rev. Jack A. Gleason; Sr. Marie Pierre Fleming, O.S.B., Pastoral Assoc.; Deacon Robert DeWeese.
Res.: 3188 E. 22nd St., 74114. Tel: 918-744-0023; Fax: 918-744-0024.
Catechesis/Religious Program—Tel: 918-744-9417. Mrs. Kay Bashaw, D.R.E. Students 104.

8—ST. FRANCIS XAVIER (1926), (Hispanic), [JC] Revs. Jose Maria Briones (Mexico); Festus Maliwa.
Mailing Address: 2434 E. Admiral Blvd., 74110.
Res. & Church: 2515 E. 1st St., 74110. Tel: 918-592-6770; Fax: 918-592-2208.
Catechesis/Religious Program—Sr. Marcelina Santos, D.R.E. Students 520.

9—IMMACULATE CONCEPTION (1923), Unassigned.

10—ST. JOSEPH CHURCH (1977), (Vietnamese), Rev. Hoang Viet Le.
Res.: 14905 E. 21st St., 74134. Tel: 918-438-1380.
Catechesis/Religious Program—Tel: 918-438-6325. Students 81.

11—ST. MONICA'S (1926), (African American), Rev. Desmond Okpogba (Nigeria).
Church: 633 Marshall Pl., 74106. Tel: 918-587-2965 (Office); Fax: 918-582-0699.
Catechesis/Religious Program—Students 22.

12—OUR LADY OF GUADALUPE, Closed., For inquiries for sacramental records contact St. Francis Xavier, Tulsa.

13—PARISH OF SAINT PETER (1996), Rev. Robert Ferguson, F.S.S.P. (SCR).
Mailing Address: 1720 E. Apache, 74110. Tel: 918-425-0486; Fax: 918-425-2077.
Res.: 1728 E. Apache, 74110.
Catechesis/Religious Program—Students 47.

14—SS. PETER AND PAUL (1950), [JC] Revs. Timothy L. Davison; Miguel Diaz De Lara (Mexico); Deacon Tommy Young.
Res.: 1436 N. 67th E. Ave., 74115. Tel: 918-836-2596; Fax: 918-836-2597.
School—1428 N. 67th E. Ave., 74115. Tel: 918-836-2165. Patrick Martin, Prin. Lay Teachers 17; Students 162.
Catechesis/Religious Program—Karen Campbell, D.R.E. Students 60.

15—ST. PIUS X (1955), [JC] Rev. Thomas M. Hildebrand; Deacons Kasper Weigant; Anthony H. Tran.
Office—1727 S. 75 E. Ave., 74112. Tel: 918-622-4488; Fax: 918-622-1239.
Res.: 7628 E. 17th St., 74112. Tel: 918-664-9723.
School—1717 S. 75 E. Ave., 74112. Tel: 918-627-5367. Karen Arras, Prin. Lay Teachers 27; Students 377.
Catechesis/Religious Program—Debbie Fields, D.R.E. Students 100.

16—RESURRECTION (1968), Revs. Michael J. Knipe; Kenneth Schumacher.
Office—P.O. Box 33169, 74153. Tel: 918-663-1907; Fax: 918-663-2533.
Res.: 4338 S. Braden Pl., 74135. Tel: 918-664-8319.
Church: 4804 S. Fulton, 74135. Tel: 918-663-1907.
Catechesis/Religious Program—Laura Hassell, D.R.E. Students 240.

17—ST. THOMAS MORE (1972), Rev. Carl Kerkemeyer.
Church and Res.: 2720 S. 129 E. Ave., 74134-2411. Tel: 918-437-0168; Fax: 918-437-0681.
Catechesis/Religious Program—Becky Bryant, D.R.E. Students 28.

OUTSIDE CITY OF TULSA

ANTLERS, PUSHMATAHA CO., ST. AGNES (1897), Rev. Joe C. Townsend.
Church: 504 E. Main, 74523.
Res.: HC 69, Box 36-1, Hugo, 74743. Tel: 580-298-6113.
Catechesis/Religious Program—Students 35.
Station—McLeod Correctional Center Farris. Tel: 405-889-6651; Fax: 405-889-2264.

BARTLESVILLE, WASHINGTON CO.

1—THE COMMUNITY OF ST. JAMES (1965), Rev. William K. Skeehan.
Res.: 5510 Douglas Ln., 74006. Tel: 918-333-5307.
Church: 5500 Douglas Ln., 74006.
Catechesis/Religious Program—Tel: 918-335-0844; Fax: 918-335-0856. Students 60.
Mission—St. Catherine 217 W. Modoc, Nowata, Nowata Co. 74048. Tel: 918-273-0737.

2—ST. JOHN'S (1906), [CEM] Revs. Stephen E. Austin; Hung Viet Le; Deacons Joseph Richard; Dan Willis.
Res.: 715 S. Johnstone Ave., 74003. Tel: 918-336-4353; Fax: 918-336-4354.
School—Tel: 918-336-0603; Fax: 918-336-0603. Kurt Nelson, Prin. Lay Teachers 10; Students 142.
Catechesis/Religious Program—Rachel Becker, D.R.E. Students 99.

BIXBY, TULSA CO., ST. CLEMENT OF ROME (1958), Rev. Daniel M. Mueggenborg.
Mailing Address: P.O. Box 8, 74008.
Res.: 21 W. Stadium Rd., 74008. Tel: 918-366-3166; Fax: 918-365-3164.
Catechesis/Religious Program—Students 150.

BROKEN ARROW, TULSA CO.

1—ST. ANNE (1936), [JC] Rev. Dovan Nguyen.
Res.: 301 S. 9th St., 74012. Tel: 918-251-4000; Fax: 918-251-8719.
Catechesis/Religious Program—Tel: 918-251-5414. Deborah Solano, D.R.E. Students 130.

2—ST. BENEDICT (1980), Revs. Patrick J. Gaalaas; Richard Cristler; Deacon John Donnelly.
Res.: 2305 S. Chestnut, 74102. Tel: 918-455-7353.
Church: 2200 W. Ithica St., 74012. Tel: 918-455-4451; Fax: 918-451-2199.
Catechesis/Religious Program—Students 665.

CLAREMORE, ROGER CO., ST. CECILIA (1911), Rev. Paul E. Eichhoff; Deacon Vincent Mrasek.
Res.: 1304 N. Dorothy, 74017. Tel: 918-341-2343; Fax: 918-343-2893.
Catechesis/Religious Program—Tel: 918-341-4238. Students 311.

CLEVELAND, OSAGE, ST. JOSEPH (1905), (Native American), Rev. Bruce Brosnahan.
Mailing Address: 333 S. 8th St., Fairfax, 74637. Tel: 918-358-2333.
Catechesis/Religious Program—Students 20.
Church: Osage & C Ave., 74020.
Mission— (1929), 421 S. Petit, Hominy, Osage Co. 74035.

COALGATE, COAL CO., BLESSED SACRAMENT ORATORY (1889), [CEM] Rev. Michael E. Cashen.
Mailing Address: P.O. Box 72, 74538.

COLLINSVILLE, TULSA CO., ST. THERESE (1906), [CEM] Rev. Patrick M. Brankin.
Res.: 1007 N. 19th St., Box 297, 74021. Tel: 918-371-2704; Fax: 918-371-3895.
Catechesis/Religious Program—Jane Webb, D.R.E. Students 94.

COWETA, WAGONER CO., ST. VINCENT DE PAUL (1981), Deacon James A. Pierret, Admin.
Mailing Address: P.O. Box 771, 74429-0771. Tel: 918-486-4757.
Catechesis/Religious Program—Students 19.

CUSHING, PAYNE CO., SS. PETER AND PAUL (1894), [CEM] Rev. Paul O. Amaliri; Deacon Alfonso A. Cardenas.
Mailing Address: P.O. Box 828, 74023.
Res.: 214 N. Steele St., 74023. Tel: 918-225-0644; Fax: 918-225-6569.
Catechesis/Religious Program—Students 46.
Mission—St. Mary Cimarron & Wood, Drumright, Creek Co. 74030. Tel: 918-352-9327 (Parish Hall).
Mission—St. John 8th & Oak, Pawnee, Pawnee Co. 74058.

DEWEY, WASHINGTON CO., OUR LADY OF GUADALUPE (1955), Rev. Stephen E. Austin; Deacons Richard Chamberlain; James Black.
400 W. Ninth St., 74029. Tel: 918-534-3420; Fax: 918-534-3013.
Catechesis/Religious Program—Students 64.

DURANT, BRYAN CO., ST. WILLIAM (1914), Rev. Valerian Gonsalves, O.S.B. (India); Deacon Albert Miller.
802 University Blvd., 74701. Tel: 580-924-1989; Fax: 580-931-3044.
Catechesis/Religious Program—Students 58.
Mission—St. Patrick Church Hwy. 69 S., Atoka, Atoka Co. 74701. Tel: 580-889-2846.

FAIRFAX, OSAGE CO., SACRED HEART (1925), (Osage Indian), Rev. Bruce C. Brosnahan; Deacon Vernon Butler.
Mailing Address: 333 S. 8th St., 74637. Tel: 918-642-5053.
Catechesis/Religious Program—Students 9.

GROVE, DELAWARE CO., ST. ELIZABETH (1949), Rev. Alex Kennedy.
Office:—1653 113th St., N.W., 74344. Tel: 918-256-2281.
Catechesis/Religious Program—Students 74.

HARTSHORNE, PITTSBURG CO., HOLY ROSARY (1895), [CEM] [JC] Rev. Leonard Ahanotu (Nigeria); Deacon Sid Starr.
Mailing Address: P.O. Box 621, Krebs, 74554.
Church: 912 Cherokee, 74547.
Catechesis/Religious Program—Students 23.
Mission—St. Catherine of Siena Second & Gann Sts., Talihina, Leflore Co. 74571. Tel: 918-567-2587.
Mission—Sacred Heart 102 Center Point Rd., Wilburton, Latimer Co. 74578. Rev. Chris Daigle; Deacon Clement Bradley.
Mission—Holy Trinity P.O. Box 747, Clayton, Pushmataha Co. 74523. Tel: 918-569-4767.

HENRYETTA, OKMULGEE CO., ST. MICHAEL (1912), [JC] Rev. Joseph Vadake Chirayath (India).
1004 W. Gentry St., P.O. Box 148, 74437. Tel: 918-652-3445; Fax: 918-652-3445.
Mission—St. Paul's 6th & Forest, Eufaula, McIntosh Co. 74554.

HOLDENVILLE, HUGHES CO., ST. STEPHEN'S (1905), Rev. Anselm Maniakupara, O.S.B. (India), Admin.
Res.: 515 E. Highway, 74848. Tel: 405-379-2512; Fax: 405-379-2512.
Catechesis/Religious Program—Students 20.
Mission—St. Teresa (1927), 8th and Broadway, Okemah, Okfuskee Co. 74859.

HOMINY, OSAGE CO., ST. JOSEPH (1929),, Now a mission under St. Joseph, Cleveland.

HUGO, CHOCTAW CO., IMMACULATE CONCEPTION (1903), Rev. Joe C. Townsend. In Res., Bro. Lawrence Jochim, G.H.M.
Res.: HC69, Box 36-1, 74743. Tel: 580-326-7300.
Catechesis/Religious Program—Students 43.
Mission—St. Jude 511 11th St., Boswell, Choctaw Co. 74727.

IDABEL, MCCURTAIN CO., ST. FRANCIS DE SALES (1945), Rev. John T. Brown, G.H.M.
Res.: 13 S.E. Jefferson, 74745. Tel: 580-286-3275.
Catechesis/Religious Program—Students 80.
Mission—Good Shepherd P.O. Box 1016, Valiant, McCurtain Co. 74764. Tel: 580-933-4742.
Mission—St. Henry [CEM] Watson. HC 15, P.O. Box 1250, Plunketville, McCurtain Co. 74963. Tel: 580-244-3157. In Res., Rev. Francisco Schenk, G.H.M.

KREBS, PITTSBURG CO., ST. JOSEPH'S (1886), [CEM] Rev. Leonard Ahanotu (Nigeria); Deacon Bill Anderson.
Res.: P.O. Box 621, 74554. Tel: 918-423-6695; Fax: 918-426-4255.
Catechesis/Religious Program—Tel: 918-423-7130. Sharon Dunbar, D.R.E. Students 74.
Station—Jackie Brannon Correctional Center, Tel: 918-426-4470; Fax: 918-426-0004.

LANGLEY, MAYES CO., ST. FRANCES OF ROME (1950), [CEM] [JC] Rev. Alex Kennedy, Admin.; Deacon Charles Toppins, Coord. Parish Life.
Res.: Hwy. 28, P.O. Box 267, 74350-0267. Tel: 918-782-2248.

MCALESTER, PITTSBURG CO., ST. JOHN (1895), [CEM] Rev. Michael E. Cashen.
Res.: 300 E. Washington Ave., Box 220, 74502. Tel: 918-423-0810; Fax: 918-423-0825.
Catechesis/Religious Program—Susan Hewitt, D.R.E.; Nancy Massaro, D.R.E.; Vicky O'Neil, D.R.E.; Laura Stizz, D.R.E.; Diane Willis, D.R.E. Students 107.
Mission—St. Edwards Hwy. 63, Pittsburg, Pittsburg Co. 74560.
Station—Oklahoma State Penitentiary, Tel: 918-423-4700; Fax: 918-423-3862.

MIAMI, OTTAWA CO., SACRED HEART (1900), Rev. W. Gregg Elliott; Deacon Marvin Morris.
Res.: 2515 N. Main, 74354. Tel: 918-542-5281; Fax: 918-542-7591.
Catechesis/Religious Program—Tel: 918-542-5898. Karen Painter, D.R.E. Students 70.
Mission—St. Ann P.O. Box 25, Welch, Craig Co. 74369. Tel: 918-788-3771.

MUSKOGEE, MUSKOGEE CO.
1—ASSUMPTION, Closed., For inquiries for sacramental records contact Saint Joseph Church, Muskogee.
2—SAINT JOSEPH CHURCH (1992), [CEM] Rev. Bryan Brooks; Deacons William Miller; Edwin Falleur; Billie Tindall.
Mailing Address: P.O. Box 189, 74402. Tel: 918-687-1351; Fax: 918-687-5541. In Res., Rev. Robert M. Dye.
Church: 321 N. Virginia, 74402.
Res. & Parish Office: 2228 E. Okmulgee, 74403. Tel: 918-687-1351; Fax: 918-687-5541.
School—(Grades PreK-8), 323 N. Virginia, 74403. Tel: 918-683-1291; Fax: 918-682-5374. Beth Stafford, Prin. Lay Teachers 13; Students 144.
Catechesis/Religious Program—Joanne Beach, D.R.E. Students 180.
Chapel—Sacred Heart
3—SACRED HEART, Closed., For inquiries for sacramental records contact Saint Joseph Church, Muskogee.

OKMULGEE, OKMULGEE CO., ST. ANTHONY'S (1910), [JC] Rev. Amalor Vima (India).
Res.: 515 S. Morton Ave., P.O. Box 698, 74447. Tel: 918-756-4385; Fax: 918-756-3719.
School—Marian Academy, (Grades PreK-5) Tel: 918-756-9042; Fax: 918-756-6578. Sr. Loretta McIluenna, O.P., Prin. Religious 2; Lay Teachers 7; Students 61.
Catechesis/Religious Program—Sr. Mary Fox, O.P., D.R.E. Students 36.
Mission—Uganda Martyrs 808 E. 3rd, Okmulgee Co. 74447.

OWASSO, TULSA CO., ST. HENRY (1957), Revs. J. Richard Bradley; J. Paul Donovan, Pastor Emeritus (Retired); Deacons Vernon Foltz; Donald LeMieux; Edmundo Martinez.
Mailing Address: P.O. Box 181, 74055-0181. Tel: 918-272-3710; Fax: 918-272-1966.
Res.: 104 E. 16th St., 74055. Tel: 918-272-7387.
Church: 8500 Owasso Expy., 74055.
Catechesis/Religious Program—Tel: 918-272-3740. Elizabeth Gagner, D.R.E. Students 418.

PAWHUSKA, OSAGE CO., IMMACULATE CONCEPTION (1887), (Osage Indian), [JC] Rev. Leonard H. Higgins.
Res.: 1314 N. Lynn Ave., 74056. Tel: 918-287-1414.
Catechesis/Religious Program—Students 64.
Mission—St. Mary 3rd and Chestnut, Barnsdall, Osage Co. 74002.
Mission—St. Ann Gypsy St. & Taylor St., Shidler, Osage Co. 74652.

PAWNEE, PAWNEE CO., ST. JOHN (1907), Rev. Paul O. Amaliri.
Mailing Address: P.O. Box 828, Cushing, 74023. Tel: 405-372-6408.
Church: 8th St. & Oak, 74058.

POTEAU, LEFLORE CO., IMMACULATE CONCEPTION (1903), Rev. Charles M. Vincent (India).
Mailing Address: P.O. Box 237, 74953.
Res.: 502 N. Bagwell St., 74953. Tel: 918-647-3475.
Church: 410 Bagwell St., 74953. Tel: 918-647-3475.
Catechesis/Religious Program—Students 15.
Mission—St. Joseph 126 S. Broadway, Stigler, Haskell Co. 74462.
Mission—St. Elizabeth Seton Hwy. 9, Spiro, Leflore Co. 74959.
Station—Ouachita Correctional Training Center [JC] Hodgens.
Catechesis/Religious Program—Students 37.

PRYOR, MAYES CO., ST. MARK'S (1942), Rev. Chi Peter Phung.
Res.: 1507 S. Vann, P.O. Box 576, 74362. Tel: 918-824-1470; Fax: 918-825-2338.
Catechesis/Religious Program—Tel: 918-825-4186. Lissa Rosebrough, D.R.E. Students 60.

SALLISAW, SEQUOYAH CO., ST. FRANCIS XAVIER (1952), Rev. Jeffrey S. Polasek; Deacon Robert Barnes.
Church: 2110 N. Dogwood, 74955. Tel: 918-775-6217; Fax: 918-775-6217.
Catechesis/Religious Program—Students 31.
Mission—St. John the Evangelist P.O. Box 4, Cookson, Cherokee Co. 74427.
Mission—St. Joseph P.O. Box 53, Webbers Falls, Muskogee Co. 74470. Tel: 918-464-2422.
Mission—Blessed Kateri Tekakwitha P.O. Box 17, Roland, Sequoyah Co. 74954.

SAND SPRINGS, TULSA CO., ST. PATRICK'S (1919), [JC] Rev. Martin Morgan; Deacons Bob Garrett; Noel Hollingshead.
Res.: 204 E. Fourth, 74063. Tel: 918-245-5254; Fax: 918-241-3100.
Catechesis/Religious Program—Students 75.
Mission—Our Lady of the Lake 400 Cimarron Dr., Mannford, Creek Co. 74044.

SAPULPA, CREEK CO., SACRED HEART (1907), [JC] Rev. Stuart Crevcoure; Deacons Francis Decker; Mark Pittman.
Church: 1777 E. Grayson Ave., 74066. Tel: 918-224-0944; Fax: 918-248-4935.
Catechesis/Religious Program—Students 75.

SKIATOOK, OSAGE CO., SACRED HEART (1921),, (Formerly St. William). Rev. James D. White; Deacon Don Tucker.
Res.: 109 W. 5th St., 74070. Tel: 918-396-1179; Fax: 918-396-0267.
Catechesis/Religious Program—Students 63.

STILLWATER, PAYNE CO.
1—ST. FRANCIS XAVIER (1895), [JC] Revs. Kenneth J. Harder, J.C.L.; David Medina; Vincent Jayarara (Sri Lanka); Deacons Paul Govek; Bill Moler.
Church: 601 West St., 74074.
Res.: 623 S. West St., Box 909, 74076. Tel: 405-372-6886; Fax: 405-372-8013.
Catechesis/Religious Program—Tel: 405-372-7987. Robert Wilson, D.R.E. Students 34.
2—ST. JOHN UNIVERSITY PARISH AND CATHOLIC STUDENT CENTER (1965), Revs. Kenneth J. Harder, J.C.L.; David Medina; Vincent Jayarara (Sri Lanka); Deacons Bill Dunbar; Tom Haan; Richard Berberet.
Res.: 201 N. Knoblock, 74075. Tel: 405-372-6408; Fax: 405-372-6409.
Catechesis/Religious Program— Twinned with St. Francis Xavier, Stillwater Tel: 405-372-7987. Students 220.

TAHLEQUAH, CHEROKEE CO., ST. BRIGID (1966), Rev. Kenneth Iheanaho (Nigeria); Deacons Joseph Faulds; Mark Keeley.
Res.: 807 Crafton St., 74464. Tel: 918-456-8388; Fax: 918-456-8880.
Catechesis/Religious Program—Tel: 918-456-4204. Patsy Clifford, D.R.E. Students 87.

VINITA, CRAIG CO., HOLY GHOST (1892), Rev. Alex Kennedy.
Res.: 120 W. Sequoyah Ave., 74301. Tel: 918-256-2281.
Catechesis/Religious Program—Tel: 918-256-3118. Sr. Mary Grace Sieben, D.R.E. Students 60.
Station—Eastern State Hospital
Station—Northeastern Correctional Facility

WAGONER, WAGONER CO., HOLY CROSS (1895), Rev. Chi Peter Phung.
Mailing Address: P.O. Box 710, 74477. Tel: 918-485-5145; Fax: 918-485-0656.
Church: S.W. 15th & Pierce, 74477.
Catechesis/Religious Program—Sherry Ruyle, D.R.E. Students 25.

Special Assignment:
Revs.—
Dye, Robert M., Hispanic Ministry
Edward, Yew, Graduate Studies
Khiet, Nquyen, Graduate Studies

On Duty Outside the Diocese:
Revs.—
Cain, Robert K.C., U.S. Navy Chaplain
Minh, Vu Duc, U.S. Air Force Chaplain
Wells, Peter B., Vatican Diplomatic Corps, assigned to Secretary of State Office, Vatican

Graduate Studies:
Rev.—
LaChance, Matthew G., Pontifical North American College, Vatican City

Retired:
Rev. Msgr.—
Halpine, James F., P.O. Box 3204, 74101.
Revs.—
Casey, Denis, 2121 S. Yorktown # 503, 74114.
Courtright, Lawrence P., 1921 S. Xanthus Ave., 74104.
Dally, Peter F., 1605 8th Ave. S. E., Olympia, WA 98501.
Donovan, J. Paul, P.O. Box 181, Owasso, 74055.
Eastman, Patrick W.
Foken, Herman J., Franciscan Villa, 17110 E. 51st St., S., Broken Arrow, 74012.
Fulton, Kenneth S., 8437 E. 58th St., 74145.
King, Kenneth A., P.O. Box 7206, Grove, 74344.
Lundberg, John W., 43 California Ave., Middletown, NY 10940.
MacAuley, Stephen A., Franciscan Villa, 17110 E. 51st St. S., Apt. 2, Broken Arrow, 74012.
Males, Jake A., Franciscan Villa, 17110 E. 51st St., S., Broken Arrow, 74012.
McCarthy, Jerry, Franciscan Villa, 17110 E. 51st St. S., Broken Arrow, 74012.
McGlinchey, James J., 1767 S. Wheeling, 74104.
Melton, Thomas K., P.O. Box 151, Wilburton, 74578.
O'Neil, Lee E., P.O. Box 515, Gulf Shores, AL 36542.
Perlinski, Daniel A., 1735 S. Wheeling Ave., 74104.
Pickett, Robert T., 1414 E. 49th St., 74105-4798.
Richard, Edward, 1594 S. Chamberlain Blvd., North Port, FL 34286.
Swett, Charles J., 2009 Xanthus, 74104.
Swift, William V., 1779 S. Wheeling, 74104.

Permanent Deacons:
Anderson, Bill, St. Joseph, Krebs
Barnes, Robert, Blessed Kateri Tekakwitha, Roland
Bender, Richard F., Church of St. Mary, Tulsa
Berberet, Richard, St. John University Parish, Stillwater
Black, James, St. John, Bartlesville
Bradley, Clement W., Sacred Heart, Wilburton
Breazille, James E., Unassigned
Butler, Vernon, Sacred Heart, Fairfax
Campbell, Richard, St. Bernard, Tulsa
Campbell, Sam, Immaculate Conception, Pawhuska
Cardenas, Alfonso, SS. Peter & Paul, Cushing
Chamberlain, Richard, Our Lady of Guadalupe, Dewey
Decker, Francis I., Sacred Heart, Sapulpa
DeLeon, Felix, (Retired), St. Francis, Tulsa
DeWeese, Robert, Church of the Madalene, Tulsa
Donnelly, John E., St. Benedict, Broken Arrow
Doty, Edward, St. Catherine, Tulsa
Dunbar, Bill, Stillwater Parishes
Falleur, Edwin E., St. Joseph, Muskogee
Faulds, Joseph M., St. Brigid, Tahlequah
Foltz, Vernon, St. Henry, Owasso
Garrett, James R., St. Patrick, Sand Springs
Govek, Paul, St. Francis Xavier, Stillwater
Haan, Tom, St. John University Parish, Stillwater
Hollingshead, Noel, St. Patrick, Sand Springs
Johnson, Dave, St. Bernard, Tulsa
Keeley, Mark, St. Brigid, Tahlequah
Kizzia, Millard H., Holy Family Cathedral, Tulsa
LeMieux, Donald J., St. Henry, Owasso
Litwack, Stephen J., St. Augustine, Tulsa
Loney, Tom, St. Joseph, Bristow
Luschen, Loren F., Christ the King, Tulsa
Martin, Robert, St. Bernard of Clairvaux, Tulsa
Martinez, Edmundo S., St. Henry, Owasso
Mattox, Jerry, Holy Family Cathedral, Tulsa
Mikell, Alan G., St. Bernard, Tulsa
Miller, Albert J., St. William, Durant
Miller, Bill, St. Joseph, Muskogee
Moler, William J., St.Francis Xavier, Stillwater
Morris, Marvin D., Sacred Heart, Miami
Mrasek, Vincent J., St. Cecilia, Claremore
Perez, Jose, (Retired)
Pierret, James A., St. Vincent de Paul, Coweta
Pittman, Mark, Sacred Heart, Sapulpa

Richard, Joseph N., St. John, Bartlesville
Rutherford, Gerard, St. John, Bartlesville
Schumacher, Kenneth, Church of the Resurrection, Tulsa
Starr, Sid, Holy Rosary, Hartshorne
Sullivan, Timothy, Dir. Catholic Charities
Tindall, Billie D., St. Joseph, Muskogee
Toppins, Charles A., St. Frances of Rome, Langley
Tran, Anthony, St. Pius X, Tulsa
Tucker, Donel, Sacred Heart, Skiatook
Weigant, Kasper E., St. Pius X, Tulsa
Willis, Daniel H., St. John, Bartlesville
Young, Thomas, SS. Peter & Paul, Tulsa

INSTITUTIONS LOCATED IN THE DIOCESE

[A] HIGH SCHOOLS, DIOCESAN

TULSA. *Bishop Kelley High School*, 3905 S. Hudson, 74135-5699. Tel: 918-627-3390; Fax: 918-664-2134. Email: aweyland@bkelleyhs.org. Web: www.bkelleyhs.org. Alan V. Weyland, Pres./Prin.; Marianne Stich, Campus Min. Brothers 2; Lay Teachers 83; Students 930.

[B] HIGH SCHOOLS, PRIVATE

TULSA. *Cascia Hall Preparatory School*, (Grades 6-12), Mailing Address: Box 52247, 74152. Tel: 918-746-2600; Fax: 918-746-2636. Email: info@casciahall.org. Web: www.casciahall.org. 2520 S. Yorktown Ave., 74114. Tel: 918-746-2600; Fax: 918-746-2636. Revs. Bernard C. Scianna, O.S.A., Headmaster; John H. Gaffney, O.S.A.; William A. Hamill, O.S.A.; Henry V. Spielmann, O.S.A.; Theodore E. Tack, O.S.A.; Philip C. Cook, O.S.A.; John J. Sotak, O.S.A.; William A. Perez, O.S.A. Augustinians (Order of St. Augustine), Coed College Preparatory School. Priests 8; Sisters 1; Lay Teachers 46; Students 587.

[C] ELEMENTARY SCHOOLS, DIOCESAN

BROKEN ARROW. *All Saints School*, 299 S. 9th St., 74012. Tel: 918-251-3000; Fax: 918-258-9879. Email: office@allsaintsba.com. Tracey Robinson, Prin. Lay Teachers 25; Students 276.

[D] ELEMENTARY SCHOOLS, PRIVATE

TULSA. *Monte Cassino School*, (Grades PreK-8), 2206 S. Lewis, 74114. Tel: 918-743-4471; Fax: 918-742-5206. Web: www.montecasino.org. Sr. Mary Clare Buthod, O.S.B., School Dir. Sisters 3; Lay Teachers 74; Students 1,036.

[E] GENERAL HOSPITALS

TULSA. *Saint Francis Hospital*, 6161 S. Yale Ave., 74136. Tel: 918-494-2200; Fax: 918-494-7175. Web: www.saintfrancis.com. Mr. Jake Henry Jr., Pres. & CEO; Revs. Joseph Thoonkuzhy; John V. Choorackunnel, C.M.I.; Michael Rooney. Bed Capacity 589; Bassinets 40; Patients Assisted Annually 418,884.

St. John Health System, Inc., 1923 S. Utica, 74104. Tel: 918-744-2180; Fax: 918-744-2716. Web: www.stjohnhealthsystem.com. Sr. M. Therese Gottschalk, Pres.

St. John Medical Center, Inc., 1923 S. Utica Ave., 74104. Tel: 918-744-2345; Fax: 918-744-2716. Web: www.sjmc.org. David Pynn, Pres.; Revs. Gary Sherman, Chap.; Gerald J. Coleman, Chap. Sisters of the Sorrowful Mother (Third Order of St. Francis) Sisters 11; Bed Capacity 579; Patients Assisted Annually 70,000.

Marian Health System, Inc., P.O. Box 4753, 74159-0753. Tel: 918-742-9988; Fax: 918-744-2716. Web: www.marianhealthsystem.com. Sr. M. Therese Gottschalk, Pres.

BARTLESVILLE. **Jane Phillips Health Corp.*, 3500 E. Frank Phillips Blvd., 74006.

[F] HOMES FOR THE AGED

TULSA. *Frances Streitel Senior Care Corporation*, 1923 S. Utica Ave., 74104. Tel: 918-744-2471.

St. John Villas, Inc., 1923 S. Utica, 74104. Tel: 918-744-2180; Fax: 918-744-2716. Web: www.stjohnhealthsystem.com/departments/seniorliving. Sr. Catherine Marie Hanegan, Pres.; Revs. Stephen A. MacAuley, Chap. (Retired); Gary D. Sherman, Chap. Sisters of the Sorrowful Mother, Retirement Residence and Health Care Center for Intermediate Nursing Care. Bed Capacity 304; Apartments 186; Residents 430; Total Staff 305.

[G] MONASTERIES FOR MEN

HULBERT. *Our Lady of the Annunciation of Clear Creek Monastery*, 5804 W. Monastery Rd., 74441. Tel: 918-772-2454; Fax: 918-772-1044. Web: www.clearcreekmonks.org. Rev. Philip Anderson, O.S.B., Prior.

[H] CONVENTS AND RESIDENCES FOR SISTERS

TULSA. *St. Joseph Monastery*, 2200 S. Lewis, 74114-3100. Tel: 918-742-4989; Fax: 918-744-1374. Email: sisters@tulsaosb.org. Web: www.tulsaosb.org. Sr. Barbara Austin, O.S.B., Prioress. Motherhouse of Benedictine Sisters (Federation of St. Scholastica) Sisters in Community 29.

Sisters of Saint Joseph, 3942 S. Trenton, 74105. Tel: 918-749-8954. Sisters in Community 2.

BROKEN ARROW. *St. Clare Convent*, 17600 E. 51st St., 74012. Tel: 918-355-5581; Fax: 918-355-3534. Sisters in Community 12.

Sisters of the Sorrowful Mother - Our Lady of Sorrows Convent, 17600 E. 51st St., 74012. Tel: 918-355-5581; Fax: 918-355-3534. Email: ssmdirkx@ols-ba.org. Sr. Paula Jacobs, Coord. Sisters 10.

Sisters of the Sorrowful Mother - U.S./Caribbean Province, Inc., 17600 E. 51st St., 74012. Tel: 918-355-1148; Fax: 918-355-3534. Email: ssmdirkx@ols-ba.org. Web: www.ssmfranciscans.org. Sr. Dorothy Ann M. Dirkx, U.S. & Caribbean Prov. Sisters 154.

SAND SPRINGS. *Benedictine Sisters of Perpetual Adoration*, 18701 W. Monastery Rd., 74063. Tel: 918-245-2734; Fax: 918-245-9360. Email: benitausb@inteon.net. Web: www.benedictinesisters.org. Sr. Benita Luetkemeyer, O.S.B., Supr. Osage Monastery, OM Forest of Peace Benedictine Convent of Perpetual Adoration in Oklahoma, Inc. Sisters 6.

[I] NEWMAN CENTERS

TULSA. *St. Philip Neri Newman Center at The University of Tulsa* 440 S. Florence, 74104. Tel: 918-599-0204; Fax: 918-587-0115. Email: tu-newman@utulsa.edu. Web: www.tu-newman.org. Rev. Stuart Crevcoure; Steve Nelson, Campus Min.; Suzanne Curtin, Dir. Opers.

STILLWATER. *St. John's University Parish and Catholic Student Center* 201 N. Knoblock, 74075. Tel: 405-372-6408; Fax: 405-372-6409. Email: saintjohnparish@yahoo.com. Web: www.stjohn.stillwater.org. Rev. Kenneth Harder; Cathy Perry, Campus Min.

TAHLEQUAH. *Northeastern State University Catholic Student Organization* 807 Crafton St., 74464. Tel: 918-456-8388. Rev. Kenneth Iheanaho (Nigeria).

[J] MISCELLANEOUS

TULSA. *Bishop Kelley High School Endowment Trust*, 3905 S. Hudson Ave., 74135. Tel: 918-627-3390; Fax: 918-664-2134. Email: aweyland@bkelleyhs.org. Web: bkelleyhs.org. Alan Weyland, Prin.

Catholic Foundation of Eastern Oklahoma, Inc., Mailing Address: P.O. Box 690240, 74169. Tel: 918-294-1904.

Saint Francis of Assisi Tuition Assistance Trust, Diocese of Tulsa, P.O. Box 690240, 74169-0240.

St. John Medical Center Foundation, Inc., 1923 S. Utica, 74104. Tel: 918-749-3553; Fax: 918-744-2716.

Saint John Vianney Seminary Trust, Diocese of Tulsa, P.O. Box 690240, 74169-0240.

St. Joseph Residence, Inc., P.O. Box 6429, 74148. Tel: 918-587-6456; Fax: 918-587-3560. Total Assisted 36; Total Staff 6.

Priest Retirement Trust of the Roman Catholic Diocese of Tulsa, c/o Diocese of Tulsa, P.O. Box 690240, 74169-0240. Tel: 918-294-1904; Fax: 918-294-0920. Rev. Msgr. Dennis C. Dorney, V.G.

CLAREMORE. *Apostolate for the Most Holy Rosary and the Brown Scapular Association*, P.O. Box 291, Haskell, 74436. Tel: 918-482-1712. Email: highlandhaven@aol.com.

HULBERT. *Foundation for the Annunciation Monastery of Clear Creek*, 5804 W. Monastery Rd., 74441. Tel: 918-772-2454; Fax: 918-772-1044. Web: www.clearcreekmonks.org.

MUSKOGEE. *St. Joseph School Endowment Trust*, P.O. Box 189, 74402. Tel: 918-687-1351.

RELIGIOUS INSTITUTES OF MEN REPRESENTED IN THE DIOCESE

For further details refer to the corresponding bracketed number in the Religious Institutes of Men or Women section.

[0140]—*The Augustinians (Province of Our Mother of Good Counsel)*—O.S.A.
[0200]—*Benedictine Monks (Solesmes Congregation)*—O.S.B.
[0330]—*Brothers of the Christian Schools* (MIdwest Province, Burr Ridge, IL)
[]—*Carmelites of Mary Immaculate*—C.M.I.
[0570]—*Glenmary Home Missioners*—G.H.M.
[0650]—*Holy Ghost Fathers*—C.S.Sp.
[1065]—*Priestly Order of St. Peter*—F.S.S.P.

RELIGIOUS INSTITUTES OF WOMEN REPRESENTED IN THE DIOCESE

[0220]—*Benedictine Sisters of Perpetual Adoration*
[0380]—*Carmelite Sisters of St. Therese (OKC)*—C.S.T.
[1010]—*Congregation of Divine Providence (San Antonio, TX)*—C.D.P.
[0230]—*Congregation of the Benedictine Sisters of the Sacred Hearts*—O.S.B.
[]—*Little Sisters of Jesus, Mexico*
[2970]—*School Sisters of Norte Dame*
[1070-03]—*Sinsinawa Dominican Congregation*
[1570]—*Sisters of St. Francis of the Holy Family*—O.S.F.
[1640]—*Sisters of St. Francis of the Martyr of St. George*
[3830]—*Sisters of St. Joseph*—S.S.J.
[4100]—*Sisters of the Sorrowful Mother (Third Order of St. Francis)*—S.S.M.

CEMETERIES

TULSA. *Calvary*, P.O. Box 2009, 74101. Tel: 918-587-3115. 9101 S. Harvard, 74136. Tel: 918-743-5571.

NECROLOGY

† Maszkiewicz, Rev. Msgr. Mark, (Retired)—Died Sept., 2003
† Howell, Joseph W., (Retired)—Died Feb. 4, 2003
† Lange, Lawrence P., (Retired)—Died Aug. 22, 2003
† Mazaika, Joseph J., (Retired)—Died Jan. 27, 2003
† McMahon, Finton P.—Died Feb. 6, 2003

Diocese of Tyler

(Dioecesis Tylerensis)

Most Reverend

ALVARO CORRADA DEL RIO, S.J., D.D.

Bishop of Tyler; ordained July 6, 1974; consecrated August 4, 1985; on assignment, as Apostolic Administrator, Diocese of Caguas; appointed Bishop of Tyler December 5, 2000; installed January 30, 2001. *Office: Diocese of Tyler*, 1015 E.S.E. Loop 323, Tyler, TX 75701-9663. Tel: 903-534-1077; Fax: 903-534-1370.

Chancery: 1015 E.S.E. Loop 323, Tyler, TX 75701-9663. Tel: 903-534-1077; Fax: 903-534-1370.

ESTABLISHED DECEMBER 12, 1986.

Square Miles 23,443.

Comprises the following Counties in the State of Texas: Anderson, Angelina, Bowie, Camp, Cass, Cherokee, Delta, Franklin, Freestone, Gregg, Harrison, Henderson, Hopkins, Houston, Lamar, Leon, Madison, Marion, Morris, Nacogdoches, Panola, Rains, Red River, Rusk, Sabine, San Augustine, Shelby, Smith, Titus, Trinity, Upshur, Van Zandt, and Wood.

For legal titles of parishes and diocesan institutions, consult the Chancery Office.

STATISTICAL OVERVIEW

Personnel	
Bishop	1
Priests: Diocesan Active in Diocese	38
Priests: Diocesan Active Outside Diocese	3
Priests: Diocesan in Foreign Missions	1
Priests: Retired, Sick or Absent	7
Number of Diocesan Priests	49
Religious Priests in Diocese	16
Total Priests in Diocese	65
Extern Priests in Diocese	38
Ordinations:	
Diocesan Priests	3
Transitional Deacons	2
Permanent Deacons in Diocese	62
Total Brothers	3
Total Sisters	62
Parishes	
Parishes	42
With Resident Pastor:	
Resident Diocesan Priests	14
Missions	23
Pastoral Centers	1
Professional Ministry Personnel:	
Brothers	1
Sisters	15
Lay Ministers	58
Welfare	
Catholic Hospitals	4
Total Assisted	964,682
Health Care Centers	38
Total Assisted	8,101
Special Centers for Social Services	1
Total Assisted	120
Educational	
Diocesan Students in Other Seminaries	8
Total Seminarians	8
High Schools, Diocesan and Parish	1
Total Students	208
Elementary Schools, Diocesan and Parish	3
Total Students	878
Catechesis/Religious Education:	
High School Students	1,113
Elementary Students	2,610
Total Students under Catholic Instruction	4,817
Teachers in the Diocese:	
Brothers	2
Lay Teachers	88
Vital Statistics	
Receptions into the Church:	
Infant Baptism Totals	1,070
Adult Baptism Totals	165
Received into Full Communion	138
First Communions	1,456
Confirmations	369
Marriages:	
Catholic	131
Interfaith	49
Total Marriages	180
Deaths	39
Total Catholic Population	55,934
Total Population	1,304,746

Former Bishops—Most Revs. CHARLES E. HERZIG, D.D., First Bishop of Tyler; ord. May 31, 1955; appt. Bishop of Tyler Dec. 12, 1986; consecrated Feb. 24, 1987; died Sept. 7, 1991; EDMOND CARMODY, D.D., Second Bishop of Tyler; ord. June 8, 1957; appt. Auxiliary Bishop of San Antonio, Nov. 8, 1988; consecrated Dec. 15, 1988; appt. Bishop of Tyler, March 24, 1992; installed May 25, 1992; transferred to Diocese of Corpus Christi, March 17, 2000.

Office of Bishop—Most Rev. ALVARO CORRADA DEL RIO, S.J., D.D., V.G., 1015 ESE Loop 323, Tyler, 75701-9663. Tel: 903-534-1077; Fax: 903-534-1370. Email: bishopoffice@dioceseoftyler.org. Secretaries: Mrs. KATHY MELER. Tel: 903-534-1077, Ext. 132. Email: bishopoffice@dioceseoftyler.org; Mrs. VIRGINIA MEDRANO. Tel: 903-534-1077, Ext. 160. Email: vmedrano@dioceseoftyler.org.

Vicar General—Rev. XAVIER PAPPU, St. Matthew, 2800 Pine Tree Rd., Longview, 75604-1647. Tel: 903-295-3890. Email: vg@dioceseoftyler.org.

Chancery—1015 E.S.E. Loop 323, Tyler, 75701-9663. Tel: 903-534-1077; Fax: 903-534-1370. Office Hours: Mon.-Fri. 8:30-5

Chancellor—Rev. Msgr. JAMES E. YOUNG, Sacred Heart Catholic Church, 2508 Appleby Sand Rd., Nacogdoches, 75961-4524. Tel: 936-564-7807. Email: chancellor@dioceseoftyler.org.

Archivist—Rev. Msgr. JAMES E. YOUNG, Chancellor. Tel: 903-534-1077. Email: chancellor@dioceseoftyler.org.

College of Consultors—Rev. XAVIER PAPPU, V.G.; Rev. Msgrs. JOSEPH E. STRICKLAND, J.C.L.; GERALD A. PRIEST; JAMES E. YOUNG; Revs. BERNARD BOTEJU; RONALD DIEGEL; ZACHARIAS S. KUNNAKKATTUTHARA; LUIS E. LARREA, M.F.E.; GAVIN N. VAVEREK, J.C.L.

Deans—Rev. DENZIL VITHANAGE, S.S.S., East Central Deanery; Rev. Msgr. GERALD PRIEST, Northeast Deanery; Rev. RONALD L. DIEGEL, Northwest Deanery; Rev. Msgr. JAMES E. YOUNG, Southeast Deanery; Rev. ZACHARIAS S. KUNNAKKATTUTHARA, Southwest Deanery; Rev. Msgr. JOSEPH E. STRICKLAND, J.C.L., West Central Deanery.

Tribunal Office—1015 E.S.E. Loop 323, Tyler, 75701-9663. Tel: 903-534-1077; Fax: 903-534-1370.

Judicial Vicar—Rev. Msgr. JOSEPH E. STRICKLAND, J.C.L.. Email: tribunal@dioceseoftyler.org.

Judges—Rev. Msgrs. SIDNEY MARCEAUX, J.C.D.; JOSEPH E. STRICKLAND, J.C.L.; JOHN FLYNN.

Administrator—Mrs. MARGARET OPPENHEIMER.

Defenders of the Bond—Rev. GAVIN N. VAVEREK, J.C.L.; Rev. Msgr. ANTHONY MCLAUGHLIN.

Advocates—Revs. JOSE CORTEZ; STEPHEN J. DUYKA; Rev. Msgr. JOHN FLYNN.

Ecclesiastical Notaries—Mrs. MARGARET OPPENHEIMER; Mrs. KATHY MELER; Mrs. CINDY PLUMMER.

DIOCESAN ADMINISTRATION

Finance Officer—Mr. JIM SMITH, 1015 E.S.E. Loop 323, Tyler, 75701-9663. Tel: 903-534-1077. Email: businessoffice@dioceseoftyler.org.

Diocesan Finance Council—Rev. Msgr. JAMES E. YOUNG, Ex Officio; Mr. BILL SULLIVAN, Chm.; Mr. JAMES CHIARIZIO; Mr. LOUIS OWEN; Mr. JAMES KENNEDY; Rev. Msgr. XAVIER PAPPU, Ex Officio; Mr WESLEY RIVERS; Mr. JIM SMITH, Ex Officio.

Diocesan Building Board—Mr. BILLY CORDOVA, Chm.; Deacon RUBEN NATERA; Mr. TOM DEIBEL; Rev. GAVIN N. VAVEREK, J.C.L. Ex Officio: Rev. XAVIER PAPPU; Mr. JIM SMITH.

East Texas Catholic Foundation—Mr. JIM SMITH, Dir., 1015 E.S.E. Loop 323, Tyler, 75701-9663. Email: businessoffice@dioceseoftyler.org; Mr. DAVID CARLILE; Mrs. SUZIE HAIR; Mr. VINCE RICHBOURG; Mr. WALTER VOLZ; Mr. PAUL WALSH; Mr. TOM WOLF.

Priests' Pension Board—Rev. Msgr. JAMES E. YOUNG; Rev. XAVIER PAPPU; Mr. JIM SMITH, Treas.; Revs. ZACHARIAS S. KUNNAKKATTUTHARA; BERNARD BOTEJU; RONALD DIEGEL; Rev. Msgrs. GERALD A. PRIEST; JOSEPH E. STRICKLAND, J.C.L.; Rev. GAVIN N. VAVEREK, J.C.L.

Catholic Campaign for Human Development—Mrs. KATHY MELER. Tel: 903-534-1077.

Catholic School Office—Deacon VIC BONNAFFEE, Interim Supt.; Mrs. MARY ELLIOTT, Sec., 1015 E.S.E. Loop 323, Tyler, 75701-9663. Email: schooloffice@dioceseoftyler.org.

Diocesan Catholic School Advisory Council—Mrs. SUZI STREIT, Chm.; Mr. STEVE KENNEDY, Chm. Elect; Mrs. MARTHA CARNEY, Sec.; Mrs. SYLVESTER GUERRA; Mr. CHUCK HEIMERDINGER; Mr. KEN WILSON; Deacon VIC BONNAFFEE, Exec. Officer; Mrs. MARY ELLIOTT, Recording Sec.

Religious Education Office—Mrs. LINDA PORTER, Dir.. Email: religioused@dioceseoftyler.org; Ms. CECILIA ALLGOOD, Sec.

Diocesan Christian Initiation Team—LINDA PORTER; Revs. GAVIN VAVEREK, J.C.L., Consultant; MARK DUNN, Longview - St. Mary's; Sisters INEZ ARGUELLO, E.F.M.S., Kilgore - Christ the King; SUSAN SEITZ, O.S.F., Tyler - Cathedral; GEMA DE LA TRINIDAD, E.F.M.S., Kilgore - Christ the King; Deacon DAVID DARBY, Nacog. - Sacred Heart; TERESA DARBY, Nacog. - Sacred Heart; Deacons JIM FINEGAN, Hilltop Lakes - St. Thomas More; AUBREY FISK, Mineola - St. Peter the Apostle; BILLY MITCHELL, Lufkin - St. Patrick; RUBEN NATERA, Tyler - Cathedral.

Pastoral Ministries—Rev. XAVIER PAPPU, V.G., Coord.; Mrs. VIRGINIA MEDRANO, Sec., 1015 E.S.E. Loop 323, Tyler, 75701-9663. Tel: 903-534-1077. Email: pastoralmin@dioceseoftyler.org.

Diocesan Pastoral Team - DPT—Most Rev. ALVARO CORRADA DEL RIO, S.J., D.D., V.G.; Rev. XAVIER PAPPU, V.G., Vicar General; Rev. Msgrs. JAMES E. YOUNG, Chancellor; JOSEPH E. STRICKLAND, J.C.L.; Revs. STEPHEN J. DUYKA, Liturgical Office; EDUARDO NEVARES, M.S., Vocation Office; GAVIN VAVEREK, J.C.L., Promoter of Justice; Deacons DON BROWN, Prison Ministry; JOHN SHAFFER, Deacon Office; RUBEN NATERA, Hispanic Mission; Mr. JIM H. D'AVIGNON, Catholic East Texas; Mrs. VIRGINIA MEDRANO, Recording Sec.; Mrs. KATHY MELER, Bishop Sec.; Mrs. LUPE NATERA, Hispanic Mission; Mrs. LINDA PORTER, Relg. Education; Mr. EDWARD RUESEWALD, Youth Ministry; Mr. JIM SMITH, Business Office.

Family Life/Youth Ministry—Mr. EDWARD RUESEWALD, Dir.; Mrs. DARLENE BARTUSH, Sec., 1015 E.S.E. Loop 323, Tyler, 75701-9663. Tel: 903-534-1077.

Tyler Catholic Committee on Scouting—Rev. FRANCIS O'DOWD, Chap., P.O. Box 1071, Lindale, 75771-1078. Tel: 903-228-4079; Mrs. MARGARITA DE LA GARZA GRAHM, M.D., Chm.; Mr. MIKE CONNOR, Professional Scouter, 905 Happiness St., Longview, 75601. Tel: 903-757-7524.

Young Adult/Campus Ministries—Rev. STEPHEN J. DUYKA, St. Mary Chapel, 211 E. College, Nacogdoches, 75965. Tel: 936-564-0661. Email: sjduyka@catholicweb.com.

Mission & Hispanic—Deacon RUBEN NATERA, Dir.; Mrs. LUPE NATERA, Asst. Dir. Tel: 903-534-1077.

Hispanic Ministry Advisory Council—Revs. RUBEN C. FIGUEROA, O.F.M., Chm.; LUIS E. LARREA, M.F.E.; Deacon RUBEN NATERA, Dir.; Mrs. LUPE NATERA, Asst. Dir.

Priests' Personnel Board—Rev. Msgr. JAMES E. YOUNG, Chm.; Rev. XAVIER PAPPU; Rev. Msgrs. GERALD A. PRIEST; JOSEPH E. STRICKLAND, J.C.L., Sec.; Revs. BERNARD BOTEJU; RONALD DIEGEL; RUBEN FIGUEROA; LUIS E. LARREA, M.F.E.; ZACHARIAS S. KUNNAKKATTUTHARA.

Presbyteral Council—Rev. Msgrs. JOSEPH E. STRICKLAND, J.C.L., Chm.; JAMES E. YOUNG, Chancellor & Vice Chm.; GERALD PRIEST; Revs. XAVIER PAPPU, V.G.; RONALD L. DIEGEL; OCTAVIO SUAREZ; GAVIN N. VAVEREK, J.C.L.; DENZIL VITHANAGE, S.S.S.; MARK DUNNE; EDUARDO NEVARES, M.S.

Office of Clergy Development/Continuing Education—Rev. Msgr. JAMES E. YOUNG, Chancellor, 1015 E.S.E. Loop 323, Tyler, 75701-9663. Tel: 903-534-1077. Email: chancellor@dioceseoftyler.org.

Permanent Diaconate—Deacons JOHN K. SHAFFER, Dir.; LOREN SEELY, Formation Dir., 2108 Ridgewood, Longview, 75605-5199. Tel: 903-757-5855.

Deacon Council—Most Rev. ALVARO CORRADA, S.J., Pres. Executive Officers: Deacon JOHN SHAFFER; Mrs. NANCY SHAFFER; VACANT, Chm.; Deacon SAM MULLEN; Mrs. NANCY MULLEN; Mrs. SUSAN WELLS, Recording Sec.; Deacon JERRY BEEZE; Mrs. MARY BEEZE; Deacon LARRY BENZMILLER; Mrs. GLORIA BENZMILLER; Deacon JIM FINEGAN; Mrs. CLAUDETTE FINEGAN; Deacon BILL KENNEDY; Mrs. SUSAN KENNEDY; Deacon JUAN MIRJARES; MARY MIRJARES; Deacon JESUS REYES; LEANDRA REYES; Deacon LEN SANCHEZ; ELOISE SANCHEZ.

Vocations—Revs. FRANCIS O'DOWD, Dir.; EDUARDO NEVARES, M.S., Asst. Dir.; Sr. GABRIELA DELGADO, Sec., 1015 E.S.E. Loop 323, Tyler, 75701-9663. Tel: 903-534-1077. Email: vocations@dioceseoftyler.org.

Diocesan Vocations Awareness Board—Revs. FRANCIS O'DOWD; EDUARDO NEVARES, M.S.; Deacon JIM FINEGAN; Mr. BILL ELLIOTT; Mrs. DIANE JAGER; Mrs. MARY M. LEE; Mr. DAN MACY; Mrs. SARA MACY; Mrs. LINDA PORTER.

Communications Director—Mr. JIM H. D'AVIGNON, 1015 E.S.E. Loop 323, Tyler, 75701-9663. Tel: 903-534-1077.

Bishop's Annual Appeal—Mrs. JUDY GREEN, Dir.; Mrs. JIMMIE COCKRELL, Sec., 1015 E.S.E. Loop 323, Tyler, 75701-9663. Tel: 903-534-1077.

Newspaper "Catholic East Texas"—Mr. JIM H. D'AVIGNON, Editor. Reporters: Mrs. SUSAN DEMATTEO NECESSARY, Reporter; Mrs. JOANNE FLORES EMBLETON, Reporter, 1015 E.S.E. Loop 323, Tyler, 75701-9663. Tel: 903-534-1077; Fax: 903-534-1370.

DIOCESAN OFFICES

Diocesan Council of Catholic Women—Mrs. SHELIA COTE, Pres., 929 W. Main, Van, 75790; Rev. GAVIN N. VAVEREK, J.C.L., Moderator, 2108 Ridgewood, Longview, 75605-5199. Tel: 903-757-5855.

Respect Life Program—Rev. GAVIN N. VAVEREK, J.C.L., 2108 Ridgewood, Longview, 75605-5199. Tel: 903-757-5855. Co-Directors: Mr. JOE DUDAS; Mrs. MARGE DUDAS, 1605 H.G. Mosley, Longview, 75604. Tel: 903-297-3767.

Disaster Relief Director—Mr. ROY SHEAR, 621 Bentley Ct., Tyler, 75703. Tel: 903-561-0425.

Youth Office—Mr. EDWARD RUESEWALD, Dir.; Mrs. DARLENE BARTUSH, Sec.. Email: youth@dioceseoftyler.org.

Victim Assistance Coordinator—Rev. GAVIN N. VAVEREK, J.C.L. Tel: 903-266-2159. Email: promoter@dioceseoftyler.org.

Diocesan Deanery Representatives On Ethics and Integrity Policy for Church Personnel—Rev. GAVIN N. VAVEREK, J.C.L., Promoter of Justice; Rev. Msgr. JOSEPH E. STRICKLAND, J.C.L., Judicial Vicar; Deacon LARRY BENZMILLER, Northeast Deanery; Mrs. GLORIA BENZMILLER, Northeast Deanery; Deacon JERRY BESZE, Northwest Deanery; MARY BESZE, Northwest Deanery; Deacons JIM FINEGAN, Southwest Deanery; RUBEN NATERA, Spanish Resources; Mrs. LUPE NATERA, Spanish Resources; Deacon JOHN SHAFFER, East Central Deanery; Mrs. LINDA PORTER, West Central Deanery.

Diocesan Liturgical Commission—Revs. STEPHEN J. DUYKA, Chm.; XAVIER PAPPU, V.G., Ex Officio; MORGAN WHITE; WILLIAM PALMER; GAVIN N. VAVEREK, J.C.L.; Deacons GERARDO TREVINO; TREVOR WELLS; Mr. BRIAN BRAQUET; Mrs. DIANNA BRAQUET; Mrs. PEGGY HAMMETT; Mrs. LINDA PORTER; Mrs. ANN SEELY.

CLERGY, PARISHES, MISSIONS AND PAROCHIAL SCHOOLS

CITY OF TYLER
(SMITH COUNTY)

1—CATHEDRAL OF THE IMMACULATE CONCEPTION (1987), Rev. Msgr. Joseph E. Strickland, J.C.L.; Revs. Amal Punganoor (India); Victor Hamon (Colombia); Augustine Tharappel, M.S.F.S. (India); William Palmer; Sr. Susan Seitz, O.S.F., Pastoral Assoc.; Deacons Ramiro Martinez; Ruben Natera; Bob Wanless; Bill Necessary.
Social Services:—Office, 423 S. Broadway, 75702. Tel: 903-592-0027; Fax: 903-593-7326.
Res.: 114 W. Front St., 75702. Tel: 903-592-5462.
School—St. Gregory School, 500 S. College St., 75702. Tel: 903-595-4109; Fax: 903-592-8626. Mrs. Kathy Shieldes Harry, Prin. Lay Teachers 26; Students 347.
School—Bishop T. K. Gorman Middle School, 1405 E.S.E. Loop 323, 75701. Tel: 903-561-2424; Fax: 903-561-2645. Mr. Jim Franz, Prin. Students 175.
High School—Bishop Gorman High School, Tel: 903-561-2424. Priests 1; Lay Teachers 37; Students 209.
Catechesis/Religious Program—Tel: 903-592-1317. Lay Teachers 81; Students 443.
Chapel—St. Paul 1015 E.S.E. Loop 323, 75702.
Mission—St. Joseph the Worker Church 1015 E.S.E. Loop 323, 75701. Tel: 903-939-3221. Email: st.joseph@cox-internet.com. Rev. Carlos S. Casavantes, F.S.S.P. (SCR).
Station—St. Mary Magdalene Flint.

2—OUR LADY OF GUADALUPE (1996), (Hispanic), Rev. Ruben Figueroa.
Church & Mailing Address: 922 Old Omen Rd., 75701-3709. Tel: 903-593-2006; Fax: 903-593-6033.
Catechesis/Religious Program—Students 320.

3—ST. PETER CLAVER (1936), [CEM] [JC] Rev. Luis Eduardo Larrea, M.F.E.
Res.: 1403 N. Tenneha Ave., 75702. Tel: 903-595-2612; Fax: 903-596-9659.
Catechesis/Religious Program—Fax: 903-596-9659. Students 143.

OUTSIDE THE CITY OF TYLER

ATHENS, HENDERSON CO., ST. EDWARD CHURCH (1947), [JC] Revs. Pancras Savarimuthu (India); Raymundo Garcia (Mexico).
Res.: 800 E. Tyler, 75751-2140. Tel: 903-675-2509; Fax: 903-675-8805.
Catechesis/Religious Program—Robin Haynie, D.R.E. Tel: 903-677-2174. Students 352.
Mission—St. Boniface (1997), 318 S. Broad St., P.O. Box 762, Chandler, Van Sand Co. 75758-0762. Rev. Luke U. Clerical, M.S.F.S.

ATLANTA, CASS CO., ST. CATHERINE OF SIENA CHURCH (1965), [JC] Rev. Devaraj Arulappa (India).
Res.: 309 N. Louise St., P.O. Box 985, 75551-0985. Tel: 903-796-4494; Fax: 903-796-9990.
Catechesis/Religious Program—Tel: 903-756-5723. Irene Webster, D.R.E. Students 41.

BUFFALO, LEON CO., BLESSED KATERI TEKAKWITHA CHURCH (1979), Rev. Theodore F. Rydelek.
Mailing Address: 208 N. Merrill, P.O. Box 878, 75831. Tel: 903-322-3705; Fax: 903-322-3155.
Catechesis/Religious Program—Students 42.

CANTON, VAN ZANDT CO., ST. THERESE (1980), Rev. Bernard Boteju, S.R.I. (Sri Lanka), Admin.
Mailing Address: 14786 FM 859, 75103-3676. Tel: 903-567-4286; Fax: 903-567-0586.
Catechesis/Religious Program—Students 96.
Mission—St. Luke 450 E. James St., Wills Point, Van Zandt Co. 75169. Tel: 903-873-1238. Rev. Ouseph Thekumthala (India).

CARTHAGE, PANOLA CO., ST. WILLIAM OF VERCELLI (1948), Rev. Morgan White (Ireland).
Res.: 4088 N.W. Loop, 75633-3346. Tel: 903-693-5586; 903-693-3766; Fax: 903-693-3759.
Catechesis/Religious Program—Students 80.

CENTER, SHELBY CO., ST. THERESE (1951), Rev. M. Jones Jayaraj.
Res.: 717 FM 2974, 75935-6006. Tel: 936-598-8458; Fax: 936-598-5599.
Catechesis/Religious Program—Students 65.
Mission—Epiphany 3072 US Hwy. 59 S., Timpson, Shelby Co. 75975. Tel: 936-254-9662.

CLARKSVILLE, RED RIVER CO., ST. JOSEPH (1870), (Hispanic), [CEM] Rev. Jose G. Marin.
Res.: 406 E. Broadway, 75426-3110. Tel: 903-427-5044; Fax: 903-427-5044.
Catechesis/Religious Program—Students 8.

CROCKETT, HOUSTON CO., ST. FRANCIS OF THE TEJAS (1931), Rev. Jose George (India).
Res.: 609 N. 4th, 75835-4001. Tel: 936-544-5338; Fax: 936-544-7914.
Catechesis/Religious Program—Students 72.
Mission—St. Leo the Great P.O. Box 356, Centerville, Leon Co. 75833-0356. Tel: 903-536-5012; Fax: 903-536-1549. Rev. Carlos Rangel, Contact Person.
Station—St. Thomas More Hilltop Lakes. Tel: 936-855-2640; Fax: 936-855-2935. Rev. Carlos Rangel, Contact Person.

DAINGERFIELD, MORRIS CO., OUR LADY OF FATIMA (1951), (Hispanic), [CEM] Rev. Ambrose Chinnappa.
Mailing Address: 1305 Bert St., 75638-9704.
Res.: Bert & Tiger Streets, 75638. Tel: 903-645-5637.
Catechesis/Religious Program—Students 84.

DIBOLL, ANGELINA CO., OUR LADY OF GUADALUPE (1971), (Hispanic), [CEM] Rev. Diego Ossa; Deacons Catarino Perez Jr.; Jesus Reyes.
Mailing Address: P.O. Box 310, 75941-0310. Tel: 936-829-3650; Fax: 936-829-3659.
Res.: 100 Maynard St., 75941.
Catechesis/Religious Program—Tel: 409-829-2981. Mrs. Valerie Maynard, D.R.E. Students 92.

FAIRFIELD, FREESTONE CO., ST. BERNARD OF CLAIRVAUX (1976), Rev. Msgr. Samuel Metzger, Admin.
Res.: 630 W. Main, 75840-1418. Tel: 903-389-4616; Fax: 903-389-3844.
Catechesis/Religious Program—Tel: 903-389-2444. Students 62.
Mission—St. Mary 609 Cedar, Teague, Freestone Co. 75840-1617. Tel: 254-739-3692. Rev. Said Dunan (Colombia).

GILMER, UPSHUR CO., ST. FRANCIS OF ASSISI (1994), Rev. Amal Punganoor (India).
Mailing Address: P.O. Box 704, 75644-0704. Tel: 903-797-3303.
Res.: 208 S. Montgomery, 75644. Tel: 903-843-9030.
Catechesis/Religious Program—Tel: 903-797-3303. Students 50.
Mission—Holy Spirit Church 1612 S. FM 2869, Holly Lake Rach, Sulphur Co. 75755-9604. Tel: 903-769-3235; Fax: 903-769-1611.

GUN BARREL CITY, HENDERSON CO., ST. JUDE (1975), Rev. Msgr. John A. Brennan; Deacon Richard Sykora.
Res.: 172 Luther Ln., 75156. Tel: 903-887-1452 (Office); 903-887-5803 (Res.); Fax: 903-887-4906 (Office).
Catechesis/Religious Program—Tel: 903-887-5252; 903-887-9795 (Office). Mrs. Edna Beltz, D.R.E. Students 120.
Mission—Mary Queen of Heaven P.O. Box 508, 2269 CR 1703, Malakoff, Henderson Co. 75148-4905. Tel: 903-489-2366; Fax: 903-489-3533. Rev. Joseph Kallookalam, C.M.I. (India).

HEMPHILL, SABINE CO., ST. PIUS I (1939), [CEM] Rev. Basil P. Hoan.
Corner Hwy. 184 & Barber St., P.O. Box 1925, 75948-1925. Tel: 409-787-4189 (Res.).
Catechesis/Religious Program—Students 2.
Mission—San Augustine Hwy. 21, St. Augustine, San Augustine Co. 75972.

HENDERSON, RUSK CO., ST. JUDE (1934), Rev. Jayaseelanraj Lucas.
Res.: 200 Morningside, 75652. Tel: 903-657-4398; Fax: 903-657-0078.
Catechesis/Religious Program—Students 90.

JACKSONVILLE, CHEROKEE CO., OUR LADY OF SORROWS (1954), Revs. Matthew Edassery; Julian Villegas; Deacon Juventino Torres.
Res.: 1023 Corinth Rd., 75766-9801. Tel: 903-586-4538; Fax: 903-586-4996.
Catechesis/Religious Program—Tel: 903-586-1559. Charles Paul, D.R.E. Students 265.
Mission—Sacred Heart P.O. Box 947, Rusk, Cherokee Co. 75785. Tel: 903-683-1862. Rev. Mark Kusmirek.
Mission—Our Lady of Guadalupe Rt. 5, P.O. Box 357, New Summerfield, Cherokee Co. 75780-9351. Tel: 903-726-7272. Rev. Jose Cortez.

JEFFERSON, MARION CO., IMMACULATE CONCEPTION (1867), [CEM] Rev. Mani Mathai (India), Admin.
Res.: 201 N. Vale St., 75657-2143. Tel: 903-665-2869; Fax: 903-665-8778.
Catechesis/Religious Program—Tel: 903-665-8805. Students 28.
Mission—St. Lawrence Brindisi P.O. Box 928, Waskom, Harrison Co. 75292-0928. Tel: 903-687-2385; Fax: 903-687-4503. Rev. Peter Stanialus (India).

Catechesis/Religious Program—Tel: 903-687-2951. Students 38.

KILGORE, GREGG CO., CHRIST THE KING (1936), [JC] Revs. Matias Rodriquez; John Whitsell; Deacons Dennis Gilchrist; Alejandro Cisneros; William Holda; Michael Heglin.
Res.: 1407 Broadway, 75662-3209. Tel: 903-984-3716; Fax: 903-984-1426.
Catechesis/Religious Program—Tel: 903-986-3573; Fax: 903-984-3716. Sr. Gemma de la Trinidad, E.F.M.S., D.R.E. Students 218.
Mission—Our Lady Queen of Angels 707 Bradford, P.O. Box 322, Overton, Rusk Co. 75684-0322. Tel: 903-984-0537.

LINDALE, SMITH CO., HOLY FAMILY (1994), Rev. Francis O'Dowd.
Mailing Address: P.O. Box 1071, 75771. Tel: 903-882-4079; Fax: 903-882-8382.
Catechesis/Religious Program—Students 29.

LONGVIEW, GREGG CO.
CATECHESIS/RELIGIOUS PROGRAM—PAULINE B. GREEN, D.R.E.; ERIN LEE, D.R.E.

1—ST. ANTHONY (1880), (Hispanic), Revs. Bruce Lincon; Mark Dunne; Deacons Gonzalo Rojas; Joseph Pipak; Manuel Villalobos.
Mailing Address: 908 E. Olive St., 75601-6730. Tel: 903-758-0116; Fax: 903-758-9066.
Res.: 908 E. Olive, 75601. Tel: 903-758-9550; Fax: 903-758-0116.
Church: 508 N. 6th St., 75601.
Catechesis/Religious Program—Students 51.

2—ST. MARY (1982), Revs. Gavin Vaverek, J.C.L.; Gary Rottman; Deacons John Borens; John Shaffer; William H. Bridwell; Trevor Wells.
Res.: 2108 Ridgewood Dr., 75605-5199. Tel: 903-757-5855; Fax: 903-758-5074.
School—405 Hollybrook Dr., 75605-2464. Tel: 903-753-1657; Fax: 903-758-7347. Mrs. Becky Chenevert, Prin. Lay Teachers 12; Students 182.
Catechesis/Religious Program—Tel: 903-757-5891; Fax: 903-758-5074. Colleen Medley, D.R.E. Students 165.
Mission—Our Lady of Grace P.O. Box 782, Hallsville, Harrison Co. 75650-0782. Tel: 903-668-5279; Fax: 903-668-5220. Rev. Selveraj Sinnappa (India).

3—ST. MATTHEW CATHOLIC CHURCH (1999), Revs. Xavier Pappu; Cristians Zelaya.
Res.: 2800 Pine Tree Rd., 75604. Tel: 903-295-3890; Fax: 903-295-7559.

LUFKIN, ANGELINA CO.

1—ST. ANDREW (1998), Rev. Michael Doyle.
Office:—1611 Feagin Dr., 75904. Tel: 936-632-9100; 936-632-9812 (Res); Fax: 936-632-0627.
Catechesis/Religious Program—Students 110.

2—ST. PATRICK (1928), Revs. William J. Slight, M.S.; James Kalliathu Parambil, M.S.; Kalliathu Parambill. In Res., Rev. Eduardo Nevares, M.S.
Res.: 2118 Lowry St., 75901-1316. Tel: 409-634-6833; Fax: 409-634-6891.
School—St. Patrick School, (Grades PreK-7) Tel: 409-634-6719; Fax: 936-639-2776. Larry Gaudet, Prin. Lay Teachers 15; Students 175.
Catechesis/Religious Program—Tel: 936-639-3676; Fax: 936-634-1090. Rosie Vasquez, D.R.E. (PreK-12). Students 300.

MADISONVILLE, MADISON CO., ST. ELIZABETH ANN SETON (1978), [JC] Rev. Michael J. Barone.
Mailing Address: 100 S. Tammye Lane, 77864. Tel: 936-348-6368; Fax: 936-348-5377.
Catechesis/Religious Program—Students 90.

MARSHALL, HARRISON CO., ST. JOSEPH (1874), [CEM] Revs. Denzil Vithanage, S.S.S.; Luis Roncancio (Colombia); Deacons Santiago Suarez; Felipe Pena.
Res.: 410 N. Alamo Blvd., 75670-3450. Tel: 903-935-2536; Fax: 903-938-1591.
Catechesis/Religious Program—Students 300.
Mission—San Pedro the Fisherman Hwy. 43, P.O. Box 430, Tatum, Panola Co. 75691-0430. Tel: 903-947-6358; Fax: 903-947-2876. Rev. Cristians Zelaya.

MINEOLA, WOOD CO., ST. PETER THE APOSTLE (1937), [JC] Rev. J. Felix Chirapurathel (India).
Res.: 1520 N. Newsom, P.O. Box 1022, 75773-7022. Tel: 903-569-3665; Fax: 903-569-3631.
Catechesis/Religious Program—Students 82.
Mission—St. Celestine 116 W. Frank, Grand Saline, Van Zandt Co. 75140. Tel: 903-962-6350. Rev. Lionel Fernando (Sri Lanka).
Mission—St. John the Evangelist Church 551 E. FM 2795, Emory, Rains Co. 75140. Rev. Lionel Fernando (Sri Lanka).

MOUNT PLEASANT, TITUS CO., ST. MICHAEL (1917), Revs. Octavio Suarez, Admin.; Luis F. Arroyave (Colombia).
Mailing Address: 1403 E. 1st St., 75455-4715. Tel: 903-572-5227; Fax: 903-572-9659.
Res.: 310 Denman Dr., 75455-4157. Tel: 903-572-5611; Fax: 903-572-9659.
Catechesis/Religious Program—Ofelia Valdez, D.R.E. Students 284.

MOUNT VERNON, FRANKLIN CO., SACRED HEART (1986), Rev. Mariasusai J. Avula (India).
Mailing Address: P.O. Box 918, 75457. Tel: 903-537-2174; Fax: 903-537-2174.
Church: Hwy 37 S. & Rutherford St., 75457.
Catechesis/Religious Program—Tel: 903-537-7280. Students 65.

NACOGDOCHES, NACOGDOCHES CO., SACRED HEART (1716), [CEM] [JC 2] Rev. Msgr. James E. Young; Rev. Raymundo Chavez Vasquez; Deacons David Darby; Michael Doyle; Gary Giese; Ray Shaw; Librado Sosa.
Res.: 2508 Appleby Sand Rd., 75965-3632. Tel: 936-564-7134; 936-564-7807; Fax: 936-564-8777.
Catechesis/Religious Program—Tel: 936 564-5321. Tommy Cordova, D.R.E. Students 360.
Mission—Our Lady of Lourdes Chireno Nacogdoches Co. 75961. Tel: 936-598-8458. Rev. Martin Gerber (WDC).
Mission—Immaculate Conception [CEM] [JC 3] Moral, Nacogdoches Co. Tel: 936-560-1533; Fax: 936-462-8825. Rev. Martin Gerber (WDC).
Mission—Our Lady of Guadalupe 4401 Old Lufkin Rd., Nacogdoches Co. 75964. Tel: 936-560-1902. Rev. Raymundo Chavez-Vasquez, Contact Person.
Chapel—Nacogdoches, St. Mary's Chapel, Stephen F. Austin State University 211 E. College, 75961. Tel: 936-564-0661. Rev. Stephen J. Duyka.

NEW BOSTON, BOWIE CO., ST. MARY OF THE CENACLE (1918), [JC] Rev. Lawrence Chellaian (India).
Mailing Address: 216 W. Magnolia St., 75570-0914. Tel: 903-628-2323; Fax: 903-628-2323.
Res.: 216 Magnolia St., 75570. Tel: 903-628-6186.
Catechesis/Religious Program—Tel: 903-628-2323. Students 49.

PALESTINE, ANDERSON CO., SACRED HEART (1893), [CEM] Revs. Zacharias S. Kunnakkattuthara (India); Alvaro Jimenez (Colombia); Deacons Alex Kobar; Daniel Rose, Prison Chap.
Res.: 503 N. Queen St., 75801-2718. Tel: 903-729-2463; Fax: 903-723-9799.
Catechesis/Religious Program—Tel: 903-729-5375. David Bunch, D.R.E.; Don Cumm, D.R.E. Students 428.
Mission—St. Charles Borromeo 1101 Hwy. 155 N., Frankston, Anderson Co. 75763. Tel: 903-876-3309; Fax: 903-876-3309. Rev. Zacharias S. Kunnakkattuthara (India).

PARIS, LAMAR CO., OUR LADY OF VICTORY (1880), [JC] Rev. Ronald Diegel.
Res.: 3300 Clarksville St., 75460. Tel: 903-784-1000; Fax: 903-784-3946.
Catechesis/Religious Program—Nellie Denman, D.R.E. Students 343.

PITTSBURG, CAMP CO., HOLY CROSS (1987), [JC] Rev. Augustine J. Mailadiyil (India).
501 Hill Ave., 75686-1810. Tel: 903-856-7609.
Catechesis/Religious Program—Students 138.

SULPHUR SPRINGS, HOPKINS CO., ST JAMES (1880), Rev. Joe Kannampuzha, Admin.; Deacons Jerry Besze; Jose Hernandez; William O'Brien; Loren G. Seely.
Mailing Address: P.O. Box 93, 75483-0093. 297 Texas St., 75483. Tel: 903-885-1222; Fax: 903-885-5855.
Res.: 303 Texas St., 75483. Tel: 903-885-2873.
Catechesis/Religious Program—Tel: 903-885-0157. Susie Thesing, D.R.E. Students 72.
Mission—St. Ann Church Hwy. 515 W. Coke Rd., Winnsboro, Wood Co. 75494-0733. Tel: 903-629-7884; Fax: 903-629-3347. Rev. Jose Kumblumkal, C.M.I.
Mission—St. Clare Mission 10 E. Side Sq., Cooper, Delta Co. 75432.

TEXARKANA, BOWIE CO., SACRED HEART (1874), [CEM 2] Rev. Msgr. Gerald Priest; Rev. William Gerard Foley; Deacons Keith A. Woods; Larry Benzmiller.
Res.: 4505 Elizabeth St., 75503-2998. Tel: 903-794-4444; Fax: 903-792-1529.
Catechesis/Religious Program—Tel: 903-792-6846. Students 238.

TRINITY, TRINITY CO., MOST HOLY TRINITY (1972), [JC] Rev. Tom Edelen, Contact Person; Deacon John Milton.
Res.: Rte. 1, Box 61-X, 75862-9801. Tel: 936-594-6364; Fax: 936-594-5244.
Catechesis/Religious Program—Students 58.

UNION GROVE-GLADEWATER, UPSHUR CO., ST. THERESA OF THE INFANT JESUS (1945), [JC] Rev. Ronald G. Demski; Deacon Guy Blasingame.
Mailing Address: 10138 Union Grove Rd., Gladewater, 75647-0967. Tel: 903-845-2306; Fax: 903-845-5256.
Catechesis/Religious Program—Tel: 903-895-5256. Students 45.

WHITEHOUSE, SMITH CO., PRINCE OF PEACE (1996), Rev. Daniel L. Daugherty.
Mailing Address: P.O. Box 456, 75791-0456. Tel: 903-581-9600; Fax: 903-561-4946.
Res.: 903 Langford Lane, 75791. Tel: 903-839-7599.
Catechesis/Religious Program—Students 66.

Chaplains of Public Institutions

CROCKETT. *Crockett State School.* Attended by St. Francis of the Tejas Church, Crockett

GROVETON. *Hope Center Wilderness Program for Girls*, P.O. Box 760, 75845-0760. Tel: 936-642-2384. Attended by Most Holy Trinity Church, Trinity

HENDERSON. *Bradshaw State Facility, Texas Department of Corrections.* Rev. Lucas Jayaselanraj. Attended by St. Jude Church, Henderson

LOVELADY. *Eastham Unit, Texas Department of Corrections*, P.O. Box 16, 75851-0016. Tel: 936-636-7321, Ext. 7204. P.O. Box 16, 75851-0016. Rev. Jose George (India), Chap.

NEW BOSTON. *Telford Unit, Texas Department of Corrections*, P.O. Box 9200, 75570. Tel: 903-628-3171. Rev. Lawrence Chellaian (India).

OVERTON. *Billy Max Moore Pre-release Facility*, 800 N. FM 3053, 75684-1000. Rev. John L. Whitsell, Chap.

PALESTINE. *Beto I Unit and Louie C. Powledge Unit, Texas Department of Corrections*, P.O. Box 2250, 75801. Rev. Zacharias S. Kunnakkattuthara (India), Chap.

RUSK. *Jerry H. Hodge Unit and Sky view Unit, Texas Department of Corrections*, P.O. Box 999, 75785-0999. Tel: 903-683-5784. Revs. Mark Kusmirek, Chap., Jose Cortez, Chap.

TEAGUE. *Boyd Unit, Texas Department of Correction*, Rt. 2 Box 500, 75860. Tel: 254-739-5555. Rev. Said Duran.

TENNESSEE COLONY. *Coffield Unit, Texas Department of Corrections*, Rt.1 Box 150, 75861-9710. Tel: 903-928-2211. Rev. Zacharias S. Kunnakkattuthara (India), Chap.
Gurney Unit. Rev. Zacharias S. Kunnakkattuthara (India), Chap. Attended by Sacred Heart, Palestine
Michael Unit, P.O. Box 4500, 75886-4500. Tel: 903-928-2311. Rev. Zacharias S. Kunnakkattuthara (India), Chap.

TEXARKANA. *Federal Corrections Institution*, P.O. Box 9500, 75505-9500. Tel: 903-838-4587. Rev. Msgr. Gerald Priest, Chap. Attended by Sacred Heart, Texarkana

WINNSBORO. *Clyde Johnston Unit, Texas Department of Corrections*, 703 Airport Road, 75494-9999. Tel: 903-342-6166. Rev. Jose Kumblumkal, C.M.I.

On Duty Outside the Diocese:
Revs.—
Gonzalez, Daniel I., Ecuador.
Kelly, Timothy J., Rome, Italy.
McLaughlin, Anthony K., Washington, DC.

Retired:
Revs.—
Dean, Joseph, 1106 S. Merritt St., Mt Pleasant, 75455.
O'Donnell, Robert Patrick, 1106 S. Merritt St., Mount Pleasant, 75455. Tel: 903-572-2529
Whitney, Peter A., Queen of Peace, 1224 Cedar Dr., La Marque, 77568-3932. Tel: 936-938-7000 (Parish)
Zakshesky, Francis, 8409 CR 31, Sinton, 78387.

Absent on Sick Leave:
Rev.—
Zakshesky, Francis (Retired), 8409 CR 31, Sinton, 78387.

Permanent Deacons:
Adams, Michael, St. Augustine Church, San Augustine
Benzmiller, Lawrence, Sacred Heart Church, Texarkana
Besze, Jerry, St. James the Apostle Church, Sulphur Springs
Blasingame, Guylan, St. Theresa, Union Grove
Borens, John, St. Mary, Longview
Bridwell, William H., St. Mary, Longview
Brown, Donald R., Telford Unit, New Boston
Cisneros, Alejandro, Christ the King, Kilgore
Cordero, Abelino, St. Patrick, Lufkin
Darby, David, Sacred Heart Church, Nacogdoches
Doyle, Micheal, St. Augustine Church, San Augustine
Faber, William, St. Peter the Apostle Church, Mineola; and St. Celestine Church, Grand Saline.
Finegan, James, St. Thomas More Church in Hilltop Lakes, St. Leo the Great Church in Centerville and St. Elizabeth Ann Seton Church in Madisonville.
Fisk, Aubrey, St. Peter the Apostle Church, Mineola
Flores, William, St. Edward, Athens
Giese, Gary, Sacred Heart Church, Nacogdoches
Gilchrist, Dennis S., Christ the King, Kilgore
Gonzales, Pedro, Sacred Heart, Nacogdoches
Hall, Dwight S., (Inactive)

Hernandez, Jose, St. James, Sulphur Springs
Heslin, Mike, Christ the King Church in Kilgore, Bradshaw State Prison in Henderson and Bill Magmore Correctional Facility, Overton.
Kennedy, William C., III, Sacred Heart Church, Nacogdoches
Kobar, Alex, Sacred Heart, Palestine
Landry, Burke J., St. Elizabeth Ann Setor, Madisonville
Lawrence, Richard, St. Therese Church, Canton
Martinez, Ramiro, Cathedral of the Immaculate Conception, Tyler
Mijares, Juan, St. Patrick, Lufkin
Miller, Carl, St. Ann, Winnsboro
Milton, John, Assignment Outside diocese
Mireles, Jose Luis, Assignment Outside Diocese
Mitchell, Billy, St. Patrick Church, Lufkin
Moreno, Joe Ibarra, St. Michael, Mt. Pleasant
Mullen, Sam, Sacred Heart, Mt. Vernon
Natera, Ruben, Dir. of Mission & Hispanic Min., Cathedral of the Immaculate Conception, Tyler
Necessary, William, Tyler Cathedral, with additional ministry to St. Peter Claver Church, Tyler.
O'Brien, William E., St. James, Sulphur Springs
Panuco, Ignacio, Sacred Heart, Rusk
Pena, Felipe, St. Joseph, Marshall
Perez, Catarino, Jr., Our Lady of Guadalupe, Diboll
Pipak, Joseph, St. Anthony, Longview
Ramos, Manuel J., St. Patrick, Lufkin
Roden, John Adrian, St. Joseph, Marshall
Rojas, Gonzalo, St. Anthony, Longview
Rose, Daniel, Beto I & Powledge Unit, TDC, Palestine
Sanchez, Len, St. Ann, Winnsboro
Seely, Loren G., St. James, Sulphur Springs
Shaffer, John K., St. Mary, Longview
Shaw, Ray, Sacred Heart Church, Nacogdoches
Sosa, Librado Cruz, Sacred Heart, Nacogdoches
Suarez, Santiago, St. Joseph, Marshall
Sykora, Richard L., St. Jude, Gun Barrel City
Tapia, Ezequiel, Sacred Heart, Nacogdoches
Torres, Juventino, Our Lady of Sorrows, Jacksonville
Trevino, Gerardo, St. Patrick, Lufkin
Villalobos, Manuel, St. Anthony, Longview
Wanless, Robert, Tyler Cathedral, Tyler
Wells, Trevor, St. Mary Church, Longview
Woods, Keith A., Sacred Heart, Texarkana

INSTITUTIONS LOCATED IN THE DIOCESE

[A] GENERAL HOSPITALS

TYLER. *Trinity Mother Frances Health System*, 800 E. Dawson St., 75701. Tel: 903-593-8441; Fax: 903-531-4067. Web: www.tmfhs.org. Mr. J. Lindsey Bradley Jr., Pres.; Rev. Thomas Kandathil, Chap. Sisters of the Holy Family of Nazareth 6; Bed Capacity 475; Staff 3,331; Annually Assisted 950,000.

MADISON. *Madison Acquisition Company* dba Madison St. Joseph Health Center , P.O. Box 698 - 100 W. Cross St., 77864-2432. William F. Hyer Jr., Trustee & Contact Person; Mr. Reed Edmundson, Admin.

MADISONVILLE. *St. Joseph Health Center*, 100 W. Cross St., 77864-2432. Tel: 936-348-2631. Reed Edmundson, Admin. Sponsored by the Sisters of St. Francis of Sylvania, OH.

TEXARKANA. *Christus St. Michael Health System*, 2600 St. Michael Dr., 75503. Tel: 903-614-1000; Fax: 903-614-2030. Email: nancy.burleson@christushealth.org. Web: www.christusstmichael.org. Chris Karam, Pres & CEO. General Hospital, Operated by Christus Health (Merged 2/1/1999). Annually Assisted 12,869; Staff 1,441; Bed Capacity 270.

St. Michael Rehabilitation Hospital, 2400 St. Michael Dr., 75503. Tel: 903-614-4000; Fax: 903-614-4064. Web: www.christusstmichael.org. Claudia Eisenmann, Admin. Operated by Christus Health, Houston Texas Health Care Centers, Ancillary Care Systems: Total Staff 146; Bed Capacity 80; Patients Assisted Annually 1,209.

[B] MONASTERIES AND RESIDENCES OF PRIESTS

PALESTINE. *Hermitage*, 10020 An. Co. Rd. 404, 75803. Email: dhpvcsl@hotmail.com. Rev. Denis Walsh. Other Institutions: Houses of Religious Men 1; Total in Residence 1; Total Staff 1.

Prayer Mountain Hermitage, 10089 An. Co. Rd. 404, 75803. Sr. Mary Vogel, H.S.S.R.

[C] CONVENTS AND RESIDENCES FOR SISTERS

LUFKIN. *Monastery of the Infant Jesus*, 1501 Lotus Ln., 75904-2699. Tel: 936-634-4233; Fax: 936-634-2156. Sr. Mary Annunciata, O.P., Prioress; Rev. John Raymond Corr, O.P. Cloistered Dominican Nuns Professed Sisters 26.

[D] CAMPUS MINISTRY

TYLER. *Tyler Junior College and The University of Texas at Tyler Newman Center* 423 S. Broadway, 75702. Tel: 903-592-1617. Attended from the Cathedral of the Immaculate Conception.

NACOGDOCHES. *Stephen F. Austin University Catholic Student Center* P.O. Box 7051, SFASU, 75962. Tel: 936-564-0661; Fax: 936-564-0661. Email: stduyka@catholicweb.com. Web: www.sfacatholic.net. Rev. Stephen J. Duyka, Chap. Other Institutions: Newman Centers 0; Total in Residence 1; Total Staff 1.

[E] MISCELLANEOUS

TYLER. **Tyler Catholic School Foundation*, 401 E. Front, Ste. 221A, 75701-9663. Tel: 903-526-5988; Fax: 903-526-5988. P.O. Box 131175, 75713. D. V. Emery, Exec. Dir.

LONGVIEW. **Longview Catholic School Endowment Fund*, 405 Hollybrook, 75605. Tel: 903-753-1657; Fax: 903-758-7347. Web: www.stmaryslgv.org.

LUFKIN. **St. Patrick School Foundation*, 2118 Lowry, 75901. Tel: 936-634-6833; Fax: 936-634-6891. Email: stpatrick@xucom.net. Web: www.stpatricklufkin.com.

**St. Patrick School Fund*, 2118 Lowry, 75901. Tel: 936-634-6833; Fax: 936-634-6891. Email: stpatrick@ltxucom.net. Web: www.stpatricklufkin.com.

RELIGIOUS INSTITUTES OF MEN REPRESENTED IN THE DIOCESE

For further details refer to the corresponding bracketed number in the Religious Institutes of Men or Women section.

[0600]—*Brothers of the Congregation of the Holy Cross*—C.S.C.

[]—*Carmelite of Mary Immaculate*—C.M.I.

[0220]—*Congregation of the Blessed Sacrament*—S.S.S.

[]—*Franciscan*—O.F.M.

[]—*Holy Cross of Notre Dame*—C.S.C.

[]—*Indian Missionary Society*—I.M.S.

[0720]—*The Missionaries of Our Lady of La Salette*—M.S.

[]—*Missionaries of St. Francis de Sales*—M.S.F.S.

[]—*Missionary Franciscans of the Eucharist*—M.F.E.

[]—*Norbertine Fathers*—O.Praem

[0430]—*Order of Preachers - Dominicans*—O.P.

[]—*Order of the Imitation of Christ*—O.I.C.

RELIGIOUS INSTITUTES OF WOMEN REPRESENTED IN THE DIOCESE

[0230]—*Benedictine Sisters of Pontifical Jurisdiction*—O.S.B.

[]—*Congregation of the Mother of Carmel*—C.M.C.

[0470]—*Congregation of the Sisters of Charity of the Incarnate Word. Houston, Texas* (San Antonio, TX)—C.C.V.I.

[1050]—*Dominican Contemplative Nuns*—O.P.

[1070-19]—*Dominican Sisters of Houston, Texas (Congregation of the Sacred Heart)*—O.P.

[]—*Eucharistic Franciscan Sisters of Los Angeles*—E.F.M.S.

[]—*Franciscan Sisters of Dubuque*—O.S.F.

[]—*Hermit Sisters of St. Romuald*—H.S.S.R.

[]—*Instituto Santa Mariana de Jesus*—I.S.M.J.

[0990]—*Sisters of Divine Providence*—C.D.P.

[1570]—*Sisters of St. Francis of the Holy Family*—O.S.F.

[1970]—*Sisters of the Holy Family of Nazareth*—C.S.F.N.

NECROLOGY

(No Deaths)

Diocese of Venice

(Dioecesis Venetiae in Florida)

Most Reverend

JOHN J. NEVINS, D.D.

Bishop of Venice; ordained June 6, 1959; appointed Titular Bishop of Rusticiana and Auxiliary of Miami February 6, 1979; consecrated March 24, 1979; appointed First Bishop of Venice July 17, 1984; installed October 25, 1984 *Res.: P.O. Box 2006, Venice, FL 34284.*

To Serve with Mercy

Catholic Center: P.O. Box 2006, Venice, FL 34284. Tel: 941-484-9543; Fax: 941-484-1121.

Web: dioceseofvenice.org

Email: info@dioceseofvenice.org

ESTABLISHED OCTOBER 25, 1984.

Square Miles 9,035.

Comprises the Counties of Charlotte, Collier, DeSoto, Glades, Hardee, Hendry, Highlands, Lee, Manatee and Sarasota in the State of Florida.

For legal titles of parishes and diocesan institutions, consult the Chancellor.

STATISTICAL OVERVIEW

Personnel	
Bishop	1
Priests: Diocesan Active in Diocese	65
Priests: Diocesan Active Outside Diocese	8
Priests: Diocesan in Foreign Missions	1
Priests: Retired, Sick or Absent	16
Number of Diocesan Priests	90
Religious Priests in Diocese	84
Total Priests in Diocese	174
Extern Priests in Diocese	88
Ordinations:	
Diocesan Priests	2
Transitional Deacons	5
Permanent Deacons in Diocese	74
Total Brothers	28
Total Sisters	114
Parishes	
Parishes	54
With Resident Pastor:	
Resident Diocesan Priests	41
Resident Religious Priests	13
Missions	4
Pastoral Centers	10
Professional Ministry Personnel:	
Brothers	3
Sisters	20
Lay Ministers	72
Welfare	
Catholic Hospitals	2
Total Assisted	505,546
Homes for the Aged	9
Total Assisted	38,569
Day Care Centers	1
Total Assisted	84
Specialized Homes	1
Total Assisted	78
Special Centers for Social Services	18
Total Assisted	46,288
Other Institutions	2
Total Assisted	10,467
Educational	
Diocesan Students in Other Seminaries	13
Total Seminarians	13
High Schools, Diocesan and Parish	3
Total Students	1,616
Elementary Schools, Diocesan and Parish	9
Total Students	3,662
Catechesis/Religious Education:	
High School Students	601
Elementary Students	9,227
Total Students under Catholic Instruction	15,119
Teachers in the Diocese:	
Priests	3
Brothers	3
Sisters	9
Lay Teachers	423
Vital Statistics	
Receptions into the Church:	
Infant Baptism Totals	4,178
Adult Baptism Totals	205
Received into Full Communion	333
First Communions	3,851
Confirmations	2,900
Marriages:	
Catholic	544
Interfaith	275
Total Marriages	819
Deaths	2,658
Total Catholic Population	217,585
Total Population	1,718,925

Catholic Center—1000 Pinebrook Rd., Venice, 34285. Tel: 941-484-9543; Fax: 941-484-1121. *Mailing Address, P.O. Box 2006, Venice, 34284.*

Office of the Bishop—Rev. NORMANDO FELIZ, Asst. to the Bishop; Mrs. JOHANNA MARONE, Exec. Sec.; Ms. DOROTHY VIEIRA, Receptionist & Sec.

Vicar General—Very Rev. EDWARD D. MORETTI, V.G.

Chancellor—Dr. VOLODYMYR SMERYK, M.A., J.C.D., J.D.

Assistant to the Chancellor/Notary—Miss JEANNE C. HICKEY.

Treasurer Pro Tempore—Rev. PHILIP SCHEFF.

College of Consultors—Rev. THOMAS G. ANGLIM; Very Revs. EDWARD D. MORETTI, V.G.; ROBERT D. TABBERT, V.F.; Revs. JOSEPH STEARNS; THOMAS G. ANGLIM; GERARD FINEGAN; JEROME A. CAROSELLA; VINCENT SHEEHY.

Deans—Very Revs. ESTEBAN SOY, V.F., Eastern Deanery; STEPHEN E. MCNAMARA, V.F., Central Deanery; ROBERT TABBERT, V.F., Southern Deanery; EDWARD PICK, V.F., Northern Deanery.

Presbyteral Council—Rev. THOMAS G. ANGLIM; Very Revs. EDWARD D. MORETTI, V.G.; EDWARD PICK, V.F.; GEORGE RATZMANN; ROBERT TABBERT, V.F.; Revs. THOMAS G. ANGLIM; JEROME A. CAROSELLA; JOSEPH CONNOLLY, T.O.R.; JOHN F. COSTELLO, S.J.; ERNEST A. FEARS; JANUSZ JANCARZ, S.T.L.; ROBERT KANTOR; JEROME P. KAYWELL; VICENTE LLARIA; ROBERT B. MATTINGLY; Very Rev. STEPHEN E. MCNAMARA, V.F.; Rev. TIMOTHY NAVIN; Very Rev. ESTEBAN SOY, V.F.

Theologian to the Bishop—Rev. FAUSTO STAMPIGLIA, S.A.C.

Vicar for Priests—Rev. GERARD FINEGAN.

Vicar for Deacons—Deacon FRANCIS J. CAMACHO.

Vicar for Religious—Sr. REGIS KRUSNIEWSKI, S.S.N.D.

Priest Personnel Board—Very Rev. STEPHEN E. MCNAMARA, V.F., Chm.

Continuing Education of Clergy—Rev. NORMANDO FELIZ.

Official Archivist—Dr. VOLODYMYR SMERYK, M.A., J.C.D., J.D., Interim Chancellor.

Historical Archivist—Mrs. GAIL M. MCGRATH.

Victim Assistance Coordinator—Mrs. BEVERLY ZEISS, R.N., D.Min. Tel: 941-416-6114.

Diocesan Tribunal— All Pastoral Center searches for information prior to October 25, 1984 should be directed to the Diocese of St. Petersburg for Manatee, Hardee, Sarasota, DeSoto, Glades, Charlotte and Lee Counties; to the Diocese of Orlando for Highlands Co. and to the Archdiocese of Miami for Hendry and Collier Counties

Judicial Vicar—Very Rev. JOHN V. DOLCIAMORE, S.T.L., J.C.L.

Adjutant Judicial Vicars—Very Rev. ROBERT R. CANNON, J.C.L., M.Th.; Rev. JOSEPH AMATO, J.C.L.

Auditors—Rev. RAFAEL PADILLA, J.C.L.; Mr. PETER VERE, J.C.L., M.C.L.

Defenders of the Bond—Rev. RAFAEL PADILLA, J.C.L.; Mr. PETER J. VERE, J.C.L., M.C.L.

Promoters of Justice—Very Rev. ROBERT R. CANNON, J.C.L., M.Th.; Rev. RAFAEL PADILLA, J.C.L.

Judges—Very Revs. ROBERT R. CANNON, J.C.L., M.Th.; JOHN V. DOLCIAMORE, S.T.L., J.C.L.; Revs. JOSEPH S. AMATO, J.C.L.; DENNIS C. KLEMME, J.C.D.; RAFAEL PADILLA, J.C.L.

Ecclesiastical Notaries/Case Assessors—Mrs. ANN MANRODT; Mrs. MARIANA BARTOLILLO; Mrs. JANINE M. MCCARTHY.

Vicar for Marriage Matters—Very Rev. JOHN V. DOLCIAMORE, S.T.L., J.C.L.

Diocesan Offices

African Caribbean American Ministry (AFCAAM)—Mr. ISMAEL HERNANDEZ, M.A., Exec. Dir.. Email: lael@aol.com. Web: www.afcaam.org.

Building Department—Mr. RAYMOND HADDAD, Dir.

Campaign for Human Development—Mrs. BRIDGET SHEEHAN, Dir.

**Catholic Charities of the Diocese of Venice, Inc.*—Mr. PETER ROUTSIS-ARROYO, CEO.

Catholic Relief Services/Operation Rice Bowl—Mrs. BRIDGET SHEEHAN, Dir.

Communications Department—Mrs. GAIL M. MCGRATH, Dir. Tel: 941-486-4702; Fax: 941-486-4761.

Technology—Mrs. PAMELA MANN, Deputy Dir. & IT Mgr.

Catholic Mass on Television—Mrs. NAOMI ZOELLER, Production Coord.

Internet/Intranet—Mrs. JUDY PIPER, Coord.

The Florida Catholic, Venice Edition—Most Rev. JOHN J. NEVINS, D.D., Publisher; Mrs. HEATHER FELTON, Editor. Tel: 941-486-4701; Fax: 941-486-4763.

The Florida Catholic of Venice, Inc.—Rev. JEROME A. CAROSELLA, Pres. & Dir.; Mrs. GAIL M. MCGRATH, Sec. & Dir.; Mr. JOHN G. BAUER, Treas. & Dir.

Venice Catholic Communications, Inc.—1000 Pinebrook Rd., Venice, 34292. Most Rev. JOHN J. NEVINS, D.D., Pres. & Dir.; Rev. JEROME A. CAROSELLA, Vice Pres. & Dir.; Mrs. GAIL M. MCGRATH, Sec. & Treas. & Dir.

Development Office/Annual Bishop's Appeal—Mr. WILLIAM MCCARTHY, Dir.; Mr. DAVID HARTING, Assoc. Dir.

Diaconate—Rev. FAUSTO STAMPIGLIA, S.A.C., Dir.

Ecumenical and Interreligious Affairs—Co-Directors:: Revs. WILLIAM ADAMS; JOEL SCHEVERS, O.Carm.; Ms. JOANNE WEBER, Assoc. Dir.

Education—Sr. ROBERTA SCHMIDT, C.S.J., Dir.; Mrs. ROSEMARY BRATTON, Supt. of Schools; Mrs. KATHY KLEINLEIN, Dir., Catechetical Ministry; Bro. PAUL HENNESSY, C.F.C., Pres., Blessed Edmund Rice School for Pastoral Ministry. Migrant Education Apostolates: Bros. THOMAS MORONEY, C.F.C.; CHRISTIAN VOLLMER, C.F.C.

Finance Department—Rev. PHILIP SCHEFF, Treasurer Pro Tempore; Mr. JOHN BAUER, Dir.; Mrs. MARY MOORE, Controller.

Human Resources—Mr. ARTHUR FLEISCHER, Dir.

Insurance—Mr. DAN DURKIN, Mgr.; Ms. JOANNE COYNE, Admin.

Internal Financial Services—Mrs. LEIGH MORROW, Dir.

Legal— DiVito and Higham, P.A., Gen. Counsel Mrs. GLYNDA L. WHITE, Paralegal.

Ministry to Cultural Groups—

Hispanic, Migrant and Spanish Speaking Apostolates/National Migration Week—Rev. CELESTINO GUTIERREZ, Dir.; Very Rev. ESTEBAN SOY, V.F.; Revs. VICTOR CAVIEDES; JOSE GONZALEZ; RAFAEL PADILLA.

Juventud Hispana (Hispanic Youth Ministry)—Rev. JOSE GONZALEZ, Dir. Espiritual. Coord. Laicos: Mr. JUVENCIO ILDEFONSO; Mrs. BLANCA ILDEFONSO.

Ministry to Haitian People—Rev. JEAN-MARIE "FRITZ" LIGONDE, Dir.

Ministry to Haitian People in Collier County—Rev. TONY CHERMEIL, Priest-in-Charge.

Ministry to Haitian People in Lee County—Rev. ANTONIO JEAN, Priest-in-Charge.

Ministry to Haitian People in Manatee and Sarasota Counties—Rev. JEAN RONALD JOSEPH, Priest-in-Charge.

Ministry to Haitian People in Glades, Hardee, Highlands & DeSoto Counties—Rev. JEANNOT JEAN FRANCOIS SIMEON, Priest-in-Charge.

Ministry to People with HIV/AIDS—Most Rev. PRIAMO ROSARIO-TEJEDA, D.D.; Mr. DERICK FABIAN, Sarasota County; Sisters JUDY H. SIMONIS, C.S.J., Charlotte County; MARY JOHN FRANEY, O.L.C., Lee County.

Department of Ministries—Directors: Dr. MIMI REILLY, D.Min.; Dr. TERRY H. REILLY, D.Min.

Black Catholic Ministry, Office of—Mr. ISMAEL HERNANDEZ, M.A., Acting Dir. Tel: 941-344-0570.

Campus Ministry— The Newman House at the New College Campus *524 58th St., Sarasota, 34243-2104*. Tel: 941-355-6952.

Charismatic Renewal—Rev. MICHAEL SCHEIP, Spiritual Dir.; Mrs. EM WEIS, Lay Dir.

Contemplative Prayer Commission—Rev. ROBERT MATTINGLY, Spiritual Moderator; Dr. MIMI REILLY, D.Min., Chm.

Criminal Justice Ministry—Mr. LOUIE FAUSTINO, Coord.

Evangelization—Directors: Dr. MIMI REILLY, D.Min.; Dr. TERRY H. REILLY, D.Min.

Family Life Office— (includes Parenting and all Marriage Enrichment and Marriage Preparation programs) Dr. MIMI REILLY, D.Min.; Dr. TERRY REILLY, D.Min.

Divorced and Separated Ministry—Rev. GERARD BENSON, O.Carm., Spiritual Moderator; Mr. MICHAEL POSSOBY JR., Coord.

Lay Ministry Office—Directors: Dr. MIMI REILLY, D.Min.; Dr. TERRY H. REILLY, D.Min.

Youth Ministry Office—Mr. RON DUQUETTE, Coord.

Scouting—Deacon FRANCIS COLE, Dir.

Peace and Social Justice Department—Mr. NEIL MICHAUD, M.S.W., Dir.

Respect Life Department—Rev. NICHOLAS MCLOUGHLIN, Moderator. Associate Moderators: Very Rev. ROBERT R. CANNON, J.C.L., M.Th.; Rev. DENNIS COONEY; Mrs. JEANNE BERDEAUX, Dir.; Ms. MARINA KOPKO, Asst. Dir.

Project Rachel—Tel: 877-908-1212 (Toll Free).

Older Catholics, Apostolate for—VACANT.

Persons with Disabilities, Apostolate for—VACANT.

Real Estate Department—Dr. VOLODYMYR SMERYK, M.A., J.C.D., J.D.; Sr. CATHY BUSTER, S.P., Dir. & HUD Specialist.

Vocations/Seminarian Formation—Most Rev. JOHN J. NEVINS, D.D., Dir.; Rev. ROBERT KANTOR, Assoc. Dir.; Ms. BRIDGET OLSON, Asst. Dir.

Other Offices

Propagation of the Faith/Mission Cooperative Program—Very Rev. EDWARD PICK, V.F., Dir.

Organizations

Cursillo Movement—Rev. JOHN DEARY, O.S.A., Spiritual Advisor; Mr. GENE VENDITTO, Lay Dir.

Secretariado Hispano de Cursillos—Mr. CARMELO ORTEGA, Dir. Laico.

Holy Childhood Association—Rev. EUGENE MCCARTHY, Dir.

International Order of Alhambra, Diego Caravan 255—Rev. WILLIAM SEARS, Chap.; Mr. MARVIN A. PESCHEL, Rgnl. Dir.

Legion of Mary—Rev. VINCENT CLEMENTE, Manasota Curia.

Serra International, Punta Gorda Club—Mr. ROBERT HADLEY, Pres. Tel: 941-639-6662.

St. Vincent DePaul Society—Mr. GARDNER S. TRASK, Pres.

Venice Diocesan Council of Catholic Women—Rev. CLAUDE BRUBAKER, Spiritual Dir.; Ms. MARIANNE TORGLER, Pres.

Advisory Groups to the Bishop

Audit Committee—Mr. ERNEST SKINNER, Chm.

Finance Advisory Board—Mr. ERNEST SKINNER, Chm.

Executive Investment Committee—Mr. ERNEST SKINNER, Chm.

Insurance Committee—Rev. JEROME A. CAROSELLA, Chm.

Pension Plan Board of Trustees (Archdiocese of Miami/Dioceses of St. Petersburg and Venice)—Mr. JOHN G. BAUER, Finance Dir.

Planning and Development Committee—Very Rev. EDWARD D. MORETTI, V.G., Chm.

Priest Personnel Board—Very Rev. STEPHEN E. MCNAMARA, V.F., Chm.

Real Estate Board—Rev. PHILIP SCHEFF, Chm.; Sr. CATHY BUSTER, S.P.

Review Board—Mr. JACK DELLORTO, Chm.

CLERGY, PARISHES, MISSIONS AND PAROCHIAL SCHOOLS

CITY OF VENICE
(SARASOTA COUNTY)

1—EPIPHANY CATHEDRAL (1955), [CEM] Very Rev. George Ratzmann, V.F., Rector; Revs. Jacek Mazur; Joel Schevers, O.Carm.; Peter F. Brudzynski (BO) (Retired); James Shea (BUR); Deacons John L. Blackburn, (Retired); Terry Farrell; Robert Tomasso; Francis Cole; William J. Hanlon. In Res., Rev. Jack Cosentino (FAR).
Res.: 310 Sarasota St., 34285. Tel: 941-484-3505; Fax: 941-488-9333.
School—316 Sarasota St., 34285. Tel: 941-488-2215; Fax: 941-480-1565. Dewayne Byrnes, Prin. Lay Teachers 23; Students 313.
Catechesis/Religious Program—Tel: 941-485-2325. Sr. Frances Lalor, R.S.M., D.R.E. Students 470.

2—OUR LADY OF LOURDES (1986), Revs. Vincent J. Sheehy; Rafael Padilla; Deacon Joseph Mercurio.
Res.: 1301 Center Rd., 34292. Tel: 941-497-2931; Fax: 941-497-5849.
Catechesis/Religious Program—Students 163.

OUTSIDE THE CITY OF VENICE

ARCADIA, DE SOTO CO., ST. PAUL (1885), Revs. Stanislaus Pierog; Luis Hurtado Pacheco.
Res.: 1208 E. Oak St., 34266. Tel: 863-494-2611; Fax: 863-494-6385.
Catechesis/Religious Program—Tel: 863-494-2835. Students 175.
Mission—Blessed Juan Diego 52417 S.W. Hwy. 17, Nocatee, De Soto Co. 34266. Tel: 863-993-4095.

AVON PARK, HIGHLANDS CO., OUR LADY OF GRACE (1956), Rev. Gerald P. Grogan.
Res.: 595 E. Main St., 33825. Tel: 863-453-4757; Fax: 863-453-2620.
Catechesis/Religious Program—Tel: 863-453-7537. Students 139.

BOCA GRANDE, LEE CO., OUR LADY OF MERCY (1988), Rev. Jerome A. Carosella.
Res.: P.O. Box 181, 33921. Tel: 941-964-2254; Fax: 941-964-1124.
Catechesis/Religious Program—Students 6.

BOKEELIA, LEE CO., OUR LADY OF THE MIRACULOUS MEDAL (1965), Rev. J. Thomas Pohto, O.S.A.; Deacon Frank Urrico.
Res.: 12175 H. Stringfellow Rd., 33922. Tel: 239-283-0456; Fax: 239-283-1118.
Catechesis/Religious Program—Tel: 239-574-3239. Students 51.

BONITA SPRINGS, LEE CO., ST. LEO (1962), Revs. Ernest Fears, Temp. Admin.; Jozef Mitek; Louis Jasper; Lorenzo Gonzalez.
Res.: 28290 Beaumont Rd., 34134. Tel: 239-992-0901; Fax: 239-992-5282.
Catechesis/Religious Program—Tel: 239-267-8718. Cyndi Rypl, D.R.E. Students 207.

BRADENTON, MANATEE CO.

1—ST. JOSEPH (1927), Revs. John F. Costello, S.J. (CHI); Robert G. Tierney; Ronald J. Joseph; Deacon Robert R. Nimon.
Res.: 2704 33rd Ave. W., 34205. Tel: 941-756-3732; Fax: 941-758-1244.
School—Tel: 941-755-2611; Fax: 941-755-2611. Sr. Christine Patrick, S.P., Prin. Sisters 1; Lay Teachers 30; Students 434.
Catechesis/Religious Program—Tel: 941-755-4335; Fax: 941-753-5634. Michael John, D.R.E. Students 173.

2—OUR LADY OF THE ANGELS (1999), [CEM] Rev. Damian Vincent Amantia, T.O.R.
12905 SR 70 E., 34202. Tel: 941-752-6770; Fax: 941-752-6821.

3—SS. PETER AND PAUL THE APOSTLES (1987), Very Rev. Edward D. Moretti, V.G.; Revs. Robert Joseph Kantor; Philip Joly.
Office—2850 75th St. W., 34209. Tel: 941-795-1228; Fax: 941-794-0127. (Memorial Garden)
Catechesis/Religious Program—Tel: 941-798-9705; Fax: 941-794-3012. AnnaLuisa Huffman, D.R.E. Students 454.

4—SACRED HEART (1969), Revs. Julio B. Rivero, T.O.R.; Gerald Gordon, T.O.R. (ORL).
Res.: 1220 15th St. W., 34205. Tel: 941-748-2221; Fax: 941-748-1744.
Catechesis/Religious Program—Tel: 941-746-3650. Students 161.

CAPE CORAL, LEE CO.

1—ST. ANDREW (1964), Revs. Mark Heuberger, M.A.; Sofonias Ortez; Thomas A. Heck. In Res., Revs. Marc Lussier, M.S.A.; Thomas Bouchard.
Res.: 2628 Del Prado Blvd., 33904. Tel: 239-574-4545; Fax: 239-574-2450.
School—(Grades K-8) Tel: 239-772-3922; Fax: 239-772-7182. Peg Horan, Prin. Lay Teachers 30; Students 537.
Catechesis/Religious Program—Tel: 239-574-2411. Mr. Carmine Macedonio, D.R.E. Students 801.

2—SAINT KATHARINE DREXEL (1990), Rev. John F. Deary, O.S.A.
Office—1922 S.W. 20th Ave., 33991. Tel: 239-283-9501; Fax: 239-283-9502.
Catechesis/Religious Program—Theresa Idler, D.R.E. Students 426.

CLEWISTON, HENDRY CO., ST. MARGARET (1932), (Hispanic), Rev. Marcial Garcia (Dominican Republic), Admin.
315 E. Pasadena Ave., 33440. In Res., Most Rev. Priamo P. Tejeda (Dominican Republic).
Res.: 208 N. Deane Duff Ave., 33440. Tel: 863-983-8585; Fax: 863-983-9673.
Catechesis/Religious Program—Tel: 863-983-8844. Students 112.
Chapel—Montura Rach 208 N. Deane Duff Ave., 33440.

ENGLEWOOD, SARASOTA CO., ST. RAPHAEL (1957), Rev. Morris F. Wells, O.Carm.
Res.: 770 Kilbourne Ave., 34223. Tel: 941-474-9595; Fax: 941-475-5697.
Catechesis/Religious Program—Tel: 941-473-2359. Jean Dezort, O.P., D.R.E. Students 91.

FORT MYERS BEACH, LEE CO., ASCENSION (1962), Revs. Robert M. Murphy; William Adams; Deacon Charles Kiesel. In Res., Rev. Russell Wright.
Res.: 6025 Estero Blvd., 33931. Tel: 239-463-6754; Fax: 239-463-0690.
Catechesis/Religious Program—Students 10.

FORT MYERS, LEE CO.

1—BLESSED POPE JOHN XXIII (2002), Revs. Charles K. Sullivan; Thomas Palko; Deacon Jack Gilbert.
Res.: 6401 Techster Blvd., 33912. Tel: 239-561-2245; Fax: 239-561-3713.
Catechesis/Religious Program—Tel: 239-561-7499. Students 70.

2—ST. CECILIA (1965), [CEM] Revs. Stanley J. Dombrowski, O.S.F.S.; Paul Dechant. In Res., Rev. John T. Doyle, O.S.F.S. (Retired); Deacons Bill Brodeur; Lorin Fortier.
Res.: 5632 Sunrise Dr., 33919. Tel: 239-936-3635; Fax: 239-936-2108.
Catechesis/Religious Program—Michele Salko, D.R.E. Students 180.

3—CHURCH OF THE RESURRECTION OF OUR LORD (1974), Very Rev. Stephen E. McNamara, V.F.; Rev. Oliver Toner; Deacon Michael Esper.
Parish Center & Mailing Address: 8121 Cypress Lake Dr., 33919. Tel: 239-481-7172; Fax: 239-481-8007.
Church: 8051 Cypress Lake Dr., 33919. Tel: 239-481-7171.
Catechesis/Religious Program—Tel: 239-482-6883. Joanne Macpeek, D.R.E. Students 239.

4—ST. COLUMBKILLE (1993), [CEM] Rev. Joseph G. Clifford.
Church: 12171 Iona Rd., 33908. Tel: 239-489-3973; Fax: 239-432-0066.
Catechesis/Religious Program—Tel: 239-466-5020. Students 105.

5—ST. FRANCIS XAVIER (1910), Revs. Thomas G. Anglim; Mario Kono; Michael Mullen (Ireland);

Anthonio Jean.
Res.: P.O. Box 912, 2133 Heitman St., 33902. Tel: 239-334-2161; Fax: 239-332-4178.
School—Tel: 239-334-7707; Fax: 239-334-8605. Sr. Betty Anderson, Prin. Franciscan Sisters of Allegany 1; Lay Teachers 30; Students 655.
Catechesis/Religious Program—2048 Heitman St., 33902. Tel: 239-334-7636. Students 190.
Mission—Tel: 239-567-2315.
Oratory—Our Lady of Perpetual Help 2063 Lafayette St., Lee Co. 33901. Tel: 239-334-2234.

6—JESUS THE WORKER MISSION (JESUS OBRERO) (1973), (Hispanic), Rev. Remigious Ssekiranda.
Office—881 Nuna Ave., 33905. Tel: 239-693-5333; Fax: 239-693-5333.
Catechesis/Religious Program—Students 183.

7—OUR LADY OF LIGHT (1990), [CEM] Revs. Angelo F. Maraldo, O.S.F.S.; Hugh J. McGuigan, O.S.F.S.
Office—19680 Cypress View Dr., 33912. Tel: 239-267-7088; Fax: 239-267-5481.
Res.: 9404 Windlake Dr., 33912. Tel: 239-267-2228.
Catechesis/Religious Program—Students 240.

8—ST. PETER CLAVER MISSION (1999), Rev. Edward J. Galvin, S.M.A.
Church Address: 3681 Michigan Ave., 33994. Tel: 239-461-0669; Fax: 239-461-0669.
Catechesis/Religious Program—Students 21.

9—SAN JOSE MISSION (1968), (Hispanic), Rev. Remigious Ssekiranda, Admin.
10750 Gladiolus Dr., 33908. Tel: 239-481-1143; Fax: 239-693-5333. Email: mmlcjo@earthlink.net.
Catechesis/Religious Program—Students 54.

10—ST. VINCENT DE PAUL (1986), Rev. David Arle.
Church & Mailing Address: 13031 Palm Beach Blvd., 33905. Tel: 239-693-0818; Fax: 239-693-8459.
Catechesis/Religious Program—Students 152.

GOLDEN GATE, COLLIER CO., ST. ELIZABETH SETON (1975), Revs. Joseph A. Spinelli, O.S.A.; Dennis Harten, O.S.A.
Res.: 2760 52 Ter., S.W., Naples, 34116. Tel: 239-455-3900; Fax: 239-455-6895.
School—Tel: 239-455-2262; Fax: 239-455-0549. Ms. Paula Lombardo, Prin. Lay Teachers 18; Students 290.
Catechesis/Religious Program—Tel: 239-455-9598. Cecelia Andretta, D.R.E. Students 252.

GROVE CITY, CHARLOTTE CO., ST. FRANCIS OF ASSISI (1978), Revs. Bartholomew Larkin, O.Carm.; Marcel Dube, O.Carm.
Res.: 80 Oakland Hills Pl., Rotonda West, 33947. Tel: 941-697-4899; Fax: 941-697-0602.
Church: 5265 Placida Rd., 34224.
Catechesis/Religious Program—Mary Sedonic, D.R.E. Students 95.

HOLMES BEACH, MANATEE CO., ST. BERNARD (1956), Revs. John H.R. Ellis; Aloysius Hribsek (BGP); Deacon Alfred Gaspari.
Res.: 248 S. Harbor Dr., 34217, P.O. Box 1036, 34218. Tel: 941-778-4769; Fax: 941-778-4644.
Catechesis/Religious Program—Tel: 941-778-0277. Alice White, D.R.E. Students 72.

IMMOKALEE, COLLIER CO., OUR LADY OF GUADALUPE (1957), Revs. Ettore Rubin, C.S.; Onorio Benacchio, C.S.; Jean Woady Louis.
Res.: 207 S. 9th St., 34142. Tel: 239-657-2666; Fax: 239-657-3431.
Catechesis/Religious Program—Mrs. Maria Marquez, D.R.E. Students 185.

LABELLE, HENDRY CO., OUR LADY QUEEN OF HEAVEN (1975), Revs. Chester Domaszewicz; Victor Caviedes.
Res.: 355 S. Bridge St., P.O. Box 357, 33935. Tel: 863-675-0030; Fax: 863-675-0756.
Catechesis/Religious Program—Rita Schoene, D.R.E. Students 414.

LAKE PLACID, HIGHLAND CO.

1—COMMUNIDAD CATOLICA HISPANA SANTIAGO APOSTOL (SANTIAGO MISSION) (1991), (Hispanic), [JC] Rev. Jose Gonzalez.
Mailing Address: P.O. Box 899, 33862. Tel: 863-385-6762; Fax: 863-385-5169. 685 CR 621 E, 33852. Tel: 863-699-1561.
Catechesis/Religious Program—Tel: 863-465-1800. Students 180.

2—ST. JAMES (1962), [JC] Rev. Vincent Llaria (Spain); Deacon Philip Coniglio.
Mailing Address: 3380 Placid View Dr., 33852. Tel: 863-465-3215; Fax: 863-465-0649. 779 Hawk Ave., 33852.
Catechesis/Religious Program—Students 45.

LEHIGH ACRES, LEE CO., ST. RAPHAEL (1962), Revs. Dennis J. Cooney; Juan Lorenzo; Deacons James Jacob; Lambert Kuhr; Armindo Guzman; Dean Tucker.
Res.: 2514 Lee Blvd., 33971. Tel: 239-369-1831; Fax: 239-369-1039.
Catechesis/Religious Program—Tel: 239-369-6424. Students 214.

LONGBOAT KEY, MANATEE CO., ST. MARY STAR OF THE SEA (1973), Very Rev. Edward Pick, V.F.
Res. & Church: 4280 Gulf of Mexico Dr., 34228. Tel: 941-383-1255; Fax: 941-383-8758.
Catechesis/Religious Program—P.O. Box 9110, 34228.

MARCO ISLAND, COLLIER CO., SAN MARCO (1971), Revs. Eugene McCarthy; J. Patrick Boghan, M.S.A.; Joseph T. Gomolski.
Res.: 851 San Marco Rd., 34145. Tel: 239-394-5181; Fax: 239-394-1385.
Catechesis/Religious Program—Tel: 239-394-4068. David Swierczek, D.R.E. Students 185.
Mission—St. Finbarr Naples, Collier Co.
Mission—Holy Family Everglades City, Collier Co.

MOORE HAVEN, GLADES CO., ST. JOSEPH THE WORKER (1960), (Spanish), [JC] Rev. Esteban G. Soy.
Res.: 1800 N. Hwy. 27 NW, P.O. Box 1109, 33471. Tel: 863-946-0696; Fax: 863-946-3444.
Catechesis/Religious Program—Students 25.
Mission—St. Theresa of the Child Jesus Buckhead Ridge. Hwy. 78 & Chobee Loop, Box 1109, Glades Co. 33471. Tel: 863-946-0696.

MURDOCK, CHARLOTTE CO., ST. MAXIMILIAN KOLBE (1988), Rev. Robert Mattingly; Deacons Louis Cosentino, M.D.; Robert Godlewsky; Max Wendel.
Office & Res.: 1441 Spear St., Port Charlotte, 33948. Tel: 941-743-6877; Fax: 941-743-9176.
Catechesis/Religious Program—Sr. Delores Wehle, S.N.J.M., D.R.E. Students 135.

NAPLES, COLLIER CO.

1—ST. ANN (1955), Very Rev. Robert D. Tabbert, V.F.; Revs. Jaroslaw Sniosek; Joseph Moffatt, C.S.B.
Res.: 475 Ninth Ave. S., 34102. Tel: 239-262-4256; Fax: 239-262-4296.
School—542 Eighth Ave. S., 34102. Tel: 239-262-4110; Fax: 239-262-3991. Mr. James Stiber. Sisters 1; Lay Teachers 48; Students 442.
Catechesis/Religious Program—Students 216.

2—ST. JOHN THE EVANGELIST (1988), Revs. Thomas J. Glackin; Arnold Zebrowski; Richard Mueller (PIT); Jerry Kaywell; Deacons Al Groh; Norm LaLone; Ralph Catanese; Frank Loafman.
Mailing Address: 5633 Strand Blvd. #317, 34110.
Res.: 625 111th Ave. N., 34108. Tel: 239-566-8740; Fax: 239-566-9117.
Catechesis/Religious Program—Tel: 239-514-2927; Fax: 239-566-9117. Dr. Roberta Horton, D.R.E. Students 783.
Chapel—St. Agnes Chapel 151 Rte. 951.

3—ST. PETER THE APOSTLE (1974), Revs. Timothy M. Navin; Tony Chermeil; Andrew Malarz (GRY); Carlos Mundet; Deacons David Nolan; Michael F. Cristiforo; Robert L. Tetrault; Michael Salerno.
Res.: 5130 Rattlesnake Hammock Rd., 34113-7448. Tel: 239-774-3337; Fax: 239-774-3077.
Catechesis/Religious Program—Students 210.

4—ST. WILLIAM (1973), Revs. Joseph E. Stearns; John Fitch.
Res.: 750 Seagate Dr., 34103-2886. Tel: 239-261-4883; Fax: 239-261-8729.
Catechesis/Religious Program—Tel: 239-263-5429. Debra Mahr, D.R.E. Students 430.

NORTH PORT, SARASOTA CO., SAN PEDRO (1964), Revs. Patrick C. Organ (Ireland); Tomasz M. Ochej (Poland).
Res.: 14380 Tamiami Tr., 34287. Tel: 941-426-2500; 941-426-6810; Fax: 941-423-8710.
Catechesis/Religious Program—Tel: 941-426-2893. Students 357.

OSPREY, SARASOTA CO., OUR LADY OF MOUNT CARMEL (2000), Revs. Lukas J. Schmidt, O.Carm.; Leo McCarthy, O.Carm.
Church: 838 S. Tamiami Tr., 34229. Tel: 941-966-0807; Fax: 941-966-3909.
Res.: 554 Pine Ranch E. Rd., 34229. Tel: 941-918-2032.
Catechesis/Religious Program—Students 50.

PALMETTO, MANATEE CO., HOLY CROSS (1956), (Hispanic), Revs. Teofilo Useche; Richard York (PH).
Res.: 506-26th St. W., 34221. Tel: 941-729-3891; Fax: 941-721-9402.
Catechesis/Religious Program—Tel: 941-729-1558. Students 306.

PARRISH, MANATEE CO., ST. FRANCES XAVIER CABRINI (1992), Revs. Janusz Jancarz, S.T.L.; Joseph J. Ryan (STL) (Retired).
Res.: 12001 69th St. E., 34219. Tel: 941-776-9097; Fax: 941-776-1307.
Catechesis/Religious Program—Tel: 941-776-8613. Students 183.

PORT CHARLOTTE, CHARLOTTE CO.

1—ST. CHARLES BORROMEO (1959), Revs. Nicholas McLoughlin; John J. Ludden; Jean-Marie "Fritz" Ligonde (NEW); Thomas Wantland (MAR); Leo P. Riley (DUB).
Office and Church: 21505 Augusta Ave., 33952. Tel: 941-625-4754; Fax: 941-625-0256.
School—Tel: 941-625-5533; Fax: 941-625-7359. Dr. Mary Santini, Prin. Lay Teachers 16; Students 315.
Catechesis/Religious Program—21505 Augusta Ave., 33952. Tel: 941-625-5407. Nancy Lauer, D.R.E. Students 295.

2—SAN ANTONIO (1993), Revs. Thomas J. Zedar; Philip Scheff; Sr. M. Colleen McGinnity, Pastoral Min.
24445 Rampart Blvd., 33980. Tel: 941-624-3799; Fax: 941-624-6184.
Catechesis/Religious Program—Tel: 941-624-5156; Fax: 941-624-6631. Students 244.

PUNTA GORDA, CHARLOTTE CO., SACRED HEART (1954), Revs. Robert Mongiello; Vicente Martin; Jan Antonik; Robert M. Murphy; Deacon Edward D. Lundy.
Res.: 211 W. Charlotte Ave., 33950-5546. Tel: 941-639-3957; Fax: 941-639-2061.
Catechesis/Religious Program—Tel: 941-639-9545. Sr. Josine Perez, D.R.E. Students 122.

SANIBEL, LEE CO., ST. ISABEL (1973), Rev. Christopher Senk.
Res.: 3559 Sanibel-Captiva Rd., 33957. Tel: 239-472-2763; Fax: 239-472-5351.
Catechesis/Religious Program—Fax: 239-472-2763. Students 144.

SARASOTA, MANATEE CO., OUR LADY QUEEN OF MARTYRS (1959), Revs. Joseph F. Connolly, T.O.R.; Louis McIntyre, T.O.R.; Thomas Stabile, T.O.R. In Res., Rev. Sean Sullivan, T.O.R. (Retired).
Res.: 833 Magellan Dr., 34243. Tel: 941-755-1826; Fax: 941-753-1654.
Catechesis/Religious Program— 34243. Tel: 941-755-3497. Geoff Brophy, D.R.E. Students 378.

SARASOTA, SARASOTA CO.

1—INCARNATION (1958), Revs. Gerard Finegan; Gregg Caggianelli; Dominic Szabajkowicz; Deacons Joseph Cirieco; John Crescitelli.
Res.: 2929 Bee Ridge Rd., P.O. Box 5516, 34277-5516. Tel: 941-921-6631; Fax: 941-927-2521.
School—Tel: 941-924-8588; Fax: 941-925-1248. Sr. Monica Paul Fraser, Prin. Sisters 3; Lay Teachers 20; Students 292.
Catechesis/Religious Program—Tel: 941-924-9566. John Garisto, D.R.E. Students 660.

2—ST. MARTHA (1912), Revs. Fausto Stampiglia, S.A.C.; Benedict Abraham, S.A.C.; James Palakudy, S.A.C.; Gangolu Bob Babu, S.A.C.; Paul Coutinha (India) (FTW); Vincent L. Clemente, Hospital Min.; Celestino Gutierrez, Spanish Min.; Daniel Rodriguez; George Hogan, Circus Min.; Deacons John D. Wren Jr., (Retired); William Ladroga.
Mailing Address: 200 N. Orange Ave., 34236. Tel: 941-366-4210; Fax: 941-954-8434.
School—4380 Fruitville Rd., 34232. Tel: 941-953-4181; Fax: 941-366-5580. Mr. Richard Lynn, Prin.; Dorothy Novak, Asst. Prin. Religious 1; Lay Teachers 23; Students 389.
Catechesis/Religious Program—Bro. R. Patrick Wilson, D.R.E. Students 190.

3—ST. MICHAEL THE ARCHANGEL (1958), Rev. Claude E. Brubaker.
Res.: 5394 Midnight Pass Rd., 34242. Tel: 941-349-4174; Fax: 941-349-6388.
Catechesis/Religious Program—Tel: 941-349-4174, Ext. 14. Alexandra Stocking, D.R.E. Students 30.

4—ST. PATRICK (1988), Revs. Michael A. Scheip; George Brennan, Admin.
Res.: 7900 Bee Ridge Rd., 34241. Tel: 941-378-1703; Fax: 941-378-2153.
Catechesis/Religious Program—Tel: 941-378-1521; Fax: 941-342-0543. Students 396.

5—ST. THOMAS MORE (1979), Rev. Donald H. Henry; Deacon Robert Horvath.
Mailing Address: 2506 Gulf Gate Dr., 34231. Tel: 941-923-1691; Fax: 941-923-1692.
Res.: 2612 Regatta Dr., 34231. Tel: 941-923-2095.
Catechesis/Religious Program—Students 134.

SEBRING, HIGHLANDS CO., ST. CATHERINE (1929), [JC] Rev. Jose Gonzalez, Admin.
Res.: 882 Bay St., 33870. Tel: 863-385-0049; Fax: 863-385-5169.
Catechesis/Religious Program—Tel: 863-385-7844. Sr. Julia Zilka, V.S.C., D.R.E. Students 139.

WAUCHULA, HARDEE CO., ST. MICHAEL (1969), (Spanish—Creole), Revs. Peter E. Sousa, C.SS.R.; Edmund Regensburger, C.SS.R.; James J. Burke, C.SS.R.; Jeannot Jean Simeon.
Res.: 408 Heard Bridge Rd., 33873. Tel: 863-773-4089; Fax: 863-773-5641.
Catechesis/Religious Program—Tel: 863-773-4215. Students 320.
Convent—Vincentian Sisters of Charity, 409 Alice St., 33873. Sisters 3.
Mission—Holy Child Chester Ave., Bowling Green, Hardee Co. 33834. Tel: 863-375-4881.
Mission—San Alfonso Catholic Center Schoolhouse Rd., Zolfo Springs, Hardee Co. 33890. Tel: 863-773-5889.

On Special Assignment:
Rev. Msgr.—
La Femina, Anthony A., S.T.L., J.C.D., Diocese of Charleston, 119 Broad St., Charleston, SC 29401. Tel: 843-577-5848

Rev.—
Rourke, John

Graduate Studies:
Revs.—
Gibbons, Edward
Hewitt, Anthony
McLoughlin, Nicholas
Menzies, Scott
Strycharz, Stanley

Military Chaplains:
Very Rev.—
Cannon, Robert R., J.C.L., M.Th., U.S. Air Force, 4100 W. Street, #106, Washington, DC 20007.
Revs.—
Kowalik, Jacek, Stationed in Germany.
McLaughlin, Paul E., U.S. Navy

Unassigned:
Revs.—
Ryan, Eugene, Catholic Center, 1000 Pinebrook Rd., 34292.
Sison, Ronnie

Absent on Leave:
Revs.—
Smith, Daniel
Walk, Donald J.
Zawadzki, Piotr
Deacon—
Wren, John, Jr.

Absent on Sick Leave:
Revs.—
Morillo, Jose
Noboa, Origines

Retired:
Rev. Msgr.—
Mouch, Frank M.
Revs.—
Baier, Donald
Duggan, Joseph P.
Flemming, Neil
Gonzalez, Mario
Gorr, Benjamin
Hickey, Michael
Murphy, Thomas
Murphy, Timothy
O' Connell, William
Swiatecki, Emilian

Permanent Deacons:
Allen, Eugene
Arnold, Maurice
Attridge, James
Blackburn, John L.
Brodeur, Wilfred, Leave of Absence
Burnell, Gary
Cabrera, Crescencio
Camacho, Francis
Catanese, Ralph
Cirieco, Joseph
Cole, Francis
Coniglio, Philip
Cook, James
Cooper, James
Cosentino, Louis A.
Costello, John L.
Costello, John
Crant, Ellis
Crescitelli, John
Cristoforo, Michael
DiMeglio, Michael
DiSalvo, Aldo
Doerr, George
Doughty, Gerald
Egendoerfer, Eugene
Farrell, Terry
Fortier, W. Lorin
Fox, Leonard
Gaspari, Alfred
Gilbert, John
Godlewsky, Robert
Gratkowski, Daniel
Groh, Al
Guzman, Armindo
Hanlon, William J.
Harkin, John
Hedge, Dennis, Leave of Absence
Horan, Francis
Horvath, Robert
Jackson, O. Thomas
Jacob, James
Jolin, Joseph
Kiesel, Charles
King, Loren
Kruk, Leonard
Kuhr, Lambert
Ladroga, William
Lalone, Norman
Loafman, Frank
Lundy, Edward
McGreen, Michael, Leave of Absence
Mercurio, Joseph
Minicozzi, John
Moncsko, Walter
Mullin, Paul
Mulvey, John
Nimon, Robert
Nolan, David W.
O'Grady, Lowell, Serving Outside of the Diocese
Ochner, Ronald
Pipher, Jessie, Leave of Absence
Prince, Norman A.
Salerno, Michael
Schaupp, Larry
Seaton, George L.
Stevens, Robert
Tetrault, Robert
Thoresen, Norman
Tirelli, Raymond
Tomasso, Robert
Tucker, Dean H.
Urrico, Francis
Wendell, Max
Wren, John, Jr.
Zammett, Antony

INSTITUTIONS LOCATED IN THE DIOCESE

[A] HIGH SCHOOLS

FORT MYERS. *Bishop Verot High School*, 5598 Sunrise Dr., 33919. Tel: 239-274-6700; Fax: 239-936-1753. Email: chris.beretta@bvhs.org. Web: www.bvhs.org. Revs. J. Christian Beretta, O.S.F.S, Prin., Supr.; Joseph A. Beattie, O.S.F.S.; John A. Beattie, O.S.F.S. Oblates of St. Francis de Sales Priests 3; Lay Teachers 45; Students 784; Total Staff 30.

NAPLES. *St. John Neumann High School*, 3000 53rd St., S.W., 34116. Tel: 239-455-3044; Fax: 239-455-2966. Email: lcampbell@sjnceltics.org. Web: www.sjnceltics.com. Laura J. Campbell, Prin. Congregation of Christian Brothers Lay Teachers 30; Students 297.

SARASOTA. *Cardinal Mooney High School*, 4171 Fruitville Rd., 34232. Tel: 941-371-4917; Fax: 941-371-6924. Email: schristie@cmhs-sarasota.org. Web: www.cmhs-sarasota.org. Sr. Mary Lucia Haas, S.N.D., Pres.; Mr. Stephen J. Christie, Prin. Sisters of Notre Dame of Chardon, OH Sisters 1; Lay Teachers 45; Total Staff 65; Students 545.

[B] SCHOOLS FOR THEOLOGICAL, SPIRITUAL, PASTORAL AND PERSONAL FORMATION

ARCADIA. *Blessed Edmund Rice School for Pastoral Ministry*, 10299 S.W. Peace River St., 34269-4068. Tel: 941-766-7334; Fax: 941-629-8555. Email: riceschool@juno.com. Web: www.riceschool.org. Bro. Paul K. Hennessy, C.F.C., Pres.; Rev. C. Gerard Austin, O.P. Priests 1; Sisters 2; Brothers 2; Lay Teachers 4; Total Staff 9; Students 112.

[C] MIGRANT EDUCATION

BONITA SPRINGS. *Migrant Education Apostolate*, P.O. Box 716, 34133. Tel: 239-947-9098. Brothers 2.

[D] GENERAL HOSPITALS

VENICE. *Bon Secours-Venice Healthcare Corp.*, 540 The Rialto, 34285. Tel: 941-483-7773; Fax: 941-483-7699. Email: Michael_Guley@bshsi.com. Web: www.bshsi-florida.com. Sr. Mary Catherine Rogers, C.B.S., Pres.; Mr. Michael G. Guley, F.A.C.H.E., CEO. Sisters 1; Acute Care Beds 276; LTC Beds 120; ALF Beds 104; Total Staff 1,625; Patients Assisted Annually 215,574.

PORT CHARLOTTE. *Bon Secours-St. Joseph Hospital*, 2500 Harbor Blvd., 33952. Tel: 941-766-4122; Fax: 941-766-4556. Email: art_schute@bshsi.com. Web: www.bonsecours.org/florida. Mr. Michael Harrington, CEO. Sisters 1; Bed Capacity 212; Total Staff 901; Patients Assisted Annually 46,038.

Bon Secours-St. Joseph Healthcare Group, Inc., 2500 Harbor Blvd., 33952. Tel: 941-766-4122; Fax: 941-766-4140. Sr. Mary Catherine Rogers, C.B.S., Senior Vice Pres., Sponsorship; Mr. Michael Harrington, CEO; Revs. Arthur B. Schute, NACC Cert., Dir., & Chap.; Robert M. Murphy, Chap.; Karen Riley, Chap. & Coord. Parish Nurse, NACC Cert. Bed Capacity 426; Total Assisted Annually 289,972; Total Staff 1,220.

Bon Secours-St. Joseph Healthcare Group Foundation, Inc. Tel: 941-766-4285; Fax: 941-766-4287.

[E] NURSING AND CONVALESCENT HOMES

PORT CHARLOTTE. *Bon Secours-St. Joseph Nursing and Rehabilitation Center, Inc.*, 2370 Harbor Blvd., 33952. Tel: 941-624-5966; Fax: 941-624-3963. Daniel Freed, Admin. Total Staff 144; Patients Assisted Annually 37,960.

[F] RESIDENCES FOR THE AGED

VENICE. *St. Mark's Housing of Venice, Inc.* dba Villa San Marcos , 1030 Albee Farm Rd., 34292. Tel: 941-483-1960; Fax: 941-483-3934. Email: villamarcos@comcast.net. Yvonne Heckler, Resident Mgr. (aka Villa San Marcos) Total Staff 3.

FORT MYERS. *Villa Francisco*, 2140 Cottage St., 33901. Tel: 941-332-3229; Fax: 941-332-4178. Rev. Thomas G. Anglim, Pres.; Sr. Marie Vincent Chiaravalle, O.S.F., Admin. Total in Residence 65; Total Staff 2.

PORT CHARLOTTE. *St. Charles Housing I, Inc.*, 2550 Easy St., 33952. Tel: 941-624-2266; Fax: 941-624-2283. Email: villasancarlos@comcast.net. Dr. Roseanne Samson, Pres. (aka Villa San Carlos) Total in Residence 52; Total Staff 6.

St. Charles Housing II, Inc., 22250 Vick St., 33980. Tel: 941-624-4404; Fax: 941-624-5556. Email: villasancarlosii@comcast.net. Suzanne Bergeron, Resident Mgr.; Michael Horner, Pres. (dba Villa San Carlos II) Residents 55; Total Staff 8.

SARASOTA. *St. Martha's Housing II, Inc.* (Casa Santa Marta II) , 800 N. Lemon Ave., 34236. Tel: 941-365-7913; Fax: 941-365-8887. Email: casasantamarta.csm@verizon.net. Rev. Fausto Stampiglia, S.A.C., Pres.; Cora Beals, Site Mgr. Total in Residence 55; Total Staff 3.

St. Martha's Housing, Inc. (Casa Santa Marta) , 1576 Eighth St., 34236. Tel: 941-366-4448; Fax: 941-366-2544. Email: casasantamarta.csm@verizon.net. Rev. Fausto Stampiglia, S.A.C., Pres.; Ms. Darlene Ehrhart, Mgr. Total in Residence 78; Total Staff 4.

[G] MONASTERIES AND RESIDENCES OF PRIESTS AND BROTHERS

VENICE. *St. Alphonsus Residence*, 1230 Schooner Ln., 34292. Tel: 941-485-3673; Fax: 941-486-1524. Email: olphmallen@aol.com. Revs. John L. Smyth, C.SS.R., Supr.; Charles Mallen, C.SS.R.

Carmel in Venice, 244 Harbor Dr. S., 34285. Tel: 941-485-0606. Revs. Clyde Ozminkowski, O.Carm.; Kurt Holdereid, O.Carm.; Simon Kenny, O.Carm. Priests 4.

Xavieran Brothers, 609 Cornwell on the Gulf, 34285. Tel: 941-484-9641; Fax: 941-412-1461. Email: xbprayer@att.net. Web: www.xaverianbrothers.org. Brothers of St. Francis Xavier - Sabbath House Brothers 1.

ENGLEWOOD. *Society of St. Edmund Residence*, 617 W. Harvard St., 34223. Tel: 941-473-9256. Revs. Gerald Grace, S.S.E., Facilitator; Joseph L. Hart, S.S.E.; Bro. George Francis Huyer, S.S.E.

FORT MYERS. *Oblates of St. Francis de Sales*, 5598 Sunrise Dr., 33919. Tel: 239-939-5334. Revs. Joseph A. Beattie, O.S.F.S.; John A. Beattie, O.S.F.S.; J. Christian Beretta, O.S.F.S; Hugh McGuigan, O.S.F.S. Priests 4.

NOKOMIS. *Carmel at Mission Valley*, 955 Laurel Rd. E., 34275-4507. Tel: 941-412-0678; Fax: 941-485-5716. Email: franktask@earthlink.com. Revs. John C. Fogarty, O.Carm.; Joel Schevers, O.Carm.; David Murphy, O.Carm.; Franklin R. Tasker, O.Carm.; Thomas J. Walsh, O.Carm.; Eamon Carroll, O.Carm.; Casimir Zielinski, O.Carm.; Gerard M. Benson.

SARASOTA. *Congregation of the Holy Ghost*, 459 Beach Rd., 34242. Tel: 941-349-0398. Revs. Robert N. Roach, C.S.Sp. (PIT), Supr.; Edward Raszewski, C.S.Sp.; Stephen J. Lasko, C.S.Sp.; Francis R. Duffy, C.S.Sp.; Anthony A. Bacher, C.S.Sp.; W. Robert Graves, C.S.Sp.; H. Eugene Hillman, C.S.Sp. Total in Residence 7.

Holy Cross Florida Regional Center, 1635 4th St., 34236. Tel: 941-365-0722. Email: sarasotacsc@aol.com. Bros. William Geenen, C.S.C.; Charles Krupp, C.S.C.; William Schu, C.S.C. Holy Cross Brothers Residence.

[H] CONVENTS AND RESIDENCES FOR SISTERS

FORT MYERS BEACH. *San Damiano Monastery of St. Clare.* (Solemn Vows, Papal Enclosure) , 6029 Estero Blvd., 33931-4325. Tel: 239-463-5599; Fax: 239-463-4993. Email: bellachair@aol.com. Web: www.poorclare.org/fmb. Sr. Mary Emmanuel Kilkenny, O.S.C., Abbess. Poor Clares Cloistered Sisters 4.

[I] RETREAT CENTERS

VENICE. *Our Lady of Perpetual Help Retreat and Spirituality Center*, 3989 S. Moon Dr., 34292. Tel: 941-486-0233; Fax: 941-486-1524. Email: olphsct@aol.com. Web: www.olph-retreat.org. Rev. Charles Mallen, C.SS.R., Dir.; Sr. Carmella T. DeCosty, S.N.J.M., Admin.

LAKE PLACID. *Campo San Jose*, P.O. Box 899, 33862-0899. 170 Sun 'n' Lake Blvd., 33862-0899. Tel: 863-385-6762; Fax: 863-385-5169. Email: frjose@camposanjose.com. Web: www.camposanjose.com. Rev. Jose Gonzalez, Dir.

[J] CATHOLIC CHARITIES

VENICE. *Catholic Charities of the Diocese of Venice, Inc.*, 1000 Pinebrook Rd., 34285. Tel: 941-488-5581. Email: prarroyo@dioceseofvenice.org. Peter Routsis-Arroyo, Exec. Dir.

Catholic Charities, District I (Sarasota and Manatee Counties) , 4930 Fruitville Rd., Sarasota, 34232. Tel: 941-379-5119; Fax: 941-379-3611. Email: srqdisdir@comcast.net.

Catholic Charities, District II (Lee, Glades and Hendry Counties) , 2116 Monroe St., Fort Myers, 33901. Tel: 239-334-4007; Fax: 239-334-3707. Email: catholiccharitiesofc@earthlink.net.

Catholic Charities, District III (Collier County) , 2210 Santa Barbara Blvd., Naples, 34116. Tel: 239-455-2655; Fax: 239-455-7235. Email: drobinski@naples.net.

Catholic Charities, District IV (Charlotte, Highland, Hardee and Manatee Counties) , 23081 Harborview Rd., Ste. 201, Port Charlotte, 33980. Tel: 941-629-9990; Fax: 941-629-7744. Email: cathchar@peganet.com.

[K] FOUNDATIONS

FORT MYERS. *The Bishop Verot High School Foundation*, 5598 Sunrise Dr., 33919. Tel: 239-274-6700; Fax: 239-936-1753. Email: chris.beretta@bvhs.org. Web: www.bvhs.org. Rev. J. Christian Beretta, O.S.F.S.

St. Francis Xavier School Foundation, 2133 Heitman St., 33901. Tel: 239-334-2161; Fax: 239-332-4178. Email: stfxch@aol.com. Rev. Thomas G. Anglim, Pres.; Dr. Michael Kyle, Chm.

SARASOTA. *Cardinal Mooney High School Foundation*, c/o Cardinal Mooney High School, 4171 Fruitville Rd., 34232. Tel: 941-371-4917; Fax: 941-371-6924.

Incarnation School Foundation, 2911 Bee Ridge Rd., 34239. Tel: 941-924-8588; Fax: 941-925-1248.

St. Martha School Foundation, 200 N. Orange Ave., 34230. Tel: 941-366-4210; Fax: 941-954-8434. Email: pastor@mycomcast.com. Web: www.stmartha-school.org.

[L] MISCELLANEOUS LISTINGS

VENICE. *St. Vincent de Paul Housing, Inc.*, P.O. Box 2006, 34284-2006. Tel: 941-484-9543; Fax: 941-485-6344. Email: buster@dioceseofvenice.org. Most Rev. John J. Nevins, D.D.

FORT MYERS. *Societies of St. Vincent de Paul*, 11799 S. Cleveland Ave., 33907-2883. Tel: 239-274-0660; Fax: 239-274-0659. Mr. Gardner S. Trask Trustee. District Council of Fort Myers, District Council of Manasota, District Council of Naples.

NORTH PORT. *Bon Secours-St. Joseph Home Health Agency, Inc.*, 15121 Tamiami Tr., 34287. Tel: 941-423-5100; Fax: 941-423-5113. Email: denise_ma[illegible]ot@bshsi.com.

SARASOTA. *Bethesda House* (AIDS Ministry) , 1670 Fourth St., 34236. Tel: 941-366-1886; Fax: 941-362-9733. Email: bethesdahouse@excite.com. Derick Fabien. Total Assisted Annually 8,939; Total Staff 4.

Joseph's Place (AIDS Ministry) , 7810 S. Tamiami Tr., SCRC, Ste. 14A, 34293. Tel: 941-408-9692; Fax: 941-408-7[illegible]91. Staff 2; Total Assisted 1,528.

RELIGIOUS INSTITUTES OF MEN REPRESENTED IN THE DIOCESE

For further details refer to the corresponding bracketed number in the Religious Institutes of Men or Women section.

[0140]—*The Augustinians*—O.S.A.
[1350]—*Brothers of St. Francis Xavier*—C.F.X.
[]—*Brothers of the Catholic Apostolate*—S.A.C.
[0600]—*Brothers of the Congregation of Holy Cross*—C.S.C.
[0470]—*Capuchin Friars*—O.F.M.Cap.
[0270]—*Carmelite Fathers & Brothers*—O.Carm.
[0310]—*Congregation of Christian Brothers*—C.F.C.
[]—*Congregation of St. Basil*—C.S.B.
[]—*Congregation of the Resurrection*—C.R.
[0430]—*Dominican Fathers*—O.P.
[0650]—*Holy Ghost Fathers*—C.S.Sp.
[0690]—*Jesuit Fathers*—S.J.
[0720]—*Missionaries of Our Lady of La Salette*—M.S.
[1210]—*Missionaries of St. Charles Scalabrians*—C.S.
[0590]—*Missionaries of the Holy Apostles*—M.Ss.A.
[0920]—*Oblates of St. Francis de Sales*—O.S.F.S.
[1000]—*Passionist Fathers*—C.P.
[1070]—*Redemptorist Fathers*—C.SS.R.
[0110]—*Society of African Missions*—S.M.A.
[0440]—*Society of St. Edmund*—S.S.E.
[0990]—*Society of the Catholic Apostolate*—S.A.C.
[1200]—*Society of the Divine Savior*—S.D.S
[0700]—*St. Joseph's Society of the Sacred Heart*—S.S.J.
[0560]—*Third Order Regular of St. Francis*—T.O.R.

RELIGIOUS INSTITUTES OF WOMEN REPRESENTED IN THE DIOCESE

[0270]—*Congregation of Bon Secours* (Marriotsville, MD)—C.B.S.
[1070-15]—*Congregation of St. Dominic (Sisters of St. Dominic of Blauvelt, NY)*—O.P.
[]—*Congregation of the Sisters of St. Dominic of the Immaculate Heart of Mary*—O.P.
[1105]—*Dominican Sisters of Hope*—O.P.
[1070-02]—*Dominican Sisters of St. Mary of the Springs*—O.P.
[1070-13]—*Dominican Sisters/Congregation of the Most Holy Rosary (Adrian Dominicans)*—O.P.
[1070-03]—*Dominican Sisters/Sinsinawa Dominican Congregation of the Most Holy Rosary*—O.P.
[1180]—*Franciscan Sisters of Allegheny, NY*—O.S.F.
[1820]—*Institute of the Blessed Virgin Mary (Sisters of Loretto)*—I.B.V.M.
[2420]—*Marist Missionary Sisters*—S.M.S.M.
[]—*Missionaries Daughters of Our Blessed Lady of the Light, Yucatan, Mexico*—M.H.M.L.
[1360]—*Missionary Franciscan Sisters of the Immaculate Conception* (Newton, MA)—O.S.F.
[2800]—*Missionary Sisters of the Most Sacred Heart of Jesus of Hilltrup*—M.S.C.
[3070]—*North American Union of Sisters of Our Lady of Charity*—N.A.U.-O.L
[3760]—*Order of St. Clare*—O.S.C.
[3465]—*Religious of the Sacred Heart of Mary* (Eastern North American Province)—R.S.H.M.
[2970]—*School Sisters of Notre Dame* (Baltimore Prov., St. Louis Prov., Northeastern Prov.)—S.S.N.D.
[0590]—*Sisters of Charity of St. Elizabeth, Convent Station*—S.C.
[0430]—*Sisters of Charity of the Blessed Virgin Mary*—B.V.M.
[2575]—*Sisters of Mercy of the Americas* (New Jersey Prov.)—R.S.M.
[2549]—*Sisters of Mercy, Co. Sligo, Ireland*—R.S.M.
[2990]—*Sisters of Notre Dame* (Chardon, OH)—S.N.D.
[3360]—*Sisters of Providence of St. Mary-of-the-Woods, IN*—S.P.
[3720]—*Sisters of St. Ann* (Marlboro, MA)—S.S.A.
[1630]—*Sisters of St. Francis of Penance and Christian Charity*—O.S.F.
[1650]—*Sisters of St. Francis of Philadelphia*—O.S.F.
[3830-01]—*Sisters of St. Joseph of Boston*—C.S.J.
[3840]—*Sisters of St. Joseph of Carondelet*—C.S.J.
[]—*Sisters of St. Joseph of Chestnut Hill, Philadelphia*—S.S.J.
[3830-08]—*Sisters of St. Joseph of Cleveland*—C.S.J.
[1990]—*Sisters of the Holy Name of Jesus and Mary*—S.N.J.M.
[1490]—*Sisters of the Third Franciscan Order* (Syracuse, NY)—O.S.F.
[1710]—*Sisters of the Third Order of St. Francis*—O.S.F.
[4060]—*Society of the Holy Child Jesus*—S.H.C.J.
[4070]—*Society of the Sacred Heart*—R.S.C.J.
[4160]—*Vincentian Sisters of Charity*—V.S.C.

NECROLOGY

† Schiefen, Rev. Msgr. Robert, (Retired)—Died March 25, 2003
† Dittman, Bernard F., (Retired)—Died Oct. 17, 2003
† Hannaway, Arthur W., Sarasota, FL St. Patrick—Died Sept. 15, 2003
† Ruiz, Jose H., Sebring, FL St. Catherine—Died April 20, 2003

Diocese of Victoria in Texas

(Dioecesis Victoriensis in Texia)

Most Reverend

DAVID E. FELLHAUER, PH.D., J.C.D.

Bishop of Victoria; ordained May 29, 1965; appointed Second Bishop of Victoria in Texas April 7, 1990; consecrated and installed May 28, 1990. *Res.: 302 East Red River, Victoria, TX 77901. P.O. Box 4070, Victoria, TX 77903.*

Chancery Office: P.O. Box 4070, Victoria, TX 77903. Tel: 361-573-0828; Fax: 361-573-5725.

ESTABLISHED AND CREATED A DIOCESE, MAY 29, 1982.

Square Miles 9,609.

Comprises the Counties of Calhoun, DeWitt, Goliad, Jackson, Lavaca, Matagorda, Victoria, Wharton and Colorado; also Fayette County west of the Colorado River in the State of Texas.

Legal Title: Diocese of Victoria in Texas.

For legal titles of parishes and diocesan institutions, consult the Chancery Office.

STATISTICAL OVERVIEW

Personnel	
Bishop	1
Priests: Diocesan Active in Diocese	42
Priests: Diocesan Active Outside Diocese	2
Priests: Retired, Sick or Absent	13
Number of Diocesan Priests	57
Religious Priests in Diocese	8
Total Priests in Diocese	65
Extern Priests in Diocese	7
Ordinations:	
Transitional Deacons	1
Permanent Deacons in Diocese	26
Total Brothers	1
Total Sisters	90
Parishes	
Parishes	50
With Resident Pastor:	
Resident Diocesan Priests	35
Resident Religious Priests	3
Without Resident Pastor:	
Administered by Priests	12
Administered by Religious Women	1
Missions	18
Professional Ministry Personnel:	
Sisters	22
Lay Ministers	11
Welfare	
Homes for the Aged	1
Total Assisted	59
Specialized Homes	1
Total Assisted	405
Educational	
Diocesan Students in Other Seminaries	7
Total Seminarians	7
High Schools, Diocesan and Parish	2
Total Students	187
High Schools, Private	1
Total Students	337
Elementary Schools, Diocesan and Parish	11
Total Students	1,773
Elementary Schools, Private	1
Total Students	245
Catechesis/Religious Education:	
High School Students	3,314
Elementary Students	6,389
Total Students under Catholic Instruction	12,252
Teachers in the Diocese:	
Priests	1
Sisters	19
Lay Teachers	220
Vital Statistics	
Receptions into the Church:	
Infant Baptism Totals	1,608
Adult Baptism Totals	68
Received into Full Communion	97
First Communions	1,362
Confirmations	1,069
Marriages:	
Catholic	315
Interfaith	130
Total Marriages	445
Deaths	928
Total Catholic Population	106,441
Total Population	208,736

Former Bishops—Most Rev. CHARLES V. GRAHMANN, D.D., ord. March 17, 1956; appt. Titular Bishop of Equilio and Auxiliary of San Antonio, June 30, 1981; consecrated Aug. 29, 1981; appt. First Bishop of Victoria, April 14, 1982; installed May 29, 1982; appt. Coadjutor of Dallas, Dec. 18, 1989; succeeded to See, July 14, 1990.

Chancery Office—1505 E. Mesquite Ln., Victoria, 77901. Mailing Address, P.O. Box 4070, Victoria, 77903. Tel: 361-573-0828; Fax: 361-573-5725. Office Hours: Mon.-Fri. 8:30-4:30

Vicars General—Rev. Msgrs. THOMAS C. MCLAUGHLIN, V.G., P.O. Box 4070, Victoria, 77903. Fax: 361-572-8204; JAMES C. BRUNNER, V.G., P.O. Box 2448, Victoria, 77902.

Chancellor—Rev. Msgr. THOMAS C. MCLAUGHLIN, V.G., P.O. Box 4070, Victoria, 77903. Fax: 361-572-8204.

Vice-Chancellor—Rev. GARY W. JANAK, J.C.L., St. Philip the Apostle Church, 304 W. Church St., El Campo, 77437-3317. Tel: 979-543-3770.

Diocesan Consultors—Rev. Msgrs. THOMAS C. MCLAUGHLIN, V.G.; JAMES C. BRUNNER, V.G.; MICHAEL HARROLD, V.F.; Revs. DAN MORALES; TIMOTHY KOSLER, V.F.; JOHN C. PETERS, V.F.; DONALD R. RUPPERT; FRANK LENZ.

Vicars Forane—Victoria Deanery: Rev. Msgr. MICHAEL HARROLD, V.F., Our Lady of Victory Cathedral, 1309 E. Mesquite Ln., Victoria, 77901. Tel: 361-575-4741. Cuero Deanery: VACANT. Edna Deanery: Rev. DAN MORALES, Our Lady of Gulf Church, P.O. Box 87, Port Lavaca, 77979. Tel: 361-552-6140. El Campo Deanery: Rev. DONALD RUPPERT, V.F., Holy Cross Church, P.O. Box 1325, East Bernard, 77435-1325. Tel: 979-335-7551. Hallettsville Deanery: Rev. JOHN C. PETERS, V.F., Sacred Heart Church, P.O. Box H, Hallettsville, 77964. Tel: 361-798-5888. Schulenburg Deanery: Rev. TIMOTHY KOSLER, V.F., St. Rose of Lima Church, 1010 Lyons Ave., Schulenburg, 78956. Tel: 979-743-3117.

Presbyteral Council—Rev. Msgrs. THOMAS C. MCLAUGHLIN, V.G.; JAMES C. BRUNNER, V.G.; Revs. JOHN C. PETERS, V.F.; DAN MORALES; FRANK LENZ; JOHN BILY; Rev. Msgr. MICHAEL HARROLD, V.F.; Revs. TIMOTHY KOSLER, V.F.; CHARLES SONNIER; CHARLES DWOMOH; GREG KORENEK; MICHAEL PETERING; WAYNE FLAGG; DONALD RUPPERT, V.F.

Diocesan Tribunal—1505 E. Mesquite Ln., Victoria, 77901. Tel: 361-573-0760; Fax: 361-572-8204.

Judicial Vicar—Rev. Msgr. THOMAS C. MCLAUGHLIN, V.G.

Judges—Rev. JOHN C. BILY; Rev. Msgr. MICHAEL HARROLD, V.F.; Revs. GARY W. JANAK, J.C.L.; GABRIEL MAISON, J.C.D.; CELESTINO SAY.

Promoter of Justice— Appointed as needed.

Procurator Advocate—Rev. Msgr. BENTON THURMOND (Retired); Revs. MICHAEL LYONS; CHARLES DWOMOH; MATTHEW HUEHLEFELD; SAMUEL APPIASI.

Defenders of the Bond—Rev. Msgr. EUSTACE HERMES (Retired); Revs. DAN MORALES; TIMOTHY KOSLER, V.F.; DANIEL P. KAHLICH; FRANK LENZ; GREG KORENEK.

Notaries—Mrs. MINNIE BOCHAT; Mrs. MARY HAAS.

Priests' Personnel Board—Rev. Msgrs. THOMAS C. MCLAUGHLIN, V.G., Chancellor; JAMES C. BRUNNER, V.G.; Rev. JOHN C. PETERS, V.F.; Rev. Msgr. MICHAEL HARROLD, V.F.; Revs. DONALD RUPPERT, V.F.; TIMOTHY KOSLER, V.F.; DAN MORALES.

Building Board—Deacon A. R. WEARDEN; Mr. AL HESSLER; Mr. HENRY SCHROEDER; Mr. CHARLES BLUNTZER; Mr. JAMES MIORI; Mr. ED MARTINKA.

Business Administration Office—Deacon A. R. WEARDEN, Mgr.; Mrs. SHARON JONES; Mrs. JERI JOSEPH, P.O. Box 4070, Victoria, 77903. Tel: 361-573-0828.

Campaign For Human Development and Catholic Relief Services—Rev. DAN MORALES, Dir., Our Lady of Gulf Church, P.O. Box 87, Port Lavaca, 77979. Tel: 361-552-6140.

Catholic Youth Ministry—Mrs. DEBBIE VANELLI, Dir., 1505 E. Mesquite Ln., P.O. Box 4070, Victoria, 77901. Tel: 361-573-0828.

Catholic Outreach Prison Ministry—P.O. Box 697, Cuero, 77954.

Council of Catholic Women (DCCW)—Rev. Msgr. MICHAEL O'SHAUGHNESSEY, V.F., Moderator, 506 N. Allen, Edna, 77957. Tel: 361-782-3588; Mrs. JANICE OHRT, Chm., 2221 FM 237, Victoria, 77905. Tel: 361-575-2056.

Diocesan Cemeteries—GARY RANGNOW, Dir., P.O. Box 4070, Victoria, 77903. Tel: 361-573-0828.

Diocesan Finance Board—Deacon A. R. WEARDEN; Mrs. BEATRICE GONZALEZ; Mr. OTTO KALISHKO; Mr. ROMAN SHIMEK; Mr. MARK WESTERMAN; Mrs. NANCY SUMMERS; Mr. JOHN HALL; Mr. GLEN VILLAFRANCA; Mr. JOHN STEVENSON; Rev. DONALD RUPPERT, V.F.; Rev. Msgrs. THOMAS C. MCLAUGHLIN, V.G.; JAMES C. BRUNNER, V.G.

Diocesan Services Appeal—Mrs. JERI JOSEPH, Dir., 1505 E. Mesquite Ln., P.O. Box 4070, Victoria, 77901. Tel: 361-573-0828.

Diocesan Office of Spiritual Renewal Center—AMADOR AMADOR; CONNIE AMADOR. Tel: 361-572-0836.

Ecumenical Commission—Rev. WAYNE FLAGG, SS. Peter & Paul Church, Rte. 2, Box 26, New Ulm, 78950. Tel: 979-732-3430.

Presidio of La Bahia—Mr. NEWTON WARZECHA, P.O. Box 57, Goliad, 77963. Tel: 361-645-3752.

Liturgical Commission—Rev. EDWARD J. WINKLER, P.O. Box 307, Eagle Lake, 77434. Tel: 979-234-2842.

Office of Catholic Schools—Sr. GLORIA CAIN, S.N.N.D., Supt., P.O. Box 4070, Victoria, 77903.

Permanent Diaconate Program—Rev. GABRIEL MAISON, J.C.D., Dir., 1505 E. Mesquite Ln., P.O. Box 4070, Victoria, 77903. P.O. Box 399, Moulton, 77975.

Propagation of the Faith, Holy Childhood Association—Rev. Msgr. THOMAS C. MCLAUGHLIN, V.G., Dir.

Mission Cooperative Plan—Rev. Msgr. THOMAS C. MCLAUGHLIN, V.G., Dir., Chancery Office, P.O. Box 4070, Victoria, 77903.

Religious Education—Sr. DIGNA VELA, I.W.B.S., Dir., 1505 E. Mesquite Ln., P.O. Box 4070, Victoria, 77903. Tel: 361-573-0828.

Respect Life-Pro Life—Rev. Msgr. JAMES C. BRUNNER, V.G., P.O. Box 2448, Victoria, 77902. Tel: 361-573-4328.

Rural Life Conference—VACANT.

Scouting—VACANT.

"The Catholic Lighthouse", Diocesan Newspaper—Mrs. CINDY BREWER, P.O. Box 4070, Victoria, 77903. Tel: 361-573-0828.

Vietnamese American Apostolic Center—Rev. JOSEPH PHAM DUC TRIN, St. Anthony Church, P.O. Box 900, Palacios, 77465. Tel: 361-972-2685.

Vocations Committee—Revs. MATTHEW HUEHLEFELD, Chm.; JOSEPH HYBNER; KIRBY HLAVATY; Sisters MILDRED TRUCHARD, I.W.B.S.; JACINTA BENAVIDEZ, I.W.B.S.; F. A. STEVENSON, M.D., P.O. Box 4070, Victoria, 77903. Tel: 361-573-0828.

Director of Seminarians—Rev. MATTHEW HUEHLEFELD, St. Patrick Church, P.O. Box 217, Bloomington, 77951. Tel: 361-897-1155.

Victim Assistance Coordinator—Rev. GARY W. JANAK, J.C.L. Tel: 979-543-3770. Email: apostle@sephilipapostle.org.

CLERGY, PARISHES, MISSIONS AND PAROCHIAL SCHOOLS

CITY OF VICTORIA
(VICTORIA COUNTY)

1—OUR LADY OF VICTORY CATHEDRAL, Rev. Msgr. Michael Harrold, V.F.; Rev. Dominic Antwi-Boasiako.
Res.: 1309 E. Mesquite Ln., 77901. Tel: 361-575-4741; Fax: 361-575-3473.
School—Tel: 361-575-5391; 361-578-5454; Fax: 361-575-3474. Sr. M. Leonita Barron, I.W.B.S., Prin. Sisters 1; Lay Teachers 31; Students 432.
Catechesis/Religious Program—Tel: 361-575-8132. Betty Mitchell, D.R.E. Students 458.

2—HOLY FAMILY OF JOSEPH, MARY & JESUS, [JC] Rev. Gregory E. Korenek; Deacon Steve Borowicz.
Office—704 Mallette Dr., 77904. Tel: 361-573-5304; Fax: 361-573-6053.

3—ST. MARY'S, [JC] Rev. Msgr. James C. Brunner, V.G.; Rev. Gabriel Oduro Tawiah; Deacons Richard Wearden; Jim Koenig.
Res.: 402 S. Main, P.O. Box 2448, 77902. Tel: 361-573-4328; Fax: 361-573-4308.

4—OUR LADY OF LOURDES, Rev. Celestino Say, Admin.
Res.: 105 N. William, 77901. Tel: 361-575-3813.

5—OUR LADY OF SORROWS, [JC] Revs. Victor Scocco, O.SS.T.; Alberto Rodriguez, O.SS.T.; Wolfgang Mimms, O.SS.T.; Tom Dymowski, O.SS.T.; Gabriel O'Too; Deacons Edward Molina; Jesus Perez.
Res.: 208 W. River St., P.O. Box 2548, 77901.
Catechesis/Religious Program—Tel: 361-573-2681. Sr. Susana Islas, M.C., D.R.E. Students 1,143.
Convent—Missionary Catechists of the Sacred Hearts of Jesus and Mary (Violetas), 209 W. Murray St., 77901. Tel: 361-575-7654. Sisters 4.
Mission—Holy Trinity 2511 Ozark, Victoria Co. 77901. Tel: 361-575-2293; Fax: 361-582-0405.

OUTSIDE THE CITY OF VICTORIA

AMMANNSVILLE, FAYETTE CO., ST. JOHN THE BAPTIST, [CEM] Rev. Timothy Kosler, Admin.
Mailing Address: 7745 Mensik Rd., Schulenburg, 78956.
Mission—St. Wenceslaus [CEM] Holman, Fayette Co.

BAY CITY, MATAGORDA CO.

1—HOLY CROSS, [CEM 2] [JC] Rev. Casimir Jarzombek; Deacon Guadalupe Rodriguez.
Res.: 2001 Katy St., 77414. Tel: 979-245-6379; Fax: 979-244-5481.
School—Tel: 979-245-5632; Fax: 979-245-6120. Sr. M. Geraldine Pavlik, I.W.B.S., Prin. Lay Teachers 11; Students 115; Aides 2.
Convent—Tel: 979-245-3173; Fax: 979-245-6120.
Mission—Sacred Heart Wadsworth, Matagorda Co.

2—OUR LADY OF GUADALUPE, Rev. Gerard Cernoch.
Res.: 1412 12th St., 77414. Tel: 979-245-2010; 979-245-0774 (CCD Office); Fax: 979-245-1038.

BLESSING, MATAGORDA CO., ST. PETER'S, [CEM] [JC] Rev. Samuel Appiasi.
Res.: Box 395, 77419. Tel: 361-588-6241; Fax: 361-588-1421.
Mission—St. Robert Markham, Matagorda Co.

BLOOMINGTON, VICTORIA CO., ST. PATRICK, Rev. Matthew Huehlefeld; Deacon Fred Soto.
Res.: P.O. Box 400, 77951. Tel: 361-897-1155; Fax: 361-897-1064.

CISTERN, FAYETTE CO., SS. CYRIL AND METHODIUS, [CEM 2] [JC 2] Rev. Charles B. Carolan.
Mailing Address: P.O. Box 186, Flatonia, 78941. Tel: 361-865-3568.
Church: 113 Manchester St., Flatonia, 78941. Tel: 361-865-2222.

COLUMBUS, COLORADO CO., ST. ANTHONY'S, [CEM] Rev. Daniel P. Kahlich.
Res.: P.O. Box 669, 78934. Tel: 979-732-2562; Fax: 979-732-8636.
School—635 Bonham, 78934. Tel: 979-732-5505; Fax: 979-732-9758. John O'Leary, Prin. Lay Teachers 12; Students 146.

CUERO, DEWITT CO.

1—ST. MICHAEL, Rev. Kirby Hlavaty; Deacon Anthony B. Warzecha.
Res.: 302 E. Church St., 77954-2906. Tel: 361-275-3554; Fax: 361-277-3924.
School—208 N. McLeod, 77954. Tel: 361-277-3854; Fax: 361-275-3618. Lay Teachers 8; Students 60.

2—OUR LADY OF GUADALUPE, Rev. Kirby Hlavaty.
Res.: 705 W. Broadway, P.O. Box 547, 77954. Tel: 361-277-9062; Fax: 361-275-3135.

EAGLE LAKE, BRAZORIA CO., PARISH OF THE NATIVITY (1995), Rev. Edward J. Winkler.
Res.: 545 S. Austin Rd., P.O. Box 307, 77434. Tel: 979-234-2842; Fax: 979-234-5828.
Catechesis/Religious Program—Students 42.

EAST BERNARD, WHARTON CO., HOLY CROSS, [CEM] Rev. Donald R. Ruppert.
Res.: 839 Church St., P.O. Box 1325, 77435-1325. Tel: 979-335-7551; Fax: 979-335-7038.
Convent—Tel: 979-335-4071.

EDNA, JACKSON CO., ST. AGNES, Rev. Msgr. Michael A. O'Shaughnessy.
Res.: 506 N. Allen, 77957. Tel: 361-782-3588; Fax: 361-782-8827.

EL CAMPO, WHARTON CO.

1—ST. PHILIP THE APOSTLE, [CEM] Revs. Gary W. Janak, J.C.L.; Ty Bazar; Deacons Jarrel Mohavitza; Jerome Grahmann.
Res.: 304 W. Church St., 77437. Tel: 979-543-3770; Fax: 979-578-8831.
School—Tel: 979-543-2901; Fax: 979-578-8835. Lay Teachers 14; Students 177.
Catechesis/Religious Program—Students 198.

2—ST. ROBERT BELLARMINE, Rev. Lawrence Matula; Deacon Margarito Cervantez Jr.
Res.: 512 Tegner St., 77437. Tel: 979-543-4298; Fax: 979-541-5399.

FLATONIA, FAYETTE CO., SACRED HEART, [CEM] [JC] Rev. Charles B. Carolan.
Res.: P.O. Box 186, 78941. Tel: 361-865-3568; Fax: 361-865-2518.

FRELSBURG, COLORADO CO., SS. PETER AND PAUL (1836), [CEM] Rev. Wayne N. Flagg.
Res.: 1031 Church Lane, New Ulm, 78950. Tel: 979-732-3430; Fax: 979-732-9204.

GANADO, JACKSON CO., ASSUMPTION OF THE B.V.M., [CEM] Rev. Joseph Hybner.
Mailing Address: P.O. Box 369, 77962. Tel 361-771-3425; Fax: 361-771-3526.
Res.: 108 S. Sixth St., 77962.

GOLIAD, GOLIAD CO., IMMACULATE CONCEPTION, [CEM 2] Rev. Raphael Baidoo, O.SS.T.
Res.: P.O. Box 49, 77963. Tel: 361-645-3095.
Mission—Our Lady of Guadalupe Charco, Goliad Co.
Mission—Our Lady of Assumption Fannin, Goliad Co.
Shrine—Our Lady of Loreto (Old Franciscan Mission)

HALLETTSVILLE, LAVACA CO.

1—ST. MARY, [CEM 4] Rev. John C. Peters, V.F.
Church: 1648 FM 340, 77964. Tel: 361-798-2128; Fax: 361-798-4970.

2—SACRED HEART, [CEM] Revs. John C. Peters, V.F.; Robert Guerra; Deacons Joey Targac; W.S. (Sonny) Rogers.
Res.: P.O. Box H, 77964. Tel: 361-798-5388; Fax: 361-798-4970.
School—Tel: 361-798-4251; Fax: 361-798-4970. Mr. David Smolik, Prin. (Elementary & High School). Sisters 1; Lay Teachers 15; Students 160.
High School—313 S. Texana, 77964. Sisters 1; Lay Teachers 10; Students 112.

HIGH HILL, FAYETTE CO., NATIVITY OF THE BLESSED VIRGIN MARY, [CEM] Rev. Timothy Kosler, Admin.
Mailing Address: 2833 FM 2672, Schulenburg, 78956-5608. Tel: 979-561-8455.
Res.: 1010 Lyons Ave., Box 310, Schulenburg, 78956. Tel: 979-743-3117.

HILLJE, WHARTON CO., ST. ANDREW, [CEM] Rev. Clement Quainoo; Deacon Edward Wendel.
Mailing Address: Rte. 3, Box 39, El Campo, 77437. Tel: 979-643-2864; Fax: 979-648-2024.
Mission—St. Procopius [CEM] Louise, Wharton Co.

HOSTYN, FAYETTE CO., HOLY ROSARY, [CEM] Rev. Msgr. Stanley J. Petru.
Res.: 936 FM 2436, La Grange, 78945. Tel 979-247-4441; Fax: 979-247-5008.

HUNGERFORD, WHARTON CO., ST. JOHN THE BAPTIST, [CEM] Rev. Henry C. Rachunek.
Res.: P.O. Box 121, 77448. Tel: 979-532-4747; Fax: 979-532-8713.

INEZ, VICTORIA CO., ST. JOSEPH'S, [CEM] [JC 5] Sr. Barbara J. Bacak, S.S.N.D., Pastoral Life Delegate.
Res.: P.O. Box 337, 77968. Tel: 361-782-5181; Fax: 361-782-3181.

KOERTH, LAVACA CO., ST. JOHN THE BAPTIST, [CEM] [JC] Rev. Charles Sonnier.
Res.: P.O. Box 201, Sweet Home, 77987. Tel: 361-741-3206; Fax: 361-741-3206.

MENTZ, COLORADO CO., ST. ROCH (1850), [CEM] Rev. Wayne N. Flagg; Deacon Douglas B. Tromblee.
Mailing Address: 1600 Frelsburg Rd., Alleyton, 78935. Tel: 979-732-3460; Fax: 979-733-0908.

MEYERSVILLE, DEWITT CO., SS. PETER & PAUL, Rev. Michael Petering, Admin.
Res.: 11220 FM 237, 77974. Tel: 361-275-3868; Fax: 361-277-8972.
Mission—St. Aloysius Westhoff, DeWitt Co.

MOULTON, LAVACA CO., ST. JOSEPH'S, [CEM] Rev. Gabriel Maison, J.C.D.
Res.: P.O. Box 399, 77975. Tel: 361-596-4674; Fax: 361-596-4826.

NADA, COLORADO CO., NATIVITY OF THE BLESSED VIRGIN MARY, [CEM] Rev. Joseph A. Koebel.
Res.: P.O. Box 97, 77460. Tel: 979-758-3218; Fax: 979-758-3267.

NEW TAITON, WHARTON CO., ST. JOHN NEPOMUCENE, [CEM] Rev. Joseph A. Koebel, Admin.
Res.: Rte. 1, Box 250, El Campo, 77437. Tel: 979-543-6985; Fax: 979-543-3434.

PALACIOS, MATAGORDA CO., ST. ANTHONY'S, Rev. Charles Dwomoh; Deacon Michael Vieira.
Res.: 1004 Magnusson, Box 900, 77465. Tel: 361-972-2446; Fax: 361-972-2606.
Vietnamese Apostolate—100 Vietnam, 77465. Tel: 361-972-2685. Rev. Joseph Pham duc Trin.

PLUM, FAYETTE CO., SS. PETER AND PAUL, [CEM 2] Rev. Msgr. Stanley J. Petru.
Res.: 936 FM 2436, La Grange, 78945. Tel: 979-247-4441; Fax: 979-247-5008.

PORT LAVACA, CALHOUN CO., OUR LADY OF THE GULF, Revs. Dan Morales; Ty Bazar; Deacon Kenneth Ryan.
Res.: 319 S. Nueces St., P.O. Box 87, 77979. Tel: 361-552-6140; Fax: 361-552-4300.
School—Preschool/Day Care, 412 W. Austin St., 77979. Kim Windham, Dir. Lay Teachers 11; Students 80.
School—Tel: 361-552-2774; Fax: 361-552-7485. Sr. Mary Ana Steele, O.S.F., Prin. Sisters 3; Lay Teachers 7; Students 90.
Catechesis/Religious Program— Linda Beard, D.R.E. Students 434.
Mission—St. Ann Point Comfort, Calhoun Co.
Mission—St. Joseph Port O'Connor, Calhoun Co.
Mission—St. Patrick Seadrift, Calhoun Co.

PRAHA, FAYETTE CO., ST. MARY'S, [CEM] Rev. Edward C. Bartsch.
Res.: 821 FM 1295, Flatonia, 78941. Tel: 361-865-3560.

ST. JOHN, FAYETTE CO., ST. JOHN THE BAPTIST, [CEM] Revs. John C. Peters, V.F.; Robert Guerra.
Res.: P.O. Drawer H, Hallettsville, 77964. Tel: 361-798-5888; Fax: 361-798-4970.
Mission—Ascension of Our Lord [CEM] Moravia, Lavaca Co.

SCHULENBURG, FAYETTE CO., ST. ROSE OF LIMA, [CEM] Revs. Timothy Kosler, V.F.; Frank B. Lenz.
Res.: 1010 Lyons Ave., Box 310, 78956. Tel: 979-743-3117; Fax: 979-743-4712.
School—405 Black, 78956. Tel: 979-743-3080; Fax: 979-743-4228. Mrs. Peggy Kusy, Prin. Lay Teachers 14; Students 133.

SHINER, LAVACA CO., SS. CYRIL AND METHODIUS, [CEM] Revs. Robert E. Knippenberg; Donald Hayden, O.SS.T.; Deacon Paul Patek.
Res.: 306 S. Ave. F, P.O. Box 66, 77984. Tel: 361-594-3836; Fax: 361-594-2850.
School—Elementary School, Tel: 361-594-3843; Fax: 361-594-8599. Mr. James Herndon, Prin. Sisters 1; Lay Teachers 11; Students 188.
High School—Tel: 361-594-2313. Mr. James Herndon, Prin. Sisters of the Incarnate Word and Blessed Sacrament 1; Lay Teachers 8; Students 75.

SWEET HOME, LAVACA CO., QUEEN OF PEACE, [CEM] [JC] Rev. Charles Sonnier.
Res.: P.O. Box 201, 77987. Tel: 361-741-3206; Fax: 361-741-3206.

VANDERBILT, JACKSON CO., ST. JOHN BOSCO, Rev. Johnson Owusu-Boateng.
Office—232 Main St., P.O. Box 337, 77991-0337. Tel: 361-284-3361.
Res.: 121 Garcitas St., P.O. Box 337, 77991. Tel: 361-284-3361.
Mission—St. Theresa [CEM] LaSalle, Jackson Co.

WEIMAR, COLORADO CO., ST. MICHAEL, [CEM] Rev. John C. Bily.
Res.: Box 36, 78962. Tel: 979-725-6714.
School—Tel: 979-725-8461; Fax: 979-725-8344. Sr. M. Laura Toman, I.W.B.S., Prin. Sisters of the Incarnate Word and Blessed Sacrament 2; Lay Teachers 9; Students 133.
Mission—SS. Cyril and Methodius Dubina, Fayette Co.

WHARTON, WHARTON CO.

1—HOLY FAMILY, [JC] Rev. Joseph L. Vrana; Deacon

Alvin Matthys.
Res.: 2011 Briar Ln., 77488. Tel: 979-532-3593.
Mission—St. Joseph Boling, Wharton Co.
2—OUR LADY OF MT. CARMEL, [JC] Rev. Raymond A. Jackson, C.S.B.
Res.: 506 S. East Ave., 77488. Tel: 979-532-3492; Fax: 979-532-2321.
YOAKUM, LAVACA CO., ST. JOSEPH, [CEM] Rev. Roger Hawes.
Res.: 210 Schrimscher St., Box 734, 77995. Tel: 361-293-3518; 361-741-5302; Fax: 361-293-3004.
School—Tel: 361-741-5362; Fax: 361-293-3004. Sr. Isabel Estrada, I.W.B.S., Prin. Sisters of the Incarnate & Blessed Sacrament 2; Lay Teachers 18; Students 139.
Mission—St. Ann [CEM] Hochheim, DeWitt Co.
YORKTOWN, DEWITT CO., HOLY CROSS, [CEM 2] Rev. Donald Hayden, O.SS.T., Admin. Pro. Tem.
Res.: 1214 Zorn Rd., 78164-1907. Tel: 361-564-2893; Fax: 361-564-9315.
Mission—San Luis, DeWitt Co.
Mission—St. Ann's Nordheim, DeWitt Co.

On Special or Other Diocesan Assignment:
Rev. Msgr.—
McLaughlin, Thomas C., V.G., Vicar Gen. & Chancellor. Tel: 361-573-0828

Rev.—
Franks, Gabriel, Hospital Chap., 103 D Sherwood Dr., 77901. Tel: 361-579-6895

On Duty Outside the Diocese:
Rev. Msgr.—
Anders, Arnold
Revs.—
Henninger, George, Indianapolis, IN
Mensah, Gabriel, Military Chap., U.S. Navy
Olguin, Jacinto, Laredo

On Leave of Absence:
Revs.—
Lyons, Michael
Nguyen, Thu Van

Retired:
Rev. Msgrs.—
Bernasconi, Gino
Hermes, Eustace
Schmidtzinsky, Victor
Thurmond, Benton
Revs.—
Caponi, Jerome
Higgins, Peter
Janson, Eugene
O'Brien, Daniel
Quiroz, Guido M.

Permanent Deacons:
Borowicz, Stephen James Michael
Calzada, Alonzo Farias
Cervantez, Margarito Candelario, Jr.
Grahmann, Jerome J.
Harper, Linard
Holesovsky, Bennie
Koenig, James Nicholas
Matthys, Alvin
Molina, Edwardo Pina
Nohavitza, Jarrel Joseph
Patek, Paul, Sr.
Perez, Jesus Castillo
Rodriguez, Guadalupe
Rogers, Walter Smith, Jr.
Ryan, Ken
Soto, Fred
Targac, Joseph
Tran, Luan Van
Tromblee, Douglas B.
Vieira, Michael
Warzecha, Anthony
Wearden, Arthur R.
Wendel, Edward

INSTITUTIONS LOCATED IN THE DIOCESE

[A] HIGH SCHOOLS, PRIVATE

VICTORIA. *St. Joseph High School*, 110 E. Red River, 77901. Tel: 361-573-2446; Fax: 361-573-4221. Email: bmcardle@stjvic.org. Web: www.stjvic.org. Mr. William H. McArdle Jr., Pres./Prin. Lay Teachers 31; Students 337.

[B] ELEMENTARY SCHOOLS, PRIVATE

VICTORIA. *Nazareth Academy*, 206 W. Convent, 77901. Tel: 361-573-6651; Fax: 361-573-1829. Email: nazareth@icsi.net. Web: www.nazareth.academy.org. Sr. Kathleen Goike, I.W.B.S., Prin. Attended from St. Mary's, Our Lady of Lourdes, Our Lady of Victory, Holy Family and Our Lady of Sorrows' Churches Sisters of the Incarnate Word and Blessed Sacrament 8; Lay Teachers 27; Students 245.

[C] HOMES FOR AGED

HILLJE. *Czech Catholic Home For The Aged*, Rte. 3, Box 40, El Campo, 77437. Tel: 979-648-2628; Fax: 979-648-2884. Email: czechome@wcnet.net.

[D] PERSONAL PRELATURES

SCHULENBURG. *Opus Dei, Featherock Conference Center*, 934 Holub Rd., 78956-5324. Tel: 979-743-4642.

[E] CONVENTS AND RESIDENCES FOR SISTERS

PORT LAVACA. *Vietnamese Community, Our Lady of the Gulf Convent*, 415 W. Austin St., 77979. Tel: 361-552-3670. Sr. Theresa Hoa Trinh, O.P., Supr.

VICTORIA. *Franciscan Monastery of St. Clare*, 107 N. Depot St., 77901. Tel: 361-576-6347. Email: poorclares@cox-internet.com. Web: www.poorclaresvictoria.org. Sr. Katherine Vallone, O.S.C., Supr.

Incarnate Word Convent, 1101 N.E. Water St., 77901-9298. Tel: 361-575-2266; Fax: 361-575-2165. Sisters Evelyn Korenek, I.W.B.S., Supr. Gen.; Lois Marie Etzler, Local Supr. Sisters 52.

Missionary Catechists of the Sacred Hearts of Jesus and Mary, 209 W. Murray St., 77901. Tel: 361-575-7654. Sr. Susana Islas, M.C., Supr. Sisters 4.

[F] MONASTERIES & RESIDENCES OF PRIESTS & BROTHERS

VICTORIA. *Trinity House* Novitiate Holy Trinity Fathers. , 1511 E. Commercial St., 77901. Tel: 361-573-7059. Email: damonosst@aol.com. Rev. Damon Geiger, O.SS.T.

[G] MISCELLANEOUS

VICTORIA. *Endowment Fund for the Catholic Diocese of Victoria in Texas*, P.O. Box 4070, 77903-4070. Tel: 361-573-0828; Fax: 361-573-5725. Email: jjoseph@victoriadiocese.org. Web: www.victoriadiocese.org. Mr. Arthur R. Wearden, Mailing Contact.

Jeanne Chezard De Matel Fund, 1101 N.E. Water St., 77901-9298. Tel: 361-575-2266; Fax: 361-575-2165. Email: srevelynk@yahoo.com.

Sisters of the Incarnate Word and Blessed Sacrament of Victoria, Texas, Medical and Retirement Trust, 1011 N.E. Water St., 77901-9298. Tel: 361-572-9321; Fax: 361-575-2165.

Sisters of the Incarnate Word and Blessed Sacrament, Victoria, Texas, Inc., 1101 N.E. Water St., 77901-9298. Tel: 361-575-2266; Fax: 361-575-2165. Email: srevelynk@yahoo.com. Sr. Evelyn Korenek, I.W.B.S., Supr. Gen. & Mailing Contact.

RELIGIOUS INSTITUTES OF WOMEN REPRESENTED IN THE DIOCESE

For further details refer to the corresponding bracketed number in the Religious Institutes of Men or Women section.

[2200]—*Congregation of the Incarnate Word and Blessed Sacrament*—I.W.B.S.

[2700]—*Missionary Catechists of the Sacred Hearts of Jesus and Mary*—M.C.SS.CC.

[3760]—*Order of St. Clare*—O.S.C.

[]—*School Sisters of Notre Dame*

[]—*School Sisters of St. Francis*—S.S.S.F.

[0460]—*Sisters of Charity of Incarnate Word*—C.C.V.I.

[1010]—*Sisters of the Divine Providence of San Antonio, Texas*—C.D.P.

[]—*Sisters of the Sacred Heart of Jesus*—S.S.H.J.

[]—*Vietnamese Dominican Sisters*—O.P.

NECROLOGY

† Crookes, Brian—Died Feb. 24, 2003
† Kaplinski, Peter, Yorktown, TX Holy Cross—Died April 7, 2003

Archdiocese of Washington

(Archidioecesis Washingtonensis)

His Eminence

JAMES CARDINAL HICKEY, S.T.D., J.C.D.

Archbishop Emeritus of Washington; ordained June 15, 1946; appointed Titular Bishop of Taraqua and Auxiliary Bishop of Saginaw, February 18, 1967; Episcopal ordination April 14, 1967; appointed Bishop of Cleveland May 31, 1974; installed July 16, 1974; appointed Archbishop of Washington June 17, 1980; installed August 5, 1980; created Cardinal June 28, 1988 *Office: Archdiocesan Pastoral Center,* 5001 Eastern Ave., Hyattsville, MD 20782-3447. *Mailing Address: P.O. Box 29260, Washington, DC 20017-0260.* Tel: 301-853-4500; Fax: 301-853-5346.

Most Reverend

LEONARD J. OLIVIER, S.V.D., D.D., V.G.

Auxiliary Bishop of Washington; ordained June 29, 1951; appointed Auxiliary Bishop of Washington and Titular Bishop of Legia November 10, 1988; Episcopal ordination December 20, 1988 *Res.: 2657 Woodley Rd., N.W., Washington, DC 20008.* Tel: 202-667-2553; Fax: 202-667-3690.

His Eminence

THEODORE CARDINAL McCARRICK, Ph.D., D.D.

Archbishop of Washington; ordained May 31, 1958; appointed Auxiliary Bishop of New York and Titular Bishop of Rusibisir May 24, 1977; Episcopal ordination June 29, 1977; appointed First Bishop of Metuchen November 19, 1981; installed January 31, 1982; appointed Archbishop of Newark May 30, 1986; installed July 25, 1986; appointed Archbishop of Washington November 21, 2000; installed January 3, 2001; created Cardinal priest of Saints Nereus and Achilleus February 21, 2001 *Office: Archdiocesan Pastoral Center,* 5001 Eastern Ave., Hyattsville, MD 20782-3447. *Mailing Address: P.O. Box 29260, Washington, DC 20017-0260.* Tel: 301-853 4540; Fax: 301-853-5359.

Archdiocesan Pastoral Center: 5001 Eastern Ave., P.O. Box 29260, Washington, DC 20017. Tel: 301-853-4500; Fax: 301-853-5346.

Email: chancery@adw.org

Most Reverend

KEVIN J. FARRELL, D.D., V.G.

Auxiliary Bishop of Washington; ordained December 24, 1978; appointed Auxiliary Bishop of Washington and Titular Bishop of Rusuccuru December 28, 2001; Episcopal ordination February 11, 2002 *Office: 5001 Eastern Ave., P.O. Box 29260, Washington, DC 20017.*

Most Reverend

FRANCISCO GONZALEZ, S.F., D.D., V.G.

Auxiliary Bishop of Washington; ordained May 1, 1964; appointed Auxiliary Bishop of Washington and Titular Bishop of Lamfua December 28, 2001; Episcopal ordination February 11, 2002 *Office: 5001 Eastern Ave., P.O. Box 29260, Washington, DC 20017.*

Square Miles 2,104.

Established Archdiocese July 22, 1939; Separated from Baltimore November 15, 1947; Became a Metropolitan See October 12, 1965.

Comprises the District of Columbia and Montgomery, Prince George's, St. Mary's, Calvert and Charles Counties in Maryland.

The Province of Washington has as a Suffragan, the Diocese of St. Thomas in the Virgin Islands.

For legal titles of parishes and archdiocesan institutions, consult the Chancery Office.

STATISTICAL OVERVIEW

Personnel	
Cardinals	1
Retired Cardinals	1
Auxiliary Bishops	3
Abbots	1
Retired Abbots	2
Priests: Diocesan Active in Diocese	201
Priests: Diocesan Active Outside Diocese	29
Priests: Diocesan in Foreign Missions	1
Priests: Retired, Sick or Absent	78
Number of Diocesan Priests	309
Religious Priests in Diocese	606
Total Priests in Diocese	915
Extern Priests in Diocese	196
Ordinations:	
Diocesan Priests	9
Religious Priests	3
Transitional Deacons	14
Permanent Deacons	1
Permanent Deacons in Diocese	237
Total Brothers	136
Total Sisters	734
Parishes	
Parishes	140
With Resident Pastor:	
Resident Diocesan Priests	124
Resident Religious Priests	16
Missions	9
Pastoral Centers	1
Professional Ministry Personnel:	
Brothers	3
Sisters	34
Lay Ministers	420
Welfare	
Catholic Hospitals	3
Total Assisted	502,000
Health Care Centers	7
Total Assisted	209,414
Homes for the Aged	16
Total Assisted	1,364
Residential Care of Children	1
Total Assisted	402
Day Care Centers	7
Total Assisted	437
Specialized Homes	13
Total Assisted	386
Special Centers for Social Services	76
Total Assisted	137,343
Residential Care of Disabled	49
Total Assisted	213
Other Institutions	22
Total Assisted	6,754
Educational	
Seminaries, Diocesan	2
Students from This Diocese	18
Students from Other Diocese	64
Diocesan Students in Other Seminaries	38
Seminaries, Religious	30
Students Religious	158
Total Seminarians	214
Colleges and Universities	3
Total Students	20,215
High Schools, Diocesan and Parish	1
Total Students	610
High Schools, Private	15
Total Students	8,760
Elementary Schools, Diocesan and Parish	85
Total Students	22,140
Elementary Schools, Private	10
Total Students	1,987
Non-residential Schools for the Disabled	1
Total Students	157
Catechesis/Religious Education:	
High School Students	2,103
Elementary Students	21,098
Total Students under Catholic Instruction	77,284
Teachers in the Diocese:	
Priests	29
Brothers	28
Sisters	66
Lay Teachers	2,464
Vital Statistics	
Receptions into the Church:	
Infant Baptism Totals	5,640
Adult Baptism Totals	2,001
Received into Full Communion	496
First Communions	6,821
Confirmations	5,333
Marriages:	
Catholic	1,210
Interfaith	788
Total Marriages	1,998
Deaths	3,139
Total Catholic Population	567,266
Total Population	2,614,128

Former Bishops—Most Rev. MICHAEL J. CURLEY, D.D., consecrated Bishop of St. Augustine, June 30, 1914; promoted to the See of Baltimore, Aug. 10, 1921; named Archbishop of Baltimore and Washington, July 22, 1939; died May 16, 1947; His Eminence PATRICK CARDINAL O'BOYLE (Retired), consecrated Jan. 14, 1948; retired March 3, 1973; died Aug. 10, 1987; WILLIAM CARDINAL BAUM, installed May 8, 1973; appt. Prefect, Congregation for Catholic Education in the Vatican, Jan. 15, 1980; Major Penitentiary; appt. April 6, 1990; JAMES CARDINAL HICKEY, S.T.D., J.C.D. (Retired), ord. Auxiliary Bishop of Saginaw April 14, 1967; appt. Bishop of Cleveland June 5, 1974; appt. Archbishop of Washington June 17, 1980; installed Aug. 5, 1980; created Cardinal June 28, 1988; retired Nov. 21, 2000.

Unless otherwise indicated, all Archdiocesan Offices, including the Chancery and the Tribunal, are located in the Archdiocesan Pastoral Center, 5001 Eastern Ave., P.O. Box 29260, Washington, 20017. Tel: 301-853-4500; Fax: 301-853-5346.; Office Hours: Mon.-Fri. 8:30-5

Vicars General—Most Revs. LEONARD J. OLIVIER, S.V.D., D.D.; KEVIN FARRELL, Vicar Gen. Admin.; FRANCISCO GONZALEZ, S.F., D.D., V.G., Episcopal Vicar for Hispanic Catholics; Rev. Msgr. GODFREY MOSLEY, Vicar Gen. for the Apostolate, Our Lady Queen of the Americas, 2200 California St., N.W., Washington, 20008-3902. Tel: 202-332-8838; Fax: 202-332-2967.

Moderator of the Curia—Bro. KEVIN FARRELL, V.G.

Chancellor—Mrs. JANE GOLDEN BELFORD, Esq. Tel: 301-853-4520; Fax: 301-853-7676.

Delegate to Ordinary—Rev. Msgr. BERNARD C. GERHARDT, S.T.L., J.C.D., P.A. Tel: 301-853-4520; Fax: 301-853-5346.

Canonical Consultant to the Cardinal—Sr. ELIZABETH McDONOUGH, O.P., J.C.D., S.T.L.

Archivist—Deacon BERNARD A. BERNIER. Tel: 301-853-5316.

Secretary To The Archbishop—Rev. Msgr. BARRY KNESTOUT; Rev. EDWARD J. FILARDI. Tel: 301-853-4539; 301-853-4540; Fax: 301-853-5359.

Secretariats—Sr. BERNADETTE GLODEK, S.N.D.,

Catholic Education; Rev. WALTER J. TAPPE, Parish Life & Worship; Rev. Msgr. MICHAEL J. MELLONE, Clergy; Sr. REBECCA BURKE, O.S.F., Women Religious; Most Rev. KEVIN FARRELL, Finance & Mgmt.; Mr. CHARLES SHORT, Social Concerns, Communications (See Separate sections below).

Executive Directors—Rev. Msgr. RAYMOND EAST, Office of Black Catholics; Sr. ONELLYS VILLEGAS, M.H.S.H., Office of Hispanic Pastoral Affairs, (See separate sections below).

Office of Child Protection Services—MARIA D. ZVARA, M.S.W., LCSW-C. Tel: 301-853-5328; Fax: 301-853-2787. Email: mzvara@adw.org.

The Tribunal

Tribunal—Tel: 301-853-4543; Fax: 301-853-7674.

Judicial Vicar—Rev. Msgr. JOSEPH F. SADUSKY, M.Div., M.Ch.A., J.C.D. Tel: 301-853-4544.

Assistant Judicial Vicar—Rev. Msgr. GODFREY T. MOSLEY, J.C.D. Tel: 301-853-4543.

Judges—Rev. Msgrs. BERNARD C. GERHARDT, S.T.L., J.C.D., P.A. Tel: 301-853-4535; GEORGE E. DOBES, J.C.L. Tel: 301-853-4543; Revs. CHARLES V. ANTONICELLI, J.C.L. Tel: 301-853-4543; G. PAUL HERBERT, J.C.L. Tel: 301-853-5326; FRANCIS G. HORN, O.S.A., J.C.D. Tel: 301-853-4543; VINCENT RIGDON, M.A., J.C.L. Tel: 301-853-4528; Fax: 301-853-7684; GEORGE E. STUART, J.C.L. Tel: 301-853-5327; MARK E. TUCKER, C.SS.R., J.C.L. Tel: 301-853-5322; Sr. ELIZABETH MCDONOUGH, O.P., J.C.D., S.T.L. Tel: 301-853-4543.

Promoter of Justice—Rev. DAVID F. O'CONNOR, S.T., J.C.D. Tel: 301-853-5319.

Defenders of the Bond—Revs. DAVID F. O'CONNOR, S.T., J.C.D. Tel: 301-853-5319; JOSEPH BUI TRANGH-NGHIEM, M.S., S.T.L., J.U.D. Tel: 301-853-5320; Rev. Msgr. KEVIN T. HART, J.C.D. Tel: 301-853-4543; Rev. MICHAEL J. KING, J.C.D. Tel: 301-853-4543.

Advocates—Rev. Msgr. PETER VAGHI, J.D. Tel: 301-853-4543; Revs. ROBERT G. AMEY. Tel: 301-853-4543; MARK E. BRENNAN. Tel: 301-853-4543; DONALD BRICE. Tel: 301-853-4536; JOHN T. DAKES, S.T.L. Tel: 301-853-4543; GEORGE E. GOLDEN, M.Div. Tel: 301-853-4543; PAUL D. LEE, S.T.D. Tel: 301-853-4543.

Notaries—Mrs. PATRICIA A. PERKINSON. Tel: 301-853-4544; Mrs. DENISE SMITH. Tel: 301-853-5324; Sr. MARY PAUL, O.P. Tel: 301-853-4543; Mr. MARK ADKINSON. Tel: 301-853-4515.

Consultative Groups

Archdiocesan College of Consultors—Bro. KEVIN FARRELL, V.G.; Most Revs. LEONARD J. OLIVIER, S.V.D., D.D.; FRANCISCO GONZALEZ, S.F.; Rev. Msgrs. THOMAS M. DUFFY; RAYMOND G. EAST; WILLIAM J. ENGLISH; JOHN J. ENZLER; DONALD S. ESSEX; BERNARD C. GERHARDT, S.T.L., J.C.D., P.A.; KEVIN HART; W. RONALD JAMESON; WILLIAM J. KANE; THOMAS A. KANE; GODFREY T. MOSLEY, J.C.D.

Archdiocesan Pastoral Council—His Eminence THEODORE CARDINAL MCCARRICK, Ph.D., D.D.; Mr. JOHN BADEN; Mr. CHARLES J. BIEBERICH; Ms. SARA BETH BODENHORN; Mr. JAMES CURTIS; Mr. EARL HAMILTON; Ms. BRENDA JOHNSON; Mr. PETER A. LALENA; Mr. MICHAEL MORA; Ms. MARGE NEAL; Ms. CAROLYN NG; Ms. MARY ANNE PATCHAN; Mr. JUAN PROANO; Mrs. DOLORES STEINHILBER; Mr. BINH TRAN; Mr. JOSEPH WARD; Mr. ED WHALEN; Ms. CATHERINE ZEGOWITZ.

Archdiocesan Finance Council—His Eminence THEODORE CARDINAL MCCARRICK, Ph.D., D.D. Staff: Most Rev. KEVIN FARRELL; Rev. Msgr. GODFREY MOSLEY; Mrs. JANE GOLDEN BELFORD, Esq.; RICHARD GRAVES; ROBERT B. MCCAIN; W. SHEPHERDSON ABELL, Esq.; JEREMIAH C. COLLINS; Sr. CAROL KEEHAN, D.D.; THOMAS P. RODDY; B. FRANCIS SAUL II; CAROL BATES; LOUIS J. FREEH, Esq.; WILLIAM J. SHAW; KATHY MCKINLESS.

Deans—Revs. MICHAEL WILSON, Northern Prince George's County; J. WILLIAM HINES, Middle Prince George's County; CHARLES MCCANN, Southern Prince George's County; THOMAS KALITA, Upper Montgomery County; JAMES P. MEYERS, Middle Montgomery County; FRANCIS KAZISTA, Lower Montgomery County; EDDIE TOLENTINO, Northeast, D.C.; Rev. Msgrs. PETER J. VAGHI, Northwest East, D.C.; W. RONALD JAMESON, Northwest West, D.C.; Rev. CHARLES POPE, Southeast, D.C.; Rev. Msgr. PAUL DUDZIAK, Calvert County; VACANT, Charles County; Rev. FRANCIS J. EARLY, St. Mary's County.

Council of Priests—His Eminence THEODORE CARDINAL MCCARRICK, Ph.D., D.D., Pres.; Rev. Msgr. PETER J. VAGHI, Exec. Dir.

Secretariat For Education

Secretary for Catholic Education—Sr. BERNADETTE GLODEK, S.N.D. Tel: 301-853-4519; Fax: 301-853-7691.

Superintendent of Schools—PATRICIA WEITZEL-O'NEILL, Ph.D. Tel: 301-853-5348; Fax: 301-853-7670.

Assistant Superintendent for Secondary Schools—MICHAEL CARUSO, Ph.D. Tel: 301-853-5357.

Assistant Superintendent for Elementary Schools—KATHLEEN SCHWARTZ, Ph.D. Tel: 301-853-4553.

Director of Curriculum Services—DENISE HUNT. Tel: 301-853-5353.

Director of School Personnel—Rev. JOSEPH R. SILEO. Tel: 301-853-4549.

Director of Instructional Services—Tel: 301-853-4590.

Director of Professional Development—Rev. JOSEPH SILEO, Ph.D. Tel: 301-853-4552.

Director of Student Services—Rev. JOSEPH SILEO, Ph.D. Tel: 301-853-4569.

Director of Educational Support Services—Ms. PAMELA ALLEN. Tel: 703-461-7802; 301-853-4569.

Director of Latino and Multicultural Student Initiatives—Ms. BETTY RIVERA. Tel: 301-853-4552.

Tuition Assistance Coordinator—Ms. LILLIAN RODRIGUEZ. Tel: 301-853-5356.

Executive Director Center City Consortium—Mrs. MARY ANNE STANTON, 1317 Eighth St., N.W., Washington, 20001. Tel: 202-234-4611; Fax: 202-234-4740.

Board of Education—Ms. LIDIA CARRERA, Pres. Tel: 301-424-5813.

Office of Youth Ministry/CYO—DEBBIE MCDONALD, Exec. Dir. Tel: 202-281-2467; Fax: 202-281-2470.

Our Lady of Mattaponi Retreat Center—Rev. ROBERT MORDINO, Dir. Tel: 301-952-9074; Fax: 301-952-0609.

CYO Programs—THOMAS J. MANCO, Dir. Tel: 202-281-2463; JAMES QUINN, Asst. to Dir. Tel: 202-281-2465.

Coordinator for Young Adult Ministry—PETER NEWBURN. Tel: 301-853-4559.

Ministry Development Coordinator Adult Training—DEBBIE MCDONALD. Tel: 202-281-2466.

Hispanic Youth Ministry—Rev. FRANCO LIPORACE. Tel: 202-281-2476.

African American Youth Ministry—DARREN FOSTER. Tel: 202-281-2469.

Scouting—Rev. Msgr. JOHN BRADY, Chap. Coord. Tel: 301-769-3332; FRANK ROSSOMONDO, Arch. Lay Coord., Catholic Comm. Boy Scouts & Camp Fire. Tel: 301-770-7450; ROBERT KAMMER, Arch. Lay Chm., Catholic Comm. Boy Scouting. Tel: 301-942-0882; JOAN TREACY, Arch. Chm., Girl Scouts. Tel: 301-924-0394; ROSE MARY PEZUTTO, Camp Fire Lay Coord. Tel: 301-262-1631.

Our Lady of Mattaponi Youth Retreat and Conference Center—Tel: 301-952-9074; Fax: 301-952-0609.

Office for Religious Education—Mr. LAWRENCE RILLA, S.T.L., Dir. Tel: 301-853-5368; Fax: 301-853-7687.

Hearts Aflame Program—Rev. R. SCOTT HURD, Dir. Tel: 301-853-5386.

Catechist Formation Coordinator—CAROLYN MCCART. Tel: 301-853-4531.

At-Large Field Representative—Tel: 301-853-5384.

Hispanic Catholics Religious Education—Sr. MARIA LUZ ORTIZ, M.H.S.H. Tel: 301-853-5384.

Special Religious Education—DOLORES WILSON, Coord. Tel: 301-853-4560.

Propagation of the Faith—Rev. VINCENT J. RIGDON, J.C.L., Archdiocesan Dir. Tel: 301-853-4528; Fax: 301-853-7674.

Mission Education Coordinator—Sr. MARIE DELA TRINITE, S.S.V.M. Tel: 301-853-4534.

Holy Childhood Association—Rev. VINCENT J. RIGDON, J.C.L., Dir. Tel: 301-853-4528.

Sacred Heart Basic Adult Education Center—JOSEPH SHERMAN, Dir.; KRISTINA BOYLAN, Asst. Dir. Tel: 202-462-6499.

Secretariat For Parish Life and Worship

Secretary for Parish Life and Worship—Rev. WALTER J. TAPPE, Sec. Tel: 301-853-4558; Fax: 301-853-7685; Mrs. MARGARET POLLARD, Admin. Asst. Tel: 301-853-4558; Fax: 301-853-7685.

Office for Adult Religious Formation—Mr. THOMAS BURNFORD, Dir. Tel: 301-853-5331; Fax: 301-853-7660.

Ministry to Young Adults—Mr. JOHN GRAVELINE, Coord. Tel: 301-853-4559.

Office for Ecumenical and Interreligious Affairs—Rev. PAUL LEE, Dir. Tel: 202-337-4835.

Office for Evangelization—Ms. MARTHA FERNANDEZ-SARDINA, Dir. Tel: 301-853-4596.

Office of Family Life—Mr. NICK BAGILEO, Dir. Tel: 301-853-4561; Fax: 301-853-7660; Mr. JOAQUIN TREJO, Coord., Marriage Prep & Hispanic Family Life. Tel: 301-853-4551.

Natural Family Planning—Mr. WILLIAM GORMAN, Coord. Tel: 301-853-4567.

Office for Ministry to Persons with Disabilities—Ms. DOLORES WILSON, Dir. Tel: 301-853-4560.

Office of Worship—Rev. WALTER J. TAPPE, Dir. Tel: 301-853-4594; JEFFREY MCGARRITY, Coord., RCIA Initiation of Children. Tel: 301-853-5335; Sr. CONSTANCE WARD, S.S.J., Admin. Asst. Tel: 301-853-4594; Fax: 301-853-7684; MAGDALENA GUTTIEREZ, Coord., Hispanic Liturgy & RCIA. Tel: 301-853-5334.

Charismatic Renewal Regional Service Committee—Deacon DONALD DEROZE; Mrs. DONALD DEROZE, 13103 Tamarack Rd., Silver Spring, MD 20994. Tel: 301-384-5568.

Cursillo Movement—Rev. PETER ALLIATA, Spiritual Dir., St. James Parish, 3628 Rhode Island Ave., Mount Rainier, MD 20712. Tel: 301-927-0567. Directors: LAVERNIS STEEN. Tel: 202-529-5817; VINCENT JORDAN. Tel: 301-630-0865.

St. Francis of Assisi Catholic Church and Center for the Deaf—Rev. GERARD A. TRANCONE, Dir., 7202 Buchanan St., Landover Hills, MD 20784. Tel: 301-459-7464; Fax: 301-459-8186.

Ministry for the Deaf—Rev. GERARD A. TRANCONE, Gallaudet University, 800 Florida Ave., N.E., Washington, 20002. Tel: 301-577-3527 (Voice & TDD).

Holy Name Society—Rev. Msgr. THOMAS A. KANE, 4101 Norbeck Rd., Rockville, MD 20853. Tel: 301-924-2284; Fax: 301-929-3017.

Ancient Order of Hibernians—Mr. JAMES CLARKE, 7108 Plantation Ln., Rockville, MD 20852. Tel: 301-881-4512.

Archdiocesan Council of Catholic Women—Rev. ROBERT G. AMEY, Spiritual Dir., 11801 Claridge Rd., Wheaton, MD 20705. Tel: 301-946-3636; Fax: 301-946-5061; Mrs. ELIZABETH JONES, Pres., 2713 Henderson Ave., Silver Spring, MD 20902. Tel: 301-942-3681.

Blue Army of Our Lady of Fatima—Rev. CHARLES E. POPE, Spiritual Dir., St. Thomas More Parish, 4275 Fourth St., S.E., Washington, 20032. Tel: 202-562-0431; Mrs. HARRIET NOYE, 11223 Woodson Ave., Kensington, MD 20895.

Catholic Daughters of the Americas Court District of Columbia No. 212—Mrs. EDNA WAGNER, Regent, 4445 S. Dakota Ave., N.E., Washington, 20017. Tel: 202-526-7635.

Catholic Hospital Chaplains—Rev. Msgr. LEONARD F. HURLEY, Res.: Carl O'Boyle Residence, 1150 Varnum St., N.E., Washington, 20017. Tel: 202-219-7100.

Health Care Concerns Coordinator—Rev. JOSEPH B. PIERCE, St. Ambrose Parish, 3107 63rd Ave., Cheverly, MD 20785. Tel: 301-773-9300.

Catholic Interracial Council of Washington, DC—Mrs. MADELINE FURTH, Pres., 3224 Northampton St. N.W., Washington, 20015. Tel: 202-966-6794. Email: nlfurth@aol.com.

Catholic War Veterans of the United States—Mr. JOSEPH SATRIANO, Natl. Commander, 441 N. Lee St., Alexandria, VA 23314-2344. Tel: 703-549-3622; Fax: 703-684-5196; Ms. DOLORES STADLER, Pres., National War Veterans, 441 N. Lee St., Alexandria, VA 22314. Tel: 703-549-3622; Fax: 703-684-5196.

St. Francis de Sales Association—Rev. LEWIS FIORELLI, O.S.F.S., Moderator, 1621 Otis St., N.E., Washington, 20018. Tel: 202-269-5677. Region I - USA East: DOROTHY GIBULA, Regl. Dir., 118 Reef Rd., #22, Vero Beach, FL 32963. Tel: 561-231-5988. Region II - USA East: Mrs. HAYDEE VAN STERNBERG, 98 80th Ave., #3D, Brooklyn, NY 11215. Tel: 718-230-3781. Region III - USA East: Mrs. MARY O'CONNELL, 3132 Kincorss Circle, Herndon, VA 20171. Tel: 703-435-8334. Western United States - USA West: Mrs. KAY CHARLES, 3961 E. St. Andrews Dr., Springfield, MO 65809. Tel: 417-866-2542. Mississippi River Valley: JOANNE PRIGGEL, 10140 Chaucer Ave., #3, St. Louis, MO 63114. Tel: 314-428-8542; Mrs. JOYCE BLADES, 2727 E. Ottawa St., Springfield, MO 65804. Tel: 417-881-4367.

First Friday Club—Rev. EVERETT PEARSON, Spiritual Dir., 920 Eleventh St., Washington, 20002. Tel: 202-397-2525; Fax: 202-397-6639.

John Carroll Society—Tel: 703-573-3043. Rev. Msgr. PETER VAGHI, Chap., 619 10th St. N.W., Washington, 20001. Tel: 202-347-2713; JOHN M. FACCIOLA, 2614 Stirrup Ln., Alexandria, VA 22308. Tel: 202-354-3117.

Knights of Columbus—Mr. EDWARD SRSIC, Master of the Archdiocese of Washington, 321 University Blvd., Apt. 229, Silver Spring, MD 20901. Tel: 301-593-8966.

Knights of St. Jerome—St. Peter Claver, St. Inigoes, MD 20684.

Knights of St. John—THOMAS DODSON, Grand Pres.

Womens Retreat League—Ms. ANNE PORTER, Pres., 4000 Harewood Rd. N.E., Washington, 20017. Tel: 202-529-1111; Fax: 202-529-2102.

Engaged Encounter— Contact the Office of Family Life Tel: 301-853-4561.

Marriage Encounter-Worldwide— Contact the Office of Family Life Tel: 301-853-4561.

Sodality Union—Rev. JOSEPH A CALIS, Moderator, St. John the Baptist, 12319 New Hampshire Ave., Silver Spring, MD 20904-2998; ALICE WILSON, Pres., 311 Wren Court, Upper Marlboro, MD 20774. Tel: 301-249-4770.

Secretariat for Social Concerns

Secretary—Mr. CHARLES SHORT. Tel: 301-853-4556; Fax: 301-853-7671.

Associated Catholic Charities—EDWARD J. ORZECHOWSKI, M.S.W., Pres., 924 G St., N.W., Washington, 20001-4532. Tel: 202-772-4300.

A.C.C. Housing & Initiative Corp.—924 G St., N.W., Washington, 20001-4532. Tel: 202-772-4308.

A.C.C. Model Cities Corp.—1125 Neal St. N.E., Washington, 20002. Tel: 202-396-8100.

A.C.C. Otis Street Corp.—924 G St., N.W., Washington, 20001-4532. Tel: 202-526-4100.

SHARE, DC, Inc.—5170 Lawrence Pl., P.O. Box 768, Hyattsville, MD 20781. Tel: 301-864-3115.

Anchor Mental Health Association, Inc.—KERRY SMITH, Dir., P.O. Box 29058, Washington, 20017-0058. Tel: 202-635-5900.

Pro-Life Office—Mr. THOMAS GRENCHIK, Dir. Tel: 301-853-5318; Fax: 301-853-7671.

Birthing & Care Center—Ms. MICHELLE WILLIAMS, 817 Varnum St., N.E., Washington, 20017. Tel: 202-526-2229; Fax: 202-526-1226.

Catholic Campaign for Human Development—Mr. CHRISTOPHER WAINWRIGHT. Tel: 301-853-5341.

Office of Social Development—Mr. CHARLES SHORT. Tel: 301-853-4556; Fax: 301-853-7671.

St. Vincent de Paul Society—STANLIE BARTON, Pres., 5004 2nd St., N.W., #11, Washington, 20011. Tel: 202-723-3035.

Project Rachel—817 Varnum St., N.E., Suite 260, Washington, 20017. Tel: 202-269-4673; Fax: 202-526-1226.

Ladies of Charity—ETHEL HAND, Pres., P.O. Box 10038, Washington, 20018. Tel: 301-630-4127; Rev. CARL F. DIANDA, Spiritual Dir., St. Francis de Sales Parish, 2021 Rhode Island Ave., N.E., Washington, 20018. Tel: 202-529-7451. Providence Hospital, 1150 Varnum St., N.E., Washington, 20017. Tel: 202-269-7000.

Lt. Joseph P. Kennedy Institute—MICHAEL WARD, Pres. & CEO, 801 Buchanan St. N.E., Washington, 20017. Tel: 202-529-7600.

St. Ann's Infant & Maternity Home—Sr. JOSEPHINE MURPHY, D.C., Admin., 4901 Eastern Ave., Hyattsville, MD 20782. Tel: 301-559-5500.

Christ Child Society—ANN EASBY SMITH, Pres.; Rev. Msgr. W. LOUIS QUINN, Spiritual Dir. (Retired), 5101 Wisconsin Ave. N.W., Washington, 20016. Tel: 202-966-9250.

Community Center of the Missionaries of Charity—Sr. LUCIANA, M.C., Supr., 3310 Wheeler Rd. S.E., Washington, 20032. Tel: 202-562-6890.

Missionaries of Charity—Sisters M. REGIS, M.C., Supr., Gift of Peace Home, 2800 Otis St. N.E., Washington, 20017. Tel: 202-269-3313; M. EVA SHALINI, M.C., Supr., Mother Teresa's Infant Home, Gift of Love, 5649 Western Ave. N.W., Washington, 20015. Tel: 202-237-6633.

Cambridge Apartments, Inc., c/o Victory Housing, Inc.—MARGORIE KRASKE, 676 Houston Ave., Takoma Park, MD 20912. Tel: 301-585-3750.

Andrew Kim House, Inc., c/o Victory Housing, Inc.—JEANNE HENDRICKS, 2100 Olney-Sandy Spring Rd., Olney, MD 20832. Tel: 410-224-0100.

Marian Assisted Living—MARGARET SMITH, 19109 Georgia Ave., Brookeville, MD 20833.

Byron House, Inc.—SUZANNE BEALS, Dir., 7210 Kentsdale Dr., Potomac, MD 20854.

Raphael House, Inc.—MICHELINE BUCHANAN, Dir.

Malta House, Inc.—JERRY FULTON, Dir., 4918 La Salle Rd., Hyattsville, MD 20782.

Faith House—Sr. JOSEPHINE MURPHY, D.C., Admin., 4903 Eastern Ave., Hyattsville, MD 20782. Tel: 301-559-5500.

Bartholomew House, Inc.—CATHLEEN CAMERON, Dir., 6904 River Rd., Bethesda, MD 20817.

Avondale Park Apartments, Inc.—TARA RUSSELL, Site Supvr.

Manor Apartments, Inc.—TARA RUSSELL, 4907 Eastern Ave., Hyattsville, MD 20782.

Trinity Terrace, Inc., c/o Victory Housing, Inc.—DAVID PARRISH, Vice Pres., 5430 Grosvenor Lane, Ste. 210, Bethesda, MD 20814-2142. Tel: 301-493-6991. Email: dparrish@victoryhousing.org.

Takoma Tower, Inc.—5430 Grosvenor, Bethesda, MD 20814-2142.

Victory Terrace, Inc., c/o Victory Housing, Inc.—DAVID L PARRISH, Vice Pres., 5430 Grosvenor Lane, Ste. 210, Bethesda, MD 20814-2142. Tel: 301-493-6991. Email: dparrish@victoryhousing.org.

Winslow House, Inc.—JOHN SPENCER, Vice Pres., c/o Victory Housing, Inc., 5430 Grosvenor Lane, Ste. 210, Bethesda, MD 20814-2142. Tel: 301-493-5507. Email: jspencer@victoryhousing.org.

Palmer Park Seniors Housing, Inc.—JOHN SPENCER, Vice-Pres., 5430 Grosvenor Ln., Suite 210, Bethesda, MD 20814-2142. Tel: 301-493-5507. Email: jspencer@victoryhousing.org.

District of Columbia Catholic Conference—Mr. RONALD JACKSON. Tel: 301-853-5342; Fax: 301-853-7671.

Victim Assistance Coordinator—MARCIA D. ZVARA. Tel: 301-853-5328. Email: mzvara@adw.org.

Secretariat for The Clergy

Secretary for Services for Clergy, Religious Men and Secular Institutes—Rev. Msgr. MICHAEL J. MELLONE. Tel: 301-853-4550; Fax: 301-853-7668.

Director of Priests Personnel—Rev. Msgr. MICHAEL J. MELLONE. Tel: 301-853-4550.

Coordinator, Pastoral Care of Priests—Rev. Msgr. JOSEPH RANIERI. Tel: 301-853-5361.

Director, Vocations for Men—Rev. ROBERT PANKE. Tel: 301-853-4580.

Continuing Education for Clergy—Rev. Msgr. R. CARY HILL. Tel: 301-853-5378.

St. John Vianney House—Rev. MICHAEL J MURRAY, Dir., 4214 Saul Rd., Kensington, MD 20895. Tel: 301-942-1191.

Executive Director, Permanent Diaconate—Rev. MICHAEL J. MURRAY. Tel: 301-853-4582.

Director of Deacon Personnel—Deacon LEON J. BECHET. Tel: 301-853-4591.

Director of Formation—Deacon WILLIAM BOESMAN. Tel: 301-853-4583.

Priests Retirement Board—Rev. Msgr. KEVIN HART, Chm. Tel: 301-292-0527.

Cardinal O'Boyle Residence for Priests—Rev. Msgr. LEONARD J. HURLEY, P.O. Box 29206, Washington, 20017. Tel: 202-269-7818.

Serra Club of Washington—Mrs. BEVERLY PONTON, 14700 Elissa Dr., Rockville, MD 20853. Tel: 301-460-5876.

Serra Club of Downtown Washington—ADAM CARTER, Esq., 2015 Q St., N.W., Washington, 20009. Tel: 202-265-8722.

Serra Club of Prince George's Co.—Mrs. MARY DONALDSON, 4906 Sheridan St., Riverdale, MD 20737. Tel: 301-927-2954.

Serra Club of Southern Maryland—Mr. JIM LONG, 39242 Danielle Way, Mechanicsville, MD 20659. Tel: 301-884-5861.

Liaison with Council of Priests— (see Consultative Bodies) Religious priests and brothers, Secular Institutes, Consultant on Alcoholism

Secretary for Women Religious

Secretary for Services to Women Religious and Secular Institutes—Sr. REBECCA BURKE, O.S.F. Tel: 301-853-4576 Fax: 301-853-7669.

Accounting and Financial Management—Mr. RICHARD B. GRAVES, Controller. Tel: 301-853-4525.

Parish Accounting—Mr. TERENCE FARRELL, C.P.A. Tel: 301-853-4511; Fax: 301-853-7664.

Parish Audit Department—Mr. TERENCE FARRELL, C.P.A. Tel: 301-853-4511.

Office of Investments & Real Estate—ROBERT B. MCCAIN, Dir. Tel: 301-853-5350; Fax: 301-853-7690.

Facilities Management—Mr. RICHARD DE STWOLINSKI. Tel: 202-281-2491; Fax: 202-281-2498; SCOTT SULLIVAN, Project Mgr. Tel: 202-281-2492.

Materials and Pastoral Center Management—Ms. ALESSANDRA STYLES. Tel: 301-853-4532; Fax: 301-853-7673.

Personnel and Benefits—DOROTHY MOORE, Dir. Tel: 301-853-4513; Fax: 301-853-7680.

Secretary for Development—Rev. Msgr. JOHN ENZLER, Dir. Cardinals Appeal & Parish Stewardship. Tel: 301-853-4574; Fax: 301-853-7678.

Archdiocesan Building Commission—Rev. Msgr. JOSEPH A. RANIERI, Chm.

Cardinal's Stewardship Appeal—Mr. GREGORY F. GANNON, Dir. Tel: 301-853-4575; Fax: 301-853-7678.

Paul VI Institute for the Arts—Rev. Msgr. MICHAEL DI TECCIA FARINA, Dir., 924 G St. N.W., Washington, 20017. Tel: 202-347-1450.

Office of Planned Giving—Ms. GRETCHEN KOCH. Tel: 301-853-4573.

Archdiocesan Finance Council— (see Consultative Bodies)

Carroll Publishing Company— (see Secretariat for Communications)

Archdiocesan Sacred Arts Committee—Rev. Msgr. W. RONALD JAMESON, 1725 Rhode Island Ave. N.W., Washington, 20036. Tel: 202-347-3215; Fax: 202-347-7184.

Cornerstone for Tomorrow, Inc.—Most Rev. KEVIN FARRELL, P.O. Box 29260, Washington, 20017. Tel: 301-853-4523.

Priest Retirement Fund of the Archdiocese of Washington, Inc.—Most Rev. KEVIN FARRELL, P.O. Box 29260, Washington, 20017. Tel: 301-853-4523.

Development Office

Cardinal's Stewardship Appeal—Tel: 301-853-4575.

Office of Communications

Director—Ms. SUSAN GIBBS. Tel: 301-853-4516; Fax: 301-853-7672. Email: sgibbs@adw.org.

TV Mass Producer—Mr. JOHN CAPOBIANCO. Tel: 301-853-4515.

Carroll Publishing Company—His Eminence THEODORE CARDINAL MCCARRICK, Ph.D., D.D., Publisher; Mr. THOMAS SCHMIDT, Pres. Tel: 202-281-2405; Fax: 202-281-2408.

Newspaper—Mr. MARK ZIMMERMAN, Editor. Tel: 202-281-2412; Fax: 202-281-2418. Email: mark@cathstan.org; Mr. OSCAR REYES, Editor. Tel: 202-281-2441; Fax: 202-281-2448. Email: oscar@elpreg.org. "The Catholic Standard"

Office of Black Catholics

Executive Director—Rev. Msgr. RAYMOND EAST. Tel: 301-853-4579; Fax: 301-853-7671. Email: obc@adw.org. Coordinating Office for Black Catholic History; Combating Racism; Black Catholic Congress; REJOICE! Conference on Black Catholic Liturgy; Archdiocesan Mass Choir; Other Programs & Resources for Leadership and Evangelization in the Black Community.

Council of Black Catholics—

Contact—Rev. Msgr. RAYMOND EAST, Chm.

Office of Hispanic Pastoral Affairs

Executive Director—Sr. ONELLYS VILLEGAS M.H.S.H. Tel: 301-853-4566; Fax: 301-853-7671.

Spanish Catholic Center—Rev. DONALD LIPPERT, O.F.M.Cap, Dir., 1618 Monroe St. N.W., Washington, 20010. Tel: 202-939-2437; Fax: 202-234-7323.

CLERGY, PARISHES, MISSIONS AND PAROCHIAL SCHOOLS

DISTRICT OF COLUMBIA

1—ST. MATTHEW CATHEDRAL (1840), Rev. Msgr. W. Ronald Jameson; Rev. John J. Hurley; Deacons Ulysses Rice; Lawrence C. Gordon; Matthew B. Reilly; Boyd Work; Pamela Erwin, Business Mgr. In Res., Rev. Msgr. Bernard C. Gerhardt, S.T.L., J.C.D., P.A.
Res.: 1725 Rhode Island Ave., N.W., 20036. Tel: 202-347-3215; Fax: 202-347-7184.
Catechesis/Religious Program—Students 61.

2—ST. ALOYSIUS (1859), Revs. R. Bruce Bavinger, S.J.; Edward M. Ifkovits, S.J.; John A. Conlin, S.J.; Deacon Willis Daniels.
Res.: 19 Eye St., N.W., 20001. Tel: 202-336-7200; Fax: 202-842-3693.
Father McKenna Center—Tel: 202-842-1112; Fax: 202-842-7401. Paul J. Magno, Dir.
Catechesis/Religious Program—Tel: 202-336-7219. Students 18.

3—ST. ANN (1869), Rev. Msgr. Kevin T. Hart, J.C.D.; Rev. Keith A. Woods; Deacons Robert W. Whitaker; Gerald Cooke.
Res.: 4001 Yuma St., 20016. Tel: 202-966-6288; Fax: 202-966-7722.
School—Grades PreK-8) Tel: 202-363-4460; Fax: 202-362-5560. Mrs. Barbara Kelly, Prin.
Catechesis/Religious Program—Students 272.

4—ANNUNCIATION (1948), Rev. V. James Lockman.
Res.: 3125 39th St., N.W., 20016-5409. Tel: 202-362-3323; Fax: 202-237-0652.
School—3825 Klingle Pl., 20016-5434. Tel: 202-362-1408; Fax: 202-363-4057. Mrs. K. Marguerite Conley, Prin. Lay Teachers 16; Students 158.
Catechesis/Religious Program—Sr. Kathleen O'Neill, S.H.C.J., D.R.E. Students 90.
Convent—3200 39th St., N.W., 20016. Tel: 202-362-1464.

5—ST. ANTHONY (1892), Rev. Msgr. Richard Burton; Rev. Berard L. Marthaler, O.F.M. (SD) (Retired); Deacon John Kelly. In Res., Revs. Tesfay Woldemarian Fesuh; Gary S. Chamberland, C.S.C. (FTW); Stephen S. Wilbricht, C.S.C. (FTW).
Res.: 1029 Monroe St., N.E., 20017. Tel: 202-526-8822; Fax: 202-526-1543.
School—Tel: 202-526-4657; Fax: 202-832-5567. Lay Teachers 20; Students 251.
Catechesis/Religious Program—Students 34.

6—ASSUMPTION (1916), Rev. Msgr. T. Ansgar Laczko.
Res.: 3401 Martin Luther King Jr. Ave., S.E., 20032-1597. Tel: 202-561-4178; Fax: 202-561-0336.
School—Tel: 202-562-7070; Fax: 202-574-5829. Mr.

Christopher Kelly, Prin. Lay Teachers 10; Students 173.
Catechesis/Religious Program—Students 38.

7—ST. AUGUSTINE (1858), (African American), Revs. Charles C. Green; Lowell D. Case, S.S.J., Admin.
Parish Office—1419 V St., N.W., 20009. Fax: 202-234-1787.
Res.: 1425 V St., N.W., 20009. Tel: 202-265-1470.
School—1421 V St., N.W., 20009. Tel: 202-667-2608. Donna Edwards, Prin. Lay Teachers 18; Students 173.
Catechesis/Religious Program—Students 155.

8—ST. BENEDICT THE MOOR (1946), (African American), Unassigned. Rev. Michael T. Jones.
Res.: 320 21st St., N.E., 20002. Tel: 202-397-3895; Fax: 202-398-3415.
School—Tel: 202-397-3897; Fax: 202-388-7874. Rose Thomas, Prin. Lay Teachers 17; Students 200.
Catechesis/Religious Program—Students 17.

9—ST. BLAISE (1984), (Croatian),, (Croatian Pastoral Mission) Rev. Elvis Razov (Croatia).
Mailing Address: *Our Lady of Victory*, 4835 Macarthur Blvd. N.W., 20007. Tel: 202-492-9088; Fax: 202-338-4759.
Catechesis/Religious Program—Students 10.

10—BLESSED SACRAMENT, SHRINE OF THE MOST (1911), Rev. Msgr. Thomas M. Duffy; Revs. Percival L. D'Silva; Anthony K. McLaughlin (TYL); Robert Wieckowski; Deacons John M. Leonard; Joseph B. McGrath; Daniel Thompson; John Thaddeus Hemsworth.
Res.: 6001 Western Ave., N.W., 20015. Tel: 202-966-6575; Fax: 202-966-9255.
School—5841 Chevy Chase Pkwy., N.W., 20015. Tel: 202-966-6682; Fax: 202-966-4938. Mrs. Frances Scango, Prin. Lay Teachers 44; Students 494.
Catechesis/Religious Program—Tel: 202-363-8938. Rob Maro, D.R.E. Students 420.

11—CHURCH OF ST. LOUIS (1972), (French),, (Paroisse St. Louis de France-French-speaking Parish of Washington) Rev. Antoine De Romanet.
Res.: 4125 Garrison St., N.W., 20016. Tel: 202-537-0709; Fax: 202-244-9649.
Catechesis/Religious Program—Students 240.

12—ST. DOMINIC CHURCH & PRIORY (1852), Very Rev. George Muller, O.P., Prior; Revs. William A. Newman, O.P., Subprior; Gregory Salomone, O.P.; John A. McMahon, O.P.; Robert D. Riley, O.P.; Robert L. Walker, O.P.; Edmund J. Way, O.P.; Kenneth A. France-Kelly, O.P.; Cornelius T. Kane, O.P.; Guy B. Dupont, O.P; John T. Carrigan, O.P.; V. F. McHenry, O.P.; Patrick F. Connolly, O.P.; Adrian L. Dionne, O.P.; James D. Keating, O.P.; J. Andrew Nicolicchia, O.P.; Robert Leo Pelkington; Eugene Cahourt, O.P.; Donald P. Thibault, O.P.; Joseph Hugh Mulhern, O.P. (NY); Richard Farmer, O.P.; David A. Butler, O.P. (NY); Raymond Vandegrift, O.P.; Aaron J. Cote, O.P (PRO).
Res.: 630 E St., S.W., 20024. Tel: 202-554-7863; Fax: 202-554-0231.

13—EPIPHANY (1923), Rev. Winthrop Brainerd.
Res.: 2712 Dumbarton St., N.W., 20007. Tel: 202-965-1610; Fax: 202-337-8377.

14—ST. FRANCIS DE SALES (1722), (African American), Rev. Carl F. Dianda; Deacon Floyd H. Agostinelli. In Res., Revs. John S. Wintermyer; Henry Slevin; Romanus Kyomya (Uganda); Alphonsus Oha (Nigeria).
Res.: 2021 Rhode Island Ave., N.E., 20018. Tel: 202-529-7451; Fax: 202-529-0050.
School—Tel: 202-529-5394; Fax: 202-529-1620. Sisters 1; Lay Teachers 10; Students 190.
Catechesis/Religious Program—2019 Rhode Island Ave., N.E.. Tel: 202-529-2147; Fax: 202-529-1630. Students 19.

15—ST. FRANCIS XAVIER (1924), Rev. C. Gregory Butta. In Res., Rev. Msgr. Raymond G. East.
Res.: 2800 Pennsylvania Ave., S.E., 20020. Tel: 202-582-5021; Fax: 202-581-7224.
School—Tel: 202-581-2010; 202-234-4611; Fax: 202-582-5244. Harold Thomas, Prin. Lay Teachers 12; Students 240.
Catechesis/Religious Program—Tel: 202-582-2607. Mr. Robert Fuller, D.R.E. Students 57.
Convent—Sisters of St. Joseph, 2812 Pennsylvania Ave., S.E., 20020. Tel: 202-584-5621. Sr. M. Brigid, S.S.J., Supr.

16—ST. GABRIEL (1919), Revs. Mark Hughes; Mauricio Henriquez; Sr. Maria Faina, S.N.J.M., Pastoral Assoc.; Deacons Robert L. Berry; Morris Williams. In Res., Revs. Tesfamariam Baraki; Jonathan D. Lao (Philippines).
Res.: 26 Grant Cir., N.W., 20011. Tel: 202-726-9092; Fax: 202-291-0334.
School—Tel: 202-726-9212; Fax: 202-726-1881. Mrs. Monica Arce, Prin. Lay Teachers 9; Students 165.
Catechesis/Religious Program—Tel: 202-882-5470. Students 100.

17—HOLY COMFORTER--ST. CYPRIAN (1893), (African American), Rev. Eddie Tolentino III; Deacons Charles Edelin; Kevin Butler; Ralph Cyrus; Ronald Ealey. In Res., Rev. F. Michael Bryant.
Res.: 1357 E. Capitol St., S.E., 20003. Tel: 202-546-1885; Fax: 202-544-1385.
School—Tel: 202-547-7556; Fax: 202-547-5686. Valerie Swain, Prin. Lay Teachers 13; Students 138.
Catechesis/Religious Program—Tel: 202-547-2510. Mrs. Catherine Ealey, D.R.E. Students 60.

18—HOLY NAME (1891), (African American), Revs. Everett Pearson; Robert Guilka; Deacon William Thomas. In Res., Rev. Francis M. Walsh.
Res.: 920 11th St., N.E., 20002. Tel: 202-397-2525; Fax: 202-397-6639.
School—Tel: 202-397-1614; Fax: 202-398-4832. Sr. Patricia Ralph, S.S.J., Prin. Sisters of St. Joseph 1; Lay Teachers 18; Students 202.
Catechesis/Religious Program—Tel: 202-397-4782. Students 225.

19—HOLY REDEEMER (1922), (African American), Rev. David Bava.
Res.: 206 New York Ave., N.W., 20001. Tel: 202-347-7510; Fax: 202-628-0401.
School—Holy Redeemer School, (Grades PreK-8), 1135 New Jersey Ave., N.W., 20001. Tel: 202-638-5789. Mrs. Mildred Tyler, Prin. Priests 1; Sisters 3; Deacons 1; Lay Teachers 14; Students 180.
Catechesis/Religious Program—Students 54.

20—HOLY ROSARY (1913), (Italian), Rev. Charles Zanoni, C.S.
Res.: 595 Third St., N.W., 20001-2703. Tel: 202-638-0165; Fax: 202-638-0793.
Catechesis/Religious Program—Students 19.

21—HOLY TRINITY (1787), Revs. William J. Byron, S.J.; Bert Akers, S.J.; Vincent Curtin, S.J.; Gerard J. Campbell, S.J.; Robert Poirier, S.J.; Vincent G. Conti, S.J.
Church: 36th St., N.W., between N and O Sts., 20007.
Parish Center Offices—3513 N St., N.W., 20007.
Res.: 3514 O St., N.W., 20007. Tel: 202-337-2840; Fax: 202-337-9048.
School—Tel: 202-337-2339; Fax: 202-337-0368. Sisters of St. Joseph (Chestnut Hill, PA) 2; Lay Teachers 38; Students 340.
Catechesis/Religious Program—Students 594.

22—IMMACULATE CONCEPTION (1864), (African American), Rev. James D. Watkins.
Res.: 1315 8th St., N.W., 20001. Tel: 202-332-8888; Fax: 202-332-0173.
School—(Grades PreK-5), 711 N St., N.W., 20001. Tel: 202-234-1093; Fax: 202-462-6875. Sr. Gillian Pratt, Prin. Lay Teachers 7; Students 124.
Catechesis/Religious Program—Students 16.

23—INCARNATION (1934), (African American), Rev. John A. Carroll, S.S.J.; Deacon Joseph E. Bell. In Res., Rev. Angelo Meselle, O.S.B.
Res.: 880 Eastern Ave., N.E., 20019. Tel: 202-396-0942; Fax: 202-396-6064.
Catechesis/Religious Program—Students 123.

24—ST. JOSEPH ON CAPITOL HILL (1869), Revs. Charles V. Antonicelli, J.C.L.; Christopher T. Begg. In Res., Rev. Eugene Hemrick (JOL).
Res.: 313 Second St., N.E., 20002. Tel: 202-547-1223; Fax: 202-547-4189.
Catechesis/Religious Program—Students 18.

25—KIDANE-MEHRET GE'EZ RITE CATHOLIC CHURCH (1984), (Ethiopian-Eritrean), Rev. Tesfamariam Baraki.
Mailing Address: 1001 Lawrence St., N.E., P.O. Box 29616, 20017. Tel: 202-529-8420.
Res.: 26 Grant Cir., N.W., 20011. Tel: 202-726-9092; Fax: 202-529-8523.
Catechesis/Religious Program—Students 127.

26—ST. LUKE (1957), (African American), Revs. Roderick J.D. Coates, S.S.J. (GAL); Joseph N. Begay, S.S.J.; Deacons Earle W. Coleman; Joseph M. Conrad.
Res.: 4925 E. Capitol St., 20019-5202. Tel: 202-584-8322; Fax: 202-584-3421.
Catechesis/Religious Program—Students 134.

27—ST. MARTIN OF TOURS (1901), (African American), Rev. Michael J. Kelley.
Res.: 1908 N. Capitol St., 20002. Tel: 202-232-1144; Fax: 202-832-6772.
Catechesis/Religious Program—Students 62.

28—ST. MARY, MOTHER OF GOD (1845), [CEM] Rev. David Conway. In Res., Revs. Bruce Harbert; Peter Nguyen Kham (Vietnam).
Res.: 727 Fifth St., N.W., 20001. Tel: 202-289-7771; Fax: 202-408-1989.
Catechesis/Religious Program—Tel: 202-289-7770.

29—NATIONAL SHRINE OF THE IMMACULATE CONCEPTION,

30—NATIVITY (1901), (African American), Revs. Stephen Schenck, S.D.B. (MIA); James Berning, S.D.B. (NO); Quesnel Delvard, S.D.B.; Deacon Al Douglas Turner; Bro. Bruno Busatto, S.D.B.
Res.: 6000 Georgia Ave., N.W., 20011. Tel: 202-726-6262; Fax: 200-722-7170.
School—Tel: 202-723-3322; Fax: 202-291-0219. Dr. Thomas M. Simpson, Prin. Sisters 2; Lay Teachers 16; Students 220.
Catechesis/Religious Program—Students 60.

31—NIGERIAN CATHOLIC COMMUNITY (1994), (Nigerian), Rev. Pius T. Ajiki.
Res.: 5700 St. Bernard's Dr., Riverdale, MD 20737. Nativity Parish: 6000 Georgia Ave., N.W., 20011. Tel: 301-277-1000; Fax: 301-277-3464.

32—OUR LADY OF FATIMA PARISH (1999),, (Portuguese-speaking Community) Rev. Nelson Grandi (Brazil) (MIA).
Mailing Address: 70 University Blvd. E., Silver Spring, MD 20901. Tel: 301-593-9212; Fax: 301-593-3088.
Catechesis/Religious Program—10830 Eastwood Ave., Silver Spring, MD 20901. Tel: 301-949-2488. Students 80.

33—OUR LADY OF PERPETUAL HELP (1920), (African American), Very Rev. Donald M. Fest, S.S.J.; Rev. Sidney Speaks, S.S.J.; Bro. Marx Tyree, S.S.J., Pastoral Assoc.; Deacon Thomas Jones.
Res.: 1600 Morris Rd., S.E., 20020. Tel: 202-678-4999; Fax: 202-610-3189.
School—Tel: 202-889-1662 (Grades PreK-4); 202-678-0211 (Grades 5-8); Fax: 202-610-1519. Mrs. Charlene Hursey, Prin.; Mr. Bernard Toomer, Vice Prin. School Sisters of Notre Dame 1; Lay Teachers 18; Students 164.
Catechesis/Religious Program—Students 85.

34—OUR LADY OF VICTORY (1906), Rev. Paul Lee; Deacons Leo Flynn; Michael W. Om; Jane Zilles-Sobrano, Pastoral Assoc. In Res., Rev. Msgr. Harry A. Echle (Retired).
Res.: 4835 MacArthur Blvd., N.W., 20007. Tel: 202-337-4835; Fax: 202-338-4759.
School—4755 Whitehaven Pkwy., N.W., 20007. Tel: 202-337-1421; Fax: 202-338-4759. Susan Milloy, Prin. Lay Teachers 19; Students 169.
Catechesis/Religious Program—Students 48.

35—OUR LADY QUEEN OF PEACE (1948), (African American), Rev. Alfred J. Harris; Deacon Alfred Miller; Mr. Ernest Adams, Pastoral Assoc.
Res.: 3800 Ely Pl., S.E., 20019. Tel: 202-582-8600; Fax: 202-575-3317.
Catechesis/Religious Program—Tel: 202-581-4986. Students 52.
Convent—3740 Ely Pl., S.E., 20019. Tel: 202-581-4963; Fax: 202-584-1922.

36—OUR LADY QUEEN OF THE AMERICAS (1986), (Hispanic), Most Rev. Francisco Gonzalez, S.F.; Rev. Agustin Mateo; Deacons Jorge Vargas; Bart Serafeni.
Catechesis/Religious Program—Tel: 202-332-8838, Ext. 224. Sr. Felipa Blazquez, D.R.E. Students 275.

37—ST. PATRICK (1794), Rev. Msgr. Peter J. Vaghi; Rev. Patrick Dempsey; Deacon John J. McGinness. In Res., Rev. Msgrs. Michael diTeccia Farina; Salvatore A. Criscuolo; Rev. Robert J. Panke.
Res.: 619 Tenth St., N.W., 20001-4587. Tel: 202-347-2713; Fax: 202-347-1401.

38—ST. PETER (1821), Rev. Michael J. O'Sullivan. In Res., Rev. Msgr. Joseph F. Sadusky, M.Div., M.Ch.A., J.C.D.; Revs. Thomas J. Sheehan (Retired); Joseph R. Sileo.
Res.: 313 Second St., S.E., 20003. Tel: 202-547-1430; Fax: 202-547-5732.
School—422 Third St., S.E., 20003. Tel: 202-544-1618; Fax: 202-547-5101. Pamela J. Klobukowski, Prin. Lay Teachers 23; Students 229.
Catechesis/Religious Program—Tel: 202-544-1618. Students 44.

39—SHRINE OF THE SACRED HEART (1899), Revs. Stephen Carter, O.F.M.Cap.; Paul Zaborowski, O.F.M.Cap.; Kevin Thompson, O.F.M.Cap.; Andre Pierre, O.F.M.Cap. (Haiti), (Haitian Apostolate); Francis Hgi, (Vietnamese Apostolate); Deacons Sylvester Brown, (Retired); James Quander, (Retired). In Res., Bro. Thomas Wells, O.F.M.Cap.
Res.: 3211 Pine St., 20010. Tel: 202-234-8000 (Day); 202-234-8002 (Night); Fax: 202-234-9159.
School—1625 Park Rd., N.W., 20010. Tel: 202-265-4828; Fax: 202-265-0595. Juana Brown, Prin. Lay Teachers 16; Students 228.
Catechesis/Religious Program—Tel: 202-667-2446. Students 225.

40—ST. STEPHEN MARTYR (1867), Revs. Robert Cary Hill; Patrick J. McCaffrey, (Senior Priest); Lancelot McGrath, L.C.; Deacon John W. Bobbitt. In Res., Rev. John Ceferino Ledesma, S.D.B.
Res.: 2436 Pennsylvania Ave., N.W., 20037. Tel: 202-785-0982; Fax: 202-785-1574.

41—ST. TERESA OF AVILA (1879), Rev. Patrick A. Smith; Deacons Ralph Cyrus; Lawrence Miles.
Res.: 1430 Minnesota Ave., S.E., 20020. Tel: 202-678-3709; Fax: 202-678-3325.
Church: 1244 V. St. SE, 20020.
Catechesis/Religious Program—Students 76.

42—ST. THOMAS APOSTLE (1913), Rev. Msgr. Michael J. Mellone; Deacon William C. Boesman. In Res., Rev. Msgr. William F. O'Donnell.
Res.: 2665 Woodley Rd., N.W., 20008. Tel: 202-234-1488; Fax: 202-234-1480.
Catechesis/Religious Program—Students 36.

43—ST. THOMAS MORE (1952), (African American),

Rev. Charles E. Pope; Deacon Nerus O. Martin Jr. In Res., Rev. John P. Kinter.
Res.: 4275 4th St., S.E., 20032. Tel: 202-562-0431; Fax: 202-563-7347.
School—Tel: 202-561-1189; Fax: 202-562-2336. Mr. Wilford Graham, Prin. Lay Teachers 14; Students 178.
Catechesis/Religious Program—Students 78.

44—ST. VINCENT DE PAUL (1903), (African American), Deacon Francis Kraemer. In Res., Bro. Marx Tyree, S.S.J.
Res.: 14 M St., S.E., 20003-3511. Tel: 202-488-1354; Fax: 202-488-7899.
Catechesis/Religious Program—Students 75.

CHURCHES IN MARYLAND

AVENUE, ST. MARY'S CO., HOLY ANGELS (1906), [JC] Rev. Msgr. John B. Brady.
Res.: 21340 Colton Point Rd., MD 20609-2422. Tel: 301-769-3332; Fax: 301-769-2541.
School—Holy Angels-Sacred Heart, Tel: 301-769-3389; Fax: 301-769-4948. Priests 2; Lay Teachers 11; Students 96.
Catechesis/Religious Program—Students 50.

BADEN, PRINCE GEORGES CO., ST. MICHAEL (1957), Rev. Louis J. Faust; Deacon Harvey Ballard.
Catechesis/Religious Program—Tel: 301-579-6409; Fax: 301-579-0019. Students 90.
Mission—St. Dominic's [CEM] 22300 Aquasco Rd., Aquasco, Prince Georges Co., MD 20608.

BARNESVILLE, MONTGOMERY CO., ST. MARY CHURCH AND SHRINE OF OUR LADY OF FATIMA (1807), [CEM] Revs. Walter L. Lawrence; George B. Reid, Pastor Emeritus (Retired); Deacon David Cahoon.
Res.: 18230 Barnsville Rd., P.O. Box 67, MD 20838. Tel: 301-972-8660; Fax: 301-428-8464.
Catechesis/Religious Program—Students 122.

BELTSVILLE, PRINCE GEORGES CO., ST. JOSEPH (1963), Rev. Roderick D. McKee; Deacon Andrew J. Betz. In Res., Rev. Joseph F. Mozer Jr. (BO).
Res.: 11007 Montgomery Rd., MD 20705. Tel: 301-937-7183; Fax: 301-937-7780.
School—Tel: 301-937-7154; Fax: 301-937-1467. Lay Teachers 18; Students 265.
Catechesis/Religious Program—Tel: 301-937-7419. Students 154.

BENEDICT, CHARLES CO., ST. FRANCIS DE SALES (1903), Rev. Saverio T. Vitturino.
Res.: 7185 Benedict Ave., P.O. Box 306, MD 20612-0306. Tel: 301-274-3416; 301-870-4991; Fax: 301-274-0689.
Catechesis/Religious Program—7209 Benedict Ave., MD 20612. Students 63.

BETHESDA, MONTGOMERY CO.

1—ST. BARTHOLOMEW (1960), (Spanish), Rev. Msgr. James T. Beattie; Revs. Lancelot Mcgrath, L.C.; Luis G. Salcedo (Retired).
Res.: 7212 Blacklock Rd., MD 20817. Tel: 301-229-7933; Fax: 301-229-7998.
School—6900 River Rd., MD 20817. Tel: 301-229-5586; Fax: 301-229-8654. Mrs. Kathleen Miller, Prin. Sisters 2; Lay Teachers 17; Students 205.
Catechesis/Religious Program—Tel: 301-229-3431; Fax: 301-229-7998. Students 336.

2—ST. JANE FRANCES DE CHANTAL (1950), Rev. Msgr. Donald S. Essex; Revs. Alan R. Helwig; Klaus J. Sirianni; Christopher K. O'Connor (BO); Deacon Kenneth Angell.
Res.: 9701 Old Georgetown Rd., MD 20814. Tel: 301-530-1550; Fax: 301-493-8953.
School—9525 Old Georgetown Rd., MD 20814. Tel: 301-530-1221; Fax: 301-530-1688. Mrs. Betsy Hamilton, Prin. Lay Teachers 27; Students 512.
Catechesis/Religious Program—Tel: 301-530-1640; Fax: 301-530-5881. Students 200.

3—LITTLE FLOWER (1948), Rev. Msgr. William J. Kane; Revs. John J. Dillon, S.T.B., Ph.D.; George Stuart; Deacons Gary Davies; Richard Schopfer.
Res.: 5607 Massachusetts Ave., MD 20816. Tel: 301-320-4538; Fax: 301-320-4541.
School—Tel: 301-320-3273; Fax: 301-320-2867. Sisters of the Immaculate Heart of Mary 5; Lay Teachers 22; Students 250.
Catechesis/Religious Program—Tel: 301-320-5233. Students 212.

4—NATIVITY OF THE BLESSED VIRGIN (GERMAN MISSION) (1992), Rev. Msgr. Bernd Kaut (Germany).
Rectory—6330 Linway Ter., McLean, VA 22101-4150. Tel: 703-356-4473; Fax: 703-356-4558.

5—OUR LADY OF LOURDES (1926), (Spanish), Revs. James P. Meyers; Mario E. Dorsonville; Deacon John Shewmaker. In Res., Rev. Msgr. W. Louis Quinn (Retired); Rev. Robert Bozek.
Res.: 7500 Pearl St., MD 20814. Tel: 301-654-1287; Fax: 301-986-8716.
School—Tel: 301-654-5376; Fax: 301-654-2568. Edward J. Lindekugel, Prin. Sisters 1; Lay Teachers 26; Students 209.
Catechesis/Religious Program—Tel: 301-654-5954. Students 241.

6—OUR LADY OF VIETNAM (1990), (Vietnamese), Revs. Peter Nguyen-Thanh-Long; Hilary Tran-Khac Hy (Retired); Deacon John Huong Nguyen.
Res.: 11812 New Hampshire Ave., Silver Spring, MD 20904. Tel: 301-622-4895; Fax: 301-625-9384.

BOWIE, PRINCE GEORGES CO.

1—ASCENSION (1893), [CEM] Revs. James S. Betz; Samuel L. Craig; Deacons Finis E. Thompson; Ted R. Pillman.
Mailing Address: P.O. Box 96, MD 20719. Tel: 301-262-2227; Fax: 301-805-5053.
Catechesis/Religious Program—Tel: 301-262-8604. Mrs. Hope A. Benson, D.R.E. Students 125.

2—ST. EDWARD (1972), Rev. William E. Foley; Deacons Kevin Barry; David Barnes; Stephen Hueste.
Res.: 16304 Pond Meadow Ln., MD 20716. Tel: 301-249-9199.
Catechesis/Religious Program—Tel: 301-249-9599; Fax: 301-249-1303. Students 300.

3—ST. PIUS X (1962), Revs. W. Paul Hill; Tam Tran; Deacons Andrew Nosacek; Donald Sparling. In Res., Rev. Paul Lyttle (Ireland).
Res.: 3300 Moreland Pl., MD 20715. Tel: 301-262-2141; Fax: 301-262-2632.
Church: 14720 Annapolis Rd., MD 20715.
School—Tel: 301-262-0203; Fax: 301-805-8875. Lay Teachers 48; Students 846.
Catechesis/Religious Program—Tel: 301-262-3644. Debbie Langdon, D.R.E. Students 254.

4—SACRED HEART (1729), [CEM] Revs. Charles J. Parry; Timothy R. McMorland; Deacons H. Jeffrey Raffensperger; Edward J. Danko, Sr. In Res., Rev. Walter J. Tappe.
Res.: 16501 Annapolis Rd., MD 20715. Tel: 301-262-0704; Fax: 301-805-4686.
Catechesis/Religious Program—Tel: 301-262-1221. Mrs. Mimi Shea, D.R.E. Students 203.

BRYANTOWN, CHARLES CO., ST. MARY (1793), [CEM] Rev. Joseph J. Kleinstuber; Deacons Eugene Burroughs; Henry Middleton.
Res.: 13715 Notre Dame Pl., MD 20617-2224. Tel: 301-870-2220; 301-274-3187; Fax: 301-274-0253.
School—Tel: 301-932-6883; Fax: 301-274-0626. School Sisters of Notre Dame 1; Lay Teachers 13; Students 227.
Catechesis/Religious Program—Tel: 301-274-3800. Students 154.

BURTONSVILLE, MONTGOMERY CO., RESURRECTION PARISH (1981), Revs. Robert F. Keffer; Charles E. Brown; Deacon Donald DeRoze.
Res.: 3315 Greencastle Rd., MD 20866. Tel: 301-236-5200; Fax: 301-236-5204.
Catechesis/Religious Program—Tel: 301-236-5200. Students 363.

BUSHWOOD, ST. MARY'S CO., SACRED HEART (1755), [JC] Rev. Francis J. Early.
Res.: 23080 Maddox Rd. (Rte. 238), P.O. Box 37, MD 20618. Tel: 301-769-3100; Fax: 301-769-2251.
Catechesis/Religious Program— See Holy Angels-Sacred Heart School, Avenue, MD, for details. Students 57.

CAMP SPRINGS, PRINCE GEORGES CO., ST. PHILIP THE APOSTLE (1957), Revs. Charles McCann; Bernard R. Ihrie Jr. Senior Priest (Retired); Deacon Robert L. Gignilliat. In Res., Rev. Jeffrey F. Samaha.
Res.: 5416 Henderson Way, MD 20746. Tel: 301-423-4244; Fax: 301-423-1226.
School—Tel: 301-423-4740; Fax: 301-423-4716. Lay Teachers 17; Students 254.
Catechesis/Religious Program—Tel: 301-423-0166. Students 45.

CHAPEL POINT, CHARLES CO., ST. IGNATIUS (1641), [CEM] Revs. Salvador Jordan, S.J.; Edward P. O'Connell, S.J.; Thomas E. Peacock; Bro. Joseph M. Connor.
St. Thomas Manor: 8855 Chapel Point Rd., Port Tobacco, MD 20677. Tel: 301-934-8245; Fax: 301-934-0944.
Catechesis/Religious Program—Tel: 301-392-0604. Angela Hume, D.R.E. Students 148.

CHAPTICO, ST. MARY'S CO., OUR LADY OF THE WAYSIDE (1938), Rev. John P. Stack.
Mailing Address: Rte. 238, Helen, MD 20638. Tel: 301-884-3165; Fax: 301-884-3165.
Res.: Rte. 238, P.O. Box 97, MD 20621. Tel: 301-884-2502; Fax: 301-884-0381.
School—Mother Catherine Spalding Tri Parish School, Tel: 301-884-3165. Lay Teachers 17; Students 213.
Catechesis/Religious Program—Students 110.

CHEVERLY, PRINCE GEORGES CO., ST. AMBROSE (1886), Revs. Joseph B. Pierce; Timothy K. Baer; Deacon Edwin Beller, (Retired).
Res.: 3107 63rd Ave., MD 20785. Tel: 301-773-9300; Fax: 301-773-2611.
School—Tel: 301-773-0223; Fax: 301-773-9218. Mr. Vincent Spadoni, Prin. Lay Teachers 14; Students 307.
Catechesis/Religious Program—Tel: 301-773-0627. Students 111.

CHILLUM, PRINCE GEORGES CO., ST. JOHN BAPTIST DE LA SALLE (1951), Rev. Robert C. Richardson.
Res.: 5706 Sargent Rd., MD 20782. Tel: 301-559-3636; Fax: 301-559-3062.
Catechesis/Religious Program—Tel: 301-559-3637. Students 47.

CLINTON, PRINCE GEORGES CO., CHURCH OF ST. JOHN THE EVANGELIST (1875), [CEM] Revs. Thomas W. Pollard; Stephen F. Nash; Deacon Anthony Moll.
Res.: 8908 Old Branch Ave., MD 20735. Tel: 301-868-1070; Fax: 301-868-7915.
School—Tel: 301-868-2010; Fax: 301-856-8941. Sisters of the Immaculate Heart of Mary 1; Lay Teachers 15; Students 239.
Catechesis/Religious Program—Tel: 301-868-3026. Students 140.

COLLEGE PARK, PRINCE GEORGES CO.

1—ST. ANDREW KIM (1974), (Korean), Unassigned.
Res.: 17615 Old Baltimore Rd., Olney, MD 20832. Tel: 301-924-8330; Fax: 301-924-8332.
Catechesis/Religious Program—Tel: 301-275-3734. Students 280.

2—HOLY REDEEMER (1912), Rev. William F. Berry.
Res.: 4902 Berwyn Rd., MD 20740. Tel: 301-474-3920; Fax: 301-441-4054.
School—Tel: 301-474-3993; Fax: 301-441-8137. Gregory E. Jones, Prin. Religious 2; Lay Teachers 17; Students 263.
Catechesis/Religious Program—Tel: 301-474-4299. Mrs. Sandra Tucker, D.R.E. Students 109.

DAMASCUS, MONTGOMERY CO., ST. PAUL (1957), Rev. Peter J. Sweeney; Deacons John Finerty; David Terrar; Charles Weschler.
Res.: 9240 Damascus Rd., MD 20872. Tel: 301-253-2027; Fax: 301-391-6755.
Catechesis/Religious Program—Tel: 301-253-5941. Students 770.

DARNESTOWN, MONTGOMERY CO.

1—MARY OF NAZARETH ROMAN CATHOLIC ELEMENTARY SCHOOL (1994), Mr. Michael J. Friel, Prin.
Res.: 14131 Seneca Rd., MD 20874. Tel: 301-869-0940; Fax: 301-869-0942.
Catechesis/Religious Program—Students 435.

2—OUR LADY OF THE VISITATION (1991), Rev. Raymond L. Fecteau; Deacon Paul DiDuca.
Res.: 14200 Darnestown Rd., MD 20874-3008. Tel: 301-948-5536; Fax: 301-948-7452.
Church & Mailing Address: 14139 Seneca Rd., MD 20874.
Catechesis/Religious Program—Students 291.

DERWOOD, MONTGOMERY CO., ST. FRANCIS OF ASSISI (1972), Revs. Lee J. Fangmeyer; Mark D. Knestout; Deacons Wilbur Pinder; Pascal Hong. In Res., Rev. Msgr. Ralph J. Kuehner.
Res.: 6701 Muncaster Mill Rd., MD 20855. Tel: 301-840-1407; Fax: 301-258-5080.
Catechesis/Religious Program—Tel: 301-258-9193. Students 643.

DUNKIRK, CALVERT CO., JESUS THE GOOD SHEPHERD (1985), Rev. Paul M. Dudziak; Deacons Emmett (Chad) Martin; John Verdon.
Res.: 1555 Mount Harmony Rd. W., Owings, MD 20736. Tel: 301-855-4400; Fax: 410-257-6334.
School—Cardinal Hickey Academy, 1601 W. Mt. Harmony Rd., Owings, MD 20736. Tel: 410-286-0404; Fax: 410-286-6334. Ms. Lynn Leaf, Prin.; Sr. Christine Born, O.P., Assoc. Prin.
Catechesis/Religious Program—Tel: 301-855-5694. Students 713.

FORESTVILLE, PRINCE GEORGE CO.

1—CHURCH OF THE HOLY SPIRIT (1966), Rev. Joseph A. Jenkins.
Res.: 1717 Ritchie Rd., MD 20747. Tel: 301-336-3707; Fax: 301-324-1649.
Catechesis/Religious Program—Students 31.

2—MT. CALVARY (1942), [CEM] Revs. George E. Golden, M.Div.; Thomas A. Gude; Deacon Lawrence Miles.
Res.: 6700 Marlboro Pike, MD 20747. Tel: 301-735-5532; Fax: 301-735-2005.
School—Tel: 301-735-5262; Fax: 301-736-5044. Lay Teachers 21; Students 267.
Catechesis/Religious Program—6704 Marlboro Pike, MD 20747. Tel: 301-420-4499. Students 103.

FORT WASHINGTON, PRINCE GEORGES CO., ST. IGNATIUS (1849), [CEM] Rev. Robert A. Finamore. In Res., Rev. Robert P. Wummer (Retired).
Res.: 2315 Brinkley Rd., Oxon Hill, MD 20744. Tel: 301-567-4740; Fax: 301-567-0156.
School—2317 Brinkley Rd., Oxon Hill, MD 20744. Tel: 301-567-4090. Ms. Linda Bourne, Prin. Lay Teachers 12; Students 200.
Catechesis/Religious Program—Students 41.

GAITHERSBURG, MONTGOMERY CO.

1—ST. JOHN NEUMANN (1978), Revs. Michael W. Fisher; Scott Woods; Deacon Robert Allen.
Mailing Address: 8900 Lochaven Dr., MD 20882-4460.
Church: 9000 Warfield Rd., MD 20882. Tel: 301-977-5492; Fax: 301-977-3559.
Catechesis/Religious Program—Tel: 301-977-7990; Fax: 301-330-3235. Students 695.

2—ST. MARTIN (1920), (Spanish), Revs. Mark E.

Brennan; Daniel P. Leary; Francisco Javier Santaballa; Deacons Lawrence Bell; Eugene J. Cummins Jr.; Ronald J. Meyer; Kenneth Barrett.
Res.: 201 S. Frederick Ave., MD 20877. Tel: 301-840-1830; Fax: 301-990-7538.
School—Tel: 301-840-1748; Fax: 301-840-1733. Mr. Donald Jackson, Prin. Lay Teachers 17; Students 272.
Catechesis/Religious Program—Tel: 301-840-1838; Fax: 301-840-2008. M. Patricia Dorney, D.R.E. (English); Elizabeth Rosales, D.R.E. (Spanish). Students 1,336.

3—ST. ROSE OF LIMA (1972), [CEM] Rev. Robert D. Duggan.
Mailing Address: 11701 Clopper Rd., MD 20878-1024. Tel: 301-948-7545; Fax: 301-869-2170.
Catechesis/Religious Program—Tel: 301-948-7545. Patricia Lawlor, D.R.E. Tel: 301-948-7545, Ext. 228; Tom Hild, D.R.E. Tel: 301-948-7545, Ext. 224. Students 471.

GARRETT PARK, MONTGOMERY CO., HOLY CROSS (1960), Rev. Msgr. Vincent S. Gatto; Rev. Joseph F. Perkins. In Res., Rev. Tobias Unnerstal (Sweden).
Res.: 4900 Strathmore Ave., P.O. Box 249, MD 20896. Tel: 301-942-1020; Fax: 301-949-3543.
School—Tel: 301-949-0053; Fax: 301-949-5074. Sr. Sharon Mihm, Prin. Lay Teachers 20; Students 268.
Catechesis/Religious Program—Tel: 301-942-8790. Students 268.

GERMANTOWN, MONTGOMERY CO., MOTHER SETON PARISH (1974), Revs. Ronald A. Potts; Mathew Punchayil (India) (SYM); Deacons William Vita; Timothy Enright; Robert Huber.
Res.: 19951 Father Hurley Blvd., MD 20874. Tel: 301-924-3838; Fax: 301-428-4951.
Catechesis/Religious Program—Tel: 301-444-3496; 301-444-3495. Students 606.

GREAT MILLS, ST. MARY'S CO., HOLY FACE (1879), [CEM] Rev. Kevin O'Reilly.
Mailing Address: P.O. Box 106, MD 20634.
Res.: 20476 Point Lookout Rd., MD 20634. Tel: 301-994-0525; Fax: 301-994-1547.
School—Little Flower, Tel: 301-994-0404; Fax: 301-994-2055. Lay Teachers 20; Students 308.
Catechesis/Religious Program—Students 359.

GREENBELT, PRINCE GEORGES CO., ST. HUGH (1947), Rev. Thomas F. Crowley.
Res.: 135 Crescent Rd., MD 20770. Tel: 301-474-4322; Fax: 301-474-9263.
School—145 Crescent Rd., MD 20770. Tel: 301-474-4071; Fax: 301-474-3950. Mrs. Mary Elizabeth Whelan, Prin. Lay Teachers 17; Students 240.
Catechesis/Religious Program—Tel: 301-474-0239. Students 55.

HILLCREST HEIGHTS, PRINCE GEORGES CO., HOLY FAMILY (1952), (African American), Rev. Raymond J. Wadas.
Res.: 2210 Callaway St., MD 20748. Tel: 301-894-2222; Fax: 301-894-2938.
School—2200 Callaway St., MD 20748. Tel: 301-894-2323.
Catechesis/Religious Program—Students 280.

HILLTOP, CHARLES CO., ST. IGNATIUS LOYOLA (1851), [CEM] Rev. Robert J. Kosty; Deacon Frank L. Hopson.
Mailing Address: P.O. Box 278, Port Tobacco, MD 20677. Tel: 301-934-9630; Fax: 301-934-8320.
Catechesis/Religious Program—Tel: 301-934-9080. Students 23.

HOLLYWOOD, ST. MARY'S CO., ST. JOHN (1690), [CEM] Rev. Msgr. Martin P. Harris; Rev. Martin E. Flum.
Res.: P.O. Box 69, MD 20636. Tel: 301-373-2281; Fax: 301-373-8984.
School—Tel: 301-373-2142; Fax: 301-373-4500. Patricia T. Suit, Prin. Students 219.
Catechesis/Religious Program—Rev. John J. Dillon, S.T.B., Ph.D., D.R.E. Students 270.

HUNTINGTOWN, CALVERT CO., JESUS THE DIVINE WORD PARISH (1994), Rev. Milton E. Jordan, Ph.D., S.T.M., M.Div. (PH).
Res.: 885 Cox Rd., MD 20639-9239. Tel: 301-855-1825; Fax: 410-535-9057.
Catechesis/Religious Program—Students 198.

HYATTSVILLE, PRINCE GEORGES CO.

1—ST. JEROME (1886), Rev. James M. Stack; Rev. Msgr. Joseph L. Teletchea, Pastor Emeritus (Retired); Deacons Jerome Tintle; David Duggin. In Res., Revs. Joseph Abah (Nigeria); Joseph Elamparayil, O.C.D.; Jesudoss Thomas.
Res.: 5205 43rd Ave., MD 20781. Tel: 301-927-6684; Fax: 301-927-9167.
School—Tel: 301-277-4568; Fax: 301-779-2428. Sr. Joyce Volpini, S.N.D., Prin. Sisters of Notre Dame de Namur 4; Lay Teachers 24; Students 510.
Convent—5300 43rd Ave., MD 20781. Tel: 301-864-2016.
Child Center—Tel: 301-699-1314.
Catechesis/Religious Program—Students 55.

2—ST. MARK (1958), Revs. John T. Dakes, S.T.L.; Paul Sullins; Deacons Antonio Chaves; Philip Ricker; Mark Gallagher.
Res.: 7501 Adelphi Rd., MD 20783. Tel: 301-422-8300; Fax: 301-422-2313.
School—Tel: 301-422-7440; Fax: 301-422-7710. Lay Teachers 24; Students 485.
Catechesis/Religious Program—Tel: 301-422-7822. Students 430.

INDIAN HEAD, CHARLES CO., ST. MARY STAR OF THE SEA (1918), [CEM] Rev. William F. Goode; Deacons Thomas O. Hill; Albert S. Tompa.
Res.: 30 Mattingly Ave., MD 20640. Tel: 301-753-9177; Fax: 301-753-6995.
School—Tel: 301-283-6151; Fax: 301-283-4368. Lay Teachers 13; Students 205.
Catechesis/Religious Program—Tel: 301-375-9466. Students 108.

ISSUE, CHARLES CO., HOLY GHOST (1880), [CEM] Rev. Karl A. Chimiak; Deacon Walter Rourke.
Res.: 15848 Rock Point Rd., Newburg, MD 20664. Tel: 301-259-2515; Fax: 301-259-2289.
Catechesis/Religious Program—Tel: 301-259-0237. Students 75.
Mission—St. Francis de Sales Newburg, MD. 13675 Furbush Rd., Rock Point, Charles Co., MD 20664. Tel: 301-259-0254.

KENSINGTON, MONTGOMERY CO., HOLY REDEEMER (1948), Revs. Michael A. Salah; Zygmunt Kurzawinski. In Res., Rev. Joseph E. Bonafed (GBG).
Res.: 9705 Summit Ave., MD 20895. Tel: 301-942-2333; Fax: 301-942-1041.
School—9715 Summit Ave., MD 20895. Tel: 301-942-3701; Fax: 301-942-4981. Mrs. Harriann Walker, Prin. Lay Teachers 30; Students 485.
Catechesis/Religious Program—Tel: 301-942-3430. John Buchanan, D.R.E. Students 97.

LA PLATA, CHARLES CO., SACRED HEART (1901), [CEM] Revs. Raymond F. Schmidt; George A. Wilkinson Jr.; Deacon Anthony Barrasso.
Res.: 201 St. Mary's Ave., P.O. Box 1390, MD 20646. Tel: 301-934-2261; Fax: 301-934-5435.
School—Archbishop Neale School, Tel: 301-934-9595; Fax: 301-753-1717. Sr. Helene Fee, Prin. Sisters of the Immaculate Heart of Mary 2; Lay Teachers 29; Students 522.
Catechesis/Religious Program—Tel: 301-934-3386. Deacon Anthony T. Barrasso, D.R.E. Students 198.

LANDOVER HILLS, PRINCE GEORGE'S CO.

1—ST. MARY'S CATHOLIC CHURCH (1948), Revs. J. William Hines; Michael J. Blackwell (Retired); Deacons B. Paul Blaine, (Retired); Stephen M. Robinson; Sr. M. Roberta Kerins, S.C., Pastoral Assoc. In Res., Rev. Charuvilayil Jacob Geevarughese (India).
Res.: 7401 Buchanan St., MD 20784-2323. Tel: 301-577-8844; Fax: 301-306-5543.
School—7207 Annapolis Rd., MD 20784. Tel: 301-577-0031; Fax: 301-577-5264. Susan Junge Varrone, Prin. Lay Teachers 15; Students 290.
Catechesis/Religious Program—Tel: 301-577-2478. Students 114.

2—SYRO-MALANKARA MISSION (1985), (Indian), Rev. Charuvilayil Jacob Geevarughese (India).
Res.: 7401 Buchanan St., MD 20784-9998. Tel: 301-577-8844; Fax: 301-306-5543.
Catechesis/Religious Program—Students 26.

LANHAM, PRINCE GEORGES CO., ST. MATTHIAS APOSTLE (1960), Revs. Jeffrey M. Defayette; Jaroslaw Gamrot, M.I.C.; Deacon Ronald W. Schneider.
Res.: 9475 Annapolis Rd., MD 20706-3020. Tel: 301-459-4814; Fax: 301-306-4582.
School—Tel: 301-577-9412; Fax: 301-577-2060. Ms. Mary F. Frey, Prin. Lay Teachers 19; Students 239.
Catechesis/Religious Program—Tel: 301-459-4814, Ext. 205; Fax: 301-306-4582. Students 117.

LARGO, PRINCE GEORGES CO., ST. JOSEPH (1922), (African American), Rev. Raymond H. Moore, M.A.; Deacons Leon Bechet; Alton Davis.
Res.: 2020 St. Joseph Dr., MD 20774. Tel: 301-773-4838; Fax: 301-773-6832.
Catechesis/Religious Program—Tel: 301-773-2480. Students 118.

LAUREL, PRINCE GEORGES CO.

1—ST. MARY (1843), [CEM] Revs. Michael Wilson; Lawrence A. Young; Rev. Msgr. Robert L. Keesler, Pastor Emeritus (Retired); Rev. John Ming Ruan; Deacons Donald Parker; Perfecto Santiago; Douglas Sinchak.
Res.: 114 St. Mary's Pl., MD 20707. Tel: 301-725-3080; 301-953-3255; Fax: 301-725-2409.
School—Tel: 301-498-1433; Fax: 301-498-1170. Darcy Tomko, Prin. Lay Teachers 28; Students 489.
Catechesis/Religious Program—Tel: 301-490-8770. Sr. Loretta Primus, S.F.C.C., D.R.E. Students 464.

2—ST. NICHOLAS (1967), Rev. Robert P. Buchmeier; Deacons Francis Hannagan; Perry Iannaconi.
Res.: 8603 Contee Rd., MD 20708. Tel: 301-490-5116; 301-490-5117; Fax: 301-490-1527.
Catechesis/Religious Program—Tel: 301-776-8303. Students 175.

LEONARDTOWN, ST. MARY'S CO., ST. ALOYSIUS (1710), [CEM] Revs. Rory T. Conley; Daniel J. Malaver.
Res.: 22800 Washington St., P.O. Box 310, MD 20650. Tel: 301-475-8064; Fax: 301-475-8762.
School—The Father Andrew White, S.J., Tel: 301-475-9795; Fax: 301-475-3537. Lay Teachers 18; Students 267.
Catechesis/Religious Program—Students 155.

LEXINGTON PARK, ST. MARY'S CO., IMMACULATE HEART OF MARY (1947), [CEM] Rev. Michael F. Dolan.
Mailing Address: P.O. Box 6, MD 20653. Tel: 301-863-8144; Fax: 301-863-8180.
Catechesis/Religious Program—Tel: 301-863-8793. Janet Harmon, D.R.E. Students 244.

MCCONCHIE, CHARLES CO., ST. CATHERINE OF ALEXANDRIA (1911), [CEM] Rev. Robert J. Kosty; Deacon Frank L. Hopson.
Mailing Address: P.O. Box 278, Port Tobacco, MD 20677. Tel: 301-934-9630; Fax: 301-934-8320.
Catechesis/Religious Program—Tel: 301-934-9080. Students 43.

MECHANICSVILLE, ST. MARY'S CO., IMMACULATE CONCEPTION (1876), Rev. Msgr. Paul J. Gozaloff; Deacons James E. Conner; Allen J. Trichel; William Kyte.
Mailing Address: 28297 Old Village Rd., P.O. Box 166, MD 20659. Tel: 301-884-3123; Fax: 301-884-7437.
Catechesis/Religious Program—Tel: 301-884-3016. Students 255.

MEDLEY'S NECK, ST. MARY'S CO., OUR LADY'S (1776), [CEM] Rev. John M. Barry; Deacon Thomas C. Spalding Sr.
Mailing Address: P.O. Box 111, Leonardtown, MD 20650. Tel: 301-475-8403; Fax: 301-475-6632.
Catechesis/Religious Program—Students 79.

MITCHELLVILLE, PRINCE GEORGES CO., HOLY FAMILY (1938), [CEM] Rev. Michael C. Kidd; Deacon Henry D. Dardy.
Mailing Address: P.O. Box 1599, MD 20717. Tel: 301-249-2266; Fax: 301-249-2524.
Catechesis/Religious Program—Tel: 301-249-1167. Students 109.

MORGANZA, ST. MARY'S CO., ST. JOSEPH (1700), [CEM 2] [JC] Rev. David H. Werning; Deacons James A. Somerville; Robert Fortney.
Res.: P.O. Box 175, MD 20660. Tel: 301-884-4229; Fax: 301-884-7248.
Catechesis/Religious Program—Students 127.

MOUNT RAINIER, PRINCE GEORGES CO., ST. JAMES (1905), (Hispanic), Rev. Peter R. Alliata; Deacons Rodney R. Forbes; John H. Turner. In Res., Rev. Frank V. Du Preez (South Africa) (ATL).
Res.: 3628 Rhode Island Ave., MD 20712. Tel: 301-927-0567; Fax: 301-927-5289.
Catechesis/Religious Program—Tel: 301-927-0567. Students 545.

NEWPORT, CHARLES CO., ST. MARY (1674), [CEM] Rev. Frederick H. MacIntyre.
Res.: 11555 St. Mary's Church Rd., Charlotte Hall, MD 20622. Tel: 301-934-8825; Fax: 301-934-0245.
Catechesis/Religious Program—Students 99.

NEWTOWNE, ST. MARY'S CO., ST. FRANCIS XAVIER (1640), [CEM] Rev. John S. Mattingly; Deacon William H. Nickerson.
Res.: 21370 Newtowne Neck Rd., Leonardtown, MD 20650. Tel: 301-475-9885; Fax: 301-475-5662.
Catechesis/Religious Program—Students 114.

NORBECK, MONTGOMERY CO., ST. PATRICK (1966), Rev. Msgr. Thomas A. Kane; Revs. John R. Clark; Donald P. Worch; Deacons Ronald C. Crowley; James T. Nalls.
Res.: 4101 Norbeck Rd., Rockville, MD 20853. Tel: 301-924-2284; 301-924-2285; Fax: 301-929-3017.
Catechesis/Religious Program—Tel: 301-929-9314. Students 366.

NORTH BEACH, CALVERT CO., ST. ANTHONY (1905), Rev. David P. Russell; Deacon John F. Lynch.
Res.: 8900 Bay Ave., MD 20714. Tel: 410-257-2368; 301-855-7756 (Washington); Fax: 301-855-6839.
Catechesis/Religious Program—Tel: 202-855-0897. Sr. Anne Parker, D.R.E. Students 354.

OLNEY, MONTGOMERY CO., ST. PETER (1953), Revs. Thomas M. Kalita; Peter M. Giovanoni; Thomas G. LaHood; Deacons James Cadigan; Thomas Cioffi; Mrs. Elizabeth Harper, Business Mgr.
Res.: 2900 Sandy Spring Rd., MD 20832. Tel: 301-924-3774; Fax: 301-774-5259.
School—Tel: 301-774-9112; Fax: 301-924-6698. Mrs. Carol Mikoni, Prin. Lay Teachers 30; Students 487.
Catechesis/Religious Program—Tel: 301-570-4952. Dorothy O. Fosu, D.R.E. (Grades K-4); Ms. Julia Ruthman, D.R.E. (Grades 5-8). Students 863.

OXON HILL, PRINCE GEORGES CO., ST. COLUMBA (1960), Rev. Michael J. King, J.C.D.; Deacons Richard A. Fisher; David J. Hoen.
Res.: 7804 Livingston Rd., MD 20745. Tel: 301-567-5506; Fax: 301-567-6546.
School—7800 Livingston Rd., MD 20745. Tel: 301-567-6212; Fax: 301-567-6907. Lay Teachers 17; Students 281.

Catechesis/Religious Program—Tel: 301-567-6113. Students 71.

PISCATAWAY, PRINCE GEORGES CO., ST. MARY (1640), [CEM] Revs. Y. David Brault; Frederick J. Close Jr.; Deacon George Ames.
Res.: 13401 Piscataway Rd., Clinton, MD 20735. Tel: 301-292-0527; Fax: 301-292-8786.
School—Tel: 301-292-2522; Fax: 301-292-2534. Lay Teachers 15; Students 199.
Catechesis/Religious Program—Tel: 301-292-2486. Students 110.

POMFRET, CHARLES CO., ST. JOSEPH (1763), [CEM] Rev. J. Michael Quill.
Mailing Address: 4590 St. Joseph Way, MD 20675. Tel: 301-870-3041; 301-609-4670; Fax: 301-609-7564.
Catechesis/Religious Program—Students 201.

POOLESVILLE, MONTGOMERY CO., OUR LADY OF THE PRESENTATION (1992), Rev. G. Paul Herbert, J.C.L.
Mailing Address: P.O. Box 428, MD 20837. Tel: 301-349-2045; 301-972-7504; Fax: 301-349-5423.
Catechesis/Religious Program—Students 244.

POTOMAC, MONTGOMERY CO., OUR LADY OF MERCY (1959), (Korean), [CEM] Rev. Msgr. John J. Enzler; Rev. Kevin J. Kennedy; Deacons F. Ian Ravenscroft; James Yun. In Res., Rev. Msgr. William J. Awalt (Retired).
Res.: 9200 Kentsdale Dr., MD 20854. Tel: 301-365-1415; Fax: 301-365-3104.
School—9222 Kentsdale Dr., MD 20854. Tel: 301-365-4477; Fax: 301-365-3423. Mrs. Joan C. Hosmer, Prin. Lay Teachers 27; Students 291.
Catechesis/Religious Program—Tel: 301-365-1318. Students 354.

PRINCE FREDERICK, CALVERT CO., ST. JOHN VIANNEY (1965), [CEM] Rev. Peter J. Daly.
Res.: 105 Vianney Ln., MD 20678-4123. Tel: 410-535-0223; 301-855-1928; Fax: 410-535-4422.
Catechesis/Religious Program—Tel: 410-535-4395. Jeanette M. Pedone, D.R.E. Students 432.

RIDGE, ST. MARY'S CO., ST. MICHAEL (1824), [CEM] Rev. Maurice V. O'Connell.
Res.: , MD 20680. Tel: 301-872-4321.
School—P.O. Box 429, MD 20680. Tel: 301-872-5454. Sisters of St. Joseph of Chambery (Hartford, CT) 3; Lay Teachers 8; Students 220.
Catechesis/Religious Program—Students 98.

RIVERDALE PARK, PRINCE GEORGES CO., ST. BERNARD (1950), Revs. John F. McKay; James P. Holloway; Deacon Alfredo Hidalgo. In Res., Rev. Pius T. Ajiki.
Res.: 5700 St. Bernard Dr., MD 20737-2185. Tel: 301-277-1000; Fax: 301-277-3464.
School—Tel: 301-864-3801; Fax: 301-864-2912. Philip Buckley, Prin. Lay Teachers 14; Students 242.
Catechesis/Religious Program—Tel: 301-277-4220; Fax: 301-277-3464. Mrs. Lucille Kolodrubetz, D.R.E. Students 349.

ROCKVILLE, MONTGOMERY CO.

1—ST. ELIZABETH (1964), Rev. John F. MacFarlane. In Res., Rev. Robert Richler.
Res.: 917 Montrose Rd., MD 20852. Tel: 301-881-1380; Fax: 301-881-3068.
School—Tel: 301-881-1824; Fax: 301-881-6035. Lay Teachers 26; Students 480.
Catechesis/Religious Program—Students 200.

2—ST. MARY (1813), [CEM] Revs. John F. Myslinski; L. James Downs; Deacons Daniel Kostka; Robert A. Fischer.
Res.: 520 Veirs Mill Rd., MD 20852. Tel: 301-424-5550; Fax: 301-424-5579.
School—Tel: 301-762-4179; Fax: 301-762-8507. Lay Teachers 27; Students 267.
Catechesis/Religious Program—Tel: 301-424-7751. Students 341.
Mission—Our Lady of China 1001 Grandin Ave., Montgomery Co., MD 20851. Tel: 202-210-0358; Fax: 202-635-7563. Email: fathertsau@yahoo.com. Rev. Paul Tsau, 3017 Fourth St. N.E., 20017.

3—ST. RAPHAEL (1966), Revs. G. William Finch; Mark D. White; Peter Reynierse; Deacons Lawrence Gordon; Richard Mattocks; Frank Salatto.
Mailing Address: 1592 Kimblewick Rd., MD 20854.
Res.: 1590 Kimblewick Rd., MD 20854. Tel: 301-762-2143; Fax: 301-762-0719.
Catechesis/Religious Program—Students 900.

4—SHRINE OF ST. JUDE (1956), Revs. Oliver McGready; G. Ralph Duffy (Retired); Alphonso Carew (Sierra Leone); Francisco Alves, S.J. (India); Jose Lobaton; Jaime B. Hernandez; Deacons Nicholas E. Scholz; Donald Mays; Nathaniel Cordova.
Res.: 12701 Veirs Mill Rd., MD 20853. Tel: 301-946-8200; Fax: 301-946-4527.
School—Tel: 301-946-7888; Fax: 301-929-8927. Lay Teachers 26; Students 511.
Catechesis/Religious Program—Tel: 301-949-2336. Students 249.

ROSARYVILLE, PRINCE GEORGE'S CO., CHURCH OF THE MOST HOLY ROSARY (1966), [CEM] Rev. J. Isidore Dixon.
Res.: 11704 Duley Station Rd., Upper Marlboro, MD 20772. Tel: 301-856-3880; 301-856-3881; Fax: 301-856-3944.
Catechesis/Religious Program—Tel: 301-868-5475. Mary Farrmond, D.R.E. Students 43.

ST. INIGOES, ST. MARY'S CO., ST. PETER CLAVER (1903), (African American), [CEM] Rev. Damian Shadwell.
Res.: P.O. Box 240, MD 20684. Tel: 301-872-5460; Fax: 301-872-5672.
Catechesis/Religious Program—Students 74.

ST. MARY'S CITY, ST. MARY'S CO., ST. CECILIA (1974), [JC] Rev. Damian Shadwell.
Res.: 47950 Mattapany Rd., P.O. Box 429, MD 20686-0067. Tel: 301-862-4600.
Catechesis/Religious Program— Clustered with St. Michael's, Ridge. Students 7.

SEAT PLEASANT, PRINCE GEORGES CO., ST. MARGARET (1908), (African American), Rev. Benedict Folger, SS.CC.; Deacons Sam Minor; Robert Price; John Somerville.
Res.: 408 Addison Rd. S., MD 20743. Tel: 301-336-3344; Fax 301-336-5501.
School—410 Addison Rd. S., MD 20743. Tel: 301-336-3113; Fax: 301-350-1322.
Catechesis/Religious Program—Tel: 301-336-5976. Students 225.
Mission—St. Matthias

SILVER SPRING, MONTGOMERY CO.

1—ST. ANDREW APOSTLE (1959), Revs. Joseph P. Kennedy; Roger A. Soley; Deacon Kevin M Mukri.
Res.: 11600 Kemp Mill Rd., MD 20902. Tel: 301-649-3700; Fax: 301-681-3527.
School—Tel: 301-649-3555; Fax: 301-649-2352. Mrs. Catherine Medlock, Prin. Lay Teachers 32; Students 516.
Catechesis/Religious Program—Tel: 301-649-4200. Students 136.

2—ST. BERNADETTE (Four Corners) (1948), Revs. William J. Thompson; John P. Caulfield; Deacon Thomas E. Roszkowski. In Res., Rev. Nelson Grandi (Brazil) (MIA), (Portuguese Min.).
Res.: 70 University Blvd., E., MD 20901. Tel: 301-593-0357; Fax: 301-593-3088.
School—Tel: 301-593-5611; Fax: 301-593-9042. Lay Teachers 29; Students 490.
Catechesis/Religious Program—Tel: 301-593-5104. Mrs. Jane Baily, D.R.E. Students 113.

3—ST. CAMILLUS (1951), Revs. Lawrence J. Hayes, O.F.M.; Michael Johnson, O.F.M.; William McIntyre, O.F.M. (NY); Deacon Peter Barbernitz. In Res., Rev. Michael Perry, O.F.M.
Res.: 1600 St. Camillus Dr., MD 20903. Tel: 301-434-3400; Fax: 301-434-8041.
School—1500 St. Camillus Dr., MD 20903. Tel: 301-434-2344; Fax: 301-434-7726. Lay Teachers 14; Students 260.
Catechesis/Religious Program—Tel: 301-434-2111. Mrs. Rosa Diaz, D.R.E. Students 616.
School—Child Care, (Four Corners). Tel: 301-439-1640; Fax: 301-439-7078.

4—ST. CATHERINE LABOURE (Wheaton) (1951), Revs. Robert G. Amey; Thomas G. Morrow; Luis Marroquin; Bogumil Kosciesza; Deacons Carlos Contreras; Raymond L. Chaput.
Res.: 11801 Claridge Rd., MD 20902. Tel: 301-946-3636; Fax: 301-946-5064.
School—Tel: 301-946-1717; Fax: 301-946-9572. Daughters of Charity 2; Lay Teachers 27; Students 480.
Catechesis/Religious Program—Tel: 301-946-3010. Students 656.

5—CHRIST THE KING (Wheaton) (1961), Rev. John F. Plans, S.F.
Res.: 2300 East-West Hwy., 2301 Colston Dr., MD 20910. Tel: 301-589-8616; Fax: 301-587-1929.
Catechesis/Religious Program—Tel: 301-589-8620. Mary Ann Hoffman, D.R.E. Students 244.

6—ST. JOHN THE BAPTIST (Spring Brook) (1960), Revs. Francis G. Kazista; Joseph A Calis; Deacons Norman Keller; Bernard Bernier.
Res.: 12319 New Hampshire Ave., MD 20904. Tel: 301-622-1122; Fax: 301-625-9266.
School—Tel: 301-622-3076; Fax: 301-622-2453. Marianne Moore, Prin. Lay Teachers 23; Students 265.
Catechesis/Religious Program—Tel: 301-622-3933. Sr. Carmen Marie D'Adamio, D.R.E. Students 295.

7—ST. JOHN THE EVANGELIST (Wheaton) (1774), [CEM] Rev. Msgr. William J. English; Revs. Thomas A. Meighan (Retired); Mark E. Tucker, C.SS.R., J.C.L.; Scott R. Hahn; Sr. Theresa McElroy, I.H.M., Pastoral Min.; Deacon Dan P. Stallings.
Res.: 10103 Georgia Ave., MD 20902. Tel: 301-681-7663; Fax: 301-681-8793.
School—Tel: 301-681-7656; Fax: 301-681-0754. Sr. Kathleen Lannak, I.H.M., Prin. Lay Teachers 14; Students 336.
Catechesis/Religious Program—Tel: 301-681-7634. Sr. Roberta Harding, I.H.M., D.R.E. Students 255.

8—ST. MICHAEL (1930), Revs. Vincent J. Rigdon, J.C.L.; Fidel A. de Ramos; Claudes Kisuka-Kilumbu; Deacons Tom C. Newman, (Retired); Roberto Salgado. In Res., Rev. Paz Alexander Martinez-Diaz (El Salvador).
Res.: 824 Pershing Dr., MD 20910-4471. Tel: 301-589-1155; Fax: 301-589-3470.
School—810 Wayne Ave., MD 20910. Tel: 301-585-6873; Fax: 301-587-1142. Sr. Mary Raymond, S.S.N.D., Prin. Lay Teachers 13; Students 240.
Catechesis/Religious Program—Students 322.

9—OUR LADY OF GRACE (Leisure World) (1983), Rev. Msgr. John J. Madigan.
Mailing Address: 15661 Norbeck Blvd., MD 20906. Tel: 301-924-0067; Fax: 301-924-6809.
Res.: 15665 Norbeck Blvd., MD 20906. Tel: 301-924-4928.

10—OUR LADY QUEEN OF POLAND AND SAINT MAXIMILIAN KOLBE (Leisure World) (1983), (Polish), Rev. Klemens Dabrowski, S.Chr. (Poland).
Res.: 9700 Rosensteel Ave., MD 20910. Tel: 301-589-1857; Fax: 301-589-4401.
Catechesis/Religious Program—Students 50.

SOLOMONS, CALVERT CO., OUR LADY STAR OF THE SEA (1888), [CEM] Rev. Richard E. Gardiner; Deacons John G. Etzel; Robert L. Connelly.
Mailing Address: Box 560, MD 20688. Tel: 410-326-3535; Fax: 410-326-3679.
School—Tel: 410-326-3171; Fax: 410-326-9478. Sr. Rosella Summe, C.D.P., Prin. Sisters 2; Lay Teachers 12; Students 197.
Catechesis/Religious Program—Beth Oster, D.R.E. Students 324.

SUITLAND, PRINCE GEORGE'S CO., ST. BERNARDINE (1966), Rev. Arnold W. DePorter.
Res.: 2400 Brooks Dr., MD 20746-1144. Tel: 301-736-0707; Fax: 301-736-2984.
Catechesis/Religious Program—Students 39.

TAKOMA PARK, PRINCE GEORGES CO., OUR LADY OF SORROWS (1932), Revs. Luis P. Gonzalez (NEW); Sergio Ramos (Italy); Deacon James Wilson Jr. In Res., Rev. Manuel Ingelmo.
Res.: 1006 Larch Ave., MD 20912. Tel: 301-891-3500; Fax: 301-891-1523.
School—1010 Larch Ave., MD 20912. Tel: 301-891-2555; Fax: 301-270-6919. Mrs. Gail Ruffin, Prin. Lay Teachers 15; Students 210.
Catechesis/Religious Program—Tel: 301-891-2033. Students 173.

UPPER MARLBORO, PRINCE GEORGES CO., SAINT MARY OF THE ASSUMPTION (1848), [CEM] Rev. Msgr. Richard A. Hughes; Rev. An Vu; Deacons Frank Klco; William Walker.
Res.: 14908 Main St., MD 20772. Tel: 301-627-3255; Fax: 301-627-5533.
School—Tel: 301-627-4170; Fax: 301-627-6383. Mrs. Patricia Petruzzelli, Prin. Sisters - Servants of the Immaculate Heart of Mary 2; Students 288.
Catechesis/Religious Program—Tel: 301-627-4542. Mr. Charles Long, D.R.E. Students 85.

VALLEY LEE, ST. MARY'S CO., ST. GEORGE (1851), [CEM] Rev. Mark W. Ervin; Deacon George H. L'Heureux.
Mailing Address: P.O. Box 9, MD 20692. Tel: 301-994-0607; Fax: 301-994-1793.
Catechesis/Religious Program—Tel: 301-994-0737. Students 80.
Chapel—St. George's Island, St. Francis Xavier

WALDORF, CHARLES CO.

1—OUR LADY HELP OF CHRISTIANS (1980), Rev. Eamon Dignan.
Mailing Address: 100 Village St., MD 20602-2838. Tel: 301-645-7112; Fax: 301-645-3635.
Res.: 930 Barrington Dr., MD 20602-2838. Tel: 301-843-8823; Fax: 301-645-3635.
Catechesis/Religious Program—Mrs. Kathleen White, D.R.E. Students 454.

2—ST. PETER (1700), [CEM] Rev. John R. Pennington; Rev. Msgr. Henry Otero; Rev. David Beaubein; Rev. Msgr. Andrew Cassin, Pastor Emeritus; Deacons Charles J. Wilson; Robert A. Lyons.
Res.: 3320 St. Peter's Dr., MD 20601. Tel: 301-843-8916; Fax: 301-843-3163.
School—Tel: 301-843-1955; Fax: 301-843-6371. Judith DeLucco, Prin. Lay Teachers 34; Students 450.
Catechesis/Religious Program—Tel: 301-843-9583; Fax: 301-843-8548. Alice Culbreth, D.R.E. Students 231.

Chaplains of Public Institutions

WASHINGTON. *Children's Medical Center*, 111 Michigan Ave. N.W., 20010. Tel: 202-884-5050. Rev. Dominic Eshikena, O.P., Chap.

St. Elizabeth's Hospital (Government Operated), 2700 Martin Luther King Jr. Ave. S.E., 20032. Tel: 202-671-1218. Rev. Maximo J. Ortiz, O.S.A., Chap.

National Rehabilitation Hospital, 102 Irving St. N.W., 20010. Tel: 202-877-1000. Sr. Mary Leo Bryan, S.H.C.J.

Providence Hospital, 1150 Varnum St., N.E., 20017-2180. Tel: 202-269-7000. Revs. Carlo Napoli, T.O.R., Chap., Phelim Jordan, S.V.D. (Ireland), Chap.

Washington Hospital Center, 110 Irving St. N.W., 20010. Tel: 202-877-6691. Revs. John S. Wintermyer,

Chap., James Moran, Dominic Eshikena, O.P.
BETHESDA. *National Institutes of Health, Clinical Center*, MD. Tel: 301-496-3407. Revs. Henry Hefferman, S.J., Vincent J. O'Brien, S.J., Chap.
LANHAM. *Doctor's Hospital of Prince Georges County*, MD 20706. Served by the priests of St. Matthias Parish.

Special Ministries:
Rev. Msgrs.—
Criscuolo, Salvatore A., Chap., Police and Fire Dept.
Hurley, Leonard F., Rector, Cardinal Boyle Residence
O'Donnell, William F., Priest Dir., Catholic Cemeteries
Revs.—
Adams, John E., Dir., S.O.M.E.
Begg, Christopher T., Catholic University of America
Bryant, Michael, Chap., District of Columbia Jail
Byrne, William D., Chap., Newman Center, University of Maryland
Conley, Rory T., Archdiocesan Historian
Hurd, R. Scott, Hearts Aflame Program
Kemp, Raymond B., Fellow, Woodstock Theological Center, Georgetown University
Kuhn, John G., Dir. Emeritus, Anchor Mental Health Assoc.
Martin, Francis, Chap., Mother of God Community; Instructor, John Paul II Institute
Mcgrath, Lancelot, L.C., Chap., George Washington University Newman Medical Center
Montgomery, William L., Teacher, Carroll High School
Mordino, Robert F., Dir. CYO Retreats
Mudd, John, Dir., of Devel., Carroll High School
O'Brien, Raymond C., J.D., Asst. Dean, Catholic University
Trancone, Gerard A., Chap., Center for the Deaf & Gallaudet University
Woods, Keith, Chap., American Univ.

Pastoral Center Special Ministries:
Most Rev.—
Farrell, Kevin J., D.D., V.G., Vicar Gen. & Sec., Finance & Mgmt.
Rev. Msgrs.—
Gerhardt, Bernard C., S.T.L., J.C.D., P.A., Delegate to Ordinary
Hill, R. Cary, Sec. for Clergy
Knestout, Barry, Sec., Archbishop Cardinal McCarrick
Mellone, Michael J., Sec. for Clergy
Mosley, Godfrey, Vicar General
Ranieri, Joseph A., Coord. of Pastoral Care of Priests
Sadusky, Joseph F., M.Div., M.Ch.A., J.C.D., Judicial Vicar Tribunal
Revs.—
Bui, Joseph (OAK), Tribunal
Filardi, Edward J., Sec. to Cardinal
Herbert, G. Paul, J.C.L., Tribunal
Hurd, R. Scott, Hearts Aflame Program
Lee, Paul D., S.T.D., Office for Interreligious & Ecumenical Affairs.
Murray, Michael J., Exec. Dir., Office of the Permanent Diaconate
Panke, Robert J., Dir. of Priestly Vocations
Rigdon, Vincent J., J.C.L., Dir., Propagation of the Faith
Sileo, Joseph R.
Stuart, George E., J.C.L., Tribunal
Tappe, Walter J., Dir., Office of Worship

Hospital & Nursing Home Ministries:
Rev. Msgr.—
Hurley, Leonard F.
Revs.—
Kinter, John P.
Samaha, Jeffrey F.
Valentine, Keveny M.
Wintermyer, John S.

On Duty Outside the Archdiocese:
Rev. Msgrs.—
Albacete, Lorenzo, New York
Langsfeld, Paul J., S.T.D., Pontifical College Josephinum, Columbus, OH
Roensch, Roger, Vatican City State
Revs.—
Culkin, Michael, Lancaster, PA
Gancayco, Richard K., Honduras
Giese, Samuel C., West Virginia
Holt, Paul-Stephen, Iowa
Izac, Andre C. (R), North Carolina
Kuebler, A.M. Seamus, Maine
Metzdorf, William C., California
Murray, Paul, New York
Oberle, James P., S.S., Baltimore, MD
Sanz, Jose, D.L.P., California
Slevin, Henry, Vietnam
Smith, K. Bartholomew, Rome
Twohig, Christopher T., Ireland
Ulshafer, Thomas, S.S., Baltimore, MD
Walsh, Francis M.

Graduate Studies:
Revs.—
Coan, Gregory S., North American College, Rome
Golas, Robert W., North American College, Rome

Military Chaplains:
Revs.—
Cusick, Kevin M.
Fitz-Patrick, David M.
Lee, Matthew
Mudd, David A.
Passamonti, Paul G.
Studniewski, Gary R.

Absent On Leave:
Rev.—
Cocca, Stephen M.

Retired:
Rev. Msgrs.—
Awalt, William J., Our Lady of Mercy, 9200 Kentsdale Dr., Patomac, MD 20854.
Bailey, John L., O'Boyle Residence.
Bazan, Joaquin, Jeanne Jugan Residence.
Cassin, Andrew J., St. Peter, Waldorf, MD.
Echle, Harry A., Our Lady of Victory, 20007.
Farina, Michael F., St. Patrick, 20001.
Gillen, James G., Rome, Italy.
Jimenez, Armando, Cardinal O'Boyle Residence.
Joy, James B.
Keesler, Robert L., St. Mary, Laurel, MD.
Mohan, Robert Paul, Ph.D., Catholic University of America.
Quinn, W. Louis, Our Lady of Lourdes, Bethesda, MD.
Teletchea, Joseph L., Cardinal O'Boyle Residence.
Revs.—
Alvarez-Garcia, Julio, Carroll Manor, Miami, FL.
Barry, Paul, 5404 Bye St., Capitol Heights, MD 20743.
Bender, Lawrence A., S.S., Fort Washington, MD.
Bober, Francis J., 2475 Virginia Ave., N.W., #407, 20037.
Branch, Leslie, Carroll Manor, 1150 Varnum St., N.E., 20017.
Brogan, Hugh T., 678 Main St., Sugar Notch, PA 18706.
Caimi, Luke A., 9840 Sodus Manor Pl., P.O. Box 208, Faulkner, MD 20632.
Duffy, G. Ralph, Shrine of St. Jude, Rockville, MD.
Evans, Edward, Sunapee, NH.
Flaherty, Francis T., The Townhouse, 860 Arnold Ave., Pt. Pleasant, NJ 08742.
Gallagher, Roger P., Cardinal O'Boyle Residence, P.O. Box 29206, 20017.
Grace, Robert S., 4842 Willows Rd., Chesapeake Beach, MD 20732.
Higgins, John J., 300 Ocean Ave., Seabright, NJ 07760.
Ihrie, Bernard R., Jr., 3637 Bay Dr., Edgewater, MD 21037.
Jacobs, Harry W., 3134 Adderley Ct., Silver Spring, MD 20906.
Januszkiewicz, Henry, 4281 Inca Dove Ct., Naples, FL 34119.
Joyce, George V., 577 Carew St., Springfield, MA 01104.
Kehoe, Thomas F.
Kemp, Patrick W., 2900 Shipmaster Way, #301, Annapolis, MD 21401.
Liston, Paul F., 2657 Woodley Rd., NW.
McCormack, Brendan, Raphael House, 1515 Dunster Rd., Rockville, MD 20854.
McManus, Eamon, 215 E. Church St., Frederick, MD 21701.
Meighan, Thomas A., St. John the Evangelist, Silver Spring, MD.
Morel, Paul A.
Murphy, Francis J., 2875 Idlewood Dr., #29, Reno, NV 89509.
Muzzey, Charles H., Friendship Terrace, 4201 Buerworh Pl. NW # 522, 20016-4562.
Newman, Aloysius T., 6260 Crain Hwy., P.O. Box 2225, LaPlata, MD 20646.
Panares, Auxentivs, 5972-2 Pine Straw Ln., Jacksonville, FL 32221.
Powderly, James J., Cardinal O'Boyle Residence.
Quinones, Miguel P., Apartado, P.O. Box 40579, Bucaramanga-Santander, Colombia.
Reid, George B., St. Mary, Barnesville, MD 20838.
Roy, J. Jean, 15 Talmuth Ave., Haverhill, MA 01830.
Salcedo, Luis G., St. Bartholomew, Bethesda, MD.
Schellenberg, Milton A., Bartholomew House, 6904 River Rd., Bethesda, MD 20817.
Sheehan, Thomas J., St. Peter, 20069.
Torsiello, Ralph C., 4 Winchester Dr., Ocean View, DE 19970.
Tou, Louis A., 510 Edmonston Dr., Rockville, MD 20851.
Tran-Khac-Hy, Hilarius, Boyds, MD.
Twiddy, Paul, Charlotte Hall Veteran's Home, Rte. 5, Charlotte Hall, MD 20622.
Ward, Neal A., Taylor Farm Assisted Living, Bushwood, MD.
Wilson, George W., Hyattsville, MD.
Winnenberg, John O., San Pedro, CA 90732.
Wummer, Robert P., St. Ignatius, Oxon Hill, MD 20744.

Permanent Deacons:
Abbate, Paul J., (Retired), Archdiocese of Agana, Guam
Agostinelli, Floyd D., (On Leave of Absence)
Allen, David A., (Retired)
Allen, Robert F., St. John Neumann, Gaithersburg, MD
Ames, George B., Jr., St. Mary, Piscataway, MD
Angell, Kenneth, St. Jane Frances de Chantal, Bethesda, MD
Barbernitz, Peter M., St. Camillus, Silver Spring, MD
Barnes, John R., St. Joseph, Pomfret, MD
Barrasso, Anthony T., Sacred Heart, La Plata, MD
Barrett, Kenneth, St. Martin, Gaithersburg, MD
Barrett, Raymond J., Little Sisters of the Poor, Washington, D.C.
Barry, T. Kevin, St. Edward the Confessor, Bowie, MD
Battaglia, Thomas D., (Retired)
Bechet, Leon J., St. Joseph, Largo, MD
Begg, George B., Jr., (Retired)
Bell, Joseph, Incarnation, Washington, DC
Bell, Lawrence G., St. Martin, Gaithersburg, MD
Beller, Edwin J., (Retired)
Bernier, Bernard A., St. John the Baptist, Silver Spring, MD
Berry, Robert L., St. Gabriel, Washington, DC
Betz, Andrew J., St. Joseph, Beltsville, MD
Birkel, Richard, (On Leave of Absence)
Blaine, B. Paul, (Retired)
Bobbitt, John W., (Retired)
Boesman, William C., St. Thomas the Apostle, Washington, DC
Brink, Edward J., (Leave of Absence)
Briscoe, John A., (Retired)
Brokenborough, Alfred T., (Retired)
Brown, James E., Holy Redeemer, Washington, DC
Brown, Sylvester, (Retired)
Burroughs, Eugene, St. Mary, Bryantown, MD
Butler, Kevin A., Sr., Holy Comforter-St. Cyprian, Washington, DC
Cadigan, James, St. Peter, Olney, MD
Cahoon, David L., Jr., St. Mary, Barnesville, MD
Cain, Leonard F., (Retired)
Carroll, Donald T., (Leave of Absence)
Chaput, Raymond L., St. Catherine Laboure, Wheaton, MD
Chase, Ira E., Basilica of the National Shrine of the Immaculate Conception, Washington, DC
Chaves, Antonio, (Retired)
Chrzanowski, Edmund A., Jr., St. John Vianney, Prince Frederick, MD
Cioffi, Thomas, St. Peter, Olney, MD
Coates, Vincent J., Jr., (Leave of Absence)
Coleman, Earle W., (Retired)
Collins, Gerald A., Holy Family, Hillcrest Hts., MD
Connelly, Robert L., Our Lady Star of the Sea, Solomons, MD
Conner, James E., Immaculate Conception, Mechanicsville, MD
Connor, John E., (Leave of Absence)
Conrad, Joseph M., St. Luke, Washington, DC
Contreras, Carlos E., St. Catherine Laboure, Wheaton, MD
Cooke, Gerald F., St. Ann, Wahington, DC
Cooper, Philip J., (Leave of Absence)
Cordova-Ferrer, Nathaniel, St. Mark the Evangelist, Hyattsville, MD
Crowley, Ronald C., St. Patrick, Rockville, MD
Cummins, Don E., (Leave of Absence)
Cummins, Eugene J., Jr., St. Martin, Gaithersburg, MD
Curtis, Joseph F., Jr., St. Francis Xavier, Washington, D.C.
Cyrus, Ralph W., Holy Comforter-St. Cyprian, Washington, DC
Daniels, Willis, St. Aloysius, Washington, DC
Danko, Edward, Sacred Heart, Bowie, MD
Dardy, Henry, Holy Family, Mitchellville, MD
Davies, Gary, Little Flower, Bethesda, MD
Davis, Alton, Jr., St. Joseph, Largo, MD
Davis, William E., (Leave of Absence)
DeRoze, Donald G., Resurrection, Burtonsville, MD
DiDuca, Paul, Our Lady of the Visitation, Darnestown, MD

Ditewig, William, (Leave of Absence)
Donlon, Jerome A., Holy Cross, Garrett Park, MD
Draper, Harry R., (Retired)
Duggin, David, St. Jerome, Hyattsville, MD
Dunne, Joseph E., (Leave of Absence)
Ealey, Ronald R., Holy Comforter-St. Cyprian, Washington, D.C.
Edelin, Charles E., Jr., Holy Comforter-St. Cyprian, Washington, DC
Elliott, Thomas B., (Leave of Absence)
Emley, William P., (Leave of Absence)
Enderle, Francis X., (Leave of Absence)
Enright, Timothy D., Mother Seton, Germantown, MD
Etzel, John G., (Retired)
Feneis, Albert G., (Leave of Absence)
Finerty, John F., St. Paul, Damascus, MD
Fisher, Richard A., St. Columba, Oxon Hill, MD
Fisher, Robert A., St. Mary, Rockville, MD
Flynn, Leo, Our Lady of Victory, Washington, DC
Forbes, Rodney R., St. James, Mt. Rainier, MD
Fortney, Charles R., St. Joseph, Morganza, MD
Gallagher, Mark J., St. Mark, Hyattsville, MD
Garcia, David F., (Leave of Absence)
Genis, Thomas P., Immaculate Conception, Washington, DC
Gignilliat, Robert L., St. Joseph, Pomfret, MD
Glenn, Clark, St. Ignatius, Oxon Hill, MD
Gordon, Lawrence C., (Retired)
Hannagan, Francis L., St. Nicholas, Laurel, MD
Haywood, Hiram H., Jr., (Retired)
Hidalgo, Alfredo, (Retired)
Hill, Charles, (Retired)
Hill, Thomas O., Sr., (Retired)
Hoen, David J., St. Columba, Oxon Hill, MD
Hoffman, Michael R., St. Anthony, North Beach, MD
Holson, Edward, (Leave of Absence)
Hong, Pascal, St. Francis of Assisi, Derwood, MD
Hopson, Frank, (Retired)
Huber, Robert T., Mother Seton, Germantown, MD
Huete, Stephen, (Leave of Absence)
Hume, W. Michael, (Leave of Absence)
Iannaconni, Perry F., St. Nicholas, Laurel, MD
Interlandi, Joseph S., (Leave of Absence)
Jackson, Harold I., (Leave of Absence)
Johnson, Bernard C., (Retired)
Jones, Thomas R., Our Lady of Perpetual Help, Washington, DC
Keller, Grafton T., (Retired)
Keller, Norman B., (Retired)
Kelly, John D., St. Anthony, Washington, DC
Kelly, Richard F., St. Augustine, Washington, DC
Kemp, William, Holy Angels, Avenue, MD
Klco, Frank, St. Mary of the Assumption, Upper Marlboro, MD
Kostka, Daniel S., St. Mary, Rockville, MD
Kraemer, Francis W., Sr., (Retired)
Kronschnabel, Michael C., (Leave of Absence)
Kube, Carl B., (Leave of Absence)
Kunsemiller, John H., (Leave of Absence)
Kyte, William, Immaculate Conception, Mechanicsville, MD
L'Heureux, George G., St. George, Valley Lee, MD
Lacovaro, James G., (Leave of Absence)
Lemon, John, (Leave of Absence)
Lennon, Joseph M., (Retired)
Leonard, John M., (Retired)
Levy, Richard A., Jr., (Leave of Absence)
Locke, John W., (Retired)
Luetjen, Palmer, (Retired)
Lynch, John F., St. Anthony, North Beach, MD
Lyons, Robert A., St. Peter, Waldorf, MD
Lyons, Robert R., St. Bartholomew, Bethesda, MD
Mangold, Charles C., (Retired)
Marinari, A. John, (On Leave of Absence)
Martin, E. Chad, Jesus the Good Shephard, Dunkirk, MD
Martin, J. Murry, (Retired)
Martin, Nerus O., Jr., (Retired)
Mastrangelo, Eugene K., St. John Vianney, Prince Frederick, MD
Mattocks, Richard E., St. Raphael, Rockville, MD
Mays, Donald, Shrine of St. Jude, Rockville, MD
McAskill, Donald K., (Leave of Absence)
McCann, James C., St. Rose of Lima, Gaithersburg, MD
McGinness, John J., St. Patrick, Washington, DC
McGrath, Joseph B., (Retired)
Merella, Bartholomew J., St. Joseph, Washington, DC
Meyer, Ferdinand, (Retired)
Meyer, Ronald J., St. Martin, Gaithersburg, MD
Middleton Henry D., III, St. Mary, Bryantown, MD
Migliorini Louis, Sr., (Retired)
Miles, Lawrence A., Mount Calvary, Forestville, MD
Miller, Alfred A., Jr., Our Lady Queen of Peace, Washington, DC
Miller, Lawrence L., (Leave of Absence)
Minor, Samuel L., Jr., St. Margaret, Seat Pleasant, MD
Moll, Anthony W., St. John the Evangelist, Clinton, MD
Moore, James, St. Ignatius, Chapel Point, MD
Moskaitis J. Vincent, Holy Redeemer, Kensington, MD
Mukri, Kevin, St. Andrew the Apostle, Silver Spring, MD
Murati, George, (Leave of Absence)
Nalls, James T., St. Patrick, Rockville, MD
Newman, C. Thomas, (Retired)
Nguyen, John H., Our Lady of Vietnam, Silver Spring, MD
Nickerson, William J., St. Francis Xavier, Newtowne, MD
Nosacek, Andrew J., St. Pius X, Bowie, MD
Oettinger, Frank F., (Leave of Absence)
Om, Michael W., Our Lady of Mercy, Potomac, MD
Paolucci, Robert J., (Leave of Absence)
Parker, Donald A., St. Mary of the Mills, Laurel, MD
Picard, Adrien D., (Leave of Absence)
Pillman, Theodore, Ascension, Bowie, MD
Pinder, Wilbur L., Jr., St. Francis of Assisi, Derwood, MD
Powell, David R., (Leave of Absence)
Price, Robert, St. Margaret of Scotland, Seat Pleasant, MD
Pyle, Jay Allen, (Leave of Absence)
Quander James W., (Retired)
Raffensperger, Jeffrey, Sacred Heart, Bowie, MD
Ravenscroft, F. Ian, Our Lady of Mercy, Potomac, MD
Reilly, Matthew B., Cathedral of St. Matthew, Washington, DC
Rice, Ulysses, (Retired)
Ricker, Philip W., St. Mark, Hyattsville, MD
Robinson, John, Jr., (Leave of Absence)
Robinson, Stephen M., St. Mary, Landover Hills, MD
Roszkowski, Thomas E., St. Bernadette, Silver Spring, MD
Rourke, Walter G., Holy Ghost, Issue, MD
Ruffo, Paul, (Leave of Absence)
Salatto, Frank J., Jr., St. Raphael, Rockville, MD
Salgado, Roberto, St. Michael, Silver Spring, MD
Santiago, Perfecto, St. Mary of the Mills, Laurel, MD
Schneider, Ronald W., St. Matthias, Lanham, MD
Scholz, Nicholas E., Shrine of St. Jude, Rockville, MD
Schopfer, Richard J., Little Flower, Bethesda, MD
Serafini, Bartolo, Hispanic Center, Washington, DC
Sferrella, Joseph J., (Leave of Absence)
Shewmaker, John B., Our Lady of Lourdes, Bethesda, MD
Sinchak, J. Douglas, St. Mary of the Mills, Laurel, MD
Smith, Anthony S., (Retired)
Somerville, James, St. Joseph, Morganza, MD
Somerville, John W., Basilica of the National Shrine of the Immaculate Conception, Washington, DC
Soto, Alfredo, St. Bartholomew, Bethesda, MD
Spalding, Thomas C., Sr., (Retired)
Sparling, Donald, St. Pius X, Bowie, MD
Springer, James R., (Leave of Absence)
Stackpole, Terrell U., Archbishop Carroll High School, Washington, D.C.
Stallings, Dan P., St. John the Evangelist, Silver Spring, MD
Sweeney, Anthony J., III, Immaculate Heart of Mary, Lexington Park, MD
Tan, Domingo, Our Lady of China, Rockville, MD
Terrar, David B., St. Paul, Damascus, MD
Testudine, Joseph, (Retired)
Thomas, Reginald A., Our Lady Help of Christians, Waldorf, MD
Thomas, William, (Retired)
Thompson, Daniel R., Shrine of the Most Blessed Sacrament, Washington, D.C.
Thompson, Finis E., Ascension, Bowie, MD
Tintle, Jerome A., St. Jerome, Hyattsville, MD
Tompa, Albert S., St. Mary, Star of the Sea, Indian Head, MD
Trichel, Allen J., (Leave of Absence)
Turner, Al Douglas, Nativity, Washington, D.C.
Turner, John H., (Retired)
Vargas, Jorge W., Our Lady Queen of the Americas, Washington, DC
Verdon, John, Jesus the Good Shepherd, Dunkirk, MD
Vita, William A., Jr., Mother Seton, Germantown, MD
Wakefield, Walter W., III, (Leave of Absence)
Walker, William, St. Mary of the Assumption, Upper Marlboro, MD
Welch, Joseph, Holy Spirit, Forestville, MD
Weschler, Charles A., St. Paul, Damascus, MD
Whitaker, Robert W., St. Ann, Washington, DC
White, Robert C., Sr., St. Augustine, Washington, DC
Williams, Morris, (Retired)
Wilson, Charles J., St. Peter, Waldorf, MD
Wilson, James, (Retired)
Work, Boyd, Jr., Cathedral of St. Matthew, DC
Yates, Paul F., (Retired)
Yun, James, Our Lady of Mercy, Potomac, MD
Ziemianski, Lawrence L., (Leave of Absence)
Zusi, J. Michael, (Leave of Absence)

INSTITUTIONS LOCATED IN THE ARCHDIOCESE

[A] SEMINARIES, ARCHDIOCESAN

WASHINGTON

Faculty: Revs. Thomas R. Hurst, S.S., Ph.D., Rector; Edward J. Frazer, S.S., M.A., S.T.L.; Albert C. Giaquinto, S.S., M.A., S.T.L.; David D. Thayer, S.S., S.T.L., Ph.D., Vice Rector; Chorbishop Seely Beggiani, S.T.D.; Revs. Anthony J. Pogorelc, M.Div., M.S., Ph.D.; Jon J. O'Brien, S.J., D.O.; Jerome M. Hall, S.J., S.T.L., Ph.D.

Theological College of the Catholic University of America, 401 Michigan Ave., N.E., 20017. Tel: 202-756-4900; Fax: 202-756-4909. Email: decker@theologicalcollege.org. Web: www.theologicalcollege.org.

Legal Title: *Theological College, Inc.* Sulpician Fathers Faculty: Priests 6; Religious 2; Students 80.

[B] SEMINARIES, RELIGIOUS OR SCHOLASTICATES

WASHINGTON. *Atonement Seminary-Franciscan Friars of the Atonement*, 5207 Colorado Ave., N.W., 20011. Tel: 202-722-1893; Fax: 202-722-1716. Rev. John J. Keane, S.A., Admin. Priests 3. In Res. Revs. Kenneth Cienik, S.A.; Clement St. Jacques, S.A. (Retired).

Augustinian College, Order of St. Augustine, 3700 Oakview Ter., N.E., 20017-2591. Tel: 202-635-5299; Fax: 202-635-5296. Web: www.augustinian.org. Revs. Francis J. Horn, O.S.A., Treas.; Luis A. Vera, O.S.A. Prior, Dir. Pre-Novices. Solemnly Professed Friars 9; Simply Professed Friars 5; Prenovices 2. In Res. Revs. Francis J. Caponi, O.S.A.; Mark A. Garrett, O.S.A.; Joseph A. Genito, O.S.A., Dir. Professed Students; James V. Vitali, O.S.A.

St. Bonaventure Friary, 3514 15th St., N.E., 20017. Tel: 202-529-5324; 202-832-0953; Fax: 202-635-4871. Revs. Berard L. Marthaler, O.F.M. (SD) (Retired); John Kuziol, O.F.M.Conv., M.Div.; Martin Day, O.F.M.Conv., M.A., Guardian; Bros. Robert Roddy, O.F.M.Conv., Treas. & Procurator; William Pineda, O.F.M.Conv.; Andrew Santamauro, O.F.M.Conv.; Daniel Lutolf, O.F.M.Conv. Priests 3; Brothers 12.

Deshairs Community-Oblates of St. Francis de Sales Residence, 1621 Otis St., N.E., 20018-2321. Tel: 202-526-7403. Revs. Lewis S. Fiorelli, O.S.F.S.; Donald J. Heet, O.S.F.S.; John W. Crossin, O.S.F.S. (ARL); James R. Yeakel, O.S.F.S. Brothers 1.

Diocesan Laborer Priests, House of Studies (1966), 3706 15th St., N.E., 20017. Tel: 202-832-4217; Fax: 202-526-5692. Email: dlpriests@hotmail.com. Revs. Juan L. Garcia, Dir.; Ovidio Pecharroman, Delegate; Gabriel Calvo; Juan A. Paigbo. Priests 4; Total Enrollment 4.

Discalced Carmelite Friars, 2131 Lincoln Rd., N.E., 20002-1199. Tel: 202-832-6622; Fax: 202--83--571. Revs. John Sullivan, O.C.D., Prior; Marc Foley, O.C.D.; Regis Jordan, O.C.D.; Kieran Kavanaugh, O.C.D.; Francis Miller, O.C.D. (Retired); Steven Payne, O.C.D.; Bros. Antonine DiSabella, O.C.D.; Joseph Girouard, O.C.D.; Edward O'Donnell, O.C.D.; Bryan Paquette, O.C.D.; Michael Stoegbauer, O.C.D.

Legal Title: *Discalced Carmelite Friars, Inc.* Priests 6; Brothers 5.

Dominican House of Studies, 487 Michigan Ave., N.E., 20017. Tel: 202-529-5300; Fax: 202-636-4460. Very Rev. John C. Vidmar, O.P., Prior; Revs. Brian J. Shanley, O.P., Subprior; Vincent Wiseman, O.P., Student Master; Very Rev. Thomas P. McCreesh, O.P., Pres., Pontifical Faculty; Bro. Martin Downey, O.P., Economic Admin.; Revs. John W. Burke, O.P., Dir. Word of God Institute; Joseph Augustine DiNoia, O.P., Dir., Intercultural Forum, Pope John Paul II Cultural Center; Stephen Paul Alcott, O.P.; Mario Juan Diego Brunetta, O.P.; Basil Burr Cole, O.P.; Pierre H. Conway, O.P.; John Dominic Corbett, O.P.; Giles Richard Dimock, O.P.; Henry Thomas Donoghue, O.P.; Lawrence J. Donohoo, O.P.; John Martin Egan, O.P.; Joseph Peter Fegan, O.P.;

Norman H. Fenton, O.P.; Dominic Fields, O.P.; Kenneth Harkins, O.P.; William J. Hill, O.P.; John Frederick Hinnebusch, O.P.; John Gregory Maturi, O.P.; John Patrick McGovern, O.P.; Albert Paretsky, O.P.; Kurt Pritzl, O.P., Ph.D.; Stephen Desmond Ryan; Matthew Rzeczkowski, O.P.; Malcolm Sylvester Willoughby, O.P. Priests 30; Brothers 1; Clerical Students 23; Seminarians 23. In Res. Revs. Vincent Li, O.P.; Anthony Walsh, O.P.

St. Francis Friary-Capuchin College, 4121 Harewood Rd., N.E., 20017-1593. Tel: 202-529-2188; Fax: 202-526-6664. Web: www.capcollege.net. Revs. Francis Yacobi, O.F.M.Cap., Supr.; William Graham, O.F.M.Cap., Treas.; Donald F. Lippert, O.F.M.Cap; Sebastian F. Miklas, O.F.M.Cap.; J. Daniel Mindling, O.F.M.Cap.; Christopher Rengers, O.F.M.Cap. (RCK); Joseph Mindling, O.F.M.Cap.; William Wiethorn, O.F.M.Cap., Vicar; Moises Villalta, O.F.M.Cap.; Paul Winter, O.F.M.Cap. (Australia); Charles Knoll, O.F.M.Cap.; Bros. Michael Letosak, O.F.M.Cap.; Alfred Vincent, O.F.M.Cap.; Robert Toomey, O.F.M.Cap. Priests 11; Scholastics 6; Brothers 3; Total Enrollment 6.

Franciscan Mission Service of North America, 1323 Quincy St., N.E., P.O. Box 29034, 20017. Tel: 202-832-1762; Fax: 202-832-1778. Email: fms5@juno.com. Web: www.franciscanmissionservice.catholic.edu. Rev. Joseph J. Nangle, O.F.M., Co-Dir.; Megeen White Testa, Co-Dir. Priests 1; Religious Women 1; Lay Staff 2.

St. Joseph's Seminary, 1200 Varnum St., N.E., 20017. Tel: 202-526-4231; 202-526-4229 (Student); Fax: 202-526-7811. Email: filippellissj@aol.com. Very Revs. John L.M. Filippelli, S.S.J., Spiritual Dir.; Thomas Frank, S.S.J., Rector; Revs. James A. Hayes, S.S.J., Dir. of Maintenance; John Raphael, S.S.J.; James McLinden, S.S.J., Dir. Josephite Pastoral Center; Joseph L. Waters, S.S.J.; Robert DeGrandis, S.S.J.; Bros. Earl Kent, S.S.J.; Thomas Vincent, S.S.J. St. Joseph's Society of the Sacred Heart-Josephite Fathers & Brothers Priests 6; Franciscan Sisters of St. Joseph 5; Seminarians 7. In Res. Revs. Howard Johnson (JKS) (Retired); Joseph Kamanda (Sierra Leone); Nicholas Nnabuaku, C.S.S.P. (Nigeria).

Josephite Pastoral Center, 1200 Varnum St., N.E., 20017. Tel: 202-526-9270; 202-526-9271; Fax: 202-526-7811. Email: ssjpastrcntr@aol.com. Rev. James E. McLinden, S.S.J., Dir.; Maria M. Lannon, Admin. Priests 1; Brothers 1; Deacons 1; Lay Women 3.

Marian Fathers Scholasticate, 3885 Harewood Rd., N.E., 20017. Tel: 202-526-8884; Fax: 202-832-6551. Email: fjoe@juno.com. Web: www.marian.org. Revs. Joseph Roesch, M.I.C., Supr. & Formation Dir.; Lawrence Dunn, M.I.C.; Bro. Leonard Konopka, M.I.C., Asst. Supr. Priests 2; Brothers 1; Novices 3; Seminarians 5.

Marist College, The Scholasticate, 815 Varnum St., N.E., 20017-2199. Tel: 202-529-2821; Fax: 202-635-4627. Revs. Mark G. Kenney, S.M., Rector & Supr.; Joseph C. Hurtuk, S.M., Formation Team. Priests 2; Scholastics 2.

Maryknoll Fathers and Brothers, 4834 16th St., N.W., 20011. Tel: 202-726-4252; Fax: 202-726-0466. Email: mkldc@aol.com. Web: www.maryknoll.org. Revs. Richard S. Czajkowski, M.M., Dir.; John Sullivan, M.M., Dir. Affiliates.

Office of Justice and Peace, P.O. Box 29132, 20017. Tel: 202-832-1780; Fax: 202-832-5159. Email: mknolldc@igc.org. Marie Dennis, Dir.; Rev. James W. Kofski, M.M.; Sisters Mary Duffy, M.M., Assoc.; Mercedes Roman, M.M., Assoc.; Judy Coode, Communications Dir.; Deidre E. Point, Admin. Asst.

Oblates of St. Francis de Sales, 721 Lawrence St., N.E., 20017. Tel: 202-269-9410; Fax: 202-526-4323. Web: www.oblates.org. Priests 5; Brothers 1; Professed 3; Postulants 5.

DeSales Hall Residence: Revs. James J. Greenfield, O.S.F.S., Supr. & Dir. Formation; William F. Davis, O.S.F.S.; Robert M. Rutledge, O.S.F.S.; Dominic G. Ciriaco; Kevin M. Nadolski, O.S.F.S. (ARL); Bro. Michael O'Neill McGrath, O.S.F.S., Artist, Bee Still Studio.

Vocation Office Tel: 202-526-5651; Fax: 202-526-5653. Email: knadolski@oblates.org.

Bee Still Studio Tel: 202-526-7074.

St. Paul's College, 3015 Fourth St., N.E., 20017-1199. Tel: 202-832-6262; Fax: 202-269-2507. Revs. James W. Donovan, C.S.P., Supr.; Charles A. Martin, C.S.P., Assoc. Dir. of Formation; Kenneth G. Boyack, C.S.P., D.Min.; John E. Hurley, C.S.P., D.Min.; John E. Lynch, C.S.P., Ph.D. (Retired); Neil J. McEleney, C.S.P., S.S.L.; Robert E. Moran, C.S.P., Dir. of Novices; Robert S. Rivers, C.S.P.; Ronald G. Roberson, C.S.P., S.E.O.D. Paulist Fathers Priests 9; Sisters 5; Laity 7; Students 10.

Queen of Pious Schools House of Studies-Piarist Fathers, 1339 Monroe St., N.E., 20017-2510. Tel: 202-529-7734; Fax: 202-526-4014. Email: piarist@earthlink.net. Revs. Andrew C. Buechele, Sch.P., Ph.D., Rector & Master of Clerics; David B. Powers, Sch.P., Prov.; Leonard Gendernalik, Sch.P., Prov. Sec. Priests 3.

Washington Theological Union, 6896 Laurel St., N.W., 20012. Tel: 202-726-8800; Fax: 202-726-1716. Web: www.wtu.edu. Revs. Daniel McLellan, O.F.M., Pres.; Marion Moeser, O.S.F., Vice Pres. Academic Affairs & Academic Dean.

Legal Title: *Washington Theological Union, Inc.*, Established in 1968 as the Coalition of Religious Seminaries. The Union is a school of theology and ministry owned by seven religious communities: Order of Carmelites, Provinces of the Most Pure Heart of Mary and St. Elias; Congregation of the Sacred Hearts of Jesus and Mary, US East Coast Province; Order of Friars Minor, Province of the Most Holy Name of Jesus; Order of St. Augustine, Province of St. Thomas of Villanova; Redemptorist Fathers and Brothers, Baltimore Province; Order of Friars Minor Conventual, Province of the Immaculate Conception. Priests 17; Sisters 6; Lay Teachers 1; Students 281.

Whitefriars Hall, 1600 Webster St., N.E., 20017. Tel: 202-526-1221; Fax: 202-526-9217. Email: egavin@carmelnet.org. Revs. Emmett Gavin, O.Carm., Prior & Formation Dir.; David Blanchard, O.Carm.; Donald W. Buggert, O.Carm.; Stefanus Buyung, O.Carm. (Indonesia); Quinn Conners, O.Carm.; Christopher J. Kulig, O.Carm. (GAL); Joseph Lucchesi, O.Carm. (JOL); Raymond Maher, O.Carm. (PMB), Co-Dir. Formation; Patrick McMahon, O.Carm., Ph.D.; Craig Morrison, O.Carm.; Joseph Mothersill, O.Carm. (Ireland); Benny Phang, O.Carm. (Indonesia); Godlif Sianipar, O.Carm. (Indonesia); Joachim Smet, O.Carm. (JOL); Wilson Varikatt, O.Carm. (India); John Welch, O.Carm.; Lambert Yore, O.Carm.; Bro. Daryl Moresco, O.Carm. (Australia), Assoc. Dir. Formation. Friars in Solemn Profession 16; Friars in First Profession 6.

The Carmelitana Library Tel: 202-526-1221, Ext. 121; Fax: 202-526-9217. Rev. Patrick McMahon, O.Carm., Ph.D.

BELTSVILLE. *The Saint LaSalle Auxiliary*, P.O. Box 1710, MD 20704-1710. Tel: 301-210-7444; Fax: 301-210-0614. Email: lsauxiliary@hotmail.com. Bro. Thomas Chadwick, F.S.C., Dir. The Auxiliary is the Development Office for the Christian Brothers of the Baltimore Province. Brothers 2; Lay Staff 3.

CHEVERLY. *Damien House*, 6013 Inwood St., MD 20785. Tel: 301-386-4840. Email: ssccdc@aol.com. Revs. Marisi Palpale, SS.CC.; Ambrose Forgit, SS.CC.; Bro. Johnathan Hurrell, SS.CC. Congregation of the Sacred Hearts Priests 2; Brothers 1.

SILVER SPRING. *Austin Friars Hall, Order of St. Augustine*, 2123 Edgewater Pkwy., MD 20903-1210. Tel: 301-445-2583; Fax: 301-445-0565. Email: wimmer@erols.com. Revs. William R. Faix, O.S.A.; Joseph F. Wimmer, O.S.A., Treas.; William M. Cleary, O.S.A., Prior; Maximo J. Ortiz, O.S.A.; Cedric M. Wilson, O.S.A. Priests 6. In Res. Rev. John Burkhard, O.F.M.Conv.

Holy Family Seminary, 401 Randolph Rd., P.O. Box 4138, MD 20914-4138. Tel: 301-622-3582; Fax: 301-622-2959. Email: HolyFamSem@aol.com. Web: members.aol.com/holyfamsem. Very Rev. Miguel Mateo, S.F., Vice Prov. Supr.; Revs. Jose Maria Conde, S.F. (SFE); John A. Sierra, S.F.; Nicholas Rodriguez, S.F. Priests 3; Students 5.

Holy Name College (Residence) , 1650 St. Camillus Dr., MD 20903. Tel: 301-434-3400; Fax: 301-434-4624. Rev. Joseph G. Rozansky, O.F.M., Supr. & Dir. Formation; Bro. Thomas E. Conway, Vicar & Asst. Dir. Formation; Revs. James P. Scullion, O.F.M.; Lawrence Ford, O.F.M.; Peter C. Sheridan, O.F.M.; Russel Murray, O.F.M.; Bro. Juniper Capece, O.F.M. House of Studies for Holy Name Province of the Order of Friars Minor Solemnly Professed Friars 7; Simply Professed Friars 9.

Salvatorian Community, 104 Bishop Dr., MD 20905. Tel: 301-933-3451; Fax: 301-933-3330. Email: gwillis@frostcenter.com. Web: www.sds.org. Revs. Glen Willis, S.D.S., Area Coord.; Richard Maloney, S.D.S.; Eliot Nitz, S.D.S., First Consultor; Roman Stadtmueller, S.D.S.; F. Philip Vogel, S.D.S.; David J. Bergner, S.D.S.; Robert Nugent, S.D.S.; Donald Skwor, S.D.S.; Julian Guzman, S.D.S.; Bogdan Palka, S.D.S.; Bros. Roger Nelson, S.D.S., Vicar Coord.; Marvin Kluesner, S.D.S.; James Rieden, S.D.S.; Nickolas Crosby, S.D.S.; Sean McLaughlin, S.D.S. Society of the Divine Savior/ Salvatorians Priests 9; Brothers 5; Lay Members 20.

WEST HYATTSVILLE. *Pallottine Seminary at Green Hill*, 2009 Van Buren St., MD 20782-1761. Tel: 301-422-3777; Fax: 301-422-4070. Rev. Bernard P. Carman, S.A.C., Rector, Formation Dir. Society of the Catholic Apostolate Priests 1.

[C] COLLEGES AND UNIVERSITIES

WASHINGTON. *Catholic University of America, The* (1887), Nugent Hall/Executive Offices, 20064. Tel: 202-319-5000; Fax: 202-319-4441. Email: webmaster@cua.edu. Web: www.cua.edu. Most Revs. Theodore Cardinal McCarrick, Chancellor; William E. Lori, Chm., Bd. of Trustees; Very Rev. David M. O'Connell, C.M., J.C.D., Pres.; John J. Convey, Ph.D., Provost; Ralph H. Beaudoin, M.B.A., Vice Pres. Finance & Treas.; Susan D. Pervi, M.A., Vice Pres. Students Life; Frank G. Persico, M.A., Vice Pres. & Chief of Staff; Rev. Msgr. Brian Ferme, D.Phil., J.C.D., Dean School of Canon Law; Rev. Kurt Pritzl, O.P., Ph.D., Dean School of Philosophy; Lawrence R. Poos, Ph.D., Dean School of Arts & Sciences; Charles C. Nguyen, Sc.D., Dean School of Engineering; William F. Fox Jr., J.D., LL.M., Dean Columbus School of Law; Ann Marie T. Brooks, Ph.D., Dean School of Nursing; Murry Sidlin, M.M., Dean Benjamin T. Rome School of Music; Martha L. Hale, Ph.D., Dean School of Library & Information Science; James R. Zabora, S.C.D., Dean Natl. Catholic School of Social Svc.; Randall Ott, M.Arch., Dean School of Architecture & Planning; Sara M. Thompson, Ph.D., Dean Metropolitan College; Rev. Thomas R. Hurst, S.S., Ph.D., Rector, Theological College; Christopher J. Wheatley, Ph.D., Vice Provost & Dean of Undergraduate Studies; Dr. Peter Cimbolic, Ph.D., Vice Provost & Dean of Graduate Studies; Ziaeddin Mafaher, M.A., M.S., CIO; James W. Mayo, Ph.D., Assoc. Provost for Sponsored Research; Rev. Robert Schlageter, O.F.M.Conv., S.T.L., Univ. Chap. & Dir. Campus Ministry; Adele Chwalek, M.S.L.S., Dir. Libraries; Mary Ellen Flaherty, J.D., Registrar; Victor Nakas, M.Phil., Exec. Dir. Office of Public Affairs; David J. McGonagle, Ph.D., Dir., CUA Press; Shahin Mafaher, B.S., Acting Dean, Enrollment Mgt.; Carl A. Petchik, M.Arch., M.C.R.P., Exec. Dir. Facility Opers.; Paul K. Brooks, B.A., J.D., LL.M., Dir. Devel. Priests 35; Sisters 12; Lay Teachers 312; Students 5,527.

Priests Associated with the University Full-Time: Rev. Msgrs. Thomas J. Green, J.C.D. (BGP); Kevin W. Irwin, S.T.D. (NY); Robert S. Sokolowski, Ph.D. (HRT); Robert F. Trisco, Hist.Eccl.D. (CHI), Prof. Emeritus, Church History; John Wippel, Ph.D. (STU); Revs. Regis Armstrong, O.F.M.Cap., M.Div., M.Theo., M.S.Ed., Ph.D.; John P. Beal, J.C.D.; Christopher T. Begg; Walter J. Burghardt, S.J., S.T.D.; William Cenkner, O.P., Ph.D. (Retired); Raymond F. Collins, S.T.D.; Francis W. Danella, O.S.F.S., D.Min.; Alexander A. Di Lella, O.F.M., S.T.L., S.S.L., Ph.D.; John T. Ford, C.S.C., M.A., S.T.D. (FTW); Edward J. Frazer, S.S., M.A., S.T.L.; Robert M. Friday, S.T.D. (PIT); Timothy Friedrichsen, Ph.D., S.T.D.; John P. Galvin, D.Th. (BO); Albert C. Giaquinto, S.S., M.A., S.T.L.; Francis T. Gignac, S.J., S.T.L., D.Phil.; Patrick Granfield, O.S.B., Ph.D., S.T.D.; Jacques Gres-Gayer, D.Theo., S.T.D. (France); Sidney H. Griffith, S.T.D., Ph.D.; Jerome M. Hall, S.J., S.T.L., Ph.D.; Thomas P. Halton, Ph.D. (Ireland), Prof. Emeritus (Retired); Rev. Msgr. Stephen W. Happel, s.t.d.; Revs. Donald J. Heet, O.S.F.S.; Joseph Jensen, O.S.B., S.S.L., S.T.D.; David W. Johnson, S.J., Ph.D. (Retired); Thomas C. Kane, O.P., S.T.D. (Retired); Robert J. Kaslyn, C.P., J.C.D.; Robert T. Kennedy (NY); Joseph A. Komonchak (NY); Louis M. LaFavia, C.PP.S., Ph.D. (Retired); John E. Lynch, C.S.P., Ph.D. (Retired); Berard L. Marthaler, O.F.M. (SD), Prof. Emeritus (Retired); Frank J. Matera (HRT); Gerald D. McBrearity, S.S., M.A., S.T.B., D.Min.; Francis J. Moloney, S.D.B., S.T.L., S.S.L., D.Phil., S.T.B. (Australia); William J. Moorman, O.SS.T.; Mark Morozowich, S.E.O.D. (SJP); Hy Khac Nguyen; Raymond C. O'Brien, J.D.; Jon J. O'Brien, S.J., D.O.; Anthony J. Pogorelic, S.S., M.Div., Ph.D.; David N. Power, O.M.I., S.T.D. (Retired); Kurt Pritzl, O.P., Ph.D.; Dominic F. Serra, S.T.D.; Brian J. Shanley, O.P.; Raymond Studzinski, O.S.B., Ph.D.; David Thayer, S.S., S.T.L., Ph.D.; James A. Wiseman, O.S.B., M.A., S.T.D.

Priests Associated with the University Part-Time: Very Rev. Seely Beggiani, S.T.D. (SAM); Rev. Joseph A. Fitzmyer, S.J., S.T.L., S.S.L., Ph.D., Prof. Emeritus, Biblical Studies; Rev. Msgrs. George G. Higgins, Ph.D. (CHI) (Retired); Robert Paul Mohan, Ph.D., Prof. Emeritus, Philosophy (Retired); Rev. Raymond H. Potvin, Ph.D. (SPR), Prof. Emeritus, Sociology (Retired); Rev. Msgr. Gerald Sloyan, S.T.D., Ph.D.; Rev. John F. Smolko (BGP).

Clerical Members, Board of Trustees: Most Rev. Robert J. Banks; Rev. Msgr. Michael Bransfield; Most Revs. Daniel M. Buechlein, O.S.B., D.D.

(MEM); Charles J. Chaput, D.D. (RC); Thomas V. Daily, D.D. (PMB), Bishop Emeritus; Harry J. Flynn, D.D. (STP); His Eminence Francis Cardinal George, O.M.I., Ph.D., S.T.D. (CHI); William Cardinal Keeler (BAL); Most Rev. William E. Lori, Chm.; His Eminence Adam Cardinal Maida; Theodore Cardinal McCarrick, Chancellor; Most Revs. William Francis Murphy; Frances B. Shulte, Bishop Emeritus; Terry J. Steib; Donald W. Wuerl, S.T.D. (PIT); Philip M. Hannan, Bishop Emeritus; Roger Cardinal Mahony; Justin Cardinal Rigali; His Eminence Edward Cardinal Egan (NY); Most Revs. Gregory M. Aymond, D.D. (AUS); Daniel N. Dinardo; John C. Favalora, D.D. (MIA); Edward P. Cullen, D.D. (ALN); Timothy M. Dolan (NO); Allen H. Vigneron, D.D. (OAK).

Georgetown University (1789), 37th and O Sts., N.W., 20057. Tel: 202-687-0100. Web: www.georgetown.edu. John J. DeGioia, Ph.D., Pres.; James J. O'Donnell, Ph.D., Provost; Daniel D. Sedmak, M.D., Exec. Vice Pres. & Exec. Dean, Medical Center; Judith C. Areen, Vice Pres. Law Center Affairs & Dean of the Law Center; Spiros Dimolitsas, Ph.D., Senior Vice Pres.; Edward M. Quinn, Univ. Sec.; Christopher Joyce, M.B.A., Senior Vice Pres., CFO & Treas.; Michael Goodwin, Vice Pres., Alumni & Univ. Rels.; Todd A. Olson, Ph.D., Interim Vice Pres. Student Affairs; Jo-Ann Henry, Vice Pres. & Chief Human Resources Officer; Daniel R. Porterfield, Ph.D., Vice Pres. Public Affairs & Strategic Devel.; H. David Lambert, Vice Pres. for Information Services & CIO; Jane E. Genster, Vice Pres. & Gen. Counsel; Rev. Philip L. Boroughs, S.S.J., Vice Pres., Mission & Ministry; Michael D. McGuire, Exec. Dir. Planning & Institute Research.

The following are the Schools and Colleges which compose the University:

Georgetown College (1789), Jane Dammen McAuliffe, Ph.D., Dean.

Graduate School of Arts & Sciences (1820), David W. Lightfoot, Ph.D., Dean.

School of Medicine (1851), 3900 Reservoir Rd., N.W., 20007. Ray Mitchell, M.D., Senior Assoc. Dean Academic Affairs.

Law Center (1870), 600 New Jersey Ave., N.W., 20001. Judith C. Areen, Dean.

School of Nursing & Health Studies (1903), 3700 Reservoir Rd., N.W., 20007. Bette Keltner, R.N., F.A.A.N., Ph.D., Dean.

Edmund A. Walsh School of Foreign Service (1919), Hon. Robert L. Gallucci, Ph.D., Dean.

Robert Emmett McDonough School of Business (1957), John Mayo, Ph.D., Dean.

Georgetown Public Policy Institute (1990), 3600 N. St. N.W., Ste. 200, 20007. Judith Feder, Ph.D., Dean.

School of Summer and Continuing Education (1974), Robert J. Thomas, Ph.D., Dean.

Joseph Mark Lauinger Library Artemus G. Kirk, M.A., Univ. Librarian.

Office of the University Registrar John Q. Pierce IV, M.A., University Registrar.

Office of Alumni & University Relations, Georgetown University, Box 571253, 20057. Tel: 202-687-4111.

Affirmative Action Programs, G-10 Darnall Hall, 37th St. & O St., N.W., 20057. Tel: 202-687-4798; Fax: 202-687-7778. Rosemary Kilkenny, J.D., Special Asst. to Pres. for AAP. Jesuits 23; Sisters 5; Lay Teachers 1,067; Total Enrollment 12,688.

Trinity College, 125 Michigan Ave., N.E., 20017. Tel: 202-884-9000; Fax: 202-884-9229. Email: pauleya@Trinitydc.edu. Web: www.trinitydc.edu. Patricia A. McGuire, Pres.; Sr. Mary Johnson, S.N.D., Community Representative; Dr. Robert Preston, Vice Pres. Academic Affairs. Sisters of Notre Dame de Namur Priests 1; Sisters 5; Lay Professors 54; Students 1,600.

[D] HIGH SCHOOLS, ARCHDIOCESAN

WASHINGTON. *Archbishop Carroll High School*, 4300 Harewood Rd., N.E., 20017. Tel: 202-529-0900; Fax: 202-529-5989. Email: archbishopcarroll.org. Web: www.archbishopcarroll.org. Mr. John T. Butler, Pres.; Mr. James Mumford, Prin.; Revs. William Cleary; William L. Montgomery; John Mudd. (Coed) Priests 2; Sisters 1; Lay Teachers 58; Students 625.

[E] HIGH SCHOOLS, PRIVATE

WASHINGTON. *St. Anselm's Abbey School*, (Grades 6-12), 4501 South Dakota Ave., N.E., 20017. Tel: 202-269-2350; Fax: 202-269-2373. Email: mainoffice@saintanselms.org. Web: www.stanselms.org. Rev. Dom Peter Weigand, O.S.B., Headmaster. Operated by the Benedictine Monks of St. Anselm's Abbey, Seven year college preparatory courses. Priests 8; Sisters 1; Brothers 2; Lay Teachers 45; Students 255.

Georgetown Visitation Preparatory School, 1524 35th St., N.W., 20007. Tel: 202-337-3350; Fax: 202-342-5733. Email: name@visi.org. Web: www.nisi.org. Sr. Mary Berchmans Hannan, V.H.M., Pres.; Mr. Dan Kerns, Headmaster. Sisters 4; Lay Teachers 45; Students 457

Gonzaga College High School, 19 Eye St., N.W., 20001. Tel: 202-336-7100; Fax: 202-336-7172. Email: anovotny@gonzaga.org. Web: www.gonzaga.org. Rev. Allen P. Novotny, S.J., Pres.; Michael Pakenham, Headmaster; Revs. Robert J Rokusek (DET), Chap.; James R. Conroy, S.J., Rector. Society of JesusJesuit Community Priests 20; Brothers 2; Lay Teachers 66; Scholastics 2; Students 890. In Res. Revs. R. Bruce Baringer, S.J., Pastor; John A. Conlin, S.J.; Olivier de Fromage, S.J.; Henry B. Haske, S.J.; Henry G. Heffernan, S.J.; Robert J. Keslyn, S.J.; Raymond M. Lelii, S.J.; Joseph M. McCloskey, S.J.; Bro. Donald Dixon, S.J.

St. John's College High School (1851), (Boys Grade 8, Coed Grades 9-12) , 2607 Military Rd., N.W., 20015. Tel: 202-363-2316; Fax: 202-686-5162. Email: stjohnschs@stjohns-chs.org. Web: stjohns-chs.org. Bro. Thomas Gerrow, F.S.C., Pres.; Mr. Jeffrey Mancabelli, Prin.

Legal Title: *St. John's College* Brothers of the Christian Schools, College Preparatory, Elective Army Junior ROTC. Brothers 8; Sisters 1; Lay Teachers 78; Students 1,056.

BETHESDA. *Mater Dei School, Inc.*, 9600 Seven Locks Rd., MD 20817. Tel: 301-365-2700; 301-365-2701; Fax: 301-365-2710. Mr. Edward N Williams, Headmaster; Mr. Christopher S. Abell, Pres. Students 225.

Stone Ridge School of the Sacred Heart, 9101 Rockville Pike, MD 20814. Tel: 301-657-4322; Fax: 301-657-2381. Email: adyer@stoneridge.org. Web: www.stoneridge.org. Sr. Anne Dyer, Headmistress. Religious of the Sacred Heart Sisters 3; Lay Teachers 68; Students 792.

BLADENSBURG. *Elizabeth Seton High School*, 5715 Emerson St., MD 20710-1844. Tel: 301-864-4532; Fax: 301-864-8946. Email: 460@setonhs.org. Web: www.setonhs.org. Sr. Virginia Ann Brooks, D.C., Pres.; Mrs. Sharon Pasterick, Prin. Daughters of Charity of St. Vincent de Paul 4; Lay Staff 32; Lay Teachers 43; Administration & Staff 34; Girls 538.

FORESTVILLE. *Bishop McNamara High School* (Coed) , 6800 Marlboro Pike, MD 20747. Tel: 301-735-8401; Fax: 301-735-0934. Email: clarkm@bmhs.org. Web: www.bmhs.org. Ms. Heather Gossart, Pres.; Mr. Marco Clark, Prin. Holy Cross Brothers Brothers 8; Lay Teachers 72; Students 806.

GAITHERSBURG. *Mother of God School*, 20501 Goshen Rd., P.O. Box 2418, MD 20879. Tel: 301-990-2088; Fax: 301-947-0574. Email: mogsadmin@erols.com. Web: www.mogschool.com. Students 245.

HYATTSVILLE. *De Matha Catholic High School*, 4313 Madison St., MD 20781. Tel: 301-864-3666; Fax: 301-864-0248. Email: dmmail@dematha.org. Web: www.dematha.org. Rev. William J. Sullivan, O.SS.T., Rector; Dr. Daniel J. McMahon, Prin. Conducted by the Trinitarian Fathers of the Province of the Immaculate Heart of Mary Priests 4; Lay Teachers 75; Students 973.

KENSINGTON. *The Academy of the Holy Cross, Inc.*, 4920 Strathmore Ave., MD 20895. Tel: 301-942-2100; Fax: 301-929-6440. Email: ahcadmin@erols.com. Web: academyoftheholycross.org. Sr. Katherine Kase, C.S.C., Prin.

Legal Title: *The Academy of the Holy Cross, Inc.* Sisters 9; Lay Teachers 30; Students 520.

LAUREL. *St. Vincent Pallotti High School* , MD 20707. Tel: 301-725-3228; Fax: 301-776-4343. Email: admissions@pallottins.org. Web: www.pallottihs.org. Stephen J. Edmonds, Prin. Missionary Sisters of the Catholic Apostolate Priests 1; Sisters 2; Lay Teachers 30; Students 480.

LEONARDTOWN. *St. Mary's Ryken High School*, 22600 Camp Calvert Rd., MD 20650. Tel: 301-475-2814; 301-932-4422; Fax: 301-475-7972. Web: www.smrhs.org. Rev. Paul S. Tipton (MOB), Pres.; Mrs. Mary Joy Hurlburt, Prin. Sponsored by the Xaverian Brothers Brothers 1; Lay Teachers 45; Students 641.

NORTH BETHESDA. *Georgetown Preparatory School* , MD 20852. Tel: 301-493-5000; Fax: 301-530-9531. Email: jesuit@gprep.org. Web: www.gprep.org. Dr. James P. Power, Headmaster; Dr. Peter J. Relic, Acting Headmaster; Revs. Garrett D. Orr, S.J., Supr.; William L. George, Pres.; David A. Sauter, S.J.; Gregory J. Eck, S.J.; William J. Elliott, S.J.; Aloysius C. Galvin, S.J.; Eugene J. Linehan, S.J.; Vincent M. O'Brien, S.J. Jesuit CommunitySociety of Jesus Priests 5; Lay Teachers 43; Students 445

POTOMAC. *Connelly School of the Holy Child*, (Grades 6-12), 9029 Bradley Blvd., MD 20854. Tel: 301-365-0955; Fax: 301-365-0981. Web: www.holychild.org. Maureen K. Appel, Headmistress. Sisters of the Holy Child Jesus, College Preparatory for Girls. Sisters 1; Lay Teachers 53; Students 441.

WHEATON. *Good Counsel High School*, 11601 Georgia Ave., MD 20902. Tel: 301-942-1155; Fax: 301-942-3656. Email: raimo@olgchs.org. Web: olgchs.org. Mr. Arthur Raimo, Pres.; Mr. John Graham, Prin.; Revs. Michael T. Jones, Chap.; Barry R. Gross (LFT). Xaverian Brothers Priests 1; Brothers 1; Lay Teachers 84; Students 1,073.

[F] ELEMENTARY SCHOOLS, PRIVATE

BETHESDA. *The Woods Academy*, 6801 Greentree Rd., MD 20817. Tel: 301-365-3080; Fax: 301-469-6439. Email: mworch@woodsacademy.org. Web: www.woodsacademy.org. Mary Worch, Head of School. Students 301; Lay Teachers 26.

POTOMAC. *The Heights School*, 10400 Seven Locks Rd., MD 20854. Tel: 301-365-4300; Fax: 301-365-4303. Email: bstetson@mail.com. Mr. Alvaro de Vicente, Headmaster; Rev. William H. Stetson, Chap.; Mr. Andrew Reed, Middle School Head; Mr. Jeff Presberg, Lower School Head. Private, Independent, Spiritual Formation and Religious Education provided by the Prelature of Opus Dei.

[G] SPECIAL SCHOOLS

WASHINGTON. *Lt. Joseph P. Kennedy, Jr., Institute*, 801 Buchanan St., N.E., 20017. Tel: 202-529-7600; Fax: 202-529-2028. Email: gadair@kennedyinstitute.org. Web: www.kennedyinstitute.org. Deacon Richard C. Birkel, Ph.D., Pres. & CEO.

Nonprofit Organization Serving Children and Adults With Developmental Disabilities:

Adult Learning & Employment Services Tel: 202-529-0500; Fax: 202-529-8211. Participants 364.

Family & Personal Support Services Tel: 301-251-2860; Fax: 301-251-8559. Staff 25; Participants 102.

Early Intervention & Preventive Services Tel: 202-529-7600; Fax: 202-529-2028. Staff 45; Participants 82.

Kennedy Education Tel: 202-529-7600; Fax: 202-529-2028. (Includes Kennedy School, Outreach Program to Catholic Schools and Inclusion 2000) Staff 52; Students 140.

Residential Division Tel: 202-529-7600; Fax: 202-529-2028. Staff 81; Residents 61.

Administration Division Tel: 202-529-7600; Fax: 202-529-2028. Staff 25.

Community Living Partnership Staff 3; Families 50.

ROCKVILLE. *The Frost Center, Society of the Divine Savior*, 4915 Aspen Hill Rd., MD 20853. Tel: 301-933-3451; Fax: 301-933-3330. Email: seanmcl@frostcenter.com. Web: www.frostcenter.com. Bro. Sean McLaughlin, S.D.S., Dir.; Gregory Headen, Prin.; Rev. Glen Willis, S.D.S., Business Mgr.; Bros. Roger Nelson, S.D.S.; Peter Farnesi, S.D.S., Plant Mgr. A School and Therapy Program for Emotionally Disturbed Students and Families. Grades 1-12. Priests 1; Brothers 3; Staff 37; Students 67.

[H] CATHOLIC CHARITIES OF THE ARCHDIOCESE

WASHINGTON. *Catholic Charities of the Archdiocese of Washington, Inc.*, 924 G St., N.W., 20001. Tel: 202-772-4300; Fax: 202-772-4308. Web: catholiccharitiesdc.org. Mr. Edward Orzechowski, M.S.W., Pres.

Montgomery County Family Center, 11160 Veirs Mill Rd., Ste. 700, Wheaton, MD 20902. Tel: 301-942-1856; Fax: 301-942-3793.

Prince George's County Family Center, 6706 Marlboro Pike, Forestville, MD 20747. Tel: 301-568-9529; Fax: 301-568-9567.

Calvert County Family Center, 855 Main St., Prince Frederick, MD 20678. Tel: 410-535-0309; Fax: 410-257-1002.

Charles County Family Center, The Charles Bldg., 513 E. Charles St., La Plata, MD 20646. Tel: 301-934-2582; Fax: 301-934-3439.

St. Clement's Family Center, P.O. Box 113, Avenue, MD 20609. Tel: 301-769-2788; Fax: 301-769-2789.

Southeast Family Center, 220 Highview Place, S.E., 20032. Tel: 202-574-3442; Fax: 202-574-3474. Total Assisted 80,438; Total Staff 401.

[I] ARCHDIOCESAN VOLUNTEER ORGANIZATIONS

WASHINGTON. *Archdiocesan Association of Ladies of Charity*, P.O. Box 10038, 20018. Mrs. Patricia Y. Camp, Pres. Purpose: Individual charity work, usually of emergency nature and support various other agencies, foodbanks, child care centers and pregnancy aid centers.

Society of St. Vincent de Paul, Archdiocesan Council of Washington, 1357 E. Capitol St. SE, 20003.

Office of Archdiocesan Council Tel: 301-699-3410.

[J] ORPHANAGES AND INFANT HOMES

HYATTSVILLE. *St. Ann's Infant and Maternity Home*, 4901 Eastern Ave., MD 20782. Tel: 301-559-5500; Fax: 301-853-6985. Email: questions@saint-anns.com. Web: www.saint-anns.com. Sisters Josephine Murphy, D.C., Admin.; Virginia Ann, Local Supr. Daughters of Charity Sisters 9; Residential Children 60; Day Care 75; Teen Mother-Baby Program: Mothers 20; Babies 15.

[K] GENERAL HOSPITALS

WASHINGTON. *Center for Life of Providence Hospital*, 1150 Varnum St., N.E., 20017. Tel: 202-269-7074; Fax: 202-267-7470. Email: ghassin@provhosp.org. Non-Profit Corporation to Render Service, Support and Assistance in the Provision of Community Services Which Foster Human Dignity, Family Unity and Respect for Life. Services Include: Reduced Fee Maternity Programs. Total Assisted 109,400; Total Staff 1,586.

De Paul Foundation, Inc., 1150 Varnum St., N.E., 20017. Tel: 202-269-7039; Fax: 202-269-7029. Email: jboland@provhosp.org. De Paul Foundation, Inc. was Organized to Provide Fund Development, Financial and Other Assistance to Provide Hospital and Other Subsidiaries of De Paul Foundation for the Health Care, Medical, Educational and Human Needs of the District of Columbia and Vicinity, by Functioning as a Charitable Nonprofit, Nonstock Corporation.

Providence Health Foundation, 1150 Varnum St., N.E., 20017. Tel: 202-269-7776; Fax: 202-269-7687. Providence Health Foundation, Inc. (PHF), a District of Columbia Charitable Nonprofit Corporation, was Organized to Support the Mission of Providence Hospital by Conducting Fundraising and Development Activities, by Receiving and Managing Donations, by Making Grants, and by Promoting Educational Activities and Scientific Research.

Georgetown University Hospital, 3800 Reservoir Rd., N.W., 20007. Tel: 202-784-3000; Fax: 202-784-3095. Email: sheamj@gunet.georgetown.edu. Web: www.georgetown.edu. Joy Drass, M.D., Pres.; Rev. James M. Shea, S.J., Dir. Pastoral Care; Sr. Patricia Parachini, S.N.J.M., Chap.; Revs. Joy Alappat, Chap.; Gustaaf M. Keppens, S.J., Chap. Bed Capacity 535; Total Staff 3,833; Patients Assisted Annually 195,060.

Providence Health Services, Inc., 1150 Varnum St., N.E., 20017. Ambulatory-Outpatient Care, Promote Wellness and Carry Out of Educational Activities and Scientific Research.

Providence Hospital, 1150 Varnum St., N.E., 20017. Tel: 202-269-7000; Fax: 202-269-7160. Email: srcarol@provhosp.org. Web: www.provhosp.org. Sr. Carol Keehan, D.C., Pres.; Revs. Phelim Jordan, S.V.D. (Ireland), Chap.; Carlo Napoli, T.O.R., Chap. Daughters of Charity of St. Vincent de Paul Sisters 10; Bed Capacity 576; Patients Assisted Annually 180,000; Total Staff 2,340.

SILVER SPRING. *Holy Cross Hospital of Silver Spring, Inc.*, 1500 Forest Glen Rd., MD 20910. Tel: 301-754-7000; Fax: 301-754-7413. Web: www.holycrosshealth.org. Mr. Kevin J. Sexton, CEO; Sr. Virginia McLaughlin, C.S.C., Dir. Pastoral Care; Revs. Eliot Nitz, S.D.S.; George Markwell, M.Afr.; Lamberto Pasion, O.P. Sisters of the Holy Cross Sisters 14; Bed Capacity 340; Patients Assisted Annually 186,000; Total Staff 2,330.

[L] HOMES FOR AGED

WASHINGTON. *Cardinal O'Boyle Residence for Priests*, 1150 Varnum St., N.E., 20017. Tel: 202-269-7100; Fax: 202-269-7820. P.O. Box 29206, 20017-0206. In Res. Rev. Msgrs. John L. Bailey (Retired); Leonard F. Hurley, Chap., Carroll Manor & Rector; Armando Jimenez (Retired); Hugh J. Philips; Joseph L. Teletchea (Retired); Revs. Joseph Bui-Trang-Nghiem, Tribunal; James Finan; Roger P. Gallagher (Retired); James J. Powderly (Retired).

Jeanne Jugan Residence-St. Joseph's Villa, 4200 Harewood Rd., N.E., 20017-1554. Tel: 202-269-1831; Fax: 202-269-1134. Email: mswashlsp@earthlink.net. Sr. Cecilia Mary Sartorius, L.S.P., Admin.; Rev. Msgr. Joaquin Bazan (Retired). Little Sisters of the Poor Sisters 13; Residents 76; Apartments 23; Total Staff 79.

BELTSVILLE. *Ammendale Normal Institute of Prince George's County-La Salle Hall* (1880), 6001 Ammendale Rd., MD 20705. Tel: 301-210-7443; Fax: 301-210-0614. Email: kevinerb20@hotmail.com. Bros. Kevin Erb, F.S.C., Dir.; Robert Wise, F.S.C., Assoc. Dir. Brothers of the Christian Schools, Residence for Retired and Convalescent Brothers. Brothers 19.

BETHESDA. *Palmer Park Senior Housing, Inc.*, c/o Victory Housing, Inc., 5430 Grosvenor Ln., Ste. 210, MD 20814-2142. Tel: 301-493-6000; Fax: 301-493-9788. Email: info@victoryhousing.org. Web: www.victoryhousing.org. John Spencer, Vice Pres.

Takoma Tower, Inc., c/o Victory Housing, Inc., 5430 Grosvenor Ln., Ste. 210, MD 20814-2142. Tel: 301-493-6000; Fax: 301-493-9788. Email: info@victoryhousing.org. Web: www.victoryhousing.org. John D. Spencer, Vice Pres.

Winslow House, Inc., c/o Victory Housing, Inc., 5430 Grosvenor Ln., Ste. 210, MD 20814-2142. Tel: 301-493-5507. Email: jspencer@victoryhousing.org. John Spencer, Vice Pres.

HYATTSVILLE. *Sacred Heart Home Inc.*, 5805 Queens Chapel Rd., MD 20782. Tel: 301-277-6500; Fax: 301-277-3181. Email: sistervacha@sacredhearthome.org. Web: www.sacredhearthome.org. Sr. Waclawa Kludziak; Rev. Clifford Aniefuna. Sisters, Servants of Mary Immaculate Sisters 5; Residents 102.

MITCHELLVILLE. *Villa Rosa Nursing Home, Inc.*, 3800 Lottsford Vista Rd., MD 20721-4026. Tel: 301-459-4700; Fax: 301-459-0754. Rev. Anthony Dal Balcon, C.S., Dir.; Mr. Eugene L. Zibrat, Admin.; Sr. Teolide Cecagno, M.S.C.S., Supr. Comprehensive Care Nursing Facility. Sisters 4; Residents 100.

[M] MONASTERIES AND RESIDENCES OF PRIESTS AND BROTHERS

WASHINGTON. *St. Anselm's Abbey*, 4501 South Dakota Ave., N.E., 20017. Tel: 202-269-2300; Fax: 202-269-2312. Web: www.stanselms.org. Rt. Revs. Aidan Shea, O.S.B., Abbot; Alban Boultwood, O.S.B.; Revs. James A. Wiseman, O.S.B., M.A., S.T.D., Prior; Thomas Fahy, O.S.B.; John Farrelly, O.S.B.; David Granfield, O.S.B.; Patrick Granfield, O.S.B., Ph.D., S.T.D.; Michael Hall, O.S.B.; Hilary Hayden, O.S.B.; Edmund Henkels, O.S.B.; Benet Hill, O.S.B.; Joseph Jensen, O.S.B., S.S.L., S.T.D.; Daniel Kirk, O.S.B.; Giles LeVasseur, O.S.B.; Paul McKane, O.S.B.; Gabriel Myers, O.S.B.; Urban Schnaus, O.S.B.; Mark Sheridan, O.S.B.; Philip Simo, O.S.B.; Boniface von Nell, O.S.B.; Peter Weigand, O.S.B.; Christopher Wyvill, O.S.B.; Bros. Dunstan Robidoux, O.S.B.; Matthew Nylund, O.S.B. Benedictine Foundation at Washington, DC, Order of St. Benedict Priests 21; Brothers 2.

Center for Assisted Living Dominican Fathers and Brothers. , 630 E St., S.W., 20024. Tel: 202-484-0149; Fax: 202-554-5735. Email: JMCMOP@aol.com. Rev. John A. McMahon, O.P., Dir.

Commissariat of the Holy Land, Franciscan Monastery - Mount St. Sepulchre, 1400 Quincy St., N.E., 20017. Tel: 202-526-6800; Fax: 202-529-9889. Email: sebastian@pressroom.com. Web: www.pressroom.com/franciscan/. Bro. Fabian Adkins, O.F.M., Guardian; Revs. James Brabandt, O.F.M., Dir. of Candidates, Mod. Knights; Kevin Treston, O.F.M., Almanac Editor, Spiritual Asst. to Sec. Franciscan Order; Bro. Callistus Welch, O.F.M., Commissary of the Holy Land & Procurator; Revs. Manuel Ybarra, O.F.M., Asst. Procurator; Patrick Flannigan, O.F.M.; Brian McTommoney, O.F.M.; Sabin Plechta, O.F.M.; Stephen F. Sabbagh, O.F.M.; Francis X. Sihuay, O.F.M. (Peru). Priests 8; Brothers 14; Solemnly Professed 25; Simple Professed 4; Postulants 4; Novices 1; Missionaries in the Holy Land 20.

Divine Word College, 1025 Michigan Ave., N.E., 20017. Tel: 202-526-5047; Fax: 202-529-4489. Email: dcrector@juno.com. Rev. Phelim Jordan, S.V.D. (Ireland), Rector; Bros. G. Raker, S.V.D., Treas.; Daniel Holman, S.V.D., Formation Dir.; Revs. John Szukalski, S.V.D. (MIL); Antionius Eko Yuliantoro, S.V.D. (Indonesia); Phelim Jordan, S.V.D. (Ireland); John Rodney, S.V.D.; John Prempeh (Ghana); Joseph Keladu (Indonesia); Rejimon Varghese (India); Konrad Kebung (Indonesia); Bro. Henry Miller, S.V.D. Divine Word College has 32 Priests and Brothers in Residence. 12 of these are members of the S.V.D.; the other 20 are from other religious communities or dioceses in the U.S.A., and are studying at the Catholic University, the John Paul II Institute, or Dominican House of Studies. We offer them our House for the duration of their studies. Residents 32.

Holy Redeemer College (1930), 3112 Seventh St., N.E., 20017. Tel: 202-529-4410; 202-529-4484; Fax: 202-832-1321. Very Rev. James P. Brennan, C.SS.R., Rector & Dir. Formation; Revs. Kevin O'Neil, C.SS.R., Asst. Dir. Formation; James Wallace, C.SS.R., Vicar; Thomas Forrest, C.SS.R. Legal Title: *Holy Redeemer College*, Opened in 1930. Redemptorist Theology Residence Since 1985. Priests 5; Religious Students 7. In Res. Rev. Julio Delgado, C.SS.R.

The Jesuit Community at Georgetown University, 37th and O Sts., N.W., 20057-1200. Tel: 202-687-1700; Fax: 202-687-7679. Email: jbhgu@aol.com. Rev. Brian O. McDermott, S.J., Rector; Bro. Joseph M. Ritzman, S.J., Admin. & Treas.; Rev. Francisco Alves, S.J. (India); Bro. Steven Alvey, S.J.; Revs. Edward W. Bodnar, S.J.; Philip L. Boroughs, S.J. (SEA); Dr. John M. Braverman, S.J.; Revs. Thomas J. Buckley, S.J.; Gerard J. Campbell, S.J.; Martin J. Casey, S.J.; Paul L. Cioffi, S.J.; T. Byron Collins, S.J.; Brian J. Conley, S.J. (BO); Patrick J. Conroy, S.J. (Oregon); James A. Devereux, S.J. (R); Robert F. Drinan, S.J. (BO); Joseph T. Durkin, S.J.; Stephen M. Fields, S.J.; Kevin T. Fitzgerald, S.J.; Thomas R. Fitzgerald, S.J.; Joseph A. Fitzmyer, S.J., S.T.L., S.S.L., Ph.D.; Gerald P. Fogarty, S.J.; Francis T. Gignac, S.J. (DET); Joseph A. Haller, S.J.; Patrick A. Heelan, S.J. (Ireland); Otto H. Hentz, S.J.; Robert M. Hussey, S.J.; Mr. Benedict Jung, S.J.; Revs. Josef Kadlec, S.J.; Gustaaf M. Keppens, S.J.; Thomas M. King, S.J.; James G. Knapp, S.J. (STL); John P. Langan, S.J. (DET); Lawrence J. Madden, S.J.; Ryan J. Maher, S.J.; Cesar Maldonado, S.J. (Bolivia); James A. Martin, S.J.; John F. Martin, S.J.; William C. McFadden, S.J.; Gerard J. McGlone, S.J.; Dennis L. McNamara, S.J. (Wisconsin); Paul D. McNelis, S.J.; Ralph E. Metts, S.J.; Joseph M. Moffitt, S.J.; Keith F. Muccino, S.J.; G. Ronald Murphy, S.J.; Jon J. O'Brien, S.J., D.O.; Joseph F. O'Connell, S.J.; Ladislas Orsy, S.J. (Hungary); Kevin P. Quinn, S.J. (New York); Jocelyn Rabeson, S.J.; Alvaro Ribeiro, S.J. (China); Solomon I. Sara, S.J. (New England); Mr. John E. Sauer, S.J.; Revs. James V. Schall, S.J. (California); Francis Schemel, S.J.; James M. Shea, S.J.; Dr. John R. Siberski, S.J.; Revs. Christopher W. Steck, S.J. (NO); Joseph F. Sweeney, S.J.; James P.M. Walsh, S.J.; Kevin W. Wildes, S.J.; John W. Witek, S.J. (CHI); Eric A. Zimmer, S.J. (DET). Priests 63; Brothers 3.

La Salette Community, 1243 Monroe St., N.E., 20017. Tel: 202-526-8070; Fax: 202-529-6577. Email: jawelchms@aol.com. Web: www.lasalette.org.
Legal Title: *Missionaries of La Salette Corporation*

Leonard Neale House, 1726 New Hampshire Ave., N.W., 20009. Tel: 202-387-5375; 202-387-5376; Fax: 202-387-8220. Revs. John F. Armstrong, S.J.; Carlos G. Cenzon, S.J.; Charles L. Currie, S.J.; Thomas P. Gaunt, S.J.; Kenneth J. Gavin, S.J. (NY); David J. Haschka, S.J.; James E. Hug, S.J.; James M. McCann, S.J.; T. Michael McNulty, S.J.; Stephen J. Sauer, S.J.; Bradley M. Schaeffer, S.J.; James R. Stormes, S.J. (CHI); Michael J. Vjecha, S.J. (DET); Thomas C. Widner, S.J. Priests 14; Total Staff 14.

St. Louis Friary, 831 Varnum St., N.E., 20017-2144. Tel: 202-529-0171; Fax: 202-832-8513. Revs. Thomas Bourque, T.O.R.; Joseph Lehman, T.O.R.; Carlo Napoli, T.O.R.; Ambrose Phillips, T.O.R. House of Post-Novitiate Formation for Franciscan Friars, T.O.R., Province of the Most Sacred Heart of Jesus. Friars in Post-Novitiate Formation 9; Brothers in Postulat Program 2; Total in Residence 15.

Marist Center, 4408 8th St., N.E., 20017-2298. Tel: 202-529-4800; Fax: 202-526-2295. Email: maristprov@aol.com. Revs. Thomas E. Dubay, S.M.; Philip S. Gage, S.M.; John H. Harhager, S.M.; George M. Lepping, S.M.; Howard C. Smith, S.M.; Timothy F. Sugrue, S.M., Business Mgr. & Admin. The Marist Finance Center of the Atlanta Province of the Society of Mary, Fathers and Brothers.

723 Palisades Beach Rd., Unit 211, Santa Monica, CA 90402-2648. Tel: 301-451-2479; Fax: 301-939-9562. Rev. Stanley W. Hosie, S.M.

1497 Ashford Pl., N.E., Atlanta, GA 30319-5105. Tel: 770-455-4457. Rev. Eugene E. Hughes, S.M. (Retired).

6200 Westchester Park Dr., Apt. 1113, College Park, MD 20740-2840. Tel: 301-588-4030. Rev. Timothy G. Keating, S.M.

Mary Joseph Residence, 4201 Woodland Dr., New Orleans, LA 70131-7398. Tel: 504-394-2200; Fax: 504-391-3347. Rev. Leonard P. Kellerman, S.M. (Retired).

1497 Ashford Pl., N.E., Atlanta, GA 30319-5105. Tel: 770-455-4457. Rev. Andrew G. McCormack, S.M. (Retired).

150 Burns St, #6-C, Forest Hills, NY 11375-6111. Tel: 718-544-8054; Fax: 718-990-1907. Rev. Patrick D. Primeaux, S.M.

2424 W.Tampa Bay Blvd., Apt M-408, Tampa, FL 33607-1310. Tel: 813-877-7971. Rev. John F. Beckley, S.M.

Malta Court Apartments, 3500 Saint Claude Ave., New Orleans, LA 70117-6152. Tel: 504-943-6776; Fax: 504-948-9123. Rev. Raymond J. Carr, S.M., Chap.

Three Palms Pointe, Unit 801-W, 400 64th Ave., St. Petersburg Beach, FL 33706-2138. Tel: 727-367-8744. Rev. Richard K. Colbert, S.M.

8630 Shell Dr., Tampa, FL 33615-1439. Tel:

813-249-5307. Rev. Robert Fahey, S.M. (Retired). P.O. Box 34, Fort Knox, NY 40121-0034. Tel: 502-942-3438. Rev. Joseph M. Fleury, S.M., Army Chap.

263 Courtyard Blvd., apt. 207, Sun City Center, FL 33573-4706. Tel: 813-633-8350. Rev. Fortune C. Frenoy, S.M. (Retired).

Marian Estates, 424 SE Oak Grove Loop, Sublimity, OR 97385-9533. Tel: 503-767-3704; Fax: 503-769-3569. Rev. W. Thomas Jones, S.M. (Retired).

Welty Apartments, Apt. 409, 1276 National Rd., Wheeling, WV 26003-5770. Tel: 304-242-5177. Rev. H. Joseph Wilhelm, S.M. (Retired).

Missionaries of Africa, 1624 21st St., N.W., 20009-1003. Tel: 202-232-5154; Fax: 202-332-8640. Email: r.roy-lapia1@juno.com. Revs. Richard P. Roy, Asst. Prov.; John Philip Reed, M.Afr., Coord. Justice & Peace Office; Sjef Donders, M.Afr. (Holland); John Lynch, M.Afr., Treas. & Planned Giving Office; George Markwell, M.Afr. Province of North America. Priests 6; Total Staff 6.

Missionary Oblates of Mary Immaculate Tel: 202-529-4505; Fax: 202-529-4572. Email: province@omiusa.org. Web: www.omiusa.org.

Provincial Offices of the United States Province of the Missionary Oblates of Mary Immaculate, 391 Michigan Ave., N.E., 20017-1516. Tel: 202-529-4505; Fax: 202-529-4572. Very Revs. David A. Kalert, O.M.I., Prov.; Charles D. Banks, O.M.I., Vicar Prov.; Revs. David Ullrich, O.M.I., Councilor; Thomas Singer, O.M.I., Gen. Councilor; Robert Moosbrugger, O.M.I., Treas.; Charles Hurkes, O.M.I., Dir. Communications; Seamus P. Finn, O.M.I., Dir. Justice & Peace; Jose Arong, O.M.I., Councilor; Normand Bonneau, O.M.I.; Richard G. Cote, O.M.I.; Salvatore DeGeorge, O.M.I., Councilor; Joseph H. Hitpas, O.M.I., Councilor; Allen Maes, O.M.I., Councilor; William O'Donnell, O.M.I., Councilor; Dale Schlitt, O.M.I.; Richard Sudlik, O.M.I., Councilor.

Legal Titles and Holdings:

The United States Province of the Missionary Oblates of Mary Immaculate, Inc. Tel: 202-529-4505; Fax: 202-529-4572.

Oblate Service Corporation Tel: 202-529-4505; Fax: 202-529-4572.

Oblate Shrines and Renewal Centers, Inc. Tel: 202-529-4505; Fax: 202-529-4572.

Oblate Title Holding Corporation Tel: 202-529-4505; Fax: 202-529-4572.

Oblate Continuing Care Trust Tel: 202-529-4505; Fax: 202-529-4572.

Oblate Education and Formation Trust Tel: 202-529-4505; Fax: 202-529-4572.

Oblate Annuity Trust Tel: 202-529-4505; Fax: 202-529-4572.

Oblate Endowment Trust Tel: 202-529-4505; Fax: 202-529-4572.

Oblate Patrimony Trust Tel: 202-529-4505; Fax: 202-529-4572.

Oblate Service Trust Tel: 202-529-4505; Fax: 202-529-4572.

Oblate Real Estate Trust Tel: 202-529-4505; Fax: 202-529-4572.

Oblate Community, 391 Michigan Ave., N.E., 20017-1587. Tel: 202-281-1617; Fax: 202-636-9444. Rev. William McSweeney, O.M.I., Dir. & Supr.; Very Rev. Charles D. Banks, O.M.I., Vicar Provincial; Revs. Seamus P. Finn, O.M.I.; Charles Hurkes, O.M.I.; Very Rev. David A. Kalert, O.M.I., Prov.; Revs. Raymond Lebrun, O.M.I.; Ruben Martinez, O.M.I. (OAK); George F. McLean, O.M.I., Ph.D.; Robert Moosbrugger, O.M.I., Prov. Treas.; David N. Power, O.M.I., S.T.D. (Retired); Andrew Small, O.M.I. (GAL); Louis Songderoth, O.M.I.; David Ullrich, O.M.I., Prov. Councillor; Bros. Benjamin Juarez, O.M.I.; Paul Hoemeke, O.M.I. Priests 13; Brothers 2.

Piarist Fathers, 1339 Monroe St., NE, 20017-2519. Tel: 202-529-7734; 202-529-6792 (Provincial Sce.); Fax: 202-526-4014. Email: dariff@hotmail.com. Web: www.calasanz.net; www.piarists.us. Very Rev. David Powers, Sch.P., Prov. Supr.; Revs. Leonard J. Gendernalik, Sch.P. (MA), Prov. Sec. Fax: 202-526-4014; Andrew C. Buechele, Sch.P., Ph.D., Rector.

Woodstock Jesuit Community, 1419 35 St., N.W., 20007. Tel: 202-337-7750; Fax: 202-687-5835. Email: woodstock@georgetown.edu. Revs. Gasper F. LoBiondo, S.J., Supr.; J. Leon Hooper, S.J.; Joseph M. Palacios, S.J.; James Redington, S.J. (OAK). Priests 4.

ADELPHI. *Missionary Servants of the Most Holy Trinity*, 1733 Metzerott Rd., MD 20783. Tel: 301-439-3171; Fax: 301-434-0848. Email: fjmcmd@aol.com. Revs. Gabriel Hannan, S.T.; Gerald Swift, S.T.; Charles Tague, S.T.; Maurice Haiss, S.T.; Luke Mikschl, S.T.; Shaun McCarty, S.T.; Edwin Dill, S.T.; Martin VanTrieste, S.T.; Hugh Marshall, S.T.; Bros. Robert Conway, S.T.; Jonathan Daneski, S.T.; Richard McCann, S.T., Dir.; William Coombs, S.T., Asst. Dir.; Loughlan Sofield, S.T.; Daniel Rezmer, S.T.; Gregory Martin, S.T.; Boris Farrah, S.T.; Basil Phillips, S.T. Senior Ministry Residence.

Our Lady Missionary Cenacle, 2717 Curry Dr., MD 20783-1725. Tel: 301-422-6100; Fax: 301-422-6199. Email: sthilarymet@aol.com. Bros. Hilary Mettes, S.T., Supr. Howard Piller, S.T.

BROOKEVILLE. *Marian Monastery-Brookeville* Marian Residence & Marian Assisted Living , 19101 Georgia Ave., Box 220, MD 20833. Tel 301-774-4478; 301-774-2242; Fax: 301-570-8645. Web: www.marian.org. Revs. John Kobza, M.I.C.; Joseph Sielski, M.I.C. Priests 2.

HYATTSVILLE. *St. John de Matha Monastery, Order of Most Holy Trinity*, 4310 Madison St., MD 20781. Tel: 301-927-6418; Fax: 301-927-8458. Revs. Damian Anuszewski, O.SS.T., Supr.; Albert M. Anuszewski, O.SS.T., Vicar. Priests 2.

POTOMAC. *Legionaries of Christ*, 10211 Norton Rd., MD 20854. Tel: 301-299-0806; Fax: 301-299-0809. Email: rgill@legionaries.org. Revs. William Izquierdo L.C., Supr.; Richard Gill, L.C.; Steven Reilly, L.C.; Michael Sliney, L.C.; James Swanson, L.C.; Bros. Nicholas McMillan; Michael Macaborski.

RIVERDALE. *Holy Spirit Missionary Cenacle* (1996), 5809 Riverdale Rd., MD 20737. Tel: 301-277-7442; Fax: 301-209-0355. Rev. Seraphim Molina, S.T., Dir. Formation In Res. Rev. Sidney H. Griffith, S.T.D., Ph.D., Semantics & Early Christian Studies. Tel: 301-927-4919 Faculty Catholic University of America; Pre-Novitiate Jacobus Glas.

SILVER SPRING. *Gemelli House* Franciscan Friars-Holy Name Province , 10400 Lorain Ave., MD 20901. Tel: 301-681-9478; Fax: 301-681-7170. Revs. Kenneth R. Himes, O.F.M., Guardian; Vincent de Paul Cushing, O.F.M.; Garret Galvin, O.F.M.; Romuald Green, O.F.M.; Richard Kelly, O.F.M.; Daniel McLellan, O.F.M.; Jame Sabak, O.F.M. (W.D.C); Bros. Gregory Jakubowicz, O.F.M.; Joseph LaGressa, O.F.M.; Charles Raymond Selker, O.F.M. Priests 7; Brothers 3.

TAKOMA PARK. *Redemptoris Mater Archdiocesan Missionary Seminary*, 1006 Larch Ave., MD 20912. Tel: 301-891-3259; Fax: 301-891-3356. Email: RMSWashington@juno.com. Revs. Luis P. Gonzalez; Manuel Ingelmo; Sergio Ramos (Italy). Seminarians 24.

Society of African Missions (S.M.A.)

House of Studies, 209 Lincoln Ave., MD 20912-5738. Tel: 301-270-2008; Fax: 301-270-0132. Email: smausa-o@smafathers.org. Web: www.smafathers.org. Rev. Austin Charles Ochu, S.M.A., Local Supr.

Lay Missionary Program, 256 N. Manor Cir., MD 20912-4551. Tel: 301-270-2009 (Home); 301-891-2037; Fax: 301-270-6370. Email: smausa-v@smafathers.org. Rev. Daniel Lynch, S.M.A.; Theresa Hicks, Dir.; Dr. Steve Price; Lucy McGovern.

UNIVERSITY PARK. *Holy Trinity Missionary Cenacle* (1995), 4001 Van Buren St., MD 20782. Tel: 301-779-0939; Fax: 301-699-1745. Bro. Jordan Baxter, S.T., Custodian; Revs. Ralph Frisch, S.T. Tel: 301-864-3470; Louis E. Murphy, S.T. Tel: 301-779-0939; David O'Connor, S.T. Tel: 301-699-3508; Conrad Schmitt, S.T. Tel: 301-779-0939; Bro. Alexis Norton, S.T. Tel: 301-699-1729

[N] MINISTRY TO PRIESTS

KENSINGTON. *St. John Vianney House*, 4214 Saul Rd., MD 20895. Tel: 301-942-1191; Fax: 301-942-1191. Rev. Michael J. Murray.

[O] CONVENTS AND RESIDENCES FOR SISTERS

WASHINGTON. *St. Dominic's Monastery*, 4901 16th St., N.W., 20011-3839. Tel: 202-726-2107; Fax: 202-829-7999. Sr. Mary Paul, O.P., Prioress. Dominican Nuns, a Contemplative Community with Solemn Vows and Papal Enclosure Sisters 11.

Franciscan Sisters of Atonement, 4000 Harewood Rd., N.E., 20017. Tel: 202-529-1111 Sr. Margaret Mullin, S.A., Dir. Sisters 7; Total Staff 9.

Georgetown Visitation Monastery, 1500 35th St., N.W., 20007. Tel: 202-337-0350; Fax: 202-965-3845. Email: geoviscon@aol.com. Web: www.ee.cua.edu~georgvis. Sr. Mary Philomena Tisinger, Supr. Professed Sisters 20

Institute of Our Lady of Mount Carmel, 4415 Eighth St., N.E., 20017. Tel: 202-526-9180 Fax: 202-526-3608. Total Assisted 45; Total Staff 8.

Little Sisters of Jesus, 1740 Euclid St., N.W., Apt. 1, 20009. Tel: 202-265-6177. Email: littlesrs.dc@juno.com. Sisters 4.

Little Sisters of the Poor, 4200 Harewood Rd., N.E., 20017. Tel: 202-269-1831; Fax: 202-269-1134. Email: mswashlsp@earthlink.net. Sisters 13.

Missionaries of Charity, 3310 Wheeler Rd., S.E., 20032. Tel: 202-562-6890. Sisters 6; Total Assisted 16,181.

Missionaries of Charity, Gift of Peace Convent, 2800 Otis St., N.E., 20018. Tel: 202-269-3313. Sr. M. Regis, M.C., Supr. Total Assisted 75; Total in Residence 38; Total Staff 25.

Oblates Sisters of the Most Holy Eucharist, 2907 Ellicott Ter., N.W., 20008. Tel: 202-244-7714. Email: oblatesl@juno.com. Sr. M. Stella Symanski, O.S.S.E., Supr. Sisters 7.

Poor Clares of Perpetual Adoration, 3900 13th St., N.E., 20017-2699. Tel: 202-526-6808; Fax: 202-526-0678. Email: claresdcpray4u@starpower.net. Cloistered Monastery of Perpetual Adoration Cloistered Nuns 11.

Religious of the Sacred Heart, 1235 Otis St., N.E., 20017. Tel: 202-832-1598; Fax: 202-526-3506. Email: kcollins@rscj.org. Web: www.rscj.org. Sr. Catherine Collins, R.S.C.J., Dir. Center for Educational Design & Communication. Tel: 202-635-7987. Sisters 3.

Religious of the Sacred Heart Perry Street Community , 1201 Perry St., N.E., 20017. Tel: 202-526-9398. Sr. Marion Duffy, Contact Person.

Religious of the Sacred Heart Oakview Community. , 1215 Perry St., N.E., 20017. Tel: 202-832-0071. Sr. Fleisa Garcia, Contact Person.

Religious Sisters of Mercy of Alma, MI, 1211 Lawrence St., N.E., 20017. Tel: 202-832-7111; Fax: 202-832-6325. Sr. Dolora Keating, R.S.M., Contact Person.

Rosary House of Studies-Dominican Sisters of The Presentation, 1201 Monroe St., N.E., 20017. Tel: 202-529-1768; Fax: 202-526-7526. Email: lapointe2@juno.com. Sisters 4.

Sisters of Notre Dame de Namur, 145 Taylor St., N.E., 20017. Tel: 202-832-6240; Fax: 202-832-6270. Email: jbilliartr@aol.com. Sr. Elizabeth Ann McFadden, S.N.D., Contact Person. Residence for Sisters. Sisters 8.

Sisters of the Holy Child Jesus, 1033 Newton St., N.E., 20017. Tel: 202-526-6832. Web: www.shcj.org. Novitiate Community Sisters 3.

Other Convents:

1244 Monroe St., N.E., 20017. Tel: 202-832-3237. Sisters 4.

St. Anthony's School Sisters 1.

Sisters of the Third Franciscan Order-Syracuse, NY Emmaus Convent , 1334 Perry St., N.E., 20017-2531. Tel: 202-526-8017. Email: mlsalerno@aol.com smcosf@aol.com. Web: www.osfsyr.org. Sisters 2.

ANACOSTIA, WASHINGTON. *Missionaries of Charity (Contemplatives)*, 1244 V St., S.E., 20020-7016. Tel: 202-889-6100. Sr. M. Andrea, M.C., Supr.

CHEVY CHASE. *Missionary Sisters of Our Lady of Africa*, 3715 Williams Ln., MD 20815. Tel: 301-654-2047. Email: msolachevch@aol.com. Web: www.smnda.org.

CLINTON. *Religious Sisters of Mercy of Alma, MI* St. Andrew Home of Mercy , 6100 Wolverton Lane, MD 20735. Tel: 301-297-5617; Fax: 301-297-5618. Email: misericordia@acninc.net. Sr. Dolora Keating, R.S.M., Contact Person. Sisters 7.

FORT WASHINGTON. *The Missionary Catechists of St. Therese of the Infant Jesus, Inc.*, 2400 Brinkley Rd., MD 20744. Tel: 301-839-7751; Fax: 301-839-7751. Email: mcstusa@erols.com. Sr. Editha E. Basa, M.C.S.T., Pres. Sisters 4.

HYATTSVILLE. *Carmelite Sisters of Charity*, 8138 15th Ave. # 203, MD 20783. Email: vedvune@aol.com. Sisters Maria Pilar Chamorro, C.C.V., Regl. Supr.; Miren A. Lapazaran, First Councilor; Claudia Paredes, C.C.V., Second Councilor; Carmen Banegas, C.C.V., Sec.; M. Carmen de Juan, C.C.V., Treas.; Amaya Duralde, C.C.V., Formation Dir. U.S. Delegation Regional House

DeMatha Convent, 4318 Madison St., MD 20781. Tel: 301-927-6418; Fax: 301-927-8458.

KENSINGTON. *Sisters of the Holy Cross*, St. Angela Hall, 4910 Strathmore Ave., MD 20895. Tel: 301-946-7750; Fax: 301-946-7751.

Legal Title: *Sisters of the Holy Cross, Inc.*, Retirement House for the Sisters of the Holy Cross. Sisters 20.

Academy of the Holy Cross Convent, 4920 Strathmore Ave., MD 20895. Tel: 301-942-2102.

Legal Title: *The Academy of the Holy Cross, Inc.* Sisters 9.

1271 Twig Tr., Silver Spring, MD 20904. Tel: 301-236-4967.

Sisters of the Holy Cross, 3809 Woodridge Ave., Silver Spring, MD 20902-2354. Tel: 301-933-2213. Sisters 3.

Our Lady of Lourdes Convent, 4511 East-West Hwy., Bethesda, MD 20814. Tel: 301-986-5741. Sisters 2.

LANHAM-SEABROOK. *Mission Helpers of the Sacred Heart*, 9471 Annapolis Rd., MD 20706. Tel: 301-459-8078. Email: srsusanne@stmatthias.org. Sisters 6.

LAUREL. *Pallotti Convent*, 404 Eighth St., MD 20707. Tel: 301-725-1717. Sr. M. Karen Lester, S.A.C., Local Supr. Professed Sisters 8; Total Staff 1.

MOUNT RAINIER. *Congregation of Jesus and Mary, Provincialate*, 3706 Rhode Island Ave., MD 20712-2009. Tel: 301-277-3594; Fax: 301-277-8656. Email: janetsrjm@aol.com. Sr. Janet Stolba, R.J.M., Prov. Administrative Team 4; Staff 2.
Other Residences:
Religious of Jesus and Mary, 6709 41st Ave., University Park, MD 20782. Tel: 301-779-0662; Fax: 301-779-3843. Sisters 5.
4602 Clemson Rd., College Park, MD 20740. Tel: 301-699-3931; Fax: 301-927-4157. Sisters 3.
3521 13th St., N.W., 20010. Tel: 202-265-8812; Fax: 202-265-1842. Sisters 2.
Jesus Mary Provincialate, St. James Convent, 3706 Rhode Island Ave., MD 20712-2009. Tel: 301-277-3334; Fax: 301-277-8656. Sisters 6.

NORTH BEACH. *Sisters of St. Dominic of St. Cecilia of Nashville, TN*, St. Anthony Convent, 4104 First St., P.O. Box 600, MD 20714. Tel: 410-286-3393; Fax: 410-286-3275. Sr. Christine Born, Convent Supr. Sisters 4.

PORT TOBACCO. *Carmel of Port Tobacco* (1790), 5678 Mount Carmel Rd., MD 20646-9611. Tel: 301-934-1654; Fax: 301-934-0958. Email: steresa@erols.com. Web: www.erols.com/carmel-of-port-tobacco. Professed 11; Professed Novice 1; Novices 3.

SILVER SPRING. *Religious of the Sacred Heart* St. Michael Community. , 2524 Locustwood Pl., MD 20905. Tel: 301-879-2441. Sr. Victoria Rajca, Contact Person.
Sisters of Mercy of the Americas Administrative Center, 8300 Colesville Rd., Ste. 300, MD 20910. Tel: 301-587-0423; Fax: 301-587-0533. Email: srsofmercy@aol.com. Web: www.sistersofmercy.org. Sr. Marie Chin, R.S.M., Pres. Legal Holdings; Mercy Action, Inc.; McAuley Institute, Inc.; Mercy Corps., Inc. Administrative Team 5.
Sisters of the Good Shepherd, 504 Hexton Hill Rd., MD 20904-3300. Tel: 301-384-1169; Fax: 301-384-8889. Web: www.goodshepherdsisters.org. Sisters 4.
Sisters of the Holy Names (S.N.J.M.), 9603 Flower Ave., MD 20901. Tel: 301-587-1717; Fax: 301-587-1718. Email: kksnjml@aol.com. Web: www.snjm.org. Sr. Ann Marean, Supr. Sisters 3.
Other Convents:
519 Varnum St., N.W., 20011. Tel: 202-829-8671. Sisters 3.
9212 Glenville Rd., MD 20901. Tel: 301-445-0309.
10705 Torrance Dr., MD 20902.

[P] RETREAT HOUSES

WASHINGTON. *Washington Retreat House, Inc.* (1930), 4000 Harewood Rd., N.E., 20017. Tel: 202-529-1111; Fax: 202-259-2102. Email: washretreat@juno.com. Sr. Margaret Mullin, S.A., Dir. Franciscan Sisters of the Atonement Sisters 7; Total in Residence 7; Total Staff 10.

FAULKNER. *Loyola Retreat House*, P.O. Box 9, MD 20632. Tel: 301-934-8862; 301-870-3515; Fax: 301-392-0808. Email: director@loyolaretreat.org. Web: www.loyolaretreat.org. Revs. Timothy J. Stephens, S.J., Dir.; Frank T. Kaminski, S.J., Supr. Total in Residence 6; Total Staff 7.
Staff: Revs. Robert J. Braunreuther, S.J.; Francis J. Miles, S.J.; Richard C. Schmidt, S.J.; Bro. Thomas R. Williams, S.J.; Sr. Patricia McDermott, I.H.M.

UPPER MARLBORO. *Our Lady of Mattaponi Youth Retreat and Conference Center*, 11000 Mattaponi Rd., MD 20772. Tel: 301-952-9074; Fax: 301-952-0609. Email: mattaponi@adw.org. Rev. Robert F. Mordino. Total in Residence 1; Total Staff 3.

[Q] NATIONAL SHRINE

WASHINGTON. *Basilica of the National Shrine of the Immaculate Conception* 400 Michigan Ave., N.E., 20017-1566. Tel: 202-526-8300; Fax: 202-526-8313. Email: info@nationalshrine.com. Web: www.nationalshrine.com. Rev. Msgr. Michael J. Bransfield (PH), Rector; Revs. Walter R. Rossi (SCR), Dir. Pilgrimages; Raymond A. Lebrun, O.M.I., Spiritual Dir.; Leo J. Ovian, m.s.a., Spiritual Counselor; Andrew J. Fisher (ARL), Dir. Liturgy.

[R] HOUSES OF PRAYER

WASHINGTON. *Catholic Information Center*, 1501 K St., NW Ste. 175, 20005-1401. Tel: 202-783-2062; Fax: 202-783-6667. Email: frcjm@aol.com. Web: www.cicdc.org. Total Staff 4.
Madonna House, 220 C St., N.E., 20002. Tel: 202-547-0177; Fax: 202-547-8117. Web: www.madonnahouse.org. Catherine A. Mitchell, Dir. Total in Residence 4; Total Staff 4.

[S] OFFICES OF CAMPUS MINISTRY

WASHINGTON. *Archdiocesan Campus Ministry*
American University Catholic Community Kay Spiritual Life Center, 4400 Massachusetts Ave., N.W., 20016-8010. Tel: 202-885-3327; Fax: 202-885-3317. Email: frwoods@stanndc.org. Rev. Keith A. Woods, Chap. Tel: 202-885-3327; Dr. Karin Thornton, Assoc. Chap. Tel: 202-885-3326.
Gallaudet University Catholic Community 800 Florida Ave., N.E., 20002. Tel: 202-651-5102. Rev. Gerard A. Trancone, Chap.
7202 Buchanan St., Landover Hills, MD 20784. Tel: 301-459-7467; 301-459-7464; Fax: 301-459-8186.
George Washington Univ. Newman Center 2210 F St., N.W., 20037. Tel: 202-676-6855; Fax: 202-676-6859. Rev. James J. Greenfield, O.S.F.S., Chap.
Howard Univ. Newman Center 818 Newman Center, 20059. Tel: 202-238-2687; Fax: 202-806-4641. Rev. John Raphael, S.S.J., Chap.
University of Maryland Catholic Student Center 4141 Guilford Dr., College Park, MD 20740. Tel: 301-864-6223; 301-864-6224; Fax: 301-864-8411. Rev. William D. Byrne, Chap.; Sr. Rita Ricker, R.J.M., Assoc.
St. Mary's College Campus Ministry P.O. Box 67, St. Mary's City, MD 20686. Tel: 301-862-4600. Rev. Francis W. Krastel.

[T] PERSONAL PRELATURES

WASHINGTON. *Prelature of the Holy Cross and Opus Dei*, 2301 Wyoming Ave., N.W., 20008. Tel: 202-234-1567; Fax: 202-238-0621. Web: www.opusdei.org. Revs. William H. Stetson; Lawrence A. Kutz; C. John McCloskey.
Other Centers:
Tenley Study Center, 4300 Garrison St., N.W., 20016. Tel: 202-362-2419; Fax: 202-362-0318. Revs. Gregory Coyne; Paul Kaiss.
4955 Linnean Ave., N.W., 20008. Tel: 202-237-6894; Fax: 202-277-7396. Rev. Ronald S. Gillis, S.T.L., J.C.D.

[U] SECULAR INSTITUTES

WASHINGTON. *Caritas Christi*, Bladensburg Rd., N.E., P.O. Box 41372, 20018. Tel: 301-459-6754; Fax: 202-319-6536. Email: stdenis@cua.edu. Dr. Helen St. Denis, C.C., Former Pres. US-CSI. A Secular Institute of Pontifical Right.
Community of Christ, 1003 Kearney St., N.E., 20017. Tel: 202-832-9710; 202-797-8806; Fax: 202-265-3849. Email: frjohn@some.org. Rev. John Adams (RIC), Moderator. A Private Association Community of Archdiocesan Right for Priests, Lay Men and Lay Women. The Community of Christ Purpose is Simple Lifestyle, Poverty Ministry, Spiritual Growth and Prayer of Community Members.

WEST BETHESDA. *Missionaries of the Kingship of Christ*, P.O. Box 34513, MD 20827-0513. Tel: 301-990-8630; Fax: 978-342-1481. Email: cdahlin@aol.com. Web: www.simkc.org.
A Francisan Secular Institute of Pontifical Right. Tel: 301-990-8630; Fax: 978-342-1481. Rev. Dominic V. Monti, O.F.M. Tel: 716-375-2532.

[V] MISCELLANEOUS

WASHINGTON. **Africa Faith & Justice Network*, 3035 Fourth St., N.E., 20017. Tel: 202-832-3412; Fax: 202-832-9051. Email: afjn@afjn.org. Web: www.afjn.cua.edu. Marcel Kitissou, Ph.D., Exec. Dir.
"The Americas", Catholic University of America, Gibbons Hall, Room B 17, 20064. Tel: 202-319-5890; Fax: 202-319-5569. Email: americas@cua.edu. Web: www.theamericasjournal.org.
Archbishop Carroll High School Records Center for the Archdiocese of Washington. , 4300 Harewood Rd., N.E., 20017. Tel: 202-529-0900; Fax: 202-529-5989. Email: jbutler@archbishopcarroll.org. Web: www.archbishopcarroll.org.
Alumni Office Tel: 202-529-0900; Fax: 202-529-5989. Mark Savercool, Dir. Tel: 202-529-0900, Ext. 160.
Archdiocese of Cotabato, 391 Michigan Ave., N.E., 20017. Tel: 202-529-4572; Fax: 202-529-4505. Most Rev. Orlando Quevedo, O.M.I., D.D.; Rev. Robert Moosbrugger, O.M.I.
Archivists for Congregations of Women Religious, ACWR National Office, Trinity College, 125 Michigan Ave, N.E., 20017. Tel: 202-884-9441; Fax: 202-884-9229. Email: acwr@juno.com. Web: www.homestead.com/acwr. Purpose: Professional Preservation of the archives of Roman Catholic women religious congregations and collaboration with historians in making known the lives and works of women religious.
Association of Catholic Colleges & Universities, One Dupont Cir., Ste. 650, 20036. Tel: 202-457-0650; Fax: 202-728-0977. Email: accu@accunet.org. Web: www.accunet.org. Dr. Monika K. Hellwig, Pres.
Black Leadership and Christ's Kingdom Society, P.O. Box 4579, 20017. Tel: 202-529-4860; 301-888-2566; Fax: 202-529-7214. Rev. Robert S. Pittman, S.S.S., Dir. Total in Residence 8; Total Staff 15.
CARA, Center for Applied Research in the Apostolate, Georgetown University, 20057-1203. Tel: 202-687-8080; Fax: 202-687-8083. Email: cara@georgetown.edu. Web: cara.georgetown.edu. Sr. Mary E. Bendyna, R.S.M., Interim Exec. Dir.
Carmelite Institute, 1600 Webster St., N.E., 20017. Tel: 202-635-3534; Fax: 202-635-3538. Email: mail@carmeliteinstitute.org. Web: www.carmeliteinstitute.org. Rev. Steven Payne, O.C.D., Pres. Tel: 202-832-6622; Mary E. Rodriguez-Harrington, O.C.D.S., Exec. Dir.
Carroll Manor Nursing & Rehabilitation Center, 1150 Varnum St., N.E., 20017-2180. Tel: 202-269-7100; Fax: 202-269-7816. Rev. Msgr. Leonard F. Hurley, Chap.
Catholic Biblical Association, Catholic University of America, 314 Caldwell Hall, 20064. Tel: 202-319-5519; Fax: 202-319-4799. Email: cua-cathbib@cua.edu. Web: cba.cua.edu. Rev. Joseph Jensen, O.S.B., S.S.L., S.T.D., Exec. Sec.
Catholic Historical Society of Washington, 619 10th St., N.W., 20001. Mr. Paul Liston, Dir.
Center of Concern, 1225 Otis St., N.E., 20017-2516. Tel: 202-635-2757; Fax: 202-832-9494. Email: coc@coc.org. Web: www.coc.org. Rev. James E. Hug, S.J., Pres.
Centro Maria, 650 Jackson St., N.E., 20017. Tel: 202-635-1697; Fax: 202-635-7246. Email: rmiwashington@rcn.com. Web: www.religiosasdemariainmaculada.org. Sr. Luisa L. (Marisa) Gomez, Dir.
Christ Child Society of Washington, DC , Inc., 5101 Wisconsin Ave., N.W., #304, 20016. Tel: 202-966-9250; Fax: 202-966-2880. Email: info@christchilddc.org. Web: www.charityadvantage.com/christchilddc. Colleen Delaney Eubanks, Exec. Dir. A nonprofit, volunteer organization of approximately 600 persons serving needing children, regardless of race or creed, through layette distribution, school counseling, camp and camperships and uniform and shoe programs. Total Assisted 16,000; Total staff 21.
Christian Life Communities, Washington Area Promoters: 5040 Nebraska Ave., N.W., 20008-2938. Tel: 202-363-4593. Ms. Margaret Fox.
201 E. Wayne Ave., Silver Spring, MD 20901-3808. Tel: 301-495-2969; Fax: 301-495-7318. Fred and Betty Leone.
Communio: International Catholic Review, 487 Michigan Ave., N.E., 20017. Tel: 202-526-0251; Fax: 202-526-1934. Email: communio@aol.com. Web: www.communio-icr.com. David L. Schindler, Contact Person.
The Community of St. John, 247 A St., N.E., #202, 20002. Tel: 202-547-1380; Fax: 202-547-1380. Email: walker_adrian@msn.com. Adrian Walker, Contact Person. Total in Residence 4.
Consolata Missionaries House of Studies, 1321 Otis St., N.E., 20017. Tel: 202-832-3582; Fax: 202-832-3583. Email: imcwash@aol.com. Web: www.geocities.com/imcwash. Revs. Mario Barbero, I.M.C., Rector; David Kamau Gikonyo, I.M.C.; Cyrus Karuthi, I.M.C.; Erasto C. Mgalama, I.M.C.; Ugo Pozzoli, I.M.C.; Deacon Javier Castro, I.M.C.; Bros. Benedict Ngala, I.M.C.; Felix O. Wao, I.M.C.
Council for Research in Values and Philosophy, The Catholic University of America, 20064. Tel: 202-319-6089; Fax: 202-319-6089; 800-659-9962. Email: mclean@cua.edu. Web: www.crvp.org. Rev. George F. McLean, O.M.I., Ph.D., Sec.
**Culture of Life Foundation*, 1412 K St., N.W., 20005. Tel: 202-289-2500. Email: clf@culture-of-life.org. Web: www.colfi.org.
District of Columbia Detention Facility, Office of Chaplain, 1901 D St., S.E., 20003. Tel: 202-547-1715; 202-673-8400 (Office); Fax: 202-544-1385. Rev. F. Michael Bryant, Chap. Total in Residence 2,500; Total Staff 15.
Dorothy Day Catholic Worker, 503 Rock Creek Church Rd., N.W., 20010. Tel: 202-882-9649. Total Assisted 300; Total Staff 3.
**Education for Parish Service Programs*, Trinity College, 125 Michigan Ave., N.E., 20017-1094. Tel: 202-884-9020; Fax: 202-483-0253. Email: WaltzB@TrinityDC.edu. Web: eps.trinitydc.edu. Sr. Mary Ann Cook, S.N.D.deN., Pres.
Equestrian Order of the Holy Sepulchre of Jerusalem - Middle Atlantic Lieutenancy of the U.S., P.O. Box 29260, 20017-0260. Tel: 301-853-5309; Fax: 301-853-7681. His Eminence James Cardinal Hickey, Grand Prior; John C. Piunno, Lieutenant.
Ethiopian and Eritrean Catholic Mission, USA, 1001 Lawrence St., N.E., 20017. Tel: 202-829-3934; Fax: 202-529-8523. Rev. Tesfamariam Baraki (Ethiopia), Dir.
Fellowship of Catholic Scholars, John Paul II Institute, 487 Michigan Ave., N.E., 20017. Tel: 219-631-8385; Fax: 219-631-6371. Email:

wmay975874@aol.com. Web: www.catholicscholars.org. Gerard V. Bradley, Pres.

The Franciscan Federation, Third Order Regular of the Sisters and Brothers of the United States, 817 Varnum St., N.E., P.O. Box 29080, 20017. Tel: 202-529-2334; Fax: 202-529-7016. Email: franfed@aol.com. Web: www.franfed.org.

**Friends of the Pontifical Irish College, Rome, Inc.*, 2121 K St., Ste. 800, 20037. Tel: 202-261-6585; Fax: 202-261-3501. Frank J. Cain, Pres.

**Institute for Pastoral Renewal, Inc.*, c/o Jesuit Community, Georgetown University, 20057. Tel: 202-687-4164; Fax: 202-687-2045. Email: paulcioffi@cs.com. Web: http://ipr.zramp.com. Rev. Paul L. Cioffi, S.J., Dir. 455 priests attended retreats, workshops, and seminars on liturgical renewal last year. None in residence. Two part-time staff members.

Institute of Carmelite Studies and ICS Publications, 2131 Lincoln Rd., N.E., 20002-1199. Tel: 800-832-8489; Fax: 202-832-8967. Email: brpaquette@aol.com. Web: www.icspublications.org. Revs. John Sullivan, O.C.D., Publisher; Kieran Kavanaugh, O.C.D., Editorial Asst.; Bro. Bryan Paquette, O.C.D., Business Mgr. & Promotion Dir.

Jesuit Conference, Inc., 1616 P St., N.W., Ste. 300, 20036-1420. Tel: 202-462-0400; Fax: 202-328-9212. Email: usjc@jesuit.org. Web: www.jesuit.org. Revs. Bradley M. Schaeffer, S.J., Pres.; Thomas P. Gaunt, S.J., Exec. Sec.

Jesuit Missions, Inc., 1616 P St., N.W., #300, 20036. Tel: 202-462-0400; Fax: 202-328-9212. Email: outreach@jesuit.org. Rev. Richard J. Ryscavage, S.J., Exec. Dir.

Jesuit Refugee Service, 1616 P St., N.W., Ste. 300, 20036-2286. Tel: 202-462-0400; Fax: 202-328-9212. Email: aborja@jesuit.org. Web: www.jesref.org; www.jrsusa.org. Rev. Kenneth J. Gavin, S.J. (NY), Natl. Dir.

Jesuit Secondary Education Association, 1616 P St., N.W., Ste. 400, 20036-1405. Tel: 202-667-3888; Fax: 202-387-6305. Email: jsea@jsea.org. Web: www.jsea.org. Revs. Joseph F. O'Connell, S.J., Pres.; Ralph E. Metts, S.J., Vice Pres.; Bernard L. Bouillette, Ph.D., Vice Pres.; Gretchen Z. Kane, Assoc. Vice Pres.; Liletha A. Davidson, Admin. Coord.; Shana L. Stepp, Exec. Sec. Total Staff 6.

Jesuit Social and International Ministries-National Office, 1616 P St., N.W., Ste. 300, 20036-1405. Tel: 202-462-0400; Fax: 202-328-9212. Email: outreach@jesuit.org. Web: www.jesuit.org. Ms. British Robinson, Natl. Dir.

Jesuit Volunteers International, P.O. Box 3756, 20027-0256. Tel: 202-687-1132; Fax: 202-687-5082. Email: jvi@JesuitVolunteers.org. Web: www.JesuitVolunteers.org. Dennis Heaphy, Exec. Dir. Staff 8; Lay Volunteers 75; Foreign Missions 11.

The John Carroll Society, P.O. Box 50188, 20091. Tel: 703-573-3043; Fax: 703-573-3043. Email: johncarrollsociety@hotmail.com. Web: www.johncarrollsociety.org. John M. Facciola, Pres.; Rev. Msgr. Peter J. Vaghi.

McKenna House, 1501 Park Rd., N.W., 20010. Tel: 202-332-7333. Hagos Weldegiorgis, Prog. Mgr.

**Missionary Vehicle Association, Inc.* MIVA America. , 1400 Michigan Ave., N.E., 20017. Tel: 202-635-3444; Fax: 202-526-0830. Email: miva@miva.org. Web: www.miva.org. Rev. Philip DeRea, M.S.C., Natl. Dir.

Morley Publishing Group, Inc., 1814 1/2 N St., N.W., 20036. Tel: 202-861-7790; Fax: 202-861-7788. Email: hudson@crisismagazine.com. Web: www.crisismagazine.com.

Mount Carmel House, 471 G Pl., N.W., 20001. Tel: 202-289-6315; Fax: 202-289-1710. Web: www.mtcarmelhouse.org. Sr. Ann Forrest, O.S.F., Dir. Transitional Rehabilitative Housing for Women with 21 beds.

National Black Sisters' Conference, 101 Q St., N.E., 20002-2166. Tel: 202-529-9250; Fax: 202-529-9370. Email: nbsc@igc.org. Web: www.nbsc68.tripod.com. Sr. Donna Banfield, S.B.S., Pres. Total Staff 3.

National Catholic Conference for Interracial Justice, 1200 Varnum St., N.E., 20017-2796. Tel: 202-529-6480; Fax: 202-526-1262. Deacon Joseph M. Conrad Jr., Exec. Dir.

National Institute for the Family, Inc., 3019 Fourth St., N.E., 20017. Tel: 202-462-2591; Fax: 202-462-6534. Email: nacre@earthlink.net. Rev. Donald B. Conroy, S.T.L., Ph.D. (GBG), Exec. Dir.; Dr. Carolyn Gutowski, M.A.T., Ph.D., Assoc. Dir. Research Program: Intergenerational Parish Ministry. Seminary and Lay Leadership Training in association with the Washington Theological Union.

**Notre Dame Education Center*, 101 Q St., N.E., 20002. Tel: 202-526-6420; Fax: 202-526-6423. Nonprofit, tax exempt adult education program for low income people. The center enables adults to earn a high school diploma and trains them in computers.

Paul VI Institute for the Arts, 619 10th St., N.W., 20001-4587. Tel: 202-347-1450; Fax: 202-347-1401. Rev. Msgr. Michael diTeccia Farina.

Paulist Media Works, 3055 4th St., N.E., 20017-1102. Tel: 202-269-6064; Fax: 202-269-4304. Email: sdonovan@paulist.org. Web: www.paulist.org/pmw. Sue Donovan, Pres. & Exec. Producer; Jeanean Merkel, Vice Pres. Operations.

Paulist National Catholic Evangelization Assoc., 3031 Fourth St., N.E., 20017-1102. Tel 202-832-5022; Fax 202-269-0209. Email: pncea@pncea.org. Web: www.pncea.org. Rev. Kenneth C. Boyack, C.S.P., D.Min., Pres.; Sr. Susan Wolf, S.N.D., Senior Vice Pres. & Exec. Dir.; Rev. Robert S. Rivers, C.S.P., Vice Pres., Dir. of Diocesan & Parish Svcs.; Mr. Anthony Bosnick, Dir. Publications; Mr. Joseph Feakes, Dir. Devel.; Ms. Mary Weaver, Dir. Finance & Human Resources; Mr. Denny Marcotte, Dir. Production, Fulfillment & Facilities; Roderick Loss, Dir. of Prison Ministry; Ms. Kim Fuhrman, Dir. Mktg.; Rev. Anthony F. Krisak, S.S. (TR), Co-Dir. Envision.

Pax Romana/Catholic Movement for Intellectual and Cultural Affairs-USA, 3025 Fourth St., N.E., 20017. Tel: 202-269-6672. Email: paxromanausa@aol.com. Edward Holland, Ph.D., Pres.

Rosary Shrine of St. Jude Dominican Fathers and Brothers , St. Dominic's Church, 501 Sixth St., S.W., 20024. Tel: 202-554-7863; Fax: 202-554-3492. Rev. Kenneth A. France-Kelly, O.P., Dir.

S.N.D.B.C. Charitable Trust, 1233 Quincy St., N.E., 20017. Tel: 202-526-2303; Fax: 202-526-2303. Email: sndbcunit@aol.com. Sisters Ann Gormly, S.N.D., Trustee; Ann Theresa Sciannella, S.N.D., Trustee; Teresa McElwee, S.N.D., Trustee.

Sisters of Notre Dame de Namur Base Communities, Inc., 3037 Fourth St., N.E., 20017-1102. Tel: 202-832-8770; Fax: 202-635-4912. Email: sndbcunit@aol.com. Web: www.SNDdeN.org. Sisters 18.

Sovereign Military Order of Malta-Federal Association, 1730 M St., N.W., Ste. 403, 20036. Tel: 202-331-2494; Fax: 202-331-1149. Email: info@smom.org. Web: www.smom.org. G. Patrick Clancy, Pres.; Joseph J. Dempsey Jr., Exec. Dir.

Spanish Catholic Center, Administrative Office, P.O. Box 11150, 20008-0650. Tel: 202-939-2437; Fax: 202-234-7323. Email: infoscc@yahoo.com. Web: www.centrocatolicohispano.org. Rev. Donald F. Lippert, O.F.M.Cap.

Mt. Pleasant Branch, 1618 Monroe St., N.W., 20010. Tel: 202-939-2437; Fax: 202-234-7323.

Medical Clinic Tel: 202-939-2400; Fax: 202-232-1970.

Dental Clinic Tel: 202-939-2423; Fax: 202-234-7349.

Social Services Tel: 202-939-2414; Fax: 202-232-1970.

Immigration Services Tel: 202-939-2420; Fax: 202-234-7349.

Maryland Locations:

Langley Park Office, 1015 University Blvd. E., Silver Spring, MD 20903. Tel: 301-431-3773 Fax: 301-431-0886.

Adult Clinic Tel: 301-434-8381; Fax: 301-434-8067.

Pediatric Clinic Tel: 301-434-3999; Fax: 301-434-5160.

Piney Branch Office, 8545 Piney Branch Rd., Silver Spring, MD 20901.

Social, Employment & Immigration Services Tel: 301-587-0582; Fax: 301-587-8209.

Medical Clinic Tel: 301-929-0207; Fax: 301-929-0594

Gaithersburg Branch, 117 N. Frederick Ave., Gaithersburg, MD 20877. Tel: 301-417-9113; Fax: 301-417-9895.

Social, Employment & Immigration Services Tel: 301-417-9113; Fax: 301-417-9895.

Spiritual Life, 2131 Lincoln Rd., N.E., 20002-1199. Tel: 888-616-1713; Fax: 202-832-5711. Email: editor@spiritual-life.org. Web: www.spiritual-life.org. Rev. Regis Jordan, O.C.D., Notice Editor; Bros. Edward O'Donnell, O.C.D., Editor; Bryan Paquette, O.C.D., Business Mgr.; Joseph Girouard, O.C.D., Book Review Editor. A Quarterly of Contemporary Spirituality.

The Catholic Charities Foundation of the Archdiocese of Washington, 924 G St. N.W., 20001-4532. Tel: 202-772-4380; Fax: 202-772-4407. Email: orzechowskie@catholiccharitiesdc.org. Edward J. Orzechowski, M.S.W., Pres.

St. Vincent Pallotti Center for Apostolic Development, Inc., 415 Michigan Ave., N.E., 20017-1518. Tel: 202-529-3330; 877-865-5465 (Toll free); Fax: 202-529-0911. Email: pallotti@pallotticenter.org. Web: www.pallotticenter.org. Dr. Andrew D. Thompson, Natl. Dir. Total Assisted 15,000; Total Staff 4.

Woodstock Theological Center, Georgetown University, Box 571137, 20057-1137. Tel: 202-687-3532; Fax: 202-687-5837. Email: woodstock@georgetown.edu. Web: www.georgetown.edu/centers/woodstock. Revs. J. Leon Hooper, S.J.; Raymond B. Kemp; Gasper F. LoBiondo, S.J., Dir.; James Redington, S.J. (OAK).

BETHESDA. *Alpha Omega, Inc. The Legion of Christ Inc.*, Our Lady of Bethesda Retreat Center, 7007 Bradley Blvd., MD 20817. Tel: 301-365-0612; Fax: 301-469-7522. Web: www.outladuofbethesda.org. Rev. Richard Gill, L.C.

Avondale Park Apartments, Inc., c/o Victory Housing, 5430 Grosvenor Ln., Ste. 210, MD 20814-2142. Tel: 301-493-6000; 301-493-5507; Fax: 301-493-9788. Email: jspencer@victoryhousing.org. Web: www.victoryhousing.org.

Catholic Institute for the Psychological Science, Inc., 7007 Bradley Blvd., MD 20817. Tel: 203-281-4798. Bro. Juan Sabadell, L.C., Sec. & Treas.

Conquest NA, Inc., 7007 Bradley Blvd., MD 20817. Tel: 301-365-7614; Fax: 301-299-0809. Email: msliney@legionaries.org. Rev. Juan Sabadell, Sec. & Treas.

Holy Family Hospital of Bethlehem Foundation, c/o James E. Murray, 4706 Fort Sumner Dr., MD 20816. Tel: 301-320-1600; Fax: 301-320-0844. Email: info@hfhfoundation.org. Web: www.hfhfoundation.org.

Institute for Evangelization, Inc., 7007 Bradley Blvd., Ste. 300, MD 20817. Tel: 301-365-0612; Fax: 301-469-7522. Email: ife@familink.com. Rev. Jose Felix Ortega, L.C. (HRT).

Lay Women's Association, P.O. Box 34513, MD 20827. Tel: 301-990-8630; Fax: 978-342-1481. Email: cdahlin@aol.com. Web: www.sinkc.org. National Headquarters of the LWA.

National Christ Child Society, Inc., 6900 Wisconsin Ave., N.W., Ste. 604, MD 20815. Tel: 800-814-2149; Fax: 301-718-8822. Email: msaffell@nationalchristchildsoc.org. Web: www.nationalchristchildsoc.org. Roseann Anderson, Pres.; Mrs. Margaret Saffell, Exec. Dir. A national non-profit organization with 40 affiliate chapters consisting of over 7,000 member volunteers serving needy children since 1887.

Natural Family Planning Center of Washington, DC, Inc., 8514 Bradmoor Dr., MD 20817-3810. Tel: 301-897-9323; Fax: 301-571-5267. Email: hklaus@dgsys.com. Web: www.teenstar-international.org. Sr. Hanna Klaus, M.D., Exec. Dir. Teen STAR & Holistic Sexuality Programs. Total in Residence 2; Total Staff 6.

Victory Youth Centers, Inc., 7201 Wisconsin Ave., Ste. 780, MD 20854. Tel: 301-654-6200. Email: gdyer@dyercpa.com. Gregory B. Dyer, Pres.

FORT WASHINGTON. *Birhen Ng Antipolo, USA, Inc.*, 8504 Oxon Hill Road, MD 20744. Tel: 202-274-7357; Fax: 301-567-4914. Web: www.antipolo.org. Eddie D. Caparas, Pres. & Chm.

GAITHERSBURG. *Emmanuel, Inc.*, P.O. Box 2418, MD 20886-2418.

Mother of God School, 20501 Goshen Rd., MD 20879. Tel: 301-990-2088; Fax: 301-947-0574. Email: mogsadmn@erols.com. Web: www.mogschool.com. Total Staff 25; Students 204.

HYATTSVILLE. *Faith House, Inc.*, 4901 Eastern Ave., MD 20782. Tel: 301-559-5500; Fax: 301-853-6985. Email: questions@saint-anns.com. Web: www.saint-anns.com. Sr. Josephine Murphy, D.C., CEO. Total Assisted 8.

Prison Outreach Ministry, P.O. Box 2173, MD 20784. Tel: 301-773-1926; Fax: 301-773-7017. Rev. Michael Bryant, Chap. Total in Residence 2,200.

KENSINGTON. *Inter Mirifica*, P.O. Box 241, MD 20895. Tel: 301-942-9577; Fax: 301-942-9577 (Call first). Email: jdhoconnell@cs.com. Web: www.intermirifica.org. Rev. John Hardon, S.J., Founder; John O'Connell, Contact Person. Religious publications.

LANDOVER HILLS. *The Center for Deaf Ministries of the Archdiocese of Washington*, 7202 Buchanan, MD 20784. Tel: 301-459-7464 (TTY/Voice); Fax: 301-459-8186. Email: deafmindc@aol.com. Web: www.hometown.aol.com/deafmindc. Rev. Gerard A. Trancone, Dir. Total in Residence 1; Total Staff 3.

LAUREL. *Pallotti Early Learning Center, Inc.*, 113 Saint Mary's Pl., MD 20707. Tel: 301-776-6471; Fax: 301-776-0019. Email: sr-eileen@yahoo.com. Web: pallottidaycare.com. Sr. Eileen Connor, Pres.

MCLEAN. *Physical Location*, 6330 Linway Ter., VA 22101. Tel: 703-356-4473; Fax: 703-356-4558. Rev. Msgr. Bernd Kaut (Germany).

POMFRET. *Ministr-O-Media, Inc.*, St. Joseph Church, MD 20675. Tel: 301-870-3990. Rev. Msgr. John B. Brady, Pres.

POTOMAC. *Youth for the Third Millennium*, P.O. Box 60001, MD 20859. Tel: 301-365-3205; Fax: 301-365-4241. Email: info@ytm.org. Web: www.ytm.org. 7007 Bradley Blvd., Bethesda, MD 20817. Tel: 301-365-3205; Fax: 301-365-4241. Mr. Paul Bernetsky, Exec. Dir. YTM is a Catholic organization that trains young adult lay missionaries through parish and campus-based chapters - strengthening their Catholic identity, their baptismal call to evangelize, their role in works of Christian charity and their commitment to Christ and His Church.

ROCKVILLE. *Conference for Mercy Higher Education*, 8380 Colesville Rd., MD 20850. Tel: 202-361-7833. Email: mercyhighered@aol.com. Web: www.mercyhighered.org. Mary Kathryn Grant, Exec. Dir.

SILVER SPRING. *All Hallows Mission Fund, Inc.*, P.O. Box 3691, MD 20918. Tel: 301-593-4461; Fax: 301-593-4461.

Apostleship of Prayer, League of the Sacred Heart, 15107 Interlachen Dr. #722, MD 20906-5632. Tel: 301-438-3753; Fax: 301-441-4954. Web: www.apostlesofprayer.org/insignis. Rev. Gerard P. Bell, S.J. (NY), Archdiocesan Dir.

Archdiocese of Washington Division, The Blue Army World Apostolate of Fatima , P.O. Box 4934, MD 20914. Tel: 301-949-4951; Fax: 301-933-3829. Harriet Noye, Pres.; Rev. Charles E. Pope, Spiritual Dir.

Camp St. Charles, Inc., 104 Bishop Dr., MD 20905. Tel: 301-384-5432; 301-259-2645 (Summer); Fax: 301-384-5432; 301-259-4165 (Summer). Email: gwillis@frostcenter.com. Web: www.campstcharles.org. Rev. Glen Willis, S.D.S. Total Assisted 600; Total Staff 35.

Catholics Committed to Support the Pope, 9402 Stateside Ct., MD 20903. Tel: 301-434-3245; 301-434-7763; Fax: 301-434-5486. Email: patmorse@comcast.net. George P. Morse, K.G.C.S.G., Pres. & Publisher; His Eminence Edward Cardinal Egan (NY), Councilor; Edouard Cardinal Gagnon, p.s.s., Councilor; George Cardinal Pell, Councilor; Josef Cardinal Tomko, Councilor; Alfonso Cardinal Lopez Trujillo, Councilor; Most Revs. Timothy M. Dolan (NO), Councilor; William E. Lori, Councilor; Rev. Msgr. Peter J. Elliott, Councilor; Rev. Robert L. Stern, Councilor; Dr. William E. May, Councilor. Prepares, publishes and distributes world-wide twelve-volume series of PRECIS OF OFFICIAL CATHOLIC TEACHING for use by rectors and faculty of seminaries, for seminarians, bishops , Catechetical Directors and DRE's, theologians and academics, for Catholic education courses and teaching, writers and teachers, Catholic Study Groups and laity. CCSP publishes and distributes "THE MASS: ITS MYSTERIES REVEALED."

Friends of John Paul II Foundation, 9700 Rosensteel Ave., MD 20910. Tel: 301-589-1857; Fax: 703-536-8371. Email: mflan90753@aol.com. Web: friendsofjohnpaul2foundation.org. Rev. Klemens Dabrowski, S.Ch.; Mary E. Flanagan, Pres.

Holy Cross Health Corp., 1500 Forest Glen Rd., MD 20910-1484. Tel: 301-754-7000; Fax: 301-754-7413. Web: www.holycrosshealth.org. Mr. Kevin J. Sexton, Pres. & CEO. Includes Holy Cross Hospital, Home Health Agency, and other services.

Leadership Conference of Women Religious in the U.S.A., 8808 Cameron St., MD 20910. Tel: 301-588-4955; Fax: 301-587-4575. Email: director@lcwr.org. Web: www.lcwr.org. Sisters Constance Phelps, S.C.L., Pres.; Christine Vladimiroff, O.S.B., Vice Pres.; Mary Ann Zollmann, B.V.M., Past Pres.; Anne Hennessy, C.S.J., Sec.; Rose Jochmann, O.S.F., Treas.; Carole Shinnick, S.S.N.D., Exec. Dir.

Little Sisters of the Holy Family, 14000 New Hampshire Ave., MD 20904-6202. Tel: 301-236-4009. Sr. Domina Son, L.S.H.F., Supr.

Saint Luke Institute, Inc., 8901 New Hampshire Ave., MD 20903. Tel: 301-445-7970; Fax: 301-422-5400. Email: stever@sli.org. Rev. Stephen J. Rossetti, Ph.D., D.Min., Pres. The Institute is a licensed and accredited treatment center for priests and religious, and a center for education and research. Total Assisted 650; Total Staff 65.

Lumen Catechetical Consultants, Inc., P.O. Box 1761, MD 20915. Tel: 301-593-1066; Fax: 301-593-1689. Email: lumen@lifeaftersunday.com. Web: lifeaftersunday.com. Mr. John M. Capobianco, Pres. Provides Consulting & Production Services to Catholic Organizations; Assist in Development and Production of Catechetical Materials in Various Media. Publishes "Life After Sunday."

National Association for Treasurers of Religious Institutes, 8824 Cameron St., MD 20910-4152. Tel: 301-587-7776; Fax: 301-589-2897. Email: natri@natri.org. Web: www.natri.org. Rev. Allan Da Corte, O.F.M., Pres.; Sr. Laura Reicks, R.S.M., Exec. Dir.

North American Conference of Provincials, Corporation Sisters of the Good Shepherd. , 504 Hexton Hill Rd., MD 20904. Tel: 301-622-6838; Fax: 301-384-1025. Sr. Gayle Lwanga Crumbley, R.G.S., Natl. Coord.

Sister of Charity of St. Charles Borromeo, Inc., 11320 Classical Ln., MD 20901. Tel: 301-681-9665. Email: sistersofcb@aol.com. Sr. Caecilia H. Hadiwijana, Pres.

SOAR (Support Our Aging Religious) , 1400 Spring St., Ste. 320, MD 20910-2735. Tel: 301-589-9811; Fax: 301-589-2482. Email: info@soar-usa.org. Web: www.soar-usa.org. Timothy P. Hamer, Pres.; Diane T. Waldo, Grants Program Coord.

Washington Catholic Charismatic Service Committee, 13103 Tamarack Rd., MD 20904. Tel: 301-384-5568; Fax: 301-236-5204. Email: lderoze@cs.com. Deacon Donald DeRoze, Dir.

WALDORF. *Body of Christ Farm Community, Inc.*, 3325 Martha Pl., MD 20601. Tel: 301-888-2566; Fax: 301-888-2566. Email: r.pittman@erols.com. Rev. Robert S. Pittman, S.S.S., Dir.

WEST HYATTSVILLE. *Dominican Province of Nigeria*, Development and Mission Office, P.O. Box 5087, MD 20782. Tel: 301-927-0387; Fax: 301-927-0388. Email: nigopmissions@comcast.net. Web: www.op.org/nigeriaop/default.htm. Rev. Dominic Eshikena, O.P., Dir.

WHEATON. *U.S. Foundation for the Congregation of the Holy Ghost and the Immaculate Heart of Mary, Inc.* (The Spiritan Foundation) , 11411 Amherst Ave., MD 20902. Tel: 301-933-6130; Fax: 301-942-5993. Email: spiritan@thespiritans.org. Web: www.thespiritans.org. Rev. Noel P. O'Meara, C.S.Sp., Pres.

RELIGIOUS INSTITUTES OF MEN REPRESENTED IN THE ARCHDIOCESE

For further details refer to the corresponding bracketed number in the Religious Institutes of Men or Women section.

[0140]—*The Augustinians*—O.S.A.
[0200]—*Benedictine Monks*—O.S.B.
[1350]—*Brothers of St. Francis Xavier*—C.F.X.
[0330]—*Brothers of the Christian Schools* (Baltimore Prov.)—F.S.C.
[0600]—*Brothers of the Congregation of Holy Cross*—C.S.C.
[0400]—*Canons Regular of the Order of the Holy Cross*—O.S.C.
[0470]—*The Capuchin Friars* (Prov. of St. Augustine)—O.F.M.Cap.
[0270]—*Carmelite Fathers & Brothers*—O.Carm.
[1140]—*Congregation of the Sacred Hearts of Jesus and Mary*—SS.CC.
[0480]—*Conventual Franciscans*—O.F.M.Conv
[0260]—*Discalced Carmelite Fathers (Prov. of the Immaculate Heart of Mary)*—O.C.D.
[0520]—*Franciscan Friars (Commissariat of the Holy Land)*—O.F.M.
[0530]—*Franciscan Friars of the Atonement*—S.A.
[0650]—*Holy Ghost Fathers (Eastern Prov.)*—C.S.Sp.
[0690]—*Jesuit Fathers and Brothers (Prov. of Maryland)*—S.J.
[0730]—*Legionaries of Christ*—L.C.
[0740]—*Marian Fathers*—M.I.C.
[0770]—*The Marist Brothers*—F.M.S.
[0780]—*Marist Fathers*—S.M
[0800]—*Maryknoll*—M.M.
[0850]—*Missionaries of Africa*—M.Afr.
[0720]—*The Missionaries of Our Lady of La Salette*—M.S.
[1210]—*Missionaries of St. Charles (Scalabrinians)*—C.S.
[0590]—*Missionaries of the Holy Apostle*—M.Ss.A.
[0840]—*Missionary Servants of the Most Holy Trinity*—S.T.
[0870]—*Montfort Missionaries*—S.M.M.
[0910]—*Oblates of Mary Immaculate (Eastern Prov.)*—O.M.I.
[0920]—*Oblates of St. Francis de Sales*—O.S.F.S.
[0430]—*Order of Preachers (Dominican) (Prov. of St. Joseph)*—O.P.
[1310]—*Order of the Holy Trinity (American Prov.)*—O.SS.T.
[1030]—*Paulist Fathers*—C.S.P.
[1040]—*Piarist Fathers*—Sch.P.
[0610]—*Priests of the Congregation of Holy Cross* (Indiana Prov.)—C.S.C.
[1070]—*Redemptorist Fathers* (Baltimore Prov.)—C.SS.R.
[0110]—*Society of African Missions*—S.M.A.
[1260]—*Society of Christ*—S.Ch.
[0990]—*Society of the Catholic Apostolate (Immaculate Conception Prov.)*—S.A.C.
[1200]—*Society of the Divine Savior* (Milwaukee, WI)—S.D.S.
[0420]—*Society of the Divine Word*—S.V.D.
[1290]—*Society of the Priests of Saint Sulpice*—S.S.
[0640]—*Sons of the Holy Family*—S.F.
[0700]—*St. Joseph Society of the Sacred Heart*—S.S.J.
[0560]—*Third Order Regular of Saint Francis (Prov. of the Immaculate Conception)*—T.O.R.

RELIGIOUS INSTITUTES OF WOMEN REPRESENTED IN THE ARCHDIOCESE

[1810]—*Bernardine Franciscan Sisters*—O.S.F.
[0340]—*Carmelite Sisters of Charity*—C.Ch
[3803-05]—*Congregation of the Sisters of St. Joseph* (Rockville Center, Brentwood, NY)—C.S.J.
[1920]—*Congregation of the Sisters of the Holy Cross*—C.S.C.
[0760]—*Daughters of Charity of St. Vincent de Paul*—D.C.
[0960]—*Daughters of Wisdom*—D.W.
[0420]—*Discalced Carmelite Nuns*—O.C.D.
[1070-13]—*Dominican Congregation of the Most Holy Rosary* (Adrian, MI)—O.P.
[1050]—*Dominican Contemplative Nuns*—O.P.
[1070-03]—*Dominican Sisters* (Sinsinawa, WI)—O.P.
[1100]—*Dominican Sisters of Charity of the Presentation of the Blessed Virgin*—O.P.
[1470]—*Franciscan Sisters of St. Joseph*—H.F.S.J.
[1190]—*Franciscan Sisters of the Atonement*—S.A.
[1250]—*The Institute of the Franciscan Sisters of the Eucharist*—F.S.E.
[0410]—*Institute of the Sisters of Our Lady of Mt. Carmel*—O.Carm.
[2330]—*Little Sisters of Jesus*—L.S.J.
[2340]—*Little Sisters of the Poor*—L.S.P.
[2345]—*Little Workers of the Sacred Hearts of Jesus and Mary*—P.O.S.C.
[2490]—*Medical Mission Sisters*—M.M.S,
[2720]—*Mission Helpers of the Sacred Heart*—M.H.S.H.
[2710]—*Missionaries of Charity*—M.C.
[2820]—*Missionary Sisters of Our Lady of Africa*—M.S.O.L.A.
[2900]—*Missionary Sisters of St. Charles Borromeo*—M.S.C.S.
[2760]—*Missionary Sisters of the Immaculate Conception of the Mother of God*—S.M.I.C.
[2865]—*Missionary Sisters of the Sacred Heart of Our Lady of Guadalupe*—M.S.C.Gpe.
[3530]—*Missionary Sisters, Servants of the Holy Spirit*—S.Sp.S.
[3040]—*Oblate Sisters of Providence*—O.S.P.
[]—*Oblate Sisters of the Most Holy Eucharist*—O.S.S.E.
[3210]—*Poor Clares of Perpetual Adoration*—P.C.P.A.
[3450]—*Religious of Jesus and Mary*—R.J.M.
[3460]—*Religious of Mary Immaculate*—R.M.I.
[2519]—*Religious Sisters of Mercy* (Alma, MI)—R.S.M.
[3430]—*Religious Teachers Filippini*—M.P.F.
[2970]—*School Sisters of Notre Dame*—S.S.N.D.
[3520]—*Servants of the Holy Heart of Mary*—S.S.C.M.
[3620]—*Sister Servants of Mary Immaculate*—S.S.M.I.
[0500]—*Sisters of Charity of Nazareth*—S.C.N.
[0570]—*Sisters of Charity of Seton Hill, Greensburg, Pennsylvania*—S.C.
[1000]—*Sisters of Divine Providence* (Melbourne, KY)—C.D.P.
[2575]—*Sisters of Mercy of the Americas*—R.S.M.
[2990]—*Sisters of Notre Dame*—S.N.D.
[3000]—*Sisters of Notre Dame de Namur* (Maryland, Chesapeake & Base Communities Prov.)—S.N.D.deN.
[3360]—*Sisters of Providence of St. Mary-of-the-Woods, IN*—S.P.
[3893]—*Sisters of Saint Joseph of Chestnut Hill, Philadelphia*—S.S.J.
[4090]—*Sisters of Social Service*—S.S.S.
[3718]—*Sisters of St. Ann*—S.S.A.
[3740]—*Sisters of St. Casimir*—S.S.C.
[1070-07]—*Sisters of St. Dominic of St. Cecilia* (Nashville, TN)—O.P.
[1650]—*Sisters of St. Francis of Philadelphia*—O.S.F.
[1600]—*Sisters of St. Francis of the Martyr St. George*—O.S.F.
[3830-13]—*Sisters of St. Joseph*—C.S.J.
[3850]—*Sisters of St. Joseph of Chambery*—C.S.J.
[3890]—*Sisters of St. Joseph of Peace*—C.S.J.P.
[3980]—*Sisters of St. Paul de Chartres*—S.P.C.
[3150]—*Sisters of the Catholic Apostolate (Pallotine)*—S.A.C.
[1830]—*Sisters of the Good Shepherd*—R.G.S.
[1950]—*Sisters of the Holy Family*—S.S.F.
[1990]—*Sisters of the Holy Names of Jesus and Mary*—S.N.J.M.
[2110]—*Sisters of the Humility of Mary*—H.M.
[3320]—*Sisters of the Presentation of the Blessed Virgin Mary*—P.B.V.M.
[1490]—*Sisters of the Third Franciscan Order*

(Syracuse, NY)—O.S.F.

[1720]—*Sisters of the Third Order Regular of St. Francis of the Congregation of Our Lady of Lourdes*—O.S.F.

[2160]—*Sisters, Servants of the Immaculate Heart of Mary*—I.H.M.

[4060]—*Society of the Holy Child Jesus*—S.H.C.J.

[4070]—*Society of the Sacred Heart*—R.S.C.J.

[4120-06]—*Ursuline Nuns of the Congregation of Paris* (Toledo, OH)—O.S.U.

[4190]—*Visitation Nuns*—V.H.M.

ARCHDIOCESAN CEMETERIES

WASHINGTON. *The Catholic Cemeteries of the Archdiocese of Washington, Inc.*, 13801 Georgia Ave., Silver Spring, MD 20906. Tel: 301-871-1300 (All offices 9-4:30 P.M.). Rev. Msgr. William F. O'Donnell, Dir.; Mr. Frank Markowski, Dir.

St. Mary's, 2121 Lincoln Rd., N.E., 20002. Tel: 202-635-7444. Warren A. Meny.

Mount Olivet, 1300 Bladensburg Rd., N.E., 20002. Tel: 202-399-3000. Warren A. Meny.

CLINTON. 8000 Woodyard Rd., MD 20735. Tel: 301-868-5141. Harry S. Lancaster Jr.

LEONARDTOWN. Box 379, MD 20650. Tel: 301-475-5005. Mr. John A. Spalding.

SILVER SPRING. *Gate of Heaven*, 13801 Georgia Ave., MD 20906. Tel: 301-871-6500. Samuel E. French Jr., Mgr.

St. John's Forest Glen, Rosensteel Ave., MD 20910. Tel: 301-871-6500. Samuel E. French Jr.

NECROLOGY

† Albert, Rev. Msgr. Louis W., (Retired)—Died Dec. 23, 2002

† Grodavent, Rev. Msgr. Thomas J., (Retired)—Died May 25, 2003

† McMain, Rev. Msgr. Robert O., St. Ann. (Retired)—Died Dec. 20, 2002

† Holden, Paul, (Retired)—Died March 16, 2003

† Siekierski, Matthew J., LaPlata, MD Sacred Heart—Died Aug. 3, 2003

† Treacy, Canice, St. Peter, Olney, MD. (Retired)—Died Jan. 6, 2003

Diocese of Wheeling-Charleston

(Dioecesis Vhelingensis carolopolitanus)

Most Reverend

BERNARD W. SCHMITT, D.D.

Bishop of Wheeling-Charleston; ordained May 28, 1955; appointed Titular Bishop of Walla Walla and Auxiliary Bishop of Wheeling-Charleston May 31, 1988; ordained to the Episcopacy August 1, 1988; appointed Seventh Bishop of Wheeling-Charleston March 30, 1989; installed May 17, 1989 *1300 Byron St., P.O. Box 230, Wheeling, WV 26003.*

Chancery Office: 1300 Byron St., P.O. Box 230, Wheeling, WV 26003. Tel: 304-233-0880; Fax: 304-233-4086.

Web: www.dwc.org

Email: jgallagher@dwc.org

Square Miles 24,282.

Established as Diocese of Wheeling July 19, 1850; Redesignated Diocese of Wheeling-Charleston October 4, 1974.

Comprises the entire State of West Virginia.

For legal titles of parishes and diocesan institutions, consult the Chancery Office.

STATISTICAL OVERVIEW

Personnel	
Bishop	1
Priests: Diocesan Active in Diocese	75
Priests: Diocesan Active Outside Diocese	1
Priests: Retired, Sick or Absent	39
Number of Diocesan Priests	115
Religious Priests in Diocese	66
Total Priests in Diocese	181
Extern Priests in Diocese	9
Ordinations:	
Diocesan Priests	1
Transitional Deacons	2
Permanent Deacons in Diocese	32
Total Brothers	18
Total Sisters	223
Parishes	
Parishes	112
With Resident Pastor:	
Resident Diocesan Priests	68
Resident Religious Priests	23
Without Resident Pastor:	
Administered by Priests	8
Administered by Deacons	1
Administered by Professed Religious Men	3
Administered by Religious Women	4
Missions	24
Pastoral Centers	4
New Parishes Created	1
Closed Parishes	1
Professional Ministry Personnel:	
Brothers	8
Sisters	43
Lay Ministers	28
Welfare	
Catholic Hospitals	3
Total Assisted	559,556
Health Care Centers	2
Total Assisted	4,130
Homes for the Aged	4
Total Assisted	851
Residential Care of Children	1
Total Assisted	19
Day Care Centers	4
Total Assisted	432
Specialized Homes	1
Total Assisted	19
Special Centers for Social Services	4
Total Assisted	19,905
Educational	
Diocesan Students in Other Seminaries	19
Total Seminarians	19
Colleges and Universities	1
Total Students	1,462
High Schools, Diocesan and Parish	7
Total Students	1,559
High Schools, Private	1
Total Students	60
Elementary Schools, Diocesan and Parish	25
Total Students	4,849
Elementary Schools, Private	1
Total Students	150
Catechesis/Religious Education:	
High School Students	1,195
Elementary Students	4,216
Total Students under Catholic Instruction	13,510
Teachers in the Diocese:	
Priests	2
Brothers	2
Sisters	4
Lay Teachers	489
Vital Statistics	
Receptions into the Church:	
Infant Baptism Totals	929
Adult Baptism Totals	288
Received into Full Communion	213
First Communions	1,363
Confirmations	1,190
Marriages:	
Catholic	207
Interfaith	230
Total Marriages	437
Deaths	1,150
Total Catholic Population	100,648
Total Population	1,801,916

Former Bishops—Rt. Revs. RICHARD VINCENT WHELAN, D.D., consecrated March 21, 1841; Bishop of Richmond; transferred to Wheeling in 1850; died July 7, 1874; JOHN JOSEPH KAIN, D.D., consecrated May 23, 1875; transferred to June 15, 1893, to the Titular Archiepiscopal See of Oxyrynchia; appt. July 6, 1893; Coadjutor ""cum jure successionis" to the Most Rev. Archbishop of St. Louis, MO; created Archbishop of St. Louis, May 21, 1895; died Oct. 13, 1903; PATRICK JAMES DONAHUE, D.D., consecrated April 8, 1894; died Oct. 4, 1922; Most Revs. THOMAS J. MCDONNELL, D.D., LL.D., consecrated Sept. 15, 1947; appt. Auxiliary Bishop of New York, June 21, 1947; appt. Coadjutor of Wheeling, "cum jure successionis," March 7, 1951; died Feb. 25, 1961; JOHN J. SWINT, D.D., LL.D., appt. Auxiliary Bishop of Wheeling Feb. 22, 1922; consecrated May 11, 1922; appt. Bishop of Wheeling Dec. 11, 1922; promoted to rank of Archbishop "ad personam," March 12, 1954; died Nov. 23, 1962; JOSEPH H. HODGES, D.D., ord. Dec. 8, 1935; appt. Titular Bishop of Rusadus and Auxiliary of Richmond Aug. 8, 1952; consecrated Oct. 15, 1952; transferred to Wheeling See as Coadjutor, "cum jure successionis", May 24, 1961; succeeded to the See Nov. 23, 1962; died Jan. 27, 1985; FRANCIS B. SCHULTE, D.D., ord. May 10, 1952; appt. Titular Bishop of Afufenia and Auxiliary Bishop of Philadelphia June 27, 1981; consecrated Bishop Aug. 12, 1981; transferred to Wheeling July 31, 1985; transferred to Archdiocese of New Orleans Feb. 14, 1989.

Vicar General—Very Rev. JOHN R. GALLAGHER, V.G., V.G., P.O. Box 230, Wheeling, 26003. Tel: 304-233-0880; Fax: 304-233-4086.

Chancery Office—P.O. Box 230, Wheeling, 26003. Tel: 304-233-0880; Fax: 304-233-0890. Office Hours: Mon.-Fri. 8:30-4:30

Chancellor—Very Rev. JOHN R. GALLAGHER, V.G., V.G.

Assistant to the Bishop—Very Rev. KEVIN M. QUIRK, J.C.D.

Diocesan Tribunal— All Rogatory Commissions should be addressed to the office of the Diocesan Tribunal *P.O. Box 230, Wheeling, 26003.* Tel: 304-233-0880.

Judicial Vicar—Very Rev. KEVIN M. QUIRK, J.C.D.

Promoter Justitiae—Rev. PATRICK A. CONDRON, J.C.L.

Defensores Vinculi—Rt. Rev. JOHN M. LOGAN, O.Praem., J.C.L.; Sr. MARY BYRON, S.S.J., J.C.L.

Diocesan Consultors—Very Revs. WILLIAM A. ANDERSON, V.F.; STEPHEN D. DUBE, V.F.; JOHN R. GALLAGHER, V.G., V.G.; Revs. JAMES LACROSSE, S.M.; JOHN H. MCDONNELL; JEROME MCKENNA, C.P.; P. EDWARD SADIE.

Vicar for Religious—Sr. MARIAN MADDEN, S.C., P.O. Box 230, Wheeling, 26003-0010. Tel: 304-233-0880; Fax: 304-230-2231.

Delegate for Clergy—Rev. ROBERT G. PARK, P.O. Box 230, Wheeling, 26003-0010. Tel: 304-233-0880.

Episcopal Vicar for Clergy—Very Rev. FREDERICK P. ANNIE, V.E., P.O. Box 230, Wheeling, 26003-0010. Tel: 304-233-0880; Fax: 304-230-2231.

Vicars Forane—Very Revs. STEPHEN D. DUBE, V.F., Wheeling Vicariate; RICHARD SHODA, J.C.L., V.F., Beckley Vicariate; F. LEON ALEXANDER, V.F., Charleston Vicariate; MARK WARD, C.P., V.F., Clarksburg Vicariate; JOHN V. DIBACCO JR., V.F., Martinsburg Vicariate; EDWARD M. BELL, V.F., Parkersburg Vicariate; WILLIAM A. ANDERSON, V.F., Weston Vicariate.

Finance Council—P.O. Box 230, Wheeling, 26003.

Finance Officer—Very Rev. JOHN R. GALLAGHER, V.G., V.G., P.O. Box 230, Wheeling, 26003. Tel: 304-233-0880.

Diocesan Offices and Directors

Apostleship of Prayer—Very Rev. KEVIN M. QUIRK, J.C.D., P.O. Box 230, Wheeling, 26003.

Archivist—Ms. TRACEY RASMER, P.O. Box 230, Wheeling, 26003.

Behavioral Counseling and Ministry—Rev. ROBERT G. PARK, P.O. Box 230, Wheeling, 26003. Tel: 304-233-0880.

Diocesan School Board of Advisors—Mr. JOHN YELENIC, Supt. Schools & Chm., P.O. Box 230, Wheeling, 26003. Tel: 304-233-0880.

Buildings and Properties—Mr. DARRYL COSTANZO, Dir., P.O. Box 230, Wheeling, 26003. Tel: 304-233-0880.

Catholic Community Services, Inc.—Mr. GEORGE E. SMOULDER, Exec. Dir., P.O. Box 230, Wheeling, 26003. Tel: 304-233-0880; Fax: 304-233-9293. Email: gsmoulder@dwc.org; Northern Regional Office, P.O. Box 230, Wheeling, 26003-0030. Tel: 304-233-0880. Western Regional Office, 352 Mansion St., Hamlin, 25523. Tel: 304-824-5069.

Central Regional Office, 235 High St., Ste. 210, Morgantown, 26505. Tel: 304-292-6597. Southern Regional Office, P.O. Box 386, 601 Harrison St., Princeton, 24740-2909. Tel: 304-425-4306. Eastern Regional Office, 320 Elm Place, Romney, 26757. Tel: 304-822-5414. Parkersburg Regional Office, P.O. Box 13, 130 4th St., Parkersburg, 26102. Tel: 304-422-1120.

Catholic Community Homemaker Services, Inc.—Mr. GEORGE E. SMOULDER, Exec. Dir., 1300 Byron St., P.O. Box 230, Wheeling, 26003. Tel: 304-233-0880; Fax: 304-233-0890. Email: gsmoulder@dwc.org.

Catholic University, Friends of—Very Rev. JOHN R. GALLAGHER, V.G., V.G., P.O. Box 230, Wheeling, 26003. Tel: 304-233-0880.

Cemeteries—Very Rev. JOHN R. GALLAGHER, V.G., V.G., Dir., P.O. Box 230, Wheeling, 26003. Tel: 304-233-0880.

Censor Librorum—VACANT.

West Virginia Council of Catholic Women—Sr. MARIAN MADDEN, S.C., Diocesan Moderator, P.O. Box 230, Wheeling, 26003. Tel: 304-233-0880; JANE ANN GRISHABER, Pres., 1652 Fourth Ave., #101, Charleston, 25312. Tel: 304-346-6255.

Stewardship and Development, Office of—Mr. BRYAN MINOR, Dir., P.O. Box 230, Wheeling, 26003. Tel: 233-0880; Ms. KRISTEN BENSON, Asst. Dir., P.O. Box 230, Wheeling, 26003. Tel: 304-233-0880.

Diaconal Council—Deacon JOHN W. LOCKE, Chm., 110 Arrowhead Ridge, Hedgesville, 25427-5345. Tel: 304-754-5993; Fax: 304-754-5906. Email: jlockewv@intrepid.net.

Finance Office—Very Rev. JOHN R. GALLAGHER, V.G., V.G., Finance Officer; Mr. WILLIAM G. FISHER, C.P.A., Finance Dir.; Mr. JOHN L. HOFFMAN, Parish Finance Mgr., P.O. Box 230, Wheeling, 26003-0010. Tel: 304-233-0880; Fax: 304-233-4086.

Hispanic Affairs—Rev. JEROME MCKENNA, C.P., Acting Dir., 1300 Byron St., P.O. Box 230, Wheeling, 26003. Tel: 304-233-0880.

Holy Childhood Association—Mrs. ROBYN HAMMOND, P.O. Box 230, Wheeling, 26003. Tel: 304-233-0880.

Home and Foreign Missions, Society for the Propagation of the Faith— Catholic Students' Mission Crusade Very Rev. JOHN R. GALLAGHER, V.G., V.G., Diocesan Dir., P.O. Box 230, Wheeling, 26003.

Hospitals, Representative for Catholic—Sr. DIANE BUSHEE, S.A.C., St. Mary's Hospital, 2900 First Ave., Huntington, 25702. Tel: 304-526-1234.

Human Resources, Office of—Mr. MICHAEL NAU, Dir., P.O. Box 230, Wheeling, 26003. Tel: 304-233-0880.

Infirm Priests Association—Most Rev. BERNARD W. SCHMITT, D.D., Pres.; Very Rev. JOHN R. GALLAGHER, V.G., V.G., Sec. & Treas. P.O. Box 230, Wheeling, 26003. Tel: 304-233-0880.

Justice and Life, Office of—Ms. CAROL WARREN, Dir., 600 Shrewsbury St., #6, Charleston, 25302. Tel: 304-343-3360.

Migration and Refugee Services, Office of—Mrs. KIM KEENE, Dir., 1033 Quarrier St., Room 105, Charleston, 25301. Tel: 304-343-1036.

Natural Family Planning—Ms. NANCY J. BOTKIN, R.N. Tel: 304-343-1036.

Office of Diocesan Planning and Pastoral Services—Rev. JEROME MCKENNA, C.P., P.O. Box 230, Wheeling, 26003. Tel: 304-233-0880, Ext. 260.

Parish Care & Empowerment—Ms. BARBARA SUTTON, Dir., P.O. Box 230, Wheeling, 26003-0030. Tel: 304-233-0880, Ext. 376.

Pastoral Services Liaisons for Office of Diocesan Planning & Pastoral Services—

Wheeling Vicariate—Ms. BEVERLY NICKERSON, Holy Family Mission, P.O. Box 386, Beech Bottom, 26030. Tel: 304-394-5500; Fax: 304-394-5500.

Charleston Vicariate—Deacon JOHN HANNA, John XXIII Pastoral Center, 100 Hodges Rd., Charleston, 25314-2281. Tel: 304-342-0051; Fax: 304-347-9298.

Beckley Vicariate—Sr. CLARA CHANDLER, H.M., 601 Harrison St., Princeton, 24740. Tel: 304-431-2677; Fax: 304-425-7515.

Clarksburg Vicariate—Mrs. KATHY KERZAK, 46 Beechurst Ave., Morgantown, 26505. Tel: 304-296-0061; Fax: 304-296-0062.

Parkersburg Vicariate—Dr. MEG WATZEK, Ph.D., 521 Market St., #12, Parkersburg, 26101. Tel: 304-424-3457, Ext. 207; Fax: 304-422-1025.

Weston Vicariate—Mrs. CAROLYN SANTILLI, P.O. Box 278, Buckhannon, 26201. Tel: 304-472-5698; Fax: 304-472-3170.

Martinsburg Vicariate—Ms. MARY POFFENBERGER, P.O. Box 808, Charleston, 25414. Tel: 304-724-7074; Fax: 304-724-7175.

Presbyteral Council—Rev. DEAN G. BORGMEYER, Chm., P.O. Box 4204, Star City, 26504. Tel: 304-599-3747.

Priests Eucharistic League—VACANT.

Public Affairs Representative—Rev. CHARLES MCCALLISTER (Retired), P.O. Box 1309, Elkins, 26241. Tel: 304-636-2452; G. NICHOLAS CASEY JR. ESQ., Ste 700, One Valley Square, P.O Box 1746, Charleston, 25326. Tel: 304-345-2000.

Religious Unity, Diocesan Commission for—Rev. JOHN H. MCDONNELL, Chm., 4807 Staunton Ave. S.E., Charleston, 25304-1951. Tel: 304-925-2864.

Resettlement of Displaced Persons—Mrs. KIM KEENE, Dir., 1033 Quarrier St., Rm. 105, Charleston, 25301. Tel: 304-343-1036.

Scholarship Association—Mr. JOHN ELCESSER, Sec. & Treas., P.O. Box 230, Wheeling, 26003. Tel: 304-233-0880.

Scouting—Very Rev. STEPHEN D. DUBE, V.F., 229 California Ave., Weirton, 26062-3729. Tel: 304-723-2054.

Catholic Charities, Department of—Mr. GEORGE SMOULDER, Exec. Dir., P.O. Box 230 Wheeling, 26003. Tel: 304-233-0880.

Victim Assistance Coordinator—Very Rev. JOHN R. GALLAGHER, V.G., V.G. Tel: 304-233-0880. Email: jgallagher@dwc.org.

Vocations, Office of—Very Rev. JOHN R. GALLAGHER, V.G., V.G., Dir., P.O. Box 230, Wheeling, 26003. Tel: 304-233-0880; Rev. CASEY B. MAHONE, Assoc. Dir., Immaculate Conception Parish, 329 Maryland Ave., P.O. Box 1726 - E, Fairmont, 26555. Tel: 304-363-1840.

West Virginia State Catholic Conference—Very Rev. JOHN R. GALLAGHER, V.G., V.G., Exec. Dir., P.O. Box 230, Wheeling, 26003. Tel: 304-233-0880.

Women, Office of—Sr. MARIAN MADDEN, S.C., Dir., P.O. Box 230, Wheeling, 26003-0010. Tel: 304-233-0880.

Catholic Education and Parish Life

Catholic Education and Parish Life, Dept. of—Mr. JOHN F. ELCESSER, Exec. Dir., P.O. Box 230, Wheeling, 26003-0030. Tel: 304-233-0880.

Catholic Charismatic Renewal—Rev. PATSY J. IAQUINTA, Liaison, P.O. Box 608, Bluefield, 24701. Tel: 304-327-5623.

Cursillo—Mr. EDWARD A. MARN, Lay Dir., 200 Church St., Paden City, 26159. Tel: 304-337-8005.

Communications & Technology—VACANT, Dir., P.O. Box 230, Wheeling, 26003-0030. Tel: 304-233-0880.

Resource Library/Audio-Visual Center—Mrs. CONNIE GORDER, P.O. Box 230, Wheeling, 26003-0030. Tel: 304-233-0880.

"Catholic Spirit, The"—Mr. THOMAS PAPEIKA, Editor; Ms. COLLEEN DUNCAN, Assoc. Editor, P.O. Box 230, Wheeling, 26003-0030. Tel: 304-233-0880, Ext. 347.

Catechetical Ministries—CHERYL J. FOURNIER, Dir., P.O. Box 230, Wheeling, 26003-0030. Tel: 304-233-0880.

Evangelization—Mr. BRYAN S. REISING, Dir., P.O. Box 230, Wheeling, 26003-0030. Tel: 304-233-0880.

Family Life—Ms. KATHLEEN "KATHI" PROBO, Dir., P.O. Box 230, Wheeling, 26003-0030. Tel: 304-233-0880.

Parenting and Pregnancy Program—Ms. JACQUELINE HAMILTON, Dir.

Liturgical Practices—Mrs. MARIANNE ENGELMANN, Dir., P.O. Box 230, Wheeling, 26003-0030. Tel: 304-233-0880.

Liturgical Art and Architecture Commission—Very Rev. WILLIAM A. ANDERSON, V.F., Chm.

Schools, Superintendent of—Mr. JOHN YELENIC, Supt.; VACANT, Asst. Supr., Admin. & Finance, P.O. Box 230, Wheeling, 26003-0030. Tel: 304-233-0880.

Advancement Director for Catholic Schools—Mr. GARY W. MULHERN, P.O. Box 230, Wheeling, 26003. Tel: 304-233-0880.

Director of Curriculum and Instruction—Sr. MARY LOU PALAS, S.C., Diocesan Dir.

Director of Religious Education in Schools—Mrs. ROBYN HAMMOND, Dir., P.O. Box 230, Wheeling, 26003-0030. Tel: 304-233-0880.

Instructional Technology—Ms. JENNIFER L. HORNYAK, Coord., P.O. Box 230, Wheeling, 26003. Tel: 304-233-0880.

Office of Ministry with Persons with Disabilities—Ms. ROSE WILKINS, Dir., P.O. Box 230, Wheeling, 26003-0030. Tel: 304-233-0880; 304-230-2230 TTY.

Youth, Young Adult, and Camp Ministry—Mr. MICHAEL R. HALL, Dir., P.O. Box 230, Wheeling, 26003-0030. Tel: 304-233-0880.

Teens Encounter Christ (TEC)—Mr. MICHAEL R. HALL.

CLERGY, PARISHES, MISSIONS AND PAROCHIAL SCHOOLS

CITY OF WHEELING
(OHIO COUNTY)

1—ST. JOSEPH'S CATHEDRAL (1828),, Including former parishes: Blessed Trinity, St. Joan of Arc, and Sacred Heart. Rev. Larry W. Dorsch Rector. In Res., Very Rev. John R. Gallagher, V.G., V.G.; Revs. Robert G. Park; Frederick P. Annie.
Res.: 14 13th St., 26003-0051. Tel: 304-233-4121; Fax: 304-233-4129.
School—Wheeling Catholic Elementary School 26003. Tel: 304-233-1515.

2—ST. ALPHONSUS (1856),, Including former parishes St. Mary and St. Ladislaus. Rev. Patrick A. Condron, J.C.L.; Bro. David Cooney, F.M.S., Pastoral Assoc.
Church & Res. Address: 2111 Market St., 26003-3827. Tel: 304-232-4353; Fax: 304-232-0914.
School—Wheeling Catholic Elementary School 26003. Tel: 304-233-1515.
Catechesis/Religious Program—Students 122.

3—BLESSED TRINITY (1931), Closed., Merged with St. Joseph's Cathedral.

4—CORPUS CHRISTI (1916), Rev. Eugene S. Ostrowski.
Res.: 1516 Warwood Ave., 26003-7197. Tel: 304-277-2911; Fax: 304-277-2823.
School—Tel: 304-277-1220; Fax: 304-277-2823. Mr. Dick Taylor, Prin. Dominican Sisters 1; Lay Teachers 11; Students 188.
Catechesis/Religious Program—Students 65.

5—IMMACULATE CONCEPTION (ST. MARY) (1873), Closed., Merged with St. Alphonsus.

6—ST. JOAN OF ARC (1923), Closed., Merged with St. Joseph's Cathedral.

7—ST. LADISLAUS (1902), Closed., Merged with St. Alphonsus.

8—ST. MICHAEL'S (1897), Revs. James M. Sobus; Robert Eric Hall IV, Assoc. Rector; Deacon Paul J. Smith.
Res.: 1225 National Rd., 26003-5791. Tel: 304-242-1560; Fax: 304-243-5710.
School—1221 National Rd., 26003. Tel: 304-242-3966. Lay Teachers 29.
Catechesis/Religious Program—Tel: 304-242-5897. Students 94.

9—OUR LADY OF PEACE (Mt. Olivet) (1962), Rev. Francis A. O'Kruta.
Res.: 2 Allendale Rd., Mt. Olivet, 26003-4601. Tel: 304-242-6575.
School—Tel: 304-242-1383; Fax: 304-243-1383. Mrs. C'Ann Reilly, Prin. Lay Teachers 12; Students 235.

10—SACRED HEART (1903), Closed., Merged with St. Joseph's Cathedral.

11—ST. VINCENT DE PAUL'S (1895), Rev. James LaCrosse, S.M. In Res., Rev. William Seli, S.M.; Bro. John Hunt.
Res.: 2244 Marshall Ave., 26003-7440. Tel: 304-242-0406; Fax: 304-243-0837.
School—Tel: 304-242-5844; Fax: 304-243-1624. Sisters 3; Lay Teachers 17; Students 206.
Catechesis/Religious Program—Students 195.
Mission—Our Lady of Seven Dolors [CEM] Chapel Hill Rd., Triadelphia, Ohio Co. 26059. Tel: 304-547-5342.

CITY OF CHARLESTON
(KANAWHA COUNTY)

1—ST. AGNES (1923), Rev. John H. McDonnell.
Res.: 4807 Staunton Ave., S.E., 25304. Tel: 304-925-2836; Fax: 304-925-2854.
School—4801 Staunton Ave., S.E., 25304. Tel: 304-925-4341; Fax: 304-925-4423. Sr. Judith Ann Teufel, S.S.J., Prin. Sisters of St. Joseph 1; Lay Teachers 19; Students 182.
Catechesis/Religious Program—Students 51.
Convent—300 49th St., S.E., 25304. Tel: 304-925-2480.

2—ST. ANTHONY (1905), Rev. Dismas Young, O.F.M-.Cap.; Deacon David Wuletich. In Res., Rev. Kieran Quinn, O.F.M.Cap.
Res.: 1000 Sixth St., 25302. Tel: 304-342-2716; Fax: 304-344-1678.
School—Tel: 304-346-8441. Ms. Myrtolyn English. Lay Teachers 18; Students 107.
Catechesis/Religious Program—Students 39.

3—SACRED HEART CO-CATHEDRAL (1866), [CEM] Revs. P. Edward Sadie, Rector; Timothy J. Grassi, Assoc. Rector; Paul Hudock; Deacon John J. Lynch.
Res.: 1032 Virginia St. E., 25301-2879. Tel: 304-342-8175; Fax: 304-344-3907.
School—Tel: 304-346-5491. Mrs. Jean M. Cavalier, Prin. Lay Teachers 24; Students 472.
Catechesis/Religious Program—Students 133.

OUTSIDE THE CITIES OF WHEELING AND CHARLESTON

BARRACKVILLE, MARION CO., ALL SAINTS, Merged,

with St. Joseph, Fairmont; St. Anthony, Grant Town, and Our Lady of the Assumption, Rivesville to form St. Peter the Fisherman, Fairmont

BECKLEY, RALEIGH CO., ST. FRANCIS DE SALES (1907), [CEM] Revs. Samuel S. Sacus; Pericles P. Malacaman; Deacons W. Donald Wise; John F. Ziolkowski.
Res.: 614 S. Oakwood Ave., 25801. Tel: 304-253-3695 (Parish Office); 304-256-3594 (Rectory); Fax: 304-253-3694.
School—Tel: 304-252-4087; Fax: 304-252-4087. Lay Teachers 13; Students 121.
Catechesis/Religious Program—626 S. Oakwood Ave., 25801. Tel: 304-255-4694. Students 124.

BEECH BOTTOM, BROOKE CO., HOLY FAMILY, Closed., See St. John, Wellsburg.

BELINGTON, BARBOUR CO., RESURRECTION MISSION (1978), [CEM] Sr. Teresa Reddington, S.S.J., Dir.
Res.: 701 Brown Ave., 26250. Tel: 304-823-1576.
Catechesis/Religious Program—Students 4.

BELLE, KANAWHA CO., ST. JOHN (1951), Rev. Albert Alexandrunas, O.F.M.Cap.
Res.: 321 E. Tenth St., 25015. Tel: 304-949-3063.
Catechesis/Religious Program—Students 22.
Mission—Good Shepherd East Bank. Box 16, Coalburg, Kanawha Co. 25067. Tel: 304-595-6002. Sr. Clara Lill, R.C., Parochial Coord.

BENWOOD, MARSHALL CO., ST. JOHN'S (1875), Rev. Joseph Hayden, S.J.
Res.: 622 Main St., 26031. Tel: 304-232-6455.
School—Sts. James and John Consolidated School, Tel: 304-232-1587. Mrs. Jennifer Marsh, Prin. Lay Teachers 7; Students 50.

BERKELEY SPRINGS, MORGAN CO., ST. VINCENT DE PAUL (1931), [CEM] Rev. Cyprian Joseph Mercieca, T.O.R.; Deacons John W. Locke; Robert B. Lilly.
Res.: P.O. Box 634, 25411-0634. Tel: 304-258-3935; Fax: 304-258-7559.
Catechesis/Religious Program—Tel: 304-258-1311; Fax: 304-258-7559. Students 52.

BLUEFIELD, MERCER CO., SACRED HEART (1895), Very Rev. Patsy Iaquinta, V.F.
Res.: 1003 Wyoming St., P.O. Box 608, 24701-0608. Tel: 304-327-5623; Fax: 304-327-7769.

BRIDGEPORT, HARRISON CO., ALL SAINTS (1946), Rev. Harry N. Cramer.
Res.: 317 E. Main St., 26330-1750. Tel: 304-842-2283; Fax: 304-842-2283.
School—Harrison Co. Catholic School System, Tel: 304-624-5129.
Catechesis/Religious Program—Students 288.

BUCKHANNON, UPSHUR CO., HOLY ROSARY (1921), Rev. James B. McCafferty, S.M.
Church: 35 Franklin St., P.O. Box 848, 26201-0848. Tel: 304-472-3414; Fax: 304-472-6502.
Rectory:—9 Lincoln Heights, 26021.
Catechesis/Religious Program—Students 56.
Mission—Sacred Heart (1902), [CEM] Pickens, Randolph Co. 26230.

CAMDEN, LEWIS CO., ST. BONIFACE (Leading Creek) (1875), [CEM] Rev. John H. Finnell.
Res.: 9140 U.S. Hwy. 33 W., 26338-8256. Tel: 304-269-1767.
Catechesis/Religious Program—Students 5.
Chapel—St. Clara, St. Clare [CEM]
Catechesis/Religious Program—Students 3.

CAMERON, MARSHALL CO., ST. MARTIN (1871), [CEM] Rev. Francois Gonda Babulu.
Church: 5 Fitzgerald Ave., 26033. Tel: 304-686-3847.

CHARLES TOWN, JEFFERSON CO., ST. JAMES (1889), [CEM], Includes St. Peter, Harper's Ferry. Revs. S. Brian Owens; George Pucciarell.
Res.: 311 S. George St., P.O. Box 370, 25414-0370. Tel: 304-725-5558; Fax: 304-725-1685.
Catechesis/Religious Program—Students 400.

CHEAT LAKE, MONONGALIA CO., ST. LUKE (1980), Rev. Giles Le Vasseur, O.S.B.
Res.: 19 Jo Glen Dr., Morgantown, 26508-4434. Tel: 304-594-2353; Fax: 304-594-2359.
School—St. Francis Central Catholic School, 375 Birch St., Morgantown, 26505. Tel: 304-598-0133; Fax: 304-598-2690.
Catechesis/Religious Program—Students 196.
Mission—Mary Help of Christians (1983), Bruceton Mills, Preston Co. 26525. Tel: 304-379-4220.

CHESTER, HANCOCK CO., SACRED HEART (1902), Rev. F. Rodger Hughes.
Res.: 424 Fourth St., Box 313, 26034-0313. Tel: 304-387-0198.

CLARKSBURG, HARRISON CO.

1—IMMACULATE CONCEPTION (1864), [CEM] Rev. Cesidio J. Federico.
Res.: 126 E. Pike St., 26301-2155. Tel: 304-622-8280.
Parish Office—Tel: 304-622-8243.
Catechesis/Religious Program—Tel: 304-622-8257. Students 155.

2—ST. JAMES (1924), Rev. Robert A. Perriello.
Res.: 2107 Pride Ave., 26301-1819. Tel: 304-622-1668; Fax: 304-622-4618.
School—Harrison County Catholic School System, Tel: 304-623-1026; 304-622-9831; Fax: 304-623-1026.
Catechesis/Religious Program—Tel: 304-624-5811. Students 62.

COALTON, RANDOLPH CO., ST. PATRICK CHURCH (1918), [CEM 4] Very Rev. William A. Anderson, V.F.; Rev. Thomas W. Dagle.
Res.: 200 Church St., P.O. Box 99, 26257-0099. Tel: 304-636-5754.
Catechesis/Religious Program—Students 12.

DUNBAR, KANAWHA CO., CHRIST THE KING (1942), Rev. Richard Chirichiello, O.S.B.
Mailing Address: P.O. Box 339, Nitro, 25143. Tel: 304-755-0791; Fax: 304-768-8547.
Church: 1504 Grosscup Ave., 25064-2925. Tel: 304-768-2527; Fax: 304-768-8547. Students 35.
Catechesis/Religious Program—Students 42.

ELKINS, RANDOLPH CO., ST. BRENDAN (1897), [CEM] Very Rev. William A. Anderson, V.F.; Rev. Thomas W. Dagle.
Res.: P.O. Box 2205, 26241-2205. Tel: 304-636-0467; 304-636-0546.
Catechesis/Religious Program—Students 133.

ELKVIEW, KANAWHA CO., OUR LADY OF THE HILLS (1977), Rev. Roy Schuster, O.F.M.Cap.
Res.: 4084 Indian Creek Rd., 25071-9366. Tel: 304-965-7670; Fax: 304-965-7670.
Catechesis/Religious Program—Students 40.
Mission—St. Anne 63 Elk River Rd. S., Clendenin, Kanawha Co. 25045-9710. Tel: 304-548-7147. Sisters Jacqueline Le Boeuf, S.S.A., Co-Dir.; Marguerite St. Amand, S.S.A., Co-Dir.

FAIRMONT, MARION CO.

1—ST. ANTHONY (1964), Rev. Gary P. Naegele; Sr. Gale Bednarek, O.S.F., Pastoral Assoc.
Res.: 1660 Mary Lou Retton Dr., 26554-2099. Tel: 304-363-1328.
School—Fairmont Catholic Grade School, Tel: 304-363-5313.
Catechesis/Religious Program—Students 23.

2—IMMACULATE CONCEPTION (1960), Rev. Casey B. Mahone; Sisters Stella Cronauer, C.S.J., Pastoral Assoc.; Judith Udechukwu, Pastoral Assoc.; Arinzechukwu Anyaso, Pastoral Assoc.
Church: 329 Maryland Ave., P.O. Box 1726-E, 26555-1726. Tel: 304-363-5796; Fax: 304-366-4937.
School—Fairmont Catholic Grade School, Tel: 304-363-5313.
Catechesis/Religious Program—Students 145.

3—ST. JOSEPH'S (1909), Merged, with St. Peter's, Fairmont to form The New St. Peter the Fisherman, Fairmont.

4—ST. PETER THE FISHERMAN (1873), [CEM 2], (Formerly St. Peter's, Fairmont.) Merged with St. Joseph, Fairmont; St. Anthony, Grant Town; Our Lady of the Assumption, Rivesville, and All Saints, Barrackville Rev. Leonard A. Smith.
Res.: 407 Jackson St., 26554-2941. Tel: 304-363-7434; Fax: 304-363-7516.
School—Fairmont Catholic Grade School, Tel: 304-363-5313.
Catechesis/Religious Program—Students 248.

FARMINGTON, MARION CO., ST. PETER'S (1921), Rev. Franklin A. Neville; Sisters Miriam Sitarz, O.S.F., Pastoral Assoc.; Grace Koszela, O.S.F., Pastoral Assoc.
Mailing Address: 204 Furbee Ave., Mannington, 26582-1399. Tel: 304-986-2321; Fax: 304-986-1419.
Catechesis/Religious Program—Tel: 304-986-1624. Students 20.

FOLLANSBEE, BROOKE CO., ST. ANTHONY (1906), (Italian), Rev. Anthony Cincinnati.
Res.: 1017 Jefferson St., 26037-1334. Tel: 304-527-2286; Fax: 304-527-2548.
Catechesis/Religious Program—Tel: 304-527-3966. Students 175.

FORT ASHBY, MINERAL CO., ANNUNCIATION OF OUR LORD (1981), Rev. Paul D. Yuenger.
Res.: P.O. Box 553, 26719-0553. Tel: 304-298-3392; Fax: 304-298-3419.
Catechesis/Religious Program—Students 64.

FRANKLIN, PENDLETON CO., ST. ELIZABETH ANN SETON (1975), Revs. Mario R. Claro; Alex Jebadu; Bros. William Lavigne, F.M.S.; Philip Oullette, F.M.S.; Luke Reddington, F.M.S.
Church & Res.: P.O. Box 890, 26807. Tel: 304-358-7012.
Catechesis/Religious Program—Students 22.

GARY, MCDOWELL CO., OUR LADY OF VICTORY (1904), [CEM] Revs. Stanley Uroda, S.V.D.; Thomas Tran, S.V.D.; Sr. Mary Denise Thomas, I.H.M., Parochial Coord.
Church: Church St., P.O. Box 130, 24836-0130. Tel: 304-448-2749.
Res.: HC 76, P.O. Box 402, Powhatan, 24877-0167. Tel: 304-862-3494; Fax: 304-862-3999.

GASSAWAY, BRAXTON CO., ST. THOMAS (1973), Rev. Elmer Nadicksbernd, S.V.D.; Sr. Mary Kriley, C.D.P., Pastoral Assoc.
Res.: 624 Kanawha St., 26624-1208. Tel: 304-364-5895; Fax: 304-364-8099.
Catechesis/Religious Program—Students 40.

GLEN DALE, MARSHALL CO., ST. JUDE (1968), Rev. Thomas E. Schiffer.
Res.: 710 Jefferson Ave., P.O. Box 147, 26038-0147. Tel: 304-845-8165 (Rectory); 304-845-2646 (Office); Fax: 304-845-3015.
Catechesis/Religious Program—Students 77.

GLENVILLE, GILMER CO., GOOD SHEPHERD (1958), Rev. Edwin G. Daschbach, S.V.D.
Res.: 701 Mineral Rd., 26351-1310. Tel: 304-462-7130; Fax: 304-462-7130.
Catechesis/Religious Program—Tel: 304-462-7130. Students 24.

GRAFTON, TAYLOR CO., ST. AUGUSTINE (1852), (Irish), [CEM 2] Rev. Ronald G. Prechtl.
Res.: 17 W. Washington St., 26354-1398. Tel: 304-265-1848; 304-265-3861 (Office); Fax: 304-265-2810.
Catechesis/Religious Program—Students 60.

GRANT TOWN, MARION CO., ST. ANTHONY'S (1907), Merged, with St. Joseph, Fairmont; Our Lady of the Assumption, Rivesville and All Saints, Barrackville to form St. Peter the Fisherman, Fairmont.

HARPERS FERRY, JEFFERSON CO., ST. PETER (1830), Closed., Merged with St. James, Charles Town.

HARRISVILLE, RITCHIE CO., CHRIST OUR HOPE (1980), Rev. Thomas Karachira (India); Sr. Kathryn Holohan, O.S.F., Pastoral Assoc.
Res.: Rte. 1, Box 44A, 26362-9707. Tel: 304-643-4261.
Church: Pullman Rd. & E. Main, 26362-9707.
Catechesis/Religious Program—Students 20.
Chapel—Pennsboro, St. Joseph (1870), [CEM]

HINTON, SUMMERS CO., ST. PATRICK (1874), (Irish), [CEM] [JC 2] Rev. Vincent Elhanikatt Joseph (India).
Res.: 309 Second Ave., 25951-0008. Tel: 304-466-3966.
Mission—St. Mary of the Greenbrier David St., P.O. Box 441, Alderson, Greenbrier Co. 24910. Tel: 304-445-7967.
Catechesis/Religious Program—Students 30.

HOLDEN, LOGAN CO., ST. MARY'S (1961), Consolidated, with Our Lady of Mount Carmel, Logan, to form St. Francis of Assisi, Logan.

HUNTINGTON, CABELL CO.

1—ST. JOSEPH'S (1872), [CEM] Rev. Msgr. Lawrence J. Luciana; Rev. Julian Marneni.
Res.: 1304 Sixth Ave., P.O. Box 369, 25708. Tel: 304-525-5202; Fax: 304-525-0951.
School—520 Thirteenth St., 25701. Tel: 304-522-2644; Fax: 304-522-2512. Karen Elk, Prin. Lay Teachers 10; Students 131.

2—OUR LADY OF FATIMA (1952), Rev. Joseph L. Peterson; Deacon Lawrence E. French; Michael R. Prestera, Pastoral Assoc.
Res.: 545 Norway Ave., 25705. Tel: 304-525-0866; Fax: 304-525-0390.
School—535 Norway Ave., 25705. Tel: 304-523-2861; 304-523-2863. Mr. Kenneth C. Poritt, Prin. Lay Teachers 18; Students 174.
Catechesis/Religious Program—Students 71.

3—ST. PETER CLAVER (1937), (African American), Revs. Andrew G. Kranyc; Livinus Uba, Assoc. Pastor.
Res.: 828 Fifteenth St., 25701. Tel: 304-523-7311.
Catechesis/Religious Program—Students 16.

4—SACRED HEART (1934), Rev. Andrew G. Kranyc; Sr. Mary Terence Wall, S.A.C., Pastoral Assoc.
Res.: 2015 Adams Ave., 25704-1419. Tel: 304-429-5088 (Rectory); 304-429-4318 (Office); Fax: 304-429-4319.

HURRICANE, PUTNAM CO., CATHOLIC CHURCH OF THE ASCENSION (1980), Rev. Neil R. Buchlein.
Res.: 905 Hickory Mill Rd., 25526. Tel: 304-562-5816; Fax: 304-562-3589.
Catechesis/Religious Program—Students 215.

HUTTONSVILLE, RANDOLPH CO., ST. JOHN BOSCO (1948), Very Rev. William A. Anderson, V.F.; Rev. Thomas W. Dagle, Assoc. Pastor; Deacon Louis J. Belldina.
Res.: Rte. 1, Box 9D, 26273-9737. Tel: 304-335-2165; Fax: 304-335-2165.
Station—Huttonsville Correctional Center, Tel: 304-338-6323.

INWOOD, BERKELEY CO., ST. LEO (1982), Rev. D. Brian Shoda.
Res.: 2109 Sulphur Springs Rd., P.O. Box 93, 25428-0093. Tel: 304-229-8945; Fax: 304-229-9755.
Catechesis/Religious Program—Students 360.

KEYSER, MINERAL CO., ASSUMPTION (1874), [CEM] Rev. Ivan M. Lebar, T.O.R.; Bro. Luke D. Stone, T.O.R., Pastoral Assoc.
Res.: 34 James St., 26726-2721. Tel: 304-788-2488; Fax: 304-788-0647. Email: Ldstor@mindspring.com.
Catechesis/Religious Program—Students 70.

KINGWOOD, PRESTON CO., ST. SEBASTIAN'S (1914), [CEM 3] Revs. Mark Ward, C.P.; Vincent Segotta, C.P., Assoc. Pastor; Deacon Truman A. Lipscomb. In Res., Rev. John Michael Lee, C.P.
Res.: P.O. Box 519, 26537. Tel: 304-329-1519; Fax: 304-329-2546.
Church: 324 E. Main St..
Catechesis/Religious Program—Students 90.
Mission—St. Edward Terra Alta, Preston Co.

Logan, Logan Co., St. Francis of Assisi (1996), Rev. Dave Glockner, G.H.M.; Mrs. Connie Bazzilla, Pastoral Assoc.
Res.: 561 Main St., 25601-3899. Tel: 304-752-3017; Fax: 304-752-3017.
Church: Stratton St., 25601.
Catechesis/Religious Program—Students 20.

Lubeck, Wood Co., St. Monica's (1976), [CEM] Rev. John H. Fahey.
Res.: R.R. 1, Box 362, Washington, 26181-9615. Tel: 304-863-5580.
Church: State Rte. 68, Lubeck Washington.
Catechesis/Religious Program—Students 74.

Madison, Boone Co., St. Mary, Queen of Heaven (1957), Rev. James E. O'Connor.
Res.: P.O. Box 467, 25130-0467. Tel: 304-369-4538; Fax: 304-369-6268.
Church: 51 Madison Ave., 25130.
Catechesis/Religious Program—Students 16.
Mission—St. Joseph the Worker (1958), P.O. Box 444, Whitesville, Boone Co. 25209-0444. Tel: 304-854-2997; Fax: 304-854-1258. Sisters Marcan Freking, O.S.F.; Conall O'Connell, O.S.F.
Mission—St. Barbara (1979), *Crawley Creek*, HC 74, Box 3018, Chapmanville, Logan Co. 25508. Tel: 304-855-7962. Rev. Dave Glockner, G.H.M.

Man, Logan Co., St. Edmund (1961), Rev. Dave Glockner, G.H.M.
Mailing Address: 110 Bridge St., 25635.
Res.: 561 Main St., Logan, 25601-3899. Tel: 304-752-3017.
Church: 110 S. Bridge St., 25635. Tel: 304-583-2476; Fax: 304-239-3131.
Catechesis/Religious Program—Students 5.

Mannington, Marion Co., St. Patrick's (1897), (Irish), Rev. Franklin A. Neville; Sisters Miriam Sitarz, O.S.F., Pastoral Assoc.; Grace Koszela, Pastoral Assoc.
Res.: 204 Furbee Ave., 26582-1399. Tel: 304-986-2321; Fax: 304-986-1419.
Catechesis/Religious Program—Tel: 304-986-1624. Students 34.
Mission—Assumption of the Blessed Virgin Mary (1859), [CEM 2] Long Drain Rd., Littleton, Wetzel Co. 26581. (Suppressed Sept. 1, 2001)

Marlinton, Pocahontas Co., St. John Neumann (1977), [CEM] Rev. Nguyen That Son.
Res.: 714 10th Ave., 24954-1314. Tel: 304-799-6778; Fax: 304-799-6778.
Mission—St. Mark the Evangelist (1977), Rt. 92-250, Bartow, Pocahontas Co. 24920.
Catechesis/Religious Program—Students 23.

Martinsburg, Berkeley Co., St. Joseph's (1803), [CEM] Very Rev. John V. DiBacco Jr., V.F. In Res., Rev. Robert K. Judge, S.J. (BAL).
Res.: 219 S. Queen St., 25401-3213. Tel: 304-264-8947; Fax: 304-263-7357.
School—Tel: 304-267-6447; Fax: 304-267-6573. Daughters of Charity of Vincent de Paul 1; Lay Teachers 24; Students 368.
Catechesis/Religious Program—Students 135.
Mission—St. Bernadette 205 W. Main St., P.O. Box 11, Hedgesville, Berkeley Co. 25427. Tel: 304-754-7830; Fax: 304-754-7830.

Masontown, Preston Co., St. Zita's (1962), Revs. Mark Ward, C.P.; Vincent Segotta, C.P., Assoc. Pastor; Deacon Truman A. Lipscomb. In Res., Rev. John Michael Lee, C.P.
Res.: P.O. Box 519, Kingwood, 26537-0519. Tel: 304-329-1519; Fax: 304-329-2546.
Church: Tel: 304-864-5512.
Catechesis/Religious Program—Tel: 304-329-1063. Students 29.

Maysel, Clay Co., Risen Lord (1972), Rev. Elmer Nadicksbernd, S.V.D.; Sr. Ruth Nadicksbernd, C.D.P.
Mailing Address: HC 60, Box 7, 25133. Tel: 304-587-4740; Fax: 304-587-4886.
Res.: 624 Kanawha St., Gassaway, 26624. Tel: 304-364-5895.

McMechen, Marshall Co., St. James (1900), Rev. Joseph Hayden, S.J.
Mailing Address: 328 Logan St., 26040. Tel: 304-232-1227.
School—Sts. James and John Consolidated Schools, Tel: 304-232-1587. Mrs. Jennifer Marsh, Prin. Lay Teachers 7; Students 60.
Catechesis/Religious Program—Students 10.

Monongah, Marion Co., Holy Spirit (1975), (Polish—Italian), [CEM] Rev. Larry Wrenn.
Res.: 687 Maple Ter., 26554-1116. Tel: 304-534-3020; Fax: 304-534-5910.
Catechesis/Religious Program—Students 62.

Montgomery, Fayette Co., Immaculate Conception (1888), Rev. Paul J. Wharton.
Res.: P.O. Box 65, 25136. Tel: 304-442-2101.
Mission—St. Anthony Shrine (1928), P.O. Box 428, Boomer, Fayette Co. 25031. Tel: 304-779-2561.
Catechesis/Religious Program—Tel: 304-442-5224. Students 50.

Moorefield, Hardy Co., Epiphany of the Lord (1980), [CEM] [JC] Revs. Mario R. Claro; Alex Jebadu; Bro. Philip Ouellette.
Church: 2029 State Rd. 55, 26836. Tel: 304-434-2547.
Catechesis/Religious Program—Tel: 304-257-1057; Fax: 304-257-9442. 16

Morgantown, Monongalia Co.
1—St. John University Parish, Newman Hall (1966), Revs. Donald X. Higgs; Paul Hudock; Deacon Joseph Prentiss.
Res.: 1481 University Ave., 26505-5598. Tel: 304-296-8231; Fax: 304-296-4650.
School—St. Francis Central Catholic School, 375 Birch St., 26505. Tel: 304-598-0133; Fax: 304-598-2690.
Catechesis/Religious Program—Students 166.

2—St. Francis De Sales Catholic Church, Formerly The New St. Theresa & St. Elizabeth Ann Seton (2003),, (Formerly St. Theresa's Morgantown. Merged with St. Elizabeth Ann Seton, Westover to form The New St. Theresa & St. Elizabeth Ann Seton, Morgantown.) ; (Formerly The New St. Theresa & St. Elizabeth Ann Seton) Rev. Colombo F. Bandiera (Retired); Sr. Nancy White, S.S.J., Pastoral Assoc.
Res.: One Guthrie Ln., 26508. Tel: 304-296-5353; Fax: 304-296-8200.
School—St. Francis Central Catholic School, 375 Birch St., 26505. Tel: 304-598-0133.
Catechesis/Religious Program—Students 98.

Moundsville, Marshall Co., St. Francis Xavier's (1857), Revs. Ronan J. Deegan, T.O.R.; Albert Driesch, T.O.R.; Terrance Adams, T.O.R.
Res.: 912 Seventh St., 26041. Tel: 304-845-1593; Fax: 304-845-2006.
School—(Grades K-8) Tel: 304-845-2562 Fax: 304-845-0016. Mrs. Catherine Frame. Lay Teachers 13; Students 112; Preschool 22.
Catechesis/Religious Program—Students 58.
Station—Northern Regional Jail and Correctional Facility , NJ. Tel: 304-843-4067.

Mullens, Wyoming Co., St. John the Evangelist (1923), Rev. John C. Reich.
Res.: 13 Terry St., 25882-1624. Tel: 304-294-8128; Fax: 304-294-8128.
Catechesis/Religious Program—Students 9.
Mission—Holy Cross Rte. 10, P.O. Box 375, Pineville, Wyoming Co. 24874. Tel: 304-732-6199; 304-732-8302 (Rectory).

New Cumberland, Hancock Co., Immaculate Conception (1904), Rev. Ronald A. Getsinger.
Res.: 1016 Ridge Ave., P.O. Box 666, 26047-0666. Tel: 304-564-5068.
Catechesis/Religious Program—Students 28.

New Martinsville, Wetzel Co., St. Vincent de Paul (1901), Rev. J. Stephen Vallelonga.
Res.: 21 Rosary Rd., 26155-1602. Tel: 304-455-4615; Fax: 304-455-4617.
Catechesis/Religious Program—Students 130.

Nitro, Kanawha Co., Holy Trinity (1962), Rev. Richard Chirichiello, O.S.B.
Mailing Address: P.O. Box 339, 25143-0339. Tel: 304-755-0792; Fax: 304-755-3473.
Res.: 2219-22nd St., 25143-0339. Tel: 304-755-0791; Fax: 304-755-3473.
Catechesis/Religious Program—Students 84.
Mission—St. Patrick 207 Jefferson St., P.O. Box 238, Bancroft, Putnam Co. 25011. Tel: 304-586-3485; Fax: 304-586-3485.

Oak Hill, Fayette Co., SS. Peter and Paul (1906), [CEM] Rev. John P. McDonough.
Res.: 129 Elmore St., 25901-2628. Tel: 304-465-5445; Fax: 304-465-5445.
School—Tel: 304-465-5045; Fax: 304-465-8726. Mrs. Rebecca Aldridge, Prin. Lay Teachers 8; Students 100.
Catechesis/Religious Program—Students 97.

Ona, Cabell Co., St. Stephen (1980), Rev. Bert W. Valdes.
Res.: 2491 James River Tpke., 25545-9722. Tel: 304-743-3234.
Catechesis/Religious Program—Students 31.

Paden City, Tyler and Wetzel Cos., Mater Dolorosa (1921), Rev. Joseph Ezharath (India); Deacon N. Rollin Fagert.
Res.: 302 E. Main St., 26159-1736. Tel: 304-337-9837.
Catechesis/Religious Program—Students 31.
Mission—St. Lawrence P.O. Box 267, Middlebourne, Tyler Co. 26149. Tel: 304-758-4649.

Parkersburg, Wood Co.
1—St. Francis Xavier's (1853), [CEM 3] Rev. William K. Matheny Jr.; Deacons Douglas A. Deem; James R. Kelly.
Res.: 532 Market St., 26101-5144. Tel: 304-422-3142.
Catechesis/Religious Program—Tel: 304-422-6786; Fax: 304-422-6786. Students 85.

2—St. Margaret Mary (1923), Very Rev. Edward M. Bell, V.F.; Revs. John Rice; Benedict E. Kapa; Deacons George B. Showalter; John Maher.
Res.: 2500 Dudley Ave., 26101-2695. Tel: 304-428-1262; Fax: 304-422-4905.
Catechesis/Religious Program—Tel: 304-422-4905. Students 115.

Petersburg, Grant Co., St. Mary's (1971), [JC] Rev. Mario R. Claro; Bros. William Lavigne, F.M.S., Parochial Coord.; Philip Oullette, F.M.S., Parochial Coord.; Luke Reddington, F.M.S., Parochial Coord.
Rectory—5 Pierpont St., 26847-1633. Tel: 304-257-1057; Fax: 304-257-9442.
Church: 4 Grant St., 26847.
Catechesis/Religious Program—Students 23.

Philippi, Barbour Co., St. Elizabeth Parish and Newman Center (1953), Rev. Damian P. Drass, T.O.R.
College Hill: Rte. 3, Box 257, 26416-9581. Tel: 304-457-2641. Deacon A. Ray Shaw III.
Res.: Rte. 3, Box 38-I, 26416-9581. Tel: 304-457-1408.
Catechesis/Religious Program—Students 39.

Point Pleasant, Mason Co., Sacred Heart (1948), Rev. Regis Schlick, O.F.M.Cap.
Res.: 2222 Jackson Ave., 25550-2004. Tel: 304-675-4602.
Catechesis/Religious Program—Students 30.
Mission—St. Joseph (1856), [CEM] 3rd St. & Pomeroy St., Mason, Mason Co. 25260.

Powhatan, McDowell Co., Sacred Heart (1895), Revs. Stanley Uroda, S.V.D.; Thomas Tran, S.V.D.
Res.: HC 76, Box 402, 24877. Tel: 304-862-3494.
Catechesis/Religious Program—Students 6.

Princeton, Mercer Co., Sacred Heart (1915), Rev. Manuel Gelido (Philippines).
Res.: 507 Harrison St., 24740-3198. Tel: 304-425-3664; Fax: 304-425-3676.
Catechesis/Religious Program—Students 115.
Campus Ministry, Concord College—Athens, 24712. Tel: 304-384-9502.

Rainelle, Greenbrier Co., Sacred Heart (1951), Rev. Vincent Elhanikatt Joseph (India), Admin.
Res.: 309-2nd Ave., Hinton, 25951. Tel: 304-466-3966.
Chapel—Springdale, Sacred Heart [CEM], (1876)
Catechesis/Religious Program—Students 10.

Ravenswood, Jackson Co., St. Matthew (1957), Rev. John H. Fahey; Sr. Rosanne Fogarty, O.S.M., Parochial Coord.
Res.: 600 Crooks Ave., 26164-1312. Tel: 304-273-2175; Fax: 304-273-2175.

Richwood, Nicholas Co., Holy Family (1902), [CEM] Rev. Jerome D. Rawa, S.M.; Bro. Richard McKenna, S.M.
Res.: 4 Maple St., 26261-1318. Tel: 304-846-2873; Fax: 304-846-2873.
Catechesis/Religious Program—Students 16.

Ridgeley, Mineral Co., St. Anthony (1916), Rev. Paul D. Yuenger.
Res.: Box 553, Fort Ashby, 26719-0553. Tel: 304-298-3392; Fax: 304-298-3419.
Catechesis/Religious Program—Students 21.

Rivesville, Marion Co., Our Lady of the Assumption, Merged, with St. Joseph, Fairmont; St. Anthony, Grant Town; Our Lady of the Assumption, Rivesville, and All Saints, Barrackville to form St. Peter the Fisherman, Fairmont

Romney, Hampshire Co., Our Lady of Grace (1951), Rev. William J. Kuchinsky.
Res.: 299 School St., P.O. Box 871, 26757-0871. Tel: 304-822-5561; Fax: 304-822-5561.
Catechesis/Religious Program—Students 62.

Ronceverte, Greenbrier Co., St. Catherine of Siena (1892), Very Rev. Richard W. Shoda, V.F., J.C.L.
Res.: 407 Walnut St., 24970-1233. Tel: 304-647-4515; Fax: 304-647-4520.
Mission—St. Louis, King of France (1977), Lewisburg, Greenbrier Co.
Mission—St. Andrew the Apostle (1977), P.O. Box 347, Union, Monroe Co. 24983-0347. Tel: 304-772-5849. Sr. Molly Bauer, S.S.J., Pastoral Assoc.
Chapel—The Immaculate Conception of the Blessed Virgin Mary [CEM]
Chaplaincy—WV School of Osteopathic Medicine, Lewisburg.

St. Albans, Kanawha Co., St. Francis of Assisi (1947), [CEM] Rev. Patrick M. McDonough.
Res.: 1023 Sixth Ave., 25177. Tel: 304-727-3033; Fax: 304-727-6640.
School—Tel: 304-727-5690; Fax: 304-727-5690. Priests 1; Lay Teachers 7; Students 108.
Catechesis/Religious Program—Students 45.

St. Joseph Settlement, Marshall Co., St. Joseph's (1853), (German), [CEM] Rev. Francois Gonda Babulu.
Res.: R.D. 1, Box 203, Proctor, 26055. Tel: 304-455-4303; Fax: 304-455-4303.
Catechesis/Religious Program—Students 15.

St. Marys, Pleasants Co., St. John (1913), [JC] Rev. Thomas Karachira (India).
Mailing Address: P.O. Box 338, 26170-0338.
Res.: 310 Washington St., 26170-1313. Tel: 304-684-7669.
Catechesis/Religious Program—Students 23.

Salem, Harrison Co., Sacred Heart (1915), [CEM] Rev. Saju Puthenpurackal Joseph.
Res.: Rte. 23 S. off Rte. 50, RR5 Box 1424, 26426. Tel: 304-782-2277.

Catechesis/Religious Program—Students 8.
SHEPHERDSTOWN, JEFFERSON CO., ST. AGNES (1794), Rev. T. Matthew Rowgh.
Res.: 108 S. Duke, P.O. Box 1603, 25443-1603. Tel: 304-876-6436.
Catechesis/Religious Program—Students 87.
SHINNSTON, HARRISON CO., ST. ANN'S (1923), Rev. Karl R. Wohinc.
Res.: 610 Pike St., 26431-1451. Tel: 304-592-2733.
Mission—Holy Family (1925), Spelter, Harrison Co. 26438.
SISTERSVILLE, TYLER CO., HOLY ROSARY (1898), Rev. Joseph Ezharath (India); Deacon N. Rollin Fagert.
Church: 519 Main St., 26175-1405. Tel: 304-652-6381; 304-337-9837 (Rectory).
Catechesis/Religious Program—Students 22.
SOUTH CHARLESTON, KANAWHA CO., BLESSED SACRAMENT (1941), Very Rev. F. Leon Alexander, V.F.; Deacon John J. Hanna.
Res.: 305 E St., 25303-1597. Tel: 304-744-5523; Fax: 304-744-5669.
Catechesis/Religious Program—Students 131.
SPENCER, ROANE CO., HOLY REDEEMER (1957), Rev. David J. Schmitt.
Res.: 602 Parkersberg Rd., 25276-1024. Tel: 304-927-2013.
Catechesis/Religious Program—Students 47.
Mission—St. Elizabeth of Hungary (1977), Hwy. 14, P.O. Box 191, Elizabeth, Wirt Co. 26143. Tel: 304-275-4226; Fax: 304-275-4821. Sr. Nancy Fortkort, O.S.F., Pastoral Assoc.
Mission—Jesus Christ, Prince of Peace (1977), Hwy. 16, P.O. Box 416, Grantsville, Calhoun Co. 26147. Tel: 304-354-7937. Sisters Mary Keane, S.S.J., Pastoral Assoc.; Loretta Scully, S.S.J., Pastoral Assoc.
STAR CITY, MONONGALIA CO., ST. MARY'S (1953), [CEM] Rev. Dean G. Borgmeyer.
Res.: 3344 University Ave., P.O. Box 4204, 26504-4204. Tel: 304-599-3747; Fax: 304-599-3769.
School—St. Francis Central Catholic School, 375 Birch St., Morgantown, 26505. Tel: 304-598-0133; Fax: 304-598-2690.
Catechesis/Religious Program—Tel: 304-296-0061. Students 140.
STONEWOOD, HARRISON CO., OUR LADY OF PERPETUAL HELP (1955), Rev. John S. Ledford.
Res.: 707 3rd St., 26301-4854. Tel: 304-623-2334; Fax: 304-623-9988.
Catechesis/Religious Program—Students 40.
SUMMERSVILLE, NICHOLAS CO., ST. JOHN THE EVANGELIST (1849), [CEM] Rev. Xavier Cooney, S.V.D.
Res.: 1704 Webster Rd., 26651-1096. Tel: 304-872-2554; Fax: 304-872-0580.
Catechesis/Religious Program—Students 58.
THOMAS, TUCKER CO., ST. THOMAS AQUINAS (1897), [CEM] Rev. Lino P. Ebejer.
Res.: P.O. Box 300, 26292-0300. Tel: 304-463-4488; Fax: 304-463-4488.
Church: Brown St. & Third St., 26292.
Catechesis/Religious Program—Tel: 304-478-4575. Students 15.
Mission—Our Lady of Mercy (1960), 221 Water St., P.O. Box 97, Parsons, Tucker Co. 26287-0097. Tel: 304-478-4575. Sr. Electa Schmidt, I.H.M., Parochial Coord.
VIENNA, WOOD CO., ST. MICHAEL'S (1956), [JC] Rev. James J. Chetock.
Res.: 5501 Fourth Ave., 26105-2007. Tel: 304-295-6109.
Catechesis/Religious Program—Students 180.
WAR, MCDOWELL CO., CHRIST THE KING (1942), Revs. Stanley Uroda, S.V.D.; Thomas Tran, S.V.D.; Bro. Rogers Hannan, S.V.D.
Church: P.O. Box 728, 24892-0728. Tel: 304-875-3827.
WAYNE, WAYNE CO., NATIVITY OF OUR LORD (1980), Rev. Julian Marneni.
Church: Rte. 4, Box 2502, 25570-9738. Tel: 304-272-5832; 304-525-5202; Fax: 304-272-6176.
Catechesis/Religious Program—Students 12.
Station—Genoa Christian Center P.O. Box 67, Genoa, 25517. Tel: 304-385-4583; Fax: 304-385-4583. Sr. Monica Schieber, C.PP.S., Dir.
WEBSTER SPRINGS, WEBSTER CO., ST. ANNE'S (1920), Rev. David Cornett, S.V.D.
Res.: 160 McGraw, 26288-1134. Tel: 304-847-5512; Fax: 304-847-5512.
WEIRTON, BROOKE CO.
1—ST. PAUL'S (1910), [CEM] Rev. Msgr. Patrick L. Fryer; Rev. Anthony Thurston.
Res.: 140 Walnut St., 26062-4521. Tel: 304-748-6710 (Rectory); 304-748-4118.
School—Tel: 304-748-5225; Fax: 304-748-4163. Mr. Frank Carey, Prin. Lay Teachers 11; Students 210.
WEIRTON, HANCOCK CO.
1—ST. JOSEPH THE WORKER (1957), Very Rev. Stephen D. Dube, V.F.; Rev. Douglas B. Sutton.
Res.: 229 California Ave., 26062-3790. Tel: 304-723-2054; 304-723-2057; Fax: 304-723-3961.
School—Tel: 304-723-1970; Fax: 304-723-5122. Mr. Alfred Boniti, Prin. Lay Teachers 15; Students 268.
Catechesis/Religious Program—Students 139.
2—SACRED HEART OF MARY (1916), (Polish), Rev. D. Kent Durig; Deacon Richard W. Mankowski.
Office—200 Preston Ave., 26062-3994. Tel: 304-723-7175; 304-723-0707 (Rectory); Fax: 304-723-7176.
Catechesis/Religious Program—Students 27.
WELCH, MCDOWELL CO., ST. PETER (1923), Revs. Thomas Tran, S.V.D.; Stanley Uroda, S.V.D.
Res.: 111 Virginia Ave., 24801-2424. Tel: 304-436-2014; Fax: 304-436-2332.
Chapel—Kimball, Our Lady Queen of the Apostles, (1959)
Catechesis/Religious Program—Students 9.
WELLSBURG, BROOKE CO., ST. JOHN THE EVANGELIST (1857), [CEM] Rev. Walter M. Jagela, Acting Prin.
Res.: 1300 Charles St., 26070-1408. Tel: 304-737-0429.
School—Tel: 304-737-0511; Fax: 304-737-0511. Lay Teachers 10; Students 126.
Catechesis/Religious Program—Students 45.
Mission—Holy Family (1980),, (Formerly Power) , Beech Bottom. Box 7, Beech Bottom, Brooke Co. 26030-0007. Tel: 304-394-5929; Fax: 304-394-1256. Sr. Ellen Dunn, O.P., Parochial Coord.
WEST UNION, DODDRIDGE CO., ST. PATRICK'S (1856), Rev. Saju Puthenpurackal Joseph.
Res.: 503 W. Main St., 26456-1129.
Catechesis/Religious Program—Students 6.
WESTON, LEWIS CO., ST. PATRICK'S (1845), Rev. Jeremiah F. McSweeney.
Res.: 222 Center Ave., 26452-2029. Tel: 304-269-3048; Fax: 304-269-5547.
School—Tel: 304-269-5547. Sr. Eileen Marie Sinnott, S.S.J., Prin. Lay Teachers 7; Students 105.
Catechesis/Religious Program—Students 76.
Chapel—Loveberry, St. Bernard [CEM]
Chapel—Roanoke, St. Bridget [CEM]
Chaplaincy—Weston State Hospital. Tel: 304-269-3048.
WESTOVER, MONOGALIA CO., ST. ELIZABETH ANN SETON (1977), Merged, with St. Theresa, Morgantown, to form The New St. Theresa & St. Elizabeth Ann Seton, Morgantown.
WHITE SULPHUR SPRINGS, GREENBRIER CO., ST. CHARLES BORROMEO (1903), [CEM] [JC] Rev. Benedict E. Kapa; Deacon William B. Strange. Tel: 304-536-2333.
Res.: 325 W. Main, P.O. Box 609, 24986. Tel: 304-536-1813; Fax: 304-536-1813.
Catechesis/Religious Program—St. Louis Church, Lewisburg, 24901. Students 12.
Chapel—Sweet Springs, St. John The Evangelist [CEM 2] [JC 2]Tel: 304-647-4515; Fax: 304-647-4520. (1859)
WHITESVILLE, BOONE CO., ST. JOSEPH THE WORKER (1958), Closed., See St. Mary Queen of Heaven, Madison.
WILLIAMSON, MINGO CO., SACRED HEART (1911), Rev. Harold Dunn.
Res.: 110 W. Fourth Ave., 25661-3112. Tel: 304-235-2982; Fax: 304-235-3027.
School—126 W. Fourth Ave., 25661. Tel: 304-235-3027. Sisters 1; Lay Teachers 4; Students 32.
Catechesis/Religious Program—Students 50.

On Duty Outside the Diocese:
Rev.—
Cullinane, Jeremiah J., Neuhoff Catholic Center, Southern Methodist University, 3057 University Blvd., Dallas, TX 75205. Tel: 214-987-0044

Absent on Sick Leave:
Revs.—
Cupp, Edwin
Lee, Michael G.
McCormick, Michael

Absent on Leave:
Rev.—
Meuret, Donald

Retired:
Rev. Msgr.—
Staud, Sylvester W., Hickory Mill Apts., 31 Hickory Mill Dr., Hurricane, 25526.
Revs.—
Arnold, Andrew L., Welty Apartments #402, 1276 National Rd., 26003.
Bandiera, Colombo F., 442 Ash St., Morgantown, 26505-6668.
Bauer, Carl E., 106 Johnstone St., Hampton, SC 29924.
Beyer, Leroy O., 889 Wess Rd., Mineral Point, PA 15942.
Briggs, Everett F., Maple Terrace, P.O. Box 9066, Monongah, 26555-9066.
Brunner, Frank J., Welty Apartments #404, 1276 National Rd., 26003.
Campi, Vincent L., P.O. Box 856, Frederick, MD 21701.
Cann, Hilarion V., 174 Ridgeway Dr., Bridgeport, 26330.
Chalany, Robert, 17 Cedar Lake Rd., Chester, CT 06412.
Conlon, Anthony J., 8 Beech Park, Swinford Co., Mayo, Ireland.
Dene, Joseph, 6 Cool View Ln., Bridgeport, 26330.
Duhaime, John N., 327-13th Ave., P.O. Box 116, Rainelle, 25962.
Gillooly, Patrick J., 517 S. Green St., Berkeley Springs, 25411.
Jacobs, Eugene S., Box 54, Loretto, PA 15940.
Lombard, Roy A., Welty Apartments, #405, 1276 National Rd., 26003-5743.
Lukas, Andrew F., P.O. Box 201, Fairmont, 26555-0201.
Lydon, Leo B., 236 Parkway Dr., Clarksburg, 26301.
Maguire, Seamus J., Church of Our Lady of Perpetual Help, Harris Promenade, San Fernando, Trinidad and Tobago.
Mascioli, Joseph M., P.O. Box 11, Morgantown, 26505.
McCallister, Charles, P.O. Box 1309, Elkins, 26241.
McGinnity, John C., 604 Geddings Dr., Myrtle Beach, SC 29577-6029.
Murphy, James J., 32 Elm Rd., Donnycarney, Dublin 9, Ireland.
Nash, Robert C., P.O. Box 1093, Deltaville, VA 23043.
O'Donovan, Donal, Westwood, Chapel St., Dummanway, Co. Cork Ireland.
O'Loughlin, Eugene P., 362 Redford Ct., Greystone, Co. Wicklow Ireland.
O'Reilly, Joseph F., P.O. Box 22303, Hilton Head Island, SC 29926.
Ralph, John, 1757 State St., Biloxi, MS 39531.
Schneider, Charles J., Welty Apts. #403, 1276 National Rd., 26003.
Snincak, Stephen A., 2104 Hyde Park St., Sarasota, FL 33579.
Teufel, Charles B., Welty Apartments, 1276 National Rd., #401, 26003.
Weber, Eugene J., Welty Apartments, #408, 1276 National Rd., 26003.
Werner, Leo E., Welty Home, 21 Washington Ave., Rm. 113, 26003.
Wojtus, Anthony, P.O. Box 3803, 24338-3803.

Permanent Deacons:
Belldina, Louis J., St. John Bosco, Huttonsville
Bishof, Paul H., Jr., (Retired)
Deem, Douglas A., St. Francis Xavier, Parkersburg
Divita, John, Immaculate Conception, Montgomery
Doerr, George J., St. Luke, Cheat Lake & Good Counsel Friary, Morgantown
Fagert, Rollin N., Mater Dolorosa, Paden City & Holy Rosary, Sistersville
Goetemann, Gerald B., (Retired)
Grant, Russell J., St. William, Naples, FL
Hanna, John J., Blessed Sacrament, South Charleston
Higgs, Henry F., (On Leave of Absence)
Iafrate, Albert L., Catholic Charities Neighborhood Center, Wheeling
Kelly, James R., St. Francis Xavier, Parkersburg
Lilly, Robert B., St. Vincent De Paul, Berkeley Springs
Lipscomb, Truman A., St. Sebastian, Kingwood
Locke, John W., St. Vincent de Paul, Berkeley Springs
Lynch, John J., Sacred Heart, Charleston
Maher, John F., Christ Our Hope, Harrisville; St. John, St. Marys
Mankowski, Richard W., Sacred Heart of Mary, Weirton
Molinari, Donald F., (On Duty Outside the Diocese)
Moses, John T., St. Joseph Cathedral, Wheeling
Nedeff, George A., (On Leave of Absence)
Prentiss, Joseph J., St. John University, Morgantown
Santilli, Anthony P., St. James, Clarksburg
Shaw, A. Ray, III, St. Elizabeth, Phillipi
Showalter, George B., St. Margaret Mary, Parkersburg
Shultz, John A., (Retired)
Smith, Paul J., St. Michael, Wheeling
Strange, William B., St. Charles Borromeo, White Sulphur Springs
Wise, W. Donald, St. Francis De Sales, Beckley
Wojcicki, Ronald J., (Retired)
Wuletich, David E., St. Anthony, Charleston
Ziolkowski, John F., St. Francis De Sales, Beckley

INSTITUTIONS LOCATED IN THE DIOCESE

[A] COLLEGES AND UNIVERSITIES

WHEELING. *Wheeling Jesuit University*, 316 Washington Ave., 26003-6243. Tel: 304-243-2000; Fax: 304-243-4349. Email: jhacala@wju.edu. Web: www.wju.edu. Revs. Joseph R. Hacala, S.J., Pres., University; James J. Ditillo, S.J.; Terrence Toland, S.J., Rector, Jesuit Community; Brian P. O'Donnell, S.J.; Walter A. Buckius, S.J.; John J. Coll, S.J.; Joseph J. Hayden, S.J.; George R. Hohman, S.J.; Edward A. Jarvis, S.J.; Daniel R.J. Joyce, S.J.; John J. Karwin, S.J.; Joseph E. Kolb, S.J.; Vincent J. Lagomarsino, S.J.; James A. O'Brien, S.J.; Douglas F. Peduti, S.J.; Donald M. Serva, S.J.; Paul V. Stark, S.J.; Michael F. Steltenkamp, S.J. Jesuit Fathers Priests 18; Lay Teachers 78; Students 1,627.

[B] HIGH SCHOOLS, CENTRAL

WHEELING. *Central Catholic High School*, 75-14th St., 26003. Tel: 304-233-1660; Fax: 304-233-3187. Web: www.cchsknights.org. Dr. Joseph F. Viglietta, Ph.D., Prin. Sisters of St. Joseph 1; Lay Teachers 33; Students 485.

CHARLESTON. *Charleston Catholic High School*, 1033 Virginia St. E., 25301. Tel: 304-342-8415; Fax: 304-342-1259. Web: www.charlestoncatholic-crw.org. Mrs. Debra K. Sullivan, Prin. Lay Teachers 34; Students 469.

CLARKSBURG. *Harrison Co. Catholic School System. Notre Dame High School*, (Grades 7-12), 127 E. Pike St., 26301. Tel: 304-623-1026; Fax: 304-623-1026. Email: ndhs@iolinc.net. Dr. Carroll Kelly Morrison, Prin. Lay Teachers 16; Students 144.

HUNTINGTON. *St. Joseph Catholic High School*, 600 13th St., 25701. Tel: 304-525-5096; Fax: 304-525-0781. Email: jashworth@stjosephhs.org. Web: www.stjosephhs.org. Rev. Msgr. Lawrence Luciana, Pastor & Prin.; James Isaac, Admin. Lay Teachers 14; Students 121.

MCMECHEN. *Bishop Donahue Memorial High School*, 325 Logan St., 26040. Tel: 304-233-3850; Fax: 304-233-8677. Email: royrene@hotmail.com. Web: www.bishopdonahue.org. Bro. Rene D. Roy, F.M.S., Prin. (For Marshall Co.) Brothers 2; Sisters 1; Lay Teachers 8; Students 84.

PARKERSBURG. *Parkersburg Catholic Junior-Senior High School*, 3201 Fairview Ave., 26101. Tel: 304-485-6341; Fax: 304-485-4697. Email: pchs@pchs1.com. Web: pchs1.com. Lay Teachers 16; Students 189.

WEIRTON. *Madonna High School*, 150 Michael Way, 26062. Tel: 304-723-0545; Fax: 304-723-0564. Email: csistilli@weirtonmadonna.org. Web: www.weirtonmadonna.org. Cathy Sistilli, Prin. Lay Teachers 14; Students 132.

[C] HIGH SCHOOLS, PRIVATE

WHEELING. *Mount de Chantal Visitation Academy, Inc.*, 410 Washington Ave., 26003. Tel: 304-233-3771; Fax: 304-233-8598. Email: kvicker@access.k12.wv.us. Web: www.mountdechantal.org. Visitation Nuns, Day School. (Girls Grades PreK-12, Boys Grades PreK-6) / Resident School. (Girls Grades 9-12) Sisters 5; Lay Teachers 49; Students 208.

[D] ELEMENTARY SCHOOLS, CENTRAL

WHEELING. *Wheeling Catholic Elementary School* Consolidation of the following parishes: St. Alphonsus; St. Ladislaus; St. Mary; St. Joseph; Sacred Heart; Blessed Trinity; St. Joan of Arc & Blessed Martin De Porres. , 77-14th St., 26003. Tel: 304-233-1515; Fax: 304-233-1516. Email: jstechly@access.k12.wv.us. Web: wheelingcatholicschool.com. Lay Teachers 10; Students 122.

BENWOOD. *SS. James and John Elementary School*, (Grades PreK-8), 52 Seventh St., 26031. Tel: 304-232-1587; Fax: 304-232-4707. Email: saintjj@stratuswave.net. Mrs. Nannette Kennedy, Prin. Consolidation of the following parishes: St. John, Benwood; St. James, McMechen. Lay Teachers 8; Students 64.

CLARKSBURG. *Harrison County Catholic School System. St. Mary's Central Grade School*, (Grades PreK-6), 107 E. Pike St., 26301. Tel: 304-622-9831; Fax: 304-622-9831. Email: smgs@iolinc.net. Consolidation of the following parishes: All Saints, Bridgeport; Immaculate Conception, Clarksburg; St. James, Clarksburg; Our Lady of Perpetual Help, Stonewood; St. Ann, Shinnston; Sacred Heart, Salem. Lay Teachers 11; Students 130.

FAIRMONT. *Fairmont Catholic Grade School*, (Grades K-8) , Consolidation of the following parishes: St. Peter; Immaculate Conception; St. Anthony. , 416-A Madison St., 26554. Tel: 304-363-5313; Fax: 304-363-7701. Email: FCSSSchool@aol.com. Sr. Mary DiDomenico, S.S.J., Prin. Sisters 1; Lay Teachers 15; Students 221.

MORGANTOWN. *St. Francis de Sales Central Elementary School*, 375 Birch St., 26505. Tel: 304-598-0133; Fax: 304-598-2690. Email: pfoley@access.k12.wv.us. Web: www.falcon.sfcc.pvt.k12.wv.us. Sr. Patricia Ann Foley, C.S.J., Prin. Sisters 2; Lay Teachers 24; Students 385.

PARKERSBURG. *Parkersburg Catholic Elementary School*, 810 Juliana St., 26101. Tel: 304-422-6694; Fax: 304-422-2469. Email: pces@pchs1.com. Mr. Kevin Simonton, Prin. Lay Teachers 9; Students 188.

[E] PASTORAL CENTERS

WHEELING. *Paul VI Pastoral Center*, 667 Stone & Shannon Rd., 26003. Tel: 304-277-3300; Fax: 304-277-4320. Email: paulvi@hgo.net. Capacity 72.

CHARLESTON. *John XXIII Pastoral Center*, 100 Hodges Rd., 25314. Tel: 304-342-0507; Fax: 304-342-4786. Email: jchnxxiii@charter.net. Deacon John J. Lynch, Dir. Capacity 166.

HUTTONSVILLE. *Bishop Hodges Pastoral Center*, Rte. 1, Box 9D, 26273. Tel: 304-335-2165; Fax: 304-335-2165. Email: bhpc@sunlitsurf.com. Web: www.neumedia.net~bhpc. Deacon Louis J. Belldina, Dir. Capacity 72.

KEARNEYSVILLE. *Priest Field Pastoral Center*, 4030 Middleway Pike, 25430. Tel: 304-725-1435; Fax: 304-725-1437. Email: priestfieldpc@aol.com. Rev. William P. Linhares, T.O.R., Dir. Capacity 110.

[F] ASSOCIATED SPIRITUAL AND PASTORAL LIFE CENTERS

WHEELING. *St. Joseph Center-Mount St. Joseph*, 137 Mount St. Joseph Rd., 26003-1799. Tel: 304-232-8160; Fax: 304-232-1404. Email: ssjwhgsjc@aol.com. Web: www.ssjwhg.org. Sr. Mary Clark, S.S.J., Dir. Overnight Capacity & Daytime Capacity 25.

Maryhill Hermitage, 2264 Marshall Ave., 26003.

St. Thomas More Center, P.O. Box 230, 26003. Tel: 304-233-0880; Fax: 304-233-0890. Email: jelerick@dwc.org. Accommodations for youth retreats, cursillo and area retreats.

MORGANTOWN. *Our Lady of Good Counsel Franciscan Friary*, 493 Tyrone Rd., 26508-2960. Tel: 304-594-1714; Fax: 304-594-9247. Rev. Jude J. Mili, O.F.M., S.T.D., Dir. In Res. Rev. John Agapito, C.P.M.; Deacon George J. Doerr.

OLD FIELDS. *Holy Spirit Hermitage*, H.C. 66, Box 20, 26845-9201. In Res. Rev. Richard B. Hite, M.S.A.; Sr. Joan Sutherland, Diocesan Hermit.

[G] GENERAL HOSPITALS

WHEELING. *Bishop Joseph H. Hodges Continuous Care Center*, 600 Medical Park, P.O. Box 6316, 26003. Tel: 304-243-3800; Fax: 304-243-3898. Email: gcouch@whellinghosp.com. Web: www.wheelinghospital.com. George G. Couch, Admin. Skilled and Intermediate Care. Bed Capacity 120; Total Annually Assisted 385; Total Staff 152.

Wheeling Hospital, Medical Park, 26003. Tel: 304-243-3000; Fax: 304-243-3060. Web: www.wheelinghospital.com. Donald H. Hofreuter, M.D., Admin.; Sr. Mary Ann Rosenbaum, S.S.J., Dir. of Pastoral Care Dept.; Rev. Michael McKay, O.S.B. Chap.; Sisters Maireao Scanlon, S.S.J., Chap.; Mona Farthing, S.S.J., Chap. Sisters of St. Joseph 3; Patients Assisted Annually 290,250; Total Staff 2,031; Bed Capacity 276.

BUCKHANNON. *St. Joseph's Hospital of Buckhannon, Inc.*, 1 Amalia Dr., 26201. Tel: 304-473-2000; Fax: 304-472-6620. Web: www.stj.net. Mr. Wayne B. Griffith, Admin. Attended by Marist Fathers Sisters of the Pallottine Missionary Society 4; Bed Capacity 95; Patients Assisted Annually 68,631; Home Health Care & Hospice Patients 7,760; Total Staff 300.

St. Joseph's Foundation of Buckhannon, Inc., 1 Amalia Dr., 26201.

HUNTINGTON. *St. Mary's Hospital of Huntington, Inc.*, 2900 First Ave., 25702. Tel: 304-526-1234; Fax: 304-526-1538. Web: www.st-marys.org. Michael G. Sellards, Exec. Dir. Pallottine Missionary Sisters 13; Bed Capacity 440; Patients Assisted Annually 139,953.

School of Nursing Tel: 304-526-1415; Fax: 304-526-1517. Student Nurses 121; Total Staff 1,951.

[H] NURSING HOMES

WHEELING. *Good Shepherd Nursing Home*, 159 Edgington Ln., 26003. Tel: 304-242-1093; Fax: 304-242-1121. Mr. Donald R. Kirsch, Admin.; Rev. John Weiglein, S.M., Chap. Sisters 2; Bed Capacity 192; Total Staff 220.

[I] HOMES FOR AGED

WHEELING. *Welty Home for the Aged, Inc.*, 21 Washington Ave., 26003-6261. Tel: 304-242-5233; Fax: 304-242-1312. Residents 52.

Welty Trust, Inc., P.O. Box 230, 26003. Trustees: Most Rev. Bernard W. Schmitt, D.D., Pres.; Very Rev. John R. Gallagher, V.G., V.G., Vice Pres. & Sec.; Richard G. Herndon Esq., Treas.

Welty Retirement Apartments, 1276 National Rd., 26003. Tel: 304-242-5820.

[J] HEALTH SERVICES

HUNTINGTON. *Pallottine Health Services, Inc.*, 2900 First Ave., 25702. Tel: 304-526-8915; Fax: 304-526-8918. Email: sister.celeste@st-marys.org. Web: www.st-marys.org. Sponsored by the Pallottine Missionary Sisters.
Parent Corp. for:

St. Mary's Hospital of Huntington, Inc., 2900 First Ave., 25702. Tel: 304-526-1270; Fax: 304-526-1538.

St. Joseph's Hospital of Buckhannon, Inc., 1 Amalia Dr., Buckhannon, 26201. Tel: 304-473-2111; Fax: 304-472-6620. Bed Capacity 535; Total Annually Assisted 217,691; Total Staff 2,311.

PINEVILLE. *Children's Health Care, Inc.*, Pineville Children's Clinic, Box 430, 24874. Tel: 304-732-7069; Fax: 304-732-7098. Email: ecatters@marshall.edu. Sr. Eileen Catterson, D.W.M.D., Dir. Total Annually Assisted 6,040; Total Staff 13.

RHODELL. *Rhodell Health Clinic*, P.O. Box 158, 25915. Tel: 304-683-4318.
Legal Title: *Appalachian Health Cooperative, Inc.*

[K] SOCIAL SERVICE INSTITUTIONS

WHEELING. *Catholic Charities Neighborhood Center*, 125-18th St., P.O. Box 6176, 26003-0713. Tel: 304-232-7157; Fax: 304-232-4323. Email: doddc2@stratuswave.net. Sr. Constance Dodd, S.M., Dir.

Sisters of St. Joseph House of Hospitality, Inc., 110-15th St., 26003. Tel: 304-232-3129; Fax: 304-232-1404. Email: ssjwhg@aol.com. Web: www.ssjwhg.org.

Society of St. Vincent de Paul, Society of St. Vincent de Paul Store, 348 National Rd., P.O. Box 6115, 26003. Tel: 304-232-4230; Fax: 304-232-4230. Email: flubic50@hotmail.com.

HUTTONSVILLE. *Camp Tygart*, Rte. 1, Box 9D, 26273. Tel: 304-335-2130 (In Season); 304-233-0880 (Out of Season); Fax: 304-233-9293. Email: mhall@dwc.org. Mr. Michael Hall, Admin. Diocesan Children's Camp.

KERMIT. *A.B.L.E. Families, Inc.*, P.O. Box 1249, 25674. Tel: 304-393-4987; Fax: 304-393-4987. Email: jpeterworth@ablefamilies.org. Web: www.ablefamlies.org.

SALEM. *Nazareth Farm*, Rte. 2, Box 194-3, 26426. Tel: 304-782-2742; Fax: 304-782-4358. Email: nazarethfarm@citynet.net. Web: www.nazarethfarm.org.

[L] HOMES FOR DEPENDENT CHILDREN

WHEELING. *St. John's Home for Children*, 141 Key Ave., 26003-7412. Tel: 304-242-5633; Fax: 304-243-4911. Email: stjohns@stratuswave.net. Terence A. McCormick, Exec. Dir. Children 8; Total Assisted 20.

[M] MONASTERIES AND RESIDENCES OF PRIESTS AND BROTHERS

WHEELING. *Capuchin Hermitage of St. Joseph*, Formerly Webb Farm Residence *St. Joseph of Leonissa Capuchin Heritage*, 665 Stone & Shannon Rd., 26003. Tel: 304-277-2971; Fax: 304-277-2972. Email: caphermitage@att.net. Revs. Michael Greb, O.F.M.Cap. (PIT); Gregory Chervenak, O.F.M.Cap.; Bro. James Allman, O.F.M.Cap.

CHARLESTON. *Capuchins-St. Anthony Friary*, 1000 Sixth St., 25302. Tel: 304-342-2716. Email: tonycap@citynet.net. Web: home.att.net/~stanthony/capuchinfranciscan.html. Revs. Dismas Young, O.F.M.Cap., Guardian; Kieran Quinn, O.F.M.Cap., Chap.; Albert Alexandrunas, O.F.M.Cap., Vicar; Regis Schlick, O.F.M.Cap.

HINTON. *Monastery of Christ on the Mountain*, P.O. Box 429, 25951-0429. Tel: 304-466-4782; Fax: 304-466-1176. Email: Regisocd@citynet.Net. Rev. Bonaventure Lussier, O.C.D.; Bro. Gilbert Tovares, O.C.D. Discalced Carmelite Hermits

[N] CONVENTS AND RESIDENCES FOR SISTERS

WHEELING. *Mt. St. Joseph*, 137 Mount St. Joseph Rd., 26003-1799. Tel: 304-232-8160; Fax: 304-232-1404. Email: SSJWHG@aol.com. Web: www.ssjwhg.org. Sr. Marguerite O'Brien, S.S.J., Pres. Motherhouse of the Sisters of St. Joseph Professed Sisters 90. Attended by Wheeling Jesuit University.

North America Union Sisters of Our Lady of Charity, Inc., 141 Edgington Ln., 26003. Tel: 304-242-7070; Fax: 304-242-8221. Sisters Carol

Pregno, Local Supr.; Deana Kohlman, Business Mgr.
Legal Title: *North American Union Sisters of Our Lady of Charity, Inc.*

Sisters of the Visitation, Mount de Chantal, 410 Washington Ave., 26003. Tel: 304-232-1283; Fax: 304-233-8598. Email: sisters@mountdechantal.org. Web: www.mountdechantal.org; www.visitationsisters.org. Sr. Catherine Marie Paumier, V.H.M., Supr.
Legal Title: *Sisters of the Visitation of Holy Mary of Mount de Chantal, Inc.*, Attended by Wheeling Jesuit University. Professed Sisters 14.

[O] FOUNDATIONS

WHEELING. *Central Catholic High School Educational Foundation, Inc.*, 75-14th St., 26003. Tel: 304-233-1660; Fax: 304-233-3187.

Common Fund for Schools, P.O. Box 230, 26003. Tel: 304-233-0880, Ext. 317; Fax: 304-233-8551. Email: epajak@dwc.org. Web: dwc.org.

John S. Thoner Family Charitable Trust, 1300 Byron St., P.O. Box 230, 26003. Tel: 304-233-0880; Fax: 304-233-0890. Email: jgallagher@dwc.org. Very Rev. John R. Gallagher, V.G., V.G., Chancellor & Trustee.

Medical Park Foundation, One Medical Park, 26003. Tel: 304-243-4438; Fax: 304-234-2169. Email: lgood@wheelinghospital.com.

The Sisters of St. Joseph Health & Wellness Foundation, 137 Mount St. Joseph Rd., 26003-1799. Tel: 304-233-4500; Fax: 304-232-1404. Email: ssjhwf@aol.com helenssj@aol.com. Web: www.ssjhealthandwellnessfoundation.org. Sisters Judith Minear, S.S.J., Co-Exec. Dir.; Helen Skormisley, S.S.J., Co-Exec. Dir.

Sisters of St. Joseph of Wheeling Foundation, Inc., 137 Mount St. Joseph Rd., 26003-1799. Tel: 304-232-8160; Fax: 304-232-1404. Email: SSJWHG@aol.com. Web: www.ssjwhg.org.

West Virginia Catholic Foundation, P.O. Box 230, 26003. Tel: 304-233-0880; Fax: 304-233-0890. Email: bminor@dwc.org. Web: wvcf.dwc.org. Mr. Bryan E. Minor, Exec. Dir.

CLARKSBURG. *Harrison County Catholic Education Foundation, Inc.*, 126 E. Pike St., 26301-2720.

PARKERSBURG. *Parkersburg Catholic Schools Foundation, Inc.*, 3201 Fairview Ave., 26104-2111. Tel: 304-428-7528; Fax: 304-428-8159. Email: pcsf@netassoc.net. Web: pchs1.com.

Sisters of St. Joseph Charitable Fund, Inc., 4420 Rosemar Rd., Ste. 204, P.O. Box 4440, 26104-4440. Tel: 304-424-6080; Fax: 304-424-6081. Email: ssjcf@wirefire.com. Web: www.ssjcharitablefund.org. Sr. Jane Harrington, S.S.J., Exec. Dir.

[P] NEWMAN CENTERS

ATHENS. *Concord College Newman Center* 301 Vermillion, P.O. Box 447, 24712. Tel: 304-384-9502. Email: sacheapar@citlink.net. Rev. Manuel T. Gelido.

BETHANY. *St. John Fisher Catholic Chapel* 201 Richardson St., Box W, 26032. Tel: 304-829-4622. Very Rev. Kevin M. Quirk, J.C.D.

BUCKHANNON. *West Virginia Wesleyan College Newman Center* 35 Franklin St., Box 848, 26201-0848. Tel: 304-472-3414. Email: hrchurch@msys.net. Rev. James B. McCafferty, S.M.

FAIRMONT. *Fairmont State College Newman Center* 1200 College Park, 26554. Tel: 304-363-2300. Email: fatherjz@juno.com. Rev. Jude Molnar, T.O.R.

HUNTINGTON. *Marshall Newman Center* 1609 Fifth Ave., 25703. Tel: 304-525-4618. Email: catholic-center@marshall.edu. Web: www.marshall.edu/catholic-center.

PHILIPPI. *Alderson-Broaddus College Newman Center* College Hill, Rte. 3, Box 257, 26416. Tel: 304-457-2641. Rev. Damian P. Drass, T.O.R.

WEST LIBERTY. *West Liberty State College, St. Thomas Aquinas Campus Ministry* 134 Chatham St., 26074. Tel: 304-336-7751; 304-829-4622 (Bethany). Box W, Bethany, 26032. Very Rev. Kevin M. Quirk, J.C.D.

[Q] CHILD CARE CENTERS

WHEELING. *Holy Family Child Care Center, Inc.*, 161 Edgington Ln., 26003. Tel: 304-242-5222; Fax: 304-242-5379. Email: drp6713@aol.com. Debra Ponsetti, Exec. Dir. Total Assisted 107; Total Staff 28.

CLARKSBURG. *Madonna Day Care Center* 444 E. Pike St., 26031. Tel: 304-622-4453. Total Staff 6.

[R] MISCELLANEOUS

WHEELING. *St. Joseph Health Initiative, Inc.*, 137 Mount St. Joseph Rd., 26003-1799. Tel: 304-232-8160; Fax: 304-232-1404. Email: SSJWHG@aol.com. Sr. Marguerite O'Brien, S.S.J., Pres.

Retirement Trust Agreement of the Infirm Priests' Association of the Diocese of Wheeling-Charleston, 1300 Bryon St., 26003. Tel: 304-233-0880; Fax: 304-233-0890. Email: jgallagher@dwc.org. Very Rev. John R. Gallagher, V.G., V.G., Trustee.

Sisters of St. Joseph Health System, Inc, 137 Mount St. Joseph Rd., 26003-1799. Tel: 304-232-8160; Fax: 304-232-1404. Email: SSJWHG@aol.com. Sr. Marguerite O'Brien, S.S.J., Pres.

CHARLESTON. *West Virginia Council of Catholic Women*, 1652 Fourth Ave. #101, 25312. Tel: 304-346-6255; Fax: 304-346-6255. Sr. Marian Madden, S.C., Diocesan Moderator; Jane A. Grishaber, Pres. Tel: 304-346-6255; Kelly Sadd, Treas. Tel: 304-344-0651.

RELIGIOUS INSTITUTES OF MEN REPRESENTED IN THE DIOCESE

For further details refer to the corresponding bracketed number in the Religious Institutes of Men or Women section.

[0200]—*Benedictine Monks*—O.S.B.
[0470]—*The Capuchin Friars*—O.F.M.Cap.
[1000]—*Congregation of the Passion*—C.P.
[0260]—*Discalced Carmelite Fathers*—O.C.D.
[0820]—*Fathers of Mercy*—C.P.M.
[0520]—*Franciscan Friars*—O.F.M.
[0570]—*Glenmary Home Missioners*—G.H.M.
[]—*Heralds of Good News Missionary Society* (Eluru, India)—H.G.N.
[0690]—*Jesuit Fathers and Brothers*—S.J.
[0770]—*Marist Brothers*—F.M.S.
[0780]—*Marist Fathers*—S.M.
[0590]—*Missionaries of the Holy Apostles*—M.S.A.
[0840]—*Missionary Servants of the Most Holy Trinity*—S.T.
[0420]—*Society of the Divine Word*—S.V.D.
[0560]—*Third Order Regular of St. Francis*—T.O.R.

RELIGIOUS INSTITUTES OF WOMEN REPRESENTED IN THE DIOCESE

[3110]—*Congregation of Our Lady of the Retreat in the Cenacle* (North American Prov.)—R.C.
[3710]—*Congregation of Sisters of St. Agnes*
[2100]—*Congregation of the Humility of Mary*—C.H.M.
[1730]—*Congregation of the Sisters of the Third Order of St. Francis* (Oldenburg, IN)—O.S.F.
[0760]—*Daughters of Charity of St. Vincent De Paul* (Emmitsburg Prov.)—D.C.
[0960]—*Daughters of Wisdom*—D.W.
[1105]—*Dominican Sisters of Hope* (Ossining, NY)—O.P.
[1070-02]—*Dominican Sisters of St. Mary of the Springs* (Columbus, OH)—O.P.
[1430]—*Franciscan Sisters of Our Lady of Perpetual Help*—O.S.F.
[2430]—*Marist Sisters*—S.M.
[2490]—*Medical Mission Sisters*—M.M.S.
[3070]—*North American Union Sisters of Our Lady of Charity*—N.A.U.-O.L
[3150]—*Pallottine Missionary Sisters*—S.A.C.
[2970]—*School Sisters of Notre Dame*—S.S.N.D.
[1680]—*School Sisters of St. Francis*—O.S.F.
[3590]—*Servants of Mary (Servite Sisters)*—O.S.M.
[0570]—*Sisters of Charity of Seton Hill, Greensburg, PA*—S.C.
[0990]—*Sisters of Divine Providence (Marie de la Roche Prov.)*—C.D.P.
[2360]—*Sisters of Loretto at the Foot of the Cross*—S.L.
[2575]—*Sisters of Mercy of the Americas*—R.S.M.
[3720]—*Sisters of St. Anne*—S.S.A.
[1630]—*Sisters of St. Francis of Penance and Christian Charity*—O.S.F.
[1650]—*Sisters of St. Francis of Philadelphia*—O.S.F.
[1530]—*Sisters of St. Francis of the Congregation of Our Lady of Lourdes*—O.S.F.
[3830-13]—*Sisters of St. Joseph of Pittsburgh*—C.S.J.
[3830-05]—*Sisters of St. Joseph of Rockville Centre*—C.S.J.
[3830-17]—*Sisters of St. Joseph of Wheeling*—S.S.J.
[2110]—*Sisters of the Humility of Mary*—H.M.
[3270]—*Sisters of the Most Precious Blood, O'Fallon, MO*—C.PP.S.
[3220]—*Sisters of the Poor Child Jesus*—P.C.J.
[1760]—*Sisters of the Third Order of St. Francis of Penance and Charity*—O.S.F.
[1720]—*Sisters of the Third Order Regular of St. Francis of the Congregation of Our Lady of Lourdes*—O.S.F.
[2160]—*Sisters, Servants of the Immaculate Heart of Mary* (Scranton)—I.H.M.
[4120-03]—*Ursuline Nuns of the Congregation of Paris*—O.S.U.
[4190]—*Visitation Nuns* (Wheeling, WV)—V.H.M.

DIOCESAN CEMETERIES

WHEELING. *Mount Calvary* (1872), 1685 National Rd., 26003-5599. Tel: 304-242-0460. Very Rev. John R. Gallagher, V.G., V.G

NECROLOGY

† Dobosz, Emil J., (Retired)—Died July 31, 2003
† O'Reilly, Michael P., Romney, WV Our Lady of Grace—Died April 17, 2003
† Schmitt, Eugene A., (Retired)—Died Feb. 20, 2003

Diocese of Wichita

(Dioecesis Wichitensis)

Most Reverend

EUGENE J. GERBER, D.D.

Bishop Emeritus of Wichita; ordained May 19, 1959; appointed Bishop of Dodge City October 16, 1976;ordained December 14, 1976; installed December 15, 1976; appointed Bishop of Wichita November 23, 1982; installed February 9, 1983; retired October 4, 2001. *Res.: 505 Sandtrap, Wichita, KS 67235.*

ESTABLISHED AUGUST 2, 1887.

Square Miles 20,021.

New boundaries established by Apostolic Letters dated May 19, 1951. Bounded on the west by the west lines of Rice, Reno, Kingman and Harper counties, south by Oklahoma, east by Missouri, and north by the north lines of Bourbon, Allen, Woodson, Greenwood, Morris, Marion, McPherson and Rice Counties in Kansas.

For legal titles of parishes and diocesan institutions, consult the Chancery Office.

(VACANT SEE)

The Chancery: 424 N. Broadway, Wichita, KS 67202. Tel: 316-269-3900; Fax: 316-269-3936.

STATISTICAL OVERVIEW

Personnel	
Bishop.	1
Retired Bishops.	1
Priests: Diocesan Active in Diocese.	79
Priests: Diocesan Active Outside Diocese	6
Priests: Retired, Sick or Absent.	44
Number of Diocesan Priests.	129
Religious Priests in Diocese.	4
Total Priests in Diocese.	133
Ordinations:	
Diocesan Priests.	3
Transitional Deacons.	3
Permanent Deacons in Diocese.	1
Total Sisters.	314
Parishes	
Parishes.	91
With Resident Pastor:	
Resident Diocesan Priests.	66
Resident Religious Priests.	1
Without Resident Pastor:	
Administered by Priests.	24
Professional Ministry Personnel:	
Brothers.	1
Sisters.	12
Lay Ministers.	35
Welfare	
Catholic Hospitals.	7
Total Assisted.	670,624
Health Care Centers.	2
Total Assisted.	40,406
Homes for the Aged.	2
Total Assisted.	442
Day Care Centers.	1
Total Assisted.	175
Specialized Homes.	1
Total Assisted.	45
Special Centers for Social Services.	1
Total Assisted.	25,484
Other Institutions.	1
Total Assisted.	3,645
Educational	
Diocesan Students in Other Seminaries	31
Total Seminarians.	31
Colleges and Universities.	1
Total Students.	1,929
High Schools, Diocesan and Parish.	4
Total Students.	2,335
Elementary Schools, Diocesan and Parish	33
Total Students.	7,974
Catechesis/Religious Education:	
High School Students.	3,215
Elementary Students.	8,007
Total Students under Catholic Instruction	23,491
Teachers in the Diocese:	
Priests.	2
Sisters.	18
Lay Teachers.	619
Vital Statistics	
Receptions into the Church:	
Infant Baptism Totals.	2,240
Adult Baptism Totals.	302
Received into Full Communion.	419
First Communions.	2,515
Confirmations.	2,309
Marriages:	
Catholic.	457
Interfaith.	339
Total Marriages.	796
Deaths.	973
Total Catholic Population.	116,913
Total Population.	959,389

Former Bishops—Most Revs. JAMES O'REILLY, D.D., Bishop-Elect; died July 26, 1887; JOHN JOSEPH HENNESSY, D.D., consecrated Nov. 30, 1888; died July 13, 1920; AUGUSTUS JOHN SCHWERTNER, D.D., ord. June 12, 1897; consecrated June 8, 1921; installed June 22, 1921; died Oct. 2, 1939; CHRISTIAN HERMAN WINKELMANN, S.T.D., ord. June 11, 1907; consecrated Auxiliary Bishop of St. Louis, Nov. 30, 1933; installed March 5, 1940; died Nov. 18, 1946; MARK K. CARROLL, S.T.D., ord. June 10, 1922; appt. Feb. 15, 1947; consecrated April 23, 1947; installed May 6, 1947; resigned Sept. 27, 1967; died Jan. 12, 1985; LEO C. BYRNE, D.D., ord. June 10, 1933; appt. Titular Bishop of Sabidia and Auxiliary of St. Louis, May 21, 1954; consecrated June 29, 1954; transferred to Wichita, "cum jure successionis" 1961; appt. Apostolic Administrator, Feb. 25, 1963; transferred to St. Paul and Minneapolis, Sept. 27, 1967; died Oct. 21, 1974; DAVID M. MALONEY, S.S., S.T.L., J.C.D., former Bishop of Wichita; ord. Dec. 8, 1936; appt. Titular Bishop of Ruspae Auxiliary of Denver, Nov. 9, 1960; consecrated Jan. 4, 1961; transferred to Wichita, Dec. 6, 1967; resigned July 16, 1982; died Feb. 15, 1995; EUGENE J. GERBER, D.D., Bishop of Wichita; ord. May 19, 1959; appt. Bishop of Dodge City Oct. 16, 1976; ord. Dec. 14, 1976; installed Dec. 15, 1976; appt. Bishop of Wichita Nov. 23, 1982; installed Feb. 9, 1983; resigned Oct. 4, 2001.

Chancery Office—424 N. Broadway, Wichita, 67202. Tel: 316-269-3900; Fax: 316-269-3902.

Vicars General—Rev. Msgr. ROBERT E. HEMBERGER, J.C.L.; Rev. DWIGHT J. BIRKET, 424 N. Broadway, Wichita, 67202.

Moderator of the Diocesan Curia—Rev. Msgr. ROBERT E. HEMBERGER, J.C.L., 424 N. Broadway, Wichita, 67202.

Vicar for Priests—Rev. Msgr. JOHN P. GILSENAN, V.G., J.C.L.

Director of Diocesan Planning—Rev. Msgr. ROBERT E. HEMBERGER, J.C.L.

Chancellor—Rev. Msgr. ROBERT E. HEMBERGER, J.C.L.

Vice Chancellor—Sr. JACINTA LANGLOIS, A.S.C.

Presbyteral Council/Diocesan Consultors—Most Revs. EUGENE J. GERBER, D.D.; THOMAS J. OLMSTED, D.D; Rev. Msgrs. JOHN P. GILSENAN, V.G., J.C.L.; ROBERT E. HEMBERGER, J.C.L., Chm.; WILLIAM M. CARR; Revs. JOHN V. HOTZE; DWIGHT J. BIRKET; MICHAEL MAYBRIER; ANDREW EUYKENDALL; H. PATRICK MALONE; SHAWN MCKNIGHT; WAYNE SCHMID; JOHN P. SHERLOCK; THOMAS A. WELK, C.PP.S.

Parish Priest Consultors—Rev. Msgrs. CHARLES F. WALSH; JOHN P. GILSENAN, V.G., J.C.L.; CHARLES W. REGAN.

Tribunal—424 N. Broadway, Wichita 67202. Tel: 316-269-3960.

Judicial Vicar—Rev. JOHN V. HOTZE.

Adjutant Judicial Vicar—Rev. MICHAEL E. NOLAN.

Promoter of Justice—Rev. Msgr. JOHN P. GILSENAN, V.G., J.C.L.

Judges—Revs. STEPHEN R. BAXTER, J.C.L.; DOUGLAS CAMPBELL, J.C.L.; ROBERT E. HEMBERGER, J.C.L.; JOHN V. HOTZE; MICHAEL E. NOLAN; STUART M. SMELTZER.

Defenders of the Bond—Rev. Msgr. JOHN P. GILSENAN, V.G., J.C.L.; Revs. J. PATRICK MANNION (Retired); STUART M. SMELTZER.

Procurator-Advocates—Sr. JACINTA LANGLOIS, A.S.C.

Notaries—Mrs. ROBERTA RAU; Mrs. CLAUDINE WALD.

Deans—Revs. WAYNE SCHMID, North Wichita; DWIGHT J. BIRKET, South Wichita; Rev. Msgr. JOHN P. GILSENAN, V.G., J.C.L., East Wichita; Revs. JAMES BILLINGER, West Wichita; IVAN C. ECK, Hutchinson; PAUL J. OBORNY, Newton; JEROME BEAT, St. Patrick, North Wichita; THOMAS J. STROOT, Pittsburg; THOMAS F. SCALETTY, Chanute.

Ongoing Formation of the Clergy Committee—Revs. PAUL S. COAKLEY; KENT HEMBERGER; Rev. Msgr. ROBERT E. HEMBERGER, J.C.L., Prog. Consultant; Revs. DAVID J. LIES; JEROME L. SPEXARTH; WAYNE L. SCHMID; DANIEL L. VACCA; KENNETH S. VAN HAVERBEKE, Prog. Dir.

Diocesan Offices and Directors

Catholic Diocese of Wichita—Most Revs. THOMAS J. OLMSTED, D.D., Pres.; EUGENE J. GERBER, D.D., Vice Pres.

Apostleship of Prayer—6900 E. 45th St., N., Wichita, 67226.

Catholic Charities—Ms. JANET PAPE, Dir., 437 N. Topeka, Wichita, 67202. Tel: 316-264-8344.

Catholic Life Center—424 N. Broadway, Wichita, 67202. Tel: 316-269-3900.

Cemeteries—Mr. JEROME GERBER, 424 N. Broadway, Wichita, 67202. Tel: 316-269-3900.

Commission for Communications—VACANT, 424 N. Broadway, Wichita, 67202. Tel: 316-269-3900; Fax: 316-269-3902.

Cursillo—Rev. JEROME A. BEAT, 2007 Arkansas, Wichita, 67203. Tel: 316-262-4683.

Diocesan Synod Office—Rev. JOHN P. SHERLOCK, Gen. Sec.; Ms. RHONDA LOHKAMP, Assoc. Gen. Sec., 424 N. Broadway, Wichita, 67202. Tel: 316-269-3900; Fax: 316-269-3902.

Wichita Diocesan Charismatic Services—Revs. JAMES WELDON, Moderator, St. Thomas Aquinas, 1321 Stratford Lane, Wichita, 67206; JAMES S. MAINZER, Assoc. Moderator, St. James Church, 813 State St., Augusta, 67010. Tel: 316-775-2155.

Diocesan Apostolate to Engaged Encounter—Rev. DAVID J. LIES, 124 N. Roosevelt, Wichita, 67208. Tel: 316-682-4557.

Catholic Marriage Preparation-Evenings for Engaged—Rev. H. PATRICK MALONE, 1425 N. Chautauqua, Wichita, 67214. Tel: 316-682-8712.

Diocesan Apostolate to Marriage Encounter—Rev. DANIEL J. SPEKARTH, St. Thomas Aquinas Church, 1321 Stratford Lane, Wichita, 67206. Tel: 316-683-6569.

Diocesan Building Commission—Rev. JAMES J. BILLINGER; Mr. WILMER FREUND; Rev. KENT A. HEMBERGER; Rev. Msgr. ROBERT E. HEMBERGER, J.C.L., Exec. Sec.; Mr. CHARLES G. BEAN; Ms. BRONWEN LEWIS; Mr. DANIEL L. LOUGHMAN; Rev. W. SHAWN MCKNIGHT, S.T.D.; Mrs. LINDA SNOOK; Mrs. THERESA WHITE.

Diocesan Director of Stewardship and Finance—Mr. DANIEL L. LOUGHMAN, 424 N. Broadway, Wichita, 67202. Tel: 316-269-3900.

Diocesan Finance Committee—Most Rev. THOMAS J. OLMSTED, D.D.; Mr. MICHAEL AYLWARD; Rev. DWIGHT J. BIRKET; Rev. Msgr. ROBERT E. HEMBERGER, J.C.L.; Mr. RICHARD KERSCHEN; Ms. JOYE HANEBERG; Mr. DANIEL L. LOUGHMAN; Mr. ALBERT LIEBERT; Mr. FRANK REMAR; Mr. DALE WIGGINS.

Diocesan Liaison for Health Affairs—Rev. Msgr. ROBERT E. HEMBERGER, J.C.L., 424 N. Broadway, Wichita, 67202. Tel: 316-269-3962.

Diocesan Office for Ministry with Persons with Disabilities—Mr. GEORGE GERBER, Dir., 424 N. Broadway, Wichita, 67202. Tel: 316-269-3900.

Education—Mr. ROBORT VOBORIL, Supt., 424 N. Broadway, Wichita, 67202. Tel: 316-269-3950.

Office of Religious Education—Ms. RHONDA LOHKAMP, Dir., 424 N. Broadway, Wichita, 67202. Tel: 316-269-3940.

Latin America Mission and Volunteer Services—Sr. URSULA FOTOVICH, C.S.J., Dir., 424 N. Broadway, Wichita, 67202. Tel: 316-269-3946.

Legion of Mary—Rev. JOHN C. REINKEMEYER, 638 Ave. D. W., Kingman, 67068. Tel: 316-532-5440.

Marriage and Family Life Services—Ms. SARA SPLICHAL, Dir.

Natural Family Planning Office—Ms. JUDITH LEONARD, Dir., 1515 S. Clifton, Ste. 400, Wichita, 67218. Tel: 316-685-6776; Fax: 316-685-7540.

Newspaper: "The Catholic Advance" Diocesan Weekly—Mr. CHRISTOPHER M. RIGGS, Editor; Mr. DANIEL L. LOUGHMAN, Business Mgr., 424 N. Broadway, Wichita, 67202. Tel: 316-269-3965.

Office of Development and Planned Giving—Ms. BRONWEN LEWIS, 424 N. Broadway, Wichita, 67202.

Office of Pastoral Life and Ministry—424 N. Broadway, Wichita, 67202. Tel: 316-269-3947.

Office of Worship—Revs. W. SHAWN MCKNIGHT, S.T.D., Dir.; JASON BORKENHAGEN, Assoc. Dir., 424 N. Broadway, Wichita, 67202. Tel: 316-269-3945.

Presbyteral Council—Most Revs. THOMAS J. OLMSTED, D.D., Bishop; EUGENE J. GERBER, D.D., Bishop Emeritus; Rev. Msgrs. JOHN P. GILSENAN, V.G., J.C.L.; ROBERT E. HEMBERGER, J.C.L., Chm.; WILLIAM M. CARR; Revs. DWIGHT J. BIRKET; JOHN V. HOTZE; ANDREW KUYKENDALL; MICHAEL MAYBRIER; H. PATRICK MALONE; SHAWN MCKNIGHT; WAYNE SCHMID; JOHN P. SHERLOCK; THOMAS WELK, C.PP.S.

Propagation of the Faith and Holy Childhood Assn.—Sr. URSULA FOTOVICH, C.S.J., Dir., 424 N. Broadway, Wichita, 67202. Tel: 316-269-3946.

Respect Life and Social Justice Office—Rev. JOHN B. BRUNGARDT, Dir.; Mr. JOHN MCCORMICK, Assoc. Dir., 424 N. Broadway, Wichita, 67202. Tel: 316-269-3935.

Retreats—Rev. PAUL S. COAKLEY, Dir., Spiritual Life Center, 7100 E. 45th St. N., Wichita, 67226. Tel: 316-744-0167.

Rural Life Ministry—Rev. BERNARD GORGES, St. Patrick Church, 638 Avenue D, W., Kingman, 67068. Tel: 316-532-5440.

Social Service—Ms. JANET PAPE, 437 N. Topeka, Wichita, 67202. Tel: 316-264-8344.

Technology Coordinator—Mr. RICK GALLAGHER, 424 N. Broadway, Wichita, 67202. Tel: 316-269-3900.

Victim Assistance Coordinator—KATHERINE J. LAMBERTZ. Tel: 316-264-8344, Ext. 230. Email: klambertz@wkscatholiccharities.org.

Vocations—Rev. MATTHEW C. MCGINNESS, Dir., 424 N. Broadway, Wichita, 67202. Tel: 316-269-3900.

Wichita Diocesan Hispanic Council—Rev. JOSE MACHADO, Dir., 424 N. Broadway, Wichita, 67202. Tel: 316-269-3900.

Youth and Young Adult Ministry—Ms. CHRISTINE EDMONDS, Dir., 424 N. Broadway, Wichita, 67202. Tel: 316-269-3930.

CLERGY, PARISHES, MISSIONS AND PAROCHIAL SCHOOLS

CITY OF WICHITA
(SEDGWICK COUNTY)

1—CATHEDRAL OF THE IMMACULATE CONCEPTION (1887), Revs. John P. Sherlock, Rector; Juan P. Garza.
Res.: 307 E. Central Ave., 67202. Tel: 316-263-6574; Fax: 316-269-2909.
Catechesis/Religious Program—Students 265.

2—ALL SAINTS (1946), [JC 3] Rev. Dwight J. Birket.
Res.: 3205 E. Grand St., 67218. Tel: 316-682-1415; Fax: 316-682-1096.
School—Tel: 316-682-6021; Fax: 316-682-8734. Ann Kathleen Patterson, Prin. Lay Teachers 13; Students 225.
Catechesis/Religious Program—Sandra Nettleton, D.R.E. Students 135.

3—ST. ANNE (1955), Rev. Kent A. Hemberger; Mary Beth Steiner, Pastoral Assoc.
Office—2801 S. Seneca, 67217-2399. Tel: 316-522-2383; Fax: 316-524-2370.
School—(Grades K-8) Tel: 316-522-6131. Sr. Margaret Nugent, C.S.J. Sisters 2; Lay Teachers 14; Students 200.
Catechesis/Religious Program—Students 102.

4—ST. ANTHONY (1887), (German), Rev. Hung Q. Pham.
Res. & Mailing Address: 325 Ohio, 67214. Tel: 316-269-4641.
Catechesis/Religious Program—Students 10.

5—BLESSED SACRAMENT (1927), [JC] Rev. Msgr. John P. Gilsenan, V.G., J.C.L.; Rev. John F. Jirak.
Rectory—Rectory: 401 S. Roosevelt Ave., 67218. Tel: 316-681-2204; 316-682-4557 (Office); Fax: 316-682-4558.
Church Office: 124 N. Roosevelt, 67218.
School—Tel: 316-684-3752; Fax: 316-687-1082. Jim Grogan, Prin. Sisters of St. Joseph 1; Lay Teachers 30; Students 413.
Catechesis/Religious Program—Cindy Honton, D.R.E. Students 42.
Convent—132 N. Quentin, 67208. Tel: 316-684-3977.

6—CHRIST THE KING (1950), [JC] Rev. Michael Schemm.
Res.: 4411 Maple Ave., 67209. Tel: 316-943-4353; Fax: 316-943-8196.
School—4501 Maple Ave., 67209. Tel: 316-943-7361. Richard Sleefe, Prin. Sisters, Adorers of the Blood of Christ 1; Lay Teachers 13; Students 248.
Catechesis/Religious Program—Students 40.

7—CHURCH OF THE MAGDALEN (1950), Revs. Kenneth S. VanHaverbeke; Michael A. Klag; Sr. Connie Beiriger, C.S.J., Pastoral Assoc.
Res.: 12626 E. 21st St. N., 67206. Tel: 316-634-2315; Fax: 316-634-3948.
School—Tel: 316-634-1572; Fax: 316-634-6957. Candida Spacil, Prin. Lay Teachers 22; Students 497.
Catechesis/Religious Program—Students 140.

8—CHURCH OF THE RESURRECTION (1965), Rev. Kenneth J. Schuckman.
Res.: 4910 N. Woodlawn, 67220. Tel: 316-744-2776; Fax: 316-744-3027.
School—(Grades PreK-8) Tel: 316-744-3576; Fax: 316-744-1582. Thomas Heiman, Prin. Lay Teachers 14; Students 250.
Catechesis/Religious Program—Susie Asbridge, D.R.E.; Julie Kaiser, D.R.E.; Joanne Haiman, D.R.E. Students 98.

9—ST. ELIZABETH ANN SETON (1982), Revs. James J. Billinger; Jeffrey A. Fasching; Nicholas A. Voelker.
Res.: 645 N. 119th St. W., 67235. Tel: 316-721-1686; Fax: 316-721-1723.
School—Tel: 316-721-5693. Mr. David Charles, Prin.; Mrs. Kitty Garcia, Asst. Vice Prin. Lay Teachers 36; Students 749.
Catechesis/Religious Program—Students 427.

10—ST. FRANCIS OF ASSISI (1959), Revs. Daryl Befort; Brian Nelson; Robert J. Hartmann.
Res.: 861 N. Socora, 67212. Tel: 316-722-4404; Fax: 316-722-4738.
School—Tel: 316-722-5171; Fax: 316-722-0492. Ms. Candace Buser, Prin.; Larry Geist, Vice Prin. Adorers of the Blood of Christ 3; Lay Teachers 40; Students 762.
Catechesis/Religious Program—Tel: 316-729-1350. Students 487.

11—HOLY SAVIOR (1948), (African American), Rev. H. Patrick Malone.
Res.: 1425 N. Chautauqua, 67214. Tel: 316-682-8712; Fax: 316-682-4797.
School—Tel: 316-684-2141; Fax: 316-684-4318. Mr. Paul Spacil, Prin.; Mrs. Delia Baenett, Prog. Admin. Lay Teachers 8; Students 106.
Catechesis/Religious Program—Students 26.

12—ST. JOSEPH (1886), [JC] Revs. Ivan Dawson, C.SS.R.; John Willett, C.SS.R.; Walter C. Karrer, C.SS.R.; Bro. Marvin Hamann, C.SS.R.
Res.: 145 S. Millwood Ave., 67213. Tel: 316-261-5800; Fax: 316-261-5806.
School—Tel: 316-261-5801; Fax: 316-261-5804. Dan McAdam, Prin. Sisters 1; Lay Teachers 11; Students 114.
Catechesis/Religious Program—Tel: 316-261-5811. Mrs. Betty Ewing, D.R.E. Students 36.
Convent—Sister Adorers (ASC), St. Joseph's, 128 S. Vine Ave., 67213. Tel: 316-261-5802; Fax: 316-261-5805.

13—ST. JUDE (1958), Rev. Douglas Campbell.
Res.: 3130 Amidon Ave., 67204. Tel: 316-838-1963; Fax: 316-838-8513.
School—Tel: 316-838-0800; Fax: 316-838-0866. Mr. Michael Skaggs, Prin. Lay Teachers 14; Students 251.
Catechesis/Religious Program—Dawn Day, D.R.E. Students 149.

14—ST. MARGARET MARY (1954), Rev. Richard Stuchlik, S.T.L.
Res.: 2701 Pattie, 67216. Tel: 316-262-1821; Fax: 316-262-4057.
School—(Grades PreK-8) Tel: 316-267-4911; Fax: 316-267-1707. Mary Samms, Prin. Lay Teachers 12; Students 171.
Catechesis/Religious Program—Tel: 316-262-5344. Anne Schock, D.R.E. Students 108.

15—OUR LADY OF GUADALUPE, Closed., For sacramental records contact St. Margaret Mary, Wichita.

16—OUR LADY OF PERPETUAL HELP (1927), [JC] Rev. Jose Machado.
Res.: 2351 N. Market St., 67219. Tel: 316-838-8373; Fax: 316-821-9250.
Catechesis/Religious Program—Students 323.
Convent—2354 N. Market St., 67219. Tel: 316-838-3190. Congregation of the Daughters of the Passion of Our Lord Jesus Christ and the Sorrows of Mary 3.
Parish Center—2409 N. Market St., 67219. Tel: 316-838-5750.

17—ST. PATRICK (1895), [JC] Rev. Eric M. Weldon.
Res.: 2007 Arkansas Ave., 67203. Tel: 316-262-4683; Fax: 316-262-6217.
School—2023 Arkansas Ave., 67203. Tel: 316-262-4071. Sr. Eloise Hertel, O.P., Prin. Dominican Sisters 1; Lay Teachers 13; Students 217.
Catechesis/Religious Program—Linda F. Gosche, D.R.E., (English); Trini Gonzalez, D.R.E., (Spanish). Students 216.
Convent—2045 Arkansas Ave., 67203. Tel: 316-267-0021.

18—ST. PAUL PARISH (1970), Rev. Matthew C. McGinness.
Res.: 1810 N. Roosevelt, 67208. Tel: 316-684-6896; Fax: 316-684-2679.

19—ST. THOMAS AQUINAS (1957), Revs. Daniel J. Spexarth; Michael M. Simone; Mary Ewers, Business Mgr. In Res., Rev. James F. Weldon.
Res.: 1321 Stratford Ln., 67206. Tel: 316-683-6569; Fax: 316-683-6569.
School—Tel: 316-684-9201; Fax: 316-684-7421. Miss Mary Sweet, Prin.; Mrs. Vanessa Harshberger, Asst. Prin. Lay Teachers 42; Students 715.
Catechesis/Religious Program—Students 150.

20—ST. VINCENT DE PAUL (1955), Rev. Michael E. Baldwin.
Res.: 123 N. Andover Rd., Andover, 67002. Tel: 316-733-1423; Fax: 316-733-1687.
Catechesis/Religious Program—Gayle Beuke, D.R.E.; Teresa Marshall, D.R.E.; Karen Kroupa, D.R.E. Students 662.

OUTSIDE THE CITY OF WICHITA

ALEPPO, SEDGWICK CO., IMMACULATE CONCEPTION (1900), (German), [CEM] Revs. David W. Linnebur; John C. Reinkemeyer.
Church: 25741 W. 13th St. N., Garden Plain, 67050. Tel: 316-531-2662.
Catechesis/Religious Program—Students 64.

ANDALE, SEDGWICK CO., ST. JOSEPH (1890), (German), [CEM] Rev. Reinhard C. Eck.
Res.: 318 Rush Ave., Box 8, 67001. Tel: 316-444-2196.
Catechesis/Religious Program—Mary Jo Hieger, D.R.E. Students 330.

ANTHONY, HARPER CO., SACRED HEART (1934), Closed., For inquiries for parish records contact St. Joan of Arc, 1023 W. Main St., Box 218, Harper, KS 67058.

ARKANSAS CITY, COWLEY CO., SACRED HEART (1886), Rev. John Balthasar Brungardt.
Res.: 302 S. B. St., 67005. Tel: 620-442-0566; Fax: 620-441-0935.
School—308 S. B St.. Tel: 620-442-6550; Fax: 620-441-0935. Sr. Jacklyn Duncan, Prin. Sisters of St. Joseph 1; Dominican Sisters 1; Lay Teachers 4; Students 60.
Catechesis/Religious Program—Sr. Jacklyn Duncan, D.R.E. Students 101.

ARMA, CRAWFORD CO., ST. JOSEPH (1934), Rev. Donald R. Thissen.
Res.: 310 W. South St., P.O. Box 948, 66712. Tel:

620-347-4525.
Catechesis/Religious Program—Students 2.
AUGUSTA, BUTLER CO., ST. JAMES (1879), [CEM] Rev. Samuel J. Pinkerton.
Res.: 1012 Belmont Ave., 67010. Tel: 316-775-2155; Fax: 316-775-2131.
School—(Grades K-5) Tel: 316-775-5721. Richard Guy, Prin. Lay Teachers 10; Students 91.
Catechesis/Religious Program—Tel: 316-733-5247. Bonnie Toombs, D.R.E.; Lizzie Payne, D.R.E. Students 239.
BAXTER SPRINGS, CHEROKEE CO., ST. JOSEPH (1868), [JC] Rev. Chrysostom Ah Maung.
307 Galena, P.O. Box 296, Galena, 66739.
Res.: 115 W. Walnut, Columbus, 66725. Tel: 620-429-2639.
Catechesis/Religious Program—Students 27.
BURNS, MARION CO., IMMACULATE CONCEPTION, Closed., For sacramental records contact Holy Family, Marion.
BUSHTON, RICE CO., HOLY NAME OF JESUS (1878), (German), [CEM] Rev. Steven Scheier.
Res.: 296 3rd Rd., 67427. Tel: 316-562-3427.
Catechesis/Religious Program—Tel: 620-562-3662. Students 27.
CALDWELL, SUMNER CO., ST. MARTIN OF TOURS (1888), [JC] Rev. Josephat Lwin.
Res.: 428 N. Main, 67022. Tel: 620-845-6763; Fax: 620-845-6733.
Catechesis/Religious Program—Students 54.
CANEY, MONTGOMERY CO., SACRED HEART (1914), Rev. Sixtus ye Myint (Burma).
Res.: P.O. Box 276, Moline, 67353-0276. Tel: 620-647-3577.
Catechesis/Religious Program—Tel: 620-879-2355. Students 23.
CAPALDO, CRAWFORD CO., ST. ALICE, Closed., For sacramental records contact Sacred Heart, Frontenac.
CASTLETON, RENO CO., ST. AGNES (1872), Closed., For inquiries for sacramental records contact St. Teresa, Hutchinson.
CEDAR VALE, CHAUTAUQUA CO., ST. JOSEPH, Closed. For inquiries for parish records contact the chancery.
CHANUTE, NEOSHO CO., ST. PATRICK (1873), [CEM 2] Rev. Thomas F. Scaletty.
Res.: 424 S. Central, 66720. Tel: 620-431-3165; Fax: 620-431-6587.
School—(Grades PreK-5) Tel: 620-431-4020. Frank Kennedy, Prin. Sisters 1; Lay Teachers 6; Students 116.
Catechesis/Religious Program—Tel: 620-431-4287. Students 100.
CHASE, RICE CO., ST. MARY (1888), (German), Closed., For inquiries for sacramental records contact St. Paul, Lyons.
CHEROKEE, CRAWFORD CO., ST. ANASTASIA, Closed., For sacramental records contact Our Lady of Lourdes, Pittsburg.
CHERRYVALE, MONTGOMERY CO., ST. FRANCIS XAVIER'S (1871), (German), [CEM] Revs. Stephen M. Thapwa (Burma); Kevin Trayers (Retired).
Res.: 202 S. Liberty St., 67335. Tel: 620-336-2941.
Catechesis/Religious Program—Tel: 620-336-2310. Students 34.
CHETOPA, LABETTE CO., SACRED HEART (1873), [CEM] Rev. Larry Parker.
Res.: 1112 W. Third., Oswego, 67356. Tel: 620-795-2262.
Catechesis/Religious Program—Students 15.
CHICOPEE, CRAWFORD CO., ST. BARBARA, Closed., For sacramental records contact Our Lady of Lourdes, Pittsburg.
CLONMEL, SEDGWICK CO., ST. JOHN (1879), [CEM] Rev. Philip J. Allen.
Res.: 18630 W. 71st St., Viola, 67149. Tel: 316-545-7171; 316-794-2784; Fax: 316-794-2784.
Parish Hall—Tel: 316-545-7211.
Catechesis/Religious Program—Sylvia Kerschen, D.R.E.; Art Gentry, D.R.E. Students 106.
COFFEYVILLE, MONTGOMERY CO., HOLY NAME (1869), [CEM 2] Rev. Michael J. Maybrier.
Res.: 408 Willow St., 67337. Tel: 620-251-0475; Fax: 620-251-0475.
School—409 Willow St., 67337. Tel: 316-251-0480; Fax: 316-251-1651. Sr. Janice Roberts, Prin. Sisters of St. Joseph 2; Lay Teachers 9; Students 121.
Catechesis/Religious Program—Students 121.
COLUMBUS, CHEROKEE CO., ST. ROSE (1887), [JC] Rev. Chrysostom Ah Maung.
Res.: 115 W. Walnut St., 66725. Tel: 620-429-2639.
Catechesis/Religious Program—Tel: 620-429-2938. Students 26.
COLWICH, SEDGWICK CO., SACRED HEART (1901), [CEM] Rev. Brian D. Bebak.
Res.: 231 S. Fifth St., P.O. Box 578, 67030. Tel: 316-796-1224; Fax: 316-796-0735.
Catechesis/Religious Program—Students 335.
CONWAY SPRINGS, SUMNER CO., ST. JOSEPH (1886), (German), [CEM] Rev. Thomas M. Hoisington.
Res.: 217 N. Sixth St., Box 157, 67031. Tel: 316-456-2276; Fax: 316-456-3317.
School—Tel: 316-456-2270; Fax: 316-456-2272. Mr. Pat Carl, Prin. Lay Teachers 7; Students 163.
Catechesis/Religious Program—Fax: 316-456-3276. Renee Means, D.R.E. Students 216.
COUNCIL GROVE, MORRIS CO., ST. ROSE (1883), [CEM] [JC 2] Rev. Jeffery A. Fasching.
Res.: 316 Spencer St., 66846. Tel: 316-767-6412; Fax: 316-767-5370.
Catechesis/Religious Program—Cheryl Downs, D.R.E. Tel: 620-767-6638. Students 100.
CUNNINGHAM, KINGMAN CO., SACRED HEART (1908), (German), [CEM] Rev. John Miller.
Res.: P.O. Box 216, 67035. Tel: 316-298-2601; Fax: 316-298-2926.
Catechesis/Religious Program—Tel: 316-246-5241. Linda Kerschen, D.R.E. Students 45.
DANVILLE, HARPER CO., IMMACULATE CONCEPTION (1883), Closed., For inquiries for parish records contact St. Joan of Arc, 1023 W. Main St., Box 218, Harper, KS 67058.
DERBY, SEDGWICK CO., ST. MARY'S (1954), Rev. Wayne Schmid; Kathleen Parisio, Admin.; Sr. Marie Zoglman, A.S.C., Pastoral Assoc.
Parish Office:—P.O. Box 325, 722 N. Derby, 67037. Tel: 316-788-5525; Fax: 316-788-1577.
School—700 N. Derby, 67037. Tel: 316-788-3151; Fax: 316-788-6895. Mr. Richard Montgomery, Prin. Sisters of St. Joseph 1; Lay Teachers 20; Students 258.
Catechesis/Religious Program—Tel: 316-788-1253. Janet Clark, D.R.E. Students 160.
EL DORADO, BUTLER CO., ST. JOHN (1915), Rev. Michael E. Nolan.
Res.: 302 N. Denver Ave., 67042. Tel: 316-320-4796; Fax: 316-321-1709.
Catechesis/Religious Program—Tel: 316-321-4933. Bonnie Toombs, D.R.E. Students 170.
ERIE, NEOSHO CO., ST. AMBROSE (1915), Rev. Daniel L. Vacca.
Res.: 519 N. Main, P.O. Box 116, 66733. Tel: 620-244-3216.
Catechesis/Religious Program—Students 64.
EUREKA, GREENWOOD CO., SACRED HEART (1881), (German), [JC] Rev. Leo A. Kerschen.
Res.: 514 N. Elm St., 67045. Tel: 316-583-7100.
Catechesis/Religious Program—Students 69.
Mission—*St. John* Hamilton, Greenwood Co.
Mission—*St. Teresa Of Avila* Madison, Greenwood Co. Tel: 316-437-2504.
FLORENCE, MARION CO., ST. PATRICK, Closed., Merged with St. Mark, Marion; St. John Nepomucene, Pilsen; and Holy Redeemer, Tampa to form Holy Family, Marion.
FORT SCOTT, BOURBON CO., MARY QUEEN OF ANGELS (1860), [CEM] Rev. Darrin M. May.
Res.: 716 S. Eddy St., 66701-2534. Tel: 620-223-4340; Fax: 620-223-4340.
School—(Grades K-5) Tel: 620-223-6060; Fax: 620-223-6060. Gary Eckert, Prin. Lay Teachers 6; Students 47.
Catechesis/Religious Program—Tel: 620-223-4336. Dan Meara, D.R.E. Students 66.
FREDONIA, WILSON CO., SACRED HEART (1906), [CEM] Rev. Stephen R. Baxter, J.C.L.
Res.: 428 N. 12th St., 66736. Tel: 620-378-2694; Fax: 620-378-2694.
Catechesis/Religious Program—Tel: 620-378-3565. Judy Puckett, D.R.E. Students 77.
FRONTENAC, CRAWFORD CO., SACRED HEART (1891), (Italian), [CEM] Rev. Robert W. McElwee.
Res.: 100 S. Cherokee St., 66763.
Parish Hall—102 S. Cherokee St., 66763. Tel: 620-231-7747; Fax: 620-232-7006.
Catechesis/Religious Program—Students 105.
FULTON, BOURBON CO., ST. PATRICK, Closed., For sacramental records contact Mary Queen of Angels, Fort Scott.
GALENA, CHEROKEE CO., ST. PATRICK (1879), [JC] Rev. Chrysostom Ah Maung.
Res.: 115 W. Walnut, Columbus, 66725. Tel: 620-429-2639.
Church: 307 Galena, 66739.
Catechesis/Religious Program—Students 28.
GARDEN PLAIN, SEDGWICK CO., ST. ANTHONY (1901), (German), [CEM] Rev. David W. Linnebur.
Res.: 615 N. Main, 67050. Tel: 316-531-2252; Fax: 316-531-2694.
Catechesis/Religious Program—Tel: 316-535-2593. Students 320.
GIRARD, CRAWFORD CO., ST. MICHAEL (1925), (Irish—German), Rev. Donald R. Thissen.
Res.: 106 N. Western, 66743. Tel: 620-724-8717.
Catechesis/Religious Program—Jean Davied, D.R.E. Students 168.
GODDARD, SEDGWICK CO., HOLY SPIRIT (1998), Rev. H. Setter.
Res.: 18218 W. Hwy. 54, P.O. Box 787, 67052. Tel: 316-794-3496; Fax: 316-794-3795.
School—Tel: 316-794-8139; Fax: 316-794-2055. Miss Mickey Wasinger, Prin. Teachers 3; Students 33.
Catechesis/Religious Program—Students 102.
GREENBUSH, CRAWFORD CO., ST. ALOYSIUS, Closed., For sacramental records contact St. Michael, Girard.
HALSTEAD, HARVEY CO., SACRED HEART OF JESUS (1874), [JC] Rev. Thomas Than Wai (Burma).
Res.: 419 Poplar, 67056. Tel: 316-835-2173; Fax: 316-830-2889.
Catechesis/Religious Program—Box 307, Sedgwick, 67135. Tel: 316-772-5841. Gary Crow, D.R.E. Tel: 316-830-2703. Students 138.
HAMILTON, GREENWOOD CO., ST. JOHN (1888), (German), Rev. Leo A. Kerschen.
Res.: 514 N. Elm St., Eureka, 67045. Tel: 316-583-7100.
Catechesis/Religious Program—Students 2.
HARPER, HARPER CO.
1—ST. JOAN OF ARC (1997), (Irish—German), Rev. Michael Peltzer.
Res.: 1023 W. Main, P.O. Box 218, 67058. Tel: 620-896-7886; Fax: 620-896-2249.
Catechesis/Religious Program—Tel: 620-896-7119. Pam Gorges, D.R.E. Students 112.
Mission— (1883), 116 Ashman, Danville, Harper Co. 67036. Tel: 620-962-5466.
Mission— (1879), 121 S. Madison, Anthony, Harper Co. 67003. Tel: 620-842-5537.
2—ST. PATRICK (1882), Closed., For inquiries for parish records contact St. Joan of Arc, 1023 W. Main St., Box 218, Harper, KS 67058.
HAYSVILLE, SEDGWICK CO., ST. CECILIA (1959), Rev. Andy Kuykendall.
Res.: 1802 W. Grand, 67060. Tel: 316-524-7801; Fax: 316-524-6183.
School—(Grades K-6), 1912 W. Grand, 67060. Tel: 316-522-0461. Mary Carter, Prin. Lay Teachers 8; Students 120.
Catechesis/Religious Program—JoAnne Audley, D.R.E. Students 80.
HUMBOLDT, ALLEN CO., ST. JOSEPH (1867), [CEM] Rev. Thomas F. Scaletty.
Church: 514 Central St., 66748. Tel: 620-473-2129; Fax: 620-431-6587.
Res.: 424 S. Central Ave., Chanute, 66720. Tel: 620-431-3165.
Catechesis/Religious Program—Tel: 620-431-4287. Students 35.
HUTCHINSON, RENO CO.
1—HOLY CROSS (1957), [CEM 3] [JC] Rev. Joseph A. Eckberg.
Res.: 2631 Independence Rd., 67502. Tel: 620-665-5163; Fax: 620-662-5085.
School—2633 Independence Rd., 67502. Tel: 316-665-6168; Fax: 316-665-6168. Mrs. Amy Wagoner, Prin. Lay Teachers 18; Students 273.
Catechesis/Religious Program—Students 536.
2—OUR LADY OF GUADALUPE (1927), (Hispanic), Rev. Ned J. Blick.
Res.: 612 S. Maple, South Hutchinson, 67505-2099. Tel: 620-662-6443; Fax: 620-662-6443.
Catechesis/Religious Program—551 E. Ave. A, 67501. Tel: 620-669-1403. Mrs. Cathy Jones, D.R.E. Students 280.
3—ST. TERESA (1897), [CEM] Rev. Stuart M. Smeltzer.
Res.: 211 E. Fifth St., 67501. Tel: 620-662-7812; Fax: 620-662-7812.
School—215 E. Fifth St., 67501. Tel: 620-662-5601; Fax: 620-662-5601. Ms. Ellen Albert, Prin. Lay Teachers 9; Students 166.
Catechesis/Religious Program—Tel: 620-665-7102. Nora Reinecker, D.R.E. Students 95.
INDEPENDENCE, MONTGOMERY CO., ST. ANDREW (1869), (German—Mexican), [CEM 2] Rev. Stephen M. Thapwa (Burma).
Res.: 210 N. Fourth St., 67301. Tel: 620-331-1789; Fax: 620-331-6496.
School—Tel: 620-331-2870. Rebecca Brown, Admin. Lay Teachers 10; Students 154.
Catechesis/Religious Program—Tel: 620-331-8401. Students 80.
IOLA, ALLEN CO., ST. JOHN (1897), [CEM] [JC] Rev. Leon J. Kerschen.
Res.: 310 S. Jefferson Ave., 66749. Tel: 316-365-3454.
Catechesis/Religious Program—Tel: 316-365-8278. Mrs. Annette Rexwinkle, D.R.E. Students 182.
KINGMAN, KINGMAN CO., ST. PATRICK (1885), (Irish), [JC] Rev. Joseph C. Tatro.
Res.: 638 Ave. D W., 67068. Tel: 316-532-5440; Fax: 316-532-5549.
School—Tel: 316-532-2791; Fax: 316-532-2966. Mrs. Kristin Schmitz, Prin. Lay Teachers 12; Students 204.
Catechesis/Religious Program—Tel: 316-532-5440. Students 220.
LIBERTY, MONTGOMERY CO., ALL SAINTS, Closed. For inquiries for parish records contact the chancery.
LINDSBORG, MCPHERSON CO., ST. BRIDGET OF SWEDEN (1985), Rev. Paul J. Oborny.
Church: 206 W. Swensson, P.O. Box 268, 67456. Tel: 785-227-3588; Fax: 620-245-9677.

Res.: 520 E. Northview, McPherson, 67460. Tel: 620-241-0821; Fax: 620-241-8497.
Catechesis/Religious Program—Mary Patrick, D.R.E. Students 75.

LITTLE RIVER, RICE CO., HOLY TRINITY (1885), [JC] Rev. Thomas Leland.
Res.: 415 St. Francis St., Lyons, 67554. Tel: 620-257-3503; Fax: 620-257-3021.
Catechesis/Religious Program—Tel: 620-489-6436. Cynthia Wright, D.R.E. Tel: 620-257-2969. Students 46.

LYONS, RICE CO., ST. PAUL (1927), [JC] Revs. Thomas Leland; James N. Hoagland (Retired).
Res.: 415 St. Francis St., 67554. Tel: 620-257-3503; Fax: 620-257-3021.
Catechesis/Religious Program—Tel: 620-257-3183. Julie McClure, D.R.E. Students 163.

MADISON, GREENWOOD CO., ST. TERESA OF AVILA (1954), (German), [JC] Rev. Leo A. Kerschen.
Res.: 514 N. Elm St., Eureka, 67045. Tel: 316-583-7100; 316-437-2504 (Church).
Catechesis/Religious Program—Students 3.

MARION, MARION CO., HOLY FAMILY (1992), [CEM 5] [JC 2], Parish formed from merger of St. Mark, Marion; St. John Nepomucene, Pilsen; St. Patrick, Florence; Holy Redeemer, Tampa; and Immaculate Conception, Burns. Rev. Stephen F. Gronert.
Residence and Mailing: 415 N. Cedar St., 66861. Tel: 620-382-3422; 620-382-3369 (Office).
Catechesis/Religious Program— Dr. Jessica Laurin, D.R.E., Florence; Ed Davies, D.R.E., Marion; Gemma Davies, D.R.E.; Denice Bina, D.R.E., Pilsen; Mary Jirak, D.R.E., Tampa; Jean Rziha, D.R.E., Tampa. Students 162.
Mission—Holy Redeemer Tampa, Marion Co. 66861.

MCPHERSON, MCPHERSON CO., ST. JOSEPH (1880), Rev. Paul J. Oborny.
Res.: 520 E. Northview, 67460. Tel: 620-241-0821; Fax: 620-245-9677.
School—Tel: 620-241-3913. Penny Stoss, Prin. Lay Teachers 9; Students 80.
Catechesis/Religious Program—Anna Ruxlow, D.R.E. Students 250.
Mission—St. Bridget of Sweden Box 268, Lindsborg, McPherson Co. 67456. Tel: 785-227-3588.

MOLINE, ELK CO., ST. MARY'S (1899), [CEM] Rev. Sixtus ye Myint (Burma).
Res.: Box 276, 67353-0276. Tel: 620-647-3577.
Catechesis/Religious Program—Students 19.

MOUNT VERNON, KINGMAN CO., ST. ROSE (1911), (German—Irish), [CEM] Rev. Ivan C. Eck.
Res.: 13015 E. Maple Grove Rd., Mount Hope, 67108. Tel: 316-444-2210.
Catechesis/Religious Program—Tel: 316-542-3990. Students 125.

MULBERRY, CRAWFORD CO., ST. GABRIEL, Closed., For sacramental records contact Sacred Heart, Frontenac.

MULVANE, SUMNER CO., ST. MICHAEL THE ARCHANGEL (1948), Rev. James S. Mainzer.
Res.: 545 E. Main, 67110. Tel: 316-777-4221; Fax: 316-777-9456.
Catechesis/Religious Program—Tel: 316-777-0444. Karen Oblinger, D.R.E. Students 263.

NEODESHA, WILSON CO., ST. IGNATIUS (1873), [CEM] Rev. Stephen R. Baxter, J.C.L.
Res.: P.O. Box 186, 66757. Tel: 620-378-2694; Fax: 620-378-2694.
Catechesis/Religious Program—Tel: 620-325-3709. Students 42.

NEWTON, HARVEY CO.
1—ST. MARY (1872), [CEM] Rev. John V. Hotze.
Res.: 106 E. Eighth St., 67114. Tel: 316-282-0459; Fax: 316-283-0036.
School—Tel: 316-282-1974; Fax: 316-283-3642. Mrs. Leasa Coufal, Prin. Lay Teachers 16; Students 157.
Catechesis/Religious Program—Mrs. Marie Morford, D.R.E. Students 101.
2—OUR LADY OF GUADALUPE (1919), (Hispanic), [JC] Rev. Floyd E. McKinney.
Res.: 415 S. Ash St., 67114. Tel: 316-283-3499; Fax: 316-283-6813.
Catechesis/Religious Program—Students 56.

OST, RENO CO., ST. JOSEPH (1880), (German), [CEM] Rev. Ivan C. Eck.
Res.: 13015 E. Maple Grove Rd., Mount Hope, 67108. Tel: 316-444-2210.
Catechesis/Religious Program—Tel: 316-444-2637. Students 95.

OSWEGO, LABETTE CO., MOTHER OF GOD (1878), [JC] Rev. Larry Parker.
Res.: 1112 W. Third, 67356. Tel: 620-795-2262.
Catechesis/Religious Program—Students 31.

OXFORD, SUMNER CO., ST. MARY (1872), [JC] Rev. Bernard X. Gorges.
Res.: 412 E. Eighth St., Winfield, 67156. Tel: 620-221-3610; Fax: 316-221-3528.
Catechesis/Religious Program—Myra Jacobs, D.R.E. Students 35.

PARSONS, LABETTE CO.
1—MARY QUEEN OF PEACE (1909), Closed., For inquiries for parish records contact St. Patrick, Parsons.
2—ST. PATRICK (1872), [CEM 2] [JC] Rev. Robert B. Wachter.
Res.: 1807 Stevens Ave., 67357. Tel: 620-421-6762; Fax: 620-421-4032.
School—1831 Stevens Ave., 67357. Tel: 620-421-0710; Fax: 620-421-2429. Mr. Harry Heppler, Prin. Sisters of St. Joseph 1; Lay Teachers 11; Students 154.
Catechesis/Religious Program—Tel: 620-421-1628. Students 105.

PILSEN, MARION CO., ST. JOHN NEPOMUCENE, Closed., Merged with St. Mark, Marion; St. Patrick, Florence; and Holy Redeemer, Tampa to form Holy Family, Marion.

PIQUA, WOODSON CO., ST. MARTIN (1884), (German), Closed., For inquiries for sacramental records contact St. John, Iola.

PITTSBURG, CRAWFORD CO., OUR LADY OF LOURDES (1881), [CEM] Revs. Thomas J. Stroot; Jerome J. Spexarth.
Res.: 916 N. Locust St., P.O. Box 214, 66762. Tel: 620-231-2135; Fax: 620-231-4804.
School—St. Mary's Elementary, (Grades K-6), 213 E. Ninth, 66762. Tel: 620-231-6941. Mr. Patrick Forbes, Prin. Sisters of St. Joseph 2; Lay Teachers 18; Students 293.
School—St. Mary Junior High School, 212 E. 9th, P.O. Box 266, 66762. Tel: 620-231-4690. (Grades 7-8) Lay Teachers 5; Students 85.
High School—St. Mary-Colgan High School Priests 1; Lay Teachers 15; Students 157.
Catechesis/Religious Program—Tama Dutton, D.R.E. Tel: 620-347-8992. Students 49.
Convent—821 N. Locust St., 66762. Tel: 620-231-6014.

ST. LEO, KINGMAN CO., ST. LEO THE GREAT (1906), (German), [CEM] Rev. John Miller.
Res.: 8035 S.W. 160 Ave., Nashville, 67112. Tel: 316-246-5370.
Catechesis/Religious Program—P.O. Box 216, Cunningham, 67035. Tel: 316-298-2601. Students 32.

ST. MARK'S, SEDGWICK CO., ST. MARK (1876), (German), [CEM] Rev. David J. Lies.
Res.: 19230 W. 29th St. N., Colwich, 67030. Tel: 316-796-1604; Fax: 316-769-0511.
Catechesis/Religious Program—Tel: 316-640-8527. Vanessa Condreay, D.R.E. Students 253.

ST. PAUL, NEOSHO CO., ST. FRANCIS (1847), [CEM 2] Rev. Daniel L. Vacca.
Res.: 208 Washington St., P.O. Box 216, 66771-0216. Tel: 620-449-2224; Fax: 620-449-8986.
Catechesis/Religious Program—Tel: 620-449-2672. Suzan Diskin, D.R.E. Students 153.

SCAMMON, CHEROKEE CO., ST. BRIDGET'S (1868), [CEM] Rev. Chrysostom Ah Maung.
Res.: 115 W. Walnut, Columbus, 66725. Tel: 620-429-2639.
Catechesis/Religious Program—Tel: 620-479-2236. Students 59.

SCHULTE, SEDGWICK CO., ST. PETER THE APOSTLE (1905), [CEM] Rev. Patrick G. York. In Res., Rev. Eric M. Weldon.
Parish Offices—11000 S.W. Blvd., 67215. Tel: 316-524-4259; Fax: 316-524-0932.
Res.: 10980 S.W. Blvd., 67215. Tel: 316-522-4728.
School—Tel: 316-524-6585; Fax: 316-524-1656. Betty Hunt, Prin.; Bob Lyall, Assoc. Prin. Lay Teachers 21; Students 367.
Catechesis/Religious Program—Tel: 316-529-1681. Bob Benoit, D.R.E.; Kayleen Benoit, D.R.E. Students 167.

SEDAN, CHAUTAUQUA CO., ST. ROBERT BELLARMINE (1962), Rev. Sixtus ye Myint (Burma).
Res.: P.O. Box 276, Moline, 67353-0276. Tel: 620-647-3577.
Catechesis/Religious Program—Tel: 620-725-5198. Students 19.

STRONG CITY, CHASE CO., ST. ANTHONY OF PADUA (1880), [CEM] [JC] Rev. Jeffery A. Fasching.
Res.: 316 Spencer, Council Grove, 66846. Tel: 316-767-6412; Fax: 316-767-5370.
Catechesis/Religious Program—Tel: 316-273-8617. Jeanette Black, D.R.E. Students 37.

TAMPA, MARION CO., HOLY REDEEMER, , Now an oratory of Holy Family, Marion.

WALNUT, CRAWFORD CO., ST. PATRICK, Closed., For sacramental records contact St. Francis Church, St. Paul.

WATERLOO, KINGMAN CO., ST. LOUIS (1881), (German—Irish), [CEM] Rev. Ivan C. Eck.
Res.: 13015 E. Maple Grove Rd., Mt. Hope, 67108. Tel: 316-444-2210.
Catechesis/Religious Program—Students 5.

WEIR, CHEROKEE CO., SACRED HEART, Closed., For sacramental records contact St. Rose of Lima, Columbus.

WELLINGTON, SUMNER CO.
1—ST. ANTHONY (1884),, All information is for both St. Anthony and St. Rose. Rev. Andrew J. Seiler.
Mailing Address: 210 N. B St., 67152. Tel: 620-326-2522; Fax: 620-326-2527.
Catechesis/Religious Program—Tel: 620-326-3480. Pam Montenegro, D.R.E. Students 240.
2—ST. ROSE OF LIMA (1949), (Hispanic), Rev. Andrew J. Seiler.
Mailing Address: 210 N. B St., Wellington, 67152. Tel: 316-326-2522.
Church: 1205 E. Harvey, 67152. Tel: 316-326-3572.
Catechesis/Religious Program—Tel: 316-326-3480. Students 292.

WEST MINERAL, CHEROKEE CO., IMMACULATE CONCEPTION, Closed., For sacramental records contact St. Rose of Lima, Columbus.

WILLOWDALE, KINGMAN CO., ST. PETER'S (1884), (German), [CEM] Rev. John P. Miller.
Res.: P.O. Box 86, Zenda, 67159. Tel: 316-243-5451.
Catechesis/Religious Program—Students 12.

WINFIELD, COWLEY CO., HOLY NAME (1878), [JC] Rev. Bernard X. Gorges.
Res.: 412 E. Eighth St., 67156. Tel: 620-221-3610; Fax: 316-221-3528.
School—Tel: 620-221-0230; Fax: 620-221-4047. Mr. James Wessling, Prin. Lay Teachers 4; Students 55.
Catechesis/Religious Program—Students 68.

YATES CENTER, WOODSON CO., ST. JOSEPH (1957), [JC] Rev. Leon J. Kerschen.
Res.: 107 E. Bell St., 66783.
Catechesis/Religious Program—Tel: 316-625-2672. Students 57.

ZENDA, KINGMAN CO., ST. JOHN (1908), (German), [CEM] Rev. John P. Miller.
Res.: P.O. Box 86, 67159. Tel: 316-243-5451.
Catechesis/Religious Program—Linda Kerschen, D.R.E. Students 22.

Chaplains of Public Institutions

WICHITA. *El Dorado Correctional Facility*. Rev. Michael E. Nolan.
Sedgwick County Adult Local Detention Facility. Rev. John P. Sherlock.
Veterans Administration Hospital. Rev. Richard Stuchlik, S.T.L. Vacant.

HUTCHINSON. *Kansas State Industrial Reformatory*. Rev. Floyd E. McKinney.

On Duty Outside the Diocese:
Rev. Msgr.—
Conley, James, Villa Stritch, Via della Nocetta, 63, Rome 00164 Italy.
Revs.—
Gile, Joseph M., North American College, Casa Santa Maria, Via dell' Umilta, 30, Rome 00187 Italy.
Nolan, Joseph T.
Siewert, Charles F., Catholic University of America, 1025 Michigan Ave. N.E., Washington, DC 20017.

Retired:
Rev. Msgrs.—
Carr, William, 6900 E. 45th St. N., Apt. F-4, 67226.
Hogan, J. Vincent, 6900 E. 45th St. N., Apt. D-3, 67226.
Lampe, Irvin F., 13014 La Terraza Dr., Sun City West, AZ 85375.
McGread, Thomas, 6900 E. 45th St. N., 67226.
Regan, Charles, 6900 E. 45th St. N., Apt. E-2, 67226.
Schmidt, George N., 6900 E. 45th St. N., 67226.
Walsh, Charles, 6900 E. 45th St. N., 67226.
Revs.—
Bieberle, Victor, 29 Tiburon Way, Hot Springs, AR 71909.
Busch, Arthur, 6900 E. 45th St. N., Apt. G-2, 67226.
Cox, Francis, 6900 E. 45th St. N., 67226.
Curran, John, 6900 E. 45th St. N., 67226.
Dinan, John, 1915 N. Porter, Apt. A-78, 67203.
Freed, Robert, Macungie Village Apartments, 26 W. Chestnut St., Macungie, PA 18062.
Garrahy, Michael, 6900 E. 45th St. N., 67226.
Harvey, Charles K., 6900 E. 45th St. N., 67226.
Hay, Francis J., 6900 E. 45th St. N., 67226.
Hoagland, James N., 1205 E. Harvey, Wellington, 67152.
Kocour, Robert F., Apartado 407, Barquisimeto Lara 3001-A Venezuela.
Larkin, Patrick, 6900 E. 45th St. N., 67226.
Mannion, J. Patrick, 6900 E. 45th St., Apt. G-3, 67226.
Metcko, Leo E., Catholic Care Center, 6700 E. 45th St. N., 67226.
Mulvihill, Daniel R., 6900 E. 45th St. N., 67226.
O'Hare, Donald J., 6900 E. 45th St., FL 67226.
O'Leary, David A., 6900 E. 45th St. N., 67226.
O'Malley, Michael W.
O'Shea, John J., 6900 E. 45th St., 67226.
Pepe, Robert F., 4 Circle Dr., Port Duncan, Afton, OK 74331.
Reinkemeyer, John, St. Mary, 25741 W. 13th St. N.,

Garden Plains, 67050.
Rusteika, John B., 6900 E. 45th St. N., 67226.
Slomski, Joseph P., 6900 E. 45th St. N., Apt. A-4, 67226.
Spexarth, James, R.R. 1, P.O. Box 30, Marion, 66861.
Stremel, Adolph, c/o P.A. Sullivan, 801 Main St., Victoria, 67671.
Trayers, Kevin, 202 S. Liberty, Cherryvale, 67335.
Walsh, Ulich
Wilkinson, James, 6900 E. 45th St., Wichita 67226.
York, Edward, 46 Leicester Dr., Bella Vista, AR 72714.

INSTITUTIONS LOCATED IN THE DIOCESE

[A] COLLEGES AND UNIVERSITIES

WICHITA. *Newman University*, 3100 McCormick Ave., 67213-2097. Tel: 316-942-4291; Fax: 316-942-4483. Web: www.newmanu.edu. Rev. Sherman Orr, Chap.; Aidan O. Dunleavy, Ph.D., Pres.; B. Lee Cooper, Ph.D., Provost & Vice Pres. Acad. Affairs; Mark Dresselhaus, Vice Pres. Finance & Admin.; Kim Miller Jacobs, Vice Pres. Enrollment Mgmt.; Shirley Rueb, Registrar. Coeducational liberal arts college, founded in 1933 by the Sisters Adorers of the Blood of Christ. (Accredited by the North Central Association of Colleges and Secondary Schools). Sisters 11; Lay Teachers 69; Total Staff 187; Students 1,929.

[B] HIGH SCHOOLS, DIOCESAN

WICHITA. *Bishop Mark K. Carroll Catholic High School*, 8101 W. Central, 67212. Tel: 316-722-2390; Fax: 316-722-6670. Email: nielsenleticia@bcchs.org. Web: www.bcchs.com. Leticia C. Nielsen, Prin.; Rev. Jarrod Lies, Chap. & Instructor. Tel: 316-682-1415. Priests 1; Sisters 3; Lay Teachers 62; Total Staff 66; Students 988.

Kapaun Mt. Carmel Catholic High School, 8506 E. Central, 67206. Tel: 316-634-0315; Fax: 316-636-2437. Email: mburrus@kapaun.org. Web: www.kapaun.org. Revs. Jim Weldon; Jason Borkenhagen. Sisters 2; Priests 1; Lay Teachers 54; Total Staff 82; Students 843.

HUTCHINSON. *Trinity High School*, 1400 E. 17th, 67501. Tel: 316-662-5800; Fax: 316-662-1233. Email: bcordel@trinity-hutch.com. Web: www.trinity-hutch.com. Mr. Brian Cordel, Prin.; Rev. Ned J. Blick, Chap. Priests 1; Sisters 3; Lay Teachers 17; Total Staff 20; Students 261.

The Trinity High School Education Endowment Fund, 1400 E. 17th, 67501. Tel: 620-662-5800; Fax: 316-662-1233. Email: suehall@trinity-hutch.com. Web: hutch-trinity.coxkansas.com. *c/o Eugene J. Gerber*, 424 N. Broadway, 67202. Tel: 316-269-3950. Priests 1; Sisters 3; Lay Teachers 19; Total Staff 23; Total Enrollment 260.

PITTSBURG. *St. Mary-Colgan High School*, 212 E. 9th St., 66762. Tel: 620-231-4690; Fax: 620-231-0690. Email: smcolgan@stmary-colgan.org. Web: www.stmarys.colgan.org. Rev. Thomas J. Stroot, Admin.; Mr. Patrick Forbes, Prin. Priests 1; Lay Teachers 20; Total Staff 26; Students 242.

[C] SPECIAL EDUCATION

WICHITA. *Art of Learning Center*, 201 S. Millwood, 67213. Tel: 316-265-6853. Sr. Sibyllina Mueller, O.P., Dir. Speech, Language, Reading Therapy. Total Assisted 1,770; Total Staff 2.

[D] GENERAL HOSPITALS

WICHITA. *Via Christi Regional Medical Center, Inc.* Tel: 316-268-5000; Fax: 316-268-7999. Web: www.Via-Christi.org. Mr. Randall G. Nyp, Pres. & CEO; Sisters Sherri Marie Kuhn, S.S.M., Vice Pres. of Mission Svcs.; Marie Veronica Janousek, Vice Pres. of Mission Svcs.; Rev. Raymond Joyce. Licensed Beds 1,532; In Patients 322,946; Out Patients 305,887; Total Staff 4,231.

St. Francis Campus, 929 N. St. Francis, 67124. Tel: 316-268-5000. Rev. Peter Leigh. Tel: 316-268-8522.

St. Joseph Campus, 3600 E. Harry, 67218. Tel: 316-685-1111.

Via Christi Rehabilitation Center, Inc., Our Lady of Lourdes Campus, 1151 N. Rock Rd., 67206. Tel: 316-634-3400; Fax: 316-634-1141. Email: laura_klusener@via-christi.org. Web: www.via-christi.org. Mr. Bob O'Brien, Bd. Chm.; Ms. Laurie Labarca, COO; Sr. Anne Dolores LaPlante, Mission Svcs. Staff 245; Bed Capacity 60; Patients Assisted Annually 4,758.

Via Christi Riverside Medical Center, Inc. Frank Creeden, COO2622 W. Central, 67203. Tel: 316-268-5084. Bed Capacity 125; Patients Assisted Annually 133,563; Total Staff 482.

COLUMBUS. *Maude Norton Memorial Hospital (MNMCH, Inc.)*, 220 N. Pennsylvania St., 66725. Tel: 620-429-2545; Fax: 316-429-1984. Email: cneely@stj.com. Cynthia Neely, Admin. Bed Capacity 25; Patients Assisted Annually 10,179; Total Staff 53.

FORT SCOTT. *Mercy Health System of Kansas, Inc.*, 821 Burke St., 66701. Tel: 316-223-7057; Fax: 316-223-5327. Jerry Stevenson, Pres. & CEO. Sisters of Mercy 19; Lay Staff 474; Bed Capacity 78; Bassinets 6; Patients Assisted Annually 36,159; Home Health Visits 11,252.

INDEPENDENCE *Mercy Health Systems of Kansas, Inc.-Independence*, 800 W. Myrtle St., P.O. Box 388, 67301. Tel: 620-331-2200; Fax: 620-332-3270. Email: abrau@mhsk.smhs.com. Web: terraworld.net/mercy/. Jerry Stevenson, CEO. Sisters of Mercy 2; Total Staff 270; Bed Capacity 58; Patients Assisted Annually 38,500.

OSWEGO. *Oswego Health Center, Inc.*, 800 Barker Dr., 67356-9461. Tel: 620-795-2921; Fax: 316-795-4903. Email: kathym@oswego.net. Ms. Kathy Moyer, Admin. Total Staff 32; Bed Capacity 12; Patients Assisted Annually 59.

PITTSBURG. *Mount Carmel Regional Medical Center*, 1102 E. Centennial, 66762. Tel: 620-231-6100; Fax: 620-232-0493. Web: www.mtcarmel.org. Dan Lingor, Pres. & CEO. Sisters of St. Joseph 4; Total Staff 841; Bed Capacity 188; Patients Assisted Annually 86,097.

Mount Carmel Foundation

[E] HOMES FOR AGED

WICHITA. *Catholic Care Center, Inc.*, 6700 E. 45th St. N., 67226. Tel: 316-744-2020; Fax: 316-744-2182. Web: www.catholiccarecenter.org. Thomas Church, CEO. Operated by Catholic Diocese of Wichita & the Via Christ Health System. Sisters 14; Total Staff 296; Residents 298; Total assisted 341.

Georgetown Village, Inc., 1655 Georgetown St., 67218. Tel: 316-685-0400; Fax: 316-685-0174. Email: maggie_rader@via-christi.org. Web: www.georgetown-village.org. Staff 80; Total Assisted 80; Independent Living 130; Condominiums 17.

Sheridan Village, Inc., 1051 S. Bluffview, 67218. Tel: 316-858-4903. Robert W. Harvey, Pres. & Contact Person.

MULVANE. *Villa Maria*, 116 S. Central, 67110. Tel: 316-777-1129; Fax: 316-777-4406. Email: chmathis@hotmail.com. Charlene Mathis, Admin. Home for Aging Men and Women. Adorers of the Blood of Christ 2; Total Staff 75; Guests 82; Total Assisted 101.

[F] MONASTERIES AND RESIDENCES FOR PRIESTS AND BROTHERS

WICHITA. *Priests Retirement Center*, 6900 E. 45th St. N., 67226. Tel: 316-744-2020; Fax: 316-744-2182. Thomas M. Church, CEO. Residents 24.

Redemptorist Mission House, 145 S. Millwood Ave., 67213. Tel: 316-262-5800; Fax: 316-262-5803. Web: www.stjosephparish.ws/. Revs. John Willett, C.SS.R., Supr.; Walter C. Karrer, C.SS.R.; Ivan Dawson, C.SS.R.; Bro. Marvin Hamann, C.SS.R. Legal Title: *Society of the Redemptorist Fathers of Wichita, Kansas*. Residents 4; Staff 4.

[G] CONVENTS AND RESIDENCES FOR SISTERS

WICHITA. *Adorers of the Blood of Christ U.S. Province*, Wichita Center, 1165 Southwest Blvd., 67213. Tel: 316-942-2201; Fax: 877-942-0859. Email: stewartj@newmanu.edu. Web: www.adorers.org. Rev. Thomas Welk, C.PP.S., Chap. Professed Sisters 200; Novices 3.

Dominican House of Studies, 201 S. Millwood, 67213. Tel: 316-267-4551. Residents 7.

Medical Sisters of St. Joseph-United States Foundation, 3435 E. Funston, 67218. Tel: 316-686-4746; Fax: 316-686-4746. Email: msjkansas@aol.com. Sr. Audrey, Supr. Professed Sisters 9.

Mt. St Mary Convent, Motherhouse and Novitiate of the Sisters of St. Joseph, 3700 E. Lincoln, 67218-2099. Tel: 316-686-7171; Fax: 316-689-4056. Email: sistersofstjoseph@csjwichita.org. Web: www.csjwichita.org. Sr. Helene Lentz, C.S.J., Pres.; Rev. Robert E. Hemberger, Chap. Professed Sisters 167.

Sisters of the Immaculate Heart of Mary of Wichita, Inc. (I.H.M.), 605 N. Woodchuck, 67212. Tel: 316-722-9316; Fax: 316-722-4568. Email: mmb@sistersihmofwichita.org. Web: www.sistersihmofwichita.org. Sr. Marie Bernadette Mertens, I.H.M., Supr. Professed Sisters 13; Novices 6.

[H] RETREAT HOUSES

WICHITA. *Spiritual Life Center*, 7100 E. 45th N., 67226. Tel: 316-744-0167; Fax: 314-744-8072. Email: slc@wichita.org. Web: www.slcwichita.org. Revs. Paul S. Coakley, Dir.; John P. Lanzrath. Residents 2; Staff 25. Ministry Staff: Jim Rundell, Admin.; Chuck Weber, Prog. & Publicity Dir.; Jerrilyn Szelle Holladay, Dir. for Adult Education; Ms. Sara Splichal, Dir. for Family Life.

[I] COMMUNITY CENTERS

WICHITA. **Center of Hope, Inc.*, 400 N. Emporia, 67202-2514. Tel: 316-267-3999; Fax: 316-267-7778. Email: george@centerofhopeinc.org. Web: www.centerofhopeinc.org. Sr. Stella Rosenhamer, A.S.C., Dir. Tel: 316-267-0222; Fax: 316-267-7778. Sponsored by Adorers of the Blood of Christ Staff 3; Total Assisted 3,645.

CSJ "Dear Neighbor" Ministries, Inc. Sr. Helene Lentz, C.S.J., Pres.3700 E. Lincoln, 67218. Tel: 316-689-4001.

Guadalupe Clinic, 940 S. St. Francis, 67211. Tel: 316-264-8974; Fax: 316-262-4938. Email: guadalupe@guadalupeclinic.kscoxmail.com. Ms. Marlene Dreiling, M.N., R.N., Dir. Staff 12; Total Assisted 35,648.

The Lord's Diner, 520 N. Broadway, 67214. Tel: 316-266-4966; Fax: 316-265-6646. Email: wendyg@thelordsdiner.org. Scott Dryden, Admin. Meals Served: 202,994.

[J] NEWMAN CENTERS

WICHITA. *Wichita State University* , Newman Center , 1810 N. Roosevelt, 67208. Tel: 316-684-6896; Fax: 316-684-2679. Rev. Matthew C. McGinness, Chap.

PITTSBURG. *St. Pius X Center (Pittsburg State University)* 301A E. Cleveland, 66762. Tel: 316-235-1138. Email: newmancenter@mobil1.net. Web: www.pittstate.edu/union/organization/newman. Rev. Robert W. McElwee, Chap.

[K] CATHOLIC CHARITIES

WICHITA. *Catholic Charities, Inc.*, 437 N. Topeka, 67202. Tel: 316-264-8344; Fax: 316-264-4442. Email: jvpape@wkscatholiccharities.org. Web: www.wkscatholiccharities.org. Ms. Janet Valente Pape, Exec. Dir. Total Agency Staff 111; Total Individuals Assisted 22,447.

Foster Grandparent Program, 437 N. Topeka, 67202. Tel: 316-264-8344; Fax: 316-264-4442. Provides 101,260 hours of service Staff 3; Total Children Assisted 1,725; Total Foster Grandparents 163.

Harvest House Program, 437 N. Topeka, 67202. Tel: 316-264-8344; Fax: 316-264-4442. Staff 2; Centers 31; Members Assisted 1,795.

Emergency Services, 437 N. Topeka, 67202. Tel: 316-262-8898; Fax: 316-264-4442. Total Assisted 9,660; Total Staff 3.

Immigration & Refugee Services, 437 N. Topeka, 67202. Tel: 316-264-0282; Fax: 316-264-4442. Staff 3; Total Assisted 2,367.

Pregnancy and Adoption Services, 425 N. Topeka, 67202. Tel: 316-263-0507; Fax: 316-263-5259. Total Assisted 402; Total Staff 3; Adoptions Completed 8.

Counseling Services, 425 N. Topeka, 67202. Tel: 316-263-6941; Fax: 316-263-5259. Individuals Served 3,312; Total Staff 13.

Adult Day Services, 5920 W. Central, 67212. Tel: 316-942-2008; Fax: 316-942-2260. Staff 22; Total Assisted 175.

Anthony Family Shelter, 256 N. Ohio, 67214. Tel: 316-264-7233; Fax: 316-267-3774. Staff 14; Individuals Assisted 494.

Harbor House Shelter, P.O. Box 3759, 67201. Tel: 316-263-6000; Fax: 316-263-8347. Staff 18; Women & Children Assisted 521; Victim's Advocate Program 1,000.

Adult Education Center, 522 S. Market, 67202. Tel: 316-262-5350; Fax: 316-262-5356. Students Served 313; Total Staff 4.

St. Dismas Missioners, 437 N. Topeka, 67202. Tel: 316-264-8344; Fax: 316-264-4442. Total Staff 1; Inmates Served 750.

Interpreter Services, 437 N. Topeka, 67202. Tel: 316-264-8344; Fax: 316-264-4442. Clients Served 107; Total Staff 7.

Hispanic Social Services, 437 N. Topeka, 67202. Tel: 316-269-5851; Fax: 316-264-4442. Clients Served 1,334; Total Staff 1.

[L] MISCELLANEOUS

WICHITA. *Cornerstone Assisted Living, Inc.*, 3720 E. Bayley, 67218. Tel: 316-858-4902; Fax: 316-858-4199. Email: Mark_Bailey@via-christi.org. Web: www.via-christi.org/cornerstonebroadmoor. Mr. Mark Bailey, CEO.

Diocesan Office, Ministry with Persons with Disabilities, 424 N. Broadway, 67202. Tel: 316-269-3900; Fax: 316-269-3902. Email: ginnys@cdowk.org.

Gerard House, Inc., 3144 N. Hood, 67204. Tel: 316-832-0777; Fax: 316-832-1327. Deneen Dryden, Dir. Shelter for Needy Pregnant Women. Education Program 51; Total Assisted 45.

Leaven International Corporation, 1400 S. Sheridan, 67213. Tel: 316-943-1203; Fax: 316-943-1427. Email: peterg@adorers.edu. Web: www.adorers.org. Greg Peter, Financial Officer; Sr. Barbara Jean Franklin, A.SC., Pres. A charitable organization of the Adorers of the Blood of Christ.

The Mary Magdalen Foundation, 12626 E. 21st St. N., 67206. Tel: 316-634-2315; Fax: 316-634-3948. Email: prange@magdalenwichita.com. Web: www.magdalenwichita.com.

Priests' Retirement and Education Fund of Wichita Rev. Wayne Schmid, Contact Person100 N. Broadway, Ste. 700, 67202. Tel: 316-262-5043.

The Redemptorist Community in Wichita, Kansas, Inc., Redemptorist Mission House, 145 S. Millwood Ave., 67213. Tel: 316-261-5800; Fax: 316-261-5803.

Legal Title: *Society of Redemptorist Fathers of Wichita, Kansas.*

Riverside Village Inc. Mark Mains, CEO777 N. McLean Blvd., 67203. Tel: 316-942-7000; Fax: 316-946-5727. Web: www.via-christi.org/riversidevillage.

Serra Club of Reno County, 424 N. Broadway, 67202. Rev. Joseph A. Eckberg, Chap.

Serra Club of Wichita - Downtown, 424 N. Broadway, 67202. Tel: 316-269-3900. Rev. Kenneth J. Schuckman, Chap.

Serra Club of Wichita - Metro, 424 N. Broadway, 67202. Tel: 316-269-3900. Rev. Msgr. Thomas McGread, Chap. (Retired).

Totus Tuus, Inc., 424 N. Broadway, 67202. Tel: 316-269-3900; Fax: 316-269-3902. Sr. Jacinta Langlois.

Via Christi Foundation, Inc., 2622 W. Central, 67203. Tel: 316-946-5020; Fax: 316-946-5034. Email: james_barber@via-christ.org. Mr. James N. Barber, Pres. A subsidiary of Via Christi Regional Medical Center. Staff 11.

Via Christi Health Partners, Inc., 3720 E. Bayley, 67218. Tel: 316-858-4909. Web: www.Via-Christi.org.

Via Christi Health System, Inc., 3720 E. Bayley, 67218. Tel: 316-858-4900. Web: www.Via-Christi.org. Mr. LeRoy Rheault, Pres. & CEO. Owned and operated by Marian Health System (sponsored by the Sisters of the Sorrowful Mother of Broken Arrow, Oklahoma) and the Sisters of St. Joseph of Wichita, Kansas. Participating organizations include five acute care facilities, eight senior care facilities, and one 50% owned, managed acute care facility, located in three states.

Via Christi Healthcare Outreach Program for Elders, Inc. (HOPE), 935 S. Glendale, 67218. Tel: 316-858-1111; Fax: 316-858-1166. Email: mark_bailey@via-christi.org. Web: viachristihope.org.

Via Christi Home Health Inc., 1122 N. Topeka, 2nd Floor, 67214. Tel: 316-268-8588; Fax: 316-269-1556. Email: brian_koehn@via-christi.org. Web: www.via-christi.org.

Via Christi Property Services, Inc., 3720 E. Bayley, 67218. Tel: 316-858-4909. Web: www.Via-Christi.org.

Via Christi Senior Services, Inc., 3720 E. Bayley, 67218. Tel: 316-858-4910; Fax: 316-858-4199. Email: Bob_Harvey@via-christi.org. Web: www.via.christi.org.

PITTSBURG. *Cornerstone Village Inc.*, 1502 E. Centennial, 66762. Tel: 620-235-0020. Email: Evelyn_Walters@via-christi.org. Web: www.via-christi.org. Ms. Evelyn Walters, Contact Person.

RELIGIOUS INSTITUTES OF MEN REPRESENTED IN THE DIOCESE

For further details refer to the corresponding bracketed number in the Religious Institutes of Men or Women section.

[1070]—*Redemptorist Fathers* (Province of Denver)—C.Ss.R.

[1060]—*Society of the Precious Blood* (Kansas City Prov.)—C.PP.S.

RELIGIOUS INSTITUTES OF WOMEN REPRESENTED IN THE DIOCESE

[0100]—*Adorers of the Blood of Christ*—A.S.C.

[]—*Carmelite Sisters of St. Teresa*—C.S.S.T.

[]—*Congregation of the Daughters of the Passion of Our Lord Jesus Christ and the Sorrows of Mary*—C.F.P.

[]—*Discalced Carmelite Sisters*

[1070-24]—*Dominican Sisters*—O.P.

[2575]—*Institute of the Sisters of Mercy of the Americas*—R.S.M.

[2500]—*Medical Sisters of St. Joseph*—M.S.J.

[0430]—*Sisters of Charity of the Blessed Virgin Mary*—B.V.M.

[3830-18]—*Sisters of St. Joseph*—C.S.J.

[2185]—*Sisters of the Immaculate Heart of Mary of Wichita*—I.H.M.

[4100]—*Sisters of the Sorrowful Mother (Third Order of St. Francis)*—S.S.M.

[2150]—*Sisters, Servants of the Immaculate Heart of Mary*—I.H.M.

NECROLOGY

† Tonne, Rev. Msgr. Arthur, (Retired)—Died May 20, 2003

† Blanpied, Rev. Msgr. Robert, (Retired)—Died Oct. 6, 2003

Diocese of Wilmington

(Dioecesis Wilmingtoniensis)

Most Reverend

MICHAEL A. SALTARELLI, D.D.

Bishop of Wilmington; ordained May 28, 1960; appointed Titular Bishop of Mesarfelta and Auxiliary Bishop of Newark, June 12, 1990; Episcopal ordination July 30, 1990; appointed Eighth Bishop of Wilmington November 21, 1995; installed January 23, 1996

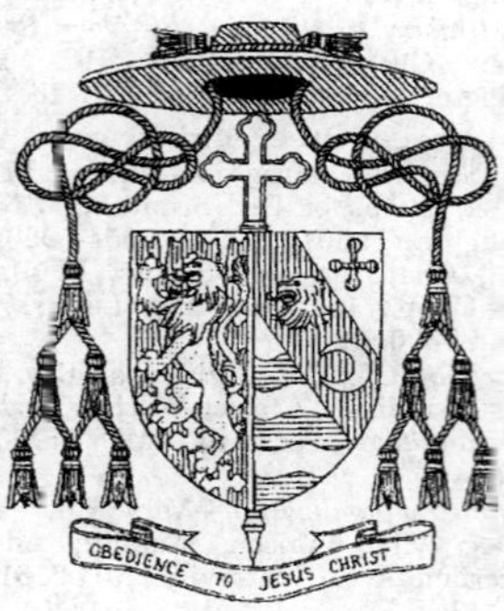

Chancery Office: P.O. Box 2030, Wilmington, DE 19899-2030. Tel: 302-573-3100; Fax: 302-573-3128.

Web: www.cdow.org

Email: ccurtis@cdow.org

ESTABLISHED MARCH 3, 1868.

Square Miles Delaware 1,932; Maryland 3,375; Total 5,307.

Comprises the State of Delaware and the Counties of Caroline, Cecil, Dorchester, Kent, Queen Anne's, Somerset, Talbot, Wicomico and Worcester in Maryland.

For legal titles of parishes and diocesan institutions, consult the Chancery Office.

STATISTICAL OVERVIEW

Personnel	
Bishop	1
Priests: Diocesan Active in Diocese	88
Priests: Diocesan Active Outside Diocese	12
Priests: Retired, Sick or Absent	19
Number of Diocesan Priests	119
Religious Priests in Diocese	86
Total Priests in Diocese	205
Extern Priests in Diocese	16
Ordinations:	
Diocesan Priests	3
Transitional Deacons	3
Permanent Deacons	5
Permanent Deacons in Diocese	77
Total Brothers	29
Total Sisters	259
Parishes	
Parishes	57
With Resident Pastor:	
Resident Diocesan Priests	52
Resident Religious Priests	4
Without Resident Pastor:	
Administered by Priests	1
Missions	19
Pastoral Centers	8
Professional Ministry Personnel:	
Sisters	26
Lay Ministers	81
Welfare	
Catholic Hospitals	1
Total Assisted	177,740
Health Care Centers	2
Total Assisted	352
Homes for the Aged	5
Total Assisted	354
Residential Care of Children	3
Total Assisted	89
Day Care Centers	2
Total Assisted	205
Specialized Homes	3
Total Assisted	425
Special Centers for Social Services	17
Total Assisted	519,436
Other Institutions	3
Total Assisted	12,587
Educational	
Diocesan Students in Other Seminaries	16
Total Seminarians	16
High Schools, Diocesan and Parish	5
Total Students	2,953
High Schools, Private	3
Total Students	1,724
Elementary Schools, Diocesan and Parish	27
Total Students	9,630
Elementary Schools, Private	5
Total Students	995
Non-residential Schools for the Disabled	1
Total Students	102
Catechesis/Religious Education:	
High School Students	1,294
Elementary Students	10,887
Total Students under Catholic Instruction	27,601
Teachers in the Diocese:	
Priests	14
Brothers	5
Sisters	44
Lay Teachers	983
Vital Statistics	
Receptions into the Church:	
Infant Baptism Totals	2,874
Adult Baptism Totals	185
Received into Full Communion	285
First Communions	2,776
Confirmations	2,032
Marriages:	
Catholic	467
Interfaith	294
Total Marriages	761
Deaths	1,539
Total Catholic Population	220,000
Total Population	1,215,685

Former Bishops—Rt. Revs. THOMAS A. BECKER, D.D., consecrated Aug. 16, 1868; transferred to Savannah, 1886; died July 29, 1899; ALFRED A. CURTIS, D.D., consecrated Nov. 14, 1886; resigned 1896; named Titular Bishop of Echinus; died July 11, 1908; Most Revs. JOHN J. MONAGHAN, D.D., consecrated May 9, 1897; resigned and named Titular Bishop of Lydda, July 10, 1925; died Jan. 7, 1935; EDMOND JOHN FITZMAURICE, D.D., consecrated Nov. 30, 1925; resigned March 2, 1960 and named Titular Archbishop of Tomi; died July 25, 1962; HUBERT J. CARTWRIGHT, D.D., consecrated Coadjutor "with right of succession," Oct. 24, 1956; Titular Bishop of Neve; died March 6, 1958; MICHAEL W. HYLE, D.D., consecrated Sept. 24, 1958 as Titular Bishop of Christopolis and Coadjutor with right of succession; succeeded to See, March 2, 1960; died Dec. 26, 1967; THOMAS J. MARDAGA, D.D., consecrated Jan. 25, 1967; named Titular Bishop of Mutugenna; appt. Bishop of Wilmington, March 13, 1968; installed April 6, 1968; died May 28, 1984; JAMES C. BURKE, O.P., consecrated May 25, 1967; named Titular Bishop of Lamigiggia; Vicar Apostolic of Chimbote, Peru, 1962-1978; Served in Diocese of Wilmington, 1978-1994;; died May 28, 1994; ROBERT E. MULVEE, D.D., J.C.D., ord. June 30, 1957; Auxiliary Bishop of Manchester and Titular Bishop of Summa, Feb. 15, 1977; consecrated April 14, 1977; appt. Bishop of Wilmington, Feb. 19, 1985; installed April 11, 1985; appt. to Diocese of Providence as Coadjutor Bishop of Providence, Feb. 7, 1995; installed March 27, 1995; succeeded to See, June 11, 1997.

Office of the Bishop—P.O. Box 2030, Wilmington, 19899. PATRICIA SLEPESKY-BOSSI, Sec. to Bishop & Notary for the Curia. Tel: 302-573-3100; Fax: 302-573-2391.

Vicar General for Administration and Moderator of the Curia—Very Rev. Msgr. J. THOMAS CINI, V.G., 1925 Delaware Ave., P.O. Box 2030, Wilmington, 19899. Tel: 302-573-3118; Fax: 302-573-3128.

Vicar General for Pastoral Services—Rev. Msgr. JOSEPH F. REBMAN, V.G., S.T.L., J.C.L., C.C.C.E., 1925 Delaware Ave., P.O. Box 2030, Wilmington, 19899. Tel: 302-573-3100; Fax: 302-254-4044.

Vicar for Priests—Rev. Msgr. CLEMENT P. LEMON, 1925 Delaware Ave., P.O. Box 2030, Wilmington, 19899. Tel: 302-573-3144; Fax: 302-573-3128.

Pastoral Services Department

Secretary, Pastoral Services Department—Rev. Msgr. JOSEPH F. REBMAN, V.G., S.T.L., J.C.L., C.C.C.E.

Chancery Office—Rev. Msgr. JOHN O. BARRES, S.T.D., J.C.L., Chancellor, Mailing Address, P.O. Box 2030, Wilmington, 19899. Office, 1925 Delaware Ave., Wilmington, 19806. Tel: 302-573-3100; Fax: 302-254-4044. Email: ccurtis@cdow.org. Web: www.cdow.org. Office Hours: Mon.-Fri. 8:30-4:30; Send all marriage dispensation requests to Chancery Office.

Archives—Mr. DONN DEVINE, Archivist, 8 Old Church Rd., Greenville, 19807. Tel: 302-655-0597.

Diocesan Tribunal—Mailing Address, P.O. Box 2030, Wilmington, 19899. 1925 Delaware Ave., Wilmington, 19806. Tel: 302-573-3107; Fax: 302-573-3128.

Judicial Vicar—Very Rev. GEORGE J. BRUBAKER, J.C.L.

Office Supervisor—Mrs. JOANN KUBASKO.

Court of First Instance Judges—Rev. STANLEY R. DRUPIESKI, O.S.F.S.; Very Rev. GEORGE J. BRUBAKER, J.C.L.; Sr. JEANNE HAMILTON, O.S.U., J.C.L.; Ms. JACQUELINE E. HANNEM, J.C.L.

Auditor—Deacon FRANCIS STAAB.

Defenders of the Bond—Mr. JACK D. ANDERSON, J.C.D.; Sr. PATRICIA SMITH, O.S.F., J.C.D.

Secretaries/Notaries—Mrs. MARIE BRADLEY; Mrs. GAIL ESPOSITO; Mrs. PATRICIA KILLEN.

Catholic Cemeteries—Rev. Msgr. JOSEPH F. REBMAN, V.G., S.T.L., J.C.L., C.C.C.E., Dir.; Mr. MARK A. CHRISTIAN, C.C.C.E., Exec. Dir., Mailing Address, P.O. Box 2506, Wilmington, 19805. Tel: 302-656-3323; Fax: 302-656-1069.

Coordinator of Institutional Chaplains—

Priest Personnel Committee—Tel: 302-328-1790.

Vocation Office—Revs. JOSEPH M.P.R. COCUCCI, Dir.; RALPH L. MARTIN, Dir. Seminarians, 1626 N. Union St., P.O. Box 2030, Wilmington, 19899. Tel: 302-573-3113; Fax: 302-573-2393.

Office for Deacons—Deacon HAROLD D. JOPP JR., Dir., 1626 N. Union St., P.O. Box 2030, Wilmington, 19899. Tel: 302-573-2390; Fax: 302-573-2393.

Office of Worship—Rev. MICHAEL J. CARRIER, Dir., 1626 N. Union St., Wilmington, 19899. Tel: 302-573-3137; Fax: 302-573-2393.

Delegate for Religious—Sr. CELESTE CRINE, O.S.F.,

1626 N. Union St., P.O. Box 2030, Wilmington, 19899. Tel: 302-573-3124; Fax: 302-573-2393.

Mission Office— Propagation of the Faith and Holy Childhood Association, Rev. JOHN P. KLEVENCE, Dir., 1626 N. Union St., P.O. Box 2030, Wilmington, 19899. Tel: 302-573-3104; Fax: 302-573-2393.

Apostolate for Ethnic Ministries—P.O. Box 2030, Wilmington, 19899. Tel: 302-573-3100.

Ministry of Black Catholics—DARRYL S. SIMMS, Dir.

Hispanic Community—

Wilmington Office—Rev. CHRIS POSCH, O.F.M., Dir. Associate Directors: Rev. JOSEPH GIRONE, O.S.A.; Sr. AGNES OMAN, C.S.B., 1010 W. Fourth St., Wilmington, 19805. Tel: 302-655-0518; Fax: 302-655-7684.

Korean Catholics—Rev. PETER LEE HAE, Pastoral Min.; Mr. JOHN KO, Lay Leader, 2710 Duncan Rd., Wilmington, 19808. Tel: 302-998-7609.

Native American Community—Ms. GAIL RANDO, Contact, 1200 Windon Dr., Wilmington, 19803. Tel: 302-478-5412.

Catholic Education Department

Secretary—Mr. EDMUND F. GORDON.

Catholic Schools—Bro. JAMES MALONE, C.F.X., Supt.; Sr. KATHLEEN CALLAGHAN, S.S.J., Asst. Supt.; Ms. CATHERINE WEAVER, Asst. Supt., 1626 N. Union St., Wilmington, 19806. Tel: 302-573-3133; Fax: 302-573-3143.

Religious Education—Mr. EDMUND F. GORDON, Diocesan Dir.; Sr. SALLY RUSSELL, S.S.J., Assoc. Dir., 1626 N. Union St., Wilmington, 19806. Tel: 302-573-3130; Fax: 302-573-2393.

Education Ministry for Persons With Special Needs—Mrs. JO-ANN DORA, Coord. Spec. Rel. Educ. Tel: 302-573-3130; Mrs. MARGARET WYNN, Coord. Hearing Impaired, 1626 N. Union St., Wilmington, 19806. Tel: 302-573-3130.

Catholic Youth Ministry—Mr. PATRICK DONOVAN, Dir.; ANTHONY ALBENCE, Training Specialist; JOE McNESBY, Coord. Athletics, 1626 N. Union St., Wilmington, 19806. Tel: 302-658-3800; Fax: 302-658-7617. Web: www.cdow.org.

Catholic Campus Ministry—Rev. MICHAEL F. SZUPPER, Ph.D., Dir., University of Delaware, 45 Lovett Ave., Newark, 19711. Tel: 302-368-4728; Fax: 302-368-2548.

Communications Department

Secretary—Mr. ROBERT KREBS.

Office of Public Relations, Radio and T.V.—Mr. ROBERT KREBS, Dir., 1626 N. Union St., Wilmington, 19899. Tel: 302-573-3116; Fax: 302-573-2393.

Finance Department

Chief Financial Officer and Secretary—Mr. JOSEPH P. CORSINI, Mailing Address, P.O. Box 2030, Wilmington, 19899. 1925 Delaware Ave., Wilmington, 19806. Tel: 302-573-3105; Fax: 302-573-3129.

Development Department

Secretary and Diocesan Development Director—Mrs. DEBORAH A. FOLS, P.O. Box 2030, Wilmington, 19899. Tel: 302-573-3121; Fax: 302-573-3128.

Annual Catholic Appeal—Mrs. DEBORAH A. FOLS, Dir., P.O. Box 2030, Wilmington, 19899. Tel: 302-573-3100; Fax: 302-573-3128.

Catholic Charities Department

Catholic Charities—Ms. BARBARA GRIECO, M.C., M.B.A., Acting Dir., Fourth St. & Greenhill Ave., P.O. Box 2610, Wilmington, 19805. Tel: 302-655-9624; Fax: 302-655-9753 (Refer to separate listings in the Institutions for detailed information on Catholic Charities and related organizations.).

Parish Social Ministry—Mr. ANDREW ZAMPINI, Dir., Fourth St. & Greenhill Ave., P.O. Box 2610, Wilmington, 19805. Tel: 302-655-9624; Fax: 302-655-9753.

Offices Reporting to Vicar General for Adminstration/Moderator of the Curia

Catholic Press Inc., "The Dialog"—Most Rev. MICHAEL A. SALTARELLI, D.D., Publisher; Mr. JIM GRANT, Editor & Gen. Mgr., P.O. Box 2208, Wilmington, 19899. 1925 Delaware Ave., Wilmington, 19806. Tel: 302-573-3109 (Newsroom); 302-573-3112 (Advertising); Fax: 302-573-2397. Email: news@thedialog.org.

Human Resources Office—Sr. SUZANNE DONOVAN, S.C., Dir., P.O. Box 2030, Wilmington, 19899. Tel: 302-573-3126.

Management Information System (MIS)—Mrs. NANCY MOORE, Dir., P.O. Box 2030, Wilmington, 19899. 1925 Delaware Ave., Wilmington, 19806. Tel: 302-573-3122.

Legal Services—JAMES P. COLLINS SR., Esq., Diocesan Attorney, P.O. Box 2030, Wilmington, 19899. 1626 N. Union St., Wilmington, 19806. Tel: 302-573-3138; Fax: 302-573-2351.

Diocesan Planning—Very Rev. Msgr. J. THOMAS CINI, V.G., P.O. Box 2030, Wilmington, 19899. Tel: 302-573-3118.

Diocesan Real Estate Committee—Very Rev. Msgr. J. THOMAS CINI, V.G., Sec., P.O. Box 2030, Wilmington, 19899. Tel: 302-573-3118.

Catholic Ministry to the Elderly—Very Rev. Msgr. J. THOMAS CINI, V.G., Sec., P.O. Box 2030, Wilmington, 19806. Tel: 302-573-3118.

Other Ministries

Catholic Scouting Program—Revs. MICHAEL J. CARRIER, Chap. for Girl Scouts, 500 N. West St., Wilmington, 19801. Tel: 302-654-5920; JAMES D. HREHA, Chap. for Boy Scouts; MICHAEL DARCY, Assoc. Chap., 152 Tulip Dr., Lewes, 19958. Tel: 302-644-7300.

Liaison for Non-Christian Religions—Rev. LEONARD J. KEMPSKI, Liaison, Church of the Good Shepherd, 828 Aiken Ave., Perryville, MD 21903. Tel: 410-642-6534.

Liaison for Evangelization—Very Rev. WILLIAM J. LAWLER, V.F., Liaison, Mailing Address, 303 Chesterfield Ave., Centreville, MD 21617. Tel: 410-758-0140.

Ecumenical Liaison—Rev. Msgr. JOSEPH F. REBMAN, V.G., S.T.L., J.C.L., C.C.C.E., Dir., Mailing Address, P.O. Box 2030, Wilmington, 19899. Tel: 302-573-3100.

Marian Devotions—Rev. Msgr. JOSEPH F. REBMAN, V.G., S.T.L., J.C.L., C.C.C.E., Dir. Associate Directors: Rev. Msgr. JOHN O. BARRES, S.T.D., J.C.L.; Rev. JOSEPH J. PIEKARSKI, Mailing Address, P.O. Box 2030, Wilmington, 19899. Tel: 302-573-3100.

Volunteer Liaison for the Physically Challenged—Mr. BOB CICHOCKI, M.H.S., 260 Christiana Rd., #B-3, New Castle, 19720. Fax: 302-325-2131.

Principal Advisory Groups to the Bishop

College of Consultors—Rev. Msgr. JOSEPH F. REBMAN, V.G., S.T.L., J.C.L., C.C.C.E.; Very Rev. Msgr. J. THOMAS CINI, V.G.; Rev. Msgrs. PAUL J. TAGGART (Retired); CLEMENT P. LEMON; JOHN O. BARRES, S.T.D., J.C.L.; Revs. JOHN J. KAVANAUGH; PHILIP P. SHEEKEY; JOHN P. HOPKINS; JOSEPH J. PIEKARSKI; BARRY LANGLEY, O.F.M., P.O. Box 2030, Wilmington, 19899.

Priests' Council—Rev. JOHN P. HOPKINS, Exec. Officer; Rev. Msgr. JOHN O. BARRES, S.T.D., J.C.L., Sec., P.O. Box 2030, Wilmington, 19899. Tel: 302-573-3100.

Deans—Very Revs. DANIEL W. GERRES, V.F.; WILLIAM J. LAWLER, V.F.; ARTHUR B. FIORE, V.F.; RAYMOND L. FORESTER, V.F.; CHARLES L. BROWN, V.F.; CHRISTOPHER LABARGE, V.F.; Rev. STANLEY J. RUSSELL.

Finance Council—Mr. JOSEPH P. CORSINI, Sec., P.O. Box 2030, Wilmington, 19899. Tel: 302-573-3105.

Parish Priest Consultors—Very Rev. CHARLES L. BROWN, V.F.; Revs. CHARLES C. DILLINGHAM; THOMAS E. HANLEY; JOHN J. KAVANAUGH; Very Rev. CHRIS LABARGE, V.F.; Rev. STANLEY J. RUSSELL.

Priests' Personnel Committee—Rev. JOHN J. MINK, Dir., P.O. Box 2030, Wilmington, 19899. Tel: 302-328-1790.

Women's Commission—Co-Chairs: Sr. CELESTE CRINE, O.S.F., 1925 Delaware Ave., Wilmington, 19806; KIM ZITZNER, 45 Lovett Ave., Newark, 19711.

Other Advisory Groups

Priests' Continuing Formation Committee—Rev. JOHN P. HOPKINS, Chm., St. Margaret of Scotland, 230 Executive Dr., Ste. 8, Newark, 19702. Tel: 302-369-8100; Fax: 302-369-6200.

Council of Religious—Sr. CELESTE CRINE, Contact, Mailing Address, P.O. Box 2030, Wilmington, 19899. Tel: 302-573-3124; Fax: 302-573-3128.

Diocesan School Board—Bro. JAMES MALONE, C.F.X., Sec., Mailing Address, P.O. Box 2030, Wilmington, 19899. Tel: 302-573-3133.

Diocesan Religious Education Board—Mr. EDMUND F. GORDON, Sec., Mailing Address, 1626 N. Union St., Wilmington, 19806. Tel: 302-573-3130; Fax: 302-573-2393.

Diocesan Building Committee—Mr. PAUL S. ADAMS JR., Chm.; Very Rev. Msgr. J. THOMAS CINI, V.G., Episcopal Liaison, P.O. Box 2030, Wilmington, 19899. Tel: 302-573-3118; Fax: 302-573-3128.

Office for Pro-Life Activities—Mr. THOMAS JEWETT, Chm., P.O. Box 2610, Wilmington, 19805. Tel: 302-655-9624; Fax: 302-655-9753.

Pastoral Council—Co Executive Officers: Mr. LAWRENCE BUCCI; BILLY LARSON; Rev. Msgr. JOHN O. BARRES, S.T.D., J.C.L., Sec., Mailing Address, P.O. Box 2030, Wilmington, 19899. Tel: 302-573-3100; Fax: 302-254-4044.

Public Affairs Advisory Committee—Very Rev. Msgr. J. THOMAS CINI, V.G., Chm., P.O. Box 2030, Wilmington, 19899. Tel: 302-573-3118; Fax: 302-573-3128.

Respect Life Committee—Mr. THOMAS JEWETT, Chm., Fourth St. & Greenhill Ave., Wilmington, 19805. Tel: 302-655-9624; Fax: 302-655-9753.

Due Process Commission—Contact: Very Rev. GEORGE J. BRUBAKER, J.C.L., Clerk, P.O. Box 2030, Wilmington, 19899. Tel: 302-573-3107; Fax: 302-573-3128.

Diocesan Corporations

Catholic Cemeteries, Inc.—Rev. Msgr. JOSEPH F. REBMAN, V.G., S.T.L., J.C.L., C.C.C.E., Vice Pres.; Mr. MARK A. CHRISTIAN, C.C.C.E., Sec., P.O. Box 2506, Wilmington, 19805. Tel: 302-656-3323.

Catholic Diocese of Wilmington, Inc.— A corporation sole under the laws of the State of Delaware Rev. Msgr. JOSEPH F. REBMAN, V.G., S.T.L., J.C.L., C.C.C.E., Vice Pres.; Very Rev. Msgr. J. THOMAS CINI, V.G., Sec., Mailing Address, P.O. Box 2030, Wilmington, 19899. Tel: 302-573-3118. Office, 1925 Delaware Ave., Wilmington, 19899.

Catholic Diocese Foundation—Mr. JOSEPH P. CORSINI, Exec. Dir., P.O. Box 2030, Wilmington, 19899. Tel: 302-573-3105.

Catholic Ministry to the Elderly, Inc.—Very Rev. Msgr. J. THOMAS CINI, V.G., Vice Pres., P.O. Box 2030, Wilmington, 19899. Tel: 302-573-3118.

Catholic Press of Wilmington, Inc.—Very Rev. Msgr. J. THOMAS CINI, V.G., Vice Pres., P.O. Box 2208, Wilmington, 19899. Tel: 302-573-3118.

Catholic Charities, Inc.—VACANT, Sec., Fourth St. & Greenhill Ave., P.O. Box 2610, Wilmington, 19806. Tel: 302-655-9624.

Catholic Youth Organization, Inc.—Very Rev. Msgr. J. THOMAS CINI, V.G., Vice Pres., Mailing Address, P.O. Box 2030, Wilmington, 19899. Tel: 302-573-3118.

Children's Home, Inc.—VACANT, Sec., Fourth St. & Greenhill Ave., P.O. Box 2610, Wilmington, 19806. Tel: 302-655-9624.

Diocese of Wilmington Schools, Inc.—Bro. JAMES MALONE, C.F.X., Sec., 1626 N. Union St., Wilmington, 19806. Tel: 302-573-3133.

Seton Villa, Inc.—VACANT, Sec., Fourth St. & Greenhill Ave., P.O. Box 2610, Wilmington, 19806. Tel: 302-655-9624.

Siena Hall, Inc.—VACANT, Sec., Fourth St. & Greenhill Ave., P.O. Box 2610, Wilmington, 19806. Tel: 302-655-9624.

Activities

Apostleship of Prayer—Rev. JOSEPH R. MCMAHON, 7 Sharpley Rd., Wilmington, 19803. Tel: 302-652-6800.

Campaign for Human Development—VACANT, Diocesan Dir., Fourth St. & Greenhill Ave., P.O. Box 2610, Wilmington, 19806. Tel: 302-655-9624.

Catholic Charismatic Renewal—Rev. THOMAS A. FLOWERS, Chap., St. Polycarp, 135 Ransom Lane, Smyrna, 19977. Tel: 302-653-8279.

Catholic Relief Services, Inc.—Very Rev. GEORGE J. BRUBAKER, J.C.L., Diocesan Dir., 506 Seabury Ave., Milford, 19963. Tel: 302-422-5123.

Commission for the Catholic Missions Among the Colored People and the Indians—Rev. JOSEPH F. REBMAN, V.G., Diocesan Dir., P.O. Box 2030, Wilmington, 19899. Tel: 302-573-3100; Fax: 302-573-3128.

Cursillo Movement—Rev. THOMAS E. HANLEY, Spiritual Dir., 631 S. State St., Dover, 19901. Tel: 302-674-5787; Mr. HANK WISNIEWSKI, Lay Dir., 128 Rutherford Rd., Newark, 19715. Tel: 302-737-6837.

Delmarva Catholic Network, Inc.—Mr. ROBERT KREBS, Contact Person, P.O. Box 2030, Wilmington, 19899. Tel: 302-573-3116.

Diocesan Healing Ministry—JEANNE CASEY, Lay Dir., 533 Waterford Dr., Hockessin, 19707. Tel: 302-239-5982.

KAIROS Ministries, Inc.—Rev. GREGORY CORRIGAN, Contact Person, St. Mark's High School, 2501 Pike Creek Rd., Wilm, 19808. Tel: 302-994-2922.

Korean Catholic Community, Inc.—Rev. PETER LEE HAE, Chap.; Mr. JOHN KO, Lay Leader, 2712 Duncan Rd., Wilmington, 19808. Tel: 302-998-7730.

St. Thomas More Society—Rev. Msgr. PAUL J. TAGGART, Chap. (Retired); Rev. JOHN S. GRIMM, Assoc. Chap., Mailing Address, P.O. Box 1320, Wilmington, 19899. Tel: 302-573-3100.

St. Vincent dePaul Society—Mr. PAUL COLLINS, 312 Hazlett Rd., New Castle, 19720. Tel: 302-328-5166.

Organizations With Which Diocese Has Liaison

**Birthright of Delaware, Inc.*—Mrs. MARY JO FROHLICH, Dir., 1311 N. Scott St., Wilmington, 19806. Tel: 302-656-7080.

**Delaware Citizens for Life*—Mr. THOMAS JEWETT, Chm., 4019 Greenmount Rd., Wilmington, 19810.

Delawareans United for Education—Very Rev. Msgr.

J. THOMAS CINI, V.G., P.O. Box 2030, Wilmington, 19899. Tel: 302-573-3118.

Jesus House—Mr. CHRISTIAN MALMGREN, Dir.; ANGELA MALMGREN, Assoc. Dir.; Deacon JOSEPH CONTE, Chap., 2501 Milltown Rd., Wilmington, 19808. Tel: 302-995-6859; Fax: 302-995-6833.

Maryland Catholic Conference— (An agency of the Archdiocese of Baltimore, Washington and the Diocese of Wilmington) Mr. RICHARD J. DOWLING, Exec. Dir., 309 Cathedral St., Baltimore, MD 21201. Tel: 301-322-0901; Very Rev. Msgr. J. THOMAS CINI, V.G., Diocesan Liaison, P.O. Box 2030, Wilmington, 19899. Tel: 302-573-3118.

National Catholic Ministry to the Bereaved—Mr. THOMAS R. JEWETT, M.C., Contact, P.O. Box 2610, Wilmington, 19805. Tel: 302-655-9624; Fax: 302-655-9753.

National Conference for Community and Justice—Rev. CLEMENS D. MANISTA, 3200 Philadelphia Pike, Claymont, 19703. Tel: 302-798-2904.

Operation Help, Inc.—Rev. PATRICK SHAULES, S.J., Pres.; MARCINDA HAEDGE, Sec. & Treas. P.O. Box 134, Hartly, 19953. Tel: 302-397-7065; Fax: 302-397-7065.

Regina Coeli Society—Rev. ROBERTO BALDUCELLI, Chap., 901 N. Dupont St., Wilmington, 19805. Tel: 302-421-3700.

Victim Assistance Coordinator—MARY ELIZABETH "BETH" KRIEGER. Tel: 302-655-9624. Email: bkrieger@ccwilm.org.

World Wide Marriage Encounter—Contact Persons: MIKE RABASCA; KAREN RABASCA. Tel: 410-742-7284; Fax: 410-376-0427.

CLERGY, PARISHES, MISSIONS AND PAROCHIAL SCHOOLS

DELAWARE, CITY OF WILMINGTON
(NEW CASTLE COUNTY)

1—CATHEDRAL OF ST. PETER (1796), Rev. Michael J. Carrier, Rector; Deacon George M. Taylor Jr. In Res., Revs. Carlos R. Vazquez; Mark W. Kopacz.
Res.: 500 West St., 19801. Tel: 302-654-5920; Fax: 302-654-3197.
School—310 W. 6th St., 19801. Tel: 302-656-5234; Fax: 302-658-6489. Daughters of Charity of St. Vincent de Paul 2; Lay Teachers 13; Students 216.
Catechesis/Religious Program—Students 216.

2—ST. ANN (1887), Very Rev. Msgr. J. Thomas Cini, V.G.; Rev. James S. Lentini, St. Ann Church, 2013 Gilpin Ave., 19806; Sisters John Regina Lang, M.S.B.T., Pastoral Assoc.; Marie Bernadette Lang, M.S.B.T., Pastoral Assoc.
Res.: 2013 Gilpin Ave., 19806. Tel: 302-654-5519; 302-652-0152; Fax: 302-654-5527.
School—Tel: 302-652-6567; Fax: 302-652-4156. Mr. Ronald Bogia, Prin. Lay Teachers 17; Students 260.
Catechesis/Religious Program—Tel: 302-654-8504. Anita Wood, D.R.E. Students 115.

3—ST. ANTHONY OF PADUA (1924), (Italian), Revs. John F. McGinley, O.S.F.S.; Charles C. Garst, O.S.F.S.; James M. Turner, O.S.F.S.; Bro. Michael J. Rosenello, O.S.F.S. In Res., Revs. Roberto Balducelli, O.S.F.S.; Mario Bugliosi, O.S.F.S.; Deacon Robert J. Leonzio.
Res.: 901 N. DuPont St., 19805. Tel: 302-421-3700; Fax: 302-421-3709.
School—9th & Scott Sts., 19805. Tel: 302-421-3743; Fax: 302-421-3796. Mr. Bernard J. Fisher, Prin. Sisters of St. Francis of Philadelphia 2; Lay Teachers 24; Students 398.
High School—Padua Academy, 905 N. Broom St., 19805. Tel: 302-421-3739; Fax: 302-421-3748. Sr. Ann Michele Zwosta, O.S.F., Prin. Sisters 2; Lay Teachers 57; Brothers 1; Students 628.
Catechesis/Religious Program—Tel: 302-421-3706; Fax: 302-421-3705. Students 53.
Convent—1710 W. 9th St., 19805. Tel: 302-421-3754. Sisters 2.
Convent—1401 W. 10th St., 19806. Tel: 302-421-3739. Sisters 5.
St. Anthony's Education Fund, Inc.—901 N. Du-Pont St., 19805. Tel: 302-421-3700; Fax: 302-421-3709.

4—CHRIST OUR KING (1926), Revs. James Nash; Theodore E. Olson, J.C.L., M.S.; Deacon William J. Maloney Jr.
Res.: 2810 N. Monroe St., 19802. Tel: 302-762-4140; Fax: 302-762-8414.
School—28th & Madison Streets, 19802. Tel: 302-762-4031; Fax: 302-762-5571. Daughter of Charity 1; Lay Teachers 9; Students 105.
Catechesis/Religious Program—Mr. Robert Leonzio, D.R.E. Students 2.

5—ST. ELIZABETH (1908), Revs. Charles C. Dillingham; Jay R. McKee; Deacon David M. De Ghetto.
Res.: 809 S. Broom St., 19805-4296. Tel: 302-652-3626; Fax: 302-658-5957.
School—1500 Cedar St., 19805-4249. Tel: 302-655-8208; Fax: 302-655-5457. Mr. Francis Corrigan, Prin. Sisters of St. Benedict 2; Lay Teachers 27; Aides 10; Students 491.
High School—Tel: 302-656-3369; Fax: 302-656-7513. Sr. Mary Ellen, O.S.B., Prin. Sisters 5; Lay Teachers 31; Students 422.
Catechesis/Religious Program—St. Hedwig, 408 S. Harrison St., 19805. Tel: 302-594-1400, Ext. 3; Fax: 302-594-1407. Students 32.

6—ST. HEDWIG (1890), (Polish), Revs. Andrew Molewski; Anthony T. Schelich, O.S.F.S.
Res.: 408 S. Harrison St., 19805. Tel: 302-594-1400; Fax: 302-594-1415.
School—Linden & Harrison Sts., 19805. Tel: 302-594-1402; Fax: 302-594-1407. Felician Sisters 1; Lay Teachers 16; Students 241.
Catechesis/Religious Program—Students 48.

7—ST. JOSEPH'S R.C. CHURCH OF WILMINGTON, INC. (1889), Franciscan Pastoral Team:, Rev. Barry J. Langley, O.F.M., Pastoral Moderator; Bro. David W. Schlatter, O.F.M., Admin.; Deacons Robert J. Cousar Jr.; Robert J. Levesque.
Church: 1012 French St., 19801. Tel: 302-658-4535; Fax: 302-656-2167.
Res.: 1010 W. 4th St., 19805.

8—ST. MARY OF THE IMMACULATE CONCEPTION (1858), Rev. David F. Murphy, Admin.
Res.: 1414 King St., 19801. Tel: 302-652-0743; Fax: 302-652-7378.
Church: 6th & Pine Sts., 19801.

9—ST. PATRICK (1880), Rev. David F. Murphy, Admin.
Res.: 1414 King St., 19801. Tel: 302-652-0743; Fax: 302-652-7678.

10—ST. PAUL'S (1869), Rev. John J. Heffernan, O.F.M. (R). In Res., Revs. Barry J. Langley, O.F.M.; Christopher J. Posch, O.F.M.; Bro. David Schlatter, O.F.M.; Revs. Flavian A. Walsh, O.F.M.; Thomas M. Gallagher, O.F.M.; Deacons Angel L. Rivera; Estaban R. Velasquez.
Res.: 1010 W. 4th St., 19805. Tel: 302-655-6596; Fax: 302-655-7684.
School—3rd & Van Buren Sts., 19805. Tel: 302-656-1372; Fax: 302-656-5238. Mrs. Kathleen Connor, Prin. Lay Teachers 16; Students 245.

11—SACRED HEART (1874),, Reopened as Sacred Heart Oratory, Inc. (1998) A Center for Evangelization Revs. Ronald Giannone, O.F.M-.Cap.; Robert Longo, O.F.M.Cap., Admin.; Sr. Christa Rowe, C.S.C., Assoc.
Res.: 917 N. Madison St., 19801. Tel: 302-428-3658; Fax: 302-428-3655.

12—ST. STANISLAUS KOSTKA (1912), (Polish), Rev. Edward J. Kaczorowski.
Mailing Address: P.O. Box 30110, 19805-7110.
Res.: 901 E. 7th St., 19801. Tel: 302-571-0622; Fax: 302-571-1508.

13—ST. THOMAS (1903), Very Rev. Daniel W. Gerres, V.F.; Deacon Francis A. Quinlan.
Res.: 301 N. Bancroft Pkwy., 19805. Tel: 302-658-5131; Fax: 302-652-6222.
School—201 Bayard Ave., 19805. Tel: 302-654-0746; Fax: 302-426-1738. Lay Teachers 13; Students 213.

DELAWARE

OUTSIDE THE CITY OF WILMINGTON

BEAR, NEW CASTLE CO., ST. ELIZABETH ANN SETON (1978), Very Rev. Charles L. Brown, V.F.; Rev. Roger F. DiBuo; Deacons Thomas H. Miller; William Kibler.
Res.: 345 Bear-Christiana Rd., 19701-1048. Tel: 302-322-6430; Fax: 302-322-6297.
Catechesis/Religious Program—Tel: 302-322-8194. Sr. Kathleen Ruszkowski, O.S.B., D.R.E. Students 523.

BELLEFONTE, NEW CASTLE CO., ST. HELENA (Wilmington P.O.) (1936), Revs. Stanley J. Russell; John L Taggart.
Res.: 602 Philadelphia Pike, 19809. Tel: 302-764-0325 Fax: 302-764-1068.
School—210 Bellefonte Ave., 19809. Tel: 302-762-5595 Fax: 302-762-6329. Lay Teachers 11; Assistants 2; Students 210.
Catechesis/Religious Program—Tel: 302-762-4280. Hummy Pennell, D.R.E. Students 111.
Convent—610 Philadelphia Pike, 19809. Tel: 302-764-3427.

BETHANY BEACH, SUSSEX CO., ST. ANN (1955), Rev. David F. Kelley; Deacons Edward Brink; Robert Tracy; Donald Lydick; Dennis Hayden.
Res.: 691 Garfield Ave., P.O. Box 149, 19930. Tel: 302-539-6449; Fax: 302-539-0657.
Catechesis/Religious Program—Tel: 302-539-5443; Fax: 302-539-5509. Students 350

BRANDYWOOD, NEW CASTLE CO., CHURCH OF THE HOLY CHILD (Wilmington P.O.) (1969), Revs. James T. Kirk Jr.; William D. Melnick; Deacon Joseph Cilia Jr.; Sr. Ann Hughes, S.S.J., Pastoral Assoc.
Res.: 2500 Naamans Rd., 19810. Tel: 302-475-6486; Fax: 302-475-3458.
Catechesis/Religious Program—Tel: 302-475-3458. Sr. Margaret Cunniffe, O.S.F., Admin. Asst. Students 310.

CLAYMONT, NEW CASTLE CO., HOLY ROSARY (1921), Revs. Clemens D. Manista; John J. Gayton; Deacons Richard J. Maichle; Allen Wolf. In Res., Rev. William F. Graney.
Res.: 3200 Philadelphia Pike, 19703. Tel: 302-798-2904; 302-798-2987; Fax: 302-798-3609.
School—3110 Philadelphia Pike, 19703. Tel: 302-798-5584; Fax: 302-798-1603. Sisters of St. Joseph 1; Lay Teachers 17; Students 275.
Catechesis/Religious Program—Tel: 302-798-0123. Ms. Maryanne Bemiller, D.R.E. Students 198.

DELAWARE CITY, NEW CASTLE CO., ST. PAUL (1852), Rev. Philip L. Siry.
Res.: 209 Washington St., P.O. Box 544, 19706. Tel: 302-834-4321; Fax: 302-834-7517.

DOVER, KENT CO., HOLY CROSS (1870), [CEM] Revs. Daniel J. McGlynn; James B. Smith; Michael P. Darcy; Maximo Clemente; Deacons Anthony Vinciguerra; Weston "Pete" Nellius; Robert McMullen.
Res.: 631 S. State St., 19901. Tel: 302-674-5780; Fax: 302-674-5783.
School—Tel: 302-674-5784. Mr. William Farley, Prin. Lay Teachers 37; Students 685.
Catechesis/Religious Program—Tel: 302-674-5786. Carmella Jones, D.R.E. Students 600.

ELSMERE, NEW CASTLE CO., CORPUS CHRISTI (Wilmington P.O.) (1948), Revs. Gregory M. Corrigan; Joseph J. Narimattam; Deacons John G. Parisi; William J. Johnston Jr. In Res., Rev. William B. Kauffman.
Res.: 901 New Rd., Elsmere, 19805. Tel: 302-994-2922; Fax: 302-892-3315.
School—907 New Rd., Elsmere, 19805. Tel: 302-995-2231; Fax: 302-993-0767. Sr. Donna Desien, O.S.F., Prin. Sisters 4; Lay Teachers 24; Students 522.
Catechesis/Religious Program—Tel: 302-998-2864. Debbie Ciafre, D.R.E. Students 45.
Convent—912 New Rd., Elsmere, 19805. Tel: 302-994-5641.

FAIRFAX, NEW CASTLE CO., ST. MARY MAGDALEN (Wilmington P.O.) (1951), Revs. Joseph R. McMahon; Stanislao Esposito, St. Mary Magdalen Church, 7 Sharpley Rd., 19803.
Res.: 7 Sharpley Rd., 19803. Tel: 302-652-6800; Fax: 302-652-4771.
School—9 Sharpley Rd., 19803. Tel: 302-656-2745; Fax: 302-656-7889. Barbara Wanner, Prin. Lay Teachers 40; Students 526.
Catechesis/Religious Program—Tel: 302-652-7141. Sheila Meara, D.R.E. Students 148.

GARFIELD PARK, NEW CASTLE CO., HOLY SPIRIT (New Castle P.O.) (1954), Rev. Roy F. Pollard; Deacon Patrick Johnston. In Res., Rev. Philip P. Sheekey.
Res.: 12 Winder Rd., Garfield Park, New Castle, 19720. Tel: 302-658-1069; Fax: 302-658-6890.
School—Church Dr., New Castle, 19720. Tel: 302-658-5345. Sisters 6; Lay Teachers 11; Students 182.
Catechesis/Religious Program—Students 91.

GEORGETOWN, SUSSEX CO., ST. MICHAEL THE ARCHANGEL (1956), Revs. Daniel J. McCloskey Jr.; Edmund Coppinger (Retired); Cesar Gomez (Honduras); Deacon Donald Carroll.
Res.: 202 Edward St., 19947. Tel: 302-856-6451; Fax: 302-856-2353.
Catechesis/Religious Program—Students 109.
Mission—Mary Mother of Peace Rte. 24, Millsboro, Sussex Co. 19966. Tel: 302-945-4044.

GLASGOW, NEW CASTLE CO., ST. MARGARET OF SCOTLAND (1999), Rev. John P. Hopkins; Deacons Raymond R. Zolandz Jr.; Thomas E. Watts.
Res.: 230 Executive Dr., Ste. #8, Newark, 19702. Tel: 302-369-8100; Fax: 302-369-6200.
Catechesis/Religious Program—Tel: 302-369-8100, Ext. 13; Fax: 302-369-6200. Students 525.

GREENVILLE, NEW CASTLE CO., ST. JOSEPH ON THE BRANDYWINE (1841), [CEM 2] Rev. Msgr. Joseph F. Rebman, V.G., S.T.L., J.C.L., C.C.C.E.; Deacon F. Edmund Lynch. In Res., Rev. Msgr. John O. Barres, S.T.D., J.C.L.; Rev. Stephen J. Connell.
Res.: 10 Old Church Rd., 19807. Tel: 302-658-7017; Fax: 302-428-0639.
Catechesis/Religious Program—Tel: 302-656-7185; Fax: 302-658-8723. Sr. Imelda P. Dooley, O.S.F., D.R.E. Students 230.

HOCKESSIN, NEW CASTLE CO., ST. MARY OF THE ASSUMPTION (1882), [CEM] Revs. Stephen C. Lonek; John S. Grimm; Michael J. McDermott; Deacons John W. Freebery Jr.; John Giacci; Joseph W. Jackson Sr.
Res.: 7200 Lancaster Pike, 19707. Tel: 302-239-7100; Fax: 302-239-8219.
Catechesis/Religious Program—Tel: 302-239-7100, Ext. 17. Students 835.

LEWES, SUSSEX CO., ST. JUDE THE APOSTLE (2002), Rev. James D. Hreha; Deacon John A. Smith.

Office:—152 Tulip Dr., 19958. Tel: 302-644-7300; Fax: 302-644-7415.
Catechesis/Religious Program—Tel: 302-644-7413.

LIFTWOOD, NEW CASTLE CO., IMMACULATE HEART OF MARY (Wilmington P.O.) (1955), Rev. Msgr. Clement P. Lemon; Rev. Robert A. Wozniak; Deacon Austin M. Snow Jr.; Theresa H. Gerlach, Pastoral Assoc. In Res., Rev. John Lunness.
Res.: 4701 Weldin Rd., Liftwood, 19803. Tel: 302-764-0357; Fax: 302-764-4381.
School—1000 Shipley Rd., Liftwood, 19803. Tel: 302-764-0977; Fax: 302-764-0375. Carol McCarry, Prin. Lay Teachers 32; Students 522.
Catechesis/Religious Program—Tel: 302-762-5550. Sharon B. Hayes, D.R.E. Students 215.

MIDDLETOWN, NEW CASTLE CO., ST. JOSEPH (1883), [CEM 2] Revs. Steven B. Giuliano; Paul J. Campbell, O.S.F.S.; Deacon John J. Falkowski.
Res.: 115 Cleaver Farm Rd., P.O. Box 630, 19709. Tel: 302-378-5800; Fax: 302-378-5808.
Catechesis/Religious Program—Susan Pascoe, Co-ord.; Tracie Reinhart, Coord. Students 700.
Mission—St. Rose of Lima Lock St., Chesapeake City, Cecil Co., MD 21915.
Shrine—St. Francis Xavier-Old Bohemia Warwick.

MILFORD, KENT AND SUSSEX COS., ST. JOHN THE APOSTLE (1910), Very Rev. George J. Brubaker, J.C.L.; Revs. Rene A. Mangahas; Thomas J. Protack; Deacons James D. Malloy; Anthony Bianco.
Res.: 506 Seabury Ave., 19963-2217. Tel: 302-422-5123; Fax: 302-422-5720.
Catechesis/Religious Program—Tel: 302-422-5123; Fax: 302-422-5720. Students 375.
Mission—St. Bernadette 109 Dixon, Harrington, Kent Co. 19952. Tel: 302-398-8269; Fax: 302-398-0253.

NEW CASTLE, NEW CASTLE CO., ST. PETER (1845), [CEM] Very Rev. Arthur B. Fiore, V.F.; Deacon Thomas G. Halko.
Church, Mailing & Res. address: 521 Harmony St., 19720. Tel: 302-328-2335; Fax: 302-328-0519.
School—6th & Harmony Sts., 19720. Tel: 302-328-1191; Fax: 302-328-8049. Lay Teachers 13; Students 264.
Catechesis/Religious Program—Sr. Joan Lewis, S.S.J., D.R.E. Students 75.

NEWARK, NEW CASTLE CO.
1—ST. JOHN THE BAPTIST-HOLY ANGELS (1891), [CEM] Revs. Richard A. Reissmann; Michael J. Cook; Mark A. Kelleher; Deacons Hugh J. McCann; Francisco Hernandez.
Res.: 82 Possum Park Rd., 19711. Tel: 302-731-2200; Fax: 302-731-2434.
School—Tel: 302-731-2210; Fax: 302-731-2211. Lay Teachers 25; Students 508.
Catechesis/Religious Program—Tel: 302-731-2209. Students 451.
2—ST. THOMAS MORE ORATORY (1975),, (Personal Parish for Students & Faculty of University of Delaware) Rev. Michael F. Szupper, Ph.D.; Kim Zitzner, Pastoral Assoc.
Res.: 155 Haines St., 19711. Tel: 302-368-4728; Fax: 302-368-2548.
Church & Mailing: 45 Lovett Ave., 19711. Tel: 302-368-4728.
Catechesis/Religious Program—Tel: 302-368-4728. Students 35.

NEWARK, NEWCASTLE CO., PARISH OF THE RESURRECTION (1969), Rev. Paul Mast; Deacons Joseph J. Conte; Francis J. Huhn; Tom Bailey.
Office:—3000 Videre Dr., Skyline Ridge, 19808. Tel: 302-368-0146; Fax: 302-368-3536.
Res.: 119 Larkspur Dr., Skyline Ridge, 19711. Tel: 302-737-3066; Fax: 302-368-3536.
Catechesis/Religious Program—Tel: 302-366-1596. Joanne Huhn, D.R.E. Students 312.

OGLETOWN, NEW CASTLE CO., HOLY FAMILY (Newark P.O.) (1979), Revs. Michael Angeloni; John Grasing; Shawn Mahon; Deacons Joseph F. Certesio Sr.; William Murrian; Martin J. Barrett.
Res.: 15 Gender Rd., Newark, 19713. Tel: 302-368-4665; Fax: 302-368-4667.
Catechesis/Religious Program—Tel: 302-368-8976; Fax: 302-368-5184. Melody Duffy, D.R.E.; Donna Wakeman, D.R.E. Students 346.

REHOBOTH, SUSSEX CO., ST. EDMOND (1952), Very Rev. Raymond L. Forester, V.F.
Office—409 King Charles St., P.O. Box 646, Rehoboth Beach, 19971. Tel: 302-227-4550; Fax: 302-227-4557.
Res.: 402 King Charles St., P.O. Box 646, Rehoboth Beach, 19771.
Catechesis/Religious Program—Tel: 302-227-4553. Mrs. Geraldine Buckley, D.R.E. Students 395.

SEAFORD, SUSSEX CO., OUR LADY OF LOURDES (1945), [CEM] Revs. John Harrison, C.SS.R.; Pasquale Tremonte, C.SS.R.; Deacon Arcy Passwaters.
Res.: 528 Stein Hwy., P.O. Box 719, 19973-0719. Tel: 302-629-3591; Fax: 302-629-6758.
Catechesis/Religious Program—Tel: 302-629-7999. Sr. Debra Depta, D.R.E. Students 305.

SHERWOOD PARK, NEW CASTLE CO., ST. JOHN THE BELOVED (1955), Revs. John J. Kavanaugh; Joseph Kandathiparampil; Richard Smith. In Res., Deacon James Haley.
Res.: 907 Milltown Rd., 19808. Tel: 302-999-0211; Fax: 302-999-9184.
School—903 Milltown Rd., 19808. Tel: 302-998-5525. Sisters of St. Francis of Philadelphia 2; Lay Teachers 29; Students 612.
Catechesis/Religious Program—Tel: 302-994-7757. Pauline Berlingieri, D.R.E. Students 614.

SMYRNA, KENT CO., ST. POLYCARP (1883), Rev. Thomas A. Flowers; Deacon Charles Robinson.
Res.: 135 Ransom Ln., 19977. Tel: 302-653-8279; Fax: 302-653-3509.
Catechesis/Religious Program—Tel: 302-653-4101. Sr. Ellen Gerlach, D.R.E. Students 200.

WILMINGTON MANOR, NEW CASTLE CO., OUR LADY OF FATIMA (New Castle P.O.) (1948), Revs. John J. Mink; Timothy M. Nolan; Steven P. Hurley, Our Lady of Fatima Church, 801 DuPont Blvd., New Castle, 19720; Deacon Joseph C. Romans.
Res.: 801 Dupont Blvd., New Castle, 19720. Tel: 302-328-3431; 302-328-5773; Fax: 302-328-6318.
School—Tel: 302-328-2803; Fax: 302-328-5427. Lay Teachers 27; Students 491.
Catechesis/Religious Program—Tel: 302-328-0307. Patricia Walker, D.R.E. Teachers 20; Students 182.

WILMINGTON, NEW CASTLE CO., ST. CATHERINE OF SIENA (Wilmington P.O.) (1960), Rev. John M. Hynes; Deacon Francis J. Staab. In Res., Rev. Christopher H. Plokhooy (Retired).
Res.: 2503 Centerville Rd., 19808. Tel: 302-633-4900; Fax: 302-633-4960.
School—Tel: 302-633-4901; Fax: 302-633-4902. Lay Teachers 16; Students 278.
Catechesis/Religious Program—2503 Centerville Rd.. Tel: 302-633-4903; Fax: 302-633-4960. Sr. Theresa Cappelli, D.R.E. Students 346.

WOODCREST, NEW CASTLE CO., ST. MATTHEW (1941), Revs. Joseph J. Drobinski; William M. Hazzard; William J. Klapps, (Retired U.S.N.) (Retired); Deacons Harold Chalfant; Michael T. Wilber; William A. Kaper.
Res.: 3 Curtis Ave., 19804. Tel: 302-633-5850; Fax: 302-633-6022.
School—One Fallon Ave., 19804. Tel: 302-633-5860; Fax: 302-633-3787. Lay Teachers 23; Students 488.
Catechesis/Religious Program—811 Newport Pk, 19804. Tel: 302-633-5858. Students 171.

MARYLAND

CAMBRIDGE, DORCHESTER CO., ST. MARY REFUGE OF SINNERS (1885), [CEM] Rev. Bruce Byrolly.
Res.: 1515 Glasgow St., Box 218, MD 21613. Tel: 410-228-4770; Fax: 410-228-0969.
Catechesis/Religious Program—Tel: 410-228-2701. Sr. Kathleen Winkleman, O.S.F., D.R.E. Students 68.
Mission—St. Mary, Star of the Sea [CEM] Meekin's Neck, Dorchester Co., MD.

CENTREVILLE, QUEEN ANNE CO., OUR MOTHER OF SORROWS (1890), [CEM] Very Rev. William J. Lawler, V.F.; Deacon Kenneth M. Hanbury.
Res.: 303 Chesterfield Ave., MD 21617. Tel: 410-758-0140; Fax: 410-758-5463.
Catechesis/Religious Program—Tel: 410-758-0143. Sr. Elaine McCarron, S.C.N., D.R.E. Students 215.
Mission—St. Peter Gateway, MD. 5319 Ocean, Queenstown, Queen Anne Co., MD 21658. Tel: 410-827-8084.

CHESTER, KENT ISLAND, QUEEN ANNE CO., ST. CHRISTOPHER (1954), Revs. Paul F. Jennings Jr.; Joseph V. Bozzelli; Deacon John Robinson Jr.
Res.: Box 660, 1861 Harbor Dr., MD 21619. Tel: 410-643-6220; Fax: 410-643-4055.
Catechesis/Religious Program—Tel: 410-643-8489. Students 500.

CHESTERTOWN, KENT CO., SACRED HEART (1876), [CEM] Rev. Leonard J. Blakely.
Res.: 508 High St., MD 21620. Tel: 410-778-3160; Fax: 410-810-0427.
Catechesis/Religious Program—Tel: 410-778-4650. Sr. Elaine McCarron, S.C.N., D.R.E. Students 108.
Mission—St. John W. Main St., Rock Hall, Kent Co., MD 21661. Tel: 410-778-3160.
Mission—Most Precious Blood 1910 Main St., Betterton, Kent Co., MD 21610.

EASTON, TALBOT CO., SS. PETER AND PAUL (1868), [CEM] Revs. Robert E. Coine; Cornelius J. Breslin.
Res.: 215 Goldsborough St., MD 21601. Tel: 410-822-2344; Fax: 410-770-5080.
School—900 High St., MD 21601. Tel: 410-822-2251; Fax: 410-820-0136. Lay Teachers 30; Students 507.
High School—Tel: 410-822-2275; Fax: 410-822-1767. Lay Teachers 25; Students 194.
Catechesis/Religious Program—Tel: 410-822-6581; Fax: 410-822-6581. Mrs. Marianne Wegener, D.R.E. Students 1,022.
Mission—St. Joseph 13209 Church Lane, Cordova, Talbot Co., MD 21625. Tel: 410-364-5543.
Mission—St. Michael 109 Lincoln Ave., St. Michaels, Talbot Co., MD 21663. Tel: 410-745-2822.

ELKTON, CECIL CO., IMMACULATE CONCEPTION (1849), [CEM 2] Revs. Joseph J. Piekarski; Francis P. Kenney; Deacon Joseph J. Kosman.
Office—455 Bow St., P.O. Box 345, MD 21922. Tel: 410-398-1100; Fax: 410-398-1175.
Res.: 300 Maryland Ave., MD 21922.
School—452 Bow St., MD 21921. Tel: 410-398-2636; 410-398-4161; Fax: 410-398-1190. Sisters of St. Francis of Philadelphia 3; Lay Teachers 20; Students 266.
Catechesis/Religious Program—Tel: 410-392-3551; Fax: 410-392-9917. Sr. Grace Andrew, D.R.E. Students 488.
Mission—St. Jude 928 Turkey Point, North East, Cecil Co., MD 21901.

GALENA, KENT CO., ST. DENNIS (1856), [CEM] Rev. Thomas J. Peterman.
Mailing Address: P.O. Box 249, MD 21635. Tel: 410-648-5145; Fax: 410-648-5767.
Catechesis/Religious Program—Tel: 410-648-5287. Students 143.

MARYDEL, CAROLINE CO., IMMACULATE CONCEPTION (1916), Very Rev. Christopher LaBarge, V.F.
Res.: 522 Main St., Box 399, MD 21649. Tel: 410-482-7687; Fax: 410-482-7253.
Catechesis/Religious Program—Tel: 410-482-8939. Students 128.

OCEAN CITY, WORCESTER CO.
1—ST. LUKE AND ST. ANDREW (1985), Revs. Raymond F. Weisman; Edward J. Fahey; Thomas J. Protack; Deacons Jack H. Campbell; Edward Holson; John Lemon.
Office—144th St. & Lighthouse Ave., P.O. Box 3400, MD 21843. Tel: 410-250-0300; 410-250-0301; Fax: 410-250-0417.
Res.: 403 141st St., MD 21843. Tel: 410-250-0399; Fax: 410-250-0417.
Catechesis/Religious Program—Tel: 410-250-0342. Mrs. Mary Anne Blatzheim, D.R.E. Students 285.
Mission—St. John Neumann Rt. 589 & Beauchamp Rd., Ocean Pines, Worcester Co., MD 21811. Tel: 410-208-2956.
2—ST. MARY, STAR OF THE SEA (1877), Rev. John P. Klevence; Deacon Edward Gardner Sr.
Res.: 208 S. Baltimore Ave., MD 21842-4106. Tel: 410-289-9419.
Office: 212 Kingfish St., MD 21842. Tel: 410-289-0652.
Catechesis/Religious Program—Tel: 410-289-7038. Elizabeth A. Sacca-Kuczinski, D.R.E. Students 195.
Mission—Holy Saviour Philadelphia Ave. & 17th St., Worcester Co., MD 21842.

PERRYVILLE, CECIL CO., CHURCH OF THE GOOD SHEPHERD (1949), Rev. Leonard J. Kempski.
Res.: 810 Aiken Ave., MD 21903. Tel: 410-642-6534; Fax: 410-642-2234.
School—800 Aiken Ave., MD 21903. Tel: 410-642-6265; Fax: 410-642-6522. Lay Teachers 17; Students 225.
Catechesis/Religious Program—Tel: 410-642-6534. Students 205.
Mission—St. Teresa 162 N. Main St., Port Deposit, Cecil Co., MD 21904.
Mission—St. Patrick Pilottown, Cecil Co., MD.
Mission—St. Agnes 150 S. Queen St., Rising Sun, Cecil Co., MD 21911. Tel: 410-658-9422.

POCOMOKE CITY, WORCESTER CO., HOLY NAME OF JESUS (1943), Rev. William J. Porter.
Res.: 1913 Old Virginia Rd., P.O. Box 179, MD 21851. Tel: 410-957-1215; Fax: 410-957-1214.
Catechesis/Religious Program—Nancy Atkinson, D.R.E. Students 85.
Mission—St. Elizabeth 8734 Old Westover Rd., Westover, Somerset Co., MD 21871. Tel: 410-651-9117.

RIDGELY, CAROLINE CO., ST. BENEDICT (1896), [CEM 2] Rev. Norman P. Carroll; Deacons Harold D. Jopp Jr.; William G. Nickum; Bradley D. Taylor.
Res.: 408 Central Ave., P.O. Box 459, MD 21660. Tel: 410-634-2253; Fax: 410-634-1997.
Catechesis/Religious Program—Tel: 410-634-1921; Fax: 410-634-1997. Students 196.
Mission—St. Elizabeth [CEM] First St. & Franklin St., Denton, Caroline Co., MD 21629.

SALISBURY, WICOMICO CO., ST. FRANCIS DE SALES (1910), Revs. Edward M. Aigner Jr.; Ralph T. Castelow; Michael B. Roark; Deacons Carl R. Beers; Ron R. Siers; James E. Dean; Stephen Kuczma. In Res., Rev. Johnny Laura Lazo.
Res.: 514 Camden Ave., MD 21801. Tel: 410-742-6443; Fax: 410-742-9410.
School—500 Camden Ave., MD 21801. Tel: 410-749-9907; Fax: 410-749-9507. Sr. M. Jane Veldof, R.S.M., Prin. Lay Teachers 20; Students 298.
Catechesis/Religious Program—Tel: 410-546-2908. Michele Harris, D.R.E. Students 630.
Convent—417 Wicomico St., MD 21801. Tel: 410-742-9343.

Mission—Holy Redeemer Bi-State Blvd. & Chestnut St., Delmar, Wicomico Co., MD 21875.

SECRETARY, DORCHESTER CO., OUR LADY OF GOOD COUNSEL (1891), [CEM] Rev. Anthony F. Greco. Res.: 109 Willow Street, P.O. Box 278, MD 21664. Tel: 410-943-4300; Fax: 410-943-1357.

Catechesis/Religious Program—Students 74.

Mission—Holy Child P.O. Box 278, Bethlehem, Caroline Co., MD 21664.

Chaplains of Public Institutions

National Guard

WILMINGTON. *Delaware Air National Guard.* 506 Seabury Ave., Milford, 19963. Tel: 302-422-5123. Very Rev. George J. Brubaker, J.C.L.

Delaware Army National Guard. Revs. John J. Mink, Chap., David F. Murphy, Chap.

Health Care

WILMINGTON. *St. Francis Hospital,* 7th St. & Clayton St., 19805. Tel: 302-421-4577. Revs. John Finn, O.S.F.S., Joseph J. McKenna, O.S.F.S.

DELAWARE CITY. *Governor Bacon Health Center.* Rev. Philip L. Siry, Chap. Tel: 302-834-4321.

ELSMERE. *Veteran's Hospital,* 1601 Kirkwood Hwy.. Tel: 302-994-2511. Revs. Sean P. Connery, O.S.F.S., Chap., William J. Dougherty, O.S.F.S., Chap., William B. Kauffman, Chap.

NEW CASTLE. *Delaware Psychiatric Hospital.* Rev. Carlos R. Vazquez, Chap. Tel: 302-577-4360.

NEWARK. *Christiana Care Health Services, Inc.,* 4755 Ogletown-Stanton Rds.. Tel: 302-733-1900; 302-733-1280.

Wilmington Hospital. 14th & Washington Sts., 19805. Tel: 302-733-1280. Rev. William F. Graney, Chap.

PERRY POINT. *Veterans Admin..* Rev. Jeffrey Reynolds.

SMYRNA. *Delaware Home & Hospital for the Chronically Ill.* Rev. Thomas A. Flowers, Chap. Tel: 302-653-8279.

Correctional Facilities

WILMINGTON. *Ferris School and Bridge House.* (Vacant)

Gander Hill Correctional Center. Very Rev. Daniel W. Gerres, V.F., Chap. Tel: 302-764-0357.

SMYRNA. *Delaware State Correctional Center.* Rev. James M. Jackson, Chap. Tel: 302-653-9261, Ext. 487.

WESTOVER. *Eastern Correctional Institution.* Rev. Edward M. Aigner Jr., Chap. Tel: 410-742-6443.

Campus Ministry

CHESTERTOWN. *Washington College,* Sacred Heart, 508 High St., MD 21620. Tel: 410-778-3160. Deacon Joseph J. Kosman, Chap.

DOVER. *Wesley College.* Rev. Michael F. Szupper, Ph.D., Chap. Tel: 302-368-4728.

NEWARK. *University of Delaware,* St. Thomas More Oratory, 45 Lovett Ave., 19711. Tel: 302-368-4728. Rev. Michael F. Szupper, Ph.D., Chap. & Dir. Campus Ministry.

SALISBURY. *Salisbury State College,* 211 W. College Ave., MD 21801. Tel: 410-219-3376. Mrs. Regina Yankalunas, Campus Min.

University of Maryland, Eastern Shore, 211 W. College Ave., MD 21801. Tel: 410-219-3376. Mrs. Regina Yankalunas, Campus Min.

Apostleship of the Sea:
Rev.—
Kauffman, William B., Chap., 901 New Rd., 19805. Tel: 302-994-2922

Nursing Homes:
Rev.—
Sheekey, Philip P., Chap., NCC Health Care Facilities, 10 Winder Rd., New Castle, 19720. Tel: 302-658-1069

Special or Other Diocesan Assignment:
Revs.—
Glapiak, Edward, 3 Towne Estates, Apt. G3, 19805.
Richardson, James E., 2504 Blackwood Rd., 19810. Tel: 302-475-6252

On Duty Outside the Diocese:
Rev. Msgr.—
Koper, Francis B., SS. Cyril and Methodius Seminary, Orchard Lake, MI 48033.
Revs.—
Gallagher, Michael J., Trinity College, Theology Dept., 125 Michigan Ave., Washington, DC 20017.
McMahon, Kevin T., S.T.B., S.T.L., S.T.D., St. Charles Borromeo Seminary, 1000 E. Wynnewood Rd. Overbrook, Philadelphia, PA 19096.
Mullen, Owen J., Holy Family Church, 830 Main St., Honolulu, HI 96818.
O'Neill, Patrick J., P.O. Box 2030, W, 19899.
Pagano, Bernard T., St. Mary of Mt. Virgin, 190 Sanford St., New Brunswick, NJ 08901
Turley, Sean F., SS. Michael and James, Haunton near Tamworth, Staffordshire B799HL (1848) England.

Military Chaplains:
Revs.—
Kopec, Christopher A., Box 33422, Fort Lewis, WA 98433-0422.
Volmi, Dennis G., 4WGHC, 1505 Vermont Garrison St., Seymour Johnson AFB, NC 27531-2449.

Absent on Sick Leave:
Revs.—
Casari, Michael T., P.O. Box 2030, 19899
Gomolski, Joseph T., 241 Balboa Dr., Kissimmee, FL 34753.
Hanley, Thomas E., P.O. Box 2030, 19899.
Mathesius, William P., P.O. Box 2030, 19899.
McDermott, Michael J., P.O. Box 2030, W, 19899.
O'Neill, Patrick J., P.O. Box 2030, 19899
Trainor, James F., Jeanne Jugan Residence, 185 Salem Church Rd., Newark, 19713-2997.

Retired:
Rev. Msgrs.—
Brady, Patrick A., Vianney House, 905 Milltown Rd., 19808.
Dewson, John H., Vianney House, 905 Milltown Rd., 19808. (Retired)
Taggart, Paul J., 1401 Pennsylvania Ave., #1411, 19806.
Revs.—
Clark, Howard T., P.O. Box 147, Essington, PA 19029.
Coppinger, Edmund, 225 28th St., Richmond, CA 94804. (Retired)
Eckrich, James P., 773 Paper Mill Rd., Newark, 19711.
Frundt, Oscar H., 417 Delaware Ave., 19803.
Gardocki, Thomas F., 4620 Sylvanus Dr., 19803.
Jennings, William E., 2303 Inglewood Dr., 19803.
Klapps, William J., Caravel Farms, 260 Benjamin Blvd., Bear, 19701.
Kochan, Frederick A., 2201-A Baltimore Ave., Lavellette, NJ 08735.
McGann, L. Philip, 316 Cedar Lane, Mount Laurel, NJ 08054. (Retired)
Plokhooy, Christopher H., 2505 Center Ville Rd., 19808. (Retired)
Rhodes, George V., Vianney House, 905 Milltown Rd., 19808.
Storck, Edward J., 1504-2 N. Broom St., #17, 19806.

Permanent Deacons:
Bailey, Thomas A., Resurrection Parish, Newark, DE
Baker, Joseph G., (Retired)
Barrett, Martin J., Holy Family Parish, Newark, DE
Beers, Carl, St. Francis de Sales, Salisbury, MD
Bianco, Anthony A., St. Bernadette, Milford, DE
Brink, Edward J., St. Ann, Bethany Beach, DE
Campbell, Jack H., (Retired)
Carroll, Donald T., St. Michael the Archangel, Georgetown, DE
Certesio, Joseph F., Sr., Holy Family Parish, Newark, DE
Chalfant, Harold F., St. Matthew, Wilmington, DE
Cilia, Joseph A., Jr., Asst. Chap., Next Step Group, Church of the Holy Childhood, Wilmington, DE
Cimino Thomas S., Eastern Correctional Institute, Westover, MD; Holy Name of Jesus, Pocomoke City, MD
Conte, Joseph J., (Retired)
Costello, John L., (Retired)
Cousar, Robert J., Jr., St. Joseph Parish, Wilmington, DE
Dean, James E., St. Francis de Sales Parish, Salisbury, MD
DeGhetto, David M., St. Elizabeth Parish, Wilmington, DE
Dunning, Edward A., (Retired)
Falkowski, John J., St. Joseph, Middletown, DE
Freebery, John W., Jr., St. Mary of the Assumption, Hockessin, DE
Gardner, Edward, Sr., St. Mary Star of the Sea, Ocean City, MD
Giacci, John, St. Mary of the Assumption, Hockessin, DE
Haley, James J., St. John the Beloved, Wilmington, DE
Halko, Thomas G., St. Peter the Apostle Parish, New Castle, DE
Hanbury, Kenneth M., Our Mother of Sorrows, Centreville, MD
Handlir, James, Jeanne Jugan Residence, Newark, DE
Hayden, Dennis L., St. Ann, Bethany Beach, DE
Holson, Edward G., St. Luke/St. Andrew, Ocean City, MD
Huhn, Francis J., Parish of the Resurrection, Newark, DE
Jackson, Joseph W., Sr., St. Mary of the Assumption Parish, Hockessin, DE; Jesus House, Wilmington, DE
Johnston, Patrick K., Holy Spirit Parish, New Castle, DE
Johnston, William J., Corpus Christi Parish, Elsmere, DE
Jopp, Harold D., Jr., St. Benedict's, Ridgely, MD
Kaper, William A., St. Matthew Parish, Wilmington, DE
Kibler, William, III, St. Elizabeth Ann Seton, Bear, DE
Kosman, Joseph J., Immaculate Conception Parish, Elkton, MD; Washington College, Chestertown, MD
Kuczma, Stephen, St. Francis de Sales Parish, Salisbury, MD
Lafferty, James J., Jr., (Retired)
Lemon, John, St. Luke/St. Andrew, Ocean City, MD
Leonzio, Robert J., St. Anthony of Padua Parish, Wilmington, DE
Levesque, Robert J., St. Joseph Parish, Wilmington, DE
Lydick, Donald E., St. Ann, Bethany Beach, DE
Lynch, Edmund F., St. Joseph on the Brandywine, Greenville, DE
Maichle, Richard J., Holy Rosary, Claymont, DE
Malloy, James D., St. John the Apostle, Milford, DE
Maloney, William, Jr., (Retired)
McCann, Hugh J., (Retired)
McMullen, Robert E., Holy Cross Parish, Dover, DE
Miller, Thomas H., St. Elizabeth Ann Seton, Bear, DE
Murrian, William J., Holy Family, Newark, DE
Nellius, Weston E., Holy Cross Parish, Dover, DE
Nickum, William G., St. Benedict Parish, Ridgely, MD
Normoyle, Robert H., (Retired)
O'Connor, Howard J., (Retired)
Paolucci, Robert, St. Mary Refuge of Sinners, Cambridge, MD
Parisi, John G., Corpus Christi, Wilmington, DE
Passwaters, Arcy A., Our Lady of Lourdes, Seaford, DE
Quinlan, Francis A., St. Thomas the Apostle, Wilmington, DE
Recce, Richard L., (Retired)
Rivera, Angel, St. Paul, Wilmington, DE
Robinson, Charles, St. Christopher, Chester, MD
Romans, Joseph C., Our Lady of Fatima, New Castle and Christiana Div., Christiana Care Health System, Newark, DE
Rose, Albert F., (Retired)
Siers, Ronald, St. Francis de Sales, Salisbury, MD
Smith, John A., St. Jude The Apostle, Lewes, DE
Snow, Austin M., Jr., Immaculate Heart of Mary, Wilmington, DE; Chap., Seton Villa & Siena Hall, Wilmington, DE
Staab, Francis J., St. Catherine of Siena, Wilmington, DE
Taylor, Bradley D., St. Benedict Parish, Ridgely, MD
Taylor, George M., Jr., Cathedral of St. Peter, Wilmington, DE
Tracy, Robert, St. Ann, Bethany Beach, DE
VanBourgondien, Cornelius J., (Retired)
Velasquez, Estaban, St. Paul, Wilmington, DE
Vinciguerra, Anthony P., Holy Cross, Dover, DE
Watts, Thomas, St. Margaret of Scotland, Newark, DE
Wilber, Michael T., St. Matthew Parish, Wilmington, DE
Wolf, Allen S., Claymont, DE, Holy Rosary; Christiana Div., Christiana Care Health System, Newark, DE
Zolandz, Raymond R., Jr., St. Margaret of Scotland Parish, Glasgow, DE

INSTITUTIONS LOCATED IN THE DIOCESE

[A] HIGH SCHOOLS, DIOCESAN

WILMINGTON. *St. Mark's High School,* 2501 Pike Creek Rd., 19808. Tel: 302-738-3300; Fax: 302-738-5132. Email: mfreund@stmarkshs.org. Mr. Mark John Freund, Prin.; Rev. Gregory M. Corrigan. Priests 1; Sisters 4; Lay Teachers 115; Students 1,566.

MAGNOLIA. *St. Thomas More Academy* 133 Thomas More Dr., 19962. Tel: 302-697-8100; Fax: 302-697-8122. Email: jgrant@saintmore.org. Web: www.saintmore.org. Jonathan M. Grant, Ph.D., Prin.; Rev. Michael P. Darcy, Chap. Priests 1; Lay

Teachers 12; Students 150.

[B] HIGH SCHOOLS, PRIVATE

WILMINGTON. *Salesianum School*, 1801 N. Broom St., 19802. Tel: 302-654-2495; Fax: 302-654-7767. Email: saloblates@aol.com. Web: www.salesianum.org. Revs. John J. Fisher, O.S.F.S., Prin.; Thomas B. Curran, O.S.F.S., Pres.; James Dalton, O.S.F.S., Asst. Prin.; Stephen E. Shott, O.S.F.S.; Thomas J. Tucker, O.S.F.S., Supr.; Sean P. Connery, O.S.F.S.; Stanley R. Drupieski, O.S.F.S.; Robert D. Kenney, O.S.F.S.; John A. Kolodziej, O.S.F.S.; John A. Kowalewski, O.S.F.S.; William T. McCandless, O.S.F.S.; John M. Mokluk, O.S.F.S.; Francis J. Pileggi, O.S.F.S.; Edward J. Roszko, O.S.F.S., B.A.; John P. Spellman, O.S.F.S.; Bro. Joseph G. Schodowski, O.S.F.S.; Rev. Mark J. Wrightson, O.S.F.S. Priests 16; Brothers 2; Lay Teachers 69; Boys 1,009. In Res. Bro. Edward F. Ogden, O.S.F.S.

Ursuline Academy of Wilmington, DE, Inc., 1106 Pennsylvania Ave., 19806. Tel: 302-658-7158; Fax: 302-658-4297. Email: jkeegan@ursuline.org. Web: www.ursuline.org. James M. Keegan, Interim Pres. (Coed Grades Early Childhood-3, All Girls Grades 4-12) Lay Faculty 80; Ursuline Nuns 1; Students 653.

CLAYMONT. *Archmere Academy*, 3600 Philadelphia Pike, 19703. Tel: 302-798-6632; Fax: 302-798-7290. Email: generale-mailbox@archmereacademy.com. Web: www.archmereacademy.com. Revs. Timothy F. Mullen, O.Praem., Headmaster; Joseph P. McLaughlin, O.Praem., Chap.; Very Rev. Michael T. Collins, O.Praem.; Rev. Blaise P. Krautsack, O.Praem. Coed College Prepatory High School. Priests 4; Lay Teachers 52; Students 495.

[C] INTERPAROCHIAL SCHOOLS

BERLIN. *Most Blessed Sacrament Catholic School*, 11242 Racetrack Rd., MD 21811. Tel: 410-208-1600; Fax: 410-208-4757. Ms. Amy Mike, Prin.

NEWARK. *Christ the Teacher Catholic School*, (Grades K-6), 2451 Frazer Rd., 19702. Tel: 302-838-8850; Fax: 302-838-8854. Email: slking@christtheteacher.org. Lay Teachers 19; Students 519; Total Staff 46.

[D] ELEMENTARY SCHOOLS, PRIVATE

WILMINGTON. *Saint Edmond's Academy*, (Grades 4-8), 2120 Veale Rd., 19810. Tel: 302-475-5370; Fax: 302-475-2256. Email: jhart@stedmondsacademy.org. Web: stedmondsacademy.org. Bros. Michael A. Smith, C.S.C., Headmaster; Joseph Ash, C.S.C.; James DeTemple, C.S.C.; Thomas Meany, C.S.C.; Edward Quintal, C.S.C. Brothers of Holy Cross 5; Lay Teachers 22; Boys 270.

CHILDS. *Mount Aviat Academy*, (Grades PreK-8), 399 Childs Rd., MD 21916. Tel: 410-398-2206; Fax: 410-398-8063. Email: school@mountaviat.org. Web: www.mountaviat.org. Sr. John Elizabeth, O.S.F.S., Prin. Oblate Sisters of St. Francis de Sales Sisters 3; Lay Teachers 8; Students 263.

RIDGELY. *The Benedictine School for Exceptional Children*, 14299 Benedictine Ln., MD 21660. Tel: 410-634-2112; Fax: 410-634-2640. Email: benefound@aol.com. Web: www.benschool.com. Sr. Jeannette Murray, O.S.B., Dir. Sisters of St. Benedict Sisters 7; Lay Teachers 20; Students 102.

Benedictine School for Exceptional Children Foundation, Inc., 14299 Benedictine Ln., MD 21660. Tel: 410-634-2292; Fax: 410-634-1855. Email: benefound@aol.com. Web: benschool.com. Sr. Jeannette Murray, O.S.B., Dir. Sisters 1; Lay Staff 4.

[E] DIOCESAN CATHOLIC CHARITIES PROGRAM

WILMINGTON. *Catholic Charities, Inc.*, 2601 W. 4th St., P.O. Box 2610, 19805-0610. Tel: 302-655-9624; Fax: 302-655-9753. Web: www.cdow.org/charities.html. Ms. Barbara Grieco, M.C., M.B.A., Acting Dir.; Katrina Furlong, B.A., Dir. Community & Family Support Svcs.; Mr. Frederick Jones, M.S., Dir. of Children's Svcs.; Ms. Laura Hummel, M.S.N., R.N.C.S., C.A.D.C., Dir. Behavioral Healthcare Svcs.; Ms. Donna Connor, B.A., C.F.R.E., Dir. Devel. & Community Rels. Staff 172; Individuals Served 54,500; Fuel Program 30,410.

Energy Assistance Program

New Castle Office Tel: 302-654-9295.

Sussex Office Tel: 302-856-6310.

Kent Office Tel: 302-674-1782.

Counseling and Social Services

Wilmington Office, 4th St. & Greenhill Ave., P.O. Box 2610, 19805-0610. Tel: 302-656-0651.

Dover Office, 1155 W. Walker Rd., Dover, 19904. Tel: 302-674-1600.

Georgetown Office, 406 S. Bedford St., Ste. 9, Georgetown, 19947. Tel: 302-856-9578.

Sailsbury Office, 1405 Wesley Dr., Salisbury, MD 21801. Tel: 410-749-1121.

Children's Services (Adoption & Foster Care), 4th St. & Greenville Ave., P.O. Box 2610, 19805-0610. Tel: 302-665-9624. Ms. Neomi Litonjua, L.C.S.W., Supvr.

Family & Individual Services (including Family Life Bureau), 4th St. & Greenhill Ave., P.O. Box 2610, 19805-0610. Tel: 302-665-9624. Mr. Thomas R. Jewett, M.C., Dir., Family Life Bureau.

HIV Family Resource Center (AIDS Ministry), 2825 Madison St., 19802. Tel: 302-762-9244. Michael Hassler, Prog. Mgr.

Community and Family Support Services

Crisis Alleviation

4th St. & Greenhill Ave., P.O. Box 2610, 19805-0610. Tel: 302-654-6473. Sharon Truitt, Contact Person.

1155 W. Walker Rd., Dover, 19904. Tel: 302-674-4016. Sheena Naber, Contact Person; Katrina Furlong, B.A., Dir. Community Svcs.

New Castle Co. Tel: 302-654-6473.

Kent Co. Tel: 302-674-4016.

Sussex Co. Tel: 302-856-6310.

Energy Assistance

New Castle Co. Tel: 302-654-9295.

Kent Co. Tel: 302-674-1782.

Sussex Co. Tel: 302-856-6310.

Immigration & Refugee Services

4th St. and Greenhill Ave., P.O. Box 2610, 19805-0610. Tel: 302-654-6460. Mabel Surgeon, Supvr.

406 S. Bedford St., Ste. 9, Georgetown, 19947. Tel: 302-856-9578. Leila Krouse, Contact Person.

Catholic Charities Thrift Center, 1320 E. 23rd St., 19802. Tel: 302-764-2717. Diane Giovannozzi, Mgr.

Child & Adult Care Food Program

1155 W. Walker Rd., Dover, 19904. Tel: 302-674-1600; 800-239-2839. Donna Costilow, Contact Person.

New Castle Co. Tel: 302-655-9624. Joanne Varnes, Contact Person.

Sussex Co. Tel: 302-856-3414. Karen Adams, Contact Person.

Counseling and Substance Abuse Services, Fifth St. & Greenhill Ave., P.O. Box 2610, 19805-0610. Tel: 302-665-0651. Ms. Laura Hummel, M.S.N., R.N.C.S., C.A.D.C., Dir., Behavioral Health Svcs.

Residential Services, 2901 Green St., Claymont, 19703. Tel: 302-798-0601. Frederick Jones, M.S., Dir. Children's Svcs.

Siena Hall, Inc., P.O. Box 2610, 19805. Tel: 302-655-9624. Frederick Jones, M.S., Dir. Children's Svcs.

Seton Villa, Inc., 800 Bellevue Rd., 19809. Tel: 302-762-2982. Mr. Fritz Jones, M.S., Dir. Children's Svcs.

Children's Home, 2901 Green St., Claymont, 19703. Tel: 302-798-0601. Frederick Jones, M.S., Dir. Children's Svcs.

Casa San Francisco, 127 Broad St., P.O. Box 38, Milton, 19968. Tel: 302-684-8694; Fax: 302-684-2808. Elizabeth Moore, Prog. Mgr.

Seton Center, 30632 Hampden Ave., P.O. Box 401, Princess Anne, MD 21853. Tel: 410-651-9608.

Office for Parish Social Ministry, 4th St. & Greenhill Ave., P.O. Box 2610, 19805-0610. Tel: 302-655-9624. Andrew Zampini, S.F.O., Dir.

[F] RESIDENCES FOR CHILDREN

WILMINGTON. *Seton Villa, Inc.*, 800 Bellevue Rd., 19809. Tel: 302-762-2982; Fax: 302-762-3187. Email: fjones@ccwilm.org. Web: www.cdow.org. Ms. Fritz Jones, Dir. of Children's Svcs. Capacity 16; Total Assisted 20; Total Staff 20.

Siena Hall, Inc., P.O. Box 2610, 19805. Tel: 302-655-9624. Ms. Fritz Jones, Dir. of Children's Svcs. Capacity 12; Total Assisted 20; Total Staff 20.

CLAYMONT. *Children's Home, Inc. - Adolescent Program* Children (ages 12-18) , 2901 Green St., 19703. Tel: 302-798-0601; Fax: 302-798-0604. Email: fjones@ccwilm.org. Web: www.cdow.org. Ms. Fritz Jones, Dir. of Children's Svcs.

Children's Home Pre-Adolescent Program for Boys Tel: 302-798-0738; Fax: 302-798-7354. Boys (ages 9-12) Combined Capacity of Both Programs 40; Total Assisted (Combined Programs) 29; Total Combined Staff 41.

[G] OTHER WELFARE AGENCIES (Not under jurisdiction of Department of Social Concerns)

WILMINGTON

Home of Divine Providence, Inc.-Bayard House, 300 Bayard Ave., 19805. Tel: 302-654-1184; Fax: 302-654-8570. Email: Cheryl.McConnell@Bayardhouse.org. Web: bayard-house.org. Cheryl McConnell, Exec. Dir. Pregnant Teens & Women (12-35) 0; Residents 25; Staff 13; Total Assisted Annually 400.

Ministry of Caring, Inc., 506 N. Church St., 19801-4812. Tel: 302-652-5523; Fax: 302-652-1919. Email: mail@ministryofcaring.org. Arthur G. Connolly III, Esq., Pres., Bd. of Directors; Rev. Ronald Giannone, O.F.M.Cap., Exec. Dir.; Ms. Louisa Teoli, Exec. Personal Asst.; Debbe Philips, Senior Exec. Asst.

Our Lady of Guadalupe, 1801 W. 6th St., 19805. Tel: 302-428-3702; Fax: 302-428-3707. Mary Anne Matarese, Deputy Dir.; Gene Bradley, CFO.

Sacred Heart House, 917 N. Madison St., 19801. Tel: 302-428-3652; Fax: 302-428-3655. Marie Keefer, Human Resources Dir.

Child Care Center, 221 N. Jackson St., 19805-3649. Tel: 302-652-8992; Fax: 302-652-8945. Email: childcarecenter@ministryofcaring.org. Peggy Sudler, Dir. Child care for homeless children, from infancy to 4 years old.

St. Clare Medical Outreach, 7th & Clayton Sts., 19805-3156. Tel: 302-575-8218. Eileen Schmitt, M.D., Medical Dir.; Maryann Fagan, R.N. Mobile medical van which provides health services for the poor.

Mary Mother of Hope House Transitional Residence, 818-820 Jefferson St., 19801-1432. Tel: 302-427-9170; Fax: 302-594-9434. Email: hopehouseI@ministryofcaring.org. Debbie Snyder, Dir. Transitional residence for single women. Capacity 12.

House of Joseph II, 7-9 W. 18th St., 19802-4833. Tel: 302-594-9473; Fax: 302-594-9494. Email: houseofjosephII@ministryofcaring.org. Rev. Robert Longo, O.F.M.Cap., Dir. Hospice for people with AIDS. Capacity 8.

House of Joseph III, Rehabilitation for formerly incarcerated young men live-in program. 822 Jefferson St., 19801. Tel: 302-652-1758; Fax: 302-652-1759. Rebecca Hurst, Dir. Capacity 5.

Pierre Toussaint Dental Office, 830 Spruce St., 19801-4205. Tel: 302-652-8947; Fax: 302-652-8994. Email: pierretoussaint@ministryofcaring.org. Gary Isaacs, D.M.D. Dental office for the homeless.

Angela Merici House, 1105 W. 8th St., 19806-4605. Tel: 302-655-4817. Residence for Religious Sisters. Religious Sisters 3.

St. Francis Transitional Residence, 103-107 & 111 N. Jackson St., 19805-3648. Tel: 302-652-1935; Fax: 302-594-9475. Email: hopehouseII@ministryofcaring.org. Ms. Marva King, Dir. Transitional living for women and children.

House of Joseph Transitional Residence, 704 West St., 19801-1523. Tel: 302-652-0904; Fax: 302-652-9472. Email: houseofjosephI@ministryofcaring.org. Francis Kamau, Dir. Transitional residence for men.

Samaritan Outreach, 1410 N. Claymont St., 19802-5227. Tel: 302-594-9476; Fax: 303-594-9478. Email: samaritanoutreach@ministryofcaring.org. Ms. Karen Lienau, Dir. Social outreach for the homeless.

Mary Mother of Hope House I, 1103 W. 8th St., 19806-4605. Tel: 302-652-8532; Fax: 302-594-9434. Email: hopehouseI@ministryofcaring.org. Debbie Snyder, Dir. Emergency shelter for homeless women. Capacity 21.

Mary Mother of Hope House II, 121 N. Jackson St., 19805-3670. Tel: 302-652-1935; Fax: 302-594-9475. Email: hopehouseII@ministryofcaring.org. Ms. Marva King, Dir. Emergency shelter for women with children. Capacity 23.

Mary Mother of Hope House III, 515 N. Broom St., 19805-3114. Tel: 302-652-0970; Fax: 302-594-9496. Email: hopehouseIII@ministryofcaring.org. Ms. Marva King, Dir.; Ms. Linda Richardson, Mgr. Emergency shelter for women with children. Capacity 21.

Job Placement Center, 1100 Lancaster Ave., 19805-4009. Tel: 302-652-5518; Fax: 302-652-0917. Email: jobplacementcenter@ministryofcaring.org. Ms. Karen Lienau, Dir. Employment agency to assist the poor.

House of Joseph I, 1328 W. Third St., 19805-3662. Tel: 302-652-0904; Fax: 302-594-9496. Email: houseofjosephI@ministryofcaring.org. Francis Kamau, Dir. Shelter for homeless employable men who are seeking employment. Capacity 13.

Emmanuel Dining Room, West, 121 N. Jackson St., 19805-3670. Tel: 302-652-3228; Fax: 302-652-2576. Email: emmanueldiningroom@ministryofcaring.org. Patrick Gaffney, Dir.

Emmanuel Dining Room, East, 226 N. Walnut St., 19801-3934. Tel: 302-652-2577; Fax: 302-652-2576. Mr. Odell Parker, Mgr.

Emmanuel Dining Room, South, 500 Rogers Rd., New Castle, 19720. Tel: 302-577-2951; Fax: 302-652-2576. Sr. Bernadette McGoldrick, O.S.F., Co-mgr.; Michael Smith, Co-mgr.

Ministry of Caring Distribution Center, 1410 N. Claymont St., 19802-5227. Tel: 302-652-0969; Fax: 302-594-9478. Mr. Eugene McLaughlin, Dir.

Ministry of Caring Guild, 506 N. Church St., 19801. Tel: 302-235-7256. Elaine Vignola, Pres.

Sacred Heart Housing, Inc., 506 N. Church St.,

19801. Tel: 302-652-5523; Fax: 302-652-1919. Susan Canning, Pres., Board of Directors.

Guardian Angel Child Care, 1000 Wilson St., 19801. Tel: 302-428-3620; Fax: 302-428-3622. Email: guardianangel@ministryofcaring.org. Peggy Sudler, Dir.

Nazareth House I, 106 N. Broom St., 19805. Tel: 302-652-0790; Fax: 302-594-9496. Email: nazarethhouse@ministryofcaring.org. Ms. Marva King, Dir. Capacity 3 Families 0.

Bethany House, 601 N. Jackson St., 19805-3241. Tel: 302-594-9458. Email: hopehouseI@ministryofcaring.org. Debbie Snyder, Dir. Transitional residence for single women Capacity 8.

Nazareth House II, 898 Linden St., 19805-4423. Tel: 302-428-3635; Fax: 302-428-3636. Ms. Marva King, Dir. Transitional residence for families. Capacity 4.

Nazareth House III, 203 N. Jackson St., 19805-3649. Tel: 302-652-1935; Fax: 302-594-9475. Ms. Marva King, Dir. Transitional residence for families.

Nazareth House IV, 807 W. 6th St., 19805. Tel: 302-652-1935; Fax: 302-594-9475. Transitional residence for families. Capacity 1.

Francis X. Norton Center, 917 N. Madison St., 19801. Tel: 302-594-9449; Fax: 302-594-9450. Emma Terrell, Dir. Multigenerational community center.

Il Bambino, 903 N. Monroe St., 19801. Tel: 302-594-9455; Fax: 302-594-9456. Peggy Sudler, Dir. Infant day care program. Infants 24.

NEWARK

Our Lady of Grace Home for Children, Inc., 487 E. Chestnut Hill Rd., 19713. Tel: 302-738-4658; 302-737-6650; Fax: 302-369-1395. Email: OLGHCH@cs.com. Sr. Mary Antonea Slowik, C.S.S.F., Admin. & Supr. Felician Sisters 6; Children 12; Total Assisted 12.

RIDGELY

St. Martin's Ministries, 14259 Benedictine Ln., MD 21660. Tel: 410-634-2497; Fax: 410-634-1410. Email: corta@juno.com. Web: www.stmartinsministries.org. Sr. Patricia Gamgort, O.S.B., Exec. Dir. Sisters of St. Benedict

St. Martin's Barn, 14376 Benedictine Ln., MD 21660. Tel: 410-634-1140; Fax: 410-634-2684. Bill Reep, Dir. Volunteers 40; Staff 5; Total Assisted 8,342.

St. Martin's House, 14374 Benedictine Ln., MD 21660. Tel: 410-634-1293. Sr. Veronica Daniels, O.S.B. Volunteers 10; Staff 11; Total Assisted 53.

[H] HOMES FOR AGED

WILMINGTON. *The Antonian*, 1701 W. 10th St., 19805. Tel: 302-421-3758; Fax: 302-421-3759. Tori Daniello, Mgr.; Rev. Mario Bugliosi, O.S.F.S., Chap. Congregate Housing for the Elderly Residents 143; Apartments 136; Total Staff 6.

Franciscan Health System / Care at Wilmington, 801 N. Broom St., 19806. Tel: 302-652-3861; Fax: 302-652-1854. Email: connolly@che_east.org. Web: www.stfrancishealthcare.org. Jane Connolly, I.H.M., Chap.

St. Patrick's House, Inc., 115 E. 14th St., 19801. Tel: 302-654-6908. Rev. James F. Trainor, Chm. of the Bd. Affiliated with St. Patrick Parish. Congregate Independent Living Facility for the elderly Capacity 15; Total in Residence 15; Total Staff 3.

Vianney House, 905 Milltown Rd., 19808. Tel: 302-636-0200. Lisa Winnington, Dir. Residents 3.

HOCKESSIN. *Franciscan Health System / Care at Brackenville*, 100 St. Clare Dr., 19707. Tel: 302-234-5420; Fax: 302-234-5424. Email: jconnolly@che_east.org. Web: www.stfrancishealthcare.org. Jane Connolly, I.H.M., Chap. A 104-bed skilled nursing facility

NEWARK. *Jeanne Jugan Residence*, 185 Salem Church Rd., 19713. Tel: 302-368-5886; Fax: 302-738-5610. Email: msnewarklsp@mycomcast.com. Sr. Edward Marie, L.S.P., Supr. Conducted by the Little Sisters of the Poor Residents 81; Sisters 9.

Marydale Retirement Village, 135 Jeandell Dr., 19713. Tel: 302-368-2784; Fax: 302-731-0584. Email: rpierce384@aol.com. Mr. Ronald Pierce, Admin.; Sr. Mary Sheehan, I.H.M., Pastoral Care Coord. Apartments for Elderly. Apartments 108; Residents 112; Total Assisted 98.

[I] GENERAL HOSPITALS

WILMINGTON. *St. Francis Hospital, Inc.*, 7th and Clayton Sts., P.O. Box 2500, 19805-0500. Tel: 302-575-8301; Fax: 302-575-8320. Email: jmcdevitt@chi-east.org. Web: www.stfrancishealthcare.org. Richard Long, Pres. & CEO; Sr. Jean Margaret McDevitt, O.S.F., V.P. Mission & Ministry; Revs. John Finn, O.S.F.S.; Joseph J. McKenna, O.S.F.S.; Sr. Seton Connolly, S.S.C.M., Chap.; Timothy Duff, STM Dir.; Sisters Margaret Culbert, S.S.J., Chap.; Karen O'Neill, I.H.M., Chap. Bed Capacity 395; Staff 1,164; Patients Assisted Annually 143,228.

[J] MONASTERIES AND RESIDENCES OF PRIESTS AND BROTHERS

WILMINGTON. *Brothers of Holy Cross, St. Edmond's Academy*, 2120 Veale Rd., 19810. Tel: 302-475-5321. Email: veal2120@aol.com. Bro. Joseph W. Ash, C.S.C., Dir. Religious. Brothers 5.

Capuchin Franciscan Friars, St. Francis Renewal Center, 1901 Prior Rd., 19809. Tel: 302-798-1454; Fax: 302-798-3360. Revs. Cyprian Rosen, O.F.M.Cap., Guardian, Dir.; Thomas Pietrantonio, O.F.M.Cap., Vicar; Edmund Walker, O.F.M.Cap.; Bros. William Arlia, O.F.M.Cap.; Michael Ascione, O.F.M.Cap.; Jack Boehm, O.F.M.Cap.

DeSales House, 1600 Brinckle Ave., 19806. Tel: 302-656-4342; Fax: 302-656-6108. Email: wjuergens@oblates.org. Web:. Revs. Francis J. Hanlon, O.S.F.S.; William J. Dougherty, O.S.F.S. John A. Finn, O.S.F.S.; William R. Gore, O.S.F.S.; John J. Hurley, O.S.F.S.; William H. Juergens, O.S.F.S.; William J Keech, O.S.F.S.; Richard D. Leone, O.S.F.S.; Joseph J. McKenna, O.S.F.S. Priests 9.

St. Felix Friary, 119 N. Jackson St., 19805-3670. Tel: 302-652-7010; Fax: 302-652-8948. Email: stfelix@ministryofcaring.org. Revs. Ronald Giannone, O.F.M.Cap., Guardian; Robert Longo, O.F.M.Cap. Brothers 2.

Oblates of St. Francis De Sales, Residence of the Provincial, 2200 Kentmere Pkwy., 19806 Tel: 302-656-8529; Fax: 302-658-8052. Email: efitzpatrick@oblates.org. Web: www.oblates.org. Very Rev. Joseph G. Morrissey, O.S.F.S., Prov.; Revs. Edward T. Fitzpatrick, O.S.F.S., Asst. Prov. & Dir. Personnel; Michael T. Cavanaugh, O.S.F.S., Rel.-in-Charge; Richard R. De Lillio, O.S.F.S., Dir. Devel.; Francis J. Hanlon, O.S.F.S., Dir. Senior Oblates, (Staff member -- not in residence); Robert A. Mancini, O.S.F.S., Treas.; Michael S. Murray, O.S.F.S., Dir. Spirituality Center. Priests 16.

Rev. Oblates Attached to the Provincial Residence: Revs. Walter R. Dean, O.S.F.S.; William J. Hultberg, O.S.F.S.; George S. Salzmann, O.S.F.S.; James J. MacNew, O.S.F.S., Military Chap.; John W. Lyle, O.S.F.S., Military Chap.; Anthony J. Pinizzotto, O.S.F.S., Education; John A. Gilvey, O.S.F.S.; Mark A. Hushen, O.S.F.S.; William R. Gore, O.S.F.S.

CHILDS. *Oblates of St. Francis De Sales*, MD. Tel: 410-398-3040; Fax: 410-620-6131. Email: jjocco@dol.net. Web: www.oblates.org. Retirement and Assisted Care Facility.

Retirement and Assisted Care Facility, 1120 Blue Ball Rd., MD 21916-0043. Tel: 410-398-3040; Fax: 410-620-6131. Rev. Joseph P. Jocco, O.S.F.S., Supr. In Res. Priests 25; Brothers 10. In Res. Revs. Joseph A. Baird, O.S.F.S.; Joseph Bananiewicz, O.S.F.S.; Joseph D. Bowler, O.S.F.S.; John W. Brennan, O.S.F.S.; George J. Brownholtz, O.S.F.S.; Vincent dePaul Burke, O.S.F.S.; Richard E. Cleary, O.S.F.S.; Raymond G. Collins, O.S.F.S.; John J. Conmy, O.S.F.S.; John P. Connolly, O.S.F.S.; Nicholas O. DiIenno, O.S.F.S.; Michael B. Donovan, O.S.F.S.; Hugh E. Duffy, O.S.F.S.; Francis J. Greene, O.S.F.S.; Robert P. Hanlon, O.S.F.S.; Robert J. Hermley, O.S.F.S.; John F. Kenny, O.S.F.S.; Anthony J. Larry, O.S.F.S.; George W. Martyn, O.S.F.S.; John J. Mozdakis, O.S.F.S.; Edward F. O'Rourke, O.S.F.S.; William O. Seelaus, O.S.F.S.; Joseph A. Travers, O.S.F.S.; Joseph E. Woods, O.S.F.S.; Bros. John M. Carroll, O.S.F.S.; Robert M. Carter, O.S.F.S.; John J. Dochkus, O.S.F.S.; Henry J. Fiegl, O.S.F.S.; Joseph H. Hayden, O.S.F.S.; Frank J. Konstanty, O.S.F.S.; Harry F. McGovern, O.S.F.S.; Eugene J. Rehrman, O.S.F.S.; Paul A. Schuler, O.S.F.S.; Gerald M. Sweeney, O.S.F.S.

MIDDLETOWN. *Immaculate Conception Priory of the Canons Regular of Premontre*, 1269 Bayview Rd., 19709. Tel: 302-449-1840; Fax: 302-449-1217. Revs. John M. Logan, O.Praem.; James D. Bagnato, O.Praem., Admin.; Walter J. Burke, O.Praem. Jeffrey T. Cesarone, O.Praem., Interim Dir. Vocation; Francis J. Ciliberti, O.Praem.; Martin A. Frigo, O.Praem. Priests 10; Brothers 10.

Norbertine Fathers of Delaware, Inc., 1269 Bayview Rd., 19709. Tel: 302-449-1840; Fax: 302-449-1217. Rt. Rev. E. Thomas DeWane, O.Praem., Pres.; Rev. James D. Bagnato, O.Praem., Vice Pres

[K] CONVENTS AND RESIDENCES FOR SISTERS

WILMINGTON. *St. Benedict*, 113 Canterbury Dr., 19803. Tel: 302-478-3754; Fax: 302-478-9305. Email: margosb@aol.com. Sisters of St. Benedict 3.

St. Francis Convent, 701 N. Rodney St., 19805. Tel: 302-652-8489. The Sisters of St. Francis of Philadelphia 9.

Monastery of St. Veronica Giuliani (Strict Enclosure) , 816 Jefferson St., 19801. Tel: 302-654-8727. Fax: 302-652-3929. Email: stveronicagiuliani@MSN.com. Sr. Maria del Carmen Quiroz, O.S.C.Cap., Abbess; Rev. Ronald Giannone, O.F.M.Cap., Chap. Capuchin Poor Clare Nuns of Delaware Sisters 11.

Our Lady of Peace Convent, 1801 W. 8th St., 19805. Tel: 302-426-1809. Web: www.osfphila.org. The Sisters of St. Francis of Philadelphia 2.

Ursuline Academy Inc., The, 1104 Pennsylvania Ave., 19806. Tel: 302-656-5890; Fax: 302-656-2315. Sr. Mildred Haipt, O.S.U., Supr. Sisters 18.

CHILDS. *Villa Aviat Convent*, 399 Childs Rd., MD 21916. Tel: 410-398-3699; Fax: 410-398-5801. Email: oblatesisters@mountaviat.org. Web: www.oblatesisters.org. Sr. Anne Elizabeth, O.S.F.S., Supr. Oblate Sisters of St. Francis de Sales Sisters 11.

EASTON. *Eastern Shore Co-op*, 304 Prospect Ave., MD 21601. Tel: 410-820-7437. Sisters 2.

PRINCESS ANNE. *St. Joseph Novitiate*, 10572 Anderson Rd., MD 21853. Tel: 410-651-5309. Sisters Mary Elizabeth Gintling, Foundress; Constance R. Ladd, Supr. Gen. Sisters 2; Postulants 2.

Seton Center, Sisters of Charity (Convent Station) , P.O. Box 401, MD 21853. Tel: 410-651-9608; Fax: 410-651-1437. Email: seton-center@juno.com. Sisters 4; Assisted 8,000.

RIDGELY. *St. Gertrude's Monastery, Motherhouse and Novitiate of the Sisters of St. Benedict*, 14259 Benedictine Ln., MD 21660. Tel: 410-634-2497; Fax: 410-634-1410. Email: sgfalkowsk@aol.com. Web: www.ridgelybenedictines.org. Sr. M. Gerard Falkowska, O.S.B., Prioress. Sisters 32.

SALISBURY. *Joseph House, Little Sisters of Jesus & Mary.*, P.O. Box 1755, MD 21802. Tel: 410-543-1645; Fax: 410-742-3390. Email: convent@thejosephhouse.org. Web: www.thejosephhouse.org. Sr. Constance R. Ladd, Supr. Gen. Sisters 3.

[L] SECULAR INSTITUTES

WILMINGTON. *Secular Franciscan Order* (St. Patrick's Fraternity) , 1901 Prior Rd., 19809. Tel: 302-737-7884. Therese Schaffer, S.F.O., Min.; Rev. Edmund Walker, O.F.M.Cap., Spiritual Asst.

BEAR. *Secular Order of Discalced Carmelites*, 769 Fox Chase Cir., 19701. Tel: 302-836-3843. Email: malove@comcast.net. Mary An Love, Pres.; Bro. Bryan Paquette, O.C.D., Spiritual Asst. (Annunciation Community)

DOVER. *Secular Institute of the Two Hearts*, P.O. Box 1719, 19903. Tel: 302-678-1358; Fax: 302-678-3246. Email: sith76usa@aol.com. Agnes Frias, Intl. Supr.; Deanna Crisologo, Intl. Vicar; Revs. Edgardo M. Arellano, Spiritual Dir.; John R. Santos, Asst. Spiritual Dir.

KENNETT SQUARE. *Secular Franciscan Order* (San Damiano Fraternity) , 412 Harrum Dr., PA 19348. Email: carisio@yahoo.com. Sr. Elise Betz, O.S.F., Spiritual Asst.

MIDDLETOWN. *De Sales Secular Institute*, 108 W. Cochran St., 19709. Tel: 302-378-2423. Web: www.secularinstitutes.org/sfs.htm. Jacquelyn Delaporte, Contact; Therese Keyes, Dir. U.S.A. Tel: 203-469-3277.

SALISBURY. *Secular Order of Discalced Carmelites* (Mary, Mother of Life Community) , 631 Ridge Rd., MD 21811. Tel: 410-742-1777. Mrs. Marianne Chapin; Bro. Bryan Paquette, O.C.D., Spiritual Asst.

[M] RETREAT HOUSES, GENERAL

WILMINGTON. *St. Francis Renewal Center*, 1901 Prior Rd., 19809. Tel: 302-798-1454; Fax: 302-798-3360. Revs. Cyprian Rosen, O.F.M.Cap., Guardian, Dir.; Thomas Pietrantonio, O.F.M.Cap., Vicar; Edmund Walker, O.F.M.Cap.; Bros. William Arlia, O.F.M.Cap.; Michael Ascione, O.F.M.Cap.; Jack Boehm, O.F.M.Cap. Priests 3; Brothers 3.

CHILDS. *De Sales Spirituality Center*, Formerly De Sales Centre, 1120 Blue Ball Rd., MD 21916-0043. Tel: 410-398-3383; Fax: 410-398-0116. Email: mmurray@osfs.org. Web: www.oblates.org/spirituality. Rev. Michael S. Murray, O.S.F.S., Dir.

[N] RETREAT HOUSES, WOMEN

CHILDS. *Oblate Sisters of St. Francis de Sales*, Villa Aviat, 399 Childs Rd., MD 21916. Tel: 410-398-3699; Fax: 410-398-5801. Email: oblatesisters@mountaviat.org. Web: www.oblatesisters.org.

RIDGELY. *Berg Retreat Center*, St. Gertrude's Monastery, 14259 Benedictine Ln., MD 21660. Tel: 410-634-2497; Fax: 410-634-1410. Email: sgfakowsk@aol.com. Web: www.ridgelybenedictines.org. Benedictine Sisters

[O] INFORMATION CENTERS

WILMINGTON. *The Franciscan Center*, 833 N. Market St., 19801-3078. Tel: 302-656-0711; Fax: 302-656-2167. Bro. David W. Schlatter, O.F.M., Dir.; Revs. Barry J. Langley, O.F.M., Asst. Dir.; James Richardson, C.A.D.C.

[P] NEWMAN CENTERS

NEWARK. *Catholic Campus Ministry, Univ. of*

Delaware St. Thomas More Oratory, 45 Lovett Ave., 19711. Tel: 302-368-4728; Fax: 302-368-2548. Email: szuptmo@udel.edu. Web: udel.edu/stu-org/catholic. Rev. Michael F. Szupper, Ph.D., Chap. & Diocesan Dir. Campus Ministry.

Delmar Organization of Catholic Students - DOCS Tel: 302-368-4728; Fax: 302-368-2548. Kimberly S. Zitzner, B.A., Dir.

Salisbury University 211 W. College Ave., Salisbury, MD 21801. Tel: 410-219-3376; Fax: 410-219-3376. Mrs. Regina YankaLunas, M.P.S., Campus Min.

University of Maryland Eastern Shore 211 W. College Ave., Salisbury, MD 21801. Tel: 410-219-3376; Fax: 410-219-3376. Email: campusministry@hotmail.com. Mrs. Regina YankaLunas, M.P.S., Campus Min.

Wesley College Newman Center Tel: 302-368-4728; Fax: 302-368-2548. Email: szuptmo@udel.edu. Rev. Michael F. Szupper, Ph.D., Chap.

Washington College 45 Lovett Ave., 19711. Tel: 302-368-4728; Fax: 302-368-2548. Email: joe@delanet.com. Rev. Michael F. Szupper, Ph.D.; Deacon Joseph Kosman, Chap. Tel: 302-834-8792.

Wesley College Catholic Campus Ministry St. Thomas More Oratory, 45 Lovett Ave., 19711. Tel: 302-368-4728. Email: szuptmo@udel.edu.

RELIGIOUS INSTITUTES OF MEN REPRESENTED IN THE DIOCESE

For further details refer to the corresponding bracketed number in the Religious Institutes of Men or Women section.

[1350]—*Brothers of St. Francis Xavier*—C.F.X.

[0600]—*Brothers of the Congregation of Holy Cross* (Eastern Province)—C.S.C.

[0900]—*Canons Regular of Premontre*—O.Praem.

[0470]—*The Capuchin Friars* (Prov. of the Stigmata)—O.F.M.Cap.

[0520]—*Franciscan Friars* (Holy Name Province)—O.F.M.

[0690]—*Jesuit Fathers and Brothers* (California Prov.)—S.J.

[]—*Oblate Apostles of the Two Hearts*—O.A.T.H.

[0920]—*Oblates of St. Francis de Sales*—O.S.F.S.

[1070]—*Redemptorist Fathers* (Baltimore, MD)—C.SS.R.

RELIGIOUS INSTITUTES OF WOMEN REPRESENTED IN THE DIOCESE

[0100]—*Adorers of the Blood of Christ*—A.S.C.

[0230]—*Benedictine Sisters of Pontifical Jurisdiction*—O.S.B.

[3765]—*Capuchin Poor Clare Sisters*—O.S.C.Cap.

[]—*Carmelites of Charity of Verduna*—C.C.V.

[3735]—*Congregation of St. Brigid*—C.S.B.

[0760]—*Daughters of the Charity of St. Vincent de Paul*—D.C.

[1070-11]—*Dominican Sisters*—O.P.

[1170]—*Felician Sisters*—C.S.S.F.

[]—*Leaven of the Immaculate Heart of Mary Sisters*—L.I.H.M.

[2331]—*Little Sisters of Jesus and Mary*—L.S.J.M.

[2340]—*Little Sisters of the Poor*—L.S.P.

[2720]—*Mission Helpers of the Sacred Heart* (Prov. of Baltimore)—M.H.S.H.

[2790]—*Missionary Servants of the Most Blessed Trinity*—M.S.B.T.

[3060]—*Oblates Sisters of St. Francis de Sales*—O.S.F.S.

[2575]—*Religious Sisters of Mercy of the Americas* (Baltimore, MD; Merion, PA)—R.S.M.

[2970]—*School Sisters of Notre Dame*—S.S.N.D.

[0440]—*Sisters of Charity of Cincinnati*—S.C.

[0500]—*Sisters of Charity of Nazareth*—S.C.N.

[0590]—*Sisters of Charity of Saint Elizabeth, Convent Station* (Southern, Western Provs.)—S.C.

[3000]—*Sisters of Notre Dame* (Base Communities Prov.; Maryland Prov.)—S.N.D.deN.

[3780]—*Sisters of Saints Cyril and Methodius*—SS.C.M.

[3770]—*Sisters of St. Clare*—O.S.C.

[1650]—*Sisters of St. Francis of Philadelphia*—O.S.F.

[3893]—*Sisters of St. Joseph of Chestnut Hill, Philadelphia*—S.S.J.

[3890]—*Sisters of St. Joseph of Peace*—C.S.J.P.

[3730]—*Sisters of the Order of St. Basil the Great*—O.S.B.M.

[2160]—*Sisters, Servants of Immaculate Heart of Mary*—I.H.M.

[4110]—*Ursuline Nuns (Roman Union)* (Eastern Prov.)—O.S.U.

DIOCESAN CEMETERIES

WILMINGTON. *All Saints*, Box 2506, 19805. Tel: 302-737-2524; Fax: 302-737-4091. *Office*, Kirkwood Hwy., 19805. Mr. Mark A. Christian, C.C.C.E., Exec. Dir.; Thomas J. Kane, Supt.

Cathedral, P.O. Box 2506, 19805. Tel: 302-656-3323; Fax: 302-656-1069. *Office*, 2400 Lancaster Ave., 19805. Mr. Mark A. Christian, C.C.C.E., Exec. Dir. & Supt.

DAGSBORO. *Gate of Heaven*, P.O. Box 940, Ocean View, 19970. *Office*, Oak Square Professional Center, Ocean View, 19970. Tel: 302-537-8953; Fax: 302-537-8955. Mr. Mark A. Christian, C.C.C.E., Exec. Dir.; Donald Suter, Supt.

NECROLOGY

† Baumgartel, David A., Wilmington, DE Parish of the Resurrection—Died Oct. 8, 2002

† O'Brien, John F., Wilmington, DE St. Mary Magdalen—Died Jan. 7, 2003

Diocese of Winona

(Dioecesis Vinonaensis)

Most Reverend

BERNARD J. HARRINGTON, D.D.

Bishop of Winona; ordained June 6, 1959; appointed Auxiliary Bishop of the Archdiocese of Detroit and Titular Bishop of Uzali November 23, 1993; Transferred to Winona November 5, 1998; installed January 6, 1999.

Most Reverend

LORAS J. WATTERS, D.D.

Retired Bishop of Winona; ordained June 7, 1941; appointed Titular Bishop of Fidoloma and Auxiliary Bishop of Dubuque June 23, 1965; consecrated August 26, 1965; Transfered to Winona January 8, 1969; retired October 14, 1986; appointed Apostolic Administrator October 14, 1986. *Res.: 618 Forest, Apt. D, Pacific Grove, CA 93950.* Tel: 408-373-3715.

Pastoral Center: 55 W. Sanborn St., P.O. Box 588, Winona, MN 55987. Tel: 507-454-4643; Fax: 507-454-8106.

Web: www.dow.org

Email: diocese@dow.org

ESTABLISHED NOVEMBER 26, 1889.

Square Miles 12,282.

Comprises the Counties of Winona, Wabasha, Olmsted, Dodge, Steele, Waseca, Blue Earth, Watonwan, Cottonwood, Murray, Pipestone, Rock, Nobles, Jackson, Faribault, Martin, Freeborn, Mower, Fillmore and Houston in the State of Minnesota.

For legal titles of parishes and diocesan institutions, consult the Pastoral Center.

STATISTICAL OVERVIEW

Personnel	
Bishop	1
Retired Bishops	1
Retired Abbots	1
Priests: Diocesan Active in Diocese	66
Priests: Diocesan Active Outside Diocese	2
Priests: Retired, Sick or Absent	50
Number of Diocesan Priests	118
Religious Priests in Diocese	8
Total Priests in Diocese	126
Extern Priests in Diocese	4
Permanent Deacons in Diocese	9
Total Brothers	22
Total Sisters	511
Parishes	
Parishes	115
With Resident Pastor:	
Resident Diocesan Priests	52
Resident Religious Priests	3
Without Resident Pastor:	
Administered by Priests	51
Administered by Lay People	7
Completely Vacant	2
Pastoral Centers	2
Closed Parishes	3
Professional Ministry Personnel:	
Brothers	2
Sisters	12
Lay Ministers	72
Welfare	
Catholic Hospitals	2
Total Assisted	76,517
Health Care Centers	1
Total Assisted	6,200
Homes for the Aged	10
Total Assisted	1,001
Day Care Centers	3
Total Assisted	10,169
Special Centers for Social Services	7
Total Assisted	5,496
Other Institutions	1
Total Assisted	99
Educational	
Seminaries, Diocesan	1
Students from This Diocese	8
Students from Other Diocese	48
Diocesan Students in Other Seminaries	3
Total Seminarians	11
Colleges and Universities	1
Total Students	1,357
High Schools, Diocesan and Parish	4
Total Students	1,218
Elementary Schools, Diocesan and Parish	26
Total Students	4,707
Catechesis/Religious Education:	
High School Students	4,529
Elementary Students	9,734
Total Students under Catholic Instruction	21,556
Teachers in the Diocese:	
Priests	1
Brothers	2
Sisters	27
Lay Teachers	352
Vital Statistics	
Receptions into the Church:	
Infant Baptism Totals	1,714
Adult Baptism Totals	53
Received into Full Communion	218
First Communions	1,732
Confirmations	1,728
Marriages:	
Catholic	329
Interfaith	270
Total Marriages	599
Deaths	1,074
Total Catholic Population	130,527
Total Population	557,684

Former Bishops—Rt. Revs. JOSEPH B. COTTER, D.D., consecrated Dec. 27, 1889; died June 28, 1909; PATRICK R. HEFFRON, D.D., consecrated May 19, 1910; died Nov. 23, 1927; Most Revs. FRANCIS M. KELLY, D.D., consecrated June 9, 1926; transferred to Diocese of Winona, Feb. 10, 1928; transferred to Titular See of Nasal, Oct. 17, 1949; died June 24, 1950; EDWARD A. FITZGERALD, D.D. (Retired), consecrated Sept. 12, 1946; Auxiliary Bishop of Dubuque; transferred to Winona, Oct. 20, 1949; retired and transferred to the Titular See of Zerta, Jan. 8, 1969; died March 30, 1972; LORAS J. WATTERS, D.D. (Retired), ord. June 7, 1941; appt. Titular Bishop of Fidoloma and Auxiliary Bishop of Dubuque, June 23, 1965; consecrated Aug. 26, 1965; transferred to Winona, Jan. 8, 1969; retired Oct. 14, 1986; appt. Apostolic Administrator, Oct. 14, 1986; JOHN G. VLAZNY, D.D., ord. Dec. 20, 1961; appt. Auxiliary Bishop of Chicago and Titular Bishop of Stagno, Oct. 31, 1983; consecrated Dec. 13, 1983; appt. Bishop of Winona, May 19, 1987; installed July 29, 1987; appt. Archbishop of Portland, Oct. 28, 1997.

Vicar General and Moderator of the Curia—Very Rev. MICHAEL J. HOEPPNER, J.C.L., V.G., 55 W. Sanborn St., P.O. Box 588, Winona, 55987. Tel: 507-454-4643; Fax: 507-454-8106.

Chancellor—Rev. MICHAEL J. CRONIN, J.C.L., 55 W. Sanborn St., P.O. Box 588, Winona, 55987. Tel: 507-454-4643; Fax: 507-454-8106.

Deans—Very Rev. JOHN M. SAUER, Winona; VACANT, Rochester; Very Revs. GREGORY P. LEIF, Austin-Albert Lea; JOHN M. KUNZ, Mankato GERALD C. KOSSE, Worthington.

Diocesan Consultors—Rev. Msgrs. ROY E. LITERSKI (Retired); DONALD P. SCHMITZ, M.Ch.A.; Revs. THOMAS J. JENNINGS; JOSEPH L. KEEFE; ROBERT G. MEYER; JAMES D. RUSSELL.

Finance Council—Very Rev. MICHAEL J. HOEPPNER, J.C.L., V.G.; Rev. JOHN OZBUN; Mr. LAWRENCE J. DOSE, Dir. & Exec. Sec.; Sr. JEAN KENIRY, O.S.F.; Mr. ROBERT HOODECHECK; Mrs. SHARON WAGNER; Mr. JAMES ANDERSON; Mr. JAMES WIEKAMP.

Diocesan Board of Administration— (Civil Corporation): Most Rev. BERNARD J. HARRINGTON, D.D., Pres.; Very Rev. MICHAEL J. HOEPPNER, J.C.L., V.G., Vice Pres.; Rev. MICHAEL J. CRONIN, J.C.L., Sec.; Mr. ROBERT HOODECHEK; Mrs. SHARON WAGNER.

Deposit and Loan Board—Very Rev. MICHAEL J. HOEPPNER, J.C.L., V.G., Vice Pres.; Rev. MICHAEL J. CRONIN, J.C.L., Sec.; Mr. LAWRENCE DOSE, Treas.; Rev. Msgr. DONALD W. GRUBISCH; Mr. ROBERT HOODECHECK; Mrs. SHARON WAGNER; Ms. CAROL ORLOWSKI; Mr. MICHAEL KIEFFER.

Tribunal—*55 W. Sanborn St., P.O. Box 588, Winona, 55987.* Tel: 507-454-4643.

Judicial Officers—Very Rev. R. PAUL HEITING, J.C.L., Vicar Judicial; Mr. LAWRENCE G. PRICE, J.D., J.C.L., Dir.

Censors of Books and Periodicals—Rev. WILLIAM M. BECKER, S.T.D.; JOHN M. SAUER, S.T.L.; TIMOTHY T. REKER, S.T.L.; Rev. ANDREW J. BEERMAN, S.T.L.

Associate Judges—Revs. WILLIAM KULAS, J.C.L.; DAVID WECHTER, O.Cist., J.C.L.; Very Rev. MICHAEL J. HOEPPNER, J.C.L., V.G.; Rev. MARK MALLAK, J.C.L.; Mr. LAWRENCE G. PRICE, J.D., J.C.L.

Defenders of the Bond—Rev. Msgr. DONALD P. SCHMITZ, M.Ch.A.; Revs. MICHAEL J. CRONIN, J.C.L.; DONALD J. SCHMITZ, M.A.; Sr. VICTORIA VONDENBERGER, R.S.M., J.C.L.; Mr. GEORGE NIX, J.C.L.

Advocates—Very Rev. GERALD C. KOSSE; Rev. MARTIN T. SCHAEFFER; Mr. THOMAS HEALY, J.D.

Auditors—Revs. RICHARD M. COLLETTI; CHARLIE I. COLLINS; DONALD F. CONNELLY; CLAYTON J. HABERMAN (Retired); GERALD C. KOSSE; JOSEPH LAMANTE; GREGORY P. LEIF; THOMAS A. LOOMIS; MARTIN T. SCHAEFER; PAUL W. SURPRENANT; DONALD W. ZENK (Retired); Sisters SEVERINA CARON, O.S.F.; ROSE MARY SCHWALBE, S.S.N.D.; MARGARET GILLARD; THERESE GRANER; DONNA HARRIS; CHARLES JACOBSON; MARGARET

JACOBSON; ROXANNE KEMPER; DEE LIBERA; THOMAS PARLIN; MARY SCHNEIDER; RANDY ZELLMER.

Auditors-in-Training—Rev. KEVIN CONNOLLY; Deacon LEONARD FULLER; BETTY SINGER-TOWNES; BERNARD MCNAB.

Outside Auditors—

Metropolitan Tribunal—

Second Instance Court Judges—Very Rev. R. PAUL HEITING, J.C.L.; Mr. LAWRENCE G. PRICE, J.D., J.C.L.; Revs. WILLIAM J. KULAS, J.C.L.; MARK MALLAK, J.C.L.; Very Rev. MICHAEL J. HOEPPNER, J.C.L., V.G.

Promoter of Justice—Rev. Msgr. DONALD P. SCHMITZ, M.Ch.A.

Ecclesiastical Notaries—Mrs. LACINDIA THEIS; Ms. PAULA WATEMBACH; Mrs. JULIE WRIGHT.

Diocesan Offices and Directors

All Diocesan Offices and Directors are located at the Pastoral Center (unless otherwise indicated), 55 W. Sanborn St., P.O. Box 588, Winona, 55987. Tel: 507-454-4643; Fax: 507-454-8106. Please send all matrimonial dispensations and permissions to The Chancellor's Office *55 W. Sanborn St., P.O. Box 588, Winona, 55987*. Tel: 507-454-4643; Fax: 507-454-8106. Web: www.dow.org.

Curia—

Vicar General—Very Rev. MICHAEL J. HOEPPNER, J.C.L., V.G.

Chancellor—Rev. MICHAEL J. CRONIN, J.C.L.

Pastoral Planning—Very Rev. MICHAEL J. HOEPPNER, J.C.L., V.G.

Finances—Mr. LAWRENCE J. DOSE, Dir.

Catholic Charities—Mr. ROBERT TEREBA, Exec. Dir., 111 Market St., P.O. Box 379, Winona, 55987. Tel: 507-454-2270; Fax: 507-457-3027.

Communications - "The Courier"—Mr. IVAN KUBISTA.

Office of RCIA, Liturgy and Evangelization—Ms. PEGGY LOVRIEN.

Education, Human Resources and Schools—Mrs. P. J. THOMPSON.

Faith Formation—Mr. MARK NUEHRING.

Youth and Family Life—Mrs. ALMA RICHARD.

Diaconate Formation—Rev. TIMOTHY T. REKER, S.T.L., St. Francis of Assisi Church, 1114 3rd St., S.E., Rochester, 55904. Tel: 507-288-7313; Mr. TODD GRAFF, Contact Person.

Vocations—Revs. THOMAS P. MELVIN, Dir., Diocese of Winona, 55 W. Sanborn St., P.O. Box 588, Winona, 55987. Tel: 507-454-4643; Fax: 507-454-8106; THOMAS E. COOK, Vocations Promoter, Our Lady of Mt. Carmel Church, 27 Main St., P.O. Box 8, Easton, 56025. Tel: 507-787-2303.

Lay Ministry Formation—Mr. TODD GRAFF.

Stewardship and Development—Deacon LEONARD FULLER.

Additional Ministries—

Annual Diocesan Appeal—Ms. DIANE M. ZITTEL, Dir.

Continuing Education for Clergy—Rev. MICHAEL J. CRONIN, J.C.L., Dir.

Ecumenism—Mr. TODD GRAFF.

Emmaus House of Formation—Rev. TIMOTHY E. BIREN, Dir., 1502 Warren St., Mankato, 56001. Tel: 507-385-0647. Email: timbiren@yahoo.com.

Emmaus House—Rev. THOMAS P. MELVIN, Dir., 706 W. Broadway, Winona, 55987. Tel: 507-454-4643; 507-474-6485. Email: tmelvin@dow.org.

Propagation of the Faith—Rev. CHARLIE I. COLLINS, Christ the King Church, 202 4th St., N.W., P.O. Box 1000, Byron, 55920-1000. Tel: 507-775-6455.

Hispanic Ministry—Very Rev. KURT FARRELL, Vicar, Queen of Angels Church, 1001 E. Oakland Ave., Austin, 55912. Tel: 507-434-4085.

Coordinator of Diocesan Health Ministry—Rev. JAMES F. BURYSKA, Diocesan Dir. of Hospitals, Rochester Methodist Hospital Chaplain Services, 201 W. Center St., Rochester, 55902. Tel: 507-255-5551; Fax: 507-255-3125.

Advisory Bodies—

Presbyteral Council—

Ex Officio—Very Rev. MICHAEL J. HOEPPNER, J.C.L., V.G.

Elected Senior Member—Rev. GERALD W. CONWAY (Retired).

Appointed Members—Rev. Msgrs. ROY E. LITERSKI (Retired); DONALD P. SCHMITZ, M.Ch.A.; Revs. THOMAS J. JENNINGS; JOSEPH L. KEEFE; THOMAS E. COOK, Sec.

Elected At-Large Representatives—Revs. THOMAS J. HARGESHEIMER; JOSEPH B. FOGAL.

Elected Deanery Representatives—Revs. WILLIAM M. BECKER, S.T.D.; MARTIN T. SCHAEFER; JOHN OZBUN, Vice Pres.; THOMAS A. LOOMIS; STEVEN J. PETERSON.

Priest Assignments Committee—Very Rev. MICHAEL J. HOEPPNER, J.C.L., V.G.; Rev. Msgr. DONALD P. SCHMITZ, M.Ch.A.; Rev. JOSEPH B. FOGAL.

Diocesan Pastoral Council—Very Rev. MICHAEL J. HOEPPNER, J.C.L., V.G.; Rev. JOSEPH B. FOGAL; Bro. PATRICK CONWAY; Sisters JOAN LEWISON, O.S.F.; BRENDA PENNING, S.S.N.D.; Mrs. JOYCE ARNDORFER; Mrs. ROSEMARY MURPHY; Mr. MARK OLDENBURG.

Bishop's Council—Very Revs. MICHAEL J. HOEPPNER, J.C.L., V.G.; GERALD C. KOSSE; JOHN M. KUNZ; GREGORY P. LEIF; JOHN M. SAUER; Sisters CATHERINE BERTRAND, S.S.N.D.; MONIQUE SCHWIRTZ, O.S.F.

Priests' Pension Board—Revs. WILLIAM J. KULAS; LAVERN E. TROCINSKI; STEVEN J. PETERSON; Bro. LOUIS DETHOMASIS; Mr. TIMOTHY GEISLER; Mr. LAWRENCE J. DOSE, Treas.; Mr. THOMAS CROWLEY.

Commission on Sacred Liturgy—Ms. PEGGY LOVRIEN, Ex Officio; Very Revs. JOHN M. SAUER, Consultant; GERALD C. KOSSE; Mr. ROBERT HACKMEISTER; Mrs. SUSAN SHEPHARD; Ms. THERESA HOFFMAN; Ms. BETSY DIERCKS; Ms. RACHEL KIMMAN.

Vocations Advisory Council—Revs. THOMAS P. MELVIN, Dir.; THOMAS E. COOK, Vocations Promoter; ANDREW J. BEERMAN; TIMOTHY E. BIREN; Sisters JOYCE KOLBET, S.S.N.D.; WANDA METTES, O.S.F.; MARY BETH SCHRAML, S.S.N.D.; Mr. DICK BREITER; Mrs. THERESA BREITER; Mrs. PAMELA J. THOMPSON.

Winona Diocesan Organizations-Agencies-Programs

Archives—Rev. MICHAEL J. CRONIN, J.C.L., Pastoral Center, 55 W. Sanborn St., P.O. Box 588, Winona, 55987. Tel: 507-454-4643; Fax: 507-454-8106.

Boy Scouts—Mrs. ALMA RICHARD, Coord., Pastoral Center, 55 W. Sanborn St., P.O. Box 588, Winona, 55987. Tel: 507-454-4643; Fax: 507-454-8106.

Chaplain—Rev. THOMAS A. LOOMIS, Church of the Resurrection, 1600 11th Ave. SE, Rochester, 55904. Tel: 507-288-5528.

Catholic Charities—Mr. ROBERT TEREBA, Exec. Dir., Administrative and Winona Regional Office, 111 Market St., P.O. Box 379, Winona, 55987. Tel: 507-454-2270; Fax: 507-457-3027. Email: rtereba@ccwinona.org. Web: www.ccwinona.org.

Catholic Charities Board—JOHN SMITH, Chm.

Regional Offices—Mankato: 816 Hubbell Ave., Mankato, 56001. Tel: 507-387-5586; Fax: 507-387-5587. *Rochester: 117 E. Center St., Ste. B, Rochester, 55904*. Tel: 507-287-2047; Fax: 507-287-2050. *Worthington: 1118 Oxford St., Worthington, 56187*. Tel: 507-376-9757; Fax: 507-376-9758.

Field Offices—Albert Lea: 308 E. Fountain, Albert Lea, 56007. Tel: 507-377-3664. *Austin: 405 4th St., N.W., Austin, 55912*. Tel: 507-433-3062. *Owatonna: 577 State Ave., Owatonna, 55060*. Tel: 507-455-2008.

Parish and Community Social Action Office—Ms. SUZANNE BELONGIA, Supvr., 111 Market St., P.O. Box 379, Winona, 55987. Tel: 507-454-2270; Fax: 507-457-3027. Email: sbelongia@ccwinona.org. Coordination of: Parish Social Ministry, Rural Life Ministry, Catholic Campaign for Human Development, Catholic Relief Services, HIV-AIDS Ministry, Disaster Relief Services.

Hispanic Ministry—111 Market St., P.O. Box 379, Winona, 55987. Tel: 507-454-2270; Fax: 507-457-3027. JUAN VALENCIA, Coordinator, 816 Hubbell Ave., Mankato, 56001. Tel: 507-387-5586; Fax: 507-387-5587. Email: jvalencia@ccwinona.org.

Refugee Resettlement—Deacon GORDON RICHARD, Dir., 117 E. Center St., Ste. B, Rochester, 55904. Tel: 507-287-2047; Fax: 507-287-2050.

Clinical and Child Welfare—Mrs. VALERIE CUNNINGHAM, Supvr., 117 E. Center St., Ste. B, Rochester, 55904. Tel: 507-287-2047; Fax: 570-287-2050. Email: rgen@ccwinona.org.

Adult Community Services—Mr. WES BRANDENBURGER, Supvr., 111 Market St., P.O. Box 379, Winona, 55987. Tel: 507-454-2270; Fax: 507-457-3027. Email: wbrandenburger@ccwinona.org.

Child and Family Evaluation/Mediation Services—Mrs. MARY BORGEN, Supvr., 111 Market St., P.O. Box 379, Winona, 55987. Tel: 507-454-2270; Fax: 507-457-3027.

Cemeteries—Rev. MICHAEL J. CRONIN, J.C.L., Pastoral Center, 55 W. Sanborn St., P.O. Box 588, Winona, 55987. Tel: 507-454-4643; Fax: 507-454-8106.

Charismatic Renewal—Very Rev. MICHAEL J. HOEPPNER, J.C.L., V.G., Pastoral Center, 55 W. Sanborn St., P.O. Box 588, Winona, 55987. Tel: 507-454-4643; Fax: 507-454-8106.

Council of Catholic Women—Ms. ROSE SCHWALBACH, Pres., 1305 2nd St., Windom, 56101. Tel: 507-831-3490; Rev. THOMAS J. HARGESHEIMER, Diocesan Moderator, St. Joseph Church, 512 S. Elm Ave., Owatonna, 55060. Tel: 507-451-4845.

Diocesan Self-Insurance Plan—Mr. MIKE SAFFEL, Catholic Mutual Group, 111 Riverfront, Ste. 209, Winona, 55987. Tel: 507-454-6452; 800-494-6452; Fax: 800-335-8141; 507-454-8141.

Diocese of Winona Foundation—Deacon LEONARD FULLER, Exec. Dir., 55 W. Sanborn St., P.O. Box 588, Winona, 55987. Tel: 507-454-4643; Fax: 507-454-8106. Email: 1fuller@dow.org. Web: www.dow.org.

Hospitals—Rev. JAMES F. BURYSKA, Rochester Methodist Hospital, 201 W. Center St., Rochester, 55902. Tel: 507-255-5551; Fax: 507-255-3125.

Catholic Medical Association—Dr. JOHN I. LANE, M.D., 200 First St., S.W., Rochester, 55905. Tel: 507-266-1206. Email: lane.john@mayo.edu.

Girl Scouts—Mrs. ALMA RICHARD, Coord., 55 W. Sanborn St., P.O. Box 588, Winona, 55987. Tel: 507-454-4643; Fax: 507-454-8106.

Marriage Preparation/Enrichment—Mrs. ALMA RICHARD, 55 W. Sanborn St., P.O. Box 588, Winona, 55987. Tel: 507-454-4643; Fax: 507-454-8106.

Pathways TEC (Teens Encounter Christ)—Mrs. ALMA RICHARD, Diocesan Liaison, 55 W. Sanborn St., P.O. Box 588, Winona, 55987. Tel: 507-454-4643; Fax: 507-454-8106; Rev. ANDREW J. BEERMAN, S.T.L., Spiritual Dir., Church of St. Catherine, 203 E. Brown St., Luverne, 56156. Tel: 507-283-8502.

Respect Life—Mrs. ALMA RICHARD, 55 W. Sanborn St., P.O. Box 588, Winona, 55987. Tel: 507-454-4643; Fax: 507-454-8106.

Misconduct Issues—Very Rev. MICHAEL J. HOEPPNER, J.C.L., V.G.; Rev. MICHAEL J. CRONIN, J.C.L.; Mrs. PAMELA J. THOMPSON, 55 W. Sanborn St., P.O. Box 588, Winona, 55987. Tel: 507-454-4643; Fax: 507-454-8106; Mr. ROBERT TEREBA, Catholic Charities, 111 Market St., P.O. Box 379, Winona, 55987. Tel: 507-454-2270; Fax: 507-457-3027. Email: rtereba@ccwinona.org.

Southern Minnesota Retrouvaille—Rev. THEODORE J. HOTTINGER, S.J., Dir., Ss. Peter & Paul Church, 105 N. 5th St., Mankato, 56001-4442. Tel: 507-388-2995; 507-386-1369 (Couple Contact).

Victim Assistance Coordinator—Mrs. P. J. THOMPSON. Tel: 507-454-4643, Ext. 223. Email: pjthompson@dow.org.

CLERGY, PARISHES, MISSIONS AND PAROCHIAL SCHOOLS

CITY OF WINONA
(WINONA COUNTY)

1—CATHEDRAL OF THE SACRED HEART (1950), [JC] Very Rev. John M. Sauer, Rector; Rev. Eugene M. Klein. In Res., Rev. Cyril Fabian, O.P. Tel: 507-452-5428 (Res); 507-457-1539; Very Rev. Michael J. Hoeppner, J.C.L., V.G. Tel: 507-454-4643.
Res.: 360 Main St., 55987-3299. Tel: 507-452-4770; Fax: 507-454-1974.
School— See listings under Centralized Catholic Schools.
Catechesis/Religious Program—Students 199.

2—ST. CASIMIR'S (1906), [JC] Attended by, Cathedral of the Sacred Heart, 360 Main St., Winona. Very Rev. John M. Sauer.
Church: 624 W. Broadway, 55987-2721. Tel: 507-452-3434; Fax: 507-474-1980.
Catechesis/Religious Program—Tel: 507-454-7311. Students 50.

3—ST. JOHN NEPOMUCENE (1888), Attended by, St. Stanislaus, Winona. , 625 E. Fourth St., 55987-4297. Tel: 507-452-5430; Fax: 507-452-3355.
Catechesis/Religious Program—602 E. Fifth St., 55987. Students 29.

4—ST. MARY'S (1911), [JC] Rev. William M. Becker, S.T.D.; Deacon Gordon D. Richard.
Res.: 1303 W. Broadway, 55987-2395. Tel: 507-452-5656; Fax: 507-452-5477.
School— See listings under Centralized Catholic Schools.
Catechesis/Religious Program—Tel: 507-452-5656; Fax: 507-452-5477. Students 168.

5—ST. STANISLAUS (1871), Rev. Daniel R. Dernek.
Res.: 625 E. Fourth St., 55987-4297. Tel: 507-452-5430; Fax: 507-452-3355.
School—Tel: 507-452-3766. See listings under Centralized Catholic Schools.
Catechesis/Religious Program—602 E. Fifth St., 55987. Students 100.

OUTSIDE THE CITY OF WINONA

ADAMS, MOWER CO., SACRED HEART (1886), [CEM] Very Rev. Gregory P. Leif.
Res.: 412 Main St., P.O. Box 352, 55909-9998. Tel: 507-582-3321; Fax: 507-582-1033.
School—(Grades 1-8) Tel: 507-582-3120. Mr. Shawn

Kennedy, Prin. Sisters 1; Lay Teachers 7; Students 121.
Catechesis/Religious Program—Tel: 507-582-3321. Students 63.
Convent—Tel: 507-582-3304.

ADRIAN, NOBLES CO., ST. ADRIAN (1877), [CEM] Very Rev. Gerald C. Kosse.
Res.: 512 Maine Ave., P.O. Box 475, 56110-0475. Tel: 507-483-2317; Fax: 507-483-2460.
Catechesis/Religious Program—108 E. Sixth St., 56110. Tel: 507-483-2480; Fax: 507-483-2480. Students 179.

ALBERT LEA, FREEBORN CO., ST. THEODORE'S (1882), [CEM] Rev. Robert J. Schneider.
Res.: 308 E. Fountain, 56007-2456. Tel: 507-373-0603; Fax: 507-373-0603.
Parish Center & School—323 E. Clark St., 56007. Tel: 507-373-9657. See listings under Centralized Catholic Schools.
Catechesis/Religious Program—Tel: 507-373-2987; Fax: 507-373-9657. Students 437.

ALTURA, WINONA CO., ST. ANTHONY'S (1919), [JC] Attended by, St. Rose of Lima. Rev. Shawn T. Haremza.
180 S. Fremont, P.O. Box 727, Lewiston, 55952-0727. Tel: 507-796-6271; 507-523-2428 (Rectory).
Catechesis/Religious Program—Students 85.

AUSTIN, MOWER CO.
1—ST. AUGUSTINE'S (1857), [JC] Attended by, St. Edward, Austin. Rev. Joseph B. Fogal.
Res.: 405 Fourth St., N.W., 55912-3091. Tel: 507-437-4537; Fax: 507-437-4537.
School— See listings under Centralized Catholic Schools.
Catechesis/Religious Program—Tel: 507-437-3250. Students 171.
2—ST. EDWARD'S (1960), [JC] Rev. Joseph B. Fogal. In Res., Very Rev. Kurt Farrell; Rev. Richard P. Loomis (Retired).
Res.: 2000 Oakland Ave. W., 55912-1599. Tel: 507-433-1841; Fax: 507-433-9680.
School— See listings under Centralized Catholic Schools.
Catechesis/Religious Program—Tel: 507-437-3250. Students 92.
3—QUEEN OF ANGELS (1936), [JC] Rev. Dale E. Tupper.
Res.: 1001 Oakland Ave. E., 55912-3896. Tel: 507-433-1888; Fax: 507-433-1889.
School—Tel: 507-433-8745. See listings under Centralized Catholic Schools.
Catechesis/Religious Program—511 4th Ave., N.W., 55912. Tel: 507-437-3250. Students 182.
Catechesis/Religious Program—Spanish Catechesis, 912 1st Ave., N.W., 55912. Tel: 507-433-8474. Total Enrollment 8.
Queens of Angels Hermitage—1009 E. Oakland Ave., 55912. Tel: 507-437-4015. Rev. Jon H. Moore.

BLOOMING PRAIRIE, STEELE CO., ST. COLUMBANUS (1878), [CEM] Rev. Richard J. Dernek.
Res.: 114 E. Main, 55917-1427. Tel: 507-583-2529; 507-583-2784; Fax: 507-583-7738.
Catechesis/Religious Program—Tel: 507-583-2784. Students 145.

BLUE EARTH, FARIBAULT CO., SS. PETER AND PAUL'S (1866), [CEM] Rev. John W. Ozbun.
Res.: 214 S. Holland, 56013-1331. Tel: 507-526-5626.
Catechesis/Religious Program—Tel: 507-526-2816. Students 209.

BREWSTER, NOBLES CO., SACRED HEART (1901), [CEM] Attended by, St. Francis Xaiver, Windom Rev. Andrew D. Olsem.
548 17th St., Windom, 56101-1217. Tel: 507-831-3300; Fax: 507-831-3300.
Catechesis/Religious Program—P.O. Box 187, 56119. Tel: 507-842-5584; Fax: 507-842-5523. Loretta Smith, D.R.E. Students 70.

BROWNSDALE, MOWER CO., OUR LADY OF LORETTO (1946), Attended by, Queen of Angels, Austin. Rev. Dale E. Tupper.
1001 Oakland Ave. E., Austin, 55912-1599. Tel: 507-433-1888; Fax: 507-433-1889.
Catechesis/Religious Program—Tel: 507-567-2602. Students 29.

BROWNSVILLE, HOUSTON CO., ST. PATRICK'S (1871), [CEM] [JC 2] Attended by, St. Peter. Rev. Paul J. Breza.
Mailing Address: P.O. Box 355, Hokah, 55941-0355. Tel: 507-894-4242; Fax: 507-894-4375.
Catechesis/Religious Program—P.O. Box 155, 55919. Tel: 507-482-6769. Students 40.

BYRON, OLMSTED CO., CHRIST THE KING (1965), Rev. Charlie I. Collins.
Res.: 202 Fourth St., N.W., P.O. Box 1000, 55920-1000. Tel: 507-775-6455; Fax: 507-775-6473.
Catechesis/Religious Program—Tel: 507-775-0501. Students 268.

CALEDONIA, HOUSTON CO., ST. MARY (1975), [CEM] Rev. Donald J. Schmitz, M.A.
Res.: 513 S. Pine St., P.O. Box 406, 55921-0406. Tel: 507-725-3804; Fax: 507-725-2001.
School—(Grades K-8) Tel: 507-725-3355. Mrs. Gail Trocinski, Prin. Priests 1; Lay Teachers 14; Students 180.
Catechesis/Religious Program—Tel: 507-725-4408. Students 196.
Convent—308 E. South, 55921.

CANTON, FILLMORE CO., THE ASSUMPTION (1891), [CEM] [JC] Attended by, Nativity of B.V.M. Rev. Msgr. Donald P. Schmitz, M.Ch.A.
640 First Ave., S.W., Harmony, 55939-0596. Tel: 507-886-2393; Fax: 507-886-2393.
Catechesis/Religious Program— (Students attend Rel. Educ programs at Nativity, Harmony or St. Olaf, Mabel). Total Enrollment 18.

CHATFIELD, FILLMORE CO., ST. MARY'S (1856), [CEM 2] Rev. Russell G. Scepaniak.
405 Twiford St., 55923. Tel: 507-867-3148; Fax: 507-867-0073.
Catechesis/Religious Program—Tel: 507-867-3138. Students 150.

CLAREMONT, DODGE CO., ST. FRANCIS DE SALES (1869), [CEM] [JC] Attended by, St. John Baptist de La Salle, Dodge Center. Rev. James J. Seitz.
20 Second St., N.E., P.O. Box 310, Dodge Center, 55927-0310. Tel: 507-374-6830; Fax: 612-605-4315.
Catechesis/Religious Program—Tel: 507-528-2200. Students 27.

CURRIE, MURRAY CO., IMMACULATE HEART OF MARY (1883), Rev. Msgr. Paul C. Evers.
Res.: 510 Mill St., P.O. Box 174, 56123-0174. Tel: 507-763-3145.
Catechesis/Religious Program—Students 107.

DAKOTA, WINONA CO., HOLY CROSS (1890), Attended by, Crucifixion Church, LaCrescent. Rev. Msgr. Donald W. Grubisch; Rev. Eugene M. Klein.
Church: 320 River St., 55925. Tel: 507-895-4720; Fax: 507-895-6880.
Catechesis/Religious Program—Tel: 507-452-7261. Students 24.

DEERFIELD, STEELE CO., CORPUS CHRISTI (1869), Attended by, Christ the King, Medford. Ms. Amy Hellevik Parish Dir.
205 N.W. Second Ave., P.O. Box 120, Medford, 55049-0120. Tel: 507-451-6353; Fax: 507-451-6353.
Catechesis/Religious Program—Tel: 507-451-8898. Students 20.

DELAVAN, FARIBAULT CO., MATER DOLOROSA (1889), Closed. For inquiries for parish records contact the chancery.

DODGE CENTER, DODGE CO., ST. JOHN BAPTIST DE LA SALLE (1945), Rev. James J. Seitz.
Res.: 20 Second St. N.E., P.O. Box 310, 55927-0310. Tel: 507-374-6830; Fax: 612-605-4315.
Catechesis/Religious Program—Tel: 507-374-6765. Students 55.

DUNDEE, NOBLES CO., ST. MARY, Closed. For inquiries for parish records contact the chancery.

EAST CHAIN, MARTIN CO., HOLY FAMILY (1897), [CEM] [JC] Attended by, St. John Vianney, Fairmont. Rev. Kevin Connolly.
Res.: 901 S. Prairie Ave., Fairmont, 56031-3098. Tel: 507-235-5535; Fax: 507-235-5639.
Catechesis/Religious Program—Tel: 507-773-4491. Students 52.

EASTON, FARIBAULT CO., OUR LADY OF MOUNT CARMEL (1866), [CEM] Rev. Thomas E. Cook.
Res.: 27 Main St., P.O. Box 8, 56025-0008. Tel: 507-787-2303; Fax: 507-787-2221.
Catechesis/Religious Program—Students 28.

ELBA, WINONA CO., ST. ALOYSIUS (1877), [CEM] Attended by, St. Charles Borromeo, St. Charles. Rev. James F. Callahan, S.M.A.
736 Church Ave., St. Charles, 55972-1426. Tel: 507-932-3294; Fax: 507-932-3393.
Catechesis/Religious Program— Attend St. Charles Borromeo program, Tel: 507-932-3303. Students 30.

ELLENDALE, FREEBORN CO., ST. AIDAN (1857), [CEM] Attended by, All Saints, New Richland. Rev. Thein Van Nguyen.
Mailing Address: 307 SW First St., P.O. Box 185, New Richland, 56072-0185. Tel: 507-465-8217.
Catechesis/Religious Program—Tel: 507-684-2245. Students 82.

ELLSWORTH, NOBLES CO., ST. MARY'S (1885), [CEM] Attended by, St. Catherine, Luverne. 203 E. Brown St., Luverne, 56156-1599. Tel: 507-283-8502; Fax: 507-283-3638.
Catechesis/Religious Program—Tel: 712-479-2444. Students 18.

EYOTA, OLMSTED CO., HOLY REDEEMER (1891), Attended by, St. Charles Borromeo, St. Charles. Rev. James F. Callahan, S.M.A.
Mailing Address: 736 Church Ave., St. Charles, 55972-1426. 761 Whitewater Ave. St. Charles, 55972-1426. Tel: 507-932-3294; Fax: 507-932-3393.
Catechesis/Religious Program—Tel: 507-545-2161; Fax: 507-545-2161. Students 167.

FAIRMONT, MARTIN CO., ST. JOHN VIANNEY (1952), [CEM] Rev. Kevin Connolly; Deacon Edwin C. Bonnarens.
Parish Office—901 S. Prairie Ave., 56031-3098. Tel: 507-235-5535; Fax: 507-235-5536. Email: sjv@frontiernet.net.
School—(Grades PreK-7), 911 S. Prairie Ave., 56031. Tel: 507-235-5304; Fax: 507-235-9099. Email: sjv@frontiernet.net. Joan Schaffer, Prin. Priests 1; Lay Teachers 11; Students 149.
Catechesis/Religious Program—Tel: 507-235-5903. Students 243.

FOUNTAIN, FILLMORE CO., ST. LAWRENCE O'TOOLE (1872), Closed. For inquiries for parish records contact the chancery.

FULDA, MURRAY CO., ST. GABRIEL'S (1882), [CEM] Attended by, Immaculate Heart of Mary, Currie. Rev. Msgr. Paul C. Evers.
501 Mill St., P.O. Box 174, Currie, 56123-0174. Tel: 507-763-3145.
Res.: 309 W. Lake Ave., 56131-9402. Tel: 507-425-2595.
Catechesis/Religious Program—Tel: 507-425-2369. Students 177.

GENEVA, FREEBORN CO., ST. MARY (1867), [CEM] Attended by, All Saints, New Richland. Rev. Thein Van Nguyen.
307 1st St., S.W., P.O. Box 185, New Richland, 56072-0185. Tel: 507-465-8217; 507-465-8381.
Catechesis/Religious Program—Tel: 507-583-7530. Students 43.

GOOD THUNDER, BLUE EARTH CO., ST. JOSEPH (1879), [CEM] Attended by, St. Teresa, Mapleton. Tom Johnson, Parish Dir.
104 Silver St. W., P.O. Box 305, Mapleton, 56065. Tel: 507-524-3127; Fax: 507-524-4423.
Catechesis/Religious Program—Tel: 507-278-3444. Students 56.

GRAND MEADOW, MOWER CO., ST. FINBARR'S (1878), [CEM] Attended by, St. Ignatius, Spring Valley. Rev. Steven J. Peterson.
213 W. Franklin St., Spring Valley, 55975-1312. Tel: 507-346-7565.
Church: 504 1st St. S.W., P.O. Box 326, 55951. Tel: 507-754-5190.
Catechesis/Religious Program—Students 89.

GUCKEEN, FARIBAULT CO., OUR LADY OF MERCY (1902), Closed.

HAMMOND, WABASHA CO., ST. CLEMENT'S, Closed., For inquiries for parish records contact SS. Peter and Paul, Mazeppa.

HARMONY, FILLMORE CO., THE NATIVITY OF THE BLESSED VIRGIN (1906), Rev. Msgr. Donald P. Schmitz, M.Ch.A.
Res.: 640 First Ave., S.W., 55939-0596. Tel: 507-886-2393; Fax: 507-886-2394.
Catechesis/Religious Program—Students 53.

HAYFIELD, DODGE CO., SACRED HEART (1935), Attended by, St. Columbanus, Blooming Prairie. Rev. Richard J. Dernek.
114 E. Main St., Blooming Prairie, 55917-1427. Tel: 507-583-2529; Fax: 507-583-7738.
Catechesis/Religious Program—Tel: 507-477-2297. Students 79.

HERON LAKE, JACKSON CO., SACRED HEART (1884), [CEM] Attended by, St. Francis Xavier, Windom. Rev. Andrew D. Olsem.
548 17th St., Windom, 56101-1217. Tel: 507-831-3300; Fax: 507-831-3300.
Catechesis/Religious Program—Tel: 507-793-2773. Students 120.

HOKAH, HOUSTON CO., ST. PETER'S (1876), [CEM] [JC 2] Rev. Paul J. Breza.
Res.: 34 Main St., P.O. Box 355, 55941-0355. Tel: 507-894-4242.
School—(Grades K-8) Tel: 507-894-4375; 507-894-4944. Email: nativity@means.net. Mrs. Rachel Evenson, Prin. Students 64.
Catechesis/Religious Program—Students 23.

HOUSTON, HOUSTON CO., ST. MARY'S (1873), [CEM] Attended by, St. Joseph, Rushford. Rev. William J. Kulas.
101 Rushford Ave. W., P.O. Box 577, Rushford, 55971-0557. Tel: 507-864-2257; Fax: 507-864-2257.
Catechesis/Religious Program—Students 77.

IONA, MURRAY CO., ST. COLUMBA'S (1891), [CEM] Attended by, St. Ann, Slayton. Rev. Mark C. McNea.
2747 29th St., Slayton, 56172-1485. Tel: 507-836-8030; Fax: 507-836-6261.
Catechesis/Religious Program—Students 59.

JACKSON, JACKSON CO., GOOD SHEPHERD (1891), [CEM] Rev. Charles J. Quinn.
Res.: 311 N. Sverdrup Ave., P.O. Box 65, 56143-1329. Tel: 507-847-2504; Fax: 507-764-7831.
Catechesis/Religious Program—Tel: 507-847-2719. Susanne Foster, D.R.E. Students 150.

JANESVILLE, WASECA CO., ST. ANN'S (1876), [CEM] Rev. Glenn K. Frerichs.
307 W. Second St., P.O. Box 218, 56048-0218. Tel: 507-234-6244; Fax: 507-234-6237.
Catechesis/Religious Program—Tel: 507-234-5753. Students 153.

JASPER, PIPESTONE CO., ST. JOSEPH'S (1890), [CEM]

Attended by, St. Leo's, Pipestone. Rev. Martin T. Schaefer.
106 4th St., S.E., P.O. Box 36, Pipestone, 56154-0036. Tel: 507-825-3152; Fax: 507-825-4492.
Catechesis / Religious Program—Students 32.

JEFFERS, COTTONWOOD CO., ST. AUGUSTINE'S (1912), Closed. For inquiries for parish records contact the chancery.

JOHNSBURG, MOWER CO., ST. JOHN'S (1859), [CEM] Attended by, Sacred Heart, Adams. Rev. Gregory P. Lief.
412 Main St., P.O. Box 352, Adams, 55909. Tel: 507-582-3321; Fax: 507-582-1033.
Catechesis / Religious Program—Students 32.

KASSON, DODGE CO., HOLY FAMILY (1976), [CEM] Attended by, Christ the King, Byron. Rev. Charlie I. Collins.
202 Fourth St., N.W., P.O. Box 1000, Byron, 55920-1000. Tel: 507-775-6455; Fax: 507-775-6473.
Catechesis / Religious Program—Tel: 507-634-7599. Students 252.

KELLOGG, WABASHA CO.
1—ST. AGNES (1900), Attended by, St. Felix, Wabasha. Rev. Donald J. Lovas.
117 3rd St. W., Wabasha, 55981-1201. Tel: 651-565-3931; Fax: 651-565-4363.
Catechesis / Religious Program—Tel: 507-767-4780. Students 56.
2—IMMACULATE CONCEPTION (1881), Attended by, St. Felix, Wabasha. , 117 3rd St. W., Wabasha, 55981-1201. Tel: 651-565-3931; Fax: 651-565-4363.
Catechesis / Religious Program—Tel: 507-534-3588. Students 104.

LA CRESCENT, HOUSTON CO., THE CRUCIFIXION (1856), [CEM 2] Rev. Msgr. Donald W. Grubisch.
Res.: 407 S. Second St., 55947-1326. Tel: 507-895-4720; Fax: 507-895-6880.
School—(Grades K-6), 420 S. Second St., 55947. Tel: 507-895-4402; Fax: 507-895-4403. Lay Teachers 10; Students 125.
Catechesis / Religious Program—1380 Lancer Blvd., 55947. Tel: 507-895-2700. Students 278.
Convent—423 S. Second St., 55947. Tel: 507-895-6867.

LAKE CITY, WABASHA CO., ST. MARY'S OF THE LAKE (1877), Rev. James D. Russell; Mr. Michael Kieffer, Admin.
Res.: 419 Lyon Ave., 55041-1649. Tel: 651-345-4134; Fax: 651-345-6134.
Catechesis / Religious Program—Tel: 651-345-3535. Students 270.

LAKE CRYSTAL, BLUE EARTH CO., HOLY FAMILY (1900), [CEM] Attended by, St. Joseph the Worker, Mankato. Rev. John P. Wilmot.
Res.: 423 W. 7th St., Mankato, 56001-2197. Tel: 507-388-3766; Fax: 507-388-2101.
Catechesis / Religious Program—Tel: 507-726-2725. Students 108.

LAKE WILSON, MURRAY CO., ST. MARY (1916), [JC] Attended by, St. Ann, Slayton. Rev. Mark C. McNea.
2747 29th St., Slayton, 56172-1485. Tel: 507-836-8030; Fax: 507-836-6261.
Catechesis / Religious Program—Students 41.

LAKEFIELD, JACKSON CO., ST. JOSEPH (1897), [CEM] Attended by, Good Shepherd, Jackson. Rev. Charles J. Quinn.
311 N. Sverdrup Ave., P.O. Box 65, Jackson, 56143-1329. Tel: 507-847-2504; Fax: 507-847-3734.
Catechesis / Religious Program—410 Broadway Ave., Box 517, 56150. Tel: 507-662-5819. Students 104.

LAMOILLE, WINONA CO., PRECIOUS BLOOD (1900), Closed. For inquiries for parish records contact the chancery.

LANESBORO, FILLMORE CO., ST. PATRICK (1871), [JC] Attended by, St. Mary's, Chatfield. Rev. Russell G. Scepaniak.
Church: 408 N.W. Preston St., Preston, 55965. Tel: 507-867-3148; Fax: 507-867-0073.
Catechesis / Religious Program—Tel: 507-467-2610. Students 30.

LE ROY, MOWER CO., ST. PATRICK'S (1878), [CEM] Attended by, St. Ignatius, Spring Valley. Rev. Steven J. Peterson.
213 W. Franklin St., Spring Valley, 55975-1312. Tel: 507-346-7565; Fax: 507-324-5203.
Catechesis / Religious Program—Tel: 507-324-5575. Students 141.

LEWISTON, WINONA CO., ST. ROSE OF LIMA (1876), [CEM] Rev. Shawn T. Haremza.
Res.: 180 S. Fremont, P.O. Box 727, 55952-0727. Tel: 507-523-2428.
Catechesis / Religious Program—Tel: 507-523-3548. Students 184.

LISMORE, NOBLES CO., ST. ANTHONY'S (1887), [CEM] Very Rev. Gerald C. Kosse, Priest Moderator; Roxanne Lisnak Kemper.
Mailing Address: 310 Third Ave. S., P.O. Box 158, 56155-0158. Tel: 507-472-8262; Fax: 507-472-8454.
Catechesis / Religious Program—Tel: 507-472-8262; Fax: 507-472-8454. Students 56.

LITOMYSL, STEELE CO., HOLY TRINITY (1877), Attended by, Sacred Heart, Owatonna. Rev. Peter J. Klein.
Church: 2000 Oakland Ave. W., Austin, 55912-1599. Tel: 507-451-1588.
School—St. Isidore, (Grades K-8) Tel: 507-451-5876; Fax: 507-433-9680. Ann Nylund, Prin. Priests 1; Lay Teachers 3; Students 39.
Catechesis / Religious Program—Tel: 507-583-7591. Students 42.

LUVERNE, ROCK CO., ST. CATHERINE'S (1881), [CEM] Rev. Andrew J. Beerman, S.T.L.
203 E. Brown, 56156-1599. Tel: 507-283-8502; Fax: 507-283-3638.
Catechesis / Religious Program—Tel: 507-283-8071. Students 216.

LYLE, MOWER CO., QUEEN OF PEACE (1946), (German), Attended by, St. Peter, Rose Creek. Rev. Ruben C. Spinler.
302 Maple St., S.W., Rose Creek, 55970-9701. Tel: 507-433-1532.
Catechesis / Religious Program—Tel: 507-325-4677. Students 54.

MABEL, FILLMORE CO., ST. OLAF (1954), [JC] Attended by, Nativity of B.V.M., Harmony. Rev. Msgr. Donald P. Schmitz, M.Ch.A.
640 First Ave., S.W., Harmony, 55939-0596. Tel: 507-886-2393; Fax: 507-886-2394.

MADELIA, WATONWAN CO., ST. MARY (1872), Rev. James C. Berning.
Res.: 212 First St., N.E., 56062-1702. Tel: 507-642-8305.
School—(Grades PreK-6) Tel: 507-642-3324. Mrs. Bridgette McMichael, Prin. Priests 1; Lay Teachers 3; Students 62.
Catechesis / Religious Program—Students 123.

MADISON LAKE, BLUE EARTH CO., ALL SAINTS (1894), [CEM] Rev. Patrick O. Arens.
Parish Endowment Fund, Inc. of All Saints Church—600 3rd St., P.O. Box 217, 56063-0217. Tel: 507-243-3319; Fax: 507-243-4308.
School—(Grades PreK-6), P.O. Box 158, 56063-0158. Tel: 507-243-3819. Sr. Mary Beth Schraml, S.S.N.D., Prin. Priests 1; Sisters 2; Lay Teachers 4; K-6 37; Preschool 19.
Catechesis / Religious Program—Students 136.
Convent—Tel: 507-243-3010.

MANKATO, BLUE EARTH CO.
1—ST. FRANCIS XAVIER MISSION CHAPEL, Closed. For inquiries for parish records contact the chancery.
2—ST. JOHN THE BAPTIST'S (1884), [JC] Revs. Richard M. Colletti; Shawn T. Haremza.
Res.: 632 S. Broad St., 56001-3890. Tel: 507-625-3131; Fax: 507-625-3270.
School— See listings under Centralized Catholic Schools.
Catechesis / Religious Program—Students 726.
3—ST. JOSEPH THE WORKER (1957), [JC] Rev. John P. Wilmot.
Res.: 423 W. 7th St., 56001-2197. Tel: 507-388-3766; Fax: 507-388-2101.
School— See listings under Centralized Catholic Schools.
Catechesis / Religious Program—423 W. 7th St., 56001. Tel: 507-625-3450. Students 172.
Convent—Tel: 507-388-2515.
4—SS. PETER AND PAUL'S (1854), Revs. Karl J. Voelker, S.J.; Theodore J. Hottinger, S.J.
Res.: 105 N. Fifth St., 56001-4442. Tel: 507-388-2995; Fax: 507-388-7661.
School—Tel: 507-387-3316. See listings under Centralized Catholic Schools.
Pastoral Center—512 Mulberry St., 56001-4442. Tel: 507-388-1664.
Catechesis / Religious Program—Tel: 507-387-6228. Students 263.

MAPLETON, BLUE EARTH CO., ST. TERESA'S (1876), [CEM] Rev. Timothy E. Biren, Priest Moderator; Mr. Tom Johnson, Parish Dir.
Res.: 104 Silver St., P.O. Box 305, 56065. Tel: 507-524-3127; Fax: 507-524-4423.
Catechesis / Religious Program—Tel: 507-524-4606. Students 116.

MAZEPPA, WABASHA CO., SS. PETER AND PAUL (1860), Rev. Robert G. Meyer.
Res.: 1st St. S., P.O. Box 224, 55956-0224. Tel: 507-843-3885; Fax: 507-843-3900.
Catechesis / Religious Program—Tel: 507-843-4600. Students 87.

MEDFORD, STEELE CO., CHRIST THE KING (1943), Ms. Amy Hellevik, Parish Dir.; Rev. Robert D. Herman (Retired).
Res.: 205 N.W. Second Ave., P.O. Box 120, 55049-0120. Tel: 507-451-6353; Fax: 507-451-6353.
Catechesis / Religious Program—Tel: 507-451-8898. Students 80.

MINNEISKA, WABASHA CO., ST. MARY'S (1867), Attended by, Holy Trinity, Rollingstone. Rev. Michael J. Cronin, J.C.L.
83 Main St., Rollingstone, 55969-9759. Tel: 507-689-2351; Fax: 507-689-2251.
Catechesis / Religious Program—Total Enrollment 8.

MINNESOTA CITY, WINONA CO., ST. PAUL'S (1924), [CEM] Rev. Edward Cunningham, O.M.I.
Res.: 132 Anderson St., P.O. Box 26, 55959-0026. Tel: 507-689-2485; Fax: 507-689-4559.
Catechesis / Religious Program—Students 13.

MINNESOTA LAKE, FARIBAULT CO., ST. JOHN THE BAPTIST (1865), [CEM] Attended by, Our Lady of Mount Carmel, Easton. Rev. Thomas E. Cook.
Mailing Address: 27 Main St., P.O. Box 8, Easton, 56025-0008. Tel: 507-787-2303; Fax: 507-787-2221.
Church: 100 Park St., P.O. Box 158, 56068. Tel: 507-462-3636; Fax: 507-462-3212.
Catechesis / Religious Program—Tel: 507-462-3791. Students 73.

NEW RICHLAND, WASECA CO., ALL SAINTS (1879), [CEM] Rev. Thein Van Nguyen.
Res.: 307 1st St., S.W., P.O. Box 185, 56072-0185. Tel: 507-465-8217.
Catechesis / Religious Program—Students 104.

OAK RIDGE, WINONA CO., IMMACULATE CONCEPTION (1875), Closed., For inquiries about sacramental records contact Holy Trinity, Rollingstone.

OWATONNA, STEELE CO.
1—ST. JOSEPH'S (1891), Rev. Thomas J. Hargeshemer; Deacon Paul Hillyer.
Res.: 512 S. Elm St., 55060-3399. Tel: 507-451-4845; Fax: 507-451-4651.
School— See listings under Centralized Catholic Schools.
Catechesis / Religious Program—Students 411.
2—SACRED HEART (1866), [JC] Rev. Peter J. Klein; Deacon George Anderberg, Pastoral Assoc.
Res.: 810 S. Cedar Ave., 55060-3297. Tel: 507-451-1588; Fax: 507-446-9979.
School—Tel: 507-446-2300; Fax: 507-446-2304. See listings under Centralized Catholic Schools.
Catechesis / Religious Program—Marian Dr., 55060. Tel: 507-446-2302. Students 400.

PIPESTONE, PIPESTONE CO., ST. LEO'S (1887), [CEM] Rev. Martin T. Schaefer.
Res.: 106 Fourth St., S.E., P.O. Box 36, 56164-0036. Tel: 507-825-3152; Fax: 507-825-4492.
Catechesis / Religious Program—Students 235.

PLAINVIEW, WABASHA CO., ST. JOACHIM'S (1858), [CEM] Rev. Donald F. Connelly.
Res.: 900 W. Broadway, 55964-1039. Tel: 507-534-3321; Fax: 507-534-3687.
Catechesis / Religious Program—Tel: 507-534-2887. Students 428.

PRESTON, FILLMORE CO., ST. COLUMBAN (1869), [CEM 2] [JC] Attended by, St. Mary's, Chatfield. Rev. Russell G. Scepaniak.
Church: 408 N.W. Preston St., 55965. Tel: 507-765-3886.
Catechesis / Religious Program—Students 60.

ROCHESTER, OLMSTED CO.
1—ST. BRIDGET'S (1857), [CEM] Attended by, St. Bernard, Stewartville. Rev. Gregory G. Havel.
116 4th Ave., S.E., Stewartville, 55976. Tel: 507-533-8257.
Catechesis / Religious Program—Tel: 507-533-8192. Students 68.
2—ST. FRANCIS OF ASSISI (1937), [JC] Rev. Timothy T. Reker, S.T.L.; Deacons Michael Mangas; Placedo Zavala.
Res.: 1114 3rd St., S.E., 55904-7293. Tel: 507-288-7313; Fax: 507-281-5997.
School—Tel: 507-288-4816; Fax: 507-288-4815. See listings under Centralized Catholic Schools.
Catechesis / Religious Program—Tel: 507-289-2427. Students 242.
3—HOLY SPIRIT (1990), [JC] Rev. Donald J. Schmitz, M.A.
Office:—5455 50th Ave., N.W., 55901. Tel: 507-280-0638; Fax: 507-292-9547.
Res.: Tel: 507-281-8323.
School— See listings under Centralized Catholic Schools.
Catechesis / Religious Program—Students 227.
4—ST. JOHN'S (1863), [JC] Rev. Msgr. Gerald A. Mahon; Deacon John DeStazio.
Res.: 11 4th Ave., S.W., 55902-3098. Tel: 507-288-7372; Fax: 507-288-7373.
School—Tel: 507-282-5248. See listings under Centralized Catholic Schools.
Catechesis / Religious Program—Students 200.
5—PAX CHRISTI (1973), [JC] Rev. Joseph L. Keefe.
Res.: 4135 18th Ave., N.W., 55901-0460. Tel: 507-282-8542; Fax: 507-289-8741.
School—Tel: 507-280-0349; Fax: 507-289-4008. See listings under Centralized Catholic Schools.
Catechesis / Religious Program—Students 610.
6—ST. PIUS X (1954), [JC] Revs. Paul W. Surprenant; Paul E. Nelson.
Res.: 1315 12th Ave., N.W., 55901-1744. Tel: 507-288-8238; Fax: 507-286-8769.
School—Tel: 507-282-5161; Fax: 507-282-5107. See listings under Centralized Catholic Schools.
Catechesis / Religious Program—Tel: 507-289-6317;

Fax: 507-286-8769. Students 229.
7—RESURRECTION (1967), [JC] Revs. Thomas A. Loomis; Robert Horihan.
Res.: 1600-11th Ave., S.E., 55904-5499. Tel: 507-288-5528; Fax: 507-252-0763.
School— See listings under Centralized Catholic Schools.
Catechesis/Religious Program—Students 530.
ROLLINGSTONE, WINONA CO., HOLY TRINITY (1862), [CEM] Rev. Michael J. Cronin, J.C.L.; Sr. Anne Walch, O.S.F., Pastoral Assoc.
Res.: 83 Main St., 55969-9759. Tel: 507-689-2351; Fax: 507-689-2251.
Catechesis/Religious Program—Students 54.
Oratory—Immaculate Conception Chapel Oak Ridge.
ROSE CREEK, MOWER CO., ST. PETER'S (1885), [CEM] Rev. Ruben C. Spinler.
Res.: 302 Maple St., S.W., 55970-9701. Tel: 507-433-1532.
Catechesis/Religious Program—Tel: 507-433-6472. Students 87.
RUSHFORD, FILLMORE CO., ST. JOSEPH'S (1868), [CEM] Rev. William J. Kulas.
Res.: 101 Rushford Ave. W., P.O. Box 577, 55971-0577. Tel: 507-864-2257; Fax: 507-864-3716.
Catechesis/Religious Program—Students 89.
ST. CHARLES, WINONA CO., ST. CHARLES BORROMEO (1867), [CEM] Rev. James F. Callahan, S.M.A.
Mailing Address: 736 Church Ave., 55972-1426. Tel: 507-932-3294; Fax: 507-932-3393.
Church: 761 Whitewater Ave., 55972-1426.
Catechesis/Religious Program—Tel: 507-932-3303. Students 275.
ST. CLAIR, BLUE EARTH CO., IMMACULATE CONCEPTION (1874), [CEM] Attended by, All Saints Church, 600 3rd St., P.O. Box 217, Madison Lake 56063-0217. Rev. Patrick O. Arens.
Tel: 507-243-3319.
Catechesis/Religious Program—Students 196.
ST. JAMES, WATONWAN CO., ST. JAMES (1876), [CEM] Attended by, St. Mary Church, 212 First St., N.E., Madelia, MN, 56062. Rev. James C. Berning. Tel: 507-642-8305; Sr. Lucille Hass, O.S.F., Pastoral Assoc.
Church: 707 4th St. S., 56081-1824. Tel: 507-375-3542; Fax: 507-375-4170.
Catechesis/Religious Program—Nonnie Hanson, D.R.E.; Mary Christensen, D.R.E. Students 200.
ST. KILIAN, NOBLES CO., ST. KILIAN (1903), [CEM] Attended by, St. Anthony, Lismore. Roxanne Lisnak Kemper, Parish Dir.
Mailing Address: 310 Third Ave. S., P.O. Box 158, Lismore, 56155-0158. Tel: 507-472-8262; Fax: 507-472-8454.
Catechesis/Religious Program—Tel: 507-472-8206. Students 23.
SHERBURN, MARTIN CO., ST. LUKE'S (1888), [CEM] Attended by, Good Shepherd, Jackson. Rev. Charles J. Quinn.
Res.: 311 N. Sverdrup Ave., P.O. Box 65, Jackson, 56143-1329. Tel: 507-847-2504; Fax: 507-847-5322.
Catechesis/Religious Program—Tel: 507-764-7831; Fax: 507-764-7831. Students 75.
SLAYTON, MURRAY CO., ST. ANN'S (1897), [CEM] Rev. Mark C. McNea.
Res.: 2747 29th St., 56172-1485. Tel: 507-836-8030; Fax: 507-836-6261.
Catechesis/Religious Program—Students 162.
SPRING VALLEY, FILLMORE CO., ST. IGNATIUS (1878), [CEM] Rev. Steven J. Peterson.
Res.: 213 Franklin St., 55975-1312. Tel: 507-346-7565.
Catechesis/Religious Program—Tel: 507-346-7194. Students 110.
STEWARTVILLE, OLMSTED CO., ST. BERNARD'S (1894), [CEM] Rev. Gregory G. Havel.
Res.: 116 Fourth Ave., S.E., 55976. Tel: 507-533-8257.
Catechesis/Religious Program—Tel: 507-533-8192. Students 324.
THEILMAN, WABASHA CO., ST. JOSEPH'S (1903), [CEM] Attended by, St. Mary of the Lake, Lake City. Rev. James D. Russell.
419 Lyon Ave., Lake City, 55041-1649. Tel: 651-345-4134; Fax: 507-345-6134.
TRIMONT, MARTIN CO., ST. JOSEPH, Closed. For inquiries for parish records contact the chancery.
TRUMAN, MARTIN CO., ST. KATHERINE (1954), Attended by, St. Mary, Madelia. Rev. James C. Berning.
212 First St., N.E., Madelia, 56062-1702. Tel: 507-642-8305; Fax: 507-375-4170.
Catechesis/Religious Program—Students 50.
TWIN LAKES, FREEBORN CO., ST. JAMES (1876), Attended by, St. Theodore, Albert Lea. Rev. Robert J. Schneider.
Church: 602 31st St., N.W., Austin, 55912. Tel: 507-373-0603; Fax: 507-373-9657.
VERNON CENTER, BLUE EARTH CO., ST. MATTHEW (1911), [CEM] Attended by, St. Teresa, Mapleton. Tom Johnson, Parish Dir.
104 Silver St. W., P.O. Box 305, Mapleton, 56065.
Tel: 507-524-3127; Fax: 507-524-4423.
Catechesis/Religious Program—Tel: 507-549-3358. Students 65.
WABASHA, WABASHA CO., ST. FELIX (1858), [CEM] Rev. Donald J. Lovas.
Res.: 117 W. Third St., 55981-1201. Tel: 651-565-3931; Fax: 651-565-4363.
School—(Grades PreK-6), 130 Third St. E., 55981. Tel: 651-564-4446; Fax: 651-565-0244. Sr. M. Joann McMahon, S.S.N.D., Prin. Priests 1; Sisters 2; Lay Teachers 7; Students 184.
Catechesis/Religious Program—Tel: 651-565-3718; Fax: 651-565-4363. Students 150.
Convent—36 Bailey Ave., 55981. Tel: 651-565-4578.
WALDORF, WASECA CO., ST. JOSEPH'S (1878), [CEM] Attended by, St. Ann, Janesville, 307 W 2nd St., P.O. Box 218, Janesville, MN 56048-0218. Rev. Glenn K. Frerichs.
Tel: 507-234-6244; Fax: 507-234-6237.
Catechesis/Religious Program—Students 64.
WASECA, WASECA CO., SACRED HEART (1869), [JC 2] Very Rev. John M. Kunz.
Res.: 111 Fourth St., N.W., 56093-2413. Tel: 507-835-1222; Fax: 507-833-1498.
School—(Grades PreK-4), 308 W. Elm Ave., 56093. Tel: 507-835-2780. LeAnn Dahle, Prin. Priests 1; Lay Teachers 11; Students 187.
School—Sacred Heart Children's House (Grades PreSchool-PreSchool), 400 Second Ave., N.W., 56093. Tel: 507-835-1044. Students 94.
Catechesis/Religious Program—Tel: 507-835-1500. Students 475.
WELLS, FARIBAULT CO., ST. CASIMIR'S (1880), [CEM] Rev. Eugene F. Stenzel.
Res.: 320 Second Ave., S.W., 56097-1399. Tel: 507-553-5391.
School—(Grades K-8), 330 Second Ave., S.W., 56097. Tel: 507-553-5822. Joanne Tibodeau, Prin. Lay Teachers 12; Students 112.
Catechesis/Religious Program—Students 151.
WEST ALBANY, WABASHA CO., ST. PATRICK OF WEST ALBANY (1865), [CEM] Attended by, SS. Peter and Paul, Mazeppa. Rev. Robert G. Meyer.
1st St. S., P.O. Box 224, Mazeppa, 55956-0224. Tel: 507-843-3885.
Catechesis/Religious Program—Tel: 507-753-2424; Fax: 507-843-3900. Students 62.
WEST CONCORD, DODGE CO., ST. VINCENT DE PAUL (1945), [CEM] Attended by, St. John Baptist de La Salle, Dodge Center. Rev. James J. Seitz.
20 Second St., N.E., P.O. Box 310, Dodge Center, 55927-0310. Tel: 507-374-6830.
Catechesis/Religious Program—P.O. Box 117, 55985. Tel: 507-527-2384; Fax: 612-605-4315. Students 59.
WESTBROOK, COTTONWOOD CO., ST. ANTHONY'S (1909), [CEM] Attended by, Immaculate Heart of Mary, Currie. Rev. Msgr. Paul C. Evers.
501 Mill St., P.O. Box 174, Currie, 56123-0174. Tel: 507-763-3145.
Church: 1153 1st. Ave., 56183.
WILMONT, NOBLES CO., OUR LADY OF GOOD COUNSEL (1903), [CEM] Attended by, St. Adrian Adrian. Very Rev. Gerald C. Kosse.
512 Main Ave., P.O. Box 475, Adrian, 56110-0475. Tel: 507-483-2317; Fax: 507-483-2460.
Catechesis/Religious Program—Tel: 507-926-5305. Students 56.
WILSON, WINONA CO., IMMACULATE CONCEPTION (1874), Attended by, St. Rose of Lima, Lewiston. Rev. Shawn T. Haremza.
180 S. Fremont St., P.O. Box 727, Lewiston, 55952-0727. Tel: 507-523-2428.
WINDOM, COTTONWOOD CO., ST. FRANCIS XAVIER'S (1898), Rev. Andrew D. Olsem.
Res.: 548 17th St., 56101-1217. Tel: 507-831-3300; Fax: 507-831-3300.
Catechesis/Religious Program—532 17th St., 56101. Tel: 507-831-1985. Students 163.
WINNEBAGO, FARIBAULT CO., ST. MARY'S (1893), [CEM] Attended by, Ss. Peter and Paul, Blue Earth Rev. John W. Czbun.
Church: 32 1st St., N.E., 56098-0308. Tel: 507-526-5626; Fax: 507-526-2456.
Catechesis/Religious Program—Students 54.
WOODSTOCK, PIPESTONE CO., ST. MARTIN'S (1882), [CEM] Attended by, St. Leo, Pipestone. Rev. Martin T. Schaefer.
Mailing Address: 106 Fourth St., S.E., P.O. Box 36, Pipestone 56164-0036. Tel: 507-825-5152; Fax: 507-825-4492.
Church: 101 Smith St., N., 56186.
Catechesis/Religious Program—Students 22.
WORTHINGTON, NOBLES CO., ST. MARY'S (1886), [CEM] Rev. Hilary R. Brixius.
Res.: 1215 Seventh Ave., 56187-2297. Tel: 507-376-6005; Fax: 507-376-9167.
School—(Grades PreK-6), Twelfth St. & Eighth Ave., 56187. Tel: 507-376-5236; Fax: 507-376-6159. Barbara Daly, Prin. Sisters 1; Lay Teachers 10; Students 129.
Catechesis/Religious Program—1206 Eighth Ave., 56187. Tel: 507-372-2090. Students 379.
Convent—1221 Seventh Ave., 56187. Tel: 507-376-4035.
WYKOFF, FILLMORE CO., ST. KILIAN'S (1887), Closed. For inquiries for parish records contact the chancery.

Chaplains of Public Institutions

WINONA. *Winona County Law Enforcement Center*. Deacon Justin Green, Chap.466 Chestnut St., 55987. Tel: 507-452-4723.
ROCHESTER. *Federal Medical Center*, Bureau of Prisons, 2110 Center St. E., 55904. Sr. Emile Bormann, P.B.V.M., Chap.
WASECA. *Federal Correctional Institution*. Vacant.

On Special or Other Diocesan Assignment:
Revs.—
Buryska, James F., Rochester Methodist Hospital, 201 W. Center St., Rochester, 55902. Tel: 507-255-5551
Byrne, David, Chap., Mayo Medical Center, 1216 2nd St. S.W., Rochester, 55902.
Kunz, James H., Mayo Medical Center, 1216 2nd St., S.W., Rochester, 55902. Tel: 507-285-5123
Marek, Dean V., Mayo Medical Center, 1216 2nd St., S.W., Rochester, 55902. Tel: 507-255-5780

On Duty Outside the Diocese:
Rev.—
Brandenhoff, Peter B., 8859 Spring Lane, Woodbury, 55125. Tel: 612-578-0957

Military Chaplains:
Rev.—
Arnoldt, David M., 20 A Sheridan Ave., Fort Riley, KS 66442. Tel: 785-239-4691 (LTC)

Absent on Leave:
Revs.—
Cashman, Joseph C.
Hodapp, Timothy L., 224 Lexington Pkwy. S., St. Paul, 55105. Tel: 651-848-0805
Taylor, Robert H., Diocese of Winona, P.O. Box 588, 55987.

Retired:
Rev. Msgrs.—
Egan, Eugene E., 401 N. Maple St., Ellsworth, 56129. Tel: 507-967-2382
Galles, Francis A., 500 Preston St., N.W., Preston, 55965. Tel: 507-765-2756
Habiger, James D., Univ. of St. Thomas, 2115 Summit Ave., Box 4174, St. Paul, 55105. Tel: 612-962-8065 (Res); 612-227-8777
Klein, Frank W., Callista Court, 1455 W. Broadway, Apt. 215, 55987.
Literski, Roy E., 1328 D. McNally Dr., 55987. Tel: 507-452-7685
McGinnis, Joseph R., 12262 W. Grant Blvd., Wabasha, 55981-1098. Tel: 651-565-5513
Mountain, Joseph W., 2143 Kennedy Dr., Faribault, 55021.
Ploof, Thomas M., 12301 W. Grant Blvd., Wabasha, 55981.
Revs.—
Brown, Sylvester F., 302 N.W. 4th St., P.O. Box 232, Elysian, 56028.
Conway, Gerald W., 728 First Ave. S.W., #404, Rochester, 55902-3307. Tel: 507-285-1279
Cook, Louis G., 495 8th St. S.W., Plainview, 55964.
Dandelet, James D., P.O. Box 46, Easton, 56025-0046. Tel: 507-787-2520
Duellman, Virgil S., 84 Teepeota Cir., Wabasha, 55981. Tel: 651-565-4623
Eikens, Leroy F., 728 First Ave., S.W. #403, Rochester, 55902-3307. Tel: 507-280-7692
Engels, Richard J., 205 Dugan St., Wabasha, 55981.
Ernster, Milo L., 163 Pioneer Dr., Wabasha, 55981. Tel: 612-565-2191
Gavin, Harold E., St. Elizabeth Home Health Care #117, 1200 Grant Blvd. W., Wabasha, 55981. Tel: 651-565-5577
Ginther, Lawrence P., 5125 W. Seventh St., Apt. 8, 55987-5616. Tel: 507-454-4789
Gits, Douglas J., 1420 4th St. S.E., Rochester, 55904-4716. Tel: 507-286-7874
Haberman, Clayton J., 5371 Elkton Tr., Faribault, 55021-8453. Tel: 507-334-0610
Halloran, Paul F., 7646 Sixth Lake Rd., N.W., Akeley, 56433-9507.
Hennessy, James W.
Herman, Robert D., 205 N.W. 2nd Ave., P.O. Box 120, Medford, 55049. Tel: 507-451-6353
Jewison, Harry P., 1024 Ninth St., N.E., Rochester, 55906. Tel: 507-285-5515
Kellen, Elmer W., 12104 W. Grant Blvd., Wabasha,

55981. Tel: 651-565-5679
Kerrigan, Bernard A., St. Elizabeth Health Care Center, 626 Shields Ave., Wabasha, 55981.
Kulas, Robert A., 7510 Cahill Rd., #201B, Edina, 55439. Tel: 952-946-8972
Kunz, Francis P., 240 Hudson Ave. E., Mankato, 56001. Tel: 507-625-6217
LaPlante, Joseph A., 31 Robinson Dr., Wabasha, 55981-3016. Tel: 651-565-2441
Leary, Donald G., 220 S. Broadway, #1504, Rochester, 55902. Tel: 507-288-5813
Loomis, Richard P., St. Edward Church, 2000 Oakland Ave. W., Austin, 55912. Tel: 507-433-1841
Loosbrock, Donald L., 149 Pioneer Dr., Wabasha, 55981-3214. Tel: 651-565-6531
Maher, Robert G., 9505 Salem Hills Court, Las Vegas, NV 89134-4600. Tel: 702-804-2718
McCauley, James A., P.O. Box 203, Brownsville, 55919. Tel: 507-482-6631
Mountain, Edward C., 420 11th St., S.E., Owatonna, 55060-4008. Tel: 507-451-6752
Mountain, Harold B., 50 Teton Ln., #124, Mankato, 56001-4813. Tel: 507-345-8933
Murtagh, Lawrence J., 839 Park Ave., Brookings, SD 57006. Tel: 605-692-1919
Quesnel, Raymond, O.M.I., Madonna Towers, 4001 19th Ave., N.W., Rochester, 55901-0553. Tel: 507-288-3911
Schaefer, Edgar J., 9659 111th Ave. N, Sun City, AZ 85351. Tel: 602-875-9749
Schiltz, Roger J., 1532 Glenrosa Dr., North Las Vegas, NV 89031-5548.
Smith, Leland J., 468 Center St., 55987. Tel: 507-454-8464
Speck, James A., 528 Maceman St., Apt. 108, 55987-2479. Tel: 507-454-2129
Stamschror, Robert P., 2480 Goodview Rd., 55987. Tel: 507-452-4202
Traufler, John F., 200 18th St. N.W., Austin, 55912. Tel: 507-434-7702
Trocinski, LaVern F., 4513 Ruby Lane, N.W., Rochester, 55901.
Verdick, Jerome F., 210 E. Paddock, P.O. Box 87, Alpha, 56111-0087. Tel: 507-847-2939
Vincent, John F., St. Anne of Winona, 1347 W. Broadway, 55987.
Zenk, Donald W., 602 31st St., N.W., Austin, 55912. Tel: 507-437-3579

Permanent Deacons:
Anderberg, George T., Sacred Heart, Owatonna.
Bonnarens, Edwin C., St. John Vianney, Fairmont
DeStazio, John, St. John the Evangelist, Rochester
Fuller, Leonard, Diocese of Winona, Winona
Green, Justin, St. Casimir Church, Winona.
Hillyer, Paul, St. Joseph, Owatonna.
Mangas, Michael, St. Francis of Assisi, Rochester.
Richard, Gordon, Catholic Charities, Rochester.
Zavala, Placedo, St. Francis of Assisi, Rochester.

INSTITUTIONS LOCATED IN THE DIOCESE

[A] SEMINARIES, DIOCESAN

WINONA. *Immaculate Heart of Mary Seminary*, 700 Terrace Hts. #43, 55987-1399. Tel: 507-457-7373; Fax: 507-457-8601. Email: ihms@smumn.edu. Web: www.ihmseminary.org. Very Rev. James P. Steffes, Rector; Revs. Thomas J. Jennings, Vice Rector; Jon H. Moore, Spiritual Dir.; Very Rev. R. Paul Heiting, J.C.L., Resident Spiritual Dir.; Revs. Joseph A. LaPlante, Extern Spiritual Dir. (Retired); Thomas P. Melvin, Extern Spiritual Dir.; Rev. Msgr. Donald P. Schmitz, M.Ch.A., Extern Spiritual Dir.; Rev. David Wechter, O.C.S.O., Extern Spiritual Dir.; Mr. Lawrence G. Price, J.D., J.C.L., Coord. of Liturgical Music. Affiliated with Saint Mary's University of MN. Priests 4; Lay Staff 4; Students 56.

[B] COLLEGES AND UNIVERSITIES

WINONA. *Saint Mary's University of Minnesota* (Coed), 700 Terrace Hts., 55987-1399. Tel: 507-457-1600; Fax: 507-457-1722. Email: admissions@smumn.edu. Web: www.smumn.edu. Bro. Louis De Thomasis, F.S.C., Pres.; Dr. Jeffrey Highland, University Provost & Vice Pres. of College; Mr. Anthony Piscitiello, Exec. Vice Pres. Admissions; Bro. Patrick Conway, F.S.C., Vice Pres. Student Dev.; Mr. Tim Burchill, Vice Pres. Univ. Rel. & Pres., Metanoia; Cynthia Marek, Vice Pres. Fin. Affairs; Loras Sieve, Vice Pres. Corporate and Community Rels.; Bro. Robert Smith, Assoc. Vice Pres. for Mission; Ann Merchlewitz, Vice Pres. Gen. Counsel; Dr. James Towers, Dean School of Educ.; Lawrence Gorrell, Dean School of the Arts; James Bedtke, Vice Pres. Graduate & Special Programs, Associate Provost; Dr. Joseph Shields, Assoc. Vice Pres. of College; Robert Conover, Vice Pres. Communications & Mktg.; Linka Holey, Assoc. Vice Pres. Graduate & Special Programs, Academic Dean; John Pyle, Assoc. Vice Pres. Graduate & Special Programs, Dean of Enrollment; Robert Connor, Dean of Intl Studies. DeLaSalle Christian Brothers Priests 4; Brothers 13; Sisters 4; Lay Faculty 92; Students 1,357.

[C] CENTRALIZED CATHOLIC SCHOOLS

WINONA. *Cotter High School & Junior High School*, (Grades 7-12), 1115 W. Broadway, 55987. Tel: 507-453-5002; Fax: 507-453-5006. Email: sblank@winonacotter.org dforney@winonacotter.org. Web: www.winonacotter.org. Craig Junker, Pres.; Sandra Blank, Prin.; Dave Forney, Dir. Cotter Junior High School; Mary Ann Miller, Campus Min.; Patrick Bowler, Dean of Students. Priests 1; Sisters 1; Lay Teachers 45; Students 471.
Winona Area Catholic Schools, 352 Center St., 55987. Tel: 507-452-4936; Fax: 507-454-1473. Email: swalker@wacsl.org. Web: www.wacsl.org. Scott Walker, Prin. Lay Teachers 31.
St. Mary's Primary School (Grades PreK-K), 1315 W. Broadway, 55987. Tel: 507-452-2890; Fax: 507-452-2898. Email: swalker@wacsl.org. Scott Walker, Prin. Students 96.
Cathedral Elementary School (Grades 1-3), 352 Center St., 55987. Tel: 507-452-4936; Fax: 507-454-1473. Email: swalker@wacsl.org. Scott Walker, Prin. Students 168.
St. Stanislaus Middle School (Grades 4-6), 602 E. Fifth St., 55987. Tel: 507-452-3766; Fax: 507-452-5497. Email: swalker@wacsl.org. Scott Walker, Prin. Students 172.
Winona Area Catholic Schools Foundation, 360 Main St., 55987. Tel: 507-454-7449; Fax: 507-454-1473.

ALBERT LEA. *St. Theodore School*, (Grades K-6), 323 E. Clark St., 56007. Tel: 507-373-9657; Fax: 507-373-9657. Email: jfc@sttheo.org. Web: www.sttheo.org. Mr. Tom Klipfel, Prin. Lay Teachers 7; Students 88.

AUSTIN. *Austin Area Catholic Schools*, 511 N.W. Fourth Ave., 55912. Tel: 507-433-6630; Fax: 507-433-6630.
St. Augustine's - St. Edward (Grades PreK-4), 511 N.W. Fourth Ave., 55912. Tel: 507-433-8859; Fax: 507-433-6630. Email: winqoa@impresso.com. Richard J. Cook, Prin. Lay Teachers 14; Students 184.
Queen of Angels (Grades 5-8), 912 First Ave., N.E., 55912. Tel: 507-433-8745; Fax: 507-433-6630. Email: winqoa@impresso.com. Richard J. Cook, Prin. Lay Teachers 9; Students 114.
Pacelli Senior High School (Grades 9-12), 311 Fourth St., N.W., 55912. Tel: 507-437-3278; Fax: 507-433-5693. Email: ladwell@hotmail.com. Norman Blazer, Dean of Students; Alice Duffy-Meyer, Campus Min. Lay Teachers 9; Students 91.
United Catholic Schools Foundation of Austin, MN, Inc., 511 N.W. Fourth Ave., 55912. Tel: 507-433-6630; Fax: 507-433-6630. Mrs. Alice Snater, Fin. Sec.

MANKATO. *Mankato Area Catholic Schools*, 145 Good Counsel Dr., 56001-3146. Tel: 507-388-2997; Fax: 507-388-3081. Email: sschultz@macsmn.com. Web: www.MankatoAreachCatholicSchools.org. Sr. Katherine DuVal, S.S.N.D., Supt. Total Enrollment 681.
Notre Dame Elementary School (Grades K-3), 135 Good Counsel Drive, 56001. Tel: 507-388-2997; Fax: 507-387-1490. Email: shogan@macsmn.com. Mr. Shawn Hogan, Prin. Sisters 1; Lay Teachers 11; Students 187.
Fitzgerald Middle School (Grades 6-8), 110 N. Fifth St., 56001-4499. Tel: 507-388-9344; Fax: 507-388-2750. Email: marydonaldssnd@yahoo.com. Sr. Mary Donald Miller, S.S.N.D., Prin. Sisters 2; Lay Teachers 12; Students 162.
Loyola High School (Grades 9-12), 145 Good Counsel Dr., 56001-3146. Tel: 507-388-2997; Fax: 507-388-3081. Email: sschultz@macsmn.com. Rev. Neal Wilkinson; Sr. Bridget Waldorf, S.S.N.D., Campus Min.; Shelley Schultz, Prin. Priests 1; Sisters 2; Lay Teachers 21; Students 202.
Holy Rosary School (Grades 4-5), 546 Grant Ave., North Mankato, 56003. Tel: 507-345-6765; Fax: 507-388-2017. Email: shogan@macsmn.com. Mr. Shawn Hogan, Prin. Lay Teachers 4; Students 80.

OWATONNA. *St. Mary's School*, (Grades PreK-8), 730 South Cedar St., 55060. Tel: 507-446-2300; Fax: 507-446-2304. Email: stmarys-owatonna.org. Web: www.stmarys-owatonna.org. Mr. Gerald Kent, Admin.; Mr. Thomas Donlon, Asst. Admin. Lay Teachers 30; Students 421.

ROCHESTER. *Rochester Catholic Schools*, 621 W. Center St., 55902. Tel: 507-280-0349; Fax: 507-289-4008. Email: www.DSchwinghammer@RochesterCatholic.k12.mn.us. Mrs. Diane Schwinghammer, Supt.
St. Francis of Assisi School (Grades PreK-8), 318 11th Ave., S.E., 55904. Tel: 507-288-4816; Fax: 507-288-4815. Email: bplenge@rochestercatholic.k12.mn.us. Mrs. Barb Plenge, Prin. Priests 3; Lay Teachers 34; Students 442.
St. John School (Grades K-8), 424 W. Center St., 55902. Tel: 507-282-5248; Fax: 507-282-1343. Email: dkutzke@rochestercatholic.k12.mn.us. Mrs. Denise Kutzke, Prin. Priests 1; Sisters 1; Lay Teachers 26; Students 373.
St. Pius X School (Grades PreK-8), 1205 12th Ave., 55901. Tel: 507-282-5161; Fax: 507-282-5107. Email: mklebe@rochestercatholic.k12.mn.us. Mr. Matthew Klebe, Prin. Priests 4; Lay Teachers 22; Students 239.
Lourdes High School of Rochester, Inc. (Grades 9-12), 621 W. Center St., 55902. Tel: 507-289-3991; Fax: 507-289-4008. Email: dnigon@rochestercatholic.k12.mn.us. Mr. Dennis Nigon, Prin.; Rita Hendrickson, Campus Min. Priests 1; Lay Teachers 46; Students 563.
Holy Spirit School (Grades K-8), 5455 50th Ave., N.W., 55901. Tel: 507-288-8818; Fax: 507-288-5155. Email: rgaines@rochestercatholic.k12.mn.us. Ronald Gaines, Prin. Priests 1; Lay Teachers 29; Students 424.

[D] GENERAL HOSPITALS

ROCHESTER. *Catholic Medical Association*, 200 First St., S.W., 55905. Tel: 507-266-1206; Fax: 507-266-1657. Email: lane.john@mayo.edu. Dr. John I. Lane, M.D.
**Saint Mary's Hospital* 55902-1970. Tel: 507-255-5123; Fax: 507-255-3125. B. Lynn Frederick, Admin.; Revs. James H. Kunz. Tel: 507-255-4743; James F. Buryska. Tel: 507-255-5551; Dean V. Marek. Tel: 507-266-7283; William D. Byrne. Tel: 507-255-5123; Joseph C. Perumpuzha. Tel: 507-255-9025. Sisters of the Third Order Regular of St. Francis of the Congregation of Our Lady of Lourdes 32; Bed Capacity 1,157; Patients Assisted Annually 49,017.

WABASHA. *Saint Elizabeth's Medical Center*, 1200 Grant Blvd., W., 55981. Tel: 651-565-4531; Fax: 651-565-2482. Email: Tiffany.Carmen@StElizabethsWabasha.org. Web: www.StElizabethsWabasha.org. Mr. Thomas Crowley, Pres.; Rev. Elmer W. Kellen (Retired). Corporate Sponsor: Ministry Health Care, Inc. (Milwaukee, WI); Sponsored by Sisters of the Sorrowful Mother Sisters of the Third Order of St. Francis of the Sorrowful Mother 1; Bed Capacity 25; Patients Assisted Annually 27,500; Staff 160.

[E] SPECIAL HOSPITALS AND REHABILITATION FACILITIES

ROCHESTER. *Guest House*, 4800 48th St., N.E., P.O. Box 954, 55903. Tel: 800-634-4155; 507-288-4693; Fax: 507-288-1240. Email: ghousemn@infonet.isl.net. Web: www.guesthouse.org. William C. Morgan, Dir. A State licensed, JCAHO accredited and ecclesiastically endorsed residential treatment center for priests, brothers, deacons and seminarians. (Corporate headquarters located in Lake Orion, MI 48361) Bed Capacity 39; Total Assisted 99.

[F] HOMES FOR AGED

WINONA. *Saint Anne of Winona*, 1347 W. Broadway, 55987. Tel: 507-454-3621; Fax: 507-454-8626. Constance Schein, Admin. Subsidiary of Benedictine Health Systems. Bed Capacity 121; Residents 121; Nursing Care for the aged, chronically ill or invalid (resident days) 46,334; Total Staff 220.
Callista Court, 1455 W. Broadway, 55987. Tel: 507-457-3810; Fax: 507-494-5117. Independent and assisted living for seniors. Units 75; Residents 75; Total Staff 45.
Benedictine Adult Day Center, 1455 W. Broadway, 55987. Email: memarkey@bhshealth.org. Bernadette Rogers, Dir. Guest Days 4,310.
St. Anne Extended Health Care, 1347 W. Broadway, 55987. Tel: 507-454-3621; Fax: 507-452-2556. Email: fbmiezio@bhshealth.org. Constance Schein, CEO & Admin.; Kathy Schams, Dir. of Nursing Svcs.
Saint Anne Training Center, 1455 W. Broadway, 55987. Tel: 507-457-3811; Fax: 507-494-5117. Email: constance.schein@bhshealth.org. Margaret Markey, Contact Person.

AUSTIN. *Sacred Heart Care Center, Inc.*, 1200 Twelfth St., S.W., 55912. Tel: 507-433-1808; Fax: 507-433-8012. Rebecca Mathews Halverson, Admin. Sisters of the Third Order of St. Francis of the Congregation of Our Lady of Lourdes 1; Bed Capacity 59; Residents 59; Assisted Living

Apartments (filled) 24; Adult Day Care (client days) 3,697; Alzheimer's Day Program (client days) 2,393; Total Staff 150; Home Health Care (clients) 128.

PLAINVIEW. *Green Prairie Place*, 810 2nd Ave., N.W., 55964. Tel: 507-534-4204; Fax: 507-534-0139. Email: joann.klavetter@bhshealth.org. Joanne Klavetter, Resident Services Mgr.; Bob Ferk, Admin. Benedictine Health System, sponsored by Srs. of St. Scholastica Monastery Total Assisted 70; Total Staff 15.

Hillcrest Community Care Center, 800 2nd Ave., N.W., 55964. Tel: 507-534-3191; Fax: 507-534-2778. Email: bob.ferk@bhshealth.org. Bob Ferk, Admin. Benedictine Health System, sponsored by Srs. of St. Scholastica Monastery Total Assisted 155; Total Staff 83.

ROCHESTER. *Madonna Meadows of Rochester*, 3035 Salem Meadows Dr., S.W., 55902. Tel: 507-252-5400. Mark Cairns, Admin. & Corp. Exec. Officer. Sponsored by: Benedictine Health System and Sisters of St. Scholastica Monastery

Madonna Towers of Rochester, Inc., 4001 19th Ave., N.W., 55901. Tel: 507-288-3911; Fax: 507-288-0393. Email: mark.cairns@bhshealth.org. Mark Cairns, Admin. & Corp. Exec. Officer. Subsidiary of Benedictine Health System. Guests 180; Total Staff 180.

Chapel of St. Benedict and Chapel of St. Scholastica Tel: 507-288-3911; Fax: 507-288-0393.

Madonna Towers Foundation, Formerly Madonna Towers Health Care Endowment Fund 4001 19th Ave., N.W., 55901. Tel: 507-288-3911; Fax: 507-288-0393.

WABASHA. *St. Elizabeth's Health Care Center*, 626 Shields Ave., 55981. Tel: 651-565-4581; Fax: 651-565-3414. Web: www.ministryhealth.org. Thomas Crowley, Admin.; Rev. Bernard A. Kerrigan (Retired). (Conducted in connection with St. Elizabeth's Hospital of Wabasha, Inc.) Skilled Beds 85; Admissions 150; Total Assisted 160; Staff 100.

St. Elizabeth's Nursing Home, 1200 Grant Blvd., W., 55981. Tel: 651-565-4531; Fax: 651-565-5679. Thomas Crowley, Admin.; Rev. Elmer W. Kellen (Retired). (Conducted in connection with St. Elizabeth's Medical Center) Bed Capacity 30; Residents 29; Admissions 50; Total Assisted 220; Staff 30.

[G] CONVENTS AND RESIDENCES FOR SISTERS

HOUSTON. *Hermits of St. Mary of Carmel, (H.S.M.C.)* Carmelite Eremitical Community of Diocesan Right , R.R. 1, Box 143, 55943-9737. Tel: 507-896-2125; Fax: 507-896-4349. Sr. Rosemary Therese Quinn, H.S.M.C., Prioress; Rev. David Wechter, O.C.S.O. (DUB). Tel: 507-896-2125. Sisters 5.

JACKSON. *Convent of Religious Sisters of Mercy*, 51437 800th St., 56143. Tel: 507-847-5498; Fax: 507-847-5689. Sr. Marie Paul Lockerd, R.S.M., Local Supr. Sisters 2.

MANKATO. *Provincial House of the School Sisters of Notre Dame*, Convent of Our Lady of Good Counsel, 170 Good Counsel Dr., 56001-3138. Tel: 507-389-4200; Fax: 507-345-6679. Email: cbertrand@ssndmankato.org. Web: www.ssndmankato.org. Sisters Catherine Bertrand, Prov. Leader; Joyce Kolbert, S.S.N.D., Vocation Dir. Religious in Province 398; Sisters in Motherhouse 134; Lay Staff 121.

School Sisters of Notre Dame at Mankato, MN, Inc. Tel: 507-389-4200; Fax: 507-345-6679.

School Sisters of Notre Dame at Mankato MN, Inc. Charitable Trust Tel: 507-389-4200; Fax: 507-345-6679.

School Sisters of Notre Dame Cooperative Investment Fund Tel: 507-389-4200; Fax: 507-345-6679.

ROCHESTER. *Sisters of the Third Order Regular of St. Francis of the Congregation of our Lady of Lourdes*, Assisi Heights Admin. Ctr., 1001 14th St., N.W., Ste. 100, 55901-2511. Tel: 507 282-7441; Fax: 507-282-7762. Email: assisiheights@compuserve.com. Web: www.rochesterfranciscan.org. Sr. Delore M. Rockers, O.S.F., Pres. & Community Min.

Legal Title: *Academy of Our Lady of Lourdes* Religious in Prov. 323; Sisters in Motherhouse 132; Lay Staff 122.

[H] RETREAT HOUSES AND CENTERS OF SPIRITUALITY

AUSTIN. *Queen of Angels Hermitage, Monastic Fraternity of St. Joseph*, 1009 Oakland Ave. E., 55912. Tel: 507-437-4015. Rev. Jon H. Moore. Brothers 2.

JANESVILLE. *Holy Spirit Retreat Center*, 3864 420th Ave., 56048. Tel: 507-234-5712; Fax: 507-234-6188. Email: retreat@frontiernet.net. Web: www.RochesterFranciscan.org. Sisters Elaine Frank, O.S.F., Dir.; Colleen Bryon, O.S.F., Dir.

MANKATO. *Good Counsel Education Center*, 151 Good Counsel Dr., 56002. Tel: 507-389-4291. Email: dhodapp@juno.com. Sr. Dolores Hodapp S.S.N.D., Dir.

ROCHESTER. *Assisi Community Center*, Assisi Heights., 1001 14th St., N.W., Ste. 200, 55901-2511. Tel: 507-280-2180; Fax: 507-282-7762. Email: acomc@aol.com. Web: www.acomc.org. Sr. Joy Barth, O.S.F., Contact Person. Total Staff 6.

I] NEWMAN CENTERS

WINONA. *St. Thomas Aquinas Newman Center* 475 Huff St. 55987. Tel: 507-452-2781. Email: newman@hbci.com. Web: http://studentsclubs.winona.edu/cnc. Mr. Thomas Parlin, Dir.; Rev. Eugene M. Klein, Chap.

MANKATO. *St. Thomas More Newman Center, Minnesota State University* 1331 Warren St., 56001. Tel: 507-387-4154. Email: mccabes@mnsu.edu Ms. Sydelle McCabe, Dir.; Rev. Timothy E. Biren, Chap.

[J] MISCELLANEOUS LISTINGS

WINONA. *Diocese of Winona Deposit & Loan*, 55 W. Sanborn St., P.O. Box 588, 55987. Tel: 507-454-4643; Fax: 507-454-8106.

Diocese of Winona Foundation, 55 W. Sanborn St., P.O. Box 588, 55987. Tel: 507-454-4643 Fax: 507-454-8106. Email: lfuller@dow.org. Web: www.dow.org. Deacon Leonard Fuller, Exec. Dir.

Saint Mary's Press, Christian Brothers Publications, 702 Terrace Hts., 55987. Tel: 800-533-8095; Fax: 800-344-9225. Email: smpress@smp.org. Web: www.smp.org. Bro. Damian Steger, F.S.C., CEO; John M. Vitek, Pres., COO.

ALBERT LEA. *St. Theodore Catholic School Endowment*, 308 E. Fountain St., 56007-2456. Tel: 507-373-0603; Fax: 507-373-0603. Email: rjs@sttheo.org. Web: www.sttheo.org. Rev. Robert J. Schneider, Contact.

JACKSON. *Sacred Heart Mercy Health Care Center* (Pro Life Clinic, N.F.P. Family Practice) , 803 Fourth St., 56143. Tel: 507-847-3571; Fax: 507-847-5664. Email: sacredheartmercl@qwest.net. Sr. Cecelia Marie Scaduto, R.S.M., Admin. Patients Assisted Annually 6,200; Total Staff 9.

ROCHESTER. *Poverello Foundation*, St. Mary's Hospital, 1216 S.W. Second St., 55902. Tel: 507-255-5158; Fax: 507-255-3125. Email: meyer.carol@mayo.edu. Sr. Generose Gervais, O.S.F., Pres.

The Roman Catholic Pontifical Lay Association Memores Domini, 6006 Woodridge Ct., 55906. Tel: 507-292-0551; Fax: 507-288-7373. Email: mdrochester@hotmail.com. Web: www.comunioneliberazione.org.

RELIGIOUS INSTITUTES OF MEN REPRESENTED IN THE DIOCESE

For further details refer to the corresponding bracketed number in the Religious Institutes of Men or Women section.

[0330]—*Brothers of the Christian Schools*—F.S.C.

[0340]—*Cistercian Fathers* (Abbey of Our Lady of New Malleray)—O.Cist.

[0690]—*Jesuit Fathers and Brothers* (Wisconsin Province)—S.J.

[0910]—*Oblates of Mary Immaculate* (Central Province)—O.M.I.

[0430]—*Order of Preachers (Dominicans)* (Chicago Province)—O.P.

[0110]—*Society of African Missions*—S.M.A.

RELIGIOUS INSTITUTES OF WOMEN REPRESENTED IN THE DIOCESE

[0230]—*Benedictine Sisters of Pontifical Jurisdiction*—O.S.B.

[1780]—*Congregation of the Sisters of the Third Order of St. Francis of Perpetual Adoration* (Eastern, Central Regions)—F.S.P.A.

[1310]—*Franciscan Sisters of Little Falls*—O.S.F.

[]—*Hermits of St. Mary of Carmel (Contemplative Community)*—H.S.M.C.

[2470]—*Maryknoll Sisters of St. Dominic*—M.M.

[2519]—*Religious Sisters of Mercy of Alma, Michigan*—R.S.M.

[2970]—*School Sisters of Notre Dame*—S.S.N.D.

[1680]—*School Sisters of St. Francis*—O.S.F.

[0430]—*Sisters of Charity of the Blessed Virgin Mary*—B.V.M.

[1705]—*The Sisters of St. Francis of Assisi*—O.S.F.

[1570]—*Sisters of St. Francis of the Holy Family*—O.S.F.

[3320]—*Sisters of the Presentation of the B.V.M.*—P.B.V.M.

[4100]—*Sisters of the Sorrowful Mother (Third Order of St. Francis)*—S.S.M.

[1720]—*Sisters of the Third Order Regular of St. Francis of the Congregation of Our Lady of Lourdes*—O.S.F.

[]—*Third Order Regular Common Franciscan*—S.S.S.F.

DIOCESAN CEMETERIES

WINONA. *Catholic Cemeteries of Winona*, 55 W. Sanborn St., P.O. Box 588, 55987. Rev. Michael J. Cronin, J.C.L.

NECROLOGY

† Tighe, Rev. Msgr. Emmett F., (Retired)—Died June 7, 2003

† Halloran, Jerome D., (Retired)—Died Sept. 1, 2003

Diocese of Worcester

(Dioecesis Wigorniensis)

Most Reverend

ROBERT J. MCMANUS

Bishop of Worcester; ordained May 27, 1978; appointed Auxiliary Bishop of Providence and Titular Bishop of Allegheny December 1, 1998; consecrated February 22, 1999; appointed Bishop of Worcester March 9, 2004; installed May 14, 2004 *Chancery Office: 49 Elm St., Worcester, MA 01609.*

Most Reverend

DANIEL P. REILLY, D.D.

Retired Bishop of Worcester; ordained May 30, 1953; appointed Bishop of Norwich June 17, 1975; consecrated August 6, 1975; appointed Bishop of Worcester October 27, 1994; installed December 8, 1994; retired March 9, 2004 *Res.: 2 High Ridge Rd., Worcester, MA 01602.*

Chancery Office: 49 Elm St., Worcester, MA 01609. Tel: 508-791-7171; Fax: 508-754-2768.

Web: www.worcesterdiocese.org

Most Reverend

GEORGE E. RUEGER, D.D., V.G.

Auxiliary Bishop of Worcester; ordained January 6, 1958; appointed Auxiliary Bishop of Worcester and Titular Bishop of Maronana January 19, 1987; consecrated February 25, 1987 *Res.: St. Stephen's Rectory,* 16 Hamilton St., Worcester, MA 01604.

ESTABLISHED JANUARY 14, 1950.

Square Miles 1,532.

Comprises the County of Worcester in the State of Massachusetts.

For legal titles of parishes and diocesan institutions, consult the Chancery Office.

STATISTICAL OVERVIEW

Personnel	
Bishop	1
Auxiliary Bishops	1
Abbots	3
Priests: Diocesan Active in Diocese	157
Priests: Diocesan Active Outside Diocese	17
Priests: Diocesan in Foreign Missions	2
Priests: Retired, Sick or Absent	51
Number of Diocesan Priests	227
Religious Priests in Diocese	111
Total Priests in Diocese	338
Ordinations:	
Diocesan Priests	1
Transitional Deacons	4
Permanent Deacons	5
Permanent Deacons in Diocese	74
Total Brothers	78
Total Sisters	447
Parishes	
Parishes	126
With Resident Pastor:	
Resident Diocesan Priests	125
Without Resident Pastor:	
Administered by Deacons	1
Missions	2
Professional Ministry Personnel:	
Brothers	74
Sisters	450
Lay Ministers	88
Welfare	
Catholic Hospitals	1
Total Assisted	200,000
Homes for the Aged	2
Total Assisted	125
Day Care Centers	12
Total Assisted	2,000
Specialized Homes	2
Total Assisted	285
Special Centers for Social Services	21
Total Assisted	40,000
Residential Care of Disabled	1
Total Assisted	180
Other Institutions	1
Total Assisted	80
Educational	
Diocesan Students in Other Seminaries	12
Total Seminarians	12
Colleges and Universities	3
Total Students	6,825
High Schools, Diocesan and Parish	4
Total Students	2,697
High Schools, Private	4
Total Students	1,434
Elementary Schools, Diocesan and Parish	23
Total Students	6,167
Elementary Schools, Private	2
Total Students	375
Non-residential Schools for the Disabled	2
Total Students	95
Catechesis/Religious Education:	
High School Students	1,925
Elementary Students	8,166
Total Students under Catholic Instruction	27,696
Teachers in the Diocese:	
Priests	2
Brothers	1
Sisters	30
Lay Teachers	697
Vital Statistics	
Receptions into the Church:	
Infant Baptism Totals	4,160
Adult Baptism Totals	117
Received into Full Communion	314
First Communions	4,309
Confirmations	2,907
Marriages:	
Catholic	749
Interfaith	170
Total Marriages	919
Deaths	3,777
Total Catholic Population	369,096
Total Population	762,207

Former Bishops—His Eminence JOHN CARDINAL WRIGHT, D.D., ord. Dec. 8, 1935; appt. Titular Bishop of Aegea and Auxiliary Bishop of Boston, May 10, 1947; consecrated June 30, 1947; transferred to new See of Worcester, Jan. 28, 1950;; enthroned March 7, 1950;; appt. Bishop of Pittsburgh, Jan. 28, 1959; created Cardinal, April 28, 1969; transferred to the Roman Curia Prefect, Sacred Congregation for the Clergy; died Aug. 10, 1979; Most Revs. BERNARD J. FLANAGAN, D.D., J.C.D. (Retired), resigned March 31, 1983; died Jan. 28, 1998; TIMOTHY J. HARRINGTON, D.D. (Retired), retired Oct. 27, 1994; died March 23, 1997; DANIEL P. REILLY, D.D., ord. May 30, 1953; appt. Bishop of Norwich June 17, 1975; cons. Aug. 6, 1975; appt. Bishop of Worcester Oct. 27, 1994; installed Dec. 8, 1994; retired March 9, 2004.

Vicar General—Most Rev. GEORGE E. RUEGER, D.D., V.G., Moderator of the Curia, St. Stephen's Rectory, 16 Hamilton St., Worcester, 01604. Tel: 508-791-7171.

Chancery Office—Rev. Msgr. THOMAS J. SULLIVAN, Chancellor, 49 Elm St., Worcester, 01609. Tel: 508-791-7171; Fax: 508-753-7180.

Diocesan Director of Educational Services—Most Rev. GEORGE E. RUEGER, D.D., V.G., 49 Elm St., Worcester, 01609. Tel: 508-791-7171.

Diocesan Director of Fiscal Affairs—Rev. Msgr. EDMOND T. TINSLEY, V.G., 49 Elm St., Worcester, 01609. Tel: 508-791-7171.

Diocesan Director for Human Services (and Catholic Relief Services)—Rev. Msgr. EDMOND T. TINSLEY, V.G., Res.: 8 Berwick St., Worcester, 01602. Tel: 508-754-5314.

Diocesan Expansion Fund—Most Rev. GEORGE E. RUEGER, D.D., V.G.; Mr. DENNIS F. GORMAN, Chm., 49 Elm St., Worcester, 01609. Tel: 508-791-7171.

Diocesan Finance Committee—JOSEPH GIOVINO, Chm., 49 Elm St., Worcester, 01609.

Diocesan Tribunal—Address all communications to, 49 Elm St., Worcester, 01609. Tel: 508-791-7171.

Judicial Vicar and Vicar for Canonical Affairs—Rev. Msgr. F. STEPHEN PEDONE, J.C.L., 49 Elm St., Worcester, 01609.

Associate Judicial Vicar—Rev. PAUL T. O'CONNELL, J.C.L.

Judges—Rev. PAUL T. O'CONNELL, J.C.L.; Rev. Msgr. F. STEPHEN PEDONE, J.C.L.; Sr. MARY L. WALSH, S.N.D., J.C.L.

Promoter of Justice—Sr. MARY L. WALSH, S.N.D., J.C.L.

Psychologist—Sr. MARY DANIEL MALLOY, R.S.M.

Secretary to the Tribunal—Deacon ANTHONY R. SUROZENSKI.

Defenders of the Bond—Rev. Msgr. ANTHONY S. CZARNECKI, J.C.L.; Deacon GEORGE L. O'TOOLE.

Advocates—Revs. ROLAND L. GAMACHE; THOMAS E. MAHONEY; LEO BARRY; JAMES P. KERRIGAN; GEORGE J. RIDICK; WILLIAM F. SANDERS; MICHAEL A. DIGERONIMO; TERRENCE T. KILCOYNE.

Notary—JUDITH M. GAUTHIER Address all requests for dispensations to: Diocesan Tribunal, 49 Elm St., Worcester, 01609.

Diocesan College of Consultors—Most Rev. GEORGE E. RUEGER, D.D., V.G.; Rev. Msgr. THOMAS J. SULLIVAN; Revs. H. EDWARD CHALMERS; JOSEPH NALLY; FRANCIS T. GOGUEN; GEORGE L. O'BRIEN; BRIAN P. O'TOOLE; Rev. Msgr. F. STEPHEN PEDONE, J.C.L.; Rev. ROCCO M. PICCOLOMINI; Rev. Msgr. FRANCIS J. SCOLLEN; Rev. JOSEPH SZWACH; Rev. Msgr. EDMOND T. TINSLEY, V.G.

Deans—Revs. MICHAEL A. DIGERONIMO, Area I; MICHAEL BAFARO, Area II; JOSEPH A. ADAMO, Area III; MARTIN P. DONAHUE, Area IV; BRIAN P. O'TOOLE, Area V; PAUL J. TOUGAS, Area VI; MICHAEL J. ROY, Area VII; C. MICHAEL BRODERICK, Area VIII; RICHARD T. CAREY, Area IX; FRANCIS T. GOGUEN, Area X; H. EDWARD

CHALMERS, Area XI; GEORGE O'BRIEN, Area XII; ARTHUR C. OUILLETTE, Area XIII.

Vicar for Clergy—Rev. ROCCO M. PICCOLOMINI, Res.: Our Lady of Mt. Carmel-St. Ann, 53 E. Central St., Worcester, 01605.

Vicar for Religious—Sr. PAULA KELLEHER, S.S.J., 49 Elm St., Worcester, 01609. Tel: 508-791-7171.

Diocesan Offices and Directors

The Adopt-A-Student Endowment Trust—VACANT, 49 Elm St., Worcester, 01609. Tel: 508-791-7171.

Ethnic Ministries, Office for—Sr. MARIE PREFONTAINE, S.N.D., Dir., 49 Elm St., Worcester, 01609. Tel: 508-791-7171, Ext. 328; Fax: 508-753-7180.

African Ministry—Rev. ANTHONY OGUNLEYE, Contact Person, St. Peter, 929 Main St., Worcester, 01610. Cell: 508-981-7571.

Haitian Apostolate—CONNIE BARNA, Dir. Tel: 508-234-9115.

Asian Ministries—Sr. MARIE PREFONTAINE S.N.D., Contact Person. Tel: 508-791-7171, Ext. 328 Cambodian, Chinese, Filipino, Indian, Japanese, Korean, Laotian.

Hmong Ministry—St. Anthony, Fitchburg, 01420. Tel: 978-342-4706. Rev. ROBERT D. BRUSO, Contact Person.

Vietnamese Ministry—Our Lady of Vilna, Worcester, 01610. Tel: 508-752-1825. Rev. PHUONG VAN NGUYEN, Admin.

Brazilian Ministry—Rev. AMERICO DALBELO C.SS.R., Chap. Tel: 978-660-0180 Holy Name of Jesus, Worcester; Holy Trinity, Leominster; St. Mary, Milford.

European Ministries—

New Irish Ministry—Sr. MARIE PREFONTAINE, S.N.D., Contact Person.

Lithuanian Churches— St. Casimir, Worcester; Our Lady of Vilna, Worcester

Polish Ministry—St. Joseph, Webster, 01570. Tel: 508-943-0467. Rev. Msgr. ANTHONY CZARNECKI, Natl. Delegate, Our Lady Czestochowa, Worcester; Jasna Gora, Clinton; St. Andrew Bobola, Dudley; St. Joseph, Gardner; St. Hedwig, Southbridge; St. Stanislaus, West Warren.

Portuguese Ministry—St. Mary, Milford, 01757. Tel: 508-473-2000. Rev. EUSIQUIO-ARRANZ MUNOZ.

Hispanic Ministry—

St. Paul—19 Chatham St., Worcester, 01609. Tel: 508-754-3195. Rev. JOSEPH P. MAHONEY; Sr. MARIA DALLARI, X.M.M.; Deacon FRANCISCO ESCOBAR.

St. Peter—929 Main St., Worcester, 01610. Tel: 508-752-4674. Rev. Msgr. FRANK SCOLLENS; Sr. ANN MARSHALL, R.S.M.

St. Joan of Arc—570 Lincoln St., Worcester, 01605. Tel: 508-852-3232. Rev. JOSE A. RODRIGUES; Sr. SOLEDAD CHACON, R.O.D.A.

Our Lady of Fatima—7 Auburn St., Worcester, 01605. Tel: 508-755-3820. Rev. WILLIAM E. REISER, S.J.; Sr. STEPHANIE LOI, X.M.M.

St. John—149 Chestnut St., Clinton, 01510. Tel: 978-368-0366. Rev. KENNETH CARDINALE; Sr. PATRICIA VENEGAS, S.S.A.

St. Francis—63 Sheridan St., Fitchburg, 01420. Tel: 978-342-9651. Rev. ANGEL MATOS; Deacon WILLIAM COLON.

Holy Spirit—45 Metcalf St., Gardner, 01440. Tel: 978-632-3333.

St. Joseph—46 Woodland St., Fitchburg, 01420. Tel: 978-342-7907.

Holy Trinity—69 Lincoln Terr., Box 667, Leominster, 01453. Tel: 978-534-5258. Rev. DONALD B. GOTHING; Sr. CECILIA QUESADA, R.O.D.A.

St. Leo—108 Main St., Leominster, 01453. Rev. JESUS E. MARTINEZ.

St. Mary—27 Pearl St., Milford, 01757. Tel: 508-473-2000. Rev. EUSIQUIO-ARRANZ MUNOZ.

St. Mary—263 Hamilton St., Southbridge, 01550. Tel: 978-764-3226. Rev. PETER JOYCE; Sr. MARY ESTELLA, R.O.D.A.

St. Louis—15 Lake St., Webster, 01570. Tel: 508-943-0240. Rev. CONRAD S. PECEVICH.

Black Catholics: African American—St. Peter, 929 Main St., Worcester, 01610. Tel: 508-752-4674. Rev. Msgr. FRANCIS J. SCOLLEN, Contact Person.

Catholic Charities—10 Hammond St., Worcester, 01609. Tel: 508-798-0191.

Refugee Apostolate—731 Main St., Worcester, 01609. Tel: 508-831-7455.

Apostleship of Prayer and Eucharistic Crusade—Rev. THADDEUS X. STACHURA, Our Lady of Czestochowa, 34 Ward St., Worcester, 01610. Tel: 508-755-5959.

Apostolate Office of Divine Mercy and Healing—Rev. RALPH A. DIORIO, Dir., P.O. Box 668, Worcester, 01613-0663. Tel: 508-791-0427.

Archivist—Most Rev. GEORGE E. RUEGER, D.D., V.G., 49 Elm St., Worcester, 01609. Tel: 508-791-7171.

Brazilian Pastoral Ministry—Rev. AMERICO DALBELO, C.SS.R., 49 Elm St., Worcester, 01609. Fax: 508-753-7180.

Bishop's Fund—VACANT, 49 Elm St., Worcester, 01609. Tel: 508-791-7171.

Diocesan Building Commission Members—Most Rev. GEORGE E. RUEGER, D.D., V.G.; Rev. Msgr. EDMOND T. TINSLEY, V.G.; Revs. JOHN FOLEY, Chm.; ROBERT JOHNSON; THADDEUS STACHURA; JOHN THOMAS; Mr. NORMAND MAROIS; Mr. JORDAN O'CONNOR; Mrs. MARY SLOCUM, 49 Elm St., Worcester, 01609. Tel: 508-791-7171.

Campus Ministry—Rev. PETER J. SCANLON, Vicar for College Communities, Diocesan Office, P.O. Box 903, Worcester, 01613. Tel: 508-757-6097. Newman Center, 281 Highland Ave., Fitchburg, 01420. Tel: 508-345-2688. Res.: The Center, 19 Schussler Rd., Worcester, 01609. Tel 508-757-6097.

Catholic Charities—CATHERINE LOEFFLER, Dir., 10 Hammond St., Worcester, 01610-1513. Tel: 508-798-0191 (Refer to separate listings for detailed information on Catholic Charities and related organizations).

Cemeteries—Mr. ROBERT ACKERMAN, Dir.; Rev. JOHN CAHILL, Priest Liaison, 260 Cambridge St., Worcester, 01610. Tel: 508-757-7415.

Charismatic Renewal, Office of—Mr. MICHAEL FREEL, Liaison, St. Joseph, West St., P.O. Box 284, Berlin, 01503. Tel: 508-365-6492.

Clergy Benefit Plan—Rev. JOHN J. FOLEY, 1052 Pleasant St., Worcester, 01602.

Collaborative for Education and Ministry: Institute for Academic and Pastoral Development—Most Rev. GEORGE E. RUEGER, D.D., V.G., Chm.

Communication Office—RAYMOND L. DELISLE, Dir., 49 Elm St., Worcester, 01609. Tel: 508-791 5357.

Continuing Education of the Clergy—Rev. MICHAEL ROSE, Dir., 89 Main St., South Grafton, 01560. Tel: 508-839-5354.

Cursillo—Rev. ROBERT A. GRATTAROTI, Dir., 37 Worcester Rd., Charlton City, 01508. Tel: 508-248-7862.

Development Office— Bishop's Fund, Good Shepherd Endowment Fund, Adopt-A-Student, Annual Catholic School Appeal, Project Share for Christ, The Adopt-A-Student Endowment Trust VACANT, Dir., 49 Elm St., Worcester, 01609. Tel: 508-791-7171; Fax: 508-754-2768.

Diocesan Expansion Fund—Members: JANET S. SIMONDS Revs. RICHARD REIDY; PAUL W. LEMIRE; Most Rev. GEORGE E. RUEGER, D.D., V.G.; Rev. Msgr. EDMOND T. TINSLEY, V.G.; JANET CHAMBERS; Mr. DENNIS F. GORMAN, Chm.; Mr. ANDREW STANHOPE; Mr. JEROME JUSSAUME; Mr. JAMES O'COIN; PETER J. DAWSON, Attorney.

Diocesan Scouts—Boy Scout Office / Girl Scout Office, 120 Hill St., Whitinsville, 01588. Tel: 508-234-0346. Rev. RICHARD REIDY, 19 Chatham St., Worcester, 01609.

Ecumenical and Interreligious Affairs, Diocesan Office for—Sr. THERESE DION, S.S.A., 49 Elm St., Worcester, 01609.

Evangelization, Office of—Rev. LAWRENCE J. ESPOSITO, Chm.; VACANT, Evangelization & Stewardship, 49 Elm St., Worcester, 01609.

Family Life Ministry—CYNTHIA DOBRZNSKI, Dir., 49 Elm St., Worcester, 01609. Tel: 508-791-7171.

Finance Office—Rev. Msgr. EDMOND T. TINSLEY, V.G., Fiscal Affairs; JEROME D. JUSSAUME, Mgr. Finance, 49 Elm St., Worcester, 01609. Tel: 508-791-7171.

Haitian Ministries Coalition of the Diocese of Worcester—Deacon PETER R. FAFORD, Co-Chm.; LINDA M. FAFORD, Co-Chm. & Treas.; Mrs. CONNIE BARNA, Sec.; Dr. SITA RAM UPADHYAY; Rev. BRIAN O'TOOLE; Mrs. LOIS KOLOSKY, Adopt-A-Student; Rev. OLIVER BLANCHETTE, Advisory Board; Sr. ALICE RICHARDS, Advisory Board; ROBERT LANGLOIS, Micro Loan Project, Office for Youth Ministry, 120 Hill St., Whitinsville, 01588. Tel: 508-234-0346; Fax: 508-234-0348.

Holy Childhood Association—Most Rev. GEORGE E. RUEGER, D.D., V.G., Dir., 353 Grove St., Worcester, 01605. Tel: 508-754-8419.

Meet-the-Father Ministry, Inc.—Mrs. EILEEN GEORGE, Contact Person, 363 Greenwood St., Millbury, 01527.

Newspaper—Mrs. MARGARET M. RUSSELL, Exec. Editor, 51 Elm St., Worcester, 01609. Tel: 508-757-6387. "The Catholic Free Press"

Office for Worship—Rev. ROBERT JOHNSON, Dir., 19 Chatham St., Worcester, 01609. Tel: 508-798-0417.

Pastoral Associate Ministry Consultative Board—Sr. PAULA KELLEHER, S.S.J., Chm., 49 Elm St., Worcester, 01609. Tel: 508-791-7171.

Permanent Diaconate—Co-Directors: Revs. ROCCO M. PICCOLOMINI; JAMES AQUINO, 49 Elm St., Worcester, 01609.

Presbyteral Council—Most Revs. DANIEL P. REILLY, D.D., Pres.; GEORGE E. RUEGER, D.D., V.G.; Rev. Msgrs. F. STEPHEN PEDONE, J.C.L.; THOMAS SULLIVAN; Revs. GEORGE L. O'BRIEN, Chm.; MICHAEL A. DIGERONIMO, Vice Chm.; Rev. Msgr. EDMOND T. TINSLEY, V.G., Sec.; Revs. RICHARD T. CAREY, Treas.; JAMES J. AQUINO; BRIAN O'TOOLE; ROCCO M. PICCOLOMINI; JOSEPH F. SZWACH; JOSEPH M. NALLY, Chancery Bldg.: 49 Elm St., Worcester, 01609. Tel: 508-791-7171.

Priests' Personnel Board—Rev. ROCCO M. PICCOLOMINI, Our Lady of Mt. Carmel-St. Ann, 53 E. Central St., Worcester, 01605. Tel: 508-792-4574.

Ministry to Retired Priests—Sr. MARY ANN BARTELL, C.S.E., 188 Old Worcester Rd., Charlton, 01507. Tel: 508-868-9239.

Priests' Retirement Residence—Rev. JOHN F. CAHILL, Admin., 222 June St., Worcester, 01602. Tel: 508-791-0311.

Pro-Life—ALLISON LEDOUX, 49 Elm St., Worcester, 01609. Tel: 508-791-7171.

Propagation of the Faith—Most Rev. GEORGE E. RUEGER, D.D., V.G., Dir., 353 Grove St., Worcester, 01605. Tel: 508-754-8419.

Religious Education Office—Rev. Msgr. LOUIS R. PIERMARINI, Dir., 49 Elm St., Worcester, 01609. Tel: 508-791-7171. Res.: St. Roch, 334 Main St., Oxford, 01540.

North County Office Fitchburg—VACANT, Assoc. Dir. & North Country Coord., 89 Sheridan St., Fitchburg, 01420. Tel: 508-345-6636.

School Department—Mr. CHARLES E. MCMANUS, Supt. Associate Superintendents: PATRICIA M. HALPIN; Sisters ANNE MARIE LANDRY, C.N.D.; MARGUERITE TIMOTHY YOUNG, S.N.D., 49 Elm St., Worcester, 01609. Tel: 508-791-7171.

Office of Justice & Peace—49 Elm St., Worcester, 01609. Tel: 508-791-7171.

Spanish Apostolate—Rev. JOSE A. RODRIGUEZ, Bishop's Liaison, 570 Lincoln St., Worcester, 01605. 49 Elm St., Worcester, 01609. Tel: 508-791-7171.

St. Vincent dePaul Society—- Central and Greater Worcester District Council: FRANCES PIKE, Pres.; Rev. Msgr. EDMOND T. TINSLEY, V.G., Spiritual Dir., Res.: 8 Berwick St., Worcester, 01602. Tel: 508-754-5314.

Northern Worcester County District Council—JOHN YOVINO, Pres.; Rev. Msgr. LEO J. BATTISTA, Chap.

Southern Worcester County District Council—ALFRED E. BALLARD, Pres.; Rev. J. NORMAND TREMBLAY, Chap.

Tri-Conference Retirement Fund for Religious—Sr. PAULA KELLEHER, S.S.J., Diocesan Coord., 49 Elm St., Worcester, 01609. Tel: 508-791-7171.

Vicar for Priests—Rev. ROCCO M. PICCOLOMINI, 53 E. Central St., Worcester, 01605.

Vicar for Religious—Sr. PAULA KELLEHER, S.S.J., 49 Elm St., Worcester, 01609. Tel: 508-791-7171.

Vietnamese Apostolate—Rev. PHUONG VAN NGUYEN, 153 Sterling St., Worcester, 01610. Tel: 508-752-1825.

Victim Assistance Coordinator—FRANCES J. NUGENT. Tel: 508-929-4363. Email: fnugent@worcesterdiocese.org.

Vocation Office—Rev. Msgr. THOMAS SULLIVAN, Dir., 49 Elm St., Worcester, 01609. Tel: 508-791-7171.

Worcester Diocesan Commission for Women—Mrs. MARY DONOVAN, Chm., 49 Elm St., Worcester, 01609. Tel: 508-791-7171.

Youth Ministry—Sr. BETTY PAUL, S.P., Dir. Youth Ministry, Office, 120 Hill St., Whitinsville, 01588. Tel: 508-234-0346.

CLERGY, PARISHES, MISSIONS AND PAROCHIAL SCHOOLS

CITY OF WORCESTER
(WORCESTER COUNTY)

1—ST. PAUL'S CATHEDRAL (1866), Revs Richard F. Reidy, Rector; Joseph P. Mahoney; William G. Gallagher (RVC) (Retired); Deacon Francisco Escobar. In Res., Revs. David E. Doiron; Robert K. Johnson.

Res.: 38 High St., 01609. Tel: 508-799-4193; Fax: 508-752-6308.

Catechesis/Religious Program—Tel: 508-755-1414; Fax: 508-755-1414. Students 301.

2—ST. ANDREW THE APOSTLE (1954), Rev. James F. Carmody; Sr. Therese Gosselin, S.S.A., Pastoral Assoc.

Res.: 16 Vineyard St., 01603. Tel: 508-754-6057; Fax: 508-754-0830.

Catechesis/Religious Program—Tel: 508-752-4701. Students 100.

3—ASCENSION (1911), Rev. Joseph A. Adamo. In Res., Rev. Conrad S. Pecevich.
Res.: 48 Vernon St., 01610. Tel: 508-752-4459; Fax: 508-752-8821.
Catechesis/Religious Program—Students 22.

4—ST. BERNARD (1916), Rev. Richard F. Trainor.
Res.: 236 Lincoln St., 01605. Tel: 508-791-3104; Fax: 508-791-7124.
Catechesis/Religious Program—One Harlow St., 01605. Students 65.

5—BLESSED SACRAMENT (1912), Rev. Charles J. Dumphy. In Res., Rev. Thomas Landry.
Res.: 551 Pleasant St., 01602. Tel: 508-755-5291; Fax: 508-755-6891.
Catechesis/Religious Program—Epiphany House, Tel: 508-752-4368. Students 160.

6—ST. CASIMIR'S (1894), (Lithuanian), Rev. Richard A. Jakubauskas.
Res.: 41 Providence St., 01604-4258. Tel: 508-754-5142; Fax: 508-770-8060.

7—ST. CATHERINE OF SWEDEN (1952), Rev. George J. Ridick; Sr. Ann Miriam, Pastoral Assoc.; Deacon James Denning.
Res.: 3 Wiser Ave., 01607. Tel: 508-752-1624; Fax: 508-797-1196.
Catechesis/Religious Program—Tel: 508-793-2187. Students 73.

8—ST. CHARLES BORROMEO (1954), Rev. Chester J. Misiewicz; Deacon Peter R. Faford.
Res.: 341 June St., 01602. Tel: 508-799-4031; Fax: 508-792-6675.
Catechesis/Religious Program—Sr. Elaine Potvin, S.S.A., D.R.E. Students 123.

9—CHRIST THE KING (1936), Rev. John J. Foley; Sr. Bernadette Lavoie, S.S.A., Pastoral Assoc.; Deacon Joseph M. Banieukiewicz.
Res.: 1052 Pleasant St., 01602. Tel: 508-754-5361; Fax: 508-753-0448.
Catechesis/Religious Program—Tel: 508-752-5514. Carol A. Bertel, D.R.E. Students 379.

10—ST. CHRISTOPHER (1956), Rev. Martin P. Donahue.
Res.: 950 W. Boylston St., 01606. Tel: 508-853-1492; Fax: 508-853-4338.
Catechesis/Religious Program—Tel: 508-853-3302; Fax: 508-854-4338. Students 101.

11—ST. GEORGE (1951), Rev. Henry A. Donoghue. In Res., Rev. Msgr. F. Stephen Pedone, J.C.L.
Res.: 40 Brattle St., 01606. Tel: 508-853-0183; Fax: 508-854-0864.
Catechesis/Religious Program—Tel: 508-852-1784. Peggy Moynahan, D.R.E. Students 533.

12—HOLY NAME OF JESUS (1893), (French), Rev. Msgr. Joseph V. Sirois.
Res.: 51 Illinois St., 01610. Tel: 508-799-2792; Fax: 508-799-2368.
Catechesis/Religious Program—Tel: 508-756-6370. Students 50.

13—IMMACULATE CONCEPTION (1873), Rev. William E. Champlin.
Res.: 353 Grove St., 01605. Tel: 508-754-8419.
Catechesis/Religious Program—Father Connor Center, Tel: 508-791-5887; Fax: 508-754-8508. Students 89.

14—ST. JOAN OF ARC (1950), Rev. Jose A. Rodriguez; Sisters Soledad Chacon, R.O.D.A., Pastoral Assoc.; Mary Christopher Power, S.S.J., Pastoral Assoc.; Lucille Pleau, S.A.S.V., Pastoral Assoc.
Res.: 570 Lincoln St., 01605. Tel: 508-852-3232; Fax: 508-852-3223.
Catechesis/Religious Program—Students 220.

15—ST. JOHN'S (1834), Rev. Msgr. Edmond T. Tinsley, V.G. In Res., Rev. Joseph P. Mahoney.
Res.: 44 Temple St., 01604. Tel: 508-756-7165; Fax: 508-754-5153.
Catechesis/Religious Program—Mrs. Donna Mastrovito, D.R.E. Students 213.

16—ST. MARGARET MARY (1922), Rev. Patrick J. Hawthorne; Deacon Bruce Vidito.
Res.: 77 Alvarado Ave., 01604. Tel: 508-753-5788; Fax: 508-797-1644.
Catechesis/Religious Program—Students 85.

17—NOTRE DAME DES CANADIENS - ST. JOSEPH (1869), (French), [CEM] Rev. Richard G. Roger; Mary G. Guerin, Pastoral Assoc.
Res.: 5 Whitman Rd., 01609. Tel: 508-754-6722; 508-757-0830; Fax: 508-438-0368.
Catechesis/Religious Program—Students 66.

18—OUR LADY OF CZESTOCHOWA (1903), (Polish), Revs. Thaddeus X. Stachura; Krzystof Korcz.
Res.: 34 Ward St., 01610. Tel: 508-755-5959; Fax: 508-767-1644.
School—St. Mary's, (Grades K-6), 50 Richland St.. Tel: 508-753-0484; Fax: 508-795-0506. Sr. Roberta Garczynska, Prin. & D.R.E. Sisters of the Holy Family of Nazareth 2; Lay Teachers 7; Students 140.
School—St. Mary's Jr. & Sr. High School, Tel: 508-753-1170; Fax: 508-795-0560. Gregory Marcotte, Prin. Sisters 1; Lay Teachers 15; Students 163.
Catechesis/Religious Program—Fax: 508-767-1384. Students 93.

19—OUR LADY OF FATIMA (1952), (Spanish), Rev. Edward M. Ryan; Sr. Gloria Enciso, X.M.M., Spanish Apostolate; Deacon Vincent Librandi.
Res.: 7 Auburn St., 01605. Tel: 508-755-3820; Fax: 508-755-7196.
Catechesis/Religious Program—Tel: 508-755-3830. Students 75.

20—OUR LADY OF LORETO (1966), (Italian), Rev. James J. Aquino; Deacons Pasquale G. Mussulli; Paul T. Audette.
Res.: 33 Massasoit Rd., 01604. Tel: 508-753-5001; Fax: 508-754-1537. Res.: Email: aloreto@aol.com.
Catechesis/Religious Program—37 Massasoit Rd., 01604. Tel: 508-799-2445. Students 87.

21—OUR LADY OF LOURDES (1949), Rev. James B. O'Shea. In Res., Rev. Francis J. Roach.
Res.: 1290 Grafton St., 01604. Tel: 508-757-0789; Fax: 508-757-0048.
Catechesis/Religious Program—Tel: 508-753-5773. Jo-Ann Bafaro, D.R.E. Students 220.

22—OUR LADY OF MT. CARMEL AND ST. ANN (1872), (Italian—Irish), Rev. Michael P. Bafaro. In Res., Rev. Rocco Piccolomini.
Res.: 53 E. Central St., 01605. Tel: 508-752-2964; Fax: 508-755-3506.
Catechesis/Religious Program—Tel: 508-791-6139. Joan D'Argenis, D.R.E. Students 311.

23—OUR LADY OF THE ANGELS (1916), Rev. Charles F. Monroe; Deacon Alphonse Desautels, Pastoral Assoc.; Karen Barrows, Pastoral Assoc. In Res., Rev. Terrence Dougherty, O.C.D.
Res.: 1222 Main St., 01603. Tel: 508-791-0951; Fax: 508-753-9531.
School—1220 Main St., Rear, 01603. Tel: 508-752-5609; Fax: 508-798-9634. Doreen J. Albert, Prin.; Jodi L. Zaparakas, Asst. Prin. Lay Teachers 17; Students 296.
Catechesis/Religious Program—Tel: 508-754-4165. Students 369.

24—OUR LADY OF THE ROSARY (1911), Rev. William F. Sanders. In Res., Rev. Leo J. O'Neil.
Res.: 23 Fales St., 01606. Tel: 508-853-1640; Fax: 508-853-2426.
Catechesis/Religious Program—Father Riley Center, 9 Emerson Rd., 01604. Sr. Irene Moran, M.P.V., D.R.E. Students 403.

25—OUR LADY OF VILNA (1925), (Lithuanian—Vietnamese), Rev. Phuong Van Nguyen, Admin.
Res.: 153 Sterling St., 01610. Tel: 508-752-1825; Fax: 508-756-1267.

26—ST. PETER (1884), Rev. Msgr. Francis J. Scollen; Rev. Anthony Ogunleye, African Ministry.
Res.: 929 Main St., 01610. Tel: 508-752-4674; Fax: 508-767-1511.
Catechesis/Religious Program—Tel: 508-752-0797; Fax: 508-767-1511. Students 211.

27—SACRED HEART (1880), (Irish), Rev. Edward J. Hanlon. In Res., Rev. Peter J. Scanlon.
Res.: 596 Cambridge St., 01610. Tel: 508-752-1608; 508-753-2555; Fax: 508-757-2462.
Catechesis/Religious Program—Students 105.

28—ST. STEPHEN'S (1887), Rev. Joseph M. Nally; Deacon James F. DiPadua Jr. In Res., Most Rev. George E. Rueger, D.D., V.G.
Res.: 16 Hamilton St., 01604. Tel: 508-755-3165; Fax: 508-755-0937.
School—(Grades PreK-8), 355 Grafton St.. Tel: 508-755-3209; Fax: 508-770-1052. Ruth O. McGinn, Prin. Sisters 2; Lay Teachers 14; Students 262.
Catechesis/Religious Program—Ramona Kneeland, D.R.E. Students 185.

OUTSIDE THE CITY OF WORCESTER

(In the County of Worcester)

ASHBURNHAM, ST. DENIS (1951), [CEM] Rev. Joseph J. Jurgelonis; Deacons Michael P. Connor; Richard DesJardins.
Res.: 85 Main St., P.O. Box 418, 01430. Tel: 978-827-5806; Fax: 978-827-1191.
Catechesis/Religious Program—Tel: 978-827-4892. Students 325.

ATHOL

1—ST. FRANCIS (1912), (Lithuanian), Rev. Stephen D. Johnson.
Res.: 105 Main St., 01331. Tel: 978-249-3361; Fax: 978-534-9318.
Catechesis/Religious Program— Combined with Our Lady Immaculate, Athol.

2—OUR LADY IMMACULATE (1882), Revs. Stephen D. Johnson; James B. Callahan; Deacons James L. Linderman; Robert Dio.
Res.: 192 School St., 01331-2399. Tel: 978-249-2738; Fax: 978-249-0447.
Catechesis/Religious Program—Tel: 978-249-7690. Sharon Maher, D.R.E. Students 231.
Mission—Our Lady Queen of Heaven Rte. 68, South Royalston, Worcester Co. 01368. Tel: 978-249-4103.

AUBURN

1—ST. JOSEPH'S (1907), Revs. Lawrence J. Esposito; Joseph M. Dolan; Paul W. Lemire; Deacon Peter Ryan.
Res.: 194 Oxford St., 01501. Tel: 508-832-2074; Fax: 508-832-8894.
Catechesis/Religious Program—Tel: 508-832-5975; Fax: 508-721-7607. Lisa Wass, D.R.E. Students 712.

2—NORTH AMERICAN MARTYRS (1952), Rev. John F. Gee.
Res.: 8 Wyoma Dr., 01501. Tel: 508-798-8779; Fax: 508-791-6614.
Catechesis/Religious Program—Tel: 508-798-0612. Joan Sundstrom, D.R.E. Students 140.

BALDWINVILLE, ST. VINCENT DE PAUL (1955), Rev. John E. Kelley; Deacon Robert J. Leger.
Res.: 18 Pleasant St., 01436. Tel: 978-939-8851; Fax: 978-939-2120.
Catechesis/Religious Program—Tel: 978-939-8290. Students 196.

BARRE, ST. JOSEPH'S (1896), [CEM] Rev. Thomas H. Hultquist.
Res.: 90 Common St., 01005. Tel: 978-355-4463; Fax: 978-355-0136.
Catechesis/Religious Program—Tel: 978-355-6402. Students 128.
Mission—St. Augustine 98 Church Ln., Wheelwright, Hardwick Co. 01094. Tel: 978-355-4463.

BERLIN, ST. JOSEPH THE GOOD PROVIDER (1973), Rev. Robert M. Spellman.
Res.: 52 West St., Box 284, 01503-0284. Tel: 978-838-9922; Fax: 978-838-9933.
Catechesis/Religious Program—Students 167.

BLACKSTONE

1—ST. PAUL'S (1850), [CEM] Rev. James D. Champion.
Res.: 48 St. Paul St., 01504. Tel: 508-883-6726; Fax: 508-883-2079.
Catechesis/Religious Program—Tel: 508-883-2590; Fax: 508-883-2079. Students 397.

2—ST. THERESA (1929), (French), Rev. Dennis J. Rocheford.
Res.: 630 Rathbun St., 01504. Tel: 508-883-7206; Fax: 508-883-5250.
Catechesis/Religious Program—Tel: 508-883-7527. Students 134.

BOLTON, ST. FRANCIS XAVIER (1953), Rev. Thomas B. Fleming.
Res.: 808 Main St., 01740. Tel: 978-779-2750; Fax: 978-779-0337.
Catechesis/Religious Program—Students 116.

BOYLSTON, ST. MARY OF THE HILLS (1952), Rev. Paul J. Tougas; Deacon Eduardus Meilus.
Res.: 620 Cross St., 01505. Tel: 508-869-6771.
Catechesis/Religious Program—Tel: 508-869-6776; Fax: 508-869-0418. Marcella Wilson, D.R.E. Students 345.

BROOKFIELD, ST. MARY'S (1885), Rev. John G. Hillier.
Res.: 4 Howard St., 01506. Tel: 508-867-3188; Fax: 508-867-4313.
Catechesis/Religious Program—Students 77.

CHARLTON CITY, ST. JOSEPH'S (1900), Revs. Robert A. Grattaroti; J. Normand Tremblay; Deacons Lawrence F. Miskell; William S. Miller.
Res.: Box 338, 01508. Tel: 508-248-7862; Fax: 508-248-5832.
Catechesis/Religious Program—Tel: 508-248-7986. Elizabeth Cotrupi, D.R.E. (High School); Cheryl Kingston, D.R.E. (Elementary); Joanne Powell, D.R.E. (Grades 1-5). Students 490.

CLINTON

1—ST. JOHN THE EVANGELIST (1849), (Irish), [CEM] Revs. Thomas V. Walsh; Kenneth R. Cardinale; Sisters Patricia Venegas, S.S.A., Pastoral Assoc.; Sheila Finnegan, S.N.D., Pastoral Assoc.
Res.: 149 Chestnut St., 01510. Tel: 978-368-0366; Fax: 978-368-4359.
Catechesis/Religious Program—Tel: 508-368-0052; Fax: 978-368-4360. Students 478.

2—OUR LADY OF JASNA GORA (1913), (Polish), Revs. Tomasz J. Borkowski; John F. Madden; Deacon George O'Connor.
Res.: 128 Franklin St., 01510. Tel: 978-365-2724; Fax: 978-365-5705.
School—St. Mary's, 128 Franklin St., 01510. Tel: 978-365-3137; Fax: 978-365-3380. Marilyn Blanchard, Prin. Lay Teachers 13; Students 110.
Catechesis/Religious Program—Tel: 508-393-3431. Students 28.

3—OUR LADY OF THE ROSARY (1909), Rev. J. Brendan Nally.
Res.: One Cross St., 01510. Tel: 508-365-3621; Fax: 508-368-3082.
Catechesis/Religious Program—Students 86.

DUDLEY

1—ST. ANDREW BOBOLA (1963), (Polish), [JC] Revs. Joseph F. Szwach; Joseph Bielonko.
Res.: 54 W. Main St., P.O. Box 98, 01571. Tel: 508-943-5633; Fax: 508-949-6701.
Catechesis/Religious Program—Students 84.

2—ST. ANTHONY'S (1905), [CEM] Rev. Paul F. Campbell.
Res.: 22 Dudley Hill Rd., Box 277, 01571-0277. Tel:

508-943-0470; Fax: 508-943-5663.
Catechesis/Religious Program—Tel: 508-949-0335; Fax: 508-943-5663. Linda Brink, D.R.E. Students 243.

EAST BROOKFIELD, ST. JOHN THE BAPTIST (1952), Rev. George A. Charland.
Res.: 121 Blaine Ave., 01515. Tel: 508-867-3738; Fax: 508-867-3301.
Catechesis/Religious Program—Tel: 508-885-4506. Students 101.

EAST DOUGLAS, ST. DENIS (1870), [CEM] Rev. William N. Cormier.
Res.: 23 Manchaug St., 01516. Tel: 508-476-2002; Fax: 508-476-2022.
Catechesis/Religious Program—Students 520.

EAST TEMPLETON, HOLY CROSS (1952), Revs. George L. O'Brien; Joachim Son Nguyen, Pastoral Assoc.
Res.: 25 Lake Ave., P.O. Box 418, 01438. Tel: 978-632-2121; Fax: 978-630-3890.
Catechesis/Religious Program—Tel: 978-632-2194. Students 253.

FISKDALE, ST. ANNE'S AND ST. PATRICK'S (1886), [CEM] Revs. Norman Meiklejohn, A.A.; Aidan M. Furlong, A.A.
Res.: 16 Church St., 01518. Tel: 508-347-7338; Fax: 508-347-2982.
Catechesis/Religious Program—Tel: 508-347-9353; Fax: 508-347-9353. Students 187.

FITCHBURG

1—ST. ANTHONY OF PADUA (1908), (Italian), Rev. Robert D. Bruso; Deacon Salvatore Tantillo.
Res.: 2 Beekman St., 01420. Tel: 978-342-4706; Fax: 978-342-8160.
School—(Grades PreK-8) Tel: 978-345-7785; Fax: 978-342-5110. Rosemary Thibodeau, Prin. Sisters 2; Lay Teachers 14; Students 258.
Catechesis/Religious Program—Tel: 978-342-2491. Ellen DePatie, D.R.E. Students 97.

2—ST. BERNARD'S (1847), (Irish), [CEM] Revs. H. Edward Chalmers; Thiel X. Nguyen. In Res., Revs. Thomas M. Tierney; Theodore R. Laperle (Retired).
Res.: 240 Water St., 01420. Tel: 978-343-7459; Fax: 978-343-0193.
School—254 Summer St., 01420. Tel: 978-342-1948; Fax: 978-342-1153. Sisters of the Presentation of the Blessed Virgin Mary 2; Lay Teachers 10; Students 250.
Catechesis/Religious Program—Students 188.

3—ST. CAMILLUS DE LELLIS (1953), Rev. Richard P. Lewandowski; Deacon Benjamin A. Nogueira.
Res.: 333 Mechanic St., 01420. Tel: 978-342-7921; Fax: 978-345-2688.
Catechesis/Religious Program—Students 55.

4—ST. FRANCIS OF ASSISI (1903), (French), Rev. Gerald A. Dorais; Deacon William Colon, Spanish Ministry. In Res., Rev. Angel Matos, Spanish Ministry.
Res.: 63 Sheridan, 01420. Tel: 978-342-9651; Fax: 978-342-7936.
Catechesis/Religious Program—Tel: 978-342-3521. Robert Jones, D.R.E. Students 73.

5—IMMACULATE CONCEPTION (1886), (French), Rev. Thien Nguyen.
Res.: 59 Walnut St., 01420. Tel: 978-342-5851; Fax: 978-345-2491.
Catechesis/Religious Program—Students 42.

6—ST. JOSEPH'S (1890), [CEM] Rev. Thomas G. Sickler, M.S.; Deacon Andre W. Croteau. In Res., Revs. Laurie L. Leger, M.S.; John Hughes, M.S.; Bro. Bob Belliveau, M.S.
Res.: 49 Woodland St., 01420. Tel: 978-345-7997; Fax: 978-345-7678.
School—35 Columbus St., 01420. Tel: 978-343-3630; Fax: 978-343-2671. Cheryl Slattery, Prin. Lay Teachers 10; Students 182.
Catechesis/Religious Program—Tel: 978-345-7997. Bette Brunell, D.R.E. Students 100.

7—MADONNA OF THE HOLY ROSARY (1955), Rev. Frank J. Liistro.
Res.: 118 Theresa St., 01420. Tel: 978-342-1290; Fax: 978-345-3032.
Catechesis/Religious Program—Tel: 978-345-4906. Judy A. Alario, D.R.E. Students 160.

8—SACRED HEART OF JESUS (1878), (Irish), Rev. John A. Dwyer.
Res.: 22 Cottage St., 01420. Tel: 978-342-9606; Fax: 978-342-7131.
Catechesis/Religious Program—Students 42.

GARDNER

1—HOLY SPIRIT (1955), Revs. Andre M. Gariepy; Angel Matos, Spanish Ministry.
Res.: 45 Metcalf St., 01440. Tel: 978-632-3333; Fax: 978-632-3630.
Catechesis/Religious Program—Students 191.

2—ST. JOSEPH'S (1908), (Polish), [CEM] Rev. Thomas M. Tokarz.
Res.: 358 Pleasant St., 01440. Tel: 978-632-0375; Fax: 978-632-1282.
Catechesis/Religious Program—Students 12.

3—OUR LADY OF THE HOLY ROSARY (1884), (French), [CEM] Rev. Andre Dargis, A.A., Admin.
Res.: 135 Nichols St., 01440. Tel: 508-632-0253; Fax: 508-630-1773.
School—99 Nichols St., 01440. Tel: 508-632-8656; Fax: 508-630-1433. Lay Teachers 19; Students 321.
Catechesis/Religious Program—Students 144.

4—SACRED HEART OF JESUS (1874), [CEM] Rev. Donald H. Baker; Deacon Paul J. Carrier.
Res. & Parish Hall: 166 Cross St., 01440. Tel: 978-632-0237; Fax: 978-630-2459.
Parish Center—100 Central St., 01440. Tel: 978-632-0217 (Deacon's Office).
School—Sacred Heart, (Grades K-8), Lynde St., 01440. Tel: 978-632-0950; Fax: 978-630-2448. Maureen Lapan, Prin. Lay Teachers 13; Students 203.
Catechesis/Religious Program—Tel: 978-632-0218. Students 302.
School—Day Care, Tel: 978-632-5745. Mrs. Jane Pineo, Dir.

GILBERTVILLE, ST. ALOYSIUS (1894), [CEM] Rev. Paul M. LaPalme.
Res.: 58 Church St., P.O. Box 542, 01031-0542. Tel: 413-477-6493; Fax: 413-477-0140.
Catechesis/Religious Program—Students 55.

GRAFTON, ST. PHILIP'S (1869), [CEM] Rev. Anthony T. Marteka.
Res.: 12 West St., 01519. Tel: 508-839-3325; Fax: 508-839-1310.
Catechesis/Religious Program—Tel: 508-839-9130. Students 180.

HARVARD, ST. THERESA'S (1950), Rev. Normand R. Gaumond.
Res.: 15 Still River Rd., P.O. Box 746, 01451. Tel: 978-456-3563; Fax: 978-456-8352.
Catechesis/Religious Program—Tel: 978-456-8807. Lorretta DiPietro, D.R.E. Students 309.

HOPEDALE, SACRED HEART OF JESUS (1935), Rev. William C. Konicki; Deacon Joseph Manella.
Res.: 187 Hopedale St., 01747. Tel: 508-473-1900; Fax: 508-473-1745.
Catechesis/Religious Program—Tel: 508-473-1701. Marie Venaglia, D.R.E. Students 483.

JEFFERSON, ST. MARY'S (1884), [CEM] Rev. Andre N. Remillard; Sr. Jacquelyn Alix, Pastoral Assoc.; Pamela Reidy, Pastoral Assoc.
Res.: 114 Princeton St., 01522. Tel: 508-829-4508; Fax: 508-829-0429.
Catechesis/Religious Program—Tel: 508-829-6758. Students 523.

LANCASTER, IMMACULATE CONCEPTION (1915), Rev. Edward P. Lettic.
Res.: 28 Packard St., P.O. Box 95, 01523. Tel: 978-365-6582; Fax: 978-365-3097.
Catechesis/Religious Program—Students 174.

LEICESTER

1—ST. JOSEPH'S (1851), [CEM] Rev. Michael A. DiGeronimo; Carol Cornacchioli, Pastoral Assoc.
Res.: 759 Main St., 01524. Tel: 508-892-7407; Fax: 508-892-4753.
Catechesis/Religious Program—Tel: 508-892-0660. Tony McCaffrey, D.R.E. Combined with St. Pius X. Students 242.
School—Day Care, Caring Place, Tel: 508-892-3168. Students 43.

2—ST. PIUS X (1956), Rev. Michael A. DiGeronimo; Carol A. Cornacchioli, Pastoral Assoc
Mailing Address: 759 Main St., 01524 Tel: 508-892-7407; Fax: 508-892-4753.
Church: 1161 Main St., 01524.
Catechesis/Religious Program—Tony McCaffrey, D.R.E. Combined with St. Joseph's, Leicester. Students 242.

LEOMINSTER

1—ST. ANNA'S (1937), (Italian), Rev. Ronald G. Falco.
Res.: 199 Lancaster St., 01453. Tel: 978-537-5293; Fax: 978-537-2950.
School—Tel: 978-534-4770; Fax: 978-466-1167. Rita Bernard, Prin. Priests 1; Lay Teachers 10; Students 182.
Catechesis/Religious Program—Tel: 978-537-2945. Students 343.

2—ST. CECILIA'S (1900), (French), [CEM] Rev. Francis T. Goguen; Rev. Msgr. George E. Deromme; Deacon Ronald J. Aubuchon.
Res.: 170 Mechanic St., 01453. Tel: 978-537-6541; Fax: 978-840-1965.
Catechesis/Religious Program—Tel: 978-537-4673. Patricia Secino, D.R.E. Students 309.

3—HOLY FAMILY OF NAZARETH (1963), Rev. Thomas F. Egan
Res.: 750 Union St., 01453. Tel: 978-537-3016; Fax: 978-534-1119.
Catechesis/Religious Program—Tel: 978-537-5660. Anne Booth, D.R.E. Students 230.

4—ST. LEO'S (1872), [CEM] Revs. John E. Doran; Jesus E. Martinez.
Res.: 108 Main St., 01453. Tel: 978-537-7257; Fax: 978-840-6182.
School—120 Main St., 01453. Tel: 978-537-1007; Fax: 978-537-2828. Mrs. Carolyn Polselli, Prin. Sisters of the Presentation of the Blessed Virgin Mary 2; Lay Teachers 29; Students 325.
Catechesis/Religious Program—Tel: 978-537-1194. Students 370.

5—OUR LADY OF THE LAKE (1952), Rev. Timothy M. Brewer; Sr. Paulette Gariepy, D.H.S., Pastoral Assoc.; Deacon Fred A. Harkins.
Res.: 1400 Main St., 01453. Tel: 978-342-2978; Fax: 978-342-8738.
Catechesis/Religious Program—Tel: 978-345-7469. Lisa Sciacca, D.R.E. Students 532.

LINWOOD, GOOD SHEPHERD (1904), Rev. Daniel R. Mulcahy Jr.; Deacon Donald Webster.
Res.: 121 Linwood St., P.O. Box 517, 01525. Tel: 508-234-7726; Fax: 508-234-0964.
Catechesis/Religious Program—Tel: 508-234-5340. Carol Trainque, D.R.E. & Coord. Students 261.

LUNENBURG, ST. BONIFACE (1950), Rev. Edward D. Niccolls; Sr. Mary E. LeBlanc, P.B.V.M., Pastoral Assoc.; Deacon Joseph M. Cieri.
Res.: 817 Massachusetts Ave., 01462. Tel: 978-582-4008; Fax: 978-582-9355.
Catechesis/Religious Program—Tel: 978-582-6650; Fax: 978-582-9355. Maura L. Sweeney, D.R.E. Students 290.

MANCHAUG, ST. ANNE'S (1900), Rev. Stanley F. Krutcik.
Res.: 31 Main St., P.O. Box 311, 01526. Tel: 508-476-2405; Fax: 508-476-4443.
Catechesis/Religious Program—Students 38.

MENDON, ST. MICHAEL'S (1952), Rev. Thomas E. Mahoney; Deacon Ernest E. Desmarais.
Res.: 29 North Ave., P.O. Box 33, 01756. Tel: 508-478-4456; Fax: 508-634-2664.
Catechesis/Religious Program—Students 340.

MILFORD

1—ST. MARY OF THE ASSUMPTION (1848), (Portuguese—Spanish), [CEM] Revs. Michael G. Foley; Tam A. Bui; Eusiquio-Arranz Munoz; Sr. Theresa Lucier, S.P., Pastoral Assoc.
Res.: 27 Pearl St., 01757. Tel: 508-473-2000; Fax: 508-473-6907.
Catechesis/Religious Program—St. Mary's Parish Center, 17 Winter St., 01757. Tel: 508-478-7440. Martha LaFreniere Harris, D.R.E. Students 880.

2—SACRED HEART (1905), [CEM] Rev. Richard Scioli, C.S.S. (BO); Sr. Claire Belforti, S.S.J., Pastoral Min. In Res., Rev. Leonard J. Ferrecchia, C.S.S. (BO).
Res.: 5 E. Main St., 01757. Tel: 508-634-5435; Fax: 508-478-4993.
Catechesis/Religious Program—Tel: 508-473-1036. Sr. Catherine Walsh, R.S.M., D.R.E. Students 560.

MILLBURY

1—ASSUMPTION (1884), (French), Rev. Richard A. Fortin.
Res.: 12 Waters St., 01527. Tel: 508-865-2657; Fax: 508-865-4866.
School—17 Grove St., 01527. Tel: 508-865-5404; Fax: 508-581-8974. Sr. Gertrude Lanouette, D.H.S., Prin. Lay Teachers 13; Students 222.
Catechesis/Religious Program—Students 76.

2—ST. BRIGID (1849), Revs. John E. Horgan; Emerito Ortiz.
Res.: 59 Main St., 01527. Tel: 508-865-6624; Fax: 508-865-3101.
Catechesis/Religious Program—Tel: 508-865-2752. Mrs. Gloria Schimke, D.R.E. Students 560.

MILLVILLE, ST. AUGUSTINE'S (1884), Deacon William Lucier.
Res.: 17 Lincoln St., 01529. Tel: 508-883-6678; Fax: 508-883-5878.
Catechesis/Religious Program—15 Lincoln St., 01529. Tel: 508-883-8794. Students 130.

NORTH BROOKFIELD, ST. JOSEPH'S (1867), [CEM] Rev. Richard T. Carey.
Res.: 28 Mt. Pleasant St., 01535. Tel: 508-867-6811; Fax: 508-867-7756.
Catechesis/Religious Program—27 Mt. Pleasant St., 01535. Tel: 508-867-9302. Students 262.

NORTH GRAFTON, ST. MARY'S (1952), Rev. Raymond F. Goodwin; Deacon Nicholas M. CaraDonna Jr.
Res.: 17 Waterville St., 01536. Tel: 508-839-3993; Fax: 508-839-1330.
Catechesis/Religious Program—Tel: 508-839-3993, Ext. 12. Patricia Verderese, D.R.E. Students 340.

NORTH OXFORD, ST. ANN'S (1906), Rev. James M. Steuterman; Sr. Jeanne Rouillard, S.A.S.V., Pastoral Assoc.
Res.: 652 Main St., P.O. Box 488, 01537. Tel: 508-987-8892; Fax: 508-987-1598.
Catechesis/Religious Program—P.O. Box 488, 01537. Tel: 508-987-1869. Students 282.

NORTHBORO

1—ST. BERNADETTE (1959), Rev. Stephen M. Gemme, Admin.
Res.: 258 Main St., 01532. Tel: 508-393-2223; Fax: 508-393-2718.
School—(Grades PreK-8), 266 Main St., 01532. Tel: 508-351-9905. Paul DiDomenico, Prin. Sisters 2; Lay Teachers 31; Students 501.
Catechesis/Religious Program—Tel: 508-393-7445. Students 115.

2—ST. ROSE OF LIMA (1883), Rev. James A. Houston.

Res.: 244 W. Main St., P.O. Box 685, 01532. Tel: 508-393-2413; Fax: 508-393-4922.
Catechesis/Religious Program—P.O. Box 387. Tel: 508-393-6444. Mrs. Maria Gasser, D.R.E. Students 808.

NORTHBRIDGE, ST. PETER (1904), Rev. John F. Connell.
Res.: 39 Church Ave., 01534. Tel: 508-234-2156; Fax: 508-234-5123.
Catechesis/Religious Program—Tel: 508-234-6355. Students 161.

OTTER RIVER, ST. MARTIN'S (1864), Revs. Cornelius F. O'Leary; Son Anh Nguyen (Vietnam), Pastoral Assoc.
Res.: 248 State Rd., 01436. Tel: 978-939-5588; Fax: 978-939-2305.
Church: 247 State Rd., 01436.
Catechesis/Religious Program—Students 68.

OXFORD, ST. ROCH'S (1886), [CEM] Rev. Msgr. Louis R. Piermarini.
Res.: 334 Main St., 01540. Tel: 508-987-8987; Fax: 508-987-8938.
Catechesis/Religious Program—Tel: 508-987-2382. Students 356.

PAXTON, ST. COLUMBA'S (1951), Rev. James M. Shea.
Res.: 10 Richards Ave., 01612. Tel: 508-755-0408; Fax: 508-767-0759.
Catechesis/Religious Program—Tel: 508-755-0601. Students 255.

PETERSHAM, ST. PETER (1968), Revs. Stephen D. Johnson; James B. Callahan.
Mailing Address: Main St., 01366. Tel: 978-249-3361; Fax: 978-249-0447.
Res.: 192 School St., Athol, 01331. Tel: 978-249-2738.
Catechesis/Religious Program—Tel: 978-249-7690. Students 27.

PRINCETON, PRINCE OF PEACE (1967), Rev. James J. Caldarella; Sr. Teresa Rose Carchidi, Pastoral Assoc.
Res.: 5 Worcester Rd., P.O. Box 305, 01541. Tel: 508-464-2871; Fax: 508-464-0449.
Catechesis/Religious Program—Students 196.

ROCHDALE, ST. ALOYSIUS-ST. JUDE (1904), Rev. Peter H. White.
Res.: 2 Church Pl., P.O. Box 296, 01542-0296. Tel: 508-892-8296; Fax: 508-892-8296.
Catechesis/Religious Program—Mrs. Ann Listenic, D.R.E. Students 155.

RUTLAND, ST. PATRICK'S (1938), Rev. James P. Kerrigan; Deacon William J. Vigliotti.
Res.: 290 Main St., Box 939, 01543. Tel: 508-886-4309; Fax: 508-886-2897.
Church: 258 Main St., 01543. Tel: 508-886-6131.
Catechesis/Religious Program—Tel: 508-886-4984; Fax: 508-886-7414. Michele Curtis, D.R.E. Students 497.

SHREWSBURY
1—ST. ANNE'S (1950), [CEM] Rev. Edward J. Moran; Sr. Charlene O'Leary, P.B.V.M., Pastoral Assoc.
Res.: 130 Boston Tpke., 01545. Tel: 508-757-5154; Fax: 508-797-9520.
Catechesis/Religious Program—Tel: 508-752-5040. Karen Weigold, D.R.E. Students 998.
2—ST. MARY'S (1922), Revs. Paul T. O'Connell, J.C.L.; Dennis J. O'Brien; Leo Lancaster.
Res.: 18 Summer St., 01545. Tel: 508-845-0161; Fax: 508-842-9132.
School—Tel: 508-842-1601; Fax: 508-845-1535. Joanne Gannon, Prin. Sisters 1; Lay Teachers 25; Students 247.
Catechesis/Religious Program—Tel: 508-845-1154. Students 967.

SOUTH ASHBURNHAM, ST. ANNE (1895), Rev. Joseph J. Jurgelonis; Deacons Michael P. Connor; Richard DesJardins.
Pastoral Office—85 Main St., P.O. Box 418, Ashburnham, 01430-0418. Tel: 978-827-5806; Fax: 978-827-1191.
Catechesis/Religious Program—Tel: 978-827-4892. Combined with St. Denis.

SOUTH BARRE, ST. THOMAS-A-BECKET (1923), Rev. Ernest Allega.
Res.: P.O. Box 186, Vernon Ave., 01074. Tel: 978-355-2228; Fax: 978-355-0042.
Catechesis/Religious Program—Tel: 508-882-3353. Students 145.

SOUTH GRAFTON, ST. JAMES (1887), Rev. Michael F. Rose; Deacon Edward Richards.
Res.: 89 Main St., 01560. Tel: 508-839-5354; Fax: 508-839-5430.
Catechesis/Religious Program—Tel: 508-839-6800. Students 465.

SOUTHBOROUGH
1—ST. ANNE (1886), Rev. Thirburse F. Millott.
Res.: 20 Boston Rd., P.O. Box 403, 01772. Tel: 508-485-0141; Fax: 508-481-9374.
Catechesis/Religious Program—Tel: 508-481-3159. Cynthia dela Pena, D.R.E.; Anthony Nachef, D.R.E. Students 492.
2—ST. MATTHEW (1956), [JC] Rev. James B. Flynn.
Res.: 105 Southville Rd., 01772. Tel: 508-485-2285; Fax: 508-485-4437.
Catechesis/Religious Program—Tel: 508-229-2429; Fax: 508-229-0837. Students 603.

SOUTHBRIDGE
1—ST. HEDWIG'S (1916), (Polish), [CEM] Rev. Charles E.J. Borowski.
Res.: 29 Summer St., 01550. Tel: 508-764-6947; Fax: 508-764-7707.
Catechesis/Religious Program—Students 34.
2—ST. MARY'S (1861), [CEM] Rev. Peter Joyce; Deacons Richard Olson; Teodoro Camacho.
Res.: 263 Hamilton St., 01550. Tel: 508-764-3226; Fax: 508-764-3209.
Catechesis/Religious Program—Tel: 508-765-0245; 508-765-0394 (Spanish). Sr. Estelia Viquez, R.O.D.A., D.R.E.; Antonia Martinez, D.R.E. Students 421.
3—NOTRE DAME (1869), (French-Canadian), Revs. Maurice L. Gilbert; Leo-Paul J. LeBlanc; Deacon Michael J. Corby.
Res.: 61 Marcy St., 01550. Tel: 508-765-0601; Fax: 508-764-4148.
Catechesis/Religious Program—Religious Education Center, 20 Marcy St., 01550. Tel: 508-764-8018. Students 206.
4—SACRED HEART (1908), (French), Rev. Charles R. Armey; Deacon Thomas Skonieczny.
Res.: 40 Charlton St., 01550. Tel: 508-764-6964; Fax: 508-764-3320.
Catechesis/Religious Program—Tel: 508-765-5597. Students 105.

SPENCER
1—MARY, QUEEN OF THE ROSARY (1994), [CEM], Merger of St. Mary, Spencer and Our Lady of the Rosary, Spencer. Revs. James F. Hoey; Thomas M. Barry; Deacon Harry M. Sweet.
Office—60 Maple St., 01562. Tel: 508-885-3111; Fax: 508-885-4905.
Res.: 46 Maple St., 01562. Tel: 508-885-3806.
Catechesis/Religious Program—Tel: 508-885-0211. Mrs. Carol St. John, D.R.E. Students 446.
2—OUR LADY OF THE ROSARY (1854), Merged, with St. Mary's, Spencer to form Mary, Queen of the Rosary, Spencer.

STERLING, ST. RICHARD OF CHICHESTER (1953), Rev. Thomas B. Garlick; Sr. Anne Marie Wildenhain, S.S.J., Pastoral Assoc.; Jeanne A. Whitford, Business Mgr.
Res.: 4 Bridge St., P.O. Box 657, 01564. Tel: 508-422-8881; Fax: 508-422-0291.
Catechesis/Religious Program—Tel: 508-422-8921. Patricia Cole, D.R.E. Students 494.

SUTTON, ST. MARK (1966), [CEM] Revs. Brian P. O'Toole; Joseph W. McKiernan; Deacons Walter Doyle; John Dugan.
Res.: 356 Boston Rd., 01590. Tel: 508-865-3860; Fax: 508-865-5095.
Catechesis/Religious Program—Tel: 508-845-3860, Ext. 16. Patricia Morin, D.R.E. Students 596.

UPTON, HOLY ANGELS (1900), Rev. Laurence V. Brault.
Res.: 2 Nelson St., 01568. Tel: 508-529-6981; Fax: 508-529-6317.
Catechesis/Religious Program—Tel: 508-529-3109. Simone Caron, D.R.E. Students 587.

UXBRIDGE, ST. MARY'S (1853), [CEM] Rev. Paul J. Doherty; Deacon Paul Brown; Mrs. Rosemary Seibold, Pastoral Assoc.
Res.: 77 Mendon St., 01569. Tel: 508-278-2226; Fax: 508-278-7949.
Catechesis/Religious Program—Tel: 508-278-3777. Students 512.

WARREN, ST. PAUL'S (1872), [CEM] Rev. Daniel J. Becker, Admin.
Res.: 1082 Main St., P.O. Box 1027, 01083-1027. Tel: 413-436-7327; Fax: 413-436-9677.
Catechesis/Religious Program—Tel: 413-436-7492. Clustered with St. Thomas Aquinas, West Warren. Students 160.

WEBSTER
1—ST. JOSEPH'S BASILICA (1887), (Polish), [CEM] Rev. Msgr. Anthony Czarnecki; Rev. Edward Michalski.
Res.: 53 Whitcomb St., 01570. Tel: 508-943-0467; Fax: 508-943-0808.
School—Tel: 508-943-0378; Fax: 508-949-0581. Sr. Marie JoAnn Lewko, C.S.S.F., Prin. Felician Sisters 3; Lay Teachers 12; Students 255.
Catechesis/Religious Program—Tel: 508-943-2738. Students 63.
2—ST. LOUIS (1853), Revs. Joseph A. Marcotte; Bernard Davenport.
Res.: 15 Lake St., 01570. Tel: 508-943-0240; Fax: 508-943-0801.
School—Tel: 508-943-0257; Fax: 508-943-0257. Lay Teachers 12; Students 230.
Catechesis/Religious Program—Tel: 508-943-0817. Students 506.
3—SACRED HEART OF JESUS (1870), [CEM] [JC] Rev. Michael J. Roy; Deacons Roland R. Michaud; Laurent Mongeau, (Retired).
Res.: 18 E. Main St., 01570. Tel: 508-943-3140; Fax: 508-943-2213.
School—St. Anne, Day St., 01570. Tel: 508-943-2735; Fax: 508-943-6215. Sr. Constance Bayeur, S.S.A., Prin. Sisters of St. Anne 2; Lay Teachers 12; Students 256.
Catechesis/Religious Program—Tel: 508-943-0113. Students 105.

WEST BOYLSTON, OUR LADY OF GOOD COUNSEL (1869), [CEM] Rev. John F. Burke. In Res., Rev. Francis A. Roberge.
Res.: 111 Worcester St., 01583. Tel: 508-835-3606; Fax: 508-835-5456. Email: goodcounsel@charter.net.
Catechesis/Religious Program—Tel: 508-835-6336. Thomas Faucher, D.R.E. Students 471.

WEST BROOKFIELD, SACRED HEART OF JESUS (1950), Rev. David B. Galonek.
Res.: 10 Milk St., 01585-0563. Tel: 508-867-6469; Fax: 508-867-3670.
Parish Center—Tel: 508-867-4460.
Catechesis/Religious Program—Tel: 508-867-4460. Students 120.

WEST WARREN
1—ST. STANISLAUS (1913), (Polish), Rev. John M. Lizewski.
Res.: 2270 Main St., P.O. Box 723, 01092-0503. Tel: 413-436-5110; Fax: 413-436-0556.
Catechesis/Religious Program—Students 62.
2—ST. THOMAS AQUINAS (1893),
St. Paul's Rectory: 1082 Main St., P.O. Box 1027. Tel: 413-436-7327; Fax: 413-436-7324.
Catechesis/Religious Program—Fax: 413-436-7492. Clustered with St. Paul, Warren. Students 98.

WESTBOROUGH, ST. LUKE THE EVANGELIST (1870), [CEM] Revs. George O. Lange; Steven M. LaBaire.
Res.: 70 W. Main St., 01581. Tel: 508-366-5502; Fax: 508-366-6049.
Catechesis/Religious Program—One Ruggles St., 01581. Tel: 508-366-8509. Mary Sanning, D.R.E. Students 853.

WESTMINSTER, ST. EDWARD THE CONFESSOR (1951), Rev. Terence T. Kilcoyne, D.Min.; Deacon Roderick F. Cashes.
Res.: 10 Church St., 01473. Tel: 978-874-2362; Fax: 978-840-1024.
Catechesis/Religious Program—Tel: 978-874-1559. Students 325.

WHITINSVILLE, ST. PATRICK'S (1889), [CEM] Rev. C. Michael Broderick; Deacons Anthony R. Surozenski; Steve Miller.
Res.: 7 East St., P.O. Box 60, 01588. Tel: 508-234-5656; Fax: 508-234-6845.
Catechesis/Religious Program—Tel: 508-234-3511. MaryAnn DiGregorio, D.R.E. Students 524.

WINCHENDON, IMMACULATE HEART OF MARY (1870), [CEM] Rev. Roland L. Gamache; Sr. Anne O'Shea, P.M., Pastoral Asst.; Deacon Mark J. Carrier.
Res.: 52 Spruce St., 01475. Tel: 508-297-0280; Fax: 508-297-3577.
Catechesis/Religious Program—Tel: 508-297-2699. Sr. Pauline Grenier, P.M., D.R.E. Students 200.
Convent—Our Lady of Sorrows. Tel: 508-297-0275. Sisters of the Presentation of Mary 2.

Chaplains of Public Institutions

WORCESTER. *ADCARE Hospital of Worcester*. Vacant.
Air National Guard. Serviced by Catholic Charities priests.
Hahnemann Hospital. Serviced by Priests of St. Bernard, St. Joan of Arc, Immaculate Conception, Our Lady of the Rosary Churches.
Memorial Hospital. Rev. Thomas Landry, Catholic Pastoral Ministry.
University of Mass Medical Center. Rev. Francis Roach.
Worcester Belmont House. Serviced by St. Margaret Mary Church.
Worcester Detention Center. Serviced by Urban Ministry.
Worcester State Hospital. Vacant

BOYLSTON. *Worcester County Jail and House of Correction*. Deacon Gary Miller.
Worcester County Sanitarium. Vacant.

GARDNER. *Massachusetts Correctional Institution*. Rev. Thomas M. Tierney, Chap.

LANCASTER. *Massachusetts Correctional Institution*. Vacant.

OTTER RIVER. *Templeton Developmental Center*. Rev. George L. O'Brien.

On Special or Other Diocesan Assignment:
Revs.—
Banach, Michael, Vatican Diplomatic Corp.
Ciambelli, Blase A.
DiOrio, Ralph A., Apostolate of Healing
Doiron, David E., Pastoral Counseling
Gothing, Donald B., Admin., Capilia de la Santisima Trinidad, 69 Lincoln Ter. P.O. Box 667, Leominster, 01453. Tel: 978-534-5258

On Duty Outside the Diocese:
Rev. Msgrs.—
Banach, Michael, Nunciatura Apostolica, Avenida

Arce 2990, Casilla Postal 136, La Paz, Bolivia.
Gelineau, Raymond H.
Kelly, Francis D., Rector
Mattimore, William F., St. George, 41-1323 Kalanianole Hwy., Waimanalo, HI 96795. Tel: 808-259-7188; Fax: 808-259-0169
Mongelluzzo, James A., P.O. Box 2545, 01613.
Moroney, James P., Exec. Dir., National Conference of Catholic Bishops, Secretariat for the Liturgy, 3211 4th St., N.E., Washington, DC 20017-1194. Tel: 202-541-3060; Fax: 202-541-3088

Revs.—
Carr, David W., 740 Palm Trail, Delray Beach, FL 33447.
Damian, Ronald
Dunkley, George
Hill, George H., Abbey of the Genesee, Piffard, NY 14533.
Kelly, David F., Duquesne Univ., Theology Dept., Pittsburgh, PA 15219.
Roy, F. Gilles, Apartado 46, Sicuani (Via Cuzco), Peru.

Military Chaplains:
Revs.—
Bomba, Paul M.
Boucher, Roger R.

Retired:
Rev. Msgrs.—
Battista, Leo, 30 Julio Dr., Shrewsbury, 01545.
Collette, Richard, Southgate, 30 Julio Dr., Shrewsbury, 01545.
Daley, Thomas J., Vianney House, 222 June St., 01602.
Dyer, John J., 72 Goldthwaite Rd., 01605.
Haddad, Edmond G., Vianney House, 222 June St., 01602.

Revs.—
Anger, Raymond G., 30 Julio Dr., Apt. 317, Shrewsbury, 01545.
Banach, Henry S., 64 Oakwood Ln., 01604.
Barrett, John W., 49 Elm St., 01609.
Barry, Leo, The Seasons Assisted Living, 5 Saint Elizabeth Way, East Greenwich, RI 02818.
Bedard, J. Raymond, 401 Lake Shore Dr., West Palm Beach, FL 33401.
Berthiaume, Eugene F., P.O. Box 415, West Warren, 01092.
Clifford, James J., St. Ann, North Oxford, 01537.
Conlin, Bernard J., Southgate of Shrewsbury, 30 Julio Dr., Shrewsbury, 01545.
Debitetto, Ronald E., 66 Stetson St., Hyannis, 02601.
Dutram, Charles J., 880 School St., Webster, 01570.
Dyer, Edward J., 30 Apricot St., 01603.
Falvey, Edmund F., Southgate, 35 Julio Dr., Shrewsbury, 01545.
Fontaine, John-Paul, 5 Harbor Lights Rd., Bourne, 02532.
Gallagher, William J., 49 Elm, 01609.
Galligan, Eymard P., S.S.E., 58 Main St., P.O. Box 119, Southborough, 01772.
Gariepy, Robert E., 320 Sprice Dr., Ashburnham, 01453.
Gilgun, Bernard E., St. Anne's, Shewsbury.
Gionet, Urbain J., Southgate of Shrewsbury, 30 Julio Dr., Apt. 112, Shrewsbury, 01545.
Grochowski, Bernard J., Box 9839, Las Vegas, NV 89191.
Hamernik, Peter P., Immaculate Conception Rectory, 25 Parker St., Indian Orchard, 01151.
Hebert, Roland G., Southgate of Shrewsbury, 30 Julio Dr. Apt. 109, Shrewsbury, 01545.
Holland, George G., Box 488, North Oxford, 01537.
Labonte, Richard H., P.O. Box 207, Hope Valley, RI 02832.
Lamothe, C. Romero, Southgate of Shewsbury, 30 Julio Dr., Shrewsbury, 01545.
Lange, Raymond L., 22 Surrey Ln., Brookfield, 01506.
Laperle, Theodore R., St. Bernard Rectory, 240 Water St., Fitchburg, 01420.
LeBeau, Cyril A., Southgate of Shewsburyianney House, 30 Julio Dr., Shrewsbury, 01545.
Loiselle, Joseph G., 48 W. Main St., Millbury, 01527.
McGovern, William W., Vianney House, 222 June St., 01602.
McKenna, John J., Sisters of Providence, 1233 Maint St., Holyoke, 01040.
McNamara, Philip D., 30 Julio Dr., Shrewsbury, 01545.
O'Brien, Thomas F., 7 Woodland Dr., Paxton, 01612.
O'Brien, William G., 362 West Brookfield, West Brookfield, 01585.
O'Donoghue, Brendon W., 30 Julio Dr. Apt. 246, Shrewsbury, 01545.
Ouillette, Arthur A., 165 Sunset Dr., P.O. Box 1285, Charlton City, 01508.
Pelletier, Edgar A., 4308 Oklawaha Ln., New Port Richey, FL 34655.
Prunier, Arthur J., Southgate of Shewsbury, 30 Julio Dr., Shrewsbury, 01545.
Raftery, William J., Southgate of Shewsbury, 30 Julio Dr., Shrewsbury, 01545.
Yankauskas, Albin J., Radius Healthcare Center, 119 Providence St., 01604.

Permanent Deacons:
Aliskevicz, John J., St. Vincent Hospital, Worcester
Archibald, Norbert, St. George, Worcester, MA
Arsenault, Roger D., (Retired), Holy Rosary, Gardner
Aubuchon, Ronald J., St. Cecilia, Leominster
Audette, Paul T., Our Lady of Loreto Worcester, MA
Baniukiewicz, Joseph M., Christ the King, Worcester
Benvenuti, Clement E., (Retired)
Blackwelder, Edgar B., (Retired)
Bosse, Raymond J., (Retired)
Brown, Paul E., Deaf Ministry Catholic Charities, Worcester; St. Mary, Uxbridge
Camacho, Theodoro, St. Mary, Southbridge
CaraDonna, Nicholas M., Jr., St. Mary's, North Grafton
Carrier, Mark, Immaculate Heart of Mary, Gardner
Carrier, Paul J., Sacred Heart of Jesus, Gardner
Cashes, Roderick F., St. Edward the Confessor, Westminster
Cieri, Joseph M., St. Boniface, Lunenburg
Colon, William B., Hispanic Community, St. Francis, Fitchburg
Connor, Michael P., St. Dennis, Ashburnham; St. Ann, South Ashburnham
Corby, Michael P., Notre Dame, Southbridge
Couture, James, St. Francis Athol
Croteau, Andre W., (Retired)
Daluga, Richard B., St. Mary, Milford
Denning, James, St. Catherine of Sweden, Worcester
Desautels, Alphonse T., Our Lady of the Angels, Worcester
Desjardin, Richard C., St. Dennis/St. Ann, Ashburnham
Desmarais, Ernest E.
Devine, Philip E., St. Mary, Shrewsbury
DeVito, Frederick A., (Retired)
Dio, Robert F., Our Lady Queen of the Rosary, South Royalston
DiPadua, James F., Jr., 49 Elm St., Worcester
Doyle, Walter F., Refugee Apostolate, Worcester; St. Mark's, Sutton
Dugan, John, St. Mark, Sutton
Dunphy, Melvin A., On Duty Outside the Diocese
DuVarney, Joseph T., 49 Elm St., Worcester
Escobar, Francisco, St. Paul Cathedral, Worcester
Faford, Peter R., St. Charles Borromeo
Fenner, Harry, (Retired)
Gendron, Steven P., St. Anna, Leominster
Giard, Arthur J., Jr., (Retired)
Green, Amos H., Sr., (Retired)
Harkins, Frederick A., Our Lady of the Lake, Leominster
Hayes, Myles, St. Bernard, Worcester
Isabel, David R., Souza-Baranouski Correction Center, Lancaster
King, Loren M., (Retired)
Ladroga, William J., On Duty Outside the Diocese
Leger, Robert, St. Vincent DePaul, Baldwinville
Librandi, Vincent A., Our Lady of Fatima, Worcester
Linderman, James L., Our Lady Immaculate, Athol
Lucier, William J., St. Augustine, Millville
Manella, Joseph R., Sacred Heart, Hopedale
Martel, Clarence H., (Retired), (Retired)
McCaffrey, Joseph A., (Retired)
Meilus, Eduardas, St. Mary of the Hills, Boylston, MA
Michaud, Roland R., Sacred Heart, Webster
Miller, Gary, Worcester County Jail and House of Corrections
Miller, William S., St. Patrick, Whitinsville
Miskell, Lawrence F., St. Joseph, Charlton
Mongeau, Laurent M., (Retired)
Montiverdi, Gerald M., University of Massachusetts Medical Center, Worcester
Mussulli, Pasquale, Our Lady of Loreto, Worcester
Nogueira, Benjamin A., Campus Ministry, Fitchburg State College, Fitchburg
O'Connor, George, Our Lady of Jasna Gora, Clinton
O'Connor, Richard J., Office for Worship, Worcester
O'Toole, George L., (Retired)
Olson, Richard V., St. Mary, Southbridge
Packard, Lee, St. Rose, Northboro
Prince, Norman A., (Retired), Immaculate Conception, Fitchburg
Richards, Edward J., St. James, South Grafton
Ryan, Peter, St. Joseph, Auburn
Skonieczny, Thomas A., Sacred Heart, Southbridge
Stevens, Wesley, St. Roch, Oxford
Surozenski, Anthony R., St. Patrick, Whitinsville
Sweet, Harry M., Mary Queen of the Rosary, Spencer
Tantillo, Salvatore, St. Anthony di Padua, Fitchburg
Tatro, Leo J., (Retired)
Vidito, Bruce R., St. Margaret Mary, Worcester
Vigliotti, William J., St. Patrick, Rutland
Wagner, Thomas A., (On Duty Outside the Diocese)
Webster, Donald, Good Shepard, Linwood
Weiss, Stephen J., Our Lady of the Rosary, Worcester

INSTITUTIONS LOCATED IN THE DIOCESE

[A] SEMINARIES, RELIGIOUS, OR SCHOLASTICATES

SPENCER. *St. Joseph's Abbey School of Theology and Institute of Monastic Studies* 01562. Tel: 508-885-8700; Fax: 508-885-8701. Email: sjasecrt@mindspring.com. Web: www.spencerabbey.com. Rt. Rev. Damian Carr, Abbot & Rector; Revs. Dominic Whedbee, O.C.S.O., Prior; Gabriel Bertoniere, O.C.S.O., Novice Master; James Palmigiano; Luke Truhan, O.C.S.O., Dean of Studies; James Palmigiano, Dean of Juniors; Bro. Robert Robinson, O.C.S.O., Subprior. Priests 6; Brothers 2; Professors 8; Students 3.

[B] COLLEGES AND UNIVERSITIES

WORCESTER. *Assumption College*, 500 Salisbury St., 01615-0005. Tel: 508-767-7000; Fax: 508-756-1780. Email: info@assumption.edu. Web: www.assumption.edu. Dr. Thomas R. Plough, Pres.; Rev. Wilfred J. Dufault, A.A., Chancellor; Francis P. Gurley, Exec. Vice Pres.; Joseph E. Gower, Provost; Rev. Dennis Gallagher, A.A., Vice Pres. Mission; Thomas E. Ryan, Vice Pres. Institutional Advancement; Catherine M. Woodbrooks, Vice Pres. Student Life. A Catholic Liberal Arts College under the Auspices of the Augustinians of the Assumption (Assumptionists). Priests 2; Sisters 1; Lay Teachers 145; Students 2,770; Total Enrollment 3,999.

College of the Holy Cross, Inc. 01610. Tel: 508-793-2011; Fax: 508-793-3030. Email: atebo@holycross.edu. Web: www.holycross.edu. Rev. Michael C. McFarland, S.J., Pres. A College for Boarders and Day Scholars. Sisters 1; Lay Teachers 257; Students 2,779; Jesuit Teachers 10.

PAXTON. *Anna Maria College*, Sunset Ln., 01612. Tel: 508-849-3300; Fax: 508-849-3334. Email: jprice@annamaria.edu. Web: www.annamaria.edu. William McGarry, Pres.; Sr. Rollande Quintal, S.S.A., Registrar. Sisters of St. Anne, A Coeducational Catholic College. Sisters 1; Lay Teachers 37; Total Staff 365; Students 1,142.

[C] HIGH SCHOOLS, CENTRAL

WORCESTER. *Holy Name Central Catholic Junior/Senior High School*, 144 Granite St., 01604. Tel: 508-753-6371; Fax: 508-831-1287. Email: mriordan@holyname.net. Web: www.holyname.net. Mrs. Mary E. Riordan, Headmaster; Mr. Edward M. Reynolds, Prin.; Mr. George Olson, Vice Prin.; Mrs. Arlene Maurello, Asst. Prin.; Rev. James B. Flynn, Senior Counselor. Priests 1; Sisters 1; Lay Teachers 56; Students 912.

St. Peter-Marian Central Catholic Junior/Senior High School, 781 Grove St., 01605-3196. Tel: 508-852-5555; Fax: 508-852-7238. Email: spmoffice@netscape.net. Mr. Matthew R. Sturgis, Headmaster; Miss Patricia Aubertine, Prin.; Mrs. Joanne Ethier, Asst. Prin.; Mr. John Pace, Asst. Prin.; Rev. Kenneth Cardinale. Priests 1; Sisters 2; Lay Teachers 80; Students 1,139.

FITCHBURG. *St. Bernard's Central Catholic High School*, 45 Harvard St., 01420. Tel: 978-342-3212; Fax: 978-345-8067. Email: stbhs@net1plus.com. Web: stb.echalk.com. James Conry, Headmaster; John Hoogasian, Ph.D., Prin. Priests 1; Sisters 1; Lay Teachers 30; Students 483.

SOUTHBRIDGE. *Trinity Catholic Academy* Elementary School , 11 Pine St., 01550. Tel: 508-765-5991; Fax: 508-765-0017. Email: mbrouillar@aol.com. Mrs. Madeleine Brouillard, Prin. Lay Teachers 11; Students 245; Total Staff 22.

[D] HIGH SCHOOLS, PAROCHIAL

WORCESTER. *St. Mary's Junior/Senior High School*, 50 Richland St., 01610. Tel: 508-753-1170; Fax: 508-795-0560. Email: GSKMarcotte@msn.com. Congregation of the Sisters of the Holy Family of

Nazareth Sisters 1; Lay Teachers 16; Students 161.

[E] HIGH SCHOOLS, PRIVATE

WORCESTER. *Notre Dame Academy*, 425 Salisbury St., 01609. Tel: 508-757-6200; Fax: 508-757-7200. Email: morrisoa@nda.mec.edu. Web: www.nda.mec.edu. Sr. Ann Morrison, S.N.D., Prin. A Private Day School for Girls. Sisters of Notre Dame de Namur 5; Other Religious Orders 2; Lay Teachers 31; Girls 322.

FITCHBURG. *Notre Dame Preparatory School*, (Grades 7-12), 171 South St., 01420. Tel: 978-343-7635; Fax: 978-343-6579. Email: jheffh@hotmail.com. Web: www.ndprepfitchburg.org. Mr. Jeff Hammond, Headmaster. Lay Teachers 10; Students 44.

LANCASTER. *Trivium School*, 471 Langen Rd., 01523. Tel: 978-365-4795; Fax: 978-365-4795. Email: triviumschool@aol.com. Web: triviumschool.com. P.O. Box 597, South Lancaster, 01561. Dr. William M. Schmitt, Headmaster. Lay Teachers 14; Students 76.

SHREWSBURY. *St. John's High School*, 378 Main St., 01545. Tel: 508-842-8934; Fax: 508-842-3670. Email: sgregory@stjohnshigh.org. Web: www.stjohnshigh.org. Mr. Michael W. Welch, Headmaster. Xaverian Brothers Brothers 2; Lay Teachers 64; Boys 1,104.

STILL RIVER. *Immaculate Heart of Mary School*, 282 Still River Rd., Box 1000, 01467. Tel: 978-456-8877; Fax: 978-456-9052. Email: sme@saintbenedict.com. Web: www.saintbenedict.com. Sr. Mary Elizabeth, Prin. Sisters 8; Students 132; Total Staff 18.

[F] MIDDLE SCHOOLS, PRIVATE

WORCESTER. *The Nativity School of Worcester*, 10 Irving St., 01606. Tel: 508-799-0100; Fax: 508-799-3951. Email: infor@nativityworcester.org. Web: www.nativityworcester.org. Joanne G. McClatchy, Exec. Dir. Tel: 508-799-0100; Alex Zequeira, Prin. Tel: 508-799-0100. Boys 25; Teachers 8.

[G] ELEMENTARY SCHOOLS, CENTRAL

WORCESTER. *St. Peter's Central Catholic Elementary School*, 865 Main St., 01610. Tel: 508-791-6496; Fax: 508-770-0818. Email: spcc@choiceonemail.com. Mrs. Meg Kursonis, Head of School. Sisters of St. Joseph Lay Teachers 20; Students 366; Preschool Students 44; Total Enrollment 410.

MILFORD. *Milford Catholic Elementary School*, 11 E. Main St., 01757. Tel: 508-473-7303; Fax: 508-478-4902. Email: milfordcatholic@comcast.net. Web: milfordcatholic.org. Sr. Patricia Murphy, S.S.J., Prin. Sisters of St. Joseph 1; Lay Teachers 14; Students 286; Aids 2.

UXBRIDGE. *Our Lady of Valley Regional Elementary School*, 75 Mendon St., 01569. Tel: 508-278-5851; Fax: 508-278-0391. Email: secretary+ourladyvalley.com. Sr. Gloria Corriveau, S.S.J., Prin. Sisters 1; Lay Teachers 9; Students 219; Part-Time Teachers 4.

[H] ELEMENTARY SCHOOLS, PRIVATE

WORCESTER. *Venerini Academy*, 27 Edward St., 01605. Tel: 508-753-3210; Fax: 508-754-6050. Email: snap@venerini.org. Web: www.venerini.org. Sr. Sandra Napier, S.N.D., Prin. Sisters 4; Lay Teachers 16; Students 383.

LEOMINSTER. *Julie Country Day School*, 365 Lindell Ave., 01453. Tel: 978-537-4939; Fax: 978-534-0347. Email: jcdcoed@aol.com. Sr. Judith Ward, S.N.D., Prin. Lay Teachers 22; Students 184.

[I] CATHOLIC CHARITIES

WORCESTER. *Catholic Charities*, 10 Hammond St., 01610-1513. Tel: 508-798-0191; Fax: 508-797-5659. Web: www.ccworc.org. Catherine Loeffler, Diocesan Dir.; Louise L. Myer, Dir. Financial Mgmt.; Heather McDonald, Admin., Quality Assurance & Program Development; Judith Zeh, Manager, Personnel & Training.

Northern Worcester Co. Offices, 53 Highland Ave., Fitchburg, 01420-7896. Tel: 978-343-4879; Fax: 978-345-4161.

12 Riverbend St., Athol, 01331-2520. Tel: 978-249-4563; Fax: 978-249-2545. Jacqueline Hager, Area Admin.

Southern Worcester Co. Offices

Southbridge Office, 79 Elm St., Southbridge, 01550-2601. Tel: 508-765-5936; Fax: 508-764-4153. Edelmira A. Spence, Area Admin.

Blackstone Valley/Greater Milford Area Office, 9 Spring St., Whitinsville, 01588-1409. Tel: 508-234-3800; Fax: 508-234-2321.

126 Main St., Rm. 6, Milford, 01757. Tel: 508-478-9632; Fax: 508-478-9632. Noreen Landry, Area Admin.

Senior Employment Service, 10 Hammond St., 01610-1513. Tel: 508-798-0191; Fax: 508-797-5659. Robert Holmes, Admin.

Refugee Resettlement, 10 Hammond St., 01610-1513. Tel: 508-798-0191; Fax: 508-797-5659. Debra Spangler, Admin.

Family & Community Services, 10 Hammond St., 01610-1513. Tel: 508-798-0191; Fax: 508-797-5659. Sara Glenn, Admin.

Home Care Services, 10 Hammond St., 01610-1513. Tel: 508-798-0191; Fax: 508-797-5659. Heather McDonald, Interim Admin.

Literacy Volunteers, 10 Hammond St., 01610-1513. Tel: 508-798-0191; Fax: 508-797-5659. Madelyn Hennessy, Admin.

Crozier House, 10 Hammond St., 01610-1513. Tel: 508-798-0191; Fax: 508-797-5659. J. David Mulrooney, Admin. A Half-Way House for Substance Abusing Men.

Mercy Centre (Developmental Disabilities), 25 W. Chester St., 01605-1136. Tel: 508-852-7165; Fax: 508-856-9755. Doris Dyer, Admin. Special Education Day Program and Sheltered Workshop for Developmentally Disabled Youngsters and Adults

Youville House Shelter for Homeless Families, 133 Granite St., 01604-4500. Tel: 508-753-3084; Fax: 508-754-0139. Kenneth Michaud, Admin. Total Assisted 40,000; Total Staff 335.

[J] CHILD CARE AGENCIES

WORCESTER. *Guild of St. Agnes*, 133 Granite St., 01604. Tel: 508-755-2238; Fax: 508-754-2026. Email: swood016@aol.com. Web: www.guildofstagnes.org. Mr. Edward Madaus, Dir. Day Care Centers for Infants, Toddlers, Preschoolers & School-age Children. Children aged 4 weeks-12 years. ; Family Day Care Program ages 6 weeks-5 years. Children 850; Children 320; For all: Total Staff 225.

FITCHBURG. *Guild of St. Agnes*, 62 Dover St., 01420. Tel: 978-343-3042; Fax: 978-343-2610. Total Assisted 145; Total Staff 11.

LEICESTER. *McAuley Nazareth Home for Boys* 01524. Tel: 508-892-4886; Fax: 508-892-9736. Email: naz1901@aol.com. Sisters Mary T. Barry, R.S.M., Exec. Dir.; Janet Ballentine, R.S.M., Exec. Dir.; Rev. Msgr. Edmond T. Tinsley, V.G., Chap. Sisters of Mercy Sisters 3; Boys 20; Special Education School: Boys 24; Lay Teachers 5.

[K] GENERAL HOSPITALS

WORCESTER. *Saint Vincent Hospital, Inc.*, 20 Worcester Center Blvd., 01604-4015. Tel: 508-363-5000; Fax: 508-363-5387. Email: dennis.irish@tenethealth.com. Web: www.stvincenthospital.com. Mr. Barry C. Dykes, Pres. & CEO; Rev. Peter R. Beaulieu, Dir. Pastoral Care; Sr. Peggy Kicras, CPE Supvr.; Rev. Louis J. Gould, Chap.; Sr. Mary O'Leary, S.P., Chap.; Deacon John Aliskevicz, Chap. Sisters 2; Bed Capacity 348; Patients Assisted Annually 177,250; Total Staff 1,947.

[L] SPECIAL HOSPITALS AND SANATORIA

WORCESTER. *Saint Francis Home*, 101 Plantation St., 01604. Tel: 508-791-6954; Fax: 508-798-0625. Email: ceo@saintfrancishome.org. Sr. Anna Marie Tag, R.S.M., Admin. Bed Capacity 137; Employees 210.

Notre Dame Health Care Center, Inc., 559 Plantation St., 01605. Tel: 508-852-3011; Fax: 508-852-0397. Email: klemay@lightband.com. Web: www.notredameltcc.org. Katherine Lemay, Admin. Bed Capacity 123; Total Staff 170.

MILLBURY. *Providence House Nursing Home of Millbury*, 29 Main St., 01527. Tel: 508-865-6106. Member of St. Vincent Healthcare System, Inc. Bed Capacity 138; Total Assisted 138; Total Staff 180.

WHITINSVILLE. *St. Camillus Hospice, Inc.*, 447 Hill St., 01588. Tel: 508-234-7306; Fax: 508-234-7597. Rev. John J. Gallagher, O.S.Cam.; Bro. Thomas J. Farrell, O.S.Cam., Treas.

St. Camillus Nursing Home Inc., 447 Hill St., 01588. Tel: 508-234-7306. Mr. David C. Turner; Bro. Thomas Farrell, O.S.Cam., Dir. Pastoral Care. Priests 1; Brothers 2; Bed Capacity 123; Patients Assisted Annually 43,070.

St. Camillus Institute, 497 Hill St., 01588.

St. Camillus Rectory: 495 Hill St., 01588. Rev. Jack Gallagher, O.S.Cam.

[M] HEALTH SERVICES

WORCESTER. *Compassion House*, 36 King St., 01610. Tel: 508-756-2713. Rev. Thomas B. Fleming, Dir.; Mrs. Nancy Price, House Mgr.

Our Lady of Mercy Health Care Center, Inc., 101 Barry Rd., 01609. Tel: 508-798-3727; Fax: 508-757-9415. Email: olmadm@aol.com. Sisters Suzanne Elloitt, R.S.M., Pres. Regl. Community; Catherine M. Cumming, Board Chair; Anne Bradley Roy, Licensed Admin. Bed Capacity 28; Total Annually Assisted 26; Total Staff 56.

Pernet Family Health Service, 237 Millbury St., 01610. Tel: 508-755-1228; Fax: 508-797-3477. Email: sdooley@pernetfamilyhealth.org. Web: pernetfamilyhealth.org. Sheilah Dooley, Exec. Dir. Mission of the Little Sisters of the Assumption.; Certified Home Health and Social Service Agency. Focus of services toward the parent and young child. Parenting groups, family activities available, Early Childhood Development services also available. Total Staff 27; Little Sisters of the Assumption 2; Total Volunteers 7.

[N] HOMES FOR AGED

WORCESTER. *Notre Dame du Lac*, 555 Plantation St., 01605. Tel: 508-852-5800; Fax: 508-852-1700. Email: csessions@charter.net. Web: www.notredamedulac.org. Candace Turgeon, Exec. Dir. Apartments 108; Total Staff 97.

Vianney House, 222 June St., 01602. Tel: 508-791-0311. Rev. Msgrs. Thomas J. Daley (Retired); Edmond G. Haddad (Retired). Retired Priests' Home. Total Staff 4.

c/o 49 Elm St., 01609. Revs. William W. McGovern (Retired); John F. Cahill, Admin.; Robert E. Kelley; James J. Clifford (Retired); Alphonse A. Volungis.

LEOMINSTER. *Presentation Health Care Center*, 99 Church St., 01453-3147. Tel: 978-537-7856; Fax: 978-840-1564. Sr. Catherine Cleary, P.B.V.M., Pres. Purpose: To operate and maintain a nursing home for aged and/or infirmed persons at Presentation Convent. Total in Residence 17; Total Staff 30.

[O] MONASTERIES AND RESIDENCES OF PRIESTS AND BROTHERS

WORCESTER. *Assumptionists (Augustinians of the Assumption)*, 50 Old English Rd., 01609. Tel: 508-754-6276; Fax: 508-797-1789. Revs. Alexis A. Babineau, A.A.; Albert E. Brochu, A.A.; Bernard Guillet, A.A.; Roland O. Guilmain, A.A.; Joseph Richard, A.A.; Wilfred J. Dufault, A.A.; Bros. Omer Gemme, A.A.; Armand Lemaire, A.A.; John-Thomas McHugh, A.A.; Richard Gagnon, A.A., Treas. Priests 6; Brothers 4; Total Staff 2.

Assumptionists of Assumption College, Emmanuel House, 512 Salisbury St., 01609-1326. Tel: 508-767-7523; Fax: 508-793-9701. Email: dgallagh@assumption.edu. Web: www.assumption.edu. Revs. Donat R. Lamothe, A.A., Treas.; Barry Bercier, A.A.; Donald Espinosa, A.A.; Dennis Gallagher, A.A., Supr.; Jerome Lively, A.A.; Omer Mbusa Sivendire, A.A.; Peter Precourt, A.A.; Bro. Paul Henry, A.A. Total in Residence 8; Total Staff 1.

Jesuits of Holy Cross College, Inc. 01610. Tel: 508-793-2011; Fax: 508-793-2624. Email: akuzniew@Holycross.edu. Web: www.holycross.edu/index.html. Revs. John E. Brooks, S.J.; William A. Clark, S.J.; Terence W. Curry, S.J.; Alfred R. Desautels, S.J.; Charles J. Dunn, S.J.; Michael F. Ford, S.J.; J. Thomas Hamel, S.J.; Lionel P. Honore, S.J.; Anthony J. Kuzniewski, S.J., Rector; Vincent A. Lapomarda, S.J.; Brian F. Linnane, S.J.; John J. MacDonnell, S.J.; Michael C. McFarland, S.J.; Earle L. Markey, S.J.; Francis X. Miller, S.J.; James J. Miracky, S.J.; Paul J. Nelligan, S.J.; William J. O'Halloran, S.J.; Joseph B. Pomeroy, S.J.; John P. Reboli, S.J.; William E. Reiser, S.J.; Philip C. Rule, S.J.; William E. Stempsey, S.J.; Edward J. Vodoklys, S.J.; Thomas W. Worcester, S.J.; Dennis J. Yesalonia, S.J. Priests 27.

Casa Santa Maria del Camino, Inc., 6 Claremont St., 01610. Tel: 508-798-0104. Rev. William E. Reiser, S.J., Pres.

FITCHBURG. *Missionaries of Our Lady of LaSalette Corp.*, St. Joseph, 46 Woodland St., 01420. Tel: 978-342-7907; Fax: 978-345-7678. Bro. Claude F. Rheaume, M.S., Treas. & Contact Person. Total in Residence 6.

PETERSHAM. *St. Mary's Monastery*, N. Main St., P.O. Box 345, 01366. Tel: 978-724-3350; Fax: 978-724-3549. Email: franselm@one800.net. Web: www.stmarysmonastery.org. Revs. Anselm Atkinson, O.S.B., Supr.; Bede Kierney, O.S.B.; Gregory Phillips, O.S.B. Priests-Monks 3; Monks 4.

SHREWSBURY. *Calvary Retreat Center, Passionist Fathers of Shrewsbury, Inc.*, 59 South St., P.O. Box 219, 01545-0219. Tel: 508-842-8821; Fax: 508-842-5356. Email: jpowers@cpprov.org. Web: calvaryretreat.org. Very Rev. John Powers, C.P., Retreat Community Dir.; Revs. Brice Edwards, C.P., Vicar; Fidelis Connolly, C.P.; Malcolm Cornwell, C.P.; John O'Brien, C.P.; Edward Wolanski, C.P.; Bonaventure Moccia, C.P.; Ernie Rivard, Admin. Priests 7.

Xaverian Brothers, 378 Main St., 01545. Tel: 508-845-1878; Fax: 508-842-3670. Email: pfeeney@stjohnshigh.org. Bros. Paul Feeney, C.F.X., Dir.;

Paul Feeney, C.F.X.; Thomas Klar, C.F.X.; James Mahoney, C.F.X.; Plunket Doherty, C.F.X.; Regis Moynihan, C.F.X.; J. Conal Owens, C.F.X. Brothers 6.

SPENCER. *St. Joseph's Abbey* 01562-1233. Tel: 508-885-8700; Fax: 508-885-8701. Email: spenabby@spencerabbey.org. Web: www.spencerabbey.org. Rt. Rev. Damian Carr, O.C.S.O.; Revs. Dominic Whedbee, O.C.S.O., Prior; Laurence Bourget, O.C.S.O.; Adrian Proback, O.C.S.O.; Raphael Simon, O.C.S.O.; Pius Rivera-Martinez, O.S.C.O.; Basil Byrne, O.C.S.O.; Eugene Lacasse, O.C.S.O.; Robert Kevin Anderson, O.C.S.O., (In Service Outside the Community); Simon Sansone, O.C.S.O.; Edward Steriti, O.C.S.O.; Basil Pennington, O.C.S.O.; Matthew Flynn, O.C.S.O.; Gabriel Bertoniere, O.C.S.O.; Patrick Brown, O.C.S.O.; Kevin Hunt, O.C.S.O.; Robert Morhous, O.C.S.O.; Henry Scarborough, O.C.S.O.; Peter Schmidt, O.C.S.O.; Gerald Sears, O.C.S.O.; Edward John Mullaney, O.C.S.O.; Kizito Thompson, O.C.S.O.; Marius Granato, O.C.S.O.; Aquinas Keane, O.C.S.O., (In Service Outside the Community); Joseph Chu Cong, O.C.S.O.; Luke Truhan, O.C.S.O.; Aidan Archur H. Logan, O.C.S.O., (On Leave to Military Ordinariate); Francis Rodriguez, O.C.S.O.; Andrew Johnson, O.C.S.O., (In Service Outside Community); Dominic Whedbee, O.C.S.O.; David Lavich, O.C.S.O., (In Service Outside the Community); James Palmigiano.
Legal Title: *Cistercian Abbey of Spencer, Inc.* Cistercian Order of the Strict Observance (Trappists) Solemnly Professed 73; Simply Professed 1; Novices 3; Total Priests in Community 33; Total in Community 78.

STILL RIVER. *Benedictine Monks, St. Benedict Abbey* (Harvard) , 252 Still River Rd., P.O. Box 67, 01467. Tel: 978-456-3221; Fax: 978-456-8181. Email: abbey@abbey.org. Web: www.abbey.org. Rt. Rev. Gabriel Gibbs, O.S.B., Abbot; Very Rev. Xavier Connelly, O.S.B., Prior; Revs. Basil Rechenburg, O.S.B.; Peter Connelly, O.S.B.; Anthony Kloss, O.S.B.; Marc Crilly, O.S.B.; Andrew Koch, O.S.B.; James Doran, O.S.B. Priests 8; Brothers 8; Oblates 1. In Res. Rev. Francis Xavier (Sri Lanka).

WHITINSVILLE. *St. Camillus Community*, 447 Hill St., 01588. Tel: 508-266-1045; Fax: 508-234-7597. Email: bgraves@stcamillus.com. Web: www.stcamillus.com. Bro. Thomas Farrell, O.S.Cam.; Rev. John Gallagher, O.S.Cam., Supr. Priests 1; Brothers 1.

[P] CONVENTS AND RESIDENCES FOR SISTERS

WORCESTER. *Harper Residence*, Res., 11 Beechmont St., 01609. Tel: 508-792-1619; Fax: 508-792-2067. Email: lcsasv@yahoo.com. Sisters 3.
Little Franciscans of Mary, 55 Moore Ave., 01602-1819. Tel: 508-755-0878; Fax: 508-755-6822. Email: sjalix@yahoo.com. Sr. Jacqueline Alix, P.F.M., Regl. Supr. Tel: 508-755-0878. Sisters 17.
Little Franciscans of Mary, 101 Plantation St., 01604. Tel: 508-755-8605; Fax: 508-798-0271. Email: pfmsfh@yahoo.com. Sr. Adrienne Lamoureux, P.F.M., Supr. Sisters 10.
Little Sisters of the Assumption, Pernet Family Health Service, Inc., 237 Millbury St., 01610. Tel: 508-755-1228; Fax: 508-797-3477. Family Health Agency. Nursing and Family Development Services-Home Based.
Religious Venerini Sisters Provincial Office, 23 Edward St., 01605. Tel: 508-745-1020; Fax: 508-745-6715. Email: zaccari@venerini.org. Web: www.venerinisisters.org. Sr. Mary Rose Zaccari, M.P.V., Prov. Sisters 31; Total in Residence 23.
Sisters of Mercy, 101 Barry Rd., 01609. Tel: 508-798-3727; Fax: 508-757-9415. Email: mercyma@aol.com. Sisters 20.
Sisters of St. Anne, Esther House, 1015 Pleasant St., 01602. Tel: 508-757-6053. Email: smdugas@hotmail.com. Web: www.sistersofsaintanne.org. Sisters 5; Total in Residence 5; Total Staff 5.
Sisters of St. Joseph, S.S.J., 783 Grove St., 01605. Tel: 508-852-1659. Sisters 2.
Sisters of the Assumption of the Blessed Virgin, 316 Lincoln St., 01605. Tel: 508-856-9383; Fax: 508-853-0881. Email: lono9595@aol.com. Sr. Lorraine Normand, S.A.S.V., Treas. Tel: 508-856-9450.
Sisters of the Holy Family of Nazareth, 119 Endicott St., 01610. Tel: 508-753-3835. Sr. M. Roberta, C.S.F.N., Supr. Sisters 3.
Xaverian Missionary Society of Mary, Headquarters: 242 Salisbury St., 01609-1639. Tel: 508-757-0514; Fax: 508-757-0514. Email: xavsistersusa@aol.com. Sr. Stefanina Loi, X.M.M., Delegate Gen. & Supr. Sisters 5.

CHARLETON. *Carmelite Sisters of the Eucharist of Worcester, MA*, 188 Old Worcester Rd., 01507. Tel: 508-248-2936; Fax: 508-248-3814. Sisters 5.

LEOMINSTER. *The Sisters of the Presentation of the Blessed Virgin Mary, New Windsor, NY*, 99 Church St., 01453. Tel: 978-537-7108; Fax: 978-340-1564. Email: presentationconvent@juno.com. Ministries are in the areas of education in parochial elementary and high schools; pastoral services; health care; social services. Professed Sisters 165.
Mt. St. Joseph, 880 Jackson Ave., New Windsor, NY 12553. Tel: 845-564-6630; 914-564-0513 (Admin. Office); Fax: 845-567-0219 (Admin. Office). Sisters Catherine Cleary, Pres.; Brian Elizabeth Barnicle, House Coord.

PETERSHAM. *Assumption Residence of the Sisters of the Assumption of the Blessed Virgin*, 211 N. Main St., Box 128, 01366. Tel: 978-724-3468; Fax: 978-724-0200. Email: alparent2000@yahoo.com. Sisters Estelle Dube, S.A.S.V., Co-Admin.; Alice Parent, S.A.S.V., Co-Admin. Professed Sisters 57.
St. Scholastica Priory, 271 N. Main St., Box 606, 01366. Tel: 978-724-3213; Fax: 978-724-3216. Sisters Mary Clare Vincent, O.S.B., Prioress; Mary Frances Wynn, O.S.B., Subprioress. Benedictine Nuns (Cloistered) Nuns in Solemn Vows 9; in Simple Vows 2; Claustral Oblates 2.

STILL RIVER. *Sisters of Saint Benedict Center, Slaves of the Immaculate Heart of Mary Inc.*, St. Ann House, 254 Still River Rd., P.O. Box 22, 01467. Tel: 978-456-8017; Fax: 978-456-8508. Email: micm@bicnet.net. Professed Sisters 15; Live-In Oblates 1; Novices 1.

WEBSTER. *St. Joseph Convent*, 5 Maynard St., 01570. Tel: 508-943-2228. Email: cssfwebster@yahoo.com. Sr. Marie JoAnn Lewko, C.S.S.F., Supr. Felician Sisters 3.

[Q] RETREAT HOUSES AND HOUSE OF PRAYER

SPENCER. *St. Joseph Abbey*, 167 N. Spencer Rd., 01562-1233. Tel: 508-885-8710; Fax: 508-885-8701. Email: spenabby@spencerabbey.org. Web: www.spencerabbey.org. Rev. Peter Schmidt, O.C.S.O. Guestmaster. Guest house and Retreat house.
Mary House, Inc., 186 N. Spencer Rd. (Rte. 31), P.O. Box 20, 01562. Tel: 508-885-5450. Ms. Joyce Thomasmeyer, Pres. House of Prayer and Contemplation.

STILL RIVER. *Benedictine Monks, St. Benedict Abbey* (Harvard) ; (See separate listing under Monasteries and Residences for Men. , 252 Still River Rd., P.O. Box 67, 01467. Tel: 978-456-3221; Fax: 978-456-8181. Email: abbey@abbey.org. Web: www.abbey.org. Rt. Rev. Gabriel Gibbs, O.S.B., Abbot.

[R] NEWMAN CHAPLAINS AND CENTERS

WORCESTER. *Campus Ministry* P.O. Box 903, 01613. Tel: 508-757-6097. Email: priest@WPI.edu. Web: www.wpi.edu/~newman. Rev. Peter J. Scanlon, Vicar. Total Staff 23.
Assumption College, 500 Salisbury St. 01609. Tel: 508-767-7419. Email: godonline@assumption.edu. Rev. Roland O. Guilmain, A.A.; Mr. Peter Hart; Mr. John Fleming; Sr. Cecilia Hervas, R.A.; Frank Corbin, Ph.D.
Becker College, 19 Schussler Rd., 01609. Tel: 508-757-6097. Email: priest@wpi.edu. Rev. Peter J. Scanlon, Chap., Religious Center at W.P.I.
Clark University, Box A-62, 01610. Tel: 508-793-7737. Email: eschaper@clark.edu. Beth Duffy Schaper, M.Ed.
Holy Cross College, The Office of the College Chaplain. Tel: 508-793-2448. Email: kmcelane@holycross.edu. Ms. Katherine McElaney, Dir.; Revs. Joseph J. LaBran, S.J.; Gerard R. McKeon, S.J.; Michael F. Ford, S.J. Sisters 1.
Becker College at Leicester Tel: 508-757-6097. Email: priest@wpi.edu. Refer to Diocesan Office.
Quinsigamond Community College, 670 W. Boylston St., 01606. Tel: 508-853-2300, Ext. 300. Email: helene@qcc.mass.edu. Sr. Helen Egan, S.S.J., M.A.
University of Massachusetts Medical School Tel: 508-757-6097. Email: priest@wpi.edu. Refer to Diocesan Office.
Worcester State College, Campus Ministry Center, 486 Chandler St., 01602. Tel: 508-793-8017. Email: froberge@juno.com. Rev. Francis A. Roberge.
Worcester Polytechnic Institute, Religious Center at WPI, 19 Schussler Rd., 01609. Tel: 508-757-6097. Email: priest@wpi.edu. Rev. Peter J. Scanlon.
Nichols College (Dudley), 01570. Tel: 508-943-1560. Email: pecevics@nichols.edu. Rev. Conrad S. Pecevich.
Fitchburg State College (Fitchburg), Newman Center, 231 Highland Ave., 01420. Tel: 508-345-2688. Email: loisnc@fsc.edu. Rev. Richard P. Lewandowski; Deacon Benjamin A. Nogueira; Lois I. Nogueira, Chap.
Mt. Wachusett Community College (Gardner), Campus Ministry at MW CC, 419 Green St., Gardner, 01440. Tel: 508-632-6600, Ext. 193. Email: watkin@juno.com. Ms. Corrine Watkins.
Anna Maria College, Box 35, Paxton, 01612. Tel: 508-849-3399. Sr. Yvette E. Bellerose, S.S.A.

PAXTON. *Anna Maria College* Office of Campus Ministry, 01612-1198. Tel: 508-849-3399; Fax: 508-849-3319. Web: www.annamaria.edu. Sr. Sarah Landis, I.H.M. Total Staff 1.

[S] MISCELLANEOUS

WORCESTER. *Casa Santa Maria del Camino, Inc.*, 52 Queen St., #1, 01610. Tel: 508-798-0104. Email: wreiser@holycross.edu. Rev. William E. Reiser, S.J., Pres. Pastoral Outreach Center for the Hispanic Community. Total Staff 1.
The Charlton Charitable Corporation, Inc. Diocese of Worcester. , 49 Elm St., 01609. Tel: 508-791-7171; Fax: 508-754-2768.
Dismas House of Central Massachusetts, To provide transition for those who are leaving prison.P.O. Box 30125, 01603. Tel: 508-799-9389; Fax: 508-767-9930. Web: www.dismashouse.org. David McMahon, Co-Dir.; Colleen Hilferty, Co-Dir.; Doug Klier, Program Advocate.
The Guild of Our Lady of Providence, Tel: 508-791-7171. *Chancery Office of the Diocese of Worcester*, 49 Elm St., 01609. Tel: 508-791-7171; Fax: 508-753-7180.
Mendon Charitable Corporation, Inc., 49 Elm St., 01609. Tel: 508-791-7171; Fax: 508-754-2768. Most Rev. George E. Rueger, D.D., V.G., Contact Person.
Monsignor Thomas Griffin Foundation, 49 Elm St., 01609. Tel: 508-791-7171; Fax: 508-753-7180. Rev. Msgr. Edmond T. Tinsley, V.G., Contact Person.
Notre Dame Development Fund, Inc., 340 Plantation St., 01604-1637. Tel: 508-770-1744; Fax: 508-770-1745. Email: SNDNEdev@aol.com. Web: www.SNDDEN.org/dev/ne. Sr. Anne-Louise Nadeau, S.N.D., Pres.; Mr. Paul Carr, Dir. Devel.
Office for Ethnic Ministries, 49 Elm St., 01609. Tel: 508-791-7171; Fax: 508-753-7180. Email: sprefontaine@worcesterdiocese.org. Web: www.worcesterdiocese.org. Sr. Marie Prefontaine, S.N.D., Dir.
St. Peter-Marian Endowment Trust, c/o St. Peter-Marian Central Catholic Junior/Senior High School, 781 Grove St., 01605. Tel: 508-852-5555; Fax: 508-852-7238. Email: alumspm@aol.com.

CHARLTON. *Ministry to Retired Priests*, 188 Old Worcester Rd., 01507. Tel: 508-868-9239.

FITCHBURG. *PACE - Parents Alliance for Catholic Education*, 124 Summer St., 01420. Tel: 617-723-9890; Fax: 617-723-9892. Email: sperla@paceorg.net. Web: www.pacesite.org. Stephen A. Perla, Exec. Dir.

GARDNER. *House of Peace & Education, Inc.*, 20 Barthel Ave., 01440. Tel: 978-630-4752; Fax: 978-630-4752. Email: hope@net1plus.com. Maxyne D. Schneider, S.S.J., Exec. Dir. Purpose: Neighborhood educational center for disadvantaged women and children.

PETERSHAM. *St. Bede's Publications*, 271 N. Main St., P.O. Box 545, 01366-0545. Tel: 978-724-3217; Fax: 978-724-3216. Web: www.fordhampress.com. Sr. Mary Clare Vincent, O.S.B.
St. Mary and St. Scholastica Church, Inc., 271 N. Main St., 01366-9503.

SHREWSBURY. *New England Intercommunity Support Services (NEISS)*, 89 Hill St., 01545-1930. Tel: 508-842-3555; Fax: 508-852-0397. Email: marnasnd@aol.com. Sr. Marna Rogers, S.N.D., Contact Person.

SPENCER. *Cistercian Publications, Inc.*, St. Joseph's Abbey, 01562. Tel: 508-885-8730; Fax: 508-885-4687. Email: spenabby@spencerabbey.org. Web: www.spencerabbey.org/cistpub. Dr. Ernst Breisach, Pres.; Dr. E. Rozanne Elder, Exec. Vice Pres. & Mng. Editor; Rev. M. Basil Pennington, O.C.S.O., Sec.
St. Joseph's Abbey Resident Care Facility, Inc., 167 North Spencer Rd., 01562-1233. Tel: 508-885-8702; Fax: 508-885-8701. Email: gsapl@hotmail.com. Web: www.spencerabbey.org. Bro. Gregory Sampl, O.C.S.O., Admin.

WHITINSVILLE. *St. Camillus Institute, Inc.*, 447 Hill St., 01588. Tel: 617-234-7306. Very Rev. William F. Cronin, O.S.Cam., Pres. Order of the Servants of the Sick (St. Camillus)

RELIGIOUS INSTITUTES OF MEN REPRESENTED IN THE DIOCESE

For further details refer to the corresponding bracketed number in the Religious Institutes of Men or Women section.

[0130]—*Assumptionists*—A.A.

[0200]—*Benedictine Monks* (Petersham; Still River)—O.S.B.

[1350]—*Brothers of St. Francis Xavier*—C.F.X.

[0350]—*Cistercians Order of the Strict Observance (Trappists)*—O.C.S.O.

[0790]—*Congregation of Maronite Monks*—O.Mar.
[1000]—*Congregation of the Passion*—C.P.
[0690]—*Jesuit Fathers and Brothers*—S.J.
[0740]—*Marian Fathers*—M.I.C.
[0720]—*Missionaries of Our Lady of LaSalette* (Seven Dolors Prov.)—M.S.
[0240]—*Order of St. Camilus - Camillian Fathers and Brothers*—O.S.Cam.
[1280]—*Stigmatine Fathers and Brothers*—C.S.S.

RELIGIOUS INSTITUTES OF WOMEN REPRESENTED IN THE DIOCESE

[0230]—*Benedictine Sisters of Pontifical Jurisdiction* (Petersham; Rutland; Eau Clare, WI)—O.S.B.
[0192]—*Carmelite Sisters of the Eucharist, Inc.*—C.S.E.
[0820]—*Daughters of the Holy Spirit*—D.H.S.
[1070-06]—*Dominican Sisters* (Newburgh, NY)—O.P.
[1170]—*Felician Sisters*—C.S.S.F.
[2575]—*Institute of the Sisters of Mercy of the Americas* (New York, NY)—R.S.M.
[2280]—*Little Franciscans of Mary*—P.F.M.
[2310]—*Little Sisters of the Assumption*—L.S.A.
[2790]—*Missionary Servants of the Most Blessed Trinity*—M.S.B.T.
[2420]—*Missionary Sisters of the Society of Mary (Marist)*—S.M.S.M.
[3390]—*Religious of the Assumption*—R.A.
[2070]—*Religious of the Holy Union of the Sacred Hearts*—S.U.S.C.
[4180]—*Religious Venerini Sisters*—M.P.V.
[]—*Sisters Oblates to Divine Love*—R.O.D.A.
[3000]—*Sisters of Notre Dame de Namur* (Boston, Ipswich, Japan and Connecticut Provs.)—S.N.D.deN.
[3340]—*Sisters of Providence*—S.P.
[3720]—*Sisters of Saint Anne*—S.S.A.
[1650]—*The Sisters of St. Francis of Philadelphia*—O.S.F.
[3830-01]—*Sisters of St. Joseph* (Boston, Brighton)—C.S.J.
[3830-16]—*Sisters of St. Joseph*—S.S.J.
[3815]—*Sisters of Ste. Jeanne D'Arc*—S.J.A.
[0150]—*Sisters of the Assumption*—S.A.S.V.
[1970]—*Sisters of the Holy Family of Nazareth*—C.S.F.N.
[3310]—*Sisters of the Presentation of Mary*—P.M.
[3320]—*Sisters of the Presentation of the B.V.M.*—P.B.V.M.
[4230]—*Xaverian Missionary Society of Mary, Inc.*—X.M.M.

DIOCESAN CEMETERIES

WORCESTER. *St. John's*

NECROLOGY

† Haddad, Rev. Msgr. Edmund G., (Retired)—Died Nov. 21, 2003
† Kelliher, Rev. Msgr. John J., (Retired)—Died Oct. 18, 2003
† Archey, Eugene C., (Retired)—Died Dec. 20, 2003
† Bowen, Henry G.—Died Dec. 2, 2002
† Devaney, Roy J., (Retired)—Died Jan. 8, 2003
† Howes, Robert G.—Died June 23, 2003
† Kurzawski, Casimir J., (Retired)—Died Oct. 12, 2003
† Manahan, Martin J.—Died Oct. 28, 2003
† Shea, Peter D., (Retired)—Died Jan. 20, 2003
† Sullivan, Andrew J., (Retired)—Died Aug. 19, 2003

Diocese of Yakima

(Dioecesis Yakimensis)

Most Reverend

CARLOS A. SEVILLA, S.J., D.D.

Bishop of Yakima; ordained June 3, 1966; appointed Auxiliary Bishop of San Francisco December 6, 1988; Episcopal ordination January 25, 1989; appointed Bishop of Yakima December 31, 1996; installed February 17, 1997 *Address all correspondence to: 5301-A Tieton Dr., Yakima, WA 98908.*

Pastoral Office (Chancery): 5301-A Tieton Dr., Yakima, WA 98908. Tel: 509-965-7117; Fax: 509-966-8334.

Email: info@yakimadiocese.org

ESTABLISHED JUNE 23, 1951.

Square Miles 17,787.

Comprises the following Counties in the State of Washington: Benton, Chelan, Douglas, Grant, Kittitas, Klickitat and Yakima.

Legal Title: Corporation of the Catholic Bishop of Yakima.

For legal titles of parishes and diocesan institutions, consult the Pastoral Office.

STATISTICAL OVERVIEW

Personnel	
Bishop	1
Priests: Diocesan Active in Diocese	42
Priests: Diocesan Active Outside Diocese	14
Priests: Retired, Sick or Absent	16
Number of Diocesan Priests	72
Religious Priests in Diocese	12
Total Priests in Diocese	84
Extern Priests in Diocese	2
Ordinations:	
Diocesan Priests	3
Permanent Deacons in Diocese	24
Total Brothers	3
Total Sisters	48
Parishes	
Parishes	41
With Resident Pastor:	
Resident Diocesan Priests	37
Resident Religious Priests	4
Missions	3
Pastoral Centers	1
Professional Ministry Personnel:	
Sisters	2
Lay Ministers	15
Welfare	
Catholic Hospitals	1
Total Assisted	75,436
Day Care Centers	2
Total Assisted	224
Special Centers for Social Services	5
Total Assisted	42,664
Educational	
Diocesan Students in Other Seminaries	20
Total Seminarians	20
High Schools, Private	1
Total Students	172
Elementary Schools, Diocesan and Parish	6
Total Students	1,792
Catechesis/Religious Education:	
High School Students	2,456
Elementary Students	5,150
Total Students under Catholic Instruction	9,590
Teachers in the Diocese:	
Brothers	4
Sisters	4
Lay Teachers	109
Vital Statistics	
Receptions into the Church:	
Infant Baptism Totals	2,726
Adult Baptism Totals	185
Received into Full Communion	112
First Communions	2,346
Confirmations	698
Marriages:	
Catholic	328
Interfaith	114
Total Marriages	442
Deaths	542
Total Catholic Population	68,561
Total Population	600,055

Former Bishops—Most Revs. JOSEPH P. DOUGHERTY, D.D., First Bishop of Yakima; ord. June 14, 1930; appt. July 9, 1951; consecrated Sept. 26, 1951; resigned Feb. 5, 1969; died July 10, 1970; CORNELIUS M. POWER, D.D., Second Bishop of Yakima; ord. June 3, 1939; appt. Feb. 5, 1969; consecrated May 1, 1969; elevated to Metropolitan See of Portland in Oregon, Jan. 24, 1974; died May 22, 1997; NICOLAS E. WALSH, D.D., Third Bishop of Yakima; ord. June 6, 1942; appt. Sept. 5, 1974; consecrated Oct. 28, 1974; installed Oct. 30, 1974; transferred to Archdiocese of Seattle as Auxiliary Bishop, Aug. 10, 1976; resigned Sept. 6, 1983; died April 22, 1997; WILLIAM S. SKYLSTAD, D.D., Fourth Bishop of Yakima; ord. May 21, 1960; appt. Feb. 22, 1977; consecrated May 12, 1977; transferred to Spokane as Bishop of Spokane, April 17, 1990; FRANCIS E. GEORGE, O.M.I., Ph.D., S.T.D., Fifth Bishop of Yakima; ord. Dec. 21, 1963; appt. July 10, 1990; consecrated Sept. 21, 1990; appt. Metropolitan See of Portland in Oregon, April 30, 1996; appt. Metropolitan See of Chicago, April 8, 1997; created Cardinal Priest, Feb. 21, 1998.

Pastoral Office (Chancery)—5301-A Tieton Dr., Yakima, 98908. Tel: 509-965-7117; Fax: 509-966-8334.

Vicar General—Rev. Msgr. JOHN A. ECKER, 5301-A Tieton Dr., Yakima, 98908-3493.

Vicar for Priests—Rev. Msgr. JOHN J. MCDONNELL (Retired); Rev. MARIO A. SALAZAR.

Chancellor and Moderator of the Curia—Rev. Msgr. RONALD W. METHA.

Vice-Chancellor—Mrs. GAYLE A. MILLER.

Office of Canonical Concerns—5301-D Tieton Dr., Yakima, 98908. Tel: 509-965-7123.

Judicial Vicar—Very Rev. MICHAEL J. IBACH, J.C.L.

Adjutant Judicial Vicars—Rev. JESUS ANTONIO CASTANEDA, J.C.D.

Co-Director—Ms. ANGELITA T. GRANILLO.

Judges—Very Rev. MICHAEL J. IBACH, J.C.L.; Revs. JOHN F. HENEGHAN, J.C.L.; JESUS ANTONIO CASTANEDA, J.C.D.; Ms. ANGELITA T. GRANILLO.

Defenders of the Bond—Revs. THOMAS C. CHAMPOUX; SALOMON COVARRUBIAS-PINA; Deacon LEROI RICE; Ms. KAY SHEPHERD.

Advocates— Clergy and pastoral ministers by appointment

Notaries—Mrs. VIRGINIA SANTILLANES; Mrs. EILEEN M. WALKER.

Diocesan Consultors—Revs. JOSE DE LOZA; THOMAS C. CHAMPOUX; Rev. Msgrs. JOHN A. ECKER; RONALD W. METHA; Revs. JOSE DE JESUS RAMIREZ; RICHARD D. SEDLACEK.

Diocesan Offices, Commissions, Committees

Adults with Developmental Disabilities—MICHELE WALL, 12203 Klendon Dr., Yakima, 98908. Tel: 509-965-4642.

Calvary Cemetery—KATHY DEAN, Dir., 1405 S. 24th Ave., Yakima, 98902. Tel: 509-457-8432; Fax: 509-457-6267.

CYO—DON ERICKSON, 410 S. 47th Ave., Yakima, 98908. Tel: 509-965-3382.

Campaign for Human Development—Mr. JOHN L. YOUNG, 5301-C Tieton Dr., Yakima, 98908.

Catholic Charities—Mr. JOHN L. YOUNG, Exec. Dir., Office, 5301-C Tieton Dr., Yakima, 98908. Tel: 509-965-7130.

Charismatic Renewal, English—5301-A Tieton Dr., Yakima, 98908. Tel: 509-965-7117.

Charismatic Renewal, Spanish—5301-A Tieton Dr., Yakima, 98908. Tel: 509-965-7117.

Cursillo, English—Rev. JOHN SHAW, Spiritual Dir. (English), 213 N. Beech, Toppenish, 98948. Tel: 509-865-4725; DON CURET, Coord., 30 Vienna Ct., Richland, 99352.

Spanish—Deacon FRANK MARTINEZ, Spiritual Dir., 3790 Rd. 10.4 S.W., Royal City, 99357. Tel: 509-346-9536; HECTOR HERNANDEZ, Coord., 615 S. Ironwood Dr., Moses Lake, 98837.

Native American—Rev. JOHN M. SHAW, Spiritual Dir.; JIM ARNOUX, Liaison.

Director of Planned Giving—Rev. SAMUEL P. BELLINO, S.J., 5301-A Tieton Dr., Yakima, 98908. Tel: 509-965-7117.

Development Office/Stewardship—Mr. DONALD M. KLIPPSTEIN, Dir., 5301-A Tieton Dr., Yakima, 98908. Tel: 509-965-7117.

Diocesan Coordinator for Health Affairs—Rev. THOMAS C. CHAMPOUX, 5301-C Tieton Dr., Yakima, 98908. Tel: 509-965-7100.

Diocesan Commission for the Catechumenate—Most Rev. CARLOS A. SEVILLA, S.J., D.D.; Revs. MICHAEL E. BRZEZOWSKI; JUAN M. FLORES; Mrs. BETTY JO LEVAD; Ms. KAY SHEPARD; Mrs. JACQUE LOYND; Deacon ROBERT SCHROM.

Diocesan Commission on Public Worship—Revs. JUAN FLORES; THOMAS S. KUYKENDALL, Chm.; Mrs. PAT MANDELAS; Deacon RAY MILLER.

Diocesan Pastoral Council—Most Rev. CARLOS A. SEVILLA, S.J., D.D.; Deacon BERNEY ALVARADO; Rev. Msgr. DESMOND P. DILLON (Retired); LUPE SANCHEZ; CHUCK GRAFF; JOE GALLEGOS; JANE SCHNEIDER; ISIDRO LEPEZ; RITA KEENE; JAMES PERKO; Mr. RUSSELL SHJERVEN; Sr. MAE CRUIKSHANK, S.N.J.M.; DON WHITE; AGATHA DURAZO; JERRY WALTON.

Ecumenical Liaison—Rev. Msgr. JOHN A. ECKER, 15 S. 12th Ave., Yakima, 98902. Tel: 509-575-3713.

Engaged Encounter—Mrs. BRENDA BIRNBAUM; Mr. JEROME BIRNBAUM, 109 Center Blvd., Richland, 99352. Tel: 509-627-9284.

Diocesan Finance Council—Most Rev. CARLOS A. SEVILLA, S.J., D.D., Pastoral Center, 5301-A Tieton Dr., Yakima, 98908; Rev. Msgrs. RONALD W. METHA, 5301-A Tieton Dr., Yakima, 98908; JOHN A. ECKER; Mr. J. RICHARD GOLOB; Rev. SAMUEL P. BELLINO, S.J.; Mr. NICANOR DELEON; Ms. ANN DRADER; Mr. JOHN KRANZ; Mrs. COLLEEN KELLEHER; Mr. DONALD M. KLIPPSTEIN; Mrs. PAT MYERS; Mr. ALEX SANTILLANES; Rev. DAN DUFNER; JEFF PETERSON, Consultant; Mrs. PEGGY ROY; Mr.

PETER SPADONI.

Gang Outreach Ministry—ALEX SANTILLANES, 1704 Grant Ave., Yakima, 98902. Tel: 509-469-7138; Fax: 509-469-7098.

Home Schooling—Deacon DUANE BERGER, Chap., 1706 Lower Ahtanum, Yakima, 98903. Tel: 509-457-1926; JONELLA LEADON; SUSAN SCHELL.

Lay Advisory Board—Mr. RUSSELL MAZZOLA, Chm. Tel: 888-276-4490; Mr. JAMES DANIELSON; Mr. THOMAS DITTMAR; Rev. Msgr. JOHN A. ECKER; Mr. MARIO MAGANA; Ms. CAITLIN P. NEWMAN; Dr. ROY SIMMS; Mrs. YVONNE SMITH.

Marriage Encounter, English—Mrs. MARY ANN BRESHEARS; Mr. RICH BRESHEARS, 1840 W. 23rd, Kennewick, 99337. Tel: 509-582-4804.

Spanish—Rev. JOSE DE JESUS RAMIREZ, P.O. Box 340, Royal City, 99357-0340. Tel: 509-346-2730.

Natural Family Planning Advisory Committee—JANE VILLANUEVA, Coord.; ALFRED ARROYO; ANNA ARROYO; BRIAN HEINE; ANN HEINE; ALEX KEENE; GINA KEENE; KATHERINE MELTON, N.F.P.P.; ANNE NEALEN, M.D.; THEODORE F. O'DONNELL, M.D.; Rev. RONALD PATNODE; Dr. JAN. HEMSTAD; Mrs. JAN HEMSTAD.

Ministry & Education Center—Mrs. CATHY COLVER, Supt. of Schools, 5301-B Tieton Dr., Yakima, 98908. Tel: 509-965-7110.

Hispanic Religious Education—Mr. PEDRO ROMO, Dir.

Evangelization and Lay Formation, Deacon Formation, Pastoral Council, Small Church Communities—Mr. ROBERT FONTANA, Dir.

Family Ministries—Sr. SUSANNE THIBAULT, M.S.B.T., 5301-C Tieton Dr., Yakima, 98908-3493. Tel: 509-965-7100.

Religious Education—Ms. REE KEARNS, Dir.

Youth/Young Adult Director—Mrs. MARIA ELENA PONCE.

Youth/Young Adult Hispanic Ministry—Mr. CARLOS CARRILLO.

Deacon Council—Deacons FRANK MARTINEZ; BOB DAVALLE; SHIRLEY DAVALLE; Deacon DON GRIEK; ROSIE GRIEK; Deacon JIM KRAMPER; PAT KRAMPER; Deacon BILL MICH; MARGO MICH; Deacon ANTONIO OSORIO; CARMEN OSORIO.

Permanent Diaconate Liaison—Deacon FRANK MARTINEZ, 3790 Rd. 10.4 S.W., Royal City, 99357. Tel: 509-346-9536.

Clergy Personnel Board—Most Rev. CARLOS A. SEVILLA, S.J., D.D.; Rev. Msgrs. JOHN A. ECKER; RONALD W. METHA; Revs. THOMAS S. KUYKENDALL; WILLIAM E. SHAW; MARIO A. SALAZAR; ROBERT M. SILER; RICARDO VILLARREAL.

Press (Central Washington Catholic)—Rev. Msgr. RONALD W. METHA, Moderator; Mr. PAUL PAYNE, Production Editor, 5301-A Tieton Dr., Yakima, 98908. Tel: 509-965-7117. Email: mtaoblate311@msn.com.

Presbyteral Council Executive Committee—Most Rev. CARLOS A. SEVILLA, S.J., D.D.; Rev. Msgrs. JOHN A. ECKER; RONALD W. METHA; Revs. RICARDO VILLARREAL; JUAN M. FLORES; THOMAS KUYKENDALL; ANTONIO CASTANDEA-SERNA; Revs. SEAMUS KERR; JOHN MORSE, S.J.; ARGEMIRO OROZCO; RONALD PATNODE; EMMETT SARSFIELD; RICHARD SEDLACEK; JOHN SHAW.

Native American Ministries—Rev. JOHN M. SHAW, 213 N. Beech, Toppenish, 98948. Tel: 509-865-4725.

Natural Family Planning—Mrs. JANE VILLANUEVA, 5301-B Tieton Dr., Yakima, 98908. Tel: 509-965-7110.

Jail Ministry—Rev. GEORGE PURDY, S.J., P.O. Box 128, Naches, 98937. Tel: 509-653-2534; Deacon NESTOR CHAVEZ, 710 E. Race St., Yakima, 98901.

St. Peter the Apostle Retreat Center—*15880 Summitview Rd., Cowiche, 98923*. Tel: 509-678-4935.

Respect Life Committee—Mr. RUBEN BEEDLE; Mr. MIKE BRIGGS; Mr. GEORGE BRIGGS; Mrs. JEANNE HALL; Dr. ANNE NEALEN; Sr. SUSANNE THIBAULT, M.S.B.T.; Mrs. JANE VILLANUEVA, 5301-B Tieton Dr., Yakima, 98908. Tel: 509-965-7110.

Diocesan Catholic Committee on Scouting—Deacon WILLIAM A. DRONEN, Chap., 306 Railroad Ave., Cashmere, 98815. Tel: 509-782-3976; Mr. MARC DESGROSEILLIER, Chm.; Mr. CARLOS CARRILLO; Mrs. CINDY DESGROSEILLIER; Mrs. CHARLENE DRONEN; Mrs. ILIANA GARZA; Mr. JOHN WARREN.

Social Justice and Human Life Commission—Mrs. JANE VILLANUEVA; Mr. JOHN YOUNG; Mr. CHRIS CASSIDY; Mr. JOHN PARRISH; Mr. MARIO VILLANUEVA; Mr. RUSSELL SHJERVEN; Sr. SUSANNE THIBAULT, M.S.B.T.; Rev. WILLAIM VOGEL, S.J., 5301-B Tieton Dr., Yakima, 98908. Tel: 509-965-7110.

St. Joseph Mission at the Ahtanum—Directors: ED CAMPBELL; CARY CAMPBELL, 17740 Ahtanum Rd., Yakima, 98903. Tel: 509-966-0865; Fax: 509-966-5649. Email: cascprus2Aprodigy.net.

St. Vincent de Paul Society—Rev. THOMAS C. CHAMPOUX, Spiritual Dir., 1126 Long Ave., Richland, 99352. Tel: 509-946-1675.

St. Vincent de Paul Stores—THOMAS GEHLEN, Dir., 305 North Ave., Sunnyside, 98944. Tel: 509-837-7968.

Serra Club—HARRY (BUD) KOHL, Pres., 212 North, 25th Ave., Yakima, 98902. Tel: 509-457-5373.

Victim Assistance Coordinators—LINDA BERNARD. Tel: 509-965-7100. Email: lbernard@cfcsyakima.org; SUSAN M. ROMZEK. Tel: 509-965-7100. Email: sromzek@cfcsyakima.org.

Vocations—Rev. Msgr. JOHN A. ECKER, Dir., 15 S. 12th Ave., Yakima, 98902. Tel: 509-575-3713.

CLERGY, PARISHES, MISSIONS AND PAROCHIAL SCHOOLS

CITY OF YAKIMA
(YAKIMA COUNTY)

1—ST. PAUL CATHEDRAL (1914), [CEM] Rev. Msgr. John A. Ecker; Rev. Juan Manuel Flores; Deacon Ray Miller; Jack Pain, Pastoral Assoc.
Res.: 15 S. 12th Ave., 98902. Tel: 509-575-3713; Fax: 509-453-7497.
School—(Grades PreK-8), 1214 W. Chestnut Ave., 98902. Tel: 509-575-5604; Fax: 509-577-8817. Lay Teachers 20; Students 349.
Catholic Student Center—810 S. 16th Ave., 98902. Tel: 509-249-6238.
Catechesis/Religious Program—Students 390.

2—HOLY FAMILY (1959), Very Rev. Michael J. Ibach, J.C.L.; Rev. Robert D. Inman; Deacons John Cornell; Jim Kramper.
Res.: 5315 Tieton Dr., 98908. Tel: 509-966-0830; Fax: 509-965-1742.
Catechesis/Religious Program—(Grades PreSchool-8) Tel: 509-966-0788; Fax: 509-965-0288. Students 510.
Mission—*St. Joseph Mission at the Ahtanum* 17740 Ahtanum Rd., Yakima Co. 98908. Tel: 509-966-0865; Fax: 509-966-5649.

3—HOLY REDEEMER (1962), (Hispanic), [JC] Rev. Nicholas Milich; Deacon Duane Berger.
Res.: 1609 Landon Ave., 98902. Tel: 509-248-2241; Fax: 509-457-3312.
Catechesis/Religious Program—Tel: 509-457-3435. Students 245.

4—ST. JOSEPH'S, Revs. Michael Pope, S.J.; Thomas R. Royce, S.J.; Virgilio Zea, S.J.; Mary E. Bischoff, Admin.
212 N. 4th St., 98901-2499. Tel: 509-248-1911; Fax: 509-248-2604. In Res., Revs. Neill R. Meany, S.J.; Charles E. Schmitz, S.J.; Robert Saenz, S.J.
School—*St. Joseph/Marquette*, Tel: 509-575-5555; Fax: 509-457-5621. Sisters of Providence 1; Lay Teachers 25; Students 387.
Catechesis/Religious Program—Students 295.

OUTSIDE THE CITY OF YAKIMA

BENTON CITY, BENTON CO., ST. FRANCES XAVIER CABRINI (1963), Rev. James Spezzano.
Mailing Address: P.O. Box 179, 99320-0179. Fax: 509-588-3636.
Church: Horn Rd., 99320. Tel: 509-588-3636.
Catechesis/Religious Program—Tel: 509-588-4235. Students 83.

BRIDGEPORT, DOUGLAS CO., ST. ANNE'S (1964), (Hispanic), Rev. Daniel G. Dufner.
Mailing Address: P.O. Box 1089, Chelan, 98816-1089. Tel: 509-682-2433; Fax: 509-682-9147.
Catechesis/Religious Program—Students 30.
Mission—*St. Mary* (1909), Mansfield Blvd. & 2nd, Mansfield, Douglas Co. 98830.

CASHMERE, CHELAN CO., ST. FRANCIS XAVIER (1915), Rev. Ricardo Villarreal; Deacon Bill Dronen.
Res.: 307 Angier, 98815. Tel: 509-782-2643; Fax: 509-782-2686.
Catechesis/Religious Program—Tel: 509-782-5916. Students 85.

CHELAN, CHELAN CO., ST. FRANCIS DE SALES (1904), Rev. Daniel G. Dufner.
215 W. Allen Ave., P.O. Box 1089, 98816-1089. Tel: 509-682-2433; Fax: 509-682-9147.
Catechesis/Religious Program—Students 131.

CLE ELUM, UPPER KITTITAS CO., ST. JOHN THE BAPTIST (1913), Rev. Lawrence T. Reilly.
Office—303 W. 2nd St., 98922. Tel: 509-674-2531; Fax: 509-674-1894.
Catechesis/Religious Program—Students 30.

COWICHE, YAKIMA CO., ST. JUAN DIEGO, Formerly St. Peter's (1959), (Spanish),, (Formerly known as St. Peter the Apostle). Rev. Jesus Antonio Castaneda, S.J.C.D.
Res.: 15880 Summitview Rd., 98923. Tel: 509-678-4164; Fax: 509-678-4165.
Catechesis/Religious Program—Students 75.

EAST WENATCHEE, DOUGLAS CO., HOLY APOSTLES (1962), Revs. Francisco P. Higuera; Gustavo Gomez; Deacon Bill Loranger.
Res.: P.O. Box 7279, 98802. Tel: 509-884-5444; Fax: 509-886-3424.
Catechesis/Religious Program—1315 8th St. N.E., 98802. Tel: 509-884-5444. Students 250.

ELLENSBURG, KITTITAS CO., ST. ANDREW'S (1884), [CEM] Rev. Robert M. Siler; Deacon Jack Spence.
Res.: 401 S. Willow St., 98926. Tel: 509-962-9819; Fax: 509-962-9846.
Catechesis/Religious Program—Students 190.

EPHRATA, GRANT CO., ST. ROSE OF LIMA (1941), [CEM] Rev. Seamus Kerr.
Parish Office—323 D St., S.W., 98823. Tel: 509-754-3640; Fax: 509-754-4064.
School—(Grades PreK-6), 520 S.E. Blvd., 98823. Tel: 509-754-4901; Fax: 509-754-9274. Lay Teachers 5; Students 80.
Catechesis/Religious Program—Students 130.

GOLDENDALE, KLICKITAT CO., HOLY TRINITY (1884), [CEM] Rev. William Byron.
Res.: 210 S. Schuster St., 98620. Tel: 509-773-4516; Fax: 509-773-6983.
Catechesis/Religious Program—Jackie Bugler, D.R.E. Students 55.

GRAND COULEE, GRANT CO., ST. HENRY'S (1955), [JC] Rev. Robert P. Himes; Deacon Dan Farrell.
Res.: 590 Grand Coulee Ave. W., P.O. Box P, 99133. Tel: 509-633-1180; Fax: 509-633-6859.
Catechesis/Religious Program—Students 26.

GRANDVIEW, YAKIMA CO., BLESSED SACRAMENT (1954), Revs. Gary L. Desharnais; Alvaro Drez.
Res.: 1201 Missouri, 98930. Tel: 509-882-1657; Fax: 509-882-1107.
Catechesis/Religious Program—Students 251.

GRANGER, YAKIMA CO., OUR LADY OF GUADALUPE (1966), (Hispanic), [JC] Rev. Mario P. Salazar.
Res.: 608 Ave. E., P.O. Box 308, 98932. Tel: 509-854-1558; Fax: 509-854-7326.
Catechesis/Religious Program—Tel: 509-854-2164. Students 60.

HARTLINE, GRANT CO., ST. PATRICK'S (1955), [CEM], Served from St. Henry's, P.O. Box P, Grand Coulee 99133. Revs. Robert P. Himes; Daniel J. Farrell.
Mailing Address: P.O. Box 925, Coulee City, 99115. Tel: 509-633-1180; Fax: 509-633-6859.
Catechesis/Religious Program—Students 13.
Mission—*Holy Angels* P.O. Box 925, Coulee City, Grant Co. 99115.

KENNEWICK, BENTON CO.

1—HOLY SPIRIT (1980), Rev. John G. O'Shea; Deacon John E. Powers.
Office—7409 W. Clearwater, 99336. Tel: 509-735-8558; Fax: 509-735-8559.
Catechesis/Religious Program—Lori Casey, D.R.E.; Pat Moore, D.R.E. Students 194.

2—ST. JOSEPH'S (1911), Revs. Richard D. Sedlacek; Jorge Granados Lopez; Sr. Robert Joseph, C.S.J., Pastoral Assoc.; Deacon William Mich. In Res., Rev. Msgr. Desmond P. Dillon (Retired).
Res.: 520 S. Garfield, 99336. Tel: 509-586-3820; Fax: 509-586-3558.
School—(Grades PreSchool-8), 901 W. 4th Ave., 99336. Tel: 509-586-0481; Fax: 509-585-9781. Sisters of St. Joseph of Carondelet 3; Lay Teachers 15; Students 400.
Catechesis/Religious Program—Tel: 509-582-8460. Students 357.

LEAVENWORTH, CHELAN CO., OUR LADY OF THE SNOWS (1912), Rev. Ricardo Villarreal; Deacon Don Griek.
Res.: 145 Wheeler St., 98826. Tel: 509-548-5119; Fax: 509-548-5051.
Catechesis/Religious Program—Tel: 509-548-8314. Students 37.

MABTON, YAKIMA CO., IMMACULATE CONCEPTION (1910), Revs. Gary L. Desharnais; Alvaro Drez.
Mailing Address: P.O. Box 275, 98935. Tel: 509-882-1657; Fax: 509-882-1107.
Res.: 1201 Missouri, Grandview, 98930. Tel: 509-882-1657; Fax: 509-882-1107.
Catechesis/Religious Program—Students 169.

MATTAWA, GRANT CO., OUR LADY OF THE DESERT (1987), [JC] Rev. Jose de Loza.
Mailing Address: P.O. Box 2268, 99349. Tel: 509-932-5424; Fax: 509-932-4055.
Catechesis/Religious Program—Students 87.

MOSES LAKE, GRANT CO., OUR LADY OF FATIMA (1955), (Spanish), Revs. John Morse, S.J.; Felipe Pulido, Pastoral Assoc.; Deacon Robert Schrom. In Res., Rev. Msgr. Martin O. Skehan (Retired).
Res.: 200 N. Dale Rd., 98837. Tel: 509-765-6729; Fax: 509-765-0114.
Parish Center—210 N. Dale Rd., 98837. Tel: 509-765-6729.
Catechesis/Religious Program—Tel: 509-766-1930. Annemarie Hermann, D.R.E. (K-8); Ray Towry, D.R.E. (High School); Shannon Towry, D.R.E. (High School). Students 258.

MOXEE CITY, YAKIMA CO., HOLY ROSARY (1900), [CEM]

Rev. Thomas V. Lane. In Res., Rev. Msgr. Edmund G. McGrath, Assoc. Pastor (Retired).
Res.: 201 N. Iler., P.O. Box 279, 98936. Tel: 509-453-4061; Fax: 509-576-6290.
Catechesis / Religious Program—Tel: 509-453-6754. Students 215.

NACHES, YAKIMA CO., ST. JOHN'S (1959), Rev. George Purdy, S.J.
Res.: 204 Moxee Ave., P.O. Box 128, 98937. Tel: 509-653-2534; Fax: 509-653-2534.
Catechesis / Religious Program—Tel: 509-658-2150. Students 26.

PROSSER, BENTON CO., SACRED HEART (1899), Rev. Michael Brzezowski.
Res.: 1905 Highland Dr., 99350. Tel: 509-786-1783; Fax: 509-786-1747.
Catechesis / Religious Program—Cynthia O'Brien, D.R.E., (English Prog.). Tel: 509-973-2265; Juanita Lopez, D.R.E., (Spanish Program). Tel: 509-882-5460. Students 308.

QUINCY, GRANT CO., ST. PIUS X (1955), (Hispanic), Rev. Mario A. Salazar.
Res.: 805 N. Central Ave., P.O. Box 308, 98848. Tel: 509-787-2622; 509-787-3116; Fax: 509-787-6068.
Catechesis / Religious Program—Rita Keene, D.R.E.; Esperanza Hernandez, D.R.E., (Spanish). Students 287.

RICHLAND, BENTON CO., CHRIST THE KING (1946), Revs. Thomas C. Champoux; Wilmar Zabala; Vandennis Nguyen, Pastoral Assoc.; Deacons Robert DaValle; LeRoi Rice; Alfred Rizzo.
Office—1126 Long Ave., 99352. Tel: 509-946-1675; Fax: 509-946-9940.
School—1122 Long Ave., 99352. Tel: 509-946-6158; Fax: 509-943-8402. Lay Teachers 30; Students 465.
Catechesis / Religious Program—Tel: 509-946-1154. Lori Wasner, D.R.E. Students 503.

ROSLYN, UPPER KITTITAS CO., IMMACULATE CONCEPTION (1887), Rev. Lawrence T. Reilly.
Mailing Address: 303 W. 2nd St., Cle Elum, 98922. Tel: 509-674-2531; Fax: 509-674-1894.
Res.: 211 N. 8th St..
Catechesis / Religious Program— Twinned with St. John the Baptist, Cle Elum. Students 24.

ROYAL CITY, GRANT CO., ST. MICHAEL THE ARCHANGEL (1966), (Hispanic), Rev. J. Jesus Ramirez; Deacon Francisco Martinez.
Res.: 145 Daisy St., N.W., P.O. Box 340, 99357. Tel: 509-346-2730; Fax: 509-346-2901.
Catechesis / Religious Program—Tel: 509-246-2730. Students 186.

SELAH, YAKIMA CO., OUR LADY OF LOURDES (1975), Rev. Ronald Patnode; Deacon William D. Hudson.
Res.: 1112 W. Fremont, 98942. Tel: 509-697-4633; Fax: 509-697-3134.
Catechesis / Religious Program—Mary Payment, (Elementary) D.R.E. Students 120.

SUNNYSIDE, YAKIMA CO., ST. JOSEPH'S (1936), Revs. Alberto Magana; Alejandro E. Trejo.
Res.: 920 S. 6th St., 98944. Tel: 509-837-2243; Fax: 509-839-4720.
Catechesis / Religious Program—Tel: 509-839-4758. Students 545.
Convent—Tel: 509-837-2242. Missionary Daughters of the Most Pure Virgin Mary 4.

TOPPENISH, YAKIMA CO., ST. ALOYSIUS (1908), Rev. Argemiro Orozco; Deacon Berny Alvarado.
Mailing Address: 213 N. Beech St., 98948. Tel: 508-865-4725; Fax: 508-865-7882. In Res., Revs. Bill Vogel, S.J.; John Shaw.
Religious Education Center—214 N. Beech St., 98948. Tel: 509-865-2565.
St. Vincent De Paul Center—11 S. B, 98948. Tel: 509-865-5311.
Catechesis / Religious Program—Fax: 509-865-3077. Darlene Riojas, D.R.E. Students 620.

WAPATO, YAKIMA CO., ST. PETER CLAVER (1908), Rev. Salomon Cevarrubias-Pina; Deacons John Kassinger; Antonio Osorio.
Res.: 509 S. Satus Ave., 98951. Tel: 509-877-2813; Fax: 509-877-6207.
Catechesis / Religious Program—Tel: 509-877-4881. Students 300.

WARDEN, GRANT CO., QUEEN OF ALL SAINTS (1966), (Spanish), Revs. John Morse, S.J.; Felipe Pulido, Pastoral Assoc.
200 N. Dale Rd., Moses Lake, 98837. Tel: 509-765-6729; Fax: 509-765-0114.
Catechesis / Religious Program—Tel: 509-349-2757. Students 200.

WATERVILLE, DOUGLAS CO., ST. JOSEPH'S (1892), (German), [CEM] [JC] Rev. John C. Vogl.
Res.: Poplar St., P.O. Box 519, 98858. Tel: 509-745-8205.
Catechesis / Religious Program—Tel: 509-745-8728. Jacque Clements, D.R.E. Students 58.

WENATCHEE, CHELAN CO., ST. JOSEPH'S (1903), Revs. Thomas Kuykendall; Francisco Gutierrez; Deacon Bill Osborn.
Res.: 504 S. Chelan, P.O. Box 2138, 98807. Tel: 509-662-4539; Fax: 509-663-8437.
School—(Grades PreK-5) Tel: 509-663-2644; Fax: 509-663-8474. Lay Teachers 11; Students 151.
Catechesis / Religious Program—600 St. Joseph Pl., 98801. Students 395.

WHITE SALMON, KLICKITAT CO., ST. JOSEPH (1912), (Spanish), Rev. Felix M. Rodriguez, Admin.
Res.: 240 N.W. Washington., P.O. Box 2049, 98672. Tel: 509-493-2828; Fax: 509-493-2175.
Catechesis / Religious Program—Tel: 509-493-8836. Students 76.

WHITE SWAN, YAKIMA CO., ST. MARY'S (1847), [CEM] Rev. William Shaw.
Res.: P.O. Box 417, 98952. Tel: 509-874-2436; Fax: 509-874-1197.
Catechesis / Religious Program—Students 30.

ZILLAH, YAKIMA CO., RESURRECTION (1963), Rev. Emmett Sarsfield; Deacon Bernie Alvarado.
Mailing Address: P.O. Box 567, 98953-0567. Tel: 509-829-5433; 509-829-5312 (Spanish Ministries); Fax: 509-829-5312.
Catechesis / Religious Program—Tel: 509-829-5433; 509-969-3289 Maria Sears.

Special Assignment:
Revs.—
Aguirre, Osmar R., Casa Santa Maria, Via dell Umitla, 30, Rome, Italy. (Italy)
Bunnell, Thomas J., S.J., P.O. Box 4744, Tri Cities, 99302-4744.
Jimenez, David J., Colonia St., Ursula Xitla, Tlalpan 14420 Mexico.
McCreedy, Justin D., O.S.B., 711 W. Walnut Ave., #203, 98902.
Minder, Kevin, Casa Santa Maria, Via dell'Umilta .30, Rome 00187 Italy.
Mitchell, Darell J., 5301-A Tieton Dr., 98908.
Peterson, Maurice F., c/o 5301-A Tieton Dr., 98908.

On Duty Outside the Diocese:
Revs.—
Auve, Perron J., Mount Angel Seminary, 119 Anselm, St. Benedict, OR 97373.
Hernandez, Francisco J., 3213 Stop 32 A, Zapata, TX 78076.
Kenna, Joseph J., 929 Lakefront Dr., Bowie, MD 20721.
Keolker, Richard F., Mount Angel Seminary, St. Benedict, OR 97373.
Murtagh, John J., 5315 Tieton Dr., 98908.
Norman, Gary, 615 Mine St., Roseville, CA 95678.
Sewvello, Robert, P.O. Box 6, Plentywood, MT 59254.
Surman, Darrell, P.O. Box 12523, Thorndon Wellington, New Zealand.

Military Chaplains:
Rev.—
House, Richard M., U.S.S. Ronald Reagan CVN 76, 3311 West Ave. #608, Newport News, VA 23607.

Retired:
Rev. Msgrs.—
Dillon, Desmond P., St. Joseph Parish, 520 S. Garfield, Kennewick, 99336.
Marasciulo, John, 70043 Monopoli, Via Ricasoli No 110, (Bari), Italy.
McDonnell, John J., 5315 Tieton Dr., 98908.
McGrath, Edmund G., P.O. Box 279, Moxee City, 98936-0279.
Skehan, Martin O., W. 318 Northshore Dr., Moses Lake, 98837.
Revs.—
Camacho, Enrique, Apartado Postal 7 Cocula, Jalisco CP 48500 Mexico.
Cerezo, Alberto F., 11637 100th Ave., N.E., #C2W, Kirkland, 98034.
Dahlquist, Thomas S., 5301-A Tieton Dr., 98908.
Dorian, Brendan, Duffy's Cross, Readpenny, Co. Louth Ireland.
Gallagher, Brian T., P.O. Box 1601, Duarte, CA 91009.
Greene, Daniel (ORL), 9724 Cross Creek Blvd., Tampa, FL 33647-3408.
Hannick, Anthony S., 1600 Roosmoor Pkwy., Walnut Creek, CA 94553.
Heneghan, John F., Waverly Collacoon, Mayo, Ireland.
Shields, Robert J., 4602 Tieton Dr., Apt. D 24, 98908.
Tholen, John, 5301-A Tieton Dr., 98908.
Wawrzynski, Edward A., U.S.A.F.R., 5856 106th Ter. N., Pinellas Park, FL 34666.

Permanent Deacons:
Alvarado, Berney, 15 S. Date St., Toppenish, 98948.
Berger, Duane, 1706 Lower Ahtanum, 98903.
Chavez, Nestor, 710 E. Race St., 98901.
Cornell, John, 2504 W. Chestnut, 98902.
DaValle, Robert, 1837 Marshall Ave., Richland, 99352.
Dronen, Bill, 306 Railroad Ave., Cashmere, 98815.
Garcia, Gilberto, P.O. Box 6185, Kennewick, 99336.
Griek, Don, P.O. Box 1023, Leavenworth, 98826.
Henn, Thomas W., 22402 N. Vega Dr., Sun City, AZ 85375-2046.
Hudson, William D., 1404 W. Yakima Ave., 98902.
Kassinger, John, 1314 N. Ave., #4, Sunnyside, 98944.
Kramper, James, 7304 Tieton Dr., 98908.
Loranger, Bill, 613 Briarwood Dr., East Wenatchee, 98802.
Martinez, Frank, 3790 Rd. 10.4 S.W., Royal City, 99357.
Mich, William, 601 N. Reed, Kennewick, 99336.
Miller, Ray, 2412 W. Chestnut, 98902.
Osborn, Bill, 410 Cottage Ave., Cashmere, 98815.
Osorio, Antonio, 14 S. I St., Toppenish, 98948.
Powers, John, 3614 S. Green St., Kennewick, 99337.
Reyna, Lupe, 1130 S. Grand, Moses Lake, 98837.
Rice, LeRoi, 1845 Mahan Ave., Richland, 99352.
Rizzo, Al, 135 MacArthur St., Richland, 99352.
Schrom, Robert, 7240 Rd. 17, S.W., Royal City, 99357.
Spence, Jack, 350 Hanson Rd., Ellensburg, 98926.

INSTITUTIONS LOCATED IN THE DIOCESE

[A] COLLEGES AND UNIVERSITIES

TOPPENISH. **Heritage College* (Interdenominational University with an Independent Board) , 3240 Fort Rd., 98948. Tel: 509-865-8600; Fax: 509-865-7976. Email: ross_k@heritage.edu. Web: www.heritage.edu. Sisters 5; Lay Teachers 40; Students 1,250.

[B] HIGH SCHOOLS

UNION GAP. *La Salle High School*, 3000 Lightning Way, 98903. Tel: 509-225-2900; Fax: 509-225-2950. Email: lasallehs@aol.com. Web: www.lasalleyakima.com. Timothy McGree, Pres.; Mary Klarich, Prin. Brothers 3; Sisters 1; Lay Teachers 12; Total Staff 20; Students 172.

[C] HOSPITALS

RICHLAND. *Lourdes Counseling Center*, 1175 Carondelet Dr., 99352. Tel: 509-943-9104; Fax: 509-943-7206. Email: bmead@lourdesonline.org. Web: lourdesonline.org. Barbara Mead, Exec. Dir. Bed Capacity 32; Total Assisted Annually 75,436; Total Staff 136.

[D] CATHOLIC SOCIAL SERVICE CATHOLIC CHARITIES

YAKIMA. *Carroll Children's Center*, 5301 Tieton Dr., Ste. C, 98908. Tel: 509-965-7104; Fax: 509-966-9750. Email: khelseth@cfcsyakima.org. Kathy Helseth, Prog. Mgr. Capacity 140; Total Assisted Annually 174; Total Staff 25.
Catholic Charities of the Diocese of Yakima, 5301-C Tieton Dr., 98908. Tel: 509-965-7100; Fax: 509-972-0167. Email: jlyhd28@aol.com. Mr John L. Young, Exec. Dir.
Catholic Family and Child Service, 5301 Tieton Dr., Ste. C, 98908. Tel: 509-965-7100; Fax 509-966-9750. Email: info@cfcsyakima.org. Web: www.cfcsyakima.org. Mrs. Darlene Darnell, M.S.W., Agency Dir. Total Assisted Annually 37,489; Total Staff 125.
Child Care Nutrition, P.O. Box 2399, 98907. Tel: 509-965-7107; Fax: 509-966-9750. Email: coliphant@cfcsyakima.org.
St. Vincent de Paul Store, 2629 S. First St., 98903. Tel: 509-457-5111; Fax: 509-457-3526. Thomas Gehlen, Mgr. (Of All Stores in Diocese). Total Staff 14.

CHELAN. *St. Vincent de Paul Store*, 404 E. Woodin, P.O. Box 2387, 98816. Tel: 509-682-3655; Fax: 509-682-3655.

ELLENSBURG. *St. Vincent de Paul Store*, 1200 Canyon St., 98926. Tel: 509-925-2167; Fax: 509-925-9547. Total Staff 8.

GRANDVIEW. *Catholic Family and Child Service of Yakima*, 322 Division, P.O. Box 22, 98930. Tel: 509-882-3050; Fax: 509-882-5026. Email: rrgrand@aol.com. Total Assisted 1,200; Total Staff 6.

KENNEWICK. *St. Vincent de Paul Store*, 1401 W. Kennewick Ave., 99336. Tel: 509-586-1053; Fax: 509-586-6910.

MOSES LAKE. *Catholic Family and Child Service of Moses Lake-Ephrata*, 414 Burress St., 98837. Tel: 509-765-1875; Fax: 509-766-1836. Email: jval001@

msn.com. Total Assisted 1,500; Total Staff 7.

RICHLAND. *Catholic Family and Child Service*, 2139 Van Giesen, P.O. Box 1504, 99352. Tel: 509-946-4645; Fax: 509-943-2068. Email: mmcgrath@cfcs3cities.org. Maureen C. McGrath, M.A. Total Assisted 3,087; Total Staff 42.

SUNNYSIDE. *St. Vincent de Paul Store*, 305 North Ave., 98944. Tel: 509-837-2055; Fax: 509-837-2033. Total Staff 12.

WENATCHEE. *Catholic Family and Child Service*, 23 S. Wenatchee Ave., #320, 98801. Tel: 509-662-6761; Fax: 509-663-3182. Email: stryon@cfcs.net. Total Assisted 2,500; Total Staff 24.

St. Vincent de Paul Store, 330 S. Wenatchee Ave., 98801. Tel: 509-662-6010; Fax: 509-662-2810. Total Staff 9.

[E] RETIREMENT HOMES

YAKIMA. **The Gamelin Association-Providence House*, 312 N. 4th St., 98901-2459. Tel: 509-452-5017; Fax: 509-452-1947. Email: Dawn_Rodrigues@providence.org. Web: www.providence.org/Long_Term_Care/Housing/e20ProvHouse.htm. Dawn Rodrigues, Dir. Low income housing for elderly.

[F] VOLUNTEER SERVICES

YAKIMA. *Holy Family Parish Conference*, 5315 Tieton Dr., 98908. Tel: 509-966-0830; Fax: 509-965-1742.

Holy Redeemer Parish Conference, 1609 Landon Ave., 98902. Tel: 509-248-2241; Fax: 509-457-3312. Email: holyredeemer2002@aol.com. Web: diocese.net. Raymond Faith, Pres.

St. Joseph's Parish Conference, 212 N. 4th St., 98901. Tel: 509-248-1911; Fax: 509-248-2604. Mrs. O. Gress, Pres.

St. Paul's Parish Conference, 15 S. 12th Ave., 98902. Tel: 509-575-3713; Fax: 509-453-7497. Email: stpaul@wolfenet.com. Bob Rogers, Pres.; Fred Baur, Treas.

Society of St. Vincent de Paul, Particular Council of Yakima, 305 North Ave., Sunnyside, 98944. Tel: 509-837-7968; Fax: 509-837-2033. Email: director@stvincentyakima.org. Tom Gehlen, Pres. Total Staff 15.

EAST WENATCHEE. *Holy Apostles Parish Conference*, P.O. Box 7279, 98801. Tel: 509-884-5444; Fax: 509-886-3424. Steve Piccirillo, Pres.; Revs. Francisco P. Higuera; Gustavo Gomez; Deacon William F. Loranger.

KENNEWICK. *St. Joseph Parish Conference*, 520 S. Garfield, 99336. Tel: 509-586-3820; Fax: 509-586-3558. Email: parish.office@stjosephs-kennewick.com.

MOSES LAKE. *Our Lady of Fatima Parish Conference*, 200 N. Dale Rd., 98837. Tel: 509-765-6729; Fax: 509-765-0114. Email: jmorse@nwi.net. Don Tibbets, Pres.

RICHLAND. *Christ the King Parish Conference*, 1126 Long Ave., 99352. Tel: 509-946-1675; Fax: 509-946-9940. Email: bulletin@ckparish.org. Web: www.ckparish.org. Bob Morford, Pres.

TOPPENISH. *St. Aloysius Parish Conference*, 213 N. Beech St., 98948. Tel: 509-865-4725; Fax: 509-865-7882. Adrianna Hede, Pres.

St. Vincent de Paul Center, 213 N. Beech St., 98948. Tel: 509-865-5311; Fax: 509-865-7882. Total Assisted 5,771; Total Staff 1.

11 S. B St., 98948. Tel: 509-865-5311. Adriana Hede, Dir.

WENATCHEE. *St. Joseph Parish Conference, St Vincent de Paul*, 504 S. Chelan, 98801. Tel: 509-662-4569. V. E. Houck, Pres.

[G] RETREAT HOUSES

COWICHE. *St. Peter the Apostle Retreat Center*, 15880 Summitview Rd., 98923. Tel: 509-678-4935; Fax: 509-678-8758. Email: stpetersretreat@juno.com. Juan Gonzalez, Admin. Total in Residence 3; Total Staff 4.

[H] CAMPUS MINISTRY

ELLENSBURG. *Catholic Campus Ministry at Central Washington University* 706 N. Sprague, 98926. Tel: 509-925-3043. Email: ccm-cwu@elltel.net. Mr. Joseph Kiesel-Nield, Dir. & Campus Min. Total in Residence 5; Total Staff 1.

[I] MISCELLANEOUS LISTINGS

YAKIMA. *Catholic In Action*, 5301-A Tieton Dr., 98908. Tel: 509-829-6257. Email: cia@yakimadiocese.org. Web: www.yakimadiocese.org/cia/main.html. Richard Sevigny, Pres.

**Central Washington Catholic Foundation*, 5301-A Tieton Dr., Ste. A, 98908-3497. Rev. Samuel P. Bellino, S.J., Exec. Dir.

**Diocese of Yakima Housing Services*, 5301 Tieton Dr., Ste. C, 98908-3478. Tel: 509-965-7100; Fax: 509-972-0167. Email: mvillanueva@cfcsyakima.org. Mr. John L. Young, Pres.; Mario Villanueva, Dir.

La Salle Foundation of Yakima, 402 E. Yakima Ave., Ste. 370, 98901. Tel: 509-248-7886; Fax: 206-248-2641. Email: jcolgan@lasalleyak.org. Web: www.lasalleyakima.com. John Colgan, Exec. Dir.; Timothy McGree, Pres.

Simmer Down Productions, 5301-A Tieton Dr., 98908. Tel: 509-829-6257. Email: 4life@newyorknet.net. Richard Sevigny, Pres.

COWICHE. *REACH Youth Ministry*, P.O. Box 130, 98923-0130. Tel: 509-678-8754; Fax: 509-678-8758. Email: reachym@prodigy.net. Web: pages.prodigy.net/reachym. Gina Morrissey, Dir. Total Assisted 8,000; Total Staff 4.

TOPPENISH. *Association of Catholic Sisters for Educational Opportunities for the Poor*, 3240 Fort Rd., 98948. Tel: 509-877-7977. Sr. Kathleen Ross, S.N.J.M., Pres.

RELIGIOUS INSTITUTES OF MEN REPRESENTED IN THE DIOCESE

For further details refer to the corresponding bracketed number in the Religious Institutes of Men or Women section.

[0200]—*Benedictine Monks (American Cassinese Congregation)*—O.S.B.

[0330]—*Brothers of the Christian Schools* (Prov. of San Francisco)—F.S.C.

[0690]—*Jesuit Fathers and Brothers (Oregon Providence)*—S.J.

RELIGIOUS INSTITUTES OF WOMEN REPRESENTED IN THE DIOCESE

[0230]—*Benedictine Sisters of Pontifical Jurisdiction*—O.S.B.

[1070-20]—*Dominican Sisters*—O.P.

[]—*Missionary Daughters of the Most Pure Virgin Mary*

[2790]—*Missionary Servants of the Most Blessed Trinity*—M.S.B.T.

[3350]—*Sisters of Providence* (Mother Joseph Prov.)—S.P.

[3840]—*Sisters of St. Joseph of Carondelet*—C.S.J.

[1990]—*Sisters of the Holy Names of Jesus and Mary*—S.N.J.M.

[2160]—*Sisters, Servants of the Immaculate Heart of Mary*—I.H.M.

NECROLOGY

(No Deaths)

Diocese of Youngstown

(Dioecesis Youngstoniensis)

Most Reverend

THOMAS J. TOBIN, D.D.

Bishop of Youngstown; ordained July 21, 1973; appointed Titular Bishop of Novica and Auxiliary Bishop of Pittsburgh, November 3, 1992; appointed Fourth Bishop of Youngstown installed February 2, 1996

Most Reverend

BENEDICT C. FRANZETTA, D.D.

Retired Auxiliary Bishop of Youngstown; ordained April 29, 1950; appointed Titular Bishop of Oderzo and Auxiliary July 29, 1980; consecrated September 4, 1980; retired September 4, 1996 *Res.: St. Columba Rectory*, 159 W. Rayen Ave., Youngstown, OH 44503.

ESTABLISHED MAY 15, 1943.

Square Miles 3,404.

Canonically Erected July 22, 1943.

Comprises six Counties in the northeastern part of the State of Ohio, namely, Ashtabula, Columbiana, Mahoning, Portage, Stark and Trumbull Counties.

For legal titles of parishes and diocesan institutions, consult the Chancery Office.

Chancery Office: 144 W. Wood St., Youngstown, OH 44503. Tel: 330-744-8451; Fax: 330-742-6448; 330-744-2848

Web: www.doy.org

Email: chancery@doy.org

STATISTICAL OVERVIEW

Personnel	
Bishop	1
Retired Bishops	1
Priests: Diocesan Active in Diocese	112
Priests: Diocesan Active Outside Diocese	5
Priests: Diocesan in Foreign Missions	1
Priests: Retired, Sick or Absent	59
Number of Diocesan Priests	177
Religious Priests in Diocese	22
Total Priests in Diocese	199
Extern Priests in Diocese	8
Ordinations:	
Diocesan Priests	1
Transitional Deacons	1
Permanent Deacons in Diocese	68
Total Brothers	18
Total Sisters	226
Parishes	
Parishes	116
With Resident Pastor:	
Resident Diocesan Priests	94
Resident Religious Priests	3
Without Resident Pastor:	
Administered by Priests	19
Missions	2
Professional Ministry Personnel:	
Sisters	30
Lay Ministers	103
Welfare	
Catholic Hospitals	3
Total Assisted	442,633
Health Care Centers	15
Total Assisted	671,163
Homes for the Aged	9
Total Assisted	886
Day Care Centers	7
Total Assisted	1,024
Specialized Homes	7
Total Assisted	614
Special Centers for Social Services	21
Total Assisted	44,668
Other Institutions	3
Total Assisted	144
Educational	
Diocesan Students in Other Seminaries	12
Total Seminarians	12
Colleges and Universities	1
Total Students	1,801
High Schools, Diocesan and Parish	6
Total Students	2,704
Elementary Schools, Diocesan and Parish	42
Total Students	9,406
Elementary Schools, Private	1
Total Students	295
Catechesis/Religious Education:	
High School Students	1,509
Elementary Students	13,660
Total Students under Catholic Instruction	29,387
Teachers in the Diocese:	
Sisters	25
Lay Teachers	862
Vital Statistics	
Receptions into the Church:	
Infant Baptism Totals	2,485
Adult Baptism Totals	218
Received into Full Communion	409
First Communions	3,031
Confirmations	3,231
Marriages:	
Catholic	577
Interfaith	437
Total Marriages	1,014
Deaths	3,138
Total Catholic Population	235,541
Total Population	1,227,633

Former Bishops—Most Revs. JAMES A. MCFADDEN, S.T.D., LL.D., appt. Titular Bishop of Bida and Auxiliary of Cleveland, May 13, 1932; consecrated Sept. 8, 1932; appt. Bishop of Youngstown, June 2, 1943; died Nov. 16, 1952; EMMET M. WALSH, D.D., ord. Jan. 15, 1916; appt. Bishop of Charleston, June 20, 1927; appt. Titular Bishop of Rhaedestus and Coadjutor, Sept. 8, 1949; succeeded to See, Nov. 16, 1952; died March 16, 1968; JAMES W. MALONE, D.D. (Retired), ord. May 26, 1945; appt. Titular Bishop of Alabanda and Auxiliary, Jan. 2, 1960; appt. Apostolic Administrator, Jan. 22, 1966; succeeded to See, May 2, 1968; retired Dec. 4, 1995; died April 9, 2000.

All Diocesan offices and personnel can be reached at 144 W. Wood St., Youngstown, OH, 44503. Tel: 330-744-8451, Fax: 330-742-6448; 744-2848 unless otherwise indicated.

Chancery Office

Vicar General and Moderator of the Curia—Rev. Msgr. ROBERT J. SIFFRIN.

Chancellor—Mrs. NANCY YUHASZ.

"The Catholic Exponent", Diocesan Newspaper—Most Rev. THOMAS J. TOBIN, D.D., Publisher; Mr. LOUIS JACQUET, Editor & Gen. Mgr. Tel: 330-744-5251.

College of Consultors—Rev. Msgr. MICHAEL CARIGLIO; Rev. GERALD DELUCIA; Rev. Msgrs. JOHN DEMARINIS; JOHN FINNIGAN; JAMES A. CLARKE; Revs. CHARLES CRUMBLEY; RONALD KLINGLER; RAYMOND THOMAS; Rev. Msgr. ROBERT SIFFRIN.

Communications—

Catholic Television Network of Youngstown (CTNY)—Bro. DOMINIC CALABRO, S.S.P., Pastoral Dir.; BOB GAVALIER, Gen. Mgr., P.O. Box 430, Canfield, 44406-0430. Tel: 330-533-2243.

Public-Media Relations—NANCY YUHASZ.

Development/Stewardship—Mr. PAT PALOMBO, Dir., The Foundation of the Roman Catholic Diocese of Youngstown.

Ecumenism—Rev. JOSEPH WITMER, Dir., Ecumenical Commission, 342 S. Chillicothe, Aurora, 44202. Tel: 330-562-8519.

Office of Missions/Propagatoin of Faith—Bro. THOMAS AQUINAS DOLAN, O.P., Dir.

Office of Pro-Life Activities—MELINDA KNIGHT, Dir.

Scouting, Diocesan Office—Rev. LEO WEHRLIN, Dir., 323 S. 15th St., Sebring, 44672. Tel: 330-938-2033.

Department of Canonical Services

Department of Canonical Services—Rev. Msgr. MICHAEL CARIGLIO, J.C.L., Exec. Dir., 141 W. Rayen Ave., Youngstown, 44503. Tel: 330-744-8451; Fax: 330-742-6450.

Office of Conciliation—

Matrimonial Dispensations—

Tribunal—

Judicial Vicar—Rev. Msgr. MICHAEL CARIGLIO, J.C.L.

Adjutant Judicial Vicar—Rev. Msgr. PETER POLANDO, J.C.L.

Judges—Rev. Msgrs. FRANK A. CARFAGNA; DAVID W. RHODES; MARTIN S. SUSKO; LAWRENCE C. FYE, M.Ed., V.F.; Revs. ROBERT G. GIBAS; JOHN E. KEEHNER, J.C.L.; DANIEL J. KULESA; THOMAS J. MCCARTHY; JOHN NAGELE, C.PP.S.; JOHN R. OLSAVSKY, J.C.L.; ROBERT F. PFEIFFER, J.C.L.; GARY D. YANUS, J.C.D.

Defenders of the Bond—Rev. Msgr. JOHN ZURAW, J.C.L.; Revs. TERRENCE HAZEL; RAYMOND PAUL; JOHN F. WARNER.

Advocates—Rev. BERNARD N. GAETA; PHYLLIS KULICS; Mrs. BARBARA ROGICH.

Promoter of Justice—Rev. Msgr. JOHN A. ZURAW, J.C.L.

Notaries—PHYLLIS KULICS; BARBARA ROGICH; JULIE TABAKA; VICKI KIDD.

Department of Catholic Charities Services

Department of Catholic Charities Services—Mr. BRIAN CORBIN, Exec. Dir., Health & Human Svcs. Commission; Liaison to St. Vincent DePaul Society.

Office of Social Action—Mr. BRIAN CORBIN, Dir. Environment, Hunger & Rural Life Committee; Housing & Community Devel. Committee; Minorities Commission; Respect Life Committee; Parish Social Ministry; Criminal Justice Ministry.

Office of Social Services—Mrs. MARY ELLEN ANDERSEN, Pres., Diocese of Youngstown Catholic Charities Corp.; Dir., Aging Svcs.

St. Vincent DePaul Society—WILLIAM DUNLAP, Pres., Particular Council of Youngstown, 235 Wick Ave., Youngstown, 44503. Tel: 330-746-5222; Mr. VINCENT SCHUYLER, Pres., Particular Council of Trumbull Deanery, 2415 Niles Rd., S.E., Warren, 44484. Tel: 330-369-4198.

Department of Clergy and Religious Services

Department of Clergy and Religious Services—Rev. Msgr. JOHN ZURAW, J.C.L., Exec. Dir.

Office of Vocations—Rev. LEO WEHRLIN, Dir., 323 S. 15th St., Sebring, 44672. Tel: 330-938-2033.

Serra Club of Trumbull County—Rev. FREDERICK LUKEHART, Chap., 1000 Tod Ave., Warren, 44485. Tel: 330-395-3747.

Serra Club of Mahoning County—Rev. G. DAVID WEIKART, Chap., 3165 S. Schenley Ave., Youngstown, 44511. Tel: 330-792-3829.

Serra Club of Stark County—Rev. NICHOLAS MANCINI, Chap., 1515 California Ave., Louisville, 44641. Tel: 330-875-4635.

Office of Clergy Services—Rev. Msgr. JOHN ZURAW, J.C.L., Dir.

Priests' Council—Rev. BERNARD R. SCHMALZRIED, Exec. Sec., 232 Seneca St., N.E., Warren, 44481. Tel: 330-393-8721.

Office of Continuing Education and Formation of Priests—Rev. STEPHEN POPOVICH, Dir., 4490 Norquest Blvd., Youngstown, 44515. Tel: 330-793-9988.

Office of Priests' Personnel Advisor—Rev. THOMAS MCCARTHY, 935 E. State St., Salem, 44460. Tel: 330-332-0336.

Office of Permanent Diaconate—Rev. Msgr. JOHN ZURAW, J.C.L., Dir.

Office of Religious—Sr. JOYCE CANDIDI, O.S.H.J., Dir.

Diocesan Conference of Religious—Sr. JOYCE CANDIDI, O.S.H.J., Dir.

Department of Financial Services

Department of Financial Services—Mr. ROBERT A. HOFFMAN, C.F.O.

Office of Finance—Mr. JOHN DIDEK JR., Dir. Finance; Mrs. MARGARET FISHER, Dir. Finance; Mr. LEONARD W. DERSHAW, Dir. Auditing; Mr. KEVIN C. O'DONNELL, Financial Accountant.

Office of Management Information Systems—Mr. LOUIS ORBIN, Dir.; Ms. MARIJO ORBIN, Assoc. Dir.

Department of Pastoral and Educational Services

Pastoral and Educational Services—Sr. M. BRENDON ZAJAC, S.N.D., Exec. Dir.

Office of Catholic Schools—Dr. MICHAEL SKUBE, Supt.; Dr. ALAN DIGIANANTONIO, Dir. Curriculum Instruction & Technology; Mrs. JUDY BOGDAN, Dir. Certificated Personnel; Mr. WALLACE DUNNE, Dir., Govt. Programs & Resource Devel.

The Catholic Diocese of Youngstown Educational Fund, Inc.—

Office of Religious Education—BARBARA WALKO, Diocesan Dir., 225 Elm St., Youngstown, 44503. Tel: 330-744-8451; THOMAS SAULINE, Consultant; CARLETTE CHORDAS, Consultant; JANET CRISPI, Media Resources.

Council for Catechesis—Sr. MARY AGNES O'MALLEY, S.N.D., Chm.; ANN MARIE VEGA, Vice Chm.

Office of Youth and Young Adult Ministry—CINDEE CASE, Dir.; FAYE ABBONDANZA, Assoc. Dir.

Office of Campus Ministry—Rev. JOHN JEREK, Diocesan Dir., 1424 Horning Rd., Kent, 44240. Tel: 330-678-0240.

Hiram College—Rev. RICHARD J. PENTELLO, St. Ambrose Parish, 10692 Freedom St., Garrettsville, 44231. Tel: 330-527-4105.

Immaculate Heart of Mary University Parish (Kent State Newman Center)—Rev. JOHN JEREK, Pastor; Mrs. CARMEN ROEBKE, Campus Min., 1424 Horning Rd., Kent, 44240. Tel: 330-678-0240.

Stark State College of Technology/Kent State Stark Campus—THOMAS DOUCE, Dir.; KEVIN O'BRIEN, Campus Minister, Interfaith Campus Ministry, 6200 Frank Ave., N.W., Canton, 44720. Tel: 330-499-9935.

Walsh University—Rev. Msgr. LEW GAETANO, Ph.D.; PAUL KELLY; LYNN DALSKY, 2020 Easton St., N.W., North Canton, 44720. Tel: 330-490-7344; 330-490-7341; 330-490-7182.

Youngstown State University—Rev. JOHN KEEHNER, J.C.L., Dir., 254 Madison Ave., Youngstown, 44504. Tel: 330-747-9202.

Office of Worship—FRAN AMER, Dir.

Office of Lay Ministry Formation—EILEEN NOVOTNY, Dir.

Office of Marriage & Family Ministry—Mr. JOHN DAMICO, Dir.

Other Ministries

Bishop's Delegate for Retired Priests—Rev. THOMAS MCCARTHY.

Catholic Alumni Club of Youngstown, Inc.—Rev. VINCENT FREEH, M.S.C., Chap., 1602 Market Ave., S., Canton, 44707-3778. Tel: 330-453-2110.

Catholic Women, Diocesan Council of—Rev. Msgr. JAMES A. CLARKE, Moderator, 241 S. Main St., North Canton, 44720. Tel: 330-499-2201.

Charismatic Prayer Group—Rev. ROBERT EDWARDS, Dir., 271 Chestnut St., Lisbon, 44432. Tel: 330-424-7648.

Disabled Services—

Physically and Developmentally—Rev. TERRENCE HAZEL, Chap., 281 Glenview Dr., Canfield, 44406. Tel: 330-533-6839.

Deaf and Hearing Impaired—Rev. TERRENCE HAZEL, Chap., 281 Glenview Dr., Canfield, 44406. Tel: 330-533-6839.

Spanish Speaking—BRIAN CORBIN, Office of Social Action, 144 W. Wood St., Youngstown, 44503. Tel: 330-744-8451.

Hispanic Immigrant Services and Outreach Ministries—Sr. TERESA ANN WOLF, O.S.B., Coord. Pastoral Care for Migrants and Refugees, Tri-Diocesan Migrant Ministry Project; JEFF STEWART, Dir., Immigration Svcs., Centro San Jose, 1500 Market Street, N., Canton, 44714. Tel: 330-454-2220; Fax: 330-454-2255.

Victim Assistance Coordinator—NANCY YUHASZ. Tel: 330-744-8451. Email: nyuhasz@youngstowndiocese.org.

CLERGY, PARISHES, MISSIONS AND PAROCHIAL SCHOOLS

CITY OF YOUNGSTOWN
(MAHONING COUNTY)

1—CATHEDRAL OF ST. COLUMBA (1847), [JC] Rev. Msgr. Lawrence C. Fye, M.Ed., V.F.; Rev. John Keehner, J.C.L., Vice Rector. In Res., Most Rev. Benedict C. Franzetta, D.D., V.G. (Retired).
Res.: 159 W. Rayen Ave., 44503. Tel: 330-744-5233; Fax: 330-744-2282.
Catechesis/Religious Program—Tel: 330-744-4233. Students 51.

2—ST. ANTHONY'S (1898), (Italian), Rev. Msgr. John H. DeMarinis; Deacon Nicholas Boccieri.
Res.: 1125 Turin Ave., 44510. Tel: 330-744-5091; Fax: 330-744-1407.
Catechesis/Religious Program—Students 21.

3—ST. BRENDAN (1923), Rev. James M. Daprile, Ph.D. In Res., Rev. Msgr. Robert Siffrin.
Res.: 2800 Oakwood Ave., 44509. Tel: 330-792-3875; Fax: 330-792-9080.
School—144 N. Schenley Ave., 44509. Tel: 330-799-9741; Fax: 330-799-1113.
Catechesis/Religious Program—Tel: 330-792-3875, Ext. 13. Students 205.

4—ST. CASIMIR (1906), Rev. Msgr. Lawrence C. Fye, M.Ed., V.F., Admin.
Church: 145 Jefferson St., P.O. Box 2209, 44510-1325. Tel: 330-743-3951.

5—ST. CHRISTINE (1953), [CEM] Rev. Msgr. David W. Rhodes; Rev. G. David Weikart; Sr. Ann McManamon, Pastoral Assoc.; Deacons David Beil; Ronald Layko; Robert Cuttica, M.D.; Jim Brown.
Res.: 3165 S. Schenley Ave., 44511. Tel: 330-792-3829; Fax: 330-792-6587.
School—3125 S. Schenley Ave., 44511. Tel: 330-792-4545; Fax: 330-792-6888. Lay Teachers 22; Students 470.
Catechesis/Religious Program—Tel: 330-793-0544; Fax: 330-792-3820. Colleen Boyle, D.R.E. Students 520.

6—SS. CYRIL AND METHODIUS (1896), (Slovak), Unassigned.
Res.: 252 E. Wood St., 44503. Tel: 330-743-5291; Fax: 330-746-1207.
Catechesis/Religious Program— Twinned with St. Stephen of Hungary. Students 15.

7—ST. DOMINIC (1923), Revs. Joseph P. Allen, O.P.; William J. Rock, O.P.; Gerard Lessard, O.P. (NEW); Robert R. Heuschkel.
Res.: 77 E. Lucius Ave., 44507. Tel: 330-783-1900; Fax: 330-783-2396.
Parish Center—3403 Southern Blvd., 44507. Tel: 330-782-1123.
Catechesis/Religious Program—Students 110.

8—ST. EDWARD (1917), Rev. Frank M. Lehnerd.
Res.: 240 Tod Ln., 44504. Tel: 330-743-2308; Fax: 330-743-8321.
Catechesis/Religious Program—Students 47.

9—ST. ELIZABETH (1922), (Slovak), Revs. Michael Swierz; Howard Ziemba.
Res.: 124 Keystone St., Campbell, 44405. Tel: 330-747-4085; Fax: 330-747-8647.
Catechesis/Religious Program—Tel: 330-726-7775. Students 31.

10—HOLY NAME (1916), (Slovak), Rev. John E. Reiss.
Res.: 613 N. Lakeview Ave., 44509. Tel: 330-799-8873.
Catechesis/Religious Program—Students 46.

11—IMMACULATE CONCEPTION (1882), Rev. Msgr. John A. Zuraw, J.C.L., Admin.; Sr. Mary Lee Nalley, O.S.U., Pastoral Min.
Res.: 811 Oak St., 44506. Tel: 330-747-3533; Fax: 330-747-0219.
School—810 Oak St., 44506. Tel: 330-747-9471; Fax: 330-747-5022. Mrs. Amy Ellis, Prin. Lay Teachers 7; Students 125.
Catechesis/Religious Program—Sr. Kathleen McCarragher, O.S.U., D.R.E. Students 35.

12—IMMACULATE HEART OF MARY (1954), Rev. Stephen Popovich.
Res.: 4490 Norquest Blvd., 44515. Tel: 330-793-9988; Fax: 330-799-9269.
School—Tel: 330-799-1944; Fax: 330-799-0151. Sisters 2; Lay Teachers 12; Students 161.
Catechesis/Religious Program—Tel: 330-799-4202. Students 243.

13—ST. JOSEPH (1966), Rev. J. James Korda; Deacon Michael Roberts.
Res.: 4545 New Rd., Austintown, 44515. Tel: 330-792-1919; Fax: 330-792-5233.
School—Tel: 330-793-1250; Fax: 330-793-2377. Lay Teachers 13; Students 236.
Catechesis/Religious Program—Tel: 330-792-1934. Students 400.

14—ST. MATTHIAS (1914), (Slovak), Rev. Msgr. Peter M. Polando, J.C.L.; Deacon Salvatore DiFrancesco. In Res., Rev. Msgr. Michael E. Ronik.
Res.: 915 Cornell St., 44502-2765. Tel: 330-788-5082; Fax: 330-788-2383.
School—2800 Shady Run Rd., 44502-2700. Tel: 330-788-0241; Fax: 330-788-0534. Vincentian Sisters of Charity 2; Lay Teachers 14; Students 157.
Catechesis/Religious Program—Tel: 330-788-5732. Students 90.
Convent—937 Cornell St., 44502-2765.

15—OUR LADY OF HUNGARY (1929), (Hungarian), Rev. John E. Reiss.
Office—545 N. Belle Vista Ave., 44509. Tel: 330-799-6829; Fax: 330-799-6829.
Catechesis/Religious Program—Students 20.

16—OUR LADY OF MT. CARMEL (1908), (Italian), Rev. Msgr. Michael J. Cariglio, J.C.L.; Deacon Joseph Nohra.
Res.: 343 Via Mt. Carmel, 44505. Tel: 330-743-4144; Fax: 330-743-1035.
Catechesis/Religious Program—Tel: 330-743-3508. Students 182.

17—ST. PATRICK (1911), Rev. Edward P. Noga.
Res.: 1420 Oak Hill Ave., 44507. Tel: 330-743-1109; Fax: 330-743-8810.
Catechesis/Religious Program—Students 80.

18—SS. PETER AND PAUL (1911), (Croatian), Rev. Joseph Rudjak.
Res.: 421 Covington St., 44510. Tel: 330-747-6762.
Catechesis/Religious Program—Students 55.

19—ST. ROSE OF LIMA (1961), (Hispanic), Rev. Charles Poore, Admin.; Deacons Felipe Colon; John Rentas; Enrique Santiago.
Res.: 50 Struthers-Coitsville Rd., 44505. Tel: 330-755-3633; Fax: 330-755-3683.
Catechesis/Religious Program—Students 72.

20—SACRED HEART OF JESUS (1888), Rev. Charles Poore.
Res.: 400 Lincoln Park Dr., 44506. Tel: 330-747-6080; Fax: 330-747-7003.
School—Tel: 330-747-9471; Fax: 330-747-0219. Combined with Immaculate Conception.
Catechesis/Religious Program—Tel: 330-747-3533. Sr. Kathleen McCarragher, O.S.U., D.R.E. Students 26.

21—ST. STANISLAUS KOSTKA (1902), (Polish), Rev. Edward J. Neroda; Deacon Michael Schlais.
Res.: 430 Williamson Ave., 44507. Tel: 330-747-8503; Fax: 330-747-6334.
Catechesis/Religious Program—Tel: 330-747-3015. Students 35.

22—ST. STEPHEN OF HUNGARY (1905), (Hungarian), Rev. Melvin E. Rusnak; Deacon Al Medvez.
Church: 854 Wilson Ave., 44506. Tel: 330-743-1905; Fax: 330-743-1905.
Catechesis/Religious Program— Twinned with SS. Cyril and Methodius, 252 E. Wood St., Youngstown Tel: 330-743-5291; Fax: 330-746-1207.

OUTSIDE THE CITY OF YOUNGSTOWN

ALLIANCE, STARK CO.

1—ST. JOSEPH (1859), [CEM] Rev. Donald L. Feicht.

Res.: 427 E. Broadway, 44601. Tel: 330-821-5760; Fax: 330-821-5783.
Catechesis/Religious Program—Students 92.

2—REGINA COELI (1958), [JC] Rev. J. Patrick Manning; Sr. Yvonne Horning, O.P., Pastoral Assoc.
Res.: 663 Fernwood Blvd., 44601-2796. Tel: 330-821-5880; Fax: 330-821-8837.
School—733 Fernwood Blvd., 44601-2796. Tel: 330-829-9239; Fax: 330-823-1877. Lay Teachers 14; Students 250.
Catechesis/Religious Program—Amy Benedetti, D.R.E. Students 90.

ANDOVER, ASHTABULA CO., OUR LADY OF VICTORY (1949), Rev. David L. Misbrener.
Res.: 481 S. Main St., P.O. Box 669, 44003-9778. Tel: 440-293-6218; Fax: 440-293-7778.
Catechesis/Religious Program—Students 37.

ASHTABULA, ASHTABULA CO.

1—ST. JOSEPH (1862), [CEM] Rev. Philip Miller; Deacons Richard Johnson; Alan Prasek; Donald Johnson; Peter Olsen, Business Mgr.
Res.: 3330 Lake Ave., 44004. Tel: 440-992-0330; Fax: 440-993-3579.
Mission—Our Lady of Miracles (St. Joseph Mission) 4317 West Ave., Ashtabula Co. 44004. Tel: 440-997-7121.
Catechesis/Religious Program—Students 170.

2—MOTHER OF SORROWS (1890), (Irish—Finnish), [JC] Rev. Kevin Peters.
Res.: 1514 W. 6th St., 44004. Tel: 440-964-3277 (Office); Fax: 440-964-6780.
Catechesis/Religious Program—Students 123.

3—OUR LADY OF MT. CARMEL (1902), (Italian), Rev. Joseph Ruggieri; Sr. Laurie Divoky, S.N.D., Pastoral Min.
Res.: 1200 E. 21st St., 44004. Tel: 440-998-4111; Fax: 440-998-7829.
Catechesis/Religious Program—Students 130.

AURORA, PORTAGE CO., OUR LADY OF PERPETUAL HELP (1955), Rev. Joseph W. Witmer; Sisters Lu Haidnick, C.D.P., Pastoral Assoc.; Therese Ann Rich, O.S.U., Pastoral Assoc.; Deacon Joseph Pepoy.
Res.: 342 S. Chillicothe Rd., 44202-7814. Tel: 330-562-8519; Fax: 330-562-2529.
Catechesis/Religious Program—Dr. Thomas Brozich, D.R.E. Students 616.

BOARDMAN, MAHONING CO.

1—ST. CHARLES BORROMEO (1926), Revs. Daniel M. Venglarik; Maciej Mankowski; Deacon Michael A. Kocjancic; Paul Hershey, Business Mgr.; Sue Heher, Pastoral Assoc.; Linda O'Brien, Pastoral Assoc.
Res.: 7345 Westview Dr., 44512. Tel: 330-758-2325; Fax: 330-758-2004.
School—7325 Westview Dr., 44512. Tel: 330-758-6689; Fax: 330-758-7404. Sr. Mary Alyce Koval, O.S.U., Prin. Sisters 1; Lay Teachers 31; Students 580.
Catechesis/Religious Program—Tel: 330-758-8063. Mrs. Judy Magielski, D.R.E. Students 948.
Convent—7515 Oregon Tr., 44512. Tel: 330-758-2396.

2—ST. LUKE (1962), Revs. Joseph A. Fata; Richard A. Brobst; Deacon Richard Milanek.
Res.: 5235 South Ave., 44512. Tel: 330-782-9783; Fax: 330-782-1574.
School—Tel: 330-782-4060; Fax: 330-782-4842. Lay Teachers 12; Students 174.
Catechesis/Religious Program—Students 169.

BREWSTER, STARK CO., ST. THERESE (1928), [JC] Rev. Robert W. Kaylor, Admin.
Res.: 456 Wabash Ave. S., 44613. Tel: 330-767-3622; Fax: 330-478-6086.
Catechesis/Religious Program—Students 60.

CAMPBELL, MAHONING CO.

1—ST. JOHN THE BAPTIST (1919), (Slovak), [CEM] Revs. Michael Swierz; Howard Ziemba; Deacon Ronald J. Bunofsky.
Res.: 159 Reed Ave., 44405. Tel: 330-755-4141; Fax: 330-755-1022.
Catechesis/Religious Program—Tel: 330-755-1367. Marge O'Malley, D.R.E. Students 32.

2—ST. JOSEPH THE PROVIDER (1919), (Polish), Revs. Michael Swierz; Howard Ziemba.
Res.: 633 Porter Ave., 44405. Tel: 330-755-0266; Fax: 330-755-1988.
School—Tel: 330-755-4747; Fax: 330-755-4749. Lay Teachers 9; Students 128.
Catechesis/Religious Program—Tel: 330-747-4085; Fax: 330-747-8647.

3—ST. LUCY (1937), (Italian), Rev. Msgr. John P. Ashton, Ph.D.
Res.: 394 Tenney Ave., 44405-1695. Tel: 330-755-4132.
Catechesis/Religious Program—Tel: 330-755-1367. Students 72.

CANAL FULTON, STARK CO., SS. PHILIP AND JAMES (1845), [CEM] Rev. John Warner.
Res.: 412 High St., 44614. Tel: 330-854-2332; Fax: 330-854-2599.
School—Tel: 330-854-2823; Fax: 330-854-1109. Sharon Parrish, Prin. Lay Teachers 12; Students 221.
Catechesis/Religious Program—Tel: 330-854-3988. Students 160.

CANFIELD, MAHONING CO., ST. MICHAEL (1952), Rev. Terrence J. Hazel; Sr. Brendan Sherlock O.S.U., Pastoral Min.; Deacon Tom Soich; Mrs. Barbara Spencer, Pastoral Min.; Mrs. Lori Pugh, Pastoral Min.
Res.: 281 Glenview Dr., 44406. Tel: 330-533-6839; Fax: 330-702-0432. Email: info@stmichaelcanfield.org. Web: www.stmichaelcanfield.org.
Catechesis/Religious Program—Tel: 330-533-5275. Jim Merhaut, D.R.E. Students 728.

CANTON, STARK CO.

1—ALL SAINTS (1920), (Polish—Hispanic), Rev. Thomas G. Bishop, Admin.
Res.: 1386 Henry Ave., S.W., 44706. Tel: 330-453-6429; Fax: 330-453-2071.
Catechesis/Religious Program—Tel: 330-452-9539; 330-453-9722 (Hispanic Ministry); Fax: 330-452-4870. Mary Lou Vega, D.R.E.; Nazario Mendoza, Coord. Hispanic Min. Students 38.

2—ST. ANTHONY (1908), (Italian), Rev. Thomas G. Bishop.
Res.: 1530 11th St., S.E., 44707. Tel: 330-452-9539; Fax: 330-452-4870.
Catechesis/Religious Program—Students 190.

3—ST. BENEDICT (1923), Rev. John E. Zuzik
Res.: 2207 Third St., S.E., 44707. Tel: 330-452-0751; Fax: 330-452-7299.
Benedict Center—Tel: 330-453-3642.
Church: E. Tuscarawas St. & Girard Ave., S.E., 44707.
Catechesis/Religious Program—Students 89.

4—ST. JOAN OF ARC (1944), Revs. Thomas P. Dyer; Osward Mbendi Murungi, A.J. (Kenya); Deacon David Conversino. In Res., Rev. Msgr. John J. Daum (Retired).
Res.: 4940 Tuscarawas St. W., 44708-5012. Tel: 330-477-6796; 330-477-6797; Fax: 330-477-0594.
School—120 Bordner Ave., S.W., 44710. Tel: 330-477-2972; Fax: 330-478-2606. Lay Teachers 24; Students 435.
Catechesis/Religious Program—166 Bordner Ave., S.W., 44710. Students 323.

5—ST. JOHN THE BAPTIST (1823), [CEM] Rev. Ronald M. Klingler; Deacon Carl Burkhardt.
Res.: 627 McKinley Ave., N.W., 44703. Tel: 330-454-8044; Fax: 330-454-1397.
Catechesis/Religious Program—Tel: 330-453-5418. Students 96.

6—ST. JOSEPH (1902), Rev. Msgr. Frank A. Carfagna; Rev. Edward L. Beneleit; Deacon Wilbur J. Bagley.
Res.: 2427 W. Tuscarawas St., 44708. Tel: 330-453-2526.
School—126 Columbus Ave., N.W., 44708. Tel: 330-454-9737; Fax: 330-454-9866. Lay Teachers 15; Students 208.
Catechesis/Religious Program—Tel: 330-454-2144. Students 100.

7—ST. MARY (1899), Rev. Gerald J. Sommer, M.S.C.
Res.: 1602 Market Ave. S., 44707. Tel: 330-453-2110; Fax: 330-453-4008.
Catechesis/Religious Program—Students 110.

8—ST. MICHAEL THE ARCHANGEL (1952), Revs. Bradford N. Helman; Joseph Zamary; Sisters Carol McHenry, S.N.D., Pastoral Assoc.; Dorothy Fuchs, S.N.D., Pastoral Assoc.; Deacon Peter P. Pohl; Mrs. Faith Wackerly, Pastoral Assoc.; Mrs. Mary Germain, Parish Admin.; Miss Emily Niese, Youth Min.
Res.: 3430 St. Michael Blvd., N.W., 44718. Tel: 330-492-3119; Fax: 330-492-0339.
School—3431 St. Michael's Blvd., N.W., 44718. Tel: 330-492-2657; Fax: 330-492-9618. Mrs. Sally Roden, Prin. Sisters 1; Lay Teachers 26; Students 518.
Catechesis/Religious Program—Tel: 330-492-2034. Mr. Michael Ress, D.R.E. Students 595.

9—OUR LADY OF PEACE (1952), Rev. John Hentwick.
Res.: 833 39th St., N.W., 44709. Tel: 330-492-0757; Fax: 330-492-1214.
School—1001 39th St., N.W., 44709. Tel: 330-492-0622; Fax: 330-492-0959. Lay Teachers 28; Students 340.
Catechesis/Religious Program—Tel: 330-492-0929. Students 156.

10—ST. PAUL (1907), [JC] Rev. Joseph Gleixner, M.S.C., Admin.
Res.: 1459 Superior Ave., N.E., 44705. Tel: 330-456-7555; Fax 330-452-7716.
Catechesis/Religious Program—Students 44.

11—ST. PETER (1845), [CEM] Rev. Msgr. John C. Finnigan; Deacon Robert Klein.
Res.: 726 Cleveland Ave., N.W., 44702. Tel: 330-453-8493; Fax 330-453-8083.
School—702 Cleveland Ave., N.W., 44702. Tel: 330-452-0125; Fax: 330-456-8606. Sisters of Notre Dame 1; Lay Teachers 10; Students 186
Catechesis/Religious Program—Students 169.

12—SACRED HEART (1922), (Slovak), Rev. William Shipe; Deacon Edward Briestensky.
Res.: 1620 Clark Ave., S.W., 44706. Tel: 330-453-1028.

CHAMPION, TRUMBULL CO., ST. WILLIAM (1963), Rev. Michael J. Smar; Sr. Mary Cora Skrivan, S.N.D., D.R.E.
Res.: 5411 Mahoning Ave., N.W., Warren, 44483. Tel: 330-847-8677.
Catechesis/Religious Program—Tel: 330-847-8627. Students 164.

COLUMBIANA, COLUMBIANA CO., ST. JUDE (1966), Rev. Thomas G. Ziegler.
Res.: 180 7th St., 44408. Tel: 330-482-2351; Fax: 330-482-0993.
Catechesis/Religious Program—Tel: 330-482-2888. Ms. Mary Glasser, D.R.E. Students 262.

CONNEAUT, ASHTABULA CO.

1—ST. FRANCES CABRINI (1954), [JC] Rev. Raymond J. Thomas.
Res.: 744 Mill St., P.O. Box 619, 44030. Tel: 440-599-8570; Fax: 440-593-6772.
School—(Grades PreK-PreK) Tel: 440-593-1677; Fax: 440-599-9576.
Catechesis/Religious Program—Students 89.

2—ST. MARY'S (1888), [CEM] [JC] Rev. Raymond J. Thomas.
Res.: 480 State St., P.O. Box 619, 44030. Tel: 440-599-8855; Fax: 440-593-6772.
Catechesis/Religious Program—Tel: 440-599-8570. Students 89.

CORTLAND, TRUMBULL CO., ST. ROBERT BELLARMINE PARISH (1952), [CEM] Rev. Carl Kish.
Res.: 4659 Niles-Cortland Rd., N.E., 44410. Tel: 330-637-4886; Fax: 330-637-0608.
Catechesis/Religious Program—Students 500.

DUNGANNON, COLUMBIANA CO., ST. PHILIP NERI (1817), [CEM] Rev. John P. Tully.
Mailing Address: P.O. Box 309, Hanoverton, 44423-0309.
Office & Res.: 16017 Smith Rd., Summitville, 43962. Tel: 330-223-1871.
Church: 11328 Gavers Rd., 44423. Tel: 330-223-1973.

EAST LIVERPOOL, COLUMBIANA CO.

1—ST. ALOYSIUS (1838), (Irish), [CEM] Rev. Bernard N. Gaeta.
Res.: 235 W. 5th St., 43920. Tel: 330-385-7131; Fax: 330-385-3025.
School—335 W. 5th St., 43920. Tel: 330-385-5963; Fax: 330-385-6455. Lay Teachers 11; Students 137.
Catechesis/Religious Program—Tel: 330-385-6472. Students 73.

2—ST. ANN (1915), Rev. George J. Balasko.
Res.: 1506 Pennsylvania Ave., 43920. Tel: 330-385-5582; Fax: 330-386-5246.

EAST PALESTINE, COLUMBIANA CO., OUR LADY OF LOURDES (1880), [CEM] Rev. Msgr. Dezso Torok, Pastor Emeritus; Rev. Daniel Cipar.
Res.: 200 E. Main St., 44413. Tel: 330-426-9346; Fax: 330-426-9846.
Catechesis/Religious Program—20 N. James St., 44413. Tel: 330-426-2254. Students 117.

GARRETTSVILLE, PORTAGE CO., ST. AMBROSE (1944), Rev. Richard J. Pentello; Deacon Robert Rapp.
Res.: 10692 Freedom St., 44231. Tel: 330-527-4105; Fax: 330-527-2500.
Catechesis/Religious Program—Students 123.

GENEVA, ASHTABULA CO., ASSUMPTION B.V.M. (1915), Rev. Paul R. Tobin.
Res.: 594 W. Main St., 44041. Tel: 440-466-3427; Fax: 440-466-4670.
School—Tel: 440-466-2104. Deacon Michael Cahill, Prin. Lay Teachers 10; Students 134.
Catechesis/Religious Program—Students 150.

GIRARD, TRUMBULL CO., ST. ROSE (1892), Rev. Msgr. Martin S. Susko; Rev. Peter Haladej; Deacons Paul Milligan; Matthew W. Shelton.
Res.: 48 E. Main St., 44420. Tel: 330-545-4351; Fax: 330-545-0119.
School—65 E. Main St., 44420. Tel: 330-545-1163. Sr. Patricia Yacucci, Prin. Sisters 1; Lay Teachers 18; Students 310.
Catechesis/Religious Program—Tel: 216-545-1216. Sam Rose, D.R.E. Students 390.

HUBBARD, TRUMBULL CO., ST. PATRICK (1869), [CEM] Revs. Timothy H. O'Neill; Robert M. Miller; John A. Murray (Retired); Robert Friedman.
Mailing Address & Res.: 225 N. Main St., 44425. Tel: 330-534-1928; Fax: 330-534-0820.
School—38 E. Water St., 44425. Tel: 330-534-2509; Fax: 330-534-0305. Lay Teachers 15; Students 196.
Catechesis/Religious Program—225 N. Main St., 44425. Tel: 330-534-8304. Karen Bartos, D.R.E. Students 440.

JEFFERSON, ASHTABULA CO., ST. JOSEPH CALASANCTIUS (1858), Rev. Stephen M. Wassie.
Res.: 32 E. Jefferson St., 44047. Tel: 440-576-3651.
Catechesis/Religious Program—Tel: 440-576-3339. Students 120.

KENT, PORTAGE CO.

1—IMMACULATE HEART OF MARY (1953), Rev. John M.

Jerek.
Res.: 1424 Horning Rd., 44240. Tel: 330-678-0240; Fax: 330-678-7780.
Catechesis/Religious Program—Students 80.
2—ST. PATRICK'S (1864), [JC] Deacon Timothy DeFrange.
Res.: 313 N. Depeyster St., 44240. Tel: 330-673-5849; Fax: 330-673-5849.
School—127 Portage St., 44240. Tel: 330-673-7232; Fax: 330-678-6612. Lay Teachers 21; Students 338.
Catechesis/Religious Program—Tel: 330-677-4453. Students 230.
KINGSVILLE, ASHTABULA CO., ST. ANDREW (1936), [CEM] Rev. Stephen Wassie, Admin.
Res.: 3700 Rte. 193, 44048. Tel: 440-224-0987 (Church).
Catechesis/Religious Program—Students 66.
KINSMAN, TRUMBULL CO., ST. PATRICK (1957), Attended by, Our Lady of Victory, Andover. Rev. David L. Misbrener.
Mailing Address: 6397 State Rte. 87, N.E., 44428. Tel: 440-293-6218; Fax: 440-293-7778.
Res.: 481 S. Main St., P.O. Box 669, 44003-9778.
Catechesis/Religious Program—Students 35.
LAKE MILTON, MAHONING CO., ST. CATHERINE (1956), Rev. David W. Merzweiler.
Res.: 1254 Grandview Rd., 44429-9542. Tel: 330-654-4001.
Catechesis/Religious Program—Sr. Janice Kusick, O.S.U., D.R.E. Students 41.
LEETONIA, COLUMBIANA CO., ST. PATRICK (1861), [CEM] Rev. Edward R. Brienz, Admin.
Res.: 167 W. Main St., P.O. Box 67, East Palestine, 44431. Tel: 330-427-6577; Fax: 330-427-6573.
Catechesis/Religious Program—Students 34.
LISBON, COLUMBIANA CO., ST. GEORGE (1820), Rev. Robert Edwards.
Res.: 271 W. Chestnut St., 44432. Tel: 330-424-7648.
Catechesis/Religious Program—Tel: 330-424-0109. Students 80.
Mission—St. Agatha, Tel: 330-424-0155.
LOUISVILLE, STARK CO.
1—ST. LOUIS (1838), (French—German), [CEM] Revs. Kenneth E. Miller; Homer G. Oliver.
Res.: 300 N. Chapel St., 44641. Tel: 330-875-1658; Fax: 330-875-1657.
School—Tel: 330-875-1467; Fax: 330-875-2511. Lay Teachers 12; Students 128.
Catechesis/Religious Program—Students 260.
2—SACRED HEART OF MARY (1833), [CEM] Rev. William B. Kraynak.
Res.: 8277 Nickelplate Ave., N.E., 44641. Tel: 330-875-2827; Fax: 330-875-5511.
School—8267 Nickelplate Ave., N.E., 44641. Tel: 330-875-5167; Fax: 330-875-2410. Jane Burgess, Prin. Lay Teachers 12; Students 97.
Catechesis/Religious Program—Tel: 330-875-7705. Students 60.
LOWELLVILLE, MAHONING CO., OUR LADY OF THE HOLY ROSARY (1867), [CEM] Rev. Gerald M. DeLucia.
Res.: 131 E. Wood St., 44436. Tel: 330-536-6436; Fax: 330-536-9188.
Catechesis/Religious Program—Students 186.
MANTUA, PORTAGE CO., ST. JOSEPH'S (1923), Rev. Michael D. Balash.
Res.: 11045 St. Joseph Blvd., 44255. Tel: 330-274-2114.
Parish Center—Tel: 330-274-2253; Fax: 330-274-2254.
School—Tel: 330-274-2268; Fax: 330-274-2412. Lay Teachers 16; Students 182.
Catechesis/Religious Program—Students 240.
MASSILLON, STARK CO.
1—ST. BARBARA (1867), (German), [CEM] Rev. Thomas Cebula; Mrs. Marcia Popovich, Pastoral Assoc.
Res.: 2813 Lincoln Way, N.W., 44647. Tel: 330-833-6898; Fax: 330-833-5164.
School—2825 Lincoln Way, N.W., 44647. Tel: 330-833-9510; Fax: 330-833-3297. Sisters 1; Lay Teachers 10; Students 181; Preschool Children 17.
Catechesis/Religious Program—Students 115.
2—ST. JOSEPH (1863), [CEM] Rev. Raymond L. Paul; Deacons Steven A. Wyles; Donald F. Molinari.
Res.: 322 Third St., S.E., 44646. Tel: 330-833-2607.
Parish Center and Office—330 Fourth St., S.E., 44646. Tel: 330-833-4907; 330-833-6088; Fax: 330-833-3907.
Catechesis/Religious Program—Students 155.
3—SAINT MARY (1839), [CEM] Revs. A. Edward Gretchko; James Johnson, S.P.; Deacons Edwards Kurkas; Joseph Fries.
Parish Office—726 1st St., N.E., 44646. Tel: 330-833-8501; Fax: 330-833-3359.
Res.: 206 Cherry Rd., N.E., 44646.
School—640 First St., N.E., 44646. Tel: 330-832-9355; Fax: 330-832-9030. Sisters 1; Lay Teachers 19; Students 350.
Catechesis/Religious Program—Tel: 330-832-5719; Fax: 330-832-9020. Students 178.
MASURY, TRUMBULL CO., ST. BERNADETTE (1940), Rev. John Lody.
Res.: 7800 Locust St., 44438. Tel: 330-448-8015; Fax: 330-448-6653.
Catechesis/Religious Program—Brookfield Junior High, Brookfield. Tel: 330-448-3003. Students 57.
MAXIMO, STARK CO., ST. JOSEPH (1850), [CEM] Rev. Thomas Ungashick.
Res.: 12055 Easton St., N.E., P.O. Box 219, 44650. Tel: 330-823-7809.
Catechesis/Religious Program—Tel: 330-823-5233. Students 106.
MCDONALD, TRUMBULL CO., OUR LADY OF PERPETUAL HELP (1943), Rev. Daniel J. Kulesa.
Res.: 618 Ohio Ave., 44437. Tel: 330-530-6929; Fax: 330-530-2488.
Catechesis/Religious Program—601 Indiana Ave., 44437. Tel: 330-530-1111. Students 205.
MIDDLEBRANCH, STARK CO., ST. THERESE LITTLE FLOWER (1929), Revs. Kevin L. Fete; Edward F. Varble, Pastor Emeritus (Retired); Mr. David R. Schmidt, Pastoral Assoc.
Res.: 2040 Diamond St., N.E., North Canton, 44720. Tel: 330-494-2759; Fax: 330-494-2536.
Catechesis/Religious Program—Students 302.
MINERAL RIDGE, TRUMBULL CO., ST. MARY (1870), [CEM] Rev. Richard Murphy.
Res.: 3504 Main St., 44440. Tel: 330-652-7761; Fax: 330-652-7765.
Catechesis/Religious Program—Students 103.
NAVARRE, STARK CO., ST. CLEMENT (1830), [CEM] Rev. Robert G. Gibas.
Res.: 216 Wooster St. E., 44662. Tel: 330-879-5900; Fax: 330-879-5138.
School—Tel: 330-879-2645; Fax: 330-879-3242. Lay Teachers 9; Students 131.
Catechesis/Religious Program—Students 40.
NEW MIDDLETOWN, MAHONING CO., ST. PAUL THE APOSTLE (1952), [JC] Rev. Nicholas R. Shori.
Res.: 10143 Main St., P.O. Box 515, 44442. Tel: 330-542-3466; Fax: 330-542-2448.
Catechesis/Religious Program—Tel: 330-542-3824. Students 389.
NEWTON FALLS, TRUMBULL CO.
1—ST. JOSEPH (1923), (Slovak), [CEM] Rev. John P. Madden.
Res.: 131 W. Quarry St., 44444-1560. Tel: 330-872-5742; Fax: 330-872-5744.
School—Tel: 330-872-7676; Fax: 330-872-1013. Students 211.
Catechesis/Religious Program—Tel: 330-872-9947. Students 177.
2—ST. MARY (1928), (Polish), [JC] Rev. John P. Madden.
Res.: 131 West Quarry St., 44444. Tel: 330-872-5742; Fax: 330-872-5744.
Catechesis/Religious Program—Tel: 330-872-9947. Students 16.
NILES, TRUMBULL CO.
1—OUR LADY OF MT. CARMEL (1907), (Italian), Revs. Lawrence Frient; John D. Mulqueen.
Res.: 381 Robbins Ave., 44446. Tel: 330-652-5825; Fax: 330-544-1872.
School—Tel: 330-652-5547; Fax: 330-652-1921. Sisters 1; Lay Teachers 10; Students 170.
Catechesis/Religious Program—Students 181.
2—ST. STEPHEN (1853), [CEM] Rev. John H. Gubser.
Res.: 129 W. Park Ave., 44446. Tel: 330-652-4396; Fax: 330-652-9317.
School—(Grades PreK-8), 45 S. Chestnut, 44446. Tel: 330-652-5511; Fax: 330-652-4264. Lay Teachers 14; Students 182; Preschool 65.
Catechesis/Religious Program—Students 150.
NORTH CANTON, STARK CO., ST. PAUL (1845), [CEM] Rev. Msgr. James A. Clarke; Revs. James E. McKarns (Retired); Donald J. Oser (Retired); Thomas J. Kraszewski; Judy Piero, Pastoral Min.; Deacons William Lambert; Ron Reolfi; Ron Reolfi, Business Admin.
Res.: 241 S. Main St., 44720. Tel: 330-499-2201; Fax: 330-499-8106.
School—303 S. Main St., 44720. Tel: 330-494-0223; Fax: 330-494-3226. Jackie Zufall, Prin. Lay Teachers 21; Students 417.
Catechesis/Religious Program—Tel: 330-494-4036. Kathy Weber, D.R.E. Students 621.
NORTH JACKSON, MAHONING CO., ST. JAMES PARISH FAMILY (1943), Rev. David W. Merzweiler.
Mailing & Office Address: 50 Rosemont Rd., 44451. Tel: 330-538-2602.
Res.: 1254 Grandview Rd., Lake Milton, 44429. Tel: 330-654-4001.
Catechesis/Religious Program—Sr. Janice Kusick, O.S.U. Students 107.
ORWELL, ASHTABULA CO., ST. MARY (1922), [CEM] Rev. Gregory F. Fedor.
Res.: 103 N. Maple, Box 217, 44076. Tel: 440-437-6262; Fax: 440-437-8216.
Catechesis/Religious Program—Tel: 440-437-8216. Students 103.
POLAND, MAHONING CO., HOLY FAMILY (1956), Rev. Msgr. William J. Connell; Rev. Benson Claret Okpara (Nigeria); Deacon Ray Hatala.
Res.: 2729 Center Rd., 44514. Tel: 330-757-1545; Fax: 330-757-4443.
School—Tel: 330-757-3713; Fax: 330-757-7648. Sisters 1; Lay Teachers 24; Students 316.
Catechesis/Religious Program—Students 542.
RANDOLPH TOWNSHIP, PORTAGE CO., ST. JOSEPH (1831), [CEM] Rev. Edward R. Wieczorek; Deacons James White; Steven Gies.
Res.: 2643 Waterloo Rd., Mogadore, 44260. Tel: 330-628-9941; Fax: 330-628-9942.
School—Tel: 330-628-9555. Lay Teachers 10; Students 194.
Catechesis/Religious Program—Tel: 330-628-4844. Linda Shaw, D.R.E. Students 269.
RAVENNA, PORTAGE CO., IMMACULATE CONCEPTION (1854), [CEM] Revs. John-Michael Lavelle; Kevin McCaffrey; Sr. Julia Baluch, Pastoral Min.; Deacon Russell J. Brode.
Res.: 409 W. Main St., 44266. Tel: 330-296-6434; Fax: 330-296-9193.
School—225 S. Sycamore St., 44266. Tel: 330-296-4817; Fax: 330-296-2925. Lay Teachers 6; Students 71.
Catechesis/Religious Program—Tel: 330-296-4549. Students 277.
ROCK CREEK, ASHTABULA CO., SACRED HEART (1956), [JC] Rev. Gregory F. Fedor; Deacon John D. Pallo.
Office: 3409 SR 45, P.O. Box 310, 44084. Tel: 440-563-3010.
Catechesis/Religious Program—Tel: 440-563-5253. Students 60.
ROOTSTOWN, PORTAGE CO., ST. PETER OF THE FIELDS (1868), [CEM] Rev. Thomas J. Crum; Sr. Regina Zeleznik, S.N.D., Pastoral Min.; Deacon Thomas Shay.
Res.: 3487 Old Forge Rd., 44272. Tel: 330-325-7543.
Catechesis/Religious Program—Students 194.
SALEM, COLUMBIANA CO., ST. PAUL (1881), Rev. Thomas Eisweirth; Donna Lynn, Pastoral Assoc.; Amanda Raymond, Pastoral Assoc. In Res., Rev. Thomas McCarthy.
Res.: 157 Ohio Ave., 44460. Tel: 330-332-0336; Fax: 330-332-7982.
Parish Administration Center—935 E. State St., 44460.
School—925 E. State St., 44460. Tel: 330-337-3451; Fax: 330-337-3452. Lay Teachers 12; Students 151.
Catechesis/Religious Program—Joan Reedy, D.R.E.; Donna Dermotta, D.R.E.; Sondra O'Donnell, Youth Min. Students 248.
SALINEVILLE, COLUMBIANA CO., ST. PATRICK (1873), [CEM] Rev. John P. Tully.
Mailing Address: P.O. Box 309, Hanoverton, 44423-0309.
Office & Res.: 16017 Smith St., Summitville, 43962. Tel: 330-223-1871.
Church: 611 Jefferson St., 43945.
Catechesis/Religious Program—Students 3.
SEBRING, MAHONING CO., ST. ANN (1908), Rev. Leo Wehrlin; Deacon Ralph Chase.
Res.: 323 S. 15th St., 44672. Tel: 330-938-2033; Fax: 330-938-2033.
Catechesis/Religious Program—Students 90.
STREETSBORO, PORTAGE CO., ST. JOAN OF ARC (1965), Rev. Pat Ferraro; Deacon John F. Carney.
Res.: 8894 State Rte. 14, 44241. Tel: 330-626-3424; Fax: 330-626-3422.
Catechesis/Religious Program—Tel: 330-626-2050. Students 267.
STRUTHERS, MAHONING CO.
1—HOLY TRINITY (1907), (Slovak), Rev. William Petrunak, Admin.
Res.: 250 N. Bridge St., 44471. Tel: 330-755-2115; Fax: 330-750-9431.
Catechesis/Religious Program—Tel: 330-755-4133. Students 32.
2—ST. NICHOLAS (1865), Revs. Philip E. Rogers; Martin Celuch; Deacons John Terranova; Paul Lisko; Mrs. Rita DeFrance, Pastoral Min.
Res.: 775 5th St., 44471-1795. Tel: 330-750-2555.
Parish Office—764 5th St., 44471-1704. Tel: 330-755-9819; Fax: 330-755-9949.
School—762 5th St., 44471-1704. Tel: 330-755-2128. Lay Teachers 17; Students 215.
Catechesis/Religious Program—Tel: 330-755-6245. Miss Stephanie Tarajack, D.R.E. Students 400.
SUMMITVILLE, COLUMBIANA CO., ST. JOHN (1846), [CEM] Rev. John P. Tully.
Mailing Address: P.O. Box 309, Hanoverton, 44423-0309.
Office & Res.: 16017 Smith Rd., 43962. Tel: 330-223-1871.
Catechesis/Religious Program—Students 49.
UNIONTOWN, STARK CO., HOLY SPIRIT (1979), Rev. John Zapp.
Res.: 2952 Edison St., N.W., 44685. Tel: 330-699-4500; Fax: 330-699-9270.
Catechesis/Religious Program—Students 261.
VIENNA, TRUMBULL CO.
1—QUEEN OF THE HOLY ROSARY (1997), Rev. Joseph R. Valentine, F.S.S.P.

Res.: 291 Scoville Dr., 44473. Tel: 330-856-4204; Fax: 330-856-9587.
Catechesis/Religious Program—Students 56.
2—St. Vincent de Paul (1879), Rev. Frank L. Zanni.
Res.: 4453 Warren-Sharon Rd., 44473. Tel: 330-394-2461; Fax: 330-609-0320.
Catechesis/Religious Program—Tel: 330-394-2361. Students 170.
Warren, Trumbull Co.
1—Blessed Sacrament (1959), Rev. Donald E. King.
Res.: 3020 Reeves Rd., N.E., 44483. Tel: 330-372-2215; Fax: 330-372-6380.
School—Notre Dame, (Grades PreK-3), 3000 Reeves Rd., N.E., 44483. Tel: 330-372-2375; Fax: 330-372-2465. Mrs. Theresa A. Dolan-Dixon, Prin. Queen of All Saints Building Lay Teachers 14; Students 207.
Catechesis/Religious Program—Tel: 330-372-6930. Students 502.
2—Christ Our King (1951), Rev. Frederick Lukehart.
Res.: 1000 Tod Ave., S.W., 44485. Tel: 330-395-3747; Fax: 330-395-1631.
Catechesis/Religious Program—Tel: 330-395-3737. Students 21.
3—SS. Cyril and Methodius (1928), (Slovak), Rev. James P. Walker.
Res.: 185 Laird Ave., N.E., 44483. Tel: 330-393-9766; Fax: 330-393-0555.
Catechesis/Religious Program—Tel: 330-393-0781. Students 64.
4—St. James (1947), Rev. Charles W. Crumbley.
Res.: 2532 Burton St., S.E., 44484. Tel: 330-369-3518; Fax: 330-369-2761.
School—Queen of Angels Building, (Grades 4-5) 44484. Tel: 330-369-4218; Fax: 330-369-2541. Lay Teachers 10; Students 112.
School—Notre Dame Queen of Peace, (Grades 5-8), 261 Elm Rd., 44483. Tel: 330-399-5154; Fax: 330-399-2499. Mrs. Kathleen Victor, Prin.
Catechesis/Religious Program—2106 Arbor St., S.E., 44484. Tel: 330-369-3518. Sr. Immaculata Pavlik, V.S.C., D.R.E. Students 95.
5—St. Joseph (1928), (Polish), [CEM] Rev. Fred E. Trucksis.
Res.: 1346 Vernon St., N.W., 44483. Tel: 330-393-0226; Fax: 330-393-4764.
Catechesis/Religious Program—Students 39.
6—St. Mary (1835), [CEM] Rev. Bernard R. Schmalzried.
Res.: 232 Seneca St., N.E., 44481. Tel: 330-393-8721; 330-394-3426.
Catechesis/Religious Program—Students 83.
7—St. Pius X (1959), Rev. William J. Loveless.
Res.: 1401 Moncrest Ave., N.W., 44485. Tel: 330-399-8881; 330-399-8882; Fax: 330-399-1361.
School—Notre Dame System, (Grades PreK-3) Tel: 330-399-5411; Fax: 330-399-7364. Mary Jo Dugan, Prin. Lay Teachers 10; Students 106.
Catechesis/Religious Program—Tel: 330-394-4343. Students 48.
Waynesburg, Stark Co., St. James (1928), Rev. Michael D. Seifert.
Res.: 400 W. Lisbon St., 44688. Tel: 330-866-9449; Fax: 330-866-1750.
School—Tel: 330-866-9556; Fax: 330-866-4075. Lay Teachers 84.
Catechesis/Religious Program—Tel: 330-866-9449. Students 78.
Wellsville, Columbiana Co., Immaculate Conception (1842), [CEM] Rev. Bernard N. Gaeta; Mary E. Frost, Business Mgr.
Res.: 1021 Riverside Ave., 43968. Tel: 330-532-3445; Fax: 330-532-3445.
Catechesis/Religious Program—Tel: 330-532-2382. Mr. Robert Barto, D.R.E. Students 96.
Windham, Portage Co., St. Michael's (1943), Rev. James Paul Lang.
Res.: 9736 E. Center St., 44288. Tel: 330-326-3531.
Catechesis/Religious Program—Students 35.

On Duty Outside the Diocese:
Revs.—
Bonnot, Bernard R., Studio City, CA
Dailey, John, El Salvador, Central America
Deffenbaugh, Joseph T., Pensacola, FL
Nuzzi, Ronald, Notre Dame, IN

Military Chaplains:
Revs.—
Garvey, Michael, U.S. Navy
Mikstay, Michael, U.S. Marines

Absent on Leave:
Revs.—
Bliss, Dennis
Trimbur, John

Retired:
Rev. Msgrs.—
Adamko, Cyril A.
Daum, John J.
Kelly, Thomas F.
Kolp, James
Oliver, Homer G.
Reagan, Donald
Reidy, Robert
Ronik, Michael
Sabatino, Robert
Slaven, Frederick
Torok, Dezso
Revs.—
Bakos, Stephen
Bantz, William
Bruce, Robert J.
Cavanaugh, James K.
Chonko, Michael J.
Coccarelli, August
Curran, Gerald X.
Czaja, Joseph S.
Dobosiewicz, Leon W.
Duritsa, George M.
Esposito, Anthony
Fasline, Anthony
Forgach, Carl J.
Franko, George M.
Friedrich, Ralph
Gubser, Paul
Herttna, Matthew M.
Hill, Robert
Horvath, Stephen
Karas, Stephen
Lettau, David
Lyons, John F.
McKarns, James E.
Mintjal, Frank
Murphy, Thomas
Murray, John
Nachtigal, Fred
Nist, Arthur
O'Brien, James E.
O'Leary, Patrick D.
Oser, Donald
Pierce, Blaine F.
Platt, Stewart
Pleban, Leo
Rath, John G.
Santucci, Louis
Sargent, John
Slipski, William P.
Snock, Francis
Spitale, John
Summers, John
Tamburrini, Joseph
Varble, Edward F.
Willis, Nathan
Witt, William
Yablonsky, Gabriel

Permanent Deacons:
Arend, David H., St. George, Lisbon
Bagley, Wilbur J., St. Joseph, Canton
Beil, David C., St. Christine, Youngstown
Boccieri, Nicholas J., St. Anthony, Youngstown
Brechbill, Kenneth W., (Retired)
Briestensky, Edward L., Sacred Heart, Canton
Brode, Russell J., Immaculate Conception, Ravenna
Brown, James, St. Christine, Youngstown
Bunofsky, Ronald J., St. John, Campbell
Burkhardt, Carl R., St. John the Baptist, Canton
Carney, John F., St. Joan of Arc, Streetsboro
Centric, Louis, On Duty Outside the Diocese.
Chase, Ralph, St. Ann, Sebring
Colon, Felipe, St. Rose of Lima, Youngstown
Conversino, David, St. Joan of Arc, Canton
Cosentino, Louis A., St. Jude, Columbia
Coulter, Terry L., St. Jude, Columbiana
Cuttica, Robert J., St. Christine, Youngstown
DeFrange, Tim, St. Patrick, Kent
DiFrancesco, Salvatore, St. Matthias, Youngstown
Dubois, Bartley, St. William, Warren
Friedman, Robert J., St. Patrick, Hubbard
Fries, Joseph K., St. Mary, Massillon
Gies, Steven R., Immaculate Conception, Ravenna
Harvey, James G., St. William, Warren
Hatala, Ray H., Office of Permanent Diaconate
Hawkins, Edward, St. Patrick, Youngstown
Heinz, Edward, Sts. Peter and Paul, Youngstown
Ivan, Ellis C., Holy Spirit, Uniontown
Jaskiewicz, Albert F., St. Pius X, Warren
Johnson, Don, St. Joseph, Ashtabula
Johnson, Richard M., St. Joseph, Ashtabula
Klein, Robert E., St. Peter, Canton
Kocjancic, Michael A., St. Charles, Boardman
Krause, Harold R., (On Duty Outside the Diocese)
Kurkas, Edward G., St. Mary, Massillon
Lamar, Kevin T., St. Vincent dePaul, Vienna
Lambert, William H., St. Paul, North Canton
Layko, Ronald J., St. Christine, Youngstown
Lewis, David, St. James, Warren
Lisko, Paul, St. Nicholas, Struthers
Mastrovich, George, St. Ann, East Liverpool & Immaculate Conception, Wellsville
Medvez, Alvin A., St. Stephen, Youngstown
Milanek, Richard, St. Luke, Boardman
Milligan, Paul, St. Rose, Girard
Nohra, Joseph S., St. Maron & Mt. Carmel, Youngstown
O'Neill, Russell, Holy Spirit, Uniontown
Pallo, John D., Sacred Heart, Rock Creek
Pasko, Lawrence, St. Patrick, Leetonia
Pepoy, Joseph E., Our Lady of Perpetual Help, Aurora
Pfleger, James W., (On Duty Outside the Diocese)
Pohl, Peter P., SS. Philip & James, Canal Fulton
Prasek, Alan, St. Joseph, Ashtabula
Rapp, Robert, St. Ambrose, Garrettsville
Rentas, John, St. Rose of Lima, Youngstown
Reolfi, Ron, St. Paul, North Canton
Roberts, Michael R., Jr., St. Joseph, Austintown
Rohr, Thomas J., SS. Philip & James, Canal Fulton
Schlais, Michael, St. Stanislaus, Youngstown
Shay, Thomas R., Sr., St. Peter of the Fields, Rootstown
Sherwood, Ronald D., St. Benedict, Canton
Smith, James, St. Edward, Youngstown
Soich, Thomas G., St. Michael, Canfield
Terranova, John, St. Nicholas, Struthers
Toth, Joseph P., Blessed Sacrament, Warren
White, James A., St. Joseph, Randolph
Williams, Don, Our Lady of Peace, Canton
Wyles, Steve, St. Joseph, Massillon

INSTITUTIONS LOCATED IN THE DIOCESE

[A] SEMINARIES, RELIGIOUS, OR SCHOLASTICATES

Canfield. *Society of St. Paul*, 9531 Akron-Canfield Rd., P.O. Box 595, 44406. Tel: 330-533-5503; 330-533-1076; Fax: 330-533-1076. Email: paultheapostle@msn.com. Web: www.albahouse.org. Revs. Matthew Roehrig, S.S.P., Supr.; Thomas Fogarty, S.S.P.; Jeffrey Mickler, S.S.P.; Arthur Palisada, S.S.P.; Francis J. Parella, S.S.P.; Angelo Y. Sye, S.S.P.; Bros. Luke Bedard, S.S.P.; Dismas Beique, S.S.P.; Richard Brunner, S.S.P.; Dominic Calabro, S.S.P.; Paschal Duesman, S.S.P.; Peter Scalise, S.S.P.; Joshua Seidl, S.S.P. Priests 6; Brothers 7; Total Staff 13.

[B] COLLEGES AND UNIVERSITIES

North Canton. *Walsh University* (Coed) , 2020 Easton St., N.W., 44720-3396. Tel: 330-490-7090; Fax: 330-490-7165. Email: admissions@walsh.edu. Web: www.walsh.edu. Rev. Msgr. Lew Gaetano, Ph.D., Dir. Campus Min.; Richard Jusseaume, Pres.; Mr. Dale Howard, Vice Pres. for Student Affairs; Brett Freshour, Dean Enrollment Mgmt.; John Wray, Vice Pres. Business & Finance; Joanne Matika, Vice Pres. Devel. & Univ. Rels. Brothers of Christian Instruction Priests 2; Brothers 8; Lay Teachers 67; Total Staff 211; Students 1,801.

[C] HIGH SCHOOLS, DIOCESAN

Youngstown. *Cardinal Mooney High School*, 2545 Erie St., 44507. Tel: 330-788-5007; Fax: 330-788-4511. Email: jmkudlacz@aol.com. Web: www.cardinalmooney.com. Sr. Jane Marie Kudlacz, H.M., Prin. Sisters 1; Lay Teachers 44; Students 575.
Ursuline High School, 750 Wick Ave., 44505. Tel: 330-744-4563; Fax: 330-744-3358. Email: ygnursuline@doy.org. Web: www.ursuline.com. Patricia Fleming, Prin. Priests 1; Sisters 2; Lay Teachers 33; Students 495.

Ashtabula. *SS. John & Paul School*, (Grades 7-12) , St. John High School Building , 541 W. 34th St., 44004. Tel: 440-997-5531; Fax: 440-998-1661. Email: ssjp@knownet.net. Web: www.knownet.net/users/ssjp. Miss Albina Larson, Prin. Lay Teachers 14; Students 188.

Canton. *Central Catholic High*, 4824 Tuscarawas St. W., 44708-5198. Tel: 330-478-2131; Fax: 330-478-6086. Email: rkaylor@crusader.stark.k12.oh.us. Web: www.cchsweb.com. Rev. Robert W. Kaylor, Prin.; Mr. John Korecki, Asst. Prin.; Mr. Leo DeMatteis, Dean of Students; Mr. James Naegeli, Campus Ministry Dir. Priests 1; Lay Teachers 47; Total Staff 48; Students 615.

Louisville. *St. Thomas Aquinas High School*, 2121 Reno Dr., N.E., 44641. Tel: 330-875-1631; Fax: 330-875-8469. Web: www.aquinas-knights.com. Rev. Thomas P. Dyer, Prin.; Mr. Joseph Vagedes, Vice Prin.; Miss Cindi Eby, Dir. of Student Svcs. Lay Teachers 30; Religious 2; Total Staff 50; Students 413.

WARREN. *John F. Kennedy High School* Girard-Niles-Youngtown. , 2550 Central Pkwy., S.E., 44484. Tel: 330-369-1804; Fax: 330-369-1125. Email: firstclass@doy.org. Web: www.warrenjfk.com. Rev. William Petrunak, Chap.; Mrs. June Drennen, Prin.; Mr. James Boyle, Asst. Prin. Priests 1; Lay Teachers 28; Students 407.

[D] ELEMETARY SCHOOLS, DIOCESAN

ASHTABULA. *SS. John & Paul School*, (Grades K-6) , Our Lady of Mt. Carmel Building , 2150 Columbus Ave., 44004. Tel: 440-997-5821; Fax: 440-998-0514. Email: thomas.thornton@neomin.org. Web: www.knownet.net/users/ssjp. Lay Teachers 8; Students 175.
Consolidated school for Mother of Sorrows, St. Joseph & Our Lady of Mt. Carmel. Mr. Thomas Thornton, Prin.

[E] MIDDLE SCHOOLS, DIOCESAN

WARREN. *Notre Dame School* Queen of Peace Building , 261 Elm Rd., N.E., 44483. Tel: 330-399-5154; Fax: 330-399-2499. Email: ygnpeace@firstclass.com. Sr. Judith Anne Sabau, S.N.D., Prin.; Thomas L. Shilling, Vice Prin. Sisters 1; Lay Teachers 18; Students 160.

[F] PRIVATE SCHOOLS

CANFIELD. *Ursuline Preschool & Kindergarten*, 4300 Shields Rd., 44406. Tel: 330-792-4150; Fax: 330-792-9553. Sr. Jan Gier, O.S.U., Dir. & Prin. Ursuline Sisters 1; Lay Teachers 7; Students 295.

[G] GENERAL HOSPITALS

YOUNGSTOWN. *Humility of Mary Health Partners, St. Elizabeth Health Center*, 1044 Belmont Ave., Box 1790, 44501. Tel: 330-746-7211; Fax: 330-480-7974. Web: www.hmpartners.org. Mr. Robert W. Shroder, Pres. & CEO; James R. Davis, Exec. Vice Pres., HMHP; COO, SEHC. Sisters of the Humility of Mary 3; Bed Capacity 580; Bassinets 60; Patients Assisted Annually 327,397; Total Staff 2,756.

CANTON. **CSAHS/UHHS - Canton, Inc.,*, Mercy Medical Center, 1320 Mercy Dr., N.W., 44708. Tel: 330-489-1000; Fax: 330-489-1312. Email: mail@cantonmercy.com. Web: www.thequalityhospital.com. Thomas Cecconi, Pres. & CEO. Bed Capacity 475; Bassinets 48; Total assisted annually 0; 605,544; Total Staff 2,460.

WARREN. *Humility of Mary Health Partners, HM Hospice*, 2460 Elm Rd., 44483. Tel: 330-372-0259; Fax: 330-372-5035. Robert Shroder, Pres. & CEO; Rodney Carnifax, Dir. Home Care. Patients Assisted Annually 3,000; Total Staff 120.

St. Joseph Health Center, 667 Eastland Ave., S.E., 44484. Tel: 330-841-4000; Fax: 330-841-4019. Web: www.hmpartners.org. Mr. Robert W. Shroder, Pres. & CEO; William A. Young, Sr. Vice Pres. & SJHC Admin.; Rev. George Popovich, Chap. Sisters of the Humility of Mary 4; Bed capacity 202; Bassinets 17; Patients Assisted Annually 160,607; Total Staff 852.

[H] SPECIAL CARE FACILITIES

NORTH LIMA. *The Assumption Village*, 9800 Market St., 44452. Tel: 330-549-0740; Fax: 330-549-0701. Rocco Parro, Dir.; Lisa Peretto, R.N., Dir. Nursing. Sponsorship: Sisters of the Humility of Mary, Member: Catholic Healthcare Partners.; Special Care Unit for residents with Alzheimer's or Dementia; Skilled Nursing Unit with Subacute Care Program; Intermediate Care. Residents 282; Total Staff 73; Assisted Living Residents 63; Assisted Living Total Staff 196.

[I] HOMES FOR AGED

AUSTINTOWN. *Humility House*, 755 Ohltown Rd., 44515. Tel: 330-505-0144; Fax: 330-544-5694. Warren Harris, Vice Pres. Long Term Care. Total Staff 127; Nursing Home Beds 70; Assisted Living Apartments 32; Total Assisted 206.

CANTON. *House of Loreto*, 2812 Harvard Ave., N.W., 44709. Tel: 330-453-8137; Fax: 330-453-8140. Email: marysacres@aol.com. Sisters Gladys Spengler, C.D.S., Exec. Dir.; Claire Batterson, C.D.S., Admin. Administered by the Congregation of the Divine Spirit. Sisters of the Congregation of the Divine Spirit 18; Residents 50; Total Assisted 68; 71; Total Staff 61. In Res. Rev. Msgr. Homer C. DeWalt (E) (Retired); Rev. Norbert R. West.

HUBBARD. *Villa Maria Teresa*, 50 Warner Rd., 44425. Tel: 330-759-9329 (Villa); 330-875-4635 (Emmaus House); Fax: 330-759-7290. Email: jcoblate@aol.com. Web: www.oblatesister.org. Retired Priests' Residence. Villa Residents 5; Emmaus House Residents 3; Total Assisted 8; Total Staff 4.

LOUISVILLE. *Emmaus House*, 1515 California Ave., 44641. Tel: 330-875-4635. Email: rsacred@neo.rr.com. Rev. William B. Kraynak, Admin. Retired Priests' Residence. Residents 3; Total Staff 4.

St. Joseph Care Center, 2308 Reno Dr., 44641. Tel: 330-875-5562; Fax: 330-875-8947. Email: sjcc@neo.rr.com. Web: www.thealsatian.com. John T. Banks, Admin. Sisters of St. Joseph of St. Mark 4; Sisters of the Humility of Mary 1; Sisters of St. Joseph of the Third Order of St. Francis 1; Nursing Home 100; Assisted Living 40; Independent Living 66; Total Staff 210; Adult Day Care 25.

NORTH LIMA. *The Assumption Village*, 9800 Market St., 44452. Tel: 330-549-0740; Fax: 330-549-0701. Phyllis Anderson, Admin.; Lisa Peretti, R.N., Dir. Nursing. Sponsorship: Sisters of the Humility of Mary, Member: Catholic Healthcare Partners.; Skilled Nursing Unit with Subacute Care Program; Special Care Unit for residents with Alzheimer's or cognitive impairment Total Assisted 282; Total Staff 73.

[J] MONASTERIES AND RESIDENCES OF PRIESTS AND BROTHERS

YOUNGSTOWN. *Mt. Alverna Friary*, 517 S. Belle Vista Ave., 44509. Tel: 330-799-1888; Fax: 330-799-0723. Email: brvit@hotmail.com. Revs. Vit Fiala, O.F.M., Dir.; Jules Wong, O.F.M.; Bros. Reginald Antal, O.F.M.; Emery Kish, O.F.M.; James T. Welch II, O.F.M. Franciscan Friars Total in Residence 5; Total Staff 5.

[K] CONVENTS AND RESIDENCES FOR SISTERS

CANFIELD. *Motherhouse and Educational Center of the Ursuline Sisters*, 4250 Shields Rd., 44406. Tel: 330-792-7636; Fax: 330-792-9553. Email: admainosuyo@yahoo.com. Web: www.theursulines.org. Sr. Regina Rogers, O.S.U., Gen. Supr. Total in Community 62; Total in Residence 37; Total Staff 5.

Ursuline Center, 4280 Shields Rd., 44406. Tel: 330-799-4941; Fax: 330-792-9553.

CANTON. *Sancta Clara Monastery*, 4200 N. Market Ave., 44714. Tel: 330-492-1171; Fax: 330-492-2227. Email: sisters@poorclares.org. Web: www.poorclares.org. Rev. Nickolas Lohkamp, O.F.M., Chap.; Sr. Marion Zeltmann, Abbess. Poor Clares of Perpetual Adoration Cloistered Professed Nuns 7.

HUBBARD. *Villa Maria Teresa*, 50 Warner Rd., 44425. Tel: 330-759-9329; Fax: 330-759-7290. Email: jcoblate@aol.com. Web: www.oblatesister.org. Sr. Teresina Rosa, O.S.H.J., Regl. Supr. & Convent Supr. Novitiate and American Headquarters of Oblate Sisters of the Sacred Heart of Jesus Sisters 16; Total Staff 10.

[L] CATHOLIC CHARITIES SOCIAL SERVICE AGENCIES

YOUNGSTOWN. *Catholic Charities Housing Opportunities Corporation*, 225 Elm St., 44503. Tel: 330-744-4419; Fax: 330-744-3677. Email: ccho@cboss.com. Web: www.rc.net/youngstown.catholic_charities. Mr. Brian Corbin, Pres.; George Garchar, Exec. Dir. Purpose: Provides coordination, integration and leadership in the provisions of housing services which promote affordable housing in the community. Total Families Assisted 490; Total Staff 5.

Diocese of Youngstown Catholic Charities Corporation, 144 W. Wood. St., 44503. Tel: 330-744-8451; Fax: 330-742-6447. Email: charities@youngstowndiocese.org. Web: www.doy.org.

ASHTABULA. *Catholic Charities of Ashtabula County*, 4200 Park Ave., 3rd Floor, 44004. Tel: 440-992-2121; Fax: 440-992-5974. Email: ccac_cccs@alltel.net. Web: www.catholiccharitiesashtabula.org. Danita M. Eartly, Exec. Dir. Total Assisted 10,000; Total Staff 29.

CANTON. *Catholic Charities of Stark County*, 3112 Cleveland Ave., N.W., 44709. Tel: 330-491-0896; Fax: 330-491-1298. Email: ccstark@neo.rr.com. Sr. Edwardine Baznik, S.J.S.M., Exec. Dir. Total Assisted 3,500.

RAVENNA. *Catholic Charities of Portage County*, 206 W. Main St., 44266. Tel: 330-297-7745; Fax: 330-297-7763. Email: ccpc206@aol.com.

WARREN. *Catholic Charities Regional Agency*, P.O. Box 1740, 44482. Tel: 330-393-4254; Fax: 330-393-4050. Email: nancy-ccs@cboss.com. Nancy Voitus, Exec. Dir. Family and child welfare work in various social services and counseling in Mahoning, Trumbull and Columbiana Counties. Total Staff 120.

[M] HOMES FOR WOMEN

YOUNGSTOWN. *Beatitude House*, 287 Lora Ave., 44504. Tel: 330-744-3147; Fax: 330-744-3991. Email: beatitudehouse@juno.com. Web: www.beatitudehouseonline.org. Sr. Patricia McNicholas, O.S.U., Exec. Dir. Transitional housing, job preparation, job training, counseling, education and case management for economically disadvantaged women. Total Assisted 200; Total Staff 24.

[N] RETREAT HOUSES

YOUNGSTOWN. *Sacred Heart Retreat and Renewal Center*, 144 W. Wood St., 44503. 3128 Logan Way, 44501. Tel: 330-759-9539; Fax: 330-759-8235. Email: MSCYNG@aol.com. Society of the Missionaries of the Sacred Heart Total Staff 3.

[O] NEWMAN CENTERS

YOUNGSTOWN. *Newman Center at Youngstown State University* 254 Madison Ave., 44504-1627. Tel: 330-747-9202; Fax: 330-747-1667. Email: usunewmancenter@sbcglobal.net. Web: www.ysu.edu/newmancenter/. Total Staff 2.

KENT. *Kent State University Newman Center* 1424 Horning Rd., 44240. Tel: 330-678-0240; Fax: 330-678-7780. Email: jjerek@kent.edu. Web: dept.kent.edu/newman. Rev. John M. Jerek; Mrs. Carmen Roebke, Pastoral & Campus Min. Total in Residence 1; Total Staff 4.

[P] MISCELLANEOUS LISTINGS

YOUNGSTOWN. *Caritas Communities*, 225 Elm St., 44503. Tel: 330-744-4419; 330-384-1555; Fax: 330-744-3677. Email: ccho@cboss.com. Web: www.rc.net/youngstown/catholic_charities. George Garchar, Pres. & CEO; Ken Radigan, Chm. As a member of Corporation of Catholic Charities Housing Opportunities and the Humility of Mary Housing Program, Caritas Communities will serve as Property Management Corporation for low income and special needs housing. Families Assisted 154; Total Staff 5.

"The Catholic Exponent", P.O. Box 6787, 44501-6787. Tel: 330-744-5251; Fax: 330-744-5252. Email: exponent@cboss.com. Web: www.doy.org.

Declaration of Trust of Trumbull, Department of Education,144 W. Wood St., 44503. Tel: 330-744-8451; Fax: 330-742-6448. Email: mskube@doy.org. County Catholic School Endowment Fund.

St. Elizabeth Development Foundation, 1044 Belmont Ave., P.O. Box 1790, 44501-1790. Tel: 330-480-3349; Fax: 330-480-2957. Email: edward_toth@hmis.org. Web: www.hmpartners.org. Edward R. Toth Jr., Pres. & CEO. Total Staff 2.

Humility of Mary Information Systems, Inc., 250 Federal Plaza E., 2nd Fl., 44503. Tel: 330-884-6603; Fax: 330-746-6824. Email: chuck_folkwein@hmis.org. Web: www.hmpartners.org. Chuck Folkwein, Senior Vice Pres. & CIO.

Roman Catholic Diocese of Youngstown Foundation, Inc., 144 W. Wood St., 44503. Tel: 330-744-8451; Fax: 330-744-2848. Mr. Robert A. Hoffman, CFO.

Roman Catholic Diocese of Youngstown Property Corporation, 144 W. Wood St., 44503. Tel: 330-744-8451; Fax: 330-744-2848. Mr. Robert A. Hoffman, CFO.

CANFIELD. *The Ursuline Center*, 4280 Shields Rd., 44406. Tel: 330-799-4941; Fax: 330-792-9553. Email: ursulinecenter@aol.com. Web: www.theursulines.org. Resource and outreach services for the poor, including prison ministry, AIDS ministry, retreats, water therapy, adult formation, speech and hearing services, school of music, massage therapy, college courses, preschool, and kindergarten. Total Assisted 25,000; Sisters 12; Total Staff 20.

CANTON. *CSA Mercy Ministries*, 3114 Cleveland Ave., N.W., 44709. Tel: 216-696-5560. Web: www.csahealthsystem.org. Sr. Judith Ann Karam, C.S.J., Pres. & CEO.

Sisters of Charity Foundation of Canton, Unizan Plaza, Ste. 310, 220 Market Ave. S., 44702. Tel: 330-454-5800; Fax: 330-454-5909. Email: vconley@scfcanton.org. Web: www.scfcanton.org. Victoria Conley, Exec. Dir.

LOUISVILLE. *St. Thomas Aquinas High School Endowment Fund*, 2121 Reno Drive, N.E., 44641. Tel: 330-875-1631; Fax: 330-875-8469. Rev. Thomas P. Dyer, Pres.; Victoria Frustaci, Business Mgr.

MASSILLON. *National Shrine of St. Dymphna* (1938), 3000 Erie St. S., P.O. Box 4, 44648-0004. Tel: 330-833-8478; Fax: 330-833-5193. Rev. Matthew M. Herttna, Chap. & Dir. (Retired). Located on the grounds of Heartland Behavioral Healthcare.

WARREN. *St. Joseph Development Foundation*, 667 Eastland Ave., S.E., 44484. Tel: 330-841-4198; Fax: 330-841-4019. Email: edward_toth@hmis.org. Web: www.hmpartners.org. Edward R. Toth Jr., Pres. & CEO. Total Staff 2.

[Q] DIOCESAN CEMETERIES

YOUNGSTOWN. *Calvary*, 248 S. Belle Vista Ave., 44509.
Catholic Cemeteries of the Diocese of Youngstown, 144 W. Wood St., 44503. Tel: 330-744-8451; Fax: 330-742-6448. Rev. Msgr. Frank A. Carfagna, Dir.
Resurrection, 300 N. Racoon Rd., 44515. Tel: 330-799-1900.

CORTLAND. *All Souls*, 3823 Hoagland Blackstub Rd., 44410. Tel: 330-637-2761.

MASSILLON. *Calvary*, 3469 Lincoln Way E., 44647.

RELIGIOUS INSTITUTES OF MEN REPRESENTED IN THE DIOCESE

For further details refer to the corresponding bracketed number in the Religious Institutes of Men or Women section.

[0320]—*Brothers of Christian Instruction*—F.I.C.
[]—*Congregation of the Apostles of Jesus*—A.J.
[0520]—*Franciscan Friars* (Immaculate Conception Prov. of New York)—O.F.M.
[]—*Franciscans-Province of St. John the Baptist*—O.F.M.
[1110]—*Missionaries of the Sacred Heart*—M.S.C.
[0430]—*Order of Preachers (Dominicans)* (Prov. of St. Joseph)—O.P.
[1020]—*Pauline Fathers and Brothers*—S.S.P.
[1065]—*Priestly Fraternity of St. Peter*—F.S.S.P.
[1230]—*Servants of the Paraclete*—S.P.

RELIGIOUS INSTITUTES OF WOMEN REPRESENTED IN THE DIOCESE

[0100]—*Adorers of the Blood of Christ*—A.S.C.
[]—*Antonine Sisters*—A.S.
[]—*Benediction Sisters (Byzantine Sisters)*—O.S.B.
[1040]—*Congregation of the Divine Spirit*—C.D.S.
[1710]—*Congregation of the Third Order of St. Francis of Mary Immaculate, Joliet, IL*—O.S.F.
[1070-28]—*Dominican Sisters*—O.P.
[]—*Little Sisters of Mary Immaculate*
[3050]—*Oblate Sisters of the Sacred Heart of Jesus*—O.S.H.J.
[]—*Order of St. Benedict*
[3210]—*Poor Clares of Perpetual Adoration*—P.C.P.A.
[0580]—*Sisters of Charity of St. Augustine*—C.S.A.
[0990]—*Sisters of Divine Providence*—C.D.P.
[2990]—*Sisters of Notre Dame*—S.N.D.
[]—*Sisters of Our Lady of Kilimanjaro*
[]—*Sisters of St. Francis of Millvale*—O.S.F.
[3830-08]—*Sisters of St. Joseph*—C.S.J.
[3910]—*Sisters of St. Joseph of St. Mark*—S.J.S.M.
[]—*Sisters of St. Joseph of the Third Order of St. Francis*—S.S.J.-T.O.S.F.
[2110]—*Sisters of the Humility of Mary*—H.M.
[3730]—*Sisters of the Order of St. Basil the Great*—O.S.B.M.
[]—*Ursuline Sisters of Cleveland*—O.S.U.
[4120-07]—*Ursuline Sisters of Youngstown*—O.S.U.
[4160]—*Vincentian Sisters of Charity*—V.S.C.

NECROLOGY

† Kenney, Rev. Msgr. Timothy, Kent, OH St. Patrick—Died March 23, 2003
† Radetic, Rev. Msgr. Branimir—Died Feb. 15, 2003
† Barrett, Robert P.—Died March 17, 2003
† Kaminski, Sylvester, (Retired)—Died July 26, 2003
† Schmidt, John W.—Died Feb. 10, 2003
† Spisak, Thomas M., Warren, OH St. Mary—Died Feb. 20, 2003

Apostolate to Hungarians

Most Reverend

ATTILA MIKLOSHAZY, S.J., S.T.D.

Titular Bishop of Castel Minore and Bishop for the Spiritual Assistance to the Hungarian Emigrant People; ordained June 18, 1961; appointed August 12, 1989; consecrated November 4, 1989 *Res.: St. Augustine's Seminary*, 2661 Kingston Rd., Scarborough ON M1M 1M3 Canada. Tel: 416-261-7207; Fax: 416-261-2529.

ESTABLISHED MAY 20, 1983.

The Apostolate of the Bishop of Hungarians living outside of Hungary extends territorially to all the Hungarian communities existing outside of Hungary. The main purpose of the Apostolate is to give spiritual assistance to them through and in cooperation with the local ordinary and pastors.

Former Bishop—Most Rev. LADISLAUS A. IRANYI, Sch.P., ord. March 13, 1938; appt. May 20, 1983; consecrated July 27, 1983; died March 6, 1987.

Bishop's Office—2661 Kingston Rd., Scarborough ON M1M 1M3 Canada. Tel: 416-261-7202; Fax: 416-261-2529.

Delegate of the Bishop in Europe—Rev. FERENC CSERHATI, Ung.Kath.Delegatur, Landwehrst.66, D-80336, Munchen, Germany. Tel: 49-89-532-8288; Fax: 49-89-532-8245.

Delegate of the Bishop in the U.S.A.—Rev. STEPHEN N. MUSTOS, Sch.P., 223 Third St., Passaic, NJ 07055. Tel: 973-779-0332; Fax: 973-778-4263.

American Hungarian Catholic Priests' Association—East Coast Division: Rev. STEPHEN N. MUSTOS, Sch.P., 223 Third St., Passaic, NJ 07055. Tel: 973-779-0332; Fax: 973-778-4263. Middle East Division:: Rev. BARNABAS G. KISS, O.F.M., 8423 South St., Detroit, MI 48209. Tel: 313-842-1133; Fax: 313-842-2773.

Hungarian Catholic League of America, Inc.—Rev. Msgr. WILLIAM I. VARSANYI, P.A., Chm., One Cathedral Sq., Providence, RI 02903. Tel: 401-278-4520; Fax: 401-278-4548.

Hungarian Priests' Association in Canada—Rev. CSABA CABAFI, S.J., 432 Sheppard Ave. E., Toronto ON M2N 3B7 Canada. Tel: 416-225-3300; Fax: 416-225-3814.

Newspapers & Magazines—Rev. FERENC CSERHATI, Editor, Landwehrstrasse 66, D-80336, Munchen 2, Germany. Tel: 49-89-532-8288; Fax: 49-89-532-8245. "Eletunk" (Our Life)

"HIS- Press Service"— published by the Hungarian Institute for Sociology of Religion. Rev. EMERIC ANDRAS, S.J., Editor, Gerlgasse 10/3, A-1030, Wien, Austria. Tel: 43-1-798-0233; Fax: 43-1-798-4181.

"Tavlatok"— (Perspectives), Quarterly on Worldview, Spirituality and Culture, ed. by the Unio Cleri Hungarici. Revs. FERENC SZABO, S.J.; FERENC NAGY, S.J., Sodras u. 13, H-1026, Budapest, Hungary. Tel: 36-1-176-7062; Fax: 36-1-275-0269.

"A Sziv"— (Sacred Heart Messenger), monthly, published by the Hungarian Jesuit Fathers. Rev. VERTESALJAI LASILO, S.J., Editor, Pf. 586, H-1398, Budapest, Hungary. Tel: 36-1-176-7062; Fax: 36-1-275-0269. Address in Canada, 432 Sheppard Ave. E., Toronto ON M2N 3B7 Canada.

INSTITUTIONS LOCATED IN THE DIOCESE

STATISTICS

Most personnel and institutions are under the jurisdiction of their local ordinaries.

NECROLOGY

Incorporated in diocesan and archdiocesan listings.

Apostolate For Lithuanian Catholics

Living Outside Lithuania

Reverend Monsignor

EDMUND PUTRIMAS, J.C.L.

Delegate of the Lithuanian Bishops Conference appointed August 19, 2003 to coordinate the pastoral care of Lithuanian Catholics living outside of Lithuania *Office: 1 Resurrection Rd., Toronto ON M9A 5G1 Canada*. Tel: 416-233-7819; Fax: 416-233-5765. Email: uzsielovadas@rogers.com.

Most Reverend

PAUL A. BALTAKIS, O.F.M.

Former Bishop For Lithuanian Catholics; ordained August 24, 1952; appointed Titular Bishop of Egara and Bishop for Spiritual Assistance of Lithuanian Catholics June 1, 1984; cons. Sept. 14, 1984; retired July 12, 2003 *Res.: 64-14 Clinton Ave., Maspeth, NY 11378*. Tel: 718-326-3199; Fax: 718-326-5206. Email: lcra@earthlink.net.

ESTABLISHED JUNE 1, 1984.

The Apostolate for Lithuanian Catholics, extends worldwide to all Lithuanian communities existing outside Lithuania. Seventy-five percent of them in the U.S.A. The purpose of the apostolate is to give spiritual assistance to them in cooperation with the local ordinaries and pastors.

(VACANT SEE)

Email: lcra@earthlink.net

Former Lithuanian Bishops—Most Revs. VINCENTAS BRIZGYS, Ph.D., J.C.D., cons. May 19, 1940; Titular Bishop of Bosana; Auxiliary Bishop of Kaunas, Lithuania (Impeditus); died April 23, 1992; ANTANAS DEKSNYS, Ph.D., cons. Jan. 15, 1969; Titular Bishop of Lavello; died May 5, 1999; PAUL A. BALTAKIS, O.F.M. ordained Aug. 24, 1952; appt. Titular Bishop of Egara and Bishop of Spiritual Assistance of Lithuanian Catholics in diaspora June 1, 1984; cons. Sept. 14, 1984; retired July 12, 2003.

Office of General Counsel—SAULIUS V. KUPRYS, 150 S. Wacker Dr., Ste. 1050, Chicago, IL 60606. Tel: 312-346-5275; Fax: 312-346-5640. Email: viskas@aol.com.

Lithuanian R. Catholic Priests' League of Canada—Rev. AGUSTINAS SIMANAVICIUS, O.F.M., Pres., 1 Resurrection Rd., Toronto M9A 5G1 Canada. Tel: 416-533-0621; Fax: 416-532-4816.

Lithuanian R. Catholic Priests' League of America—Rev. Msgr. ALBERT CONTONS, Pres., P.O. Box 1025, Humarock, MA 02047. Tel: 781-834-4079.

Lithuanian Franciscan Province of St. Casimir—Very Rev. PLACIDAS BARIUS, O.F.M., Delegate, Kennebunkport, ME 04046. Tel: 207-967-2031; Fax: 207-967-5721.

Lithuanian Jesuit Province—Very Rev ANTANAS GRAZULIS, S.J., Delegate, 2345 W. 56th St., Chicago, IL 60636. Tel: 773-737-8400.

Lithuanian Marian Province of St. Casimir—Very Rev. DONALD PETRAITIS, M.I.C., Prov., 6336 Kilbourn Ave., Chicago, IL 60636. Tel: 773-582-8191.

Pontifical Lithuanian College of St. Casimir—Rev. Msgr. ALGIMANTAS BARTKUS, J.C.L., Rector, via Casalmonferrato 20, Rome 00182 Italy Tel: 06-70-24-908; Fax: 06-70-11-659.

Sisters of the Immaculate Conception of the Blessed Virgin Mary—Sr. PAULE SAVICKAITE, Prov., Rte. 21, R.D. 2, Putnam, CT 06260. Tel: 860-928-7955; Fax: 860-928-1930.

Poor Sisters of Jesus Crucified and the Sorrowful Mother—Sr. MARY J. VALLERE, Supr Gen., 261 Thatcher St., Brockton, MA 02402. Tel: 617-588-5070.

Sisters of St. Casimir—Sr. IMMACULATA WENDT, Gen. Supr., 2601 W. Marquette Rd., Chicago, IL 60609. Tel: 773-776-1324.

Sisters of St. Francis—Sr. JOAN BRAZINSKI, Dir., 3603 McRoberts Rd., Pittsburgh, PA 15234. Tel: 412-882-9911.

**Lithuanian R. Catholic Religious Aid, Inc.*—Most Rev. PAUL A. BALTAKIS, O.F.M., Pres.; Mrs. VIDA JANKAUSKAS, Mgr., 64-25 Perry Ave., Maspeth, 11378. Tel: 718-326-5202; Fax: 718-326-5206. Email: lcra@earthlink.net.

Lithuanian American R. Catholic Federation—Youth Camp, 15100 Austin Rd., Manchester, MI 48158.

Lithuanian Roman Catholic Charities, Inc.—4545 W. 63rd St., Chicago, IL 60629.

Publications— Darbininkas (Brooklyn, NY); Draugas (Chicago, IL); The Observer (Chicago, IL); Teviskes Ziburiai (Toronto, Ontario, Canada); Teviskes Aidai (Adelaide, Australia)

INSTITUTIONS LOCATED IN THE DIOCESE

[A] SCHOOLS

CHICAGO. *Maria High School*
THOMPSON. *Marionapolis Prep School*

[B] HOSPITALS

CHICAGO. *Holy Cross Hospital*

[C] NURSING HOMES AND HOMES FOR THE AGED

BROCKTON. *St. Joseph Manor Nursing Home*
ELMHURST. *St. Mary's Villa*
HOLLAND. *St. Joseph Nursing Home*
LEMONT. *Holy Family Villa*
PUTNAM. *Maulaitis Nursing Home*

[D] MISCELLANEOUS

CHICAGO. *Catholic Action Fund*
Jesuit Lithuanian Center
Lithuanian Roman Catholic Charities, 4545 W. 63rd St., IL 60629.
Matulaitis Institute

MANCHESTER. *Lithuanian American R. Catholic Federation Youth Camp*, 15100 Austin Rd., MI 48158.
PUTNAM. *American Lithuanian Catholic Archives*
WEST BRATTLEBORO. *Camp Neringa*

[E] CEMETERIES

CHICAGO. *St. Casimir Lithuanian*

RELIGIOUS INSTITUTES OF MEN REPRESENTED IN THE DIOCESE

For further details refer to the corresponding bracketed number in the Religious Institutes of Men or Women section.

[]—*Congregation of the Marians Province of St. Casimir* (Chicago, IL)

[]—*Franciscan Fathers of the Lithuanian Province of St. Casimir* (Kennebunkport, ME)

[]—*Jesuit Fathers of Della Strada* (Chicago, IL)

RELIGIOUS INSTITUTES OF WOMEN REPRESENTED IN THE DIOCESE

[3240]—*Poor Sisters of Jesus Crucified and the Sorrowful Mother* (Brockton, MA)—C.J.C.

[2140]—*Sisters of Immaculate Conception of the Blessed Virgin Mary* (Putnam, CT)

[3740]—*Sisters of St. Casimir* (Chicago, IL)—S.S.C.

[1690]—*Sisters of St. Francis* (Pittsburgh, PA)—O.S.F.

STATISTICS

Most personnel and institutions are under the jurisdiction of their local ordinaries.

NECROLOGY

(No Deaths)

Personal Prelatures

Personal prelatures are jurisdictional structures of a secular type which are established by the Holy See as an instrument within the hierarchical pastoral work of the Church to carry out special pastoral or missionary tasks. Personal prelatures are based on the principle of insertion into the local Church. In this they differ essentially from the personal dioceses, such as those constituted for the faithful of a particular rite, which are based on the principle of independence or autonomy in regard to local Churches.

Vatican II provided for setting up personal prelatures (see Decree, Presbyterorum ordinis, no. 10). Additional norms were established in subsequent pontifical legislation (see Motu proprio Ecclesiae Sanctae no. 1, no. 4, August 6, 1966 and the Apostolic Constitution Regimini Ecclesiae Universae, no. 49, no. 1, Aug. 15, 1967). General legislation concerning personal prelatures is contained in canons 294 to 297 of the 1983 Code of Canon Law.

Personal prelatures are to be established by the Holy See after hearing the views of the respective Episcopal Conferences (can. 294). They are governed by a Prelate according to statutes given by the Holy See. The Prelate is their proper Ordinary, who may incardinate priests and must look after their spiritual and temporal welfare (can. 295). Lay people can dedicate themselves by means of a contractual agreement, to the apostolic activities of the prelature; the statutes are to specify the manner of this organic cooperation (can. 296). And the statutes are also to determine the relations of the prelature with the Ordinaries of the places in which the prelature works, with the prior consent of the Ordinaries (can. 297).

Eastern Church

Eastern Catholic Association (ECA)

The Eastern Catholic Associates is the association of all Eastern Catholic Bishops in the United States. All Eastern Catholic Bishops, diocesan bishops (and their equivalent in law) and auxiliaries are members. The Association represents the Armenian, Chaldean, Maronite Melkite, Romanian, Ruthenian and Ukrainian Churches. The Syriac, Syro-Malabar and Russian churches are also represented but without a bishop member since they presently have no established hierarchy in the United States. Officers of the Association are—President: Most Rev. Nicholas J. Samra, D.D., V.G., Auxiliary Bishop of Newton, 8525 Cole, Warren MI 48093-5239. Tel: 810-558-0143; Fax: 810-558-0144. Vice President: Most Rev. Robert M. Moskal, D.D., Bishop of the Ukrainian Diocese of St. Josaphat in Parma, 5720 State Rd., Parma, OH 44134-7180. Tel: 216-888-1522; Fax: 216-888-3477. Secretary: Most Rev. John Botean, Bishop of Romanian Catholic Diocese of St. George, Canton, 1121 44th St., N.E., Canton, OH 44714-1297. Tel: 330-492-4086; Fax: 330-493-1416.

Religious Education Department

The ECA has established the ECDD - The Eastern Catholic Conference of Diocesan Directors of Religious Education which oversees, through God With Us Publications, all publications of catechetical materials published by it and used in Eastern Catholic Churches, mainly of Byzantine tradition. Rev. John S. Kachuba, M.A., Chm.-ECDD & Dir.-Religious Education, Eparchy of Parma, 532 Lloyd R., Euclid, OH 44132. Tel: 216-732-7292; Fax: 216-732-9434. Rev. Fred Saato, Asst. Chm./Dir.-Publications & Dir.-Education Services, Eparchy of Newton, 27 Lake Ave., Yonkers, NY 10703. Tel: 914-968-2428; Fax: 914-423-9239. Sr. Ann Laszok, O.S.B.M., Treas. & Bus. Mgr.-ECDD, 204 Olivia St., McKeesrocks, PA 15136. Tel: 412-481-9778; Fax: 412-331-8140. God With Us Publications, P.O. Box 99203, Pittsburgh, PA 15233. Tel: 412-771-9119; Fax: 412-766-8244.

In addition to the Eastern Churches listed below there are other Eastern Churches in communion with Rome which do not have Ordinaries of their own in the United States. Consequently they are under the jurisdiction of the local Ordinary and the various parishes and institutions are incorporated in the Archdiocesan and Diocesan listings. Please consult these pages for full information regarding churches, personnel and statistics. For convenience, however, listed below are the Russian Eastern Churches and the cities in which they are located.

RUSSIAN

California

El Segundo (LA), St. Andrew

San Francisco (SFR), Our Lady of Fatima Center

New York

New York (NY), St. Michael Chapel (St. Patrick's Old Cathedral)

U.S. Territorial Sees

Dioceses located on territory of the United States of America, but are members of episcopal conferences other than the United States Conference of Catholic Bishops.

Personal Prelatures

Personal Prelatures

PRELATURE OF OPUS DEI
(Praelatura Sanctae Crucis et Operis Dei)

Most Reverend

JAVIER ECHEVARRIA, J.D., J.C.D.

Prelate of the Prelature of the Holy Cross and Opus Dei; ordained August 7, 1955; appointed April 20, 1994; episcopal ordination January 6, 1995. *Curia of the Prelature, Viale Bruno Buozzi 73, 00197, Rome, Italy. Tel: 39-06-808-961.*

Erected by the Apostolic Constitution, "Ut sit," on November 28, 1982 by Pope John Paul II.

Opus Dei was founded on October 2, 1928 by Saint Josemaria Escriva, to spread in all sectors of society a profound awareness of the universal call to sanctity in ordinary life and, more specifically, in the exercise of one's work.

Curia of the Prelature—Viale Bruno Buozzi, 73, 00197. Rome, Italy. Tel: 39-06-808-961.

Vicar General—Rev. Msgr. Fernando Ocariz, Ph.D., S.T.D., *Viale Bruno Buozzi 73, 00197. Rome, Italy.*

Regional Vicar for the United States—Very Rev. Thomas G. Bohlin, Ph.D., S.T.D., *139 East 34th St., New York, NY 10016.* Tel: 646-742-2700.

Vicar for the Midwest—Very Rev. Peter V. Armenio, B.S., Ph.D., *5800 N. Keating Ave., Chicago, IL 60646.* Tel: 312-283-5800. Embracing the states of Illinois, Indiana, Missouri and Wisconsin.

Vicar for California—Very Rev. John R. Meyers, D.D.S., S.T.D., *765 14th Ave., San Francisco, CA 94118.* Tel: 415-386-0431.

Vicar for Texas—Very Rev. Gerald S. Kolf, B.S., M.B.A., S.T.D., *5505 Chaucer Dr., Houston, TX 77005.* Tel: 715-523-4351.

Represented in the Archdioceses of Boston, Chicago, Los Angeles, Milwaukee, Newark, New York, St. Louis, San Antonio, San Francisco, Washington and in the Dioceses of Burlington, Dallas, Fort Wayne-South Bend, Galveston-Houston, Gary, Oakland, Palm Beach, Peoria, Pittsburgh, Providence, Trenton and Victoria.

Regional Vicar for Puerto Rico—Very Rev. Vicente Ariza, Ph.D., *35 A St., Villa Caparra, Guaynabo, P.R. 00966.* Tel: 787-781-9123.

Represented in the Archdiocese of San Juan and the Dioceses of Mayaguez and Ponce.

CHAPLAINS FOR THE UNITED STATES

State of New York

New Rochelle—Revs. Bradley K. Arturi; Martin Heneghan. *99 Overlook Circle, New Rochelle, NY 10804.* Tel: 914-235-0199.

New York—Very Rev. Thomas G. Bohlin, Reg. Vicar; Very Rev. Arne A. Panula, Ph.D., S.T.D.; Rev. Msgr. Javier Garcia de Cardenas; Revs. James Albrecht; Robert Brisson. *139 East 34th St., New York, NY 10016.* Tel: 646-742-2700; Rev. Malcolm M. Kennedy. *330 Riverside Dr., New York, NY 10025.* Tel: 212-222-3285.

District of Columbia

Washington—Revs. William H. Stetson; Lawrence A. Kutz; C. John McCloskey, III. *2301 Wyoming Ave. N.W., Washington, DC 20008.* Tel: 202-234-1567; Revs. Gregory Coyne; Paul D. Kaiss. *4300 Garrison St. N.W., Washington, DC 20016.* Tel: 202-362-2419; Rev. Ronald S. Gillis, *4955 Linnean Ave., N.W., Washington, DC 20008.* Tel: 202-237-6894.

State of Massachusetts

Cambridge—Revs. Deo G. Rosales; David J. Cavanagh. *25 Follen St., Cambridge, MA 02138.* Tel: 617-354-3204.

Chestnut Hill—Revs. Raphael F. Caamano; Richard W. Rieman; José P. Ruisanchez; Alvaro Silva (in res., St. Patrick, Duxbury, MA). *481 Hammond St., Chestnut Hill, MA 02167.* Tel: 617-738-7348.

State of New Jersey

Princeton—Rev. Juan Velez. *34 Mercer St., Princeton, NJ 08540.* Tel: 609-497-9448.

South Orange—Rev. Robert A. Connor. *170 Montrose Ave., South Orange, NJ 07079.* Tel: 201-763-8397.

State of Pennsylvania

Pittsburgh—Revs. Rene J. Schatteman; Martin J. Miller. *5090 Warwick Ter., Pittsburgh, PA 15213.* Tel: 412-683-8448.

State of Florida

Delray Beach—Rev. Christopher Schmitt., *4409 Frances Dr., Delray Beach, FL 33445.* Tel: 305-498-1249.

Miami—Revs. Salvador S. Vahi; Orestes Gonzalez., *4415 S.W. 88th Ave., Miami, FL 33165.* Tel 305-551-7965.

State of Rhode Island

Providence—Rev. George A. Crafts, *224 Bowen St., Providence, RI 02906.* Tel: 401-272-7834.

State of Illinois

Chicago—Very Rev. Peter V. Armenio, Ph.D., Vicar for the Midwest; Revs. John C. Agnew; Edward G. Maristany; Frank J. Hoffman. *5800 N. Keating Ave., Chicago, IL 60646.* Tel: 312-283-5800; Rev. Joseph P. Landauer. *7225 N. Greenview Ave., Chicago IL 60646.* Tel: 312-465-3486; Revs. John P. Debicki; Hilary F. Mahaney; Charles Ferrer; Fred M. Piegl. *1825 N. Wood St., Chicago, IL 60622.* Tel: 312-278 2644.

Oak Park—Revs. Richard L. Schendt; James Socias; Martin J. Miller. *829 S. Euclid, Oak Park IL 60304.* Tel: 708-383-0928.

Urbana—Rev G. Barry Cole. *715 W. Michigan, Urbana, IL 61801.* Tel: 217-367-6650.

State of Indiana

South Bend—Rev. Mark S. Mannion, *1121 N. Notre Dame Ave., South Bend, IN 46617.* Tel: 219-232-0550.

State of Missouri

Kirkwood—Revs. Michael E. Giesler; John J. Alvarez. *100 E. Essex Ave., Kirkwood, MO 63122.* Tel: 314-821-1608.

State of Wisconsin

Brookfield—Revs. Timothy J. Uhen; John Kubeck. *12900 W. North Ave., Brookfield, WI 53005.* Tel: 414-784-1523.

State of California

San Francisco—Very Rev. John R. Meyer, D.D.S., S.T.D., Vicar for California; Rev Msgr. James A. Kelly; Rev. Jerome L. Jung. *765 14th Ave., San Francisco, CA 94118.* Tel: 415-386-0431.

Menlo Park—Rev. Torlach C. Delargy. *1160 Santa Cruz Ave., Menlo Park, CA 94025.* Tel: 415-32*-1675.

Mill Valley—Rev. William G. Shaughnessy. *108 Kipling Dr., Mill Valley, CA 94941.* Tel: 415-388-4531.

Los Angeles—Revs. Paul A. Donlon; John E. Waiss. *655 Levering Ave., Los Angeles, CA 90024.* Tel: 213-208-0941.

Berkeley—Rev. Matthew Bloomer. *2710 College Ave., Berkeley, CA 94705.* Tel: 510-548-2819.

State of Texas

Houston—Very Rev. Gerald S. Kolf, B.S., M.B.A, S.T.D., Vicar for Texas; Revs. Michael J. Barrett; John E. Solarski. *5505 Chaucer Dr., Houston, TX 77005.* Tel: 713-523-4351.

Irving—Revs. Michael J. Manz; Victor Cortés. *3610 Wingren, Irving, TX 75062.* Tel: 214-650-0064.

San Antonio—Rev. Thomas J. Lamb. *345 E. Summit Ave., San Antonio, TX 78212.* Tel: 210-732-3065.

Puerto Rico

Guaynabo—Rev. Msgr. Vicente Ariza, J.C.D., Reg. Vicar; Revs. Juan Aramendi; Javier Bennaola; Andrés Eiroa. 35 A St., Villa Caparra, Guaynabo, P.R. 00966. Tel: 787-781-9123. Revs. Gonzalo Díaz; Alfredo Gastalver, 48 A St., Villa Caparra, Guaynabo, P.R. 00966. Tel: 787-783-1987.

San Juan—Revs. Martin Llambías. *51 Margarita St., Santa Rita, San Juan, P.R. 00925.* Tel: 787-759-6193.

Ponce—Revs. Ramón Álvarez; José Francisco Tejeda; 8 Alcázar St., La Alhambra, Ponce, P.R. 00731. Tel: 787-844-2661.

Mayagüez—Rev. Pablo Concepción. 69 Orquídeas St., Ensanche Martinez, Mayagüez, P.R. 00680. Tel: 787-833-6461.

Armenian Catholic Exarchate of U.S.A. and Canada

Most Reverend

MANUEL BATAKIAN

Apostolic Exarch for Armenian Catholics in the United States and Canada; born November 5, 1929; ordained December 8, 1954; appointed Titular Bishop of Caesarea of Cappadocia January 8, 1995; ordained March 12, 1995; appointed Apostolic Exarch for Armenian Catholics in United States and Canada November 30, 2000; installed January 20, 2001. *Office: 167 N. 6th St., Brooklyn, NY 11211.*

Chancery & Vicar General Office: 167 N. 6th St., Brooklyn, NY 11211. Tel: 718-388-4218; Fax: 718-486-0615.

Legal Title: Apostolic Exarchate for Armenian Catholics in the United States of America.

STATISTICAL OVERVIEW

Personnel	
Bishop	1
Priests: Diocesan Active in Diocese	3
Number of Diocesan Priests	3
Religious Priests in Diocese	8
Total Priests in Diocese	11
Ordinations:	
Diocesan Priests	1
Permanent Deacons	1
Permanent Deacons in Diocese	1
Total Sisters	11
Parishes	
Parishes	7
With Resident Pastor:	
Resident Diocesan Priests	3
Resident Religious Priests	4
Educational	
Elementary Schools, Private	4
Total Students	935
Catechesis/Religious Education:	
Elementary Students	23
Total Students under Catholic Instruction	958
Teachers in the Diocese:	
Priests	2
Sisters	10
Lay Teachers	79
Vital Statistics	
Receptions into the Church:	
Infant Baptism Totals	128
Adult Baptism Totals	13
First Communions	57
Confirmations	140
Marriages:	
Catholic	13
Interfaith	90
Total Marriages	103
Deaths	47
Total Catholic Population	25,000

Former Bishop—Most Revs. HOVHANNES TERTZAKIAN, O.M.Ven. (Retired), ord. Sept. 8, 1948; appt. Titular Bishop of Trebisonda and Apostolic Exarch for Armenian Catholics in the United States and Canada Jan. 6, 1995; ord. April 29, 1995; installed May 7, 1995; retired Nov. 30, 2000; died Jan. 28, 2002; NERSES MIKAEL SETIAN (Retired), ord. April 13, 1941; appt. Titular Bishop of Ancera and Apostolic Exarch for the Armenian Catholics in the U.S.A. and Canada July 3, 1981; ord. Dec. 5, 1981; installed Dec. 27, 1981; retired Sept. 18, 1993; died Sept. 9, 2002.

Chancery & Vicar General Office—167 N. 6th St., Brooklyn, 11211. Tel: 718-388-4218; Fax: 718-486-0615.

Vicar General—Rev. GEORGES ZABARIAN. Tel: 212-477-2030.

Business Chancellor—Rev. RAPHAEL ANDONIAN, O.Mech. Tel: 212-477-2030.

Newspaper Diocesan Bulletin—Office, 110 E. 12th St., New York, 10003-5395. Tel: 212-477-2030. "The Eternal Flame"

Newspaper Diocesan Bulletin "VERELK"—Office, 1327 Pleasant Ave., Los Angeles, CA 90033-2328. Tel: 323-267-1740.

CLERGY, PARISHES, MISSIONS AND PAROCHIAL SCHOOLS

STATE OF NEW YORK

NEW YORK, NEW YORK CO., ST. ANN'S CATHEDRAL (1983), Rev. Thomas Garabedian; Most Rev. Manuel Batakian.
Res.: 167 N. 6th St., Brooklyn, 11211. Tel: 718-388-4218; Fax: 718-486-0615.

STATE OF CALIFORNIA

GLENDALE, LOS ANGELES CO., ST. GREGORY (1998), Rev. Raphael Minassian.
Res.: 1504-10 E. Mountain St., CA 91207-1226. Tel: 818-243-8400; Fax: 818-243-0095.

LOS ANGELES, LOS ANGELES CO., OUR LADY QUEEN OF MARTYRS (1951), Revs. Raphael Minassian; Antoine Noradounghian (NY).
Res.: 1327 Pleasant Ave., CA 90033-2328. Tel: 323-261-9898; Fax: 323-261-0522.

STATE OF MASSACHUSETTS

BOSTON, MIDDLESEX CO., HOLY CROSS (1940), Revs. Armenaq Bedrossian; Charles Oduke, S.J.; Deacon M.J. Connolly.
Res.: 200 Lexington St., Belmont, MA 02478-1241. Tel: 617-489-2280; Fax: 617-489-0218.

STATE OF MICHIGAN

DETROIT, WAYNE CO., ST. VARTAN'S (1948), Rev. Antoine Saroyan.
Res.: 8541 Greenfield Rd., MI 48228-2224. Tel: 313-584-3345; Fax: 313-582-7012.

STATE OF NEW JERSEY

PATERSON, PASSAIC CO., SACRED HEART (1927), Rev. George Kalousieh.
Res.: 155 Long Hill Rd., Little Falls, NJ 07424-2374. Tel: 973-890-0447; Fax: 973-890-0292.

STATE OF PENNSYLVANIA

PHILADELPHIA, PHILADELPHIA CO., ST. MARK'S ARMENIAN CATHOLIC (1924), Rev. Antranik Atamian.
Res.: 400 Haverford Rd., Wynnewood, PA 19096-2699. Tel: 610-896-7789; Fax: 610-896-0915.

INSTITUTIONS LOCATED IN THE DIOCESE

[A] SCHOOLS

STATE OF CALIFORNIA

MONTROSE. *Armenian Sisters of the Immaculate Conception*, 2361 Florencita Dr., CA 91020-1817. Tel: 626-249-8783; Fax: 626-249-7288. Sr. Lucia Al-Haik, Prin.

TUJUNGA. *Mekhitarist School*, 6470 Foothill Blvd., CA 91042-2729. Tel: 818-353-3003; Fax: 818-353-0815. Revs. Augustin Szekula, O.Mech., Prin.; David Ghazarian.
6507 Alta Gracia Dr., CA 91042-3403. Tel: 818-352-3048; Fax: 818-352-2647.

STATE OF MASSACHUSETTS

LEXINGTON. *Armenian Sisters Academy*, 20 Pelham Rd., MA 02421-5702. Tel: 781-861-8303; Fax: 781-862-8479. Sr. Genevieve Davidian, Prin.

STATE OF PENNSYLVANIA

RADNOR. *Armenian Sisters Academy*, 440 Upper Gulph Rd., PA 19087-4699. Tel: 610-687-4100; Fax: 610-687-2430. Web: ameniansrsacademy.org. Sr. Louisa Kassarjian, Supr. & Prin.

[B] RELIGIOUS INSTITUTES AND CONVENTS FOR WOMEN

STATE OF CALIFORNIA

MONTROSE. *Armenian Sisters of the Immaculate Conception*, 2361 Florencita Dr., CA 91020-1817. Tel: 626-249-8783; 818-249-7493 (convent); Fax: 626-249-7288; 818-242-4610 (convent). Sr. Lucia Al-Haik, Prin.

STATE OF MASSACHUSETTS

LEXINGTON. *Armenian Sisters of the Immaculate Conception*, 6 Eliot Rd., MA 02173. Tel: 781-863-5962; Fax: 781-674-0410. Sr. Genevieve Davidian, Prin.

STATE OF PENNSYLVANIA

RADNOR. *Armenian Sisters of the Immaculate Conception*, 440 Upper Gulph Rd., PA 19087-4699. Tel: 610-687-4100; 610-688-9360 (convent); Fax: 610-687-2430. Sr. Louisa Kassarjian, Supr. & Prin.

[C] EDUCATIONAL FOUNDATIONS

STATE OF CALIFORNIA

GLENDALE. **Mekhitarian Educational Foundation*, 702 E. Glenoaks Blvd., CA 91207-1714. Tel: 818-546-1967; Fax: 818-548-1166. Rev. Dadjad Yardemian, O.Mech., Exec. Dir.

NECROLOGY

(No Deaths)

Diocese of Newton (Melkite-Greek Catholic)

Most Reverend

JOHN A. ELYA, B.S.O., D.D.

Eparch of Newton; ordained February 17, 1952; appointed Auxiliary Bishop of Newton April 2, 1986; appointed Eparch of Newton November 25, 1993; installed January 25, 1994 *Res.: 3 VFW Pkwy., Roslindale, MA 02131.* Tel: 617-323-9922; Fax: 617-323-0944.

Most Reverend

NICHOLAS J. SAMRA, D.D.

Auxiliary Bishop of Newton; ordained May 10, 1970; appointed Auxiliary Bishop of Newton June 29, 1989 *Res.: 8525 Cole, Warren, MI 48093.* Tel: 586-756-1971; Fax: 586-756-1976.

The Chancery: 3 VFW Pkwy., Roslindale, MA 02131. Tel: 617-323-9922; Fax: 617-323-0944.

Web: melkite.org

Email: dioceseofnewton@aol.com

ESTABLISHED AS AN APOSTOLIC EXARCHATE JANUARY 10, 1966.

Elevated to Eparchy, June 28, 1976; Embraces all members of the Melkite Greek Catholic Church in the United States.

For legal titles of parishes and institutions, consult the Chancery Office.

STATISTICAL OVERVIEW

Personnel	
Bishop	1
Auxiliary Bishops	1
Priests: Diocesan Active in Diocese	36
Priests: Diocesan Active Outside Diocese	2
Priests: Retired, Sick or Absent	9
Number of Diocesan Priests	47
Religious Priests in Diocese	15
Total Priests in Diocese	62
Extern Priests in Diocese	2
Ordinations:	
Diocesan Priests	1
Permanent Deacons	3
Permanent Deacons in Diocese	39
Total Sisters	3
Parishes	
Parishes	35
With Resident Pastor:	
Resident Diocesan Priests	28
Resident Religious Priests	6
Without Resident Pastor:	
Administered by Deacons	1
Missions	7
Educational	
Seminaries, Diocesan	1
Students from This Diocese	2
Seminaries, Religious	1
Total Seminarians	2
Catechesis/Religious Education:	
High School Students	326
Elementary Students	1,309
Total Students under Catholic Instruction	1,637
Vital Statistics	
Receptions into the Church:	
Infant Baptism Totals	401
Adult Baptism Totals	21
Received into Full Communion	32
First Communions	444
Confirmations	458
Marriages:	
Catholic	100
Interfaith	16
Total Marriages	116
Deaths	166
Total Catholic Population	29,024

Former Bishops—Most Revs. JUSTIN A. NAJMY, B.A.O., D.D., born April 23, 1898;; ord. Dec. 25, 1926; consecrated May 29, 1966; installed June 4, 1966; died June 11, 1968; JOSEPH E. TAWIL, D.D., LL.D., ord. July 20, 1936; consecrated Jan. 1, 1960; appt. Apostolic Exarch, Oct. 30, 1969; appt. Eparch, June 28, 1976; became emeritus Dec. 2, 1989.; died Feb. 17, 1999; IGNATIUS GHATTAS, B.S.O., D.D., born Dec. 25, 1920;; ord. July 7, 1946; appt. Dec. 2, 1989; consecrated Feb. 23, 1990; died Oct. 11, 1992.

Diocesan Administration

Chancery Office—3 VFW Pkwy., Roslindale, 02131. Tel: 617-323-9922; Fax: 617-323-0944. Office Hours: Mon.-Fri. 9-5

Protosyncellus—Most Rev. NICHOLAS J. SAMRA, D.D.

Chancellor—Deacon PAUL F. LAWLER.

Diocesan Tribunal—3 VFW Pkwy., Roslindale, 02131.

Judicial Vicar—Rev. GERASIMOS MURPHY, B.S.O., 6458 Tapestry Cir., Spring Hill, FL 34606.

Judge and Adjutant Judicial Vicar—Rev. MICHAEL SKROCKI, J.C.L.

Judges—Revs. JOSEPH KOURY, J.C.D.; JOHN FARAJ, J.C.D.; HERBERT MAY, J.C.L.

Defender of the Bond and Promoter of Justice—Rev. JOSEPH S. HAGGAR, M.A., J.C.L.

Notaries—Deacons GEORGE YANY; PAUL LAWLER; LUCILLE LAROCHE.

Economos—Rev. ANDRE ST. GERMAIN. Fax: 617-323-0692.

Protopresbyters—Revs. JOSEPH S. HAGGAR, M.A., J.C.L., New England; JOHN FARAJ, B.S.O., Mid-Atlantic; FRANK MILIENEWICZ, Southeast; PHILIP RACZKA, Great Lakes; ALEXEI SMITH, West.

Consultative Bodies

College of Eparchial Consultors—Most Rev. NICHOLAS J. SAMRA, D.D.; Revs. JOSEPH S. HAGGAR, M.A., J.C.L.; GERASIMOS MURPHY, B.S.O., D.Min., J.C.D.; ROMANOS V. RUSSO; FRANK J. MILIENEWICZ; ANDRE ST. GERMAIN; JOHN FARAJ, B.S.O.; EUGENE MITCHELL, B.S.O.

Presbyteral Council—Most Revs. JOHN A. ELYA, B.S.O., D.D., Pres.; NICHOLAS J SAMRA, D.D.; Revs. CHARLES ABOODY; JOSEPH S. HAGGAR, M.A., J.C.L.; FRANK MILIENEWICZ; PHILIP RACZKA; ANDRE ST. GERMAIN; ALEXEI SMITH; Very Rev. DANIEL MUNN; Revs. JAMES BABCOCK; PETER BOUTROS; GREGORY EL-THOM; JOHN FARAJ, B.S.O.; EMMANUEL CHARLES MCCARTHY; MARK MELONE; EUGENE MITCHELL, B.S.O.; THOMAS STEINMETZ; YOUSSEF YOUSSEF, B.S.O.

Diocese of Newton for the Melkites in the USA, Inc., a Massachusetts Corporation—Most Revs. JOHN A. ELYA, B.S.O., D.D.; NICHOLAS J. SAMRA, D.D.; Revs. JOSEPH S. HAGGAR, M.A., J.C.L.; GERASIMOS MURPHY, B.S.O.; ANDRE ST. GERMAIN; YOUSSEF YOUSSEF, B.S.O.; Deacon PAUL F. LAWLER.

Finance Council—Most Rev. NICHOLAS J. SAMRA, D.D.; Rev. ANDRE ST. GERMAIN, Economos; Mr. STANLEY SABA; Dr. JOHN NAZARIAN; Deacon ROBERT SHALHOUB; GILBERT SHASHA; RAYMOND KAYAL; EDMUND NAHOM; BASIL ZALOOM.

Priest's Sickness & Disability, and Retirement Plans—Most Rev. NICHOLAS J. SAMRA, D.D.; Revs. JOSEPH FRANCAVILLA; JOSEPH S. HAGGAR, M.A., J.C.L.; FRANK MILIENEWICZ; PHILIP RACZKA; ANDRE ST. GERMAIN; JOHN FARAJ, B.S.O.; ALEXEI SMITH.

Canonical Consultants—Revs. VICTOR J. POSPISHIL, J.C.D.; JOHN FARAJ, B.S.O.; JOHN D. FARIS, J.C.O.D.; GEORGE D. GALLARO, J.C.O.D.

Legal Consultant—CAMILLE F. SARROUF JR., Esq., 95 Commercial Wharf, Boston, 02110. Tel: 617-227-5800.

Liturgical Consultants—Revs. ROBERT TAFT, S.J.; EUTHIMIOS SKAFF, B.S.O.

Pastoral Offices and Commissions

Continuing Education of Clergy Office—Revs. PAUL FRECHETTE; GABRIEL GHANOUM, B.S.O.; ALEXEI SMITH; IGNATIUS HARRINGTON.

National Association of Melkite Youth—Deacon GEORGE YANY, 1 Valley St., Central Falls, RI 02863. Tel: 401-722-0017.

MAYA (Melkite Assoc. of Young Adults)—Rev. JUSTIN ROSE, 923 W. Congress St., San Bernardino, CA 92410. Tel: 909-889-3579.

Ambassadors—Rev. THOMAS STEINMETZ, 161 S. Beech St., Manchester, NH 03102. Tel: 603-622-0206.

National Association of Melkite Women—Rev. EDWARD KAKATY, 41 Cross Rd., Waterford, CT 06385. Tel: 860-442-2211.

Liturgical Commission—Most Rev. NICHOLAS SAMRA, Chm.; Revs. JOSEPH HAGGAR; VICTOR SAMAHA, B.C.O.; EDWARD KAKATY; ROMANOS RUSSO; MARK MELONE.

Office of Communications—PAUL LEONARCZYK, Dir.. Email: leonarczyk1@aol.com.

Educational Services—FRANCES COLIE, Ph.D., Dir.; ROBERT SPENCER, Assoc. Dir., 1710 Surf Ave., Belmar, NJ 07719. Tel: 732-280-1774.

Vocations Office—Revs. PHILIP RACZKA, Coord., 600 W. Exchange St., Akron, OH 44302. Tel: 330-535-7364; Fax: 330-535-8037; EDWARD KAKATY; FRANK MILIENEWICZ; ALEXEI SMITH; SAMI BAROODY; IGNATIUS HARRINGTON.

"Sophia" (A Journal)—Rev. ROBERT RABBAT, Editor-in-Chief. Associates:: Rev. JAMES GRAHAM; Deacon

ELIAS SAHYOUNI; JOSEPH A. BOU-SLIMAN, 200 E. North Ave., Northlake, IL 60164. Tel: 708-865-7050; Fax: 708-345-4211.

Ecumenical & Interreligious Commission—Rev. EDWARD G. KAKATY, 41 Cross Rd., Waterford, CT 06385.

Order of St. Nicholas—Most Rev. NICHOLAS J. SAMRA, D.D., Grand Advisor; GREGORY OUSSANY, National Chm.; Revs. ANDRE ST. GERMAIN, Treas.; GABRIEL GHANOUM, B.S.O., Chap., Mailing Address, 3 VFW Pkwy., Roslindale, 02131. Tel: 617-323-9922; Fax: 617-323-0692.

Associated Melkite Charities—Rev. PHILARET LITTLEFIELD, 1617 W. State St., Milwaukee, WI 53233. Tel: 414-342-1543.

Sophia Press—Rev. ANDRE ST. GERMAIN, 3 VFW Pkwy., Roslindale, 02131. Tel: 617-323-9922; Fax: 617-323-0692.

Victim Assistance Coordinator—Rev. ANDRE. Tel: 603-674-4049. Email: abounaandre@msn.com.

CLERGY, PARISHES, MISSIONS AND PAROCHIAL SCHOOLS

STATE OF MASSACHUSETTS

BOSTON, SUFFOLK CO., ANNUNCIATION CATHEDRAL, Rev. Eugene Mitchell, B.S.O., Rector; Deacons Paul F. Lawler, Protodeacon; John Moses.
Res.: 7 V.F.W. Pkwy., 02131. Tel: 617-323-5242; Fax: 617-325-2662.

LAWRENCE, ESSEX CO., ST. JOSEPH, Rev. Alam Alam; Deacons Bryan McNeil; John MacMillan.
Res.: 241 Hampshire St., 01841. Tel: 978-682-8152; Fax: 978-682-6114.

WORCESTER, WORCESTER CO., OUR LADY OF PERPETUAL HELP, Rev. Paul G. Frechette.
Res.: 256 Hamilton St., 01604. Tel: 508-752-4174; Fax: 508-752-8351.

STATE OF ALABAMA

BIRMINGHAM, JEFFERSON CO., ST. GEORGE, Rev. Frank J. Milienewicz; Deacon Seraphim Ritchey.
Res.: 425 Sixteenth Ave. S., AL 35205. Tel: 205-252-5788; Fax: 205-252-0063.

STATE OF ARIZONA

PHOENIX, MARICOPA CO., ST. JOHN OF THE DESERT, Rev. Peter Boutros; Deacon Marion Rimmer.
Res.: 3718 E. Greenway Rd., AZ 85032. Tel: 602-787-4787.

STATE OF CALIFORNIA

EL SEGUNDO, LOS ANGELES CO., ST. PAUL, Rev. Alexei R. Smith, Admin.; Deacon Irenaeus Dionne.
Res.: 538 Concord St., CA 90245. Tel: 310-322-1892; Fax: 310-322-1919.

LA MESA, SAN DIEGO CO., ST. JACOB MISSION, , Sevices at Holy Angels Church, San Diego. Rev. George Said Bisharat; Deacon Edward Bagdasar.
Mailing Address: 5707 Baltimore Dr., Apt. #5, CA 91942. Tel: 619-460-0444; Fax: 619-667-3860.

NORTH HOLLYWOOD, LOS ANGELES CO., ST. ANNE, Rev. Albert Wehby, B.A.O.; Deacons George Sayegh; George Karout; Tareq Nasrallah.
Res.: 11245 Rye St., CA 91602. Tel: 818-761-2034; Fax: 818-761-2922.

OAKLAND, ALAMEDA CO., ST. JOHN THE THEOLOGIAN, Revs. Owen Carroll (OAK); Eugene M. Ludwig, O.F.M.Cap. (OAK).
Res.: 5 Gleneden Ave., CA 94611. Tel: 510-428-2234.

PLACENTIA, ORANGE CO., HOLY CROSS, Rev. James K. Babcock.
Church & Res.: 451 W. Madison Ave., CA 92870. Tel: 714-985-1710; Fax: 714-985-1765.

RIVERSIDE, RIVERSIDE CO., VIRGIN MARY MISSION, , Services at St. Mark Church, San Marcos. Rt. Rev. Nassir Matta, Admin.
Mailing Address: 33881 Orange St., Wildomar, CA 92595. Tel: 909-674-3162.

SACRAMENTO, SACRAMENTO CO., ST. GEORGE, Rev. Mark E. Melone.
Church: 1620 Bell St., CA 95825. Tel: 916-920-2900; Fax: 916-920-2900.

SAN BERNARDINO, SAN BERNARDINO CO., ST. PHILIP, Rev. Justin Rose; Deacon Saad Ghandour.
Mailing Address: 923 W. Congress St., CA 92410. Tel: 909-889-3579; Fax: 909-889-5461.

SAN JOSE, SANTA CLARA CO., ST. ELIAS, Rev. James K. Graham.
Res. & Church: 4411 Hyland Ave., CA 95127. Tel: 408-259-0259.

STATE OF CONNECTICUT

DANBURY, FAIRFIELD CO., ST. ANN, Rev. Basil R. Parent.
Mailing Address: 181 Clapboard Ridge Rd., CT 06811. Tel: 203-743-5119.

WATERFORD, NEW LONDON CO., ST. ANN, Rev. Edward G. Kakaty; Deacon Dennis J. McCarthy.
Res.: 41 Cross Rd., CT 06385. Tel: 860-442-2211; Fax: 860-442-2211.

STATE OF FLORIDA

DELRAY BEACH, PALM BEACH CO., ST. NICHOLAS, , Served by Miami. Revs. Gabriel Ghanoum, B.S.O.; Naim Khalil, B.S.O.; Deacon Magdi Negm.
Res.: 126 S.E. 15 Rd., Miami, FL 33129. Tel: 305-856-8666.

MIAMI, DADE CO., ST. JUDE, Revs. Gabriel Ghanoum, B.S.O.; Naim Khalil, B.S.O.; Deacon Magdi Negm.
Res.: 126 S.E. 15 Rd., FL 33129. Tel: 305-856-8666; Fax: 305-859-7982.

STATE OF GEORGIA

ATLANTA, DEKALB CO., ST. JOHN CHRYSOSTOM, Rev. John Azar. In Res., Rev. Basil Samra.
Res.: 1428 Ponce de Leon Ave., N.E., GA 30307. Tel: 404-373-9522; Fax: 404-373-9755.

AUGUSTA, RICHMOND CO., ST. IGNATIOS OF ANTIOCH, Very Rev. Daniel Munn; Rev. Miguel Grave de Peralta; Deacon Kent Plowman.
Mailing Address: P.O. Box 3351, GA 30914-3351.
Church: 1003 Merry St., GA 30904. Tel: 706-738-9388; Fax: 706-738-6559.
Res.: 967 Meigs St., GA 30904. Tel: 706-738-5623.

STATE OF ILLINOIS

NORTHLAKE, COOK CO., ST. JOHN THE BAPTIST, Rev. Robert Rabbat; Deacons Elias Sahyouni; Habib Khasho; Antoine Shehata.
Res.: 200 E. North Ave., IL 60164. Tel: 708-865-7050; Fax: 708-345-4211.

STATE OF INDIANA

HAMMOND, LAKE CO., ST. MICHAEL THE ARCHANGEL, Rev. Saba Shofany, Admin.
Mailing Address: 606 141st St., IN 46327. Tel: 219-933-1457.

SOUTH BEND, ST. JOSEPH CO., ST. JOHN OF DAMASCUS, Rev. Robert L. Kerby; Deacon Lawrence Farhat.
Church: 839 Woodcliff Dr., IN 46615. Tel: 574-282-2140.
Res.: 918 Simon Ct., IN 46615. Tel: 574-233-5338.

STATE OF MICHIGAN

LANSING, INGHAM CO., ST. JOSEPH, Rt. Rev. Victor M. Samaha, B.C.O.
Res.: 921 Westover Circle, MI 48917. Tel: 517-327-6394; Fax: 517-327-6965.

PLYMOUTH, WAYNE CO., ST. MICHAEL, Rev. Edmond J. Ghazal, B.C.O., Admin.; Deacon Joseph Daratony.
Church: 585 N. Mill St., MI 48170. Tel: 734-414-6110.

WARREN, MACOMB CO., OUR LADY OF REDEMPTION, Most Rev. Nicholas J. Samra, Protosyncellus; Revs. George D. Gallaro, J.C.O.D.; Gregory El-Thom, B.C.O.; Deacon James Soloman.
Res.: 8525 Cole, MI 48093. Tel: 586-751-6017; Fax: 586-751-1877.

STATE OF NEW HAMPSHIRE

MANCHESTER, HILLSBOROUGH CO., OUR LADY OF THE CEDARS, Revs. Andre St. Germain; Thomas P. Steinmetz.
Res.: 161 S. Beech St., NH 03103. Tel: 603-623-8944; Fax: 603-645-6017.

STATE OF NEW JERSEY

CLIFFSIDE PARK, BERGEN CO., ST. DEMETRIUS, , Administered from St. Ann Church, West Paterson.
Church: 184 Cliff St., NJ 07010. Tel: 201-840-8554; 201-785-4144 (Res.).

WEST PATERSON, PASSAIC CO., ST. ANN, Rev. Sami W. Baroody; Deacons Edward Bsarany; Roland Basinski; Robert Shalhoub.
Res.: 802 Rifle Camp Rd., NJ 07424. Tel: 973-785-4144; Fax: 973-890-9599.

STATE OF NEW YORK

BROOKLYN, KINGS CO., CHURCH OF THE VIRGIN MARY, Revs. John Faraj, B.S.O.; Jean Ghaby.
Res.: 216 Eighth Ave., NY 11215. Tel: 718-788-5454; Fax: 718-499-7702.

ROCHESTER, MONROE CO., ST. NICHOLAS, Rev. Kenneth Sherman; Deacon Edmond Elhilow.
Res.: 1492 Spencerport Rd., NY 14606. Tel: 716-426-4218.

UTICA, ONEIDA CO., ST. BASIL, Rt. Rev. Julien A. Eliane; Deacon Daniel A. Klockowski.
Res.: 901 Sherman Dr., NY 13501. Tel: 315-732-4662; Fax: 315-797-4895.

YONKERS, WESTCHESTER CO., CHRIST THE SAVIOR CHURCH, Rev. Romanos V. Russo, Economos; Protodeacon Saleem Naber; Deacon Ibrahim S. Marji.
Res.: 491 Palisade Ave., NY 10703. Tel: 914-963-6680; Fax: 914-963-1058.

STATE OF OHIO

AKRON, SUMMIT CO., ST. JOSEPH, Rev. Philip Raczka.
Res.: 600 W. Exchange St., OH 44302. Tel: 330-535-7364; Fax: 330-535-8037.

BROOKLYN, CUYAHOGA CO., ST. ELIAS, Rev. Youssef A. Youssef, B.S.O.
Res.: 8023 Memphis Ave., OH 44144. Tel: 216-661-1155; Fax: 216-661-3838.

COLUMBUS, FRANKLIN CO., HOLY RESURRECTION, Rev. Ignatius Harrington.
Res.: 7752 Deercrest Ct., Dublin, OH 43016. Tel: 614-761-7975; Fax: 614-761-7975.

ZANESVILLE, MUSKINGUM CO., HOLY TRINITY, Rev. Ignatius Harrington.
Res.: 7752 Deercrest Ct., Dublin, OH 43016. Tel: 614-761-7975; Fax: 614-761-7975.
Church: 317 Wayne Ave., P.O. Box 2116, OH 43701.

STATE OF PENNSYLVANIA

SCRANTON, LACKAWANNA CO., ST. JOSEPH, Protodeacon Michael Jolly, Admin.
130 N. Cabrini Ave., PA 18504. Tel: 570-343-6092; Fax: 570-969-0862.

STATE OF RHODE ISLAND

LINCOLN, PROVIDENCE CO., ST. BASIL THE GREAT, Rt. Rev. Joseph S. Haggar; Deacons George M. Yany; Edmond Raheb.
Church: 15 Skyview Dr., RI 02865.
Res.: 111 Cross St., Central Falls, RI 02863. Tel: 401-722-1345; Fax: 401-722-2436.

WOONSOCKET, PROVIDENCE CO., ST. ELIAS, Rt. Rev. Joseph S. Haggar.
Church: 80 Hamilton St., RI 02895.
Res.: 111 Cross St., Central Falls, RI 02863. Tel: 401-722-1345.

STATE OF VIRGINIA

MCLEAN, FAIRFAX CO., HOLY TRANSFIGURATION, Revs. Joseph F. Francavilla; Ephrem Handal; Protodeacon Paul Weyrich; Deacons David Baroody; Nicholas Rosov.
Res.: 8501 Lewinsville Rd., VA 22102. Tel: 703-734-9198; Fax: 703-734-5148.

STATE OF WISCONSIN

MILWAUKEE, MILWAUKEE CO., ST. GEORGE, Rev. Philaret Littlefield.
Res.: 1617 W. State St., WI 53233. Tel: 414-342-1543; Fax: 414-933-3755.

Military Chaplains:
Revs.—
Brown, Shaun S.
Gosselin, Lawrence

Leave of Absence:
Revs.—
Golini, Ronald
Kirk, David
Koury, James
Saato, Fred
Samra, Basil
Deacon—
Negm, Magdi

Retired:
Revs.—
Aboody, Charles
Azoon, Philip
Badaoui, Adib, B.S.O.
Dagher, George, B.S.O.
Hage, Simon, B.S.O.
Hassey, Athanase
Jadaa, John, B.S.O.
King, James E.
Moloney, Patrick W.
Murphy, Gerasimos, B.S.O.

Deacons:
Deacons—
Bagdasar, Edward, El Cajon, CA
Baroody, David, McLean, VA
Basinski, Roland, West Paterson, NJ
Bsarany, Edward, West Paterson, NJ
Daratony, Joseph, Plymouth, MI
Dionne, Irenaeus, El Segundo, CA
Elhilow, Edmond, Rochester, NY
Farhat, Lawrence, South Bend, IN
Ghandour, Stephen, San Bernardino, CA
Heinemeyer, Carl, (Retired)
Jolly, Michael, Scranton, PA
Karout, George, North Hollywood, CA
Khasho, Habib, Northlake, IL
Klockowski, Daniel, Utica, NY
Lawler, Paul, Boston, MA

MacMillan, John, Lawrence, MA
Marji, Ibrahim, Yonkers, NY
McCarthy, Dennis, Waterford, CT
McNeil, Bryan, Lawrence, MA
Moses, John, Boston, MA
Naber, Saleem, Yonkers, NY
Nasrallah, Tareq, North Hollywood, CA
Plowman, Kent M., Augusta, GA
Raheb, Edmond, Lincoln, RI
Rimmer, Marion, Phoenix, AZ
Ritchey, Seraphim, Birmingham, AL
Rosov, Nicholas, McLean, VA
Sahyouni, Elias, Northlake, IL
Sayegh, George, North Hollywood, CA
Shalhoub, Robert, West Paterson, NJ
Shehata, Antoine, Northlake, IL
Soloman, James, Warren, MI
Weyrich, Paul, McLean, VA
Yany, George, Central Falls, RI

Deacons Serving Outside the Eparchy:
Deacons—
Haddad, Gregory
Hill, James A.
Nasser, Andre P.
Richardson, David W.
Versage, Joseph V.

INSTITUTIONS LOCATED IN THE DIOCESE

[A] SEMINARIES

STATE OF MASSACHUSETTS

METHUEN. *Seminary of St. Basil the Great*, 30 East St., 01844. Tel: 978-683-2471. Rev. Martin A. Hyatt, B.S.O., Dean. Priests 4.

ROSLINDALE. *Seminary of St. Gregory the Theologian*, 3 VFW Pkwy., 02131. Rev. Emmanuel Charles McCarthy, Rector. Priests 1.

[B] MONASTERIES AND RESIDENCES FOR PRIESTS AND BROTHERS

STATE OF MASSACHUSETTS

METHUEN. *Basilian Salvatorian Order*, 30 East St., 01844. Tel: 978-683-2471; Fax: 978-794-3452. Revs. John Faraj, B.S.O., Regl. Supr.; Eugene Mitchell, B.S.O., Gen. Economos; Martin A. Hyatt, B.S.O., Local Supr.; Lawrence Tumminelli, B.S.O.; Rt. Revs. George Dagher, B.S.O. (Retired); Simon Hage, B.S.O. (Retired).

[C] CONVENTS AND RESIDENCES FOR SISTERS

STATE OF CONNECTICUT

DANBURY. *Community of The Mother of God of Tenderness*, 79 Golden Hill Rd., CT 06811-4631. Tel: 203-794-1486. Email: sophiam@comcast.net. Sr. Mary Ann Socha, C.M.G.T., Pres. Sisters 3.

[D] MISCELLANEOUS

STATE OF ALABAMA

BIRMINGHAM. *National Shrine of St. George*, 425 16th Ave. S., AL 35205. Tel: 205-252-5788. Rev. Frank J. Milienewicz.

STATE OF MASSACHUSETTS

METHUEN. *St. Basil's Salvatorian Center*, 30 East St., 01844. Tel: 978-683-2959; Fax: 978-794-3379. Patricia Paduano, Contact Person.

STATE OF NEW YORK

YONKERS. *The Friends of the Holy Land, Inc.*, 347 Mile Sq. Rd., NY 10701. Tel: 914-969-0887; 914-949-2106; Fax: 914-476-8196. Ernest F. Russo, Governor Gen., Patriarchal Order of the Holy Cross of Jerusalem.

RELIGIOUS INSTITUTES OF MEN REPRESENTED IN THE EPARCHY

For further details refer to the corresponding bracketed number in the Religious Institutes of Men or Women section.

[]—*Basilian Aleppian Order* (Deir-es-Chir, Lebanon)—B.A.O.

[]—*Basilian Chouerite Order* (St. John Monastery, Khonchara, Lebanon)—B.C.O.

[0190]—*Basilian Salvatorian Order* (Holy Saviour Monastery, Sidon, Lebanon)—B.S.O.

NECROLOGY

(No Deaths)

Diocese of Our Lady of Deliverance

For Syriac Catholics in the United States and Canada

Most Reverend

JOSEPH YOUNAN, D.D.

Bishop of Our Lady of Deliverance; ordained September 12, 1971; ordained Bishop January 7, 1996; installed February 10, 1996. *Chancery Office: 502 Palisade Ave., Union City, NJ 07087-5213.*

Chancery Office: 502 Palisade Ave., Union City, NJ 07087-5213P.O. Box 8366, Union City, NJ 07087-8262

Web: www.syriac-catholic.org

Email: frsyriac@aol.com

DIOCESE ESTABLISHED NOVEMBER 18, 1995.

Comprises the United States and Canada.

STATISTICAL OVERVIEW

Statistical report was not submitted for 2004.

Personnel	
Bishop	1
Priests: Diocesan Active in Diocese	9
Priests: Diocesan Active Outside Diocese	3
Number of Diocesan Priests	12
Total Priests in Diocese	12
Parishes	
Parishes	8
With Resident Pastor:	
Resident Diocesan Priests	8
Without Resident Pastor:	
Administered by Priests	3
Administered by Lay People	1
Missions	3
Educational	
Students from This Diocese	2
Total Seminarians	2
Catechesis/Religious Education:	
High School Students	10
Elementary Students	333
Total Students under Catholic Instruction	513
Vital Statistics	
Receptions into the Church:	
Infant Baptism Totals	82
Adult Baptism Totals	4
Received into Full Communion	4
First Communions	112
Confirmations	86
Marriages:	
Catholic	41
Interfaith	4
Total Marriages	45
Deaths	34
Total Catholic Population	12,610

Chancery—502 Palisade Ave., Union City, 07087-5213. Tel: 201-583-1067; Fax: 201-583-0212. *P.O. Box 8366, Union City, 07087-8262.*

Vicar General—Rev. Msgr. TOMA B. AZIZO.

Chancellor—Rev. ST SUTTON. Tel: 201-583-1067.

Secretary—Rev. ST SUTTON. Tel: 201-583-1067.

Officialis—Rev. ST SUTTON. Tel: 201-583-1067.

CLERGY, PARISHES, MISSIONS AND PAROCHIAL SCHOOLS

STATE OF NEW JERSEY

OUR LADY OF DELIVERANCE (1986), Rev. Fahd Tabban, Admin.; Mr. Nabil Cherbaka, Parish Council Chair.
Res.: 502 Palisade Ave., 07087-5213. Tel: 201-583-9590; Fax: 201-583-9639.
Catechesis/Religious Program—Mrs. Nahla Mensi, D.R.E. Students 49.

STATE OF CALIFORNIA

LOS ANGELES, LOS ANGELES CO., SACRED HEART PARISH, Revs. Yousif Habash; Youssef Abdulmasih; Deacon George Qatto; Mr. Elian Maida, Parish Council Chair.
Res.: 10837 Collins St., North Hollywood, CA 91601-2009. Tel: 818-766-7001; Fax: 818-766-7254.
Catechesis/Religious Program—Mrs. Layla Touma, D.R.E. Students 52.

OCEANSIDE, SAN DIEGO CO., SAINT JOSEPH'S MISSION, Rev. Emad Hanna Al-Shaikh, Admin.

SAN DIEGO, SAN DIEGO CO., OUR MOTHER OF PERPETUAL HELP PARISH, Rev. Emad Hanna Al-Shaikh, Admin.
Mailing Address: 9911 Bonnie Vista Dr., La Mesa, CA 91941. Fax: 619-660-1492.
Res.: 9800 San Juan St., Spring Valley, CA 91977.
Catechesis/Religious Program—Mrs. Khouloud Habbosh, D.R.E. Students 42.

STATE OF FLORIDA

JACKSONVILLE, DUVAL CO., SAINT EPHREM, Rev. Selwan A. Sulaiman; Mr. Jack Albanna, Parish Council Chair.
Res.: 14608 Stacey Rd., FL 32250. Tel: 904-992-0025.
Catechesis/Religious Program—Mrs. Emtethal Yazji, D.R.E. Students 64.

STATE OF ILLINOIS

TECHNY, COOK CO., SAINT MARY VIRGIN IMMACULATE MISSION, , Served by Chancery personnel
Res.: 2001 Waukegan Rd., IL 60082. Tel: 847-272-2700; Fax: 847-272-1233.

STATE OF MICHIGAN

FARMINGTON HILLS, OAKLAND CO., SAINT TOMA'S, Rev. Msgr. Tomas B. Azizo; Mr. Charles Halabo, Parish Council Chair.
Mailing Address: 18290 W. 12 Mile Rd., Southfield, MI 48076. Tel: 248-569-3107; Fax: 248-478-0814.
Res.: 29000 W. 11 Mile Rd., MI 48336.
Catechesis/Religious Program—Mrs. Dhamia Albert Mansour, D.R.E. Students 68.

STATE OF PENNSYLVANIA

ALLENTOWN, LEHIGH CO., OUR MOTHER OF MERCY MISSION, Rev. Samer Saegh, Admin.

STATE OF RHODE ISLAND

PROVIDENCE, PROVIDENCE CO., SAINT JAMES SYRIAC MISSION, Mr. Samir Mansourati, Admin.
Mailing Address: *Saint Francis Chapel*, 58 Weybosset St., RI 02903.

CANADA

HAMILTON, SYRIAC MISSION, Rev. Yousif Mansour, Admin.

LAVAL, PAROISSE SAINT EPHREM, Rev. Paskal Kassis; George Chahine, Parish Council Chair.
Mailing Address: 3000 Edouard Monpetit QC H7T 2T5 Canada. Tel: 450-682-7546; Fax: 450-682-7603.
Res.: 7055 Jean Bourdon, Montreal QC Canada.
Catechesis/Religious Program—Michel Jiji, D.R.E. Students 160.

MONTREAL, NOTRE DAME DE L'ASSOMPTION, , Served by Chancery personnel

TORONTO, SAINT JOSEPH'S, Rev. Yousif Mansour.
Res.: 222 Ridley Blvd. ON M5M 3M6 Canada. Tel: 416-487-0960; Fax: 416-489-4183.
Catechesis/Religious Program—Mrs. Samira Raffi, D.R.E. Students 78.

Special Assignment:

Rev.—

Sutton, ST, Chancellor & Sec. to the Bishop

NECROLOGY

(No Deaths)

Eparchy of Our Lady of Lebanon of Los Angeles

Most Reverend

ROBERT J. SHAHEEN

Bishop of Our Lady of Lebanon of Los Angeles; ordained May 2, 1964; appointed December 5, 2000; consecrated February 15, 2001

Pastoral Center: 1021 S. 10th St., St. Louis, MO 63104.
Tel: 314-231-1021; Fax: 314-231-1418.

Web: www.usamaronite.org

Email: mdenny@usamaronite.org

Comprises the States of Ohio, West Virginia, Illinois, Alabama, Michigan, Minnesota, Missouri, Texas, Utah, Arizona, Nevada, Oregon, California, Alaska, Hawaii, Indiana, Kentucky, Tennessee, Mississippi, Wisconsin, Iowa, Arkansas, Louisiana, North Dakota, South Dakota, Kansas, Oklahoma, Nebraska, Montana, Wyoming, Colorado, New Mexico, Idaho and Washington.

STATISTICAL OVERVIEW

Personnel	
Bishop	1
Retired Bishops	1
Priests: Diocesan Active in Diocese	24
Priests: Diocesan Active Outside Diocese	1
Priests: Retired, Sick or Absent	4
Number of Diocesan Priests	29
Religious Priests in Diocese	16
Total Priests in Diocese	45
Ordinations:	
Diocesan Priests	1
Transitional Deacons	1
Permanent Deacons	9
Permanent Deacons in Diocese	9
Total Sisters	7
Parishes	
Parishes	32
With Resident Pastor:	
Resident Diocesan Priests	20
Resident Religious Priests	12
Missions	6
Professional Ministry Personnel:	
Lay Ministers	1
Welfare	
Residential Care of Children	1
Total Assisted	12
Day Care Centers	1
Total Assisted	30
Educational	
Seminaries, Diocesan	1
Students from This Diocese	2
Diocesan Students in Other Seminaries	2
Total Seminarians	4
Elementary Schools, Diocesan and Parish	1
Total Students	80
Catechesis/Religious Education:	
Elementary Students	89
Vital Statistics	
Receptions into the Church:	
Infant Baptism Totals	405
Adult Baptism Totals	47
Received into Full Communion	103
First Communions	327
Confirmations	301
Marriages:	
Catholic	84
Interfaith	33
Total Marriages	117
Deaths	161
Total Catholic Population	38,415

Former Bishop—Most Rev. JOHN GEORGE CHEDID, D.D. (Retired), ord. Dec. 21, 1951; appt. Titular Bishop of Callinicum and Auxiliary Bishop of St. Maron of Brooklyn, Oct. 28, 1980; consecrated Jan. 25, 1981; appt. Bishop of Our Lady of Lebanon of Los Angeles, Feb. 19, 1994; retired Dec. 5, 2000.

Pastoral Center—Rev. GREGORY J. MANSOUR, S.T.L., Protosyncellus and Chancellor; Mrs. MARY DENNY, Vice Chancellor & Chief Fiscal Officer; Deacon WISSAM G. AKIKI, Pastoral Assoc., 1021 S. 10th St., St. Louis, 63104. Tel: 314-231-1021; Fax: 314-231-1418.

College of Consultors—Chorbishop FAOUZI ELIA; Rev. Msgrs. WILLIAM BONCZWESKI; RICHARD SAAD; Revs. ABDALLAH ZAIDAN, M.L.M.; ANTOINE BAKH; ANTHONY SPINOSA; GREGORY J. MANSOUR, S.T.L.

Commission for Lebanon—Rev. ABDALLAH ZAIDAN, M.L.M.

Tribunal—

Defender of the Bond—Rev. ROBERT BISHOP, S.T.L., C.F.M.

Judicial Vicar—Chorbishop WILLIAM LESER, S.T.B.

Moderator of the Tribunal—Most Rev. ROBERT J. SHAHEEN.

Procurator/Advocate—Revs. ABDALLAH E. ZAIDAN, M.L.M.; ELIAS S. LEIMAN, M.L.M.

Promoter of Justice—Rev. ROBERT BISHOP, S.T.L., C.F.M.

Notary—Ms. KATARINA LEIGH.

Eparchial Newsletter—Rev. DONALD J. SAWYER, Editor, P.O. Box 1891, Austin, TX 78767. "Maronites Today"

Office for Immigration—Chorbishop FAOUZI ELIA.

Office for Missions—Revs. DONALD J. SAWYER; ANTHONY SPINOSA.

Office of Communications—Rev. Msgr. RICHARD SAAD.

Office of Inter-faith/Ecumenical Affairs—Rev. ANTHONY SPINOSA.

Office of Liturgy—Chorbishop MICHAEL KAIL.

Office of Ministries—Deacon LOUIS PETERS.

Office of Priestly Vocations—Rev. SHARBEL MAROUN; Sr. SAMIA ABOU-SHAMRA, A.S., Assoc. Dir.

Office of Religious Education—Rev. ANTHONY SALIM.

Office of Youth Ministries—Rev. GARY GEORGE, C.SS.R.

Master of Ceremonies—Rev. ANDRE MHANNA.

Office of Young Adult Ministry—Rev ANDRE MHANNA.

Presbyteral Council—Chorbishop FAOUZI ELIA; Rev. Msgr. RICHARD SAAD; Revs. ABDALLAH ZAIDAN, M.L.M.; ALFRED BADAWI; ANTOINE BAKH; ANTHONY SALIM; JOHN NAHAL, M.L.M.; ANTHONY SPINOSA; Rev. Msgr. WILLIAM BONCZWESKI; Chorbishop GREGORY J. MANSOUR, S.T.L., Ex Officio.

Pro-Life & Family Life Office—VACANT.

Office for the Third Millenium—Rev. ANTHONY SPINOSA.

Eparchial Webmaster—Mr. FADI MOUHANNA.

Properties Owned—

St. Maron Office Building— Detroit, MI

Los Angeles Chancery Office— Los Angeles, CA

Father Tobia Retirement Home— North Jackson, OH

Bishop's Residence— Bel Air, CA

Maronite Catholic Pastoral Center— St. Louis, MO

Protopresbyters—Chorbishop FAOUZI ELIA, Mid-America Region; Revs. ANTHONY SPINOSA, Midwest Region; ABDALLAH ZAIDAN, M.L.M., Southwest Region; Rev. Msgr. RICHARD SAAD, Southern Region.

Spiritual Director for the National Apostolate of Maronites—Rev. DON JOSEPH SAWYER.

Order of St. Sharbel—PAUL KASSOUF, Pres.; VACANT, Vice Pres., Eparchy of Our Lady of Lebanon of Los Angeles, 1021 S. 10th St., St. Louis, 63104.

Victim Assistance Coordinator—Deacon PHILIP R. HENGEN. Tel: 636-391-6837. Email: harvath@kennrick.edu.

CLERGY, PARISHES, MISSIONS AND PAROCHIAL SCHOOLS

STATE OF CALIFORNIA

ANAHEIM, ORANGE CO., ST. JOHN MARON (1988), Rev. Antoine Bakh; Deacon Alfred Harb.
Mailing Address: 1546 E. La Palma Ave., CA 92805. Tel: 714-520-5303; Fax: 714-520-4273.
Res.: 601 N. Woods Ave., Fullerton, CA 92832. Tel: 714-525-4216.
Catechesis/Religious Program—Students 40.
Mission—Maronite Catholic Community of Riverside

LOS ANGELES, LOS ANGELES CO.

1—OUR LADY OF MT. LEBANON-ST. PETER CATHEDRAL (1923), (Lebanese), Rev. Abdallah E. Zaidan, M.L.M., Rector; Deacon Edward Corey; Rev. Elias Sleiman, M.L.M.
Res.: 333 S. San Vicente Blvd., CA 90048. Tel: 310-275-6634; Fax: 310-858-0856.
Catechesis/Religious Program—Students 65.

2—ST. JUDE MISSION (1999), (Lebanese), Rev. Georges Bou Msallem, M.L.M.
Res.: 553A E. Bonita, San Dimas, CA 91773. Tel: 909-592-9090; Fax: 909-592-9494.
Catechesis/Religious Program—P.O. Box 885, San Dimas, CA 91773. Tel: 626-848-4134. Students 27.

MILLBRAE, SAN MATEO CO., OUR LADY OF LEBANON (1979), (Lebanese), [JC] Rev. Toufic M. Nasr.
Mailing Address: P.O. Box 896, CA 94030.
Res.: 600 El Camino Real, CA 94030. Tel: 650-589-9653; Fax: 650-866-3091.
Mission—Maronite Catholic Community of Stockton Stockton, San Joaquin Co., CA. Tel: 650-652-5644.

SAN DIEGO, SAN DIEGO CO., SAINT EPHREM (1989), [CEM] Rev. Nabil Mouannes.
Mailing Address: 750 Medford St., El Cajon, CA 92020. Tel: 619-697-3040; Fax: 619-654-1888.
Res.: 766 Medford St., El Cajon, CA 92020. Tel: 619-697-3040.

THOUSAND OAKS, VENTURA CO., SAINTS PETER AND

PAUL MISSION, Rev. Pierre Albalaa, M.L.M.
P.O. Box 4455, CA 91359-1455. Tel: 818-219-7605; Fax: 818-889-3405.

STATE OF ALABAMA

BIRMINGHAM, JEFFERSON CO.
1—ST. ELIAS (1910), (Lebanese), Rev. Msgr. Richard D. Saad; Deacons Joseph Stephens; Samuel Wehby.
Res.: 836 Eighth St. S., AL 35205-4567. Tel: 205-251-5057; 205-252-3867; Fax: 205-251-5028.
Catechesis / Religious Program—Students 105.
2—MARONITE CATHOLIC COMMUNITY OF MOBILE (1910), (Lebanese), Rev. Msgr. Richard D. Saad, Contact Person.
Mailing Address: St. Elias Church, 836 8th St. S., AL 35205. Tel: 205-251-5057; Fax: 205-251-5028.

STATE OF ARIZONA

PHOENIX, MARICOPA CO., ST. JOSEPH MISSION (1992), Rev. Ghassan Mattar, M.L.M.
Res.: 5406 E. Virginia Ave., AZ 85008. Tel: 602-667-3280; Fax: 602-468-0174.
Catechesis / Religious Program—Students 35.

STATE OF COLORADO

DENVER, DENVER CO., ST. RAFKA MISSION, Rev. Shane Wasinger (DEN), Admin.
Res.: 4950 S. Logan St., Englewood, CO 80112. Tel: 720-833-0354; Fax: 720-833-0354.
Catechesis / Religious Program—Students 11.

STATE OF ILLINOIS

HILLSIDE, COOK CO., OUR LADY OF LEBANON CHURCH (1952), (Lebanese), Rev. Alfred Badawi.
Res.: 17 W. 730 Butterfield Rd. Apt. 218, Oakbrook Terrace, IL 60181. Tel: 630-932-9640; Fax: 630-932-9463.
Catechesis / Religious Program—Tel: 708-442-1127. Students 72.
Mission—Maronite Catholic Community Sacred Heart Church, Eighth St., Michigan City, La Porte Co., IN 46360.
PEORIA, PEORIA CO., ST. SHARBEL (1973), Chorbishop Faouzi Y. Elia; Deacons James Siedlecki; Bechara Anada.
Res.: 2914 W. Scenic Dr., IL 61615. Tel: 309-688-5555; Fax: 309-688-0431.
Catechesis / Religious Program—Students 46.

STATE OF KENTUCKY

LOUISVILLE, JEFFERSON CO., MARONITE CATHOLIC COMMUNITY OF LOUISVILLE (1910), (Lebanese), Rev. Antoine Elghazal, Admin.
Mailing Address: 2530 Victory Pkwy., Cincinnati, OH 45206. Tel: 513-961-0120; Fax: 513-861-5075.

STATE OF LOUISIANA

BATON ROUGE, EAST BATON ROUGE PARISH, MARONITE CATHOLIC COMMUNITY, Rev. Msgr. Richard D. Saad, Admin.
Tel: 205-251-5057; Fax: 205-251-5028.
LAFAYETTE, CONTRA COSTA CO., MARONITE CATHOLIC COMMUNITY, Rev. Msgr. Richard D. Saad, Admin.
Tel: 205-251-5057; Fax: 205-251-5028.
LAKE CHARLES, CALCASIEU PARISH, MARONITE CATHOLIC COMMUNITY, Rev. Msgr. Richard D. Saad, Admin.
Tel: 205-251-5057; Fax: 205-251-5028.
NEW ORLEANS, ORLEANS PARISH, MARONITE CATHOLIC COMMUNITY, Rev. Msgr. Richard D. Saad, Admin.
Tel: 205-251-5057; Fax: 205-251-5028.

STATE OF MICHIGAN

DETROIT, WAYNE CO.
1—ST. MARON (1909), (Lebanese), [CEM] Rev. Ghattas Khoury.
Res.: 11466 Kercheval, MI 48215. Tel: 313-824-0196; Fax: 313-824-6418.
Catechesis / Religious Program—Students 9.
2—ST. RAFKA MARONITE MISSION, Formerly Maronite Community of Detroit (Westside) Chorbishop Michael Kail.
Mailing Address: c/o 31601 Schoenherr Rd., Warren, MI 48093-1977. Tel: 586-826-9688; Fax: 586-826-3521.
FLINT, GENESEE CO., OUR LADY OF LEBANON (1973), Rev. Msgr. William D. Bonczewski; Deacons Martin J. Rachid; Earl Matte.
Res.: 4133 Calkins Rd., MI 48532. Tel: 810-733-1259; Fax: 810-732-2760.
Catechesis / Religious Program—Students 50.
WARREN, MACOMB CO., ST. SHARBEL (1987), Chorbishop Michael Kail.
Res.: 31601 Schoenherr Rd., MI 48093-1977. Tel: 586-826-9688; Fax: 586-826-3521.
Catechesis / Religious Program—Students 230.

STATE OF MINNESOTA

MINNEAPOLIS, HENNEPIN CO., ST. MARON (1948), (Lebanese), [CEM] [JC] Rev. Sharbel G. Maroun.
Res.: 600 University Ave., N.E., MN 55413. Tel: 612-379-2758; Fax: 612-379-7647.
Catechesis / Religious Program—Tel: 612-631-2182. Students 80.
ST. PAUL, RAMSEY CO., HOLY FAMILY CHURCH (1918), (Lebanese), [CEM] Revs. Steve Bonian, S.J.; Rodrigue Constantin.
Res.: 203 E. Robie St., MN 55107. Tel: 651-291-1116; Fax: 651-222-3033.

STATE OF MISSOURI

COLUMBIA, BOONE CO., MARONITE CATHOLIC COMMUNITY (1998), Chorbishop Gregory J. Mansour, S.T.L.
Tel: 314-621-0056; Fax: 314-231-9057.
ST. LOUIS, ST. LOUIS CITY CO., ST. RAYMOND'S CATHEDRAL (1913), (Lebanese), Chorbishop Gregory J. Mansour, S.T.L., Rector; Rev. Andre Mhanna; Deacons Louis Peters; George Simon.
Res.: 931 Lebanon Dr., 63104. Tel: 314-621-0056; Fax: 314-231-9057.
Catechesis / Religious Program—Students 130.

STATE OF NEVADA

LAS VEGAS, CLARK CO., ST. SHARBEL MISSION (1991), Rev. Nabil Mouannes, Admin. Tel: 619-337-1350.
766 Medford St., El Cajon, CA 92020. Tel: 619-697-3040; Fax: 619-654-1888.

STATE OF OKLAHOMA

TULSA, TULSA CO., ST. EPHREM MISSION (1998), Rev. Elias Abi-Sarkis.
Res.: 12300 E. 91st S., Broken Arrow, OK 74012. Tel: 918-740-5463; Fax: 918-254-0375.

STATE OF OHIO

CINCINNATI, HAMILTON CO., ST. ANTHONY OF PADUA (1910), (Lebanese), [CEM] [JC] Revs. Anthony Salim; Antoine El-Ghazal; Deacons Joseph Mousie; Arthur Evans.
Res.: 2530 Victory Pkwy., OH 45206. Tel: 513-961-0120; Fax: 513-961-6058.
Catechesis / Religious Program—Students 2.
CLEVELAND, CUYAHOGA CO., ST. MARON (1915), [JC] Chorbishop Bernard C. Khachan; Deacons George M. Khoury; James Peters.
Res.: 1245 Carnegie Ave., OH 44115. Tel: 216-781-6161; Fax: 216-781-6162.
Catechesis / Religious Program—Students 125.
COLUMBUS, FRANKLIN CO., OUR LADY OF LEBANON MARONITE MISSION, Rev. Pierre Bassil, Admin.
Contact—Fax: 937-253-2525.
DAYTON, MONTGOMERY CO., SAINT IGNATIUS MISSION (1993), [JC] Rev. Pierre Bassil.
Mailing Address: 727 Beckman St., OH 45410. Tel: 937-256-3134; Fax: 937-253-2525.
FAIRLAWN, SUMMIT CO., OUR LADY OF THE CEDARS OF MT. LEBANON (1937), Rev. Msgr. Louis Baz; Deacon Robert Foster.
Res.: 507 S. Cleveland-Massillon Rd., OH 44333-3019. Tel: 330-666-3598; Fax: 330-666-3897.
Catechesis / Religious Program—Students 58.
TOLEDO, LUCAS CO., MARONITE CATHOLIC COMMUNITY (1999), Rev. Anthony Spinosa.
Mailing Address: 4133 Calkins Rd., Flint, MI 48523. Tel: 810-733-1259.
YOUNGSTOWN, MAHONING CO., ST. MARON (1902), Rev. Gary George, C.SS.R., Admin.; Deacons Joseph Nohra; Thomas Craven.
Res.: 1555 S. Meridian Rd., OH 44511-1199. Tel: 330-792-2371; 330-792-7671 (Center); Fax: 330-792-3026.
Catechesis / Religious Program—Tel: 330-538-2567; Fax: 330-538-9820. Students 131.

STATE OF OREGON

PORTLAND, MULTNOMAH CO., SAINT SHARBEL (1970), Rev. Jonathan Decker, S.J. M.J.
Res.: 1804 S.E. 16th Ave., OR 97214. Tel: 503-231-3853; Fax: 503-533-8524.
Catechesis / Religious Program—Students 24.

STATE OF TEXAS

AUSTIN, TRAVIS CO., OUR LADY'S MARONITE PARISH (1982), Rev. Donald Sawyer, D.Min.; Deacon Joseph Crowley.
Mailing Address: 1320 E. 51st St., TX 78723. Tel: 512-458-3693; Fax: 512-451-9554.
Catechesis / Religious Program—Students 48.
EL PASO, EL PASO CO., ST. ANTHONY OF THE DESERT MISSION (1997), (Lebanese), Rev. Georges Chaanine.
Res.: 3617 Breckenridge St., TX 79936. Tel: 915-593-3121; Fax: 915-594-8515.
Catechesis / Religious Program—Students 5.
HOUSTON, HARRIS CO., OUR LADY OF THE CEDARS MARONITE MISSION (1990), (Lebanese), [JC] Revs. Milad T. Yaghi, M.L.M.; Andre Estephan, M.L.M.
Res.: 11935 Belfort Village, TX 77031. Tel: 281-568-6800; Fax: 281-564-6961.
Catechesis / Religious Program—Students 75.
LEWISVILLE, DENTON CO., OUR LADY OF LEBANON MISSION (1990), (Lebanese), Rev. Assaad El-Bacha, M.L.M.
Res.: 719 University Pl., TX 75067. Tel: 972-436-7617; Fax: 972-221-3430.
Catechesis / Religious Program—Students 70.
SAN ANTONIO, BEXAR CO., ST. GEORGE MARONITE (1925), (Maronite), [JC] Revs. John Nahal, M.L.M.; Fadi Helwangi, M.L.M.; Deacon Raymond E. Casillas.
Church: 6070 Babcock Rd., TX 78240. Tel: 210-690-9569; Fax: 210-690-5093.
Catechesis / Religious Program—Students 173.

STATE OF UTAH

MURRAY, SALT LAKE CO., SAINT JUDE CHURCH (1975), (Lebanese), Rev. Gebran Bou-Merhi.
Res.: 4893 Wasatch St., UT 84107. Tel: 801-268-2820.
Church: 4900 Wasatch St., UT 84107. Tel: 801-268-2820; Fax: 801-268-4404.
Catechesis / Religious Program—Students 20.

STATE OF WEST VIRGINIA

WHEELING, OHIO CO., OUR LADY OF LEBANON (1906), (Lebanese), [JC] Rev. Bakhos Chidiac.
Res.: 2216 Eoff St., WV 26003. Tel: 304-233-1688; Fax: 304-233-4714.
Catechesis / Religious Program—Students 7.

STATE OF WASHINGTON

SEATTLE, KING CO., ST. JOSEPH MARONITE MISSION, Formerly Maronite Catholic Community of Seattle (2001), Rev. Peter Karam, Admin.
Res.: 1240 N.E. 127th St., WA 98125-0177. Tel: 206-363-6767; Fax: 206-362-4863.

Special Assignment:
Revs.—
Fisher, David, Adjunct Prof. of Theology, Marianist University of Dayton
Kimes, John Paul, Rome, Italy.

Retired:
Rev. Msgr.—
Michael, Kenneth
Rev.—
Hitti, Michael

INSTITUTIONS LOCATED IN THE DIOCESE

[A] MONASTERIES AND RESIDENCES OF PRIESTS AND BROTHERS

ANN ARBOR. *Maronite Order of Blessed Virgin Mary*, 4405 Earhart Rd., MI 48105. Tel: 734-662-4822; Fax: 734-662-4822. Email: frziad@avemariafoundation.org. Revs. Ziad Antoun, O.M.M.; Antonio El-Feghali, O.M.M.; Jihad Youness, O.M.M. Total in Residence 3.

HOUSTON. *The Congregation of Maronite Lebanese Missionaries*, Our Lady of the Cedars, 11935 Bellfort Village, TX 77031. Tel: 281-568-6800; Fax: 281-564-6961. Email: azaidan@earthlink.net. Revs. Abdallah E. Zaidan, M.L.M., Supr.; Pierre Al-Balaa, M.L.M.; Milad T. Yaghi, M.L.M.; Andre S. Estephan, M.L.M.; John Nahal, M.L.M.; Assaad El-Bacha, M.L.M.; Ghassan Mattar, M.L.M.; George Bou Msallem, M.L.M.; Elias Sleiman, M.L.M.; Fadi Helwangi, M.L.M.

[B] CONVENTS AND RESIDENCES FOR SISTERS

NORTH JACKSON. *Antonine Maronite Sisters of Youngstown, Inc.*, 2691 N. Lipkey Rd., OH 44451. Tel: 330-538-2567; Fax: 330-538-9820. Email: anto9srs@aol.com. Sisters 6.
Antonine Sisters Adult Day Care, Inc., 2675 N. Lipkey Rd., OH 44451. Tel: 330-538-9822; Fax: 330-538-9820. Total Staff 21; Total Assisted 79.

[C] NATIONAL SHRINES

NORTH JACKSON. *National Shrine of Our Lady of Lebanon* 2759 N. Lipkey Rd., OH 44451. Tel: 330-538-3351; Fax: 330-538-0455. Web: www.nationalshrine.org. Rev. Msgr. William D. Bonczewski.

[D] RELIGIOUS COMMUNITIES OF MEN

PHILIPPI. *Our Lady of Solitude Maronite Hermitage, Inc.*, 334 S. Main St., WV 26416. Tel: 304-457-3330; Fax: 304-457-3303. Email: monkbg7@aol.com. Rev. Bernard Grunewald, Er.O.L.S, Supr. Total in Residence 1.

[E] RESIDENCES FOR CLERGY

NORTH JACKSON. *Father Tobia Retirement Home*, 2759 N. Lipkey Rd., OH 44451. Tel: 330-538-3351; Fax: 330-538-0455. Web: www.nationalshrine.org.

[F] MISCELLANEOUS

LOS ANGELES. *Bishop's Retirement Home*, 850 Stone Canyon Rd., CA 90077. Tel: 310-472-3903.

ST. LOUIS. *Bishop's Charities*, 1021 S. 10th St., 63104. Tel: 314-231-1021; Fax: 314-231-1418. Email: moenny@usamaronite.org. Most Rev. Robert Shaheen, Chm.

Bishop's Retirement Trust Fund, 1021 S. 10th St., 63104. Tel: 314-231-1021; Fax: 314-231-1418. Chorbishop Gregory J. Mansour, S.T.L.

Caritas Lebanon, 1021 S. 10th St., 63104. Tel: 314-231-1021; Fax: 314-231-1418. Email: eparchy@aol.com.

Catholic School Assistance Fund, 1021 S. 10th St., 63104. Tel: 314-231-1021; Fax: 314-231-1418. Email: moenny@usamaronite.org eparchy@aol.com. Web: www.eparchyla.org. Most Rev. Robert J. Shaheen.

Eparchial Endowments, 1021 S. 10th St., 63104. Tel: 314-231-1021; Fax: 314-231-1418. Chorbishop Gregory J. Mansour, S.T.L.

Our Lady of Smiles Orphanage, 1021 S. 10th St., 63104. Tel: 314-231-1021; Fax: 314-231-1418. Email: eparchy@aol.com. Rev. Mansour Labaky, Pres.

Priest's Retirement Fund, 1021 S. 10th St., 63104. Tel: 314-231-1021; Fax: 314-231-1418. Email: eparchy@aol.com. Web: eparchyla.org.

RELIGIOUS INSTITUTES OF MEN REPRESENTED IN THE DIOCESE

For further details refer to the corresponding bracketed number in the Religious Institutes of Men or Women section.

[0785]—*The Congregation of Maronite Lebanese Missionaries* (San Antonio, TX)—M.L.M.

[0782]—*Maronite Order of Blessed Virgin Mary* Ann Arbor, MI—O.M.M.

NECROLOGY

(No Deaths)

Byzantine Eparchy of Parma

Most Reverend

JOHN M. KUDRICK

Bishop of Parma; ordained May 3, 1975; consecrated and installed July 10, 2002.

Chancery Office: *1900 Carlton Rd., Parma, OH 44134.* Tel: 216-741-8773; Fax: 216-741-9356.

Web: www.parma.org

ESTABLISHED FEBRUARY 21, 1969.

Embraces all Byzantine Ruthenian Rite Catholics in the States of Illinois, Indiana, Iowa, Kansas, Michigan, Minnesota, Missouri, Nebraska, North Dakota, South Dakota and Wisconsin. Also the entire State of Ohio excluding the Counties of Ashtabula, Trumbull, Mahoning, Columbiana, Carroll, Harrison, Guernsey, Noble, Morgan, Athens, Meigs, Gallia and Lawrence.

Legal Title: For legal titles of parishes and diocesan institutions, consult the Chancery Office.

STATISTICAL OVERVIEW

Personnel	
Bishop	1
Priests: Diocesan Active in Diocese	25
Priests: Diocesan Active Outside Diocese	1
Priests: Retired, Sick or Absent	11
Number of Diocesan Priests	37
Religious Priests in Diocese	1
Total Priests in Diocese	38
Extern Priests in Diocese	6
Ordinations:	
Diocesan Priests	1
Transitional Deacons	1
Permanent Deacons	2
Permanent Deacons in Diocese	8
Total Sisters	13
Parishes	
Parishes	31
With Resident Pastor:	
Resident Diocesan Priests	26
Resident Religious Priests	1
Without Resident Pastor:	
Administered by Priests	4
Missions	6
Closed Parishes	1
Professional Ministry Personnel:	
Sisters	13
Lay Ministers	1
Welfare	
Day Care Centers	2
Total Assisted	81
Special Centers for Social Services	5
Total Assisted	10,000
Educational	
Elementary Schools, Diocesan and Parish	2
Total Students	239
Catechesis/Religious Education:	
High School Students	185
Elementary Students	676
Total Students under Catholic Instruction	1,100
Teachers in the Diocese:	
Sisters	3
Lay Teachers	17
Vital Statistics	
Receptions into the Church:	
Infant Baptism Totals	111
Adult Baptism Totals	17
Received into Full Communion	42
First Communions	81
Confirmations	67
Marriages:	
Catholic	38
Interfaith	15
Total Marriages	53
Deaths	186
Total Catholic Population	12,401

Former Bishops—Most Revs. EMIL J. MIHALIK, D.D., ord. Sept. 21, 1945; appt. first Bishop of the Ruthenian Eparchy of Parma, March 22, 1969; installed June 12, 1969; died Jan. 27, 1984; ANDREW PATAKI, D.D., appt. Titular Bishop of Tellmisus and Auxiliary of Passaic, NJ, May 30, 1983; installed Aug. 23, 1983; succeeded to See, June 19, 1984; transferred to Parma See, Aug 16, 1984; transferred to Byzantine Eparchy of Passaic, Nov. 21, 1995; BASIL SCHOTT, O.F.M., ord. Aug. 29, 1965; consecrated and installed as Bishop of Parma July 11, 1996; transferred to Archeparchy of Pittsburgh July 9, 2002.

Chancery Office—1900 Carlton Rd., Parma, 44134. Tel: 216-741-8773; Fax: 216-741-9356.

Protosyncellus—Very Rev. JOHN KACHUBA, M.A.

Syncellus for Clergy and Religious—Very Rev. STEVEN KOPLINKA.

Syncellus for Parishes and Laity—Very Rev. THOMAS LOYA.

Syncellus for Doctrine and Worship—Very Rev. MICHAEL HAYDUK.

Chancellor—Very Rev. DENNIS HRUBIAK.

Notary—Rev. ROBERT KELLY.

Presbyteral Council—Very Revs. JOHN KACHUBA, M.A.; DAVID HANNES, J.C.L.; MICHAEL HAYDUK; DENNIS HRUBIAK; STEVEN KOPLINKA; THOMAS LOYA; BRYAN EYMAN, D.Min.; Revs. BASIL HUTSKO; JOHN KAPITAN JR., O.F.M.; ROBERT KELLY; DAVID PETRAS, S.E.O.D.; JOSEPH REPKO, M.Div.

Eparchial Pastoral Council—Very Revs. JOHN KACHUBA, M.A.; MICHAEL HAYDUK; STEVEN KOPLINKA; THOMAS LOYA; Revs. BASIL HUTSKO; JOSEPH REPKO, M.Div.; Deacon JOHN PETRUS, M.D.; DANIEL BANDURA; KATHERINE BARANKO; VIRGILDEE DANIEL; NICHOLAS J. NAGRANT; LORETTA NEMETH; BERNARD PAUL; MICHAEL ROBUSTO; ANN SEABRIGHT; KATHRYN SZILAGYE.

Eparchial Finance Council—Rev. ROBERT KELLY.

Eparchial Finance Officer—Very Rev. JOHN KACHUBA, M.A.; Sr. HELEN MILLOW, Sec.; JEROME J. LUCAS; EDWARD MAHER; THOMAS PERCIAK.

Eparchial Consultors—Very Revs. JOHN KACHUBA, M.A.; DENNIS HRUBIAK; Revs. BASIL HUTSKO; MICHAEL EVANICK; DAVID PETRAS, S.E.O.D.; Very Rev. DAVID HANNES, J.C.L.

Protopresbyters—Ohio: Very Rev. BRYAN EYMAN, D.Min. Midwest: Rev. Msgr. FRANK KORBA. Great Lakes: Very Rev. JAMES KUBAJAK, M.Div.

Vicar Judicialis—Very Rev. DAVID HANNES, J.C.L.

Vicar Adjutant—Rev. MICHAEL J. HUSZTI.

Judge—Rev. NICHOLAS R.A. RACHFORD, J.C.L.

Secretary of the Tribunal—Rev. NICHOLAS R.A. RACHFORD, J.C.L.

Defender of the Bond—Very Rev. JAMES KUBAJAK, M.Div.

Promoter of Justice—Very Rev. JAMES KUBAJAK, M.Div.

Notary—MARY LIZANICH.

Eparchial Censor—Rev. DAVID PETRAS, S.E.O.D.

Eparchial Commissions

Sacred Liturgy—Revs. DAVID PETRAS, S.E.O.D., Chm.; ROBERT BARTER; Very Revs. MICHAEL HAYDUK; STEVEN KOPLINKA.

Building Commission—Rev. DAVID PETRAS, S.E.O.D.; Very Rev. BRYAN EYMAN, D.Min.

Cantors' Institute—NICOLETTE BOROS, Dir., Cantors' Institute Faculty:; Rev. DAVID PETRAS, S.E.O.D.; Very Revs. DENNIS HRUBIAK; MICHAEL HAYDUK; Revs. MICHAEL J. HUSZTI; JAMES BATCHA; NICHOLAS RACHFORD.

Office of Religious Education—Very Rev. JOHN KACHUBA, M.A., Dir. Tel: 216-741-4102. Associates: Rev. BASIL HUTSKO, Great Lakes; Rev. Msgr. FRANK KORBA, Midwest; Sr. SUSAN HARVEY, O.S.B.M., Ohio.

Catechetical Board—Very Rev. Msgr. FRANK KORBA; BETTY BARANKO; MELVIN CANNON; RENA FULKA; Deacon RICHARD GUIDEN; LISA STANICH.

Office of Youth Ministry—Revs. BRUCE RIEBE, Dir.; BASIL HUTSKO, Great Lakes; Very Rev. THOMAS LOYA, Midwest.

Young Adults—Rev. TERRENCE FARMER.

Office of Family Life—VIRGILDEE DANIEL, Dir.

Office of Lay Apostolate—ROBERT SHIRILLA, Dir.; DAVID BASALLA.

Office of Evangelization and Missionary Activity—Rev. JAMES BATCHA, Dir.

Office of Vocations—Very Rev. DENNIS HRUBIAK, Dir.; Deacon JOSEPH MARQUIS.

Seminary Education Formation Board—Rev. DAVID PETRAS, S.E.O.D., Chm.; Very Revs. MICHAEL HAYDUK; DENNIS HRUBIAK; JOHN KACHUBA, M.A.; STEVEN KOPLINKA.

Priest's Pension Board—Very Revs. JOHN KACHUBA, M.A.; MICHAEL HAYDUK; Revs. JAMES ATKINS; ROBERT BARTER; BRUCE RIEBE; BASIL HUTSKO; JOSEPH POHORLAK; ROBERT KELLY.

Office of Ecumenical Activity—Rev. DAVID PETRAS, S.E.O.D., Dir.

Stewardship Office—MARY S. LIZANICH.

Eparchial Shrine of the Weeping Madonna of Mariapoch— (Burton, OH): President, The Most Rev. Ordinary of the Parma Eparchy. Assisted by the Social Mission Sisters Tel: 440-834-8807. Sr. M. FLORA, S.M.S., Supr. Tel: 440-834-4078.

Respect Life Office—PATRICK PEROTTI.

Pre-Cana Office—Very Rev. MICHAEL HAYDUK.

Victim Assistance Coordinator—SHARON DILAURO, M.D. Tel: 330-659-3195. Email: jpetrus@adelphia.net.

CLERGY, PARISHES, MISSIONS AND PAROCHIAL SCHOOLS

STATE OF OHIO

AKRON, SUMMIT CO., ST. MICHAEL THE ARCHANGEL, [CEM] Rev. Alan Kapron, Admin.; Deacon John Petrus.

Res.: 847 Crouse St., 44306-1125. Tel: 330-376-6633; Fax: 330-376-4149.

BARBERTON, SUMMIT CO., ST. NICHOLAS, [CEM] Rev. Alan Kapron.
Res.: 1051 E. Robinson St., 44203-3852. Tel: 330-753-2031; Fax: 330-753-1188.

BEDFORD, CUYAHOGA CO., ST. EUGENE, Rev. Joseph Repko, M.Div.
Res.: 264 Warrensville-Center Rd., 44146-2741. Tel: 440-232-7302; Fax: 440-439-9537.

BRECKSVILLE, CUYAHOGA CO., ST. JOSEPH, Rev. Bruce Riebe.
Res.: 8111 Brecksville, 44141-1204. Tel: 440-526-1818; Fax: 440-526-6464.

BRUNSWICK, MEDINA CO., ST. EMILIAN, Very Rev. Stephen Koplinka, Admin.; Rev. Terrence Farmer.
Res.: 1231 Substation Rd., 44212-0843. Tel: 330-225-9857; Fax: 330-220-5963.

BURTON, GEAUGA CO., CHURCH OF MARIAPOCH, Unassigned.
Church: 17486 Mumford Rd., 44021-9640.
Shrine—Shrine of Mariapoch, Tel: 440-834-4078.
Social Mission Sisters of Hungary 2.

CLEVELAND, CUYAHOGA CO.
1—HOLY GHOST, Rev. Michael J. Huszti, Admin.
Res.: 2420 W. 14th St., 44113-4406. Tel: 216-861-2177.
2—ST. MARY, Very Rev. Steven Koplinka; Rev. Terrence Farmer.
Res.: 4600 State Rd., 44109-5243. Tel: 216-741-7979; Fax: 216-741-6622.
School—Tel: 216-749-7980; Fax: 216-749-7981. Rita Basalla, Prin. Sisters of St. Basil the Great 3; Lay Teachers 11; Students 276.
3—ST. NICHOLAS, (Croatian), Rev. Michael J. Huszti.
Res.: 3431 Superior Ave., 44114-4160. Tel: 216-361-5069; Fax: 216-361-2455.

COLUMBUS, FRANKLIN CO., ST. JOHN CHRYSOSTOM, Rev. James Batcha.
Res.: 5858 Cleveland Ave., 43231-2862. Tel: 614-882-7578; Fax: 614-890-6048.

DAYTON, MONTGOMERY CO., ST. BARBARA, Rev. John Kapitan Jr., O.F.M., Admin.
Res.: 5915 Springboro Pk., 45449-3249. Tel: 937-434-9205.

EUCLID, CUYAHOGA CO., ST. STEPHEN, Very Rev. Archpriest John S. Kachuba.
Res.: 532 Lloyd Rd., 44132-1721. Tel: 216-732-7292; Fax: 216-732-9434.

FAIRPORT HARBOR, LAKE CO., ST. MICHAEL, Very Rev. Bryan R. Eyman, D.Min.
Mailing Address: *St. Andrew*, c/o 5768 Andrews Rd., Mentor-on-the-Lake, 44060-2608.
Res.: 630 Plum St., 44077-5660. Tel: 440-257-3620; Fax: 440-257-6524.

FAIRVIEW PARK, CUYAHOGA CO., ST. MARY MAGDALENE, Very Rev. Dennis M. Hrubiak; Rev. John Kovach, Admin.
Res.: 5390 W. 220th St., 44126-2968. Tel: 440-734-4644; Fax: 440-734-4645.

LAKEWOOD, CUYAHOGA CO., ST. GREGORY THE THEOLOGIAN, Rev. Robert D. Kelly.
Res.: 2035 Quail Ave., 44107-5217. Tel: 216-521-1081; Fax: 216-521-1026.

LORAIN, LORAIN CO.
1—ST. MICHAEL, Closed. For inquiries for parish records contact the chancery.
2—ST. NICHOLAS, Rev. Nicholas Rachford.
Res.: 2711 W. 40th St., 44053-2252. Tel: 440-282-7525; Fax: 440-282-9185.
School—2707 W. 40th St., 44053-2252. Tel: 440-282-3289; Fax: 440-282-3289. Mr. Russell Tabak, Prin. Lay Teachers 5; Students 44.

MARBLEHEAD, OTTAWA CO., ST. MARY, [CEM] Rev. Joseph R. Radvansky.
Res.: 506 E. Main St., 43440-2232. Tel: 419-798-4283; Fax: 419-798-4095.

MENTOR-ON-THE-LAKE, LAKE CO., ST. ANDREW THE APOSTLE, Very Rev. Bryan R. Eyman, D.Min.
Res.: 5768 Andrews Rd., 44060-2608. Tel: 440-257-3620; Fax: 440-257-6524.

NORTHWOOD, LUCAS CO., ST. MICHAEL THE ARCHANGEL, Very Rev. James Kubajak; Deacon James Sofalvi.
Res.: 2526 Skagway Dr., 43619. Tel: 419-691-5656; Fax: 419-691-7669.
Church: 4001 Navarre Ave., Oregon, 43616.

PARMA, CUYAHOGA CO.
1—SAINT JOHN THE BAPTIST, CATHEDRAL, Very Rev. Michael Hayduk.
Church: 1900 Carlton Rd., 44134-3129. Tel: 216-661-8658; Fax: 216-661-8221.
Res.: 1703 Carlton Rd., 44134.
2—HOLY SPIRIT, [CEM 2] Very Rev. Dennis M. Hrubiak; Rev. John Kovach; Deacon Sidney Sidor.
Res.: 5500 W. 54th St., 44129-2274. Tel: 440-884-8452; Fax: 440-884-8453.

SOLON, CUYAHOGA CO., ST. JOHN THE BAPTIST, Rev. Joseph Repko, M.Div.
Res.: 36125 Aurora Rd., 44139-3841. Tel: 440-248-0417; Fax: 440-248-8044.

STATE OF ILLINOIS

CHICAGO, COOK CO., ST. MARY, Closed. For inquiries for parish records contact the chancery.

HOMER GLEN, WILL CO., ANNUNCIATION BYZANTINE CATHOLIC CHURCH, [CEM] Very Rev Thomas J. Loya; Deacons Michael Kenes; J. Timothy Tkach.
Res.: 14610 S. Will-Cook Rd., IL 60491-9212. Tel: 708-645-0241; Fax: 708-645-0243.

JOLIET, WILL CO., ST. MARY ASSUMPTION, Closed. For inquiries for parish records contact the chancery.

STATE OF INDIANA

EAST CHICAGO, LAKE CO., ST. BASIL'S, Closed. For inquiries for parish records contact the chancery.

INDIANA HARBOR CO., HOLY GHOST, Closed. For inquiries for parish records contact the chancery.

INDIANAPOLIS, MARION CO., ST. ATHANASIUS CHURCH, Rev. John Kapitan Jr., O.F.M.
Res.: 1117 S. Blaine Ave., IN 46221-1110. Tel: 317-632-4157; Fax: 317-632-2988.

MERRILLVILLE, LAKE CO., ST. MICHAEL, Very Rev. Michael Evanick.
Res.: 557 W. 57th Ave., IN 46410-2540. Tel: 219-980-0600; Fax: 219-980-0127.

MUNSTER, LAKE CO., SAINT NICHOLAS [CEM] Rev. Msgr. Frank Korba, V.F.
Res.: 8103 Columbia Ave., IN 46321-1802. Tel: 219-838-9380; Fax: 219-838-1265.

WHITING, LAKE CO., ASSUMPTION OF THE BLESSED VIRGIN, [CEM] Rev. Joseph Pohorlak; Deacon Richard Guiden.
Res.: 2011 Clark St., IN 46394-2023. Tel: 219-659-0277; Fax: 219-659-1687.

STATE OF MICHIGAN

ALLEN PARK, WAYNE CO., ST. STEPHEN, Rev. Cyril Attak; Deacon Lawrence Hendricks.
Res.: 4141 Laurence Ave., MI 48101-3049. Tel: 313-382-5901; Fax: 313-382-5902.

BAY CITY, BAY CO., SAINT GEORGE, Rev. Robert Stash.
Res. 204 N. Van Buren St., MI 48706-6519. Tel: 989-892-0763; Fax: 989-892-8941.

DETROIT, WAYNE CO.
1—ST JOHN THE BAPTIST, Closed. For inquiries for parish records contact the chancery.
2—ST NICHOLAS, Rev. Robert J. Barter; Deacon Joseph Marquis.
Church: 19130 Beaconsfield St., MI 48224-1177. Tel: 313-521-6827; Fax: 313-521-5704.

FLUSHING, GENESEE CO., ST. MICHAEL, Very Rev. David A. Hannes, J.C.L.
Res.: 2333 N. Elms Rd., MI 48433-9426. Tel: 810-659-4887; Fax: 810-659-8363.

LIVONIA, WAYNE CO., SACRED HEART, Rev. Nicholas Ivan.
Res.: 29125 W. Six-Mile Rd., MI 48152-3661. Tel: 734-522-3166.

OMER, ARENAC CO., ST. JOHN, Rev. Robert Stash.
Mailing Address: P.O. Box 236, MI 48749-0236. Tel: 989-892-0763.
Res.: 204 N. Van Buren St., Bay City, MI 48706-6519.

STERLING HEIGHTS, MACOMB CO., ST. BASIL, Rev. Basil J. Hutsko.
Res.: 4700 Metropolitan Pkwy., MI 48310-3905. Tel: 586-268-1082; Fax: 586-268-2548.

TAYLOR, WAYNE CO., CHRIST THE KING, Closed. For inquiries for parish records contact the chancery.

STATE OF MINNESOTA

MINNEAPOLIS, HENNEPIN CO., ST. JOHN THE BAPTIST, Rev. James Atkins. In Res., Rev. Edward C. Wojciechowski (Retired).
Res.: 2215 Third St., N.E., MN 55418-3422. Tel: 612-789-6252.

STATE OF MISSOURI

ST. LOUIS, ST. LOUIS CO., ST. LOUIS MISSION, Revs. Eugene P. Selzer; Paul Niemann; Joseph A. Weber.
Mailing Address: 2001 Shepard Rd., Wildwood, MO 63038. Tel: 636-458-2977; Fax: 636-405-1276.
Blessed John XXIII Center: 8300 Morganford Rd., MO 62123.

SUGAR CREEK, JACKSON CO., ST. LUKE, BYZANTINE CATHOLIC PARISH, Rev. Stephen Muth.
Mailing Address: 1029 Bennington, Kansas City, MO 64126-2299.
Church: 11411 Chicago, MO 64054. Tel: 816-254-5532.

STATE OF WISCONSIN

BRISTOL, KENOSHA CO., ST. IRENE, Closed., For information regarding the Byzantine Catholic Community contact the Chancery.

On Duty Outside the Diocese:
Rev.—
Petras, David M., Byzantine Catholic Seminary, 3605 Perrysville Ave., Pittsburgh, PA 05214. Tel: 412-321-5133; Fax: 412-321-9936

Absent on Leave:
Revs.—
Chelena, Thomas
Francisko, Gary
Rebovich, John
Ruglovsky, Robert
St. Germain, Brian

Retired:
Rev. Msgrs.—
Smochko, Basil, 66399 Estrella Ave., Desert Hot Springs, CA 82240-4525. Tel: 760-251-0802
Yarnovitz, Robert, 876 Tippecanoe, Akron, 44319. Tel: 330-645-6086
Very Rev.—
Zavell, Edward, V.F., 11644 Katherine, Taylor, MI 48180. Tel: 734-374-0346
Revs.—
Jadwisiak, Edmund, 3964 E. State Rd., Port Clinton, 43452. Tel: 419-734-9923
Linowski, Eugene R., 2660 Montcalm Rd., Columbus, 43231. Tel: 614-488-0427
Wojciechowski, Edward C., 2215 Third St., N.E., Minneapolis, MN 55418-3422. 2215 Third St., N.E., Minneapolis, MN 55418-3422. Tel: 612-789-6252

Permanent Deacons:
Ackley, Randall
Guiden, Richard, Assumption of the Blessed Virgin Mary, Whiting, IN
Hendricks, Lawrence, St. Stephen, Allen Park, MI
Kenes, Michael, Annunciation Byzantine Church, Lockport, IL
Marquis, Joseph, St. Nicholas, Detroit, MI
Petrus, John, St. Michael, Akron, OH
Sofalvi, James, St. Michael, Northwood, OH
Tkach, J. Timothy, Annunciation Byzantine Church, Lockport. IL

INSTITUTIONS LOCATED IN THE DIOCESE

[A] CONVENTS AND RESIDENCES FOR SISTERS

NORTH ROYALTON. *Motherhouse and Novitiate*, 6688 Cady Rd., 44133. Tel: 440-237-6800. Sr. Mary Philomena Horkavi, B.N.S.C., Supr.

[B] RELIGIOUS SHRINES

BURTON. *Shrine of Mariapoch* 17486 Mumford Rd., 44021. Tel: 440-834-8807. Sr. Flora, Supr. Tel: 440-834-4078.

[C] MISCELLANEOUS

CLEVELAND. *St. Mary Hospitality House*, 5500 W. 54th St., 44129. Tel: 440-884-8453. Email: frdennis@megsinet.net. Dorothy Papke, Dir.

RELIGIOUS INSTITUTES OF WOMEN REPRESENTED IN THE DIOCESE

For further details refer to the corresponding bracketed number in the Religious Institutes of Men or Women section.

[]—*Byzantine Nuns of St. Clare* (Parma Eparchy)—B.N.S.C.

[3730]—*Sisters of the Order of St. Basil the Great*—O.S.B.M.

[]—*Social Mission Sisters of Mariapoch*—S.M.S.

NECROLOGY

† Keblesh, John W., Brunswick, OH St. Emilian—Died April 4, 2003

Byzantine Catholic Eparchy of Passaic

Most Reverend

ANDREW PATAKI, J.C.L., D.D.

Bishop of Passaic; appointed Titular Bishop of Tellmisus and Auxiliary Bishop of Passaic, May 30, 1983; consecrated August 23, 1983; appointed Bishop June 19, 1984; Transferred to Parma See August 16, 1984; Transferred to Passaic November 21, 1995.

Most Reverend

MICHAEL J. DUDICK, D.D.

Retired Bishop of Passaic; ordained November 13, 1945; appointed Bishop August 21, 1968; consecrated and installed October 24, 1968; retired November 21, 1995. *Res.: 445 Lackawanna Ave., West Paterson, NJ 07424.*

Chancery Office: 445 Lackawanna Ave., West Paterson, NJ 07424. Tel: 973-890-7777; Fax: 973-890-7275.

Web: members.aol.com/byzruth/index/htm

Email: eclnews@aol.com

ESTABLISHED JULY 31, 1963.

Embraces all Catholics of the Byzantine-Ruthenian Rite in the States of New Jersey, Connecticut, Delaware, District of Columbia, Florida, Georgia, Maine, Maryland, Massachusetts, New Hampshire, New York, North Carolina, Rhode Island, South Carolina, Vermont, Virginia and all Eastern Pennsylvania within the western boundaries of the Counties of Franklin, Juniata, Lycoming, Mifflin, Union and Tioga.

For legal titles of parishes and diocesan institutions, consult the Chancery Office.

STATISTICAL OVERVIEW

Personnel	
Bishop	1
Retired Bishops	1
Priests: Diocesan Active in Diocese	60
Priests: Diocesan Active Outside Diocese	6
Priests: Retired, Sick or Absent	13
Number of Diocesan Priests	79
Religious Priests in Diocese	9
Total Priests in Diocese	88
Extern Priests in Diocese	3
Ordinations:	
Permanent Deacons	6
Permanent Deacons in Diocese	21
Total Brothers	1
Total Sisters	14
Parishes	
Parishes	92
With Resident Pastor:	
Resident Diocesan Priests	55
Resident Religious Priests	6
Without Resident Pastor:	
Administered by Priests	31
Missions	4
Educational	
Diocesan Students in Other Seminaries	2
Total Seminarians	2
Catechesis/Religious Education:	
High School Students	448
Elementary Students	1,679
Total Students under Catholic Instruction	2,129
Vital Statistics	
Receptions into the Church:	
Infant Baptism Totals	263
Adult Baptism Totals	14
Received into Full Communion	27
First Communions	323
Confirmations	240
Marriages:	
Catholic	57
Interfaith	14
Total Marriages	71
Deaths	569
Total Catholic Population	24,031

Former Bishops—Most Revs. STEPHEN J. KOCISKO, D.D. (Retired), ord. March 30, 1941; appt. Titular Bishop of Theveste and Auxiliary of Exarchate of Pittsburgh, July 20, 1956; appt. First Eparch of Passaic, July 31, 1963; appt. Eparch of Pittsburgh, Dec. 21, 1967; installed March 5, 1968; elevated to Metropolitan Archbishop of Pittsburgh, Feb. 21, 1969; retired June 12, 1991; died March 7, 1995; MICHAEL J. DUDICK, D.D. (Retired), ord. Nov. 13, 1945; appt. Bishop of Passaic, Aug. 21, 1968; installed Oct. 24, 1968; retired Nov. 21, 1995.

Protosyncellus-Vicar General—Very Rev. GERALD N. DINO, O.E.S.L.

Syncellates and Protopresbyterates—

Susquehanna Valley Syncellate—

Syncellus—Very Rev. FRANCIS M. TWARDZIK, S.D.B., St. Mary's Church, 310 Mifflin Ave., Scranton, PA 18503. Tel: 570-342-8429.

Northern Pennsylvania/Northern New York Protopresbyterate—Rev. Msgr. JOHN T. SEKELLICK, J.C.L., Protopresbyter, Holy Ghost Church, 313 First St., Jessup, PA 18434. Tel: 570-489-2353.

Wyoming Valley Protopresbyterate—Very Rev. JAMES HAYER, Protopresbyter, St. Mary's Church, 695 N. Main St., Wilkes-Barre, PA 18705. Tel: 570-822-6028.

Central Pennsylvania Syncellate—

Syncellus—Very Rev. RONALD BARUSEFSKY, SS. Peter & Paul Church, 107 S. Fourth St., Minersville, PA 17954. Tel: 570-544-2074.

Mid-Pennsylvania Protopresbyterate—VACANT.

South Pennsylvania Protopresbyterate—Very Rev. PETER J. HOSAK, M.S., Protopresbyter, SS. Peter & Paul Church, 1140 Johnston Dr., Bethlehem, PA 18017-1934. Tel: 610-867-2322.

New Jersey Syncellate—

Syncellus—Very Rev. MICHAEL MONDIK, St. Thomas the Apostle Church, 1410 Church St., Rahway, 07065. Tel: 732-382-5300.

Northern New Jersey Protopresbyterate—Very Rev. MARCEL SZABO, Protopresbyter, St. Michael Cathedral, 96 First St., Passaic, 07055. Tel: 973-777-2553.

Central New Jersey Protopresbyterate—Very Rev. GREGORY J. NOGA, M.A., Protopresbyter, St. Mary Church, 411 Adeline St., Trenton, 08611. Tel: 609-394-5004.

New York-New England Syncellate—

Syncellus—Very Rev. ROBERT J. HOSPODAR, J.C.L., St. Mary Church, 246 E. 15th St., New York, NY 10003. Tel: 212-677-0516.

New York/New England Protopresbyterate—VACANT.

Middle States Syncellate—

Syncellus—Very Revs. JOHN G. BASARAB, M.A., Epiphany of Our Lord Church, 3410 Woodburn Rd., Annandale, VA 22003. Tel: 703-573-3986; CONAN TIMONEY, Ph.D., Protopresbyter, Patronage of Mother of God Church, 1260 Stevens Ave., Baltimore, MD 21227. Tel: 410-247-4936.

Southern States Syncellate—

Syncellus—Very Revs. PETER LICKMAN, St. Basil Church, 1475 N.E. 199th Street, Miami, FL 33179. Tel: 305-651-0991; ROBERT EVANCHO, Protopresbyter, St. Therese Church, 4265 13th Ave. N., St. Petersburg, FL 33713. Tel: 727-323-4022.

Chancery Office—Eparchial Center, 445 Lackawanna Ave., West Paterson, 07424. Tel: 973-890-7777; Fax: 973-890-7175. Office Hours: Mon.-Fri. 9-12 & 1-4

Chancellor—Very Rev. ROBERT J. HOSPODAR, J.C.L.

Eparchial Finance Officer—Very Rev. ROBERT RADVANSKY.

Eparchial Finance Council—Very Revs. GERALD N. DINO, O.E.S.L.; ROBERT RADVANSKY; Mr. THOMAS P. DEVITA, Attorney at Law; Mr. BERT REIMAN; Mr. JERRY LUCAS, C.P.A.; Ms. VICKI WINDSOR.

Eparchial College of Consultors—Very Revs. GERALD N. DINO, O.E.S.L.; FRANCIS M. TWARDZIK, S.D.B.; BASIL RAKACZKY, O.S.B.M., S.T.L.; MICHAEL MONDIK; JOHN G. BASARAB, M.A.; PETER LICKMAN; RONALD BARUSEFSKY; ROBERT J. HOSPODAR, J.C.L., Sec.

Presbyteral Council—Ex Officio Members: Very Revs. GERALD N. DINO, O.E.S.L.; FRANCIS M. TWARDZIK, S.D.B.; BASIL RAKACZKY, O.S.B.M., S.T.L.; MICHAEL MONDIK; ROBERT J. HOSPODAR, J.C.L., Sec.; JOHN G. BASARAB, M.A.; PETER LICKMAN; RONALD BARUSEFSKY; Rev. Msgr. JOHN T. SEKELLICK, J.C.L. Elected Members: Very Revs. GREGORY J. NOGA, M.A.; ROBERT RADVANSKY; CONAN TIMONEY, Ph.D.; JAMES HAYER; Revs. EDWARD G. CIMBALA, D.Min.; EDWARD J. HIGGINS; MICHAEL KANE, Ph.D.; THEODORE KREPP; MICHAEL POPSON. Appointed Member: Very Rev. BASIL RAKACZKY, O.S.B.M., S.T.L.

Eparchial Tribunal—445 Lackawanna Ave., West Paterson, 07424. Tel: 973-890-7777.

Judicial Vicar—Rev. Msgr. JOHN T. SEKELLICK, J.C.L.

Defender of the Bond—Very Rev. ROBERT J. HOSPODAR, J.C.L.

Auditors—Revs. ANDOR RAKACZKI, S.T.D.; VOLODYMYR ZABLOTSKYY.

Advocate—Very Rev. BASIL RAKACZKY, O.S.B.M., S.T.L.

Promoter of Justice—Very Rev. ROBERT J. HOSPODAR, J.C.L.

Notaries—Rev. VOLODYMYR ZABLOTSKYY; Mrs. MARY ELLEN GAFFNEY; Rev. GARY J. MENSINGER.

Commissions, Departments and Institutions

Building and Properties Commission—Very Rev. MICHAEL MONDIK, Chm.

Cemeteries Commission—Very Rev. GERALD N. DINO, O.E.S.L., Chm.

Clergy Continued Education—VACANT.

Commissions for Ecumenism—VACANT.

Communications and Telecommunications—Very Rev. JAMES HAYER.

Evangelization—Rev. JOSEPH BERTHA, Ph.D., Chm.

Respect Life—Very Rev. ROBERT J. HOSPODAR, J.C.L., Dir.

Family Life—Rev. Msgr. JOHN T. SEKELLICK, J.C.L., Dir.

Eparchial Historian—Very Rev. ROBERT J. HOSPODAR, J.C.L.

Holy Name Society—Rev. Msgr. ROBERT G. MONETA, Chm.

Eparchial Liturgy and Art Commission—Very Rev. MICHAEL MONDIK, Chm.

Eparchial Music Commission—Rev. Msgr. ROBERT G. MONETA, Chm.

Eparchial Newspaper—Very Rev. JAMES HAYER, Editor; Rev. GEORGE M. MALITZ, Business Mgr. "The Eastern Catholic Life" Associate Editors:: Revs. GLENN DAVIDOWICH; JAMES BADEAUX. Tel: 973-890-7794.

Office for Eastern Christian Formation (formerly: Office of Religious Education)—Very Rev. GREGORY J. NOGA, M.A., Dir.

Secretariat for Youth—Rev. GEORGE M. MALITZ, Moderator.

Retirement Plan Board—Very Revs. GERALD N. DINO, O.E.S.L.; ROBERT J. HOSPODAR, J.C.L.; ROBERT RADVANSKY, Treas.; Rev. Msgrs. ROBERT G. MONETA; NICHOLAS I. PUHAK; Revs. GEORGE M. MALITZ; JOSEPH BERTHA, Ph.D.; JAMES BADEAUX; NICHOLAS DEPROSPERO; ROBERT KEMETER; MICHAEL KERESTES; SALVATORE A. PIGNATO.

Saint Nicholas Shrine - Carpathian Village—Rev. MICHAEL SALNICKY, Dir., P.O. Box 616, Canadensis, PA 18325. Tel: 570-595-3265; Fax: 570-595-6177.

Vocations—Rev. EDWARD G. CIMBALA, D.Min., Dir.

Priesthood & Diaconate Formation Programs—Rev. EDWARD G. CIMBALA, D.Min., Dir.

Eastern Catholic Associates—445 Lackawanna Ave., West Paterson, 07424. "God With Us"

CLERGY, PARISHES, MISSIONS AND PAROCHIAL SCHOOLS

STATE OF NEW JERSEY

BAYONNE, HUDSON CO., ST. JOHN THE BAPTIST, Rev. Michael Yurista.
Res.: 15 E. 26th St., 07002. Tel: 201-339-1840; Fax: 201-339-6255.

CARTERET, MIDDLESEX CO., ST. ELIAS, Rev. Edward Semko.
Res.: 42 Cooke Ave., 07008. Tel: 732-541-5213; Fax: 732-541-9637.

DUNELLEN, MIDDLESEX CO., ST. NICHOLAS, , Administered from St. Mary's, Hillsborough, NJ. In Res., Rev. Gregory Hosler.
Res.: 121 Madison Ave., 08812. Tel: 732-968-3337.

EAST BRUNSWICK, MIDDLESEX CO., NATIVITY OF OUR LORD, Rev. Volodymyr Zablotskyy.
Res.: 700 Old Bridge Tpke., 08816. Tel: 732-238-0865; Fax: 732-238-2950.

EDISON, MIDDLESEX CO., ST. NICHOLAS, Very Rev. Robert J. Radvansky.
Res.: 215 May St., 08837. Tel: 732-661-1160; Fax: 732-661-1050.

ELIZABETH, UNION CO., SS. PETER AND PAUL, , Administered from St. George's, Linden, NJ. In Res., Rev. Michael Chubirko, S.D.B.
Res.: 316 First Ave., 07206. Tel: 908-353-7246; Fax: 908-353-7791.

FLANDERS, MORRIS CO., HOLY WISDOM, Rev. Daniel Staniskis.
Res.: 197 Emmans Rd., 07836. Tel: 973-584-0414.

HILLSBOROUGH TOWNSHIP, SOMERSET CO., ST. MARY'S, Rev. Edward G. Cimbala, D.Min.
Res.: 1900 Brook Blvd., 08844. Tel: 908-725-0615; Fax: 908-725-9615.

JERSEY CITY, HUDSON CO., ST. MARY'S, Rev. Robert J. Skurla.
Res.: 231 Pacific Ave., 07304. Tel: 201-333-2975.

LINDEN, UNION CO., ST. GEORGE'S, Very Rev. Gerald N. Dino, O.E.S.L.
Res.: 417 McCandless St., 07036. Tel: 908-486-6500; Fax: 908-486-6523.

MAHWAH, BERGEN CO., HOLY SPIRIT, , Administered from St. Michael Cathedral, Passaic, NJ. , Mailing Address: c/o 96 First St., Passaic, 07055.
Church: Island Rd. at Church St., 07430.

NEW BRUNSWICK, MIDDLESEX CO., ST. JOSEPH, Rev. Stephen J. Skinta, O.S.B.M., Admin.
Res.: 30 High St., 08901. Tel: 732-545-1686.

NEWARK, ESSEX CO., ST. GEORGE, Rev. Msgr. Robert G. Moneta.
Res.: 214 Warwick St., 07105. Tel: 973-589-7202; Fax: 973-589-7202.

PASSAIC, PASSAIC CO., ST. MICHAEL CATHEDRAL, [CEM] Very Rev. Marcel Szabo; Rev. Gregory Hosler.
Res.: 96 First St., 07055. Tel: 973-777-2553; Fax: 973-777-9474.
Chapel— 415 Lackawanna Ave., 07424. Tel: 973-256-0134; Fax: 973-777-9474.

PERTH AMBOY, MIDDLESEX CO.
1—ST. MICHAEL, [CEM] Very Rev. Basil M. Rakaczky, O.S.B.M.
Res.: 401 Hall Ave., 08861. Tel: 732-826-0792; Fax: 732-826-7993.
2—ST. NICHOLAS, [CEM], Administered from St. Nicholas, Edison.
Church: 320 Washington St., 08861. Tel: 732-442-0418.

PHILLIPSBURG, WARREN CO., SS. PETER AND PAUL, Rev. Steven Safko.
Res.: 723 S. Main St., 08865. Tel: 908-454-5482; Fax: 908-859-6174.

RAHWAY, UNION CO., ST. THOMAS THE APOSTLE, Very Rev. Michael Mondik.
Res.: 1410 Church St., 07065. Tel: 732-382-5300; Fax: 732-382-3265.

ROEBLING, BURLINGTON CO., ST. NICHOLAS, [CEM] Rev. Lawrence Robert Wolf, O.S.B.M., Admin.
Res.: 191 Norman Ave., 08554. Tel: 609-499-0058; Fax: 609-499-9539.

SOMERSET, SOMERSET CO., SS. PETER AND PAUL, Rev. Robert Kemeter.
Res.: 285 Hamilton St., 08873. Tel: 732-545-5500; Fax: 732-545-3466.

TOMS RIVER, OCEAN CO., OUR LADY OF PERPETUAL HELP, Rev. Charles Yastishock.
Res.: 1937 Church Rd., 08753. Tel: 732-255-6272; Fax: 732-279-0206.

TRENTON, MERCER CO.
1—ST. MARY OF THE ASSUMPTION, [CEM] Very Rev. Gregory J. Noga, M.A.
Res.: 411 Adeline St., 08611. Tel: 609-394-5004; Fax: 609-394-5045.
Chapel—Hamilton Township, St. Mary Chapel
2—ST. NICHOLAS, Closed., For parish records, contact St Mary of the Assumption, Trenton, NJ. , Mailing Address: *c/o*, 411 Adeline St. 08611.

STATE OF CONNECTICUT

BRIDGEPORT, FAIRFIELD CO., HOLY TRINITY, , Administered from St. John the Baptist, Trumbull, CT. , Mailing Address: c/o 100 St. John's Dr., Trumbull, CT 06611.
Church: 155 Scofield Ave., CT 06605. Tel: 203-377-5967.

DANBURY, FAIRFIELD CO., ST. NICHOLAS Rev. Michael George Popson.
Res.: 13 Pembroke Rd., CT 06811. Tel: 203-743-1106; Fax: 203-743-5326.

MERIDEN, NEW HAVEN CO., ST. NICHOLAS OF MYRA, , Administered from St. Nicholas, Danbury, CT. , Mailing Address: c/o 13 Pembroke Rd., Danbury, CT 06810.
Church: 89 Summer St., CT 06450. Tel: 203-743-1106.

NEW BRITAIN, HARTFORD CO., HOLY TRINITY, [CEM] Rev. Robert F. Slesinski, Ph.D.
Res.: 121 Beaver St., CT 06051. Tel: 860-229-2531; Fax: 860-827-0564.

TRUMBULL, FAIRFIELD CO., ST. JOHN THE BAPTIST, Rev. George M. Malitz.
Res.: 100 St. John's Dr., CT 06611. Tel: 203-377-5967; Fax: 203-377-5968.

STATE OF FLORIDA

COCONUT CREEK, BROWARD CO., OUR LADY OF THE SIGN, Rev. Michael N. Kane, Ph.D.
Res.: 7311 Lyons Rd., FL 33073. Tel: 954-429-0056.

FORT PIERCE, PORT ST. LUCIE CO., SS. CYRIL AND METHODIUS, Rev. Michael Sopoliga, Admin.
Res.: Tel: 772-595-8862.
Church: 1002 Bahama Ave., FL 34982. Tel: 561-595-1021.

JACKSONVILLE, DUVAL CO., PROTECTION OF THE MOTHER OF GOD, Closed., For parish records, contact Holy Dormition, Ormond Beach, FL.

LAKE WORTH, DUVAL CO., HOLY APOSTLES, , Administered from Our Lady of the Sign, Coconut Creek, FL. Mailing Address: c/o 7311 Lyons Rd., Coconut Creek, FL 33073.
Church: 4788 Clock Rd., FL 33463. Tel: 954-429-0056.

MIAMI, DADE CO., ST. BASIL'S, Very Rev. Peter Lickman.
Res.: 1475 N.E. 199 St., FL 33179. Tel: 305-651-0991; Fax: 305-651-4902.

NEW PORT RICHEY, PASCO CO., ST. ANNE'S, , Administered from St. Theresa, St. Petersburg, FL. , Mailing Address: 4265 13th Ave., N., St. Petersburg, FL 33713. Tel: 727-323-4022.
Church: 7120 Massachusetts Ave., FL 34653.

NORTH FORT MYERS, LEE CO., ALL SAINTS BYZANTINE CATHOLIC, Rev. James Mitchko.
Res.: 10291 Bayshore Rd., FL 33917. Tel: 239-543-6363; Fax: 239-543-6363.

ORLANDO, ORANGE CO., ST. NICHOLAS OF MYRA, Rev. Salvatore A. Pignato.
Res.: 5135 Sand Lake Rd., FL 32819. Tel: 407-351-0133; Fax: 407-351-0133.

ORMOND BEACH, VOLUSIA CO., HOLY DORMITION, , Administered from St. Nicholas of Myra, Orlando, FL , Mailing Address: P.O. Box 731197, FL 32173-1197.
Church: 17 Buckskin Ln., FL 32174. Tel: 407-351-0133; Fax: 407-351-0133.

ST. PETERSBURG, PINELLAS CO., ST. THERESE, Very Rev. Robert Evancho.
Res.: 4265 13th Ave. N., FL 33713. Tel: 727-323-4022; Fax: 727-323-8351.
Convent—1200 37th St. N., FL 33713. Tel: 727-322-0003.

STATE OF GEORGIA

ROSWELL, FULTON CO., EPIPHANY BYZANTINE CHURCH, Rev. Philip P. Scott, Ph.D.
Res.: 2030 Old Alabama Rd., GA 30076. Tel: 770-993-0973; Fax: 770-993-2419.

STATE OF MARYLAND

BALTIMORE, BALTIMORE CO., PATRONAGE OF THE MOTHER OF GOD, Very Rev. Conan H. Timoney, Ph.D.
Church: 1260 Stevens Ave., MD 21227. Tel: 410-247-4936; Fax: 410-247-1542.
Mission—St. Francis Abingdon, Harford Co., MD.
Mission—St. Ann's Hagerstown, Washington Co., MD.

BELTSVILLE, PRINCE GEORGE'S CO., ST. GREGORY OF NYSSA, Rev. Michael Kerestes.
Res.: 12420 Old Gunpowder Rd., MD 20705. Tel: 301-953-9323; Fax: 301-953-1529.

STATE OF MASSACHUSETTS

SOUTH HADLEY, HAMPSHIRE CO., ST. MICHAEL'S, Closed., For parish records, contact Holy Trinity, New Britain, CT. , Mailing Address: c/o 121 Beaver St., New Britain, CT 06051.

STATE OF NEW YORK

AMHERST, ERIE CO., ST. STEPHEN'S, Rev. Joseph Bertha, Ph.D.
Res.: 620 Ayer Rd., Williamsville, NY 14221. Tel: 716-688-9290.

BINGHAMTON, BROOME CO., HOLY SPIRIT, [CEM] Rev. John J. Cigan, J.C.B.
Res.: 360 Clinton St., NY 13905. Tel: 607-797-2122; Fax: 607-797-2167.

BROOKLYN, KINGS CO., ST. ELIAS, , Administered from St. Mary's, New York. , Mailing Address: c/o 246 E. 15th St., New York, NY 10003.
Church: 145 Kent St., NY 11232. Tel: 212-677-0516.

ENDICOTT, BROOME CO., SS. PETER AND PAUL'S, , Administered from Holy Spirit, Binghamton, NY. , Mailing Address: c/o 360 Clinton St., Binghamton, NY 13905.
Church: 106 N. Rogers Ave., NY. Tel: 607-797-2122.

GRANVILLE, WASHINGTON CO., SS. PETER AND PAUL, , Administered from St. Mary's, New York, NY. , Mailing Address: c/o 246 E. 15th St., New York, NY 10003. Tel: 212-677-0516. In Res., Rev. Harold R. Stockert.
Church: 2 Park Ave., NY 12832.

NEW YORK, NEW YORK CO.
1—EXALTATION OF HOLY CROSS, , Administered from St. Nicholas of Myra, White Plains, NY. , Mailing Address: c/o 768 North St., White Plains, NY 10605.
Church: 323 E. 82nd St., NY 10028. Tel: 914-681-0659.
2—ST. MARY'S, Very Rev. Robert J. Hospodar, J.C.L.
Res.: 246 E. 15th St., NY 10003. Tel: 212-677-0516; Fax: 212-260-6071.

OLEAN, CATTARAGUS CO., ST. MARY'S, , Administered from St. Stephen Church, Amherst, NY. , Mailing Address: c/o 620 Ayer Rd., Williamsville, NY 14221.
Church: 718 Fountain St., NY 14760. Tel: 716-688-9290.

PEEKSKILL, WESTCHESTER CO., SS. PETER AND PAUL, Rev. Msgr. Robert Senetsky, J.C.D.
Res.: 705 Shenandoah Ave., NY 10566. Tel: 914-737-8249; Fax: 914-737-8438.

SMITHTOWN, SUFFOLK CO., RESURRECTION, [CEM] Rev. Daniel J. Bitsko.
Res.: 37 Juniper Ave., NY 11787. Tel: 631-724-4979.
WESTBURY, NASSAU CO., ST. ANDREW THE APOSTLE, Rev. Daniel J. Bitsko, Admin.; Deacon Nicholas Daddona.
Church: 275 Ellison Ave., NY 11590. Tel: 516-333-3266; 631-724-4979 (Office).
WHITE PLAINS, WESTCHESTER CO., ST. NICHOLAS OF MYRA, Rev. Andor Rakaczki, S.T.D.
Res.: 768 North St., NY 10605. Tel: 914-681-0659; Fax: 914-681-0238.
YONKERS, WESTCHESTER CO., ST. NICHOLAS OF MYRA, , Administered from St. Nicholas of Myra, White Plains. , Mailing Address: 768 North St., White Plains, NY 10605.
Church: 75 Ash St., NY. Tel: 914-681-0659.

STATE OF NORTH CAROLINA

CARY, WAKE CO., SS. CYRIL & METHODIUS BYZANTINE CATHOLIC, Rev. Richard Rohrer.
Res.: 2510 Piney Plains Rd., NC 27511. Tel: 919-851-9266; Fax: 919-233-3997.

STATE OF PENNSYLVANIA

ALLENTOWN, LEHIGH CO.
1—ST. ANDREW THE APOSTLE, Closed., For parish records, contact St. Michael, Allentown.
2—ST. MICHAEL, Rev. J. Michael Venditti.
Res.: 156 Green St., PA 18102. Tel: 610-432-6773; Fax: 610-432-6773.
BEAVER MEADOWS, CARBON CO., SS. PETER AND PAUL, [CEM] Rev. James J. Demko; Deacon Michael Pataki.
Res.: P.O. Box 206, PA 18216. Tel: 570-455-1442; Fax: 570-455-7144.
BETHLEHEM, NORTHAMPTON CO., SS. PETER AND PAUL, Very Rev. Peter J. Hosak, M.S.
Res.: 1140 Johnston Dr., PA 18017. Tel: 610-867-2322; Fax: 610-867-7274.
BROCKTON, SCHUYLKILL CO., ST. MARY'S, , Administered from St. Mary's, Mahanoy City, PA. , Mailing Address: c/o 621 Mahanoy Ave., Mahanoy City, PA 17948.
Church: Green St., PA 17925.
CLARKS SUMMIT, LACKAWANNA CO., TRANSFIGURATION, , Administered from St. Mary, Scranton, PA. , Mailing Address: c/o 310 Mifflin Ave., Scranton, PA 18503.
Church: 1105 Gravel Pond Rd., PA 18411.
COATESVILLE, CHESTER CO., ST. MARY'S, , Administered from St. Michael's, Mont Clare, PA. , Mailing Address: c/o 203 Jacob St., Mont Clare, PA 19453.
Church: 82 Gap Rd., PA 19320.
DUNMORE, LACKAWANNA CO., ST. MICHAEL, [CEM] Rev. Theodore Rudy.
Res.: 511 E. Drinker St., PA 18512. Tel: 570-344-2521; Fax: 570-344-4535.
FOREST CITY, SUSQUEHANNA CO., ST. JOHN THE BAPTIST, , Administered from Holy Ghost, Jessup, PA. , Mailing Address: c/o 313 First Ave., Jessup, PA 18434.
Church: 306 Susquehanna St., PA 18421.
FREELAND, LUZERNE CO., ST. MARY'S, [CEM] Rev. Msgr. Nicholas I. Puhak.
Res.: 643 Fern St., PA 18224. Tel: 570-636-0700; Fax: 570-636-1955.
GLEN LYON, LUZERNE CO., ST. MICHAEL, , Mailing Address: 321 Chestnut Ave., Kingston, PA 18704.
Chuch: 47 Spring St., PA 18617.
HARRISBURG, DAUPHIN CO., ST. ANN, Rev. Michael P. Shear.
Res.: 5408 Locust Ln., PA 17109. Tel: 717-652-1415; Fax: 717-652-5471.
HAZLETON, LUZERNE CO.
1—ST. JOHN THE BAPTIST CHURCH, [CEM 2] Rev. Carmen Scuderi, O.F.M.
Res.: 5 E. 20th St., PA 18201. Tel: 570-454-1142; Fax: 570-454-6120.
2—ST. MARY'S, Rev. Peter M. Donish.
Res. & Church: 227 E. Beech St., PA 18201. Tel: 570-455-3232; Fax: 570-455-5654.
HILLTOWN, BUCKS CO., BYZANTINE CATHOLIC MISSION OF BUCKS COUNTY, PA, Closed., For mission records, contact Holy Ghost, Philadelphia, PA. , Mailing Address: *c/o*, 2310 S. 24th St., Philadelphia, PA 19145.
JESSUP, LACKAWANNA CO., HOLY GHOST, [CEM] Rev. Msgr. John T. Sekellick, J.C.L.
Res.: 313 First Ave., PA 18434. Tel: 570-489-2353; Fax: 570-489-7049.
School—LaSalle Academy, Tel: 570-489-2010; Fax: 570-489-3887. Dr. James Tarity Jr., Prin. Sisters 2; Lay Teachers 26; Students 391.
KINGSTON, LUZERNE CO., ST. MARY'S, [CEM] Very Rev. Theodore Krepp.
Res.: 321 Chestnut Ave., PA 18704. Tel: 570-287-0282; Fax: 570-283-0464.
LANSFORD, CARBON CO., ST. JOHN THE BAPTIST, [CEM], Administered from St. Mary's, Hazleton, PA Very Rev. Ronald Barusefski.
Mailing Address: c/o 227 E. Beech St., Hazleton, PA 18201. In Res., Rev. G. Scott Boghossian.
Church: 116 E. Bertsch St., PA 18232.
LEVITTOWN, BUCKS CO., OUR LADY OF PERPETUAL HELP, Rev. Myron M. Badnerosky.
Res.: 1787 Woodburne Rd., PA 19056. Tel: 215-945-5122.
LOPEZ, SULLIVAN CO., SS. PETER AND PAUL, , Administered from St. Mary's, Scranton, PA. , Mailing Address: c/o 310 Mifflin Ave., Scranton, PA 18503.
MAHANOY CITY, SCHUYLKILL CO., ST. MARY'S, [CEM] Rev. James Carroll, O.F.M., Admin.
Res.: 621 W. Mahanoy Ave., PA 17948. Tel: 570-773-2631.
MCADOO, SCHUYLKILL CO., ST. MICHAEL, [CEM] Rev. George A. Bujnak.
Res.: 17 E. Blaine St., PA 18237. Tel: 570-929-1062; Fax: 570-929-3239.
MINERSVILLE, SCHUYLKILL CO., SS. PETER AND PAUL, [CEM] Very Rev. Ronald Barusefsky.
Res.: 107 S. Fourth St., PA 17954. Tel: 570-544-2074; Fax: 570-544-2074.
MONT CLARE, MONTGOMERY CO., ST. MICHAEL, [CEM] Rev. Glenn M. Davidowich, Admin.
Res.: 203 Jacob St., PA 19453. Tel: 610-933-2819; Fax: 610-935-9460.
NANTICOKE, LUZERNE CO., ST. MARY'S, Closed., (Hanover) For inquiries for parish records, contact St. John's, Wilkes-Barre, PA. , Mailing Address: *c/o*, 526 Church St., Wilkes-Barre, PA 18702.
NESQUEHONING, CARBON CO., ST. MARY'S, [CEM], Administered from St. John the Baptist, Lansford, PA. , Mailing Address: *c/o*, 227 E. Beech St., Hazleton, PA 18201.
Church: 141 W. High St., PA 18240.
OLD FORGE, LACKAWANNA CO., ST. NICHOLAS, [CEM] Rev. Gary J. Mensinger. In Res., Rev. Nicholas Kraynak.
Res.: 140 Church St., PA 18518. Tel: 570-457-3042; Fax: 570-457-1906.
PALMERTON, CARBON CO., SS. PETER AND PAUL, , Administered from St. Michael's, Allentown, PA. , Mailing Address: *c/o*, 156 Green St., Allentown, PA 18102.
Church: 142 Lafayette Ave., PA 18071.
PHILADELPHIA, PHILADELPHIA CO.
1—HOLY GHOST, Rev. Edward J. Higgins.
Res.: 2310 S. 24th St., PA 19145. Tel: 215-334-5129; Fax: 215-334-1797.
2—HOLY TRINITY, , Administered from Holy Ghost, Philadelphia, PA. , Mailing Address: c/o 2310 S. 24th St., PA 19145. In Res., Rev. Austin Mohrbacher.
Church: 6801 N. 10th St., PA 19126. Tel: 215-548-2837.
PITTSTON, LUZERNE CO., ST. MICHAEL, [CEM] Rev. Michael Krulak.
Res.: 205 N. Main St., PA 18640. Tel: 570-654-4564; Fax: 570-654-5349.
POCONO SUMMIT, MONROE CO., ST. NICHOLAS, Rev. Michael J. Salnicky, Admin.
Rte. 940 & Commerce St., P.O. Box 515, PA 18346. Tel: 570-839-8090; Fax: 570-595-6177.
POTTSTOWN, MONTGOMERY CO., ST. JOHN THE BAPTIST, [CEM] Rev. Nicholas DeProspero.
Res.: 301 Cherry St., PA 19464. Tel: 610-326-1877; Fax: 610-326-1890.
ST. CLAIR, SCHUYLKILL CO., ST. MARY'S, [CEM], Administered from SS. Peter and Paul, Minersville, PA. , Mailing Address: c/o 107 S. 4th St., Minersville, PA 17954.
Church: 131 S. Morris St., PA 17970.
SCRANTON, LACKAWANNA CO.
1—ST. JOHN THE BAPTIST, , Administered from St. Mary's, Scranton, PA. , Mailing Address: c/o 310 Mifflin Ave., PA 18503.
Church: 310 Broadway, PA 18505.
2—ST. MARY'S, [CEM] Very Rev. Francis M. Twardzik, S.D.B.
Res.: 310 Mifflin Ave., PA 18503. Tel: 570-342-8429; Fax: 570-342-6773.
SHEPPTON, SCHUYLKILL CO., ST. MARY'S, [CEM], Administered from SS. Peter and Paul, Beaver Meadows. , Mailing Address: *c/o*, P.O. Box 206, Beaver Meadows, PA 18216.
SWOYERSVILLE, LUZERNE CO., ST. NICHOLAS, , Administered from St. John's, Wilkes-Barre, PA. , Mailing Address: c/o 526 Church St., Wilkes-Barre, PA 18702.
Church: 271 Tripp St., PA 18704.
TAYLOR, LACKAWANNA CO., ST. MARY'S, [CEM], Administered from St. Nicholas, Old Forge. , Mailing Address: c/o 140 Church St., Old Forge, PA 18518.
Church: 700 Oak St., PA 18517.
WILKES-BARRE, LUZERNE CO.
1—ST. JOHN'S, Rev. James Badeaux.
Res.: 526 Church St., PA 18702. Tel: 570-825-4338; Fax: 570-825-0786.
2—ST. MARY'S, [CEM] Very Rev. James Hayer.
Res.: 695 N. Main St., PA 18705. Tel: 570-822-6028; Fax: 570-822-5423.
School— Closed. For information and records contact parish office. , 522 Madison St., PA 18705.
WILLIAMSTOWN, DAUPHIN CO., HOLY SPIRIT, [CEM] Closed., For inquiries for parish records, contact SS. Peter and Paul, Minersville, PA. , Mailing Address: *c/o*, 107 S. Fourth St., Minersville, PA 17954.

STATE OF VIRGINIA

ANNANDALE, FAIRFAX CO., EPIPHANY OF OUR LORD, Very Rev. John G. Basarab, M.A.; Deacons Gerald McDonnell; Elmer Pekarik.
3410 Woodburn Rd., VA 22003. Tel: 703-573-3986; Fax: 703-573-0344. In Res., Rev. Richard Kanar.
Mission—Mother of God Community School 20501 Goshen Rd., Gaithersburg, MD 20879.
WILLIAMSBURG, YORK CO., ASCENSION OF OUR LORD, Rev. Ronald Hatton.
Mailing Address: P.O. Box 5096, VA 23188. Tel: 757-253-5641; Fax: 757-253-9423.
Church: 114 Palace Ln., VA 23185. Tel: 757-220-8098.
Mission—Our Lady of Perpetual Help 216 S. Parliament Dr., Virginia Beach, Virginia Beach Co., VA 23462. Tel: 757-456-0809.

Special or Other Diocesan Assignment:
Revs.—
DeFronzo, Anthony R.
Untereiner, Harry

On Duty Outside Diocese:
Revs.—
Custer, John S., SS. Cyril & Methodius Seminary, 3605 Perrysville Ave., Pittsburgh, PA 15214. Tel: 412-321-8383; Fax: 321-993-
Drucker, James N., Dept. of Veteran Affairs, Chillicothe VA Medical Center, 17273 State Rt. 104, Chillicothe, OH 45601. Tel: 740-773-1141
Fulton, Eugene, Larchmont Trinity Retreat, One Pryer Manor Rd., Larchmont, NY 10538. Tel: 914-632-3743
Hamperzonian, Jerry, Chap., VA Medical Center, 3350 La Jolla Village Dr., San Diego, CA 92161. Tel: 619-582-5722
Kapron, Alan, St. Nicholas, 1051 E. Robinson St., Barberton, OH 44203-3852. Tel: 303-753-2031
Zeyack, John, S.T.L., Greek Catholic Theological Academy of Uzhgorod, Patrusa Karpatskoho Str. 2A, Minaj, Uzhgorodrajon 89424 Ukraine. Tel: 00380312 664090

Leave of Absence:
Revs.—
Baran, Jody
Brady, Vincent M.
Hutter, Eugene
Siroki, David
Woytek, Robert

Absent on Sick Leave:
Revs.—
Czachor, Christopher
Paulshock, Emil

Retired:
Rev. Msgr.—
Misulich, Raymond M., J.C.L., 4 Springbrook Ter., Lake Hopatcong, 07849. Tel: 973-663-3093
Revs.—
Brown, Charles, M.D., Santa Teresita del Nino Jesus, 2 Poniente #2714, Puebla CP 72140 Mexico. Tel: 011-22-48-38-78
Eles, Joseph, 150 Horizons E., Apt. 305, Boynton Beach, FL 33435. Tel: 407-731-2682
Homa, Joseph, 25 Runnymede Rd., Colonia, 07067.
Petruska, Christopher, 15544 Bellflower Blvd., Apt. C, Bellflower, CA 90706.
Tigyer, Paul, P.O. Box 658, Hamlin, PA 18427. Tel: 717-689-2153

Permanent Deacons:
Berhens, Robert
Ciarciaglino, Joseph M.
Daddona, Nicholas
Dunlop, Richard
Erdek, Michael A.
Foran, Lawrence
Guze, John G.
Hook, Thomas
Kotlar, Anthony
Kubik, Alexander
McDonnell, Gerald E.
Obsitnik, Vincent, (On Leave of Absence)
Pataki, Michael
Pekarik, Elmer
Russo, Stephen
Senoyuit, Michael
Sotack, Michael
Sotak, Nicholas
Szewczyk, William

Thomas, David
Tizio, William
Vanisko, Thomas L.
Wolf, Daniel

INSTITUTIONS LOCATED IN THE DIOCESE

[A] MONASTERIES

MATAWAN. *Basilian Fathers of Mariapoch*, 360 Monastery Ln., 07747-9703. Tel: 732-566-8445; Fax: 732-566-8762. Very Revs. Joseph J. Erdei, O.S.B.M., Supr.; Basil M. Rakaczky, O.S.B.M.; Revs. Stephen J. Skinta, O.S.B.M.; Lawrence Robert Wolf, O.S.B.M.

SYBERTSVILLE, PA.. *Holy Dormition Friary*, P.O. Box 270, PA 18251. Tel: 570-788-1212; Fax: 570-788-2431. Revs. Carmen Scuderi, O.F.M.; Anthony Skurla, O.F.M., Guardian; James Carroll, O.F.M.; Bro. Augustine Paulik, O.F.M.

[B] CONVENTS AND RESIDENCES FOR SISTERS

SUGARLOAF, PA.. *Holy Annunciation Monastery*, 403 W. County Rd., PA 18249. Tel: 570-788-1205; Fax: 570-788-3329. Sr. Marija of the Holy Spirit, O.C.D., Prioress. Discalced Byzantine Carmelite Nuns Nuns with Solemn Vows 7; Nuns with Temporary Vows 4; Novices 4.

[C] SHRINES AND SPIRITUAL RENEWAL CENTERS

CANADENSIS, PA.. *St. Nicholas Shrine - Carpathian Village* P.O. Box 616, PA 18325. Tel: 570-595-3265; Fax: 570-595-6177. Rev. Michael Salnicky, Dir.

[D] MISCELLANEOUS

PASSAIC. *Eastern Catholic Associates*, 96 First St., 07055.

God with Us Publications, 445 Lackawanna Ave., 07424. Most Revs. Robert Moskal, Pres.; Basil Schott, Vice Pres.; Robert J. Shaheen (OLL), Sec.; Andrew Pataki, J.C.L., Registered Agent.

RELIGIOUS INSTITUTES OF MEN REPRESENTED IN THE DIOCESE

For further details refer to the corresponding bracketed number in the Religious Institutes of Men or Women section.

[0520]—*Franciscan Friars*—O.F.M.

[0180]—*Order of St. Basil the Great*—O.S.B.M.

RELIGIOUS INSTITUTES OF WOMEN REPRESENTED IN THE DIOCESE

[0420]—*Discalced Carmelite Nuns (Byzantine Rite)*—O.C.D.

[3730]—*Sisters of the Order of St. Basil the Great*—O.S.B.M.

NECROLOGY

† Jackanich, Rev. Msgr. Joseph, (Retired)—Died Nov. 10, 2003

† Danilak, John—Died April 16, 2003

Metropolitan Archdiocese of Philadelphia Ukrainian

Most Reverend

STEPHEN SOROKA

Archbishop of Philadelphia Ukrainian; ordained June 13, 1982; appointed Auxiliary Bishop of Winnipeg (Ukrainian) March 29, 1996; ordained Auxiliary Bishop of Winnipeg (Ukrainian) June 13, 1996; appointed Archbishop of Philadelphia Ukrainian November 29, 2000; installed Archbishop of Philadelphia Ukrainian February 27, 2001

Chancery Office: 827 N. Franklin St., Philadelphia, PA 19123-2097. Tel: 215-627-0143; Fax: 215-627-0377.

Email: ukmet@catholic.org

Most Reverend

STEPHEN SULYK

Archbishop Emeritus of Philadelphia Ukrainian; ordained June 14, 1952; appointed Archbishop of Philadelphia Ukrainian December 29, 1980; ordained March 1, 1981; retired November 29, 2000

Most Reverend

WALTER PASKA

Retired Auxiliary Bishop of Philadelphia Ukrainian; appointed February 4, 1992; retired November 29, 2000

ESTABLISHED MAY 28, 1913.

The jurisdiction of the Metropolitan Archdiocese of Philadelphia includes the District of Columbia, the States of Virginia, Maryland, Delaware, New Jersey and eastern Pennsylvania to the eastern boundaries of the following Counties: Potter, Clinton, Center, Mifflin, Huntington and Fulton. With regard to persons, his subjects are all Catholics of the Byzantine Rite: 1. Who immigrated to this country from Galicia, Bucovina and other Ukrainian provinces; 2. Who descend from such persons (can. 755); 3. Women married to men referable to 1. and 2. if they comply with can. 98, n. 4; 4. Who in accordance with can. 98, n. 3 changed their Rite; 5. Converts to the Catholic Church of the Byzantine Rite; 6. And in fact all other Catholics of the Byzantine Rite who are attached to parishes subject to the jurisdiction of the Archbishop.

Legal Title: For legal titles of parishes and archdiocesan institutions, consult the Chancery Office.

STATISTICAL OVERVIEW

Personnel	
Archbishops	1
Retired Archbishops	1
Retired Bishops	2
Priests: Diocesan Active in Diocese	56
Priests: Diocesan Active Outside Diocese	1
Priests: Retired, Sick or Absent	4
Number of Diocesan Priests	61
Religious Priests in Diocese	6
Total Priests in Diocese	67
Extern Priests in Diocese	12
Ordinations:	
Diocesan Priests	2
Permanent Deacons in Diocese	5
Total Sisters	81
Parishes	
Parishes	74
With Resident Pastor:	
Resident Diocesan Priests	45
Resident Religious Priests	8
Without Resident Pastor:	
Administered by Priests	21
Professional Ministry Personnel:	
Sisters	35
Lay Ministers	10
Welfare	
Homes for the Aged	1
Total Assisted	240
Day Care Centers	1
Total Assisted	10
Educational	
Seminaries, Diocesan	1
Diocesan Students in Other Seminaries	2
Total Seminarians	2
Colleges and Universities	1
Total Students	1,106
High Schools, Private	1
Total Students	377
Elementary Schools, Diocesan and Parish	7
Total Students	782
Catechesis/Religious Education:	
High School Students	193
Elementary Students	736
Total Students under Catholic Instruction	3,196
Teachers in the Diocese:	
Sisters	24
Lay Teachers	346
Vital Statistics	
Receptions into the Church:	
Infant Baptism Totals	197
Adult Baptism Totals	14
Received into Full Communion	31
First Communions	195
Confirmations	198
Marriages:	
Catholic	63
Interfaith	39
Total Marriages	102
Deaths	404
Total Catholic Population	67,159

Former Bishops—Most Revs. STEPHEN SOTER ORTYNSKY, O.S.B.M., D.D., First Ukrainian Catholic Bishop of the United States;; ord. July 18, 1891; consecrated May 12, 1907; died March 24, 1916; CONSTANTINE BOHACHEVSKY, D.D., S.T.D., appt. Bishop in the United States, May 20, 1924; appt. Metropolitan Archbishop of the Philadelphia Archeparchy, Byzantine Rite, Aug. 6, 1958; consecrated June 15, 1924; died Jan. 6, 1961; AMBROSE SENYSHYN, O.S.B.M., D.D., appt. Auxiliary Bishop to the Philadelphia Bishop, July 6, 1942; appt. Exarch of Stamford, July 20, 1956; appt. Eparch of Stamford, Nov. 1, 1958; appt. Metropolitan Archbishop of Philadelphia, Aug. 14, 1961; died Sept. 11, 1976; JOSEPH M. SCHMONDIUK, D.D., appt. Titular Bishop of Zeugma and Auxiliary of the Archeparchy of Philadelphia, July 20, 1956; consecrated Nov. 8, 1956; transferred to the Diocese of Stamford See, Nov. 9, 1961; appt. Metropolitan Archbishop of Philadelphia, Oct. 1, 1977; died Dec. 25, 1978; His Eminence MYROSLAV CARDINAL LUBACHIVSKY, D.D., appt. Metropolitan Archbishop of Philadelphia, Sept. 21, 1979; appt. Apostolic Administrator of Philadelphia, Oct. 3, 1979; consecrated in Rome, Nov. 12, 1979; named Coadjutor Major Archbishop of Lviw, March 24, 1980; transferred to Rome; Assumed position of Major Archbishop of Lviw, Sept. 7, 1984. Created Cardinal, May 25, 1985.; died Dec. 14, 2000; Most Rev. STEPHEN SULYK, D.D. (Retired), appt. Archbishop of Philadelphia for Ukrainians and Metropolitan of the Ukrainian Catholic Church in the USA, Dec. 29, 1980; ord. March 1, 1981; retired Nov. 29, 2000.

Chancellor—Sr. THOMAS HRYNEWICH, S.S.M.I. Tel: 215-627-0143.

Secretary to the Archbishop—Sr. LYDIA SAWKA, O.S.B.M.

Chancery Office—827 N. Franklin St., Philadelphia, 19123-2097. Tel: 215-627-0143; Fax: 215-627-0377.

College of Archeparchial Counsultors—Most Rev. STEFAN SOROKA, D.D., Ph.D.; Rev. Msgr. JOHN BURA; Rev. Archpriests DANIEL GUROVICH; JOHN FIELDS; Revs. MICHAEL HUTSKO; ROMAN DUBITSKY; Rev. Msgr. JAMES MELNIC; Rev. JOHN CIURPITA.

Presbyteral Council—Most Rev. STEFAN SOROKA, D.D., Ph.D.; Rev. Msgr. JOHN BURA; Rev. Archpriests DANIEL GUROVICH; JOHN FIELDS; Revs. ROMAN DUBITSKY; MICHAEL HUTSKO; Rev. Msgr. JAMES MELNIC; Rev. JOHN CIURPITA.

Archeparchial Corporation—Most Rev. STEFAN SOROKA, D.D., Ph.D., Pres.; Rev. Archpriest JOHN FIELDS; Revs. MICHAEL HUTSKO; ROMAN DUBITSKY; Sr. THOMAS HRYNEWICH, S.S.M.I.

Archdiocesan Tribunal—827 N. Franklin St., Philadelphia, 19123. Tel: 215-627-0143.

Judicial Vicar—Most Rev. WALTER PASKA, J.C.D.

Adjunct Judicial Vicar—Rev. ArchpriestDANIEL GUROVICH.

Synodal Judge—Rev. Archpriest DANIEL GUROVICH.

Defender of the Bond—Rev. JAMES GRANT.

Promoter of Justice—Rev. Msgr. RONALD POPIVCHAK, Ph.D.

Notary—Sr. THOMAS HYRNEWICH, S.S.M.I.

Archeparchial Council for Economic Affairs—Most Rev. STEFAN SOROKA, D.D., Ph.D.; Revs. MICHAEL HUTSKO; ANDREW FYLYPOWYCH; CHARLIE CHRIN; ALBERT SCHULZE; Rev. Archpriests DANIEL GUROVICH; JOHN FIELDS

Financial Officer—JOHN DROZD.

Protopresbyters (Deans)—Rev. Msgr. RONALD POPIVCHAK, Ph.D., Lehigh-Schuylhill Valley; Rev. JOHN CIURPITA, Philadelphia; Rev. Msgr. STEPHEN CHOMKO, North Anthracite; Revs. JOSEPH SZUPA, New Jersey; MICHAEL HUTSKO, South Anthracite; TARAS LONCHYNA, Delmarva.

Diocesan Offices and Directors

Youth Ministry—Sr. NATAYLA STOCZANYN, S.S.M.I., Dir.; Rev. PETRO ZVARYCH.

Pro-Life and Family Ministry—Rev. Msgr. MYRON GRABOWSKY.

Apostolate—Most Rev. STEFAN SOROKA, D.D., Ph.D.; Rev. Archpriest JOHN FIELDS.

Cemeteries—Sr. THOMAS HRYNEWICH, S.S.M.I.

Censors—Rev. Msgrs. RONALD POPIVCHAK; JOHN BURA.

Ecumenical Relations—Rev. JOHN CIURPITA.

Insurance Commission—JOHN DROZD.

League of Ukrainian Catholics—Sr. THOMAS HRYNEWICH, S.S.M.I., Archdiocesan Dir.

Press, The Way—Revs. D. GEORGE WORSCHAK, Editor; ROBERT HITCHENS, English; IVAN DEMKIV, Ukrainian; Sr. MONICA JACIUK, O.S.B.M., Copy;

Rev. MARK FESNIAK, Special Interest.

Archdiocesan Bulletin—Office, 827 N. Franklin St., Philadephia, 19123.

Priests Beneficial Fund—Most Rev. STEFAN SOROKA, D.D., Ph.D., Pres.; Rev. Archpriest DANIEL GUROVICH, Sec. & Treas. Board Members: Rev. ROMAN DUBITSKY; Rev. Archpriest MICHAEL HUTSKO; Rev. Msgr. JOHN BURA; Rev. JOSEPH SZUPA.

Office of Vocations—Rev. ROBERT HITCHENS; Sisters DOROTHY ANN BUSOWSKI, O.S.B.M.; MICHELE YAKYMOVICH, S.S.M.I.; YOSAPHATA LITVENCZUK, M.S.M.G.; Rev. PETRO ZVARYCH; Deacon PAUL MAKAR.

Archdiocesan Radio Programs— "Christ Among Us", aired Sundays 9-9:30 am WTEL, 860 AM (Phila.) Rev. Msgr. JAMES MELNIC; Rev. VASYL SIVINSKIJ.

Archeparchial Seminary Advisory and Admissions Board—Most Rev. STEFAN SOROKA, D.D., Ph.D.; Rev. Msgrs. JOHN BURA; JAMES MELNIC; Rev. Archpriest MICHAEL HUTSKO; Revs. ROBERT HITCHENS NESTOR IWASIW; TARAS LONCHYNA; Sisters THOMAS HRYNEWICH, S.S.M.I.; CECELIA SWORIN, S.S.M.I.

Sheptytsky Educational Center—Most Rev. STEFAN SOROKA, D.D., Ph.D.; Sr. THOMAS HRYNEWICH, S.S.M.I.; Rev. Msgr. JAMES MELNIC; Ms. TAISA CLARE.

Archeparchial Museum—Sisters THOMAS HRYNEWICH, S.S.M.I.; NADIA BARANICK, M.S.M.G.; EVHENIA PRUSNAY, M.S.M.G.; TIMOTHEA KONYU, M.S.M.G.

Victim Assistance Coordinator—Sr. NATALYA STOCZANYN, S.S.M.I. Tel: 215-873-6162. Email: srnatalya@catholic.org.

CLERGY, PARISHES, MISSIONS AND PAROCHIAL SCHOOLS

CITY OF PHILADELPHIA
(PHILADELPHIA COUNTY)

1—IMMACULATE CONCEPTION OF BLESSED VIRGIN MARY, CATHEDRAL, [CEM] Revs. Paul Wolensky; Ivan Turyk; Evhan Moniuk (Ukraine).
Res.: 833 N. Franklin St., 19123. Tel: 215-922-2845; Fax: 215-922-4635.
Chapel—Immaculate Conception Cathedral Convent
Chapel—Missionary Sisters of Mother God Convent
Chapel—Chapel of St. Joseph of Arimathea and the Holy Myrrh-Bearing Women

2—ST. ANDREW, Attended by, Cathedral of the Immaculate Conception, Philadelphia. , Mailing Address: 833 N. Franklin St., 19123-2097. 427 Pine St., 19106. Tel: 215-922-2845.

3—ANNUNCIATION OF THE B.V.M., Rev. Msgr. James Melnic.
Res.: 1204 Valley Rd., Melrose Park, 19027-3035. Tel: 215-635-1627; Fax: 215-635-9203.
Church: 1206 Valley Rd., Melrose Park, 19127-3035. Tel: 215-782-9865.

4—CHRIST THE KING, Rev. Yaroslav Kurpel (Ukraine).
Res.: 1629 W. Cayuga St., 19140. Tel: 215-455-2416.

5—ST. JOSAPHAT'S, Rev. D. George Worschak.
Res.: 6932 Ditman St., 19135. Tel: 215-332-8488.
School—4521 Longshore Ave., 19135. Tel: 215-332-8008. Sr. Theodosia, O.S.B.M., Prin. Sisters 2; Lay Teachers 14; Students 264.

6—ST. NICHOLAS, Rev. Ivan Demkiv (Ukraine).
Res.: 871 North 24th St., 19130.
Church: 24th & Poplar Sts., 19130-1988.

7—PROTECTION OF BLESSED VIRGIN MARY, Rev. T. Frank Patrylak.
Res.: 100 S. Penn St., Clifton Heights, 19018. Tel: 610-626-9495.

8—SACRED HEART, Closed. For inquiries for parish records contact the chancery.

STATE OF DELAWARE

WILMINGTON, NEW CASTLE CO., ST. NICHOLAS, Rev. Msgr. John Bura.
Res.: 801 Lea Blvd., DE 19802. Tel: 302-762-5511; Fax: 302-656-6108.

STATE OF MARYLAND

BALTIMORE, BALTIMORE CO., ST. MICHAEL'S, [CEM] Rev. Wasyl Kharuk (Ukraine).
Res.: 2401 Eastern Ave., MD 21224. Tel: 410-675-7557.

CHESAPEAKE CITY, CECIL CO., ST. BASIL THE GREAT, Attended by, St. Nicholas, Wilmington. , Mailing Address: 801 Lea Blvd., Wilmington, DE 19802.
Chapel—Chesapeake City, Sisters of St. Basil the Great

CURTIS BAY, BALTIMORE CO., SS. PETER AND PAUL, Attended by, St. Michael's, Baltimore. , Mailing Address: 2401 Eastern Ave., Baltimore, MD 21224.
Church: 1506 Church St., MD 21226-1440.

SILVER SPRING, MONTGOMERY CO., HOLY TRINITY, Rev. Taras R. Lonchyna, Admin.
Res.: 16631 New Hampshire Ave., MD 20905-3919. Tel: 301-989-3318; Fax: 301-989-1494.

STATE OF NEW JERSEY

BAYONNE, HUDSON CO., ASSUMPTION B.V.M., Attended by, SS. Peter and Paul, Jersey City. , Mailing Address: *c/o SS. Peter and Paul*, 30 Bentley Ave., Jersey City, NJ 07304. Tel: 201-432-3122; Fax: 201-432-0111.
Church: 30 E. 25th St., Box 260, NJ 07002.

CARTERET, MIDDLESEX CO., ST. MARY'S, Rev. Vitaliy Demyanets (Ukraine).
Res.: 719 Roosevelt Ave., NJ 07008. Tel: 732-541-7678; Fax: 732-541-7678.

CHERRY HILL, CAMDEN CO., ST. MICHAEL'S, Rev. John Ciurpita.
Res.: 675 Cooperlanding Rd., NJ 08002. Tel: 856-482-0938; Fax: 609-482-9092.

ELIZABETH, UNION CO., ST. VLADIMIR'S, [CEM] Rev. Joseph Szupa.
Res.: 312 Grier Ave., NJ 07202-3310. Tel: 908-352-8823; Fax: 908-352-7648.
Catechesis/Religious Program—Students 30.

GREAT MEADOWS, WARREN CO., ST. NICHOLAS, Attended by, Holy Ghost, West Easton, PA. Rev. James Karepin, O.P.
Mailing Address: c/o 315 Fourth St., West Easton, 18042. Tel: 610-252-4266; Fax: 610-252-3533.
Church: Rte. 46, P.O. Box 162, NJ 07838.

HILLSIDE, UNION CO., IMMACULATE CONCEPTION, Rev. Andriy Rabiy.
Mailing Address: 684 Alta Vista Pl., Perth Amboy, NJ 08861. Tel: 732-826-8954; Fax: 732-826-6744.
Church: Bloy St. and Liberty Ave., NJ 07205.

JERSEY CITY, HUDSON CO., SS. PETER AND PAUL, Rev. Vasyl Putera (Ukraine).
Res.: 30 Bentley Ave., NJ 07304. Tel: 201-432-3122; Fax: 201-432-0111.

HILLSBOROUGH, SOMERSET CO., ST. MICHAEL'S, Attended by Rev. Andriy Rabiy.
Mailing Address: 684 Alta Vista Pl., Perth Amboy, NJ 08861.
Church: 1700 Brooks Blvd., NJ 08844.

MARLBORO, MONMOUTH CO., ST. VOLODYMYR'S, Attended by, St. Mary's, Carteret. Rev. Viktor Bek (Ukraine).
Mailing Address: 719 Roosevelt Ave., Carteret, NJ 07008. Tel: 732-541-7678.
Church: 1209 W. Front St., Lincroft, NJ 07738.
Catechesis/Religious Program—Students 65.

MILLVILLE, CUMBERLAND CO., ST. NICHOLAS, [CEM] Attended by, Holy Ghost, Chester, PA Rev. Wasyl Bunik (Ukraine).
Mailing Address: 3015 W. Third St., Chester, 19013.
Church: 373 Carmel Rd., NJ 08332. Tel: 609-825-4826.

NEW BRUNSWICK, MIDDLESEX CO., NATIVITY OF B.V.M., Rev. Roman Pitula (Ukraine).
Mailing Address: 1195 Deutz Ave., Trenton, NJ 08611. Tel: 609-695-3771; Fax: 609-815-0232.

NEWARK, ESSEX CO., ST. JOHN THE BAPTIST, Revs. Bohdan Lukie, C.SS.R.; Andriy Manko, C.SS.R.
Res.: 719 Sandford Ave., NJ 07106. Tel: 973-371-1356; Fax: 973-416-0085.
School—Tel: 973-373-9359. Sr. Stephanie Sema, S.S.M.I., Prin. Sisters Servants of Mary Immaculate 2; Lay Teachers 15; Students 118.
Catechesis/Religious Program—Students 26.

PASSAIC, PASSAIC CO., ST. NICHOLAS, Rev. Ihor Royik (Canada).
Res.: 60 Holdsworth Ct., NJ 07055. Tel: 973-471-9727; Fax: 973-471-4714.
School—Tel: 973-779-0249; Fax: 973-779-6309. Sr. Kathleen, S.S.M.I., Prin. Sisters 3; Lay Teachers 8; Students 135.

PERTH AMBOY, MIDDLESEX CO., ASSUMPTION OF B.V.M., Revs. Roman Dubitsky; Augustine Molodowitz; Deacon Paul Makar.
Res.: 684 Alta Vista Pl., NJ 08861. Tel: 732-826-0767; Fax: 732-826-6744.
School—Tel: 732-826-8721. Ms. Melanie Lawrence, Prin. Missionary Sisters of Mother of God 2; Lay Teachers 10; Students 178.

RAMSEY, BERGEN CO., ST. PAUL, Attended by, St. John the Baptist, Whippany. , Mailing Address: 7 S. Jefferson Rd., Whippany, NJ 07981. Tel: 973-887-3616.

RUTHERFORD, BERGEN CO., ANNUNCIATION B.V.M., Attended by, Patronage of Mother of God, Carteret, NJ. , Mailing Address: 719 Roosevelt Ave., Carteret, NJ 07008. Tel: 732-541-7678; Fax: 732-541-7678.
Church: 70 Home Ave., NJ 07070.

TOMS RIVER, OCEAN CO., ST. STEPHEN'S, Attended by, Assumption of B.V.M., Perth Amboy Rev. Roman Dubitsky; Deacon Paul Makar.
Mailing Address: *Assumption of B.V.M.*, 684 Alta Vista Pl., Perth Amboy, NJ 08861. Tel: 732-826-0767; Fax: 732-826-6744.
Church: 1344 White Oak Bottom Rd., NJ 08755. Tel: 732-505-6293; Fax: 732-826-6744.

TRENTON, MERCER CO., ST. JOSAPHAT'S, Rev. Roman Pitula (Ukraine).
Res.: 1195 Deutz Ave., NJ 08611. Tel: 609-695-3771.

WHIPPANY, MORRIS CO., ST. JOHN THE BAPTIST, Rev. Archpriest Roman Mirchuk.
Res.: 7 S. Jefferson Rd., NJ 07981. Tel: 973-887-3616.
Church: Rte. 10, NJ 07981.

WILLIAMSTOWN, GLOUCESTER CO., SS. PETER AND PAUL, [CEM] Rev. Paul Labinsky.
Mailing Address: 1101 Heartwood Dr., Cherry Hill, NJ 08003.

WOODBINE, CAPE MAY CO., ST. NICHOLAS, Closed., For inquiries for parish records contact St. Nicholas, Millville, NJ

STATE OF PENNSYLVANIA

ALDEN STATION, LUZERNE CO., ST. VLADIMIR, Closed., For inquiries for parish records contact St. Nicholas, Glen Lyon, PA

ALLENTOWN, LEHIGH CO., IMMACULATE CONCEPTION OF B.V.M., Closed., For inquiries for parish records contact St. Josaphat, Bethlehem, PA.

BERWICK, COLUMBIA CO., SS. CYRIL AND METHODIUS, [CEM] Rev. Stephen Chomko.
Res.: 706 Warren St., 18603. Tel: 717-752-3172.
Catechesis/Religious Program—Students 66.

BETHLEHEM, LEHIGH CO., ST. JOSAPHAT'S, [CEM] Rev. Archpriest Daniel Gurovich.
Res.: 1826 Kenmore Ave., 18018-3305. Tel: 610-865-2521; Fax: 610-865-2521.
Catechesis/Religious Program—Students 169.

BRIDGEPORT, MONTGOMERY CO., SS. PETER AND PAUL, [CEM] Rev. Msgr. Ronald P. Popivchak.
Res.: 519 Union Ave., P.O. Box 126, 19405. Tel: 610-272-7035.
Catechesis/Religious Program—George Maxim, D.R.E. Students 120.

BRISTOL, BUCKS CO., ST. MARY'S, Rev. Msgr. Myron Grabowsky.
Res.: 2026 Bath Rd., 19007. Tel: 215-788-7117; Fax: 215-788-7175.

CENTRALIA, COLUMBIA CO., ASSUMPTION OF B.V.M., [CEM] Attended by, Mount Carmel. Rev. Bohdan Kudleychuk (Ukraine).
Mailing Address: 131 N. Beech St., Mount Carmel, 17851. Tel: 570-339-0650; Fax: 570-339-2715.

CHESTER, DELAWARE CO., HOLY GHOST, Rev. Wasyl Bunik.
Res.: 3015 W. Third St., 19013. Tel: 610-494-7899; Fax: 610-494-2350.

CLIFTON HEIGHTS, DELAWARE CO., SS. PETER AND PAUL, Rev. T. Frank Patrylak.
Res.: 104 S. Penn St., 19108.
Church: 100 S. Penn St., 19018. Tel: 610-626-9495.

EDWARDSVILLE, LUZERNE CO., ST. VLADIMIR'S, [CEM] Rev. Thaddeus Krawchuk, C.SS.R.
Mailing Address: 20 Turner St., Plymouth, 18651-2013. Tel: 570-779-9728.
Catechesis/Religious Program—Tel: 717-822-1589. Dr. Michael Labuda, D.R.E. Students 125.

FRACKVILLE, SCHUYLKILL CO., ST. MICHAEL'S, Rev. George J. Kuzara, C.PP.S.
Res.: 45 S. Second St., 17931. Tel: 570-874-1101; Fax: 570-874-0448.
Catechesis/Religious Program—Tel: 717-874-1101. Students 50.

GLEN LYON, LUZERNE CO., ST. NICHOLAS, Attended by, St. Nicholas, Nanticoke, PA. , Mailing Address: 240 Center St., Nanticoke, 18634.
Church: 153 Main St., 18617.

HAZLETON, LUZERNE CO., ST. MICHAEL'S, Attended by, St. Mary's, McAdoo. Rev. Gregory Maslak.
Mailing Address: 210 W. Blaine St., McAdoo, 18237.

JENKINTOWN, MONTGOMERY CO., ST. MICHAEL THE ARCHANGEL, Rev. Petro Semenych (Ukraine).
Res.: 1013 Fox Chase Rd., 19046. Tel: 215-576-5827; Fax: 215-576-8500.

LANSDALE, MONTGOMERY CO., PRESENTATION OF OUR LORD, Attended by, St. Anne's, Warrington. Rev. Archpriest John Fields.
Mailing Address: 1545 Easton Rd., P.O. Box 417, Warrington, 18976.
Church: 1564 Allentown Rd., 19446. Tel: 215-368-3993; Fax: 215-343-8060.

MAHANOY CITY, SCHUYLKILL CO., ST. NICHOLAS, [CEM] Attended by, St. Michael, Shenandoah. , Mailing Address: 114 Chestnut St., Shenandoah, 17976. Tel: 570-773-0115; Fax: 570-462-0517.

MAIZEVILLE, SCHUYLKILL CO., ST. JOHN THE BAPTIST, [CEM] Attended by, St. Michael, Frackville. , Mailing Address: 45 S. Second St., Frackville, 17931. Tel: 570-874-1821.
Church: Main St., 17934.

MARION HEIGHTS, NORTHUMBERLAND CO., PATRONAGE OF THE MOTHER OF GOD, Attended by, SS. Peter & Paul, Mount Carmel. , Mailing Address: 131 N. Beech St., Mount Carmel, 17851.

MCADOO, SCHUYLKILL CO., ST. MARY'S, Rev. Gregory

Maslak.
Church: 210 W. Blaine St., 18237. Tel: 570-929-2804; Fax: 570-462-0517.

MIDDLEPORT, SCHUYLKILL CO., NATIVITY OF B.V.M., [CEM] Rev. Archpriest Michael Hutsko.
Mailing Address: 415 N. Front St., Minersville, 17954. Tel: 570-544-4581; Fax: 570-544-9653.
Church: Kaska St., 17953.

MINERSVILLE, SCHUYLKILL CO., ST. NICHOLAS, [CEM] Rev. ArchpriestMichael Hutsko.
Res.: 415 Front St., 17954. Tel: 570-544-4581; Fax: 570-544-9653.
School—Tel: 570-544-2800; Fax: 570-544-6471. Sr. Stephanie, S.S.M.I., Prin.; Peter Zedonek, Admin. Sisters 3; Lay Teachers 13; Students 175.
Catechesis / Religious Program—Students 105.

MOSCOW, LACKAWANNA CO., HOLY GHOST, Closed., For inquiries for parish records contact St. Vladimir, Scranton, PA

MOUNT CARMEL, NORTHUMBERLAND CO., SS. PETER AND PAUL, [CEM] Rev. Bohdan Kudleychuk (Ukraine); Deacon Theodore Spotts.
Res.: 131 N. Beech St., 17851. Tel: 570-339-0650; Fax: 570-339-2715.

NANTICOKE, LUZERNE CO.
1—ST. NICHOLAS, Rev. Volodymyr Klanichka (Ukraine).
Mailing Address: 240 Center St., 18634.
Church: 111 Green St., 18634.
2—TRANSFIGURATION OF OUR LORD, Attended by Rev. Volodymyr Klanichka (Ukraine).
Res.: 240 Center St., 18634. Tel: 570-735-2262; Fax: 570-735-6020.

NORTHAMPTON, NORTHAMPTON CO., ST. JOHN THE BAPTIST, [CEM] Rev. Archpriest David Clooney.
Res.: 1343 Newport Ave., 18067. Tel: 610-262-4104.
School—Tel: 610-262-2231; Fax: 610-262-2274. Michael Duda, Prin. Lay Teachers 9; Students 90.

OLYPHANT, LACKAWANNA CO., SS. CYRIL AND METHODIUS, [CEM] Very Rev. Msgr. Stephen Hrynuck.
Res.: 135 River St., 18447. Tel: 570-489-2271.
Catechesis / Religious Program—Students 119.

PALMERTON, CARBON CO., ST. VLADIMIR'S, Rev. Evhan Moniuk (Ukraine).
Res.: 101 Lehigh Ave., 18071. Tel: 610-826-2359.

PHOENIXVILLE, CHESTER CO., SS. PETER AND PAUL, Attended by, SS. Peter and Paul, Bridgeport. Rev. Msgr. Ronald P. Popivchak.
Mailing Address: 519 Union Ave., P.O. Box 126, Bridgeport, 19405. Tel: 610-272-7035.

PLYMOUTH, LUZERNE CO., SS. PETER AND PAUL, Rev. Thaddeus Krawchuk, C.S.R.
Res.: 20 Turner St., 18651. Tel: 570-779-4411; Fax: 570-779-4411.

POTTSTOWN, MONTGOMERY CO., ST. MICHAEL'S, [CEM] Attended by Rev. Leonard Sinatra.
Res.: 425 W. Walnut St., 19464. Tel: 610-326-2150.

READING, BERKS CO., NATIVITY OF BLESSED VIRGIN MARY, [CEM] Very Rev. Archpriest Uriy Markewych.
Res.: 1814 Philadelphia Ave., 19607. Tel: 610-376-0586; Fax: 610-376-0586.

ST. CLAIR, SCHUYLKILL CO.
1—HOLY TRINITY, [CEM] Rev. John Wysochansky.
Res.: 254 N. Mill St., 17970. Tel: 570-429-2212.
2—ST. NICHOLAS, [CEM] Attended by, Holy Trinity, St. Clair. Rev. John Wysochansky.
Mailing Address: *Holy Trinity*, 254 N. Mill St., 17970. Tel: 570-429-2212.
Church: N. Morris St., 17970.

SAYRE, BRADFORD CO., ASCENSION OF OUR LORD, [CEM] Rev. Paul Guthrie, O.F.M.
Res.: 110 N. Higgins Ave., 18840. Tel: 570-888-2207.

SCRANTON, LACKAWANNA CO., ST. VLADIMIR'S, [CEM] Rev. John Seniw.
Res.: 430 N. Seventh St., 18503. Tel: 570-342-7023.

SHAMOKIN, NORTHUMBERLAND CO., TRANSFIGURATION OF OUR LORD, [CEM] Rev. Msgr. Michael Fedorowich.
Res.: 303 N. Shamokin St., 17872-5460. Tel: 570-648-5932; Fax: 570-648-5932.
School—Tel: 570-648-6435. Sr. Anne Roman, S.S.M.I., Prin. Sisters Servants of Mary Immaculate 3; Lay Teachers 9; Students 135.

SHENANDOAH, SCHUYLKILL CO., ST. MICHAEL'S, [CEM] Rev. Peter Zvarych.
Res.: 114 S. Chestnut St., 17976. Tel: 570-462-0809; Fax: 570-462-0517.

SIMPSON, LACKAWANNA CO., SS. PETER AND PAUL, [CEM] Attended by Rev. Edward Levandusky.
Res.: 43 Rittenhouse St., 18407. Tel: 570-282-0331.

WARRINGTON, BUCKS CO., ST. ANNE'S, Rev. Archpriest John Fields.
Res.: 1545 Easton Rd., Box 417, 18976. Tel: 215-343-0779; Fax: 215-343-8060.
Catechesis / Religious Program—Students 58.

WEST EASTON, NORTHAMPTON CO., HOLY GHOST, [CEM] Rev. James Karepin, O.P.
Res.: 315 Fourth St., 18042. Tel: 610-252-4266; Fax: 610-252-8533.

WILKES-BARRE, LUZERNE CO., SS. PETER AND PAUL, [CEM] Attended by, St. Vladimir's, Scranton. Rev. John Seniw, Admin.
Mailing Address: 430 N. Seventh St., Scranton, 18503-2104.
Church: 635 N. River St., 18701. Tel: 570-342-7023; Fax: 570-342-7130.
Catechesis / Religious Program—Mary Ann Mudrak, D.R.E. Students 49.

STATE OF VIRGINIA

MANASSAS, PRINCE WILLIAM CO., ANNUNCIATION OF THE BLESSED VIRGIN MARY, [CEM] Attended by, Holy Trinity, Silver Spring, MD. Rev. Taras R. Lonchyna, Admin.
Mailing Address: 16631 New Hampshire Ave., Silver Spring, MD 20905-3919.
Church: 6719 Hoadly Rd., VA 20108-0878. Tel: 301-421-1739.

RICHMOND, HENRICO CO., ST. JOHN THE BAPTIST, Attended by, Holy Trinity, Silver Spring, MD. Rev. Taras R. Lonchyna, Admin.
Mailing Address: 16631 New Hampshire Ave., Silver Spring, MD 20905-3919. Tel: 301-421-1739.
Chapel—Sisters of Verona Chapel , VA. Tel: 804-359-4934.

DISTRICT OF COLUMBIA

WASHINGTON, DISTRICT OF COLUMBIA, UKRAINIAN CATHOLIC NATIONAL SHRINE OF THE HOLY FAMILY, Rev. Nestor Iwasiw; Deacons Theophil Staruch; Donald Latrick.
Res.: 4250 Harewood Rd., N.E., DC 20017. Tel: 202-526-3737; Fax: 202-526-1327.
Catechesis / Religious Program—Students 152.

On Duty Outside the Diocese:
Rev. Msgr.—
Canavan, Martin, Pl. S. Yura, 5, Lviv 290000 Ukraine.

Absent on Leave:
Rev.—
Kin, Bohdan

Retired:
Most Rev.—
Paska, Walter
Rev. Msgrs.—
Bilanych, John, 1539 First Ave., Berwick, 18603.
Pospishil, Victor J., 6 Michigan Dr., Matawan, NJ 07747.
Rev.—
Kostiuk, Nick

Permanent Deacons:
Latrick, Donald, Holy Family Ukrainian Catholic National Shrine, Washington, DC
Makar, Paul, Perth Amboy, NJ
Spotts, Theodore, SS. Peter & Paul, Mt. Carmel, PA; Protection BVM, Marion Heights, PA; Assumption BVM, Centralia, PA
Staruch, Theophil, Holy Family Ukrainian Catholic National Shrine, Washington, DC
Waak, Michael P., Perth Amboy, NJ

INSTITUTIONS LOCATED IN THE ARCHDIOCESE

[A] SEMINARIES, ARCHEPARCHY

WASHINGTON. *St. Josaphat Seminary*, 201 Taylor St., N.E., DC 20017. Tel: 202-529-1177; Fax: 202-269-0043.

[B] COLLEGES AND UNIVERSITIES

JENKINTOWN. *Manor College*, 700 Fox Chase Rd., 19046. Tel: 215-885-2360; Fax: 215-576-6564. Email: scecilia@mail.manor.edu. Web: www.manor.edu. Sr. M. Cecilia Jurasinski, O.S.B.M., Pres.; Sally Mydlowec, Academic Dean; Olga Udvari, Contact Person. Sisters of St. Basil the Great, Approved by the Commonwealth of Pennsylvania and accredited by the Middle States Association of Colleges and Secondary Schools.

[C] HIGH SCHOOLS, PRIVATE

FOX CHASE MANOR. *St. Basil Academy*, 711 Fox Chase Rd., 19046. Tel: 215-745-5550; Fax: 215-885-4025. Email: admissions@stbasilacademy.org. Web: www.stbasilacademy.org. Sr. Carla Hernandez, O.S.B.M., Prin. Sisters 7; Lay Teachers 32; Students 350.

[D] HOMES FOR SENIOR CITIZENS

PHILADELPHIA. *Ascension Manor, Inc.*, 911 N. Franklin St., 19123. Tel: 215-922-1116. Most Rev. Stefan Soroka, D.D., Ph.D.; Rev. Msgr. James Melnic, Exec. Vice Pres.; Rev. Archpriest John Fields, Sec. & Treas.; Dr. Jaroslaw Jarymowych, Dir.; Jeanne Karbiwnyk, Dir.; Ihor Shust, Dir.; Albert Schulte, Dir.; John Siwak, Gen. Mgr.
Ascension Manor I, 911 N. Franklin St., 19123. Tel: 215-922-1116; Fax: 215-922-3735. Anna Siwak, Mgr.
Ascension Manor II, 970 N. Seventh St., 19123. Tel: 215-923-3907; Fax: 215-922-3735.

[E] MONASTERIES AND RESIDENCES OF PRIESTS AND BROTHERS

WASHINGTON. *Monastery of the Holy Cross*, 1302 Quincy St., N.E., DC 20017-2614. Tel: 202-832-8519. Rev. Joseph (Richard) Lee.

[F] CONVENTS AND RESIDENCES FOR SISTERS

PHILADELPHIA. *Immaculate Conception Convent*, 819 N. 8th St., 19123. Tel: 215-925-3059. Sr. Thomas Hrynewich, S.S.M.I., Supr.
Motherhouse of the Missionary Sisters of Mother of God, 711 N. Franklin St., 19123. Tel: 215-627-7808. Sr. Nadia Baranick, M.S.M.G., Supr. Gen.
Sacred Heart Convent, 160 W. Carpenter Ln., 19119. Tel: 215-843-2266. Sr. Daniella, P.O.S.C., Supr. Students 12.

CHESAPEAKE CITY. *St. Basil's Convent*, 415 Lock St., MD 21915. Sr. M. Augustine, Supr. Sisters O.S.B.M.

FOX CHASE MANOR. *Provincial Motherhouse of the Sisters of St. Basil the Great*, 710 Fox Chase Rd., 19046. Tel: 215-379-3998; Fax: 215-728-6129. Email: Basilians@aol.com. Web: www.basiliansfoxchase.org. Sisters Dorothy Ann Busowski, O.S.B.M., Prov. Supr.; Laura Palka, O.S.B.M., Asst. Prov.; Rev. Robert Hitchens, Chap.; Sisters Mary Cecilia Jurasinski, O.S.B.M., Councilor; Miriam Clair Kowal, O.S.B.M., Councilor; Paula Jacynyk, O.S.B.M., Councilor. Professed Sisters 60.

[G] MISCELLANEOUS

PHILADELPHIA. *Archieparchial Museum and Educational Center*, 814 N. Franklin St., 19123. Tel: 215-627-0143; Fax: 215-627-0377. Sr. Nadia Baranic, M.S.M.G., Admin.

FOX CHASE MANOR. *Basilian Spirituality Center*, 710 Fox Chase Rd., 19046. Tel: 215-780-1227; Fax: 215-728-6129. Web: basilcenter@aol.com. Sr. Marina Bochnewich, O.S.B.M., Dir.

JENKINTOWN. *The Basileiad Library*, 700 Fox Chase Rd., 19046. Brian T. Johnstone, Librarian. Sisters of St. Basil the Great

RELIGIOUS INSTITUTES OF MEN REPRESENTED IN THE ARCHEPARCHY

For further details refer to the corresponding bracketed number in the Religious Institutes of Men or Women section.

[1070]—*Redemptorist Fathers*—C.SS.R.

RELIGIOUS INSTITUTES OF WOMEN REPRESENTED IN THE ARCHEPARCHY

[2345]—*Little Workers of the Sacred Heart of Jesus and Mary*—P.O.S.C.
[2810]—*Missionary Sisters of Mother of God*—M.S.M.G.
[3730]—*Sisters of the Order of St. Basil the Great*—O.S.B.M.
[3610]—*Sisters Servants of Mary Immaculate*—S.S.M.I.

ARCHDIOCESAN CEMETERIES

LANGHORNE. *Mother of Sorrows*, Langhorne & Yardley Rd., 19047. Tel: 215-627-0143.

NECROLOGY

† Boholnick, Rev. Msgr. Theodore, Simpson, PA SS. Peter & Paul—Died Nov. 20, 2002
† Radchuk, Anthony, (Retired)—Died Oct. 27, 2003

Metropolitan Archeparchy of Pittsburgh, Byzantine

Most Reverend

BASIL M. SCHOTT, O.F.M.

Metropolitan Archbishop for Pittsburgh, Byzantine; ordained August 29, 1965; appointed Eparch of Parma May 3, 1996; enthroned July 11, 1996; appointed Metropolitan Archbishop of Pittsburgh May 3, 2002; enthroned July 9, 2002 *Chancery Office: 66 Riverview Ave., Pittsburgh, PA 15214.*

Chancery Office: 66 Riverview Ave., Pittsburgh, PA 15214. Tel: 412-231-4000; Fax: 412-231-1697.

ESTABLISHED FEBRUARY 25, 1924.

Raised to Archeparchy February 21, 1969.

Embraces all Byzantine Ruthenian Rite Catholics in that part of the State of Pennsylvania west of the western boundaries of the Counties of Tioga, Lycoming, Union, Mifflin, Juniata and Franklin. In the State of Ohio, the Counties of Ashtabula, Athens, Belmont, Carroll, Columbiana, Gallia, Guernsey, Harrison, Jefferson, Lawrence, Mahoning, Meigs, Morrow, Morgan, Noble, Trumbull and Washington and also the States of Alabama, Arkansas, Kentucky, Louisiana, Mississippi, Oklahoma, Tennessee, Texas and West Virginia.

For legal titles of parishes and diocesan institutions, consult the Chancery Office.

STATISTICAL OVERVIEW

Personnel	
Archbishops	1
Abbots	1
Priests: Diocesan Active in Diocese	52
Priests: Retired, Sick or Absent	12
Number of Diocesan Priests	64
Religious Priests in Diocese	11
Total Priests in Diocese	75
Extern Priests in Diocese	5
Ordinations:	
Diocesan Priests	1
Transitional Deacons	1
Permanent Deacons in Diocese	10
Total Brothers	4
Total Sisters	96
Parishes	
Parishes	84
With Resident Pastor:	
Resident Diocesan Priests	49
Resident Religious Priests	5
Without Resident Pastor:	
Administered by Priests	30
Missions	2
Professional Ministry Personnel:	
Brothers	2
Sisters	12
Welfare	
Homes for the Aged	2
Total Assisted	361
Educational	
Seminaries, Diocesan	1
Students from This Diocese	1
Students from Other Diocese	7
Total Seminarians	1
Elementary Schools, Diocesan and Parish	2
Total Students	334
Catechesis/Religious Education:	
High School Students	377
Elementary Students	1,228
Total Students under Catholic Instruction	1,940
Teachers in the Diocese:	
Sisters	4
Lay Teachers	22
Vital Statistics	
Receptions into the Church:	
Infant Baptism Totals	260
Adult Baptism Totals	17
Received into Full Communion	45
First Communions	264
Confirmations	288
Marriages:	
Catholic	68
Interfaith	31
Total Marriages	99
Deaths	512
Total Catholic Population	60,100

Former Bishops—Most Revs. BASIL TAKACH, ord. Dec. 12, 1902; appt. May 20, 1924; consecrated June 15, 1924; died May 13, 1948; DANIEL IVANCHO, D.D. (Retired), Titular Bishop of Europus; ord. Sept. 30, 1934; appt. Coadjutor Bishop, Aug. 29, 1946; consecrated Nov. 5, 1946; succeeded to May 13, 1948; retired Dec. 2, 1954; died Aug. 2, 1972; NICHOLAS T. ELKO, D.D., ord. Sept. 30, 1934; consecrated March 6, 1955; transferred to Rome, Dec. 22, 1967; died May 18, 1991; STEPHEN J. KOCISCKO, D.D. (Retired), ord. March 30, 1941; appt. Titular Bishop of Theveste and Auxiliary Bishop of Pittsburgh July 20, 1956; consecrated Oct. 23, 1956; appt. First Eparch of Passaic July 31, 1963; appt. Eparch of Pittsburgh Dec. 21, 1967; enthroned March 5, 1968; elevated to Metropolitan Archbishop of Pittsburgh Feb. 21, 1969; retired June 12, 1991; died March 7, 1995; THOMAS V. DOLINAY, ord. May 16, 1948; appt. Titular Bishop of Thyatira and Auxiliary of Passaic, Sept. 23, 1976; consecrated Nov. 23, 1976; appt. First Ordinary of the Byzantine Catholic Eparchy of Van Nuys; installed March 1982; appt. Coadjutor Archbishop of Pittsburgh, March 13, 1990; installed May 29, 1990; succeeded to June 12, 1991; died April 13, 1993; JOHN M. BILOCK, ord. Feb. 3, 1946; appt. Titular Bishop of Pergamo and Auxiliary Bishop to the Metropolitan Archbishop of Pittsburgh; installed March 1, 1973; consecrated May 15, 1973; appt. Archeparchial Administrator, April 20, 1993; died Sept. 8, 1994; JUDSON M. PROCYK, ord. May 19, 1957; appt. Metropolitan Archbishop of Pittsburgh Nov. 15, 1994; installed Feb. 7, 1995; died April 24, 2002.

Chancery—66 Riverview Ave., Pittsburgh, PA 15214. Tel: 412-231-4000; Fax: 412-231-1697. Email: archpitt@aol.com. Office Hours: Mon.-Fri. 9:30-12 and 12:30-4.

Protosyncellus—Rev. Msgr. RUSSELL A. DUKER, S.E.O.D.

Vicar for Canonical Services—Very Rev. RICHARD J. WHETSTONE, J.C.O.L.

Finance Officer—GREGORY S. POPIVCHAK.

Consultors—Rev. DENNIS M. BOGDA; Very Rev. JOHN J. BORODACH; Rev. Msgr. RUSSELL A. DUKER, S.E.O.D.; Revs. RICHARD I. LAMBERT; SIMEON B. SIBENIK; Very Revs. JAMES A. SPONTAK; RICHARD J. WHETSTONE, J.C.O.L.

Protopresbyters—Very Rev. JOHN J. BORODACH, Clairton; Rev. Msgr. RAYMOND A. BALTA, Johnstown; Very Rev. JOHN H. SALKO, Mon-Valley; Revs. JOHN J. MIHALCO, S.E.O.L., North-Central; EUGENE P. YACKANICH, Pittsburgh; Very Rev. JOSEPH J. JUGAN, Tri-State; Rev. RICHARD I. LAMBERT, Youngstown.

Finance Council—Most Rev. BASIL SCHOTT, O.F.M.; GREGORY S. POPIVCHAK; Very Rev. JOHN J. BORODACH; MICHAEL I. ROMAN; BERNARD J. KOSAR SR.; CATHY A. CHROMULAK, Attorney.

Tribunal—

Judicial Vicar—Very Rev. RICHARD J. WHETSTONE, J.C.O.L.

Pro-Synodal Judges—Rev. RICHARD I. LAMBERT; Very Rev. ANSELM ORLOSKY, O.S.B.; Rev. SIMEON B. SIBENIK; Rev. Msgr. PETER WASLO.

Defender of the Bond—Rev. JOHN J. MIHALCO, S.E.O.L.

Promoter of Justice—Rev. Msgr. ALEXIS E. MIHALIK.

Secretary—Sr. ELAINE KISINKO, O.S.B.M.

Notaries—Rev. GREGORY J. MICHALISIN; DONNA OBSINCS.

Archieparchial Choir—DARLENE FEJKA, Dir.

Archives—Revs. JOHN L. MINA, Ph.D., Archivist; ROBERT F. ORAVETZ, Asst.; Sr. ELAINE KISINKO, O.S.B.M., Asst.

Clergy Continuing Formation—

Presbyteral Council—VACANT.

Communications—VERONICA VARGA, Dir.

Diaconate Program—Very Rev. Archpriest JOHN G. PETRO, Dir.

Evangelization, Mission Activity and Ecumenism—Rev. ROBERT F. ORAVETZ, Dir.

Vocations—Rev. DENNIS M. BOGDA, Dir.; Sr. JEAN MARIE CIHOTA, O.S.B.M., Asst.

Priests' Pension Board— Ex Officio Members: Most Rev. BASIL SCHOTT; GREGORY S. POPIVCHAK, Finance Officer; Rev. Msgr. RUSSELL A. DUKER, S.E.O.D., Protosyncellus & Chancellor.

Elected Deanery Representatives—Revs. JOSEPH R. RAPTOSH, Sec., Clairton; EUGENE P. YACKANICH, Greater Pittsburgh; DANIEL J. LOYA, Johnstown; JEROME G. BOTSKO, Mon Valley; JOHN J. MIHALCO, S.E.O.L., North Central; ANDREW CHURA, Tri State; FRANK A. FIRKO, S.T.L., Youngstown.

Office of Religious Education—Sr. MARION DOBOS, O.S.B., Dir.; Rev. ELIAS L. RAFAJ, Asst. Dir., Archeparchial Catechetical Center, 3605 Perrysville Ave., Pittsburgh, 15214. Tel: 412-322-8773; Fax: 412-322-8737.

Revitalization and Renewal Commission—Revs. DENNIS M. BOGDA; JOSEPH KAPUSNAK; ROBERT J. KARL; ANDREW DESKEVICH; HELEN KENNEDY; Deacon DENNIS M. PRESTASH; SANDRA SIMKO; Deacon RAYMOND J. ZADZILKO.

Archieparchial Newspaper—VERONICA VARGA, Editor; Sr. ELAINE KISINKO, O.S.B.M., Copy Editor, 66 Riverview Ave., Pittsburgh, 15214. Tel: 412-231-4000; Fax: 412-231-1697. Byzantine Catholic World

Byzantine Catholic Seminary Press—Sr. SERAPHIM OLSAFSKY, O.S.B.M., Dir., 3643 Perrysville Ave., P.O. Box 7626, Pittsburgh, 15214. Tel: 412-322-8307; Fax: 412-322-9530.

Victim Assistance Coordinator—Sr. SERAPHIM, O.S.B.M., M.S.W. Tel: 412-322-8307. Email: sseraphim@aol.com.

CLERGY, PARISHES, MISSIONS AND PAROCHIAL SCHOOLS

STATE OF LOUISIANA

NEW ORLEANS, ORLEANS PARISH, ST. NICHOLAS OF MYRA MISSION (1984), Rev. Ellis De Priest, S.M., Admin.

2435 S. Carrollton Ave., LA 70118. Tel: 504-524-5192; Fax: 504-524-9796.

Res.: 1706 Jackson Ave., LA 70113-1510.

STATE OF PENNSYLVANIA

ALIQUIPPA, BEAVER CO., ST. GEORGE THE GREAT MARTYR, Rev. Elias O'Brien, O.Carm.
Res.: 1001 Clinton St., 15001. Tel: 724-375-2742; Fax: 724-375-8776.

AMBRIDGE, BEAVER CO., ST. MARY'S, Rev. Msgr. Edward V. Rosack.
Res.: 624 Park Rd., 15003. Tel: 724-266-2030; Fax: 724-266-2030.

ARCADIA, INDIANA CO., ASCENSION, [CEM] Attended by, Northern Cambria. , 719 Chestnut Ave., Northern Cambria, 15714-1459. Tel: 814-948-8242; Fax: 814-948-8252.

AVELLA, WASHINGTON CO., ST. JOHN THE BAPTIST, [CEM] Attended by, St. Mary's, Weirton, WV.
Res.: P.O. Box 565, 15312. Tel: 304-748-2087; Fax: 304-748-7550.

BEAVER, BEAVER CO., SAINT NICHOLAS CHAPEL, Very Rev. Archpriest John G. Petro, Admin.
5400 Tuscarawas Rd., 15009-9513. Tel: 724-495-3400.

BEAVERDALE, CAMBRIA CO., ST. MARY'S, [CEM] Rev. Edward J. Pyo.
Res.: P.O. Box 610, 15921. Tel: 814-487-7458; Fax: 814-487-4830.

BRADDOCK, ALLEGHENY CO., SS. PETER AND PAUL, Rev. Msgr. Russell A. Duker, S.E.O.D.; Rev. David A. Bosnich.
Res.: 431 George St., 15104. Tel: 412-271-1297.

BRADENVILLE, WESTMORELAND CO., ST. MARY'S, [CEM] Very Rev. Archpriest Joseph Borodach.
Res.: R.R. #1, Box 75, 15620-9711. Tel: 724-537-5839; Fax: 724-532-1499.

BROWNSVILLE, FAYETTE CO., ST. NICHOLAS, [CEM] Rev. Jerome G. Botsko.
Res.: 302 Third Ave., 15417. Tel: 724-785-7573; Fax: 724-785-4649.

CANONSBURG, WASHINGTON CO., ST. MICHAEL, [CEM] Very Rev. Joseph Jugan; Deacon Lance D. Weakland.
Res.: 166 E. College St., 15317. Tel: 724-745-7117; Fax: 724-745-3097.

CHARLEROI, WASHINGTON CO., HOLY GHOST, Very Rev. James A. Spontak.
Res.: 828 Meadow Ave., 15022. Tel: 724-483-8622; Fax: 724-483-0696.

CLAIRTON, ALLEGHENY CO., ASCENSION OF OUR LORD, [CEM] Rev. John L. Mina, Ph.D.
Res.: 318 Park Ave., 15025. Tel: 412-233-7422; Fax: 412-233-0529.

CLARENCE, CENTRE CO., ST. MARY'S, [CEM] Attended by, St. John the Baptist Church, Hawk Run. , Mailing Address: c/o St. John the Baptist Church, P.O. Box 2, Hawk Run, 16840. Tel: 814-342-4315.

CLYMER, INDIANA CO., ST. ANNE, Attended by, St. Jude Thaddeus, Ernest. , Mailing Address: P.O. Box 130, Ernest, 15739. Tel: 724-463-3397; Fax: 724-465-5773.

COAL RUN, INDIANA CO., HOLY CROSS, Attended by, Holy Protection of Mary, Homer City. , 279 Yellow Creek St., Homer City, 15748. Tel: 724-479-2206.

CONEMAUGH, CAMBRIA CO., HOLY TRINITY, [CEM] Rev. Ronald W. Borsuk.
Res.: 217 Fourth St., 15909. Tel: 814-535-5231; Fax: 814-535-2417.

DONORA, WASHINGTON CO., ST. MICHAEL, [CEM] Very Rev. Archpriest John J. Borodach.
Res.: 511 Murray Ave., 15033. Tel: 724-379-9751; Fax: 724-379-9752.

DU BOIS, CLEARFIELD CO., NATIVITY OF THE MOTHER OF GOD, Attended by, Holy Trinity, Sykesville. Rev. John J. Mihalco, S.E.O.L.; Deacons Paul M. Boboige; George M. Fatula.
Res.: 200 McCullough St., 15801. Tel: 814-894-5440; Fax: 814-894-2412.

DUNLO, CAMBRIA CO., SS. PETER AND PAUL, [CEM] Attended by, St. Mary's, Beaverdale. , Mailing Address: P.O. Box 610, Beaverdale, 15921. Tel: 814-487-7458.

DUQUESNE, ALLEGHENY CO.
1—ST. MARY'S, Attended by, St. Elias, Munhall.
Res.: 1209 Kennedy Ave., 15110. Tel: 412-461-1712; Fax: 412-461-1712.
2—SS. PETER AND PAUL, [CEM] Rev. Msgr. Russell A. Duker, S.E.O.D.; Revs. David A. Bosnich; Stephen J. Wahal, Admin.
Res.: 701 Foster Ave., 15110. Tel: 412-466-3578; Fax: 412-466-3578.

EAST PITTSBURGH, ALLEGHENY CO., ST. MARY'S, Rev. George Evancho.
Res.: 317 Howard St., 15112. Tel: 412-824-1622.

ERIE, ERIE CO., SS. PETER AND PAUL, Rev. Andrew J. Deskevich.
Res.: 3415 Wallace St., 16504. Tel: 814-825-8140.

ERNEST, INDIANA CO., ST. JUDE THADDEUS, Rev. James A. Ragan.
Res.: Box 130, 15739. Tel: 724-463-3397; Fax: 724-465-5773.

GIBSONIA, ALLEGHENY CO., ST. ANDREW THE APOSTLE, Very Rev. Richard J. Whetstone, J.C.O.L.
Res.: 235 Logan Rd., 15044. Tel: 724-625-1160; Fax: 724-625-1085.

GIRARD, ERIE CO., SS. CYRIL AND METHODIUS, Attended by, Sts. Peter and Paul, Erie
Res.: 1022 Tilden Ave., 16417. Tel: 814-774-3281; Fax: 814-774-5405.

GREENSBURG, WESTMORELAND CO., ST. NICHOLAS OF MYRA, Rev. Regis Dusecina.
Res.: 622 E. Pittsburgh St., 15601. Tel: 724-837-0295; Fax: 724-837-9042.

HANNASTOWN, WESTMORELAND CO., ST. MARY'S, Attended by, St. Nicholas of Myra, Greensburg. , 622 E. Pittsburgh St., Greensburg, 15601. Tel: 724-837-0295.

HAWK RUN, CLEARFIELD CO., ST. JOHN THE BAPTIST, [CEM] Rev. Robert F. Oravetz; Deacons John A. Custaney; Dennis M. Prestash.
Mailing Address: P.O. Box 2, 16840. Tel: 814-342-4315.

HERMINIE, WESTMORELAND CO., ST. MARY'S, Attended by, St. Stephen's, North Huntington. , 7 Second St., 15637. Tel: 724-446-0262.

HERMITAGE, MERCER CO., ST. MICHAEL, [CEM] Rev. Frank A. Firko, S.T.L.
Res.: 2230 Highland Rd., 16148. Tel: 724-981-6680; Fax: 724-981-7422.

HOMER CITY, INDIANA CO., HOLY PROTECTION OF MARY, THE MOTHER OF GOD, Rev. Cuthbert A. Jack, O.S.B. (GBG).
Res.: 279 Yellow Creek St., 15748. Tel: 724-479-2206; Fax: 724-479-9506.

JEROME, SOMERSET CO., SS. PETER AND PAUL, [CEM] Attended by, St. Mary, Windber. Rev. Daniel J. Loya; Deacon Paul J. Pipta.
803 Somerset Ave., Windber, 15963. Tel: 814-467-8044; Fax: 814-467-8044.

JOHNSTOWN, CAMBRIA CO., ST. MARY'S, [CEM] Rev. Msgr. Raymond A. Balta.
Res.: 411 Power St., 15906. Tel: 814-535-4132; Fax: 814-536-9017.

LEISENRING, FAYETTE CO., ST. STEPHEN, [CEM] Rev. Joseph Kapusnak.
Res.: P.O. Box 128, 15455. Tel: 724-628-6611; Fax: 724-628-5009.

LYNDORA, BUTLER CO., ST. JOHN THE BAPTIST, [CEM] Rev. Dennis M. Bogda; Deacon Paul Simko.
Res.: 105 Kohler Ave., 16045. Tel: 724-287-5000; Fax: 724-287-6769.

MCKEES ROCKS, ALLEGHENY CO., HOLY GHOST, Revs. Ronald P. Larko; Jason R. Dolan.
Res.: 225 Olivia St., 15136. Tel: 412-771-3324; Fax: 412-331-1870.

MCKEESPORT, ALLEGHENY CO.
1—ST. NICHOLAS, [CEM] Rev. Donald J. Voss.
Res.: 410 Sixth Ave., 15132. Tel: 412-664-9131; Fax: 412-664-0854.
2—TRANSFIGURATION OF OUR LORD, Attended by, St. Nicholas, McKeesport.
Res.: 121 Sixth Ave., 15132. Tel: 412-672-0728.

MONESSEN, WESTMORELAND CO., ASSUMPTION OF THE BLESSED VIRGIN, [CEM] Rev. Msgr. Andrew D. Parvensky; Deacon John M. Hanchin.
Res.: 125 McKee Ave., 15062. Tel: 724-684-5662; Fax: 724-684-3301.

MONONGAHELA, WASHINGTON CO., ST. MACRINA, Closed. For inquiries for parish records contact the chancery.

MONROEVILLE, ALLEGHENY CO., CHURCH OF THE RESURRECTION, Rev. Richard Joseph Raptosh, Admin.
Res.: 455 Center Rd., 15146. Tel: 412-372-8650; Fax: 412-372-1442.

MUNHALL, ALLEGHENY CO.
1—ST. JOHN THE BAPTIST CATHEDRAL, [CEM] Rev. Simeon B. Sibenik, Rector.
Res.: 210 Greentree Rd., 15120. Tel: 412-461-0944; Fax: 412-462-3495.
2—ST. ELIAS, [CEM] Rev. Eugene P. Yackanich.
Res.: 4200 Homestead-Duquesne Rd., 15120. Tel: 412-461-1712; Fax: 412-461-1712.

NANTY-GLO, CAMBRIA CO., ST. NICHOLAS, Attended by, Holy Trinity, Conemaugh.
Res.: 1191 Second St., 15943. Tel: 814-749-0421.

NEW SALEM, FAYETTE CO., ST. MARY'S, [CEM] Attended by, St. Nicholas, Brownsville. , Mailing Address: P.O. Box 487, 15468. Tel: 724-245-7188.

NORTH HUNTINGDON, WESTMORELAND CO., ST. STEPHEN'S, Rev. Gregory Michalisin.
Res.: 90 Bethel Rd., 15642. Tel: 724-863-6776; Fax: 724-864-9685.

NORTHERN CAMBRIA, CAMBRIA CO., ST. JOHN THE BAPTIST, [CEM] Rev. Oliver J. Hebert, T.O.R.
Res.: 719 Chestnut Ave., 15714-1459. Tel: 814-948-8242; Fax: 814-948-8252.

PATTON, CAMBRIA CO., SS. PETER AND PAUL, [CEM] Attended by, St. John, Northern Cambria. Rev. Oliver J. Hebert, T.O.R.; Deacon Raymond J. Zadzilko.
Church: 516 Palmer Ave., 16668. Tel: 814-674-5552.

PERRYOPOLIS, FAYETTE CO., ST. NICHOLAS, [CEM] Rev. Robert E. Halus.
Res.: 102 Railroad St., 15473. Tel: 724-736-4344; Fax: 724-736-4642.

PITTSBURGH, ALLEGHENY CO.
1—HOLY GHOST, Very Rev. Richard J. Whetstone, J.C.O.L.
Res.: 1437 Superior Ave., 15212. Tel: 412-321-5072; Fax: 412-321-0260.
2—HOLY SPIRIT, Rev. Msgr. Russell A. Duker, S.E.O.D.; Rev. David A. Bosnich.
Res.: 4815 Fifth Ave., 15213. Tel: 412-687-1220; Fax: 412-687-1520.
3—ST. JOHN CHRYSOSTOM, Rev. John J. Cuccaro.
Res.: 506 Saline St., 15207. Tel: 412-421-0243; Fax: 412-422-3624.
4—ST. JOHN THE BAPTIST, [CEM] Rev. Elias L. Rafaj.
Res.: 1720 Jane St., 15203. Tel: 412-431-1090; Fax: 412-431-2059.
5—NATIVITY OF B.V.M., Attended by, St. John Chrysostom, Pittsburgh
Res.: 4027 Beechwood Blvd., 15217. Tel: 412-421-5231.
6—ST. PIUS X, Rev. Msgr. Nicholas X. Smiciklas.
Res.: 2336 Brownsville Rd., 15210. Tel: 412-881-8344; Fax: 412-884-7504.

PORTAGE, CAMBRIA CO., SS. PETER AND PAUL, [CEM] Rev. Robert J. Karl.
Res.: 143 Church Rd., 15946. Tel: 814-736-9780; Fax: 814-736-8701.

PUNXSUTAWNEY, JEFFERSON CO., SS. PETER AND PAUL, [CEM 2] Rev. Robert K. Yetsko, T.O.R.
Res.: 714 Sutton St., 15767. Tel: 814-938-6564; Fax: 814-938-6551.

RANKIN, ALLEGHENY CO., ST. JOHN'S, Attended by, St. Mary's, East Pittsburgh. Rev. George Evancho.
317 Howard St., East Pittsburgh, 15112. Tel: 412-824-1622.
Church: 44 Miller Ave., 15104.

SAGAMORE, ARMSTRONG CO., ST. MARY'S, [CEM] Attended by, St. Jude Thaddeus, Ernest. , Mailing Address: Box 130, Ernest, 15739. Tel: 724-463-3397.

SCOTTDALE, WESTMORELAND CO., ST. JOHN THE BAPTIST, [CEM] Very Rev. John H. Salko.
Res.: 525 Porter Ave., 15683. Tel: 724-887-5072; Fax: 724-887-3365.

SHEFFIELD, WARREN CO., ST. MICHAEL, [CEM] Very Rev. Leo R. Schlosser, O.S.B.
Res.: 407 School St., 16347. Tel: 814-968-5478; Fax: 814-968-4445.

SOUTH FORK, CAMBRIA CO., ST. MICHAEL'S, [CEM] Attended by, SS. Peter and Paul Church, Portage. Rev. Robert J. Karl, Admin.
143 Church Rd., Portage, 15946. Tel: 814-736-9780; Fax: 814-736-8701.

SYKESVILLE, JEFFERSON CO., HOLY TRINITY, [CEM] Rev. John J. Mihalco, S.E.O.L.
Res.: 104 Shaffer St., 15865. Tel: 814-894-5440; Fax: 814-894-2412.

TARENTUM, ALLEGHENY CO., STS. PETER AND PAUL, Rev. Wesley M. Mash (HBG).
Res.: 339 E. 10th Ave., 15084-1003. Tel: 724-224-3026; Fax: 724-224-5242.

TRAUGER, WESTMORELAND CO., ST. MARY'S, [CEM] Rev. Christopher R. Burke.
Res.: R.D. 3, Box 373-C, Latrobe, 15650. Tel: 724-423-3673; Fax: 724-423-1808.

UNIONTOWN, FAYETTE CO., ST. JOHN THE BAPTIST, [CEM] Rev. Thomas J. Wesdock.
Res.: 185 E. Main St., 15401. Tel: 724-438-6027; Fax: 724-438-1382.

UPPER ST. CLAIR, ALLEGHENY CO., ST. GREGORY NAZIANZUS, Rev. Bruno Asturi.
Res.: 2005 Mohawk Rd., 15241. Tel: 412-835-7800; Fax: 412-835-7890.

WALL, ALLEGHENY CO., HOLY TRINITY, Very Rev. Anselm Orlosky, O.S.B.
Res.: 470 Wall Ave., 15148. Tel: 412-824-9803; Fax: 412-824-9803.

WINDBER, SOMERSET CO., ST. MARY (DORMITION) CHURCH, [CEM] Rev. Daniel Loya.
Res.: 803 Somerset St., 15963. Tel: 814-467-8044; Fax: 814-467-8044.

STATE OF OKLAHOMA

OKLAHOMA CITY, OKLAHOMA CO., BYZANTINE CATHOLIC COMMUNITY OF OKLAHOMA CITY, Rev. Philip M. Seeton, Admin.
Res.: 1010 N.W. 82nd St., Lawton, OK 73506. Tel: 580-531-2607; Fax: 580-531-2608.

STATE OF OHIO

ASHTABULA, ASHTABULA CO., ST. NICHOLAS, Rev. A. Edward Gretchko.
Res.: 206 Cherry Rd., N.E., Massillon, OH 44646.
Church: 1104 E. Fifteenth St., OH 44004. Tel: 330-833-8501; Fax: 330-833-3359.

BOARDMAN, MAHONING CO., INFANT JESUS OF PRAGUE, Rev. Msgr. Alexis E. Mihalik.
Res.: 7754 S. Ave. Extension, P.O. Box 7006, OH 44512. Tel: 330-758-6019; Fax: 330-758-6776.

CAMPBELL, MAHONING CO., ST. MICHAEL, [CEM] Rev. Msgr. Victor G. Romza.
Res.: 463 Robinson Rd., Box 426, OH 44405. Tel: 330-755-4831; Fax: 330-755-1818.

MINGO JUNCTION, JEFFERSON CO., ST. JOHN THE

BAPTIST, Attended by, St. Joseph, Toronto. Church: 207 Standard St., OH 43938. Tel: 740-535-0271; Fax: 740-537-9802.

NEWTON FALLS, TRUMBULL CO., ST. MICHAEL, [CEM] Rev. John Kasarda.
Res.: 737 Ridge Rd., OH 44444. Tel: 330-872-5216; Fax: 330-872-0200.

PLEASANT CITY, GUERNSEY CO., ST. MICHAEL, [CEM] Rev. Dennis Logue, S.V.D.
Res.: 408 Walnut St., OH 43772. Tel: 740-685-3292; Fax: 740-685-1015.

TORONTO, JEFFERSON CO., ST. JOSEPH, Rev. Andrew Chura.
Res.: 814 N. Fifth St., OH 43964. Tel: 740-537-1026; Fax: 740-537-9802.

WARREN, TRUMBULL CO., SS. PETER AND PAUL'S, [CEM] Rev. Sylvester Hladky.
Res.: 180 Belvedere Ave., N.E., OH 44483. Tel: 330-372-1875; Fax: 330-372-5965.
School—195 Belvedere Ave., N.E., OH 44483. Tel: 330-372-1312; Fax: 330-372-5965. Sr. Margaret Mary, O.S.B., Ph.D., Prin. Sisters of the Order of St. Benedict 2; Lay Teachers 15; Students 141.

YOUNGSTOWN, MAHONING CO.
1—ASSUMPTION OF THE BLESSED VIRGIN, [CEM] Rev. Richard I. Lambert.
Res.: 356 S. Belle Vista, OH 44509. Tel: 330-799-8163; Fax: 330-793-5360.
2—ST. GEORGE, Attended by, St. Nicholas, Youngstown. , 1726 Canfield Rd., OH 44511. Tel: 330-782-2865.
3—ST. JOHN THE BAPTIST, Closed., For inquiries for parish records contact St. Nicholas, 1898 Wilson Ave., Youngstown, OH 44506. Tel.: 330-743-0419.
4—ST. NICHOLAS, [CEM] Rev. David J. Shortt.
Res.: 1898 Wilson Ave., OH 44506. Tel 330-743-0419; Fax: 330-743-6888.
School—Byzantine Catholic Central, 5512 Youngstown-Poland Rd., OH 44514. Tel: 330-757-9185; Fax: 330-757-8150. Sisters 2; Lay Teachers 7; Students 193.

STATE OF TEXAS

HOUSTON, HARRIS CO., ST. JOHN CHRYSOSTOM, Rev. Julian Anthony.
Res.: 5402 Acorn St., TX 77092-4255. Tel: 713-681-3580; Fax: 713-681-3466.

IRVING, DALLAS CO., ST. BASIL THE GREAT, Rev. Stephen J. Wahal.
Res.: 1118 E. Union Bower Rd., TX 75061. Tel: 972-438-5644; Fax: 972-721-0696.

STATE OF TENNESSEE

SEYMOUR, SEVIER CO., HOLY RESURRECTION MISSION, Rev. Thomas P. O'Connell, Admin.
Res.: 407 Overlook Dr., TN 37865. Tel: 865-609-1081; Fax: 865-579-3645.

STATE OF WEST VIRGINIA

MORGANTOWN, MONONGALIA CO., ST. MARY HOLY PROTECTION, Attended by, St. John the Baptist, Uniontown, PA. , Mailing Address: 2115 Listravia Ave., WV 26505.
Church: Tel: 304-296-2455.

WEIRTON, HANCOCK CO., ST. MARY'S, Rev. Edward Lucas.
Res.: 3116 Elm St., WV 26062. Tel: 304-748-2087; Fax: 304-748-7550.

Retired:
Rev. Msgrs.—
Macko, John, 101 Whitestown Rd., Lyndora, 16045.
Tay, Peter P., 1200 San Pedro St., 15212.
Revs.—
Chewning, Seraphim John, 821 Clark St., Cambridge, OH 43725.
Chornyak, Joseph I., P.O. Box 338, Perryopolis, 14573-0338.
Gnall, Julian M., O.S.B., Chap., U.S. Navy, San Diego, CA.
Gran, Thomas, 401 Cambria Ave., Windber, 15963.
Kolcun, Stephen J., 4469 Country Club Dr., 15236.
Kubinyi, Julius, 6458 Highland Rd., Kane, 16735.
Mokris, Michael, 472 Church St., Swoyersville, 18704.

INSTITUTIONS LOCATED IN THE ARCHDIOCESE

[A] SEMINARIES, ARCHDIOCESAN

PITTSBURGH. *Byzantine Catholic Seminary of SS. Cyril and Methodius*, 3605 Perrysville Ave., 15214-2297. Tel: 412-321-8383; Fax: 412-321-9936. Email: byzcathsem@att.net. Very Rev. John G. Petro, Rector. Tel: 412-321-7550; Revs. David M. Petras, Spiritual Dir. Tel: 412-321-5133; John S. Custer, Dean. Tel: 412-321-5993. Students for Priesthood 6.

[B] HOMES FOR AGED

UNIONTOWN. *Mt. Macrina Manor*, 520 W. Main St., 15401-2602. Tel: 724-437-1400; Fax: 724-430-1095. Christina M. Yakich, Admin. Brothers of the Holy Spirit 1; Sisters of St. Basil the Great 3; Bed Capacity 141.

WARREN. *Infant of Prague Manor*, 169 Kenmore, N.E., OH 44483. Tel: 330-372-4700; Fax: 330-372-5965. Email: smm@netdotcom.com. Web: www.stspeterandpaulbyz.org. Sr. Margaret Mary, O.S.B., Ph.D., Admin. Housing for the elderly. Apartments 46; Staff 4; In Residence 33.

[C] MONASTERIES AND RESIDENCES OF PRIESTS AND BROTHERS

BUTLER. *Holy Trinity Monastery*, P.O. Box 990, 16003. Tel: 724-287-4461; Fax: 724-287-6160. Rt. Rev. Leo R. Schlosser, O.S.B., Abbot/Hegumen; Very Rev. Anselm Orlosky, O.S.B., Prior; Bro. Michael Zetzer, O.S.B., Procurator. Priests 5; Brothers 3.

[D] CONVENTS AND RESIDENCES FOR SISTERS

ALIQUIPPA. *St. George Convent*, 1000 Clinton St., 15001. Tel: 724-378-0238. Sr. Mary Virginia Ermay, O.Carm., Dir. of Catechetics.

UNIONTOWN. *Motherhouse and Novitiate of the Sisters of St. Basil the Great*, 500 W. Main St., P.O. Box 878, 15401. Tel: 724-438-8644; Fax: 724-438-8660. Email: osbmolph@stargate.net. Sr. Ruth Plante, O.S.B.M., Prov. Supr.; Rev. Innokentij Stikhin, Chap. Professed Sisters 85.

WARREN. *Queen of Heaven Monastery*, 3640 Squires Ln., N.E., OH 44484. Tel: 330-856-1813; Fax: 330-856-9528. Email: qohm@netdotcom.com. Web: www.benedictinebyzantine.org. Sr. Margaret Mary Schima, O.S.B., Prioress. Benedictine Sisters of the Byzantine Rite 9.

YOUNGSTOWN. *Byzantine Convent*, 5512 Youngstown-Poland Rd., OH 44514. Tel: 330-757-9186; Fax: 330-757-1950. Sisters of St. Basil the Great 2.

[E] MISCELLANEOUS

UNIONTOWN. *Mt. St. Marcina Retreat Center*, 510 W. Main St., P.O. Box 878, 15401-0878. Tel: 724-438-7149; Fax: 724-438-7149. Email: macrina@sgi.net. Sr. Carol Petrasovich, O.S.B.M., Dir.

RELIGIOUS INSTITUTES OF MEN REPRESENTED IN THE ARCHDIOCESE

For further details refer to the corresponding bracketed number in the Religious Institutes of Men or Women section.

[0200]—*Benedictine Monks*—O.S.B.

RELIGIOUS INSTITUTES OF WOMEN REPRESENTED IN THE ARCHDIOCESE

[0230]—*Benedictine Sisters of the Byzantine Rite*—O.S.B.

[3730]—*Sisters of the Order of St. Basil the Great*—O.S.B.M.

NECROLOGY

(No Deaths)

Romanian Catholic Diocese of Saint George's in Canton

Most Reverend

JOHN MICHAEL BOTEAN, D.D.

Bishop for the Romanian Byzantine Faithful; ordained May 18, 1986; appointed Bishop for the Romanian Byzantine Faithful of the United States July 15, 1996; Episcopal Ordination August 24, 1996 *Res.: 1123 44th St., N.E., Canton, OH 44714-1297.* Tel: 330-493-9355; Fax: 330-493-9963.

Most Reverend

LOUIS PUSCAS, D.D.

Bishop Emeritus for the Romanian Byzantine Faithful; ordained May 14, 1942; appointed Exarch for the Romanian Byzantine Faithful of the United States December 4, 1982; Episcopal ordination June 26, 1983; installed August 28, 1983; promoted first Eparch April 16, 1987; retired July 15, 1993 *111 W. Park Ave., Apt. 407, Aurora, IL 60506.* Tel: 630-859-3961.

Chancery: P.O. Box 7189, Canton, OH 44705-0189. Tel: 330-493-9355; Fax: 330-493-9963.

Web: www.romaniancatholic.org

Email: chancery@romaniancatholic.org

ESTABLISHED DECEMBER 4, 1982

Elevated from Apostolic Exarchate for Romanian Byzantine to the Rank of an Eparchy (Diocese) March 26, 1987.

The Jurisdiction of the Romanian Catholic Diocese of Canton extends territorially to all of the United States.

Legal Title: The Romanian Catholic Diocese of Canton.

STATISTICAL OVERVIEW

Personnel	
Bishop	1
Retired Bishops	1
Priests: Diocesan Active in Diocese	11
Priests: Retired, Sick or Absent	6
Number of Diocesan Priests	17
Religious Priests in Diocese	2
Total Priests in Diocese	19
Extern Priests in Diocese	4
Ordinations:	
Transitional Deacons	1
Permanent Deacons in Diocese	2
Parishes	
Parishes	15
With Resident Pastor:	
Resident Diocesan Priests	9
Resident Religious Priests	2
Without Resident Pastor:	
Administered by Priests	4
Missions	4
Educational	
Diocesan Students in Other Seminaries	3
Total Seminarians	3
Catechesis/Religious Education:	
High School Students	17
Elementary Students	63
Total Students under Catholic Instruction	83
Vital Statistics	
Receptions into the Church:	
Infant Baptism Totals	30
Adult Baptism Totals	5
Received into Full Communion	6
First Communions	27
Confirmations	30
Marriages:	
Catholic	6
Interfaith	3
Total Marriages	9
Deaths	23
Total Catholic Population	5,000

Former Bishop—Most Rev. LOUIS PUSCAS, D.D. (Retired), ord. May 14, 1942; appt. Exarch, Dec. 4, 1982; Episcopal ordination, June 26, 1983;; installed Aug. 28, 1983; promoted to first Eparch, April 16, 1987; retired July 15, 1993.

Chancery—Mailing Address, P.O. Box 7189, Canton, 44705-0189.

Chancellor—Rev. EMMANUEL G. SAMAYOA.

Vice Chancellor—Very Rev. CHARLES A. MEZZOMO.

Economos—Mr. JAMES P. DERSHAW, C.P.A.

Board of Consultors—Very Revs. GEORGE DAVID, V.G.; AUREL PATER; Revs. MICHAEL MOISIN; MICHAEL KIRILA; GEORGE GAGE; ANDRE MATTHEWS.

Protosyncellus—Very Rev. GEORGE DAVID, V.G.

Vicar for Theological Affairs—Sr. THERESA KOERNKE, I.H.M., Ph.D.

Director of Religious Education—ANNAMARIA SILVERI.

Pro-Life Commission—Rev. MICHAEL KIRILA.

Director of Scouting Svcs.—Deacon GARY A. BOYCE, Dir.

Formation Council—Rev. RICHARD J. MUCOWSKI, O.F.M., Ph.D.; Sr. THERESA KOERNKE, I.H.M., Ph.D.; Revs. AUGUST J. DEASIO, M.A. (Retired); EMMANUEL G. SAMAYOA.

Director of Vocations—VACANT.

Office to Aid the Church in Romania—Rev. MICHAEL MOISIN, Coord.

Diocesan Collections Coordinator—Rev. GEORGE GAGE.

Evangelization—IPODIACON PAUL VOIDA.

Victim Assistance Coordinator—CAROL ANN GALL. Tel: 216-444-4095. Email: gallc@ccf.org.

CLERGY, PARISHES, MISSIONS AND PAROCHIAL SCHOOLS

STATE OF CALIFORNIA

LOS ANGELES, LOS ANGELES CO., ST. MARY ROMANIAN CATHOLIC MISSION, , Congregating at the Monastery of the Angels, 1977 Carmen Ave., Los Angeles, CA 90068-4098. Rev. Calin Tamiian.

STATE OF ILLINOIS

AURORA, DU PAGE CO., ST. MICHAEL, Very Rev. Aurel Pater.
Res. & Church: 609 N. Lincoln Ave., IL 60505-2112. Tel: 630-897-8115; Fax: 630-897-5923.

AURORA, KANE CO., ST. GEORGE, Rev. Frederick Peterson, O.S.B.
Res.: 850 Butterfield Rd., IL 60504-8609. Tel: 630-897-7215, Ext. 346; Fax: 630-897-0393.
Church: 720 Rural St., IL 60505-2551. Tel: 630-851-4002; Fax: 630-851-4002.

CHICAGO, COOK CO., SS. PETER AND PAUL MISSION, Rev. Sergiu Cornea, Admin.
Res.: 1472 Burr Oak Cir., Aurora, IL 60506-1396. Tel: 630-896-4807; Fax: 630-896-4807.
Mission—Holy Redeemer Church 3107 Fullerton Ave., Cook Co., IL 60647. Tel: 773-342-7373; Fax: 773-342-7373.

STATE OF INDIANA

EAST CHICAGO, LAKE CO., ST. NICHOLAS, Very Rev. Charles A. Mezzomo.
Church & Res.: 4309 Olcott Ave., IN 46312-2649. Tel: 219-398-3760; Fax: 219-391-0919.

STATE OF MASSACHUSETTS

BOSTON, MIDDLESEX CO., ROMANIAN CATHOLIC MISSION OF BOSTON, Rev. Michael Moisin, Admin.
Res. & Mailing Address: 8 Druce St., Brookline, MA 02445-4213. Tel: 617-566-4345; Fax: 617-566-3073.

STATE OF MICHIGAN

DEARBORN, WAYNE CO., ST. MARY, Rev. Gheorghe Opris, Admin.
Church & Res.: 823 S. Military, MI 48124-2109. Tel: 313-274-2347; Fax: 313-274-9130.

DETROIT, WAYNE CO., ST. JOHN THE BAPTIST, Rev. Michael Kirila.
Res.: 2371 Woodstock Dr., MI 48203-1060. Tel: 313-386-1046; Fax: 313-368-5358.

STATE OF NEW JERSEY

ROEBLING, BURLINGTON CO., ST. MARY, Attended by, St. Basil, Trenton. Very Rev. George David, V.G.
Church: 181 Norman Ave., NJ 08554-1125. Tel: 609-695-6093.

TRENTON, MERCER CO., ST. BASIL, Very Rev. George David, V.G.
Church & Res.: 238 Adeline St., NJ 08611-2420. Tel: 609-695-6093; Fax: 609-695-6093.

STATE OF NEW YORK

ASTORIA, QUEENS CO., ST. MARY ROMANIAN CATHOLIC MISSION,
Holy Cross Church: 31-12 30th St., Long Island City, NY 11106-2802. Tel: 718-845-5366. Rev. Vasile Tivadar (STF).

STATE OF OHIO

ALLIANCE, STARK CO., ST. THEODORE, Attended by, St. George, Canton. Rev. Emmanuel G. Samayoa.
Mailing Address: 1121 44th St. N.E., 44714-1297. Tel: 330-492-8413; Fax: 330-493-9963.
Church: 820 S. Linden St., 44601.

CANTON, STARK CO., ST. GEORGE CATHEDRAL, Revs. Emmanuel G. Samayoa, Rector; John J. Skala (Retired); Most Rev. John Michael Botean, D.D.
Church & Res.: 1121 44th St., N.E., 44714-1297. Tel: 330-492-8413; Fax: 330-493-9963.
Bishop's Residence:—1123 44th St., N.E., 44714-1297. Tel: 330-493-9355; Fax: 330-493-9963.

CHESTERLAND, GEAUGA CO., MOST HOLY TRINITY, Rev. Albert M. Marflak, O.S.B., Admin.
Res.: 10510 Buckeye Rd., Cleveland, 44104-3725. Tel: 216-721-5300, Ext. 208; Fax: 216-721-1253.
Church: 8549 Mayfield Rd., 44026-2625. Tel: 216-729-7636.

CLEVELAND, CUYAHOGA CO., ST. HELENA, Rev. Andre Matthews.
Church & Res.: 1367 W. 65th St., 44102-2109. Tel: 216-651-0965; Fax: 216-631-3853.

LORAIN, LORAIN CO., ST. BASIL, , Served from St. Helena, Cleveland. Rev. Andre Matthews.
St. Helena: 1367 W. 65th St., Cleveland, 44102-2109. Tel: 216-651-0965; Fax: 216-631-3853.
Church: 2305 E. 31st St., 44052-2015. Tel 216-277-5646.

YOUNGSTOWN, MAHONING CO., ST. MARY, Rev. George D. Gage.
Church & Res.: 7782 Glenwood Ave., Boardman, 44512-5823. Tel: 330-726-8573; Fax: 330-726-8573.

STATE OF PENNSYLVANIA

MCKEESPORT, ALLEGHENY CO., ST. MARY, Revs. John M. Elanjileth; James E. Reiter (Canada).
Church & Res.: 318 26th St., PA 15132-7014. Tel: 412-673-5552. Rev. James E. Reiter (Canada).
Res.: 1105 10th Ave., Irwin, PA 15642-3827. Tel: 412-863-6837; Fax: 412-863-6997.

SHARON, MERCER CO., ST. JOHN THE BAPTIST, Attended by, St. Mary, Youngstown. Rev. George D. Gage.
Res.: 7782 Glenwood Ave., Boardman, 44512-5823. Tel: 330-726-8573; Fax: 330-726-8573.
Church: 3056 Morefield Rd., Hermitage, PA 16148.

Unassigned:
Revs.—
Brown, Konstantin K.
Tamiian, Calin
Yossa, Kenneth F.

Retired:
Most Rev.—
Puscas, Louis, D.D. Tel: 630-859-3961
Revs.—
Buga, John
Skala, John J.
Streza, Charles V.

NECROLOGY

† Ciungu, John, (Retired)—Died Feb. 3, 2003

Ukrainian Catholic Diocese of St. Josephat in Parma

Most Reverend

ROBERT M. MOSKAL, D.D.

Bishop of St. Josaphat in Parma; ordained March 25, 1963; appointed Titular Bishop of Agathopolis and Auxiliary Bishop of the Archeparchy of Philadelphia August 3, 1981; consecrated October 13, 1981; appointed First Bishop of St. Josaphat in Parma December 5, 1983 *Res.: 5720 State Rd., P.O. Box 347180, Cleveland, OH 44134.*

Chancery: 5720 State Rd., P.O. Box 347180, Parma, OH 44134-7180. Tel: 440-888-1522; Fax: 440-888-3477.

Email: josaphateparchy@cs.com

ESTABLISHED DECEMBER 3, 1983.

The jurisdiction of the Bishop of St. Josaphat in Parma extends territorially through all the States of Ohio, Mississippi, West Virginia, Kentucky, Tennessee, Alabama, Georgia, North Carolina, South Carolina, Florida and western Pennsylvania. With regards to persons, his subjects are Catholics of the Byzantine Ukrainian Rite: 1. Who immigrated to this country from Galicia, Bucovina and other Ukrainian provinces; 2. Who descend from such persons (Can. 755); 3. Women married to men referable to 1 and 2, if they comply with (Can. 98, n.4); 4. Who in accordance with (Can. 98, n.3) changed their Rite; 5. Converts to the Catholic Church of the Byzantine Ukrainian Rite; 6. And in fact, all other Catholics of the Byzantine Ukrainian Rite who are attached to parishes subject to the jurisdiction of the Bishop of St. Josaphat in Parma.

For legal titles of parishes and diocesan institutions, consult the Chancery.

STATISTICAL OVERVIEW

Personnel	
Bishop	1
Priests: Diocesan Active in Diocese	32
Priests: Diocesan Active Outside Diocese	2
Priests: Retired, Sick or Absent	6
Number of Diocesan Priests	40
Religious Priests in Diocese	1
Total Priests in Diocese	41
Extern Priests in Diocese	8
Ordinations:	
Diocesan Priests	1
Permanent Deacons in Diocese	5
Total Brothers	10
Total Sisters	5
Parishes	
Parishes	38
With Resident Pastor:	
Resident Diocesan Priests	31
Resident Religious Priests	1
Without Resident Pastor:	
Administered by Priests	6
Missions	2
Professional Ministry Personnel:	
Sisters	2
Welfare	
Homes for the Aged	2
Total Assisted	169
Educational	
Diocesan Students in Other Seminaries	3
Total Seminarians	3
Elementary Schools, Diocesan and Parish	2
Total Students	241
Catechesis/Religious Education:	
High School Students	52
Elementary Students	447
Total Students under Catholic Instruction	743
Teachers in the Diocese:	
Sisters	1
Lay Teachers	27
Vital Statistics	
Receptions into the Church:	
Infant Baptism Totals	93
Adult Baptism Totals	7
Received into Full Communion	2
First Communions	95
Confirmations	99
Marriages:	
Catholic	46
Interfaith	12
Total Marriages	58
Deaths	206
Total Catholic Population	11,058

Vicar General—Rev. Msgr. LEO ADAMIAK.

Vicar General in Curia—Rev. Msgr. THOMAS A. SAYUK.

Chancellor—Rev. Msgr. THOMAS A. SAYUK.

Vice Chancellor—Rev. Msgr. PETER WASLO.

Diocesan Treasurer—Rev. Msgr. THOMAS A. SAYUK.

Chancery—5720 State Rd., P.O. Box 347180, Parma, 44134-7180. Tel: 440-888-1522; Fax: 440-888-3477. Office Hours: Mon.-Fri. 10-12 & 2-4

Secretary—Sr. JUDITH PISZYK, O.S.B.M.

Diocesan Consultors—Rev. Msgrs. LEO ADAMIAK; MICHAEL POLOWAY; MICHAEL REWTIUK; GEORGE APPLEYARD; THOMAS A. SAYUK; Very Rev. Canon JAROSLAW MYCHAJLENKO; ROBERT HNATYSHYN; Rev. Msgr. PETER WASLO.

Diocesan Corporation—Most Rev. ROBERT M. MOSKAL, D.D., Pres.; Rev. Msgrs. PETER WASLO, Vice Pres.; THOMAS A. SAYUK, Sec. & Treas.

Diocesan Administrative Council—Most Rev. ROBERT M. MOSKAL, D.D.; Rev. Msgrs. LEO ADAMIAK; PETER WASLO; THOMAS SAYUK; Rev. MARK MOROZOWICH, S.E.O.D.

Protopresbyters-Deans—

Western Deanery—Very Rev. Canon JAROSLAW MYCHAJLENKO, Dean.

Central Deanery—Rev. Msgr. MICHAEL POLOWAY, Dean.

Eastern Deanery—Very Rev. JAMES POORMAN, Dean.

Southern Deanery—Rev. Msgr. JOHN STEVENSKY, Dean.

Vicar for Clergy—Rev. Msgr. PETER WASLO.

Vicar for Religious—Rev. Msgr. GEORGE APPLEYARD.

Liturgical Commission—Most Rev. ROBERT MOSKAL; Rev. Msgrs. THOMAS SAYUK; GEORGE APPLEYARD; Rev. MARK MOROZOWICH, S.E.O.D.

Diocesan Offices and Directors

Acolyte Confraternity—Deacon MICHAEL LEVY.

Catechetical Planning Committee—Sr. ANN LASZOK, O.S.B.M., Chm.; Rev. Msgr. GEORGE APPLEYARD; Sr. OLGA MARIE FARYNA, O.S.B.M.; Very Rev. Canon JAROSLAW MYCHAJLENKO; Revs. XAVIER ELAMBASSERY; ANTHONY BALISTRERI; Rev. Msgr. PETER WASLO; Sr. LUBA BELEY, O.S.B.M.

Clergy Examiners—Rev. Msgr. LEO ADAMIAK; Rev. MARK MOROZOWICH, S.E.O.D.; Rev. Msgrs. PETER WASLO; THOMAS A. SAYUK.

Department of Religious Education—Sr. ANN LASZOK, O.S.B.M., Dir., 726 Washington Ave., Carnegie, PA 15106. Tel: 412-279-4652.

Diocesan Ecumenical Office—Rev. Msgr. GEORGE APPLEYARD, Dir.

Diocesan Promoter for the Cause of Metropolitan Andrew Sheptytsky—Rev. Msgr. THOMAS A. SAYUK.

Diocesan Resource Committee—Rev. Msgr. GEORGE APPLEYARD, Spiritual Dir.; NICKOLAUS KOTOW, Chm.; DAVID HODOWANEC, Vice Chm.; LILLIAN MISKO COURY, Sec.; PETER HLUTKOWSKY, Treas.

Director of Liturgical Chant—STEPHEN ZINSKI; LILLIAN MISKO COURY; BRUCE SCILENY.

Director of Youth Ministries—Rev. ANTHONY BALISTRERI.

Lay Ministries—Sisters ANN LASZOK, O.S.B.M.; OLGA MARIE FARYNA, O.S.B.M.; LUBA BELEY, O.S.B.M.

League of Ukrainian Catholics (LUC)—Rev. MICHAEL POLOSKY, Spiritual Dir. of Western PA Council; Rev. Msgr. JOHN STEVENSKY, Organizer of Southern Deanery LUC.

League of Ukrainian Catholic Youth (LUCY)—Rev. ANTHONY BALISTRERI, Spiritual Dir.

Lector Training Team—Sr. ANN LASZOK, O.S.B.M., Dir.

Marian Sodalities—Sr. OLGA MARIA FARYNA, O.S.B.M.

Obnova—Rev. WOLODYMYR WOLOSZCZUK, Dir. (Retired).

Office for Evangelization—Rev. MICHAEL POLOSKY, Liaison.

Pastoral Ministry Office—Sr. ANN LASZOK, O.S.B.M., Coord. Adult Religious Education: Dr. VERA KROKONKO; Deacon JEFFREY SMOLILO, 727 E. Carson St., Pittsburgh, PA 15203. Tel: 412-481-9778.

Permanent Diaconate Program—Rev. Msgrs. GEORGE APPLEYARD, Dir.; MICHAEL POLOWAY; PETER WASLO; Rev. JOHN ROPKE.

Prayer League for Canonization of Metropolitan Andrew Sheptytsky—Rev. Msgr. THOMAS SAYUK.

Presbyteral Council—Rev. Msgrs. LEO ADAMIAK; THOMAS A. SAYUK; MICHAEL POLOWAY; MICHAEL REWTIUK; Very Rev. Canons JAMES POORMAN; WALTER WYSOCHANSKY; Rev. XAVIER ELAMBASSERY; Rev. Msgr. PETER WASLO; Revs. STEVEN PALIWODA; ANTHONY BALISTRERI; MICHAEL POLOSKY; MICHAEL KRUPKA; JOHN ROPKE; Rev. Msgrs. JOHN STEVENSKY; GEORGE APPLEYARD.

Priests' Continuing Education—Rev. CanonJOHN A. ROPKE.

Vocation Director—Rev. STEVEN PALIWODA.

Diocesan Personnel Board—Revs. ANTHONY BALISTRERI, Chm.; JOHN ROPKE, Sec.; Very Rev. Canon WALTER WYSOCHANSKY; Revs. MICHAEL POLOSKY; VALERIAN MICHLIK.

Tribunal—

Judicial Vicar—Rev. Msgr. PETER WASLO.

Judge—Rev. W. BECKETT SOULE, O.P.

Defender of the Bond—Rev. MARK Q. FEDOR, J.C.D.

Notary—Very Rev. Canon JAROSLAW MYCHAJLENKO.

Victim Assistance Coordinator—KRISTIN LIGUS. Tel: 330-273-8244. Email: liguskrm@ notes.udayton.edu.

CLERGY, PARISHES, MISSIONS AND PAROCHIAL SCHOOLS

STATE OF OHIO

AKRON, SUMMIT CO., HOLY GHOST, Rev. Peter Tomas. Res.: 1859 Carter Ave., 44301. Tel: 330-724-8277.

AUSTINTOWN, MAHONING CO., ST. ANNE, Rev. Msgr. George Appleyard; Rev. Andrew Marko; Deacon Donald Billy.
Res.: 3055 S. Raccoon Rd., 44515-5351. Tel: 330-792-8555; Fax: 330-793-5436.
Church: 4310 Kirk Rd., 44511-1899.
School—Tel: 330-792-9806; Fax: 330-792-3995. Lay Teachers 10; Students 106.

CANTON, STARK CO., ST. NICHOLAS, Attended by,

Akron. Rev. Steven Paliwoda.
Res.: 1859 Carter Ave., Akron, 44301. Tel: 330-724-8277.
Church: 1020 Lippert Rd., 44704.

CLEVELAND, CUYAHOGA CO., SS. PETER AND PAUL, [CEM] Rev. Steven Zarichny.
Res.: 2280 W. 7th St., 44113. Tel: 216-861-2176.

LORAIN, LORAIN CO., ST. JOHN THE BAPTIST, Rev. Peter Tomas.
Res.: 3038 Charleston Ave., 44055-2164. Tel: 440-277-7114.
Church: 2445 E. 31st St., 44055.

PARMA

1—ST. JOSAPHAT CATHEDRAL, Rev. Msgr. Michael Rewtiuk, Archpriest; Rev. Canon Andrew Hanowsky; Rev. Matthew Schroeder; Deacon Jefrey Smolilo.
Res.: 5720 State Rd., 44134-2536. Tel: 440-886-2108.
School—Tel: 440-884-1812; Fax: 440-884-3435.
Sisters of St. Basil the Great 1; Lay Teachers 17; Students 135.

2—ST. ANDREW, Rev. Canon John A. Ropke; Rev. Ihor Kasayan; Deacon Michael Kulick.
Res.: 7700 Hoertz Rd., 44134-6404. Tel: 440-843-9149; Fax: 440-845-2986.

3—POKROVA UKRAINIAN CATHOLIC PARISH, [CEM] Rev. Vasil Petriv.
Office—6812 Broadview Rd., 44134. Tel: 216-524-0918; Fax: 216-524-0919.
Res.: 6810 Broadview Rd., 44134-4804. Tel: 440-524-0918.

ROSSFORD, WOOD CO., ST. MICHAEL, Rev. George Mullonkal.
Res.: 133 Walnut St., 43460-1248. Tel: 419-666-5627.

SOLON, CUYAHOGA CO., PROTECTION B.V.M., Very Rev. Canon Jaroslaw Mychajlenko.
Res.: 27275 Aurora Rd., 44139-1804. Tel: 440-248-4549.

YOUNGSTOWN, MAHONING CO., HOLY TRINITY, Rev. Msgr. Leo Adamiak, V.G.; Rev. Joseph Tamburro.
Res.: 526 W. Rayen Ave., 44502-1124. Tel: 330-744-5820.

STATE OF FLORIDA

APOPKA, ORANGE CO., ST. MARY'S, Rev. Ivan Kubishyn.
Res.: 20 E. Nightingale St., FL 32712-2710. Tel: 407-880-1640.
Mission— Daytona Beach, Volusia Co., FL.

MIAMI, DADE CO., ASSUMPTION OF B.V.M., Rev. John Chirovsky.
Res.: 11000 S.W. 128th St., FL 33126. Tel: 305-262-4192; Fax: 305-261-9759.
Mission— Lantana, Palm Beach Co., FL.

NORTH PORT, SARASOTA CO., ENTRANCE OF B.V.M. INTO THE TEMPLE, Revs. Wolodymyr Woloszczuk; Severyn Kovalyshin, Pastor Emeritus.
Res.: 1078 N. Biscayne Dr., FL 34286. Tel: 941-426-7931.

ST. PETERSBURG, PINELLAS CO., EPIPHANY OF OUR LORD, Rev. Msgr. John Stevensky; Rev. Andrew Krasulski.
Res.: 434 90th Ave. N., FL 33702. Tel: 727-576-1001 (Res.); Fax: 727-576-6821.

SPRING HILL, HERNANDO CO., ST. ANDREW, Rev. Boris Dukeley.
Mailing Address: 8064 Weeping Willow St., Brooksville, FL 34613. Tel: 352-597-4366.
Res.: 415 Montpellier Ct., FL 34608. Tel: 352-684-4876.

STATE OF GEORGIA

CONYERS, ROCKDALE CO., MOTHER OF GOD, Rev. Michael Eliszcz.
Res.: 2880 Hwy. 138, N.E., GA 30013. Tel: 770-760-1111.

STATE OF PENNSYLVANIA

ALIQUIPPA, BEAVER CO., SS. PETER AND PAUL, Rev. Michael Derbish, O.F.M.
Res.: 2001 Main St., PA 15001. Tel: 412-375-7016.

ALTOONA, BLAIR CO., IMMACULATE CONCEPTION, [CEM], Served by Northern Cambria
Res.: 2020 20th St., PA 16601.

AMBRIDGE, BEAVER CO., SS. PETER AND PAUL, Rev. Michael Polosky; Rev. Canon Walter Wysochansky.
Res.: 404 6th St., PA 15003. Tel: 412-266-2262; Fax: 412-266-2262.

CARNEGIE, ALLEGHENY CO., HOLY TRINITY, [CEM] Rev. Msgr. Peter Waslo; Rev. John Smereka.
Res.: 730 Washington Ave., PA 15106. Tel: 412-279-4652.
Res.: 407 W. Main St., PA 15106. Tel: 412-279-5973.

FORD CITY, ARMSTRONG CO., ST. MARY, [CEM] Rev. Michael Sopp, Admin.
Res.: 514 Ninth St., PA 16226. Tel: 724-763-1203.

JEANNETTE, WESTMORELAND CO., ST. DEMETRIUS, Rev. John Gribik.
Res.: 1013 Gaskill Ave., PA 15644-3307. Tel: 724-523-9389.

JOHNSTOWN, CAMBRIA CO., ST. JOHN THE BAPTIST, [CEM] Rev. Michael Krupka.
Res.: 606 Maple Ave., PA 15901. Tel: 814-535-2634.

LATROBE, WESTMORELAND CO., ASSUMPTION OF B.V.M., Rev. Xavier Elambassery.
Res.: 526 Hillview Ave., PA 15650. Tel: 412-537-6450.

LYNDORA, BUTLER CO., ST. MICHAEL, Rev. Douglas Lorance.
Res.: 610 Hansen Ave., PA 16045-1325. Tel: 724-283-6230; Fax: 724-283-0363.

MCKEES ROCKS, ALLEGHENY CO., ST. JOHN THE BAPTIST, Rev. Roman Harwas.
Res.: 204 Olivia St., PA 15136. Tel: 412-331-5605.

MCKEESPORT, ALLEGHENY CO., ST. JOHN THE BAPTIST, Very Rev. Robert Hnatyshyn.
Res.: 1907 Eden Park Blvd., PA 15132. Tel: 412-672-0923.

NEW ALEXANDRIA, WESTMORELAND CO., NATIVITY B.V.M., [CEM] Attended by, Latrobe , 526 Hillview Ave., Latrobe, PA 15650. Tel: 412-537-6450.
Church: Shersburg Rd., PA 15670.

NEW KENSINGTON, WESTMORELAND CO., ST. VLADIMIR, Rev. Anthony Balistreri.
Res.: 1601 Kenneth Ave., Arnold, PA 15068. Tel: 724-339-9622; Fax: 724-339-9622.

NORTHERN CAMBRIA, CAMBRIA CO., IMMACULATE CONCEPTION, Rev. Emanuel Rathapilly.
Res.: 300 Campbell Ave., P.O. Box 1066, PA 15714. Tel: 814-948-9193.

PITTSBURGH, ALLEGHENY CO.

1—ST. GEORGE, Rev. Valerian Michlik.
Res.: 3455 California Ave., PA 15212. Tel: 412-766-8801; Fax: 412-766-3379.

2—ST. JOHN THE BAPTIST, [CEM] Rev. Msgr. Michael Poloway; Deacon Joseph M. Levy.
Res.: 109 S. Seventh St., PA 15203. Tel: 412-431-2531; Fax: 412-431-6404.

RAMEY, CLEARFIELD CO., ANNUNCIATION B.V.M., [CEM] Very Rev. Canon James E. Poorman.
Res.: P.O. Box 205, PA 16671. Tel: 814-378-7688.

REVLOC, CAMBRIA CO., PROTECTION BLESSED VIRGIN MARY, Attended by, Johnstown. , 606 Maple Ave., Johnstown, PA 15901. Tel: 814-535-2634.
Church: 560 Cambria Ave., P.O. Box 194, PA 15948-0914.

WEST LEECHBURG, ARMSTRONG CO., ST. MICHAEL, Attended by, Ford City, PA. , Mailing Address: 514 Ninth St., Ford City, PA 16226. Tel: 724-763-1203.
Church: Main St., PA 15656.

WILMERDING, ALLEGHENY CO., SS. PETER AND PAUL, Attended by, Jeannette, PA. , Mailing Address: 1013 Gaskill Ave., Jeannette, PA 15644-3307. Tel: 724-523-9389.
Church: 163 State St., PA 15148-1323. Tel: 724-829-1833.

STATE OF WEST VIRGINIA

WHEELING, OHIO CO., OUR LADY OF PERPETUAL HELP, Rev. Canon Philip Bumbar.
Res.: 4136 Jacob St., WV 26003. Tel: 304-232-2168; Fax: 304-232-8719.

On Assignment Outside the Diocese:
Revs.—
Kachur, Oleh, 251 Bolton St., Apt. 20, Ottawa ON K1N5B5 Canada.
Morozowich, Mark, S.E.O.D., St. Paul College, 3015 Fourth St., NE, Washington, DC 20017.

Retired:
Rev. Msgrs.—
Kachmar, Walter, Green Meadows, 500 Brouwers Dr., #70, Latrobe, PA 15650. Tel: 724-459-8614
Nestor, Michael, 867 N. Concord St., Gilbert, AZ 85234. Tel: 602-507-5015
Revs.—
Adamiak, Stephen, 6000 21st St. N., St. Petersburg, FL 33714.
Balaban, Oryst, 1532 Fourth Ave., Arnold, PA 15068-4402.
Griffiths, James, 111 S. Cliff St., Apt. 6B6, Butler, PA 16001-6045.
Woloszczuk, Wolodymyr, 4240 Timberline Blvd., Venice, FL 34293.

Permanent Deacons:
Billy, Donald, 2515 McCollum Rd., Youngstown, 44509. Tel: 330-792-3166
Boyce, Gary, 6976 S. Evening Glow Pl., Gold Canyon, AZ 85219-2946. Tel: 480-288-6854
Kulick, Michael, 8455 Sunnydale Dr., Brecksville, 44141. Tel: 440-526-4517
Levy, Joseph M., 5216 Kerrington Dr., Gibsonia, PA 15044. Tel: 724-443-8764
Smolilo, Jeffery, 4546 Shelly Dr., Seven Hills, 44131. Tel: 216-328-0743

INSTITUTIONS LOCATED IN THE DIOCESE

[A] CONVENTS

PARMA. *St. Josaphat Convent*, 5720 State Rd., 44134-2536. Tel: 440-885-1245. Sisters of St. Basil the Great

[B] HOMES FOR THE AGED

PARMA. *Shevchenko Manor*, 5620 W. 24th St., 44134-2751. Tel: 216-459-1440; Fax: 216-459-1442. Jennie Bochar, Mgr.

PITTSBURGH. *Sheptytsky Arms*, 3505 Mexico St., PA 15212. Tel: 412-766-8802; Fax: 412-766-0938.

NECROLOGY

† Tylawskyj, Mitrat Iwan, (Retired)—Died Oct. 18, 2003

Eparchy of St. Maron of Brooklyn

Most Reverend

GREGORY J. MANSOUR

Bishop of Saint Maron of Brooklyn; ordained September 18, 1982; appointed Bishop of Saint Maron of Brooklyn January 10, 2004; consecrated March 2, 2004; installed April 27, 2004 *109 Ramsen St., Brooklyn, NY 11201.*

Most Reverend

STEPHEN HECTOR DOUEIHI, S.T.D.

Retired Bishop of Saint Maron of Brooklyn; born June 25, 1927; ordained August 14, 1955; appointed Second Eparchial Bishop of the Eparchy of Saint Maron of Brooklyn November 23, 1996; consecrated January 11, 1997; enthroned February 5, 1997; retired January 10, 2004 *Res.: 8070 Harbor View Ter., Brooklyn, NY 11209.*

Most Reverend

FRANCIS M. ZAYEK, D.D., S.T.D., J.C.D.

Retired Archbishop and Former Eparch of St. Maron of Brooklyn; born October 18, 1920; ordained March 17, 1946; appointed Titular Bishop of Callinicum May 30, 1962; consecrated August 5, 1962; appointed Eparch of the Diocese of Saint Maron November 11, 1971; installed June 4, 1972; elevated to Archbishop December 22, 1982; retired November 11, 1996 *Res.: 4010 Galt Ocean Dr., Apt. 1203, Fort Lauderdale, FL 33308.*

Established as an Apostolic Exarchate January 10, 1966; Elevated to a Diocese November 11, 1971.

The jurisdiction of the Diocese extends to all the Maronite Catholics in New York, New Jersey, Pennsylvania, Florida, Georgia, North Carolina, South Carolina, Delaware, Virginia, District of Columbia, Maine, New Hampshire, Vermont, Massachusetts, Rhode Island, Connecticut and Maryland.

For legal titles of parishes and diocesan institutions, consult the Chancery Office.

Chancery Office: 109 Remsen St., Brooklyn, NY 11201. Tel: 718-237-9913; Fax: 718-243-0444.

STATISTICAL OVERVIEW

Personnel	
Retired Archbishops	1
Bishop	1
Priests: Diocesan Active in Diocese	36
Priests: Diocesan Active Outside Diocese	7
Priests: Retired, Sick or Absent	14
Number of Diocesan Priests	57
Religious Priests in Diocese	12
Total Priests in Diocese	69
Extern Priests in Diocese	6
Permanent Deacons in Diocese	13
Total Brothers	7
Total Sisters	2
Parishes	
Parishes	34
With Resident Pastor:	
Resident Diocesan Priests	34
Missions	5
Educational	
Seminaries, Diocesan	1
Students from This Diocese	1
Students from Other Diocese	2
Diocesan Students in Other Seminaries	1
Total Seminarians	2
Catechesis/Religious Education:	
High School Students	338
Elementary Students	1,554
Total Students under Catholic Instruction	1,894
Vital Statistics	
Receptions into the Church:	
Infant Baptism Totals	453
Adult Baptism Totals	17
Received into Full Communion	57
First Communions	321
Confirmations	320
Marriages:	
Catholic	101
Interfaith	23
Total Marriages	124
Deaths	248
Total Catholic Population	30,000

Protosyncellus (Vicar General)—Chorbishop JOSEPH F. KADDO.

Chancellor—Chorbishop JOSEPH F. KADDO.

Vicar for Canonical Services/Administration—Very Rev. FRANCIS J. MARINI, J.D., J.C.O.D.

The Chancery—109 Remsen St., Brooklyn, 11201. Tel: 718-237-9913; Fax: 718-243-0444. Office Hours: Mon.-Fri. 9-12 & 1-4. Closed on Maronite holy days and national holidays

Tribunal of the Eparchy of Saint Maron of Brooklyn—

Tribunal—2055 Coral Way, Miami, FL 33145. Tel: 305-762-1269; Fax: 305-856-5740.

Judicial Vicar—Rev. Msgr. MICHAEL G. THOMAS, J.C.D.

Adjutant Judicial Vicar—Very Rev. FRANCIS J. MARINI, J.D., J.C.O.D.

Judges—Rev. Msgrs. ANDREW L. ANDERSON, J.C.D.; MICHAEL SOUCKAR, J.C.D.; Rev. KENNETH SCHWANGER, J.C.D.

Promoter of Justice—Rev. Msgr. TOMAS MARIN, J.C.L.

Defender of the Bond—Rev. CARL MORRISON, J.C.L.

Approved Advocates—Rev. Msgr. NEVIN KLINGER, J.C.L.; Rev. TANIOS AKOURY, J.C.L.

Notaries—Mrs. JOAN MATELIS; Mrs. VICTORIA LOPEZ.

Presbyteral Council-Ex Officio Members—Most Rev. STEPHEN HECTOR DOUEIHI, S.T.D. (Retired); Chorbishop JOSEPH F. KADDO; Very Rev. FRANCIS J. MARINI, J.D., J.C.O.D.; Chorbishop SEELY BEGGIANI; Rev. Msgr. IGNACE SADEK; Chorbishop JOSEPH LAHOUD; Rev. Msgrs. PETER FAHED AZAR; GEORGE SEBAALI.

Elected Members—Chorbishop JOSEPH LAHOUD; Very Rev. FRANCIS J. MARINI, J.D., J.C.O.D.; Rev. Msgr. DAVID M. GEORGE.

Appointed Members—Chorbishop NORMAN J. FERRIS (Retired); Rev. EDWARD T. NEDDER.

Protopresbyters— Chorbishop JOSEPH LAHOUD, (Northern); Rev. Msgrs. PETER FAHED AZAR, (Central); GEORGE SEBAALI, (Southern).

Lebanon Commission—Chorbishop SEELY BEGGIANI, Chm., 7164 Alaska Ave., N.W., Washington, DC 20012. Tel: 202-723-8831.

National Apostolate of Maronites National Office—BEVERLY MIKE-NARD, Pres.; ED SHINER, Exec. Dir., P.O. Box 280126, Brooklyn, 11228-0126. Tel: 718-630-5868; Fax: 718-630-5191.

Diocesan Offices and Directors

Communications—Rev. Msgr. GEORGE SEBAALI, 4611 Sadler Rd., Glen Allen, VA 23060. Tel: 804-270-7234; Fax: 804-273-9914.

(Diocesan Newspaper) "The Maronite Voice"—Rev. Msgr. GEORGE SEBAALI, Editor, 4611 Sadler Rd., Glen Allen, VA 23060. Tel: 804-762-4301; Fax: 804-273-9914.

Finance Council—Most Rev. STEPHEN HECTOR DOUEIHI, S.T.D., Chm. (Retired).

Liturgy—Most Rev. STEPHEN HECTOR DOUEIHI, S.T.D., Chm. (Retired); Rev. CLAUDE W. FRANKLIN JR., Asst., 109 Remsen St., Brooklyn, 11201. Tel: 718-237-9913; Fax: 718-243-0444.

Ministries (Permanent Deacons and Subdeacons)—Rev. EDWARD T. NEDDER, 375 Island Pond Rd., Springfield, MA 01118. Tel: 413-732-0589.

Order of Saint Sharbel—Mr. ALBERT ALBERT, National Office, 109 Remsen St., Brooklyn, 11201.

Office of Outreach—Rev. Msgr. RONALD BESHARA, Dir., 55 N. Lakeshore Dr., Hypoluxo, FL 33462-6077. Tel: 561-840-6196; Fax: 561-882-1025.

Pro-Life Director—Rev. KEVIN BEATON, 2 W. Reynolds St., New Castle, PA 16101. Tel: 724-658-0787.

Religious Education—Rev. GEORGES EL-KHALLI, 2040 Wehrle Dr., Williamsville, 14221. Tel: 716-634-0669; Fax: 716-634-0674.

Victim Assistance Coordinator—ROSANNE SOLOMON. Tel: 781-828-5183. Email: rosannesolomon@hotmail.com.

Vocations—Rev. JAMES ROOT, 1000 Lindsay Rd., Carnegie, PA 15106. Tel: 412-278-0841; Fax: 412-278-0846.

Youth Ministry Office—Rev. JOHN MORRISON, 806 Arsenal Ave., Fayetteville, NC 28305. Tel: 910-484-1531; Fax: 910-484-5387.

CLERGY, PARISHES, MISSIONS AND PAROCHIAL SCHOOLS

STATE OF NEW YORK

BROOKLYN, KINGS CO., CATHEDRAL OF OUR LADY OF LEBANON, Rev. Msgr. Ignace Sadek, Rector.
Res.: 113 Remsen St., 11201. Tel: 718-624-7228; Fax: 718-624-8034.

OLEAN, CATTARAUGUS CO., ST. JOSEPH, Rev. Joseph G. Akiki.
Res.: 331 N. Fourth St., 14760. Tel: 716-372-4311.

TROY, RENSSELAER CO., ST. ANN, Rev. Elie G. Kairouz.
Church: 184 Fourth St., 12180. Tel: 518-272-6073.

UTICA, ONEIDA CO., ST. LOUIS GONZAGA, Rev. Bassam Saade.
Res.: 520 Rutger St., 13501. Tel: 315-732-6019; Fax: 315-732-3047.

WILLIAMSVILLE, ERIE CO., ST. JOHN MARON, Rev. Georges El-Khalli, Ph.D.
Res.: 2040 Wehrle Dr., 14221-7041. Tel: 716-634-0669; Fax: 716-634-0674.

STATE OF CONNECTICUT

DANBURY, FAIRFIELD CO., ST. ANTHONY, Rev. Larry Jensen.
Res.: 17 Granville Ave., CT 06810. Tel: 203-744-3372; Fax: 203-794-0949.

TORRINGTON, LITCHFIELD CO., ST. MARON, Rev. Lawrence P. Michael.
Res.: 613 Main St., CT 06790. Tel: 860-489-9015; Fax: 860-482-1614.

WATERBURY, NEW HAVEN CO., OUR LADY OF LEBANON, Rev. Msgr. David M. George.
Res.: 8 E. Mountain Rd., CT 06706. Tel: 203-753-6633; 203-753-9428; Fax: 203-573-8384.

STATE OF FLORIDA

JACKSONVILLE, DUVAL CO., ST. MARON MARONITE,

Rev. Elie Abi-chedid.
Res.: 7032 Bowden Rd., FL 32216. Tel: 904-448-0203; Fax: 904-448-8277.

MIAMI, DADE CO., OUR LADY OF LEBANON (1973), Rev. Msgr. Michael G. Thomas, J.C.D.; Rev. Jorge I. Perales (MIA).
Mailing Address: 2055 Coral Way, FL 33145. Tel: 305-856-7449; Fax: 305-856-7740.
Res.: 420 Como Ave., Coral Gables, FL 33146.

ORLANDO, ORANGE CO., ST. JUDE MISSION, Rev. George Zina.
Res.: 5555 Dr. Phillips Blvd., FL 32819. Tel: 407-363-7405; Fax: 407-363-7793.

TAMPA, HILLSBOROUGH CO.
MISSION—MARONITE MISSION OF TAMPA Maronite Mission of Tampa, c/o St. Mary's R.C. Church, 15520 N. Blvd., Miami, FL 33163. Tel: 813-964-0368. Rev. Paul E. Damien.

WEST PALM BEACH, PALM BEACH CO., MARY MOTHER OF LIGHT MARONITE MISSION, Rev. Msgr. Ronald Beshara.
Mailing Address & Church: 4891 Lake Worth Rd., Greenacres, FL 33467.

STATE OF GEORGIA

ATLANTA, FULTON CO., ST. JOSEPH'S MARONITE CHURCH, Rev. Peter Boulos.
Res.: 502 Seminole Ave., N.E., GA 30307. Tel: 404-525-2504; Fax: 404-589-1744.

STATE OF MAINE

WATERVILLE, KENNEBEC CO., ST. JOSEPH, Rev. Samuel A. Najjar; Deacon Peter P. Joseph.
Res.: 3 Appleton St., ME 04901. Tel: 207-872-8515; Fax: 207-872-8089.

STATE OF MASSACHUSETTS

BROCKTON, PLYMOUTH CO., ST. THERESA, Rev. Tanios K. Akoury.
Mailing Address: P.O. Box 2567, MA 02305-2567. Fax: 508-587-8139.
Res.: 343 N. Main St., MA 02301. Tel: 508-586-1428.

FALL RIVER, BRISTOL CO., ST. ANTHONY OF THE DESERT, Chorbishop Joseph F. Kaddo; Deacons Donald P. Massoud; Andre Nasser.
Res.: 300 N. Eastern Ave., MA 02723. Tel: 508-672-7653; Fax: 508-678-1474.

JAMAICA PLAIN, SUFFOLK CO., OUR LADY OF THE CEDARS OF LEBANON, Chorbishop Joseph F. Lahoud.
Res.: 61 Rockwood St., MA 02130. Tel: 617-522-0225; Fax: 617-522-0194.

LAWRENCE, ESSEX CO., ST. ANTHONY, [CEM] Rev. Msgr. James T. Khoury; Rev. Elie Hares Mikhael.
Res.: 145 Amesbury St., MA 01841. Tel: 617-685-7233; Fax: 978-688-4475.

NEW BEDFORD, BRISTOL CO., OUR LADY OF PURGATORY, Rev. Charbel T. Semaan.
Res.: 11 Franklin St., MA 02740. Tel: 508-996-8934; Fax: 508-996-2744.

SPRINGFIELD, HAMPDEN CO., ST. ANTHONY, Rev. Edward T. Nedder; Deacons Terrence O'Connell; Charles Gebron.
Mailing Address: 375 Island Pond Rd., MA 01118-1002.
Res.: 419 Island Pond Rd., MA 01118-1002. Tel: 413-732-0589.

WORCESTER, WORCESTER CO., OUR LADY OF MERCY, Rev. Msgr. Assad Awad.
Res.: 74 Mulberry St., MA 01605. Tel: 508-752-4287.

STATE OF NEW HAMPSHIRE

DOVER, STRAFFORD CO., ST. GEORGE, Rev. Joseph Khoueiry.
Mailing Address: P.O. Box 2210, NH 03821-2210.
Res.: 46 Hough St., NH 03820.
Church: 15 Chapel St., NH 03821. Tel: 603-742-1149 (Rectory); 603-740-4287 (Church); Fax: 603-740-9624.

STATE OF NEW JERSEY

SOMERSET, SOMERSET CO., ST. SHARBEL, Rev. Maroun Asmar.
Res.: 7 Reeve St., NJ 08873. Tel: 732-828-2055; Fax: 732-328-5488.

STATE OF NORTH CAROLINA

FAYETTEVILLE, CUMBERLAND CO., ST. MICHAEL THE ARCHANGEL, Rev. John Morrison.
Res.: 806 Arsenal Ave., NC 28305. Tel: 910-484-1531; Fax: 910-484-5387.

FUQUAY-VARINA, WAKE CO., SAINT SHARBEL MISSION, Rev. Joseph Thomas, B.S.O., Admin.
2104 Piney Plains Rd., Cary, NC 27511. Tel: 919-852-0800.

STATE OF PENNSYLVANIA

CARNEGIE, ALLEGHENY CO., OUR LADY OF VICTORY, Rev. James A. Root.
Res.: 1000 Lindsay Rd., PA 15106. Tel: 412-278-0841; Fax: 412-278-0846.

EASTON, NORTHAMPTON CO., OUR LADY OF LEBANON, Rev. Msgr. Sami Hayek.
Res.: 54 S. Fourth St., PA 18042. Tel: 610-252-5275; Fax: 610-252-1737.

NEW CASTLE, LAWRENCE CO., ST. JOHN THE BAPTIST, Rev. Kevin J. Beaton; Deacon Richard E. Stone.
Res.: 2 W. Reynolds St., PA 16101. Tel: 724-658-0787.

NEWTOWN SQUARE, DELAWARE CO., ST. SHARBEL, Rev. Paul Mooradd.
Res.: 3679 Providence Rd., Newton Square, PA 19073-3006. Tel: 610-353-5952.

PHILADELPHIA, PHILADELPHIA CO., ST. MARON, Rev. Msgr. Sharbel Lischaa; Deacon Joseph Regan.
Res.: 1010 Ellsworth St., PA 19147. Tel: 215-389-2000.

SCRANTON, LACKAWANNA CO., ST. ANN, Very Rev. Francis J. Marini, J.D., J.C.O.D.
Res.: 1320 Price St., PA 18504-3336. Tel: 570-344-2129; Fax: 570-344-3920.

UNIONTOWN, FAYETTE CO., ST. GEORGE, Rev. Joseph David.
Res.: 5 Lebanon Ter., PA 15401. Tel: 724-437-5589; Fax: 724-437-3819.

WILKES-BARRE, LUZERNE CO.
1—ST. ANTHONY, Merged, with St. George, Wilkes-Barre to form St. Anthony/St. George, Wilkes-Barre
2—ST. ANTHONY/ST. GEORGE, Rev. Msgr. Peter F. Azar.
Res.: 79 Loomis St., PA 18702. Tel: 570-824-3599; Fax: 570-824-1747.
3—ST. GEORGE, Merged, with St. Anthony, Wilkes-Barre to form St. Anthony/St. George, Wilkes-Barre

STATE OF RHODE ISLAND

PAWTUCKET, PROVIDENCE CO., HOLY TRINITY-ST. GEORGE, Rev. Paul Mouawad.
Res.: 50 Summit St., RI 02860. Tel: 401-723-8444.
Church: 50 Main St., RI 02860.

STATE OF SOUTH CAROLINA

SPARTANBURG, SPARTANBURG CO., ST. RAFKA MARONITE, Rev. Bartholomew Leon, O.S.B.
Res.: *St. Mary's Catholic Church*, 111 Hampton Ave., Greenville, SC 29601. Tel: 864-271-8422; Fax: 864-370-9880.

STATE OF VIRGINIA

GLEN ALLEN, HENRICO CO., ST. ANTHONY, Rev. Msgr. George M. Sebaali.
Res.: 4611 Sadler Rd., VA 23060. Tel: 804-270-7234; Fax: 804-273-9914.

ROANOKE, ROANOKE CITY CO., ST. ELIAS, Rev. Rodolph Wakim.
Res.: 4730 Cove Rd., N.W., VA 24017. Tel: 540-562-0012; Fax: 540-562-1300.

DISTRICT OF COLUMBIA

WASHINGTON, DISTRICT OF COLUMBIA, OUR LADY OF LEBANON CHURCH, Chorbishop Dominic F. Ashkar.
Res.: 7164 Alaska Ave., N.W., DC 20012. Tel: 202-829-5554.

On Duty Outside the Diocese:
Chorbishop—
Faris, John D
Rev. Msgr.—
Beshara, Ronald N.
Revs.—
Amar, Joseph P.
Bartoul, William
Coover, Thomas .
Michael, David C. (BO)

Graduate Studies:
Rev.—
Franklin, Claude W., Jr.

Unassigned:
Revs.—
Basinow, Leonard
Henderson, Christopher

Retired:
Most Rev.—
Zayek, Francis M.
Chorbishop—
Abi-Nader, Joseph
Ferris, Norman J.
Rev. Msgrs.—
Antoun, Elie
Bistany, Joseph
Revs.—
Andary, John S.
Boackle, Paul H.
El-Hayek, Nehmatallah
Hitti, Michael
Mahfoud, Peter
Saad, Antoun
Saidi, Joseph
Shaheen, Joseph
Thomas, Donald N.
Zogheib, Hares

Permanent Deacons:
Calabrese, Robert, Danbury, CT
Caporiccio, Richard, Springfield, VA
Gebron, Charles, Springfield, MA
Joseph, Peter P., Waterville, ME
Koury, Anthony, Easton, PA
Massoud, Donald P., Fall River, MA
Mattar, Jean E., New Bedford, MA
Nasser, Andre, Fall River, MA
O'Connell, Terrence J., Springfield, MA
Ramey, Al, Lawrence, MA
Regan, Joseph W., Sewell, NJ
Salamy, Paul A., Utica, NY
Shami, Elias, Jacksonville, FL
Stone, Richard E., New Castle, PA

INSTITUTIONS LOCATED IN THE DIOCESE

[A] SEMINARIES, DIOCESAN

WASHINGTON. *Our Lady of Lebanon Maronite Seminary*, 7164 Alaska Ave., N.W., DC 20012. Tel: 202-723-8831; Fax: 202-829-6053. Email: seebeggiani@comcast.net. Chorbishop Seely Beggiani, S.T.D., Rector.

[B] CONVENTS AND RESIDENCES FOR SISTERS

NORTH BROOKFIELD. *Hermits of Jesus The Eternal Priest*, P.O. Box 216, MA 01535. Tel: 508-867-0134. Email: hjep@juno.com. Sr. Elias, Supr.

[C] RELIGIOUS COMMUNITIES OF MEN

PETERSHAM. *Most Holy Trinity Monastery*, 67 Dugway Rd., MA 01366. Tel: 978-724-3347. Revs. William J. Driscoll, O.Mar., Abbot; Giles R. Goyette, O.Mar., Vicar; Michael Cermak, O.Mar.; John Marie Choiniere, O.Mar.; Louis Marie Dauphinais, O.Mar.; Elias Havel, O.Mar.; Francis DeGuzman, O.Mar.; Maron Morgan, O.Mar. Martin Ferland, O.Mar.; Anthony Kramer, O.Mar. Priests 10; Brothers 7.

[D] RESIDENCES FOR CLERGY

BROOKLYN. *Bishop's Residence*, 8070 Harbor View Ter., 11209. Chorbishop Joseph F. Kaddo.

[E] MISCELLANEOUS

BROOKLYN. *Bishops Retirement Trust Fund*, 109 Remsen St., 11201.
Order of St. Sharbel Trust Fund, 109 Remsen St., 11201.
Priest Retirement Trust Fund, 109 Remsen St., 11201.
Tele Lumiere International, 109 Remsen St., 11201. Tel: 718-237-9913; Fax: 718-243-0444. Email: chancerystmaron@earthlink.net. Most Rev. Stephen Hector Doueihi, S.T.D. (Retired).

NEW BEDFORD. *Cedar Holdings, Inc.*, P.O. Box 51021, MA 02745-0035. Tel: 508-996-8934; Fax: 508-996-2744. Email: ctscedars@aol.com.

SHELBURNE. *Saint Rafka Retreat Center*, 6420 Rte. 116, VT 05482-7191. Tel: 802-660-2528; Fax: 802-660-0868. Rev. Anthony Weiler.

NECROLOGY

(No Deaths)

Diocese of St. Nicholas in Chicago for Ukrainians

Most Reverend

RICHARD S. SEMINACK

Bishop of St. Nicholas in Chicago; ordained May 25, 1967; appointed Bishop of St. Nicholas in Chicago March 25, 2003; ordained June 4, 2003. *Office: 2245 W. Rice St., Chicago, IL 60622.* Tel: 773-276-5080.

Most Rev.

INNOCENT LOTOCKY, O.S.B.M., D.D., PH.D.

Retired Bishop of St. Nicholas in Chicago; ordained November 24, 1940; appointed Second Bishop of Chicago January 29, 1981; consecrated March 1, 1981; installed April 2, 1981; retired September 28, 1993. *2245 W. Rice St., Chicago, IL 60622.* Tel: 773-276-8981.

Comprises all of the United States west of the western borders of Ohio, Kentucky, Tennessee and Mississippi.

For legal titles of parishes and diocesan institutions, consult the Chancery Office.

Chancery Office: 2245 W. Rice St., Chicago, IL 60622. Tel: 773-276-5080; Fax: 773-276-6799.

Email: sneparchy@iols.com

STATISTICAL OVERVIEW

Statistical report was not submitted for 2004.

Personnel	
Bishop	1
Retired Bishops	1
Abbots	1
Priests: Diocesan Active in Diocese	16
Priests: Diocesan Active Outside Diocese	1
Priests: Retired, Sick or Absent	3
Number of Diocesan Priests	20
Religious Priests in Diocese	13
Total Priests in Diocese	33
Extern Priests in Diocese	19
Ordinations:	
Permanent Deacons	2
Permanent Deacons in Diocese	12
Total Sisters	2
Parishes	
Parishes	36
With Resident Pastor:	
Resident Diocesan Priests	23
Resident Religious Priests	3
Without Resident Pastor:	
Administered by Priests	9
Administered by Deacons	2
Missions	7
Educational	
Diocesan Students in Other Seminaries	2
Total Seminarians	2
High Schools, Diocesan and Parish	1
Elementary Schools, Diocesan and Parish	2
Total Students	380
Catechesis/Religious Education:	
High School Students	152
Elementary Students	325
Total Students under Catholic Instruction	935
Teachers in the Diocese:	
Sisters	2
Lay Teachers	52
Vital Statistics	
Receptions into the Church:	
Infant Baptism Totals	255
Adult Baptism Totals	5
Received into Full Communion	7
First Communions	250
Confirmations	260
Marriages:	
Catholic	52
Interfaith	15
Total Marriages	67
Deaths	180
Total Catholic Population	10,000

Former Bishops—Most Revs. JAROSLAV GABRO, D.D., appt. First Bishop of Chicago, July 12, 1961; consecrated Oct. 26, 1961; died March 28, 1980; INNOCENT LOTOCKY, O.S.B.M., D.D., Ph.D. (Retired), ord. Nov. 24, 1940; appt. Second Bishop of Chicago, Jan. 29, 1981; consecrated March 1, 1981; installed April 2, 1981; retired Sept. 28, 1993; MICHAEL WIWCHAR, C.SS.R., D.D., ord. June 28, 1959; appt. Third Bishop of St. Nicholas July 2, 1993; ord. Sept. 28, 1993; appt. Bishop of Saskatoon (Ukrainian), Nov. 29, 2000; secondary appt. Apostolic Administrator of St. Nicholas in Chicago, Dec. 9, 2000.

Protosyncellus—Very Rev. WAYNE RUCHGY.

Chancellor—Rev. MYKHAILO KUZMA.

Chief Financial Officer—Rev. WILLIAM H. MACKINNON III, S.O.L.T.

Chancery Office—2245 W. Rice St., Chicago, 60622. Tel: 773-276-5080; Fax: 773-276-6799. Email: sneparchy@iols.com. Office Hours: Mon.-Fri. 9-4

Diocesan Consultors—Very Rev. WAYNE RUCHGY; Revs. BASIL SALKOVSKI, O.S.B.M.; MYRON PANCHUK; RICHARD JANOWICZ; Very Rev. Canon MICHAEL STELMACH; Rev. MYKHAILO KUZMA.

Presbyteral Council—Most Rev. RICHARD S. SEMINACK, D.D., Ex Officio; Very Rev. WAYNE RUCHGY, Chm.; Revs. ABRAHAM MILLER; MYRON PANCHUK; MYKHAILO KUZMA; PAVLO HAYDA, Vice Chm.; RICHARD JANOWICZ, Sec. & Treas.; BASIL SALKOVSKI, O.S.B.M.; Very Rev. Canon MICHAEL STELMACH; Revs. WALTER RYBICKY, O.S.B.M.; BOHDAN NALYSNYK.

Personnel Board—Most Rev. MICHAEL WIWCHAR, C.SS.R.; Very Rev. WAYNE RUCHGY, Chm.; Revs. MYKHAILO KUZMA; ABRAHAM MILLER; RICHARD JANOWICZ; MYRON PANCHUK.

Tribunal— Through Special Permission of the Holy See, Local Latin Rite Tribunals Handle the Cases Within the Diocese

Protopresbyteries (Deans)—Detroit: Very Rev. BASIL SALKOVSKY, O.S.B.M., Protopresbyter; Rev. ROBERTO LUCAVEI, O.S.B.M., Vice Protopresbyter. Chicago: Rt. Rev. Mitred Archpriest IVAN KROTEC, Protopresbyter; Revs. MYKHAILO KUZMA, Vice Protopresbyter. Minneapolis: Very Rev. Canon MICHAEL STELMACH, Protopresbyter; Rev. PETER LEIGH, Vice Protopresbyter. South-West: Rev. RICHARD JANOWICZ, Protopresbyter; Very Rev. Canon THOMAS GLYNN, Vice Protopresbyter.

Eparchial Censor—Rev. DEMETRIUS WYSOCHANSKY, O.S.B.M.

Eparchial Office of Religious Education & Catechesis—Rev. OLEH KRYVOKULSKY, Dir.; JAROSLAVA VATASHCHUK, Asst., 2208 W. Chicago Ave., Chicago, 60622. Tel: 773-227-3970; Fax: 773-227-3971.

Stewardship and Development Office—Rev. THEODORE WROBLICKY, Dir. Devel.. Email: twroblicky@aol.com; BARBARA WROBLICKY, Dir., Stewardship. Email: bwroblicky@aol.com; 2245 W. Rice St., Chicago, 60622. Tel: 773-276-9500; Fax: 773-276-9502.

CLERGY, PARISHES, MISSIONS AND PAROCHIAL SCHOOLS

STATE OF ILLINOIS

CHICAGO, COOK CO.

1—ST. NICHOLAS UKRAINIAN CATHOLIC CATHEDRAL (1906), (Ukranian), [CEM] Revs. Bogdan Nalysnyk, Rector; Volodymyr Hudzan; Deacon Mychajlo Horodysky.
Res.: 2238 W. Rice St., 60622. Tel: 773-276-4537; Fax: 773-276-5558.
School—2200 W. Rice St., 60622. Tel: 773-384-7243; Fax: 773-384-7283. Sr. Irenea Hankewych, O.S.B.M., Supr. & Prin. Sisters 4; Lay Teachers 15; Students 186.
Convent—Sisters of St. Basil the Great, 2230 W. Rice St., 60622. Tel: 773-486-6820.

2—ST. JOSEPH (N.W. Chicago) (1956), (Ukranian), Rev. Pavlo Hayda; Very Rev. Canon Thomas Glynn.
Res.: 5000 N. Cumberland Ave., 60656. Tel: 773-625-4833; 773-625-4805 (Office); Fax: 773-625-4148.
Catechesis/Religious Program—Students 36.

3—ST. MICHAEL'S (1917), (Ukranian), [JC] Rev. Abraham Miller, Admin.
Mailing Address: 12211 S. Parnell, 60628. Tel: 773-334-4512.
Church: 2238 W. Rice St., 60622. Tel: 773-276-4537; Fax: 773-276-5558.

4—SS. VOLODYMYR AND OLHA (1968), (Ukranian), [JC] Rt. Rev. Mitred Archpriest Ivan Krotec. Tel: 312-455-0178; Revs. Myron Panchuk. Tel: 312-666-6051; Yaroslav Mendyuk. Tel: 773-384-0247; Mykola Buryadnyk. Tel: 312-421-5230; Deacon Michael Szyjan. Tel: 773-252-1711.
Parish Office—2245 W. Superior St., 60612. Tel: 312-829-5209; Fax: 312-829-4113.

MADISON, MADISON CO., ST. MARY'S, [JC]
Res.: 1312 Iowa St., 62060. Tel: 616-452-9118.

PALATINE, COOK CO., IMMACULATE CONCEPTION (1963), (Ukranian), Very Rev. Mykhailo Kuzma; Deacon Andrew Plishka.
Res.: 745 S. Benton, 60067. Tel: 847-991-0820; Fax: 847-991-7873.
Catechesis/Religious Program—Tel: 847-639-9188. Students 71.

PALOS PARK, COOK CO., NATIVITY OF B.V.M. (1911), (Ukranian), Revs. Walter Rybicky, O.S.B.M.; Demetrius Wysochansky, O.S.B.M.
Res.: 8530 W. 131 St., 60464. Tel: 708-361-8876; 708-361-8820; Fax: 708-361-8820.

STATE OF ARIZONA

PHOENIX, MARICOPA CO., ASSUMPTION OF B.V.M. (1959), Rev. Hugo Soutus.
Res.: 3730 W. Maryland Ave., AZ 85019. Tel: 602-973-3667; Fax: 602-973-3667.
Church: 3720 W. Maryland Ave., AZ 85019.

TUCSON, PIMA CO., ST. MICHAEL (1978), (Ukranian), [JC] Rev. Basil Buchek.
Res.: 1557 N. Brown Way, AZ 85715-5578. Tel: 520-298-4967.

STATE OF CALIFORNIA

LOS ANGELES, LOS ANGELES CO., NATIVITY OF B.V.M. (1947), (Ukranian), Rev. Oleh Romanenko.
Res.: 5154 De Longpre Ave., Hollywood, CA 90027. Tel: 323-663-6307; Fax: 323-663-0369.

SACRAMENTO, SACRAMENTO CO., ST. ANDREW THE APOSTLE, Rev. Valeriy Kandyuk, Admin.
Res.: 7001 Florin Rd., CA 95828. Tel: 415-468-2601; 415-486-0632; Fax: 415-715-0291.
Catechesis/Religious Program—Tel: 916-381-2529; Fax: 916-381-2529.

SAN DIEGO, SAN DIEGO CO., OUR LADY OF PERPETUAL HELP (1960), (Ukranian), Rev. John Hritzko.
Church: 4400 Palm Ave., La Mesa, CA 92041. Tel: 619-697-5085; Fax: 619-269-2303.
Res.: 4061 Winona Ave., CA 92105.

SAN FRANCISCO, SAN FRANCISCO CO., IMMACULATE CONCEPTION (1957), (Ukranian), Rev. Alexander Avramenko, Admin.
Res.: 215 Silliman, CA 94134. Tel: 415-468-2601; Fax: 415-715-0291.
Catechesis/Religious Program—Tel: 415-468-2601; Fax: 415-468-0291.

SANTA CLARA, SANTA CLARA CO., ST. VLADIMIR, Attended by, San Francisco. Rev. Alexander Avramenko.

UKIAH, UKIAH CO., UKRAINIAN CATHOLIC MISSION (1999), (Ukranian), Rev. David Anderson.
Res.: 2975 Mill Creek Rd., CA 95482. Tel: 707-468-4348; Fax: 707-467-0505.

STATE OF COLORADO

DENVER, DENVER CO., TRANSFIGURATION OF OUR LORD (1954), (Ukranian), [JC] Rev. Peter A. Bohdanowycz (DEN); Deacon Michael Bozio, Admin.
Res.: 4118 Shoshone St., CO 80211. Tel: 303-433-2347.

STATE OF HAWAII

HONOLULU, BYZANTINE MISSIONS, Rev. Thomas D. Marick.
Res.: 1121 Ala Napunani, 704, HI 96818. Tel: 808-833-2472.

WAIANAE, ST. SOPHIA BYZANTINE MISSIONS (1996), (Ukranian), Revs. Philip Gregory Harmon; Thomas Marick, Pastoral Assoc.; Damian Higgins, Pastoral Assoc.
Res.: 86-660 Lua Lualei Homestead Rd., HI 96792. Tel: 808-696-2244; 808-696-2655; 808-833-2474; Fax: 808-696-6608.
Catechesis/Religious Program—Students 2.

STATE OF INDIANA

MISHAWAKA, ST. JOSEPH CO., ST. MICHAEL (1962), Rev. Thomas Dobrowolski.
Res.: 712 E. Lawrence St., IN 46544. Tel: 219-259-7173.

MUNSTER, LAKE CO., ST. JOSAPHAT (1958), (Ukranian), Rev. John Hritzko.
Res.: 8624 White Oak Ave., IN 46321. Tel: 219-923-0984; Fax: 219-923-0984.
Catechesis/Religious Program—Students 11.

STATE OF MICHIGAN

DEARBORN HEIGHTS, WAYNE CO., OUR LADY OF PERPETUAL HELP (1963), (Ukranian), Very Rev. Archpriest John Lazar.
Res.: 26606 Ann Arbor Trail, MI 48127. Tel: 313-278-0470; Fax: 313-278-2266.
Catechesis/Religious Program—Students 20.

DEARBORN, WAYNE CO., ST. MICHAEL'S (1962), Very Rev. Canon Wayne J. Ruchgy.
Res.: 6340 Chase Rd., MI 48126. Tel: 313-582-1424; Fax: 313-582-8157.
Mission—Holy Ascension Salem Township.

DETROIT, WAYNE CO., ST. JOHN THE BAPTIST (1918), (Ukranian), Rev. Volodymyr Petriv.
Res.: 3877 Clippert Ave., MI 48210. Tel: 313-897-7300; Fax: 313-897-7304.

FLINT, GENESEE CO., ST. VLADIMIR'S (1950), Rev. Mykola Dovzhuk, Admin.
Res.: c/o 3877 Clippert Ave., Detroit, MI 48210. Tel: 313-897-7300.

GRAND RAPIDS, KENT CO., ST. MICHAEL'S (1949), (Ukranian), [JC] Rev. Stepan Vasyliv, Admin.; Deacon Jaroslaw Bohatch, Asst.
Mailing Address: 4390 Woodside Oaks Dr., S.E., MI 49546-6216. Fax: 616-949-1151.

HAMTRAMCK, WAYNE CO., IMMACULATE CONCEPTION OF B.V.M. (1914), (Ukranian), Very Rev. Tarcisio Lucavei, O.S.B.M., Pastor & Supr.; Revs. Constantine Wysochansky, O.S.B.M.; Lauro Schaicoski, O.S.B.M.
Res.: 11700 McDougall St., MI 48212. Tel: 313-893-1710; Fax: 313-893-0770.
School—29500 Westbrook, Warren, MI 48093. Tel: 810-574-2480; Fax: 810-574-0867. Rosemary Sobol, Prin. Lay Teachers 17; Students 238.
High School—29400 Westbrook, Warren, MI 48092. Tel: 810-574-0510; Fax: 810-574-2723. Michalene Weigle, Prin. Priests 1; Lay Teachers 14; Students 81.

WARREN, MACOMB CO., ST. JOSAPHAT (1961), (Ukranian), [CEM] Revs. Basil Salkovski, O.S.B.M.; Sebastian Sabol, O.S.B.M.; Roman Hylavy, O.S.B.M.
Res.: 26401 St. Josaphat Dr., MI 48091. Tel: 810-755-1740; Fax: 810-755-1399.

STATE OF MINNESOTA

MINNEAPOLIS, HENNEPIN CO., ST. CONSTANTINE (1913), (Ukranian), [CEM] Rev. Michael Stelmach.
Res.: 515 University Ave., N.E., MN 55413-1944. Tel: 612-379-2394; Fax: 612-379-2470.

ST. PAUL, RAMSEY CO., ST. STEPHEN (1951), (Ukranian), Attended by, St. Constantine Church, Minneapolis.
Church: 1260 Greenbrier St., MN 55106. Tel: 612-379-2394; Fax: 612-379-2470.

STATE OF MISSOURI

ST. JOSEPH, BUCHANAN CO., ST. JOSEPH'S (1918), (Ukranian), Attended by, Omaha, NE. Rev. William H. MacKinnon III, S.O.L.T.
Church: 526 Virginia, MO 64504 Tel: 816-238-1187; Fax: 402-345-1552.

ST. LOUIS, ST. LOUIS CO., ASSUMPTION B.V.M. (1894), (Ukranian), Rev. Robert Piorkowski, Admin.
Church: 11363 Oak Branch Dr., MO 63129.

STATE OF NEBRASKA

LINCOLN, LANCASTER CO., ST. GEORGE'S (1950), (Ukranian), Rev. William H. MacKinnon III, S.O.L.T.
Res.: 1513 Martha St., Omaha, NE 68108.
Church: 3330 N. 13th St., NE 68521. Tel: 402-435-5882; 402-345-1552.

OMAHA, DOUGLAS CO., ASSUMPTION OF B.V.M. (1950), (Ukranian), Rev. William H. MacKinnon III, S.O.L.T.
Res.: 1513 Martha St., NE 68108. Tel: 402-345-1552.

STATE OF NORTH DAKOTA

BELFIELD, STARK CO., ST. JOHN THE BAPTIST (1946), (Ukranian), [CEM 2] Rev. Michael Taras Miles.
Res.: P.O. Box 428, ND 58622-0428. Tel: 701-575-4281; Fax: 701-575-4281.
Catechesis/Religious Program—Tel: 701-575-8645. Students 5.

FAIRFIELD, BILLINGS CO., ST. DEMETRIUS (1905), (Ukranian), [CEM 2] Rev. Michael Taras Miles; Deacon Leonand Kordonowy.
Res.: P.O. Box 428, Belfield, ND 58622-0428. Tel: 701-575-4281.
Catechesis/Religious Program—Students 22.

WILTON, MCLEAN CO., SS. PETER AND PAUL (1906), (Ukranian), [CEM] Rev. George L. Pruys, Admin.
Res.: 106 N. 7th St., P.O. Box 275, ND 58579. Tel: 701-734-6464.
Catechesis/Religious Program—Students 14.
Mission—St. Michael 812 N. Main St., Minot, Ward Co., ND 58703. Tel: 701-839-4756.

STATE OF OREGON

SPRINGFIELD, LANE CO., NATIVITY OF THE MOTHER OF GOD (1981), (Ukranian), Rev. Richard Janowicz.
Res.: 704 Aspen St., OR 97477. Tel: 541-726-7309; Fax: 541-726-7309.

STATE OF TEXAS

HOUSTON, HARRIS CO., PROTECTION OF THE MOTHER OF GOD (1957), (Ukranian), [JC] Rev. Andrij Taras Dwulit, Admin.
Res.: 9102 Meadowshire St., TX 77037. Tel: 713-447-2749; Fax: 713-447-2749.
Catechesis/Religious Program—Students 27.

THE COLONY, ST. SOPHIA UKRAINIAN CATHOLIC CHURCH (1999), (Ukranian), Rev. Vasyl Savchyn.
Church & Res.: 5600 N. Colony Blvd., TX 75056-1927. Tel: 972-379-4700; Fax: 972-379-4700.

STATE OF WISCONSIN

MILWAUKEE, MILWAUKEE CO., ST. MICHAELS (1950), (Ukranian), [JC] Rev. Volodymyr Zaiats.
Res.: 1025 S. 11th St., P.O. Box 64012, WI 53204. Tel: 414-672-5616; Fax: 414-672-5616.

Chaplains of Public Institutions
Hospitals

Rev. Msgr. William M. Bilinsky, Chap., Dir. of Clinical Ethics, 4000 Forest Dr., Delavan, WI 53115. Tel: 262-728-9930.

CHICAGO. *St. Mary of Nazareth Hospital Center*. Rev. Abraham Miller, Chap.

On Duty Outside the Diocese:
Very Rev.—
Klimchuk, Walter, Winnipeg, Canada
Rev.—
Leigh, Peter, 4032 West 10th St., Wichita, KS 67212.

Absent on Sick Leave:
Rev.—
Prodywus, Alexander

Retired:
Very Rev. Canons—
Bobersky, Michael, 6209 E. McKellips, Mesa, AZ 85205. Tel: 602-985-7620
Kurylo, Michael, 3821-49th St., San Diego, CA 92105. Tel: 619-282-7958
Revs.—
Kmech, John, Rest Haven, 16300 Wausau Ave., South Holland, 60473.
Pedelesky, Nestor, Lakefront Health Care Center, 7618 N. Sheridan Rd.. Tel: 773-743-7711

Permanent Deacons:
Bankston, James, Holy Spirit Seminary, Ottawa, ON
Bohatch, Jaroslav, St. Michael, Grand Rapids, MI
Bozio, Michael, Transfiguration of Our Lord, Denver, CO
Chabin, Nicholas, Milwaukee, WI
Horodysky, Mychajlo, St. Nicholas Cathedral, Chicago, IL
Huskey, Michael, Christ the Redeemer, Chicago, IL
Kordonowy, Leonard, St. John the Baptist, Belfield, ND; St. Demetrius, Fairfield, ND
Kostivk, Stephan, St. Nicholas Cathedral, Chicago, IL
May, Andrew, Downers Grove, IL
Plishka, Andrew, St. Joseph, Chicago, IL
Russell, Anthony, St. Michael, Grand Rapids, MI
Szyjan, Michael, SS. Volodymyr & Olha, Chicago, IL
Wasylyna, E., (Retired), Denver, CO

INSTITUTIONS LOCATED IN THE DIOCESE

[A] MONASTERIES

EAGLE HARBOR. *Skete of Holy Transfiguration Monastery* Society of St. John , Star Rte. 1, P.O. Box 226, MI 49950. Tel: 906-289-4384; Fax: 906-289-4388. Email: skete@societystjohn.com. Web: societystjohn.com. Very Rev. Nicholas Glenn, Hegumen; Deacon Ambrose; Rev. Basil Paris. Priests 2; Professed Monks 3; Novices 1.

REDWOOD VALLEY. *Holy Transfiguration Monastery*, 17001 Tomki Rd., CA 95470. Tel: 707-485-8959; Fax: 707-485-1122. Email: mttabor@pacific.net. Web: www.byzantines.net/monastery. P.O. Box 217, CA 95470. Very Rev. Joseph Homick, Abbot; Rev. Theodore Zientek. Monks of Mount Tabor Priests 3; Deacons 1; Professed Monks 9.

[B] MISCELLANEOUS

Ukrainian Catholic Education Foundation, 2247 W. Chicago Ave., 60622. Tel: 773-235-8462; Fax: 773-235-8464. Email: ucef@ucef.org. Web: www.ucef.org. Mr. John Kurey Esq., Pres.

RELIGIOUS INSTITUTES OF MEN REPRESENTED IN THE DIOCESE

For further details refer to the corresponding bracketed number in the Religious Institutes of Men or Women section.

[]—*Monks of Mt. Tabor*
[0180]—*Order of St. Basil the Great*—O.S.B.M.
[]—*Skete of Mt. Tabor*

RELIGIOUS INSTITUTES OF WOMEN REPRESENTED IN THE DIOCESE

[3730]—*Sisters of the Order of St. Basil the Great*—O.S.B.M.

NECROLOGY

† Kurylo, Michael, (Retired)—Died 2003

Eparchy of St. Peter the Apostle (Chaldean)

ESTABLISHED JULY 25, 2002.

The Jurisdiction of the Eparchy extends territorially to all Western States in the United States of America inclusive. With regards to persons, its subjects are all Catholics of the Chaldean or Assyrian Ancestry: (1) Who immigrated to this country from the Middle East, especially from Iraq and Iran; (2) Who descends from such persons (can. 755); (3) Women married to men referable to (1) & (2) if they comply with can. 98, n.4; (4) Who in accordance with can. 98, n. 3, changed their Rite; (5) converts to the Catholic Church of the Chaldean Rite; (6) And in fact, all other Catholics of the Chaldean Rite who are attached to the parishes subject to the jurisdiction of the Eparch. For legal titles of parishes and diocesan institutions, consult the Chancery Office.

Most Reverend

SARHAD Y. JAMMO

First Bishop-Eparch of the Eparchy of Saint Peter the Apostle-Chaldean; ordained December 19, 1964; appointed Chaldean Bishop May 4, 2002; consecrated Bishop July 18, 2002 in Detroit, Michigan; installed July 25, 2002 in San Diego, California; appointed First Bishop Eparch to the Eparchy of Saint Peter the Apostle-Chaldean Catholic Diocese of America July 25, 2002. *Res.: St. Peter Chaldean Diocese*, 1627 Jamacha Way, El Cajon, CA 92019.

Chancery Office: 1627 Jamacha Way, El Cajon, CA 92019. Tel: 619-579-7913; Fax: 619-588-8281.

Email: sjammo@aol.com

STATISTICAL OVERVIEW

Personnel		Resident Diocesan Priests	8	Adult Baptism Totals	4
Bishop	1	**Welfare**		First Communions	248
Priests: Diocesan Active in Diocese	7	Homes for the Aged	2	Confirmations	387
Priests: Diocesan Active Outside Diocese	1	Total Assisted	113	Marriages:	
Number of Diocesan Priests	8	Special Centers for Social Services	2	Catholic	72
Religious Priests in Diocese	3	Total Assisted	110	Interfaith	5
Total Priests in Diocese	11	**Vital Statistics**		Total Marriages	77
Parishes		Receptions into the Church:		Deaths	69
Parishes	7	Infant Baptism Totals	383	Total Catholic Population	35,000
With Resident Pastor:					

Chancery Office—1627 Jamacha Way, El Cajon, 92019. Tel: 619-579-7913; Fax: 619-588-8281.

Vicar General—Rev. SABRI A. KEJBO, 799 E. Washington Ave., El Cajon, 92020. Tel: 619-444-9911; Fax: 619-444-7989.

Episcopal Vicar for Assyrian Affairs—Rev. KAMAL WARDA BIDAWID.

Director of Finance—Rev. YOSHIA SANA.

Judicial Officer—Rev. MICHAEL J. BAZZI.

Victim Assistance Coordinator—Rev. SABRI A. KEJBO. Tel: 619-444-9911. Email: st.michaels@cox.net.

CLERGY, PARISHES, MISSIONS AND PAROCHIAL SCHOOLS

STATE OF CALIFORNIA

EL CAJON, SAN DIEGO CO.

1—*ST. PETER CHALDEAN CATHEDRAL*, Formerly St. Peter Chaldean Parish (1973), (Chaldean), Revs. Michael J. Bazzi; Felix Al-Shabi.
Res.: 1627 Jamacha Way, 92019. Tel: 619-579-7913; 619-588-9921; Fax: 619-588-8281.
Catechesis/Religious Program—Tel: 619-447-8876; Fax: 615-588-8281. Khelood Allos, D.R.E. Students 710.
Convent—Chaldean Sisters, 1591 Jamacha Way, 92019. Tel: 619-447-4842; Fax: 619-590-0052.

2—ST. MICHAEL CHALDEAN CATHOLIC CHURCH (1999), (Chaldean), Rev. Sabri A. Kejbo.
Church: 799 E. Washington Ave., 92020. Tel: 619-444-9911; Fax: 619-444-7989.
Catechesis/Religious Program—Nadia Najor, D.R.E. Students 120.

NORTH HOLLYWOOD, LOS ANGELES CO., ST. PAUL ASSYRIAN-CHALDEAN CATHOLIC PARISH (1980), (Chaldean—Assyrian), [JC] Revs. Noel Gorgis, Admin.; Tomy Tomiekha.
Res.: 13050 Vanowen St., 91605. Tel: 818-765-3665; Fax: 818-765-0493.

SAN JOSE, SANTA CLARA CO., ST. MARY ASSYRIAN-CHALDEAN PARISH (1987), Rev. Yoshia Sana.
Church & Rectory: 109 N. First St., Campbell, 95008. Tel: 408-378-6212; Fax: 408-379-0496.
Catechesis/Religious Program—Students 40.

SANTA ANA, ORANGE CO., ST. GEORGE CHALDEAN CATHOLIC CHURCH (2001), (Chaldean), [JC] Rev. Zuhair G. Toma, Admin.
Church: 4807 W. McFadden, 92704. Tel: 714-531-7760; Fax: 714-531-3409.
Catechesis/Religious Program—Students 20.

TURLOCK, STANISLAUS CO., ST. THOMAS ASSYRIAN-CHALDEAN PARISH (1964), (Chaldean), [CEM] [JC] Rev. Kamal Warda Bidawid.
Res.: 2901 N. Berkeley Ave., 95380. Tel: 209-668-4500; Fax: 209-668-2762.
Convent—Chaldean Sisters, 2937 N. Berkeley Ave., 95380. Tel: 209-634-2043; Fax: 209-668-2762.
St. Thomas Retirement Center—Tel: 209-634-7252.

STATE OF ARIZONA

SCOTTSDALE, MARICOPA CO., MAR AURAHA CHALDEAN CATHOLIC PARISH (1992), (Chaldean), [JC] Rev. Poulos Ghozairan, Admin.
Res.: 6816 E. Cactus Rd., AZ 85254. Tel: 480-596-6798; Fax: 480-596-9067.
Catechesis/Religious Program—Students 140.
Convent—6308 East Shea Blvd., AZ 85254. Tel: 480-596-1012. Sisters 2.

NECROLOGY

(No Deaths)

Eparchy of Saint Thomas the Apostle (Chaldean)

Most Reverend

IBRAHIM N. IBRAHIM, D.D.

First Bishop-Eparch of the Eparchy of Saint Thomas the; ordained December 30, 1962; appointed Chaldean Apostolic Exarch and Titular Bishop of Anbar January 26, 1982; consecrated Bishop March 7, 1982 in Baghdad, Iraq; installed April 18, 1982 in Detroit; appointed First Bishop Eparch to the Eparchy of Saint Thomas the Apostle-Chaldean Catholic Diocese of America September 14, 1985 *Res.: St. Thomas the Apostle, Chaldean Diocese of U.S.A.*, 25603 Berg Rd., Southfield, MI 48034.

Chancery Office: 25603 Berg Rd., Southfield, MI 48034. Tel: 248-351-0440; Fax: 248-351-0443.

Email: chaldeandiocese@aol.com

Exarchate Erected January 26, 1982. Elevated to the Rank of Eparchy September 14, 1985.

The Jurisdiction of the Eparchy extends territorially to all Eastern States in the United States of America inclusive. With regard to persons, its subjects are all Catholics of the Chaldean or Assyrian Ancestry: (1) Who immigrated to this country from the Middle East, especially from Iraq and Iran; (2) Who descends from such persons (can. 755); (3) Women married to men referable to (1) & (2) if they comply with can. 98, n. 4; (4) Who in accordance with can. 98, n. 3., changed their Rite; (5) Converts to the Catholic Church of the Chaldean Rite; (6) And in fact, all other Catholics of the Chaldean Rite who are attached to the parishes subject to the jurisdiction of the Eparch.

Legal Title: For legal titles of parishes and diocesan institutions, consult the Chancery Office.

STATISTICAL OVERVIEW

Personnel	
Bishop	1
Priests: Diocesan Active in Diocese	9
Priests: Retired, Sick or Absent	2
Number of Diocesan Priests	11
Total Priests in Diocese	11
Total Sisters	9
Parishes	
Parishes	7
With Resident Pastor:	
Resident Diocesan Priests	7
Welfare	
Homes for the Aged	1
Total Assisted	60
Special Centers for Social Services	1
Total Assisted	100
Educational	
Students from This Diocese	2
Total Seminarians	2
Total Students under Catholic Instruction	2
Vital Statistics	
Receptions into the Church:	
Infant Baptism Totals	820
Adult Baptism Totals	11
First Communions	720
Marriages:	
Catholic	339
Interfaith	21
Total Marriages	360
Deaths	157
Total Catholic Population	75,000

Chancery Office—25603 Berg Rd., Southfield, 48034. Tel: 248-351-0440; Fax: 248-351-0443. Email: chaldeandiocese-detroit@comcast.net. Web: www.chaldeandiocese.org.

*Vicar General—*Rev. MANUEL Y. BOJI, 25585 Berg Rd., Southfield, 48034. Tel: 248-356-0565; Fax: 248-356-5235.

*Eparchial College of Consultors—*Revs. MANUEL BOJI; STEPHEN KALLABAT; JACOB YASSO; SULEIMAN DENHA; JIRJIS ABRAHIM; WISAM MATTI; EMANUEL ISHO; FRANK KALABAT.

*Diocesan Corporation-The Chaldean Catholic Church of U.S.A.—*Most Rev. IBRAHIM N IBRAHIM, D.D., Pres.; Revs. MANUEL Y. BOJI, Treas.; FRANK KALABAT, Sec.

*Eparchial Tribunal—*Rev. STEPHEN H. KALLABAT, Court of the First Instance, Chancery Office, 25603 Berg Rd., Southfield, 48034. Tel: 248-351-0440.

CLERGY, PARISHES, MISSIONS AND PAROCHIAL SCHOOLS

STATE OF MICHIGAN

DETROIT, WAYNE CO., SACRED HEART CHALDEAN PARISH (1973), (Chaldean), Rev. Jacob O. Yasso.
Res.: 310 W. Seven Mile Rd., 48203. Tel: 313-368-6214 (Church); Fax: 313-891-0132.
*Catechesis/Religious Program—*Tel: 248-548-0066. Students 140.
Convent—Chaldean Sisters, 24900 Middlebelt Rd., Farmington, 48336. Tel: 248-615-2951; Fax: 248-615-3482.

OAK PARK, OAKLAND CO., MAR ADDAI CHALDEAN PARISH (1979), (Chaldean), Revs. Stephen Kallabat; Suleiman Denha.
Res.: 24010 Coolidge Hwy., 48237. Tel: 248-547-4648; Fax: 248-399-9089.
*Catechesis/Religious Program—*Students 220.

SOUTHFIELD, OAKLAND CO., OUR LADY OF CHALDEANS CATHEDRAL, MOTHER OF GOD CHALDEAN PARISH (1948), (Chaldean), Revs. Manuel Y. Boji, Rector; Wisam Matti.
Res.: 25585 Berg Rd., 48034. Tel: 248-356-0565; 248-356-0569; 248-356-9809 (Hall); Fax: 248-356-5235.
*Catechesis/Religious Program—*Tel: 248-356-2448. Joyce Appelt, D.R.E. Students 180.
Convent—Chaldean Sisters
*Chaldean Manor Housing for Elders—*25775 Berg Rd., 48034. Tel: 248-355-9491. (Middle Age & up)

TROY, OAKLAND CO., ST. JOSEPH CHALDEAN PARISH (1981), (Chaldean), Revs. Emanuel Isho Shaleta; Jirjis Abrahim, Vicar.
Res.: 2442 E. Big Beaver Rd., 48083. Tel: 248-528-3676; 248-524-1144 (Church); Fax: 248-524-1957.
Convent—Chaldean Sisters, Tel: 248-615-2951; Fax: 248-615-3482.

WEST BLOOMFIELD, OAKLAND CO., ST. THOMAS CHALDEAN CATHOLIC PARISH (1992), (Chaldean), Rev. Frank Y. Kalabat.
Mailing Address: 6900 Maple Rd., 48322. Tel: 248-788-2460; Fax: 248-788-2153.
Res.: 6900 Maple Rd., 48322. Tel: 248-788-2460.
*Catechesis/Religious Program—*Tel: 248-306-6004. Students 170.

STATE OF ILLINOIS

CHICAGO, COOK CO.

1—ST. EPHREM'S CHURCH (1904), (Chaldean-Assyrian), [JC] Rev. Msgr. Edward J. Bikoma.
Res.: 2537 W. Bryn Mawr Ave., IL 60659-4996. Tel: 773-271-8899; Fax: 773-271-8866.
*Catechesis/Religious Program—*Tel: 773-506-9957. Students 145.
Convent—Chaldean Sisters, 2626 W. Rascher Ave., IL 60625.

2—MART MARIAM PARISH (1986), (Chaldean-Assyrian), [JC] Rev. Msgr. Edward J. Bikoma.
Mailing Address: 2537 W. Bryn Mawr, IL 60659. Tel: 773-271-8899; Fax: 773-271-8866.
Res.: 2847 W. Chase Ave., IL 60645. Tel: 773-761-9401; Fax: 773-271-8866.

Retired:
Revs.—
Ablahad, Najor, 28454 Red Leaf, 48076. Tel: 248-569-5736
Rayes, Emanuel, 6900 Maple Rd., West Bloomfield, 48322. Tel: 248-788-2460

INSTITUTIONS LOCATED IN THE DIOCESE

RELIGIOUS INSTITUTES OF WOMEN IN THE EPARCHY

For further details refer to the corresponding bracketed number in the Religious Institutes of Men or Women section.

[]—*Daughters of Mary Immaculate* (Baghdad, Iraq); (Farmington Hills, MI; Chicago, IL)—D.M.I.

NECROLOGY

(No Deaths)

St.Thomas Syro-Malabar Catholic Diocese of Chicago

Most Reverend

JACOB ANGADIATH

Bishop of St. Thomas Syro-Malabar; ordained January 5, 1972; appointed Bishop of St. Thomas Syro-Malabar Catholic Diocese of Chicago March 13, 2001; Episcopal Ordination July 1, 2001. *Office: 717 N. Eastland, Elmhurst, IL 60126.*

ESTABLISHED MARCH 13, 2001.

Comprises all of the United States and Canada.

Diocesan Office: 3009 S. 49th Ave., Cicero, IL 60804. Tel: 708-656-3362; Fax: 708-656-8663.

STATISTICAL OVERVIEW

Personnel	
Bishop	1
Priests: Diocesan Active in Diocese	28
Number of Diocesan Priests	28
Religious Priests in Diocese	9
Total Priests in Diocese	37
Total Sisters	7
Parishes	
Parishes	7
With Resident Pastor:	
Resident Diocesan Priests	5
Resident Religious Priests	2
Missions	32
Pastoral Centers	1
New Parishes Created	3
Closed Parishes	2
Educational	
Catechesis/Religious Education:	
High School Students	1,095
Elementary Students	1,436
Total Students under Catholic Instruction	2,531
Vital Statistics	
Receptions into the Church:	
Infant Baptism Totals	112
Adult Baptism Totals	1
Received into Full Communion	1
First Communions	214
Confirmations	217
Marriages:	
Catholic	44
Interfaith	14
Total Marriages	58
Deaths	31
Total Catholic Population	80,000

Diocesan Office—3009 S. 49th Ave., Cicero, 60804. Tel: 708-656-3362; Fax: 708-656-8663.

Administration

Vicar General (Protosyncellus)—Rev. GEORGE MADATHIPARAMPIL, V.G., 3009 S. 49th Ave., Cicero, 60804-3664. Tel: 708-656-3287.

Vicar General (Syncellus)—Rev. ABRAHAM MUTHOLATH JACOB, Our Lady of Victory Church, 5212 W. Agatite Ave., Chicago, 60630. Tel: 773-286-2556.

Chancellor & Secretary to Bishop—Rev. ROY JOSEPH KADUPPIL, 3009 S. 49th Ave., Cicero, 60804-3664. Tel: 708-656-3362.

Procurator—Rev. ANTONY PERUMANOOR, 3009 S. 49th Ave., Cicero, 60804-3664. Tel: 708-656-3362.

Eparchial Consultors—Revs. GEORGE MADATHIPARAMPIL, V.G.; ABRAHAM MUTHOLATH, V.G.; ROY JOSEPH KADUPPIL; ANTONY PERUMANOOR; ANTONY THUNDATHIL; JOS KANDATHIKUDY; PHILIP THODUKAYIL; JOHN MELEPURAM.

Cathedral Church—Mar Thoma Shleeha Church, 5000 St. Charles Rd., Bellwood, 60104. Tel: 708-544-7250; Fax: 708-544-5890.

Victim Assistance Coordinator—Dr. PAUL CHERIAN. Tel: 630-769-9603 (USA); 01144-158-2415517 (London). Email: pcherian14@hotmail.com.

CLERGY, PARISHES, MISSIONS AND PAROCHIAL SCHOOLS

STATE OF ILLINOIS

BELLWOOD, COOK CO.

1—MAR THOMA SHLEEHA CATHEDRAL (1985), (Indian), [JC 2] Revs. Antony Thundathil; Varghese Naickomparambil.
5000 St. Charles Rd., 60104. Tel: 708-544-7250; Fax: 708-544-5890.
Catechesis/Religious Program—Mr. Thomas Moolayil, Contact Person. Students 524.

2—SYRO-MALABAR CATHOLIC MISSION OF THE ARCHDIOCESE OF CHICAGO (1985), (Indian), Closed. For inquiries for parish records contact the chancery.

CHICAGO, COOK CO., KNANAYA SYRO-MALABAR CATHOLIC MISSION, CHICAGO (1983), (Indian), Rev. Phillip Thodukayil.
Immaculate Heart of Mary—3817 N. Christiana, 60618. Tel: 773-509-9147; Fax: 773-509-9174.
Catechesis/Religious Program—Students 156.

STATE OF CALIFORNIA

CHATSWORTH, LOS ANGELES CO., BL. ALPHONSA SYRO-MALABAR CATHOLIC MISSION OF LOS ANGELES (2002), (Asian—Indian), Rev. Paul Kottackal.
Mailing Address: *St. Eude*, 9901 Mason Ave., CA 91311.
Rancho San Antonio Chaple—21000 Plummer St., CA 91311. Tel: 818-341-3680; Fax: 818-882-4326.

FREMONT, ALAMEDA CO., SYRO-MALABAR CATHOLIC COMMUNITY OF SAN FRANCISCO (2001), (Indian), Rev. James Thottapally.
St. Leonard—3600 St. Leonard's Way, CA 94538. Tel: 925-709-1307; Fax: 925-458-3161.

LOS ANGELES, LOS ANGELES CO., ST. PIUS X (KNANAYA CATHOLIC) MISSION OF LOS ANGELES (2001), (Indian), Rev. Thomas Animoottil.
St. Mary Magdalen—Formerly St. Jerome, 1241 Corning St., CA 90035. Tel: 310-652-2444; Fax: 310-652-4885.

SAN JOSE, SANTA CLARA CO., KNANAYA CATHOLIC COMMUNITY OF NORTHERN CALIFORNIA (1997), (Indian), Rev. Dominic Joseph.
St. Francis Cabrini—15333 Woodard Rd., CA 95124. Tel: 408-879-1123; Fax: 408-377-3587.
Catechesis/Religious Program—Tel: 510-745-9244. Students 60.

STANTON, ORANGE CO., ST. THOMAS THE APOSTLE CHURCH, STANTON, CA, , Mailing Address: 336 E. Truslow St., Fullerton, CA 92832.
Sacred Heart Church—Formerly St. Polycarp, 314 W. Workman St., Covina, CA 91723. Tel: 714-893-2766; Fax: 714-898-6675. Deacon Jacob Kattackal, Contact Person.

STATE OF CONNECTICUT

HARTFORD, HARTFORD CO., ST. THOMAS SYRO-MALABAR MISSION OF HARTFORD (1998), (Indian), Rev. Thomas Puthiyadom.
133 Woodland St., Apt. 10, CT 06105. Tel: 860-247-4549; Fax: 860-247-4549.

STATE OF FLORIDA

POMPANO BEACH, BROWARD CO., OUR LADY OF HEALTH PARISH, FLORIDA, Formerly Our Lady of Health Indian Mission, Florida (2002), (Asian—Indian), Rev. John Melepuram (India) (MIA).
Mailing Address: 201 N. University Dr., Coral Springs, FL 33071.
St. Malachy's Church—6200 John Horan Ter., Tamarac, FL 33321.
Catechesis/Religious Program—Students 22.

STATE OF GEORGIA

LAWRENCEVILLE, GWINNETT CO., BLESSED ALPHONSA SYRO-MALABAR CATHOLIC MISSION, ATLANTA (2001), (Indian), Rev. Joseph Mullakara, Dir.
Mailing Address: 4721 Crain Creek Tr., Lilburn, GA 30047.
St. Lawrence—319 Grayson Hwy., GA 30045. Tel: 678-442-0914; Fax: 770-963-1251.
Catechesis/Religious Program—Students 430.

STATE OF MARYLAND

BALTIMORE, BALTIMORE CO., INDIAN CATHOLIC SOCIETY OF BALTIMORE (1979), (Asian—Indian), Rev. George Kallampally, C.M.F. (India).
2612 Wilkens Ave., MD 21223. Tel: 410-947-4988; Fax: 410-947-6009.

STATE OF MICHIGAN

ROSEVILLE, MACOMB CO., ST. THOMAS INDIAN CATHOLIC MISSION, DETROIT (1995), (Indian), [JC] Rev. Joy Chakian.
Mailing Address: 25001 Chippendale, MI 48066. Tel: 586-445-6365; Fax: 586-445-6366.

STATE OF MINNESOTA

ST. PAUL, RAMSEY CO., SYRO-MALABAR CATHOLICS OF MINNESOTA (1999), (Indian), Rev. Joseph J. Arackal, V.C.
Mailing Address: *Syro-Malabar Catholics of MN*, 106 W. Main St., P.O. Box 22, Vermillion, MN 85085. Tel: 651-437-7103.

STATE OF NEW JERSEY

FLORAL PARK, NASSAU CO., KNANAYA CATHOLIC MISSION OF LINDEN, NJ OUR LADY OF SNOWS, Formerly Knanaya Catholic Mission of NJ Our Lady of Snows (1996), (Indian), [JC] Rev. Michael Nedumthuruthil.
258-15 80th Ave., NY 11004. Tel: 718-831-0249.

JERSEY CITY, HUDSON CO., SYRO-MALABAR CATHOLIC SOCIETY, JERSEY CITY, NJ (1990), (Indian), Rev. Thomas Thottungal.
St. Alosius Rectory—691 Westside Ave., NJ 07304. Tel: 201-433-6365; Fax: 201-451-6438.

LINDENWOLD, CAMDEN CO., SOUTH JERSEY INDIAN CATHOLIC COMMUNITY (1999), (Indian), Rev. Josekutty Manjakunnel (India).
Mailing Address: *St. Lawrence Catholic Church*, South & Cleveland Aves.,, NJ 08021. Tel: 856-566-1812; Fax: 856-627-8210.

MILLTOWN, MIDDLESEX CO., SYRO-MALABAR CATHOLIC COMMUNITY OF MILLTOWN, NJ (2000), (Indian), Revs. Thomas V. Perunilam; Philip Vadakekara.

Our Lady of Lourdes—233 N. Main St., NJ 08850. Tel: 732-828-0011; Fax: 732-828-3133.

NEW MILFORD, BERGEN CO., SYRO-MALABAR CATHOLIC MISSION OF NEW JERSEY ASCENTION CHURCH, Formerly Syro-Malabar Catholic Mission of New Milford Ascention Church (1987), (Indian), Rev. Joy Alappat (NEW). Tel: 201-951-1701; 201-801-0281. Mailing Address: 256 Azalea Dr., NJ 07646. Tel: 201-836-8961; Fax: 201-836-5896.
Catechesis/Religious Program—Students 40.

NUTLEY, ESSEX CO., SYRO-MALABAR CATHOLIC COMMUNITY OF NUTLEY, NJ, (Indian), Merged, with Syro-Malabar Catholic Mission of New Jersey Ascention Church.

PARAMUS, BERGEN CO., SYRO-MALABAR CATHOLIC COMMUNITY OF DUMONT (1999), (Indian), Rev. Sebastian Kunnath.
Mailing Address: 234 Fairview Ave., NJ 07652. Tel: 201-261-3077; Fax: 201-261-2995.

SCOTCH PLAINS, UNION CO., SYRO-MALABAR CATHOLIC COMMUNITY OF SCOTCH PLAINS, NJ, (Indian), Rev. Joy Alookaran.
St. Bartholomew—2032 Westfield Ave., NJ 07067. Tel: 908-490-0025.

STATE OF NEW YORK

BRONX, WESTCHESTER CO., ST. THOMAS SYRO-MALABAR CATHOLIC CHURCH (2002), (Asian—Indian), Rev. Jos Kandathikudy, Contact Person.
Mailing Address: 810 E. 221 St., NY 10467. Tel: 718-944-4747; Fax: 718-944-3717.
Catechesis/Religious Program—Tel: 914-963-2959. Students 88.

ELMONT, NASSAU CO., SYRO-MALABAR CATHOLIC COMMUNITY OF LONG ISLAND, NY (1980), (Indian), Merged, with Indian Catholic Community of Floral Park, NY, Floral Park to form St. Mary Syro-Malabar Catholic Church, West Hempstead.

FLORAL PARK, NASSAU CO.
1—INDIAN CATHOLIC COMMUNITY OF FLORAL PARK, NY, Merged, with Syro-Malabar Catholic Community of Long Island, NY, Elmont to form St. Mary Syro-Malabar Catholic Church, West Hempstead.
2—KNANAYA CATHOLIC MISSION OF BROOKLYN, NY (1993), (Asian—Indian), [JC] Rev. Michael Nedumthuruthil.
Our Lady of the Snows—258-15 80th Ave., NY 11004. Tel: 718-831-0249; Fax: 718-343-3221.

NANUET, ROCKLAND CO., SYRO-MALABAR CATHOLIC MISSION OF ROCKLAND COUNTY, SPRING VALLEY AND ORANGEBURG, NY (1999), (Indian), Rev. Abraham Vallayil, C.M.I. (NY).
St. Catherine Church—Formerly St. Anthony, 523 Western Hwy., Blauvelt, NY 10913. Tel: 845-627-8569.

STATEN ISLAND, RICHMOND CO., KERALA CATHOLIC ASSOCIATION, STATEN ISLAND, NY (1988), (Indian), Rev. Mathew Eraly.
St. Ann—101 Cromwell Ave., NY 10304. Tel: 718-980-2506; Fax: 718-980-4731.

WEST HEMPSTEAD, NASSAU CO., ST. MARY SYRO-MALABAR CATHOLIC CHURCH, Rev. Abraham Karott, M.C.B.S.
Mailing Address: 24 W. Minister Rd., NY 11552. Tel: 914-738-4436.

YONKERS, WESTCHESTER CO.
1—KNANAYA CATHOLIC MISSION OF ROCKLAND, NY (1993), (Indian), [JC] Rev. Abraham K. Chacko, Mission Dir.
740 N. Broadway, NY 10701. Tel: 914-966-0340; Fax: 914-963-7548.
Catechesis/Religious Program—Students 113.
2—KNANAYA CATHOLIC MISSION OF WESTCHESTER AND BRONX, NY (1994), (Indian), [JC] Rev. Abraham K. Chacko, Dir.
Mailing Address: 740 N. Broadway, NY 10701. Tel: 914-966-0340; Fax: 914-963-7548.
Catechesis/Religious Program—Students 90.

STATE OF OKLAHOMA

OKLAHOMA CITY, OKLAHOMA CO., SYRO-MALABAR MISSION, , Mailing Address: *St. Joseph Old Cathedral*, 307 N.W. 4th St., P.O. Box 408, OK 73101. Tel: 405-815-6650.

STATE OF PENNSYLVANIA

AMBLER, MONTGOMERY CO., KNANAYA CATHOLIC MISSION OF GREATER PHILADELPHIA (1999), (Indian), Rev. Thomas Vattothuparambil.
St. Anthony Rectory—259 Forest Ave., PA 19002. Tel: 215-646-4742; Fax: 215-646-4864.

JENKINTOWN, MONTGOMERY CO., ST. THOMAS CATHOLIC MISSION (1985), (Asian—Indian), Rev. Jacob Christy.
Mailing Address: *Immaculate Conception Church*, 604 West Ave., PA 19046-2708. Tel: 215-572-0987; Fax: 215-887-4163.

STATE OF TEXAS

GARLAND, DALLAS CO., ST. THOMAS THE APOSTLE CATHOLIC CHURCH (SYRO-MALABAR) (1984), (Indian), Rev. Zacharias Thottuvelil.
4922 Rosehill Rd., TX 75043. Tel: 972-303-5404; Fax: 469-366-5204.
Catechesis/Religious Program—Sophia Joseph, Contact Person. Students 265.

HOUSTON, HARRIS CO., KNANAYA CATHOLIC MISSION OF DALLAS AND FORT WORTH (1996), (Indian), [JC] Rev. Joseph Manapuram.
11027 S. Gessner Dr., TX 77071. Tel: 713-778-1201; Fax: 713-720-0441.

HOUSTON, TX
CATECHESIS/RELIGIOUS PROGRAM—STUDENTS 143KNANAYA CATHOLIC MISSION OF HOUSTON (1994), (Indian), [JC] Rev. Joseph Manapuram.
St. Albert—11027 S. Gessner Dr., TX 77071. Tel: 713-778-1201; Fax: 713-720-0441.

SUGAR LAND, FORT BEND CO., ST. JOSEPH SYRO-MALABAR CATHOLIC CHURCH, Formerly Syro-Malabar Catholic Mission, Sugar Land, TX (2001), (Indian), Rev. Ligory Philip.
Mailing Address: 211 Present St., Missouri City, TX 77489. Tel: 281-261-7700.
St. Theresa—115 7th St., Sugarland, TX 77478. Tel: 281-261-7700; Fax: 281-242-1393.
Catechesis/Religious Program—Students 110.

DISTRICT OF COLUMBIA

SYRO-MALABAR CATHOLIC MISSION, Formerly Catholic Association of Greater Washington (1980), (Indian), Rev. Mathew Punchayil (India).
Mother Seton Parish—, Formerly St. Patrick, 19951 Father Hurley Blvd., Germantown, MD 20874-1003. Tel: 202-924-3838, Ext. 211; Fax: 301-428-4951.

NECROLOGY

(No Deaths)

Ukrainian Catholic Diocese of Stamford

Most Reverend

BASIL H. LOSTEN, D.D., S.T.L., LL.D. (HON.)

Bishop of Stamford; ordained June 10, 1957; appointed Titular Bishop of Arcadiopolis and Auxiliary of Ukrainian Catholic Archeparchy of Philadelphia March 15, 1971; consecrated May 25, 1971; appointed Apostolic Administrator of Archeparchy of Philadelphia June 8, 1976; Transferred to the Stamford See September 20, 1977 *Res.: 161 Glenbrook Rd., Stamford, CT 06902.*

Chancery Office: 14 Peveril Rd., Stamford, CT 06902-3019. Tel: 203-324-7698; Fax: 203-967-9948.

Email: basileos@aol.com

ESTABLISHED AUGUST 8, 1956.

The jurisdiction of the Bishop of Stamford extends territorially throughout all of New York State and the New England States. With regard to persons, his subjects are all members of the Ukrainian Catholic Church (Byzantine Rite), irrespective of where they received Baptism.

For legal titles of parishes and diocesan institutions, consult the Chancery Office.

STATISTICAL OVERVIEW

Personnel	
Bishop	1
Priests: Diocesan Active in Diocese	27
Priests: Diocesan Active Outside Diocese	1
Priests: Retired, Sick or Absent	8
Number of Diocesan Priests	36
Religious Priests in Diocese	15
Total Priests in Diocese	51
Extern Priests in Diocese	27
Ordinations:	
Diocesan Priests	1
Permanent Deacons in Diocese	9
Total Brothers	3
Total Sisters	32
Parishes	
Parishes	51
With Resident Pastor:	
Resident Diocesan Priests	41
Resident Religious Priests	4
Without Resident Pastor:	
Administered by Priests	10
Missions	4
Welfare	
Homes for the Aged	1
Total Assisted	30
Day Care Centers	1
Total Assisted	44
Special Centers for Social Services	2
Total Assisted	125
Educational	
Seminaries, Diocesan	1
Students from Other Diocese	12
Diocesan Students in Other Seminaries	17
Total Seminarians	17
High Schools, Diocesan and Parish	1
Total Students	150
Elementary Schools, Diocesan and Parish	3
Total Students	199
Catechesis/Religious Education:	
High School Students	218
Elementary Students	772
Total Students under Catholic Instruction	1,356
Teachers in the Diocese:	
Sisters	3
Lay Teachers	22
Vital Statistics	
Receptions into the Church:	
Infant Baptism Totals	196
Received into Full Communion	1
First Communions	166
Confirmations	197
Marriages:	
Catholic	58
Interfaith	4
Total Marriages	62
Deaths	357
Total Catholic Population	16,000

Former Bishops—Most Revs. AMBROSE SENYSHYN, O.S.B.M., D.D., installed as first Bishop of Stamford, Dec. 15, 1956; transferred to the Archeparchy of Philadelphia, Oct. 26, 1961; died Sept. 11, 1976; JOSEPH M. SCHMONDIUK, D.D., Bishop of Stamford, Nov. 9, 1961; transferred to the Archeparchy of Philadelphia, Sept. 20, 1977; died Dec. 25, 1978.

Chancery Office—14 Peveril Rd., Stamford, 06902-3019. Tel: 203-324-7698; Fax: 203-967-9948. Office Hours: Mon.-Fri. 9-12 & 1-5

Vicar General—Rev. IHOR MIDZAK.

Econome—Rt. Rev. Mitred Msgr.JOHN TERLECKY.

Vice Econome—Rev. MIHAI DUBOVICI.

Chancellor & Archivist—Rev. Msgr. LEON A. MOSKO.

Vice Chancellor and Secretary—OKSANA DRAGAN.

Chancery Secretary—Rev. MYKHALO DOSIAK.

Notary Publics—Rev. MIHAI DUBOVICI; OKSANA DRAGAN.

Diocesan Consultors—Rev. IHOR MIDZAK; Very Rev. Msgrs. LEON MOSKO; Rt. Rev. Mitred Msgr. JOHN TERLECKY; GEORGE BINKOWSKI; Very Revs. PAUL LUNIW; KIRIL ANGELOV; Rev. PHILIP SANDRICK, O.S.B.M.

Diocesan Tribunal—14 Peveril Rd., Stamford, 06902-3019. Tel: 203-324-7698.

Judicial Vicar—Very Rev. PAUL LUNIW.

Judges—Very Rev. Msgr. GEORGE BINKOWSKI, B.S., M.S., B.D.; Rev. TEODOSIUS ILNICKI, O.S.B.M.

Defender of the Bond— "Ad Hoc" Appointment

Notary—Rev. PHILIP WEINER.

Diocesan Protopresbyters (Deans)—Albany: Rev. VLADIMIR MARUSCEAC. Boston: Rev. JAROSLAW NALYSNYK. Brooklyn: Very Rev. Msgr. GEORGE BINKOWSKI, B.S., M.S., B.D. Buffalo: Very Rev. MARIJAN PROCYK. Hartford: Very Rev. PAUL LUNIW. New York: Rev. PHILIP WEINER. Syracuse: Rev. IVAN KASZCZAK.

Presbyteral Council—Most Rev. BASIL LOSTEN; Rev. IHOR MIDZAK; Very Rev. Msgrs. LEON MOSKO; GEORGE BINKOWSKI; Revs. MICHAEL BUNDZ; IVAN KASZCZAK; Rev. Msgrs. JOHN SQUILLER, B.A., S.T.L.; ROMAN GOLEMBA; Revs. ZBIGNIEW BRZEZICKI;Rt. Rev. Mitred Msgr. JOHN TERLECKY, B.A., M.A., M.L.S.; Very Rev. PAUL LUNIW; Revs. KIRIL ANGELOV; BOHDAN DANYLO; PHILIP SANDRICK, O.S.B.M.

Diocesan Offices and Directors

All offices are located at the following address unless otherwise noted *14 Peveril Rd., Stamford, 06902-3019.* Tel: 203-325-2116; Fax: 203-967-9948.

Administrative Council—Most Rev. BASIL H. LOSTEN, D.D., S.T.L., LL.D. (Hon.); Very Rev. Msgr. LEON MOSKO; Rt. Rev. Mitred Msgr. JOHN TERLECKY; Revs. KIRIL ANGELOV; MIHAI DUBOVICI; IHOR MIDZAK.

Apostolate—VACANT.

Apostleship of Prayer—Very Rev. MARIJAN PROCYK.

Catechetics (Heritage Schools)—MARYANA GERMAN; Deacon VASILE COLOPELNIC.

Cemeteries—Holy Spirit Ukrainian Catholic Cemetery, 141 Sarah Wells Trail, Campbell Hall, NY 10916. Tel: 845-496-5506. Directors:: Most Rev. BASIL H. LOSTEN, D.D., S.T.L., LL.D. (Hon.), Pres. & Chm.; Rev. JAROSLAW KOSTYK, Exec. Dir.; Very Rev. Msgr. LEON MOSKO, Sec.; Revs. IHOR MIDZAK; JOHN TERLECKY; Mr. LOUIS NIGRO; Mr. JOHN SENKO; Mr. ROMAN KOZICKY ESQ.

Censors—Very Rev. Archpriest EDWARD YOUNG; Rev. JONATHAN MORSE.

Communications—Very Rev. Msgr. LEON MOSKO.

Development Office—Ms. ALEXANDRA LENCYK.

Diaconate, Permanent—Deacon WILLIS HOMICK.

Diocesan Charities and Missions—Most Rev. BASIL H. LOSTEN, D.D., S.T.L., LL.D. (Hon.).

Ecumenical Commission—Most Rev. BASIL H. LOSTEN, D.D., S.T.L., LL.D. (Hon.); Revs. MIHAI DUBOVICI; THEODOSIUS ILNICKI, O.S.B.M., J.C.L.; Very Rev. Archpriest EDWARD YOUNG.

Educational Institutions—Most Rev. BASIL H. LOSTEN, D.D., S.T.L., LL.D. (Hon.); Rev. JAMES MORRIS; Sr. JONATHAN DUCHENSKY, S.S.M.I.; Very Rev. Msgr. GEORGE BINKOWSKI, B.S., B.D., M.S.W., Supt. of Diocesan Schools.

Family Life—Rev. JONATHAN MORSE.

Holy Name Societies—Rev. PHILIP WEINER.

League of Ukrainian Catholics—Rev. PAWLO MARTYNIUK, Spiritual Dir. (New England); Very Rev. MARIJAN PROCYK, Spiritual Dir. (New York).

Liturgical Commission—Very Rev. Msgr. LEON MOSKO; Rev. PHILIP WEINER.

Missionaries, Diocesan—Rev. PHILIP SANDRICK, O.S.B.M.

Ukrainian Museum and Library of Stamford, Inc.—161 Glenbrook Rd., Stamford, 06902. Museum Library Research Center, 39 Clovelly Rd., Stamford, 06902. Tel: 203-327-7899. LUBOW WOLYNETZ, Curator, Librarian & Archivist; Rev. JOHN TERLECKY, Librarian.

Press, Diocesan: "The Sower"—Very Rev. Msgr. LEON MOSKO, Editor-in-Chief; Ms. MYROSLAVA ROZDOLSKA, Ukrainian Editor; Deacon VOLODYMYR SYBIRNYY, Assoc. Ukrainian Editor.

Priests' Benevolent Association—Rev. MIKHAIL MYSHCHUK, Sec. & Treas.

Religious Communities, Vicar—Rev. MAURICIO POPADIUK, O.S.B.M.

Religious Education—Rev. JONATHAN MORSE.

Sodalities, B.V.M.—Rev. STEPHEN YANOWSKI.

Ukrainian Catholic Relief, Inc.—Rev. JONATHAN MORSE.

Vocations—Rev. BOHDAN DANYLO.

Youth Apostolate—Rev. IVAN MAZURYK; MARYANA GERMAN.

Youth-For-Christ Association—MARYANA GERMAN.

CLERGY, PARISHES, MISSIONS AND PAROCHIAL SCHOOLS

STATE OF CONNECTICUT

ANSONIA, NEW HAVEN CO., SS. PETER AND PAUL (1897), (Ukranian), [CEM] Rev. Pawlo Martyniuk.
Res.: 105 Clifton Ave., 06401. Tel: 203-734-3895; Fax: 203-732-3191.

BRIDGEPORT, FAIRFIELD CO., PROTECTION OF B.V.M. (1950), (Ukranian), Rev. Stepan Yanovski.
Holy Protection of B.V.M. Ukrainian Catholic Church: 457 Noble Ave., 06608. Tel: 203-367-5054; Fax: 203-367-5054.
Res.: 255 Barnum Ave., 06608. Tel: 203-367-5054.

COLCHESTER, NEW LONDON CO., ST. MARY DORMITION (1948), (Ukranian), [CEM] Rev. Kiril Manolev.
Res.: 178 Linwood Ave., 06415. Tel: 860-537-2069; Fax: 860-537-2069.

GLASTONBURY, HARTFORD CO., ST. JOHN THE BAPTIST (1925), (Ukranian), Attended by, St. Mary Dormition, Colchester. Rev. Kiril Manolev.
Church: 26 New London Tpke., 06033.
Res.: 178 Linwood Ave., Colchester, 06415. Tel: 860-537-2069.

HARTFORD, HARTFORD CO., ST. MICHAEL (1907), (Ukranian), [CEM] Revs. Ihor Midzak; Peter Hronsky.
Church: 125 Wethersfield Ave., 06114.
Res.: 135 Wethersfield Ave., 06114. Tel: 860-525-7823; Fax: 860-548-1049.
School—Saturday Ukrainian School, Tel: 860-728-8792. Priests 1; Lay Teachers 11; Students 75.

NEW BRITAIN, HARTFORD CO., ST. JOSAFHAT (1951), (Ukranian), Rev. Stepan Bereza.
Res.: 303 Eddy Glover Blvd., 06053. Tel: 860-225-7340; Fax: 860-229-5490.
Catechesis/Religious Program—Priests 1; Lay Teachers 2; Students 18.

NEW HAVEN, ST. MICHAEL (1909), (Ukranian), Rev. Iura Godenciuc.
Res.: 569 George St., 06511. Tel: 203-865-0388; Fax: 203-752-0327.
School—St. Michaels Ukrainian Heritage School Myron Melnyk, Prin. (Saturdays) Priests 1; Lay Teachers 5; Students 29.

STAMFORD, FAIRFIELD CO., ST. VLADIMIR CATHEDRAL (1916), (Ukranian), Rev. John Terlecky.
Res.: 24 Wenzel Ter., 06902. Tel: 203-324-0242; Fax: 203-316-8284.
Catechesis/Religious Program—Priests 1; Lay Teachers 1; Students 27.

TERRYVILLE, LITCHFIELD CO., ST. MICHAEL (1910), (Ukranian), [CEM] Rev. Paul Luniw.
Res.: 35 Allen St., 06786. Tel: 860-583-7588; Fax: 860-582-8064.
Catechesis/Religious Program—Tel: 860-582-1850. Frank Dziubek, D.R.E. Priests 1; Lay Teachers 1; Students 4.

WILLIMANTIC, WINDHAM CO., PROTECTION OF B.V.M. (1950), (Ukranian), Rev. Ivan Bilyk.
Res.: 69 Oak St., 06226. Tel: 860-423-5031; Fax: 860-423-5031.

STATE OF MASSACHUSETTS

BOSTON, SUFFOLK CO., CHRIST THE KING (1968), [CEM] Rev. Jaroslaw Nalysnyk, Admin.
Res.: 146 Forest Hills St., Jamaica Plain, MA 02130. Tel: 617-522-9720; Fax: 617-983-0309.
School—Saturday Ukrainian School Priests 1; Lay Teachers 3; Students 40.
Catechesis/Religious Program—Priests 1; Lay Teachers 2; Students 25.

FALL RIVER, BRISTOL CO., ST. JOHN-THE-BAPTIST (1914), [JC] Attended by, Woonsocket, RI. Rev. Msgr. Roman Golemba.
Church: 339 Center St., MA 02724. Tel: 508-673-2353; Fax: 401-762-2733.
Res.: 394 Blackstone St., Woonsocket, RI 02895. Tel: 401-762-2733.

LUDLOW, HAMPDEN CO., SS. PETER AND PAUL (1912)(1924), (Ukranian), Very Rev. Archpriest Edward P. Young.
Res.: 45 Newbury St., MA 01056. Tel: 413-583-2140; Fax: 413-583-2140.
Catechesis/Religious Program—Priests 1; Students 1.

PITTSFIELD, BERKSHIRE CO., ST. JOHN THE BAPTIST (1921), (Ukranian), Rev. Robert Markowitch.
Res.: Tel: 518-828-5226; Fax: 518-828-6749.

SALEM, ESSEX CO., ST. JOHN THE BAPTIST (1918), (Ukranian), Rev. James Morris, Admin.
Mailing Address: P.O. Box 206, MA 01970-0206. Tel: 978-745-3151.
Church: 124 Bridge St., MA 01970.
Catechesis/Religious Program—Tel: 617-599-8138. Students 6.

SOUTH DEERFIELD, FRANKLIN CO., HOLY GHOST (1920), (Ukranian), Very Rev. Archpriest Edward P. Young.
Res.: 44 Sugarloaf St., MA 01373. Tel: 413-665-3880.
Catechesis/Religious Program—Priests 1; Lay Teachers 2; Students 15.

STATE OF NEW HAMPSHIRE

MANCHESTER, HILLSBORO CO., PROTECTION OF B.V.M. (1908), (Ukranian), Rev. Zbigniew Brzezicki.
Church: 54 Walnut St., NH 03104. Tel 603-622-0034; Fax 603-642-8961.
Catechesis/Religious Program—Priests 1; Lay Teachers 6; Students 32.

STATE OF NEW YORK

AMSTERDAM, MONTGOMERY CO., ST. NICHOLAS (1909), (Ukranian), [CEM] Rev. Marian Kostyk.
Res.: 24 Pulaski St., NY 12010. Tel: 518-842-8731; Fax: 518-342-1384.

AUBURN, CAYUGA CO., SS. PETER AND PAUL (1901), (Ukranian), Rev. Robert Batcho.
Res.: 132 Washington St., NY 13021. Tel: 315-252-5573; Fax: 315-252-7469.
School—(Grades K-8) Tel: 315-252-5567. William LoCastro, Co-Prin.; Mary Ann Dec, Co-Prin. Lay Teachers 8; Students 99.
Catechesis/Religious Program—Lay Teachers 3; Students 15.

BATH, STEUBEN CO., CHRIST THE KING, Closed. For inquiries for parish records contact the chancery.

BRONX, BRONX CO., ST. MARY PROTECTRESS (1943), (Ukranian), [JC] Rev. Mauricio Popadiuk, O.S.B.M.
Church: 1745 Washington Ave., NY 10457. Tel: 718-731-9392.
Res.: East Beach Dr., Glen Cove, NY 11542. Tel: 516-671-0545; Fax: 516-676-7465.

BROOKLYN, KINGS CO.
1—HOLY GHOST (1913), (Ukranian), Revs. Ivan Tykhovytch, (On leave - military duty); Nicolau Korczagin.
Mailing Address: 161 N. Fifth St., NY 11211.
Church: 160 N. 5th St., NY 11211. Tel: 718-782-9592; Fax: 718-599-2905.
2—ST. NICHOLAS (1916), (Ukranian), Rev. Mykhaylo Dosiak, Admin.
256 19th St., NY 11215. Tel: 718-389-8744.

BUFFALO, ERIE CO., ST. NICHOLAS (1894), (Ukranian), Very Rev. Marijan Procyk; Rev. Raymond Palko.
Res.: 308 Fillmore Ave., NY 14206. Tel: 716-852-7566; Fax: 716-855-1319.
Catechesis/Religious Program—Elaine P. Nowadly, D.R.E. Priests 2.

COHOES, ALBANY CO., SS. PETER AND PAUL (1907), (Ukranian), Rev. Vladimir Marusceac.
Res.: 198 Ontario St., NY 12047. Tel: 518-237-0535; Fax: 518-237-2397.

ELMIRA HEIGHTS, CHEMUNG CO., ST. NICHOLAS (1895), (Ukranian), Rev. Vasile Godenciuc.
Res.: 410 E. McCanns Blvd., NY 14903. Tel: 607-734-1221; Fax: 607-737-7569.
Catechesis/Religious Program—Irene Moffe, D.R.E. Priests 1; Lay Teachers 4; Students 20.

FRESH MEADOWS, QUEENS CO., ANNUNCIATION OF THE B.V.M. (1957), (Ukranian), Rev. Msgr. George Binkowski.
Res.: 48-26 171st St., NY 11365. Tel: 718-939-4116; Fax: 718-939-3696.

GLEN SPEY, SULLIVAN CO., ST. VOLODYMYR (1961), (Ukranian), [JC] Rev. Mark Hirniak.
Res.: 2105 Rte. 41, NY 12737-5618. Tel: 845-856-5500; Fax: 845-856-5500.

HAMPTONBURGH, ORANGE CO., ST. ANDREW'S (1983), (Ukranian), Rev. Yaroslaw Kostyk.
Res.: 141 Sarah Wells Tr., Campbell Hall, NY 10916. Tel: 845-496-5506; Fax: 845-496-5564.
Catechesis/Religious Program—Priests 1; Lay Teachers 1; Students 4.

HEMPSTEAD, NASSAU CO., ST. VLADIMIR (1944), (Ukranian), Very Rev. Maxim Kobasuk, O.S.B.M.
Res.: 709 Front St., NY 11550. Tel: 516-481-7717; Fax: 516-481-3435.
Parish Center—226 Uniondale Ave., Uniondale, NY 11553. Tel: 516-485-0775.
School—Saturday Ukrainian School Priests 1; Lay Teachers 8; Students 60.
Catechesis/Religious Program—Priests 1; Lay Teachers 9; Students 64.

HUDSON, COLUMBIA CO., ST. NICHOLAS (1923), (Ukranian), Rev. Robert Markowitch.
Res.: 29 S. Second St., NY 12534. Tel: 518-828-5226; Fax: 518-828-6749.

HUNTER, GREENE CO., ST. JOHN THE BAPTIST (1962), (Ukranian),, Rte 23A, P.O. Box 284, NY 12442. Tel: 518-263-3862.

JOHNSON CITY, BROOME CO., SACRED HEART UKRAINIAN CATHOLIC CHURCH (1944), (Ukranian), [CEM] Rev. Wasyl Hrynkiw.
Res.: 230 Ukrainian Hill Rd., NY 13790. Tel: 607-797-6293; Fax: 607-797-6295.
School—Saturday Ukrainian School, Tel: 607-797-6294. Lay Teachers 3; Students 11.
Catechesis/Religious Program—Tel: 607-797-6294. Luba Woytew, D.R.E. Lay Teachers 3; Students 20.

KENMORE, ERIE CO., ST. JOHN THE BAPTIST (1902), (Ukranian), Rev. Stepan Kuklich.
Res.: 3275 Elmwood Ave., NY 14217. Tel: 716-873-5011; Fax: 716-871-8804.

KERHONKSON, ULSTER CO., HOLY TRINITY (1965), (Ukranian), Rev. Volodymyr Pyso.
Mailing Address: 211 Foordmore Rd., NY 12446.
Church: 211 Foordmore Rd., NY 12446. Tel: 845-626-2864.
School—Saturday Ukrainian School Priests 1; Lay Teachers 2; Students 26.

LACKAWANNA, ERIE CO., OUR LADY OF PERPETUAL HELP (1925), (Ukranian), Rev. Andriv Kasiyan.
Res.: 1182 Ridge Rd., NY 14218. Tel: 716-823-6182; Fax: 716-823-6550.
Catechesis/Religious Program—Annette M. Nayda, D.R.E.; Maria Slabyk, D.R.E. Priests 1; Lay Teachers 2.

LANCASTER, ERIE CO., ST. BASIL (1921), (Ukranian), Rev. Robert Moreno.
Res.: 12 Embry Pl., NY 14086. Tel: 716-683-0313; Fax: 716-651-9873.
Church: 3657 Walden Ave., NY 14086.

LITTLE FALLS, HERKIMER CO., ST. NICHOLAS (1912), Attended by, Amsterdam. Rev. Marian Kostyk.
Res.: 150 Furnace St., NY 13365. Tel: 315-823-4474.

LONG ISLAND CITY, QUEENS CO., HOLY CROSS (1944), (Ukranian), Revs. Bernard J. Panczuk, O.S.B.M.; Christopher Woytyna, O.S.B.M.
Res.: 31-12 30th St., NY 11106. Tel: 718-932-4060; Fax: 718-932-6370.
Catechesis/Religious Program—Priests 1; Lay Teachers 2; Students 6.

NEW YORK, NEW YORK CO., ST. GEORGE (1905), (Ukranian), Revs. Philip Sandrick, O.S.B.M.; Mario Daechen, O.S.B.M.; Teodosij Ilnicki, O.S.B.M.; Bro. Emil Turko, O.S.B.M.
Res.: 30 E. Seventh St., NY 10003. Tel: 212-674-1615; Fax: 212-475-7017.
School—215 E. Sixth St., NY 10003. Tel: 212-473-3130; Fax: 917-534-0819. Sr. Chrysostom, O.S.B.M., Prin. Sisters of St. Basil the Great 2; Lay Teachers 8; Students 100.
High School—Tel: 212-473-3323; Fax: 917-534-0819. Peter Shyshka, Prin. Sisters 1; Lay Teachers 12; Students 150.

NIAGARA FALLS, NIAGARA CO., PROTECTION OF B.V.M. (1920), (Ukranian), Rev. Demetrius Laptuta, C.SS.R.
Res.: 2713 Ferry Ave., NY 14301. Tel: 716-284-7066; Fax: 716-282-6902.

OZONE PARK, QUEENS CO., ST. MARY PROTECTRESS (1954), (Ukranian), Rev. Vasile Tivadar.
Res.: 97-06 87th St., NY 11416. Tel: 718-845-5366; Fax: 718-529-1477.

RIVERHEAD, SUFFOLK CO., ST. JOHN THE BAPTIST (1924), (Ukranian), [CEM] Rev. Ihor Tarasiw.
Res.: 820 Pond View Rd., NY 11901. Tel: 631-727-2766; Fax: 631-727-4141.
Church: Franklin St., NY 11901.

ROCHESTER, MONROE CO.
1—EPIPHANY OF OUR LORD (1958), (Ukranian), [JC] Rev. Janusz Jedrychowski.
Res.: 202 Carter St., NY 14621. Tel: 585-266-4036; Fax: 585-323-9691.
2—ST. JOSAPHAT (1909), (Ukranian), Very Rev. Kiril Angelov.
Res.: 940 Ridge Road E., NY 14621. Tel: 585-467-6457; Fax: 585-467-7296.
School—95 Stanton Ln., NY 14621. Tel: 585-266-8700; Fax: 585-266-8837. Priests 2; Lay Teachers 14; Students 80.
Catechesis/Religious Program—Lay Teachers 9; Students 55.
Convent—910 Ridge Rd. E., NY 14621. Tel: 585-266-1540.

ROME, ONEIDA CO., ST. MICHAEL (1914), (Ukranian), [CEM] Attended by, St. Vladimir, Utica. Rev. Michael Bundz.
Res.: 296 Genessee St., Utica, NY 13502. Tel: 315-735-5138; Fax: 315-735-0443.
Church: 133 River St., NY 13440.

SPRING VALLEY, ROCKLAND CO., SS. PETER AND PAUL (1913), (Ukranian), Rev. Stepan Bilyk.
Res.: 41 Collins Ave., NY 10977. Tel: 845-356-1634; Fax: 845-425-2749.
Catechesis/Religious Program—Tel: 201-529-4208. Irene Gojdycz, D.R.E. Lay Teachers 2; Students 14.

STATEN ISLAND, RICHMOND CO., HOLY TRINITY (1949), (Ukranian), Rev. Mykhaylo Dosiak.
Res.: 288 Vanderbilt Ave., NY 10304. Tel: 718-442-2555.

SYRACUSE, ONONDAGA CO., ST. JOHN THE BAPTIST (1900), Revs. Ivan Kaszczak; Wasyl Kadylo.
Res.: 207 Tompkins St., NY 13204. Tel: 315-478-5109; Fax: 315-471-9867.
Catechesis/Religious Program—Priests 1; Lay Teachers 9; Students 50.

TROY, RENSSELAER CO., PROTECTION OF B.V.M. (1952), (Ukranian), [JC] Attended by, SS. Peter and Paul, Cohoes. Rev. Vladimir Marusceac.
Res.: 198 Ontario St., Cohoes, NY 12047. Tel:

518-237-0535; Fax: 518-237-2397.
Church: 459 Second St., NY 12180. Tel: 518-274-5318.

UTICA, ONEIDA CO., ST. VOLODYMYR THE GREAT (1950), (Ukranian), [CEM] Rev. Michael Bundz, Admin.
Res.: 296 Genessee St., NY 13502. Tel: 315-735-5138; Fax: 315-735-0443.
School—Saturday Ukrainian School Priests 1; Lay Teachers 1; Students 8.

WATERVLIET, ALBANY CO., ST. NICHOLAS (1905), (Ukranian), [CEM] [JC] Rev. Mikhail Myshchuk.
Res.: 2410-4th Ave., NY 12189. Tel: 518-273-6752; Fax: 702-446-5439.
School—Saturday Ukrainian School & C.C.D. Lay Teachers 8; Students 34.

WEST ISLIP, SUFFOLK CO., HOLY FAMILY (1924), (Ukranian), Rev. Olvian Popovichi.
Res.: 471 Montauk Hwy., NY 11795-4475. Tel: 631-661-0031; Fax: 631-321-4368.

YONKERS, WESTCHESTER CO., ST. MICHAEL (1899), (Ukranian), Revs. Philip Weiner; Wolodymr Kucaj.
Res.: 21 Shonnard Pl., NY 10703. Tel: 914-963-0209; Fax: 914-969-6269.
Catechesis/Religious Program—Priests 2; Students 186.
Mission—Holy Protection of the Mother of God Bedford Hills, Westchester Co., NY.

STATE OF RHODE ISLAND

WOONSOCKET, PROVIDENCE CO., ST. MICHAEL (1908), [CEM] [JC] Rev. Msgr. Roman Golemba.
Res.: 394 Blackstone St., RI 02895. Tel: 401-762-2733; Fax: 401-762-2733.
Church: 396 Blackstone St., RI 02895.

Special Assignment:
Rev. Msgr.—
Mosko, Leon A., Chancellor
Revs.—
Morse, Jonathan K., Ukrainian Catholic Relief, Inc.
Shubiak, Stephen, U.S. Chap. Corps

Military Services:
Rev.—
Tykhovych, Ivan

On Leave of Absence:
Rev.—
Smolley, Robert

Retired:
Rev. Msgr.—
Skrincosky, Peter, 222 Broad St., Arnot, St. Clair, PA 17970.
Rev. Canon—
Sharanevych, Emile, 332 Foordmore Rd., Kerhonkson, NY 12446. Tel: 914-626-4947
Revs.—
Andrushkiw, Vladimir, 195 Glenbrook Rd., 06902.
Chomko, Stephen, 706 Warren St., Berwick, PA 18603.
Mudry, Lubomyr, 195 Glenbrook Rd., 06902.
Pelensky, Ihor, P.O. Box 533, Westmoreland, NY 13490.

Permanent Deacons:
Coleman, Paul, SS. Peter & Paul, Auburn, NY
Evans, Michael, SS. Peter & Paul, Auburn, NY
Hobczuk, John, St. Nicholas, Elmira Heights, NY
Homick, Willis, SS. Peter & Paul, Auburn, NY
Kotch, Myron, Syracuse, NY
Malachowsky, Yourij, Holy Cross, Long Island City, NY

INSTITUTIONS LOCATED IN THE DIOCESE

[A] SEMINARIES, DIOCESAN

STAMFORD. *Ukrainian Catholic Seminary Inc. St. Basil College*, 195 Glenbrook Rd., 06902-3099. Tel: 203-324-4578; Fax: 203-357-7681. Most Rev. Basil H. Losten, D.D., S.T.L., LL.D., Chm., Bd. of Directors; Rev. Msgr. John Squiller, B.A., S.T.L., Pres. & Rector; Revs. Bohdan Danylo, B.A., S.T.B., Vice Rector; Marian Struc, Dir. of Spiritual Formation; John Terlecky, B.A., M.A., M.L.S., Librarian; Ivan Mazuryk, Dean of Men & Procurator; Mihai Dubovici, B.A., S.T.B., Bursar; Edward J. Bordeau, M.A., Ph.B., Ph.D., Dean & Registrar; Ms. Lubow Wolynetz, B.A., M.L.S., Asst. Librarian.

[B] SEMINARIES, RELIGIOUS

GLEN COVE. *Basilian Fathers Novitiate of the Order of St. Basil the Great*, E. Beach Dr., NY 11542. Tel: 516-671-0545; Fax: 516-676-7465. Very Rev. Cyril Izczuk, O.S.B.M., Supr. & Master of Novices; Revs. Januario Lucavei, O.S.B.M., Asst. Master of Novices; Hilarion Benedik, O.S.B.M.; Athanasius B. Pekar, O.S.B.M.; Taras Prokopiw, O.S.B.M. Priests 5; Brothers 2; Scholastics 4.

[C] NURSERY SCHOOLS

STAMFORD. *St. Ann's Nursery School*, 111 W. North St., 06902. Tel: 203-323-1237; 203-348-5675; Fax: 203-323-0262. Missionary Sisters of Mother of God 6; Nursery 44; Staff 3.

[D] ADULT FACILITIES

SLOATSBURG. *St. Joseph's Adult Care Home, Inc.*, Formerly St. Joseph's Home, 125 Sisters Servants Ln., NY 10974-0008. Tel: 845-753-2555; Fax: 845-753-6910. Sr. Bernardine Symionow, S.S.M.I., Admin. Sisters Servants of Mary Immaculate 13; Residents 30; Total Staff 13.

[E] MONASTERIES AND RESIDENCES OF PRIESTS AND BROTHERS

NEW YORK. *Provincialate of Basilian Fathers* , NY. Priests 23; Scholastics 7; Brothers 3.
Res.: 29 Peacock Ln., Locust Valley, NY 11560. Tel: 516-609-3262; Fax: 516-609-3264. Rev. Mauricio Popadiuk, O.S.B.M., Protohegumen.

WEST BURKE. *Mary Theotokos Centre*, P.O. Box 88, VT 05871-0088. Tel: 802-467-1132. Email: stefan@sover.net. Rev. Stephen C. von Fauer, Supr.

[F] MONASTERIES OF NUNS

STAMFORD. *Missionary Sisters of Mother of God*, 111 W. North St., 06902. Tel: 203-323-1237; Fax: 203-323-0262. Sr. Nadia Baranik, M.S.M.G., Supr.; Rev. Jonathan Morse, Chap.

MIDDLETOWN. *Nuns of St. Basil the Great*, Sacred Heart Monastery, 209 Keasel Rd., NY 10940-6287. Tel: 845-343-1308. Sr. M. Bernadette Reshetylo, O.S.B.M., Supr. Sisters 5.

SLOATSBURG. *Sister Servants of Mary Immaculate, Inc.*, Formerly Immaculate Conception Provinciate, Sisters Servants Ln., 9 Emmanuel Dr., P.O. Box 9, NY 10974-0009. Tel: 845-753-2840; Fax: 845-753-1956. Sr. Michele Yakymovitch, S.S.M.I., Prov. Supr. Sisters Servants of Mary Immaculate Conception Province Sisters 20.

[G] MISCELLANEOUS

STAMFORD. *Institute of Catechists of the Heart of Jesus*, 161 Glenbrook Rd., 06902. Tel: 203-327-6374. Cecilia Daciuk, Supr. Total Members 6.
Providence Association of Ukrainian Catholics in America, Branch #188, 14 Peveril Rd., 06902. Tel: 203-324-7698; Fax: 203-967-9948. Cecilia Daciuk, Branch Sec.
**Ukrainian Catholic Relief, Inc.*, 14 Peveril Rd., 06902. Email: morseucrstamford@worldnet.att.net.

SLOATSBURG. *St. Mary's Villa Spiritual, Cultural & Educational Center*, 150 Sisters Servants Ln., P.O. Box 9, NY 10974-0009. Tel: 845-753-5100; Fax: 845-753-1956. Sr. Albina Gregory, S.S.M.I., Coord.

RELIGIOUS INSTITUTES OF MEN REPRESENTED IN THE DIOCESE

For further details refer to the corresponding bracketed number in the Religious Institutes of Men or Women section.

[0180]—*Order of St. Basil the Great*—O.S.B.M.
[1070]—*Redemptorists*—C.Ss.R.

RELIGIOUS INSTITUTES OF WOMEN REPRESENTED IN THE DIOCESE

[]—*Institute of Catechists of the Heart of Jesus*
[2810]—*Missionary Sisters of Mother of God*—M.S.M.G.
[3730]—*Sisters of the Order of St. Basil the Great*—O.S.B.M.
[3610]—*Sisters Servants of Mary Immaculate*—S.S.M.I.

NECROLOGY

† Chrepta, Rev. Msgr. Stephen J., (Retired)—Died May 16, 2003

Byzantine Eparchy of Van Nuys

Most Reverend

GEORGE M. KUZMA, D.D.

Retired Bishop of Van Nuys; ordained May 29, 1955; appointed Auxiliary Bishop of the Byzantine Eparchy of Passaic, November 11, 1986; consecrated February 4, 1987; appointed Bishop of Eparchy of Van Nuys October 23, 1990; installed Second Bishop of Van Nuys, January 15, 1991; retired December 5, 2000.

Most Reverend

WILLIAM C. SKURLA

Bishop of Van Nuys; ordained May 23, 1987; appointed Bishop of Eparchy of Van Nuys February 19, 2002; ordained April 23, 2002 *Office: 8105 N. 16th St., Phoenix, AZ 85020.*

Chancery Office: 8105 N. 16th St., Phoenix, AZ 85020. Tel: 602-861-9778; Fax: 602-861-9796.

Web: eparchy-of-van-nuys.org

Email: eparchyvannuys@aol.com

ESTABLISHED DECEMBER 3, 1981.

Embraces all Catholics of the Byzantine-Ruthenian Church in the States of California, Oregon, Washington, Idaho, Nevada, Arizona, Utah, Wyoming, Montana, Colorado, New Mexico, Alaska and Hawaii.

Principal Patron-Patronage of the Mother of God (Pokrov).

For legal titles of parishes and diocesan institutions, consult the Chancery Office.

STATISTICAL OVERVIEW

Personnel	
Bishop	1
Retired Bishops	1
Priests: Diocesan Active in Diocese	13
Priests: Diocesan Active Outside Diocese	2
Priests: Retired, Sick or Absent	3
Number of Diocesan Priests	18
Religious Priests in Diocese	7
Total Priests in Diocese	25
Extern Priests in Diocese	3
Ordinations:	
Permanent Deacons	3
Permanent Deacons in Diocese	8
Total Brothers	7
Total Sisters	4
Parishes	
Parishes	19
With Resident Pastor:	
Resident Diocesan Priests	13
Resident Religious Priests	5
Without Resident Pastor:	
Administered by Priests	1
Professional Ministry Personnel:	
Brothers	7
Sisters	4
Welfare	
Other Institutions	1
Total Assisted	24
Educational	
Diocesan Students in Other Seminaries	2
Total Seminarians	2
Catechesis/Religious Education:	
High School Students	135
Elementary Students	432
Total Students under Catholic Instruction	569
Vital Statistics	
Receptions into the Church:	
Infant Baptism Totals	57
Adult Baptism Totals	9
Received into Full Communion	19
First Communions	81
Confirmations	98
Marriages:	
Catholic	10
Interfaith	5
Total Marriages	15
Deaths	33
Total Catholic Population	2,849

Former Bishops—Most Revs. THOMAS V. DOLINAY, D.D., ord. May 16, 1948; consecrated Nov. 23, 1976; appt. Tutular Bishop of Thyatira and Auxiliary of Passiac, Sept. 23, 1976; appt. First Ordinary of the Byzantine Catholic Diocese of Van Nuys, CA; installed March 9, 1982; appt. Coadjutor Archbishop of Pittsburgh Byzantine Rite, March 13, 1990; succeeded to June 12, 1991; died April 13, 1993; GEORGE M. KUZMA, D.D. (Retired), ord. May 29, 1955; appt. Auxiliary Bishop of the Byzantine Eparchy of Passaic, Nov. 11, 1986; consecrated Feb. 4, 1987; appt. Bishop of Eparchy of Van Nuys Oct. 23, 1990; installed as Second Bishop of Van Nuys, Jan. 15, 1991; retired Dec. 5, 2000.

Chancery Office—Byzantine Catholic Eparchy of Van Nuys, Pastoral Center, 8105 N. 16th St., Phoenix, 85020. Tel: 602-861-9778; Fax: 602-861-9796. Email: eparchyvannuys@aol.com. Web: www.eparchy-of-van-nuys.org. Office Hours: Mon.-Thurs. 10-3; Fri. 10-1

Chancellor and Protosyncellus—Rev. STEPHEN G. WASHKO.

Treasurer—Sr. CELESTINE PETRUSKA, O.S.B.M.. Email: evntreasurer@aol.com.

Eparchial Consultors - Presbyteral Council—Rev. WESLEY IZER, S.D.B.; Very Rev. MICHAEL MORAN, J.C.D.; Rev. JOSEPH HUTSKO; Rev. Msgr. GEORGE VILA; Revs. STEPHEN WASHKO; FRANCIS M. VIVONA, S.T.M., J.C.L.

Diocesan Matrimonial Tribunal—Office of the Tribunal Eparchy of Van Nuys, 2120 Lindell Rd., Las Vegas, NV 89146. Tel: 702-873-5102; Fax: 702-873-5104.

Judicial Vicar—Rev. FRANCIS M VIVONA, S.T.M., J.C.L.

Promoter of Justice—Very Rev. MICHAEL MORAN, J.C.D.

Secretary—Mr. ROBERT BUSSEY, M.A.

Defender—Rev. PHILIP ACQUARO, C.S.B., J.C.L.

Judge—Rev. FRANCIS VIVONA, J.C.L.

Notary—Deacon STEPHEN CASMUS, M.A.

Building Commission—Revs. STEPHEN G. WASHKO; WESLEY IZER, S.D.B.; Deacon JOHN MONTALVO III; Mr. JOEL WEISHEIT.

Director of Religious Education—Rev. ANTHONY HERNANDEZ.

Director of Evangelization—Rev. JOSEPH STANICHAR.

Eparchial Finance Commission—Revs. STEPHEN G. WASHKO, Chm.; WESLEY IZER, S.D.B.; Sr. CELESTINE PETRUSKA, O.S.B.M.; Mrs. JOSEFINA DANOVICH.

Safe Environment Coordinator—Sr. JOANNE LICKVAR, O.S.B.M.

Victim Assistance Coordinators—HELEN VOGEL. Email: cath7@sbcglobal.net; ROSEMARIE LUDWIG, Ph.D. Tel: 602-997-1550. Email: rlstussy@hotmail.com.

Victim Rights Advocates—ROSEMARIE LUDWIG, Ph.D.; JAN VOGEL.

Vocation Director—Rev. ROBERT M. PIPTA.

Ecclesiatical Notary—Mrs. DIANE RABIEJ; Rev. STEPHEN WASHKO.

Liturgy & Music Commission—Revs. STEPHEN WASHKO, Chm.; JOSEPH HUTSKO; ROBERT M. PIPTA; Sr. CHRISTOPHER MALCOVSKY, O.S.B.M.; Mr. BASIL RABAYDA JR.

Newsletter—Mrs. DIANE RABIEJ. Email: evnsecretary@aol.com. "Eparchial Newsletter"

Director of Development & Stewardship—Sr. CHRISTOPHER MALCOVSKY, O.S.B.M.

Director of Ecumenical Affairs—Rev. STEPHEN WASHKO.

Censor—Rev. FRANCIS VIVONA, J.C.L.

Administrative Secretary—Mrs. DIANE RABIEJ. Email: evnsecretary@aol.com.

Commission for the Implementation of the Particular Law—Very Rev. MICHAEL MORAN, J.C.D., Chm.; Revs. PHILIP ACQUARO, C.S.B., J.C.L.; FRANCIS VIVONA, J.C.L.; STEPHEN G. WASHKO.

CLERGY, PARISHES, MISSIONS AND PAROCHIAL SCHOOLS

STATE OF ARIZONA

GILBERT, MARICOPA CO., ST. THOMAS THE APOSTLE (1982), Rev. Philip A. Acquaro, C.S.B., J.C.L., Admin.
Mailing Address: P.O. Box 667, 85299-0667. Tel: 480-497-5799; Fax: 480-497-6726. 19 W. Bruce Ave., 85233. Tel: 480-497-6726.

PHOENIX, MARICOPA CO., ST. STEPHEN (1968),, (Byzantine Catholic Pro-Cathedral), Rev. Stephen G. Washko, Rector; Sr. Christopher Malcovsky, O.S.B.M., Pastoral Assoc.; Deacon John Montalvo III.
Res.: 8141 N. 16th St., 85020-3999. Tel: 602-943-5379; Fax: 602-997-4093. Rev. Nils F. Thompson, O.F.M.

Convent—St. Stephen Convent, 8141 N. 16th St. #27, 85020. Tel: 602-944-5121; Fax: 602-861-9796. Sisters 3.

TUCSON, PIMA CO., ST. MELANY (1974), Rev. Robert Rankin, Admin.; Deacon Michael Milazzo.
Church: 1212 N. Sahuara, 85712-5018. Tel: 520-886-4225; Fax: 520-751-4574.

STATE OF ALASKA

ANCHORAGE, ANCHORAGE CO., SAINT NICHOLAS OF MYRA (1957), Rev. Wesley Izer, S.D.B.
Res.: 2200 Arctic Blvd., AK 99503-1909. Tel: 907-277-6731; Fax: 907-222-6891.

STATE OF CALIFORNIA

SHERMAN OAKS, LOS ANGELES CO., CATHEDRAL OF ST. MARY (1956), Very Rev. Archpriest Michael Moran, J.C.D., Rector; Deacon Michael Hladky, (Retired).
Res.: 5329 Sepulveda Blvd., CA 91411-3441. Tel: 818-907-5511; Fax: 818-981-7107.

ANAHEIM, ORANGE CO., ANNUNCIATION (1969), Rev. Msgr. George N. Vida.
Res.: 995 N. West St., CA 92801-4305. Tel: 714-533-6292; Fax: 714-991-9738.

FONTANA, SAN BERNARDINO CO., ST. NICHOLAS (1958), Rev. Joseph Hutsko.
Res.: 9112 Oleander Ave., CA 92335-5599. Tel: 909-822-9917; Fax: 909-822-7663.

FRESNO, FRESNO CO., BYZANTINE CATHOLIC COMMUNITY OF FRESNO, CA, Closed. For inquiries for parish records contact the chancery.

LOS GATOS, SANTA CLARA CO., ST. BASIL THE GREAT (1986), Rev. Anthony Hernandez.
Res.: 14263 Mulberry Dr., CA 95032-1208. Tel: 408-871-0919; Fax: 408-871-0911.

PALM SPRINGS, RIVERSIDE CO., BYZANTINE CATHOLIC COMMUNITY OF PALM SPRINGS, CA, Closed. For inquiries for parish records contact the chancery.

SACRAMENTO, SACRAMENTO CO., ST. PHILIP THE APOSTLE (1971), Rev. Anthony Hernandez, Admin.
Church: 3866 65th St., CA 95820-2033. Tel: 916-452-1888 (Office); Fax: 916-452-6333.

SAN DIEGO, SAN DIEGO CO., HOLY ANGELS (1958), Rev. Melvin Rybarczyk, C.R., Admin.; Deacon David Hess.
Mailing Address: 2235 Galahad Rd., CA 92123-3931. Tel: 858-277-2511; Fax: 858-277-5792.

SAN LUIS OBISPO, SAN LUIS OBISPO CO., SAINT ANNE (1986), Rev. Edmund M. Idranyi, Admin.; Mr. Paul Sawko, Financial Admin.
Mailing Address: 222 Foothill Blvd., CA 93405-1540. Tel: 805-543-8883 (Voice/Fax).

SAN MATEO, SAN MATEO CO., ST. MACRINA, Closed., All records at the Chancery Office.

STOCKTON, SAN JOAQUIN CO., BYZANTINE CATHOLIC COMMUNITY OF STOCKTON, Closed. For inquiries for parish records contact the chancery.

STATE OF COLORADO

COLORADO SPRINGS, EL PASO CO., BYZANTINE CATHOLIC MISSION, Closed. For inquiries for parish records contact the chancery.

DENVER, DENVER CO., HOLY PROTECTION OF THE MOTHER OF GOD (1974), Rev. Archimandrite Januarius Izzo, O.F.M., M.A., J.C.D., Admin.; Deacon Andrew Bodnar.
Mailing Address: 1074 S. Cook St., CO 80209-4923. Tel: 303-778-8283; Fax: 303-778-8283.
Church: 1201 S. Elizabeth St., CO 80210.

STATE OF NEVADA

LAS VEGAS, CLARK CO.

1—ST. GABRIEL THE ARCHANGEL (1977), Rev. Robert M. Pipta, Admin.
Church: 2250 E. Maule Ave., NV 89119-4607. Tel: 702-361-2431; Fax: 702-361-3772.

2—OUR LADY OF WISDOM ITALO-GREEK (1993), Rev. Francis Vivona, J.C.L.; Deacon Stephen Casmus.
Church: 2120 Lindell Rd., NV 89146. Tel: 702-873-5101; Fax: 702-873-5104.

STATE OF NEW MEXICO

ALBUQUERQUE, BERNALILLO CO., OUR LADY OF PERPETUAL HELP (1974), Rev. Christopher L. Zugger; Deacon Gerald Sondergaard.
Church: 1837 Alvarado Dr., N.E., NM 87110. Tel: 505-256-1539; 505-256-1787 (Res.); Fax: 505-256-1278.
Catechesis/Religious Program—1838 Palomas N.E., NM 87110.

LAS CRUCES, DONA ANA CO., BYZANTINE CATHOLIC MISSION, Closed., Records are located at Albuquerque Parish.

STATE OF OREGON

PORTLAND, MULTNOMAH CO., ST. IRENE BYZANTINE CATHOLIC CHURCH, Rev. Kurt Burnette, Admin.
Mailing Address: 8261 S.E. Clatsop, OR 97266. Tel: 503-777-1814.
Church: 4630 N. Maryland Ave., OR 97217.

STATE OF UTAH

SALT LAKE CITY, SALT LAKE CO., BYZANTINE CATHOLIC MISSION, Closed. For inquiries for parish records contact the chancery.

STATE OF WASHINGTON

OLYMPIA, THURSTON CO., ST. GEORGE BYZANTINE (1989), Rev. Ashley Perry, S.S.J., Admin.; Deacon Joseph Wargacki.
Res.: 9730 Yelm Hwy., WA 98513. Tel: 360-413-5651.

SEATTLE, KING CO., ST. JOHN CHRYSOSTOM (1981), Rev. Joseph Stanichar, Pastor.
Res.: 1305 S. Lander St., WA 98144-5038. Tel: 206-329-9219; Fax: 206-322-6930.

SPOKANE, SPOKANE CO., SS. CYRIL & METHODIUS (1979), Rev. William O'Brien.
Mailing Address: P.O. Box 15314, WA 99215-5314.
Res.: 4315 N. Evergreen Rd., WA 99216-1298. Tel: 509-922-4527.

WALLA WALLA, WALLA WALLA CO., BYZANTINE CATHOLIC MISSION, Closed., For inquiries for parish records contact the Spokane parish.

On Special Assignment:
Revs.—
Kovach, John, St. Mary Magdalene, 5390 W. 220 St., Fairview Park, OH 44126.
Michalenko, Alexei, Chap., Georgetown Law Center, 600 New Jersey Ave., N.W., Washington, DC 20001.

On Leave:
Revs.—
Barrand, James
Greskowiak, Stephen

Retired:
Revs.—
Dorich, John M., 8141 N. 16th St., #2, 85020-3999.
Ridella, Joseph, 66295 Hacienda Ave., Desert Hot Springs, CA 92240.

Permanent Deacons:
Bodnar, Andrew, Denver, CO
Casmus, Stephen, Las Vegas, NV
Hess, David, San Diego, CA
Hladky, Michael, (Retired)
Milazzo, Michael, Tucson, AZ
Montalvo, John, III, Phoenix, AZ
Sondergaard, Gerald, Albuquerque, NM
Wargacki, Joseph, Olympia, WA

INSTITUTIONS LOCATED IN THE DIOCESE

[A] RELIGIOUS COMMUNITIES

PHOENIX. *Congregation of Saint Basil*, 8141 N. 16th St., #22, 85020-3901. Tel: 602-395-0457; Fax: 602-257-5646. Revs. Philip A. Acquaro, C.S.B., J.C.L.. Email: frphil@diocesephoenix.org; Paul F. O'Connor, C.S.B.

St. Stephen Convent, 8141 N. 16th St., #27, 85020. Tel: 602-944-5121; Fax: 602-861-9796. Sisters Christopher Malcovsky, O.S.B.M.; Celestine Petruska, O.S.B.M.; Joanne Lickvar, O.S.B.M.

NEWBERRY SPRINGS. *Holy Resurrection Monastery* (Monastic Community of Men est. Aug. 4, 1995) , 45704 Valley Center Rd., P.O. Box 130, CA 92365. Tel: 760-257-4008; Fax: 760-257-3362. Email: holyresurrection@mscomm.com. Web: www.hrmonline.org. Rev. Nicholas Zachariadis, Hegumen.
Monks: Bros. Maximos Davies, Protos; Basil Doty; Moses Wright.

RAMONA. *Good Shepherd Monastery* (Monastic Community of Men est. Oct. 1, 1998) , P.O. Box 251, Santa Ysabel, CA 92070. Tel: 760-782-9232. Email: goodshepherdmonastery@mail.com. 26922 Mesa Grande Rd., Santa Ysabel, CA 92070. Rev. Jon Jensen-Rieser, Supr.; Bros. Francisco Gallegos Marin; Jorge Ortega Cordova.

REDLANDS. *Byzantine Brothers of St. Francis*, 9458 Buckeye St., CA 92374. Tel: 909-793-1127. Email: brmike_7@msn.com. Bros. Michael Sullivan, B.B.S.F., Supr.; John Gray, B.B.S.F., Treas.

[B] RETIREMENT HOMES

PHOENIX. *St. Stephen Senior Citizen Apartments*, 8141 N. 16th St., 85020. Tel: 602-943-5379. Sr. Christopher Malcovsky, O.S.B.M., Contact Person.

RELIGIOUS INSTITUTES OF MEN REPRESENTED IN THE DIOCESE

For further details refer to the corresponding bracketed number in the Religious Institutes of Men or Women section.

[0170]—*Basilian Fathers*—C.S.B.
[]—*Byzantine Brothers of St. Francis*—B.B.S.F.
[1080]—*Congregation of the Resurrection*—C.R.
[0520]—*Franciscan Friars*—O.F.M.
[1190]—*Salesians of Don Bosco*—S.D.B.
[0700]—*Society of St. Joseph*—S.S.J.

RELIGIOUS INSTITUTES OF WOMEN REPRESENTED IN THE DIOCESE

[3730]—*Sisters of the Order of St. Basil the Great*—O.S.B.M.

NECROLOGY

(No Deaths)

Archdiocese of Agana

Most Reverend

ANTHONY SABLAN APURON, O.F.M.CAP., D.D.

Archbishop of Agana; ordained August 26, 1972; appointed Auxiliary Bishop December 8, 1983; ordained Titular Bishop of Muzuca February 19, 1984; appointed Apostolic Administrator to the Archdiocese October 27, 1985; succeeded to Metropolitan See May 11, 1986 *Res.: Archbishop's Residence*, 196-B Cuesta San Ramon, Agana, GU 96910. Tel: 671-472-6116; 671-472-6573; Fax: 671-477-3519.

Erected by Pope Pius X, March 1, 1911 and Committed to the Order of Friars Minor Capuchin. Extended to all the Marianas Islands, July 4, 1946, Wake Island, June 14, 1948. Elevated to a Diocese, October 14, 1965, as a Suffragan of San Francisco. Elevated to Metropolitan Archdiocese, May 20, 1984 with a Suffragan See, Diocese of Caroline-Marshalls and Diocese of Chalan Kanoa (subsequently added January 13, 1985). Member of CEPAC Conference. Member of Federation of Catholic Bishops Conference of Oceania. Observer to NCCB-USCC Conference.

Guam is a Territory of the U.S.A. by Act of the U.S. Congress July 21, 1949.

Legal Title: Archbishop of Agana, a Corporation Sole.

STATISTICAL OVERVIEW

Personnel	
Archbishops	1
Priests: Diocesan Active in Diocese	30
Priests: Diocesan Active Outside Diocese	2
Priests: Retired, Sick or Absent	3
Number of Diocesan Priests	35
Religious Priests in Diocese	13
Total Priests in Diocese	48
Ordinations:	
Diocesan Priests	1
Permanent Deacons	12
Permanent Deacons in Diocese	19
Total Brothers	2
Total Sisters	101
Parishes	
Parishes	24
With Resident Pastor:	
Resident Diocesan Priests	17
Resident Religious Priests	7
Welfare	
Homes for the Aged	1
Total Assisted	59
Day Care Centers	3
Total Assisted	408
Special Centers for Social Services	1
Total Assisted	12,760
Educational	
Seminaries, Diocesan	1
Students from This Diocese	15
Diocesan Students in Other Seminaries	1
Students Religious	1
Total Seminarians	17
High Schools, Diocesan and Parish	2
Total Students	791
High Schools, Private	1
Total Students	339
Elementary Schools, Diocesan and Parish	11
Total Students	2,385
Catechesis/Religious Education:	
High School Students	1,672
Elementary Students	3,081
Total Students under Catholic Instruction	8,285
Teachers in the Diocese:	
Brothers	1
Sisters	22
Lay Teachers	187
Vital Statistics	
Receptions into the Church:	
Infant Baptism Totals	1,631
Adult Baptism Totals	33
Received into Full Communion	91
First Communions	1,106
Confirmations	677
Marriages:	
Catholic	192
Interfaith	3
Total Marriages	195
Deaths	454
Total Catholic Population	131,430
Total Population	154,623

Former Vicars-Apostolic—Most Revs. FRANCIS X. VILLA Y MATEU, O.F.M.Cap., D.D., consecrated Titular Bishop of Adraha, Oct. 1, 1911; died at Agana, Jan. 1, 1913; AUGUSTIN BERNAUS Y SERRA, O.F.M.Cap., D.D., consecrated Titular Bishop of Milopotamo, May 9, 1913; transferred to Vicariate-Apostolic of Bluefields, Nicaragua, 1914; JOAQUIN FELIPE OLAIZ Y ZABALZA, O.F.M.Cap., D.D., consecrated Titular Bishop of Docimeo, Nov. 30, 1914; died at Pamplona, Spain, Dec. 8, 1945; MIGUEL ANGEL OLANO Y URTEAGA, O.F.M.Cap., D.D., consecrated Titular Bishop of Lagina, May 5, 1935; resigned and made Asst. at Pontifical Throne Aug. 20, 1945; died at Agana, Guam May 21, 1970; APOLLINARIS W. BAUMGARTNER, O.F.M.Cap., D.D., consecrated Sept. 18, 1945; appt. First Bishop of Agana, Oct. 14, 1965; died at Agana, Guam Dec. 18, 1970; FELIXBERTO CAMACHO FLORES, ord. April 30, 1949; appt. Apostolic Admin., Diocese of Agana, May 2, 1969; appt. Titular Bishop of Stonj, March 19, 1970; consecrated May 17, 1970; succeeded to See, May 15, 1971; died Oct. 25, 1985.

Chancery Office—196 B Cuesta San Ramon, Hagatna, 96910. Tel: 671-472-6116; 671-472-6573; Fax: 671-477-3519. Office Hours: Mon.-Fri. 8-12 & 1-4

Moderator of the Curia and Vicar General—Rev. DAVID C. QUITUGUA, J.C.D.

Chancellor—Rev. ADRIAN L.F. CRISTOBAL.

Finance Officer and Business Mgr.—Mr. JOSEPH T. DUENAS.

Archdiocesan College of Consultors—Revs. DAVID C. QUITUGUA, J.C.D.; ADRIAN L.F. CRISTOBAL; Very Rev. ERIC FORBES, O.F.M.Cap.; Revs. KENNETH HEZEL, S.J.; RAY CEPEDA, J.C.L.; JAMES L.G. BENAVENTE.

Archdiocesan Finance Council—Revs. DAVID C. QUITUGA, J.C.D.; JAMES L.G. BENAVENTE; Mr. JOSEPH T. DUENAS; RICHARD UNTALAN, Pres.; Mr. JOSEPH RIVERA; Sr. MARY STEPHEN TORRES, R.S.M.

Archdiocesan Presbyteral Council—Revs. DAVID C. QUITUGUA, J.C.D.; ADRIAN L.F. CRISTOBAL; Very Rev. ERIC FORBES, O.F.M.Cap.; Revs. KENNETH HEZEL, S.J.; JAMES L.G. BENAVENTE; DAVID I.A. QUITUGUA; JOSEPH ENGLISH, O.F.M.Cap.; AGUSTIN GUMATAOTAO, O.F.M.Cap.; RAY CEPEDA, J.C.L.; PATRICK CASTRO, O.F.M.Cap.; BRIGIDO ARROYO.

Metropolitan Tribunal—

Judicial Vicar—Rev. DAVID C. QUITUGUA, J.C.D.

Promoter of Justice—Rev. JOSE VILLAGOMEZ, O.F.M.Cap.

Defender of the Bond—Rev. CARLOS S. VILA, J.C.L.

Associate Judges—Rev. Msgr. ZOILO CAMACHO; Rev. RAYMOND F. CEPEDA, J.C.L.; Sr. LEE, O.P., J.C.L.

Advocate—Rev. JAMES L.G. BENAVENTE.

Notary—Rev. FELIXBERTO LEON GUERRERO, O.F.M.Cap.

Chancery Records Department—Mrs. JUNE UNGACTA.

Computer Systems—MANNY CRUZ.

Catholic Schools Office—Ms. LEA SANTOS, Supt.; Sr. ANA LEE, O.P., Assoc. Supt.

Division of Pastoral Ministries—Sr. MARIAN ARROYO, R.S.M., Exec. Dir. Tel: 671-472-5116; Fax: 671-472-4406.

Office of Faith Formation—CONNIE P. GUERRERO, Dir.

Office of Family and Youth Ministry—CONNIE P. GUERRERO, Dir.

Office of Pastoral Planning—Sr. MARIAN ARROYO, R.S.M., Dir.

Office of Worship—Sr. MARIAN ARROYO, R.S.M., Dir.

Office of Communications—Mr. TONY DIAZ, Dir., 196 B Cuesta San Ramon, Hagatna, 96910. Tel: 671-472-6427; Fax: 671-477-5656.

Catholic Educational Radio, KOLG—196 B Cuesta San Ramon, Hagatna, 96910. Tel: 671-477-5654; Fax: 671-477-5656.

Pacific Voice—Mr. TONY DIAZ, Editor, 193 B Cuesta San Ramon, Hagatna, 96910. Tel: 671-472-6427; Fax: 671-477-5224. Email: pacvoice@ite.net.

Other Archdiocesan Pastoral Offices and Directors

Catholic Campus Ministry, Newman Center, University of Guam—VACANT, Dir., P.O. Box 23142, GMF Barrigada, 96921. Tel: 671-734-3507; Fax: 671-734-2943.

Catholic Cemetery Office—Rev. JAMES L.G. BENAVENTE, Dir., 196 B Cuesta San Ramon, Hagatna, 96910. Tel: 671-472-6201; Fax: 671-472-1729.

Office of Vocations—Rev. ADRIAN L.F. CRISTOBAL, Dir. Tel: 671-472-6116; Fax: 671-477-3519.

Associations and Charitable Organizations in the Archdiocese

Alee Shelter Program for Spousal Abuse—Sr. BRIGID PEREZ, R.S.M., Dir., c/o Catholic Social Service, 234-A US Army Juan C. Fejeran St., Barrigada, 96913. Tel: 671-635-1409; Fax: 671-635-1444.

Catholic Charities Appeal—Rev. ADRIAN L.F. CRISTOBAL, Chm., 196 B Cuesta San Ramon, Hagatna, 96910. Tel: 671-472-6116; Fax: 671-477-3519.

Catholic Pro-Life Committee—

Gentle Refuge Crisis Pregnancy Center—

Project Rachel (Abortion Aftermath Counseling)—Deacon FRANCISCO TENORIO, Exec. Dir., P.O. Box 23006, GMF, 96921. Tel: 671-477-1724.

Catholic Social Service—Mrs. CERILA RAPADAS, Exec. Dir.; Sr. CALLISTA CAMACHO, R.S.M., Deputy Dir., 234-A US Army Juan C. Fejeran St., Barrigada, 96913. Tel: 671-635-1410; Fax: 671-635-1444. Email: css@kuentos.guam.net. Web: www.css.org.

Kamalen Karidat—Deacon FRANCISCO TENORIO, Gen. Mgr., P.O. Box 23006, GMF, 96921. Tai Thrift Shop. Tel: 671-734-2479. Quality Thrift Shop. Tel: 671-734-2483. Kusinan Kamalen Karidad. Tel: 671-472-6068.

Pontifical Holy Childhood Association & Pontifical Society for the Propagation of the Faith—Rev. DAVID C. QUITUGUA, J.C.D., Contact Person, 196 B Cuesta San Ramon, Hagatna, 96910. Tel: 671-472-6116; 671-472-6573; Fax: 671-477-3519.

Groups, Ecclesial Movements and other Organizations in the Archdiocese

Catholic Daughters of the Americas—Rev. BRIGIDO ARROYO, Chap., P.O. Box 7707, Tamuning, 96931. Tel: 671-646-7181.

Court 2047, Our Lady of Camarin—Mrs. MAE QUINATA, Regent.

Court 2450, Maria Rainan I Familia—Mrs. JULIE BLAZ, Regent.

Confraternity of Christian Mothers—Rev. FELIXBERTO LEON GUERRERO, O.F.M.Cap., Spiritual Dir.; Mrs. MAE QUINATA, Island Bd. Pres., c/o St. Fidelis Friary, 135 Chalan Kapuchino, Agana Heights, 96910.

United Catholic Charismatic Community—

Catholic Covenant Community—CARLOS SAN AGUSTIN. Tel: 671-477-9118.

Cell Prayer Community—ROQUE MENDIOLA.

El Shaddai DWXII, Prayer Partner International, Guam Chapter—IGNACIO MERCADO. Tel: 671-632-5659.

Our Lady of Lourdes Catholic Charismatic Group—LINDA ESTRELLA. Tel: 671-653-2584.

Worship and Praise—FLO SANCHEZ. Tel: 671-646-8044.

Cursillo in Christianity—Rev. JOEL DELOS REYES, Spiritual Dir., c/o 229 San Roke St., Barrigada, 96913. Tel: 671-734-4573; Fax: 671-734-5858; Mr. JOHN CONCEPCION, Pres.

Evenings for the Engaged—Coordinators: FRANCIS GUERRERO; CONNIE GUERRERO, 229 San Roke St., Barrigada, 96913. Tel: 671-734-4573; Fax: 671-734-5858.

Knights of Columbus—Sir Knight ART SALOME, State Deputy; Sir Knight BERT UNPINGCO, Master of the 4th Degree. Tel: 671-472-8725 Pale' San Vitores Council, No. 5666; Mr. EDWIN CARBONEL, P.O. Box 1252, Tamuning, 96911; Most Rev. ANTHONY SABLAN APURON, O.F.M.Cap., D.D., State Chaplain.

Knights of St. Gregory the Great—Sir Knight CRISTOBAL DUENAS.

Knights of St. Sylvester—Sir Knights CRISTOBAL DUENAS; FRANK CRUZ; PEDRO M. CAMACHO; RICHARD UNTALAN; FRANK SANTOS.

Legion of Mary—Rev. DAVID C. QUITUGUA, J.C.D., Spiritual Dir.; Mrs. JUANITA ULLOA, Pres., 196 B Cuesta San Ramon, Hagatna, 96910. Tel: 671-472-6116; 671-472-6573; Fax: 671-477-3519.

Marriage Encounter—Coordinators: RAY HERNANDEZ; JOSEPHINE HERNANDEZ, L.S.C.S.W., 196 B Cuesta San Ramon, Hagatna, 96910. Tel: 671-472-6116; 671-472-6573; Fax: 671-477-3519.

Neo Catechumenal Way— Dulce Nombre de Maria Cathedral-Basilica; Most Rev. ANTHONY SABLAN APURON, O.F.M.Cap., D.D., 207 Archbishop Flores St., Agana, 96910. Tel: 671-472-6201; Fax: 671-472-1729. San Vicente Ferrer Parish: Rev. ADRIAN CRISTOBAL, Presbyter, 229 San Roke St., Barrigada, 96913. Tel: 671-734-4573; Fax: 671-734-5858. Saint Anthony Parish: Rev. BRIGIDO ARROYO, Presbyter, P.O. Box 7707, Tamuning, 96931. Tel: 671-646-8044; Fax: 671-649-1039. Our Lady of Lourdes Parish: Rev. JEFFREY SAN NICOLAS, Presbyter, P.O. Box 11001, Yigo, 96929. Tel: 671-653-2584; Fax: 671-653-4746. Nino Perdido Parish (Asan): Rev. RUDOLFO AREJOLA, Presbyter, P.O. Box 45, Agana, 96910. Tel: 671-477-2211.

Secular Franciscans (Third Order)—Rev. DANIEL CRISTOBAL, O.F.M.Cap., Spiritual Dir.; Mrs. CARMEN MANIBUSAN, Pres., 135 Chalan Kapuchino, Agana Heights, 96910.

Sponsor Couple Program—

Natural Family Planning Program—CONNIE GUERRERO, Coord., 196 B Cuesta San Ramon, Hagatna, 96910. Tel: 671-472-6116; 671-472-6573; Fax: 671-477-3519.

CLERGY, PARISHES, MISSIONS AND PAROCHIAL SCHOOLS

CITY OF AGANA
ISLAND OF GUAM

1—DULCE NOMBRE DE MARIA CATHEDRAL - BASILICA (1669), Most Rev. Anthony Sablan Apuron, O.F.M.Cap., D.D., Pastor; Revs. James L.G. Benavente, Rector; David C. Quitugua, J.C.D.; Thomas B. McGrath, S.J.; Domingo-James B. Bejer, S.S.J.; Deacons John Dierking; Ronald San Nicolas.
Res.: 207 Archbishop Felixberto C. Flores St., 96910. Tel: 671-472-6201; 671-477-1842; Fax: 671-472-1729.
Catechesis / Religious Program—Students 110.

2—ST. ANDREW KIM (1998), (Korean),, Under the Jurisdiction of Santa Barbara Parish, Dededo. , Mailing Address: P.O. Box 1555, 96910. Tel: 671-637-4148; Fax: 671-637-4149.

OUTSIDE THE CITY OF AGANA

AGANA HEIGHTS, OUR LADY OF THE BLESSED SACRAMENT (1948), Rev. Michael Tenorio, O.F.M.Cap.
Res.: 135 Chalan Kapuchino, 96919. Tel: 671-472-6246.
Catechesis / Religious Program—Eleanor Cruz, D.R.E. Students 260.

AGAT, OUR LADY OF MOUNT CARMEL (1957), [CEM] Revs. Jose Villagomez, O.F.M.Cap.; Agustin Gumataotao, O.F.M.Cap.; Randy Nowak, O.F.M.Cap.
Res.: 135 Chalan Kapuchino, Agana Heights, 96910. Tel: 671-565-2136; Fax: 671-565-9678.
Catechesis / Religious Program—Tel: 671-565-9676. Students 241.

ASAN, HOLY FAMILY, NINO PERDIDO, Rev. Rodolfo Arejola.
Res.: P.O. Box 45, 96932. Tel: 671-477-2211; Fax: 671-477-1510.
Catechesis / Religious Program—Students 100.

BARRIGADA, SAN VICENTE FERRER (1947), Rev. Msgr. Domingo Tanalgo (Philippines); Revs. Adrian F. Cristobal; Joel de los Reyes (Philippines); Mariano Garrido (Philippines).
Res.: 229 San Roke St., 96913. Tel: 671-734-4573; Fax: 671-734-5858.
Catechesis / Religious Program—Sr. Mary Gertrude Quitugua, R.S.M., D.R.E. Students 352.

CHALAN PAGO, NUESTRA SENORA DE LA PAZ Y BUEN VIAJE (1945), Rev. Vito B. San Andres.
Res.: 135 Chalan Kapuchino, Agana Heights, 96910. Tel: 671-734-3723; Fax: 671-734-3722.
Catechesis / Religious Program—Tel: 671-734-4223. Students 110.

DEDEDO, SANTA BARBARA (1947), Rev. Raymond F. Cepeda, J.C.L.; Rev. Msgr. Zoilo L.G. Camacho, Pastor Emeritus (Retired); Revs. Joseph Anore; James McDonough; Tony Camora; Edgar Momay; Deacons Ramon Diaz; Herbert Cruz; Peter L. Kaai.
Res.: 3372 Gloria Cir., 96929. Tel: 671-632-5659; 671-632-9534; Fax: 617-632-1713.
Catechesis / Religious Program—Vangie Cepeda, D.R.E.; Ann Tydingco, D.R.E.; Virginia Avaricio, D.R.E.; Cristeta Deliquina, D.R.E.; Leslie Gonzales, D.R.E. Students 1,131.

INARAJAN, ST. JOSEPH (1680), (Chamorro), [CEM] Rev. Manuel Ombao.
Res.: P.O. Box 170022, 96917. Tel: 671-828-8102; Fax: 671-828-7062.
Catechesis / Religious Program—Students 206.

MAINA, OUR LADY OF THE PURIFICATION (1949), Rev. Simeon Balmeo.
Res.: P.O. Box 4477, 96910. Tel: 671-477-7256; Fax: 671-477-0221.
Catechesis / Religious Program—Students 33.

MALOJLO, SAN ISIDRO (1977), [JC] Rev. Manuel Trenchera Jr.
Res.: HCR Box 17083, Inarajan, 96917. Tel: 671-828-8454; Fax: 671-828-8455.
Catechesis / Religious Program—Students 118.

MANGILAO, SANTA TERESITA (1951), Rev. Felixberto C. Leon Guerrero, O.F.M.Cap.
Res.: 192 Vietnam Veteran's Hwy., 96910. Tel: 671-734-2171; 671-734-2100.
Catechesis / Religious Program—Students 651.

MERIZO, SAN DIMAS AND OUR LADY OF THE ROSARY (1680), (Chamorro), [CEM] Rev. Michael Crisostomo; Deacon Jeff Barcinas.
Res.: P.O. Box 6099, 96916. Tel: 671-828-8056; Fax: 671-828-3100.
Catechesis / Religious Program—Students 268.

MONGMONG, NUESTRA SENORA DE LAS AQUAS (1969), Rev. Manuel Trenchera Jr.
Res.: P.O. Box 163, 96932. Tel: 671-477-6754; Fax: 671-477-3766.
Catechesis / Religious Program—Tel: 671-477-3422. Maria Rosario L.G. Perez, D.R.E. Students 127.

ORDOT, SAN JUAN BAUTISTA (1947), (Chamorro), Revs. David I.A. Quitugua; Danilo C. Bien (Philippines).
Res.: P.O. Box 49, 96910. Tel: 671-472-8341; Fax: 671-472-2324.
Catechesis / Religious Program—Students 134.

PITI, ASSUMPTION OF OUR LADY (1930), (Chamorro), Rev. Wilfredo Lorilla.
Mailing Address: 314 Assumption Dr., 96925. Tel: 671-472-2272; Fax: 671-477-1955.
Res.: 96910. Tel: 671-472-2272; Fax: 671-477-1955.
Catechesis / Religious Program—Students 124.

SANTA RITA, OUR LADY OF GUADALUPE (1944), Rev. Agustin Gumataotao, O.F.M.Cap.; Deacon Anthony Leon Guerrero.
Res.: P.O. Box 4632, 96910. Tel: 671-565-2160; Fax: 671-565-7078.
Catechesis / Religious Program—Mrs. Cecilia Cruz, D.R.E. Students 405.

SINAJANA, SAINT JUDE THADDEUS (1962), Rev. Robert Phelps, O.F.M.Cap.
Church & St. Jude Rectory: 122 Avenida Bien Venida, 96910. Tel: 671-475-6530; Fax: 671-477-5353.
Catechesis / Religious Program—John Blasczcek, D.R.E. Students 450.

TALOFOFO, SAN MIGUEL (1945), (Chamorro), Rev. Daniel Cristobal, O.F.M.Cap.
Res.: 71 San Miguel St., 96930. Tel: 671-789-1069; Fax: 671-789-7665.
Catechesis / Religious Program—Tel: 671-789-0130. Marie E. Meno, D.R.E.; Goring Duenas, D.R.E. Students 259.

TAMUNING, ST. ANTHONY AND ST. VICTOR (1946), Revs. Brigido U. Arroyo; James Ch'e; Jorge Carao (Philippines); Carlos S. Vila, J.C.L. (Philippines); Deacon Mario L. Celis. In Res., Revs. Antonio Bobis (Philippines); Jovito Cordero (Philippines).
Res.: P.O. Box 7707, 96931. Tel: 671-646-7181; 671-646-8044; Fax: 671-646-1039.
Catechesis / Religious Program—Students 290.

TOTO, IMMACULATE HEART OF MARY (1948), Rev. Alfonso Asis; Deacon Jose Santos.
Res.: P.O. Box 2552, 96910. Tel: 671-477-9118; Fax: 671-472-2514.
Catechesis / Religious Program—Tel: 671-472-6754. Students 96.

TUMON BAY, BLESSED DIEGO LUIS DE SAN VITORES CHURCH (1970), Rev. Jose Antonio P. Abad, Pastor; Deacons William Hagen; Jeff Barcinas.
Res.: 884 Pale' San Vitores Rd., 96913-4013. Tel: 671-646-5649; Fax: 671-649-6887.
Catechesis / Religious Program—Students 137.

UMATAC, SAN DIONISIO (1680), (Chamorro), [CEM] Rev. Michael Crisostomo.
Res.: P.O. Box 6099, Merizo, 96915. Tel: 671-828-8056; Fax: 671-828-3100.
Catechesis / Religious Program—Students 123.

YIGO, OUR LADY OF LOURDES (1947), Revs. Jeffrey C. San Nicolas; William G. Ybanez; Deacons Fred Otte; Len Stohr; David Richards.
Res.: P.O. Box 11001, 96929. Tel: 671-653-2584; Fax: 671-653-4746.
Catechesis / Religious Program—Tel: 671-653-1102. Femy Castro, D.R.E.; Thelma Lumbre, D.R.E.; Veronica Lizama, Coord.; Glenda Luke, Coord.; Josephine Perez, Coord. Students 769.
Mission—Santa Bernadita Mission Chapel Sta. Bernadita Dr., Agafa Gumas, 96929.

YONA, SAN FRANCISCO D'ASSISI (1954), [CEM] Rev. Patrick Castro, O.F.M.Cap.
San Fidelis Friary: 135 Chalan Kapuchino, Agana Heights, 96910. Tel: 671-789-1491; 671-789-1492; Fax: 671-789-1400; 671-789-1404.
Catechesis / Religious Program—Josephine L.G. Santos, D.R.E. Students 396.

On Duty Outside the Archdiocese:
Revs.—
Adversario, Efren, Military Chap., U.S. AF
Perez, Antonio, St. Mary's Seminary, Baltimore, MD

Retired:
Rev. Msgr.—
Camacho, Zoilo L.G., 315 W. Santa Barbara Ave., Dededo, 96912. Tel: 671-632-5659
Rev.—
Brouillard, Louis A., 525 9th St., Pine City, MN 55063.

Permanent Deacons:
Agbulos, Louis T., Jr.
Barcinas, Jeff
Barcinas, Joseph
Borja, Eddie A.
Celis, Mario
Claros, Larry
Cruz, Herbert
Diaz, Ramon
Dierking, John
Hagen, William
Kaai, Peter L.
Leon Guerrero, Anthony
Martinez, Steve
Otte, Fred
Rama, Louis
Richards, David
Ruda, Itoi
San Nicolas, Ronald
Santos, Jose
Stohr, Leonard
Tenorio, Francisco

INSTITUTIONS LOCATED IN THE ARCHDIOCESE

[A] SEMINARIES

YONA. *Redemptoris Mater Archdiocesan Missionary Seminary*, 130 Chalan Seminariu, 96915. Tel: 671-789-2400; Fax: 671-789-2800. Email: rmsguam@ite.net. Web: www.seminaryguam.com. Rev. James E. Starasinich (NEW), Rector. Seminarians 22.

[B] HIGH SCHOOLS

AGANA. *Academy of Our Lady of Guam*, 233 W.

Archbishop Felixberto C. Flores St., 96910. Tel: 671-477-8203; Fax: 671-477-8555. Email: acad@aolg.edu.gu. Web: www.aolg.edu.gu. Sr. Francis Jerome Cruz, R.S.M., Prin. Sisters of Mercy Sisters 2; Lay Teachers 24; Staff 12; Students 406.

HAGATNA. *The Father Duenas Memorial School*, P.O. Box FD, 96932. Tel: 671-734-2261; 671-734-2263; Fax: 671-734-5738. Email: fdms2@ite.net. Web: www.fatherduenas.com. Mr. William Roth, Prin. Sisters 1; Lay Teachers 23; Students 362.

TALOFOFO. *Notre Dame High School*, 480 S. San Miguel St., 96915-3540. Tel: 671-789-1676; 671-789-1745; Fax: 671-789-4847. Email: ndhs@netpci.com. Sr. Regina Paulino, S.S.N.D., Ed.D., Pres.; Pilar Perez Williams, Prin. Sisters 2; Lay Teachers 16; Students 250.

[C] ELEMENTARY AND JUNIOR HIGH SCHOOLS

AGAT. *Our Lady of Mt. Carmel School*, P.O. Box 7830, 96928. Tel: 671-565-5128; Fax: 671-565-3539. Email: mtcarmel@ite.net. Sr. Regina Paulino, S.S.N.D., Ed.D., Prin. Sisters 3; Lay Teachers 9; Students 84.

BARRIGADA. *San Vicente School*, 196 Bejong St., 96913. Tel: 671-735-4240; Fax: 671-734-8718; 735-424-. Email: svc-braces@netpci.com. Web: www.geocities.com/sanvicentebraves2000/index.htm. Sr. Mary Juan Camacho, S.S.N.D., Prin. Sisters 2; Lay Teachers 18; Students 245.

DEDEDO. *Santa Barbara School*, 274-A W. Santa Barbara Ave., 96929. Tel: 671-632-2789; Fax: 671-632-1414. Email: info@sbs.edu.gu. Web: www.sbs.edu.gu. 274-B W. Santa Barbara Ave., 96929-5308. Sr. Jeanette Marie Pangelinan, R.S.M., Prin. Sisters 4; Lay Teachers 32; Students 435.

GMF. *St. Francis School*, P.O. Box 22199, 96921. Tel: 671-789-1270; 671-789-1350; Fax: 671-789-3900. Email: sfcsyona@ite.net. Web: www.sfguam.com. Sr. Marcia Nededog, S.S.N.D., Prin. Sisters 3; Lay Teachers 12; Students 212.

SINAJANA. *Bishop Baumgartner Memorial School*, 281 Calle Angel Flores St., 96910. Tel: 671-472-6670; 671-477-2677; 671-477-4010; 671-477-4003; Fax: 671-477-4028; 671-477-9256. Email: mcharlesc@bbms.edu.gu. Web: www.bbms.edu.gu. Sr. Mary Charles Cameron, R.S.M., Pres.; Mrs. Rita Duenas, Prin.; Sr. Elizabeth Ann Uncangco, R.S.M., Vice Prin. Cathedral Grade School merged with Bishop Baumgartner Middle School to form Bishop Baumgartner Memorial School. Sisters 5; Lay Teachers 32; Students 625.

TAMUNING. *Saint Anthony School*, 529 Chalan San Antonio, 96911. Tel: 671-647-1140; Fax: 671-649-7130. Email: sasadm@ite.net. Web: www.stanthonyschoolguam.org. Sr. Doris San Agustin, R.S.M., Prin. Sisters 3; Lay Teachers 39; Students 544.

YIGO. *Dominican School*, 114 Chalan Pale Ramon-Lagu, Rte. 1, 96929. Tel: 671-653-3021; Fax: 671-653-3090. Sr. Zenaida Ancheta, O.P., Prin. Sisters 6; Lay Teachers 14; Students 175.

[D] KINDERGARTEN AND NURSERY SCHOOLS

AGANA HEIGHTS. *Maria Artero Catholic Preschool & Kindergarten*, 161 A Sunset Dr., 96919. Tel: 671-472-8777; Fax: 671-472-2326. Email: manprinc@ite.net. Sr. Katherine E. Bromwell, M.M.B., Prin. Sisters 3; Lay Teachers 3; Students 64.

ORDOT. *Dominican Child Development Center*, P.O. Box 5668, 96932. Tel: 671-477-7228; 671-472-1524; Fax: 671-472-4282. Email: dcdc@ite.net. Sr. Josefina Manago, O.P., Contact Person. Sisters 4; Lay Teachers 6; Aides 3; Students 68.

PEREZVILLE-TAMUNING. *Mercy Heights Nursery and Kindergarten, Inc.*, 211 San Vitores St., 96913. Tel: 671-646-1185; Fax: 671-649-1822. Sr. Mary Roberta Taitano, R.S.M., Admin. Sisters 2; Lay Teachers 12; Students 172.

TAI. *Infant of Prague Nursery and Kindergarten, Inc.*, P.O. Box 22865, GMF, 96921. Tel: 671-734-2785; Fax: 671-734-2785. Email: sbu@ite.net. Sr. Barbara Ungacta, R.S.M., Admin. Sisters of Mercy Lay Teachers 7; Students 177.

[E] CATHOLIC CHARITIES

BARRIGADA. *Catholic Social Services of Guam*, 234A U.S. Army Juan C. Fejeran St., 96913. Tel: 671-635-1409; Fax: 671-635-1444. Email: css@kuentos.guam.net. Web: www.css.org. Mrs. Cerila Rapadas, Exec. Dir.; Sr. Callista Camacho R.S.M., Deputy Dir. Total Elderly Assisted 3,027; Total Adults Assisted 4,511; Total Children Assisted 5,237; Total Families Assisted 4,927; Total Staff 262.

Alee Shelter Program for Spouse Abuse Sr. Brigid Perez, R.S.M., Dir.

[F] MONASTERIES AND RESIDENCES OF PRIESTS

AGANA HEIGHTS. *St. Fidelis Friary*, 135 Chalan Kapuchino 96910. Tel: 671-472-6339; Fax: 671-472-3335. Web: www.pacificaps.org. Very Rev. Eric Forbes, O.F.M.Cap., Vice Prov., Guardian; Revs. Felix Leon Guerrero, O.F.M.Cap., Councilor; George Maddock, O.F.M.Cap., Councilor; Robert Phelps, O.F.M.Cap.; Jose Villagomez, O.F.M.Cap.; Agustin Gumataotao, O.F.M.Cap.; Randolph Nowak, O.F.M.Cap.; Lee Friel, O.F.M.Cap.; Daniel Cristobal, O.F.M.Cap.; Patrick Castro, O.F.M.Cap.; Joseph English, O.F.M.Cap.; Michael Tenorio, O.F.M.Cap.; Bro. Brian Champoux, O.F.M.Cap. Headquarters of Capuchin Friars (Vice Province, Star of the Sea).

AGAT. *Capuchin Fraternity*, P.O. Box 7787, 96928. Tel: 671-565-2136; Fax: 671-565-9678. Revs Randolph Nowak, O.F.M.Cap., Senior Friar; Jose Villagomez, O.F.M.Cap.; Agustin Gumataotao, O.F.M.Cap.

YIGO. *St. Ignatius of Loyola House of Studies*, P.O. Box 20516, GMF, 96921. Tel: 671-653-5348; Fax: 671-653-6348. Email: sihs@ite.net. Rev. Basilio Dilipiy (CI), Dir. Seminarians 4.

[G] CONVENTS AND RESIDENCES FOR SISTERS

AGANA HEIGHTS. *Mercedarian Missionaries of Berriz*, 161 A Sunset Dr., 96910-6451. Tel: 671-477-8303; Fax: 671-472-2326. Email: mmbm cro@ite.net. P.O. Box 3487, 96932. Sisters Mary Pilar Latasa, M.M.B., Regl. Coord.; Jacintha Marsil, M.M.B., Regl. Vicar; Sinia Paulis, M.M.B., Councilor; Anotia Addy, M.M.B., Local Coord. Sisters 5.

AGAT. *Mt. Carmel Community*, P.O. Box 7705, 96928. Tel: 671-565-2369. Sisters teach at Mt. Carmel Elementary & Jr. High. Sisters 4.

BARRIGADA. *San Vicente Community*, 201 Bejong St., 96913. Tel: 671-734-3010; Fax: 671-734-8718. Email: ssndbarr@ite.net. Sisters teach at San Vicente Elementary, St. Francis School. Sisters 3.

DEDEDO. *Santa Barbara Convent*, 274 B. W. Santa Barbara St., 96929-5308. Tel: 671-632-2384; Fax: 671-632-1414. Email: jmariep@sbs.edu.gu. Web: www.sbs.edu.gu. Institute of the Sisters of Mercy of the Americas, North Carolina Region. Sisters 4.

Kamalin House, P.O. Box 4678, Hagatna, 96932. Tel: 671-637-3211.

HAGATNA. *Sisters of Mercy-Cathedral Mercy Convent*, 221 Archbishop Felixberto C. Flores St., 96910. Tel: 671-477-9291; Fax: 671-477-9293. Email: mercy@aolg.edu.gu. Sisters of Mercy 7.

INARAJAN. *Sisters of Mercy*, c/o St. Joseph Convent, P.O. Box 17211, 96915. Tel: 671-828-8285. Institute of Sisters of Mercy of the Americas, North Carolina Region 3.

MALOJLO. *Discalced Order Of Carmelites Monastery*, P.O. Box 17084, Inarajan, 96915. Tel: 671-828-8280; Fax: 671-828-8972. Email: guam@carmelite-nuns.org. Web: www.stormpages.com/carmelofguam. Sr. Dawn Marie, O.C.D., Prioress. Order of Discalced Carmelites Sisters 10.

ORDOT. *Religious Missionaries of St. Dominic* Tel: 671-477-7228; 671-472-1524; Fax: 671-472-4282. P.O. Box 5668, 96932. Total in Residence 5; Total Staff 5.

PEREZVILLE-TAMUNING. *Mercy Heights Convent*, 211 San Vitores St., 96913. Tel: 671-646-7246; Fax: 671-649-1822. Email: guamrsm@ite.net. Sr. Mary Angela Perez, R.S.M., Guam Region Pres. Administrative Residence and Offices of the Institute of the Sisters of Mercy of the Americas, North Carolina Region.; Sisters in residence teaching and working in Tamuning and Agana. Sisters 17.

SINAJANA. *St. Jude Thaddeus Convent*, P.O. Box 394, Hagatna, 96932. Tel: 671-472-9687; Fax: 671-472-9687. Email: sgamakaka@netpci.com. Franciscan Sisters of Perpetual Adoration

TAI. *Mercy Convent and Formation House*, P.O. Box 22865, Barrigada, 96921. Tel: 671-734-3312; Fax: 671-734-2260. Institute of the Sisters of Mercy of the Americas, North Carolina Region.; Professed Sisters in various Apostolates and Sisters in basic formation. Sisters 12.

TALOFOFO. *Notre Dame Community*, 480 S. San Miguel St., 95915-3540. Tel: 671-789-1629; Fax: 671-789-3810.

S.S.N.D. Regional House, 480 San Miguel St., 96930. Tel: 671-789-7763; 671-789-0501; Fax: 671-789-3810. Email: guamsrjo@ite.net. Sisters 28.

St. Augustine Community Tel: 671-789-5965; Fax: 671-789-3810.

Mother Theresa Tel: 671-789-0501; Fax: 671-789-3810.

Notre Dame Community Tel: 671-789-1629; Fax: 671-789-3810.

Mt. Carmel Community Tel: 671-565-2369. Sr. Joseph Ann Quinene, S.S.N.D., Regl. Leader.

[H] MISCELLANEOUS LISTINGS

AGANA. *Our Lady of the Waters House of Prayer* (Retreat Center) , P.O. Box 163, 96932. Tel: 671-477-3422; Fax: 671-477-3766. Rev. Manuel Trenchera Jr., Dir.

Secular Franciscans, 135 Chalan Kapuchino, 96910. Tel: 671-472-6023; 671-472-6339; Fax: 671-789-7665. Rev. Daniel Cristobal, O.F.M.Cap., Spiritual Dir.; Mrs. Carmen Manibusan, Pres.

Saint Vincent de Paul Society, c/o Santa Teresita Parish, P.O. Box 306, 96910. Tel: 671-734-2100. Mr. John Lizama, Pres. Tel: 671-472-6068.

BARRIGADA. *Saint Dominic's Senior Care Home*, 350 N. Sabana Barrigada Dr., Barrigada Heights, 96913-1262. Tel: 671-632-9370; 671-632-9378; Fax: 671-637-1679. Email: stdom@ite.net. Sr. Emelita Cinco, O.P., Admin. Total in Residence 59; Total Staff 75.

MANGILAO. *Campus Ministry, Newman Center, University of Guam*, Tel: 671-734-3507; Fax: 671-734-2943. Email: info@campusminguam.org. Web: www.campusminguam.org.

RELIGIOUS INSTITUTES OF MEN REPRESENTED IN THE ARCHDIOCESE

For further details refer to the corresponding bracketed number in the Religious Institutes of Men or Women section.

[0470]—*The Capuchin Friars* (Vice Prov. of Mary, Star of the Sea)—O.F.M.Cap.

[0690]—*The Society of Jesus- Jesuit Fathers and Brothers* (N.Y. Prov.)—S.J.

RELIGIOUS INSTITUTES OF WOMEN REPRESENTED IN THE ARCHDIOCESE

[1780]—*Congregation of the Sisters of the Third Order of St. Francis of Perpetual Adoration* (La Crosse, WI)—F.S.P.A.

[0420]—*Discalced Carmelite Nuns*—O.C.D.

[2510]—*Mercedarian Missionaries of Berriz*—M.M.B.

[]—*Order of Saint Benedict*—O.S.B.

[]—*Religious Missionaries of St. Dominic*—O.P.

[2970]—*School Sisters of Notre Dame* (Mequon, WI)—S.S.N.D.

[2575]—*Sisters of Mercy of the Americas* (Belmont, NC)—R.S.M.

NECROLOGY

(No Deaths)

Diocese of Arecibo, Puerto Rico

(Dioecesis Arecibensis)

Most Reverend

INAKI MALLONA TXERTUDI, C.P.

Bishop of Arecibo; ordained March 27, 1956; appointed December 14, 1991; consecrated January 6, 1992; installed January 25, 1992 *Res.: 206 Dr. Salas St., P.O. Box 616, Arecibo, PR 00613.*

The Chancery: 206 Dr. Salas St., P.O. Box 616, Arecibo, PR 00613. Tel: 787-878-3180; Fax: 787-880-2661.

Email: obispado@xsn.net

ESTABLISHED APRIL 30, 1960.

Square Miles 833.

Comprises the mid-northern part of the Island.

STATISTICAL OVERVIEW

Personnel	
Bishop	1
Priests: Diocesan Active in Diocese	61
Priests: Diocesan Active Outside Diocese	8
Priests: Diocesan in Foreign Missions	4
Priests: Retired, Sick or Absent	14
Number of Diocesan Priests	87
Religious Priests in Diocese	44
Total Priests in Diocese	131
Extern Priests in Diocese	14
Ordinations:	
Transitional Deacons	1
Permanent Deacons in Diocese	6
Total Brothers	8
Total Sisters	161
Parishes	
Parishes	59
With Resident Pastor:	
Resident Diocesan Priests	41
Resident Religious Priests	18
Missions	241
Welfare	
Homes for the Aged	4
Total Assisted	352
Residential Care of Children	3
Total Assisted	100
Specialized Homes	1
Total Assisted	23
Special Centers for Social Services	1
Total Assisted	1,697
Educational	
Seminaries, Diocesan	1
Students from This Diocese	3
Diocesan Students in Other Seminaries	5
Total Seminarians	8
Colleges and Universities	1
Total Students	867
High Schools, Diocesan and Parish	9
Total Students	1,337
High Schools, Private	5
Total Students	1,705
Elementary Schools, Diocesan and Parish	9
Total Students	4,356
Elementary Schools, Private	5
Total Students	4,656
Catechesis/Religious Education:	
High School Students	463
Elementary Students	1,449
Total Students under Catholic Instruction	14,541
Teachers in the Diocese:	
Priests	17
Brothers	3
Sisters	30
Lay Teachers	520
Vital Statistics	
Receptions into the Church:	
Infant Baptism Totals	3,994
Adult Baptism Totals	259
First Communions	3,787
Confirmations	2,770
Marriages:	
Catholic	763
Interfaith	45
Total Marriages	808
Deaths	1,740
Total Catholic Population	370,000
Total Population	603,469

Former Bishops—Most Revs. ALFRED F. MENDEZ, C.S.C. (Retired), ord. 1935; consecrated Oct. 28, 1960; retired Jan., 1974; died Jan. 28, 1995; MIGUEL RODRIQUEZ, C.S.S.R., D.D. (Retired), ord. June 22, 1958; appt. Jan. 21, 1974; consecrated March 23, 1974; retired March, 1990; died Aug. 13, 2001.

Secretary to the Bishop—Miss SYLVIA HERNANDEZ.

Chancery Office—206 Dr. Salas St., P.O. Box 616, Arecibo, 00613-0616. Tel: 787-878-3180; 787-878-3110; Fax: 787-880-2661.

Vicar General—Rev. JOSE D. SOBERAL, V.G., P.O. Box 616, Arecibo, 00613. Tel: 787-878-3180; 787-878-3110.

Administrator—Mr. MIGUEL GONZALEZ.

Accountant—CARMEN MERCADO, C.P.A.

Chancellor—Rev. JOSEPH D. SCHRECK, O.F.M.Cap., P.O. Box 616, Arecibo, 00613. Tel: 787-878-3180.

Vice Chancellor & Secretary—Miss SYLVIA VARGAS.

Diocesan Tribunal of Arecibo—Revs. EDWIN MERCADO VIERA, J.C.L., Judicial Vicar & Presiding Judge; JORGE L. VIRELLA SANCHEZ, J.C.L., Official, P.O. Box 143964, Arecibo, 00613. Tel: 787-816-5614; Fax: 787-816-5614.

Promoter of Justice—Rev. GABRIEL MADURO LOPEZ.

Defenders of the Bond—Revs. ALBERTO DIAZ COLON; GABRIEL MADURO; JOSEPH SCHRECK, O.F.M.Cap.

Advocate—Miss SARAH R. LOPEZ ALBERTI.

Notary—Mrs. JOSEPHINE BURGOS.

Secretary—Mrs. LIVIA E. SERRANO.

Vicar of Diocesan Pastoral Affairs—Rev. JOSE D. SOBERAL, V.G.

Diocesan Consultors—Rev. Msgr. FRANCISCO CONCEPCION; Revs. JOSE D. SOBERAL, V.G.; DANIEL FERNANDEZ; ELIAS FERNANDEZ, O.SS.T.; JOSEPH D. SCHRECK, O.F.M.Cap.; EDWIN MERCADO; CARMELO URARTE; VICTOR ROJAS.

Priest's Senate (Consejo Presbiteral)—Rev. Msgr. FRANCISCO CONCEPCION; Revs. JOSE D. SOBERAL, V.G.; EDWIN MERCADO; VICTOR ROJAS; ELIAS FERNANDEZ, O.SS.T.; CARMELO URARTE; DANIEL FERNANDEZ; NEIL MCQUILLAN, C.S.Sp.; JESUS MONREAL, O.Carm.; GILBERTO GARCES; LUIS VELAZQUEZ; TOMAS SANTOS; JORGE VIRELLA; ANGEL DIAZ MARRERO.

Diocesan Offices and Directors

Ayuda Social Movimiento Juan XXIII—MARIA S. SANTIAGO, Coord., P.O. Box 241, Sabana Hoyos, 00688-0241. Tel: 787-881-7141; 787-881-2342; Fax: 787-881-7141. Email: ayudasoc@coqui.net.

Confraternity of Christian Doctrine—Sr. MARIA ELISA GONZALEZ, H.C., 5 Calle Mariano Abril, Box 1151, Arecibo, 00613. Tel: 787-878-8401. Email: catequesis_arecibo@hotmail.com.

Cursillos de Cristiandad—Rev. VICTOR ROJAS, P.O. Box 1826, Arecibo, 00613. Tel: 787-872-2563.

Diocesan Council of Catholic Women—VACANT.

Propagation of Faith—Rev. MANUEL P. CARDENAS, M.N.M.

Holy Childhood—Rev. MANUEL P. CARDENAS, M.N.M.

Director of Youth—Rev. CARLOS E. GRANADOS.

Legion of Mary—VACANT.

Movimiento Familiar Cristiano (CFM)—VACANT.

Prison Services—Rev. ELVIN A. IRIZARRY, Box 775, Vega Alta, Vega Alta, 00692. Tel: 787-878-4910.

Seminario Jesus Maestro College Seminary—Rev. DANIEL FERNANDEZ, Dir., Box 2164, Arecibo, 00613. Tel: 787-878-1528.

Seminary Board—Rev. JORGE L. VIRELLA.

Pastoral Vocational Program—Revs. DANIEL FERNANDEZ; CARLOS E. GRANADOS; RAMON OLIVENCIA; VICTOR ROJAS; ROBERTO VEGA.

Superintendent of Schools—Miss LYDIA HERNANDEZ; Mrs. TRINIDAD GONZALEZ, Sec., P.O. Box 1683, Arecibo, 00613. Tel: 787-878-1095; Fax: 787-878-1095.

Promotion of Human Development Office—

Catholic Charities—Sisters ROBERTA GRZELAK, C.D.P., Dir.; VERONICA ORAVEC, C.D.P., Admin.; EURELIA PEREZ, Prog. Dir., P.O. Box 353, Arecibo, 00613. Tel: 787-817-6951; Fax: 787-817-7597.

Programs—

Women Head of Household—NEIDA MARTINEZ.

Domestic Violence Unit—NEIDA MARTINEZ.

Parenting with Love—MICHELLE ACEVEDO.

Community Development—CLAUDIA ROGGENHOFER.

Improving Your Self Esteem—NYDIA VAZQUEZ.

Retreat House, Centro Diocesano Mons. Mendez—Rev. DANIEL FERNANDEZ, Apdo. 2164, Arecibo, 00613. Tel: 787-878-4796.

Boy Scouts—VACANT.

Hospital Chaplains—

Arecibo Hospital—Dr. COLL Y TOSTE; Rev. DELFIN RODRIGUEZ; Miss ESTHER COSTA.

Buen Pastor Hospital—Revs. P. GABRIEL MADURO and priests of Cathedral of San Felipe Apostol:; ROBERTO VEGA.

Susoni Hospital—Rev. P. GABRIEL MADURO.

Vocations—Rev. DANIEL FERNANDEZ, Apdo. 2164, Arecibo, 00613. Tel: 787-878-1528.

Police Chaplain—Rev. LUIS A. VAZQUEZ.

Sociedad San Vincente de Paul (Vincentinos)—Mr. ANGEL GINES, Pres. Consejo Diocesano. Tel: 787-884-5087; 787-854-2562.

CLERGY, PARISHES, MISSIONS AND PAROCHIAL SCHOOLS

CITY OF ARECIBO

1—CATHEDRAL OF SAN FELIPE APOSTOL (1616), [JC] Revs. Roberto Vega, Rector; Gabriel Maduro; Omar A. Bedodya.
De Diego St.: Box 577, 00613. Tel: 809-878-1149; Fax: 787-816-5719. Email: catedralarecibo@hotmail.com.
Chapel—Islote II, Sagrada Familia
Chapel—Islote III (Sector Vibora), San Juan Evangelista
Chapel—Sector Boam, Maria Reina
Chapel—Islote I (Vigia), N.S. del Carmen

2—CHURCH OF CHRIST THE KING (1967), Rev. Serapio Fernandez.
Res.: Box 1932, 00613. Tel: 809-878-9214.
Catechesis / Religious Program—Students 155.
Chapel—Bo. Hato Arriba, Maria Auxiliadora

3—CHURCH OF SAGRADO CORAZON DE JESUS (1961), [JC] Rev. Cesar Ramirez, Admin. In Res., Rev. Msgr. Buenaventura Ballester, P.H. (Retired).
Res.: Box 140637, 00614. Tel: 787-878-4910; Fax: 787-879-2124.
School—Colegio San Felipe, Box 673, 00613. Tel: 809-878-3532. Mercedes Cardona, Prin. Lay Teachers 37; Students 436.
Catechesis / Religious Program—Students 87.
Chapel—Bo. Obrero, Inmaculada Concepcion

4—CHURCH OF SAN MARTIN DE PORRES (1973), Rev. Edwin Mercado.
Res.: Calle 6 F-12, Box 14-2142, Urb. Univ. Gardens, 00613. Tel: 787-878-1822.
Catechesis / Religious Program—Students 225.
Chapel—Victor Rojas II, San Jose Obrero

5—CHURCH OF SANTA CECILIA (1981), [JC] Rev. Carlos E. Granados.
Res.: HC-02 Box 13674, 00612. Tel: 787-879-3364. Email: peregrino59@aol.com.
Catechesis / Religious Program—Students 120.
Chapel—Calichosa, San Jose
Chapel—Los Canos, San Martin de Porres
Chapel—La Guinea, La Milagrosa

6—CHURCH OF SANTA TERESITA (1980), [JC] Rev. Luis A. Vazquez.
Res.: Road 492, KM 1.9, P.O. Box 9242, Cotto Station, 00613. Tel: 787-878-7015.
Catechesis / Religious Program—Students 60.
Chapel—Hato Arriba, N.S. La Providencia
Chapel—Barrancas, La Milagrosa

7—INMACULADO CORAZON DE MARIA (1987), [JC] Revs. Cornelius T. McQuillan, C.S.Sp.; Christopher Chukwu, C.S.Sp.
Res.: Box 1282, Sabana Hoyos, 00688.
Chapel—Bo. Asomante, San Isidro
Chapel—Bo. Carolina, Sagrado Corazon de Jesus
Chapel—Bo. Arrozal, San Jose
Chapel—Los Muertos, San Francisco

8—LA MILAGROSA (1973), [JC] Rev. Angel M. Santos.
Res.: Box 204, Bajadero, 00616. Tel: 787-881-0295.
Catechesis / Religious Program—Students 310.
Chapel—Bajadero, Immaculada Concepcion
Chapel—Domingo Ruiz, N.S. La Providencia
Chapel—Carreras, San Judas
Chapel—Biafara, N.S. La Virgen del Carmen

9—NUESTRA SENORA DE FATIMA (1967), [JC] Revs. Gilberto Da Silva, C.M.V.; Jesus Gonzalez, C.M.V.; Raul Mamani.
Res.: Box 667, Sabana Hoyos, 00688. Tel: 787-881-8274.
Catechesis / Religious Program—Students 145.
Chapel—Garrochales, S. Fco. de Asis
Chapel—Ballaja, N.S. del Carmen
Chapel—Garrochales, La Milagrosa, San Luis
Chapel—Espino, Immaculada Concepcion

10—NUESTRA SENORA DEL CARMEN (1961), [JC] Revs. Alberto Diaz; Delfin Rodriguez.
Res.: Bo. Cotto No. 985, P.O. Box 9949, Cotto Sta., 00613. Tel: 787-878-1268; Fax: 787-817-5062.
School—Hogar-Colegio La Milagrosa, Ave., Cotto, 00613. Tel: 809-878-0341. Sisters of Charity 4; Lay Teachers 27; Students 424.
Catechesis / Religious Program—Students 218.
Chapel—Abra S. Francisco, San Antonio
Chapel—Rodriguez Olmo, San Francisco

11—OUR LADY OF HOPE (1986), [JC] Rev. David Rivas.
Res.: Box 489, 00613. Tel: 787-880-1943.
Catechesis / Religious Program—Students 37.
Chapel—Cantagallo, Sgdo. Corazon de Jesus
Chapel—Plan Bonito, San Rafael

12—SAN JUAN BOSCO (1971), Revs. Melquiades Rojas; Juan R. Mora.
Res.: Urb. Jardines de Arecibo, Calle R-Y-26, 00612. Tel: 787-879-1070; Fax: 787-817-4107.
School—Tel: 809-879-2069. Nilda Gonzalez, Prin. Sisters 3; Lay Teachers 29; Students 460.
Catechesis / Religious Program—Students 194.
Chapel—Las Canelas, N.S. La Dolorosa, San Daniel
Sisters of Mercy 3.

13—SANTA ANA (1961), [JC] Revs. Victor Rojas; Abel A. Plaza.
Res.: Bo. Santana, Box 318, 00612. Tel: 787-881-6005.
Catechesis / Religious Program—Tel: 787-881-6882. Students 119.
Chapel—Factor II, N.S. del Carmen
Chapel—Santuario Cristo de los Milagros

14—SANTISIMO SACRAMENTO (1990), [JC] Rev. Felix Rivera.
Res.: Ste. 109, P.O. Box 4015, 00613. Tel: 787-880-65[illegible]3.
Catechesis / Religious Program—Students 65.
Chapel—Del Valle, La Milagrosa
Chapel—Jobos, San Pascual

OUTSIDE OF ARECIBO

BARCELONETA

1—CHURCH OF OUR LADY OF MT. CARMEL (1882), [JC] Revs. Augusto Concha; Steve Perzan.
Res.: P.O. Box 2062, 00617. Tel: 809-846-5625; Fax: 787-846-5690. Email: senoradelcarmen@coqui.net.
Catechesis / Religious Program—Tel: 787-846-7343. Students 209.
Chapel—Garrochales I, N.S. de Fatima
Chapel—Palmas Altas, San Antonio
Chapel—Punta Palma, N.S. del Mar

2—OUR LADY OF VICTORY (1963), [JC] Rev. Leon Perez.
Res.: Ste. 125, Call Box 2020, 00617. Tel: 809-846-6120.
Catechesis / Religious Program—Students 107.
Chapel—Parcelas Imberry, San Jose Obrero
Chapel—Quebrada, Immaculate Heart of Mary
Chapel—Tiburones, N.S. de Fatima
Chapel—Palenque, San Juan Bautista

CAMUY

1—ST. JOSEPH (1827), [JC] Revs. Adrian Jimenez; Pedro N. Montoya.
Res.: P.O. Box 414, 00627. Tel: 787-898-3620; Fax: 787-898-3620.
Catechesis / Religious Program—Students 451.
Convent—San Jose Hermanas Terciarias Capuchinas 4.
Chapel—Membrillo, N.S. La Monserrate
Chapel—Puente (Zarzas), Sagrado Corazon
Chapel—Puente (Zarza Parcelas), N.S. La Milagrosa
Chapel—Puente (Sector Pica), N.S. del Rosario
Chapel—Abra Honda, Espiritu Santo
Chapel—Zanjas, Immaculada Concepcion

2—OUR LADY OF ASUMPTION (1984), [JC] Rev. Martin A. Bustos, M.N.M.
Res.: HC-02 Box 8047, 00627. Tel: 787-898-8038.
Catechesis / Religious Program—Students 372.
Chapel—Cibao Ocasio, N.S. del Perpetuo Socorro
Chapel—Callejones, Sagrado Corazon
Chapel—Callejones II, San Pablo de la Cruz
Chapel—Cibao Lugo, Maria Auxiliadora

3—OUR LADY OF MONSERRATE (1961), [JC] Rev. Victor Lugo, M.N.M.
Res.: HC-03 Box 16512, Quebradillas, 00678-9820. Tel: 787-898-6784.
Catechesis / Religious Program—Students 200.
Convent—Tel: 787-896-6176. Hermanes Angeles Custodios 2.
Chapel—Piletas (Lares), N.S. del Carmen
Chapel—Guajataca (Queb.), N.S. de Fatima
Chapel—Aibonito Beltran, San Antonio
Chapel—Cibao (S. Sebastian), Santa Ana
Chapel—Planas I (Isabela), Santa Cruz
Chapel—Planas II, N.S. del Rosario

4—OUR LADY OF THE MIRACULOUS MEDAL (1962), [JC], (El Calvario) Rev. Jose Carmona, M.N.M.
Res.: HC-01 Buzon 5240, 00627. Tel: 787-898-5825.
Catechesis / Religious Program—Tel: 787-898-4841. Students 436.
Chapel—Planas II, Santiago Apostol
Chapel—Puertos, Sagrado Corazon
Chapel—Cienaga, Cristo Rey
Chapel—Camuy Arriba, N.S. del Carmen
Chapel—Sector Riego, Santa Clara
Chapel—Sector Mani, Sagrado Corazon

CIALES

1—HOLY ROSARY (1820), [JC] Revs. Jose Oliveras; Elias Pascual; Luis Miranda, O.Carm.; Gabriel M. Torres, Pastor.
Res.: P.O. Box 26, 00638. Tel: 787-871-2205; 787-871-3485.
School—P.O. Box 1334, 00638. Tel: 787-871-1318. Blanca Marrero, Prin. Lay Teachers 22; Students 340.
Catechesis / Religious Program—Tel: 787-871-1492. Students 760.
Chapel—Pozas, San Elias
Chapel—Cialitos, Buen Pastor
Chapel—Hato Viejo, Corazon de Jesus
Chapel—Hato Viejo, San Antonio
Chapel—Jaguas, Santa Clara
Chapel—Pesa, San Ignacio
Chapel—Cialitos-Cruces, Corazon de Maria
Chapel—Toro Negro, N.S.
Chapel—Bo. Marias, Maternidad de la Virgen

2—N.S. MADRE DEL REDENTOR (1988), [JC] Rev. Wiktor Tarnawski.
Res.: P.O. Box 1181, 00638. Tel: 787-871-2404.
Catechesis / Religious Program—Students 200.
Chapel—Yunes, San Jose
Chapel—Fronton (Sabana), Perpetuo Socorro
Chapel—Cordillera 5, N.S. La Providencia
Chapel—Limon, Smo. Rosario
Chapel—Cordillera 7, Sagrada Familia

COROZAL, HOLY FAMILY (1804), [JC] Revs. Eugenio Gayarre; Jesus M. Munoz.
Res.: P.O. Box 474, 00783. Tel: 787-859-2595; Fax: 787-859-5018.
School—Tel: 787-859-2420. Sisters of St. Joseph 12; Lay Teachers 45; Students 1,101.
Catechesis / Religious Program—Students 1,025.
Chapel—Guarico Palmarejo I, San Judas Tadeo
Chapel—Palmarejo II, San Vicente
Chapel—Palmarejo II, San Francisco de Asis
Chapel—Dos Bocas II, Santa Teresita
Chapel—Cibuco, N.S. del Carmen
Chapel—Abras, San Jose
Chapel—Urb. Sylvia, Perpetuo Socorro

COROZAL-PADILLA, OUR LADY OF THE SEVEN SORROWS (1984), Revs. Ramon Olivencia, Admin.; Miguel Rivera.
Res.: P.O. Box 740, 00783-0740. Tel: 787-859-1900. Email: 7dolores@catholicnet.zzn.co.
Catechesis / Religious Program—Students 700.
Chapel—Padilla Hermita, San Rafael
Chapel—Padilla Hormiga, San Martin
Chapel—Cieneguita (V.A.), N.S. del Perpetuo Socorro

COROZAL-PALMARITO, LA MILAGROSA, Revs. Domingo Figueroa, C.R.L., Vicar; Manuel Rabadan, C.R.L.
Res.: HC-03 Box 13976, 00783-9803. Tel: 787-859-5306. Email: crl-milagrosa@hotmail.com.
Catechesis / Religious Program—Students 514.
Convent—HC-03 Box 14048, 00783. Tel: 787-859-8151. Hnas. de San Francisco (Secular Institute) 2.
Chapel—Maguelles, Cristo Rey
Chapel—Mana, N.S. de Fatima
Chapel—Radio Oro, Nuestra Senora del Carmen

COROZAL-PALOS BLANCOS, CHRIST THE KING (1968), [JC] Rev. Rafael J. Gonzalez, C.R.L., Pastor.
Res.: P.O. Box 1091, 00783-1091. Tel: 787-859-7313.
Catechesis / Religious Program—Students 725.
Chapel—Cuchillas, N.S. del Perpetuo Socorro
Chapel—Negros, N.S. del Rosario
Chapel—Palos Blancos, Santa Teresita
Chapel—Palos Blancos, San Antonio

FLORIDA, OUR LADY OF MERCY (1887), [JC] Rev. Jorge Paredes.
Res.: P.O. Box 437, 00650. Tel: 787-822-2670; Fax: 787-822-2670.
Catechesis / Religious Program—Tel: 787-822-2045. Students 100.
Chapel—Monte Bello, N.S. del Carmen
Chapel—Pajornal (Bta.), Santa Rosa de Lima

HATILLO

1—OUR LADY OF GUADALUPE (1961), [JC] Rev. Luis A. Curbelo, Admin.; Sr. Teresa Maria V. de la Eucaristia.
Res.: Carr. Ins. 129, Arecibo to Lares, P.O. Box 1131, 00613. Tel: 787-898-8035. Email: laguadalupe@prtc.net.
Catechesis / Religious Program—Students 296.
Chapel—Pajuil, Santa Rosa de Lima
Chapel—Buena Vista, Inmaculada Concepcion
Chapel—Bda Colon, N.S. La Providencia
Chapel—Sector Naranjito, San Jose

2—OUR LADY OF MT. CARMEL (1830), [JC] Revs. Fernando Morell, Pastor; Julio A. Anglada.
Res.: P.O. Box 2, 00659. Tel: 809-898-5300.
School—Tel: 787-898-2800. Carmen Diaz, Prin. Lay Teachers 53; Students 922.
Catechesis / Religious Program—Tel: 787-898-3302. Students 610.
Chapel—Carrizales, Sagrado Corazon
Chapel—Corcovados, Immaculada Concepcion
Chapel—Capaez, N.S. Perpetuo Socorro
Chapel—Carrizales, San Jose
Chapel—Santa Rosa, Santa Rosa de Lima
Chapel—Lechuga: San Pio X
Chapel—Palma Gordo: Sagrada Familia

3—PERPETUAL HELP (1961), [JC] Rev. Jose Estensoro.
Res.: Ste. 393, P.O. Box 69001, 00659. Tel: 787-898-7771.
Catechesis / Religious Program—Tel: 787-820-2819. Students 140.
Chapel—Aibonito, Cristo Rey
Chapel—Berrocal, Sagrado Corazon de Jesus
Chapel—Sonadora, La Milagrosa
Chapel—Mariposa, N.S. del Carmen
Chapel—Cantera, Ntra. Sra. de la Providencia

ISABELA

1—ST. ANTHONY (1835), [JC] Revs. Elias Fernandez, O.SS.T.; Wilfredo Echevarria, O.SS.T.

Res.: Box 525, 00662. Tel: 787-872-2563; Fax: 787-872-4393.
School—Sisters of St. Dominic 3; Lay Teachers 32; Students 511.
Catechesis/Religious Program—Students 608.
Chapel—Medina, Sma. Trinidad
Chapel—Curva, Santa Rosa de Lima
Chapel—Cotto, San Martin de Porres
Chapel—Arenales Bajo, N.S. La Monserrate
Chapel—Vendrel, N.S. La Providencia
Chapel—Jobos, Buen Pastor
Chapel—Guayabos, Espiritu Santo
Chapel—Arenales A., El Salvador
Chapel—Arenales Alto, Sagrado Corazon, Tel: 787-872-0015. Sister of Trinity (Valencia) 4.
Chapel—Hogar Infantil/Jesus Nazareno, Isabella

2—OUR LADY OF MOUNT CARMEL (1983), [JC] Rev. Francisco Pildain, O.SS.T.
Res.: Box 1555, 00662. Tel: 787-872-5550.
Catechesis/Religious Program—Students 390.
Chapel—Poncito, Santos Inocentes
Chapel—Planas, San Juan Bautista
Chapel—La Tuna, San Juan de Mata
Chapel—Galateo Bajo, La Milagrosa

LARES

1—ST. JOSEPH (1827), [JC] Revs. Esteban Barrueta-bena; Juan B. Bengurria, C.P.; Carlos L. Rodriguez, C.P.
Res.: P.O. Box 103, 00669-0103. Tel: 787-897-2067.
School—Tel: 809-897-2640. Maritza Lopez Pol, Prin. Hermanas Pasionistas 2; Lay Teachers 18; Students 211.
Catechesis/Religious Program—Tel: 787-897-2717. Students 850.
Chapel—Piletas II, San Carlos
Chapel—Sebruguillo, La Resurreccion
Chapel—Piletas Arece, La Milagrosa
Chapel—Piletas, Saint Maria Goretti
Chapel—Tabonuco, La Providencia Hermanas Josefinas de Mexico 6.

2—ST. JUDAS TADEOS (1986), [JC] Rev. Angel R. Diaz, Admin.
Res.: P.O. Box 1109, 00669. Tel: 809-897-3540.
Catechesis/Religious Program—Students 240.
Chapel—Palmar Llano, Perpetuo Socorro
Chapel—Vega de los Acevedo, La Dolorosa
Chapel—Buenos Aires, Sgda. Familia de Nazaret
Chapel—Matilde, San Antonio

MANATI

1—LA CANDELARIA (1738), [JC] Revs. Emilio Tovar, C.M.; Tomas de la Puebla, C.M.
Res.: Calle Padial #2, 00674. Tel: 787-854-2013. Email: manaticm@atenas.com.
School—Sisters of Charity 4; Lay Teachers 45; Students 976.
Catechesis/Religious Program—Tel: 787-854-4021. Students 77.
Chapel—Pugnado, N.S. del Perpetuo Socorro
Chapel—Villa Amalia, La Milagrosa
Chapel—Cortes, Sagrado Corazon
Chapel—Polvorin, La Monserrate
Chapel—Ceiba, Espiritu Santo

2—NUESTRA SENORA DEL MAR (1978), [JC] Rev. Jesus A. Rodriguez.
Res.: Apdo. 1183, 00674. Tel: 787-854-5388.
Catechesis/Religious Program—Tel: 787-854-9252. Students 276.
Chapel—Tierras Nuevas, Santa Rosa de Lima
Chapel—Sector Cantito, La Milagrosa
Chapel—Boquillas, Nuestra Senora de Lourdes

3—OUR SAVIOR, Rev. Victor Sanchez.
Res.: P.O. Box 465, 00674. Tel: 787-884-3664. Email: parrelsalv@ad.com.
School—Colegio Marista, P.O. Box 462, 00764. Tel: 787-854-1075. Margarita Santiago, Prin. Marist Brothers 2; Lay Teachers 25; Students 477.
Catechesis/Religious Program—Students 100.
Chapel—San Jose, San Jose
Chapel—Lagunas Tierra Nueva, N.S. de Lourdes
Chapel—Guayaney, San Martin de Porres

4—SAGRADA FAMILIA (1972), [JC] Revs. Francisco J. Marrodan, C.M.; Manuel Araujo, C.M.
Res.: P.O. Box 704, 00674. Tel: 787-854-2858.
Catechesis/Religious Program—Students 216.
Chapel—Parcelas Marquez, San Judas Tadeo
Chapel—Palo Alto, N.S. La Monserrate
Chapel—Polvorin, La Milagrosa

MOROVIS

1—NUESTRA SENORA DEL CARMEN (1820), [JC] Revs. Jesus Monreal, O.Carm.; Enrique Oria, O.Carm.; Jorge Rivera, O.Carm.
Res.: Box 428, 00687. Tel: 787-862-2620.
Catechesis/Religious Program—Students 2,176.
Chapel—San Lorenzo, N.S. del Rosario
Chapel—Perchas, N.S. del Carmen
Chapel—Pastos, N.S. del Carmen
Chapel—Rio Grande, La Milagrosa
Chapel—Morovis Sur, San Jose
Chapel—Unibon, San Miguel
Chapel—Vaga III, La Milagrosa
Chapel—MPatron I, Sagrada Familia
Chapel—Cuchillas, Segrado Corazon
Chapel—Morovis Sur, Inmaculada Concepcion

2—ST. PAUL APOSTLE (1985), [JC] Rev. Tomas Santos.
Res.: P.O. Box 537, 00687. Tel: 787-862-3445.
Catechesis/Religious Program—Students 313.
Chapel—Franquez, Nino de Praga
Chapel—Franquez Carretera, La Providencia
Chapel—Torrecillas, Senor de los Milagros

OROCOVIS

1—OUR LADY OF FATIMA (1975), [JC] Revs. Jose Alamo, C.S.Sp.; Toselle Giangiacomo, C.S.S.p.
Res.: Box 2118, 00720. Tel: 787-867-3277. Email: fatimaorocovis@hotmail.com.
Catechesis/Religious Program—Students 475.
Chapel—Bermejales, Cristo de la Salud
Chapel—Bauta, N.S. La Dolorosa
Chapel—Damian Arriba, N.S. del Perpetuo Socorro
Chapel—Pellejas I, Espiritu Santo
Chapel—Miraflores, San Martin

2—SAN JUAN BAUTISTA (1838), [JC] Revs. Jorge Santiago, S.D.B.; Demetrio Coello, S.D.B.; Antonio Robles, S.D.B.; Elmon Hernandez, S.D.B.
Res.: P.O. Box 2114, 00720. Tel: 787-867-2210; Fax: 787-867-5675. Email: sdboro@coqui.net.
School—Tel: 787-867-2295. Salesians Sisters 2; Lay Teachers 26; Students 259.
Catechesis/Religious Program—Students 991.
Chapel—Sabana, Angeles Custodios
Chapel—Botijas I, Cristo Resucitado
Chapel—Botijas II, Santa Clara
Chapel—El Puente, San Pablo
Chapel—Mata de Cana, Sagrado Corazon
Chapel—Damian Arriba, Espiritu Santo
Chapel—Montebello, N.S. del Carmen
Chapel—Guadalupe, N.S. La Guadalupe
Chapel—Gato Bajura, N.S. La Providencia
Chapel—Gato, San Judas Tadeo

QUEBRADILLAS

1—SACRED HEART (1977), [JC] Rev. Carmelo Urarte.
Res.: Box 1569, 00678. Tel: 787-895-3033; Fax: 787-895-3033.
Catechesis/Religious Program—Students 250.
Chapel—San Antonio, San Miguel
Chapel—Yeguada, N.S. del Perpetuo Socorro
Chapel—El Verde, Madre Dolorosa

2—SAN RAPHAEL (1828), [JC] Revs. Miguel Mercado; Rafael Mendez.
Res.: Box 57, 00678. Tel: 787-895-2035.
School—Tel: 809-895-2280. Brigida Valle, Prin. Lay Teachers 23; Students 307.
Catechesis/Religious Program—Students 450.
Chapel—San Jose, San Jose
Chapel—Quebrada, N.S. del Carmen
Chapel—Chivos, Santa Cruz
Chapel—Cacao, La Milagrosa
Chapel—Parcelas San Antonio, N.S. La Monserrate
Chapel—San Antonio, San Antonio
Chapel—Charcas, N.S. del Perpetuo Socorro
Chapel—Las Talas, La Guadalupe

UTUADO

1—NUESTRA SENORA DEL MONTE CARMELO (1981), [JC] Rev. Pedro Hernandez.
Res.: P.O. Box 299, Caonillas-Utuado, 00641. Tel: 787-894-7340. Email: parrmontecarmelo@yahoo.com.
Catechesis/Religious Program—Students 8.
Chapel—Mameyes, San Antonio
Chapel—Tetuan III, Sagrado Corazon
Chapel—Tetuan I, Cristo Salvador
Chapel—Don Alonso, La Milagrosa

2—OUR LADY OF ANGELS (1967), [JC] Rev. Salomon J. Morales.
Res.: Box 98, Angeles, 00611. Tel: 809-894-7722.
Catechesis/Religious Program—Students 59.
Chapel—Corcho, San Jose
Chapel—Santa Isabela, N.S. La Monserrate
Chapel—Las Vegas, Sagrada Familia

3—OUR LADY OF SORROWS (1983), [JC] Rev. Bertulfo Acevedo.
Res.: P.O. Box 2525, CMB-70, 00641-2525. Tel: 787-894-7144.
Catechesis/Religious Program—Students 54.
Chapel—Roncador, San Martin de Porres
Chapel—Cayuco, Cristo Rey
Chapel—Jacanas, N.S. la Monserrate

4—SAN MIQUEL (1746), [JC] Revs. Roy Martinez, O.F.M.Cap., Pastor; Joseph Schreck, O.F.M.Cap.; Ricardo Colon; Edward Madonado. In Res., Bros. Bernardo Ayala, O.F.M.Cap.; Jose E. Sanchez, O.F.M.Cap.; Reynaldo Saliva, O.F.M.Cap.
Res.: 8 Barcelo St., P.O. Box 10, 00641-0010. Tel: 787-894-2696; 787-894-3108; Fax: 787-894-3812. Email: parroquiasanmiguel@utuadoweb.com.
School—Elementary School, Progreso St., Box 10, 00641. Lay Teachers 22; Students 198.
School—Intermediate and High School, San Miguel Ave., Box 10, 00641. Tel: 809-894-9386. Mrs. Lydia M. Giusti, Prin.
Catechesis/Religious Program—Students 536.
Chapel—Puente Blanco, San Fidel
Chapel—Arenas, San Martin
Chapel—Sabana Grande, N.S. del Perpetuo Socorro

5—SAN PEDRO Y SAN PABLO (1988), [JC] Rev. Rafael Nuno.
Res.: Box 679, 00641. Tel: 787-894-0696.
Catechesis/Religious Program—Students 146.
Chapel—Las Palmas, San Francisco
Chapel—Vivi Arriba, Immalculada Concepcion
Chapel—La Pica, La Milagrosa
Chapel—Consejo, San Jose
Chapel—Vivi Abajo, Nuestra Senora de la Divina Providencia Monastery Mother of God Cloistered 33.

VEGA-ALTA

1—IMMACULATE CONCEPTION OF BLESSED VIRGIN MARY (1805), Rev. Msgr. Francisco Concepcion; Rev. Elvin A. Irizarry.
Res.: P.O. Box 775, 00692. Tel: 787-883-4875.
Catechetical Center—Calle Colon 17, 00692. Sisters of Charity 4; Students 464.
Chapel—Maricao IV, Sagrado Corazon
Chapel—Bajura II, San Vicente
Chapel—Bajura I, Santa Ana
Chapel—Candelaria, Inmaculado Corazon de Maria
Chapel—Maricao II, N.S. La Guadalupe

2—PERPETUO SOCORRO (1975), [JC] Rev. Edward Santana, J.C.D. (CGS).
Res.: Box 9018, Sabana Branch, Vega-Baja, 00694-9018. Tel: 787-883-5776; Fax: 787-270-3103.
Catechesis/Religious Program—Students 111.
Chapel—Sabana (V.B.), San Vicente
Chapel—Cerro Gordo, N.S. del Carmen

3—SANTA ANA (1967), Rev. Gilberto G. Garces. In Res., Rev. Jesus Diaz (Retired).
Res.: Urb. Santa Ana, Apartado 2105, Calle 3H9, 00692. Tel: 787-883-2502.
Catechesis/Religious Program—Students 190.
Chapel—Espinosa, N.S. del Carmen

VEGA-BAJA

1—THE BLESSED TRINITY (1971), Rev. Francisco Tejada, Admin.
Res.: P.O. Box 58, Almirante Sur Station, 00694-0058. Tel: 809-858-8743.
Catechesis/Religious Program—Students 310.
Chapel—Almirante Norte, Sagrada Familia
Chapel—Patron II, N.S. La Providencia

2—HOLY ROSARY (1794), [JC] Revs. Jose A. Rodriguez; William Cesar Chaparro.
Res.: P.O. Box 1388, 00694. Tel: 787-858-2969.
School—Principals: Jorge Adrover; Nilda Fontan. Sisters 1; Lay Teachers 41; Students 678.
Catechesis/Religious Program—Students 232.
Chapel—Arenales, San Jose
Chapel—Almirante, N.S. de Fatima

3—N.S. DE LA PROVIDENCIA (1970), [JC] Rev. Angel Diaz.
Res.: Box 4056, Vega Baja, 00694-4056. Tel: 809-858-2171; Fax: 809-858-2171.
Catechesis/Religious Program—Students 356.
Chapel—Brisas de Tortuguero, San Jose
Chapel—Vega Baja Lakes, San Pedro

4—OUR LADY OF CARMEN-PLAYA (1976), [JC] Rev. Cesar E. Santos, Admin.
Res.: Apdo. 4095, 00694-4095. Tel: 787-855-5226; Fax: 787-855-5115.
Catechesis/Religious Program—Students 122.
Chapel—Naranjos, San Judas Tadeo
Chapel—San Demetrio, Divino Nino Jesus

5—OUR LADY OF LOURDES (1984), [JC] Rev. Jose A. Acaba.
Res.: P.O. Box 4414, 00694-4414. Tel: 787-855-4942; Fax: 787-807-9249.
Catechesis/Religious Program—Students 515.
Convent—Tel: 787-855-0341. Hermanas Terciarias Capuchinas 3.
Chapel—Rio Abajo, Santa Rosa de Lima
Chapel—Quebrada Arenas, San Juan Bautista
Chapel—Las Granjas, S. Francisco de Asis

6—OUR LADY OF MT. CARMEL (1968), [JC] Rev. Luis Velazquez.
Res.: P.O. Box 1417, 00694-1417. Tel: 787-855-0159; Fax: 787-855-0159.
Catechesis/Religious Program—Students 490.
Chapel—Pueblo Nuevo, La Milagrosa
Chapel—Sabana Hoyos, San Judas
Chapel—Santa Rosa, La Guadalupe

7—PARROQUIA DE SAN MARTIN DE PORRES (1967), [JC] Rev. Efrain Montesino.
Res.: P.O. Box 254, Vega Baja, 00694. Tel: 787-858-1485; Fax: 787-858-1485.
Catechesis/Religious Program—Tel: 787-858-8651. Students 271.
Chapel—Panaini, Del Carmen
Chapel—Pugnado Adentro, San Jose
Chapel—Vila Colombo, St. Anthony

On Duty Outside the Diocese:
Revs.—
Davila, Andres, Mexico

Gomez, Walter, Archdiocese of San Juan
Guerrero, Jose Ma., Espana
Lopez, Juan J., Lyons, CA
Nunez, Philip, III, Miami, FL
Pagan, Angel M., Archdiocese of San Juan
Rios Capiello, Luis B., Archdiocese of San Juan
Rosario, Luis A. Guatemala
Vazquez, Antonio J., Archdiocese of San Juan

Graduate Studies:

Revs.—
Colon, Jose, Rome, Italy
Perez, Ovidio
Portalatin, Antonio, Rome, Italy

Retired:
Rev. Msgrs.—
Diaz, Jesus, Vega Alta, Puerto Rico
Salvador, Antonio, Espana
Revs.—
Burgos, Jose Casco, Espana
Caraballo, Antonio, Spain
Hernandez, Jimmy, Quebradillas, Puerto Rico
Irizarry, Rafael, Quebradillas, Puerto Rico
Jimenez, Francisco, Camuy, Puerto Rico
Jimenez, Victorino, Spain
Martinez, Francisco, Spain
Munoz, Rafael, Spain
San Llorente, Ricardo, Spain
Zayas, Hector, Utando, Puerto Rico

INSTITUTIONS LOCATED IN THE DIOCESE

[A] EDUCATIONAL

ARECIBO. *Pontificia Universidad Catholica de Puerto Rico, Recinto de Arecibo*, Mailing Address: P.O. Box 144045, 00614-4045. Tel: 787-881-1212. Rev. Victor Rojas, Chap. Sisters 1; Brothers 1; Lay Teachers 52; Students 857.

Seminario de Jesus Maestro, Mailing Address: P.O. Box 2164, 00613. Tel: 787-878-1528; Fax: 787-880-2661. Rev. Daniel Fernandez. Total Enrollment 7.

[B] HOMES FOR AGED AND ORPHANS

ARECIBO. *Hogar de Ancianos San Vicente de Paul*, P.O. Box 4196, Vega Baja, 00694. Bo. Almirante Sur-Carr 645 Km. 6.6, Vega Baja, 00763. Tel: 787-855-0487; Fax: 787-858-3103. Email: svpaulpr@aol.com. Nelson De Leon, Dir. Tel: 787-862-5257; Cell: 787-318-6695.

Hogar Sta. Maria Eufrasia - Hnq. Francisca Torres Calvo Email: hbpsme86@mailhost.tld.net. P.O. Box 1909, 00613. Fax: 787-880-2632. Carr. Est. 651-10 Hato Abajo, 00612. Tel: 787-878-5166. House for Unwed Mothers. Good Shepard Sisters 5; Unwed Mothers 16; Babies 7.

La Milagrosa Home for Orphan Girls, Ave. Francisco Jimenez Gonzalez #662, 00612. Tel: 809-878-6231. Sisters of Charity 4; Girls 20.

San Rafael Home for Aged - Sor. Engracia Colon Diaz 00612. Tel: 787-878-3813; Fax: 787-879-4592. Sr. Milagros Olivencia, H.C. Sisters of Charity 5; Guests 30.

Hogar Geriatrico San Rafael, Calle Cervantes, 00612. Tel: 787-878-3813; Fax: 787-879-4592.

ISABELA. *Hogar Infantil Jesus Nazareno, Inc.*, P.O. Box 1671, 00662. Tel: 787-872-0015; Fax: 787-872-0015. Email: hijn@coqui.net. Sisters 4; Residential Care of Children 50.

LARES. *Hogar Envejecientes Irma Fe Pol Mendez, Inc.*, P.O. Box 1185, 00669. Tel: 787-897-6090; Fax: 787-897-0612. Charity Sisters of St. Joseph (Mexico) 5; Guests 61.

VEGA-ALTA. *Centro Actividades Multiples/Conferencia San Vicente de Paul*, P.O. Box 1613, 00692. Tel: 787-504-7488. Orlando Garcia, Dir. Tel: 787-504-7488. Sisters of Charity 6; Guests 227.

Centro Geriatrico Juan de los Olivos, P.O. Box 1613, 00692. Tel: 787-883-2370; Fax: 787-883-2370.

[C] MISCELLANEOUS

ARECIBO. *Hogar Infantil Santa Teresita del Nino Jesus, Inc*, P.O. Box 140057, 00614-0057. Tel: 787-817-6651; Fax: 787-817-6651. Email: hogarsantateresita@hotmail.com. Hnas. Dominicas de la Presentacion 4; Kids 45.

UTUADO. *Fondita Santa Marta*, P.O. Box 10, 00631-0010. Tel: 787-894-3108; Fax: 787-894-3812. Bro. Jose Enrique Sanchez, O.F.M.Cap.

RELIGIOUS INSTITUTES OF MEN REPRESENTED IN THE DIOCESE

For further details refer to the corresponding bracketed number in the Religious Institutes of Men or Women section.

[]—*Canonigos Regulares Lateranenses de San Agustin* (Bronx, NY)—C.R.L.
[0470]—*Capuchin Friars* (Province of Pittsburgh)—O.F.M.Cap.
[0270]—*Carmelite Fathers and Brothers* (Province de Aragon, Valencia, Espana)—O.Carm.
[1330]—*Congregation of the Mission* (Vice Province of Puerto Rico)—C.M.
[1000]—*Congregation of the Passion* (Bilbao, Spain)—C.P.
[]—*Esclavos de la Eucaristia y Maria Virgen*—E.E.M.V.
[0650]—*Holy Ghost Fathers* (Eastern Province)—C.S.Sp.
[0770]—*Marist Brothers*—F.M.S.
[]—*Misioneros de Villa Regia-Italia*—C.M.V.
[]—*Misioneros Natividad de Maria* (Mexico)—M.N.M.
[1310]—*Order of the Holy Trinity* (Viscaya, Spain Province)—O.SS.T.
[1190]—*Salesians of Don Bosco* (Province of Madrid)—S.D.B.

RELIGIOUS INSTITUTES OF WOMEN REPRESENTED IN THE DIOCESE

[]—*Congregation of Sisters of Passion* (Mexico)
[0760]—*Daughters of Charity of St. Vincent de Paul*—D.C.
[1070-05]—*Dominican Sisters*—O.P.
[]—*Dominican Sisters of Amityville, N.Y*
[1100]—*Dominican Sisters of Charity of the Presentation of the Blessed Virgin*—O.P.
[]—*Dominican Sisters of Fatima* (Yauco PR)
[]—*Dominicas Divina Misericordia* (Lares, Puerto Rico)
[]—*Hermanas de San Jose de Corozal* (Corozal)
[]—*Hermanas del Buen Pastor*
[]—*Hermanas Esclaves del Santisimo y la Inmaculada*
[]—*Hermanas Josefinas* (Mexico)
[]—*Hermanas San Francisco* (Instituto Secular)
[]—*Hnas. Apostolado Corzon de Jesus* (Madrid)—R.A.
[]—*Hnas. Carmelitas* (Madrid, Spain)
[2460]—*Hnas. Carmelitas Madre Candelaria, Carmelite Nuns* (Venezuela)
[]—*Hnas. de Nazaret* (El Salvador)
[]—*Hnas. Religiosas Angeles Custodios* (Madrid, Spain)
[]—*Instituto Sma. Trinidad* (Valencia, Spain)
[]—*Mercedarias Caridad* (Roma)
[]—*Misioneras de la Sagrada Familia* (Instituto Secular)
[]—*Misioneras Sagrado Corazon* (Santo Domingo)
[]—*Misioneras Villa Regia-Italia*
[]—*Monasterio La Immaculada* (Espana)
[]—*Monasterio Madre de Dios - Cloistered Dominican Nuns*
[]—*Salesian Sisters* (Roma)
[]—*Siervas de Maria* (Roma)
[0990]—*Sisters of Divine Providence* (Pittsburgh)—C.D.P.
[]—*Sisters of Mercy* (Spain)
[3930]—*Sisters of St. Joseph of the Third Order of St. Francis* (South Bend, IN)—S.S.J.-T.O
[]—*Terciarias Capuchina Sgda. Familia* (Roma)

NECROLOGY

(No Deaths)

Diocese of Caguas, Puerto Rico

(Dioecesis Caguana)

Most Reverend

RUBEN ANTONIO GONZALEZ MEDINA, C.M.F.

Bishop of Caguas; ordained February 9, 1975; appointed Bishop of Caguas December 12, 2000; consecrated February 4, 2001

Most Reverend

ENRIQUE HERNANDEZ RIVERA, D.D.

Bishop Emeritus of Caguas; ordained June 8, 1968; appointed Titular Bishop of Vanalla, North Africa and Auxiliary Bishop of San Juan June 11, 1979; consecrated August 17, 1979; appointed Bishop of Caguas February 13, 1981; officially installed March 8, 1981; retired July 28, 1998 *Res.: Bishop's House*, Box 8698, Caguas, PR 00726. Tel: 787-747-5885; 787-747-5787; Fax: 787-747-5616; 787-747-5767.

Web: *www.home.coqui.net/obicag*

Email: *obicag@coqui.net*

ESTABLISHED NOVEMBER 1964.

Square Miles 737.

Comprises east and southeast portion of Puerto Rico and the Islands of Culebra and Vieques.

Patroness of the Diocese: Maria, Madre de la Iglesia - November 12, 1988.

STATISTICAL OVERVIEW

Personnel	
Bishop	1
Retired Bishops	2
Abbots	1
Retired Abbots	1
Priests: Diocesan Active in Diocese	53
Priests: Diocesan Active Outside Diocese	6
Priests: Retired, Sick or Absent	5
Number of Diocesan Priests	64
Religious Priests in Diocese	35
Total Priests in Diocese	99
Extern Priests in Diocese	2
Ordinations:	
Diocesan Priests	1
Transitional Deacons	2
Permanent Deacons in Diocese	66
Total Brothers	17
Total Sisters	133
Parishes	
Parishes	43
With Resident Pastor:	
Resident Diocesan Priests	28
Resident Religious Priests	9
Without Resident Pastor:	
Administered by Priests	7
Welfare	
Specialized Homes	3
Total Assisted	1,252
Educational	
Seminaries, Diocesan	1
Students from This Diocese	6
Diocesan Students in Other Seminaries	12
Total Seminarians	18
High Schools, Diocesan and Parish	1
Total Students	120
High Schools, Private	6
Total Students	3,182
Elementary Schools, Diocesan and Parish	4
Total Students	665
Elementary Schools, Private	12
Total Students	3,998
Catechesis/Religious Education:	
High School Students	3,289
Elementary Students	5,201
Total Students under Catholic Instruction	16,473
Teachers in the Diocese:	
Priests	10
Scholastics	4
Brothers	4
Sisters	15
Lay Teachers	380
Vital Statistics	
Receptions into the Church:	
Infant Baptism Totals	5,322
Adult Baptism Totals	479
First Communions	5,425
Confirmations	2,739
Marriages:	
Catholic	972
Interfaith	46
Total Marriages	1,018
Deaths	2,366
Total Catholic Population	515,000
Total Population	653,012

Former Bishops—Most Revs. RAFAEL GROVAS, D.D., S.T.D., Ph.D., J.C.L. (Retired), ord. April 7, 1928; appt. Jan. 19, 1965; consecrated March 28, 1965; retired Feb. 13, 1981; died Sept. 9, 1991; ENRIQUE HERNANDEZ RIVERA, D.D. (Retired), ord. June 8, 1968; consecrated Aug. 17, 1979; appt. Feb. 13, 1981; retired July 28, 1998.

Vicar General—Rev. ANTONIO CARTAGENA.

Sec. Chancellor—Rev. ANGEL MOLINA.

Sec. Vice Chancellor—VACANT.

Diocesan Consultors—Revs. HIPOLITO TORRES; AURELIO ADAN; ANTONIO CARTAGENA; EUSEBIO RAMOS; OSCAR RIVERA, O.S.B.; CAMPO E. ARIZA; ABOD OSCAR RIVERA, O.S.B.; ISRAEL BERRIOS.

Diocesan Tribunal of Caguas—Rev. FELIX NUNEZ, Judicial Vicar; Sr. CARMEN GONZALEZ, C.D.P., J.C.L., Dir., P.O. Box 9779, Caguas, 00726. Tel: 787-286-8595; Fax: 787-286-8620.

Board of Diocesan Government—Rev. FELIX OLIVERAS VILLANUEVA; Deacon JOSE RODRIGUEZ.

Priests Senate—Revs. EUSEBIO RAMOS; HIPOLITO TORRES; ANTONIO CARTAGENA; AURELIO ADAN; FELICIANO RODRIGUEZ; ANGEL MOLINA; LUIS RIVERA; RAUL MORALES; OSCAR RIVERA, O.S.B.; CAMPO E. ARIZA; FELIX NUNEZ; MIGUEL ARROYO, O.C.D.; ISRAEL BERRIOS; OSCAR RIVERA, O.S.B.; MIGUEL MERCED; HENRY BEAUCHAMP, C.SS.R.

Diocesan Offices and Directors

Economic Administrator—Rev. FELIX OLIVERAS VILLANUEVA, P.O. Box 8698, Caguas, 00726. Tel: 787-747-5885; 787-747-5787, Ext. 227.

Planning Vicar—VACANT, P.O. Box 8698, Caguas, 00726. Tel: 787-747-5885; 787-747-5787.

Movimientos y Organizaciones Diocesanas—

Cursillos de Cristiandad—GILDO MASSO. Tel: 787-734-7068.

Legion de Maria—ANTONIO RODRIGUEZ.

Renovacion Carismatica—ADELAIDA CRUZ. Tel: 787-736-4871.

Juan XXIII—MAXIMILIANO RIVERA. Tel: 787-747-3748.

Apostolado de la Cruz—ELVIN PENA. Tel: 787-715-1768.

Caballeros de Colon—JOSE SOTO CARMONA. Tel: 787-746-4747.

Equipos Ntra. Sra.—GUILLERMO TORRES; MILAGROS ORTIZ; LUIS Y AMPARO URBINA.

Equipo Ntra. Sra.—LUIS Y AMPARO URBINA. Tel: 787-739-8581.

Hijas Catolicas—GLORIA M. BENITEZ SOLA.

Hnos. Cheos—ESTEBAN RIVERA. Tel: 787-850-5224.

Misioneros Padre Ntro.—RAMON L. RAMOS.

Schoenstatt—JOSE N. BRACERO. Tel: 787-722-3941.

Vicentinos—CARMENCITA COLON. Tel: 787-747-6546.

Talleres de Oracion y Vida—LUZ ADDARICH. Tel: 787-745-4123.

Sociedad del Santo Nombre—EVARISTO RUIZ. Tel: 787-744-6641.

Guerra Contra el Hambre—MAGALY MILLAN. Tel: 787-747-5767.

VACS—Hna. CARMEN D. ROSADO. Tel: 787-286-3333.

Comisiones Diocesanas—

Pastoral de Multitudes—OSCAR LOPEZ. Tel: 787-738-1941.

Pastoral Familiar—Diac. VICTOR M. CRUZ. Tel: 787-733-3592.

Pastoral Preadolescentes—Hnas. SALESIANAS. Tel: 787-744-0858.

Pastoral Social—RICARDO DIAZ. Tel: 787-745-8183.

Espiritualidad Comunitaria—HERMINIA FONSECA. Tel: 787-746-2669.

Misiones—Diac. JOSE BERRIOS. Tel: 787-869-3042.

Pastoral Penitenciaria—D. ANIBAL GONZALEZ. Tel: 787-263-0976.

Pastoral Nec. Especiales—OLGA V. VAZQUEZ. Tel: 787-852-3257.

Formacion Diac. Permanentes—Deacon CARLOS COLON BERNARDI.

Catholic Youth—Rev. PEDRO R. ORTIZ, P.O. Box 8698, Caguas, 00726. Tel: 787-744-6738, Ext. 229.

Catholic Social Action—VACANT, P.O. Box 8698, Caguas, 00726. Tel: 787-747-5885; 787-747-5787.

Catholic School Consultors—DOMICIANO GARCIA, P.O. Box 8699, Caguas, 00726. Tel: 787-743-1171.

Catechetical Vicar—Rev. HERMENEGILDO ALAYON.

Building Commission—VACANT, P.O. Box 8698, Caguas, 00726. Tel: 787-747-5885; 787-747-5787.

Liturgical Consultor—VACANT, P.O. Box 8698, Caguas, 00626. Tel: 787-747-5885, Ext. 222.

Communication Office—Mrs. ISABEL CRUZ, P.O. Box 8698, Caguas, 00726. Tel: 809-746-3783.

Guerra Contral el Hambre (War on Hunger)—VACANT, P.O. Box 8698, Caguas, 00726. Tel: 787-747-5767.

Vincentian Society—CARMENCITA COLON, P.O. Box 8698, Caguas, 00726.

Hospitals—Rev. JAVIER HERNANDEZ, P.O. Box 8698, Caguas, 00726.

Legion of Mary—Rev. CLEMENTE CAHILL, C.SS.R., P.O. Box 967, Caguas, 00726; Mr. ISABELO HUERTAS, P.O. Box 8698, Caguas, 00726.

Master of Ceremonies—Rev. JOSE A. AROCHO, P.O. Box 8698, Caguas, 00726. Tel: 809-747-5885.
Pastoral Vicar—Rev. FELICIANO RODRIGUEZ, P.O. Box 8698, Caguas, 00726. Tel: 787-286-0075, Ext. 245.
Schools—P.O. Box 8699, Caguas, 00726. Tel: 787-743-1171.
School Superintendent—DOMICIANO GARCIA.
Vocations—Revs. JORGE D. CARDONA; FLOYD MERCADO, P.O. Box 8698, Caguas, 00726. Tel: 787-747-5885, Ext. 243; Fax: 787-857-3585.
Catholic Charities—VACANT, P.O. Box 8698, Caguas, 00726. Tel: 787-703-0775; Fax: 787-747-5616.
Commission of Permanent Deacons—Deacon CARLOS COLON BERNARDI.

CLERGY, PARISHES, MISSIONS AND PAROCHIAL SCHOOLS

CITY OF CAGUAS

1—CATHEDRAL DULCE NOMBRE DE JESUS (1771),, Redemptorist Fathers. Revs. Hipolito Torres, Rector; David Matos. School Sisters of Notre Dame In Res., Rev. Javier Hernandez.
Res.: 44 Betances St., Box 665, 00726-0665. Tel: 787-743-4311; 787-743-2927; Fax: 787-746-5399.
School—Colegio Catolico de Caguas, Acosta St., Box 967, 00726. Tel: 787-743-2385; Fax: 787-743-7567. Sr. Bernardine Marie, S.S.N.D. School Sisters of Notre Dame. Sisters 2; Lay Teachers 43; Students 1,031; Aids 10.
High School—Notre Dame, Urb. Borinquen, Box 541, 00726. Tel: 787-743-3693; 787-743-5501; Fax: 787-258-9648. Mr. Jose G. Grillo. School Sisters of Notre Dame. Priests 2; Sisters 4; Lay Teachers 68; Students 1,200.
Chapel—Nuestra S. Perpetuo Socorro (1929), 24 Aguayo St., 00726.
Chapel—San Gerardo (1940), 221 B St., B-14, Jardines de Caguas, 00726.
Chapel—San Vicente de Paul 221 B St., Brooklyn, NY 11209.
Chapel—La Sagrada Familia (1978), 1004 P St., Bda. Morales.

2—DIVINO NINO (1995), Revs. Campo Emilio Ariza; Luis Ruiz; Deacons Leonardo Matos; Rolando Rocafort.
Mailing Address: P.O. Box 9416, 00726. Tel: 787-746-1450; Fax: 787-744-3497.
Catechesis/Religious Program—Fax: 787-744-3497. Students 120.
Chapel—San Francisco Javier, Tel: 787-286-0440.

3—EL SALVADOR (1970), Rev. Orlando De Jesus Gomez; Deacon Pablo Gonzalez.
Parcelas Bo. Boringuen: HC 03, Buzon 38888, 00725-9723. Tel: 787-747-0091; Fax: 787-747-0091 (call first).
Catechesis/Religious Program—Students 300.
Chapel—Bo. San Salvador, Cristo Rey (1922),
Chapel—Sector Anon, San Alfonso (1929),
Chapel—Sector Hato, Nuestra S. del Carmen (1911),

4—INMACULADO CORAZON DE MARIA (1971), [JC] Revs. Jose Vicente Martinez, C.M.F. (Spain) (SJN); Danilo deJesus Martinez, C.M.F.; Deacon Jose A. Velez Velazquez.
Mailing Address: HC 05, P.O. Box 57564, 00725-9233. Tel: 787-747-6336; Fax: 787-258-4910.
Catechesis/Religious Program—Students 435.
Chapel—Bo. La Barra, Cristo Rey (1971),
Chapel—San Antonio (1950),
Chapel—Bo. La Mesa, N.S. Providencia (1982),
Chapel—Bo. La Mesa, Nuestra S. del Carmen
Chapel—Bo. Quebrada Arenas, San Felipe
Chapel—Guasabara, Sta. Teresa del Nino Jesus (1995),

5—MARIA MADRE DE LA IGLESIA (1972), Rev. Javier Hernandez; Deacons Genaro Estrella Martinez; Francisco Gonzalez; Hipolito Montanez; Felix Cotto Velez.
Calle Juan M. Morales D-23 Urb Valle Tolima, 00725. Tel: 787-258-4481; Fax: 787-747-5616.
Chapel—Bo. Canabon, Maria Reina
Chapel—Las Carolinas, Ntra. Sra. del Carmen

6—NUESTRA SENORA DE LA PROVIDENCIA (1966), Rev. Pedro Ortiz, Admin.; Deacon Ruben Villodas.
Res.: Urb. Villa del Carmen, Box 6318, 00726. Tel: 787-743-8200; Fax: 787-743-8200.
Station—Urb. Mariolga
Station—Caserio Publico
Station—Los Flamboyanes
Station—Rio Verde
Station—Villa Carmen
Station—Villa del Rey I
Station—Residencial San Carlos 00726.
Station—Residencial San Alfonso

7—NUESTRA SENORA DEL PERPETUO SOCORRO (1968), Revs. Angel Molina; Francisco Hernandez (OM).
Res.: Calle 2, A-13, Villa Nueva, 00725. Tel: 787-744-1420; Fax: 787-258-4341.
Station—San Patricio (1926), Bo. Canaboncito.
Station—San Judas Tadeo (1960), Villa Esperanza.
Station—Sagrado Corazon Bo. Canaboncito (Las Parcelas).
Station—Nuestra S. del Carmen (1988), Urb. Turabo Gardens.

8—SAGRADO CORAZON DE JESUS (1963), Rev. Felix Oliveras Villanueva.
Res.: HC 04, Box 45078, Bo. Beatriz, 00726. Tel: 787-747-5170.
Chapel—Bo. Beatriz, Cristo Rey (1960),
Chapel—San Martin (1994),

9—SAN JOSE (1960),, (Discalced Carmelites from Spain) Revs. Miguel A. Arroyo, O.C.D. Antonio Mata, O.C.D.; Alejandro Moral, O.C.D.
Res.: Coral St., Villa Blanca, Box 1749, 00726. Tel: 787-743-5889; Fax: 787-258-0683.
School—Box 806, 00725. Tel: 787-743-2032; Fax: 787-258-0683. Sr. Nelly O. Rodriguez, C.M., Prin. (Spanish Discalced Carmelite Sisters) Priests 2; Sisters 5; Lay Teachers 29; Students 596.
High School—Tel: 787-744-8993; Fax: 787-744-4111. Mrs. Brenda Figueroa de Soler, Prin. Priests 1; Lay Teachers 21; Students 450.
Chapel—Bairoa, Nuestra Senora de Rosario (1981),Tel: 787-743-5889.

10—SAN JUAN APOSTOL Y EVANGELISTA (1982), Rev. Antonio Cartagena; Deacons Francisco Gonzalez; Jose Rodriquez; Ruben Huertas.
Res.: Apartado 459, Avenida Bairoa, 00726. Tel: 787-744-6359; Fax: 787-743-8266.
Catechesis/Religious Program—Tel: 787-743-8266. Students 200.

11—SAN PABLO APOSTOL (1980), (Hispanic), Rev. Edwin R. Hernandez; Deacon Asuncion Concepcion.
Res.: Kennedy U-32-B Urb. Jose Mercado, 00725. Tel: 787-743-3546; Fax: 787-743-3546.
Chapel—Bo. Tomas de Castro I, Nuestra S. de Guadalupe (1928),
Chapel—Bo. Tomas de Castro II, Santa Rose de Lima
Chapel—Sector Ramal, San Martin (1969),
Chapel—Sector Buenos Aires, San Juan Bautista
Chapel—Sector RM5, Virgen de la Monserrate
Catechesis/Religious Program—Students 134.

12—SAN PEDRO APOSTOL (1982), Rev. Antonio Munoz Alcarria.
Res.: Urb. Bonneville, P.O. Box 8878, 00726. Tel: 787-744-2036; Fax: 787-743-4695.

13—SANTISIMA TRINIDAD (1986), Rev. Efrain Zabala; Deacon Esteban Dominquez.
Res.: P.O. Box 9630, 00726. Tel: 787-747-6967; Fax: 787-747-6967.

14—SANTISIMO SACRAMENTO (1967),, Blessed Sacrament Fathers. Revs. Jose Martin Eguiguren; Jesus Maria Maiza, S.S.S.; Domingo Gayarre, S.S.S.
Res.: Calle Caney A-11, Caguax, 00725. Tel: 787-743-8444; Fax: 787-745-5165.
Chapel—Urb. Caguas Norte, San Antonio de Padua
Chapel—Nuestra S. de Guadalupe 5th St., 00725.

OUTSIDE THE CITY OF CAGUAS FROM LAS AMERICAS EXPRESS WAY TOWARD THE WEST

AGUAS BUENAS, AGUAS BUENAS CO.

1—CHURCH OF TRES SANTOS REYES (1838),, Redemptorist Fathers. Revs. Jose J. Rached, C.SS.R.; Antonio Hernandez, C.SS.R.; Clemente Cahill, C.SS R.; Federico Consla, C.SS.R.
Res.: 4 Munoz Rivera St., P.O. Box 1, 00703. Tel: 787-732-2741; Fax: 787-732-2185.
School—Academia San Alfonso, Tel: 787-732-8288; Fax: 787-732-4115. Mrs. Carmen N. Diaz, Prin. Lay Teachers 12; Students 186.
Chapel—Bo. Sumidero, Nuestra S. del Perpetuo Socorro (1933),
Chapel—Sector Las Corujas del Barrio Sumidero, Buen Pastor (1984),
Chapel—Bo. Sonadora, Sagrado Corazon (1937),
Chapel—Bo. Jagueyes Abajo, San Jose (1939),
Chapel—Bo. Jagueyes Quinta, Santisimo Redentor (1947),
Chapel—Bo. Caguitas, Madre del Perpetuo Socorro (1941),
Chapel—Bo. Caguitas, Sector La Brusca, Ntra. De Fatima (1996),
Chapel—Parcelas Santa Clara, Santa Clara (1974),

2—ESPIRITU SANTO (1991), Rev. Baltazar Nunez; Deacons Juan Lopez; Jose Rivera.
Res.: P.O. Box 1250, 00703. Tel: 787-732-1270.
Chapel—Carr. 156, Santa Teresita (1929),
Chapel—Bo. Mulitas Alvelo, De Todos los Santos (1974),
Chapel—Bo. Mulitas Tiza, San Gerardo Mayela (1974),
Chapel—Bo. Juan Ascencio, San Alfonso

AIBONITO, AIBONITO CO., CHURCH OF ST. JOSEPH (1897), Revs. Enrique Gomez; Israel Berrios; Deacons Modesto Reyes; Ezequiel Collazo; Cristobal Rolon; Otilio Rivera.
Res.: P.O. Box 2038, 00705. Tel: 787-735-3741; Fax: 787-735-4436.
Catechesis/Religious Program—Tel: 787-735-4856. Students 1,900.
Mission—Barrio Algarrobo Barrio La Plata, Amoldadero. Tel: 787-735-5032.
Chapel—Bo. Asomante (Cuadritos), Nuestra S. del Carmen (1959),Tel: 787-735-1811.
Chapel—Bo. Asomante (Abejas), Inmaculada Concepcion (1965), Tel: 787-735-6455.
Chapel—Bo. Pasto, Nuestra S. de Guadalupe (1970),Tel: 787-735-6977.
Chapel—Nuestra S. de la Providencia (1982), Palestina St.. Tel: 787-735-3072.
Chapel—Bo. Rabanal (Parcelas), Nuestra S. de Fatima (1972),Tel: 787-735-0395.
Chapel—Ext. San Luis, Nuestra S. del Carmen (1986),Tel: 787-735-7189.
Chapel—La Plata, La Milagrosa (1986),Tel: 787-735-4038.
Chapel—Llanos, Sector El Juicio, Tel: 787-735-1973.
Chapel—La Sierra, San Judas Tadeo, Tel: 787-735-2835.

BARRANQUITAS, BARRANQUITAS CO.

1—CHURCH OF ST. ANTHONY OF PADUA (1808; 1988), Revs. Juan Colon Pineiro; Miguel Merced; Deacon Carlos Colon Bernardi.
Res.: P.O. Box 1099, 00794. Tel: 787-857-3585; Fax: 787-857-3585.
Catechesis/Religious Program—Students 1,800.
Chapel—San Francisco de Asis (1960),
Chapel—Bo. Mana, Virgen del Carmen (1963),
Chapel—Bo. Canabon, Virgen de la Providencia (1968),
Chapel—Bo. Helechal, San Jose Obrero (1968),
Chapel—Bo. Quebrada Grande, Nuestra Sra. de la Monserrate (1968),
Chapel—Bo. Palo Hincado, Virgen del Perpetuo Socorro (1975),
Chapel—Bo. Lajitas, Nuestra S. del Pilar (1970),
Chapel—Sector La Torre, Santa Cruz (1975),
Chapel—Bo. Helechal, San Martin de Porres (1950),

2—SAN ANDRES APOSTOL (1986), Rev. Jose A. de Leon; Deacons Optaciano Rivera Ortiz; Angel Mercado. In Res., Rev. Jose Luis Ortiz.
Res.: Bo. Quebradillas, Box 490, 00794. Tel: 787-875-5424; Fax: 787-875-5424.
Catechesis/Religious Program—Students 241.
Chapel—Bo. Palomas, Comerio, San Jose (1925),
Chapel—Bo. Quebradillas, Barranquitas, Corazon de Jesus (1940; 1987),
Chapel—Bo. Cedro Arriba, Naranjito, San Antonio de Padua (1864),
Chapel—Bo. Quebradillas, Barranquitas, Inmaculada Concepcion y Santa Cruz (1957),
Chapel—Bo. Cedro Arriba, Naranjito, Santuario Maria Auxiliadora (1992),

CAYEY, CAYEY CO.

1—NUESTRA SENORA DE LA ASUNCION (1787),, Mercedarian Fathers. Revs. Jose Munoz, O.M.; Jesus Saez, O.M.
Casa Parroquial: P.O. Box 37 2887, 00737-2887. Tel: 787-738-2763; Fax: 787-738-2763.
Catechesis/Religious Program—Students 1,069.
Chapel—Bo. Jajome, Sagrado Corazon de Jesus (1935),
Chapel—Bo. Pasto Viejo, Nuestra S. del Carmen (1937; 1988),
Chapel—Bo. Toita, Nuestra S. de la Merced (1946),
Chapel—Res. Brisas de Cayey, San Ramon Nonato (1978),
Chapel—Bo. Maton Arriba, Santa Teresita del Nino Jesus (1987),

2—NUESTRA SENORA DE LA MERCED (1968), Revs. Jesus Saez Castrillo, O.de.M.; Benigno Lopez; Wilfredo Riveros; Fidel Fernandez.
Reparto Montellano: P.O. Box 1840, 00737. Tel: 787-738-3872; Fax: 787-263-1810.
Chapel—Bo. Vegas, San Ramon Nonato (1961),
Chapel—Bo. Culebras, Nuestra S. del Carmen (1973),
Chapel—Bo. Farallon, San Pedro Nolasco (1980),
Chapel—San Pedro Armengol (La Plata) (1994),

3—SAN ESTEBAN PROTOMARTIR (1985), Rev. Jose Antonio Ortiz; Deacons Anibal Gonzalez Vazquez; Felix Montanez Perez; Silvestre Rodriguez Flores; Jesus M. Felix.
Res.: Bo. Guavate, 22601 Sector Nieves, 00736-9522. Tel: 787-747-4555.
Chapel—Bo. Borinquen Pradera, Nuestr Senora del Carmen (1910),
Chapel—Bo. Guavate, San Jose de la Montana (1951; 1990),

CIDRA, CIDRA CO.

1—NUESTRA SENORA DE FATIMA (1963), Rev. Juan B. Medina; Deacons Reyes Santos; Israel Santiago.
Bo. Rabanal: Box 214, 00739. Tel: 787-739-0633.

Catechesis / Religious Program—Students 596.
Chapel—Bo. Toita, Sagrado Corazon de Jesus (1960),
Chapel—Bo. Salto, San Vicente (1965),
Chapel—Bo. Honduras, Perpetuo Socorro (1970),
Chapel—Bo. Rabanal, Jesus Salvador (1970),
Chapel—Bo. Parcelas, La Milagrosa (1978),
Chapel—Bo. Salto, Nuestra Senora de la Providencia
Chapel—Bo. Salto, Santa Teresita (1982),
Chapel—Santo Cristo de Los Milagros (1987),

2—NUESTRA SENORA DEL CARMEN (1818), Revs. Raul Morales Berrios; Felix Rivera, O.C.D.; Deacons Diego Reyes Vasquez; Carlos Antonio Sola Fonseca.
Centro Plaza Municipal: P.O. Box 359, 00739. Tel: 787-739-2406; Fax: 787-739-4991.
Chapel—Bo. Rio Abajo, Madre del Salvador
Chapel—Urb. Treasure Valley, La Milagrosa
Chapel—Bo. Bayamon-Centenejas I, La Inmaculada
Chapel—Bo. Montellano, Santa Teresa del Nino Jesus
Chapel—Bo. Bayamon-Certenejas II, Perpetuo Socorro
Chapel—Bo. Bayamon-Juan del Valle, Nuestra Senora del Rosario
Chapel—Bo. Arena-Santa Clara, San Joaquin
Chapel—Bo. Ceiba-Hevia, Nuestra Senora del Rosario
Chapel—Bo. Arenas, Nuestra Senora de la Providencia
Chapel—Bo. Ceiba, Cristo Rey
Chapel—Bo. Bayamon-San Jose, San Jose
Chapel—Bo. Rincon, San Francisco de Asis
Chapel—Bo. Sud, La Milagrosa
Chapel—Bo. Sud, San Pablo

COMERIO, COMERIO CO., SANTO CRISTO DE LA SALUD (1832), Revs. John Alicea; Alirio Araque Galvis; Deacon Manuel Rivera Gonzalez.
Mailing Address: P.O. Box 1139, 00782. Tel: 787-875-4525; Fax: 787-875-3481.
Res.: Calle Santiago R Palmer #12, 00782.
Chapel—Bo. Sabana, Nuestra Senora del Santisimo Rosario (1966),
Chapel—Bo. Rio Hondo, Nuestra Senora de Fatima (1953),
Chapel—Bo. Palomas, Santa Ceceilia (1954),
Chapel—Bo. Cedrito, Virgen de la Providencia (1958),
Chapel—Bo. Rio Hondo-Sector Las Parcelas, San Pablo (1965),
Chapel—Bo. Pinas Arriba, Nuestra Senora del Carmen (1973),
Chapel—Bo. Naranjo-Sector Las Parcelas, San Antonio de Padua (1977),
Chapel—Bo. Vega Redonda, San Francisco de Asis (1977),
Chapel—Bo. Cejas, Santa Rose de Lima (1980),
Chapel—Bo. Dona Elena, San Martin de Porres (1950),
Chapel—Rio Hondo II, Maria Madre de la Iglesia

NARANJITO, NARANJITO CO., SAN MIGUEL ARCANGEL (1831), Revs. Oscar Rivera; Floyd Mercado; Floyd Mercado Vidro, Centro Parroquial, Box 68, 00719; Deacons Abigail Matos; Jose Berrios; Angel Oyola.
Res.: Centro Parroquial, P.O. Box 68, 00719. Tel: 787-869-2840; Fax: 787-869-3050.
Chapel—Bo. Nuevo, Santa Rosa de Lima (1953),
Chapel—Bo. Lomas Centro, Virgen del Carmen (1954),
Chapel—Bo. Anones, La Milagrosa (1962),
Chapel—Bo. Lomas Valles, San Judas Tadeo (1963),
Chapel—Bo. Guadiana, La Monserrate (1967),
Chapel—Bo. Achiote, Sagrado Corazon (1978),
Chapel—Bo. Nuevo Parcelas, San Vicente de Paul (1981),
Chapel—Bo. Cedro Abajo, San Jose (1981),

OUTSIDE THE CITY OF CAGUAS FROM LAS AMERICAS EXPRESS WAY TOWARD THE EAST COAST

CEIBA, CEIBA CO., SAN ANTONIO DE PADUA (1840), Rev. Jose A. Arocho.
Res.: 561 Escolastico Lopez St., P.O. Box 77, 00735. Tel: 787-885-2530; Fax: 787-885-2218.
Mission—Sagrado Corazon de Jesus Parcelas Aguas Claras, 00735.
Mission—N.S. del Perpetuo Socorro Ceiba, Bo. Rio Abajo, Ceiba Co. 00735.
Chapel—Nuestra Senora de Fatima (1968), Bo. Daguao, 00735.
Catechesis / Religious Program—Students 112.

FAJARDO, FAJARDO CO.

1—SANTIAGO APOSTOL (1766),, Redemptorist Fathers. Revs. Henry Beachamp, C.SS.R.; Joseph Checchia, C.SS.R.; Gerardo McSwigan, C.SS.R.
Res.: 16 Garrido Morales St., P.O. Box 806, 00738. Tel: 787-863-2365; Fax: 787-860-1837.
Chapel—Bo. Florencio, Santa Elena (1962),
Chapel—Bo. Quebrada Vueltas, Perpetuo Socorro (1965),
Chapel—La Milagrosa (1978),
Chapel—Santa Isidra, Santiago Apostol

2—SANTISIMO REDENTOR (1993), Rev. Ramon Santana.
Urb. Monte Brisas: Calle C-V-19, 00738. Tel: 787-863-5227; Fax: 787-860-0560.
Catechesis / Religious Program—Students 140.
Chapel—Puerto Real, Ntra. Sra. de Carmen
Chapel—Sardinera, San Juan Bautista
Chapel—Las Croabas, Maria, Madre del Senor
Chapel—Fajardo Gardens, Maria, Madre de la Providencia

GURABO, GURABO CO., SAN JOSE (1822), Rev. Angel Colon.
Res.: 7 Santiago Iglesias St., P.O. Box 733, 00778. Tel: 787-737-2656; Fax: 787-737-2656.
Chapel—Bo. Jagual, Sagrado Corazon de Jesus (1951),
Chapel—Bo. Jaguas Llano, Virgen del Carmen (1967),
Chapel—Bo. Santa Rita, Santa Rita (1968),
Chapel—La Milagrosa (1973), Bo. Hato Nuevo, 00778.
Chapel—Bo. Celada, Santa Francisca Javier Cabrini (1967),
Chapel—Bo. Hato Nuevo, La Milagrosa (1982),
Chapel—Bo. Jaguas Loma, San Miguel (1989),
Chapel—Bo. Mamey II, Ntra. Sra. del Carmen
Catechesis / Religious Program—Students 240.

HUMACAO PLAYA, HUMACAO CO., NUESTRA SENORA DEL CARMEN (Punta Santiago) (1970), Rev. Roberto Solivan.
Res.: P.O. Box 91, Punta Santiago, 00741. Tel: 787-850-2125; Fax: 787-850-2125.
Catechesis / Religious Program—Calle 5 #103 Verde Mar, P.O. Box 91, Punta Santiago, 00741. Tel: 787-852-3882. Students 125.
Chapel—Bo. Pasto Viejo, Sector El batey, Nuestra Senora del Perpetuo Socorro (1937; 1986),Tel: 787-852-4421.

HUMACAO, HUMACAO CO.

1—DULCE NOMBRE DE JESUS (Pueblo) (1763), [CEM 3] [JC] Revs. Hermenegildo Alayon; Renelmo Ramirez Vilela; Deacons Angel Cruz Cruz; Justino Cruz; Pablo Ortiz.
Res.: 3 Font Martelo St., Box 9087, 00791. Tel: 787-852-0868; Fax: 787-850-6448.
Catechesis / Religious Program—Students 670.
Chapel—San Agustin (1955), Parcela No. 44, Bo. Anton Ruiz.
Chapel—Nuestra Senora de la Candelaria (1956), Parcela No. 30, Candelero Arriba.
Chapel—San Jose (1957), Carr. 922 Cotto Mabu.
Chapel—Nuestra Senora de Fatima (1962), Bo. Juniquito.
Chapel—Santa Teresita (1965), Bo. Candelero Abajo.
Chapel—San Pedro y San Pablo (1986), Caserio Roig.
Chapel—Nuestra Senora de la Providencia (2000), Bo. Catano.
Chapel—Perpetuo Socorro (1944), Bo. Buena Vista.
Chapel—Inmaculada Concepcion (1996), Urbanizacion Villa.
Chapel—Maria Auxiliadora (1999), Bo. Candelero Abajo, Parcelas Martinez.

2—MARIA REINA DE LA PAZ (Pueblo) (1989), Revs. Kharlosg Lopez; Ignacio Aguirre, O.S.B.; Enrique Asencio; Deacon Rafael Ulfret.
Mailing Address: Correo Villa PMB 102, 00791-4349.
Villa Universitaria: Calle 4 A20, 00792. Tel: 787-850-3081; 787-285-0351; Fax: 787-850-3080.
Catechesis / Religious Program—Students 120.
Chapel—Sagrado Corazon de Jesus (1940),
Chapel—San Martin de Porres (1962),
Chapel—Bo. Mariana IV
Chapel—Buen Pastor (1970),
Chapel—Bo. Tejas, Cristo Rey (1976),
Chapel—Bo. Mariana II, Santa Rosa de Lima (1978),
Chapel—Comunidad Vista Hermosa

JUNCOS, JUNCOS CO., INMACULADA CONCEPCION (1797), Revs. Feliciano Rodriquez, Admin.; Felix Nunez Hernandez.
Res.: Almodovar St. #18, P.O. Box 1728, 00777. Tel: 787-734-2431; Fax: 787-734-0350.
Catechesis / Religious Program—Students 200.
Chapel—Bo. Canta Gallo, Cristo Redentor (1975),
Chapel—Bo. Ceiba Sur, Sagrado Corazon (1976),
Chapel—Bo. Valenciano Sector Amigo, Espiritu Santo (1976),
Chapel—Bo. Ceiba Norte, Cristo Rey (1978),
Chapel—Bo. Valenciano Arriba, San Juan Bautista (1979),
Chapel—Bo. Ceiba Norte Sector Chinos, Buen Pastor (1979),
Chapel—Bo. Pinas, Santa Cruz (1981),
Chapel—Bo. Lirios, San Jose (1978),
Chapel—Bo. Canta Gallo Secto Reparto Valenciano, Maria Reina De La Paz (1993),
Mission— Bo. Placita.

LAS PIEDRAS, LAS PIEDRAS CO.

1—INMACULADA CONCEPCION (1801), Revs. Boris Espinoza Perez; Carlos R. Soto.
Res.: Box 324, 00771. Tel: 787-733-2381; Fax: 787-733-1180.
Catechesis / Religious Program—Tel: 787-733-8325. Sor Miriam Nieves, D.R.E.; Hnas Fatima, D.R.E. Students 450.
Chapel—Bo. Montones I, Perpetuo Socorro (1935),
Chapel—Bo. Tejas Asomonte, Nuestra Senora de la Providencia (1955),
Chapel—Bo. La Fermina, Jesus de Nazaret (1979),
Chapel—Bo. Montones IV, Santa Teresa del Nino Jesus (1980),
Chapel—Bo. Montones II, San Juan Bautista (1982),
Mission— Salon Usos Multiples-Urb. April Gardens, Las Piedras.

2—SAN JUAN BAUTISTA (Bo. Pueblito del Rio) (1971), Rev. Angel L. Cintron; Deacons Angel Luis Santiago; Efrain Gomez.
Bo. Pueblito del Rio: HC 02, Buzon 4467, 00771. Tel: 787-733-6444.
Chapel—Finca Roig, San Juan Bautista (1911; 1940),
Chapel—Bo. Boqueron, La Sagrada Familia (1957),
Chapel—Bo. Pena Pobre, Santo Tomas de Aquino (1964),
Chapel—Bo. Rio Blanco, La Milagrosa (1972),
Chapel—Bo. Mango, San Francisco Javier
Chapel—Bo. Pasto Seco, El Buen Pastor 00771.

MAUNABO, MAUNABO CO., SAN ISIDRO LABRADOR (1799), Revs. Luis Antonio Alicea; Eusebio Ramos Morales.
Res.: P.O. Box 248, 00707. Tel: 787-861-2595; Fax: 787-861-2595.
Chapel—Nuestra Senora del Carmen (1962),
Chapel—Bo. Calzada, Nuestra Senora de la Providencia (1971),
Chapel—Bo. Matuyas, Nuestra Senora de la Candelaria (1974),
Chapel—Bo. Palo Seco, San Judas Tadeo (1975),
Chapel—Bo. Emajaguas, San Antonio de Padua (1977),
Mission— Bo. Quebrada Arenas.
Mission— Bo. Lizas.
Mission— Bo. Talante.
Mission— Bo. Paloseco.
Mission— Bo. Talante (La Pica).
Mission— Bo. Calzada.

NAGUABO, NAGUABO CO., NUESTRA SENORA DEL ROSARIO (1794), (Hispanic), [CEM 2] [JC] Rev. P. Jose A. Rivera Maldonado.
Res.: Box 665, 00718. Tel: 787-874-2235; Fax: 787-874-0150.
Chapel—Nuestra Senora del Perpetuo Socorro (1946),
Chapel—Bo. Maizales, Nuestra Senora de la Altagracia (1963),
Chapel—Bo. Duque, Nuestra Senora de Fatima (1965),
Chapel—Bo. Florida, Nuestra Senora del Perpetuo Socorro (1942),
Chapel—Nuestra Senora del Carmen Playa Hucares (1920),
Chapel—Bo. Mariana, Nuestra Senora de la Providencia (1965),
Chapel—Bo. Santiago y Lima (Botija), Santa Rosa de Lima (1975),
Mission— Barrio Rio, Sector Brazo Seco.
Mission— Barrio Cecilia, Sector La Fe.

SAN LORENZO, SAN LORENZO CO.

1—NUESTRA SENORA DE LA MERCEDES (1810), (Hispanic), Revs. Angel Lopez, C.SS.R.; Juan Ramon Hernandez, C.SS.R.; Hector Colon, C.SS.R.; Santiago Mallen, C.SS.R.
Res.: Munoz Rivera 55, Apartado 1280, 00754-1280. Tel: 787-736-2571; Fax: 787-736-1213.
Chapel—Bo. Jagual, Nuestra Senora del Carmen (1952),
Chapel—Bo. Quemados, Nuestra Senora del Perpetuo Socorro (1957),
Chapel—Bo. Cerro Gordo Abajo, Cristo Redentor (1965),
Chapel—Bo. Quebrada, Jesus Maestro
Chapel—Bo. Florida, Santa Monica
Chapel—Bda. Roosevelt, Nuestra Senora del Carmen (1968),
Chapel—Bo. Hato Km. 6, Nuestra Senora del Perpetuo Socorro (1968),
Chapel—Bo. Cerro Gordo Arriba, Nuestra Senora del Perpetuo Socorro (1977),
Chapel—Bo. Lorenzo del Valle, Inmaculado Corazon de Maria (1978),
Chapel—Bo. Santa Clara, San Gerardo (1986),
Chapel—Urb. Los Flamboyanes, Bo. Florida, Nuestra Senora de Lourdes (1988),
Catechesis / Religious Program—Students 1,115.

2—SAGRADO CORAZON DE JESUS Y 12 APOSTOLES (Bo. Espino) (1986), Revs. Luis Antonio Rivera Cruz; Franklin Rodriguez; Giovanni Ruiz.
Bo. Espino: HC 30, Box 32716, 00754-9726. Tel: 787-715-6947; Fax: 787-715-6947.
Chapel—San Francisco de Asis (1988), Carr. 181, 00754.
Chapel—Santa Rosa de Lima (1989), Carr. 181, 00754.

Chapel—San Jose (1959), Carr. 181, 00754.
Chapel—Nstra. Sra. del Rosario (1994), Carr. 181, Ramal 745, 00754.
Chapel—Maria Madre de la Iglesia (1990), Carr. 181, 00754.
Chapel—San Pedro (1998), 00754.
Chapel—Santa Teresita del Nino Jesus (1950), 00754.

YABUCOA, YABUCOA CO., SANTOS ANGELES CUTODIOS (1793), Revs. Rafael A. Rodriguez; P. Rafael Mateo; Freddy Celano; Jose A. Flores; Deacons Genaro Rodriguez; Carlos M. Ramos; Juan R. Delgado; Rev. Parroguis San Miguel.
Res.: P.O. Box 7, 00767. Tel: 787-893-2250 (Res.); 787-893-3347 (Office); Fax: 787-266-0841.
Catechesis/Religious Program—Students 930.
Chapel—Bo. Rosa Sanchez, Santa Rosa de Lima
Chapel—Bo. Jacanas Granjas, San Juan Evangelista
Chapel—Bo. Jac. Piedra Blanca, Sagrado Corazon (1976),
Chapel—Bo. Tejas Piedra Azul, Sta. Maria Reina Paz
Chapel—Bo. Martorell, Santa Teresita del Nino Jesus
Chapel—Bo. Tejas, Ntra. Sra. de la Divina Providencia
Chapel—Bo. Playita Cuesta, San Bernardo
Chapel—Bo. Playita Arriba, S. Antonio de Padua (1947),
Chapel—Bo. Playita Parcelas, Virgen Milagrosa
Chapel—Bo. Quebradillas, Ntra. Sra. del Carmen
Chapel—Bo. Guayabota, La Sagrada Familia (1948),
Chapel—Bo. Calabazas Arriba, San Jose (1942),
Chapel—Bo. Quebrada Grande, San Benito
Chapel—Bo. Playa Guayanes, Ntra. Sra. de Carmen
Chapel—Bo. Aguacate, Ntra. Sra. del Perpetuo Socorro (1987),
Chapel—Bo. Jagueyes, Inmaculada Concepcion (1910),
Chapel—Bo. Ingenio, Santisima Trinidad
Chapel—Bo. Camino Nuevo, San Jeronimo
Chapel—Bo. Jacanas Sur, Divino de Jesus y Beato Diego (1999),
Chapel—Bo. Tejas Valerio, Corpus Christi.

OUTSIDE THE MAIN ISLAND OF PUERTO RICO, THE SMALL ISLANDS

CULEBRA, CULEBRA CO., NUESTRA SENORA DEL CARMEN (1889; 1990), Rev. Hilario Rivera Gonzalez.
Mailing Address: P.O. Box 236, 00775. Tel: 787-742-0133.

VIEQUES, VIEQUES CO., INMACULADA CONCEPCION (1844), (Hispanic), Rev. Nelson Lopez Aponte; Deacon Justino Lopez Ortiz.
Res.: 442 Lebrum St., 00765. Tel: 787-741-2241; Fax: 787-741-2241.
Chapel—Bo. Puerto Real, Sagrado Corazon de Jesus (1949),
Chapel—Bo. Esperanza, San Gerardo (1952),
Chapel—Bo. Monte Santo, Nuestra Senora del Perpetuo Socorro (1945),
Chapel—Bo. Santa Maria, Virgen del Carmen (1942),
Chapel—Bo. Destino, Nuestra Senora de Fatima (1950),

Chaplains of Public Institutions

CAGUAS. *Government Regional Hospital*. Rev. Javier Hernandez.
Hospital Hima. Rev. Javier Hernandez.

Retired:
Revs.—
Chocarro, Antonio
Martinez, Alfredo
Santos, Raul

INSTITUTIONS LOCATED IN THE DIOCESE

[A] PAROCHIAL SCHOOLS

CAGUAS. *Academia Cristo de los Milagros*, Box 7618, 00726-7618. Tel: 787-743-4855; 787-743-3131; 787-743-4242; Fax: 787-746-1428. Email: acdlm@caribe.net. Priests 1; Deacons 1; Lay Teachers 62; Students 1,406.
Colegio Catolico Notre Dame Elemental, P.O. Box 967, 00726. Tel: 787-743-2385; 787-743-2524; Fax: 787-743-7567; 787-744-6464. Email: tecumsa@coguinet.com. Web: www.prsbm@yahoo.com. Priests 1; Sisters 2; Lay Teachers 65; Aides 14; Students 1,045.
Colegio Catolico Notre Dame Superior, Box 541, 00726. Tel: 787-743-3693; 787-743-5501; Fax: 787-258-9648. Web: www.ccnd.org. Priests 2; Sisters 4; Lay Teachers 80; Students 1,185.
Colegio San Jose Elemental, P.O. Box 806, 00726. Tel: 787-743-2032; Fax: 787-258-0683. Email: csje-sec@csje-sec.org. Web: www.csje-sec.org. Priests 2; Sisters 5; Lay Teachers 26; Students 560.
Colegio San Jose Superior, P.O. Box 1101, Y/O 1749, 00726. Tel: 787-744-8993; Fax: 787-744-4111. Email: san.jose@prw.net. Priests 1; Lay Teachers 22; Students 397.
Colegio San Juan Apostol y Evangelista, P.O. Box 459, 00726-0459. Tel: 787-743-8266; Fax: 787-743-8266. Wilma Roman, Admin. Lay Teachers 27; Students 486.

AGUAS BUENAS. *Academia San Alfonso*, (Grades PreK-9), Pio Rechani St., P.O. Box 1, 00703. Tel: 787-732-8288; Fax: 787-732-2188. Lay Teachers 13; Students 200.

AIBONITO. *Colegio Parroquial San Jose*, P.O. Box 812, 00705. Tel: 787-735-7235; Fax: 878-735-7235. Priests 2; Brothers 1; Sisters 1; Lay Teachers 15; Students 200.

BARRANQUITAS. *Colegio San Francisco de Asis Elemental y Superior*, P.O. Box 789, 00794. Tel: 787-857-2123. Deacon Carlos Colon Bernardi, Dir. Brothers 3; Students 118.

CAYEY. *Colegio Nuestra Senora de la Merced*, Lucia Vazquez St., 00736. Tel: 787-738-3438; Fax: 787-263-5837. (Nuestra Senora de la Asuncion Parish) Priests 1; Lay Teachers 23; Students 423.

FAJARDO. *Colegio Santiago Apostol*, (Grades K-12), Call Box 70007, 00738. Tel: 787-863-0524; 787-863-0445; Fax: 787-860-6655. Students 425; Lay Teachers 22.

GURABO. *Colegio Ntra. Sra. De Pilar*, P.O. Box 1332, 00778. Tel: 787-737-1400. Mrs. Ramonita Quinones Santos. Priests 1; Lay Teachers 15; Total Staff 25; Students 203.

HUMACAO. *Colegio Nuestra Senora del Perpetuo Socorro de Humacao, Inc.*, P.O. Box 9107, 00792. Tel: 787-852-0845; 787-850-0025; Fax: 787-852-8706. Email: perpetuo@east-net.net. Web: www.psocorroacaribe.net. Lay Teachers 19; Students 413.
Colegio San Antonio Abad (Benedictines), P.O. Box 729, 00792. Tel: 787-852-1616; Fax: 787-852-1920. Email: santabad@east-net.net. Glenda Bermudez, Prin. Students 455; Priests 2; Lay Teachers 29.
Colegio San Benito, P.O. Box 728, 00792. Tel: 787-852-1365; 787-850-7075; Fax: 787-285-8137. Students 771; Sisters 6; Lay Teachers 40.

JUNCOS. *Colegio Corazon de Maria*, (Grades PreK-12), P.O. Box 1776, Carr. #935 Bo. Cieba Norte, 00777-1776. Tel: 787-734-5551; 787-734-5565; Fax: 787-734-2724. Email: ccm_sec@ccm_sec.org. Web: www.ccm_sec.org. Priests 1; Sisters 3; Lay Teachers 36; Students 397.

NARANJITO. *Academia Santa Teresita*, P.O. Box 244, 00719. Tel: 787-869-7968; 787-869-6731; 787-869-8357; Fax: 787-869-8357. Email: astnar@prtc.net. Lay Teachers 25; Students 390.

[B] RETREAT HOUSES

AGUAS BUENAS. *Casa Cristo Redentor* (1967), P.O. Box 8, 00703-0008. Tel: 787-732-5161; Fax: 787-732-1115. Email: pdamian@coqui.net. Revs. Terence Damian Wall, C.SS.R., S.T.D., Supr.; Hipolito Vicens, C.SS.R., Dir.; Bro. Mateo Perez, C.SS.R. In Res. Rev. Harold Spacht, C.SS.R.

AIBONITO. *Casa Manresa*, P.O. Box 1319, 00705. Tel: 787-735-8016; 787-735-8017; Fax: 787-735-2421. Email: manresa@caribe.net. Web: www.netdial.caribe.net/~manresa. Revs. Aurelio Adan, Dir.; Alberto Martinez; Sr. Mercedes Cadena, R.M., Supr.

JUNCOS. *Casa Cursillos de Cristiandad de Caguas* (Lay Corp. of Cursillistas), Salida de Juncos Carretera 919, P.O. Box 1761, 00777. Tel: 787-734-7068.

SAN LORENZO. *Casa Charlie Rodriguez*, P.O. Box 1190, 00754. Tel: 787-736-5750. Rev. Edward Santana, J.C.D

[C] MONASTERIES AND RESIDENCES OF PRIESTS

CAGUAS. *Misioneros Hijos del Inmaculado Corazon de Maria (Claretianos)*, Bo. Rio Canas HC-05 Box 57564, 00725-9233. Tel: 787-747-6336; Fax: 787-258-4910. Email: jvicente@coqui.net jvmsg@hotmail.com.

AIBONITO. *Casa Salesiana de Retiros*, P.O. Box 2019, 00705. Tel: 787-735-2486; Fax: 787-735-5501. Email: sdbaibon@coqui.net. Revs. Adan Luis Marrero Berrios, Dir.; Luis Dalbon; Franklin Santana.

HUMACAO. *San Antonio Abad Abbey of the Order of St. Benedict*, P.O. Box 729, 00792. Tel: 787-852-1616; Fax: 787-852-1920. Email: santabad@east-net.com. Revs. Oscar Rivera, O.S.B., Abbot; Jose Rodriguez, O.S.B. (Retired); Very Rev. Eduardo Torrelas, Prior; Revs. Rafael Perez, O.S.B.; Jaime Reyes, O.S.B.; Eric Buermann, O.S.B.; Mauro Simpson, O.S.B.; Bros. Aristedes Pacheco, Subprior; Felix Neussendorfer; Tarcisio Medina; Gregorio Valentin; Randolph Perkins; Roberto Rossi; Jaime Trevino; Ricardo Padilla; Gerardo Suarez; Alfredo Vallejo; Antonio Hernandez. Brothers 8; Novices 2.

[D] CLOISTER SISTERS

AGUAS BUENAS. *Reina de la Paz Convent*, P.O. Box 1183, 00703. Tel: 787-732-5339.

[E] SHRINES

SAN LORENZO. *Diocesan Shrine Our Lady of Mount Carmel* P.O. Box 1190, 00754. Tel: 787-736-5750. Rev. Edward Santana, J.C.D., Rector.

[F] MISCELLANEOUS

CAGUAS. *Diocesan Tribunal of Caguas*, P.O. Box 9779, 00726. Tel: 787-286-8595; Fax: 787-286-8620. Rev. Felix Nunez, Judicial Vicar.
Instituto Secular de Ntra. Sra. de la Altagracia, Calle 13, L23. Urb. Delgado, 00725. Tel: 787-744-3628; Fax: 787-744-3628. Isabel Vazquez Rivera; Maria Melendez Sanchez; Ramonita Lopez Diaz; Zoraida Santos Santos; Judith Colon Cruz; Olga Rodriguez Berrios; Maria Isabel Colon; Prixda Santos Agosto; Doris Roque Julia; Natividad Ramos Ramos; Evelyn Rosado Rivera.
Movimiento Juan XXIII, P.O. Box 7229, 00726. Tel: 787-747-3748. Rev. Hector Bruno de Jesus.
Voluntarios y Acompanantes Comprometidos con el SIDA (VACS), P.O. Box 656, 00726. Tel: 747-286-3333; Fax: 787-286-3612. Email: vacs@coqui.net.

NARANJITO. *Seminario Pablo VI - Propedeutico*, P.O. Box 302, 00719. Tel: 787-869-0861; Fax: 787-869-0861. Email: jcardona@prtc.net. Revs. Jorge Cardona, Rector; Felix Nunez, Vocation Dir.

RELIGIOUS INSTITUTES OF MEN REPRESENTED IN THE DIOCESE

For further details refer to the corresponding bracketed number in the Religious Institutes of Men or Women section.

[0200]—*Benedictine Monks* (Collegeville, MN)—O.S.B.
[]—*Claretian Fathers*—C.M.F.
[0220]—*Congregation of the Blessed Sacrament* (N. Spain Prov.)—S.S.S.
[]—*Mercedarian Fathers* (Spain)
[]—*Order of Carmelites*—O.Carm.
[1070]—*Redemptorist Fathers* (San Juan Prov.)—C.SS.R.
[1190]—*Salesians of Don Bosco* (Cuba)—S.D.B.

RELIGIOUS INSTITUTES OF WOMEN REPRESENTED IN THE DIOCESE

[0230]—*Benedictine Sisters of Pontifical Jurisdiction* (St. Joseph, MN)—O.S.B.
[0420]—*Discalced Carmelite Nuns* (Spain)—O.C.C.
[]—*Franciscan Nuns (Cloistered)*
[2790]—*Missionary Servants of the Most Holy Trinity* (Spain)—M.S.B.T.
[3760]—*Order of St. Clare*—P.C.C.
[]—*Sacred Heart Sisters*
[]—*Salesian Sisters*
[2970]—*School Sisters of Notre Dame* (Wilton, CT)—S.S.N.D.
[]—*Siervas de Maria* (Spain)
[0640]—*Sisters of Charity of St. Vincent de Paul* (Puerto Rico Prov.)—S.C.
[]—*Sisters of Fatima* (Diocesan)
[1650]—*The Sisters of St. Francis of Philadelphia*—O.S.F.
[2150]—*Sisters Servants of the Immaculate Heart of Mary*—I.H.M.

NECROLOGY

† Gutierrez y Alvarez, Julio, (Retired)—Died May 11, 2003

Diocese of the Caroline Islands

Most Reverend

AMANDO SAMO, D.D.

Bishop of the Caroline Islands; ordained Priest December 10, 1977; appointed Titular Bishop of Libertina and Auxiliary Bishop of the Caroline and Marshalls May 10, 1987; ordained Bishop August 15, 1987; named Coadjutor February 3, 1994; named Bishop of the Diocese March 25, 1995; installed June 6, 1995. *Res.: P.O. Box 939, Chuuk, FM 96942.* Tel: 691-330-2399; Fax: 691-330-4585.

Most Reverend

MARTIN J. NEYLON, S.J., D.D.

Retired Bishop of the Caroline Islands; ordained June 18, 1950; appointed Titular Bishop of Libertina October 2, 1969, "cum jure successionis"; consecrated February 2, 1970; succeeded as Vicar Apostolic September 20, 1971; appointed First Bishop of Carolines-Marshalls May 3, 1979; installed February 3, 1980; retired June 6, 1995. *Res.: St. Ignatius Loyola Residence*, 53 E. 83rd St., New York, NY 10028. Tel: 212-288-3588; Fax: 212-734-3671.

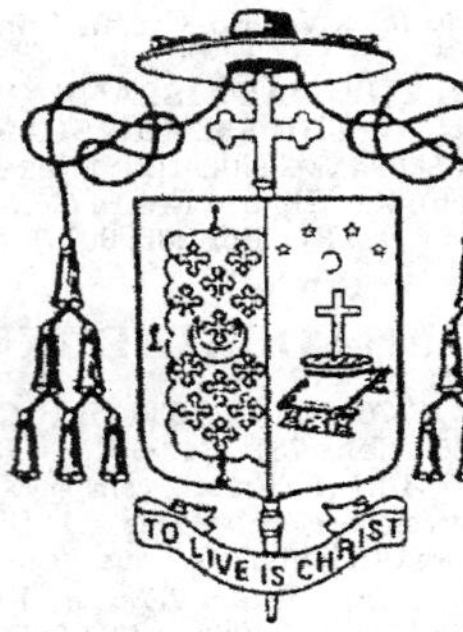

Chancery Office: P.O. Box 939, Chuuk, FM 96942. Tel: 691-330-2399; Fax: 691-330-4585.

Web: www.diocesecarolines.org

Email: diocese@mail.fm

Square Miles Ocean 1,725,000.

Total Population of 135,831.

Vicariate of the Caroline Islands erected December 10, 1905 and committed to the Order of Friars Minor Capuchin, extended to the Mariana Islands March 1, 1911.

Vicariate of the Marianas and Caroline and Marshall Islands erected May 4, 1923 and committed to the Society of Jesus. Marianas Islands separated July 4, 1946. Diocese of the Caroline-Marshalls created February 3, 1980. The Marshalls made a separate Prefecture Apostolic August 15, 1993, and the Diocese renamed "Diocese of the Caroline Islands."

Civilly it includes the four Federated States of Micronesia (Chuuk, Kosrae, Pohnpei and Yap) and the Republic of Palau.

STATISTICAL OVERVIEW

Statistical report was not submitted for 2004.

Personnel	
Bishop	1
Retired Bishops	1
Priests: Diocesan Active in Diocese	12
Priests: Retired, Sick or Absent	1
Number of Diocesan Priests	13
Religious Priests in Diocese	18
Total Priests in Diocese	31
Extern Priests in Diocese	13
Ordinations:	
Diocesan Priests	1
Religious Priests	2
Transitional Deacons	1
Permanent Deacons	43
Total Brothers	1
Total Sisters	33
Parishes	
Parishes	26
With Resident Pastor:	
Resident Diocesan Priests	8
Resident Religious Priests	5
Without Resident Pastor:	
Administered by Priests	3
Administered by Deacons	9
Administered by Lay People	3
Missions	4
Pastoral Centers	8
Professional Ministry Personnel:	
Sisters	3
Educational	
Diocesan Students in Other Seminaries	5
Total Seminarians	5
High Schools, Diocesan and Parish	3
Total Students	455
High Schools, Private	1
Total Students	343
Elementary Schools, Diocesan and Parish	5
Total Students	1,309
Catechesis/Religious Education:	
High School Students	798
Elementary Students	1,309
Total Students under Catholic Instruction	4,219
Teachers in the Diocese:	
Priests	6
Scholastics	2
Brothers	1
Sisters	24
Lay Teachers	134
Vital Statistics	
Receptions into the Church:	
Infant Baptism Totals	1,804
Adult Baptism Totals	307
Received into Full Communion	20
First Communions	1,071
Confirmations	657
Marriages:	
Catholic	347
Interfaith	78
Total Marriages	425
Total Catholic Population	72,940
Total Population	149,225

Former Bishops—Most Revs. SALVADOR WALLAESER, O.F.M.Cap., consecrated Vicar Apostolic and Titular Bishop of Tanagra, Aug. 21, 1912; resigned June 23, 1919; died Jan. 1, 1946; SANTIAGO LOPEZ DE REGO, S.J., consecrated Vicar Apostolic and Titular Bishop of Dionisiopolis, Aug. 26, 1923; resigned June 2, 1939; died Aug. 5, 1940; THOMAS J. FEENEY, S.J., consecrated Vicar Apostolic and Titular Bishop of Agno, Sept. 8, 1951; died Sept. 9, 1955; VINCENT I. KENNALLY, S.J., consecrated Vicar Apostolic and Titular Bishop of Sassura, March 25, 1957; resigned Sept. 20, 1971; died April 12, 1977; MARTIN J. NEYLON, S.J., D.D. (Retired), ord. Bishop, Feb. 2, 1970; succeeded to as Vicar Apostolic, Sept. 20, 1970; named to be Bishop of the new diocese, May 3, 1979; installed as first Bishop of the Diocese of the Carolines-Marshalls, Feb. 3, 1980; retired June 6, 1995.

Chancery Office—P.O. Box 939, Chuuk, 96942. Tel: 691-330-2399; Fax: 691-330-4585.

Vicar General—Rev. JOHN F. CURRAN, S.J., J.C.L.

Chancellor—Rev. NICHOLAS P. RAHOY.

Diocesan Consultors—Revs. JOHN F. CURRAN, S.J., J.C.L.; RUSK SABURO; JOHN S. HAGILEIRAM, S.J.; ADALBERT UMWECH.

Finance Committee—Rev. JOHN F. CURRAN, S.J., J.C.L.; Mr. SANTI ASANUMA; Mr. ANGKEN XYMOON; Mr. TONY GANNGIYAN; Mr. ALBINO KERMAN; Rev. NICHOLAS P. RAHOY.

Episcopal Vicars—

Chuuk—Rev. DAVID LEWIS, P.O. Box 337, Chuuk, 96942. Tel: 691-330-2672; Fax: 691-330-4394.

Palau—Rev. JOHN PAUL ILILAU, P.O. Box 128, Palau, PW 96940. Tel: 680-488-6539; 680-488-2226; Fax: 680-488-1819.

Pohnpei-Kosrae—Rev. JOHN F. CURRAN, S.J., J.C.L., P.O. Box 160, Pohnpei, 96941. Tel: 691-320-4661; Fax: 691-320-5876.

Yap—Rev. JOHN S. HAGILEIRAM, S.J., P.O. Box "A", Yap, 96943. Tel: 691-350-2265; Fax: 691-350-2784.

Diocesan Tribunal—

Judical Vicar—Rev. WILLIAM J. RAKOWICZ, S.J., P.O. Box 128, Palau, PW 96940. Tel: 680-488-2226; Fax: 680-488-1819.

Defenders of the Bond—Revs. FLORENTINUS AKKIN; NEIL POULIN, S.J.; RUSK SABURO.

Notaries—Rev. JOHN F. CURRAN, S.J., J.C.L.; Mrs. MIRIAM CHIN; Ms. FILIPANA PHILLIP.

Vocations—Rev. JULIO ANGKEL.

CLERGY, PARISHES, MISSIONS AND PAROCHIAL SCHOOLS

CHUUK (TRUK) STATE, CAROLINE ISLANDS

Mailing Address for the Vicariate of Chuuk: Rev. David Lewis, P.O. Box 250, Chuuk, Caroline Islands, FM 96942. Tel: 691-330-2672; Fax: 691-330-4394 (unless otherwise noted).

FEFAN, SACRED HEART, Rev. John Ikataere, M.S.C.

Mission— Parem.

MORTLOCK ISLANDS, MORTLOCK, Rev. Florentinus Akkin.

Mission— Satowan.
Mission— Kuttu.
Mission— Moch.
Mission— Ettal.
Mission— Namoluk.
Mission— Lukunor.
Mission— Oneop.
Mission— Ta.
Mission— Nama.
Mission— Piis.
Mission— Losap.

NEEPWUKOS, HOLY FAMILY CHURCH, Rev. Julio Angkel; Deacons Eliot Cholymay; Bername Itiraw.

TOL, ASSUMPTION OF THE BLESSED VIRGIN MARY, Rev. Adalbert Umwech; Deacons Angken Rapun; Roke Rokop; Kintin Rawit; Itoi Ruta; Oiken Victus; Missa Sewell; Francisco Ykuta; Lukas Paulus.
School—St. Julia Sr. Yolanda Delgadillo, M.M.B., Prin. Mercedarian Missionaries of Berriz 6; Lay Teachers 6; Students 91.

TOLOWAS, ST. ANTHONY'S, Rev. David Lewis; Deacon Tobias Soram.

TUNNUK, IMMACULATE HEART OF MARY CATHEDRAL, Rev. Basilio Dilipiy; Deacons Chitaro William; Yostaro Noporu; Edwin Shuru, (Retired).
School—St. Cecilia's, Tel: 691-330-4525; Fax: 691-330-4394. Mr. Mariano Marcus, Prin. Mercedarian Missionaries of Berriz 2; Peace Corps Volunteer 1; Lay Teachers 30; Students 634.

UDOT, ST. FRANCIS ASSISI, Rev. Mathews Abraham; Deacons John Fritz; Eichy Karsom.
Mission—St. Joseph Romanum.

UMAN, HOLY CROSS, Rev. Edmond Luwich; Deacons Audreas Nimas; Carlos Sam; Salvador Mailos; Akiuo Meisa; Joseph Albert; Nori Oneitam.

POHNPEI STATE, CAROLINE ISLANDS

Mailing Address for the Vicariate of Pohnpei: Rev. John F. Curran, S.J., P.O. Box 160, Pohnpei, Caroline Islands, FM 96941. Tel: 691-320-4661; Fax: 691-320-5876 (unless otherwise noted).

AWAK, ST. JOSEPH, Deacons Adelino Lorens, Admin.; Manuel Amor, (Retired).
Tel: 691-320-6025.

IPWUTEK, ST. AUGUSTINE, Deacon Tarsisio Amon, Admin.
Tel: 691-320-8930.

KOLONIA, OUR LADY OF MERCY, Revs. Cuthbert Yiftheg; Kasiano Paul; Deacons Edgar Martin; Martiniano Rodriguez; Geronimo Victor.
Tel: 691-320-2557; Fax: 691-320-5876.
School—Pohnpei Catholic School, Tel: 691-320-2556. Sisters 3; Lay Teachers 11; Students 213.

PALIKIR, STS. PAUL AND BARNABAS, Deacon Thomas Santos, Admin.
Tel: 691-320-5822.

PORRASSAPW, CHRIST THE KING, Deacons Saulus Olbet, Admin.; Koropin Kermen.
Tel: 691-320-3744.

SEINWAR, MOST PURE HEART OF MARY, Deacon Luciano Iowanis.
Tel: 691-320-3573.

SOKEHS, ST. PETER'S, Deacon Albert Linny, Admin.
Tel: 691-320-4667; 691-320-6923.

TAMOROI, SACRED HEART, Rev. Edward A. Soucie, S.J.; Deacon Darris Amor, Admin.
Tel: 691-320-5742.
Mission— Metip.

YAP STATE, CAROLINE ISLANDS

Mailing Address for the Vicariate of Yap: Rev. Apollinaris Thall, S.J., Vicar, P.O. Box A, Yap, FM 96943. Tel: 691-350-2265; Fax: 350-2784.

GAGIL-TOMIL, ST. JOSEPH, Rev. Neil C. Poulin, S.J.
Tel: 691-350-2598.

NEMAR, ST. MARY, Rev. Apollinaris I. Thall, S.J.
School—St. Mary's Sr. Vincent Marie Balajadia, S.S.N.D., Prin. Priests 1; Sisters 1; Lay Teachers 13; Students 310.

ULITHI AND NEIGHBORING ISLANDS, QUEEN OF HEAVEN, Deacon John Rulmal.
Mission— Ngulu.

WOLEAI AND NEIGHBORING ISLANDS, ST. IGNATIUS, Revs. John S. Hagileiram, S.J.; Kenneth Urumolug, S.J.

REPUBLIC OF PALAU, CAROLINE ISLANDS

Mailing Address for the Vicariate of Palau: Rev. John Paul Iliau, Vicar, P.O. Box 128, Koror, Palau PW 96940. Tel: 680-488-1758; Fax: 680-488-1819.

BABELDAOB, ST. THOMAS APOSTLE, Rev. John Paul Ililau, Admin.

IOUELDOAB, ST. JOHN BAPTIST, Rev. John Paul Ililau.

KOROR, SACRED HEART, Rev. Rusk R. Saburo.
School—Maris Stella Mr. Felix Okabe, Prin. Mercedarian Missionaries of Berriz 6; Lay Teachers 23; Students 330.
Mission— Ngcheangl.
Mission— Sonsorol.
Convent—Our Lady of Lourdes Mercedarian Missionaries of Berriz 7.
Manresa Jesuit Novitiate—Very Rev. Felix K. Yaoch, S.J., Dir.

Permanent Deacons:
- Albert, Joseph, Uman, Chuuk
- Amor, Manuel, Awak, Pohnpei
- Amor, Tarsisio, Ipwutek, Pohnpei
- Cholymay, Eliot, Neepwokos, Moen, Chuuk
- Edgar, Martin, Kolonia, Pohnpei
- Else, Pelsiano, Sapwuahfik, Pohnpei
- Elukan, Augustine, (Retired), Maap, Yap
- Felichoo, Francisco, Gagil-Tomil, Yap
- Fichiman, Donald, Gagil-Tomil, Yap
- Fritz, John, Udot, Chuuk
- Iowanis, Tuciano, Seinwar, Pohnpei
- Itiraw, Bername, Neepwukos, Chuuk
- Karsom, Eichy, Udot, Chuuk
- Kermen, Koropin, Kiti, Pohnpei
- Linny, Albert, Sokehs, Pohnpei
- Lorens, Adelino, Uh, Pohnpei
- Mailos, Salvador, Uman, Chuuk
- Meisa, Akiuo, Uman, Chuuk
- Nimas, Andreas, Uman, Chuuk
- Noporu, Yostaro, Fono, Chuuk
- Olbet, Saulus, Porrassapw, Pohnpei
- Oneitam, Nory, Uman, Chuuk
- Paulus, Lucas, Fanapanges, Chuuk
- Rapun, Angken, Tol, Chuuk
- Rawit, Kintin, Wonei, Chuuk
- Rodriguez, Martiniano, Kolonia, Pohupei
- Rokop, Roke, Tol, Chuuk
- Rulmal, John B., Ulithi, Yap
- Ruta, Itoi, Tol, Chuuk
- Sam, Karlos, Uman, Chuuk
- Santos, Thomas, Palikir, Pohnpei
- Sewell, Meisa, Tol, Chuuk
- Shuru, Edwin, (Retired), Moen, Chuuk
- Silbanuz, Peter, Tamworoi, Pohnpei
- Soram, Tobias, Tolowas, Chuuk
- Sos, Iakim, Uman, Chuuk
- Victor, Geronimo, Kolonia, Pohnpei
- Victus, Oiken, Pwene, Chuuk
- William, Chitaro, Tunnuk, Moen, Chuuk
- Ykuta, Francisco, Pwene, Chuuk

INSTITUTIONS LOCATED IN THE DIOCESE

[A] PASTORAL RESEARCH INSTITUTE

POHNPEI. *Micronesian Seminar*, P.O. Box 160, 96941. Tel: 691-320-4067; Fax: 691-320-5876. Rev. Francis X. Hezel, S.J., Dir. Lay Assistants 2.

[B] HIGH SCHOOLS

CHUUK. *Saramen Chuuk Academy*, P.O. Box 662, 96942. Tel: 691-330-4442; Fax: 691-330-4452. Julia William, Prin. Sisters 1; Lay Teachers 22; Students 258.
Xavier High School, P.O. Box 220, 96942. Tel: 691-330-4266; Fax: 691-330-4753. Revs. James P. Croghan, S.J., Dir.; Richard S. McCouch, S.J.; Mrs. Lynn Polloi, Prin. Lay Teachers 13; Scholastics 2; Students 163.

PALAU. *Mindszenty High School*, P.O. Box 69. Tel: 680-488-2437. Ms. Justa Polloi, Prin. Priests 1; Mercedarian Sisters 1; Lay Teachers 17; Students 197.

POHNPEI. *Our Lady of Mercy Vocational Training School*, P.O. Box 73, 96941. Tel: 691-320-3168. Sr. Maria Perez-Caballero, M.M.B., Prin. Mercedarian Sisters 2; Lay Teachers 6; Students 61.
PATS (Pohnpei Agriculture and Trade School), P.O. Box 39, 96941. Tel: 691-320-2991; Fax: 691-320-6046. Revs. Gregory F. Muckenhaupt, S.J., Dir.; Paul L. Horgan, S.J., Chap.; Akilina Soram, Prin.; Bro. Terence N. Todd, S.J., Asst. Dir. Priests 2; Brother Teaching 1; Lay Teachers 30; Students 148.

[C] RESIDENCES OF PRIESTS AND BROTHERS

KOLONIA, POHNPEI. *Jesuit House*, P.O. Box 160, 96941. Tel: 691-320-2317; Fax: 691-320-5876. In Res. Revs. Joseph A. Cavanagh, S.J.; John F. Curran, S.J., J.C.L., Vicar Gen. & E. Vicar; Francis X. Hezel, S.J., Supr.; Edward A. Soucie, S.J.

KOROR, PALAU. *Manresa Jesuit House*, P.O. Box 128. Tel: 680-488-2226; Fax: 680-488-1319; 680-488-1725 Very Rev. Felix K. Yaoch, S.J., Regl. Supr.; Revs. William J. Rakowiez, S.J.; Fusk R. Saburo; John P. Flilau; Wayne Tkel, S.J.; Simplicio Sumpayco, S.J.

TUNNUK, CHUUK. *Vicariate Residence* P.O. Box 250, 96942. Tel: 691-330-2313; Fax: 691-330-4394. In Res Revs. Mathews Abraham; Julio Angkel; Basilio Dilipy; David Lewis; Edmond Ludwick, Admin.; Nicholas P. Rahoy; Adalbert Umwech.

[D] RESIDENCES OF SISTERS

AWAK, POHNPEI. *Sisters of Marie Auxiliatrice*, P.O. Box 1375, 96942. Tel: 691-320-2626. Sr. Keiko Akaiwa, M.A., Supr. Sisters 6.

COLONIA, YAP. *Maryknoll Sisters*, P.O. Box 26, 96943. Tel: 691-350-2148 (Colonia). Sr. Joanne McMahon, M.M., Contact Person. Sisters 3.
School Sisters of Notre Dame, P.O. Box 111, 96943. Tel: 691-350-2345. Sr. Vincent Marie Balajadia, S.S.N.D., Contact Person. Sisters 2.

KOLONIA, POHNPEI. *Mercedarian Missionaries of Berriz*, P.O. Box 73, 96941. Tel 691-320-2558. Sr. Maria Perez-Caballero, M.M.B. Coord. Sisters 4.

KOROR, PALAU. *Mercedarian Missionaries of Berriz*, P.O. Box 56. Tel: 680-488-2272. Sr. Micaela Udui, M.M.B., Coord. Sisters 7.

NEEPWUKOS, CHUUK. *Religious Sisters of Mercy* 96942. Tel: 691-330-3363. Sr. Grace Joseph, R.S.M., Coord. Sisters 1.

TOL, CHUUK. *Mercedarian Missionaries of Berriz*, P.O. Box 190, 96942. Sr. Yolanda Delgadillo, M.M.B., Coord. Sisters 6.

WENO, CHUUK. *Mercedarian Missionaries of Berriz*, P.O. Box 67, 96942. Tel: 691-330-4587. Sr. Faustina Nedelec, M.M.B., Coord. Sisters 4.

RELIGIOUS INSTITUTES OF MEN REPRESENTED IN THE DIOCESE

For further details refer to the corresponding bracketed number in the Religious Institutes of Men or Women section.

[0690]—*Jesuit Fathers and Brothers* (New York Prov.)—S.J.

[1110]—*Missionaries of the Sacred Heart*—M.S.C.

RELIGIOUS INSTITUTES OF WOMEN REPRESENTED IN THE DIOCESE

[2470]—*Maryknoll Sisters of St. Dominic*—M.M.

[2510]—*Mercedarian Missionaries of Berriz*—M.M.B.

[2970]—*School Sisters of Notre Dame*—S.S.N.D.

[]—*Sisters of Marie Auxiliatrice*—M.A.

[2575]—*Sisters of Mercy of the Americas*—R.S.M.

NECROLOGY

(No Deaths)

Diocese of Chalan Kanoa

(Dioecesis Vialenbensis)

Most Reverend

TOMAS A. CAMACHO, D.D.

Bishop of Chalan Kanoa; ordained June 14, 1961; appointed Prelate of Honor by Pope Paul VI in 1974; appointed Bishop of Chalan Kanoa November 8, 1984; consecrated and installed January 13, 1985. *Res.: Bishop's Residence*, P.O. Box 500745 CK, Saipan, MP 96950. Tel: 670-234-3000.

ESTABLISHED NOVEMBER 8, 1984.

Square Miles 184.

Corporate Title: "Bishop of Chalan Kanoa, a Corporation Sole."

Comprises the Mariana Island chain except for Guam, known legally as the Commonwealth of the Northern Mariana Islands.

Legal Title: For legal titles of parishes and diocesan institutions, consult the Diocesan Curia.

Web: www.cnmicatholic.org

Email: diocese@vzpacifica.net

STATISTICAL OVERVIEW

Personnel	
Bishop	1
Priests: Diocesan Active in Diocese	14
Priests: Diocesan Active Outside Diocese	1
Number of Diocesan Priests	15
Religious Priests in Diocese	2
Total Priests in Diocese	17
Ordinations:	
Diocesan Priests	2
Parishes	
Parishes	11
With Resident Pastor:	
Resident Diocesan Priests	7
Resident Religious Priests	2
Missions	2
Welfare	
Special Centers for Social Services	1
Total Assisted	4,345
Educational	
Diocesan Students in Other Seminaries	1
Total Seminarians	1
High Schools, Diocesan and Parish	1
Total Students	176
Elementary Schools, Diocesan and Parish	3
Total Students	525
Catechesis/Religious Education:	
High School Students	264
Elementary Students	820
Total Students under Catholic Instruction	1,786
Teachers in the Diocese:	
Sisters	7
Vital Statistics	
Receptions into the Church:	
Infant Baptism Totals	779
Adult Baptism Totals	29
First Communions	501
Confirmations	301
Marriages:	
Catholic	16
Interfaith	4
Total Marriages	20
Deaths	115
Total Catholic Population	43,000
Total Population	71,850

Diocesan Curia—P.O. Box 500745, Saipan, 96950. Tel: 670-234-3000; Fax: 670-235-3002.

Vicar General—Rev. JOSEPH E. BILLOTTI, S.J.

Chancellor—Rev. MANUEL CORCUERA.

Finance Officer—Rev. JOSEPH E. BILLOTTI, S.J.

Personnel Officer—VACANT.

Director of Vocations—Rev. FLORENTINO E. RECAIDO JR., Dir.

Director of Religious Education—Sr. ESTELA V. ALTEA, S.G.B.P.

Superintendent of Catholic Schools—VACANT.

Director of Worship—VACANT.

Director of Youth Ministry—Rev. FLORENTINO E. RECAIDO JR.

Diocesan Curia Staff—Mrs. LOLITA M. BABAUTA, Office Mgr.; VACANT, Bishop's Sec.; Mr. NICHOLAS J. ROLLS, Finance Mgr.

Consultative Bodies

Presbyteral Council—Rev. RYAN JIMENEZ; Rev. Msgr. LOUIS ANTONELLI; Revs. MANUEL CORCUERA; SALVADOR DUMAS; ISAAC AYUYU; MATTHEW BLOCKLEY; CHARLITO BORJA; ROLANDO JOSON; MANUEL IGROBAY JR.; ANGELO PARK; BERNARDO BANAL; JOSEPH E. BILLOTTI, S.J.; ISIDRO T. OGUMORO; FLORENTINO E. RECAIDO JR.; FRANCISCO SANTOS.

College of Consultors—Revs. MANUEL CORCUERA; SALVADOR DUMAS; JOSEPH E. BILLOTTI, S.J.; MANUEL IGROBAY JR.; BERNARDO BANAL.

Diocesan Finance Council—Mr. MICHAEL JOHNSON; Mr. KARL REYES; Mr. JESUS Q. GUERRERO; JOAQUIN Q. DELA CRUZ.

Diocesan Pastoral Council— Representatives from every Parish, Clergy and Religious. Rev. MANUEL CORCUERA; Sr. MARYANN HARTMAN, M.M.B.; CHRISTOPHER TENORIO; VIRGINIA C. VILLAGOMEZ; HERBERT S. DELROSARIO; JAMES LG. SABLAN; ROSIKY F. CAMACHO; JOSEFA C. TAITANO; MARIE T. MUNA; Sr. VERONICA A. BENAVENTE; FRANCES T. JOHNSON; TRICIA T. TENORIO; FRANCISCO LG. CAMACHO; NIEVES L. BABAUTA; NOMINANDA L. KOSAKA; PRESCILLA SN. MUNA; MARGARET C. DELACRUZ; MARCELINA P. CEPEDA; MARIA MALUA T. PETER; FRANCISCO M. DIAZ; BAE IN HWA; HAN GI YANG; RITA A. MANGLONA; ROSA P. ACQUININGOC; ANICETO MUNDO; FRANCISCO S. CALVO; VINCENT M. CALVO.

Diocesan Tribunal

Judicial Vicar—Rev. DAVID C. QUITUGUA, J.C.D.

Marriage Tribunal Judge—VACANT.

Defender of the Bond—VACANT.

Tribunal Auditor—VACANT.

Diocesan Commissions

Commission on Worship—VACANT, Chm.

Commission on Justice and Development—Rev. JOSEPH E. BILLOTTI, S.J., Chm.

Commission on Evangelization—VACANT, Chm.

Commission on Family Life—Rev. MANUEL CORCUERA, Chm.

Commission on Ministerial Development—Rev. PATRICK GARCIA, Chm.

Apostolic Works of the Diocese

Diocesan Publications Office—Rev. JOSEPH E. BILLOTTI, S.J., Dir.; Mr. RUY V. POLISTICO, Editor of "North Star" (Diocesan Newspaper); Mrs. MARGRET T. CABRERA, Advertising Mgr.

Electronic Media—Rev. JOSEPH E. BILLOTTI, S.J.

Hospital Chaplaincy (Saipan)—Rev. MANUEL IGROBAY JR.

Mt. Carmel Catholic Cemetery—Mr. MARLON CARLOS, Consultant.

Prison Chaplaincy—Rev. JOSEPH E. BILLOTTI, S.J.

Police and Fire Departments Chaplaincy—Rev. JOSEPH E. BILLOTTI, S.J.

St. Joseph Catholic School (Tinian)—Sr. DOROTHEA PAMPLONA, O.P., Admin. & Prin.

Civilly Incorporated Activities of the Diocese

Mount Carmel School, Inc. (Saipan)—Mr. EDWARD MANIBUSAN, Chm.; Mrs. MARGARET C. DELA CRUZ, Pres.; Mr. TODD BLAHNIK, Prin.; VACANT, School Chap.

Eskuelan San Francisco de Borja School, Inc. (Rota)—Mr. LAWRENCE MESNGON, Chm.; Sr. ASCENSION ZAMBRA, O.P., Admin.

Karidat, Inc.—Mr. NED ARRIOLA, Pres. Bd. Directors; Ms. ANGIE V. GUERRERO, Exec. Dir.

Associations of the Faithful

A.G.A.P.E. (Almighty God and People Encounter)—Adult Leaders: CRIS SABLAN; LUCINDA SABLAN; Rev. FLORENTINO E. RECAIDO JR., Spiritual Dir.

Catholic Daughters of America—Mrs. THOMASA T. ADA, Regent.

Children of God the Father, Inc.—Mrs. ROMA DIAZ-ARANDA, Pres.; VACANT, Spiritual Dir.

Confraternity of Christian Mothers—Mrs. CARMEN S. TAIMANAO, Diocesan Bd. Pres.; Rev. PATRICK GARCIA, Spiritual Dir.

Couples for Christ—Mr. RUFO MAFNAS, Household Leader; VACANT, Spiritual Dir.

Cursillo Movement—Mr. ESTANISLAO K. BENAVENTE, Pres.; Rev. MANUEL CORCUERA, Spiritual Dir.

El Shaddai Movement—Mr. EDUARDO I. BALLESTEROS, Leader; Rev. MANUEL IGROBAY JR., Spiritual Dir.

Eucharistic Adoration Society—Most Rev. TOMAS A. CAMACHO; ELIZABETH CHO; FRANCISCO PALACIOS.

Knights of Columbus—Sir Knight ANTONIO L. TAISACAN, District Deputy; Rev. ISIDRO T. OGUMORO, Spiritual Dir. for Rev. Msgr. Vicente T. Martinez Council; VACANT, Spiritual Dir. for Pale Luis Medina Council.

Legion of Mary—Rev. MANUEL CORCUERA, Diocesan Spiritual Dir.

San Roque Parish - Mother of Divine Love Praesidium—Rev. FLORENTINO E. RECAIDO JR., Spiritual Dir.

Legion of Mary at San Antonio Parish—Rev. MANUEL IGROBAY JR., Spiritual Dir.

Light & Salt Catholic Charismatic Community—FRANCIS FLORES, Head Servant; Rev. FRANCISCO SANTOS, Spiritual Dir.

Marriage Encounter—Main Contact: Mr. JESUS SONODA; Mrs. ANICIA SONODA; Rev. ISAAC M. AYUYU, Spiritual Dir.

CLERGY, PARISHES, MISSIONS AND PAROCHIAL SCHOOLS

ISLAND OF SAIPAN

CHALAN KANOA VILLAGE, CATHEDRAL OF OUR LADY OF MT. CARMEL, Most Rev. Tomas A. Camacho; Revs. Charlito Borja; Isaac M. Ayuyu.
Mt. Carmel Rectory: P.O. Box 500745, 96950. Tel: 670-234-3000.
Mission—Korean Catholic Community P.O. Box 693, 96950. Tel: 670-235-1449; 670-235-1450. Rev. Angelo Park.
Oratory—Mercedarian Missionary Sisters of Berriz, Formation House and Little House.

GARAPAN VILLAGE, DISTRICT 11, KRISTO RAI PARISH, Revs. Joseph E. Billotti, S.J.; Ryan Jimenez.
Oratory—Maturana House of Prayer
Oratory—Navy Hill, Commonwealth Health Center Chapel

KAGMAN VILLAGE, SANTA SOLEDAD MISSION PARISH, Rev. Francisco Santos.
Mailing Address: P.O. Box 500745, 96950. Tel: 670-256-7767; 670-234-3000.

SAIPAN, SAN JUDE PARISH, Rev. Patrick Garcia.
Rectory—P.O. Box 500745, 96950. Tel: 670-288-0269; Fax: 670-235-3002.

SAN ANTONIO VILLAGE, DISTRICT 6, SAN ANTONIO PARISH, Rev. Manuel Igrobay Jr.
San Antonio Rectory: P.O. Box 500745, 96950. Tel: 670-235-4515.

SAN JOSE VILLAGE, DISTRICT 7, SAN JOSE PARISH, Rev. Isidro T. Ogumoro.
Rectory—P.O. Box 500745, 96950. Tel: 670-234-3000.

SAN ROQUE VILLAGE, DISTRICT 9, SAN ROQUE PARISH, Rev. Florentino E. Recaido Jr.
Cathedral Rectory: P.O. Box 500745, 96950. Tel: 670-234-3000.

SAN VICENTE VILLAGE, DISTRICT 10, SAN VICENTE PARISH, Rev. Manuel Corcuera.
San Vicente Rectory: P.O. Box 500745, 96950. Tel: 670-235-8208.
Oratory—Dominican Sisters of the Most Holy Rosary Convent
Oratory—Our Lady of the Most Holy Rosary Dandan, Malta.

TANAPAG VILLAGE, DISTRICT 8, SANTA REMEDIOS PARISH, Rev. Florentino E. Recaido Jr.
Cathedral Rectory: P.O. Box 500745, 96950. Tel: 670-234-3000.

ISLAND OF ROTA

SONGSONG VILLAGE
1—SAN FRANCISCO DE BORJA PARISH, Rev. Bonifacio Espeleta.
San Francisco de Borja Rectory: Songsong Village, P.O. Box 542, Rota, 96951. Tel: 670-532-3522.
2—SAN ISIDRO PARISH (Sinapalo), Rev. Msgr. Louis Antonelli.
Rectory—Sinapalo Village, P.O. Box 590, Rota, 96951. Tel: 670-532-0720.

ISLAND OF TINIAN

SAN JOSE VILLAGE, SAN JOSE, Rev. Salvador Dumas.
Catholic Rectory, San Jose Village: Tinian, 96952. Tel: 670-433-3000.
School—St. Joseph Catholic School, P.O. Box 282, Tinian, 96952. Tel: 670-433-7527; Fax: 670-433-7527. Sr. Dorothea Pamplona, O.P., Admin. & Prin.

DIOCESAN MISSIONS

San Ignacio Chapel, (Island of Pagan) San Jose Chapel, (Island of Anatahan) anta Cruz Chapel, (Island of Alamagan)Santa Cruz Chapel, (Island of Agrihan)

INSTITUTIONS LOCATED IN THE DIOCESE

[A] ELEMENTARY AND HIGH SCHOOLS

TINIAN. *St. Joseph Catholic School*, P.O. Box 282, 96952. Tel: 670-433-7527; Fax: 670-433-7527. Sr. Dorothea Pamplona, O.P., Admin. & Prin.

[B] RESIDENCES OF SISTERS

SAIPAN. *M.M.B. Formation House*, P.O. Box 136, 96950. Tel: 670-234-6214. Sr. Martha Ramarui, M.M.B., Local Coord. Sisters 6; Apostulants 3.
M.M.B. Little House, P.O. Box 245, 96950. Tel: 670-234-6127. Sr. Mary Louise Balzarini, M.M.B., Local Coord. Sisters 4.
M.M.B. Maturana Hill Community, P.O. Box 1178-CK, 96950. Tel: 670-322-9713; Fax: 670-323-4673. Sr. Mary Ann, M.M.B., Local Coord. Sisters 10.
Pastorelle Sisters Convent (San Antonio Parish), P.O. Box 745, 96950. Tel: 670-234-1213. Sisters Estela Altea, S.G.B.P., Local Coord.; Edna Apolonio Local Coord.; Argell Baguio, Local Coord.

ROTA. *Dominican Sister Convent*, P.O. Box 542, 96951. Tel: 670-532-5683; Fax: 670-532-3151. Sisters Mariana Salmo, O.P., Local Coord. Ascension Zambra, O.P., Local Coord. Sisters 2.

RELIGIOUS INSTITUTES OF MEN REPRESENTED IN THE DIOCESE

For further details refer to the corresponding bracketed number in the Religious Institutes of Men or Women section.

[0690]—*The Society of Jesus*—S.J.

RELIGIOUS INSTITUTES OF WOMEN REPRESENTED IN THE DIOCESE

[]—*Dominican Sisters of the Holy Rosary*—O.P.
[]—*Dominican Sisters of the Philippines-Rota*—O.P.
[]—*Dominican Sisters of the Philippines-Saipan*—O.P.
[]—*Dominican Sisters of the Philippines-Tinian*—O.P.
[2510]—*Mercedarian Missionaries of Berriz*—M.M.B.
[]—*Pastorelle Sisters*
[0420]—*Religious Sisters of Mercy*—R.S.M.

NECROLOGY

† Tenorio, Roger P.T., Saipan, MP Kristo Rai—Died Dec. 6, 2002

Prefecture Apostolic of the Marshall Islands

Reverend Monsignor

JAMES C. GOULD, S.J.

First Prefect Apostolic of the Marshall Islands; appointed First Prefect Apostolic of the Marshall Islands April 23, 1993; installed August 15, 1993. *Res.: Cathedral of the Assumption*, P.O. Box 8, Majuro, MH 96960. Tel: 692-625-6675; Fax: 692-625-5520.

Square Miles 500,000.

Total Population (est.) 59,000.

Prefecture Apostolic of the Marshall Islands divided from the Diocese of the Carolines-Marshalls and erected on August 15, 1993 and committed to the Society of Jesus, New York Province. Area is that of the Republic of the Marshall Islands which is related by a Compact of Free Association to the United States.

P.O. Box 8, Majuro, MH 96960. Tel: 692-625-6675; Fax: 692-625-5520.

Email: diocesemarshalls@yahoo.com

STATISTICAL OVERVIEW

Personnel	
Priests: Diocesan Active Outside Diocese	1
Number of Diocesan Priests	1
Religious Priests in Diocese	4
Total Priests in Diocese	5
Ordinations:	
Permanent Deacons	2
Permanent Deacons in Diocese	2
Total Brothers	1
Total Sisters	11
Parishes	
Parishes	4
With Resident Pastor:	
Resident Religious Priests	3
Without Resident Pastor:	
Administered by Priests	1
Professional Ministry Personnel:	
Brothers	1
Sisters	11
Educational	
Diocesan Students in Other Seminaries	2
Total Seminarians	2
High Schools, Diocesan and Parish	2
Total Students	360
Elementary Schools, Diocesan and Parish	5
Total Students	963
Catechesis/Religious Education:	
High School Students	370
Elementary Students	1,200
Total Students under Catholic Instruction	2,895
Teachers in the Diocese:	
Brothers	1
Sisters	10
Lay Teachers	48
Vital Statistics	
Receptions into the Church:	
Infant Baptism Totals	88
Adult Baptism Totals	10
Received into Full Communion	22
First Communions	73
Marriages:	
Catholic	8
Interfaith	2
Total Marriages	10
Total Catholic Population	4,602
Total Population	52,894

Prefecture Consultors—Rev. R. RICHARD MCAULIFF, S.J.; Sr. JOAN CREVCOURE, M.M.; Mrs. NEIMAT REIMERS; Mr. DONALD CAPELLE; Mrs. ROSITA CAPELLE; Mr. DENNIS MOMOTARO; Mrs. DAISEY MOMOTARO.

Finance Committee—Sr. ROSE LAUREN EARL, M.M.; Mr. ALAN FOWLER; Mr. DENNIS MOMOTARO.

Judicial Vicar—Rev. WILLIAM J. RAKOWICZ, S.J., P.O. Box 128, Koror, Palau, PW 96940-0128.

Defender of the Bond—Rev. R. RICHARD MCAULIFF, S.J.

Notary—Mrs. VERONICA KILUWE.

Vocations—Rev. Msgr. JAMES C. GOULD, S.J., P.O. Box 8, Majuro, 96960.

CLERGY, PARISHES, MISSIONS AND PAROCHIAL SCHOOLS

MARSHALL ISLANDS

Mailing Address for the Marshalls: P.O. Box 8, Majuro, MH 96960. Tel: (011) 692-625-6675; Fax: (011) 692-625-5520, unless otherwise noted.

MAJURO, CATHEDRAL OF THE ASSUMPTION, Rev. Msgr. James C. Gould, S.J.; Rev. R. Richard McAuliff, S.J. Tel: 692-625-8307; Fax: 692-625-6507.
School—Sisters 2; Lay Teachers 16; Students 380.
High School—Sisters 3; Lay Teachers 10; Students 200.
Mission—Laura Majuro Atoll.

EBEYE, QUEEN OF PEACE, Rev. Simione Volavola, M.S.C.
Mailing Address: P.O. Box 5065, Marshall Islands, 96960. Tel: 692-329-3826; Fax: 692-625-3689.
School—Lay Teachers 28; Students 325.
High School—Lay Teachers 13; Students 160.
Mission—Santo Kwajalein.

KWAJALEIN

1—BLESSED SACRAMENT, Rev. William Sullivan, S.J. Mailing Address: P.O. Box 1711, Apo, AP 96555. Tel: 805-355-2116; 805-355-4535; Fax: 805-355-8404.

2—OUTER ISLAND PARISH, Rev. Msgr. James C. Gould, S.J.
School—Arno Lay Teachers 5; Students 101.
School—Jaluit Lay Teachers 5; Students 85.
School—Wotje Lay Teachers 4; Students 81.
Mission—Arno
Mission—Ailinglaplap
Mission—Buoj, Woja
Mission—Jaluit
Mission—Likiep
Mission—Namorik
Mission—Wotje

Special Assignment:
Rev.—
Young, David, Military Chap. (Retired)

INSTITUTIONS LOCATED IN THE DIOCESE

[A] MISCELLANEOUS

MAJURO. *Catholic Pastoral Center: Ajeltake*, P.O. Box 8, 96960. Tel: 011-692-247-; Fax: 011-692-625-. Mrs. Adella Hone, Contact Person.

NECROLOGY

(No Deaths)

Diocese of Mayaguez, Puerto Rico

(Dioecesis Maiaguezensis)

Most Reverend

ULISES AURELIO CASIANO VARGAS, D.D.

Bishop of Mayaguez; ordained May 30, 1967; appointed Bishop March 4, 1976; ordained April 30, 1976. *Res.: P.O. Box 2272, Mayaguez, PR 00681.* Tel: 787-831-2942; 787-833-5411 (Office).

Erected by the Bull "Qui arcano Dei" on March 1, 1976, by Pope Paul VI.

Comprises a portion of the southwest of the Island.

STATISTICAL OVERVIEW

Personnel	
Bishop	1
Priests: Diocesan Active in Diocese	33
Priests: Diocesan Active Outside Diocese	3
Priests: Retired, Sick or Absent	6
Number of Diocesan Priests	42
Religious Priests in Diocese	27
Total Priests in Diocese	69
Extern Priests in Diocese	5
Ordinations:	
Diocesan Priests	1
Religious Priests	1
Permanent Deacons in Diocese	4
Total Brothers	2
Total Sisters	130
Parishes	
Parishes	29
With Resident Pastor:	
Resident Diocesan Priests	22
Resident Religious Priests	7
Pastoral Centers	158
Professional Ministry Personnel:	
Sisters	16
Lay Ministers	736
Welfare	
Catholic Hospitals	1
Total Assisted	42,381
Homes for the Aged	1
Total Assisted	145
Day Care Centers	3
Total Assisted	156
Special Centers for Social Services	2
Total Assisted	15,500
Educational	
Diocesan Students in Other Seminaries	8
Total Seminarians	8
Colleges and Universities	1
Total Students	1,680
High Schools, Diocesan and Parish	5
Total Students	789
High Schools, Private	5
Total Students	1,193
Elementary Schools, Diocesan and Parish	6
Total Students	1,419
Elementary Schools, Private	5
Total Students	1,220
Catechesis/Religious Education:	
Elementary Students	10,485
Total Students under Catholic Instruction	16,794
Teachers in the Diocese:	
Priests	1
Brothers	2
Sisters	1
Lay Teachers	283
Vital Statistics	
Receptions into the Church:	
Infant Baptism Totals	3,859
Adult Baptism Totals	166
Received into Full Communion	56
First Communions	3,133
Confirmations	2,914
Marriages:	
Catholic	622
Interfaith	33
Total Marriages	655
Deaths	2,305
Total Catholic Population	350,000
Total Population	491,518

Vicar General—Rev. Msgr. GONZALO DIAZ.

Episcopal Vicars—

For Pastoral—Rev. ROGELIO MUR, O.Carm.

For Diocesan Administration—Rev. Msgr. GONZALO DIAZ.

Chancery Office—*P.O. Box 2272, Mayaguez, 00681.* Tel: 787-833-5411.

Chancellor—Rev. Msgr. GONZALO DIAZ.

Diocesan Consultors—Rev. Msgrs. GONZALO DIAZ; ROGELIO MUR, O.Carm; Revs. RAFAEL SASTRE; ANGEL MENDEZ; HUMBERTO LOPEZ; JOSE F. BAEZ.

Diocesan Board of Administration—Rev. Msgr. GONZALO DIAZ HERNANDEZ; Revs. ROGELIO MUR, O.Carm.; ALBERTO CASTRO, P.D.

Administrator—Mr. ALBERTO RODRIGUEZ.

Censor Librorum—Rev. JULIO FERNANDEZ.

Parish Priests Consultors—Rev. Msgr. GONZALO DIAZ HERNANDEZ; Rev. ROGELIO MUR, O.Carm.; Rev. Msgr. HECTOR RIVERA RAMOS.

Diocesan Offices and Directors

Youth Apostolate—Rev. RAFAEL MENDEZ.

Communications Media—Rev. NOMAR J. CALERO; Sr. MARIA LOURDES MERCADO, O.P.

Cursillos de Cristiandad—Rev. Msgr. GONZALO DIAZ.

Holy Childhood—Most Rev. HERMIN NEGRON.

Legion of Mary—Rev. HECTOR RIVERA.

Supt. of Schools—Sr. VIVINA GRACIA, C.S.J.

Religious Consultor—Rev. JULIO FERNANDEZ.

Catechetics—Sr. CARLETA MUNOZ, C.S.J.

Christian Family Movement—Rev. LEONIDES SOTO.

Religious Coordinator—Rev. JULIO FERNANDEZ.

Development and Planification—Rev. ROGELIO MUR, O.Carm.

Vocations—Revs. ORLANDO ROSAS; DELROY THOMAS SCOTT; EDGAR CARLO.

Catholic Social Services—Sr. LOURDES T. TORO, M.S.B.T., Dir., Carr. 108 Km. 2.8 Int., Calle Obispado Final, Bo. Miradero, Mayaguez, 00681. Tel: 787-833-3627; 787-833-3638; Fax: 787-833-3627. Email: sscdmaya@caribe.net.

Seasonal Head Start Program—*Calle Dr. Veve #44, San German, 00683.* Tel: 787-892-3800; Fax: 787-892-3866.

CLERGY, PARISHES, MISSIONS AND PAROCHIAL SCHOOLS

CITY OF MAYAGUEZ

1—CATHEDRAL OF OUR LADY OF PURIFICATION (1763), Revs. Hector E. Rivera Ramos; Nomar J. Calero; Rene J. Hernandez.

Res.: P.O. Box 220, 00681-0220. Tel: 787-831-2444.

School—Academy of the Immaculate Conception, Tel: 787-834-5400; 787-834-7824 (High School). Mrs. Marlene Rosa, Elementary Prin.; Mr. Rene Torres, High School Prin. Lay Teachers 42; Students: Elementary 410; High School 400.

School—Colegio La Milagrosa, Tel: 787-834-0350. Sr. Trinidad Irizarry, Prin. Sisters of Charity 6; Lay Teachers 27; Students: Elementary 280; High School 159.

Mission—Maria Socorro de los Cristianos Barrio Leguisamo.

Mission—Santa Ana Quebrada Grande.

Catechesis/Religious Program—Students 143.

2—ASCENSION (1968), Rev. Jose Fco. Baez Camacho.

Res.: Box 4361, Salud Sta., 00681-4361. Tel: 787-832-0766; Fax: 787-832-0766.

Mission—St. Teresita Bo. Limon.

Mission—Our Lady of Perpetual Help Bo. Las Vegas.

Mission—Ntra. Sra. de la Providencia (Rep. Masias) Bo. El Porvenir.

Catechesis/Religious Program—Students 160.

3—CHURCH DE EL BUEN PASTOR (1986), Rev. Patrick O. Erwin.

Res.: Urb. Mayaguez Ter., 5000 Calle San Gerardo, 00682-6627. Tel: 787-833-8800; Fax: 787-805-3660.

Catechesis/Religious Program—Students 151.

Mission—El Senor de Los Milagros Alturas de Mayaguez. Tel: 787-265-5936.

Mission—Sta. Teresita Parcelas Soledad.

4—CHURCH OF THE RESURRECTION (1988), Rev. Marcelino Arocho, Admin.

Res.: Balboa 285, 00680. Tel: 787-831-6180.

Catechesis/Religious Program—Students 56.

Chapel—Consumo, Jesus Redentor

Chapel—Rio Canas, Nuestra Senora del Perpetuo Socorro

Chapel—Barrio Quemado, Nuestra Senor del Carmen

5—NUESTRA SENORA DE FATIMA (1986), [JC] Rev. Edwin Lugo Silva, Admin.

Res.: Parcelas Castillo C-2, 00680. Tel: 787-833-0794.

Catechesis/Religious Program—Students 101.

Mission—Cristo Rey Andalucia St., Sultana, 00680.

Mission—Espiritu Santo Sagitario St., Villa del Oeste, Sabalos, 00680.

Mission—Corpus Christi Urb. Vista Verde, 00680.

6—OUR LADY OF MT. CARMEL, Rev. Harry Lopez Vazquez, Admin.

Res.: Box 3166, 00681. Tel: 787-831-6544; 787-832-2036 (Office); Fax: 787-834-2777.

Mission—Infant of Prague Mani.

Mission—Perpetuo Socorro Jardines del Caribe.

Catechesis/Religious Program—Students 207.

7—SACRED HEART (1959), Revs. Cristobal Jose Amate Guerrero, O.S.B.; Toribio Pascual Diez, O.S.B.; Paulino Mazuelas, O.S.B.; Gerardo Ibarra Rodriguez, O.S.B.; Frank Perez Martinez, O.S.B.

Res.: R.F.D. 348 Buzon 400, 00680. Tel: 787-832-1464.

School—St. Benedict, Tel: 787-832-9626. Rev. Paulino Mazuelas, O.S.B., Prin. Lay Teachers 31; Students: Elementary 347; High School 225.

Catechesis/Religious Program—Students 320.

Mission—San Jose Rosario.

Mission—San Carlos y San Antonio Rio Hondo.

Mission—La Milagrosa Bo. Malezas.

8—SAN VICENTE (1965), [JC] Revs. Encarnacion M. Rodriguez, C.M.; Prudencio Sanchez, C.M.

Res.: Ave. Guanajibo, No. 401, 00680. Tel:

787-832-8874.
Catechesis/Religious Program—Students 63.
9—SANTA TERESITA (1970), Rev. Rafael Sastre, Admin. Res.: Principe St., 203 Bo. Colombia, 00680. Tel: 787-806-0881; Fax: 787-806-0881.
Catechesis/Religious Program—Students 88.

OUTSIDE THE CITY OF MAYAGUEZ

AGUADA

1—ST. FRANCIS OF ASSISI (1692), Revs. Jose Luis Diez Gabela, O.S.A. (Spain); Lesmes Bernabe Lazaro, O.S.A. (Spain); German Lombo, O.S.A. (Spain); Isaias Revilla, O.S.A. (Spain); Ildefonso Blanco, O.S.A. (Spain).
Res.: P.O. Box 608, 00602. Tel: 787-868-2630; Fax: 787-868-8561.
Catechesis/Religious Program—Students 2,124.
Convent—Hermanas de la Caridad del Cardenal Sancha, Calle Jose Hernandez, Box 1136, 00602. Tel: 787-868-8257; Fax: 787-868-8257.
Mission—San Jose Sabana.
Mission—Santa Rita Laguna.
Mission—Santa Monica Cruces.
Mission—Santo Tomas de Villanueva Galicia-Columbani.
Mission—San Augustin Jaguey Chiquito.
Mission—Perpetuo Socorro Rio Grande.
Mission—Ntra. Madre de la Consolacion Naranjo Militar.
Mission—Ntra. Sra. de Altagracia Atalaya.
Mission—San Pablo Naranjo-Guanabanas.
Mission—Asuncion de Maria Marias.
Mission—Buen Consejo Cerro Gordo.
Mission—Perpetuo Socorro Mamey.
Mission—Ntra. Sra. del Carmen Guaniquilla.
Mission—Ntra. Sra. de las Mercedes Carrizales.
Mission—Immaculada Concepcion Malpaso-Cesar Ruiz.
Mission—Sagrada Familia Bajio.
Mission—Sgdo. Corazon de Jesus Quebrada Larga.
Mission—Ntra. Sra. del Carmen Rio Grande-Playa.
Mission—El Buen Pastor Guayabo.
Mission—Ntra. Sra. Reina de la Paz Piedras Blancas.

2—SANTUARIO PROTOMARTIRES DE LA CONCEPCION (1524), Rev. Roberto Soler.
Res.: Bo. Espinar, Buzon 1162, 00602. Tel: 787-891-2889.
Chapel—Bo. Palmar, El Buen Pastor
Chapel—Bo. Tablonar, El Nino Jesus
Catechesis/Religious Program—Students 88.

AGUADILLA

1—ST. CHARLES BORROMEO, [CEM] Revs. Angel Mendez; Rafael Sanchez.
Res.: P.O. Box 238, 00605. Tel: 787-891-0575; Fax: 787-891-3622.
School—Tel: 787-891-1445; Fax: 787-882-3270. Mrs. Lizzette Ortiz, Prin. Lay Teachers 41; Students: Elementary 448; High School 210.
Catechesis/Religious Program—Students 652.
Convent—Tel: 787-882-3629. Sr. Magda Marrero, Supr. Salesian Sisters 4.
Convent—Tel: 787-891-7496. Sr. M. Assisi, M.C. Missionaries of Charity 4.
Chapel—Bo. Corrales, Our Lady of Perpetual Help
Chapel—Caimital Alto, St. John Baptist
Chapel—Victoria-Nuestra, Senora de la Victoria
Chapel—Esteves, N. S. del Rosario
Chapel—Bda. Caban, Ntra. Sra. de la Sagrada Familia

2—LA MILAGROSA (1920), Rev. Ramon E. Albino.
Res.: Urb. Marbella, Calle 1 Num. 379, 00605. Tel: 787-891-7014.
School—Corpus Christi, Tel: 787-891-1445. Students 44.
Catechesis/Religious Program—Students 198.
Mission—Our Lady of Victory Borinquen.
Mission—Our Lady of Fatima Camaseyes.
Mission—Playuelas San Judas Tadeo.

3—SAN JOSE OBRERO (1975), Revs. Cristian Jose Then Henriquez, S.D.B.; Hiram Santiago, S.D.B.; Mario Ghietti, S.D.B.
Res.: Poblado San Antonio, P. O. Box 787, San Antonio, 00690-0787. Tel: 787-890-2449; Fax: 787-826-2494.
Catechesis/Religious Program—Students 225.
Mission—La Providencia Bo. Guerrero.
Mission—Los Santos Reyes Ramey-Maleza.

ANASCO, ST. ANTHONY ABBOT (1730), Revs. Rogelio Mur Aguilar, O.Carm.; Juan Maria Amoros, O.Carm.
Res.: Box 392, 00610. Tel: 787-826-2215.
School—LaSalle, Tel: 787-826-6071. Students 262.
Catechesis/Religious Program—Students 450.
Mission—Chapel of Our Lady of Perpetual Help Miraflores.
Mission—Our Lady of Carmel La Playa.
Mission—St. Lawrence Martyr Bo. Espino.
Mission—La Immaculade Bo. Pinales.
Mission—La Providencia Bo. Carreras.
Mission—Our Lady of Monserrat Bo. Cerro Gordo.
Mission—St. Rita Bo. Marias.
Mission—Cristo Redentor Bo. Oveja.
Mission—Santa Rosa de Lima Bo. Pozo Hondo.
Jesus Maestro Casa de Formaction—

CABO ROJO, ST. MICHAEL (1783), Revs. Angel Ortiz, Admin.; Jose R. Linares; Edgardo Lopez.
Res.: Box 625, 00623. Tel: 787-851-1283; Fax: 787-851-1970.
School—San Agustin Miss Olivia Laracuente, Dir. Lay Teachers 42; Students: High School 267; Elementary 385.
Catechesis/Religious Program—Students 652.
Mission—Our Lady of Mt. Carmel Puerto Real.
Mission—St. John the Baptist Joyuda.
Mission—St. Joseph Boqueron.
Mission—Our Lady of Good Counsel Llanos Tunas.
Mission—St. Rita Las Palmas.
Mission—St. Jude Thaddeus Monte Grande.
Mission—Cristo Rey El Corozo.
Mission—Our Lady of Fatima Betances.
Mission—St. Martin de Porres Conde Avila.
Mission—Ntro. Sra. de la Providencia Bo. Miradero.

HORMIGUEROS

1—EL SALVADOR (1969), Rev. Omar Yanez, Admin.
Res.: Box 567, 00660. Tel: 787-834-1993.
Catechesis/Religious Program—Students 80.
Chapel—Valle Hermoso Arriba, San Judas Tadeo
Chapel—Parcelas S. Romualdo, Sta. Teresita

2—SHRINE OF OUR LADY OF MONSERRATE (1874), Rev. Msgr. Gonzalo Diaz Hernandez; Rev. Jose Juan Cardona Diaz.
Res.: Box 24, 00660. Tel: 787-849-2260.
Convent—Box 185, 00660. Tel: 787-849-2055; Fax: 787-849-2035. Sr. Digna Acosta, O.P. Sisters of Fatima for Social Work 3.
Mission—Sagrado Corazon de Jesus Bo. Lavadero.
Mission—Ntra. Sra. de la Paz Bo. Jaquitas.
Mission—La Asuncion Bo. Carretera Nueva.
Mission—San Martin de Porres Bo. Guanajibo.
Mission—Santa Rosa de Lima Bo. El Hoyo.

LAJAS

1—DE LA MERCED PARISH (1971), Rev. Edgar Carlo, Admin.; Deacon Ramon Cardona, P.D.
Res.: P.O. Box 1023, 00667-1063. Tel: 787-899-1910.
Catechesis/Religious Program—Students 110.
Mission—Ntra. Sra. de la Monserrate Carr. 101 Ramal 303 K.2.4, Bo. Maguayo, 00667.
Mission—San Pedro Carr. 304 Calle Principal, Bo. Parguera, 00667.
Mission—Ntra. Sra. de Monserrate Carr. 116 Parcellas Cuesta Blanca #264, Bo. Cuesta Blanca, 00667.
Mission—Ntra. Sra. del Carmen Carr. 324 K. 5.6, Bo. Salinas, 00667.
Mission—Ntra Sra. del Perpetuo Socorro Carr. 306, Bo. Paris, 00667.

2—OUR LADY OF THE PURIFICATION (1883), Revs. Rafael Mendez, Admin.; P. Floyd McCoy.
Res.: Box 425, 00667. Tel: 787-899-1911; Fax: 787-899-2455.
School—St. Louis Academy Sisters of St. Joseph, Tel: 787-899-4080. Sr. Delia Inzarry, Prin. (Brooklyn) Sisters 2; Lay Teachers 29; Students: Elementary 198; High School 175.
Catechesis/Religious Program—Students 202.
Convent—La Providencia, Tel: 787-899-5180.
Mission—Sagrado Corazon de Jesus Parcelas #201, Bo. La Plata, 00667.
Mission—Ntra. Sra. del Perpetuo Socorro Carretera 118 Km 0, Bo. Lajas Arriba (La Tea), 00667.
Mission—San Pablo Parcelas #48, Bo. Lajas Arriba (Parcelas), 00667.
Mission—Santa Rosa de Lima Comunidad Sta. Rosa #35, Bo. Parcelas Santa Rosa, 00667.
Mission—San Judas Tadeo Parcelas #172, Bo. Parcelas Palmarejo, 00667.
Mission—San Juan Bautista Parcela #80, Bo. Palmarejo II, 00667.
Mission—Santa Rosa de Lima Bo. La Haya.

LAS MARIAS, IMMACULATE HEART OF MARY (1863), Rev. Edward Acevedo, Admin.
Res.: Box 126, 00670. Tel: 787-827-3300.
Catechesis/Religious Program—Students 177.
Mission—San Jose Carr. 406, Km. 3.9, Anones, 00607.
Mission—La Milagrosa Carr. 124, R. 370, Km. 6.8 Int Buena Vista, Buena Vista, 00670.
Mission—N.S. de Fatima Palma Escrita.

MARICAO, ST. JOHN THE BAPTIST (1864), Rev. Orlando Rosas Muniz, Admin.
Res.: Box 453, 00606. Tel: 787-838-2014.
Catechesis/Religious Program—Students 142.
Mission—Sagrado Corazon Bucarabones.
Mission—Santa Rosa Indiera Fria.
Chapel—Montoso, Immaculado Corazon de Maria, Tel: 787-838-2272. Sr. Inocencia Olmeda, O.P., Supr. Dominican Sisters of Our Lady of Fatima 6.

MOCA, OUR LADY OF MONSERRATE (1772), Revs. Santiago Rivera Allende; David Perez Mendez; Daniel Enrique Hernandez Velez; Juan Bautista Morales.
Res.: P.O. Box 435, 00716. Tel: 787-877-2765.
School—Students 205.
Catechesis/Religious Program—Carmen O. Soto, D.R.E. Students 1,738.
Mission—San Judas Bo. Plata.
Mission—Espiritu Santo Bo. Voladoras Lomas.
Mission—Sagrada Familia Bo. Voladoras Parcelas.
Mission—Corazon de Jesus Bo. Naranjo.
Mission—Santos Guillermo y Mateo Bo. Cuchillas La Salle.
Mission—Corazon de Jesus Bo. Chucillas Sabana.
Mission—Virgen del Rosario Bo. Limon.
Mission—Cristo Rey Bo. Cuchillas Loperena.
Mission—Virgen Monserrate Bo. Cordero.
Mission—La Providencia Bo. Rocha Magueyes.
Mission—San Pedro Bo. Punta Brava.
Mission—Perpetuo Socorro Bo. Capa Barreto.
Mission—Cristo Salvador Bo. Capa Bosque.
Mission—Inmacula Corazon de Maria Bo. Cerro Gordo.
Mission—San Martin de Porres Bo. Aceituna.

RINCON, ST. ROSE OF LIMA (1789), Revs. Delroy Thomas Scott, Admin.; Angel Roman Ramos.
Res.: Box 128, 00677. Tel: 787-823-2650; Fax: 787-823-4400.
Catechesis/Religious Program—Students 600.
Mission—Santa Rosa Bo. Calvache.
Mission—El Cristo de la Reconciliacion Bo. Atalaya.
Mission—La Milagrosa Bo. Corcega.
Mission—Sagrado Corazon de Jesus Bo. Cruces.
Mission—Nuestra Senora del Carmen Bo. Puntas.
Mission—San Jose Bo. Jaguey.

ROSARIO, ROSARY, Rev. Vicente Perez Roig.
Res.: Box 692, 00636. Tel: 787-832-3533.
Mission—Nuestra Senora del Rosario
Mission—La Monserrate Bo. Rosario Penon, 00680.
Catechesis/Religious Program—Students 40.

SABANA GRANDE, CHURCH OF SAN ISIDRO (1813), Revs. Jorge L. Caro Morales; Julio Vera; Edgardo Acosta.
Res.: Box 817, 00637. Tel: 787-873-4475.
Catechesis/Religious Program—Students 889.
Convent—Tel: 787-873-2750. Sr. Angeles Marie, O.P., Supr. Sisters 4.
Mission—Cristo Rey Carr.368 R.367 KM.2.0, El Papayo, 00637.
Mission—La Resurreccion Carr.121 Calle Azucena, Susua, 00637. Tel: 809-873-0382.
Mission—Sagrado Corazon de Jesus Calle Rable #44-Carr.121 K. 5.0, Bo. Maginas, 00637. Tel: 809-873-1368.
Mission—San Jose Carr.121 Km. 4.1, Bo. La Pica, 00637. Tel: 809-873-4231.
Mission—San Francisco de Asis Carr.369 Km.1.4, Bo. Cerro Gordo, 00637. Tel: 809-873-8048.
Mission—Ntra. Sra. de Monserrate Carr.2 R.365 Km.2.8 Int., Bo. Molinas, 00637. Tel: 809-873-2656.
Mission—Ntra. Sra. de Fatima Carr.328 Km.3.6, Bo. Guaras, 00637. Tel: 809-873-0886.
Mission—Santa Catalina de Siena Carr.388 Km.5.9 Int., Bo. La Torre, 00637. Tel: 809-873-7591.
Mission—Santa Ana Carr.114 R.363 Km.2.4, Bo. La Maquina, 00637.
Mission—Ntra. Sra. del Rosario Carr.120 Km.6, Bo. Santana Pichel, 00637. Tel: 809-873-3707.
Mission—La Virgen Milagrosa Carr.364 Km.7 Interior, Bo. El Hoyo, 00637.
Mission—San Judas Tadeo Carr.117 Km.10.7, Bo. Rayo Plata, 00637.
Mission—Sta Lucia Carr.120 Km.3.1, Bo. Sta. Ana Moreno, 00637. Tel: 809-873-7962.

SAN GERMAN

1—ST. ROSE OF LIMA (1967), Revs. Urbano Saenz, O.S.A.; Francisco Larran, O.S.A.; Edwin Lorenzo Muniz, O.S.A.
Res.: Box 364, 00683. Tel: 787-892-1276.
Catechesis/Religious Program—Students 542.
Mission—N. Sra. de la Consolacion Bo. Guama.
Mission—Perpetuo Socorro Bo. Minillas Carretera.
Mission—Santa Rita Bo. Retiro Tea.
Mission—Santa Monica Bo. Minillas Valle.
Mission—St. Martin de Porres Bo. Cain.

2—SAN GERMAN DE AUXERRE, Revs. Humberto Lopez; Urian Perez Zapata; Fernando Palacio Salazar; Angel Leonides Soto.
Res.: Box 305, 00683. Tel: 787-892-1027.
School—Tel: 787-892-1009. Sr. Maria Ines Martin, C.S.J., Prin. Sisters of St. Joseph (Brooklyn) 1; Lay Teachers 37; Students: Elementary 400; High School 245.
Catechesis/Religious Program—Students 318.
Mission—Chapel of St. Augustin Duey.
Mission—Chapel of St. Joseph Hoconuco.
Mission—Gruta de Lourdes Maresua.
Mission—Our Lady of Fatima Cotuy.
Mission—San Judas Tadeo Sabana Eneas.

SAN SEBASTIAN, SAN SEBASTIAN MARTIR (1752), Revs. Angel Antonio Perez, C.P.; Bernardo Onaindia, C.P.; Anibal Rodriguez, C.P.; Jose Lizarralde, C.P.; Dennys Walter Cruz, C.P.
Res.: P.O. Box 801, 00685. Tel: 787-896-1028.
School—San Sebastian Martir, Tel: 787-896-5728.

Jose Joaquin Rivera, Prin. Lay Teachers 32; Students: Elementary 327; High School 75.
Catechesis/Religious Program—Students 1,181.
Mission—Cristo Rey Bo. Perchas I.
Mission—La Pasion Bo. Perchas II.
Mission—San Gabriel de la Dolorosa Bo. Calabazas.
Mission—La Asuncion Bo. La Lechuza.
Mission—Santa Teresita Bo. Juncal.
Mission—Ntra. Sra. del Carmen Bo. Aibonito Guerrero.
Mission—San Judas Tadeo Bo. Saltos.
Mission—San Patricio Bo. Hato Arriba.
Mission—San Pablo de la Cruz Bo. Hato Arriba (Parcelas).
Mission—Ntra. Sra. de Fatima Bo. Altozano.
Mission—Sagrado Corazon Bo. Robles.
Mission—San Jose Obrero Bo. Hoyamala.
Mission—Santa Cruz Bo. Parcelas Guacio (Parcelas).
Mission—Espiritu Santo Bo. Culebrinas.
Mission—Cristo Resucitado Bo. Sonadur.
Mission—Ntra. Senora de la Providencia Bo. Eneas.
Mission—Sagrada Familia Bo. Pozas.

On Special Assignment:
Rev.—
Diaz, Gonzalo, Chancellor & Vicar Gen., Box 24, Hormingueros.

INSTITUTIONS LOCATED IN THE DIOCESE

[A] COLLEGES AND UNIVERSITIES

ANASCO. *De La Salle Catholic College*, Apartado 61, 00610. Tel: 787-826-6071; Fax: 787-826-5185. Rene Hernandez Perez, Contact Person.

AQUADILLA. *Corpus Christi College*, Apartado 4021, 00605-4021. Tel: 787-882-8433; Fax: 787-891-4555. Rev. Ramon E. Albino.

MOCA. *Nuestra Senora de la Monserrate College*, Apartado 435, 00676. Tel: 787-877-2765; Fax: 787-877-7795. Hilda Perez, Prin.

[B] HOSPITALS

SAN GERMAN. *Hospital of the Immaculate Conception*, Box 285, 00683. Tel: 787-892-1860; Fax: 787-892-6465. Email: maest@caribe.net. Web: www.hospconcepcion.org. Sr. Ana Delia Vega, Supr.; Rev. Fernando Palacio Salazar, Chap.; Jaime Maestre, Admin. Sisters of Charity Sisters 7; Bed Capacity 167; Patients assisted annually Admission 8,381; Emergency Visits 34,000.

[C] INSTITUTIONS

MAYAGUEZ. *Asylum for the Poor and Aged*, Calle Post 62, 00680. Sr. Cruz M. Fontan, Supr. Sisters of Charity (Spanish) Sisters 4; Bed Capacity 112; Residents 87.

Convent of the Servants of Mary, Hostos Ave., 401, 00708. Tel: 787-832-0391. Sr. Aurea Fernandez Fontan, Supr. Sisters care for the sick in their homes and hospital. Sisters 13.

HORMIGUEROS. *Residence for the Aged, San Jose*, Valle Hermoso, 00660. Tel: 787-832-4243; Fax: 787-833-4529. Sr. Hilda M. Rodriquez, Supr. Sisters 13; Residents 145.

[D] PERSONAL PRELATURES

MAYAGUEZ. *Opus Dei (Prelature of the Holy Cross and Opus Dei)*, 69 Orquideas St., Ensanche Martinez, 00680. Tel: 787-833-6461. Rev. Pablo Concepcion.

RELIGIOUS INSTITUTES OF MEN REPRESENTED IN THE DIOCESE

For further details refer to the corresponding bracketed number in the Religious Institutes of Men or Women section.

[]—*Acies Christi* (Spain)
[0140]—*Augustinians*—O.S.A.
[0200]—*Benedictine Monks* Spain—O.S.B.
[0270]—*Carmelite Fathers and Brothers* (Spain)—O.Carm.
[1330]—*Congregation of the Mission* (Vice Province of Puerto Rico)—C.M.
[1000]—*Congregation of the Passion*—C.P.
[]—*Salesian Fathers*

RELIGIOUS INSTITUTES OF WOMEN REPRESENTED IN THE DIOCESE

[]—*Acies Christi* (Spain)
[]—*Carmelitas de Clausura* (Spain)
[]—*Hermanas de la Caridad*
[]—*Hermanas Salesianas* (Spain)
[]—*Hermanas Teatinas* (Spain)
[2340]—*Little Sisters of the Poor*—L.S.P.
[2790]—*Missionary Servants of the Most Blessed Trinity*—M.S.B.T.
[]—*Monasterio Santa Maria del Monte Carmelo*
[3580]—*Servants of Mary* (Spain)—O.S.M.
[0650]—*Sisters of Charity of St. Vincent de Paul* (Spanish)—S.C.
[]—*Sisters of Fatima* (Puerto Rico)
[]—*Sisters of Schoenstatt* (Germany)
[]—*Sisters of St. Joseph* (Brooklyn)

NECROLOGY

(No Deaths)

Diocese of Ponce, Puerto Rico

(Dioecesis Poncensis)

Most Reverend

FELIX LAZARO, SCH.P.

Bishop of Ponce; ordained April 9, 1961; appointed Coadjutor Bishop of Ponce March 20, 2002; consecrated April 25, 2002; appointed Bishop of Ponce June 11, 2003 *Res.: Bishop's House*, P.O. Box 32205, Ponce, PR 00732-2205. Tel: 787-848-5265; Fax: 787-841-1778.

Web: www.pucpr.edu

Email: obispadoponce@pucpr.edu

Most Reverend

FREMIOT TORRES OLIVER, D.D.

Bishop Emeritus of Ponce; ordained April 10, 1950; appointed Bishop November 4, 1964; consecrated December 21, 1964; retired November 10, 2000 *Res.: C. Marques de Mondejar 24, 3B, Madrid 28028 Spain.*

Most Reverend

RICARDO SURINACH CARRERAS

Bishop Emeritus of Ponce; ordained April 13, 1957; appointed Auxiliary Bishop of Ponce May 26, 1975; consecrated July 25, 1975; appointed Bishop of Ponce November 10, 2000; installed November 30, 2000; retired June 11, 2003 *Res.: Bishop's House*, P.O. Box 32205, Ponce, PR 00732-2205. Tel: 787-848-5265; Fax: 787-841-1778.

ESTABLISHED NOVEMBER 21, 1924.

Square Miles 830.

Comprises the south portion of the Island of Puerto Rico and is in the Ecclesiastical Province of Puerto Rico.

STATISTICAL OVERVIEW

Personnel	
Bishop	1
Retired Bishops	2
Priests: Diocesan Active in Diocese	60
Priests: Diocesan Active Outside Diocese	17
Priests: Retired, Sick or Absent	14
Number of Diocesan Priests	91
Religious Priests in Diocese	55
Total Priests in Diocese	146
Ordinations:	
Diocesan Priests	1
Transitional Deacons	2
Permanent Deacons	17
Permanent Deacons in Diocese	89
Total Brothers	7
Total Sisters	230
Parishes	
Parishes	42
With Resident Pastor:	
Resident Diocesan Priests	26
Resident Religious Priests	14
Without Resident Pastor:	
Administered by Priests	2
Missions	2
Pastoral Centers	231
Professional Ministry Personnel:	
Brothers	6
Sisters	230
Lay Ministers	1,500
Welfare	
Homes for the Aged	2
Total Assisted	351
Specialized Homes	2
Total Assisted	3,124
Special Centers for Social Services	2
Total Assisted	4,280
Other Institutions	1
Total Assisted	1,671
Educational	
Seminaries, Diocesan	1
Students from This Diocese	6
Students from Other Diocese	5
Seminaries, Religious	3
Students Religious	8
Total Seminarians	14
Colleges and Universities	1
Total Students	9,862
High Schools, Diocesan and Parish	20
Total Students	9,422
Elementary Schools, Diocesan and Parish	22
Total Students	7,619
Total Students under Catholic Instruction	26,917
Teachers in the Diocese:	
Priests	21
Sisters	33
Lay Teachers	635
Vital Statistics	
Receptions into the Church:	
Infant Baptism Totals	6,528
Adult Baptism Totals	626
First Communions	5,901
Confirmations	5,199
Marriages:	
Catholic	1,047
Interfaith	32
Total Marriages	1,079
Total Catholic Population	474,759
Total Population	593,448

Former Bishops—Most Revs. EDWIN V. BYRNE, D.D., consecrated in Philadelphia, Nov. 30, 1925; transferred to San Juan, PR; promoted to Archbishop of Santa Fe, NM, June 15, 1943; died July 25, 1963; ALOYSIUS J. WILLINGER, C.SS.R., D.D., ord. July 2, 1911; appt. Bishop of Ponce March 8, 1929; consecrated Oct. 28, 1929; appt. Titular Bishop of Bida and Coadjuctor of Monterey-Fresno (cum jure successionis), Dec. 12, 1946; installed Bishop of Monterey-Fresno, Jan. 3, 1953; resigned Oct. 25, 1967; died July 25, 1973; JAMES E. MCMANUS, C.SS.R., D.D., J.C.D., transferred to the Archdiocese of New York, Nov. 18, 1963; died July 1, 1976; His Eminence LUIS CARDINAL APONTE MARTINEZ, D.D., ord. April 10, 1950; appt. Titular Bishop of Lares and Auxiliary of Ponce, July 23, 1960; consecrated Oct. 12, 1960; appt. Coadjutor Bishop of Ponce, April 16, 1963; appt. Bishop of Ponce, Nov. 18, 1963; installed Feb. 20, 1964; promoted to Archbishop of San Juan, Nov. 4, 1964; installed Jan. 15, 1965; created Cardinal, March 5, 1973; resigned May 8, 1999; Most Revs. FREMIOT TORRES OLIVER, D.D. (Retired), ord. April 10, 1950; appt. Bishop Nov. 4, 1964; consecrated Dec. 21, 1964; retired Nov. 10, 2000; RICARDO SURINACH CARRERAS, D.D. (Retired), ord. April 13, 1957; appt. Auxiliary Bishop of Ponce May 26, 1975; consecrated July 25, 1975; appt. Bishop of Ponce Nov. 10, 2000; installed Nov. 30, 2000; retired June 11, 2003.

Vicar General—Rev. Msgr. ROBERTO GARCIA BLAY.

Pro-Vicar General—VACANT.

Chancellor—Rev. Msgr. HERMINIO DE JESUS.

Episcopal Vicar for Diocesan Administration—Rev. Msgr. HERMINIO DE JESUS.

Episcopal Vicar for Pastoral Coordination—Rev. Msgr. JUAN RODRIGUEZ ORENGO.

Episcopal Vicar for Religious—Rev. MARIO MASTRANGELO, O.F.M.Cap.

Episcopal Vicar for Education—Rev. JOSE MATEO, Sch.P.

Tribunal Interdiocesano de Puerto Rico—P.O. Box 32229, Calle Isabel No. 31, Ponce, 00732-2229. Tel: 787-843-4630; Fax: 787-841-7483. First instance for the Dioceses of Mayaguez and Ponce. Second Instance for the Archdiocese of San Juan.

Judicial Vicar—Rev. Msgr. ELIAS MORALES.

Associate Judicial Vicars—Rev. MANUEL SANTIAGO.

Moderator—Most Rev. FELIX LAZARO, Sch.P.

Judge—Mayaguez:: Rev. Msgr. GONZALO DIAZ.

Diocesan Consultors—Rev. Msgrs. ROBERTO GARCIA BLAY; HERMINIO DE JESUS; MARCOS A. PANCORBO; JESUS R. DIEZ ANTONANZAS; ANDRES GUERRERO; JOSE LOZANO; JUAN RODRIGUEZ ORENGO.

Diocesan Board of Administration—Rev. Msgrs. ROBERTO GARCIA BLAY; MARCOS PANCORBO; Deacon ALBERTO CASTRO; Mr. SANTIAGO RAMOS; Mr. JAIME SANTIAGO CANET.

Parish Priests Consultors—Rev. Msgrs. MARCOS PANCORBO; ANDRES GUERRERO; HERMINIO DE JESUS; JOSE LOZANO.

Notaries—Mrs. LUZ DELIA MEDINA; Miss IRIS YOLANDA PAGAN, M.J.; Miss NANCY MENDEZ GARCIA.

Censores Librorum—Revs. EDUARDO TORRES; BRIAN HARRISON, O.S.

Administrator—Rev. Msgr. ROBERTO GARCIA BLAY.

Diocesan Offices and Directors

Catechesis—Sr. CARIDAD ORTIZ, O.P., P.O. Box 331064, Ponce, 00733-1064. Tel: 787-842-9178; Fax: 787-259-1718.

Catholic Youth Organization—Rev. JERY RIVERA.

Children of Mary—Rev. Msgr. JUAN RODRIGUEZ ORENGO.

Committee for Community Planning—Rev. Msgr. HERMINIO DE JESUS.

Communications—Sr. NATIVIDAD LUGO, O.P., P.O. Box 330986, Ponce, 00733-0986. Tel: 787-843-1548.

Cursillos de Cristiandad—Rev. SAMUEL SANTIAGO, La Rambla, 4072 Ave. Tito Castro, Ste. 201, Ponce, 00716-4702.

Ecumenism—Rev. Msgr. JUAN RODRIGUEZ ORENGO, P.O. Box 32205, Ponce, 00732-2205.

Legion of Mary—Rev. Msgr. JUAN RODRIGUEZ ORENGO, P.O. Box 32205, Ponce, 00732-2205.

Liturgical Commission—Most Rev. FELIX LAZARO MARTINEZ, Sch.P., P.O. Box 32205, Ponce, 00732-2205.

Sacred Music Commission—Rev. Msgr. ABEL DI MARCO.

St. Vincent de Paul Conferences—Mr. IBRAHIM MALDONADO, Cristo Rey Parish, Urb La Rambla, 2933 Calle Valladolid, Ponce, 00730-4011.

Superintendent of Schools—Sr. MARIA UNA, R.A.D., P.O. Box 32552, Ponce, 00732-2552. Tel: 787-848-4020; Fax: 787-844-5987.

Vigilance for the Faith—Most Rev. FELIX LAZARO MARTINEZ, Sch.P.

Vocations—Rev. Msgr. JESUS R. DIEZ ANTONANZAS, P.O. Box 32110, Ponce, 00732-2110. Tel: 787-848-4380; Fax: 787-848-4380.

Institute of Family Orientation—Deacon FRANCISCO LUGO, P.O. Box 32214, Ponce, 00732-2214. Tel: 787-840-6018; Fax: 787-848-4523.

CLERGY, PARISHES, MISSIONS AND PAROCHIAL SCHOOLS

CITY OF PONCE

1—CATHEDRAL OF OUR LADY OF GUADALUPE (1692), Rev. Msgr. Marcos A. Pancorbo; Rev. Orlando Rivera; Deacons Jose Mercado; Carlos J. Rodriguez.
Res.: 28 Cristina St., Box 32210, 00732-2210. Tel: 787-842-0134; Fax: 787-848-9104.

2—CHRIST THE KING (1964), Rev. Msgr. Juan Rodriguez Orengo; Rev. Jose A. Barrera Hernandez; Deacons Anibal Rosario; Eduardo A. Dosal; Manuel Roman.
Res.: Urb La Rambla, 2933 Calle Valladolid, 00730-4011. Tel: 787-843-3028; Fax: 787-848-1861.
School—Urb. La Rambla, c/o San Judas, 3011, 00730-4091. Tel: 787-843-0766; Fax: 787-843-6443. Sr. Maria Ortiz Osorio, S.S.N.D., Prin.
Catechesis/Religious Program—Students 426.
Mission—Santa Teresita Calle 33, Parque Central, Ponce Co. 00730.
Mission—Nino Jesus de Praga Bo. Los Claves, Rio Chiquito, Ponce Co.
Mission—La Dolorosa Villa Ponce - Rambla, Calle Castellana Final, Ponce Co. 00730-4011. Tel: 787-840-8380.

3—CHURCH OF THE GOOD SHEPHERD (1968), Rev. Msgr. Elias Morales; Deacons David Ramos; Rafael D. Ruiz; Luis Gonzalez.
Res.: Calle 40-NN25, Jardines del Caribe, 00731. Tel: 787-843-6202; Fax: 787-843-4422.
Mission—La Milagrosa Bo. Quebrado del Agua, Ponce Co. 00731.

4—CHURCH OF THE RESURRECTION (1967), Rev. Msgr. Roberto Garcia Blay; Revs. Esteban Santaella; Jose M. Herrero; Jose R. Gomez; Deacon Rafael Castro.
Glenview Gardens: PMB-98, P.O. Box 2000, Mercedita, 00715. Tel: 787-842-7167; Fax: 787-841-8718.
Mission—Immaculate Heart of Mary Bo. La Yuca, Ponce Co.
Mission—Our Lady of Monserrate Bo. Collado, Ponce Co.
Mission—San Lucas Bo. Las Vallas, Ponce Co.
Mission—Saint Joseph Bo. La Yuca, Ponce Co.
Mission—Our Lady of Carmel Bo. Carmelita, Ponce Co.

5—CHURCH OF THE SACRED HEART (1969), Rev. Jose M. Galan; Deacon Reinaldo Rivera.
Res.: P.O. Box 577, Mercedita, 00715-0577. Tel: 787-843-4891; Fax: 787-848-9212.
Catechesis/Religious Program—Students 100.

6—CHURCH SANTISIMO SACRAMENTO (1984), Revs. Jesus de Duenas, L.D.; Alberto Llavila, L.D.
Res.: Urb. Vistas del Mar, 2238 Calle Marlin, 00716-0834. Tel: 787-843-0245; Fax: 787-284-1032.

7—LA MERCED (1928), Revs. Jose Estevez Iglesias, O.deM.; Gregorio Dafonte Vaz, O.deM.; Silvino Gonzalez, O.deM.; Javier Gutierrez Fernandez, O.deM.; Deacons Carlos M. Rodriguez-Guilbe; Jose D. Ruiz; Antonio Victor Fabre.
Res.: 4632 Luna St., 00717-2000. Tel: 787-842-0069; Fax: 787-842-0603.

8—LA MILAGROSA (1928), Revs. Juan Lamela, C.M.; Manuel Prado, C.M.; Deacons Ramon L. Vazquez; Carlos Burgos.
Res.: Guadalupe No. 2, 00730-3110. Tel: 787-842-3188; Fax: 787-284-1100.
School—Tel: 787-842-1164; Fax: 787-284-1100. Liz Marie Santiago, Prin.
Catechesis/Religious Program—Students 500.

9—LA SANTISIMA TRINIDAD (1971), Revs. Jose Luis Fernandez, O.SS.T.; Alfonso Rementeria, O.SS.T.; German Rementeria, O.SS.T.; Deacons Francisco Lugo; Jose Rodriguez.
Las Delicias: Box 8226, 00732. Tel: 787-842-6073; Fax: 787-842-6073.
Catechesis/Religious Program—Students 171.
Mission—San Juan de Mata Box 8226, Bo. Magueyes, Ponce Co. 00732.
Mission—San Andres Bo. Guaragoa, Ponce Co. 00732.
Mission—Santa Ana Bo. Guaragoa, Arriba, Ponce Co. 00732.
Mission—N.S. Fatima Bo. Marueno, Arriba, Ponce Co. 00732.
Mission—San Antonio de Padua Parcelas de Marueno, Ponce Co. 00732.
Mission—N.S. del Rosario Bo. Madrigal, Ponce Co. 00732.
Mission—Inmaculada Bo. Pastillo, Ponce Co. 00732.
Mission—Cristo Rey Bo. Corral Viejo, Ponce Co. 00732.
Mission—San Miguel de los Santos Las Delicias 11, Ponce Co. 00732.
Mission—Resurreccion Bo. Santas Pascuas, Ponce Co. 00732.

10—OUR LADY OF MT. CARMEL (1883), Revs. Miguel Alvarez, Sch.P.; Jose Mateo, Sch.P.; Cecilio Lacruz, Sch.P. (Spain) (SJN); Francisco Aisa; Deacon Jose Rivera.
Res.: P.O. Box 34118, Playa de Ponce, 00734-4118. Tel: 787-842-1333; Fax: 787-841-6861.
School—Tel: 787-842-5018; Fax: 787-842-5018. Mrs. Paquita Alvarado, Prin.
Mission—San Martin de Porres Constancia Ave., Villa del Carmen, Ponce Co. 00734. Tel: 787-848-4355.
Mission—Santa Marta c/o Santa Marta #8, Bo. Salistral, Ponce Co. 00732.

11—OUR LADY OF MT. CARMEL (1973), Rev. Jose Antonio Lopez Vega; Deacon Juan R. Vargas.
Res.: Box 187, Coto Laurel, 00780. Tel: 787-848-2030.
Mission—Santa Maria Virgen Bo. Hoyos, Ponce Co. 00780.
Mission—Sagrado Corazon de Jesus Carr. 511 K. 15, Bo. Las Raices, Ponce Co. 00780.
Mission—San Mateo Bo. Real Anon Abajo, Ponce Co. 00780.
Mission—San Martin de Porres Bo. Real Anon Arriba, Ponce Co. 00780.

12—SAN CONRADO (1948), Rev. Jose R. Alvarado de Jesus; Deacon Emerito Lopez. In Res., Rev. Msgr. Pedro J. Ballester.
Res.: Box 7362, 00732. Tel: 787-843-0560; Fax: 787-843-0600.
School—P.O. Box 7111, 00732. Tel: 787-843-1405; 787-843-2293; Fax: 787-841-7303. Sr. Nildred Rodriguez, C.S.J., Prin.
Catechesis/Religious Program—Students 749.

13—SAN JOSE (1965), Revs. Juan Alberto Torres, O.C.D.; Mariano Fraile, O.C.D.; Alexio Jose de Armas, O.C.D.; Deacons David Rodriguez; Benjamin Pagan; Edgardo Muniz; Arnaldo Gierbolini.
Res.: Urb. San Jose, 416 Calle Beato Francisco Palau Box 8414, 00728-1905. Tel: 787-843-3910; Fax: 787-843-1994.

14—SAN JOSE OBRERO (1979), Rev. Manuel Santiago; Deacons Nestor Rentas; Angel R. Mendez; Vicente Aponte Arroyo.
Res.: Parcelas El Tuque, Calle Ramos Antonini #632, P.O. Box 8027, 00732-8027. Tel: 787-843-9072; Fax: 787-290-5339.
Mission—Ntra. Sra. del Pilar 616 M #7, Punto Oro, Ponce Co. 00728.

15—SAN VICENTE-CANTERA (1964), Revs. Santiago Arribas, C.M.; Bernardo Hernandez, C.M.; Deacon Jorge Almodovar Capielo.
Res. Paseo La Cantera No. 67, 00730-3026. Tel: 787-843-1976; Fax: 787-812-0212.
Catechesis/Religious Program—Students 100.
Mission—San Vicente Rio Chiquito, Ponce Co.
Mission—Santos Reyes Bo. La Mocha, Ponce Co.
Mission—Santa Luisa Bo. Nuevo Mameyes, Ponce Co.
Mission—La Inmaculada Sector San Patricio, Ponce Co.

16—SANTA MARIA (1952), Revs. Romeo Salcido, M.J.; Michael J. Diemer, M.J.
Res.: P.O. Box 32101, 00732-2101. Tel: 787-848-5370; 787-848-3313; Fax: 787-290-4189.
School—Tel: 787-842-1164; Fax: 787-843-6755 (Elem.); 787-290-3711 (H.S.). Mrs. Nancy Ghigliotti, Prin., Elem.; Mrs. Lydia Otero, Prin., H.S.

17—SANTA TERESITA (1930), Revs. Jose A. Torres, O.F.M.Cap.; Mario Mastrangelo, O.F.M.Cap.; Francisco Garcia, O.F.M.Cap.; Deacons Casildo Rodriguez; Ildefonso Gonzalez Plaza; Luis A. Lopez Quirindongo.
Res.: Box 7244, 342 Victoria St., 00732. Tel: 787-842-3137; 787-842-5055 (Friary); Fax: 787-844-7267.
School—342 Victoria St., 00732. Tel: 787-842-4110; Fax: 787-842-4300. Mrs. Mildred Reyes, Prin.

18—SANTUARIO SAN JUDAS TADEO (1964), Revs. Jose Maria Reyes, O.de.M.; Modesto Vaca, O.de.M.; Angel Cuadrado Calvo, O.de.M.; Vicente Salas Avello, O.de.M.
Res.: P.O. Box 7046, 00732. Tel: 787-843-0572; Fax: 787-842-0148.
School—San Judas Tadeo, Tel: 787-844-2610; Fax: 787-843-3802. Migdonia Serrano, Prin.
Catechesis/Religious Program—Urb. Constancia Calle Coloso 2929. Students 369.

PARISHES IN FORMATION

1—CHURCH OUR LADY OF MIRACULOUS MEDAL, Rev. Msgr. Marcos A. Pancorbo, Admin.
Res.: P.O. Box 32210, 00732-2210. Tel: 787-842-0134.

2—CHURCH SAN PATRICIO, Rev. Esteban Santaella, Admin.
Res.: La Pica, Cr. Buzon 234-B, 00730. Tel: 787-828-6350.

OUTSIDE THE CITY OF PONCE

ADJUNTAS, ADJUNTAS CO., ST. JOACHIM (1815), Revs. Jaime Martinez Gonzalez, O.R.C.; Luis Jusino Flores; Deacons Samuel Sepulveda; Radames Marcucci; Edwin Figueroa.
Res.: 14 Rius Rivera St., 00601. Tel: 787-829-3145; Fax: 787-829-3145.
School—San Joaquin Elementary and Intermediate, 12 Primo Delgado St., 00601. Tel: 787-829-3040; Fax: 787-829-3040. Mrs. Carmen Zelideth Ortiz Reyes, Prin.
Mission—San Francisco Garzas, Adjuntas Co.
Mission—Sta. Ana Vegas Arriba, Adjuntas Co.
Mission—Santa Teresita Tres de Jayuya, Adjuntas Co.
Mission—Santa Rosa Pellejas, Adjuntas Co.
Mission—Virgen del Carmen Yahuecas, Adjuntas Co.
Mission—Sagrado Corazon Tanama, Adjuntas Co.
Mission—San Antonio Guilarte, Adjuntas Co.
Mission—La Milagrosa Vegas Abajo, Adjuntas Co.
Mission—Inm. Corazon de Maria Limani, Adjuntas Co.

AGUIRRE, SALINAS CO., SACRED HEART (1946), Rev. Juan J. Saliva; Deacon Pedro Rivera.
Res.: Box 260, 00704-0260. Tel: 787-853-3620; Fax: 787-853-2131.
School—Perpetuo Socorro, Box 260, 00704. Tel: 787-853-2270. Sr. Aurea M. Fuentes, R.A., Prin. Students 672.
Mission—St. Judas Las Mareas, Salinas Co.
Mission—Our Lady of Perpetual Help Coqui, Salinas Co.
Mission—St. Martin de Porres San Felipe, Salinas Co.
Mission—La Milagrosa, Salinas Co.

ARROYO, ARROYO CO., OUR LADY OF MT. CARMEL (1855), Revs. Felix Emilio Alvarado; Winston Reinaldo Mendez Silvagnoli.
Res.: Box 388, 00714. Tel: 787-839-3465; Fax: 787-839-1552.
Mission—Ntra Sra. del Carmen Bo. Pitahaya, Arroyo Co.
Mission—La Milagrosa Bda. Marin, Arroyo Co.
Mission—San Jose Bo. Yaurel Palmarejo, Arroyo Co.
Mission—Ntra Sra. de Fatima Bo. Palmas, Arroyo Co.
Mission—San Martin Bo. Yaurel Santa Clara, Arroyo Co.

CASTANER, LARES CO., OUR LADY OF THE MIRACULOUS MEDAL (1969), Rev. Carlos Alberto Reinoso, O.R.C.; Deacon Wilfredo Torres.
Res.: Box 1006, 00631. Tel: 787-897-5843.
Catechesis/Religious Program—Tel: 787-829-6389.
Mission—Immaculate Conception c/o 128 Int. 135, Bartolo, Rio Grande Co. 00669.
Mission—La Virgen Bo. Mirasol, Lares Co. 00669.
Mission—Milagrosa Bo. Rio Prieto, Lares Co. 00669.

COAMO, COAMO CO.

1—ST. BLASE (1616), Revs. Jose Diego Rodriguez; Eluid Aponte Rivera; Cristobal Reilly, S.T.; Deacons Angel A. Negron; Pedro Garcia; Orlando Martinez; Alfredo Rivera Cardona.
Res.: Box 196, 00769. Tel: 787-825-1122; Fax: 787-825-7006.
School—Ntra. Sra. de Valvanera, Box 1903, 00769. Tel: 787-825-1145; Fax: 787-825-1145. Noemi Torres, Prin.
Mission—Sacred Heart of Mary Palmarejo, Coamo Co. 00769.
Mission—Christ the King Pulguillas, Coamo Co. 00769.
Mission—Our Lady of Mt. Carmel Hayales, Coamo Co. 00769.
Mission—Miraculous Virgin Santa Catalina, Coamo Co. 00769.
Mission—Sacred Heart Sector Descalabrado, Santa Catalina, Coama Co. 00769.
Mission—Saint James Cilantro, Coamo Co. 00769. Fax: 787-825-1122.
Mission—Miraculous Virgin Pedro Garcia, Coamo Co. 00769.
Mission—Santa Ana Santa Ana, Coamo Co. 00769.
Mission—San Diego San Diego, Coamo Co. 00769.
Mission—Holy Family Emanueli, Coamo Co. 00769.

Mission—Our Lady of Fatima Melendez, Coamo Co. 00769. Fax: 787-825-1122.

2—SAN ANTONIO DE PADUA (2002), Rev. Msgr. Andres Guerrero; Deacon Angel R. Morales Colon.
Res.: P.O. Box 2227, 00769. Tel: 787-803-4801.
Mission—San Martin Las Flores, Coamo, Coamo Co. 00769.
Mission—Our Lady of Lourdes Rio Jueyes, Coamo, Coamo Co. 00769.

ENSENADA, GUANICA CO., SACRED HEART (1963), Rev. Samuel Santiago; Deacon Wallis S. Sanchez.
Res.: Box 179, 00647. Tel: 787-821-2857.
Mission—Divina Providencia Salinas-Providencia, Guanica Co.
Mission—Monserrate Bo. Fuig., Guanica Co.
Mission—Virgen del Rosario Bo. Guaypao, Guanica Co.

GUANICA, GUANICA CO., ST. ANTHONY ABBOT (1888), Rev. Jose Carlos Vargas; Deacon Reinaldo Galarza.
Res.: Box 804, 00653. Tel: 787-821-2147; Fax: 787-821-8896.
School—Blessed Imelda, Dr. Veve Str. 26, 00653. Tel: 787-821-2714; Fax: 787-821-2714.
Mission—Cristo Rey Bo. Belgica, Guanica Co.
Mission—N. Sra. Rosario Bo. Santa Juanita, Guanica Co.
Mission—San Judas Bo. La Laguna, Guanica Co.
Mission—N. Sra Fatima Bo. La Luna, Guanica Co.
Mission—La Providencia Bda. Esperanza, Guanica Co.

GUAYAMA, GUAYAMA CO., ST. ANTHONY OF PADUA (1736), Revs. J. Joseph Dionne, C.SS.R.; Mark Wise, C.SS.R.; Miguel A. Garcia, C.SS.R.; Deacons Alberto Montanez; Genaro Rivera; Francisco Carrasquillo; Juan B. Garcia.
Res.: Box 2820, 00785. Tel: 787-864-4100; Fax: 787-864-5494.
School—St. Anthony, Box 777, 00785. Tel: 787-864-2062; Fax: 787-864-1450. Mrs. Evelyn Adams, Prin.
Mission—Our Lady of Perpetual Help Caimital, Guayama Co.
Mission—SS. Peter and Paul P.O. Box 837, Bo. Puente Jobos, Guayama Co. 00785. Tel: 787-864-2912; 864-330-. Revs. Jose Roberto Gandara, C.SS.R.; Miguel A. Torres, C.SS.R.
Mission—St. Gerard Palmas, Guayama Co.
Mission—Our Lady of Mt. Carmel Carmen, Guayama Co.
Mission—Cristo Rey Bo. Olimpo, Guayama Co.
Mission—La Candelaria Bo. Corazon, Guayama Co.
Mission—Perpetuo Socorro Colonia Villodos, Guayama Co.
Mission—San Francisco de Asis Bo. Puerto Jobos, Guayama Co.
Mission—Sgdo. Corazon Bo. Guamani, Guayama Co.
Mission—San Martin Bo. Carite, Guayama Co.
Mission—La Monserrate Bo. Barrancas, Guayama Co.

GUAYANILLA, GUAYANILLA CO., IMMACULATE CONCEPTION (1841), Revs. Raymond L. Rivera; Jery Rivera; Deacon Saba Gonzalez.
Res.: P.O. Box 560573, 00656-0573. Tel: 787-835-3035; Fax: 787-835-3082.
School—Immaculate Conception, P.O. Box 560573, 00656-0573. Maria S. Hernandez Perez, Prin.
Catechesis/Religious Program—Tel: 787-835-2230. Students 220.
Mission—Our Lady of Mt. Carmel Barrio Sierra Baja, Guayanilla Co.
Mission—Perpetuo Socorro Magas Arriba, Guayanilla Co.
Mission—San Francisco de Asis Quebradas, Guayanilla Co.
Mission—San Juan Bosco Barrio Indios, Guayanilla Co.
Mission—La Monserrate Consejo Alto, Guayanilla Co.
Mission—Virgen de Fatima Macana Rio, Guayanilla Co.
Mission—Nuestra Senora Quebrada Honda, Guayanilla Co.
Mission—San Martin de Porres Macana Parcelas, Guayanilla Co.

JAYUYA, JAYUYA CO., OUR LADY OF MONSERRATE (1883), Revs. Pedro Faustino Echevarria; Manuel de la Cruz Sanchez Rivera; Deacon Jose De Jesus Simancas; Revs. Esteban Santaella; Hector Zayas (ARE) (Retired); Deacons Luis Rosario; Carlos Orama; Jose A. Perez.
Res.: Calle Figueras 13, 00664. Tel: 787-828-6350; Fax: 787-828-5062.
Mission—Cristo Rey Bo. Collares, Jayuya Co. 00664.
Mission—San Jorge Bo. Coabay, Jayuya Co. 00664.
Mission—La Milagrosa Canalizo, Jayuya Co. 00664.
Mission—Buen Pastor Gripinas, Jayuya Co. 00664.
Mission—Santa Cecila Zama, Jayuya Co. 00664.
Mission—Esp. Santo Hoyo Planas, Jayuya Co. 00664.
Mission—S. Antonio Mameyes, Jayuya Co. 00664.
Mission—Santos Reyes Salto, Jayuya Co. 00664.
Mission—San Francisco Saliente, Jayuya Co. 00664.
Mission—San Juan Puerto Plata, Jayuya Co. 00664.
Mission— La Pica, San Patricio Co. 00664.
Mission— Hogares Seguros, San Antonio Co. 00664.

JUANA DIAZ, JUANA DIAZ CO.

1—NUESTRA SENORA DE LOURDES (Aguilita) (1984), Rev. Msgr. Herminio de Jesus; Deacons Cirilo Carmona; Ruperto Reyes; Jaime Velez; Fernando Perez; Marcelino Lebron Romero.
Res.: P.O. Box 1824, 00795. Tel: 787-837-1097.
Mission—Virgen del Carmen Bo. Tiburones, Juana Diaz Co. 00795.
Mission—Sagrado Corazon Bo. Buyones, Juana Diaz Co. 00795.
Mission—San Pedro Nolasco Bo. La Cuarta, 00795.

2—ST. RAYMOND NONATO (1798), Rev. Msgr. Jose Lozano; Revs. Santiago Solla; Edwin Vazquez-Vega; Deacons Narciso Ortiz; Norberto Santiago; William Santiago Figueroa.
Res.: Box 1426, 00795. Tel: 787-837-2390; Fax: 787-837-2390.
Mission—Santiago Apostol Pastillo, Cotopaso Co.
Mission—San Judas Rio Canas Abajo, Juana Diaz Co.
Mission—N.S. de Fatima Bo. Jacaquas, Juana Diaz Co.
Mission—La Milagrosa Bo. Jacaguas. Collores, Juana Diaz Co.
Mission—Santiago, Ap. Las Margaritas, Bo. Collores Arriba.
Mission—P. Socorro Corral, Juana Diaz Co.
Mission—Our Lady of the Rosary Bo. Guayabal, Juana Diaz Co.
Mission—San Ramon Callabo, Bo. Callabo.
Mission—La Merced Bo. Rio Cana Arriba, Juana Diaz Co.

3—SANTA TERESITA (Arus) (1984), Rev. Adalin Rivera; Deacon Secundino Torres.
Res.: P.O. Box 32131, 00732-2131. Tel: 787-844-4823.
Mission—San Martin de Porres, (Singapur)
Mission—Divine Mercy Piedra Aguza, Juana Diaz Co.
Mission—Our Lady of Carmel Pastillito, Manzanilla, Juana Diaz Co. (Galicia)

PATILLAS, PATILLAS CO., INMACULADO CORAZON DE MARIA (1811), Revs. Gerardo Ramirez; Benito Aranda Ballestin; Deacons Ruben Pabon; Luis Melendez.
Res.: Box 635, 00723. Tel: 787-839-5333.
Mission—Perpetuo Socorro Bo. Marin Alto, Patillas, Patillas Co.
Mission—Madre Cabrini Bo. Guarderraya, Patillas, Patillas Co.
Mission—Sto. Cristo de Los Milagros Bo. Recio, Patillas, Patillas Co.
Mission—Carmen Bo. Jacaboa, Patillas, Patillas Co.
Mission—Cristo Rey Bo. El Bajo, Patillas, Patillas Co.
Mission—Providencia Bo. Providencia, Patillas, Patillas Co.
Mission—Santa Rosa de Lima Bo. Los Pollos, Patillas, Patillas Co.
Mission—S. Juan Evangelista Bo. Los Barros, Patillas, Patillas Co.
Mission—San Guillermo Bo. El Real, Patillas, Patillas Co.
Mission—Carmen Bo. Jagual, Patillas, Patillas Co.

PENUELAS, PENUELAS CO.

1—ST. JOSEPH (1793), Revs. Gioacchino Basile; Jorge Acosta; Diego Di Modugno; Deacons Carmelo Vazquez; Jose E. Gelpi; Glidden R. Perez; Jose A. Rosario; Jose Torres; Joaquin Massoller.
Res.: Box 25, 00624. Tel: 787-836-1038; Fax: 787-836-0167.
Catechesis/Religious Program—Students 260.
Mission—La Milagrosa Carr. #391, El Rucio, Penuelas Co. 00624.
Mission—San Antonio Carr. #132, El Alto, Penuelas Co. 00624.
Mission—Fatima Carr. #131, Macana, Penuelas Co. 00624.
Mission—Santa Ana Carr. #132, Tallaboa Alta, Penuelas Co. 00624.
Mission—Santa Cruz Carr. #386, Bo. Barreal, Penuelas Co. 00624.
Mission—Milagrosa Carr. #387, Quebrada Ceiba, Penuelas Co. 00624.
Mission—Milagrosa Carr. #391, Bo. Rucio, Penuelas Co.
Mission—Carmen Carr. #132, Bo. Santo Domingo, Penuelas Co.
Mission—San Judas Tadeo Carr. #132, Bo. Cotto Mato, Penuelas Co.
Mission—San Martin de Porres Carr. Panoramica, Bo. Caracoles III, Penuelas Co.
Mission—Divino Nino Calle #8, Bo. Tallaba Alta, Sector La Moca, Penuelas Co.

2—SACRED HEART (Tallaboa) (1928), Rev. Gioacchino Basile (NEW), Admin., Penuelas, Pr Sacred Heart of Jesus Parish; Deacon Carmelo Vazquez.
Res.: HC 01, Box 13063, 00624. Tel: 787-836-1164.
Mission—Holy Family Bo. Buena Vista, Penuelas Co.

SALINAS, SALINAS CO., OUR LADY OF MONSERRAT (1854), Revs. Alberto Muniz; Hilario Avendano; Deacon Pablo F. Miranti.
Res.: Box 1172, 00751. Tel: 787-824-2215.
Mission—San Jose Plena, Salinas Co.
Mission—Santa Ana Coco, Salinas Co.
Mission—Esp. Santo Parcelas Vazquez, Salinas Co.
Mission—Virg. del Carmen Bo. Las Palmas, Salinas Co.
Mission—Santa Marta Naranjo, Salinas Co.
Mission—Inmaculada Concepcion Las Ochenta, Salinas Co.
Mission—Virgen Milagrosa Bo. Playita, Salinas Co.
Mission—Carmen Bo. Playa, Salinas Co.
Mission—Perpetuo Socorro Sabana Llana, Salinas Co.

SANTA ISABEL, SANTA ISABEL CO., ST. JAMES (1854), Revs. Ismael Larena; Angel Berrios; Moises Navascues, Sch.P.; Deacon Jaime Martinez.
Res.: Box 137, 00757. Tel: 787-845-2450; Fax: 787-845-2485.
Mission—San Patricio Playita Cortada, Santa Isabel Co.
Mission—Virgen del Rosario Bo. Penuelas, Penuelas Co.
Mission—Virgen del Perpetuo Socorro Bo. Paso Seco, Santa Isabel Co.
Mission—Monserrate Bo. Ollas, Santa Isabel Co.
Mission—San Ignacio de Loyola Jauca, Santa Isabel Co.

VILLALBA, VILLALBA CO.

1—OUR LADY MOTHER OF DIVINE PROVIDENCE (Mission Noell) (1962), Revs. Raymond D. Middendorf, S.M.; Vincent A. Plassenthal, S.M.
Res.: HC 01 Box 3471, 00766. Tel: 787-867-2052.
Catechesis/Religious Program—
Mission—Our Lady of Mt. Carmel Bo. Alturita, Cacao Co.
Mission—Imm. Concepcion Bo. Cacao, Cacao Co.
Mission—Nino de Praga Bo. El Frio, Ala de La Piedra Co.
Mission—Santa Ana Bo. Guineo, Ala de La Piedra Co.
Mission—N.S. del Rosario Bo. Bauta, Bauta Abajo Co.
Mission—N.S. del Pilar Bo. Damian Abajo, Damian Abajo Co.
Mission—N.S. Monserrate Bo. Pozas, Damian Abajo Co.
Mission—O.L. of Perp. Help La Piedra, Ala de La Piedra Co.
Mission—Sacred Heart of Jesus Matrullas, Cacao Co.
Mission—San Mateo Ortiga, Bauta Abajo Co.

2—OUR LADY OF MT. CARMEL (1917), Revs. Angel Sanchez; Emiliano Alamo; Christopher de Herrera; Deacons Javier Gonzalez; Ramon A. Resto; Jose A. Pagan.
Res.: Box 432, 00766. Tel: 787-847-0695; Fax: 787-847-8137.
School—Box 1033, 00766. Tel: 787-847-2875. Sr. Ana M. Santamarta, R.A.D., Prin.
Convent—Sisters of the Love of God, Tel: 787-847-2874; 787-847-2391.
Mission—Sagrado Corazon HC01 Box 5081, Romero, Villalba Co. 00766. Tel: 787-847-1591.
Mission—Jesus Crucificado Bo. Vista Alegre, Villalba Co. 00766.
Mission—Santisima Tinidad Bo. Mogote, Villalba Co. 00766.
Mission—Espiritu Santo Bo. Cerro Gordo, Villalba Co. 00766.
Mission—La Milagrosa, Villalba Co. 00766.
Mission—San Pedro Bo. Corillo, Villalba Co. 00766.
Mission—San Jose Bo. Palmarejo, Villalba Co. 00766.
Mission—Santisimo Sacramento Bo. Higuero, Villalba Co. 00766.
Mission—Jesus Crucificado Bo. Camarones, Villalba Co. 00766.
Mission—Maria Madre de la Iglesia Bo. Canonilla Abajo, Villalba Co. 00766.
Mission—Cristo de la Salud Bo. Sierrita Caonillas, Villalba Co. 00766.
Mission—Madre Cabrini Barrio Jaguey, Villalba Co. 00766.
Mission—Santa Cecilia Barrio Semil, Villalba Co. 00766.
Mission—San Alfonso Barrio Apeadero, Villalba Co. 00766.
Mission—Sagrada Familia Barrio Hatillo, Villalba Co. 00766.
Mission—San Antonio Bo. Camarones-Los Robles, Villalba Co. 00766.
Mission—La Milagrosa Bo. Hatillo Viejo, Villalba Co. 00766.

Mission—La Asuncion Bo. Cuchilla del Limon, Villalba Co. 00766.
Mission—Virgen de la Amargura Bo. Limon, Villalba Co. 00766.
Mission—N.S. del Carmen Bo. Dajas, Villalba Co. 00766.
Mission—San Francisco de Asis Bo. La Sierrita de Vacas, Villalba 00766.
Mission—La Milagrosa Bo. El Pino, Villalba 00766.
Mission—San Juan Evangelista Bo. Chichon, Villalba 00766.

YAUCO, YAUCO CO.

1—HOLY ROSARY (1756), Revs. Juan Burgos Acevedo, O.P.; Victor Perez Aviles, O.P.; Jose Fernandez, O.P.; Roberto Arzola Maisonet, O.P.; Deacon Jesus Vazquez.
Res.: Box 46, 00698. Tel: 787-856-1222; Fax: 787-856-6845.
School—Box 26, 00698. Tel: 787-856-1001; Fax: 787-267-1238. Mrs. Judith Negron, Prin.
Catechesis/Religious Program—Tel: 787-856-1573. Students 617.
Convent—Sisters of Fatima for Social Work, Tel: 787-856-1573. Sr. Julia Cintron, O.P., Supr. Sisters 4.
Mission—Virgin of Mt. Carmel Duey, Yauco Co.
Mission—St. James Barinas, Yauco Co.
Mission—Our Lady of Perpetual Help Cambalaches, Yauco Co.
Mission—Our Lady of Montserrat Carrizales, Hatillo Co.
Mission—St. Lucy Sierra Alta, Yauco Co.
Mission—St. Anthony Naranjo, Yauco Co.
Mission—St. Anthony Diego Hdez, Yauco Co.
Mission—Sacred Heart Quebradas, Yauco Co.
Mission—St. Martin Aguas, Yauco Co.

2—ST. MARTIN DE PORRES (1969), Rev. Segismundo Cintron.
Res.: Las Palomas, Box 2005, 00698. Tel: 787-856-3617.
Convent—Sisters of Fatima-Motherhouse, P.O. Box 62, Santa Rita, 00698. Tel: 787-856-1476; Fax: 787-821-2439. Sr. Celeste Ortiz, O.P., Mother Gen. Sisters 123; Novices 11; Postulants 4.
Mission—Ntra. Sra. de Lourdes Bo. Susua, PR, Guanica Co.
Mission—N.S. de La Providencia Bo. Susa, Guanica Co.
Mission—S. Martin de Porres Bo. Arenas de Guancia, Guanica Co.
Mission—S. Francisco de Asis Bo. Susa, Yauco Co.
Mission—N.S. de La Monserrate Bo. Susa, Yauco Co.

3—SANTO DOMINGO DE GUZMAN, Revs. Julio Rolon; Carlos Roman; Deacon Victor Sanchez.
Mailing Address: P.O. Box 3036, 00698-3036. Tel: 787-856-8212; Fax: 787-856-8138.
Mission—Sacred Heart Collores, Yauco.
Mission—Sta. Teresita Las Vegas, Yauco.
Mission—St. Joseph Lluberas, Yauco.
Mission—Our Lady of Fatima Algarrobos, Yauco.
Mission—St. Martin de Porres Almacigo Bajo, Yauco.
Mission—St. Juan Macias Almacigo Alto, PR, Yauco.
Mission—Our Lady of Montserrat Rio Loco, PR, Yauco.
Mission—St. Rosa de Lima El Cafetal, PR, Yauco.

On Duty Outside the Diocese:
Revs.—
Alvarez, Pablo D., F.S.S.P., 13780 S.W. 17 Ter., Miami, FL 33175.
Arguinzoniz, Francisco, Apartado 70 Durango, Vizcaya, Spain.
Barrett, Kevin S., Chap., Apostolate of Family Consecration, P.O. Box 151, Bloomingdale, OH 43910-0151.
Colon, Jose E., Colinas Montecarlo, Bldg. D-35, San Juan, 00927.
Fletcher Patrick, 62 AW/Chapel, 746 Main St., McChord AFB, WA 98438.
Gusiora Alphonsus, P.O. Box 61, Enugwu-Ukwu (Anambra State), Nigeria.
Kelty, Edward J., O.S., Via Antonio Zanoni 44, Rome 00134 Italy.
MacIssac, Charles S., O.S., c/o J. Joseph MacIsaac, 281 York St., Canton, MA 02021.
Malachowski, Christopher, O.S., Bethlehem-Domus Panis Vitae, Nadliwie 05-281 Urb Poland.
Medina, George, P.O. Box 286, East Boston, MA 02128.
Mezquida, Ramon, San Jose 4, Alqueria Condesa 46715, Valencia, Spain.
Morales, Francisco, P.O. Box 9023477, Viejo San Juan, 00902.
Munoz, Rafael, P.O. Box 187, Barceloneta, 00657.
Nieves, Carlos, HC763, Buzon 4240, Patillas, 00723.
Nischan, James R., 1625 Mayo Ave., Owensboro, KY 42301.
Quinones, Leoncio, Urb. Apolo, Guaynabo, 00657.
Sancho Piquer, Enrique, Calvario 49, 2, 4, Pafelbunoli, Valencia, Spain.
Serrano, Dionisio, Maestro Ripoll 14, 28006 Madrid, Spain.
Sirvent, Francisco, Capitan Cortes 8-2, Valencia, Spain.
Tyrrell, Anthony, Catholic Pastoral Center, P.O. Box 32180, Oklahoma City, OK 73132.
Weslin, Norman U., O.S., 3290 William Dr., Dalenan, NY 14042.
Zayas, Antonio, Naranjito, 00719.

Retired:
Most Revs.—
Carreras, Ricardo Surinach, D.D., Bishop's House, P.O. Box 32205, 00732-2205. Tel: 787-848-5265
Oliver, Fremiot Torres, D.D., C. Marquez de Mondejar 24, 3 B, 28028 Madrid, Spain. Tel: 91-726-0008 (34)
Rev. Msgrs.—
Colon, Jose, Box 242, Merceditas, 00715.
Santiago, Rafael, Calle Estrella #62, 00730.
Revs.—
Cano, Emilio, P.O. Box 21012, Rio Piedras, 00928.
Pacho, Jesus, 2065 Ave. Las Americas, Apt. 207, P.O. Box 9010, 00731-9427.

Permanent Deacons:
Almodovar Capielo, Jorge
Altori Vargas, Juan
Aponte Arroyo, Vicente
Burgos Roca, Joseph
Garcia Rivera, Juan B.
Gierbolini Rodriguez, Arnaldo
Gonzalez Plaza, Ildefonso
Lebron Romero, Marcelino
Lopez Quirindongo, Luis A.
Lopez Sanchez, Benjamin
Morales Colon, Angel R.
Muniz Rivera, Edgardo
Rivera Cardona, Alfredo
Sanchez, Carlos Rodriguez
Santiago Negron, Norberto
Torres, Antonio Victor Fabre

INSTITUTIONS LOCATED IN THE DIOCESE

[A] SEMINARIES

PONCE. *Diocesan Seminary* (Major) , P.O. Box 32110, 00732-2110. Tel: 787-848-4380; 787-812-3024; Fax: 787-848-4380. Email: regcleri@caribe.net. Rev. Msgr. Jesus R. Diez Antonanzas, Rector; Rev. Melvin Diaz Aponte. Priests 2; Lay Staff 3; Seminarians 11.

[B] COLLEGES & UNIVERSITIES

PONCE. *The Pontifical Catholic University of Puerto Rico*, 2250 Avenida de las Americas, 00717-0777. Tel: 787-841-2000; Fax: 787-651-2034. Web: www.pucpr.edu. The University is composed of the following: College of Arts and Humanities and Graduate Studies in Hispanic Studies; College of Business Administration and Graduate Studies; College of Education and Graduate Studies; College of Science and Graduate Studies; School of Law; Institute of Graduate Studies in Behavioral Science and Community Affairs; Institute of Social Doctrine of the Church; Program for Special Services; Post-Baccalaureate Achievement Program; Upward Bound Program. Priests 29; Sisters 4; School of Law 42; Lay Teachers 575; Students 9,862.
Administration: Most Revs. Felix Lazaro, Sch.P., Grand Chancellor; Ulises Casiano, Chm. Bd. Trustees; Mrs. Marcelina Velez, Pres.; Mr. Carl Sauder, Vice Pres. Academic Affairs; Mrs. Irma Rodriguez, Vice Pres Fin. Affairs; Mrs. Caridad C. de Frau, Vice Pres Student Affairs; Mr. Carlos Maldonado, Dir. Continuing Education; Dr. Gabriel A. Infante, Dir. Institute Devel., Research & Planning; Mr. Alfonso Santiago, Dean College of Arts and Humanities; Mr. Jaime Santiago Canet, Dean College of Business Admin.; Dr. Lillian Negron, Dean College of Education; Miss Carmen L. Velazquez, Dean College of Science; Charles R. Cuprill Esq., Dean School of Law; Mr. Ivan E. Davila, Registrar; Mrs. Ana Bonilla de Sanchez, Dir. Admissions; Mrs. Irem C. Poventud, Dir. Devel.; Mrs. Carmen Gonzalez, Dir. Guidance Center; Mrs. Esther Irizarry, Dir. Libraries; Mrs. Noelia Padua Esq., Dir. Law Library; Dr. Nilda Cordolisai, Institute of Graduate Studies; Mrs. Gilda Rivera, Exec. Dir. Information Technology & Telecommunications.
Faculty: Rev. Msgrs. Herminio de Jesus; Roberto Garcia; Jesus R. Diez Antonanzas; Abel A. DiMarco; Elias Morales; Revs. Eduardo Torres; Jose Luis Larreategui, Sch.P.; Perfecto Alvarez, O.S.A.; Jose M. Herrero; Moises Navascues, Sch.P.; Adalin Rivera; Alvaro Huerga, O.P.; Diego Di Modugno; Luis A. Mendez; Melvin Diaz; Carlos Roman; Mario Mastrangelo, O.F.M.Cap.; Brian W. Harrison, O.S.
Mayaguez Revs. Jose F. Baez Camacho; Edgardo Lopez Hernandez; Delroy Thomas Scott (MGZ); Floyd L. McCoy Jordan; Edgardo Acosta.
Ponce: Revs. Segismundo Cintron; Julio Rolon; Jose Luis Alonso, O.P.; Jesus Pacho; Felix E. Alvarado.
Guayama: Rev. Juan Saliva.

[C] SCHOOLS - INSTITUTES OF EDUCATION

PONCE. *Centro San Francisco* Tel: 787-842-2776; Fax: 787-342-2776. Email: sisterscsf@aol.com. Box 10479, 00732. Tel: 787-844-2434 Fax: 787-842-2776. Sisters of St. Joseph Lay Teachers 20; Librarians 2; Social Workers 1; Counselor 1.
Colegio Del Sagrado Corazon De Jesus, 2511 Avenida Obispado, 00716-3836. Tel: 787-842-0339; Fax: 787-843-0250. Email: sagrado@coqui.net. Web: www.home.coqui.net/sagraco. Mrs. Maria Serrano, Prin. Religious of the Sacred Heart Priests 2; Brothers 2; Sisters 5; Lay Teachers 49; Total Staff 77; Total Enrollment 879.
Colegio El Ave Maria, 4506 Dr. Bartolomei, Reparto Valle Alegre, 00728-3151. Tel: 787-284-2453; Fax: 787-284-2953. Email: avemaria@pucpr.edu. Sr. Milagros Pizarro, O.D.M., Dir. & Prin. Operarias del Divino Maestro (Avemarianas) Sisters 5; Lay Teachers 13; Total Staff 18; Total Enrollment 13.
Holy Family School, 1270 Ave. Hostos, 00717-0928. Tel: 787-842-3208; Fax: 787-344-6773. Email: oficinap@coqui.net. Sr. Maria Dolores Vicens, H.C., Prin. Sisters of Charity - Saint Vincent de Paul Sisters 5; Lay Teachers 24; Total Staff 29.

COTO LAUREL. *Colegio Ponceno* (Day School) , 999 Carr 14, 00780-2147. Tel: 787-848-2525; Fax: 787-259-4282. Email: colegio@copin.net. Web: www.copin.net. Revs. Angel Garralda, Sch.P.; Juan L. Cabrerizo, Sch.P.; Jose A. Basols, Sch.P.; Fernando Torres, Sch.P. Piarists Fathers Priests 3; Deacons 2; Lay Teachers 67; Total Staff 75; Total Enrollment 1,145.

PLAYA PONCE. *Centros Sor Isolina Ferre, Inc.*, P.O. Box 34360, 00734-4360. Tel: 787-842-0000; Fax: 787-840-5020. Email: mperez@csifpr.org. Web: www.csifpr.org. Sr. Silvia Arias, M.S.B.T., Custodian of the mission. Missionary Servants of the Most Blessed Trinity, Multiservice center that promotes the integral development of children, youth and adults in all areas: health, education, arts, culture, values, spiritual development, strategies of intercessors and community empowerment. Priests 1; Sisters 6; Total Staff 400.

[D] HOMES FOR THE AGED

PONCE. *Residencia Santa Marta* Home for Aged and Infirm , Barrio Sabenetas, P.O. Box 242, Mercedita, 00715. Tel: 787-840-7575; Fax: 787-840-1649. Sr. Araceli Villa, Supr.; Rev. Jose Esteves, O.deM., Chap. Total Staff (Religiosas) 17; Residents 196.

[E] MONASTERIES AND RESIDENCES OF PRIESTS AND BROTHERS

PONCE. *Fraternidad Santa Teresita, Frailes Capuchinos* (Postulantado) , 342 Victoria St., Box 7244, 00732. Tel: 787-842-5055; Fax: 787-844-7267. Email: jose.torres@email.pucpr.edu. Web: www.loscapuchinos.com. Revs. Jose Angel Torres, O.F.M.Cap., Guardian & Dir. Postulantado; Mario Mastrangelo, O.F.M.Cap.; Francisco Garcia, O.F.M.Cap., Dir. Hogar La Providencia & Casa Cristo Pobre; Jose R. Gonzalez, O.F.M.Cap. Postulants 3.

[F] CONVENTS & RESIDENCES OF SISTERS

PONCE. *Blessed Trinity Missionary Cenacle*, P.O. Box 34213, 00734-4213. Tel: 787-844-1627; Fax: 787-842-6748. Email: msbtponce@coqui.net. Web: www.msbt.org. Sr. Silvia Arias, M.S.B.T., Mission Custodian. Sisters 4.
Convent of Servants of Mary, Urb. La Rambla, 1703 Calle Siervas de Maria, 00730-4027. Tel: 787-842-2336; Fax: 787-844-5449. Sr. Lucrecia Pichardo Rodriguez, S.M., Supr. Religious 23; Postulants 2; Novices 5; Administered in the home 2,300.
Religiosas del Apostolado del Sagrado Corazon de Jesus, P.O. Box 8300, 00732-8300. Tel: 787-842-4340; Fax: 787-813-2066. Email: apostoladoponce@hotmail.com. Sisters Apostolate of the Sacred Heart of Jesus 25.
Colegio N. S. Perpetuo Socorro, Bo. Coqui, Aguirre, 00704. Tel: 787-853-2270; Fax: 787-853-2531. Sr. Aurea M. Fuentes, R.A., Supr., Delegada Regl.

Representante de la Superiora Gen.

[G] PERSONAL PRELATURES

PONCE. *Prelature of the Holy Cross and Opus Dei*, Urb. Alhambra, 1814 calle Alcazar, 00716-3829. Tel: 787-844-2661; Fax: 787-844-2661. Revs. Ramon Alvarez; Jose F. Tejeda.

[H] MISCELLANEOUS

COTO LAUREL. *Diocesan Fathers of Schoenstatt-Santuary of Schoenstatt*, P.O. Box 371, 00780-0771. Tel: 787-837-8907. Rev. Guillermo Esters.

PONCE. *Albergue La Providencia, Inc.*, P.O. Box 10142, 00732. Tel: 787-841-2119; Fax: 787-840-6641. Email: alp@prtc.net. Web: www.laprovidencia.org. Rev. Francisco Garcia, O.F.M.Cap., Dir. Refuge Center for AIDS patients. Total Assisted 37; Total Staff 27.

Apostolate for Family Consecration, Tel: 787-315-5587. *Our Lady of Guadalupe Center*, P.O. Box 32132, 00732-2132.

Centro Madre Dominga, Casa Belen, Urb. San Jorge, 3504 Calle Andino Apt. 2, 00717-0777. Tel: 787-290-3627; Fax: 787-290-3627. Email: centromadredominga@hotmail.com. Sr. M. Amada Rios, O.P., M.S.W., Dir.

Institucion Magdalena Aulina - Operarias Parroquiales (Secular Institute) , Simon de la Torre 43, 00731. Tel: 787-842-7209; Fax: 787-842-1935. Email: jiaulina@hotmail.com.

Jardin Infantil Aulina I, II and III, (I) Calle Simon de la Torre #43; (II) Calle Torre #48, Esq. Juan Seix, (III) Calle Juan Seix, Esq. Mendez Vigo #35, 00731. Grades: (I) 19-30 months; (II) 2-5 years; (III) 0-18 months

Memores Domini, P.O. Box 32197, 00732-2197. Tel: 787-844-0464; Fax: 787-844-0464. Email: zaffagiu@yahoo.com.

Miles Jesu, Ladies House, P.O. Box 32165, 00732-2165. Tel: 787-840-9436; Fax: 787-840-9436.

Men's House, Parroquia Santa Maria Reina, P.O. Box 32166, 00732-2166. Tel: 787-848-5370; Fax: 787-290-4189.

Oblates of Wisdom, Pontifical Catholic University of PR, 2250 Ave Las Americas, Ste. 601, 00717-0777. Tel: 787-842-6384. Email: materdei@pucpr.edu. Web: www.rtforum.org. Rev. Brian W. Harrison, O.S., Regl. Dir.

Pastoral Care of the Sick, Convento San Jose, 2250 Ave. Las Americas, Ste. 591, 00717-0777. Tel: 787-848-5600, Ext. 202. Sr. Maria Teresa Jensen, C.S.J., Dir.

Shelter for the Homeless, Tel: 787-841-5443. *Hna. Eulalia Antony, M.C.*, P.O. Box 32177, 00732-2177. Sr. M. Eulalia Antony, M.C., Supr. Missionaries of Charity (Mother Theresa of Calcutta) Sisters 6; Residents 44; Total Assisted 57.

PENUELAS. *Training School for the Lay Apostolate (Hermanos Cheos)*, P.O. Box 120, 00624. Tel: 787-836-1512; Fax: 787-836-1512. Rev. Msgr. Marcos A. Pancorbo, Dir.; Bro. Sixto Rivera Flores, Pres. Brothers 106.

YAUCO. *Instituto Especial para el Desarrollo Integral del Individuo, la Familia y la Communidad, Inc.*, Apartado 1241, 00968-1241. Tel: 787-856-3798; Fax: 787-856-4192. Email: instyco@coqui.net. Sr. M. Rosa Emilia del Valle Rivera, O.P., Dir.

RELIGIOUS INSTITUTES OF MEN REPRESENTED IN THE DIOCESE

For further details refer to the corresponding bracketed number in the Religious Institutes of Men or Women section.

[0470]—*The Capuchin Friars (Vice Province of Puerto Rico)*—O.F.M.Cap.
[0270]—*Carmelite Fathers & Brothers*—O.Carm
[1330]—*Congregation of the Mission*—C.M.
[0650]—*Holy Ghost Fathers* (Eastern Prov.)—C.S.Sp.
[]—*Lumen Dei*—L.D.
[]—*The Marist Priest (Mision Noel)*—S.M.
[]—*Mercedarian Fathers.*—O.deM.
[]—*Operarios Del Reino De Cristo*—O.R.C.
[0430]—*Order of Preachers-Dominicans* (Holland Prov.)—O.P.
[1310]—*Order of the Holy Trinity* (Spain)—O.SS.T.
[1040]—*Piarist Fathers* (Spain)—Sch.P.
[1070]—*Redemptorist Fathers* (San Juan Prov.)—C.SS.R.
[]—*Santuario Nuestra Senora Del Encuentro Con Dios Hislaterio Masculino Lumen Dei*

RELIGIOUS INSTITUTES OF WOMEN REPRESENTED IN THE DIOCESE

[0130]—*Apostles of the Sacred Heart of Jesus*—A.S.C.J.
[0340]—*Carmelite Sisters of Charity*—C.ach.
[1070-05]—*Dominican Sisters*—O.P.
[]—*Hermanas de los Ancianos Desamparados*
[]—*Hermanas del Servicio Social*
[]—*Hermanas Del-Amor De Dios*
[]—*Hermanas Dominicas de Fatima*—O.P.
[]—*Hermanas Ntra. Sra. del Perpetuo Socorro* Juana Diaz, Ponce—N.S.P.S.
[]—*Hnas. Clarisas*—O.S.C.
[2340]—*Little Sisters of the Poor*—L.S.P.
[2710]—*Missionaries of Charity*—M.C.
[2790]—*Missionary Servants of the Most Blessed Trinity*—M.S.B.T.
[]—*Operarias del Divino Maestro (Avemarianas)*
[]—*Religious de los Santos Angeles Custodios (Adjuntas, Ponce)*—R.A.C.
[]—*Santuario Nuestra Senora Del Encuentro Con Dios Hislaterio Femenino Lumen Dei*
[]—*School Sisters of Notre Dame*—S.S.N.D.
[3580]—*Servants of Mary*—O.S.M.
[]—*Sisters of Charity of St. Vincent de Paul*—H.C.
[]—*Sisters of St. Joseph*—S.S.J.
[2150]—*Sisters, Servants of the Immaculate Heart of Mary*—I.H.M.

NECROLOGY

† Ferre, Antonio, (On Duty Outside the Diocese)—Died Sept., 2003
† Grinena, Agustin, Penuelas, PR Sacred Heart of Jesus—Died Aug., 2003
† Margola, Joseph F., (On Duty Ourside the Diocese)—Died Sept., 2003

Diocese of St. Thomas in the Virgin Islands

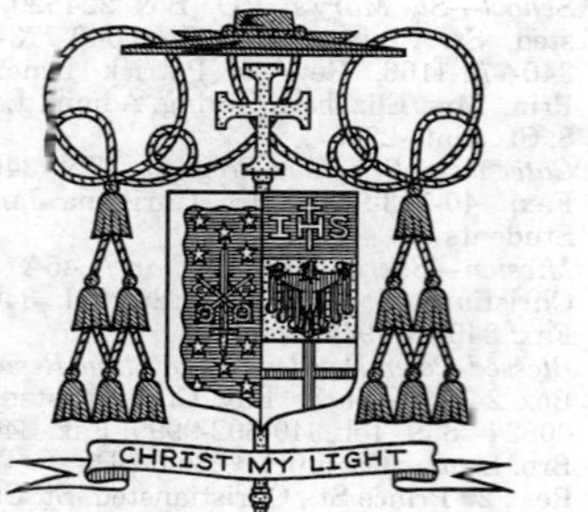

Most Reverend

GEORGE V. MURRY, S.J.

Bishop of St. Thomas in the Virgin Islands; ordained June 9, 1979; appointed May 5, 1998; installed June 30, 1999

Chancery Office: P.O. Box 301825, Charlotte Amalie, VI 00803. Tel: 340-774-3166; 340-776-1865; Fax: 340-774-5816.

Web: www.islands.vi/~chancery

Email: chancery@islands.vi

ESTABLISHED AS PRELATURE OF VI, JULY 23, 1960.

Established as Diocese of St. Thomas in the Virgin Islands April 20, 1977.

Comprises the Islands of St. Thomas, St. Croix, St. John and Water Island.

STATISTICAL OVERVIEW

Personnel	
Bishop	1
Retired Bishops	1
Priests: Diocesan Active in Diocese	11
Priests: Diocesan Active Outside Diocese	3
Priests: Retired, Sick or Absent	1
Number of Diocesan Priests	15
Religious Priests in Diocese	5
Total Priests in Diocese	20
Permanent Deacons in Diocese	28
Total Brothers	3
Total Sisters	17
Parishes	
Parishes	8
With Resident Pastor:	
Resident Diocesan Priests	6
Resident Religious Priests	2
Missions	2
Professional Ministry Personnel:	
Sisters	4
Lay Ministers	3
Welfare	
Special Centers for Social Services	2
Total Assisted	530
Other Institutions	1
Total Assisted	94
Educational	
Diocesan Students in Other Seminaries	1
Total Seminarians	1
High Schools, Diocesan and Parish	2
Total Students	217
Elementary Schools, Diocesan and Parish	3
Total Students	585
Catechesis/Religious Education:	
High School Students	123
Elementary Students	699
Total Students under Catholic Instruction	1,625
Teachers in the Diocese:	
Brothers	1
Sisters	1
Lay Teachers	57
Vital Statistics	
Receptions into the Church:	
Infant Baptism Totals	239
Adult Baptism Totals	15
Received into Full Communion	10
First Communions	196
Confirmations	141
Marriages:	
Catholic	78
Interfaith	17
Total Marriages	95
Deaths	147
Total Catholic Population	30,000
Total Population	108,612

Former Bishops—Most Revs. EDWARD J. HARPER, C.SS.R., D.D. (Retired), ord. June 18, 1939; appt. July 23, 1960; consecrated Oct. 6, 1960; named first residential bishop of Diocese of St. Thomas in the Virgin Islands, April 20, 1977; retired Oct. 15, 1985; died Dec. 2, 1990; SEAN P. O'MALLEY, O.F.M.Cap., ord. Aug. 29, 1970; named coadjutor, May 30, 1984; ord. Bishop, Aug. 2, 1984; installed Oct. 16, 1985; transferred to Fall River Aug. 11, 1992; ELLIOTT G. THOMAS, D.D. (Retired), ord. June 6, 1986; consecrated and installed as Bishop Dec. 12, 1993; retired June 30 1999.

Chancery Office—P.O. Box 301825, Charlotte Amalie, 00803. Tel: 340-774-3166; 340-776-1865; Fax: 340-774-5816.

Chancellor—Rev. Msgr. JEROME FEUDJIO. Tel: 340-774-3166.

Fiscal Officer—ANTHONY OLIVE.

Diocesan Consultors—Rev. SIMON PETER OPIRA; Rev. Msgr. JEROME FEUDJIO; Very Rev. KENNETH GADDY, C.SS.R., V.G.; Rev. Msgr. MICHAEL KOSAK; Revs. NEIL SCANTLEBURY; CECIL CORNEILLE.

Youth Coordinator—Very Rev. KENNETH GADDY, C.SS.R., V.G., P.O. Box 547, Frederiksted, St. Croix, 00841. Tel: 340-772-0138.

Hispanic Ministry—Revs. JOHN MARK, P.O. Box 301767, St. Thomas, 00803. Tel: 340-774-0201; Fax: 340-776-9586; MICHAEL HOUSTON, C.SS.R., 45 A Queen St., St. Croix, 00820. Tel: 340-773-7564; Fax: 340-713-9149.

Catholic Charities of the Virgin Islands, Inc.—Mr. MICHAEL AKIN, Exec. Dir., P.O. Box 10736, Charlotte Amalie, 00801. Tel: 340-777-8518; Fax: 340-777-4875.

Catholic Schools Office—Mr. DAVID COREY, Supt., P.O. Box 301825, Charlotte Amalie, 00803. Tel: 340-774-3166; Fax: 340-774-5816.

Vocations—Rev. CECIL CORNEILLE, P.O. Box 2150, Kingshill, St. Croix, 00851. Tel: 340-692-2005; Fax: 340-692-2748.

Charismatic Movement—Deacon HYACINTHE GEORGE, St. Croix, VI; Rev. Msgr. MICHAEL KOSAK, P.O. Box 1160 - Kingshill, St. Croix, 00851. Tel: 340-778-0484; Fax: 340-779-3151.

Caribbean Catholic Network (CCN)— Channel 7, Rev. Msgr. MICHAEL KOSAK, Gen. Mgr., P.O. Box 1160, Kingshill, St. Croix, 00851. Tel: 340-779-3000; Fax: 340-779-3151.

Catholic Television Network (CTN)— Channel 16, Rev. Msgr. JEROME FEUDJIO, P.O. Box 301825, Charlotte Amalie, 00803. Tel: 340-777-4828; Fax: 340-776-9586.

Diocesan Newspaper—Rev. CHARLES CRESPO, Editor, P.O. Box 241 - Cruz Bay, St. John, 00831-0241. Tel: 340-776-6339; Fax: 340-693-7685. "The Catholic Islander"

Communications Coordinator—Rev. Msgr. MICHAEL KOSAK, P.O. Box 1160 - Kingshill, St. Croix, 00851. Tel: 340-778-0484; Fax: 340-779-3151.

Prison Ministry—Sr. CLAUDIA PALACIOS, R.G.S., St. Croix. Tel: 340-773-7564; Fax: 340-713-9149; Rev. Msgr. JEROME FEUDJIO, St. Thomas. Tel: 340-774-3166; Fax: 340-774-5816.

Natural Family Planning Coordinator—Rev. TROY SCHUSTER, P.O. Box 304983, St. Thomas, 00803-4983. Tel: 340-774-0885; Fax: 340-774-5896.

Permanent Diaconate—Very Rev. KENNETH GADDY, C.SS.R., V.G., Dir. Tel: 340-772-0138; Fax: 340-772-0142.

Shelters for the Homeless—Mr. MICHAEL AKIN, Exec. Dir., Bethlehem House, P.O. Box 10736, Charlotte Amalie, 00801. Tel: 340-774-4663. St. Croix. Tel: 340-778-1227. Administration. Tel: 340-777-8518; Fax: 340-777-4475.

CLERGY, PARISHES, MISSIONS AND PAROCHIAL SCHOOLS

ISLAND OF ST. THOMAS

(CATHOLIC POPULATION, 12,500)

1—CATHEDRAL OF STS. PETER AND PAUL (1773), (West Indian), Revs. Neil Scantlebury; John K. Mark; Deacons Jose Vasquez; William Kenny.

Mailing Address: P.O. Box 301767, 00803. Tel: 340-774-0201; 340-776-7384; Fax: 340-776-9586.

In Res., Rev. Msgr. Jerome Feudjio; Revs. George Franklin; Jean Marie Degraff.

Res.: 22A Kronprindsens Gade (Main St.), 00803.

School—Sts. Peter and Paul School, (Grades PreK-12), P.O. Box 301706, St. Thomas, 00803. Tel: 340-774-5662; 340-774-2199; Fax: 340-777-5355. Mrs. Barbara Kenny, Asst. Prin. Sisters 1; Lay Teachers 12; Students (Grades Jr.K-6) 122.

School—Tel: 340-774-2199. Bro. Lawrence Lavallee, F.M.S., Prin. Lay Teachers 12; Students (Grades 7-12) 134.

Catechesis/Religious Program—Students 90.

Convent—Sisters of Charity of St. Elizabeth, 31 A Prindcesse Gade, P.O. Box 303785, 00803. Tel: 340-774-0248; Fax: 340-776-9586.

Mission—Chapel of St. Anne P.O. Box 306810, Carenage, 00803. Tel: 340-714-1101; Fax: 340-714-1101. Rev. Msgr. Jerome Feudjio; Deacon Alberto Olive.

2—HOLY FAMILY PARISH (1969), (West Indian), [JC] Revs. Simon Peter Opira; John K. Mark; Deacon Roy Bruney.

Res.: Cassi Hill, P.O. Box 502218, St. Thomas, 00805. Tel: 340-775-1650; Fax: 340-775-1750.

Catechesis/Religious Program—Tel: 340-775-5466. Gloria Etienne, D.R.E. Students 120.

3—OUR LADY OF PERPETUAL HELP (1926), (West Indian), [CEM] Rev. Troy Schuster; Deacon William Summer.

Mailing Address: P.O. Box 304983, 00803. Tel: 340-774-0885; Fax: 340-774-5896.

Catechesis/Religious Program—Students 43.

ISLAND OF ST. JOHN

(CATHOLIC POPULATION 300)

OUR LADY OF MT. CARMEL PARISH (1962), Rev. Charles Crespo; Deacons Austin Medina; Jose Vasquez.
Res.: P.O. Box 241, St. John, 00831. Tel: 340-776-6339 (Res. & Office); Fax: 340-693-7685.
Catechesis/Religious Program—Ms. Nausica Antoine, D.R.E. Students 38.

ISLAND OF ST. CROIX

(CATHOLIC POPULATION, APPROX. 17,200)

1—CHURCH OF ST. JOSEPH (1947), [JC] Rev. Cecil C. Corneille; Deacons James Verhoff; Conrad Williams; Neville Charles; Raymond Leonce; Guillermo Huertas.
Mailing Address: P.O. Box 2150, Kingshill, St. Croix, 00851-2150. Tel: 340-692-2005; Fax: 340-692-2748. In Res., Bro. James A. Petrait, O.S.F.S.
Res.: Mt. Pleasant, Frederiksted, St. Croix, 00841.
Catechesis/Religious Program—Students 170.
Convent—West Indian Franciscans, P.O. Box 1847, Kingshill, St. Croix, 00851. Tel: 340-778-5773; Fax: 340-719-3037.

2—CHURCH OF ST. PATRICK (1846), (African-Caribbean), Rev. Joseph Bertrand, C.SS.R.; Very Rev. Kenneth Gaddy, C.SS.R., V.G.; Rev. John Mcloughlin, C.SS.R.; Deacons Ed Cave; Emith Fludd; Lambert Heyliger.
Mailing Address: P.O. Box 547, Frederiksted, St. Croix, 00841. Tel: 340-772-0138; Fax: 340-772-0142.
School—P.O. Box 988, Frederiksted, St. Croix, 00841. Tel: 340-772-5052; Fax: 340-772-4488. Sr. Claina LaTang, L.C.M, Prin. Lay Teachers 16; Students 240.
Catechesis/Religious Program—Students 80.
Convent—Missionary Sisters of the Immaculate Heart of Mary, Caribbean Center, P.O. Box 95, Frederiksted, St. Croix, 00841. Tel: 340-772-0341; Fax: 340-772-4908.
DeMeester Residence—P.O. Box 52, St. Croix, 00841. Tel: 340-772-0132.
Light of Christ Retreat Center—301 New St., P.O. Box 547, St. Croix, 00841. Tel: 340-772-4782; Fax: 340-772-0142.

3—CHURCH OF THE HOLY CROSS (1755), (West Indian), [CEM 3] [JC] Revs. E. Patrick Lynch, C.SS.R.; Michael Houston, C.SS.R.; Bro. Leonard Samuel, C.SS.R.; Deacons Ulric Benjamin; James Matthews; David Capriola; Vincent Colianni; Hector Rivera; Angel Maldonado.
Res.: 45A Queen St., Christiansted, 00820. Tel: 340-773-7564; Fax: 340-713-9149.
School—St. Mary's, P.O. Box 224620, Christiansted, St. Croix, 00822. Tel: 340-773-0117; Fax: 340-773-1166. Rev. E. Patrick Lynch, C.SS.R., Prin.; Mrs. Elizabeth Hering, Admin. Lay Teachers 8; Students 223.
Catechesis/Religious Program—Tel: 340-773-7564; Fax: 340-713-9149. Mrs. Christina James, Coord. Students 90.
Mission—Sacred Heart Chapel 45A Queen St., Christiansted, U.S.V.I. 00820. Tel: 340-773-7564; Fax: 340-713-9149.
Blessed Peter Donder's Formation Residence—P.O. Box 24839-Gallows Bay, Christiansted, St. Croix, 00824-0839. Tel: 340-692-9999; Fax: 340-692-9997. Bro. Leonard Samuel, C.Ss.R., Dir.
Res.: 20 Prince St., Christiansted, St. Croix, 00820. Tel: 340-692-9999; Fax: 340-692-9997.
Convent—Missionaries of Charity, P.O. Box 3058, Christiansted, St. Croix, 00821. Tel: 340-773-1950; Fax: 340-713-9149.
Convent—Sisters of the Good Shepherd, P.O. Box 222984, Christiansted, 00822. Tel: 340-713-8724.

4—CHURCH ST. ANN (1823), (Caribbean), Rev. Msgr. Michael F. Kosak; Rev. Louis Kemayou; Deacons Arnold Helenese; Joseph Mark; Norbert Xavier; Hyacinthe George, Admin. Asst.; Robert Gibson; Denis Griffith; Eugene Thompson; Robert Brady.
Mailing Address: 42 Barrenspot Hill, P.O. Box 1160, Kingshill, St. Croix, 00851-1160. Tel: 340-778-0484; Fax: 340-779-3151. In Res., Rev. Msgr. Bernard Campbell (Retired).
Catechesis/Religious Program—Deacon Hyacinthe George, D.R.E. Students 191.
School—School of Evangelization, Tel: 340-778-0484; Fax: 340-779-3151. Rev. Msgr. Michael F. Kosak, Coord.; Deacon Joseph Mark, Prin.; Sr. Patricia Alexander, W.I.F., Spiritual Dir.; Deacon Hyacinthe George, Asst. Prin. Students 75.
Chaplaincy—Herbert Grigg Home for the Aged, Kingshill, 00851. Tel: 340-778-0708.
Shrine—Our Lady of Barrenspot Hill

Chaplaincies

These chaplaincies only pertain to the Island of St. Thomas.

ST. THOMAS. *Lucinda Millin Home for the Aged.*
Queen Louise Home for the Aged.
Seaview Nursing and Rehabilitation Center.
St. Thomas Hospital and Community Health Center.

On Duty Outside the Diocese:
Revs.—
Herrera, Jose
Obeng, Simon
Sanchez, Alejandro

Permanent Deacons:
Benjamin, Ulric
Brady, Robert
Bruney, Roy
Capriola, David
Cave, Edward
Charles, Neville
Colianni, Vincent
Fludd, Emith
George, Hyacinthe
Gibson, Robert
Griffith, Denis
Helenese, Arnold
Heyliger, Lambert
Huertas, Guillermo
Kenny, William
Leonce, Raymond
Maldonado, Angel
Mark, Joseph T.
Matthew, James
Medina, Austin
Olive, Alberto
Rivera, Hector
Summer, William
Thompson, Eugene
Vazquez, Jose
Verhoff, James
Williams, Conrad
Xavier, Norbert

INSTITUTIONS LOCATED IN THE DIOCESE

[A] INTERPAROCHIAL HIGH SCHOOLS

ST. CROIX. *St. Joseph High School*, 3 Mt. Pleasant, Rte. 2, Frederiksted, 00840. Tel: 340-692-2455; Fax: 340-692-2458. Email: sjhs@islands.vi. Web: www.islands.vi/~sjhs. Susan Diverio, Ed.D., Prin. Brothers 1; Lay Teachers 5; Students 83.

[B] ORGANIZATIONS IN THE DIOCESE

ST. THOMAS. *Miscellaneous Organizations* (For further information contact the Chancery Office) , Box 301825, 00803. Tel: 340-774-3166; Fax: 340-774-5816. Email: chancery@islands.vi.
Catholic Charismatic Renewal Tel: 340-778-0484; Fax: 340-779-3151. Rev. Msgr. Michael F. Kosak, Dir.; Sr. Patricia Alexander, Asst. Dir.
Catholic Daughters of the Americas Fax: 340-776-9586. Mrs. Marlene Adams, Regent. Tel: 340-776-2550.
Children of Mary Fax: 340-775-1750. Wende Rouse. Tel: 340-775-1351; Fax: 340-775-1750.
COR (Christ in Others Retreat) Fax: 340-772-0142. Very Rev. Kenneth Gaddy, C.SS.R., V.G. Tel: 340-772-0138.
Gabriel Project/Rachel Project/Good Shepherd Center Tel: 340-719-0264; Fax: 340-713-9149. Sr. Claudia Palacios, R.G.S., Dir.
Hispanic Ministry, St. Croix. Tel: 340-773-7564; Fax: 340-713-9149. Rev. Michael Houston, C.SS.R.
Knights of Columbus, St. Croix. Juan Cruz, Sgt. & Grand Knight. Tel: 340-773-7564.
Knights of Columbus Tel: 340-775-1650; Fax: 340-775-1750.
Legion of Mary, St. Croix. Rev. Michael Houston, C.SS.R. Tel: 340-773-7564.
Legion of Mary, St. John, 00831. Tel: 340-776-6054; Fax: 340-693-7685. Maggie Metor.
Legion of Mary, St. Thomas Tel: 340-775-3503; Fax: 340-775-1750. Eubald Rene. Tel: 340-775-3503.
Lumen 2000/Caribbean Region Rev. Msgr. Michael F. Kosak. Tel: 340-778-0484; Fax: 340-779-3151.
Magnificat Ministry Carmen Grant, Asst. Coord. Tel: 340-775-5369.
Propagation of the Faith Fax: 340-775-1750. Rev. Simon Peter Opira, Dir. Tel: 340-775-1650.
Secular Franciscans Sr. Patricia Alexander, W.I.F., Spiritual Asst. Tel: 340-778-5773; Fax: 340-719-3037.
Fraternity Our Lady of the Angels Deacon Raymond Leonce. Tel: 340-772-9131; Mrs. Cleo Hobson, Min. Tel: 340-775-0666.
St. Vincent de Paul Society, St.Thomas. Fax: 340-775-1750. Alma Wells. Tel: 340-775-0839.
Catholic Charities of the Virgin Islands Tel: 340-777-8518; Fax: 340-777-4475. Debra Brown-Roumo, Exec. Dir.
Disciples of the Holy Spirit, Inc., P.O. Box 1160, Kingshill, St. Croix, 00851. Tel: 340-778-0484; Fax: 340-779-3151. Rev. Msgr. Michael F. Kosak, Dir.
St. Joseph Workers Fax: 340-775-1750. Orville Rouse. Tel: 340-775-1351.
Secular Order Discalced Carmelites, St. Croix. Barbara O'Dea, Dir. Tel: 340-778-0933.
Men's Fellowship, St. Ann-Barrenspot, St. Croix. Tel: 340-778-0484; Fax: 340-779-3151.
Cursillo Movement, St. Croix. Tel: 340-692-2005; Fax: 340-692-2748. Victoria Soto. Tel: 340-772-1118.
Young Adults, St. John. Tel: 340-776-3339. Mrs. Simonia Athanase, Contact Person.
Prayer Group, St. John. Tel: 340-776-6339. Deacon Austin Medina, Contact Person.
Men's Fellowship, St. John, 00831. Tel: 340-776-6339. Deacon Austin Medina, Contact Person.
Youth Group, St. John. Tel: 340-776-6339. Ms. Catherine Celaire-Morton, Contact Person.
Hispanic Ministry, P.O. Box 301767, 00803. Tel: 340-774-0201; Fax: 340-776-9586. Rev. John K. Mark, Contact Person.

RELIGIOUS INSTITUTES OF MEN REPRESENTED IN THE DIOCESE

For further details refer to the corresponding bracketed number in the Religious Institutes of Men or Women section.

[0770]—*Marist Brothers*—F.M.S.
[0920]—*Oblates of St. Francis De Sales*—O.S.F.S.
[1070]—*Redemptorist Fathers*—C.SS.R.

RELIGIOUS INSTITUTES OF WOMEN REPRESENTED IN THE DIOCESE

[]—*Association of West Indian Franciscans*—W.I.F.
[2710]—*Missionaries of Charity*—M.C.
[2750]—*Missionary Sisters of the Immaculate Heart of Mary*—I.C.M.
[0590]—*Sisters of Charity of Saint Elizabeth (Convent Station)*—S.C.
[1830]—*Sisters of the Good Shepherd*—R.G.S.

NECROLOGY

(No Deaths)

Diocese of Samoa-Pago Pago

Most Reverend

JOHN QUINN WEITZEL, M.M.

Bishop of Samoa-Pago Pago; ordained June 11, 1955; appointed First Bishop of Samoa-Pago Pago October 29, 1986 *Fatuoaiga: P.O. Box 596, Pago Pago, AS 96799*. Tel: 684-699-1402; Fax: 684-699-1459.

Email: quinn@samoatelco.com

CREATED A DIOCESE NOVEMBER, 1982.

The Diocese of Samoa-Pago Pago includes the islands of Tutuila; Swains; Manu'a Is., Ofu, Olosega & Ta'u; Aunu'u and Rose Island.

STATISTICAL OVERVIEW

Personnel	
Bishop	1
Priests: Diocesan Active in Diocese	8
Priests: Diocesan in Foreign Missions	1
Priests: Retired, Sick or Absent	1
Number of Diocesan Priests	10
Religious Priests in Diocese	5
Total Priests in Diocese	15
Ordinations:	
Diocesan Priests	1
Permanent Deacons	19
Permanent Deacons in Diocese	16
Total Sisters	13
Parishes	
Parishes	13
With Resident Pastor:	
Resident Diocesan Priests	6
Resident Religious Priests	1
Without Resident Pastor:	
Administered by Priests	4
Administered by Deacons	1
Administered by Lay People	1
Missions	1
Pastoral Centers	1
New Parishes Created	1
Professional Ministry Personnel:	
Sisters	11
Lay Ministers	42
Welfare	
Homes for the Aged	1
Total Assisted	26
Day Care Centers	1
Total Assisted	100
Special Centers for Social Services	1
Total Assisted	310
Educational	
Diocesan Students in Other Seminaries	8
Total Seminarians	8
High Schools, Diocesan and Parish	1
Total Students	128
Elementary Schools, Diocesan and Parish	2
Total Students	394
Catechesis/Religious Education:	
High School Students	836
Elementary Students	2,000
Total Students under Catholic Instruction	3,366
Teachers in the Diocese:	
Sisters	8
Lay Teachers	84
Vital Statistics	
Receptions into the Church:	
Infant Baptism Totals	261
Adult Baptism Totals	127
Received into Full Communion	57
First Communions	284
Confirmations	175
Marriages:	
Catholic	52
Interfaith	20
Total Marriages	72
Deaths	59
Total Catholic Population	14,550
Total Population	60,000

Vicar General of Diocese—Very Rev. VIANE ETUALE.

Chancellor—Mrs. IVONA T. MAUGA.

Diocesan Consultors—Most Rev. J. QUINN WEITZEL, M.M.; Rev. Msgr. MASELINO PAULO; Very Revs. VIANE ETUALE, V.G.; PETELO SILIAKO, V.G.; Rev. SETEFANO TUISEA.

Diocesan Pastoral Council—Very Rev. VIANE ETUALE, Chm.; Rev. KELEMETE PUA'AULI, Sec.

Fatuoaiga Multipurpose Cultural and Pastoral Center—Very Rev. VIANE ETUALE, Dir. Faculty Members: Revs. VIANE ETUALE; KELEMETE PUA'AULI; FALANIKO ATONIO; KOLIO ETUALE; Deacon NIUATOA PULETASI.

St. Anne Society—Mrs. VERONIKA TAVALE, Pres.; Mrs. NELLIE TOILOLO, Vice Pres.; Mrs. MALIA PEPE, Treas.

Sacred Heart Society—Mrs. SUSANA LUTALI, Pres.; Mrs. FATUIVA TE'O, Vice Pres.; Mrs. JOANNE KIMOTO, Treas.; Ms. MAGGIE CRADDICK, Sec.

Vicar for Diocesan Youth—Rev. IOSEFO TIMU, M.F., Dir.

Director of Vocations—Rev. VIANE ETUALE.

Port Chaplain—Deacon NIKOLAO PULA.

Hospital Chaplain—Deacon FELISE TOILOLO, F.K., Catechist.

Director of Propagation of the Faith—Rev. ELADIO B. OLIVER, M.S.P.

CLERGY, PARISHES, MISSIONS AND PAROCHIAL SCHOOLS

SAMOA-PAGO PAGO

1—CATHEDRAL OF THE HOLY FAMILY (1986), Most Rev. John Quinn Weitzel, M.M.; Revs. Ricarte Galo, M.S.P.; Kelemete Pua'auli; Deacons Anetele'a Puletasi; Francis Leasiolagi; Felise Toilolo.
Mailing Address: *Fatuoaiga*, P.O. Box 3594, AS 96799-3594. Tel: 684-699-1446; Fax: 684-699-1459.
Catechesis/Religious Program—Tel: 684-699-2209; Fax: 684-699-1459. Miss Christina Iosefo, D.R.E.; Mrs. Cecilia Solofa, D.R.E. Students 550.
Mission—Mary, Star of the Sea Manu'a Island, AS. Tel: 684-677-3103.

2—CHRIST THE KING (Amanave), Rev. Falaniko Atonio.
Mailing Address: P.O. Box 5408, AS 96799. Tel: 684-688-1542.
Catechesis/Religious Program—Students 60.

3—CHRIST THE KING (Malaeloa) (1997), Very Rev. Petelo Siliako, V.G.; Deacon August Gabriel.
Mailing Address: P.O. Box 596, AS 96799. Tel: 684-688-2438; Fax: 684-699-1459.
Catechesis/Religious Program—Students 134.

4—CHRIST THE KING (Nu'uuli) (1983), Rev. Eladio B. Oliver, M.S.P. (Philippines), Admin.
Mailing Address: P.O. Box 596, AS 96799. Fax: 684-699-1459.
Catechesis/Religious Program—Malaki Timu, D.R.E. Students 80.

5—CHURCH OF SACRED HEART (Alao) (1989), Rev. Iosefo Timu, M.F.; Deacons Sogimaletavai Leo; Uikirifi Auelua.
Mailing Address: *Alao*, P.O. Box 4175, AS 96799. Tel: 684-622-7029; Fax: 684-699-1459.
Catechesis/Religious Program—Students 215.
Mission— Aoa, AS. Tel: 684-622-7416.
Mission— Amouli, AS. Tel: 684-622-7613.

6—CHURCH OF ST. PETER AND PAUL (Lauli'i) (1969), Revs. Iosefo Timu, M.F.; Etuale To'alepai, M.F.; Deacons Setefano Lesa; Fred Pele.
Mailing Address: P.O. Box 985, AS 96799. Tel: 684-644-5581.
Catechesis/Religious Program—Tel: 684-644-4697. Students 150.
Mission— Masefau, AS. Tel: 684-622-7131. Samuelu Aoelua, D.R.E.
Mission— Faga'itua, AS. Tel: 684-622-7130.
Mission— Sa'ilele, AS.

7—CHURCH OF THE HOLY CROSS (Leone) (1861), Rev. Kolio Etuale, Admin.
Mailing Address: *Leone*, P.O. Box 1206, AS 96799. Tel: 684-688-7663; Fax: 684-699-1459.
Mission— Amaluia, AS.
Catechesis/Religious Program—Anitele'a Iese, D.R.E. Students 300.

8—CHURCH OF THE IMMACULATE CONCEPTION (Lepua) (1867), Rev. Tagaloa Tatino.
Mailing Address: *Lepua*, P.O. Box 398, AS 96799. Tel: 684-644-5512.
Catechesis/Religious Program—Tel: 684-644-2411. Asalemo Taulamano, D.R.E.; Deacons Toetofi Tavale; Kalini Folau. Students 70.
Mission— Afono, AS. Tel: 684-644-4797.
Mission— Aua, AS. Tel: 684-644-5826.

9—CO-CATHEDRAL OF ST. JOSEPH THE WORKER (Fagatogo) (1974), Rev. Setefano Tuisea, Admin.; Deacons Lutia Timoteo; Nikolao Pula.
Mailing Address: *Fagatogo*, P.O. Box AA, AS 96799. Tel: 684-633-1548.
Catechesis/Religious Program—Students 622.
Mission— Utulei, AS.
Mission— Faga'alu, AS. Tel: 684-633-2560.

10—OUR LADY OF FATIMA (2002), Rev. Alefosio Uelese, Admin.
Mailing Address: *Aua Parish*, P.O. Box 4052, AS 96799. Tel: 684-644-5826; Fax: 684-699-1459.
Catechesis/Religious Program—Students 215.

11—ST. PAUL (Ili'ili) (1974), Rev. Viane Etuale; Deacon Sagapolutele Malaeola.
Mailing Address: *Ili'ili*, P.O. Box 2004, AS 96799. Tel: 684-699-7572; Fax: 684-699-1459.
Office—Fatuoaiga, P.O. Box 596, AS 96799. Tel: 684-699-7575.
Catechesis/Religious Program—Students 260.
Mission— Faleniu, AS.
Mission— Futiga, AS.
Mission— Pava'ia'i, AS. Tel: 684-699-7613.
Mission— Aasu/Aoloau, AS. Tel: 684-699-9766.

12—STS. PETER & PAUL (Asili), Rev. Falaniko Atonio; Deacon Taleo Sitama.
Mailing Address: P.O. Box 7286, AS 96799. Tel:

684-688-7236.
Catechesis/Religious Program—Students 70.

13—SACRED HEART PARISH-PAGO PAGO (2001), Deacon David Pereira, Admin.
Res.: P.O. Box 596, AS 96799. Tel: 684-633-4035.
Catechesis/Religious Program—Total Enrollment 110.

Permanent Deacons:

Auelua, Uikirifi
Folau, Kalini
Gabriel, August
Lafaele, Setefano
Leasiolagi, Francis
Leo, Herman Sogimaletavai
Ma'ileoi, Naisina
Maugaotega, Tagataese, (On leave)
Pele, Tupuaga Fred
Pereira, Tavita
Pula, Taafulisia Nikolao
Puletasi, Niuatoa Andy
Sagapolutele, Anthony Malaeola
Tavale, Toetofi
Timoteo, Lutia Laupapa
Toilolo, Felise, F.K.

INSTITUTIONS LOCATED IN THE DIOCESE

[A] PRESCHOOLS

PAGO PAGO. *Mary The Mother Montessori Early Education Center*, c/o Diocese of Samoa-Pago Pago, Fatuoaiga-P.O. Box 596, AS 96799. Tel: 684-644-1311; Fax: 684-699-1459. Sr. Marilyn Evans, M.M., Prin. & Supr. Sisters 1; Lay Teachers 7; Students 60.

[B] ELEMENTARY SCHOOLS, PAROCHIAL

LEONE. *St. Theresa*, P.O. Box 883, AS 96799-0596. Tel: 684-688-1105; Fax: 684-688-1114. Mrs. Makerita Satele, Prin. Missionary Sisters of the Society of Mary Sisters 3; Lay Teachers 12; Students 192.

LEPUA. *Marist St. Francis*, Fatuoaiga, P.O. Box 429, AS 96799-0429. Fax: 684-699-1459. Sr. Sesilia Sala, F.M.A., Prin. Lay Teachers 17; Students 200.

[C] HIGH SCHOOLS, PAROCHIAL

LEPUAPUA. *Faasao Marist College Preparatory School*, P.O. Box 729, AS 96799. Tel: 684-688-7731; Fax: 684-688-2055. Email: courgars@faasao.com. Sue Ozar, Prin. Sisters 1; Volunteer Lay Missionaries 5; Students 128.

[D] HOMES FOR AGED & SPECIAL CARE FOR CHILDREN

PAGO PAGO. *Nazareth House*, P.O. Box 1510, AS 96799. Tel: 684-699-2101; Fax: 684-699-1459. Sr. Sheila Collingborn, Admin. Aged Residents 18; Special Care Children 8; Montessori Early Education 80; Day Care Center 100; Total Staff 60.

[E] MISCELLANEOUS

PAGO PAGO. *Catholic Social Services, Inc.*, P.O. Box 596, AS 96799. Tel: 684-699-5683; Fax: 684-699-1340. Email: ccs1@samoatelco.com. Bud Ozar, S.T.L., Dir. Total Assisted 310; Total Staff 3.

RELIGIOUS INSTITUTES OF MEN REPRESENTED IN THE DIOCESE

For further details refer to the corresponding bracketed number in the Religious Institutes of Men or Women section.

[0800]—*Maryknoll*—M.M.

[]—*Missionaries of the Faith*—M.F.

[]—*Missionaries of the Society of the Philippines*—M.S.P.

RELIGIOUS INSTITUTES OF WOMEN REPRESENTED IN THE DIOCESE

[]—*Congregation of the Sisters of Nazareth*—C.S.N.

[2420]—*Marist Missionary Sisters, Inc. (Missionary Sisters of the Society of Mary)*—S.M.S.M.

[2470]—*Maryknoll Sisters of St. Dominic*—M.M.

[]—*Religious Sisters of the Virgin Mary*—R.V.M.

[]—*Salesian Sisters(Daughters of Mary Help of Christians)*—F.M.A.

NECROLOGY

(No Deaths)

Archdiocese of San Juan, Puerto Rico

(Sancti Joannis Portoricensis)

His Eminence

LUIS CARDINAL APONTE MARTINEZ, D.D.

Retired Archbishop of San Juan; ordained April 10, 1950; appointed Titular Bishop of Lares and Auxiliary of Ponce July 23, 1960; consecrated October 12, 1960; appointed Coadjutor Bishop of Ponce April 16, 1963; appointed Bishop of Ponce November 18, 1963; installed February 22, 1964; promoted to Archbishop of San Juan November 4, 1964; installed January 15, 1965; Created Cardinal March 5, 1973; retired March 26, 1999

Most Reverend

TIMOTHY BROGLIO

Apostolic Delegate for Puerto Rico *Ponce de Leon Ave. #256, San Juan, PR 00907. P.O. Box 191771, San Juan, PR 00907.* Tel: 787-723-1280; Fax: 787-723-1280.

Most Reverend

ROBERTO O. GONZALEZ NIEVES, O.F.M.

Archbishop of San Juan; ordained May 8, 1977; appointed Titular Bishop of Ursona and Auxiliary Bishop of Boston July 19, 1988; consecrated October 3, 1988; appointed Coadjutor Bishop of Corpus Christi May 16, 1995; Transferred to Corpus Christi June 26, 1995; succeeded to See April 1, 1997; appointed Archbishop of San Juan March 26, 1999; installed May 8, 1999

Chancery Office: P.O. Box 9021967, San Juan, PR 00902-1967. Tel: 787-977-0672; 787-727-7373; Fax: 787-723-4040; 787-728-1719.

Most Reverend

HECTOR M. RIVERA, D.D.

Auxiliary Bishop of San Juan PR; ordained June 12, 1966; appointed Titular Bishop of Tubune in Numidia and Auxiliary Bishop of San Juan PR June 11, 1979; consecrated August 17, 1979 *Res.: Valle Arriba Heights,* Calle Alamo, BF #20, Carolina, PR 00983. Tel: 787-276-1413. *P.O. Box 31155, San Juan, PR 00929-2155.*

Most Reverend

HERMIN NEGRON SANTANA, D.D.

Auxiliary Bishop of San Juan, PR; ordained May 30, 1969; appointed Titular Bishop of Gegi, North Africa and Auxiliary Bishop of San Juan, PR June 30, 1981; consecrated September 7, 1981 *Res.: Urb. Caparra Heights, 1562 C. Encarnacion, San Juan, PR 00920.* Tel: 787-277-5680.

ERECTED AUGUST 8, 1511.

Square Miles 353.

Erected an Archdiocese April 30, 1960.

Comprises the northeast portion of the Island of Puerto Rico, with a Total Population of 1,460,593.

STATISTICAL OVERVIEW

Personnel	
Retired Cardinals	1
Archbishops	1
Auxiliary Bishops	2
Priests: Diocesan Active in Diocese	139
Priests: Diocesan Active Outside Diocese	5
Priests: Retired, Sick or Absent	14
Number of Diocesan Priests	158
Religious Priests in Diocese	189
Total Priests in Diocese	347
Extern Priests in Diocese	59
Permanent Deacons in Diocese	242
Total Brothers	32
Total Sisters	480
Parishes	
Parishes	154
With Resident Pastor:	
Resident Diocesan Priests	102
Resident Religious Priests	52
Without Resident Pastor:	
Administered by Priests	1
Missions	173
Professional Ministry Personnel:	
Brothers	32
Welfare	
Catholic Hospitals	1
Total Assisted	215
Health Care Centers	2
Total Assisted	1,685
Homes for the Aged	7
Total Assisted	892
Residential Care of Children	11
Total Assisted	1,024
Day Care Centers	39
Total Assisted	1,252
Specialized Homes	10
Total Assisted	17,849
Special Centers for Social Services	2
Total Assisted	153,781
Educational	
Seminaries, Diocesan	1
Students from This Diocese	3
Students from Other Diocese	3
Diocesan Students in Other Seminaries	3
Students Religious	8
Total Seminarians	14
Colleges and Universities	2
Total Students	8,586
High Schools, Diocesan and Parish	20
Total Students	4,300
High Schools, Private	28
Total Students	6,668
Elementary Schools, Diocesan and Parish	28
Total Students	9,623
Elementary Schools, Private	40
Total Students	13,379
Non-residential Schools for the Disabled	1
Total Students	138
Catechesis/Religious Education:	
High School Students	10,967
Elementary Students	27,415
Total Students under Catholic Instruction	81,090
Teachers in the Diocese:	
Priests	30
Brothers	23
Sisters	93
Lay Teachers	2,295
Vital Statistics	
Receptions into the Church:	
Infant Baptism Totals	9,378
Adult Baptism Totals	1,248
First Communions	7,155
Confirmations	4,700
Marriages:	
Catholic	1,775
Interfaith	106
Total Marriages	1,881
Total Catholic Population	1,001,178
Total Population	1,697,435

Former Bishops—Most Revs. ALONSO MANSO, D.D., appt. May 1511; JAMES H. BLENK, S.M.D.D., appt. Bishop of Puerto Rico, June 12, 1899; died April 20, 1917; WILLIAM A. JONES, O.S.A., consecrated Feb. 24, 1907; died Jan. 1921; GEORGE J. CARUANA, D.D., appt. Bishop 1921; promoted to the Apostolic Delegation of Mexico, 1925; promoted to Nunciature Apostolic of Cuba, 1927; EDWIN VINCENT BYRNE, D.D., former Bishop of Ponce, Puerto Rico; consecrated Nov. 30, 1925; appt. March 1929; promoted to Archdiocese of Santa Fe, June 15, 1943; died July 25, 1963; JAMES PETER DAVIS (Retired), appt. 1943; consecrated Oct. 9, 1943; transferred to Archdiocese of Santa Fe, June, 1963; installed Feb. 25, 1964; retired Oct. 1974; His Eminence LUIS CARDINAL APONTE MARTINEZ, D.D. (Retired), appt. Auxiliary Bishop of Ponce July 23, 1960; consecrated Oct. 12, 1960; appt. Coadjutor Bishop of Ponce April 16, 1963; succeeded to Nov. 18, 1963; installed Feb. 22, 1964; appt. Archbishop of San Juan Nov. 4, 1964; installed Jan. 15, 1965; created Cardinal March 5, 1973; retired March 26, 1999.

Vicars General—Most Revs. HECTOR RIVERA, D.D.; HERMIN NEGRON SANTANA, D.D.; Rev. Msgr. CELESTINO LINERA.

Episcopal Moderator—

for Administration of Temporalities—Rev. LEONARDO J. RODRIGUEZ, Moderator.

Office of Economic Affairs—Mr. RICARDO F. GONZALEZ, Economist; Mrs. SANDRA RODRIGUEZ, Asst. to Economist.

for Education—Rev. Msgr. BAUDILIO MERINO. Email: www.escueloscatolicos-sj.org.

for Pastoral Affairs—Rev. Msgr. EMILIO TORO.

for Geographic-Pastoral Zones—San Juan-Santurce: Rev. R. JAIME CASELLAS, O.F.M.Cap. Bayamon: Rev. DANIEL TRUJILLO-MEJIA. Carolina: Rev. NESTOR YULFO-HOFFMAN Rio Piedras: Rev. MARIO MESA-CAPARROS, C.F.M.Cap. Rio Grande: Rev. VICENTE PASQUALETTO, S.T. Guaynabo-Puerto Nuevo: Rev. Msgr. MARIO A. GUIJARRO DEL CORZO.

*Chancery Office—P.O. Box 9021967, San Juan, 00902-1967*Web: www.arqsj.org.

Chancery Affairs—Dr. ANIBAL COLON ROSADO, Chancellor. Email: cancilleria@arqsj.org.

Metropolitan Curia—

Moderator—Rev. LEONARDO RODRIGUEZ-JIMENES.

Secretary to the Archbishop—Rev. ALFONSO D. GUZMAN, O.F.M. Tel: 787-725-4975; 787-977-0672.

Executive Assistant to the Archbishop—Mr. SAMUEL SOTO-ALONSO. Tel: 787-725-4975; 787-977-0672.

Assistant to the Archbishop and Secretary to the Cardinal—Miss MIRIAM RAMOS. Tel: 787-725-4975.

Judicial Vicar—Rev. LUIS O. CAPACETTI-CARABALLO.

Adjunct Vicar—Rev. PEDRO REYES-LEBRON.

Judges—Miss MARIA LUCIA SANCHEZ; Revs. REINALDO SAGARDIA-PEREZ; CARLOS ORTIZ; RICARDO A. ROIG.

Defender of the Bond—Rev. FLORENTINO SANZ.

Instructors—Mr. RIGOBERTO HIRALDO; Mr. JOSE GARCIA; Mr. ROLANDO QUEVEDO; Mr. PLINIO RODRIGUEZ. Email: tribunal@arqsj.org.

Diocesan Consultors—Most Revs. HERMIN NEGRON SANTANA, D.D.; HECTOR RIVERA-PEREZ, D.D.; Rev. Msgrs. CELESTINO LINERA-TORMOS; BAUDILIO MERINO-MERINO; Revs. LUIS O. CAPACETTI-CARABALLO; EDDIE RIVERA-MARZAN; R. JAIME CASELLAS-RIVERA, O.F.M.Cap.

Censor Librorum—Rev. PEDRO REYES.

Vicar for Pastoral Affairs—Rev. Msgr. R. EMILIO TORO.

Vicar for Education—Rev. Msgr. BAUDILIO MERINO.

Vicar for Religious—Rev. ALFONSO D. GUZMAN, O.F.M.

Examinatores Cleri—VACANT.

Vicar for Vocations—Rev. IVAN LUIS HUERTAS-COLON.

Vicar for Communications—Rev. Msgr. WILFREDO PENA-MORENO.

Pro-Synodal Examiner—VACANT.
Vicar for Priests—Rev. ALBERTO LOPEZ-FIGUEROA.
Vicar for Youth—Rev. MIGUEL ANGEL TRINIDAD-FONSECA.

Archdiocesan Offices and Directors

Boy Scouts—Prof. AMERICO LOPEZ, P.O. Box 8812, San Juan, 00910-0812.

Catechetics—Most Rev. HECTOR RIVERA, Archdiocesan Coord., Calle San Jorge 201, Santurce, 00914.

Catechetics Center—San Juan-Santurce, P.O. Box 9021967, San Juan, 00902-1967. Tel: 787-727-7373. Bayamon: Sr. IMELDA MORALES, M.SS.S., P.O. Box 4152, Bayamon, 00958. Tel: 787-780-1173. Rio Piedras: Sr. AILEEN BARDEN, C.S.J., P.O. Box 20884, San Juan, 00920. Tel: 787-761-4280. Guaynabo-PtoNuevo: Sr. ROSE MORALES, M.S.B.T., P.O. Box 9021967, San Juan, 00902-1967. Tel: 787-731-6100. Rio Grande: Sr. ISABEL SOTO, M.SS.S., P.O. Box 1793, Rio Grande, 00745. Tel: 787-888-5317. Carolina: Urb. Valle Arriba Heights, Calle Alamo BF-20, Carolina, 00983. Tel: 787-276-1413.

Catholic Charities—Mr. AMERICO P. LOPEZ ORTIZ, P.O. Box 8812, San Juan, 00910-0812. Tel: 787-727-7373; Fax: 787-728-4100. Email: ssc@arqsj.org.

"El Visitante"— Weekly Catholic Paper for All Dioceses (Interdiocesan). Published By The P.R., Episcopal Conference. Most Rev. ROBERTO GONZALEZ NIEVES, O.F.M., Pres.; Rev. EFRAIN ZABALA, Editor; Dr. JOSE R. ORTIZ-VALLADARES, Dir., Mailing Address, P.O. Box 41305, Minillas Sta., San Juan, 00940-1305. Tel: 787-728-3710; Fax: 787-268-1748. Offices, Pumarada St. 1704, Santurce, 00914.

Radio Stations— WORO-FM and WKVM-AM 81, VACANT, Dir., Urb. Baldrich, 415 Calle Ingeniero Carbonell, San Juan, 00918. c/o P.O. Box 9021967, San Juan, 00902-1967. Tel: 787-731-1380; 787-751-1018; Fax: 787-758-9967. Email: radiooro@arqsj.org.

Television Station— WPRV-TV CHANNEL 13, Tele Oro, Rev. Msgr. WILFREDO PENA-MORENO, Exec. Dir.; Mr. JUAN M. MUNIZ, Gen. Mgr., Ave Iturregui Esq. Marginal, Baldorioty De Castro Ave., Carolina, 00982. Tel: 787-276-1300; Fax: 787-276-1307. P.O. Box 9021967, San Juan, 00902-1967.

Commission for Sacred Liturgy and Popular Piety—Rev. LEONARDO J. RODRIGUEZ.
- *Subcommission for Sacred Art*—Rev. RODOLFO LAMAR; Dr. ARTURO DAVILA, Urb. Baldrich, Calle Rossy #202, San Juan, 00918. Tel: 787-763-9154.
- *Subcommission for Sacred Music*—Rev. MIGUEL TRINIDAD.
- *Subcommission for Popular Piety*—Rev. TARSICIO GOTAY FIGAREDO, O.Carm.
- *Subcommission for Ministries*—Rev. LEONARDO J. RODRIGUEZ.

Clergy Social Security (Prevision Social del Clero)—Rev. Msgr. EMILIO TORO, Pres.; Revs. CARLOS QUINTANA-PUENTE, Treas.; ALBERTO DIAZ; Miss TAHIRA VARGAS, Sec., CEP, P.O. Box 4682, San Juan, 00940-0682. Tel: 787-728-1650; Fax: 787-728-1654.

Istepa—Rev. FRANCISCO MEDINA, Camino Alejandrino KM 3.4, Antiguo, Guaynabo, 00969. Mailing Address, Edificio 2021, Carretera #177, Guaynabo, 00969-5140. Tel: 787-731-6100; Fax: 787-731-0000.

San Juan Bautista Regional Seminary—Revs. JUAN LUIS NEGRON, Rector; IVAN L. HUERTAS-COLON, Vice Rector; DANIEL FERNANDEZ, Dean of Studies; PEDRO L. REYES, Spiritual Dir., P.O. Box 11714, San Juan, 00922-1714. Tel: 787-783-0645; 787-273-8090; Fax: 787-783-0645. Ave. De Diego 930, Urb. La Riviera, Rio Piedras, 00921. Email: seminary@coqui.net.

San Jose Minor Seminary—Rev. CARLOS ORTIZ, Rector, Demetrio O'Dally St. 1000, Country Club, San Juan, 00924. Tel: 787-768-3157; Fax: 787-752-2410.

Serra Club—VACANT.

Vocations Promoter—Rev. IVAN L. HUERTAS-COLON, P.O. Box 11714, San Juan, 00922-1714. Tel: 787-706-9455; 787-273-8090.

Superintendent of Schools—Mrs. MARIA COLON DE MARSUACH, Supt.; Mrs. BLANCA MARQUEZ, Asst.; Sr. MARY ELLEN GEMMELL, C.S.F.N., Religion Program Dir., Mailing Address, Edificio 2021, Carretera 177, Guaynabo, 00969-5140. Tel: 787-731-6100; Fax: 787-731-0000. Web: www.esculelascatolicas-sj.org.

Archdiocesan Historical Archive—Mrs. ELSE ZAYAS LEON, Calle San Sebastian 5-N, San Juan, 00902. P.O. Box 9021967, San Juan, 00902-1967. Tel: 787-977-1447.

Youth Ministries—Rev. MIGUEL ANGEL TRINIDAD-FONSECA, Parroquia N. Sra. Rosario, Urb. Villa Espana, Bayamon, 00961.

Police Chaplains—Rev. Msgr. BAUDILIO MERINO. Tel: 787-767-6552; Revs. VALERIANO MIGUELEZ. Tel: 787-754-0570; LUIS ANGEL TORRES. Tel: 787-769-5665; GREGORIO BRAVO. Tel: 787-765-0600; Deacon JOSE A. TORRES. Tel: 787-785-6029; Rev. ANTONIO GARCIA CASTEJON. Tel: 787-757-4454; Deacon JOSE PENA GONZALEZ. Tel: 787-786-5309.

Society for the Protection of Children—Most Rev. ROBERTO GONZALEZ NIEVES, O.F.M., Mailing Address, P.O. Box 9021967, San Juan, 00902-1967. Tel: 787-727-7373.

United Against Hunger (Unidos Contra El Hambre)—Mrs. LAURA BLIZZARD DE APONTE, San Jorge St., No. 201, Santurce, 00914. Mailing Address, P.O. Box 11547, San Juan, 00910-2647. Tel: 787-727-7373, Ext. 240; Fax: 787-727-7938. Email: uch@arqsj.org.

Propagation of the Faith—Rev. PRISCILIANO CARDENAS-RUIZ, 106 Ruiz Belvis St., Floral Park, P.O. Box 191882, San Juan, 00919.

Pius Union of the Clergy—Rev. Msgr. CELESTINO LINERA, Mailing Address, P.O. Box 9021967, San Juan, 00902-1967. Tel: 787-727-7373.

Catholic Charismatic Renewal—Rev. Msgr. BANDILIO MERINO, Dir., Arzobispado de San Juan. Tel: 787-765-6240; 787-727-7373.

Master of Ceremonies to the Archbishop—VACANT.

Pre Cana Conferences—VACANT, Dir., Parroquia Santa Rosa Lima, 1765 Calle Lesbos, San Juan, 00926. Tel: 787-761-6586; Mr. MANUEL SANCHEZ, Urb. Country Club, 1031 Calle Genoveva De Lugo, San Juan, 00924. Tel: 787-769-3565.

Catholic Social Services—Dr. AMERICO LOPEZ-ORTIZ, Exec. Dir., P.O. Box 8812, San Juan, 00910-0812. Tel: 787-727-7373; Fax: 787-728-4100.

Cursillos De Cristiandad—Revs. LUIS O. CAPACETTI; TOMAS GONZALEZ-GONZALEZ; VICENTE FERNANDEZ-MARINO, P.O. Box 361809, San Juan, 00936-1809. Tel: 787-789-7596; Fax: 787-790-7596.

Inmigrant Aid—Sr. MARIA MERCEDES ALEJANDRO, M.H.S.H., Catholic Social Services, P.O. Box 9021967, San Juan, 00902-1967. Tel: 787-727-7373.

Holy Childhood Association—Rev. PRISCILIANO CARDENAS-RUIZ, 106 Ruiz Belvis St., Floral Park, San Juan, 00919-1882. Tel: 787-754-0995; Fax: 787-754-0749. P.O. Box 191882, San Juan, 00919-1882.

Holy Name Society—Rev. OMAR MARTINEZ, O.P., Parroquia Invencion De La Santa Cruz, Calle Degetau #12, Bayamon, 00961; Mr. MIGUEL A. RODRIGUEZ, Archdiocesan Dir., P.O. Box 31164, San Juan, 00929. Tel: 787-276-2212; 787-764-4813; Mr. FRANCISCO FIGUEROA, Sec. Tel: 787-768-4787.

Renovacion Conyugal (Fundacion Fernando Martinez Calle, Inc.)—Rev. BAUDILIO GUZMAN, S.J., Dir., Urb. Ext. Roosevelt, 576 Calle Eddie Gracia, San Juan, 00918. Tel: 787-751-6001; 787-766-1363. Email: ambertsj@aol.com. Web: www.renovacion.net.

Legion of Mary—Mrs. ROSITA SANTANA, Pres.; Rev. ANGEL CIAPPI, Spiritual Dir., Urb. Munoz Rivera, C. Betania #34, Guaynabo, 00969. Tel: 787-360-0508.

Marriage Encounter—Mr. RICARDO PACHECO; Mrs. RICARDO PACHECO, Mansiones De Rio Piedras, 1795 C. Gardenia, San Juan, 00926-7212. Tel: 787-761-1868.
- *Spiritual Director*—Rev. RICKY ROIG, San Juan de Dios Parish. Tel: 787-757-5060.

Head Start-Municipality of Carolina—Rev. SILVERIO RUEDA, Dir., P.O. Box 9689, Carolina, 00988-9689. Tel: 787-752-3040; Fax: 787-276-2420.

Head Start-Municipality of San Juan—Mrs. IVETTE SEPULVEDA, Dir., Urb. Country Club, Calle Eider #800, San Juan, 00924. Tel: 787-757-1913; 787-768-0580; Fax: 787-257-6680.

Catholic Daughters of America—Mrs. TERESA COLON DE CARDONA, P.O. Box 256, Humacao, 00792. Tel: 787-852-0661.

Knights of Columbus—Mr. JUAN R. NIEVES-BONILLA; Rev. Msgr. RAFAEL FONTANEZ, Chap., P.O. Box 40175, San Juan, 00940-0175. Tel: 787-728-2690; 787-630-1167.

Movimiento "Por Un Mundo Mejor"—Rev. JUAN J. GENOVARD, M.SS.CC., Calle Duke 211, University Gardens, Rio Piedras, 00927. Tel: 787-282-9062; 787-282-0501; Fax: 787-282-9063.

Nocturnal Adoration—Mr. ANGEL PAGAN, Pres., P.O. Box 190199, San Juan, 00919-0199. Tel: 787-749-0502.
- *Spiritual Director*—VACANT.

Talleres De Oracion y Vida P. Larranaga—Mrs. LEONOR PITA, Dir., Urb. Baldrich, 168 Calle Presidente Ramirez, San Juan, 00918. Tel: 787-766-0743; 787-781-5247.

Tourism and Apostleship of the Sea—Casamar—VACANT.

UPR Catholic Student Center—Rev. JUAN J. SANTIAGO, S.J., Mariana Bracetti 10, Rio Piedras, 00925-2201. Tel: 787-767-3348; Fax: 787-758-4145.

San Juan International Airport Chapel—Deacon EDUARDO GONZALEZ.

Carmelite Third Order—Rev. LUIS MIRANDA, O.Carm. Tel: 787-726-2631.

Casa San Clemente—
- *Psychological and Pastoral Counseling—257 Ponce De Leon, San Juan, 00906*. Tel: 787-723-6915.

Couple to Couple League—Mr. TONY FEBLES; Mr. TONY FEBLES, 5 C. Arzuaga, Ste. 333, San Juan, 00925-3701. Tel: 787-276-4951.

Pro-Life Center (Human Life International)—Rev. MATEO MATEO, SS.CC., Dir., Centro San Jose, P.O. Box 916, Guaynabo, 00970-0916. Tel: 787-272-5404.

Pro-Life Pharmacists International—Miss SANDRA FABREGAS, Dir. Tel: 787-724-0232, Ext. 5317.

Consejo De Accion Social Arquidiocesano—Most Rev. HECTOR RIVERA, Dir.; Mrs. IDIS OTERO, Coord. Tel: 787-374-8952.

Servicios Pastorales Paules—VACANT, Dir., 1650, Ave. Fernandez Juncos, San Juan, 00910-0118. Tel: 787-727-3963. P.O. Box 19118, San Juan, 00910.

Franciscan Third Order (Secular Franciscan Order)—Rev. RAMON H. NEGRON, O.F.M.Cap., Spiritual Dir.; Mrs. AWILDA VASQUEZ, Natl. Minister, P.O. Box 3915, Carolina, 00984. Tel: 787-752-7363.

Focolares—LUIS NOEL SOTO, Dir., Q2 Calle 21, Ciudad Universitaria, Trujillo Alto, 00976. Tel: 787-761-5721; 787-767-2346; Fax: 787-761-5721.

Secretariado Sagrado Corazon—Most Rev. HECTOR M. RIVERA, Spiritual Dir.; Mrs. ANA M. BONET, Pres., Urb. Prado Alto, C6 Calle 4, Guaynabo, 00966. Tel: 787-781-6295.

Grupo Reina De La Paz—Miss IVETTE PACHECO, Pres., PMB 258, Ste. 2, Ave. Esmeralda 405, Guaynabo, 00969. Tel: 787-644-8256; Fax: 787-731-8256; Mrs. IVONNE MELENDEZ, Sec. Tel: 787-754-8383; Rev. MANUEL GAMARRA CORTIJO, Spiritual Dir.

Union Eucaristica Reparadora (UNER)—Rev. VICTORINO RAMOS, Spiritual Dir. (Retired); Mrs. MARIA MERCEDES MAIZ, Dir., Urb. Villa Canales, C. Saure #1514, San Juan, 00927. Tel: 787-751-1821.

Sociedad San Vicente De Paul—Mrs. PETRIN, Pres., 938 Calle Azabache, San Juan, 00924.

Maranatha House of Prayer—Mrs. MARISA MENDEZ, Dir., Urb. Villa Nevarez, 353 Calle 4, San Juan, 00927-5311. Tel: 787-759-7734. Mailing Address, Urb. La Arboleda, C. Alameda, B #13, Guaynabo, 00966.

Juventud Mariana Vicenciana (JMV)—VACANT, Dir., Seminario San Vicente De Paul. Tel: 787-727-4110; Sr. MILAGROS OLIVENCIA, H.C., Archdiocesan Representative, Hospital Auxilio Mutuo.

Hermandad N. Sra. De La Caridad—Rev. NICANOR VALDES, Dir., P.O. Box 10151, San Juan, 00922-0151. Tel: 787-783-3522.

Movimiento Juan XXIII—Mr. ANGEL L. RIOS, Pres., Villa Contessa, F35 Calle Aragon, Bayamon, 00976. Tel: 787-787-5984; Fax: 787-785-1024.

Movimiento De Schoenstatt—Mr. CARLOS A. FALCON, Urb. Paseo Real, Calle B, D-2, San Juan, 00926. Tel: 787-748-7436.

Fatima Blue Army—Mr. AMERICO LOPEZ-ORTIZ, P.O. Box 19671, Fernandez Juncos Station, San Juan, 00910. Tel: 787-727-7373.

Neocatecumenal Way—Mr. JULIO ALVAREZ, Dir., Urb. Lago Alto, F81 Calle Loiza, Trujillo Alto, 00976. Tel: 787-755-4320.

Our Lady of Providence Association—Mrs. DAPHNE ROJO. Tel: 787-722-0524.

Perpetual Adoration—Mrs. VIRGINIA ALVAREZ, Asst., Mailing Address, Box S-763, San Juan, 00902. Tel: 787-725-7734.

Padre Nuestro—Mr. SAMUEL VALENTIN, Pres., Urb. Las Colinas, Calle 6, F. 35, Toa Baja, 00949. Tel: 787-368-3810.

Movimiento De Seglares Claretianos—Mrs. ISABEL RIVERA, Dir., San Antonio Maria Claret Parish. Tel: 787-797-3337.

Apostolado Del Cenaculo Misionero—Mrs. ALMA ROBLES; Rev. VICENTE PASQUALETTO, S.T., Spiritual Dir., Urb. Los Colobos, Calle Robles #516, Carolina, 00987. Tel: 787-752-9327.

Conferencia Mariana De Puerto Rico—Mr. RICARDO HERNANDEZ; Mrs. RICARDO HERNANDEZ.

CLERGY, PARISHES, MISSIONS AND PAROCHIAL SCHOOLS

CITY OF SAN JUAN

1—Catedral de San Juan Bautista (1522),, (Nuestra Sra. de los Remedios). Revs. Jose Emilio Cummings, C.M., Rector; Miguel Esquerro (Spain); Deacons Louis Marin; Rafael Morales; Luis Echegaray Martinez.
Res.: 151 Cristo St., Box 9022145, 00902-2145. Tel: 787-722-0861; Fax: 787-722-0861.
Chapel—Santo Cristo
Chapel—San Jose, Tel: 787-725-7501.
Chapel—Santa Ana

2—Asuncion de La Virgen (1972), Rev. Carlos Jimenez.
Res.: Calle Calve No. 1484, Urb. Antonsanti, Rio Piedras, 00928. Tel: 787-250-6771.

3—Corpus Christi (1972), Rev. Pablo Valenzuela (Spain); Deacons Francisco Gierbolini; Miguel Mendez; Luis R. Perez; Juan Figueroa; Reinaldo Del Valle; Jose Perez; Casiano Lugo; Luis Fernando Amador.
Res. & Mailing Address: Calle Jose Abad, 1224 Urb. Club Manor, 00924. Tel: 787-757-5821; Fax: 787-257-2741.
Mission—Santo Domingo de Guzman Carretera 849 Km. 8.7, Sector Santo Domingo, Penuelas Co.

4—Cristo Redentor (1971), Rev. Damian Carvajal (Spain); Deacon Wilfredo Rodriguez.
Res. & Mailing Address: Calle Ganges 140, Urb. El Paraiso, 00926. Tel: 787-764-1583; Fax: 787-761-6617.

5—Cristo Rey (1956), Rev. Msgr. Antonio Gomez (Spain); Deacons Victor Reyes; Miguel Roman Del Valle.
Mailing Address: P.O. Box 29695, 65 Inf. Sta., 00929-0695.
Res.: Calle Jaime Drew, No. 789, Urb. Los Maestros, Rio Piedras, 00923. Tel: 787-767-3289.

6—Espiritu Santo (1941), Rev. Valeriano Miguelez (Spain).
Mailing Address: P.O. Box 190259, 00919-0259. Calle Pachin Marin, Esq. Suiza, Hato Rey.
Res.: 75 Ruiz Belvis St., Floral Park, Hato Rey, 00919. Tel: 787-754-0570.
School—P.O. Box 191715, 00917. Tel: 787-754-0490; 787-754-0555; Fax: 787-754-7154. Sr. Enedina Santos, Prin.; Olga Iris Torres, Assoc. Prin. Priests 1; Lay Teachers 46; Students 756.

7—Francisca Javiera Cabrini (1968),, (Mother Cabrini) Rev. Angel Ciappi-Azcorra.
Res.: 1564 Encarnacion St., 00920. Tel: 787-783-7447; Fax: 787-706-2073.
Catechesis/Religious Program—Students 90.

8—Inmaculado Corazon de Maria (1961), Revs. Norberto Lopez, O.S.B.; Dennis Alexander, O.M.I. (Canada); Deacons Benjamin Totti; Jose Rodriguez; Israel Suarez.
Urb. Santiago Iglesias, #1740 Calle Rodriguez Vera, Rio Piedras, 00921. Tel: 787-782-4176; Fax: 787-782-4176.
Res.: Rodriguez Vera y Ferrer St., Urb. Santiago Iglesias, 00922.
Catechesis/Religious Program—Students 260.
Mission—Monacillos San Fernando, San Juan Co.
Chapel—Colegio Ntra. Sra. de la Providencia
Chapel—N. Sra. del Camino, Metropolitan Hospital [JC]

9—Jesus Maestro (1969), Revs. Higinio Madrazo, C.M. (Spain); Eugenio Villafranca, C.M. (Spain); Deacons Rafael Velazquez; William Gomez Soto.
Res.: Segre 1725 Urb. Rio Piedras Heights, 00926. Tel: 787-763-8291.
Mission—Jesus Nazareno Calle Guadiana #1666, Urb. El Cerezal.

10—Jesus Mediador (1988), Rev. Carlos Ortiz-Mejias; Deacons Candido Martinez; Edwin Rivera.
Res. & Mailing Address: Calle Demetrio O'Daly 1000, Urb. Country Club, 00924. Tel: 787-752-2410; Fax: 787-752-2410.

11—Maria Auxiliadora (1962), Revs. Nicolas Navarro, S.D.B.; Wilfredo Calderon, S.D.B.; Rogelio Barranco, S.D.B.; Andres Rivera, S.D.B.; Antonio Polo, S.D.B.; Jose Luis Gomez, S.D.B.; Bro. Jose Cabo.
Mailing Address: P.O. Box 14367, 00916.
Res.: C. Constitucion Esq. Sta. Elena, Cantera. Tel: 787-727-5346; 787-726-1995, Ext. 267.
Catechesis/Religious Program—Students 300.
Mission—Sagrado Corazon, Sector Buenavista.
Mission—Nra. Sra. del Altagracia, Sector Buenavista.
Mission—Ntra. Sra. de Fatima, Sector Ultimo Chance-Cerro.
Mission—Santisima Trinidad Ave. Borinquen Final.

12—Maria Madre de La Iglesia (1967), Rev. Gregorio Bravo (Spain); Deacons George Gonzalez; Eugenio Torres.
Res.: 1120 Calle 5, Urb. Villa Nevarez, 00927. Tel: 787-765-0600.

13—Maria Reina del Mundo (1971), Rev. Msgr. Felix Varas (Spain).
Mailing Address: G.P.O. Box 3828, 00936-3828. Tel: 787-767-1572; 787-781-0303.
Res.: Caserio Nemesio Canales, Roosevelt Ave. Puerto Nuevo, Rio Piedras.

14—Ntr. Sra. de la Caridad del Cobre (1969), Rev. Jaime Oliver Marques (Spain).
Res.: Urb. Buena Vista, Calle 5, No. 124, 00917. Tel: 787-753-0108.
Mission—Sma. Trinidad Calle Buenos Aires, No. 25, Parada 27, Hato Rey, San Juan Co. 00919.

15—Ntra. Sra. de Fatima (1967), Revs. Julio Fernandez Dominguez, O.M. (Spain); Martin Garamendi, O.M. (Spain); Jose M. Gallego, O.M. (Spain); Ramon Conde-Ocampo, O.M. (Spain); Antonio Garcia-Martinez, O.M. (Spain).
Mailing Address: P.O. Box 190396, 00919-0396. Tel: 787-753-6334; Fax: 787-764-3571.
Res.: 608 Munoz Rivera Ave., Stop 34, Urb. Baldrich, Hato Rey, 00919.
School—La Merced (1949), P.O. Box 364048, 00936-4048. Tel: 787-765-7342; 787-754-1162; Fax: 787-765-3970. Mrs. Rosa M. Figueroa, Prin. Lay Teachers 36; Students 485.
Mission—Egida del Maestro

16—Ntra. Sra. de la Medalla Milagrosa (1957), Rev. Antonio Jose Vazquez Colon (AFE).
Mailing Address: Urb. Perez Moris, Calle Mayaguez 209, 00917.
Res.: 209 Mayaguez St., 00917. Tel: 787-751-2335; Fax: 787-274-0939.

17—Ntra. Sra. de la Monserrate (1916), Revs. Saturnino Juan Vega, O.S.A. (Spain); Heber Nazario, O.S.A.; David Vargas Grajales, O.S.A.
Mailing Address: P.O. Box 13726, 00908-3726.
Res.: 1058 Fernandez Juncos Ave., 00907. Tel: 787-722-3134; Fax: 787-723-7838.
School—Santa Monica, Tel: 787-723-2573 (Elem.); 787-723-3845 (H.S.); Fax: 787-723-3992. Deacon Jorge Rivera, Prin. Lay Teachers 45; Students 549.
Catechesis/Religious Program—Students 64.
Mission—Trastalleres Santa Ana, San Juan Co.

18—Ntra. Sra. del Perpetuo Socorro (1941), Revs. Armando Alvarez; Joaquin Mansilla (Spain).
Res.: Calle Marti 704, Miramar, Santurce, 00907-3227. Tel: 787-721-1015; 787-721-1016.
School—Jose Marti St. 704, 00907. Tel: 787-724-1447; 787-721-4540; Fax: 787-725-8104 (Elem.); 787-723-4550 (H.S.). Sr. Armand Marie, S.S.N.D., Prin. Priests 1; Lay Teachers 102; Students 1,312.

19—Nuestra Senora de Belen (1950), Rev. Reinaldo Sagardia.
Mailing Address: P.O. Box 10845, 00922-0845. Tel: 787-793-2485; Fax: 787-792-8541.
Res.: Calle Jacinto Galib Final, Avda San Patricio, Guaynaro.

20—Nuestra Senora de la Altagracia (1958), Rev. Franco Gutierrez (Spain); Deacons Ildefonso Lugo; Rafael Colon.
Mailing Address: Apartado 29493, 00929-0493. Tel: 787-765-0281.
Res.: Calle Felipe Gutierrez 672, Urb. Villa Prades, Rio Piedras, 00924. Tel: 787-765-0281.
Catechesis/Religious Program—Tel: 787-764-0614. Students 376.

21—Nuestra Senora de la Caridad del Cobre, Rev. Pedro Luis Zaballa.
Res.: Urb. La Riviera, Calle 3 S.O. 1027, 00921-2517. Tel: 787-268-1325.

22—Nuestra Senora de la Esperanza (1962), Rev. Francisco Morales Feliu (PCE).
Mailing Address: P.O. Box 8532, 00910-8532.
Res.: Calle Republica No. 854, Urb. Hipodromo, Parada 20, Santurce, 00910. Tel: 787-723-5998; Fax: 787-723-5998.
Mission—Ntra. Sra. de la Providencia Barriada Figueroa.
Chapel—Doctors Hospital, Tel: 787-723-2950; Fax: 787-721-3155.

23—Nuestra Senora de la Merced (1940), Revs. Elias Lorenzana, O.de.M. (Spain); Jose Benito Osorio Mowrino, O.de.M. (Spain); Jose Luis Garcia Diaz, O.de.M. (Spain); Javier Errecalde, O.de.M. (Spain).
Mailing Address: P.O. Box 364133, 00936-4133.
Res.: C/Pedro Espada 430 Urb. Roosevelt, Hato Rey. Tel: 787-763-3657.
Catechesis/Religious Program—Students 50.

24—Nuestra Senora de La Piedad (1956), Revs. Lionel Pacheco Padilla, C.P.; Manuel Elejalde, C.P. (Spain); Jose Ramon Zubizarreta, C.P. (Spain), Supr.; Florencio Landa, C.P. (Spain).
Mailing Address: Box 6277, Loiza Sta., 00914-6277.
Res.: Calle Marginal, AB-1, Ext. Villamar, Isla Verde, 00979. Tel: 787-726-2880; Fax: 787-982-2155.
School—Tel: 787-727-7585 (H.S.); 787-727-2460 (Elem.); Fax: 787-268-0634 (H.S.); 787-728-0125 (Elem.). Mrs. Nilda Ramos, Prin. (High School); Mrs. Lizette Matos, Assoc. Prin.; Rev. Florencio Landa, C.P. (Spain), Dir. Priests 1; Lay Teachers 77; Students 685.

25—Nuestra Senora de la Providencia (1959), Rev. Msgr. Baudilio Merino (Spain); Deacons Luis Vazquez; Pedro Rivera; Ricardo Martinez.
Res. & Mailing Address: Santa Agueda St., No. 1730, Urb. San Gerardo, Rio Piedras, 00926. Tel: 787-765-6240; 787-765-8613; Fax: 787-765-4821.
School—Carretera #176, Km. 2.7, Calle Santa Agueda 1733, Urb. San Gerardo, Rio Piedras, 00926. Tel: 787-767-6552; 787-767-6755; Fax: 787-765-4821. Dr. Rafael L. Morales, D.P., Ed.D., Prin. Lay Teachers 35; Students 429.
Catechesis/Religious Program—Students 400.

26—Nuestra Senora de la Providencia (1973), Rev. Hermenegildo Vicedo (Spain).
Res. & Mailing Address: 219 Aponte St., 00912. Tel: 787-727-1878.

27—Nuestra Senora de Lourdes (1969), Rev. Msgr. Efrain Rodriguez; Deacon Dionilo Torres.
Mailing Address: P.O. Box 14452, Bo. Obrero Sta., 00916.
Res.: Gilberto Monroig Ave., Cr. of Colton St., 288, 00916. Tel: 787-726-4643.

28—Nuestra Senora del Carmen (1923), Rev. Mariano Martinez, O.M.I. (Peru).
Mailing Address: P.O. Box 7275, 00916-7275. Tel: 787-727-0737; Fax: 787-728-4860.
Res.: Ave., Borinquen, Esq., Calle Tapia, Num. 609, Barrio Obrero, Santurce, 00916.
School—Padre Berrios, P.O. Box 7717, 00916. Tel: 787-726-4851. Sr. Ana L. Munoz, H.C.C.S., Prin. Sisters 5; Lay Teachers 10; Students 249.
Mission—San Martin de Porres Calle: Tito Rodriguez #719 Barrio Obrero, Barrio Obrero, 00916.

29—Nuestra Senora del Pilar (1714), Revs. Ignacio Alonso, C.M. (Spain); Maximiano Santos, C.M. (Spain); Teodoro Calzada, C.M. (Spain); Deacons Cesar Guiven; Jose L. Velazquez.
Mailing Address: Box 21134, 00928-1134.
Res.: Plaza de Recreo, Rio Piedras, 00928. Tel: 787-764-5088; 787-763-3161.
Mission—Santa Teresita de Nino Jesus Calle, Tanque #37, Bda. Venezuela, Rio Piedras, San Juan Co. 00925.
Chapel—Colegio La Milagrosa De Diego St. 107, Rio Piedras. Tel: 787-765-6114.
Chapel—Hogar Crea Barriada Venezuela.

30—Nuestra Sra. de Guadalupe (1951), Unassigned., Mailing Address: G.P.O. Box 4125, 00936-4125. Tel: 787-782-0016; Fax: 787-782-0016.
Res.: Calle 19 N.E. No. 1, Puerto Nuevo, 00920.
School—Tel: 787-782-0330; Fax: 787-782-0454. Mrs. Genevieve Zayas, Prin. Lay Teachers 37; Students 702.
Catechesis/Religious Program—Students 60.

31—Resurreccion del Senor (1968), Revs. Samuel Azcona, O.F.M. (Spain); Cruz Ajuria, O.F.M. (Spain); Luis Zabala, O.F.M. (Spain).
Res. & Mailing Address: Calle 31, S.O. #797, Urb. Las Lomas, 00921-1205. Tel: 787-792-1416; 787-792-5939; Fax: 787-792-1416.

32—Sagrada Familia (1971), Rev. Msgr. Tomas Su (China).
Mailing Address: P.O. Box 29311, 00929.
Res.: Ave 65 de Inf., Esquina Calle 7, No. 112, Hills Brothers, Sabana Llana, 00924. Tel: 787-767-1723.

33—Sagrado Corazon de Jesus (1971), Revs. Basilio Roldan, C.M. (Spain); Jaime Vergara, C.M. (Spain); Jose Yanez, C.M. (Spain).
Res. & Mailing Address: Calle Oxford 251, Esq. Howard Urb. University Gardens, 00927. Tel: 787-765-4798; Fax: 787-765-5456.
School—Esq. Iteramericana y Palma Real: Urb. University Gardens, Rio Piedras, 00927-4826. Tel: 787-765-9430; Fax: 787-765-5267. Mary Andreen, O.S.F., Prin.
Catechesis/Religious Program—Students 37.

34—Sagrado Corazon de Jesus (1909), Rev. Ovidio Ortega Lemus (Cuba); Deacon Francisco Martinez.
Mailing Address: Box 8312, F. Juncos Sta., 00910-8312.
Res.: Ponce de Leon Ave., #1308, Stop 19, Santurce, 00910. Tel: 787-722-0235; Fax: 787-722-4845.

35—San Agustin (1889), Revs. Terry Tull, C.SS.R.; Carlos R. Valles, C.SS.R.; Alfonso Amador, C.SS.R. Mailing Address: P.O. Box 9066557, 00906-6557.
In Res., Bro. Mateo Perez, C.SS.R.; Revs. Robert Gaugler, C.SS.R.; Manuel Rodriguez Delgado, C.SS.R., Prov. Supr.
Res.: 265 Ponce de Leon Ave., Pta. de Tierra, 00906. Tel: 787-722-4289; Fax: 787-725-7737.
School—Colegio San Agustin, 225 Ponce de Leon Ave., Box 9066547, 00906. Tel: 787-722-4544; Fax: 787-977-1700. Marie Benitez Alonso, Prin. Lay Teachers 30; Students 484.
Catechesis/Religious Program—Students 14.

36—San Antonio (1908), [JC] Revs. Luis Francisco Gonzalez, O.F.M.Cap.; Pedro Silva Bisbal,

O.F.M.Cap.
Res.: Calle Arzuaga #218, Esq. Frailes Capuchinos, Apartado 21350, 00928. Tel: 787-765-0606; Fax: 787-765-1180.
School—Tel: 787-764-0090; Fax: 787-763-7592. John Bartemes, Admin.; Rosalina Burgos, Academic Prin.; Fe Villafane, Administrative Prin.; Miguel Rosa, Prin. (Intermediate & High School). Priests 2; Sisters 2; Lay Teachers 102; Students 1,411.
Catechesis/Religious Program—Students 51.
Mission—Nuestra Senora del Buen Consejo Calle Alto, 00926.

37—SAN FRANCISCO DE ASIS (1858), Revs. Ramon Jaime Casellas, O.F.M.Cap.; Jose Fernando Irizzary, O.F.M.Cap.; Alberto Figueroa, O.F.M.Cap., Vice Prov.; Bros. Jorge Macias, O.F.M.Cap.; Juan Rolando Gonzalez, O.F.M.Cap.
Res.: 301 San Francisco St., Box 9024231, 00902-4231. Tel: 787-724-1131; Fax: 787-721-4616.
Catechesis/Religious Program—Students 12.
Mission—Capilla San Conrado Bo. La Perla, 00902.

38—SAN FRANCISCO DE MONTE ALVERNIA (1985), Rev. Perfecto Fondevilla (Spain); Deacon Juan Bautista Perez.
Res.: Calle 10, #15 Ext. San Agustin, 00926. Tel: 787-765-8824.

39—SAN FRANCISCO JAVIER (1967), Rev. Felipe Nunez Carrion; Deacons Abel De Varona; Jose Hernandez.
Res.: Calle 19, G46. Urb. Fair View, 00926. Tel: 787-761-2115; Fax: 787-755-9294.
Catechesis/Religious Program—Students 48.

40—SAN IGNACIO DE LOYOLA (1956), Revs. Lawrence P. Searles, S.J.; Donald M. Vega, S.J.; Jorge R. Ambert, S.J.; Francisco X. Santiago, S.J.
Res. & Mailing Address: Calle Narciso 1904, 00927-6706. Tel: 787-751-7680; 787-751-7512; Fax: 787-758-0124.
School—Academia San Ignacio de Loyola, 1908 Calle Narciso, Rio Piedras. Tel: 787-765-8190; Fax: 787-765-3635. Glorimar Soegaard, Prin.; Blanca I. Esteves, Ed.D., Dir. Students 631.
Chapel—Hospital Psiquiatria

41—SAN JORGE (1965), Rev. Msgr. Jesus Santoalla.
Mailing Address: P.O. Box 6427, Loiza Sta., 00914-6427.
Res.: Calle San Jorge 157, Santurce, 00914. Tel: 787-724-7780.

42—SAN JOSE (Villa Caparra) (1948), Rev. Msgr. Rafael Fontanez; Rev. Walter Gomez (ARE); Deacons Luis Colon; Luis Cordero; Ramon Rodriguez.
Res.: Urb. Villa Caparra, Bloque ZM 215, Guaynabo, 00966. Tel: 787-781-1155; Fax: 787-774-8985.
School—Calle Josemaria Escriva 32, Guaynabo (Villa Caparra), 00966-2209. Tel: 787-783-1995 (H.S.); 787-792-7489 (Elem.); Fax: 787-792-7440 (Elem.); 787-781-3029 (H.S.). Sisters Catherine Ortiz, O.P., Prin. (Elementary); John Christian, Prin. (High School). Priests 2; Sisters 4; Lay Teachers 90; Students 1,600.

43—SAN JOSE OBRERO (1956), Rev. Angel M. Pagan Torres (ARE); Deacons Eugenio Rivera; J. Francisco Ubarri-Mestres.
Mailing Address: Calle Belmonte 470, 00923. Tel: 787-767-1448; Fax: 787-753-5392.
Res.: Urb. San Jose, Calle Belmonte 470, Rio Piedras, 00923.
Catechesis/Religious Program—Students 65.
Mission—San Antonio Ma. Claret, Embalse Sector.
Mission—San Martin de Porres, Bitumul 435 Carrillas St., 00923.

44—SAN JUAN BOSCO (1945), Revs. Juan J. Gregorio Roman, S.D.B.; Miguel Rivera, S.D.B.; Enrique Mendez, S.D.B.; Lorenzo Ruiz.
Mailing Address: P.O. Box 14125 Barrio Obrero Sta., 00915.
Res.: 370 Lutz St., Villa Palmeras, 00915. Tel: 787-726-1420; 787-726-0232; Fax: 787-726-7317.
Mission—La Milagrosa Villa Palmeras, C. Lutz 300 Final, Santurce, Mayaguez Co. 00915. Tel: 787-728-2175; Fax: 787-726-7313.
Mission—Ntra. Sra. del Rosario Fajardo St., 00915.
Mission—San Martin de Porres Union St. #58, Playita, Yabucoa Co. 00915.

45—SAN JUAN DE LA CRUZ (1990), Rev. Mario Mesa, O.F.M.Cap. (Spain); Deacon Martin Nieves.
Mailing Address: MSC 216, Urb. La Cumbre, Emiliano Pol Sta., 00926.
Res.: Urb. La Cumbre, Calle Julio Ruedas #1935, Borinquen Gardens, Rio Piedras, 00926. Tel: 787-731-2016; Fax: 787-708-0812.

46—SAN JUAN M. VIANNEY (1972),, (Santo Cura de Ars) Rev. Florentino Sanz (Spain); Deacon Manuel Caban.
Res. & Mailing Address: Calle 2, F-14, Urb. Hillside, 00926. Tel: 787-790-2014.
Mission—La Milagrosa, San Juan Co.
Mission—Cristo del Perdon Parcelas Canejas, Bo. Caimito Bajo.
Mission—Dulce Nombre de Maria Bo. Dulce, Caimito Bajo.
Mission—Ntra. Sra. del Carmen Calle Fidalgo, Sector Corea, Bo. Caimito Bajo.

47—SAN LUCAS (1972), Rev. Tomas Gonzalez; Deacons Jose Rodriguez; Hector Cruz DeChoudens.
Mailing Address: Urb. El Senorial, Calle Pio Baroja 380, 00926.
Res.: Pio Baroja St., No. 380, Urb. El Senorial, 00926. Tel: 787-761-5476; Fax: 787-761-5476.
Catechesis/Religious Program—Students 72.

48—SAN LUIS GONZAGA (1965), Rev. Virgilio Martinez (Spain).
Res. & Mailing Address: Calle Ronda A-17, Urb. Villa Andalucia, 00926. Tel: 787-761-9438; Fax: 787-761-9438.

49—SAN LUIS REY (1968), Rev. Edwin Hernandez Relat.
Mailing Address: P.O. Box 71325, Ste. #65, 00936-8425.
Res.: Calle 43 S.E. Final, Urb. Reparto Metropolitano, Rio Piedras. Tel: 787-767-6235.
School—Calle 43 S.E. #869, Reparto Metropolitano, Rio Piedras, 00921. Tel: 787-767-4006; Fax: 787-767-6235. Silvia Almenas, Prin. Sisters 1; Lay Teachers 10; Students 213.

50—SAN MATEO (1773), Rev. Eddie Rivera.
Mailing Address: P.O. Box 6081, 00914-6081.
Res.: Calle San Mateo, Esq. San Jorge, Stop 25, Santurce, 00912. Tel: 787-722-4158; 787-759-1255; Fax: 787-518-3251.

51—SAN PABLO (1965), Rev. Ramon Orlando Tirado, C.M.; Deacons Tomas Ramirez; Orlando Sanchez.
Res.: Duero St., No. 370, Urb. Villa Borinquen, Puerto Nuevo, 00920. Tel: 787-706-0412; Fax: 787-706-0412.
Mission—Ntra. Sra. de la Caridad Del Cobre Borinquen Towers, Puerto Nuevo, San Juan Co. 00920.

52—SAN VICENTE DE PAUL (1940), [CEM] Revs. Faustino Burgos (Dominican Republic), Prov. Supr.; Evaristo Oliveras, C.M.; Higinio Madrazo, C.M. (Spain); Manuel Aznar, C.M. (Spain); Pascual Sota, C.M. (Spain); Bros. Wilfredo Acevedo, C.M.; Jean Kettel Bonhomette, C.M. (Haiti).
Mailing Address: P.O. Box 19118, 00910-0118.
Res.: 1650 Ave Fernandez Juncos, Stop 24, Santurce, 00910. Tel: 787-727-3963; Fax: 787-726-7986.
School—709 Bolivar St., Box 8699, 00910. Tel: 787-727-4273; Fax: 787-728-2263. Mrs. Isabel Casanas, Prin. Lay Teachers 31; Students 658.
Catechesis/Religious Program—Students 80.

53—SANTA BERNARDITA SOUBIROUS (1982), Rev. Msgr. Wilfredo Pena Moredo; Deacons Ismael Colon; Angel Rivera; Rafael Sanabria; Ramon Santiago.
Mailing Address: P.O. Box 29826, 65 Infanteria Sta., 00929-0826. Tel: 787-762-0375; 787-257-7643; Fax: 787-257-6642.
Res.: Calle Espioncela, Esquina Calle Torcaza, Country Club, Rio Piedras, 00924.

54—SANTA CATALINA LABOURE (1977), Rev. Eusebio C. Fernandez Salazar (Colombia); Deacon Jacinto Ortiz.
Mailing Address: Urb. La Cumbre 497 Emiliano Pol, Ste. 507, 00926-5636. Tel: 787-720-0303; Fax: 787-731-7166.
Res.: Carretera 842 Km. 3.6 Barrio Caimito, Rio Piedras.
Mission—Medalla Milagrosa Barrio Los Romeros, Bo. Caimito 00926-5636. Tel: 787-720-2215.
Mission—San Pablo Carretera 842, Bo. Caimito 00926.

55—SANTA CECILIA (1969), Rev. Jose Maria Lopez Mairal (Spain); Deacon Victor Merced de la Paz.
Mailing Address: P.O. Box 415, El Senorial Sta., 00926-0415.
Res.: Avenida Ceciliana #1, Urb. Rivieras de Cupey, Rio Piedras. Tel: 787-755-8670; 787-761-5461 (Parish House).
Catechesis/Religious Program—Students 33.
Chapel—Hogar Santa Teresa Jornet, Tel: 787-761-5805; Fax: 787-755-5575.
Chapel—Capilla San Agustin Carretera 844, Cupey Bajo.

56—SANTA LUISA DE MARILLAC (1962), Rev. Yesid Ricardo Castellanos Ruiz (Colombia); Deacon Francisco Colon.
Mailing Address: Urb. La Cumbre Ave., Emiliano Pol Sta. 497, Ste. #17, 00926-5636.
Res.: Ave. Emiliano Pol, Urb. La Cumbre, Rio Piedras, 00926. Tel: 787-720-3150; Fax: 787-720-8779.

57—SANTA MARIA DE LOS ANGELES (1954), Rev. Anibal R. Torres-Ortiz; Deacons Rafael Reyes Crespo; Manuel Camacho.
Mailing Address: Box 10716, 00922-0716. Tel: 787-792-2640; Fax: 787-792-2640.
Res.: De Diego Ave., No. 930, Urb. La Rivera, Rio Piedras.

58—SANTA ROSA DE LIMA (1971), Rev. Angel Raul Saez; Deacons Pedro Costa; Angel Pabon.
Res. & Mailing Address: Calle Lesbos No. 1765, Urb. Venus Gardens, 00926. Tel: 787-761-6586.

59—SANTA TERESA JORNET (1985), Rev. Ivan Serrano Rivera, C.S.Sp.; Deacons Vicente Lasanta; Martin Cuevas.
Mailing Address: Aptdo. 415, El Senorial Mail Sta., 00926-0415.
Res.: Carr. 176 Camino el Mudo, Km. 10.0 Cupey Alto, 00926. Tel: 787-748-2978.
Mission—San Martin de Porres Camino El Mudo, Cupey.
Mission—Virgen de la Salud Camino Guayabos Carr. 176, Km. 9.5, Cupey.
Mission—Ermita N. Sra. Providencia [CEM] Camino Los Gonzalez, Km. 5.3. Tel: 787-760-8376.

60—SANTA TERESITA DEL NINO JESUS (1930), Revs. Tarsicio Gotay Figaredo, O.Carm.; Tomas Ciscar, O.Carm. (Spain), Supr. Regl.; Francisco Armell, O.Carm.; Salvador Rodrigo, O.Carm. (Spain).
Res.: 2059 Loiza St., 00911-1799. Tel: 787-727-0181; 787-727-0030; Fax: 787-728-0056.
School—Tel: 787-727-4260; 787-727-4317; 787-727-4358. Ana R. Castro, Prin. Priests 1; Sisters 1; Lay Teachers 47; Students 360.
Mission—Sagrada Familia Residencial, Luis Llorens Torres, San Juan Co. 00913. Tel: 809-726-0570.

61—SANTISIMO SALVADOR (1966), Revs. Benito Forcano, Sch.P. (Spain), Supr.; Leopoldo Laredo, Sch.P. (Spain); Francisco Javier Lopez, Sch.P. (Spain), Supr.; Agustin Lopez, Sch.P. (Spain); Miguel Angel Medina, Sch.P. (Spain); Deacons Julio Alvarez; Luis M. Medina; Luis O. del Rio.
Res.: Niza St., 575, Urb. Villa Capri, 00924. Tel: 787-761-3314; Fax: 787-755-1595.
School—Calasanz (1968), Ave. Montecarlo, Esq. Z, Urb. Montecarlo, P.O. Box 29067, 65 Inf. Sta., Rio Piedras, 00929-0067. Tel: 787-750-2500; Fax: 787-257-0450. Ana Celia Santos, Prin. (High School); Leticia Santiago Orria, Prin. (Elementary). Priests 4; Lay Teachers 34; Students 468.
Catechesis/Religious Program—Students 65.
Mission—N. Sra. Reina de la Paz Calle #1 Esq. C-8 Urb. Berwind States, Rio Piedras, San Juan Co. 00924.
Mission—San Jose de Calasanz Calle #23 408, Parc. Hills Brothers, Rio Piedras, San Juan Co. 00924.

62—SANTISMO SACRAMENTO (1967), Rev. Manuel Gamarra Cortijo (Peru); Deacon Gegorio Ayala.
Res.: 500 Jerusalem St., Urb. Matienzo Cintron, Rio Piedras, 00923. Tel: 787-764-3448.
Catechesis/Religious Program—Students 40.

63—SANTOS PEDRO Y PABLO LOS APOSTOLES (1980), Rev. Vicente Egurrola (Spain).
Mailing Address: Las Teresas II Apt. 7F, Calle Azabache 905, 00924-3244.
Res.: Urb. Jardines De Berwind, Calle Las Casitas, Lote K, 65 Infanteria, Rio Piedras, 00929. Tel: 787-768-1424.

64—STELLA MARIS (1965), Rev. Efrain Lopez (CGS).
Res.: 69 Cervantes St., Condado, San Juan, 00907-1947. Tel: 787-723-2240; 787-723-2359; Fax: 787-722-3200.

OUTSIDE THE CITY OF SAN JUAN

BAYAMON

1—ASCENSION DEL SENOR (1984), Rev. Epi Fanio Fernandez, O.SS.T. (Spain); Deacon Juan Perez del Valle.
Mailing Address: P.O. Box 3367, 00958-3367. Tel: 787-799-6120; Fax: 787-799-1977. In Res., Revs. Pedro Gorena, O.SS.T. (Spain); Javier Elorriaga, O.SS.T.
Res.: Calle 31, Final, Urb. Rexville, 00957.

2—CATALINA DE SIENA (1963), Revs. Hector Lopez-Rodriguez, O.P.; Angel Valentin, O.P.; Deacons Francisco Cruz; Victor Lopez; Antonio Santiago; Jose Rios; Agapito Diaz; Nicomedes Cosme.
Mailing Address: P.O. Box 4188, 00959-4188.
Res.: Urb. Hermanas Davila, Calle 10, Q-3, 00959. Tel: 787-785-2381; Fax: 787-269-5065.
Catechesis/Religious Program—Students 145.

3—CRISTO SALVADOR (1998), Rev. Luis Rios Capiello (ARE).
Mailing Address: Casa Linda del Sur Apto C-104, 00959.
Church: Carr. 177, Los Filtros, 00959. Tel: 787-287-5678.

4—ESPIRITU SANTO (2002), Rev. Pedro Gorena, O.SS.T. (Spain).
Res. & Mailing Address: Urb. Bella Vista Gardens, Calle 24, Y-300, 00957. Tel: 787-799-6120; Fax: 787-799-1977.

5—INVENCION DE LA SANTA CRUZ (1772), Revs. Edgardo Sanabria, O.P.; Marcos Espinel (Spain).
Res.: 12 Degetau St., 00961. Tel: 787-785-2134.

6—LA RESURRECCION DEL SENOR (1987), Rev. Juan Santa (CGS); Deacon Nicanor Mercado.
Res. & Mailing Address: Calle 12 F-1, Urb. Royal Town, 00956. Tel: 787-730-4310.
Catechesis/Religious Program—Students 60.

7—NTRA. SRA. DE LA MONSERRATE (1985), Revs. Mario Gonzalez, O.S.A. (Spain); Domingo Aller, O.S.A. (Spain); Deacons Luis A. Rodriguez; Jesus Lopez.

Mailing Address: P.O. Box 3948, 00958-3948.
Res.: Carr. 829, Km. 6.2, Bo. Santa Olaya, Bayamon Gardens, 00958. Tel: 787-797-0708; 787-799-7340; Fax: 787-797-9953.
Mission—Cristo Rey Bo. Guaraguao, Sector La Morenita.
Mission—Santa Monica Bo. Guaraguao, Sector Pena, Bayamon Co. 00619.

8—NUESTRA SENORA DE LA MILAGROSA (1968), Rev. Edgaro Pinto (Peru).
Mailing Address: P.O. Box 2104, 00960-2104.
Res.: Carr. 864, No. 82, Bo. Hato Tejas, 00960. Tel: 787-785-6620.

9—NUESTRA SENORA DEL PERPETUO SOCORRO (1976), Rev. Edgardo Sanabria; Deacons Ramon L. Ramon; Miguel Velez; Rafael Ortiz.
Res. & Mailing Address: Comerio St. No. 190, 00956. Tel: 787-785-2381; 787-780-4367; Fax: 787-785-2134.

10—NUESTRA SENORA DEL ROSARIO (1971), Rev. Miguel Angel Trinidad-Fonseca; Deacon Luis A. Navedo.
Res.: Calle Zaragoza, Bloque, B No. 34, Esq. Calle Vizcaya, Urb. Villa Espana, 00961. Tel: 787-787-0418; Fax: 787-787-0418.
Mission—Minillas San Jose.
Mission—N. Sra. del Carmen Bella Vista.
Mission—Sagrado Corazon de Jesus

11—NUESTRA SRA. DE LOS DOLORES (1976), Rev. Edwin Cruz, O.S.A.; Deacon Francisco Hernandez.
Res. & Mailing Address: Bloque DD-25, 18th St., Urb. Alturas de Flamboyan, 00957. Tel: 787-786-7494.
Catechesis/Religious Program—Students 12.

12—NUESTRA SRA. DEL ROSARIO (1993), Rev. Heriberto Londono (Colombia); Deacon Hector Rivera.
Mailing Address: Box 3917, 00958.
Res.: Carr. 816 Km. 5.6, Barrio Nuevo. Tel: 787-730-6000; Fax: 787-730-6000.
Mission—San Juan Bautista, Montellano Co.
Mission—Jesus Maestro, Dajaos Co.
Mission—La Providencia, Dajaos Co.

13—SAGRADA FAMILIA (1976), Rev. Leonardo J. Rodriguez; Deacons Americo Arroyo; Gumersindo Colon; Ramon L. Ortiz.
Mailing Address: P.O. Box 8478, 00960-8478.
Res.: Calle Caracas and Valparaiso, Urb. Ext. Forest Hills, 00960. Tel: 787-798-2010; Fax: 787-798-2010.
Catechesis/Religious Program—Students 170.

14—SAN AGUSTIN (1964), Revs. Carlos Cordero, O.S.A.; Felipe Fernandez, O.S.A. (Spain); Benigno Palomo, O.S.A. (Spain); Deacons Ignacio Perez; Cristobal Rivera.
Mailing Address: P.O. Box 4263, Bayamon Gardens Sta., 00958-4283.
Res.: Urb. Lomas Verdes, Calle Duende, Bloque 2, E #21, 00956. Tel: 787-785-8611; Fax: 787-785-8611.
School— (1964), Box 4263, Bayamon Gardens Sta., 00958. Tel: 787-786-8055. Mrs. Mary Jo Duran, Prin. Lay Teachers 28; Students 406.
Mission—San Martin de Porres c/1 Barrio Juan Sanchez, Bayamon Co. 00959.
Mission—N. Sra. del Buen Consejo Villas de San Agustin, Bayamon Co. 00959.

15—SAN ANTONIO MARIA CLARET (1966), Revs. Norberto Padilla, C.M.F.; Marcelino Romero, C.M.F. (Spain); Jose Nieto, C.M.F.; Deacon Jose Dolores Rivera.
Mailing Address: P.O. Box 3292, 00958-3292.
Res.: D-24 Castiglioni Ave., Urb. Bayamon Gardens, 00957. Tel: 787-797-3337.
Catechesis/Religious Program—Students 250.

16—SAN JOSE (1964), [CEM] Revs. Hector F. Cuadrado, C.M.F.; Jose Armengol, C.M.F. (Spain); Camilo Riano, C.M.F. (Spain); Severiano Garcia, C.M.F. (Spain); Fausto Cruz, C.M.F. (Dominican Republic).
Res. & Mailing Address: Dakar, F-169, Forest View, 00956. Tel: 787-785-6675; Fax: 787-785-0670.
School—Academia Claret, Tel: 787-787-6685; 787-786-7976. Israel Irizarry, Prin. Priests 3; Lay Teachers 30; Students 444.

17—SAN JUAN BAUTISTA DE LA SALLE (1979), Revs. Jesus M. Ciriza, M.SS.CC. (Spain); Jose M. Garcia Bazton, M.SS.CC. (Spain); Deacons Francisco Ortiz; Jose Vega; Jorge Rivera.
Res. & Mailing Address: A-19 Rio Cialitos St., 1ra. Secc. Estancias de Rio Hondo, 00961. Tel: 787-787-9567; Fax: 787-798-5071.

18—SAN MIGUEL ARCANGEL (1962), Rev. Francisco Medina.
Mailing Address: P.O. Box 361714, 00936-1714. Tel: 787-787-4459; Fax: 787-787-4459.
Res.: Urb. Jardines de Caparra, Calle 12A Bloque AB., No. 32, 00959.
Mission—San Miguel Barriada San Miguel, Guaynabo, Guaynabo Co. 00657.

19—SANTA ELENA (1978), Rev. Daniel Trujillo (Colombia).
Mailing Address: P.O. Box 366, 00960-0366.
Res.: Calle 6, H-14, Urb. Sta. Elena, 00957. Tel: 787-785-6604; Fax: 787-785-6604.

20—SANTA MARIA (1984), Revs. Salvador Salgado, C.M.F.; Pedro Lopez Moran, C.M.F. (Spain); Vicente Penalba, C.M.F. (Spain); Romualdo Fernandez, C.M.F. (Spain); Deacons Jose Ramon Cruz; Rafael Araya.
Mailing Address: Urb. Cana, Calle 24 #II-1, 00957.
Res.: Calle 24, Esq. 23, Urb. Cana, 00957. Tel: 787-797-7248; 787-797-8230; Fax: 787-279-5292.
Mission—San Gerardo Mayela Bo. Buena Vista, Bayamon Co. 00957.
Mission—Sagrado Corazon Bo. Cerro Gordo, Bayamon Co. 00956.

21—SANTA RITA DE CASIA (1967), Revs. Eliseo Garcia, O.S.A. (Spain), Supr.; Isaias Alvarez, O.S.A.; Gonzalo Gonzalez O.S.A. (Spain); Bro. Agustin Sanchez, O.S.A; Deacons Eliezer Toro; Ramon Luis Rivera; Noel Vasquez.
Res. & Mailing Address: Ave. Hostos NS-8, Urb. Santa Juanita, 00956. Tel: 787-786-3971; Fax: 787-778-3806.
Retired House—Ntra. Sra. del Buen Consejo, 00956.
Mission—San Jose Carretera 831, Bo. Minillas, Bayamon Co. 00619.
Mission—N. Sra. Del Carmen Calle Reno P-54, Urb. Vista Bella, Bayamon Co. 00619.
Mission—Sagrado Corazon De Jesus

22—SANTA ROSA DE LIMA (1976), Rev. Pedro Campana (Spain); Deacons Ricardo D'Auria; Ricardo Longueira; Juan R. Santos.
Mailing Address: Calle 12, Bloque No. 28 No. 9, Urb. Santa Rosa, 00959. Tel: 787-798-2300; 787-787-1676; Fax: 787-780-3680.
Res.: Urb. Sta. Rosa, Av. Main, Calles 11, 12, 13. Tel: 787-798-2300; Fax: 787-780-3680.
School—Ave. Main, Urb. Santa Rosa. Tel: 787-798-2829; 787-798-2539; Fax: 787-780-3380; 787-288-4996. Sr. Selenia Quinones, O.P., Prin. Sisters 7; Lay Teachers 37; Students 854.
Catechesis/Religious Program—Students 854.

23—SANTA TERESA DE JESUS (1983), Rev. Angel Figueroa Sanchez; Deacon Eugenio Torres.
Mailing Address: P.O. Box 9204, 00960-9204.
Res.: Calle 12 F #10, Urb. Teresita, 00960. Tel: 787-269-6749.
Mission—San Martin de Porres Rio Plantation Urb. Toa Baja, 00950.
Mission—Convento Missioneras de La Caridad Sector Punta Brava.

24—SANTIAGO APOSTOL (1966), [CEM] Revs. Jesus Jordan, M.SS.C. (Spain); Antonio Picornell, M.SS.CC. (Spain); Deacon Angel Fabon.
Res.: Urb. Sierra Bayamon, Calle 23, Bloque 23, Num. 17, 00961. Tel: 787-786-9679; 787-288-1966; Fax: 787-269-3965.
School—Tel: 787-786-9179; Fax: 787-269-3965. Mrs. Zoraida N. de Alonso, Prin. Priests 3; Lay Teachers 11; Students 330.
Catechesis/Religious Program—Students 330.

25—SANTO DOMINGO DE GUZMAN (1976), Rev. Angel Diaz, O.P.; Deacons Hector Negron; William Rodriguez.
Mailing Address: P.O. Box 4188, 00960-4188.
Res.: Ext. La Milagrosa Calle 2, 00960. Tel: 787-786-8592; 787-785-2381; Fax: 787-269-5065.
Catechesis/Religious Program—Students 64.

26—SANTO DOMINGO DE GUZMAN (1984), Rev. Orlando de Jesus Londono Arango (Colombia); Deacons Virgilio Andino; Ramon Ramos.
Mailing Address: P.O. Box 3342, 00958-3342.
Res.: Parcelas Van Scoy, Calle Principal Esquina Calle, #3, 00957. Tel: 787-797-5510; 787-799-2377.
Catechesis/Religious Program—Students 173.
Mission—Santisima Trinidad Carretera 167 Km. 10, Bo. Ortiz, Corozal Co.
Mission—N. Sra. de la Providencia Urb. Los Dominicos, 00958.

CANOVANAS

1—NUESTRA SENORA DEL PILAR (1960), Rev. Fabio Moncada (Colombia); Deacon Jose R. Rivera.
Mailing Address: P.O. Box 1615, 00729-1615.
Res.: Luis Hernaiz St., #3, 00729. Tel: 787-876-2655; 787-876-3020; Fax: 787-256-5767.
School—3 Luis Hernaiz St., 00729. Tel: 787-876-3020. Mr. Victor Hernandez, Dir. Lay Teachers 19; Students 804.
Mission—San Francisco Javier Bo. Cambalache, Canovanas Co. 00629.

2—RESURRECCION DEL SENIOR (1978), Rev. Luis E. Villada (Colombia); Deacons Pedro Flores; Miguel Roman.
Mailing Address: P.O. Box 896, 00729-0896.
Res.: Las Parcelas de San Isidro, Carret. 188 Km. 2.0, 00729. Tel: 787-876-3917; Fax: 787-256-4836.
Mission—Ntra. Sra. de la Providencia Villas De Loiza.

3—SAGRADO CORAZON DE JESUS (1991), Rev. Rodney Algarin-Rosado; Deacon Anthony Calderon.
Mailing Address: P.O. Box 35000, PMB 20147, 00729-0014. Tel: 787-876-1355; Fax: 787-886-3668.
Res.: Bo. Cubuy, Carretera 186 Km. 77, 00729. Tel: 787-876-1355; Fax: 787-886-3668.
Mission—La Milagrosa Bo. Cuatrocientos, Canovanas Co. 00729.
Mission—San Pedro Apostol Bo. Las Lomas, Canovanas Co.

4—SAN JOSE (1971), Rev. Rodney Algarin Rosado; Deacon Felipe Rivera.
Mailing Address: P.O. Box 807, 00729-0807.
Res.: Bo. Campo Rico, Carretera 185, 00729. Tel: 787-876-7167.
Mission—Ntra. Sra. de la Asuncion Carrt. 957 Km. 6.8, Palma Sola, Villalba Co.
Mission—Ntra. Sra. del Carmen Carrt. 185 Km. 5.3, Alturas de Campo Rico.

5—SANTA MARIA MADRE DE DIOS (1971), Rev. Vicente Pasqualetto, S.T.; Deacon Jose L. Casaigne.
Mailing Address: E-189 Girasol St., Urb. Loiza Valley, 00729. Tel: 787-876-0827; Fax: 787-256-2142.
Res.: Urb. Loiza Valley, Calle Girasol #189, 00729.
Mission—Capilla Cristo Salvador Sector Pueblo Indio.

CAROLINA

1—CRISTO REY (1971), Rev. Miguel A. Corrales (Colombia).
Mailing Address: P.O. Box 1215, 00986-1215.
Res.: Urb. Parque Ecuestre, Calle Dulce Sueno U-8, 00987. Tel: 787-757-8712.
Mission—S. Francisco de Asis Entre las calles Tinajero y Dulce Sueno, Parque Encuestre.
Mission—Maria Auxiliadora Carrt. 857 Km. 3.6, Bo. Canovanillas.
Mission—Divino Nino Jesus Ubanizaciones: Ciudad Jardin y Colobos Park, Bo. Cambute, Carolina Co.
Mission—Cristo Rey Bo. Carruzos.

2—EPIFANIA DEL SENOR (1982), Rev. Juan Patron Kastner (Peru); Deacon Miguel Roman.
Mailing Address & Res.: Calle Calais 425, Ext. El Comandante, 00982-3601. Tel: 787-752-1149.
Catechesis/Religious Program—Students 19.

3—INMACULADA CONCEPCION (1966), Rev. Hernan Berdugo (Colombia).
Mailing Address: Apartado 3562, 00984-3562.
Res.: Urb. Valle Arriba Heights, Calle Almendro A-15, 00984. Tel: 787-276-1527; Fax: 787-276-1527.

4—NTRA. SRA. DE FATIMA (1998), Rev. Alberto Pagan, O.P.; Deacons Domingo Ocasio; Orlando Rodriguez.
Mailing Address: HC-3 Box 12076, Barrio Cedros, 00985.
Res.: Bo. Cedros, Carr 853, Km. 13.6. Tel: 787-750-8562; Fax: 787-750-8562.
Mission—N. Sra. del Carmen, Barrazas Co.
Mission—Santa Teresa, Cacao Co.

5—NTRA. SRA. DEL CARMEN (1984), Rev. Antonio Garcia (Spain); Deacons Ernie Diaz; Cesar Avila.
Mailing Address: P.O. Box 299, 00986-0299.
Res.: Urb. Lomas de Carolina, Monte Membrillo Km. 8, 00987. Tel: 787-752-8708; 787-752-4454; Fax: 787-762-6656.
School—Academia del CarmenMonte Britton:, Esq. Monte Membrillo, Lomas de Carolina, 00987. Tel: 787-757-4489; 787-757-4454. Zoraida Batista, Prin. Priests 1; Lay Teachers 20; Students 270.
Catechesis/Religious Program—Students 120.

6—NTRA. SRA. REINA DE LA PAZ (1969), Rev. Jesus A. Garcia (Venezuela); Deacons Euripides Lugo; Miguel Marrero; Manuel Reyes; Efigenio Rivera.
Mailing Address: P.O. Box 3688, 00984-6388.
Res.: Calle 6, Final, Urb. Sabana Gardens, 00983. Tel: 787-752-5607; Fax: 787-762-4277.
Mission—Divino Nino Jesus

7—NTRA. SRA. REINA DE LOS ANGELES (1960), Rev. Richard Marmol (Venezuela); Deacon Ildefonso Berrios.
Res. & Mailing Address: 17A Bloque W Calle N, Urb. Los Angeles, 00979-1154. Tel: 787-791-2594; Fax: 787-791-2594.

8—NUESTRA SENORA DE LOURDES (1956), Rev. David Arrieta (Spain); Deacons Emilio Caceres; Nelson Soto.
Mailing Address: Urb. El Comandante, 1173 Calle Alejo Cruzado, 00924.
Res.: 1173 Alejo Cruzado, Ext. El Comandante. Tel: 787-752-3716.

9—SAN ANDRES (1982), Rev. Nestor Yulfo; Deacons Marino Hernandez; Gilberto Mejias.
Res. & Mailing Address: MF-15 Calle 482, Urb. Country Club (4 Ta. Extension), 00982. Tel: 787-769-7076; Fax: 787-769-7076.

10—SAN FELIPE APOSTOL (1971), Rev. Rafael Suazo; Deacons Eugenio Balasquide; Jose Rafael Vazquez.
Mailing Address: P.O. Box 1494, 00984-1494.
Res.: Calle 419, Bloque 165, No. 3, 4 ta. Ext. Villa Carolina, 00964. Tel: 787-762-6520; Fax: 787-257-8995. Email: sanfelipepr@hotmail.com.

11—SAN FERNANDO (1851), Most Rev. Hector Rivera Perez, D.D.; Deacons Jose Birriel; Enrique Colon; Santiago Diaz Rosa; Prebistero Rivera.
Mailing Address: P.O. Box 128, 00986-0128.
Res.: Calle Munoz Rivera, No. 65, frente a Plaza de Recreo, 00986. Tel: 787-769-0170; Fax: 787-769-5223.

12—SAN FRANCISCO DE ASIS (1988), Rev. Frank de la

Rosa Peguero (Dominican Republic); Deacon Justo Montanez.
Res. & Mailing Address: Calle 22 #0-31 A, Urb. Metropolis, 00987. Tel: 787-768-8860.

13—SAN JUAN DE DIOS (1971), Rev. Ricardo A. Roig; Deacon Luis R. O'Neill.
Mailing Address: P.O. Box 3179, 00984-3179.
Res.: R-19-A Canaria St., Jardines de Borinquen, 00984. Tel: 787-757-5060; Fax: 787-757-5060.
Mission—La Sagrada Familia C. Progreso A-79A, Villa Esperanza, Carolina Co. 00985.

14—SAN VALENTIN (1971), Rev. Francisco Jose Quiceno (Colombia); Deacons Miguel Diaz; Antonio Quintana; Jose A. Pappaterra.
Mailing Address: P.O. Box 9382, 00988-9382.
Res.: Calle San Luis 128, Urb. Rolling Hills, 00988. Tel: 787-750-5277; Fax: 787-750-5277.
Catechesis/Religious Program—Students 66.
Mission—Jardines de Carolina Calle E, esq. Calle F, Santa Rosa, 00987. Tel: 787-750-5272.
Mission—San Antonio Urb. San Anton, Calle Tomas Ortiz, esq. Kercado, Carolina Co. 00987.

15—SANTA CLARA DE ASIS (1966), Revs. Fernando Hortiguela, O.F.M. (Spain); Leandro Abarrategui, O.F.M. (Spain); Luis S. Olmo, O.F.M. (Spain); Deacons Luis Del Rio Pitre; Jose A. Morales; Luis Montes.
Mailing Address: Urb. Villa Fontana, JL-456 Via 14, 00983.
Res.: Via 14 JL No. 456 Urb. Villa Fontana, 00983. Tel: 787-768-1708; Fax: 787-750-2898.
School— (1968),Tel: 787-768-7110; Fax: 787-757-5044. Mrs. Lillivette Torres, Prin.; Rev. Leanadro Abarratelegui, O.F.M., Dir. Lay Teachers 23; Students 355.
Mission—San Francisco de Asis
Mission—Parque Boliviano 5-JL Villa Fontana Park, Carolina Co. 00983.

16—SANTA GEMA GALGANI (1971), Revs. Jose R. Montanez Lopez, C.P. (MGZ); Felix Barruetabena, C.P. (Spain).
Mailing Address: P.O. Box 2789, 00984-2789.
Res.: Av. Galicia Final, Urb. Vistamar, 00984. Tel: 787-769-5663; Fax: 787-750-3090.
School—Tel: 787-768-3082; 787-757-2505; Fax: 787-750-3090. Mrs. Lilia Luna de Anaya, Prin. Lay Teachers 32; Students 631.

17—SANTISIMA TRINIDAD (1982), Rev. Luis Angel Torres; Deacons Ibrahim Suarez; Esteban Valle; Bienvenido Domenech; Gaspar Orozco.
Mailing Address: Urb. Country Club, 3 ra Ext., Ave. Campo Rico PA-16, 00982. Tel: 787-769-5665.
Res.: Avenida Campo Rico PA-16, Urb. Country Club.
Catechesis/Religious Program—Students 175.

18—SANTO CRISTO DE LA AGONIA (1971), Rev. Jorge J. Castillejo-Llusia (Spain); Deacons Ernesto Rivera; Miguel A. Marrero-Nieves.
Mailing Address: P.O. Box 5108, 00984-5108.
Res.: Calle Robles 29, Urb. Eduardo J. Saldana (Ceramica), 00984. Tel: 787-768-0374.
Catechesis/Religious Program—Students 60.
Mission—N. Sra. de la Esperanza Sabana Abajo, Carolina Co.

19—SANTO CRISTO DE LOS MILAGROS (1971), Rev. Msgr. Ramon E. Toro (Colombia).
Mailing Address: P.O. Box 834, 00986-0834. Fax: 787-768-3810. In Res., Rev. Alejandro Sanchez (STV).
Res.: Ave. Sanchez Castano, Urb. Villa Carolina, 00985. Tel: 787-768-3810.

CATANO

1—NUESTRA SENORA DEL CARMEN (1893), Revs. Alfredo Vallina-Vega, O.P. (Spain); Felix A.P. Struik, O.P. (Holland); Deacons Angel Oquendo; Enrique Rivera.
Mailing Address: P.O. Box 427, 00963-0427. In Res., Revs. Malachi Clune, O.P. (Ireland); Oscar Morales, O.P.
Res.: Calle Tren Num. 42, 00963. Tel: 787-275-1309; Fax: 787-788-5905.
Mission—San Martin de Porres Urb. Bayview.
Mission—San Jose Obrero Rev. Juan A. Matos.

2—SAN FRANCISCO DE SALES (1969), Revs. Juan Martinez, S.D.B.; Jorge L. Gonzalez, S.D.B., Supr.; Francisco Juan Garcia, S.D.B.
Mailing Address: P.O. Box 567, 00963-8163.
Res.: Ave. Flor del Valle Bloque BB-No. 108, Urb. Las Vegas, 00963. Tel: 787-788-5036; Fax: 787-788-8163.
Mission—Santo Domingo De Guzman Puente Blanco, Catano Co.
Mission—Maria Auxiliadora Urb. Vistas Del Morro.
Mission—San Judas Tadeo (Santuario) Parcelas Bo. Palmas.
Mission—Immaculada Concepcion Sector La Cucharilla.

DORADO

1—NTRA. SRA. DE LA SALUD (1982), Rev. Manuel Garcia (Spain); Deacons Hilario De Leon; Cresencio Rosario.
Mailing Address: Bo. Higuillar, P.O. Box 470, 00646-0470.
Res.: Parcela 202, Calle Principal 210, Sector San Antonio, 00646. Tel: 787-796-3418; Fax: 787-796-3418.

2—SAN ANTONIO DE PADUA (1842), Rev. Angel Luis Morales; Deacons Jose Marrero; Romulo Rodriguez.
P.O. Box 602, 00646-0602. Tel: 787-278-1416; 787-278-1154 (Res.); Fax: 787-278-4759.
Res.: Paseo del Cristo, Lot #8, Urb. Martorell, 00646.
Shrine—Christ of Reconciliation (2001), Paseo Del Cristo Lot #8, Urb. Martorell, 00646.

GUAYNABO

1—BUEN PASTOR (1965), Rev. Jaime Vazquez Rojas.
Res. & Mailing Address: Avenida Apolo, Urb. Apolo, 00969. Tel: 787-789-2653; Fax: 787-789-2653.

2—CORAZON DE JESUS (1992), Rev. Luis A. Sada Izaguirre, SS.CC. (Spain); Deacon Andres Figueroa Acevedo.
Mailing Address: P.O. Box 225, 00970-0225. Tel: 787-789-2014.
Res.: Carr. 834 Km. 4.0, Bo. Sonadora, 00970.
Mission—San Juan Bosco Bo. Mamey 1.
Mission—Sagrada Familia Bo. Sonadora, Sagrados Corazones, Bo. Sonadora.

3—DIVINO NINO JESUS (1992), Rev. Rodolfo Lamas (Cuba); Deacons Gerardo Comulada; Milton Valladares.
Mailing Address: PBM 143, HC-01, Box 29030, Caguas, 00725. Tel: 787-720-0203; Fax: 787-720-0203.
Res.: Urb. Lomas Del Sol, Calle Principal Y-6.
Mission—San Rafael Arcangel Barrio Camarones, Carr. #20, Guaynabo Co. 00970.
Mission—Jesus Nazareno Bo. Mamey, Guaynabo Co. 00970.
Mission—El Buen Pastor Carr. #1, Guaynabo Co. 00970. Tel: 787-798-9596.
Mission—N. Sra. de la Paz Bo. Quebrada Arenas, Guaynabo Co.

4—MARIA MADRE DE LA MISERICORDIA (1995), Revs. Eliades Petit (Cuba); Vicente Fernandez.
Mailing Address: Ave. Santa Ana. #150, 00969.
Res.: Carretera 833 Km. 13.2, Bo. Santa Rosa 3, 00969. Tel: 787-789-0090; Fax: 787-790-7596.

5—MARIA MADRE DE MI SENOR (1988), Rev. Francisco Javier Quinones.
Mailing Address: P.O. Box 2150, 00970-2150. Tel: 787-789-1837; 787-720-1709.
Res.: Bo. Tortugos, Carretera 873, #1904, 00970.
Mission—Ntra. Sra. del Carmen Bo. Frailes Llanos, Sector Los Baez, Guaynabo Co. 00657.

6—NUESTRA SENORA DE LA PAZ (1992), Rev. Jesus Vietes, SS.CC. (Spain); Deacons Porfirio Franco; Jose M. Castillo.
Mailing Address: P.O. Box 225, 00970-0225. Tel: 787-789-2014.
Res.: Bo. Guaraguao, 00970.
Mission—Sta. Rosa de Lima Bo. Santa Rosa III, Guaynabo Co.
Mission—N. Sra. de la Divina Providencia Cantagallo, Juncos Co.
Mission—Espiritu Santo Bo. Santa Rosa I.
Mission—Inmaculada Concepcion Bo. Camarones Centro, Ciales Co.
Mission—San Jose Obrero Bo. Sta. Rosa II.

7—SAGRADOS CORAZONES (1968), Revs. Esteban Beltran de Otalora, SS.CC.; Mateo Mateo, SS.CC.; Jose Ma. Garcia, SS.CC.; Deacons Ivan E. Dominguez; Ulpiano H. Rivera; Julio Toro.
Mailing Address: P.O. Box 3902, 00970-3902.
Res.: Urb. Ponce de Leon, 208 Ave. Esmeralda, 00969. Tel: 787-720-6151; Fax: 787-720-6035.
School—Avenue A.. Tel: 787-720-2585; 787-720-6316; Fax: 787-720-6035. Edith Casiano, Prin. (High School); Maria V. Rivera, Prin. (Elementary). Sisters 3; Lay Teachers 35; Students 796.
Mission—Virgen de la Paz Bo. Cruz Melendez. Tel: 787-789-2014.

8—SAN JUAN EVANGELISTA (1962), Rev. Nicanor Valdes (Cuba); Deacon Miguel De La Sota.
Mailing Address: P.O. Box 10151, 00922-0151.
Res.: Calle Church Hill, J-5, Urb. Torrimar, 00966. Tel: 787-783-3522; Fax: 787-781-0236.
School—Tel: 787-781-5325; Fax: 787-793-8076. Rev. Nicanor Valdes (Cuba), Dir. Priests 1; Lay Teachers 12; Students 103.
Mission—San Francisco de Asis [CEM] Carretera 19, La Marina, Guaynabo Co. 00966.

9—SAN PEDRO MARTIR DE VERONA (1769), Rev. Msgr. Mario A. Guijarro de Corzo (Cuba); Deacons Carlos Rivera Martinez; Gumersindo Negron Morales; Humberto Reyes Anciano; Angel Loyola Zayas; Gregory A. Guijarro; Jorge Encarnacion; Jose Falon.
Mailing Address: P.O. Box 32, 00970-0032.
Res.: Calle Tapia No. 5, 00970. Tel: 787-720-2361; 787-272-6739; 787-287-1791; Fax: 787-287-2833.
School—Alpierre St. Final, Urb. Colimar, P.O. Box 2560, 00970-2560. Tel: 787-720-2219; Fax: 787-272-8770. Mrs. Ivonne D. Carlo, Prin.; Deacon Gregory A. Guijarro, Prof. & Vice Dir. Priests 2; Sisters 9; Lay Teachers 45; Students 610.
Catechesis/Religious Program—Students 267.

10—SANTA ROSA DE LIMA (1973), Rev. Johnny Cruz Velazquez, O.SS.T.; Deacon Filiberty De Jesus.
Mailing Address & Res.: 16 Parque St., Barrio Amelia, 00965. Tel: 787-781-5855; 787-783-9731; Fax: 787-781-5855; 787-783-9731.
Mission—La Milagrosa Barriada Vietnam.

LOIZA

1—SAN PATRICIO (1719), Rev. Harold Stone, S.T.; Deacons Santiago Acosta; Marcos Penaloza; Pastor Perez.
Mailing Address: Box 504, 00772-0504.
Res.: Calle Espiritu Santo #10, 00772. Tel: 787-876-2229; Fax: 787-876-7828.
Mission—Santa Rosa Bo. Pinones, Loiza Co.
Mission—Ntra. Sra. del Perpetuo Socorro Bo. La Torre, Loiza Co.
Mission—Santisima Trinidad Bo. Mediana Baja.
Mission—San Antonio Bo. Las Cuevas.
Mission—Ntra. Sra. de Fatima Villa Canona.
Mission—San Rafael Villa Alvarez.

2—SANTIAGO APOSTOL, EL MAYOR (1971), Revs. Francis J. Conkle, S.T.; Eduardo Sittinger, S.T.
Mailing Address: P.O. Box 118, 00772-0118.
Res.: Carretera 187 Km. 6.0, Bo. Mediania Alta, 00772. Tel: 787-876-1879; Fax: 787-876-3060.
Mission—Ntra. Sra. Perpetuo Socorro Parcelas Suarez, Loiza Co.
Mission—La Milagrosa Bo. El Jobos.
Mission—La Providencia Bo. Mini Mine.
Mission—N. Sra. De Fatima Parcelas Vieques, Loiza Co.

LUQUILLO

1—MADRE DEL REDENTOR (1997), Rev. Luis H. Quinonez-Murillo (Colombia).
Mailing Address: P.O. Box 591, 00773-0591. Tel: 787-889-0733; Fax: 787-889-0733.
Res.: Barrio Pitaya, Sector Casablanca, Carr. 173, Km. 1.5, 00773.
Mission—N. Sra. del Carmen Bo. Pitahaya, Luquillo Co.
Mission—N. Sra. Milagrosa Bo. Sabana, Luquillo Co.
Mission—S. Vicente de Paul Bo. Juan Martin.
Mission—N. Sra. del Perpetuo Socorro San Martin, San Juan Co.

2—SAN JOSE (1797), Rev. Leonardo Rodriguez Ochoa; Deacons Jesus Ramos; Frank Rivera.
Mailing Address: P.O. Box 493, 00773-0493.
Res.: Calle Soledad No. 15, fronte a Plaza de Recreo, 00773. Tel: 787-889-2590; Fax: 787-889-6180.
Mission—San Judas Bo. Mata de Platano.
Mission—Ntra. Sra. del Cobre Parcelas Fortuna, Luquillo Co.

RIO GRANDE

1—CRISTO REY (1970), Rev. Julio Ortiz-Mangual.
Mailing Address: P.O. Box 382, Palmer, 00721-0382.
Res.: Calle Principal, #50, Palmer, 00721. Tel: 787-887-3552.
Mission—La Milagrosa Palmer. Parcela 69 Hato Rio Grande, Bo. Carola, Rio Grande Co. 00721.
Mission—Ntra. Sra. de la Providencia [CEM] Bloque S-1 #7, Palmer, Rio Grande Co. 00721.

2—NUESTRA SENORA DEL CARMEN (1840), Revs. Mario Lopez, S.O.L.T.; Juan Perez, S.O.L.T.; Deacons Jose Carrasquillo; Vidal Diaz; Juan Rodriguez.
Mailing Address: P.O. Box 845, 00745-0845. Tel: 787-887-2365; Fax: 787-887-2365.
Res.: No. 9 del Carmen St., 00745. Tel: 787-888-3991.
School—Calle 14 Urb. Alturas de Rio Grande, P.O. Box 818, 00745. Tel: 787-887-4099; Fax: 787-887-0872. Mrs. Maria Guzman, Prin.
Catechesis/Religious Program—Students 95.
Mission—Nuestra Senora de Fatima Bo. El Verde, Rio Grande Co. 00745.
Mission—Ntra. Sra. de Guadalupe Jardines de Rio Grande, Rio Grande Co. 00745.
Mission—San Pedro Bo. Bartolo, Rio Grande Co. 00745.
Mission—La Milagrosa Calle 14, Alturas de Rio Grande, Rio Grande Co. 00745.
Mission—Sagrado Corazon de Jesus Coco Beach, Rio Grande Co. 00745.

3—SAN FRANCISCO DE ASIS (1986), Rev. Francisco J. Zipasuca Quemba (Colombia); Deacon Manuel Llanos.
Mailing Address: P.O. Box 1449, Bo. Malpica, 00745-1449.
Res.: Barrio Malpica, 00745. Tel: 787-888-5302; Fax: 787-888-5302.

TOA ALTA

1—N. SRA. DE LA PROVIDENCIA (1988), Rev. Carlos Verdia; Deacons Gregorio Cuevas; Jose C. Pacheco.
Mailing Address: P.O. Box 3836, Bayamon Gardens Sta., Bayamon, 00958-3836. Tel: 787-797-1618; Fax: 787-279-8439.
Res.: Bo. Pinas, Carretera 861 Km. 5.6.

Mission—N. Sra. de Fatima Sector Rincon, Bo. Pinas, Comerio Co.
Mission—La Resurreccion Villa del Rio, Bo. Pinas, Comerio Co.
Mission—N. Sra. del Carmen Sector del 7.
Mission—Sagrada Familia Villa Juventud, Bo. Pinas, Comerio Co.

2—NUESTRA SENORA DE LA MEDALLA MILAGROSA, Rev. Jairo Salazar (Colombia); Deacons German Hernandez; Santos Nieves.
Mailing Address: P.O. Box 335, 00954-0335.
Res.: Bo. Quebrada Cruz, Carretera 824, Km. 3.8, 00954. Tel: 787-870-4090; Fax: 787-870-8125.
Mission—Nuestra Senora del Carmen Sector El Cuco, Bo. Quebrada Cruz, Toa Alta Co. 00758.
Mission—Sagrado Corazon de Jesus Carretera 165 Km. 3.1, Quebrada Cruz, Toa Alta Co. 00758.

3—SAN ESTEBAN, PROTOMARTIR (1997), Rev. Jose Antonio Carrion (Cuba); Deacon Jose Ramon Perez-Bracero.
Res. & Mailing Address: Urb. Monte Sol, Ave. Hato Tejas, Esq. Carretera 861, 00953. Tel: 787-799-2925; Fax: 787-279-8439.
Catechesis/Religious Program—Students 155.
Mission—Capilla Cristo Rey Sector La Cuerda, Barrio Bucarabones, Toa Alta Co. 00953.
Mission—N. Sra. del Rosario Convento Hnas. Amityville, Bo. Pajaros, RR-5, Box 4103, Bayamon, Toa Alta Co. 00956. Tel: 787-799-7950.

4—SAN FERNANDO REY (1751), [JC] Rev. Miguel Angel Colon Marrero; Deacons Jose Narvaez; Felipe Collazo; Pablo Irene.
Mailing Address: P.O. Box 63, 00954-0063.
Res.: Calle Jose de Diego #10, 00953. Tel: 787-870-2585.
Mission—San Antonio Rio Lajas, Dorado, Dorado Co. 00646.

5—SAN JOSE (1998), Rev. Calixto Soto (Colombia); Deacons Francisco Villamil; Enrique Laureano; Rafael Morales.
Mailing Address: P.O. Box 777, 00954-0777.
Res.: Sector Jazmin, Carretera 823, Rio Lajas. Tel: 787-870-6415.
Mission—Ntra. Sra. del Camino Bo. Espinosa, Carretera #2, Dorado, Dorado Co. 00646.
Mission—S. Francisco De Asis Bo. Maguayo, Dorado, Dorado Co. 00646.
Mission—Cristo de los Milagros
Mission—Santa Teresita Bo. Rio Lajas, Toa Alta Co. 00758.
Mission—Sagrada Familia Sector Marzan, Bo. Rio Lajas, Toa Alta Co. 00758.
Mission—Sagrado Corazon Sector Los Mudos, Bo. Quebrada Arenas, Toa Alta Co. 00758.

6—SAN JUDAS TADEO (2002), Rev. Victor Torres, O.M.I. (Panama); Deacons Luis Rivera-Albino; Jose Diaz.
Mailing Address: RP-03, Box 9169, 00954.
Res.: Carretera 804 Km. 1.2, Bo. Galateo Centro. Tel: 787-870-6643; Fax: 787-870-8018.
Mission—S. Martin de Porres Bo. Galateo.
Mission—Santa Teresa De Jesus Bo. Quebrada Cruz, Toa Alta Co. 00758.

TOA BAJA

1—ESPIRITU SANTO (1965), Revs. Ricardo Hernandez Morales; Jose B. Molina Rojas (Colombia); Deacons Pablo Maldonado; Jose Miranda; Miguel A. Torres.
Mailing Address: P.O. Box 50272, Levittown Sta., 00950. Mailing Address: P.O. Box 51540, Levittown, 00949.
Res.: Paseo Damisela No. 1453, Urb. Levittown Primera Seccion, 00949. Tel: 787-784-4805; Fax: 787-784-3051.
School—Paseo Damisela 1453, 00632. Tel: 787-784-0905; Fax: 787-795-5418. Jose A. Ruiz, Dir.; Ines Y. Elias, Prin. Lay Teachers 46; Students 645.
Catechesis/Religious Program—Students 195.
Mission—N. Sra. del Carmen Calle Carmen, Bo. Palo Seco, Toa Baja Co. 00759.

2—NTRA. SRA. DE LA CANDELARIA (1960), Rev. Jose Dario Martinez Tobon (Colombia); Deacons Anselmo Miranda; Roberto Ortiz; Camildo Ortiz.
Mailing Address: P.O. Box 892, 00951-0892.
Res.: Carretera No. 863, Km. 0.6, Bo. Pajaros, 00951. Tel: 787-251-0503.
Mission—Cristo Rey Calle 10, Bo. Bucarabones, Toa Alta, Toa Alta Co. 00758.
Mission—Santa Maria La Mayor Carretera #2 R.063, Bo. Macun, Bo. Macun, Toa Baja Co. 00759.
Mission—Santisima Trinidad Urb. Las Colinas, Toa Baja Co. 00759.
Mission—Buen Pastor Urb. Sta. Maria, Toa Baja Co. 00759.

3—NUESTRA SENORA DE COVADONGA (1984), Rev. Francisco Arana (Spain); Deacon Efrain Narvaez.
Mailing Address: P.O. Box 9076, Bayamon, 00960-9076. Tel: 787-251-6466; Fax: 787-251-6466.
Res.: Calle 13, 2-C-4, Esq. Calle 14, Urb. Covadonga, 00949.
Mission—Ntra. Sra. de Lourdes Bo. Candelaria Arenas, Toa Baja Co. 00759.
Mission—San Martin de Porres Bo. Kennedy, Toa Baja Co. 00759.
Mission—Divino Nino Jesus Urb. El Plantio, Toa Baja Co. 00759.

4—SAN JOSE OBRERO (1965), Revs. Angel Dario Carrero, O.F.M., Supr.; Juan Luis Belaustegui (Spain); Alfonso D. Guzman, O.F.M.; Deacon Ramon L. Colon.
Mailing Address: Box 173, Sabana Seca, 00952-0173.
Res.: Carretera 2-R 866, Km. 3 #6, 00952. Tel: 787-784-1400; 787-795-3141; Fax: 787-261-3469.
Mission—Ntra. Sra. del Carmen Sector Los Bravos.
Mission—San Martin de Porres Villa Marisol.

5—SAN PEDRO APOSTOL (1745), Revs. Miguel Angel Colon Marrero; Jairo Gelvez Tarazona (Colombia); Deacon Gerardo Trujillo.
Mailing Address: P.O. Box 513, 00951-0513.
Res.: 45 Las Flores St., 00951. Tel: 787-794-1327.
Catechesis/Religious Program—Students 260.
Mission—St. Teresita Calle Quintero.
Mission—Ntra. Sra. de Guadalupe Calle Crisantemo, Parcela 137-A.
Mission—San Jose Calle San Jose #303.
Mission—San Pablo Calle Universo, Parcela #9, Toaville.
Mission—La Virgen de la Providencia Bo. Villa Calma

6—SANTISIMA TRINIDAD (1978), Rev. Juan M. Beristain (Spain); Deacons Eusebio Jaca; Justo Ortiz; Edwin Negron.
Mailing Address: Apartado 50378, Levittown, 00950-0378. Tel: 787-784-2889; Fax: 787-261-2911.
Res.: Ave. Los Dominicos, Esquina Dr. Sanchez Cardona, Levittown, 00950.

TRUJILLO ALTO

1—BIENVENTURADA VIRGEN MARIA DE LOURDES (1975), Most Rev. Pedro Reyes Lebron; Rev. Francisco Javier Munoz (Colombia); Deacons Oscar Sanchez; Pablo Torres.
Mailing Address: P.O. Box 1081, 00976-1081.
Res.: Santuario, Gruta de Lourdes, Carretera 876 Km. 1.6, Barrio Cuevas, 00977. Tel: 787-761-0571; Fax: 787-761-0571.

2—EXALTACION DE LA SANTA CRUZ (1801), Rev. Jose Miguel Cardona Matta; Deacon Domingo Vargas.
Mailing Address: Box 1808, 00977-1808.
Res.: J. Diaz St., #515, frente a la Plaza de Recreo, 00977. Tel: 787-761-0507; Fax: 787-761-0507.

3—MARIA LLENA DE GRACIA (1997), Rev. Silverio Rueda (Colombia).
Mailing Address: P.O. Box 1618, 00977-1618. Tel: 787-283-0364.
Res.: Urb. Rincon Espanol, Calle 1, Esq. Calle 4, 00977.

4—SAN BARTOLOME (1985), Rev. P. Jose Alcocer Corbaton, M.SS.CC. (Spain); Deacon Alberto Gomez.
Mailing Address & Res.: Urb. Ciudad Universitaria, X-1 Calle 16, 00976. Tel: 787-755-0120.

5—SAN FRANCISCO DE ASIS (1992), Rev. Raul Quesada (Cuba); Deacons Hector Rivera; Alfredo Aponte; William Rios.
Mailing Address: P.O. Box 1316, 00977-1316.
Res.: Parcela Ramon T. Colon, Calle 2, Parcelas #32, Quebrada Negrito, 00977. Tel: 787-748-5584.
Mission—Espiritu Santo Bo. Kennedy Hills, Carretera 181 Km. 10.
Mission—San Jose de la Montana Carretera #181 R-851, Bo. Sabana.
Mission—La Inmaculada Concepcion Bo. Talanco, Carretera #181 R-852.

6—SAN JUDAS TADEO (1980), Rev. Miguel Pons; Deacons Jose Baez; Jose Ramon Oliveras.
Mailing Address: Apartado 1535, 00977-1535.
Res.: Calle 7, Esq. 8, Urbanizacion El Conquistador, 00977-1535. Tel: 787-755-5993.
Catechesis/Religious Program—Students 75.
Mission—El Divino Pastor Carretera 844 Km. 0.2, Parcelas Carraizo, Trujillo Alto Co. 00760.
Mission—Ntra. Sra. del Carmen Carretera 175, Bo. Carraizo Alto, Trujillo Alto Co. 00760.

7—SAN PIO X (1971), Rev. Alberto Lopez; Deacon Julio Sanchez.
Mailing Address: P.O. Box 631, St. Just, 00978.
Res.: Carretera 848, K-1.4, Bo. Sain Just, 00978. Tel: 787-761-5040.
Mission—N. Sra. del Rosario Calle Lirio, Esq. Orquidea, Urb. Round Hill, Rio Piedras, San Juan Co. 00923.

Chaplains of Public Institutions

SANTURCE. *Ashford Presbyterian Community Hospital*, 1451 Ave. Ashford, Condado. Tel: 787-725-8820; 787-724-8320. Rev. Freddy Alecio Rodriguez.
Doctors Community Hospital, 1395 Calle San Rafael. Tel: 787-723-2950. Rev. Francisco Morales Feliu (PCE). Tel: 787-723-5998.
Hospital Del Nino San Jorge, 255 Calle San Jorge. Tel: 787-727-1000. Rev. Eddie Rivera. Tel: 787-722-4158.
Hospital Pavia-Santurce, 1462 Calle Asia. Tel: 787-727-6060. Rev. Evaristo Oliveras, C.M. Tel: 787-727-3963.

Resident Chaplains:
Rev. Msgr.—
Valdes, Angel, Hospital del Maestro, Hato Rey, 00919.
Revs.—
Lopez Mairal, Jose Maria (Spain), Hogar de Sta. Teresa Jornet, Bo. Cupey, Rio Piedras, Trujillo Alto.
Ortega, Ovidio, Hogar de Ntra. Sra. de la Providencia, Ave. Ponce de Leon, Puerta de Tierra.

On Duty Outside the Archdiocese:
Revs.—
Alecio-Rodriguez, Freddy Sabbatical
Cruz Davila, Carlos D., Sabbatical
Del Valle, Tomas
Ferrer Martinez, Miguel, Sick Leave
Garcia Padron, Victor Julio, Sabbatical
Landrau Roman, Jose Antonio, Sabbatical
McCoy, Floyd
Parello, Joseph J., Miami.
Pierino, Vicente, U.S. Dept. of Justice, Coleman, FL.
Quintana-Puente, Carlos, Treas., Celam, Colombia.
Rivas Campis, Jose, Sabbatical
Roldan, Juan
Soto Tanon, Carmelo, Sabbatical
Sutil, Florencio
Torres Graciano, Ivan, Rochester, NY.

Graduate Studies:
Rev. Msgrs.—
Felices, Fernando B., Rome.
Hernandez, Jose G., Madrid, Spain.
Revs.—
Mejias, Carlos Ortiz, Rome.
Rodriguez Jimenes, Leonardo, Rome, Italy.
Saez Munoz, Raul
Toro, Carlos Perez, Rome, Italy.
Torres, William, Madrid, Spain.

Military Services:
Revs.—
Castillejo, Jorge, (Army)
Perez Vazquez, Juan De La Cruz, (Army)
Tirado, Orlando, C.M., (Air Force)

Awaiting Assignment:
Rev.—
Betancourt Ramirez, Jorge

Retired:
Rev. Msgrs.—
Cruz, Remberto
Maisonet-Ortiz, Tomas
Valdes-Valdes, Angel
Revs.—
Coroztieta, Jose Madoz
Cruz, Gilbert J. (Spain)
De Carlo Mena, Francisco
Diaz, Alvaro
Egurrola, Vicente
Fernandez-Mendez, Jose R.
Fuentes Rodriguez, Josi
Gonzalez, Cruz Gil
Gonzalez Chao, Luis
Gray Marks, Teodoro
Quijones-Rivera, Leoncio
Ramos, Victorino
Ribera-Ribo, Francisco J.

Permanent Deacons:
Acosta Osorio, Santiago
Alicea Rivera, Angel L.
Alvarez Granada, Enrique
Alvarez Torano, Julio
Amador Melendez, Luis F.
Andino Cintron, Virgilio
Andino Santos, Manuel
Aponte Diaz, Alfredo
Araya Brenes, Rafael F.
Araya Fernandez, Antonio
Arroyo Acevedo, Americo
Avila Rodriguez, Cesar
Ayala Garay, Gregorio
Baez Cotto, Pedro J.
Baez Navarro, Jose
Balasquide Vargas, Eugenio
Bermudez Martes, Jose A.
Berrios Berrios, Ildefonso
Birriel Rodriguez, Jose
Caban, Vicente
Caban Roman, Manuel
Caceres Paredes, Emilio
Calderon Rodriguez, Anthony
Camacho Rivera, Manuel

Carmona, Eduardo
Carrasquillo Rodriguez, Jose M.
Casaigne Ayala, Jose L.
Castillo Lopez, Jose M.
Claudio Flores, Pedro
Collazo Montalvo, Felipe
Colon Andino, Gumersindo
Colon Colon, Rafael
Colon Febres, Ismael
Colon Hernandez, Ramon L.
Colon Mallen, Vicente
Colon Marrero, Miguel
Colon Melendez, Enrique
Colon Ramos, Luis
Colon Rivera, Francisco
Comulada Pabon, Gerardo
Cordero Mercado, Luis
Cosme Varela, Nicomedes
Costa, Pedro Tomas
Cruz De Choudens, Hector M.
Cruz Ortiz, Francisco
Cruz Vazquez, Jose R.
Cuevas Alfonso, Martin
Cuevas Nieves, Gregorio
D'Auria, Ricardo
De Jesus Robles, Filiberty
De La Sota Pumarejo, Miguel
De Leon Sanchez, Hilario
De Varona Juarez, Abel
Del Rio del Rio, Anastasio
Del Rio Ortiz, Luis O.
Del Rio Pitre, Luis
Del Valle Gonzalez, Reinaldo
Diaz Diaz, Miguel A.
Diaz Miranda, Ernie P.
Diaz Rivera, Jose
Diaz Rivera, Vidal
Diaz Rosa, Santiago
Diaz Sifonte, Agapito
Domenech, Bienvenido
Dominguez, Ivan
Echegaray Martinez, Luis
Encarnacion Torres, Jorge
Estrada Galarza, Martin
Falcon Matos, Jose E.
Figueroa Acevedo, Andres
Figueroa Carrasquillo, Raul
Figueroa Dominguez, Nelson
Figueroa Sanchez, Juan
Flores Torres, Pedro
Franco Torres, Porfirio
Gierbolini Santiago, Francisco
Gomez Maldonado, Alberto
Gomez Soto, William
Gonzalez Rodz, Eduardo
Gonzalez Rosario, Pablo
Gonzalez Rosario, Pedro
Gonzalez Segarra, George
Guijarro del Corzo, Gregory A.
Guiven Flores, Cesar H.
Guzman Rosario, Jose A.
Hernandez Adorno, Francisco
Hernandez Hernandez, Marino
Hernandez Jorge, Jose A.
Irene Vargas, Pablo
Jaca Hernandez, Eusebio
LaSanta Arroyo, Vicente
LaTorre Rivera, Santiago
Laureano Molina, Enrique
Laureano Rivera, Juan
LLanos Calderon, Manuel Enrique
Longueira, Ricardo
Lopez Cepero, Victor
Lopez Collazo, Jesus
Lopez Echevarria, Felix
Loyola Zayas, Angel A.
Lugo Cordero, Casiano
Lugo Lugo, Euripides
Lugo Soto, Benito
Maldonado Febo, Pablo J.
Marin Mingaro, Louis
Marrero Nieves, Miguel A.
Marrero Picorneli, Jose M.
Martinez Duran, Ricardo L.
Martinez Pacini, Francisco
Martinez Santiago, Candido
Medina Nunez, Bernardino
Medina Rivera, Luis A.
Mejias Nunez, Gilberto
Melendez Lozano, Juan R.
Mendez Santiago, Miguel
Mendia Colon, Roberto
Mercado Vila, Nicanor
Merced De La Paz, Victor
Merino Raposo, Latino
Miranda Cruz, Jose
Miranda Mercado, Anselmo
Montanez, Justo
Montes Quevedo, Luis J.
Morales Gonzalez, Jose A.
Morales Maldonado, Rafael
Morales Morales, Angel
Morales Rodriguez, Carlos R.
Narvaez Hernandez, Jose R.
Narvaez Santiago, Efraim
Navedo Rodriguez, Luis A.
Negron Morales, Gumersindo
Negron Santana, Hector
Nel Arevalo, Pedro
Nieves Carbona, Luis M.
Nieves Nieves, Martin
Nieves Vazquez, Santos
Nunez, Pedro Arcadio
O'Neill Rosario, Luis R.
Ocasio Gonzalez, Domingo
Oquendo Serrano, Angel
Orlando Del Rios, Luis
Orozco Carrasquillo, Gaspar
Ortiz Alvarado, Justo
Ortiz Collazo, Francisco
Ortiz Core, Ramon L.
Ortiz Mangual, Julio
Ortiz Rodriguez, Jacinto
Ortiz Rosado, Camildo
Ortiz Rosario, Feliciano
Ortiz Rosario, Juan Rafael
Ortiz Rosario, Roberto
Ortiz Toro, Julio
Oyola Figueroa, Angel L.
Pabon Hernandez, Angel R.
Pabon Molina, Angel A.
Pacheco Diaz, Jose C.
Pappeterra Arthur, Jose A.
Pena Gonzalez, Jose
Penaloza Lacen, Marcos
Perez Ayala, Edwin
Perez Bracero, Jose R.
Perez Del Valle, Juan B.
Perez Fuentes, Raul
Perez Gonzales, Ignacio
Perez Gonzalez, Luis R.
Perez Guadalupe, Jose
Perez Pizarro, Pastor
Perez Silva, Juan B.
Pizarro Davila, Angel M.
Quintana Medina, Antonio
Ralat Saiz, Carlos
Ramirez Abreu, Tomas
Ramos Rodriguez, Ramon L.
Ramos Torres, Jesus R.
Reyes Anciano, Humberto
Reyes Crespo, Rafael
Reyes Matos, Manuel
Reyes Torres, Victor M.
Rios Aponte, William
Rios Arroyo, Jose M.
Rios Torres, Vicente
Rivera, Luis Marcial
Rivera, Prudencio I.
Rivera Albino, Luis
Rivera Alequin, Ulpiano H.
Rivera Archilla, Pedro
Rivera Baez, Eugenio
Rivera Collazo, Angel
Rivera De Jesus, Efigenio
Rivera Diaz, Hector R.
Rivera Estremera, Felipe
Rivera Fuentes, Jorge L.
Rivera Garcia, Edwin
Rivera Lopez, Hector M.
Rivera Martinez, Carlos
Rivera Matos, Frank
Rivera Mojica, Jose D.
Rivera Negron, Ernesto
Rivera Rios, Cristobal
Rivera Rivera, Jose R.
Rivera Rivera, Ramon L.
Rivera Rodriguez, Presbitero
Rivera Torres, Jose A.
Rivera Velez, Enrique
Rodriguez, Luis A.
Rodriguez Acevedo, Ramon
Rodriguez Marrero, Romulo
Rodriguez Martinez, Jose
Rodriguez Melendez, Orlando
Rodriguez Perazza, Jose R.
Rodriguez Rodriguez, Jose M.
Rodriguez Rodriguez, Juan
Rodriguez Rodriguez, Wilfredo
Rodriguez Serrano, William
Roman, Luis Ramon
Roman Del Valle, Miguel A.
Roman Maldonado, Jose M.
Roman Maldonado, Miguel A.
Rosario Rodriguez, Crescencio
Sanabria Lopez, Rafael
Sanchez, Samuel Alejandro
Sanchez Acosta, Oscar
Sanchez Munoz, Orlando
Sanchez Ortiz, Julio
Santiago Correa, Ramon
Santiago Rivera, Antonio
Santos Bello, Juan R.
Santos Negron, Marcos A.
Soto Miranda, Nelson
Suarez, Ibrahim
Suarez Molina, Israel
Toro Toro, Obed E.
Torres Acevedo, Pablo L.
Torres Burgos, Miguel A.
Torres Diaz, Eugenio
Torres Labauld, Jose A.
Torres Rodriguez, Dionilo
Torres Torres, Jose A.
Totti Lugo, Benjamin
Trujillo Cardona, Gerardo
Ubarri Mestres, Juan
Valladares Almodovar, Milton
Valle Valle, Esteban
Vargas Ramos, Domingo
Vazquez, Jose R.
Vazquez Garcia, Luis A.
Vazquez Rosario, Noel A.
Vega Vega, Jose P.
Velazquez Gonzalez, Jose L.
Velazquez Reyes, Rafael
Velez, Gregorio
Velez Roman, Miguel
Villamil Marrero, Fco. E.

INSTITUTIONS LOCATED IN THE ARCHDIOCESE

[A] COLLEGES & UNIVERSITIES

SAN JUAN. *Sacred Heart University*, Calle Rosales esq. San Antonio, Parada 26 1/2, Santurce. P.O. Box 12383, 00914-0383. Tel: 787-728-1515. Email: jjrivera@sagrado.edu. Web: www.sagrado.edu. The University has the following Departments and Programs: Departments of Communications, Humanities, Business Administration, Education, Natural Sciences and Social Sciences. The Graduate Programs include: Masters of Business Administration in Management of Systems Information, Masters of Arts & Communications, Masters of Art & Education, Masters of Occupational Nursing, Medical Technology Certificate. Faculty 136; Total Enrollment 5,234.
Governing Board: Mr. Alberto Paraccini, Pres. Bd. of Trustees; Dr. Jose Jaime Rivera, Pres.; Dr. Lydia Espinet, Dean of Academic Affairs; Ms. Lourdes Beltran, Dean of Admissions; Sr. Sororro Julia, Dean of Devel.; Pedro Fraile, Dean Student Affairs; Dr. Isabel Yamin, Dir. of Humanities; Camen Garcia, Dir. of Communications; Adalexis Rios, Dir. of Education; Arturo Figueroa, Dir. of Business Admin.; Dr. Manuel Aquino, Interino, Natural Sciences; Fernando Medina, Dir. of Social Sciences; Hylsa Silva Janer, License & Legal Counsel; Ms. Mildred Pineiro, Registrar; Mr. Luis A. Quiles, Dir. of Student Financial Aid; Rev. Jorge Castillejo, Dir. of Campus Ministry.

BAYAMON. *Bayamon Central University*, Avenida Zaya Verde, Bo. Hato Tejas, P.O. Box 1725, 00960-1725. Tel: 787-786-3030; Fax: 787-785-4365. Email: pbreyes@ucb.pr. Web: ucb.edu.pr. The University has the following Departments and Programs: Humanites; Business Administration; Natural Sciences; Education; Graduate Studies; Adult Education Program; Student Support Services; Upward Bound. Lay Teachers 60; Total Enrollment 3,200.
Governing Board: Rev. Mario Rodriguez-Leon, Pres. Council of Founders; C.P.A. Ismael Sanchez-Rivera, Pres. Bd. of Trustees.
Administration: Rev. Benito Reyes-Rivera, O.P., Pres.; Dr. Blanca Berio, Dean Academic Affairs; Mr. Mario Medina, Dean Admin. & Finances; Mr. Yanius Alvarado, Dean Student Affairs; Dr. Modesto Fernandez, Dir. Humanities; Dr. Nydia Cohen, Dir. Education; Dr. William A. Soler, Prof. & Dir. Natural Sciences; Mr. Pedro Bermudez, Dir. Institutional Devel.; Mr. Enrique Arias, Esq., Legal Counsel; Angela Ramos, Dir. of Human Resources; Mr. Victor Colon, Registrar; Mrs. Christine Hernandez, Dir. Admissions; Ms. Vivian Cintron, Dir. Student Financial Aid; Ms. Ana Medina, Dir. Academic Resource Ctr.
Faculty: Revs. Felix A.P. Struik, O.P. (Holland); Luis Espinel, O.P.; Angel Diaz Caceres; Mario Rodriguez Leon, O.P.; Angel Dario Carrero, O.F.M.; Manuel Soler Pala, M.SS.CC.; Victor Ortiz; Antonio Gonzalez Pola.

GUAYNABO. *ISTEPA (Instituto Superior de Teologia y Pastoral)*, Edificio 2021, Carretera 177, 00969-5140. Tel: 787-731-6100; Fax: 787-731-0000.

(Theology, Biblical and Pastoral courses for lay ministers and Deacons) Priests 5; Sisters 1; Deacons 9; Lay Teachers 7; Students 661.

[B] ELEMENTARY & HIGH SCHOOLS

SAN JUAN. *Academia San Ignacio de Loyola*, Urb. Santa Maria, 1908 Calle Narciso, 00927-6716. Tel: 787-765-8190; Fax: 787-765-3635. Email: asi-rpii@asi-rpii.org. Web: www.asi-rpii.org. Rev. Lawrence P. Searles, S.J., Chap.; Blanca I. Esteves, Ed.D., Dir.; Glorimar Soegaard, Prin.; Mrs. Dacita Bruno, Asst. Prin. Lay Teachers 49; Total Enrollment 631.

Colegio Angeles Custodios, Calle Sicilia Num. 13, San Jose, 00923. Tel: 787-763-3829; Fax: 787-764-9496. Email: cac-rpi@cac-rpi.org. Maria Aranzazu Labak, Dir.; Sr. Luis Roberto Rivera Cepeda, Prin.; Rev. Angel Pagan, Religion Dir. Students (K-8) 355; Students (9-12) 117.

Colegio Corazon De Maria, Calle Ferrer y Ferrer, Urb. Santiago Igesias, 00922. Tel: 787-783-3275. GPO Box 70359, 00936. (Archdiocesan School) Priests 1; Lay Teachers 18; Students 349.

Colegio de Parvulos, Inmaculado Corazon de Maria, 263 San Sebastian St., 00901. Tel: 787-722-1334; Fax: 787-724-2043. Sr. Luz Maria Arzuaga, H.C. Sisters 4; Lay Teachers 8; Students 102.

Colegio Maria Auxiliadora, 2273 Eduardo Conde, 00915. Tel: 787-726-8288; Fax: 787-727-6497. Email: fmasanturce@hotmail.com. Sr. Maritza Ortiz, F.M.A., Prin. Sisters 7; Lay Teachers 20; Students 435.

Colegio Nuestra Senora Del Carmen, R.R. 2, Box 15, 00926-9701. Tel: 787-761-8010; Fax: 787-748-2505. Email: melisea@coqui.net. Sisters Arlyn Medina Vazquez, Dir.; Elizabeth Andino, Prin.; Lissette Torres, Prin.; Liliana Santiago, Prin. Sisters 8; Lay Teachers 38; Students 510.

Colegio San Ignacio de Loyola, Urb. Santa Maria, 1940 Calle Sauco. Tel: 787-765-3814; Fax: 787-758-4145. Rev. Mario Alberto Torres, S.J., Dir.; Mr. Rafael Fernandez, Prin. Priests 3; Students 762.

Cristo Rey (Archdiocesan School) , Urb. Los Maestros, 789 Calle Jaime Drew, 00923. Tel: 787-767-0922; Fax: 787-764-9164. Email: acadcristorey@rp.org. Sr. Irene Martin, H.T.F. Sisters 4; Lay Teachers 15; Students 222.

Nuestra Senora De Belen (Archdiocesan School) , P.O. Box 10845, 00922-0845. Tel: 787-792-3115; Fax: 787-781-4920. Eleonor Marrero, Prin. (Elementary); Janet Hernandez, Prin. (High School); Mayra Mendez Barreto, Dir. Priests 0; Lay Teachers 73; Students 853.

Nuestra Senora de la Altagracia (Archdiocesan School) , P.O. Box 29493, 00929-0493. Tel: 787-763-7755; 787-763-7057; Fax: 787-756-5195. Mrs. Mirta Alicea, Prin.; Mr. Angel Castillo, Dir. Students 375.

San Jorge (Archdiocesan School) , 1701 Colon St., 00911. Tel: 787-722-3182; Fax: 787-725-4580. Email: sanjorge@iname.com. Mrs. Maritza Rosario, Prin.; Mrs. Vanesa Valdes, Dir. Lay Teachers 70; Students 681.

BAYAMON. *Colegio Beato Carlos Manuel Rodriguez*, Esq. Millones 2na. Ext. Lomas Verdes. Tel: 787-798-5260; 787-798-2329; 787-798-2747; Fax: 787-798-2620. Email: escb@crcnet.net. Web: familyeducation.com/pr. P.O. Box 4225, 00956. Mrs. Luisa Molina, Dir. & Prin. Students 663.

Colegio Ntra. Sra. del Rosario, Calle 5, AA-7, Repto. Valencia, 00659. Tel: 787-798-5100; Fax: 787-269-7551. Sr. Ma. Ana Jimenez Maldonado, O.P., Dir.; Elba I. Soto, Prin. Students 300.

Colegio Santa Rosa, Calle Marti 15, P.O. Box 6032, Estacion #1, 00960. Tel: 787-785-1195 (H.S.); 787-785-0381 (Elem.); Fax: 787-740-0115 (H.S.); 787-785-3791 (Elem.). Mrs. Luz Valentin, Prin. (High School); Mrs. Nilsa Gonzales, Prin. (Elementary). Priests 1; Lay Teachers 30; Total Enrollment 976.

Sagrada Familia (Archdiocesan School) , P.O. Box 4153, Bayamon Garden Sta., 00961. Tel: 787-785-2792; Fax: 787-787-7700. Sr. Rosario Morales Urrutia, C.S.J., Prin. & Dir. Priests 1; Sisters 1; Lay Teachers 18; Students 315.

Santo Tomas de Aquino, P.O. Box 1557, 00960-1557. Tel: 787-786-5015 (High School); 787-785-3838 (Elementary); Fax: 787-786-5015 (H.S.); 787-798-0180 (Elem.). Lay Teachers 50; Students 1,311.

P.O. Box 4098, 00958-1098. Mrs. Carmen J. Acosta, Elementary Prin.; Miss Micaela Hurtado, High School Prin.

CAROLINA. *Colegio Maria Auxiliadora*, Box 7770, 00986-7770. Tel: 787-762-0350; Fax: 787-257-3760. Email: maux@coqui.net. Web: www.colegiomariaux_car.org. Rosa Perez, Dir. Priests 1; Sisters 1; Lay Teachers 75; Students 1,500.

GUAYNABO. *Colegio Marista*, Alturas de Torrimar, 00969. Tel: 787-720-2186; 787-720-2187; Fax: 787-720-7020. Email: marista1@prtc.net. Bro. Ricardo Herrero, Dir. Priests 1; Brothers 7; Lay Teachers 89; Students 1,385.

Colegio Ntra. Sra. De La Caridad, Carretera Estatal #19, X-19, Villa Caparra., 00966 Tel: 787-781-8835; 787-781-1744; Fax: 787-781-8835. Email: caridad@coqui.net. P.O. Box 11164, 00922-1164. Sr. Rosa Maria Merino, S.J., Prin. St. Joseph of the Mountain Sisters Sisters 5; Lay Teachers 15; Students 177.

HATO REY. *Colegio Lourdes*, 87 Mayaguez St., 00917. Tel: 787-767-6106; 787-756-5436; Fax: 787-767-5282. Email: clourdes@coqui.net. Web: colegiolourdes.net. P.O. Box 190847, 00919-0847. Sr. Maria Paz Asiain, O.P., Dir. Sisters 5; Lay Teachers 44; Students 840.

RIO PIEDRAS. *Colegio La Milagrosa*, 107 De Diego Ave., 00925. Tel: 787-765-6114; Fax: 787-763-5324. Sr. Cecilia Serrano Guzman, H.C., Prin. Sisters 8; Lay Teachers 24; Students 467.

Colegio Nuestra Senora De La Providencia (Girls) , Ave. San Ignacio #1358, Urb. Altamesa, 00921. Tel: 787-781-7506; Fax: 787-792-7388. Email: zegri@coqui.net. Sr. Enriqueta Hernandez, Prin. Spanish Mercedarian Sisters Priests 1; Sisters 4; Lay Teachers 44; Students 965.

Colegio Sagrado Corazon de Jesus, (Grades PreK-8), Calle Palma Real 215 Esq. Interamericana, University Gardens, Rio Peidras, 00927. Tel: 787-765-9430; Fax: 787-765-5267. Rev. Jaime Vergara, C.M. (Spain), Dir.; Sr. Mary Andreen Rusin, O.S.F., Prin.; Rev. Jose Yanez, C.M. (Spain), Religion Dir. Students 943.

Colegio San Jose Tel: 787-751-8177; Fax: 787-767-1746. Email: sanjose@csj-pr.org. Web: www.csj-pr.org Box 21300, 00928-1300. Bro. Francisco T. Gonzalez, S.M., M.D., Dir. & Prin. Priests 1; Brothers 2; Lay Teachers 43; Students 520.

SANTURCE. *Academia Sagrado Corazor* Tel: 787-721-3300; Fax: 787-725-1865. Email: nawita@prtc.net. Box 11368, Fernandez Juncos Sta., 00910. Rev. Francisco Quinones, Spiritual Dir.; Mrs. Consuelo Mercado de Bou, Prin. Priests 1; Lay Teachers 21; Students 365.

Colegio La Inmaculada Tel: 787-727-6673; Fax: 787-727-5330. Stop 26, Ave. Ponce de Leon #1711, 00909-1997. Sr. Luz Mary Arzuaga, H.C., Dir.; Mr. Jose Acevedo, Prin. Sisters 6; Lay Teachers 20; Students 425.

Colegio Sagrada Familia (Archdiocesan School) Tel: 787-726-1742; Fax: 787-726-0718. Urb. Llorens Torres, Calle Loiza #2059, 00911. Ines Y. Elias, Prin.; Vanessa Valdes, Dir. Lay Teachers 6; Students 164.

Colegio San Juan Bosco, Carpenter Rd.. Rev. Nicolas Navarro, S.D.B., Dir.; Mrs. Lissette M. Ruiz. Priests 2; Religious 15; Lay Teachers 12; Students 288.

TRUJILLO ALTO. *Santa Cruz* (Archdiocesan School) , Dr. Fernandez St., #203, 00977. Tel: 787-761-1100; Fax: 787-755-3065. Box 1809, 00977-1809. Sr. Maria Ramon Santiago, O.S.F., Dir.; Mrs. Ana L. Monzon de Matos, Prin. Sisters 3; Lay Teachers 25; Students 430.

[C] SPECIAL SCHOOLS AND SEMINARIES

SAN JUAN. *Instituto Psicopedagogico De P.R.*, P.O. Box 363744, 00936-3744. Tel: 787-782-4640; 787-783-5431; Fax: 787-792-3610. Sr. Isabel Lauado, Supr. Jesus Nazarene Sisters Sisters 4; Bed Capacity 134; Patients Assisted Annually 134.

Seminario Menor San Jose (Diocesan) , Demetrio O'Dally St. 1000 Country Club, 00924. Tel: 787-768-3157; Fax: 787-752-2410. Rev. Carlos Ortiz-Mejias, Rector. (Diocesan) Priests 1; Lay Teachers 2.

BAYAMON. *Casa Beato Pedro Donders* (Redemptorists) , Carretera 864 #127, Hato Tejas, 00959. Tel: 787-785-2867.

Centro Vocational Claretiano (Claretians) , Urb. Cana, Calle 24 esq. Calle 23 00957. Tel: 787-797-8230.

Convento Del Santisimo Rosario (Dominicans) , Calle Capitan Corpea N-27, Reparto Flamingo, P.O. Box 1968, 00960. Tel: 787-785-6542; Fax: 787-798-2712. P.O. Box 1968, 00960-1968.

Seminario Agustiniano Sto. Tomas De Villanueva, Carretera 830 km 5.1, Camino Los Muleros, Barrio Santaolaya. P.O. Box 3948, 00958. Tel: 787-797-0708; Fax: 787-797-9953. Email: d_aller@hotmail.com. Rev. Domingo Aller, O.S.A., Prior. (Augustinians) Priests 4; Brothers 1.

Seminario Misionero del Espiritu Santo (Holy Spirit Fathers) , Calle Zaya Verde #44-A, Hato Tejas, 00959. Tel: 787-786-8233; Fax: 787-787-2398. Email: opgcssp@caribe.net. Rev. Osualdo Perez Gonzalez, C.S.Sp., M.Div., Prin. Supr.

CATANO. *Prenoviciado Salesiano* (Don Bosco Salesians) , Ave. Flor Del Valle, Bloque BB #108, Urb. Las Vegas. Tel: 787-275-1921; Fax: 787-788-8163. Email: sanfasal@coqui.net. P.O. Box 567, 00963-8163. Tel: 787-275-1921. Rev. Adan Marrero, S.D.B.

DORADO. *Estudiantado Pasionista* (Passionists) , Carretera 695 km. 3.3, Sector Los Puertos, Barrio Higuillar. Tel: 787-278-0517. P.O. Box 593, 00646-0593. Rev. Ramon Gurtubay, C.P. (Spain), Supr. Priests 2; Students 6.

GUAYNABO. *Casa Padre Damian*, Calle P. Damian Final, Aptdo. 225, 00970-0225. Tel: 787-789-2014. Email: esparza@prtc.net. Priests 3.

RIO PIEDRAS. *Fraternidad San Lorenzo de Brindis* (Capuchin Postnovitiate) , Calle Arzuaga #216. Tel: 787-761-8060; Fax: 787-761-8410. P.O. Box 21350, 00928-1350.

Fraternidad Santa Maria de Los Angeles (Centro Capuchins) , Expreso Trujillo Alto, Km. 1 Hm. 1. Tel: 787-761-8060; 787-761-8410; Fax: 787-293-1682. Aptdo. 29882, 00929-0882. Rev. Roberto Martinez, O.F.M.Cap., Dir.; Bro. Jaime Perez Munoz, O.F.M.Cap.

Jesuit Community, 2106 Calle Jose Fidalgo Diaz, Sector Chapero, Bo. Caimito Bajo. Tel: 787-790-3557; Fax: 787-790-3162. R.R. 10, Buzon 5348, 00926-9675. Revs. Jorge R. Ambert, S.J., Supvr.; John F. Talbot, S.J.; Fabian Rodriguez, S.J.; Fernando A. Pico, S.J. Priests 4.

Seminario Mayor Regional San Juan Bautista (Diocesan) , Ave. De Diego No. 930, Urb. La Riviera, 00922-1714. Tel: 787-273-8090; 787-783-0645; Fax: 787-783-0645. Email: seminary@coqui.net. P.O. Box 11714, 00922-1714. Revs. Juan Luis Negron (CGS), Rector; Ivan L. Huertas-Colon, Vice Rector. Priests 9; Brothers 1; Lay Teachers 7; Total Staff 17.

SANTUCE. *Seminario San Vicente De Paul* (Vincentians) , C. Victoria 1658, Pda. 24. Tel: 787-727-4110. P.O. Box 19119, 00910.

TOA BAJA. *Post-Noviciado San Jose Obrero* (Franciscans) , Carretera 866 Km. 3.4, Sabana Seca. P.O. Box 173, Sabana Seca, 00952.

[D] SPECIAL CENTERS

SAN JUAN. *Renovacion Conyugal dba Fundacion Fernando Martinez*, 576 Calle Eddie Gracia, 00918. Tel: 787-751-6001; Fax: 787-766-1363. Email: ambertsj@aol.com. Web: www.renovacion.net. Rev. Jorge Ambert, S.J., Dir.

Santa Ana Chapel Perpetual Adoration , Calle Tetuan 203, Box 763, 00902. Tel: 787-725-7734. Rev. Jose Emilio Cummings, C.M., Rector.

PUERTO NUEVO. *San Gabriel School For The Deaf*, Prolongacion Calle 19 NE. Tel: 787-783-3455; Fax: 787-781-3770. P.O. 360347, 00936-0347. Sr. Amparo Blasco, Dir.

RIO PIEDRAS. *Centro De Espiritualidad Ignaciana Pedro Arrupe (CEIPA)*, Tel: 787-272-3524; Fax: 787-790-3162. Email: fabsj10@hotmail.com. Web: geocites.com/ceipasj. RR 10, Buzon 5348, 00926. Rev. Fabian Rodriguez, S.J., Dir.

Centro Universitario Catolico, 10 Mariana Bracetti St., 00925-2201. Tel: 787-767-3348; 787-763-5432. Email: coqui02@hotmail.com. Revs. Jose A. Borges, S.J., Dir.; Fernando Gomez, S.J., Coop.

[E] CLINICS, HEALTH CENTERS

SAN JUAN. *Casa La Providencia, Inc.* Drug Rehabilitation Center. Tel: 787-725-5358; Fax: 787-725-0058. Email: casalaprovidencia@hotmail.com. Web: casalaprovidencia.org. P.O. Box 9020614, 00902-0614. Tel: 787-725-5358; Fax: 787-725-0058. Sr. Adela Dominguez, Dir. Sisters Oblates of the Most Holy Redeemer 4; Bed Capacity 36; Annually Assisted 110; Total Staff 23.

Centro Medico de P.R., Calle 10 #1030, Puerto Nuevo, 00920. Apdo. 347, 00936. Tel: 787-763-7272. Rev. Antonio Jose Vazquez Colon (ARE), Vicario. Tel: 787-751-2335; Cell: 787-562-4065; Rev. Msgr. Angel Valdes, Hosp. Del Maestro. Tel: 787-765-1572; Revs. Francisco Arana, Chap., Hospital Oncologico. Tel: 787-251-6466; Pedro Luis Zaballa, Chap., Hospital Universitario; Manuel Garcia (Spain), Chap. Hospital Municipal. Tel: 787-796-3418; Bartolome Vanrell, Chap., Hospital Cardiovascular. Tel: 787-740-3425; Luis B. Rios, Hosp. San Pablo. Tel: 787-455-3599; Evaristo Oliveras, C.M., Hosp. Pavia, Santurce. Tel: 787-727-3963; Francisco Morales, Doctor's Hosp. Tel: 787-723-5998; Jesus Laraneta, Hosp. Auxilio Mutuo. Tel: 787-758-2000, Ext. 3024; Valeriano Miguelez (Spain), Hosp. Pavia, Hato Rey. Tel: 787-754-0570; Hector Diaz, Hosp. Veteranos. Tel: 787-641-7582, Ext. 3350; Neil Macaulay, O.M.I. (Canada), Hosp. Metropolitano. Tel: 787-782-4176; Luis Francisco Gonzalez, O.F.M.Cap., Hosp. San Francisco. Tel: 787-765-0606; Carlos Cordero, O.S.A., Hosp. Regional, Bayamon. Tel: 787-786-8611; Deacons Jose R. Rivera, Hosp. Pediatrico. Tel: 787-475-7849;

Andres Figueroa, Hosp. Pediatrico. Tel: 787-505-9973; Angel Pabon, Hosp. San Jorge, Santurce; Carlos Morales, Hosp. San Juan Capestrano. Tel: 787-757-2114.

VA Medical Center, 10 Calle Casia, 00921-3200. Tel: 787-641-3624; 787-641-7575. Email: luis.lopez_alvarado@med.va.org. Rev. Luis Lopez Alvardo (CGS), Chap. Bed Capacity 535.

BAYAMON. *Hospital Hermanos Melendez* Tel: 787-785-6542. Rev. Carlos Pijnenburg, O.P., Chap.

Hospital Matilde Brenes Tel: 787-785-2381. Rev. Angel A. Diaz Perez, O.P., Chap.

Hospital Regional Tel: 787-785-8611. Dr. Ramon Ruiz Arnau, Dir.; Rev. Gonzalo Gonzalez, O.S.A. (Spain), Chap.

Hospital San Pablo Tel: 787-785-2134. Deacon Hector Negron, Chap. Tel: 787-785-6874.

CAROLINA. *Hospital Regional* Tel: 787-752-5607. Rev. Jesus Garcia Rodriguez (Venezuela), Chap.

HATO REY. *Hospital Auxilio Mutuo* Tel: 787-758-2000, Ext. 3070; Fax: 787-771-7960. Web: www.auxiliomutuo.com. P.O. Box 1277, 00919. Rev. Jesus Larraneta, C.M., Chap. Bed Capacity 591; Total Staff 1,750.

Hospital Pavia, Ave. Ponce De Leon. Tel: 787-754-0570. Rev. Valeriano Miguelez (Spain).

RIO PIEDRAS. *Hospital del Maestro*, Calle Flamboyanes #218, Hyde Park, 00929. Tel: 787-763-8383. Rev. Msgr. Angel Valdes, Chap.

Hospital San Francisco Tel: 787-765-0606. Rev. Luis Gonzalez, O.F.M.Cap., Chap.

Hospital San Juan Capestrano Tel: 787-757-2114. Deacon Carlos Morales, Chap.

SANTURCE. *Doctor's Community Hospital* Tel: 787-723-5998. Rev. Francisco Morales, Chap.

Hospital Del Nino San Jorge Tel: 787-722-4158. Rev. Eddie Rivera, Chap.

Hospital Pavia Tel: 787-727-3963. Vincentian Fathers (Chaplains)

[F] HOMES AND RESIDENCES

SAN JUAN. *Casa La Providencia* (Drug Addicted Women) , Calle Norzagaray #200. Tel: 787-725-5358; Fax: 787-725-0058. Email: casalaprovidencia@hotmail.com. P.O. Box 9020614, 00902-0614. Sr. Adela Dominguez, Dir. Total Staff 23; Patients Assisted Annually 136.

Centro De Orientacion Vocacional Nuestra Senora del Consuelo (Teenagers/Single Mothers) , Floral Park, 20 C. Matienzo Citron, 00919. Tel: 787-250-6323; Fax: 787-250-6323. Email: oblaheher@coqui.net.

BAYAMON. *Hogar Del Nino "El Ave Maria"* (For Abused Children) , Carretera 861, km 2.0, Bo. Pajaros Americanos. Tel: 787-797-2382; 787-279-3003; Fax: 787-799-1977. Mailing Address: BMS 239 P.O. Box 607061, 00960-7061. Rev. Pedro Gorena, O.SS.T. (Spain), Dir.

Hogar Escuela Sor Maria Rafaela (Girls with Problems) , Carretera 871, km 1.0, Bo. El Volcan, Hato Tejas, 00961. Tel: 787-785-9586; Fax: 787-787-5324. Email: sormaria@caribe.net. P.O. Box 3024, PR 00961. Sr. Nelida Gonzalez, Dir.

Hogar Fatima (Girls) , Ave. Santa Juanita Final, Camino Esteban Cruz. Fax: 787-779-3999. Email: fatima001@prttc.net. Web: www.osrhogarfatimainc.com. P.O. Box 4228, Bayamon Garden Sta., Bayamon, 00958-4228. Tel: 787-787-2580; Fax: 787-787-2580. Sr. Maria Saez, Dir. Patients Assisted Annually 53; Staff 17.

CANOVANAS. *Hogar Teresa Toda* (For Girls) , P.O. Box 868, 00729. Tel: 787-886-2060; Fax: 787-886-2075. Email: htodapr@isla.net. Web: www.teresatodapr.org. Calle 5-A, R-14, Villas De Loiza, Loiza, 00729. Tel: 787-886-2060; Fax: 787-886-2075. Sr. Ines Pena, Dir.

DORADO. *Santuario del Espiritu Santo*, Box 187, 00646-0187. Tel: 787-796-2798; Fax: 787-796-1359. Email: espiritanos@espiritanos.com. Web: www.espiritanos.com. Revs. Eduardo Caron, C.S.Sp.; Jonas Rivera Martinez, C.S.Sp.; Orlando Camacho Torres, C.S.Sp.

PUERTA DE TIERRA. *Asylum For The Aged and Infirm* (Hogar de la Providencia) , Stop 5, 00906-6571. Tel: 787-722-1331; Fax: 787-725-4308. P.O. Box 9066571, 00906-6571. Sr. Ana Maria Hidalgo, Supr.; Rev. Ovidio Ortega, Chap. Sisters of the Poor Sisters 18; Patients Assisted Annually 203.

RIO PIEDRAS. *Asylum For Orphan Girls*, 107 Jose de Diego St., 00925. Tel: 787-765-6114. Sr. Virginia Torres, H.C., Supr.; Rev. Higinio Madrazo, C.M. (Spain), Chap. Daughters of Charity Sisters 15; Bed Capacity 70.

Centro N. Sra. de la Providencia Sisters of Notre Dame. , R.F.D. #2, Box 16T, 00928. Tel: 787-761-0273.

Centro Santa Luisa (Day Care Center for the Elderly) , Carretera 842, Camino Los Romeros km 1.9, Bo. Caimito, 00926. Tel: 787-720-2764; Fax: 787-731-7795. Email: centrosantaluisa@yahoo.com. Web: www.geocities.com/centrosantaluisa. RR6, Box 9492, 00926. Sr. Catalina Sanchez, H.C., Dir. Patients Assisted Annually 178; Staff 17.

Hogar Carmelitano Julian Bengochea Final (Elderly Retirement Hospice) , Urb. San Martin, 00924. Tel: 787-769-6510; 787-769-3110; Fax: 787-768-1240. Sr. Maribelle Mejias Muniz, Admin. Carmelite Sisters (Spain) Bed Capacity 224; Patients Assisted Annually 160; Total Staff 76.

Hogar Rafaela Ibarra (Orphan or Abused Girls) , Calle Torrelaguna 432, 00926. Tel: 787-763-1204; Fax: 787-763-6266. Email: hrybarra@coqui.net. Web: www.hogaresrafaelaybarra.com. 432 Calle Torrelaguna, 00923-1773. Sr. Julia Jose, Dir. Patients Assisted Annually 90; Staff 21.

Hogar Santa Teresa Jornet for the Aged, Cupey Alto, Ave. Las cumbres, Km. 3, Hm. 8. Tel: 787-761-5805; Fax: 787-755-5575. P.O. Box 21012, 00928. Sr. Gladys Rosario Gomez, Mother Supr.; Rev. Jose Maria Lopez, Chap. Sisters of the Poor Sisters 18; Bed Capacity 215; Residents 215; Total Staff 80.

SANTURCE. *Casa Manuel Fernandez Juncos* (Orphans and Abused Boys) , Calle Villa Verde Esq. Refugio, PdA 11, Miramar. Tel: 787-724-2904; 787-725-6328; Fax: 787-724-0908. P.O. Box 9020163, 00902-0163. Revs. Vicente Gregori Costa, RR.T.C.; Candido Lizarraga, RR.T.C.; Bros. Eliecer Balladares; Abner Hiram Picon; Deacon Pablo Osorio Carmona. Total Staff 22.

Politecnico Amigo (For School Dropout Boys) , Calle Refugio #960, Pda II. Tel: 787-725-2059; Fax: 787-722-3436. Email: polam@prtc.net. P.O. Box 13204, 00908.

TOA ALTA. *Hogar Santisima Trinidad* (Drug Addiction Rehabilitation Home) , Lote A y Lote D, km 7.0, Bo Mucarabones, Carr. 861. Tel: 787-799-6208; Fax: 787-799-1977. BMS 326 P.O. Box 607061, Bayamon, 00960-7061. Rev. Pedro Gorena, O.SS.T. (Spain). Patients Assisted Annually 91; Total Staff 15.

TOA BAJA. *Hogar Divino Nino Jesus (Drug Addict Rehabilitation)*, Carretera 854, Km. 3.5. Tel: 787-794-0020; Fax: 787-794-0020. Email: divinoninojesus@yahoo.es. P.O. Box 2464, 00951. Julio Pachelo, Dir.

[G] PERSONAL PRELATURES

GUAYNABO. *Opus Dei* (Prelature of the Holy Cross and Opus Dei), Region of Puerto Rico of the Prelature , Calle Josemaria Escriva 35, Urb. Villa Caparra, 00966. Tel: 787-783-6206; Fax: 787-783-1201. Email: prricoinfo@coqui.net. Very Rev. Vicente Ariza, Regl. Vicar; Revs. Alfredo Gastalver; Gonzalo Diaz; Martin Llambias; Jaime Guixa; Andres Eiroa Sanchez.

[H] MONASTERIES AND RESIDENCES FOR PRIESTS AND BROTHERS

SAN JUAN. *The Capuchin Formation Trust of Puerto Rico*

Capuchin Health and Retirement Trust of Puerto Rico

Legal Title: *Asociacion Frailes Capuchinos, Inc.*

Comunidad Jesuita, Colegio San Ignacio, Urb. Santa Maria, 1940 Calle Sauco, 00927-6718. Tel: 787-758-1717, Ext. 1721; Fax: 787-750-8640. Revs. Jose R. Aponte, S.J., Supr.; Jose A. Borges, S.J.; Jorge Ferrer, S.J.; Francisco J. Marrero, S.J.; Mario A. Torres, S.J.; Donald M. Vega, S.J.

The Viceprovince of Saint John the Baptist, Puerto Rico, of the Order Friars Minor Capuchin (1905), 216 Arzuaga St., P.O. Box 21350, 00928-1350. Tel: 787-764-3090; Fax: 787-764-4070. Bros. Alberto Figueroa Morales, O.F.M.Cap., Vice Prov. Min.; Roy F. Martinez Negron, O.F.M.Cap., First Councillor; Ramon H. Negron Cruz, O.F.M.Cap., Second Councillor; Jorge Macias de Cespedes, O.F.M.Cap., Vice Prov. Sec. & Treas. & Dir. Capuchin Mass Assoc.

Legal Title: *Asociacion De Frailes Capuchinos, Inc.; Asociacion Misionera Capuchina; Capuchin Formation Trust of Puerto Rico; Capuchin Health and Retirement Trust of Puerto Rico* Friars 27; Postulants 3.

HATO REY. *Jesuit Community - Casa Claver*, 398 Francisco Sein, 00917. Tel: 787-759-7654; Fax: 787-790-3162. Apto. 22634 U.P.R. Sta., 00931-2634. Rev. Fernando Pico, S.J.

Casa Spinola De Angelis

Urb. Baldrich, 580 Hostos Ave.. Tel: 787-282-8522; Fax: 787-282-6087. Revs. Alberto Villa Verde, S.J.; Juan J. Santiago, S.J.; Rafael Rodriguez, S.J.

TRUJILLO ALTO. *Carmelite Monastery of St. Joseph* (1651), (Monasterio Carmelita De San Jose) , 00977-0568. Tel: 787-761-9548; Fax: 787-283-7235. Email: mcsjose@prdigital.com. P.O. Box 568, 00977-0568. Sr. Rosa M. Estremera, O.Carm., Prioress.

[I] MISCELLANEOUS

SAN JUAN. *Casa San Clemente* (Spiritual, Personal, Pastoral, and Psychological Counseling) , Ave. Ponce De Leon 257, Puerta De Tierra, 00901. Tel: 787-723-6915; Fax: 787-977-8156. P.O. Box 9066315, 00906-6315. Rev. Terence Damian Wall, C.SS.R., S.T.D. (CGS), Exec. Dir.; Bro. Mateo Perez, C.SS.R., Ph.D.; Ms. Ela Iglesias, Exec. Dir.

Centro Sor Isolina, R.R. 6, Box 9541, 00928. Tel: 787-731-5700; Fax: 787-272-3390. Email: sister@prtc.net. Mrs. Lourdes M. Ortiz, M.T.S. (Social Improvement of the Poor)

Hogar Buen Pastor (Homeless Shelter) , Ave. Ponce De Leon #250, Pueroa De Tierra, 00901. Tel: 787-721-8579. P.O. Box 9066547, 00906-6547. Sr. Rose Mary Gonzalez, S.S.N.D.

MEDIANIA ALTA, LOIZA. *Centro Esperanza, Inc.*, 1st St., Parcelas Vieques Development, 00772. Tel: 787-876-1545; Fax: 787-876-1545. Email: cesperanza@coqui.net. P.O. Box 482, Loiza, 00772-0482. Tel: 787-876-1545. Sr. Carmen Gloria Alayon, H.C., Dir. & Contact Person. Sponsored by: Sisters of Charity, Saint Vincent de Paul.

RIO PIEDRAS. *Paulinas Multimedia* (Books, Cassettes and Catholic Publications) , Calle Arzuaga # 164, 00925-3322. Tel: 787-764-4885; 787-765-4390; Fax: 787-767-6214. Email: paulinas@yunque.net. Web: www.paulinaspr.com.

SANTURCE. *Beth Yash'ah* (Spiritual and Psychological Counseling) , 1708 Calle Pumarada, 00912. Tel: 787-763-6708; 787-268-2661; 787-727-4100; Fax: 787-268-2661. Dr. Lucy Lopez-Roig, Dir.; Dr. Cecilia Arias.

Fondita De Jesus (Supportive, spiritual and psychosocial services and transitional/permanent housing) , Calle Monserrate 704, PDA 16 1/2. Tel: 787-724-4051; Fax: 787-722-0992. Email: lfdj@coqui.net. P.O. Box 19384, 00910-1384. Maria M. Juanarena, Exec. Dir. Total Assisted 3,100.

Servicios Pastorales Paules (Books, Leaflets and Catholic Publications) , P.O. Box 19118, 00910. Rev. Juan Javier Inigo, C.M., Dir.

RELIGIOUS INSTITUTES OF MEN REPRESENTED IN THE ARCHDIOCESE

For further details refer to the corresponding bracketed number in the Religious Institutes of Men or Women section.

[0140]—*Augustinian Friars* (Spain)—O.S.A.
[0470]—*The Capuchin Friars* (Vice Prov. of Puerto Rico)—O.F.M.Cap
[0270]—*Carmelite Fathers & Brothers* (Prov. of Aragon, Valentina, Spain)—O.Carm.
[0360]—*Claretian Missionaries* (Spain)—C.M.F.
[0310]—*Congregation of Christian Brothers* (Antilles Prov.)—C.F.C.
[0820]—*Congregation of the Fathers of Mercy* (Madrid, Spain)—C.P.M.
[1330]—*Congregation of the Mission* (Prov. of Puerto Rico)—C.M.
[1000]—*Congregation of the Passion* (Bibao)—C.P.
[]—*Congregation of the Sacred Heart* (Spain)—C.SS.CC.
[]—*Congregation of the Terciarios Capuchinos Ntra. Sra. de los Dolores* (Spain)—T.C.
[0520]—*Franciscan Friars* (Spain)—O.F.M.
[0650]—*Holy Ghost Fathers* (American Prov.)—C.S.Sp.
[0690]—*Jesuit Fathers and Brothers* (Prov. of Puerto Rico)—S.J.
[0740]—*Marian Fathers*—M.I.C.
[0770]—*The Marist Brothers*—F.M.S.
[1120]—*Missionaries of the Sacred Hearts of Jesus and Mary* (Spain)—M.SS.CC.
[0840]—*Missionary Servants of the Most Holy Trinity*—S.T.
[0910]—*Oblates of Mary Immaculate* (Peru Prov.)—O.M.I.
[0430]—*Order of Preachers-Dominicans* (Gen. Vicariate of P.R.)—O.P.
[1310]—*Order of the Holy Trinity* (Spain)—O.SS.T.
[1040]—*Piarist Fathers* (Spain)—Sch.P.
[1070]—*Redemptorist Fathers* (San Juan Prov.)—C.SS.R.
[1190]—*Salesians of Don Bosco* (Antilles Prov.)—S.D.B.
[0760]—*Society of Mary* (New York Prov.)—S.M.
[0975]—*Society of Our Lady of the Most Holy Trinity*—S.O.L.T.

RELIGIOUS INSTITUTES OF WOMEN REPRESENTED IN THE ARCHDIOCESE

[1070-06]—*Dominican Sisters*—O.P.
[1070-05]—*Dominican Sisters*—O.P.
[1070-13]—*Dominican Sisters*—O.P.
[]—*Dominicanas Terciarieas del Santisimo Sacramento* (Cadiz, Spain)
[]—*Eumen Dei* (Madrid, Spain)—U.L.D.

[]—*Hermanas Carmelitas de la Caridad* (Rome, Italy)—C.ach.
[]—*Hermanas Carmelitas de Madre Candelaria (Venezuela)*
[]—*Hermanas Carmelitas Teresas de San Jose (Barcelona, Spain)*
[]—*Hermanas de la Amistad Misionera en Cristo Obrero* (Amico and Madrid, Spain)
[]—*Hermanas de la B.V. Maria del Monte Carmelo* (Madrid, Spain)—H.Carm.
[]—*Hermanas de la Caridad del Cardenal Sancha* (San Domingo)—HCCS
[]—*Hermanas de la Caridad Del Sagrado Corazon De Jesus* (Madrid, Spain)
[]—*Hermanas de la Compania del Salvador* (Spain)
[]—*Hermanas de Santos Angeles Custodios* (Bilbao, Spain)
[]—*Hermanas Dominicas de la Presentacion* (Tours, France; Colombia)
[]—*Hermanas Dominicas de Nuestra Senora del Rosario de Fatima* (Yauco)
[]—*Hermanas Hospitalarias de Jesus Nazareno* (Cordoba, Spain)
[]—*Hermanas Mercedarias de la Caridad* (Madrid, Spain)
[]—*Hermanas Misioneras de la Madre Dolorosa y San Francisco de Asis* Buga, Colombia
[]—*Hermanas Misioneras de los Sagrados Corazones* (Palma de Mallorca, Spain)
[]—*Hermanitas de los Ancianos Desamparados* (Valencia, Spain)
[]—*Hermans De La Divina Providencia* (Rome, Italy)—CDP
[]—*Hijas de Maria Auxiliadora* (Torino, Italy)
[]—*Hijas Del Corazon Misericordioso De Maria* (Bogota, Colombia)
[0950]—*Instituto Misionero Hijas de San Pablo* (Rome, Italy)
[]—*Instituto Santa Mariana de Jesus Hermanas Marianites)* (Ecuador)—R.M.
[]—*Madres de Desamparados y San Jose de la Montana* (Valencia, Spain)
[]—*Madres Escolapis* (Rome)
[]—*Misioneras de Cristo Salvador*
[2710]—*Misioneras De La Capidad* (Calcutta, India)—M.C.
[]—*Misioneras del Buen Pastor* (San Juan)
[]—*Misioneras del Santisimo Sacramento y Maria Inmaculada* (Spain)
[]—*Misioneras Dominicas del Santisimo Rosario* (Madrid, Spain)
[2720]—*Mission Helpers of the Sacred Heart*—M.H.S.H.
[2790]—*Missionary Servants of the Most Blessed Trinity* (Philadelphia, PA)—M.S.B.T.
[]—*Monjas de la Orden de la Bienventurada Virgen Maria de Monte Carmelo*—O.Carm.
[]—*Oblates De La Santisima Trinidad* (Spain)
[]—*Oblates del Santisimo Redenteor* (Madrid, Spain)
[]—*Operarias Del Divino Maestro* (Valencia, Spain)
[]—*Religiosas del Sagrado Corazon* (Rome, Italy)
[]—*Religiosas Oblates del Divino Amor*
[]—*Religiosas Teatinas de la Inmaculada Concepcion* (Rome)—R.T.
[]—*Religiosas Terciarias de San Francisco de Asis y de la Inmaculada Concepcion* (Valencia, Spain)
[2970]—*School Sisters of Notre Dame* (Wilton, CT)—S.S.N.D.
[]—*Siervas De La Verdad* (Bayamon, Puerto Rico)
[3600]—*Siervas de Maria y Ministras de los Enfermos* (Rome, Italy)—S.M.
[2570]—*Sisters of Mercy* (Pittsburgh, PA)—R.S.M.
[1620]—*Sisters of Saint Francis of Millvale, Pennsylvania*—O.S.F.
[1650]—*Sisters of St. Francis of Philadelphia*—O.S.F.
[1800]—*Sisters of St. Francis of the Third Order Regular* (Williamsville, New York)—O.S.F.
[3830]—*Sisters of St. Joseph* (Brentwood)—C.S.J.
[3930]—*Sisters of St. Joseph of the Third Order of St. Francis*—S.S.J.-T.O.S.F.
[1970]—*Sisters of the Holy Family of Nazareth*—C.S.F.N.
[1490]—*Sisters of the Third Franciscan Order*—O.S.F.
[2150]—*Sisters, Servants of the Immaculate Heart of Mary*—I.H.M.
[]—*Terciarias Franciscanas de la Purisima* (Murcia, Spain)

NECROLOGY

† Miranda, Rev. Msgr. Juan, San Juan, PR Nuestra Sra. de Guadalupe—Died Nov. 8, 2003
† Gutierrez, Julio, (Retired)—Died 2003

American Foreign Missions

AUGUSTINIAN MISSIONS (O.S.A.)

Foreign Missions of the Midwestern Provinces of the Order of St. Augustine (O.S.A.)

Foreign Missions

Provincial Headquarters

Province of Our Mother of Good Counsel (Midwestern): *Tolentine Center,* 20300 Governors Highway, Olympia Fields, IL 60461-1081. Phone: 708-748-5435; Fax: 708-481-2090. Very Rev. David L. Brecht, O.S.A. Ord: '65, Prov. Bro. John J. Stobba, O.S.A., Mission Procurator.

Midwestern Augustinian Religious serving in Foreign Missions: Most Rev. Daniel T. Turley, O.S.A. Ord: '68, Peru; Revs. Alfred M. Burke, O.S.A. Ord: '57, Japan; Charles J. Bodden, O.S.A. Ord: '78, Peru; John J. Dowling, O.S.A. Ord: '68, Peru; Richard Palmer, O.S.A. Ord: '87, Peru; John P. Tasto, O.S.A. Ord: '67, Mexico; John A. Tyma, O.S.A. Ord: '59, Peru; Christopher C. Steinle, O.S.A. Ord: '98, Peru.

Province of St. Thomas of Villanova (Eastern): P.O. Box 340, Villanova, PA 19085-0340. Phone: 610-525-3330; Fax: 610-520-0618. Very Rev. Donald F. Reilly, O.S.A. Ord: '74, Prior Prov.; Revs. Richard D. Appicci, O.S.A. Ord: '60, Dir. Missions. Anthony P. Burrascano, O.S.A. Ord: '79, Mission Procurator.

U.S. Religious serving in Foreign Missions: Revs. John J. Lydon, O.S.A. Ord: '84; Maurice J. Mahoney, O.S.A. Ord: '60; Thomas P. Dwyer, O.S.A. Ord: '53; Aquilino D. Gonzalez, O.S.A. Ord: '72; Robert P. Terranova, O.S.A. Ord: '73; Michael J. Hilden, O.S.A. Ord: '73; Edward V. Hattrick, O.S.A. Ord: '56; Thomas P. Purcell, O.S.A. Ord: '43.

AMERICAN BENEDICTINE FOREIGN MISSIONS (O.S.B.)

American - Cassinese Congregation Foreign Missions

St. Vincent Archabbey: 300 Fraser Purchase Rd., Latrobe, PA 15650-2690. Phone: 724-532-6600. Rt. Rev. Douglas R. Nowicki, O.S.B. Ord: '72, Archabbot; Rev. Noel H. Rothrauff, O.S.B. Ord: '54, Mission Dir.

U.S. Religious serving in Taiwan: Bros. Nicholas Koss, O.S.B. Prior; David Liang Ho, O.S.B.

St. John's Abbey: Box 2015, Collegeville, MN 56321-2015. Fax: 320-363-3082.

U.S. Religious serving Abroad: Revs. Kieran Nolan, O.S.B. Ord: '59, Japan; Neal Henry Lawrence, O.S.B. Ord: '60, Japan; Fintan Bromenshenkel, O.S.B. Ord: '45, Nassau; George Wolf, O.S.B. Ord: '44, Nassau; Thomas Wahl, O.S.B. Ord: '58, Japan; Cyprian Weaver, O.S.B. Ord: '72, Taiwan.

St. Benedict's Abbey: Atchison, KS 66002. Phone: 913-367-7853; Fax: 913-367-6230. Rt. Rev. Barnabas Senecal, O.S.B., Abbot.

U.S. Religious serving in Brazil: Most Rev. Herbert Hermes; Revs. Kieran McInerney, O.S.B. Ord: '52; Denis Meade, O.S.B. Ord: '55; Duane Roy, O.S.B. Ord: '67.

St. Procopius Abbey: 5601 College Rd., Lisle IL 60532. Phone: 630-969-6410; Fax: 630-969-6426. Very Rev. Alban Hrebic, O.S.B. Ord: '52, Prior.

U.S. Religious serving in China: Very Rev. Alban Hrebic, O.s.B. Ord: '52, Prior.

Assumption Abbey: P.O. Box A, Richardton, ND 58652. Phone: 701-974-3315.

U.S. Religious serving in South America: Very Rev. Philip Vanderlin, O.S.B. Ord: '80, Prior; Revs. Gonzalo Blanco, O.S.B., Subprior; Efraim Villegas, O.S.B. Ord: '88; Carlos Suarez, O.S.B. Ord: '86; Francis Wehri, O.S.B. Ord: '61; Gonzalo Blanco, O.S.B. Ord: '92; Nicolas Cano Ord: '97; Bros. Fabio Mejia; Manuel Cely; Roberto Duarte.

St. Paul's Abbey: Newton, NJ 07860-0007. Phone: 973-383-2470; Fax: 973-383-5782.

U.S. Religious serving Abroad: Revs. Damian Milliken, O.S.B. Ord: '58, Tanzania; Peter W. Blue, O.S.B. Ord: '70, Namibia.

Blue Cloud Abbey: Marvin, SD 57251. Phone: 605-398-9200; Fax: 605-398-9201. Rt. Rev. Thomas Hillenbrand Ord: '65, Supr. & Mission Dir.

U.S. Religious serving in Guatemala: Revs. Basil Dilger, O.S.B. Ord: '61; Cletus Miller, O.S.B. Ord: '44; Bernardine Ness, O.S.B. Ord: '64.

Swiss-American – Congregation Foreign Missions

Mount Angel Abbey: St. Benedict, OR 97373. Phone: 503-845-3030; Fax: 503-845-3594.

U.S. Religious serving in Mexico: Very Rev. Konrad Shaefer, O.S.B. Ord: '80; Bro. James Bartos, O.S.B.

Marmion Abbey: Aurora, IL 60504.

U.S. Religious serving in Central America: Very Rev. John Brahill, O.S.B. Ord: '82, Prior; Revs. Matthias Zinkan, O.S.B. Ord: '40.

AMERICAN CAPUCHIN MISSIONS (O.F.M.CAP.)

Missions of the American Provinces of the Order of Friars Minor Capuchin (The Capuchin Friars) in the United States and other countries.

General Headquarters: Via Piemonte, 70, 00187, Rome, Italy. Most Rev. John Corriveau, O.F.M.Cap., Gen. Min.; Rev. Linus Faeh, O.F.M.Cap., Sec. Gen. for the Missions.

Provincial Headquarters

Capuchin Foreign Missions

Province of St. Joseph: 1740 Mt. Elliott Ave., Detroit, MI 48207. Fax: 313-579-2275. Revs. Daniel Anholzer, O.F.M.Cap. Ord: '80, Prov. Minister; James Zelinski, O.F.M.Cap. Ord: '61, Mission Sec.

U.S. Religious serving Abroad: Revs. Evarist Bertrand, O.F.M.Cap. Ord: '63, Nicaragua; Paul Craig, O.F.M.Cap. Ord: '66, Middle East; Francis Solanus Fary, O.F.M.Cap. Ord: '67, Nicaragua; Ralph Fellenz, O.F.M.Cap. Ord: '68, Panama; Carmel Flora, O.F.M.Cap. Ord: '53, Australia; Glenn Gessner, O.F.M.Cap. Ord: '60, Nicaragua; Kevin Heagerty, O.F.M.Cap. Ord: '61, Panama; Walter Kasuboski, O.F.M.Cap. Ord: '74, Panama; Wilbert Lanser, O.F.M.Cap. Ord: '59, Nicaragua; Benjamin Markwell, O.F.M.Cap. Ord: '66, Middle East; John Myers, O.F.M.Cap. Ord: '54, Australia; Theodore Niehaus, O.F.M.Cap. Ord: '65, Nicaragua; Most Rev. Paul Schmitz, O.F.M.Cap. Ord: '70, Bishop-Vicar Apostolic of Bluefields, Nicaragua; Revs. August Seubert, O.F.M.Cap. Ord: '57, Nicaragua; Jozef Timmers, O.F.M. Cap. Ord. '00, Panama; Bernard Wagner, O.F.M.Cap. Ord: '63, Nicaragua; Lawrence Webber, O.F.M.Cap. Ord: '80, Honduras; Andre Weller, O.F.M.Cap. Ord: '63, Panama; Nicholas Widhammer, O.F.M.Cap. Ord: '63, Middle East; Joseph Wolf, O.F.M.Cap. Ord: '64, Nicaragua; Most Rev. David Zywiec, O.F.M.Cap. Ord: '74, Auxiliary Bishop, Vicariate of Bluefields, Nicaragua.

Province of Mid-America: 3553 Wyandot St., Denver, CO 80211-2948. Phone: 303-477-0296; Fax: 303-477-6925. Revs. Michael Scully, O.F.M.Cap. Ord: '65, Prov. Min.; Mark Schenk, O.F.M.Cap., Mission Sec.

U.S. Religious serving in Papua New Guinea: (St. Michael the Archangel Vice Provice of Papua New Guinea and the Solomon Islands) Most Rev. Stephen Reichert, O.F.M.Cap. Ord: '69, Bishop of Mendi; Revs. Peter Meis, O.F.M.Cap. Ord: '67; Donald Debes, O.F.M.Cap. Ord: '70; Bro. Gerald Wintz, O.F.M.Cap.

U.S. Religious serving in Mexico: Rev. William Kraus, O.F.M.Cap. Ord: '73.

Province of St. Augustine: 220 37th St., Pittsburgh, PA 15201. Phone: 412-682-6011; Fax: 412-682-0506. Very Rev. Paul Kuppe, O.F.M.Cap. Ord: '70, Prov. Min. Rev. Francis Fugini, O.F.M.Cap. Ord: '54, Coord. of Misssions.

U.S. Religious serving in Papua New Guinea (St. Michael the Archangel Vice Province of Papua New Guinea and the Solomon Islands): Revs. Cyril Repko, O.F.M.Cap. Ord: '62, Vice-Prov.; Emilio Biosca, O.F.M.Cap. Ord: '94; Samuel Driscoll, O.F.M.Cap. Ord: '59; William Fey, O.F.M.Cap. Ord: '68; Dunstan Jones, O.F.M.Cap. Ord: '61; Benjamin Madden, O.F.M.Cap. Ord: '58; Brian Newman, O.F.M.Cap. Ord: '61 Colman Studeny, O.F.M.Cap. Ord: '61; William Talentino, O.F.M.Cap. Ord: '67; Allan Wasiecko, O.F.M.Cap. Ord: '68; Roger White, O.F.M.Cap. Ord: '65; Jonathan Williams, O.F.M.Cap. Ord: '71; Bro. Raymond Ronan, O.F.M.Cap.

U.S. Religious serving in Puerto Rico (St. John the Baptist Vice Province): Rev. Mario Mastrangelo, O.F.M.Cap. Ord: '58.

Province of St. Mary: 30 Gedney Park Dr., White Plains, NY 10605. Phone: 914-761-3008. Very Rev. Michael Banks, O.F.M.Cap. Ord: '84, Prov.; Rev. Francis Gasparik, O.F.M.Cap. Ord: '86, Mission Sec.

U.S. Religious serving in Guam: Revs. Lee G. Friel, O.F.M.Cap. Ord: '56; George Maddock, O.F.M.Cap. Ord: '64; Randolph Nowak, O.F.M.Cap. Ord: '52; Robert Phelps, O.F.M.Cap. Ord: '66; Bro. Brian Champoux, O.F.M.Cap.

U.S. Religious serving in Japan: Revs. Wayne Berndt, O.F.M.Cap. Ord: '83; Louis Chiusano, O.F.M.Cap. Ord: '57; Roland Daigle, O.F.M.Cap. Ord: '84; Peter Von Essen, O.F.M.Cap. Ord: '56; John Szamreta, O.F.M.Cap. Ord: '81; Bartholomew Minson, O.F.M.Cap. Ord: '64; LaSalle Parsons, O.F.M.Cap. Ord: '57; Bro. Martin de Porres Schmitt, O.F.M.Cap.

U.S. Religious serving in Central America: Revs. John Clermont, O.F.M.Cap. Ord: '53, Honduras; Raymond Richard, O.F.M.Cap. Ord: '72, Honduras.

The Seraphic Mass Association-Capuchin Mission Association: St. Mary's Province, 210 West 31st St., New York, NY 10001-2876.

This Association supports the Capuchin Foreign Mission.

AMERICAN CARMELITE MISSIONS (O.CARM)

Carmelite Foreign Missions

Foreign Missions of the American Province of the Most Pure Heart of Mary

Provincial Headquarters: Carmelite Provincial Office, 1317 Frontage Rd., Darien, IL 60561. Fax: 630-971-0195. Very Rev. John F. Russell, O.Carm. Ord: '60, Prov.

Mission Office: Carmelite Missions, 8501 Bailey Rd., Darien, IL 60561-8418. Phone: 630-969-5220; Fax: 630-969-5266. Very Rev. John Malley, O.Carm. Ord: '56, Mission Dir.

U.S. Religious serving in Peru: Revs. Kevin Lafey, O.Carm. Ord: '72; Alban Quinn, O.Carm. Ord: '49; Most Rev. Michael LaFay, O.Carm. Ord: '60; Revs. James Geaney, O.Carm. Ord: '59; Enrique Laguna, O.Carm. Ord: '90; Edward Adelmann, O.Carm. Ord: '75.

U.S. Religious serving in Mexico: Revs. John Hertel, O.Carm., Ord: '53; Thomas Jordan, O.Carm. Ord: '70; Joel Moelter, O.Carm. Ord: '51; William Smith, O.Carm. Ord: '54; Thomas Alkire, O.Carm. Ord: '63.

COMBONI MISSIONARIES (VERONA FATHERS) (M.C.C.J.)

Comboni Foreign Missions

Legal Title: *Comboni Missionaries of the Heart of Jesus, Inc.*

U.S. Headquarters: Comboni Mission Center, 1318 Nagel Rd., Cincinnati, OH 45255-3120. Phone: 513-474-4997; Fax: 513-474-0382. Revs. Dennis Conway, M.C.C.J. Ord: '68, Prov. Supr.; Joseph Bragotti, M.C.C.J. Ord: '62, Mission Dir. E-mail: info@combonimissionaries.org.

U.S. Religious Serving Abroad: Revs. Albert Anichini, M.C.C.J. Ord: '62, Uganda; Manuel Baeza, M.C.C.J. Ord: '96, South Africa; David Baltz, M.C.C.J. Ord: '67, Uganda; Michael Barton, M.C.C.J. Ord: '75, Sudan; David Bohnsack, M.C.C.J. Ord: '94, Sudan; Angel Camorlinga, M.C.C.J. Ord: '96, Ecuador; James Francez, M.C.C.J. Ord: '57, Mexico; Raymond Pax, M.C.C.J. Ord: '65, Sudan; John Converset, M.C.C.J. Ord: '71, South Africa.

AMERICAN CONVENTUAL FRANCISCAN MISSIONS (O.F.M.CONV.)

Conventual Franciscan Foreign Missions

General Headquarters: Convento SS. XII Apostoli Piazza SS. Apostoli 51, 00187, Roma, Italia. Most Rev. Tadeusz Swiatkowski, O.F.M.Conv. Sec. Gen. for the Missions.

Provincial Headquarters

Province of the Immaculate Conception: P.O. Box 629, 517 Washington Ave., Rensselaer, NY 12144. Very Rev. Canice Connors, O.F.M.Conv. Ord: '61, Prov. & Mission Dir. Phone: 518-472-1000.

U.S. Religious serving Abroad: Revs. Bertrand Hodes, O.F.M.Conv. Ord: '39; Maury Marhafer, O.F.M.Conv. Ord: '54; Andre John Lambert, O.F.M.Conv. Ord: '54; Most Rev. Elias Manning, O.F.M.Conv. Bishop of Valenca, Brazil.

Province of Saint Anthony of Padua: Provincial House & Office of Mission Procurator, 12300 Folly Quarter Rd., Ellicott City, MD 21042-1419. Phone: 410-531-9200; Fax: 410-531-4881. Very Rev. Michael Kolodziej, O.F.M.Conv. Ord: '70, Minister Prov. Rev. Martin Kobos, O.F.M.Conv. Ord: '76, Mission Procurator.

Franciscan Mission Association: 12300 Fully Seuarter Rd., Ellicott City, MD 21042. Prov. Rev. Martin Kobos, O.F.M.Conv. Ord: '76, Mission Dir.

U.S. Religious serving Abroad: Revs. David Blowey, O.F.M.Conv. Ord: '87, Kenya; Vincent Lachendro, O.F.M.Conv. Ord: '63, Japan; Dominic Slemba, O.F.M.Conv. Ord: '51, Ghana. Giles Zakowicz, O.F.M.Conv. Ord: '75, Ghana.

Province of Our Lady of Consolation: Provincial Office, Mt. St. Francis, IN 47146. Rev. Peter Dauian Massengill, O.F.M.Conv. Ord: '67, Min. Prov.

Religious serving Abroad: Revs. Juniper Cummings, O.F.M.Conv. Ord: '50, Vicar Custos; Kamil Wenzel, O.F.M.Conv. Ord: '66, Zambia; Efisio Steri, O.F.M.Conv. Ord: '60, Zambia; Werner Iten, O.F.M.Conv. Ord: '74, Zambia; Emil Cook, O.F.M.Conv. Ord: '66, Honduras; Ronald Roll, O.F.M.Conv. Ord: '80, Honduras; Pius Uitendaal, O.F.M.Conv. Ord: '63, Zambia; Terence Tobin, O.F.M.Conv. Ord: '55, Zambia; Mark Weaver, O.F.M.Conv. Ord: '77; Honduras; Fritz O'Kelly, O.F.M.Conv. Ord: '56, Zambia; Jude Rochford, O.F.M.Conv. Ord: '55, Zambia. Bros. Joseph Weissling, O.F.M.Conv., Guardian; John Doyle, O.F.M.Conv., Zambia; Anthony Droll, O.F.M.Conv., Zambia.

Province of Saint Bonaventure: Provincial Office, 6107 N. Kenmore Ave., Chicago, IL 60660-2797. Phone: 773-274-7681; Fax: 773-274-9751. Very Rev. Anthony Labedis, O.F.M.Conv. Ord: '60, Minister Prov.

U.S. Religious serving Abroad: Revs. John Calgaro, O.F.M.Conv. Ord: '74, Mexico; Abraham Crisostomo, O.F.M.Conv. Ord: '96; Bros. Paschal Metzger, O.F.M.Conv., Mexico; Stanislaus Zabkiewicz, O.F.M.Conv., Zambia.

CROSIER FATHERS MISSIONS (O.S.C.)

Crosier Foreign Missions

Crosier Fathers and Brothers: (Canons Regular of the Order of the Holy Cross)

U.S. Address: Crosier Missions, 3510 Vivian Ave., St. Paul, MN 55126-3852. Phone: 651-486-7456; Fax: 651-287-1130. Very Rev. Thomas Carkhuff, O.S.C. Ord: '76, Prov.; Mr. David Kostik, Mission Coord.

U.S. Religious serving Abroad: Revs. Ernest Martello, O.S.C. Ord: '70, Congo; Virgil Petermeier, O.S.C. Ord: '77, Indonesia; Robert Rossi, O.S.C. Ord: '70, Congo.

AMERICAN DIVINE WORD MISSIONARIES (S.V.D.)

Society of the Divine Word Foreign Missions

Missions of the American Provinces of the Society of the Divine Word (S.V.D.) commonly known as Divine Word Missionaries.

Latin: Societas Verbi Divini

Provincial Headquarters in the U.S.A.

*Chicago Province:*Society of the Divine Word-Province of Blessed Joseph Freinademetz, S.V.D., 1985 Waukegan Rd., P.O. Box 6038, Techny IL 60082-6038. Phone: 847-272-2700; Fax: 847-272-2517. Very Rev. Thomas A. Krosnicki, S.V.D. Ord: '66, Prov. Supr.; Bro. Dennis Newton, S.V.D., Mission Dir. for all three Provinces.

Publication: *Divine Word Missionaries*

*Southern Province:*Society of the Divine Word-Province of St. Augustine, 201 Ruella Ave., Bay St. Louis, MS 39520-4638. Phone: 228-467-4322. Very Rev. Clifton Labbe, S.V.D. Ord: '69, Prov. Supr.

*Western Province:*Society of the Divine Word, P.O. Box 7195, Los Angeles, CA 90007. Phone: 323-735-8130. Very Rev. Joseph A. Miller, S.V.D. Ord: '68, Prov. Supr.

American Divine Word Missionaries in Overseas Missions: Revs. Thomas Ascheman, S.V.D. Ord: '82, Italy; Daniel Bauer, S.V.D. Ord: '74, Taiwan; Francis Beemsterboer, S.V.D. Ord: '51, Ghana; Andrew Biller, S.V.D. Ord: '61, Philippines; Joseph Bisson, S.V.D. Ord: '63, Papua New Guinea; Michael Blume, S.V.D. Ord: '72, Rome; Bro. William Brennan, S.V.D., Australia; Revs. Francis Budenholzer, S.V.D. Ord: '72, Taiwan; Most Rev. John Bukovsky, S.V.D., Austria; Revs. Francis Bures, S.V.D. Ord: 53, Japan; Dennis Callan, S.V.D. Ord: '87, Korea; Thomas Cassidy, S.V.D. Ord: '45, Philippines; Richard Daschbach, S.V.D. Ord: '64, East Timor; Anthony Dugay, S.V.D. Ord: '62, Ghana; Bro. Xavier Eshman, S.V.D., Paraguay; Revs. Lloyd Fiedler, S.V.D. Ord: '70, Philippines; Patrick Fincutter, S.V.D. Ord: '55, Papua New Guinea; Kenneth Feehan, S.V.D. Ord: '59, Papua New Guinea; Dennis Flynn, S.V.D. Ord: '61, Philippines; Bro. Ronald Fratzke, S.V.D., Australia; Revs. Paul Gootee, S.V.D. Ord: '55, Indonesia; Robert Grochowski, S.V.D. Ord: '96, Japan; Lawrence Hambach, S.V.D. Ord: '61, Indonesia; James Heisig, S.V.D. Ord: '69, Japan; Edward Herberger, S.V.D. Ord: '60, Anguilla; Raymond Hober, S.V.D. Ord: '60, Philippines; Alan Jenkins, S.V.D. Ord: '73, Mexico; Robert Johnson, S.V.D. Ord: '92, Montserrat – Caribbean; Most Rev. Raymond Kalisz, S.V.D., Papua New Guinea; Bro. Lawrence Kieffer, S.V.D., Papua New Guinea; Revs. Jon Kirby, S.V.D. Ord: '71, Ghana; Robert Kisala, S.V.D. Ord: '85, Japan; Ronald Lange, S.V.D. Ord: '71, Ghana; Paul LaForge, S.V.D. Ord: '58, Japan; Lawrence LaPlante, S.V.D. Ord: '67, Philippines William Liebert, S.V.D. Ord: '57, Papua, New Guinea; James Liebner, S.V.D. Ord: '85, Taiwan; Michael Lindstrom, S.V.D. Ord: '82, Japan; Bro. Damien Lunders, S.V.D., Thailand; Revs. Matthew Lunzer, S.V.D. Ord: '45, Papua New Guinea; John Khien Luu, S.V.D. Ord: '92, Australia; Adam MacDonald, S.V.D. Ord: '00, Philippines; David Mayer, S.V.D. Ord: '66, Japan; Dennis McKillip, S.V.D. Ord: '47, Philippines; John McSherry, S.V.D. Ord: '61, Philippines; Peter Michael, S.V.D. Ord: '40, Philippines; Bro. Henry Miller, S.V.D., Antigua – Caribbean; Revs. Theodore Murnane, S.V.D. Ord: '59, Philippines; John Musinsky, S.V.D. Ord: '44, Rome; Paul Nadolny, S.V.D. Ord: '89, Mozambique; Lawrence Nemer, S.V.D. Ord: '60, England; Joseph Trong Nguyen, S.V.D. Ord: '91, Vietnam; Peter Sam Cao Nguyen, S.V.D. Ord: '86, Korea; Van Hiep Nguyen, S.V.D. Ord: '99, Ecuador; Cuong Hung Nguyen, S.V.D. Ord: '00, Argentina; Nick Hien Nguyen, S.V.D. Ord: '00, Taiwan; Michael Van Nhan Tran, S.V.D. Ord: '00, Argentina; Joseph Minh Vu Nguyen, S.V.D. Ord: '96, Australia; Donald O'Connor, S.V.D. Ord: '64, Papua New Guinea; Stanley Plutz, S.V.D. Ord: '53, Philippines; Robert Pung, S.V.D. Ord: '44, Rome; Bro. Mark Rastall, S.V.D. Australia, Revs. Robert Riemer, S.V.D. Ord: '60, Japan; Roger Risse, S.V.D. Ord: '54, Indonesia; James Risse, S.V.D. Ord: '61, Philippines; Charles Scanlon, S.V.D. Ord: '54, Philippines; Bartley Schmitz, S.V.D. Ord: '44, Taiwan; Eugene Schmitz, S.V.D. Ord: '67, Indonesia; Charles Schneider, S.V.D. Ord: '46, Ghana; William Seifert, S.V.D. Ord: '67, Papua New Guinea; John Seland, S.V.D. Ord: '68, Japan; Werner Shadeg, S.V.D. Ord: '45, Papua New Guinea; Norbert Shadeg, S.V.D. Ord: '49, Indonesia; Otto Shelly, S.V.D. Ord: '42, Australia; Arnold Steffen, S.V.D. Ord: '57, Papua New Guinea; Victor Stevko, S.V.D. Ord: 57, Australia; Nicholas Strawn, S.V.D. Ord: '62, Indonesia; David Streit, S.V.D. Ord: '69, Rome; Richard Szippl, S.V.D. Ord: '81, Japan; Gerald Theis, S.V.D. Ord: '80, Papua New Guinea; Richard Thibeau, S.V.D. Ord: '57, Mexico; Frederick Timp, S.V.D. Ord: 71, Ghana; Joseph Huynh Tran, S.V.D. Ord: '93, Taiwan; Cong Bang Tran, S.V.D. Ord: '00, Togo; Peter Tam Tran, S.V.D. Ord: '98, Australia; Thomas Umbras S.V.D. Ord: '81, Mexico; James Vorwek, S.V.D. Ord: '69, Argentina; Lawrence Wagner, S.V.D. Ord: '44, Mexico; Wilbert Wagner, S.V.D. Ord: '40, Mexico; Joseph Tri Van Vu, S.V.D Ord: '85, Vietnam; John Khien Mai Luu, S.V.D. Ord: '92, Vietnam.

AMERICAN DOMINICAN MISSIONS (O.P.)

Dominican - Order of Preachers Foreign Missions

Foreign Missions of the American Provinces of the Order of Preachers

Provincial Headquarters

*Province of St. Joseph (Eastern):*141 E. 65th St., New York, NY 10021. Phone: 212-861-8776. Very Rev. D. Dominic Izzo, O.P. Ord: '94, Prov.; Rev. Scott Matthew Erickson, O.P. Ord: '90, Mission Sec.

U.S. Religious serving in Pakistan: Revs. J. M. Connors, O.P. Ord: '51; J. Nuttall, O.P. Ord: '59; G. L. Sukovaty, O.P. Ord: '51.

U.S. Religious serving Elsewhere: Rev. D. G. Doherty, O.P. Ord: '57, Philippines; Most Rev. Christopher Cardone, O.P. Ord: '86, Auxiliary Bishop -Solomon Islands.

U.S. Religious serving in Peru: Rev. Thomas Kraft, O.P. Ord: '84.

U.S. Religious serving in Kenya: Very Rev. M. B. Schepers, O.P. Ord: '56, Vicar Prov.; Revs. Vincent Wiseman, O.P. Ord: '71; Kenneth Andrew Hofer, O.P. Ord: '02; Kieran J. Healy, O.P. Ord: '61; Leon Martin A. Martiny, O.P. Ord: '98'; Lewis M. Shea, O.P. Ord: '52; Thomas R. Heath, O.P. Ord '50; John B. Croell, O.P. Ord: '98.

*Province of St. Albert the Great (Central):*1909 S. Ashland Ave., Chicago, IL 60608-2994. Fax: 312-829-8471. Very Rev. Edward M. Ruane, O.P. Ord: '69, Prov. Rev. Bede Jagoe, O.P. Ord: '60, Dir.-St. Dominic Mission Society.

U.S. Religious serving in Kenya: Rev. Lewis M. Shea, O.P. Ord: '52.

U.S. Religious serving in Nigeria: Revs. Peter Otillio, O.P. Ord: '57, Joseph H. Kenny, O.P. Ord: '50; Thomas K. McDermott, O.P. Ord: '83; Justus Pokrzewinski, O.P. Ord: '60; Edward H. Riley, O.P. Ord: '60; Gilbert Thesing, O.P. Ord: '75; Bro. Stephen Lucas, O.P.

U.S. Religious serving in Bolivia Revs. Thomas Lynch, O.P. Ord: '86, Daniel Roach O.P. Ord: '56; Mark Paraday, O.P. Ord: '83.

Province of the Holy Name:(Western Dominican Province), 5877 Birch Court, Oakland, CA 94618. Very Rev. Roberto Corral, O.P. Ord: '88, Prov.

U.S. Religious serving in Mexico: Revs. David Bello, O.P. Ord: '81, Thomas Kraft, O.P. Ord: '86; Jose Ricardo Garcia, O.P. Ord: '73; Kieran Healy, O.P. Ord: '61, Kenya.

*St. Martin de Porres Province: (Southern Dominican Province),*1421 N. Causeway Blvd., Ste. 200, Metairie, LA 70001-4144. Phone: 504-837-2129; Fax: 504-837-6604. Very Rev. Martin J. Gleeson, O.P. Ord: '98, Prov.; Rev. Brian J. Pierce, O.P. Ord: '83.

U.S. Religious serving Abroad: Revs. James L. Dolan, O.P. Ord: '60, Peru. Emanuel Camilleri, O.P. Ord: '37, Malta; Jesus Guerra, O.P. Ord: '57, Venezuela; Luis Roberto Aguilar Leal, O.P. Ord: '92, Honduras; George Dyer, O.P. Ord: '61, Belgium; Rafael Proenza, O.P. Ord: '96, Cuba; Michael O'Rourke, O.P. Ord: '96, Italy; Alfred Wilder, O.P. Ord: '65, Italy.

AMERICAN FRANCISCAN MISSIONS (O.F.M.)

Franciscan Foreign Missions

Missions of the American Provinces of the Order of Friars Minor (Franciscans) in the United States and other countries.

*Holy Name Province:*135 W. 31st St., New York, NY 10001-3439. Phone: 212-924-1451. Rev. Russell C. Becker, O.F.M., Prov. Promoter of the Missions, Sec. Missionary Evangelization; Bro. D. Gordon Clark, O.F.M., Dir.-Emeritus.

U.S. Religious serving in Africa: Revs. Roy Corrigan, O.F.M. Ord: '55; Joseph B. Ehrhardt, O.F.M. Ord: '67; Finian A. Riley, O.F.M. Ord: '55.

U.S. Religious serving in Bolivia: Revs. Ignatius Harding, O.F.M. Ord: '65; William R. Keenan, O.F.M. Ord: '56; Thomas J. Kornacki, O.F.M. Ord: '88; Clement Comesky, O.F.M. Ord: '55.

U.S. Religious serving in Brazil: Most Rev. John Burke O.F.M.; Most Rev. Benedict D. Coscia, O.F.M.; Most Rev. Capistran F. Heim, O.F.M.; Revs. David J. Babcock, O.F.M. Ord: '53; Donald J. Chin, O.F.M. Ord: '67; Alexander F. Eustace, O.F.M. Ord: '50; Berard J. Hanlon, O.F.M. Ord: '63; Juvenal F. Leahy, O.F.M. Ord: '58; Ignatius J. McGeady, O.F.M. Ord: '48; Aloysius Siracuse, O.F.M. Ord: '47.

U.S. Religious serving in Japan: Revs. Bede Fitzpatrick, O.F.M. Ord: '55; Campion Lally, O.F.M. Ord: '53; Bartholomew McMahon, O.F.M. Ord: '62; Donnon P. Murray, O.F.M. Ord: '56; Callistus Sweeney, O.F.M.; Stanislaus Widomski, O.F.M. Ord: '62.

U.S. Religious serving in Peru: Revs. Mariano Gagnon, O.F.M. Ord: '58; Mariano Guzman, O.F.M. Ord: '57; Christopher J. Dunn, O.F.M. Ord: '82; Anthony Wilson, O.F.M. Ord: '87; Paul Breslin, O.F.M. Ord: 88; Bros. Declan McCabe, O.F.M.; James McIntosh, O.F.M.

U.S. Religious serving in Puerto Rico: Rev. Alfonso D. Guzman, O.F.M. Ord: '71.

U.S. Religious serving in Taiwan: Rev. Pius Lui, O.F.M. Ord: '53.

*Franciscan Province of the Immaculate Conception:*125 Thompson St., New York, NY 10012. Bro. Courtrand A. Campbell, O.F.M., Sec./Missionary Evangelization & Franciscan Missionary Union.

Province-affiliated Religious serving in Honduras: Revs. Peter Paul Meilak, O.F.M. Ord: '49; Albert Gauci, O.F.M. Ord: '71; Most Rev. Maurice Muldoon, O.F.M.; Most Rev. Gerald Scarpone, O.F.M.; Most Rev, Roberto Camilleri, O.F.M. Ord: '75; Revs. Angelo Falzon, O.F.M. Ord: '84; Joseph Bonello, O.F.M. Ord: '85; Donald Salazar, O.F.M. Ord: '67; Valentine Gesuale, O.F.M. Ord: '65; Bro. Guillermo Salgado, O.F.M.

Province-affiliated Religious serving in El Salvador: Revs. Flavian Mucci, O.F.M. Ord: '63; Guy Vellardita, O.F.M. Ord: '58, San Pedro; Rafael Fernandez, O.F.M. Ord: '87.

Province-affiliated Religious serving in Guatemala: Revs. Rocco Famiglietti, O.F.M. Ord: '47; Ottaviano Battolini, O.F.M. Ord: '43; Robert Siguere, O.F.M. Ord: '73.

Sacred Heart Province: 3140 Meramec St., St. Louis, MO 63118. Phone: 314-353-3421. Revs. John L. Doctor, O.F.M. Ord: '76, Prov.; Kenneth Capalbo, O.F.M. Ord: '74, Prov. Vicar; Bro. Joseph Rogenski, O.F.M., Promoter of the Missions.

Franciscan Missionary Union: Phone: 314-353-7729

U.S. Religious serving Elsewhere: Revs. Albert Haase, O.F.M. Ord: '83, Taiwan; James Perluzzi, O.F.M. Ord: '65, Italy; Jesus Aguirre Garza, O.F.M. Ord: '96, Egypt; James Edmiston, O.F.M. Ord: '98, Russia; Bro. Jeffrey Haller, O.F.M., Taiwan.

U.S. Religious serving in Alaska: Revs. William E. Cardy, O.F.M. Ord: '72; Joseph Hemmer, O.F.M. Ord: '54; Bros. Robert Ruzicka, O.F.M.; Justin Huber, O.F.M.

U.S. Religious serving in Brazil: Revs. Michael Grawe, O.F.M. Ord: '70; Gregory Kemner, O.F.M. Ord: '55; Nestor Windolph, O.F.M. Ord: '55; Richard Duffy, O.F.M. Ord: '58.

St. Barbara Province: 1500 34th Ave., Oakland, CA 94601. Fax: 510-536-3970.

U.S. Religious serving Overseas: Revs. Ignatius DeGroot, O.F.M. Ord: '64, Peru; David Gaa, O.F.M. Ord: '98, Kazakhstan; Elias Galvez, O.F.M. Ord: '56, Mexico; John Gibbons, O.F.M. Ord: '01, Russia; Thomas King, O.F.M. Ord: '93, Peru; Bros. Edward Dunn, O.F.M., Mexico; Miguel Lozano, O.F.M., Mexico; Leo Gonzalez, O.F.M., Israel; Gerard Saunders, O.F.M., Peru.

Assumption B.V.M. Province: Franklin WI 53132. Phone: 414-525-9253; Fax: 414-525-9289. Revs. Thomas Luczak, O.F.M. Ord: '70, Minister Prov.; Hugh Zurat, O.F.M. Ord: '62.

Franciscan Evangelization Center - Assumption Province: Chicago, IL 60659. Phone: 773-539-4042; Fax: 773-539-9553.

Publication: *Mission Newsletter.*

U.S. Religious serving Abroad: Revs. Laurian Wegner, O.F.M. Ord: '78, Japan; Lyle Chrobak, O.F.M. Ord: '62, Mexico; Most Rev. Henry Howaniec, O.F.M. Ord: '56, Kazakhstan; Revs. John Liczner, O.F.M. Ord: '66, Papua, New Guinea; Barnabas Gorski, O.F.M. Ord: '60, Morocco; Sergius Wroblewski, O.F.M. Ord: '46, South Africa. ; Bros. Augustine Fraszczak, O.F.M., Philippines;. Mario Nagy, O.F.M., Russia; John Brice, O.F.M., South Africa.

Province of St. John the Baptist: 1615 Vine St., Cincinnati, OH 45202-6400. Phone: 513-721-4700; Fax: 513-421-9672. Bro. Scott Obrecht, O.F.M. Dir.-Secretariat for Missionary Evangelization & Franciscan Missionary Union.

Publication: *Mission Newsletter, Friarworks.*

U.S. Religious serving Abroad: Revs. Malachy Brogan, O.F.M. Ord: '57, Holy Land; John Joseph Gonchar, O.F.M. Ord: '57, Jamaica, West Indies; Harold Geers, O.F.M. Ord: '60, Philippines; Joseph Hund, O.F.M. Ord: '89, Jamaica, West Indies; Carl Kemphues, O.F.M. Ord: '56, Philippines; Daniel Kroger, O.F.M. Ord: '73, Philippines; Max Langenderfer, O.F.M. Ord: '73, Kenya; Elgar Nadon, O.F.M. Ord: '59, Philippines; Bernardin Schneider, O.F.M. Ord:'44, Japan; Bertram Tiemeyer, O.F.M. Ord:'47, Philippines; David Turnbull, O.F.M. Ord:'57, Philippines; Francis Wendling, O.F.M. Ord:'59; Bros. Philip Wilhelm, O.F.M., Philippines; Roger Covero, O.F.M., Philippines; Mark Gehret, O.F.M., Jamaica, West Indies; Louis Zant, O.F.M. Ord: '73, Jamaica, West Indies.

VI SLAV-BYZANTINE MISSIONS, U.S.A.

Custody of St. Mary of the Angels. Byzantine-Slavonic Rite (New Canaan, CT)

Established by decree of the Most Rev. Minister General of the Order of Friars Minor on November 7, 1947, with the approbation of the Sacred, Congregation for the Oriental Church on October 28, 1947, among the peoples of the Byzantine Rite.

Commissariats of the Holy Land: 1400 Quincy St. N.E., Washington, DC 20017. Phone: 202-526-6800; Fax: 202-529-9889. Bros. Callistus Welch, O.F.M., Commissary; David Wathen, O.F.M.; James Paul Brabandt, O.F.M.; Revs. Joshua Doyle, O.F.M.; Brian McTommoney, O.F.M. Ord: '53.

Commissary Custody of the Holy Land: Jordan, Israel, Lebanon, Syria, Cyprus, Egypt and Rhodes.

U.S. Religious serving Abroad: Revs. Xavier Geiser, O.F.M. Ord: '55; Jerusalem, Israel; Peter Vasko, O.F.M. Ord: '87, Jerusalem, Israel; George Lewett, O.F.M. Ord: '88, Bethlehem, Isreal; Athanasius Macora, O.F.M. Ord: '92, Jerusalem, Israel; Matthias Rendon, O.F.M. Ord: '92, Jerusalem, Israel; Danielmose Shroeder, O.F.M. Ord: '91, Jerusalem, Israel; Bros. Leo Gonzales, O.F.M., Mt. Tabor, Israel; Angel Beda Ison, O.F.M., Jerusalem, Israel; Aloysius Florio, O.F.M., Rome, Italy; Michael Raum, O.F.M., Jerusalem, Israel; Thomas Courtney, O.F.M., Syria.

FRANCISCAN FRIARS OF THE ATONEMENT (S.A.)

General Headquarters: Graymoor, P.O. Box 300, Garrison, NY 10524. Phone: 845-424-2113; Fax: 845-424-2166.

For detailed information on the U.S. Religious working in foreign missions, please refer to the listings under the Archdiocese of New York section entitled "Monasteries and Residences of Priests and Brothers", Graymoor, Garrison, NY.

HOLY CROSS MISSION CENTER (C.S.C.)

U.S. Headquarters and Procure: Holy Cross Mission Center, P.O. Box 543, Notre Dame IN, 46556. Phone: 574-631-5477; Fax: 574-631-6813. Revs. Thomas W. Smith, C.S.C. Ord: '72, Dir.; David E. Schlaver, C.S.C. Ord: '71, Assoc. Dir.

Legal Title: *Holy Cross Foreign Mission Society, Inc.*

Holy Cross Foreign Missions

Indiana Province: Congregation of Holy Cross, P.O. Box 1064, Notre Dame, IN 46556-1064.

Midwest Province: Congregation of Holy Cross, P.O. Box 460, Notre Dame, IN 46556-0460

Eastern Province: Congregation of Holy Cross, 835 Clinton Ave., Bridgeport, CT 06604-2393.

South-West Province: Congregation of Holy Cross, 1101 St. Edward's Dr., Austin, TX 78704-6512.

Eastern Province of Brothers: Congregation of Holy Cross, 85 Overlook Cir., New Rochelle, NY 10804-4501.

Southern Province of Priests: Congregation of Holy Cross, 2111 Brackenridge St., Austin, TX 78704-4322.

U.S. Religious serving in Foreign Missions: Revs. Robert R. Baker, C.S.C. Ord: '70, Peru; James T. Banas, C.S.C. Ord: '57, Bangladesh; Gerald R. Barmasse, C.S.C. Ord: '76, Chile; Leonard J. Collins, C.S.C. Ord: '69, Mexico; Charles A. Delaney, C.S.C. Ord: '49, Chile; Philip T. Devlin, C.S.C. Ord: '56, Peru; Joseph A. Dorsey, C.S.C. Ord: '57, Chile; David E. Farrell, C.S.C. Ord: '68, Peru; Donald Fetters, C.S.C. Ord: '76, Chile; James Ferguson, C.S.C. Ord: '65, Kenya; Robert Gilbo, C.S.C. Ord: '67, Chile; Robert G. Gilmour, C.S.C. Ord: '68, Ghana; Robert T. Hesse, C.S.C. Ord: '58, Uganda; Eugene E. Homrich, C.S.C. Ord: '55, Bangladesh; James W. Irwin, C.S.C. Ord: '65, Mexico; Malcolm D. Johnson, C.S.C. Ord: '59, Chile; James Kelly, C.S.C. Ord: '58, Uganda; Joseph Lehane, C.S.C. Ord: '57, Bangladesh; L. Peter Logsdon, C.S.C. Ord: '68, Mexico; George Lucas, C.S.C. Ord: '72, Uganda; James E. McDonald, C.S.C. Ord: '84, Chile; Russell McDougall, C.S.C. Ord: '91, Uganda; Francis Murphy, C.S.C. Ord: '86, Uganda; Daniel A. Panchot, C.S.C. Ord: '65, Mexico; Gerald T. Papen, C.S.C. Ord: '63, Chile; Joseph S. Peixotto, C.S.C. Ord: '61, Bangladesh, William Persia, C.S.C. Ord: '62, Peru; James H. Phalan, C.S.C. Ord: '92, Peru; Robert Plasker, C.S.C. Ord: '57, Chile; George F. Pope, C.S.C. Ord: '58, Bangladesh; Richard L. Potthast, C.S.C. Ord: '67, Uganda; Francis Quinlivan, C.S.C. Ord: '70, Bangladesh; Most Rev. Charles A. Schleck, C.S.C. Ord: '51, Italy; Revs. Thomas Shea, C.S.C. Ord: '67; Peru, Robert G. Simon, C.S.C. Ord: '61, Chile; Richard E. Stout, C.S.C. Ord: '71, Uganda; Richard W. Timm, C.S.C. Ord: '49, Bangladesh; Gerald J. Whelan, C.S.C. Ord: '55, Chile. Bros. Thomas More Beere, C.S.C., Bangladesh; Donald Becker, C.S.C., Bangladesh; John Benesh, C.S.C., Peru; Richard Burgie, C.S.C., Brazil; Thomas Dillman, C.S.C., Ghana; Ronald Drahozal, C.S.C., Bangladesh; John Flood, C.S.C., Uganda; Vincent Gross, C.S.C., Ghana; Thomas Giumenta, C.S.C., Chile; Alan Gugel, C.S.C., Uganda; Alan Harrod, C.S.C., Uganda; Ronald Hein, C.S.C., Brazil; Joseph Kinsman, C.S.C., Brazil; Bernard Klim, Uganda; Jerome F. Kroetsch, C.S.C., Ghana; Alfred Ledet, C.S.C., Brazil; Dismas Lenzi, C.S.C., Brazil; Norbert Lengerich, C.S.C., Brazil; Harold Naudet, C.S.C., Brazil; James Nichols, C.S.C., Uganda; Leonard Reeson, C.S.C., Brazil; Frank Robinson, C.S.C., Brazil; Paul Schaefer, C.S.C., Brazil; Sergio Stolf, C.S.C., Brazil; Gerard Suddick, C.S.C., Uganda; J. Rodney Struble, C.S.C., Bangladesh; Nicholas Thielman, C.S.C., Bangladesh; Ernest Turk, C.S.C., Brazil; Robert Weinmann, C.S.C., Brazil; Robert Nebus, C.S.C., Uganda; Joseph Walsh, C.S.C., Uganda. Revs. Geroge J. Whelan, C.S.C. Ord: '55, Chile.

Priests 42; Brothers 32.

JESUIT MISSIONS (S.J.)

Jesuit Foreign Missions

Jesuit Mission Inc. An official missionary organization of the Provinces of the United States Assistancy of the Society of Jesus.

National Headquarters: Jesuit Missions, 1616 P St., N.W., #300, Washington, DC 20036. Phone: 202-462-0400; Fax: 202-328-9212. Revs. Thomas H. Smolich, S.J. Ord: '86, Pres.; Thomas Gaunt, S.J. Ord: '81, Sec.; Jean-Marc Laporte, S.J. Ord: '67, Treas.

Provinces

Society of Jesus: California Province, 300 College Ave., Los Gatos, CA 95030. Revs. Thomas H. Smolich, S.J. Ord: '86, Prov.; Theodore E. Gabrielli, S.J. Ord: '96, Mission Dir.

Legal Title: *California Jesuit Missionaries.*

U.S. Religious serving in Foreign Missions: Revs. Louis G. Aldrich, S.J. Ord: '86, Republic of China; Ferdinand T. Azevedo, S.J. Ord: '70, Brazil; Robert R. Becka, S.J. Ord: '60, Japan; Philip L. Bourret, S.J. Ord: '41, Republic of China; Walter G. Brennan, S.J. Ord: '60, Japan; Robert E. Chiesa, S.J. Ord: '68, Japan; Robert W. Cunningham, S.J. Ord: '55, Philippines; John R. Donahue, S.J. Ord: '79, Honduras; John R. Donald, S.J. Ord: '72, Honduras; Gustavo D. Fernandez, S.J. Ord: '67, Guatemala; Fred J. Green, S.J. Ord: '58, Peru; Robert B. Grimaldi, S.J. Ord: '68, Honduras; Kieth Barry Martinson, S.J. Ord: '75, Republic of China; George G. Martinson, S.J. Ord: '73, Republic of China; Edward J. Murphy, S.J. Ord: '43, Republic of China; John B. Palm, S.J. Ord: '41, Republic of China; Paul E. Pollock, S.J. Ord: '73, Thailand; Robert J. Ronald, S.J. Ord: '65, Republic of China; Daniel J. Ross, S.J. Ord: '66, Republic of China; Richard J. Schneck, S.J. Ord: '72, Ecuador; Edward J. Thylstrup, S.J. Ord: '67, Republic of China; Charles A. Welsh, S.J. Ord: '72, Republic of China; Bros. Richard J. Devine, S.J., Japan; Donald J. Poetzl, S.J., Mexico. Priests 22; Brothers 2.

Society of Jesus: Chicago Province, 2050 N. Clark St., Chicago, IL 60614. Phone: 773-975-6363. Revs. Richard J. Baumann, S.J. Ord: '75, Prov.; George E. Von Kaenel, S.J. Ord: '58, Prov. Asst. Intl. Ministries.

Legal Title: *Jesuit International Missions, (Formerly, Jesuits in Peru, Chicago Province, and Patna Jesuit Mission Society).*

U.S. Religious serving in Foreign Missions: Revs. Robert E. Beckman, S.J. Ord: '56, Peru; Theodore B. Bowling, S.J. Ord: '53, India; Lawrence V. Brooks, S.J. Ord: '74, Nepal; Patrick M. Casey, S.J. Ord: '72, Peru; Francis M. Chamberlain, S.J. Ord: '68, Peru; Terrence P. Charlton, S.J. Ord: '76, Kenya; Martin P. Coyne, S.J. Ord: '66, Nepal; Edwin J. Daly, S.J. Ord: '59, India; Robert M. Deiters, S.J. Ord: '58, Japan; Robert L. Dolan, S.J. Ord: '73, Peru; James J. Donnelly, S.J. Ord: '59, Nepal; Jerome F. Durack, S.J. Ord: '60, India; William J. Everett, S.J. Ord: '53, Japan; Kevin H. Flaherty, S.J. Ord: '83, Peru; Charles J. Fox, S.J. Ord: '44, India; Kevin E. Gallagher, S.J. Ord: '61, Peru; Anthony J. Grollig, S.J., Ord: '55, India; John J. Kenealy, S.J. Ord: '58, India; Jeffrey L. Klaiber, S.J. Ord: '74, Peru; Richard T. Lambert, S.J. Ord: '67, India; Roman B. Lewicki, S.J. Ord: '65, India; John K. Locke, S.J. Ord: '64, Nepal; Charles L. Murtaugh, S.J. Ord: '69, Peru; James M. O'Leary, S.J. Ord: '91, Peru; John L. O'Malley, S.J. Ord: '63, Japan; Edward Schmidt, S.J. Ord: '71, Peru; Ludwig F. Stiller, S.J. Ord: '62, Nepal; Eugene L. Watrin, S.J. Ord: '52, Nepal; Joseph F. Willmes, S.J. Ord: '48, India.

Priests 44.

Detroit Province: 303 West Seven Mile Rd., Detroit, MI 48221-2121. Phone: 313-861-7500.

Legal Title: *Jesuit International Missions, (Formerly, Patna Jesuit Mission Society),* Revs. Robert J. Scullin, S.J. Ord: '76, Prov.; Richard H. Twohig, S.J. Ord: '65, Mission Dir.

U.S. Religious serving in Foreign Missions: Revs. Paul H. Besanceney, S.J. Ord: '56, Sudan; Richard W. Cherry, S.J. Ord: '69, Tanzania; Gerald A. Drinane, S.J. Ord: '62, India; Michael A. Evans, S.J. Ord: '83, Kenya; William G. Goudreau, S.J., Ord: '52, India; Eugene F. Hattie, S.J. Ord: '53, Uganda; Paul S. Kehres, S.J. Ord: '51, India; Norman Langenderfer, S.J. Ord: '54, India; John A. Lucal, S.J. Ord: '61, Turkey; Casper J. Miller, S.J. Ord: '64, Nepal; Joseph E. Mulligan, S.J. Ord: '73, Nicaragua; James J. Regan, S.J. Ord: '67, Peru; Robert H. Schmidt, S.J. Ord: '69, India; Thomas F. Tobin, S.J. Ord: '65, India; Theodore W. Walters, S.J. Ord: '56, Tanzania; Bro. Richard L. Cure, S.J., Japan.

Priests 15; Brothers 1.

Society of Jesus: Maryland Province, 5704 Roland Ave., Baltimore, MD 21210. Phone: 410-532-1400; Fax: 410-532-1419. Rev. Timothy B. Brown, S.J. Ord: '79, Prov.; Mr. Stephen J. Callahan, Asst. Prov. International Apostolate.

Legal Titles: *Jesuit Mission Inc. An official missionary organization of the Provinces of the United States Assistancy of the Society of Jesus.*

U.S. Religious serving in Foreign Missions: Revs. Eugene J. Barber, S.J. Ord: '63, Chile; Gerard S. Barry, S.J. Ord: '63, Japan; Edward J. Brady, S.J. Ord: '59, Kenya; Vincent J. Capuano, S.J. Ord: '98, Argentina; Jeffrey G.L. Chang, S.J. Ord: '99, China; Robert F. Currie, S.J. Ord: '71, Nicaragua; William J. Currie, S.J. Ord: '67, Japan; Angelo D'Agostino, S.J. Ord: '66, Kenya; Edgar J. Debany, S.J. Ord: '84, Nigeria; John J. Deeney, S.J. Ord: '52; India; James M. Desjardins, S.J. Ord: '77, Russia; Carl L. Dincher, S.J. Ord: '57, India; Edward C.A. Dougherty, S.J. Ord: '72, South Africa; Thomas M. Gavin, S.J. Ord: '75, Chile; John F. Guidera, S.J. Ord: '56, India; Robert E. Hamm, S.J.

Ord: '68, Nigeria; John F. Henry, S.J. Ord: '55, Chile; George A. Hess, S.J. Ord: '50, India; F. Scott Howell, S.J. Ord: '77, Japan; Richard A. Kenna, S.J. Ord: '57, India; Sigmund J. Laschenski, S.J. Ord: '55, Thailand; Richard S. McCouch, S.J. Ord: '93, Micronesia; Edward H. McGrath, S.J. Ord: '53, India; Edward H. Nash, S.J. Ord: '46, India; John J. Nissel, S.J. Ord: '56, Japan; George W. Quickley, S.J. Ord: '80, Nigeria; Eugene M. Rooney, S.J. Ord: '57, Chile; Dominic J. Totaro, S.J. Ord: '67, Nigeria; David L. Ungerleider, S.J. Ord: '77, Mexico; Eugene A. Welch, S.J. Ord: '60, India; Robert D. Wiesenbaugh, S.J. Ord: '71, Bolivia; Charles E. Wolf, S.J. Ord: '49, Philippines.

Priests 33.

Society of Jesus: Missouri Province, 4511 W. Pine Blvd., St. Louis, MO 63108. Phone: 314-361-7765; Fax: 314-758-7164. Rev. Timothy M. McMahon, S.J. Ord: '87, Prov.

Legal Title: *The Jesuits of the Missouri Province.*

U.S. Religious serving in Foreign Missions: Revs. Robert T. Costello, S.J. Ord: '63, Britain; Mauricio Gaborit, S.J. Ord: '78, El Salvador; Steven B. Hawkes-Teeples, S.J. Ord: '93, Italy; John L. Maher, S.J. Ord: '74, Belize; Keith P. McMillan, S.J. Ord: '93, Britain; Maurice M. Murray, S.J. Ord: '66, Belize; William T. Dulvey, S.J. Ord: '85, Belize; Raymond A. Pease, S.J. Ord: '68, Honduras; Richard D. Perl, S.J., Ord: '78, Belize; Donald W. Reck, S.J. Ord: '65, Spain; Jesus R. Riveroll, S.J. Ord: '88, Belize; Thomas M. Rochford, S.J. Ord: '76, Italy; James M. Short, S.J. Ord: '61, Belize; William J. Snyders, S.J. Ord: '66, Belize; Ricardo Steinmetz, S.J. Ord: '55, Mexico; John J. Stochl, S.J. Ord: '54, Belize; James H. Swetnam, S.J. Ord: '58, Italy; Bros. Karl D. Swift, S.J., Belize; Harold A. Teel, S.J., Belize; Revs. J. Timothy Thompson, S.J. Ord: '70, Belize; Jorge R. Toruno, S.J. Ord: '44, Guatemala; Jose Antonio Vega, S.J. Ord: '00, Belize; Bro. N. Aloysius Vogt, S.J., Belize; Revs. Robert D. Voss, S.J. Ord: '72, Honduras; Jarrell D. Wade, S.J. Ord: '65, Honduras; Francis K. Wallace, S.J. Ord '46, Panama; John B. Warner, S.J. Ord: '74, Honduras; Robert A. White, S.J. Ord: '62, Italy; John H. Willmering, S.J. Ord: '68, Honduras; Stephen T. Yavorsky, S.J. Ord: '77, Rwanda-Burundi; John H. Zupez S.J. Ord: '67, Nigeria.

Priests 28; Brothers 3.

Society of Jesus: New England Province. 85 School St., Watertown, MA 02472-4251. Phone: 617-607-2800; Fax: 617607-2888.

Legal Title: *The Society of Jesus of New England.* Revs. Robert J. Levens, S.J. Ord: '81, Prov.; Michael J. Linden, S.J. Ord: '80, Prov. Asst.-International Ministries.

U.S. Religious serving in Foreign Missions: Revs. John A. Carty, S.J. Ord: '59, Egypt; Denis R. Como, S.J. Ord: '66, Jordan; John J. Donohue, S.J. Ord: '59, Lebanon; Theodore A. Dziak, S.J. Ord: '83, Jamaica; Thomas J. Fitzpatrick, S.J. Ord: '68, Israel; James A. Gillon, S.J. Ord: '74, Tanzania; Louis L. Grenier, S.J. Ord: '49, Jamaica; Richard P. Guerrera, S.J. Ord: '73, Mozambique; Alfred J. Hicks, S.J. Ord: '66, Jordan; Donald L. Larkin, S.J. Ord: '66, Jamaica; Joseph A. MacWade, S.J. Ord: '61, ; Jamaica; Martin F. McDermott, S.J. Ord: '64, Lebanon; Joseph F. McHugh, S.J. Ord: '83, Jamaica; Gerald L. McLaughlin, S.J. Ord: '59, Jamaica; Oliver E. Nickerson, S.J. Ord: '54, Jamaica; Kevin G. O'Connell, S.J. Ord: '69, Jordan; William J. Raftery, S.J. Ord: '57, Bahamas; William C. Russell, S.J. Ord: '65, Jamaica; Francis J. Ryan, S.J. Ord: '56, Jamaica; Paul A. Schweitzer, S.J. Ord: '70, Brazil; Gregory C. Sharkey, S.J. Ord: '88, Nepal; David A. Skelskey, S.J. Ord: '80, Ethiopia; Thomas Vallamattam, S.J. Ord: '64, Jamaica.

Priests 23; Seminarians 2.

Society of Jesus: New Orleans Province, 211 Pere Marquette Bldg., New Orleans, LA 70112. Phone: 504-525-4043.

Legal Title: *Jesuit Mission Bureau.* Rev. Edward B. Arroyo, S.J. Ord: '75, Prov.

U.S. Religious serving in Foreign Missions: Revs. Donald G. Bahlinger, S.J. Ord: '59, Paraguay; Edward G. Benya, S.J. Ord: '84, Brazil; David C. Borbridge, S.J. Ord: '63, Brazil; Bro. Anthony S. Coco, S.J., Brazil; Revs. Fred Cooley, S.J. Ord: '54, Sri Lanka; Claude Daly, S.J. Ord: '43, Sri Lanka; Carlos E. de la Cruz, S.J. Ord: '75, Paraguay; Alfonso Del Marmol, S.J. Ord: '51, Sri Lanka; Edward J. Dougherty, S.J. Ord: '70, Brazil; A. Gerard Fineran, S.J. Ord: '50, Brazil; Bro.Robert E. Hollingsworth, S.J., Brazil; Revs. O. Kenneth Johnson Ord: '92, Zambia; Leo V. Leise, S.J. Ord: '94, Paraguay; Roland J. Lesseps, S.J. Ord: '65, Zambia; Lloyd Lorio, S.J. Ord: '56, Sri Lanka; Patrick S. Madigan S.J. Ord: '83, Zimbabwe; Francis X. Mayer, S.J. Ord: '50, Sri Lanka; Joseph H. Meyer, S.J. Ord: '46, Sri Lanka; Harry Miller, S.J Ord: '54, Sri Lanka; Harold J. Rahm, S.J. Ord: '50, Brazil; David H. Romero, S.J. Ord: '91, Brazil; Stephen C. Rowntree, S.J. Ord: '75, Kenya; John F. Schroder, S.J. Ord: '53, Belize; John Stacer, S.J. Ord: '63, Zimbabwe; Charles B. Thibodeaux, S.J. Ord: '59, Paraguay; Bro. Terence N. Todd, S.J., Micronesia; Rev. Harold J. Weber, S.J. Ord: '44, Sri Lanka.

Priests 25; Brothers 3; Scholastics 1.

Society of Jesus: New York Province, 39 E. 83rd St., New York, NY 10028. Phone: 212-774-5500. Very Rev. Gerald J. Chojnacki, S.J. Ord: '73, Prov.; Rev. Thomas E. Smith, S.J. Ord: '74, Asst. Prov.-International Apostolates.

U.S. Religious Serving in Foreign Missions: Revs. William M. Abbott, S.J. Ord: '72, Philippines; Gerald W. Aman, S.J. Ord: '73, Nigeria; Joseph E. Billotti, S.J. Ord: '63, Micronesia; J. Dean Brackley, S.J. Ord: '76 El Salvador; John J. Carroll, S.J. Ord: '55, Philippines; Matthew J. Cassidy, S.J. Ord: '99, Ghana; Joseph A. Cavanagh, S.J. Ord: '62, Micronesia; John E. Chambers, S.J. Ord: '64, Philippines; Francis X. Clark, S.J. Ord: '43, Philippines; James P. Croghan, S.J. Ord: '85, Micronesia; John F. Curran, S.J. Ord: '59, Micronesia; Thomas R. Fitzpatrick, S.J. Ord: '61, Philippines; Robert P. Flynn, S.J. Ord: '50, Japan; Joseph a. Galdon, S.J. Ord: '59, Philippines; Pasquale T. Giordano, S.J. Ord: '72, Philippines; Francis N. Glover, S.J. Ord: '58, Philippines; Very Rev. James C. Gould, S.J. Ord: '74, Micronesia – Pref. Apostolic Marshall Islands; Revs. George R. Graziano, S.J. Ord: '59, Japan; Thomas H. Green, S.J. Ord: '63, Philippines; John J. Halligan, S.J. Ord: '61, Ecuador; Gerald W. Healy, S.J. Ord: '46, Philippines; Victor J. Helly, S.J. Ord: '54, Philippines; Francis X. Hezel, S.J. Ord: '69, Micronesia; Very Rev. Kenneth J. Hezel, S.J. Ord: '66, Guam – Reg. Supr.-Micronesia; Donald J. Hinfey, S.J. Ord: '63, Ghana; Robert C. Hogan, S.J. Ord: '64, Philippines; Raymond T. Holscher, S.J Ord: '72, Philippines; Paul L. Horgan, S.J. Ord: '68, Micronesia; John E. Hyatt, S.J. Ord:'77, Dominican Republic; William P. Klintworth, S.J. Ord: '61, Philippines; John G. Krebs, S.J. Ord: '65, Philippines; William H. Kreutz, S.J. Ord: '69, Philippines; Dennis M. Leder, S.J. Ord: '76, Guatemala; John J. Madden, S.J. Ord: '69, Ghana; Paul J. Maher, S.J. Ord: '64, Nigeria; William J. Malley, S.J. Ord: '64, Philippines; R. Richard McAuliff, S.J. Ord: '92, Micronesia; Daniel F. McCoy, S.J. Ord: '45, Japan; James A. McDonough, S.J. Ord: '42, Guam; William J. McGarry, S.J. Ord: '58, Micronesia; Thomas B. McGrath, S.J. Ord: '64, Guam; James A. McKeough, S.J. Ord: '54, Philippines; Daniel J. McNamara, S.J. Ord: '80, Philippines; James T. Meehan, S.J. Ord: '63, Philippines; Michael D. Moga, S.J. Ord: '64, Philippines; Gregory F. Muckenhaupt, S.J. Ord: '88, Micronesia; Ugo R. Nacciarone, S.J. Ord: '64, Zambia; James A. O'Donnell, S.J. Ord: '61, Philippines; Thomas H. O'Gorman, S.J. Ord: '63, Philippines; John J. Phelan, S.J. Ord: '58, Philippines; Calvin H. Poulin, S.J. Ord: '62, Philippines; Neil C. Poulin, S.J. Ord: '66, Micronesia; William J. Rakowicz, S.J. Ord: '80, Micronesia; James B. Reuter, S.J. Ord: '46, Philippines; Robert A. Rice, S.J. Ord: '52, Philippines; Joseph L. Roche, S.J. Ord: '58, Philippines; Michael F. Rooney, S.J. Ord: '72, Philippines; Marc J. Roselli, S.J. Ord: '85, Nigeria; Patrick J. Ryan, S.J. Ord: '68, Nigeria; Very Rev. Ramon A. Salomone, S.J. Ord: '65, Nigeria & Reg. Supr.-Nigeria-Ghana; J. Peter Schineller, S.J Ord: '70, Kenya; Herbert Schneider, S.J. Ord: '70, Philippines; John N. Schumacher S.J. Ord: '57, Philippines; John R. Sheehan, S.J. Ord: '92, Nigeria; Joseph J. Smith, S.J. Ord: '57, Philippines; Edward A. Soucie, S.J. Ord: '62, Micronesia; Thomas B. Steinbugler, S.J. Ord: '61, Philippines; Robert J. Suchan, S.J. Ord: '56, Philippines; William M. Sullivan, S.J.

Society of Jesus: Oregon Province, Mailing Address: P.O. Box 86010, (3215 S.E. 45th Ave.,) Portland, OR 97286-0010. Phone: 503-226-6977. Revs. John D. Whitney, S.J. Ord: '94, Prov.; Dan T. Mai, S.J. Ord: '63, Prov. Liaison for Jesuit Interntl. Ministries.

Legal Title: *American Jesuits in Africa.*

U.S. Religious serving in Foreign Missions: Revs. Joseph E. Danel, S.J. Ord: '52, Zambia; Peter J. Henriot, S.J. Ord: '70, Zambia; Ronald E. Hidaka, S.J. Ord: '74, Zambia; Gary N. Smith, S.J. Ord: '71, Uganda; James P. McGloin, S.J. Ord: '74, Zambia; Bartholomew J. Murphy, S.J. Ord: '72., Tanzania; Michael J. Schultheis, S.J. Ord: '65, Ghana; Roy W. Thaden, S.J. Ord: '73, Zambia; Peter R. Titland, S.J. Ord: '70, Zambia.

Priests 9.

Society of Jesus: Wisconsin Province, 3400 W. Wisconsin Ave., P.O. Box 080288, Milwaukee, WI 53208-0288. Phone: 414-937-6949; Fax: 414-937-6950. Revs. James E. Grummer, S.J. Ord: '82, Prov.; John M. Paul, S.J. Ord: '80, Socius.

U.S. Religious serving in Foreign Missions: Revs. Francis X. Buchmeier, S.J. Ord: '73, Korea; John V. Daly, S.J. Ord: '66, Korea; Emil J. Denemark, S.J. Ord: '81, Korea; James A. Egan, S.J. Ord: '65, Uganda; Jonathan Haschka, S.J. Ord: '75, Tanzania; Robert J. Kelly, S.J. Ord: '52, Korea; John D. Mace, S.J. Ord: '68, Philippines; Peter E. Marchetti, S.J. Ord: '77, Honduras; H. Francis Mathy, S.J. Ord: '58, Japan; Robert K. McIntosh, S.J. Ord: '72, Korea; Philip E. Pick, S.J. Ord: '50, Honduras; Basil M. Price, S.J. Ord:'54, Korea; John R. Schak, S.J. Ord: '61, Argentina; Nicholas E. Schiel, S.J. '55, Honduras; Christopher A. Spalatin, S.J. Ord: '71, Korea; James J. Strzok, S.J. Ord: '70, Kenya; Anthony J. Wach, S.J. Ord: '72, Uganda.

Priests 17.

CONGREGATION OF THE HOLY SPIRIT (C.S.Sp.)

Holy Spirit Foreign Missions

U.S.A. - East Province: Spiritans, 6230 Brush Run Rd., Bethel Park, PA 15102. Fax: 412-831-0970. Very Rev. James P. McCloskey, C.S.Sp. Ord: '80, Prov.

U.S. Religious serving Abroad: Revs. Remo J. Bonifazi, C.S.Sp. Ord: '45, Republic of South Africa; William H. Christy, C.S.Sp. Ord: '92, Arusha, Tanzania; Paul M. Flamm, C.S.Sp. Ord: '99, Kasulu-Kigoma; Adrien T. Hebert, C.S.Sp. Ord: '58, Pomeroy, RSA; Joseph M. Herzstein, C.S.Sp. Ord: '63, Arusha; Richard J. LeClair, C.S.Sp. Ord: '51, Arusha, Tanzania; Edward T. Marchessault, C.S.Sp. Ord: '64, Arusha, Tanzania; Josaphat Msongore, C.S.Sp. Ord: '63, Arusha, Tanzania; Patrick A. Patten, C.S.Sp. Ord: '78, Arusha, Tanzania; Vincent G. Stegman, C.S.Sp. Ord: '62, Ethiopia; Most Rev. Bernard M. Ngaviliau, C.S.Sp. Ord: '49, Arusha, Tanzania; Bro. Francis Sullivan, C.S.Sp., Arusha, Tanzania.

JESUIT VOLUNTEERS INTERNATIONAL (S.J.)

U.S. Headquarters: Jesuit Volunteers International, P.O. Box 3756, Washington, DC 20027-0256. Phone: 202-687-1132; Fax: 202-687-5082. Mr. Dennis Heaphy, Dir.

A Christian service organization offering young College educated lay men and women an opportunity to volunteer in a developing country in collaboration with Jesuits. Volunteers serve for two years without returning to the U.S.

MARYKNOLL (M.M.)

A community of American secular priests and brothers. Established in 1911 by action of the United States Hierarchy. Authorized by Pope Pius X, with later approvals by Pope Benedict XV and Pope Pius XI.

U.S. Foundation: *Maryknoll Society Center & Administrative Offices Catholic Foreign Mission Society of America,* P.O. Box 303, Maryknoll, NY 10545-0303, Phone: 914-941-7590; Fax: 914-762-0316. Revs. John C. Sivalon, M.M. Ord: '65, Supr. Gen. & Pres.; Francis T. McGourn, M.M. Ord: '64, Vicar Gen. & Vice Pres.; John C. Barth, M.M. Ord: '91, Asst. Gen.; John J. McAuley, M.M. Ord: '81, Asst. Gen.

The Society is incorporated in New York, under the Legal Title: *Catholic Foreign Mission Society of America, Incorporated.* It is also incorporated in California, Hawaii, Illinois, Massachusetts, Minnesota, and Missouri.

For detailed information regarding statistics, activities in the Archdioceses and Dioceses in the United States, Properties owned or sponsored and Houses in the United States, and the placement of the Maryknollers in the various Archdioceses and Dioceses, please refer to the sections for Religious Institutes of Men and the designated Archdioceses and Dioceses.

Maryknoll Foreign Missions

Maryknollers serving Overseas: Province Office

Religious serving in Bangladesh: Revs. Robert T. McCahill, M.M. Ord: '64; William J. McIntire, M.M. Ord: '67; Douglas F. Venne, M.M. Ord: '59. Priests 3.

Religious serving in Bolivia: Revs. Denis P. Browne, M.M. Ord: '47; Joseph M. Everson, M.M. Ord: '99; John F. Gorski, M.M. Ord: '63; Michael A. Gould, M.M. Ord: '54; Thomas P. Henehan, M.M. Ord: '65; Sigmund S. Jamroz, M.M. Ord: '66; Stephen P. Judd, M.M. Ord: '78; Mark A. Meyer, Ord: '97; Paul A. O'Brien, M.M. Ord: '59; John J. Ogurchock, M.M. Ord: '54; Arthur J.

Prall, M.M. Ord: '52; Eugene W. Toland, M.M. Ord:'64, Reg. Supr.; Joseph C. Tran, M.M. Ord:'03; Juan M. Zuniga, M.M. Ord:'64.
Priests 13; Brothers 6; Associates 1.
Religious serving in Brazil: Revs. Daniel F. McLaughlin Ord: '61; Dennis Moorman, M.M. Ord: '98; Francis B. Higdon, M.M. Ord:'67; James L. Hilgeman, M.M., M.D. Ord: '65; Gerald M. Wickenhauser, M.M. Ord: '62.
Priests 5.
Religious serving in Cambodia: Revs. James P. Noonan, M.M. Ord: '60; Charles R. Dittmeier Ord: '70; Ramone St.Vil, M.M. Ord:'03; Hung T. Nguyen Ord: '94.
Priests 1; Priest Associates 2.
Religious serving in Chile: Revs. Dale F. Barron, M.M. Ord: '65; Richard L. Brooker, M.M. Ord: '55; Joseph H. Cappel, M.M. Ord: '35; John J. Gallahue, M.M. Ord: '62; Frederick J. Hegarty, M.M. Ord: '53; John A. Jensen, M.M. Ord: '44; Ernest C. Lukaschek, M.M. Ord: '64; Elmer J. Meyer, M.M. Ord: '54; George F. Painter, M.M. Ord: '44; Richard J. Sammon, M.M. Ord: '56; J. Lawrence Schanberger, M.M. Ord: '49; Paul M. Sykora, M.M. Ord:'76; James R. Weckesser, M.M. Ord: '55.
Priests 13; Brothers 1.
Religious serving in Egypt: Rev. Douglas E. May, M.M. Ord: '86.
Religious serving in El Salvador: Revs. David C. Kelly, M.M. Ord: '57; James M. Lynch, M.M. Ord: '74; Gerald J. Persha, M.M. Ord: '70; John H. Spain, M.M. Ord: '70.
Priests 4.
Religious serving in Ethiopia: Rev. George C. Cotter, M.M. Ord: '60. Priests 1.
Religious serving in Guatemala: Revs. William J. Donnelly, M.M. Ord: '65; Thomas R. Amarillas, M.M. Ord: '68; William F. Mullan, M.M. Ord: '62; Robert F. Crohan, M.M. Ord: '62; Joseph W. Halpin, M.M. Ord: '52; James P. LaCoste, M.M. Ord: '56; Kevin A. Lynch, M.M. Ord: '61; John J. McGovern, M.M. Ord: '54; Joseph C. Nerino, M.M. Ord: '50; John J. Ruessmann, M.M. Ord: '79.
Priests 10.
Religious serving in Honduras: Revs. Robert F. Coyne, M.M.; Ord: '83; Richard C. Frank, M.M. Ord: '53; Thomas F. Goekler, M.M. Ord: '67; David E. LaBuda, M.M. Ord: '71; Ronald J. Potter, M.M. Ord: '61; William Senger, M.M. Ord:'73.
Priests 6.
Religious serving in Hong Kong: Revs. Sean P. Burke, M.M. Ord: '78, Reg. Supr.; Jose A. Aramburu, M.M. Ord: '84; John F. Ahearn, M.M. Ord: '73; Robert F. Astorino, M.M. Ord: '70; Peter J. Barry, M.M. Ord: '65: Robert C. Bayne, M.M. Ord:'63; Anthony V. Brennan, M.M. Ord: '61; John J. Casey, M.M. Ord: '56; John A. Cioppa, M.M. Ord: '59; Vincent F. Corbelli, M.M. Ord: '60; Thomas E. Danaher, M.M. Ord: '62; Scott T. Harris, M.M. Ord: '78; Stephen B. Edmonds, M.M. Ord: '40; John P. Grady, M.M. Ord: '55; John E. Geitner, M.M. Ord: '53; Adam B. Gudalefsky, M.M. Ord: '59; Denis J. Hanly, M.M. Ord: '59; Lawrence J. Lewis, M.M. Ord: '75; Michael J. McKeirnan, M.M. Ord: '41; Edward F. Malone, M.M. Ord: '52; Thomas A. Peyton, M.M. Ord: '58; Ronald R. Saucci, M.M. Ord: '65; J. Edward Szendrey, M.M. Ord: '62; Eugene A. Thalman, M.M. Ord: '60; Elmer P. Wurth, M.M. Ord: '56.
Priests 25; Brothers 2.
Religious serving in Indonesia: Rev. Vincent P. Cole, M.M. Ord: '71.
Priests 1.
Religious serving in Italy: Rev. Edward M. Dougherty, M.M. Ord: '79, Procurator. Collegio Maryknoll, Via Sardegna, 83, Rome, Italy 00187.
Priests 1.
Religious serving in Japan: Revs. Patrick F. O'Donoghue, M.M. Ord: '50; Roy C. Assenheimer, M.M. Ord: '65; Gerald L. Beausoleil, M.M. Ord: '52; John T. Brinkman, M.M. Ord: '71; Anthony B. Brodniak, M.M. Ord: '54; LoXuan Dam, M.M. Ord: '00; John F. Felago, M.M. Ord: '68; Regis B. Ging, M.M. Ord: '66; James H. Gorman, M.M. Ord: '52; William J. Grimm, M.M. Ord: '77; Joseph L. Hamel, M.M. Ord: '85; Kevin J. Hanlon, M.M. Ord: '89; Joseph H. Hermes, M.M. Ord: '62; James R. Jackson, M.M. Ord: '58; Joseph V. Maynard, M.M. Ord: '48; James J. Mylet, M.M. Ord: '75; Robert V. Nehrig, M.M. Ord: '54; Bryce T. Nishimura, M.M. Ord: '56; James W. O'Neill, M.M. Ord: '55; Francis A. Riha, M.M. Ord: '68, Reg. Supr.; Kenneth C. Sleyman, M.M. Ord: '90; Louis J. Wolken, M.M. Ord: '46; Robert R. Zahn, M.M. Ord: '55.
Religious serving in Kenya: Revs. John E. Conway, M.M. Ord: '73; Donald F. Donovan, M.M. Ord: '55; William Fryda, M.M. Ord: '88; Michael C. Kirwen, M.M. Ord: '63; John J. Lange, M.M. Ord: '58; Lance P. Nadeau, M.M. Ord: '90; Edward J. Phillips, M.M. Ord: '74; Richard J. Quinn, M.M. Ord: '54; Robert W. Vujs, M.M. Ord: '61; Maurice J. Zerr, M.M. Ord: '51.
Priests 12; Brothers 5; Priest Associate 1.
Religious serving in Korea: Revs. Edward J. Whalen, M.M. Ord: '61; Richard Agustin, M.M. Ord: '85; Carl A. Costa, M.M. Ord: '71; Gerald J. Farrell, M.M. Ord: '57; Russell J. Feldmeier, M.M. Ord: '80; Alfred J. Fleming, M.M. Ord: '60; James M. Gilligan, M.M. Ord: '55; Gerard E. Hammond, M.M. Ord: '60, Reg. Supr.; Robert M. Lilly, M.M. Ord: '60; Philip W. Mares, M.M. Ord: '86; Gerald P. O'Connor, M.M. Ord: '69; Fernand Paquet, M.M. Ord: '56; Robert R. Pellini, M.M. Ord: '59; David L. Pfeiffer, M.M. Ord: '66; Joseph A. Slaby, M.M. Ord: '66; James P. Sinnott, M.M. Ord:'60; Joseph Turowski, M.M. Ord:'84; Michael O. Zunno, M.M. Ord: '53.
Priests 17; Bishops 1.
Religious serving in Mexico: Revs. Richard L. Clifford, M.M. Ord: '53; Thomas E. Lavelle, M.M. Ord: '55; John P. Martin, M.M. Ord: '66; Charles A. Murray, M.M. Ord: '51; Peter J. Petrucci, M.M. Ord: '49; Eugene A. Theisen, M.M. Ord: '53; Robert E. Tobin, M.M. Ord: '57.
Religious serving in Mozambique: Revs. Jose Padin, M.M. Ord: '97; Kenneth F. Thesing, M.M. Ord: '69.
Priests 2; Brothers 2.
Religious serving in Namibia: Revs. Richard P. Albertine, M.M. Ord: '66; Richard W. Bauer, M.M. Ord:'85.
Priests 2.
Religious serving in Nepal: Revs. John J. Corcoran, M.M. Ord: '63; Joseph L. Thaler, M.M. Ord: '77.
Priests 2.
Religious serving in Nicaragua: Revs. Edward O. Custer, M.M. Ord: '72; Miguel F. d'Escoto, M.M. Ord: '61; John C. Moynihan, M.M. '67.
Priests 3.
Religious serving in the Philippine Islands: Revs. James H. Kroeger, M.M. Ord: '75; Jeremiah R. Burr, M.M. Ord:'67; Herman W. Cisek, M.M. Ord: '65; John F. Coholan, M.M. Ord: '46; Robert L. Depinet, M.M. Ord: '61; Francis J. Felter, M.M. Ord: '69; James T. Ferry, M.M. Ord: '56; William P. Heffernan, M.M. Ord: '55; James C. Kalchthaler, M.M. Ord: '56; Ralph S. Kroes, M.M. Ord: '58; William J. LaRousse, M.M. Ord: '80; James D. McAuley, M.M. Ord: '80; Donald P. McQuade, M.M. Ord: '65; Walter J. Maxcy, M.M. Ord: '47; Edward D. Shellito, M.M. Ord: '80; J. David Sullivan, M.M. Ord: '60; Reg. Supr. John D. Walsh, M.M. Ord: '56.
Religious serving in Peoples Republic of China: Revs. Donald L. Allen, M.M. Ord: '69; Brian Barrons, M.M. Ord: '84; Francis H. Beninati, M.M. Ord: '55; John P. Cuff, M.M. Ord: '69; Laurence A. Dugas, M.M. Ord: '54; Thomas R. Egan, M.M. Ord: '74; Francis J. Flynn, M.M. Ord:'76; William J. Galvin, M.M. Ord:'56; Carmen G. La Mazza, M.M. Ord: '55; Francis J. Leong, M.M. Ord:'87; James T. Najmowski, M.M. Ord:'76; Lawrence D. Radice, M.M. Ord:'85; Richard S. Rolewicz, M.M. Ord:'65; John C. Tynan, M.M. Ord:'62.
Priests 14; Brothers 1.
Religious serving in Peru: Revs. Thomas J. Burns, M.M. Ord: '69; Michael J. Briggs, M.M. Ord: '76; Charles H. Cappel, M.M. Ord: '44; Edmund L. Cookson, M.M. Ord: '65; Stephen T. De Mott, M.M. Ord: '76; Joseph J. Donovan, M.M. Ord: '79; Joseph Fedora, M.M. Ord: '84; James J. Madden, M.M.; Ord: '60; Philip N. Erbland, M.M. Ord: '66; Robert E. Hoffman, M.M. Ord: '60; Richard G. Laszewski, M.M. Ord: '51; James V. Roth, M.M. Ord: '54; James J. Stefaniak, M.M. Ord: '50; Kyungsu Son, M.M. Ord: '79. Priests 14.
Religious serving in Russia: Revs. Emile E. Dumas, M.M. Ord: '67; Fernand L. Gosselin, M.M. Ord: '70; Joseph V. McCabe, M.M. Ord: '77.
Priests 3.
Religious serving in Samoa: Most Rev. J. Quinn Weitzel, M.M. Ord: '55.
Priests 1.
Religious serving in Taiwan: Revs. Kurt J. Anderson, M.M. Ord: '72; Paul J. Brien, M.M. Ord: '60; Peter C. Brien, M.M. Ord: '60, Reg. Supr.; Robert F. Crawford, M.M. Ord: '61; Richard M. Devoe, M.M. Ord: '56; Alan T. Doyle, M.M. Ord: '64; Paul J. Duffy, M.M. Ord: '79; Clarence A. Engler, M.M. Ord: '59; Edward J. Flanigan, M.M. Ord: '56; Donald F. Glover, M.M. Ord: '70; Delos A. Humphrey, M.M. Ord: '54; John B. Keaney, M.M. Ord: '55; Raymond H. Kelley, M.M. Ord: '58; John F. Kennedy, M.M. Ord: '55; J. Donald McGinnis, M.M. Ord: '53; John P. McKernan, M.M. Ord: '52; James T. Manning, M.M. Ord: '48; Leonard J. Marron, M.M. Ord: '57; Eugene M. Murray, M.M. Ord: '58; Nhuan D. Nguyen, M.M. Ord: '93; Brendan M. O'Connell, M.M. Ord: '63; Francis T. O'Donnell, M.M. Ord: '55; Norbert A. Pacheco, M.M. Ord: '79; Anthony V. Polyak, M.M. Ord: '62; Louis B. Rost, M.M. Ord: '55; Francis F. Schexnayder, M.M. Ord: '64; R. Joyalito F. Tajonera, M.M. Ord: '02; Peter A. Wu, M.M. Ord: '61; Richard E. Zeimet, M.M. Ord: '64.
Priests 29; Brothers 1.
Religious serving in Tanzania: Revs. Thomas A. Tiscornia, M.M. Ord: '73, Reg. Supr.; James A. Conard, M.M. Ord: '56; William F. Daley, M.M. Ord: '56; Edward V. Davis, M.M. Ord: '61; James E. Eble, Jr., M.M. Ord: '88; John W. Eybel, M.M. Ord: '70; Paul E. Fagan, M.M. Ord: '60; J. Francis Flynn, M.M. Ord: '52; Edward A. Hayes, M.M. Ord: '59; Joseph G. Healey, M.M. Ord: '66; Richard A. Hochwalt, M.M. Ord: '51; Leo R. Kennedy, M.M. Ord: '59; Donald E. Larmore Ord: '63; Ramon J. McCabe, M.M. Ord: '56; Howard E. O'Brien, M.M. Ord: '55; Daniel F. Ohmann, M.M. Ord: '55; Edward J. Quinn, M.M. Ord: '51; David A. Smith, M.M. Ord: '85; William S. Stanley, M.M. Ord: '92; Kenneth J. Sullivan, M.M. Ord: '57; Donald F. Sybertz, M.M. Ord: '55.
Priests 20; Brothers 2; Priest Associates 1.
Religious serving in Thailand: Revs. Michael Bassano, M.M. Ord: '75; Daniel A. Boyd, M.M. Ord: '82; Thomas J. Dunleavy, M.M. Ord: '75; William T. O'Leary, M.M. Ord: '61.
Priests 4.
Religious serving in Vietnam: Revs. Charles P. Robak, M.M. Ord: '70; Thomas J. O'Brien, M.M. Ord: '74.
Priests 2.

MISSIONARIES OF AFRICA (M.AFR.)

Missionaries of Africa Foreign Missions

U.S. Headquarters: *Province of North America*, 1624 21st St. N.W., Washington, DC 20009-1003. Phone: 202-232-5154; Fax: 202-332-8640. Rev. Richard Roy, M.Afr. Ord: '71, Asst. Prov.
U.S. Religious serving in Africa: Revs. Richard Archambault, M.Afr. Ord: '73; William Curran, M.Afr. Ord: '66; Rene Dionne, M.Afr. (Spain) Ord: '61; William Dyer, M.Afr. Ord: '70; David Goergen, M.Afr. Ord: '69, Great Britain; Roger A. LaBonte, M.Afr. Ord: '62; Michel J. Lavoie, M.Afr. Ord: '70; Robert McGovern, M.Afr. Ord: '63; William Moroney, M.Afr. Ord:'61, France; Thomas Reilly, M.Afr. Ord: '78; Bros. Vernon Zachman, M.Afr.; Martin Chapper, James Heintz, M.Afr.

MISSIONARIES OF THE SACRED HEART (M.S.C.)

Missionaries of the Sacred Heart Foreign Missions

Missionaries of the Sacred Heart: P. O. Box 270, 305 S. Lake St., Aurora, IL 60507. Phone: 630-892-2371; 892-8400 (Prov. Supr.); Fax: 630-892-1678. Very Rev. David Foxen, M.S.C. Ord: '67, Prov. Supr.; Revs. Gerald Paul, M.S.C. Ord: '60, Treas.; Raymond Diesbourg, M.S.C. Ord: '74, Sec. & Editor, M.S.C. Spotlite.
Publication: *M.S.C. Spotlite.*
Religious serving in Papua New Guinea: Revs. Hilary Fischer, M.S.C. Ord: '57; Bernard Miller, M.S.C. Ord: '59; Leon Weisenberger, M.S.C. Ord: '59; Richard Kennedy, M.S.C. Ord: '67; Bros. James Miller, M.S.C.; Patrick O'Hara, M.S.C.; Daniel Rakow, M.S.C.; Joseph Tesar, M.S.C.; Anton Feitas, M.S.C.
Religious serving in Colombia, South America: Very Rev. German Barona Monsalve, M.S.C. Ord: '86, Section Supr.; Revs. Wilson Tascon, M.S.C. Ord: '90; Michael Miller, M.S.C. Ord: '85; Tito Medina Mora, M.S.C. Ord: '92; Javier Bautista Pinillos, M.S.C. Ord: '95.

OBLATES OF ST. FRANCIS DE SALES MISSIONS (O.S.F.S.)

Oblates of St. Francis de Sales Foreign Missions

U.S. Mission Headquarters: *Office of the Mission Procurato Oblates of St. Francis de Sales*, 1801 N. Broom St., Wilmington, DE 19802. Revs. Francis D. Dougherty, O.S.F.S. Ord: '38; Procurator, Phone: 302-652-3202; John J. Hurley, O.S.F.S. Ord: '68, Procurator, Phone: 302-654-2238; Francis J. Gross, O.S.F.S., Mission Procurator, Toledo-Detroit Prov., 69 O'Hara Rd., Tonawanda, NY 14150. Phone: 716-694-4950.
U.S. Religious serving in Africa & South America: Revs. Leon V. Bonikowski, O.S.F.S. Ord: '65, George J. Brownholtz, O.S.F.S. Ord: '69; Edward P. Canavan, O.S.F.S.; John J. Coyne, O.S.F.S. Ord: '71; Walter DeSa, O.S.F.S.; Walter J. Hartlove, O.S.F.S. Ord: '48; Peter J. Harvey, O.S.F.S. Ord: '60; Robert J. Hindley, O.S.F.S. Ord: '58; Most Rev. John B. Minder, O.S.F.S., D.D.; Revs. Michael Moore, O.S.F.S.; Edmund F. O'Rourke, O.S.F.S.; Harry J. Schlight, O.S.F.S. Ord: '44; Most Rev. Edward J. Schlotterback, O.S.F.S., D.D.; Revs. Alfred J. Smuda, O.S.F.S.

AMERICAN PASSIONIST MISSIONS (C.P.)

Passionist Foreign Missions

Home and Foreign Missions of the American Provinces of the Congregation of the Passion.

General Motherhouse: St.Giovanni e Paolo 13, Rome, 00184, Italy. Provincial Headquarters U.S.A. Most Rev. Ottaviano D/Egidio, C.P., Supr. Gen.

Provincial Headquarters U.S.A.

St. Paul of the Cross Province :Province Pastoral Center, 80 David St., South River, NJ 08882. Phone: 732-257-7177. Very Rev. Terence Kristofak, C.P. Ord: '69, Prov. Supr.; Very Rev. Gerald Laba, C.P. Ord: '73, Vice Prov. & Consultor; Very Rev. Joseph Jones, C.P. Ord: '65, Mission Procurator & Sec.

U.S. Religious Serving Abroad: Revs. Richard Award, C.P. Ord:'81, West Indies; Thomas Brislin, C.P. Ord:'68, Bahamas; Herbert Eberly, C.P. Ord:'58, Philippines; Richard Frechette, C.P. Ord:'79, Haiti; Henry Free, C.P. Ord:'58, Philippines; Aelred Lacomara, C.P. Ord:'57, Africa; Richard Leary, C.P. Ord:'46, West Indies; Lawrence Rywalt, C.P. Ord:'92, Rome; Hilarion Walters, C.P. Ord:'47, Philippines; Bros. Robert McKenna, C.P., Philippines; Michael Stomber, C.P., West Indies; Kingsley Asphall, C.P. Ord:'91, West Indies.

Priests 13; Brothers.

Mission Procurators

Eastern: Revs. Joseph Jones, C.P. Ord: '65, Dir., 80 David St. South River, NJ 08882; Sebastian Kolinovsky, C.P. Ord: '51; Passionist Missionaries, Monastery Pl., Union City, NJ 07087; Bro. Leo DiFiore, C.P. Passionist.

Overseas Missions: 148 Monastery Ave., Pittsburgh, PA 15203.

Canada: 2102 Kipling Ave., Rexdale, ON, M9W 4K5.

Philippines: Procurator, P.O. Box 1290 MCCPO, Metro Manila 1252, Makati, China; Passionist Mission Procurator, Maryknoll House, Stanley, Hong Kong.

Holy Cross Province (Western): 5700 N. Harlem Ave., Chicago, IL 60631. Phone: 773-631-6336; Fax: 773-631-8059. Very Rev. Michael Higgins, C.P. Ord: '70, Prov.; Very Rev. Donald Webber, C.P. Ord: '73, Consultor & Sec.; Rev. Luke Connolly, C.P. Ord: '52

Mission Appeals

Japan: Rev. Leonard Kosatka, C.P. Ord: '42, Passionist Community-Japan Passionist Missions, Passionist Monastery, 10-1 Mefuyamate-cho, Takarazuka-shi 665-0854, Japan. Phone: 011-81-797-84-3111.

U.S. Religious serving Abroad: Revs. Justin Bartoszek, C.P. Ord: '64, Korea; Ward Biddle, C.P. Ord: '51, Japan; Most Rev. Paul M. Boyle, C.P. Ord: '53, West Indies; Revs. Gabriel Brecheteau, C.P. Ord: '48, Japan; Christopher Gibson, C.P. Ord: '75, Rome; David Colhour, C.P. Ord: '94, India; Robert Coward, C.P. Ord: '68, Rome; Blaise Czaja, C.P. Ord: '64, South India; Leonard Kosatka, C.P. Ord: '59, Japan; Denis McGowan, C.P. Ord: '55, Japan; Clement Paynter, C.P. Ord: '52, Japan; Richard Thomson, C.P. Ord: '69, Korea; Joseph VanLeeuwen, C.P. Ord: '64, India; Matthew Vetter, C.P. Ord: '38, Japan; Bro. Laurence Finn, C.P., Korea.

AMERICAN REDEMPTORIST FATHERS (C.SS.R.)

Mission of the Provinces and Vice-Provinces on the United States and other countries and lands

Redemptorist Foreign Missions

Baltimore Province: *Redemptorist Fathers of New York*, 7509 Shore Rd., Brooklyn, NY 11209. Fax: 718-630-5666. Very Rev. Kevin J. Moley, C.Ss.R. Ord: '70, Prov.

Publication: *Perpetual Help World*, 294 E. 150th St., New York, NY 10051.

U.S. Religious serving in Dominica, W.I.: Revs. Jerome Moody, C.Ss.R. Ord: '73; Joseph F. Krastel, C.Ss.R. Ord: '64; John F. McLoughlin, C.Ss.R. Ord: '92.

U.S. Religious serving in Paraguay: Revs. Antonio Cannoles, C.Ss.R. Ord: '69; Robert Hopwood, C.Ss.R. Ord: '52.

U.S. Religious serving in St. Lucia, W.I.: Revs. Edmund J. Faliskie, C.Ss.R. Ord: '91; John P. Gallagher, C.Ss.R. Ord: '95; Rodney J. Olive, C.Ss.R. Ord: '86; Matthew T. Allman, C.Ss.R. Ord: '00; Bruce A. Lewandowski, C.Ss.R. Ord: '94; Kevin M. MacDonald, C.Ss.R. Ord: '91.

Denver Province: P.O. Box 300399, Denver, CO 80203-0399 Phone: 303-370-0036; Fax: 303-370-0036. Very Rev. Richard Thibodeau, C.Ss.R. Ord: '76, Prov.; Rev. Patrick O'Brien, C.Ss.R. Ord: '64, Dir.-Foreign Missions, P.O. Box 6, Glenview, IL 60025, Phone: 847-724-0425; Fax: 847-724-8953.

U.S. Religious serving in Brazil: Revs. Vince Aggeler, C.Ss.R. Ord: '58; Joseph Butz, C.Ss.R. Ord '70; William Fitzgerald, C.Ss.R. Ord: '43; John Gouger, C.Ss.R. Ord: '65; Donnell Kirchner, C.Ss.R. Ord: '66; Patrick McBride, C.Ss.R. Ord: '85; John McCarthy, C.Ss.R. Ord: '62; Thomas McIntosh, C.Ss.R. Ord: ' 66; Most Rev. Alfred Novak, C.Ss.R., Bishop of Paranagua, Brazil; Most Rev. Gutemberg Regis, C.Ss.R., Bishop of Coari, Brazil; Revs. William Steiner, C.Ss.R. Ord: 54; Joseph Stenger, C.Ss.R. Ord: '57; Andrew Thompson, C.Ss.R. Ord: '81; Bro. Leo Patin, C.Ss.R.

U.S. Religious serving in Nigeria: Revs. William M. Cleary, C.Ss.R. Ord: '62; William A. Peterson, C.Ss.R. Ord: '67; Richard Thiele, C.Ss.R. Ord: 54; Robert Wirth, C.Ss.R. Ord: '64.

U.S. Religious serving in Thailand: Revs. Raymond Brennan, C.Ss.R. Ord: '59; Charles Cotant, C.Ss.R. Ord: '41; Francis Gautreaux, C.Ss.R. Ord '50; Joseph Maier, C.Ss.R. Ord: '65; Robert Martin, C.Ss.R. Ord: '50; Patrick Morrissy, C.Ss.R. Ord: '55; Lawrence Patin, C.Ss.R. Ord: '63; Most Rev. George Phimphisan, C.Ss.R., Bishop of Udon Thani; Revs. Michael Shea, C.Ss.R. Ord: '64; Leo Travis, C.Ss.R. Ord: '54; William Wright, C.Ss.R. Ord: '60.

ST. COLUMBAN'S FOREIGN MISSION SOCIETY (S.S.C.)

(THE COLUMBAN FATHERS)

Founded in 1918 with the approval of Pope Benedict XV. Placed under the patronage of St. Columban and made a Pontifical Society by Pope Pius XI.

Generalate: *St. Columban's*, Grange Rd., Donaghmede, Dublin 13, Ireland. Very Rev. Brendan O'Sullivan, S.S.C. Ord: '70, Supr. Gen.

U.S. Foundation & Administration: Columban Fathers, St. Columbans, NE 68056. Phone: 402-291-1920. Very Revs. John Burger, S.S.C. Ord: '73, Dir.; Rev. Thomas P. Reynolds, S.S.C. Ord: '61, Vice Dir.

Publication: *Columban Mission.*

Legal Title: *St. Columban Mission Society.*

The Society is incorporated in California, Illinois, Massachusetts, Nebraska, New York, Rhode Island, and registered in Pennsylvania.

St. Columban's Foreign Mission

House of Post-Graduate Studies: Collegio Colombano, Corso Trieste, 57, Roma Italy. 00198, Very Rev. Padhraic O'Loughlin, S.S.C. Ord: '57, Procurator Gen.

U.S. Religious serving Overseas: Revs. William D. Bourke, S.S.C. Ord: '54, Philippines; Thomas Browning, S.S.C. Ord: '90, Taiwan; John A. Buckley, S.S.C. Ord: '68, Brazil; Vincent J. Busch, S.S.C. Ord: '74, Philippines; Francis P. Carroll, S.S.C. Ord: '62, Japan; David J. Clay, S.S.C. Ord: '62, Philippines; John Comiskey, S.S.C. Ord: '68, Philippines; Neil Boyle, S.S.C. Ord: '43, Ireland; Charles Duster, S.S.C. Ord: '61, Fiji; Otto Imholte, S.S.C. Ord: '63, Ireland; Michael Hoban, S.S.C. Ord: '70, Chile; Quentin F. Kalick, S.S.C. Ord: '42, Philippines; David Padrnos, S.S.C. Ord: '71, Japan; Ronald Kelso, S.S.C. Ord: '73, Japan; Donald Kill, S.S.C. Ord: '72, Philippines; Charles Lintz, S.S.C. Ord: '70, Korea; James J. McCaslin, S.S.C. Ord: '54, Hong Kong; Joseph McSweeny, S.S.C. Ord: '90, Taiwan; John P. Moran, S.S.C. Ord: '50, Philippines; William Morton, S.S.C. Ord: '85, Mexico; Robert E. Mosher, S.S.C. Ord: '82, Chile; Brendan O'Sullivan, S.S.C. Ord: '70, Ireland; Richard L. Pankratz, S.S.C. Ord: '74, Philippines; Desmond Quinn, S.S.C. Ord: '54, Ireland; Edward I. Quinn, S.S.C. Ord: '55, Fiji; Francis A. Regan, S.S.C. Ord: '66, Britain; Paul Richardson, S.S.C. Ord: '54, Philippines; Christopher Saenz, S.S.C. Ord: '00, Chile; David M. Sheehan, S.S.C. Ord: '53, Korea; Thomas Walsh, S.S.C. Ord: '57, Chile; John Wanaurny, S.S.C. Ord: '59, Mexico; Vincent J. Youngkamp, S.S.C. Ord: '59, Japan.

Priests 29.

BROTHERS OF THE SACRED HEART (S.C.)

Brothers of the Sacred Heart Foreign Missions

Provincial House: 685 Steere Farm Rd., Pascoag, RI 02859-4601. Phone: 401-568-3361; Fax: 401-568-1450. Bros. Raymond F. Reinsant, S.C., Prov. Supr.; Paul Hebert S.C., Mission Procurator. The Brothers of the Sacred Heart have mission schools and stations in Kenya, Lesotho, Uganda, Zambia and Zimbabwe.

Brothers 82; Brothers in Africa 50.

SALESIANS OF DON BOSCO (S.D.B.)

Salesians of Don Bosco Foreign Missions

Salesian Provincial House: 148 Main St., Box 639, New Rochelle, NY 10802-0639. Phone: 914-636-4225. Very Rev. James Heuser, S.D.B. Ord: '84, Prov.; Bro. Emile Dube, S.D.B., Procurator.

U.S. Religious serving Abroad: Revs. Henry Bonetti, S.D.B. Ord: '73, Korea; Dominic DeBlase, S.D.B. Ord: '61, Sierra Leone; Robert Falk, S.D.B. Ord: '63, Korea; Lawrence Gilmore, S.D.B. Ord: '84, Liberia; Edward Liptak, S.D.B. Ord: '59, Tanzania; Harry Peterson, S.D.B. Ord: '61, Chile; John Thompson, S.D.B. Ord: '79, Sierra Leone; John Trisolini, S.D.B. Ord: '67, Korea; John Cosgrove, S.D.B. Ord:'02, Sierra Leone.

Salesian Provincial House: 1100 Franklin St., San Francisco, CA 94109. Phone: 415-441-7144; Fax: 415-441-7155. Very Rev. David T. Purdy, S.D.B. Ord: '70, Prov.

U.S. Religious serving Abroad: Revs. Albert Mengon, S.D.B. Ord: '66, Sierra Leone; Wjociech Mroczek, S.D.B. Ord: '03, Sierra Leone; Thomas Thodukulam, S.D.B. Ord:'00, Sierra Leone; Bros. Joseph Reza, S.D.B., Ethiopia; William Regner, S.D.B., Sierra Leone.

SALVATORIAN MISSIONS (S.D.S.)

Salvatorian Foreign Missions

U.S.A. Provincial Headquarters: *Salvatorian Provincial Offices*, 1735 N. Hi-Mount Blvd., Milwaukee, WI 53208-1720. Phone: 414-258-1735. Very Rev. Peter Schuessler, S.D.S. Ord: '80, Prov.

U.S.A. Procurator: 1735 N. Hi-Mount Blvd., Milwaukee, WI 53208-1720 Phone: 414-258-1735. Rev. Eric Middlecamp, S.D.S. Ord: '52, Mission Dir.

Publication: *The Salvatorian Newsletter.*

U.S. Religious serving in Tanzania: Revs. Carl Gleason, S.D.S. Ord: '56; Daniel Pekarske, S.D.S. Ord: '90; James Weyker, S.D.S. Ord: '69; Bro. Donald Maurer, S.D.S.

SOCIETY OF AFRICAN MISSIONS (S.M.A.)

Society of African Missions

U.S. Provincial Headquarters: 23 Bliss Ave., Tenafly, NJ 07670. Phone: 201-567-0450; 567-9085; Fax: 201-567-7156; 541-1280. Rev. Thomas M. Wright, S.M.A. Ord: '92, Prov. Supr.

U.S. Religious serving Abroad: Revs. Albert Cooney, S.M.A. Ord: '55, Kenya; Frank Allen Wright, S.M.A. Ord: '93; Kenya.

SOCIETY OF ST. EDMUND (S.S.E.)

Edmundite Foreign Missions

U.S. Foundation: 270 Winooski Park, Colchester, VT, 05439. Phone: 802-654-3400; Fax: 802-654-3409. Very Rev. Richard M. Myhalyk, S.S.E. Ord: '71, Supr. Gen.

U.S. Religious serving Abroad: Revs. Edward J. Dubriske, S.S.E. Ord: '64, Venezuela; Philippe Simonnet, S.S.E. Ord: '52, France.

THE SOCIETY OF MARY (S.M.)

MARIST FATHERS

Marist Foreign Missions

General Motherhouse: Via Alesandro Poerio, 63, Rome, Italy, 00152. Very Revs. Jan Hulshof, S.M. Ord: '66, Supr. Gen.; Craig Larkin, S.M. Ord: '67, Vicar Gen.

U.S. Mission Promoter: *Marist Missions*, 29 Isabella St., Boston, MA 02116-5216. Phone: 617-482-0832; Fax: 617-482-1570. Rev. J. Armand Robichaud, S.M. Ord: '50, Dir.; Missions in Brazil, Fiji, Japan, New Caledonia, Norway, Papua New Guinea, Peru, Philippine Islands, Samoa, Senegal, Solomon Islands, Tonga, Vanuatu, Venezuela, Wallis & Futuna, Republic of Cameroon.

U.S. Religious serving abroad: Revs. Paul Frechette, S.M. Ord: '76, Italy; John Galvin, S.M., Ord: '63, Solomon Islands; Joseph J. McLaughlin, S.M. Ord: '72, Philippines; Louis Morosini, S.M. Ord: '56, Solomon Islands; Alfred Puccinelli, S.M. Ord: '66, Brazil; Joseph Pusateri, S.M. Ord: '65, Samoa; Bertrand Soucy, S.M. Ord: '53, Vanuatu; Neil Soucy, S.M. Ord: '62, New Caldonia.

Society of St. James the Apostle

Society of St. James the Apostle, Inc.: 24 Clark St. Boston, MA 02109. Phone: 617-742-4715; Fax: 617-723-7389. Revs. Robert Thomas, Ord: '03 Dir.; Milton Eggerling (OAK) Ord: '54.

Founded by His Eminence Richard Cardinal Cushing, in 1958 to recruit Diocesan priest volunteers for South America.

Serving in Bolivia: Revs. Raymond Cowell (CHI) Ord: '56; Harold Holbrook (BGP) Ord: '57; Paul M. Koch (DM) Ord: '61; Thomas Oates (BO) Ord: '63.

Serving in Ecuador: Revs. James Coleman (P) Ord: '85; Cornelius Kiely (BAK) Ord: '67; John J. Moriarty (JOL) Ord: '62.

Serving in Peru: Revs. John E. Davis (FAR) Ord: '69; George Flynn (BO) Ord: '56; Donald Gorski (CHR) Ord: '59; Kevin Hays (CHI) Ord: '77; Eugene K. Kirke

(BO) Ord: '62; Joseph I. Martin (BO) Ord: '56; J. Joseph McCarthy (BO) Ord: '66; John O'Leary (MIA) Ord: '67; Gerard O'Meara (BO) Ord: '76; Raymond O'Sullivan (BO) Ord: '68; John J. Pashby (BO) Ord: '60; Jules Roos (PIT) Ord: '56; Desmond Tynan (BO) Ord: '67.

THIRD ORDER REGULAR MISSIONS (T.O.R.)

THIRD ORDER REGULAR OF ST. FRANCIS

T.O.R. Foreign Missions

Provincial Residence: *Province of the Most Sacred Heart of Jesus,* 128 Woodshire Dr., Pittsburgh, PA 15215-1714. Phone: 412-781-8333. Very Rev. Edmund F. Carroll, T.O.R. Ord: '57, Minister Prov.; Bro. Mark McBride, T.O.R., Prov. Dir. of Foreign Missions.

U.S. Religious serving Abroad: Revs. Gerald J. King, T.O.R. Ord: '71, Brazil; Joseph Markalonis, T.O.R. Ord: '66, Brazil; Paul R. Pavlik, T.O.R. Ord: '59, Brazil.

MISSIONARY SERVANTS OF THE MOST HOLY TRINITY (S.T.)

Trinity Missions

International Headquarters

Generalate: 1215 N. Scott St., Arlington, VA 22209-3009. Phone: 703-276-8646; Fax: 703-522-2656. Rev. Austin Walsh, S.T. Ord: '65, Supr. Gen.; Bro. Steven Vesely, S.T., Sec. Gen.

U.S. Religious serving Abroad: Revs. Rudy Breunig, S.T. Ord: '65, Costa Rica; Charles Gordon, S.T. Ord: '67, Costa Rica; Kevin Nugent, S.T. Ord: '51, Costa Rica; Victor Santiago Mateo, S.T. Ord: '82, Colombia; Eugene Mueller, S.T. Ord: '55, Mexico; Bruce Ward, S.T. Ord: '60, Mexico; Guy Wilson, S.T. Ord: '78, Costa Rica.

AMERICAN VINCENTIAN MISSIONS (C.M.)

Provincial Headquarters

Vincentian Foreign Missions

Eastern Province: *St. Vincent's Seminary,* 500 East Chelten Ave., Philadelphia, PA 19144. Phone: 215-848-1985; Fax: 215-844-2085. E-mail: cmphila88@aol.com. Very Rev. Thomas F. McKenna, C.M. Ord: '67, Prov.; Rev. Charles P. Strollo, C.M. Ord:'73, Asst. Prov.

U.S. Religious serving Abroad: Revs. Osvaldo Ayala, C.M. Ord: '01, Puerto Armuelles, Panama; Elmer Bauer, III, C.M. Ord: '93, Rome, Italy; Thomas M. Byrnes, C.M. Ord: '50, Balboa, Panama; Gilberto Caballero, C.M. Ord:'03, Concepcion, Panama; John J. Carney, C.M. Ord: '82, Colon, Panama; Edison Famania, C.M. Ord: '94, Concepcion, Panama; G. Gregory Gay, C.M. Ord: '80, Guatemala, Central America; Alcibiades Guerra, C.M. Ord: '90, Centro Vicentino, Panama; Jose Pio Jimenez, C.M. Ord: '68, Balboa, Panama; Teodoro Justavino, C.M. Ord: '90, Santa Fe, Panama City; Alan J. McLellan, C.M. Ord: '65, Colon, Panama; John J. MacGillivray, C.M. Ord: '76, Volcan, Panama; Robert P. Maloney, C.M. Ord: '66, Rome; Geovany Morales, C.M. Ord: '01, Concepcion, Panama; Emmet J. Nolan, C.M. Ord: '92, Centro Vicentino, Panama; Panama; John P. Prager, C.M. Ord: '82, Puerto Armuelles, Panama; Teodoro A. Rios, C.M. Ord: '76, Concepcion, Panama; Secundino Rios, C.M. Ord: 01, Panama; Charles G. Schuster, C.M. Ord: '55, Soloy Puerto Armuelles, Panama; Thomas Sendlein, C.M. Ord: '72, Taipei, Taiwan, Republic of China; Harold G. Skidmore, C.M. Ord: '50, Balboa, Panama; Ernesto Urbina, C.M. Ord:'03, Darien, Panama. Bros. G. Edgardo Lopez, C.M., Puerto Armuelles, Panama; A. Alberto Mendoza, C.M., Centro Vicentino, Panama.

Midwest Province: *Vincentian Fathers and Brothers,* 13663 Rider Trail N., Earth City, MO 63045-1512. Phone: 314-344-1184; Fax: 314-344-2989. Very Rev. James E. Swift, C.M. Ord: '78, Prov.

U.S. Religious serving in Foreign Missions: Revs. Gary A. Mueller, C.M. Ord: '95; Stephen Gallegos, C.M. Ord: '88; Very Rev. Robert Wood, C.M. Ord: '56, Supr.; Revs. W. Barry Moriarty, C.M. Ord: '67; Thomas G. O'Hern, C.M. Ord: '77; John T. Richardson, C.M. Ord: '49; Hugh F. O'Donnell, C.M. Ord: '61; Jacob Johnson, C.M. Ord: '47; Robert W. Chap, C.M. Ord: '66; Richard Preuss, C.M. Ord:'73; Arthur L. Trapp, C.M.; Bro. James Donlevy, C.M.

Southern Province: *Congregation of the Mission,* 3826 Gilbert Ave., Dallas, TX 75219-4346. Phone: 214-526-0234; Fax: 214-526-3477. Very Rev. Dan Paul Borlik, C.M. Ord: '76, Prov.

U.S. Religious serving in Foreign Missions: Rev. Gilbert R. Walker, C.M. Ord:'87, Havana.

XAVERIAN MISSIONARY FATHERS (S.X.)

Xaverian Foreign Missions

U.S. Foundation: *Xaverian Missionary Fathers,* 12 Helene Ct., Wayne, NJ 07470. Phone: 201-942-2975; Fax: 201-942-5012. Revs. Ivan Marchesin, S.X. Ord: '66, Prov.; Dario Maso, S.X. Ord: '82, Local Supr. & Dir.-Vocation Ministry; Frank B. Grappoli, S.X. Ord: '63, Prov., Local Treas. & Mission Procurator.

Religious Serving in Brasil: Revs. Francis Gugliotta, S.X. Ord: '52; Danilo Lago, S.X. Ord: '77; Mario Pezzotti, S.X. Ord: '59; Gino Nasini, S.X. Ord: '65.

Religious serving in Cameroon: Revs. Rene Lovat, S.X. Ord: '57; Pierino Zoni, S.X. Ord: '61.

U.S. Religious serving in Colombia: Revs. Mark Marangone, S.X. Ord: '84, Mauro Loda, S.X. Ord: '99.

U.S. Religious serving in Indonesia: Revs. Bruno Orru, S.X. Ord: '63; Franco Qualizza, S.X. Ord: '71.

U.S. Religious serving in Japan: Revs. Paolo Gobbo, S.X. Ord: '94; Greg Holm, S.X. Ord: '87.

U.S. Religious serving in Mexico: Rev. Adolph Menendez, S.X. Ord: '68.

U.S. Religious serving in Philippines: Revs. Carl Chudy, S.X. Ord: '86; Kenneth Cannon, S.X. Ord: '97.

U.S. Religious serving in Sierra Leone: Most Rev. George Biguzzi, S.X.; Revs. Luciano Peterlini, S.X. Ord: '63; Graziano Rossato, S.X. Ord: '66.

U.S. Religious serving in Taiwan: Revs. Joseph Matteucig, S.X. Ord: '84; Martino Roia, S.X.

MISSIONHURST (C.I.C.M.)

Missionhurst Foreign Missions

American Headquarters (1946): *Congregation of the Immaculate Heart of Mary,* 4651 N. 25th St., Arlington, VA 22207. Phone: 703-528-3800; Fax: 703-528-5355. E-mail: provincial@missionhurst.org. Rev. William G. Quigley, C.I.C.M. Ord: '74, Prov. Supr.

Publication: *Missionhurst.*

U.S. Religious serving Abroad: Revs. Timothy Atkin, C.I.C.M. Ord: '74, Prov. Supr., Haiti; Paul Delaere, C.I.C.M. Ord: '43, Belgium; Clement DeMeersman, C.I.C.M. Ord: '52, Belgium; Frans Holscher, C.I.C.M. Ord: '56, Belgium; Luke Moortgat, C.I.C.M. Ord: '65, Philippines; John B. Peters, C.I.C.M. Ord: '53, Brazil; Alphonse Rigouts, C.I.C.M. Ord: '48, Belgium; Gerard Rogmans, C.I.C.M. Ord: '55, Dominican Republic; Roy Shea, C.I.C.M. Ord: '86, Brazil; Stan Szarwark, C.I.C.M. Ord: '64, Dominican Republic; Vincent VandeWeyer, C.I.C.M. Ord: '48, Belgium; Joseph Verswyvel, C.I.C.M. Ord: '52, Belgium; Bros. Leon Delanoy, C.I.C.M., Dominican Republic; Robert Dixon, C.I.C.M., Brazil; Jerry Galloway, C.I.C.M., Kinshasa, Democratic Republic of Congo.

AMERICAN OBLATE MISSIONS (O.M.I.)

Home and Foreign Missions of the United States Province of the Missionary Oblates of Mary Immaculate (Oblate Fathers).

United States Province: 391 Michigan Ave., N.E., Washington, DC 20017. Phone: 202-529-4505; Fax: 202-529-4572. Very Rev. David Kalert, O.M.I. Ord: '64, Prov.

Religious in Scandinavian Missions: Revs. Michael Bradley, O.M.I. Ord: '66; Allen Courteau, O.M.I. Ord: '76; Frank Jobst, O.M.I. Ord: '72; Leo Kertz, O.M.I. Ord: '63; Paul Marx, O.M.I. Ord: '65; Carroll Parker, O.M.I. Ord: '61; Clyde Rausch, O.M.I. Ord: '68; John Schoeberle, O.M.I. Ord: '61; Bros. Olof Asblom, O.M.I.; Daniel Bozek, O.M.I.

U.S. Religious serving in Brazil: Revs. James Gibbons, O.M.I. Ord: '69; Thomas Brown, O.M.I. Ord: '55; Peter Curran, O.M.I. Ord: '71; Thomas Delaney, O.M.I. Ord: '60; John Drexel, O.M.I. Ord: '62; Edward Figueroa, O.M.I. Ord: '60; Robert Fitzpatrick, O.M.I. Ord: '71; Bro. Daniel Hayes, O.M.I.; Revs. Bruce Heit, O.M.I. Ord: '64; James Kohmetscher, O.M.I. Ord: '55; Edmund Leising, O.M.I. Ord: '46; Paul Medeiros, O.M.I. Ord: '64; Robert Mayer, O.M.I. Ord: '67; Daniel Meehan, O.M.I. Ord: '61; David O'Brien, O.M.I. Ord: '59; Thomas O'Brien, O.M.I. Ord: '55; William Reinhard, O.M.I. Ord: '61; Anthony Rendon, O.M.I. Ord: '67; Charles Tierney, O.M.I. Ord: '73.

U.S. Religious serving in Canada: Revs. Richard G. Cote, O.M.I. Ord: '60; Normand Bonneau, O.M.I. Ord: '76; Dale Schlitt, O.M.I. Ord: '69.

U.S. Religious serving in Haiti: Revs. Alfred Charpentier, O.M.I. Ord: '71; Real Corriveau, O.M.I. Ord: '61; Omer Duplessis, O.M.I., Ord: '43; Prov.; John Henault, O.M.I. Ord: '63; Roland Gagnon, O.M.I. Ord: '51; Charles Heon, O.M.I. Ord: '64; Raymond Marquis, O.M.I. Ord: '74; Francis Mitchell, O.M.I. Ord: '44; Mauril Rancourt, O.M.I. Ord: '60; John St. Cyr, O.M.I. Ord: '61; Joseph Vaillancourt, O.M.I. Ord: '46; Marc Boisvert, O.M.I. Ord: '84.

U.S. Religious serving in Indonesia: Rev. Lucien Bouchard, O.M.I. Ord: '55.

U.S. Religious serving in Japan: Revs. John Mahoney, O.M.I. Ord: '54, Raymond Bourgoin, O.M.I. Ord: '66; John Deely, O.M.I. Ord: '70; Francis Hahn, O.M.I. Ord: '72; Thomas Maher, O.M.I. Ord: '57; William Maher, O.M.I. Ord: '66; Jerome Novotny, O.M.I. Ord: '68; Angelo Siani, O.M.I. Ord: '65; Bertram Silver, O.M.I. Ord: '54; Edward Williams, O.M.I. Ord: '57.

U.S. Religious serving in Mexico: Revs. Daniel Gagnon, O.M.I. Ord: '87; Robert Hickl, O.M.I. Ord: '79; Richard Junius, O.M.I. Ord: '56; Charles Krzewinski, O.M.I. Ord: '52; James Lyons, O.M.I.; Augustine Petru, O.M.I. Ord: '53; Francis Pfeifer, O.M.I.; Gilberto Pinon, O.M.I. Ord: '71, Cuba; Lawrence Rosebaugh, O.M.I. Ord: '63, Guatemala; Jose Torres, O.M.I. Ord: '74; Gerald Kapustka, O.M.I. Ord: '65, Guatemala.

U.S. Religious serving in other countries: Revs. Robert Durette, O.M.I. Ord: '60, Bolivia; Ruben Elizondo, O.M.I. Ord: '62, Guatemala; Roger Hallee, O.M.I. Ord: '63 Colombia; Paul Hughes, O.M.I. Ord: '73, Colombia; Leo Guilmette, O.M.I. Ord: '63, Paraguay; Bro. Valmond LeClerc, O.M.I., Colombia.

U.S. Religious serving in the Philippine Islands: Revs. Armand Carignan, O.M.I. Ord: '53; Maurice Hemann, O.M.I. Ord: '50; Richard Pommier, O.M.I. Ord: '66; Cletus Ternes, O.M.I. Ord: '61; Richard Weixelman, O.M.I. Ord: '65.

U.S. Religious serving in Tahiti: Rev. Patrice Morel, O.M.I. Ord: '54.

U.S. Religious serving in Zambia: Most Rev. Paul Duffy, O.M.I. Ord: '62; Archbishop of Mongu; Revs. Patrick Gitzen, O.M.I. Ord: '75; Ronald Carignan, O.M.I. Ord: '59; Leo Dummer, O.M.I. Ord: '59; John Staak, O.M.I. Ord: '95; Paul Waldie, O.M.I. Ord: '65; Ronald Walker, O.M.I. Ord: '61.

Missionary Activities

RELIGIOUS SOCIETIES ENGAGED IN MISSIONARY WORK

Augustinian Recollect Fathers: *Province of St. Nicholas of Tolentine U.S. Delegation,* 3201 Central Ave., Union City, NJ 07087. Rev. Francisco Legarra, O.A.R., Prov. Delegate.

Engaged in missionary work among Spanish-speaking people. Sustains mission personnel in the Archdiocese of New York, Newark and in the Dioceses of Las Cruces and El Paso.

Augustinian Recollect Fathers and Brothers (1944): *Province of St. Augustine,* 29 Ridgeway Ave., West Orange, NJ 07052. Very Rev. John A. Gruben, O.A.R., Prov. Supr.

Missionary work among Spanish-speaking people established in colonies throughout a notable part of the U.S. and active in cursillo and retreat work in the Archdiocese of New York.

Blessed Sacrament Fathers and Brothers: *Province of St. Ann,* 5384 Wilson Mills Rd., Cleveland, OH 44143.

Brothers of the Christian Schools: *U.S.A. & Toronto Regional Office of the De La Salle Christian Brothers Conference,* 4351 Garden City Dr., Ste. 200, Landover, MD 20785. Phone: 301-459-9410; Fax: 301-459-8056.

The missionary activities administered by The Christian Brothers Conference include Bethlehem University, West Bank; Kenya, Nigeria, South Africa; Eritrea/Ethiopia. Individual Province Mission responsibilities include San Francisco; Mexico, and Tijuana.Christian Brothers also serve as missionaries in the Philippines & Central America.

* **Christian Foundation for Children and Aging:** One Elmwood Ave., Kansas City, KS 66103. Phone: 913-384-6500; 800-875-6564. Web site: www.cfcausa.org. Robert K. Hentzen, Pres.; Paco Wertin, CEO; Bill Cordaro, Contact Person.

Christian Foundation for Children and Aging (CFCA) is an international Catholic mission organization dedicated to raising mission consciousness here at home and helping the poor at Catholic mission sites abroad. Founded by Catholic lay people in 1981, CFCA develops support through "sponsorship" — linking a child or aging friend in need with a sponsor in a mutually beneficial relationship. Sponsor assistance helps provide food, medical care, opportunity for education while at the same time permitting the sponsor to get to know the culture and life of their sponsored friend. CFCA currently works with over 40 missionary orders and the local church in 25 developing countries and also sponsors an extensive lay volunteer program.

Claretian Missionaries: *Headquarters of Western Province,* 1119 Westchester Pl., Los Angeles, CA 90019. Phone: 323-734-1824; Fax: 323-737-0301. Very Rev. Roland Lozano C.M.F., Prov.

Headquarters of Eastern Province, 400 N. Euclid Ave., Oak Park, IL 60302. Phone: 708-848-2076. Very Rev. Len Brown, C.M.F., Prov.

Please refer to the Religious Institutes of Men section for activities and representation in the United States.

Claret Center: 5536 S. Everett Ave., Chicago, IL. Resources for Counseling and Spiritual Directions. Chicago, IL.

Missions outside the United States entrusted to the Claretians: Guatemala, Cameroons, Mexico.

Publications: monthly magazine, U.S. Catholic; extensive line of Pamphlets and Paperback Books; bimonthly Newsletter; Fides-Claretian.

Columban Sisters (1922 Ireland): 73 Mapleton St., Brighton, MA 02135. Phone: 617-782-5683; Fax: 617-789-3569. Sr. Maura Ryan, S.S.C., U.S. Area Coord.

The Missionary Sisters of Saint Columban are also known as the Columban Sisters. The Columban Sisters are religious women called to bring the good news of Christ to all in need, particularly the poor and the oppressed and those who have not yet had the Gospel proclaimed to them. The congregation strives to respond to the needs of the people by dedication to the work of evangelization through pastoral, educational, medical, and social ministries, and supporting the efforts of the local church where its members are sent. The congregation also endeavors, through programs of mission education and animation, to deepen an awareness of global vision and world justice.

Active in the U.S. in the Archdioceses of Boston, Los Angeles and in the Dioceses of Buffalo, Raleigh. Active outside the U.S. in Ireland, Myanmar, China,England, Scotland, Hong Kong, Korea, Philippines Peru, Chile and Pakistan.

Comboni Missionaries of the Heart of Jesus, Inc. (Verona Fathers): *Provincial Headquarters: Comboni Mission Center,* 1318 Nagel Rd., Cincinnati, OH 45255-3120. Phone: 513-474-4997. Revs. Dennis Conway, M.C.C.J., Prov.; Joseph Bragotti, M.C.C.J., Mission Dir.; Paul Donohue, M.C.C.J., Communications Dir. E-mail: info@combonimissionaries.org. Web site: www.combonimissionaries.org.

Foreign mission society, both priests and brothers, founded by Bishop Daniel Comboni, Vicar Apostolic of Central Africa.

Active in the Archdioceses of Chicago, Cincinnati, Los Angeles and Newark.

Comboni Missionaries work with local churches in: Africa—Benin, Central African Republic, Egypt, Eritrea, Ethiopia, Ghana, Kenya, Malawi, Mozambique, South Africa, Sudan, Chad, Togo, Uganda, Zambia and Democratic Republic of the Congo; Asia—Philippines, China; Latin America—Brazil, Chile, Colombia, Costa Rica, Ecuador, El Salvador, Guatemala, Mexico, Nicaragua, and Peru; North America—Canada and the United States.

Training Centers: Africa—Eritrea, Ethiopia, Kenya, Malawi, Mozambique, South Africa, Togo, Egypt, Sudan, Uganda, Democratic Republic of the Congo; Asia—Philippines; Europe— Austria, England, France, Germany, Italy, Poland, Portugal and Spain; Latin America—Brazil, Colombia, Costa Rica, Ecuador, Mexico and Peru; North America—United States.

Publications: Comboni Press Network Newsletter; Comboni Press Feature Service; Comboni Mission Newsletter.

Comboni Missionary Sisters: *American Headquarters,* 1307 Lakeside Ave., Richmond, VA 23228. Phone: 804-262-8827; Fax: 804-264-2906. Sr. Maria Teresa Goffi, Prov. Supr.

An international congregation of 1,700 sisters founded by Bishop Daniel Comboni in 1872 in Verona, Italy. Engaged in pastoral and catechetical work; education; social services; health services; building Christian communities; training of local church leaders in Africa, Latin America and Middle East.

The American Province recruits and trains sisters for the foreign mission, mission education, fundraising for missions, pastoral ministry among the poor, and day care centers.

Congregation of Alexian Brothers: *Immaculate Conception Province, U.S. Provincial Headquarters,* 600 Alexian Way, Elk Grove Village, IL 60007. Bro. Lawrence Krueger, Provincial.

Missionary healthcare work in Davao City, Philippines directed by Alexian Brothers. Please refer to the Religious Institutes of Men section for activities and representation in the United States.

Congregation of Christian Brothers: *Eastern American Province, United States Headquarters,* 21 Pryer Terr. New Rochelle, NY 10804. Bro. Brian M. Walsh, C.F.C.,Prov. Leader; Bro. Kevin G. Cawley, C.F.C., Deputy Prov. Leader.

Missionary and educational work in Peru.

Congregation of the Holy Ghost and of the Immaculate Heart of Mary (1872) 6230 Brush Run Rd., Bethel Park, PA 15102. Phone: 412-831-0302; Fax 412-831-0970. Holy Ghost Fathers and Brothers (C.S.Sp.), Eastern Province, Very Rev. Donald J. McEachin, C.S.Sp., Prov. Western Province (1963) 1700 W. Alabama St., Houston, TX 77098-2808. Phone: 713-522-2882; 713-522-2667; Fax: 713-522-8063. Very Rev. Michael T. White, C.S.Sp., Prov.

Missionary work among the abandoned, including first evangelization, teaching, care of homeless children, and pastoral ministry.

Missionaries serve in 17 (Arch)Dioceses in the United States: the Archdiocese of San Juan and the Dioceses of Arecibo in Puerto Rico; the Dioceses of Ciudad Valles, Tampico, the Archdiocese of San Luis Potosi in Mexico; Archdiocese of Arusha, and Dioceses of Moulu and Zanzibar in Tanzania. Nairobi in Kenya; Bethlehem in South Africa; and Awasa in Ethiopia. Other establishments in North and South America, Europe, Africa and Australia.

Missionaries of Our Lady of La Salette: *Province of Mary, Mother of the Americas,* 915 Maple Ave., Hartford, CT 06114-2330. Phone: 860-956-8870. Very Rev. Dennis J. Loomis, M.S., Prov. Supr.; Rev. John R. Nuelle, M.S., Procurator, 85 New Park Ave., Hartford, CT 06106-2184.Tel: 860-523-4017; Fax: 860-523-4074.

Active in Archdioceses of Buenos Aires, Argentina; Cochabamba, Bolivia; Cordoba, Argentina; and Diocese of Santiago del Estero, Argentina.

Please refer to the Religious Institutes of Men section for activities and representation in the United States.

Congregation of the Priests of the Sacred Heart, The: *U.S. Provincialate Offices,* P.O. Box 289, Hales Corners, WI 53130-0289. Phone: 414-425-6910. Very Rev. Richard MacDonald, S.C.J., Prov. Supr.

Please refer to the Religious Institutes of Men section for other activities and representation in the United States.

Missionary work in the home and foreign missions; educational activities; welfare work, especially in industrial centers. Home Missions: Lower Brule and Cheyenne Indian Reservations, South Dakota; Black Missions, Diocese of Jackson, Mississippi; Spanish-speaking Apostolate, Dioceses of Brownsville, Galveston-Houston, and Archdiocese of San Antonio. Foreign Missions: Zaire, Cameroon, Mozambique, South Africa, Brazil, Argentina, Uruguay, Chile, Venezuela, India, Indonesia and Finland.

Congregation of the Resurrection: *Resurrection Catholic Missions of the South, Inc.,* 2815 Forbes Dr., Montgomery, AL 36110. Phone: 334-263-4221; Fax: 334-263-4999.

The Resurrection Catholic Missions ministries includes a home for handicapped and severely mentally retarded children, an early childhood development facility for preschoolers, a church and elementary school, a 65-bed geriatric nursing facility; post pediatric nursing facility; 24 bed assisted living facility; as well as an outreach program to homebound elders and an addictions counseling/prevention program.

Please refer to the Religious Institutes of Men section for activities and representation in the United States. Active also in Australia, Brazil, Bolivia, Bulgaria, Canada, Germany, Jamaica, Mexico, Poland and Tanzania.

Consolata Missionaries (1901): *Provincial Headquarters,* 2301 Hwy. 27, P.O. Box 5550, Somerset, NJ 08875-5550. Phone: 732-297-9191; Fax: 732-940-3121. Rev. Leonard DePasquale, I.M.C., Reg. Supr.

Legal Title: *Consolata Society for Foreign Missions.*

Serving in 22 countries around the world including the United States.

Publication: Consolata Missionaries.

Consolata Missionary Sisters (1910): 6801 Belmont Ave., N.E., P.O. Box 371, Belmont, MI 49306. Phone: 616-361-2072; Fax: 616-361-2049. Sr. Zelia M. Cordeiro, M.C., Supr.

The congregation is committed to all types of missionary apostolate, primarily in African and South American countries.

Corpus Christi Carmelites: 516 Broadway, Newport, RI 02840. Sr. Teresa Winefride, O.Carm., Supr.

Sisters work as catechists and social workers in America and abroad; own and/or operate homes for the aged, girls, and sick children; hostels; day nurseries; do ministry work in prisons and hospitals andeducational work in kindergartens, primary and secondary schools.

Crosier Fathers and Brothers: *Crosier Missions,* 3510 Vivian Ave., St. Paul, MN 55126-3852. Phone: 651-486-7456; Fax: 651-287-1130. Mr. David Kostik, Mission Coord.

Legal Title: *Canons Regular of the Order of the Holy Cross.*

Missionary work among the Asmat tribes of Irian Jaya Indonesia, since 1958.

Publication: quarterly, Crossview.

Daughters of Mary Help of Christians: *St. Philip Apostle Province,* 655 Belmont Ave., Haledon, NJ 07508. Mother Judith Suprys, F.M.A., Prov.

Legal Title: *Missionary Society of the Salesian Sisters, Inc.*

Missionary work in home and foreign countries; catechetical, educational and training centers; social services; hostels, hospitals, clinics and dispensaries; mission centers, and youth centers.

Active in U.S. within the Archdioceses of Newark, New Orleans, New York, Miami and the Dioceses of Paterson, St. Petersburg.

Eucharistic Missionaries of St. Dominic: 3801 Canal Street, Ste. 400, New Orleans, LA 70119. Phone: 504-486-1133; Fax: 504-486-6547. Sr. Dorothy Troclair, O.P., Pres.

Missionary work and ministry in religious education; forensic social work; pastoral associates; social service; parish administrators; spirituality-retreat center; home & clinic nursing; hospital chaplaincy; counseling; pastoral care of the sick in homes; literacy ministry to Mayan immigrants.

Franciscan Friars of the Atonement-Generalate: *Graymoor,* P.O. Box 300, Garrison, NY 10524-0005. Phone: 845-424-2113; Fax: 845-424-2166.

Mission activities outside of the U.S.: Japan. Also staff parishes in Canada, England and the United States. The Friars mission of reconciliation is promoted through preaching of the Gospel, ecumenism and inter-religious activity and missionary activity.

Please refer to the Religious Institutes of Men section for activities and representation in the United States.

Franciscan Missionaries of Mary, The: *U.S. Provincial House,* 3305 Wallace Ave., Bronx, NY 10467. Phone: 718-547-4693; 102. Fax: 718-325-5102. Sr. Mary Motte, F.M.M., Prov.

Founded in India in 1877, for the work of evangelization and development in non-Christian and de-Christianized countries. Active mission apostolate is centered in daily adoration of the Blessed Sacrament exposed.

This international congregation serves 865 missions in 54 provinces.

Missionary work of evangelization and development, catechetics, social work, nursing, community development programs, educational and public health programs, pastoral activity and various forms of ministry and service.

Franciscan Missionary Sisters for Africa: *American Headquarters Center for Promotion and Formation,* 172 Foster St., Box 35095, Brighton, MA 02135. Phone: 617-254-4343; Fax: 617-787-8007, E-mail:sisters172@aol.com. Sr. Miriam Duggan, F.M.S.A., Supr. Gen.

Missions in Kenya, Uganda, South Africa, Zambia and Zimbabwe.

Publication: The Daystar.

Franciscan Mission Association: *Franciscan Mission House,* 517 Washington Ave., Rensselaer, NY 12144. Phone: 518-465-0062; Fax: 518-465-3673. Web site: The FMA.org. Rev. Henry Madigan, O.F.M.Conv., Dir.

The American branch of the Franciscan Mission Crusade founded in 1924, approved by Pope Pius XI to further the work of the Conventual Franciscan Missionary Apostolate. The purpose is to aid the Mission of the Order in every possible way. The revenues of the Association accrue from the annual and perpetual enrollments in the Association, bequests, other free-will offerings and donations, membership in monthly mission club appeal.

Franciscan Mission Association (1953): *Franciscan Missions,* 322 West St., Carey, OH 43316. Phone: 419-396-6455. Bro. Bryan Hoban O.F.M.Conv., Dir.

The purpose of the association, which is part of the Province of Our Lady of Consolation, is to give financial and other material aid to the missionaries of Africa: the Dioceses of Ndola and Solwezi, Zambia; missionaries in the Dioceses of Olancho, Tegucigalpa and Comayagua in Honduras and San Jose in Costa Rica; and missionaries of the Southwestern United States. Both living and deceased may be enrolled as members. Members of the laity have an active part in promoting the growth of the association as outlined in Vatican II.

Franciscan Mission Association, Inc.: *Province of St. Anthony of Padua,* 12300 Folly Quarter Rd., Ellicott City, MD 21042. Phone: 410-531-3695; Fax: 410-531-4881. Rev. Martin Kobos, O.F.M.Conv., Dir. E-mail: devdir@saprov.org.

Founded to support the domestic and foreign missions of the Conventual Franciscans of St. Anthony Province.

Franciscan Sisters of Allegany: *St. Elizabeth Motherhouse,* Allegany, NY 14706. Sr. Margaret Mary Kimmins, O.S.F., Gen. Minister; Sr. Marie Dolores Gionta, O.S.F., Mission Society Dir.

Sisters serve in areas of education; health-care; pastoral ministry; social ministries; and other missionary work in the Archdiocese of Kingston and Dioceses of Montego Bay, Jamaica; the Archdioceses of Brasilia and Goiania, and Palmas, Brazil; Prelacy of Cristalandia, Brazil; Dioceses of Anapolis, Ipameri, Goias, Rui Barbosa, Miracema do Tocantins and Jatai, Brazil. Archdiocese of La Paz and Dioceses of Cochabamba, Bolivia; Diocese of Caceres, Philippines.

Congregation 382; foreign missions 87.

Publication: Zeal.

Franciscan Sisters, Daughters of the Sacred Hearts of Jesus and Mary: *Province of St. Clara,* P.O. Box 667, Wheaton, IL 60189-0667. Phone: 630-462-7422; Fax: 630-462-7148. Sr. Margaret Grempka, O.S.F., Prov. Dir.

Active in the United States ministering in home health care; counseling, housing; education; pastoral ministry; care of elderly; wellness; long-term care; social services; spiritual direction and retreats in Archdioceses of Milwaukee, St. Louis, Dubuque, Denver and Chicago; in Dioceses of Joliet, Green Bay, Springfield-Cape Girardeau and Gary. Outside the U.S.: Brazil and Italy.

Franciscan Sisters of Little Falls, MN: *Motherhouse,* Little Falls, MN 56345. Phone: 320-632-2981. Sr. Beatrice Eichten, Pres.

Serving in Catholic and non-sectarian hospitals; Catholic and non-sectarian nursing homes; group homes; apartments for the elderly; home health nursing; public health nursing; Catholic high schools; Catholic elementary schools; special education; Spirituality Farm, Native Americans; community colleges; state colleges and universities; religious education; parish ministry; liturgical music ministry; music center; health and recreation center; retreat ministry; counseling; spiritual direction; social service; ministry to the poor; ministry to the migrants; clinics; consultant for healthcare & related organizations; art therapist, computer programmer; pastoral ministry; education, health, social services in Quito, Ecuador, S.A., Tanzania, Africa.

Franciscan Sisters of the Poor: *Congregational Office,* 133 Remsen St., Brooklyn, NY 11201. Phone: 718-643-1919; Fax: 718-643-9710. Sr. Jeanne M. Glisky, S.F.P., Pres.

Sisters serve in healing ministry; health care; social welfare; pastoral ministry in the U.S.; pastoral ministry and health care in the Dioceses of Rome, Padua and Messina in Italy. Mission ministry is represented in the Archdiocese of Goiania and in the Dioceses of Jatai and Ipameri in Brazil and in Kaolack and Dakar in Senegal, West Africa.

Number in Congregation 171; Mission Ministry 28.

Glenmary Home Missioners (1939): *National Headquarters,* P.O. Box 465618, Cincinnati, OH 45246. Phone: 513-874-8900. Rev. Dan Dorsey, G.H.M., Pres. Web site: www.glenmary.org.

Glenmary is an apostolic society of priests and brothers who, along with lay coworkers establish the Catholic Church in small towns and rural America. Glenmary is the only religious community dedicated exclusively to serving the spiritually and materially poor in Appalachia, the rural South and Southwest. Glenmary missioners serve in areas where less than three percent of the population is Catholic, a significant percent have no church affiliation, and the poverty rate is almost twice the national average. The missionary activities include nurturing Catholic communities, fostering ecumenism, evangelizing the unchurched, working for justice and social outreach. Glenmary staffs 60 missions, a pastoral center, a research center, a group volunteer program at Glenmary Farm and commissions on evangelization and justice.

Please refer to the Religious Institutes of Men section for activities and representation in the United States.

Publication: Glenmary Challenge.

Glenmary Home Mission Sisters of America (1941): *Glenmary Sisters,* P.O. Box 22264, Owensboro, KY 42304-2264. Fax: 270-686-8759. Sr. Patricia Leighton, Pres. Glenmary is a community of women religious of diocesan right -a home mission community dedicated to bringing mission presence and activity to the rural, small town areas of the United States. The sisters live and work among the poor, the sick, the oppressed and unchurched in Appalachia and the South in areas where less than 2% of the total population is Catholic. When possible the sisters work in collaboration with the Glenmary Priests and Brothers. The Glenmary Sisters believe in a holistic approach to mission - the caring of the whole person - through their ministries of evangelization, pastoral outreach, religious education, home visitations, and a wide variety of social services for the very poor.

Please refer to the Religious Institutes of Women section for activities in the United States.

Publications: Kinship; Kinship for Kids.

Institute of Charity (Rosminian Fathers): *Rosmini House,* 2327 W. Heading Ave., Peoria, IL 61604.

Active in the Dioceses of Peoria, and St. Petersburg. Missions and missionary work in Tanga, Tanzania; New Zealand; Venezuela; and Kerala, India.

Jesuit Volunteers International: P.O. Box 3756, Washington, DC 20027-0256. Phone: 202-687-1132; Fax: 202-687-5082. Mr. Dennis Heaphy, Exec. Dir.

A Christian service organization offering young college educated lay men and women an opportunity to volunteer in a developing country in collaboration with Jesuits. Volunteers serve for two years without returning to the U.S. in the interim.

Mariannhill, Congregation of Missionaries of (1882): 23715 Ann Arbor Tr., Dearborn Hts., MI 48127. Rev. Gervais Giguere, C.M.M., Provincial Supr.

The American-Canadian province recruits and trains young men as priests and lay brothers for foreign missions, secures funds for the foreign missions, and does a limited amount of pastoral work at home.

Active in the Archdiocese of Detroit.

Outside the U.S.: Austria, Canada, Germany, Kenya, Mozambique, Netherlands, Papua New Guinea, Poland, South Africa, Spain, Switzerland, Zambia and Zimbabwe.

Worldwide membership: Bishops 3; Priests 215; Brothers 100; Students Professed 71; Total Members 389.

Publication: Leaves.

Marist Missionary Sisters: *North American Provincial Office,* 349 Grove St., Waltham, MA 02453. Phone: 781-893-0149; Fax: 781-894-7610. Web site: www.maristmissionarysmsm.org. Sr. Georgeanne M. Donovan, S.M.S.M., Prov.; Sr. Claire Rheaume, S.M.S.M., Mission Promotor; Sr. Avelina Raiwaleta, S.M.S.M., Vocation Directress.

Legal Title: *Missionary Sisters of the Society of Mary, Inc.*

Founded in France in 1845 for mission in the South Pacific, today, the International Missionary Congregation consist of 568 sisters (in seven provinces), serving the people of God in 28 countries around the world. The American Province has 112 sisters working in Massachusetts, Tennessee, Texas, Florida, California, and Jamaica, W.I. The mission is to bring the good news of God's love through spiritual and corporal works of mercy; catechetical, medical, educational and social services; pastoral ministry; formation of laity for leadership and a great concern for the poorest and most neglected. Working by preference among people of different cultures and languages, to bring about greater understanding, dignity and mutual respect.

Formation is international with a French-speaking novitiate in Senegal, an English-speaking novitiate in New Zealand and a Spanish-speaking novitiate in Peru.

Province headquarters are in the United States, Italy, Australia, New Zealand, Peru, France and New Caledonia.

Please refer to the Religious Institutes of Women section for activities and representation in the United States.

Maryknoll Sisters of St. Dominic, Inc.: P.O. Box 311, Maryknoll, NY 10545-0311. Sr. Suzanne Moore, M.M., Community Pres.; Sr. Ellen McDonald, M.M., Vice Pres.; Sr. Connie Krautkremer, M.M., Gen. Sec.; Sr. Jeanne Rancourt, M.M., Team Member.

A Pontifical Institute under the jurisdiction of the Congregation for the Institutes of Consecrated Life. The purpose of the Maryknoll Sisters Congregation is to participate in the mission presence and activity of the universal Church so that God's reign of peace, justice and love may be proclaimed and witnessed to throughout the world. The Maryknoll Sisters embrace a plurality of ministries while giving a clear sign of Christian community; faith-sharing; self-gift in service through pastoral and catechetical work; basic ecclesial communities; education; social services; medical and health promotion work; services through hostels; services to refugees; and ministries that promote human rights, social justice and the dignity and equality of women.

Please refer to the Religious Institutes of Women section for activities in the United States.

Active in Bangladesh, Bolivia, Brazil, Cambodia, Central Pacific, Chile, China, East Timore, Ecuador, El Salvador, Guatemala, Japan, Kenya, Korea, Micronesia, Mexico, Nepal, Namibia, Nicaragua, Panama, Peru, Philippines, Sudan, Taiwan, Tanzania, Thailand, USA and Zimbabwe.

Medical Missionaries of Mary: 563 Minneford Ave., City Island, NY 10464-1118. Phone: 718-885-0945; Fax: 718-885-0010. Sr. Margaret Quinn, M.M.M., Congregational Ldr.; Sr. Siobhan Corkery, M.M.M., Zonal Coord.; Sr. Therese McDonough, M.M.M., Area Leader USA.

Missionary work in hospitals, clinics and leprosy treatment; public health and pastoral ministry centers in Africa, South America and Clinchco, VA.

Please refer to the Religious Institutes of Women section for activities and representation in the United States.

Active also in Angola, Benin, Rwanda, Nigeria, Uganda, Tanzania, Honduras, Kenya, Malawi, Ethiopia, England, Ireland and Brazil.

Publication: quarterly, The Mini MMM.

Medical Mission Sisters: *North American Headquarters*, 8400 Pine Rd., Philadelphia, PA 19111. Fax: 215-342-3948. Sr. Carmelita Perez, M.M.S., Society Coord.; Sr.Joan Foley, M.M.S., North American Sector Coord.; Monica M. McGinley, Pub. Rels. Dir.

Legal Titles: *Society of Catholic Medical Missionaries, Inc.; Society of Catholic Medical Missionaries Generalate, Inc.*, (effective 1991).

Medical Mission Sisters have the special call in the Church of "being a healing presence at the heart of a wounded world." Members commit themselves "to promote healing and wholeness in all aspects of life" in the spirit of Jesus. They share life with those who are sick and have been made poor, trying to help them to live fully as human beings. Medical Mission Sisters' healing presence today involves a full range of preventative, curative and promotive health services; health training programs; and development and social justice activities in Ghana, Uganda, Kenya, Ethiopia, Malawi, Pakistan, India, Belgium, Venezuela, Brazil, Peru, Indonesia, Philippines, Italy, Holland, Germany, England, Mexico and the United States.

Medical Mission Houses in the United States are listed under the Religious Institutes of Women Section.

Publication: Medical Mission Sisters News.

Mill Hill Missionaries: *St. Joseph's Missionary Society*, 222 W. Hartsdale Ave., Hartsdale, NY 10530. Phone: 914-682-0645; Fax: 914-682-0862. Very Rev. Robert J. O'Neil, M.H.M., Reg. Rep.; Counselors: Revs. Emile Frische, M.H.M.; Bartholomew Daly, M.H.M.; Very Rev. Theo M. Feldbrugge, M.H.M., Reg. Bursar.

An international society of priests and brothers, founded in 1866, devoted entirely to the missionary needs of the Church.

Active in the U.S. in the Archdioceses of New York and Los Angeles.

Active outside the United States. Canada: Diocese of Kingston, ONT. Cameroon: the Archdiocese of Bamenda and the Dioceses of Buea, Kumbo, Mamfe and Ngaoundere. Congo: Diocese of Basankusu. Kenya: Archdioceses of Kisumu, Nairobi, and the Dioceses of Bungoma, Kakamega, Kisii, Malindi, Nakuru and Ngong. Uganda: Archdioceses of Kampala, Tororo and the Dioceses of Jinja, Soroti, Kotido and Lugazi. South Africa: Diocese of Kroonstad, Rustenburg. Sudan: Archdiocese of Khartoum, and the Diocese of Malakal. China: Diocese of Hong Kong. India: Archdioceses of Hyderabad, Bangalore, and the Dioceses of Jammu-Srinagar and Varanasi. Pakistan: Dioceses of Islamabad-Rawalpindi and Hyderabad. Malaysia: Archdiocese of Kuching, and the Dioceses of Kota Kinabalu, Miri and Sibu. Brunei: Prefecture Apostolic of Brunei. Philippines: Archdioceses of Manila, Jaro, and the Dioceses of San Jose and Infanta. Australia: Diocese of Geraldton. New Zealand: Dioceses of Aukland and Hamilton. Brazil: Dioceses of Governador Valadares and Itaquai. Also Ecaudor: Archdiocese of Guayaquil. Bolivia: Archdiocese of Cochabamba.

Mission Helpers of the Sacred Heart: 1001 W. Joppa Rd., Baltimore, MD 21204-3787. Phone: 410-823-8585, Fax: 410-825-6355. Sr. M. Judith Waldt, M.H.S.H., Pres.

A Pontifical, missionary congregation with principal work of evangelization and catechesis; adult religious education; instruction of youth and children; D.R.E. programs; pastoral ministers; pastoral associates; pastoral social ministers; special ministers of the Eucharist; ministry in homes and institutions; ministry to the elderly and infirm; catechesis of blind, deaf, retarded; campus ministry; Hispanic pastoral ministry to adults and youth; spiritual direction and retreat work.

Please refer to the Religious Institutes of Women for activities and representation in the United States.

Activities also in the Archdioceses of Barquisimeto, Venezuela, and San Juan.

Publication: 3 times yearly, The Mission Helper.

Mission International, Inc.: 2301 Hwy. 27, Somerset, NJ 08873. Phone: 732-297-9191; Fax: 732-940-3121. Rev. Leonard DePasquale, Chm.

Missionaries of Africa (M.Afr.): *U.S. Province of North America Headquarters,* 1624 21st St.,N.W., Washington, DC 20009-1003. Fax: 202-332-8640. Rev. Richard Roy, M.Afr., Asst. Prov.

International and interracial missionary society of priests and brothers working in teams almost exclusively in Africa.

Active in the Archdioceses of Washington and the Diocese of St. Petersburg.

Training centers and mission promotion centers in Brazil, Canada, Belgium, France, Germany, Great Britain, Holland, India, Ireland, Italy, Mexico, Philippines, Poland, Spain and Switzerland.

Missionary work in Algeria, Burundi, Ethiopia, Ghana, Kenya, Malawi, Mali, Mozambique, Nigeria, Rwanda, Senegal, Sudan, Tanzania, Tunisia, Uganda, Burkina Faso, Democratic Republic of Congo, Zambia, South Africa, Ivory Coast, and Nigeria. Totaling 99 Dioceses and Archdioceses in Africa; also special team working in Jerusalem.

Publication: newsletter, Missionaries of Africa Report.

Missionaries of the Holy Apostles, Society of the: 22 Prospect Hill Rd., Cromwell, CT 06416. Phone: 860-632-3039; Fax: 860-635-4823. Very Rev. Raymond Halliwell, M.S.A., Prov. Animator.

Apostolic works consist in the promotion and training of adults for Christian leadership and for the diocesan or religious priesthood.

Please refer to the Religious Institutes of Men section for activities and representation in the United States.

Activities also in Brazil, Venezuela, Cameroon, Colombia, Canada, and Peru.

Missionary Benedictine Sisters: *Provincial Motherhouse & Novitiate-Immaculata Monastery,* 300 N. 18th St., Norfolk, NE 68701-3687. Phone: 402-371-3438; Fax: 402-379-2877. Sr. Kevin Hermsen, O.S.B., Prioress.

Missionary work in elementary schools; catechetical programs; pastoral ministry; nursing homes; hospitals in the Archdiocese of Omaha and Diocese of New Ulm, Minnesota; Indian Mission, Northeast Nebraska; Hispanic ministry .

Missionary work outside the U.S. the Philippine Islands, Korea, Brazil, Argentina, Australia, China, India, Tanzania, Namibia, Kenya, Angola, Portugal, Germany, Italy, Spain, Switzerland, Bulgaria and Uganda.

Missionary Servants of the Most Blessed Trinity: *Motherhouse, Novitiate and Generalate,* 3501 Solly Ave., Philadelphia, PA 19136. Fax: 215-335-7559. Sr. Barbara De Moranville, M.S.B.T., Gen. Custodian.

The congregation's mission is the preservation of the faith. This involves nourishing the faith life of those of the Roman Catholic tradition, cooperating in ecumenical endeavors, strengthening life-giving faith among all people, evangelization, actively promoting human development and social justice. The special apostolic intent is to advance and support the ministry of the laity in the mission of the Church, accomplished through the ministries of education, social work and health care on parish and diocesan levels.

Please refer to the Religious Institutes of Women section for activities and representation in the United States.

Active also in the Archdiocese of San Juan, Mexico City and the Dioceses of Ponce, Caguas and Mayaguez in Puerto Rico as well as the Dioceses of Apatzingan and Texcoco in Mexico.

Missionary Servants of the Most Holy Trinity (Trinity Missions): 1215 N. Scott St., Arlington, VA 22209-3009. Phone: 703-276-8646; Fax: 703-522-2656. Rev. Austin Walsh, S.T., Gen. Custodian; Bros. Steven Vesely, S.T., Sec. Gen.; Jordan Baxter, S.T., Treas. Gen.; Rev. Domingo Rodriguez, S.T., Mission Procurator. Mailing Address: P.O. Box 7130, Silver Spring, MD 20907-7130.

A clerical congregation of Pontifical Right founded for the preservation of the faith and missionary work wherever the Church directs. The major fields are the missionary areas of the southern United States and the Spanish-speaking people in the United States, Puerto Rico, Colombia, Costa Rica and Mexico. The principal work is the development of Catholic lay leaders. There is also training for the missionary priesthood and brotherhood of the congregation.

Please refer to the Religious Institutes of Men section for activities and representation in the United States.

Publication: Trinity Missions.

Missionary Sisters of Our Lady of Africa: *American Headquarters,* 47 W. Spring St., Winooski, VT 05404. Sr. Claire Bernier, Liaison.

Missionary activities in Africa and Yemen: catechetical, pastoral ministry, social work, education and health programs, and the founding and forming of African Religious Congregations.

Missionary Sisters of the Immaculate Conception of the Mother of God: *Generalate,* 47 Garden Ave., West Paterson, NJ 07424-3337. Phone: 973-279-1484; Fax: 973-279-2991. Sr. Corona Chung, S.M.I.C., Coord. Gen.

Missionary work in homes for the aged, catechetical and social service centers, schools, dispensaries and hospitals.

Active in the U.S. in the Archdioceses of Newark, San Antonio and the Dioceses of Austin, Gallup, Galveston-Houston, Paterson, Portland, and San Bernardino.

Active outside the U.S. in Brazil, Germany, Namibia, Philippines and Taiwan.

Missionary Sisters of St. Peter Claver (1894): *American Headquarters,* P.O. Box 6067, 667 Woods Mill Rd., S. Chesterfield, MO 63006. Phone: 314-434-8084. Sr. Mary Irene Brahmakulath.

Legal Title: The Sodality of St. Peter Claver for the African Missions.

The congregation is of Pontifical Jurisdiction, fostering interest in and obtaining funds and requisites for the missions. Apostolate of the press in Africa.

Publications: monthly magazine, Echo from Africa, annual, Claver Almanac.

Missionary Sisters of Our Lady of the Holy Rosary: 205 Cricket Ave., Ardmore, PA 19003. Phone: 610-896-1786. Sr. Monica Devine, Congregational Ldr.; Sr. Terry Shields, M.S.H.R., Reg. Ldr.

Founded for the evangelization of people in Africa and Latin America through educational, medical, social, pastoral and catechetical work.

Active in the U.S. in the Archdiocese of Philadelphia.

Active outside the U.S. in England, Ireland, Scotland, Nigeria, Sierra Leone, Cameroon, Ethiopia, Kenya, South Africa, Zambia, Ghana, Mexico and Brazil.

Missionary Sisters of the Immaculate Heart of Mary (1919): 238 E. 15th St.,# 5, New York, NY 10003. Phone: 212-677-2959. Sr. Annie Claes, Dist. Supr.

Please refer to the Religious Institutes of Women section for further details.

Missionary Sisters Servants of the Holy Spirit (1901): Techny, IL 60082-6026. Fax: 847-441-5587. Sr. Margaret Anne Norris, Prov. Supr.; Sr. Maryann Regensburger, Supr.

Home and foreign missions including teaching, nursing and social work.

Please refer to the Religious Institutes of Women section for activities and representation in the United States.

Also active in the Philippine Islands, New Guinea, China, Indonesia, Japan, India, Africa, Australia, Europe, Russia, South America, Taiwan, Mexico, Cuba and Korea.

Publication: SSpS Mission.

Operation Help, Inc.: P.O. Box 134, Hartly, DE 19953. Phone: 302-697-7065; Fax: 302-697-7065. Rev. Patrick Shaules, S.J., Pres.; Marcinda Haedge, Admin. For Contributions: Mailing Address: P.O. Box 384. Camden-Wyoming, DE 19934.

Operation Help, Inc., is an independently incorporated nonprofit organization dedicated to helping Catholic priests and sisters bring spiritual and material salvation to the destitute poor. It offers advice and funding and places a special emphasis on Asian and African mission areas.

Our Lady of Victory Missionary Sisters: *Victory-Noll,* P.O. Box 109, Huntington, IN 46750-0109. Phone: 260-356-0628. Sr. Jeanette Halbach, O.L.V.M., Pres.; Sr. Melanie Persche, O.L.V.M., Gen. Sec.

Legal Title: *Our Lady of Victory Missionary Sisters, Inc.*

A Marian congregation proclaiming the Gospel in a personal, non-institutional way through pastoral ministry, religious education, social service and health-care programs in favor of the poor and oppressed.

Please refer to the Religious Institutes of Women section for activities and representation in the United States. Active also in foreign missions in Cochabamba, Oruro, Bolivia.

Parish Visitors of Mary Immaculate: *Motherhouse Generalate and Novitiate-Marycrest,* P.O. Box 658, Monroe, NY 10950-0658. Phone: 845-783-2251. Sr. Mary Gemma Spoldi, Gen. Supr.; Sr. Dolores Marie, Novice Dir.

Founded for the missionary visitation of families and individuals in the parish and for religious instruction of children and adults; assists parish priests in their ministry of evangelization, catechetical programs, spiritual surveys, census, follow-up religious counseling, religious social services, training laity.

Please refer to the Religious Institutes of Women section for activities and representation in the United States and overseas.

Publication: The Parish Visitor.

Passionist Sisters (1924): *Sisters of the Cross and Passion American Provincialate,* Holy Family Convent, One Wright Ln., North Kingstown, RI 02852. Sr. Rosemary Traynor, C.P., Prov. Supr.

Diversified apostolic works according to the needs of the Church; catechetical, pastoral and social work; educational functions; retreats; missionary work in the United States and Africa, Argentina, Bosnia, Botswana, Europe, England, Ireland, Jamaica, Latin America, Chile, Papua New Guinea, Peru, Romania, Scotland, Wales, and West Indies.

Please refer to the Religious Institutes of Women section for activities and representation in the United States.

Pontifical Institute for Foreign Missions, P.I.M.E., Inc.: *U.S. Region,* 17330 Quincy Ave., Detroit, MI 48221. Phone: 313-342-4066; Fax: 313-342-6816. Very Rev. Bruno Piccolo P.I.M.E., Prov. Supr.

Legal Title: *Pontifical Institute for Foreign Missions (P.I.M.E.), Inc.*

American Province recruits and trains priests and brothers for foreign missionary work; secures funds for foreign mission work and mission education activities.

Active in the Archdiocese of Detroit and the Dioceses of Columbus, Lansing, Paterson and Palm Beach.

Outside the U.S.— Bangladesh, Brazil, Cambodia, Cameroon, Hong Kong, India, Ivory Coast, Japan, Guinea-Bissau, Mexico, Papua New Guinea, Philippines, Taiwan, and Thailand.

Publication: national magazine, PIME World.

St. Joseph's Society of the Sacred Heart (Josephites): *Headquarters,* 1130 North Calvert St., Baltimore, MD 21202. Phone: 410-727-3386; Fax: 410-727-1006. E-mail: josephite1@aol.com. Web Site: josephite.com. Very Rev. Edward J. Chiffriller, S.S.J., Supr. Gen.

An organization of priests and brothers doing missionary work in the African American community of the United States.

Publication: The Josephite Harvest.

St. Patrick's Missionary Society: 70 Edgewater Rd., Cliffside Park, NJ 07010. Fax: 201-943-2946. Rev. Michael Morris, Supr.; Rev. Karl Langsdorf, Supr. Chicago, IL; Rev. Stephen Donohue, U.S.-Supr., Saratoga, CA.

A society of secular priests devoted entirely to the missionary needs of the Church.

Activities in the Archdioceses of Newark, Chicago and the Dioceses of San Jose, and Paterson.

Outside the U.S. in Nigeria—Archdiocese of Lagos, Dioceses of Abakaliki, Calabar, Abuja, Minna, Ogoja, Warri, Port Harcourt and Missio Sui Juris Bomadi. Kenya—Archdiocese of Nairobi, Dioceses of Eldoret, Kitui, Lodwar and Nakuru. Sudan—Diocese of Torit. Malawi—Dioceses of Lilongwe, Chikwawa, Zomba and Mzuzu. Zambia—Archdiocese of Lusaka, Diocese of Chipata. Brazil—Archdioceses of Sao Paulo, Dioceses of Campo Limpo, Osasco, Santo Amaro, Sao Miguel Paulista and Campina Grande. Grenada—Diocese of St. George's. South Africa—Dioceses of Tzaneen and Witbank. Zimbabwe—Archdiocese of Harare and Diocese of Mutare. Cameroon—Archdiocese of Bamenda.

Publication: Africa, St. Patrick's Mission.

Salesian Missions: 2 Lefevre Ln., New Rochelle, NY 10801. Phone: 914-633-8344.

The Salesians were founded to help bring the Faith to all people, and contribute to their social and economic development through education, especially in trade and agricultural schools. The purpose of the society is the recruitment and preparation of vocations for the missions and the education of the American public on the needs of other people through lectures, mass media, direct mail and the magazine, Salesian. It is also the purpose of the society to educate the American public on the unique system of education developed by the society's founder, St. John Bosco, as well as to spread knowledge of his life and accomplishments. Funds are raised to implement the religious, educational and technical assistance projects of the society.

Please refer to the Religious Institutes of Men section for activities and representation in the United States. Represented in over 125 countries throughout the world.

Publication: Salesian.

School Sisters of Notre Dame: *Milwaukee Province,* 13105 Watertown Plank Rd., Elm Grove, WI 53122-2291. Phone: 262-782-9850; Fax: 262-782-5725. Sr. Marilyn Kesler, Prov. Leader.

Please refer to the Religious Institutes of Women section I.D.# [2970] for provinces, activities and representations in the United States and overseas.

Sisters of the Blessed Sacrament for Indians and Colored People (1891): *St. Mary Generalate,* Bensalem, PA 19020-5796. Phone: 215-244-9900; Fax: 215-244-8174. Sr. Monica Loughlin, Pres.

Missionary work in the educational, catechetical and social services among Black and Native Americans as well as Haitians in the U.S., Guatemala and Haiti.

Please refer to the Religious Institutes of Women section for activities and representation in the United States.

Publication: Mission; The Peacemaker.

Society of African Missions: *SMA Fathers American Province,* 23 Bliss Ave., Tenafly, NJ 07670. Phone: 201-567-9085 & 567-0450; Fax: 201-567-7156 & 541-1280. Very Rev. Thomas M. Wright, S.M.A., Prov.

Please refer to the Religious Institutes of Men section for activities and representation in the United States.

Active also in: Liberia—Diocese of Cape Palmas, Archdiocese of Monrovia, Diocese of Gbarnga; Ivory Coast—Archdiocese of Abidjan; Dioceses of Abengourou, Bondoukou, Bouake, Daloa, Gagnoa, Katiola, Grand-Bassam, Korhogo, Odienne, Man, San Pedro, Yamoussoukro, and Yopougon; Ghana—Archdiocese of Cape Coast; Dioceses of Accra, Konongo-Mampong, Keta-Akatsi, Kumasi, Sekondi-Takoradi, Obuasi; Togo—Archdiocese of Lome; Dioceses of Kara, and Sokode; Benin—Archdiocese of Cotonou & Parakou; Dioceses of Abomey, Kandi, Djougou, Natitingou, Dassa-Zoume and Porto-Novo; Nigeria—Archdioceses of Kaduna, Abuja (Benin City) Jos, Lagos, Ibadan; Dioceses of Abeokuha, Bauchi, Ilorin, Issele-Uku, Kafanchan, Kano, Kontagor, Makurdi, Ondo and Warri; Niger—Diocese of Niamey; Central African Republic—Archdiocese of Bangui; Dioceses of Berberati. Zambia-Archdiocese of Lusaka, Dioceses of Ndola, Solwezi. Egypt—Vicarate Apostolic of Alexandria Morocco-Rabat; Congo-Kinshasa, Kikwit. Tanzania—Dioceses of Mwanza and Shinyanga. Kenya—Archdiocese of Nairobi; Diocese of Ngong & Lodwar. Argentina—Archdiocese of Cordoba. Australia—Archdiocese of Perth. South Africa—Diocese of Rustenburg, Archdiocese of Pretoria. Philippines—Archdiocese of Manila. South India: Tamilnadu. Poland-Warsaw.

Society of Mary: *Marianist Province of the United States,* 4425 W. Pine Blvd., St. Louis, MO 63108. Phone: 314-533-1207; Fax: 314-533-0778. Bro. Stephen Glodek, S.M., Prov.

Educational, parish and development work in the following territories: Archdiocese of San Juan and Diocese of Ponce, Puerto Rico. Also in Africa in Karonga, Malawi; Mzuzu, Malawi; Mombasa, Kenya; Nairobi, Kenya; and Lusaka, Zambia. Archdiocese of Nairobi, Mombasa, Kenya and the Dioceses of Karonga, Malawi, Lusaka, Zambia, Africa; Archdioceses of Ranchi & Bangalore and the Dioceses of Patna and Khunti; (Mexico) Dioceses of Coatzacoalcos and Queretaro; Diocese of Dhaka, Korea: Archdiocese of Seoul and Kwangu and the Diocese of Incheon.

Society of St. Edmund: *Edmundite Generalate,* 270 Winooski Park, Colchester, VT 05439. Phone: 802-654-3400; Fax: 802-654-3409. Very Rev. Richard M. Myhalyk, S.S.E., Supr. Gen.

Legal Title: *Society of St. Edmund, Inc.*

Major missionary endeavors in the United States are in Selma, Alabama and surrounding areas, and in the inner city of New Orleans (LA).

See the Foreign Mission section for the list of priests serving abroad.

Publications: Edmundite Missions.

Society of the Precious Blood: *Cincinnati Province,* 431 E. Second St., Dayton, OH 45402. Fax: 937-228-6878. Very Rev. Angelo Anthony, C.PP.S., Prov. Dir.; Rev. Larry Hemmelgarn, C.PP.S., Prov. Sec.; Bro. Joseph J. Fisher, C.PP.S., Mission Procurator; Rev. William Nordenbrock, C.PP.S., Mission Coord.

Mission activities outside the U.S. in Chile, Peru, South America, Guatemala, Central America; Missions in La Tinta, Tucuru, Santiago, Purranque, Valdivia, LaOroya, Lima, Guatemala City, La Labor.

Priests, brothers and deacons in foreign missions 34.

Publication: C.PP.S. Today.

Sons of Mary Missionary Society (1952): 567 Salem End Rd., Framingham, MA 01702-5599. Phone: 508-879-2541. Web Site: www.sonsofmary.com. Rev. John Murphy, F.M.S.I., Major Coord.; Bro. Kevin Courtney, F.M.S.I., Finance Coord.; Rev. John Coss, F.M.S.I., Councilor.

Legal Title: *Sons of Mary, Health of the Sick, Inc.*

Dedicated to the ministry of healing: medical, catechetical and social apostolates in the home and foreign missions.

Third Order Regular of St. Francis: *Province of the Most Sacred Heart of Jesus, Franciscan T.O.R. Missions,* P.O. Box 188, Loretto, PA 15940. Phone: 814-472-3348. Bro. Mark McBride, T.O.R., Prov. Dir. of Foreign Missions; Very Rev. Edmund Carroll, T.O.R., Minister Prov., Phone: 412-781-1232.

Secures missionaries and material aid to missions.

Active in the Archdioceses of Manaus and Sao Paulo; the Prelacy of Borba, Brazil; the Diocese of Bhagalpur, Bihar, India; and Diocese of Vice Province of Saint Joseph, Republic of South Africa.

Xaverian Missionary Fathers: *Provincial Headquarters,* 12 Helene Ct., Wayne, NJ 07470-2813. Phone: 973-942-2975; Fax:973-942-5012. Very Rev. Ivan Marchesin, S.X.

A religious society of priests and brothers dedicated exclusively to foreign mission work and the training of candidates for missionary life.

Active in Brazil, Democratic Republic of Congo, Burundi, Chad, Cameroon, Bangladesh, Indonesia, Japan, Mexico, Sierra Leone, Colombia, Philippines, Mozambique, Taiwan, Italy, Spain, Great Britain and the United States of America.

Please refer to the Religious Institutes of Men section for activities and representation in the United States.

Publication: Xaverian Mission Newsletter.

Pontifical Mission Societies

A. The Pontifical Society for the Propagation of the Faith (1822): *National Office,* 366 Fifth Ave., New York, NY 10001. Phone: 212-563-8700; Fax: 212-563-8725. E-mail: pmsusa@propfaith.org. Web site: www.worldmissions-catholicchurch.org. Rev. Msgr. John E. Kozar, Natl. Dir. & Pres.; Rev. Msgr. James A. Moloney, Vice Pres.; Rev. Robert F. Sharman, Treas.; Rev. Vincent J.Rigdon, Asst. Treas.; Rev. Msgr. Ferdinando D. Berardi, Sec.; Mr. James R. Borut, Asst. Sec.

International Officers: His Eminence Crescenzio Cardinal Sepe, Prefect of the Congregation for Evangelization of Peoples; Rev. Fernando Galbiati, P.I.M.E., Interim Sec. Gen., Vatican City.

The Propagation of the Faith, under the direction of the Congregation for the Evangelization of Peoples, is established in every country where the Church is free to operate; it has a two-fold goal of promoting a universal missionary spirit and encouraging prayer and financial support for the local churches of the missions.

Each diocese in the United States has a director appointed by the Ordinary to promote the work of the Society through programs such as World Mission Sunday (the next-to-last Sunday in October) and Membership, presentations in seminaries, lesson plans and materials for mission animation in schools (grades 9-12) and parishes, news media and personal contact with parishes and diocesan organizations.

Offerings received by the Propagation of the Faith in the United States are joined with offerings from all other countries and distributed annually to more than 1,100 mission Dioceses and Vicariates.

Publication: quarterly, Mission, Rev. John E. Kozar, Publisher.

B. The Society of St. Peter Apostle (1889): *National Office,* 366 Fifth Ave., New York, NY 10001. Phone: 212-563-8700. Rev. Msgr. John E. Kozar, National Dir. & Pres. International Officers: His Eminence Crescenzio Cardinal Sepe, Prefect of the Congregation for Evangelization of Peoples; Rev. Msgr. Jose Antonio S. Galvez, Sec. Gen., Vatican City.

The Society of St. Peter Apostle, under the direction of the Congregation for the Evangelization of Peoples, is established for the support of seminarians and novices in the missions. During 2002, there were 32,103 major seminarians, 45,294 minor seminarians and some 10,000 novices receiving assistance from the Society of St. Peter Apostle. The Society also helps support local religious communities and retired native clergy. Each diocese in the United States has a local director who is also the Director of the Propagation of the Faith.

C. The Pontifical Missionary Union (1916): *National Office,* 366 Fifth Ave., New York, NY 10001. Phone: 212-563-8700. Rev. Msgr. John E. Kozar, Natl. Dir. & Pres.

International Officers: His Eminence Crescenzio Cardinal Sepe, Prefect of the Congregation for Evangelization of Peoples; Rev. Fernando Galbiati, P.I.M.E., Sec.-Gen., Vatican City.

The Missionary Union, under the direction of the Congregation for the Evangelization of Peoples, is established to inspire, deepen and sustain a mission spirit among priests, deacons, religious, seminarians, candidates for the religious life and others in the pastoral ministry of the Church. The director in each diocese is also the Director of the Propagation of the Faith.

D. Holy Childhood Association: *National Office,* 366 Fifth Ave., New York, NY 10001. Phone: 212-563-8700; Fax: 212-994-8569. Rev. John E. Kozar, Natl. Dir. & Pres.

International Officers: His Eminence Crescenzio Cardinal Sepe, Prefect of the Congregation for Evangelization of Peoples; Most Rev. Albert Malcolm Ranjith, Pres.; Rev. Patrick Byrne, Sec. Gen., Vatican City.

Founded in 1843 by Bishop Charles de Forbin Janson. It is the official agency of the Church by which Catholic children of the world contribute through their prayers and sacrifices to the welfare of other children in more than 100 mission countries. Since its beginning, it has become the personal favorite of every Pope. In 1926, Pope Pius XI elevated the society to Pontifical rank. Holy Childhood endeavors to attain its ends through the united efforts of all Catholic children who are taught to recognize that sensitivity to others is an essential dimension of Christianity. Funds raised through children's efforts are directed to the Association's two-fold mandate, the majority being distributed annually to every part of the mission world by a Pontifical Commission and a portion being directed to catechetical education of children in the United States.

The Education and Promotion Fund solicits adult donations for the purpose of underwriting HCA educational efforts so that a greater portion of children's donations reach children in need.

All allocations sent to the missions through the agency of the Holy Childhood are used solely in the interests of the children of these missions. The Association is officially established in all Archdioceses and Dioceses of the United States.

Missionary Societies, Mission Boards and their Diocesan Branches.

Committee on the Home Missions: *U.S Conference of Catholic Bishops,* 3211 Fourth St. N.E., Washington, DC 20017. Phone: 202-541-3011; Fax: 202-722-8752. Most Rev. J. Peter Sartain, Chm.; Dr. David M. Byers, Exec. Dir.

A committee of the U.S. Conference of Catholic Bishops dedicated to support of the home missions. The CHM makes grants to extend the Church's presence as a means of salvation and to strengthen the Church's presence where it is weak. Grantees include Dioceses, religious institutes and national, regional and interdiocesan Catholic organizations in the United States and its dependencies. The CHM funds a wide range of mission and evangelization activities; examples include parish support, seminary formation, lay ministry training, religious education, and ministry with ethnic groups. Application materials are available August 1 of each year; the deadline for submission of completed applications is October 1. The CHM makes grant decisions once a year in March, and grants are disbursed in quarterly payments July through April. The CHM's funds come from the Catholic Home Missions Appeal.

American Conventual Franciscan Missions:
Refer to the American Foreign Mission section of the Directory and the Religious Institutes of Men section I.D. #[0480] for detailed information on provinces and activities.

Bureau of Catholic Indian Missions (1874): 2021 H St., N.W., Washington, DC 20006-4207. Phone: 202-331-8542; Fax: 202-331-8544. His Eminence William Cardinal Keeler, Pres.; His Eminence Edward Cardinal Egan; His Eminence Justin Cardinal Rigali; Rev. Msgr. Paul A. Lenz, D.D., Exec. Dir.; Patricia L. O'Rourke, Asst. Sec./Treas.

Collecting and distribution of funds for the support of American Indian missions. The Bureau represents the missions in Government relations, specifically in Washington, DC.

Active throughout the United States, where American Indian, Eskimo and Aleute missions are present.

Promotes cause for canonization of Blessed Kateri Tekakwitha.

Publication: bi-monthly newsletter; monthly Kateri Circle Agenda.

Catholic Missionary Union: 86-11 Midland Pkwy., Jamaica Estates, NY 11432. Phone: 718-291-5995. His Eminence Edward Cardinal Egan, Pres.; Rev. John J. Foley, C.S.P., Sec. & Treas.

The corporation subsidizes Evangelization activities.

Catholic Church Extension Society of the United States of America, The (1905): 150 S. Wacker Dr.-20th Flr., Chicago, IL 60606-4200. Phone: 888-473-2484; Fax: 312-236-5276. Web site: www.catholic-extension.org. His Eminence Francis E. George, O.M.I., Chancellor; Most Rev. William R. Houck, Pres.; Mr. Richard A. Ritter, Vice Pres. & Gen. Sec.

Catholic Extension is a Papal fundraiser that helps to support the Church in rural, remote and poor areas of the United States and its territories. Catholic Extension raises money through freewill donations, charitable gift annuities, trusts and will bequests to support missionary work in America.

Requests for funds are submitted by Bishops in designated America mission Dioceses. Funding is for religious purposes: construction of chapels and other mission buildings; living expenses of priests, religious and lay people working for missions; seminarian education; campus ministry; scholarships in religious education at Fordham University to those working in mission catechetical programs; chapel furnishings; evangelization; religious education, including sponsorship of parish calendars, videotapes on mission work in the U.S., and evangelization booklets.

Publications: EXTENSION Magazine; Catholic Extension Parish Calendars.

Catholic Near East Welfare Association (1926): 1011 First Ave., New York, NY 10022. His Eminence Edward Cardinal Egan, Pres. & Treas. Most Rev. William F. Keeler, Vice Pres.; Rev. Msgr. Robert L. Stern, Sec. Gen.; Rev. Msgr. Denis Madden, Assoc. Sec. Gen.; Chorbishop John D. Faris, Asst. Sec. Gen.

A papal agency for humanitarian and pastoral support established by Pope Pius XI in 1926. It promotes awareness of the condition and the needs of the churches, institutions and persons under the jurisdiction of the Congregation for the Eastern Churches and the Permanent Interdiscasterial Commission for the Church on Eastern Europe. It raises and distributes funds to help meet the material and spiritual needs of the people it serves.

The Association works for people in those lands in which from ancient times the majority of Christians have been members of the various eastern churches. Its mandate extends to the churches and peoples of the Middle East, Northeast Africa, India and Eastern Europe. It encourages and provides assistance to projects and programs of pastoral support, humanitarian assistance, interfaith communication and public awareness.

Publication: bimonthly magazine, Catholic Near East.

Catholic Negro American Mission Board (1907): 2021 H St., N.W., Washington, DC 20006-4207. Phone: 202-331-8542. His Eminence William Cardinal Keeler, Pres.; His Eminence Edward Cardinal Egan; His Eminence Justin Cardinal Rigali; Rev. Msgr. Paul A. Lenz, D.D., Exec. Dir.; Patricia L. O'Rourke, Asst. Sec./Treas.

Engaged in the support of priests and sisters throughout the states below Mason and Dixon Line, especially support in poor black schools.

Active in the United States, particularly all states in the South.

Commissariat of the Holy Land: 3140 Meramec St., St. Louis, MO 63118-4339. Phone: 314-353-7729; Fax: 314-655-0563. Bro. Joseph Rogenski, O.F.M., Commissary.

Established for collecting and distributing funds for the support of the sacred places in the Holy Land. Regional Commissariat for the Ecclesiastical Provinces of Chicago, Cincinnati, Detroit, Dubuque, Indianapolis, Kansas City, Louisville, Milwaukee, Mobile, New Orleans, Oklahoma City, Omaha, St. Louis, St. Paul-Minneapolis and San Antonio.

Commissariat of the Holy Land: 28-3 San Fernando Rd., Los Angeles, CA 90065-1320. Phone: 323-254-7764 ext.208. Rev. Martial Luebke, O.F.M., Commissary; Rev. Warren Rouse, O.F.M., Vice Commissary.

Established to collect and distribute funds for support of the Sacred Shrines and educational and charitable institutions in the Holy Land. Assigned Territory: Ecclesiastical Provinces of Denver, Los Angeles, Portland (OR), San Francisco, Santa Fe and Seattle.

Commission for Catholic Missions Among the Colored People and the Indians (Black and Indian Mission Office)(1884): 2021 H St., N.W., Washington, DC 20006-4207. Phone: 202-331-8542; Fax: 202-331-8544. Board of Directors: His Eminence William Cardinal Keeler, Pres.; His Eminence Edward Cardinal Egan; His Eminence Justin Cardinal Rigali; Rev. Msgr. Paul A. Lenz, D.D., Exec. Dir.; Patricia L. O'Rourke, Dir. Collection & Asst. Sec./Treas.

Organized by the Third Plenary Council as trustee of the funds collected in the churches for support of Black, Indian, Eskimo and Aleute evangelization programs in the United States. Grant applications are sent to Ordinaries each year and grant disbursements made in January and June.

The Commission is financial support for the National Black Catholic Congress and also the National Catholic Tekakwitha Conference. Both national organizations have been able to grow rapidly in the last decade as a result of the Commission.

Publication: annual, Annual Report.

Commissariat of the Holy Land: *Franciscan Monastery,* 14th and Quincy Sts., N.E., Washington, DC 20017. Phone: 202-526-6800; Fax: 202-529-9889. Bro. Fabian Adkins, O.F.M.

Collecting funds for support of the sacred places, educational and charitable institutions in the Holy Land through the Good Friday collection, and educating young men for the Missions of the Custody of the Holy Land in Syria, Jordan, Lebanon, Cyprus, Rhodes, Israel and Egypt.

Dominican Mission Secretariate: 141 E. 65th St., New York, NY 10021-6607. Phone: 212-861-3776; Fax: 212-639-9823. Rev. Matthew Erickson, O.P. Dir.

Legal Title: *St. Jude Dominican Foreign Missions, Inc. (formerly Rosary Foreign Mission Society, Inc.).*

Founded by the Order of Preachers (Dominican Friars), Province of St. Joseph for the purpose of promoting American Dominican activity in the foreign missions throughout the world. Presently the Mission Office aids and supports work in the Archdioceses of Karachi and Lahore, the Dioceses of Multan, Faisalabad and Islamabad-Rawalpindi in Pakistan. The Archdioceses of Lima, Peru. Nairobi and Kisumu in Kenya; Calayan Island, Philippines, and the Solomon Islands.

Assumption B.V.M. Province: *Holy Dormition Friary,* P.O. Box 270, Sybertsville, PA 18251. Fax: 717-788-2431. Rev.Anthony Skurlai, O.F.M., Guardian.

Preparing missionaries to work among the people in the Byzantine Church.

General Secretariat of the Franciscan Missions, Inc.: P.O. Box 130, Waterford, WI 53185. Phone: 262-534-5470; Fax: 262-534-4342. E-mail: framis@wi.net. Web site: www.franciscanmissions.org. Revs. Sereno Baiardi, O.F.M., Dir.; Sante de Angelis, O.F.M., Assoc. Dir.

General American office for assistance to Franciscan Missions under the auspices of the General Minister of the Order of Friars Minor.

Catholic Network Of Volunteer Service: 6930 Carroll Ave.-Ste. 506, Takoma Park, MD 20912-4423. Phone: 301-270-0900; Fax: 301-270-0901. Most Rev. John J. Snyder, Episcopal Advisor; James G. Lindsay, Exec. Dir.

Catholic Network of Volunteer Service promotes, recruits and refers volunteers to missions in the United States and overseas. We represent over 210 faith-based volunteer programs worldwide and work with the U.S. Dioceses, religious communities and the private sector to determine their needs for help. Catholic Network of Volunteer Service (CNVS) is committed to the goal that every Catholic man and woman be invited to consider a period of service in the missions, as a vital and important manifestation of the baptismal call of all Catholic people. Currently, 9,600 men and women are serving in CNVS member mission programs offering their gifts and abilities in full-time service to people in need and living their Catholic faith more fully than many had imagined possible. These volunteers are serving domestically for a summer, six months, a year or more, and they are serving internationally for two or more years at a time. They are single and married, recent college graduates and early retirees, doctors and teachers, parish ministers and social workers, community organizers, computer programmers, legal aides and more.

Gatherings: Annual Conference; Formation Workshops, Training Seminars.

Awards: The Father George Mader Award, given annually to honor organizations and individuals who promote the value of lay mission service.

Publications: annual, Response: Directory of Volunteer Opportunities; monthly, How Can I Help?; quarterly, Lay Mission Handbook.

Missionary Association of Catholic Women (1916): *National Office,* 3501 S. Lake Dr. - Box 070912, Milwaukee, WI 53207-0912. Phone: 414-769-3406. E-mail: wmo@archmil.org. Sr. Frances P. Cunningham, O.S.F., Contact Person.

Association providing material and financial aid to home and foreign missions.

MIVA-America Missionary Vehicle Association Inc: *National Office,* 1400 Michigan Ave.,N.E., Washington, DC 20017. Phone: 202-635-3444; Fax: 202-526-0830. Web site: www.miva.org. Rev. Philip DeRea, M.S.C., Natl. Dir.; Larry Nigh, Office Admin.; Michele Marth, M.S.C., Appeal Coord.

The Missionary Vehicle Association (MIVA America) is a non-profit organization whose sole purpose is to raise money to fund the purchase of reliable transportation for American missionaries working around the world. Without dependable transportation, missionaries are often unable to reach the people that most need their help. MIVA America's funds allow American Missionaries to purchase cars, trucks, jeeps, bicycles, motorcycles, boats, buses and ambulances.

Oblates of St. Francis de Sales (O.S.F.S.) (1906): *Wilmington-Philadelphia Province,* 2200 Kentmere Pkwy., Wilmington, DE 19806. Phone: 302-656-8529; Fax: 302-658-8052. Very Rev. Joseph G. Morrissey, O.S.F.S., Prov. ;Very Rev. David Whelan, O.S.F.S., Prov., American Mission Dir.

Missionary work in Republic of South Africa, Diocese of Keimeos; Nambia, Diocese of Keetmamshoop; South America — Uruguay, Archdiocese of Montevideo; Brazil, Archdioceses of Rio de Janeiro and Porto Alegre (Rio Grande de Sol), Dioceses of Bage (RGS), Cruz Alta (RGS), Frederico Westphalen (RGS), and Senhor do Bofim (Bahia); India, Archdiocese of Bangalore (province of Karnataka); Haiti — Diocese of Les Gonaives; Mexico — Archdiocese of Merida.

Please refer to the Religious Institutes of Men section for activities and representation in the United States.

Provinces outside the United States: France, Germany, Austria, Switzerland, Italy, and Holland.

Pontifical Mission for Palestine (1949): 1011 First Ave., New York, NY 10022. Phone: 212-826-1480. Rev. Msgr. Robert L. Stern, Pres.; Rev. Msgr. Denis Madden, Vice Pres.; Ms. Patricia Molloy, Admin.-Vatican Office; Mr. Issam Bishara, Dir.-Beirut Office; Rev. Guido Gockel, Dir.-Jerusalem Office; Mr. Ra Banou, Dir.-Amman Office.

A papal agency for humanitarian and charitable assistance established by Pope Pius XII in 1949. Its mission is to assist, without regard to nationality or religion, all who suffer as a result of the repeated conflicts which have devastated Palestine and neighboring regions of the Middle East.

It encourages and supports projects and programs of relief, rehabilitation, development; collaboration with other agencies; and education.

St. Paul's Guild, Inc.: *Attn: Chancellors office,* 1011 First Ave., Rm. 1940, New York, NY 10022.

Formerly National Catholic Converts' League, now interested in assisting former Protestant clergymen and former Protestant religious.

Tekakwitha Conference (1939): *National Center,* P.O. Box 6768, Great Falls, MT 59406. Phone: 406-727-0147; 800-842-9635; Fax: 406-452-9845. E-mail: tekakwitha.conference@worldnet.att.net. Web Site: www.tekconf.org.

Nonprofit organization established for evangelization within the Catholic Church with American Indians, Eskimos and missionaries working together at a national level to develop a Native American identity voice and presence in the Catholic Church. Catechesis, liturgy, youth ministry, Inculturation and related areas within the Catholic Church are goals of the Conference.

Publication: 5 issues annually, Cross & Feathers.

Catholic Medical Mission Board, Inc. (1928): 10 W. 17th St., New York, NY 10011-5765. Members of the Board: Rev. Msgr. Ferdinando D. Berardi, Rev. William J. Scanlan, S.J., John A. Donnelly, Sr. Marilyn Fischer, S.F.P., Rev. Msgr. Robert J. Fuhrman, Dr. Thomas G. Flynn, M.D., Dr. Patricia Smith, M.D., Mr. Thomas P. Melady, Most Rev. William Skylstad, Sr. Peggy Egan, O.S.F., Mr. James A. Cunningham, Mr. Terry Kirch, Rev. Charles J. Casamento.

The Catholic Medical Mission Board (CMMB), founded in 1928, provides pharmaceuticals and health care supplies for organizations and clinical facilities that make health care available to the world's needy. In addition to its schedule of shipments, CMMB responds to health care emergencies. In 1999, over $43 million in medicines and related supplies were shipped to clinical faciltites in 52 countries. Financial aid is also granted to students in accredited health care training programs. CMMB's Medical Volunteer Program places health providers interested in volunteering for short-term and long-term tours of service at selected clinical sites around the world. Catholic Medical Mission Board publishes "Medical Mission News," a quarterly journal magazine which provides in-depth information on its programs.

United States Conference of Secular Institutes

U.S.C.S.I. Attn: Ms. Carol Winkler, Pres. P.O. Box 4556, 12th St. N.E., Washington, DC 20017. Members of the U.S.C.S.I. are Secular Institutes of Diocesan or Pontifical Right, canonically erected since 1947, following the promulgation of the Apostolic Constitution, "Provida Mater Ecclesia," by Pope Pius XII. The Institutes are listed on this page by the Congregation for the Institutes of Consecrated Life and for Societies of Apostolic Life. The purpose of the U.S.C.S.I., canonically erected by the Congregation as of its 1976 statutes, is to offer the Institutes an opportunity to exchange experiences, conduct research, and promote ways to make the vocation and Institutes known. The executive council includes: Carol Winkler, President (Schoenstatt); Rev. John F. Lorenz, Vice-President (Institute of the Heart of Jesus); Marjorie L. Baker, Secretary (Missionaries of the Kingship of Christ); Anita H. Plourde, Treasurer (Oblate Missionaries of Mary Immaculate).

Caritas Christi: P.O. Box 5162, River Forest, IL 60305. Mary Jane McCarthy, Natl. Sponsor. Forms and gives to the Church laywomen who according to their callings, talents and professional skills seek to respond to the love of Christ in their providential environment by following the demands of the Gospel.

Company of St. Paul: 52 Davis Ave., White Plains, NY 10605.Rev. Stuart Sandberg, Contact Person. (Lay People and Priests).
Founded in Milan, Italy November 17, 1920, under the auspices of Cardinal Andrew Ferrari; approved as a Secular Institute of Pontifical Right on June 30, 1950.
Aim: The practice of evangelical counsels is the expression of consecration to God. Professional work becomes the main means of the apostolate.

Diocesan Laborer Priests: 3706 15th St. N.E., Washington, DC 20017. Phone: 202-832-4217; Fax: 202-526-5692. Rev. Ovidio Pecharrohan, Delegate.
A Secular Institute of Pontifical Right founded in Spain in 1883.
The aim of the Institute is the promotion, sustenance and cultivation of apostolic, religious and priestly vocations.

Secular Institute of St. Francis de Sales: 87 Gerrish Ave. T2, East Haven, CT 06512. Therese Keyes, Dir.
Founded in Vienna, Austria by Rev. Franz Reisinger, O.S.F.S., in 1946. Approved as a Secular Institute in 1964. Aim: Personal sanctification of its members living in the world according to the spirituality of St. Francis de Sales. Open to women: single, widowed and divorced who wish to embrace the consecrated life by the profession of vows.

Don Bosco Volunteers: P.O. Box 588, Hawthorne, NJ 07507-0588. Cathy Sylvester, Contact Person.
Founded as a Secular Institute for Women by Blessed Philip Rinaldi, S.D.B., in Turin, Italy in 1917.
Approved as an Institute of Pontifical Right in 1978. Existing in 35 countries, with over 1,200 members.
Aim: To live in the spirit of St. John Bosco, in a wide variety of apostolates in one's own environment, and in the service of the local church, particularly on behalf of youth. An Institute for Men was founded in Rome in November, 1994. For information, see address above.

Handmaids of Divine Mercy: 2410 Hughes Ave., Bronx, NY 10458.
A Secular Institute for women who, through the practice of the evangelical, counsel in a faithful imitation of Jesus Christ. The members commit themselves to the service of the Church by a parish- or diocesan-oriented apostolate under the leadership of and in collaboration with the clergy.

Institute of Secular Missionaries: 2710 Ruberg, Cincinnati, OH 45211. Evelyn Dilger, Contact Person. (Women).
Founded in Vitoria, Spain in 1939, approved as Secular Institute in 1955 Working for the integral good of humankind, specifically for the poor who need and claim most of the Church's support at this time. This endeavor is taken within the spirit of the Beatitudes and in communion with the Church.

Missionaries of the Kingship of Christ: P.O. Box 34513, Bethesda, MD 20827-0513.
Under this title are included three distinct and juridically separate institutes following the spirituality of St. Francis of Assisi.
Women Missionaries of the Kingship of Christ:
Founded in Italy in 1919 and approved as an Institute of Pontifical Right in 1953. Existing in twenty-nine countries, the American branch began in 1950 and has spread to 25 states. Through a consecrated life in the world they work individually in professions and apostolates for the reign of Christ in the world. Rev. Dominic Monti, O.F.M., Ecclesiastical Asst.
Men Missionaries of the Kingship of Christ:
Founded in Italy in 1928 and approved as an institute of Pontifical Right in 1998. It was established in the United States in 1962. Their purpose is spreading the social reign of Christ through individual professions and occupations.

Oblate Missionaries of Mary Immaculate: P.O. Box 303, Manville, RI 02838. Women: P.O. Box 764, Lowell, MA 01853.
Founded in Canada on July 2, 1952. Approved of Pontifical Right March 24, 1984.
International Membership: The members profess the evangelical counsels. Unique spirituality based on five attitudes of life: presence of God, absence of criticism and complaints, service and Charism.
Aim: A constant availability to the will of the Father to live everywhere the charity of Christ, through service, with the help of Mary.

Opus Spiritus Sancti: 421 E. Bluff St., Carroll, IA 51401. Phone: 712-792-4386. Rev. James D. McCormick, Regional Coord. Pius X: 553. Phone: 603-641-9789.
Founded in New Hampshire in 1939.
Approved as a Secular Institute of Diocesan Right on Dec. 8, 1959.
Aim: The general end is the perfection of its members. The members strive to achieve this aim through the effective practice in the world of the three evangelical counsels of perfection, and by making the promise to dedicate themselves totally to the particular apostolate of the Institute. The Institute also admits married or unmarried men as associate members.

Secular Institute of Schoenstatt Fathers: W 284 N 746 Cherry Ln., Waukesha, WI 53188. Rev. Gerold M. Langsch, Supr.
Founded by Father Joseph Kentenich in 1965, approved as a Secular Institute of Pontifical Right, June 24, 1988.
Aim: To aid the moral and religious renewal of society and the realization of the post-Vatican II mission of the Church, especially through priestly service to the International Schoenstatt Movement. About 240 ordained members in 20 nations worldwide.

Secular Institute of Schoenstatt Sisters of Mary: W 284 N 404 Cherry Ln., Waukesha, WI 53188-9416. Phone: 262-542-4384 & 542-1544; Fax: 262-542-5730. (Women). E-mail: schoenstattsisters@schsrsmary.org.
Founded in Germany in 1926 by Father Joseph Kentenich; approved as a Secular Institute of Pontifical Right in 1948.
Aim: The moral and religious renewal of society. The members practice a Marian lay asceticism as a means of growing in love for God, and consecrating the world to Him. They are active within the Schoenstatt Movement and in a wide variety of professional spheres.

Servitum Christi (Women): Mailing Address: 1209 Greenwood Ave., Pueblo, CO 81003. 184 East 76th St., New York, NY 10021. Ms. Elaine Kozlowski, Contact Person.
Founded Origin inspired by St. Peter Julian Eymard (1868), founder of the Congregation of the Blessed Sacrament. Founded in Holland, 1952; approved as a Secular Institute of Diocesan Right May 8, 1963.
Aim: To live the mystery of the Eucharist fully as consecrated lay persons and to make known its meaning so that the reign of Christ may come and the glory of God be revealed to the world.

Society of Our Lady of the Way: 2339 N. Catalina St., Los Angeles, CA 90027.
Additional Members in Cleveland, OH; Daly City & Lancaster, CA; Bridgeport, CT; Green Bay, WI; Jersey City, NJ; Tokyo, Japan; and New Orleans.
Founded in Vienna, Austria in 1936; approved as a Secular Institute of Pontifical Right in 1953. To Christianize the secular order, members are consecrated to God through the vows of chastity, obedience and poverty. They pursue individual apostolates, seeking to manifest Christ in all the circumstances of their life and work. Spirituality is Marian and Ignatian.

Voluntas Dei Institute (1958): 615 Palm Ave., Los Altos, CA 94022. E-mail: Director@voluntasdeiusa.org. Rev. George F. Hazler, Contact Person.
Approved as a Secular Institute of Pontifical Right in 1987.
The Institute assembles together within a common apostolic project both clerics and celibate laymen. The Institute directs its members to discover the will of God, adhere to it and cherish it through the profession of the vows of poverty, chastity, and obedience. The Institute also includes married couples as Associate Members. These commit themselves to live according to their state in life the same ideal and apostolic project as the clerics and celibate laymen, through commitment to living poverty, chastity and apostolic obedience. Members of the Institute regularly gather as a team which is the place for listening to the Word and discerning the Will of God.

Alphabetical Listing of Mission Churches in the United States

A

Aasu/Aoloau, AS, c/o Pago Pago, AS, St. Paul. (SPP)
Abernathy, TX, Hale Co., St. Isidore, c/o Petersburg, TX, Sacred Heart. (LUB)
Abeytas, NM, Socorro Co., San Antonio, c/o La Joya, NM, Our Lady of Sorrows. (SFE)
Abie, NE, Butler Co., SS. Peter and Paul, c/o Bruno, NE, St. Anthony. (LIN)
Abingdon, MD, Harford Co., St. Francis, c/o Baltimore, MD, Patronage of the Mother of God. (PSC)
Abo, NM, Torrance Co., c/o Mountainair, NM, St. Alice. (SFE)
Abram, TX, Hidalgo Co., St. Mary Magdalene, c/o La Joya, TX, Our Lady, Queen of Angels. (BWN)
Absarokee, MT, Stillwater Co., St. Michael, c/o Columbus, MT, St. Mary's. (GF)
Acomita, NM, Cibola Co., St. Anne, c/o Pueblo of Acoma, NM, San Esteban, Acoma Catholic Indian Mission. (GLP)
Acton, CA, Los Angeles Co., Our Lady of the Desert, c/o Palmdale, CA, St. Mary. (LA)
Adel, GA, Cook Co., St. Margaret Mary, c/o Lakeland, GA, Queen of Peace. (SAV)
Adel, OR, Lake Co., St. Richard, c/o Lakeview, OR, St. Patrick's. (BAK)
Adona, AR, Conway Co., St. Elizabeth's, c/o Bigelow, AR, St. Boniface's. (LR)
Adrian, OR, Malheur Co., Our Lady of Guadalupe, c/o Nyssa, OR, St. Bridget of Kildare. (BAK)
Afono, AS, c/o Pago Pago, AS, Church of the Immaculate Conception. (SPP)
Afton, NY, Chenango Co., St. Agnes, c/o Bainbridge, NY, St. John the Evangelist. (SY)
Afton, WY, Lincoln Co., Holy Family, c/o Jackson, WY, Our Lady of the Mountains. (CHY)
Agafa Gumas, GU, Santa Bernadita Mission Chapel, c/o Yigo, GU, Our Lady of Lourdes. (AGN)
Aguas, PR, Yauco Co., St. Martin, c/o Yauco, PR, Holy Rosary. (PCE)
Aguila, AZ, Maricopa Co., Our Lady of Guadalupe, c/o Wickenburg, AZ, St. Anthony of Padua. (PHX)
Aguirre, PR, Salinas Co., La Milagrosa, c/o Aguirre, PR, Sacred Heart. (PCE)
Ak–Chin, AZ, Pinal Co., St. Francis, c/o Laveen, AZ, St. John The Baptist. (PHX)
Alamillo, NM, Socorro Co., c/o Socorro, NM, San Miguel. (SFE)
Alapaha, GA, Berrien Co., St. Ann, c/o Tifton, GA, Our Divine Saviour. (SAV)
Albany, NY, Albany Co., Albany Medical Center, c/o Albany, NY, St. Teresa of Avila. (ALB)
Alberton, MT, Mineral Co., St. Albert the Great, c/o Frenchtown, MT, St. John the Baptist. (HEL)
Albin, WY, Laramie Co., St. Joseph, c/o Pine Bluffs, WY, St. Paul's. (CHY)
Albuquerque, NM, Bernalillo Co., Morada de San Jose, c/o Albuquerque, NM, St. Anne. (SFE)
Albuquerque, NM, Bernalillo Co., Our Lady of Mount Carmel, c/o Albuquerque, NM, Nativity of the Blessed Virgin Mary. (SFE)
Albuquerque, NM, Bernalillo Co., San Jose de los Duranes, c/o Albuquerque, NM, San Felipe de Neri. (SFE)
Alcalde, NM, Rio Arriba Co., c/o San Juan Pueblo, NM, St. John the Baptist. (SFE)
Alderson, WV, Greenbrier Co., St. Mary of the Greenbrier, c/o Hinton, WV, St. Patrick. (WH)
Alexander, ND, McKenzie Co., Our Lady of Consolation, c/o Watford City, ND, Epiphany. (BIS)
Alexandria, NE, Thayer Co., St. Mary's, c/o Fairbury, NE, St. Michael's. (LIN)
Algarrobos, PR, Yauco, Our Lady of Fatima, c/o Yauco, PR, Santo Domingo de Guzman. (PCE)
Algodones, NM, Sandoval Co., c/o Bernalillo, NM, Our Lady of Sorrows. (SFE)
Alice, TX, Jim Wells Co., Sacred Heart, c/o Alice, TX, St. Joseph. (CC)
Alice, TX, Jim Wells Co., Santo Nino De Atocha, c/o Alice, TX, Our Lady of Guadalupe. (CC)
Allaben, NY, Ulster Co., Our Lady of Lourdes, c/o Phoenicia, NY, St. Francis de Sales. (NY)
Allen, SD, Bennett Co., St. John of the Cross, c/o Kyle, SD, Our Lady of Sorrows. (RC)
Allendale, SC, Barnwell Co., St. Mary, c/o Orangeburg, SC, Holy Trinity. (CHR)
Alma, GA, Bacon Co., St. Raymond, c/o Hazlehurst, GA, Good Shepherd. (SAV)
Alma, NE, Harlan Co., St. Kathrine Drexel, c/o Alma, NE, St. Joseph's. (LIN)
Almacigo Alto, PR, , Yauco, St. Juan Macias, c/o Yauco, PR, Santo Domingo de Guzman. (PCE)
Almacigo Bajo, PR, Yauco, St. Martin de Porres, c/o Yauco, PR, Santo Domingo de Guzman. (PCE)
Almont, ND, Morton Co., St. Mary, Queen of Peace, c/o New Salem, ND, St. Pius V. (BIS)
Alpine, CA, San Diego Co., Nativity of BVM, c/o Lakeside, CA, Blessed Kateri Tekakwitha. (SD)
Alto, TN, Franklin Co., St. Margaret Mary, c/o Decherd, TN, Good Shepherd. (NSH)
Alturas de Campo Rico, PR, Ntra. Sra. del Carmen, c/o Canovanas, PR, San Jose. (SJN)
Alturas de Mayaguez, PR, El Senor de Los Milagros, c/o Mayaguez, PR, Church De El Buen Pastor. (MGZ)
Alvord, IA, Lyon Co., Sacred Heart, c/o Rock Valley, IA, St. Mary's. (SC)
Amado, AZ, Santa Cruz Co., Assumption Chapel, c/o Tubac, AZ, St. Ann. (TUC)
Amagansett, NY, Suffolk Co., St. Peter the Apostle, c/o East Hampton, NY, Most Holy Trinity. (RVC)
Amalia, NM, Taos Co., c/o Questa, NM, St. Anthony. (SFE)
Amaluia, AS, c/o Pago Pago, AS, Church of the Holy Cross. (SPP)
Amargosa Valley, NV, Nye Co., Christ the Desert, c/o Pahrump, NV, Our Lady of the Valley. (LAV)
Amelia, NE, Holt Co., St. Joseph, c/o O'Neill, NE, St. Patrick. (OM)
Amherst, NE, Buffalo Co., St. John Capistran, c/o Elm Creek, NE, Immaculate Conception. (GI)
Amouli, AS, c/o Pago Pago, AS, Church of Sacred Heart. (SPP)
Anaheim, CA, Orange Co., Sacred Heart, c/o Anaheim, CA, St. Justin Martyr. (ORG)
Andes, NY, Delaware Co., St. Ann, c/o Margaretville, NY, Sacred Heart. (ALB)
Andrews, SC, Georgetown Co., St. Leo the Great, c/o Georgetown, SC, St. Mary's. (CHR)
Angoon, AK, c/o Sitka, AK, St. Gregory of Nazianzen. (JUN)
Anguilla, MS, Sharkey Co., Our Mother of Mercy, c/o Belzoni, MS, All Saints. (JKS)
Annapolis, MD, Anne Arundel Co., St. John Neuman, c/o Annapolis, MD, St. Mary. (BAL)
Anones, PR, San Jose, c/o Las Marias, PR, Immaculate Heart of Mary. (MGZ)
Anselmo, NE, Custer Co., St. Anselm's, c/o Broken Bow, NE, St. Joseph's. (GI)
Ansley, NE, Custer Co., Sacred Heart, c/o Broken Bow, NE, St. Joseph's. (GI)
Antelope, OR, Wasco Co., St. Mary's, c/o Wasco, OR, St. Mary's. (BAK)
Anthony, KS, Harper Co., c/o Harper, KS, St. Joan of Arc. (WCH)
Antwerp, NY, Jefferson Co., St. Michael, c/o Evans Mills, NY, St. Mary. (OG)
Anza, CA, Riverside Co., Cahuilla Indian Reservation, c/o Anza, CA, Sacred Heart. (SB)
Anza, CA, Riverside Co., Our Lady of the Snows, c/o Anza, CA, Sacred Heart. (SB)
Anza, CA, Riverside Co., Santa Rosa Reservation, c/o Anza, CA, Sacred Heart. (SB)
Aoa, AS, c/o Pago Pago, AS, Church of Sacred Heart. (SPP)
Apache, OK, Caddo Co., Mother of Sorrows, c/o Elgin, OK, St. Ann. (OKL)
Aquasco, MD, Prince Georges Co., St. Dominic's, c/o Brandywine, MD, St. Michael. (WDC)
Aquin, OH, Haiti Parish Twinning Program, c/o Marysville, OH, Our Lady of Lourdes. (COL)
Arago, NE, Richardson Co., St. Mary's, c/o Rulo, NE, Immaculate Conception. (LIN)
Arapahoe, NE, Furnas Co., St. Germanus, c/o Cambridge, NE, St. John's. (LIN)
Arboles, CO, Archuleta Co., SS. Peter & Rose, c/o Ignacio, CO, St. Ignatius Parish. (PBL)
Arbuckle, CA, Colusa Co., Holy Cross, c/o Maxwell, CA, Sacred Heart. (SAC)
Archcape, OR, Clatsop Co., St. Peter the Fisherman, c/o Seaside, OR, Our Lady of Victory. (P)
Argyle, MN, Marshall Co., St. Rose of Lima, c/o Warren, MN, SS. Peter and Paul. (CR)
Arivaca, AZ, Pima Co., St. Ferdinand, c/o Tubac, AZ, St. Ann. (TUC)
Arlee, MT, Lake Co., Sacred Heart, c/o St. Ignatius, MT, St. Ignatius Mission. (HEL)
Armagh, MO, Franklin Co., St. Patrick, c/o Catawissa, MO, St. James. (STL)
Arnold, CA, Arnold Co., Our Lady of the Sierra, c/o Angels Camp, CA, St. Patrick Church of Angels Camp (Pastor of). (STO)
Arnold, NE, Custer Co., St. Agnes, c/o Stapleton, NE, St. John the Evangelist. (GI)
Arnot, PA, Tioga Co., St. Stanislaus Kostka, c/o Blossburg, PA, St. Mary's. (SCR)
Arock, OR, Malheur Co., Holy Family, c/o Jordan Valley, OR, St. Bernard's. (BAK)
Arroyo Hondo, NM, Taos Co., Nuestra Senora de Dolores, c/o Arroyo Seco, NM, La Santisima Trinidad. (SFE)
Arvada, CO, Coal Creek Catholic Community, c/o Arvada, CO, St. Joan of Arc. (DEN)
Ashdown, AR, Little River Co., St. Elizabeth Ann Seton, c/o Texarkana, AR, St. Edward's. (LR)
Ashfork, AZ, Yavapai Co., St. Anne, c/o Seligman, AZ, St. Francis. (PHX)
Ashland, AL, Clay Co., St. Mark, c/o Alexander City, AL, St. John the Apostle. (BIR)
Ashland, NY, Greene Co., St. Joseph's Chapel, c/o Windham, NY, St. Theresa of Child Jesus. (ALB)
Ashtabula, OH, Ashtabula Co., Our Lady of Miracles (St. Joseph Mission), c/o Ashtabula, OH, St. Joseph. (Y)
Ashton, NE, Sherman Co., St. Francis, c/o Loup City, NE, St. Josaphat's. (GI)
Aspen, CO, Pitkin Co., Snowmass in Snowmass Village, c/o Aspen, CO, St. Mary. (DEN)
Aspermont, TX, Stonewall Co., St. Mary, c/o Rotan, TX, St. Joseph. (LUB)
Asti, CA, Our Lady of Mt. Carmel, c/o Cloverdale, CA, St. Peter's. (SR)
Astor, FL, Lake Co., St. Hubert of the Forest, c/o Ocala, FL, Our Lady of the Springs. (ORL)
Atalaya, PR, Ntra. Sra. de Altagracia, c/o Aguada, PR, St. Francis of Assisi. (MGZ)
Athena, OR, Umatilla Co., Sacred Heart, c/o Milton Freewater, OR, St. Francis of Assisi. (BAK)
Atlanta, IL, Logan Co., St. Mary, c/o Lincoln, IL, Holy Family. (PEO)
Atlantic Mine, MI, Houghton Co., St. Mary, c/o Houghton, MI, St. Ignatius Loyola. (MAR)
Atoka, OK, Atoka Co., St. Patrick Church, c/o Durant, OK, St. William. (TLS)
Atwood, CA, Orange Co., St. Theresa Chapel, c/o Placentia, CA, St. Joseph. (ORG)
Aua, AS, c/o Pago Pago, AS, Church of the Immaculate Conception. (SPP)
Auburn, CA, Placer Co., St. Teresa of Avila, c/o Auburn, CA, St. Joseph. (SAC)
Auburn, PA, Susquehanna Co., St. Bonaventure, c/o Meshoppen, PA, St. Joachim's. (SCR)
Augusta, MT, Lewis and Clark Co., St. Matthias, c/o Fairfield, MT, St. John. (HEL)
Aurora, NM, San Miguel Co., c/o Villanueva, NM, Our Lady of Guadalupe. (SFE)
Austin, NV, Lander Co., St. Augustine, c/o Battle Mountain, NV, St. John Bosco. (RNO)
Austwell, TX, Refugio Co., St. Anthony of Padua, c/o Tivoli, TX, Our Lady of Guadalupe. (CC)
Autrain, MI, Alger Co., St. Therese, c/o Trenary, MI, St. Rita. (MAR)
Ava, MO, Douglas Co., St. Leo the Great, c/o Ava, MO, Immaculate Heart of Mary. (SPC)
Avoca, NE, Cass Co., Holy Trinity, c/o Syracuse, NE, St. Paulinus. (LIN)
Avon, MT, Powell Co., St. Theodore, c/o Deer Lodge, MT, Immaculate Conception. (HEL)
Avondale, LA, Jefferson Civil Parish, Assumption of Mary, c/o Marrero, LA, St. Agnes Le Thi Thanh. (NO)
Avondale, PA, Chester Co., Santa Maria, Madra de Dios, c/o West Grove, PA, Assumption B.V.M.. (PH)
Ayrshire, IA, Palo Alto Co., Sacred Heart, c/o Ruthven, IA, Sacred Heart. (SC)
Azle, TX, Tarrant Co., Holy Trinity, c/o Forth Worth, TX, St. Thomas. (FWT)

B

Babb, MT, Glacier Co., St. Mary, Queen of the World, c/o Browning, MT, Church of the Little Flower.

(HEL)
Badger, MN, Roseau Co., St. Mary's, c/o Roseau, MN, Sacred Heart. (CR)
Baggs, WY, Carbon Co., Our Lady of the Sage, c/o Rawlins, WY, St. Joseph's. (CHY)
Bagley, MN, Clearwater Co., St. Joseph, c/o Red Lake, MN, St. Mary's Mission Church. (CR)
Bahner, MO, Pettis Co., St. John, c/o Sedalia, MO, Sacred Heart. (JC)
Bainville, MT, Roosevelt Co., Sacred Heart, c/o Sidney, MT, St. Matthew's. (GF)
Bajio, PR, Sagrada Familia, c/o Aguada, PR, St. Francis of Assisi. (MGZ)
Baker, CA, San Bernardino Co., Our Lady of the Desert, c/o Barstow, CA, St. Joseph. (SB)
Bakersfield, CA, Kern Co., Holy Spirit, c/o Bakersfield, CA, Our Lady of Guadalupe. (FRS)
Bakersfield, CA, Kern Co., San Clemente, c/o Bakersfield, CA, Our Lady of Perpetual Help. (FRS)
Bakersfield, CA, Kern Co., St. Jude, c/o Bakersfield, CA, Our Lady of Guadalupe. (FRS)
Bald Knob, AR, White Co., St. Richard, c/o Searcy, AR, St. James. (LR)
Ballantine, MT, Yellowstone Co., Sts. Cyril & Methodius, c/o Billings, MT, St. Bernard's. (GF)
Ballardville, MA, St. Joseph's, c/o Andover, MA, St. Augustine. (BO)
Bancroft, WV, Putnam Co., St. Patrick, c/o Nitro, WV, Holy Trinity. (WH)
Banquete, TX, Nueces Co, St. Michael the Archangel, c/o Agua Dulce, TX, St. Frances of Rome. (CC)
Barberville, FL, Volusia Co., San Jose Mission, c/o De Land, FL, St. Peter's. (ORL)
Barinas, PR, Yauco Co., St. James, c/o Yauco, PR, Holy Rosary. (PCE)
Barneston, NE, Gage Co., St. Joseph's, c/o Wymore, NE, St. Mary's. (LIN)
Barnesville, GA, Lamar Co., St. Ann, c/o Griffin, GA, Sacred Heart. (ATL)
Barnsdall, OK, Osage Co., St. Mary, c/o Pawhuska, OK, Immaculate Conception. (TLS)
Barriada Vietnam, PR, La Milagrosa, c/o Guaynabo, PR, Santa Rosa de Lima. (SJN)
Barrineau Park, FL, Escambia Co., St. Elizabeth of Hungary, c/o Cantonment, FL, St. Jude Thaddeus. (PT)
Barrington, NH, Strafford Co., Chapel of the Nativity, c/o Dover, NH, St. Joseph. (MAN)
Barrio Apeadero, PR, Villalba Co., San Alfonso, c/o Villalba, PR, Our Lady of Mt. Carmel. (PCE)
Barrio Cecilia, Sector La Fe, PR, c/o Naguabo, PR, Nuestra Senora del Rosario. (CGS)
Barrio Hatillo, PR, Villalba Co., Sagrada Familia, c/o Villalba, PR, Our Lady of Mt. Carmel. (PCE)
Barrio Indios, PR, Guayanilla Co., San Juan Bosco, c/o Guayanilla, PR, Immaculate Conception. (PCE)
Barrio Jaguey, PR, Villalba Co., Madre Cabrini, c/o Villalba, PR, Our Lady of Mt. Carmel. (PCE)
Barrio La Plata, Amoldadero, PR, Barrio Algarrobo, c/o Aibonito, PR, Church of St. Joseph. (CGS)
Barrio Obrero, PR, San Martin de Porres, c/o San Juan, PR, Nuestra Senora del Carmen. (SJN)
Barrio Rio, Sector Brazo Seco, PR, c/o Naguabo, PR, Nuestra Senora del Rosario. (CGS)
Barrio Semil, PR, Villalba Co., Santa Cecilia, c/o Villalba, PR, Our Lady of Mt. Carmel. (PCE)
Barrio Sierra Baja, PR, Guayanilla Co., Our Lady of Mt. Carmel, c/o Guayanilla, PR, Immaculate Conception. (PCE)
Barstow, TX, Ward Co., Our Lady of Refuge, c/o Pecos, TX, Santa Rosa Church. (ELP)
Bartolo, PR, Rio Grande Co., Immaculate Conception, c/o Castaner, PR, Our Lady of the Miraculous Medal. (PCE)
Bartow, WV, Pocahontas Co., St. Mark the Evangelist, c/o Marlinton, WV, St. John Neumann. (WH)
Basile, LA, Evangeline Parish, Assumption, c/o Basile, LA, St. Augustine. (LAF)
Basin, WY, Big Horn Co., St. Philip, c/o Greybull, WY, Sacred Heart. (CHY)
Bass Lake, CA, Madera Co., St. Dominic Savio, c/o Oakhurst, CA, Our Lady of the Sierra. (FRS)
Bassett, NE, Rock Co., Holy Cross, c/o Ainsworth, NE, St. Pius X. (GI)
Basye, VA, Shenandoah Co., Our Lady of the Shenandoah, c/o Woodstock, VA, St. John Bosco. (ARL)
Batesville, TX, Zavala Co., St. Patrick, c/o La Pryor, TX, St. Joseph. (LAR)
Baxley, GA, Appling Co., St. Rose of Lima, c/o Hazlehurst, GA, Good Shepherd. (SAV)
Bay Mills, MI, Chippewa Co., Blessed Kateri Tekakwitha, c/o Brimley, MI, St. Francis Xavier. (MAR)
Bay St. Louis, MS, Hancock Co., St. Joseph's Chapel, c/o Bay St. Louis, MS, Our Lady of the Gulf. (BLX)
Bayamon, PR, Bayamon Co., N. Sra. Del Carmen, c/o Bayamon, PR, Santa Rita de Casia. (SJN)
Bayamon, PR, N. Sra. de la Providencia, c/o Bayamon, PR, Santo Domingo De Guzman. (SJN)
Bayamon, PR, Bayamon Co., N. Sra. del Buen Consejo, c/o Bayamon, PR, San Agustin. (SJN)
Bayamon, PR, Toa Alta Co., N. Sra. del Rosario, c/o Toa Alta, PR, San Esteban, Protomartir. (SJN)
Bayamon, PR, Bayamon Co., Sagrado Corazon, c/o Bayamon, PR, Santa Maria. (SJN)
Bayamon, PR, Bayamon Co., San Gerardo Mayela, c/o Bayamon, PR, Santa Maria. (SJN)
Bayamon, PR, Bayamon Co., San Jose, c/o Bayamon, PR, Santa Rita de Casia. (SJN)
Bayamon, PR, Bayamon Co., San Martin de Porres, c/o Bayamon, PR, San Agustin. (SJN)
Bayamon, PR, Bayamon Co., Santa Monica, c/o Bayamon, PR, Ntra. Sra. de la Monserrate. (SJN)
Bayard, NE, Morrill Co., Sacred Heart, c/o Bridgeport, NE, All Souls. (GI)
Bayside, TX, Refugio Co., St. Mary, c/o Woodsboro, TX, St. Therese The Little Flower. (CC)
Bda. Esperanza, PR, Guanica Co., La Providencia, c/o Guanica, PR, St. Anthony Abbot. (PCE)
Bda. Marin, PR, Arroyo Co., La Milagrosa, c/o Arroyo, PR, Our Lady of Mt. Carmel. (PCE)
Beach Haven, NJ, Ocean Co., St. Thomas Aquinas, c/o Brant Beach, NJ, St. Francis of Assisi. (TR)
Beach Lake, PA, Wayne Co., St. Bernard, c/o White Mills, PA, St. Joseph's. (SCR)
Beardsley, KS, Rawlins Co., St. John's, c/o St. Francis, KS, St. Francis. (SAL)
Beaulieu, MN, Mahnomen Co., St. Joseph, c/o Mahnomen, MN, St. Michael's. (CR)
Beaver, OK, Beaver Co., St. Frances Cabrini, c/o Woodward, OK, St. Peter's. (OKL)
Beaver Creek, CO, Eagle Co., Beaver Creek Chapel, c/o Edwards, CO, St. Clare of Assisi. (DEN)
Bedford Hills, NY, Westchester Co., Holy Protection of the Mother of God, c/o Yonkers, NY, St. Michael. (STF)
Bedford Hills, NY, Westchester Co., St. Matthias, c/o Katonah, NY, St. Mary of the Assumption. (NY)
Bee, NE, Seward Co., St. Wenceslaus, c/o Dwight, NE, Assumption. (LIN)
Beech Bottom, WV, Brooke Co., Holy Family, c/o Wellsburg, WV, St. John The Evangelist. (WH)
Bel Air, MD, Harford Co., St. Mary Magdalen, c/o Bel Air, MD, St. Margaret. (BAL)
Belaire Cove, LA, Sacred Heart, c/o Ville Platte, LA, Sacred Heart of Jesus. (LAF)
Belfair, WA, Mason Co., Prince of Peace, c/o Port Orchard, WA, St. Gabriel. (SEA)
Belgrade, MT, Gallatin Co., Valley of Flowers, c/o Three Forks, MT, Holy Family. (HEL)
Belgrade Lakes, ME, Kennebec Co., St. Helena, c/o Oakland, ME, St. Theresa. (PRT)
Bellevue, LA, St. Landry Parish, Christ the King, c/o Grand Coteau, LA, St. Charles Borromeo. (LAF)
Bellflower, IL, McLean Co., St. John, c/o Farmer City, IL, Sacred Heart. (PEO)
Bellwood, NE, Butler Co., St. Joseph's, c/o Bellwood, NE, St. Peter's. (LIN)
Bemidji, MN, Beltrami Co., Holy Spirit Newman Center, c/o Bemidji, MN, St. Philip's. (CR)
Bennettsville, SC, Marlboro Co., St. Denis, c/o Cheraw, SC, St. Peter's. (CHR)
Bennington, NY, Wyoming Co., Our Lady Help of Christians, c/o Darien Center, NY, Our Lady of Good Counsel. (BUF)
Bent, NM, Otero Co., Our Lady of Guadalupe, c/o Mescalero, NM, St. Joseph. (LSC)
Benton, LA, Bossier Parish, Mary, Queen of Heaven, c/o Bossier City, LA, St. Jude. (SHP)
Benton, PA, Columbia Co., Christ the King, c/o Bloomsburg, PA, St. Columba. (HBG)
Benwood, MN, Roseau Co., St. Joseph, The Worker, c/o Roseau, MN, Sacred Heart. (CR)
Bergland, MI, Ontonagon Co., St. Ann, c/o White Pine, MI, St. Jude. (MAR)
Berino, NM, Dona Ana Co., Immaculate Conception, c/o Anthony, NM, St. Anthony's. (LSC)
Bermuda, LA, Natchitoches Parish, St. Charles, c/o Natchez, LA, St. Augustine's. (ALX)
Berne, NY, Albany Co., St. Bernadette, c/o Altamont, NY, St. Lucy. (ALB)
Berrien Springs, MI, Berrien Co., St. Gabriel Mission Church, c/o Niles, MI, St. Mary. (KAL)
Berryville, AR, Carroll Co., St. Anne, c/o Eureka Springs, AR, St. Elizabeth of Hungary. (LR)
Berryville, VA, Clarke Co., St. Bridget of Ireland, c/o Winchester, VA, Sacred Heart of Jesus. (ARL)
Berthold, ND, Ward Co., St. Ann, c/o Foxholm, ND, St. Mary. (BIS)
Bertram, TX, Burnet Co., Holy Cross, c/o Burnet, TX, Our Mother of Sorrows. (AUS)
Betances, PR, Our Lady of Fatima, c/o Cabo Rojo, PR, St. Michael. (MGZ)
Bethel, ME, Oxford Co., Our Lady of the Snows, c/o Norway, ME, St. Catherine of Sienna. (PRT)
Bethlehem, MD, Caroline Co., Holy Child, c/o Secretary, MD, Our Lady of Good Counsel. (WIL)
Bethlehem, NH, Grafton Co., Christ the King, c/o Littleton, NH, St. Rose of Lima. (MAN)
Betterton, MD, Kent Co., Most Precious Blood, c/o Chestertown, MD, Sacred Heart. (WIL)
Beulah, CO, Pueblo Co., Our Lady of Lourdes, c/o Pueblo, CO, St. Francis Xavier. (PBL)
Bevier, MO, Macon Co., Sacred Heart, c/o Macon, MO, Immaculate Conception. (JC)
Bibo, NM, Cibola Co., Our Lady of Loretto, c/o Seboyeta, NM, Our Lady of Sorrows. (GLP)
Biddeford Pool, ME, York Co., St. Brendan, c/o Biddeford, ME, St. Mary's. (PRT)
Bieber, CA, Lassen Co., St. Stephen, c/o Burney, CA, St. Francis of Assisi. (SAC)
Big Bay, MI, Marquette Co., St. Mary, c/o Marquette, MI, St. Peter Cathedral. (MAR)
Big Elbow Lake, MN, Becker Co., St. Francis Cabrini, c/o Waubun, MN, St. Ann. (CR)
Big Lake, AK, Matanuska–Susitna Borough, Our Lady of the Lake, c/o Wasilla, AK, Sacred Heart. (ANC)
Big Oak Flat, CA, Tuolumne Co., Our Lady of Mt. Carmel, c/o Sonora, CA, St. Patrick Church of Sonora (Pastor of). (STO)
Big Pine, CA, Inyo Co., St. Stephen, c/o Bishop, CA, Our Lady of Perpetual Help. (FRS)
Big Piney, WY, Sublette Co., St. Anne, c/o Pinedale, WY, Our Lady of Peace. (CHY)
Big Spring, TX, Howard Co., St. Joseph, c/o Big Spring, TX, Immaculate Heart of Mary. (SAN)
Big Sur, CA, Monterey Co., St. Francis of the Redwoods, c/o Carmel, CA, San Carlos Borromeo Basilica. (MRY)
Big Wells, TX, Dimmit Co., St. Michael, c/o Asherton, TX, Immaculate Conception. (LAR)
Billings, OK, Noble Co., Sacred Heart, c/o Perry, OK, St. Rose of Lima. (OKL)
Binger, OK, Caddo Co., Our Lady of the Most Holy Rosary, c/o Anadarko, OK, St. Patrick's. (OKL)
Bird City, KS, Cheyenne Co., St. Joseph's, c/o St. Francis, KS, St. Francis. (SAL)
Birmingham, AL, Jefferson Co., Holy Rosary (Gate City), c/o Birmingham, AL, St. John Bosco. (BIR)
Biscoe, NC, Montgomery Co., Our Lady of the Americas, c/o Albemarle, NC, Our Lady of the Annunciation. (CHL)
Bismarck, MO, St. Francois Co., St. John, c/o Park Hills, MO, Immaculate Conception. (STL)
Bison, SD, Perkins Co., Blessed Sacrament, c/o Lemmon, SD, St. Mary's. (RC)
Black Canyon City, AZ, Yavapai Co., St. Philip Benizi, c/o Camp Verde, AZ, St. Frances Cabrini. (PHX)
Black Horse, PA, Montgomery Co., Our Lady of Mount Carmel, c/o Norristown, PA, Holy Saviour. (PH)
Black Lake, LA, Natchitoches Parish, Our Lady of the Holy Rosary, c/o Campti, LA, Nativity of The Blessed Virgin Mary. (ALX)
Black Lake, NM, Colfax Co., St. Anthony, c/o Cimarron, NM, Immaculate Conception Church. (SFE)
Black Pipe–Corn Creek, SD, Melette Co., St. Joseph Hall, c/o Parmelee, SD, St. Agnes. (RC)
Blackduck, MN, Beltrami Co., St. Ann, c/o Kelliher, MN, St. Patrick. (CR)
Blackville, SC, Barnwell Co., Sacred Heart, c/o Barnwell, SC, St. Andrew. (CHR)
Blackwater, AZ, Pinal Co., Holy Family, c/o Sacaton, AZ, St. Peter's. (PHX)
Blackwell's Corner, CA, Kern Co., Nuestra Senora de la Paz, c/o Wasco, CA, St. John the Evangelist. (FRS)
Blaine, WA, Whatcom Co., St. Anne, c/o Ferndale, WA, St. Joseph. (SEA)
Blanca, CO, Costilla Co., St. James, c/o San Luis, CO, Sangre de Cristo. (PBL)
Blencoe, IA, Monona Co., St. Bernard, c/o Onawa, IA, St. John. (SC)
Blooming Grove, PA, Good Shepherd, c/o Hawley, PA, St. John Neumann. (SCR)
Bloomingburgh, NY, Sullivan Co., Our Lady of the Assumption, c/o Middletown, NY, Our Lady of Mt. Carmel. (NY)
Bloomington, NE, Franklin Co., Sacred Heart, c/o Alma, NE, St. Joseph's. (LIN)
Blowing Rock, NC, Epiphany, c/o Boone, NC, St. Elizabeth. (CHL)
Blue Hill, NE, Webster Co., Holy Trinity, c/o Campbell, NE, St. Anne. (LIN)
Blue Lake, CA, St. Joseph, c/o Arcata, CA, St. Mary's. (SR)
Blue Mountain Lake, NY, Hamilton Co., St. Paul, c/o Indian Lake, NY, St. Mary's. (OG)
Bluetown, TX, Cameron Co., Cristo Rey, c/o Progreso, TX, Holy Spirit. (BWN)
Bluewater, NM, McKinley Co., Risen Savior, c/o Crownpoint, NM, St. Paul. (GLP)
Bly, OR, Klamath Co., St. James the Apostle, c/o Chiloquin, OR, Our Lady of Mt. Carmel. (BAK)
Bo. Aceituna, PR, San Martin de Porres, c/o Moca, PR, Our Lady of Monserrate. (MGZ)
Bo. Aibonito Guerrero, PR, Ntra. Sra. del Carmen, c/o San Sebastian, PR, San Sebastian Martir. (MGZ)
Bo. Altozano, PR, Ntra. Sra. de Fatima, c/o San Sebastian, PR, San Sebastian Martir. (MGZ)
Bo. Alturita, PR, Cacao Co., Our Lady of Mt. Carmel, c/o Villalba, PR, Our Lady Mother of Divine Providence. (PCE)
Bo. Arenas de Guancia, PR, Guanica Co., S. Martin de Porres, c/o Yauco, PR, St. Martin de Porres. (PCE)
Bo. Atalaya, PR, El Cristo de la Reconciliacion, c/o

Rincon, PR, St. Rose of Lima. (MGZ)
Bo. Barrancas, PR, Guayama Co., La Monserrate, c/o Guayama, PR, St. Anthony of Padua. (PCE)
Bo. Barreal, PR, Penuelas Co., Santa Cruz, c/o Penuelas, PR, St. Joseph. (PCE)
Bo. Bartolo, PR, Rio Grande Co., San Pedro, c/o Rio Grande, PR, Nuestra Senora del Carmen. (SJN)
Bo. Bauta, PR, Bauta Abajo Co., N.S. del Rosario, c/o Villalba, PR, Our Lady Mother of Divine Providence. (PCE)
Bo. Belgica, PR, Guanica Co., Cristo Rey, c/o Guanica, PR, St. Anthony Abbot. (PCE)
Bo. Buena Vista, PR, Penuelas Co., Holy Family, c/o Penuelas, PR, Sacred Heart. (PCE)
Bo. Cacao, PR, Cacao Co., Imm. Concepcion, c/o Villalba, PR, Our Lady Mother of Divine Providence. (PCE)
Bo. Cain, PR, St. Martin de Porres, c/o San German, PR, St. Rose of Lima. (MGZ)
Bo. Calabazas, PR, San Gabriel de la Dolorosa, c/o San Sebastian, PR, San Sebastian Martir. (MGZ)
Bo. Calvache, PR, Santa Rosa, c/o Rincon, PR, St. Rose of Lima. (MGZ)
Bo. Calzada, PR, c/o Maunabo, PR, San Isidro Labrador. (CGS)
Bo. Camarones, PR, Villalba Co., Jesus Crucificado, c/o Villalba, PR, Our Lady of Mt. Carmel. (PCE)
Bo. Camarones Centro, PR, Ciales Co., Inmaculada Concepcion, c/o Guaynabo, PR, Nuestra Senora de la Paz. (SJN)
Bo. Camarones–Los Robles, PR, Villalba Co., San Antonio, c/o Villalba, PR, Our Lady of Mt. Carmel. (PCE)
Bo. Cambute, PR, Carolina Co., Divino Nino Jesus, c/o Carolina, PR, Cristo Rey. (SJN)
Bo. Canonilla Abajo, PR, Villalba Co., Maria Madre de la Iglesia, c/o Villalba, PR, Our Lady of Mt. Carmel. (PCE)
Bo. Canovanillas, PR, Maria Auxiliadora, c/o Carolina, PR, Cristo Rey. (SJN)
Bo. Capa Barreto, PR, Perpetuo Socorro, c/o Moca, PR, Our Lady of Monserrate. (MGZ)
Bo. Capa Bosque, PR, Cristo Salvador, c/o Moca, PR, Our Lady of Monserrate. (MGZ)
Bo. Caracoles III, PR, Penuelas Co., San Martin de Porres, c/o Penuelas, PR, St. Joseph. (PCE)
Bo. Carite, PR, Guayama Co., San Martin, c/o Guayama, PR, St. Anthony of Padua. (PCE)
Bo. Carola, PR, Rio Grande Co., La Milagrosa, c/o Palmer, PR, Cristo Rey. (SJN)
Bo. Carreras, PR, La Providencia, c/o Anasco, PR, St. Anthony Abbot. (MGZ)
Bo. Carretera Nueva, PR, La Asuncion, c/o Hormigueros, PR, Shrine of Our Lady of Monserrate. (MGZ)
Bo. Cerro Gordo, PR, Villalba Co., Espiritu Santo, c/o Villalba, PR, Our Lady of Mt. Carmel. (PCE)
Bo. Cerro Gordo, PR, Inmacula Corazon de Maria, c/o Moca, PR, Our Lady of Monserrate. (MGZ)
Bo. Cerro Gordo, PR, Our Lady of Monserrat, c/o Anasco, PR, St. Anthony Abbot. (MGZ)
Bo. Cerro Gordo, PR, San Francisco de Asis, c/o Sabana Grande, PR, Church of San Isidro. (MGZ)
Bo. Chucillas Sabana, PR, Corazon de Jesus, c/o Moca, PR, Our Lady of Monserrate. (MGZ)
Bo. Coabay, PR, Jayuya Co., San Jorge, c/o Jayuya, PR, Our Lady of Monserrate. (PCE)
Bo. Collado, PR, Ponce Co., Our Lady of Monserrate, c/o Mercedita, PR, Church of the Resurrection. (PCE)
Bo. Collares, PR, Jayuya Co., Cristo Rey, c/o Jayuya, PR, Our Lady of Monserrate. (PCE)
Bo. Corazon, PR, Guayama Co., La Candelaria, c/o Guayama, PR, St. Anthony of Padua. (PCE)
Bo. Corcega, PR, La Milagrosa, c/o Rincon, PR, St. Rose of Lima. (MGZ)
Bo. Cordero, PR, Virgen Monserrate, c/o Moca, PR, Our Lady of Monserrate. (MGZ)
Bo. Corillo, PR, Villalba Co., San Pedro, c/o Villalba, PR, Our Lady of Mt. Carmel. (PCE)
Bo. Corral Viejo, PR, Ponce Co., Cristo Rey, c/o Ponce, PR, La Santisima Trinidad. (PCE)
Bo. Cotto Mato, PR, Penuelas Co., San Judas Tadeo, c/o Penuelas, PR, St. Joseph. (PCE)
Bo. Cruces, PR, Sagrado Corazon de Jesus, c/o Rincon, PR, St. Rose of Lima. (MGZ)
Bo. Cuchilla del Limon, PR, Villalba Co., La Asuncion, c/o Villalba, PR, Our Lady of Mt. Carmel. (PCE)
Bo. Cuchillas La Salle, PR, Santos Guillermo y Mateo, c/o Moca, PR, Our Lady of Monserrate. (MGZ)
Bo. Cuchillas Loperena, PR, Cristo Rey, c/o Moca, PR, Our Lady of Monserrate. (MGZ)
Bo. Cuesta Blanca, PR, Ntra. Sra. de Monserrate, c/o Lajas, PR, De la Merced Parish. (MGZ)
Bo. Culebrinas, PR, Espiritu Santo, c/o San Sebastian, PR, San Sebastian Martir. (MGZ)
Bo. Dajas, PR, Villalba Co., N.S. del Carmen, c/o Villalba, PR, Our Lady of Mt. Carmel. (PCE)
Bo. Damian Abajo, PR, Damian Abajo Co., N.S. del Pilar, c/o Villalba, PR, Our Lady Mother of Divine Providence. (PCE)
Bo. El Bajo, Patillas, PR, Patillas Co., Cristo Rey, c/o Patillas, PR, Inmaculado Corazon de Maria. (PCE)
Bo. El Frio, PR, Ala de La Piedra Co., Nino de Praga, c/o Villalba, PR, Our Lady Mother of Divine Providence. (PCE)
Bo. El Hoyo, PR, La Virgen Milagrosa, c/o Sabana Grande, PR, Church of San Isidro. (MGZ)
Bo. El Hoyo, PR, Santa Rosa de Lima, c/o Hormigueros, PR, Shrine of Our Lady of Monserrate. (MGZ)
Bo. El Jobos, PR, La Milagrosa, c/o Loiza, PR, Santiago Apostol, El Mayor. (SJN)
Bo. El Porvenir, PR, Ntra. Sra. de la Providencia (Rep. Masias), c/o Mayaguez, PR, Ascension. (MGZ)
Bo. El Real, Patillas, PR, Patillas Co., San Guillermo, c/o Patillas, PR, Inmaculado Corazon de Maria. (PCE)
Bo. El Verde, PR, Rio Grande Co., Nuestra Senora de Fatima, c/o Rio Grande, PR, Nuestra Senora del Carmen. (SJN)
Bo. Eneas, PR, Ntra. Senora de la Providencia, c/o San Sebastian, PR, San Sebastian Martir. (MGZ)
Bo. Espino, PR, St. Lawrence Martyr, c/o Anasco, PR, St. Anthony Abbot. (MGZ)
Bo. Fuig., PR, Guanica Co., Monserrate, c/o Ensenada, PR, Sacred Heart. (PCE)
Bo. Guama, PR, N. Sra. de la Consolacion, c/o San German, PR, St. Rose of Lima. (MGZ)
Bo. Guamani, PR, Guayama Co., Sgdo. Corazon, c/o Guayama, PR, St. Anthony of Padua. (PCE)
Bo. Guanajibo, PR, San Martin de Porres, c/o Hormigueros, PR, Shrine of Our Lady of Monserrate. (MGZ)
Bo. Guaragoa, PR, Ponce Co., San Andres, c/o Ponce, PR, La Santisima Trinidad. (PCE)
Bo. Guaragoa, Arriba, PR, Ponce Co., Santa Ana, c/o Ponce, PR, La Santisima Trinidad. (PCE)
Bo. Guaras, PR, Ntra. Sra. de Fatima, c/o Sabana Grande, PR, Church of San Isidro. (MGZ)
Bo. Guarderraya, Patillas, PR, Patillas Co., Madre Cabrini, c/o Patillas, PR, Inmaculado Corazon de Maria. (PCE)
Bo. Guayabal, PR, Juana Diaz Co., Our Lady of the Rosary, c/o Juana Diaz, PR, St. Raymond Nonato. (PCE)
Bo. Guaypao, PR, Guanica Co., Virgen del Rosario, c/o Ensenada, PR, Sacred Heart. (PCE)
Bo. Guerrero, PR, La Providencia, c/o San Antonio, PR, San Jose Obrero. (MGZ)
Bo. Guineo, PR, Ala de La Piedra Co., Santa Ana, c/o Villalba, PR, Our Lady Mother of Divine Providence. (PCE)
Bo. Hatillo Viejo, PR, Villalba Co., La Milagrosa, c/o Villalba, PR, Our Lady of Mt. Carmel. (PCE)
Bo. Hato Arriba, PR, San Patricio, c/o San Sebastian, PR, San Sebastian Martir. (MGZ)
Bo. Hato Arriba (Parcelas), PR, San Pablo de la Cruz, c/o San Sebastian, PR, San Sebastian Martir. (MGZ)
Bo. Higuero, PR, Villalba Co., Santisimo Sacramento, c/o Villalba, PR, Our Lady of Mt. Carmel. (PCE)
Bo. Hoyamala, PR, San Jose Obrero, c/o San Sebastian, PR, San Sebastian Martir. (MGZ)
Bo. Hoyos, PR, Ponce Co., Santa Maria Virgen, c/o Coto Laurel, PR, Our Lady of Mt. Carmel. (PCE)
Bo. Jacaboa, Patillas, PR, Patillas Co., Carmen, c/o Patillas, PR, Inmaculado Corazon de Maria. (PCE)
Bo. Jacaquas, PR, Juana Diaz Co., N.S. de Fatima, c/o Juana Diaz, PR, St. Raymond Nonato. (PCE)
Bo. Jagual, Patillas, PR, Patillas Co., Carmen, c/o Patillas, PR, Inmaculado Corazon de Maria. (PCE)
Bo. Jaguey, PR, San Jose, c/o Rincon, PR, St. Rose of Lima. (MGZ)
Bo. Jaquitas, PR, Ntra. Sra. de la Paz, c/o Hormigueros, PR, Shrine of Our Lady of Monserrate. (MGZ)
Bo. Juncal, PR, Santa Teresita, c/o San Sebastian, PR, San Sebastian Martir. (MGZ)
Bo. La Haya, PR, Santa Rosa de Lima, c/o Lajas, PR, Our Lady of the Purification. (MGZ)
Bo. La Laguna, PR, Guanica Co., San Judas, c/o Guanica, PR, St. Anthony Abbot. (PCE)
Bo. La Lechuza, PR, La Asuncion, c/o San Sebastian, PR, San Sebastian Martir. (MGZ)
Bo. La Luna, PR, Guanica Co., N. Sra Fatima, c/o Guanica, PR, St. Anthony Abbot. (PCE)
Bo. La Maquina, PR, Santa Ana, c/o Sabana Grande, PR, Church of San Isidro. (MGZ)
Bo. La Mocha, PR, Ponce Co., Santos Reyes, c/o Ponce, PR, San Vicente–Cantera. (PCE)
Bo. La Pica, PR, San Jose, c/o Sabana Grande, PR, Church of San Isidro. (MGZ)
Bo. La Plata, PR, Sagrado Corazon de Jesus, c/o Lajas, PR, Our Lady of the Purification. (MGZ)
Bo. La Torre, PR, Loiza Co., Ntra. Sra. del Perpetuo Socorro, c/o Loiza, PR, San Patricio. (SJN)
Bo. La Torre, PR, Santa Catalina de Siena, c/o Sabana Grande, PR, Church of San Isidro. (MGZ)
Bo. La Yuca, PR, Ponce Co., Immaculate Heart of Mary, c/o Mercedita, PR, Church of the Resurrection. (PCE)
Bo. Lajas Arriba (La Tea), PR, Ntra. Sra. del Perpetuo Socorro, c/o Lajas, PR, Our Lady of the Purification. (MGZ)
Bo. Lajas Arriba (Parcelas), PR, San Pablo, c/o Lajas, PR, Our Lady of the Purification. (MGZ)
Bo. Las Palmas, PR, Salinas Co., Virg. del Carmen, c/o Salinas, PR, Our Lady of Monserrat. (PCE)
Bo. Las Raices, PR, Ponce Co., Sagrado Corazon de Jesus, c/o Coto Laurel, PR, Our Lady of Mt. Carmel. (PCE)
Bo. Las Vallas, PR, Ponce Co., San Lucas, c/o Mercedita, PR, Church of the Resurrection. (PCE)
Bo. Las Vegas, PR, Our Lady of Perpetual Help, c/o Mayaguez, PR, Ascension. (MGZ)
Bo. Lavadero, PR, Sagrado Corazon de Jesus, c/o Hormigueros, PR, Shrine of Our Lady of Monserrate. (MGZ)
Bo. Limon, PR, St. Teresita, c/o Mayaguez, PR, Ascension. (MGZ)
Bo. Limon, PR, Villalba Co., Virgen de la Amargura, c/o Villalba, PR, Our Lady of Mt. Carmel. (PCE)
Bo. Limon, PR, Virgen del Rosario, c/o Moca, PR, Our Lady of Monserrate. (MGZ)
Bo. Lizas, PR, c/o Maunabo, PR, San Isidro Labrador. (CGS)
Bo. Los Barros, Patillas, PR, Patillas Co., S. Juan Evangelista, c/o Patillas, PR, Inmaculado Corazon de Maria. (PCE)
Bo. Los Pollos, Patillas, PR, Patillas Co., Santa Rosa de Lima, c/o Patillas, PR, Inmaculado Corazon de Maria. (PCE)
Bo. Macun, PR, Toa Baja Co., Santa Maria La Mayor, c/o Toa Baja, PR, Ntra. Sra. de la Candelaria. (SJN)
Bo. Madrigal, PR, Ponce Co., N.S. del Rosario, c/o Ponce, PR, La Santisima Trinidad. (PCE)
Bo. Maginas, PR, Sagrado Corazon de Jesus, c/o Sabana Grande, PR, Church of San Isidro. (MGZ)
Bo. Maguayo, PR, Ntra. Sra. de la Monserrate, c/o Lajas, PR, De la Merced Parish. (MGZ)
Bo. Magueyes, PR, Ponce Co., San Juan de Mata, c/o Ponce, PR, La Santisima Trinidad. (PCE)
Bo. Malezas, PR, La Milagrosa, c/o Mayaguez, PR, Sacred Heart. (MGZ)
Bo. Marias, PR, St. Rita, c/o Anasco, PR, St. Anthony Abbot. (MGZ)
Bo. Marin Alto, Patillas, PR, Patillas Co., Perpetuo Socorro, c/o Patillas, PR, Inmaculado Corazon de Maria. (PCE)
Bo. Marueno, Arriba, PR, Ponce Co., N.S. Fatima, c/o Ponce, PR, La Santisima Trinidad. (PCE)
Bo. Minillas Carretera, PR, Perpetuo Socorro, c/o San German, PR, St. Rose of Lima. (MGZ)
Bo. Minillas Valle, PR, Santa Monica, c/o San German, PR, St. Rose of Lima. (MGZ)
Bo. Miradero, PR, Ntro. Sra. de la Providencia, c/o Cabo Rojo, PR, St. Michael. (MGZ)
Bo. Mirasol, PR, Lares Co., La Virgen, c/o Castaner, PR, Our Lady of the Miraculous Medal. (PCE)
Bo. Mogote, PR, Villalba Co., Santisima Tinidad, c/o Villalba, PR, Our Lady of Mt. Carmel. (PCE)
Bo. Molinas, PR, Ntra. Sra. de Monserrate, c/o Sabana Grande, PR, Church of San Isidro. (MGZ)
Bo. Naranjo, PR, Corazon de Jesus, c/o Moca, PR, Our Lady of Monserrate. (MGZ)
Bo. Nuevo Mameyes, PR, Ponce Co., Santa Luisa, c/o Ponce, PR, San Vicente–Cantera. (PCE)
Bo. Olimpo, PR, Guayama Co., Cristo Rey, c/o Guayama, PR, St. Anthony of Padua. (PCE)
Bo. Ollas, PR, Santa Isabel Co., Monserrate, c/o Santa Isabel, PR, St. James. (PCE)
Bo. Ortiz, PR, Corozal Co., Santisima Trinidad, c/o Bayamon, PR, Santo Domingo De Guzman. (SJN)
Bo. Oveja, PR, Cristo Redentor, c/o Anasco, PR, St. Anthony Abbot. (MGZ)
Bo. Palmarejo, PR, Villalba Co., San Jose, c/o Villalba, PR, Our Lady of Mt. Carmel. (PCE)
Bo. Palmarejo II, PR, San Juan Bautista, c/o Lajas, PR, Our Lady of the Purification. (MGZ)
Bo. Palmas, PR, Arroyo Co., Ntra Sra. de Fatima, c/o Arroyo, PR, Our Lady of Mt. Carmel. (PCE)
Bo. Paloseco, PR, c/o Maunabo, PR, San Isidro Labrador. (CGS)
Bo. Parcelas Guacio (Parcelas), PR, Santa Cruz, c/o San Sebastian, PR, San Sebastian Martir. (MGZ)
Bo. Parcelas Palmarejo, PR, San Judas Tadeo, c/o Lajas, PR, Our Lady of the Purification. (MGZ)
Bo. Parcelas Santa Rosa, PR, Santa Rosa de Lima, c/o Lajas, PR, Our Lady of the Purification. (MGZ)
Bo. Parguera, PR, San Pedro, c/o Lajas, PR, De la Merced Parish. (MGZ)
Bo. Paris, PR, Ntra Sra. del Perpetuo Socorro, c/o Lajas, PR, De la Merced Parish. (MGZ)
Bo. Paso Seco, PR, Santa Isabel Co., Virgen del Perpetuo Socorro, c/o Santa Isabel, PR, St. James. (PCE)
Bo. Pastillo, PR, Ponce Co., Inmaculada, c/o Ponce, PR, La Santisima Trinidad. (PCE)
Bo. Penuelas, PR, Penuelas Co., Virgen del Rosario, c/o Santa Isabel, PR, St. James. (PCE)
Bo. Perchas I, PR, Cristo Rey, c/o San Sebastian, PR, San Sebastian Martir. (MGZ)
Bo. Perchas II, PR, La Pasion, c/o San Sebastian, PR, San Sebastian Martir. (MGZ)
Bo. Pinales, PR, La Immaculade, c/o Anasco, PR, St. Anthony Abbot. (MGZ)

Bo. Pinas, PR, Comerio Co., La Resurreccion, c/o Bayamon, PR, N. Sra. de la Providencia. (SJN)
Bo. Pinas, PR, Comerio Co., N. Sra. de Fatima, c/o Bayamon, PR, N. Sra. de la Providencia. (SJN)
Bo. Pinas, PR, Comerio Co., Sagrada Familia, c/o Bayamon, PR, N. Sra. de la Providencia. (SJN)
Bo. Pinones, PR, Loiza Co., Santa Rosa, c/o Loiza, PR, San Patricio. (SJN)
Bo. Pitahaya, PR, Luquillo Co., N. Sra. del Carmen, c/o Luquillo, PR, Madre del Redentor. (SJN)
Bo. Pitahaya, PR, Arroyo Co., Ntra Sra. del Carmen, c/o Arroyo, PR, Our Lady of Mt. Carmel. (PCE)
Bo. Placita, PR, c/o Juncos, PR, Inmaculada Concepcion. (CGS)
Bo. Plata, PR, San Judas, c/o Moca, PR, Our Lady of Monserrate. (MGZ)
Bo. Playa, PR, Salinas Co., Carmen, c/o Salinas, PR, Our Lady of Monserrat. (PCE)
Bo. Playita, PR, Salinas Co., Virgen Milagrosa, c/o Salinas, PR, Our Lady of Monserrat. (PCE)
Bo. Pozas, PR, Damian Abajo Co., N.S. Monserrate, c/o Villalba, PR, Our Lady Mother of Divine Providence. (PCE)
Bo. Pozas, PR, Sagrada Familia, c/o San Sebastian, PR, San Sebastian Martir. (MGZ)
Bo. Pozo Hondo, PR, Santa Rosa de Lima, c/o Anasco, PR, St. Anthony Abbot. (MGZ)
Bo. Providencia, Patillas, PR, Patillas Co., Providencia, c/o Patillas, PR, Inmaculado Corazon de Maria. (PCE)
Bo. Puente Jobos, PR, Guayama Co., SS. Peter and Paul, c/o Guayama, PR, St. Anthony of Padua. (PCE)
Bo. Puerto Jobos, PR, Guayama Co., San Francisco de Asis, c/o Guayama, PR, St. Anthony of Padua. (PCE)
Bo. Punta Brava, PR, San Pedro, c/o Moca, PR, Our Lady of Monserrate. (MGZ)
Bo. Puntas, PR, Nuestra Senora del Carmen, c/o Rincon, PR, St. Rose of Lima. (MGZ)
Bo. Quebrada Arenas, PR, c/o Maunabo, PR, San Isidro Labrador. (CGS)
Bo. Quebrado del Agua, PR, Ponce Co., La Milagrosa, c/o Ponce, PR, Church of the Good Shepherd. (PCE)
Bo. Rayo Plata, PR, San Judas Tadeo, c/o Sabana Grande, PR, Church of San Isidro. (MGZ)
Bo. Real Anon Abajo, PR, Ponce Co., San Mateo, c/o Coto Laurel, PR, Our Lady of Mt. Carmel. (PCE)
Bo. Real Anon Arriba, PR, Ponce Co., San Martin de Porres, c/o Coto Laurel, PR, Our Lady of Mt. Carmel. (PCE)
Bo. Recio, Patillas, PR, Patillas Co., Sto. Cristo de Los Milagros, c/o Patillas, PR, Inmaculado Corazon de Maria. (PCE)
Bo. Retiro Tea, PR, Santa Rita, c/o San German, PR, St. Rose of Lima. (MGZ)
Bo. Rio Abajo, PR, Ceiba Co., N.S. del Perpetuo Socorro, c/o Ceiba, PR, San Antonio de Padua. (CGS)
Bo. Rio Cana Arriba, PR, Juana Diaz Co., La Merced, c/o Juana Diaz, PR, St. Raymond Nonato. (PCE)
Bo. Rio Prieto, PR, Lares Co., Milagrosa, c/o Castaner, PR, Our Lady of the Miraculous Medal. (PCE)
Bo. Robles, PR, Sagrado Corazon, c/o San Sebastian, PR, San Sebastian Martir. (MGZ)
Bo. Rocha Magueyes, PR, La Providencia, c/o Moca, PR, Our Lady of Monserrate. (MGZ)
Bo. Rosario Penon, PR, La Monserrate, c/o Rosario, PR, Rosary. (MGZ)
Bo. Rucio, PR, Penuelas Co., Milagrosa, c/o Penuelas, PR, St. Joseph. (PCE)
Bo. Sabana, PR, Luquillo Co., N. Sra. Milagrosa, c/o Luquillo, PR, Madre del Redentor. (SJN)
Bo. Sabana, PR, San Jose de la Montana, c/o Trujillo Alto, PR, San Francisco de Asis. (SJN)
Bo. Salinas, PR, Ntra. Sra. del Carmen, c/o Lajas, PR, De la Merced Parish. (MGZ)
Bo. Salistral, PR, Ponce Co., Santa Marta, c/o Playa de Ponce, PR, Our Lady of Mt. Carmel. (PCE)
Bo. Saltos, PR, San Judas Tadeo, c/o San Sebastian, PR, San Sebastian Martir. (MGZ)
Bo. Santa Juanita, PR, Guanica Co., N. Sra. Rosario, c/o Guanica, PR, St. Anthony Abbot. (PCE)
Bo. Santa Rosa I, PR, Espiritu Santo, c/o Guaynabo, PR, Nuestra Senora de la Paz. (SJN)
Bo. Santa Rosa III, PR, Guaynabo Co., Sta. Rosa de Lima, c/o Guaynabo, PR, Nuestra Senora de la Paz. (SJN)
Bo. Santana Pichel, PR, Ntra. Sra. del Rosario, c/o Sabana Grande, PR, Church of San Isidro. (MGZ)
Bo. Santas Pascuas, PR, Ponce Co., Resurreccion, c/o Ponce, PR, La Santisima Trinidad. (PCE)
Bo. Santo Domingo, PR, Penuelas Co., Carmen, c/o Penuelas, PR, St. Joseph. (PCE)
Bo. Sierrita Caonillas, PR, Villalba Co., Cristo de la Salud, c/o Villalba, PR, Our Lady of Mt. Carmel. (PCE)
Bo. Sonadora, PR, Sagrada Familia, c/o Guaynabo, PR, Corazon de Jesus. (SJN)
Bo. Sonadur, PR, Cristo Resucitado, c/o San Sebastian, PR, San Sebastian Martir. (MGZ)
Bo. Sta. Ana Moreno, PR, Sta Lucia, c/o Sabana Grande, PR, Church of San Isidro. (MGZ)
Bo. Susa, PR, Yauco Co., N.S. de La Monserrate, c/o Yauco, PR, St. Martin de Porres. (PCE)
Bo. Susa, PR, Guanica Co., N.S. de La Providencia, c/o Yauco, PR, St. Martin de Porres. (PCE)
Bo. Susa, PR, Yauco Co., S. Francisco de Asis, c/o Yauco, PR, St. Martin de Porres. (PCE)
Bo. Susua, PR, , Guanica Co., Ntra. Sra. de Lourdes, c/o Yauco, PR, St. Martin de Porres. (PCE)
Bo. Talante, PR, c/o Maunabo, PR, San Isidro Labrador. (CGS)
Bo. Talante (La Pica), PR, c/o Maunabo, PR, San Isidro Labrador. (CGS)
Bo. Tallaba Alta, Sector La Moca, PR, Penuelas Co., Divino Nino, c/o Penuelas, PR, St. Joseph. (PCE)
Bo. Vista Alegre, PR, Villalba Co., Jesus Crucificado, c/o Villalba, PR, Our Lady of Mt. Carmel. (PCE)
Bo. Voladoras Lomas, PR, Espiritu Santo, c/o Moca, PR, Our Lady of Monserrate. (MGZ)
Bo. Voladoras Parcelas, PR, Sagrada Familia, c/o Moca, PR, Our Lady of Monserrate. (MGZ)
Bo. Yaurel Palmarejo, PR, Arroyo Co., San Jose, c/o Arroyo, PR, Our Lady of Mt. Carmel. (PCE)
Bo. Yaurel Santa Clara, PR, Arroyo Co., San Martin, c/o Arroyo, PR, Our Lady of Mt. Carmel. (PCE)
Bodega, CA, St. Teresa, c/o Occidental, CA, St. Philip. (SR)
Boiceville, NY, Ulster Co., Our Lady of La Salette, c/o Phoenicia, NY, St. Francis de Sales. (NY)
Boise City, OK, Cimarron Co., Good Shepherd, c/o Guymon, OK, St. Peter's. (OKL)
Boles Acres, NM, Otero Co., Our Lady of the Desert, c/o Alamogordo, NM, Immaculate Conception. (LSC)
Bolinas, CA, Marin Co., St. Mary Magdalen, c/o Olema, CA, Sacred Heart. (SFR)
Boling, TX, Wharton Co., St. Joseph, c/o Wharton, TX, Holy Family. (VIC)
Bon Secour AL, Baldwin Co., Our Lady of Bon Secour, c/o Magnolia Springs, AL, St. John the Baptist. (MOB)
Bonanza, OR, Klamath Co., St. Frances Cabrini, c/o Merrill, OR, St. Augustine. (BAK)
Bongard, IL, Champaign Co., Immaculate Conception, c/o Philo IL, St. Thomas. (PEO)
Bonhamtown, NJ, Middlesex Co., St. Margaret Mary Alacoque, c/o Edison, NJ, Guardian Angels. (MET)
Bonneau, SC, Berkeley Co., Our Lady of Peace, c/o Moncks Corner, SC, St. Philip Benizi. (CHR)
Booker, TX, Lipscomb Co., St. Peter, c/o Perryton, TX, Immaculate Conception. (AMA)
Boomer, WV, Fayette Co., St. Anthony Shrine, c/o Montgomery, WV, Immaculate Conception. (WH)
Boone, CO, Pueblo Co., St. William, c/o Avondale, CO, Sacred Heart. (PBL)
Booneville, KY, Owsley Co., Booneville Catholic Church of the Holy Family, c/o Beattyville, KY, Queen of All Saints. (LEX)
Boonsboro, MD, Washington Co., St. James, c/o Williamsport, MD, St. Augustine. (BAL)
Boonville, CA, Mendocino Co., St. Elizabeth Seton, c/o Ukiah, CA, St. Mary of the Angels. (SR)
Boqueron, PR, St. Joseph, c/o Cabo Rojo, PR, St. Michael. (MGZ)
Borica, NM, Guadalupe Co., c/o Santa Rosa, NM, St. Rose of Lima. (SFE)
Borinquen, PR, Our Lady of Victory, c/o Aguadilla, PR, La Milagrosa. (MGZ)
Bosque, NM, Valencia Co., c/o Belen, NM, Our Lady of Belen. (SFE)
Boswell OK, Choctaw Co., St. Jude c/o Hugo, OK, Immaculate Conception. (TLS)
Boulder Valley, MT, Jefferson Co., St. John the Evangelist, c/o Boulder, MT, St. Catherine. (HEL)
Bowie, AZ, Cochise Co., Our Lady of Guadalupe, c/o Willcox, AZ, Sacred Heart. (TUC)
Bowling Green, FL, Hardee Co., Holy Child, c/o Wauchula, FL, St. Michael. (VEN)
Box Elder, MT, Hill Co., St. Anthony, c/o Box Elder, MT, St. Margaret Mary. (GF)
Bozrah, CT, New London Co., St. John, c/o Norwichtown, CT, Sacred Heart. (NOR)
Braddock, ND, Emmons Co., St. Katherine, c/o Hazelton, ND, St. Paul. (BIS)
Bradley, CA, Monterey Co., Our Lady of Guadalupe, c/o San Miguel, CA, San Miguel. (MRY)
Brainardsville, NY, Franklin Co., St. Jude, c/o Chateaugay, NY, St. Patrick. (OG)
Braithwaite, LA, Plaquemines Parish, Assumption of the Blessed Virgin, c/o Pointe a la Hache, LA, St. Thomas. (NO)
Branch, LA, French Parish, St. Edmund, c/o Rayne, LA St. Leo IV. (LAF)
Brant Lake, NY, Warren Co., St. Teresa of Avila, c/o Hague, NY, Blessed Sacrament. (ALB)
Briarcliff, TX, Travis Co., Queen of Angels, c/o Lakeway, TX, Emmaus Catholic Church. (AUS)
Bridgeport, CA, Mono Co., Infant of Prague Mission Church, c/o Mammoth Lakes, CA, St. Joseph Church of Mammoth Lakes. (STO)
Bridger, SD, Ziebach Co., Immaculate Conception, c/o Eagle Butte, SD, All Saints. (RC)
Bridger, SD, Ziebach Co., Immaculate Conception, c/o Eagle Butte, SD, Cheyenne River Reservation. (RC)
Bridport, VT, Addison Co., St. Bernadette, c/o Middlebury, VT, Assumption of the Blessed Virgin Mary. (BUR)
Brier Hill, NY, St. Lawrence Co., Our Lady of Grace, c/o Morristown, NY, St. John the Evangelist. (OG)
Brisbane, CA, San Mateo Co., Our Lady of Guadalupe, c/o San Francisco, CA, Visitacion, Church of the. (SFR)
Bristol, CO, Prowers Co., St. Mary, c/o Holly, CO, St. Frances of Rome. (PBL)
Bristow, OK, Creek Co., St. Joseph, c/o Tulsa, OK, St. Catherine. (TLS)
Broadview, MT, Yellowstone Co., Little Flower, c/o Roundup, MT, St. Benedict's. (GF)
Brockton, MT, Roosevelt Co., St. Thomas, c/o Poplar, MT, Our Lady of Lourdes. (GF)
Bronte, TX, Coke Co., St. James, c/o Ballinger, TX, St. Mary Star of the Sea. (SAN)
Brookline, NH, Hillsborough Co., Infant Jesus, c/o Milford, NH, St. Patrick. (MAN)
Brooklyn, NY, Queens Co., Our Lady of Mount Carmel, c/o Corona, NY, St. Leo. (BRK)
Brooklyn, NY, Kings Co., Regina Pacis Votive Shrine, c/o Brooklyn, NY, St. Rosalia–Regina Pacis. (BRK)
Brooks, MN, Red Lake Co., St. Joseph, c/o Red Lake Falls, MN, St. Joseph's. (CR)
Brown City, MI, Sanilac Co., Sacred Heart, c/o North Branch, MI, St. Mary's Burnside. (DET)
Brownstown, IN, Jackson Co., Our Lady of Providence, c/o Seymour, IN, St. Ambrose. (IND)
Brownsville, OR, Linn Co., Holy Trinity, c/o Sweet Home, OR, St. Helen. (P)
Brownsville, TN, Haywood Co., St. John Church, c/o Jackson, TN, St. Mary's. (MEM)
Brownsville, TX, Cameron Co., Sacred Heart, c/o Brownsville, TX, Immaculate Conception Cathedral. (BWN)
Brownsville, TX, Cameron Co., St. Thomas, c/o Brownsville, TX, Immaculate Conception Cathedral. (BWN)
Bruceton Mills, WV, Preston Co., Mary Help of Christians, c/o Morgantown, WV, St. Luke. (WH)
Bruni, TX, Jim Hogg Co., Sacred Heart, c/o Hebbronville, TX, Our Lady of Guadalupe. (LAR)
Brunswick, NE, Antelope Co., St. Ignatius, c/o Creighton, NE, St. Ludger. (OM)
Bryan, TX, Brazos Co., San Salvador, c/o Bryan, TX, St. Anthony's. (AUS)
Bucarabones, PR, Sagrado Corazon, c/o Maricao, PR, St. John the Baptist. (MGZ)
Buckhorn, CA, Amador Co., Our Lady of the Pines, c/o Jackson, CA, St. Patrick's. (SAC)
Buena Vista, GA, Marion Co., St. Mary Magdalen, c/o Columbus, GA, Our Lady of Lourdes. (SAV)
Buena Vista, PR, La Milagrosa, c/o Las Marias, PR, Immaculate Heart of Mary. (MGZ)
Buenavista, NM, Mora Co., c/o Mora, NM, St. Gertrude. (SFE)
Bueyeros, NM, Harding Co., c/o Roy, NM, Holy Family–St. Joseph. (SFE)
Buffalo, OK, Harper Co., St. Joseph, c/o Woodward, OK, St. Peter's. (OKL)
Buffalo Creek, CO, Jefferson Co., St. Elizabeth, c/o Conifer, CO, Our Lady of The Pines. (DEN)
Buhach, CA, Merced Co., Immaculate Conception, c/o Atwater, CA, St. Anthony. (FRS)
Bullhead, SD, Corson Co., St. Aloysius, c/o McLaughlin, SD, St. Bernard. (RC)
Bullhead, SD, Corson Co., St. Aloysius, c/o McLaughlin, SD, Standing Rock Reservation. (RC)
Bullville, NY, Orange Co., St. Paul, c/o Middletown, NY, Our Lady of Mt. Carmel. (NY)
Bunker, MO, Reynolds Co., Christ the King, c/o Salem, MO, Sacred Heart. (SPC)
Burchard, NE, Pawnee Co., Sacred Heart, c/o Steinauer, NE, St. Anthony. (LIN)
Bureau, IL, Bureau Co., St. Francis Xavier, c/o Granville, IL, Sacred Heart Of Jesus. (PEO)
Burkesville, KY, Cumberland Co., Holy Cross Catholic, c/o Albany, KY, Emmanuel Catholic. (L)
Burlington, TX, Milam Co., St. Michael's, c/o Burlington, TX, St. Ann's. (AUS)
Burlington Junction, MO, Nodaway Co., St. Benedict Catholic Church, c/o Tarkio, MO, St. Paul the Apostle. (KC)
Burnsville, NC, Yancey Co., Sacred Heart, c/o Mars Hill, NC, St. Andrew the Apostle. (CHL)
Burwell, NE, Garfield Co., Sacred Heart, c/o Ord, NE, Our Lady of Perpetual Help. (GI)
Busby, MT, Big Horn Co., Christ the King, c/o Lame Deer, MT, Blessed Sacrament. (GF)
Bush, LA, St. Tammany Parish, St. Michael the Archangel, c/o Abita Springs, LA, St. Jane de Chantal. (NO)
Butler, AL, Washington Co., St. Paul, c/o Butler, AL, St. John The Evangelist. (MOB)
Butner, NC, St. Bernadette, c/o Roxboro, NC, SS. Mary and Edward. (R)
Butte La Rose, LA, St. Martin Parish, Sacred Heart, c/o Breaux Bridge, LA, Our Lady of Mercy. (LAF)

Bylas, AZ, Graham Co., Blessed Kateri Tekakwitha, c/o San Carlos, AZ, San Carlos Catholic Mission. (TUC)

C

Cabezon, NM, Sandoval Co., San Jose, c/o Cuba, NM, Immaculate Conception. (GLP)
Cabool, MO, Texas Co., St. Michael, c/o Mountain Grove, MO, Sacred Heart. (SPC)
Cactus, TX, Sherman Co., Our Lady of Guadalupe, c/o Stratford, TX, St. Joseph's. (AMA)
Cade, LA, St. Anthony, c/o Broussard, LA, St. Joseph. (LAF)
Caimital, PR, Guayama Co., Our Lady of Perpetual Help, c/o Guayama, PR, St. Anthony of Padua. (PCE)
Cairo, GA, Grady Co., St. Elizabeth Ann Seton, c/o Thomasville, GA, St. Augustine. (SAV)
Caldwell, TX, Burleson Co., Holy Rosary, c/o Caldwell, TX, St. Mary's. (AUS)
Calhoun, LA, Ouachita Parish, St. Francis of Assisi, c/o West Monroe, LA, St. Paschal. (SHP)
Callabo, PR, Bo. Callabo, San Ramon, c/o Juana Diaz, PR, St. Raymond Nonato. (PCE)
Callaway, MN, Becker Co., Assumption, c/o Frazee, MN, Sacred Heart. (CR)
Callaway, NE, Logan Co., St. Boniface, c/o Stapleton, NE, St. John the Evangelist. (GI)
Calvert, TX, Robertson Co., St. Mary, c/o Hearne, TX, St. Mary's. (AUS)
Camaseyes, PR, Our Lady of Fatima, c/o Aguadilla, PR, La Milagrosa. (MGZ)
Cambalaches, PR, Yauco Co., Our Lady of Perpetual Help, c/o Yauco, PR, Holy Rosary. (PCE)
Cambridge, IL, Henry Co., St. John Vianney, c/o Kewanee, IL, St. Francis of Assisi. (PEO)
Camden, AL, Wilcox Co., St. Joseph, c/o Monroeville, AL, Annunciation. (MOB)
Cameron, LA, Cameron Parish, St. Rose of Lima, c/o Creole, LA, Sacred Heart of Jesus. (LKC)
Camilla, GA, Mitchell Co., St. John Vianney, c/o Moultrie, GA, Immaculate Conception. (SAV)
Camp Sacramento, CA, El Dorado Co., Our Lady of the Sierra, c/o South Lake Tahoe, CA, St. Theresa. (SAC)
Camp Summit, NY, Schoharie Co., N.Y.S. Correctional Facility, c/o Summit, NY, St. Anna. (ALB)
Camp Summit, NY, Schoharie Co., S.U.N.Y. Cobleskill College, c/o Summit, NY, St. Anna. (ALB)
Camp Wood, TX, Real Co., St. Mary Magdalen, c/o Rocksprings, TX, Sacred Heart of Mary. (SAT)
Campbell, NY, Steuben Co., St. Joseph, c/o Addison, NY, St. Stanislaus. (ROC)
Campbellton, TX, Atascosa Co., Sacred Heart, c/o Pleasanton, TX, St. Andrew. (SAT)
Campo, CA, San Diego Co., St. Adelaide at Cameron Corners, c/o El Cajon, CA, Our Lady of Grace. (SD)
Campton, KY, Wolfe Co., Catholic Church of the Good Shepherd, c/o Hazard, KY, Mother of Good Counsel. (LEX)
Canaan, NH, Grafton Co., St. Mary, c/o Enfield, NH, St. Helena. (MAN)
Canaan, PA, Wayne Co., St. Patrick, c/o Waymart, PA, St. Mary's. (SCR)
Canadohta Lake, PA, Crawford Co., Our Lady of Fatima, c/o Union City, PA, St. Teresa of Avila. (E)
Canalizo, PR, Jayuya Co., La Milagrosa, c/o Jayuya, PR, Our Lady of Monserrate. (PCE)
Candelaria, TX, Presidio Co., Our Lady of Peace, c/o Presidio, TX, Santa Teresa de Jesus. (ELP)
Canjilon, NM, Rio Arriba Co., San Juan Nepumoceno, c/o Chama, NM, St. Patrick. (SFE)
Cannon Ball, ND, Sioux Co., St. Elizabeth, c/o Fort Yates, ND, St. Peter – Catholic Indian Mission. (BIS)
Canon de Vallecitos, NM, Rio Arriba Co., c/o El Rito, NM, San Juan Nepomuceno. (SFE)
Canoncito, NM, Mora Co., c/o Mora, NM, St. Gertrude. (SFE)
Canoncito, NM, Santa Fe Co., c/o Pecos, NM, St. Anthony. (SFE)
Canoncito, NM, Bernalillo Co., c/o Tijeras, NM, Holy Child. (SFE)
Canones, NM, Rio Arriba Co., c/o Abiquiu, NM, St. Thomas Apostle. (SFE)
Canovanas, PR, Canovanas Co., La Milagrosa, c/o Canovanas, PR, Sagrado Corazon de Jesus. (SJN)
Canovanas, PR, Canovanas Co., San Francisco Javier, c/o Canovanas, PR, Nuestra Senora del Pilar. (SJN)
Cantagallo, PR, Juncos Co., N. Sra. de la Divina Providencia, c/o Guaynabo, PR, Nuestra Senora de la Paz. (SJN)
Canton, NC, Haywood Co., Immaculate Conception, c/o Waynesville, NC, St. John the Evangelist. (CHL)
Cantwell, , c/o Healy, AK, Holy Mary of Guadalupe. (FBK)
Canyon, NM, Sandoval Co., c/o Jemez Pueblo, NM, San Diego Indian Missions. (SFE)
Canyon Ferry, MT, Lewis and Clark Co., Our Lady of the Lake, c/o East Helena, MT, SS. Cyril and Methodius. (HEL)
Capitan, NM, Lincoln Co., Sacred Heart, c/o Carrizozo, NM, St. Rita. (LSC)
Capulin, NM, Rio Arriba Co., c/o Abiquiu, NM, St. Thomas Apostle. (SFE)
Carbondale, CO, Garfield Co., St. Mary of the Crown, c/o Carbondale, CO, St. Vincent. (DEN)
Carenage, VI, Chapel of St. Anne, c/o Charlotte Amalie, VI, Cathedral of Sts. Peter and Paul. (STV)
Carmen, PR, Guayama Co., Our Lady of Mt. Carmel, c/o Guayama, PR, St. Anthony of Padua. (PCE)
Carnation, WA, King Co., St. Anthony, c/o Snoqualmie, WA, Our Lady of Sorrows. (SEA)
Carnegie, OK, Caddo Co., St. Richard, c/o Anadarko, OK, St. Patrick's. (OKL)
Carnuel, NM, Bernalillo Co., Holy Child, c/o Tijeras, NM, Holy Child. (SFE)
Carolina, PR, Barrazas Co., N. Sra. del Carmen, c/o Carolina, PR, Ntra. Sra. de Fatima. (SJN)
Carolina, PR, Carolina Co., Parque Boliviano 5–JL, c/o Carolina, PR, Santa Clara de Asis. (SJN)
Carolina, PR, Carolina Co., San Antonio, c/o Carolina, PR, San Valentin. (SJN)
Carolina, PR, Cacao Co., Santa Teresa, c/o Carolina, PR, Ntra. Sra. de Fatima. (SJN)
Carpenter, WY, Laramie Co., St. Peter, c/o Pine Bluffs, WY, St. Paul's. (CHY)
Carrissa Plains, CA, San Luis Obispo Co., St. James Mission, c/o Paso Robles, CA, Santa Margarita de Cortona. (MRY)
Carrizales, PR, Ntra. Sra. de las Mercedes, c/o Aguada, PR, St. Francis of Assisi. (MGZ)
Carrizales, PR, Hatillo Co., Our Lady of Montserrat, c/o Yauco, PR, Holy Rosary. (PCE)
Carroll, NH, Coos Co., St. Patrick, c/o Whitefield, NH, St. Matthew. (MAN)
Carson, MS, Jefferson Davis Co., St. Elizabeth, c/o Bassfield, MS, St. Peter. (BLX)
Casa Colorada, NM, Valencia Co., c/o Tome, NM, Immaculate Conception. (SFE)
Cascade, CO, El Paso Co., Holy Rosary, c/o Colorado Springs, CO, Sacred Heart. (COS)
Cascade, MT, Cascade Co., Sacred Heart, c/o Fort Shaw, MT, St. Ann. (GF)
Cascade, PA, Lycoming Co., Assumption of the B.V.M., c/o Williamsport, PA, St. Ann's. (SCR)
Castine, ME, Hancock Co, Our Lady of Holy Hope, c/o Stonington, ME, St. Mary Star of the Sea. (PRT)
Catarina, TX, Dimmit Co., St. Henry, c/o Asherton, TX, Immaculate Conception. (LAR)
Cathlamet, WA, Wahkiakum Co., St. Catherine, c/o Longview, WA, St. Rose de Viterbo. (SEA)
Cave Junction, OR, Josephine Co., St. Patrick, c/o Grants Pass, OR, St. Anne. (P)
Cazadero, CA, St. Colman, c/o Guerneville, CA, St. Elizabeth. (SR)
Cebolla, NM, Rio Arriba Co., Santo Nino, c/o Chama, NM, St. Patrick. (SFE)
Cedar Bluffs, NE, Saunders Co., St. Mary, c/o Colon, NE, St. Joseph's. (LIN)
Cedar Creek, AZ, Gila Co., St. Anthony, c/o Cibecue, AZ, St. Catherine. (GLP)
Cedar Hill, NE, Saunders Co., Sacred Heart, c/o Morse Bluff, NE, St. George. (LIN)
Cedar Hill, TN, Robertson Co., St. Michael, c/o Springfield, TN, Our Lady of Lourdes. (NSH)
Cedaredge, CO, Delta Co., St. Philip Benizi, c/o Delta, CO, St. Michael. (PBL)
Cedarville, CA, Modoc Co., St. James, c/o Alturas, CA, Sacred Heart. (SAC)
Ceiba, PR, Sagrado Corazon de Jesus, c/o Ceiba, PR, San Antonio de Padua. (CGS)
Celina, TN, Clay Co., Divine Savior, c/o Cookeville, TN, St. Thomas Aquinas. (NSH)
Center, MO, Ralls Co., St. Paul (Historic Church), c/o Perry, MO, St. William. (JC)
Centermoreland, PA, Luzerne Co., Blessed Sacrament, c/o Wyoming, PA, St. Frances Cabrini. (SCR)
Centerville, MT, Cascade Co., Holy Trinity, c/o Belt, MT, St. Mark the Evangelist. (GF)
Centerville, TX, Leon Co., St. Leo the Great, c/o Crockett, TX, St. Francis of the Tejas. (TYL)
Central City, CO, Gilpin Co., St. Mary of the Assumption, c/o Idaho Springs, CO, St. Paul. (DEN)
Centreville, MI, St. Joseph Co., St. Clare, c/o Three Rivers, MI, Immaculate Conception. (KAL)
Cerrito, NM, San Miguel Co., c/o Villanueva, NM, Our Lady of Guadalupe. (SFE)
Cerro, NM, Taos Co., c/o Questa, NM, St. Anthony. (SFE)
Cerro Gordo, PR, Buen Consejo, c/o Aguada, PR, St. Francis of Assisi. (MGZ)
Chacon, NM, Mora Co., c/o Mora, NM, St. Gertrude. (SFE)
Chalmette, LA, St. Bernard Parish, Chapel of St. Lawrence, c/o Chalmette, LA, Our Lady of Prompt Succor. (NO)
Chama, CO, Costilla Co., Immaculate Conception, c/o San Luis, CO, Sangre de Cristo. (PBL)
Chama, CO, Huerfano Co., Our Lady of Guadalupe, c/o Walsenburg, CO, St. Mary. (PBL)
Chamisal, NM, Taos Co., Santa Cruz Mission, c/o Penasco, NM, San Antonio de Padua. (SFE)
Chamita, NM, Rio Arriba Co., c/o San Juan Pueblo, NM, St. John the Baptist. (SFE)
Chandler, TX, Van Sand Co., St. Boniface, c/o Athens, TX, St. Edward Church. (TYL)
Chaparral, NM, Dona Ana Co., St. Thomas More, c/o Anthony, NM, St. Anthony's. (LSC)
Chapmanville, WV, Logan Co., St. Barbara, c/o Madison, WV, St. Mary, Queen of Heaven. (WH)
Charco, TX, Goliad Co., Our Lady of Guadalupe, c/o Goliad, TX, Immaculate Conception. (VIC)
Charlemont, MA, Franklin Co., St. Christopher, c/o Shelburne Falls, MA, St. Joseph's. (SPR)
Charlestown, RI, Washington Co., St. James, c/o Carolina, RI, St. Mary. (PRO)
Charley Creek, MT, Richland Co., St. Bernard's, c/o Sidney, MT, St. Matthew's. (GF)
Charlo, MT, Mount Lake Co., St. Joseph's, c/o Ronan, MT, Sacred Heart. (HEL)
Cherokee, NC, Swain Co., Our Lady of Guadalupe, c/o Bryson City, NC, St. Joseph. (CHL)
Cherokee, OK, Alfalfa Co., St. Cornelius, c/o Alva, OK, Sacred Heart. (OKL)
Cherry Creek, SD, Ziebach Co., St. Joseph, c/o Eagle Butte, SD, All Saints. (RC)
Cherry Creek, SD, Ziebach Co., St. Joseph, c/o Eagle Butte, SD, Cheyenne River Reservation. (RC)
Cherryfield, ME, Washington Co., St. Michael's, c/o Machias, ME, Holy Name of Jesus. (PRT)
Chesapeake City, MD, Cecil Co., St. Rose of Lima, c/o Middletown, DE, St. Joseph. (WIL)
Chester, CA, Plumas Co., Christ the King, c/o Westwood, CA, Our Lady of the Snows. (SAC)
Chester, MA, Hampden Co., St. John, c/o Huntington, MA, St. Thomas. (SPR)
Chester, PA, Delaware Co., St. Hedwig Chapel, c/o Clifton Heights, PA, Sacred Heart. (PH)
Chesterfield, NH, Cheshire Co., Our Lady of the Lake, c/o Keene, NH, St. Margaret Mary. (MAN)
Chicago, IL, Angel Guardian Croatian Catholic Mission, c/o Chicago, IL, Archdiocese of Chicago's Joseph Cardinal Bernardin Archives and Records Center. (CHI)
Chicago, IL, Cook Co., Holy Redeemer Church, c/o Aurora, IL, Ss. Peter and Paul Mission. (ROM)
Chicago, IL, Our Lady of Fatima Mission, c/o Chicago, IL, Archdiocese of Chicago's Joseph Cardinal Bernardin Archives and Records Center. (CHI)
Chicago, IL, Our Lady of the Cross Mission Chapel, c/o Chicago, IL, Archdiocese of Chicago's Joseph Cardinal Bernardin Archives and Records Center. (CHI)
Chicago, IL, Passionist Missions of India, c/o Chicago, IL, Passionist Provincial Office. (CHI)
Chicago, IL, Cook Co., Sacred Heart, c/o Chicago, IL, Holy Name of Mary. (CHI)
Chicago, IL, San Marcello Mission, c/o Chicago, IL, Archdiocese of Chicago's Joseph Cardinal Bernardin Archives and Records Center. (CHI)
Chicago, IL, Santa Lucia Mission, c/o Chicago, IL, Archdiocese of Chicago's Joseph Cardinal Bernardin Archives and Records Center. (CHI)
Chicago, IL, St. Florian Mission, c/o Chicago, IL, Archdiocese of Chicago's Joseph Cardinal Bernardin Archives and Records Center. (CHI)
Chicago, IL, St. Hedwig Mission, c/o Chicago, IL, Archdiocese of Chicago's Joseph Cardinal Bernardin Archives and Records Center. (CHI)
Chicago, IL, St. Hyacinth Mission, c/o Chicago, IL, Archdiocese of Chicago's Joseph Cardinal Bernardin Archives and Records Center. (CHI)
Childersburg, AL, Talladega Co., Holy Name of Jesus, c/o Sylacauga, AL, St. Jude. (BIR)
Chilili, NM, Bernalillo Co., San Juan de Nepumoceno, c/o Tijeras, NM, Holy Child. (SFE)
China Lake, ME, Kennebec Co., St. Peter, c/o North Vassalboro, ME, St. Bridget's. (PRT)
Chino Valley, AZ, Yavapai Co., St. Catherine Laboure, c/o Prescott, AZ, Sacred Heart. (PHX)
Chippewa Lake, OH, Medina Co., Jesus Divine Redeemer, c/o Litchfield, OH, Our Lady Help of Christians Parish. (CLV)
Chireno, TX, Nacogdoches Co., Our Lady of Lourdes, c/o Nacogdoches, TX, Sacred Heart. (TYL)
Chittenden, VT, Rutland Co., St. Robert, c/o Pittsford, VT, St. Alphonsus Liguori. (BUR)
Choctaw, LA, Lafourche Parish, St. James, c/o Thibodaux, LA, St. Lawrence the Martyr. (HT)
Christiansted, VI, U.S.V.I., Sacred Heart Chapel, c/o Christiansted, VI, Church of the Holy Cross. (STV)
Christine, TX, Atascosa Co., St. Ignatius, c/o Jourdanton, TX, St. Matthew's. (SAT)
Christmas Valley, OR, Lake Co., Holy Family, c/o La Pine, OR, Holy Redeemer. (BAK)
Chualar, CA, Monterey Co., Chualar Mission, c/o Gonzales, CA, St. Theodore. (MRY)
Chugwater, WY, Platte Co., Mary Queen of Heaven, c/o Wheatland, WY, St. Patrick's. (CHY)
Cilantro, PR, Coamo Co., Saint James, c/o Coamo, PR, St. Blase. (PCE)
Cincinnatus, NY, Cortland Co., Our Lady of Perpetual Help, c/o Marathon, NY, St. Stephen. (SY)

Citra, FL, Marion Co., Christ the King, c/o Candler, FL, Immaculate Heart of Mary. (ORL)
Clallam Bay, WA, Clallam Co., St. Thomas the Apostle, c/o Forks, WA, St. Anne Parish. (SEA)
Clancy, MT, Jefferson Co., St. John's, c/o East Helena, MT, SS. Cyril and Methodius. (HEL)
Clanton, AL, Chilton Co., Church of the Resurrection, c/o Montevallo, AL, St. Thomas the Apostle. (BIR)
Clark, WY, Park Co., Our Lady of the Valley, c/o Powell, WY, St. Barbara. (CHY)
Clarkdale, AZ, Yavapai Co., St. Cecilia, c/o Cottonwood, AZ, Immaculate Conception. (PHX)
Clarksville, MO, Pike Co., Mary Queen of Peace, c/o Louisiana, MO, St. Joseph. (JC)
Clatskanie, OR, Columbia Co., St. John the Baptist, c/o Rainier, OR, Nativity B.V.M.. (P)
Claudell, KS, Smith Co., St. Francis, c/o Phillipsburg, KS, SS. Philip and James. (SAL)
Claybanks, MI, Oceana Co., St. John, c/o Montague, MI, St. James. (GR)
Claypool, AZ, Gila Co., St. Joseph, c/o Miami, AZ, Our Lady of the Blessed Sacrament. (TUC)
Clayton, AL, Barbour Co., Ventress Correctional Facility, c/o Eufaula, AL, Holy Redeemer. (MOB)
Clayton, GA, Rabun Co., St. Helena, c/o Clarkesville, GA, St. Mark. (ATL)
Clayton, OK, Pushmataha Co., Holy Trinity, c/o Krebs, OK, Holy Rosary. (TLS)
Clear Lake, IN, Steuben Co., St. Paul Chapel, c/o Angola, IN, St. Anthony. (FTW)
Clear Spring, MD, Washington Co., St. Michels, c/o Hagerstown, MD, St. Mary. (BAL)
Clearmont, WY, Johnson Co., St. Mary, c/o Buffalo, WY, St. John the Baptist. (CHY)
Clendenin, WV, Kanawha Co., St. Anne, c/o Elkview, WV, Our Lady of the Hills. (WH)
Cleveland, GA, White Co., St. Paul the Apostle, c/o Blairsville, GA, St. Francis of Assisi. (ATL)
Cleveland, NM, Mora Co., c/o Mora, NM, St. Gertrude. (SFE)
Cleveland, OH, c/o Cleveland, OH, Our Lady of Mount Carmel. (CLV)
Clifford, MI, Lapeer Co., St. Patrick's, c/o North Branch, MI, SS. Peter and Paul. (DET)
Clifton, AZ, Greenlee Co., St. Mary, c/o Clifton, AZ, Sacred Heart. (TUC)
Climax Springs, MO, Camden Co., Our Lady of the Snows, c/o Holts Summit, MO, St. Andrew. (JC)
Clinton, AR, Van Buren Co., St. Jude, c/o Fairfield Bay, AR, St. Francis Assisi. (LR)
Clinton Corners, NY, Dutchess Co., St. Joseph, c/o Bangall, NY, Immaculate Conception. (NY)
Clintonville, , St. Catherine of Sienna, c/o Keeseville, NY, Church of the Immaculate Conception. (OG)
Cloudcroft, NM, Otero Co., Sacred Heart, c/o Alamogordo, NM, Immaculate Conception. (LSC)
Cloverdale, OR, Tillamook Co., St. Joseph, c/o Tillamook, OR, Sacred Heart. (P)
Clyde, TX, Callahan Co., Sts. Joachim and Ann, c/o Abilene, TX, Sacred Heart. (SAN)
Clyde Park, MT, Park Co., St. Margaret, c/o Livingston, MT, St. Mary's. (GF)
Coal Mine, TX, Atascosa Co., Immaculate Conception, c/o Lytle, TX, St. Andrew. (SAT)
Coalburg, WV, Kanawha Co., Good Shepherd, c/o Belle, WV, St. John. (WH)
Coaldale, PA, Schuylkill Co., St. Patrick (Seek), c/o Tamaqua, PA, St. Jerome. (ALN)
Cochiti, NM, Sandoval Co., Indian Pueblo, c/o Pena Blanca, NM, Nuestra Senora De Guadalupe. (SFE)
Cochranton, PA, Crawford Co., Our Lady of Lourdes, c/o Guys Mills, PA, St. Hippolyte. (E)
Coco, PR, Salinas Co., Santa Ana, c/o Salinas, PR, Our Lady of Monserrat. (PCE)
Coeburn, VA, Wise Co., St. Mary, c/o Norton, VA, St. Anthony. (RIC)
Coffman Cove, AK, c/o Craig, AK, St. John by the Sea. (JUN)
Cohoes, NY, Albany Co., Sacred Heart of Jesus, c/o Cohoes, NY, St. Rita–Sacred Heart. (ALB)
Cokeville, WY, Lincoln Co., St. Dominic, c/o Kemmerer, WY, St. Patrick's. (CHY)
Cole Camp, MO, Benton Co., SS. Peter & Paul, c/o Warsaw, MO, St. Ann. (JC)
Collegeville, AL, Jefferson Co., Sacred Heart, c/o Birmingham, AL, Our Lady Queen of the Universe. (BIR)
Collores, PR, Juana Diaz Co., La Milagrosa, c/o Juana Diaz, PR, St. Raymond Nonato. (PCE)
Collores, PR, Yauco, Sacred Heart, c/o Yauco, PR, Santo Domingo de Guzman. (PCE)
Colon, MI, St. Joseph Co., St. Barbara, c/o Bronson, MI, St. Mary's. (KAL)
Colonia Nueva, TX, Hidalgo Co., Christ the King, c/o Donna, TX, St. Joseph. (BWN)
Colonia Villodos, PR, Guayama Co., Perpetuo Socorro, c/o Guayama, PR, St. Anthony of Padua. (PCE)
Colonias, NM, Guadalupe Co., c/o Santa Rosa, NM, St. Rose of Lima. (SFE)
Colorado Springs, CO, El Paso Co., Immaculate Conception, c/o Colorado Springs, CO, St. Mary's Cathedral. (COS)
Colrain, MA, Franklin Co., St. John the Baptist, c/o Shelburne Falls, MA, St. Joseph's. (SPR)
Columbia, CA, Tuolumne Co., St. Anne, c/o Sonora, CA, St. Patrick Church of Sonora (Pastor of). (STO)
Columbia, KY, Adair Co., Good Shepherd, c/o Jamestown, KY, Holy Spirit. (L)
Columbia, LA Caldwell Parish, St. John, c/o Winnsboro, LA, St. Mary. (ALX)
Columbia, NC Tyrrell, All Souls, c/o Edenton, NC, St. Anne. (R)
Columbus, NM, Luna Co., Holy Family, c/o Deming, NM, St. Ann's. (LSC)
Comal, TX, Comal Co., St. Joseph, c/o New Braunfels, TX, SS. Peter and Paul. (SAT)
Commerce, GA, Jackson Co., St. Catherine Laboure, c/o Toccoa, GA, St. Mary's. (ATL)
Comstock, TX, Valverde Co., Mary, Queen of the Universe, c/o Del Rio, TX, Sacred Heart. (SAT)
Concepcion, TX, Duval Co., Immaculate Conception, c/o Premont, TX, St. Theresa of the Infant Jesus. (CC)
Concrete, WA, Skagit Co., St. Catherine, c/o Sedro Woolley, WA, Immaculate Heart of Mary. (SEA)
Conde Avila, PR, St. Martin de Porres, c/o Cabo Rojo, PR, St. Michael. (MGZ)
Conehatta, MS, Newton Co., St. Catherine, c/o Philadelphia, MS, Holy Rosary. (JKS)
Congress Junction, AZ, Yavapai Co., Good Shepherd of the Desert, c/o Prescott, AZ, Sacred Heart. (PHX)
Consejo Alto, PR, Guayanilla Co., La Monserrate, c/o Guayanilla, PR, Immaculate Conception (PCE)
Constantia, NY, Oswego Co., St. Bernadette, c/o Cleveland, NY, St. Mary of the Assumption. (SY)
Contoocook, NH, Merrimack Co., St. Mary, c/o Henniker, NH, St. Theresa. (MAN)
Contreras, NM, Socorro Co., San Jose, c/o La Joya, NM, Our Lady of Sorrows. (SFE)
Conway, MA, Franklin Co., St. Mark, c/o South Deerfield, MA, St. James. (SPR)
Cookson, OK, Cherokee Co., St. John the Evangelist, c/o Sallisaw, OK, St. Francis Xavier. (TLS)
Cooper, TX Delta Co., St. Clare Mission c/o Sulphur Springs, TX, St. James. (TYL)
Cooper Landing, AK, Kenai Peninsula Borough, St. John Neumann Church, c/o Seward, AK, Sacred Heart. (ANC)
Copper Harbor, MI, Keweenaw Co., Our Lady of the Pines, c/o Mohawk, MI, Our Lady of Peace. (MAR)
Coqui, PR, Salinas Co., Our Lady of Perpetual Help, c/o Aguirre, PR, Sacred Heart. (PCE)
Coral, MI, Montcalm Co., St. Clara, c/o Sand Lake, MI, Mary Queen of Apostles. (GR)
Cordell, OK, Washita Co., St. Anne, c/o Clinton, OK, St. Mary's. (OKL)
Cordova, MD, Talbot Co., St. Joseph, c/o Easton, MD, SS. Peter and Paul. (WIL)
Cordova, NM, Rio Arriba Co., San Antonio, c/o Chimayo, NM, Holy Family. (SFE)
Corning, AR, Clay Co., St. Joseph, c/o Paragould, AR, St. Mary's. (LR)
Corona, NM, Lincoln Co., St. Therese of the Little Flower, c/o Carrizozo, NM, St. Rita. (LSC)
Corozal Town, , Catholic Mission Corozal, c/o Bogota 10, D.C., , (CHI)
Corpus Christi, TX, Nueces Co., St. Helena of the True Cross of Jesus, c/o Corpus Christi, TX, Our Lady of Perpetual Help. (CC)
Corpus Christi, TX, Nueces Co., St. Mary, c/o Corpus Christi, TX, St. Peter Prince of Apostles. (CC)
Corral, PR, Juana Diaz Co., P. Socorro, c/o Juana Diaz, PR, St. Raymond Nonato. (PCE)
Costilla, NM, Taos Co., c/o Questa, NM, St. Anthony. (SFE)
Cotton City, NM, Hidalgo Co., St. Jude, c/o Lordsburg, NM, St. Joseph. (LSC)
Cottonwood, CA, Shasta Co., St. Anne, c/o Anderson, CA, Sacred Heart. (SAC)
Cottonwood, MT, Hill Co., St. John the Baptist, c/o Havre, MT, St. Jude Thaddeus. (GF)
Cotuy, PR, Our Lady of Fatima, c/o San German, PR, San German de Auxerre. (MGZ)
Coupeville, WA, Island Co., St. Mary, c/o Oak Harbor, WA, St. Augustine. (SEA)
Coushatta, LA, Red River Parish, St. George, c/o Bossier City, LA, Mary, Queen of Peace. (SHP)
Covelo CA, Mendocino Co., Our Lady Queen of Peace, c/o Willits, CA, St. Anthony. (SR)
Covington, KY, Kenton Co., St. Ann, c/o Covington, KY, St. John. (COV)
Cox, SD, Harding Co., St. Agnes, c/o Buffalo, SD, St. Anthony. (RC)
Coyanosa, TX, Pecos Co., St. Isidore, c/o Crane, TX, Good Shepherd. (SAN)
Coyanosa, TX, Pecos Co., St. Isidore, c/o Fort Stockton, TX, St. Agnes. (SAN)
Coyote, NM, Rio Arriba Co., c/o Abiquiu, NM, St. Thomas Apostle. (SFE)
Craftsbury, VT, Orleans Co., Our Lady of Fatima, c/o Hardwick, VT, St. Norbert. (BUR)
Crane, OR, Harney Co., St. Thomas, c/o Burns, OR, Holy Family. (BAK)
Cranfield, MS, Adams Co., St. John the Baptist, c/o Natchez, MS, Holy Family. (JKS)
Crates, PA, Clarion Co., St. Nicholas, c/o New Bethlehem, PA, St. Charles. (E)
Crawfordsville, AR, Crittenden Co., Sacred Heart, c/o West Memphis, AR, St. Michael's. (LR)
Creede, CO, Mineral Co., Immaculate Conception, c/o Del Norte, CO, Holy Name of Mary. (PBL)
Crescent, OK, Logan Co., St. Margaret Mary, c/o Guthrie, OK, St. Mary's. (OKL)
Crescent City, IL, Iroquois Co., St. Joseph, c/o Watseka, IL, St. Edmund. (JOL)
Creswell, OR, Lane Co., St. Philip Benizi, c/o Cottage Grove, OR, Our Lady of Perpetual Help. (P)
Cripple Creek, CO, Teller Co., St. Peter's, c/o Woodland Park, CO, Our Lady of the Woods. (COS)
Cristo Rey, TX, Starr Co., La Victoria, c/o Grulla, TX, Holy Family. (BWN)
Crittenden, NY, Erie Co., St. Patrick, c/o Corfu, NY, St. Francis of Assisi. (BUF)
Crook, CO, Logan Co., St. Peters, c/o Julesburg, CO, St. Anthony. (DEN)
Crosbyton, TX, Crosby Co., St. Joseph, c/o Ralls, TX, St. Michael. (LUB)
Cross City, FL, Dixie Co., Holy Cross, c/o Chiefland, FL, St. John the Evangelist. (STA)
Crosstown, MO, Perry Co., St. James, c/o Perryville, MO, St. Vincent De Paul. (STL)
Crows Landing, CA, Stanislaus Co., Immaculate Heart of Mary, c/o Patterson, CA, Sacred Heart Church of Patterson (Pastor of). (STO)
Cruces, PR, Santa Monica, c/o Aguada, PR, St. Francis of Assisi. (MGZ)
Crucible, PA, Greene Co., St. Mary, c/o Carmichael, PA, Our Lady of Consolation. (PIT)
Crystal Beach, TX, Galveston Co., St. Therese of Lisieux, c/o Port Bolivar, TX, Our Mother of Mercy. (GAL)
Cuadrilla, TX, El Paso Co., San Jose, c/o Fabens, TX, Our Lady of Guadalupe. (ELP)
Cuba, OH, Putnam Co., St. Isidore, c/o Kalida, OH, St. Michael. (TOL)
Cube Cove, AK, c/o Yakutat, AK, St. Ann. (JUN)
Cuchillo, NM, Sierra Co., St. Joseph, c/o Truth or Consequences, NM, Our Lady of Perpetual Help. (LSC)
Cuervo, NM, Guadalupe Co., c/o Santa Rosa, NM, St. Rose of Lima. (SFE)
Culbertson, MT, Roosevelt Co., St. Anthony's, c/o Sidney, MT, St. Matthew's. (GF)
Cundiyo, NM, Rio Arriba Co., Santo Domingo, c/o Chimayo, NM, Holy Family. (SFE)
Cuny Table, SD, Shannon Co., St. Joseph, c/o Pine Ridge, SD, Holy Rosary. (RC)
Cupey, PR, San Martin de Porres, c/o San Juan, PR, Santa Teresa Jornet. (SJN)
Cupey, PR, Virgen de la Salud, c/o San Juan, PR, Santa Teresa Jornet. (SJN)
Curtis, MI, Mackinac Co., St. Timothy, c/o Grand Marais, MI, Holy Rosary Church. (MAR)
Custer, MT, Yellowstone Co., St. Mary, c/o Hardin, MT, St. Joseph's. (GF)
Cuthbert, GA, Randolph Co., St. Luke, c/o Blakely, GA, Holy Family. (SAV)

D

Dahlia, NM, Guadalupe Co., c/o Anton Chico, NM, San Jose. (SFE)
Dallas City, IL, Hancock Co., Sacred Heart, c/o Nauvoo, IL, SS. Peter and Paul's. (PEO)
Dalton, NE, Cheyenne Co., St. Mary, c/o Bridgeport, NE, All Souls. (GI)
Danby, VT, Rutland Co., Holy Trinity, c/o Manchester Center, VT, St. Paul's. (BUR)
Dandan, , Our Lady of the Most Holy Rosary, c/o Saipan, MP, San Vicente Parish. (CHK)
Danforth, ME, Washington Co., St. Ann, c/o Lincoln, ME, St. Mary. (PRT)
Danville, KS, Harper Co., c/o Harper, KS, St. Joan of Arc. (WCH)
Danville, VT, Caledonia Co., Our Lady Queen of Peace, c/o Lyndonville, VT, St. Elizabeth. (BUR)
Darby, MT, Ravalli Co., St. Philip Benizi, c/o Hamilton, MT, St. Francis. (HEL)
Dardanelle, AR, Yell Co., St. Augustine, c/o Atkins, AR, Assumption B.V.M.. (LR)
Darien, GA, McIntosh Co., Nativity of Our Lady, c/o Brunswick, GA, St. Francis Xavier. (SAV)
Darlington, SC, Darlington Co., St. Joseph the Worker, c/o Hartsville, SC, St. Mary the Virgin Mother. (CHR)
Darrington, WA, Snohomish Co., St. John Mary Vianney, c/o Arlington, WA, Immaculate Conception. (SEA)
David City, NE, Butler Co., Assumption, c/o David City, NE, St. Mary's. (LIN)
Dawsonville, GA, Dawson Co., Christ Redeemer, c/o Dahlonega, GA, St. Luke Catholic. (ATL)
Dayton, OR, Yamhill Co., St. Martin de Porres, c/o McMinnville, OR, St. James. (P)

Daytona Beach, FL, Volusia Co., c/o Apopka, FL, St. Mary's. (SJP)
De Bruce, NY, Sullivan Co., Sacred Heart, c/o Livingston Manor, NY, St. Aloysius. (NY)
De Ridder, LA, Beauregard Parish, St. Jude, c/o De Ridder, LA, St. Joseph's. (LKC)
De Ruyter, NY, Madison Co., St. Lawrence, c/o Truxton, NY, St. Patrick. (SY)
Decatur, NE, Burt Co., Holy Family, c/o Tekamah, NE, St. Patrick. (OM)
Deep Creek Lake, MD, Garrett Co., St. Peter of the Lake, c/o Oakland, MD, St. Peter the Apostle. (BAL)
Deerfield, KS, Kearny Co., Christ the King, c/o Lakin, KS, St. Anthony. (DOD)
Del City, OK, Mission Co., c/o Del City, OK, St. Paul, Apostle. (OKL)
Del Rey, CA, Fresno Co., St. Katherine's, c/o Sanger, CA, St. Mary. (FRS)
Del Rio, TX, Valverde Co., San Juan Diego Chapel, c/o Del Rio, TX, Our Lady of Guadalupe. (SAT)
Delhi, CA, Merced Co., Blessed Teresa of Calcutta, c/o Livingston, CA, St. Jude Thaddeus. (FRS)
Delhi, LA, Richland Parish, St. Theresa, c/o Rayville, LA, Sacred Heart. (SHP)
Dell City, TX, Hudspeth Co., San Isidro, c/o Van Horn, TX, Our Lady of Fatima. (ELP)
Delmar, MD, Wicomico Co., Holy Redeemer, c/o Salisbury, MD, St. Francis De Sales. (WIL)
Delmas Dedeaux, MS, Harrison Co., Our Lady of Chartres, c/o Gulfport, MS, St. Ann. (BLX)
Delta, UT, Millard Co., St. John Bosco, c/o Milford, UT, St. Bridget. (SLC)
Deming, WA, Whatcom Co., St. Peter, c/o Lynden, WA, St. Joseph. (SEA)
Dennis Port, MA, Barnstable Co., Our Lady of the Annunciation, c/o West Harwich, MA, Holy Trinity. (FR)
Denton, MD, Caroline Co., St. Elizabeth, c/o Ridgely, MD, St. Benedict. (WIL)
Denton, MT, Fergus Co., St. Anthony, c/o Stanford, MT, St. Rose of Lima. (GF)
Des Moines, NM, Union Co., Our Lady of Guadalupe, c/o Clayton, NM, St. Francis Xavier. (SFE)
Detroit, OR, Marion Co., St. Christopher, c/o Sublimity, OR, St. Boniface. (P)
Deweese, NE, Clay Co., Assumption, c/o Lawrence, NE, Sacred Heart. (LIN)
Dexter, NY, Jefferson Co., St. Elizabeth Seton, c/o Brownville, NY, Immaculate Conception of the B.V.M.. (OG)
Dexter, OR, Lane Co., St. Henry, c/o Oakridge, OR, St. Michael. (P)
Diego Hdez, PR, Yauco Co., St. Anthony, c/o Yauco, PR, Holy Rosary. (PCE)
Diener Ranch At Five Points, CA, Fresno Co., Holy Family Chapel, c/o Riverdale, CA, St. Ann. (FRS)
Dilia, NM, Guadalupe Co., c/o Anton Chico, NM, San Jose. (SFE)
Dilley, TX, Frio Co., St. Mary, c/o Dilley, TX, St. Joseph's. (SAT)
Dillon Valley, CO, Summit Co., Our Lady of Peace, c/o Frisco, CO, St. Mary. (DEN)
Dilworth, MN, Clay Co., St. Elizabeth, c/o Moorhead, MN, St. Francis de Sales. (CR)
Dimmick Township, IL, Sacred Heart, c/o La Salle, IL, Resurrection. (PEO)
Diomede, AK, St. Jude, c/o Nome, AK, St. Joseph. (FBK)
Dividing Ridge, KY, Pendleton Co., St. John's, c/o Williamstown, KY, St. William. (COV)
Dixfield, ME, Oxford Co., St. Joseph, c/o Mexico, ME, St. Theresa. (PRT)
Dixon, NE, Dixon Co., St. Anne, c/o Laurel, NE, St. Mary. (OM)
Dobbins, CA, Yuba Co., Sacred Heart Church, c/o Marysville, CA, St. Joseph. (SAC)
Dockton, WA, King Co., St. Patrick, c/o Vashon, WA, St. John Vianney. (SEA)
Dodson, MT, Phillips Co., Sacred Heart, c/o Malta, MT, St. Mary's. (GF)
Doe Run, PA, Chester Co., St. Malachy, c/o Parkesburg, PA, Our Lady of Consolation. (PH)
Dolan Springs, AZ, Mohave Co., Our Lady of the Desert, c/o Kingman, AZ, St. Mary's. (PHX)
Dollar Bay, MI, Houghton Co., St. Francis of Assisi, c/o Hancock, MI, Resurrection. (MAR)
Dolores, CO, Montezuma Co., Our Lady of Victory Church, c/o Cortez, CO, St. Rita. (PBL)
Donaldson, IN, Maria Center, c/o Donaldson, IN, Convent Ancilla Domini. (FTW)
Donalsonville, GA, Seminole Co., Church of the Incarnation, c/o Bainbridge, GA, St. Joseph's. (SAV)
Doniphan, KS, Doniphan Co., St. John the Baptist, c/o Atchison, KS, St. Benedict's. (KCK)
Donken, MI, Houghton Co., Immaculate Heart of Mary, c/o Chassell, MI, St. Anne. (MAR)
Donnybrook, ND, Ward Co., St. Anthony, c/o Kenmare, ND, St. Agnes. (BIS)
Dorado, PR, Dorado Co., Ntra. Sra. del Camino, c/o Toa Alta, PR, San Jose. (SJN)
Dorado, PR, Dorado Co., S. Francisco De Asis, c/o Toa Alta, PR, San Jose. (SJN)
Dorado, PR, Dorado Co., San Antonio, c/o Toa Alta, PR, San Fernando Rey. (SJN)
Doraville, GA, Dekalb Co., Our Lady of the Americas, c/o Atlanta, GA, Immaculate Heart of Mary. (ATL)
Dorothy, NJ, Atlantic Co., St. Bernard, c/o Mays Landing, NJ, St. Vincent de Paul. (CAM)
Dorrance, KS, Russell Co., St. Joseph, c/o Wilson, KS, St. Wenceslaus. (SAL)
Dorris, CA, Siskiyou Co., Our Lady of Good Counsel, c/o Tulelake, CA, Holy Cross. (SAC)
Douglas, NE, Otoe Co., St. Martin's, c/o Palmyra, NE, St. Leo's. (LIN)
Dove Creek, CO, Dolores Co., St. Jude, c/o Cortez, CO, St. Margaret Mary. (PBL)
Downey, CA, Los Angeles Co., Los Padrinos Juvenile Hall, c/o Downey, CA, St. Raymond. (LA)
Downey, CA, Los Angeles Co., Rancho Los Amigos Hospital, c/o Downey, CA, St. Raymond. (LA)
Downs, KS, Osborne Co., St. Mary's, c/o Osborne, KS, St. Aloysius. (SAL)
Downsville, NY, Delaware Co., Holy Family, c/o Walton, NY, St. John the Baptist. (ALB)
Doylesburg, PA, Franklin Co., Our Lady of Refuge, c/o Chambersburg, PA, Corpus Christi. (HBG)
Doyline, LA, Webster Parish, Mary, Queen of the Most Holy Rosary Chapel, c/o Bossier City, LA, Christ the King. (SHP)
Draper, SD, Jones Co., St. Anthony of Padua, c/o Presho, SD, Christ the King. (RC)
Drew, SD, Perkins Co., St. James, c/o Lemmon, SD, Blessed Sacrament. (RC)
Drewsey, OR, Harney Co., Our Lady of Loretto, c/o Burns, OR, Holy Family. (BAK)
Drexel, MD, Frederick Co., St. Katharine, c/o Frederick, MD, St. John the Evangelist. (BAL)
Drifting, PA, Clearfield Co., St. Severin, c/o Frenchville, PA, St. Mary of the Assumption. (E)
Driftwood, PA, Cameron Co., St. James, c/o Emporium, PA, St. Mark. (E)
Driscoll, TX, Nueces Co., St. James, c/o Bishop, TX, St. James. (CC)
Drummond Island, MI, Chippewa Co., St. Florence, c/o DeTour, MI, Sacred Heart. (MAR)
Drumright, OK, Creek Co., St. Mary, c/o Cushing, OK, SS. Peter and Paul. (TLS)
Dubina, TX, Fayette Co., SS. Cyril and Methodius, c/o Weimar, TX, St. Michael. (VIC)
Dubois, WY, Fremont Co., Our Lady of the Woods, c/o Riverton, WY, St. Margaret's. (CHY)
Dubuisson, MS, Harrison Co., St. Ann, c/o Pass Christian, MS, The Catholic Church in DeLisle. (BLX)
Duchesne, UT, Duchesne Co., Holy Spirit, c/o Roosevelt, UT, St. Helen's. (SLC)
Duey, PR, Chapel of St. Augustin, c/o San German, PR, San German de Auxerre. (MGZ)
Duey, PR, Yauco Co., Virgin of Mt. Carmel, c/o Yauco, PR, Holy Rosary. (PCE)
Dulce, NM, Rio Arriba Co., St. Anthony, c/o Dulce, NM, St. Francis of Assisi. (GLP)
Dumas, AR, Desha Co., Holy Child, c/o Lake Village, AR, Our Lady of the Lake. (LR)
Duncannon, PA, Perry Co., St. Bernadette, c/o Marysville, PA, Our Lady of Good Counsel. (HBG)
Dundee, NY, Yates Co., St. Andrew, c/o Penn Yan, NY, St. Michael. (ROC)
Dungannon, VA, Scott, St. Patrick, c/o Gate City, VA, St. Bernard. (RIC)
Dupree, SD, Ziebach Co., Sacred Heart, c/o Eagle Butte, SD, All Saints. (RC)
Dupree, SD, Ziebach Co., Sacred Heart, c/o Eagle Butte, SD, Cheyenne River Reservation. (RC)
Dupuyer, MT, Pondera Co., Holy Cross, c/o Valier, MT, St. Francis. (HEL)
Duran, NM, Torrance Co., c/o Vaughn, NM, St. Mary. (SFE)
Durham, CA, Butte Co., St. James, c/o Chico, CA, St. John the Baptist. (SAC)
Duvall, WA, King Co., Holy Innocents, c/o Snoqualmie, WA, Our Lady of Sorrows. (SEA)

E

Eagle, CO, Eagle Co., St. Mary Chapel, c/o Edwards, CO, St. Clare of Assisi. (DEN)
Eagle Harbor, MI, Keweenaw Co., Holy Redeemer, c/o Mohawk, MI, Our Lady of Peace. (MAR)
Eagle Nest, NM, Colfax Co., St. Mel, c/o Cimarron, NM, Immaculate Conception Church. (SFE)
Eagles Mere, PA, Sullivan Co., St. Francis of Assisi, c/o Dushore, PA, St. Basil's. (SCR)
Eagleville, CT, Tolland Co., St. Joseph, c/o Coventry, CT, St. Mary. (NOR)
Earth, TX, Lamb Co., St. Mary Magdalen, c/o Muleshoe, TX, Immaculate Conception. (LUB)
Easley, SC, Anderson Co., St. Luke, c/o Pickens, SC, Holy Cross. (CHR)
East Barre, VT, Washington Co., St. Cecilia & St. Frances Cabrini, c/o Graniteville, VT, St. Sylvester. (BUR)
East Berkshire, VT, Franklin Co., Our Lady of Lourdes, c/o Richford, VT, All Saints. (BUR)
East Brewster, MA, Barnstable Co., Immaculate Conception, c/o Brewster, MA, Our Lady of the Cape. (FR)
East Dorset, VT, Bennington Co., St. Jerome, c/o Manchester Center, VT, St. Paul's. (BUR)
East Durham, NY, Greene Co., Our Lady of Knock Shrine, c/o Cairo, NY, Sacred Heart. (ALB)
East Durham, NY, Greene Co., St. Mary, c/o Cairo, NY, Sacred Heart. (ALB)
East Fairfield, VT, Franklin Co., St. Anthony–St. George, c/o Fairfield, VT, St. Patrick. (BUR)
East Glacier, MT, Glacier Co., Church of the Ascension, c/o Browning, MT, Church of the Little Flower. (HEL)
East Highlands, CA, San Bernardino Co., St. John Bosco, c/o Highland, CA, St. Adelaide. (SB)
East Huntsville, OH, Logan Co., St. George Chapel Marianists of Ohio, c/o Russells Point, OH, St. Mary of the Woods. (CIN)
East Killingly, CT, Windham Co., Our Lady of Peace, c/o Danielson, CT, St. James. (NOR)
East Longmeadow, MA, Hampden Co., St. Joseph's, c/o Springfield, MA, St. Paul. (SPR)
East Otto, NY, Cattaraugus Co., St. Isidore, c/o Cattaraugus, NY, St. Mary. (BUF)
East Quogue, NY, Suffolk Co., c/o Hampton Bays, NY, St. Rosalie's. (RVC)
East Raymond, ME, Cumberland Co., St. Raymond Chapel, c/o Windham, ME, Our Lady of Perpetual Help. (PRT)
East Sebago, ME, Cumberland Co., Our Lady of Sebago, c/o Gorham, ME, St. Anne. (PRT)
Eatonville, WA, Pierce Co., Our Lady of Good Counsel, c/o Puyallup, WA, Holy Disciples. (SEA)
Eden, VT, Lamoille Co., St. Gabriel, c/o Morrisville, VT, Holy Cross. (BUR)
Eden, WY, Sweetwater Co., St. Christopher, c/o Pinedale, WY, Our Lady of Peace. (CHY)
Edenville, MI, Gladwin Co., St. Anne, c/o Coleman, MI, St. Philip Neri. (SAG)
Edgemont, SD, Fall River Co., St. James, c/o Hot Springs, SD, St. Anthony's. (RC)
Edgewater, FL, Volusia Co., St. Gerard, c/o New Smyrna Beach, FL, Sacred Heart. (ORL)
Edgewood, NM, Santa Fe Co., St. Elizabeth Ann Seton, c/o Moriarty, NM, Estancia Valley Catholic Parish. (SFE)
Edison, NJ, Middlesex Co., St. Theresa of the Infant Jesus, c/o New Brunswick, NJ, St. Mary of Mount Virgin. (MET)
Edisto Island, SC, Charleston Co., SS. Frederick & Stephen, c/o Yonges Island, SC, St. Mary. (CHR)
Edmeston, NY, Otsego Co., Nativity of B.V.M., c/o Morris, NY, Holy Cross. (ALB)
Effie, LA, Avoyelles Parish, St. Winifred, c/o Deville, LA, St. John the Baptist. (ALX)
Egan, LA, Acadia Parish, St. Michael, c/o Iota, LA, St. Joseph. (LAF)
Ekalaka, MT, Carter Co., St. Joan of Arc, c/o Baker, MT, St. John the Evangelist. (GF)
El Alto, PR, Penuelas Co., San Antonio, c/o Penuelas, PR, St. Joseph. (PCE)
El Cafetal, PR, , Yauco, St. Rosa de Lima, c/o Yauco, PR, Santo Domingo de Guzman. (PCE)
El Cajon, CA, San Diego Co., Immaculate Conception of BVM, c/o Lakeside, CA, Blessed Kateri Tekakwitha. (SD)
El Carmen, NM, Mora Co., c/o Mora, NM, St. Gertrude. (SFE)
El Corozo, PR, Cristo Rey, c/o Cabo Rojo, PR, St. Michael. (MGZ)
El Duende, NM, Rio Arriba Co., c/o Espanola, NM, Sacred Heart. (SFE)
El Guache, NM, Rio Arriba Co., c/o Espanola, NM, Sacred Heart. (SFE)
El Guique, NM, Rio Arriba Co., c/o San Juan Pueblo, NM, St. John the Baptist. (SFE)
El Macho, NM, San Miguel Co., c/o Pecos, NM, St. Anthony. (SFE)
El Papayo, PR, Cristo Rey, c/o Sabana Grande, PR, Church of San Isidro. (MGZ)
El Paso, TX, El Paso Co., Santa Teresita, c/o El Paso, TX, San Judas Tadeo. (ELP)
El Pueblo, NM, San Miguel Co., San Antonio de Padua, c/o Ribera, NM, San Miguel Del Vado. (SFE)
El Rancho, NM, Santa Fe Co., c/o Santa Fe, NM, N.S. de Guadalupe del Valle de Pojoaque. (SFE)
El Rio, CA, Ventura Co., Santa Clara Chapel, c/o Oxnard, CA, Santa Clara. (LA)
El Rucio, PR, Penuelas Co., La Milagrosa, c/o Penuelas, PR, St. Joseph. (PCE)
El Santuario, NM, Santa Fe Co., El Santuario Shrine, c/o Chimayo, NM, Holy Family. (SFE)
El Sauz, TX, Starr Co., Our Lady of Guadalupe, c/o Roma, TX, Sacred Heart. (BWN)
El Valle, NM, Taos Co., San Miguel Archangel, c/o Chimayo, NM, Holy Family. (SFE)
Elba, NE, Howard Co., St. Joseph, c/o St. Paul, NE, SS. Peter and Paul. (GI)

Elberta, UT, Utah Co., San Isidro, c/o Orem, UT, St. Francis of Assisi. (SLC)
Elberton, GA, Elbert Co., St. Mary's, c/o Washington, GA, St. Joseph's. (ATL)
Elbridge, MI, Oceana Co., Kateri Tekawitha Native American Center & St. Joseph Center, c/o Hart, MI, St. Gregory's. (GR)
Eleele, HI, Kauai Co., Sacred Heart, c/o Kalaheo, HI, Holy Cross. (HON)
Elfin Cove, AK, c/o Yakutat, AK, St. Ann. (JUN)
Elizabeth, IN, Harrison Co., St. Peter, c/o Corydon, IN, St. Joseph. (IND)
Elizabeth, LA, Allen Parish, St. Frances, c/o Oakdale, LA, Sacred Heart. (LKC)
Elizabeth, WV, Wirt Co., St. Elizabeth of Hungary, c/o Spencer, WV, Holy Redeemer. (WH)
Elizabethtown, NC, Bladen Co., Our Lady of the Snows, c/o Whiteville, NC, Sacred Heart. (R)
Elk, TX, McLennon Co., St. Joseph, c/o West, TX, St. Martin. (AUS)
Elka Park, NY, Greene Co., St. Francis de Sales, c/o Haines Falls, NY, Immaculate Conception. (ALB)
Elkhorn City, KY, Pike Co., St. Joseph the Worker, c/o Pikeville, KY, St. Francis of Assisi. (LEX)
Elkin, NC, Surry Co., St. Stephen, c/o North Wilkesboro, NC, St. John Baptist de LaSalle. (CHL)
Ellijay, GA, Gilmer Co., Good Samaritan, c/o Blue Ridge, GA, St. Anthony's. (ATL)
Elmer, LA, Rapides Parish, St. Peter, c/o Glenmora, LA, St. Louis. (ALX)
Elmwood, NE, Cass Co., St. Mary's, c/o Manley, NE, St. Patrick's. (LIN)
Elsie, NE, Perkins Co., Resurrection of Our Lord, c/o Wallace, NE, St. Mary's. (LIN)
Emanueli, PR, Coamo Co., Holy Family, c/o Coamo, PR, St. Blase. (PCE)
Eminence, KY, Henry Co., St. John Chrysostom, c/o Shelbyville, KY, Annunciation of the Blessed Virgin Mary. (L)
Eminence, MO, Shannon Co., St. Sylvester, c/o Mountain View, MO, St. John Vianney. (SPC)
Emmanuel, LA, Natchitoches Parish, Holy Rosary, c/o Cloutierville, LA, St. John the Baptist. (ALX)
Emory, TX, Rains Co., St. John the Evangelist Church, c/o Mineola, TX, St. Peter the Apostle. (TYL)
Empire, LA, Plaquemines Parish, St. Ann, c/o Buras, LA, Our Lady of Good Harbor. (NO)
Empire, NV, Washoe Co., St. Joseph the Worker, c/o Fernley, NV, St. Robert Bellarmine. (RNO)
Encinal, NM, Valencia Co., Nativity of the Blessed Virgin Mary, c/o Laguna, NM, St. Joseph. (GLP)
Encino, NM, Torrance Co., c/o Vaughn, NM, St. Mary. (SFE)
Encino, TX, Brooks Co., St. Ann, c/o Falfurrias, TX, Sacred Heart. (CC)
England, AR, Lonoke Co., Holy Trinity, c/o Carlisle, AR, St. Rose of Lima Church. (LR)
Ensenada, NM, Rio Arriba Co., c/o Los Ojos, NM, San Jose. (SFE)
Ephraim, UT, Sanpete Co., St. Jude, c/o Monroe, UT, St. Elizabeth's. (SLC)
Ericson, NE, St. Theresa of the Child Jesus, c/o Spalding, NE, St. Michael's. (GI)
Ericson, NE, Wheeler Co., St. Theresa of the Child Jesus, c/o Burwell, NE, Sacred Heart. (GI)
Erie, IL, Whiteside Co., St. Ambrose, c/o Prophetstown, IL, St. Catherine. (RCK)
Errol, NH, Coos Co., St. Pius X, c/o Colebrook, NH, St. Brendan. (MAN)
Erving, MA, Franklin Co., St. Blanche, c/o Millers Falls, MA, St. John's. (SPR)
Escalalute, UT, Wayne Co., St. Sylvester, c/o Cedar City, UT, Christ the King. (SLC)
Escobosa, NM, Bernalillo Co., San Isidro, c/o Tijeras, NM, Holy Child. (SFE)
Esopus, NY, Ulster Co., Sacred Heart, c/o Port Ewen, NY, Presentation of the Virgin Mary. (NY)
Esparto, CA, Yolo Co., St. Martin, c/o Winters, CA, St. Anthony. (SAC)
Essex, IL, Kankakee Co., St. Lawrence O'Toole, c/o Braidwood, IL, Immaculate Conception. (JOL)
Estaca, NM, Rio Arriba Co., c/o San Juan Pueblo, NM, St. John the Baptist. (SFE)
Estancia, NM, Torrance Co., Sts. Peter & Paul, c/o Moriarty, NM, Estancia Valley Catholic Parish. (SFE)
Esther, LA, Vermilion Parish, St. James, c/o Erath, LA, St. John. (LAF)
Estherwood, LA, Acadia Parish, St. Margaret, c/o Mermentau, LA, St. John the Evangelist. (LAF)
Ethete, WY, Fremont Co., St. Joseph, c/o St. Stephens, WY, St. Stephen's. (CHY)
Etna, CA, Siskiyou Co., St. Mary's, c/o Fort Jones, CA, Sacred Heart. (SAC)
Euclid, MN, Polk Co., St. Mary, c/o Crookston, MN, Cathedral of the Immaculate Conception. (CR)
Eufaula, OK, McIntosh Co., St. Paul's, c/o Henryetta, OK, St. Michael. (TLS)
Eureka, CA, St. Joseph, c/o Eureka, CA, St. Bernard. (SR)
Eutaw, AL, Greene Co., St. Mary, c/o Demopolis, AL, St. Leo. (BIR)
Everglades City, FL, Collier Co., Holy Family, c/o Marco Island, FL, San Marco. (VEN)
Everly, IA, Clay Co., St. Mary's, c/o Royal, IA, St. Louis. (SC)
Expressway Heights, TX, Hidalgo Co., Nuestra Senora de Guadalupe, c/o Weslaco, TX, San Martin de Porres. (BWN)

F

Fabius, NY, Onondaga Co., St. Paul, c/o Pompey, NY, Immaculate Conception. (SY)
Faga'alu, AS, c/o Pago Pago, AS, Co–Cathedral of St. Joseph the Worker. (SPP)
Faga'itua, AS, c/o Pago Pago, AS, Church of St. Peter and Paul. (SPP)
Fair Haven, NY, Cayuga Co., St. Jude Chapel, c/o Wolcott, NY, St. Thomas the Apostle. (ROC)
Fairacres, NM, Dona Ana Co., San Jose Mission, c/o Mesilla, NM, St. Albino. (LSC)
Fairfield, AL, Jefferson Co., St. Mary's, c/o Birmingham, AL, Holy Family. (BIR)
Fairford, AL Washington Co., Our Lady of Sorrows, c/o Mount Vernon, AL, St. Peter the Apostle (MOB)
Fairplay, CO, Park Co., St. Joseph, c/o Buena Vista, CO, St. Rose of Lima. (COS)
Fairview, MT, Richland Co., St. Catherine, c/o Sidney, MT, St. Matthew's. (GF)
Fairview, OK, Major Co., St. Ann, c/o Bison, OK, St. Joseph's. (OKL)
Falcon, TX, Zapata Co., Santa Ana, c/o Zapata, TX, Our Lady of Lourdes. (LAR)
Falcon Heights, TX, Starr Co., Holy Trinity, c/o Roma, TX, Our Lady of Refuge. (BWN)
Faleniu, AS, c/o Pago Pago, AS, St. Paul. (SPP)
Fall River Mills, CA, Shasta Co., Our Lady of the Valley, c/o Burney, CA, St. Francis of Assisi. (SAC)
Falun, MN, Roseau Co., St. Philip, c/o Warroad, MN, St. Mary's. (CR)
Fannin, TX, Goliad Co., Our Lady of Assumption, c/o Goliad, TX, Immaculate Conception. (VIC)
Farmersville, CA, Tulare Co., St. Anthony of Egypt, c/o Exeter, CA, Sacred Heart. (FRS)
Farmerville, LA, Union Parish, Our Lady of Perpetual Help, c/o West Monroe, LA, St. Paschal. (SHP)
Farnam, NE, Dawson Co., St. Joseph's, c/o Curtis, NE, St. James. (LIN)
Farwell, NE, Howard Co., St. Anthony of Padua, c/o St. Paul, NE, SS. Peter and Paul. (GI)
Fashing, TX, Atascosa Co., St. Elizabeth, c/o Karnes City, TX, St. Cornelius. (SAT)
Fayette, AL, Fayette Co., Holy Family, c/o Winfield, AL, Holy Spirit. (BIR)
Faysville, TX, Hidalgo Co., St. Therese, c/o Edinburg, TX, St Joseph the Worker. (BWN)
Faywood, NM, Luna Co., San Jose, c/o Hurley, NM, Infant Jesus. (LSC)
Fellsmere, FL, Indian River Co., c/o Fellsmere, FL, Our Lady of Guadalupe Mission. (PMB)
Fence Lake, NM, Valencia Co., El Morro, c/o Ramah, NM, San Lorenzo. (GLP)
Fillmore, UT, Millard Co., Holy Family c/o Milford, UT, St. Bridget. (SLC)
Fine, NY, St. Lawrence Co., St. Michael, c/o Star Lake, NY, St. Hubert. (OG)
Fish Creek, NY, SS. Peter & Paul, c/o West Leyden, NY, St. Mary's Nativity. (OG)
Fish Lake, NV, Esmeralda Co., Our Lady of Guadalupe, c/o Tonopah, NV, St. Patrick. (LAV)
Fisher, MN, Polk Co., St. Francis, c/o East Grand Forks, MN, Sacred Heart. (CR)
Fishville, LA, Grant Parish, St. Edward, c/o Jena, LA, St. Mary. (ALX)
Fitzgerald, GA, Ben Hill Co., St. William, c/o Douglas, GA, St. Paul's. (SAV)
Flagler, CO, Kit Carson Co., St. Mary, c/o Limon, CO, Our Lady of Victory. (COS)
Flatwoods, LA, Rapides Parish, St. Cyril, c/o Boyce, LA, St. Margaret. (ALX)
Flaxville, MT, Daniels Co., St. Louis, c/o Scobey, MT, St. Philip Bonitus. (GF)
Fleming, CO, Logan Co., St. Peter the Apostle, c/o Holyoke, CO, St. Patrick. (DEN)
Florence, MT, Ravalli Co., St. Joseph, c/o Stevensville, MT St. Mary. (HEL)
Florian, MN, Marshall Co., Assumption, c/o Stephen, MN, St. Stephen's. (CR)
Florida, NY, Orange Co., St. Edward, c/o Warwick, NY, St. Stephen. (NY)
Floyd, VA, Floyd Co., Church of All Saints, c/o Woodlawn, VA, St. Joseph's. (RIC)
Folkston, GA, Charlton Co., St. Francis of Assisi, c/o St. Marys, GA, Our Lady Star of the Sea. (SAV)
Folsom, NM, Union Co., St. Joseph, c/o Clayton, NM, St. Francis Xavier. (SFE)
Fordyce, AR, Dallas Co., Good Shepherd, c/o Camden, AR, St. Louis. (LR)
Foreman, AR, Little River Co., Sacred Heart, c/o Texarkana, AR, St. Edward's. (LR)
Forest City, MO, Holt Co., St. Patrick, c/o Savannah, MO, St. Rose of Lima. (KC)
Forest Park, GA, Clayton Co., San Felipe de Jesus, c/o Atlanta, GA, Sacred Heart of Jesus. (ATL)
Forestville, MI, Sanilac Co., St. John Chrysostom, c/o Port Sanilac, MI, St. Mary. (SAG)
Forked Island, LA, Vermilon Parish, Immaculate Conception, c/o Abbeville, LA, St. Anne. (LAF)
Forrest, IL, Livingston Co., St. James, c/o Chatsworth, IL, SS. Peter and Paul. (PEO)
Fort Adams, MS, Wilkinson Co., St. Patrick, c/o Woodville, MS, St. Joseph. (JKS)
Fort Belknap Agency, MT, Blaine Co., Sacred Heart, c/o Hays, MT, St. Paul's Indian Mission. (GF)
Fort Bridger, WY, Uinta Co., St. Helen, c/o Evanston, WY, St. Mary Magdalen. (CHY)
Fort Duchesne, UT, Uintah Co., Blessed Kateri Tekakwitha, c/o Roosevelt, UT, St. Helen's. (SLC)
Fort Garland, CO, Costilla Co., Holy Family, c/o San Luis, CO, Sangre de Cristo. (PBL)
Fort Meade, FL, Polk Co., St. Elizabeth Ann Seton, c/o Bartow, FL, St. Thomas Aquinas. (ORL)
Fort Montgomery, NY, Orange Co., Blessed Sacrament, c/o Highland Falls, NY, Sacred Heart of Jesus. (NY)
Fort Myers, FL, Lee Co., Our Lady of Perpetual Help, c/o Fort Myers, FL, St. Francis Xavier. (VEN)
Fort Peck, MT, Valley Co., Our Lady of the Lake, c/o Glasgow, MT, St. Raphael's. (GF)
Fort Stanton, NM, Lincoln Co., Sacred Heart, c/o Ruidoso, NM, St. Eleanor. (LSC)
Fort Totten, ND, Benson Co., St. Jerome, c/o Tokio, ND, (Spirit Lake Sioux). (FAR)
Fort Totten Reservation, ND, Benson Co., Seven Dolors Indian Mission, c/o Tokio, ND, (Spirit Lake Sioux). (FAR)
Fort Valley, GA, Peach Co., St. Juliana, c/o Perry, GA, St. Patrick. (SAV)
Fort Washakie, WY, Fremont Co., Blessed Sacrament, c/o St. Stephens, WY, St. Stephen's. (CHY)
Fort Yates, ND, Sioux Co., Sacred Heart, c/o Fort Yates, ND, St. Philomena. (BIS)
Fossil, OR, Wheeler Co., St. Catherine, c/o Condon, OR, St. John's. (BAK)
Fosston, MN, Polk Co., St. Mary, c/o Oklee, MN, St. Francis Xavier's. (CR)
Foster City, MI, Dickinson Co., St. Joseph, c/o Channing, MI, St. Rose. (MAR)
Fountain, FL, Bay Co., Our Lady Queen of Peace, c/o Panama City, FL, Our Lady of the Rosary. (PT)
Fowler, CO, Otero Co., Mary Queen of Heaven, c/o Rocky Ford, CO, St. Peter. (PBL)
Frances, CO, Archuleta Co., St. Francis, c/o Pagosa Springs, CO, Immaculate Heart of Mary. (PBL)
Frances, WA, Pacific Co., Holy Family, c/o Pe Ell, WA, St. Joseph. (SEA)
Franconia, MN, Chisago Co., St. Francis Xavier, c/o Taylors Falls, MN, St. Joseph's. (STP)
Franconia, NH, Grafton Co., Our Lady of the Snows, c/o Littleton, NH, St. Rose of Lima. (MAN)
Franklin, NY, Delaware Co., St. Paul, c/o Sidney, NY, Sacred Heart. (ALB)
Franklin, VT, Franklin Co., St. Mary, c/o Sheldon Springs, VT, St. Anthony. (BUR)
Frankston, TX, Anderson Co., St. Charles Borromeo, c/o Palestine, TX, Sacred Heart. (TYL)
Frazer, MT, Valley Co., St. Joseph, c/o Wolf Point, MT, Immaculate Conception. (GF)
Fredericksburg, TX, Gillespie Co., Our Lady of Guadalupe, c/o Fredericksburg, TX, St. Mary's. (SAT)
Fredericksburg, VA, Spotsylvania Co., St. Jude, c/o Fredericksburg, VA, St. Mary. (ARL)
Freeport, FL, Walton Co., Christ the King Catholic Mission, c/o Santa Rosa Beach, FL, St. Rita. (PT)
Freeport, ME, Cumberland Co., St. Jude's, c/o Yarmouth, ME, Sacred Heart. (PRT)
Freiburg, MI, Sanilac Co., St. Ignatius, c/o Argyle, MI, St. Joseph. (SAG)
French Camp, CA, San Joaquin Co., Good Shepherd, c/o Stockton, CA, St. George Church (Pastor of). (STO)
French Village, MO, St. Francois Co., St. Anne, c/o Bonne Terre, MO, St. Joseph's. (STL)
Fresno, CA, Fresno Co., St. Francis, c/o Fresno, CA, St. John Cathedral. (FRS)
Friendship, NY, Allegany Co., Sacred Heart, c/o Cuba, NY, Our Lady of the Angels. (BUF)
Frilot Cove, LA, Evangeline Co., St. Ann, c/o Opelousas, LA, St. Joseph. (LAF)
Fromberg, MT, Carbon Co., St. Joseph, c/o Bridger, MT, Sacred Heart. (GF)
Fronton, TX, Starr Co., Lamb of God, c/o Roma, TX, Our Lady of Refuge. (BWN)
Fryeburg, ME, Oxford Co., St. Elizabeth Ann Seton, c/o Bridgton, ME, St. Joseph. (PRT)
Fulton, MS, Itawamba Co., Christ the King, c/o Amory, MS, St. Helen. (JKS)
Futiga, AS, c/o Pago Pago, AS, St. Paul. (SPP)

G

Gabriels, NY, Franklin Co., Assumption of the B.V.M., c/o Bloomingdale, NY, St. Paul. (OG)

Gainesville, MO, Ozark Co., St. William, c/o Ava, MO, Immaculate Heart of Mary. (SPC)
Gaithersburg, MD, Mother of God Community School, c/o Annandale, VA, Epiphany of Our Lord. (PSC)
Galicia–Columbani, PR, Santo Tomas de Villanueva, c/o Aguada, PR, St. Francis of Assisi. (MGZ)
Galisteo, NM, Santa Fe Co., c/o Cerrillos, NM, St. Joseph. (SFE)
Gallatin, MO, Daviess Co., Mary Immaculate, c/o Hamilton, MO, Sacred Heart. (KC)
Gallegos, NM, Harding Co., c/o Roy, NM, Holy Family–St. Joseph. (SFE)
Gallina, NM, Rio Arriba Co., c/o Abiquiu, NM, St. Thomas Apostle. (SFE)
Gallinas, NM, San Miguel Co., Santo Nino, c/o Las Vegas, NM, Our Lady of Sorrows Church. (SFE)
Galveston, TX, Galveston Co., Queen of Peace Mission, c/o Galveston, TX, St. Patrick. (GAL)
Galway, NY, Saratoga Co., St. Mary, c/o Broadalbin, NY, St. Joseph. (ALB)
Gamerco, NM, McKinley Co., St. Joseph the Worker, c/o Gallup, NM, St. Francis of Assisi. (GLP)
Ganado, AZ, Apache Co., St. Anne, c/o Ganado, AZ, All Saints. (GLP)
Garcia, CO, Costilla Co., Sacred Heart of Jesus, c/o San Luis, CO, Sangre de Cristo. (PBL)
Gardiner, MT, Park Co., St. William, c/o Livingston, MT, St. Mary's. (GF)
Gardner, CO, Huerfano Co., Sacred Heart, c/o Walsenburg, CO, St. Mary. (PBL)
Garrison, ND, St. Nicholas, White Shield, Sacred Heart, c/o Garrison, ND, St. Nicholas. (BIS)
Garrison, NY, Putnam Co., St. Joseph's Chapel, c/o Cold Spring, NY, Our Lady of Loretto. (NY)
Gary, IN, St. Hedwig, c/o Merrillville, IN, St. Andrew. (GRY)
Garzas, PR, Adjuntas Co., San Francisco, c/o Adjuntas, PR, St. Joachim. (PCE)
Genesee, PA, Potter Co., Sacred Heart, c/o Galeton, PA, St. Bibiana. (E)
Geneva, AL, Geneva Co., St. Mary, c/o Enterprise, AL, St. John. (MOB)
Gentilly, MN, Polk Co., St. Peter, c/o Crookston, MN, Cathedral of the Immaculate Conception. (CR)
George West, TX, Live Oak Co., c/o George West, TX, St. George. (CC)
Georgetown, CA, El Dorado Co., St. James, c/o Placerville, CA, St. Patrick's. (SAC)
Georgetown, CO, Clear Creek Co., Our Lady of Lourdes, c/o Idaho Springs, CO, St. Paul. (DEN)
Georgetown, MN, Clay Co., St. John, c/o Moorhead, MN, St. Francis de Sales. (CR)
Georgia, VT, Franklin Co., Ascension, c/o Fairfax, VT, St. Luke. (BUR)
Geraldine, MT, Chouteau Co., St. Margaret, c/o Fort Benton, MT, Immaculate Conception. (GF)
Germfask, MI, Schoolcraft Co., St. Therese, c/o Grand Marais, MI, Holy Rosary Church. (MAR)
Geyser, MT, Judith Basin Co., St. Cyril, c/o Stanford, MT, St. Rose of Lima. (GF)
Gila, NM, Grant Co., St. Isidore, c/o Silver City, NM, St. Vincent de Paul. (LSC)
Gila Bend, AZ, Maricopa Co., San Lucy, c/o Laveen, AZ, St. John The Baptist. (PHX)
Gila River, AZ, Yuma Co., Indian Care Center, c/o Laveen, AZ, St. John The Baptist. (PHX)
Gilberts, IL, Kane Co., St. Mary, c/o Dundee, IL, St. Catherine of Siena. (RCK)
Gilchrist, OR, Klamath Co., Our Lady of the Snows, c/o La Pine, OR, Holy Redeemer. (BAK)
Gilman, VT, Essex Co., St. Theresa, c/o St. Johnsbury, VT, St. John the Evangelist. (BUR)
Giltner, NE, Hamilton Co., St. Joseph's, c/o Aurora, NE, St. Mary's. (LIN)
Girdwood, AK, Anchorage Co., Our Lady of Snows, c/o Anchorage, AK, St. Elizabeth Ann Seton. (ANC)
Gladstone, ND, Stark Co., St. Thomas the Apostle, c/o New England, ND, St. Mary. (BIS)
Glasgo, CT, New London Co., St. Anne, c/o Voluntown, CT, St. Thomas Apostle. (NOR)
Glen Ullin, ND, Grant Co., St. Joseph, c/o Glen Ullin, ND, Sacred Heart of Jesus. (BIS)
Glencoe, LA, St. Mary Parish, St. Joan of Arc, c/o Franklin, LA, St. Peter the Apostle. (LAF)
Glencoe, NM, Lincoln Co., San Ysidro, c/o Ruidoso, NM, St. Eleanor. (LSC)
Glendale, OR, Douglas Co., Holy Family, c/o Myrtle Creek, OR, All Souls. (P)
Glendale, RI, Providence Co., St. Louis Chapel, c/o Harrisville, RI, St. Patrick. (PRO)
Glendo, WY, Platte Co., Our Lady of Lourdes, c/o Douglas, WY, St. James. (CHY)
Glenmont, OH, Holmes Co., SS. Peter and Paul, c/o Millersburg, OH, St. Peter. (COL)
Glenmore, NY, Oneida Co., St. Anne, c/o Taberg, NY, St. Patrick. (SY)
Glennon, MO, Bollinger Co., St. Anthony, c/o Leopold, MO, St. John. (SPC)
Glennville, GA, Tattnall Co., St. Jude, c/o Claxton, GA, St. Christopher. (SAV)
Glentana, MT, Valley Co., Holy Family, c/o Scobey, MT, St. Philip Bonitus. (GF)
Glenwood, NM, Catron Co., Santo Nino, c/o Alpine, AZ, St. Helena. (GLP)
Glidden, IA, Carroll Co., St. Elizabeth Seton Church, c/o Lidderdale, IA, Holy Family. (SC)
Glorieta, NM, Santa Fe Co., c/o Pecos, NM, St. Anthony. (SFE)
Gloster, MS, Amite Co., Holy Family, c/o Woodville, MS, St. Joseph. (JKS)
Gluckstadt, MS, Madison Co., St. Joseph, c/o Madison, MS, St. Francis of Assisi. (JKS)
Gobles, MI, Van Buren Co., St. Jude's Church, c/o Paw Paw, MI, St. Mary. (KAL)
Gold Beach, OR, Curry Co., St. Charles Borromeo, c/o Brookings, OR, Star of the Sea. (P)
Goldcreek, MT, Powell Co., St. Mary, c/o Drummond, MT, St. Michael. (HEL)
Golden, NM, Santa Fe Co., c/o Cerrillos, NM, St. Joseph. (SFE)
Goldens Bridge, NY, Westchester Co., St. Michael, c/o Croton Falls, NY, St. Joseph. (NY)
Golondrinas, NM, Mora Co., c/o Mora, NM, St. Gertrude. (SFE)
Goltry, OK, Alfalfa Co., St. Michael, c/o Enid, OK, St. Gregory the Great. (OKL)
Golva, ND, Golden Valley Co., St. Mary, c/o Beach, ND, St. John the Baptist. (BIS)
Gonzales, TX, Gonzales Co., Sacred Heart, c/o Gonzales, TX, St. James. (SAT)
Gonzales Ranch, NM, San Miguel Co., c/o Villanueva, NM, Our Lady of Guadalupe. (SFE)
Goodhue, MN, Goodhue Co., Holy Trinity, c/o Goodhue, MN, St. Columbkill. (STP)
Goodridge, MN, Pennington Co., St. Anne, c/o Oklee, MN, St. Francis Xavier's. (CR)
Gorum, LA, Natchitoches Parish, St. Margaret Mary, c/o Boyce, LA, St. Margaret. (ALX)
Goshen, NJ, Cape May Co., St. Elizabeth, c/o Woodbine, NJ, St. Casimir's. (CAM)
Gothenburg, NE, Dawson Co., Our Lady of Good Counsel, c/o Cozad, NE, Christ the King. (GI)
Goudeau, LA, Avoyelles Parish, St. Charles, c/o Evergreen, LA, Little Flower. (ALX)
Grady, AR, Lincoln Co., Blessed Sacrament, c/o Star City, AR, St. Justin's. (LR)
Granby, CO, Grand Co., Our Lady of the Snow, c/o Granby, CO, St. Anne. (DEN)
Grand Chenier, LA, Cameron Parish, Immaculate Conception, c/o Grand Chenier, LA, St. Eugene. (LKC)
Grand Gorge, NY, Delaware Co., St. Philip Neri, c/o Stamford, NY, Sacred Heart. (ALB)
Grand Isle, VT, Grand Isle Co., St. Joseph, c/o South Hero, VT, St. Rose of Lima. (BUR)
Grand Junction, IA, Greene Co., St. Brigid, c/o Jefferson, IA, St. Joseph's. (SC)
Grand Ridge, IL, La Salle Co., St. Mary's, c/o Ottawa, IL, St. Columba. (PEO)
Grand Saline, TX, Van Zandt Co., St. Celestine, c/o Mineola, TX, St. Peter the Apostle. (TYL)
Grandfalls, TX, Ward Co., St. Gertrude, c/o Monahans, TX, St. John the Apostle and Evangelist. (ELP)
Grandfield, OK, Tillman Co., Our Lady of Perpetual Help, c/o Frederick, OK, St. Helen. (OKL)
Grandin, MO, Carter Co., St. Anne, c/o Doniphan, MO, St. Benedict. (SPC)
Granite Falls, WA, Snohomish Co., Holy Cross, c/o Snohomish, WA, St. Michael. (SEA)
Granjeno, TX, Hidalgo Co., Our Lady of Fatima, c/o Mission, TX, Our Lady of the Holy Rosary. (BWN)
Grant, MI, Newaygo Co., Our Lady of Guadalupe Church, c/o Newaygo, MI, St. Bartholomew's. (GR)
Grantsville, WV, Calhoun Co., Jesus Christ, Prince of Peace, c/o Spencer, WV, Holy Redeemer. (WH)
Grass Flats, PA, Clearfield Co., SS. Peter & Paul, c/o Frenchville, PA, St. Mary of the Assumption. (E)
Grass Valley, OR, Sherman Co., St. John the Baptist, c/o Wasco, OR, St. Mary's. (BAK)
Grassy Butte, ND, McKenzie Co., St. Peter Canisius, c/o Watford City, ND, Epiphany. (BIS)
Greasewood, AZ, Navajo Co., Our Lady of the Rosary, c/o Ganado, AZ, All Saints. (GLP)
Great Bend, KS, Great Bend Dominican Sisters Office of Mission and Ministry, c/o Great Bend, KS, Immaculate Conception Convent. (DOD)
Great Falls, SC, Chester Co., St. Michael, c/o Lancaster, SC, St. Catherine's. (CHR)
Greeley, PA, Pike Co., Sacred Heart of Jesus, c/o Shohola, PA, St. Ann's. (SCR)
Green Lake, ME, Hancock Co., Our Lady of the Lake, c/o Ellsworth, ME, St. Joseph's. (PRT)
Green River, UT, Emery Co., St. Michael, c/o East Carbon, UT, Good Shepherd. (SLC)
Greene, ME, Androscoggin Co., St. Francis, c/o Sabattus, ME, Our Lady of the Rosary. (PRT)
Greenfield, MO, Dade Co., St. Patrick, c/o Mount Vernon, MO, St. Susanne. (SPC)
Greensboro, AL, Hale Co., Our Lady of Lourdes, c/o Demopolis, AL, St. Leo. (BIR)
Greensboro Bend, VT, Orleans Co., St. Michael, c/o Hardwick, VT, St. Norbert. (BUR)
Greenup, KY, St. Lawrence, c/o Ashland, KY, Holy Family. (LEX)
Greenville, CA, Plumas Co., St. Anthony, c/o Quincy, CA, St. John. (SAC)
Greenwich, CT, Fairfield Co., St. Timothy's, c/o Greenwich, CT, St. Michael the Archangel. (BGP)
Greenwood, NE, Cass Co., St. Joseph's, c/o Ashland, NE, St. Mary's. (LIN)
Greig, NY, Lewis Co., St. Thomas, c/o Lowville, NY, St. Mary. (OG)
Gripinas, PR, Jayuya Co., Buen Pastor, c/o Jayuya, PR, Our Lady of Monserrate. (PCE)
Gruver, TX, Hansford Co., Cristo Redentor, c/o Spearman, TX, Sacred Heart. (AMA)
Grygla, MN, Marshall Co., St. Clement, c/o Oklee, MN, St. Francis Xavier's. (CR)
Guachupanque, NM, Rio Arriba Co., c/o Espanola, NM, Sacred Heart. (SFE)
Guadalupita, NM, Mora Co., c/o Mora, NM, St. Gertrude. (SFE)
Gualala, CA, Mary, Star of the Sea, c/o Point Arena, CA, St. Aloysius. (SR)
Guaniquilla, PR, Ntra. Sra. del Carmen, c/o Aguada, PR, St. Francis of Assisi. (MGZ)
Guayabo, PR, El Buen Pastor, c/o Aguada, PR, St. Francis of Assisi. (MGZ)
Guaynabo, PR, Guaynabo Co., El Buen Pastor, c/o Caguas, PR, Divino Nino Jesus. (SJN)
Guaynabo, PR, Guaynabo Co., Jesus Nazareno, c/o Caguas, PR, Divino Nino Jesus. (SJN)
Guaynabo, PR, Guaynabo Co., N. Sra. de la Paz, c/o Caguas, PR, Divino Nino Jesus. (SJN)
Guaynabo, PR, Guaynabo Co., Ntra. Sra. del Carmen, c/o Guaynabo, PR, Maria Madre de Mi Senor. (SJN)
Guaynabo, PR, Guaynabo Co., San Miguel, c/o San Juan, PR, San Miguel Arcangel. (SJN)
Guaynabo, PR, Guaynabo Co., San Rafael Arcangel, c/o Caguas, PR, Divino Nino Jesus. (SJN)
Guaynabo, PR, Virgen de la Paz, c/o Guaynabo, PR, Sagrados Corazones. (SJN)
Guilarte, PR, Adjuntas Co., San Antonio, c/o Adjuntas, PR, St. Joachim. (PCE)
Gulf Breeze, FL, Santa Rosa Co., Our Lady of the Assumption, c/o Gulf Breeze, FL, St. Ann. (PT)
Gulliver, MI, Schoolcraft Co., Divine Infant of Prague, c/o Engadine, MI, Our Lady of Lourdes. (MAR)
Gulnare, CO, Las Animas Co., San Jose, c/o Aguilar, CO, St. Anthony. (PBL)
Gussetville, TX, Live Oak Co., St. Joseph, c/o George West, TX, St. George. (CC)
Gustavus, AK, c/o Yakutat, AK, St. Ann. (JUN)

H

Hagerman, NM, Chavez Co., St. Catherine, c/o Dexter, NM, Immaculate Conception. (LSC)
Hagerstown, MD, Washington Co., St. Ann's, c/o Baltimore, MD, Patronage of the Mother of God. (PSC)
Hague, VA, Westmoreland Co., St. Paul, c/o Kilmarnock, VA, St. Francis de Sales. (ARL)
Haines Falls, NY, Greene Co., Wayside Shrine, c/o Haines Falls, NY, Immaculate Conception. (ALB)
Halaula, HI, Hawaii Co., Our Lady of Grace, c/o Kapaau, HI, Sacred Heart. (HON)
Haleyville, AL, Winston Co., Our Lady of Guadalupe, c/o Jasper, AL, St. Cecilia. (BIR)
Halfway, OR, Baker Co., St. Therese, c/o Baker, OR, Cathedral of St. Francis De Sales. (BAK)
Hallsville, TX, Harrison Co., Our Lady of Grace, c/o Longview, TX, St. Mary. (TYL)
Halstad, MN, Norman Co., Holy Family, c/o Ada, MN, St. Joseph's. (CR)
Hamburg, AR, Ashley Co., c/o Crossett, AR, Holy Cross. (LR)
Hamilton, IL, Hancock Co., St. Mary, c/o Warsaw, IL, Sacred Heart. (PEO)
Hamilton, KS, Greenwood Co., St. John, c/o Eureka, KS, Sacred Heart. (WCH)
Hamilton City, CA, Glenn Co., St. Mary, c/o Orland, CA, St. Dominic. (SAC)
Hamlin, TX, Jones Co., Holy Trinity, c/o Anson, TX, St. Michael's. (LUB)
Hammond, OR, Clatsop Co., St. Francis de Sales, c/o Astoria, OR, St. Mary, Star of the Sea. (P)
Hampton, CT, Windham Co., Our Lady of Lourdes, c/o Hampton, CT, Our Lady of La Salette. (NOR)
Hampton, IL, Rock Island Co., St. Mary, c/o Rapids City, IL, St. John the Baptist. (PEO)
Hampton, SC, Hampton Co., St. Mary, c/o Ridgeland, SC, St. Anthony's. (CHR)
Hanalei, HI, Kauai Co., St. William, c/o Kapaa, HI, St. Catherine. (HON)
Hanceville, AL, Cullman Co., St. Boniface, c/o Cullman, AL, Sacred Heart. (BIR)
Hanna, WY, Carbon Co., St. Joseph, c/o Saratoga, WY, St. Ann's. (CHY)
Hanover, NM, Grant Co., Holy Family, c/o Bayard, NM, Our Lady of Fatima. (LSC)
Happy Camp, CA, Siskiyou Co., All Saints, c/o Fort Jones, CA, Sacred Heart. (SAC)
Hargill, TX, Hidalgo Co., St. Frances Xavier Cabrini,

c/o Raymondville, TX, Our Lady of Guadalupe. (BWN)
Harlem, MT, Blaine Co., St. Thomas the Apostle, c/o Chinook, MT, St. Gabriel's. (GF)
Harmon, NY, Westchester Co., Church of the Good Shepherd, c/o Croton–on–Hudson, NY, Holy Name of Mary. (NY)
Harmony, WA, Lewis Co., St. Yves, c/o Morton, WA, Sacred Heart. (SEA)
Harpswell, ME, Cumberland Co., St. Katharine Drexel, c/o Brunswick, ME, St. Charles. (PRT)
Harquahala Valley, AZ, Maricopa Co., San Isidoro Labrador, c/o Buckeye, AZ, Saint Henry. (PHX)
Harrington, DE, Kent Co., St. Bernadette, c/o Milford, DE, St. John the Apostle. (WIL)
Harrison, NE, Sioux Co., Church of the Nativity of the Blessed Virgin Mary, c/o Crawford, NE, St. John the Baptist. (GI)
Hart, TX, Castro Co., St. John's, c/o Dimmitt, TX, Immaculate Conception. (AMA)
Hartford, AR, Sebastian Co., St. Leo's, c/o Fort Smith, AR, Immaculate Conception. (LR)
Hartley, IA, O'Brien Co., St. Joseph's, c/o Sutherland, IA, St. Cecilia's. (SC)
Harvard, MI, Kent Co., St. Margaret, c/o Greenville, MI, St. Charles. (GR)
Harwood, PA, Luzerne Co., St. Michael, c/o West Hazleton, PA, St. Francis of Assisi. (SCR)
Haskell, TX, Haskell Co., St. George, c/o Stamford, TX, St. Ann. (LUB)
Hastings–on–Hudson, NY, Westchester Co., Andrus Nursing Home, c/o Hastings–on–Hudson, NY, St. Matthew. (NY)
Hato Rey, PR, San Juan Co., Sma. Trinidad, c/o San Juan, PR, Ntr. Sra. de la Caridad del Cobre. (SJN)
Hawkinsville, CA, Siskiyou Co., Immaculate Conception, c/o Yreka, CA, St. Joseph. (SAC)
Hawley, MN, Clay Co., St. Andrew, c/o Detroit Lakes, MN, Holy Rosary. (CR)
Hawthorne, FL, Alachua Co., St. Philip Neri, c/o Gainesville, FL, St. Patrick's. (STA)
Haxtun, CO, Phillips Co., Christ the King, c/o Holyoke, CO, St. Patrick. (DEN)
Hay Springs, NE, Sheridan Co., St. Columbkille, c/o Gordon, NE, St. Leo's. (GI)
Hayales, PR, Coamo Co., Our Lady of Mt Carmel, c/o Coamo, PR, St. Blase. (PCE)
Hayden, NM, Quay Co., Holy Trinity, c/o Clayton, NM, St. Francis Xavier. (SFE)
Hayes, LA, Calcasieu Parish, St. Daniel Chapel, c/o Bell City, LA, St. John Vianney. (LKC)
Hayesville, NC, Clay Co., Immaculate Heart of Mary, c/o Murphy, NC, St. William. (CHL)
Hayfork, CA, Trinity Co., Holy Trinity, c/o Weaverville, CA, St. Patrick. (SAC)
Haymarsh, ND, Morton Co., St. Clement, c/o Hebron, ND, St. Ann. (BIS)
Hazard, NE, St. Gabriel, c/o Loup City, NE, St. Josaphat's. (GI)
Hazlehurst, MS, Copiah Co., St. Martin, c/o Crystal Springs, MS, St. John. (JKS)
Hazleton, PA, Luzerne Co., St. Ladislaus, c/o Hazleton, PA, St. Joseph's. (SCR)
Healdton, OK, Carter Co., St. Cecilia, c/o Ardmore, OK, St. Mary. (OKL)
Heart Butte, MT, Glacier Co., Holy Family Mission, c/o Heart Butte, MT, St. Anne. (HEL)
Heartwell, NE, Kearney Co., Holy Family, c/o Minden, NE, St. John's. (LIN)
Heber, CA, Imperial Co., Sacred Heart, c/o El Centro, CA, Our Lady of Guadalupe. (SD)
Heber City, UT, Wasatch Co., St. Lawrence, c/o Park City, UT, St. Mary of the Assumption. (SLC)
Heber Springs, AR, Cleburne Co., St. Albert, c/o Searcy, AR, St. James. (LR)
Hedgesville, WV, Berkeley Co., St. Bernadette, c/o Martinsburg, WV, St. Joseph's. (WH)
Heidelberg, KY, Lee Co., St. Therese c/o Beattyville, KY, Queen of All Saints. (LEX)
Helena, TX, Karnes Co., St. Helena, c/o Panna Maria, TX, Immaculate Conception of the Blessed Virgin Mary. (SAT)
Hemingford, NE, Box Butte Co., St. Bridget, c/o Alliance, NE, Holy Rosary. (GI)
Henderson, NY, Jefferson Co., Queen of Heaven, c/o Sackets Harbor, NY, St. Andrew. (OG)
Henryville, IN, Clark Co., St. Francis Xavier, c/o Charlestown, IN, St. Michael. (IND)
Hermeleigh, TX, Scurry Co., St. John, c/o Snyder, TX, St. Elizabeth's. (LUB)
Hermosa, SD, Custer Co., St. Michael's, c/o Rapid City, SD, Cathedral of Our Lady of Perpetual Help. (RC)
Hernandez, NM, Rio Arriba Co., c/o Espanola, NM, Sacred Heart. (SFE)
Hershey, NE, Lincoln Co., Our Lady of Guadalupe, c/o North Platte, NE, Holy Spirit. (GI)
Hershey, NE, Lincoln Co., Our Lady of Guadalupe, c/o Paxton, NE, Sacred Heart. (GI)
Hesperia, MI, Oceana Co., Christ the King, c/o Fremont, MI, St. Michael's. (GR)
Hessel, MI, Mackinac Co., Our Lady of the Snows, c/o Goetzville, MI, St. Stanislaus Kostka. (MAR)
Hickory Hill, LA, Avoyelles Parish, St. Richard, c/o Marksville, LA, Holy Ghost. (ALX)
High Falls, NY, Ulster Co., Our Lady Help of Christians, c/o Rosendale, NY, St. Peter. (NY)
Highland, MO, Perry Co., St. Joseph, c/o Perryville, MO, St. Vincent De Paul. (STL)
Highlands, NC Macon Co., Our Lady of the Mountains, c/o Franklin, NC, St. Francis of Assisi. (CHL)
Hill City, SD, Pennington Co., St. Rose of Lima, c/o Rapid City, SD, Blessed Sacrament. (RC)
Hill Top, PA, Wayne Co., St. Cecilia, c/o Pleasant Mount, PA, St. James. (SCR)
Hillsboro, NM Sierra Co., Our Lady of Guadalupe, c/o Garfield, NM, San Isidro. (LSC)
Hinsdale, MT, Valley Co., St. Albert, c/o Glasgow, MT, St. Raphael's. (GF)
Hinton, OK, Caddo Co., Sacred Heart, c/o Weatherford, OK, St. Eugene's. (OKL)
Hobart Bay, AK, c/o Yakutat, AK, St. Ann. (JUN)
Hobson, MT, Judith Basin Co., Sacred Heart, c/o Stanford, MT, St. Rose of Lima. (GF)
Hochheim, TX, DeWitt Co., St. Ann, c/o Yoakum, TX, St. Joseph. (VIC)
Hoconuco, PR, Chapel of St. Joseph, c/o San German, PR, San German de Auxerre. (MGZ)
Hode, KY, Martin Co., St. John Neumann, c/o Louisa, KY, St. Jude. (LEX)
Hogares Seguros, PR, San Antonio Co., c/o Jayuya, PR, Our Lady of Monserrate. (PCE)
Hogeland, MT, Blaine Co., St. Thomas Aquinas, c/o Chinook, MT, St. Gabriel's. (GF)
Hollandale, MS, Washington Co., Immaculate Conception, c/o Leland, MS, St. James. (JKS)
Hollis, AK, c/o Craig, AK, St. John by the Sea. (JUN)
Hollis, OK, Harmon Co., Our Lady of Guadalupe, c/o Altus, OK, Prince of Peace. (OKL)
Holly Beach, LA, Cameron Parish, Holy Trinity, c/o Hackberry, LA, St. Peter Apostle. (LKC)
Holly Lake Rach, TX, Sulphur Co., Holy Spirit Church, c/o Gilmer, TX, St. Francis of Assisi. (TYL)
Holman, NM, Mora Co., c/o Mora, NM, St. Gertrude. (SFE)
Holman, TX, Fayette Co., St. Wenceslaus c/o Schulenburg, TX, St. John The Baptist. (VIC)
Holualoa, HI, Hawaii Co., Immaculate Conception, c/o Kailua–Kona, HI, St. Michael The Archangel. (HON)
Holyoke, MA, Hampden Co., Holyoke Soldier's Home Chapel, c/o Holyoke, MA, Blessed Sacrament. (SPR)
Homer, IL, Champaign Co., St. Charles Borromeo, c/o Tolono, IL, St. Patrick's. (PEO)
Homer, LA, Claiborne Parish, St. Margaret, c/o Minden, LA, St. Paul. (SHP)
Homer, NE, Dakota Co., St. Cornelius, c/o South Sioux City, NE, St. Michael. (OM)
Hominy, OK, Osage Co., c/o Fairfax, OK, St. Joseph. (TLS)
Honalo, HI, Hawaii Co., St. Paul, c/o Kailua–Kona, HI, St. Michael The Archangel. (HON)
Honaunau, HI, Honaunau Co., c/o Captain Cook, HI, St. Benedict. (HON)
Honokahua (Kapalua), HI, Maui Co., Sacred Hearts of Jesus and Mary, c/o Lahaina, HI, Maria Lanakila. (HON)
Honomu, HI, Hawaii Co., Good Shepherd, c/o Papaikou, HI, Immaculate Heart of Mary. (HON)
Hooker, OK, Texas Co., Sacred Heart, c/o Guymon, OK, St. Peter's. (OKL)
Hopedale, IL, Tazewell Co., St. Joseph's, c/o Delavan, IL, St. Mary's. (PEO)
Hopeton, CA, Merced Co., St. John the Baptist, c/o Merced, CA, Our Lady of Mercy/St. Patrick's. (FRS)
Hopkins Park, IL, Kankakee Co., Sacred Heart, c/o Momence, IL, St. Patrick. (JOL)
Hopland, CA, St. Francis Rancheria, c/o Ukiah, CA, St. Mary of the Angels. (SR)
Hornitos, CA, Mariposa Co., St. Catherine of Sienna, c/o Mariposa, CA, St. Joseph. (FRS)
Horse Cave, KY, Hart Co., Our Lady of the Caves Church, c/o Glasgow, KY, St. Helen. (L)
Horse Springs, NM, Catron Co., St. Anne, c/o Reserve, NM, Santo Nino. (GLP)
Horseshoe Bend, AR, Izard Co., St. Mary of the Mount Church, c/o Cherokee Village, AR, St. Michael's. (LR)
Horseshoe Lake, AR, Crittenden Co., St. Mary's of the Lake, c/o West Memphis, AR, St. Michael's. (LR)
Hostyn Hill, TX, Fayette Co., St. Mary's, c/o Fayetteville, TX, St. John's. (AUS)
Hot Springs, MT, Sanders Co., Sacred Heart, c/o Plains, MT, St. James. (HEL)
Hot Springs, NC, Madison Co., Chapel of the Redeemer, c/o Mars Hill, NC, St. Andrew the Apostle. (CHL)
Hotchkiss, CO, Delta Co., St. Margaret Mary, c/o Paonia, CO, Sacred Heart. (PBL)
Houston, MS, Chickasaw Co., Immaculate Heart of Mary, c/o Aberdeen, MS, St. Francis of Assisi. (JKS)
Hoyo Planas, PR, Jayuya Co., Esp. Santo, c/o Jayuya, PR, Our Lady of Monserrate. (PCE)
Hubbard, NE, Dakota Co., St. Mary, c/o Jackson, NE, St. Patrick. (OM)
Hubbard, OR, Marion Co., St. Agnes, c/o Woodburn, OR, St. Luke. (P)
Hudson, WY, Fremont Co., Ascension, c/o Lander, WY, Holy Rosary. (CHY)
Huff, ND, Morton Co., St. Martin, c/o Mandan, ND, Christ the King. (BIS)
Hugo, CO, Lincoln Co., St. Anthony of Padua, c/o Limon, CO, Our Lady of Victory. (COS)
Hulberton, NY, Orleans Co., St. Rocco, c/o Holley, NY, St. Mary. (BUF)
Hulett, WY, Crook Co., St. Matthew's, c/o Newcastle, WY, Corpus Christi. (CHY)
Humansville, MO, Polk Co., St. Catherine, c/o Bolivar, MO, Sacred Heart. (SPC)
Humarock, MA, St. Theresa's, c/o Marshfield, MA, St. Christine. (BO)
Hume, IL, Edgar Co., St. Michael's, c/o Villa Grove, IL, Sacred Heart. (SFD)
Huntingdon, TN, Carroll Co., Holy Family Church, c/o Camden, TN, St. Mary Church. (MEM)
Huntington, UT, Emery Co., San Rafael, c/o Price, UT, Notre Dame de Lourdes. (SLC)
Huntsville, UT, Weber Co., St. Florence, c/o Ogden, UT, St. Joseph's. (SLC)
Hurley, MS, Jackson Co., St. Ann, c/o Moss Point, MS, St. Joseph. (BLX)
Hurricane Branch, MO, Chariton Co., St. Joseph, c/o Marceline, MO, St. Bonaventure. (JC)
Hyannis, NE, Grant Co., All Saint's, c/o Mullen, NE, St. Mary's. (GI)
Hydaburg, AK, c/o Craig, AK, St. John by the Sea. (JUN)
Hyde Park, VT, Lamoille Co., St. Teresa, c/o Morrisville, VT, Holy Cross. (BUR)
Hysham, MT, Treasure Co., St. Joseph, c/o Forsyth, MT, Immaculate Conception. (GF)

I

Imperial, TX, Pecos Co., Our Lady of Lourdes, c/o Crane, TX, Good Shepherd. (SAN)
Imperial, TX, Pecos Co., Our Lady of Lourdes, c/o Fort Stockton, TX, St. Agnes. (SAN)
Independence, CA, Inyo Co., St. Vivian, c/o Lone Pine, CA, Santa Rosa. (FRS)
Indian Village, LA, Sacred Heart Parish, Sacred Heart, c/o Kinder, LA, St. Philip Neri. (LKC)
Indiera Fria, PR, Santa Rosa, c/o Maricao, PR, St. John the Baptist. (MGZ)
Industry, TX, Austin Co., Immaculate Conception, c/o Bellville, TX, SS. Peter & Paul. (GAL)
Ingleside, IL, St. Mary of the Lake Mission, c/o Chicago, IL, Archdiocese of Chicago's Joseph Cardinal Bernardin Archives and Records Center. (CHI)
Inglis, FL, Levy Co., St. Anthony the Abbot, c/o Williston, FL, Holy Family. (STA)
Ingold, NC, Sampson Co., San Juan, c/o Clinton, NC, Immaculate Conception. (R)
Interior, SD, Jackson Co., Holy Rosary, c/o Wall, SD, St. Patrick's. (RC)
Inverness, MT, Hill Co., Sacred Heart, c/o Chester, MT, Our Lady of Ransom. (GF)
Ione, CA, Amador Co., Mule Creek State Prison, c/o Ione, CA, Sacred Heart. (SAC)
Ione, CA, Amador Co., Preston School of Industry, California Youth Authority, c/o Ione, CA, Sacred Heart. (SAC)
Iowa, LA, Calcasieu Parish, St. Peter Claver, c/o Welsh, LA, St. Joseph. (LKC)
Iraan, TX, Pecos Co., St. Francis, c/o Big Lake, TX, St. Margaret of Cortona. (SAN)
Irasburg, VT, Orleans Co., St. John Vianney, c/o Orleans, VT, St. Theresa of Child Jesus. (BUR)
Irish Grove Rd., IL, Stephenson Co., St. Patrick, c/o Durand, IL, St. Mary. (RCK)
Irishtown, MI, Gratiot Co., St. Patrick, c/o Shepherd, MI, St. Vincent De Paul. (SAG)
Isabel, SD, Dewey Co., St. Mary, c/o Timber Lake, SD, Holy Cross. (RC)
Island Heights, NJ, Ocean Co., St. Gertrude, c/o Toms River, NJ, St. Joseph. (TR)
Isle La Motte, VT, Grand Isle Co., St. Joseph, c/o Alburg, VT, St. Amadeus. (BUR)
Isle of Hope, GA, Chatham Co., Our Lady of Good Hope, c/o Savannah, GA, St. James. (SAV)
Isleboro, ME, Waldo Co., St. Mary of the Isles, c/o Belfast, ME, St. Francis of Assisi. (PRT)
Islesford, ME, Hancock Co., Our Lady Star of the Sea, c/o Bar Harbor, ME, St. Ignatius. (PRT)
Italy, TX, Ellis Co., Epiphany, c/o Waxahachie, TX, St. Joseph. (DAL)
Iuka, MS, Tishomingo Co., St. Mary, c/o Booneville, MS, St. Francis of Assisi. (JKS)
Ivanhoe, CA, Tulare Co., San Felipe de Jesus, c/o Visalia, CA, Holy Family. (FRS)

J

Jackpot, NV, Elko Co., Our Lady of Guadalupe, c/o

Elko, NV, St. Joseph's. (RNO)
Jackson, AL, Clarke Co., Visitation, c/o Grove Hill, AL, Sacred Heart. (MOB)
Jackson, GA, Butts Co., St. Mary's, c/o McDonough, GA, St. James The Apostle. (ATL)
Jacksonville, OR, Jackson Co., St. Joseph, c/o Medford, OR, Sacred Heart of Jesus. (P)
Jacumba, CA, San Diego Co., St. Mary Magdalene, c/o El Cajon, CA, Our Lady of Grace. (SD)
Jaguey Chiquito, PR, San Augustin, c/o Aguada, PR, St. Francis of Assisi. (MGZ)
Jamaica Beach, TX, Galveston Co., Mary, Star of the Sea, c/o Galveston, TX, St. Peter the Apostle. (GAL)
Jamestown, PA, Mercer Co., St. Margaret, c/o Greenville, PA, St. Michael. (E)
Jamestown, TN, Fentress Co., Mission Catholic Community of Fentress County, c/o Harriman, TN, Blessed Sacrament. (KNX)
Jarales, NM, Valencia Co., c/o Belen, NM, Our Lady of Belen. (SFE)
Jardines del Caribe, PR, Perpetuo Socorro, c/o Mayaguez, PR, Our Lady of Mt. Carmel. (MGZ)
Jasper, FL, Hamilton Co., St. Therese of Jesus, c/o Live Oak, FL, St. Francis Xavier. (STA)
Jasper, GA, Pickens Co., Our Lady of the Mountains, c/o Canton, GA, Our Lady of LaSalette. (ATL)
Jauca, PR, Santa Isabel Co., San Ignacio de Loyola, c/o Santa Isabel, PR, St. James. (PCE)
Jayton, TX, Kent Co., Epiphany, c/o Spur, TX, St. Mary. (LUB)
Jefferson, NH, Coos Co., St. Agnes, c/o Lancaster, NH, All Saints. (MAN)
Jefferson, OR, Marion Co., St. Thomas, c/o Scio, OR, St. Bernard. (P)
Jeffrey City, WY, Freemont Co., St. Brendan, c/o Lander, WY, Holy Rosary. (CHY)
Jenny Lind, AR, SS. Sabina & Mary Church, c/o Barling, AR, Sacred Heart of Mary. (LR)
Jersey City, NJ, Hudson Co., St. Thomas Malankara, c/o Jersey City, NJ, St. John the Baptist. (NEW)
Jessenland, MN, Sibley Co., St. Thomas, c/o Henderson, MN, St. Joseph. (NU)
Jessup, PA, Lackawanna Co., St. Stanislaus, c/o Jessup, PA, St. James. (SCR)
Jobstown, NJ, Burlington Co., St. Andrew, c/o Mount Holly, NJ, Sacred Heart. (TR)
Jocko, MT, Lake Co., St. John Berchman's, c/o St. Ignatius, MT, St. Ignatius Mission. (HEL)
Johnson, VT, Lamoille Co., St. John the Apostle, c/o Morrisville, VT, Holy Cross. (BUR)
Johnson Bayou, LA, Cameron Parish, Our Lady of the Assumption, c/o Hackberry, LA, St. Peter Apostle. (LKC)
Johnson City, TX, Blanco Co., Good Shepherd, c/o Blanco, TX, St. Ferdinand's. (AUS)
Johnsonville, SC, Florence Co., St. Patrick, c/o Lake City, SC, St. Philip's. (CHR)
Joliet, MT, Carbon Co., St. John, c/o Bridger, MT, Sacred Heart. (GF)
Jolon, CA, Monterey Co., South Shore of Lake San Antonio, c/o Jolon, CA, San Antonio Mission. (MRY)
Jones, OK, Oklahoma Co., St. Robert Bellarmine, c/o Oklahoma City, OK, Corpus Christi. (OKL)
Jonesville, LA, Catahoula Parish, St. Gerard, c/o Ferriday, LA, St. Patrick. (ALX)
Jordan, MT, Garfield Co., St. John the Baptist, c/o Circle, MT, St. Francis Xavier. (GF)
Joyuda, PR, St. John the Baptist, c/o Cabo Rojo, PR, St. Michael. (MGZ)
Juana Diaz, PR, Juana Diaz Co., Sagrado Corazon, c/o Juana Diaz, PR, Nuestra Senora de Lourdes. (PCE)
Juana Diaz, PR, San Pedro Nolasco, c/o Juana Diaz, PR, Nuestra Senora de Lourdes. (PCE)
Juana Diaz, PR, Juana Diaz Co., Virgen del Carmen, c/o Juana Diaz, PR, Nuestra Senora de Lourdes. (PCE)
Judith Gap, MT, Wheatland Co., Immaculate Conception, c/o Harlowton, MT, St. Joseph. (HEL)
Julian, NE, Nemaha Co., St. Bernard's, c/o Nebraska City, NE, St. Joseph's. (LIN)
Juniata, NE, Adams Co., Assumption, c/o Roseland, NE, Sacred Heart. (LIN)
Juntura, OR, Malheur Co., St. Charles, c/o Burns, OR, Holy Family. (BAK)

K

Kahakuloa, HI, Maui Co., St. Francis Xavier, c/o Waihee, HI, St. Ann. (HON)
Kahaluu, HI, Hawaii Co., St. Peter, c/o Kailua–Kona, HI, St. Michael The Archangel. (HON)
Kahuku, HI, Honolulu Co., St. Joachim, c/o Kahuku, HI, St. Roch. (HON)
Kake, AK, c/o Petersburg, AK, St. Catherine of Siena. (JUN)
Kalama, WA, Cowlitz Co., St. Joseph, c/o Woodland, WA, St. Philip. (SEA)
Kalaoa, HI, Hawaii Co., Holy Rosary, c/o Kailua–Kona, HI, St. Michael The Archangel. (HON)
Kalawao, HI, Molokai Co., St. Philomena, c/o Kalawao, HI, St. Francis. (HON)
Kalskag, AK, c/o Aniak, AK, St. Theresa. (FBK)
Kannapolis, NC, Cabarrus Co., St. Joseph, c/o Concord, NC, St. James. (CHL)
Kansas, OH, Seneca Co., St. James, c/o Helena, OH, St. Mary. (TOL)
Kaplan, LA, Vermilion Parish, St. Frances Xavier Cabrini, c/o Kaplan, LA, Our Lady of the Holy Rosary. (LAF)
Karlstad, MN, Marshall Co., St. Edward, c/o Greenbush, MN, Blessed Sacrament. (CR)
Kasaan, AK, c/o Craig, AK, St. John by the Sea. (JUN)
Kaumakani, HI, Kauai Co., St. Joseph, c/o Kekaha, HI, St. Theresa. (HON)
Kaupo, HI, Maui Co., St. Joseph, c/o Hana, HI, St. Mary. (HON)
Kaycee, WY, Johnson Co., St. Hubert, c/o Buffalo, WY, St. John the Baptist. (CHY)
Keaau, HI, Hawaii Co., Holy Rosary, c/o Mountain View, HI, St. Theresa. (HON)
Keanae, HI, Maui Co., St. Gabriel, c/o Haiku, HI, St. Rita. (HON)
Keenesburg, CO, Weld Co., Holy Family, c/o Roggen, CO, Sacred Heart. (DEN)
Keithsburg, IL, Mercer Co., St. Mary's, c/o Aledo, IL, St. Catherine's Church. (PEO)
Kelly, NM, Socorro Co., c/o Socorro, NM, San Miguel. (SFE)
Kelseyville, CA, St. Peter, c/o Lakeport, CA, St. Mary. (SR)
Kenel, SD, Corson Co., Assumption of the Blessed Virgin Mary Church, c/o McLaughlin, SD, Standing Rock Reservation. (RC)
Kenel, SD, Corson Co., Our Lady of the Assumption Parish, c/o McLaughlin, SD, St. Bernard. (RC)
Kerhonkson, NY, Ulster Co., Our Lady of Lourdes, c/o Ellenville, NY, St. Mary and St. Andrew. (NY)
Keswick, IA, Keokuk Co., Our Lady of Lourdes, c/o Sigourney, IA, St. Mary's. (DAV)
Kettleman City, CA, Kings Co., St. Cecilia, c/o Avenal, CA, St. Joseph. (FRS)
Kewanna, IN, Fulton Co., St. Ann, c/o Rochester, IN, St. Joseph. (LFT)
Keyapaha, SD, Tripp Co., St. Ann, c/o Winner, SD, Immaculate Conception. (RC)
Keystone, SD, Pennington Co., Our Lady of Mt. Carmel, c/o Rapid City, SD, Blessed Sacrament. (RC)
Kilauea, HI, Kauai Co., St. Sylvester, c/o Kapaa, HI, St. Catherine. (HON)
Killington, VT, Rutland Co., Our Lady of the Mountains, c/o Woodstock, VT, Our Lady of the Snows. (BUR)
King, NC, Stokes Co., Good Shepherd, c/o Winston–Salem, NC, St. Benedict the Moor. (CHL)
King George, VA, King George Co., St. Anthony's, c/o Colonial Beach, VA, St. Elizabeth. (ARL)
King Ranch, TX, Kleberg Co., Christ the King, c/o Kingsville, TX, St. Martin. (CC)
Kingman, ME, Penobscot Co., St. James, c/o Lincoln, ME, St. Mary. (PRT)
Kings Beach, CA, Placer Co., Our Lady of the Lake, c/o Truckee, CA, Assumption of the Blessed Virgin Mary. (SAC)
Kings Mountain, NC, Cleveland Co., Christ the King, c/o Shelby, NC, St. Mary's. (CHL)
Kingston, NH, Rockingham Co., St. Frederick, c/o Newton, NH, Mary, Mother of the Church. (MAN)
Kingsville, TX, Kleberg Co., St. Thomas Aquinas Catholic Campus Center – Texas A & M, c/o Kingsville, TX, St. Gertrude. (CC)
Kinnear, WY, Fremont Co., St. Edward, c/o Riverton, WY, St. Margaret's. (CHY)
Kipahulu, HI, Maui Co., St. Paul, c/o Hana, HI, St. Mary. (HON)
Kirtland, NM, San Juan Co., San Juan Catholic Center, c/o Waterflow, NM, Sacred Heart. (GLP)
Kit Carson, CO, Cheyenne Co., St. Augustine, c/o Cheyenne Wells, CO, Sacred Heart. (COS)
Kitzmiller, MD, Garrett Co., Immaculate Conception, c/o Oakland, MD, St. Peter the Apostle. (BAL)
Klamath, CA, St. Robert and Ann, c/o Crescent City, CA, St. Joseph. (SR)
Klawock, AK, c/o Craig, AK, St. John by the Sea. (JUN)
Knickerbocker, TX, Tom Green Co., Immaculate Conception, c/o Eldorado, TX, Our Lady of Guadalupe. (SAN)
Knippa, TX, Uvalde Co., St. Joseph, c/o Sabinal, TX, St. Patrick's. (SAT)
Koeltztown, MO, Osage Co., St. Boniface, c/o Argyle, MO, St. Aloysius. (JC)
Kolin, LA, Rapides Parish, Sts. Francis and Anne, c/o Deville, LA, St. John the Baptist. (ALX)
Koontz Lake, IN, Starke Co., St. Dominic, c/o Hamlet, IN, Holy Cross. (GRY)
Kovar, TX, Bastrop Co., Sts. Peter and Paul, c/o Smithville, TX, St. Paul the Apostle. (AUS)
Kress, TX, Swisher Co., St. Paul the Apostle, c/o Tulia, TX, Church of the Holy Spirit. (AMA)
Kwajalein, MH, Santo, c/o Marshall Islands, MH, Queen of Peace. (MI)

L

L'Erable, IL, Iroquois Co., St. John the Baptist, c/o Ashkum, IL, Assumption of the Blessed Virgin Mary. (JOL)
La Bajada, NM, Sandoval Co., c/o Pena Blanca, NM, Nuestra Senora De Guadalupe. (SFE)
La Barge, WY, Lincoln Co., La Barge Catholic Community Center, c/o Kemmerer, WY, St. Patrick's. (CHY)
La Casita, TX, Starr Co., Our Lady of the Peace, c/o Grulla, TX, Holy Family. (BWN)
La Cienega, NM, Santa Fe Co., c/o Santa Fe, NM, San Isidro. (SFE)
La Cueva, NM, Mora Co., c/o Mora, NM, St. Gertrude. (SFE)
La Grange, CA, Stanislaus Co., St. Louis, c/o Hughson, CA, St. Anthony Church of Hughson (Pastor of). (STO)
La Grange, MO, Lewis Co., Notre Dame, c/o Canton, MO, St. Joseph. (JC)
La Honda, CA, San Mateo Co., Our Lady of Refuge, c/o Half Moon Bay, CA, Our Lady of the Pillar. (SFR)
La Isla, TX, El Paso Co., San Luis, c/o Fabens, TX, Our Lady of Guadalupe. (ELP)
La Jara, CO, Conejos Co., Our Lady of the Valley, c/o Capulin, CO, St. Joseph. (PBL)
La Jara, NM, Sandoval Co., Santo Nino, c/o Cuba, NM, Immaculate Conception. (GLP)
La Lagunita, NM, San Miguel Co., c/o Ribera, NM, San Miguel Del Vado. (SFE)
La Luz, NM, Otero Co., Our Lady of the Light, c/o Alamogordo, NM, Immaculate Conception. (LSC)
La Madera, NM, Rio Arriba Co., c/o El Rito, NM, San Juan Nepomuceno. (SFE)
La Marina, PR, Guaynabo Co., San Francisco de Asis, c/o San Juan, PR, San Juan Evangelista. (SJN)
La Paloma, TX, Cameron Co., Our Lady of Lourdes, c/o San Benito, TX, St. Ignatius. (BWN)
La Pica, PR, San Patricio Co., c/o Jayuya, PR, Our Lady of Monserrate. (PCE)
La Piedra, PR, Ala de La Piedra Co., O.L. of Perp. Help, c/o Villalba, PR, Our Lady Mother of Divine Providence. (PCE)
La Playa, PR, Our Lady of Carmel, c/o Anasco, PR, St. Anthony Abbot. (MGZ)
La Puente, NM, Rio Arriba Co., c/o Los Ojos, NM, San Jose. (SFE)
La Puerta, TX, Starr Co., St. Paul, c/o Rio Grande City, TX, Immaculate Conception. (BWN)
La Union, NM, Dona Ana Co., Our Lady of Refuge, c/o Anthony, NM, St. Anthony's. (LSC)
La Veta, CO, Huerfano Co., Christ the King, c/o Walsenburg, CO, St. Mary. (PBL)
La Villa, TX, Hidalgo Co., Our Lady of Guadalupe, c/o Edcouch, TX, St. Theresa of the Infant Jesus. (BWN)
LaCrosse, IN, LaPorte Co., St. Martin, c/o Wanatah, IN, Sacred Heart. (GRY)
LaPorte, MN, Hubbard Co., St. Theodore, c/o Akeley, MN, Our Lady of the Pines. (CR)
LaSal, UT, San Juan Co., Sacred Heart, c/o Moab, UT, St. Pius X. (SLC)
LaSalle, TX, Jackson Co., St. Theresa, c/o Vanderbilt, TX, St. John Bosco. (VIC)
Lacassine, LA, Jefferson Davis Parish, St. John the Evangelist, c/o Fenton, LA, St. Charles Borromeo. (LKC)
Lacey, MI, Barry Co., Our Lady of Great Oak, c/o Delton, MI, St. Ambrose. (KAL)
Lackawaxen, PA, Pike Co., St. Mary of the Assumption, c/o Shohola, PA, St. Ann's. (SCR)
Laddonia, MO, Audrain Co., St. John, c/o Vandalia, MO, Sacred Heart. (JC)
Lafayette, LA, Lafayette Parish, Gift of Mary Chapel, c/o Lafayette, LA, St. Genevieve. (LAF)
Lafayette, LA, Lafayette Parish, Our Lady of Good Hope, c/o Lafayette, LA, St. Paul The Apostle. (LAF)
Laguna, PR, Santa Rita, c/o Aguada, PR, St. Francis of Assisi. (MGZ)
Lajitas, TX, Brewster Co., Lajitas Mission, c/o Presidio, TX, Santa Teresa de Jesus. (ELP)
Lake Arthur, NM, Chavez Co., Our Lady of Guadalupe, c/o Dexter, NM, Immaculate Conception. (LSC)
Lake Bonaparte, NY, St. Rita, c/o Harrisville, NY, St. Francis Solanus. (OG)
Lake Carmel, NY, Putnam Co., Our Lady of the Lake, c/o Carmel, NY, St. James the Apostle. (NY)
Lake Charles, LA, Calcasieu Parish, Our Lady of Fatima Chapel, c/o Lake Charles, LA, Immaculate Heart of Mary. (LKC)
Lake City, CO, Hinsdale Co., St. Rose of Lima, c/o Gunnison, CO, St. Peter. (PBL)
Lake Como, PA, Wayne Co., Assumption of the B.V.M., c/o Pleasant Mount, PA, St. James. (SCR)
Lake Hauto, PA, Carbon Co., Sacred Heart Chapel, c/o Nesquehoning, PA, Sacred Heart. (ALN)
Lake Huntington, NY, Sullivan Co., Our Lady of the Lake, c/o Narrowsburg, NY, St. Francis Xavier. (NY)

Lake Park, MN, Becker Co., St. Francis Xavier, c/o Detroit Lakes, MN, Holy Rosary. (CR)
Lake Peekskill, NY, Putnam Co., North American Martyrs, c/o Cortlandt Manor, NY, St. Columbanus. (NY)
Lake Titus, NY, Franklin Co., St. Mary, c/o Malone, NY, St. Helen. (OG)
Lake Wallenpaupack, PA, Pike Co., St. Veronica, c/o Hawley, PA, Blessed Virgin Mary, Queen of Peace. (SCR)
Lakehills, TX, Bandera Co., St. Victor's Chapel, c/o Bandera, TX, St. Stanislaus. (SAT)
Lakeshore, MS, Hancock Co., St. John, c/o Lakeshore, MS, St. Ann. (BLX)
Lakeside, CA, San Diego Co., Assumption of BVM, c/o Lakeside, CA, Blessed Kateri Tekakwitha. (SD)
Lakeside, SD, Meade Co., St. Margaret, c/o New Underwood, SD, St. John the Evangelist. (RC)
Lakeview, MI, Montcalm Co., St. Frances de Sales, c/o Howard City, MI, Christ the King. (GR)
Lakeview, NY, Nassau Co., Chapel, c/o West Hempstead, NY, St. Thomas, the Apostle. (RVC)
Lakewood, NJ, Ocean Co., Holy Family Church, c/o Lakewood, NJ, St. Mary of the Lake. (TR)
Lambert, MT, Richland Co., St. Theresa, c/o Sidney, MT, St. Matthew's. (GF)
Lamesa, TX, Dawson Co., Our Lady of Guadalupe, c/o Lamesa, TX, St. Margaret Mary. (LUB)
Lancaster, CA, Los Angeles Co., St. Elizabeth, c/o Lancaster, CA, Blessed Junipero Serra. (LA)
Lancaster, MN, Kittson Co., Holy Rosary, c/o Hallock, MN, St. Patrick's. (CR)
Lansford, ND, Bottineau Co., St. John, c/o Glenburn, ND, St. Philomena. (BIS)
Lantana, FL, Palm Beach Co., c/o Miami, FL, Assumption of B.V.M.. (SJP)
Laporte, PA, Sullivan Co., Sacred Heart, c/o Dushore, PA, St. Basil's. (SCR)
Laredo, TX, Webb Co., Santa Cruz, c/o Laredo, TX, Holy Redeemer. (LAR)
Largo, FL, Pinellas Co., Holy Martyrs of Vietnam, c/o Largo, FL, St. Matthew. (SP)
Las Colonias, NM, Taos Co., Santo Nino de Atocha, c/o Arroyo Seco, NM, La Santisima Trinidad. (SFE)
Las Colonias, NM, San Miguel Co., c/o Pecos, NM, St. Anthony. (SFE)
Las Flores, Coamo, PR, Coamo Co., San Martin, c/o Coamo, PR, San Antonio de Padua. (PCE)
Las Mareas, PR, Salinas Co., St. Judas, c/o Aguirre, PR, Sacred Heart. (PCE)
Las Margaritas, PR, Bo. Collores Arriba, Santiago, Ap., c/o Juana Diaz, PR, St. Raymond Nonato. (PCE)
Las Nutrias, NM, Socorro Co., San Isidro, c/o La Joya, NM, Our Lady of Sorrows. (SFE)
Las Ochenta, PR, Salinas Co., Inmaculada Concepcion, c/o Salinas, PR, Our Lady of Monserrat. (PCE)
Las Palmas, PR, St. Rita, c/o Cabo Rojo, PR, St. Michael. (MGZ)
Las Palomas, NM, Sierra Co., San Ysidro, c/o Truth or Consequences, NM, Our Lady of Perpetual Help. (LSC)
Las Rucias, TX, Cameron Co., Sacred Heart, c/o San Benito, TX, St. Ignatius. (BWN)
Las Tablas, NM, Taos Co., c/o El Rito, NM, San Juan Nepomuceno. (SFE)
Las Vegas, NV, c/o Las Vegas, NV, St. Paul Jung–Ha–Sang. (LAV)
Las Vegas, PR, Yauco, Sta. Teresita, c/o Yauco, PR, Santo Domingo de Guzman. (PCE)
Lasara, TX, Willacy Co., St. Patrick, c/o Raymondville, TX, Our Lady of Guadalupe. (BWN)
Latimer, MS, Jackson Co., Christ the King, c/o Vancleave, MS, Holy Spirit Catholic Church. (BLX)
Laupahoehoe, HI, c/o Laupahoehoe, HI, St. Anthony. (HON)
Laurel Lake, NJ, Our Lady of the Lake Chapel, c/o Cedarville, NJ, St. Michael's. (CAM)
Laurens, SC, Laurens Co., Holy Spirit, c/o Joanna, SC, St. Boniface. (CHR)
Lavelle, PA, Schuylkill Co., St. Elizabeth, c/o Ashland, PA, St. Mauritius. (ALN)
Lawrence, NE, Nuckolls Co., St. Stephen's, c/o Lawrence, NE, Sacred Heart. (LIN)
Le Bleu Settlement, LA, Calcasieu Parish, St. Joseph, c/o Iowa, LA, St. Raphael. (LKC)
Le Doux, NM, Mora Co., c/o Mora, NM, St. Gertrude. (SFE)
LeGrand, CA, Merced Co., Our Lady of Lourdes, c/o Planada, CA, Sacred Heart. (FRS)
Leakesville, MS, Perry Co., Holy Trinity, c/o Waynesboro, MS, St. Bernadette. (BLX)
Leakey, TX, Real Co., St. Raymond of Pennafort, c/o Rocksprings, TX, Sacred Heart of Mary. (SAT)
Leaton, MI, Isabella Co., St. Charles, c/o Rosebush, MI, St. Henry. (SAG)
Lebanon, OH, c/o Lebanon, OH, St. Francis de Sales. (CIN)
Lebanon, PA, Lebanon Co., Our Lady of Fatima, c/o Lebanon, PA, Assumption of the Blessed Virgin Mary. (HBG)
Ledgedale, PA, Wayne Co., St. Mary, c/o Lake Ariel, PA, St. Thomas More. (SCR)
Lee Vining, CA, Mono Co., Our Savior of the Mountains, c/o Mammoth Lakes, CA, St. Joseph Church of Mammoth Lakes. (STO)
Leeds, NY, Greene Co., St. Bridget, c/o Catskill, NY, St. Patrick. (ALB)
Lefor, ND, Stark Co., St. Elizabeth's, c/o New England, ND, St. Mary. (BIS)
Leggett, CA, St. Cecilia, c/o Garberville, CA, Our Lady of the Redwoods. (SR)
Lehi, AZ, Maricopa Co., St. Paschal Baylon, c/o Tempe, AZ, St. Margaret. (PHX)
Leicester, VT, Addison Co., St. Agnes, c/o Brandon, VT, St. Mary's. (BUR)
Leming, TX, Atascosa Co., Our Lady of Guadalupe, c/o Pleasanton, TX, St. Luke–Loire. (SAT)
Lemitar, NM, Socorro Co., c/o Socorro, NM, San Miguel. (SFE)
Lemont, IL, Blessed Jurgis Matulaitis Mission, c/o Chicago, IL, Lithuanian American Jesuits. (CHI)
Lenorah, TX, Martin Co., St. Isidore, c/o Stanton, TX, St. Joseph's. (SAN)
Lesterville, MO, Reynolds Co., Our Lady of Sorrows, c/o Ironton, MO, Ste. Marie Du Lac. (SPC)
Lewisburg, WV, Greenbrier Co., St. Louis, King of France, c/o Ronceverte, WV, St. Catherine of Siena. (WH)
Lewiston, CA, Trinity Co., St. Gilbert, c/o Weaverville, CA, St. Patrick. (SAC)
Lexington, IL, McLean Co., St. Mary, c/o Chenoa, IL, St. Joseph's. (PEO)
Lexington, TX, Lee Co., Holy Family, c/o Lime Box, TX, St. Joseph's. (AUS)
Leyba, NM, San Miguel Co., c/o Villanueva, NM, Our Lady of Guadalupe. (SFE)
Liberty, KY, Casey Co., Sacred Heart, c/o Liberty, KY, St. Bernard. (L)
Licking, MO, Texas Co., St. John The Baptist, c/o Houston, MO, St. Mark. (SPC)
Limani, PR, Adjuntas Co., Inm. Corazon de Maria, c/o Adjuntas, PR, St. Joachim. (PCE)
Lincoln, MT, Lewis and Clark Co., St. Jude's, c/o Helmville, MT, St. Thomas. (HEL)
Lincoln, NM, Lincoln Co., San Juan, c/o Ruidoso, NM, St. Eleanor. (LSC)
Lindsay, OK, Garvin Co., St. Peter's, c/o Pauls Valley, OK, St. Catherine of Siena. (OKL)
Lindsborg, KS, McPherson Co., St. Bridget of Sweden, c/o McPherson, KS, St. Joseph. (WCH)
Linlithgo, NY, Columbia Co., Nativity of Our Lord, c/o Germantown, NY, Resurrection. (ALB)
Linton, ND, Emmons Co., St. Michael, c/o Linton, ND, St. Anthony. (BIS)
Linville, NC, Avery Co., St. Bernadette, c/o Spruce Pine, NC, St. Lucien. (CHL)
Lisco, NE, Garden Co., St. Gall, c/o Chappell, NE, St. Joseph's. (GI)
Lisle, IL, Slav Missions, c/o Lisle, IL, St. Procopius Abbey. (JOL)
Litchfield, ME, Kennebec Co., St. Leo, c/o Winthrop, ME, St. Francis Xavier. (PRT)
Litchfield, OH, Medina Co., Jesus the Christ Child, c/o Litchfield, OH, Our Lady Help of Christians Parish. (CLV)
Little Italy, AR, Pulaski Co., St. Francis, c/o Bigelow, AR, St. Boniface's. (LR)
Little Orleans, MD, Allegany Co., St. Patrick's, c/o Hancock, MD, St. Peter's. (BAL)
Little Valley, NY, Cattaraugus Co., St. Mary, c/o Cattaraugus, NY, St. Mary. (BUF)
Littleton, WV, Wetzel Co., Assumption of the Blessed Virgin Mary, c/o Mannington, WV, St. Patrick's. (WH)
Live Oak, CA, Sutter Co., Our Lady of Guadalupe, c/o Gridley, CA, Sacred Heart. (SAC)
Llano Largo, NM, Taos Co., San Acacio Mission, c/o Penasco, NM, San Antonio de Padua. (SFE)
Llano Quemado, NM, Taos Co., N.S. del Carmel, c/o Ranchos De Taos, NM, San Francisco de Asis. (SFE)
Llano San Juan, NM, Taos Co., San Juan Nepomuceno Mission, c/o Penasco, NM, San Antonio de Padua. (SFE)
Llanos Tunas, PR, Our Lady of Good Counsel, c/o Cabo Rojo, PR, St. Michael. (MGZ)
Lluberas, PR, Yauco, St. Joseph, c/o Yauco, PR, Santo Domingo de Guzman. (PCE)
Lobatos, CO, Conejos Co., Sagrada Familia, c/o Antonito, CO, Our Lady of Guadalupe (PBL)
Loch Lomond, CA, Our Lady of the Lake, c/o Middletown, CA, St. Joseph. (SR)
Lockney, TX, Floyd Co., San Jose, c/o Plainview, TX, St. Alice. (LUB)
Loda, IL, Iroquois Co., St. Joseph, c/o Paxton, IL, St. Mary. (JOL)
Lodgepole, MT, Blaine Co., St. Thomas, c/o Hays, MT, St. Paul's Indian Mission. (GF)
Lodi, OH, Medina Co., Jesus Our Teacher, c/o Litchfield, OH, Our Lady Help of Christians Parish. (CLV)
Logan, NM, Quay Co., San Antonio, c/o Tucumcari, NM, St. Anne. (SFE)
Loleta, CA, St. Patrick, c/o Fortuna, CA, St. Joseph. (SR)
Lolo, MT, Missoula Co., Spirit of Christ, c/o Missoula, MT, Holy Family. (HEL)
Lometa, TX, Lampasas Co., Good Shepherd Catholic Church, c/o Lampasas, TX, St. Mary's. (AUS)
London, CA, Tulare Co., Santa Cruz, c/o Kingsburg, CA, Holy Family. (FRS)
Long Beach, CA, Los Angeles Co., Our Lady of Mt. Carmel Cambodian Catholic Center, c/o Long Beach, CA, St. Anthony. (LA)
Long Creek, OR, Grant Co., St. Katherine, c/o John Day, OR, St. Elizabeth's. (BAK)
Long Eddy, NY, Sullivan Co., St. Patrick, c/o Callicoon, NY, Holy Cross. (NY)
Long Island, ME, Cumberland Co., c/o Peaks Island, ME, St. Christopher's. (PRT)
Lopeno, TX, Zapata Co., San Pedro, c/o Zapata, TX, Our Lady of Lourdes. (LAR)
Lopezville, TX, Hidalgo Co., Immaculate Conception, c/o San Juan, TX, St. John the Baptist. (BWN)
Loraine, TX, Mitchell Co., San Jose, c/o Colorado City, TX, St. Ann's. (SAN)
Lorenzo, TX, Crosby Co., San Lorenzo, c/o Idalou, TX, St. Philip Benizi. (LUB)
Los Alamos, CA, Santa Barbara Co., St. Anthony's Church, c/o Santa Maria, CA, St. Louis de Montfort. (LA)
Los Angeles, CA, Old Co., Assumption, c/o Los Angeles, CA, Assumption. (LA)
Los Angeles, CA, Los Angeles Co., Blessed Alphonsa Catholic Mission, c/o Chatsworth, CA, St. John Eudes. (LA)
Los Angeles, CA, Hermanas Misioneras Servidoras de la Palabra, c/o Los Angeles, CA, Santa Isabel. (LA)
Los Angeles, CA, Los Angeles Co., La Purisima Chapel, c/o Los Angeles, CA, Our Lady of the Rosary of Talpa. (LA)
Los Angeles, CA, Los Angeles Co., San Conrado, c/o Los Angeles, CA, St. Peter. (LA)
Los Angeles, CA, Los Angeles Co., San Felipe, c/o Los Angeles, CA, Our Lady of Guadalupe. (LA)
Los Angeles, CA, Los Angeles Co., Santo Nino, c/o Los Angeles, CA, St. Vincent De Paul. (LA)
Los Angeles, CA, Los Angeles Co., St. John Bosco, c/o Los Angeles, CA, St. Odilia. (LA)
Los Angeles, CA, Los Angeles Co., St. Turibius, c/o Los Angeles, CA, St. Joseph. (LA)
Los Chavez, NM, Valencia Co., c/o Belen, NM, Our Lady of Belen. (SFE)
Los Cordovas, NM, Taos Co., San Isidro, c/o Ranchos De Taos, NM, San Francisco de Asis. (SFE)
Los Ebanos, TX, Hidalgo Co., St. Michael, c/o La Joya, TX, Our Lady, Queen of Angels. (BWN)
Los Garcias Ranch, TX, Starr Co., Sacred Heart, c/o Rio Grande City, TX, Immaculate Conception. (BWN)
Los Hueros, NM, Mora Co., c/o Wagon Mound, NM, Santa Clara. (SFE)
Los Le Febres, NM, Mora Co., c/o Wagon Mound, NM, Santa Clara. (SFE)
Los Lentes, NM, Valencia Co., San Antonio, c/o Los Lunas, NM, San Clemente. (SFE)
Los Martinez, NM, Torrance Co., Our Lady of Guadalupe, c/o Bloomfield, NM, St. Rose of Lima. (GLP)
Los Saenz, TX, Starr Co., Holy Family, c/o Roma, TX, Our Lady of Refuge. (BWN)
Los Sauces, CO, Conejos Co., St. Anthony, c/o Capulin, CO, St. Joseph. (PBL)
Los Valdeses, CO, Rio Grande Co., St. Francis of Assisi, c/o Del Norte, CO, Holy Name of Mary. (PBL)
Lott, TX, Falls Co., Sacred Heart, c/o Marlin, TX, St. Joseph's. (AUS)
Louise, TX, Wharton Co., St. Procopius, c/o El Campo, TX, St. Andrew. (VIC)
Louisville, GA, Jefferson Co., St. Joan of Arc, c/o Waynesboro, GA, Sacred Heart. (SAV)
Loveladies, NJ, Ocean Co., St. Clare, c/o Brant Beach, NJ, St. Francis of Assisi. (TR)
Lowell, VT, Orleans Co., St. Ignatius Loyola, c/o Troy, VT, Sacred Heart of Jesus. (BUR)
Lower San Francisco, NM, Catron Co., San Isidro, c/o Reserve, NM, Santo Nino. (GLP)
Loyalton, CA, Sierra Co., Holy Rosary, c/o Portola, CA, Holy Family. (SAC)
Lozano, TX, Cameron Co., St. Vincent de Paul, c/o Rio Hondo, TX, St. Helen. (BWN)
Lucedale, MS, George Co., St. Lucy, c/o Wiggins, MS, St. Francis Xavier. (BLX)
Lucerne, CA, Queen of the Rosary, c/o Clearlake, CA, Our Lady, Queen of Peace. (SR)
Lucero, NM, Mora Co., c/o Mora, NM, St. Gertrude. (SFE)
Luis Llorens Torres, PR, San Juan Co., Sagrada Familia, c/o San Juan, PR, Santa Teresita Del Nino Jesus. (SJN)
Luis Lopez, NM, Socorro Co., c/o Socorro, NM, San Miguel. (SFE)
Lull, TX, Hidalgo Co., Capilla de San Jose, c/o Edinburg, TX, Sacred Heart. (BWN)
Lummi, WA, Whatcom Co., St. Joachim (Indian Reservation), c/o Ferndale, WA, St. Joseph. (SEA)

Lunenburg, VT, Essex Co., St. Leo, c/o St. Johnsbury, VT, St. John the Evangelist. (BUR)
Luther, MI, Lake Co., St. Ignatius, c/o Baldwin, MI, St. Ann's. (GR)
Lyden, NM, Rio Arriba Co., San Jose, c/o Dixon, NM, St. Anthony. (SFE)
Lyman, NE, Scotts Bluff Co., Sacred Heart, c/o Mitchell, NE, St. Theresa's. (GI)
Lyons, OR, Linn Co., St. Patrick, c/o Jordan, OR, Our Lady of Lourdes. (P)
Lyons Falls, NY, Lewis Co., St. John, c/o Port Leyden, NY, St. Martin. (OG)

M

MacDonaldton, PA, Somerset Co., St. Gregory, c/o Meyersdale, PA, SS. Philip and James. (ALT)
Macana, PR, Penuelas Co., Fatima, c/o Penuelas, PR, St. Joseph. (PCE)
Macana Parcelas, PR, Guayanilla Co., San Martin de Porres, c/o Guayanilla, PR, Immaculate Conception. (PCE)
Macana Rio, PR, Guayanilla Co., Virgen de Fatima, c/o Guayanilla, PR, Immaculate Conception. (PCE)
Macon, MS, Noxubee Co., Corpus Christi, c/o Starkville, MS, St. Joseph. (JKS)
Macy, NE, Thurston Co., Our Lady of Fatima, c/o Walthill, NE, St. Joseph. (OM)
Madawaska, ME, Aroostook Co., St. Michael's Chapel, c/o Madawaska, ME, St. Agatha's. (PRT)
Madera, CA, Madera Co., St. Agnes, c/o Madera, CA, St. Joachim. (FRS)
Madera, PA, Clearfield Co., Immaculate Conception, c/o Houtzdale, PA, Christ the King. (E)
Madero, TX, Hidalgo Co., Our Lady of Lourdes, c/o Mission, TX, Our Lady of the Holy Rosary. (BWN)
Madill, OK, Marshall Co., Holy Cross, c/o Ardmore, OK, St. Mary. (OKL)
Madison, GA, Morgan Co., St. James, c/o Covington, GA, St. Augustine Church. (ATL)
Madison, KS, Greenwood Co., St. Teresa Of Avila, c/o Eureka, KS, Sacred Heart. (WCH)
Magas Arriba, PR, Guayanilla Co., Perpetuo Socorro, c/o Guayanilla, PR, Immaculate Conception. (PCE)
Magdalena, NM, Socorro Co., c/o Socorro, NM, San Miguel. (SFE)
Mageetown, PA, Crawford Co., Immaculate Conception, c/o Titusville, PA, St. Titus. (E)
Magnolia, AR, Columbia Co., Immaculate Heart of Mary, c/o El Dorado, AR, Holy Redeemer. (LR)
Magnolia, ID, St. Joseph's Chapel, c/o Gloucester, MA, St. Ann. (BO)
Magnolia, MS, Pike Co., St. James, c/o Chatawa, MS, St. Teresa. (JKS)
Majuro Atoll, MH, Laura, c/o Cathedral of the Assumption. (MI)
Makoti, ND, Ward Co., St. Elizabeth, c/o Parshall, ND, St. Bridget. (BIS)
Malaga, CA, Fresno Co., Christ the King, c/o Fresno, CA, St. Anthony Claret. (FRS)
Malaga, NM, Eddy Co., Cristo Rey, c/o Loving, NM, Our Lady of Grace. (LSC)
Malakoff, TX, Henderson Co., Mary Queen of Heaven, c/o Gun Barrel City, TX, St. Jude. (TYL)
Malpaso–Cesar Ruiz, PR, Immaculada Concepcion, c/o Aguada, PR, St. Francis of Assisi. (MGZ)
Mamey, PR, Perpetuo Socorro, c/o Aguada, PR, St. Francis of Assisi. (MGZ)
Mameyes, PR, Jayuya Co., S. Antonio, c/o Jayuya, PR, Our Lady of Monserrate. (PCE)
Manassa, CO, Conejos Co., St. Therese of the Child Jesus, c/o Capulin, CO, St. Joseph. (PBL)
Manchester, KY, Clay Co., St. Ann, c/o London, KY, St. William. (LEX)
Mangum, OK, Greer Co., Sacred Heart, c/o Hobart, OK, Sts. Peter and Paul. (OKL)
Mani, PR, Infant of Prague, c/o Mayaguez, PR, Our Lady of Mt. Carmel. (MGZ)
Manito, IL, Mason Co., Immaculate Conception, c/o Havana, IL, St. Patrick's. (PEO)
Manitou Springs, CO, El Paso Co., Our Lady of Perpetual Help, c/o Colorado Springs, CO, Sacred Heart. (COS)
Mannford, OK, Creek Co., Our Lady of the Lake, c/o Sand Springs, OK, St. Patrick's. (TLS)
Manning, SC, Clarendon Co., Our Lady of Hope Mission, c/o Summerton, SC, St. Mary's. (CHR)
Manset, ME, Hancock Co., St. Peter's, c/o Bar Harbor, ME, St. Ignatius. (PRT)
Mansfield, WA, Douglas Co., St. Mary, c/o Chelan, WA, St. Anne's. (YAK)
Manton, KY, Washington Co., Holy Rosary, c/o Springfield, KY, Holy Trinity. (L)
Manu'a Island, AS, Mary, Star of the Sea, c/o Pago Pago, AS, Cathedral of the Holy Family. (SPP)
Many, LA, Sabine Parish, St. Terence, c/o Many, LA, St. John the Baptist. (SHP)
Many Farms, AZ, Apache Co., St. Anthony, c/o Chinle, AZ, Our Lady of Fatima. (GLP)
Manzano, NM, Torrance Co., c/o Mountainair, NM, St. Alice. (SFE)
Manzanola, CO, Otero Co., St. Joseph the Worker, c/o Rocky Ford, CO, St. Peter. (PBL)
Maple, NC, Currituck Co., St. Katherine Drexel, c/o Elizabeth City, NC, Holy Family. (R)
Marak, TX, Milam Co., Ss. Cyril & Methodius, c/o Burlington, TX, St. Joseph's. (AUS)
Marana, AZ, Pima Co., San Juan Bautista, c/o Tucson, AZ, Blessed Kateri Tekakwitha. (TUC)
Marcellus, MI, Cass Co., St. Margaret Mary, c/o Mattawan, MI, St. John Bosco. (KAL)
Marengo, IN, Crawford Co., St. Joseph, c/o Depauw, IN, St. Bernard. (IND)
Marenisco, MI, Gogebic Co., St. Catherine, c/o Wakefield, MI, Immaculate Conception of the Blessed Virgin Mary. (MAR)
Maresua, PR, Gruta de Lourdes, c/o San German, PR, San German de Auxerre. (MGZ)
Marian, TN, Marian Co., Virgin of the Poor Shrine, c/o South Pittsburg, TN, Our Lady of Lourdes. (KNX)
Marianna, AR, Lee Co., St. Andrew, c/o Helena, AR, St. Mary's. (LR)
Marias, PR, Asuncion de Maria, c/o Aguada, PR, St. Francis of Assisi. (MGZ)
Maricopa, AZ, Pinal Co., St. Francis de Sales, c/o Casa Grande, AZ, St. Anthony of Padua. (TUC)
Marietta, OK, Love Co., Good Shepherd, c/o Ardmore, OK, St. Mary. (OKL)
Marion, NC, McDowell Co., Our Lady of the Angels, c/o Morganton, NC, St. Charles Borromeo. (CHL)
Marion, SC, Marion Co., Infant Jesus, c/o Dillon, SC, St. Louis. (CHR)
Marion, TX, Guadalupe Co., Immaculate Conception, c/o Schertz, TX, Church of the Good Shepherd. (SAT)
Marked Tree, AR, Poinsett Co., St. Norbert Church, c/o Weiner, AR, St. Anthony's. (LR)
Markham, TX, Matagorda Co., St. Robert, c/o Blessing, TX, St. Peter's. (VIC)
Marlow, OK, Stephens Co., Immaculate Conception, c/o Duncan, OK, Assumption. (OKL)
Marmarth, ND, Slope Co., Immaculate Heart of Mary, c/o Rhame, ND, St. Charles. (BIS)
Marshall, OK, Logan Co., St. Camillus, c/o Hennessey, OK, St. Joseph's. (OKL)
Marshfield, VT, Washington Co., North American Martyrs, c/o Montpelier, VT, St. Augustine. (BUR)
Marysdale, OH, Defiance Co., Immaculate Conception, c/o Defiance, OH, St. Stephen. (TOL)
Marysville, MT, Lewis and Clark Co., Our Lady of Lourdes, c/o Helena, MT, Our Lady of the Valley. (HEL)
Masefau, AS, c/o Pago Pago, AS, Church of St. Peter and Paul. (SPP)
Mason, TX, Mason Co., St. Joseph, c/o Llano, TX, Holy Trinity. (AUS)
Mason, WV, Mason Co., St. Joseph, c/o Point Pleasant, WV, Sacred Heart. (WH)
Mason City, IL, Mason Co., St. Columba, c/o Elkhart, IL, St. Patrick. (PEO)
Mason City, NE, Custer Co., St. Thomas, c/o Broken Bow, NE, St. Joseph's. (GI)
Matador, TX, Motley Co., Our Lady of Guadalupe, c/o Floydada, TX, St. Mary Magdalen. (LUB)
Matrullas, PR, Cacao Co., Sacred Heart of Jesus, c/o Villalba, PR, Our Lady Mother of Divine Providence. (PCE)
Mattingly Settlement, OH, Muskingum Co., St. Mary, c/o Dresden, OH, St. Ann's. (COL)
Mattituck, NY, Suffolk Co., Our Lady of Good Counsel, c/o Cutchogue, NY, Sacred Heart. (RVC)
Matunuck, RI, Washington Co., St. Romuald, c/o Wakefield, RI, St. Francis of Assisi. (PRO)
Maud, OK, Seminole Co., St. Cecelia, c/o Seminole, OK, Immaculate Conception. (OKL)
Maupin, OR, Wasco Co., St. Mary's, c/o Dufur, OR, St. Alphonsus. (BAK)
Max, ND, McClean Co., Immaculate Conception, c/o Garrison, ND, St. Nicholas. (BIS)
Maxwell, NM, Colfax Co., c/o Springer, NM, St. Joseph. (SFE)
Mayaguez, PR, Corpus Christi, c/o Mayaguez, PR, Nuestra Senora De Fatima. (MGZ)
Mayaguez, PR, Cristo Rey, c/o Mayaguez, PR, Nuestra Senora De Fatima. (MGZ)
Mayaguez, PR, Espiritu Santo, c/o Mayaguez, PR, Nuestra Senora De Fatima. (MGZ)
Mayaguez, PR, Maria Socorro de los Cristianos, c/o Mayaguez, PR, Cathedral of Our Lady of Purification. (MGZ)
Mayaguez, PR, Santa Ana, c/o Mayaguez, PR, Cathedral of Our Lady of Purification. (MGZ)
Mayer, AZ, Yavapai Co., St. Joseph, c/o Prescott Valley, AZ, St. Germaine. (PHX)
Maysville, MO, DeKalb Co., St. Aloysius, c/o Cameron, MO, St. Munchin. (KC)
Mayville, ND, Traill Co., State University Newman Club, c/o Mayville, ND, Our Lady of Peace. (FAR)
McCartys, NM, Cibola Co., Santa Maria de Acoma, c/o Pueblo of Acoma, NM, San Esteban, Acoma Catholic Indian Mission. (GLP)
McCook, NE, Red Willow Co., Sacred Heart, c/o McCook, NE, St. Patrick. (LIN)
McCook, NE, Red Willow Co., St. Ann's, c/o McCook, NE, St. Patrick. (LIN)
McCormick, SC, McCormick Co., Good Shepherd, c/o Abbeville, SC, Sacred Heart. (CHR)
McCrory, AR, Woodruff Co., St. Mary's, c/o Wynne, AR, St. Peter's. (LR)
McDermitt, NV, Humboldt Co., Sacred Heart, c/o Winnemucca, NV, St. Paul. (RNO)
McGehee, AR, Desha Co., St. Mary Church, c/o Lake Village, AR, Our Lady of the Lake. (LR)
McGill, NV, White Pine Co., St. Michael's, c/o Ely, NV, Sacred Heart. (LAV)
McIntosh, SD, Corson Co., St. Bonaventure, c/o McLaughlin, SD, St. Bernard. (RC)
McKee, KY, Jackson Co., St. Paul, c/o Berea, KY, St. Clare. (LEX)
McRoberts, KY, Letcher Co., Holy Angels, c/o Jenkins, KY, St. George. (LEX)
Meadow Lake, NM, Valencia Co., Juan Diego, c/o Peralta, NM, Our Lady of Guadalupe. (SFE)
Meadow Wood Acres, TX, Bexar Co., St. John Vianney, c/o LaCoste, TX, Our Lady of Grace. (SAT)
Meadville, MS, Franklin Co., St. Ann, c/o Brookhaven, MS, St. Francis. (JKS)
Mechanic Falls, ME, Oxford Co., St. Mary, c/o Mechanic Falls, ME, Our Lady of Ransom. (PRT)
Mechanicsville, CT, Windham Co., Sacred Heart, c/o North Grosvenordale, CT, St. Joseph. (NOR)
Medanales, NM, Rio Arriba Co., c/o Abiquiu, NM, St. Thomas Apostle. (SFE)
Medicine Bow, WY, Carbon Co., St. Malachy, c/o Saratoga, WY, St. Ann's. (CHY)
Medicine Lane, MT, Sheridan Co., St. Patrick, c/o Plentywood, MT, St. Joseph's. (GF)
Medicine Root, SD, Shannon Co., St. Stephens, c/o Kyle, SD, Our Lady of Sorrows. (RC)
Meeker, OK, Lincoln Co., St. Michael, c/o Prague, OK, St. Wenceslaus, National Shrine of the Infant Jesus of Prague. (OKL)
Meekin's Neck, MD, Dorchester Co., St. Mary, Star of the Sea, c/o Cambridge, MD, St. Mary Refuge of Sinners. (WIL)
Meeteetse, WY, Park Co., St. Therese, c/o Cody, WY, St. Anthony. (CHY)
Meherrin, VA, Prince Edward, Sacred Heart, c/o Crewe, VA, St. John the Baptist. (RIC)
Melendez, PR, Coamo Co., Our Lady of Fatima, c/o Coamo, PR, St. Blase. (PCE)
Melrose, MT, Silver Bow Co., St. John The Apostle, c/o Dillon, MT, St. Rose of Lima. (HEL)
Melrose, NM, Curry Co., c/o Clovis, NM, Sacred Heart. (SFE)
Melstone, MT, Musselshell Co., Our Lady of Mercy, c/o Roundup, MT, St. Benedict's. (GF)
Melvin, IL, Ford Co., St. George, c/o Gibson City, IL, Our Lady of Lourdes. (JOL)
Melvin, TX, McCullogh Co., St. Francis Xavier, c/o Brady, TX, St. Patrick's. (SAN)
Merced, CA, Merced Co., El Nido, c/o Merced, CA, Sacred Heart. (FRS)
Merced, CA, Merced Co., St. George, c/o Merced, CA, Sacred Heart. (FRS)
Mercersburg, PA, Franklin Co., St. Luke the Evangelist, c/o Greencastle, PA, St. Mark the Evangelist. (HBG)
Mereta, TX, Tom Green Co., Holy Family, c/o Wall, TX, St. Ambrose. (SAN)
Merkel, TX, Taylor Co., Our Mother of Mercy, c/o Sweetwater, TX, Holy Family. (SAN)
Merna, NE, Custer Co., St. Paul, c/o Broken Bow, NE, St. Joseph's. (GI)
Merrill, IA, Plymouth Co., St. Joseph at Ellendale, c/o Hinton, IA, Assumption Church. (SC)
Merryville, LA, Beauregard Parish, St. Bridget, c/o De Ridder, LA, St. Joseph's. (LKC)
Mertzon, TX, Irion Co., St. Peter's, c/o Eldorado, TX, Our Lady of Guadalupe. (SAN)
Mesa de Poleo, NM, Rio Arriba Co., c/o Abiquiu, NM, St. Thomas Apostle. (SFE)
Mesita, NM, Valencia Co., Sacred Heart, c/o Laguna, NM, St. Joseph. (GLP)
Mesquite, NM, Dona Ana Co., Our Lady of Perpetual Help, c/o San Miguel, NM, San Miguel. (LSC)
Metip, FM, c/o Sacred Heart. (CI)
Metlakatla, AK, Holy Family, c/o Ketchikan, AK, Holy Name. (JUN)
Metter, GA, Candler Co., Holy Family, c/o Swainsboro, GA, Holy Trinity. (SAV)
Mexico Beach, FL, Bay Co., Our Lady of Guadalupe, c/o Panama City, FL, St. Dominic. (PT)
Miami, FL, La Milagrosa, c/o Miami, FL, Corpus Christi. (MIA)
Miami, FL, Nuestra Senora de Altagracia, c/o Miami, FL, Corpus Christi. (MIA)
Miami, FL, San Francisco y Santa Clara, c/o Miami, FL, Corpus Christi. (MIA)
Miami, FL, San Juan Bautista, c/o Miami, FL, Corpus Christi. (MIA)
Michigan City, IN, La Porte Co., Maronite Catholic Community, c/o Oakbrook Terrace, IL, Our Lady of

Lebanon Church. (OLL)
Michigan City, IN, Sacred Heart, c/o Michigan City, IN, St. Mary of the Immaculate Conception. (GRY)
Mico, TX, Medina Co., St. Francis of Assisi (Medina Lake Chapel), c/o Castroville, TX, St. Louis. (SAT)
Middle River, MN, Marshall Co., St. Joseph, c/o Greenbush, MN, Blessed Sacrament. (CR)
Middlebourne, WV, Tyler Co., St. Lawrence, c/o Paden City, WV, Mater Dolorosa. (WH)
Middleport, PA, Schuylkill Co., Immaculate Heart of Mary Chapel, c/o New Philadelphia, PA, Sacred Heart. (ALN)
Middletown, IL, Logan Co., St. John the Baptist, c/o Elkhart, IL, St. Patrick. (PEO)
Middletown, PA, Susquehanna Co., St. Patrick, c/o Friendsville, PA, St. Francis Xavier. (SCR)
Middleville, NY, Herkimer Co., St. Mary of the Assumption, c/o Newport, NY, St. John the Baptist. (ALB)
Midkiff, TX, Upton Co., St. Thomas, c/o Garden City, TX, St. Lawrence. (SAN)
Midland, LA, St. Aloysius, c/o Morse, LA, Immaculate Conception. (LAF)
Midland, SD, Haakon Co., St. William, c/o Philip, SD, Sacred Heart. (RC)
Midwest, WY, Natrona Co., St. Francis Mission, c/o Casper, WY, St. Anthony of Padua. (CHY)
Mifflinburg, PA, Union Co., Saint George Church, c/o Lewisburg, PA, Sacred Heart of Jesus. (HBG)
Milagro, NM, Guadalupe Co., c/o Santa Rosa, NM, St. Rose of Lima. (SFE)
Milan, TN, Northern Gibson Co., c/o Humboldt, TN, Sacred Heart. (MEM)
Mildred, PA, Sullivan Co., St. Frances of Assisi, c/o Dushore, PA, St. Basil's. (SCR)
Milesville, SD, Haakon Co., St. Mary, c/o Philip, SD, Sacred Heart. (RC)
Milford Center, OH, Union Co., Sacred Heart, c/o Plain City, OH, St. Joseph. (COL)
Mill City, OR, Marion Co., St. Catherine of Siena, c/o Sublimity, OR, St. Boniface. (P)
Mill Rift, PA, Pike Co., Holy Family, c/o Matamoras, PA, St. Joseph's. (SCR)
Mill River, MA, Berkshire Co., Immaculate Conception, c/o Sheffield, MA, Our Lady of the Valley. (SPR)
Millcreek, FL, St. Johns Co., Our Lady of Good Counsel, c/o Elkton, FL, St. Ambrose. (STA)
Millen, GA, Jenkins Co., St. Bernadette, c/o Sylvania, GA, Our Lady of the Assumption. (SAV)
Millersview, TX, Concho C., Our Lady of Guadalupe, c/o Eden, TX, St. Charles. (SAN)
Millersville, MD, Anne Arundel Co., Church of Holy Apostles, c/o Millersville, MD, Our Lady of the Fields. (BAL)
Millerton, NY, Dutchess Co., St. Patrick, c/o Amenia, NY, Immaculate Conception. (NY)
Millett, TX, La Salle Co., Our Lady of Guadalupe, c/o Cotulla, TX, Sacred Heart. (LAR)
Milligan, NE, Fillmore Co., St. Wenceslaus, c/o Friend, NE, St. Joseph's. (LIN)
Millington, MI, Tuscola Co., St. Bernard, c/o Vassar, MI, St. Frances Xavier Cabrini. (SAG)
Millsboro, DE, Sussex Co., Mary Mother of Peace, c/o Georgetown, DE, St. Michael the Archangel. (WIL)
Millwood, NY, Westchester Co., Our Lady of the Wayside, c/o Briarcliff Manor, NY, St. Theresa. (NY)
Milo, ME, Piscataquis Co., St. Paul, c/o Dover Foxcroft, ME, St. Francis Xavier. (PRT)
Milolii, HI, Honaunau Co., c/o Captain Cook, HI, St. Benedict. (HON)
Milwaukee, WI, Milwaukee Co., St. John's Chapel, c/o Milwaukee, WI, All Saints. (MIL)
Minerva, KY, Mason Co., St. James, c/o Brooksville, KY, St. James. (COV)
Minot, ND, Ward Co., St. Michael, c/o Wilton, ND, SS. Peter and Paul. (STN)
Miraflores, PR, Chapel of Our Lady of Perpetual Help, c/o Anasco, PR, St. Anthony Abbot. (MGZ)
Mirando City, TX, Jim Hogg Co., St. Agnes, c/o Hebbronville, TX, Our Lady of Guadalupe. (LAR)
Mission, SD, Todd Co., St. Thomas, c/o St. Francis, SD, Rosebud Reservation. (RC)
Mitchell, WI, Sheboygan Co., St. Michael Chapel, c/o Eden, WI, Shepherd of the Hills (Good Shepherd). (MIL)
Mojave, CA, Kern Co., St. Francis of Assisi Church, c/o Rosamond, CA, St. Mary. (FRS)
Mokelumne Hill, CA, Calaveras Co., St. Thomas Aquinas, c/o San Andreas, CA, St. Andrew Church of San Andreas (Pastor of). (STO)
Monarch, MT, Cascade Co., St. Clement, c/o Belt, MT, St. Mark the Evangelist. (GF)
Moncla, LA, Avoyelles Parish, St. John the Baptist, c/o Fifth Ward, LA, Our Lady of Lourdes. (ALX)
Monet Ferry, LA, Natchitoches Parish, Holy Family, c/o Cloutierville, LA, St. John the Baptist. (ALX)
Mongaup Valley, NY, Sullivan Co., St. Joseph, c/o Monticello, NY, St. Peter. (NY)
Monmouth, ME, Kennebec Co., St. Stanislaus, c/o Winthrop, ME, St. Francis Xavier. (PRT)
Monroeville, AL, Dallas Co., Mission of Annunciation Parish, c/o Monroeville, AL, St. Joseph. (MOB)
Monte Alto, TX, Hidalgo Co., Christ the King, Holy Cross Catechetical Center, c/o Elsa, TX, Sacred Heart. (BWN)
Monte Aplanado, NM, Mora Co., c/o Mora, NM, St. Gertrude. (SFE)
Monte Grande, PR, St. Jude Thaddeus, c/o Cabo Rojo, PR, St. Michael. (MGZ)
Monte Rio, CA, St. Catherine, c/o Guerneville, CA, St. Elizabeth. (SR)
Montecello, NM, Sierra Co., St. Ignatius, c/o Truth or Consequences, NM, Our Lady of Perpetual Help. (LSC)
Monterey, MA, Berkshire Co., Our Lady of the Hills, c/o Sheffield, MA, Our Lady of the Valley. (SPR)
Montesano, WA, Grays Harbor Co., St. John, c/o Elma, WA, St. Joseph. (SEA)
Montezuma, GA, Macon Co., St. Michael, c/o Americus, GA, St. Mary. (SAV)
Montgomery, AL, Montgomery Co., Resurrection Catholic Mission, c/o Montgomery, AL, Resurrection Catholic Church. (MOB)
Montgomery, LA, Grant Parish, St. Patrick c/o Colfax, LA, St. Joseph. (ALX)
Montgomery Center, VT, Franklin Co., St. Isidore, c/o Richford, VT, All Saints. (BUR)
Monticello, MS, Lawrence Co., St. Lawrence, c/o Bassfield, MS, St. Peter. (BLX)
Monument, OR, Grant Co., St. Anne, c/o John Day, OR, St. Elizabeth's. (BAK)
Moody, TX, McLennan Co., Our Lady of San Juan, c/o McGregor TX, St. Eugene. (AUS)
Moorcroft, WY, Crook Co., St. Patrick, c/o Gillette, WY, St. Matthew's. (CHY)
Moore, MT, Fergus Co., St. Mathias, c/o Stanford, MT, St. Rose of Lima. (GF)
Moore Haven, FL, Glades Co., St. Theresa of the Child Jesus, c/o Moore Haven, FL, St. Joseph the Worker. (VEN)
Mooreland, OK, Woodward Co., Sacred Heart, c/o Woodward, OK, St. Peter's. (OKL)
Moorhead, MN, Clay Co., St. Thomas Newman Center, c/o Moorhead, MN, St. Joseph's. (CR)
Moquino, NM, Valencia Co., Santa Rosalia, c/o Seboyeta, NM, Our Lady of Sorrows. (GLP)
Moral, TX, Nacogdoches Co., Immaculate Conception, c/o Nacogdoches, TX, Sacred Heart. (TYL)
Moravia, TX, Lavaca Co., Ascension of Our Lord, c/o Hallettsville, TX, St. John the Baptist. (VIC)
Moretown, VT, Washington Co., St. Patrick, c/o Waterbury, VT, St. Andrew. (BUR)
Morgan City, LA, St. Mary Parish, St. Rosalie, c/o Morgan City, LA, Holy Cross. (HT)
Morning View, KY, Kenton Co., Assumption of the Blessed Virgin, c/o Kenton, KY, St. Matthew. (COV)
Morrill, NE, Scotts Bluff Co., St. Ann, c/o Mitchell, NE, St. Theresa's. (GI)
Morris, PA, Tioga Co., Sacred Heart, c/o Wellsboro, PA, St. Peter's. (SCR)
Morris Run, PA, Tioga Co., St. Joseph, c/o Blossburg, PA, St. Mary's. (SCR)
Morrison Bluff, AR, Logan Co., SS. Peter & Paul Church, c/o Clarksville, AR, Holy Redeemer. (LR)
Morristown, SD, Corson Co., Sacred Heart, c/o Lemmon, SD, St. Mary's. (RC)
Moses, NM, Union Co., Sacred Heart, c/o Clayton, NM, St. Francis Xavier. (SFE)
Mosquero, NM, Harding Co., c/o Roy, NM, Holy Family–St. Joseph. (SFE)
Mount Holly, VT, Rutland Co., Our Lady of Mercy, c/o Wallingford, VT, St. Patrick. (BUR)
Mount Ida, AR, Montgomery Co., All Saints, c/o Mena, AR, St. Agnes. (LR)
Mount Pulaski, IL, Logan Co., St. Thomas Aquinas, c/o Elkhart, IL, St. Patrick. (PEO)
Mountain View, AR, Stone Co., St. Mary Church, c/o Mountain Home, AR, St. Peter the Fisherman. (LR)
Moxham, PA, Cambria Co., St. Anne's, c/o Johnstown, PA, St. Therese of the Child Jesus. (ALT)
Mt. Olive, NC, Duplin Co., Posada Guadalupana, c/o Mount Olive, NC, St. Mary. (R)
Mt. Palatine, IL, La Salle Co., Immaculate Conception, c/o Wenona, IL, St. Mary's. (PEO)
Mud Butte, SD, Meade Co., c/o Faith, SD, St. Joseph. (RC)
Mukilteo, WA, Snohomish Co., St. John, c/o Everett, WA, St. Mary Magdalen. (SEA)
Mulvey, LA, Vermilion Parish, St. David, c/o Gueydan, LA, St. Peter. (LAF)
Mumford, NY, Monroe Co., St. Patrick, c/o Caledonia, NY, St. Columba. (ROC)
Murdo, SD, Jones Co., St. Martin of Tours, c/o Presho, SD, Christ the King. (RC)
Murphys, CA, Murphys Co., St. Patrick, c/o Angels Camp, CA, St. Patrick Church of Angels Camp (Pastor of). (STO)
Myrtle Point, OR, Coos Co., Sts. Ann and Michael, c/o Coquille, OR, Holy Name. (P)

N

Naco, AZ, Cochise Co., St. Michael, c/o Bisbee, AZ, St. Patrick. (TUC)
Nacogdoches, TX, Nacogdoches Co., Our Lady of Guadalupe, c/o Nacogdoches, TX, Sacred Heart. (TYL)
Nags Head, NC, Dare Co., Holy Trinity, c/o Kitty Hawk, NC, Holy Redeemer. (R)
Naknek, AK, Bristol Bay Borough, St. Theresa, c/o Dillingham, AK, Holy Rosary. (ANC)
Nalcrest, FL, Polk Co., St. Leo the Great, c/o Lake Wales, FL, Holy Spirit. (ORL)
Nambe, NM, Santa Fe Co., c/o Santa Fe, NM, N.S. de Guadalupe del Valle de Pojoaque. (SFE)
Nambe Indian Pueblo, NM, Santa Fe Co., c/o Santa Fe, NM, N.S. de Guadalupe del Valle de Pojoaque. (SFE)
Naper, NE, Boyd Co., Sacred Heart, c/o Butte, NE, SS. Peter and Paul. (OM)
Naperville, IL, Benedictine Chinese Mission, c/o Lisle, IL, St. Procopius Abbey. (JOL)
Naperville, IL, St. Scholastica Mission House, c/o Lisle, IL, St. Procopius Abbey. (JOL)
Naples, FL, Collier Co., St. Finbarr, c/o Marco Island, FL, San Marco. (VEN)
Naponee, NE, Franklin Co., St. Mary, c/o Red Cloud, NE, Sacred Heart. (LIN)
Nara Visa, NM, Quay Co., Sacred Heart, c/o Tucumcari, NM, St. Anne. (SFE)
Naranjo, PR, Salinas Co., Santa Marta, c/o Salinas, PR, Our Lady of Monserrat. (PCE)
Naranjo, PR, Yauco Co., St. Anthony, c/o Yauco, PR, Holy Rosary. (PCE)
Naranjo Militar, PR, Ntra. Madre de la Consolacion, c/o Aguada, PR, St. Francis of Assisi. (MGZ)
Naranjo–Guanabanas, PR, San Pablo, c/o Aguada, PR, St. Francis of Assisi. (MGZ)
Naschitti, NM, San Juan Co., St. Anthony, c/o Tohatchi, NM, St. Mary Church. (GLP)
Nashua, MT, Valley Co., Queen of the Angels, c/o Glasgow, MT, St. Raphael's. (GF)
Nashville, AR, Howard Co., St. Martin, c/o De Queen, AR, St. Barbara's. (LR)
Nashville, GA, Berrien Co., St. Mary, c/o Lakeland, GA, Queen of Peace. (SAV)
Nashville, MI, Barry Co., St. Cyril, c/o Hastings, MI, St. Rose of Lima. (KAL)
Natalia, TX, Medina Co., St. John Bosco, c/o Lytle, TX, St. Andrew. (SAT)
Natural Bridge, NY, Jefferson Co., St. Henry, c/o Harrisville, NY, St. Francis Solanus. (OG)
Naubinway, MI, Mackinac Co., St. Stephen, c/o Engadine, MI, Our Lady of Lourdes. (MAR)
Naukati, AK, c/o Craig, AK, St. John by the Sea. (JUN)
Naytahwaush, MN, Mahnomen Co., St. Anne, c/o Waubun, MN, St. Ann. (CR)
Nebish, MN, Beltrami Co., St. John, c/o Red Lake, MN, St. Mary's Mission Church. (CR)
Nederland, CO, Boulder Co., St. Rita, c/o Boulder, CO, Sacred Heart of Jesus. (DEN)
Nelson, NE, Nuckolls Co., Sacred Heart, c/o Superior, NE, St. Joseph's. (LIN)
Nenzel, NE, Cherry Co., St. Mary, c/o Nenzel, NE, St. Nicholas. (GI)
Nephi, UT, Utah Co., Our Lady of Victory Mission, c/o Payson, UT, San Andres. (SLC)
New Almelo, KS, Norton Co., St. Joseph's Church, c/o Norton, KS, St. Francis of Assisi. (SAL)
New Boston, IL, Mercer Co., St. Theresa of the Little Flower, c/o Aledo, IL, St. Catherine's Church. (PEO)
New Braunfels, TX, Comal Co., St. John, c/o Seguin, TX, Our Lady of Guadalupe. (SAT)
New Deal, TX, Lubbock Co., Our Lady Queen of Apostles, c/o Lubbock, TX, St. Patrick. (LUB)
New Dorp Beach, NY, Richmond Co., Our Lady of Lourdes, c/o Staten Island, NY, Our Lady, Queen of Peace. (NY)
New Germany, PA, Cambria Co., Immaculate Conception, c/o Summerhill, PA, St. John. (ALT)
New Hampton, NY, Orange Co., St. Andrew Bobola, c/o Florida, NY, St. Joseph. (NY)
New Haven, MO, Franklin Co., St. Gerald, c/o New Haven, MO, Holy Family. (STL)
New Hradec, ND, Dunn Co., SS. Peter and Paul, c/o Belfield, ND, St. Bernard. (BIS)
New Iberia, LA, Iberia Parish, St. Jude, c/o New Iberia, LA, St. Edward. (LAF)
New Leipzig, ND, Grant Co., St. John the Baptist, c/o Mott, ND, St. Vincent de Paul. (BIS)
New Marion, IN, Ripley Co., St. Mary Magdalen, c/o Osgood, IN, St. John. (IND)
New Middletown, IN, Harrison Co., Most Precious Blood, c/o Corydon, IN, St. Joseph. (IND)
New Milford, PA, Susquehanna Co., St. John, c/o Great Bend, PA, St. Lawrence's. (SCR)
New Orleans, LA, Orleans Civil Parish, Our Lady of Guadalupe, c/o New Orleans, LA, St. Louis Cathedral. (NO)
New Orleans, LA, Orleans Civil Parish, Our Lady of La Vang, c/o New Orleans, LA, Mary, Queen of Vietnam. (NO)
New Orleans, LA, Orleans Civil Parish, St. Joseph, c/o

Marrero, LA, St. Agnes Le Thi Thanh. (NO)
New River, AZ, Maricopa Co., Good Shepherd Mission, c/o Phoenix, AZ, St. Luke. (PHX)
New Summerfield, TX, Cherokee Co., Our Lady of Guadalupe, c/o Jacksonville, TX, Our Lady of Sorrows. (TYL)
New Village, NJ, Warren Co., St. Christopher, c/o Phillipsburg, NJ, St. Philip & St. James. (MET)
New York, NY, Richmond Co., Christ the King, c/o Staten Island, NY, St. Mary of the Assumption. (NY)
New York, NY, New York Co., Gift of Love, c/o New York, NY, St. Veronica. (NY)
Newfields, NH, Rockingham Co., Sacred Heart, c/o Newmarket, NH, St. Mary. (MAN)
Newfound Lake, NH, Grafton Co., Our Lady of Grace, c/o Bristol, NH, St. Timothy. (MAN)
Newfoundland, PA, Wayne Co., St. Anthony of Padua, c/o Gouldsboro, PA, St. Rita. (SCR)
Newport, AR, Jackson Co., St. Cecilia, c/o Batesville, AR, St. Mary's. (LR)
Newport, KY, Campbell Co., Corpus Christi, c/o Newport, KY, Holy Spirit. (COV)
Newport, KY, Campbell Co., St. Francis de Sales, c/o Newport, KY, Holy Spirit. (COV)
Newport, KY, Campbell Co., St. Stephen, c/o Newport, KY, Holy Spirit. (COV)
Newport, KY, Campbell Co., St. Vincent de Paul, c/o Newport, KY, Holy Spirit. (COV)
Newton, MS, Newton Co., St. Anne, c/o Forest, MS, St. Michael. (JKS)
Newton, PA, Lackawanna Co., St. Benedict, c/o Clarks Summit, PA, Our Lady of the Snows. (SCR)
Newton Falls, NY, St. Lawrence Co., St. Anthony of Padua, c/o Star Lake, NY, St. Hubert. (OG)
Nicasio, CA, Marin Co., St. Mary, c/o Lagunitas, CA, St. Cecilia. (SFR)
Nicolaus, CA, Sutter Co., St. Boniface, c/o Lincoln, CA, St. Joseph. (SAC)
Niland, CA, Immaculate Heart of Mary, c/o Calipatria, CA, St. Patrick. (SD)
Ninilchik, AK, Kenai Peninsula Borough, St. Peter, c/o Homer, AK, St. John the Baptist. (ANC)
Niobrara, NE, Knox Co., St. William, c/o Verdigre, NE, St. Wenceslaus. (OM)
No Water, SD, Shannon Co., Our Lady of Good Counsel, c/o Pine Ridge, SD, Holy Rosary. (RC)
Noble, LA, Sabine Parish, St. Catherine, c/o Noble, LA, St. Ann. (SHP)
Nocatee, FL, De Soto Co., Blessed Juan Diego, c/o Arcadia, FL, St. Paul. (VEN)
Noel, MO, McDonald Co., Nativity of Our Lord, c/o Neosho, MO, St. Canera. (SPC)
Noonan, ND, Divide Co., St. Luke, c/o Crosby, ND, St. Patrick. (BIS)
Norborne, MO, Carroll Co., Sacred Heart, c/o Carrollton, MO, St. Mary's. (KC)
Norcross, GA, Gwinnett Co., Mary, Our Queen, c/o Dunwoody, GA, All Saints Catholic. (ATL)
Nordheim, TX, DeWitt Co., St. Ann's, c/o Yorktown, TX, Holy Cross. (VIC)
Norias Ranch, TX, Kenedy Co., Santa Elena, c/o Sarita, TX, Our Lady of Guadalupe. (CC)
Norris, SD, Mellette Co., Sacred Heart, c/o St. Francis, SD, Rosebud Reservation. (RC)
North Bangor, NY, Franklin Co., St. Edward, c/o North Bangor, NY, St. Augustine. (OG)
North Brookfield, NY, Madison Co., St. Mary, c/o Waterville, NY, St. Bernard. (SY)
North East, MD, Cecil Co., St. Jude, c/o Elkton, MD, Immaculate Conception. (WIL)
North Eastham, MA, Barnstable Co., Visitation Church, c/o Wellfleet, MA, Our Lady of Lourdes. (FR)
North Fork, CA, Madera Co., St. Joseph the Worker, c/o Oakhurst, CA, Our Lady of the Sierra. (FRS)
North Greenbush, NY, Rensselaer Co., Van Rensselaer Manor, County Welfare Home, c/o Troy, NY, St. Michael the Archangel. (ALB)
North Haven, ME, Knox Co., Our Lady of Peace, c/o Camden, ME, Our Lady of Good Hope. (PRT)
North Hero, VT, Grand Isle Co., St. Benedict Joseph Labre, c/o South Hero, VT, St. Rose of Lima. (BUR)
North Hollywood, CA, Los Angeles Co., Our Lady of Zapopan, c/o Sun Valley, CA, Our Lady of the Holy Rosary. (LA)
North Powder, OR, Union Co., St. Anthony, c/o Baker, OR, Cathedral of St. Francis De Sales. (BAK)
North Pownal, VT, Bennington Co., Our Lady of Lourdes, c/o Bennington, VT, Sacred Heart St. Francis de Sales. (BUR)
North Salem, NY, Westchester Co., St. John, c/o Croton Falls, NY, St. Joseph. (NY)
North San Juan, CA, Nevada Co., St. John, c/o North San Juan, CA, Immaculate Conception. (SAC)
North Truro, MA, Barnstable Co., Our Lady of Perpetual Help,, c/o Provincetown, MA, St. Peter the Apostle. (FR)
Northbrook, IL, Mission of the Holy Ghost, c/o Chicago, IL, Archdiocese of Chicago's Joseph Cardinal Bernardin Archives and Records Center. (CHI)
Northland, MI, Marquette Co., St. Joseph, c/o Gwinn, MI, St. Anthony. (MAR)
Northome, MN, Koochiching Co., St. Michael, c/o Kelliher, MN, St. Patrick. (CR)
Northwood, NH, Rockingham Co., St. Joseph, c/o Pittsfield, NH, Our Lady of Lourdes. (MAN)
Norton, VT, Essex Co., St. Bernard, c/o Island Pond, VT, St. James the Greater. (BUR)
Norwich, VT, Windsor Co., St. Francis of Assisi, c/o Bradford, VT, Our Lady of Perpetual Help. (BUR)
Nova–Savannah, OH, Medina Co., Jesus the Good Shepherd, c/o Litchfield, OH, Our Lady Help of Christians Parish. (CLV)
Novinger, MO, Adair Co., St. Rose of Lima, c/o Kirksville, MO, Mary Immaculate. (JC)
Nowata, OK, Nowata Co., St. Catherine, c/o Bartlesville, OK, The Community of St. James. (TLS)
Noxon, MT, c/o Thompson Falls, MT, St. William. (HEL)
Nucla, CO, Montrose Co., Our Lady of Sorrows, c/o Telluride, CO, St. Patrick. (PBL)
Nunam Iqua, AK, St. Peter's, c/o Alakanuk, AK, St. Ignatius. (FBK)
Nuremberg, PA, Luzerne Co., St. Joseph, c/o Weston, PA, Sacred Heart. (SCR)

O

O'Connor Ranch, TX, Refugio Co., St. Dennis, c/o Tivoli, TX, Our Lady of Guadalupe. (CC)
Oak Beach, NY, Suffolk Co., c/o Babylon, NY, St. Joseph's. (RVC)
Oak Creek, CO, Routt Co., St. Martin of Tours, c/o Steamboat Springs, CO, Holy Name. (DEN)
Oak Forest, IN, Franklin Co., St. Cecilia of Rome, c/o Batesville, IN, St. Mary–of–the–Rock. (IND)
Oak Grove, MO, Jackson Co., St. Jude the Apostle, c/o Odessa, MO, St. George. (KC)
Oak Ridge, MN, Immaculate Conception Chapel, c/o Rollingstone, MN, Holy Trinity. (WIN)
Oakland, CA, Alameda Co., Mary Help of Christians, c/o Oakland, CA, St. Elizabeth's. (OAK)
Ocala National Forest, FL, Marion Co., St. Joseph of the Forest, c/o Ocala, FL, Our Lady of the Springs. (ORL)
Ocate, NM, Mora Co., c/o Wagon Mound, NM, Santa Clara. (SFE)
Ocean City, MD, Worcester Co., Holy Saviour, c/o Ocean City, MD, St. Mary, Star of the Sea. (WIL)
Ocean Pines, MD, Worcester Co., St. John Neumann, c/o Ocean City, MD, St. Luke and St. Andrew. (WIL)
Oceano, CA, San Luis Obispo Co., St. Francis of Assisi, c/o Arroyo Grande, CA, St. Patrick. (MRY)
Odell, NE, Gage Co., St. Mary's, c/o Wymore, NE, St. Mary's. (LIN)
Odessa, TX, Ector Co., Our Lady of San Juan, c/o Odessa, TX, St. Mary's. (SAN)
Odessa, TX, Ector Co., St. Martin de Porres, c/o Odessa, TX, St. Joseph. (SAN)
Oglala, SD, Shannon Co., Our Lady of Sioux, c/o Pine Ridge, SD, Holy Rosary. (RC)
Ogunquit, ME, York Co., All Saints, c/o Wells, ME, St. Mary. (PRT)
Oilton, TX, Jim Hogg Co., St. Bridget, c/o Hebbronville, TX, Our Lady of Guadalupe. (LAR)
Ojo Armarillo, NM, San Juan Co., Sacred Heart Missionary Cenacle, c/o Waterflow, NM, Sacred Heart. (GLP)
Ojo Caliente, NM, Rio Arriba Co., c/o El Rito, NM, San Juan Nepomuceno. (SFE)
Ojo Feliz, NM, Mora Co., c/o Mora, NM, St. Gertrude. (SFE)
Ojo Sarco, NM, Rio Arriba Co., Santo Tomas, c/o Chimayo, NM, Holy Family. (SFE)
Okemah, OK, Okfuskee Co., St. Teresa, c/o Holdenville, OK, St. Stephen's. (TLS)
Okmulgee, OK, Okmulgee Co., Uganda Martyrs, c/o Okmulgee, OK, St. Anthony's. (TLS)
Okolona, MS, Chickasaw Co., St. Theresa, c/o Aberdeen, MS, St. Francis of Assisi. (JKS)
Okreek, SD, Todd Co., St. Peter, c/o St. Francis, SD, Rosebud Reservation. (RC)
Okreek, SD, Todd Co., St. Peter's, c/o Mission, SD, St. Thomas the Apostle. (RC)
Old River, LA, Natchitoches Parish, St. Anne, c/o Natchez, LA, St. Augustine's. (ALX)
Old Washington, TX, Washington Co., Blessed Virgin Mary Chapel, c/o Somerville, TX, St. Ann's. (AUS)
Olean, NE, Colfax Co., Sacred Heart, c/o Dodge, NE, St. Wenceslaus. (OM)
Olla, LA, La Salle Parish, St. William, c/o Winnfield, LA, Our Lady of Lourdes. (ALX)
Olmito, TX, Cameron Co., Our Heavenly Father, c/o Los Fresnos, TX, St. Cecilia. (BWN)
Olton, TX, Lamb Co., St. Peter, Apostle, c/o Hale Center, TX, St. Theresa's. (LUB)
Olympic Valley, CA, Placer Co., Queen of the Snows, c/o Tahoe City, CA, Corpus Christi. (SAC)
Onarga, IL, Iroquois Co., Our Lady of Guadalupe, c/o Gilman, IL, Immaculate Conception. (JOL)
One Hundred Palms, CA, Riverside Co., San Felipe de Jesus, c/o Coachella, CA, Our Lady of Soledad. (SB)
Oneida, PA, Schuykill Co., St. John the Baptist, c/o Sheppton, PA, St. Joseph. (ALN)
Onset, MA, Plymouth Co., St. Mary Star of the Sea, c/o Buzzards Bay, MA, St. Margaret. (FR)
Oquawka, IL, Henderson Co., St. Andrew, c/o Monmouth, IL, Immaculate Conception. (PEO)
Oracle, AZ, Pinal Co., St. Helen, c/o San Manuel, AZ, St. Bartholomew. (TUC)
Orange Lake, NY, Orange Co., Our Lady of the Lake, c/o Newburgh, NY, St. Patrick. (NY)
Orange Park, FL, Clay Co., Moosehaven Chapel, c/o Orange Park, FL, St. Catherine's. (STA)
Ordway, CO, Crowley Co., St. Peter Chapel, c/o Rocky Ford, CO, St. Peter. (PBL)
Orlando, FL, Orange Co., St. Ignatius Kim Korean Mission, c/o Orlando, FL, St. James Cathedral. (ORL)
Ortiga, PR, Bauta Abajo Co., San Mateo, c/o Villalba, PR, Our Lady Mother of Divine Providence. (PCE)
Orting, WA, Pierce Co., SS. Cosmas and Damian, c/o Sumner, WA, St. Andrew. (SEA)
Ortiz, CO, Conejos Co., San Juan Nepomuceno y San Cayetano, c/o Antonito, CO, Our Lady of Guadalupe. (PBL)
Osceola, MO, St. Clair Co., St. Catherine's, c/o Clinton, MO, Holy Rosary. (KC)
Osceola, NE, Polk Co., St. Mary's, c/o Osceola, NE, St. Vincent Ferrer. (LIN)
Oshkosh, NE, Garden Co., St. Elizabeth, c/o Chappell, NE, St. Joseph's. (GI)
Oslo, MN, Marshall Co., St. Joseph, c/o Warren, MN, SS. Peter and Paul. (CR)
Otis, MA, Berkshire Co., St. Mary of the Lakes, c/o Lee, MA, St. Mary's. (SPR)
Otisco, NY, Onondaga Co., St. Patrick, c/o Tully, NY, St. Leo. (SY)
Oto, IA, Woodbury Co., St. Mary's, c/o Mapleton, IA, St. Mary's. (SC)
Otter Lake, NY, Oneida Co., St. Mary of the Snows, c/o Forestport, NY, St. Patrick. (SY)
Overton, NE, Dawson Co., Holy Rosary, c/o Elm Creek, NE, Immaculate Conception. (GI)
Overton, PA, Sullivan Co., St. Francis Xavier, c/o Dushore, PA, St. Basil's. (SCR)
Overton, TX, Rusk Co., Our Lady Queen of Angels, c/o Kilgore, TX, Christ the King. (TYL)
Owasco, NY, Cayuga Co., St. Ann, c/o Auburn, NY, Sacred Heart. (ROC)
Owenton, KY, Owen Co., St. Edward, c/o Warsaw, KY, St. Joseph. (COV)
Owingsville, KY, Bath Co., St. Julie Billiart, c/o West Liberty, KY, Prince of Peace. (LEX)
Owl's Head, NY, Franklin Co., St. Joseph, c/o Malone, NY, St. Helen. (OG)
Oxford, NE, Furnas Co., St. Michael's, c/o Orleans, NE, St. Mary's. (LIN)
Oxnard, CA, Ventura Co., Christ the King, c/o Oxnard, CA, Our Lady of Guadalupe Parish. (LA)

P

Paauilo, HI, Hawaii Co., St. Joseph, c/o Honokaa, HI, Our Lady of Lourdes. (HON)
Packing Town, OK, Oklahoma Co., Our Lady of Guadalupe, c/o Oklahoma City, OK, Our Lady of Mount Carmel and St. Therese Little Flower. (OKL)
Paducah, TX, Cottle Co., St. Elizabeth, c/o Floydada, TX, St. Mary Magdalen. (LUB)
Pageland, SC, Chesterfield Co., St. Ernest, c/o Cheraw, SC, St. Peter's. (CHR)
Pagosa Junction, CO, Archuleta Co., St. John Baptist, c/o Pagosa Springs, CO, Immaculate Heart of Mary. (PBL)
Paguate, NM, Valencia Co., St. Elizabeth, c/o Laguna, NM, St. Joseph. (GLP)
Painesdale, MI, Houghton Co., Sacred Heart, c/o Chassell, MI, St. Anne. (MAR)
Paisley, OR, Lake Co., St. John the Apostle, c/o Lakeview, OR, St. Patrick's. (BAK)
Palisade, CO, Mesa Co., St. Ann, c/o Grand Junction, CO, Immaculate Heart of Mary. (PBL)
Palisade, NE, Hitchcock Co., Holy Family, c/o Trenton, NE, St. James. (LIN)
Palito Blanco, TX, Jim Wells Co., St. Joseph, c/o San Diego, TX, St. Francis de Paula. (CC)
Palma Escrita, PR, N.S. de Fatima, c/o Las Marias, PR, Immaculate Heart of Mary. (MGZ)
Palma Sola, PR, Villalba Co., Ntra. Sra. de la Asuncion, c/o Canovanas, PR, San Jose. (SJN)
Palmarejo, PR, Coamo Co., Sacred Heart of Mary, c/o Coamo, PR, St. Blase. (PCE)
Palmas, PR, Guayama Co., St. Gerard, c/o Guayama, PR, St. Anthony of Padua. (PCE)
Palmer, MI, Marquette Co., Our Lady Perpetual Help, c/o Negaunee, MI, St. Paul. (MAR)
Palmer, PR, Rio Grande Co., Ntra. Sra. de la Providencia, c/o Palmer, PR, Cristo Rey. (SJN)
Palmetto, LA, St. Landry Parish, St. Thomas, the Apostle, c/o Melville, LA, St. John the Evangelist. (LAF)
Palo Blanco, NM, Colfax Co., c/o Springer, NM, St.

Joseph. (SFE)
Panguitch, UT, Garfield Co., St. Gertrude, c/o Cedar City, UT, Christ the King. (SLC)
Paoli, IN, Orange Co., Our Lord Jesus Christ the King, c/o French Lick, IN, Our Lady of the Springs. (IND)
Parachute, CO, Garfield Co., St. Brendan, c/o Rifle, CO, St. Mary's. (DEN)
Paradise, MI, Chippewa Co., Our Lady of Victory, c/o Newberry, MI, St. Gregory. (MAR)
Paradise Valley, NV, Humboldt Co., St. Alphonsus, c/o Winnemucca, NV, St. Paul. (RNO)
Paraje, NM, Valencia Co., St. Mary Margaret, c/o Laguna, NM, St. Joseph. (GLP)
Paramount, CA, Los Angeles Co., Catholic Korean Community of St. Raphael, c/o Paramount, CA, Our Lady of the Rosary. (LA)
Parcelas Fortuna, PR, Luquillo Co., Ntra. Sra. del Cobre, c/o Luquillo, PR, San Jose. (SJN)
Parcelas Soledad, PR, Sta. Teresita, c/o Mayaguez, PR, Church De El Buen Pastor. (MGZ)
Parcelas Suarez, PR, Loiza Co., Ntra. Sra. Perpetuo Socorro, c/o Loiza, PR, Santiago Apostol, El Mayor. (SJN)
Parcelas Vazquez, PR, Salinas Co., Esp. Santo, c/o Salinas, PR, Our Lady of Monserrat. (PCE)
Parcelas Vieques, PR, Loiza Co., N. Sra. De Fatima, c/o Loiza, PR, Santiago Apostol, El Mayor. (SJN)
Parcelas de Marueno, PR, Ponce Co., San Antonio de Padua, c/o Ponce, PR, La Santisima Trinidad. (PCE)
Paris, MI, Mecosta Co., St. Anne, c/o Reed City, MI, St. Philip Neri. (GR)
Paris, MO, Monroe Co., St. Frances Cabrini, c/o Perry, MO, St. William. (JC)
Parishville, NY, St. Lawrence Co., St. Michael, c/o Colton, NY, St. Patrick. (OG)
Parks, LA, St. Louis, c/o Parks, LA, St. Joseph. (LAF)
Parmelee, SD, Todd Co., St. Agnes, c/o St. Francis, SD, Rosebud Reservation. (RC)
Parque Encuestre, PR, S. Francisco de Asis, c/o Carolina, PR, Cristo Rey. (SJN)
Parsons, TN, Decatur Co., St. Regina, c/o Lexington, TN, St. Andrew. (MEM)
Parsons, WV, Tucker Co., Our Lady of Mercy, c/o Thomas, WV, St. Thomas Aquinas. (WH)
Pastillito, Manzanilla, PR, Juana Diaz Co., Our Lady of Carmel, c/o Ponce, PR, Santa Teresita. (PCE)
Pastillo, PR, Cotopaso Co., Santiago Apostol, c/o Juana Diaz, PR, St. Raymond Nonato. (PCE)
Pastura, NM, Guadalupe Co., c/o Vaughn, NM, St. Mary. (SFE)
Patrick Springs, VA, Patrick, Church of the Risen Lord, c/o Woodlawn, VA, St. Joseph's. (RIC)
Patten, ME, Aroostook Co., St. Paul, c/o Houlton, ME, St. Agnes. (PRT)
Paul Smiths, NY, Franklin Co., St. Gabriel, c/o Lake Clear, NY, St. John in the Wilderness. (OG)
Pava'ia'i, AS, c/o Pago Pago, AS, St. Paul. (SPP)
Pawnee, OK, Pawnee Co., St. John, c/o Cushing, OK, SS. Peter and Paul. (TLS)
Pawnee, TX, Bee Co., Our Lady of Guadalupe, c/o Three Rivers, TX, Sacred Heart. (CC)
Paxton, NE, Keith Co., St. Patrick, c/o Paxton, NE, Sacred Heart. (GI)
Paxton, NE, Keith Co., St. Patrick's Church, c/o Ogallala, NE, St. Luke's. (GI)
Peapack, NJ, Somerset Co., St. Brigid, c/o Far Hills, NJ, St. Elizabeth. (MET)
Pearce, AZ, Cochise Co., St. Francis of Assisi, c/o Pearce, AZ, St. Jude Thaddeus. (TUC)
Pecan Island, LA, Vermilion Parish, Sacred Heart, c/o Abbeville, LA, St. Anne. (LAF)
Peck, MI, Sanilac Co., St. John, c/o Croswell, MI, St. Patrick. (SAG)
Pedro Garcia, PR, Coamo Co., Miraculous Virgin, c/o Coamo, PR, St. Blase. (PCE)
Peerless, MT, Daniels Co., St. Ann, c/o Scobey, MT, St. Philip Bonitus. (GF)
Pejepscot, ME, Topsham Co., St. Andrew, c/o Brunswick, ME, St. John the Baptist. (PRT)
Pelican, AK, c/o Yakutat, AK, St. Ann. (JUN)
Pellejas, PR, Adjuntas Co., Santa Rosa, c/o Adjuntas, PR, St. Joachim. (PCE)
Pembroke, GA, Bryan Co., Holy Cross, c/o Claxton, GA, St. Christopher. (SAV)
Pembroke, ME, Washington Co., St. John the Evangelist, c/o Eastport, ME, St. Joseph. (PRT)
Penitas, TX, Hidalgo Co., St. Anthony, c/o La Joya, TX, Our Lady, Queen of Angels. (BWN)
Pennington, MN, Beltrami Co., St. Charles, c/o Bemidji, MN, St. Philip's. (CR)
Pensacola, FL, Escambia Co., Church of Our Savior, c/o Pensacola, FL, St. Paul. (PT)
Pentwater, MI, Oceana Co., St. Vincent, c/o Hart, MI, St. Joseph's. (GR)
Pep, TX, Hockley Co., St. Philip Neri, c/o Morton, TX, St. Ann. (LUB)
Perrineville, NJ, Monmouth Co., St. Joseph, c/o Englishtown, NJ, Our Lady of Mercy. (TR)
Perrinton, MI, Gratiot Co., St. Martin De Porres, c/o Ithaca, MI, St. Paul the Apostle. (SAG)
Perry Park, KY, Owen Co., Transfiguration, c/o Carrollton, KY, St. John the Evangelist. (COV)
Perryville, KY Boyle Co., St. Mary, c/o Harrodsburg, KY, St. Andrew. (LEX)
Peru, NE, Nemaha Co., St. Clara, c/o Auburn, NE, St. Joseph's. (LIN)
Pescadero, CA, San Mateo Co., St. Anthony, c/o Half Moon Bay, CA, Our Lady of the Pillar. (SFR)
Petaca, NM, Taos Co., c/o El Rito, NM, San Juan Nepomuceno. (SFE)
Petersville, MD, Frederick Co., St. Mary's, c/o Brunswick, MD, St. Francis of Assisi. (BAL)
Petit Mamou, LA, Acadia Parish, St. Jules, c/o Evangeline, LA, St. Joseph. (LAF)
Petrolia, CA, St. Patrick, c/o Ferndale, CA, Church of the Assumption. (SR)
Phelps, KY, Pike Co., Jesus of the Mountains Catholic Church, c/o Pikeville, KY, St. Francis of Assisi. (LEX)
Philadelphia, MS, Neshoba Co., St. Therese, c/o Philadelphia, MS, Holy Rosary. (JKS)
Philadelphia, NY, Jefferson Co., St. Joseph, c/o Evans Mills, NY, St. Mary. (OG)
Philadelphia PA, Central Shrine of the Miraculous Medal, c/o Philadelphia, PA, Immaculate Conception. (PH)
Philadelphia, PA, Philadelphia Co., Holy Redeemer Chinese Church, c/o Philadelphia, PA, St. John the Evangelist. (PH)
Philadelphia, PA, c/o Philadelphia, PA, St. Francis Xavier. (PH)
Phillipsburg, KY, Marion Co., Our Lady of Fatima, c/o Lebanon, KY, Holy Name of Mary. (L)
Philmont, NY, Columbia Co., Pine Haven Home, c/o Philmont, NY, Sacred Heart. (ALB)
Philo, OH, Muskingum Co., St. Ann, c/o Zanesville, OH, St. Thomas Aquinas. (COL)
Phoenix, AZ, Maricopa Co., Our Lady of Fatima, c/o Phoenix, AZ, SS. Anthony and Pius X. (PHX)
Phoenix, AZ, Maricopa Co., Santa Rosa Chapel, c/o Phoenix, AZ, SS. Simon and Jude Cathedral. (PHX)
Phoenix, AZ, Maricopa Co., St. Philip the Deacon Catholic Center, c/o Phoenix, AZ, St. Mark. (PHX)
Phoenix, AZ, Maricopa Co., St. Pius X, c/o Phoenix, AZ, SS. Anthony and Pius X. (PHX)
Picacho, NM, Dona Ana Co., St. Joseph, c/o Ruidoso, NM, St. Eleanor. (LSC)
Pickens, WV, Randolph Co., Sacred Heart, c/o Buckhannon, WV, Holy Rosary. (WH)
Pickwick, TN, Hardin Co., Our Lady of the Lake, c/o Savannah, TN, St. Mary's. (MEM)
Picuris Indian Pueblo, NM, Taos Co., San Lorenzo Mission c/o Penasco, NM, San Antonio de Padua. (SFE)
Piedmont, AL, Calhoun Co., St. Joachim, c/o Jacksonville, AL, St. Charles. (BIR)
Piedra Aguza, PR, Juana Diaz Co., Divine Mercy, c/o Ponce, PR, Santa Teresita. (PCE)
Piedras Blancas, PR, Ntra. Sra. Reina de la Paz, c/o Aguada, PR, St. Francis of Assisi. (MGZ)
Pilar, NM, Taos Co., Nuestra Senora de los Dolores, c/o Dixon, NM, St. Anthony. (SFE)
Pilottown, MD, Cecil Co., St. Patrick, c/o Perryville, MD, Church of the Good Shepherd. (WIL)
Pima, AZ, Graham Co., Pima Mission, c/o Safford, AZ, St. Rose of Lima. (TUC)
Pin Oak TX, Bastrop Co., St. Mary's in Pin Oak, c/o Giddings, TX, St. Margaret. (AUS)
Pine Bluff, AR, Jefferson Co., St. Raphael's, c/o Pine Bluff, AR, St. Peter's. (LR)
Pine Mountain, GA, Harris Co., Christ the King, c/o Columbus, GA, St. Anne. (SAV)
Pine Point, ME, Scarborough Co., St. Jude, c/o Scarborough, ME, St. Maximilian Kolbe. (PRT)
Pine Springs, AZ, Apache Co., St. Rose, c/o Houck, AZ, St. John the Evangelist. (GLP)
Pinedale, CA, Fresno Co., St. Agnes, c/o Fresno, CA, St. Anthony of Padua. (FRS)
Pineville, KY, Bell Co., St. Anthony, c/o Middlesboro, KY, St. Julian. (LEX)
Pineville, WV, Wyoming Co., Holy Cross, c/o Mullens, WV, St. John the Evangelist. (WH)
Pinon, AZ, Navajo Co., St. Mary of the Rosary, c/o Chinle, AZ, Our Lady of Fatima. (GLP)
Pinos Altos, NM, Grant Co., Holy Cross, c/o Silver City, NM, St. Vincent de Paul. (LSC)
Pinos Wells, NM, Torrance Co., c/o Vaughn, NM, St. Mary. (SFE)
Pintada, NM, Guadalupe Co., c/o Santa Rosa, NM, St. Rose of Lima. (SFE)
Piru, CA, Ventura Co., San Salvador, c/o Fillmore, CA, St. Francis of Assisi. (LA)
Pittsburg, OK, Pittsburg Co., St. Edwards, c/o McAlester, OK, St. John. (TLS)
Pittsfield, MA, Berkshire Co., All Souls, c/o Pittsfield, MA, Our Lady of Mt. Carmel. (SPR)
Placita, NM, Taos Co., Nuestra Senora de la Asuncion Mission, c/o Penasco, NM, San Antonio de Padua. (SFE)
Placitas, NM, Sierra Co., San Lorenzo, c/o Truth or Consequences, NM, Our Lady of Perpetual Help. (LSC)
Placitas, NM, Sandoval Co., c/o Bernalillo, NM, Our Lady of Sorrows. (SFE)
Placitas, NM, Rio Arriba Co., c/o El Rito, NM, San Juan Nepomuceno. (SFE)
Plains, TX, Yoakum Co., Sacred Heart, c/o Denver City, TX, St. William. (LUB)
Plainview, SD, Meade Co., Our Lady of Victory, c/o Faith, SD, St. Joseph. (RC)
Plaisance, LA, St. Landry Parish, St. Andrew, c/o Washington, LA, St. Peter. (LAF)
Plasi, NE, Saunders Co., SS. Cyril and Methodius, c/o Prague, NE, St. John's. (LIN)
Playita, PR, Yabucoa Co., San Martin de Porres, c/o San Juan, PR, San Juan Bosco. (SJN)
Playita Cortada, PR, Santa Isabel Co., San Patricio, c/o Santa Isabel, PR, St. James. (PCE)
Plaza, ND, Mountrail Co., Sacred Heart, c/o Parshall, ND, St. Bridget. (BIS)
Plaza Blanca, NM, Rio Arriba Co., c/o Los Ojos, NM, San Jose. (SFE)
Plaza de, NM, Sangro de Christo, c/o Anton Chico, NM, San Jose. (SFE)
Pleasant Valley, PA, Blair Co., Our Lady of the Assumption, c/o Altoona, PA, Our Lady of Mt. Carmel. (ALT)
Pleasanton, NE, Buffalo Co., St. Mary's, c/o Ravenna, NE, Our Lady of Lourdes. (GI)
Pleasantville Park, NY, Westchester Co., Our Lady of Pompeii, c/o Pleasantville, NY, Holy Innocents. (NY)
Plena, PR, Salinas Co., San Jose, c/o Salinas, PR, Our Lady of Monserrat. (PCE)
Plevna, MT, Fallon Co., St. Anthony, c/o Baker, MT, St. John the Evangelist. (GF)
Plum Bayou, AR, Jefferson Co., St. Mary's, c/o Pine Bluff, AR, St. Joseph's. (LR)
Plum Island, MA, St. James, c/o Newburyport, MA, Immaculate Conception. (BO)
Plunketville, OK, McCurtain Co., St. Henry, c/o Idabel, OK, St. Francis De Sales. (TLS)
Plush, OR, Lake Co., St. Thomas, c/o Lakeview, OR, St. Patrick's. (BAK)
Plymouth, CA, Amador Co., St. Mary of the Mountains, c/o Sutter Creek, CA, Immaculate Conception. (SAC)
Pocahontas, PA, Somerset Co., St. Mary's, c/o West Salisbury, PA, St. Michael's. (ALT)
Pocono Summit, PA, Monroe Co., St. Joan of Arc, c/o Mount Pocono, PA, St. Mary of the Mount. (SCR)
Point Comfort, TX, Calhoun Co., St. Ann, c/o Port Lavaca, TX, Our Lady of the Gulf. (VIC)
Pointblank, TX, San Jacinto Co., St. Stephen the Martyr, c/o New Waverly, TX, St. Joseph. (GAL)
Polvadera, NM, Socorro Co., c/o Socorro, NM, San Miguel. (SFE)
Ponce, PR, Ponce Co., La Dolorosa, c/o Ponce, PR, Christ the King. (PCE)
Ponce, PR, Ponce Co., Our Lady of Carmel, c/o Mercedita, PR, Church of the Resurrection. (PCE)
Ponce, PR, Ponce Co., Saint Joseph, c/o Mercedita, PR, Church of the Resurrection. (PCE)
Ponce, PR, Ponce Co., San Miguel de los Santos, c/o Ponce, PR, La Santisima Trinidad. (PCE)
Ponce, PR, Ponce Co., Santa Teresita, c/o Ponce, PR, Christ the King. (PCE)
Pond Creek, OH, Scioto Co., Holy Trinity, c/o West Portsmouth, OH, Our Lady of Sorrows. (COL)
Pond Creek, OK, Grant Co., St. Joseph's, c/o Medford, OK, St. Mary's. (OKL)
Pond Eddy, NY, Sullivan Co., Sacred Heart, c/o Yulan, NY, St. Anthony of Padua. (NY)
Ponderosa, NM, Sandoval Co., c/o Jemez Pueblo, NM, San Diego Indian Missions. (SFE)
Ponsford, MN, Becker Co., St. Theodore, c/o Ogema, MN, Most Holy Redeemer. (CR)
Pontiac, MI, Oakland Co., St. Vincent de Paul, c/o Pontiac, MI, St. Joseph. (DET)
Pontotoc, MS, Pontotoc Co., St. Christopher, c/o New Albany, MS, St. Francis of Assisi. (JKS)
Poplarville, MS, Pearl River Co., St. Joseph, c/o Lumberton, MS, Our Lady of Perpetual Help. (BLX)
Porcupine, ND, Sioux Co., St. James, c/o Fort Yates, ND, St. Peter – Catholic Indian Mission. (BIS)
Porcupine, SD, Shannon Co., St. Paul, c/o Pine Ridge, SD, Church of Christ the King. (RC)
Port Costa, CA, Contra Costa Co., St. Patrick, c/o Crockett, CA, St. Rose of Lima. (OAK)
Port Deposit, MD, Cecil Co., St. Teresa, c/o Perryville, MD, Church of the Good Shepherd. (WIL)
Port Norris, NJ, Cumberland Co., St. Anthony, c/o Cedarville, NJ, St. Michael's. (CAM)
Port O'Connor, TX, Calhoun Co., St. Joseph, c/o Port Lavaca, TX, Our Lady of the Gulf. (VIC)
Port Orford, OR, Curry Co., St. John the Baptist, c/o Bandon, OR, Holy Trinity. (P)
Port St. Joe, FL, Gulf Co., San Blas Catholic Mission, c/o Port St. Joe, FL, St. Joseph. (PT)
Portage, ME, Aroostook Co., Our Lady of the Lakes, c/o Ashland, ME, St. Mark's. (PRT)
Portal, ND, Burke Co., St. John the Baptist, c/o Crosby, ND, St. Patrick. (BIS)

Portales, NM, Roosevelt Co., University Catholic Center, c/o Portales, NM, St. Helen. (SFE)
Porterville, CA, Tulare Co., Our Lady of Guadalupe, c/o Porterville, CA, St. Anne. (FRS)
Portland, PA, Northampton Co., St. Vincent de Paul, c/o Bangor, PA, Our Lady of Good Counsel. (ALN)
Portola Valley, CA, San Mateo Co., Our Lady of the Wayside, c/o Menlo Park, CA, St. Denis. (SFR)
Poston, AZ, Kateri Tekawitha Indian Mission, c/o Parker, AZ, Sacred Heart. (TUC)
Potash, LA, Plaquemines Parish, St. Joseph, c/o Port Sulphur, LA, St. Patrick. (NO)
Potato Creek, SD, Jackson Co., St. Henry, c/o Wanblee, SD, Ignatius Loyola. (RC)
Potawatomi Reservation, KS, Jackson Co., Our Lady of Snows, c/o Perry, KS, St. Theresa's. (KCK)
Potter Place, NH, Merrimack Co., Immaculate Conception, c/o New London, NH, Our Lady of Fatima. (MAN)
Power, MT, Teton Co., Guardian Angel, c/o Dutton, MT, St. William. (HEL)
Powers, OR, Coos Co., St. Bridget, c/o Coquille, OR, Holy Name. (P)
Powers Lake, ND, Burke Co., St. James, c/o Stanley, ND, Queen of the Most Holy Rosary. (BIS)
Prairie Laurent, LA, St. Landry Parish, St. Jules, c/o Leonville, LA, St. Catherine. (LAF)
Prairie Ronde, LA, St. Landry Parish, Sacred Heart, c/o Lawtell, LA, St. Bridget. (LAF)
Prairie View, AR, Logan Co., St. Meinrad, c/o Scranton, AR, St. Ignatius. (LR)
Prentiss, MS, Jefferson Davis Co., St. Mary's, c/o Bassfield, MS, St. Peter. (BLX)
Primghar, IA, O'Brien Co., St. Anthony of Padua, c/o Sutherland, IA, Sacred Heart. (SC)
Primrose, NE, Boone Co., St. Mary, c/o Cedar Rapids, NE, St. Anthony. (OM)
Princeton, CA, Colusa Co., St. Joseph, c/o Colusa, CA, Our Lady of Lourdes. (SAC)
Princeton, MO, Mercer Co., Immaculate Heart of Mary Church, c/o Trenton, MO, St. Joseph's. (KC)
Proctorsville, VT, Windsor Co., Holy Name of Mary, c/o Ludlow, VT, Annunciation of the Blessed Virgin Mary. (BUR)
Promise, SD, Dewey Co., St. Catherine, c/o Eagle Butte, SD, All Saints. (RC)
Promise, SD, Dewey Co., St. Catherine, c/o Eagle Butte, SD, Cheyenne River Reservation. (RC)
Promised Land, PA, Monroe Co., Our Lady of Fatima, c/o Canadensis, PA, St. Bernadette. (SCR)
Prudence Island, RI, Newport Co., Our Lady of Prudence, c/o Bristol, RI, St. Mary. (PRO)
Puako, HI, Hawaii Co., Church of the Ascension, Puako, c/o Kamuela, HI, Church of the Annunciation. (HON)
Pueblitos, NM, Valencia Co., c/o Belen, NM, Our Lady of Belen. (SFE)
Pueblo West, CO, Pueblo Co., St. Paul the Apostle, c/o Pueblo, CO, St. Pius X. (PBL)
Puente Blanco, PR, Catano Co., Santo Domingo De Guzman, c/o Catano, PR, San Francisco de Sales. (SJN)
Puerto Nuevo, PR, San Juan Co., Ntra. Sra. de la Caridad, c/o Puerto Nuevo, PR, San Pablo. (SJN)
Puerto Plata, PR, Jayuya Co., San Juan, c/o Jayuya, PR, Our Lady of Monserrate. (PCE)
Puerto Real, PR, Our Lady of Mt. Carmel, c/o Cabo Rojo, PR, St. Michael. (MGZ)
Puerto de Luna, NM, Guadalupe Co., c/o Santa Rosa, NM, St. Rose of Lima. (SFE)
Pulaski, VA, Davis Co., St. Edward, c/o Wytheville, VA, St. Mary's. (RIC)
Pulguillas, PR, Coamo Co., Christ the King, c/o Coamo, PR, St. Blase. (PCE)
Punta de Agua, NM, Torrance Co., c/o Mountainair, NM, St. Alice. (SFE)
Punto Oro, PR, Ponce Co., Ntra. Sra. del Pilar, c/o Ponce, PR, San Jose Obrero. (PCE)
Puuiki, HI, Maui Co., St. Peter, c/o Hana, HI, St. Mary. (HON)

Q

Quartzsite, AZ, Queen of Peace, c/o Parker, AZ, Sacred Heart. (TUC)
Quebrada Ceiba, PR, Penuelas Co., Milagrosa, c/o Penuelas, PR, St. Joseph. (PCE)
Quebrada Honda, PR, Guayanilla Co., Nuestra Senora, c/o Guayanilla, PR, Immaculate Conception. (PCE)
Quebrada Larga, PR, Sgdo. Corazon de Jesus, c/o Aguada, PR, St. Francis of Assisi. (MGZ)
Quebradas, PR, Yauco Co., Sacred Heart, c/o Yauco, PR, Holy Rosary. (PCE)
Quebradas, PR, Guayanilla Co., San Francisco de Asis, c/o Guayanilla, PR, Immaculate Conception. (PCE)
Queen Creek, AZ, Maricopa Co., Our Lady of Guadalupe, c/o Gilbert, AZ, St. Anne. (PHX)
Queensbury, NY, Warren Co., Our Lady of the Assumption, c/o Lake George, NY, Sacred Heart. (ALB)
Queenstown, MD, Queen Anne Co., St. Peter, c/o Centreville, MD, Our Mother of Sorrows. (WIL)
Quemado, TX, Maverick Co., Our Lady of Guadalupe, c/o Eagle Pass, TX, Our Lady of Refuge. (LAR)
Quimby, IA, Cherokee Co., St. John the Baptist Church, c/o Cherokee, IA, Visitation of the B.V.M.. (SC)
Quinault, WA, Grays Harbor & Jefferson Cos., Our Lady of the Olympics, c/o Hoquiam, WA, Our Lady of Good Help. (SEA)
Quinlan, TX, Hunt Co., Our Lady of Fatima, c/o Greenville, TX, St. William. (DAL)
Quitman, MS, Clarke Co., Good Shepherd, c/o Meridian, MS, St. Patrick. (JKS)

R

Rainsville, NM, Mora Co., c/o Mora, NM, St. Gertrude. (SFE)
Raisin City, CA, Fresno Co., Mission de Guadalupe, c/o Fresno, CA, Our Lady of Mt. Carmel. (FRS)
Raleigh, MS, Smith Co., St. Paul, c/o Magee, MS, St. Stephen. (JKS)
Ralph, SD, Harding Co., St. Isidore, c/o Buffalo, SD, St. Anthony. (RC)
Ralston, PA, Lycoming Co., St. Aloysius, c/o Canton, PA, St. Michael. (SCR)
Ramey–Maleza, PR, Los Santos Reyes, c/o San Antonio, PR, San Jose Obrero. (MGZ)
Ramirez, TX, Duval Co., Our Lady of Guadalupe, c/o Premont, TX, St. Theresa of the Infant Jesus. (CC)
Ranchester, WY, Sheridan Co., St. Edmund, c/o Sheridan, WY, Holy Name. (CHY)
Ranchito, TX, Fisher Co., Sacred Heart, c/o Rotan, TX, St. Joseph. (LUB)
Ranchitos, NM, Rio Arriba Co., c/o San Juan Pueblo, NM, St. John the Baptist. (SFE)
Rancho Murieta, CA, Sacramento Co., c/o Elk Grove, CA, St. Joseph. (SAC)
Randsburg, CA, Kern Co., Santa Barbara, c/o Ridgecrest, CA, St. Ann. (FRS)
Rangeley, ME, Franklin Co., St. Luke, c/o Oquossoc, ME, Our Lady of the Lakes. (PRT)
Rankin, IL, Vermilion County, Holy Trinity, c/o Hoopeston, IL, St. Anthony's. (PEO)
Rankin, TX, Upton Co., St. Thomas, c/o Big Lake, TX, St. Margaret of Cortona. (SAN)
Ransom, IL, La Salle Co., St. Patrick, c/o Marseilles, IL, St. Joseph's. (PEO)
Rapid City, SD, Pennington Co., Indian Health Service, Sioux San Hospital and Pennington County Jail, c/o Rapid City, SD, St. Isaac Jogues. (RC)
Ray, ND, Williams Co., St. Michael, c/o Tioga, ND, St. Thomas. (BIS)
Raymond, CA, Madera Co., St. Anne, c/o Madera, CA, St. Joachim. (FRS)
Raymond, MS, Hinds Co., Immaculate Conception, c/o Clinton, MS, Holy Savior. (JKS)
Raynesford, MT, Judith Basin Co., St. Mary, c/o Belt, MT, St. Mark the Evangelist. (GF)
Reading, PA, Berks Co., Holy Rosary Chapel, c/o Reading, PA, Holy Rosary. (ALN)
Realitos, TX, Duval Co., Sacred Heart, c/o Hebbronville, TX, Our Lady of Guadalupe. (LAR)
Red Feather Lakes, CO, Larimer Co., Our Lady of the Lakes, c/o Fort Collins, CO, St. Joseph. (DEN)
Red Owl, SD, Meade Co., St. Anthony, c/o Faith, SD, St. Joseph. (RC)
Red River, NM, Taos Co., c/o Questa, NM, St. Anthony. (SFE)
Red Scaffold, SD, Ziebach Co., Sacred Heart, c/o Eagle Butte, SD, All Saints. (RC)
Red Scaffold, SD, Ziebach Co., Sacred Heart, c/o Eagle Butte, SD, Cheyenne River Reservation. (RC)
Red Shirt Table, SD, Shannon Co., St. Bernard, c/o Pine Ridge, SD, Holy Rosary. (RC)
Red Springs, NC, Robeson Co., St. Andrew, c/o Lumberton, NC, St. Francis De Sales. (R)
Reddick, IL, Kankakee Co., St. Mary, c/o Cabery, IL, St. Joseph. (JOL)
Redford, TX, Presidio Co., San Jose, c/o Presidio, TX, Santa Teresa de Jesus. (ELP)
Redwood, TX, Guadalupe Co., St. Joseph, c/o Seguin, TX, Our Lady of Guadalupe. (SAT)
Redwood City, CA, San Mateo Co., San Jose Obrero, c/o Menlo Park, CA, St. Anthony. (SFR)
Reeder, ND, Adams Co., Sacred Heart, c/o Hettinger, ND, Holy Trinity. (BIS)
Reeves, LA, Sacred Heart Parish, St. Maurice, c/o Kinder, LA, St. Philip Neri. (LKC)
Reform, AL, Pickens Co., St. Robert, c/o Tuscaloosa, AL, St. Francis of Assisi University Parish. (BIR)
Reidsville, GA, Tattnall Co., St. Andrew the Apostle, c/o Vidalia, GA, Sacred Heart. (SAV)
Reserve, NM, Catron Co., St. Francis, c/o Reserve, NM, Santo Nino. (GLP)
Retsof, NY, Livingston Co., St. Lucy, c/o Leicester, NY, St. Thomas Aquinas. (ROC)
Reva, SD, Harding Co., Our Lady of the Prairie, c/o Buffalo, SD, St. Anthony. (RC)
Rhame, ND, Bowman Co., St. Mel, c/o Rhame, ND, St. Charles. (BIS)
Rhinecliff, NY, Dutchess Co., St. Joseph, c/o Rhinebeck, NY, The Good Shepherd. (NY)
Ricardo, TX, Kleberg Co., Sacred Heart, c/o Vattman, TX, Our Lady of Consolation. (CC)
Rices Landing, PA, Greene Co., Sacred Heart, c/o Carmichael, PA, Our Lady of Consolation. (PIT)
Rich Hill, MO, Bates Co., St. Bridget's, c/o Nevada, MO, St. Mary's. (KC)
Richardton, ND, Stark Co., St. Stephen, c/o Richardton, ND, St. Mary. (BIS)
Richey, MT, Dawson Co., St. Francis de Sales, c/o Circle, MT, St. Francis Xavier. (GF)
Richgrove, CA, Tulare Co., St. Vincent, c/o Delano, CA, St. Mary's of the Miraculous Medal. (FRS)
Richlands, VA, Buchanan Co., St. Joseph, c/o Richlands, VA, St. Mary. (RIC)
Richmond, KY, Madison Co., St. Stephen the Martyr, c/o Richmond, KY, St. Mark. (LEX)
Rico, CO, Dolores Co., Immaculate Heart of Mary Chapel, c/o Cortez, CO, St. Rita. (PBL)
Rideau Settlement, LA, St. Landry Parish, Sacred Heart, c/o Lebeau, LA, Immaculate Conception. (LAF)
Ridgebury, PA, Bradford Co., Our Lady of Perpetual Help, c/o Gillett, PA, St. Ann's. (SCR)
Ridgefield, WA, Clark Co., St. Mary of Guadalupe, c/o Battle Ground, WA, Sacred Heart. (SEA)
Ridgeview, SD, Dewey Co., St. Joseph, c/o Eagle Butte, SD, All Saints. (RC)
Ridgeview, SD, Dewey Co., St. Joseph, c/o Eagle Butte, SD, Cheyenne River Reservation. (RC)
Riegelwood, NC, Columbus Co., Christ the King, c/o Wilmington, NC, St. Mark. (R)
Riley, NM, Socorro Co., c/o Socorro, NM, San Miguel. (SFE)
Rileyville, PA, Wayne Co., St. Joseph, c/o Honesdale, PA, St. John the Evangelist. (SCR)
Rimersburg, PA, Clarion Co., St. Richard, c/o East Brady, PA, St. Eusebius. (E)
Rincon, NM, Dona Ana Co., Our Lady of All Nations, c/o Hatch, NM, Our Lord of Mercy. (LSC)
Ringgold, LA, Bienville Parish, Blessed Sacrament, c/o Minden, LA, St. Paul. (SHP)
Rio Bravo, TX, Webb Co., Santa Monica Mission, c/o Rio Bravo, TX, Santa Rita de Casia Independent Mission. (LAR)
Rio Canas Abajo, PR, Juana Diaz Co., San Judas, c/o Juana Diaz, PR, St. Raymond Nonato. (PCE)
Rio Chiquito, NM, Rio Arriba Co., Sagrado Corazon, c/o Chimayo, NM, Holy Family. (SFE)
Rio Chiquito, PR, Ponce Co., Nino Jesus de Praga, c/o Ponce, PR, Christ the King. (PCE)
Rio Chiquito, PR, Ponce Co., San Vicente, c/o Ponce, PR, San Vicente–Cantera. (PCE)
Rio Grande, PR, Rio Grande Co., La Milagrosa, c/o Rio Grande, PR, Nuestra Senora del Carmen. (SJN)
Rio Grande, PR, Rio Grande Co., Ntra. Sra. de Guadalupe, c/o Rio Grande, PR, Nuestra Senora del Carmen. (SJN)
Rio Grande, PR, Perpetuo Socorro, c/o Aguada, PR, St. Francis of Assisi. (MGZ)
Rio Grande, PR, Rio Grande Co., Sagrado Corazon de Jesus, c/o Rio Grande, PR, Nuestra Senora del Carmen. (SJN)
Rio Grande–Playa, PR, Ntra. Sra. del Carmen, c/o Aguada, PR, St. Francis of Assisi. (MGZ)
Rio Hondo, PR, San Carlos y San Antonio, c/o Mayaguez, PR, Sacred Heart. (MGZ)
Rio Jueyes, Coamo, PR, Coamo Co., Our Lady of Lourdes, c/o Coamo, PR, San Antonio de Padua. (PCE)
Rio Loco, PR, , Yauco, Our Lady of Montserrat, c/o Yauco, PR, Santo Domingo de Guzman. (PCE)
Rio Lucio, NM, Taos Co., Sagrado Corazon Mission, c/o Penasco, NM, San Antonio de Padua. (SFE)
Rio Piedras, PR, San Juan Co., N. Sra. Reina de la Paz, c/o San Juan, PR, Santisimo Salvador. (SJN)
Rio Piedras, PR, San Juan Co., N. Sra. del Rosario, c/o Trujillo Alto, PR, San Pio X. (SJN)
Rio Piedras, PR, San Juan Co., San Jose de Calasanz, c/o San Juan, PR, Santisimo Salvador. (SJN)
Rio Piedras, PR, San Juan Co., Santa Teresita de Nino Jesus, c/o San Juan, PR, Nuestra Senora del Pilar. (SJN)
Rio Rancho, NM, Sandoval Co., St. John Vianney, c/o Rio Rancho, NM, St. Thomas Aquinas. (SFE)
Rio Verde, AZ, Maricopa Co., St. Dominic, c/o Fountain Hills, AZ, Ascension. (PHX)
Rio en Medio, NM, Sante Fe Co., Our Lady of Sorrows, c/o Santa Fe, NM, Our Lady of Guadalupe. (SFE)
Rios, TX, Duval Co., St. Francis of Assisi, c/o Premont, TX, St. Theresa of the Infant Jesus. (CC)
Ripley, CA, Riverside Co., Nuestra Senora de Guadalupe, c/o Blythe, CA, St. Joan of Arc. (SB)
Ripley, NY, Chautauqua Co., St. Thomas More, c/o Westfield, NY, St. James Major. (BUF)
Ripley, TN, Lauderdale Co., Ave Maria, c/o Covington, TN, St. Alphonsus. (MEM)
Rising Sun, MD, Cecil Co., St. Agnes, c/o Perryville, MD, Church of the Good Shepherd. (WIL)
River Forest, IL, St. Thomas Mission, c/o Chicago, IL, Archdiocese of Chicago's Joseph Cardinal Bernardin

Archives and Records Center. (CHI)
Riverdale, CA, Fresno Co., Our Lady of the Assumption, c/o Riverdale, CA, St. Ann. (FRS)
Riverside, CA, Riverside Co., Our Lady of Guadalupe, c/o Riverside, CA, St. Thomas the Apostle. (SB)
Riverside, MT, McCone Co., Sacred Heart, c/o Wolf Point, MT, Immaculate Conception. (GF)
Riverton, NE, Franklin Co., St. Catherine's, c/o Red Cloud, NE, Sacred Heart. (LIN)
Riviera, TX, Kleberg Co., Our Lady of Guadalupe, c/o Vattman, TX, Our Lady of Consolation. (CC)
Roanoke, AL, Randolph Co., Immaculate Conception, c/o Lanett, AL, Holy Family. (BIR)
Robbins, IL, Cook Co., St. Peter Claver, c/o Blue Island, IL, St. Benedict. (CHI)
Robbinsville, NC, Graham Co., Prince of Peace, c/o Andrews, NC, Holy Redeemer. (CHL)
Robert Lee, TX, Coke Co., Our Lady of Guadalupe, c/o Ballinger, TX, St. Mary Star of the Sea. (SAN)
Roberts, IL, Ford Co., Immaculate Conception, c/o Piper City, IL, St. Peter. (JOL)
Robinson Township, MI, Ottawa Co., St. Anthony, c/o Grand Haven, MI, St. Patrick's. (GR)
Robstown, TX, Nueces Co., St. Mary, c/o Robstown, TX, St. Anthony. (CC)
Robstown, TX, St. Vivian, c/o Corpus Christi, TX, Our Lady of Mount Carmel. (CC)
Roby, MO, Texas Co., St. Vincent de Paul, c/o Houston, MO, St. Mark. (SPC)
Rochester, VT, Windsor Co., St. Elizabeth, c/o Bethel, VT, St. Anthony. (BUR)
Rociada Abajo, NM, San Miguel Co., Santo Nino, c/o Las Vegas, NM, Our Lady of Sorrows Church. (SFE)
Rock City Falls, NY, Saratoga Co., St. Paul, c/o Greenfield Center, NY, St. Joseph. (ALB)
Rock Hall, MD, Kent Co., St. John, c/o Chestertown, MD, Sacred Heart. (WIL)
Rock Point, MD, Charles Co., St. Francis de Sales, c/o Newburg, MD, Holy Ghost. (WDC)
Rockvale, CO, Fremont Co., St. Patrick, c/o Florence, CO, St. Benedict. (PBL)
Rockville, MD, Montgomery Co., Our Lady of China, c/o Rockville, MD, St. Mary. (WDC)
Rockville, NE, Sherman Co., St. Mary's, c/o Ravenna, NE, Our Lady of Lourdes. (GI)
Rockwood, ME, Somerset Co., St. Joseph's, c/o Greenville, ME, Holy Family. (PRT)
Rocky Boys Indian Reservation, MT, Hill Co., St. Mary, c/o Box Elder, MT, St. Margaret Mary. (GF)
Rocky Mount, NC, Nash & Edgecombe Cos., Immaculate Conception, c/o Rocky Mount, NC, Our Lady of Perpetual Help. (R)
Rodarte, NM, Taos Co., Santa Barbara Mission, c/o Penasco, NM, San Antonio de Padua. (SFE)
Rodeo, NM, Hidalgo Co., San Felipe, c/o Lordsburg, NM, St. Joseph. (LSC)
Rogers, TX, Bell Co., St. Matthew, c/o Temple, TX, St. Luke's. (AUS)
Roland, OK, Sequoyah Co., Blessed Kateri Tekakwitha, c/o Sallisaw, OK, St. Francis Xavier. (TLS)
Romeo, CO, Conejos Co., Our Lady of the Immaculate Conception, c/o Capulin, CO, St. Joseph. (PBL)
Romero, PR, Villalba Co., Sagrado Corazon, c/o Villalba, PR, Our Lady of Mt. Carmel. (PCE)
Roosevelt Lake, AZ, Gila Co., St. Theresa, c/o Miami, AZ, Our Lady of the Blessed Sacrament. (TUC)
Ropesville, TX, Hockley Co., San Francisco de Asis, c/o Brownfield, TX, St. Anthony's. (LUB)
Rosario, PR, Nuestra Senora del Rosario, c/o Rosario, PR, Rosary. (MGZ)
Rosario, PR, San Jose, c/o Mayaguez, PR, Sacred Heart. (MGZ)
Roscoe, IL, Winnebago Co., Church of the Holy Spirit, c/o South Beloit, IL, St. Peter. (RCK)
Roscoe, NY, Sullivan Co., Gate of Heaven, c/o Livingston Manor, NY, St. Aloysius. (NY)
Roscoe, TX, Nolan Co., St. Albert the Great, c/o Sweetwater, TX, Immaculate Heart of Mary. (SAN)
Rosebud, SD, Todd Co., St. Bridget, c/o St. Francis, SD, Rosebud Reservation. (RC)
Roseton, NY, Orange Co., Our Lady of Mercy, c/o Marlboro, NY, St. Mary. (NY)
Rosita, TX, Starr Co., Santa Rosa de Lima, c/o Roma, TX, Sacred Heart. (BWN)
Rossie, NY, St. Lawrence Co., St. Patrick, c/o Morristown, NY, St. Peter. (OG)
Rotten Bayou, MS, Harrison Co., St. William, c/o Pass Christian, MS, The Catholic Church in DeLisle. (BLX)
Roulette, PA, Potter Co., St. Mary, c/o Port Allegany, PA, St. Gabriel the Archangel. (E)
Round Mountain, NV, Nye Co., St. Barbara, c/o Tonopah, NV, St. Patrick. (LAV)
Round Rock, AZ, Apache Co., Our Lady of Guadalupe, c/o Lukachukai, AZ, St. Isabel. (GLP)
Rouseville, PA, Venango Co., St. Venantius, c/o Oil City, PA, Assumption of the Blessed Virgin Mary. (E)
Rowe, NM, San Miguel Co., c/o Pecos, NM, St. Anthony. (SFE)
Roxbury, CT, Litchfield Co., St. Patrick's, c/o Washington Depot, CT, Our Lady of Perpetual Help. (HRT)
Roxbury, NY, Delaware Co., Our Lady of Good Counsel, c/o Margaretville, NY, Sacred Heart. (ALB)
Roxbury Pond ME, Oxford Co., St. Mary's Chapel, c/o Rumford, ME, St. Athanasius–St. John. (PRT)
Rudyard, MT, Hill Co., Holy Family Center, c/o Chester, MT, St. Mary's. (GF)
Rush Springs, OK, Grady Co., St. Francis of Assisi, c/o Duncan, OK, Assumption. (OKL)
Rushville, NE, Sheridan Co., Immaculate Conception, c/o Gordon, NE, St. Leo's. (GI)
Rushville, NY, Ontario Co., St. Mary, c/o Penn Yan, NY, St. Theresa. (ROC)
Rusk, TX, Cherokee Co., Sacred Heart, c/o Jacksonville, TX, Our Lady of Sorrows. (TYL)
Russell, NY, St. Lawrence Co., St. Rene Goupil, c/o De Kalb Junction, NY, St. Henry. (OG)
Russellville, AR, Pope Co., St. Leo The Great, c/o Russellville, AR, St. John's. (LR)
Russian Mission, AK, Wade Hampton Co., Our Lady of Guadalupe Russian Mission, c/o Marshall, AK, Immaculate Heart of Mary. (FBK)
Rutherford, CA, Holy Family, c/o Yountville, CA, St. Joan of Arc. (SR)
Ryan, OK, Jefferson Co., San Jose, c/o Duncan, OK, Assumption. (OKL)
Rye, CO, Pueblo Co., St. Aloysius, c/o Pueblo, CO, Holy Family. (PBL)
Ryegate, MT, Golden Valley Co., St Mathias, c/o Roundup, MT, St. Benedict's. (GF)

S

Sa'ilele, AS c/o Pago Pago, AS, Church of St. Peter and Paul. (SPP)
Sabana, PR, San Jose, c/o Aguada, PR, St. Francis of Assisi. (MGZ)
Sabana Eneas, PR, San Judas Tadeo, c/o San German, PR, San German de Auxerre. (MGZ)
Sabana Llana, PR, Salinas Co., Perpetuo Socorro, c/o Salinas, PR, Our Lady of Monserrat. (PCE)
Sabin, MN, Clay Co., St. Cecilia, c/o Barnesville, MN, Assumption. (CR)
Sabinal, NM, Socorro Co., San Antonio c/o La Joya, NM, Our Lady of Sorrows. (SFE)
Sabinoso, NM, San Miguel Co., c/o Roy, NM, Holy Family–St. Joseph. (SFE)
Sacaton, AZ, Pinal Co., St. Anthony, c/o Sacaton, AZ, St. Peter's. (PHX)
Sacaton Flats, AZ, Pinal Co., Our Lady of Victory, c/o Sacaton, AZ, St. Peter's. (PHX)
Saco, MT Phillips Co., St. Francis of Assisi, c/o Malta, MT, St. Mary's. (GF)
Saegertown, PA, Crawford Co., St. Bernadette, c/o Meadville, PA, St. Agatha. (E)
Sagamore, MA, Barnstable Co., St. Theresa, c/o East Sandwich, MA, Corpus Christi. (FR)
Saguache, CO, Saguache Co., St. Agnes, c/o Center, CO, St. Francis Jerome. (PBL)
Saipan, MP, Korean Catholic Community, c/o Saipan, MP, Cathedral of Our Lady of Mt. Carmel. (CHK)
Salem, IN, Washington Co., St. Patrick, c/o Scottsburg, IN, American Martyrs. (IND)
Salem, OR, Marion Co., San Jose, c/o Salem, OR, St. Joseph. (P)
Salem Township, IL, Holy Ascension, c/o Dearborn, MI, St. Michael's. (STN)
Saliente, PR, Jayuya Co., San Francisco, c/o Jayuya, PR, Our Lady of Monserrate. (PCE)
Salinas–Providencia, PR, Guanica Co., Divina Providencia, c/o Ensenada, PR, Sacred Heart. (PCE)
Salineno, TX, Starr Co., St. Joseph, c/o Roma, TX, Our Lady of Refuge. (BWN)
Salon Usos Multiples–Urb. April Gardens, PR, Las Piedras, c/o Las Piedras, PR, Inmaculada Concepcion. (CGS)
Salt River Indian, AZ, Maricopa Co., St. Francis, c/o Tempe, AZ, St. Margaret. (PHX)
Saltillo, MS, Lee Co., St. Thomas Aquinas, c/o Tupelo, MS, St. James. (JKS)
Salto, PR, Jayuya Co., Santos Reyes, c/o Jayuya, PR, Our Lady of Monserrate. (PCE)
Salton City, CA, Imperial Co., c/o Borrego Springs, CA, St. Richard. (SD)
San Acacio, CO, Costilla Co., San Acacio, c/o San Luis, CO, Sangre de Cristo. (PBL)
San Antonio, CO, Conejos Co., San Antonio de Padua, c/o Antonito, CO, Our Lady of Guadalupe. (PBL)
San Antonio, NM, San Miguel Co., Los Vigiles (Our Lady of Refuge), c/o Las Vegas, NM, Immaculate Conception. (SFE)
San Antonio, NM, Socorro Co., c/o Socorro, NM, San Miguel. (SFE)
San Antonio, NM, Bernalillo Co., c/o Tijeras, NM, Holy Child. (SFE)
San Antonio, TX, Bexar Co., Purisima Concepcion, c/o San Antonio, TX, St. Cecilia. (SAT)
San Antonio, TX, Bexar Co., San Francesco di Paola (Italian), c/o San Antonio, TX, Cathedral of San Fernando. (SAT)
San Antonio, TX, Bexar Co., Santa Maria Goretti, c/o San Antonio, TX, St. Jude. (SAT)
San Antonio, TX, Bexar Co., St. Catherine, c/o San Antonio, TX, St. Margaret Mary. (SAT)
San Antonio, TX, Bexar Co., St. Frances Cabrini, c/o San Antonio, TX, San Francisco de la Espada. (SAT)
San Ardo, CA, Monterey Co., Our Lady of Ransom, c/o San Miguel, CA, San Miguel. (MRY)
San Benito, TX, Cameron Co., St. Joseph, c/o San Benito, TX, Our Lady, Queen of the Universe. (BWN)
San Cristobal, NM, Taos Co., San Cristobal, c/o Arroyo Seco, NM, La Santisima Trinidad. (SFE)
San Diego, CA, San Diego Co., SDSU Newman Center, c/o San Diego, CA, Blessed Sacrament. (SD)
San Diego, PR, Coamo Co., San Diego, c/o Coamo, PR, St. Blase. (PCE)
San Felipe, NM, Sandoval Co., Indian Pueblo, c/o Pena Blanca, NM, Nuestra Senora De Guadalupe. (SFE)
San Felipe, PR, Salinas Co., St. Martin de Porres, c/o Aguirre, PR, Sacred Heart. (PCE)
San Felipe, TX, Austin Co., c/o Harlingen, TX, Our Lady of the Assumption. (BWN)
San Fernando, PR, San Juan Co., Monacillos, c/o Rio Piedras, PR, Inmaculado Corazon de Maria. (SJN)
San Francisco, CA, San Francisco Co., All Hallows Chapel, c/o San Francisco, CA, Our Lady of Lourdes. (SFR)
San Francisco, CO, Costilla Co., St. Francis of Assisi, c/o San Luis, CO, Sangre de Cristo. (PBL)
San Ignacio, NM, Guadalupe Co., c/o Santa Rosa, NM, St. Rose of Lima. (SFE)
San Ignacio, TX, Zapata Co., St. Ignatius, c/o Zapata, TX, Our Lady of Lourdes. (LAR)
San Isidro, CO, Costilla Co., St. Isidro, c/o San Luis, CO, Sangre de Cristo. (PBL)
San Isidro, NM, Dona Ana Co., San Isidro, c/o Dona Ana, NM, Our Lady of the Purification. (LSC)
San Isidro Norte, NM, San Miguel Co., c/o Ribera, NM, San Miguel Del Vado. (SFE)
San Isidro Sur, NM, San Miguel Co., c/o Ribera, NM, San Miguel Del Vado. (SFE)
San Joaquin, CA, Fresno Co., St. Vincent de Paul, c/o Tranquillity, CA, St. Paul. (FRS)
San Jon, NM, Quay Co., Our Lady of Guadalupe, c/o Tucumcari, NM, St. Anne. (SFE)
San Jose, AZ, Graham Co., San Jose, c/o Solomon, AZ, Our Lady of Guadalupe. (TUC)
San Jose, NM, Sierra Co., Arrey, c/o Garfield, NM, San Isidro. (LSC)
San Jose, NM, San Miguel Co., c/o Ribera, NM, San Miguel Del Vado. (SFE)
San Jose, PR, Minillas, c/o Bayamon, PR, Nuestra Senora del Rosario. (SJN)
San Jose Ranch, TX, Duval Co., St. Joseph, c/o Benavides, TX, St. Rose of Lima. (CC)
San Juan, NM, Grant Co., San Juan, c/o Hurley, NM, Infant Jesus. (LSC)
San Juan, NM, San Miguel Co., c/o Ribera, NM, San Miguel Del Vado. (SFE)
San Juan, PR, Capilla San Conrado, c/o San Juan, PR, San Francisco de Asis. (SJN)
San Juan, PR, San Juan Co., La Milagrosa, c/o San Juan, PR, San Juan M. Vianney. (SJN)
San Juan, PR, Bo. Caimito, Medalla Milagrosa, c/o San Juan, PR, Santa Catalina Laboure. (SJN)
San Juan, PR, Ntra. Sra. del Rosario, c/o San Juan, PR, San Juan Bosco. (SJN)
San Juan, PR, Nuestra Senora del Buen Consejo, c/o San Juan, PR, San Antonio. (SJN)
San Juan, PR, San Martin de Porres, Bitumul, c/o San Juan, PR, San Jose Obrero. (SJN)
San Juan, PR, Bo. Caimito, San Pablo, c/o San Juan, PR, Santa Catalina Laboure. (SJN)
San Judas Tadeo, PR, Playuelas, c/o Aguadilla, PR, La Milagrosa. (MGZ)
San Lorenzo, NM, Black Range Station, c/o Bayard, NM, Our Lady of Fatima. (LSC)
San Lorenzo, NM, Grant Co., San Lorenzo, c/o Bayard, NM, Our Lady of Fatima. (LSC)
San Lucas, CA, Monterey Co., St. Luke, c/o King City, CA, St. John the Baptist. (MRY)
San Luis, NM, Sandoval Co., Saint Aloysius Gonzaga, c/o Cuba, NM, Immaculate Conception. (GLP)
San Luis Rey, CA, San Diego Co., San Luis Rey de Francia, c/o Oceanside, CA, Mission San Luis Rey. (SD)
San Manuel, TX, Hidalgo Co., St. Anne, c/o Edinburg, TX, St. Joseph the Worker. (BWN)
San Marcos, CA, San Diego Co., c/o San Marcos, CA, St. Mark. (SD)
San Marcos, TX, Hays Co., Guadalupe Chapel, c/o San Marcos, TX, St. John the Evangelist. (AUS)
San Martin, PR, San Juan Co., N. Sra. del Perpetuo Socorro, c/o Luquillo, PR, Madre del Redentor. (SJN)
San Patricio, NM, Lincoln Co., St. Jude Thaddeus, c/o Ruidoso, NM, St. Eleanor. (LSC)
San Pedro, CO, Costilla Co., SS. Peter and Paul, c/o San Luis, CO, Sangre de Cristo. (PBL)
San Pedro, TX, Cameron Co., San Pedro, c/o Brownsville, TX, Our Lady of Good Counsel. (BWN)
San Perlita, TX, Willacy Co., St. Anne, Mother of Mary,

c/o Raymondville, TX, St. Anthony. (BWN)
San Rafael, CA, Marin Co., St. Sylvester, c/o San Rafael, CA, St. Raphael. (SFR)
San Rafael, CO, Conejos Co., San Pedro y San Rafael, c/o Antonito, CO, Our Lady of Guadalupe. (PBL)
San Simon, AZ, Cochise Co., Our Lady of Perpetual Help, c/o Willcox, AZ, Sacred Heart. (TUC)
San Ysidro, NM, Sandoval Co., c/o Jemez Pueblo, NM, San Diego Indian Missions. (SFE)
Sand Springs, IA, Immaculate Conception, c/o Hopkinton, IA, St. Luke. (DUB)
Sandersville, GA, Washington Co., St. William, c/o Dublin, GA, Immaculate Conception. (SAV)
Sandia Indian Pueblo, NM, Sandoval Co., c/o Bernalillo, NM, Our Lady of Sorrows. (SFE)
Sandy Valley, NV, Clark Co., St. Catherine of Siena, c/o Las Vegas, NV, Christ the King. (LAV)
Sangerville, ME, Piscataquis Co., Holy Family, c/o Dover–Foxcroft, ME, St. Thomas. (PRT)
Santa Ana, NM, Sandoval Co., c/o Jemez Pueblo, NM, San Diego Indian Missions. (SFE)
Santa Ana, PR, Coamo Co., Santa Ana, c/o Coamo, PR, St. Blase. (PCE)
Santa Ana, PR, San Juan Co., Trastalleres, c/o San Juan, PR, Ntra. Sra. de la Monserrate. (SJN)
Santa Catalina, PR, Coamo Co., Miraculous Virgin, c/o Coamo, PR, St. Blase. (PCE)
Santa Catalina, PR, Coama Co., Sacred Heart, c/o Coamo, PR, St. Blase. (PCE)
Santa Clara, NY, St. Peter, c/o St. Regis Falls, NY, St. Ann. (OG)
Santa Cruz, AZ, Pinal Co., St. Catherine, c/o Laveen, AZ, St. John The Baptist. (PHX)
Santa Fe, NM, Santa Fe Co., Our Lady of Guadalupe, c/o Santa Fe, NM, Cristo Rey. (SFE)
Santa Maria, AZ, Maricopa Co., Our Lady of Guadalupe, c/o Cashion, AZ, St. William. (PHX)
Santa Maria, TX, Cameron Co., St. Margaret Ann, c/o Progreso, TX, Holy Spirit. (BWN)
Santa Monica, TX, Willacy Co., Santa Monica, c/o Lyford, TX, Prince of Peace. (BWN)
Santa Rita, NM, San Miguel Co., c/o Ribera, NM, San Miguel Del Vado. (SFE)
Santa Rosa, PR, Jardines de Carolina, c/o Carolina, PR, San Valentin. (SJN)
Santan, AZ, Pinal Co., St. Anne, c/o Sacaton, AZ, St. Peter's. (PHX)
Santee, SC, Orangeburg Co., Santee Catholic Community, c/o Summerton, SC, St. Mary's. (CHR)
Santiago–Talco, NM, Mora Co., c/o Mora, NM, St. Gertrude. (SFE)
Santo Domingo, NM, Sandoval Co., Indian Pueblo, c/o Pena Blanca, NM, Nuestra Senora De Guadalupe. (SFE)
Santurce, PR, Mayaguez Co., La Milagrosa, c/o San Juan, PR, San Juan Bosco. (SJN)
Sapello, NM, San Miguel Co., Our Lady of Guadalupe, c/o Las Vegas, NM, Our Lady of Sorrows Church. (SFE)
Sapphire Valley, NC, Jackson Co., St. Jude, c/o Brevard, NC, Sacred Heart. (CHL)
Saragosa, TX, Reeves Co., Our Lady of Guadalupe, c/o Balmorhea, TX, Christ the King. (ELP)
Saratoga Lake, NY, Saratoga Co., St. Isaac Jogues, c/o Stillwater, NY, St. Peter the Apostle. (ALB)
Sardis, MS, Panola Co., St. John the Baptist, c/o Batesville, MS, St. Mary. (JKS)
Sargent, NE, Custer Co., Assumption of the Blessed Virgin Mary, c/o Ord, NE, Our Lady of Perpetual Help. (GI)
Sargent, NE, Custer Co., Assumption of the Blessed Virgin Mary, c/o Burwell, NE, Sacred Heart. (GI)
Sartwell, PA, McKean Co., St. Mary, c/o Eldred, PA, St. Raphael. (E)
Saspamco, TX, Bexar Co., Our Lady of Perpetual Help, c/o Elmendorf, TX, St. Anthony. (SAT)
Satin, TX, Satin Falls Co., Santa Rita, c/o Waco, TX, St. Francis on the Brazos. (AUS)
Savage, MT, Richland Co., St. Michael, c/o Sidney, MT, St. Matthew's. (GF)
Savannah, NY, Wayne Co., St. Patrick, c/o Clyde, NY, St. John the Evangelist. (ROC)
Savoy, LA, St. Landry Parish, St. Thomas, c/o Church Point, LA, St. Edward. (LAF)
Sawmill, AZ, Apache Co., St. Francis Mission, c/o Navajo, NM, St. Berard. (GLP)
Sawyer, MI, Berrien Co., St. Agnes, c/o Three Oaks, MI, St. Mary of the Assumption. (KAL)
Sawyer's Bar, CA, Siskiyou Co., St. Joseph, c/o Fort Jones, CA, Sacred Heart. (SAC)
Saxtons River, VT, Windham Co., St. Edmund of Canterbury, c/o Putney, VT, Our Lady of Mercy. (BUR)
Sayre, OK, Beckham Co., Queen of All Saints, c/o Elk City, OK, St. Matthew's. (OKL)
Schenectady, NY, Schenectady Co., St. Teresa Carmelite Monastery, c/o Schenectady, NY, St. Luke. (ALB)
Schenevus, NY, Otsego Co., St. Mary, c/o Worcester, NY, St. Joseph. (ALB)
Schoolcraft, NE, Madison Co., St. Francis de Sales, c/o Battle Creek, NE, St. Patrick's. (OM)
Scio, NY, Allegany Co., St. Joseph, c/o Belmont, NY, St. Mary. (BUF)
Scotia, NE, Greeley Co., St. Patrick, c/o Greeley, NE, Sacred Heart. (GI)
Scotland, CT, Windham Co., St. Margaret, c/o Willimantic, CT, St. Joseph. (NOR)
Scotland Neck, NC, Halifax Co., St. Anne, c/o Ahoskie, NC, St. Charles Borromeo. (R)
Scotts Mills, OR, Marion Co., Holy Rosary, c/o Mt. Angel, OR, St. Mary. (P)
Scranton, ND, Bowman Co., Sacred Heart, c/o Hettinger, ND, Holy Trinity. (BIS)
Scriba, NY, Oswego Co., Sacred Heart, c/o Oswego, NY, St. Peter. (SY)
Scribner, NE, Dodge Co., St. Lawrence, c/o Hooper, NE, St. Rose of Lima. (OM)
Seabrook Beach, NH, Rockingham Co., St. Elizabeth's of Hungary, c/o Hampton, NH, Our Lady of the Miraculous Medal. (MAN)
Seadrift, TX, Calhoun Co., St. Patrick, c/o Port Lavaca, TX, Our Lady of the Gulf. (VIC)
Seagraves, TX, Gaines Co., St. Paul's, c/o Seminole, TX, St. James. (LUB)
Seama, NM, Valencia Co., St. Anne, c/o Laguna, NM, St. Joseph. (GLP)
Seatonville, IL, Bureau Co., St. Gertrude, c/o Ladd, IL, St. Benedict's. (PEO)
Sebastian, TX, Willacy Co., St. Martin, c/o Lyford, TX, Prince of Peace. (BWN)
Seco Mines, TX, Maverick Co., Our Lady of Lourdes, c/o Eagle Pass, TX, Our Lady of Refuge. (LAR)
Sector La Cucharilla, PR, Immaculada Concepcion, c/o Catano, PR, San Francisco de Sales. (SJN)
Sector Punta Brava, PR, Convento Missioneras de La Caridad, c/o Bayamon, PR, Santa Teresa de Jesus. (SJN)
Sector San Patricio, PR, Ponce Co., La Inmaculada, c/o Ponce, PR, San Vicente–Cantera. (PCE)
Sector Santo Domingo, PR, Penuelas Co., Santo Domingo de Guzman, c/o San Juan, PR, Corpus Christi. (SJN)
Sedillo, NM, Bernalillo Co., San Isidro, c/o Tijeras, NM, Holy Child. (SFE)
Seeley, CA, Imperial Co., Holy Spirit, c/o Imperial, CA, St. Anthony of Padua. (SD)
Seeley Lake, MT, Missoula Co., Living Water, c/o Helmville, MT, St. Thomas. (HEL)
Segundo, CO, Las Animas Co., St. Ignatius, c/o Trinidad, CO, Most Holy Trinity, Trinidad Area Catholic Community (Trinidad Cluster). (PBL)
Seiling, OK, Dewey Co., St. Thomas, c/o Okeene, OK, St. Anthony's. (OKL)
Seldovia, AK, Kenai Peninsula Borough, St. James the Apostle, c/o Homer, AK, St. John the Baptist. (ANC)
Selinsgrove, PA, Snyder Co., Selinsgrove Center, c/o Selinsgrove, PA, St. Pius X. (HBG)
Selinsgrove, PA, Snyder Co., Snyder County Prison, c/o Selinsgrove, PA, St. Pius X. (HBG)
Selinsgrove, PA, Snyder Co., Susquehanna University, c/o Selinsgrove, PA, St. Pius X. (HBG)
Sena, NM, San Miguel Co., c/o Villanueva, NM, Our Lady of Guadalupe. (SFE)
Seneca, OR, Grant Co., St. Charles, c/o John Day, OR, St. Elizabeth's. (BAK)
Seneca, SC, Oconee Co., St. Paul the Apostle, c/o Clemson, SC, St. Andrew. (CHR)
Servilleta, NM, Taos Co., c/o El Rito, NM, San Juan Nepomuceno. (SFE)
Seville–Creston, OH, Medina Co., Jesus Emmanuel, c/o Litchfield, OH, Our Lady Help of Christians Parish. (CLV)
Shafter, TX, Presidio Co., Sgdo. Corazon de Jesus, c/o Presidio, TX, Santa Teresa de Jesus. (ELP)
Shamrock, TX, Wheeler Co., St. Patrick, c/o Wellington, TX, Our Mother of Mercy. (AMA)
Sharon, GA, Talifero Co., Purification, c/o Washington, GA, St. Joseph's. (ATL)
Sharon Springs, NY, Schoharie Co., St. Mary, c/o Cobleskill, NY, St. Vincent de Paul. (ALB)
Shasta Lake City, CA, Shasta Co., St. Michael, c/o Redding, CA, St. Joseph. (SAC)
Shattuck, OK, Ellis Co., Holy Name, c/o Woodward, OK, St. Peter's. (OKL)
Shawmut, MT, Wheatland Co., Blessed Sacrament, c/o Harlowton, MT, St. Joseph. (HEL)
Sheffield, TX, Pecos Co., Good Shepherd, c/o Ozona, TX, Our Lady of Perpetual Help. (SAN)
Shelby, IN, Lake Co., St. Theresa, c/o Lowell, IN, St. Edward. (GRY)
Shelton, NE, Buffalo Co., Sacred Heart, c/o Wood River, NE, St. Mary's. (GI)
Sheridan, AR, Grant Co., Holy Cross, c/o Camden, AR, St. Louis. (LR)
Sherman Station, ME, Penobscot Co., St. Joseph's Church, c/o Benedicta, ME, St. Benedict's. (PRT)
Sherwood, ND, Renville Co., St. James, c/o Mohall, ND, St. Jerome. (BIS)
Shickley, NE, Fillmore Co., St. Mary, c/o Geneva, NE, St. Joseph's. (LIN)
Shidler, OK, Osage Co., St. Ann, c/o Pawhuska, OK, Immaculate Conception. (TLS)
Shingletown, CA, Shasta Co., Mary Queen of Peace, c/o Anderson, CA, Sacred Heart. (SAC)
Shoreham, VT, Addison Co., St. Genevieve, c/o Middlebury, VT, Assumption of the Blessed Virgin Mary. (BUR)
Shoshone–Tecopa, CA, Inyo Co., St. John the Baptist, c/o Lone Pine, CA, Santa Rosa. (FRS)
Shoshoni, WY, Fremont Co., St. Joseph, c/o Riverton, WY, St. Margaret's. (CHY)
Shubert, NE, Richardson Co., St. Anne's, c/o Dawson, NE, St. Mary's. (LIN)
Sidnaw, MI, Houghton Co., St. Francis Xavier, c/o Ewen, MI, Sacred Heart. (MAR)
Sieper, LA, Rapides Parish, St. Jude, c/o Glenmora, LA, St. Louis. (ALX)
Sierra Alta, PR, Yauco Co., St. Lucy, c/o Yauco, PR, Holy Rosary. (PCE)
Sierra Blanca, TX, Hudspeth Co., Our Lady of Miracles, c/o Van Horn, TX, Our Lady of Fatima. (ELP)
Sigel, PA, Jefferson Co., St. Dominic, c/o Brookville, PA, Immaculate Conception. (E)
Sile, NM, Sandoval Co., c/o Pena Blanca, NM, Nuestra Senora De Guadalupe. (SFE)
Siletz, OR, Lincoln Co., St. Mary, c/o Newport, OR, Sacred Heart Parish. (P)
Silt, CO, Garfield Co., Sacred Heart, c/o Rifle, CO, St. Mary's. (DEN)
Silver Lake, PA, Susquehanna Co., St. Augustine, c/o Friendsville, PA, St. Joseph's. (SCR)
Silverton, CO, San Juan Co., St. Patrick, c/o Ouray, CO, St. Daniel the Prophet. (PBL)
Silverton, TX, Briscoe Co., Our Lady of Loreto, c/o Tulia, TX, Church of the Holy Spirit. (AMA)
Smith Valley, NV, Lyon Co., St. John the Baptist, c/o Yerington, NV, Holy Family. (RNO)
Smithfield, NE, Gosper Co., St. John's, c/o Holdrege, NE, All Saints. (LIN)
Smiths Corners, MI, Huron Co., Holy Trinity, c/o Rapson, MI, St. Joseph. (SAG)
Smiths Creek, MI, St. Clair Co., Holy Rosary, c/o Columbus, MI, St. Philip Neri. (DET)
Sodus Point, NY, Wayne Co., St. Rose, c/o Sodus, NY, Epiphany. (ROC)
Soileau, LA, Allen Parish, St. Joseph, c/o Oberlin, LA, St. Joan of Arc. (LKC)
Solana Beach, CA, San Diego Co., St. Leo, c/o Solana Beach, CA, St. James. (SD)
Soldier Creek, SD, Todd Co., St. Rose, c/o Mission, SD, St. Thomas the Apostle. (RC)
Soldier Creek, SD, Todd Co., St. Rose, c/o St. Francis, SD, Rosebud Reservation. (RC)
Soledad, CA, Monterey Co., Nuestra Senora de la Soledad, c/o Soledad, CA, Our Lady of Solitude. (MRY)
Somers, MT, St. Ann, c/o Bigfork, MT, St. Catherine. (HEL)
Sonoita, AZ, Santa Cruz Co., Our Lady of Angels, c/o Patagonia, AZ, St. Theresa. (TUC)
South Byron, NY, Genesee Co., St. Michael, c/o Bergen, NY, St. Brigid. (BUF)
South Chatham, MA, Barnstable Co., Our Lady of Grace, c/o Chatham, MA, Holy Redeemer. (FR)
South Colton, NY, St. Lawrence Co., St. Paul, c/o Colton, NY, St. Patrick. (OG)
South Fork, CO, Rio Grande Co., Holy Family, c/o Del Norte, CO, Holy Name of Mary. (PBL)
South Hartford, NY, Washington Co., St. Philip, c/o Fort Ann, NY, St. Ann. (ALB)
South Lee, MA, Berkshire Co., St. Francis of Assisi, c/o Lee, MA, St. Mary's. (SPR)
South Royalston, MA, Worcester Co., Our Lady Queen of Heaven, c/o Athol, MA, Our Lady Immaculate. (WOR)
South Salem, NY, Westchester Co., South Salem Presbyterian Church, c/o Katonah, NY, St. Mary of the Assumption. (NY)
South Sterling, PA, Wayne Co., St. Mary Magdalene, c/o Gouldsboro, PA, St. Rita. (SCR)
South Strafford, VT, Orange Co., Our Lady of Light, c/o Bradford, VT, Our Lady of Perpetual Help. (BUR)
South Tucson, AZ, Pima Co., Blessed Kateri Tekakwitha Parish Center, c/o Tucson, AZ, Blessed Kateri Tekakwitha. (TUC)
South Vallejo, CA, Solano Co., St. Louis Bertrand, c/o Vallejo, CA, St. Vincent Ferrer. (SAC)
Southton, TX, Bexar Co., St. Ann, c/o San Antonio, TX, San Juan Capistrano. (SAT)
Southwest Oswego, NY, Oswego Co., St. Joseph, c/o Hannibal, NY, Our Lady of the Rosary. (SY)
Spanish Lake, LA, Natchitoches Parish, St. Anne, c/o Powhatan, LA, St. Francis of Assisi. (ALX)
Sparta, NC, Alleghany Co., St. Frances of Rome, c/o Jefferson, NC, St. Francis of Assisi. (CHL)
Spartansburg, PA, Crawford Co., Our Lady of Victory, c/o Corry, PA, St. Elizabeth. (E)
Spelter, WV, Harrison Co., Holy Family, c/o Shinnston, WV, St. Ann's. (WH)
Spencer, OH, Medina Co., Jesus Our Savior, c/o Litchfield, OH, Our Lady Help of Christians Parish. (CLV)

Spencer Mountain, NC, Gaston Co., St. Helen, c/o Charlotte, NC, Our Lady of Consolation. (CHL)
Spencerville, OH, Allen Co., St. Patrick, c/o Delphos, OH, St. John Baptist. (TOL)
Spiro, OK, Leflore Co., St. Elizabeth Seton, c/o Poteau, OK, Immaculate Conception. (TLS)
Split Rock, NY, Onondaga Co., St. Peter, c/o Syracuse, NY, St. Michael. (SY)
Spofford Junction, TX, Kinney Co., St. Blaise, c/o Brackettville, TX, St. Mary Magdalen. (SAT)
Spring Creek, SD, Todd Co., St. Patrick, c/o St. Francis, SD, St. Charles. (RC)
Spring Creek, SD, Todd Co., St. Patrick, c/o St. Francis, SD, Rosebud Reservation. (RC)
Spring Lake, NJ, Monmouth Co., St. Margaret, c/o Spring Lake, NJ, St. Catharine. (TR)
Spring Lake Twp., MN, Scott Co., St. Catherine, c/o Jordan, MN, St. Patrick. (STP)
Springfield, GA, St. Boniface, c/o Port Wentworth, GA, Our Lady of Lourdes. (SAV)
Springfield, MA, St. Joseph, c/o Springfield, MA, St. Michael's Cathedral. (SPR)
Springfield, SC, Orangeburg Co., St. Theresa, c/o Barnwell, SC, St. Andrew. (CHR)
Springfield Center, NY, Otsego Co., Blessed Sacrament, c/o Cherry Valley, NY, St. Thomas the Apostle. (ALB)
Springhill, LA, Webster Parish, Sacred Heart, c/o Minden, LA, St. Paul. (SHP)
Squaw Valley, CA, Fresno Co., St. Rita, c/o Orange Cove, CA, St. Isidore the Farmer. (FRS)
St. Anthony, ND, Morton Co., St. Anthony, c/o Mandan, ND, Christ the King. (BIS)
St. Augustine, FL, St. Johns Co., Prince of Peace, c/o St. Augustine, FL, Cathedral – Basilica of St. Augustine. (STA)
St. Augustine, FL, St. Johns Co., St. Benedict the Moor, c/o St. Augustine, FL, Cathedral – Basilica of St. Augustine. (STA)
St. Augustine, TX, San Augustine Co., San Augustine, c/o Hemphill, TX, St. Pius I. (TYL)
St. Boniface, PA, Cambria Co., St. Boniface Chapel, c/o Hastings, PA, St. Bernard. (ALT)
St. David, IL, Fulton Co., St. Michael, c/o Lewistown, IL, St. Mary's. (PEO)
St. Denis, IN, Jennings Co., St. Denis, c/o Greensburg, IN, Immaculate Conception. (IND)
St. Elmo, IL, Fayette Co., St. Mary, c/o Altamont, IL, St. Clare. (SFD)
St. Francis, SD, Todd Co., St. Charles, c/o St. Francis, SD, Rosebud Reservation. (RC)
St. Helena Island, SC, Beaufort Co., Holy Cross, c/o Beaufort, SC, St. Peter's. (CHR)
St. James, MO, c/o St. James, MO, Immaculate Conception. (JC)
St. Landry, LA, Evangeline Parish, St. Theresa, c/o Pine Prairie, LA, St. Peter. (LAF)
St. Mary, NE, Johnson Co., St. Mary's, c/o Tecumseh, NE, St. Andrew's. (LIN)
St. Michaels, AZ, Apache Co., St. Michael's Mission for Navajo Indians, c/o St. Michaels, AZ, St. Michael. (GLP)
St. Michaels, MD, Talbot Co., St. Michael, c/o Easton, MD, SS. Peter and Paul. (WIL)
St. Paul, MN, Mission of the Mother–Coredemptrix, c/o Minneapolis, MN, St. Joseph Hien. (STP)
St. Paul, TX, San Patricio Co., St. Paul, c/o Sinton, TX, Sacred Heart. (CC)
St. Pauls, NC, Robeson Co., San Pablo, c/o Lumberton, NC, St. Francis De Sales. (R)
St. Petersburg, FL, Pinellas Co., The Mercy of God Polish Mission, c/o St. Petersburg, FL, St. Paul. (SP)
St. Pius, IN, Ripley Co., St. Pius, c/o Morris, IN, St. Anthony of Padua. (IND)
St. Xavier, MT, Big Horn Co., St. Francis Xavier, c/o Crow Agency, MT, St. Dennis. (GF)
Staatsburg, NY, Dutchess Co., St. Paul, c/o Hyde Park, NY, Regina Coeli. (NY)
Staffordville, CT, Tolland Co., St. Joseph, c/o Stafford Springs, CT, St. Edward. (NOR)
Stamford, VT, Bennington Co., St. John Bosco, c/o Readsboro, VT, St. Joachim. (BUR)
Standish, NY, Clinton Co., St. Michael, c/o Lyon Mountain, NY, St. Bernard. (OG)
Stanfield, AZ, Pinal Co., St. Mary, c/o Casa Grande, AZ, St. Anthony of Padua. (TUC)
Starks, LA, Calcasieu Parish, St. Michael, c/o Vinton, LA, St. Joseph. (LKC)
Starr School, MT, Sacred Heart, c/o Browning, MT, Church of the Little Flower. (HEL)
Starrucca, PA, Wayne Co., St. Paul, c/o Jackson, PA, St. Martin of Tours. (SCR)
Staten Island, NY, Staten Island Co., St. Nicholas, c/o Staten Island, NY, St. Teresa. (NY)
Stedman, NC, Cumberland Co., St. Isidore, c/o Hope Mills, NC, Good Shepherd. (R)
Steilacoom, WA, Pierce Co., Immaculate Conception, c/o Lakewood, WA, St. John Bosco. (SEA)
Stephentown, NY, Rensselaer Co., St. Joseph's, c/o New Lebanon, NY, Immaculate Conception. (ALB)
Stepstone, KY Pendleton Co., Immaculate Conception, c/o California, KY, Sts. Peter and Paul. (COV)
Sterling, CT, Windham Co., St. Joseph, c/o Moosup, CT, All–Hallows. (NOR)
Sterling, OK, Comanche Co., Our Lady of Perpetual Help, c/o Elgin, OK, St. Ann. (OKL)
Sterling City, TX, Sterling Co., St. Paschal Baylon, c/o Carlsbad, TX, St. Therese of the Child Jesus. (SAN)
Stevenson, WA, Skamania Co., Star of the Sea, c/o Camas, WA, St. Thomas Aquinas. (SEA)
Stevinson, CA, Merced Co., St. Mary, c/o Hilmar, CA, Holy Rosary. (FRS)
Stigler, OK, Haskell Co., St. Joseph, c/o Poteau, OK, Immaculate Conception. (TLS)
Stinnett, TX, Hutchinson Co., St. Ann's, c/o Borger, TX, St. John the Evangelist. (AMA)
Stockton, CA, San Joaquin Co., Maronite Catholic Community of Stockton, c/o Millbrae, CA, Our Lady of Lebanon. (OLL)
Stockton, MO, Cedar Co., St. Peter the Apostle, c/o El Dorado Springs, MO, St. Elizabeth. (SPC)
Stockton, NJ, Hunterdon Co., St. Agnes, c/o Lambertville, NJ, St. John the Evangelist. (MET)
Stoneham, CO, Morgan Co., St. John, c/o Brush, CO, St. Mary. (DEN)
Stonehan, TX, Grimes Co., St. Joseph, c/o Plantersville, TX, St. Mary. (GAL)
Stonewall, LA, DeSoto Parish, St. Ann's Chapel, c/o Mansfield, LA, St. Joseph. (SHP)
Stoney Point, TX, Travis Co., Blessed Juan Diego, c/o Kyle, TX, St. Anthony Marie De Claret. (AUS)
Stonyford, CA, Colusa Co., St. Mary of the Mountain, c/o Maxwell, CA, Sacred Heart. (SAC)
Story, WY, Sheridan Co., Our Lady of the Pines, c/o Sheridan, WY, Holy Name. (CHY)
Stowell, PA, Wyoming Co., St. Anthony, c/o Wyalusing, PA, St. Mary's Assumption. (SCR)
Stratford, CA, Kings Co., St. Joseph, c/o Lemoore, CA, St. Peter. (FRS)
Strathmore, CA, Tulare Co., St. James Catholic Church, c/o Lindsay, CA, Sacred Heart. (FRS)
Stratton, ME, Franklin Co., St. John, c/o Oquossoc, ME, Our Lady of the Lakes. (PRT)
Stratton, NE, Hitchcock Co., St. Josephs, c/o Benkelman, NE, St. Joseph's. (LIN)
Stratton Mountain, VT, Windham Co., Chapel of the Snows, c/o Putney, VT, Our Lady of Mercy. (BUR)
Strawn, IL, Livingston Co., St. Rose, c/o Fairbury, IL, St. John the Baptist. (PEO)
String Prairie, TX, Bastrop Co., Assumption of the Blessed Virgin Mary, c/o Bastrop, TX, Sacred Heart. (AUS)
Stroud, OK, Lincoln Co., St. Louis, c/o Chandler, OK, Our Lady of Sorrows. (OKL)
Sturgeon Bay, WI, c/o Sturgeon Bay, WI, Corpus Christi. (GB)
Sugar Island, MI, Chippewa Co., Sacred Heart, c/o Sault Sainte Marie, MI, Holy Name of Mary. (MAR)
Sugarloaf Shores, FL, Sugarloaf Firehouse, c/o Big Pine Key, FL, St. Peter. (MIA)
Sugarloaf U.S.A., ME, Franklin Co., Richard H. Bell Memorial Chapel, c/o Oquossoc, ME, Our Lady of the Lakes (PRT)
Sullivan City, TX, Hidalgo Co., St. William, c/o La Joya, TX, Our Lady, Queen of Angels. (BWN)
Sulphur, LA, Calcasieu Parish, St. Peter Claver, c/o Sulphur, LA, Our Lady of Prompt Succor. (LKC)
Sulphur, OK, Murray Co., St. Francis Xavier, c/o Ada, OK, St. Joseph. (OKL)
Sun River, OR, Deschutes Co., Holy Trinity, c/o La Pine, OR, Holy Redeemer. (BAK)
Sunapee, NH, Sullivan Co., St. Joachim, c/o Newport, NH, St. Patrick. (MAN)
Sunburst, MT, St. Thomas Aquinas, c/o Shelby, MT, St. William. (HEL)
Sundance, WY, Crook Co., St. Paul, c/o Newcastle, WY, Corpus Christi. (CHY)
Sundown, TX, Hockley Co., San Isidro, c/o Levelland, TX, St. Michael's. (LUB)
Sunland Park, NM, Dona Ana Co, Santa Teresa de Avila, c/o Sunland Park, NM, St. Martin de Porres. (LSC)
Sunray, TX, Moore Co., Christ the King, c/o Dumas, TX, SS. Peter and Paul. (AMA)
Sunrise Beach, TX, Burnet Co., Our Lady of the Lake, c/o Kingsland, TX, St. Charles Borromeo. (AUS)
Superior, MT, Mineral Co., St. Mary Queen of Heaven, c/o Frenchtown, MT, St. John the Baptist. (HEL)
Superior, WY, Sweetwater Co., St. Vivian, c/o Rock Springs, WY, Holy Spirit Catholic Community. (CHY)
Suquamish, WA, Kitsap Co., St. Peter, c/o Poulsbo, WA, St. Olaf. (SEA)
Surf City, NC, Pender Co., St. Mary, Gate of Heaven, c/o Hampstead, NC, St. Jude the Apostle. (R)
Surf City, NJ, Ocean Co., St. Thomas of Villanova, c/o Brant Beach, NJ, St. Francis of Assisi. (TR)
Susua, PR, La Resurreccion, c/o Sabana Grande, PR, Church of San Isidro. (MGZ)
Sutherland, NE, Lincoln Co., Sacred Heart, c/o North Platte, NE, Holy Spirit. (GI)
Swansea, MA, Bristol Co., Our Lady of Fatima, c/o Swansea, MA, St. Michael's. (FR)
Swartz, LA, Ouachita Parish, St. Lawrence, c/o Monroe, LA, Our Lady of Fatima. (SHP)
Sweet Lake, LA, Cameron Parish, St. Patrick's, c/o Big Lake, LA, St. Mary of the Lake. (LKC)
Sweet Springs, MO, Saline Co., Holy Family, c/o Marshall, MO, St. Peter. (JC)

T

Tabor, MN, Polk Co., Holy Trinity, c/o East Grand Forks, MN, Sacred Heart. (CR)
Tabor, NE, Colfax Co., St. Mary, c/o Dodge, NE, St. Wenceslaus. (OM)
Tache Indian Reservation, CA, Kings Co., St. Rosa, c/o Lemoore, CA, St. Peter. (FRS)
Tahoka, TX, Lynn Co., St. Jude, c/o O'Donnell, TX, St. Pius X. (LUB)
Tajique, NM, Torrance Co., c/o Moriarty, NM, Estancia Valley Catholic Parish. (SFE)
Talihina, OK, Leflore Co., St. Catherine of Siena, c/o Krebs, OK, Holy Rosary. (TLS)
Tallaboa Alta, PR, Penuelas Co., Santa Ana, c/o Penuelas, PR, St. Joseph. (PCE)
Talpa, NM, Taos Co., N.S. de San Juan de Los Lagos, c/o Ranchos De Taos, NM, San Francisco de Asis. (SFE)
Tampa, FL, Hillsborough Co., St. Joseph Vietnamese Mission, c/o Tampa, FL, Epiphany. (SP)
Tampa, KS, Marion Co., Holy Redeemer, c/o Marion, KS, Holy Family. (WCH)
Tanama, PR, Adjuntas Co., Sagrado Corazon, c/o Adjuntas, PR, St. Joachim. (PCE)
Taos, NM, Taos Co., St. Jerome, c/o Taos, NM, Nuestra Senora De Guadalupe. (SFE)
Taos Pueblo, NM, Taos Co., c/o Taos, NM, Nuestra Senora De Guadalupe. (SFE)
Tatum, NM, Lea Co., Our Lady of the Holy Rosary, c/o Lovington, NM, St. Thomas Aquinas. (LSC)
Tatum, TX, Panola Co., San Pedro the Fisherman, c/o Marshall, TX, St. Joseph. (TYL)
Taylorsville, KY, Spencer Co., All Saints Church, c/o Fairfield, KY, St. Michael. (L)
Taylorsville, NC, Alexander Co., Holy Trinity, c/o Lenoir, NC, St. Francis of Assisi. (CHL)
Teague, TX, Freestone Co., St. Mary, c/o Fairfield, TX, St. Bernard of Clairvaux. (TYL)
Tecolotito, NM, San Miguel Co., c/o Anton Chico, NM, San Jose. (SFE)
Tehama, CA, Tehama Co., St. Stanislaus, c/o Corning, CA, Immaculate Conception. (SAC)
Temple, PA, Berks Co., St. Anthony, c/o Reading, PA, Holy Guardian Angels. (ALN)
Ten Sleep, WY, Washakie Co., St. Brigid's, c/o Worland, WY, St. Mary Magdalen. (CHY)
Tenakee Springs, AK, c/o Yakutat, AK, St. Ann. (JUN)
Tenino, WA, Thurston Co., St. Peter, c/o Yelm, WA, St. Columban. (SEA)
Tennessee, IL, McDonough Co., Sacred Heart, c/o Macomb, IL, St. Paul's. (PEO)
Terlingua, TX, Brewster Co., St. Mary, c/o Alpine, TX, Our Lady of Peace. (ELP)
Terra Alta, WV, Preston Co., St. Edward, c/o Kingwood, WV, St. Sebastian's. (WH)
Terra Bella, CA, Tulare Co., Blessed Miguel Agustin Pro, c/o Porterville, CA, St. Anne. (FRS)
Terry, MT, Prairie Co., Sacred Heart, c/o Miles City, MT, Sacred Heart. (GF)
Tesuque, NM, Santa Fe Co., San Ysidro, c/o Santa Fe, NM, Our Lady of Guadalupe. (SFE)
Texico, NM, Curry Co., c/o Clovis, NM, Our Lady of Guadalupe. (SFE)
Texline, TX, Dallum Co., St. Mary's, c/o Dalhart, TX, St. Anthony's. (AMA)
Thatcher, AZ, Graham Co., Neuman Center, c/o Safford, AZ, St. Rose of Lima. (TUC)
Thayer, MO, Oregon Co., Sacred Heart, c/o West Plains, MO, St. Mary. (SPC)
Thedford, NE, Thomas Co., St. Thomas of Canterbury, c/o Mullen, NE, St. Mary's. (GI)
Theresa, NY, Jefferson Co., St. Theresa of Avila, c/o Evans Mills, NY, St. Mary. (OG)
Thermal, CA, Riverside Co., El Senor de la Misericordia, c/o Coachella, CA, Our Lady of Soledad. (SB)
Thomas, OK, Custer Co., Blessed Sacrament, c/o Weatherford, OK, St. Eugene's. (OKL)
Thomaston, GA, Upson Co., St. John the Baptist, c/o Griffin, GA, Sacred Heart. (ATL)
Thomaston, ME, Knox Co., St. James, c/o Rockland, ME, St. Bernard's. (PRT)
Thomasville, AL, Clarke Co., St. Joseph, c/o Grove Hill, AL, Sacred Heart. (MOB)
Thorne Bay, AK, c/o Craig, AK, St. John by the Sea. (JUN)
Thornhurst, PA, Luzerne Co., St. Mark, c/o Bear Creek Township, PA, St. Elizabeth. (SCR)
Thornton, CA, San Joaquin Co., Mater Ecclesiae, c/o Lodi, CA, St. Anne Church (Pastor of). (STO)
Three Rivers, CA, Tulare Co., St. Clair, c/o Woodlake, CA, St. Frances Cabrini. (FRS)

Three Rivers, NM, Otero Co., St. Patrick, c/o Mescalero, NM, St. Joseph. (LSC)
Three Rocks, CA, Fresno Co., Our Lady of Lourdes, c/o Mendota, CA, Our Lady of Guadalupe. (FRS)
Thunder Butte, SD, Ziebach Co., St. Luke, c/o Eagle Butte, SD, All Saints. (RC)
Thunder Butte, SD, Ziebach Co., St. Luke, c/o Eagle Butte, SD, Cheyenne River Reservation. (RC)
Tijeras, NM, Bernalillo Co., c/o Tijeras, NM, Holy Child. (SFE)
Tilden, TX, McMullen Co., St. Joseph, c/o Charlotte, TX, St. Rose of Lima. (SAT)
Timpson, TX, Shelby Co., Epiphany, c/o Center, TX, St. Therese. (TYL)
Tinaja, NM, Colfax Co., c/o Springer, NM, St. Joseph. (SFE)
Tioga, PA, Tioga Co., St. Mary, c/o Mansfield, PA, Holy Child. (SCR)
Tionesta, PA, Forest Co., St. Anthony, c/o Tidioute, PA, St. John. (E)
Tishomingo, OK, Johnston Co., St. Anthony, c/o Ardmore, OK, St. Mary. (OKL)
Toa Alta, PR, Toa Alta Co., Capilla Cristo Rey, c/o Toa Alta, PR, San Esteban, Protomartir. (SJN)
Toa Alta, PR, Toa Alta Co., Cristo Rey, c/o Toa Baja, PR, Ntra. Sra. de la Candelaria. (SJN)
Toa Alta, PR, Toa Alta Co., Nuestra Senora del Carmen, c/o Toa Alta, PR, Nuestra Senora de la Medalla Milagrosa. (SJN)
Toa Alta, PR, Toa Alta Co., Sagrada Familia, c/o Toa Alta, PR, San Jose. (SJN)
Toa Alta, PR, Toa Alta Co., Sagrado Corazon, c/o Toa Alta, PR, San Jose. (SJN)
Toa Alta, PR, Toa Alta Co., Sagrado Corazon de Jesus, c/o Toa Alta, PR, Nuestra Senora de la Medalla Milagrosa. (SJN)
Toa Alta, PR, Toa Alta Co., Santa Teresa De Jesus, c/o Toa Alta, PR, San Judas Tadeo. (SJN)
Toa Alta, PR, Toa Alta Co., Santa Teresita, c/o Toa Alta, PR, San Jose. (SJN)
Toa Baja, PR, Toa Baja Co., Buen Pastor, c/o Toa Baja, PR, Ntra. Sra. de la Candelaria. (SJN)
Toa Baja, PR, Toa Baja Co., Divino Nino Jesus, c/o Bayamon, PR, Nuestra Senora de Covadonga. (SJN)
Toa Baja, PR, Toa Baja Co., N. Sra. del Carmen, c/o Toa Baja, PR, Espiritu Santo. (SJN)
Toa Baja, PR, Toa Baja Co., Ntra. Sra. de Lourdes, c/o Bayamon, PR, Nuestra Senora de Covadonga. (SJN)
Toa Baja, PR, San Martin de Porres, c/o Bayamon, PR, Santa Teresa de Jesus. (SJN)
Toa Baja, PR, Toa Baja Co., San Martin de Porres, c/o Bayamon, PR, Nuestra Senora de Covadonga. (SJN)
Toa Baja, PR, Toa Baja Co., Santisima Trinidad, c/o Toa Baja, PR, Ntra. Sra. de la Candelaria. (SJN)
Tobias, NE, Saline Co., St. Joseph's, c/o Wilber, NE, St. Wenceslaus. (LIN)
Tohono O'Odham, AZ, Maricopa Co., St. Lucy, Paloma Ranch, c/o Gila Bend, AZ, St. Michael. (PHX)
Tokio, ND, Benson Co., Christ the King, c/o Tokio, ND, (Spirit Lake Sioux). (FAR)
Tollhouse, CA, Fresno Co., Infant Jesus of Prague, c/o Fresno, CA, Holy Spirit. (FRS)
Tomales, CA, Marin Co., St. Helen, c/o Tomales, CA, Church of the Assumption. (SFR)
Tompkinsville, KY, Monroe Co., Christ the King, c/o Edmonton, KY, Christ the Healer. (L)
Tonyville, CA, Tulare Co., St. Anthony Church, c/o Lindsay, CA, Sacred Heart. (FRS)
Tornillo, TX, El Paso Co., Santa Rita, c/o Fabens, TX, Our Lady of Guadalupe. (ELP)
Torreon, NM, Torrance Co., c/o Mountainair, NM, St. Alice. (SFE)
Torrey, UT, Wayne Co., St. Anthony of the Desert, c/o Monroe, UT, St. Elizabeth's. (SLC)
Toston, MT, Broadwater Co., Immaculate Conception, c/o Townsend, MT, Holy Cross. (HEL)
Touhy, NE, Saunders Co., St. Vitus, c/o Weston, NE, St. John Nepomucene. (LIN)
Townsend, TN, Blount Co., St. Francis of Assisi, c/o Alcoa, TN, Our Lady of Fatima. (KNX)
Townshend, VT, Windham Co., Our Lady of the Valley, c/o Putney, VT, Our Lady of Mercy. (BUR)
Toyah, TX, Reeves Co., St. Emily, c/o Pecos, TX, St. Catherine. (ELP)
Trail City, SD, Corson Co., Holy Rosary, c/o Timber Lake, SD, Holy Cross. (RC)
Trampas, NM, Taos Co., San Jose de Gracia, c/o Chimayo, NM, Holy Family. (SFE)
Trapper Creek, AK, Matanuska–Susitna Borough, St. Philip Benizi, c/o Talkeetna, AK, St. Bernard. (ANC)
Traver, CA, Tulare Co., St. John the Baptist Educational Center, c/o Kingsburg, CA, Holy Family. (FRS)
Tremonton, UT, Box Elder Co., Santa Ana, c/o Brigham City, UT, St. Henry. (SLC)
Trenton, ND, Williams Co., St. John the Baptist, c/o Williston, ND, St. Joseph. (BIS)
Tres Piedras, NM, Taos Co., c/o El Rito, NM, San Juan Nepomuceno. (SFE)
Tres de Jayuya, PR, Adjuntas Co., Santa Teresita, c/o Adjuntas, PR, St. Joachim. (PCE)
Triadelphia, WV, Ohio Co., Our Lady of Seven Dolors, c/o Wheeling, WV, St. Vincent de Paul's. (WH)
Trichel, LA, Natchitoches Parish, St. Joseph, c/o Campti, LA, Nativity of The Blessed Virgin Mary. (ALX)
Trinidad, CA, Holy Trinity, c/o McKinleyville, CA, Christ the King. (SR)
Trout Lake, MI, Chippewa Co., St. Mary, c/o Rudyard, MI, St. Joseph. (MAR)
Troy, MT, Lincoln Co., Immaculate Conception, c/o Libby, MT, St. Joseph. (HEL)
Troy, NY, Rensselaer Co., Hallmark Nursing Home, c/o Troy, NY, St. Michael the Archangel. (ALB)
Troy, PA, Bradford Co., St. John Nepomucene, c/o Canton, PA, St. Michael. (SCR)
Truchas, NM, Rio Arriba Co., Holy Rosary, c/o Chimayo, NM, Holy Family. (SFE)
Trujillo, CO, Archuleta Co., St. James, c/o Pagosa Springs, CO, Immaculate Heart of Mary. (PBL)
Trujillo, NM, San Miguel Co., San Isidro, c/o Las Vegas, NM, Our Lady of Sorrows Church. (SFE)
Trujillo Alto, PR, Trujillo Alto Co., El Divino Pastor, c/o Trujillo Alto, PR, San Judas Tadeo. (SJN)
Trujillo Alto, PR, Trujillo Alto Co., Ntra. Sra. del Carmen, c/o Trujillo Alto, PR, San Judas Tadeo. (SJN)
Trujillo Creek, CO, Las Animas Co., Mount Carmel, c/o Aguilar, CO, St. Anthony. (PBL)
Tsaile, AZ, Apache Co., St. Ann, c/o Lukachukai, AZ, St. Isabel. (GLP)
Tucson, AZ, Pima Co., Cristo Rey, c/o Tucson, AZ, Blessed Kateri Tekakwitha. (TUC)
Tucson, AZ, Pima Co., El Senor de los Milagros, c/o Tucson, AZ, Blessed Kateri Tekakwitha. (TUC)
Tucson, AZ, Pima Co., Our Lady of Guadalupe, c/o Tucson, AZ, Santa Cruz. (TUC)
Tucson, AZ, Pima Co., Santa Catalina, c/o Tucson, AZ, Saint Odilia. (TUC)
Tucson, AZ, Pima Co., Santa Rosa, c/o Tucson, AZ, Blessed Kateri Tekakwitha. (TUC)
Tucson, AZ, Pima Co., Santa Rosa, c/o Tucson, AZ, Holy Family. (TUC)
Tucson, AZ, Pima Co., St. Anthony's Catholic Instruction Center and Capilla, c/o Tucson, AZ, Santa Cruz. (TUC)
Tucson, AZ, Pima Co., St. Mary of the Desert, c/o Tucson, AZ, Our Lady of Fatima. (TUC)
Tulalip, WA, Snohomish Co., Tulalip Indian Reservation, St. Anne, c/o Marysville, WA, St. Mary. (SEA)
Tule Indian Reservation, CA, Tulare Co., Mater Dolorosa, c/o Porterville, CA, St. Anne. (FRS)
Tullytown, PA, Bucks Co., Sacred Heart of Jesus, c/o Bristol, PA, St. Ann. (PH)
Tunica, MS, Tunica Co., St. Anthony of Padua, c/o Walls, MS, Sacred Heart. (JKS)
Tuolumne, CA, Tuolumne Co., St. Joseph, c/o Twain Harte, CA, All Saints Church (Pastor of). (STO)
Turquillo, NM, Mora Co., c/o Mora, NM, St. Gertrude. (SFE)
Turtle Lake, ND, McLean Co., St. Catherine, c/o Underwood, ND, St. Bonaventure. (BIS)
Tuscaloosa, AL, Tuscaloosa Co., St. John, c/o Tuscaloosa, AL, Holy Spirit. (BIR)
Tuscon, AZ, Pima Co., San Ignacio, c/o Tucson, AZ, Blessed Kateri Tekakwitha. (TUC)
Tuscon, AZ, Pima Co., San Martin, c/o Tucson, AZ, Blessed Kateri Tekakwitha. (TUC)
Twin Bridges, MT, Jefferson Co., Notre Dame, c/o Whitehall, MT, St. Teresa. (HEL)
Twin Buttes, ND, Dunn Co., St. Joseph, c/o Mandaree, ND, St. Anthony. (BIS)
Twin Lakes, GA, Lowndes Co., St. Jose, c/o Lakeland, GA, Queen of Peace. (SAV)
Twin Sisters, TX, Blanco Co., Our Lady Help of Christians, c/o Blanco, TX, St. Ferdinand's. (AUS)
Twin Valley, MN, Norman Co., St. William, c/o Ada, MN, St. Joseph's. (CR)
Two Inlets, MN, Becker Co., St. Mary, c/o Park Rapids, MN, St. Peter's. (CR)
Tyler, TX, St. Joseph the Worker Church, c/o Tyler, TX, Cathedral of the Immaculate Conception. (TYL)
Tylertown, MS, Walthall Co., St. Paul the Apostle, c/o Columbia, MS, Most Holy Trinity. (BLX)
Tynan, TX, Bee Co., St. Francis Xavier, c/o Skidmore, TX, Immaculate Conception. (CC)

U

Ulster, PA, Bradford Co., Immaculate Conception, c/o Towanda, PA, SS. Peter and Paul. (SCR)
Ulupalakua, HI, Maui Co., St. James the Less, c/o Kula, HI, Our Lady Queen of the Angels. (HON)
Unadilla, NY, Otsego Co., St. Ambrose, c/o Sidney, NY, Sacred Heart. (ALB)
Unalaska, AK, Aleutian Islands Census Area, St. Christopher By the Sea, c/o Dillingham, AK, Holy Rosary. (ANC)
Union, WV, Monroe Co., St. Andrew the Apostle, c/o Ronceverte, WV, St. Catherine of Siena. (WH)
Union City, MI, Branch Co., Our Lady of Fatima, c/o Coldwater, MI, St. Charles Borromeo. (KAL)
Union Springs, AL, Bullock Co., Bullock County Correctional Facility, c/o Eufaula, AL, Holy Redeemer. (MOB)
Union Springs, AL, Bullock Co., St. Pius X, c/o Eufaula, AL, Holy Redeemer. (MOB)
Unionville, MO, Putnam Co., St. Mary, c/o Milan, MO, St. Mary. (JC)
Unionville, NY, Orange Co., Our Lady of the Scapular, c/o Middletown, NY, Holy Cross. (NY)
Unity, OR, Baker Co., St. Joseph's, c/o Baker, OR, Cathedral of St. Francis De Sales. (BAK)
Universal, IN, Vermillion Co., St. Joseph, c/o Clinton, IN, Sacred Heart. (IND)
Upper Cutmeat, SD, Todd Co., Sacred Heart, c/o Parmelee, SD, St. Agnes. (RC)
Upper Cutmeat, SD, Todd Co., Sacred Heart, c/o St. Francis, SD, Rosebud Reservation. (RC)
Upton, WY, Weston Co., St. Anthony, c/o Newcastle, WY, Corpus Christi. (CHY)
Urich, MO, Henry Co., Holy Trinity, c/o Holden, MO, St. Patrick's. (KC)
Ute, IA, Monona Co., St. Mary's, c/o Dow City, IA, St. Boniface. (SC)
Utica, NE, Seward Co., St. Patrick's, c/o Beaver Crossing, NE, Sacred Heart. (LIN)
Utulei, AS, c/o Pago Pago, AS, Co–Cathedral of St. Joseph the Worker. (SPP)

V

Vadito, NM, Taos Co., Nuestra Senora de los Dolores Mission, c/o Penasco, NM, San Antonio de Padua. (SFE)
Vado, NM, Dona Ana Co., San Pedro Del Cerro, c/o La Mesa, NM, San Jose. (LSC)
Vail, CO, Eagle Co., The Interfaith Chapel, c/o Vail, CO, St. Patrick's. (DEN)
Valdez, NM, Taos Co., San Antonio de Padua, c/o Arroyo Seco, NM, La Santisima Trinidad. (SFE)
Valencia, NM, Valencia Co., Sangre de Cristo, c/o Peralta, NM, Our Lady of Guadalupe. (SFE)
Valentine, TX, Jeff Davis Co., Sacred Heart, c/o Van Horn, TX, Our Lady of Fatima. (ELP)
Valeria, IA, Jasper Co., Sacred Heart, c/o Colfax, IA, Immaculate Conception. (DAV)
Valiant, OK, McCurtain Co., Good Shepherd, c/o Idabel, OK, St. Francis De Sales. (TLS)
Vallecitos, NM, Rio Arriba Co., c/o El Rito, NM, San Juan Nepomuceno. (SFE)
Van Alstyne, TX, Grayson Co., Holy Family, c/o McKinney, TX, St. Michael. (DAL)
Van Buren, ME, Aroostock Co., St. Rose Chapel, c/o Van Buren, ME, St. Bruno – St. Remi. (PRT)
Van Buren, MO, Carter Co., St. George, c/o Piedmont, MO, St. Catherine of Siena. (SPC)
Vanceboro, ME, Washington Co., Guardian Angel, c/o Lincoln, ME, St. Mary. (PRT)
Vandalia, NY, Cattaraugus Co., St. John the Baptist, c/o Allegany, NY, St. Bonaventure. (BUF)
Vanderpool, TX, Bandera Co., St. Mary, c/o Sabinal, TX, St. Patrick's. (SAT)
Variadero, NM, San Miguel Co., Holy Family, c/o Las Vegas, NM, Our Lady of Sorrows Church. (SFE)
Vegas Abajo, PR, Adjuntas Co., La Milagrosa, c/o Adjuntas, PR, St. Joachim. (PCE)
Vegas Arriba, PR, Adjuntas Co., Sta. Ana, c/o Adjuntas, PR, St. Joachim. (PCE)
Veguita, NM, Socorro Co., San Juan, c/o La Joya, NM, Our Lady of Sorrows. (SFE)
Velarde, NM, Rio Arriba Co., Nuestra Senora de Guadalupe, c/o Dixon, NM, St. Anthony. (SFE)
Venice, LA, Plaquemines Parish, St. Anthony, c/o Buras, LA, Our Lady of Good Harbor. (NO)
Verdunville, LA, St. Mary Parish, Immaculate Conception, c/o Franklin, LA, St. Jules. (LAF)
Verona Beach, NY, Oneida Co., St. Mary, c/o North Bay, NY, St. John. (SY)
Versailles, MO, Morgan Co., St. Philip Benizi, c/o Laurie, MO, Shrine of St. Patrick. (JC)
Viburnum, MO, Iron Co., St. Philip Benizi, c/o Ironton, MO, Ste. Marie Du Lac. (SPC)
Victor, CO, Teller Co., St. Victor's, c/o Woodland Park, CO, Our Lady of the Woods. (COS)
Victoria, TX, Victoria Co., Holy Trinity, c/o Victoria, TX, Our Lady of Sorrows. (VIC)
Vida, MT, McCone Co., St. Ann, c/o Wolf Point, MT, Immaculate Conception. (GF)
Vidrine, LA, Evangeline Parish, Holy Spirit, c/o Mamou, LA, St. Ann. (LAF)
Vigil, CO, Las Animas Co., St. Isidore, c/o Trinidad, CO, Most Holy Trinity, Trinidad Area Catholic Community (Trinidad Cluster). (PBL)
Villa Esperanza, PR, Carolina Co., La Sagrada Familia, c/o Carolina, PR, San Juan de Dios. (SJN)
Villa del Carmen, PR, Ponce Co., San Martin de Porres, c/o Playa de Ponce, PR, Our Lady of Mt. Carmel. (PCE)
Villalba, PR, Villalba Co., La Milagrosa, c/o Villalba, PR, Our Lady of Mt. Carmel. (PCE)
Villalba, PR, Villalba, La Milagrosa, c/o Villalba, PR, Our Lady of Mt. Carmel. (PCE)
Villalba, PR, Villalba, San Francisco de Asis, c/o

Villalba, PR, Our Lady of Mt. Carmel. (PCE)
Villalba, PR, Villalba, San Juan Evangelista, c/o Villalba, PR, Our Lady of Mt. Carmel. (PCE)
Villas De Loiza, PR, Ntra. Sra. de la Providencia, c/o Canovanas, PR, Resurreccion del Senior. (SJN)
Vintondale, PA, Cambria Co., SS. Timothy & Mark Chapel, c/o Twin Rocks, PA, SS. Timothy & Mark. (ALT)
Viola, IL, Mercer Co., St. John, c/o Matherville, IL, St. Anthony's Church. (PEO)
Virginia Beach, VA, Virginia Beach Co., Our Lady of Perpetual Help, c/o Williamsburg, VA, Ascension of Our Lord. (PSC)
Volcano, CA, Amador Co., St. Bernard, c/o Jackson, CA, St. Patrick's. (SAC)

W

Waco, TX, McLennan Co., St. John the Baptist, c/o Waco, TX, St. Mary of the Assumption. (AUS)
Waco, TX, McLennan Co., c/o Waco, TX, St. John the Baptist. (AUS)
Wadesboro, NC, Anson Co., Sacred Heart, c/o Hamlet, NC, St. James. (CHL)
Wadsworth, IL, St. Andrew Misson, c/o Chicago, IL, Archdiocese of Chicago's Joseph Cardinal Bernardin Archives and Records Center. (CHI)
Wadsworth, TX, Matagorda Co., Sacred Heart, c/o Bay City, TX, Holy Cross. (VIC)
Waelder, TX, Gonzales Co., St. Patrick, c/o Gonzales, TX, St. James. (SAT)
Wahneta, FL, Polk Co., Our Lady of Guadalupe, c/o Bartow, FL, St. Thomas Aquinas. (ORL)
Waiakoa, HI, Maui Co., Holy Ghost, c/o Kula, HI, Our Lady Queen of the Angels. (HON)
Waikapu, HI, Maui Co., St. Joseph, c/o Waihee, HI, St. Ann. (HON)
Waimea, HI, Kauai Co., Sacred Hearts of Jesus & Mary, c/o Kekaha, HI, St. Theresa. (HON)
Waimea Bay, HI, Honolulu Co., SS. Peter and Paul, c/o Waialua, HI, St. Michael. (HON)
Waitsfield, VT, Washington Co., Our Lady of the Snows, c/o Waterbury, VT, St. Andrew. (BUR)
Wakefield, VA, Southampton Co., Infant of Prague, c/o Franklin, VA, St. Jude. (RIC)
Wakita, OK, Grant Co., St. Mary's Assumption, c/o Medford, OK, St. Mary's. (OKL)
Wakpala, SD, Corson Co., St. Bede, c/o McLaughlin, SD, St. Bernard. (RC)
Wakpala, SD, Corson Co., St. Bede, c/o McLaughlin, SD, Standing Rock Reservation. (RC)
Walden, CO, Jackson Co., St. Ignatius, c/o Kremmling, CO, St. Peter. (DEN)
Wales, MA, Hampden Co., St. Monica, c/o Brimfield, MA, St. Christopher's. (SPR)
Walhalla, SC, Oconee Co., St. Francis of Assisi, c/o Clemson, SC, St. Andrew. (CHR)
Walker Valley, NY, Ulster Co., Our Lady of the Valley, c/o Pine Bush, NY, The Infant Saviour. (NY)
Wallace, KS, Wallace Co., St. Peter, c/o Sharon Springs, KS, Holy Ghost. (SAL)
Wallace, NC, Duplin Co., Transfiguration, c/o Burgaw, NC, St. Joseph. (R)
Wallkill, NY, Ulster Co., St. Benedict, c/o Walden, NY, Most Precious Blood. (NY)
Wallowa, OR, Wallowa Co., St. Pius X, c/o Enterprise, OR, St. Katherine's. (BAK)
Walnut Ridge, AR, Lawrence Co., Immaculate Heart of Mary, c/o Paragould, AR, St. Mary's. (LR)
Walpole, NH, Cheshire Co., St. Joseph, c/o North Walpole, NH, St. Peter. (MAN)
Walterboro, SC, Colleton Co., St. James the Greater, c/o Walterboro, SC, St. Anthony's. (CHR)
Walters, OK, Cotton Co., St. Patrick, c/o Frederick, OK, St. Helen. (OKL)
Wamsutter, WY, Sweetwater Co., St. Anthony, c/o Rock Springs, WY, Holy Spirit Catholic Community. (CHY)
Wanette, OK, Pottawatomie Co., St. Mary, c/o Konawa, OK, Sacred Heart. (OKL)
Wardsboro, VT, Windham Co., Our Lady of Hope, c/o Putney, VT, Our Lady of Mercy. (BUR)
Warm Springs, GA, Meriwether Co., St. Elizabeth Seton, c/o LaGrange, GA, St. Peter's. (ATL)
Warm Springs, OR, Jefferson Co., Blessed Kateri Tekakwitha, c/o Madras, OR, St. Patrick's. (BAK)
Warner Springs, CA, San Diego Co., St. Francis, c/o Santa Ysabel, CA, Santa Ysabel Indian Mission. (SD)
Warren, AR, Bradley Co., St. Luke, c/o Monticello, AR, St. Mark. (LR)
Warrenton, NC, Warren Co., St. Joseph, c/o Henderson, NC, St. James the Greater. (R)
Warrenton, TX, Fayette Co., St. Martin's, c/o Fayetteville, TX, St. John's. (AUS)
Warrior, AL, Jefferson Co., St. Henry, c/o Gardendale, AL, St. Elizabeth Ann Seton. (BIR)
Washburn, IL, Woodford Co., St. Elizabeth, c/o Metamora, IL, St. Mary's. (PEO)
Washburn, ME, Aroostook Co., St. Catherine, c/o Ashland, ME, St. Mark's. (PRT)
Washburn, ND, Mercer Co., St. Edwin, c/o Center, ND, St. Martin. (BIS)
Washington, VA, Rappahannock Co., St. Peter, c/o Culpeper, VA, Precious Blood. (ARL)
Washoe Valley, NV, Washoe Co., Holy Spirit, c/o Reno, NV, St. Rose of Lima. (RNO)
Waskom, TX, Harrison Co., St. Lawrence Brindisi, c/o Jefferson, TX, Immaculate Conception. (TYL)
Wataga, IL, St. Aloysius, c/o Galesburg, IL, Immaculate Heart of Mary. (PEO)
Wataga, IL, Knoxville Co., St. Aloysius, c/o Alexis, IL, St. Theresa's. (PEO)
Watauga, SD, Corson Co., St. Michael, c/o McLaughlin, SD, Standing Rock Reservation. (RC)
Waterproof, LA, Tensas Parish, St. Francis of Assisi, c/o St. Joseph, LA, St. Joseph. (ALX)
Watonga, OK, Blaine Co., St. Rose of Lima, c/o Okeene, OK, St. Anthony's. (OKL)
Watrous, NM, Mora Co., c/o Wagon Mound, NM, Santa Clara. (SFE)
Watson, MI, Allegan Co., Sacred Heart, c/o Dorr, MI, St. Stanislaus. (KAL)
Wauneta, NE, Chase Co., St. John's, c/o Imperial, NE, St. Patrick's. (LIN)
Wayland, MO, Clark Co., St. Martha, c/o Kahoka, MO, St. Michael the Archangel. (JC)
Waynoka, OK, Woods Co., Our Mother of Mercy, c/o Alva, OK, Sacred Heart. (OKL)
Webbers Falls, OK, Muskogee Co., St. Joseph, c/o Sallisaw, OK, St. Francis Xavier. (TLS)
Weirs Beach, NH, Belknap Co., St. Helena, c/o Lakeport, NH, Our Lady of the Lakes. (MAN)
Welch, OK, Craig Co., St. Ann, c/o Miami, OK, Sacred Heart. (TLS)
Welches, OR, Clackamas Co., St. John the Evangelist, c/o Sandy, OR, St. Michael the Archangel. (P)
Weldona, CO, Morgan Co., St. Francis of Assisi, c/o Fort Morgan, CO, St. Helena. (DEN)
Wellfleet, NE, Lincoln Co., St. William's, c/o Curtis, NE, St. James. (LIN)
Wells, NV, Elko Co., St. Thomas Aquinas, c/o Elko, NV, St. Joseph's. (RNO)
Wells River, VT, Orange Co., St. Eugene, c/o Bradford, VT, Our Lady of Perpetual Help. (BUR)
Wellton, AZ, Yuma Co., St. Joseph the Worker, c/o Yuma, AZ, Immaculate Conception. (TUC)
Wenden, AZ, St. John the Baptist, c/o Parker, AZ, Sacred Heart. (TUC)
Weslaco, TX, Hidalgo Co., St. Jude Chapel, c/o Weslaco, TX, San Martin de Porres. (BWN)
West Alton, MO, St. Charles Co., Immaculate Conception, c/o Portage Des Sioux, MO, St. Francis of Assisi. (STL)
West Barnstable, MA, Barnstable Co., Our Lady of Hope, c/o Centerville, MA, Our Lady of Victory. (FR)
West Castleton, VT, Rutland Co., St. Matthew of Avalon, c/o Fair Haven, VT, Our Lady of Seven Dolors. (BUR)
West Charleston, VT, Orleans Co., St. Benedict Labre, c/o Derby Line, VT, St. Edward. (BUR)
West Claremont, NH, Sullivan Co., Old St. Mary, c/o Claremont, NH, St. Mary. (MAN)
West Columbia, TX, Brazoria Co., St. John the Apostle, c/o Sweeny, TX, Our Lady of Perpetual Help. (GAL)
West Covina, CA, Los Angeles Co., St. Christopher Korean Catholic Community, c/o West Covina, CA, St. Christopher. (LA)
West Forks, ME, Somerset Co., SS. Philip & James, c/o Jackman, ME, St. Anthony. (PRT)
West Gilgo Beach, NY, Suffolk Co., c/o Babylon, NY, St. Joseph's. (RVC)
West Glacier, MT, Flathead Co., c/o Columbia Falls, MT, St. Richard. (HEL)
West Mount Vernon, AL, Mobile Co., St. Theresa, c/o Citronelle, AL, St. Thomas. (MOB)
West Pawlet, VT, Rutland Co., St. Frances Cabrini, c/o Fair Haven, VT, Our Lady of Seven Dolors. (BUR)
West Pawlet, VT, Rutland Co., St. Frances Cabrini, c/o Middletown Springs, VT, St. Anne. (BUR)
West Peru, NY, Clinton Co., St. Patrick, c/o Peru, NY, St. Augustine. (OG)
West Point, CA, Calaveras Co., Our Lady of Fatima, c/o San Andreas, CA, St. Andrew Church of San Andreas (Pastor of). (STO)
West Point, IL, Hancock Co., St. Mary, c/o Carthage, IL, Immaculate Conception. (PEO)
West Point, KY, Hardin Co., St. Patrick Church, c/o Louisville, KY, Our Lady Help of Christians. (L)
West Shokan, NY, Ulster Co., St. Augustine, c/o Woodstock, NY, St. John. (NY)
West Springfield, MA, Hampden Co., St. Ann, c/o Springfield, MA, Our Lady of Mt. Carmel. (SPR)
West Wareham, MA, Plymouth Co., St. Anthony, c/o Wareham, MA, St. Patrick's. (FR)
Westfield, PA, Tioga Co., St. Catherine, c/o Elkland, PA, St. Thomas the Apostle. (SCR)
Westhoff, TX, DeWitt Co., St. Aloysius, c/o Meyersville, TX, SS. Peter & Paul. (VIC)
Westminster, CO, Adams Co., Our Lady of Visitation, c/o Westminster, CO, Holy Trinity. (DEN)
Westover, MD, Somerset Co., St. Elizabeth, c/o Pocomoke City, MD, Holy Name of Jesus. (WIL)
Westport, WA, Grays Harbor Co., St. Paul, c/o Aberdeen, WA, St. Mary. (SEA)
Westville, NY, Franklin Co., c/o Constable, NY, The Catholic Community of Constable, Westville and Trout River. (OG)
Westway, TX, El Paso Co., Immaculate Heart of Mary, c/o Canutillo, TX, St. Patrick. (ELP)
Wetumpka, AL, Elmore Co., St. Mark's, c/o Millbrook, AL, St. Elizabeth Ann Seton. (MOB)
Wewahitchka, FL, Gulf Co., St. Lawrence Mission, c/o Port St. Joe, FL, St. Joseph. (PT)
Wewoka, OK, Seminole Co., St. Joseph, c/o Konawa, OK, Sacred Heart. (OKL)
Whale Pass, AK, c/o Craig, AK, St. John by the Sea. (JUN)
Wheatfields, AZ, Apache Co., Our Lady of the Lake, c/o Lukachukai, AZ, St. Isabel. (GLP)
Wheatland, CA, Yuba Co., St. Daniel, c/o Lincoln, CA, St. Joseph. (SAC)
Wheatville, NY, Genesee Co., St. Patrick, c/o Oakfield, NY, St. Cecilia. (BUF)
Wheeler, TX, Collingsworth Co., St. Mary, c/o Pampa, TX, Sacred Heart. (AMA)
Wheelwright, MA, Hardwick Co., St. Augustine, c/o Barre, MA, St. Joseph's. (WOR)
Whetstone, AZ, Cochise Co., Good Shepherd, c/o Sierra Vista, AZ, St. Andrew. (TUC)
White Church, MO, Howell Co., St. Joseph, c/o Willow Springs, MO, Sacred Heart. (SPC)
White Earth, MN, Becker Co., St. Benedict, c/o Ogema, MN, Most Holy Redeemer. (CR)
White Horse, SD, Dewey Co., St. Therese, c/o Eagle Butte, SD, All Saints. (RC)
White Horse, SD, Dewey Co., St. Therese, c/o Eagle Butte, SD, Cheyenne River Reservation. (RC)
White Horse Beach, MA, St. Catherine's Chapel, c/o Plymouth, MA, St. Bonaventure. (BO)
White Lake, NY, Sullivan Co., St. Anne, c/o Monticello, NY, St. Peter. (NY)
White Pigeon, MI, St. Joseph Co., St. Joseph, c/o Sturgis, MI, Holy Angels. (KAL)
White River, SD, Mellette Co., Sacred Heart, c/o St. Francis, SD, Rosebud Reservation. (RC)
White River, SD, Mellette Co., St. Ignatius, c/o St. Francis, SD, Rosebud Reservation. (RC)
White Rock, NM, Los Alamos Co., St. Joseph, c/o Los Alamos, NM, Immaculate Heart of Mary. (SFE)
White Sulphur, KY, Scott Co., St. Francis de Sales, c/o Georgetown, KY, St. John's. (LEX)
Whitesboro, TX, Grayson Co., St. Francis of Assisi, c/o Sherman, TX, St. Mary. (DAL)
Whitesville, NY, St. John of the Cross, c/o Wellsville, NY, Immaculate Conception. (BUF)
Whitesville, WV, Boone Co., St. Joseph the Worker, c/o Madison, WV, St. Mary, Queen of Heaven. (WH)
Whiteville, LA, Resurrection, c/o Morrow, LA, St. Peter. (LAF)
Whitewater, MT, Phillips Co., St. John, c/o Malta, MT, St. Mary's. (GF)
Wibaux, MT, Wibaux Co., St. Peter, c/o Glendive, MT, Sacred Heart. (GF)
Wibaux, MT, Wibaux Co., St. Philip, c/o Glendive, MT, Sacred Heart. (GF)
Wichita Falls, TX, Wichita Co., The Assumption of Mary, c/o Wichita Falls, TX, Sacred Heart. (FWT)
Wiggins, CO, Morgan Co., Our Lady of Lourdes, c/o Roggen, CO, Sacred Heart. (DEN)
Wilburton, OK, Latimer Co., Sacred Heart, c/o Krebs, OK, Holy Rosary. (TLS)
Wildwood, FL, Sumter Co., St. Vincent de Paul Mission, c/o Bushnell, FL, St. Lawrence. (ORL)
Wilkeson, WA, Pierce Co., Our Lady of Lourdes, c/o Buckley, WA, St. Aloysius. (SEA)
Willacoochee, GA, Atkinson Co., Holy Family, c/o Douglas, GA, St. Paul's. (SAV)
Willard, NM, Torrance Co., c/o Mountainair, NM, St. Alice. (SFE)
Williams, CA, Colusa Co., Annunciation, c/o Maxwell, CA, Sacred Heart. (SAC)
Williams, MN, Lake of the Woods Co., St. Joseph, c/o Baudette, MN, Sacred Heart. (CR)
Williamsfield, IL, Knox Co., St. James, c/o Brimfield, IL, St. Joseph's. (PEO)
Williamstown, NY, Oswego Co., St. Patrick, c/o Mexico, NY, St. Anne. (SY)
Williamstown, PA, Dauphin Co., Sacred Heart of Jesus, c/o Lykens, PA, Our Lady Help of Christians. (HBG)
Williamstown, VT, Orange Co., St. Edward, c/o Northfield, VT, St. John the Evangelist. (BUR)
Williamsville, MO, Wayne Co., Our Lady of Sorrows, c/o Piedmont, MO, St. Catherine of Siena. (SPC)
Willow, AK, Matanuska–Susitna Borough, St. Christopher, c/o Talkeetna, AK, St. Bernard. (ANC)
Wills Point, TX, Van Zandt Co., St. Luke, c/o Canton, TX, St. Therese. (TYL)
Wilmington, NY, Essex Co., St. Margaret, c/o Keene, NY, St. Brendan. (OG)
Wilson, TX, Lynn Co., Blessed Sacrament, c/o Post, TX, Holy Cross. (LUB)
Wilton, MN, Beltrami Co., Sacred Heart, c/o Bemidji,

MN, St. Philip's. (CR)
Windsor, MO, Henry Co., St. Bartholomew, c/o Clinton, MO, Holy Rosary. (KC)
Wingdale, NY, Dutchess Co., Our Lady of Solace Mission, c/o Dover Plains, NY, St. Charles Borromeo. (NY)
Winifred, MT, Fergus Co., Holy Family, c/o Lewistown, MT, St. Leo's. (GF)
Winn, ME, Penobscot Co., Sacred Heart, c/o Lincoln, ME, St. Mary. (PRT)
Winn, MI, Isabella Co., St. Leo, c/o Shepherd, MI, St. Vincent De Paul. (SAG)
Winnett, MT, Petroleum Co., St. Aloysius, c/o Roundup, MT, St. Benedict's. (GF)
Winnsboro, SC, Fairfield Co., St. Theresa, c/o Blythewood, SC, Transfiguration. (CHR)
Winnsboro, TX, Wood Co., St. Ann Church, c/o Sulphur Springs, TX, St. James. (TYL)
Winona, MS, Montgomery Co., Sacred Heart, c/o Lexington, MS, St. Thomas. (JKS)
Winslow, AR, Crawford Co., Our Lady of the Ozarks Shrine, c/o Van Buren, AR, St. Michael's. (LR)
Winston–Salem, NC, Forsyth Co., Our Lady of Fatima, c/o Winston–Salem, NC, Our Lady of Mercy. (CHL)
Winter Harbor, ME, Hancock Co., St. Margaret, c/o Ellsworth, ME, St. Joseph's. (PRT)
Winter Park, CO, Grand Co., St. Bernard, c/o Granby, CO, St. Anne. (DEN)
Winterhaven, CA, Imperial Co., St. Mary, c/o Winterhaven, CA, St. Thomas. (SD)
Wisdom, MT, Beaverhead Co., Our Lady of Wisdom, c/o Dillon, MT, St. Rose of Lima. (HEL)
Wolf Creek, MT, Lewis and Clark Co., Sacred Heart, c/o Helena, MT, Our Lady of the Valley. (HEL)
Wolfforth, TX, Lubbock Co., St. Francis of Assisi, c/o Lubbock, TX, San Ramon. (LUB)
Wood, SD, Melette Co., Our Lady of Good Counsel, c/o White River, SD, St. Ignatius. (RC)
Wood, SD, Mellette Co., Our Lady of Good Counsel, c/o St. Francis, SD, Rosebud Reservation. (RC)
Woodland, WI, Dodge Co., St. Mary, c/o Neosho, WI, St. Matthew. (MIL)
Woodville, CA, Tulare Co., St. Francis of Assisi, c/o Tipton, CA, St. John The Evangelist. (FRS)
Woodville, FL, Leon Co., St. Stephen the Protomartyr, c/o Crawfordville, FL, St. Elizabeth Ann Seton. (PT)
Woodward, IA, St. John of God, c/o Madrid, IA, St. Malachy's. (SC)
Woodworth, LA, Rapides Parish, Mary, Mother of Jesus, c/o Lecompte, LA, St. Martin. (ALX)
Wounded Knee, SD, Shannon Co., Sacred Heart, c/o Manderson, SD, St. Agnes. (RC)
Wright, WY, Campbell Co., Blessed Sacrament, c/o Gillette, WY, St. Matthew's. (CHY)
Wyanet, IL, Bureau Co., St. Margaret Mary, c/o Sheffield, IL, St. Patrick's. (PEO)
Wyola, MT, Big Horn Co., Blessed Kateri Tekakwitha, c/o Lodge Grass, MT, Our Lady of Loretto. (GF)

Y

Yacolt, WA, Clark Co., St. Joseph the Workman, c/o Battle Ground, WA, Sacred Heart. (SEA)
Yadkinville, NC, Yadkin Co., Cristo Rey Catholic Hispanic Center of Yadkin Valley, c/o Clemmons, NC, Holy Family. (CHL)
Yahuecas, PR, Adjuntas Co., Virgen del Carmen, c/o Adjuntas, PR, St. Joachim. (PCE)
Yakima, WA, Yakima Co., St. Joseph Mission at the Ahtanum, c/o Yakima, WA, Holy Family. (YAK)
Yancey, TX, Medina Co., Immaculate Heart of Mary, c/o D'Hanis, TX, Holy Cross. (SAT)
Yarmouth Port, MA, Barnstable Co., Sacred Heart Chapel, c/o Hyannis, MA, St. Francis Xavier's. (FR)
Yarnell, AZ, Yavapai Co., St. Mary's, c/o Prescott, AZ, Sacred Heart. (PHX)
Yellowstone National Park, WY, Park Co., c/o Cody, WY, St. Anthony. (CHY)
Yellville, AR, Marion Co., St Andrews Catholic Church, c/o Harrison, AR, Mary, Mother of God. (LR)
Yolo, CA, Yolo Co., Our Lady of Guadalupe, c/o Woodland, CA, Holy Rosary. (SAC)
York, SC, York Co., All Saints, c/o Rock Hill, SC, Divine Saviour. (CHR)
York Beach, ME, York Co., St. Mary, Star of the Sea, c/o York, ME, St. Christopher–by–the–Sea. (PRT)
Yorktown, TX, DeWitt Co., San Luis, c/o Yorktown, TX, Holy Cross. (VIC)
Youngsville, NM, Rio Arriba Co., c/o Abiquiu, NM, St. Thomas Apostle. (SFE)
Yuma, AZ, Yuma Co., Our Lady of Guadalupe, c/o Yuma, AZ, Immaculate Conception. (TUC)

Z

Zama, PR, Jayuya Co., Santa Cecila, c/o Jayuya, PR, Our Lady of Monserrate. (PCE)
Zamora, CA, Yolo Co., St. Agnes, c/o Knights Landing, CA, St. Paul. (SAC)
Zapata, TX, Zapata Co., Ntra. Sra. Del Refugio, c/o Zapata, TX, Our Lady of Lourdes. (LAR)
Zia, NM, Sandoval Co., c/o Jemez Pueblo, NM, San Diego Indian Missions. (SFE)
Zolfo Springs, FL, Hardee Co., San Alfonso Catholic Center, c/o Wauchula, FL, St. Michael. (VEN)
Zortman, MT, Phillips Co., St. Joseph, c/o Hays, MT, St. Paul's Indian Mission. (GF)

National Church Goods Association
Dealers

Alabama
Alpha Church Supply & Gifts
800-824-3887
Robert Moore Church Supply Co.
888-661-5252
Arizona
Autom
800-521-2914
602-258-8481
King's House, The
800-621-8254
Arkansas
Guardian Church Goods Store
501-372-2582
California
Ave Maria Community Book Center
800-741-6279
Cotter Church Supplies, Inc.
800-446-3366
J.R. Evans & Company
800-453-8267
Kaufer's Religious Supplies
800-874-6987
Keane's Religious Goods & Gifts
800-500-1241
McCoy Church Goods Company, Inc.
800-824-4652
San Diego Church Supply, Inc.
800-882-8234
San Joaquin Religious Goods
800-727-7373
209-523-2579
Canada
Bertrand, Foucher, Belanger, Inc.
800-263-1559
Broughton's Church Supplies
800-268-4449
Desmarais & Robitaille, Ltd.
800-363-7799
R.D. MacLean Company Ltd.
800-561-7037
St. Andrews Book, Gift & Church Supply
800-663-7161
Colorado
Gerken's Religious Supplies
800-437-5367
Connecticut
Baker & Sons, Inc., Patrick
800-243-6385
Florida
Holy Land Art Co., Inc.
800-526-1294
Moroneys' Religious Art, Inc.
800-423-7704
Shrine Religious & Church Supplies
800-342-6529
Watra Church Goods
800-282-6646
Idaho
Reilly's Church Supply
800-635-5190
Illinois
Heaven Sent Specialties
877-842-2172
J.F. Morrow & Sons, Inc.
773-631-8844
Lagron-Miller Company, Inc.
800-322-8116
Watra Church Goods
800-247-2425
Wheaton Religious Gift & Church Supply
800-837-4974

Indiana
Boric Religious Supply, Inc.
888-412-2775
Krieg Bros. Catholic Supply House
317-638-3416
Mother of Our Savior
800-451-3993
Iowa
Dubuque Religious Center, Inc.
563-556-8920
Fitzgibbon Company
712-258-1211
Religious Supply Center, Inc.
800-553-0025
Kentucky
Tonini Church Supply Co.
800-626-3545
Louisiana
Church Supply House
800-749-6528
Louisiana Church Interiors, Inc.
800-252-3328
Maryland
Gallery & Company, William J.
301-942-4700
Massachusetts
Andrew Lane Company
978-532-2025
Thomas P. Egan, Inc. Church Supplies
800-235-0003
617-436-4360
Michigan
A. Mateja Church Supply
800-662-8352
Andrzejewksi's Marian Church Supply
800-345-4694
Angelus Religious Goods
800-883-2524
E.J. McDevitt Company, Inc.
734-427-6460
Fuchs Company, G.A.
800-824-7600
Michigan Church Supply
800-521-3440
Minnesota
Leaflet Missal Company
888-532-3538
Lohmann's
800-328-1602
St. Patrick's Guild
800-652-9767
Missouri
Catholic Supply of St. Louis, Inc.
800-325-9026
Donnelly Company, I.
816-363-2828
O'Byrne Religious Goods, Inc.
800-626-9476
Nebraska
The Cosgrave Company
800-228-9785
New Hampshire
Cathedral Church Goods Co.
800-257-3014

New Jersey
Abbott Church Goods
800-522-2688
Dicocco Family St. Jude Shop, Inc.
908-429-0808
856-216-0330
Holy Land Art Co., Inc.
800-334-3621
Sikora's
800-358-5112
New Mexico
Garson & Sons, Inc.
800-835-0223
New York
Patrick Baker & Sons, Inc.
212-813-2065
Catholic Union Store
800-373-2728
Chiarelli's Religious Goods, Inc.
718-277-2990
631-271-6514
G. Siccardi & Family
888-490-4100
Good News Book Store & Religious Goods
631-757-5423
Joseph T. Reilly Church Goods
800-346-3929
Trosset Church Supply
800-342-9500
W.B. O'Connor Church Goods, Inc.
800-342-1231
Walsh/Conley Religious Goods, Inc.
800-632-2729
North Dakota
Hurley's Religious Goods, Inc.
800-437-4338
Ohio
Cathedral Bookshop
800-479-9021
Churchill's Religious Goods & Gifts
419-471-0667
800-326-0667
Dayton Church Supply, Inc.
800-553-3435
Henninger's, Inc.
800-362-0217
Mazzolini Artcraft Co., Inc.
216-431-7529
Meyer-Vogelpohl
800-543-0264
Reger Company, John A.
877-605-0561
Stanley A. McKay & Associates-East
800-228-9333
Stanley A. McKay & Associates-West
800-782-6625
Trinity Church Supply
800-327-2516
Oklahoma
Ziegler Co., F. C.
800-331-4117
Oregon
Dove Book Center
800-262-3683

Pennsylvania
The Catholic Shop
717-657-8747
Dicocco Family St. Jude Shop, Inc.
610-789-1300
215-742-6045
215-389-7694
215-563-5433
Guild, The
800-367-6610
Hofmann's Church & Religious Goods
800-422-0502
Holoviak's Church Supply, Inc.
570-759-1581
Merhaut, A.T.
800-510-7530
Paul J. Wolf Co.
800-218-4948
Robert Francis, Inc.
610-352-5338
St. Jude Religious Stores, Inc.
888-662-2356
Rhode Island
Tally's Church Supplies
800-556-7272
South Dakota
Hurley's Religious Goods, Inc.
605-334-3473
Tennessee
St. Mary's Bookstore & Church Supply
800-233-3604
Texas
Mary Regina, Inc.
800-554-4045
Sacco Church Supplies, Inc.
800-231-7513
St. Anthony's Church Supplies
800-772-5928
Utah
Mancuso's Religious Goods
800-327-0169
Vermont
Vermont Church Supply, Inc.
800-451-3453
Virginia
Peter C. Munley Church Goods
703-241-2139
Religious Goods Shop, Inc.
800-355-6634
Washington
Kaufer's Religious Supplies
800-426-3320
800-873-7375
Vercillo's Church Supply
866-471-8399
Wisconsin
Carl B. Noelke Co..
800-433-9162
F. Kaster Co., Inc.
800-726-4154
Jandrain Religious Supply, Inc.
800-242-2700
St. Patrick's Bookstore
920-731-7635
T.H. Stemper Co.
800-686-3610

NATIONAL CHURCH GOODS ASSOCIATION
NCGA

Quality, Service, & Education.

Index for Religious Institutes of Men

Religious Order Initials for Men

A.A.	Assumptionists	[0130]
B.C.S.	Brothers of Christian Service	[]
B.G.S.	Little Brothers of the Good Shepherd	[0580]
B.S.O.	Basilian Salvatorian Fathers	[0190]
C.F.A.	Alexian Brothers	[0120]
C.F.C.	Congregation of Christian Brothers	[0310]
C.F.M.M.	Brothers of Our Lady, Mother of Mercy	[0980]
C.F.P.	Brothers of the Poor of St. Francis	[0460]
C.F.R.	Franciscan Friars of the Renewal	[0535]
C.F.X.	Brothers of St. Francis Xavier	[1350]
C.I.C.M.	Missionhurst Congregation of the Immaculate Heart of Mary	[0860]
C.J.	Josephite Fathers	[0710]
C.J.M.	Congregation of Jesus and Mary	[0450]
C.M.	Congregation of the Mission	[1330]
C.M.C.	Congregation of Mother Coredemptrix	[]
C.M.F.	Claretian Missionaries	[0360]
C.M.I.	Carmelites of Mary Immaculate	[0275]
C.M.L.M.	The Congregation of Maronite Lebanese Missionaries	[0785]
C.M.M.	Congregation of Mananhill Missionaries, Marianhill Fathers & Brothers	[0750]
C. M.Vd.	Mekhitarist Fathers	[]
C.O.	Oratorians	[0950]
C.P.	Congregation of the Passion	[1000]
C.P.M.	Congregation of the Fathers of Mercy	[0820]
C.PP.S.	Society of the Precious Blood	[1060]
C.R.	Congregation of the Resurrection	[1080]
C.R.	Theatine Fathers	[1300]
C.R.I.C.	Canons Regular of the Immaculate Conception	[]
C.R.L.	Canons Regular of the Lateran	[0250]
C.R.M.	Adorno Fathers	[0100]
C.R.S.	Somascan Fathers	[1250]
C.R.S.P.	Clerics Regular of St. Paul	[0160]
C.S.	Missionaries of St. Charles Scalabrinians	[1210]
C.S.B.	Basilian Fathers	[0170]
C.S.C.	Brothers of the Congregation of Holy Cross	[0600]
C.S.C.	Priests of the Congregation of Holy Cross	[0610]
C.S.J.	Congregation of St. Joseph	[1150]
C.S.J.B.	Congregation of St. John the Baptist	[]
C.S.P.	Paulist Fathers	[1030]
C.S.P.X.	Brothers of Saint Pius X	[1180]
C.S.S.	Stigmatine Fathers and Brothers.	[1280]
C.S.Sp.	Congregation of the Holy Spirit	[0650]
C.SS.R.	Redemptorist Fathers	[1070]
C.S.V.	Clerics of St. Viator	[1320]
D.L.P.	Diocesan Labor Priests	[]
Er.Cam.	Camaldolese Hermits of the Congregation of Monte Corona	[0230]
F.C.	Brothers of Charity	[0290]
F.D.P.	Sons of Divine Providence	[0410]
F.F.I.	Franciscan Friars of the Immaculate	[0533]
F.F.S C.	Franciscan Brothers of the Holy Cross	[0510]
F.I.C.	Brothers of Christian Instruction	[0320]
F.J.	Congregation of St. John	[]
F.M.M.	Brothers of Mercy	[0810]
F.M.M.	Missionary Fraternity of Mary	[]
F.M.S.	The Marist Brothers	[0770]
F.M.S.I.	Sons of Mary Missionary Society	[1270]
F.P.M.	Presentation Brothers	[]
F.S.C.	Brothers of the Christian Schools	[0330]
F.S.E.	Brothers of the Holy Eucharist	[0620]
F.S.P.	Brothers of St. Patrick	[1160]
F.S.R.	Brothers of the Congregation of Our Lady of the Holy Rosary	[0960]
F.S.S.P.	Priestly Fraternity of St. Peter	[1065]
G.H.M.	The Glenmary Home Missioners	[0570]
H.J.D.	Los Hermanos de Juan Diego	[]
H.M.C.	Hermits of Mount Carmel	[]
I.C.	Institute of Charity	[0300]
I.C.	Incarnational Consecration	[]
I.H.M.	Brothers of the Immaculate Heart of Mary	[0680]
I.M.C.	Consolata Missionaries	[0390]
I.S.S.S.	Schoenstatt Institute of Secular Priests	[]
L.B.S.F.	Little Brothers of Saint Francis	[1144]
L.C.	Legionaries of Christ	[0730]
M.Afr.	Missionaries of Africa	[0850]
M.C.B.S.	Missionary Congregation of the Blessed Sacrament	[]
M.C.C.J.	Comboni Missionaries of the Heart of Jesus (Verona)	[0380]
M.Des.	Mercedarios Descalzos	[]
M.E.P.	Paris Foreign Mission Society	[0897]
M.G.	Guadalupe Missioners	[]
M.H.M.	Mill Hill Missionaries	[0830]
M.I.C.	Congregation of Marians of the Immaculate Conception	[0740]
M.J.	Missionaries of St. Joseph (Mexico)	[]
M.M.	Maryknoll	[0800]
M.S.	The Missionaries of Our Lady of La Salette	[0720]
M.S.A.	Missionaries of the Holy Apostles	[0590]
M.S.C.	Missionaries of the Sacred Heart	[1110]
M.S.F.	Congregation of the Missionaries of the Holy Family	[0630]
M.S.P.	Missionaries of St. Paul	[]
M.Sp.S.	Missionaries of the Holy Spirit	[0660]
M.SS.CC.	Missionaries of the Sacred Hearts of Jesus and Mary	[1120]
O.A.R.	Order of the Augustinian Recollects	[0150]
O.Carm.	Carmelite Fathers and Brothers	[0270]
O.Cart.	Order of Carthusians	[0280]
O.C.D.	Discalced Carmelite Fathers	[0260]
O.Cist.	Cistercian Fathers	[0340]
O.C.S.O.	The Cistercian Order of the Strict Observance (Trappists)	[0350]
O.de.M.	Order of Our Lady of Mercy	[0970]
O.F.M.	Franciscan Friars	[0520]
O.F.M.Cap.	The Capuchin Friars	[0470]
O.F.M.Conv.	Conventual Franciscans	[0480]
O.H.	Hospitaller Brothers of St. John of God	[0670]
O.I.C.	Order of the Imitation of Christ	[]
O.L P.	Brothers of Our Lady of Providence	[]
O.M.	Minim Fathers	[0835]
O.Mar.	Congregation of Maronite Monks	[0790]
O.M.I.	Oblates of Mary Immaculate	[0910]
O.M.V.	Oblates of the Virgin Mary	[0940]
O.P.	Order of Preachers (Dominicans)	[0430]
O.Praem.	Canons Regular of Premontre	[0900]
O.R.C.	Operarios del Reina de Cristo	[]
O.S.A.	The Augustinians	[0140]
O.S.B.	Benedictine Monks	[0200]
O.S.B.Cam.	Camaldolese Hermits	[]
O S.B.M.	Order of St. Basil the Great	[0180]
O.S.C.	Canons Regular of the Order of the Holy Cross	[0400]
O.S.Cam.	Camillian Fathers and Brothers	[0240]
O.S.F.	Congregation of the Religious Brothers of the Third Order Regular of St. Francis	[0490]
O.S.F.	Franciscan Brothers of Christ the King	[0500]
O.S.F.	Franciscan Brothers of the Third Order Regular	[0515]
O.S.F.	Franciscan Missionary Brothers of the Sacred Heart of Jesus	[0540]
O.S.F.S.	Oblates of St. Francis de Sales	[0920]
O.S.J.	Oblates of St. Joseph	[0930]
O.S.M.	Servites	[1240]
O.S.P.P.E.	Pauline Fathers	[1010]
O.Ss.S.	Brigittine Monks	[0895]
O.SS.T.	Order of the Holy Trinity	[1310]
P.I.M.E.	Pontifical Institute for Foreign Missions	[1050]
R.C.J.	Rogationist Fathers	[1090]
S.A.	Franciscan Friars of the Atonement	[0530]
S.A.C.	Society of the Catholic Apostolate	[0990]
S.C.	Brothers of the Sacred Heart	[1100]
S.C.	Servants of Charity	[1220]
S.Ch.	Society of Christ	[1260]
Sch.P.	Piarist Fathers.	[1040]
S.C.J.	Congregation of the Priests of the Sacred Heart	[1130]
S.D.B.	Salesians of Don Bosco	[1190]
S.D.S.	Society of the Divine Savior	[1200]
S.D.V.	Vocationist Fathers	[1340]
S.F.	Sons of the Holy Family	[0640]
S.F.M.	Scarboro Foreign Missions	[]
S.J.	Jesuit Fathers and Brothers	[0690]
S.M.	Society of Mary (Marianists)	[0760]
S.M.	Marist Fathers	[0780]
S.M.A.	Society of African Missions	[0110]
S.M.M.	Montfort Missionaries	[0870]
S.M.P.	Society of Our Mother of Peace	[]
S.O.Cist.	Cistercian Monks of the Strict Observance	[]
S.O.L.T.	Society of Our Lady of the Most Holy Trinity	[0975]
s.P.	Servants of the Paraclete	[1230]
S.P.S.	St. Patrick Missionary Society	[1170]
S.S.	Society of the Priests of Saint Sulpice	[1290]
S.S.C.	Society of St. Columban	[0370]
SS.CC.	Congregation of the Sacred Hearts of Jesus and Mary	[1140]
S.S.E.	Society of Saint Edmund	[0440]
S.S.J.	St. Joseph's Society of the Sacred Heart	[0700]
S.S.P.	Pauline Fathers and Brothers	[1020]
S.S.S.	Congregation of the Blessed Sacrament	[0220]
S.S.T.	Missionary Society of St. Thomas the Apostle	[]
S.T.	Missionary Servants of the Most Holy Trinity	[0840]
S.X.	Xaverian Missionary Fathers	[1360]
S.V.D.	Society of the Divine Word	[0420]
T.O.R.	Third Order Regular of Saint Francis	[0560]
V.C.	Vincentian Congregation (India)	[]
V.D.C.	Verbum Dei Community	[]

Religious Institutes of Men

The Conference of Major Superiors of Men's Institute of the United States, Inc., 8808 Cameron St., Silver Spring, MD 20910. Tel: 301-588-4030; Fax: 301-587-4575. Very Rev. Ronald D. Witherup, S.S., Pres.; Very Rev. John L. Doctor, O.F.M., Vice Pres.; Bro. Daniel F. Casey, F.S.C., Sec./Treas.; Rev. Ted Keating, S.M., Exec. Dir.

[0100] (C.R.M.)—ADORNO FATHERS

(Clerics Regular Minor)

General Motherhouse: *Via Alpi Apuane 1,* 00141 Rome, Italy. Very Rev. Nello Morrea, C.R.M., Supr. Gen.

U.S. Foundation (1936): *St. Michael's* Seminary, 575 Darlington Ave., Ramsey, NJ 07446. Tel: 201-327-7375; Fax: 201-934-5826. Revs. Americo Salvi, C.R.M., U. S. Delegate; Michael Marotta, C.R.M., Supr.

Priests 7; Brothers 5

Represented in the Archdiocese of Newark and in the Diocese of Charleston.

[0110] (S.M.A.)—SOCIETY OF AFRICAN MISSIONS

(Societas Missionum ad Afros)

Founded Dec. 8, 1856 with the approval of Pope Pius IX. A clerical society of apostolic life.

General Motherhouse: *Via della Nocetta 111,* 00164 Rome, Italy. Very Rev. Kiernan O'Reilly, S.M.A., Supr. Gen.; Revs. Lorenzo Mandirola, S.M.A., Vicar Gen.; Rev. Paul Chataigne, S.M.A. Gen. Councilor; Michael McCabe, S.M.A., Gen. Councilor.

American Province (1941): 23 Bliss Ave., Tenafly, NJ 07670. Tel: 201-567-0450; Fax: 201-541-1280. Very Rev. Thomas A. Wright, S.M.A., Prov. Supr. Tel: 201-567-9085; Fax: 201-567-7156; Revs. Thomas E. Hayden, S.M.A., Vice Prov.; Brendan Darcy, S.M.A., Local Supr.; James Gessler, S.M.A., Prov.

Legal Title: *Society of African Missions, Inc. N.J.*

Priests 35; Lay Missionary in temporary commitment 6; Lay Missionary in permanent commitment 1; Priest Associates 1; Seminarians 1.

Represented in the Archdioceses of Boston, Newark and Washington.

[0120] (C.F.A.)—ALEXIAN BROTHERS

(Congregatio Fratrum Cellitarum seu Alexianorum)

Generalate: *Signal Mountain,* TN 37377. Tel: 423-886-2969. Bros. Edward Walsh, Supr. Gen.; Warren Longo, Asst. Gen., 3910 Ohio, St. Louis, MO 63118; Kamillus Bonn, Gen. Councilor: 52001 Aachen, Germany; Dominick Champagne, C.F.A., Gen. Councilor: B-2530 Boechout, Belgium.

General Motherhouse: *Congregation of Alexian Brothers,* No. 198 James Blvd., Signal Mountain, TN

United States Province (1866): 600 Alexian Way, Elk Grove Village, IL 60007. Tel: 847-640-7550; Fax: 847-981-5561. Bro. Lawrence Krueger, C.F.A., Prov. Supr.; Prov. Councilors: Bros. Thomas Keusenkothen, C.F.A.; James Classon, C.F.A.; Richard Dube, C.F.A.; Theodore Loucks, C.F.A.; Partick Gaughan, Dir.-Vocations.

Professed Brothers 38; Novice Brothers 3.

Properties owned and or sponsored: General Hospitals 3; Continuing Care Retirement Communities 2; Alzheimers Assisted Living Facility 1; Novitiates 2; Nursing Homes 2; Residential AIDS Facility 3; HUD Housing 3; Pace 2; Mobile Clinic & Wellness Center (Davao, Philippine) 1.

Represented in the Archdioceses of Chicago, Milwaukee, and St. Louis and the Diocese of Knoxville. Also in Davao, Philippines.

[0130] (A.A.)—ASSUMPTIONISTS

(Augustinians of the Assumption)

General House: via San Pio V, 55, Rome, Italy 00165. Very Rev. Richard Lamoureux, A.A., Supr. Gen.

Province of North America (1946): 330 Market St., Brighton, MA 02135. Tel: 617-783-0400. Very Rev. John L. Franck, A.A., Prov. Supr.; Councilors: Revs. Miguel Diaz Ayllon, A.A.; Dennis Gallagher, A.A.; Christian Blance, A.A.; Stephen Goguen, A.A., Prov. Treas.

Priests 55; Brothers 10.

Parishes 3; Shrines 1; Colleges 1; Formation Centers 1; Novitiates 1; Residences 8.

Represented in the Archdioceses of Boston and New York and in the Dioceses of St. Petersburg, Nashville and Worcester. Also in Jerusalem, Kenya, Mexico, Tanzania, Italy and Canada.

[0140] (O.S.A.)—THE AUGUSTINIANS

(Ordo Fratrum Sancti Augustini)

Founded in 1244, first American foundation 1796.

Generalate: *Via Paolo VI,* 25 00193, Rome, Italy. Most Rev. Robert F. Prevost, O.S.A., Gen.

Province of St. Thomas of Villanova (1796): *Saint Augustine Friary,* 214 Ashwood Rd., P.O. Box 340, Villanova, PA 19085-0340. Tel: 610-527-3330. Very Rev. Donald F. Reilly, O.S.A., Prior Prov.; Revs. John R. Flynn, O.S.A., Prov. Sec.; Anthony P. Burrascano, O.S.A., Prov. Treas.; Prov. Counselors: Revs. William J. Donnelly, O.S.A.; William T. Garland, O.S.A.; Anthony M. Genovese, O.S.A.; James M. Paradis, O.S.A.; Jorge A. Reyes, O.S.A.; James D. McBurney, O.S.A., Dir. Vocations; Joseph S. Mostardi, O.S.A., Dir. Augustinian Volunteers; Richard D. Appicci, O.S.A., Dir. Mission Office; John J. Sheridan, O.S.A., Archivist; Joseph A. Genito, O.S.A., Counselor & Dir. Augustinian Justice & Peace Office.

Legal Title: *The Brothers of the Order of Hermits of Saint Augustine* (The Brothers of the Order of Hermits of St. Augustine, a corporation in the state of Pennsylvania.)

Priests 224; Students in Theology 12; Brothers 8; Permanent Deacon 1.

Parishes 26 (USA 21; Japan 4; South Africa 1); Major Seminary 1; Colleges 1; Universities 1; Preparatory Schools and High Schools 3; Foreign Missions.

Represented in the Archdioceses of Boston, Miami, New York, Philadelphia, and Washington and the Dioceses of Albany, Charlotte, Orlando and Venice.

Province of Our Mother of Good Counsel (Order of St. Augustine) (1941): *Tolentine College & Center,* 20300 Governors Hwy., Olympia Fields, IL 60461-1081. Tel: 708-748-9500; Fax: 708-481-2090. Web site: www.midwestaugustinians.org. Very Rev. David L. Brecht, O.S.A., Prior Prov.; Rev. G. Jerome Knies, O.S.A., Vicar Prov. & Personnel Dir.; Bros. Thomas P. Taylor, O.S.A., Prov. Sec.; William E. Lego, O.S.A., Prov. Treas.; Rev. Reinhard J. Sternemann, O.S.A., Dir. Tolentine Center; Rev. John D. Merkelis, O.S.A., Vocation Dir.

Fathers 93; Bishops 2; Permanent Deacons 1; Professed Brothers 17.

Parishes 12; High Schools 3; Retreat Centers 1; Residences 5.

Represented in the Archdioceses of Chicago, Detroit, Milwaukee, and St. Louis and in the Dioceses of Fort Worth, Joliet, Kalamazoo, Lansing and Tulsa. Also in Peru, South America.

Province of St. Augustine: 1605 28th St., San Diego, CA 92102-1417. Tel: 619-235-0247. Very Rev. Steven M. Ochoa, O.S.A., Prov.; Counselors: Revs. Patrick Keane, O.S.A.; Walter P. Vogel, O.S.A.; Thomas J.F. Whelan, O.S.A.; Kevin C. Mullins, O.S.A., Sec.

Legal Holdings or Titles: *St. Augustine High School,* San Diego, CA; *Monica House,* San Diego, CA; *Tierra del Sol,* Boulevard, CA; *Rita de Cascia House,* San Francisco, CA; *Villanova Preparatory School,* Ojai, CA; *Austin House,* San Diego, CA.

Priests 28; Deacons 1; Brothers 8.

Parishes 6; High Schools 2; Low-Income Housing 2; Orphanages 1.

Represented in the Archdioceses of Los Angeles, and Portland (OR) and the Dioceses of Oakland, Orange and San Diego.

Order of St. Augustine Province of St. Joseph: P.O. Box 333, King City, Ontario Canada. L0G 1K0

Province of St. Thomas Villanova: *St. Augustine Preparatory School,* 611 Cedar Ave., P.O. Box 279, Richland NJ 08350. Tel: 856-697-2600; Fax: 856-697-8389. Revs. Paul Galetto, O.S.A., Ph.D., Pres.; Ronald Hamaday, O.S.A., Prior.

St. Augustine Preparatory School.

Represented in the Archdiocese of Philadelphia and in the Diocese of Camden.

Region U.S.A. (1993): *Christo Rey Church,* 767 Ave. A, Beaumont, TX 77701. Tel: 409-835-7788. Rev. Luis Urriza, O.S.A., Reg. Delegate.

Fathers 6.

Represented in the Archdiocese of San Antonio and in the Diocese of Beaumont.

[0150] (O.A.R.)—ORDER OF THE AUGUSTINIAN RECOLLECTS

(Ordo Augustinianorum Recollectorum)

General Motherhouse: Rome, Italy, Viale dell' Astronomia 27 (E.U.R.). Most Rev. Javier Guerra, O.A.R., Prior Gen.

Province of St. Augustine (1944): *Augustinian Recollects,* 29 Ridgeway Ave., West Orange, NJ 07052-3297. Tel: 973-731-0616; Fax: 973-731-1033. Very Rev. John A. Gruben, O.A.R., Prior Prov.; Revs. Charles Huse, O.A.R., 1st Councilor, Vicar of Prov.; Jose Antonio Arias, O.A.R., 2nd Councilor; Marlon Beof O.A.R., 3rd Councilor; Jose Luis Martinez, O.A.R., 4th Councilor.

Priests 37; Brothers 10; Professed Clerics 5; Novices 2; Postulants 4.

Represented in the Archdioceses of Los Angeles, Newark and New York and in the Diocese of Orange. Also in Mexico.

Province of St. Nicholas of Tolentine (U.S.A. Delegation): 3201 Central Ave., Union City, NJ 07087. Rev. Francisco Legarra, O.A.R., Prov. Delegate.

Priests 24

Represented in the Archdioceses of Newark and New York and in the Dioceses of El Paso and Las Cruces.

[0160] (C.R.S.P.)—CLERICS REGULAR OF ST. PAUL

(Barnabite Fathers)

(Ordo Clericorum Regularium Sancti Pauli)

Founded in Milan, Italy in 1533. First foundation in the United States in 1952 in Buffalo, NY.

Historical Motherhouse: *Church of St. Barnabas,* Milan, since 1545.

General Motherhouse: Via Giacomo Medici, 15, Rome, Italy. Most Rev. Giovanni M. Villa, C.R.S.P., Supr. Gen.

North American Province: *Provincial Motherhouse,* 981 Swann Rd.- P.O. Box 167, Youngstown, NY 14174-0167. Tel: 716-754-7489. Very Rev. Gabriel M. Patil, C.R.S.P., Prov.

Legal Title: *Barnabite Fathers, Inc.*

Priests 16.

Fathers staff and serve: Parishes; Marian Shrine; Colleges; Spiritual Centers.

Properties Owned: *Our Lady of Fatima Shrine and Barnabite Fathers Seminary,* Youngstown, NY; *Barnabite Spiritual Center,* Bethlehem, PA.

Represented in the Dioceses of Allentown, Buffalo and San Diego. Also in Hamilton, Ontario, and Canada.

[0170] (C.S.B.)—BASILIAN FATHERS

(Congregatio Presbyterorum a S. Basilio)

General Curia: *Cardinal Flahiff Basilian Centre,* 95 St. Joseph St., Toronto, Ont. Canada. M5S 3C2, Tel: 416-921-6674; Fax: 416-920-3413.

Eastern U.S.: *Casa San Basilio,* 1910 W. Alabama, Houston, TX 77098. Tel: 713-522-1736. Very Rev. Ken Decker, C.S.B., Supr. Gen.; Rev. Alvin A. Sinasac, C.S.B., U.S. Gen. Councilor.

[0180] (O.S.B.M.)—ORDER OF ST. BASIL THE GREAT

(Ordo Sancti Basilii Magni)

General Superior "Protoarchimandrita": Rome, Italy 00153 (Aventino), Via San Giosafat 8. Rt. Rev. Dionysius Lachovicz, O.S.B.M.,

American Province (1948): 29 Peacock Lane, Locust Valley, NY 11506. Tel: 516-609-3262; Fax: 516-609-3264. Very Rev. Mauricio Popadiuk, O.S.B.M., Prov.

Fathers 24; Scholastics 7; Brothers 3; Novices 4.

Parishes 6; Community Houses 6; House of Studies; Novitiate; Monasteries 3; Retreat House; Library.

Represented in the Byzantine Rite Archdiocese of Philadelphia and in the Byzantine Rite Dioceses of Chicago, Parma, Passaic and Stamford.

[0190] (B.S.O.)—BASILIAN SALVATORIAN FATHERS

General Motherhouse: *Holy Savior Monastery,* Saida, Lebanon. Rt. Rev. Salim Ghazal, B.S.O., Supr. Gen.

American Headquarters: *Basilian Salvatorian Fathers,* 30 East St., Methuen, MA 01844. Rt. Rev. Gerasimos Murphy, B.S.O., J.C.D., Prov. Supr.; Revs. Simon Hage, B.S.O.; Lawrence Tumminelli, B.S.O.; John Jadaa, B.S.O.; Youssef Aziz, B.S.O.; Adib Badaoui, B.S.O.; George Dagher, B.S.O.; Eugene Mitchell, B.S.O., General Economos; Martin A. Hyatt, B.S.O., Local Supr.

Fathers in American Region 22.

Novitiate and House of Studies: St. Basils Seminary; Methuen, MA.

Parishes: Canada 4; U.S.A. 7.
Represented in the Archdioceses of Boston and Miami and in the Dioceses of Cleveland, Manchester, Newton and Norwich.

[0200] (O.S.B.)—BENEDICTINE MONKS
(Ordo Sancti Benedicti)

American Cassinese Congregation of the Order of Saint Benedict (Established by Pope Pius IX, August 24, 1855.)

Headquarters: *Saint John's Abbey,* Box 2015, Collegeville, MN 56321-2015. Tel: 320-363-3935; Fax: 320-363-3082. Rt. Rev. Timothy Kelly, O.S.B., Abbot Pres. Abbot.

President's Council: Rt. Rev. Douglas Nowicki, O.S.B., Saint Vincent Archabbey; Rt. Rev. Barnabas Senecal, O.S.B., Saint Benedict's Abbey; Rev. Claude Peifer, O.S.B., Saint Bede Abbey; Rev. Thomas Acklin, O.S.B., Saint Vincent Archabbey; Rev. Daniel Ward, O.S.B., Saint John Abbey.

The Abbeys and Priories belonging to this Congregation are as follows:

Saint Vincent Archabbey: 300 Fraser Purchase Rd., Latrobe, PA 15650-2690. Tel: 724-532-6600. Rt. Rev. Douglas R. Nowicki, O.S.B., Archabbot; Rt. Rev. Paul R. Maher, O.S.B., Archabbot (Resigned); Most Rev. Rembert G. Weakland, O.S.B., Resigned Archbishop of Milwaukee.
Legal Titles: *The Benedictine Society of Westmoreland County; Saint Vincent College Corporation; The Wimmer Corporation; The Saint Vincent Cemetery Corporation.*
Priests 125; Deacons 3; Solemn Professed Choir-Monks 26; Junior Professed Monks 10; Brothers 6; Choir Novices 9.
Represented in the Archdiocese of Baltimore and in the Dioceses of Altoona-Johnstown, Erie, Greensburg, Harrisburg, Pittsburgh, Richmond, Savannah and Wheeling-Charleston.

American Cassinese Congregations

St. John's Abbey: P.O. Box 2015, Collegeville, MN 56321-2015. Tel: 320-363-2011; Fax: 320-363-3082. Rt. Rev. John Klassen, O.S.B., Abbot; Very Rev. Raymond Pedrizetti, O.S.B., Prior; Very Ven. Paul Richards, O.S.B., Subprior.
Monastery Founded in 1856 and raised to an Abbey in 1866.
Fathers 121; Professed Brothers 54; Novices 1.
Abbeys 1; Dependent Priories 2; Parishes 18; Chaplaincies 11; Indian Mission Residences 1; Japanese Residences 2; School of Theology 1; University 1; High Schools 2; Novitiates 1.
Legal Holdings: *Saint John's Seminary; Saint John's University; Saint John's Preparatory School; Saint John's Abbey.*
Represented in the Archdiocese of St. Paul-Minneapolis and in the Dioceses of New Ulm, St. Cloud and San Bernardino. Also in Japan, The Bahamas and Republic of China.

St. Benedict's Abbey: 1020 North Second St., Atchison, KS 66002-1499. Tel: 913-367-7853; Fax: 913-367-6230.
Founded in 1857 and raised to an Abbey in 1876. Rt. Rev. Barnabas Senecal, O.S.B., Abbot; Rt. Rev. Owen Purcell, O.S.B., Retired Abbot; Rt. Rev. Ralph Koehler, O.S.B., Retired Abbot; Very Rev. James R. Albers, O.S.B., Prior; Rev. Meinrad Miller, Subprior.
Bishops 1; Fathers 37; Brothers Professed 11.
Abbeys 1; Parishes 13; Missions 1; Foreign Missions 1; Chaplaincies 2; Colleges 1; High Schools 1.
Represented in the Archdioceses of Chicago and Kansas City in Kansas. Also in Brazil.

St. Mary's Abbey: Delbarton, Morristown, NJ 07960. Tel: 973-538-3231; Fax: 973-538-7109. Web site: www.osbmok.org. Rt. Rev. Thomas J. Confroy, O.S.B., Abbot; Very Rev. Patrick M. Hurley, O.S.B. Prior; Rev. Rembert F. Reilly, O.S.B., Subprior; Bro. Paul Diveny, O.S.B., Novice Master.
Monastery founded in 1857 and raised to an Abbey in 1884.
Priests 38; Brothers 6; Deacons 2; Juniors 3.
Parishes 2; Schools Preparatory School; Retreat Center.
Represented in the Archdiocese of Newark and the Dioceses of Metuchen, Paterson and Trenton.

Newark Abbey: 528 Dr. Martin Luther King, Jr. Blvd., Newark NJ 07102. Tel: 973-792-5800; Fax: 973-643-6922. Abbey in 1884; Rt. Rev. Melvin J. Valvano, O.S.B., Abbot; Very Revs. Mark M. Payne, O.S.B., Prior; Matthew Wotelko, O.S.B., Subprior.
Priory founded 1857; title transferred from Newark to Morristown, N.J. in 1956; became Abbey again in 1968 and known as Newark Abbey under the patronage of the Immaculate Conception.
Priests 16; Brothers 7.
Abbeys 1; Parishes 1; Preparatory (High) School 1.
Legal Holding: *St. Benedict Preparatory School,* Newark, NJ.
Represented in the Archdioceses of Indianapolis and Newark.

Belmont Abbey: 100 Belmont-Mount Holly Rd., Belmont, NC 28012-1802. Tel: 704-825-6675; Fax: 704-825-6680. Rt. Rev. Placid D. Solari, O.S.B., Abbot; Rt. Rev. Oscar C. Burnett, O.S.B., Retired Abbot; Very Rev. David G. Brown, O.S.B., Prior; Bro. Agostino Fernandez, O.S.B., Subprior.
Monastery founded in 1876, raised to an Abbey in 1884 and erected into an Abbey Nullius in 1910; Abbey Nullius suppressed January 1, 1977 and incorporated into Diocese of Charlotte.
Legal Title: *Southern Benedictine Society of North Carolina, Incorporated.*
Priests 15; Brothers 5.
Properties owned or sponsored: *Belmont Abbey College,* Belmont, NC.

St. Bernard Abbey (1891): Cullman, AL 35055. Tel: 256-734-8291; Fax: 256-734-2925. Rt. Rev. Cletus D. Meagher O.S.B., Abbot; Very Rev. Thomas O'Connor, O.S.B., Prior; Ven. Bro. Leo Borelli, O.S.B., Subprior & Novicemaster.
Legal Title: *St. Benedictine Society of Alabama, Inc.*
Priests 16; Brothers 11.
Represented in the Archdiocese of Mobile and in the Diocese of Birmingham.

St. Procopius Abbey: 5601 College Rd., Lisle, IL 60532. Tel: 630-969-6410; Fax: 630-969-6426. Rt. Rev. Dismas Kalcic, O.S.B., Abbot; Very Ven. Columban Trojan, O.S.B., Prior; Revs. Thomas Chisholm, O.S.B., Subprior; Kevin Sheeran, O.S.B., Procurator & Business Mgr.
Monastery founded in 1885 and raised to an Abbey in 1894.
Legal Holdings or Titles: *Benedictine University,* Lisle, IL; *Benet Academy,* Lisle, IL; *Benedictine Chinese Mission,* Lisle, IL; *Slav Mission,* Lisle, IL; *St. Scholastica Mission House, Inc.,* Naperville, IL; *St.Procopius Abbey Endowment, Lisle.*
Bishops 1; Priests 31; Brothers 13; Oblates 2.
Represented in the Archdiocese of Denver and in the Dioceses of Alexandria, Joliet and Superior. Also in Taiwan.

St. Gregory's Abbey: 1900 E. Mc Arther Dr., Shawnee, OK 74804. Tel: 405-878-5491; Fax: 405-878-5189.
Monastery founded in 1875 and raised to an Abbey in 1896. Rt. Rev. Martin Lugo, O.S.B., Abbot; Rt. Rev. Philip Berning, O.S.B., Resigned; Rt. Rev. Adrian Vorderlandwehr, O.S.B., Resigned; Very Rev. Patrick McCool, O.S.B., Prior Rev. Joachim Spexarth, O.S.B., Subprior.
Legal Title: *Benedictine Fathers of Sacred Heart Mission, Inc.*
Ministries in 7 Parishes.
Priests 21; Brothers 9.
Properties owned or sponsored: *National Shrine of the Infant of Prague,* Prague, OK; *Mabee-Gerrer Museum of Art,* Shawnee, OK; *St. Gregory's University,* Shawnee, OK.
Represented in the Archdiocese of Oklahoma City and in the Diocese of Tulsa.

St. Leo Abbey: P.O. Box 2350, Saint Leo, FL 33574. Tel: 352-588-8624; Fax: 352-588-5217.
Founded in 1889 and raised to an Abbey in 1902. Very Rev. James Tingerthal, O.S.B., Admin.
Legal Title: *Order of St. Benedict of Florida, Inc.*
Fathers 14; Brothers 13; Internal Oblates 1
Represented in the Dioceses of Charlotte and St. Petersburg.

Assumption Abbey: P.O. Box A, Richardton, ND 58652. Tel: 701-974-3315.
Founded in 1893 and raised to an Abbey in 1903. Rt. Rev. Patrick Moore, O.S.B., Abbot; Rt. Rev. Lawrence Wagner, O.S.B., Resigned Abbot; Rt. Rev. Robert West, O.S.B., Resigned Abbot; Very Rev. Valerian Odermann, O.S.B., Prior; Bro. Basil Kirsch, O.S.B., Subprior; Bro. Alban Petesch, O.S.B., Formation Dir.
Priests 34; Brothers 25.
Properties owned or sponsored: Abbey; Dependent Priory; Parishes 8; Chaplaincies 4; Indian Mission.
Represented in the Dioceses of Bismarck, Fargo, Great Falls and Indianapolis. Also in Columbia.

St. Bede Abbey: Peru, IL 61354. Tel: 815-223-3140. Rt. Rev. Marion Balsavich, O.S.B., Resigned Abbot; Rt. Rev. Roger Corpus, O.S.B., Abbot; Very Ven. Nathaniel Grossman, O.S.B., Prior; Very Rev. Claude Peifer, O.S.B., Subprior.
Monastery Founded and raised to an Abbey in 1910.
Legal Title: *The Benedictine Society of Saint Bede.*
Priests 28; Brothers 6
Properties owned or sponsored: Parishes 5.
Represented in the Archdiocese of Chicago and in the Diocese of Peoria.

St. Martin's Abbey: 5300 Pacific Ave. S.E., Lacey, WA 98503-1297. Rt. Rev. Neal G. Roth, O.S.B.; Rt. Rev. Conrad R. Rausch, O.S.B., Resigned Abbot; Rt. Rev. Adrian Parcher, O.S.B., Resigned Abbot; Very Revs. Alfred J. Hulscher, O.S.B., Prior; Rev. Kieran Cunningham, O.S.B., Subprior.
Monastery Founded in 1895 and raised to an Abbey in 1914.
Legal Holdings or Titles: *St. Martin's Abbey; St. Martin's College.*
Priests 26; Brothers 12.
Represented in the Archdiocese of Seattle and in the Dioceses of San Bernadino, Spokane and Yakima.

Holy Cross Abbey: 2951 E. Hwy 50, Canon City, CO 81212. Tel: 719-275-8631.
Founded in 1886 and raised to an Abbey in 1925. Rt. Rev. Kenneth Hein, O.S.B., Retired Abbot; Rev. Ignatius Smith, O.S.B., Prior.
Fathers 11; Brothers 3; Oblates 1.
Parishes 1; Missions 1.
Represented in the Archdiocese of Portland in Oregon and in the Dioceses of Colorado Springs and Pueblo.

St. Anselm Abbey: 100 St. Anselm Dr., Manchester, NH 03102-1310. Tel: 603-641-7000; Fax: 603-641-7267. Rt. Rev. Matthew K. Leavy, O.S.B., Abbot; Most Rev. Joseph J. Gerry, O.S.B., 3rd Abbot, Tenth Bishop of Portland, ME; Very Rev. William J. Sullivan, O.S.B., Prior; Very Rev. Peter J. Guerin, O.S.B., Subprior.
Monastery Founded in 1889 and raised to an Abbey in 1927.
Legal Title: *Order of Saint Benedict of New Hampshire*
Bishops 1; Abbots 1; Fathers 27; Brothers 7.
Represented in the Archdiocese of San Francisco and in the Diocese of Manchester.

St. Andrew Abbey: 10510 Buckeye Rd., Cleveland, OH 44104. Tel: 216-721-5300.
Founded in 1922 and raised to an Abbey in 1934. Rt. Rev. Clement Zeleznik, O.S.B., Abbot; Very Rev. Albert Marflak, O.S.B., Prior; Ven. Rev. Bede Kotlinski, O.S.B., Subprior.
Legal Holdings or Titles: *Benedictine Order of Cleveland; Benedictine High School.*
Bishops 1; Priests 22; Brothers 11; Simple Vows 3; Oblates 1.
Abbeys 1; Parishes 2; High School; Chaplaincies 4.
Represented in the Dioceses of Cleveland and Great Falls-Billings.

Holy Trinity Monastery: P.O. Box 990, Butler, PA 16003. Tel: 724-287-4461. Rt. Rev. Leo R. Schlosser, O.S.B., Hegumen.
Monks 8.
Represented in the Byzantine Archdiocese of Pittsburgh.

Benedictine Priory: P.O. Box 13577, 6502 Seawright Dr., Savannah, GA 31406. Tel: 912-356-3520; Fax: 912-356-3527. Rev. Jude W. Brady, O.S.B., Prior.
Founded 1877, dependent priory of St. Vincent Archabbey, Latrobe, PA. Very Rev. Jude W. Brady, O.S.B., Prior.
Priests 6; Brothers 4.
High Schools 1.
Represented in the Diocese of Savannah.

Woodside Priory: 302 Portola Rd., Portola Valley, CA 94028. Tel: 650-851-8220. Very Rev. Martin J. Mager, O.S.B., Supr.
Founded in 1956, erected as Conventual Priory 1958, became a dependent Priory upon St. Anselm's Abbey, Manchester, NH, 1976.
Legal Title: *Benedictine Fathers of the Priory, Inc.*
Priests 4; Brothers 1.
High Schools 1; Middle Schools 1.
Represented in the Archdiocese of San Francisco.

Abadia Benedictine de San Antonio Abad: P.O. Box 729, Humacao, PR 00792. Tel: 787-852-1616; 852-1766; Fax: 787-852-1920. Rt. Rev. Oscar Rivera, O.S.B., Abbot; Rev. Eduardo Torrellas, O.S.B., Prior; Bro. Aristides Pacheco, Subprior.
Monastery Founded in 1947 and became an abbey in 1984.
Priests 8; Brothers 6.

Mary Mother of the Church Abbey: 12829 River Rd., Richmond, VA 23233-7206. Tel: 804-784-3508; Fax: 804-784-2214.
Community founded in 1911 and became an Abbey in 1989. Very Rev. Michael Naughton, O.S.B., Admin.; Rev. Donald F. Scales, O.S.B., Prior.
Priests 8; Brothers 9.
Abbeys 1; Chaplaincies 3; High Schools 1.
Legal Holdings: *Benedictine High School of Richmond; Mary Mother of the Church Abbey.*
Represented in the Diocese of Richmond.

Swiss-American Congregations

Founded by Pope Pius IX, 1870, and Pope Leo XIII, April 5, 1881.
The Abbeys and Priories belonging to this Federation are as follows:

St. Meinrad Archabbey: *Secretary to the Archabbot,* No. 100 Hill Dr., St. Meinrad, IN 47577. Tel: 812-357-6611; Fax: 812-357-6551.
Founded 1854; raised to an Abbey in 1870. Rt. Rev. Lambert Reilly, O.S.B., Archabbot; Rt. Rev. Bonaventure Knaebel, O.S.B., Retired Archabbot; Very Rev. Tobias Colgan, O.S.B., Prior.
Archbishops 1; Priests 81; Brothers 30; Novices 2.

Parishes 19; Schools of Theology 1; Chaplaincies 7.
Represented in the Archdioceses of Chicago, Hartford, Indianapolis, and Washington and in the Dioceses of Belleville, Charleston, Cheyenne, Evansville, Gary, Lexington, Owensboro and Sioux Falls.

Conception Abbey: 37174 State Hwy. VV Conception, MO 64433. Tel: 660-944-3100; Fax: 660-944-2800.
Founded December 8, 1873; Abbey April 5, 1881. Rt. Rev. Gregory Polan, O.S.B., Abbot; Very Rev. Kenneth Reichert, O.S.B., Prior; Bro. Bernard Montgomery, O.S.B., Subprior.
Legal Title: *Conception Abbey, Inc.*
Archbishops 1; Fathers 43; Brothers 19.
Parishes 13; Seminary College 1; Chaplaincies 5.
Represented in the Dioceses of Dodge City, Jefferson City, Kansas City-St. Joseph and Springfield-Cape Girardeau.

Mount Michael Abbey: 22520 Mount Michael Rd., Elkhorn, NE 68022-3400. Tel: 402-289-2541; Fax: 402-289-4539. Rt. Rev. Theodore Wolff, O.S.B., Abbot; Bro. Jerome Kmiecik, Prior; Rev. Michael Liebl, O.S.B., Subprior.
Legal Holdings & Titles: *Benedictine Fathers, Inc.; Mount Michael Benedictine High School,* Elkhorn, NE; *Mt. Michael Foundation, Inc.*
Fathers 13; Brothers 11.
Monks serve and staff: Parishes 2.
Represented in the Archdiocese of Omaha and in the Diocese of Pueblo.

Subiaco Abbey: Subiaco, AR 72865. Tel: 479-934-4295; Fax: 479-934-1000. Rt. Rev. Jerome Kodell, O.S.B., Abbot; Rev. David Bellinghausen, O.S.B., Prior; Bro. Ephrem O'Bryan, O.S.B., Subprior.
Legal Title: *Subiaco Abbey,* Subiaco, AR 72865.
Fathers 29; Perpetually Professed Brothers 29; Temporarily Professed Brothers 1.
Properties staffed or sponsored: Parishes 11; High School 1; Missions 1.
Represented in the Dioceses of Fort Worth and Little Rock. Also in Belize City-Belmopan.

St. Joseph Abbey: *St. Benedict,* LA 70457. Tel: 985-892-1800; Fax: 985-867-2270. Web site: www.stjosephabbey.org. Rt. Rev. Patrick Regan, O.S.B., Retired Abbot; Very Rev. Justin Brown, O.S.B., Prior; Rev. Matthew R. Clark, O.S.B., Subprior.
Legal Holdings: *St. Joseph Seminary College,* St. Benedict, LA.
Fathers 27; Brothers 18; Novices 4.
Parishes 4; Novitiates 4; Seminary College 1.
Represented in the Archdiocese of New Orleans.

Mt. Angel Abbey: *St. Benedict,* Mt. Angel Abbey Seminary St. Benedict, OR 97373. Tel: 503-845-3030; Fax: 503-845-3594.
Founded on Oct. 30, 1882, from Engelberg in Switzerland and raised to an abbey on March 24, 1904. Rt. Rev. Joseph Wood, O.S.B., Abbot; Very Rev. Paul Thomas, O.S.B., Prior; Very Rev. Paschal Cheline, O.S.B., Subprior.
Legal Holding or Title: *Our Lady of the Angels, Cuernavaca,* Morelos, Mexico.
Finally Professed Monks: Priests 49; Brothers 23.
Temporarily Professed Monks: Brothers 12; Novices 7.

Marmion Abbey: 850 Butterfield Rd., Aurora, IL 60504. Tel: 630-897-7215.
Founded as Dependent Priory of St. Meinrad's Abbey, June 20, 1943; Abbey since March 21, 1947. Rt. Rev. Vincent de Paul Bataille, O.S.B., Abbot; Rt. Rev. Gerald Benkert, O.S.B., Abbot Emeritus; Rt. Rev. David J. Cyr, O.S.B., Abbot Emeritus. Very Rev. Kenneth Theisen, O.S.B., Prior; Rev. Michael Burrows, O.S.B., Subprior.
Priests 33; Brothers 15.
Properties staffed or sponsored: Parishes 1; High Schools 2.
Represented in the Diocese of Rockford. Also in Quetzaltenango, Guatemala.

St. Benedict's Abbey: 12605 224th Ave., Benet Lake, WI 53102. Tel: 262-396-4311.
Monastery Founded in 1945 and raised to an Abbey in 1952. Rt. Rev. Edmund Boyce, O.S.B., Abbot; Rt. Rev. Andrew Garber, O.S.B., Abbot Resigned; Rt. Rev. Robert Schoofs, O.S.B., Abbot Resigned; Rt. Rev. Leo Ryska, O.S.B., Abbot Resigned; Very Rev. Henry Nurre, O.S.B., Prior.
Legal Titles: *Benedictine Monks, Inc.; St. Benedict's Home Missionary Society.*
Priests 7; Brothers 10.
Represented in the Archdiocese of Milwaukee.

Glastonbury Abbey: 16 Hull St., Hingham, MA 02043. Tel: 781-749-2155; Fax: 781-749-7236. Rt. Rev. Nicholas J. Morcone, O.S.B., Abbot.
Monks in Solemn Vows 10; Temporary Vows 2; Internal Oblate 1.
Property owned: *Lincoln School Apartments for the Elderly and Handicapped,* Hingham, MA.
Represented in the Archdiocese of Boston.

Blue Cloud Abbey: P.O. Box 98, Marvin, SD 57251-0098. Tel: 605-398-9200; Fax: 605-398-9201. Rt. Rev. Thomas Hillenbrand, O.S.B., Abbot. Retired Abbots: Rt. Rev. Alan Berndt, O.S.B.; Rt. Rev. Denis Quinkert, O.S.B.; Rev. George Lyon, O.S.B., Prior.
Monastery Founded June 24, 1950; raised to a Priory August 5, 1952; raised to an Abbey March 21, 1954.
Legal Title: *Blue Cloud Abbey, Inc.*
Priests 24; Brothers 18.
Represented in the Diocese of Sioux Falls. Also in Guatemala.

Corpus Christi Abbey: 101 S. Vista Dr., Sandia, TX 78383. Tel: 361-547-3257; Fax: 413-208-9281. Rt. Rev. Peter Eberle, O.S.B., Abbot; Bro. Simon Huggins, O.S.B., Prior.
Fathers 4; Professed Brothers 4.
Property owned: *Benedictine Retreat Center,* Sandia, TX.
Represented in the Diocese of Corpus Christi.

Prince Of Peace Abbey: 650 Benet Hill Rd., Oceanside, CA 92054. Tel: 760-430-1305; 430-1306. Rt. Rev. Charles Wright, O.S.B., Abbot.; Rt. Rev. Claude Ehringer, O.S.B., Abbot (Retired); Very Rev. Sharbel Ewen, O.S.B., Prior.
Fathers 9; Brothers 14; Postulants 3.

St. Benedict Abbey: 252 Still River Rd., P.O. Box 67, Still River-Harvard, MA 01467. Tel: 978-456-3221; Fax: 978-456-8181. Rt. Rev. Gabriel Gibbs, O.S.B., Abbot; Very Rev. Xavier Connelly, O.S.B., Prior.
Priests 8; Brothers 8; Oblates 1.
Represented in the Diocese of Worcester.

Congregation of St. Ottilien for Foreign Missions

St. Paul's Abbey: 289 Rt. 206, P.O. Box 7, Newton, NJ 07860. Tel: 973-383-2470; Fax: 973-383-5782. (Benedictine Missionaries)
Monastery established March 15, 1924; elevated to an Abbey June 9, 1947. Rt. Rev. Joel P. Macul, O.S.B., Abbot; Rt. Rev. Justin E. Dzikowicz, O.S.B., Resigned Abbot; Rt. Rev. Augustine J. Hinches, O.S.B., Resigned Abbot.
Solemnly professed monks 11 (10 priests).
Represented in the Diocese of Paterson.

Christ The King Priory (1985) - Benedictine Mission House: P.O. Box 528, Schuyler, NE 68661. Tel: 402-352-2177; Fax: 402-352-2176. Revs. Germar Neubert, O.S.B., Prior; Volker Futter, O.S.B.; Thomas Leitner, O.S.B.
Fathers 4; Brothers 4.
Represented in the Archdiocese of Omaha.

Congregation of the Annuciation

St. Andrew's Abbey: P.O. Box 40, Valyermo, CA 93563. Tel: 661-944-2178. Rt. Rev. Francis Benedict, O.S.B., Abbot; Revs. Simon O'Donnell, O.S.B., Prior; John Bosco Stoner, O.S.B., Subprior.
Monks solemn vows 21; Simple vows 4; Novices 2.
Represented in the Archdiocese of Los Angeles.

Houses Not In Congregations

Mount Saviour Monastery: 231 Monastery Rd., Pine City, NY 14871-9787. Tel: 607-734-1688; Fax: 607-734-1689. E-mail: info@msaviour.org. Very Rev. Martin Boler, O.S.B., Prior Rev. James Cronin, O.S.B., Subprior.
Monastery Founded in 1950, raised to Independent Priory 1957.
Professed Monks 11; Novices 2.
Represented in the Diocese of Rochester.

Weston Priory (1953): 58 Priory Hill Rd., Weston, VT 05161. Tel: 802-824-5409; Fax: 802-824-3573. Very Rev. Richard Iaquinto, O.S.B., Prior.
Monks 15.
Represented in the Diocese of Burlington.

Camaldolese Bendictine Congregation

(Congregatio Camaldulensis Ordinis Sancti Benedicti)

General Motherhouse: *The Sacred Hermitage and Monastery of Camaldoli,* Arezzo, Italy. Most Rev. Emanuele Bargellini, O.S.B.Cam., Prior Gen.

U.S. Foundation (1958): *New Camaldoli Hermitage,* 62475 Coast Hwy. One, Big Sur, CA 93920. Tel: 831-667-2456. Very Rev. Raniero Hoffman, O.S.B.Cam., Prior.
Fathers 15; Professed Brothers 9.
Represented in the Dioceses of Monterey and Oakland.

English Benedictine Congregation

St. Anselm's Abbey: 4501 S. Dakota Ave. N.E., Washington, DC 20017. Tel: 202-269-2300; Fax: 202-269-2312. Rt. Rev. Aidan Shea, O.S.B., Abbot.
Legal Title: *Benedictine Foundation at Washington DC*
Solemnly Professed Monks 23.

Abbey of St. Gregory the Great: Cory's Ln., Portsmouth, RI 02871. Tel: 401-683-2000; Fax: 401-683-5888. Rt. Rev. Mark Serna, O.S.B., Abbot; Rt. Rev. Matthew Stark, O.S.B., Abbot Emeritu & Prior.
Choir Religious 15.

Abbey of St. Mary and St. Louis: 500 S. Mason Rd., St. Louis, MO 63141-8500. Tel: 314-434-2557; Fax: 314-434-0795.
Founded as a dependent Priory 1955, granted independence 1973, raised to status of Abbey 1989. Rt. Rev. W. Thomas Frerking, O.S.B., Abbot.
Solemnly professed monks 18 (14 priests).
Simply professed monks 4; Novices 2.

Sylvestrine Benedictine Congregation

(Monachorum Silvestrinorum, O.S.B.)

General Motherhouse: Rome, Italy, S. Stefano del Cacco 26. Rt. Rev. Andrew Pantaloni, O.S.B., Abbot Gen.

Foundations in U.S. (1910): *Saint Benedict Priory,* 2711 E. Drahner Rd., Oxford, MI 48370. Tel: 248-628-2249. Very Rev. Daniel Homan, O.S.B., Conventual Prior, St. Sylvester Monastery, 17320 Rosemont Rd., Detroit, MI 48219. Tel: 313-532-6064. Holy Face Monastery, 1697 State Hwy. S-3, Clifton, NJ 07012. Tel: 201-778-1177.
Brothers 4; Priests 10.
Represented in the Archdiocese of Detroit and in the Diocese of Paterson.

Olivetan Benedictines

(Congregatio Sanctae Mariae Montis Oliveti Ordinis Sancti Benedicti)

General Motherhouse: *The Archabbey of Monte Oliveto Maggiore,* Monte Oliveto, Siena, Italy. Most Rev. Michelangelo M. Tiribilli, O.S.B., Abbot Gen.

U.S. Foundations: *Holy Trinity Monastery:* P.O. Box 298, St. David, AZ 85630. Tel: 602-720-4642. Revs. Henri Capdeville O.S.B., Prior; Lawrence Fedor, O.S.B.; Alexander Mills, O.S.B.
Solemnly Professed 7; Postulants 1.
Represented in the Diocese of Tucson.

Our Lady of Guadalupe Abbey: P.O. Box 1080, Pecos, NM 87552-1080. Tel: 505-757-6415. Rev. Christopher Zielinski, O.S.B., Temporary Admin.; Rev. Paul Meaden, O.S.B., Claustral Prior.
Priests 9; Brothers 3.
Represented in the Archdiocese of Santa Fe.

Benedictine Monastery of Hawaii: 67-290 Farrington Hwy., P.O. Box 490, Waialua, HI 96791. Tel: 808-637-7887; Fax: 808-637-8601. Rev. David Barfknecht, O.S.B., Supr.
Priests 3; Brothers 1.

Subiaco Benedictines Congregations

Monastery of Christ in the Desert (1964): Abiquiu, NM 87510. Tel: 801-545-8567. Rt. Rev. Philip Lawrence, O.S.B., Abbot.
Independent 1983; Abbey 1996.
Monks 55.
Represented in the Archdioceses of Chicago and Santa Fe. Also in Mexico.

Saint Mary's Monastery (1987): P.O. Box 345, Petersham, MA 01366. Tel: 978-724-3350. Rev. Dom Anselm Atkinson, O.S.B., Supr.
Dependent Monastery 1987.
Monks 7.
Represented in the Diocese of Worcester.

Solesmes Congregation

Benedictine Monks, Solesmes Congregation, *Our Lady of Clear Creek Monastery,* 5804 W. Monastery Rd., Hulbert, OK 74441. Tel: 918-772-2454. Rev. Philip Anderson, O.S.B., Prior.

[0220] (S.S.S.)—CONGREGATION OF THE BLESSED SACRAMENT

(Congregatio Sanctissimi Sacramenti)

General Motherhouse: 46 Via Giovanni Battista de Rossi, Rome 00161, Italy. Very Rev. Fiorenzo Salvi, S.S.S., Supr.

Province of St. Ann (1931): 5384 Wilson Mills Rd., Cleveland, OH 44143. Tel: 440-442-6311. Very Rev. Norman B. Pelletier, S.S.S., Prov.; Rev. Edward Stapleton, S.S.S., Consultor & Prov. Treas.; Consultors: Revs. Roger Bourgeois, S.S.S., Vicar Provincial; John Thomas Lane, S.S.S., Consultor for Formation; John Keenan, S.S.S.
Bishops 1; Priests 56; Permanent Deacons 1; Brothers 18.
Properties staffed or owned: Parishes 7; Seminary 1; Community Houses 9; Novitiate 1.
Represented in the Archdioceses of Chicago, New York, San Antonio, and Santa Fe and the Dioceses of Cleveland, Green Bay, Galveston-Houston and Salt Lake City.

[0230] (Er. Cam.)—CAMALDOLESE HERMITS OF THE CONGREGATION OF MONTE

(Eremitae Camaldulenses Congregationis Montis Coronae)

General Motherhouse: *Sacro Eremo,* Tuscolano 00040-Monteporzio Catone, Rome, Italy. Rt. Rev. Lanfranco Longhi, Er. Cam., Father Major.

U.S. Foundation (1959): *Holy Family Hermitage,* 1501 Fairplay Rd., Bloomingdale, OH 43910-7971. Tel: 740-765-4511. Very Rev. Basil Corriere, Er. Cam., Prior.
Hermit Priests 2; Professed 2; Oblates 1.
Represented in the Diocese of Steubenville.

[0240] (O.S.CAM.)—CAMILLIAN FATHERS AND BROTHERS or ORDER OF ST. CAMILLUS

(Order of the Servants of the Sick)
(Ordo Ministrantium Infirmis)

General Motherhouse: *Casa Generalizia,* Ministri degli Infermi, Piazza della Maddalena, 53,00186 Rome, Italy. Most. Rev. Frank Monks, O.S.Cam., Supr. Gen.; Very Rev. Renato Salvatore, O.S.Cam., Vicar Gen.; Bro. Luca Perletti, O.S.Cam., Sec. of Formation; Rev. Luigi Galvani, O.S.Cam., Sec. of Missions; Rev. Jacques Sampore, O.S.Cam., Sec. of Ministry.

North American Province (1923): *Provincialate,* 3661 S. Kinnickinnic Ave., St. Francis, WI 53235. Tel.: 414-481-3696; Fax: 414-481-8044. Very Rev. Richard O'Donnell, O.S.Cam., Prov.; Bro. Nelson Deloria, O.S.Cam., Vicar Prov.; Revs. Louis Lussier, O.S.Cam.; Joseph Bisoffi, O.S.Cam.; Bro. Mario Crivello, O.S.Cam.

Legal Titles: *St. Camillus Health Center Inc.,* Wauwatosa, WI; *St. Camillus Health System,* Wauwatosa, WI; *San Camillo, Inc.,* Wauwatosa, WI; *St. Camillus Ministries Inc.,* Wauwatosa, WI; *Order of St. Camillus Formation, Inc.,* Wauwatosa, WI; *St. Camillus Communities Inc.,* Wauwatosa, WI.

Fathers 11; Professed Brothers 5; Temporary Professed 2.

Represented in the Archdiocese of Milwaukee and in the Dioceses of Madison and Worcester.

[0250] (C.R.L.)—CANONS REGULAR OF THE LATERAN

(Ordo Canonicorum Regularium S. Augustini Congregations Ss. Salvatoris Lateranensis)

General House: *Curia Generalizia dei Canonicio Regolari Lateranensi,* Piazza S. Pietro in Vincoli, 4A 00184, Roma, Italy.

United States: *Canons Regular of the Lateran,* 2317 Washington Ave., Bronx, NY 10458. Tel: 212-295-9600. Rev. Jose L. Biain, C.R.L., Supr. Tel: 212-994-1477.

Priests 6; Brothers 4.

Represented in the Archdiocese of New York and in the Diocese of Arecibo.

[0260] (O.C.D.)—DISCALCED CARMELITE FRIARS

(Ordo Carmelitarum Discalceatorum)

Founded Mt. Carmel, Palestine in the 13th Century.

Generalate: *Carmelitani Scalzi,* Corso d'Italia, 38 00198, Rome, Italy. Very Rev. Camilo Maccise, O.C.D., Supr. Gen.

California-Arizona Province (1983): *Provincial House,* 926 E. Highland Ave., P.O. Box 2178, Redlands, CA 92373. Tel: 909-793-0424; Fax: 909-335-1304. Very Rev. Gerald Werner, O.C.D., Prov.

Legal Title: *Discalced Carmelite Province of California.*

Fathers 29; Brothers 2; Students 12; Novices 3; Postulants 6.

Properties owned, staffed or sponsored: Parishes 4; Retreat House; Novitiate; House of Studies; House of Prayer; Institute of Spirituality.

Represented in the Archdioceses of Los Angeles, Portland and Seattle and in the Dioceses of San Jose, San Bernardino, Santa Rosa and Tucson. Also in Uganda.

Province of St. Therese of Oklahoma (1935): *Provincial House,* 906 Kentucky Ave., San Antonio, TX 78201. Tel: 201-735-9127. Very Rev. Ralph Reyes, O.C.D., Prov.

Fathers 21; Brothers 1; Students of Philosophy 1; Students of Theology 2.

Properties staffed or sponsored: Parishes 3; Community Houses 1; Novitiate 1; Student House 1.

Represented in the Archdioceses of New Orleans, Oklahoma City, and San Antonio and the Dioceses of Dallas and Little Rock.

Washington Province of the Immaculate Heart of Mary (1947): *Discalced Carmelites-Prov. Office,* 1233 S. 45th St., Milwaukee, WI 53214-3693. Tel: 414-672-7212; Fax: 414-672-3138. Very Rev. Jude Peters, O.C.D., Prov.

Fathers 56; Brothers 13; Temporary Professed Brothers 15; Novices 5.

Properties owned or sponsored: Community Houses 7.

Represented in the Archdioceses of Boston, Chicago, Milwaukee and Washington and in the Diocese of Wheeling-Charleston. Also in Nairobi, Kenya.

Polish Province of the Holy Spirit, Poland (1949): *Monastery of Our Lady of Mt. Carmel,* 1628 Ridge Rd., Munster, IN 46321. Tel: 219-838-7111; Fax: 219-838-7214. Rev. Robert Andrzej Strojny, O.C.D., Prior.

Priests 10; Brothers 1.

Represented in the Diocese of Gary.

[0270] (O.CARM.)—CARMELITE FATHERS & BROTHERS

(Ordo Fratrum Beatissimae Virginis Mariae de Monte Carmelo)

General Curia: 00184, Rome, Italy, Via Giovanni Lanza, 138. Most Rev. Joseph Chalmers, O.Carm., Prior Gen.

Province of the Most Pure Heart of Mary (1864): *Carmelite Provincial Office,* 1317 Frontage Rd., Darien, IL 60561. Tel: 630-971-0050; Fax: 630-971-0195. Very Rev. John F. Russell, O.Carm., Prior Prov.; Rev. Bernhard Bauerle, O.Carm., Prov.-Midwest Commissary & Prov. Officer/Treas.; Rev. Stanley MaKacinas, O.Carm., Prov.-Western Commissary; Rev. John Welch, O.Carm., Prov.-Eastern Commissary; Provincial Officers: Revs., John Welch, O.Carm., Dir. of Education. Councilors: Revs. Daniel O'Neill, O.Carm.; Michael Sgarioto, O.Carm.; David McEvoy, O.Carm.; Emmet Gavin, O.Carm.; John-Benedict Weber, O.Carm., Lay Carmelite Dir.; Robert Colaresi, O.Carm., Dir. Little Flower Society; John Malley, O.Carm., Dir.-Carmelite Mission Office.

Ministries in 30 Parishes.

Priests 207; Clerics 10; Pre-Novitiates 15; Novices 7; Brothers 18.

Properties owned: Spiritual Centers 3; Shopping-center Chapels 2; Carefree Village, residence for senior citizens, Darien, IL; High Schools 6; Community Houses 38; House of Study 2.

Represented in the Archdioceses of Boston, Chicago, Kansas City in Kansas, Los Angeles, Louisville, Newark, and Washington and in the Dioceses of Galveston-Houston, Joliet, Pittsburgh, Phoenix, Sacramento, Tucson and Venice. Also in Canada, Peru and Mexico.

Province of The Most Pure Heart of Mary: *St. Therese Priory,* 75 E. Mariposa St., Phoenix, AZ. Revs. Stanley Makacinas, O.Carm; Kevin McBrien, O.Carm.; Valentine Boyle, O.Carm.; Michael Kwiecien, O.Carm.

Province of St. Elias (1931): P.O. Box 3079, Middletown, NY 10940-0890. Tel: 845-344-2223. Very Rev. Michael Kissane, O.Carm., Prov.

Legal Holdings or Titles: *The Missionary Society of Our Lady of Mt. Carmel of the State of New York; The Carmelite Fathers, Inc. of New York; Carmelite Fathers, Inc. of the Commonwealth of Massachusetts; Mt. Carmel Hermitage; Order of Carmelites of Palm Beach, Inc.; National Shrine of Our Lady of Mount Carmel, Inc.*

Fathers 61; Clerics 15; Brothers 5; Novices 2; Pre-Novices 2.

Properties staffed, owned or sponsored: Parishes 9; Priories 16; House of Study 2; Retreat Houses 1; Novitiate 1; High Schools 1; Hermitages 2; Shrines 1.

Represented in the Archdioceses of New York, and Washington and the Dioceses of Albany, Dodge City, Greensburg, Palm Beach, Rochester, Sioux Falls, and Trenton. Also in Trinidad & Vietnam.

Mt. Carmel Hermitage: 244 Baileys Rd., Bolivar, PA 15923. Tel: 724-238-0423.

Founded in 1970, became dependent upon St. Elias Province in 1995. Revs. Bede Mulligan, O.Carm.; Simeon Marro, O.Carm.

Fathers 2; Brothers 1.

Represented in the Diocese of Greensburg.

Carmelite Hermitage of the Blessed Virgin Mary (O.Carm), 8249 De Montreville Tr. N., Lake Elmo, MN 55042-9545. Tel: 651-779-7351; Fax: 651-779-7351. E-mail: carmelus@earthlink.net. Web site: www.decor carmeli.com. Revs. John M. Burns, O.Carm., Prior; Joseph V. Vaccaro, O.Carm.

Fathers 2; Brothers 3.

[0275] (C.M.I.)—CARMELITES OF MARY IMMACULATE

(Congregatio Fratrum Carmelitarum B.V. Mariae Immaculatae)

Founded by Blessed Kuriakose Elias Chavara and Companions at Mannanam, Kerala, India in 1831.

Generalate: *Prior General's House,* P.B. No. 1056 Ernakulam, Cochin 682 011, Kerala, India. Tel: 484-378-137; Fax: 484-378-363. Very Rev. Antony Kariyil, C.M.I., Prior Gen.

North American Headquarters: 21 Nassau Ave., Brooklyn, NY 11222. Tel: 718-388-4866. Rev. John Menonkari, C.M.I., Reg. Coord.

Legal Title: *Carmelites of Mary Immaculate, Inc.*

Ministries in Parishes; Hospitals; Universities; Prisons; Mission to the Syro-Malabar Catholics.

Priests in the United States and Canada 89.

Represented in the Archdioceses of Hartford, Los Angeles, New York, and Philadelphia and the Dioceses of Alexandria, Amarillo, Beaumont, Brooklyn, Camden, Charleston, Joliet, Lafayette, Lake Charles, Metuchen, Nashville, New Ulm, Rockville Centre, St. Augustine, Salina, San Angelo, Shreveport, Sioux Falls, Syracuse, Toledo, Tulsa and Tyler. Also in Canada.

[0280] (O.CART.)—ORDER OF ARTHUSIANS

(Ordo Cartusianorum)

Motherhouse: *Grande Chartreuse,* St. Pierre de Chartreuse (Isere), France. Rev. Father Marcellin Theeuwes, Supr. Gen.

U.S. Charterhouse of the Transfiguration (1951): *Carthusian Monastery,* 1800 Beartown Rd., Arlington, VT 05250. Tel: 802-362-2550; Fax: 802-362-3584. E mail: carthusians_in_America@juno.com. Web site: www.chartreux.org. Rev. Lorenzo Maria T. De La Rosa, Jr., O.Cart., Prior.

Legal Titles: *Carthusian Foundation in America, Inc.; Carthusian Foundation, Association Fraternelle Romande.*

In Community 16.

Represented in the Diocese of Burlington.

[0290] (F.C.)—BROTHERS OF CHARITY

(Congregatio Fratrum Caritate)

General Motherhouse (1807): Via G.B. Pagano 35, C.P.Rome, Italy. 9082 00167. Bro. Rene Stockman, F.C., Supr. Gen.

American District (1963): *District of Our Lady of Charity,* 7720 Doe Ln., Laverock, PA 19038. Bro. Michael Lonsway, District Supr.

Represented in the Archdiocese of Philadelphia.

[0300] (I.C.)—INSTITUTE OF CHARITY

Rosminians Institutum Charitatis

General Motherhouse: *Collegio Rosmini Via Porta,* Latina 17, Rome, Italy. Very Rev. James Flynn, I.C., Supr. Gen.

U.S. Foundation (1877): 2327 W. Heading Ave., Peoria, IL 61604. Tel: 309-676-6341. Rev. William T. Miller, I.C., Prov.

Fathers in the U.S. 14.

Novitiate 1; Parishes 8.

Represented in the Dioceses of Peoria and St. Petersburg.

[0305] (I.C.)—INSTITUTE OF CHRIST THE KING-SOVEREIGN PRIEST

Institute of Christ the King-Sovereign Priest
Institutum Christi Regis Summi Sacerdotis

General Motherhouse and House of Formation: *Villa Martelli, Via di Gricigliano 52,*50069, Sieci, Italy. Rev. Msgr. Gilles Wach, Prior Gen.

U.S. Mailing Address: *Institute of Christ the King-Sovereign Priest:* P.O. Box 5417, McLean, VA 22103-5417.

American Headquarters: *Immaculate Conception Priory,* 26400 CTH U, Cashton, WI 54619-9757. Tel: 608-823-7992; Fax: 608-823-7992. Rev. Timothy E. Svea, Prior/Supr.

Priory of Our Lady of the Sacred Heart: 1204 North Church St., Rockford, IL 61103. Tel: 815-965-5971; Fax: 815-965-6029. Rev. Brian A.T. Bovee, Prior.

Fathers in the U.S.: 2.

Represented in the Dioceses of La Crosse and Rockford.

[0310] (C.F.C.)—CONGREGATION OF CHRISTIAN BROTHERS

(Christian Brothers Institute)

Founded in Ireland in 1802. First foundation in the United States in 1906.

General Motherhouse: *Fratelli Cristiani,* Via Marcantonio Colonna 9, 00192, Rome, Italy. Very Rev. Bro. Joseph P. Pinto, C.F.C., Congregational Leader.

Eastern U.S. American Province (1916): 21 Pryer Terrace, New Rochelle, NY 10804. Tel: 914-636-6194. Bro. Brian M. Walsh, Prov. Leader; Councilors: Bros. Timothy D. Bray; John W. Casey; Kevin G. Cawley; Kevin M. Griffith.

Brothers 180.

Properties owned, staffed or sponsored: Colleges 2; High Schools 18; Grade Schools 4; Migrant Education Center; Care Center; Pastoral Ministry Centers 2; Parishes 2;

Represented in the Archdioceses of Boston, Miami, Newark and New York and in the Dioceses of Albany, Brownsville, Charlotte, Jackson, Orlando, Owensboro, Providence, Rochester, St. Petersburg and Venice. Also in Peru.

Brother Rice Province: (Western United States): *Brother Rice Provincialate,* 958 Western Ave., Joliet, IL 60435-6954. Tel: 815-723-5464. Bros. Charles J. Gattone, Prov.; James R. Keane, Deputy Prov.; Councilors: Bros. Daniel J. Casey; Michael S. Segvich; James R. Keane; George A. Gremley, Prov. Bursar; James McDonald, Vocations.

Legal Title: *The Christian Brothers of Ireland, Inc.*

Development Office: Christian BrothersAssociation, P.O. Box 42903, Evergreen Park, IL 60805-0903. Tel: 773-233-2949. Bro. Daniel F. McGovern, Dir.

Brothers under Vows: 86.

Properties Sponsored: *Brother Rice High School - The Christian Brothers Institute of Michigan, Inc.,* Bloomfield Hills, MI; *Brother Rice High School, Inc.,* Chicago, IL; *Damien Memorial High School - The Congregation of Christian Brothers of Hawaii, Inc.,*

Honolulu, HI; Palma Junior-Senior High School - The Christian Brothers Institute of California, Inc., Salinas, CA; *St. Laurence High School, Inc.*, Burbank, IL.
Represented in the Archdioceses of Chicago, Detroit, and Seattle and the Dioceses of Honolulu, Joliet, Monterey, Owensboro and Phoenix. Also in Peru.

[0320] (F.I.C.)—BROTHERS OF CHRISTIAN INSTRUCTION

La Mennais Brothers
(Institutum Fratrum Instructionis Christianae)

General Motherhouse: *Casa Generalizia,* Via della Divina Provvidenza, 44 00166, Rome, Italy. Tel: 66-41-5618; Fax: 66-51-0242. Rev. Jose Antonio Obeso Vega, F.I.C., Supr. Gen.

American Province (1946): *Notre Dame Province-Notre Dame Institute,* P.O. Box 159, Alfred, ME 04002. Tel: 207-324-0067. Bro. Daniel Caron, F.I.C., Prov.
Brothers 39.
College 1; High Schools 2; Retreat Center 1.
Represented in the Dioceses of Fall River, Ogdensburg, Portland (ME) and Youngstown.

[0330] (F.S.C.)— BROTHERS OF THE CHRISTIAN SCHOOLS

(Fratres Scholarum Christianarum)

General Motherhouse: *Casa Generalizia, Via Aurelia 476,* CP 9099 00100, Rome, Italy. Bros. Alvaro Rodriquez Echeverria, F.S.C., Supr. Gen.; William Mann, F.S.C., Vicar Gen.

Christian Brothers Conference: *USA / Toronto Region,* 4351 Garden City Dr., Ste. 200, Landover, MD 20785-2248. Tel: 301-459-9410. Bros. Thomas Johnson, F.S.C., Dir.; Kevin Dalmasse, F.S.C., Dir. Education; Jeffrey Calligan, F.S.C., Dir. Formation.
Organizations served by this office: Regional Conference of USA-Toronto Brother Provincials; Regional F.S.C. Education Board; Regional F.S.C. Finance Board; Regional F.S.C. Vocation and Formation Board; F.S.C. Publication Board; LaSallan Volunteers, LaSallan Association of Miguel Schools.
Organizations associated with this office: Christian Brothers Major Superiors.
Properties owned and or sponsored: *Bethlehem University of the Holy Land,* P.O. Box 9, Bethlehem, via Israel (Incorporated in the State of New Jersey); *Christian Brother Conference Community,* Hyattsville, MD; *Sangre de Cristo Center*, Santa Fe, NM.

Province of Baltimore (1845): *The Provincialate,* Box 29, Adamstown, MD 21710. Tel: 301-874-5188; Fax: 301-874-5674. Bros. Robert Schieler, F.S.C., Prov., Visitor; James Butler, F.S.C., Auxiliary-Visitor; Timothy Froehlich, F.S.C., Dir. Finance; Patrick Ellis, F.S.C., Dir. Development; Thomas Chadwick, F.S.C., Dir. St. LaSalle Auxiliary; Edward Hofmann, F.S.C., Dir. Vocations; Martin Fahey, F.S.C., Sec.
Brothers 187.
Legal Holdings or Titles: *Christian Brothers of Frederick, Inc.; Ammendale Normal Institute of Prince George's County, Inc.; Christian Brothers Community Support Charitable Trust.*
Represented in the Archdioceses of Baltimore, Newark, Philadelphia and Washington and in the Dioceses of Camden and Pittsburgh.

Brothers Of The Christian Schools (Midwest Province - 1995): *Bro. Francis Carr,* FSC, 7650 S. County Line Rd., Burr Ridge, IL 60527-4718. Tel: 630-323-3725; Fax: 630-323-3779. E-mail: info@cbmidwest.org. Bros. Francis Carr, F.S.C., Visitor; Michael Flaherty, F.S.C., Aux. Visitor; Mr. Leo F. Hirsch, Dir. Development; Joseph Saurbier, F.S.C., Dir. Finance; Robert Veselsky, F.S.C., Dir. Vocations/Formation; Nicholas Schumer, F.S.C., Dir. St. La Salle Auxiliary; Martin Spellman, F.S.C., Dir.-Senior Brothers; Karin McClelland-Anderer, Dir.-Shared Mission & Formation.
Legal Titles: *The Christian Brothers of the Midwest, Inc.; The Christian Brothers of Illinois; Brothers of the Christian Schools of the St. Louis District; The Christian Brothers of Minnesota.*
Brothers 207.
Properties owned, staffed or sponsored: Communities 39; Universities 3; High Schools 16; Middle Schools 7; Elementary Schools 2; Retreat Houses 3; Group Homes 1; Publishing House.
Represented in the Archdiocese of Chicago, Milwaukee, St. Louis, and St. Paul-Minneapolis and the Dioceses of Green Bay, Helena, Jefferson City, Joliet, Kansas City-St. Joseph, Memphis, Tulsa and Winona.

Province of New York (1848): *La Salle Provincialate Inc.,* 800 Newman Springs Rd., Lincroft, NJ 07738. Tel: 732-842-7420; Fax: 732-530-3504. Bros. Frank Byrne, F.S.C., Prov. & Chm. Bd.; Thomas Lackey, F.S.C., Assoc. Prov., Vice Pres.; Stephen Olert, F.S.C., Assoc. Prov. & Vice Pres.; Gerard Conforti, F.S.C., Treas.; Edward Cleary, F.S.C., Sec.; William Martin, F.S.C., Dir.- St. La Salle Auxiliary & Dir. Devel. Office, P.O. Box 228, Lincroft, NJ 07738.
Brothers 167.
Properties owned, staffed or sponsored: Colleges 1; High Schools 10; Elementary Schools 2 Welfare Schools 1; Community Houses 17.
Represented in the Archdioceses of Detroit, Newark and New York and in the Dioceses of Albany, Buffalo, Syracuse and Trenton.

Province of Long Island-New England (1957): *Christian Brothers' Center-Provincial Offices, St. La Salle Auxiliary and Office of Public Information and Development,* No. 635 Ocean Rd., Narragansett, RI 02882-1314. Tel: 401-789-0244; Fax: 401-783-5303. Bros. Daniel Casey, F.S.C., Prov.-Visitor; Peter Iorlano, F.S.C., Auxiliary Prov./Visitor Dir.-Formation Eugene O'Gara, F.S.C., Archivist; Bro. Frederich Mueller, F.S.C., Dir.-Education; Mr. Lee Grossi, Dir.-Finance; Mrs. Mary Yakey, Health Care Coord.
Legal Titles *Brothers of the Christian Schools; Province of the Long Island-New England, Inc.*
Brothers 88.
Properties owned, staffed or sponsored: High Schools 5; Elementary Schools 2; Community Houses 12.
Represented in the Dioceses of Brooklyn, Providence and Rockville Centre.

Province of San Francisco (1868): *Brothers of the Christian Schools Provincial Office,* P.O. Box 3720, Napa, CA 94558-0372. Tel: 707-252-0222. Bro. Stanislaw Campbell, F.S.C., Prov.
Brothers 115.
Properties owned, staffed or sponsored: Colleges 1; High Schools 11; Middle and Elementary Schools 1; Community Houses 17; House of Study 1; Retreat & Conference Center 1.
Represented in the Archdioceses of Los Angeles, Portland (OR), and San Francisco and the Dioceses of Monterey, Oakland, Sacramento, Santa Rosa, Tucson and Yakima. Also in India, Italy, Israel, Mexico, Philippines, Kenya, and England.

Province of New Orleans-Santa Fe (1921): *De La Salle - Christian Brothers Provincialate,* 1522 Carmel Dr., Lafayette, LA 70501. Tel: 337-234-1973. Bros. Clarence Fioke, F.S.C., Prov.; Richard Kovath, F.S.C., Auxiliary Prov.; Richard Hayder, F.S.C., Finance Dir.
Legal Holdings or Titles: *Brothers of the Christian Schools of Lafayette, LA., Inc.; St. La Salle Auxiliary; New Orleans-Santa Fe Retirement Plan; The Christian Brothers of J.K. Mullen High School; J.K. Mullen High School Corporation; Christian Brothers Foundation; Christian Brothers Retirement Trust.*
Brothers 98; Postulants 1.
Properties owned, staffed or sponsored: College; High Schools 6; Elementary Schools 2.
Represented in the Archdioceses of Denver, New Orleans and Santa Fe and in the Dioceses of El Paso and Lafayette (LA).

[0340] (O.CIST.)—CISTERCIAN FATHERS

(Ordo Cisterciensis)

Headquarters: Piazza del Tempio di Diana 14 I-00153, Rome, Italy. Most Rev. Maurus Esteva, O.Cist., S.T.D., Abbot Gen.

Cistercian Abbey: *Our Lady of Spring Bank,* 17304 Havenwood Rd., Sparta, WI 54656. Tel: 608-269-8138; Fax: 608-269-2800. E-Mail: Porter@Monks Online.org; Web site: www.MonksOnline.org. Very Rev. Robert Keffer, O.Cist., Prior Rt. Rev. Blaise J. Fuez, O.Cist., Abbot Emeritus; Rev. Bernard McCoy, O.Cist., Subprior.
Solemnly Professed 3; Simply Professed 2.

Cistercian Monastery: *Our Lady of Dallas,* 3550 Cistercian Rd., Irving, TX 75039. Tel: 972-438-2044. Rt. Rev. Denis Farkasfalvy, O.Cist., Abbot; Revs. Peter Verhalen, O.Cist., Prior; Bernard Marton, O.Cist., Subprior.
Priests 19; Novices 3.
Staff: Universities 2; Preparatory School 1; Novitiate 1; Chaplaincies 1.
Properties owned: *Abbey and Preparatory School.*
Represented in the Dioceses of Dallas and Fort Worth.

Cistercian Monastery of Our Lady of Fatima: 564 Walton Ave., Mt. Laurel, NJ 08054. Tel: 856-235-1330. Revs. Lino Parente, O.Cist., Prior; Maurizio Nicoletti, O.Cist.; Teclezghi Uebaghiorghis, O.Cist. Established in 1961 as a dependent Monastery of the Congregation of Casamari (Italy).
Property owned: *Fatima House and the Monastery.*

Cistercian Conventual Priory: *St. Mary's Priory,* 70 Schuylkill Rd., New Ringgold, PA 17960. Tel: 570-943-2645; Fax: 570-943-3035. Very Rev. Luke Anderson, O.Cist., Ph.D., Prior.
Legal Title: *The Cistercian Monastery of Pennsylvania.*
Monks 3.

[0350] (O.C.S.O.)—THE CISTERCIAN ORDER OF THE STRICT OBSERVANCE

(Trappists)
(Ordo Cisterciensium Strictioris Observantiae)

Generalate: *Casa Generalizia,* O.C.S.O., 33 Viale Africa, Rome 00144, Italy. Most Rev. Dom Bernardo Olivera, O.C.S.O., Abbot Gen.

Abbey of Gethsemani (1848): No. 3642 Monks Rd., Trappist, KY 40051. Tel: 502-549-3117. Rt. Rev. Damien Thompson, O.C.S.O., Abbot.
Priests 18; Brothers 50.

Abbey of Our Lady of New Melleray (1849): 6500 Melleray Cir., Peosta, IA 52068. Tel: 563-588-2319. Rt. Rev. Brendan Freeman, O.C.S.O., Abbot; Revs. Thomas MacMaster, O.C.S.O., Prior; Neil Paquette, O.C.S.O., Subprior; Stephen Verbest, O.C.S.O., Novice Dir. & Vocation Dir.
Professed Monks 36 (Priests 20).

St. Joseph's Abbey (1825): 167 North Spencer Rd., Spencer, MA 01562-1233. Tel: 508-885-8700; Fax: 508-885-8701. Rt. Rev. Damian Carr, O.C.S.O., Abbot.
Legal Title: *Cistercian Abbey of Spencer, Inc.*
Total in community 77 (Priests 32); Solemnly Professed 73; Simply Professed 1; Novices 2.

Monastery of The Holy Spirit, Inc. (1944): 2625 Hwy. 212 S.W., Conyers, GA 30094. Tel: 770-483-8705; Fax: 770-760-0989. Rev. Francis Michael Stiteler, O.C.S.O., Supr.
Professed Monks 43; Priests 23.
Represented in the Archdiocese of Atlanta.

Abbey of Our Lady of Guadalupe (1947): P.O. Box 97, Lafayette, OR 97127. Tel: 503-852-7174; Fax: 503-852-7748. Rt. Rev. Peter McCarthy, O.C.S.O., Abbot; Very Rev. Dismas Gannon, O.C.S.O., Prior; Bro. Phillip Wertman, O.C.S.O., Subprior.
Solemnly Professed 33; Priests 14; Simply Professed 2.

Abbey of Our Lady of the Holy Trinity (1947): 1250 S. 9500 E., Huntsville, UT 84317. Tel: 801-745-3784. Rt. Rev. Casimir Bernas, O.C.S.O., Abbot.
Priests 12; Brothers 9; Oblates 1.

Abbey of The Genesee (1951): 3258 River Rd.-P.O. Box 900, Piffard, NY 14533. Tel: 716-243-0660. Rt. Rev. John Denburger, O.C.S.O., Abbot; Rt. Rev. John Eudes Bamberger, O.C.S.O., Abbot Emeritus; Revs. Jerome Machar, O.C.S.O., Prior; Gerard D'Souza, O.C.S.O., Novice Master. Retreat House. Tel: 716-243-2220.
Solemnly Professed 33; Simply Professed 3; Professed Priests 10.

Mepkin Abbey (1949): 1098 Mepkin Abbey Road, Moncks Corner, SC 29461. Tel: 843-761-8509; Fax: 843-761-6719. Rt. Rev. Francis Kline, O.C.S.O., Abbot; Revs. Feliciano Manalili, O.C.S.O., Prior; Stan Gumula, O.C.S.O., Business Mgr.; Rt. Rev. Christian Aidan Carr, O.C.S.O., (Retired Abbot).
Priests 9; Monks in Community 23.

Abbey of Our Lady of the Holy Cross (1950): 901 Cool Spring Ln., Berryville, VA 22611-2700. Tel: 540-955-1425; Fax: 540-955-1356. Rt. Rev. Robert Barnes, O.C.S.O., Abbot.
Legal Title: *Community of Cistercians of the Strict Observance, Inc.*
Solemnly Professed 23; Priests 12.

Assumption Abbey: Rte. 5, Box 1056, Ava, MO 65608. Tel: 417-683-5110; Fax: 417-683-5658. Rev. Mark A. Scott, O.C.S.O., Abbot; Rt. Rev. Robert Matter, O.C.S.O., Abbot (Retired); Rt. Rev. Cyprian Harrison, O.C.S.O., Abbot (Retired).
Priests 9; Professed 12.

Abbey of New Clairvaux (1955): *Trappist-Cistercian Abbey,* Vina, CA 96092. Tel: 530-839-2161. Rt. Rev. Thomas X. Davis, O.C.S.O., Abbot.
Legal Title: *Abbey of New Clairvaux, Inc.*
Solemn Vows 17; Simple Vows 2.

St. Benedict's Monastery (1956): 1012 Monastery Rd., Snowmass, CO 81654. Tel: 970-927-3311. Rt. Rev. Joseph Boyle, O.C.S.O., Abbot; Bros. Raymond Roberts, O.C.S.O., Prior; Charles Albanese, O.C.S.O., Subprior.
Professed Monks 13.

[0360] (C.M.F.)—CLARETIAN MISSIONARIES

(Missionary Sons of the Immaculate Heart of Mary)
(Congregatio Missionariorum Filiorum Immaculati Cordis Beatae Mariae Virginis.)

General Headquarters: Rome, Via Sacro Cuore di Maria 5, Italy. Very Rev. Aquilino Bocos, C.M.F., Supr. Gen.

Western Province: *Provincial Headquarters,* 1119 Westchester Pl., Los Angeles, CA 90019. Tel: 323-734-1824; Fax: 323-737-0301. Revs. Roland Lozano, C.M.F., Prov.; Dennis G. Gallo, C.M.F., Vicar & Consultor; Frank Ferrante, C.M.F., Consultor; Art Gramaje, C.M.F., Consultor; Bro. Rene LePage, C.M.F., Treas. & Consultor.
Legal Titles: *Claretian Missionaries-Western Province, Inc. A not-for-profit corporation under the laws of the State of California having as its purpose the support of*

any Roman Catholic benevolent, charitable, educational or missionary undertakings of the Claretian Missionaries - Western Province, Inc. Other Corporations: Dominguez Seminary, Inc., Compton, CA; *Claretian Educational and Renewal Center, Inc.*, Los Angeles, CA; *Claretian Tape Ministry Inc.*, Los Angeles, CA.

Ministries in the following areas: Newman Centers; Parishes; Novitiate; House of Study; Centers for Spanish Speaking; Renewal Centers; Education; Spiritual Direction.

Fathers 77; Brothers 8; Students 5.

Represented in the Archdioceses of Los Angeles and San Antonio and in the Dioceses of Fresno and Phoenix.

Eastern Province: *Claretian Missionary Hdqtrs.*, 400 N. Euclid Ave., Oak Park, IL 60302. Tel: 708-848-2076; Fax: 708-848-2069. Very Rev. Leonard J. Brown, C.M.F., Prov. Supr.; Revs. Carl J. Quebedeaux, C.M.F., Vicar & Consultor; Mark J. Brummel, C.M.F., Treas. & Consultor; James F. Maloney, C.M.F., Sec. & Consultor; Bruce L. Wellems, C.M.F., Consultor.

Legal Holdings or Titles: *The Congregation of Sons of the Immaculate Heart of Mary of the Eastern Province, Inc.; Claret Center,* Chicago, IL; *Claretian Volunteer Program,* Chicago, IL; *Claretian Associates,* Chicago, IL; *Claretians, Inc.; St. Jude League, Inc.; St. Jude Seminary, Inc.*

Fathers 45; Brothers 4; Novices 4; House of Study 1

Represented in the Archdioceses of Atlanta and Chicago and in the Dioceses of Metuchen and Springfield-Cape Girardeau.

[0370] (S.S.C.)—SOCIETY OF ST. COLUMBAN

(Societas Sancti Columbani pro missionibus ad Exteros)

Central Administration (1918): *St. Columban's,* Grange Rd., Donaghmede, Dublin 13, Ireland. Very Rev. Brendan O'Sullivan, S.S.C., Supr. Gen.

Members 575.

Region of the United States: *Society of St. Columban,* P.O. Box 10, St. Columbans, NE 68056. Tel: 402-291-1920. Very Rev. John Burger, S.S.C., Dir.; Rev. Thomas P. Reynolds, S.S.C., Vice Dir. Council: Revs. Michael Cody, S.S.C.; Arturo Aguilar, S.S.C.; William Sullivan, S.S.C.; William Sweeney, S.S.C.

Legal Titles: *St. Columban's Foreign Mission Society; The Columban Fathers.*

Fathers 94.

Represented in the Archdioceses of Boston, Chicago, Los Angeles, Omaha, and Washington and the Dioceses of Buffalo, El Paso, Orange, Providence and San Bernardino.

[0380] (M.C.C.J.)—COMBONI MISSIONARIES OF THE HEART OF JESUS

(Verona Fathers)

(Missionarii Comboniani Cordis Jesu)

(A Pontifical World Missionary Congregation Of Priests And Brothers)

Founded by Saint Daniel Comboni in 1867, First foundation in the United States in 1939.

General Motherhouse: *Missionari Comboniani,* Via Luigi Lilio 80 Rome, Italy. 00142 Very Rev. Manuel Augusto Ferreira, M.C.C.J., Supr.

North American Province (1950): *Comboni Mission Center,* 1318 Nagel Rd., Cincinnati, OH 45255-3120. Tel: 513-474-4997; Fax: 513-474-0382. E-Mail: info@combonimissionaries.org; Web site: www.ComboniMissionaries.org. Rev. Dennis Conway, M.C.C.J., Prov.; Rev. Paul Donohue, M.C.C.J., Editor Comboni Mission Newsletter and Comboni Press Feature Service; Rev. Joseph Bragotti, M.C.C.J., Mission Office Dir.

Legal Title: *Comboni Missionaries of the Heart of Jesus, Inc.*

Priests 39; Brothers 2; College Students 1; Scholastics 18.

Home Mission Parishes 4; Mission Centers 4.

Represented in the Archdioceses of Chicago, Cincinnati, Los Angeles and Newark.

[0390] (I.M.C.)—CONSOLATA MISSIONARIES

(Institutum Missionum a Consolata)

General Motherhouse: Rome, Viale delle Mura Aurelie, 11, Italy. Very Rev. Peter Trabucco, Supr. Gen.

Headquarters in the U.S.: 2301 Rte. 27- P.O. Box 5550, Somerset, NJ 08875-5550. Tel: 732-297-9191; Fax: 732-940-3121. Rev. Leonard DePasquale, I.M.C., Reg. Supr.

Legal Title: *Consolata Society for Foreign Missions.*

Priests 19; Brothers 1.

Properties owned: Mission Community House 3; House of Studies.

Represented in the Archdiocese of Washington and in the Dioceses of Buffalo, Metuchen and San Bernardino.

[0400] (O.S.C.)—CANONS REGULAR OF THE ORDER OF THE HOLY CROSS

(Crosier Fathers and Brothers)

Canonici Regulares Ordinis Sanctae Crucis (Cruciferi)

Generalate: *Generalatus Ordinis S. Crucis,* Via del Velabro 19 00186, Rome, Italy. Most Rev. Glen Lewandowski, O.S.C., Master Gen.

United States Province: *Province of St. Odilia, Crosier National Headquarters,* 3510 Vivian Ave., Shoreview, MN 55126-3852. Tel: 651-486-7456; Fax: 651-287-1130. Very Rev. Thomas R. Carkhuff, O.S.C., Prov. Provincial Councilors: Revs. Steven Henrich, O.S.C.; Kermit Holl, O.S.C.; Timothy Conlon, O.S.C.

Legal Titles: *Crosier Fathers and Brothers Province, Inc.; Canons Regular of the Order of the Holy Cross.*

Bishops 1; Fathers 67; Brothers 20; Novices 1.

Properties owned, sponsored or staffed: Houses 6; Novitiates 2; Parishes 11; Chaplaincies 4; Foreign Mission 1.

Represented in the Archdioceses of Baltimore, Chicago, Detroit, and St. Paul-Minneapolis and the Dioceses of Duluth, Phoenix and St. Cloud. Also in Tokyo, Japan, Indonesia and the Democratic Republic of the Congo.

[0410] (F.D.P.)—SONS OF DIVINE PROVIDENCE

(Filiorum Divinae Providentiae)

General Motherhouse: *Via Etruria 6,* Rome, Italy. 00183

Founded in 1893 by Blessed Don Louis Orione. Very Rev. Roberto Simionato, F.D.P., Supr. Gen.

Delegation of Our Lady Queen of the Universe-U.S. Foundation (1953): III Orient Ave., E. Boston, MA 02128. Tel: 617-569-2100; Fax: 617-561-1138. Very Rev. Angelo Quadrini, F.D.P., Reg. Supr.

Priests 10.

Properties staffed or owned: Parishes 2; Nursing Home 2; Shrine 1.

Represented in the Archdioceses of Boston and New York and in the Diocese of Evansville.

[0420] (S.V.D.)—SOCIETY OF THE DIVINE WORD

(Societas Verbi Divini)

General Motherhouse: *Collegio del Verbo Divino,* Via Dei Verbiti 1, Rome, Italy.

Founded 1897, with Headquarters at St. Mary's Mission House (Divine Word Seminary) Techny, Illinois; later separating into four provinces. In 1985 the Eastern and Northern Provinces combined. Very Rev. Antonio Pernia, S.V.D., Supr. Gen.

Chicago Province (1985): *Province of Blessed Joseph Freinademetz, S.V.D. Province Center,* 1985 Waukegan Rd., P.O. Box 6038, Techny, IL 60082-6038. Tel: 847-272-2700; Fax: 847-272-2517. Very Rev. Thomas A. Krosnicki, S.V.D., Prov.; Bro. Dennis Newton, S.V.D., Vice Prov.; Rev. Dariuz Garbaciak, S.V.D., Treas.

Legal Titles: *Divine Word Funds, Inc.,* 1835 Waukegan Rd., P.O. Box 6099, Techny, IL 60082-6099. Tel: 847-272-7600. Bro. Dennis Newton, S.V.D., Pres. *Divine Word Missionaries, Inc.; S.V.D. Catholic Universities, Inc.; Divine Word International; Blessed Arnold Charitable Trust.*

Priests 195; Brothers 49; Theologians 43.

Minor Seminarians: College 100; Student Brothers 3; Novices 14; Associates 3.

Chaplaincies 1; Retirement Homes 2.

Properties owned: Theologate; College; Retreat House; House of Studies; Conference Center.

Represented in the Archdioceses of Boston, Chicago, Dubuque, Indianapolis, Milwaukee, Newark, St. Louis, and Washington and the Dioceses of Memphis, Pittsburgh, Trenton and Wheeling-Charleston. Also in Canada, Jamaica and the West Indies.

Eastern Province: *Amalgamated with Northern Province. See Chicago Province.*

Southern Province (1940): *Southern Province of St. Augustine Provincial Residence,* 201 Ruella Ave., Bay St. Louis, MS 39520. Tel: 228-467-4322; 467-3815. E-mail: svduss@aol.com. Very Rev. Joseph D. Simon, S.V.D., Prov.; Rev. Thomas James, S.V.D., Vice. Prov.; Bro. Richard Chanbers, S.V.D., Treas. Address applications for Retreats and Missions to: Rev. William Kelley, S.V.D. Retreat Center.

Fathers 51; Brothers 8.

Parishes 23; Mission Stations 3; Elementary Schools 5.

Represented in the Archdiocese of New Orleans and in the Dioceses of Baton Rouge, Biloxi, Galveston-Houston, Jackson, Lafayette (LA) and Little Rock.

Western Province (1964): *Province of St. Therese of the Child Jesus,* 2181 West 25th St., P.O. Box 7195, Los Angeles, CA 90007-7195. Tel: 323-735-8130; Fax: 323-735-8122. Very Rev. Joseph A. Miller, S.V.D., Prov.; Revs. Michal L. Manning, S.V.D., Vice Prov.; Gerard O'Doherty, S.V.D., Prov. Treas.

Fathers 40; Brothers 5.

Properties staffed, sponsored or owned: High Schools 2; Parishes 7; Hospitals 4; Prisons 2; Retreat Centers 1.

Represented in the Archdiocese of Los Angeles and in the Dioceses of Oakland, Orange and San Bernardino.

[0430] (O.P.)—ORDER OF PREACHERS

Dominicans Fratres Sacri Ordinis Praedicatorum

Generalitia: *Convento Santa Sabina,* Piazza Pietro d' Illiria, Aventino 00153, Rome, Italy. Most Rev. Carlos A. Azpiroz Costa, O.P., Master of the Order; Very Rev. Gerald Lee Stookey, O.P., Asst. for U.S.A. Provinces; Very Rev. Joseph Nguyen Thang, O.P., Procurator Gen.

Province of St. Joseph-Eastern Dominican Province (1805): 869 Lexington Ave., New York, NY 10021-6680. Tel: 212-737-5757; Fax: 212-861-4216. Very Revs. D. Dominic Izzo, O.P., Prior Prov.; Carleton P. Jones, O.P., Vicar Prov. and Socius to Prov.; Revs. Kenneth Sicard, O.P., Prov. Econ. Admin.; John C. Vidmar, O.P., Prov. Archivist; Brian J. Shanley, O.P., Regent of Studies; James Ferrer Quigley, O.P., Dir.-Continuing Educaiton; Ms. Janice T. Brown, M.S.N., G.N.P., R.N., Dir.-Health Services; Revs. John A. McMahon, O.P., Dir.-Center for Assisted Living; Frank I. Sutman, O.P., Dir.-Preaching; William P. Garrott, O.P., Dir.-Vocations; James M. Sullivan, O.P., Dir.-Dominican Laity; S. Matthew Erickson, O.P., Sec.-Missions & Dir.-Dominican Foreign Missions; Albino F. Barrera, O.P., Promoter-Social Justice; George L. Concordia, O.P., Promoter-Holy Name Society; Andre-Joseph LaCasse, O.P., Promoter-Rosary; R.Ferrer Halligan, O.P., Dir. Advancement & Dir.-Dominican Friars' Guild, Inc.; Deserving Poor Boys Priesthood Association, Inc.; St. Jude Dominican Missions, Inc.; St. Martin de Porres Guild, Inc.; Rosary Apostolate, Inc.; Kenneth A. France-Kelly, O.P., Dir.-Rosary Shrine of St. Jude (Washington).

Corporate Title: *Dominican Fathers Province of St. Joseph.*

Legal Titles: *Retirement Plan and Pension Plan; Dominican Fathers, Province of St. Joseph; Dominican Friars' Guilds, Inc.; Deserving Poor Boys Priesthood Association, Inc.; St. Jude Dominican Missions, Inc.; St. Martin de Porres Guild, Inc.; Dominican Foreign Missions; Handicapped Children's Fund, Peru; Rosary Shrine of St. Jude,* (Washington, DC); *Rosary Apostolate; Angelicum Fund.*

Archbishop 1; Bishops 2; Fathers 228; Cooperator Brothers 12; Professed Clerics 30; Novices 7.

Properties owned, staffed or sponsored: Priories 12; Houses 5; Parishes 16; Campus Ministries 1; Colleges 1; House of Study 1; Retreat Houses 1; Novitiates 1; Foreign Missions 1.

Represented in the Archdioceses of Boston, Cincinnati, Detroit, Hartford, Louisville, Newark, New York, and Washington and the Dioceses of Columbus, Providence, Richmond and Youngstown.

Province of the Most Holy Name of Jesus-Western Dominican Province (1912): 5877 Birch Ct., Oakland, CA 94618-1626. Tel: 510-658-8722; Fax: 510-658-1061. E-mail: WDP@opwest.org. Very Rev. Roberto Corral, O.P., Prior Prov.; Very Rev. Bartholomew J. Hutcherson, O.P., Vicar Prov. & Socius; Revs. Edward Krasevac, O.P., Vicar Prov.; Martin Walsh, O.P., Dir. Mission Foundation; Michael J. Dodds, O.P., Regent of Studies; Dominic DeDomenico, O.P., Treas.; Jose Pimentel, Dir.-Development; Jude Eli, O.P., Dir.-Preaching; Bro. Raymond Bretheaux, O.P., Archivist.

Legal Title: *Province of the Holy Name, Inc.*

Fathers 121; Brothers 7; Professed Clerics 36; Novices 7; Donatus 1.

Parishes 9; Newman Centers/Personal Parishes 10; Retreat House; House of Studies; Novitiate.

Represented in the Archdioceses of Anchorage, Denver, Los Angeles, Portland in Oregon, San Francisco, Seattle, and Washington and in the Dioceses of Fresno, Las Vegas, Oakland, Phoenix, Providence, Richmond, Sacramento, Salt Lake City, San Bernardino, San Diego, San Jose and Tucson. Also in Mexico, Kenya, Switzerland and Rome.

Province of St. Albert the Great-Central Dominican Province (1939): 1909 S. Ashland Ave., Chicago, IL 60608. Tel: 312-666-3244; Fax: 312-829-8471. Very Revs. Michael A. Mascari, O.P., Prov.; David F. Wright, O.P., Socius, Vicar Prov. – Archivist; John J. Meany, O.P., Vicar Prov.; Revs. Andrew-Carl Wisdom, O.P., Promoter of Vocations & Dir.-Society Vocational Support; Dennis C. Woerter, O.P., Promoter of Social Justice; Donald J. Goergen, O.P., Regent; Jerome M. Walsh, O.P., Dir. Society Vocational Support & Shrine of St. Jude; Bede R. Jagoe, O.P., Dir. St. Dominic Mission Society.

Legal Titles: *Dominicans, Province of St. Albert the Great, U.S.A.; Shrine of St. Jude Thaddeus, Inc.; Society for Vocational Support, Inc.; St. Dominic Mission Society; Dominican Social Action Fund;*

Dominican Laity; Dominican Central Productions; Fra Angelico Art Foundation; The Bolivian Trust of the Dominicans, Office for Mission Advancement.
Fathers 168; Professed Clerics 15; Novices 11; Brothers 20.
Properties owned, staffed or sponsored: Parishes 9; Convents 8; Houses 11; Houses of Studies 2; Novitiate; High Schools 1.
Represented in the Archdioceses of Chicago, Denver, Detroit, Military Services, St. Louis, St. Paul-Minneapolis, and Santa Fe and the Dioceses of Colorado Springs, Des Moines, Grand Rapids, Joliet, Lafayette (IN), Madison, Springfield (IL), Superior and Winona.

Southern Dominican Province of St. Martin de Porres (1979): 1421 N. Causeway Blvd., Ste. 200, Metairie, LA 70001-4144. Tel: 504-837-2129; Fax: 504-837-6604. Very Revs. Martin J. Gleeson, O.P., Prov.; Emiliano Zapata, O.P., Vicar Prov.; Joseph J. Konkel, O.P., Econ. Admin.; R.B. Williams, O.P., Promoter for Permanent Formation; John J. Markey, O.P., Regent of Studies; Henry B. Groover, O.P., Promoter of Vocations.
Legal Holdings or Titles: *Southern Dominican Foundation; Retirement and Community Support Plan, Southern Dominican Province, U.S.A.; Shrine of St. Martin de Porres.*
Fathers 105; Professed Clerics 24; Brothers 10; Novices 7; Deacons 6.
Properties owned, staffed or sponsored: Parishes 15; Priories 8; Houses 7; Shrines 1; Provincial Offices 1.
Represented in the Archdioceses of Los Angeles, Miami, New Orleans, St. Louis, San Antonio, and Washington and the Dioceses of Austin, Baton Rouge, Birmingham, Dallas, El Paso, Galveston-Houston, Houma-Thibodaux, Memphis, Raleigh, Tyler and Venice.

U.S. Foundation (1926): *Province of Spain,* P.O. Box 279, San Diego, TX 78384. Tel: 361-279-3596. Revs. Benito Retortillo, O.P.; Epifanio Rodriguez, O.P.
Priests 2.
Represented in the Diocese of Corpus Christi.

[0440] (S.S.E.)—SOCIETY OF SAINT EDMUND

(Societas Sancti Edmundi)

General Motherhouse: *Edmundite Generalate,* 270 Winooski Park, Colchester, VT 05439. Tel: 802-654-3400; Fax: 802-654-3409. Very Rev. Richard M. Myhalyk, S.S.E., Supr. Gen. Councilors: Revs. Michael P. Cronogue, S.S.E.; Carroll W. Plourde, S.S.E.; Richard N. Berube, S.S.E.; Paul G. McQuillen, S.S.E.
Legal Title: *Society of St. Edmund, Inc.*
Bishops 1; Fathers 40; Brothers 5.
Properties owned, staffed or sponsored: Parishes 17; College 1; Shrine; Novitiate; Middle School.
Represented in the Archdioceses of Detroit, Mobile and New Orleans and in the Dioceses of Burlington, Norwich and Venice. Also Venezuela and France.

[0450] (C.J.M.)—CONGREGATION OF JESUS AND MARY

(Congregatio Jesu et Mariae)
(The Eudists Fathers)

General Motherhouse: Via dei Querceti, 15 00184, Rome, Italy. Very Rev. Michel Gerard, C.J.M., Supr. Gen.

North American Province: 6125 Premiere Ave., Charlesbourg, Quebec, Canada. G1H 2V9 Tel: 418-626-6494. Very Rev. Aurele Godbout, C.J.M., Prov.

St. John Eudes Center *The Eudists:* 36 Flohr Ave., West Seneca, NY 14224-1818. Tel: 716-825-4319; Fax: 716-825-4376. E-mail: EudesCenter@cs.com. Rev. Benoit J. Drapeau, C.J.M., Supr.
Bishops 1; Fathers 88; Lay Members 3.
Represented in the Dioceses of Buffalo and San Diego.

[0460] (C.F.P.)—BROTHERS OF THE POOR OF ST. FRANCIS

(Congregatio Fratrum Pauperum)

Motherhouse: Aachen, Germany. Very Rev. Bro. Mark Gastel, C.F.P., Min. Gen.

Community of St. Joseph: *Provincial Office,* 324 Donham Ave., Cincinnati, OH 45226-2116. Tel: 513-272-6347; Fax: 513-321-3777. Bro. Joel Stern, C.F.P., USA Community Minister.
Brothers serve and staff: Development Offices; High Schools; Elementary Schools; Homes for Senior Citizens; Group Homes; Literacy Program for the Imprisoned.
Brothers' Special Mission: Care and education of neglected youth; elementary & secondary education; human services.
Professed Brothers 20.
Represented in the Archdiocese of Cincinnati and in the Dioceses of Covington, Davenport, El Paso and Little Rock.

[0470] (O.F.M.CAP.)—THE CAPUCHIN FRIARS

(Ordinis Fratrum Minorum Capuccinorum)

Generalate: *Curia Generalis Ord. Min. Cap.* via Piemonte 70, Rome, Italy 00187. Most Rev. John Corriveau, O.F.M.Cap., General Min.

Province of St. Joseph (1857): *Calvary Province* 1820 Mt. Elliott St., Detroit, MI 48207-3496. Tel: 313-579-2100; Fax: 313-579-2275. Bros. Daniel E. Anholzer, C.F.M.Cap., Prov. Minister; Robert Smith, O.F.M.Cap., Prov. Vicar. Councilors:. William Hugo, O.F.M.Cap. Alan Veik, O.F.M.Cap.; John Celichowski, O.F.M.Cap.; Mr. Mark McDonough, Corp. Sec./Treas.; Bros. Randolph Graczyk O.F.M.Cap., Sec.-Religious Affairs; Bro. T.L. Michael Auman, O.F.M.Cap., Dir.-Publications; Revs. James Wolf, O.F.M Cap., Dir.-Communications; Edward Foley, O.F.M.Cap., Dir.-Continuing Education; Richard Hart, O.F.M.Cap., Dir.-Preaching; Lloyd Thiel, O.F.M.Cap., Dir.-Public Relations Devel.; James Zelinski, O.F.M.Cap., Dir.-JPE; Campion Baer, O.F.M.Cap., Mission Sec.; Lester Bach, O.F.M.Cap., Prov. Asst.-Secular Franciscan Order; Bros. Richard Merling, O.F.M.Cap., Dir.-Solanus Guild; Leo Wollenweber, O.F.M.Cap., Vice Postulator-Cause of Ven. Solanus Casey; Rev. Michael H. Crosby, O.F.M.Cap., Corp. Responsibility Agent.
Legal Title: *Province of St. Joseph of the Capuchin Order, Inc.*
Priests 116; Perpetually Professed Lay Friars 43; Professed Friars in Temporary Vows 1.
Parishes, Hospitals, Nursing Homes, Hospices, Prisons, Retreat Centers, Soup Kitchens; Direct Services to the Poor; Educational Institutions; Home and Foreign Missions.
Represented in the Archdioceses of Chicago, Detroit, Los Angeles, Milwaukee, New York, and St. Paul-Minneapolis and in the Dioceses of Brooklyn, Fort Wayne-South Bend, Great Falls-Billings, Green Bay, LaCrosse, Las Cruces, Madison, Marquette, Oakland, Pittsburgh, Saginaw and San Bernardino. Also the vicariate of Bluefields, Nicaragua and in Dioceses of Panama, Guam, Japan, Australia, Costa Rica, Honduras and Brisbane.

Province of St. Augustine (1873): *Provincial Office,* 220 37th St., Pittsburgh, PA 15201. Tel: 412-682-6011; Fax: 412-682-0506. Very Rev. John Bednarik, O.F.M.Cap., Definitor Gen.; Very Rev. Paul Kuppe, O.F.M.Cap., Prov. Min.; Revs. John Pavlik, O.F.M.Cap., Vicar Prov.; John Petrikovic, O.F.M.Cap., Exec. Sec. & Sec. Communications; Definitors: Revs. Thomas Betz, O.F.M.Cap.; John Daya, O.F.M.Cap.; Donald Lippert, O.F.M.Cap.; R. Joseph Kusnir, Chief Fin. Officer; Dennis Klemash, O.F.M.Cap., Newsletter; Vocation Program: Thomas Betz, O.F.M.Cap.; Paul Dressler, O.F.M.Cap.; Moises Villalta, O.F.M.Cap.
Legal Titles: *Province of St. Augustine of the Capuchin Order; Headquarters of Capuchin Franciscan Volunteer Corps., Inc.; Augustine Province of the Capuchin Order; National Headquarters of Archconfraternity of Christian Mothers; Mission Office of Seraphic Mass Association; Secular Franciscan Order of St. Augustine, Province; Capuchin Friars Sick and Elderly Trust Fund; St. Fidelis, Inc.; Capuchin Friars Formation and Education Trust Fund.*
Bishops 1; Priests 129; Brothers 38; Professed in Formation 14; Novices 4; Postulants 8.
Properties owned, staffed or sponsored: Parishes 20; Formation Houses 3; Novitiate 1; Friaries 18; Postulancy Houses 1; Hospital Chaplain 11; Military Chaplain 1; Foreign Missions 2.
Represented in the Archdioceses of Baltimore, Philadelphia, and Washington and in the Dioceses of Altoona-Johnstown, Cleveland, Greensburg, Harrisburg, Pittsburgh and Wheeling-Charleston. Also in Papua New Guinea and Puerto Rico.

Province of St. Mary (1952): *St. Conrad Friary,* Attn: Rev. Jerome McHugh, O.F.M.Cap. 30 Gedney Park Dr., White Plains, NY 10605. Tel: 914-761-3008; Fax: 914-948-6429. Very Rev. Michael Banks, O.F.M.Cap., Minister Prov. Definitors: Revs. David Couturier, O.F.M.Cap.; Francis Gasparik, O.F.M.Cap.; John McHugh, O.F.M.Cap.; Bro. Timothy Jones, O.F.M.Cap.
Legal Titles: *The Province of St. Mary of the Capuchin Order; Capuchin Friars International, Inc.; St. Francis of Assisi Foundation.*
Development Office: St. John Friary, 210 W. 31st St., New York, NY 10001.
Bishops 2; Priests 119; Professed Clerical Brothers 1; Professed Lay Brothers 41; Novices 4; Postulants 1.
Properties staffed or sponsored: Parishes 13; Chaplaincies 17; Novitiate 1; Foreign Missions 3.
Represented in the Archdioceses of Agana, Boston, and New York and the Dioceses of Bridgeport, Brooklyn, Honolulu, Manchester, Norwich, Portland (ME), Rochester and Rockville Centre. Also in Japan.

Province of the Sacred Stigmata of St. Francis (1918): *Our Lady of Guadalupe Friary,* 319 - 36th St., P.O. Box 809, Union City, NJ 07087. Tel: 201-865-0611; Fax: 201-866-7035. Revs. Vincent Fortunato, O.F.M.Cap., Prov. Min.; Thomas A. Crangle, O.F.M.Cap., Prov. Vicar; Definitors: Cyprian Rosen, O.F.M.Cap.; Brian Tomlinson, O.F.M.Cap.; Jude Duffy, O.F.M.Cap., Prov. Sec.
Priests 36; Brothers 17; Temporary Professed 4; Novices 1; Postulants 3.
Parishes 8; Friaries 5; Retreat House 1; Hospital Chaplaincies 1
Represented in the Archdioceses of Newark, and New York and the Dioceses of Charlotte, Paterson, St. Petersburg and Wilmington.

Our Lady of Angels, Western American Province: 1345 Cortez Ave., Burlingame, CA 94010. Revs. Antonio Marti, O.F.M.Cap., Prov.; Definitors: Peter Banks, O.F.M.Cap.; Matthew Elshoff, O.F.M.Cap.; Jesus Vela, O.F.M.Cap. (& Treas.); Gerald Barron, O.F.M.Cap., Definitor; Camillus MacRory, O.F.M.Cap., Spiritual Asst.-Secular Franciscans; Donal Burke, O.F.M.Cap., Dir.-Devel./Finances; Miguel Angel Ortiz, O.F.M.Cap., Dir.-Foreign Missions; Miguel Angel Ortiz, O.F.M.Cap., Sec.
Ministries in Parishes, High Schools, Novitiates, Chaplaincies, House of Study, Retreats, Foreign Missions, Campus Ministry, Military Chaplaincy and Hospital Chaplaincy.
Priests 45; Brothers 12; Brothers in Formation 10; Postulants 6.
Represented in the Archdioceses of Los Angeles, and San Francisco and the Dioceses of Baker and Oakland. Also in Mexico.

Province of SS. Stanislaus and Adalbert (1948): *St. Stanislaus Friary,* 2 Manor Dr., Oak Ridge, NJ 07438. Tel: 973-697-7757. Rev. Francis Z. Majewski, O.F.M.Cap., Asst. Supr.
Fathers 4.
Represented in the Dioceses of Metuchen, Paterson and Trenton.

Vice Province of Texas: *Capuchin Franciscan Friars of Texas,* 5604 Bernal Dr., Dallas, TX 75212. Tel: 214-631-1937; Fax: 214-631-6267. Rev. Ignacio Cizur, O.F.M.Cap., Vice Prov.
Fathers 16; Brothers 2.
Parishes 4; Cursillo Centers 2.
Represented in the Dioceses of Dallas and Fort Worth.

Province of Mid-America (1977): *St. Francis of Assisi Friary,* 3553 Wyandot St., Denver, CO 80211-2948. Tel: 303-477-5436; 477-5542; Fax: 303-477-6925. Revs. Michael Scully, O.F.M.Cap., Prov. & Coord Vocation Programs; Gene Emrisek, O.F.M.Cap., Vicar Prov.; Francis X. Grinko, O.F.M.Cap., Councilor & Coord.-Formation; Harvey P. Dinkel, O.F.M.Cap., Exec. Sec. & Treas.; Blaine Burkey, O.F.M.Cap., Communications Dir.; Greg Beyer, O.F.M.Cap., Archivist. Charles Polifka, O.F.M.Cap., Councilor; Mark Schenk, O.F.M.Cap., Councilor.
Legal Titles: *Capuchin Province of Mid-America, Inc.; St. Francis Seminary Endowment Foundation, Inc.*
Bishops 3; Priests 44; Students 8; Brothers 10.
Represented in the Archdioceses of Denver, Kansas City in Kansas and St. Louis and in the Dioceses of Colorado Springs and Salina.

Vice Province of St. John The Baptist (1905): *Vice Provincial Offices,* 216 Arzuaga St., P.O. Box 21350, Rio Piedras, PR 00928-1350. Tel: 787-764-3090; Fax: 787-764-4070. Bros. Alberto Figueroa Morales, O.F.M.Cap., Vice Prov. Min.; Roy F. Martinez, O.F.M.Cap., First Councilor; Ramon H. Negron, O.F.M.Cap., Second Councilor; Jorge Macias de Cespedes, O.F.M.Cap., Vice Prov. Sec./Treas., & Dir. Capuchin Mass Assoc.
Legal Titles: *Asociacion de Frailes Capuchinos, Inc.; Capuchin Formation Trust of Puerto Rico.*
Friars 27; Postulants 3.
Properties owned, staffed and sponsored: Formation Fraternites 3; Parishes 4; Retreat Center 1; Friaries 6; Mission Office 1.
Represented in the Archdiocese of San Juan and in the Dioceses of Arecibo, Caguas and Ponce.

[0480] (O.F.M.CONV.)—CONVENTUAL FRANCISCANS

(Friars Minor Conventual)
(Ordo Fratrum Minorum S. Francisci Conventualium)

General Curia: *Piazza SS. Apostoli, 51,* Rome 00187, Italy. Most Rev. Joachim Giermach, O.F.M.Conv.; Most Rev. John Joseph Dolan, O.F.M.Conv., Asst. Gen.

Province of the Immaculate Conception B.V.M. (1852): *Provincial House-Immaculate Conception Friary,* P.O. Box 629, Rensselaer, NY 12144. Tel: 518-472-1000; Fax: 518-472-1013. Web Site: www.conventualfranciscanfriars.com. Very Rev. Canice Connors, O.F.M.Conv., Minister Prov.; Revs. Briant Cullinane, O.F.M.Conv., Guardian; Simon Mohr, O.F.M.Conv.; Bros. Andre Picotte, O.F.M.Conv., Dir.; Stephen Merrigan, O.F.M.Conv., Dir. of Elder Care; Rev. Duane Mastangelo, O.F.M.Conv., Archivist.

Legal Titles: *Order of Friars Minor Conventual Immaculate Conception; Province Charitable Trust; Franciscorps, Inc.,* Rensselaer, NY; *The Franciscan Center for Spirituality, Inc.,* Albany, NY; *Franciscans in Collaborative Ministry, Inc.,* Rensselaer, NY.
Fathers 111; Professed Brothers 18.
Parishes 21; Friaries 20; Chaplaincies 8; Filial Houses 2.
Represented in the Archdioceses of Newark, New York, Philadelphia and Washington and in the Dioceses of Albany, Charlotte, Metuchen, Raleigh, Syracuse and Trenton. Also in Canada, and Costa Rica.

Province of St. Anthony of Padua (1906): *Provincial House,* 12300 Folly Quarter Rd., Ellicott City, MD 21042-1419. Tel: 410-531-9200; Fax: 410-531-4881. Very Rev. Michael Kolodziej, O.F.M.Conv., Minister Prov. Revs. Donald Grzymski, O.F.M.Conv., Vicar Prov.; Robert Twele, O.F.M.Conv., Prov. Treas.; Definitors: Revs. Joseph Benicewicz, O.F.M.Conv.; Michael Martin, O.F.M.Conv.; Herman Czaster, O.F.M.Conv.; Dennis Grumsey, O.F.M.Conv.; Michael Lewandowski, O.F.M. Conv.
Legal Titles: *St. Francis High School of Athol Springs, NY, Inc.; The Father Justin Rosary Hour, Inc.; Franciscan Fathers Minor Conventuals of Buffalo, NY, Inc.; The Franciscan Center, Inc.; St. Anthony of Padua Province, Franciscan Fathers Minor Conventual, U.S.A., Inc.; The Friars Knights of the St. Francis High School, Inc.; Order of Friars Minor Conventual, Inc.; Conventual Franciscan Friars, St. Anthony of Padua Province, Franciscan Mission Association, Inc.; Franciscan Fathers Minor Conventual, St. Anthony of Padua Province U.S.A., MA. Inc.; Franciscan Friars, St. Anthony of Padua Province, Education Fund, Inc.; Franciscan Friars, St. Anthony of Padua Province, Fund for the Aged and Infirm, Inc.; Franciscan Minor Conventuals of Maryland, of Ellicott City, MD, Inc.; The FranciscanFathers, Minor Conventuals, of St. Stanislaus Church of Baltimore City, MD, Inc.; St. Francis of Assisi Community, Inc.; Order of Friars Minor Conventual, St. Anthony of Padua Province, U.S.A., Inc.; St. Stanislaus Cemetery, Inc.; AnthonyCorps, Inc.*
Priests 134; Brothers in Solemn Vows 16; Clerics in Temporary Vows 2; Novices 1; Candidates 2.
Friaries 27; Filial Houses 8.
Apostolates owned, staffed or sponsored: Novitiates 1; House of Study 1; Parishes 28; Campus Ministries 4; High Schools 2; Youth-Crisis Shelter 1; Sisters' Chaplaincies 3; Hospital-Nursing Home Chaplaincies 3; Apostolates Radio Apostolate; Healing Ministry; Preaching Apostolate; Foreign Missions 3; Candidate House; Youth Ministry.
Represented in the Archdioceses of Atlanta, Baltimore, Boston, and Hartford and the Dioceses of Altoona-Johnstown, Bridgeport, Brooklyn, Buffalo, Fall River, Harrisburg, Norwich, Palm Beach, Paterson, Rochester, Savannah, Springfield (MA) and Trenton.

St. Bonaventure Province (1939): 6107 N. Kenmore Ave., Chicago, IL 60660-2797. Tel: 773-274-7681; Fax: 773-274-9751. Very Rev. Anthony Labedis, O.F.M.Conv., Min. Prov.; Bro. George Searles, Treas.; Definitors: Revs. Steve McKinley, O.F.M.Conv.; Joseph Kruszynski, O.F.M.Conv., Sec.; Luke Poczworowski, O.F.M.Conv., Vicar Prov.; William Callahan, O.F.M.Conv.; Bro. Joseph Wood, O.F.M.Conv.
Legal Titles: *Conventual Franciscans of St. Bonaventure Province; Franciscan Friars Educational Corp.; Conventual Franciscan Friars of Marytown; Shrine of St. Maximillian Kolbe; St. Hedwig Cemetery and Mausoleum; The Conventual Franciscans of Saint Bonaventure Province Charitable Continuing Care Trust Fund.*
Fathers 32; Professed Clerics 3; Brothers 18.
Properties owned or sponsored: Parishes 5; Chaplaincies; Marian Center; Shrine.
Represented in the Archdioceses of Chicago, Detroit and Milwaukee and in the Dioceses of Peoria and Rockford. Also in Mexico.

Province of Our Lady of Consolation (1926): 101 Anthony Dr., Mount St. Francis, IN 47146. Tel: 812-923-8444. Very Rev. Peter Damian Massengill, O.F.M.Conv., Min. Prov.; Rev. David Lenz, O.F.M.Conv., Vicar Prov.; Bro. Robert Baxter, O.F.M.Conv., Sec.
Fathers 121; Brothers 30; Professed Clerics 2; Candidates 5; Novices 3.
Friaries 24; Parishes 22; Houses of Formation 2; Retreat-Renewal Centers 3; Missions 15; Chaplaincies 2.
Development Office: 103 St. Francis Blvd., Mt. St. Francis, IN 47146. Tel: 812-923-5250. Rev. David Lenz, O.F.M.Conv., Dir.

Province of St. Joseph of Cupertino (1981): *St. Joseph of Cupertine Friary,* P.O. Box 820, Arroyo Grande, CA 93421-0820. Tel: 805-489-1012 & 473-2256; Fax: 805-489-8303. Very Rev. Christopher Deitz, O.F.M.Conv., Min. Prov.; Revs. Ronald Rocky, O.F.M.Conv., Vicar Prov. & Prov. Sec.; Raymond Mallett, O.F.M.Conv., Definitor; John Heinz, O.F.M.Conv., Definitor; Bros. George Cherrie, O.F.M.Conv., Definitor; James Reiter, O.F.M.Conv., Custos Capitularis; Rev. Stephen Gross O.F.M.Conv., Prov. Spiritual Asst. for Secular Franciscan Order.
Legal Title: *Conventual Franciscans of California, Inc.*
Priests 42; Brothers 13; Clerics (Professed Seminarians) 16; Novices 3; Candidates 1.
Properties owned, staffed or sponsored: Parishes 7; Shrines 1; Chaplaincies 1; High Schools 1; Houses of Formation 2.
Represented in the Archdiocese of Los Angeles, Military Archdiocese, Portland in Oregon, and San Francisco and the Dioceses of Fresno, Monterey, Oakland, Reno and San Bernardino.

[0485] (M.S.F.S.)—MISSIONARIES OF ST. FRANCIS DE SALES

(Missionariorum Sancti Francisci Salesi)

Founded in Annecy, France 1838. Established in the United States of America, 1974.
Motherhouse: Chemin de Proupeine Annecy, France, F-74000
American Mission: *Villa Luyet,* 109 Johnson Rd., Lawrenceville, GA 30045-5521. Rev. Martin J. Kopchik, M.S.F.S., Mission Supr.; Revs. John F. Tiernan, III, M.S.F.S.; John C. DeVore, M.S.F.S.; Joseph Mullakkara, M.S.F.S.; Abrama Mullenkuzhy, M.S.F.S.; Augustine Tharappel, M.S.F.S.
Legal Title: *Missionaries of St. Francis de Sales, Inc.*
Fathers 6; Fathers from provinces outside U.S. 15.
Properties staffed: Parishes 2; Convents 1.
Properties owned: *Villa Luyet Mission Residence,* Lawrenceville, GA; *Wellspring House of Spirituality,* Tyler, TX.
Represented in the Archdiocese of Atlanta, Chicago, and Mobile, and the Dioceses of Alexandria, Birmingham in Alabama, Cleveland, Galveston-Houston, Lansing, Nashville, St. Augustine and Tyler.

[0490] (O.S.F.)—CONGREGATION OF THE RELIGIOUS BROTHERS OF THE THIRD ORDER REGULAR OF ST. FRANCIS

Franciscan Brothers of Brooklyn

Generalate (1858): *St. Francis Monastery,* 135 Remsen St., Brooklyn, NY 11201-4212. Tel: 212-858-8217; Fax: 718-858-8306. Bros. Kevin Smith O.S.F., Supr. Gen.; Councilors: Joseph Moloney O.S.F.; Patrick Murphy, O.S.F., Master of Novices; Vocations Dirs: James McVeigh, O.S.F.; Robert Smith, O.S.F.; Campion Lally, O.S.F.; Joshua Di Mauro, O.S.F.
Legal Titles and Holdings: *St. Francis Monastery; Franciscan Brothers' Generalate; Franciscan Brothers, Inc.,* Brooklyn, NY; *Mount Alvernia, Inc.; St. Francis Center, Inc.,*
Ministries in the field of Education at all levels; Pastoral Ministries, Social Services; Spirituality Centers.
Brothers 98.
Represented in the Dioceses of Brooklyn, Gallup, Orlando, Paterson, Raleigh, Rockville Centre and Springfield-Cape Girardeau.

[0500] (O.S.F.)—FRANCISCAN BROTHERS OF CHRIST THE KING

General Motherhouse and Novitiate (1961): 7329 E. Edgewood Ave., Indianapolis, IN 46239. Tel: 317-862-9211. Bro. Francis A. Skube, Supr. Gen.
Professed Brothers 4.
Represented in the Archdiocese of Indianapolis.

[0510] (F.F.S.C.)— FRANCISCAN BROTHERS OF THE HOLY CROSS

Generalate: *St. Josefshaus,* 53547 Hausen/Wied, Linz Rhein, West Germany. Bro. Ulrich Schmitz, Supr. Gen.
American Region (1924): 2500 St. James Rd., Springfield, IL 62707. Tel: 217-747-5947; Fax: 217-747-5950. Bros. John Francis Tyrrell, F.F.S.C., Pres./Supr.; Stephen Bissler, F.F.S.C., Vicar/Vice Pres.; Christian Guertin, F.F.S.C., Councilor/Sec.; Anthony Joseph McCoy, F.F.S.C.; Boniface Shellock, F.F.S.C.; Gerald Voycheck, F.F.S.C., Treas.
Brothers 13.
Properties owned, staffed or sponsored: Home for Mentally Handicapped; Adult Training Center for Mentally Handicapped; Schools Elementary School; Novitiate.
Represented in the Dioceses of Madison and Springfield (IL).

[0515] (O.S.F.)— FRANCISCAN BROTHERS OF THE THIRD ORDER REGULAR

Generalate: *Franciscan Brothers' Generalate,* Mountbellew, Ireland.
United States Region: 4522 Gainsborough Ave., Los Angeles, CA 90027. Tel: 323-644-2740; Fax: 323-644-2977. Bro. Hilarion O'Connor, Reg. Supr.
Ministries in the field of secondary education.
Brothers 7.
Represented in the Archdiocese of Los Angeles.

[0520] (O.F.M.)— FRANCISCAN FRIARS

(Ordinis Fratrum Minorum)

General Headquarters: Via S. Maria Mediatrice, 25 00165, Rome, Italy. *Curia Generalizia dei Frati Minori.* Most Rev. Giacomo Bini, O.F.M., Min. Gen. Tel: 011-39-6-684-91-203. Very Rev. Estevao Ottenbreit, O.F.M., Vicar Gen. Rev. Sean Collins, O.F.M., English-Speaking General Councilor.
Order of Friars Minor: *English-Speaking Conference,* 1615 Vine St., Cincinnati, OH 45202-6400. Tel: 513-721-4700; Fax: 513-421-9672. Bro. Ronald Bolfeta, O.F.M., Exec. Dir.
Includes: Order of Friars Minor Provinces 12; Custodies 1: of the United States, Canada, England, Ireland and Malta. Associate Member: Commissariat of the Holy Land, Washington DC.

Province of St. John the Baptist (1844): 1615 Vine St., Cincinnati, OH 45202-6400. Tel: 513-721-4700; Fax: 513-421-9672. Revs. Fred Link, O.F.M., Prov. Min.; Jeffrey Scheeler, O.F.M., Prov. Vicar; Councilors: Revs. Dennet Jung, O.F.M.; Gregory Friedman, O.F.M.; James Bok, O.F.M., Dir.-Devel.; Bro. Mark Ligett, O.F.M.; Bro.Gene Mayer, O.F.M., Prov. Sec.; Revs. Kenan Freson, O.F.M., Prov. Treas; Maynard Tetreault, O.F.M., Bldg. Coord.; Francis Tebbe, O.F.M., Dir.-Continuing Education/Formation Tel: 815-836-5520; Sr. Donna Graham, O.S.F., Dir.-Office of Peace, Justice & Integrity of Creation; Bros. Scott Obrecht O.F.M., Dir.-Franciscan Missionary Union; David Crank, O.F.M., Dir.-Office of Senior Friars.; Revs. Daniel Anderson, O.F.M., Prov. Archivist & Librarian; Loren Connell, O.F.M., Prov. Spiritual Asst. for Secular Order; Stanley Bir, O.F.M., Personnel Advr.; Vocation Dirs.:Revs. Donald Miller, O.F.M.; Bruno Kremp, O.F.M.; Revs. Roger Bosse, O.F.M.; Arthur Espelage, O.F.M., Prov. Canonist.
Priests 142; Temporary Professed 5; Deacons 1; Novices 2; Brothers 58.
Represented in the Archdioceses of Chicago, Cincinnati, Detroit, Indianapolis, New Orleans, Santa Fe, and Washington and the Dioceses of Allentown, Austin, Columbus, Gallup, Galveston-Houston, Gary, Greensburg, Houma-Thibodaux, Joliet, Lafayette (LA), Las Cruces, Lexington, Marquette, Peoria, Phoenix, Pittsburgh, Shreveport, St. Petersburg and Youngstown.

Province of The Sacred Heart (1858): 3140 Meramec St., St. Louis, MO 63118. Tel: 314-353-3421. Revs. John Doctor, O.F.M., Prov. Minister; Kenneth Capalbo, O.F.M., Prov. Vicar; Councilors: Revs. Mario Di Cicco, O.F.M.; Herb Jones, O.F.M.; Bertin Miller, O.F.M.; Bill Spencer, O.F.M.; Charles Gunti, O.F.M.; Larry Nickels, O.F.M., Dir.-Office of Ministries; Bro. Christopher Lambert, O.F.M., Prov. Sec.; Revs. Allan DaCorte, O.F.M., Prov. Treas.; Henry Willenborg, O.F.M., Prov. Dir. of Formation; Paul Pare, O.F.M., Dir.-Franciscan Vocation Center, 4860 W. 29th St., Cicero, IL 60650; Bro. Joseph Rogenski, O.F.M., Prov. Promoter of the Missions, Commissary of the Holy Land.
Legal Titles: *Franciscan Fathers of the State of Missouri; Franciscan Fathers of the State of Illinois; Franciscan Press; Franciscan Tertiary Province of the Sacred Heart, Incorporated; Mayslake Village; Franciscan Mayslake Village; Cloister Courts; Chariton Apartments; Employees of the Franciscan Orders.*
Solemnly Professed: Priests 198; Brothers 71; Simply Professed: Brothers 5; Permanent Deacons 1.
Properties owned, sponsored or staffed: Friaries 34; Parishes 48; Missions 18; Institutional Chaplaincies 19; Chaplaincies for Religious 4; Formation Houses 2; Novitiates 1; Colleges 1; High Schools 2; Publishing House 1.
Represented in the Archdioceses of Chicago, Indianapolis St. Louis, St. Paul-Minneapolis, and San Antonio and the Dioceses of Belleville, Cleveland, Fairbanks, Fort Worth, Gaylord, Jefferson City, Joliet, Knoxville, Little Rock, Nashville, Shreveport, Springfield (IL), Superior and Victoria.

Province of the Assumption of the Blessed Virgin Mary (1887): *Provincial Office,* P.O. Box 100, Franklin, WI 53132. Tel: 414-525-9253; Fax: 414-525-9289. Very Rev. Thomas Luczak, O.F.M., Prov.; Rev. Thomas Wojciechowski, O.F.M., Vicar; Definitors: Revs. James Gannon, O.F.M.; John Cella, O.F.M., Treas.; Robert Konkol, O.F.M.; Bro. Craig Wilking, O.F.M.; Revs. Andrew Brophy, O.F.M.; Eliot Bacia, O.F.M., Prov. Sec.; Hugh Zurat, O.F.M., Dir. of Evangelization Center; James Carroll, Prov. Spiritual Asst. of Secular Franciscan Order.
Legal Holdings or Titles: *St. Mary of the Angels Friary,* Green Bay, WI; *Queen of Peace Friary,* Burlington, WI; *Our Lady of Lourdes Friary,* Cedar Lake, IN; *San Damiano Friary,* Cedar Lake, IN; *St. Stanislaus Friary,*

Cleveland, OH; *St. Francis of Assisi School,* Greenwood, MS; *Francis and Clare House,* Franklin, WI; *Franciscan Pilgrimage Programs, Inc.,* Franklin, WI; *St. Anthony Friary and Mission House,* Pittsburgh (Ben Avon), PA; *St. Pius X Friary,* Philadelphia, PA.

Priests 127; Professed Clerics 1; Professed Brothers 51.

Properties owned or staffed: Parishes 29; Friaries 14.

Represented in the Archdioceses of Chicago, Detroit, Milwaukee, New York, Philadelphia Ukrainian, and Pittsburgh Byzantine and in the Dioceses of Brownsville, Burlington, Camden, Cleveland, Fort Wayne-South Bend, Gary, Gaylord, Green Bay, Jackson, Joliet, Parma, Pittsburgh, Rochester, Rockford, Saginaw and St. Josaphat.

Province of Our Lady of Guadalupe (1985): *Curia Juan Diego,* 1350 Lakeview Rd., S.W., Albuquerque, NM 87105. Tel: 505-877-5425; Fax: 505-877-1440. Very Rev. Larry C. Dunham, O.F.M., Min. Prov. Revs. Gino Correa, O.F.M., Prov. Vicar & Sec.-Formation & Studies; Councilors Bruce Michalek, O.F.M.; Ron Walters, O.F.M.; Ben Begin, O.F.M.; Charlie Martinez, O.F.M., Vocation Dir.; Duane Torisky, O.F.M., Sec. Prov. & Dir.-Communications; Don Billiard, O.F.M., Prov. Treas.; Bruce Michalek, O.F.M., Sec. Missionary Evangelization & Franciscan Partners Volunteer Program.

Legal Titles: *The Province of Our Lady of Guadalupe of the Order of Friars Minor, Inc.; Southwest Franciscan Missions, Inc.; Southwest Franciscan Services, Inc.*

Priests 50; Brothers 24; Postulants 7; Novices 1.

Represented in the Archdioceses of San Antonio and Santa Fe and the Dioceses of Gallup and Las Cruces. Also in Mexico and Peru.

Order of Friars Minor of the Province of the Most Holy Name (Legal Title) (1901): 158 West 27th St., 6th Fl. New York, NY 10001-6206. Tel: 212-967-6300; Fax: 212-967-6344. E-mail: hnp@hnp.org. Very Rev. John M. Felice, O.F.M., Prov. Minister, Very Rev. Charles J. Miller, O.F.M., Prov. Vicar; Provincial Councilors; Revs. Kevin Mullen, O.F.M.; Andrew Reitz, O.F.M.; David Hyman, O.F.M.; Dominic Monti, O.F.M.; John O'Connor, O.F.M.; Bros. Christopher Coccia, O.F.M.; F. Edward Coughlin, O.F.M., Prov. Sec.; Revs. Vincent Grogan, O.F.M., Canonical Counsel; Cassian A. Miles, O.F.M., Dir. Communications; Joseph Hertel, O.F.M., Dir. Office of Devel. & Public Rels.; Dennis Wilson, O.F.M., Treas.; Bro. Gordon (Denis) Clark, O.F.M., Promoter of the Missions & Sec.-Missionary Evangelization; Revs. Francis DiSpigno, O.F.M., Dir. Vocations; Richard Trezza, O.F.M., Prov.

Solemn Profession: Bishops 1; Priests 321; Brothers 74; Permanent Deacons 3; Temporary Profession: Brothers 10; Clerics 4; Novices 8.

Properties owned or sponsored: Province Parishes 28; Missions 1; Urban Ministry Centers 5; University 1; Colleges 1; Community Houses-Residences 45; Houses of Formation 5; Shrine Churches 2; Chaplaincies 14; Military Chaplain 1; Campus Ministry 8.

Represented in the Archdioceses of Atlanta, Baltimore, Boston, Chicago, Denver, Hartford, Miami, Military, Newark, New York, Philadelphia, San Juan, and Washington and the Dioceses of Albany, Arlington, Bridgeport, Buffalo, Camden, Charleston, Charlotte, Fall River, Palm Beach, Paterson, Providence, Raleigh, Rockville Centre, Salt City, San Diego, St. Petersburg, Steubenville, Trenton and Wilmington.

Province of St. Barbara (1915), *The Franciscan Friars of California (1900):* 1500 34th Ave., Oakland, CA 94601. Tel: 510-536-3722; Fax: 510-536-3970. Very Rev. Melvin A. Jurisich, O.F.M., Prov. Rev. Tom West, O.F.M., Vicar Prov.; Definitors: Revs. John Hardin, O.F.M. Michael Harvey, O.F.M.; Oscar Mendez Guzman, O.F.M.; Bros. Peter Boegel, O.F.M.; Franklin Fong, O.F.M.; John Kiesler, O.F.M.; John Summers, O.F.M., Prov. Sec.

Legal Titles: *Franciscan Friars of California; Franciscan Friars of Arizona; Franciscan Friars of Oregon.*

Priests 141; Solemnly Professed Lay Brothers 67; Simply Professed Brothers 16; Novices 4; Pre-novitiate 4.

Represented in the Archdioceses of Los Angeles, Portland (OR), and San Francisco and the Dioceses of Fresno, Gallup, Las Cruces, Monterey, Oakland, Orange, Phoenix, Las Vegas, Sacramento, San Diego, San Jose, Santa Rosa, Spokane and Tucson.

Province of the Immaculate Conception (Friars Minor of the Order of St. Francis): 125 Thompson St., New York, NY 10012. Tel: 212-674-4388. Very Rev. Robert M. Campagna, O.F.M., Prov. Rev. Patrick Boyle, O.F.M., Vicar Prov.; Definitors: Revs. Ralph Paonessa, O.F.M.; Charles Gingerich, O.F.M.; James Goode, O.F.M.; Ronald Gliatta, O.F.M.; Michael Bercik, O.F.M.; Armand Padula, O.F.M., Prov. Sec.; Mark Brown, O.F.M., SFO Prov. Spiritual Asst.; Courtland Campbell, O.F.M., Promoter of the Franciscan Missions; Madeline Bonnici, Exec. Dir., Franciscan Mission Associates, 274-280 W. Lincoln Ave., Mount Vernon, NY 10550; Rev. Robert M. Campagna, O.F.M., Pious League of St. Anthony.

Fathers 139; Bishops 4; Brothers 27; Permanent Deacons 3.

Properties owned/staffed: Parishes 41; Residences 20.

Represented in the Archdioceses of Boston Hartford, and New York and the Dioceses of Albany, Bridgeport, Brooklyn, Fall River, Manchester, Metuchen, Pittsburgh, Portland (ME), Trenton, Wheeling-Charleston and Youngstown. Also in Central America, Toronto and Italy.

Commissariat of The Holy Cross (1912): 14246 Main St., P.O. Box 608, Lemont, IL 60439. Tel: 630-257-2494; Fax: 630-257-8559. Rev. Blase Chemazar, O.F.M., Pres.; Councilors: Revs. Vendelin Spendov, O.F.M.; Athanasius Lovrencic, O.F.M.; Bernard Karmanocky, O.F.M.

Legal Titles: *The Slovene Franciscan Fathers, Order of Friars Minor, Commissariat of the Holy Cross,* Lemont, IL; *St. Mary's Retreat House,* Lemont, IL.

Fathers 8.

Parishes 3; Monastery 1; Retreat House 1; Mission Center 1.

Represented in the Archdioceses of Chicago and New York and in the Diocese of Altoona-Johnstown.

Provincial House, *Holy Family Friary,* 232 S. Home Ave., Pittsburgh, PA 15202-2899. Tel: 412-761-2550; Fax: 412-761-2959.

Franciscan Friars: *Mt. Alverna Friary,* 517 S. Belle Vista Ave., Youngstown, OH 44509. Tel: 330-799-1888. Rev. Vit Fiala, O.F.M., Guardian.

Represented in the Diocese of Youngstown.

Croatian Franciscan Custody of the Holy Family of U.S. & Canada (1926): 4851 S. Drexel Blvd., Chicago, IL 60615-1703. Tel: 773-536-0552; Fax: 773-536-2094. E-mail: Croatiancustody@aol.com. Rev. Marko Puljic, O.F.M., Custos. Councilors: Revs. Lawrence Frankovich, O.F.M.; Joseph Galic, O.F.M.; Jozo Grbes, O.F.M.; Stjepan Pandzic, O.F.M.

Fathers 33; Cleric 1.

Friaries 1; Parishes 9; Missions in Canada 7; Printery 1.

Represented in the Archdioceses of Chicago, Detroit, Milwaukee, New York and St. Louis and in the Dioceses of Allentown and Erie. Also in Canada.

Lithuanian Franciscan Vice-Province of St. Casimir: *Franciscan Friary,* 28 Beach Ave., P.O. Box 980, Kennebunkport, ME 04046-0980. Tel: 207-967-2011; Fax: 207-967-5721. Email: johnbac@adelphia.net.; Web Site www.framon.net. Revs. John Bacevicius, O.F.M., Guardian; Gabriel Baltrusaitis, O.F.M., Vicar; Placid Barius, O.F.M., Delegate Prov.

Bishops 1; Fathers 7; Seminarians 1.

Properties owned or sponsored: Friaries 3; Parishes 1; Summer Camps 1; Guest House 1.

Represented in the Dioceses of Brooklyn, Portland (ME), and St. Petersburg. Also in Toronto, Canada.

U.S. Foundation (1940): *Province of the Holy Gospel Roger Bacon College,* 2400 Marr St., El Paso, TX 79903. Rev. Raul Vazquez, O.F.M.

Priests 3.

Represented in the Diocese of El Paso.

Commissariat of the Holy Land, Franciscan Monastery of Mt. Sepulchre: 1400 Quincy St., N.E., Washington, DC 20017. Tel: 202-526-6800; Fax: 202-529-9889. Bros. Fabian Adkins, O.F.M., Guardian; Callistus Welch, O.F.M., Commissary of the Holy Land-Procurator; Revs. James Brabandt, O.F.M., Dir.-Postulants & Moderator-Knights; Stephen F. Sabbagh, O.F.M., Prov. Spiritual Asst. to the Secular Franciscan Order; Joshua Doyle, O.F.M.; Sabin Plechta, O.F.M.; Kevin Treston, O.F.M., Public Rels., Editor of Cursador's Almanac; Francis Sihuay, O.F.M. (Peru); Manuel Ybarra, O.F.M., Asst. Procurator; Patrick Flanigan, O.F.M.

Priests 9; Brothers 14; Solemnly Professed 23.

Represented in the Archdiocese of Washington.

Academy of American Franciscan History: 1712 Euclid Ave., Berkeley, CA 94709. Dr. Jeffrey M. Burns, Dir.

Legal Title: *Academy of American Franciscan History.*

Franciscan Vocational Conference (F.V.C.) (1944): *Natl. Vocation Office:* 135 West 31st St., New York, NY 10001. Tel: 920-822-5833. Rev. Francis J. DiSpigno, O.F.M., Pres.

Franciscan Society organized nationally to promote cooperative and unified vocational effort in the Franciscan Provinces, Vice-Provinces and Custodies of the U.S.A.

National Fraternity of the Secular Franciscan Order, U.S.A: *(formerly North American Federation, Third Order of St. Francis),* 136 Woods Ave., Monaca, PA 15061-2461. Tel: 1-800 FRANCIS. Web site: www.nafra-sfo.org.

Founded by St. Francis of Assisi in 1209, to give laity and diocesan clergy, an opportunity to live the Gospel intently. There are approximately 17,000 members in nearly 800 fraternities located in 31 geographic regions. Carol Gentile, S.F.O., Natl. Minister.

[0530] (S.A.)— FRANCISCAN FRIARS OF THE ATONEMENT

(Societas Adunationis T.O.R.)

Motherhouse: *St. Paul's Friary,* P.O. Box 300, Graymoor, Garrison, NY 10524-0300. Tel: 845-424-2113; Fax: 845-424-2166. Office of the Minister.

Legal Titles: *St. Chistopher's Inn; St. James Friary; St. Paul's Friary; St. Francis of Assisi Novitiate.*

Priests 87; Professed Seminarians 4; Professed Brothers 39.

Friaries 12; Novitiates 1; Parishes (U.S. and Canada) 7; Overseas Ministries: England, Italy and Japan; Ecumenical Institute 1; Pastoral Center 1; Campus Ministries; Retreat and Conference Center 1; Rehabilitation Center for Alcoholics 1; Shelter for Homeless men; Military Chaplaincies 1.

Represented in the Archdioceses of Boston, Los Angeles, New York and Washington and in the Dioceses of Arlington, Ogdensburg and Raleigh.

[0533] (F.F.I.)— FRANCISCAN FRIARS OF THE IMMACULATE

General Motherhouse: Benevento, Italy. Founded 1990.

Our Lady's Chapel: *Marian Friary of Our Lady of Guadalupe.* 199 Colonel Brown Rd., Griswold, CT 06351. Tel: 860-376-6840. Rev. Angelo Mary Geiger, F.F.I., American Supr.

Legal Title: *Marian Friary of Our Lady of Guadalupe.*

Represented in the Dioceses of Fall River, Norwich and Syracuse.

[0535] (C.F.R.)— FRANCISCAN FRIARS OF THE RENEWAL

Central House: *Saint Crispin Friary,* 420 E. 156th St., Bronx, NY 10455. Tel: 718-665-2441. Revs. Glenn Sudano, C.F.R., Community Servant; Robert Lombardo, C.F.R., Vicar; Counselors: Benedict J. Groeschel, C.F.R.; Andrew Apostoli, C.F.R.; Michael Kmiotek, C.F.R.; Bernard Murphy, C.F.R.

Represented in the Archdiocese of New York.

[0540] (O.S.F.)— FRANCISCAN MISSIONARY BROTHERS OF THE SACRED HEART OF JESUS

(Fratres Missionarii sti Francisci de Sso. Corde Jesu)

Motherhouse (1927): *Our Lady of Angels Monastery,* St. Joseph Rd., Eureka, MO 63025. Tel: 636-587-3661. Bros. Bernardo Trosa, O.S.F., Dir. Gen.; John A. Spila, O.S.F., Asst. Dir. Gen.

Legal Holdings or Titles: *The Black Madonna Shrine and Grottos (Our Lady of Czestochowa); St. Joseph's Hill Infirmary, Inc.; Price Memorial,* Eureka, MO; *Merkle-Knipprath Nursing Home and Apartment Community,* Clifton, MO.

Brothers 11.

Represented in the Archdiocese of St. Louis and in the Diocese of Joliet.

[0560] (T.O.R.)— THIRD ORDER REGULAR OF SAINT FRANCIS

(Tertius Ordo Regularis de Poenitentia)

General Motherhouse: *SS. Cosmas and Damian,* Via dei Fori Imperiali, 1, Rome, Italy. Most Rev. Ilija Zivkovic, T.O.R., Minister Gen.; Revs. Michael Higgins, T.O.R., Vicar Gen.; Counsellors: Corpus Izquierdo, T.O.R.(Sec. Gen.); Matthew Puthenparambil, T.O.R.; Fernando Scocca, T.O.R.

Province of the Most Sacred Heart of Jesus (1910): *Provincial Residence,* 128 Woodshire Dr., Pittsburgh, PA 15215-1714. Tel: 412-781-8333; Fax: 412-781-1219. Very Rev. Edmund F. Carroll, T.O.R., Minister Prov.; Rev. Thomas Bourque, T.O.R., Vicar Prov., Dir. Formation, Dir.-Continuing Education, Dir.-Post Novitiate Formation; Councilors: Revs. Brian Miller, T.O.R.; Terence Henry, T.O.R.; Richard Davis, T.O.R., Dir.-Vocations & Councilor; Bros. James Boyle, T.O.R., Prov. Sec. & Councilor; Mark McBride, T.O.R., Treas. & Dir.-Missions; Revs. Laurence Uhlman, T.O.R., Novice Master; Bernard Tickerhoof, T.O.R., Secular Franciscans Prov. Spiritual Asst.

Legal Title: *Province of the Most Sacred Heart of Jesus, Third Order Regular of Saint Francis (USA),* Loretto, PA.

Ministries in Parishes; Universities and Colleges; High Schools; Chaplaincies; House of Study 1; Novitiates 1; Laymen's Retreat League.

Fathers 110; Professed Clerics 11; Brothers 26; Novices 2; Postulants 2.

Represented in the Archdioceses of Baltimore, Philadelphia and Washington and in the Dioceses of Altoona-Johnstown, Arlington, Charlotte, Erie, Fort Worth, Pittsburgh, St. Augustine, St. Petersburg, Sioux Falls, Steubenville, Trenton, Venice and Wheeling-Charleston.

Province of The Immaculate Conception: *Saint Bridget Church,* 3811 Emerson Ave., N., Minneapolis, MN 55412-2038. Tel: 612-529-7770; Fax: 612-529-8451.

Very Rev. Anthony Criscitelli, T.O.R., Minister Prov. Very Rev. J. Patrick Quinn, T.O.R., Vicar Prov. Revs. Frank A. Scornaienchi, T.O.R.; Emile A. Gentile, T.O.R.; Edward J. Sabo, T.O.R.; William P. Linhares, T.O.R.; Prov. Councilors: Bro. David Liedl, T.O.R., Prov. Sec.; Most Rev. Ilija Zivkovic, T.O.R., Minister Gen. of the Order, Rome, Italy.

Legal Title: *Third Order Regular of St. Francis, Province of the Immaculate Conception (USA).*

Priests 43: Brothers 10; Permanent Deacons 1; Student Friars 3.

Represented in the Archdioceses of St. Paul-Minneapolis, and Washington and the Dioceses of Altoona-Johnstown, Davenport, Fort Worth, Orlando, Owensboro, and Wheeling-Charleston.

U.S.A. Franciscan Vice Province of Our Lady of Guadalupe - T.O.R.: 301 Jefferson Ave., Waco, TX 76701. Very Rev. Estaeban Jasso, T.O.R., Prov. Delegate; Rev. Lawrence Soler, T.O.R., Councilor.

Fathers 8.

Represented in the Archdiocese of San Antonio and in the Dioceses of Austin and Fort Worth.

[0570] (G.H.M.)— THE GLENMARY HOME MISSIONERS

(Societas Missionariorum Domesticorum Americas)
(The Home Missioners of America)

General Headquarters: P.O. Box 465618, Cincinnati, OH 45246-5618. Tel: 513-874-8900. Web site: www.glenmary.org. Revs. Dan Dorsey, G.H.M., Pres.; Bob Poandl, G.H.M., 1st Vice Pres.; Dominic Duggins, G.H.M., 2nd Vice Pres. &Dir.-Development; Teresa Heckenmueller, Treas.; Bro. Dennis Craig, G.H.M., House Dir.; Rev. Steve Pawelk, G.H.M., Dir.-Vocation Office.

Houses of Formation: *Candidacy and Novitiate House,* 300 Peach Alley, Hartford, KY 42347. Tel: 270-298-9886. Bro. Larry Johnson, Dir.-Candidates; Rev. Tom Charters, Dir.-Novices; Bro. Curt Kedley, Dir. House of Residency for International Studies, P.O. Box 786, Owingsville, KY 40360; Jose Grosek, Dir.-Volunteer Programs, P.O. Box 7, Vanceburg, KY 41179. Tel: 606-796-3421; The Glenmary Farm, Rt. 1, Ministry and Research Centers - 1312 Fifth Ave. N., Nashville, TN 37208. Tel: 615-256-4348. Rev. Bob Dalton, G.H.M., Dir.-Pastoral Coord. Program; Rev. Michael Langell, G.H.M., Dir.-Dept. of Pastoral Services, Tel: 615-256-1900; Dr. Kenneth Sanchagrin, Dir.-Glenmary Research Center, Tel: 615-256-1905.

Fathers 54; Candidates 3; Professed Brothers 17.

Properties owned, sponsored or staffed: Missions 60; Houses of Study 2; Pastoral and Research Centers 2; Volunteer Center.

Represented in the Archdiocese of Cincinnati and the Dioceses of Birmingham, Covington, Jackson, Knoxville, Lexington, Little Rock, Nashville, Owensboro, Raleigh, Richmond, Savannah, Tulsa and Wheeling-Charleston.

[0580] (B.G.S.)— LITTLE BROTHERS OF THE GOOD SHEPHERD

Villa Mathias: *Foundation House:* Little Brothers of The Good Shepherd, 901 Bro. Mathias Pl. N.W., P.O. Box 389, Albuquerque, NM 87102. Tel: 505-243-4238; Fax: 505-764-9721.

General Headquarters (1987): *Good Shepherd Centre,* 412 Queen St. East, Toronto, Ontario, Canada M5A 1T3. Tel: 416-869-3619. Rev. Bros. David Lynch, B.G.S., Supr. Gen.; Gerard Sullivan, B.G.S., Vicar Gen.; Savio Charron, B.G.S., Sec. Gen.; Richard MacPhee, B.G.S., Gen. Treas.; Majella Marchand, B.G.S., Dir. of Novices.

Legal Holdings and Titles: *Caritas Deus, Inc. of New Mexico; Camillus House Inc. of Florida; Camillus Health Concern Inc. of Florida; Charity Unlimited, Inc. of New Mexico; BGS Charitable of Illinois; Brother Mathias Barrett Inc. of Illinois; Brother Mathias Barrett Inc. of New Mexico; Brothers of Good Shepherd Inc. of Pennsylvania; Brothers of Good Shepherd Inc. of Florida; Brothers of The Good Shepherd Inc. of New Mexico; Brother Mathias Barrett Inc. of New Mexico (Good Shepherd Manor); Good Shepherd Center Inc. of New Mexico; Good Shepherd Center Auxiliary Inc. of New Mexico; Good Shepherd Manor, Inc.,* Momence, IL; *Little Brothers of Good Shepherd Inc.of Illinois; Villa Mathia, Inc. of New Mexico; Brothers of the Good Shepherd Inc. of California,* Los Angeles, CA.

Professed Brothers 38; Novice Brothers 5.

Properties owned and /or sponsored: temporary shelters for marginalized men and women 14; residences for the elderly 2; shelter for battered women & children 3; residences for persons with AIDS.

Represented in the Archdioceses of Miami, Philadelphia and Santa Fe and in the Diocese of Joliet.

[0590] (M.S.A.)—SOCIETY OF THE MISSIONARIES OF THE HOLY APOSTLES

General Administration: *Society of the Missionaries of the Holy Apostles,* 8594 rue Berri, Montreal, (Quebec) Canada H2P 2G4. Tel: 514-387-2222; Fax: 514-387-0863. Very Rev. Yvon Archambault, M.S.A., Supr. Gen. Animator.

Society of Missionaries of the Holy Apostles: *Provincial Administration Headquarters,* 22 Prospect Hill Rd., Cromwell, CT 06416. Tel: 860-632-3039; Fax: 860-635-4823. Very Rev. Raymond Halliwell, M.S.A., Prov. Animator

Priests 40; Brothers 3.

Properties owned, staffed or sponsored: Holy Apostles College and Seminary; 2 Parishes; Hermitage; Hospital Chaplaincies.

Represented in the Archdioceses of Denver, and Washington and in the Dioceses of Arlington, Norwich, Pennsacola-Tallahassee and Wheeling-Charleston.

[0600] (C.S.C.)—BROTHERS OF THE CONGREGATION OF HOLY CROSS

(Congregatio A Sancta Cruce)

Generalate: *Congregazione di Santa Croce,* Via Framura 85, 00168, Rome, Italy. Rev. Hugh W. Cleary, C.S.C., Supr. Gen.; Bro. John Gleason, C.S.C., First Asst. & Vicar; Rev. James T. Mulligan, C.S.C., Second Asst. & Procurator; Bro. Joseph Kofi Tsiquaye, C.S.C., Third Asst.; Rev. Arulraj Gali, C.S.C., Fourth Asst.

Midwest Province of the Brothers of Holy Cross (1841): *Province Administration,* 54515 State Rd. 933 North-P.O. Box 460, Notre Dame, IN 46556. Tel: 574-631-4000; Fax: 574-631-2999. Web site: www.hcc-nd.edu/mwp. Bros. Robert Fillmore, C.S.C., Prov. Supr.; Raymond Papenfuss, C.S.C., Asst. Prov. & Vicar; Robert Livernois, C.S.C., Sec.; Lawrence Skitzki, C.S.C., Steward & Treas.; Philip Smith, C.S.C., Councilor.

Legal Title: *Notre Dame, Ind. Brothers of Holy Cross, Inc.*

Professed Brothers 198; Temporarily Professed 17; Aspirants 6.

Properties owned, staffed or sponsored: Community Houses 2; College; High Schools 6; Scholasticates 2; Foreign Mission Schools 3.

Represented in the Archdioceses of Anchorage, Chicago, Detroit, Los Angeles, Miami, Milwaukee, New Orleans, Portland (OR), and San Antonio and the Dioceses of Austin, Cleveland, Colorado Springs, Evansville, Fort Wayne-South Bend, Gary, Grand Rapids, Lansing, Oakland, Phoenix, Providence, St. Petersburg and Venice. Also in West Africa.

South-West Province of the Brothers of Holy Cross (1956): *Brother John Baptist Province Center, St. Edward University,* 1101 St. Edwards Dr., Austin, TX 78704. Tel: 512-442-7856. Bros. Richard Critz, C.S.C., Prov.; Stephen Walsh, C.S.C., Asst. Prov.; Donald Blauvelt, C.S.C., Sec.; Harold Ehlinger, C.S.C., Steward; Councilors: Joseph Esparza, C.S.C.; Joseph Kinsman, C.S.C.; John Crowe, C.S.C.

Professed Brothers 116; Temporarily Professed 1.

Properties owned, staffed, or sponsored: Colleges 1; High Schools 5; Middle Schools 1; Home for Boys 1; Schools Foreign Mission Schools 2.

Represented in the Archdioceses of Los Angeles, Louisville, New Orleans, Portland (OR), San Antonio, and Santa Fe and in the Dioceses of Austin, Beaumont, Cheyenne, Cleveland, Fort Wayne-South Bend, Knoxville, Oakland, San Jose and Savannah.

Eastern Province of the Brothers of Holy Cross (1956): 85 Overlook Cir., New Rochelle, NY 10804. Tel: 914-632-4468; 4469; Fax: 914-632-2490. Bros. George C. Schmitz, C.S.C., Prov.; William Zaydak, C.S.C., Sec.; Councilors: Jerome Donnelly, C.S.C.; John Paige, C.S.C.; Mark Knightly, C.S.C.

Legal Title: *Brothers of Holy Cross of the Eastern Province of the United States of America, Inc.*

Professed Brothers 120; Temporarily Professed 4.

Properties owned, staffed or sponsored: High Schools 4; Foreign Mission Houses 6; Middle School; Spiritual Life Center.

Represented in the Archdioceses of Hartford, New York, and Washington and the Dioceses of Albany, Brooklyn and Wilmington.

[0610] (C.S.C.)—PRIESTS OF THE CONGREGATION OF HOLY CROSS

Congregatio a Sancta Cruce

Generalate: *Curia Generalizia di Santa Croce,* Via Framura 85 00168, Rome, Italy. Rev. Hugh W. Cleary, C.S.C., Supr. Gen., Bro. John Gleason, C.S.C., First Asst. & Vicar; Rev. James T. Mulligan, C.S.C., Second Asst.; Bro. Joseph Kofi Tsiquaye, C.S.C., Third Asst.; Revs. Arulraj Gali, C.S.C., Fourth Asst.; Paul Leblanc, C.S.C., Procurator.

Congregation of Holy Cross, Indiana Province (1841): *Provincial House,* 1304 E. Jefferson Blvd., South Bend, IN 46617. Tel: 574-289-6850. Revs. David T. Tyson, C.S.C., Prov. Supr.; Kenneth M. Molinaro, C.S.C., First Asst. Prov. & Vicar; Anthony V. Szakaly, C.S.C., Second Asst. Prov.; Thomas P. Doyle, C.S.C., Steward. Provincial Councilors; Revs. E. William Beauchamp, C.S.C.; Thomas E. Chambers, C.S.C.; Peter A. Jarret, C.S.C.; John I. Jenkins, C.S.C.; Patrick M. Neary, C.S.C.; Claude A. Pomerleau, C.S.C.; Bro. Edward C. Luther, C.S.C.

Legal Title: *Priests of Holy Cross, Indiana Province, Inc.*

Fathers 287; Professed Clerics 10; Temporarily Professed Clerics 26; Novices 10; Candidates 26; Professed Brothers 19.

Properties owned, sponsored or staffed: College Seminary; Theological Seminary; Novitiate; Mission Center; Provincial House; Postulate; Universities 2; High Schools 1; Parishes 11; Chaplaincies 17; Publishing House; Retreat House.

Holy Cross Associates Lay Missionary Program, P.O. Box 668, Notre Dame, IN 46556. Mr. John Pinter, Dir.

Holy Cross Association, Box K, Notre Dame, IN 46556. Rev. Herbert C. Yost, C.S.C., Dir.

Represented in the Archdioceses of Anchorage, Baltimore, Chicago, Detroit, Los Angeles, Military Services, New Orleans, New York, Portland (OR), San Antonio, and San Francisco and the Dioceses of Bridgeport, Cleveland, Colorado Springs, Erie, Fall River, Fort Wayne-South Bend, Gary, Kalamazoo, Monterey, Oakland, Phoenix, San Bernardino and San Jose.

Congregation of Holy Cross-Eastern Province, Inc. (1952): *Provincial Headquarters,* 835 Clinton Ave., Bridgeport, CT 06604. Tel: 203-367-7252; 367-1152; Fax: 203-366-7886. Revs. Arthur J. Colgan, C.S.C., Prov. Supr., James T. Preskenis, C.S.C., Asst. Prov. & Vicar; James Lackenmier, C.S.C., Treas & Steward; Prov. Councilors: Revs. Bradley Beaupre, C.S.C.; Thomas Bertone, C.S.C.; John Denning, C.S.C.; Charles Kociolek, C.S.C.; John J. Ryan, C.S.C.; Fred Serraino, C.S.C.; Bro. Richard F. Kyle, C.S.C.

Fathers 116; Temporarily Professed Clerics 11; Candidates 9; Novices 2; Brothers Professed 15.

Properties owned, sponsored or staffed: Colleges 2; Parishes 9; Retreat House; Chaplaincies 10; Campus Ministry 8; Family Rosary Crusade; Family Theater.

Represented in the Archdioceses of Boston, Chicago, Hartford, Los Angeles, and New Orleans, and New York and the Dioceses of Albany, Altoona-Johnstown, Austin, Bridgeport, Burlington, Fall River, Fort Wayne-South Bend, Galveston-Houston, Norwich, Oakland, Orlando, Palm Beach, Portland (ME), Rochester and Scranton.

Holy Cross Southern Province (1968): *Provincial House,* 2111 Brackenridge St., Austin, TX 78704. Tel: 512-443-3886; Fax: 512-416-1216. Revs. John S. Korcsmar, C.S.C., Prov. Supr., Bro. Thomas G. Krieter, C.S.C., Asst. Prov. & Steward; Revs. Jeffrey L. Allison, C.S.C., Prov. Sec.; Joseph A. Tomei, C.S.C., Prov. Councilor; L. Peter Logsdon, C.S.C., Prov. Councilor; Rev. Barry E. Cabell, C.S.C., Councilor.

Legal Title: *Congregation of Holy Cross, Southern Province, Inc.*

Ministries in Parishes; Foreign Missions; Chaplaincies; Social Service.

Fathers 27; Professed Brothers 1; Temporarily Professed 6.

Represented in the Archdioceses of New Orleans, St. Louis, and San Antonio and Dioceses of Austin, Fort Wayne-South Bend, Lafayette (LA) and Las Cruces.

[0620] (F.S.E.)—BROTHERS OF THE HOLY EUCHARIST

Founded in the United States 1957.

General Motherhouse and Novitiate: P.O. Box 25, Plaucheville, LA 71362. Tel: 318-922-3630; 922-3401. Rev. Bro. Andre M. Lucia, F.S.E., Supr. Gen.

Represented in the Diocese of Alexandria.

[0630] (M.S.F.)—CONGREGATION OF THE MISSIONARIES OF THE HOLY FAMILY

(Congregatio Missionariorum a Sacra Familia)

General Motherhouse: Via Odoado Beccari, 41 00154, Rome, Italy. Tel: 011-39-6-57-55-192; Fax: 011-39-6-57-55-208. Very Rev. Wim van der Weiden, M.S.F., Supr. Gen.

General Mission Office - M.S.F., Inc.: P.O. Box 918 - 260 W. Euclid Blvd., West Point, VA 23181. Tel: 804-843-2622; Fax: 804-843-3182. Rev. John Brieffies, M.S.F., Exec. Dir.

MSF Center: *Provincialate USA of the Missionaries of the Holy Family, Office:* 3014 Oregon Ave., St. Louis, MO 63118. Tel: 314-577-6300; Fax: 314-577-6301. Very Rev. Joseph P. Roelke, M.S.F., Prov. Supr.

Ministries in House of Study 2; Parishes 10.

Fathers 30; Theology Students 2; Brothers 3; Novices 1.

Represented in the Archdioceses of Louisville, St. Louis, San Antonio and the Dioceses of Brownsville, Corpus Christi, Duluth, and Richmond. Also in Canada and Mexico.

[0640] (S.F.)—SONS OF THE HOLY FAMILY

(Congregatio Filiorum Sacrae Familiae)

General Motherhouse: Entenza 301, Barcelona 08029, Spain. Very Rev., Luis Picazo, S.F., Gen. Supr.

U.S. Foundation (1920): 401 Randolph Rd., P.O. Box 4138, Silver Spring, MD 20914. Tel: 301-622-1184. Rev. Miguel Mateo, S.F., Vice Prov.

Fathers 13.

Represented in the Archdioceses of Santa Fe and Washington.

[0650] (C.S.Sp.)—CONGREGATION OF THE HOLY SPIRIT

(Congregation of the Holy Spirit under the protection of the Immaculate Heart of Mary, Spiritans.)

(Congregatio Sancti Spiritus sub tutela Immaculati Cordis Beatissimae Virginis Mariae)

Generalate: Clivo di Cinna 195, Rome 00136, Italy. Very Rev. Pierre Schouver, C.S.Sp., Supr. Gen.

Eastern Province of the United States (1872): 6230 Brush Run Rd., Bethel Park, PA 15102. Tel: 412-831-0302; Fax: 412-831-0970. Very Rev. James P. McCloskey, C.S.Sp., Prov. Supr., Councilors: Revs. Jeffrey T. Duaime, C.S.Sp.; Timothy J. Hickey, C.S.Sp.; John P. Skaj, C.S.Sp.; Christopher H. McDermott, C.S.Sp.; John A. Sawicki, C.S.Sp., Prov. Treas. & Councilor; Freddy J. Washington, C.S.Sp.

Legal Holdings: *Archconfraternity of the Holy Ghost; Provincial Residence; Duquesne University; Laval House; Holy Ghost Preparatory School; Bethel Holy Spirit Animation Center.*

Fathers in U.S. 76; Professed Brothers 1

Properties owned, sponsored or staffed: Parishes 9; Retirement Residences 2.

Represented in the Archdioceses of Chicago, Cincinnati, Detroit, New York, Philadelphia, Washington and the Dioceses of Arlington, Pittsburgh, Providence and Venice. Also in Puerto Rico.

Western Province of the United States (1964): *Congregation of the Holy Spirit,* 1700 W. Alabama St., Houston, TX 77098-2808. Tel: 713-522-2882; Fax: 713-522-8063. Web site: www.spiritans.org. Very Rev. Michael T. White, C.S.Sp., Prov. Supr.; Prov. Councilors: Revs. Michael T. Grey, C.S.Sp., 1st Asst.; Binh T. Quach, C.S.Sp., 2nd Asst.; Bro. Michael E. Suazo, C.S.Sp., Prov. Sec. & Dir. Vocations; Rev. Philip D. Evanstock, C.S.Sp., Prov. Bursar.

Priests 43; Professed Brothers 2; Candidates 5; Novices 3; Scholastics 5; Lay Spiritans 16.

Staff: Parishes 8; Training Centers 3.

Properties owned, sponsored or staffed: *Holy Spirit Provincialate and Holy Ghost Hall,* Houston, TX; *Libermann House at Spiritan Renewal Center,* New Braunfels, TX; *Casa Laval and Holy Spirit Novitiate,* Hemet, CA. Properties in Mexico: *Iglesia de Santa Ana; Mision San Juan Bautista.*

Represented in the Archdioceses of New Orleans, San Antonio and the Dioceses of Baton Rouge, Fresno, Galveston-Houston, Las Vegas, Little Rock, Phoenix, Salt Lake City, San Bernardino, and San Diego. Also in Mexico and the Philippines.

Holy Ghost Fathers of Ireland (1971): 4849 37th St., Long Island City, NY 11101. Tel: 718-729-5273; Fax: 718-729-6949. Very Rev. Patrick Doody, C.S.Sp., Prov. Delegate U.S.A. East; Very Rev. Diarmud Casey, C.S.Sp., Prov. Delegate U.S.A. West, Tel: 650-961-8600; Fax: 650-968-5633. Councilors: Revs. Thomas Basquel, C.S.Sp.; Edmond B. Duggan, C.S.Sp.; Noel O'Meara, C.S.Sp.; James Corry, C.S.Sp.

Fathers 40.

Represented in the Archdioceses of Boston, Miami, New Orleans, New York, and San Francisco and the Dioceses of Brooklyn, Fargo, Palm Beach, Peoria and St. Augustine.

[0660] (M.Sp.S.)—MISSIONARIES OF THE HOLY SPIRIT

General Motherhouse: Av. Universidad 1702 04010, Mexico, D.F., Mexico. Tel: 5-658-74-33; 5-658-7851. Very Rev. Jorge Ortiz, M.Sp.S., Supr. Gen.

American Headquarters: *Our Lady of Guadalupe,* 500 N. Juanita Ave. P.O. Box 1091, Oxnard, CA 93030. Tel: 805-483-0987.

Priests 17; Professed 17; Novices 16.

Parishes 3; House of Study 1; Novitiates 1; Theologate 1.

Represented in the Archdioceses of Los Angeles and Portland in Oregon and in the Diocese of Fresno.

[0670] (O.H.)—HOSPITALLER BROTHERS OF ST. JOHN OF GOD

General Motherhouse: *Hospitaller Brothers of St. John of God,* via della Nocetta 263, Rome, Italy 00164. Order Founded by St. John of God at Granada, Spain, in 1537. Most Rev. Bro. Pascual Piles, O.H., Prior Gen.

American Province of Our Lady Queen of Angels (1970): *Villa Maria-Provincial Curia,* 2425 S. Western Ave., Los Angeles, CA 90018. Tel: 323-734-0233; Fax: 323-731-5987. Bro. Stephen de la Rosa, O.H., Prov.

Brothers 28; Solemn Professed 28; Priests 3.

Legal Holdings: *St. John of God Retirement and Care Center,* Los Angeles, CA; *St. Joseph Health and Retirement Center,* Ojai, CA; *St. John of God Health Care Services,* Victorville, CA.

Represented in the Archdiocese of Los Angeles and in the Diocese of San Bernardino.

[0680] (I.H.M.)—BROTHERS OF THE IMMACULATE HEART OF MARY

General Motherhouse (1948): 609 N. 7th St., Steubenville, OH 43952. Tel: 740-283-2462. Bro. Dominic Carroll, I.H.M., Supr. Gen.; Bro. Anthony Motto, I.H.M., Novice Master.

Ministries in: Novitiate; Bishop's Residence; CCD Center; Pastoral Associates 3.

Professed Brothers 4.

Represented in the Diocese of Steubenville.

[0690] (S.J.)—JESUIT FATHERS AND BROTHERS

(Societas Jesu)

Generalate: *Casella Postale* 6139 00195, Rome, Italy. Very Rev. Peter-Hans Kolvenbach, S.J., Gen. Revs. Gabriel Codina, Sec.; Francis E. Case, S.J., U.S. Asst.

Jesuit Conference: *The Society of Jesus in the United States National Offices,* 1616 P St., N.W., Suite 300, Washington, DC 20036. Tel: 202-462-0400; Fax: 202-328 9212. Revs. Bradley M. Schaeffer, S.J., Pres.; Thomas P. Gaunt, S.J., Exec. Sec.; John F. Armstrong, S.J., Sec. Formation & Secondary Education; James R. Stormes, S.J., Sec.-Social International Ministries & Dir.-Jesuit Refugee Services-USA; Thomas C. Widner, S.J., Sec. for Communications; David J. Haschka, S.J., Sec.-Pastoral Ministries; Thomas P. Gaunt, S.J., Sec.-Finances Resources; Ms. British Robinson, Dir.-Social & International Ministries.

Maryland Province (1833): 5704 Roland Ave., Baltimore, MD 21210. Tel: 410-532-1400; Fax: 410-532-1419. Very Rev. Timothy B. Brown, S.J., Prov.; Revs. John W. Swope, S.J., Socius to the Prov. & Prov. Sec.; William P. Ryan, S.J., Treas.; Kevin W. Wildes, S.J., Asst. Prov. for Higher Ed.; Michael A. Hricko, S.J., Asst. Prov. for Secondary & Presecondary Ed.; Clement J. Petrik, S.J., Asst. Prov. for Pastoral Min.; D. James French, S.J., Asst. Prov. for Jesuit Students; Hugh A. Kennedy, S.J., Asst. Prov. Sec.; Mr. Stephen J. Callahan, Asst. Prov.-Social & International Apostolates; Revs. Liborio J. LaMartina, S.J., Resident Archivist; William F. Lamm, S.J., Mgr. Prov. Vehicles; Thomas P. Martin, S.J., Mgr. Investment Reporting; Harry F. Geib, S.J., Health Care Coord.; William K. McGroarty, S.J., Dir. Farm Properties; Mr. James S. Schaefer, Managing Dir.; Mr. Kevin J. O'Brien, Dir.-Ignatian Apostolic Partnerships & Mission Bureau & Jesuit Seminary Guild, Maryland Province; Revs. Robert E. Reiser, S.J., Dir. Vocations; Gerald F. Fogarty, S.J., Archivist; James A. O'Brien, S.J., Promoter, Christian Life Communities; Brian O. McDermott, S.J., Tertian Instructor; Bruce A. Maivelett, S.J., Novice Dir.

Legal Title: *Corporation of the Roman Catholic Clergymen, Maryland; Jesuit Volunteer*

Fathers 381; Scholastics 25; Brothers 21.

Properties owned, sponsored or staffed: Parishes 18; Universities 4; Colleges 1; High Schools 5; Middle and Grammar Schools 7; Houses of Retreats 3; Residences 24.

Represented in the Archdioceses of Baltimore, Philadelphia, and Washington and the Dioceses of Allentown, Camden, Charlotte, Erie, Raleigh, Richmond, Scranton, Wheeling-Charleston and Wilmington.

Province of New York (1943): 39 E. 83rd St., New York, NY 10028. Tel: 212-774-5500; Fax: 212-774-5510. Very Rev. Gerald J. Chojnacki, S.J., Prov.; Rev. Richard R. Galligan, S.J., Exec. Asst. to Prov.; Bro. Gilbert J. Scott, S.J., Asst. to the Prov.; John J. Campbell, S.J., Asst. Prov. Treas; Revs. J. Raymond Johnson, S.J., Prov. Treas.; Auditor & American Rep. for the Missions of the Society of Jesus, Vatican City; D. James French, S.J., Asst. for Formation-Maryland & New York Provs; Sr. Nora M. Cronin, P.B.V.M., Asst. for Sec. Education; Revs. Thomas E. Smith, S.J., Asst. for Intl. Apostolate; Robert E. Reiser, S.J., Dir. of Vocations; William J. Scanlon, S.J., Dir. Province Devel. Office; James J. Yannarell, S.J., Prov. Health Care Coord.; Mark C. Hallinan, S.J., Asst. for Social Ministries; Mr. Jose Ojeda, Office Mgr./ Database Admin.; John R. Raslowsky.

Legal Title: *The New York Province of the Society of Jesus,* New York, NY.

Fathers 452; Scholastics 85; Brothers 25.

Properties owned, sponsored or staffed: Parishes 8; Universities 1; Colleges 3; High Schools 8; Houses for Laymen's Retreats 3; House of Study 1; Novitiates 2; Community Houses 4.

Represented in the Archdioceses of Newark, and New York and the Dioceses of Albany, Brooklyn, Buffalo, Paterson, Rochester, Rockville Centre and Syracuse. Also in Guam, the Caroline Islands, Chalan Kanoa and the Prefecture Apostolic of Marshall Islands, West Africa - Nigeria & Ghana.

The Jesuits of the Missouri Province (Missouri Province of the Society of Jesus): *Province Offices,* 4511 W. Pine Blvd., St. Louis, MO 63108-2191. Tel: 314-361-7765; Fax: 314-758-7164. Very Rev. Timothy M. McMahon, S.J., Prov., Revs. Philip G. Steele, S.J., Socius; James J. Burshek, S.J., Treas.; David L. Fleming, S.J., Asst. for Formation; Christopher P. Pinne, S.J., Asst. for Vocations & Assoc. Dir. Jesuit Devel. Office; Thomas G. Cwik, S.J., Asst.-Social Ministries; Robert F. Weiss, S.J., Asst. to the Treas. & Delegate for Higher Education; Gerard E. Menara, S.J., Delegate for Secondary Education; L. Gene Martens, S.J., Assoc. Dir. Jesuit Devel. Office; David L. Fleming, S.J., Dir. of Publications & Editor Publication: *The Jesuit Bulletin.* Tel: 314-977-7363; Revs. William L. Mugan, S.J., Archivist; William B. Faherty, S.J., Archivist Emeritus.

Legal Titles: *Regis Jesuit High School Corporation,* Aurora, CO; *Regis University,* Denver, CO; *Rockhurst University; Rockhurst High School,* Kansas City, MO; *The Province-The Jesuits of the Missouri Province; Bellarmine House of Studies - The Jesuits of the Missouri Province; Fusz Pavilion - The Jesuits of the Missouri Province; Institute of Jesuit Sources - The Jesuits of the Missouri Province; Jesuit Mission Bureau - The Jesuits of the Missouri Province; Review for Religious - The Jesuits of the Missouri Province; DeSmet Jesuit High School; Jesuit Community Corporation at St. Louis University; Saint Louis University; St. Louis University High School; The Sacred Heart Program, Inc.; White House Retreat, Inc.; Loyola Academy,* St. Louis, MO; *Arrupe Jesuit High School,* Denver, CO; *Society of Jesus in Belize, Inc., Belize; Sacred Heart Jesuit.*

Ministries in Parishes; Universities; High Schools; Middle Schools; Novitiate; First Studies House; Curia; Retreat Houses.

Fathers 234; Students in Major Seminary 16; Novices 5; Brothers 24.

Represented in the Archdioceses of Denver, Kansas City in Kansas, and St. Louis and the Dioceses of Colorado Springs, Kansas City-St. Joseph, Pueblo and Salina. Also in Belize.

New Orleans Province (1907): 500 S. Jefferson Davis Pkwy., New Orleans, LA 70119-7192. Tel: 504-821-0334; Fax: 504-822-5322. Very Rev. Alfred C. Kammer, S.J., Prov.; Revs. James L. Lambert, S.J., Asst. for Parishes & Retreat Apostolate; Stephen C. Rowntree, S.J., Asst. for International Ministries; Thomas H. Stahel, S.J., Socius & Asst. Higher Education; Paul Deutsch, S.J., Asst. for Secondary Education; Bro. Lawrence J. Lundin, S.J., Treas.

Legal Title: *Catholic Society of Religious and Literary Education, A Louisiana Corporation.*

Fathers 193; Students in Major Seminary 21; Novices 20; Brothers 23.

Properties owned, sponsored or staffed: Parishes 10; Universities 1; Colleges 1; High Schools 4; Novitiate 1; Houses of Retreat 4.

Represented in the Archdioceses of Atlanta, Birmingham, Brownsville, Miami, New Orleans, Palm Beach, San Antonio, and Santa Fe and the Dioceses of Amarillo, Austin, Baton Rouge, Charleston, Corpus Christi, Dallas, El Paso, Fort Worth, Galveston-Houston, Gallup, Gaylord, Lafayette (LA), Las Cruces, Little Rock, Mobile, Nashville, Orlando, Venice, St. Augustine and St. Petersburg.

California Province (1909): *Executive Assistant,* 300 College Ave., P.O. Box 519, Los Gatos, CA 95031-0519. Tel: 408-884-1600. Very Rev. Thomas H. Smolich, S.J., Prov. Revs. Alfred E. Naucke, S.J., Exec. Asst.; Anthony E. Sholander, S.J., Asst. for Formation & Vocations; Robert V. Caro, S.J., Asst. for Higher Education; Theodore E. Gabrielli, S.J., Asst. for Social Ministries; Joseph G. Spieler, S.J., Asst. for Pastoral Ministries; Paul A. Soukup, S.J., Dir. Studies; Robert L. St. Clair, S.J., Prov., Treas.; Mr. William F. Masterson, Prov. Dir.-Devel; Bro. Daniel J. Peterson, S.J., Prov. Archivist; Revs. William J. Wood, S.J., Tertian Instructor; Theodore E. Gabrielli, S.J., Dir.; California Jesuit Missionaries, 284 Stanyan St., San Francisco, CA 94118-4299. Tel: 415-221-1588. Doan T. Hoang, S.J., Apostleship of Prayer; William F. Masterson, S.J., Dir. Jesuit Seminary Association.

Legal Title: *The California Province of the Society of Jesus.*
Fathers 372; Brothers 33; Scholastics 33; Scholastic Novices 13.
Properties owned, sponsored or staffed: Parishes 13; Universities 3; High Schools 6; Novitiates 1; Retreat Center 2.
Represented in the Archdioceses of Los Angeles, and San Francisco and the Dioceses of Fresno, Honolulu, Monterey, Oakland, Orange, Phoenix, Reno, Sacramento, Salt Lake City, San Diego, San Jose, Santa Rosa, Stockton and Tucson.

New England Province (1926): 85 School St., Watertown, MA 02472-4251. Tel: 617-607-2800; Fax: 617-607-2888. Revs. Thomas J. Regan, S.J., Prov.; John P. Murray, S.J.; Exec. Asst.; David I. Donovan, S.J., Prov. Asst. Formation; James M. Hayes, S.J., Dir. Vocations; Michael J. Linden, S.J., Prov. Asst. for Pastoral Social & International Ministries; William C. McInnes, S.J., Prov. Liaison for Continuing Education; James J. Keegan, S.J., Liaison for Ministry of Spiritual Exercises; Bro. George T. Williams, S.J., Prov. Coord.-Criminal Justice Ministry.
Legal Title: *The Society of Jesus of New England.*
Fathers 345; Scholastics 24; Brothers 17.
Parishes 3; Universities 2; Colleges 1; High Schools 3; Houses of Retreats 2; Seminaries 1; Novitiates 1; Residences 1.
Represented in the Archdioceses of Anchorage, Baltimore, Boston, Chicago, Los Angeles, Miami, Milwaukee, New York, Philadelphia, St. Louis, St. Paul-Minneapolis, San Francisco, Seattle, and Washington and the Dioceses of Allentown, Bridgeport, Buffalo, Burlington, Fairbanks, Gallup, Honolulu, Manchester, Nashville, Norwich, Oakland, Portland (ME), Rapid City, St. Augustine, St. Petersburg, San Diego, Scranton, Spokane, Syracuse, Tucson, Venice, Wheeling-Charleston and Worcester.

Chicago Province - Society of Jesus (S.J.) (1928): 2050 N. Clark St., Chicago, IL 60614. Tel: 773-975-6363; Fax: 773-975-0230. Very Rev. Edward W. Schmidt, S.J., Prov; Revs. Michael D. Class, S.J., Exec. Asst.; William L. Verbryke, S.J., Asst. for Formation; Daniel L. Flaherty, S.J., Prov. Treas. and Asst. for Bus. and Finance; James A. Stoeger, S.J., Asst. Secondary Education; David S. Godleski, S.J., Asst. for Vocation Promotion; Paul V. Robb, S.J., Asst. Treas.; George E. Von Kaenel, S.J., Asst.-Intl. Apostolates; Dir.-Jesuit Intl. Missions; Asst.-Social Min.; Paul J. Faulstich, S.J., Asst. for Records & Research; John J. Foley, S.J., Asst. to Devel. Dir. for Jesuit Seminary Assoc.; Richard C. Conroy, S.J., Dir. Apostleship of Prayer. Jesuit Development Office, 2059 N. Sedgwick St., Chicago, IL 60614. Tel: 773-975-8181; Fax: 773-975-2042. Quarterly Publication: Company Magazine. Offices, 1400 W. Devon Ave.-#511, Chicago, IL 60660-1312. Tel: 773-761-9432; Fax: 773-761-9443.
Legal Title: *Chicago Province of the Society of Jesus.*
Fathers 199; Scholastics 27; Brothers 15; Scholastic Novices 5.
Properties Sponsored: Parishes 3; Universities 2; High Schools 5; Retreat Houses 2; Diocesan Major Seminary 1; Residences 9; House of Writers 1.
Represented in the Archdioceses of Chicago, Cincinnati, Indianapolis and Louisville and in the Dioceses of Covington, Evansville, Fort Wayne-South Bend, Gary, Joliet, Lafayette (IN), Lexington, Peoria and Rockford.

Oregon Province - Society of Jesus (1932): 3215 S.E. 45th Ave., Portland, OR 97206. Mlg Address: P.O. Box 86010, Portland, OR 97286-0010. Tel: 503-226-6977. Very Rev. John D. Whitney, S.J., Prov; Revs. Patrick J. Ford, S.J., Socius and Legal Sec. & Chief of Staff, Asst. for Higher Education; Ignatius F. Ohno, S.J., Treas.; Dan T. Mai, S.J., Liaison for International Ministries; Joel K. Adams, S.J., Asst.-Formation & Secondary Education; Charles J. Peterson, S.J., Asst.-Native Ministries.
Legal Titles: *Society of Jesus, Oregon Province,* Portland, OR; *The Pioneer Educational Society,* Spokane, WA; *Montana Catholic Missions, SJ; The Society of Jesus, Alaska.*
Fathers 210; Scholastics 40; Brothers 11.
Properties owned, sponsored or staffed: Parishes 7; Universities 2; High Schools 4; Middle Schools 1; House of Study 1; Novitiates 1.
Represented in the Archdioceses of Anchorage, Portland in Oregon and Seattle and in the Dioceses of Baker, Boise, Fairbanks, Great Falls-Billings, Helena, Spokane and Yakima.

Detroit Province - Society of Jesus (S.J.) (1955): 7303 W. Seven Mile Rd., Detroit, MI 48221. Tel: 313-861-7500; Fax: 313-861-4230. Very Rev. Robert J. Scullin, S.J., Prov. Supr.; Revs. James F. Riley, S.J., Exec. Asst.; Walter L. Farrell, S.J., Treas.; Richard H. Twohig, S.J., Asst.-Intl. Apostolates & Secondary Education; John E. Dister, S.J., Asst.-for Social Ministries; Dennis T. Dillon, S.J., Asst. Formation; David E. Watson, S.J., Asst. Pastoral Ministries; Bro. James J. Boynton, S.J., Asst. Vocation Promotion.
Legal Titles: *Detroit Province of the Society of Jesus; Colombiere Center,* Clarkston, MI; *Jesuit Retreat House of Cleveland, Ohio; Jesuit Seminary Association; Jesuit International Missions; John Carroll University of Cleveland, Ohio; John Carroll Jesuit Community Corporation; Loyola High School,* Detroit, MI; *Loyola of the Lakes Jesuit Retreat House, Inc.; Manresa Jesuit Retreat House; Patna Jesuit Mission Society, Inc.; St. Ignatius High School of Cleveland, Ohio; St. John's Jesuit High School of Toledo, Ohio; University of Detroit Mercy; The Jesuit Community Corporation at the University of Detroit; University of Detroit Jesuit High School and Academy; Walsh Jesuit High School.*
Fathers 147; Scholastics 12; Brothers 16.
Properties owned, sponsored or staffed: Parishes 5; Universities 2; High Schools 5; Retreat Houses 3.
Represented in the Archdioceses of Boston, Chicago, Cincinnati, Detroit, Los Angeles, New Orleans, New York, St. Louis, and Washington and the Dioceses of Buffalo, Cleveland, Columbus, Gaylord, Lexington, Oakland, Toledo, Wheeling-Charleston and Worcester.

Wisconsin Province - Society of Jesus (S.J.) (1955): 3400 W. Wisconsin Ave., P.O. Box 080288, Milwaukee, WI 53208-0288. Tel: 414-937-6949; Fax: 414-937-6950. Very Rev. James E. Grummer, S.J., Prov.; Revs. John M. Paul, S.J., Asst. Prov.; James J. Gladstone, S.J., Prov. Asst.-Formation, Cross-Cultural & Pastoral Ministries; Eugene L Donahue, S.J., Prov. Asst. Education & Retreat, Renewal Ministries; Eugene M. Dutkiewicz, S.J., Prov. Asst.-Finance; Richard A. McGarrity, S.J., Pres.-Jesuit; Partnership.
Legal Title: *Wisconsin Province of the Society of Jesus.*
Fathers 285; Novices 8; Brothers 16; Scholastics 13.
Properties owned, sponsored or staffed: Parishes 10; Universities 2; High Schools 3; Middle Schools 2; Elementary Schools 2; Community Houses 18; Novitiate; Native American Missions 3; Retreat Houses 4.
Represented in the Archdioceses of Milwaukee, Omaha, and St. Paul-Minneapolis and the Dioceses of Green Bay, La Crosse, Rapid City, Winona and Cheyenne.

Province of the Antilles (1947): *Correa y Cindron,* 28; P.O. Box 76, Santo Domingo, Dominican Republic. Tel: 809-532-5628.

U.S. Address: 12725 S.W. 6th St., Miami, FL 33184. Very Rev. Jesus Zaglul, S.J., Prov.; Rev. Francisco Perez Lerena, S.J., Miami Reg. Supr.
Fathers 100; Scholastics 41; Brothers 14.
Properties owned, staffed or sponsored: High Schools: Loyola in Dominican Republic Belen Jesuit Prep in Miami; Novitiate 1; House of Retreat 3 in Santo Domingo; Juan Pablo II in Miami; Residences 2.
Represented in the Archdiocese of Miami. Also in Santo Domingo.

Puerto Rico Province - Society of Jesus (1987): *Urb. Santa Maria,* 1940 Calle Sauco, Mailing Address: RR 10, Buzon 5348, San Juan, PR 00926-9675. San Juan, PR 00927-6718. Tel: 787-790-3557; Fax: 787-790-3162. Very Rev. L. Orlando Torres, S.J., Reg. Supr.; Revs. John F. Talbot, S.J., Exec. Asst. to Reg. Supr. & Reg. Treas.; J. Raymond Johnson, S.J. Auditor.
Fathers 22; Scholastics 3; Brothers 1.
Properties owned, sponsored or staffed: Parishes 1; High Schools 1; Residences 2; Novitiates 1; Campus Ministry Centers 1; Vocation Centers 1.
Represented in the Archdiocese of Los Angeles and the Diocese of Palm Beach.

[0700] (S.S.J.)— ST. JOSEPH'S SOCIETY OF THE SACRED HEART

(The Josephites)
(Societas Sancti Joseph SSmi Cordis)

Central House of Administration: 1130 N. Calvert St., Baltimore, MD 21202. Tel: 410-727-3386; Fax: 410-727-1006. E-mail: josephite1@aol.com. Website: josephite.com. Very Rev. Edward J. Chiffriller, S.S.J., Supr. Gen.
Legal Titles: *St. Joseph's Society of the Sacred Heart, Inc.; St. Joseph Manor Foundation, Inc.; The Josephite Retirement and Disability Benfits Trust; The Josephite Seminarian*
Fathers 102; Brothers 8; Students in House of Studies 1; Seminarians 2; Novices 3; Formation in Nigeria 30.
Properties owned, staffed or sponsored: Parishes 50; Elementary Schools 18; High School; House of Study; Major Seminary; Novitiate; Nigerian Formation House.
Represented in the Archdioceses of Baltimore, Los Angeles, Mobile, New Orleans, and Washington and the Dioceses of Arlington, Baton Rouge, Beaumont, Biloxi, Birmingham, Fort Worth, Galveston-Houston, Lafayette (LA), Lake Charles, and Jackson. Also in Nigeria.

[0710] (C.J.)— JOSEPHITE FATHERS

(Institutum Josephitarum Gerardimontensium)

General Motherhouse: Geraardsbergen (Ghent), Belgium. Very Rev. Robert Hamilton, C.J., Supr. Gen.

U.S. Foundation (1963): *St. Joseph Seminary, Provincialate and Novitiate,* 180 Patterson Road, Santa Maria, CA 93455. Tel: 805-937-5378; Fax: 805-937-5759. Very Rev. Charles Hofschulte, C.J., Prov. Supr.
Ministry to: Parishes; Academic Education; Military Chaplaincy.
Fathers 13; Brothers 2.
Represented in the Archdiocese of Los Angeles.

[0720] (M.S.)— THE MISSIONARIES OF OUR LADY OF LA SALETTE

(Congregatio Missionariorum Vulgo "De la Salette")

General House: Piazza Madonna Della Salette 3, Rome 00152, Italy.
American Region was established 1892; Canonically erected 1934; Divided into other Provinces in 1945, 1958, 1967 and restructured into one Province in 2000. Very Rev. Isidro A. Perin, M.S., Supr. Gen.

Province of Mary, Mother of the Americas (2000), 915 Maple Ave., Hartford, CT 06114-2330. Tel: 860-956-8870. Very Rev. Dennis J. Loomis, M.S., Prov.; Revs. James H. Kuczynski, M.S., Vicar & Sec.; Peter D. Kohler, M.S., Asst.; John J. O'Neil, M.S., Asst.; Bro. Claude F. Rheaume, M.S., Prov. Treas.
Legal Titles: *Missionaries of LaSalette Corp.; MLS Trust.*
Priests 162; Brothers 40; Oblate Brothers 5; Scholastics 3.
Represented in the Archdioceses of Atlanta, Boston, Hartford, Milwaukee, New York, St. Louis, St.Paul-Minneapolis, and Washington and in the Dioceses of Albany, Beaumont, Fall River, Galveston-Houston, Jefferson City, Lake Charles, Manchester, Norwich, Orlando, Peoria, Pensacola-Tallahassee, Providence, Raleigh, Rockville Centre, Springfield (MA), Tucson, Tyler, Venice and Worcester. Also in Canada.

[0730] (L.C.)— LEGIONARIES OF CHRIST

Founded in Mexico 1941, first foundation in United States 1965.

General Headquarters: Via Aurelia 677, Rome, Italy. Tel: 011-39-06-664991; Fax: 011-39-06-66416553. Very Rev. Marcial Maciel, L.C., Founder and Supr. Gen.

U.S. Headquarters: 393 Derby Ave., Orange, CT 06477. Tel: 203-795-2800; Fax: 203-795-2808. Rev. Anthony Bannon, L.C., Natl. Dir. Novitiate and Juniorate, 475 Oak Ave., Cheshire, CT 06410. Tel: 203-271-0805. Rev. Christopher Brackett, L.C., Rector.
Priests 75; Religious 68; Novices 46; Juniors 56.
Represented in the Archdioceses of Atlanta, Chicago, Denver, Detroit, Hartford, Los Angeles, New York, St. Louis, and Washington and in the Dioceses of Dallas, Lincoln, Manchester, Madison, Providence, Sacramento and San Jose.

[0740] (M.I.C.)—CONGREGATION OF MARIANS OF THE IMMACULATE CONCEPTION

(Congregatio Clericorum Marianorum sub titulo Immaculatae Conceptionis Beatae Mariae Virginis)

General Motherhouse: via Corsica no. 1, Rome, Italy. Very Rev. Mark Garrow, M.I.C.; Very Rev. Jan Rokosz, M.I.C., Vicar Gen.

American Province of St. Casimir (1913): 6336 S. Kilbourn Ave., Chicago, IL 60629-5588. Tel: 773-582-8191; Fax: 773-582-8961. Very Rev. Donald S. Petraitis, M.I.C., Prov.; Councilors: Revs. Jerome Zalonis, M.I.C.; Daniel Cambra, M.I.C.; Timothy Roth, M.I.C.; Bros. Brian Manian, M.I.C.; Donald Schaefer, M.I.C., Prov. Areas.
Fathers 26; Seminarians 4; Brothers 3.
Properties owned, staff or sponsored: Parishes 6; High School 1; Community Houses 7.
Represented in the Archdioceses of Chicago and Milwaukee and in the Dioceses of Joliet and Norwich. Also in Argentina.

St. Stanislaus Kostka Province: 2 Prospect Hill Rd., Stockbridge, MA 01262-0951. Tel: 413-298-3931. Very Rev. Walter Dziordz, M.I.C., Prov. Supr.; Councilors: Revs. Joseph Roesch, M.I.C.; Seraphim Michalenko, M.I.C.; Bro. Andrew Maczynski, M.I.C., Dir. Marian Helpers Center; Rev. Daniel Papineau, M.I.C.
Legal Holdings: *Marian Helpers Center; Marian Scholasticate; John Paul II Institute of Divine Mercy; National Shrine of the Divine Mercy.*
Fathers 24; Brothers 7; Seminarians 6; Novices 1; Postulants 3.
Properties owned, staffed or sponsored: 3 Community Houses; Novitiate; Filial House; Residence.
Represented in the Archdiocese of Washington and in the Dioceses of Fairbanks, Portland (ME), Steubenville and Springfield. Also in Portugal.

[0750] (C.M.M.)—CONGREGATION OF MARIANNHILL MISSIONARIES, MARIANNHILL FATHERS AND BROTHERS

(Congregatio Missionariorum de Mariannhill)

Generalate: Via S. Giovanni Eudes 91, 00163 Rome, Italy. Very Rev. Yves LaFontaine, C.M.M., Supr.

American-Canadian Province (1938): *Our Lady of Grace Monastery,* 23715 Ann Arbor Trail, Dearborn Hts., MI 48127. Tel: 313-561-7140; Fax: 313-561-9486. Revs. Thomas Heier, C.M.M., American Reg.; Thomas Szura, C.M.M., Procurator.

Fathers 9; Brothers 3.

Legal Holdings: *Mariannhill Retreat Center,* Dearborn Heights, MI.

Represented in the Archdiocese of Detroit.

[0760] (S.M.)—SOCIETY OF MARY

(Marianists)

(Societas Mariae—Marianistae)

General Motherhouse: Via Latina 22, 00179 Rome, Italy. Very Rev. David Fleming, S.M., Supr. Gen.

The Province of Cincinnati (1849); Province of the Pacific (1948); Province of St. Louis (1908) and the Province of New York (1961) have merged June 30th, 2002 to form the Marianist Province of the United States.

Marianist Province of the United States (2002): 4425 West Pine, St. Louis, MO 63108-2301. Tel: 314-533-1207; Fax: 314-533-0778. Bro. Stephen Glodek, S.M., Prov.; Councilors: Bro. Richard Dix, S.M.; Rev. Timothy Dwyer, S.M.; Rev. James Fitz, S.M., Asst. Prov.; Rev. Joseph Lackner, S.M.; Rev. Timothy Kenney, S.M.

Legal Titles and Holdings - Properties owned: *Marianist Provincial Office,* St. Louis, MO; *St. Mary's University,* San Antonio, TX; *Central Catholic Marianist High School,* San Antonio, TX; *Chaminade Preparatory,* St. Louis, MO; *St. John Vianney High School,* St. Louis, MO; *Marianist Retreat & Conference Center,* Eureka, MO; *Marianist Community,* St. Louis; *Marianist Community,* Santa Clara, CA; *Marianist Community,* San Jose, CA; *Marianist Retreat Center; Villa St. Joseph; Marianist San Juan Community,* Cupertino, CA; *Mount St. John; Bergamo Center; University of Dayton; Chaminade-Julienne High School; Marianist Mission,* Dayton OH; *Governor's Island,* Huntsville, OH; *Marianist Communities in:* Cleveland, OH; Cincinnati, OH; Dayton, OH; *Marianist Communities,* Baltimore, MD; *Marianist Community Residence,* Baltimore, MD; *Marianist Family Center,* Cape May Point, NJ; *Marianist Community Residence,* Vernon, CT; *Marianist Community Residences,* Hollywood, FL; *Chaminade/Madonna High School,* Hollywood, FL; *Mission Noell,* Villalba, PR; *Colegio San Jose,* Rio Piedras, PR; *Chamindate University,* Honolulu, HI; *St. Louis School,* Honolulu, HI; *Marianist Center,* Honolulu, HI; *Marianist Communities,* Honolulu, HI; *Marianist Residence,* Maui, HI.

Fathers 161; Brothers 451; Brothers Perpetual Professed 356; Novices 4; Aspirants 4.

Members serve and staff: Parishes; Universities, High Schools and Middle Schools; Retreat Houses; Apostolic Centers; Missions in India, Kenya, Korea, Malawi, Mexico & Zambia.

Represented in the Archdioceses of Baltimore, Boston, Chicago, Cincinnati, Hartford, Los Angeles, Miami, New Orleans, Philadelphia, St. Louis, San Antonio, San Francisco and San Juan and in the Dioceses of Belleville, Brooklyn, Camden, Cleveland, Fort Wayne-South Bend, Fort Worth, Galveston-Houston, Honolulu, Kalamazoo, Memphis, Norwich, Monterey, Orange, Oakland, Pittsburgh, Ponce, Raleigh, Rockville Centre and San Jose. Also in Ireland.

Province of Meribah (1976): *Marianist Provincial Residence,* 240 Emory Rd., Mineola, NY 11501. Tel: 516-742-5555. Very Rev. Thomas A. Cardone, S.M., Prov.; Bro. Kenneth M. Hoagland, S.M., Asst. Prov. & Asst. for Education; Rev. James C. Williams, S.M., Councilor; Bro. Richard J. Hughes, S.M., Asst. for Temporalities; Councilors: Rev. Philip K. Eichner, S.M.; Bro. Thomas J. Cleary, S.M.

Legal Holdings: *Chaminade High School,* Mineola, NY; *Kellenberg Memorial High School,* Uniondale, NY; *Marianist Residence,* Accord, NY.

[0770] (F.M.S.)—THE MARIST BROTHERS

(Fratres Maristae a Scholis)

Generalate: Rome, Italy. Rev. Bro. Sean D. Sammon, F.M.S., Supr. Gen.; Rev. Bro. Luis Sobrado, F.M.S., Vicar Gen.

Province of the United States of America (2003): *Provincial Office,* 1241 Kennedy Blvd., Bayonne, NJ 07002. Tel: 201-823-1115; Fax: 201-823-2232. Bros. John Klein, F.M.S., Prov.; Hank Hammer, F.M.S., Asst. Prov.; Benjamin Consigli, F.M.S., Asst. Prov. Councilors: Bros. John Malich, F.M.S.; Donald Bisson, F.M.S.; Stephen Schlitte, F.M.S.; John Venturella, F.M.S.; Stephen Milan, F.M.S., Vocation Dir.; Kevin O'Neill, F.M.S., Prov. Treas.; Hugh Turley, F.M.S., Development; James Devine, F.M.S., Dir.- Marist Foreign Missions.

Brothers 218.

Properties owned, staffed or sponsored; High Schools 15; community houses 34; junior high school 1; community school in Japan 1.

Represented in the Archdioceses of Boston, Chicago, Miami, Newark, New Orleans, and New York and the Dioceses of Albany, Brooklyn, Brownsville, Laredo, Rockville Centre, St. Augustine, St. Petersburg, and Wheeling-Charleston.

[0780] (S.M.)—MARIST FATHERS

(Societas Mariae)

General Motherhouse: via Alessandro Poerio 63, Rome 00152, Italy.

The first Marist foundation in the United States was in 1863, St. Michael's in Convent, Louisiana. The first Marist Province in the United States was established in 1889 under the name of American Province. This Province was subdivided in 1924 into the Washington Province and the Boston Province; On January 1, 1962, the San Francisco Province was established. On January 1, 2000 the San Francisco and Washington Provinces merged. On September 8, 2000 the merged entity became officially known as the Atlanta Province. The Boston Province continues as a separate province. Very Rev. Jan Hulshof, S.M., Supr. Gen. Rev. John Harhager, S.M., Treas. Gen.

Atlanta Province (2000): P.O. Box 81144, Atlanta, GA 30366-1144. Tel: 770-458-1435. Very Rev. Dennis J. Steik, S.M., Prov.; Revs. Richmond J. Egan, S.M., Vicar Prov. & Councilor; H. Joseph Wilhelm, S.M., Prov. Treas.; Timothy F. Sugrue, S.M., Bus. Mgr. & Mission Promoter; Francis H. Springer, S.M., Mission Promoter; William F. Rowland, S.M., Dir. Vocations; Charles Girard, S.M., Archivist; Edwin L. Keel, S.M., & Peter R. Blanchard, S.M., Promoters of Marist Laity; Prov. Council: Revs. J. Michael Seifert, S.M.; Paul Hachey, S.M.; Timothy G. Keating, S.M.; Rene J. Iturbe, S.M.

Legal Holdings & Titles: *Marist Society, Inc.; Marist College and Marist Center,* Washington, DC; *Marist Society of GA; Marist School,* Atlanta, GA; *Marist Society of OH; Marist Society of LA; Marist Community,* New Orleans, LA; *Marist Society of PA.*

Fathers 79; Brothers 14.

Properties owned, sponsored or staffed: Community Houses 7; Parishes 11; Seminaries/Houses of Study 2. High School 1.

Represented in the Archdioceses of Atlanta, Chicago, Miami, Military Services, New Orleans, Philadelphia, Portland in Oregon, San Francisco, St. Paul-Minneapolis, and Washington and the Dioceses of Baton Rouge, Brooklyn, Brownsville, Cleveland, Honolulu, Monterey, Oakland, Orange, Savannah, St. Petersburg and Wheeling-Charleston.

Boston Province (Marist Fathers) (1924): *Marist Provincial House,* 27 Isabella St., Boston, MA 02116-5216. Tel: 617-426-5297; Fax: 617-482-1570. Very Rev. Roland A. Lajoie, S.M., Prov.; Rev. Albert DiIanni, S.M., Prov. Dir. of Third Order of Mary & Vocation Dir.; Prov. Council: Revs. John Bolduc, S.M.; Walter Gaudreau, S.M.; Albert DiIanni, S.M.; Joseph Hindelang, S.M.; James Strasz, S.M.; Raymond Arsenault, S.M., Prov. Treas.; Robert Graham, S.M., Prov. Archivist; J. Armand Robichaud, S.M., Marist Missions; Gerard Demers, S.M., Dir.- Lourdes Center. Tel: 617-247-2271.

Legal Titles: *Marist Fathers of Boston; Marist Fathers of Detroit, Inc.; Marist Fathers of New York.*

Fathers 68; Brothers 7; Seminarians 4.

Properties owned, sponsored or staffed: Community Houses 7; Parishes 6; High Schools 2; Retreat House.

Represented in the Archdioceses of Boston, Hartford, and Detroit, and in the Dioceses of Brooklyn, Burlington, Portland (ME) and Providence.

[0782] (O.M.M.)—MARONITE ORDER OF BLESSED VIRGIN MARY

Maronite Order of the Blessed Virgin Mary: 4405 Earhart Rd., Ann Arbor, MI 48105. Tel: 734-662-4822; Fax: 734-662-4822. Rev. Roger Chikri, O.M.M.; Paul Acaf, O.M.M.; Nahed Tarabay, O.M.M.

[0785] (C.M.L.M.)—THE CONGREGATION OF MARONITE LEBANESE MISSIONARIES

Founded at the Monastery of Kreim-Ghosta (Mountain of Lebanon), in the year 1865. Established in the United States March of 1991: Agreement between Archbishop Zayek of the Diocese of St. Maron and the Congregation to serve the parishes of San Antonio, Dallas and Houston.

U.S. Headquarters: *Our Lady of the Cedars Maronite Mission,* 11935 Bellfort Village, Houston, TX 77031. Tel: 281-568-6800; Fax: 281-564-6961. Rev. Abdallah Zaidan, C.M.L.M. Supr.

Bishops 2; Priests 83; Seminarians 20; Postulants 6.

Represented in the Diocese of Our Lady of Lebanon.

[0790] (O.Mar.)—MONASTERY OF MARONITE MONKS

Monastery of the Most Holy Trinity: 67 Dugway Rd., Petersham, MA 01366. Tel: 978-724-3347. Rt. Rev. William J. Driscoll, O. Mar., Abbot; Rev. Michael Cermak, O. Mar., Prior.

Priests 10; Brothers 9.

[0800] (M.M.)—MARYKNOLL

Catholic Foreign Mission Society of America, Inc.

U.S. Foundation (1911): *Maryknoll Society Center & Admin. Offices,* Maryknoll, NY 10545-0305. Tel: 914-941-7590; Fax: 914-944-3605. Revs. John C. Sivalon, M.M., Supr. Gen. & Pres.; Francis T. McGourn, M.M., Vicar Gen. & Vice Pres.; Assts. Generals: Revs. John C. Barth, M.M.; John J. McAuley, M.M.

Legal Title: *Catholic Foreign Mission Society of America Incorporated, Training Center; Maryknoll Society Center,* Maryknoll, NY 10545.

Houses in Archdioceses and Dioceses:

Boston. *Maryknoll Fathers and Brothers,* 80 Emerson Rd., East Walpole, MA 02032. Tel: 508-668-6831; Fax: 508-660-0252.

Buffalo. *Maryknoll Fathers and Brothers,* 127 Chadduck Ave., Buffalo, NY 14207. Tel: 716-875-0005; Fax: 716-875-2322.

Chicago. *Maryknoll Fathers and Brothers,* 5128 S. Hyde Park Blvd., 4 S Chicago, IL 60615-4217. Tel: 773-493-3367; Fax: 773-493-3427.

Cincinnati. *Maryknoll Fathers and Brothers,* 6930 Greenfield Dr., Cincinnati, OH 45224. Tel: 513-681-7888; Fax: 513-681-7893.

Cleveland. *Maryknoll Fathers and Brothers,* 10309 Edgewater Dr., Cleveland, OH 44102. Tel: 216-651-2121; Fax: 216-651-8242.

Denver. *Maryknoll Fathers and Brothers,* 4460 Federal Blvd., Denver, CO 80211. Tel: 303-455-5669; Fax: 303-455-5753.

Galveston-Houston. *Maryknoll Fathers and Brothers,* 2360 Rice Blvd., Houston, TX 77005. Tel: 713-529-1912; Fax: 713-529-0372. E-mail: mklhouston @maryknoll.org.

New York. *Maryknoll Fathers and Brothers,* 121 E. 39th St., New York, NY 10016. Tel: 212-697-4470; Fax: 212-697-4472.

Los Angeles. *Maryknoll Fathers and Brothers,* 745 W. Adams Blvd., Los Angeles, CA 90007. Tel: 213-747-9676; Fax: 213-747-8923.

St. Augustine. *Maryknoll Fathers and Brothers,* 2243 Saragossa Ave., Jacksonville, FL 32217-2685. Tel: 904-739-1112; Fax: 904-739-9083. Revs. Michael J. Sloboda, M.M.; Lawrence F. McCulloch, M.M.

St. Louis. *Maryknoll Fathers and Brothers,* 4542 W. Pine Blvd., St. Louis, MO 63108. Tel: 314-361-7729.

St. Paul. *Maryknoll Fathers and Brothers,* P.O. Box 16538, St. Paul, MN 55116. Tel: 651-222-5530; Fax: 651-222-2367.

San Francisco. *Maryknoll Fathers and Brothers,* 2555 Webster St., San Francisco, CA 94115. Tel: 415-921-1100; Fax: 415-775-8261.

San Jose. *Maryknoll Residence,* 23000 Cristo Rey Dr., Los Altos, CA 94024-7499. Tel: 650-967-3822; Fax: 650-965-3473.

Seattle. *Maryknoll Fathers and Brothers,* 958 16th Ave., E., Seattle, WA 98112. Tel: 206-322-8831; Fax: 206-324-6909.

Washington. *Maryknoll Fathers and Brothers,* 4834 16th St., N.W., Washington, DC 20011. Tel: 202-726-4252; 726-4281; Fax: 202-726-0466.

Priests 493; Students in Theology 25; Brothers 67; Priests Associates 4.

Properties owned or sponsored: Major Society Center; House of Formation; U.S. Community Houses 23.

Represented in the Archdioceses of Boston, Chicago, Cincinnati, Denver, Detroit, Los Angeles, New York, St. Louis, St. Paul-Minneapolis, San Francisco, Seattle and Washington and in the Dioceses of Buffalo, Cleveland, Galveston-Houston and San Jose.

[0810] (F.M.M.)—BROTHERS OF MERCY

General Motherhouse: D-56412 Montabaur, Germany. Bro. Stephen Geissler, F.M.M., Supr. Gen.

American Province: 4520 Ransom Rd., Clarence, NY 14031. Tel: 716-759-8341; Fax: 716-759-7243. Bros. Jude Holzfoerster, F.M.M., Prov. Supr.; Councilors: Bros. John McGrath, F.M.M.; Fidelis Verrall, F.M.M.

Brothers 15; Candidate 1; Novices 1.

Legal Holdings or Titles: *Brothers of Mercy Nursing Home Co., Inc.; Brothers of Mercy Housing Co., Inc.; Brothers of Mercy Sacred Heart Home, Inc.*

Represented in the Diocese of Buffalo.

[0820] (C.P.M.)—CONGREGATION OF THE FATHERS OF MERCY

(Congregatio Presbyterorum a Misericordia)

Generalate and Novitiate (1808): 806 Shaker Museum Rd., Auburn, KY 42206. Tel: 270-542-4146; Fax: 270-542-4147. Web site: www.fathersofmercy.com. Very Rev. William Casey, C.P.M., Supr. Gen.; Consultors: Revs. Wade Menezes, C.P.M.; Joel Rogers, C.P.M.; David Wilton, C.P.M.; Louis Caporiccio, C.P.M.

Priests 24; Novices 3; Students 9.

Represented in the Archdiocese of Louisville and in the Diocese of Owensboro.

[0825] M.S.S.—MISSIONARIES OF THE BLESSED SACRAMENT

Missionaries of the Blessed Sacrament

Regional Headquarters: 2933 Street Rd., Bensalem, PA 19020. Tel: 215-639-4254; Fax: 215-244-9211. Rev. Victor P. Warkulwiz, M.S.S., Supr.

Ministries in Special Apostolate: Promotion of perpetual Eucharistic adoration.

Fathers 3.

Represented in the Archdiocese of Philadelphia and in the Diocese of Lafayette.

[0830] (M.H.M.)—MILL HILL MISSIONARIES

St. Joseph's Missionary Society of Mill Hill

International Headquarters: *St. Joseph's College,* Mill Hill, London NW7 4JX, England. Very Rev. Jac Hetsen, M.H.M., Supr. Gen.

American Headquarters: *Mill Hill Missionaries,* 222 W. Hartsdale Ave., Hartsdale, NY 10530-1667. Tel: 914-682-0645; Fax: 914-682-0862. Very Rev. Robert J. O'Neil, M.H.M., Reg. Rep.

Legal Title: *Mill Hill Fathers, Inc.*

Fathers 13; Brothers 2; Associates 1.

Represented in the Archdioceses of Los Angeles and New York.

[0835] (O.M.)—MINIM FATHERS

General Motherhouse: Via S. Andrea delle Fratte, 1 00184, Rome, Italy. Tel: 011-39-6-678-0407; Fax: 011-39-6-678-0752. Very Rev. Giuseppe Morosini, O.M., Supr. Gen.

North American Delegation (1970): 3431 Portola Ave., Los Angeles, CA 90032. Tel: 323-223-1101. Friar Mario Pisano, O.M., Delegate Gen.

Legal Title: *Minim Fathers.*

Priests 3.

Vocation Center, 6043 N. Barranca Ave., Azusa, CA 91702.

Represented in the Archdiocese of Los Angeles.

[0840] (S.T.)—MISSIONARY SERVANTS OF THE MOST HOLY TRINITY

(Missionarii Servi Sanctissimae Trinitatis)

(Trinity Missions)

Generalate-Missionary Servants of the Most Holy Trinity: 1215 N. Scott St., Arlington, VA 22209-3009. Tel: 703-276-8646; Fax: 703-522-2656. Rev. Austin Walsh, S.T., Gen. Custodian, Revs. Michael Barth, S.T., Vicar Gen.; Gary Banks, S.T., Gen. Councilor; Francisco Gomez, S.T., Gen. Councilor; Bros. Steven Vesely, S.T., Sec. Gen. & Gen. Councilor; Jordan Baxter, S.T., Treas. Gen.

Legal Titles: *Missionary Servants of The Most Holy Trinity (a.k.a) Trinity Missions; Missionary Servants Charitable Trust; Father Judge Charitable Trust.*

Ministry in the following areas: Missionary Cenacles; Parishes; Missions; Stations & Specialized Apostolates; Lay Apostolate Secretariat; Halfway House; Auxiliary Military Chaplaincies; Counseling Centers; Hospitals and Rest Home Chaplains; AA Programs; Protective Institutions; Prison Chaplains; V.A. Chaplains; Community Centers; Elementary Schools.

Priests 88; Brothers 26; Student Brothers 147; Novices 10; Candidates 28; Deacon 2.

Properties owned and/or sponsored: Generalate, Arlington, VA; Parish, rectory and school, Holy Trinity, AL; Philadelphia, PA, Rio Piedras, PR; Former Seminary and Fund Raising Office Buildings, Silver Spring, MD; School Buildings, Camden, MS; St. Joseph Shrine, Stirling, NJ; Former minor seminary building, Monroe, VA; Residences: Harpers Ferry, WV; Senior Ministry Residence, Adelphi, MD and University Park, MD.

Represented in the Archdioceses of Baltimore, Los Angeles, Mobile, Newark, Philadelphia, and Washington and the Dioceses of Arlington, Biloxi, Boise, Cleveland, Jackson, Knoxville, Orange, Paterson, Pensacola-Tallahassee, San Bernardino, San Diego, Savannah and Tucson. Also in Mexico, Puerto Rico, Colombia and Costa Rica.

[0850] (M.AFR.)—MISSIONARIES OF AFRICA

(Societas Missionariorum Africae)

Generalate: 269 via Aurelia, C.P. 9078 I-00165, Rome, Italy. Rev. Francois Richard, M.Afr., Supr. Gen.

Province of North America: 1624 21st St., N.W., Washington, DC 20009-1003. Tel: 202-232-5154; Fax: 202-332-8640. Revs. Richard Roy, M.Afr., Asst. Prov.; J, M.Afr., Treas.; George Markwell, M.Afr., Hospital Chap.; John Lynch, M.Afr., Asst. Treas. & Office of Planned Giving; Phil Reed, M.Afr., Coord.-Justice & Peace.

Priests 32; Brothers 2.

Represented in the Archdiocese of Washington and in the Diocese of St. Petersburg.

[0853] (M.S.C.)—MISSIONARY SERVANTS OF CHRIST

Founded in the United States in 1979.

Headquarters and Novitiate: *Missionary Servants of Christ,* P.O. Box 1932, Ocean City, MD 21842. Tel: 410-250-3386; Fax: 410-250-3386. Bro. Edwin Baker, M.S.C., Supr.

Professed Brothers 12; Novices 2; Postulants 1.

Represented in the Diocese of Wilmington.

[0854] (M.S.P.)—MISSIONARY SOCIETY OF ST. PAUL OF NIGERIA

Generalate: *Gwagwalada,* P.O. Box 23, Abuja, Nigeria. Very Rev. Hyacinth Egbebo, M.S.P., Supr. Gen.

U.S. Region: *Missionary Society of St. Paul, Inc.,* 3607 Meriburr Ln., Houston, TX 77021-1309. Mailing Address: P.O. Box 300145, Houston, TX 77230-0145. Tel: 713-747-1722; Fax: 713-741-0245. Web site: www.mspfathers.org. Rev. Raphael Asiska, M.S.P., Local Supr. Tel: 713-747-7800.

Legal Titles: *Missionary Society of St. Paul, Inc.,* Houston, TX.

Universal number of Priests 164; Priests in U.S. 32.

Represented in the Diocese of Galveston-Houston.

[0855] (F.M.M.)—MISSIONARY FRATERNITY OF MARY

General Headquarters: 6A Calle 48-98, Zona 7-Apartado Postal 623-I, Zona 7, Guatemala, Central America. Rev. Msgr. Eduardo Aguirre-Oestmann, General Moderator.

U.S. Foundation (1991): 340 Pine St., Seaford, DE 19973. Tel: 302-629-5115. Revs. Ruben A. Soto, F.M.M., U.S. Regional Vicar; Juan Vicente Hidalgo, F.M.M.

Represented in the Diocese of Wilmington.

[0860] (C.I.C.M.)—MISSIONHURST CONGREGATION OF THE IMMACULATE HEART OF MARY

(Congregatio Immaculati Cordis Mariae)

Foreign and home missions.

Generalate: *Casa Generalizia C.I.C.M.,* Via S. Giovanni Eudes, 95, 00163 Rome, Italy. Very Rev. Jozef Lapauw, C.I.C.M., Supr. Gen.

U.S. Province (1946): *Missionhurst,* 4651 N. 25th St., Arlington, VA 22207. Tel: 703-528-3800; Fax: 703-528-5355. Rev. William G. Quigley, C.I.C.M., Prov.

Legal Titles: *American I.H.M. Province, Inc.; Immaculate Heart Missions, Inc.; Missionhurst, Inc.*

Ministries in Parishes; Prison Ministry and Hospital Pastoral Work.

Fathers 42; Brothers 1; Students 2.

Represented in the Archdioceses of Boston, Detroit, Hartford, New York, Philadelphia, and San Antonio and the Dioceses of Arlington, Brownsville and Raleigh.

[0865] (C.M.C.)—CONGREGATION OF THE MOTHER COREDEMPTRIX

Founded in the United States 1976.

U.S. Assumption Province: *Congregation of the Mother Coredemptrix,* 1900 Grand Ave., Carthage, MO 64836-3500. Tel: 417-358-7787; Fax: 417-358-9508. E-mail: cmc@dongcong.net. Very Rev. Francis Do Cao Tung, C.M.C., Prov. Supr.

Priests 26; Brothers 54; Novices 5; Postulants 7; Candidates 29.

Represented in the Diocese of Springfield-Cape Girardeau.

[0870] (S.M.M.)—MONTFORT MISSIONARIES

(Missionaries of the Company of Mary)

(Societas Mariae Montfortana)

Generalate: *Viale Dei Monfortani 65,* Rome 00135, Italy. Very Rev. William J. Considine, S.M.M.

United States Province (1948): *Montfort Missionaries,* 101-18 104th St., Ozone Park, NY 11416. Tel: 718-849-5885; Fax: 718-849-7518. Very Rev. Gerald J. Fitzsimmons, S.M.M.; Counselors: Revs. Thomas Poth, S.M.M.; Donald LaSalle, S.M.M.; George Werner, S.M.M.; Matthew Considine, S.M.M.

Legal Title: *Missionaries of the Company of Mary.*

Fathers 28; Brothers 3.

Parishes 2; Community Houses 6; Scholastics 1.

Represented in the Archdioceses of Hartford and St. Louis and in the Dioceses of Brooklyn and Rockville Centre.

[0895] (O.Ss.S.)—BRIGITTINE MONKS

(The Order of the Most Holy Savior)

Priory of Our Lady of Consolation: 23300 Walker Ln., Amity, OR 97101. Tel: 503-835-8080; Fax: 503-835-9662. E-Mail: monks@brigittine.org. Web site: www.brigittine.org. Bro. Steven Vargo, O.Ss.S., Prior.

Professed Monks 9; Novices 3.

Represented in the Archdiocese of Portland in Oregon.

[0897] (M.E.P.)—PARIS FOREIGN MISSION SOCIETY

(Societas Parisiensis Missionum Ad Exteros)

Society of secular priests, without vows, of Pontifical Right.

Headquarters: 128 Rue du Bac, Paris, France. Very Rev. Jean-Baptiste Etcharren, M.E.P., Supr. Gen.

U.S. Establishment: *Paris Foreign Mission Society,* 930 Ashbury St., San Francisco, CA 94117. Tel: 415-664-6747. Rev. Jacques R. Didier, M.E.P., Dir.

Legal Title: *American Auxiliary of Paris Foreign Missions, Inc.*

Priests 2.

Represented in the Archdiocese of San Francisco.

[0900] (O. PRAEM.)—CANONS REGULAR OF PREMONTRE

(Norbertines, Order of St. Norbert, Premonstratensians)

(Ordo Canonicorum Regularium Praemonstratensium)

Founded in France in the 12th century. First foundation in the United States in 1893. Abbot General Most Rev. Thomas A. Handgratinger, O.Praem.

Norbertine Generalate, 27 Viale Giotto 00153, Rome, Italy. Tel: 011-39-06-571-766-214 and 571-766-212; Fax: 011-39-06-574-0241.

United States: *St. Norbert Abbey,* 1016 N. Broadway, De Pere, WI 54115-2697. Tel: 920-337-4300; Fax: 920-337-4328. Rt. Rev. Gary J. Neville, O.Praem., Abbot; Rt. Rev. E. Thomas De Wane, O.Praem., Abbot Emeritus; Rt. Rev. Jerome G. Tremel, O.Praem., Abbot Emeritus; Rt. Rev. Benjamin T. Mackin, O.Praem., Abbot Emeritus; Very Rev. David M. Komatz, O.Praem., Prior; Revs. James T. Baraniak, O.Praem., Vocation Coord.; John P. Kastenholz, O.Praem, Trea.; Xavier G. Colavechio, O.Praem., Dir.-Norbertine Center for Spirituality; Thomas O. Meulemans, O.Praem., Mission Procurator; Andrew G. Cribben, O.Praem, Formation Dir./Novice Master.

Legal Titles: *The Premonstratensian Fathers; NORBERT & CO., a nominee of The Premonstratensian Fathers; Norbertine Fathers; St. Norbert Abbey, Inc.; The Walnut Markets, Inc.; Los Amigos del Peru, Inc.; Norbertine Generalate, Inc.*

Fathers 77; Brothers 4; Seminarians 9.

Properties owned, staffed or sponsored: Dependent Priories 4; House of Studies 1; Colleges 1; Chaplaincies 5; Parishes 12.

Represented in the Archdioceses of Chicago, Military Services and Santa Fe and in the Dioceses of Green Bay, Jackson, and Madison. Also in Peru.

Daylesford Abbey: *Norbertine Fathers and Brothers,* 220 S. Valley Rd., Paoli, PA 19301-1900. Tel: 610-647-2530; Fax: 610-651-0219. Rt. Rev. Ronald J. Rossi, O.Praem., Abbot; Very Rev. John J. Novielli, O.Praem., Prior; Revs. Stephen J. Albero, O.Praem, Vocation Dir.; Francis X. Cortese, O.Praem., Sub Prior; Joseph A. Serano, O.Praem., Treas.

Legal Title: *Norbertine Fathers, Inc.*

Fathers 28; Brothers 4; Oblates 1.

Properties owned, staffed or sponsored: Chaplaincies 1; Seminary; Parishes 3.

Represented in the Archdiocese of Philadelphia. Also in Peru.

St. Michael's Abbey: 19292 El Toro Rd., Silverado, CA 92676. Tel: 949-858-0222; Fax: 949-858-4583.

Legal Title: *The Norbertine Fathers of Orange, Inc.* Rt. Rev. Eugene J. Hayes, O.Praem., Abbot; Very Rev. Hugh Barbour, O.Praem., Prior; Pious Association (Aid to the Church in Need, Inc.), P.O. Box 819, El Toro, CA 92630. Tel: 949-858-0222.

Priests 42; Juniors 16; Postulants 5; Novices 3.

Properties owned: *St. Michael's College Preparatory High School,* Orange, CA; *Summer Camp,* Orange, CA.

Represented in the Archdiocese of Los Angeles and in the Diocese of Orange.

[0910] (O.M.I.)—OBLATES OF MARY IMMACULATE

General House: *Oblati di Maria Immacolata,* C.P. 9061, 00100, Roma-Aurelio, Italy. Most Rev. Wilhelm Steckling, O.M.I., Supr Gen.; Very Rev. Eugene King, O.M.I., Vicar Gen.

United States Province (1999): *Missionary Oblates of Mary Immaculate,* Provincial Admin. Office –391 Michigan Ave., N.E. Washington, DC 20017-1516. Tel: 202-529-4505; Fax: 202-529-4572. Very Rev. David Kalert, O.M.I., Prov.; Rev. Charles Banks, O.M.I., Vicar Prov.; Councilors: Revs. David Ullrich, O.M.I.; William O'Donnell, O.M.I.; Richard Sudlik, O.M.I.; Allen Maes, O.M.I.; Salvatore DeGeorge, O.M.I.; Joseph Hitpas, O.M.I.; Jose Arong, O.M.I.

Ministries in Retreat Centers, Shrines, Parishes, Chaplaincies, Religious Residences and Houses, Retirement Centers and the Media.

Fathers 390; Brothers 30; Scholastics 12.

Represented in the Archdioceses of Anchorage, Boston, Chicago, Los Angeles, Miami, New Orleans, New York, Portland, St. Louis, St. Paul-Minneapolis, San Antonio, and Washington and the Dioceses of Austin, Beaumont, Belleville, Brownsville, Columbus, Corpus Christi, Crookston, Dallas, Duluth, Galveston-Houston, Juneau, Lexington, Manchester, Monterey, Norwich, Oakland, Palm Beach, Pensacola-Tallahassee, Portland (ME), Providence, Richmond, San Angelo, San Diego, Sioux Falls, Springfield (IL), Springfield-Cape Girardeau and Winona. Also in Brazil, Canada, French Polynesia, Mexico, Natal and Zambia.

Northeast Area Office: 60 Wyman St., Lowell, MA 01852-2841. Tel: 978-458-9912; Fax: 978-458-7274. Rev. William O'Donnell, O.M.I., Area Supr.

Southeast Area Office: 6081 S.W. 21st St., Miramar, FL 33023-2920. Tel: 954-322-8596; Fax: 954-983-5569. Rev. Richard Sudlik, O.M.I., Area Supr.

North Central Area Office: 104 N. Mississippi River Blvd., St. Paul, MN 55104. Tel: 651-645-5042; Fax: 651-645-3704. Rev. Joseph Hitpas, O.M.I., Area Supr.

South Central Area Office: 224 S. DeMazenod Dr., Belleville, IL 62223. Tel: 618-394-6985; Fax: 618-394-6987. Rev. Allen Maes, O.M.I., Area Supr.

Southwest Area Office: 327 Oblate Dr., San Antonio, TX 78216-6602. Tel: 210-349-1475; Fax: 210-349-7411. Rev. Salvatore DeGeorge, O.M.I., Area Supr.

Pacific Area Office: 290 Lenox Ave., Oakland, CA 94610-4625. Tel: 510-452-1550; Fax: 510-452-3421. Rev. Jose Arong, O.M.I., Area Supr.

[0920] (O.S.F.S.)—OBLATES OF ST.FRANCIS DE SALES

(Congregatio Oblatorum Sancti Francisci Salesii)

General Motherhouse: Via Dandolo 49, Rome, Italy. In July 1966, the American Province divided into two provinces.

Wilmington-Philadelphia Province (1906): 2200 Kentmere Pkwy., Wilmington, DE 19806. Very Rev. Joseph G. Morrissey, O.S.F.S., Prov.; Provincial Councilors: Revs. Edward T. Fitzpatrick, O.S.F.S.; James E. Dalton, O.S.F.S.; Thomas B. Curran, O.S.F.S.; James J. Greenfield, O.S.F.S.; Provincial Staff: Revs. Edward T. Fitzpatrick, O.S.F.S., Dir. Personnel; Robert A. Mancini, O.S.F.S., Treas.; Richard R. De Lillio, O.S.F.S., Dir. Development; John J. Hurley, O.S.F.S., Dir. Missions; Kevin M. Nadolski, O.S.F.S., Formation & Vocations Advisor; Michael S. Murray, O.S.F.S., Dir. Spirituality Center; Michael T. Cavanaugh.

Fathers 184; Scholastics 3; Brothers 19; Postulants 5.

Properties owned, staffed or sponsored: Parishes 24; Colleges; Scholasticates; Novitiates; High Schools 5; Retreat Houses; Armed Forces; Chaplaincies 9; Foreign Missions.

Properties owned: *Provincial Residence,* Wilmington, DE; *Salesianum School,* Wilmington, DE; *DeSales House,* Wilmington, DE; *Center for New Life,* Childs, MD; *Oblate Residence,* Cape May, NJ; *DeSales Hall,* Washington, DC; *Deshairs House,* Washington, DC.

Represented in the Archdioceses of Philadelphia and Washington and Dioceses of Allentown, Arlington, Camden, Charlotte, Harrisburg, Raleigh, Venice and Wilmington.

Toledo-Detroit Province (1966): 2056 Parkwood Ave., Toledo, OH 43620-1616. Tel: 419-243-5105; Fax: 419-243-8827. Very Rev. David M. Whalen, O.S.F.S., Prov.; Revs. John J. Loughran, O.S.F.S.; Kenneth N. McKenna, O.S.F.S., Councilor; Ronald W. Olszewski, O.S.F.S., Councilor & Asst. Prov.

Legal Title: *Oblates of St. Francis de Sales, Inc.*

Ministries in Parishes; Highschools; Chaplaincies: Missionaries; Armed forces; Senior Citizens Residence

Priests 64; Brothers 14; Scholastics 1.

Properties owned, staffed or sponsored: *Provincial Residence,* Toledo, OH; *St. Francis de Sales High School,* Toledo, OH; *Oblate Residence,* Jackson, MI; *Oblate Residence,* Toronto, Canada; *Oblate Residence,* Lewiston, NY; *Oblate Residence,* Buffalo, NY.

Represented in the Archdioceses of Detroit, Miami, Military Services, and Philadelphia and the Dioceses of Buffalo, Erie, Kalamazoo, Lansing, Oakland, Saginaw, Salt Lake City, Stockton and Toledo. Also in Canada and the Virgin Islands.

[0930] (O.S.J.)—OBLATES OF ST. JOSEPH

(Congregatio Oblatorum S. Joseph)

Founded in Italy in 1878. Founder: Saint Joseph Marello (1844-1895). Cause of Beatification introduced May 28, 1948; Beatified 1993; Canonized 2001. First foundation in U.S. in 1929.

Motherhouse: *Corso Alfieri 384,* Asti, Italy.

General House: *Via Boccea, 364,* Rome, Italy. Very Rev. Lino Mela, O.S.J., Supr. Gen.; Very Rev. Sebastian Jacobi, O.S.J., Vicar Gen. Very Rev. Giocondo Bronzini, O.S.J., Procurator Gen.

Oblates of St. Joseph Eastern Province: Rte. 315, R.R. 4, Box 14, Pittston, PA 18640. Tel: 570-654-7542; Fax: 570-654-8621. Rev. Paul A. McDonnell, O.S.J., Prov.; Councilors: Revs. Gregory T. Finn, O.S.J; Daniel Schwebs, O.S.J.

Priests 8.

Parishes 2; Community Houses 4; Houses of Studies 1.

Properties owned: *St. Joseph's Oblate Seminary,* Pittston, PA.

Represented in the Diocese of Scranton.

California Province: 544 W. Cliff Dr., Santa Cruz, CA 95060. Tel: 831-457-1868; Fax: 831-457-1317. Rev. Brian Crawford, O.S.J., Prov.; Councilors: Revs. John Wurburton, O.S.J.; Carlos Esquivel, O.S.J.

Legal Title: *Oblates of St. Joseph.*

Priests 14: Brothers 5; Students 6.

Parishes 3; Community Houses 6; Houses of Study 2; Shrines 1.

Properties owned: *St. Joseph House of Studies,* Berkeley, CA; *Mount St. Joseph Seminary,* Loomis, CA; *Shrine of St. Joseph, Guardian of the Redeemer,* Santa Cruz, CA; *St. Joseph Marello House of Studies,* Oxnard CA; *St. Joseph's Villa,* Soda Springs, CA.

Represented in the Archdiocese of Los Angeles and in the Dioceses of Fresno, Monterey and Sacramento.

[0940] (O.M.V.)—OBLATES OF THE VIRGIN MARY

(Congregation of the Oblates of the Virgin Mary)
(Congregatio Oblatorum Beatae Mariae Virginis)

Generalate: *Viale XXX Aprile,* 17 00153, Rome, Italy. Very Rev. Patrice Veraquin, O.M.V., Rector Major.

St. Ignatius Province: 2 Ipswich St., Boston, MA 02215-3607. Tel: 617-536-4141. Rev. William M. Brown, O.M.V., Prov.

Ministries in Parishes; Hospital and Prison Chaplaincies; Retreats & Parish Missions; Novitiate; Community Houses; College Seminary Shrine Chaplaincies.

Priests in U.S. 36; Brothers 3.

Legal Holdings: *St. Clement's Eucharistic Shrine,* Boston, MA; *St. Joseph House,* Milton, MA; *St. Ignatius Province of the Oblates of the Virgin Mary, Inc.,* Boston, MA.

Represented in the Archdioceses of Boston, Denver, and Los Angeles and the Diocese Springfield in Illinois. Also in the Philippines.

[0950] (C.O.)—ORATORIANS

(Confederatio Oratorii S. Philippi Nerii)

A Confederation of Autonomous Houses first founded in Rome, 1575.

General Confederation: *Confederazione dell'Oratorio S. Philippi Neri,* Via S. Girolamo della Carita 63 00186, Rome, Italy. Revs. Edoardo Cerrato, C.O., Procurator Gen.; Antonio Chavez Rios, C.O., Delegate of the Holy See: The Oratory, La Professa, Isabel La Catolica, 21 Apartado Postal 7113, Mexico, DF 06000.

The Oratory of Rock Hill: P.O. Box 11586, Rock Hill, SC 29731. Tel: 803-327-2097. Very Rev. Joseph Wahl, C.O., Father Provost.

Fathers 11; Brothers 5; Novices 3.

Represented in the Diocese of Charleston.

The Oratorian Community of Monterey: P.O. Box 1688, Monterey, CA 93942. Tel: 831-373-0476. Very Rev. Peter C. Sanders, C.O., Provost & Major Supr.; Rev. Thomas A. Kieffer, C.O., Vicar & Sec.

Total in community 3.

Oratorian Foundation Inc., Arizona, P.O. Box 241, Yarnell, AZ 85362. An outreach of the Oratorian Community in Monterey.

Represented in the Diocese of Monterey.

The Pittsburgh Oratory: *Congregation of the Oratory of St. Philip Neri,* 4450 Bayard Street, Pittsburgh, PA 15213-1506. Tel: 412-681-3181. Very Rev. Bryan F. Summers, C.O., Provost; Revs. Drew P. Morgan, C.O., Vicar; David S. Abernethy, C.O., Treas.

Fathers 5; Novices 1.

Represented in the Diocese of Pittsburgh.

The Oratory of Pharr: Mailing Address, P.O. Box 1698, Pharr, TX 78577-1698 Tel: 956-843-8217; Fax: 956-843-2946. Very Rev. Leo Francis Daniels, C.O., Provost & 1st Counsel or of the Delegate of the Holy See; Revs. Mario Alberto Aviles, C.O., Vicar and Deputy for Latin American; Jose Encarnacion Losoya, C.O., Sec.; David Garcia, C.O.; Very Rev. Antonio Rios, C.O., Delegate of the Holy See.

Ministries in Parish work; Services to the poor; promotion of Mexican-American cultural services; Education at all levels; Spanish language communities.

Properties owned: *Casa Maria of the Oratory,* Pharr, TX; *Oratory Academy-Academia Oratoriana,* Pharr, TX; *Pharr Oratory of St. Philip Neri of Pontifical Right.*

Secular Oratory, Lay Institute Founded by St. Philip Neri. Principal Work; Federacion Mexicana del Oratorio de San Felipi Neri, American Office, The Oratory, Rte. 1, Box 118, Pharr, TX 78577. Rev. Antonio Ortega, C.O., Natl. Procurator. The Pharr Oratory is a member of the Mexican Federation of Oratories and at present serves as the American office of all eleven houses.

Represented in the Diocese of Brownsville. Also in Mexico and Costa Rica.

The Oratory of St. Philip Neri: 109 Willoughby St., Brooklyn, NY 11201. Tel: 718-875-2096; Fax: 718-875-4678. Very Rev. Dennis M. Corrado, C.O., Provost.

Fathers 3; Brothers 2.

[0960] (F.S.R.)—BROTHERS OF THE CONGREGATION OF OUR LADY OF THE HOLY ROSARY

Founded in the United States in 1957.

General Motherhouse and Novitiate: 232 Sunnyside Dr., Reno, NV 89503-3510. Tel: 775-747-4441. Bros. Matthew Cunningham, F.S.R., Supr.; Philip Napolitano, F.S.R., Asst. Supr.

Ministries in the field of Education and Pastoral Ministry.

Brothers 3.

Represented in the Diocese of Reno.

[0970] (O.de.M.)—ORDER OF OUR LADY OF MERCY

(Mercedarians Friars)
(Ordo de Beatae Mariae Virginis de Mercede)

Founded in Barcelona, Spain on August 10, 1218.

Generalate: *Curia Generalizia dei PP. Mercedari,* Via Monte Carmelo 3 00166, Rome, Italy. Most Rev. Pedro Mariano Labarca Araya, O.de.M., Master Gen.

U.S.A. Provincial Headquarters: *Vicariate of Mary, Co-Redemptress,* 7758 East Main Rd., LeRoy, NY 14482-9701. Tel: 585-768-7110. Very Rev. Richard S. Rasch, O.de.M., Prov. Supr.

Ministries in Parishes, education, hospital and prison chaplaincies; retreats; newman campus chaplaincies; mission word.

Priests 20; Brothers 3.

Properties owned: *St. Raymond Nonnatus Novitiate,* Le Roy, NY; *Monastery of Our Lady of Mercy,* Philadelphia, PA; *Saint Peter Nolasco Residence,* St. Petersburg, FL.

Represented in the Archdiocese of Philadelphia and in the Dioceses of Buffalo, Cleveland and St. Petersburg. Also in South India.

[0975] (S.O.L.T.)—SOCIETY OF OUR LADY OF THE MOST HOLY TRINITY

Headquarters: *Casa San Jose,* 109 W. Avenue F, P.O. Box 152, Robstown, TX 78380. Tel: 361-387-2754. Rev. Rogelio Rosalinas, S.O.L.T., Gen. Priest Servant.

Priests 75; Deacons 3; Novices 21; Seminarians 81.

Pastoral Ministries: Community House; House of Study-Novitiate; Migrant Ministry.

Represented in the Archdioceses of Hartford, San Antonio, San Juan, and Santa Fe and in the Dioceses of Albany, Austin, Cheyenne, Corpus Christi, Gallup, Galveston-Houston, Kansas City-St. Joseph, Lafayette, Laredo, Norwich, Portland ME and Wheeling-Charleston.

[0980] (C.F.M.M.)—BROTHERS OF OUR LADY, MOTHER OF MERCY

(Congregatio Fratrum Beatae Mariae Virginis, Matris Misericordiae)

Generalate: Gasthuisring 54 5041 DT, Tilburg, The Netherlands.

U.S. Region: 7140 Ramsgate Ave., Los Angeles, CA 90045. Bro. Anthony Smulders, C.F.M.M., Contact Person.

Brothers 3.

Represented in the Archdiocese of Los Angeles.

[0990] (S.A.C.)—SOCIETY OF THE CATHOLIC APOSTOLATE

(Pallottines)

Generalate: *Pallottines,* Piazza S.V. Pallotti 204 00186, Rome, Italy.

Province of the Immaculate Conception (Eastern) (1953): 204 Raymond Ave., Mailing Address, P.O. Box 979, South Orange, NJ 07079. Tel: 201-762-2926. Very Rev. Frank Amato, S.A.C., Prov. Revs. Peter T. Sticco, S.A.C., 1st Consultor; Frank Gaetano, S.A.C.,

Bursar. Consultors: Revs. Bernard Carman, S.A.C.; Michael Salerno, S.A.C.; Frank Donio, S.A.C.
Fathers 18; Professed Brothers 3.
Properties owned, sponsored or staffed: Parishes 4; Seminary; High School; Novitiate; *Shrine of St. Jude, Pallottine Center for Apostolic Causes.*
Represented in the Archdioceses of Baltimore, Newark, and Washington and the Dioceses of Brooklyn and Camden.

Mother of God Province (1946): *Pallottine Fathers and Brothers, Inc.,* 5424 W. Blue Mound Rd., Milwaukee, WI 53208. Tel: 414-259-0688; Fax: 414-258-9314. Very Rev. Robert V. Carney, S.A.C., Prov. Revs. Leon Martin, S.A.C., 1st Consultor; Richard J. Gunderman, S.A.C., Consultor.
Ministries in Parishes; Retreat House; Hospital Chaplaincies; High School.
Fathers 12; Brothers 1.
Represented in the Archdiocese of Milwaukee.

Irish Province (1909): *Homestead,* Sandyford Rd., Dundrum, Dublin 16, Republic of Ireland. Rev. John Fitzpatrick, S.A.C., Prov.
U.S. Foundation: 3352 4th St., P.O. Box 249, Wyandotte, MI 48192. Very Rev. Michael O'Dwyer, S.A.C., Prov. Delegate.
Fathers 15; Brothers 1.
Parishes 6; Missions 5.
Represented in the Archdiocese of Detroit and in the Dioceses of Fort Worth, Lubbock, Reno, and Las Vegas.

Queen of the Apostles Province (1909): Via Giuseppe Ferrari, 1-Rome, Italy. Very Rev. Gaetano Ianni, S.A.C., Prov.
U.S. Foundation: *Our Lady of Mt. Carmel Shrine and Church,* 448 E. 116th St., New York, NY 10029. Tel: 212-534-0681.
Fathers 8.
Parishes 4.
Represented in the Archdiocese of New York and in the Dioceses of Albany and Pensacola-Tallahassee.

Infant Jesus Delegature of Christ The King Province: *Mission House and Infant Jesus Shrine,* 3452 Niagara Falls Blvd., North Tonawanda, NY 14120-0563. Rev. Leslaw M. Gwareka, S.A.C., Supr. & Prov. Delegate.
Priests 13.
Represented in the Dioceses of Brooklyn and Buffalo.

[1000] (C.P.)—CONGREGATION OF THE PASSION

(Congregatio Passionis Jesu Christi)

Founded in Italy in 1720 by St. Paul of the Cross. First foundation in United States in 1852.

General Motherhouse: *SS. Giovanni e Paolo Monastery,* Rome 00184, Italy. Most Rev. Ottaviano D'Egidio, C.P., Supr. Gen.

Eastern Province, Province of St. Paul of the Cross (1852): *Province Pastoral Center,* 80 David St., South River, NJ 08882. Tel: 732-257-7177. Very Revs. Terence Kristofak, C.P., Prov.; Gerald Laba, C.P., 1st Consultor; Joseph Jones, C.P., 2nd Consultor; Francis Finnigan, C.P., 3rd Consultor; Melvin Shorter, C.P., 4th Consultor.
Legal Titles: *St. Paul's Benevolent, Educational and Missionary Institute of West Hoboken, New Jersey; Passionist Missions, Inc.; Passionist Missionaries, Inc.*
Fathers 168; Professed Clerics 1; Brothers 26.
Properties owned, sponsored or staffed: Parishes 10; Community Houses 23; House of Study.
Represented in the Archdioceses of Atlanta, Baltimore, Boston, Hartford, Newark, and New York and the Dioceses of Altoona-Johnstown, Brooklyn, Metuchen, Palm Beach, Pittsburgh, Raleigh, Rockville Centre, Scranton, Springfield (MA), Wheeling-Charleston and Worcester. Also in Canada.

Western Province, Holy Cross Province: *Passionist Provincial Office,* 5700 N. Harlem Ave., Chicago, IL 60631. Tel: 773-631-6336. Very Rev. Michael Higgins, C.P., Prov.; Consultors: Revs. Donald Webber, C.P., Asst. Prov.; James Strommer, C.P., Prov. Consultor; Alexander Steinmiller, C.P., Consultor; Philip Paxton, C.P., Consultor.
Legal Title: *Congregation of the Passion, Holy Cross Province.*
Fathers 86; Brothers 12.
Properties owned or sponsored: *Passionist Provincial Office; Stauros International; Immaculate Conception Monastery; Daneo Hall; Passionist Community CTU; Immaculate Conception Parish,* Chicago, IL.
Represented in the Archdioceses of Chicago, Detroit, Los Angeles, Louisville, and San Antonio and the Dioceses of Birmingham, Galveston-Houston, Orlando and Sacramento.

[1010] (O.S.P.P.E.)—PAULINE FATHERS

(Ordo Sancti Pauli Primi Eremitae)

Founded in Hungary in the 13th Century. First foundation in the United States in 1953.

General Motherhouse: *Ojcowie Paulini - Jasna Gora ul.* Kordeckiego 2 42-200, Czestochowa, Poland. Most Rev. Stanislaw Turek, O.S.P.P.E., Supr.

American Provincial Motherhouse (1984): *Shrine of Our Lady of Czestochowa Monastery,* Beacon Hill, P.O. Box 2049, Ferry Rd., Doylestown, PA 18901. Tel: 215-345-0607; Fax: 215-345-8071. Very Rev. Krzysztof Wieliczko, O.S.P.P.E., Prov. & Prior; Revs. Stephen Wozniczka, Shrine Dir.; Anzelm Chalupka, O.S.P.P.E., Subprior.
Priests in U.S. 22; Brothers 6.
Represented in the Archdioceses of Chicago, New York, and Philadelphia and in the Dioceses of Greensburg and Norwich.

[1020] (S.S.P.)—PAULINE FATHERS AND BROTHERS

Society of St. Paul for the Apostolate of Communications.

General Motherhouse: *Via della Fanella 39 00148,* Rome, Italy. Very Rev. Pietro Campus, S.S.P., Supr. Gen. Very Rev. Abramo Parmeggiani, S.S.P., Vicar Gen.

United States Province (1932): *Pauline Fathers & Brothers,* P.O. Box 139, Ellsworth, OH 44416-0139. Tel: 330-533-7427. Very Rev. Matthew R. Roehrig, S.S.P., Prov. Supr.; Rev. Jeffrey Mickler, S.S.P., Vicar Prov. & Vocation Dir.; Rev. Ignatius W. Staniszewski, S.S.P., Publishing Editor, Publication: *Alba House.* Tel: 718-761-0047; Rev. Matthew Roehrig, S.S.P., Editor; Publication: *Pastoral Life Magazine,* Alba House. Tel: 216-533-5503; Bro. Dismas Beique, S.S.P., Editor, Publication: *Alba House AV Communications.* Tel: 216-533-5503; Bro. Richard Brunner, S.S.P., Vocation Dir.
Priests 12; Brothers 24.
Represented in the Archdioceses of Detroit and New York and in the Diocese of Youngstown.

Los Angeles Province: 112 S. Herbert Ave., Los Angeles, CA 90063. Tel: 213-269-9814; 268-5010 (Bookstore); Fax: 213-268-4583. Revs. Gilberto Martinez, S.S.P., Supr.; Thomas Martinez, S.S.P., Vice Supr.; Valeriano Giachino, S.S.P.; Gonzalo Ponce, S.S.P.
Priests 4.

[1030] (C.S.P.)—PAULIST FATHERS

(Societas Missionaria a S. Paulo Apostolo)

Paulist Fathers Motherhouse (1858): 86-11 Midland Pkwy., Jamaica Estates, NY 11432. Tel: 718-291-5995. Very Rev. John F. Duffy, C.S.P., Pres.
Legal Title: *Missionary Society of St. Paul the Apostle in the State of New York.*
Fathers 160; Students in Major Seminary 8; Novices 2.
Properties owned or sponsored: *Newman Campus Chaplaincies; Information Centers; Paulist Press; Paulist Radio-TV-Film Communications Svcs.; Paulist National Catholic Evangelization Association; House of Study; Novitiate.*
Represented in the Archdioceses of Boston, Chicago, Denver, Los Angeles, New York, Portland (OR), St. Paul-Minneapolis, San Francisco, and Washington and the Dioceses of Austin, Brooklyn, Columbus, Grand Rapids, Knoxville, Memphis, Oakland, Paterson and Tucson.

[1040] (SCH.P.)—PIARIST FATHERS

(Ordo Clericorum Regularum Pauperum Matris Dei Scholarum Piarum)

General Motherhouse: *San Pantaleo,* Piazza De Massimi, 4, Rome, Italy 00186. Most Rev. Joseph Lecea, Sch.P., Supr. Gen.

USA Province (1975): *Piarist Fathers-USA Province,* 1339 Monroe St., N.E., Washington, DC 20017-2510. Tel: 202-529-7734 & 529-6792; Fax: 202-526-4014. E-mail: piarist@earthlink.com. Very Rev. David Powers, Sch.P., Prov. Supr.
Legal Titles and Holdings: *Piarist Fathers–USA Province, Inc.; Piarist Fathers, Inc.; Order of the Pious Schools, Inc.; Piarist Fathers House of Studies,* Washington, DC; *The Piarist School,* Martin, KY; *Piarist Fathers Residence,* Derby, NY; *Piarist Fathers Residence,* Martin, KY; *Devon Preparatory School,* Devon, PA.
Priests 22.
Represented in the Archdioceses of Miami, Philadelphia, and Washington and the Dioceses of Buffalo, Lexington and Paterson.

New York-Puerto Rico Vice Province: 999 Road 14, Coto Laurel, PR 00780-2147. Tel: 787-848-1592; Fax: 787-841-5173. Rev. Jose A. Basols, Sch.P., Vice Prov.
Bishop 1; Priests 20; Cleric Students 2; Pre Novices 4.
Houses 5; Parishes 3; High Schools 2; Schools 4.
Represented in the Archdioceses of New York and San Juan and in the Diocese of Ponce. Also, Calasanzian Fathers and Padres Escolapios de P.R.

California's Vice Province Piarist Fathers: *Piarist Fathers,* 3940 Perry St., Los Angeles, CA 90063-1174. Tel: 323-261-1386; Fax: 323-269-0883. Rev. Antonio Tort, Sch.P., Vice Prov.
Priests 20; Novices 3; Prenovices 6; Seminarians 13.
Properties owned, staffed or sponsored: Parishes 6; Grammar Schools 2; House of Formation 3.
Represented in the Archdiocese of Los Angeles.

[1050] (P.I.M.E.)—PONTIFICAL INSTITUTE FOR FOREIGN MISSIONS, INC.

General Motherhouse: Via F. D. Guerrazzi 11, Rome, Italy 00152. Very Rev. Gian Battosta Zanchi, P.I.M.E., Supr. Gen.

U.S. Region: 17330 Quincy Ave., Detroit, MI 48221. Tel: 313-342-4066; Fax: 313-342-6816. Very Rev. Bruno Piccolo, P.I.M.E., Prov. Supr.
Legal Titles and Holdings: *PIME Missionaries - PIME Mission Center; PIME College Community,* Detroit, MI; *PIME Missionaries,* Wayne, NJ & Tequesta, FL.
Fathers 25; Brothers 1; Seminarians 5.
Formation Communities 1; Mission Houses 4.
Represented in the Archdiocese of Detroit and in the Dioceses of Paterson, Columbus and Palm Beach.

[1060] (C.PP.S.)—SOCIETY OF THE PRECIOUS BLOOD

(Congregatio Missionariorum Pretiosissimi Sanguinis Domini Nostri Jesu Christi)

General Motherhouse: Viale di Porta Ardeatina 66, 1-00154 Rome, Italy. Very Rev. Barry Fischer, C.PP.S. Moderator.

Cincinnati Province: 431 E. Second St., Dayton, OH 45402. Tel: 937-228-9263. Very Rev. Angelo P. Anthony, C.PP.S., Prov. Dir.; Prov. Council: Revs. Kenneth Schnipke, C.PP.S.; Kenneth Schroeder, C.PP.S.; Thomas Hemm, C.PP.S.; James Dugal, C.PP.S. Bros. Thomas Bohman, C.PP.S.; JosephFisher, C.PP.S., Treas. & Mission Procurator.
Ministries in Parishes; Missions; Chaplaincies; Shrine; Education; Retreat Preaching; Community Houses; Houses of Study; Military Chaplains.
Fathers 158; Brothers 29; Students in Major Seminaries 18; Students in Preparatory Seminary 23; Deacons 1; Brother Candidate 1.
Represented in the Archdioceses of Chicago, Cincinnati, Detroit, Indianapolis, and Military Services and the Dioceses of Cleveland, Columbus, Fort Wayne-South Bend, Gary, Harrisburg, Lafayette in Indiana, Lansing, Orange, Orlando, Steubenville, Superior, Toledo and Youngstown.

Kansas City Province: *Precious Blood Society Provincial Office,* P.O. Box 339, Liberty, MO 64069-0339. Tel: 816-781-4344; Fax: 816-781-3639. Very Rev. James Urbanic, C.PP.S., Prov. Dir.; Revs. Aloys Ebach, C.PP.S., 1st Consultor & Prov. Sec.; Joseph Bathke, C.PP.S., 2nd Consultor; Timothy Guthridge, C.PP.S., 3rd Consultor; John Wolf, C.PP.S., 4th Consultor; William Dineen, C.PP.S., Prov. Treas.
Ministries in Parishes; Missions; Houses of Study; Community House; Chaplaincies.
Bishops 1; Fathers 59; Brothers 3.
Represented in the Archdioceses of Chicago, Cincinnati, Denver, Kansas City in Kansas, and San Antonio and the Dioceses of Davenport, Des Moines, Dodge, Jefferson City, Kansas City-St. Joseph, San Angelo, Toledo and Wichita.

Province of the Pacific: *Society of the Precious Blood Province Center,* 2337 West Avenue 134th, San Leandro, CA 94577-4132. Tel: 510-357-4982; Fax: 510-357-4036. Very Rev. Ronald P. Wiecek, C.PP.S., Prov. Dir.; Councilors: Revs. Jeffrey Finley, C.PP.S., Vice Prov.; Gary Luiz, C.PP.S., Vocation Dir.; Jeffrey Keyes, C.PP.S., Sec.; Joseph Brown, C.PP.S., Treas.
Ministries in Parishes; Chaplaincies; Community Houses; Houses of Study.
Fathers 18; Brothers 1.
Represented in the Archdioceses of Chicago, Cincinnati, and Los Angeles and in the Diocese of Oakland. Also in Mexico City.

Atlantic Province: *Society of the Precious Blood, Provincial House,* 13313 Niagara Pkwy., Niagara Falls, Ontario L2E 6S6, Canada. Tel: 905-382-0865. Very Rev. Peter Nobili, C.PP.S., Prov.; Rev. Sam D'Agelo, C.PP.S., Sec.
Priests in the U.S. 9.
Represented in the Archdiocese of Miami and in the Dioceses of Buffalo and Rochester. Also in Canada.

[1065] (F.S.S.P.)—PRIESTLY FRATERNITY OF ST. PETER

Founded in Switzerland in 1988. First foundation in United States in 1991.

General Motherhouse: *Fraternitas Sacerdotalis Sancti Petri,* Maison St. Pierre Canisius, Chemin du Schoenberg 8, CH-1700 Fribourg, Switzerland. Tel: 41-26-488-0037; Fax: 41-26-488-0038. Very Rev. Arnaud Devillers, F.S.S. P., Supr. Gen.

International Seminary: *Priesterseminar Sankt Petrus,* Kirchstrasse 16, D-88145, Opfenbach-Wigratzbad, Germany. Tel: 49-8385 9221 15; Fax: 49-8385 9221 13. Rev. Philip Creurer, F.S.S.P., Sec. Gen.

U.S. Headquarters: *Priestly Fraternity of St. Peter – North American District Headquarters,* Griffin Rd. - P.O. Box 196, Elmhurst, PA 18416. Tel: 570-842-4000; Fax: 570-842-4001. Revs. George G. Gabel, F.S.S.P., District Supr.; Neal A. Nichols, F.S.S.P., Dir.-Development; Joseph R. Howard, F.S.S.P., District Bursar.

House of Formation: *Our Lady of Guadalupe Seminary,* P.O. Box 147, Denton, NE 68339. Tel: 402-797-7700; Fax: 402-797-7705. Very Rev. James W. Jackson, F.S.S.P., Rector; Revs. Charles Van Vliet, F.S.S.P.; James B. Buckley, F.S.S.P.; Mubarak Anwar Amar, F.S.S.P.; Calvin Goodwin, F.S.S.P.; Karl Pikus, F.S.S.P.; Chad Ripperger, F.S.S.P.; Joseph Terra, F.S.S.P.

Priests 47; Seminarians 63.

Properties owned or sponsored: Houses 22; High Schools 1; Prep School 1.

Represented in the Archdioceses of Atlanta, Denver, Indianapolis, Kansas City, Oklahoma City, and Omaha and the Dioceses of Boise, Charleston, Colorado Springs, Corpus Christi, Dallas, Fort Worth, Lafayette (IN), Lincoln, Little Rock, Paterson, Rapid City, Sacramento, Scranton, Tulsa, Tyler and Youngstown. Also in Canada.

[1070] (C.SS.R.)—REDEMPTORISTS FATHERS

(Congregatio Sanctissimi Redemptoris-Redemptorists)

Generalate: *Sant'Alphonso,* Via Merulana 31. C.P. 2458 1-00100, Rome, Italy. Most Rev. Joseph Tobin, C.Ss.R., Supr. Gen.; Very Rev. George Darlix, C.Ss.R., Vicar Gen. Rev. Jose Sousa, C.Ss.R., Proc. Gen.

Province of Baltimore (1850): *Provincial Residence,* 7509 Shore Rd., Brooklyn, NY 11209. Tel: 718-833-1900. Very Rev. Kevin Moley, C.Ss.R., Prov. Supr.; Revs. Patrick F. Woods, C.Ss.R., Prov. Vicar; Alfred Bradley, C.Ss.R., Prov. Consultor; Very Rev. Francis Nelson, C.Ss.R., Prov. Procurator; Bro. Albert R. Schreiber, C.Ss.R., Prov. Sec.; Revs. Carl Hoegerl, C.Ss.R., Prov. Archivist; Gerard Knapp, C.Ss.R., Asst. Procurator; Lawrence Lover, C.Ss.R., Canonical Consultor.

Bishops 2; Priests 179; Brothers 19; Novices 1; Postulants 6.

Properties owned, staffed or sponsored: Parishes 30; Residences 3; Retreat Houses 4; Community Houses 37.

Represented in the Archdioceses of Baltimore, Boston, Hartford, New York, Philadelphia, and Washington and the Dioceses of Albany, Brooklyn, Harrisburg, Rockville Centre, Toledo, Trenton and Wilmington. Also in the West Indies.

Richmond Vice Province (1942): *Vice Provincial Headquarters,* 313 Hillman St., P.O. Box 1529, New Smyrna Beach, FL 32170. Tel: 904-427-3094. Very Rev. Edward J. Gray, C.Ss.R., Vice Prov.; Revs. Eugene S. Daigle, C.Ss.R., Vicar; Consultors: Joseph Majewski, C.Ss.R.; Michael Koncik, C.Ss.R., Vocation Dir.; Bro. Thomas Kuhn, C.Ss.R., Vice Prov. Procurator.

Legal Title: *Congregation of the Most Holy Redeemer.*

Priests 45; Brothers 4.

Properties owned, staffed or sponsored: Parishes 9; Retreat Houses 2; Retirement Home 1; Residences 1; Missions 3.

Represented in the Archdiocese of Atlanta and the Dioceses of Charleston, Charlotte, Orlando, Richmond, St. Augustine, and Venice.

The Redemptorists Denver Province (1996): *The Redemptorists Provincial Residence,* Box 300399, Denver CO 80203-0399. Tel: 303-370-0035; Fax: 303-370-0036. Very Rev. Richard Thibodeau, C.Ss.R., Prov. Supr. Revs. Paul Coury, C.Ss.R., Prov. Vicar; Peter Connolly, C.Ss.R., Prov.; Larry Sanders, C.Ss.R., Co-Dir. - Office of Financial Svcs.; Bro. Tom Wright, C.Ss.R., Co-Dir. - Office of Financial Servs.

Legal Titles: *The Redemptorists of Denver, Colorado - The Redemptorists of Greeley, Colorado, Inc.,* Denver, CO; *Redemptorist Fathers (Boise, ID),* Denver, CO; *Redemptorists Society of Oregon (Portland, OR),* Denver, CO; *The Society of the Redemptorists of the City Grand Rapids, Michigan,* Denver, CO; *The Redemptorists of Nebraska (Omaha, NE),* Denver, CO; *The Society of the Redemptorist Fathers (Detroit, MI),* Denver, CO; *The Redemptorist Fathers of Hennepin County (St.Paul-Minneapolis, MN),* Denver, CO; *Redemptorist Fathers (St. Louis, MO),* Denver, CO; *The Redemptorist Fathers of Kansas City, Missouri, The Redemptorists of Blessed Sacrament - The Redemptorist Fathers of Chicago (Chicago, IL),* Denver, CO; *Redemptorist Society of Alaska (Anchorage, AK),* Denver, CO; *The Redemptorist Society of Arizona (Tucson, AZ),* Denver, CO; *The Redemptorists Society of Washington, Palisades Retreat Association, A School of Christian Living (Seattle, WA),* Denver, CO; *The Redemptorist Community of Wichita, Kansas, Inc., Society of the Redemptorist Fathers of Wichita, Kansas,* Denver, CO.

Properties owned, sponsored or staffed: Parishes 15; Retreat Houses 5; Residences 9; Community Houses 29.

Represented in the Archdioceses of Chicago, Denver, Detroit, Los Angeles, Milwaukee, Omaha, St. Louis, St. Paul-Minneapolis, and Seattle and the Dioceses of Dodge City, Grand Rapids, Kansas City-St. Joseph, Oakland Tucson and Wichita. Also in Foreign Missions.

Bangkok Vice-Province: *Redemptorists,* 42 M004 Ramkhamhaeng Rd. Soi 184, Minburi, Bangkok, 10510, Thailand. Very Rev. Chuchart Srivichairatana, C.Ss.R., Vice Prov.

Manaus Vice-Province: *Redentoristas,* Caixa Postal 217, 69011-970 Manaus, Amazonas, Brazil, South America. Very Rev. Manuel Scares, C.Ss.R., Vice Prov.; Region of Nigeria: Redeemer House, P.O. Box 29585, Secretariat, Bodija, Ibadan, Oyo State Nigeria. Rev. William Peterson, Reg. Supr.

The Redemptorist New Orleans Vice-Province: *Redemptorist Fathers and Brothers,* 5354 Plank Rd.-P.O. Box 53900, Baton Rouge, LA 70892-3900. Tel: 504-355-2600; Fax: 504-355-6200. Very Rev. Thomas D. Picton, C.Ss.R., Vice Prov.; Revs. Richard Luberti, C.Ss.R., Local Supr.; Samuel Maranto, C.Ss.R.; Richard Luberti, C.Ss.R., Joseph Steffes, C.Ss.R.; Eugene E. Staub C.Ss.R.; John C. Vargas, C.Ss.R., (Redemptorist Generalate -Rome); Bro. Steven E. Fruge, C.Ss.R., Vice Prov.-Sec.; Clement Fumo, C.Ss.R.

Priests 39; Brothers 7; Professed Students 4.

Properties owned, staffed or sponsored: Parishes 6; Residences.

Represented in the Archdioceses of New Orleans, and San Antonio and the Dioceses of Baton Rouge, Biloxi, Corpus Christi, Galveston-Houston and Lafayette (LA).

[1080] (C.R.)— CONGREGATION OF THE RESURRECTION

(Congregatio a Resurrectione Domini Nostri Jesu Christi)

Generalate: Via San Sebastianello 11 00187, Rome, Italy. Very Rev. Sutherland MacDonald, C.R., Supr. Gen.

U.S. of America Province: 7050 N. Oakley Ave., Chicago, IL 60645. Tel: 773-465-8320. Very Rev. John H. Nowak, C.R., Prov. Supr.; Councilors: Revs. Michael Danek, C.R.; Dennis Sanders, C.R.; Eugene Szarek, C.R.; Manuel Williams, C.R.

Ministries in Parishes; Missions; High School; Retreat House; Chaplaincies.

Fathers 66; Brothers 5.

Represented in the Archdioceses of Chicago, Mobile and St. Louis and in the Dioceses of Kalamazoo, Pensacola-Tallahassee, Rockford and San Bernardino. Also in Bermuda.

Ontario Kentucky Province U.S. Address: *St. Cecilia House,* 515-D South Shelby St., Louisville, KY 40202-3609. Tel: 502-589-6113; Fax: 502-502-589-6116. Deacon Brian Karley, C.R., Supr.; Revs. Lory A. Keasey, C.R.; Timothy Unioc, C.R.; Councilors: Revs. Robert Liddy, C.R.; Jerome Kroetsch, C.R.; Jim Link, C.R.; Bro. D. Taylor, C.R., Bursar.

Properties owned, sponsored or staffed: Parishes 5; Community Houses 3; University 1.

Represented in the Archdiocese of Louisville.

[1090] (R.C.J.)—ROGATIONIST FATHERS

(Congregatio Rogationis-a-Corde-Jesu)

Generalate: *via Tuscolana 167 00182,* Rome, Italy. Very Rev. George Nalin, R.C.J., Supr. Gen.

U.S.A. Delegation: 2688 S. Newmark Ave., Box 37, Sanger, CA 93657. Tel: 559-875-5808; 875-2025; Fax: 559-875-1281. Rev. Antonio Carlucci, R.C.J., Delegation Supr.

U.S. Foundations: *St. Mary's Church,* 828 O St., P.O. Box 335, Sanger, CA 93657. Tel: 559-875-2025. Revs. Salvatore Ciranni, R.C.J.; Philip Puntrello, R.C.J.; Vito DiMarzio, R.C.J.

Legal Title: *Congregation of Rogationists, Inc.*

Ministries in Parishes; Vocation Center; Formation House; Social Service Center.

Priests 7.

Represented in the Archdiocese of Los Angeles and in the Diocese of Fresno.

[1100] (S.C.)—BROTHERS OF THE SACRED HEART

(Societas Fratrum Sacris Cordis)

Founded in Lyons, France in 1821. First foundation in the United States in Mobile in 1847.

Generalate: *Piazza Sacro Cuore,* No. 3, Rome, Italy 00151. Bro. Bernard Couvillion, S.C., Supr. Gen. Provinces.

New Orleans Province (1847): *Provincial Office,* 4540 Elysian Fields Ave., New Orleans, LA 70122. Tel: 504-282-5693; Fax: 504-288-9920. Bro. Ivy LeBlanc, S.C., Prov.; Prov. Councilors: Bros. Ronald Hingle, S.C.; Ronald Talbot, S.C.; Francis David, S.C.; Xavier Werneth, S.C.; Donnan Berry, S.C., Treas.

Legal Titles: *Brothers of the Sacred Heart, (a Louisiana Corporation); Brothers of the Sacred Heart Foundation of the New Orleans Province, Inc.*

Perpetual Professed 61; Temporary Professed 1; Ordained Brothers 5; Information 1.

Incorporated Schools: Brother Martin High School, New Orleans, LA; Catholic High School, Baton Rouge, LA; Saint Stanislaus College, Bay St. Louis, MS.

Represented in the Archdioceses of Mobile, and New Orleans and the Dioceses of Baton Rouge, Biloxi, Gallup and Houma-Thibodaux.

New England Province (1945): *Provincial House - Brothers of the Sacred Heart,* 685 Steere Farm Rd., Pascoag, RI 02859-4601. Tel: 401-568-3361; Fax: 401-568-9810. Bro. Raymond Reinsant, S.C., Prov. Supr.; Councilors: Bros. Robert Croteau, S.C.; Mark E. Hilton, S.C.; Raymond A. Hetu, S.C.; Donald O. Tardif, S.C.; Louis Laperle, S.C., Prov. Sec.; Robert T. Gagne, Accts. Mgr.

Brothers 82.

Properties owned: *Brothers of the Sacred Heart Provincial House,* Pascoag, RI; *Mt. St. Charles Academy,* Woonsocket, RI; *Bishop Guertin High School,* Nashua, NH; *St. John Residence,* Woonsocket, RI; *Brothers of the Sacred Heart Residence,* Nashua, NH.

Represented in the Archdiocese of Hartford and in the Dioceses of Manchester and Providence. Also in England, Lesotho, Zambia, Zimbabwe and Uganda, Kenya.

Province of New York (1960): *Brothers of the Sacred Heart Provincial House,* 141-11 123 Ave., South Ozone Park, NY 11436-1426. Tel: 718-322-3309; Fax: 718-529-6004. Bro. Joseph Holthaus, S.C., Prov.

Ministries in the field of Education; Spiritual Centers; Kenya Missions.

Final Professed Brothers 40; Temporary 1.

Properties owned: *Sacred Heart Center,* Belvidere, NJ; *Msgr. McClancy High School,* East Elmhurst, NY; *St.Joseph High School,* Metuchen, NJ.

Represented in the Dioceses of Brooklyn, Metuchen and Rockville Center. Also in Kenya.

[1110] (M.S.C.)—MISSIONARIES OF THE SACRED HEART

(Societas Missionarii Sacratissimi Cordis Jesu)

General Motherhouse: *Via Asmara 11 00199,* Rome, Italy. Very Rev. Michael Curran, M.S.C., Supr. Gen.

United States Province (1939): P.O. Box 270, 305 S. Lake St., Aurora, IL 60507. Tel: 630-892-8400; 892-2371; Fax: 630-892-3071. Very Rev. David Foxen, M.S.C., Prov. Supr.; Consultors: Revs. Raymond Diesbourg, M.S.C., Vice Prov.; Michael Camilli, M.S.C.; Stephen Boland, M.S.C.; Joseph Jablonski, M.S.C.; Ronald Larkin, M.S.C.

Legal Title: *Society of the Missionaries of the Sacred Heart.*

Fathers 67; Brothers 22; Foreign Missionaries 18; Professed Students 9.

Properties owned, staffed or sponsored: Renewal Centers 1; Residential Houses 6; Parishes 12; Chaplaincies 2; Foreign Missions 2.

Represented in the Archdioceses of Chicago, Philadelphia, and Washington and the Dioceses of Allentown, Ogdensburg, Rockford, San Bernardino, and Youngstown. Also in Colombia, Papua New Guinea.

U.S. Section of the Irish Province for California and Southern States: *Sectional Headquarters,* 123 W. Laurel, San Antonio, TX 78212-2916. Tel: 210-226-5514; Fax: 210-226-5725. Rev. James Dudley, M.S.C.; Pat McGlanaghy, M.S.C.

Priests 20.

Represented in the Archdioceses of Los Angeles and San Antonio and in the Dioceses of Beaumont, Charleston, Corpus Christi, Dallas San Angelo and Tyler.

[1120] (M.SS.CC.)—MISSIONARIES OF THE SACRED HEARTS OF JESUS AND MARY

(Missionarii a Sacris Cordibus Jesus et Mariae)

Founded in Italy in 1833.

General Motherhouse: Via dei Falegnami 23, Rome, Italy. Very Rev. Luigi Toscano, M.SS.CC., Supr. Gen.

American Headquarters: 2249 Shore Rd., Linwood, NJ 08221. Tel: 609-927-5600; Fax: 609-927-5262. Revs. Malcolm MacLeod, M.SS.CC., Reg. Supr.; Robert McDade, M.SS.CC., Vice-Rector & Mission Procurator.

Legal Title: *Missionaries of the Sacred Heart of Jesus and Mary.*

Priests 10; Brothers 2.

Represented in the Dioceses of Camden and Harrisburg.

[1130] (S.C.J.)—CONGREGATION OF THE PRIESTS OF THE SACRED HEART

(Priests of the Sacred Heart)

(Congregatio Sacerdotum a Corde Jesu)

General Motherhouse: *Curia Generalizia, S.C.J.,* Via Casale S. Pio v, no. 20 00165, Rome, Italy. Very Rev. Virginio Domingo Bressanelli, S.C.J., Supr. Gen.

United States Province (1933): *Provincialate Offices,* P.O. Box 289, Hales Corners, WI 53130-0289. Tel: 414-425-6910. Very Rev. Richard MacDonald, S.C.J., Prov. Supr.

Bishops 2; Priests 89; Clerics 4; Brothers 20.

Represented in the Archdioceses of Chicago, Milwaukee, and San Antonio and the Dioceses of Brownsville, Galveston-Houston, Green Bay, Jackson, Rapid City, St. Petersburg and Sioux Falls.

[1140] (SS.CC.)—CONGREGATION OF THE SACRED HEARTS OF JESUS AND MARY

(Congregatio Sacrorum Cordium)

General Motherhouse: *Casa Generalizia-Padri Dei Sacri Cuori-via,* Rivarone 85 00166, Rome, Italy. Very Rev. Enrique Losada, SS.CC., Supr. Gen.

Legal Title: *Congregation of the Sacred Hearts of Jesus and Mary.*

Eastern Province (1946): *Provincial House,* Box 111, Fairhaven, MA 02719-0111. Tel: 508-993-2442; Fax: 508-996-5499. Revs. David P. Reid, SS.CC., Prov.; William Heffron, SS.CC., Vicar Prov.; Councilors: Robert Charlton, SS.CC.; Stanley Kolasa, SS.CC.; Alphonsus McHugh, SS.CC.

Priests 57; Brothers 5; Seminarians 8; Novices 4.

Properties owned or staffed: Parishes 6; Community Houses 3; House of Studies 1.

Represented in the Archdiocese of Washington and in the Dioceses of Brownsville, Fall River and Las Cruces.

Western United States Province (1970): *Congregation of the Sacred Hearts of Jesus and Mary,* 2150 Damien Ave., La Verne, CA 91750. Tel: 909-593-5441; Fax: 909-593-3971. Very Rev. Michael W. Barry, SS.CC., Prov.

Ministries in the field of Religious and Academic Education; Parishes; Chaplaincies.

Priests 21; Brothers 1.

Represented in the Archdiocese of Los Angeles and in the Dioceses of Oakland, Orange and San Bernardino.

Hawaii Province: *Sacred Hearts Center,* Box 1365, Kaneohe, Oahu, HI 96744. Tel: 808-247-5035; Fax: 808-235-8849. Very Rev. Clarence Guerreiro, SS.CC., Prov.

Fathers 27; Brothers 10.

Properties owned, staffed or sponsored: Churches 10; Mission 1; Chaplaincies 2.

[1144] (L.B.S.F.)—LITTLE BROTHERS OF SAINT FRANCIS

Founded in the United States in 1970 by Bro. James Curran, L.B.S.F.

Regional Fraternity and Novitiate (1970): 785-789 Parker St., Roxbury, MA 02120. Tel: 617-442-2556.

Legal Title: *Little Brothers of Saint Francis - Franciscan Fraternity of Peace and Love, Inc.*

Professed Brothers 4; Novices 2; Postulants 3.

Represented in the Archdiocese of Boston.

[1150] (C.S.J.)—CONGREGATION OF ST. JOSEPH

(Congregatio Sancti Joseph)

Founded in Turin, Italy in 1873. First foundation in United States in 1951.

General Motherhouse: Via Belvedere Montello 77 00166, Rome, Italy. Very Rev. Luigi Pierini, C.S.J., Supr. Gen.

U.S. and Mexico Vice Province: *St. Leonard* House 4076 Case Rd., Avon, OH 44011. Tel: 440-934-6270. Rev. Franco Zago, C.S.J., Prov. Supr.

Priests 25; Scholastics 2.

Properties owned, staffed or sponsored: Parishes 5; High Schools 1; Youth Retreat Center.

Properties owned: *St. Leonard House,* Avon, OH.

Represented in the Archdiocese of Los Angeles and in the Diocese of Cleveland. Also in Mexico.

[1160] (F.S.P.)—BROTHERS OF ST. PATRICK

(Patrician Brothers)

Founded in Ireland 1808 by Bishop Daniel Delaney.

U.S. Foundation (1948): *St. Patrick's Novitiate,* 7820 Bolsa Ave., Midway City, CA 92655. Tel: 714-897-8181; Fax: 714-898-9020. Bro. Aquinas Cassin, F.S.P., Prov.

Brothers 8.

Represented in the Archdiocese of Los Angeles and Diocese of Orange.

[1170] (S.P.S.)—ST. PATRICK'S MISSIONARY SOCIETY

(St. Patrick Fathers)

Founded March 17, 1932 with the approval of Pope Pius XI. A Pontifical Society of secular priests devoted entirely to the missionary needs of the Church.

International Headquarters: St. Patrick's, Kiltegan, Wicklow, Ireland. Very Rev. Seamus O'Neill, S.P.S., Supr. Gen.; Rev. John Marren, S.P.S., Vicar Gen.; Rev. James Bermingham, S.P.S., Proc. Gen.-Rome; Rev. Stephen Donohue, S.P.S., Supr. for North America.

Total number of Priests 375; Priests in the U.S. 14.

U.S. Foundations (1965): *St. Patrick's (1967),* 19536 Eric Dr., Saratoga, CA 95070. Tel: 408-253-3135; Fax: 408-253-5433. Rev. Stephen Donohue, S.P.S., U.S. Supr.; Rev. Michael Morris, S.P.S., Supr.; St. Patrick's (1965), 70 Edgewater Rd., Box 3080, Cliffside Park, NJ 07010. Tel: 201-943-6575; Fax: 201-943-2946. Rev. Karl Langsdorf, S.P.S., Supr.; St. Patrick's (1968), 1347 W. Granville Ave., Chicago, IL 60660. Tel: 773-973-3737. Tel: 773-973-6049.

Legal Title: *St. Patrick Missionary Society,* Camden, NJ.

Represented in the Archdioceses of Chicago, and Newark and the Dioceses of Paterson, San Bernardino and San Jose.

[1180] (C.S.P.X.)—BROTHERS OF SAINT PIUS X

Founded in the United States in 1952.

Motherhouse: P.O. Box 217, DeSoto, WI 54624. Tel: 608-648-2087. Bro. Charles Bisenius, Dir.

Ministries in the field of Religious and Academic Education; Health Care; Community Services and Administration.

Represented in the Diocese of La Crosse.

[1190] (S.D.B.)—SALESIANS OF DON BOSCO

(Societas Sancti Francisci Salesii)

Generalate: *Salesian D. Bosco,* via Della Pisana, 1111, C.P.00163, Roma-Aurelio, Italy. Very Rev. Pascual Chavezi, S.D.B., Rector Major.

Province of St. Philip the Apostle (1902): 148 Main St., New Rochelle, NY 10802. Tel: 914-636-4225. Very Rev. James Heuser, S.D.B., Prov.; Revs. Timothy Ploch, S.D.B., Dir.-Social Communication; Bro. Thomas Dion, S.D.B., Prov. Economer & Councilor; Revs. William Keane, S.D.B., Vice Prov.; Steven Shafran, S.D.B., Dir. of Formation & Councilor; Steven Ryan, S.D.B., Dir. of Youth Ministry & Councilor.

Legal Title: *Salesian Society, Inc.,* New Rochelle, NY.

Ministries in: Parishes; High Schools; Boys Clubs; Camps.

Fathers 152; Professed Clerics 10; Students in Major Seminaries 2; Coadjutor-Brothers 26.

Represented in the Archdioceses of Boston, Chicago, Miami, Newark, New Orleans, New York, and Washington and the Dioceses of Birmingham, Columbus, Palm Beach, Passaic, Paterson, St. Petersburg and Scranton. Also in Canada.

San Francisco Province (1926): *Salesian Society - San Francisco,* 1100 Franklin St., San Francisco, CA 94109. Tel: 415-441-7144; Fax: 415-441-7155. Very Rev. David T. Purdy, S.D.B., Prov.; Revs. John Itzaina, S.D.B., Vice Prov.; Councilors: Richard Presenti, S.D.B., Treas.; Ted Montemayor, S.D.B; Mel Trinidad, S.D.B.

Ministries in Parishes; High Schools; Retreat House; Youth Centers.

Fathers 80; Professed Clerics 9; Professed Brothers 25; Seminarians 3.

Represented in the Archdioceses of Los Angeles, and San Francisco and the Dioceses of Laredo, Monterey, Oakland, San Diego, Santa Rosa and Stockton. Also in Sierra Leone.

[1200] (S.D.S.)—SOCIETY OF THE DIVINE SAVIOR

(Salvatorian Fathers and Brothers)

(Salvatorians - Societas Divini Salvatoris)

General Headquarters: *Curia Generalizia dei Salvatoriani,* Via della Conciliazione 51, I- 00193, Rome, Italy. Very Rev. Andrew Urbanski, S.D.S., Supr. Gen.

U.S.A. Province (1896): *Salvatorian Provincial Offices,* 1735 N. Hi-Mount Blvd., Milwaukee, WI 53208-1720. Tel: 414-258-1735; Fax: 414-258-1934. Very Rev. Peter Schuessler, S.D.S., Prov.; Revs. Joseph Rodrigues, S.D.S., Vicar; John Gorman, S.D.S., Dir. Personnel; Bro. Sean McLaughlin, S.D.S., Consultor; Revs. Keith Brennan, S.D.S., Consultor; David Bergner, S.D.S., Consultor.

Legal Titles: *Society of the Divine Savior; Society of the Divine Savior Ongoing Community Support Trust; Camp St. Charles, Inc.; Fund Raising and Public Relations Center; Salvatorian Center,* New Holstein, WI 53061.

Fathers 80; Brothers 38; Clerics 3.

Properties owned, staffed or sponsored: Parishes 27; Houses of Study and Formation 2.

Represented in the Archdioceses of Baltimore, Milwaukee, New York, Portland, and Washington and the Dioceses of Camden, Birmingham, Bismarck, Gallup, Green Bay, Harrisburg, LaCrosse, Madison, Nashville, Oakland, Orlando, Phoenix, Richmond, Sacramento, Savannah, St. Cloud, Tucson, Venice, Wheeling-Charleston and Wilmington.

[1210] (C.S.)—MISSIONARIES OF ST. CHARLES-SCALABRINIANS

(Congregatio Missionariorum A Sancto Carolo)

General Motherhouse: Via Calandrelli 42, 00153, Rome, Italy. Very Rev. Isaia Birollo, C.S., Supr. Gen.

Province of St. Charles Borromeo (1888): *Scalabrinians Provincial Curia,* 27 Carmine St., New York, NY 10014. Tel: 212-675-3993; Fax: 212-727-2866. Very Rev. Sergio Dall'Agnese, C.S., Prov. Supr.; Revs., Matthew Didone, C.S., Vicar & 1st Councilor; Walter Tonelotto, C.S., 2nd Councilor; Maurizio Pontin, C.S., 3rd Councilor; Horecio C. Anklan, C.S., 4th Councilor & Sec.; Joseph Fugolo, C.S., Treas.

Legal Title: *The Pious Society of the Missionaries of St. Charles Borromeo, Inc.*

Fathers 97; Brothers 3.

Properties staffed or owned: Parishes 30; Missions 7; Homes for Aged 2; Seminaries 4; Center for Migration Studies.

Represented in the Archdioceses of Boston, Hartford, Newark, New York, and Washington and the Dioceses of Brooklyn, Buffalo, Palm Beach, Providence and Venice. Also in Eastern Canada, Venezuela, Colombia, the Dominican Republic and Haiti.

Province of St. John Baptist (1903): *Missionaries of St. Charles - Fathers of St. Charles,* 546 N. East Ave., Oak Park, IL 60302. Tel: 708-386-4430; Fax: 708-386-4457. Very Rev. Antonio Tapparello, C.S., Prov.Supr.

Legal Titles: *The Fathers of Saint Charles; Scalabrinian Community Support Corp.; Scalabrinian Community Formation Corp.*

Ministries in 20 Parishes; 2 Homes for the Aged; 3 Missions; 5 Seminaries; 5 Centers for Migrants and Refugees; 2 Diocesan office for Hispanic Ministry.

Fathers 67; Brothers 5.

Represented in the Archdioceses of Chicago, Cincinnati and Los Angeles and in the Dioceses of Galveston-Houston, Kansas City-St. Joseph, San Diego and San Jose. Also in Canada, Guatemala and Mexico.

[1220] (S.C.)—SERVANTS OF CHARITY

(Guanellians)

(Congregatio Servorum a Charitate)

General Motherhouse: Vicolo Clementi 41, Rome, Italy. Very Rev. Nino Minetti, Supr. Gen.

U.S. Headquarters: *Servants of Charity,* 1795 S. Sproul Rd., Springfield, PA 19064. Tel: 610-328-3406; Fax: 610-328-1019. Rev. Battista Omodei, S.C., Supr. USA Province.

Legal Titles: *Pious Union of St. Joseph.*

Publication: *Now and At the Hour.*

Ministry for the suffering and dying: Schools for mentally handicapped boys 2; Residences for mentally handicapped adults 2; Parishes 1; House of Formation 1; Group Home 1; Chaplaincies 1.

Priests 8; Brothers 1; Theologian 1.

Represented in the Archdiocese of Philadelphia and in the Dioceses of Lansing and Providence.

[1230] (s.P.)—SERVANTS OF THE PARACLETE

Generalate, *St. Michael's Community,* 13270 Maple Dr., St. Louis, MO 63127. Tel: 314-965-0860; Fax: 314-965-7202. Web site: www.theservants.org. Very Rev. Peter Lechner, s.P., Servant Gen.; Revs. Paul Valley, s.P., Vicar Gen.; Benedict Livingstone, s.P., Treas. Gen.; Liam Hoare, s.P., Asst. for the Apostolate; Philip Taylor, s.P., Sec. Gen.

Represented in the Archdioceses of Baltimore, St. Louis and Santa Fe.

U.S. Motherhouse (1952): *Villa Louis Martin,* P.O. Box 10, Jemez Springs, NM 87025-0010. Tel: 505-829-3586; Fax: 505-829-3706. E-mail: paul@theservants .org. Rev. Paul Valley, s.P.

[1240] (O.S.M.)— SERVITES

(Order of Friar Servants of Mary)

(Ordo Fratrum Servorum Beatae Virginis Mariae)

Generalate: *Curia Generalizia dei Servi di Maria,* Piazza San Marcello al Corso, 5 00187, Rome, Italy.

Servite Friars (1999): *United States of America Province,* 3121 W. Jackson Blvd., Chicago, IL 60612-2729. Tel: 773-533-0360; Fax: 773-533-8307. Very Rev. Anthony M. O'Connell, O.S.M., Prior Prov.; Revs. Paul M. Novak, O.S.M., Asst. Prov.; James M. Dore, O.S.M.,

Prov. Councilor; John M. Fontana, O.S.M., Prov. Councilor; Luke M. Stano, O.S.M., Prov. Councilor; Bros. Edmund M. Baran, O.S.M., Prov. Treas; Michael M. Callary, O.S.M., Prov./Corporate Sec. & Province Mission Procurator; Martin M. Doherty, O.S.M., Prov. Sacristan; Joel A. Lechner, O.S.M., Pres.-Servite High School; Revs. Robert M. Anderson, O.S.M., Dir.-St. Peregrine Ministry; Conrad M. Borntrager, O.S.M., Archivist & Historian; Paul M. Gins, O.S.M., Vocation Dir.; Christopher M. Krymski, O.S.M., Dir.-St. Peregrine Ministry in Chicago; Philip M. McGlynn, O.S.M., Prov. Devel. Dir.; Vidal M. Martinez, O.S.M., Prov. Asst.-Servite Secular Order; John Topper, O.S.M., Dir.-Sanctuary of Our Sorrowful Mother; Robert M. Warsey, O.S.M., Dir.-Marian Center.

Legal Titles: *The Order of Friar Servants of Mary-U.S.A. Province, Inc.,* Chicago IL; *Retirement Plan of the Order of Friar Servants of Mary-U.S.A.,* Chicago IL; *Charitable Trust of the Order of Friar Servants of Mary-U.S.A. Province, Inc.,* Chicago, IL. *The Servite Fathers, A California Corporation; Sanctuary of Our Sorrowful Mother, Inc.,* Portland, OR.

Priests 88; Professed Brothers 14; Temporary Professed Friars 2.

Parishes 8; High Schools 1; Shrines 1; Residences 16; Chaplaincies 2.

Represented in the Archdioceses of Chicago, Denver, Los Angeles, Portland (OR), St. Louis, and Santa Fe and the Dioceses of El Paso, Oakland, Orange, Orlando, Orange, Springfield-Cape Girardeau and Phoenix. Also in Germany, Australia and South Africa.

[1250] (C.R.S.)—SOMASCAN FATHERS

(Clericorum Regularium Somaschensium)
(Order of St. Jerome Aemilian)

General Motherhouse: *Via Casal Morena,* 8 00040, Morena - Rome, Italy. Most Rev. Bruno Luppi, C.R.S., Ph.D., Father Gen.

U.S. Foundation: *Pine Haven Boys Center,* 133 River Rd.- P.O. 162, Suncook, NH 03275. Tel: 603-485-7141. Rev. Julian Gerosa, C.R.S., Supr.

Priests 9.

Represented in the Dioceses of Galveston-Houston and Manchester.

[1260] (S.Ch.)—SOCIETY OF CHRIST

(Societas Christi Pro Emigrantibus Polonis)

General Motherhouse: 60-962 Poznan Ulica Panny Marii 4, Poland. Very Rev. Tadeusz Winnicki, S.Ch., Supr. Gen. Rev. Marian Burniak, Procurator Gen.; Via Botteghe Oscure 15 00186, Rome, Italy.

American-Canadian Province: *Provincial Residence,* 3000 Eighteen Mile Rd., Sterling Heights, MI 48314. Tel: 586-939-5022. Very Rev. Andrzej Maslejak, S.Ch., Prov.; Revs. Pawel Bandurski, S.Ch., Vice-Prov.; Stanislaw Hajkowski, S.Ch., Treas.

Priests 55.

Represented in the Archdioceses of Atlanta, Baltimore, Chicago, Detroit, Los Angeles, Miami, Milwaukee, New York, Portland (OR), St. Paul-Minneapolis, San Francisco, Seattle, and Washington and the Dioceses of Dallas, Galveston-Houston, Joliet, Phoenix, San Diego, San Jose and Toledo. Also in Canada.

[1270] (F.M.S.I.)—SONS OF MARY MISSIONARY SOCIETY

(Sons of Mary, Health of the Sick)
(Filii Mariae Salutis Infirmorum)

General Headquarters: 567 Salem End Rd., Framingham, MA 01702-5599. Tel: 508-879-2541; Fax: 508-879-7667. Web site: www.sonsofmary.com. Rev. John Murphy, F.M.S.I., Major Coord.; Bro. Kevin Courtney, F.M.S.I., Financial Coord.; Rev. John Coss, F.M.S.I., Councilor.

Professed 12.

Represented in the Archdiocese of Boston. Also in the Philippines.

[1280] (C.S.S.)—STIGMATINE FATHERS AND BROTHERS

(Congregation of the Sacred Stigmata)

General Motherhouse: Via Mazzarino No. 16, Rome, Italy. Very Rev. Andrea Meschi, C.S.S., Supr. Gen.; Revs. Antonio Picciarillo, C.S.S., Vicar Gen.; Joao Carlos Seneme, C.S.S., Sec. to the Gen.

North American Province (1940): 554 Lexington St., Waltham, MA 02452. Tel: 781-209-3100; Fax: 781-894-9785. Very Rev. Gregory J. Hoppough, C.S.S., Prov. Supr.

Legal Title: *Stigmatine Fathers & Brother, Inc.*

Priests 27; Brothers 1; Temporary Professed 1.

Properties owned, staffed or sponsored: Parishes 6; Retreat & Conference Center.

Represented in the Archdioceses of Boston and New York and in the Dioceses of Springfield (MA) and Worcester.

[1290] (S.S.)—SOCIETY OF THE PRIESTS OF SAINT SULPICE

(Societas Presbyterorum a S. Sulpitio)

General Motherhouse: 6 rue du Regard, Paris 75006, France. Very Rev. Lawrence B. Terrien, S.S., Supr. Gen.

U.S. Provincial House: 5408 Roland Ave., Baltimore, MD 21210. Tel: 301-323-5070; Fax: 410-433-6524. Very Rev. Ronald D. Witherup, S.S., Prov.; Mr Joseph M. Reynolds, Exec. Asst. to Prov.; Rev. Gerald D. McBrearity, S.S., Dir.-Formation and Personnel; Thomas R. Ulshafer, S.S., Prov. Sec. & Dir. Discernment & Admissions; Rev. Michael L. Barre, S.S., Prov. Treas.

Legal Title: *The Associated Sulpicians of the United States.*

Fathers 69.

Represented in the Archdioceses of Baltimore, San Antonio, San Francisco, and Washington and in the Diocese of San Jose.

[1300] (C.R.)—THEATINE FATHERS

(Congregatio Clericorum Regularium)

General Motherhouse: *Sant'Andrea della Valle,* Piazza Vidoni, 6 00186, Rome, Italy. Most Rev. Gabriele Darida, C.R., Supr. Gen.

U.S. Headquarters: 1050 S. Birch St., Denver, CO 80222. Tel: 303-756-5522. Very Rev. Patrick Valdez, C.R.

Fathers 17; Clerics 5.

Parishes 9; House of Formation 1; Provincial House 1.

Represented in the Archdioceses of Denver and New York and in the Diocese of Pueblo.

[1310] (O.SS.T.)—ORDER OF THE MOST HOLY TRINITY

(Holy Trinity Fathers, Inc.)
(Ordo Sanctissimae Trinitatis; The Trinitarians)

Founded in France in 1198 by St. John De Matha for the ransom of Christian slaves. First settlement in the United States in 1911.

General Curia: Via Massimi, 114C 00136, Rome, Italy. Most Rev. Jose Hernandez Sanchez, Minister Gen.

U.S.A. Province (1950): *Province of the Immaculate Heart of Mary,* P.O. Box 5742 - 8400 Park Heights Ave., Baltimore, MD 21282-0742. Tel: 410-486-5171. Very Rev. Thomas J. Burke, O.SS.T., Minister Prov.; Revs. William J. Moorman, O.SS.T., Vicar Prov.; Councilors: Juan Antonio Perez, O.SS.T.; John L. Dorn, O.SS.T.; Stanley DeBoer, O.SS.T.; Bro. Richard G. Wildgen, O.SS.T., Prov. Sec.; Rev. Kurt Klismet, O.SS.T., Prov. Treas.

Ministries in 12 parishes; Seminary Facility Positions; High Schools; Prison Chaplaincies; Hospital Chaplaincies; India Foundation; Mission for Persecuted Christians.

Trinitarian Communities in the U.S. 14; Fathers 53; Brothers 9.

Properties owned: *DeMatha Catholic High School,* Hyattsville, MD; *Holy Trinity Monastery,* Pikesville, MD; *Trinity House,* Victoria, TX; *Trinitarian Residence,* Ellicott, MD; *Trinitarian Residence,* Adelphi, MD.

Represented in the Archdioceses of Baltimore, Los Angeles, New Orleans, Philadelphia, New York, and Washington and the Dioceses of Corpus Christi, Dallas, Newton, Trenton and Victoria. Also in India.

[1320] (C.S.V.)—CLERICS OF ST. VIATOR

(Congregatio Clericorum Sancti Viatoris)

General Motherhouse: Via Padre Angelo Paoli, 41, Rome, Italy. Casella Postale 10793 00144, Roma, Italia. Very Rev. Mark R. Francis, C.S.V., Supr. Gen.

Province of Chicago (1882): *Viatorians,* 1212 East Euclid St., Arlington Heights, IL 60004. Tel: 847-398-1354. Very Rev. Charles G. Bolser, C.S.V., Prov.; Revs. Thomas R. von Behren, C.S.V., Asst. Prov.; Robert E. Erickson, C.S.V., Prov. Treas. & Councilor; John E. Linnan, C.S.V., Councilor; Daniel T. Nolan, C.S.V., Councilor.

Fathers 75; Brothers 19.

Properties owned, staffed or sponsored: Parishes 15; High Schools 3; Formation Houses 2.

Represented in the Archdioceses of Chicago, and Kansas City in Kansas and the Dioceses of Joliet, Little Rock, Manchester, Monterey, Oakland, Peoria, Las Vegas, Rockford, San Diego, San Jose, Springfield (IL) and Tucson. Also in Belize, Colombia and Italy.

[1330] (C.M.)—CONGREGATION OF THE MISSION

(Vincentians)
(Congregatio Missionis Sti. Vincentii a Paulo)

Founded in France in 1625. First foundation in the United States in 1818.

General Motherhouse: *Curia Generalizia,* Via dei Capasso, 30 00164, Roma, Italia. Very Rev. Robert P. Maloney, C.M., Supr. Gen.; Rev. Elmer Bauer, III, C.M., Econome Gen.

Eastern Province of the U.S.A. (1888): *St. Vincent's Seminary,* 500 E. Chelten Ave., Philadelphia, PA 19144. Tel: 215-848-1985; Fax: 215-844-2085. Very Rev. Thomas F. McKenna, C.M., Prov.; Revs. Charles P. Strollo, C.M., Asst. Prov.; Stephen M. Grozio, C.M., Prov. Treas.; Jerry J. McGovern, Corp. Treas. Consultors: John Kettelberger, C.M.; Michael J. Carroll, C.M.; Patrick J. Griffin, C.M.; Charles T. Plock, C.M.

Legal Title: *Congregation of the Mission of St. Vincent de Paul in Germantown, Inc.*

Fathers 156; Brothers 11; Students in Major Seminaries 8; College Seminarians 10.

Properties owned, sponsored or staffed: Parishes 15; Missions in Republic of Panama 9; Universities 2; Major Seminary Residences 2; Novitiates 2; Retreat Houses 2.

Represented in the Archdioceses of Baltimore, Los Angeles, New York, Mobile, Philadelphia, and Washington and the Dioceses of Albany, Allentown, Birmingham, Brooklyn, Buffalo, Charleston, Charlotte, Galveston-Houston, Grand Rapids, Manchester, Metuchen, Portland, Rockville Centre and St. Augustine.

Midwest Province - Vincentians (1888): 13663 Rider Trail N., Earth City, MO 63045-1512. Tel: 314-344-1184; Fax: 314-344-2989. Very Rev. James E. Swift, C.M., Prov.; Revs. Raymond A. VanDorpe, C.M., Asst. Prov.; Joseph C. Geders, C.M., Prov. Treas.

Legal Title: *Motherhouse St. Mary's Seminary,* Perryville, MO.

Priests 109; Brothers 17.

Serving in 17 (arch)dioceses; Universities; Foreign Mission Stations; Houses of Apostolic Activity.

Represented in the Archdioceses of Chicago, Denver, San Francisco, and St.Louis and the Dioceses of Austin, Belleville, Colorado Springs, Evansville, Jefferson City, Kansas City-St. Joseph, Little Rock, Pueblo and Springfield-Cape Girardeau. Also in Marsabit and Nairobi, Kenya.

The New England Province of the Vincentian Fathers (1975): *DePaul Vincentian Provincial Residence,* 234 Keeney Street, Manchester, CT 06040-7048. Tel: 860-643-2828; Fax: 860-533-9462. Very Rev. John S. Sledziona, C.M., Prov.

Legal Titles: *New England Province of the Congregation of the Mission, Inc.; Charitable Trust of the New England Province of the Congregation of the Mission.*

Fathers 30; Brothers 2.

Represented in the Archdiocese of Hartford and the Dioceses of Brooklyn, Manchester and Portland (ME).

American Italian Branch (Naples, Italy) (1922): *Our Lady of Pompei Church,* 3600 Claremont St., Baltimore, MD 21224. Tel: 410-675-7790. Rev. Luigi Esposito, C.M., Supr.

Legal Title: *Vincentian Fathers of the Neapolitan Province of Maryland Charities, Inc.*

Fathers 3.

Represented in the Archdiocese of Baltimore.

American Spanish Branch (Zaragoza, Spain) (1926): *Holy Agony Church,* 1834 3rd Ave., New York, NY 10029. Tel: 212-289-5589; Fax: 212-289-8321. Revs. Victor Elia, C.M.; Candido Arrizurieta, C.M.; Venancio Goyeneche, C.M.

Legal Title: *Padres Paules Community-Vincentians Inc.*

Fathers 7.

Represented in the Archdioceses of Los Angeles and New York.

(Vincentian) Province of the West (1975): 420 Date St., Montebello, CA 90640. Tel: 323-721-5486; Fax: 323-721-5499. Very Rev. Andrew E. Bellisario, C.M., Prov.

Legal Titles: *Congregation of the Mission in California, A Corporation; Vincentian Foreign Mission Society; DePaul Center Corp. (Formerly St. Vincent's Seminary Corp.); Vincentians Province of the West Support Trust Fund.*

Fathers 43; Brothers 4; Permanent Deacons 1.

Members serve and staff, 3 Parishes, 2 Home Mission Parishes, 1 Seminarians, 2 evangelization centers and 8 community houses.

Properties owned: *DePaul Center,* Montebello, CA; *St. Mary's Seminary,* Santa Barbara, CA; *Amat House,* Los Angeles, CA; 2 Residences in California.

Represented in the Archdiocese of Chicago, Los Angeles, and Milwaukee and the Dioceses of Gallup, Phoenix, San Jose and Little Rock.

The Congregation of the Mission Southern Province (1975): 3826 Gilbert Ave., Dallas, TX 75219 4346. Tel: 214-526-0234; Fax: 214-526-3477. Very Rev. Dan Paul Borlik, C.M., Prov.; Rev. Miles Heinen, C.M., Treas.

Priests 23; Brothers 1.

Properties owned, sponsored or staffed: Parishes 6; Community Houses 5.

Represented in the Archdioceses of New Orleans, and San Antonio and the Dioceses of Alexandria, Dallas, Gallup and Little Rock.

[1335] (V.C.)—VINCENTIAN CONGREGATION
(Vincentians)

Founded by Rev. Fr. Varkey Kattarath at Thottakom, Kerala, India in 1904.

Generalate: *Vincentian Generalate,* P.B. No. 2250 - Edappally Kochi 682 024, Kerala, India. Very Rev. Antony Plackal, V.C., Supr. Gen.

St. Joseph Province: *Vincentian Provincial House,* S.H. Mouont P.O. 686 006, Kottayam, Kerala, India. Tel: 481-563-559. Very Rev. George Arackal, V.C., Prov. Supr.

North American Headquarters: *Vincentian House,* P.O. Box 252, Emery, SD 57332-0252. Revs. Joseph Thalanany, V.C., Reg. Coord.; Joseph J. Arackal, V.C., Mission Procurator.

Fathers 5.

Represented in the Archdiocese of St. Paul-Minneapolis and in the Dioceses of Sioux Falls, St. Cloud and Trenton.

[1340] (S.D.V.)—VOCATIONIST FATHERS
(The Society of Divine Vocations)

Generali: Via Cortina D'Ampezzo, 138 00135, Rome, Italy. Tel: 011 39 06 331-2758; Fax: 011 39-06-337-3685. Very Rev. Louis Caputo, S.D.V., Supr. Gen.

American Headquarters: 90 Brooklake Rd., Florham Park, NJ 07932. Tel: 973-966-6262; Fax: 973-593-8381. Rev. Michael M. Reardon, S.D.V., Delegate of Supr. Gen.

U.S. Foundations: *Our Lady of Perpetual Help Center,* 90 Broad St., Newark, NJ 07932. Tel: 973-966-6262; Fax: 973-593-8381. Revs. Mario Muccitelli, S.D.V.; Armando Palmieri, S.D.V.; Robert Vass, S.D.V.; Ugo Fraraccio, S.D.V.; James Butts, S.D.V.

Represented in the Archdiocese of Newark and in the Diocese of Paterson.

[1350] (C.F.X.)—BROTHERS OF ST. FRANCIS XAVIER
(Congregatio Fratrum Xaverianorum)

Generalate - Xaverian Brothers: 4409 Frederick Ave., Baltimore, MD 21229. Tel: 410-644-0034; Fax: 410-644-2762. Bros. Arthur Caliman, C.F.X., Supr. Gen.; Edward Driscoll, C.F.X., Vicar; Lawrence Harvey, C.F.X., Dir. Xaverian Sponsored Schools; John Fox, C.F.X., Assoc. Xaverian Sponsored Schools; Michael J. McCarthy, C.F.X., Dir.-Personnel; Richard Massa, C.F.X., Dir.-Pastoral Care; Mr. Michael Naccarato, Chief Fin. Officer; Mr. Leonard Doran, Devel. Dir.

Legal Titles: *Xaverian Brothers USA Inc.; American Northeastern Province of the Xaverian Brothers Inc.; Isidore Charitable Trust.*

Ministries in the field of: Religious and Academic Education at all levels; Diocesan Offices; Pastoral Ministry; Mission Schools; Communities; Houses and House of Formation.

Brothers 247.

Represented in the Archdioceses of Baltimore, Boston, Chicago, Los Angeles, Louisville, Milwaukee, Newark, New York, Santa Fe, and Washington and the Dioceses of Arlington, Birmingham, Brooklyn, Charleston, Fairbanks, Memphis, Norwich, Richmond, Rapid City, Venice, Wilmington and Worcester. Also in Bolivia, Belgium, Canada, Congo, England, Haiti, Kenya, Lithuania and Uganda.

[1360] (S.X.)—XAVERIAN MISSIONARY FATHERS
(Saint Francis Xavier Foreign Mission Society)
(Pia Societas Sancti Francisci Xaverii pro Exteris Missionibus)

General Motherhouse: *Istituto Saveriano Missioni Estere,* Viale Vaticano 40 00165, Rome, Italy. Very Rev. Rino Benzoni, S.X., Supr. Gen.

U.S. Province: *Xaverian Missionary Fathers,* 12 Helene Ct., Wayne, NJ 07470. Tel: 973-942-2975; Fax: 973-942-5012. Very Rev. Ivan Marchesin, S.X., Prov.

Fathers 23; Seminarians 10.

Mission Houses 2; Houses of Formation 2.

Represented in the Archdioceses of Boston, Chicago and Milwaukee and in the Diocese of Paterson.

Index for Religious Institutes of Women

(The initial D or P indicates Diocesan or Pontifical Jurisdiction.)

Religious Order Initials for Women

A.B.S.	Auxiliaries of the Blessed Sacrament	[]
A.C.J.	Handmaids of the Sacred Heart of Jesus	[1870]
A.D.	Sisters of the Lamb of God	[2260]
A.I.M.	Association of Mary Immaculate	[]
A.N.G.	A New Genesis	[]
A.P.	Nuns of Perpetual Adoration of Blessed Sacrament	[3190]
A.P.B.	Adorers of the Precious Blood	[0110]
A.P.G.	Sisters of Perpetual Adoration	[3195]
A.R.	Handmaids of the Sacred Heart of Jesus for Reparation	[1880]
A.R.	Augustinian Recollects	[]
A.S.C.	Adorers of the Blood of Christ	[0100]
A.S.C.J.	Apostles of the Sacred Heart of Jesus	[0130]
B.C.	Notre Dame du Bon Conseil (Quebec)	[]
Bethl.	Bethlemita Daughters of the Sacred Heart of Jesus	[0910]
B.V.M.	Sisters of Charity of Blessed Virgin Mary	[0430]
B.V.M.C.	Blessed Virgin Missionaries of Carmel	[]
C.ach.	Carmeilte Sisters of Charity	[0340]
Carmel.D.C.J.	Carmelite Sisters of the Divine Heart of Jesus	[0360]
C.B.S.	Congregation of Bon Secours	[0270]
C.C.	Carmel Community	[0310]
C.C.V.I.	Sisters of Charity of Incarnate Word	[0460]
C.C.V.I.	Sisters of Charity of Incarnate Word (Houston, TX)	[0470]
C.C.W.	Carmeiite Community of the Word	[0315]
C.D.P.	Sisters of Divine Providence	[0990]
C.D.P.	Sisters of Divine Providence of Kentucky	[1000]
C.D.P.	Sisters of Divine Providence of San Antonio, TX	[1010]
C.D.P.	Capuchin Sisters (Spain)	[]
C.D.S.	Congregation of Divine Spirit	[1040]
C.F.M.M.	Minim Daughters of Mary Immaculate	[2675]
C.F.P.	Feminine Congregation of the Passion	[]
C.F.P.	Mexican Passionist Sisters	[]
C.G.S.	Contemplatives of Good Shepherd	[1830]
C.H.F.	Sisters of Holy Faith	[1940]
C H.M.	Congregation of Humility of Mary	[2100]
C.H.S.	Community of the Holy Spirit	[2020]
C.I.C.	Sisters of Immaculate Conception	[2120]
C.I.J.	Congregation of Infant Jesus	[2230]
C.J.C.	Poor Sisters of Jesus Crucified and Sorrowful Mother	[3240]
C.K.	School Sisters of Christ the King	[]
C.L.H.C.	Congregation of Our Lady Help of the Clergy	[3090]
C.M.C.	Congregation of Mother of Carmel	[]
C.M.R.	Congregation of Mary Queen	[]
C.M.S.	Comboni Missionary Sisters	[0690]
C.M.S.	Cashel Mercy Sisters	[2515]
C.M.S.T.	Missionary Carmelites of St. Teresa	[0390]
C.N.D.	Congregation of Notre Dame	[2980]
C.O.C.	Companions of Christ	[]
C.P.	Religious of the Passion of Jesus Christ	[3170]
C.P.	Sisters of the Cross and Passion	[3180]
C.P.C.	Capuchin Poor Clares	[]
C.P.C.	St. Clare Capuchin Sisters	[]
C.P.P.S.	Sisters of the Precious Blood Dayton, Ohio	[3260]
C.P.P.S.	Sisters of the Most Precious Blood, (O'Fallon, MO)	[3270]
C.P.S.	Missionary Sisters of the Precious Blood	[2850]
C.R.	Sisters of the Resurrection	[3480]
C.S.	Company of the Savior	[0710]
C.S.	The Christian Sisters (Pious Union)	[]
C.S.A.	Sisters of Charity of St. Augustine	[0580]
C.S.A.	Sisters of St. Agnes	[3710]
C.S.A.	Albertine Sisters (Krakow, Poland)	[]
C.S.A.C.	Sisters of the Catholic Apostolate (Pallottine)	[3140]
C.S.B.	Congregation of St. Brigid	[3735]
C.S.C.	Congregation of Sisters of Holy Cross	[1920]
C.S.C.	Sisters of Holy Cross	[1930]
C.S.C.	Sisters of Holy Cross and Seven Dolors	[]
C.S.E.	Carmelite Sisters of the Eucharist	[]
C.S.F.N.	Sisters of Holy Family of Nazareth	[1970]
C.S.J.	Sisters of St. Joseph (Boston, Brighton)	[3830-01]
C.S.J.	Sisters of St. Joseph (Chicago, Lagrange Park)	[3830-02]
C.S.J.	Sisters of St. Joseph (Orange)	[3830-03]
C.S.J.	Sisters of St. Joseph (Rockville Centre, Brentwood)	[3830-05]
C.S.J.	Sisters of St. Joseph (Cleveland)	[3830-08]
C.S.J.	Sisters of St. Joseph (Tipton, IN)	[3830-10]
C.S.J.	Sisters of St. Joseph (Pittsburgh, Baden)	[3830-13]
C.S.J.	Sisters of St. Joseph (Salina, Concordia)	[3830-15]
C.S.J.	Sisters of St. Joseph (Wichita)	[3830-18]
C.S.J.	Sisters of St. Joseph of Carondelet	[3840]
C.S.J.	Sisters of St. Joseph of Chambery	[3850]
C.S.J.	Sisters of St. Joseph (Lyons, France)	[3870]
C.S.J.	Sisters of St. Joseph of Medaille	[3880]
C.S.JB.	Sisters of St. John the Baptist	[3820]
C.S.J.P.	Sisters of St. Joseph of Peace	[3890]
C.S.M.	Sisters of St. Martha of Antigonish N.S	[3937]
C.S.N.	Congregation of Sisters of Nazareth	[]
C.S.R.	Sisters of Holy Redeemer	[2000]
C.S.S.F.	Felician Sisters	[1170]
C.S.Sp.	Sisters of Holy Spirit	[2030]
C.S.S.T.	Carmelite Sisters of St. Teresa	[]
C.S.T.	Carmelite Sisters of St. Therese of Infant Jesus	[0380]
C.V.D.	Sisters of Bethany	[0250]
C.V.I.	Congregation of Incarnate Word and Blessed Sacrament	[2190]
C.V.I.	Religious of the Incarnate Word	[3449]
D.C.	Daughters of Charity of St. Vincent de Paul	[0760]
D.C.	Daughters of the Cross	[0770]
D.C.M.	Diocesan Carmelites of Maine	[]
D.C.P.B.	Daughters of Charity of Most Precious Blood	[0740]
D.H.M.	Daughters of Heart of Mary	[0810]
D.H.S.	Daughters of the Holy Spirit	[0820]
D.L.F.	Daughters of Our Lady of Fatima	[]
D.L.J.C.	Disciples of the Lord Jesus Christ	[0965]
D.M.	Daughters of Mary of the Immaculate Conception	[0860]
D.M.	Daughters of Our Lady of Mercy	[0890]
D.M.I.	Daughters of Mary Immaculate (Chaldean)	[]
D.M.J.	Daughters of Mary and Joseph	[0880]
D.O.M.	Daughters of Mercy (Croatian)	[]
D.S.F.	Daughters of St. Francis of Assisi	[0920]
D.S.M.P.	Daughters of St. Mary of Providence	[0940]
D.W.	Daughters of Wisdom	[0960]
E.F.M.S.	Eucharistic Franciscan Missionary Sisters	[1150]
E.M.S.	Eucharistic Missionary Society	[]
F.A.S.	Franciscan Apostolic Sisters	[]
F.C.	Daughters of the Cross of Liege	[0780]
F.C.J.	Society of Sisters Faithful Companions of Jesus	[4048]
F.C.S.C.J.	Daughters of Charity of the Sacred Heart of Jesus	[0750]
F.D.C.	Daughters of Divine Charity	[0790]
Fd.CC.	Canossian Daughters of Charity	[0730]
F.D.L.P.	Daughters of Providence	[]
F.D.N.S.C.	Daughters of Our Lady of the Sacred Heart	[0900]
F.D.P.	Daughters of Divine Providence	[0800]
F.D.Z.	Daughters of Divine Zeal	[0795]
F.H.I.C.	Franciscan Hospitaller Sisters of the Immaculate Conception	[1270]
F.H.M.	Franciscan Handmaids of the Most Pure Heart of Mary	[1260]
F.H.M.	Franciscan Sisters Daughters of Mercy	[1235]
F.J.	Congregation of the Daughters of Jesus	[0830]
F.L.G.	Franciscan Sisters of Our Lady of Grace	[]
F.M.A.	Daughters of Mary Help of Christians	[0850]
F.M.D.C.	Franciscan Missionaries of the Divine Child	[1340]
F.M.I.	Congregation of the Daughters of Mary Immaculate (Marianist Sisters)	[0870]
F.M.I.	Franciscan Sisters of Mary Immaculate of the Third Order of St. Francis of Assisi	[1500]
F.M.I.J.	Franciscan Missionaries of the Infant Jesus	[1365]
F.M.M.	The Franciscan Missionaries of Mary	[1370]
F.M.S.A.	Franciscan Missionary Sisters for Africa	[1320]
F.M.S.C.	Franciscan Missionary Sisters of the Sacred Heart	[1400]
F.M.S.J.	Mill Hill Sisters	[1410]
F.M.S.R.	Daughters of Our Lady of Holy Rosary	[]
F.N.S.S.C.	Franciscan Sisters of Our Lady of the Sacred Heart	[]
F.S.E.	The Institute of the Franciscan Sisters of the Eucharist	[1250]
F.S.J.	Religious Daughters of St. Joseph	[0930]
F.S.M.	Franciscan Sisters of Mary	[1415]
F.S.O.L.	Franciscan Sisters of Our Lady	[]
F.S.P.	Pious Society Daughters of St. Paul	[0950]
F.S.P.	Franciscan Sisters of Peace	[1425]
F.S.P.A.	Congregation of the Sisters of the Third Order of St. Francis of Perpetual Adoration	[1780]
F.S.R.	Franciscan Sisters of Ringwood	[1420]
F.S.S.C.	Franciscan Sisters of St. Clare (Pious Union)	[]
F.S.S.E.	Franciscan Sisters of St. Elizabeth	[1460]
F.S.S.J.	Franciscan Sisters of St. Joseph	[1470]
F S.S.M.	Franciscan Sisters of the Sorrowful Mother	[]
F.S.Sp.J.	Franciscan Sisters of the Spirit of Jesus	[]
G.H.M.S.	Home Mission Sisters of America (Glenmary)	[2080]
G.N.S.H.	Grey Nuns of the Sacred Heart	[1840]
H.B.S.	Hermanas Contemplativas del Buen Pastor	[]
H.C.G.	Hermanas Catequistas Guadalupanas	[1900]
H.F.deS.J.	Franciscan Sisters of St. Joseph (Mexico City)	[]
H.F.S.J.	Franciscan Sisters of St. Joseph	[1480]

H.G.S.	Congregation de Hermanas Guadalupanas de la Salle	[]
H.H.C.J.	Congregation of the Handmaids of the Holy Child Jesus	[1855]
H.H.S.	Society of Helpers	[1890]
H.J.	Hermanas Josefinas	[1910]
H.J.D.	Las Hermanas de Juan Diego	[]
H.M.	Sisters of the Humility of Mary	[2110]
H.M.C.	Hermits of Mount Carmel	[]
H.M.S.S.	Mercedarian Sisters of the Blessed Sacrament	[2590]
H.M.S.S.	Religious Sisters of the Apostolate of the Blessed Sacrament	[3370]
H.O.Carm.	Hermits of Our Lady of Mt. Carmel	[]
H.P.B.	Congregation of the Handmaids of the Precious Blood	[1860]
H.R.F.	Sisters of the Holy Rosary of Fatima (Mexico)	[]
H.S.H.	Handmaids of the Sacred Heart of Pohang	[]
H.S.M.	Hermit Sisters of Mary	[]
H.Sp.S.	Daughters of the Holy Spirit Nazareth of the Good Shepherd	[]
H.S.S.	Hermanas del Servicio Social	[]
H.S.S.R.	Hermit Sisters of Romuald	[]
H.T.	Handmaids of the Most Holy Trinity	[]
H.V.M.	Sisters, Home Visitors of Mary	[2090]
I.B.V.M.	Institute of the Blessed Virgin Mary (Loretto Sisters)	[2370]
I.B.V.M.	Institute of the Blessed Virgin Mary (Loretto Sisters)	[2380]
I.C.	Vietnamese Sisters Incarnational Consecration	[]
I.C.M.	Incarnatio-Consecratio-Missio	[2187]
I.C.M.	Missionary Sisters of the Immaculate Heart of Mary	[2750]
I.H.M.	Sisters of the Immaculate Heart of Mary at Mirinae	[2182]
I.H.M.	Sisters Servants of the Immaculate Heart of Mary	[2150]
I.H.M.	Sisters Servants of the Immaculate Heart of Mary	[2160]
I.H.M.	Sisters Servants of the Immaculate Heart of Mary	[2170]
I.H.M.	Sisters Servants of the Immaculate Heart of Mary	[2180]
I.H.M.	The California Institute of the Sisters of the Most Holy and Immaculate Heart of the Blessed Virgin Mary	[2930]
I.H.M.	Sisters of the Immaculate Heart of Mary of Wichita	[2185]
I.J.	Sisters of the Infant Jesus	[2240]
I.M.	Sisters of Charity of the Infant Mary	[]
I.S.S.M.	Secular Institute of Schoenstatt Sisters of Mary	[]
I.W.B.S.	Congregation of the Incarnate Word and Blessed Sacrament	[2200]
I.W.B.S.	Congregation of the Incarnate Word and Blessed Sacrament	[2205]
J.S.O.P.	Dominican Oblates of Jesus (Spain)	[]
L.B.	Ladies of Bethany	[]
L.C.M.	Sisters of the Little Company of Mary	[2270]
L.H.C.	Lovers of the Holy Cross Sisters	[2390]
L.H.C.	Lovers of the Holy Cross Sisters	[2392]
L.M.S.C.	Little Missionary Sisters of Charity	[2290]
L.S.	Lasallian Sisters (Vietnam)	[]
L.S.A.	Little Sisters of the Assumption	[2310]
L.S.G.	Little Sisters of the Gospel (France)	[]
L.S.I.C.	Little Servant Sisters of the Immaculate Conception	[2300]
L.S.J.	Little Sisters of Jesus	[2330]
L.S.J.M.	Little Sisters of Jesus and Mary	[2331]
L.S.P.	Little Sisters of the Poor	[2340]
M.C.	Consolata Missionary Sisters	[0720]
M.C.	Missionaries of Charity	[2710]
M.C.	Poor Clare Missionary Sisters	[2840]
M.C.D.P.	Missionary Catechists of Divine Providence, San Antonio, TX	[2690]
M.C.M.	Cordi Marian Sisters	[]
M.C.P.	Missioneras Catequestas de los Pobres	[]
M.C.S.	Missionary Sisters of the Sacred Side	[]
M.C.S.J.M.	Congregation of Missionary Catechists of the Sacred Heart of Jesus and Mary	[]
M.D.	Mothers of the Helpless	[]
M.D.P.V.M.	Missionary Daughters of the Most Pure Virgin Mary	[]
M.E.	Missionary Ecumenical (Rome)	[]
M.C.SS.CC.J.M.	Missionary Catechists of the Sacred Hearts of Jesus and Mary	[2700]
M.E.S.S.T.	Eucharistic Missionaries of the Most Holy Trinity	[]
M.E.S.T.	Eucharistic Missionaries of St. Theresa (Mexico)	[]
M.F.P.	Franciscan Missionaries Our Lady of Peace	[]
M.G.Sp.S.	Guadalupan Missionaries of the Holy Spirit	[1845]
M.H.S.	Sisters of the Most Holy Sacrament	[2940]
M.H.S.H.	Mission Helpers of the Sacred Heart	[2720]
M.I.C.	Missionary Sisters of the Immaculate Conception (Canada)	[]
M.J.	Missionary Sisters of Jesus	[]
M.J.M.J.	Missionaries of Jesus, Mary and Joseph	[2770]
M.M.	Maryknoll Sisters of St. Dominic	[2470]
M.M.B.	Mercedarian Missionaries of Berriz	[2510]
M.M.D.	Servite Missionary Sisters of the Sorrowful Mother	[]
M.M.M.	Medical Missionaries of Mary	[2480]
M.M.S.	Medical Mission Sisters	[2490]
M.O.M.	Missionary Sisters of Our Lady of Mercy	[2830]
M.P.F.	Religious Teachers Filippini	[3430]
M.P.H.	Missionary Sisters of Our Lady of Perpetual Help	[]
M.P.S.	Misioneras del Perpetual Socorro	[]
M.P.S.	Missionary Sisters of Our Lady of Perpetual Help	[]
M.P.V.	Religious Venerini Sisters	[4180]
M.R.	Marianist Sisters	[]
M.S.	Marian Sisters of the Diocese of Lincoln	[2400]
M.S.B.T.	Missionary Servants of the Most Blessed Trinity	[2790]
M.S.C.	Congregation of the Marianites of the Holy Cross	[2410]
M.S.C.	Missionary Sisters of the Most Sacred Heart of Jesus of Hiltrup	[2800]
M.S.C.	Missionary Sisters of the Sacred Heart	[2860]
M.S.C.Gpe.	Missionaries of the Sacred Heart of Jesus and of Our Lady of Guadalupe	[2865]
M.S.C.K.	Missionary Sisters of Christ the King	[2715]
M.S.F.	Missionary Sisters of the Holy Family	[]
M.S.H.F.	Missionary Sisters of the Holy Family (Poland)	[]
M.S.H.R.	Missionary Sisters of the Holy Rosary	[2730]
M.S.J.	Medical Sisters of St. Joseph	[2500]
M.S.K.C.P.	Missionary Sisters of Christ the King of Polonia	[]
M.S.M.G.	Missionary Sisters of Mother of God	[2810]
M.S.O.L.A.	Missionary Sisters of Our Lady of Africa	[2820]
M.S.S.A.	Missionary Servants of St. Anthony	[2890]
M.S.S.C.B.	Missionary Sisters of St. Charles Borromeo	[2900]
M.S.S.J.	Missionary Servants of St. Joseph (Spain)	[]
M.S.Sp.	Mission Sisters of the Holy Spirit	[2740]
M.SS.S.	Missionary Sisters of the Most Blessed Sacrament	[2780]
M.T.G.	Adorers of the Holy Cross	[4155]
M.X.Y.	The Yarumal Foreign Mission Institute (Colombia)	[]
N.A.U.-O.L.C.	North American Unions of Sisters of Our Lady of Charity	[3070]
N.D.	Notre Dame Sisters	[2960]
N.D.S.	Congregation of Notre Dame de Sion	[2950]
O.A.R.	Augustinian Recollect Sisters	[]
O.B.T.	Sisters Oblates to the Blessed Trinity	[3020]
O.C.A.	Carmelite Vietnamese of Our Lady of Mt. Carmel	[]
O.Carm.	Calced Carmelites	[0300]
O.Carm.	Carmelite Nuns of the Ancient Observance	[0320]
O.Carm.	Carmelite Sisters for Aged and Infirm	[0330]
O.Carm.	Carmelite Sisters (Corpus Christi)	[0350]
O.Carm.	Congregation of Our Lady of Mt. Carmel	[0400]
O.Carm.	Institute of the Sisters of Our Lady of Mt. Carmel	[0410]
O.C.D.	Carmelite Sisters of the Most Sacred Heart of Los Angeles	[0370]
O.C.D.	Discalced Carmelite Nuns	[0420]
O.C.D.	Carmelitas del Sagrado Corazon	[]
O.Cist.	Cistercian Nuns	[0680]
O.C.S.O.	Cistercian Nuns of the Strict Observance	[0670]
O.D.N.	Company of Mary	[0700]
O.L.C.	Sisters of Our Lady of Charity	[3071]
O.L.C.	Sisters of Our Lady of Charity	[3073]
O.L.G.	Sisters of Our Lady of the Garden	[]
O.L.L.	Sisters of Our Lady of Lourdes	[]
O.L.M.	Sisters of Charity of Our Lady of Mercy	[0510]
O.L.S.	Sisters of Our Lady of Sorrows	[3120]
O.L.V.M.	Our Lady of Victory Missionary Sisters	[3130]
O.M.M.I.	Oblate Missionaries of Mary Immaculate	[]
O.M.O.	Oblates of the Mother of Orphans	[3035]
O.P.	Dominican Contemplative Nuns (Cloistered)	[1050]
O.P.	Dominican Contemplative Sisters (Cloistered)	[1060]
O.P.	Dominican Sisters (St. Catharine, KY)	[1070-01]
O.P.	Dominican Sisters (Columbus, OH)	[1070-02]
O.P.	Dominican Sisters (Sinsinawa, WI)	[1070-03]
O.P.	Dominican Sisters (San Rafael, CA)	[1070-04]
O.P.	Dominican Sisters (Amityville, NY)	[1070-05]
O.P.	Dominican Sisters (Newburgh, NY)	[1070-06]
O.P.	Dominican Sisters (Nashville, TN)	[1070-07]
O.P.	Dominican Sisters (New Orleans, LA)	[1070-08]
O.P.	Dominican Sisters (Racine, WI)	[1070-09]
O.P.	Dominican Sisters (Springfield, IL)	[1070-10]
O.P.	Dominican Sisters (Sparkill, NY)	[1070-11]
O.P.	Dominican Sisters (San Jose, CA)	[1070-12]
O.P.	Dominican Sisters (Adrian, MI)	[1070-13]
O.P.	Dominican Sisters (Grand Rapids, MI)	[1070-14]
O.P.	Dominican Sisters (Blauvelt, NY)	[1070-15]
O.P.	Dominican Sisters (Ossining, NY)	[1070-16]
O.P.	Dominican Sisters (Elkins Park, PA)	[1070-17]
O.P.	Dominican Sisters (Caldwell, PA)	[1070-18]

O.P. Dominican Sisters (Houston, TX) [1070-19]
O.P. Dominican Sisters (Tacoma, WA) [1070-20]
O.P. Dominican Sisters (Edmonds, WA) [1070-21]
O.P. Dominican Sisters (Fall River, MA) [1070-22]
O.P. Dominican Sisters (Hawthorne, NY) [1070-23]
O.P. Dominican Sisters (Great Bend, KS) [1070-24]
O P. Dominican Sisters (Kenosha, WI) [1070-25]
O.P. Dominican Sisters (Oxford, MI) [1070-26]
O.P. Dominican Sisters (Justice, IL) [1070-27]
O.P. Dominican Sisters (Akron, OH) [1070-28]
O.P. Dominican Sisters (Spokane, WA) [1070-29]
O.P. Dominican Sisters (Oxford, South Africa) [1070-30]
O.P. Marian Society of Dominican Catechists [1090]
O.P. Dominican Sisters of Charity of the Presentation of the Blessed Virgin [1100]
O.P. Dominican Sisters of Our Lady of the Rosary and of Saint Catherine of Siena, Cabra [1110]
O.P. Dominican Sisters of the Roman Congregation [1120]
O.P. Dominican Rural Missionaries [1130]
O.P. Eucharistic Missionaries of St. Dominic [1140]
O.P. Dominican Sisters of Carondelet []
O.P. Religious Missionaries of St. Dominic (Spanish Prov.) []
O.P. Dominican Sisters of Mt. Thabor []
O.P. Dominican Sisters of Our Lady of the Most Holy Rosary []
O.P. Dominican Sisters (Vietnam) []
O.P. Dominican Contemplative Sisters []
O.P. Dominican Sisters (Colombia) []
O.P. Dominican Sisters (Ecuador) []
O.P. Hermanas Dominicanas de la Doctrine Cristiana []
O.S.A. Augustinian Nuns of Contemplative Life [0160]
O.S.A. Congregation of Augustinian Sisters Servants of Jesus and Mary [2145]
O.S.A. Sisters of St. Rita [4010]
O.S.A. Sisters of St. Augustine []
O.S.A. Augustinian Sisters of Our Lady of Consolation []
O.S.B. Benedictine Nuns of the Congregation of Solesmes [0170]
O.S.B. Benedictine Nuns of the Primitive Observance [0180]
O.S.B. Benedictine Sisters [0190]
O.S.B. Benedictine Sisters [0200]
O.S.B. Missionary Benedictine Sisters [0210]
O.S.B. Congregation of the Benedictine Sisters of Perpetual Adoration of Pontifical Jurisdiction [0220]
O.S.B. Benedictine Sisters of Pontifical Jurisdiction [0230]
O.S.B. Benedictine Nuns [0233]
O.S.B. Olivetan Benedictine Sisters [0240]
O.S.B. Congregation of Jesus Crucified [2250]
O.S.B. Benedictine Congregation of Our Lady of Monte []
O.S.B. Benedictine Sisters of Sacred Heart []
O.S.B. Contemplative Sisters of St. Benedict []
O.S.B. Benedictine Sisters of Liberty []
O.S.B. Congregation of the Benedictine Sisters of the Sacred Heart []
O.S.B.Cam. Camaldolese Benedictine Sisters []
O.S.B.M. Sisters of the Order of St. Basil the Great [3730]
O.S.B.S. Oblate Sisters of the Blessed Sacrament [3010]
O.S.C. Order of St. Clare [3760]
O.S.C.Cap. Capuchin Poor Clares [3765]
O.S.F. Franciscan Sisters of Allegany New York [1180]
O.S.F. The Franciscan Sisters of Baltimore [1200]
O.S.F. Franciscan Sisters of Chicago [1210]
O.S.F. Franciscan Sisters of Christian Charity [1230]
O.S.F. Franciscan Sister, Daughters of the Sacred Hearts of Jesus and Mary [1240]
O.S.F. Franciscan Sisters of the Immaculate Conception [1280]
O.S.F. Franciscan Sisters of the Immaculate Conception and St. Joseph for the Dying [1300]
O S.F. Franciscan Sisters of Little Falls, Minnesota [1310]
O.S.F. Franciscan Missionary Sisters of the Immaculate Conception [1350]
O.S.F. Missionary Franciscan Sisters of the Immaculate Conception [1360]
O.S.F. Franciscan Missionaries of Our Lady [1380]
O.S.F. Franciscan Missionary Sisters of Our Lady of Sorrows [1390]
O.S.F. Franciscan Sisters of Our Lady of Perpetual Help [1430]
O.S.F. Franciscan Sisters of the Sacred Heart [1450]
O.S.F. Franciscan Sisters of St. Paul [1485]
O.S.F. Sisters of the Third Franciscan Order [1490]
O.S.F. St. Francis Mission Community [1505]
O.S.F. Sisters of St. Francis [1510]
O.S.F. Sisters of St. Francis of Christ the King [1520]
O.S.F. Sisters of St. Francis of the Congregation of Our Lady of Lourdes, Sylvania, Ohio [1530]
O.S.F. Sisters of Saint Francis, Clinton, Iowa [1540]
O.S.F. Sisters of St. Francis of the Holy Cross [1550]
O.S.F. Sisters of St. Francis of the Holy Eucharist [1560]
O.S.F. Sisters of St. Francis of the Holy Family [1570]
O.S.F. Sisters of St. Francis of the Immaculate Conception [1580]
O.S.F. Sisters of St. Francis of the Immaculate Heart of Mary (Hankinson, North Dakota) [1590]
O.S.F. Sisters of St. Francis of the Martyr St. George [1600]
O.S.F. Sisters of Saint Francis of Millvale, Pennsylvania [1620]
O.S.F. Sisters of St. Francis of Penance and Christian Charity [1630]
O.S.F. Sisters of St. Francis of Perpetual Adoration [1640]
O.S.F. The Sisters of St. Francis of Philadelphia [1650]
O.S.F. Sisters of Saint Francis of the Providence of God [1660]
O.S.F. Sisters of St. Francis of Savannah, MO [1670]
O.S.F. School Sisters of St. Francis [1680]
O.S.F. School Sisters of the Third Order of St. Francis (Pittsburgh, PA) [1690]
O.S.F. School Sisters of the Third Order of St. Francis (Panhandle, TX) [1695]
O.S.F. School Sisters of the Third Order of St. Francis (Bethlehem, PA) [1700]
O.S F. The Sisters of St. Francis of Assisi [1705]
O.S.F. Congregation of the Third Order of St. Francis of Mary Immaculate (Joliet, IL) [1710]
O.S.F. Sisters of the Third Order Regular of St. Francis of the Congregation of Our Lady of Lourdes [1720]
O.S.F. Congregation of the Sisters of the Third Order of St. Francis (Oldenburg, IN) [1730]
O.S.F. Sisters of the Third Order of St. Francis of Penance and Charity [1760]
O.S.F. Sisters of the Third Order of St. Francis (Peoria, IL) [1770]
O.S.F. Sisters of St. Francis of the Third Order Regular (Williamsville, New York) [1800]
O.S.F. Bernardine Sisters of the Third Order of St. Francis [1810]
O.S.F. Hospital Sisters of the Third Order of St. Francis [1820]
O.S.F. Servants of the Holy Infancy of Jesus [1980]
O.S.F. Consolation Sisters (Highland, CA) []
O.S.F. Franciscan Sisters of Christ the Divine Teacher []
O.S.F. St. Francis Mission Community []
O.S.F.S. Oblate Sisters of St. Francis de Sales [3060]
O.S.H.J. Oblate Sisters of the Sacred Heart of Jesus [3050]
O.S.M. Mantellate Sisters, Servants of Mary of Blue Island [3570]
O.S.M. Servants of Mary [3580]
O.S.M. Servants of Mary (Servite Sisters) [3590]
O.S.M. Oblates of St. Martha []
O.S.P. Oblate Sisters of Providence [3040]
O.S.S. Sacramentine Nuns [3490]
O.SS.R. Order of the Most Holy Redeemer [2010]
O.SS.R. Oblates of the Most Holy Redeemer [3030]
O.SS.S. The Brigittine Sisters [0280]
O.SS.T. Sisters of the Most Holy Trinity [0260]
O.S.U. Ursuline Nuns (Roman Union) [4110]
O.S.U. Ursuline Nuns of the Congregation of Paris (St. Martin, OH) [4120]
O.S.U. Ursuline Nuns of the Congregation of Paris (Cincinnati, OH) [4120-01]
O.S.U. Ursuline Nuns of the Congregation of Paris (Kansas City, KS) [4120-02]
O.S.U. Ursuline Nuns of the Congregation of Paris (Louisville, KY) [4120-03]
O.S.U. Ursuline Nuns of the Congregation of Paris (Cleveland, OH) [4120-04]
O.S.U. Ursuline Nuns of the Congregation of Paris (Owensboro, KY) [4120-05]
O.S.U. Ursuline Nuns of the Congregation of Paris (Toledo, OH) [4120-06]
O.S.U. Ursuline Nuns of the Congregation of Paris (Youngstown, OH) [4120-07]
O.S.U. Ursuline Sisters of the Congregation of Tildonk, Belgium [4130]
O.S.U. Ursuline Sisters of Belleville [4140]
O.S.U. Irish Ursuline Union [4150]
P.B.V.M. Presentation of the Blessed Virgin Mary Sisters [3280]
P.B.V.M. Sisters of the Presentation of the B.V.M. [3320]
P B.V.M. Union of the Sisters of the Presentation of the Blessed Virgin Mary [3330]
P.C.C. Order of St. Clare [3760]
P.C.I. Pax Christi Institute []
P.C.J. Sisters of the Poor Child Jesus [3220]
P.C.P.A. Poor Clares of Perpetual Adoration [3210]
P.D.D.M. Pious Disciples of the Divine Master [0980]
P.F.M. Franciscans of Mary [2280]
P.H.J.C. Poor Handmaids of Jesus Christ [3230]
P.M. Sisters of the Presentation of Mary [3310]
P.O.S.C. Little Workers of the Sacred Heart [2345]
P.S.N. Poor Sisters of Nazareth [3242]
P.S.S.F. The Little Sisters of the Holy Family [2320]
P.S.S.J. Poor Sisters of St. Joseph [3250]
P.V.M.I. The Parish Visitors of Mary Immaculate [3160]
Q.M.H.C. Quinhon Missionary Sisters of the Holy Cross []
R.A. Religious of the Apostolate of the Sacred Heart [3380]
R.A. Religious of the Assumption [3390]
R.A. Antonine Sisters []
R.A.D. Sisters of the Love of God []
R.C. Congregation of Our Lady of Retreat in the Cenacle [3110]
R.C.D. Sisters of Our Lady of Christian Doctrine [3080]
R.C.E. Religious of Christian Education [3410]
R.C.M. Sisters of the Immaculate Conception [2130]
R.C.S.C.J. Sisters of the Cross of the Sacred Heart of Jesus (Mexico) []
R.D.C. Sisters of the Divine Compassion [0970]
R.F. Sisters of St. Philip Neri Missionary Teachers []
R.F.R. Sisters of Our Lady of Refuge []
R.G.S. The Sisters of the Good Shepherd [1830]
R.H.S.J. Religious Hospitallers of Saint Joseph [3440]
R.J.M. Religious of Jesus and Mary [3450]
R.M. Marianitas []
R.M.I. Claretian Missionary Sisters [0685]

Initials	Order	Code
R.M.I.	Religious of Mary Immaculate	[3460]
R.M.M.	Mercedarian Sisters	[]
R.O.D.A.	Sisters Oblates to Divine Love	[]
R.O.L.C.	Our Lady of Charity of Refuge	[3072]
R.S.C.	Religious Sisters of Charity	[3400]
R.S.C.J.	Society of the Sacred Heart	[4070]
R.S.H.M.	Religious of the Sacred Heart of Mary	[3465]
R.S.J.	Religious of St. Joseph of Australia	[]
R.S.M.	Religious Sisters of Mercy of Alma, Michigan	[2519]
R.S.M.	Sisters of Mercy	[2520]
R.S.M.	Sisters of Mercy of Ardagh & Clonmacnois	[2523]
R.S.M.	Sisters of Mercy (Galway)	[2535]
R.S.M.	Sisters of Mercy	[2540]
R.S.M.	Sisters of Mercy (Sligo)	[2549]
R.S.M.	Sisters of Mercy	[2550]
R.S.M.	Sisters of Mercy of the Americas	[2575]
R.S.M.	Sisters of Mercy (Ballyshannon, Ireland)	[]
R.S.M.	Sisters of Mercy (Mayo, Ireland)	[]
R.S.M.	Sisters of Mercy of Mississippi, Inc.	[]
R.S.M.	Sisters of Mercy of Portland	[2655]
R.S.M.	Diocesan Sisters of Mercy	[]
R.S.R.	Congregation of Our Lady of the Holy Rosary	[3100]
R.T.	Theatine Sisters of the Immaculate Conception	[]
R.V.M.	Religious of the Blessed Virgin Mary	[]
S.A.	Franciscan Sisters of the Atonement	[1190]
S.A.A.	Sisters Auxillaries of the Apostolate	[0140]
S.A.B.	Sisters of St. Anne Bangalone	[]
S.A.C.	Sisters of the Guardian Angel	[1850]
S.A.C.	Pallottine Missionary Sisters Queen of Apostles Prov	[3150]
S.A.S.V.	Sisters of the Assumption	[0150]
S.B.S.	The Sisters of the Blessed Sacrament for Indians and Colored People	[0260]
S.C.	Sisters of Charity of Cincinnati, Ohio	[0440]
S.C.	Sisters of Charity of Seton Hill, Greensburg, PA	[0570]
S.C.	Sisters of St. Elizabeth, Convent Station	[0590]
S.C.	Sisters of Charity of St. Vincent de Paul, Halifax	[0640]
S.C.	Sisters of Charity of St. Vincent de Paul, New York	[0650]
S.C.C.	Sisters of Christian Charity	[0660]
Sch.P.	Sisters of the Pious Schools	[3200]
S.C.I.C.	Sisters of Charity of the Immaculate Conception of Ivrea	[0450]
S.C.I.M.	Servants of the Immaculate Heart of Mary	[3550]
S.C.K.	Sisters of Christ the King	[]
S.C.L.	Sisters of Charity of Leavenworth, Kansas	[0480]
S.C.M.C.	Sisters of Charity of Our Lady, Mother of the Church	[0530]
S.C.M.M.	Sisters of Charity of Our Lady Mother of Mercy	[0520]
S.C.M.M.	Medical Mission Sisters	[2490]
S.C.N.	Sisters of Charity of Nazareth	[0500]
S.C.O.	Sisters of Charity of Ottawa (Grey Nuns of the Cross)	[0540]
S.C.O.	Sisters of Charity of Quebec (Grey Nuns)	[0560]
S.C.R.H.	Sisters of Charity of Rolling Meadows	[]
S.C.S.J.A.	Sisters of Charity of St. Joan Antida	[0600]
S.C.S.L.	Sisters of Charity of St. Louis	[0620]
S.C.S.H.	Sisters of Charity of St. Hyacinthe (Grey Nuns)	[0610]
S.deP.	Sister Servants of the Poor	[]
S.D.R.	Sisters of the Divine Redeemer	[1020]
S.D.S.	Sisters of the Divine Saviour	[1030]
S.D.S.H.	Sisters of the Society Devoted to the Sacred Heart	[4050]
S.D.V.	Vocationist Sisters	[4210]
S.E.	Sisters of Emanuel	[]
S.E.C.	Sisters of the Eucharistic Covenant	[]
S.F.C.C.	Sisters for Christian Community	[]
S.F.M.A.	Franciscan Missionary Sisters of Assisi	[1330]
S.F.p.	Franciscan Sisters of the Poor	[1440]
S.G.M.	Sisters of Charity of Montreal (Grey Nuns)	[0490]
S.G.S.	Hermanas del Buen Pastor	[]
S.H.C.J.	Society of the Holy Child Jesus	[4060]
S.H.F.	Sisters of the Holy Family	[1960]
S.H.J.M.	Sisters of the Sacred Hearts of Jesus and Mary	[3680]
S.H.S.	Sisters of the Holy Spirit	[2040]
S.H.Sp.	Sisters of the Holy Spirit and Mary Immaculate	[2050]
S.I.M.	Missionaries of the Kingship of Christ	[]
S.I.W.	Sisters of the Incarnate Word and the Blessed Sacrament	[2210]
S.J.	Servants of Jesus	[3560]
S.J.A.	Sisters of Ste. Jeanne D'Arc	[3815]
S.J.B.	Sisters of St. John Bosco (Taylor, TX)	[]
S.J.C.	Sisters of St. Joseph of Cluny	[3860]
S.J.S.	Servants of the Blessed Sacrament	[3499]
S.J.S.M.	Sisters of St. Joseph of St. Mark	[3910]
S.J.W.	Sisters of St. Joseph the Worker	[3920]
S.L.	Sisters of Loretto at the Foot of the Cross	[2360]
S.L.T.	Pious Society of Our Lady of the Most Holy Trinity	[]
S.L.W.	Sisters of the Living Word	[2350]
S.M.	Marist Sisters Congregation of Mary	[2430]
S.M.	Sisters of Mercy	[2516]
S.M.	Sisters of Mercy	[2518]
S.M.	Sisters of Mercy	[2570]
S.M.	Sisters of Mercy (Cork and Ross)	[2600]
S.M.	Misericordia Sisters	[2680]
S.M.	Sisters Servants of Mary	[3600]
S.M.	Sisters of Mercy (Loughrea, Ireland)	[]
S.M.	Sisters of Mercy of Tralee	[]
S.M.D.C.	Sisters of Mercy of Christian Charity of St. Vincent de Paul of Hungary	[2610]
S.M.G.	Poor Servants of the Mother of God	[3640]
S.M.I.	Sisters of Mary Immaculate	[2440]
S.M.I.C.	Missionary Sisters of the Immaculate Conception of the Mother of God	[2760]
S.M.M.G.	Sisters of Mary, Mother of God	[]
S.M.M.I.	Sisters Minor of the Mary Immaculate	[]
S.M.M.S.	Society of Mary Missionary Sisters	[]
S.M.P.	Sisters of Mary of the Presentation	[2450]
S.M.P.	Daughters of Our Mother of Peace	[]
S.M.P.	Society of Our Mother of Peace	[]
S.M.R.	Society of Mary Reparatrix	[2560]
S.M.S.H.	Sisters of Saint Marthe (of St. Hyacinthe)	[3940]
S.M.S.M.	Marist Missionary Sisters	[2420]
S.N.D.	Sisters of Notre Dame	[2990]
S.N.D.deN.	Sisters of Notre Dame de Namur	[3000]
S.N.J.M.	Sisters of the Holy Names of Jesus and Mary	[1990]
S.O.L.M.	Sisters of Our Lady of Mercy	[2670]
S.O.L.P.H.	Sisters of Our Lady of Perpetual Help	[]
S.O.L.T.	Our Lady of the Most Holy Trinity Convent	[3105]
S.P.	Sisters of Providence	[3340]
S.P.	Sisters of Providence	[3350]
S.P.	Sisters of Providence of Saint Mary-of-the-Woods, IN	[3360]
S.P.C.	Sisters of St. Paul of Chartres	[3980]
S.R.	Sisters of Reparation of the Sacred Wounds of Jesus	[3475]
S.R.C.	Servants of Our Lady Queen of Clergy	[3650]
S.R.C.M.	Sisters of Reparation of the Congregation of Mary	[3470]
S.S.A.	Sisters of St. Ann	[3718]
S.S.A.	Sisters of St. Anne	[3720]
S.S.C.	Missionary Sisters of St. Columban	[2880]
S.S.C.	Sisters of St. Casimir	[3740]
S.S.C.	Society of the Sisters of the Church	[]
SS.CC.	Congregation of the Sacred Hearts and of Perpetual Adoration	[3690]
S.S.Ch.	Sisters of St. Chretienne	[3750]
S.S.C.J.	Servants of the Most Sacred Heart of Jesus	[3630]
S.S.C.J.	Sisters of the Sacred Heart of Jesus of Saint Jacut	[3670]
S.S.C.M.	Servants of the Holy Heart of Mary	[3520]
SS.C.M.	Sisters of Saints Cyril and Methodius	[3780]
S.S.D.	Institute of the Sisters of St. Dorothy	[3790]
S.S.E.	Sisters of St. Elizabeth	[3800]
S.S.F.	Congregation of the Sisters of the Holy Family	[1950]
S.S.H.	Sisters Servants of the Most Sacred Heart	[]
S.S.H.J.P.	Servants of the Sacred Heart of Jesus and of the Poor	[3660]
S.S.J.	Servants of St. Joseph	[3595]
S.S.J.	Sisters of St. Joseph (Buffalo)	[3830-06]
S.S.J.	Sisters of St. Joseph (Burlington)	[3830-07]
S.S.J.	Sisters of St. Joseph (Erie)	[3830-09]
S.S.J.	Sisters of St. Joseph (Kalamazoo, Nazareth)	[3830-11]
S.S.J.	Sisters of St. Joseph (Ogdensburg)	[3830-12]
S.S.J.	Sisters of St. Joseph (Rochester)	[3830-14]
S.S.J.	Sisters of St. Joseph, (Springfield, MA)	[3830-16]
S.S.J.	Sisters of St. Joseph (Wheeling, Eng)	[3830-17]
S.S.J.	Sisters of Saint Joseph of Chestnut Hill, Philadelphia	[3893]
S.S.J.	Sisters of St. Joseph of St. Augustine, Florida	[3900]
S.S.J.C.	Sisters of St. Joseph Benedict Cottolengo	[]
S.S.J.-T.O.S.F.	Sisters of St. Joseph of the Third Order of St. Francis	[3930]
S.S.L.	Congregation of the Sisters of St. Louis, Juilly-Monaghan	[3935]
S.S.LOG.	Seton Sisters of Our Lady of Guadalupe, Tucson	[]
S.S.M.	Sisters of the Sorrowful Mother (Third Order of St. Francis)	[4100]
S.S.M.I.	Sisters Servants of Mary Immaculate	[3510]
S.S.M.I.	Sisters Servants of Mary Immaculate	[3610]
S.S.M.I.	Sisters Servants of Mary Immaculate	[3620]
S.S.M.N.	Sisters of Saint Mary of Namur	[3950]
S.S.M.O.	Sisters of St. Mary of Oregon	[3960]
S.S.N.D.	School Sisters of Notre Dame	[2970]
S.S.P.C.	Missionary Sisters of St. Peter Claver	[3990]
S.Sp.S.	Missionary Sisters Servants of the Holy Spirit	[3530]
S.Sp.S.deA.P.	Sister Servants of the Holy Spirit of Perpetual Adoration	[3540]
S.S.S.	Servants of the Blessed Sacrament	[3500]
S.S.S.	Sisters of Social Service of Los Angeles, Inc.	[4080]
S.S.S.	Sisters of Social Service	[4090]
S.S.S.F.	School Sisters of St. Francis	[1680]
S.S.T.V.	Congregation of Sisters of St. Thomas of Villanova	[4030]
S.T.J.	Society of St. Teresa of Jesus	[4020]
S.U.	Society of St. Ursula	[4040]
S.U.S.C.	Sisters of the Holy Union	[2070]
S.V.M.	Sisters of the Visitation of the Congregation of the Immaculate Heart of Mary	[4200]
V.D.C.	Verbum Dei Community	[]
V.H.M.	Visitation Nuns	[4190]
V.S.	Vestiarski Sisters	[]
V.S.C.	Vincentian Sisters of Charity	[4160]
V.S.C.	Vincentian Sisters of Charity	[4170]
V.Z.	Sisters of Charity of St. Vincent de Paul	[0630]
X.M.M.	Xaverian Missionary Society of Mary, Inc.	[4230]
X.S.	Catholic Mission Sisters of St. Francis Xavier	[3810]

Religious Institutes of Women

The Leadership Conference of Women Religious in the United States Office: 8808 Cameron St. Silver Spring, MD 20910. Tel: 301-587-4955; Fax: 301 587-4575. Sr. Contance Phelps, S.C.L., Pres.; Sr. Christine Vladimiroff, O.S.B., Vice Pres.; Sr. Mary Ann Zollmann, B.V.M., Past Pres.; Sr. Rose Jochmann, C.S.F., Treas.; Sr. Anne Hennessy, C.S.J., Sec.; Sr. Carole Shinnick, S.S.N.D., Exec. Dir.
Council of Major Superiors of Women Religious in the United States of America Office: 1211 Lawrence St., N.E., P.O. Box 4467, Washington, DC 20017-0467. Tel: 202-832-2575; Fax: 202-832-6325. Sr. Mary McGreevy, R.S.M., Chm.

(The initital (D) or (P) indicates Diocesan or Pontifical Jurisdiction.)

[0100] (A.S.C.)—ADORERS OF THE BLOOD OF CHRIST (P)

Founded in Acuto, Italy, in 1834. First foundation in the United States in 1870.
General Motherhouse: Via Beata Maria De Mattias 10, Rome, Italy. 00183. Sr. Vittoria Tomarelli, A.S.C., Supr. Gen.
Provincial Offices -United States Province: *Adorers of the Blood of Christ,* 721 Emerson Rd.-Ste.685, St. Louis, MO 63141. Tel: 314-991-5400; Fax: 314-989-9164. Sr. Barbara Jean Franklin, A.S.C., Prov.
Professed Sisters 451.
Legal Title: *Adorers of the Blood of Christ, Province of Columbia, PA, Inc.*
Properties owned: *St. Vincent Memorial Hospital,* Taylorville, IL; *MariaCare,* Red Bud, IL; *Villa Maria,* Mulvane, KS; *Newman University,* Wichita, KS; *St. Joseph's Villa,* David City, NE; *St. Joseph Convent-Provincial House; Precious Blood Spiritual Center; St. Anne's Retirement Community, Inc.; De Mattias Residence; St. Anne's Independent Living Retirement Village,* Columbia, PA.
Sisters serve and staff: Colleges, Secondary & Elementary Schools, Special and Religious; Education; Hospitals; Pastoral Care; Nursing Homes Domestic Service in Communities and Institutions; Administration in Religious Orders and Parishes; Prayer Ministry; Retreat Ministry; Social Service; Pastoral and Chaplaincy Ministry; Prison and Minority Ministries; Ministry to the Homeless; Diocesan Offices; Homes for the Aged & Home Nursing; Foreign Missions.
Represented in the Archdioceses of Chicago, Detroit, Kansas City in Kansas, Newark, New York, Oklahoma City, Philadelphia, St. Louis, San Antonio, San Francisco, and Washington and in the Dioceses of Alexandria, Arlington, Belleville, Dodge City, El Paso, Fort Worth, Gallup, Harrisburg, Jefferson City, Kansas City, Lexington, Lincoln, Oakland, Salina, San Diego, Springfield-Cape Girardeau, Springfield (IL), Tucson, Wilmington, Wichita and Youngstown. Also in Bolivia, Guatemala, Korea and Rome.
Ruma Center (1876): 2 Pioneer Ln., Red Bud, IL 62278. Tel: 618-282-3848.
Wichita Center (1929): 1400 S. Sheridan, Wichita, KS 67213-1394. Tel: 316-943-1203.
Columbia Center (1925): 3950 Columbia Ave., Columbia, PA 17512-9714. Tel: 717-285-4536.

[0110] (A.P.B.)—THE SISTERS ADORERS OF THE PRECIOUS BLOOD (P)
(Cloistered Contemplative Order)

American Federation: Consisting of six autonomous monasteries, 400 Pratt St., Watertown, NY 13601-4238. Tel: 315-788-1669. Sr. Marilyn McGillan, A.P.B., Pres. American Federation.
New York: 54th & Ft. Hamilton Pkwy., Brooklyn, NY 11219. Tel: 718-438-6371.
New Hampshire: 700 Bridge St., Manchester, NH 03104. Tel: 603-623-4264.
Indiana: 1106 State St., Lafayette, IN 47905. Tel: 765-742-8227.
New York: 400 Pratt St., Watertown, NY 13601. Tel: 315-788-1669.
Maine: 166 State St., Portland, ME 04101. Tel: 207-774-0861.
Canada: 9415 - 165th St., Edmonton, Alberta, Canada T5R 2S5. Tel: 403-484-6691.
Professed Sisters 75, Novices 8, Postulants 2.
Represented in the Dioceses of Brooklyn, Lafayette (IN), Manchester, Ogdensburg and Portland (ME).

[0130] (A.S.C.J.)—APOSTLES OF THE SACRED HEART OF JESUS (P)

Founded in Italy in 1894. First foundation in United States 1902.
General Motherhouse: *Via Germano Sommeiller,* Via Germano Sommeiller 38, Rome, Italy. 00185. Mother Auxiliadora deGodoy, Supr. Gen.; Sr. Leopoldina Euclidi, Archivist.
U.S. Provincial Motherhouse: *Mt. Sacred Heart,* 265 Benham St., Hamden, CT 06514. Tel: 203-248-4225. Fax: 203-230-8341.
Professed Sisters 160.
Ministry in the field of Education, Health Care, Parishes and Adult Day Care.
Properties owned: *Mary, Mother of the Church Convent,* Hamden, CT; *Mount Sacred Heart College for Sisters; Sacred Heart Academy; Sacred Heart Manor; Kindergarten and Nursery; Clelian Adult Day Care,* Hamden, CT; *Sacred Heart on the Lake,* Higganum, CT; *Cor Jesu Academy, Sacred Heart Villa Nursery,* St. Louis, MO; *Our Lady Queen of Apostles (Convent & Nursery),* Imperial, MO; *Clelian Heights School for Exceptional Children,* Greensburg, PA; *Sacred Heart Private Elementary School,* Bronx, NY.
Represented in the Archdioceses of Hartford, Newark, New York and St. Louis and in the Dioceses of Bridgeport, Greensburg, Norwich, Palm Beach, Pensacola-Tallahassee and Providence. Also in Taiwan.

[0150] (S.A.S.V.)—SISTERS OF THE ASSUMPTION (P)

Founded in Saint-Gregoire, P.Q., Canada in 1853. First foundation in the United States in 1891
General Motherhouse: Nicolet, P.Q. Canada. Sr. Aline Vadnais, S.A.S.V., Supr. Gen.
United States Region: *Regional Office,* 316 Lincoln St., Worcester, MA 01605. Tel: 508-856-9450. Sr. Lorraine Normand, S.A.S.V., Reg. Treas.
Total in Region and Professed 101.
Legal Holdings: *Assumption Residence of the Sisters of the Assumption of the Blessed Virgin,* Petersham, MA; *Harper Residence,* Worcester, MA.
Ministry in all levels of education.
Missions in Japan, Brazil and Ecuador.
Represented in the Archdioceses of Boston and Hartford and in the Dioceses of Fall River, Manchester, Portland in Maine, Providence, Springfield (MA) and Worcester.

[0160] (O.S.A.)—AUGUSTINIAN NUNS OF CONTEMPLATIVE LIFE (P)

Augustinian Contemplative Nuns: *Mother of Good Counsel Convent,* 440 N. Marley Rd., New Lenox, IL 60451. Sr. Mary Grace, O.S.A., Prioress.
Total number in community 5.
Legal Title: *Augustinian Cloistered Nuns, Inc.*
Represented in the Diocese of Joliet.

[0170] (O.S.B.)—BENEDICTINE NUNS OF THE CONGREGATION OF SOLESMES (P)

Order originated in Italy, c.529. Congregation of Solesmes formed in France in 1837.
U.S. Establishment (1981): *Monastery of the Immaculate Heart of Mary,* 4103 VT Rte. 100, Westfield, VT 05874. Tel: 802-744-6525. Rev. Mother Laurence Couture, O.S.B., Prioress.
Total in Congregation 240; Total in community 17.
Represented in the Diocese of Burlington.

[0180] (O.S.B.)—BENEDICTINE NUNS OF THE PRIMITIVE OBSERVANCE (P)

First founded in Italy in about 529. First United States establishment in 1948.
Abbey of Regina Laudis: 273 Flanders Rd., Bethlehem, CT 06751. Tel: 203-266-7727; Fax: 203-266-5915. Rt. Rev. Mother David Serna, O.S.B., Abbess; Rt. Rev. Mother Benedict Duss, O.S.B., Abbess Emerita.
Professed Nuns 29; Sisters in First Vows 5; Novices 5; Postulants 1.

[0190] (O.S.B.)—BENEDICTINE NUNS (P)

First founded in Italy c.529. Founded in the United States in 1931 from St. Walburg Abbey, Eichstatt, Bavaria, Germany.
The Sisters of St. Benedict of Westmoreland County: *St. Emma Monastery,* 1001 Harvey Ave., Greensburg, PA 15601-1494. Tel: 724-834-3060; Fax: 724-834-5772. E-mail: benedictinenuns@stemma.org. Mother Mary Anne Noll, O.S.B., Prioress.
Professed Nuns 14; Postulants 1; Novices 4.
Ministry is Monastic Life; Benedictine hospitality extended through adjacent St. Emma Retreat House; Monastic guest house.
Represented in the Diocese of Greensburg.
Benedictine Nuns: *Abbey of St. Walburga,* 32,109 N. U.S. Hwy. 287, Virginia Dale, CO 80536-8942. Tel: 970-472-0612; Fax: 970-484-4342. E-mail: abbey@walburga.org. Mother Maria Michael Newe, O.S.B., Abbess; Mother Maria-Thomas Beil, O.S.B., Retired Abbess.
Sisters 18; Novices 4.
Represented in the Archdiocese of Denver.

[0200] (O.S.B.)—BENEDICTINE SISTERS (D)
(Regina Pacis)

The Congregation of Benedictine Sisters of Kaunas, Lithuania was founded in 1621.
General Motherhouse: Benediktiniu 6-7, LT-3000 Kaunas, Lithuania. Mother Regina Petkeviciute, O.S.B., Supr. Gen.
U.S. Foundation (1957): *Benedictine Sisters of Regina Pacis,* 333 Wallace Rd., Bedford, NH 03110. Tel: 603-472-3239. Sr. Gertrude Luksaite, O.S.B., Supr.
Represented in the Diocese of Manchester.

[0210] (O.S.B.)—MISSIONARY BENEDICTINE SISTERS (P)

The Congregation of Missionary Benedictine Sisters is of Pontifical Jurisdiction. Its Constitutions were approved by Rome on June 25, 1934; Revised approval June 29, 1983.
Generalate: Rome, Italy.
Provincial Motherhouse and Novitiate: *Immaculata Monastery (1923),* 300 N. 18th St., Norfolk, NE 68701-3687. Tel: 402-371-3438; Fax: 402-379-2877. Sr. Kevin Hermsen, O.S.B., Prioress.
Professed Sisters 44; Juniorates 3; Postulants 1.
Legal Holdings or Titles: *Missionary Benedictine Sisters, Inc.,* Norfolk, NE; *Our Lady of Lourdes Hospital, Inc.,* Norfolk, NE; *St. Joseph Nursing Home, Inc.,* Norfolk, NE; *Providence Medical Center, Inc.,* Wayne, NE; *Graceville Missionary Benedictine Sisters, Inc., dba Holy Trinity Hospital - Grace Home,* Graceville, MN.
Ministry in the fields of Education; Health & Hospitals; Social Services with Hispanics; Nursing Homes.
Represented in the Archdiocese of Omaha and in the Diocese of New Ulm.

[0220] (O.S.B.)—CONGREGATION OF THE BENEDICTINE SISTERS OF PERPETUAL ADORATION OF PONTIFICAL JURISDICTION (P)

Founded from Maria Rickenbach, Switzerland, in 1874 with first monastery at Clyde, MO. Congregation erected by decree of the Holy See on June 16, 1936.
General Motherhouse: *Benedictine Convent of Perpetual Adoration,* 31970 State Highway P, Clyde, MO 64423. Tel: 660-944-2221; Fax: 660-944-2152. Sr. Ramona Varela, Prioress Gen.
Total number in community 77; Total in Congregation 110; Novices 1.
Interdependent Monasteries: 800 N. Country Club Rd., Tucson, AZ 85716. Osage Monastery, 18701 W. Monastery Rd., Sand Springs, OK 74063; San Benito Monastery, Box 510, Dayton, WY 82836.
Ministry in Monastic/Contemplative/Eucharistic Apostolate of Prayer; Liturgy of the Hours four times daily in Choir; Contemplative Prayer and Monastic Atmosphere Shared with Others; Prayer Days and Retreats for Sisters; Editing and Publishing Bimonthly Magazine: Spirit & Life; Production and Distribution of Altar Breads; Liturgical Vestments; Correspondence.
Represented in the Dioceses of Cheyenne, Kansas City-St. Joseph, Tucson and Tulsa.

[0230] (O.S.B.)—BENEDICTINE SISTERS OF PONTIFICAL JURISDICTION (P)

(I): The Federation of St. Scholastica
Erected by Decree of the Holy See, Feb. 25, 1922, with final approbation by Decree of June 10, 1930. Twenty Monasteries in the United States and two in Mexico. Total number in the Federation 971. Sr. Esther Fangman, O.S.B., Pres., residing at: Benedictines of Pontifical Jurisdiction, 3741 Forest Ave., Kansas City, MO 64109. Tel: 816-753-2514
Benedictine Sisters of Baltimore, Inc.: *Emmanuel Monastery,* 2229 W. Joppa Rd., Lutherville, MD 21093.

Tel: 410-821-5792. Fax: 410-296-9560. E-mail: bensrs@emmanuelosb.org Web site: www.emmanuelosb.org. Sr. Patricia Kirk, O.S.B., Prioress.
Total number in community 15.
Ministry in the field of Education; Parish Ministry; Retreats and Spiritual Direction; Justice Ministry; Social Services; Administrative Services; Hospital Service Ministry.
Represented in the Archdioceses of Baltimore and Newark.

Benedictine Sisters of the Byzantine Rite (1969): *Queen of Heaven Monastery,* 8640 Squires Ln., N.E., Warren, OH 44484. Tel: 330-856-1813. Sr. Margaret Mary Schima, O.S.B., Prioress.
Professed Sisters 9.
Ministry in Religious and Academic Education; Pastoral Ministry; Administration.
Represented in the Archdiocese of Pittsburgh Byzantine Rite.

Mount St. Scholastica, Inc. (1863): *Motherhouse of the Sisters of St. Benedict,* 801 S. Eighth St., Atchison, KS 66002-2778. Tel: 913-360-6200; Fax: 913-360-6190. Sr. Mary Collins, O.S.B., Prioress.
Total number in community 191.
Legal Holdings: *Dooley Center, Inc.; Mount St. Scholastica, Inc.,* Atchison, KS.
Ministry in the field of Academic Education at all levels; Special Education; Music Conservatory; Pastoral Ministry; Counseling; Retreats; Spirituality Center; Spiritual Direction; Social Services; Diocesan Offices; Hospitality; Ministry to women of all ages; Missionary Work in Brazil.
Represented in the Archdioceses of Kansas City in Kansas and in the Dioceses of Des Moines, Kansas City-St. Joseph. Also in Brazil.

Benedictine Sisters of Elk Co. (1852): *St. Joseph Monastery,* St. Marys, PA, 15857. Tel: 814-834-2267. Sr. Laura Vallimont, O.S.B., Prioress.
Professed Sisters 26; Novices 2.
Ministry in the fields of Academic and Religious Education; Pastoral Ministry; Retreats.

Benedictine Sisters (1998): *Transfiguration Monastery,* 526 Fairview St., Emmaus, PA 18049-3837. Tel: 610-965-6818. Web site: www.emmausosb.org. Sr. Martina Revak, O.S.B. Supr.
Professed Sisters 3; Affiliate 1.
Ministry in the fields of Education; Pastoral Ministry; Hospitality and Spirituality.
Represented in the Diocese of Allentown.

Benedictine Sisters of Erie (1856): *Mt. St. Benedict Monastery,* 6101 East Lake Rd., Erie, PA 16511. Tel: 814-899-0614; Fax: 814-898-4004. Sr. Christine Vladimiroff, O.S.B., Prioress.
Total in Congregation 120; Professed sisters 117; Information 2.
Properties owned: *Mount Saint Benedict Monastery; Glinodo Center; St. Benedict Education Center; Benet Center; 8 community houses.*
Sisters serve and staff: High Schools; Elementary Schools; Colleges; Day Care Centers; Residence for Elderly and Handicapped; Hospitals; Social Services; Diocesan Offices; Pastoral Ministry; Religious Education.
Represented in the Archdiocese of Milwaukee and in the Dioceses of Cleveland, Dodge, City, Erie and Syracuse. Also in Mexico and Columbia.

Benedictine Sisters of Chicago O.S.B. (1861): *St. Scholastica Monastery,* 7430 Ridge Blvd., Chicago, IL 60645. Tel: 773-764-2413. Sr. Jane Smith, Prioress; Sr. Vivian Ivantic, Community Archivist.
Professed Sisters 69.
Ministry in High Schools; Pastoral Ministry; Religious Education; University staff; Management Consultant; Campus Ministry; Spiritual Direction; Peace and Shelter Ministry; Community Center Work; Social Service Counseling.
Properties owned: *St. Scholastica Monastery,* Chicago, IL; *St. Scholastica Academy,* Chicago, IL; *St. Scholastica Academy,* Canon City, CO.
Represented in the Archdioceses of Chicago and St. Louis and in the Diocese of Pueblo.

Benedictine Sisters of the Sacred Heart O.S.B. (1895): *Sacred Heart Monastery,* 1910 Maple Ave., Lisle, IL 60532-2164. Tel: 630-969-7040. Sr. Judith Ann Heble, O.S.B., Prioress.
Professed Sisters 43.
Legal Title: *Benedictine Sisters of the Sacred Heart Charitable Trust.*
Sisters serve & staff: High Schools; Elementary Schools; Colleges; Queen of Peace Retirement Center; Religious Education; Pastoral Ministry; Nurses Administration; Independent Positions involving Secretarial, Counseling, Liturgical Works, Occupational Therapy.
Represented in the Diocese of Joliet.

Sisters of Benedict of Colorado, Inc.: 4264 W. Ponds View Dr., Littleton, CO 80123. Tel: 303-795-2378. Sr. Judith Elms, O.S.B., Supr.

Benedictine Sisters of Elizabeth, NJ O.S.B. (1868): *St. Walburga Monastery and Novitiate,* 851 N. Broad St., Elizabeth, NJ 07208. Tel: 908-352-4278. Sr. Sharon McHugh, O.S.B., Prioress; Sr. Philomena Fleck, O.S.B., SubPrioress.
Professed Sisters 57.
Legal Holdings and Titles: *Benedictine Hospital,* Kingston, NY; *Benedictine Academy,* Elizabeth, NJ; *Bender Memorial Academy,* Elizabeth, NJ.
Represented in the Archdioceses of New York and Newark and in the Diocese of Paterson.

Benedictine Sisters of Pittsburgh, PA. O.S.B. (1870): *St. Benedict Monastery,* 4530 Perrysville Ave., Pittsburgh, PA 15229-2296. Tel: 412-931-2844. Sr. Michelle Farabaugh, O.S.B., Prioress.
Professed Sisters 75.
Ministry in the field of Education in all levels; Religious and Special Education; Pastoral Ministry; Childcare; Social Service; Campus Ministry; Hospital Chaplaincy; Art Education; Ministry Resource; Outreach with Poor; Benedictine Center for Senior Citizens.
Represented in the Dioceses of Greensburg, Lexington, Pittsburgh and Steubenville.

Sisters of Benedict O.S.B. (1968): *Red Plains Monastery,* 728 Richland Rd., S.W., Piedmont, OK 73078-9324. Tel: 405-373-4565; Fax: 405-373-3392. Sr. Jan Futrell, O.S.B., Prioress.
Professed Sisters 11.
Ministry in the fields of Education, CCD and Adult Religious Education; Spiritual Formation; Spiritual Direction; Retreats.
Properties owned: *Red Plains Monastery,* Piedmont, OK.
Represented in the Archdiocese of Oklahoma City.

Benedictine Sisters O.S.B. (1879): *St. Joseph Monastery,* Priory and Novitiate, 2200 S. Lewis, Tulsa, OK 74114-3100. Tel: 918-742-4989; Fax: 918-744-1374. Sr. Barbara Austin, O.S.B., Prioress.
Professed Sisters 30; In Formation 1.
Legal Holdings & Titles: *Congregation of the Benedictine Sisters of the Sacred Hearts; Monte Cassino School.*
Ministry in the field of Academic Education; Catechetics; Evangelization; Social Work; Nursing; Pastoral Ministry; Counseling & Spiritual Direction; Prison Ministry; Religious Education & Religious Formation.
Represented in the Archdiocese of Oklahoma City and in the Dioceses of Lincoln, Tulsa and Wichita.

Benedictine Sisters of Pontifical Jurisdiction O.S.B. (1857): *St. Gertrude Monastery,* 14259 Benedictine Ln., Ridgely, MD 21660-1434. Tel: 410-634-2497. Sr. Mary Gerard Falkowska, O.S.B., Prioress.
Professed Sisters 30.
Legal Holdings and Titles: *The Benedictine School for Exceptional Children; Berg Retreat Facility; St. Martin's Barn; St. Martin House,* Ridgely, MD; *St. Benedict,* Wilmington, DE.
Ministry in Special Schools and Elementary & Secondary Education; Ministry to the poor & homeless.
Represented in the Archdiocese of Washington and in the Dioceses of Wilmington.

St. Walburg Monastery of Benedictine Sisters of Covington, KY O.S.B. (1859): *St. Walburg Monastery,* 2500 Amsterdam Rd., Villa Hills, KY 41017-5316. Tel: 859-331-6324; Fax: 859-331-2136. Motherhouse and Novitiate. Sr. Rita Brink, O.S.B., Prioress; Sr. Teresa Wolking, O.S.B., Community Archivist.
Professed Sisters 84.
Legal Titles & Holdings: *Madonna Manor Nursing-Senior Citizens Home; Villa Madonna Early Learning Center; Villa Madonna Academy; Villa Madonna Center - Spirituality Center.*
Sisters serve and staff: Diocesan Offices; Hospitals; Pastoral and Social Ministry; Home or Public Health Care; all levels of academic education.
Represented in the Archdiocese of Cincinnati and in the Dioceses of Covington, Lexington and Pueblo.

Benedictine Sisters (1902): *Sacred Heart Monastery,* P.O. Box 2040, Cullman, AL 35056. Tel: 256-734-2199; 734-4622; Fax: 256-734-8835. Sr. Veronica Ryan, O.S.B., Prioress; Sr. Mary Ruth Coffman, O.S.B., Community Archivist.
Professed Sisters 47.
Properties owned: *Benedictine Spirituality and Conference Center; Benedictine Manor Retirement Home; Sacred Heart Monastery of Cullman, AL Foundation.*
Sisters serve and staff: in all levels of Academic Education; Pastoral Ministry; Diocesan Offices; Retirement Homes; Conference Centers
Represented in the Dioceses of Birmingham and Orlando.

Benedictine Sisters of Virginia O.S.B. (1868): *St. Benedict Monastery,* Bristow, VA 20136-1217. Tel: 703-361-0106. Sr. Cecilia Dwyer, O.S.B., Prioress.
Total Professed Sisters 34.
Legal Holdings and Titles: *Benedictine Sisters of Virginia, Inc.; St. Gertrude High School,* Richmond, VA; *Linton Hall School; Benedictine Pastoral Center; Benedictine Counseling Services,* Bristow, VA; *B.E.A.C.O.N.,* Bristow, VA.
Represented in the Dioceses of Arlington and Richmond.

Benedictine Sisters (1911): *St. Scholastica's Monastery and Novitiate,* 416 W. Highland Dr., Boerne, TX 78006. Tel: 830-249-2645; Fax: 830-249-1365. Sr. Bernadine Reyes, O.S.B., Prioress.
Total number in community 20.
Properties owned: *St. Scholastica Monastery; Omega Retreat Center,* Boerne, TX; *Benedictine Sisters Charitable Trust I; Benedictine Sisters Charitable Trust II.*
Represented in the Archdiocese of San Antonio and in the Dioceses of Austin and Gallup.

Benedictine Sisters of St. Lucy's Priory Inc. O.S.B. (1956): *St. Lucy's Priory,* 19045 E. Sierra Madre Ave. Glendora, CA 91741. Tel: 626-335-1682. Sr. Elizabeth Brown, O.S.B., Prioress.
Professed Sisters 19.
Legal Holdings: *St. Lucy's Priory High School; St. Lucy's Benedictine Child Development Center.*
Sisters serve & staff: all levels of Academic Education; Continuing Education; Pastoral Ministry.
Represented in the Archdiocese of Los Angeles and in the Diocese of San Diego.

Benedictine Sisters of Florida (1889): *Holy Name Monastery,* P.O. Box 2450, St. Leo, FL 33574-2450. Tel: 352-588-8320; Fax: 352-588-8319. Sr. Mary Clare Neuhofer, O.S.B., Prioress; Sr. M. Dorothy Neuhofer, O.S.B., Community Archivist.
Professed Sisters 24; Temporary Professed 1; Novices 3.
Represented in the Diocese of St. Petersburg.

Sisters of St. Benedict (1963): *Benet Hill Monastery-Motherhouse,* 2555 N. Chelton Rd., Colorado Springs, CO 80909-1399. Tel: 719-633-0655; Fax: 719-471-0403. Sr. Rose Ann Barmann, O.S.B., Prioress; Sr. Diane Liston, Community Archivist.
Total number in community 45.
Properties owned: *Benet Hill Center; Benet Pines Retreat Center.*
Represented in the Archdiocese of Denver and Santa Fe and in the Dioceses of Colorado Springs and Pueblo. Also in Jamaica.

Benedictine Sisters O.S.B. (1989): *Queen of Angels Monastery,* 23615 N.E. 100th St., Liberty, MO 64068. Tel: 816-750-4618; Fax: 816-750-4367. Sr. Imelda Koch, O.S.B., Prioress.
Professed Sisters 9; Pre-Novitiate 1.
Ministry in Companioning, food for the hungry; prison ministry; thrift stores; Religious education and retreats; Nursing.
Represented in the Diocese of Kansas City-St. Joseph.

(II): The Federation of St. Gertrude

Erected by Decree of the Apostolic See on April 14, 1937, with final approbation by Decree of April 4, 1950. 802 E. 10th St., Ferdinand, IN 47532.

Federation Office, *Monastery Immaculate Conception (1867),* 802 E. 10th St., Ferdinand, IN 47532-9239. Tel: 812-367-1411; Fax: 812-367-2313. Sr. Kathryn Huber, O.S.B., Federation Pres.
Total in the Federation 977. Eighteen member monasteries form this Federation as follows:

Benedictine Sisters of Belcourt O.S.B.: *Queen of Peace Monastery (1963),* P.O. Box 370, Belcourt, ND 58316. Tel: 701-477-6167; Fax: 701-477-5575. Sr. Judith Emge, O.S.B., Prioress.
Professed Sisters 6.
Ministry in Counseling; Religious Education; Parish Ministry and Administration; Home Ministry; Educational Center; Indian Ministry.
Represented in the Diocese of Fargo.

Benedictine Sisters O.S.B.: *Our Lady of Peace Monastery,* 3710 West Broadway, Columbia, MO 65203-0116. Tel: 573-446-2300; Fax: 573-446-2312. Sr. Rachel Best, O.S.B.
Professed Sisters 12.
Ministry in Religious Education; Home Health Care; Pastoral Care; Parish & Social Ministries; Counseling; Legal Profession and Prison Ministry.
Represented in the Dioceses of Jefferson City and Springfield-Cape Girardeau.

Monastery of St. Gertrude (1882): HC 3 Box 121, Cottonwood, ID 83522-9408. Tel: 208-962-3224; Fax: 208-962-7212. Sr. Jean Lalande, O.S.B.
Professed Sisters 65.
Legal Title: *Idaho Corporation of Benedictine Sisters.*
Sisters serve in Education; Parish Ministry; Health Care; Retreat Ministry; Social Work; Counseling; St. Gertrude's Museum.
Represented in the Archdioceses of Indianapolis, Los Angeles, Portland (OR) and Seattle and in the Dioceses of Boise, St. Cloud and Spokane.

Sisters of St. Benedict of Crookston O.S.B.: *Mount St. Benedict Monastery (1919),* 620 E. Summit Ave., Crookston, MN 56716-2799. Tel: 218-281-3441; Fax: 218-281-6966. Sr. Catherine Merck, O.S.B., Prioress.
Professed Sisters 114.

Legal Titles or Holdings: *Villa St. Vincent,* Crookston, MN.
Sisters serve and staff: Elementary, High Schools, Colleges; Nursing Homes; Assisted Living facilities; Religious Education Center; Adult Education; Parish Ministry; Pastoral Care; Retreat Centers & Social Services; Child Care; Nursery School.
Represented in the Dioceses of Brownsville, Crookston, New Ulm and St. Cloud.

Benedictine Sisters O.S.B.: *Monastery Immaculate Conception (1867),* 802 E. 10th St., Ferdinand, IN 47532-9239. Tel: 812-367-1411; Fax: 812-367-2313. Sr. Kristine Anne Harpenau, O.S.B., Prioress.
Professed Sisters 208.
Legal Title: *Sisters of St. Benedict of Ferdinand, Indiana, Inc.*
Sisters Sponsor: *Kordes Retreat Center,* Ferdinand, IN.
Sisters serve and staff: on all levels of Academic Education; Religious Education Centers; Parish Ministry; Hospitals; Public Health-Social Service Agencies; Diocesan Offices; Foreign Missions; Hispanic Ministries; Retreat House.
Represented in the Archdioceses of Indianapolis and Louisville and in the Dioceses of Evansville, Joliet, Lexington and Owensboro. Also in Rome, Peru and Guatemala.

Benedictine Sisters, O.S.B. of St. Scholastica Monastery: *St. Scholastica Monastery (1879),* P.O. Box 3489, Fort Smith, AR, 72913. Tel: 479-783-4147; Fax: 479-782-4352. Sr. Cabrini Schmitz, O.S.B., Prioress.
Professed Sisters 89.
Ministry in the fields of Religious Education; Retreat Center; Parish Ministry; Hospital Chaplaincy; House of Prayer; Retreat Ministry; Counseling; Spiritual Direction.

Dependent Monastery: *St. Benedict Monastery,* Canyon, TX.
Represented in the Dioceses of Amarillo and Little Rock.

Sisters of St. Benedict of Riverside, California, Inc.: *Holy Spirit Monastery (1972),* 22791 Pico St., Grand Terrace, CA 92313-5725. Tel: 909-783-4446; Fax: 909-783-3525. Sr. Mary Ann Schepers, O.S.B., Prioress.
Professed Sisters 9.
Ministry in Religious Education; Parish and Diocesan Ministry; Counseling and Spiritual Direction; Retreat Ministry; Transporting and Educating the Handicapped.
Represented in the Diocese of San Bernardino.

Benedictine Sisters: *Spirit of Life Monastery,* 2430 N. Murray Blvd., Colorado Springs, CO, 80915. Tel: 715-550-3716. Sr. Katherine Wawersich, O.S.B., Prioress.
Professed Sisters 2.
Sister serve in Retreat and Prayer Ministry; Counseling and Spiritual Direction.
Represented in the Diocese of Colorado Springs.

Monastery of St. Benedict Center (1902): P.O. Box 5070, Madison, WI 53705-0070. Tel: 608-836-1631; Fax: 608-836-5586. Sr. Mary David Walgenbach, O.S.B., Prioress.
Professed Sisters 5.
Legal Titles: *Sisters of St. Benedict, Sioux City, Iowa, Inc.; Sisters of St. Benedict of Madison, Wisconsin, Inc.*
Sisters serve: Community Building, Prayer, Education, Retreat and Conference Ministries; Corporate Ministries; St. Benedict Center.
Represented in the Dioceses of Madison and Sioux City.

Benedictine Sisters of Mt. Angel, Oregon: *Queen of Angels Monastery (1882),* 840 S. Main St., Mt. Angel, OR 97362. Tel: 503-845-6141; Fax: 503-845-6585. Sr. Dorothy Jean Beyer, O.S.B., Prioress.
Professed Sisters 48.
Corporate Ministries: Shalom Prayer Center; St. Joseph's Shelter, Mt. Angel, OR.
Sisters serve: High Schools; Seminaries; Parish Ministry; Retreat and Prayer Ministry; Counseling and Spiritual Direction; Work with Handicapped and Aging; Hospital Chaplaincy; Ministry to Poor and Hispanics.
Represented in the Archdiocese of Portland (OR) and in the Diocese of Boise and Honolulu.

Benedictine Convent of St. Martin: *St. Martin Monastery (1889),* 2110-C St. Martin Dr., Rapid City, SD 57702-9660. Tel: 605-343-8011; Fax: 605-399-2723. Sr. Lorane Coffin, O.S.B., Prioress.
Professed Sisters 35.
Ministry in Religious Education; Parish Ministry; Chancery; Hospital Chaplaincies, Nursing and Child Care.
Properties owned: *St. Martin's Academy Learning Center and Community Center.*
Represented in the Archdiocese of Seattle and Dioceses of Great Falls-Billings, Helena and Rapid City.

Sisters of St. Benedict of Beech Grove, Ind., Inc.: *Our Lady of Grace Monastery (1956),* 1402 Southern Ave., Beech Grove, IN 46107. Tel: 317-787-3287; Fax: 317-780-2368. Sr. Carol Falkner, O.S.B., Prioress.
Total Professed Sisters 80.
Legal Title: *Sisters of St. Benedict of Beech Grove, Ind., Inc.; Charitable Trust of the Monastery of Our Lady of Grace; Sisters of the Order of St. Benedict.*
Ministry in Education; Parish Ministries; Retirement Home; Educational Center; Religious Education; Hospitals.
Properties owned and sponsored: *Our Lady of Grace Monastery; Benedictine Inn Retreat and Conference Center; St. Paul Hermitage; Regina Retreat.*
Represented in the Archdioceses of Cincinnati and Indianapolis and in the Diocese of Evansville.

Benedictine Sisters of Richardton, O.S.B.: *Sacred Heart Monastery (1916),* P.O. Box 364 - 8969 Hwy. 10 W, Richardton, ND 58652-0364. Tel: 701-974-2121; Fax: 701-974-2124. Sr. Marie Hunkler, O.S.B., Prioress.
Professed Sisters 32.
Legal Titles or Holdings: *St. Vincent's Nursing Home, Inc.; Marillac Manor, Inc.; Subiaco Manor Inc.; Sacred Heart Benedictine Foundation.*
Ministry in the fields of Academic Education; Hospital Chaplaincy; Native American ministry; Parish ministry; Health Care.
Represented in the Diocese of Bismarck.

The Benedictine Sisters of Mother of God Monastery O.S.B.: *Mother of God Monastery (1961),* 110 S.E. 28th Ave., Watertown, SD 57201. Tel: 605-882-6600; Fax: 605-882-6658. Sr. Judith Fischer, O.S.B., Prioress.
Professed Sisters 65; Novices 1.
Legal Titles: *The Benedictine Sisters of Mother of God Monastery,* Watertown, SD; *St. Ann's Corporation (includes Benet Place),* Watertown, SD; *Evergreen Assisted Living,* Watertown, SD; *Retirement Trust,* Watertown, SD; *Benedictine Sisters Foundation of,* Watertown, SD.
Sisters serve and staff: in Elementary and College Education; Religious Education Centers; Parish Ministry; Social Services; Hospitals and Hospices; Retreat Center; Homes for Aged; Juvenile Services; Home Health Care; Native American Ministries; Hispanic Ministries; Libraries & Archives; and Congregate Housing for Elderly.
Represented in the Archdioceses of San Antonio and St. Paul-Minneapolis and in the Dioceses of Bismarck, Fargo, La Crosse, Lincoln, Madison, New Ulm, Sioux Falls and Tyler.

St. Benedict's Monastery (1912): 225 Masters Ave., Winnipeg, Manitoba, Canada R4A 2A1. Tel: 204-338-4601; Fax: 204-339-1705. Sr. Irene Burzynski, O.S.B., Prioress.
Professed Sisters 37.
Ministry in Retreat & Conference Center; Education; Health Care; Pastoral Care.
Represented in the Dioceses of Calgary and Winnipeg Canada.

Benedictine Convent of the Sacred Heart: *Sacred Heart Monastery (1880),* 1005 W. 8th St., Yankton, SD 57078. Tel: 605-668-6000; Fax: 605-668-6153. Sr. Jacquelyn Ernster, O.S.B., Prioress.
Professed Sisters 143.
Sisters serve and staff: in Health Care Institutions; all levels of Academic Education; Social Services; Parish Ministry; Pastoral Care; Diocesan Offices; Counseling & Religious Education.
Represented in the Archdiocese of Omaha and in the Dioceses of Bismarck, Lincoln, Pueblo and Sioux Falls.

Benedictine Sisters, O.S.B.: *The Dwelling Place Monastery (1993),* 150 Mt. Tabor Rd., Martin, KY 41649. Tel: 606-886-9624. Sr. Eileen Schepers, O.S.B., Prioress.
Professed Sisters 5.
Sisters serve and staff: Elementary and Adult Education; Mentally Handicapped; Retreat Center; Parish; Social Outreach; Volunteer Program.
Represented in the Diocese of Lexington.

Benedictine Sisters of Nanaimo: *House of Bread Monastery (1993),* 2329 Arbot Rd., Nanaimo, British Columbia, Canada V9R 6S8. Tel: 250-753-1763; Fax: 250-754-3744. Sr. MaryAnn Gisler, O.S.B., Prioress.
Professed Sisters 11.
Corporate Ministries: *Bethlehem Retreat Centre; Bethlehem Counselling Centre.*
Sisters serve: Counselling; Retreat and Prayer Ministry; Nursing; Artist.
Represented in the Diocese of Victoria, Canada.

(III): The Federation of St. Benedict
Erected by decree of the Holy See March 24, 1947. 1190 Pirouy Rd., P.O. Box 66, Eau- Claire WI 54702 Tel: 715-834-3395; Fax: 715-834-4292. Sr. Michaela Hedican, O.S.B., Prioress. 104 Chapel Lane, St. Joseph, MN 56374-0220. Tel: 320-363-7070; Fax: 320-363-7130. Sr. Colleen Haggerty, O.S.B., Federation Pres.
Total number of Sisters in Federation 846. Twelve monasteries form this Federation; In addition to the nine American monasteries listed, three autonomous monasteries exist: Japan, St. Benedict's Monastery (1985); Sapporo, Hokkaido; Taiwan, St. Benedict Monastery (1988) Tanshui, Taipei; Bahamas, Saint Martin Monastery (1994) Nassau.
Legal Title: *Federation of St. Benedict.*

Sisters of St. Benedict (1994): *Mount Benedict Monastery,* 6000 South 1075 East, Ogden, UT 84405-4945. Tel: 801-479-6030. Sr. Mary Zenzen, O.S.B., Prioress.
Professed sisters 10.
Sisters serve and staff: Health Care; Campus Ministry; Diocesan Offices; Parish Ministry; Ongoing Formation of Deacons.
Represented in the Diocese of Salt Lake City.

Sisters of the Order of Saint Benedict-O.S.B. (1857): *Monasterio Santa Escolastica,* Apartado 8526, Humacao, PR 00792. Tel: 787-852-4222; Fax: 787-850-5279. Sr. Mary Ruth Santana, O.S.B.
Total Sisters 12; Novices 1.
Legal Title: *Sisters of the Order of Saint Benedict.*
Ministry in the field of Education at all levels; Parish Ministry; Social Work; Counseling.
Represented in the Dioceses of Caguas.

Sisters of the Order of Saint Benedict-O.S.B. (1857): *St. Benedict's Monastery-Motherhouse and Novitiate,* 104 Chapel Lane, St. Joseph, MN 56374-0220. Tel: 320-363-7100. Sr. Ephrem Hollermann, O.S.B., Prioress. Sr. Ruth Boedigheimer, O.S.B., Archivist.
Total Sisters in Congregation 359.
Legal Title: *Sisters of the Order of Saint Benedict,* St. Joseph, MN.
Ministry in the field of Education at all levels; Indian Missions; Hospitals; Nursing Homes; Individual Apostolates; Diocesan Marriage Tribunal; Parish Ministry; Social Work; Spirituality and Retreat Counseling.
Represented in the Archdioceses of Mobile and St. Paul-Minneapolis and in the Dioceses of Crookston, Manchester, New Ulm, St. Cloud, San Diego and Santa Rosa.

Sisters of St. Benedict - St. Scholastica Monastery O.S.B. (1892): 1001 Kenwood Ave., Duluth, MN 55811. Tel: 218-723-6555. Sr. Kathleen Hofer, O.S.B., Prioress. Sr. Aelred Roehl, Archivist.
Total number in community 136.
Ministry in the field of Academic Education at all levels; Religious Education; Indian Ministry; Residence for Elderly; Nursing Homes; Hospitals; Pastoral Care and Parish Ministries; Prison Ministry; Peace and Justice; Retreat Center.
Properties owned and/or sponsored: *McCabe Renewal Center,* Duluth, MN; *College of St. Scholastica; St. Mary's Medical Center,* Duluth, MN; *Benedictine Living Communities, Inc.,* Duluth, MN; *Benedictine Health Center; Polinsky Rehabilitation Center,* Duluth MN; *St. Joseph's Medical Center,* Brainerd, MN; *St. Mary's Regional Health Center,* Detroit Lakes, MN; *St. Francis Regional Medical Center,* Shakopee, MN; *St. Mary's Hospital,* Cottonwood, ID; *Tekakwitha Nursing Center, Inc.,* Sisseton, SD; *Madonna Towers of Rochester, Inc.,* Rochester, MN; *St. Benedict's Health Center; Prince of Peace Care Center; Benedictine Living Center of Garrison; St. Rose Care Center; St. Catherine's Living Center,* ND; *Benedictine Sisters Benevolent Association; Benedictine Health System,* Duluth, MN; *St. Gertrude's Health Center,* Shakopee, MN; *Benedictine Health Dimensions,* Cambridge, MN; *St. Mary's Hospital,* Superior, WI; *St. Anne Hospice,* Winona, MN; *St. Mary's Care Center,* Winsted, MN; *Mount Carmel Health & Rehabilitation Center,* Milwaukee, WI; *Villa St. Benedict,* Lisle, IL; *Villa St. Vincent,* Crookston, MN.
Represented in the Archdioceses of Chicago, Milwaukee, St. Paul-Minneapolis, and Seattle and in the Dioceses of Bismarck, Boise, Covington, Crookston, Duluth, Fargo, Joliet, Kansas City-St. Joseph; New Ulm, Peoria, Phoenix, St. Cloud, Superior, Sioux Falls and Winona.

St. Bede Monastery (1948): 1190 Priory Rd., P.O. Box 66, Eau Claire, WI 54702. Tel: 715-834-3176. Sr. Margaret Michaud, O.S.B., Prioress. Sr. Lorayne Andre, O.S.B. Archivist.
Total number in community 39.
Properties owned and sponsored: *St. Bede Monastery; St. Bede Retreat and Conference Center.*
Represented in the Archdiocese of San Antonio and in the Dioceses of La Crosse and Springfield-Cape Girardeau. Also in Jamaica.

Sisters of the Order of St. Benedict O.S.B. (1874): *St. Mary Monastery,* 2200 88th Ave., W, Rock Island, IL 61201-7649. Tel: 309-283-2100; Fax: 309-283-2200. Sr. Ruth Ksycki, O.S.B., Prioress; Sr. Rita Cain, Archivist.
Total number in community 64.
Ministry in the field of Religious and Academic Education; Pastoral Care; Parish Ministry.
Represented in the Dioceses of Davenport, Gary and Peoria.

Benedictine Sisters of the Annunciation, BVM (1947): *Annunciation Monastery,* 7520 University Dr., Bismarck, ND 58504-9653; Tel: 701-255-1520. Sr. Susan Berger, O.S.B., Prioress.
Professed Sisters 80.
Ministry in Hospitals; Parish Ministry and Catechetical Work; Education and Health Care.
Represented in the Dioceses of Bismarck and Fargo.

Sisters of St. Benedict (1948): *St. Paul's Monastery,* 2675 Larpenteur Ave. E., St. Paul, MN 55109. Tel: 651-777-8181; Fax: 651-777-4442. Sr. Marie Fujan, O.S.B., Prioress.
Professed Sisters 64.
Sisters serve and staff: Schools; Long term care facilities; Administration; Child Care; Retreat Center; Parish Ministry; Social Service and various other apostolic work.
Represented in the Archdiocese of St. Paul-Minneapolis and in the Diocese of Great Falls.

Sisters of St. Benedict O.S.B. (1952): *St. Placid Priory,* 500 College St., N.E., Lacey, WA 98516-5338. Tel: 360-438-1771. Sr. Laura Swan, O.S.B. Prioress.
Professed Sisters 18.
Sisters serve in the field of Education; Spirituality and Pastoral care.
Represented in the Archdioceses of Portland and Seattle.

[0233] (O.S.B.)—BENEDICTINE NUNS

Subiaco Congregation

St. Scholastica Priory, Benedictine Nuns (Cloistered): Box 606, 271 N. Main St., Petersham, MA 01366-0606. Tel: 978-724-3213; Fax: 978-724-3216. Very Rev. Mother Mary Clare Vincent, O.S.B., Prioress. Sr. Mary Frances Wynn, O.S.B., Sub-Prioress.
Nuns in Solemn vows 9; Simple vows 2; Claustral Oblates 2.

[0235] (O.S.B.Cam.)—CAMALDOLESE BENEDICTINE SISTERS

Camaldolese Congregation

First founded in Italy in the 11th century, affiliated with monastery in Rome Founded in 1722; United States foundation in 1988.

Transfiguration Monastery: *Camaldolese Benedictine Sisters,* 701 NY Rte. 79, Windsor, NY 13865. Tel: 607-655-2366. Sr. Donald Corcoran, O.S.B.Cam., Prioress.
Professed Nuns 4.
Ministry in Monastic life and Benedictine hospitality.
Represented in the Diocese of Syracuse.

[0240] (O.S.B.)—OLIVETAN BENEDICTINE SISTERS (D)

Established in the Diocese of Little Rock in 1887.

Motherhouse and Novitiate (1887): *Holy Angels Convent,* P.O. Drawer 130, Jonesboro, AR 72403-0130. Tel: 870-935-5810; Fax: 870-935-4210. Sr. M. Eileen Schneider, O.S.B., Prioress.
Professed Sisters 44; Novices 3; Postulants 4.
Properties owned: *Little Angels Day Care Center,* Little Rock, AR; *St. Bernards Healthcare, Inc.,* Jonesboro, AR; *St.Bernards Development Foundation, Inc.,* Jonesboro, AR.
Sisters serve and staff: Healthcare Ministries; High Schools; Grammar Schools; Diocesan Ministries; CCD Centers & Parish Services.
Represented in the Dioceses of Fort Worth and Little Rock.

[0250] (C.V.D.)—SISTERS OF BETHANY (P)

Founded in El Salvador in 1928.

General Motherhouse: *Instituto Bethania,* Santa Tecla El Salvador, C.A. Mother Dolores de Maria Zea; Mother foundrees Madre Luz Elena Ordonez, Supr. Gen.

U.S. Address (1949): *Bethany House,* 850 N. Hobart Blvd., Los Angeles, CA 90029. Tel: 323-669-9411; 665-6937. Sr. Leticia Gomez C.V.D., Supr.
Professed Sisters 14.
Ministry in Social Service Centers; Parish Work.
Represented in the Archdiocese of Los Angeles.

[0260] (S.B.S.)—THE SISTERS OF THE BLESSED SACRAMENT FOR INDIANS AND COLORED PEOPLE (P)

Founded in the United States in 1891.

General Motherhouse: *St. Elizabeth's Convent,* Bensalem, PA 19020-5796. Tel: 215-244-9900. Sr. Monica Loughlin, Pres.
Professed Sisters 210.
Properties owned: St. Catherine Indian School, Santa Fe, NM; St. Michael Indian School, St. Michael's, AZ; Xavier Prep, New Orleans, LA.
Sisters serve and staff in the field of Education on all levels; Catechetical Schools; Houses for Catechetical; Adult Education and Social Service; House of Prayer; Spiritual Center; Evangelization Center.
Represented in the Archdioceses of Atlanta Boston, Chicago, New Orleans, New York, Philadelphia, Santa Fe, and Washington and in the Dioceses of Baton Rouge, Birmingham, Cincinnati, Evansville, Gallup, Lafayette (LA), Palm Beach and Tucson. Also in Haiti & Guatemala.

[0270] C.B.S.)—CONGREGATION OF BON SECOURS (P)

Founded in France in 1824. First foundation in the United States in 1881.

Generalate: *Maison Mere du Bon Secours,* 20, rue N.D. des Champs, Paris, France. 75006 Sr. Nancy Glynn, C.B.S., Congregational Leader.

United States Province: *Provincial House and Novitiate,* 1525 Marriottsville Rd., Marriottsville, MD 21104. Tel: 410-442-1333; Fax: 410-442-1394. Sr. Alice M. Talone, Pres.
Total Sisters in U.S. Province 38.
Sisters own and operate: *Bon Secours Spiritual Center.*
Sisters sponsor: Bon Secours Health System, Inc. and its subsidiaries.
Represented in the Archdioceses of Baltimore, Detroit, Miami, Newark, New York and Philadelphia and in the Dioceses of Altoona-Johnstown, Charleston, Covington, Richmond, St. Petersburg and Venice.

[0280] (O.SS.S.)—THE BRIGITTINE SISTERS (P)

Founded in Sweden in 14th century.

Motherhouse: Rome, Italy.

Convent and Novitiate (1957): *Convent of St. Birgitta,* Vikingsborg, 4 Runkenhage Rd., Darien, CT 06820. Tel: 203-655-1068. Sr. M. Sabina Kavanadi, O.SS.S., Supr.
Monastic tradition, more contemplative than active.
Professed Sisters 8.
Legal Title: *Order of the Most Holy Savior of St. Bridget.*
Represented in the Diocese of Bridgeport.

[0300] (O.CARM.)—CALCED CARMELITES (P)

Carmelite Nuns of the Ancient Observance, Strictly Cloistered, belonging to the Second Order of Carmel.

Founded in Naples, Italy in 1536. First foundation in the United States in 1931.

Carmelite Monastery of St. Therese: *Little Flower of Jesus and St. M. Magdalen Di Pazzi, St. Therese's Valley,* 3551 Lanark Rd., Coopersburg, PA 18036-9324. Mother Marie Charlette, O.Carm., Prioress.
Professed Sisters 9.
Legal Title: *The Carmelite Sisters of St. Therese's Valley, Inc.*
Represented in the Dioceses of Allentown, Fargo, San Angelo and Superior.

[0315] (C.C.W.)—CARMELITE COMMUNITY OF THE WORD (D)

Motherhouse & Novitiate: *Incarnation Center (1971),* 394 Bem Rd., Gallitzin, PA, 16641. Fax: 814-886-4098. Sr. Marilyn Welch, C.C.W., Admin. Gen.
Total number in the community 18.
Ministries in Diocesan Administration; the field of Religious and Academic Education at all levels; Pastoral Care to the Imprisoned, Institutionalized, Elderly, Mentally Handicapped, Family Life Support Groups and the Poor; Parish Ministry; Mission activity in Appalacia.
Represented in the Diocese of Altoona-Johnstown.

[0320] (O.CARM.)—CARMELITE NUNS OF THE ANCIENT OBSERVANCE (P)

Carmelite Nuns of the Ancient Observance

Strictly Cloistered, belonging to the Second Order of Carmel.

Founded in Guelder, Holland, in 1453. First Foundation in the United States in 1930.

Carmel of Mary (1954): 17765 78th St., S.E., Wahpeton ND, 58075. Tel 701-642-2360. Mother Maria of Divine Mercy, O.Carm., Prioress.
Total number in community 11.
Represented in the Diocese of Fargo.

Monastery of Our Lady of Grace (1989): 6202 CR 339 Via Maria, Christoval, TX 76935-3023. Tel: 325-853-1722. Web site: carmelnet.org/christoval/christoval.htm. Sr. Mary Grace, O.Carm, Vicar Prioress.
Professed Sisters 5; Postulants 2.
Represented in the Diocese of San Angelo.

Carmel of The Sacred Heart (1963): 430 Laurel Ave., Hudson, WI 54016. Tel 715-386-2156. Sr. Mary O'Neill, O.Carm., Prioress. Sr. Lucia LaMontagne, O.Carm., Archivist.
Professed Sisters 5; Novices 1.
Legal Title: *Carmelite Nuns of the Diocese of Superior, Inc.*
Represented in the Diocese of Superior.

[0330] (O.CARM.)—CARMELITE SISTERS FOR THE AGED AND INFIRM (P)

Founded in 1929 in New York. Foundress: Mother M. Angeline Teresa, O.Carm.

Motherhouse and Novitiate: *St. Teresa's Motherhouse and Novitiate,* 600 Woods Rd., Avila on the Hudson, Germantown, NY 12526. Mother Mary Suzanne, O.Carm., Supr. Gen.
Professed Sisters 235; Novices 1.
Legal Holdings: *Carmelite System for the Aged and Infirm, Inc.,* Germantown, NY; *Carmel Terrace,* Framingham, MA; *St. Patrick Home,* Bronx, NY; *Sacred Heart Manor,* Philadelphia, PA; *Villa Teresa,* Harrisburg, PA; *St. Raphael Home,* Columbus, OH; *St. Rita's Home,* Columbus, OH; *St. Margaret's Hall,* Cincinnati, OH; *Carmel Manor,* Fort Thomas, KY; *Kahl Home for the Aged,* Davenport, IA; *St. Patrick's Manor,* Framingham, MA; *Marian Manor,* Boston, MA; *St. Patrick's Residence,* Naperville, IL; *Lourdes - Noreen McKeen Residence,* West Palm Beach, FL; *Mother Angeline McCrory Manor,* Columbus, OH; *Avila Institute of Gerontology; Our Lady's Manor,* Dublin, Ireland.
Represented in the Archdioceses of Boston, Cincinnati, New York and Philadelphia and in the Dioceses of Albany, Altoona-Johnstown, Bridgeport, Brooklyn, Columbus, Covington, Davenport, Fall River, Joliet, Harrisburg, Palm Beach, Scranton and Syracuse.

[0340] (C.aCh.)—CARMELITE SISTERS OF CHARITY (P)

Founded in 1826.

Motherhouse: Vic Spain.

Generalate: *Carlo Zucchi,*12, 00165 Rome, Italy. Tel: 06-662-03-52.

Provincial/Formation House: *Carmelite Sisters of Charity,* 701 Beacon Rd., Silver Spring, MD 20903. Tel: 301-434-6344. Sr. Maria Pilar Chamorro, Prov.
Ministry in Health Clinics; Parishes; Higher Education; Immigrants, Hispanics and Homeless, Educational Centers.
Properties owned or sponsored: *Mount Carmel House; Formation House.*
Represented in the Archdiocese of Washington and in the Diocese of Brooklyn.

[0350] (O.CARM.)—CARMELITE SISTERS (CORPUS CHRISTI) (P)

First foundation in the United States in 1920.

General Motherhouse: Tunapuna, Trinidad, West Indies. Sr. Antoinette Dickie, O.Carm., Supr. Gen.

U.S. Address: *Mount Carmel Home-Keens' Memorial,* 412 W. 18th, Kearney, NE 68847. Tel: 308-237-2287. Sr. Delphine, O.Carm., Reg. Supr.
Professed Sisters 105.
Ministry in Home and Foreign Missions; Academic and Religious Education; Social Work.
Represented in the Dioceses of Grand Island and Providence.

[0360] (Carmel D.C.J.)—CARMELITE SISTERS OF THE DIVINE HEART OF JESUS (P)

Founded in Germany in 1891. First Convent in the United States in 1912.

General Motherhouse: Sittard, Netherlands. Mother M. Angelina, Supr. Gen.

Northern Province: 1230 Kavanaugh Pl., Milwaukee, WI 53213. Tel: 414-453-4040; Fax: 414-453-6503. Sr. Maria Giuseppe, Prov.

Central Province: 10341 Manchester Rd., St. Louis, MO 63122. Tel: 314-965-7616. Sr. Mary Joseph, Prov. Supr.

South Western Province: 8585 La Mesa Blvd., La Mesa, CA 91941. Tel: 619-466-3116. Sr. Mary Angela Therese, Prov. Supr.
Professed Sisters Worldwide 457.
Total in U.S. 70; Novices 59; Postulants 34.
Sisters minister to Homes for Children 2; Homes for the Aged 9; Day Nurseries 4; Mission work in Africa, Iceland, Nicaragua, Venezuela & Brazil.
Represented in the Archdioceses of Detroit, Milwaukee, St. Louis and San Antonio and in the Dioceses of Gary, Grand Rapids, Jefferson City, Owensboro and San Diego.

[0370] (O.C.D.)—CARMELITE SISTERS OF THE MOST SACRED HEART OF LOS ANGELES (P)

General Motherhouse & Novitiate: *Carmelite Sisters of the Most Sacred Heart of Los Angeles,* 920 E. Alhambra Rd., Alhambra, CA 91801. Tel: 626-289-1353; Fax: 626-308-1913. Mother Regina Marie Gorman, O.C.D., Supr. Gen.
Total number in community 141.
Legal Titles: *Carmelite Sisters of the Most Sacred Heart of Los Angeles; Carmelite Educational Centers, Inc., dba Sacred Heart Retreat House; Mount Carmel in the*

Desert Retreat House and Day Care Center; St. Joseph Center, Alhambra, CA; *Little Flower Center, Inc., dba Little Flower Missionary House,* Los Angeles, CA; *Avila Gardens Residence for Seniors,* Duarte, CA; *Santa Teresita Hospital,* Duarte, CA; *Santa Teresita Clinic,* Asuza, CA; *Marycrest Manor, Inc.,* Culver City, CA.

Sisters serve and staff: Religious and Academic Education; General Hospital; Skilled Nursing Facility for the care of the Aged; Nursery Schools with Day Care Centers and Kindergarten; Retreat House; Directors of Religious Education; Ministry to elderly, sick and convalescents; Evangelization Center.

Represented in the Archdioceses of Denver, Los Angeles and Miami and in the Diocese of Tucson.

[0380] (C.S.T.)—CARMELITE SISTERS OF ST. THERESE OF THE INFANT JESUS (D)

Founded in the United States in 1917 at Bentley, OK.

General Motherhouse: *Villa Teresa,* 1300 Classen Dr., Oklahoma City, OK 73103-2447. Tel: 405-232-7926. Sr. Maria Francesca Forst, C.S.T., Gen.

Total number in community 22.

Legal Title: *Carmelite Sisters of St. Therese of the Infant Jesus Motherhouse.*

Ministry in the field of Academic Education; Religious Education and Parish Ministry.

Properties owned and sponsored: *Villa Teresa School,* Oklahoma City, OK; *Villa Teresa Moore,* Oklahoma City, OK.

Represented in the Archdiocese of Oklahoma City.

[0390] (C.M.S.T.)—MISSIONARY CARMELITES OF ST. TERESA (P)

Founded in Mexico City in 1903.

General Motherhouse: Fresno 150, 06400, Mexico, D.F. Mother Edith Lucia Frias De la Rosa, C.M.S.T., Supr. Gen.

U.S. Holy Family Province (1983): 9548 Deer Trail Dr., Houston, TX 77038. Tel: 281-445-5520; Fax: 281-445-5748. Sr. Ruth M. Martinez, C.M.S.T., Prov. Supr.

Professed Sisters 61.

Ministry in Pastoral; Hospital Chaplaincy; Domestic and Retreats.

Represented in the Archdioceses of St. Louis and Oklahoma City and in the Dioceses of Corpus Christi, Galveston-Houston and Little Rock.

[0397] (C.M.R.)—CONGREGATION OF MARY, QUEEN (P)

Founded in Vietnam in 1670 by Bishop Pierre Lambert de la Motte. First foundation in the United States in 1979 in Springfield MO.

U.S. Regional: 625 South Jefferson Ave., Springfield, MO 65806. Tel: 417-869-9842; Fax: 417-832-0852. Sr. Irene Dinh, C.M.R., Reg. Leader.

Professed Sisters 22.

Legal Title: *Congregation of Mary Queen, American Region.*

Represented in the Archdiocese of St. Louis and in the Dioceses of Dallas, Kansas City-St. Joseph and Springfield-Cape Girardeau.

[0400] (O.CARM.)—CONGREGATION OF OUR LADY OF MOUNT CARMEL (P)

Founded in France in 1824. First foundation in the United States in 1833.

Generalate: P.O. Box 476, Lacombe, LA 70445. Tel: 504-524-2398; Fax: 504-524-5011. Sr. Ursula Diasselliss, O.Carm., Pres.; Sr. Lawrence Habetz, O.Carm., Vice-Pres./Sec.; Sr. Therese Gregoire, O.Carm., Tres./Archivist; Sr. Paula Marie Derise, O.Carm., Devel. Dir.; Sr. Germaine Laveon, O.Carm., Asst. Archivist.

Professed Sisters 93.

Ministry in the field of Education on all levels; Hospitals; Social Service; Religious Education; Pastoral Ministry and Retreat Work; Prison Education Ministry.

Represented in the Archdiocese of New Orleans and in the Dioceses of Houma-Thibodaux, Joliet and Lafayette (LA). Also in the Philippines.

[0410] (O.CARM.)—INSTITUTE OF THE SISTERS OF OUR LADY OF MOUNT CARMEL

(Istituto delle Suore di Nostra Signora del Carmelo)

Founded in Italy in 1854, First foundation in the United States, 1947.

General Motherhouse: *Istituto di Nostra Signora del Carmelo,* Via dei Baglioni 10, Roma, Italy.

U.S. Headquarters: *Carmelite Sisters,* 5 Wheatland St., Peabody, MA 01960. Tel: 978-531-4733. Sr. Benedetta Zaccardi, Supr.

Professed Sisters 8.

Ministry in Holy Childhood Nursery and Kindergarten.

Represented in the Archdioceses of Boston and Washington.

[0420] (O.C.D.)—DISCALCED CARMELITE NUNS (P)

Founded in Spain in 1562. First foundation in the United States in 1790 in Charles County, Maryland; later this monastery was moved to Baltimore.

The Monasteries listed here are strictly contemplative and belong to the Order of Discalced Carmelites.

Carmelite Monastery (1790): 1318 Dulaney Valley Rd.,Towson, Baltimore, MD 21286-1399. Tel: 410-823-7415. Sr. Constance FitzGerald, O.C.D., Prioress.

Professed Sisters 15.

Legal Title: *Carmelite Sisters of Baltimore.*

Carmel of St. Joseph (1863): 9150 Clayton Rd., St. Louis, MO, 63124-1898. Tel: 314-993-6899; Fax: 314-993-5039. E-mail: maryjoseph@mindspring.com. Mother Stella Maris, O.C.D., Prioress.

Professed Cloistered Nuns 7; Professed Extern sisters 1; Temporary Professed 3.

Monastery of St. Joseph and St. Teresa (1877): *Discalced Carmelite Nuns,* 73530 River Rd., Covington, LA 70435-2206. Sr. Edith Turpin, O.C.D., Prioress.

Discalced Carmelite Monastery (1890): 61 Mt. Pleasant Ave., Boston, MA 02119. Tel: 617-442-1411; Fax: 617-442-0203. E-mail: bostoncarmel@juno.com. Web site: www.carmelitesofboston.org. Sr. Mary Teresa Wisniewski, O.C.D., Prioress.

Total number in community 10.

Carmelite Monastery (1902): 66th Ave. and Old York Rd. (Oak Lane), Philadelphia, PA 19126. Tel: 215-424-6143; Fax: 215-424-6143/5. Mother Barbara of the Holy Ghost, O.C.D., Prioress.

Professed Nuns 8; Novices 1.

Monastery of Our Lady of Mt. Carmel (1907): *The Chancery,* P.O. Box C, Brooklyn, NY 11202. Tel: 718-399-5900. Sr. Jane Ann Scanlon, C.N.D., Vice Chancellor (Diocese of Brooklyn).

Carmelite Monastery of the Infant Jesus (1908): 1000 Lincoln St., Santa Clara, CA 95050. Tel: 408-296-8412. Sr. Emmanuel of Bethlehem, O.C.D., Prioress.

Sisters Solemn Vows 19; Novices 1.

St. Joseph's Carmelite Monastery (1908): 2215 N.E. 147th, Shoreline, WA 98155. Tel: 206-363-7150; Fax: 206-365-7335. Sr. Michael Marie, O.C.D., Prioress.

Professed Sisters 9; Postulants 1.

Legal Title: *Carmelite Monastery of Seattle.*

Carmel of the Queen of Heaven (Formerly known as Regina Coeli Monastery) (1911): 17937 250th St., Eldridge, IA 52748. Tel: 563-285-8387; Fax: 563-285-7467. Sr. Mary Joan Loebig, O.C.D., Prioress.

Professed Sisters 11.

Discalced Carmelite Nuns (1930): *Monastery of Mary Immaculate and St. Joseph,* 1740 Newburg Rd., Louisville, KY 40205. Tel: 502-451-6796. Mother Francis, Prioress; Sr. Clare, Archivist.

Solemnly Professed Sisters 10; Temporary Professed 1; Novices 1.

Legal Title: *Carmelite Monastery of Louisville, Inc.*

Order of Discalced Carmelites O.C.D. (1913): *Carmel of St. Teresa of Los Angeles, Inc.,* 215 E. Alhambra Rd., Alhambra, CA, 91801. Tel: 626-282-2387; Fax: 626-282-2053. E-mail: teresacarm@aol.com. Mother Maria, O.C.D., Prioress.

Total number in community 16.

Carmelite Monastery (1916): 4300 Mount Carmel Dr. N.E., Ada (Parnell), MI 49301. Mother Agnes Therese, O.C.D., Prioress.

Professed 15; Novices 1; Externs 2.

Discalced Carmelite Nuns (2000): *Carmelite Monastery,* 89 Hiddenbrooke Dr., Beacon, NY 12508-2230. Tel: 845-831-5579; Fax: 845-831-5579. Sr. Marjorie Robinson, O.C.D., Prioress.

Total number in community 25.

Discalced Carmelite Monastery of St. Therese of the Child Jesus (1920): 75 Carmel Rd., Buffalo, NY 14214. Tel: 716-837-6499. Mother Miriam of Jesus, O.C.D., Prioress.

Cloistered Professed Sisters 17; Extern Professed Sisters 1; Novices 2.

Monastery of Discalced Carmelites (1922): 2500 Cold Spring Rd., Indianapolis, IN 46222. Tel: 317-926-5654. Sr. Jean Alice McGoff, O.C.D., Prioress.

Contemplative Professed Nuns 12.

Legal Title: *Monastery of the Resurrection, Discalced Carmelites, Sisters of Our Lady of Mount Carmel Carmelite Monastery.*

Carmel of the Holy Family (1923): 3176 Fairmount Blvd., Cleveland Heights, OH 44118-4199. Tel: 216-321-6568. Sr. Anne Joan Boyle, O.C.D., Prioress.

Contemplative Professed Nuns 14.

Discalced Carmelite Nuns of Schenectady, NY, Inc. (1923): *Monastery of St. Teresa of Jesus,* 428 Duane Ave., Schenectady, NY 12304. Mother Mary St. John of the Cross, O.C.D., Prioress.

Professed Nuns 12.

Discalced Carmelites of the Order of Our Lady of Mount Carmel O.C.D. (1925): *Monastery of Our Lady and St. Therese,* 27601 Hwy. 1, Carmel, CA 93923. Tel: 831-624-3043; Fax: 831-624-5495. E-mail: olmediatrix-st@carmelite-nuns.org. Mother Mercedes of Mary Immaculate, O.C.D., Prioress.

Professed Sisters 14; Novices 1.

Legal Title: *Carmelite Monastery of Carmel, California, Inc.*

Discalced Carmelites O.C.D. (1926): *Monastery of the Most Blessed Virgin Mary of Mount Carmel,* 189 Madison Ave., Morristown, NJ 07960. Mother Therese, O.C.D., Prioress.

Professed Sisters 7; Novices 1.

Order of Discalced Carmelites O.C.D. (1926): *Carmelite Monastery of the Trinity,* 5158 Hawley Blvd., San Diego, CA 92116. Tel: 619-280-5424. Sr. Ancilla Murray, O.C.D., Prioress.

Professed Nuns 12; Novices 1.

Monastery of St. Therese of the Child Jesus (1926): 35750 Moravian Dr., Clinton Township, MI 48035-2138. Tel: 586-790-7255. Mother Mary Elizabeth, O.C.D., Prioress.

Professed Nuns 9; Professed Extern Sisters 1.

Carmel of St. Therese of Lisieux, Inc. (1927): *Discalced Carmelite Nuns,* P.O. Box 57, Loretto, PA 15940-0057. Tel: 814-472-8620. Mother Teresa of Jesus, O.C.D., Prioress.

Solemn Professed Nuns 9, Temporary Professed Nuns 2, Extern Sisters 2.

Discalced Carmelite Nuns O.C.D. (1928): *Carmelite Monastery of Cristo Rey,* 721 Parker Ave., San Francisco, CA 94118-4227. Mother Elizabeth of the Trinity, O.C.D., Prioress. Sr. Maria de la Immaculada, O.C.D., Archivist.

Total number in community 14.

Monastery of Discalced Carmelites (1928): 600 Flowers Ave., Dallas, TX 75211. Reverend Mother Mary Regina, O.C.D., Prioress.

Professed Nuns 9.

Discalced Carmelite Nuns (1930): *Monastery of Our Lady and St. Joseph,* 1931 W. Jefferson Rd., Pittsford, NY 14534. Tel: 585-427-7094. Mother, John of the Cross, Prioress.

Professed Nuns with Solemn Vows 6; Professed Extern Sisters 1.

Legal Title: *Carmelite Monastery of Rochester.*

Monastery of Discalced Carmelites O.C.D. (1930): *Monastery of Our Lady of Mount Carmel and St. Therese of the Child Jesus,* 25 Watson Ave., Barrington, RI 02806. Tel: 401-245-3421. Sr. Mary Margaret Yascolt, O.C.D., Prioress.

Total number in community 16.

Discalced Carmelite Nuns O.C.D. (1934): *Monastery of the Infant Jesus of Prague and Our Lady of Guadalupe,* 6301 Culebra & St. Joseph Way, San Antonio, TX 78238-4909. Tel: 210-680-1834. Mother Therese Leonard, Prioress.

Total number in community 10.

Carmel of the Holy Family and St. Therese (1935): 6981 Teresian Way, P.O. Box 1720, Georgetown, CA 95634. Tel: 530-333-1617. Web site: www.CarmeliteMonastery.com. Mother Christine, Prioress.

Total number in community 15.

Discalced Carmelite Nuns O.C.D. (1936): *Monastery of Mary, Mother of Grace,* 1250 Carmel Dr., Lafayette LA 70501. Tel: 337-232-4651. Mother Regina Mullins, O.C.D., Prioress.

Total number in community 16.

Discalced Carmelite Nuns O.C.D. (1939): *Carmel of St. Joseph,* 20,000 N. County Line Rd., Piedmont, OK 73078. Sr. Monica Lotter, O.C.D., Prioress.

Total number in community 12.

Discalced Carmelite Nuns of Milwaukee O.C.D. (1940): *Carmel of the Mother of God,* W267 N2517, Meadowbrook Rd., Pewaukee, WI 53072. Tel: 262-691-0336; Fax: 262-695-0143. E-mail: pewaukeecarmel@aol.com. Sr. Mary Agnes Kramer, Prioress.

Total number in community 10.

Discalced Carmelite Nuns of Alexandria, South Dakota, Inc. O.C.D.: *Monastery of Our Mother of Mercy and St. Joseph,* 221 5th St., W., P.O. Box 67, Alexandria, SD 57311-0067. Tel: 605-239-4382. Mother Marie Therese of the Child Jesus, Prioress.

Total number in community 8.

Carmelite Monastery (1943): 716 Dauphin Island Pkwy., Mobile, AL 36606. Fax: 251-471-3991. Mother Marie Therese, Prioress.

Solemnly Professed Nuns 4; Novices 1.

Discalced Carmelite Monastery (1945): 49 Mount Carmel Rd., Santa Fe, NM 87505-0352. Tel: 505-983-7232. Mother Rose Teresa, O.C.D., Prioress.

Total number in community 10.

Discalced Carmelite Monastery (1946): 275 Pleasant St., Concord, NH 03301-2590. Tel: 603-225-5791. Sr. Emmanuel Sache, O.C.D., Prioress.

Solemnly Professed Nuns 8; Temporary Professed 1; Postulants 2.

Sisters of Our Lady of Mount Carmel of Terre Haute, *Carmelite Monastery,* 59 Allendale, Terre Haute, IN 47802-4751. Tel: 812-299-1410; Fax: 812-299-5820. E-mail: carmelth@heartsawake.org. Mother Anne Brackmann, O.C.D., Prioress.
Professed Nuns 11; Novices 2.

Discalced Carmelite Nuns of Colorado, Inc. (1948): *Carmel of Holy Spirit,* 6138 S. Gallup St., Littleton, CO 80120-2702. Tel: 303-798-4176. Mother Judith of the Immaculate Heart, D.C., Prioress.
Professed Nuns 9.

Order of Discalced Carmelites O.C.D. (1949): *Carmel of Mary Immaculate and St. Mary Magdalen,* 26 Harmony School Rd., Flemington, NJ 08822. Mother Mary Elizabeth of the Trinity, O.C.D., Prioress.
Total in community 16.

Discalced Carmelite Nuns O.C.D. (1950): *Monastery of the Infant Jesus of Prague,* 3501 Silver Lake Rd., Traverse City, MI 49684-8949. Tel: 231-946-4960. Mother Celine of the Cross, O.C.D., Prioress and Archivist.
Total number in community 9.

Carmelite Monastery of Christ, the Exiled King (1950): 68 Rincon Rd., Kensington, CA 94707. Sr. Mary Prioress.
Professed Nuns of Solemn Vows 5.

Discalced Carmelite Nuns O.C.D. (1951): *Monastery of the Holy Cross,* U.S. Hwy. 2, P.O. Box 397, Iron Mountain, MI 49801. Tel: 906-774-0561. Mother Maria of Jesus, O.C.D., Prioress.
Total number in community 18.

Discalced Carmelite Nuns O.C.D.: *Monastery of the Holy Name of Jesus,* 6100 Pepper Rd., Denmark, WI 54208. Tel: 920-863-5055. Mother Mary Elizabeth, O.C.D., Prioress.

Discalced Carmelite Nuns O.C.D. (1950) *Monastery of the Immaculate Heart of Mary,* 94 Main St.; P.O. Box F, Montepelier, VT 05601-1455. Tel: 914-831-5572. Sr. Jeanne Gonyon, O.C.D., Prioress.
Total number in community 10.

Discalced Carmelite Nuns O.C.D. (1950): *Monastery of St. Teresa of Jesus,* 7201 W. 32nd St., Little Rock, AR 72204-4716. Tel: 501-565-5121. Sr. Joan Monkhouse, O.C.D., Prioress.
Professed Sisters 15.
Legal Title: *Discalced Carmelite Nuns of Little Rock.*

Discalced Carmelite Nuns O.C.D. (1951): *Monastery of Our Lady of Mount Carmel and The Little Flower,* 2155 Terry Rd., Jackson, MS 39204. Tel: 601-373-1460. Sr. Margaret Mary Flynn, O.C.D., Prioress.
Professed Nuns 5.

Carmel of the Immaculate Heart of Mary (1952): 5714 Holladay Blvd., Salt Lake City, UT 84121-1599. Tel: 801-277-6075. Mother Maureen Goodwin, O.C.D., Prioress; Sr. Margaret Mary Ann Miller, O.C.D., Archivist.
Solemn Vows 6; Finally Professed Externs 1.

Discalced Carmelite Nuns of St. Paul (1952): *Carmel of Our Lady of Divine Providence,* 8251 De Montreville Trail N., Lake Elmo, MN 55042-9547. Tel: 651-777-3882. Sr. Rose of the Sacred Heart, O.C.D., Prioress.
Professed Sisters 11; Novices 3; Postulants 1.

Discalced Carmelite Nuns O.C.D. (1953): 70 Monastery Rd., Elysburg, PA 17824-9697. Tel: 570-672-2935; Fax: 570-672-0278. Sr. Angela Pikus, O.C.D., Prioress; Sr. Joan Lundy, O.C.D., Archivist.
Professed Sisters 14.

Discalced Carmelite Nuns O.C.D. (1954): *Monastery of Our Lady of the Mountains,* 1950 La Fond Dr., Reno, NV 89509-3099. Tel: 775-323-3236; Fax: 775-322-1532. Sr. Ann Weber, O.C.D., Prioress.
Professed Nuns 16.

Carmel of Maria Regina O.C.D. (1957): 87609 Green Hill Rd., Eugene, OR 97402. Tel: 541-345-8649. Mother Maria Teresa, O.C.D., Prioress; Mother Maria Teresa, O.C.D., Community Archivist.
Total number in community 8.

Monastery of the Holy Family (1957): 510 E. Gore Rd., Erie, PA 16509. Mother Emmanuel of the Mother of God, Prioress.
Professed Sisters 4; Novices 2; Postulants 2.

Discalced Carmelite Nuns (1958): *Coffee Bluff,* 11 W. Back St., Savannah, GA 31419-3219. Tel: 912-925-8505. Sr. Carmela Marolda, O.C.D., Prioress.
Total number in community 4.

Monastery of the Most Holy Trinity (1958): 5801 Mt. Carmel Dr., Arlington, TX 76017. Tel: 817-468-1781. Mother Anne Teresa of Jesus Kulinski, O.C.D., Prioress.
Total number in community 11.

Discalced Carmelite Nuns O.C.D. (1958): *Carmel of the Most Holy Trinity,* 1100 Parthenon Pl., Roman Forest, New Caney, TX 77357. Sr., Mary Ann Harrison, O.C.D., Prioress; Sr. Angel Teresa Sweeney, O.C.D., 1st Council Sister.
Total number in community 8.

Monastery of Discalced Carmelites (1959): 1101 N. River Rd., Des Plaines, IL 60016. Tel: 847-298-4241. Mother Marie Andre of the Holy Spirit, Prioress.
Total number in community 16.

Order of Discalced Carmelites O.C.D. (1958): *Carmel of St. Therese,* 15 Mt. Carmel Rd., Danvers, MA 01923-3796. Tel: 978-774-3008. Sr. Anne of the Mother of God, O.C.D., Prioress.
Legal Title: *Discalced Carmelite Nuns of Danvers.*

Discalced Carmelite Nuns O.C.D. (1960): *Monastery of The Sacred Heart and St. Joseph,* 2201 W. Main St., Jefferson City, MO 65109. Tel: 573-636-3364. Mother Therese, O.C.D., Prioress.
Solemnly Professed Nuns 8; Temporarily Professed Novices 1; Novices 3.

Carmel of the Assumption (1961): R.D. 6, Box 28, Center Dr., Latrobe, PA 15650. Tel: 724-539-1056. Sr. Barbara Sitter, O.C.D., Prioress.
Professed Sisters 13.

Discalced Carmelite Nuns, Inc. (1962): *Monastery of the Discalced Carmelite Nuns,* 2901 S. Cecelia St., Sioux City, IA, 51106-3299. Tel: 712-276-1680. Mother Kateri Marie of the Eucharist, O.C.D., Prioress.
Total number in community 10.

Carmelite Monastery of the Mother of God (1965): 530 Blackstone Dr., San Rafael, CA 94903. Tel: 415-479-6872; Fax: 415-491-4964. Mother Anna Marie, O.C.D., Prioress.
Total number in community 7.

Discalced Carmelite Nuns O.C.D. (1965): *Carmel of St. Anne,* 424 E. Monastery St., Springfield, MO 65807. Tel: 417-881-2115. Mother Mary Gemma, O.C.D., Prioress.
Total number in community 5.

Carmel of the Holy Trinity: 6301 Pali Hwy., Kaneohi, HI 96744. Tel: 808-261-6542. Mother Agnes Marie Wong, O.C.D., Prioress.
Total number in community 7.

Discalced Carmelite Nuns of the Byzantine Rite (1980): *Holy Annunciation Monastery,* 403 W. Cty. Rd., Sugarloaf, PA 18249. Tel: 570-788-1205; Fax: 570-788-3329. Mother Marija of the Holy Spirit, O.C.D., Prioress.
Professed Nuns 11; Novices 4.
Represented in the Diocese of Passaic.

Carmel of Port Tobacco (1790 and refounded 1976): 5678 Mt. Carmel Rd., La Plata, MD 20646. Mother Virginia Marie, O.C.D., Prioress.
Professed 11; Simple Professed 1; Novices 3.

[0430] (B.V.M.)—SISTERS OF CHARITY OF THE BLESSED VIRGIN MARY (P)

Founded in America in 1833.

BVM Center: *Mount Carmel,* 1100 Carmel Dr., Dubuque, IA 52003. Tel: 563-588-2351; Fax: 563-588-4832. Sr. Joellen McCarthy, B.V.M., Pres.
Total number in Congregation 712.
Sisters serve and staff: in the field of Academic Education on all levels; Health Care-Aging; Religious Education; Chaplaincies; Pastoral Care and Parish Ministry; Diocesan School Offices; Diocesan Services-Administration: Social Work; Homeless Shelters; AIDS Ministry; Social Justice; Extended Day Care.
Represented in the Archdioceses of Atlanta, Chicago, Denver, Dubuque, Indianapolis, Los Angeles, Omaha, Milwaukee, Portland (OR), St. Louis St. Paul-Minneapolis, Santa Fe, San Francisco, Seattle, and Washington and in the Dioceses of Brooklyn, Biloxi, Davenport, Des Moines, Fort Wayne-South Bend, Fresno, Helena, Honolulu, Jackson, Joliet, Kansas City-St. Joseph, La Crosse, Las Vegas, Lafayette, Lexington, Memphis, Oakland, Orange, Orlando, Peoria, Pensacola-Tallahassee, Phoenix, Richmond, Rockford, Rockville Centre, San Diego, San Bernardino, San Jose, Santa Rosa, Sioux City, Springfield-Cape Girardeau, Venice, Wichita and Winona. Also in Africa, Ecuador and Guatemala.

[0440] (S.C.)—SISTERS OF CHARITY OF CINCINNATI, OHIO (P)

Founded by Saint Elizabeth Ann Seton, Emmitsburg, MD 1809. The Cincinnati Community became independent in 1852, Papal approval in 1939.

General Motherhouse (1852): *Mount St. Joseph,* Mount St. Joseph, OH 45051. Tel: 513-347-5200; Fax: 513-347-5228 Web site: www.srcharitycinti.org. Sr. Barbara Hagedorn, Pres.
Professed Sisters 525.
Legal Title: *Sisters of Charity, Cincinnati, OH.*
Sister serve and staff: Colleges; Secondary and Elementary Schools; Parishes Healthcare Facilities and School of Nursing; Foreign Missions; Home for Profoundly Challenged Children; Senior Care Services; Social Services; Congregational Services.
Represented in the Archdioceses of Chicago, Cincinnati, Denver, Detroit, Indianapolis, Louisville, Miami, Newark, New York, St. Louis, St. Paul-Minneapolis, San Francisco, Santa Fe and Washington and in the Dioceses of Brownsville, Cleveland, Colorado Springs, Columbus, Covington, El Paso, Fort Wayne-South Bend, Helena, Kalamazoo, Lansing, Lexington, Memphis, Oakland, Orlando, Phoenix, Pueblo, Saginaw, Savannah, St. Petersburg, Spokane, Toledo and Wilmington. Also in Guatemala.

[0450] (S.C.I.C.)—SISTERS OF CHARITY OF THE IMMACULATE CONCEPTION OF IVREA (P)

Founded in Italy in the 18th Century. First Foundation in the United States in 1961.

General Motherhouse: Via della Renella 85, Rome, Italy, Tel: 396-5818145. Sr. Grazia Raffaella Rossi, Supr. Gen.
Total number in Congregation 898.

U.S. Foundation (1961): *Immaculate Virgin of Miracles Convent,* 628 Prittstow Rd., Mount Pleasant, PA 15666. Tel: 412-887-6753. Sr. Letizia Garrubai, Reg. Supr. Tel: 412-887-6753
Professed Sisters in the U.S.A. 11.
Properties owned: *Verna Montessori Children's House & Elementary School; Immaculate Virgin of Miracles Convent,* Mt. Pleasant, PA.
Sisters serve and staff: Kindergarten and Elementary Schools; Parish Services; Religious Education; Pastoral Ministry.
Represented in the Diocese of Greensburg.

[0460] (C.C.V.I.)—CONGREGATION OF THE SISTERS OF CHARITY OF THE INCARNATE WORD (P)

Founded in 1869 at San Antonio, Texas.

Generalate: 4503 Broadway, San Antonio, TX 78209-6297. Tel: 210-828-2224; Fax: 210-828-9741. Sr. Helena Monahan, C.C.V.I., Gen. Supr.

Incarnate Word Provincialate - U.S. Province: P.O. Box 15378, San Antonio, TX 78212-8578. Tel: 210-734-8310; Fax: 210-734-8369. Sr. Bette Anne Bluhm, C.C.V.I., Prov. Coord.

Incarnate Word Retirement Community: 4707 Broadway, San Antonio, TX 78209-6200. Tel: 210-829-7561; Fax: 210-828-0020. Mr. Steven Fuller, Exec. Dir.
Universal Total in Congregation 466; U.S. Province 242.
Ministry in the field of Education at all levels; Hospitals and Health Service Agencies; Nursing Homes; Pastoral Ministries; Diocesan Offices; Social Service Agencies.
Properties owned and sponsored: Universities 1; High Schools 3; Hospitals (co-sponsored) 27; Temporary shelter for homeless women & children 2; Retirement Center 1; Center for Spirituality and the Arts.
Represented in the Archdioceses of Chicago, New Orleans, St. Louis, Santa Fe, and San Antonio and in the Dioceses of Amarillo, Corpus Christi, Dallas, El Paso, Fort Worth, Grand Rapids, Jefferson City, La Crosse, Lubbock, Springfield-Cape Girardeau, San Angelo, Spokane, Tucson, Tyler, and Victoria. Also in Mexico and Peru.

[0470] (C.C.V.I.)—CONGREGATION OF THE SISTERS OF CHARITY OF THE INCARNATE WORD, HOUSTON, TEXAS

Founded in the United States in 1866, St. Mary's Infirmary, Galveston, Texas.

Motherhouse: *Villa de Matel,* 6510 Lawndale Ave., P.O. Box 230969, Houston, TX 77223-0969. Tel: 713-928-6053; Fax: 713-928-8148. Sr. Olive Bordelon, Gen. Supr.
Total number in Congregation 194.
Legal Titles: Incarnate Word Charitable Trust; The Congregation of the Sisters of Charity of the Incarnate Word, Houston, TX.
Sister serve and staff: Hospitals; Homes for Aged; Elementary Schools; Social Services.
Represented in the Archdiocese of Los Angeles and in the Dioceses of Alexandria, Beaumont, Galveston-Houston, Lake Charles, Salt Lake City, San Bernardino, Shreveport and Tyler. Also in Ireland, Guatemala, San Salvador and Kenya.

[0480] (S.C.L.)—SISTERS OF CHARITY OF LEAVENWORTH, KANSAS (P)

Founded in the United States in 1858.

Community Offices and Motherhouse: 4200 S. Fourth St., Leavenworth, KS 66048-5054. Tel: 913-758-6501; Fax: 912-682-2128. Sr. Joan Sue Miller, S.C.L., Community Dir.; Sr. Helen Forge, Archivist.
Total number in community 386.
Ministries include AIDS Victims; Cross-culture; Elderly; Prisoners, Handicapped Adults and Youth; Health Service Agencies; Mental Health; Native Americans; and Social Service Agencies.
Properties owned and sponsored: *University of Saint Mary,* Leavenworth, KS; *Residential and Day Treatment Centers for Children: Mount St. Vincent Home,* Denver, CO; *Saint John's Health Center,* Santa Monica,

CA; *Health Facilities: Sisters of Charity of Leavenworth Health System,* Lenexa, KS; *Saint John's Health Center,* Santa Monica, CA; *Saint Joseph Hospital,* Denver, CO; *St. Mary's Hospital & Medical Center,* Grand Junction, CO; *Saint John Hospital,* Leavenworth, KS; *St. Francis Health Center,* Topeka, KS; *Saint Vincent Healthcare,* Billings, MT; *St. James Healthcare,* Butte, MT; *Holy Rosary Healthcare,* Miles City, MT; *Marian Clinic,* Topeka, KS; *Marillac Clinic,* Grand Junction, CO; *Providence Medical Center,* Kansas City, KS; *Bethany Community Plaza,* Kansas City, KS; *Caritas Clinic, Inc.,* Kansas City, KS; *Saint Vincent Clinic,* Leavenworth, KS *(Div. of Caritas Clinics); Duchesne Clinic,* Kansas City, KS *(Div. of Caritas Clinics).*

Sisters serving in Elementary, Secondary and Higher Education Nursing Education; Special Education; Religious Education; Ministry Training; Hospitals; Latin American Missions; Diocesan Offices; Parish Administration and Pastoral Ministry; Liturgy-Music Ministry; Campus Ministry; Spiritual Direction; Communications; Social Justice; Housing.

Represented in the Archdioceses of Denver, Kansas City in Kansas, Los Angeles, Omaha, Portland in Oregon, St. Louis, Santa Fe, and San Antonio and in the Dioceses of Cheyenne, Cincinnati, Gallup, Great Falls-Billings, Helena, Jackson, Jefferson City, Kansas City-St. Joseph, Oakland, Pueblo, San Diego, St. Cloud and Tucson. Also in Peru.

[0490] (S.G.M.)—SISTERS OF CHARITY OF MONTREAL (Grey Nuns) (P)

Founded in 1737 by Saint Marguerite d'Youville at Montreal, Quebec, Canada. First foundation in the United States

Generalate: *General Administration,* 138 Rue Saint-Pierre, Montreal, Quebec, Canada. H2Y 2L7, Tel: 514-842-9411. Sr. Aurore Larkin, S.G.M., Supr. Gen.

St. Joseph Region U.S.A.: *Regional Admin. -SGM,* 10 Pelham Rd.-Ste. 1000, Lexington, MA 02421-8499. Tel: 781-862-4700. Sr. Jeanne Poor, S.G.M., Reg. Supr.; Sr. Helene Georges, S.G.M., Dir.-Formation.

Total number in community 49.

Legal Title: *The Grey Nuns Charities, Inc.*

Ministry in Hospitals; Nursing Homes; Parish Ministry; Social Justice; Pastoral Care; Housing for the Elderly & Handicapped; Assisted Living Residence; Religious Education; Thrift Shops.

Represented in the Archdiocese of Boston and in the Dioceses of Manchester, Portland (ME) and Toledo.

[0500] (S.C.N.)—SISTERS OF CHARITY OF NAZARETH (P)

Founded in the United States in 1812.

SCN Center: P.O. Box 172, Nazareth, KY 40048. Tel: 502-348-1555; Fax: 502-348-1502. Sr. Shalini D'Souza, S.C.N., Pres.

Total number in Congregation 695.

Legal Title: *Nazareth Literary & Benevolent Institution.*

Properties owned or sponsored: *Our Lady of Nazareth Academy,* Wakefield, MA; *Nazareth Montessori Children's Center. Retreat Facilities: Catherine Spalding Center,* Nazareth, KY; *Bethany Spring,* New Haven, KY; *Camp Maria,* Leonardtown, MD. *Facilities for the Elderly and Handicapped: Nazareth Village I, Nazareth Village II,* Nazareth, KY; *Nazareth Home,* Louisville, KY.

Nazareth Office: P.O. Box 187, Nazareth, KY 40048. Tel: 502-331-4072. Fax: 502-331-4073. Sr. Susan Gatz, S.C.N., Prov.

Louisville Office, 676 Atwood, P.O. Box 17545, Louisville, KY 40217. Tel: 502-636-0411; Fax: 502-636-0412. Sr. Theresa Knabel, S.C.N., Vice Prov.

Quincy Office, 169 Fenno St., Quincy, MA 02170. Tel: 617-479-4909; Fax: 617-786-0767. Sr. Eleanor Martin, S.C.N., Vice Prov.

Final professed sisters 508.

Sisters serve and staff: in the field of Academic Education on all levels; Special Educational Services; Social Services; Libraries; Parish Ministry; Archdiocesan Offices; Health Care Institutions; Retreat Centers; Literacy & Retirement Centers.

Represented in the Archdioceses of Chicago, Indianapolis, Louisville, Miami, and Washington and in the Dioceses of Baton Rouge, Charleston, Covington, Jackson, Knoxville, Little Rock, Lexington, Memphis, Owensboro, San Jose, St. Petersburg and Wilmington. Also in Belize City, Nicaragua and Botswana.

India Region: *Regional House,* E. Boring Canal Rd., Post Box 219, Patna, Bihar, India. 800-001 Tel: 011-91-612-532-579. Sr. Teresa Kotturan, S.C.N., Prov.

Final professed sisters 153.

Central Leadership Team: Final professed sisters 3.

[0510] (O.L.M.)—SISTERS OF CHARITY OF OUR LADY OF MERCY (D)

Founded in Charleston, South Carolina in 1829.

Generalate and Motherhouse: *Sisters of Charity of Our Lady of Mercy,* 424 Fort Johnson Rd. - P.O. Box 12410, Charleston, SC 29422. Tel: 843-795-2866; Fax: 843-795-6083. Sr. Anne Francis Campbell, O.L.M., Gen. Supr.

Total number in community 24.

Legal Title: *The Sisters of Charity of Our Lady of Mercy Charitable Trust.*

Properties owned: *Motherhouse, May Forest,* Charleston, SC; *Our Lady of Mercy Convent,* John's Island, SC; *Our Lady of Mercy Community Outreach Services, Inc.,* Johns Island, SC.

Sisters serve and staff: Parishes; Elementary Schools; Social Services.

Represented in the Archdiocese of Baltimore and in the Diocese of Charleston.

[0520] (S.C.M.M.)—SISTERS OF CHARITY OF OUR LADY, MOTHER OF MERCY (P)

Founded in Holland 1832. First foundation in the United States in 1874.

General Motherhouse: Den Bosch, Netherlands.

Universal number in Congregation 1,050.

U.S. Provincial House: 32 Tuttle Place, East Haven, CT 06512. Tel: 203-469-7872. Sr. Mary Ellen Ryley, S.C.M.M., Prov.

Total number in community 17.

Represented in the Archdioceses of Chicago, Detroit, Hartford, and St. Paul-Minneapolis and in the Diocese of San Diego.

[0530] (S.C.M.C.)—SISTERS OF CHARITY OF OUR LADY, MOTHER OF THE CHURCH (P)

First foundation in the United States in 1970.

General Motherhouse: Baltic, CT 06330. Tel: 860-822-8241; Fax: 860-822-9842. Mother M. Anthony Lemire, Supr. Gen.

Professed Sisters 72; Junior Professed 7; Novices 2.

Properties owned, staffed or sponsored: High Schools 1; Nursing Home 1; Elementary Schools 8; Home for Aged; Home for Dependent Children 1; Catechetical Schools 12; D Shelter for the Homeless 1; Hispanic Ministry 1.

Represented in the Archdiocese of Hartford and in the Dioceses of Manchester, Madison and Norwich.

[0540] (S.C.O.)—SISTERS OF CHARITY OF OTTAWA (P)

(Grey Nuns of the Cross)

Founded in Ottawa, Canada, in 1845. First foundation in the United States in 1857.

General Motherhouse: 9 Bruyere St., Ottawa, Ontario, Canada. K1N 5C9, Mother Claire Malette, S.C.O., Gen. Supr.

Total number of Sisters in Congregation based in Ottawa 750.

American Province (1950): *St. Joseph,* 559 Fletcher St., Lowell, MA 01854-3434. Tel: 978-453-4993; Fax: 978-441-1452. Sr. Prescille Malo, S.C.O., Prov. Supr., Sr. Paula Bradley, S.C.O., Archivist.

Professed U.S. Sisters 33.

Legal Title: *Sisters of Charity of Ottawa.*

Properties owned: *D'Youville Senior Care, Inc.; Bachand Hall; St. Joseph Residence,* Lowell, MA.

Sisters staff: Grammar Schools; Health Care and Pastoral Ministries; Apostolate of Aging.

Represented in the Archdioceses of Boston and Newark.

[0560] (S.C.Q.)—SISTERS OF CHARITY OF QUEBEC (P)

(Grey Nuns)

Founded in Quebec in 1849. First United States foundation in 1890.

General Motherhouse: 2655 Le Pelletier St., Beauport, Quebec, Canada. GIC 3X7, Tel: 418-628-8860. Sr. Denise Marcoux, S.C.Q., Supr.

U.S. House (1908): *Franco-American School,* 357 Pawtucket St., Lowell, MA 01854. Tel: 978-458-1251. Sr. Lorraine Richard, S.C.Q.

U.S. House (1917): *Sacred Heart Home, Inc.,* 359 Summer St., New Bedford, MA 02740. Tel: 508-996-6751. Sr. Blandine D'Amours, S.C.Q., Supr.

Professed U.S. Sisters 6.

Sisters serve and staff: The field of education and care of the elderly; Franco American School, Lowell, MA; Sacred Heart Home, New Bedford, MA.

Represented in the Archdiocese of Boston and in the Diocese of Fall River.

[0570] (S.C.)—SISTERS OF CHARITY OF SETON HILL, GREENSBURG, PENNSYLVANIA (P)

Founded in the United States in 1870.

Motherhouse: *Caritas Christi,* 459 Mount Thor Rd., Greensburg, PA 15601. Tel: 724-838-1512.

Generalate: *Sisters of Charity of Seton Hill,* 4238 North Walnut Ave., Arlington Heights, IL 60004. Tel: 847-398-1891; Fax: 847-398-1896. E-mail: marlenem@scsh.org. Sr. Marlene Mondalek, S.C., Gen. Supr.

Total number in the community 494.

Ministry in the field of Religious and Academic Education at all levels; Special Education and Rehabilitation Services for Children and Adults with physical and mental handicaps; Social and Legal Services; Health Care; Retreat Centers; Day Care Centers for Children and Adults; Pastoral and Campus Ministry; Community Service Center, Shelters for the Homeless; Spiritual Direction; Diocesan Offices; and Art Ministry.

Properties owned: *Elizabeth Seton Center,* Pittsburgh, PA; *Korea Province* in Kwangju, Korea.

U.S. Province - Provincialate: *DePaul Center,* 463 Mount Thor Rd., Greensburg, PA 15601. Tel: 724-836-0406; Fax: 724-836-8280. Sr. Vivien Linkhauer, S.C., Prov. Supr.; Sr. Mary Catherine Seli, S.C., Archivist.

Represented in the Archdioceses of Chicago, Cincinnati, Hartford, Los Angeles, and Washington and in the Dioceses of Altoona-Johnstown, Brooklyn, Erie, Greensburg, Orlando, Phoenix, Pittsburgh, Raleigh, St. Petersburg, Steubenville, Tucson and Wheeling-Charleston. Also in Israel.

[0580] (C.S.A.)—SISTERS OF CHARITY OF ST. AUGUSTINE (D)

Founded in Cleveland, Ohio in 1851.

Motherhouse: *Mount Augustine,* 5232 Broadview Rd., Richfield, OH 44286. Sr. Miriam Erb, C.S.A., Congregational Leader; Sr. Mary Denis Maher, C.S.A., Archivist.

Total number in Congregation 77.

Properties owned and sponsored: *CSA Health Network,* Cleveland, OH; *Providence Hospital,* Columbia, SC; *Regina Health Center,* Richfield, OH; *Saint Ann Foundation,* Cleveland, OH; *Saint Augustine Academy,* Lakewood, OH; *St. Vincent Charity Hospital,* Cleveland, OH; *Sisters of Charity of St. Augustine Health System, Inc.,* Cleveland, OH; *Mercy Medical Center,* Canton, OH; *Westlake Health Campus Association dba St. John West Shore Hospital,* Westlake, OH.

Represented in the Dioceses of Charleston, Cleveland, Lexington and Youngstown.

[0590] (S.C.)—SISTERS OF CHARITY OF SAINT ELIZABETH, CONVENT STATION (P)

Founded in Newark, New Jersey in 1859.

General Motherhouse: *Convent of St. Elizabeth - Administration Building,* P.O. Box 476, Convent Station, NJ 07961-0476. Tel: 973-290-5000; 290-5450 (Admin.); Fax: 973-290-5335. Sr. Maureen Shaughnessy, Gen. Supr.; Sr. Elizabeth McLoughlin, Archivist; Sr. Miriam Teresa League of Prayer.

Total number in Congregation 537.

Legal Titles and Properties: *Sisters of Charity of Saint Elizabeth Academy of Saint Elizabeth,* Convent Station, NJ; *Saint Vincent Academy,* Newark, NJ; *Academy of the Sacred Heart,* Hoboken, NJ; *Saint Frances Residence,* Paterson, NJ.

Sisters serve and staff: Academies; High Schools; Elementary Schools; Hospitals; C.C.D.; Parish Work; Social Work; Health Services; College Teaching.

Represented in the Archdioceses of Boston, Hartford, Newark, and New York, and in the Dioceses of Camden, Charlotte, El Paso, Fairbanks, Fall River, Jackson, Metuchen, Paterson, Palm Beach, Providence, Pensacola-Tallahassee, Richmond, Rochester, St. Petersburg, Syracuse, Trenton, Tucson, Venice, Wheeling-Charleston and Wilmington. Also in St. Thomas, Virgin Islands.

[0600] (S.C.S.J.A.)—SISTERS OF CHARITY OF ST. JOAN ANTIDA (P)

Founded in France in 1799 by Saint Joan Antida Thouret. First foundation in the U.S. 1932.

General Motherhouse: *Suore della Carita di Santa Giovanna Antida,* Via S. Maria in Cosmedin 5 00153 Roma, Italia. Sr. M. Luisa Colombo, Supr. Gen.

North American Province (1976): *Regina Mundi Provincial House,* 8560 N. 76th Pl., Milwaukee, WI 53223. Tel: 414-354-9233; Fax: 414-355-6463. Sr. Jennifer L. Daul, S.C.S.J.A., Prov.

Total number in Congregation 42.

Ministry in prisons; neighborhood services and parishes.

Properties owned and sponsored: *St. Joan Antida High School, Inc.; Guardian Angel Learning Center, Inc.; St. Joan Antida High School Foundation, Ltd.*

Represented in the Archdiocese of Milwaukee and in the Dioceses of Amarillo and Gallup.

[0610] (S.C.S.H.)—SISTERS OF CHARITY OF ST. HYACINTHE (P)

(Grey Nuns)

Founded in 1840 in St. Hyacinthe, P.Q., Canada. First United States foundation in 1878.

General House: 16470 Avenue Bourdages, SUD, St. Hyacinthe, P.Q., Canada J2T 4J8. Sr. Diane Beaudoin, S.C.S.H., Supr. Gen.; Sr. Claudette Jacques, S.C.S.H., Gen. Sec.

Universal number in Congregation 226.
Legal Title: *The Society of the Sisters of Charity,* Lewiston, ME.
U.S. Regional Administration: *Sisters of Charity of St. Hyacinthe,* 98 Campus Ave., Lewiston, ME 04240-6076. Tel: 207-797-8607. Sr. Diane Beaudoin, Pres.; Sr. Marguerite Carignan.
Total number in U.S. 10.
Properties owned: *St. Peter's Home,* Manchester, NH.
Represented in the Dioceses of Manchester and Portland (ME). Also in Canada and Haiti.

[0620] (S.C.S.L.)—SISTERS OF CHARITY OF ST. LOUIS (P)

Founded in France in 1803. First foundation in the United States in 1910.
Generalate: 5169 Avenue MacDonald, Montreal, (Quebec), H3X 2V9 Canada. Sr. Geraldine Hagel, Supr. Gen.
Total universal number in Congregation 722.
American Region: 4907 S. Catherine St., Plattsburgh, NY 12901. Tel: 518-563-0383; Fax: 518-563-0383. Sr. Louise Marceau, Local Supr.
Total number in community 12.
Properties owned and sponsored: *resident and Our Lady of Victory Convent,* Plattsburgh, NY.
Represented in the Diocese of Ogdensburg.

[0630] (V.Z.)—SISTERS OF CHARITY OF ST. VINCENT DE PAUL OF ZAGREB (P)

Founded in Croatia (Austria-Hungary) in 1845. First U.S. Foundation in 1955.
General Motherhouse: Zagreb, Croatia. Mother Maria Blaga Buncuga, Supr. Gen.
U.S. Foundation: *Sisters of Charity Convent,* 171 Knox Ave., West Seneca, NY 14224. Tel: 716-825-5859. Sr. M. Stella Simetich, V.Z., Supr.
Professed Sisters 17.
Properties owned: *Nursery School.*
Sisters staff: Nursery Schools; CCD Centers and Parish Services; Hospital & Health Services.
Represented in the Diocese of Buffalo.

[0640] (S.C.)—SISTERS OF CHARITY OF ST. VINCENT DE PAUL, HALIFAX (P)

Founded by Saint Elizabeth Ann Seton, Emmitsburg, Maryland in 1809. Congregation at Halifax became independent in 1856, Papal approval in 1908.
Motherhouse: *Mount Saint Vincent,* 150 Bedford Hwy., Halifax, N.S B3M 3J5, Canada. Tel: 902-457-3500; Fax: 902-457-3506. Sr. Donna Geernaert, Congregation Leader; Sr. Marie Gillen, Archivist.
Total universal number in Congregation 640.
Legal Title: *Sisters of Charity (Halifax).*
Commonwealth of Massachusetts: *Boston Branch Office,* 26 Phipps St., Quincy, MA 02169-6626. Tel: 617-773-6085; Fax: 617-472-7179. Sr. Patricia Kelly, S.C., Congregation Councilor, Tel: 617-773-6076; Fax: 617-472-7179.
Legal Title: *Sisters of Charity (Halifax) Supporting Corporation,* 125 Oakland St., Wellesley Hills, MA 02481-5338. Tel: 781-237-2161; Fax: 781-237-8152. Sr. Donna Geernaert, Congregational Leader.
Legal Title: *Sisters of Charity (Halifax) Corporate Mission, Inc.,* 26 Phipps St., Quincy, MA 02169-6626. Tel: 617-773-6085; Fax: 617-773-7179. Sr. Donna Geernaert, Congregational Leader.
Mount St. Vincent Retirement Community: 125 Oakland St., Wellesley Hills, MA 02481-5338. Tel: 781-237-2161; Fax: 781-237-8152. Community Leadership Team: Sr. Ann Marie Barry; Sr. Elizabeth Groome; Sr. Ann Regan.
Legal Titles and Holdings: *Marillac Residence, Inc.,* Wellesley Hills, MA; *Elizabeth Seton Residence, Inc.,* Wellesley Hills, MA.
State of New York: New York Branch Office, 84-32 63rd Ave., Middle Village, NY 11379-1967. Tel: 718-651-1685 & 516-783-5589; Fax: 718-651-5645. Sr. Mary Katherine Hamm, Congregational Councilor; Sr. Mary E. Moore, Congregational Councilor.
Ministering in education at all levels; homes for the aging; hospitals; parish ministry; spiritual direction/retreats/houses of prayer; social services; pastoral ministry; administration.
Represented in the Archdiocese of Boston and in the Dioceses of Brooklyn and Rockville Centre. Also in Canada, Bermuda, Dominican Republic and Peru.

[0650] (S.C.)—SISTERS OF CHARITY OF ST. VINCENT DE PAUL, OF NEW YORK (D)

Founded in Emmitsburg, MD in 1809 by Saint Elizabeth Ann Seton.
General Motherhouse: *Sisters of Charity Center, Mount Saint Vincent-on-Hudson,* 6301 Riverdale Ave., Bronx, NY 10471. Tel: 718-549-9200; Fax: 718-884-3013. Sr. Dorothy Metz, S.C., Pres.
Total number in Congregation 470.
Sisters serve and staff: Colleges; High Schools; Elementary Schools; Child Caring Homes; General Hospitals; Foundling Hospital; Schools of Nursing; Residence for Senior and Invalid Sisters; Mental Health Divisions, Rest House for Community use; Housing for Homeless.
Represented in the Archdioceses of Atlanta, Baltimore, Newark, New York and Washington and in the Dioceses of Albany, Bridgeport, Brooklyn, Camden, Gary, Rockville Centre and Shreveport. Also in the Bahamas and Guatemala.

[0660] (S.C.C.)—SISTERS OF CHRISTIAN CHARITY (P)

Daughters of the Blessed Virgin Mary of the Immaculate Conception

Founded in Germany in 1849. First foundation in the United States in 1873.
Generalate: *Suore della Carita Cristiana, Casa Generalizia,* Largo XXI Aprile, 10 00162, Roma, Italia. Tel: 011-3906-8622011. Sr. Mary Adalberta Mette, Supr. Gen.
Total universal number in Congregation 778.
North American Eastern Province (1927): *Mallinckrodt Convent Div. of North American Province,* 350 Bernardrille Rd., Mendham, NJ 07945. Tel: 973-543-6528. Sr. Mary Edward Spohrer, S.C.C., Prov. Sr. Mary Pierre Koesters, S.C.C., Archivist.
Professed Sisters 267.
Ministry in Academic Education; Retreat House; Catechetical Centers; Religion Coordinators; Health care & Parish Ministry.
Properties owned and/or sponsored: *Villa Pauline, Retreat House,* Mendham, NJ; *Divine Providence Hospital,* Williamsport, PA; *Holy Spirit Hospital,* Camp Hill, PA; *Mallinckrodt Convent Motherhouse,* Mendham, NJ; *Holy Family Convent, Home for Aged and Retired Sisters,* Danville, PA; *Muncy Valley Hospital,* Muncy, PA.
Represented in the Archdioceses of Newark, New York and Philadelphia and in the Dioceses of Allentown, Camden, Harrisburg, Metuchen, Paterson and Scranton.
North American Western Province: *Sisters of Christian Charity - Daughters of the Blessed Virgin Mary of the Immaculate Conception,* 2041 Elmwood Ave., Wilmette, IL 60091-1431. Tel: 847-920-9341; Fax: 847-920-9346. Sr. Mary Clement Eiden, Prov. Supr. Sr. Joann Kelzer, Archivist.
Professed Sisters 100.
Ministry in Academic & Religious Education; Pastoral Ministry; Parish Ministry; Ministry to Aged; Prayer Ministry; Ministry to the Poor and Multi-Cultural.
Properties owned and sponsored: *Maria Immaculata Convent; Sacred Heart Convent,* Wilmette, IL; *Josephinum High School and Convent,* Chicago, IL; *Mallinckrodt College of the North Shore,* Wilmette, IL.
Represented in the Archdioceses of Chicago, New Orleans, St. Louis and Santa Fe and in the Dioceses of Jefferson City, Rapid City, Pensacola-Tallahassee, and Tucson.

[0670] (O.C.S.O.)—CISTERCIAN NUNS OF THE STRICT OBSERVANCE (P)

Founded at Citeaux, France, in 1098. First foundation in the United States in 1949.
Generalate: Viale Africa 33, 00144, Rome, Italy.
Total Universal number of Nuns in Order 1,800. Contemplative.
U.S. Establishments:
Mount St. Mary's Abbey: 300 Arnold St., Wrentham, MA 02093-1799. Tel: 508-528-1282; Fax: 508-528-5360. Rev. Mother M. Agnes Day, O.C.S.O., Abbess.
Total number in community 46.
Represented in the Archdiocese of Boston.
Our Lady of the Mississippi Abbey: 8400 Abbey Hill Road, Dubuque, IA 52003. Tel: 563-582-2595; Fax: 563-582-5511. Rev. Mother Gail Fitzpatrick, O.C.S.O., Abbess.
Total number in community 21.
Legal Title: *Trappistine Nuns, Inc.; Iowa Cistercians of the Strict Observance.*
Represented in the Archdiocese of Dubuque.
Santa Rita Abbey: HC 1, Box 929, Sonoita, AZ 85637-9705. Tel: 520-455-5595. Mother Miriam Pollard, O.C.S.O., Prioress.
Total number in community 13.
Legal Title: *Cistercian Nuns of the Strict Observance.*
Represented in the Diocese of Tucson.
Our Lady of the Redwoods Abbey: 18104 Briceland Thorn Rd., Whitethorn, CA 95589. Tel: 707-986-7419. Web site: www.redwoodsabbey.org. Sr. Kathy DeVico, O.C.S.O., Abbess.
Total number in community 9.
Represented in the Diocese of Santa Rosa.
Our Lady of the Angels Monastery: 3365 Monastery Dr., Crozet, VA 22932. Tel: 434-823-1452; Fax: 434-823-6379. Mother Marion Rissetto, O.C.S.O., Prioress.
Legal Title: *Cistercian Nuns of the Strict Observance in Virginia, Inc.*
Represented in the Diocese of Richmond.

[0680] (O.CIST.)—CISTERCIAN NUNS (P)

Founded in 1098 at Citeaux, France, is composed of monks and nuns in independent houses.
Generalate: *Piazza del Tempio di Diana,* 14, Roma, Italia 00153. Most Rev. Maurus Esteva, O.Cist., Abbot Gen.
U.S. Headquarters: *Valley of Our Lady Monastery,* E. 11096 Yanke Dr., Prairie du Sac, WI 53578-9737. Tel: 608-643-3520; Fax: 608-643-0684. Rev. Mother Paula Hannah, O.Cist., Prioress.
Total number in community 14.

[0685] (R.M.I.)—CLARETIAN MISSIONARY SISTERS (P)

Religious of Mary Immaculate Claretian Missionary Sisters

Founded in Santiago de Cuba, August 25, 1855. Established in the United States in 1956.
Generalate: Via Calandrelli 16, 00153, Roma, Italy. Eusebia Pizarro, Supr. Gen.
U.S. Delegation: 9600 W. Atlantic Ave., Delray Beach, FL 33446. Sr. Regina Tutzo, R.M.I., Local Supr.
Sisters in the World 600; Sisters in Florida 11.
Legal Title: *Claretian Missionary Sisters of Florida, Inc.*
Ministry in Religious Education; Theological formation in Pastoral Institutes and Seminaries; Social Ministries; Parish and Diocesan Ministries.
Represented in the Archdiocese of Miami and in the Diocese of Palm Beach.

[0690] (C.M.S.)—COMBONI MISSIONARY SISTERS (P)

Founded in Italy in 1872. An international congregation of 1,700 sisters serving in the mission fields of Africa, Latin America and the Middle East. First United States Foundation in 1950.
Generalate: Rome, Italy. Mother Adele Brambilla, C.M.S., Supr. Gen.
American Headquarters: 1307 Lakeside Ave., Richmond, VA 23228. Tel: 804-262-8827; Fax: 804-264-2906. Sr. Maria Teresa Goffi, Prov.
Legal Titles & Holdings: *Provincial House, Holy Angels Day Care Center, Comboni Missionary Sisters, Inc.,* Richmond, VA.
Represented in the Archdiocese of Baltimore, and Philadelphia and in the Diocese of Richmond.

[0700] (O.D.N.)—COMPANY OF MARY (P)

Founded in Bordeaux, France, April 7, 1607, by St. Jeanne de Lestonnac. First foundation in the United States in 1926, in Douglas, Arizona.
General Motherhouse: Rome, Italy. Sr. Margarita Maria Pedraz, O.D.N., Supr. Gen.
Universal number in Congregation 1,930.
U.S. Motherhouse (1926): *Company of Mary Provincial House,* 16791 E. Main St., Tustin, CA 92780. Tel: 714-541-3125. Sr. Mary of Jesus Rodriguez, O.D.N., Prov. Supr.; Sr. Kathy Schneider, O.D.N., Community Archivist.
Total number in U.S. 51.
Properties owned: *St. Jeanne de Lestonnac Kindergarten & Day Nursery,* Los Angeles, CA; *Divine Providence Kindergarten & Day Nursery,* Los Angeles, CA; *St. Joseph Residence for Women,* Los Angeles, CA; *St. Jeanne De Lestonnac School,* Tustin, CA; *Vina de Lestonnac Ministry Center-Retreat; Lestonnac Kindergarten & Day Nursery,* Douglas, AZ; *St. Jeanne de Lestonnac School,* Temecula, CA.
Sisters serve and staff: Pre-Schools - Kindergartens; Grammar Schools; Religious Instruction Centers; Residences; Parishes & Retreat Centers.
Represented in the Archdiocese of Los Angeles and in the Dioceses of Orange, San Bernardino and Tucson.

[0710] (C.S.)—THE COMPANY OF THE SAVIOR (D)

Founded in Spain in 1952. First United States foundation in 1962.
General Motherhouse: Aravaca Madrid-23, Spain. Mother Amelia Lora-Tamayo, Supr. Gen.
U.S. Foundation: 820 Clinton Ave., Bridgeport, CT 06604. Tel: 203-368-1875.
Professed Sisters 62; Novices 8; Postulants 2.
Represented in the Diocese of Bridgeport.

[0720] (M.C.)—CONSOLATA MISSIONARY SISTERS (P)

Founded in Italy in 1910. First foundation in United States in 1954.
Motherhouse: *Istituto Suore Missionarie della Consolata,* Via Cassia Km.37, Viterbo, Nepi, Italy. 01036. Mother Gabriella Bono, Supr. Gen.

Total universal number in Congregation is approximately 900.
Represented in the Dioceses of Birmingham and Grand Rapids.
U.S. Headquarters: *Consolata Missionary Sisters,* 6801 Belmont Rd.-P.O. Box 371, Belmont, MI 49306. Tel: 616-361-2072; Fax: 616-361-2049. Sr. Zelia M. Cordeiro, M.C., Supr.
Total number in community 30.
Sisters serve and staff: Catechetical and Pastoral Work; Apostolate among Minorities; Elementary and High Schools.

[0725] (M.C-M.)—CORDI-MARIAN MISSIONARY SISTERS CONGREGATION (P)

Founded in Mexico City in 1921. First United States foundation in 1926.
General Motherhouse: Apdo. Postal #1109, Toluca, Mexico C.P. 50091. Sr. Evangelina Perez, M.C-M., Supr. Gen.
U.S. Provincial House: 11624 FM 471, Apt. 501, San Antonio, TX 78253. Tel: 210-767-1810. Sr. M. Catalina Marquez, M.C-M., Prov. Supr.
Total number in Congregation 122; Total number in U.S. community 37.
Ministry in Catechetical Centers; Pastoral Ministry Programs; Elementary Education; Kindergarten and Day Care Centers; Retreat Center; Social Service; Migrant Ministry; Prison Ministry; Vestment and Banner Making.
Properties Owned: *Cordi-Marian Villa—Retreat Center and Provincial House,* San Antonio, TX; *East St. Louis Catholic Day Care Center and Convent,* East St. Louis, IL.
Represented in the Archdioceses of Kansas City, and San Antonio and in the Diocese of Austin.

[0730] (Fd.CC.)—CANOSSIAN DAUGHTERS OF CHARITY (P)

Canossian Sisters

Founded in Verona, Italy in 1808.
General Motherhouse: via della Stazione di Ottavia 70, Rome, Italy 00135.
U.S. Provincial House: Cristo Rey-Canossian Sisters, 5625 Isleta Blvd., S.W., Albuquerque, NM 87105. Tel: 505-873-2854. Sr. E. Chambers, Prov. Supr.
Sisters in U.S. 43.
Ministry in Evangelization; Spirituality Center, Integral Promotion of the Person; Parish Pastoral Ministry; Pastoral care of the sick; Intermediate Care Facility for Developmentally Disabled Children; Lay Volunteer Program.
Represented in the Archdioceses of San Francisco and Santa Fe and in the Diocese of Sacramento. Also in Canada and Mexico.

[0740] (D.C.P.B.)—DAUGHTERS OF CHARITY OF THE MOST PRECIOUS BLOOD (P)

Founded in Pagani, Italy in 1872. First foundation in United States in 1908.
Generalate: Via Vigna Fabbri 45, Rome, Italy. Sr. Ofelia Marzocca, Mother Gen.
U.S. Address: *Daughters of Charity of the Most Precious Blood,* 1482 North Ave., Bridgeport, CT 06604. Tel: 203-334-7000. Sr. Alfonsa Kunnel, D.C.P.B., Supr.
Total number in community 18.
Represented in the Dioceses of Albany, Bridgeport and Paterson.

[0750] (F.C.S.C.J.)—DAUGHTERS OF THE CHARITY OF THE SACRED HEART OF JESUS (P)

First founded in France at La Salle de Vihiers in 1823. First founded in the United States at Newport, Vermont in October 1905.
Generalate: Montgeron, France.
General Motherhouse: La Salle de Vihiers, France. Sr. Collette Lussier, Supr. Gen.
Mount Sacred Heart Provincial House: *Daughters of the Charity of the Sacred Heart of Jesus (1949),* 226 Grove St., Littleton, NH 0356. Tel: 603-444-5346; Fax: 603-444-3970; 603-444-5348. Sr. Jeannette Roy, F.C.S.C.J., Prov.; Sr. Theresa Fournier, F.C.S.C.J., Local Supr.
Total number in Province 57.
Sisters serve and staff: Grammar Schools and Kindergarten; Catechetical Centers; Spiritual Directors; Pastoral Ministry; Preschools; Foreign Missions.
Represented in the Archdiocese of Boston and in the Dioceses of Burlington, Fall River, Lafayette, LA, Manchester, Ogdensburg and Portland (ME).

[0760] (D.C.)—DAUGHTERS OF CHARITY OF ST. VINCENT DE PAUL (P)

Founded in France in 1633. First foundation in the United States in 1809 by Saint Elizabeth Ann Seton, Emmitsburg, MD.
General Motherhouse: Paris, France. Sr. Juana Elizondo, Supr. Gen.
Emmitsburg Province (Southeast) (1809): *St. Joseph's Provincial House,* 333 South Seron Ave., Emmitsburg, MD 21727. Tel: 301-447-3121; Fax: 301-447-6038. Sr. Elyse Staab, D.C., Prov.
Total number in Province 211.
Legal Title: *Sisters of Charity of St. Joseph's.*
Sisters serve and staff: High Schools; Elementary Schools; Medical Clinics; Hospitals; Nursing Homes; Homes for unmarried Mothers; Child Caring Homes; Retreat Center; Dining Facilities for the homeless; Social Service Centers; Catholic Charities; Parish Ministries; Hispanic Ministry.
Represented in the Archdioceses of Baltimore and Washington and in the Dioceses of Charleston, Pensacola-Tallahassee, Raleigh, Richmond, Savannah, St. Augustine, St. Petersburg and Wheeling-Charleston.
West Central Province (1910): *Marillac Provincial House,* 4328 Westminster Place, St. Louis, MO 63108-2624. Tel: 314-533-3004. Sr. Marie Therese Sedgwick, Prov.; Sr. Genevieve Keusenkothen, Archivist.
Total number in the community 203.
Ministry in the field of Religious and Academic Education at all levels; Seminary Education; Hospitals; Psychiatric Hospitals; Parish Ministry; Health & Social Service Centers; Day Care Centers; Clinics; Homes for Children; Catholic Charities Offices; Housing; Peace and Justice; Diocesan Offices; State Health Care; Home Health Care; Emergency Relief Centers; Spiritual Direction and Retreats.
Sponsors: Clinics: *Centro San Vicente,* El Paso, TX; *Daughters of Charity Services of New Orleans; Daughters of Charity Services of San Antonio, Inc.; Daughters of Charity Services of San Antonio-La Mision Div.,* San Antonio, TX; *Daughters of Charity Services of San Antonio-De Paul Div.,* San Antonio, TX; *Daughters of Charity Community Services of El Paso (DCCS-EP); Daughters of Charity Health Services of Austin-Center; Daughters of Charity Health Services of Austin-Seton South,* Austin, TX. *Hospitals- Seton Medical Center,* Austin, TX, *Seton Northwest,* Austin, TX; *De Paul Center,* Waco, TX; *Providence Health Center,* Waco, TX; *Daughters of Charity Services of Arkansas-DePaul Health Center,* Dumas, AR; *Ascension Health,* St. Louis, MO; *Seton Center,* Kansas City, MO; *Daughters of Charity Foundation,* St. Louis, MO; *Daughters of Charity Healthcare Foundation of St. Louis Reardon Foundation,* Dallas, TX.
Represented in the Archdioceses of Kansas City in Kansas, New Orleans, St. Louis and San Antonio and in the Dioceses of Austin, Amarillo, Baton Rouge, Brownsville, Dallas, El Paso, Kansas City-St. Joseph, Little Rock, San Angelo and Springfield-Cape Girardeau.
East Central Province - Evansville (1969): *Daughters of Charity of St. Vincent de Paul of Indiana, Inc.,* 9400 New Harmony Rd., Evansville, IN 47720. Tel: 812-963-3341; Fax: 812-963-7589. Sr. Catherine Madigan, D.C., Prov. Supr.
Total number in the community 161.
Legal Title: *Mater Dei Provincialate, Inc.*
Ministries of Insertion Religious and Academic Education at all levels; Campus Ministry; Parish Ministry; Social Services in parishes; Catholic Charities Office; Prison Ministry; Shelters for homeless; Hispanic Ministry.
Sponsored Works: Home for Retired Sisters; General Hospitals; Skilled Nursing Facilities; Clinics; Home Health Care; Day Care Centers and Neighborhood Services; Childrens' Residence; Services to Elderly.
Co-Sponsored Organizations: Ascension Health.
Represented in the Archdioceses of Chicago, Detroit, Indianapolis, Milwaukee, and Mobile and in the Dioceses of Belleville, Birmingham, Evansville, Lafayette (IN), Nashville, Jackson, Saginaw and Springfield (IL).
Northeast Province (1969): *De Paul Provincial House,* 96 Menand Rd., Albany, NY 12204-1499. Sr. Mary Francis Martin, Prov. Supr.; Sr. Margaret Ahl, Archivist.
Total number in the community 204.
Ministry in the field of Academic Education at all levels; Hospital; Specialized Hospitals; Homes for Unmarried Mothers; Child Caring Homes; Day Care Centers; Social Service Centers; Parish Centers.
Represented in the Archdioceses of Boston, New York and Philadelphia and in the Dioceses of Albany, Allentown, Bridgeport, Brooklyn, Buffalo, Greensburg, Metuchen, Ogdensburg, Syracuse and Wilmington. Also in Canada.
Province of the West (Los Altos Hills) (1969): *Seton Provincialate,* 26000 Altamont Rd., Los Altos Hills, CA 94022-4317. Tel: 650-941-4490; Fax: 650-949-3874. Sr. Margaret Keaveney, D.C., Prov.
Total number in the community 141.
Properties owned and sponsored: *Seton Medical Center,* Daly City, CA; *Seton Provincialate,* Los Altos Hills, CA; *St. Vincent Medical Center,* Los Angeles, CA; *St. Vincent's Senior Citizen Nutrition Program,* Los Angeles, CA; *St. Francis Medical Center,* Lynwood, CA; *Maryvale,* Rosemead, CA; *Mount St. Joseph-St. Elizabeth,* San Francisco, CA; *O'Connor Hospital,* San Jose, CA; *Villa Siena,* Mountain View, CA; St. Louise Regional Hospital, *Gilroy, CA;* St. Vincent's, *Santa Barbara, CA; Robert F. Kennedy Medical Center, Hawthorne, CA.*
Represented in the Archdioceses of Anchorage, Los Angeles and San Francisco and in the Dioceses of Fresno, Gallup, Monterey, Oakland, Phoenix, Salt Lake City and San Jose.

[0770] (D.C.)—DAUGHTERS OF THE CROSS (D)

Founded in France in 1640. First foundation in the United States in 1855.
Motherhouse: *Daughters of the Cross Motherhouse,* 411 E. Flournoy-Lucas Rd., Shreveport, LA 71115-3901. Tel: 318-797-0887. Sr. Mary Louise Parisy, Supr. Gen.
Total number in community 6.
Represented in the Diocese of Shreveport.

[0780] (F.C.)—DAUGHTERS OF THE CROSS OF LIEGE (P)

Founded in Liege, Belgium in 1833. First foundation in the United States in 1958.
Principal House: *St. Bernard Convent,* 165 W. Eaton Ave., Tracy, CA 95376. Sr. M. Eugene Hagan, F.C., Supr.
Total number in community 8.
Represented in the Diocese of Stockton.

[0790] (F.D.C.)—DAUGHTERS OF DIVINE CHARITY (P)

Founded in Austria on Nov. 21, 1868. First Founded in the United States on Oct. 8, 1913, in New York City.
General Motherhouse: *Grottaferrata,* Rome, Italy.
St. Joseph Province (1921): *Provincialate:* 205 Major Ave., Staten Island, NY 10305-3734. Tel: 718-720-4377; Fax: 718-442-9247. E-mail: josiefdc@aol.com. Web site: www.godslovefdc.org. Sr. Josita, DiVita, F.D.C., Prov. Supr.
Professed Sisters 51.
Ministry in education, nursing, residences for young women.
Properties owned: *St. Mary's Residence,* NY; *St. Joseph Hill Academy,* Staten Island, NY: *Villa Madonna,* Hackettstown, NJ.
Represented in the Archdiocese of New York and the Dioceses of Bridgeport, San Bernardino and San Diego.
St. Mary Province (1950): *Provincial Motherhouse and Novitiate,* 39 N. Portage Path, Akron, OH 44303-1183. Tel: 330-867-4960. Sr. Mary Coffelt, Prov. Supr.
Total number in community 20.
Ministry in the field of Education; Home for Working Girls; Home for elderly senior Women and Men.
Properties owned: *Daughters of Divine Charity, Inc.; Leonora Hall Convent; Leonora Hall Residence; Francesca Residence.*
Represented in the Archdioceses of Miami, and Milwaukee and in the Dioceses of Cleveland.
Holy Trinity Province (1972): *Provincial House,* 39315, N. Woodward Ave., Bloomfield Hills, MI 48304. Tel: 248-645-5318. Sr. Hyacinthe Vamos, Prov. Supr.
Professed Sisters 26.
Ministry in Education; Foster Care Residence; Homes for the Aged.
Represented in the Archdiocese of Detroit and in the Diocese of Fort Wayne-South Bend.

[0793] (D.D.L.)—DAUGHTERS OF DIVINE LOVE

Founded in Ukpor, Nigeria in 1969. First United States Foundation in 1990.
General House: Fifth Avenue, P.O. Box 546, Enugu, Enugu State, Nigeria. Tel: 042-559071; 042-554450. Rev. Mother Ifechukwu Udorah, D.D.L., Mother Gen.
Total Professed Sisters 700.
U.S. Regional House: 140 North Ave., Highwood, IL 60040. Tel: 847-432-9003; Fax: 847-681-8974. E-mail: DDLoveUS@aol.com. Sr. Maria Uche Chukwu, D.D.L., Reg. Supr.
Professed Sisters in U.S. 45.
Ministry in the field of Administration; Religious and Academic Education at all levels; Special Education; Health Services; Parish and Diocesan Services; Retreat Work; Social Work.
Represented in the Archdioceses of Chicago and New Orleans and in the Dioceses of Brooklyn, Brownsville, Galveston-Houston, and Springfield, IL.

[0794] (F.D.P.)—DAUGHTERS OF DIVINE PROVIDENCE

General Motherhouse: *Daughters of Divine Providence,* Via Matteo Bartoli 255, 00143, Rome, Italy. Mother Carmen Perri, F.D.P., Supr. Gen.

U.S. Delegation: *Daughters of Divine Providence,* 3100 Mumphrey Rd., Chalmette, LA 70043, Tel: 504-279-4617; Fax: 504-279-3002. Sr. Piercarla Barone, F.D.P., Local Supr.
Total number in community 6.
Represented in the Archdiocese of New Orleans.

[0795] (F.D.Z.)—DAUGHTERS OF DIVINE ZEAL

Founded in Messina, Italy in 1887 by Blessed Hannibal Maria DiFrancia. First foundation in the United States in 1951.
Generalate: *Figlie Del Divino Zelo,* Circonvallazione Appia 144, 00179, Rome, Italy. Mother M. Diodata Guerrera, F.D.Z., Supr. Gen.
Total universal number in the Congregation 1,000.
U.S. Headquarters: *Hannibal House Spiritual Center,* 1526 Hill Rd., Reading, PA 19602. Tel: 610-375-1738 & 375-9072; Fax: 610-375-2188. Sr. Marita A. Olango, F.D.Z., Supr.
Total number in community 4.
Ministry in the field of Religious and Academic Education; Parish and Youth Ministry; Retreat, Vocation, Prayer and Apostolate.
Represented in the Diocese of Allentown.

[0810] (D.H.M.)—DAUGHTERS OF THE HEART OF MARY (P)

Founded in France in 1790. First United States foundation in 1851.
Generalate: 39 rue Notre Dame des Champs, 75006, Paris, France.
Provincialate: 1339 Northampton St., Holyoke, MA 01040-1913. Tel: 413-532-7406; Fax: 413-533-4217. Sr. Nancy Fell, D.H.M., Prov.
Professed Sisters 88; Postulants 1.
Properties owned: *Marian Center & Residence,* Holyoke, MA; *Mary Hill,* St. Paul, MN; *Nardin Academy,* Buffalo, NY; *Heart of Mary Center,* St. Louis, MO; *St. Isaac Jogues Center,* Philadelphia, PA; *Regina Maria Retreat House,* Plattsburgh, NY; *St. Joseph's School for the Deaf,* Bronx, NY; *Ephpheta Center,* Oak Park, IL.
Represented in the Archdioceses of Chicago, New York, Philadelphia, St. Louis and St. Paul-Minneapolis and in the Dioceses of Buffalo, Ogdensburg, Springfield (MA) and Trenton.

[0820] (D.H.S.)—DAUGHTERS OF THE HOLY SPIRIT (P)

Founded in France in 1706. First foundation in the U.S. in 1902.
General Motherhouse: *Congregation des Filles du Saint Esprit,* 15 boulevard Sebastopol, B.P. 50148 Rennes Cedex 3, France. 35101. Sr. Agnes Stephan, F.S.E., Supr. Gen.
Provincial House: *Daughters of the Holy Spirit, Inc.,* 72 Church St., Putnam, CT 06260. Tel: 860-928-0891. Sr. Jacqueline Robillard, D.H.S., Prov.
Total number in the community 143.
Ministry in the field of Academic Education at all levels; Home for Aged; Home/District Nursing; Health care center for Daughters of the Holy Spirit; and various social and pastoral ministries of service.
Represented in the Archdioceses of Boston, Hartford, Mobile, and Philadelphia and in the Dioceses of Birmingham, Bridgeport, Burlington, Norwich, Ogdensburg, Providence, Richmond, Sacramento, Springfield (MA), Stockton and Worcester.

[0830] (F.J.) —CONGREGATION OF THE DAUGHTERS OF JESUS (LES FILLES DE JESUS) (P)

Founded in France in 1834. First foundation in the U.S. in 1903.
U.S. Address: 4209 3rd Ave. S., Great Falls, MT 59405. Tel: 406-452-7231.
Total number in community 3.
Represented in the Diocese of Great Falls.

[0850] (F.M.A.)—DAUGHTERS OF MARY HELP OF CHRISTIANS (P)

Salesian Sisters of St. John Bosco

Founded in Mornese, Italy, in 1872. First foundation in the U.S. in 1908 at Paterson, New Jersey.
General Motherhouse: Via Ateneo Salesiano, 81, 00139, Rome, Italy. Very Rev. Mother Antonia Colombo, F.M.A., Mother Gen.
Total universal number in Congregation 15,308.
Province of St. Philip, Apostle: *Provincial House,* 655 Belmont Ave., Haledon, NJ 07508-2398. Tel: 973-790-7963. Mother Judith Suprys, F.M.A., Prov.
Total number in the community 120.
Legal Title: *Missionary Society of the Salesian Sisters, Inc.; Salesian Sisters of Tampa, Inc.*
Ministry in the field of academic and religious Education at all levels; Youth Ministry.
Properties owned: *Provincial House,* Haledon, NJ; *Mary Help of Christians Academy,* North Haledon, NJ; *Sacred Heart Center,* Newton, NJ; *Villa Madonna School-Salesian Sisters of Tampa, Inc.,* Tampa, FL; *Camp Auxilium Learning Center,* Newton, NJ.
Represented in the Archdioceses of Miami, Newark, New Orleans and New York and in the Dioceses of Paterson and St. Petersburg.
Province of Mary Immaculate: *FMA Provincial House,* 6019 Buena Vista, San Antonio, TX 78237. Tel: 210-432-0090; Fax: 210-432-4016. Sr. Phyllis Neves, F.M.A., Prov.
Total number in community 103.
Legal Title: *Institute of the Daughters of Mary Help of Christians - Salesian Sisters of St. John Bosco,* San Antonio, TX; *Salesian Sisters - Mary Help of Christians Youth Center, Inc.,* Corralitos, CA. Ministry in Education; Youth Ministry and Religious Education.
Properties owned: *FMA Provincial House & St. John Bosco School,* San Antonio, TX; *Mary Help of Christians School,* Laredo, TX; *Salesian Sisters School - Salesian Sisters: MHC Youth Center, Inc.,* Corralitos, CA.
Represented in the Archdioceses of Los Angeles, New Orleans, San Antonio, and San Francisco and in the Dioceses of Austin, Colorado Springs, Laredo, Monterey, and Phoenix.

[0860] (D.M.)—DAUGHTERS OF MARY OF THE IMMACULATE CONCEPTION (P)

Founded in New Britain in 1904.
General Motherhouse: 314 Osgood Ave., New Britain, CT 06053. Tel: 860-225-9406. Mother Mary Mark, Supr. Gen.
Total number in community 52.
Legal Title: *Congregation of the Daughters of Mary of the Immaculate Conception, Inc.*
Ministry in the field of Education; Home for the Aged; Homes for Working Girls and Students; Skilled Care
Properties owned: *St. Lucian's Home; Marian Educational Clinic; Monsignor Bojnowski Manor; Motherhouse: and Novitiate Complex,* New Britain, CT; *St. Joseph's Home, NY; St. Agnes Residence,* NY; *Our Lady's Guild House,* Boston, MA; *Sancta Maria Nursing Facility,* Cambridge, MA.
Represented in the Archdioceses of Boston, Hartford and New York and in the Diocese of Springfield (MA).

[0870] (F.M.I.)—CONGREGATION OF THE DAUGHTERS OF MARY IMMACULATE (P)

Marianist Sisters

Founded in France in 1816.
Motherhouse: Rome, Italy. Mother Jolle Bec, Supr. Gen.
U.S. Foundation (1949): *Our Lady of the Pillar Convent,* 251 W. Ligustrum Dr., San Antonio, TX 78228. Tel: 210-433-5501; Fax: 210-431-9611. Sr. Evangeline Escobar, Prov. Supr.
Total number in community 19.
Properties owned: *Our Lady of the Pillar Convent,* San Antonio, TX; *Novitiate,* Dayton, OH.
Represented in the Archdioceses of Cincinnati and San Antonio.

[0880] (D.M.J.)—DAUGHTERS OF MARY AND JOSEPH (P)

Founded in Belgium in 1817. First U.S. Foundation in 1926.
Generalate: Via Garibaldi, 28 00153, Rome, Italy. Sr. Agnes Charles, Supr. Gen.
Novitiate: 5300 Crest Rd., Rancho Palos Verdes, CA 90275. Tel: 310-377-9968; Fax: 310-541-5967. Sr. Therese Martin Schwalenberg, Formation Contact.
Provincialate: 5300 Crest Rd., Rancho Palos Verdes, CA 90274. Tel: 310-377-9968. Sr. Linda Webb, Prov.
Professed Sisters 65.
Legal Title: *Daughters of Mary and Joseph, California.*
Sisters staff: Grammar & High Schools; Parish Ministry; Health Ministry; Missionary Work; Detention Ministry; Retreat Work.
Represented in the Archdioceses of Los Angeles and San Francisco and in the Dioceses of Monterey, Orange, San Bernardino and San Diego.

[0890] (D.M.)—DAUGHTERS OF OUR LADY OF MERCY (P)

Founded in Italy in 1837 by Saint Mary Joseph Rossello. First foundation in the United States in 1919.
Generalate: Via Monte Grappa, No. 7., Savona, Italy. Rev. Mother M. Giovannina Lusso, Supr. Gen.
Provincialate and Novitiate: *Villa Rossello,* 1009 Main Rd., Newfield, NJ 08344. Tel: 856-697-2983. Sr. M. Ambrogina Aldeni, Mother Prov.; Sr. Loretta Marie Stevens, D.M., Community archivist.
Total number in community 63.
Legal Holdings: *Misericordia Convalescent Home,* York, PA; *Holy Child Nursery,* York, PA; *Our Lady of Mercy Academy,*Newfield, NJ.
Ministry in the field of Education; Health Services; Day Nursery; Convalescent Hospital; Pastoral Counselling C.C.D. and Parish Work.
Represented in the Dioceses of Camden, Harrisburg and Scranton. Also in the West Indies.

[0895] (F.M.S.R.)—DAUGHTERS OF OUR LADY OF THE HOLY ROSARY (P)

Founded in 1946 in Trung Linh, Bui Chu, North Vietnam by Bishop Dominic Maria Ho Ngoc Can. First foundation in the United States in 1967.
Motherhouse in Vietnam: Sr. Mary Cecile Vu thi Thanh, F.M.S.R.
U. S. Provincial Office: Queen of Peace Convent, 1492 Moss St., New Orleans, LA 70119-2904. Sr. Mary John Bosco Dinh Thi Kim Thanh, F.M.S.R., Prov. Supr.
Total number in community 48.
Ministry in the field of Education; Health Services; Pastoral Ministry.
Properties owned: 6 Residences.
Represented in the Archdiocese of New Orleans and in the Dioceses of Biloxi and Houma-Thibodaux.

[0900] (F.D.N.S.C.)—DAUGHTERS OF OUR LADY OF THE SACRED HEART (P)

Founded in France in 1882.
Motherhouse: Via Casale S. Pio. V, 37, Rome, Italy. Sr. Mary Ringnalda, Supr. Gen.
U.S. Foundation (1955): *St. Francis de Sales Convent,* 424 E. Browning Rd., Bellmawr, NJ 08031. Tel: 856-931-8973; Fax: 856-931 7018.
Professed Sisters in U.S. 14.
Represented in the Archdiocese of Philadelphia and in the Dioceses of Camden.

[0910] (Bethl.)—BETHLEMITA, DAUGHTER OF THE SACRED HEART OF JESUS (P)

Founded in Guatemala in 1861. First foundation in United States in Dallas, Texas.
Motherhouse: Bogota, Colombia, S.A.
U.S. Foundation: *St. Joseph Residence, Inc.,* 330 W. Pembroke St., Dallas, TX 75208. Tel: 214-948-3597. Sr. Adelaide Bocanegra, Admin.
Professed Sisters 6.
Represented in the Diocese of Dallas.

[0920] (D.S.F.)—CONGREGATION OF THE DAUGHTERS OF ST. FRANCIS OF ASSISI (P)

Founded in Austro, Hungary, 1894. First foundation in United States in 1946.
Motherhouse: *St. Joseph's Convent,* 507 N. Prairie St., Lacon, IL 61540. Tel: 309-246-2175. Sr. M. Vaclava Ballon, D.S.F., Prov. Supr.
Professed Sisters 28.
Legal Title: *Congregation of the Daughters of St. Francis of Assisi, American Province.*
Represented in the Dioceses of Peoria and Springfield-Cape Girardeau. Also in Mexico.

[0930] (F.S.J.)—RELIGIOUS DAUGHTERS OF ST. JOSEPH (P)

Founded in Gerona, Spain in 1875.
General Motherhouse: *General Asensio Cabanillas,* 18, Madrid, Spain. 28003, Mother Carmen Vela, Supr. Gen.
Total universal number in Congregation 880.
Provincial House: *Calzada Ermita Istapalapa,* Mexico, Sr. Pilar Soto, Prov.
U.S. Foundation: *Santa Marta Hospital,* 319 N. Humphreys Ave., Los Angeles, CA 90022. Sr. Eulalia Yepez, F.S.J., Supr.
Total number in community 8.
Legal Title: *Daughters of St. Joseph of California, Inc.*
Represented in the Archdiocese of Los Angeles.

[0940] (D.S.M.P.)—DAUGHTERS OF ST. MARY OF PROVIDENCE (P)

Founded in Italy in 1881. First foundation in the U.S. in 1913.
Generalate: Rome, Italy. Mother Giustina Valicenti, D.S.M.P., Supr. Gen.
Provincialate: *Daughters of St. Mary of Providence,* 4200 N. Austin Ave., Chicago, IL 60634. Tel: 773-205-1313 & 545-8300. Sr. Patricia McCafferty, Prov.
Professed Sisters 68.
Represented in the Archdioceses of Boston, Chicago, and Philadelphia and in the Dioceses of Camden, Gary, New Ulm, and Sioux Falls.

[0950] (F.S.P.)—PIOUS SOCIETY DAUGHTERS OF ST. PAUL (P)

(Missionary Sisters of the Media of Communications)

Founded in Alba, Piedmont, Italy, on June 15, 1915. First founded in the United States on June 28, 1932, in New York.
General Motherhouse: Rome, Italy. Sr. Maria Antonieta Bruscato, Supr. Gen.

Total universal number in Congregation 2,607.
Provincial House, Novitiate, Publishing House: 50 St. Paul's Ave., Boston, MA 02130. Tel: 617-522-8911. Sr. Germana Santos, F.S.P., Prov. Supr.; Sr. M. Sophie Stewart, F.S.P., Local Supr.
Total number in community 142.
Legal Title: *Daughters of St. Paul, Inc.*
Properties owned: *St. Paul Book and Media Centers, found in 17 locations throughout the States (see list of (Arch)Dioceses where represented) Provincialate,* Boston, MA; *St. Thecla Retreat House,* Billerica, MA.
Represented in the Archdioceses of Boston, Chicago, Los Angeles, Miami, New Orleans, New York, Philadelphia, St. Louis, San Antonio, and San Francisco and in the Dioceses of Arlington, Charleston, Honolulu, Memphis, Metuchen and San Diego. Also in Canada.

[0960] (D.W.)—DAUGHTERS OF WISDOM (P)

Founded in France in 1703. First foundation in the United States in 1904.
General Motherhouse: *St. Laurent-sur-Sevre,* Vendee, France. Superior General Headquarters located in Rome, Italy
U.S. Province (1949): *Provincial House,* 385 Ocean Ave., Islip, NY 11751-4600. Tel: 631-277-2660; Fax: 631-277-3274. Sr. Evelyn Eckhardt, D.W., Prov.
Professed Sisters 130.
Ministry in all levels of Education; Retreat House; Hospital & Health Services; Orphanage; Social Work; Pediatrics Clinic.
Properties owned: *Wisdom House Center for Spirituality,* Litchfield, CT; *Our Lady of Perpetual Help Convent (Rest Home for Sisters),* Sound Beach, NY; *Provincial House,* Islip, NY; *Our Lady of Wisdom Convent,* St. Agatha, ME.
Represented in the Archdioceses of Hartford, Mobile and Washington and in the Dioceses of Arlington, Brooklyn, Burlington, Charleston, Portland (ME), Raleigh, Richmond, Rockville Centre, St. Augustine, St. Petersburg and Wheeling-Charleston.

[0965] (D.L.J.C.)—DISCIPLES OF THE LORD JESUS CHRIST (D)

Founded in the United States in 1972.
Motherhouse: P.O. Box 17, Channing, TX 79018. Tel: 806-534-2312; Fax: 806-534-2223. Mother Lucy Lukasiewicz, Supr. Gen.
Total number in community 28.
Legal Holdings and Titles: *Prayertown Emmanuel Retreat House,* Channing, TX; *House of Prayer,* Alexandria, LA.
Ministry in Retreat Work and Evangelization.
Represented in the Dioceses of Alexandria and Amarillo. Also in Mexico.

[0970] (R.D.C.)—SISTERS OF THE DIVINE COMPASSION (D)

Founded in the United States in 1886.
General Motherhouse: *Good Counsel Convent,* 52 N. Broadway, White Plains, NY 10603. Tel: 914-798-1300; Fax: 914-949-5169. Sr. Alice Feeley, R.D.C., Pres.
Total number in community 103.
Legal Holdings and Titles: *Academy of Our Lady of Good Counsel High School and Elementary School,* White Plains, NY; *Preston High School,* New York, NY; *Divine Compassion Center for Spiritual Renewal,* NY; *Migrant Ministry,* Goshen, NY; *Residence,* Hampton Bays, NY; *RDC Center for Counselling and Human Development.*
Ministry in Preschool, Elementary, Secondary, College and University Education; Religious Education; Educational Consultation; Adult Education; Special Education; Pastoral Ministry; Retreat Work and Spiritual Direction; Counseling; Social Services; Migrant Ministry; Health Services; Administration and Business Services.
Represented in the Archdiocese of New York.

[0980] (P.D.D.M.)—PIOUS DISCIPLES OF THE DIVINE MASTER (P)

Founded in 1924. First foundation in the United States in 1948.
General Motherhouse: Rome, Italy. Mother Mary Paola Mancini, Supr. Gen.
Universal number in Congregation 1,400,
U.S. Headquarters: 60 Sunset Ave., Staten Island, NY 10314. Tel: 718-494-8597; Fax: 718-494-2123. Sr. M. Josephine Fallon, P.D.D.M., Reg. Supr.
Total number in region 47.
Ministry is a Three Dimensional Mission: Eucharistic, Priestly, Liturgical.
Represented in the Archdioceses of Boston, Los Angeles and New York and in the Dioceses of Fresno and San Jose.

[0990] (C.D.P.)—SISTERS OF DIVINE PROVIDENCE (P)

Founded in Germany in 1851. First foundation in United States 1876; incorporation granted Sept.17, 1881.
Amended and restated articles of incorporation on Dec. 28, 2001.
General Motherhouse: *Mother of Providence Convent,* 12 Christopher St., Wakefield, RI 02879. Tel: 401-782-1785; Fax: 401-782-6967. Sr. Myra Rodgers, C.D.P., Gen.
Marie de la Roche Province(2001): *Providence Heights,* 9000 Babcock Blvd., Allison Park, PA 15101. Tel: 412-931-5241; Fax: 412-635-5416. Sr. Mary Joan Coultas, C.D.P., Prov.; Sr. Claudia Ward, C.D.P., Area Asst.-Kingston, MA; Sr. Zita Telkamp, C.D.P., Area Asst.-St. Louis, MO.
Total number in community 310.
Ministry in the fields of Education; Social Services; Pastoral Ministry; and Health Care Services.
Properties owned and sponsored: *La Roche College,* Pittsburgh, PA; *Providence Heights Alpha,* Allison Park, PA; *Transfiguration House of Prayer,* Butler, PA; *Kearns Spirituality Center,* Allison Park, PA; *Providence Connections, Inc.; Providence Child Care Center - South,* Castle Shannon, PA; *Providence Child Care Center, North,* Pittsburgh, PA; *Providence Family Support Center,* Pittsburgh, PA; *Amelia House - Safe House,* Clarion, PA; *Room at the Inn,* St. Louis, MO; *La Posada Providencia,* San Benito, TX; *St. Elizabeth Medical Center,* Granite City, IL; *St. Elizabeth Health Foundation,* Granite City, IL; *Providence Ministry Corporation,* Bridgeton, MO; *Providence Charitable Trust,* Bridgeton, MO; *Provincial Residence; Sacred Heart Junior-Senior High School; Sacred Heart Elementary and Pre-primary School; Visitation Camp Mishannock,* Kingston, MA; *Sisters of Divine Providence of Missouri,* Bridgeton, MO.
Represented in the Archdioceses of Chicago, Boston, Denver, Detroit, Kansas City in Kansas, Miami, New York, St. Louis, Santa Fe, and San Juan and in the Dioceses of Arecibo, Bismarck, Brooklyn, Brownsville, Cleveland, Columbus, Crookston, Erie, Greensburg, Jackson, Jefferson City, Nashville, Orlando, Phoenix, Pittsburgh, Raleigh, Richmond, Wheeling-Charleston, Springfield (IL), and Youngstown. Also in Puerto Rico and the Dominican Republic.

[1000] (C.D.P.)—CONGREGATION OF DIVINE PROVIDENCE, MELBOURNE, KENTUCKY (P)

Founded in France in 1762. First foundation in the United States in 1889.
General Motherhouse: *St. Jean de Bassel,* 57930, Fenetrange, France. Sr. Marie Therese Seyler, Supr. Gen.
American Provincial House (1889): *St. Anne Convent,* Melbourne, KY 41059. Tel: 606-441-0679. Sr. Lynn Stenken, C.D.P., Prov. Supr. Sr. Mary Joan Dohmen, C.D.P., Archivist.
Total number in community 159.
Ministry in the field of Academic Education at all levels; Montessori Schools; Home for Working Women; Retreat Center; Religious Education & Pastoral Ministry; Health & Social Services.
Represented in the Archdioceses of Cincinnati, Indianapolis, Louisville, New York, and Washington and in the Dioceses of Covington, Duluth, Jackson, Lexington, Manchester, Toledo and Wheeling-Charleston. Also in West Africa.

[1010] (C.D.P.)—CONGREGATION OF DIVINE PROVIDENCE, SAN ANTONIO, TEXAS (P)

Founded in France in 1762. First Foundation in the United States in 1866.
The Generalate: P.O. Box 37345, 515 S.W. 24th St., San Antonio, TX 78237. Tel: 210-695-8721; Fax: 210-695-6033. Sr. Antoinette Billeaud, Supr. Gen.; Councilors: Sr. Diane Langford; Sr. Mary Christine Morkovsky; Sr. Patrice Sullivan; Sr. Catherine Parent; Sr. Margaret Riche, Archivist; Sr. Antoinette Keiser, Treas.
Novitiate and Formation: *Formation / Vocation Office,* 515 S.W. 24th St., San Antonio, TX 78207-4600. Tel: 210-434-1866.
Total number in community 285.
Legal Titles & Holdings: *Congregation of Divine Providence, Inc.; Providence Trust,* San Antonio, TX.
Properties owned: *The Generalate,* Helotes, TX; *Moye Center,* Castroville, TX; *Our Lady of the Lake Retirement Center,* San Antonio, TX.
Ministry in all levels of Education; Catechetical Centers; Hospitals, Clinics; Diocesan Offices; Retreat Houses; Spiritual Direction-Counseling; Pastoral; Social Work; Chaplaincies in Public Institutions; Home-Health Care; Administration.
Represented in the Archdioceses of Chicago, Denver, Los Angeles, Milwaukee, New Orleans, Oklahoma City, St. Louis, San Antonio, San Francisco, Seattle and Washington and in the Dioceses of Alexandria, Austin, Baton Rouge, Colorado Springs, Corpus Christi, Dallas, El Paso, Fort Wayne-South Bend, Fresno, Galveston-Houston, Lafayette (LA), Lake Charles, Laredo, Raleigh, St. Petersburg, San Angelo, San Bernardino, Springfield-Cape Girardeau, Tucson, Tulsa and Victoria. Also in Ghana and Mexico.

[1020] (S.D.R.)—SISTERS OF THE DIVINE REDEEMER (P)

Founded in 1849 at Niederbronn, France. First Founded in the United States on Oct. 6, 1912 at McKeesport,
Generalate: *Suore del Divin Redentore,* Via Casale Piombino 14, Rome, Italy I-00135 011-39-06-305-2512. Sr. M. Julia Zarembova, Supr. Gen.
American Province (1922): *Divine Redeemer Motherhouse,* 999 Rock Run Rd., Elizabeth, PA 15037-2613. Tel: 412-751-8600; Fax: 412-751-0355. Sr. M. Monica Kosztolnyik, Prov. Supr.; Sr. Mary Alice Varga, Archivist.
Total number in Province 44.
Legal Titles and Holdings: *Sisters of the Divine Redeemer Charitable Trust; Divine Redeemer Health Care Ministries Corp.,* Elizabeth, PA.
Sisters serve and staff: Elementary School; Personal Care Home; CCD Centers; Parish Ministry; Nursing Home.
Represented in the Archdiocese of Philadelphia and in the Diocese of Pittsburgh.

[1030] (S.D.S.)—SISTERS OF THE DIVINE SAVIOR (P)

Founded in Tivoli, Italy, in 1888. First foundation in the United States in 1895.
General Motherhouse: Rome, Italy, Viale Mura Gianicolensi 67. Sr. Therezinha Joana Rasera, Supr. Gen.
North American Province: *Sisters of the Divine Savior,* 4311 N. 100 St., Milwaukee, WI 53222-1393. Tel: 414-466-0810; Fax: 414-466-4335. Sr. Marion Etzel, S.D.S., Prov. Supr.; Sr. Aquin Gilles, S.D.S., Archivist.
Total number in U.S. Community 113.
Ministry in all levels of Education; Pastoral and Social Services; Health Care; and Homes for the Aged.
Properties owned or sponsored: *St. Anne's Home for the Elderly; Divine Savior Holy Angels High School,* Milwaukee, WI; *Divine Savior Healthcare, Inc.,* Portage, WI.
Represented in the Archdiocese of Milwaukee and in the Dioceses of Birmingham, Green Bay, La Crosse, Madison, Monterey, Nashville, Phoenix, and Tucson.

[1040] (C.D.S.)—CONGREGATION OF THE DIVINE SPIRIT (D)

First foundation in Erie, Pennsylvania in 1956.
Motherhouse: 409 W. Sixth St., Erie, PA 16507. Tel: 814-455-3590. Mother Patricia O'Connor, Supr. Gen.
Membership 40.
Sisters serve and staff: Parochial Schools; CCD Activities; Home for Aged; Social Work.
Represented in the Dioceses of Erie and Youngstown.

[1050] (O.P.)—DOMINICAN CONTEMPLATIVE NUNS (P)
(The Nuns of the Order of Preachers)

Founded in France in 1206. First foundation in the United States in 1880. Monastic contemplative branch of the Order of Preachers. Papal cloister.
Monastery of St. Dominic: 375 13th Ave., Newark, NJ 07103. Tel: 973-622-6622. Sr. Mary Christine, O.P., Prioress.
Total number in community 13.
Nuns of the Order of Preachers O.P.: *Corpus Christi Monastery,* 1230 Lafayette Ave., Bronx, NY 10474. Tel: 718-328-6996; Fax: 718-328-1974. Sr. Maria Pia, O.P., Prioress.
Total number in community 19.
Monastery of the Blessed Sacrament: *Nuns of the Order of Preachers,* 29575 Middlebelt, Farmington Hills, MI 48334-2311. Tel: 248-626-8321; 8253; Fax: 248-626-8724. Sr. Mary Rose Figura, O.P., Prioress.
Dominicans (Contemplative, Cloistered) Perpetual Adoration.
Cloistered Professed Nuns 34; Extern Professed Sisters 3; Cloistered Novices 2.
Monastery of the Angels: *Cloistered Dominican Nuns of Perpetual Adoration,* 1977 Carmen Ave., Los Angeles, CA 90068. Tel: 323-466-2186. Sr. Mary Pia, O.P., Prioress.
Sisters 23.
Legal Title: *The Monastery of the Angels.*
Monastery of the Angels: Karachi, Pakistan. Mother Mary Rose, O.P., Prioress. Sisters 13.
Queen of Angels Monastery: Bocaue, Bulacan, Philippines. Sr. Mary of the Holy Spirit, O.P., Prioress.
Sisters 20.

Corpus Christi Monastery: 215 Oak Grove Ave., Menlo Park, CA 94025. Tel: 650-322-1801; Fax: 650-322-6816. Sr. Mary of the Holy Family, O.P., Prioress.
Cloistered Total number in community 18.

Dominican Nuns O.P.: *Monastery of the Mother of God,* 1430 Riverdale St., West Springfield, MA 01089-4698. Tel: 413-736-3639; Fax: 413-736-0850. Sr. Mary of the Immaculate Conception, O.P., Prioress.
Total number in community 22.

Dominican Contemplative Nuns - O.P.: *Monastery of Our Lady of the Rosary,* 335 Doat St., Buffalo, NY 14211-2199. Tel: 716-892-0066; Fax: 716-897-1566. Mother Mary Thomas, O.P., Prioress.
Professed 29; Novices 3.
Legal Title: *Dominican Nuns of the Perpetual Rosary.*

Monastery of Our Lady of Grace: North Guilford, CT 06437-1099. Tel: 203-457-0599. Sr. Lee, O.P., Prioress.
Total number in community 37.
Legal Title: *Dominican Nuns of North Guilford, CT Inc.*

Monastery of the Infant Jesus: *Dominican Contemplative Nuns O.P.,* 1501 Lotus Ln., Lufkin, TX 75904. Tel: 936-634-4233; Fax: 936-634-2156. Sr. Mary Annunciata, O.P., Prioress.
Professed 27; Novices 1.

Monastery of Our Lady of the Rosary (Rosary Shrine): Morris Ave. & Springfield Ave., Summit, NJ 07901. Tel: 908-273-1228. Sr. Mary Martin, O.P., Prioress.
Professed Choir Sisters 16.

Nuns of the Order of Preachers O.P.: *Monastery of Mary the Queen,* 1310 W. Church St., Elmira, NY 14905. Tel: 607-734-9506; Fax: 607-734-1452. Sr. David Marie, O.P., Prioress.
Total number in community 15.

Monastery of the Dominican Nuns of the Perpetual Rosary (Cloistered): 14th St. & West St., Union City, NJ 07087. Tel: 201-866-7004. Mother Mary Clare, O.P., Prioress.
Professed Sisters 8. Aspirants 2.

Monastery of the Perpetual Rosary: 1500 Haddon Ave., Camden, NJ 08103. Mother Mary Anne, O.P., Prioress.
Professed Nuns 6.

St. Dominic's Monastery (Contemplative): 4901 16th St. N.W., Washington, DC 20011-3839. Sr. Mary Paul, O.P., Prioress.
Nuns 11.

The Dominican Nuns of the Perpetual Rosary (Cloistered- Contemplative): *Monastery of the Immaculate Heart of Mary,* 1834 Lititz Pike, Lancaster, PA 17601-6585. Tel: 717-569-2104; Fax: 717-569-1598. E-mail: monlanc@aol.com. Mother Marie Clare, O.P., Prioress.
Solemnly Professed 11.

Dominican Monastery of the Perpetual Rosary: 802 Court St., Syracuse, NY 13208. Tel: 315-471-6762. Sr. Bernadette Marie, O.P., Prioress. Solemn Vows, Papal enclosure.
Total number in community 12.

Dominican Monastery of St. Jude: P.O. Box 170, Marbury, AL 36051. Tel: 205-755-1322. Mother Mary Joseph, O.P., Prioress.
Professed Nuns 7; Postulants 1.
Legal Title: *Dominican Nuns of Perpetual Rosary and Adoration.*

[1060] (O.P.)—DOMINICAN CONTEMPLATIVE SISTERS (D)

(Cloistered Contemplative)

Founded in Calais, France in 1880.

Monastery of the Dominican Sisters of the Perpetual Rosary (Cloistered): 217 N. 68th St., Milwaukee, WI 53213. Tel: 414-258-0579. Mother Miriam Leonard, O.P., Prioress.
Professed Sisters 12.

[1070] (O.P.)—DOMINICAN SISTERS (P)

There are thirty Congregations of the Dominican Sisters of the Third Order of St. Dominic in the United States. The list of General Motherhouses follows in the order of seniority. If the Congregation is known under a more familiar name, that name is given under the name of the Congregation.

[1070-01] CONGREGATION OF ST. CATHARINE OF SIENA (1822) (P)

The first American Foundation of the Dominican Sisters in the United States founded in Kentucky in 1822.

General Motherhouse: *Congregational Offices of St. Catharine of Siena,* 2645 Bardstown Rd., St. Catharine, KY 40061-9435. Tel: 859-336-9303; Fax: 859-336-9306. Sr. Joye Gros, O.P., Pres.; Sr. Rosemary Cina, O.P., Archivist.
Total number in community 230.
Legal Title: *The Literary Society of Saint Catharine of Siena.*
Properties owned: *Rosary Manor,* Watertown, MA; *Dominican Sisters,* Plainville, MA; *Sansbury Care Center,* Louisville, KY; *St. Catharine Motherhouse; St. Catharine College,* St. Catharine, KY.
Sisters serve and staff: Colleges and Universities; High Schools; Elementary Schools; Environmental Ministry; Health Care-Facilities; Diocesan Offices; Pastoral Associates-Assistants; Parish Ministry; Chaplain-Pastoral Care; Directors Religious Education and Human Services.
Represented in the Archdioceses of Boston, Chicago, Louisville, New York, and Omaha and in the Dioceses of Brooklyn, Brownsville, Fort Wayne-South Bend, Grand Island, Jackson, Joliet, Lincoln, Memphis, Rockford, Saginaw and Worcester.

[1070-02] DOMINICAN SISTERS, ST. MARY OF THE SPRINGS (1830)

General Motherhouse: *Dominican Sisters St. Mary of the Springs,* 2320 Airport Dr., Columbus OH 43219-2098. Tel: 614-416-1900; Fax: 614-252-7435. Sr. Anne Kilbride, O.P., Prioress.
Total number in community 285.
Legal Title: *Dominican Sisters, St. Mary of the Springs,* Columbus, Ohio.
Ministry in Diocesan Offices; the field of Academic Education at all levels; Religious Education; Adult Education Programs; Congregational Infirmary; Art and Ecological/Environment; Hospitals; Home Health Care Agencies; Care of the Elderly; Parish Ministry; Pastoral Care; Justice and Peace Ministry; Family Care; Liturgy Preaching and Spirituality Programs; Research Programs; Missionaries; Counseling and Canon Law Ministry; Campus Ministry; Social Work.
Properties owned and sponsored: *Dominican Academy,* New York, NY; *Ohio Dominican University,* Columbus, OH; *Albertus Magnus College,* New Haven, CT; *Mohun Health Care Center,* Columbus, OH.
Represented in the Archdioceses of Baltimore, Cincinnati, Denver, Detroit, Hartford, New Orleans, New York, Santa Fe, and Seattle and in the Dioceses of Columbus, Fort Wayne-South Bend, Gary, Grand Rapids, Greensburg, Green Bay, Pittsburgh, Providence, Springfield, Steubenville, St. Petersburg, and Wheeling-Charleston. Also in Peru, Italy and Honduras.

[1070-03] SINSINAWA DOMINICAN CONGREGATION OF THE MOST HOLY ROSARY (1847) (P)

Generalate: *Sinsinawa Dominican Congregation of the Most Holy Rosary,* 585 County Rd. Z, Sinsinawa, WI 53824-9701. Tel: 608-748-4411. Sr. Antoinette Harris, O.P., Prioress of the Congregation. Sr. Marjorie Buttner, O.P., Archivist.

Interdependent Provinces (1987): *Eastern Province,* 7200 W. Division St., River Forest, IL 60305-1294. Tel: 708-366-0282. Sr. Mary Ellen Green, O.P., Prov.

Southern Province: *Casa San Jose,* 360 Travino Ave., St. Augustine, FL 32086-7369. Tel: 904-797-7011. Sr. Christa Cunningham, O.P., Prov.

Western Province: 3916 N. Farwell Ave., Milwaukee, WI 53211-2411. Tel: 414-332-1997. Sr. Mary Ann Nelson, O.P., Prov.
Total number in community 749.

Collaborative Dominican Novitiate: 4928 Washington Blvd., St. Louis, MO 63108. Tel: 314-454-3845. Co-Dirs: Sr. Maria Beesing, O.P.; Sr. Ann Walters, O.P.
Ministry in a variety of cultures in Preaching & Evangelization; Elementary, Secondary and Higher Education; Medical, Legal and Social Services; Adult and Religious Education; Diocesan and Parish Administration, Spiritual Direction and Counseling; Rural Migrant and Native American Services; Writing Research.
Properties owned or Institutions sponsored: *Sinsinawa Dominicans, Inc., Dominican University,* River Forest, IL; *Sinsinawa Housing, Inc., (Academy Apartments),* Sinsinawa, WI; *Bethlehem Academy* Faribault, MN; *Dominican High School,* Whitefish Bay, WI; *Queen of Peace High School,* Burbank, IL; *Trinity High School,* River Forest, IL; *Sinsinawa Nursing, Inc., (St. Dominic Villa),* Sinsinawa, WI; *Dominican Motherhouse,* Sinsinawa, WI; *Camp We-Ha-Kee,* Winter, WI; *The Bridge,* Denmark, WI; *Edgewood Campus School; Edgewood High School; Edgewood College,* Madison, WI; *Mother Samuel Coughlin Charitable Trust; Dominican Outreach Formation.*
Represented in the Archdioceses of Atlanta, Boston, Chicago, Denver, Dubuque, Indianapolis, Los Angeles, Miami, Milwaukee, Mobile, New Orleans, New York, Omaha, Portland (OR), St. Louis, St. Paul-Minneapolis, San Antonio, San Francisco, Santa Fe, Seattle and Washington and in the Dioceses of Altoona-Johnstown, Austin, Baker, Boise, Brownsville, Camden, Charleston, Cheyenne, Colorado Springs, Columbus, Crookston, Dallas, Fairbanks, Fall River, Fort Wayne-South Bend, Gallup, Gaylord, Grand Rapids, Great Falls-Billings, Grand Island, Green Bay, Helena, Honolulu, Jackson, Joliet, Juneau, Kansas City-St. Joseph, La Crosse, Lexington, Madison, Memphis, Monterey, Nashville, Oakland, Ogdensburg, Orlando, Owensboro, Palm Beach, Pensacola-Tallahassee, Peoria, Phoenix, Rapid City, Rockford, Rochester, Sacramento, Saginaw, San Angelo, San Diego, San Jose, St. Augustine, St. Cloud, St. Petersburg, Santa Rosa, Spokane, Superior, Tucson, Tulsa, Winona and Venice. Also in Bolivia, Guatemala, Switzerland and Trinidad.

[1070-04] CONGREGATION OF THE MOST HOLY NAME (1850) (P)

Generalate: *Dominican Sisters of San Rafael,* 1520 Grand Ave., San Rafael, CA 94901. Tel: 415-453-8303; Fax: 415-453-8367. Sr. Patricia Simpson, O.P.,
Total number in community 150.
Legal Holdings and Titles: *Justin Siena High School,* Napa, CA; *San Domenico School,* San Anselmo, CA; *Santa Sabina Retreat Center,* San Rafael, CA; *St. Rose Corporation,* San Francisco, CA; *St. Joseph's Regional Health System; St. Joseph's Housing Corporation,* Stockton, CA; *St. Mary's Health Network; Sisters of St. Dominic, Congregation of the Most Holy Name,* San Rafael, CA; *Mission Holding Corporation,* San Rafael, CA.
Represented in the Archdioceses of Los Angeles and San Francisco and in the Dioceses of Charleston, Monterey, Oakland, Reno, Sacramento, San Jose, Santa Rosa and Stockton. And also in Canada and Mexico.

[1070-05] CONGREGATION OF THE HOLY CROSS (1853) (D)

General Motherhouse: *Queen of the Rosary Motherhouse,* Albany Ave., Amityville, NY 11701. Tel: 631-842-6000; Fax: 631-842-0240. Sr. Virginia Maguire, O.P., Prioress; Sr. Margaret Clines, O.P., Archivist.
Total number in community 638.
Sisters are engaged in the ministry of Education at all levels; Catechetical Schools; Handicapped, Adult and Continuing Education; Hospitals; Homes for the Aged; Residence for Senior Citizens; Spiritual Life Centers; Chaplaincy; Advocacy; Communications; Social Service Institutions; Shelters; Pastoral Services; Prison ministry; Retreats; Health Services; ministry to AIDS Victims; Environmental Education Ministry.
Represented in the Archdioceses of Baltimore, Chicago, Hartford, Newark, New York and the in Dioceses of Albany, Brooklyn, Fairbanks, Kalamazoo, Orange, Providence, Rochester, Rockville Centre and Trenton. Also in Puerto Rico, Dominican Republic and Colombia.

[1070-07] CONGREGATION OF ST. CECILIA (1860) (P)

General Motherhouse: *St. Cecilia Convent,* 801 Dominican Dr., Nashville, TN 37228-1909. Tel: 615-256-5486; Fax: 615-726-1333. Mother Rose Marie Masserano, O.P., Prioress Gen.; Sr. Marian Sartain, O.P., Archivist.
Professed sisters in community 180; Novices 13; Postulants 11.
Ministry in the field of Academic Education at all levels.
Legal Holdings and Titles: *Aquinas College,* Nashville, TN.
Represented in the Archdioceses of Baltimore, Chicago, Cincinnati, Denver, New Orleans, St. Paul-Minneapolis, and Washington and in the Dioceses of Arlington, Birmingham, Knoxville, Memphis, Nashville and Richmond.

[1070-08] CONG.REGATION OF ST. MARY (1860) (P)

General Motherhouse: *Dominican Sisters,* 7300 St., Charles Ave., New Orleans, LA 70118. Tel: 504-861-8183; Fax: 504-861-8184. Sr. Angeline Magro, O.P., Prioress.
Total number in community 52.
Legal Holdings: *St. Mary's Dominican High School,* New Orleans, LA, *Dominican Conference Center,* New Orleans, LA, *Rosaryville Retreat Center,* Ponchatoula, LA.
Ministry in Education and Social Apostolates.
Represented in the Archdiocese of New Orleans and in the Diocese of Baton Rouge.

[1070-09] CONGREGATION OF ST. CATHERINE OF SIENA (1862) (P)

General Motherhouse: *Convent of St. Catherine,* Siena Center, 5635 Erie St., Racine, WI 53402-1900. Tel: 262-639-4100; Fax: 262-639-9702. Sr. Carol Wester, O.P., Pres., Sr. Diane Kenel, Archivist.
Total number in community 213.
Legal Holdings and Titles: *Sisters of St. Dominic,* Racine, WI; *Dominican College of Racine, Inc.,* Racine, WI;

St. Catherine's High School of Racine, Inc., Racine, WI; *Racine Dominican Ministries, Inc.,* Racine, WI; *St. Catherine's Infirmary, Inc.,* Racine, WI.
Properties sponsored: *Franciscan Sisters, Daughters of the Sacred Hearts of Jesus and Mary,* Wheaton, IL and the *Sisters of St. Dominic,* Racine, WI; *Catherine Marian Housing, Inc.; Villa St. Anna, Inc.,* Racine, WI.
Sisters minister in the areas of Elementary, Secondary, Higher and Music-Cultural Education; Adult Education; Religious Education; Administration; Parish and Pastoral Ministry; Prison Ministry; Social Justice; Campus Ministry; Social Services, Hospital and Health Services; Writing-Research; Hospital Chaplains; Diocesan Services; Retreats-Prayer Programs; Community Services.
Represented in the Archdioceses of Chicago, Detroit, Indianapolis, Milwaukee, Newark, St. Louis, Santa Fe and in the Dioceses of Gallup, Jackson, Green Bay, Las Cruces, Las Vegas, Little Rock, Madison, New Ulm, Toledo and Winona.

[1070-10] DOMINICAN SISTERS OF SPRINGFIELD IN ILLINOIS (1873) (P)

General Motherhouse: *Sacred Heart Convent,* 1237 W. Monroe St., Springfield, IL 62704-1680. Tel: 217-787-0481; Fax: 217-787-8169. Sr. Mary Jean Traeger, O.P., Prioress Gen.
Total number in community 287.
Legal Holdings or Titles: *Dominican Sisters of Springfield,* Illinois, Inc.; *Dominican Sisters of Springfield in Illinois Charitable Trust,* Springfield, IL; *Benincasa Ministries,* Springfield, IL; *Dominican Literacy Center,* Aurora, IL; *Marian Catholic High School,* Chicago Heights, IL; *Rosary High School,* Aurora, IL; *Sacred Heart-Griffin High School,* Springfield, IL; *St. Dominic-Jackson Memorial Hospital,* Jackson, MS.
Ministry in Elementary, Secondary Schools and College Religious & Academic Education; Daycare and Learning Centers; Hospices, Hospitals, Nursing Homes, Congregation's Infirmary and Retirement Centers; Retreat & Renewal Center; Administrative Positions in Parishes and Diocesan offices; Parish Liturgist/Musician & Pastoral Associates; Prison Ministry; Social Services; Foreign Missions.
Represented in the Archdioceses of Chicago, Dubuque, Louisville, St. Louis, and St. Paul-Minneapolis and in the Dioceses of Baton Rouge, Cleveland, Belleville, Duluth, Great Falls-Billings, Green Bay, Jackson, Joliet, Lansing, Little Rock, Peoria, Rockford and Springfield (IL). Also in Peru.

[1070-11] CONGREGATION OF OUR LADY OF THE ROSARY (1876) (D)

General Motherhouse and Novitiate: *Dominican Convent of Our Lady of the Rosary,* 175 Route 340, Sparkill, NY 10976. Tel: 914-359-6400. Sr. Maryann Summa, O.P., Pres.
Total number in community 409.
Legal Title: *Dominican Congregation of Our Lady of the Rosary.*
Ministry in High Schools and Elementary Schools; Adult Education/Literacy; Parishes; Pastoral; Colleges; House of Prayer; Housing and Community Centers; Foreign Missions; Substance Abuse Recovery.
Properties Sponsored: *Aquinas High School,* New York, NY; *Albertus Magnus High School,* Bardonia, NY; *Thorpe Family Residence,* Bronx, NY.
Represented in the Archdioceses of Chicago, New York, Newark, and St. Louis and in the Dioceses of Bridgeport, Brooklyn, Charleston, Great Falls-Billings, Helena, Jefferson City, Oakland, Rockville Centre, Rockford, San Diego, St. Petersburg, Trenton and Wilmington.

[1070-12] CONGREGATION OF THE QUEEN OF THE HOLY ROSARY (1876) D

General Motherhouse: *Dominican Convent,* P.O. Box 3908, Mission San Jose, CA 94539. Tel: 510-657-2468; Fax: 510-657-1734. Sr. Rose Marie Hennessy, Prioress Gen.; Sr. M. Evangela Balde, Community Archivist.
Profess 262; Novices 3; Postulants 5.
Legal Title: *Dominican Sisters of Mission San Jose, a Corporation, Queen of the Holy Rosary College, a Corporation, Mission* San Jose, CA; *St. Catherine's Military School, a Corporation,* Anaheim, CA; *Immaculate Conception Academy, a Corporation,* San Francisco, CA; *Flintridge Sacred Heart Academy, a Corporation,* La Canada-Flintridge, CA; *Pia Backes Support Trust,* Fremont, CA.
The Congregation's primary ministry is Catholic education. Sisters also engage in a variety of pastoral services.
Represented in the Archdioceses of Los Angeles, Portland (OR), San Francisco, and Washington and in the Dioceses of Brooklyn, Oakland, Orange, San Jose and Tucson. Also in Germany and Mexico.

[1070-13] CONGREGATION OF THE MOST HOLY ROSARY (1892) (P)

General Motherhouse: 1257 Siena Heights Dr., Adrian, MI 49221. Tel: 517-266-3400; Fax: 517-266-3545. Sr. Janet Capone, O.P., Prioress.
Mission Chapters (1982): *Florida Mission Chapter,* 810 N. Olive Ave., West Palm Beach, FL 33401. Tel: 561-832-6521. Sr. Mary Ann Caulfield, O.P., Chapter Prioress.
Adrian Crossroads Mission Chapter: 1257 Siena Heights Dr., Adrian, MI 49221 Tel: 517-266-4240. Sr. Mary Suzanne Kennedy, O.P., Chapter Prioress.
Mid-Atlantic Mission Chapter: P.O. Box 17087, Raleigh, NC 27619. Tel: 919-844-8369. Sr. Marilyn Winter, O.P., Chapter Prioress.
Dominican Midwest Mission Chapter: 8000 Linder Ave., Burbank, IL 60459. Tel: 708-636-7566. Sr. Sarah Ann Fergus, O.P., Chapter Prioress.
Holy Rosary Mission Chapter: 1257 Siena Heights Dr., Adrian, MI 49221. Tel: 517-266-4107. Sr. Joan Lawrence Sustersic, O.P., Chapter Prioress.
Great Lakes Dominican Mission Chapter: 9400 Courville St., Detroit, MI 48224. Tel: 313-343-0573. Sr. Margaret O'Flynn, O.P., Chapter Prioress.
Rosa de Lima Mission Chapter, c/o 1257 Siena Heights Dr., Adrian, MI 49221. Tel: 809-533-0272. Sr. Nancy Jurecki, O.P., Chapter Prioress.
Dominican Mission Chapter, P.O. Box 42567, Phoenix, AZ 85080. Tel: 602-938-1778. Sr. Catherine Ormond Olds, O.P., Chapter Prioress.
Total number in community 1,026.
Legal Holdings or Titles: *Dominican Sisters of Adrian, MI, Inc.,* Adrian, MI; *Camilla Madden Charitable Trust,* Adrian MI; *Adrian Dominican Sisters Office of Development,* Adrian MI; *Dominican High School,* Detroit, MI; *Dominican Santa Cruz Hospital,* Santa Cruz, CA; *Dominican Life Center,* Adrian, MI; *Regina Dominican High School,* Wilmette, IL; *Rosarian Academy,* West Palm Beach, FL; *Siena Heights University,* Adrian, MI; *St. Joseph Academy,* Adrian, MI; *St. Rose Dominican Hospital,* Henderson, NV; *Weber Retreat Center,* Adrian, MI.
Sisters minister in the areas of Formal Education–as administrators, teachers and consultants at elementary, secondary, college, state and diocesan levels; Pastoral Ministry–parishes, hospitals and campuses; Religious Education–coordinators and teachers; Social Services–case workers, administrators, counselors, therapists, consultants, care-givers for elderly and staff for retirement centers; Health Services–administrators, nurses, therapists, doctors, physician assistants, psychologists, technologists, pharmacists and dietitians; Business Services–directors, accountants, secretaries, administrative assistants, typists, bookkeepers, office managers, office staff, drivers and housekeeping staff; Spiritual Direction–retreat work, formation, congregation leadership and as diocesan Vicars for Religious; Social Justice–coordinators, staff and community organizers; other ministries including research, law, science, public relations, art, communications and full-time study.
Represented in the Archdioceses of Atlanta, Chicago, Cincinnati, Denver, Detroit, Indianapolis, Los Angeles, Louisville, Miami, New Orleans, New York, Oklahoma City, Philadelphia, Portland, St. Louis, San Antonio, San Francisco, Santa Fe, Seattle, and Washington and the Dioceses Arlington, Austin, Birmingham, Boise, Charleston, Cleveland, Columbus, Dodge City, El Paso, Fresno, Fort Wayne-South Bend, Gallup, Galveston-Houston, Gary, Gaylord, Green Bay, Helena, Jackson, Joliet, Kalamazoo, Las Vegas, Lansing,Lexington, Madison, Marquette, Monterey, Oakland, Orange, Orlando, Palm Beach, Pensacola-Tallahassee, Peoria, Phoenix, Pittsburgh, Providence, Pueblo, Raleigh, Rapid City, Richmond, Rockford, Saginaw, St. Augustine, St. Petersburg, San Bernardino, San Diego, San Jose, Superior, Toledo, Tucson and Venice. Also in South Africa, Canada, China, Dominican Republic, Mexico, and Puerto Rico.

[1070-14] CONGREGATION OF OUR LADY OF THE SACRED HEART (1877) (P)

General Motherhouse: Marywood, 2025 E. Fulton St., Grand Rapids, MI, 49503. Tel: 616-459-2910; Fax: 616-454-6105. Sr. Maribeth Holst, O.P., Prioress; Sr. Michael Ellen Carling, O.P., Archivist.
Total number in community 305.
Legal Holdings or Titles: *Sisters of the Order of St. Dominic of Grand Rapids; Marywood Academy; Sisters of St. Dominic of the Congregation of Our Lady of the Sacred Heart; Charitable Trust.*
Sisters are involved in Academic and Religious Education at all levels; Liturgy; Pastoral Ministry and Administration; Diocesan Offices; Food Service; Health Care; Congregational Services; Social Work; Sabbatical Volunteer; Public Education and Study; Foreign Missions; Justice Advocacy.
Represented in the Archdioceses of Atlanta, Baltimore, Chicago, Detroit, Newark, St. Louis, and Santa Fe and in the Dioceses of Albany, Colorado Springs, Dallas, Dodge City, Fort Wayne-South Bend, Fort Worth, Gaylord, Grand Rapids, Helena, Kalamazoo, Lansing, Lexington, Orlando, Providence, Saginaw, San Diego, Sioux Falls and Toledo. Also in Peru and Honduras.

[1070-15] CONGREGATION OF SAINT DOMINIC (1878) (D)

General Motherhouse: *Sisters of Saint Dominic of Blauvelt,* New York, 496 Western Hwy., Blauvelt, NY 10913-2097. Tel: 845-359-5600; Fax: 845-359-5773. Sr. Mary Ann Collins, O.P., Pres.; Sr., Judith Campbell, O.P., Archivist.
Total number in community 187.
Sisters serve and staff: Elementary; Secondary; Higher Education; Special Education; Hospital Care; Pastoral Care; Parish Ministry; Retreat Work; Child Care; Neighborhood Services; Services to Migrants; Services to Chemically Dependent.
Represented in the Archdioceses of Newark and New York and in the Dioceses of Orlando, Paterson, Providence, Rockville Centre and San Bernardino.

[1070-17] CONGREGATION OF ST. CATHERINE DE RICCI (1880) (P)

General Motherhouse: F anjeaux, 750 Ashbourne Rd., Elkins Park, PA 19027-2596. Tel: 215-635-6027. Sr. Carolyn Krebs, O.P., Pres.
Professed Sisters 84.
Properties owned: *Dominican Retreat House / Convent of Our Lady of Prouille,* Elkins Park, PA; *St. Dominic Hall,* Elkins Park, PA; *Dominican Retreat, Immaculate Heart of Mary Convent,* McLean, VA; *Dominican Retreat House / Our Lady of Grace Convent,* Niskayuna, NY; *Dominican Retreat House / Queen of Apostles Convent,* Miami, FL; *St. Catherine Hall,* Elkins Park, PA.
Sisters serve and staff: Retreat Houses; Religious Education Centers and Parish Services; Hospital; Pastoral Ministry; College; Diocesan Offices; Special Services; Spiritual Direction; Counseling Center; Liturgical Art Studio.
Represented in the Archdioceses of Baltimore, Cincinnati, Detroit, Miami, Philadelphia and Santa Fe and in the Dioceses of Albany, Arlington, Biloxi, Orlando, Palm Beach, Providence, Raleigh, and St. Petersburg.

[1070-18] SISTERS OF ST. DOMINIC OF THE AMERICAN CONGREGATION OF THE SACRED HEART OF JESUS (1881) (D)

Dominican Motherhouse: 1 Ryerson Ave., Caldwell, NJ 07006. Tel: 973-403-3331; Fax: 973-228-9611. Sr. Joan Doyle, O.P., Prioress; Sr. Helen Marguerite, O.P., Archivist.
Total number in community 203.
Legal Title: *Sisters of St. Dominic of Caldwell, N.J.*
Ministry in Education at all levels; Pastoral Ministry; Health and Human Services.
Properties owned: *Caldwell College,* Caldwell, NJ; *Mount Saint Dominic Academy,* Caldwell, NJ; *St. Dominic Academy,* Jersey City, NJ; *Lacordaire Academy,* Upper Montclair, NJ.
Represented in the Archdioceses of Baltimore, Boston, Newark and Portland and in the Dioceses of Metuchen, Oakland, Paterson, Savannah, Springfield (IL) and Trenton. Also in the Dominican Republic.

[1070-19] DOMINICAN SISTERS OF HOUSTON, TEXAS (CONGREGATION OF THE SACRED HEART) (1882) (P)

General Motherhouse & Novitiate: *Dominican Sisters,* 6501 Almeda Rd., Houston, TX 77021. Tel: 713-747-3310; Fax: 713-747-4707. Sr. Heloise Cruzat, O.P., Prioress.
Total number in community 115.
Legal Title: *Dominican Sisters of Houston, Texas, Inc. (aka Sacred Heart Convent of Houston).*
Ministry in the field of Academic Education at all levels and Parish Ministry.
Properties owned and sponsored: *St. Agnes Academy, St. Agnes Academy Foundation, St. Pius X High School, St. Pius X High School Foundation, Inc., The Sacred Heart Convent Retirement Trust.*
Represented in the Archdioceses of Chicago, Los Angeles, San Antonio, San Francisco, St. Louis, and Seattle and in the Dioceses of Austin, Beaumont, Brownsville, Corpus Christi, Dallas, Galveston-Houston, Lake Charles, San Angelo, San Bernardino, San Jose, Trenton and Tyler. Also in Guatemala.

[1070-20] CONGREGATION OF ST. THOMAS AQUINAS (1888) (P)

Motherhouse: *Tacoma Dominican Center,* 935 Fawcett Ave. S., Tacoma, WA 98402-5605. Tel: 253-272-9688; Fax: 253-272-8790. Sr. Patricia Morisset, O.P.

Total number in community 76.
Legal Holdings and Titles: *Sisters of St. Dominic, Tacoma Dominican Center; Sisters of St. Dominic - Tacoma Charitable Trust.*
Ministry in a variety of missions.
Represented in the Archdioceses of Los Angeles, San Francisco, and Seattle and in the Dioceses of Baker, Fresno, St. Augustine, San Diego, San Bernardino and Yakima. Also in Canada, Mexico and Nicaragua.

[1070-23] CONGREGATION OF ST. ROSE OF LIMA (1900) THE SERVANTS OF RELIEF FOR INCURABLE CANCER IN THE U.S.

General Motherhouse: *Rosary Hill Home,* Hawthorne, NY 10532. Tel: 914-769-0114. Mother Marie Edward, O.P., Supr. Gen.
Total number in community 70.
The work of these sisters is confined entirely to the incurable cancerous poor.
Represented in the Archdioceses of Atlanta, New York, Philadelphia, and St. Paul-Minneapolis and in the Diocese of Cleveland.

[1070-24] DOMINICAN SISTERS OF GREAT BEND (1902) (P)

Motherhouse & Novitiate: *Dominican Sisters, Immaculate Conception,* 3600 Broadway, Great Bend, KS 67530. Tel: 620-792-1232. Sr. Gemma Doll, O.P., Prioress.
Total number in community 116.
Legal Title: *The Nuns of the Third Order of St. Dominic.*
Properties owned and sponsored: *Heartland Center for Spirituality,* Great Bend, KS; *St. Martin de Porres Association Dominican Retreat Center,* Great Bend, KS; *Cedar Park Place, Inc. (low- and middle-income housing for the elderly and handicapped),* Great Bend, KS; *Heartland Center for Wholistic Health Association,* Great Bend, KS; *Office of Mission and Ministry,* Great Bend, KS; *Art of Learning Center,* Wichita, KS; *co-sponsor of Catholic Health initiatives.*
Properties owned: *Hospitality House,* Wichita, KS; *several residential convents; Heartland Farm,* Pawnee Rock, KS; *Novitiate House,* Great Bend, KS.
Sisters serve in Grade Schools; Colleges; Special Education; Religious Education Centers and Centers for Retreats and Spirituality; Hospitals; Nursing Homes; Infirmary; Home Health Services; Health Care Ministries; Foreign Missions; Ministry to Minorities; Ministry to Aging; Housing; Music Ministry; Parish Ministry; Office of Mission and Ministry.
Represented in the Archdioceses of Denver, Kansas City in Kansas, St. Louis and St. Paul-Minneapolis and in the Dioceses of Dodge City, Phoenix, Pueblo, Salina, San Angelo, Springfield-Cape Giradeau and Wichita. Also in Africa & Papua New Guinea.

[1070-25] CONGREGATION OF THE DOMINICAN SISTERS OF ST. CATHERINE OF SIENA OF KENOSHA (1911) (P)

General Motherhouse & Novitiate: P.O. Box 1288, Kenosha, WI 53141. Tel: 262-694-2067; Fax: 262-694-6542. Sr. Susan Anne Snyder, O.P., Prioress.
Total number in community 18.
Legal Title: *Congregation of the Dominican Sisters of St. Catherine of Siena of Kenosha, Inc.*
Properties owned: *Holy Rosary Medical Center,* Ontario, OR; *Our Lady of Fatima Villa,* Saratoga, CA; *Mercy Hospital,* Merced, CA.
Represented in the Archdiocese of Milwaukee and in the Dioceses of Baker, Columbus, Fresno and San Jose. Also in Ecuador.

[1070-26] CONGREGATION OF ST. ROSE OF LIMA (1923) (D)

General Motherhouse: *St. Joseph's Convent,* 775 Drahner Rd., Oxford, MI 48371-4866. Tel: 248-628-2872. Sr. Teresita Lipar, O.P., Prioress; Sr. Susan McMahon, O.P., Vicaress; Sr. Gene Poore, O.P., Councilor.
Total number in community 42.
Sisters minister in Nursing Homes; Retreat House; Parish Ministry; Religious Education; Senior Citizens Residence; Hospital Ministry; Pastoral Assistant.
Properties owned and sponsored: *St. Mary's Retreat House,* Oxford, MI; *St. Jude Home,* Waterford, MI; *Dominican Center (retreat house for teenagers),* Oxford, MI; *Lourdes Nursing Home Fox Manor,* Waterford, MI; *Dominican Sisters of Oxford Charitable Trust,* Oxford, MI.
Represented in the Archdioceses of Chicago, Detroit, and Milwaukee and in the Dioceses of Gary, Lansing and Saginaw.

[1070-27] CONGREGATION OF THE IMMACULATE CONCEPTION (1929) (D)

Provincial House: *Immaculate Conception Provincial House,* 9000 W. 81st. St., Justice, IL 60458. Tel: 708-458-3040. Mother M. Natalie, .O.P., Prov. Supr.
Total number in community 31.
Represented in the Archdioceses of Chicago and Milwaukee and in the Diocese of Little Rock. Also in Canada.

[1070-28] CONGREGATION OF THE SISTERS OF ST. DOMINIC OF THE IMMACULATE HEART OF MARY (1929) (D)

General Motherhouse: *Our Lady of the Elms Convent,* 1230 W. Market St., Akron, OH 44313-7108. Tel: 330-836-4908; Fax: 330-836-5913. Sr. Elizabeth Ann Schaefer, O.P., Prioress; Sr. Rebecca Betz, O.P., Archivist.
Total number in community 88.
Properties owned: *Our Lady of the Elms School, Crown Point Ecology Center,* Bath, OH.
Represented in the Archdioceses of Anchorage, Portland, St. Louis, and Seattle and in the Dioceses of Cleveland, Fort Wayne-South Bend, Lansing, Phoenix, Saginaw, Venice, Toledo and Youngstown. Also in Central America.

[1070-30] DOMINICAN SISTERS OF OAKFORD (P)

U.S. Regional Center: *Dominican Sisters of Oakford,* 980 Woodland Ave., San Leandro, CA 94577. Tel: 510-638-2822; Fax: 510-633-9734. Sr. Anna Oven, O.P., Reg.
Total number in community 21.
Ministries in Teaching; Spiritual Direction; Counselling; Parish Work; Adult Education; Care for the Elderly; Community Services and Nursing.
Properties owned: *3 residences in California; Formation House,* San Leandro, CA; *St. Catherine's Convent,* Sunnyvale, CA.
Represented in the Dioceses of Oakland, Phoenix, San Jose and Tucson.

[1100] (O.P.)—DOMINICAN SISTERS OF CHARITY OF THE PRESENTATION OF THE BLESSED VIRGIN (P)

Founded in France in 1696. First foundation in the United States in 1906.
Motherhouse: 15 Quai Portillon, 37023, Tours Cedex, France.
Universal Total in Congregation 3,000.
Provincial House: 3012 Elm St., Dighton, MA 02715. Tel: 508-669-5425; 669-5023; Fax: 508-669-6521. Sr. Joanna Fernandes, O.P., Prov. Supr.
Total number in Province 42.
Ministry in Hospitals; Homes For the Aged; Residence for Working Women & Students; Dispensaries; Migrant Clinic; Education; Pastoral Ministry.
Represented in the Archdiocese of Washington and in the Dioceses of Brownsville, Fall River and Providence. Also in India, Haiti, Honduras, Korea, Peru, Bolivia, Columbia and Mexico.

[1105] (O.P.)—DOMINICAN SISTERS OF HOPE (P)

Founded July 20, 1995, as a merging of three former Congregations: Dominican Sisters of the Congregation of the Most Holy Rosary of Newburgh, NY; Dominican Sisters of the Sick Poor of Ossining, NY and Congregation of Catherina of Siena, of Fall River, MA.
General Administrative Offices: *Dominican Sisters of Hope,* 299 N. Highland Ave., Ossining, NY 10562. Tel: 914-941-4420; Fax: 914-941-1125. Sr. Philomena Marie McCartney, O.P., Prioress.
Total number in community 286.
Legal Titles and Holdings: *Dominican Sisters of Hope Ministry Trust. Ministry in Religious & Academic Education at all levels; Health, social, community and pastoral services in low income area; Parish service, counseling, retreats and spiritual direction.*
Represented in the Archdioceses of Cincinnati, Denver, Detroit, Hartford, Newark, New York, Oklahoma City, Philadelphia and Washington and in the Dioceses of Albany, Allentown, Arlington, Bridgeport, Brooklyn, Burlington, Camden, Fall River, Gallup, Jackson, Lexington, Metuchen, Ogdensburg, Palm Beach, Paterson, Providence, Richmond, and Rockville Centre.

[1110] (O.P.)—DOMINICAN SISTERS OF OUR LADY OF THE ROSARY AND OF SAINT CATHERINE OF SIENA, CABRA (P)

Founded in Ireland in 1644.
General Motherhouse: Cabra, Dublin 7, Ireland. Region of Louisiana established in 1978.
Regional House: Dominican Sisters, Cabra, 1930 Robert E. Lee, New Orleans, LA 70122. Tel: 504-288-1593. Sr. Elizabeth Ferguson, O.P., Reg. Prioress.
Total number in local community 11.
Ministry in Academic & Religious Education; Parish Ministry; Neighborhood Social Service Agency; Diocesan Tribunal; Prison Ministry; Adult Education; Social Apostolate; Retreats; Spiritual Direction.

Represented in the Archdiocese of New Orleans and in the Dioceses of Fort Worth and Houma-Thibodaux.

[1120] (O.P.)—DOMINICAN SISTERS OF THE ROMAN CONGREGATION (P)

Founded in France in 1621. First United States foundation in 1904.
General Motherhouse: Rome, Italy. Sr. Rosario de Meer, Supr. Gen.
Universal Total in Congregation 550.
U.S. Provincial Office: 123 Dumont Ave., Lewiston, ME 04240-6107. Tel: 207-782-3535; Fax: 207-782-0435. Sr. Monique Belanger, O.P., Prov. Prioress.
Total number in community 25.
Ministry in the field of Religious & Academic Education; Adult Education; Indian Reservation; Pastoral Ministry; Health Care; Social Work.
Properties owned: *Retreat House; Residences 5.*
Represented in the Archdioceses of Chicago, New York and Portland (OR) and in the Dioceses of Davenport, Gallup, Phoenix and Portland (ME).

[1140] (O.P.)—EUCHARISTIC MISSIONARIES OF ST. DOMINIC (D)

Founded in Louisiana in 1927.
Eucharistic Missionaries of St. Dominic: *Central Office,* 3801 Canal St. - Suite 400, New Orleans, LA 70119-6048. Tel: 504-486-1133; Fax: 504-486-6547. Sr. Dorothy Trosclair, O.P., Pres.
Perpetually Professed Sisters 35; Missions 14.
Properties owned: real estate in Covington, LA; houses in New Orleans & Tucson, AZ.
Sisters serve and staff: Religious Education and Spiritual Directors at all levels; Parish and Diocesan Social Services; Parish Administrators and ministry; Home Health Nursing; Literacy ministry to immigrants; Forensic Social Work; Hospital Chaplaincies.
Represented in the Archdiocese of New Orleans and in the Dioceses of Beaumont, Biloxi, Houma-Thibodaux, Lafayette (LA), Palm Beach and Tucson.

[1145] (O.P.)—RELIGIOUS MISSIONARIES OF ST. DOMINIC

General Motherhouse: Via di Val Cannuta 138, 00166, Rome, Italy. Sr. Elvira Diez, O.P., Supr. Gen.
U.S. Delegation Office: 2237 Waldron Rd., Corpus Christi, TX 78418. Tel: 361-939-8102; Fax: 361-939-8203; Sr. Maria Paz Aribon, O.P., Delegate of the Supr. Gen.
Total number in Congregation 667; Sisters in the United States 32.
Represented in the Archdiocese of Los Angeles and in the Dioceses of Corpus Christi and Galveston-Houston.

[1150] (E.F.M.S.)—EUCHARISTIC FRANCISCAN MISSIONARY SISTERS (D)

Founded in Mexico in 1943. Mother Maria Gemma de Jesus Aranda, Founderess.
Motherhouse: *Our Lady's Convent,* 943 S. Soto St., Los Angeles, CA 90023. Tel: 323-264-6556; 1421 Cota Ave., Torrance, CA 90501. Tel: 310-328-6725. Mother Rose Seraphim, E.F.M.S., Supr. Gen.; Sr. Gloria de Jesus, E.F.M.S., Gen. Sec.
Total number in community 26.
Legal Title: *Eucharistic Franciscan Missionary Sisters of Los Angeles.*
Sisters serve and staff: The field of Education; Missionary Activities; Catechetics; Social Work; Diocesan and Administration offices.
Represented in the Archdiocese of Los Angeles and in the Dioceses of Stockton and Tyler.

[1170] (C.S.S.F.)—FELICIAN SISTERS (P)

(Congregation of Sisters of St. Felix of Cantalice, of the III Order of St. Francis)

Founded in Poland in 1855. First foundation in the United States in 1874.
General Motherhouse: Via del Casaletto 540, 00151, Rome, Italy. Sr. Mary Raymond Kasprzak, C.S.S.F., Min. Gen.
Presentation of the B.V.M. Province (1874): *Motherhouse and Novitiate-Provincialate,* 36800 Schoolcraft Rd., Livonia, MI 48150. Tel: 734-591-1730; Fax: 734-591-1710. Sr. Mary Renetta Rumpz, C.S.S.F., Prov. Min.
Professed 203; Novices 3; Postulants 1.
Ministry in the field of Academic Education at all levels; Catechetical Center; CCD Programs; Archival and Secretarial Services in Seminary; Diocesan Nursing Home; Youth Ministry Center; Pastoral Ministry Programs; DRE Offices; Hospital; Health Care Nursing Homes; Assisted Living; Hospice Inpatient and Home Care Program; Day Care Centers; Retreat Centers; House of Prayer; Senior Clergy Residence.

Properties owned: *Madonna University; Ladywood High School; Montessori Center of Our Lady St. Mary Mercy Hospital,* Livonia, MI; *St. Joseph Day Care; Presentation Prayer Center,* Jackson, MI; *Maryville Center,* Holly, MI; *Angela Hospice Home Care and Inpatient Facility, Marian Professional Building,* Livonia, MI.

Represented in the Archdiocese of Detroit and in the Dioceses of Fort Wayne-South Bend, Gaylord, Lansing, Saginaw and Toledo.

Immaculate Heart of Mary Province (1900): *Provincial House and Novitiate-Villa Maria,* 600 Doat St., Buffalo, NY 14211. Tel: 716-892-4141; Fax: 716-892-4177. Sr. Mary Ambrose Wozniak, C.S.S.F., Prov. Minister; Sr. Mary Janet Mazierski, C.S.S.F., Prov. Archivist.

Total number in community 245.

Ministry in Education on all levels; Day Care Center; School for Mentally and Multiply Handicapped; Institute of Music; Religious Education Programs; Outreach Centers; Parish Ministries; Social Services; Prison Ministries; Campus Ministries; Diocesan Office.

Properties: *Villa Maria College of Buffalo; Villa Maria Academy; Villa Maria Institute of Music,* Buffalo, NY.

Represented in the Archdioceses of Newark and New York and the Dioceses of Buffalo, Charleston, Syracuse and Rochester. Also in Canada and Italy.

Mother of Good Counsel Province (1910): *Mother of Good Counsel Provincialate, Novitiate, & Convent,* 3800 W. Peterson Ave., Chicago, IL 60659. Tel: 773-463-3020. Sr. Mary Barbara Ann Bosch, C.S.S.F., Prov. Minister. Sr. M. Adolphine Ksioszk, C.S.S.F., Community Archivist.

Total number in the community 259.

Ministry in the field of Academic and Religious Education at all levels; Homes for Aged; Independent Living for the Elderly; Assisted Living for the Elderly; Pastoral Ministry; Social Workers; Family Therapists; Day Care Centers; Hospitals; Infirmary for Sisters; Foreign Missions; Recreation House for Children.

Represented in the Archdioceses of Chicago and Milwaukee and in the Dioceses of Belleville, Green Bay, Joliet, La Crosse and Rockford.

Immaculate Conception Provincial House (1913): *Motherhouse and Novitiate-Immaculate Conception Convent,* 260 S. Main St., Lodi, NJ 07644-2196. Tel: 973-473-7447; Fax: 973-473-7126. Web site: www.feliciansisters.org. Sr. Mary Aquinas Szott, C.S.S.F., Prov. Minister; Sr. Mary Virginia Tomasiak, Prov. Sec.; Sr. Rose Marie Smiglewski, Prov.

Total number in community 207.

Properties sponsored: *Immaculate Conception High School; Felician College; Felician College Day Care Center; Felician School for Exceptional Children,* Lodi, NJ; *Felician Retreat Center; Our Lady of Grace Home St. Ignatius Nursing Home.*

Sisters serve and staff: Colleges; High Schools; Elementary Schools; Hospitals; Home for Neglected Children; Home for Aged; Infirmary for Sisters; Day Care Center; School for Exceptional Children; Religious Education; Parish Ministries.

Represented in the Archdioceses of Newark and Philadelphia and in the Dioceses of Metuchen, Paterson, and Wilmington.

Our Lady of the Sacred Heart Province (1921): *Provincial House and Novitiate, Felician Sisters of Pennsylvania,* 1500 Woodcrest Ave., Coraopolis, PA 15108. Tel: 412-264-2890; Fax: 412-264-7047. Sr. Mary Cabrini Procopio, C.S.S.F., Prov. Min.

Total number in province 113.

Legal Holdings and Titles: *Felician Sisters of Pennsylvania; Our Lady of the Sacred Heart High School.*

Ministry in the field of Academic Education at all levels; Religious Education; CCD Centers; Youth and Pastoral Ministry; Home for Mentally Retarded Children & Adults; Infirmary and Home for Aged; Missionary Work.

Represented in the Dioceses of Altoona-Johnstown, Charleston, Greensburg, Harrisburg and Pittsburgh. Also in Kenya.

Our Lady of the Angels Province (1932): *Felician Sisters Provincial Hse./Novitiate, Our Lady of the Angels Convent,* 1315 Enfield St., Enfield, CT 06082-4929. Tel: 860-745-7791; Fax: 860-741-0819. Sr. Mary Laureann Alexandrowicz, C.S.S.F., Prov. Min.

Sisters in Province 104.

Ministry in the field of Religious and Academic Education; Pastoral Ministry; Social Services; Healthcare.

Properties owned and sponsored: *Montessori School; Felician Adult Day Care,* Enfield, CT; *St. Joseph Hospital,* Bangor, ME.

Represented in the Archdioceses of Hartford and New York and in the Dioceses of Albany, Manchester, Norwich, Portland (ME), Providence, Springfield (MA) and Worcester.

Assumption of the B.V.M. Province (1953): *Provincial House - Novitiate,* 4210 Meadowlark Ln., S.E., Rio Rancho, NM 87124-1021. Sr. Mary Seraphine Moynier, C.S.S.F., Prov. Min.

Total number in community 68.

Legal Titles and Holdings: *Felician Sisters of the Southwest, Inc.; St. Felix Pantry Inc.*

Sisters serve and staff: High Schools; Elementary Schools; Foreign and Rural Missions; Religious Education Centers & Classes; Health Care; Pastoral Care; Food & Clothing Pantry; Youth Ministry; Adult Education.

Represented in the Archdioceses of Los Angeles, San Antonio, and Santa Fe and in the Dioceses of Laredo and San Bernardino. Also in Mexico.

[1180] (O.S.F.)—FRANCISCAN SISTERS OF ALLEGANY, NEW YORK (P)

Founded in the United States in 1859.

General Motherhouse (1859): *St. Elizabeth Motherhouse,* Allegany, NY 14706. Tel: 716-373-0200; Fax: 716-372-5774. Sr. Margaret Mary Kimmins, O.S.F., Gen. Minister; Sr. Noella Lachat, O.S.F., Local Minister.

Total number in community 382.

Legal Titles and Holdings: *Franciscan Sisters of Allegany, NY, Inc.; Franciscan Center, Inc.,* Tampa, FL; *Dwelling Place, Inc.,* New York, NY; *St. Joseph's Villa,* Catskill, NY; *Canticle Farm, Inc.,* Allegany, NY; *St. Elizabeth Mission Society, Inc.,* Allegany, NY; *Dr. Lyle F. Renodin Foundation, Inc.,* Allegany, NY.

Ministry to Evangelization in all levels of Education; Health Care; Social Services; Pastoral and Campus Ministries; Spiritual Ministries and Social Advocacy.

Represented in the Archdioceses of Boston, Miami, Newark, New York, and Philadelphia and in the Dioceses of Albany, Buffalo, Camden, Columbus, Fall River, Gallup, Metuchen, Norwich, Palm Beach, Providence, Rochester, Rockville Centre, St. Petersburg, Spokane, Springfield (MA), Syracuse, Trenton and Venice. Also in Bolivia, Brazil, Jamaica, and the Philippines.

Region I Office: *Franciscan Sisters of Allegany (1984),* 115 E. Main St., Allegany, NY 14706. Tel: 716-373-0200. Sr. Roberta Francis Brunner, O.S.F., Region I Minister.

Represented in the Dioceses of Albany, Buffalo, Columbus, Rochester, Spokane and Syracuse. Also in Bolivia.

Region II: *Franciscan Sisters of Allegany (1984),* 282 Suffolk St., Lowell, MA 01854. Tel: 978-452-2823. Sr. Mary Lou Lafferty, O.S.F., Region II Minister.

Represented in the Archdioceses of Boston, Newark, New York, and Philadelphia and in the Dioceses of Camden, Fall River, Gallup, Metuchen, Norwich, Providence, Rockville Centre, Springfield (MA) and Trenton.

Region III: *Franciscan Sisters of Allegany (1984),* 631 - 11th St., No., St. Petersburg, FL 33705. Tel: 727-824-0857. Sr. Marie Kathleen Stagnaro, O.S.F., Region III Minister.

Represented in the Archdiocese of Miami and in Dioceses of Palm Beach, St. Petersburg and Venice.

Region IV: *Franciscan Sisters of Allegany,* 152 Constant Spring Rd., Box 1654, Kingston, Jamaica, West Indies. Tel: 876-925-1973. Sr. Teresita Marie De Souza, O.S.F., Region IV Minister.

Region V: *Franciscan Sisters of Allegany,* C.P. 322, 75001-970 Anapolis, Goias, Brazil, South America, Tel: 011-55-62-321-0805. Sr. Maria do Socorro Rabelo, O.S.F., Region V Minister.

[1190] (S.A.)—FRANCISCAN SISTERS OF THE ATONEMENT (P)

Founded in the United States in 1898.

Motherhouse: *St. Francis Convent-Graymoor,* 41 Old Highland Trnpk., Garrison, NY 10524. Tel: 845-424-3623; Fax: 845-424-3298. Sr. Ellen Donahue, S.A., Minister Gen.; Sr. Mary Harper, S.A., Archivist.

Total number in community 197.

Properties owned: *St. Francis Convent - Complex,* Garrison, NY; *Mother Lurana House,* Garrison, NY; *Washington Retreat House,* Washington, DC.

Represented in the Archdioceses of Boston, Detroit, Newark, New York and Washington and in the Dioceses of Albany, Brooklyn, Bridgeport, Burlington, Fresno, Las Vegas, Metuchen, Monterey, Norwich, Ogdensburg, Pittsburgh, Reno, Salt Lake City, Syracuse and Trenton. Also in Canada, Brazil, Ireland, Italy and Japan.

[1210] (O.S.F.)—FRANCISCAN SISTERS OF CHICAGO (P)

Founded in Chicago, Illinois in 1894 by Mother Mary Theresa (Josephine Dudzik) Venerable Servant of God.

General Motherhouse: *Our Lady of Victory Convent,* 11400 Theresa Dr., Lemont, IL 60439-2728. Tel: 630-243-3600; Fax: 630-243-3601. Sr. Diane Marie Collins, O.S.F., Gen. Minister.

Total number in community 71.

Properties owned: *St. Anthony Home, Inc.,* Crown Point, IN; *St. Joseph Home of Chicago, Inc.,* Chicago IL; *Mount Alverna Home, Inc.; Mount Alverna Home Annex, Inc.,* Parma, OH; *Mother Theresa Home, Inc.; Franciscan Village,* Lemont, IL; *St. Francis House of Prayer; Franciscan Sisters of Chicago Service Corp. Our Lady of Victory Convent,* Lemont, IL.

Sisters serve and staff: Elementary Schools CCD Programs.

Represented in the Archdiocese of Chicago and in the Dioceses of Cleveland and Gary.

[1230] (O.S.F.)—FRANCISCAN SISTERS OF CHRISTIAN CHARITY (P)

Founded in the United States in 1869.

Motherhouse: *Holy Family Convent,* 2409 S. Alverno Rd., Manitowoc, WI 504220. Tel: 920-682-7728; Fax: 920-682-4195. Sr. Louise Hembrecht, Community Dir.; Sr. Donna Marie Kessler, Community Archivist.

Total number in community 421.

Properties owned or sponsored: Holy Family Convent, Manitowoc, WI; *Holy Family Convent of Franciscan Sisters of Christian Charity, Inc.,* Manitowoc, WI; *Holy Family Memorial, Inc.,* Manitowoc, WI; *The Retirement Trust of the Franciscan Sisters of Christian Charity,* Manitowoc, WI; *St. Francis Memorial Hospital,* West Point, NE; *Good Samaritan Medical Center,* Zanesville, OH; *St. Joseph Retirement Community,* West Point, NE; *St. Paul Villa,* Kaukauna, WI; *St. Paul Home,* Kaukauna, WI; *St. Paul Manor,* Kaukauna, WI; *Silver Lake College,* Manitowoc, WI; *Franciscan Sisters of Christian Charity HealthCare Ministry, Inc.,* Manitowoc, WI; *Holy Family Conservatory of Music,* Manitowoc, WI; *St. Clare Convent,* Manitowoc, WI; *St. Francis Convent,* Manitowoc, WI.

Represented in the Archdioceses of Chicago and Omaha and in the Dioceses of Columbus, Green Bay, Jackson, Honolulu, Marquette, Phoenix, Steubenville, Superior, and Tucson.

[1235] (F.H.M.)—FRANCISCAN SISTERS DAUGHTERS OF MERCY

Franciscanas Hijas de la Misericordia

Founded in Pina, Mallorca, Spain in 1856. First U.S. establishment in 1962.

General Motherhouse: Calle Moral 4, 07001 Palma de Mallorca, Spain. Sr. Antonia Barrilero Canadas, Supr. Gen.

Universal number in Congregation 447.

U.S. Regional Delegation: 1207 Montopolis Dr., Austin, TX 78741. Tel: 512-385-5090. Sr. Rose Moreno, F.H.M. Reg. Delegate.

Professed Sisters 6.

Ministry in Kindergarten; Catechetical Work; Pastoral Work.

Represented in the Diocese of Austin.

[1240] (O.S.F.)—FRANCISCAN SISTERS, DAUGHTERS OF THE SACRED HEARTS OF JESUS AND MARY (P)

Founded in Germany in 1860. First foundation in the United States in 1872.

Generalate: *Via di Sant'Alessio,* 22-24, 00153, Rome, Italy. Sr. Carola Thomann, O.S.F., Gen. Dir.

Universal number in Congregation 815.

St. Clara's Province (1877): *Convent of Our Lady of the Angels, Motherhouse and Novitiate,* P.O. Box 667, Wheaton, IL 60189. Tel: 630-462-7422. Sr. Margaret Grempka, O.S.F., Prov. Dir.

Total number in Province 95.

Legal Holdings and Titles: *Affinity Health System,* Oshkosh, WI; *All Saints Healthcare Foundation, Inc.,* Racine, WI; *All Saints Healthcare System, Inc.,* Racine, WI; *Assisi Homes of Neenah, Inc.,* Neenah, WI; *Assisi Homes - Batavia Apartments, Inc.,* Batavia, IL; *Assisi Homes - Colony Park, Inc.,* Carol Stream, IL; *Assisi Homes - Constitution House, Inc., Aurora, IL; Assisi Homes of Gurnee, Inc.,* Gurnee, IL; *Assisi* Homes of Illinois, Inc., *Wheaton, IL;* Assisi Homes - Jefferson Court, Inc.; Assisi Homes - Kenosha, Inc., *Kenosha, WI;* Assisi Homes - Saxony, Inc., *Kenosha, WI;* Assisi Homes of Milwaukee, Inc., *Milwaukee, WI;* Canticle Ministries, Inc., *Wheaton, IL;* Canticle Place, Inc., *Wheaton, IL;* Clare Gardens, Inc., *Denver, CO;* Clare of Assisi Homes - Westminster, Inc., *Westminster, CO;* Clara Pfaender Fund, Inc., *Wheaton, IL;* St. Joseph Regional Medical Center Foundation, Inc., *Milwaukee, WI;* Covenant Medical Center, Inc.; *Covenant Healthcare System, Inc., Milwaukee, WI; Covenant Home Health and Hospice, Inc., Milwaukee, WI;* Covenant Foundation, Inc.; Covenant Health System, Inc., *Waterloo, IA;* Marianjoy Rehabilitation Hospitals & Clinics, Inc., *Wheaton, IL;* Dayspring Villa, Inc., *Denver, CO;* Elmbrook Memorial Hospital, *Brookfield, WI;* Franciscan Care and Rehabilitation Center, Inc., *Appleton, WI;* Franciscan Shared Laboratory, Inc., *Wauwatosa, WI;* Franciscan Seniors,

Kenosha, Inc., *Kenosha, WI;* *Franciscan Ministries, Inc., *Wheaton, IL;* Francis Heights, Inc., *Denver, CO;* Franciscan *Health and Education Corporation, Inc.,* Wheaton, IL; *Franciscan Sisters Charitable Fund of Colorado, Inc.,* Denver, CO; *Marianjoy, Inc.,* Wheaton, IL; *Marian Franciscan Center, Inc.; Marian Housing Center, Inc.,* Racine, WI; *Marian Park, Inc.; Mercy Hospital of Franciscan Sisters, Inc.; Oak Park Hospital,* Oak Park, IL; *O.S.F. Services, Inc.; Ridgeway Place, Inc.,* Waterloo, IA; *Sartori Memorial Hospital, Inc.,* Cedar Falls, IA; *St. Catherine's Hospital, Inc.; St. Elizabeth Hospital Inc.,* Appleton, WI; *St. Elizabeth Hospital Community Foundation, Inc.,* Appleton, WI; *St. Joseph Regional Medical Center, Inc.,* Milwaukee, WI; *St. Michael Hospital of Franciscan Sisters of Milwaukee, Inc.,* Milwaukee, WI; *St. Michael Hospital Community Foundation, Inc.,* Milwaukee, WI; *All Saints Medical Center, Inc.,* Racine, WI; *S.E.T. Ministry, Inc.; Villa St. Anna, Inc.; Villa St. Clare, Inc.,* Neenah, WI; *Villa Maria, Inc.,* Westminster, CO; *Wheaton Franciscan Sisters Corp.; Wheaton Franciscan Sisters Religious Charitable Trust; Wheaton Franciscan Services, Inc.; Mercy Medical Center of Oshkosh, Inc.,* Oshkosh, WI.

Sisters serve, sponsor and staff: Hospitals; Housing Development; Parish Ministry; Spirituality Center; Home Health Care; Corporate Offices; System Ministries; Long-term Care; Social Services; Wellness; Spiritual Direction; Foreign Mission.

Represented in the Archdioceses of Chicago, Denver, Dubuque, Milwaukee and St. Louis and in the Dioceses of Green Bay, Joliet, La Crosse, Madison, Rockford and Springfield-Cape Girardeau. Also in Brazil, Italy and Nigeria.

[1250] (F.S.E.)—THE INSTITUTE OF THE FRANCISCAN SISTERS OF THE EUCHARIST (P)

Founded December 2, 1973.

Motherhouse: *John Lateran Center,* 405 Allen Ave., Meriden, CT 06451. Tel: 203-237-0841. Team Members, Mother Rosemae Pender; Mother Gen.; Mother Shaun Vergauwen; Mother Asst.; Mother Mary Ann Schmitz; Mother Mona Brunner; Mother Suzanne Gross; Mother Barbara Johnson.

Total number in community 80.

Legal Title: *Franciscan Sisters of the Eucharist, Inc.*

Schools and programs operated under: Franciscan Life Center Network, Incorporated.

Represented in the Archdioceses of Hartford, Portland (OR), Seattle and Washington and in the Dioceses of Boise, Duluth, Galveston-Houston and Grand Rapids. Also in Israel and Italy.

[1260] (F.H.M.)—FRANCISCAN HANDMAIDS OF THE MOST PURE HEART OF MARY (D)

Founded in the United States in 1916.

General Motherhouse: 15 W. 124th St., New York, NY 10027. Tel: 212-289-5655.

Novitiate: 444 Woodvale Ave., Pleasant Plains, Staten Island, NY 10309. Sr. Maria Goretti, Congregation Minister; Sr. Loretta Theresa, Dir. Formation; Sr. Jacqueline, Community Archivist.

Total number in community 23.

Ministry in the field of Education, Social Work and Pastoral Care.

Properties owned: *St. Benedict Day Nursery; Camp Saint Edward; Franciscan Handmaids of Mary Novitiate; Franciscan Handmaids of Mary Motherhouse.*

Represented in the Archdiocese of New York.

[1270] (F.H.I.C.)—FRANCISCAN HOSPITALLER SISTERS OF THE IMMACULATE CONCEPTION (P)

Founded in Portugal in 1876.

General Motherhouse: Linda-a-Pastora, Portugal. Sr. Maria Isilda Freitas, F.H.I.C., Supr. Gen.

U.S. Foundation (1960): *St. Joseph Novitiate,* 300 S. 17th St., San Jose, CA 95112-2245. Tel: 408-998-2896; Fax: 408-998-3407. Sr. Lucinda D. Fonseca, Supr.

Total number in community 20.

Sisters serve and staff: Parishes; Schools; Hospitals; Social Work.

Represented in the Dioceses of Fresno, Monterey and San Jose.

[1280] (O.S.F.)—FRANCISCAN SISTERS OF THE IMMACULATE CONCEPTION (P)

First foundation in United States in 1928.

General Motherhouse: Kloster Bonlanden, Germany. Sr. M. Veronica Mang, O.S.F., Supr. Gen.

Province of the Blessed Virgin Mary: 291 North St., Buffalo, NY 14201. Fax: 716-881-1578. Sr. M. Bernard, O.S.F., Prov.

Professed Sisters 2.

Represented in the Archdiocese of New York and in the Diocese of Buffalo.

[1300] (O.S.F.)—FRANCISCAN SISTERS OF THE IMMACULATE CONCEPTION AND ST. JOSEPH FOR THE DYING (D)

Founded in the United States in December, 1919 at San Carlos Parish, Monterey, California.

General Motherhouse: *St. Joseph's Convent,* 485 Church St., Monterey, CA 93940. Tel: 408-372-3579. Sr. M. Constance O.S.F., Supr. Gen.; Sr. M. Bernadette, O.S.F., Archivist.

Total number in community 5.

Legal Holding: *Ave Maria Convalescent Hospital,* Monterey, CA.

Represented in the Diocese of Monterey.

[1310] (C.S.F.)—FRANCISCAN SISTERS OF LITTLE FALLS, MINNESOTA (P)

Founded in the United States in 1891.

General Motherhouse: *St. Francis' Convent,* Little Falls, MN 56345. Tel: 320-632-2981. Sr. Beatrice Eichten, O.S.F., Pres.

Total number in community 219.

Ministry in the field of Academic Education at all levels; Health Care in Nursing Homes, Hospitals, Apartment for the Elderly, Children's Home, Clinics; Religious Education; Parish Ministry; Retreat Ministries; Liturgical Music; Music Center; Ministry to Refugees; Health and Recreation Center; Diocesan Offices; Social Services; Counseling; Spiritual Direction; Consulting; Ministry to the Poor; Ministry to Migrants; Ministry to the Hearing Impaired; Altar Bread-making and Craft Activities; Ministry in Ecology; Social Justice and Nonviolent Activities; Spirituality Farm.

Properties owned or sponsored: *St. Francis Music Center; St. Francis Health & Recreation Center; Clare's Well.*

Represented in the Archdioceses of Chicago, Los Angeles, Milwaukee, New York, St. Louis, St. Paul-Minneapolis, Santa Fe, San Francisco, and San Antonio and in the Dioceses of Arlington, Birmingham, Fargo, Jackson, La Crosse, Manchester, Memphis, New Ulm, Oakland, Phoenix, St. Cloud, St. Petersburg, San Diego, Scranton, Sioux Falls, Toledo, Tucson and Winona. Also in Ecuador, Mexico and Tanzania.

[1320] (F.M.S.A.)—FRANCISCAN MISSIONARY SISTERS FOR AFRICA (P)

Generalate: *Franciscan Missionary Sisters for Africa,* 34a Gilford Rd., Sandymount, Dublin 4, Ireland. Tel: 011-353-2838376; Fax: 011-353-1-2602049.

American Headquarters: 172 Foster St., P.O. Box 35095, Brighton, MA 02135. Tel: 617-254-4343; Fax: 617-787-8007. Sr. Maurita Kennedy, F.M.S.A.

Total number in community 7.

Represented in the Archdiocese of Boston.

[1330] (S.F.M.A.)—FRANCISCAN MISSIONARY SISTERS OF ASSISI (P)

General Motherhouse: Via San Francesco 13, Assisi, Italy. Sr. Aureliana Compostella, Mother Gen.

U.S. Viceprovince (1961): *St. Francis Convent,* 1039 Northampton St., Holyoke, MA 01040. Tel: 413-532-8156; Fax: 413-534-7741. Sr. Mary D'Angelo, Vice-Prov.

Total number in community 14.

Represented in the Archdiocese of New York and in the Diocese of Springfield (MA).

[1340] (F.M.D.C.)—FRANCISCAN MISSIONARY SISTERS OF THE DIVINE CHILD (D)

First founded in the United States on August 15, 1927 in Buffalo, New York.

Motherhouse: *Franciscan Missionary Sisters of the Divine Child Motherhouse,* 6380 Main St., Williamsville, NY 14221. Tel: 716-633-4011; Fax: 716-633-4249. Sr. Concetta DeFelice, F.M.D.C., Minister General.

Total number in community 25.

Sisters serve and staff: Catechetical Centers; CCD Coordinators; Education in High School & College; Parish Ministry; Bereavement counseling & Human Services; Vocation Formation Director.

Represented in the Archdiocese of Newark and in the Diocese of Buffalo.

[1350] (O.S.F.)—FRANCISCAN SISTERS OF THE IMMACULATE CONCEPTION (P)

Founded in Mexico in 1874. First foundation in the United States in 1926.

Provincial House: 13367 Borden Ave.-Unit A, Sylmar, CA 91342-2804. Tel: 818-364-6122 & 364-5557. Sr. Imelda Marie Gallegos, O.S.F., Prov. Supr.; Sr. Mary Gabriel De Leon, O.S.F., Community Archivist.

Total number in community 112.

Legal Holdings and Titles: *Franciscan Missionary Sisters of the Immaculate Conception, Inc.; Poverello of Assisi Retreat House,* San Fernando, CA; *St. Francis Home,* Santa Ana, CA; *Mother Gertrude Balcazar Home,* San Fernando, CA.

Ministry in the field of Education and Religious Education to Children and Adults; Health Care in Hospitals and Home Visitation to the Sick.

Represented in the Archdiocese of Los Angeles and in the Dioceses of Gallup and Orange. Also in Mexico.

[1360] (M.F.I.C.)—MISSIONARY FRANCISCAN SISTERS OF THE IMMACULATE CONCEPTION (P)

Founded in the United States in 1873 in Belle Prairie, Minnesota.

General Motherhouse: Rome, Italy. Sr. Elaine Morzone, M.F.I.C., Gen. Minister.

Provincialate: *Immaculate Conception Province,* 790 Centre St., Newton, MA 02458-2530. Tel: 617-527-1004; Fax: 617-527-2528. Sr. Suzanne Fondini, M.F.I.C., Prov.

Total number in Province 224.

Represented in the Archdioceses of Boston, Newark and New York and in the Dioceses of Bridgeport, Brooklyn, Charleston, Providence, Savannah, Syracuse and Venice. Also in Peru and Bolivia.

[1365] (F.M.I.J.)—FRANCISCAN MISSIONARY SISTERS OF THE INFANT JESUS (P)

Founded in Aquila, Italy in 1879 by Sr. Maria Giuseppa Micarelli. First Foundation in the U.S. in 1961.

Generalate: Piazza Nicoloso da Recco 13, Rome, Italy 00154. Tel: 6-575-8358. Mother Maria Felicita Decio, F.M.I.J., Supr. Gen.

U.S. Province and Novitiate: 1215 Kresson Rd., Cherry Hill, NJ 08003. Tel: 609-428-7930; Fax: 609-428-7930. Sr. Angela Pia Camillotti, F.M.I.J., Delegate Supr.

Professed Sisters 19.

Ministries of Evangelization; Education; Health Care; Social-Pastoral Services.

Represented in the Dioceses of Arlington & Camden.

[1370] (F.M.M.)—THE FRANCISCAN MISSIONARIES OF MARY (P)

Founded in India in 1877. First foundation in the United States in 1903.

General Motherhouse: 12 via Giusti, Rome, Italy. Sr. Christiane Megarbane, F.M.M., Supr. Gen.

Franciscan Missionaries of Mary-U.S. Province (1920): 3305 Wallace Ave., Bronx, NY 10467-6599. Tel: 718-547-4693. Sr. Mary Motte, F.M.M., Prov.

Total number in community 162.

Ministry in Educational Projects among Minority Group of Immigrants; Child Care Agencies; Cardiac and General Hospital; General Pediatric Hospital with Rehabilitation Specialty; Chaplaincy; Retreat Work; Day Care for Elderly; Catechetics; Mission Animation & Formation; Home Visiting & Community Development.

Represented in the Archdioceses of Boston, Chicago, New York and St. Louis and in the Dioceses of Las Cruces, Providence, Rockville Centre, Savannah and St. Petersburg.

[1380] (O.S.F.)—FRANCISCAN MISSIONARIES OF OUR LADY (P)

Founded in Calais, France in 1854. First U.S. foundation in 1913.

General Motherhouse: Paris, France.

Generalate: Paris, France.

Provincial and Novitiate House: *Maryville Novitiate,* 4200 Essen Ln., Baton Rouge, LA 70809. Tel: 225-926-1627; Fax: 225-925-5268. Sr. Barbara Arceneaux, Supr.

Total number in community 24.

Properties owned and sponsored: *Our Lady of the Lake Regional Medical Center, Inc.,* Baton Rouge, LA; *Ollie Steele Burden Manor, Inc.,* Baton Rouge, LA; *Our Lady of Lourdes Regional Medical Center, Inc.,* Lafayette, LA; *St. Francis Medical Center, Inc.,* Monroe, LA; *FMOL Health System, Inc.,* Baton Rouge, LA; *Haiti Project, Inc.,* Baton Rouge, LA.

Represented in the Dioceses of Baton Rouge, Lafayette (LA) and Shreveport.

[1390] (O.S.F.)—FRANCISCAN MISSIONARY SISTERS OF OUR LADY OF SORROWS (D)

Founded in Hunan China in 1939. First United States foundation in 1950.

Community Headquarters: *Our Lady of Peace Retreat House,* 3600 S.W. 170th Ave., Beaverton, OR 97006. Tel: 503-649-7127; Fax: 503-649-8382. Sr. Anne Marie Warren, O.S.F., Supr. Gen.

Total number in community 44.

Legal Titles and Holdings: *Our Lady of Peace Retreat,* Beaverton, OR; *St. Clare Retreat House,* Soquel, CA; *Our Lady of Mt. Carmel Group Home,* Gallup, NM.

Ministry in religious and academic education; retreat houses, group homes and foreign missions.

Represented in the Archdiocese of Portland (OR) and in the Dioceses of Gallup and Monterey.

[1400] (F.M.S.C.)—FRANCISCAN MISSIONARY SISTERS OF THE SACRED HEART (P)

Founded in Italy in 1861. First foundation in the U.S. in New York City (1865).

General Motherhouse: Rome, Italy. Sr. Ermenegilda Cavasin, Supr. Gen.

St. Francis Province (1869): *Mt. St. Francis,* 250 South St., Peekskill, NY 10566. Tel: 914-737-5409; Fax: 914-736-9614. Sr. Anne James Guerin, F.M.S.C., Prov.

Universal number in Congregation 782; Number in United States Province 54.

Legal Title: *Missionary Sisters of the Third Order of St. Francis.*

Ministry in Religious and Academic Education; Health Care for Retired Sisters; Pastoral Ministry; Prison Apostolate; Hospital Ministry.

Represented in the Archdioceses of Newark and New York and in Diocese of Brooklyn.

[1410] (F.M.S.J.)—MILL HILL SISTERS (P)

Franciscan Missionaries of St. Joseph

Founded in 1883. First United States foundation in 1952.

Generalate: *St. Joseph's Convent,* Worsley Manchester, England. Sr. Joan O'Gorman, F.M.S.J. Supr. Gen.

American Headquarters: *Franciscan House,* 1006 Madison Ave., Albany, NY 12208. Tel: 518-482-1991. Sr. Joan Kerley, F.M.S.J., Reg. Supr.

Total number in community 5.

Legal Title: *Mill Hill Sisters - New York Charitable Trust.*

Represented in the Dioceses of Albany, Norwich and Syracuse.

[1415] (F.S.M.)—FRANCISCAN SISTERS OF MARY (P)

Founded in the United States in 1872.

Administrative Offices & Novitiate: *Franciscan Sisters of Mary,* 1100 Bellevue Ave., St. Louis, MO 63117-1883. Tel: 314-768-1824; Fax: 314-768-1880. Sr. Jacqueline Motzel, F.S.M., Pres.

Total number in community 157.

Ministry in Hospitals; Skilled Nursing Facilities; Rehabilitation Unit; Hospice; Foreign Missions; Woman's Center; Social Services; Birthing Centers; Pastoral Services; Wholistic Health Services; Consultation Services.

Properties owned or sponsored: *St. Mary of the Angels,* St. Louis, MO.

Represented in the Archdioceses of Chicago, Cincinnati, Milwaukee, Oklahoma City, and St. Louis and in the Dioceses of Brownsville, Charleston, Jefferson City, Kansas City-St. Joseph, Madison, Springfield-Cape Girardeau and Tucson. Also in Brazil.

[1420] (F.S.R.)—FRANCISCAN SISTERS OF RINGWOOD (D)

Founded in the United States in Passaic, New Jersey on Nov. 21, 1929.

General Motherhouse and Novitiate: *Mt. St. Francis,* Ringwood, NJ 07456. Tel: 973-962-7411; Fax: 973-962-0445. Sr. Annette Lucchese, Gen. Coord.

Total number in community 28.

Ministry in the field of academic and religious education and as pastoral associates.

Represented in the Archdiocese of Newark and in the Diocese of Paterson.

[1425] (F.S.P.)—FRANCISCAN SISTERS OF PEACE (D)

Sisters of St. Francis of Peace: *Congregation Center,* 20 Ridge St., Haverstraw, NY 10927. Tel: 845-942-2527; Fax: 845-429-8141. Sr. Regina Holtz, F.S.P., Congregation Minister.

Total number in community 79.

Legal Titles and Holdings: *Cortlandt Manor,* New York, NY; *Congregation Center,* Haverstraw, NY.

Ministry in Youth; Care for the Aged; Pastoral; Education; Nursing; Catechetical; Social Work; Prison Ministry; Ministry to Unwed mothers; Evangelization; Social Services; Chaplaincies.

Represented in the Archdioceses of Mobile, Newark, New York, and San Francisco and in the Dioceses of Albany, Brooklyn, Paterson, Rockville Centre and Tucson.

[1430] (O.S.F.)—FRANCISCAN SISTERS OF OUR LADY OF PERPETUAL HELP (P)

Founded in the United States in 1901.

Motherhouse and Novitiate: *Franciscan Sisters of Our Lady of Perpetual Help,* 335 S. Kirkwood Rd., St. Louis, MO 63122. Tel: 314-965-3700; Fax: 314-965-3710. Sr. Monica Marie Laws, O.S.F., Supr. Gen.

Total number in community 127.

Legal Holdings and Titles: *Villa St. Joseph Motherhouse and Novitiate,* St. Louis, MO; *St. Francis Health Care Centre,* Green Springs, OH; *Perpetual Help Charitable Trust,* St. Louis, MO.

Ministry in Education; Nursing Homes; Rehabilitation Hospital; Indian Missions.

Represented in the Archdioceses of Chicago, Kansas City in Kansas, Los Angeles, Omaha, Portland in Oregon, Santa Fe, San Antonio, and St. Louis, and in the Dioceses of Cheyenne, Belleville, El Paso, Jefferson City, Las Cruces, Phoenix, Pueblo, San Angelo, Shreveport, Springfield (IL), Toledo and Wheeling-Charleston.

[1440] (S.F.P.)—FRANCISCAN SISTERS OF THE POOR (P)

Founded in Aachen, Germany in 1845. First foundation in the United States in 1858.

Congregational Office: 133 Remsen St., Brooklyn, NY 11201. Tel: 718-643-1919; Fax: 718-643-9710. Sr. Jeanne M. Glisky, S.F.P., Congregational Min.

Total number in community 171.

Congregation Sponsors: *Franciscan Health Partnership, Inc.; The Franciscan Sisters of the Poor, Inc.*

U.S. Region: 60 Compton Rd., Cincinnati, OH 45215. Tel: 513-761-9040; Fax: 513-761-6703. Sr. Mary Jacinta Doyle, S.F.P., Reg. Min.

Congregation sponsors: *St. Joseph Franciscan House, Inc.,* Brooklyn, NY; *Franciscan Sisters of the Poor Foundation, Inc.; St. Leonard Center,* Centerville, OH; *Franciscan Health System of Dayton, Inc.; Co-Sponsors: St. Anthony Medical Center, Inc.,* Columbus, OH; *West Park Retirement Community, Inc.,* Cincinnati, OH; *St. Raphael Social Service Center, Inc.,* Hamilton, OH; *West Park II, Inc.; St. John Social Service Center, Inc.; Franciscan Health System of Cincinnati, Inc. - Subsidiaries: St. Clare Retirement Community, Inc. Parent: —Subsidiaries: Mary Black Schroder Home for the Aging, Inc.,* Hamilton, OH; *Brazil Regional House and Frascati Complex,* Italy.

Represented in the Archdioceses of Cincinnati, Detroit, Newark, New York, and Philadelphia and in the Dioceses of Brooklyn, Columbus, Gallup, Lansing, Lexington, and Phoenix. Also in Italy, Senegal and Brazil.

[1450] (O.S.F.)—FRANCISCAN SISTERS OF THE SACRED HEART (P)

Congregation of the Franciscan Sisters of the Sacred Heart. Founded in Germany 1866. Established in the United States in 1876.

Motherhouse, Novitiate, Postulancy & Portiuncula Center for Prayer: *St. Francis Woods,* 9201 W. St. Francis Rd., Frankfort, IL 60423-8335. Tel: 815-469-4895; Fax: 815-464-3809. Sr. Mary Elizabeth Imler, Gen. Supr.

Total number in community 120.

Legal Titles: *An Association of Franciscan Sisters of the Sacred Heart; The Franciscan Sisters of the Sacred Heart in California; Legal Titles for Health Care entities; Provena Health; St. Anne's Maternity Home; Santa Barbara Franciscan Foundation; Franciscan Foundation.*

Sisters sponsor: *St. Joseph Medical Center,* Joliet, IL; *St. Joseph Hospital,* Elgin, IL; *St. Francis Medical Center,* Santa Barbara, CA; *St. Joseph College of Nursing,* Joliet, IL; *Villa Franciscan,* Joliet, IL; *Sacred Heart Home,* Avilla, IN; *LaVerna Terrace,* Avilla, IN; *St. Anne's Maternity Home,* Los Angeles, CA; *United Samaritans Medical Center, Logan Campus*-Danville, IL; *United Samaritans Medical Center, Sager Campus*-Danville, IL; *St. Therese Medical Center,* Waukegan, IL; *Franciscan Foundation,* Frankfort, IL.

Sisters serve and staff: Elementary Schools; High School; Religious Education Centers; Neighborhood Health Care Centers; Foreign Mission Centers; Direct Domestic Work at Retreat Houses; Canon Lawyer; Diocesan Offices; Retreat Centers; Clinics, Home Health Agencies, Health Care Systems, Hospitals, Schools of Nursing, Nursing and Retirement Homes; Home for Unwed Mothers; Apartments-Well Elderly; Parish & Youth Ministry; Hispanic Ministry; Liturgical Ministry; Social Work; Congregate Care Facility.

Represented in the Archdioceses of Chicago and Los Angeles and in the Dioceses of Fort Wayne-South Bend, Gary, Joliet, Peoria and Rockford. Also in Brazil.

[1460] (F.S.S.E.)—FRANCISCAN SISTERS OF ST. ELIZABETH (P)

(Suore Franciscane Elisabettine)

First founded in Naples, Italy, 1865. Founded in United States in Newark, New Jersey in 1919.

General Motherhouse: Via Marsico Nuovo 35, Rome, Italy. Mother Clara Capaso, Supr. Gen.

Delegate House: 499 Park Rd., Parsippany, NJ 07054. Tel: 973-539-3797. Mother Gina Maria Amico, Delegate Gen.

Total number in U.S. 50; Total in Community 300.

Ministry in Day Nurseries; Mission Houses; Elementary Schools and Montessori Schools.

Sister serve Christ in the person of the poor in Schools & Day Nursery Schools; Catechetical Instruction; Hospitals; Homes for the Poor, Aged and Disabled.

Represented in the Archdiocese of Newark and in the Dioceses of Paterson and St. Petersburg. Also in India, Indonesia, Italy, Panama, Philippines and Africa.

[1470] (F.S.S.J.)—FRANCISCAN SISTERS OF ST. JOSEPH (P)

Founded in the United States in 1897.

General Motherhouse: *Immaculate Conception Convent,* 5286 S. Park Ave., Hamburg, NY 14075. Tel: 716-649-1205; Fax: 716-649-5958. Sr. Mary Paulette Tirone, F.S.S.J., Gen. Min.

Total number in community 150.

Ministry in Education; Health Care; Parish Ministries.

Properties owned: *St. Clare Convent,* Hamburg, NY; *Immaculata Academy,* Hamburg, NY; *Marycrest Manor,* Livonia, MI; *St. Joseph Hospital,* Cheektowaga, NY.

Represented in the Archdioceses of Baltimore, Detroit, and Milwaukee and in the Dioceses of Allentown, Buffalo, Charlotte, Harrisburg, Norwich, Springfield (MA) and Trenton.

[1480] (H.F.S.J.)—FRANCISCAN SISTERS OF ST. JOSEPH (D)

Founded in Mexico.

Motherhouse: Ave. Revolucion No. 431 Delegacion, Benito Juarez, Mexico, 03801. D.F. Tel:515-1774. Rev. Madre Eva Juana Perez, H.F.S.J.

U.S. Address: *St. Paul's College,* 3015 4th St., N.E., Washington, DC 20017-1199. Tel: 202-832-6262; 269-2515. Sr. Maria de Jesus Jimenez, H.F.S.J.

Total number in community 5.

Ministry in domestic areas.

Represented in the Archdiocese of Washington.

[1485] (O.S.F.)—FRANCISCAN SISTERS OF ST. PAUL, MN. (P)

Franciscan Sisters of the Blessed Virgin Mary of the Holy Angels. (Beatae Mariae Virginis Angelorum)

Founded in Germany in 1863. First foundation in the United States in St. Paul in 1923.

General Motherhouse (1863): *St. Marienhaus, Waldbreitbach,* bei Neuwied, Rhine, Germany. Sr. Basina Kloos, O.S.F., Supr. Gen.

Universal Total in Congregation 475.

U.S. Foundation: *Franciscan Regional Center,* 1388 Prior Ave. S., St. Paul, MN 55116. Tel: 516-690-1501; Fax: 516-690-2509. Sr. Mary Lucy Scheffler, O.S.F.

Total number in community 13.

Represented in the Archdiocese of St. Paul-Minneapolis.

[1490] (O.S.F.)—SISTERS OF THE THIRD FRANCISCAN ORDER (P)

Founded in the United States in 1860.

Generalate Offices: *Sisters of the Third Franciscan Order,* 2500 Grant Blvd., Syracuse, NY 13208-1794. Tel: 315-634-7000; Fax: 315-634-7023. Sr. GraceAnne Dillenschneider, Gen. Minister.

Motherhouse: *St. Anthony Convent,* 1024 Court St., Syracuse, NY 13208-1794. Sr. Michaeleen Cabral, Gen. Sec.

Total number in community 285.

Legal Holding: *Sisters of the Third Franciscan Order-Retirement Trust Fund.*

Ministry in Academic Education at all levels; Hospitals; Schools of Nursing; Religious Education & Pastoral Ministry; Retreat House; Rehabilitation Center; Home for Dying; Adult & Child Day Care.

Properties Owned and/or Sponsored: *Sister Patricia Ann Preschool dba Gingerbread House,* Syracuse, NY; *St. Anthony Convent and Motherhouse,* Syracuse, NY; *St. Joseph's Hospital Health Center,* Syracuse, NY; *St. Elizabeth Hospital,* Utica, NY; *Stella Maris Retreat Center,* Skaneateles, NY; *St. Francis Social Adult Day Service,* Syracuse, NY; *St. Francis Health Care System,* Honolulu, HI; *St. Francis School,* Honolulu, HI; *Mercy Health and Rehabilitation Center,* Auburn, NY.

Represented in the Archdioceses of Boston, Los Angeles, Newark, and Washington and in the Dioceses of Albany, Camden, Gallup, Honolulu, Orange, Orlando, Richmond, Rochester, San Diego, St. Petersburg, Scranton, Syracuse, Trenton and Venice. Also in Peru.

[1500] (F.M.I.)—FRANCISCAN SISTERS OF MARY IMMACULATE OF THE THIRD ORDER OF ST. FRANCIS OF ASSISI (P)

Founded in Switzerland in the 16th Century. First founded in the United States on Aug. 15, 1932 at Amarillo, Texas.

General Motherhouse: Carrera 79 No. 40A-20 - Apartado Aereo 98892, Bogota, Colombia, South America. Sr. Ana Margarita Untersander, F.M.I., Supr. Gen.

Universal Total in Congregation 583.

U.S. Provincial House and Novitiate (1964): *St. Francis Convent (1932),* 4301 N.E. 18th Ave., Amarillo, TX 79107-7220. Tel: 806-383-5769; Fax: 806-383-6545. Sr. Rosa Gonzalez, F.M.I., Prov. Supr.
Total number in community 36.
Represented in the Archdioceses of Los Angeles and Santa Fe and in the Diocese of Amarillo.

[1505] (O.S.F.)—ST. FRANCIS MISSION COMMUNITY

Established 1981 in the United States of America in Amarillo, Texas, as an autonomous province of the Franciscan Sisters of Mary Immaculate.
General Motherhouse: *Our Lady of the Angels Convent,* 8202 CR 7700, Wolfforth, TX 79382. Tel: 806-863-4904. Sr. Mary Jane Alaniz, O.S.F., Prov. Min.
Professed Sisters 22.
Ministry in the field of Religious and Academic Education at all levels; Parish Work; Pastoral Care in Hospitals.
Properties owned: *La Verna Convent,* Amarillo, TX; *St. Francis Convent,* Lubbock, TX; *50 acres of real estate.*
Represented in the Archdiocese of Los Angeles and in the Dioceses of Amarillo and Lubbock. Also in Mexico.

[1510] (O.S.F.)—SISTERS OF ST. FRANCIS (D)

Sisters of St. Francis of the Mission of the Immaculate Virgin

Founded in New York in 1893.
General Motherhouse: *Sisters of St. Francis-Immaculate Conception Motherhouse,* 49 Jackson Ave., Hastings-on-Hudson, NY 10706-3217. Tel: 914-478-3930; Fax: 914-478-5470. E-mail: hastingsosf@aol.com. Sr. Roberta Stark Smith, Gen. Minister.
Total number in community 62.
Ministry in Education; Day Nurseries; Hospitals and Parishes.
Properties sponsored: *St. Francis Hospital,* Poughkeepsie, NY; *Nazareth Day Nursery,* New York, NY.
Represented in the Archdiocese of New York.

[1520] (O.S.F.)—SISTERS OF ST. FRANCIS OF CHRIST THE KING (P)

Founded in Austria in 1869. First founded in the United States at Kansas City, Kansas, in 1909.
General Motherhouse: Rome, Italy. Sr. Natalija Palac, Supr. Gen.
Universal number in Congregation 1,200.
St. Francis of Assisi of Christ the King Province (1926): *Mt. Assisi Convent,* 13900 Main St., Lemont, IL 60439. Tel: 630-257-7495. Sr. M. Paula Nasenbeny, O.S.F., Prov. Supr.
Total number in community 63.
Ministry in Education and Care in Homes for the Aged.
Properties owned and sponsored: *Mount Assisi Convent and Academy,* Lemont, IL; *Alvernia Manor,* Lemont, IL.
Represented in the Archdiocese of Chicago and in the Diocese of Joliet.

[1530] (O.S.F.)—SISTERS OF ST. FRANCIS OF THE CONGREGATION OF OUR LADY OF LOURDES, SYLVANIA, OHIO (P)

Founded in the United States in 1916 at Sylvania, Ohio. Foundation from Rochester, Minnesota.
General Motherhouse: *Convent and Novitiate,* 6832 Convent Blvd., Sylvania, OH 43560-2897. Tel: 419-882-2016; Fax: 419-885-8643. Sr. Carolyn Giera, Congregational Gen.
Total number in the Congregation 240.
Ministry in the field of Religious and Academic Education at all levels; Healthcare; Communications, Media, Producing; Counseling; Parish Ministries; Retreat Center; Social Services.
Properties owned and sponsored: *Lourdes College,* Sylvania, OH; *Franciscan Services Corp., Hospital System,* Sylvania, OH. *Sponsored Facilities: Burleson St. Joseph Health Center,* Caldwell, TX; *Trinity Community Medical Center,* Brenham, TX; *St. Joseph Regional Health Center,* Bryan, TX; *Franciscan Shelters (Bethany House),* Toledo, OH; *Franciscan Care Center,* Sylvania, OH; *Convent Park Apartments,* Sylvania, OH; *Providence Care Center,* Sandusky, OH; *The Commons of Providence,* Sandusky, OH; *Trinity Medical Center East and Trinity Medical Center West,* Steubenville, OH.
Represented in the Archdioceses of Cincinnati, Detroit, New Orleans, St. Paul-Minneapolis, and Santa Fe and in the Dioceses of Austin, Biloxi, Cleveland, Columbus, Fort Wayne-South Bend, Lansing, Palm Beach, Raleigh, Richmond, Saginaw, St. Cloud, Shreveport, Steubenville, Toledo, Tyler, and Wheeling- Charleston.

[1540] (O.S.F.)—SISTERS OF SAINT FRANCIS, CLINTON, IOWA (P)

Founded in the United States in 1866.
General Motherhouse: *Administrative Center,* 588 N. Bluff Blvd., Clinton, IA 52732. Tel: 563-242-7611; Fax: 563-243-0007. Sr. Marilyn Huegerich, O.S.F., Pres.
Ministry in the field of Academic Education at all levels; Home Health Care; Health Care in Centers and Homes for the Aged; Hospitals; Pastoral Ministry; Hospital Chaplaincy; Religious Education and Spiritual Direction; Campus Ministry; Ministry to the Poor in Legal Aid and Housing as well as to Persons with AIDS.
Legal Holdings and Properties: *The Franciscan University; The Alverno Health Care Facility; Mount St. Clare Speech and Hearing Center; Sisters of St. Francis,* Clinton, IA; *Iowa Charitable Trust,* Clinton, IA; *The Canticle,* Clinton, IA.
Represented in the Archdioceses of Chicago, Dubuque, and St. Louis and in the Dioceses of Belleville, Davenport, Des Moines, Joliet, Lexington, Kansas City-St. Joseph, Oakland, Orange, Peoria, Portland, Phoenix, San Bernardino, San Diego and Sioux City. Also in Peru.

[1550] (O.S.F.)—SISTERS OF ST. FRANCIS OF THE HOLY CROSS (D)

Founded in Wisconsin in 1881.
Motherhouse and Novitiate: *St. Francis Convent,* 3025 Bay Settlement Rd., Green Bay, WI 54311-7301. Tel: 920-468-1828; Fax: 920-468-1207. Sr. Ann Rehrauer, O.S.F., Pres.
Total number in community 83; Novices 1.
Legal Title: *Sisters of St. Francis of the Holy Cross, Inc.*
Ministries in the following areas: Education; Pastoral Ministry and Religious Education; Ministry to the Elderly; Health Care; Hospital Chaplaincy; Retreat Work; Foreign Missions.
Represented in the Archdiocese of Milwaukee and in the Diocese of Green Bay. Also in Nicaragua.

[1560] (O.S.F.)—SISTERS OF ST. FRANCIS OF THE HOLY EUCHARIST (D)

Founded in Grimmenstein, Switzerland in 1378. First foundation in United States in 1892.
Motherhouse, Novitiate and Prayer Center: *St. Francis Convent,* 2100 N. Noland Rd., Independence, MO 64050. Tel: 816-252-1673; Fax: 816-252-5574. Sr. M. Connie Boulch, O.S.F., Sister Servant; Sr. M. Lucy Lang, O.S.F., Vicar.
Total number in community 18.
Legal Title: *Franciscan Prayer Center,* Independence, MO; *Sisters of St. Francis of the Holy Eucharist Foundation,* Independence, MO.
Ministry in the following areas: Education at all levels; Retreat; Evangelization; Pastoral; Health Care.
Represented in the Archdiocese of Kansas City in Kansas and in the Diocese of Kansas City-St. Joseph.

[1570] (O.S.F.)—SISTERS OF ST. FRANCIS OF THE HOLY FAMILY (P)

Founded in Germany in 1864. First foundation in the United States in 1875.
Motherhouse and Novitiate: *Mount St. Francis,* 3390 Windsor Ave., Dubuque, IA 52001-1311. Tel: 563-583-9786; Fax: 563-583-3250. Sr. Dorothy Heiderscheit, Pres.; Sr. Elvira Kelley, Community Archivist.
Total number in community 394.
Ministry in the following areas: Academic and Religious Education at all levels; Spirituality and Parish Ministry; Health-Pastoral Care; Diocesan Offices; Social Service-Social Justice and Peace; Food Service-Dietary; Communication Centers; Clerical Work-Business; Administration; Campus Ministry; Deaf Ministry; Music and Art Studios; International Missions.
Properties owned and sponsored: *Shalom Retreat Center,* Dubuque, IA; *Sisters of St. Francis of the Holy Family Charitable Trust,* Dubuque, IA.
Represented in the Archdioceses of Anchorage, Chicago, Detroit, Dubuque, Indianapolis, Milwaukee, Omaha, Philadelphia, Portland (OR), St. Paul Minneapolis, San Antonio, and Washington and in the Dioceses of Bismarck, Charleston, Colorado Springs, Davenport, Des Moines, Fort Wayne-South Bend, Jackson, Joliet, Madison, Manchester, New Ulm, Owensboro, Phoenix, Providence, Rapid City, Rockford, St. Petersburg, San Diego, Santa Rosa, Sioux City, Springfield-Cape Girardeau, Tucson, Tulsa, Tyler, and Winona. Also in Central America.

[1580] (O.S.F.)—SISTERS OF ST. FRANCIS OF THE IMMACULATE CONCEPTION (D)

Founded in the United States in 1891.
Motherhouse: *Immaculate Conception Convent Inc.,* 2408 W. Heading Ave., West Peoria, IL 61604-5096. Tel: 309-674-6168. Sr. Irene Marie Fritch, Pres.; Sr. Louise Hynd, Archivist.
Total number in community 47.
Properties owned and sponsored: *Immaculate Conception Convent,* Peoria, IL; *St. Joseph's Home of Peoria; St. Joseph's Home of Springfield in Illinois.*
Represented in the Dioceses of Peoria, Rapid City and Springfield (IL).

[1590] (O.S.F.)—SISTERS OF ST. FRANCIS OF THE IMMACULATE HEART OF MARY (HANKINSON, NORTH DAKOTA) (P)

Founded in 1241 in Bavaria. First founded in the United States in 1913 at Collegeville, Minnesota.
General Motherhouse: Dillingen, Germany. Sr. Ann Marie Friederichs, Supr. Gen.
Province of Hankinson (1928): *Sisters of St. Francis Motherhouse,* Hankinson, ND 58041. Tel: 701-242-7195. Sr. Donna Welder, O.S.F., Prov. Supr.
Professed Sisters 56.
Legal Holdings or Titles: *St. Gerard's Community Nursing Home,* Hankinson, ND; *St. Anne's Guest Home,* Grand Forks, ND.
Ministry in the field of Religious and Academic Education; Health Care in Hospitals; Homes for the Aged.
Represented in the Diocese of Fargo.

[1600] (F.S.G.M.)—SISTERS OF ST. FRANCIS OF THE MARTYR ST. GEORGE (P)

Founded in Thuine, Germany. First United States foundation in 1923.
General Motherhouse: Thuine, Germany. Mother M. Carmen Droste, F.S.G.M., Supr. Gen.
Provincial Motherhouse: *St. Francis Convent and Novitiate,* 2120 Central Ave., P.O. Box 9020, Alton, IL 62002-9020. Tel: 618-463-2750; 463-2755. Mother M. Regina Pacis Coury, F.S.G.M., Prov.
Worldwide Total 1,555; Total in American Province 168.
Properties owned and sponsored: *Saint Anthony's Hospital,* Alton, IL; *St. Francis Day Care Center,* Alton, IL; *Mother of Good Counsel Home,* St. Louis, MO; *Saint Clare Hospital,* Alton, IL.
Sisters serve and staff: Hospitals; skilled Nursing Facility; Foreign Missions; Day Care Center; Retirement Homes for the Aged; Grade & High Schools; Retirement Homes for Priests.
Represented in the Archdioceses of St. Louis and Washington and in the Dioceses of La Crosse, Lincoln, Metuchen, Peoria, Springfield (IL), Steubenville and Tulsa.

[1620] (O.S.F.)—SISTERS OF SAINT FRANCIS OF MILLVALE, PENNSYLVANIA (P)

Motherhouse (1871): *St. Francis Convent, Mt. Alvernia,* 146 Hawthorne Rd., Millvale P.O., Pittsburgh, PA 15209. Tel: 412-821-2200; Fax: 412-821-3318. Sr. Ann Carville, O.S.F., Community Min.; Sr. Marilyn Joyce, O.S.F., Community Archivist.
Total number in community 185.
Ministry in the following areas: Academic High Schools and Elementary Schools; Day Care and Learning Center; Senior Citizen Housing; Pastoral Associates; Parish Social Work; Religious Education Directors; Missionary work in Nigeria.
Properties owned: *Mt. Alvernia High School,* Pittsburgh, PA; *Mt. Alvernia Day Care & Learning Center,* Pittsburgh, PA; *The Portiuncula Foundation of the Sisters of Saint Francis of Millvale,* Pittsburgh, PA.
Sponsored or managed facilities: Tabor House of Prayer; Alverno Apartments; Franciscan Health Wellness Ministries.
Represented in the Archdioceses of Baltimore, Chicago, Indianapolis, Los Angeles, Miami, Newark, Santa Fe, and San Juan and in the Dioceses of Altoona-Johnstown, Buffalo, Caguas, Charleston, Cleveland, Erie, Greensburg, Lubbock, Pittsburgh, Steubenville and Youngstown. Also in Canada and Nigeria.

[1630] (O.S.F.)—SISTERS OF ST. FRANCIS OF PENANCE AND CHRISTIAN CHARITY (P)

(aka Sisters of St. Francis of the Holy Name Province)

Founded in Holland in 1835. First Foundation in the U.S. in 1874.
General Motherhouse: Rome, Italy. Sr. Anisia Margareta Schneider, Gen. Min.
Universal number in Congregation 1,996.
Holy Name Province (1928): *Sisters of St. Francis,* 4421 Lower River Rd., Stella Niagara, NY 14144. Tel: 716-754-4312; Fax: 716-754-7657. Sr. Dorothy Mueller, O.S.F., Prov. Minister.
Total number in community 184.
Legal Holdings: *Stella Niagara Education Park,* Stella Niagara, NY; *Buffalo Academy of the Sacred Heart,* Buffalo, NY; *Francis Center,* Niagara Falls, NY; *St. Francis of Holy Name Province, Inc.,* Stella Niagara, NY.
Ministry in the field of Academic Education at all levels; Foreign Mission Work; Health and Hospital Care; Social Work; Pastoral Ministry.
Represented in the Archdioceses of Chicago, Cincinnati, Louisville, Miami and Santa Fe and in the Dioceses of Buffalo, Columbus, Orlando, Paterson, Steubenville, Trenton, and Wheeling-Charleston. Also in Canada.

Sacred Heart Province (1939): *Provincial Motherhouse-Marycrest,* 2851 W. 52nd Ave., Denver, CO 80221. Tel: 303-458-6270. Sr. Karen Crouse, Prov. Minister.
Total number in community 65.
Legal Holdings or Titles: *Marycrest Motherhouse; Marycrest Assisted Living; Marycrest Franciscans Development, Inc.; Queen of Peace Convent, House of Prayer ; The Damen Project - Home for Single Women & Children; Marycrest Franciscan Ministries,* Denver, CO; *St. Francis Home, (Home for Abused Native American Children),* Manderson, SD; *Marian Residence, Convent for Retired Sisters,* Alliance, NE; *St. Francis Convent; St. Clare Convent,* Alliance, NE.
Sisters serve and staff: High Schools; Parish Ministries; Apostolate of Aging; Emergency Housing; Home for Neglected Children; Retreat Ministry; Formation Programs; Administrative.
Represented in the Archdioceses of Denver and Omaha, and in the Diocese of Grand Island.

St. Francis Province (1939): *Mt. Alverno,* 3910 Bret Harte Dr., P.O. Box 1028, Redwood City, CA 94064. Tel: 650-369-1725. Sr. Maria Elena Martinez, Prov. Minister.
Total number in community 100.
Legal Title: *Sisters of St. Francis Charitable Trust; Sisters of St. Francis - Mount Alverno.*
Ministry in the following areas: Grammar Schools; Formation House; Colleges; Diocesan Offices; Parish Ministry; Pastoral Ministry; Catholic Social Services Agencies; Secondary Education; Hospitals; Residence for Retired Men and Women; Day Home; CCD Centers; Retreat-Conference Centers; Apostolic Projects; ESL.
Represented in the Archdioceses of Los Angeles, Portland (OR), San Francisco, and Seattle and in the Dioceses of Las Vegas, Monterey, Oakland, Sacramento, San Diego, San Jose and Stockton.

[1640] (O.S.F.)—SISTERS OF ST. FRANCIS OF PERPETUAL ADORATION (P)

Founded in Germany in 1863. First foundation in the United States in 1875.
Generalate: Olpe, Westfalen, Germany. Sr. Mediatrix Neis, Supr Gen.
Universal Total in Congregation 603.

Province of the Immaculate Heart of Mary (1875): *Provincial House and Novitiate, St. Francis Convent,* Box 766, Mishawaka, IN 46546-0766. Tel: 574-259-5427. Sr. M. Blanche Rausch, O.S.F., Prov.
Total number in community 135.
Ministry in the field of Academic Education at all levels; Health Care in Hospitals.
Properties owned: *Sisters of St. Francis of Perpetual Adoration, Inc.*; *St. Francis Convent*, Mishawaka, IN; *University of St. Francis, Inc.*, Fort Wayne, IN; *Sisters of St. Francis Health Services, Inc.*; *Sisters of St. Francis Health Services, Inc.*, Corporate Office, Mishawaka, IN, owns the following: *Alverno Clinical Laboratories*, Inc., Hammond, IN; *St. Anthony Medical Center of Crown Point*, Crown Point, IN; *St. Anthony Memorial Health Centers*, Michigan City, IN; *St. Clare Medical Center*, Crawfordsville, IN; *St. Francis Hospital & Health Centers*, Beech Grove, IN (including the Indianapolis, IN campus and Mooresville, IN campus); *St. James Hospital and Health Centers*, Chicago Heights, IL (including the Olympia Fields, IL campus); *St. Margaret Mercy Health Care Centers*, North Campus, Hammond, IN; *St. Margaret Mercy Health Care Centers*, South Campus, Dyer, IN; *Alverno Information Services*, Beech Grove, IN.
Represented in the Archdioceses of Chicago, Indianapolis and the Dioceses of Fort Wayne-South Bend, Gary and Lafayette (IN).

Province of St. Joseph (March 19, 1932): *Provincial House and Formation House-Mt. St. Francis,* 7665 Assisi Heights, Colorado Springs, CO 80919. Tel: 719-598-5486. Sr. Stephanie McReynolds, O.S.F., Prov.
Professed Sisters 88.
Ministry in Education; Hospitals; Homes for the Aged; Parish/Pastoral Ministry; Peace & Justice; Social Ministries; Retreat Centers.
Represented in the Archdioceses of Denver, Omaha and Santa Fe and in the Dioceses of Colorado Springs, Grand Island and Lincoln.

[1650] (O.S.F.)—THE SISTERS OF ST. FRANCIS OF PHILADELPHIA (P)

Founded in the United States in 1855.
Congregational Motherhouse: *Our Lady of Angels Convent,* 609 S. Convent Rd., Aston, PA 19014. Tel: 610-459-4125. Sr. Lynn Patrice, O.S.F. Congregational Min.; Sr. Virginia Spiegel, O.S.F., Asst. Congregational Min.; Sr. Eileen Valerie Kulacz, O.S.F., Congregational Sec.; Sr. Helen Jacobson, O.S.F., Archivist.
Total number in community 733.
Ministry in Health Care; Eldercare; Academic and Religious Education at all Levels; Specialized Education; Parish Ministry; Social Services; Family Centers; Renewal Centers; Diocesan Offices; Retreat Ministry; National Organizations.
Properties owned: *Sisters of St. Francis,* Sea Isle City, NJ; *Franciscan Residence,* Hamilton Square, NJ; *Bay House,* Tacoma, WA; *Marion House,* Tacoma, WA; *St. Ann Convent,* Tacoma, WA; *Neumann College,* Aston, PA; *Assisi House,* Aston, PA; *Portiuncula Convent,* Aston, PA; *St. Mary Convent,* Langhorne, PA; *Franciscan Residence,* Langhorne, PA; *St. Agnes Convent,* Philadelphia, PA; *Neumann Convent,* Reading, PA; *The Catholic High School of Baltimore,* Baltimore, MD; *St. Joseph Counseling Center,* Spokane, WA; *Anna Bachmann House,* Aston, PA; *Sisters of St. Francis,* Aston, PA; *Sisters of St. Francis,* Aston, PA; *Sisters of St. Francis,* Wilmington, DE; *Sisters of St. Francis of Philadelphia, Canticle House,* Philadelphia, PA; *Sisters of St. Francis of Philadelphia, TAU Convent,* Aston, PA; *St. Clare Renewal Center,* Aston, PA; *Sisters of St. Francis of Philadelphia, Our Lady of the Valley,* Aston, PA; *Mt. Alvernia Convent,* Aston, PA; *St. Clare Convent,* Trenton, NJ.
Represented in the Archdioceses of Atlanta, Baltimore, Boston, Denver, Hartford, Los Angeles, Newark, New York, Mobile, Philadelphia, Portland (OR), San Juan, Seattle, San Antonio, and Washington and in the Dioceses of Allentown, Arlington, Baker, Beaumont, Birmingham, Buffalo, Caguas (PR), Camden, Charlotte, Charleston, Cheyenne, El Paso, Fairbanks, Fresno, Fort Wayne-South Bend, Gallup, Harrisburg, Honolulu, Lexington, Manchester, Metuchen, Oakland, Orlando, Owensboro, Paterson, Pensacola-Tallahassee, Raleigh, Reno, Sacramento, San Bernardino, San Diego, St. Petersburg, Spokane, Trenton, Venice, Wheeling-Charleston and Wilmington. Also in Ireland, Central America, Zambia.

[1660] (O.S.F.)—SISTERS OF SAINT FRANCIS OF THE PROVIDENCE OF GOD (P)

Founded in Pittsburgh in 1922.
Motherhouse: *St. Francis Convent,* 3603 McRoberts Rd., Pittsburgh, PA 15234-2398. Tel: 412-882-9911; Fax: 412-885-7210. Sr. Joanne Brazinski, O.S.F., Gen. Minister; Sr. J. Lora Dambroski, O.S.F., U.S. Prov. Minister.
Total professed 104.
Ministry in the field of Education; Health Care; Social Service; Pastoral, Parish & Retreat Ministries; Retreat Directors; Prison Chaplains; Foreign Mission work in Brazil & Lithuania.
Properties owned and sponsored: *Sisters of St. Francis of the Providence of God; Sisters of St. Francis, Mt. Vernon IL, Inc.; Sisters of St. Francis of the Providence of God Ministries Corporation; St. Francis Academy; Franciscan Child Day Care Center; Franciscan Spirit and Life Center.*
Represented in the Archdiocese of Newark and in the Dioceses of Albany, Bridgeport, Buffalo, Grand Rapids, Paterson and Pittsburgh.

[1670] (O.S.F.)—SISTER OF ST. FRANCIS OF SAVANNAH, MO (P)

Founded in Austria, 1850. Founded in the United States, August 22, 1922.
Provincial House and Novitiate: 104 E. Park La Verna Heights, Box 488, Savannah, MO 64485-0488. Tel: 816-324-3179; Fax: 816-324-7264. Sr. Kathleen Reichert, Prov. Supr.
Total number in community 20.
Legal Holdings and Titles: *Sisters of St. Francis of Savannah, Inc.; Maintenance and Custodial Care Trust of the Franciscan Sisters of Savannah; La Verna Village Apartment Units for Senior Citizens and Handicapped; La Verna Village Nursing Home, Inc.; La Verna Heights Provincial House.*
Ministry in long-term care for the elderly and infirm; Academic and Religious education; Hospice care for persons with HIV and Aids; Transitional Housing and Work Programs for Prisoners with HIV; Housing for Elderly; Pastoral Care; Food Pantry.
Represented in the Diocese Kansas City-St. Joseph.

[1680] (O.S.F.)—SCHOOL SISTERS OF ST. FRANCIS (P)

Founded in the United States in 1874.
General Motherhouse: 1501 S. Layton Blvd., Milwaukee, WI 53215. Tel: 414-384-4105; Fax: 414-944-6060. Sr. Joan Puls, O.S.F., Pres.; Sr. Toni Anne Gradisnik, O.S.F., Vice Pres.; Sr. Catherine M. Ryan, O.S.F., Treas.; Sr. Charlita Foxhoven, O.S.F., Asst.Treas.; Sr. Corrine Dais, O.S.F., Archivist.
Total in Congregation 1,266; Total in U.S. 800.
Properties owned: *St. Joseph Convent,* Milwaukee, WI; *School Sisters of St. Francis, Inc.*
U.S. Province: 1515 S. Layton Blvd., Milwaukee, WI 53215. Tel: 414-384-1515. Provincial Team: Sr. Barbara Kraemer; Sr. Elizabeth Heese; Sr. Maureen McCarthy.
Properties owned and sponsored: *Alverno College,* Milwaukee, WI; *Clement Manor, Inc.,* Greenfield, WI; *Maryhill Manor,* Niagara, WI; *New Cassel,* Omaha, NE; *Clare Towers I,* Milwaukee, WI; *Clare Towers II,* Milwaukee, WI; *Telos, Inc.,* Milwaukee, WI; *St. Clare Management, Inc.,* Milwaukee, WI; *Sacred Heart Center,* Milwaukee, WI; *St. Joseph Convent,* Campbellsport, WI; *School Sisters of St. Francis of St. Joseph's Convent, Milwaukee, Wisconsin, Inc.; Convergence, Inc.* Milwaukee, WI.
Sisters serve and staff: Universities, Colleges, Seminaries, High Schools, Grade Schools, Preschools, Adult and Special Education; National and Diocesan Offices; Hospitals and Nursing Homes; School & Parish Musicians; Retreat and Spiritual Direction; Social Ministries; Campus Ministry; Psychotherapy; Home Health Care Service; Religious Education and CCD; Pastoral Ministry; Pastoral Associate; Health Pastoral Care; Retirement Homes.
Represented in the Archdioceses of Anchorage, Chicago, Denver, Dubuque, Milwaukee, New York, Oklahoma City, Omaha, St. Paul-Minneapolis, San Antonio, Santa Fe, and Washington and in the Dioceses of Charlotte, Davenport, Des Moines, El Paso, Green Bay, Jackson, Jefferson City, Joliet, Kansas City-St. Joseph, La Crosse, Lexington, Lincoln, Madison, Nashville, New Ulm, Orange, Phoenix, Rockford, San Bernardino, San Diego, Springfield (IL), St. Petersburg, Superior, Tucson, Wheeling-Charleston and Winona.

[1690] (O.S.F.)— SCHOOL SISTERS OF THE THIRD ORDER OF ST. FRANCIS (PITTSBURGH, PA.) (P)

First foundation in the U.S. in 1913.
General Motherhouse: Rome, Italy.
Motherhouse and Novitiate: *Mount Assisi Convent,* 934 Forest Ave., Bellevue, Pittsburgh, PA 15202. Tel: 412-761-6004. Sr. Bernadine Marie Stemnock, O.S.F., Prov. Minister. Tel: 412-761-2855.
Total number in community 69.
Legal Title: *School Sisters of the Third Order of St. Francis; School Sisters of the Third Order of St. Francis, of Texas.*
Ministry in the following areas: the field of academic education at all levels; CCD Centers; Pastoral Ministry; Pastoral Associate; Residence Home for the Elderly; Mission Work; Hospital Ministry; Campus Ministry; Social Ministry; House of Prayer.
Represented in the Archdiocese of San Antonio and in the Dioceses of Erie, Greensburg, Phoenix, Pittsburgh and San Angelo. Also in South Africa and Central Asia.

[1695] (O.S.F.)—SCHOOL SISTERS OF THE THIRD ORDER OF ST. FRANCIS (PANHANDLE, TEXAS) (P)

Founded in Austria, 1723; The Vienna Foundation in 1845. First founded in the United States, 1931.
General Motherhouse: Vienna, Austria.
American Center and Novitiate: P.O. Box 906, Panhandle, TX 79068. Tel: 806-537-3182. Mother M. Bernadette Black, O.S.F., Reg. Supr.
Total number in U.S. 24.
Ministry in the following areas: Elementary Schools; Confraternity Classes; Home for the Aged.
Represented in the Dioceses of Amarillo and Victoria.

[1700] (O.S.F.)—SCHOOL SISTERS OF THE THIRD ORDER OF ST. FRANCIS (BETHLEHEM, PA.) (P)

Founded in Austria, 1843. First founded in the United States, 1913.
General Motherhouse: Via Nicolo Piccolomin 27, Rome, Italy 00165. Sr. Mary Xavier Bomberger, O.S.F., Gen. Minister.
Bethlehem Province and Novitiate: 395 Bridle Path Rd., Bethlehem, PA 18017-3105. Tel: 610-866-2597 & 867-8495; Fax: 610-861-7478. Sr. M. Rosaria Shina, O.S.F., Prov. Supr.
Sisters 55.
Properties owned: *St. Francis Center for Renewal,* Bethlehem, PA.
Represented in the Archdioceses of Newark and Philadelphia and in the Dioceses of Allentown, Manchester, Metuchen, Paterson, Springfield (MA) and Trenton. Also in Chile, India, South Africa and Rome, Italy.

[1705] (O.S.F.)—THE SISTERS OF ST. FRANCIS OF ASSISI (P)

(Sisters of Penance and Charity)

Founded in the United States in 1849.
General Motherhouse: *St. Francis Convent,* 3221 S. Lake Dr., St. Francis, WI 53235-3799. Tel: 414-744-1160; Fax: 414-744-7193. E-mail: www.lakeosfs.org. Sr. Marcia Lunz, O.S.F., Dir.
Total number in community 340.

Legal Titles: *The Sisters of St. Francis of Assisi, Inc.; The Ongoing Community Support Trust of the Sisters of St. Francis, Inc.; Declaration of Trust of the Franciscan Sisters of Baltimore, Inc.*

Goals of the Congregation are to bring the healing, teaching, reconciling and liberating power of Jesus into the human situations in which we live and minister; to be in solidarity with the poor through the work of justice and peace; to appreciate and affirm and to encourage the development of each community member and each community apostolate for the sake of full effectiveness in the ministry of the Church; and to work effectively toward implementing co-responsibility, subsidiary and accountability at all levels within the Congregation.

Corporate Ministries: *Franciscan Youth Center, Inc.,* Baltimore, MD; *St. Elizabeth School, Inc.,* Baltimore, MD; *Francis House, Inc.,* Baltimore, MD; *Franciscan Center, Inc.,* Baltimore, MD; *St. Ann Center for Intergenerational Care, Inc.,* Milwaukee, WI; *St. Mary's Academy, Inc.,* Milwaukee, WI; *Cardinal Stritch University, Inc.,* Milwaukee, WI; *St. Coletta's of Wisconsin, Inc.,* Jefferson, WI; *St. Coletta School Foundation of Jefferson Charitable Trust,* Jefferson, WI; *St. Coletta's of Illinois,* Palos Park, IL; *St. Coletta's of Illinois Foundation, Inc.,* Palos Park, IL; *St. Coletta's of Massachusetts: Cardinal Cushing School and Training Center,* Hanover, MA; *Cushing Residence, Inc.,* Hanover, MA; *Cardinal Cushing School Foundation of Hanover Charitable Trust,* Hanover, MA; *Cardinal Cushing Centers, Inc. Braintree Campus and Braintree St. Coletta,* Braintree, MA. *Services to the Elderly: Alverno Housing Corporation,* Jefferson, WI; *Canticle Court, Inc.; Juniper Court, Inc.,* St. Francis, WI.

Represented in the Archdioceses of Baltimore, Boston, Chicago, Denver, Los Angeles, Milwaukee, Philadelphia, San Antonio, San Francisco, and Santa Fe and in the Dioceses of Cheyenne, Davenport, Joliet, Gary, Gallup, Green Bay, Kansas City-St. Joseph, La Crosse, Madison, Phoenix, Reno, Rockford, San Diego, Santa Rosa, Sioux City, Springfield, Steubenville, Superior, Tucson, Tulsa and Winona. Also in Taiwan.

[1710] (O.S.F.)—CONGREGATION OF THE THIRD ORDER OF ST. FRANCIS OF MARY IMMACULATE, JOLIET, IL (P)

Founded in the United States, Joliet, Illinois, in 1865.

General Motherhouse: *St. Francis Convent,* 801 N. Larkin Ave., Ste. 101, Joliet, IL 60435-3442. Tel: 815-725-8735. Sr. Maria Pesavento, O.S.F., Pres.; Sr. Marian Voelker, O.S.F., Community Archivist.

Total number in community 273.

Legal Titles: *Congregation of the Third Order of St. Francis of Mary Immaculate,* Joliet, IL; *Retirement Plan Trust of the Congregation of the Third Order of St. Francis of Mary Immaculate,* Joliet, IL.

Ministry in the following areas: School and Adult Education; Home for Emotionally Disturbed Children; Retirement Home; House of Prayer. Also engaged in Religious Education; Social Services; Spiritual Direction; Nursing and Health Services; Hospital and Parish Ministry; Food Service; and Prison ministry.

Represented in the Archdioceses of Boston, Chicago, Cincinnati, Denver, Los Angeles, Miami, Milwaukee, New York and Washington and in the Dioceses of Cleveland, Colorado Springs, Columbus, Fort Wayne-South Bend, Gary, Jackson, Joliet, Lansing, Palm Beach, Phoenix, Peoria, Rockford, St. Cloud, San Diego, St. Petersburg, Springfield-Cape Girardeau, Springfield (IL), Stockton, Superior, Toledo, Tucson and Youngstown. Also in Brazil.

[1720] (O.S.F.)—SISTERS OF THE THIRD ORDER REGULAR OF ST. FRANCIS OF THE CONGREGATION OF OUR LADY OF LOURDES (P)

Founded in the United States in 1877.

Administration Center: *Assisi Heights,* 1001 14th St., N.W., Suite 100, Rochester, MN 55901. Tel: 507-282-7441; Fax: 507-282-7762. Sr. Dolore M. Rockers, O.S.F., Pres./Community Min. Tel: 507-529-3535. Sr. Mary Lonan Reilly, Community Archivist.

Total number in community 339.

Ministry in the following areas: Education Services; Pastoral Concerns Development; Religious Life Development; Spiritual Life Development; Community Life Development; Social Concerns Development; Business Services; Health Care Services; Support Services.

Properties owned and sponsored: *Holy Spirit Retreat Center,* Janesville, MN; *Assisi Heights,* Rochester, MN.

Represented in the Archdioceses of Baltimore, Chicago, Denver, Dubuque, Indianapolis, Milwaukee, St. Paul-Minneapolis, Santa Fe, Seattle, and Washington and in the Dioceses of Brownsville, Buffalo, Charleston, Charlotte, Columbus, Great Falls-Billings, Helena, Joliet, La Crosse, Lexington, New Ulm, Oakland, Owensboro, Pueblo, Savannah, Sioux City, St. Cloud, San Bernardino, San Diego, Sioux Falls, Springfield-Cape Girardeau, Steubenville, Superior, Wheeling-Charleston and Winona. Also in Colombia.

[1730] (O.S.F.)—CONGREGATION OF THE SISTERS OF THE THIRD ORDER OF ST. FRANCIS, OLDENBURG, IN. (P)

Founded in U.S., Oldenburg, Indiana in 1851.

General Motherhouse and Novitiate: *Convent of the Immaculate Conception,* Oldenburg, IN 47036. Tel: 812-934-2475. Sr. Jean Marie Cleveland, O.S.F., Congregational Minister.

Total number in community 311.

Properties owned: *Marian College,* Indianapolis, IN; *Oldenburg Academy,* Oldenburg, IN.

Sister serve & staff: Liberal Arts College, Academy, High Schools, Elementary Schools; Navajo, Crow Indian and Cheyenne Missions; Religious Education Centers; Hospital & Parish Ministry; Apostolate of Aging; Diocesan Offices; Retreat & Counseling Ministry; Hispanic Ministry; Justice & Peace Offices; Clerical Staff; Social Services; Foreign Missions: New Guinea.

Represented in the Archdioceses of Chicago, Cincinnati, Detroit, Indianapolis, Los Angeles, Miami, New York and St. Louis and in the Dioceses of Buffalo, Charleston, Columbus, Evansville, Gallup, Great Falls-Billings, Lexington, Peoria, Springfield-IL, St. Augustine, and Wheeling-Charleston.

[1760] (O.S.F.)—SISTERS OF THE THIRD ORDER OF ST. FRANCIS OF PENANCE AND OF CHARITY (P)

Founded in Tiffin, Ohio in 1869.

General Motherhouse: *St. Francis Convent,* St. Francis Ave., Tiffin, OH 44883. Tel: 419-447-0435; Fax: 419-448-1612. Sr. Virginia Welsh, O.S.F., Community Minister.

Total number in community 131.

Legal Title: *Sisters of St. Francis of Tiffin, OH.*

Ministry in the following areas: Parochial Schools; Ministry to the Aged; Parish Ministry; Retreat and Renewal Centers; Diocese Offices; Health Care; Health-Pastoral Care; Administration.

Properties owned or sponsored: *St. Francis Villas, Inc.; St. Francis Home, Inc.,* Tiffin, OH.

Represented in the Archdioceses of Milwaukee and Santa Fe and in the Dioceses of Evansville, Cleveland, Columbus, Charlotte, Davenport, Lansing, Lexington, Madison, Owensboro, Toledo and Wheeling-Charleston. Also in Mexico.

[1770] (O.S.F.)—THE SISTERS OF THE THIRD ORDER OF ST. FRANCIS (EAST PEORIA, ILLINOIS) (P)

Founded in the United States in 1877.

Motherhouse: 1175 St. Francis Lane, East Peoria, IL 61611-1299. Tel: 309-699-7215. Sr. Mary Ellen Flannery, Major Supr.

Total number in community 52.

Properties owned and sponsored: *Saint Francis Medical Center,* Peoria, IL; *St. Joseph Medical Center,* Bloomington, IL; *St. Mary Medical Center,* Galesburg, IL; *St. James-John W. Albrecht Medical Center,* Pontiac, IL; *Saint Anthony Medical Center,* Rockford, IL; *Saint Francis Hospital,* Escanaba, MI; *OSF Healthcare System,* Peoria, IL; *OSF Healthcare Foundation,* Peoria, IL; *Motherhouse,* East Peoria, IL; *Saint Clare Home,* Peoria Heights, IL.

Represented in the Dioceses of Marquette, Peoria and Rockford.

[1780] (F.S.P.A.)—CONGREGATION OF THE SISTERS OF THE THIRD ORDER OF ST. FRANCIS OF PERPETUAL ADORATION (P)
(Franciscan Sisters of Perpetual Adoration)

Founded in the United States in 1849.

Generalate - Motherhouse and Novitiate: *St. Rose Convent,* 912 Market St., La Crosse, WI 54601-8800. Tel: 608-782-5610; Fax: 608-782-6301. Sr. Marlene Weisenbeck, F.S.P.A., Pres.; Sr. Mary Ann Gschwind, F.S.P.A., Archivist.

Total number in Congregation 409.

Properties owned and sponsored: *St Joseph Memorial Hospital, Inc.,* Hillsboro, WI; *St. Anthony Regional Hospital, Inc.,* Carroll, IA; *Viterbo University, Inc.,* La Crosse, WI; *Villa St. Joseph,* La Crosse, WI; *Franciscan Skemp Healthcare,* La Crosse, WI; *Clare Center,* Spokane, WA; *Franciscan Spirituality Center,* La Crosse, WI; *Prairiewoods - Franciscan Spirituality Center,* Hiawatha, IA; *Marywood - Franciscan Spirituality Center,* Arbor Vitae, WI; *WomanWell,* St. Paul, MN.

Represented in the Archdioceses of Agana, Chicago, Denver, Dubuque, Los Angeles, Milwaukee, Santa Fe, Seattle, and St. Paul-Minneapolis and in the Dioceses of Amarillo, Boise, Colorado Springs, Davenport, El Paso, Gallup, Green Bay, Jackson, La Crosse, Lexington, Madison, Oakland, Peoria, Las Vegas, Savannah, Sioux City, Spokane, Stockton, Superior, Tucson, and Winona. Also in Canada, El Salvador, Mexico and Zimbabwe.

[1800] (O.S.F.)—SISTERS OF ST. FRANCIS OF THE THIRD ORDER REGULAR (WILLIAMSVILLE, NEW YORK) (P)

Motherhouse: *St. Mary of the Angels Convent of Perpetual Adoration,* P.O. Box 275, Williamsville, NY 14231. Tel: 716-632-2155; Fax: 716-632-0339. Sr. Marian Rose Mansius, Gen. Minister.

Total number in community 139.

Properties owned and/or sponsored: *Mount St. Mary's LTC Facility, Inc.,* Niagara Falls, NY; *Holy Family Home,* Williamsville, NY.

Sisters serve and staff: Universities; High Schools Grammar Schools; Hospitals; Nursing Homes & Homes for the Aged; Pastoral Ministry in Parishes; Diocesan Offices; Social Service work.

Represented in the Archdioceses of Chicago and Washington and in the Dioceses of Buffalo, Charleston, Ogdensburg, Pittsburgh, and Syracuse. Also in Africa.

[1810] (O.S.F.)—BERNARDINE FRANCISCAN SISTERS (P)

Founded in the United States in 1894.

Generalate: 403 Allendale Rd., King of Prussia, PA 19406. Tel: 610-337-3864; Fax: 610-337-4359. Sr. Madonna Marie Harvath, O.S.F., Gen. Min.

Total number in community 470.

Bernardine Sisters OSF - Bernardine Franciscan Sisters: *United States Province Offices,* 460 St. Bernardine St., Reading, PA 19607-1737. Tel: 610-777-4174; Fax: 610-777-3973. Sr. Maria Korick, O.S.F., Prov. Minister; Sr. Kateri Peake, O.S.F., Prov. Minister; Sr. Mary Elena Sabalausky, O.S.F., Prov. Minister.

Total number in Province 360.

Ministry in the field of academic education at all levels - preschool to college; religious education of children & adults; hospitals, health & home care; retreat work; social work.

Represented in the Archdioceses of Boston, Detroit, Kansas City, Los Angeles, Newark, Philadelphia, San Antonio, San Juan and Washington and in the Dioceses of Allentown, Bridgeport, Buffalo, Harrisburg, Lexington, Metuchen, Providence, Richmond, Saginaw, Scranton, and Trenton. Also in Brazil, Dominican Republic, and West Africa.

Our Lady of the Rosary Convent: 27405 West Ten Mile Rd., Farmington Hills, MI 48336-2201. Tel: 248-476-4111; Fax: 248-476-6950. Sr. Mary Elena Sabalausky, O.S.F., Prov. Minister.

Total number in Province 364.

[1820] (O.S.F.)—HOSPITAL SISTERS OF THE THIRD ORDER OF ST. FRANCIS (P)

Founded in Germany in 1844. First foundation in the United States in 1875.

General Motherhouse: Muenster in Westphalia, Germany. Sr. Mary Ann Minor, O.S.F., Gen. Supr.

American Province (1875): *St. Francis Convent, Motherhouse and Novitiate,* Box 19431, Springfield, IL 62794. Tel: 217-522-3386. Sr. Joan Winkler, O.S.F., Prov. Supr.; Sr. Maureen O'Connor, O.S.F., Prov. Sec. & Contact Person.

Total number in the community 160.

Properties owned or sponsored: *Residence 14; St. Francis Convent, Motherhouse, Novitiate,* Springfield, IL; *Hospital Sisters Services, Inc.; Hospital Sisters of St. Francis Foundation; Hospital Sisters Health System; St. John's Hospital; St. John's College of Nursing,* Springfield, IL; *St. Mary's Hospital,* Decatur, IL; *St. Anthony Memorial Hospital,* Effingham, IL; *St. Joseph's Hospital,* Highland, IL; *St. Francis Hospital,* Litchfield, IL; *St. Elizabeth's Hospital,* Belleville, IL; *St. Joseph's Hospital,* Breese, IL; *St. Mary's Hospital Medical Center; St. Vincent Hospital,* Green Bay, WI; *St. Joseph's Hospital; L.E. Phillips Treatment Center for the Chemically Dependent; Hospital Sisters Health Care West, Inc.; Transitus House,* Chippewa Falls, WI; *Sacred Heart Hospital; St. Francis Apartments,* Eau Claire, WI; *St. Nicholas Hospital,* Sheboygan, WI; *St. Mary's Hospital,* Streator, IL; *Hospital Sisters Tanzania,* Springfield, IL.

Sisters serve and staff: Hospitals; Home Health Services; Catechetical; Care of Chemically Dependent; Social Ministries; Pastoral Ministries; Overseas Missions.

Represented in the Archdioceses of Dubuque, Milwaukee and St. Louis and in the Dioceses of Belleville, Green Bay, La Crosse, Peoria and Springfield (IL). Also in Tanzania, Japan and Haiti.

[1830] (R.G.S. - C.G.S.)—THE SISTERS OF THE GOOD SHEPHERD (P)

Congregation of Our Lady of Charity of the Good Shepherd

Founded in France in 1835. First foundation in the United States in Louisville, KY 1842.

Generalate for the Provinces: *Suore del Buon Pastore,* via Raffaello Sardiello 20, 00165, Rome, Italy. Sr. Liliane Tauvette, Supr. Gen.

Province of Mid-North America (2000): *Provincialate,* 7654 Natural Bridge Blvd., St. Louis, MO 63121. Tel: 314-381-3400; Fax: 314-381-7102. Sr. Barbara Beasley, Prov.

Professed Apostolic Sisters 199; Contemplative Sisters 80.

Legal Titles: *Sisters of the Good Shepherd Province of Mid-North America; Pelletier Trust, a Charitable Trust of the Sisters of the Good Shepherd; Sisters of the Good Shepherd Province of Mid-North America Foundation,* St. Louis, MO.

Properties owned and staffed: *Good Shepherd Pelletier, Inc.,* Cincinnati, OH; *Sisters of the Good Shepherd of Detroit aka Vista Maria,* Dearborn Heights, MI; *Sisters of the Good Shepherd of the City of Cleveland,* Independence, OH; *House of the Good Shepherd of Columbus,* Columbus, OH; *Good Shepherd Corporation,* Clarks Summit, PA; *Lourdesmont Good Shepherd Youth & Family Services,* Clarks Summit, PA; *CORA Services, Inc.,* Philadelphia, PA; *Euphrasia House, Inc.,* Philadelphia, PA; *Good Shepherd Corporation,* Philadelphia, PA; *Good Shepherd Neighborhood House, Mediation Program,* Philadelphia, PA; *House of the Good Shepherd,* Baltimore, MD; *Sisters of the Good Shepherd, A Corporation, Baltimore, MD; Good Shepherd Corporation,* Washington, DC; *Good Shepherd Services,* Atlanta, GA; *Good Shepherd Corporation of Orlando, Inc.,* Orlando, FL; *Good Shepherd Shelter,* Los Angeles, CA; *Gracenter,* San Francisco, CA; *Droste Residence,* St. Louis, MO; *House of the Good Shepherd of Memphis dba Casa Maria,* Memphis, TN; *Good Shepherd Services,* New Orleans, LA; *DeNeuville Learning Center,* Memphis, TN; *House of the Good Shepherd,* Chicago, IL; *Immaculate Heart Convent,* St. Louis, MO; *Good Shepherd Provincialate,* St. Louis, MO; *Home of the Good Shepherd Inc.,* St. Paul, MN.

Represented in the Archdioceses of Atlanta, Baltimore, Chicago, Cincinnati, Detroit, Los Angeles, Louisville, New Orleans, Omaha, Portland in Oregon, Philadelphia, St. Louis, St. Paul-Minneapolis, San Francisco, and Washington and in the Dioceses of Cleveland, Columbus, Covington, Gallup, Memphis, Orlando, Scranton and Springfield (IL).

Province of New York (1857): *Sisters of the Good Shepherd,* 82-31 Doncaster Pl., Jamaica, NY 11432. Tel: 718-380-3270; Fax: 718-591-9376. Sr. Yvette Arnold, Prov.

Professed Active Sisters 81; Contemplative Sisters 54.

Legal Title: *Sisters of the Good Shepherd, Province of New York.*

Legal Holdings or Titles: *Sisters of the Good Shepherd,* New York, NY; *Sisters of the Good Shepherd, Albany, NY; Sisters of the Good Shepherd,* Huntington, NY; *House of the Good Shepherd in the City of Hartford,* Hartford, CT; *The Gathering Place,* Waltham, MA; *Good Shepherd Volunteers,* New York, NY; *Madonna Hall,* Marlboro, MA; *Global Women's Exchange, Inc.,* Jamaica, NY; *Maria Droste Services (Madonna Hall).*

Ministry in Counseling Centers; Social Service Agencies; Special Education Schools; Neighborhood Family Services; Adolescent Residential Programs; Human Services Workshops; Pastoral Ministry; Prison Ministry; Hospital Chaplaincy.

Programs sponsored: *Good Shepherd Services,* New York, NY; *Maria Droste Services,* New York, NY; *Global Women's Exchange, Inc.; The Gathering Place; Collier Services,* Wickatunk, NJ; *Good Shepherd Volunteers.*

Represented in the Archdioceses of Boston, Hartford, and New York and in the Dioceses of Albany, Brooklyn, Fall River, Metuchen, Rockville Centre and Trenton.

[1840] (G.N.S.H.)—GREY NUNS OF THE SACRED HEART (P)

General Motherhouse (1921): 1750 Quarry Rd., Yardley, PA 19067-3998. Tel: 215-968-4236; Fax: 215-504-2459. Sr. Marlene G. Butler, G.N.S.H., Pres.; Ms. Eileen Dickerson, Dir. Congregational Advancement Office.

Total number in community 150.

Properties owned: *Holy Angels Academy,* Buffalo, NY; *Motherhouse Complex,* Yardley, PA.

Sisters staff: College, Secondary and Elementary Education; Hospitals; Nursing Homes; Rehabilitation Care of Aging; Pastoral Care; Personal Care Home; CCD-Parish Services; Diocesan Offices; Campus Ministry; Prison Ministry; Homeless Housing.

Represented in the Archdioceses of Anchorage, Atlanta, Baltimore, New York and Philadelphia and in the Dioceses of Brooklyn, Buffalo, Camden, Erie, Manchester, Metuchen, Ogdensburg, Paterson, Rochester, Rockville Centre and Trenton. Also in Canada.

[1845] (M.G.Sp.S.)—GUADALUPAN MISSIONARIES OF THE HOLY SPIRIT (P)

(Misioneras Guadalupanas del Espiritu Santo)

Founded in Morelia, Michoacan, Mexico in 1930 by Rev. Felix de Jesus Rougier, M.Sp.S.

General Motherhouse: Hidalgo # 7, Tlalpan 14000 Mexico, D.F., Mexico. Mother Juventina Garcia, Supr. Gen.

U.S. Delegation Headquarters: 2483 S.W. 4th St., Miami, FL 33135-2907. Tel: 305-642-9544.

U.S. Novitiate: 758 S. Dunsmuir Ave., Los Angeles, CA 90036-3811. Tel: 213-936-0135.

Total Sisters in U.S. 44.

Legal Title: *Missionary Guadalupanas of the Holy Spirit, Inc.*

Ministry in Religious Education; Pastoral and Parish Ministries.

Represented in the Archdioceses of Denver, Los Angeles and Miami and in the Dioceses of Fall River, Palm Beach, Pueblo, Stockton and Savannah. Also in San Juan, Puerto Rico.

[1850] (S.A.C.)—SISTERS OF THE GUARDIAN ANGEL

Founded in Quillan, France in 1839.

General Motherhouse: A vda, del Valle, 42, Madrid 3, Spain. Sr. Sagrario Escudero, S.A.C., Supr. Gen.

U.S. Foundation: 1245 S. Van Ness, Los Angeles, CA 90019. Tel: 213-732-7881.

Represented in the Archdiocese of Los Angeles.

[1855] (H.H.C.J.)—CONGREGATION OF THE HANDMAIDS OF THE HOLY CHILD JESUS (P)

Founded in Calabar, Nigeria in 1931 by Sister Mary Charles Magdalen Walker. Obtained Pontifical Status in 1971; first foundation in United States in 1992.

Generalate and Motherhouse: *Handmaids of the Holy Child Jesus - The Generalate, Ifuho,* P.O. Box 155, Ikot Ekpene, Nigeria. Tel: 082-775-199. Mother Mary Langley, H.H.C.J., Supr. Gen.

United States Mission House: *Ancilla Convent,* 3614 Englewood Dr., Pearland, TX 77584. Tel: 281-692-0098; Fax: 281-692-0049. Web site: www.handmaidsisters.org. Sr. Joanna Okereke, H.H.C.J., U.S. Supr.; Sr. Felicia Agibi, H.H.C.J., Development Dir.

Universal number of Professed Sisters 700; Professed Sisters in the U.S. and Canada 60.

Ministry in the field of Education at all levels; Pastoral Work; Health Care services; Women Empowerment; AIDS Education; Special Education; Youth Ministry; Clothing/Counseling Thrift Store.

Represented in the Dioceses of Galveston-Houston, Madison, Sacramento and St. Petersburg.

[1860] (H.P.B.)—HANDMAIDS OF THE PRECIOUS BLOOD (P)

Founded in Jemez Springs, New Mexico in 1947.

Motherhouse and Novitiate: *Cor Jesu Monastery,* P.O. Box 90, Jemez Springs, NM 87025. Tel: 505-829-3906. Mother John Paul, Prioress.

Professed Sisters 23; First Professed 5.

Ministry as Contemplative, Life of Eucharistic Adoration (Perpetual) for the sanctification of priests and for the entire world.

Represented in the Archdioceses of Chicago and Santa Fe. Also in Italy.

[1870] (A.C.J.)—THE HANDMAIDS OF THE SACRED HEART OF JESUS (P)

Founded in Spain in 1877. First Foundation in the United States in 1926.

General Motherhouse: *Largo dei Monti Parioli,* 3, 00197, Rome, Italy. Sr. Rita Burley, Supr. Gen.

Universal Total in Congregation 1,437.

Provincial Motherhouse: 1615 N.E. 108th St., Miami, FL 33161. Tel: 305-891-9161; Fax: 305-891-8791. Sr. Sagrario Nunez, A.C.J., Prov.

Total number in community 35.

Properties owned: *St. Raphaela Center,* Haverford, PA; *Ancillae Assumpta Academy,* Wyncote, PA; *Handmaids of Sacred Heart of Jesus,* Philadelphia, PA; facilities in Georgia and Florida.

Sister serve and staff: Elementary Schools; Retreat Center; Mission Center; Parish Ministry; CCD; Diocesan Offices; Hispanic Pastoral Ministry; Vietnamese & Cambodian Pastoral Ministry; Mission work.

Represented in the Archdioceses of Atlanta, Miami and Philadelphia.

[1880] (A.R.)—HANDMAIDS OF REPARATION OF THE SACRED HEART OF JESUS (P)

Founded in Messina, Italy in 1918.

U.S. Foundation (1958): *Sacred Heart Villa,* 36 Villa Dr., Steubenville, OH 43953-7129. Tel: 740-282-3801. Sr. Mary Ernestine Vitello, A.R., Supr.

Total number in U.S. 6.

Ministry in Apostolic Work in Religious & Academic Education: Education All Levels; Religious Education; Parish and Diocesan Ministry; CCD Work; Orphanages; Missionary Work in Africa, Brazil and Poland.

Represented in the Dioceses of Arlington and Steubenville. Also in Africa, Brazil, Italy and Poland.

[1890] (H.H.S.)—SOCIETY OF HELPERS (P)

Founded in France in 1856. First foundation in the U.S. in 1892.

Generalate: 16 rue St. J. Baptiste de la Salle, Paris, France, 75006. Sr. Elizabetta Flick, Supr. Gen.

American Provincial Office (1921): 3206 S. Aberdeen, Chicago, IL 60608. Tel: 773-523-8638. Sr. Margaret Nimbley, Prov. Supr.

Total number in U.S. province 38.

Legal Titles: *Society of the Helpers of the Holy Souls; Helpers of the Holy Souls; Province of the Helpers of the Holy Souls in the United States.*

Represented in the Archdioceses of Chicago, New York, St. Louis and San Francisco and in the Diocese of San Jose.

[1900] (H.C.G.)—HERMANAS CATEQUISTAS GUADALUPANAS (P)

Founded in Saltillo, Coahuila, Mexico in 1923. First United States foundation in 1950.

Motherhouse and Novitiate: Saltillo, Coahuila, Mexico.

U.S. Address: *Hermanas Catequistas Guadalupanas Convents,* 4110 S. Flores, San Antonio, TX 78214. Tel: 210-532-9344. Sr. Margarita Vasquez, Reg. Delegate.

Total number in the U.S. 18.

Represented in the Archdioceses of Oklahoma City and San Antonio and in the Diocese of Fort Worth.

[1910] (H.J.)—HERMANAS JOSEFINAS (P)

General Motherhouse: Condor 336, Col. las Aguilas, Delg. Alvaro Obregon, 01710, Mexico D.F. Mother Cointa Quijas, H.J., Supr. & Mother Gen.

U.S. Address: *Assumption Seminary,* 2600 W. Woodlawn Ave., P.O. Box 28240, San Antonio, TX 78284. Tel: 210-734-0039.

Sisters 8.

Represented in the Archdioceses of Chicago, Denver, Los Angeles, and San Antonio and in the Diocese of El Paso.

[1920] (C.S.C.)—CONGREGATION OF THE SISTERS OF THE HOLY CROSS (P)

Founded at Le Mans, France in 1841. First foundation in the U.S. in 1843.

General Administration: *Sisters of the Holy Cross Generalate,* Bertrand Hall-Saint Mary's, Notre Dame, IN 46556. Tel: 219-284-5550; Fax: 219-284-5779. Sr. Aline Marie Steuer, C.S.C., Pres.; Sr. M. Veronique Wiedower, C.S.C., Gen. Sec.

Professed Members 549; Temporarily Professed 21; Novices 14; Candidates 13.

Legal Titles: *Sisters of the Holy Cross, Inc.; Sisters of the Holy Cross, Inc. dba CSC Consultation Services; Holy Cross Services Corporation; Holy Cross Ministry Net-Work, Inc.; Sisters of the Holy Cross of California,* Ventura, CA; *The Academy of the Holy Cross, Inc.,* MD; *The Corporation of Saint Mary's College,* Notre Dame, IN; *Sociedade Civil Irmas da Santa Cruz,* Brazil; *Society of the Congregation of the Sisters of the Holy Cross,* Bangladesh.

Areas and Coordinators:

Area I - USA West, Los Angeles, CA. Tel: 805-641-3021. Sr. Patricia McGee, C.S.C., Coord.

Area II - USA Midwest, Notre Dame, IN. Tel: 574-284-5794; Fax: 574-284-5900. Sr. Kathryn Callahan, C.S.C., Coord.

Area III - USA South & Mexico, West Palm Beach, FL Tel: 561-681-1376;. Fax: 561-656-4539. Sr. Mary Louise Full, C.S.C., Coord.

Area IV - USA East, Wheaton, MD. Tel: 301-236-4967; Fax: 301-879-0415. Sr. M. Geraldine Blume, C.S.C., Coord.

Area V - USA Retired, Notre Dame, IN. Tel: 574-284-5636; Fax: 574-284-5593. Sr. Eileen Flavin, C.S.C., Coord.

Area VI - South America, Sao Paulo, Brazil. Tel: 011-55-11-5687-2723; Fax: 011-55-11-522-7148. Sr. Anne Veronica Horner Hoe, C.S.C.,

Area VII - West Africa, Takaradi Ghana, West Africa. Tel: 011-233-31-31321; Fax: 011-233-31-21645. Sr. M. Jane Chantal Method, C.S.C., Coord.

Area VIII - Asia, Dhaka, Bangladesh. Tel: 011-880-2-912-9600; Fax: 011-880-2-912-9600. Sr. Marian Teresa Gomes, C.S.C., Coord.

Sisters serve and staff: Colleges; High Schools; Grade Schools; Adult Education Centers; Social Service Centers; Prayer Centers; Counseling Centers; Human

Rights Centers; Women's Development Center; Hospitals and other Health Ministries including Administration of Health Systems, Primary Health Care and Long Term Health Care; Parish Ministry; Diocesan Catechetical Services; Other Parish and Diocesan Ministries; Retirement Homes; Senior Citizen Residences; Pastoral Ministry with the Deaf.

Represented in the Archdioceses of Baltimore, Boston, Chicago, Cincinnati, Denver, Indianapolis, Los Angeles, Louisville, New Orleans, Newark, San Antonio, San Francisco, Seattle, and Washington and in the Dioceses of Arlington, Austin, Beaumont, Boise, Brownsville, Cleveland, Columbus, Colorado Springs, Des Moines, Fall River, Fort Wayne-South Bend, Fresno, Gary, Harrisburg, Joliet, Kalamazoo, Knoxville, Lafayette (IN), Lexington, Manchester, Monterey, Oakland, Orange, Orlando, Palm Beach, Peoria, Phoenix, Raleigh, Richmond, Rockville Centre, Sacramento, St. Cloud, Salt Lake City, San Diego, Stockton and Tucson. Also in Brazil, Peru, Ghana, Uganda, Mexico, Bangladesh, India, and Lebanon.

[1930] (C.S.C.)—SISTERS OF HOLY CROSS (P)

Founded in Le Mans, France in 1841. First foundation in Canada in 1847.

General Administration: 905 rue Basile-Moreau, St-Laurent, Montreal, Quebec, Canada. H4L 4A1, Sr. Liette Finnerty, C.S.C., Supr. Gen.

Universal Total in Congregation 1,036.

American Regional Office: *Sisters of Holy Cross,* 377 Island Pond Rd., Manchester, NH 03109-4811. Tel: 603-622-9504; Fax: 603-622-9782. Sr. Elaine Marquis, C.S.C., Reg. Animator.

Total number in region 161.

Universal Total in Congregation 861.

Ministry in the field of Academic Education at all levels; Religious Education Centers; Social and Family Services; Counselor-Therapist; Parish Ministry; Sabbatical Programs; Adoption Agency; Clinical leader/nurses; Youth and Hospital Chaplaincies; Administrative Positions; Diocesan Services; Hispanic Ministry; Ministry to Abused Women and Children; Social Work and Elderly Assistance.

Properties owned: *Holy Cross Kindergarten,* Manchester, NH; *St. George Manor,* Manchester, NH; *Our Lady of the Sacred Heart Convent,* West Franklin, NH; *Londonderry House,* Londonderry, NH; *Sisters of the Holy Cross,* 454 Island Pond Rd., Manchester, NH 03109; 136 Lynwood Ln., Manchester, NH 03109; 113 Wedgewood Ln., Manchester, NH 03109; 969 & 971 Chestnut St., Manchester, NH 03104; 377 Island Pond Rd., Manchester, NH; Fairview Rd., R.R. 1, Box 191, Pittsfield, NH 03263; other properties in the Diocese of Manchester.

Represented in the Archdiocese of Boston, and in the Dioceses of Bridgeport, Burlington, Fall River, Manchester, Norwich, and St. Petersburg. Also in Bangladesh, Cameroon, Chile, Haiti, Mali, Rome and Peru.

[1940] (C.H.F.)—CONGREGATION OF THE SISTERS OF THE HOLY FAITH (P)

Founded in Ireland in 1856. First foundation in U.S. in 1953. St. John of God School, 13817 Pioneer Blvd., Norwalk, California, 90650.

Motherhouse: Glasnevin, Dublin, Ireland.

U.S. Province: 12322 S. Paramount Blvd., Downey, CA 90242. Tel: 562-869-6092; Fax: 562-869-4609. Sr. Colette Connelly, C.H.F., Reg. Supr.

Total number in community 240.

Represented in the Archdioceses of Los Angeles, New Orleans and San Francisco and in the Diocese of Sacramento.

[1950] (S.S.F.)—CONGREGATION OF THE SISTERS OF THE HOLY FAMILY (P)

Founded in the New Orleans, Louisiana, in 1842.

Motherhouse: 6901 Chef Menteur Hwy., New Orleans, LA 70126. Tel: 504-242-8315. Sr. Sylvia Thibodaux, S.S.F., Supr. Gen.

Total number in community 153.

Ministry in Secondary and Elementary Schools; Day Care Centers; Pastoral and Social Services; Nursing Home and Apartments for the Elderly, Disabled and Handicapped.

Represented in the Archdioceses of New Orleans and Washington and in the Dioceses of Galveston-Houston, Lafayette (LA) and Memphis. Also in Belize and Central America.

[1960] (S.H.F.)—SISTERS OF THE HOLY FAMILY (P)

Founded in San Francisco, California, in 1872.

General Motherhouse: P.O. Box 3248, Fremont, CA 94539. Tel: 510-624-4500; Fax: 510-624-4537. Sr. Sharon Flannigan, Congregational Pres.

Total number in community 112.

Ministry in the following areas: Child Care; Primary Education in Schools; School Counseling; Prison Chaplaincy; Religious Education and Pastoral Care; Social Service Agencies related to Child Protective Services; Hospital Chaplaincy; Parish Administration.

Properties owned: *St. Elizabeth's Day Home,* San Jose, CA; *Holy Family Renewal Center,* Pleasant Hill, CA.

Represented in the Archdioceses of Anchorage, Los Angeles, Louisville, San Antonio and San Francisco and in the Dioceses of Fresno, Honolulu, Las Vegas, Monterey, Oakland, Reno, Sacramento, Salt Lake City, San Diego, San Jose and Stockton.

[1970] (C.S.F.N.)—SISTERS OF THE HOLY FAMILY OF NAZARETH (P)

Founded in Italy in 1875. First foundation in the United States in 1885.

General Motherhouse: Rome, Italy. Sr. M. Janice Fulmer, C.S.F.N., Supr. Gen.

Sacred Heart Province (1885): 310 N. River Rd., Des Plaines, IL 60016-1211. Tel: 847-298-6760; Fax: 847-803-1941 Sr. Marie Kielanowicz, C.S.F.N., Prov. Supr.; Sr. M. Gemma, C.S.F.N., Archivist.

Total number in Province 121.

Ministry in Academic Education; Hospitals and Health Care.

Properties owned: *Nazarethville.*

Co-Sponsors: *Resurrection Health Care.*

Represented in the Archdiocese of Chicago and the Diocese of Joliet.

Blessed Frances Siedliska Province (1962): *Sisters of The Holy Family of Nazareth,* 1814 Egyptian Way, Box 530959, Grand Prairie, TX 75053. Tel: 972-641-4496; Fax: 972-641-1668. Sr. M. Janice Kobierowski, Prov. Supr.

Total number in community 40.

Legal Holdings or Titles: *United Regional Health Care System-11th Street Campus,* Wichita Falls, TX; *Holy Family of Nazareth Health Ministry of Wichita Falls,* Wichita Falls, TX; *Trinity Mother Frances Health System,* Tyler, TX; *Blessed Frances Siedliska Province Charitable Trust Fund,* Dallas, TX.

Ministry in Education; Health Care; Parish Ministry; Religious Education.

Represented in the Dioceses of Dallas, Fort Worth and Tyler.

Immaculate Conception BVM Province (1918): *Sisters of the Holy Family of Nazareth Provincial House and Academy,* 4001 Grant Ave., Philadelphia, PA 19114-2999. Tel: 215-268-1050; Fax: 215-1075. Sr. M. Celine Warnil, Prov. Supr.; Sr. M. Rosella Wyborska, Community Archivist.

Total number Professed Sisters in community 147.

Ministry in the field of Education; Child Care; Elder Care; Health Care; and Pastoral Ministry.

Properties owned: *Holy Family College Nazareth Academy Mount Nazareth,* Philadelphia, PA; *St. Mary Villa,* Ambler, PA; *Villa Nazareth,* Meadowbrook, PA.

Represented in the Archdioceses of Philadelphia, San Juan, and Washington and in the Diocese of Allentown.

Saint Joseph Province (1918): 285 Bellevue Rd., Pittsburgh, PA 15229-2195. Tel: 412-931 4775; Fax: 412-931-9746. Sr. Cynthia Meyer, C.S.F.N., Prov. Supr.

Professed sisters in provincialate 16: Professed sisters 96.

Sisters serve and staff: High Schools; Elementary Schools; Religious Education Centers; Hospitals; Parish Pastoral Ministry; Family Counseling; Family Life Education; Senior Citizen Apartments; Home for the Elderly; Home for Children; Learning Centers.

Legal Holdings and Titles: *Mt. Nazareth Center, Inc.,* Pittsburgh, PA; *Holy Family Institute,* Emsworth, PA; *St. Leonard's Home, Inc.,* Hollidaysburg, PA; *The Holy Family Foundation,* Emsworth, PA; *Nazareth Family Foundation,* Pittsburgh, PA.

Represented in the Archdiocese of Detroit and in the Dioceses of Altoona-Johnstown, Cleveland, Pittsburgh and Steubenville.

Immaculate Heart of Mary Province (1959): *Sisters of Holy Family of Nazareth Provincial Residence - Marian Heights,* 1428 Monroe Turnpike, Monroe, CT 06468. Tel: 203-268-7646; Fax: 203-452-9947. Sr. M. Agnese Palczynski, Prov.

Total number in Province 86.

Legal Title: *C.S.F.N. Congregation of the Sisters of the Holy Family of Nazareth.*

Ministry in Education; Child Care; Health Care; Religious Education; Retreat Work; House of Prayer; Pastoral Ministry and Hospital Chaplaincy; Prison Ministry.

Represented in the Archdioceses of Hartford and New York and in the Dioceses of Bridgeport, Brooklyn, Rockville Centre, Syracuse, Trenton and Worcester.

[1980] (O.S.F.)—CONGREGATION OF THE SERVANTS OF THE HOLY CHILD JESUS OF THE THIRD ORDER REGULAR OF SAINT FRANCIS (P)

Founded in Germany in 1855. First founded in the United States on April 9, 1929, at Staten Island, New York.

General Motherhouse (1855): Kloster Oberzell, Wuerzburg, Germany. Mother Vridiana Duerr, Supr. Gen.

Regional House: *Servants of the Holy Child Jesus-Villa Maria,* 641 Somerset St., North Plainfield, NJ 07060-4909. Tel: 908-757-3050. Fax: 908-754-9190. Sr. M. Dominic Ritter, Reg. Supr.

Total in American region 24.

Ministry in Social Work; Health Care; Teaching.

Properties owned: *Villa Maria Sanitarium, Inc.,* North Plainfield, NJ.

Represented in the Archdiocese of Newark and Diocese of Metuchen.

[1990] (S.N.J.M.)—SISTERS OF THE HOLY NAMES OF JESUS AND MARY (P)

Founded by Blessed Marie Rose Durocher, in Longueuil, Quebec, Canada in 1843. First foundation in the U.S. in 1859.

Generalate: 80, rue Saint-Charles Est, Longueuil, Quebec, Canada, J4H 1A9. Tel: 450-651-8104. Sr. Mary Pat LeRoy, Supr.

An international congregation of 1,600 religious women with missions in Lesotho, Mexico, Nicaragua, Haiti and Brazil. Congregational sponsored works include colleges; adult centers; secondary, elementary and preschools; continuing care retirement community and health clinics.

Oregon Province (1859): *Provincial Administration,* Box 25, Marylhurst, OR 97036. Tel: 503-675-2467. Sr. Lynda Thompson, Prov. Dir.

Total number in community 200.

Properties owned: *Provincial House, Marylhurst, OR; St. Mary's Academy,* Portland, OR; *Mary's Woods at Marylhurst, Inc.,* Marylhurst, OR.

Sisters ministering in works sponsored by other institutions/agencies include Formal Education in Universities, Secondary, Elementary and Preschools; Adult Basic Education/Literacy; Administration in Diocesan Offices; Campus Ministry; Pastoral Ministry; Religious Education, Health Care and Social Services.

Represented in the Archdioceses of Los Angeles, Portland (OR), San Francisco, Seattle, and Washington and in the Dioceses of Baker, Fairbanks, Jackson, Monterey, Oakland, Palm Beach, Richmond, Spokane, and Yakima.

California Province (1868): *Provincial Administration,* P.O. Box 907, Los Gatos, CA 95031. Tel: 408-395-5150. Sr. Margaret Spiller, S.N.J.M., Prov.

Total number in community 231.

Properties owned or sponsored: *Provincial House,* Los Gatos, CA; *Holy Names College; Holy Names High School,* Oakland, CA; *Ramona Convent Secondary School,* Alhambra, CA; *Villa Maria Del Mar,* Santa Cruz, CA; *Next Step Learning Center,* Oakland, CA; *Villa Holy Names,* Los Gatos, CA.

New York Province (1865): *Provincial Administration,* 1061 New Scotland Ave., Albany, NY 12208. Tel: 518-489-5469; Fax: 518-489-5804. Sr. Barbara Pavlic, Prov. Dir.

Total number in community 96.

Properties owned: *Provincial Center; Academy of the Holy Names,* Albany, NY; *Academy of the Holy Names,* Tampa, FL.

Washington Province (1962): *Provincial Administration,* 2911 W. Fort Wright Dr., Spokane, WA 99224. Tel: 509-328-7470; Fax: 509-328-9824. Sr. Ann Pizelo, S.N.J.M., Prov.

Total number in community 165.

Properties owned: *Provincial House,* Spokane, WA; *Holy Names Academy,* Seattle, WA.

[2000] (C.S.R.)—SISTERS OF THE HOLY REDEEMER (P)

First foundation in the United States on March 19, 1924 in Baltimore, Maryland.

American Province of the Immaculate Conception: 521 Moredon Rd., Huntingdon Valley, PA 19006. Tel: 215-914-4100; Fax: 215-914-4171. Sr. M. Regina Heilman, C.S.R., Prov. Supr.

Legal Holdings and Titles: *Holy Redeemer Health Care Corporation and Foundation; Holy Redeemer Health System; Holy Redeemer Hospital and Medical Center; Redeemer Center; St. Joseph's Manor; The Lafayette-Redeemer; Holy Redeemer Home Health and Hospice Services; Holy Redeemer Transitional Care Unit; Holy Redeemer Managed Care Organization; Holy Redeemer Physician and Ambulatory Services; Holy Redeemer Visiting Nurse Agency, Inc., NJ; Redeemer Village & Redeemer Village II; Drueding Center / Project Rain-*

bow; HRH Management Corporation; Redeemer Medical Supply Co., Inc. Convents— Provincialate; Angelus Convent; Emmanuel Convent; Our Lady of Peace Convent; St. Elizabeth Convent.
Represented in the Archdiocese of Philadelphia and in the Dioceses of Camden and Trenton.

[2010] (O.SS.R.)—ORDER OF THE MOST HOLY REDEEMER (P)
(Redemptoristine Nuns)

Founded 1731 by St. Alphonsus de Liguori and Ven. Marie Celeste. (Contemplative). Rule approved 1750 by Pope Benedict XIV. First United States Monastery (1957) Esopus, New York.
Monastery of St. Alphonsus (1960): *Order of the Most Holy Redeemer,* 200 Liguori Dr., Liguori, MO 63057. Tel: 636-464-1093; Fax: 636-464-9446. Sr. Joan E. Calver, O.Ss.R., Prioress.
Total number in community 16.
Represented in the Archdioceses of New York and St. Louis.
Mother of Perpetual Help Monastery: *Redemptoristine Nuns,* P.O. Box 220, Esopus, NY 12429-0220. Tel: 845-384-6533; Fax: 845-384-6654. Sr. Moira Quinn, O.SS.R., Prioress
Solemn Vows, Papal Enclosure.
Total number in community 9.

[2020] (C.H.S.)—COMMUNITY OF THE HOLY SPIRIT (D)

U.S. Foundation (1970): 6151 Rancho Mission Rd. - #205, San Diego, CA 92108. Tel: 619-584-0809. Sr. MaryJo Anderson, C.H.S.,
Total number in community 17.
Ministry in the field of Education; Health Care; and Social Services.
Represented in the Dioceses of Oakland, Orange, Portland (OR), Reno-Las Vegas, San Diego, San Jose and Wichita.

[2030] (C.S.Sp.)—SISTERS OF THE HOLY SPIRIT (D)

Founded in the United States 1929; Decree of Establishment 1932.
Motherhouse and Novitiate: 10102 Granger Rd., Garfield Heights, OH 44125. Sr. Mary Assumpta, Supr. Gen.
Total number in community 8.
Represented in the Diocese of Cleveland.

[2040] (S.H.S.)—SISTERS OF THE HOLY SPIRIT (D)

Founded in the United States in 1913 at Donora, Pennsylvania.
Motherhouse: 5246 Clarwin Ave., Ross Township, Pittsburgh, PA 15229-2208. Tel: 412-931-1917. Sr. M. Bridget Miller, S.H.S., Gen. Supr.
Total number in community 49; Novices 2.
Facilities owned and staffed: *Corporation of Sisters of the Holy Spirit of Pittsburgh; Marian Manor, Corp. Martina Spiritual Renewal Center Inc.*
Sisters serve and staff: Elementary Schools; Religious Education; Health and Social Services; Retreat Services; Child Day Care; Care Facility for the Aged.
Represented in the Dioceses of Greensburg and Pittsburgh.

[2050] (S.H.Sp.)—SISTERS OF THE HOLY SPIRIT AND MARY IMMACULATE (P)

Founded in America in 1893. Papal Approbation 1930; final Approbation, 1938.
General Motherhouse: *Convent of the Holy Spirit and Mary Immaculate,* 301 Yucca St., San Antonio, TX 78203. Tel: 210-533-5149. Sr. Veronica Cahill, S.H.Sp., Gen. Supr.
Professed Sisters 95.
Legal Holdings: *Holy Spirit Trust; Holy Spirit Motherhouse; Healy Murphy Center, Inc.,* San Antonio, TX; *Mother of Perpetual Help Nursing Home,* Brownsville, TX.
Ministry in the following areas: Education; Health Care; Pastoral Ministry; Catechetical Ministry; Social Service; Retreats.
Represented in the Archdioceses of New Orleans and San Antonio and in the Dioceses of Beaumont, Biloxi, Brownsville, Corpus Christi, Dallas, Fort Worth, Galveston-Houston, Houma-Thibadoux, Jackson and Lafayette (LA). Also in Mexico and Zambia.

[2060] (O.SS.T.)—SISTERS OF THE MOST HOLY TRINITY (P)

Founded in Rome in 1198. First foundation in the United States in 1920.
General Motherhouse: Rome, Italy.
Provincial House: *Immaculate Conception Province,* 21281 Chardon Rd., Euclid, OH 44117. Tel: 216-481-8232; Fax: 216-481-6577. Sr. Phyllis Ann Lavalle, Reg.
Total number in community 22.
Properties owned: *Our Lady of Lourdes Shrine,* Euclid, OH.
Represented in the Archdiocese of Philadelphia and in the Diocese of Cleveland.

[2070] (S.U.S.C.)—HOLY UNION SISTERS (P)

Founded in France in 1826. First foundation in the United States in 1886.
Generalate: Rome, Italy. Sr. Carol Regan, S.U.S.C., Supr. Gen.
United States Province: *Provincial Office,* P.O. Box 410 -444 Centre St., Milton, MA 02186-0006. Tel: 617-696-8765; Fax: 617-696-8571. Province Mission Team: Sr. Beverly Furtado, S.U.S.C.; Sr. Gretchen Marlatt, S.U.S.C.; Sr. Bernadette Sullivan, S.U.S.C.; Co-Archivists: Sr. Grace Donovan, S.U.S.C.; Sr. Rita Beaudoin, S.U.S.C.
Total number in community 156.
Legal Title: *Holy Union Sisters, Inc.*
Ministry in the field of Religious and Academic Education; Social Services; Pastoral Care; Pastoral Ministry; Spiritual Renewal; Day Care; Ministry Education; Family Ministry; Nursing; Peace & Justice; Spanish Apostolate; Ministry to the Handicapped; Ministry to Immigrants and Refugees; Clerical & Secretarial services; Diocesan Administrative services; Foreign Mission work in Tanzania.
Properties owned: *Holy Union Spiritual Life Center,* Groton, MA; *Holy Union Asian Center,* Lowell, MA; *Holy Union African Center,* Lowell, MA; *Holy Union House of Hospitality,* Tiverton, RI.
Represented in the Archdioceses of Baltimore, Boston, Detroit, Miami and New York and in the Dioceses of Albany, Brooklyn, Fall River, Harrisburg, Lexington, Orlando, Pensacola-Tallahassee, Providence and Rockville Centre.

[2080] (G.H.M.S.)—HOME MISSION SISTERS OF AMERICA (D)
(Glenmary Sisters)

Founded July 16, 1952.
Motherhouse: *Glenmary Sisters - Glenmary Center,* P.O. Box 22264, Owensboro, KY 42304-2264. Tel: 270-686-8401. Sr. Patricia Leighton, Pres.
Total number in community 10.
Service to Home Missions.
Represented in the Dioceses of Lexington, Owensboro and Savannah.

[2090] (H.V.M.)—SISTERS HOME VISITORS OF MARY (D)

Founded in Detroit, Michigan in 1949.
Motherhouse: 121 E. Boston Blvd., Detroit, MI 48202. Tel: 313-869-2160.
Total number in community 16.
Ministry in Urban Parishes; Senior Citizen; Prisons; Sojourner Spiritual Affirmation Center; Seminary Staff; Intercultural Center; Preschools; Religious Education, RCIA.
Represented in the Archdiocese of Detroit. Also in Nigeria.

[2100] (C.H.M.)—CONGREGATION OF THE HUMILITY OF MARY (P)

Founded in France in 1854. First United States foundation in 1864.
Motherhouse: *Humility of Mary Center,* Davenport, IA 52804. Sr. Jude Fitzpatrick, Pres.
Total number in community 161.
Legal Title: *Congregation of the Humility of Mary; Humility of Mary Shelter, Inc.; Congregation of the Humility of Mary Charitable Trust.*
Ministry in Schools and Colleges; Religious Education Centers; Migrant Programs; Pastoral Ministry; Social Services; Inner City Programs; Health Services and Ministry to the Elderly.
Represented in the Archdioceses of Chicago, Denver, Los Angeles, Seattle, and Washington and in the Dioceses of Davenport, Des Moines, Great Falls-Billings, Helena, Jackson, Lexington, Peoria, Richmond, Rockford, St. Cloud, San Angelo, Tulsa, Wheeling-Charleston and Yakima. Also in Mexico.

[2110] (H.M.)—SISTERS OF THE HUMILITY OF MARY (P)

Founded in France in 1854. First foundation in the United States in 1864 at Villa Maria, Lawrence County, Pennsylvania, 16155.
Motherhouse: *Villa Maria Community Center,* P.O. Box 914, Villa Maria, PA 16155-0914. Tel: 724-964-8861; Fax: 724-964-8082. Sr. Ruthmary Powers, H.M., Major Supr.; Sr. Mary-Joanna Huegle, H.M., Community Archivist.
Total number in community 211.
Ministry in the field of Academic and Religious Education at all levels; Hospitals and Nursing Home, Assisted Living; Parish and Pastoral Ministries; Publishing of Education Materials; Diocesan Offices; Legal Services; Social Services; Ministry to Native Americans, Migrants, Hispanics, Haitians; Housing Ministry to Rural Poor, Single Parents, Independent Elderly; Ministry to Deaf and to Prisoners; Retreat Ministry; Spirituality and Counseling; Advocacy for Eco-justice; Marketing of Creative Arts.
Legal Holdings and Titles: *Humility of Mary Health Partners, St. Elizabeth Health Center,* Youngstown, OH; *Humility of Mary Health Partners, HM Hospice,* Warren, OH; *Sisters of the Humility of Mary (Motherhouse),* Villa Maria, PA; *Sisters of the Humility of Mary Charitable Trust,* Villa Maria, PA; *Humility of Mary Health Partners, St. Elizabeth Health Center,* Youngstown, OH; *Humility of Mary Health Partners, HM Hospice,* Warren, OH; *The Assumption Village,* North Lima, OH; *Community Health Partners of Ohio,* Lorain, OH; *Community Health Partners Foundation,* Lorain, OH; *Laurel Lake Retirement Community,* Hudson, OH; *Magnificat High School,* Rocky River, OH; *Villa Montessori Center,* Cleveland, OH; *The Center for Learning,* Villa Maria, PA; *Villa Maria Education Center,* Villa Maria, PA; *Humility of Mary Housing, Inc.,* Akron, OH; *HM Housing Development Corporation, Akron, OH; HM Life Opportunity Services,* Akron, OH; *Villa Residential Services (Villa Maria Apartments),* Villa Maria, PA; *Heartbeats,* Rocky River, OH; *Common Ground Center for Community Renewal,* Oberlin, OH.
Represented in the Archdioceses of Cincinnati, San Antonio, and Washington and in the Dioceses of Cleveland, Erie, Grand Island, Lansing, Lexington, Palm Beach, Pittsburgh, Richmond, Spokane, Toledo, Trenton, Wheeling-Charleston and Youngstown. Also in Haiti.

[2120] (C.I.C.)—SISTERS OF THE IMMACULATE CONCEPTION (D)

Founded in the United States in 1874.
General Motherhouse and Convent of the Immaculate Conception: P.O. Box 50426, New Orleans, LA 70185-0426. Tel: 504-486-7426. Sr. Ada Missler, C.I.C., Contact Person.
Total number in community 17.
Ministry in Pastoral Ministry.
Represented in the Archdiocese of New Orleans and in the Diocese of Houma-Thibodaux.

[2130] (R.C.M.)—SISTERS OF THE IMMACULATE CONCEPTION (P)

Founded in Spain in 1892.
General Motherhouse: Princesa 19 y 21, Madrid, Spain. 28008, Mother Maria Luz Martinez, Mother Gen.
U.S. Delegation House (1962): 2230 Franklin, San Francisco, CA 94109. Tel: 415-474-0159. Sr. Carmen Santiuste, Reg. Supr.
Represented in the Archdiocese of San Francisco and in the Diocese of Fresno.

[2140] SISTERS OF THE IMMACULATE CONCEPTION OF THE BLESSED VIRGIN MARY (LITHUANIAN) (D)

Founded in Marijampole, Lithuania in 1918. First foundation in the United States in 1936.
American Headquarters: *Immaculate Conception Convent and Novitiate,* 600 Liberty Hwy., Putnam, CT 06260-2503. Tel: 860-928-7955; Fax: 860-928-1930. Sr. Mary Paul Savickas, Prov.
Total number in community 21.
Legal Titles & Holdings: *Immaculate Conception Convent; Matulaitis Nursing Home,* Putnam, CT; *Camp Neringa,* Marlboro, VT.
Ministry in Nursing Homes; Retreat House; Catechetical Work in Parishes; Summer Camp for Children and Young Adults.
Represented in the Archdiocese of Chicago and in the Dioceses of Burlington and Norwich. Also in Canada.

[2145] (O.S.A.)— CONGREGATION OF AUGUSTINIAN SISTERS SERVANTS OF JESUS AND MARY (P)

Generalate: via Nomentana 514, Rome, Italy. Mother Atanasia Buhagiar, Gen.
Malta Province: 208 Fleur-de-Lys, B'Kara, Malta. Mother Miriam Grech, Mother Prov.
U.S. Foundation: *St. John School,* 513 E. Broadway, Brandenburg, KY, 40108. Sr. Lydia Falzon, Supr.
Total number in community 4.
Represented in the Archdiocese of Louisville.

[2150] (I.H.M.)—SISTERS, SERVANTS OF THE IMMACULATE HEART OF MARY (P)

Founded in the United States in 1845.
SSIHM Leadership Council: 610 W. Elm, Monroe, MI 48162-7909. Tel: 734-240-9700; Fax: 734-240-9784. Sr. Virginia Pfau, I.H.M., Pres.
Total number in Congregation 618.

Legal Titles: *Marygrove College,* Detroit, MI; *Immaculate Heart of Mary High School,* Westchester, IL; *Marian High School,* Bloomfield Hills, MI; *St. Mary Center,* Monroe, MI; *Visitation House of Prayer,* Monroe, MI; *Co-Sponsor: Groundwork for a Just World,* Detroit, MI; *Institute for Communal Contemplation and Dialogue,* Detroit, MI.

Ministry in Academic and Religious Education at all levels; Pastoral Ministry (parish, healthcare, campus and prison settings); Diocesan and Parish Administration; Peace and Justice; Social Service and Counseling; Spiritual Growth and Development; Overseas Ministries.

Represented in the Archdioceses of Atlanta, Boston, Chicago, Cincinnati, Detroit, Louisville, Miami, Milwaukee, Mobile, New York, Oklahoma City, Philadelphia, St. Louis, St. Paul-Minneapolis, San Antonio, San Juan, Santa Fe, and Washington and in the Dioceses of Albany, Austin, Cleveland, Duluth, Fort Wayne-South Bend, Galveston-Houston, Gaylord, Grand Rapids, Joliet, Kalamazoo, Kansas City-St. Joseph, Lansing, Lexington, Marquette, New Ulm, Oakland, Palm Beach, Pensacola-Tallahassee, Phoenix, Portland, Raleigh, Richmond, Rockville Centre, Saginaw, St. Augustine, St. Petersburg, San Diego, Toledo and Wichita. Also in Brazil, Canada, Italy, Honduras, Mexico, Uganda, and South Africa.

[2160] (I.H.M.)—SISTERS, SERVANTS OF THE IMMACULATE HEART OF MARY (P)

Founded in 1845. Established in Scranton, Pennsylvania in 1871.

General Motherhouse: *Immaculate Heart of Mary Center,* 2300 Adams Ave., Scranton, PA 18509. Tel: 570-342-6850; Fax: 570-346-5439. Sr. Mary Persico, I.H.M., Pres.

Total number in community 573.

Ministry in the field of Academic Education; Hospitals; Early Childhood Education Centers; Congregation Retirement and Health Care Centers; Spiritual Renewal Center; Directors of Religious Education; Pastoral Ministries; Social Services; Campus Ministry; Volunteer Services; Family Ministry; Drug and Alcohol Counseling; Ministry to Hispanics; Diocesan Offices; Vicar for Religious.

Properties owned: *IHM Center; Marian Convent; Our Lady of Grace Center,* Manhasset, NY.

Represented in the Archdioceses of Baltimore, Boston, Miami, Newark, New York, Philadelphia, Santa Fe and Washington and in the Dioceses of Albany, Allentown, Altoona-Johnstown, Arlington, Boise, Bridgeport, Brooklyn, Camden, Harrisburg, Jackson, Metuchen, Paterson, Pittsburgh, Raleigh, Rochester, Rockville Centre, St. Augustine, St. Petersburg, Scranton, Syracuse, Trenton, Wheeling-Charleston, and Wilmington. Also in Peru.

[2170] (I.H.M.)—SISTERS, SERVANTS OF THE IMMACULATE HEART OF MARY (P)

Founded in 1845. Established in West Chester, Pennsylvania in 1872.

General Motherhouse: *Villa Maria,* 1140 King Rd., Immaculata, PA 19345. Tel: 610-647-2160; Fax: 610-889-4874. Sr. Rose Marie DeCarlo, I.H.M., Gen. Supr.

Total number in Congregation 1,105.

Ministry in the field of Academic Education at all levels in the U.S. as well as Peru & Chile; Pastoral Ministry; Literacy Centers; Infirmary work.

Represented in the Archdioceses of Atlanta, Boston, Hartford, Miami, and Philadelphia and in the Dioceses of Allentown, Camden, Harrisburg, Metuchen, Richmond, Savannah and Trenton.

[2180] (I.H.M.)—SISTERS OF THE IMMACULATE HEART OF MARY (P)

Founded in Spain in 1848. First foundation in United States in 1871.

General Motherhouse: Rome, Italy.

U.S. Province: 3820 N. Sabino Canyon Rd., Tucson, AZ 85750-6534. Tel: 520-886-4273. Sr. Miriam Claire Arnold, Prov. Supr.; Sr. Alice M. Martinez, Sec. & Community Archivist.

Total number in community 26.

Ministry in the field of Academic and Religious Education.

Represented in the Diocese of Tucson.

[2182] (I.H.M.M.)—SISTERS OF THE IMMACULATE HEART OF MARY OF MIRINAE (D)

Founded in 1976 by Rev. Francis Haengman Tiyeng, Marinae, Diocese of Suwon, Korea, under the motto, "through the Immaculate Heart of Mary to the Most Holy Trinity."

Motherhouse: Mirinae, Korea.

U.S. Foundation: *Immaculate Heart of Mary Pre School,* 423 South Commonwealth Ave., Los Angeles, CA 90020. Sr. Inviolata Chang, I.H.M.M., Sec.

Ministry in retreat work, school, youth and care for the aged.

Properties owned: *Sisters of the Immaculate Heart of Mary of Mirinae,* Los Angeles, CA.

Represented in the Archdiocese of Los Angeles.

[2183] (I.H.M.)—SISTERS OF THE IMMACULATE HEART OF MARY MOTHER OF CHRIST, NIGERIA (P)

Founded in Nigeria, West Africa in 1937. Classified with the Pontifical Institute Right in 1973.

Motherhouse: *Immaculate Heart Generalate,* P.O. Box 1551, Odoakpu, Onitsha, Anambra State, Nigeria. Tel: 234-46-026; 234-46-485. Rev. Mother Mary Joseph Ann Anochie, Mother Gen.

Total number in Congregation 827.

U.S.A. Regional House: *Immaculate Heart Convent,* 1209 South Walnut, Freeport, IL 61032. Tel: 612-328-0622. Sr. Mary Providentia Marinze, Reg. Supr.

Total number of Sisters in the U.S. 32.

Legal Title: *The Congregation of the Sisters of the Immaculate Heart of Mary Mother of Christ* - Nigeria.

Ministry in Education; Hospital/Clinic, Pastoral/Social Services; Care of the Aged; Diocecan House Care.

Represented in the Archdiocese of St. Paul-Minneapolis, and the Dioceses of Gallup, Rockford and Syracuse.

[2185] (I.H.M.)—SISTERS OF THE IMMACULATE HEART OF MARY OF WICHITA

Founded in Olot, Spain, in 1848. First foundation in United States in 1871. Wichita foundation in 1979.

Motherhouse: 605 N. Woodchuck, Wichita, KS 67212. Tel: 316-722-9316. Mother Marie Bernadette Mertens, I.H.M., Gen. Supr.

Total number in community 19.

Apostolate: Contemplation of the Word and the spread of His Message of salvation through the various works and levels of education and retreat work.

Represented in the Diocese of Wichita.

[2187] (I.C.M.)—INCARNATIO-CONSECRATIO-MISSIO

Founded in Vietnam in 1969. First foundation in United States in 1975.

Motherhouse: 407 Tan Han, Phuong Loc Tien, Thi Xa Bao Loc, Lam Dong, Vietnam. 011-84-63-862-177.

U.S. Regional House: *Incarnatio-Consecratio-Missio, Inc.,* 5185 Jetsail Dr., Orlando, FL 32812. Tel: 407-658-4124; Fax: 407-658-4124. E-mail: icmorlando@yahoo.com. Sr. Marie Nguyen, I.C.M., Contact Person.

Universal Membership 80.

Ministry in the areas of Education; Healthcare; Missionary Outreach; Parish Ministries and Pastoral Care.

Represented in the Dioceses of Baton Rouge and Orlando. Also in Vietnam.

[2190] (C.V.I.)—CONGREGATION OF THE INCARNATE WORD AND BLESSED SACRAMENT

Founded in France in 1625. First foundation in the United States in 1853.

Motherhouse and Novitiate: *Incarnate Word Convent,* 3400 Bradford Pl., Houston, TX 77025-1398. Tel: 713-668-0423. Sr. Lauren Beck, Supr.; Sr Dympna Lyons, Archivist; Sr. Brendan O'Donnell, Archivist.

Total number in community 62.

Ministry in the field of Academic and Religious Education; Social Service; Administration Hispanic Ministry; Diocesan Ministry - Pastoral Care; Parish Ministry; Literacy Programs.

Represented in the Dioceses of Beaumont and Galveston-Houston.

[2200] (I.W.B.S.)—CONGREGATION OF THE INCARNATE WORD AND BLESSED SACRAMENT (P)

Founded in France in 1625. First founded in the United States in 1853.

Motherhouse and Novitiate: *Incarnate Word Convent,* 1101 N.E. Water St., Victoria, TX 77901-9298. Tel: 361-575-2266; Fax: 361-575-2165. Sr. M. Evelyn Korenek, I.W.B.S., Supr. Gen.; Sr. Mary Virginia Shevlak, I.W.B.S., Community Archivist.

Total number in community 105.

Legal Titles: *Sisters of the Incarnate Word and Blessed Sacrament, Victoria, Texas, Inc.; Sisters of the Incarnate Word and Blessed Sacrament of Victoria, Texas Medical and Retirement Trust,* Victoria, TX.

Ministry in the field of Education; CCD Centers; Hospitals.

Properties owned or sponsored: *Nazareth Academy,* Victoria, TX; *Blessed Sacrament Academy,* San Antonio, TX.

Represented in the Archdiocese of San Antonio and in the Dioceses of Beaumont, Dallas, Galveston-Houston and Victoria. Also in Africa.

[2205] (I.W.B.S.)—SISTERS OF THE INCARNATE WORD AND BLESSED SACRAMENT (P)

Founded in France in 1625. First Founded in the United States in 1853.

Motherhouse and Novitiate: *Incarnate Word Convent,* 2930 S. Alameda St., Corpus Christi, TX 78404. Tel: 361-882-5413; Fax: 361-880-4152. Sr. Maria Irma Gonzalez, Supr. Gen.

Sisters 63.

Legal Titles: *Convent Academy of the Incarnate Word; Incarnate Word Academy Foundation; Fannie Bluntzer Nason Renewal Center, Inc.,* Corpus Christi, TX.

Sisters serve and staff: Private High Schools; Private Kindergartens; Montessori; Private Middle Schools; Parochial and Private Elementary Schools; Other ministries include Religious Education; Hospital Ministry; Vocation Ministry; Diocesan Offices; Adult Education; General Administration; Retreat Ministry; Parish Ministry.

Represented in the Dioceses of Brownsville, Corpus Christi, Beaumont, and Galveston-Houston.

[2210] (S.I.W.)—SISTERS OF THE INCARNATE WORD AND BLESSED SACRAMENT (D)

Founded in France in 1625. First foundation in the United States in 1853.

Motherhouse and Novitiate: 6618 Pearl Rd., (Parma Heights-U.S. Rd. 42), Cleveland, OH 44130. Tel: 216-886-6440. Sr. Carol Tobler, S.I.W., Congregational Leader.

Total number in community 32.

Ministry includes Evangelization; Elementary and Religious Education; Spiritual Ministry (Retreat and Spiritual Direction); Pastoral Ministry in Parishes, Hospitals and Nursing Homes.

Represented in the Diocese of Cleveland.

[2230] (C.I.J.)—CONGREGATION OF THE INFANT JESUS (D)

Founded in France in 1835. First foundation in the United States in 1905.

General Motherhouse: 984 N. Village Ave., Rockville Centre, NY 11570. Tel: 516-823-3800; 823-3808; Fax: 516-594-0412. Sr. Bernadette S. Downes, C.I.J., Supr. Gen.

Total number in community 61.

Corporate Title: *Nursing Sisters of the Sick Poor Inc.*

Ministry in the fields of Nursing; Social Work; Physical Therapy; Pastoral Care; Chaplains; Retreat Work; Teaching; Parish Ministry; and other works related to Health Services.

Represented in the Dioceses of Brooklyn, Lexington, Portland and Rockville Centre.

[2245] (S.J.S.)—SISTERS OF JESUS THE SAVIOR (P)

Founded in Elele, Nigeria in 1985.

U.S. Foundation: *St. Scholastica Convent,* 17305 Ashton Rd., Detroit, MI 48219. Tel: 313-541-4368.

Professed Sisters 10.

Ministry in Education and Social Assistance.

Represented in the Archdiocese of Detroit.

[2250] (O.S.B.)—CONGREGATION OF BENEDICTINES OF JESUS CRUCIFIED (P)

Founded in France in 1930. First foundation in the United States in 1955.

General Motherhouse: *Brou-sur-Chantereine,* France. Mother Godefrieda Bouwman, O.S.B., Prioress Gen.

U.S. Foundations: *Regina Mundi Priory,* 550 S. Waterloo Rd., Devon, PA 19333-1798. Tel: 610-688-5130; Fax: 610-995-0477. Sr. Marie Rita Syn, O.S.B., Prioress.

St. Paul's Priory, Newport, RI, 02840. Sr. Marie-Agathe Karunaratne, O.S.B., Prioress; Sr. Marie-Zita Wenker, O.S.B., Vocation Dir.

Total number in the U.S. 29.

Represented in the Archdiocese of Philadelphia and in the Diocese of Providence.

[2260] (A.D.)—SISTERS OF THE LAMB OF GOD (D)

Founded in France 1945.

General Motherhouse: *Institute of the Lamb of God,* 85 Rt du Vieux Saint Marc, Brest, France, 29283. Sr. Marie Francois Piriou, A.D., Supr. Gen.

U.S. Foundation (1958): *House of Formation,* 2063 Wyandotte Ave., Owensboro, KY 42301. Tel: 270-926-8656. Sr. Claire Marle, Supr.; Sr. Audrey Gold, Formation Director.

Sisters 11.

[2270] (L.C.M.)—SISTERS OF THE LITTLE COMPANY OF MARY (P)

Founded in England in 1877. First foundation in the United States in 1893.

Generalate: *Little Company of Mary Generalate,* 28 Trinity Crescent, Tooting Bec London, England, SW17 7AE.

Universal Total in Congregation: Final Professed Sisters 378; Temporary Professed Sisters 15.
Provincial Office: *Province of the Immaculate Conception, The Little Company of Mary,* 9350 S. California Ave., Evergreen Park, IL 60805. Tel: 708-422-0130. Sr. Carol Pacini, L.C.M., Prov.
Total number in community 25.
Ministry in Hospitals and Health Care; Pastoral/Parish areas.
Properties owned: *Little Company of Mary Hospital and Health Care Centers,* Evergreen Park, IL; *Memorial Hospital and Health Care Center,* Jasper, IN; *Little Company of Mary Health Services (Little Company of Mary Hospital,* Torrance, CA and *San Pedro Peninsula Hospital,* San Pedro, CA).
Represented in the Archdioceses of Chicago and Los Angeles and in the Dioceses of Evansville, Orange and Toledo.

[2280] (P.F.M.)—LITTLE FRANCISCANS OF MARY (U.S.) (P)

Founded in the United States in 1889.
General Motherhouse: *Baie St. Paul, (Charlevoix),* Diocese of Quebec, P.Q., Canada. Sr. Carmen Gravel, Supr. Gen.
American Region: *St. Francis,* 55 Moore Ave., Worcester, MA 01602. Tel: 508-755-0878. Sr. Jacquelyn Alix, Reg. Supr.
Total number in Congregation including Canada and the United States 244.
Represented in the Dioceses of Portland (ME) and Worcester.

[2300] (L.S.I.C.)—LITTLE SERVANT SISTERS OF THE IMMACULATE CONCEPTION (P)

Founded by Blessed Edmund Bojanowski in Poland on May 3, 1850. First foundation in the United States on December 8, 1926.
General Motherhouse: Stara Wies 460, 36-200 Brzozow,skr.poczt. 66,woj. podkarpackie, Poland. Mother Mariola Karas, L.S.I.C., Supr Gen.
Universal Total in Congregation 1,435.
Holy Trinity Province: *Little Servants Sisters of the Immaculate Conception Provincialate-Novitiate,* 1000 Cropwell Rd., Cherry Hill, NJ 08003. Tel: 856-424-1962; Fax: 856-424-5333. E-mail: LSICProv@aol.com. Mother Mary M. Leonarda Pyryt, L.S.I.C., Prov; Sr. M. Philomena Nowicka, L.S.I.C., Archivist.
Professed Sisters 78; Novices 1; Postulants 2.
Legal Titles: *Congregation of the Little Servant Sisters of the Blessed Virgin Mary of the Immaculate Conception, Immaculate Conception Convent, Provincialate-Novitiate,* Cherry Hill, NJ; *St. Joseph's Catholic Nursing Homes,* Woodbridge, NJ; *St. Joseph's Residences,* Woodbridge, NJ; *Edmund Child Education Center,* Cherry Hill, NJ.
Ministry: all levels of Religious and Academic Education; Pastoral Ministry; Social Work, Hospital and Prison Pastoral Care; Visiting Home Nursing Services; Senior Day Care Center; Senior Residential Homes & Assisted Living Homes, Skilled Nursing Homes; Guest House and Retreat House; Prayer Groups & Youth Ministry.
Represented in the Archdioceses of Newark, and Philadelphia and Dioceses of Camden and Metuchen.

[2310] (L.S.A.)—LITTLE SISTERS OF THE ASSUMPTION (P)

Founded in France in 1865. First foundation in the United States in 1891.
General Motherhouse: Paris, France. Sr. Mercedes Martinez, Supr. Gen., 57 rue Violet, Paris, France, 75015.
United States Province: *Little Sisters of the Assumption Provincialate,* 100 Gladstone Ave., Walden, NY 12586. Tel: 845-778-0667. Web site: www.littlesisters.org Sr. Jean McCormack, Prov. Coord.
Total number in community 39.
Legal Titles: *Family Lifeline Volunteers, Inc.,* New York, NY.
Ministry in Home Health; Community Development Supportive Family Services Located in Poverty Areas; Services are predominantly provided in the Home Setting.
Represented in the Archdioceses of Boston, New York and Philadelphia and in the Diocese of Worcester.

[2315] (L.S.G.)—LITTLE SISTERS OF THE GOSPEL (D)

Founded in 1963 in France by Rev. Rene Voillaume. First foundation in he United States in 1972 in New York.
Generalate: La Courneuve, France, 93120. Tel: 1-48361814.
U.S. House: Box 305, Mott Haven Sta., Bronx, NY 10454. Tel: 718-292-2867. Residence: 340 Willis Ave., Bronx NY, 10454.
Professed Sisters 74; Novices 7.
Ministry in Prison Ministry; Service to the Poor and Underserved.
Represented in the Archdiocese of New York.

[2320] (P.S.S.F.)—THE LITTLE SISTERS OF THE HOLY FAMILY (P)

Les Petites Soeurs de la Sainte Famille

Founded in Canada in 1880. First foundation in the United States in 1900.
General Motherhouse: *Mont Sainte-Famille,* 1820 Ouest, Rue Galt, Sherbrooke, Quebec, Canada, J1K 1H9. Tel: 819-823-0345. Sr. Jeannine Ferland, Supr.
U.S. Headquarters: *Marie Leonie Residence,* 285 Andover St., Lowell, MA 01852-1446. Tel: 508-454-7481. Sr. Gabrielle Paille, P.S.S.F., Supr.
Total number in U.S. 22.
Ministry includes Sisters dedicated to the service of priests by prayer and domestic work in rectories.
Represented in the Archdioceses of Boston and Chicago and in the Diocese of Manchester.

[2330] (L.S.J.)—LITTLE SISTERS OF JESUS (P)

Founded in the Sahara in 1939. First foundation in the United States in 1952.
General Motherhouse: Rome, Italy. Sr. Raymonde Andree, Prioress Gen.
Universal Total in Congregation 1,300.
U.S. Regional House: 400 N. Streeper St., Baltimore, MD 21224-1230. Tel: 410-327-7863. Sr. Anne-Marie Boucher, L.S.J., Reg. Dir.
Total number in U.S. 26.
Represented in the Archdioceses of Anchorage, Baltimore, Chicago and Washington and in the Dioceses of Altoona-Johnstown and Fairbanks.

[2331] (L.S.J.M.)—LITTLE SISTERS OF JESUS AND MARY (D)

Founded in the United States in 1974. Sr. Mary Elizabeth, Foundress.
Joseph House: P.O. Box 1755, Salisbury, MD 21802. Tel: 410-543-1645; Fax: 410-742-3390. Sr. Mary Elizabeth Gintling, Dir.
Total in the community 11.
Represented in the Diocese of Wilmington.

[2340] (L.S.P.)—LITTLE SISTERS OF THE POOR (P)

Founded in France in 1839. First foundation in the United States in 1868.
General Motherhouse: *La Tour St. Joseph,* St. Pern, France, 35190. Mother, Celine de la Visitation, Supr. Gen.
Province of Brooklyn (1868): *Queen of Peace Residence,* 110-30 221st St., Queens Village, NY 11429. Sr. Genevieve Regina, Prov.
Total number in Province 150.
Ministry in Homes for the Aged.
Represented in the Archdioceses of Boston, Hartford, Philadelphia and New York and in the Dioceses of Albany, Brooklyn, Metuchen, Paterson, Providence and Scranton. Also in Montreal.
Province of Baltimore: *Little Sisters of the Poor,* 601 Maiden Choice Ln., Baltimore, MD 21228-3698. Tel: 410-744-9367; Fax: 410-747-0601. Sr. Mary Bernard du St. Esprit, Prov.
Total number in Province 122.
Ministry in Homes for the Aged.
Represented in the Archdioceses of Baltimore, Cincinnati, Indianapolis, Mobile, New Orleans and Washington and in the Dioceses of Cleveland, Pittsburgh, Richmond, and Toledo.
Province of Chicago: *Little Sisters of the Poor, Chicago Province, Inc.,* 80 W. Northwest Hwy., Palatine, IL 60067-3582. Tel: 847-358-5700; Fax: 847-934-6852. Sr. Gertrude Maiorino, Prov.
Total number in Province 130.
Ministry in Homes for the Aged.
Represented in the Archdioceses of Chicago, Denver, Los Angeles, Louisville, St. Louis, St. Paul-Minneapolis and San Francisco and in the Dioceses of Evansville, Gallup and Kansas City-St. Joseph.

[2345] (P.O.S.C.)—LITTLE WORKERS OF THE SACRED HEARTS (P)

Founded in Italy in 1892. First Foundation in the U.S. in 1948.
General House: Via dei Pamphili 3, 00152, Rome, Italy.
Motherhouse and Novitiate: *Our Lady of Grace Convent,* 635 Glenbrook Rd., Stamford, CT 06906. Tel: 203-348-5531. Sr. Gesuina Gencarelli, P.O.S.C., Supr.
Ministry in Day Care Centers; Catechetics.
Represented in the Archdioceses of Philadelphia and Washington and in the Diocese of Bridgeport.

[2350] (S.L.W.)—SISTERS OF THE LIVING WORD (D)

Founded in the United States in 1975.
General Motherhouse: *The Living Word Center,* 800 N. Fernandez Ave. B, Arlington Heights, IL 60004-5336. Tel: 847-577-5972; Fax: 847-577-5980. Sr. Lea Woll, Coord. Of Spiritual Life.S.L.W., Coord. of Spiritual Life.
Total number in community 76.
Ministry in the field of Academic and Religious Education; Hospitals; Parish Ministry and Social Services.
Represented in the Archdioceses of Chicago, Detroit, New Orleans, and St. Paul-Minneapolis and in the Dioceses of Cleveland, Jackson, Lansing, Rockford, and Sioux City.

[2360] (S.L.)—SISTERS OF LORETTO AT THE FOOT OF THE CROSS (P)

Founded in America in 1812.
General Motherhouse & Novitiate: *Loretto Motherhouse and Novitiate,* Nerinx, KY 40049. Tel: 270-865-5811.
Administrative Office: 300 E. Hampden Ave., Ste. 400, Englewood, CO 80110-2661. Tel: 303-783-0450; Fax: 303-783-0611. Sr. Mary Catherine Rabbitt, S.L., Pres.
Total number in Congregation 325.
Legal Titles: *Loretto Literary and Benevolent Institution.*
Ministry in the field of Academic and Religious Education at all levels; Seminaries; Specialized Education; Health Care-Aging; Community Administration; Pastoral Ministry; Social Justice-Social Service; Administration; Diocesan Offices; Medicine and Nursing; Prayer Retreats; Clerical Offices; Consultants; Spirituality Center.
Represented in the Archdioceses of Chicago, Denver, Indianapolis, Los Angeles, Louisville, Mobile, New Orleans, New York, St. Louis, San Antonio, Santa Fe, Seattle, and Washington and in the Dioceses of Cheyenne, Colorado Springs, El Paso, Galveston-Houston, Kansas City-St. Joseph, Knoxville, Lexington, Oakland, Orange, Orlando, Portland, Pueblo, Rockford, San Diego, San Jose, Wheeling-Charleston and Worcester.

[2370] (I.B.V.M.)—INSTITUTE OF THE BLESSED VIRGIN MARY (LORETTO SISTERS) (P)

Founded in St. Omer, Belgium, 1609. First foundation in Canada in 1847; in the United States in 1880.
Generalate: *Casa Loreto,* Via Massauna 3, Roma, Italy. 00162. Sr. Mary Wright, I.B.V.M., Supr. Gen.
Universal Total in Congregation 219.
Regional Office United States: *Loretto Convent,* P.O. Box 508, Wheaton, IL 60189. Tel: 630-665-3814; Fax: 630-653-4886. Sr. Rosemary Lynch, I.B.V.M., Prov.
Total number in community 86.
Sisters serve and staff: High Schools; Grammar Schools; Missionary Work; Correspondence School; University; Pastoral Ministry; Adult Education; Social Work; Retreat Ministry; Diocesan Office; Director of Religious Education.
Properties owned: *Loretto High School,* Sacramento, CA; *Loretto Development Office; Loretto Convent,* Wheaton, IL; *Loretto Early Childhood Center,* Wheaton, IL; *Loretto Center,* Wheaton, IL.
Represented in the Archdiocese of Chicago and in the Dioceses of Joliet, Marquette, Phoenix, Sacramento and Venice.

[2380] (I.B.V.M.)—INSTITUTE OF THE BLESSED VIRGIN MARY (LORETO SISTERS) (P)

Founded in St. Omer, Belgium, in 1609. Foundation in Arizona, 1954 from the Diocese of Meath, Ireland.
Generalate: Via Massaua 3, 00162, Rome, Italy. Sr. Mary Wright, I.B.V.M., Supr. Gen.
Total number in Congregation 968.
U.S. Regional: *Mary Ward House,* 2521 W. Maryland Ave., Phoenix, AZ 85017. Tel: 602-242-2544. Sr. Raphael Quinn, I.B.V.M., Reg. Supr.
Total number in community 18.
Represented in the Diocese of Phoenix.

[2390] (L.H.C.)—LOVERS OF THE HOLY CROSS SISTERS (D)

Founded in 1670 in Viet Nam by Bishop Pierre Lambert de la Motte. First foundation in the United States in 1976.
Established as an autonomous institute of Consecrated Life of Diocesan Right in 1992.
General Motherhouse: *Holy Cross Convent,* 14700 South Van Ness Ave., Gardena, CA 90249. Tel: 310-768-1906 or 516-0271; Fax: 310-352-6435. Sr. Anne Lanh Thi Tran, L.H.C., Supr. Gen.
Sisters 51; Novices 5; Postulants 4; Aspirants 10; Oblates 2.
Legal Title: *Lovers of the Holy Cross Sisters, Inc.*
Represented in the Archdiocese of Los Angeles and in the Dioceses of Orange and San Bernardino.

[2392] (L.H.C.)—LOVERS OF THE HOLY CROSS SISTERS

(Sisters, Lovers of the Holy Cross)

Founded in Vietnam in 1670 by Bishop Pierre Lambert de la Motte. First foundation in the United States in 1975.

U.S. Foundation: *St. Theresa Convent,* 43 Crown Lane, Westbury, NY 11590. Tel: 516-333-9464. Sr. Theresa Nguyen, L.H.C., Supr.
Legal Title: *Sisters, Lovers of the Holy Cross, Inc.*
Represented in the Diocese of Rockville Centre.

[2400] (M.S.)—MARIAN SISTERS OF THE DIOCESE OF LINCOLN (D)

Marycrest Motherhouse: *Marian Center,* 6765 N. 112th, Waverly, NE 68462. Tel: 402-786-2750; Fax: 402-786-7256. Sr. Bernadette Radek, M.S., Major Supr.
Total number in community 39.
Ministry in the field of Education; Specialized Education; Health Care; Catechetics.
Represented in the Diocese of Lincoln.

[2410] (M.S.C.)—CONGREGATION OF THE MARIANITES OF HOLY CROSS (P)

Founded in France in 1841. First foundation in the United States in 1843.
Congregational Administration Headquarters: 1011 Gallier St., New Orleans, LA 70117. Tel: 504-945-1620. Web site: www.marianites.org. Sr. Mary Kay Kinberger, M.S.C., Congregational Leader.
Total number in North America 165.
Ministry in Diocesan Administration and Parishes; Social & Health Services; and the field of Education.
Legal Holdings or Titles: *Our Lady of Holy Cross Convent,* New Orleans, LA; *Our Lady of Holy Cross College,* New Orleans, LA; *Prompt Succor Nursing Home,* Opelousas, LA; *C'est la Vie (Senior Citizen Independent Living Units),* Opelousas, LA; *Holy Angels Congregational Center,* New Orleans, LA.
Represented in the Archdiocese of New Orleans, and in the Dioceses of Alexandria, Austin, Baton Rouge, Camden, Dallas, Houma-Thibodaux, Lafayette (LA), Lake Charles, Manchester, Paterson and Trenton. Also in Bangladesh, Haiti, Northern Ireland and Canada.

[2420] (S.M.S.M.)—MARIST MISSIONARY SISTERS (MISSIONARY SISTERS OF THE SOCIETY OF MARY) INC. (P)

Founded in France in 1845-1857. First foundation in the United States in Boston, Massachusetts 1922.
Motherhouse: Via Cassia, 1243, Roma, Italia 00189. Universal Total in Congregation 587.
North American Province: *Provincial Office,* 349 Grove St., Waltham, MA 02453-6018. Tel: 781-893-0149; Fax: 781-894-7610. Sr. Georgeanne M. Donovan, S.M.S.M., Prov.
Represented in the Archdioceses of Boston and Oakland and in the Dioceses of Brownsville, Memphis, St. Petersburg and Venice.

[2430] (S.M.)—MARIST SISTERS/CONGREGATION OF MARY (P)

Founded in France 1824 by Venerable John Claude Colin and Jeanne Marie Chavoin.
General Motherhouse: Via Aurelia 292, Rome, Italy, 00165. Sr. Monica O'Brien, S.M., Congregational Leader.
Universal total in Congregation 450.
U.S. Foundation (1956): *Marist Sisters - Congregation of Mary,* 9312 S. Kolmar Ave., Oak Lawn, IL 60454. Tel: 708-636-0259; Fax: 708-636-0259. Sr. Eleanor Keaney, S.M., Prov.
Total number in the community 16.
Ministry in Elementary & Adult Education; Pastoral Ministry; Counseling; Pastoral Care in Hospitals; Physical Therapy; Seminary Formation; Social Ministry.
Represented in the Archdioceses of Chicago and Detroit and in the Dioceses of Laredo and Wheeling-Charleston.

[2440] (S.M.I.)—SISTERS OF MARY IMMACULATE (P)

Catechist Sisters of Mary Immaculate, Help of Christians

Founded in India in 1948 by the late Bishop Louis LaRavoire Morrow, Bishop of Krishnagar, India.
General Motherhouse: *Krishnagar,* Nadia Dist., West Bengal, India 741 101. Sr. Marie Pothanamala, Supr. Gen.
Universal total in Congregation 520.
U.S. Foundation (1981): *Sisters of Mary Immaculate,* R.D. No.5, Box 1231, Leechburg, PA 15656. Tel: 724-845-2828; 836-0449. Sr. Francine Punneliparambil, S.M.I., Delegation Supr.; Sr. Dora Fernandes, S.M.I., Supr.
Total number in the community 6.
Legal Holdings and Titles: *St. Joseph Hall Convent,* Greensburg, PA; *Bishop Morrow Personal Care Home,* Leechburg, PA.

[2450] (S.M.P.)—SISTERS OF MARY OF THE PRESENTATION (P)

Founded in France. First foundation in the United States in 1903.
General Motherhouse: *Broons,* Cotes-du-Nord, France. Sr. Anne Grall, Supr. Gen.
U.S. Provincial House & Novitiate at Maryvale: 11550 River Rd., Valley City, ND 58072. Tel: 701-845-2864. Sr. Marlyss Dionne, S.M.P., Prov.
Total number in the community 57.
Ministry in the field of Religious and Academic Education at all levels; Parish Ministry; Hospitals and Home Health Agencies.
Properties owned: *St. Margaret's Hospital,* Spring Valley, IL; *Prairieland Home Health Agency,* Fargo, ND.
Represented in the Archdiocese of Chicago and in the Dioceses of Cheyenne, Fargo and Peoria.

[2460] (S.M.R.)—SOCIETY OF MARY REPARATRIX (P)

Founded in France in 1857. First foundation in the United States in 1908.
Generalate: *Society Di Maria Riparatrice,* Via dei Lucchesi 3, Roma, Italia 00187. Sr. Christine Barriere, Supr. Gen.
Total International Membership Sisters 900.
U.S. Region: 17320 Grange Rd., Riverview, MI, 48192. Tel: 734-285-4510; Fax: 734-285-8147. Sr. Margaret Hoey, S.M.R., Reg.
Total number in the community 29.
Represented in the Archdioceses of Detroit, Miami and New York and in the Diocese of Brooklyn.

[2470] (M.M.)—MARYKNOLL SISTERS OF ST. DOMINIC (P)

Founded in New York 1912.
Orientation Program: Maryknoll Sisters. Co-Dirs. Sr. Mary Ellen Mertens, M.M.; Sr. Beatrice Carvalho, M.M.
Center: *Maryknoll Sisters Center,* Maryknoll, NY 10545-0311. Tel: 914-941-7575. Sr. Suzanne Moore, M.M., Community Pres.; Sr. Ellen Mc Donald, M.M., Vice Pres.; Sr. Connie Krautkremer, M.M., Team Member; Sr. Jeanne Rancourt, M.M., Team Member; Sr. Carol Hassey, M.M., Center Coord.; Sr. Mary Anne O'Donnell, M.M., Center Coord.; Sr. Charlotte Hobler, M.M., Center Coord.
Total number in the Congregation 624.
Legal Titles and Holdings: *Maryknoll Sisters of St. Dominic, Inc.; Maryknoll Mission Institute.*
Represented in the Archdioceses of Baltimore, Boston, Chicago, Cincinnati, Detroit, Hartford, Los Angeles, Louisville, Newark, New York, Philadelphia, Portland (OR), St. Louis, San Francisco, and Washington and in the Dioceses of Albany, Baker, Brooklyn, Duluth, Gallup, Honolulu, Galveston-Houston, Kansas City-St. Joseph, Madison, Manchester, Oakland, Palm Beach, Phoenix, Providence, Raleigh, Rochester, Rockville Centre, Sacramento, St. Augustine, St. Petersburg, San Diego, San Jose, Scranton, Springfield, Stockton and Winona.

[2480] (M.M.M.)—MEDICAL MISSIONARIES OF MARY (P)

Founded in Nigeria in 1937. First United States Foundation in 1950.
General Motherhouse: *Rosemount,* Booterstown Ave., Blackrock, Co. Dublin, Ireland. Mother Mary Martin, M.M.M., Foundress; Sr. Philomena Sheerin, Congregational Leader.
Medical Missionaries of Mary: 563 Minneford Ave., City Island, NY 10464-1118. Tel: 718-885-0945; Fax: 718-885-0010. Sr. Siobhan Corkery, M.M.M., Zonal Coord.; Sr. Therese McDonough, M.M.M., Area Leader U.S.A.
Total number in the Congregation 414.
Represented in the Archdioceses of Boston, Chicago, and New York and in the Dioceses of Richmond and San Diego.

[2490] M.M.S.)—MEDICAL MISSION SISTERS (P)

Generalate: London, England. Sr. Elizabeth Koonthanam, M.M.S., Society Coord.
Universal total in Congregation 662.
North American Headquarters (1925): 8400 Pine Rd., Philadelphia, PA 19111. Tel: 215-742-6100; Fax: 215-342 3948. Sr. Joan Foley, M.M.S., North American Coord.
Total number in North America 134.
Legal Titles: *Society of Catholic Medical Missionaries, Inc.; Society of Catholic Medical Missionaries Generalate, Inc.*
Represented in the Archdioceses of Anchorage, Baltimore, Boston, Chicago, Cincinnati, Hartford, Louisville, New York, Philadelphia, Santa Fe, Seattle, and Washington and in the Dioceses of Arlington, Camden, El Paso, Gallup, Harrisburg, Las Cruces, Orange, Palm Beach, Richmond, St. Petersburg, San Diego, Savannah and Tucson. Also in Mexico.

[2500] (M.S.J.)—MEDICAL SISTERS OF ST. JOSEPH (P)

Founded in Kerala, South India, 1946.
General Motherhouse: *Dharmagiri,* P.O. Kothamangalam, Kerala, South India 686691. Mother Nora, M.S.J., Supr. Gen.
U.S. Foundation (1985): *Medical Sisters of St. Joseph,* 3435 E. Funston, Wichita, KS 67218. Tel: 316-686-4746. Sr. Audrey, M.S.J., Supr.
Total number in Congregation 800.
Ministry as Health Care Apostolates.
Represented in the Diocese of Wichita.

[2510] (M.M.B.)—MERCEDARIAN MISSIONARIES OF BERRIZ (P)

Order originated in Berriz, Spain 1548.Transformed into a missionary institute in 1930 in Spain. First foundation in U.S. in 1946 in Kansas City, MO.
Generalate: *Mercedarie Missionarie di Berriz,* Viale Polo 10, Rome, Italy. 00198 Tel: 39-068-41-3441. Sr. Arantzazu Lerchundi, M.M.B. Gen. Coord.
U.S. Regional House: *Mercedarian Missionaries of Berriz,* 2205 Hughes Rd. 101B, Liberty, MO 64068-7985. Tel: 816-781-8202; Fax: 816-781-8205. E-mail: mmbus@earthlink.net. Sr. Betty Preston, M.M.B. Reg. Rep.
Total number in the Region 28.
Ministries in Health and Pastoral Care.
Property sponsored: *Our Lady of Mercy Country Home.* Liberty, MO 64068.
Represented in the Dioceses of Kansas City-St. Joseph. Also in Japan, Taiwan, Philippines, Guam, Federated States of Micronesia, Republic of Palau, Commonwealth of the Northern Marianas, Peru, Ecuador, Guatemala, Nicaragua, Mexico, Democratic Republic of Congo, Spain and Rome, Italy.

[2515] (C.M.S.)—CASHEL MERCY SISTERS (D)

U.S. Foundation (St. Mel's Convent): *Congregation of the Sisters of Mercy of Ireland,* P.O. Box 1180, Fair Oaks, CA 95628. Tel: 916-967-9504. Sr. Kathleen O'Dwyer, Contact Person.
Represented in the Diocese of Sacramento.

[2516] (S.M.)—SISTERS OF MERCY (P)

Founded in Ireland in 1831.
Motherhouse: *Convent of Mercy,* Carrick-on-Suir, Ireland.
U.S. Foundation (1956): *St. John's Convent of Mercy,* 11154 San Pablo Ave., El Cerrito, CA 94530. Tel: 415-233-6769.
Other U.S. Convents (1960): *St. Nicholas Convent,* 12816 S. El Monte Ave., Los Altos Hills, CA 94022. Tel: 415-948-0775.
Professed Sisters 10.
Represented in the Dioceses of Oakland, San Jose, Santa Rosa and Sioux Falls.

[2517] SISTERS OF MERCY (P)

Founded in Dublin, 1831.
Headquarters: Dublin, Ireland.
Holy Infant Convent: 239 Nancy Pl., Ballwin, MO 63021. Tel: 636-391-1528. Sr. Laurentia Cusack, Facilitator.
Total number in the community 3.
Legal Title: *Sisters of Mercy, Ireland.*
Ministry in Education & Pastoral Ministries.
Represented in the Archdiocese of St. Louis.

[2519] (R.S.M.)—RELIGIOUS SISTERS OF MERCY OF ALMA, MICHIGAN (P)

The Religious Sisters of Mercy of Alma was officially founded on September 1, 1973; Diocesan approval on Jan. 25, 1974; Constitutions of Community approved March 17, 1978; Pontifical Status fully approved June 18, 1982. Final approval of constitution May 31, 1991.
Motherhouse and Novitiate: *Religious Sisters of Mercy,* 1965 Michigan Ave., Alma, MI 48801. Tel: 989-463-6035. Mother Mary Quentin Sheridan, R.S.M.
Total number in the community 60.
Represented in the Archdioceses of Denver, Hartford, Portland (OR) and Washington and in the Dioceses of Lansing, Saginaw, Tulsa and Winona. Also in Canada, Germany and Italy.

[2520] (R.S.M.)—SISTERS OF MERCY (P)

Founded in the United States in 1955.
General Motherhouse: *Congregation of the Sisters of Mercy,* Elblana Ave., Dun Laoghlaire, Dublin, 01-2800448 Ireland. Sr. Breege O'Neill, Supr. Gen.
U.S. Foundation: *St. Joan of Arc,* 500 S.W. Fourth Ave., Boca Raton, FL 33432. Tel: 561-368-6655. Sr. Kathleen Sweeney, Communications Coord.
Professed Sisters 4.
Represented in the Diocese of Palm Beach.
Sisters of Mercy (1971): 5392 S.W. 33rd Ave., Ft. Lauderdale, FL 33312. Tel: 954-989-8291. Sr. Maura Bane, Prov. Supr.

Total number in the community 8.
Ministry in the field of Education; Parish Work.
Represented in the Archdiocese of Miami.
U.S. Address: 2766 Navajo Rd., El Cajon, CA 92020. Tel: 619-465-2233.
Professed Sisters 2.
Ministry in Hospital, Schools and Parishes.
Represented in the Diocese of San Diego.

[2549] (R.S.M.)—SISTERS OF MERCY (SLIGO) (P)

Founded in Ireland in 1846. First foundation in United States in 1956.
Generalate: *St. Peter's Convent,* Athlone Roscommon, Ireland. Sr. Patricia Kelly, Supr. Gen.
American Region: 4825 H St., San Bernardino, CA 92447. Tel: 909-886-6172; Fax: 909-883-5954. Sr. Maura Feeley, Reg. Supr.
Total number in the community 25.
Ministry in the field of Religious and Academic Education; Parishes; Social Services; Diocesan Offices.
Represented in the Dioceses of Orange, San Bernardino and San Diego.

[2560] SISTERS OF MERCY (D)

Founded in Ireland.
General Motherhouse: *Sisters of Mercy - U.S. Province,* Redlands, CA 92374.
U.S. Address (1963): *St. James School,* 603 West Ave., Gulfport, MS 39507. Tel: 288-896-6631. Sr. Teresa O'Connell, Prov.
Total number in the community 7.
Represented in the Diocese of Biloxi.

[2575] (R.S.M.)—SISTERS OF MERCY OF THE AMERICAS

Catherine McAuley founded the Sisters of Mercy in Dublin, Ireland, in 1831. Ten years later, she received confirmation of the Rule by Pope Gregory XVI. In 1843 the Sisters of Mercy established their first U.S.A. foundation in Pittsburgh. In 1929 several of the independent congregations amalgamated to form the Sisters of Mercy of the Union. In 1991 the members of the nine provinces of the Union and of 16 other Mercy congregations founded the Sisters of Mercy of the Americas, with its 25 regional communities.
Institute Administrative Offices: 8380 Colesville Rd., #300, Silver Spring, MD 20910-6264. Tel: 301-587-0423; Fax: 301-587-0533. Sr. Marie Chin, R.S.M., Pres.
Total in the Congregation 4,888.
Legal Title: *Mercy Action, Inc. is separately incorporated to support works directed toward systemic change. McAuley Institute, Inc.* is separately incorporated to foster the development of low-income housing ministry as a work of mercy. *Mercy Volunteer Corps, Inc.* is separately incorporated to conduct a volunteer lay ministry program to further the works of mercy.

Albany (P)

Regional Community of Albany (1863): 310 S. Manning Blvd., Albany, NY 12208. Tel: 518-437-3000; Fax: 518-437-3030. Sr. Katherine Graber, R.S.M., Pres.
Total number in the community 143.
Ministry in the field of Education; Health Services; Pastoral Ministry; Social Services.
Properties owned or sponsored: *Maria College; St. Peter's Hospital; St. Peter's Health Care Services; McAuley Living Services.*
Represented in the Archdiocese of Anchorage, Hartford, New York and Washington and in the Dioceses of Albany, Portland, Rochester and Syracuse.

Auburn (P)

Auburn Regional Community: *Institute of the Sisters of Mercy of the Americas,* 535 Sacramento St., Auburn, CA 95603. Tel: 530-887-2000. Sr. Sheila Browne, R.S.M., Pres.
Total number in the community 82.
Ministry in the field of Education; Parishes; Diocesan Offices; Health Care; Pastoral Ministries; Housing; Social Ministries.
Properties owned, staffed or sponsored: *Our Lady of Mercy Convent,* Auburn, CA; *McAuley Convent Russell House; Mercy Convent,* Sacramento, CA; *Mercy Convent,* Redding, CA; *Mercy San Juan Convent,* Fair Oaks, CA; *Mercy Convent,* Folsom, CA; *Mercy Convent,* Carmichael, CA.
Represented in the Archdioceses of Washington and in the Dioceses of Fresno, Reno and Sacramento.

Baltimore (P)

Sisters of Mercy, Regional Community of Baltimore: 1322 E. Northern Pkwy, Baltimore, MD 21239-1919. Tel: 410-435-4400. Sr. Barbara Wheeley, R.S.M., Pres.
Total number in community 197.
Legal Holdings and Titles: *Sisters of Mercy, Baltimore, Inc.*
Properties owned or sponsored: High Schools 3; Hospitals 4; Retirement Facilities for Sisters 4; Leisure-Retreat Houses for Sisters 4; Residential Program for Homeless Women; Theological Center; Neighborhood Center for Families; Long-term care facilities 2.
Sisters serve and staff: USCCB post; Elementary Schools; High Schools; Institutions of Higher Education; Multi-Level Long-Term Care Facility & Health Systems; Diocesan Child Care Homes; Pastoral Ministry Programs in Parishes; Diocesan Ministries; National Conference of Catholic Bishops; United States Catholic Conference.
Represented in the Archdioceses of Atlanta, Baltimore, Mobile and Washington and in the Dioceses of Birmingham, Pensacola-Tallahassee, Savannah and Wilmington. Also in Belize & Guyana.

Brooklyn (P)

Brooklyn Regional Community (1855): 273 Willoughby Ave, Brooklyn, NY 11205. Tel: 718-622-5750. Sr. Mary Waters, Pres.
Total number in the community 242.
Properties owned or sponsored: *Angel Guardian Children and Family Services; Mercy Home for Children; Catherine McAuley H.S.,* Brooklyn, NY; *St. Mary's Children and Family Services; Our Lady of Mercy Academy,* Syosset, NY; *Mercy H.S.,* Riverhead, NY.
Sisters serve and staff: Elementary and High Schools; Institutions of Higher Education; Child Care Institutions; Pastoral Ministry Programs and Spirituality and Retreat Programs.
Represented in the Archdioceses of Baltimore, and New Orleans and in the Dioceses of Brooklyn, Orlando, Rockville Centre and Toledo. Also in Panama.

Buffalo (P)

Regional Community of Buffalo: 625 Abbott Rd., Buffalo, NY 14220. Tel: 716-826-5051; Fax: 716-826-1518. Sr. Nancy Hoff, R.S.M., Pres.
Total number in the community 178.
Ministry in the field of Education at all levels; Catholic Charities; Parish & Pastoral Ministry; Health Care; Social Services.
Legal Holdings, Titles and Sponsored Works: *Trocaire College, Mount Mercy Academy,* Buffalo, NY; *Co-sponsor: Catholic Health System,* Buffalo, NY; *Catholic Health East,* Radnor, PA.
Represented in the Archdiocese of Washington and in the Dioceses of Buffalo, Providence, Richmond and Rochester. Also in the Philippine Islands.

Burlingame (P)

Regional Community of Burlingame (1854): 2300 Adeline Dr., Burlingame, CA 94010-5599. Tel: 650-340-7410. Fax: 650-347-2550. Sr. Mary Waskowiak, Pres.; Sr. Marilyn Gouailhardou, Archivist.
Total number in the community 185.
Legal Title: *Sisters of Mercy,* Burlingame.
Ministry in Health Care; Religious and Academic Education; Prison Ministry; Spirituality and Conference Center; Foreign Missions; Social Services including housing; Retreats; Diocesan Offices.
Represented in the Archdioceses of Los Angeles, and San Francisco and in the Dioceses of Fresno, Oakland, Orange, Phoenix, Sacramento, San Diego, San Jose, Stockton and Santa Rosa. Also in Peru & Romania.

Cedar Rapids (P)

Regional Community of Cedar Rapids: *Sacred Heart Convent Motherhouse,* 1125 Prairie Dr., N.E., Cedar Rapids, IA 52402-4737. Tel: 319-364-5196; Fax: 319-364-7383. Sr. Kathy Thornton, R.S.M., Pres.; Sr. Shari Sutherland, R.S.M., Vice Pres.
Total number in the community 86.
Ministry in the field of Academic and Religious Education at all levels; Parish Ministry; Pastoral Care; Foreign Mission work; Social Services; Hospitals; Literacy Programs; Transitional Housing; Social Justice Ministries; Home.
Properties owned or sponsored: *Mount Mercy College; Mercy Medical Center; Sisters of Mercy Charitable Trust; Catherine McAuley Center for Women,* Cedar Rapids, IA; *Co-sponsor: Mercy Housing, Inc.,* Denver, CO.
Represented in the Archdioceses of Cincinnati, Dubuque, Milwaukee, New York, St. Louis, and Washington and in the Dioceses of Brownsville, Davenport, Des Moines, Helena, Sioux City, St. Cloud, Wheeling-Charleston, and Winona. Also in Peru.

Chicago (P)

Regional Community of Chicago: *Administrative Center,* 10024 S. Central Park Ave., Chicago, IL 60655-3132. Tel: 773-779-6011; Fax: 773-779-6094. Sr. Joy Clough, R.S.M. Pres.
Total number in community 260.
Legal Holdings and Titles: *Sisters of Mercy of the Americas, Regional Community of Chicago; Mercy Housing Corporation,* Chicago, IL; *Sisters of Mercy of the Americas, Regional Community of Chicago Charitable Trust.*
Properties owned and sponsored: *University 1; High Schools 1; Hospitals 1; Residence 1; Retreat Houses 1; Health System 1; co-sponsors Provena Health.*
Sisters serve and staff: Education at all Levels; Social Services; Pastoral Services; Health Care; Spirituality; Foreign Missions.
Represented in the Archdioceses of Boston, Chicago, Milwaukee and St. Louis and in the Dioceses of Charleston, Colorado Springs, Davenport, El Paso, Joliet, Knoxville, Peoria, Phoenix, Rockford, St. Petersburg, and Springfield (IL). Also in Honduras.

Cincinnati (P)

Regional Community of Cincinnati: 2335 Grandview Ave., Cincinnati, OH 45206. Tel: 513-221-1800; Fax: 513-221-0207. Sr. Marjorie Rudemiller, R.S.M. Pres.
Total number in community 314.
Sisters serve and staff: Academic Education at all levels; Parish & Diocesan Ministry; Health and Child-Care; Hospitals and Schools of Nursing; Homes for the Aged; Retreat and Renewal Center; Special Education.
Represented in the Archdioceses of Boston, Cincinnati, Detroit, Louisville, Newark, Omaha, and Washington and in the Dioceses of Brownsville, Charlotte, Cleveland, Knoxville, Las Cruces, Lansing, Memphis, Nashville, Oakland, Orlando, Owensboro, Portland, Richmond, and Toledo. Also in Jamaica, West Indies.

Connecticut (P)

Regional Community of Connecticut: *Sisters of Mercy of the Americas,* 249 Steele Rd., West Hartford, CT 06117. Tel: 860-232-8602; Fax: 860-233-0065. E-mail: edooling@mercyct.org. Sr. Eileen M. Dooling, R.S.M., Reg. Pres.; Sr. Dolores Liptak, Archivist.
Total number in the community 218.
Legal Title: *Sisters of Mercy of Connecticut, Inc.*
Ministry in the field of Religious and Academic Education at all levels; School for Exceptional Children; Spirituality and Retreat Work; Social Services and; Health Care.
Properties owned and sponsored: *Mercyknoll, Inc.; Saint Mary Home, Inc.; McAuley Center, Inc.; The Academy of Our Lady of Mercy - Lauralton Hall, Inc.; Saint Joseph College, Inc.; Our Lady of Mercy School, Inc.; Mercy Housing and Shelter, Inc.; Mercy Center, Inc.; Mercy Community Health, Inc.; Mercy Community Homecare, Inc.*
Represented in the Archdioceses of Boston, Hartford, Miami, New York, and Portland and in the Dioceses of Bridgeport, Burlington, Lexington, Manchester, Norwich, Pittsburgh, Providence, Springfield, Wheeling-Charleston, Wichita and Worcester. Also in Belize, Guatemala and Haiti.

Dallas (P)

Regional Community of Dallas: *Administrative Office,* P.O. Box 369, Dallas, PA 18612-0369. Tel: 570-675-1966; Fax: 570-675-9051. Sr. Sharon Gallagher, R.S.M., Pres. Sr. Susan Marie Nowalis, R.S.M., Community Archivist.
Total number in community 276.
Ministry in the field of Education; Hospital & Health Care; Skilled Nursing; Pastoral Services; Social Services; South American Ministries.
Properties owned or sponsored: *Mercy Center; College Misericordia; Mount Aloysius College; Mercy Center Preschool; Catherine McAuley Center; Neuman Housing Services, Inc.; Project REMAIN.*
Represented in the Archdioceses of Baltimore, Miami, New York, and Philadelphia and in the Dioceses of Altoona-Johnstown, Brooklyn, Charlotte, Greensburg, Harrisburg, Pittsburgh, Rockville Centre, Scranton, and Springfield-Cape Girardeau. Also in Guyana, South America.

Detroit (P)

Regional Community of Detroit: *Sisters of Mercy,* 29000 Eleven Mile Rd., Farmington Hills, MI 48336. Tel: 248-476-8000; Fax: 248-476-4222. Sr. Linda Werthman, R.S.M., Pres.; Sr. Michaeline Lewandowski, R.S.M., Archivist.
Total number in community 224.
Legal Title: *Sisters of Mercy - Regional Community of Detroit; Sisters of Mercy of the Americas, Regional Community of Detroit, Charitable Trusts I and II.*
Properties sponsored: *Mercy High School,* Farmington Hills, MI; *Colegio Santa Ethnea, Bella Vista, Argentina; Mercy Center,* Farmington Hills, MI; *Mercy Education Project,* Detroit, MI. *Properties Co-Sponsored: University of Detroit Mercy,* Detroit, MI; *Our Lady of Guadalupe Middle School,* Detroit, MI. *Participating Entity: Catholic Health Ministries,* Novi MI.
Represented in the Archdioceses of Baltimore, Detroit, Dubuque, Hartford, Louisville, Milwaukee, San Antonio, and Washington and in the Dioceses of Charlotte, Cleveland, Columbus, Gaylord, Grand Rapids, Kalamazoo, Kansas City-St. Joseph, Lansing, Lexington, Sacramento, and Saginaw. Also in Argentina.

Erie (P)

Regional Community of Erie: 444 E. Grandview Blvd., Erie, PA 16504. Tel: 814-824-2516; Fax: 814-824-2127.

Sr. JoAnne Courneen, Reg. Pres.; Sr. Edith Langiotti, Archivist.
Total number in the community 63.
Legal Title: *Institute of the Sisters of Mercy of the Americans - Regional Community of Erie.*
Ministry in the field of Religious and Academic Education at all levels; Prison Ministry; Health Care Ministry; Social Services.
Properties owned and or sponsored: *Mercyhurst College; Mercyhurst Preparatory School; Mercy Center for the Arts, (Preschool); Mercy Center on Aging; Mercy Terrace Apartments, (Housing for Elderly); Mercy Center for Women.*
Represented in the Archdiocese of Washington and the Dioceses of Erie and Savannah.

Merion (P)

Regional Community of Merion: *Motherhouse of the Sisters of Mercy,* Merion, PA 19066. Tel: 610-664-6650; Fax: 610-664-3429. Sr. Christine McCann, R.S.M., Reg. Pres.; Sr. Marian Francis Kelly, R.S.M., Local Coord.
Total number in the community 399.
Legal Title: *Sisters of Mercy of Merion, PA.*
Properties owned, staffed or sponsored: *Gwynedd Mercy College; McAuley Convent; Merion Mercy Academy; Waldron Mercy Academy; Gwynedd Mercy Academy; Mercy Vocational High School; St. Mary Residence; Walsingham Academy; Mercy Health System.*
Sisters serve and staff: Religious and academic education at all levels; Hospices; House of Prayer; Social service organizations.
Represented in the Archdioceses of Anchorage, Atlanta, Baltimore, New York, Philadelphia, St. Louis, and Washington and in the Dioceses of Allentown, Boise, Buffalo, Camden, Gallup, Galveston-Houston, Orlando, Providence, Raleigh, Richmond, Scranton, Trenton, Tucson, Wheeling-Charleston, Wilmington and Worcester. Also in Italy, Peru, Bolivia.

New Hampshire (P)

Motherhouse of the Sisters of Mercy Inc: *Sisters of Mercy of the Americas-Regional Community of New Hampshire (1858),* 21 Searles Rd., Windham, NH 03087-1297. Tel: 603-893-6550; Fax: 603-893-2413. Sr. Ellen Kurtz, Pres.
Total number in the community 152.
Ministry in the field of Academic Education at all levels; Nursing Homes; Hospitals.
Properties owned or sponsored: *Marian Court College,* Swampscott, MA; *Mt. St. Mary Academy,* Manchester, NH; *Manchester Convent of the Sisters of Mercy; Mount Saint Mary Corporation of the Sisters of Mercy Frances Warde House, Inc.,* Manchester, NH; *Warde Health Center, Inc.,* Windham, NH; *McAuley Commons, Inc.,* Windham, NH.
Represented in the Archdioceses of Baltimore and Boston and in the Dioceses of Fall River, Orlando, Manchester, Portland (ME), Providence, Pueblo and St. Augustine.

New Jersey (P)

Regional Community of New Jersey: 1645 U.S. Hwy 22, W., Watchung, NJ 07069-6587. Tel: 908-756-0994; Fax: 908-754-0164. Sr. Diane Szubrowski, R.S.M., Reg. Pres.; Sr. Innocent Dolan, R.S.M., Archivist.
Total number in the community 267.
Legal Title: *Sisters of Mercy of New Jersey.*
Ministry in the field of Religious and Academic Education at all levels; Health Care and Hospital Chaplaincy; Diocesan and Tribunal Administration; Parish and Prison Ministry; School for Special Education; Day Center for Senior Citizens; Child Day Care Center; House of Prayer.
Properties owned or sponsored: *McAuley Hall; McAuley School for the Exceptional Child,* Watchung, NJ; *Georgian Court College of the Sisters of Mercy,* Lakewood, NJ; *Mount Saint Mary Academy,* Watchung, NJ; *Mount Saint Mary House of Prayer,* Watchung, NJ; *Mercy Center,* Asbury Park, NJ.
Represented in the Archdioceses of New York, Newark, Philadelphia and Washington and in the Dioceses of Camden, Charlotte, Las Cruces, Metuchen, Paterson, Rochester, Santa Rosa, Trenton and Wilmington.

New York (P)

Regional Community of New York: *Sisters of Mercy,* 150 Ridge Rd., Hartsdale, NY 10530. Tel: 914-328-3200; Fax: 914-328-3761. Sr. Suzanne Elliott, R.S.M., Reg.
Total number in community 154.
Legal Title: *Sisters of Mercy, Inc.*
Ministry in the field of Academic Education at all levels; Health and Child care; Special Education; Social Services; Spirituality and Counseling centers; Catechetical services; Pastoral Ministry.
Properties owned and sponsored: *Our Lady of Victory Academy,* NY; *St. Catharine Academy,* NY; *Nazareth Home for Boys,* Leicester, MA; *Uihlein Mercy Center (Skilled Nursing Facility),* Lake Placid, NY; *Mercy Healthcare Center, Inc.,* Tupper Lake, NY; *St. Joseph's Home,* Worcester, MA; *Mercy Center,* Bronx, NY.
Represented in the Archdioceses of Hartford, Los Angeles, Newark, and New York and in the Dioceses of Ogdensburg, Rockville Centre, St. Petersburg and Worcester.

North Carolina (P)

Sisters of Mercy of the Americas - Regional Community of North Carolina: *Mercy Administration Center,* 101 Mercy Dr., Belmont, NC, 28012. Tel: 704-829-5260; Fax: 704-829-5267. Sr. Mary Rosalind Picot, R.S.M., Pres.; Sr. Mary Andrew Ray, R.S.M., Community Archivist.
Total number in the community 113.
Legal Title: *Sisters of Mercy of NC, Inc.*
Ministry in the field of Religious and Academic Education at all levels; AIDS Ministry; Pastoral Ministry; Health Care Ministry; Developmental Center for Handicapped Children; Social Work; Daycare and Preschool Centers; Transitional Housing for homeless women and children; Psycho-Spiritual Programs.
Represented in the Archdioceses of Agana, Dubuque, Hartford, and St. Louis and in the Dioceses of Albany, Arlington, Belleville, Caroline Islands Charlotte, Oakland, Orlando, Pensacola-Tallahassee and Wheeling-Charleston.

Omaha (P)

Sisters of Mercy of the Americas, Regional Community of Omaha: *Sisters of Mercy Regional Office,* 7262 Mercy Rd., Omaha, NE 68124. Tel: 402-393-8225; Fax: 402-393-8145. Sr. Patricia Forret, R.S.M., Pres.; Sr. Lynn Holmes, R.S.M., Community Archivist.
Total number in community 228; Associates 132.
Ministry in the field of Education at all levels; Hospitals; Nursing Centers and Long Term Care Facilities for the Aged; Diocesan and Parish Programs and Services Social Service; Housing for Families and Elderly.
Properties owned or sponsored: *Knowles Mercy Center,* Waterloo, NE; *Mercy High School,* Omaha, NE; *Health and Retirement Plan of the Sisters of Mercy of the Americas Health System of Mercy,* Omaha, NE; *McAuley Ministry Fund,* Omaha, NE; *Mercy Consolidated Asset Management Program,* Omaha, NE; *Regional Community of Omaha. Co-sponsor: Catholic Health Initiatives,* Denver, CO; *Mercy Housing Inc.,* Denver, CO.
Represented in the Archdioceses of Chicago, Denver, Detroit, Dubuque, Kansas City in Kansas, Omaha, Portland (OR), Santa Fe, Seattle, St. Louis, St. Paul-Minneapolis, San Francisco and Washington and in the Dioceses of Bismarck, Boise, Colorado Springs, Des Moines, Fargo, Fresno, Great Falls Billings, Kansas City-St. Joseph, Las Cruces, Lincoln, Oakland, Orange, Phoenix, Rochester, Sacramento, Salt Lake City, San Diego and Springfield-Cape Girardeau, also in Mexico.

Pittsburgh (P)

Regional Community of Pittsburgh (1843): 3333 Fifth Ave., Pittsburgh, PA 15213. Tel: 412-578-6225; Fax: 412-578-6180. Sr. Georgine Scarpino R.S.M., Pres.; Sr. Patricia Hodge, R.S.M., Community Archivist.
Total number in the community 172.
Legal Titles & Holdings: *Carlow College; Pittsburgh Mercy Health System, Inc.; The Mercy Hospital of Pittsburgh; Pittsburgh Mercy Foundation; The INTERSECTION,* Pittsburgh, PA; *St. Pius X Residence,* Pittsburgh, PA; *Holy Cross Health Ministries, Inc.; Holy Cross Hospital,* Fort Lauderdale, FL.
Ministry in the field of Education and Health Services.
Represented in the Archdiocese of Miami and in the Dioceses of Erie, Greensburg, Orlando, and Pittsburgh. Also in Honduras, Peru and Puerto Rico.

Portland (P)

Regional Community of Portland: *St. Joseph's Convent Motherhouse,* 605 Stevens Ave., Portland, ME 04103. Tel: 207-797-7861; Fax: 207-797-0146. Sr. Jean Little, R.S.M., Pres.; Sr. Mary Shaun Sevigny, R.S.M., Community Archivist.
Total number in the community 107.
Legal Title: *St. Joseph's Convent and Hospital.*
Ministry in the field of Education; Health Services; Diocesan & Pastoral Services; Social Services.
Represented in the Dioceses of Manchester, Pensacola-Tallahassee, Portland (ME) and Springfield in Massachusetts. Also in the Bahamas.

Providence (P)

Regional Community of Providence: *Sisters of Mercy of the Americas,* 15 Highland View Rd., Cumberland, RI 02864-1124. Tel: 401-333-6333; Fax: 401-333-6450. Sr. Patricia Combies, R.S.M., Pres.; Sr. Rose Marie Rocha, R.S.M., Community Archivist.
Total number in community 350.
Legal Holdings or Titles: *Sisters of Mercy of Providence, Inc.; Mount St. Rita Health Centre, Inc.; Mercymount Country Day School; Mercy Lodge House of Hospitality,* Cumberland, RI; *St. Mary Academy,* East Providence, RI; *Salve Regina University,* Newport, RI; *McAuley House McAuley Village,* Providence, RI.
Sisters serve and staff: Houses of Prayer; Hospitality Houses; Transitional House; Literacy Centers; Nursing Home; University; High Schools; Elementary Schools; Office of Peace and Justice; Diocesan Offices; Preschool and Day Care; Education for Special Groups; Health Services; Pastoral Care; Religious Education; Parish Ministry Centers; Social Service; Spirituality and Counseling Services; Foreign Missionary work.
Represented in the Archdioceses of Baltimore, Boston, Chicago, Philadelphia, St. Louis, and Washington and in the Dioceses of Brooklyn, Fall River, Honolulu, Ogdensburg, Pittsburgh, Providence, and Richmond. Also in Belize and Honduras.

Rochester (P)

Regional Community of Rochester (1857): 1437 Blossom Rd., Rochester, NY 14610. Tel: 585-228-2710, Fax: 585-288-2756. Sr. Sheila Stevenson, R.S.M.
Total number in the community 203.
Ministry in the field of Education at all levels; Inner City and Urban Renewal Programs; Religious Education Coords.; Parish Associates; Campus Ministry; Social Work; Rural Ministry; Prayer Ministry; Ministry with the Aging; Hospital Ministry; Parish Visitation; Health Apostolates; AIDS Ministry; Foreign Missions (Chile); Care of Foster Children; Ministry to Pregnant Women.
Properties owned: *Our Lady of Mercy High School,* Rochester, NY; *Mercy Prayer Center,* Rochester, NY; *Mercy Motherhouse,* Rochester, NY.
Represented in the Archdioceses of Atlanta and Washington and in the Dioceses of Buffalo, Jackson, Palm Beach, Rochester, St. Petersburg, San Jose, Toledo and Venice. Also in Chile.

St. Louis (P)

Regional Community of St. Louis: *Sisters of Mercy,* 2039 N. Geyer Rd., St. Louis, MO 63131-3399. Tel: 314-966-4313. Sr. Richard Mary Burke, R.S.M., Reg. Pres.
Total number in community 263.
Ministry in the following areas: Hospitals; Ambulatory Health Care Center; Long Term Care; Social Work Centers; Education Centers; Care and Counseling; Ministry to Elderly; Parish Ministry-Pastoral Care-Lay Ministry; Universities and Colleges; High Schools; Elementary Schools; Education Research Programs; Schools for Exceptional Children; Adult Education; Parish Directors of Religious Education-Coordinator of Religious Education; staffing of Diocesan Offices; Conference/Retreat; On-Going Development Vocation/incorporation ministry; Novitiate; Creative Spirituality Department/Office of Mercy/Associates-Volunteers.
Properties owned or sponsored: *Mercy Center,* St. Louis, MO; *Sisters of Mercy Health System; Hospitals; St. Edward Health Facilities of Logan County-dba North Logan Mercy Hospital,* Paris, AR; *St. Edward Mercy Medical Center,* Fort Smith, AR; *St. Edward Health Facilities of Franklin County dba Mercy Hospital / Turner Memorial,* Ozark, AR; *St. Joseph's Mercy Health Center,* Hot Springs, AR; *St. Edward Health Facilities of Scott County-dba Mercy Hospital of Scott County; Mercy Village,* Waldron, AR; *Mercy Health System of Kansas, Inc., dba Mercy Hospital,* Independence, KS; *Mercy Health System of Kansas, Inc.,dba Mercy Hospital,* Fort Scott, KS; *Mercy Memorial Health Center,* Ardmore, OK; *St. Francis Hospital,* Mountain View, MO; *St. John's Mercy Medical Center,* St. Louis, MO; *St. John's Regional Health Center,* Springfield, MO; *St. John's Mercy Hospital,* Washington, MO; *St. Mary-Rogers Memorial Hospital,* Rogers, AR; *Mercy Health Center, Inc.,* Oklahoma City, OK; *Mercy Crest Housing, Inc.,* Barling, AR; *Sisters of Mercy Ministries,* New Orleans, LA; *St. John's Cassville, Inc.,* Springfield, MO; *St. John's Aurora, Inc.,* Springfield, MO. *High Schools: Mount St .Mary Academy,* Little Rock, AR; *Mount St. Mary High School,* Oklahoma City, OK.
Convent Corporations: Sisters of Mercy of the St. Louis Regional Community, Inc.
Represented in the Archdioceses of Detroit, New Orleans, Oklahoma City, Omaha, St. Louis, San Antonio, and Washington and in the Dioceses of Baton Rouge, Biloxi, Brownsville, Fort Worth, Houma-Thibodaux, Jackson, Lafayette (LA), Laredo, Little Rock, Lubbock, Metuchen, Portland, Springfield-Cape Girardeau and Wichita. Also in London, Ghana, South Africa, Georgetown, Guyana.

Vermont (P)

Regional Community of Vermont: *Mt. St. Mary Motherhouse and Novitiate,* 100 Mansfield Ave., Burlington, VT 05401. Tel: 802-863-6835. Sr. Jeannine Mercure, R.S.M., Pres.
Total number in the community 69.
Ministry in the field of Education; Parish Ministry & Spirituality; Social Services.
Properties owned or sponsored: *Institute for Spiritual Development, Inc.; Mater Christi School Inc.,*

Burlington, VT; *Mercy Connections, Inc.,* Burlington, VT; *Lumen Christi Retreat House,* Benson, VT.
Represented in the Archdioceses of Hartford, Santa Fe and in the Dioceses of Burlington and Manchester.

[2590] (H.M.S.S.)—MERCEDARIAN SISTERS OF THE BLESSED SACRAMENT (P)
(Hermanas Mercedarias del Santisimo Sacramento)

Founded in Mexico in 1910. First foundation in the United States in 1926.
General Motherhouse: Fernandez Leal #130, Coyoacan Mexico. 04330, Mother Maria De La Luz Acosta Bustos, H.M.S.S., Supr. Gen.
Regional House: *Blessed Sacrament Convent,* 222 W. Cevallos St., San Antonio, TX 78204. Tel: 210-223-5013; 222-1354; Fax: 210-222-0275. Sr. Guadalupe Rosales, H.M.S.S., Reg. Supr.
Professed Sisters in U.S. 33; Novices 1.
Represented in the Archdiocese of San Antonio and in the Dioceses of Cleveland, Corpus Christi and San Diego.

[2600] (S.M.)—SISTERS OF MERCY (D)

Founded in the United States in 1960.
General Motherhouse: *Congregation of the Sisters of Mercy,* Elbana Ave., Dun Laoghlaire, Dublin, Ireland. Sr. Breege O'Neill, Supr. Gen.
U.S. Address: *Sacred Heart Convent,* 6240 105th St., Jacksonville, FL 32244. Tel: 904-771-3858. Sr. Patricia O'Hea, Contact Person.
Represented in the Diocese of St. Augustine.

[2610] (S.M.D.C.)—SISTERS OF MERCY DAUGHTERS OF CHRISTIAN CHARITY OF ST. VINCENT DE PAUL OF (HUNGARY) (P)

Founded in Hungary in 1842. Mother M. Klara Both, Supr. Gen.
U.S. Foundation: *St. Joseph Home and Convent and Novitiate,* Rte. 1, Box 353 A, 240 Longhouse Dr., Hewitt, NJ 07421. Tel: 973-853-7212. Sr. Mary Louise Horvath, Supr.
Represented in the Diocese of Paterson.

[2630] (S.C.S.C.)—SISTERS OF MERCY OF THE HOLY CROSS (P)

Founded in Switzerland in 1856. First foundation in the U.S. in 1912
General Motherhouse: Ingenbohl, Switzerland. Sr. Louise-Henri Kolly, S.C.S.C., Supr. Gen.
U.S. Provincial Residence: *Holy Cross Sisters,* 501 South Center Ave., Merrill, WI 54452. Tel: 715-539-5000; Fax: 715-539-5012. Sr. Pat Cormack, S.C.S.C., Prov.
Total number in community 45.
Legal Titles: *Sisters of Mercy of the Holy Cross of Merrill, WI, Inc.; Sponsored Institution: Bell Tower Residence, Inc.*
Ministry in the following areas: Schools; Hospitals; Social Ministries; Parishes and Diocesan Offices; Retirement Homes; Adult Education; Campus Ministries.
Represented in the Archdioceses of Cincinnati, New Orleans, and St. Paul-Minneapolis and in the Dioceses of Belleville, Baton Rouge, Gaylord, Green Bay, La Crosse, Lansing, Sioux Falls, and Superior.

[2655] SISTERS OF MERCY OF PORTLAND (D)

Motherhouse: *Diocesan Sisters of Mercy of Portland,* 265 Cottage Rd., South Portland, ME 04106. Tel: 207-767-5804. Sr. Carol Le Tourneau, R.S.M.

[2670] (S.O.L.M.)—SISTERS OF OUR LADY OF MERCY
(Mercedarians)

General Motherhouse: via Ostriana 24, Rome, Italy. Mother Igina Caddori, Supr. Gen.
Brooklyn: *Most Precious Blood,* 133 27th Ave., Brooklyn, NY 11214. Sr. Doloretta, Supr.
Sisters 6.
Represented in the Dioceses of Brooklyn and St. Petersburg.

[2675] (C.F.M.M.)—MINIM DAUGHTERS OF MARY IMMACULATE (P)

Founded in Leon, Guanajuato, Mexico 1886. Came to the United States in 1926.
U.S. Regional House: *Minim Daughters of Mary Immaculate,* 555 Patagonia Hwy., Nogales, AZ 85628. Tel: 520-287-3377; Fax: 520-287-2910. Sr. Rosa Maria Ruiz, C.F.M.M., Reg. Supr.
Total Sisters in the U.S. 22.
Ministry in Academic and Religious Education and Health Care.
Properties owned: *Lourdes Catholic School,* Nogales, AZ.
Represented in the Diocese of Tucson.

[2677] (S.M.M.I)—SISTERS MINOR OF MARY IMMACULATE (D)

First foundation in the United States June 13, 1989. Active- contemplative Franciscan Religious Congregation following the spirituality of St. Maximilian Mary Kolbe, O.F.M.Conv. and St. Terese of Liseux.
Central Motherhouse & Novitiate: Via Germanico 198, Rome, Italy 00192. Tel: 011-39-6-324-2036. Mother Maria Elisabetta Patrizi, S.M.M.I., Foundress & Mother Gen.
American Headquarters - St. Francis Villa: 138 Brushy Hill Rd., Danbury, CT 06810-8431. Tel: 203-744-8041. Sr. Mary Elizabeth Larivier, S.M.M.I., U.S. Custos/Delegate.
Legal Title: *Sisters Minor of Mary Immaculate.*
Ministry in the field of Academic and Religious Education; Health Care; Pastoral Care; Care to the elderly, youths, widows and immigrants.
Represented in the Archdiocese of Hartford and in the Dioceses of Bridgeport and Springfield (MA).

[2680] (S.M.)—MISERICORDIA SISTERS (P)

Founded in Canada in 1848. First foundation in the United States in 1887.
General Motherhouse: 12435 Misericorde Ave., Montreal, Que, Canada, H4J 2G3. Tel: 514-332-0550. Sr. Monique Lallier, S.M., Supr.
U.S. Address: 225 Carol Ave., Pelham, NY 10803. Sr. Ellen Hunt, S.M., Supr.
Represented in the Archdiocese of New York.

[2690] (M.C.D.P.)—MISSIONARY CATECHISTS OF DIVINE PROVIDENCE, SAN ANTONIO, TEXAS (P)

Autonomy with Pontifical status granted Dec. 12, 1989.
Administrative House: *St. Andrew's Convent,* 2318 Castroville Rd., San Antonio, TX 78237. Tel: 210-432-0113; Fax: 210-432-1709. Sr. Mary Lou Barba, Supr.
Total number in community 49.
Properties owned or sponsored: *Benitia Family Center,* San Antonio, TX.
Represented in the Archdioceses of Omaha, Santa Fe, and San Antonio and in the Dioceses of Austin, Brownsville, Corpus Christi, Dallas, Des Moines, Fort Worth, Galveston-Houston, Laredo, San Jose, and Tucson.

[2700] (M.C.S.H.)—MISSIONARY CATECHISTS OF THE SACRED HEARTS OF JESUS AND MARY (D)

Founded in Mexico City, D.F. in 1918. U.S. foundation in 1943 in Victoria, Texas.
Central House: Mexico City, Mexico. Sr. Rosalba Torres, Supr. Gen.
Immaculate Heart of Mary Province: 203 E. Sabine St., Victoria, TX 77901. Tel: 361-570-3332; Fax: 361-570-3377. Sr. Miriam Perez, M.C.S.H., Prov.
Total number in U.S. Region 45.
Ministry in Catechetical family ministry in parishes and missions.
Represented in the Dioceses of Fort Worth, Galveston-Houston, Lubbock, Metuchen and Victoria.

[2710] (M.C.)—MISSIONARIES OF CHARITY (P)

Founded in India, 1950.
General Motherhouse: 54A AJC Bose Rd., Calcutta India. 700016, Sr. M. Nirmala, M.C., Supr. Gen.
U.S. Foundation & Office (1971): *Missionaries of Charity,* 335 E. 145th St., Bronx, NY 10451. Tel: 718-292-0019. Sr. M. Leticia, M.C., Reg. Supr.
Professed Sisters in Congregation 4,500.
Legal Title: *Missionaries of Charity, Inc.*
Sister serve and staff: Soup Kitchens; Emergency Shelters for Women; Homes for Unwed Mothers; Shelters for Unwed Mothers; Shelters for Men; Religious Education Programs; After-School and Summer Camp Programs for Children; Homes for AIDS Patients; Prison Ministry; Nursing Homes; Hospital and Shut-in Ministry; Family Counseling and Ministry; Home for Infants for Adoption; Foreign Missionary Work.
Represented in the Archdioceses of Atlanta, Baltimore, Boston, Chicago, Denver, Detroit, Indianapolis, Los Angeles, Miami, New York, Newark, Philadelphia, San Francisco, St. Louis, St. Paul-Minneapolis, and Washington and in the Dioceses of Baton Rouge, Brooklyn, Charlotte, Dallas, Fall River, Gallup, Gary, Lafayette, Lexington, Little Rock, Memphis, Peoria, Phoenix and Trenton. Also in Canada and Mexico.

[2715] (M.CHR.)—MISSIONARY SISTERS OF CHRIST THE KING FOR POLONIA (P)

Founded in Poland on November 21, 1959 by Father Ignacy Posadzy. First foundation in the U.S. 1978.
General Motherhouse: *Siostry Misjonarki Chrystusa Krola,* ulica Siostr Misjonarek 10. 61-680 Poznan, 50 Poland. Sr. Edyta Rychel, M.Chr., Supr. Gen.
Total in Congregation 230.
Delegation Superior in the U.S.: *Missionary Sisters of Christ the King for Polonia,* 64 S. Pershing Ave., Mundelein, IL 60060. Tel: 847-837-4122. Sr. Gertruda Szymansak, M.Chr.,. Supr.; Sr. Bozena Blad, M.Chr., Sec.; Sr. Barbara Kosinska, M.Chr., Treas.
Total in Congregation 198; Professed in U.S. and Canada 35.
Legal Title: *Missionary Sisters of Christ the King for Polonia.*
Ministry among Polish immigrants and people of Polish heritage.
Represented in the Archdioceses of Chicago, Detroit, and Los Angeles and in the Dioceses of Phoenix, and San Jose. Also in Toronto, Canada.

[2717] (M.D.P.V.M.)—MISSIONARY DAUGHTERS OF THE MOST PURE VIRGIN

Founded in Mexico. First foundation in the United States in the Diocese of Corpus Christi 1916.
General Motherhouse: *Heroe de Nacocariz,* 721 Sur Aguascalientes, Mexico. Mother Virginia Quiroz, M.D.P.V.M., Supr. Gen.
Missionary Daughters of the Most Pure Virgin Mary: 919 N. 9th St., Kingsville, TX 78363. Tel: 361-595-1087. Sr. Consuelo Ramirez, M.D.P.V.M., Supr.; Sr. Rosario Armendariz, M.D.P.V.M., Sec.; Sr. Delia Zapata, M.D.P.V.M., Treas.
Total in Congregation 500; Present in U.S. 33.
Legal Title: *Missionary Daughters of the Most Pure Virgin Mary.*
Ministry in the field of Religious and Academic Education at the elementary level; Pastoral Ministry.
Represented in the Dioceses of Camden, Corpus Christi and Yakima.

[2720] (M.H.S.H.)—MISSION HELPERS OF THE SACRED HEART (P)

Founded in the United States in 1890.
Mission Helper Center: 1001 W. Joppa Rd., Baltimore, MD, 21204-3787. Tel: 410-823-8585; Fax: 410-825-6355. Sr. M. Judith Waldt, M.H.S.H., Pres.
Total number in community 93.
Legal Title: *Institute of Mission Helpers of Baltimore City.*
Represented in the Archdioceses of Baltimore, Boston, Cincinnati, Detroit, Indianapolis, San Juan (PR), San Francisco, and Washington and in the Dioceses of Erie, Norwich, Orlando, Raleigh, Pittsburgh, Rochester, St. Petersburg and Tucson. Also in Venezuela.

[2730] (M.S.H.R.)—MISSIONARY SISTERS OF THE HOLY ROSARY (P)

Generalate (1924): 23 Cross Ave., Blackrock County , Dublin, Ireland. Sr. Monica Devine, Supr. Gen.
U.S. Regional Headquarters (1954): *Missionary Sisters of the Holy Rosary,* 741 Polo Rd., Bryn Mawr, PA 19010. Tel: 610-520-1974. Sr. Terry Shields, M.S.H.R., Reg. Leader.
Total number in community 385.
Represented in the Archdiocese of Philadelphia.

[2740] (M.S.Sp.)—MISSION SISTERS OF THE HOLY SPIRIT (D)

Motherhouse and Novitiate: 1030 N. River Rd., Saginaw, MI 48609. Tel: 517-781-0934. Sr. Mary Lou Owczarzak, Community Coord.
Total number in community 11.
Legal Title: *Society of the Mission Sisters of the Holy Spirit of the Diocese of Saginaw Holy Spirit Sisters Charitable Trust,* Saginaw, MI.
Ministry in Social Services; Religious Education at all levels including Mentally Retarded; Pastoral Ministry; Pastoral Administrator.
Represented in the Diocese of Saginaw.

[2750] (I.C.M.)—MISSIONARY SISTERS OF THE IMMACULATE HEART OF MARY (P)

Founded in India in 1897. First foundation in the United States in 1919.
Generalate: Via Filogaso 40, Rome, Italy, 00173. Sr. M. Josee Cleymans, I.C.M., Supr. Gen.
Universal total of congregation 902.
American Province: 238 E. 15th St.,-#5 New York, NY 10003. Tel: 212-677-2959. Sr. Annie Claes, I.C.M., Prov.
Total number in community 29.
Missionaries Minister in Education; Catechetical; Pastoral and Social Ministry; Health Care; Ecology; Leprosaria; International Justice and the Promotion of Human Dignity.
Represented in the Archdioceses of Los Angeles, Newark, and New York and in the Dioceses of Albany and Brownsville. Also in Belgium, Brazil, Burundi, Cameroon, Guatemala, Hong Kong, India, Italy, Philippines, Taiwan, Mongolia, Tchad, Virgin Islands, West Indies and Congo.

[2760] (S.M.I.C.)—MISSIONARY SISTERS OF THE IMMACULATE CONCEPTION OF THE MOTHER OF GOD (P)

Founded in Brazil in 1910. First foundation in the United States in 1922.

Generalate: 47 Garden Ave., West Paterson, NJ 07424-3337. Tel: 973-279-1484. Sr. Corona Chung, S.M.I.C., Coord. Gen.

U.S. Province (1960): *Provincialate of the Immaculate Conception,* P.O. Box 3026, Paterson, NJ 07509-3026. Tel: 973-279-3790. Fax: 973-742-8231. Sr. Eleanor Goekler, S.M.I.C., Prov. Coord.

Professed Sisters 43.

Sisters serve and staff: Elementary Schools; Religious Education; Pastoral Ministries; Health and Social Services.

Represented in the Archdioceses of Newark, San Antonio, and Washington and in the Dioceses of Austin, El Paso, Gallup, Galveston-Houston, Metuchen, Paterson, Portland (ME) and San Bernardino.

[2770] (M.J.M.J.)—MISSIONARY SISTERS OF JESUS, MARY AND JOSEPH (P)

Founded in Spain in 1942. First foundation in United States in 1956. Mother Maria Dolores de la Cruz Domingo, Foundress.

Motherhouse: Plaza Inmaculada Concepcion 1, Madrid, Spain 28019. Sr. Maria Amparo Munoz, M.J.M.J., Supr. Gen.

Delegation Headquarters: 12940 Leopard St., Corpus Christi, TX 78410. Tel: 361-241-1955. Sr. Raquel D. Gomez, M.J.M.J., Delegation Supr.; Sr. Angela Berrozpe, M.J.M.J., Local Supr.

Sisters 25.

Properties owned: *Joseph of the Valley Preschool,* El Paso, TX.

Represented in the Archdiocese of San Antonio and in the Dioceses of Corpus Christi and El Paso. Also in Mexico.

[2780] (M.SS.S.)—MISSIONARY SISTERS OF THE MOST BLESSED SACRAMENT (P)

General Motherhouse: Calle Navarro Amandi, 11 Madrid, Spain. 28033. Mother Socorro Mugueta, Mother Gen.

U.S. Foundation: *Convent of Mary Immaculate,* 1111 Wordin Ave., Bridgeport, CT 06605. Sr. Angela Maria Zapata, M.SS.S., Prov.

[2790] (M.S.B.T.)—MISSIONARY SERVANTS OF THE MOST BLESSED TRINITY (P)

Founded in United States in 1912.

Motherhouse-Generalate-Novitiate and Candidacy: 3501 Solly Ave., Philadelphia, PA 19136. Tel: 215-335-7550. Sr. Barbara DeMoranville, M.S.B.T., Gen. Custodian.

Total number in community 191.

Properties owned and sponsored: *Blessed Trinity Mother Missionary Cenacle,* Philadelphia, PA; *Blessed Trinity Shrine Retreat Cenacle,* Holy Trinity, AL; *Trinita Ecumenical Retreat Center,* New Hartford, CT; *Blessed Trinity Mother Missionary Cenacle,* Philadelphia, PA.

Represented in the Archdioceses of Baltimore, Boston, Chicago, Hartford, Newark, Mobile, New York and Philadelphia and in the Dioceses of Arlington, Birmingham, Brooklyn, Charleston, Camden, Fall River, Gallup, Greensburg, Owensboro, Paterson, Pensacola-Tallahassee, Phoenix, Richmond, Rockville Centre, Wilmington and Yakima. Also in Puerto Rico and Mexico.

[2800] (M.S.C.)—MISSIONARY SISTERS OF THE MOST SACRED HEART OF JESUS (OF HILTRUP) (P)

Founded in Germany in 1899. First foundation in the United States in 1908.

Generalate: Via Martiri di Via Fani, Sutri (Viterbo), Italy. Sr. MaryAnne Bigos, M.S.C.

American Province-Motherhouse (1908): *St. Michael's Convent,* 51 Seminary Ave., Reading, PA 19605. Tel: 610-929-5751. Sr. Marie Raymond, M.S.C., Coord.

MSC Province Center: 2811 Moyers Ln., Reading PA, 19605. Tel: 610-929-5944. Sr. Marie Clark, M.S.C., Prov.

Total number in U.S. Province 94.

Legal Title: *Missionary Sisters of the Most Sacred Heart of Jesus, Inc.*

Ministry in Education; Health Care; Home Health Care; Parish Ministry; Pastoral Ministry to people on the move; Prison Ministry; Counseling; Social Ministry; Spiritual Ministry.

Properties owned or sponsored: *MSC Province Center; St. Michael Convent, Chevalier House, Bethany Convent, Sacred Heart Villa,* Reading, PA.

Represented in the Archdioceses of Atlanta and Philadelphia and in the Dioceses of Allentown, Galveston-Houston, Harrisburg, San Bernardino, and Venice. Also in Mexico.

[2810] (M.S.M.G.)—MISSIONARY SISTERS OF MOTHER OF GOD (D)

(Byzantine Ukrainian Rite-Stamford)

Motherhouse: 711 N. Franklin St., Philadelphia, PA 19123. Tel: 215-627-7808.

U.S. Province: 111 W. North St., Stamford, CT 06902. Tel: 203-323-1237. Sr. Josepha Kruchinsky, M.S.M.G., Treas.

Professed Sisters 12.

Ministry in the field of Education.

Represented in the Ukrainian Archdiocese of Philadelphia and in the Ukrainian Diocese of Stamford.

[2820] (M.S.O.L.A.)—MISSIONARY SISTERS OF OUR LADY OF AFRICA (P)

(Sisters of Africa)

Founded in Algiers, N. Africa, in 1869. First foundation in the United States in 1929.

General Motherhouse: Rome, Italy. Sr. Marie McDonald, Supr. Gen.

Universal Total in Congregation 1,087.

American Headquarters: 47 West Spring St., Winooski, VT 05404. Tel: 802-655-4003. Sr. Marie Claire Bernier, M.S.O.L.A., Liaison Person.

Total number in U.S. 17.

Represented in the Archdiocese of Washington and in the Diocese of Burlington.

[2830] (M.O.M.)—MISSIONARY SISTERS OF OUR LADY OF MERCY (D)

Founded in Piaui, Brazil in 1938. First foundation in United States at Lackawanna, New York 1955.

General Motherhouse: Salvador, Bahia, Brazil. Mother Felicidade Santos, M.O.M., Supr. Gen.

U.S. Headquarters: *Rainbow K,* 388 Franklin St., Buffalo, NY 14202. Tel: 716-854-5198. Sr. Therese Marie, M.O.M., Supr.

Total number in community 3.

Represented in the Diocese of Buffalo.

[2840] (M.C.)—POOR CLARE MISSIONARY SISTERS (P)

Founded in Mexico by Mother Maria Ines Teresa Arias.

General Motherhouse: Via Cardinale Garampi 17, Pineta Sachetti, Rome, Italy. Mother Maria Teresa Botello, Gen. Supr.

U.S. Foundation: *Regional House and Novitiate,* 1019 N. Newhope, Santa Ana, CA 92703.

Total number in community 42.

Ministry in Day Nurseries; Schools and; Retreat House.

Represented in the Archdiocese of Los Angeles and in the Diocese of Orange.

[2850] (C.P.S.)—MISSIONARY SISTERS OF THE PRECIOUS BLOOD (P)

Founded in South Africa on Sept. 8, 1885. First founded in the United States at Princeton, New Jersey on August 15, 1925.

Generalate: Casa Generalizia, Suore Missionarie del Preziosissimo Sangue Mariannhill, Via San Giovanni Eudes 93, Roma, Italia

Universal number in Congregation 980.

North American Province: *Precious Blood Convent,* P.O. Box 97 - 1094 Welsh Rd., Reading, PA 19607-0097. Tel: 610-777-1624. Sr. Eva A. Janning, C.P.S., Prov.

Total number in Province 50.

Represented in the Diocese of Allentown. Also in Canada.

[2860] (M.S.C.)—MISSIONARY SISTERS OF THE SACRED HEART OF JESUS (P)

(Cabrini Sisters)

Founded in Italy in 1880, by Saint Frances Xavier Cabrini. First foundation in the United States 1889.

Motherhouse: Viale Cortina D'Ampezzo, 269, Rome, Italy, 00135. Sr. Lina Colombini, M.S.C., Supr. Gen.

Provincial Office: 222 E. 19th St., 5B, New York, NY 10003. Sr. Lucille Souza, M.S.C., Prov. Supr.

Professed Sisters 406; Total in Congregation 416.

Ministry in the field of Education; Hospitals; Nursing Homes; Child Care; Retreat and Shrine Ministries; Parish Ministry; Pastoral Work; Parish Work.

Represented in the Archdioceses of Chicago, Denver, New Orleans, New York, Philadelphia, and Seattle and in the Dioceses of Galveston-Houston and Phoenix. Also in Argentina, Australia, Brazil, Central America, England, Ethiopia, France, Italy, Philippines, Portugal, Spain, Switzerland and Swaziland.

[2865] (M.S.C.Gpe.)—MISSIONARIES OF THE SACRED HEART OF JESUS AND OUR LADY OF GUADALUPE

National Address: 1212 E. Euclid Ave., Arlington Heights, IL 60004. Tel: 847-255-5616. Sr. Piedad Fernandez, Pres.; Sr. Esperansa Hernandez, Sec.; Sr. Zoila Alcala, Treas.

Ministry in Schools; Nursing Homes; Seminaries and Foreign Missions.

Represented in the Archdioceses of Boston, Chicago, San Francisco and Washington and in the Diocese of Rockford.

[2880] (S.S.C.)—MISSIONARY SISTERS OF ST. COLUMBAN (P)

(Columban Sisters)

Founded in Ireland in 1922. First Foundation in the United States in 1930.

General Motherhouse: Wicklow, Ireland. Sr. Kathleen Geaney, Congregational Leader.

U.S. Region: *Missionary Sisters of St. Columban,* 73 Mapleton St., Brighton, MA 02135. Tel: 617-782-5683. Fax: 617-789-3569. Sr. Ruth Duckert, S.S.C., U.S. Area.

Professed Sisters 23.

Represented in the Archdioceses of Boston and Los Angeles and in the Diocese of Buffalo.

[2890] (M.S.S.A.)—MISSIONARY SERVANTS OF ST. ANTHONY (D)

Founded in the United States in 1929.

General Motherhouse: 100 Peter Baque Rd., San Antonio, TX 78209-1805. Tel: 210-824-4553. Sr. Mary Ann Domagalski, M.S.S.A., Supr.

Total number in community 4.

Represented in the Archdiocese of San Antonio.

[2900] (M.S.C.S.)—MISSIONARY SISTERS OF ST. CHARLES BORROMEO

(Scalabrini Sisters)

Founded in Italy in 1895. First United States in 1941.

Motherhouse: Via Monte del Gallo 68, Rome, Italy, 00165. Sr. Maria do Rosario Onzi, M.S.C.S., Gen.

Universal Total in Congregation 810.

North American Provincial House & Bishop Scalabrini Community: 1414 N. 37th Ave., Melrose Park, IL 60160. Tel: 708-343-2162; Fax: 708-343-6452. Sr. Marissonia Daltoe, M.S.C.S., Prov.

Total number in community 64.

Ministry in the fields of Education; Pastoral Care of the Sick; Catechesis; Social Service.

Represented in the Archdioceses of Boston, Chicago, New York and Washington and in the Diocese of Springfield in MA. Also in Canada, Mexico and the Philippines.

[2920] (M.D.)—MOTHERS OF THE HELPLESS (D)

Founded in Malaga, Spain in 1881. Founded in the United States in 1916.

General Motherhouse: Avda. San Jose de la Montana No.15, Valencia, Spain, 46008. Mother Esperanza Ordonez, Supr. Gen.

U.S. Address: *Sacred Heart Residence,* 432 W. 20th St., New York, NY 10011. Mother Rocio Campana, M.D., Dir.

Professed Sisters in U.S. 6.

Properties owned and sponsored: *San Jose De La Montana Day Nursery; Sacred Heart Residence; San Jose Day Nursery,* New York, NY.

Represented in the Archdiocese of New York.

[2930] (I.H.M.)—THE CALIFORNIA INSTITUTE OF THE SISTERS OF THE MOST HOLY AND IMMACULATE HEART OF THE BLESSED VIRGIN MARY (P)

Founded in Spain in 1848. First foundation in the United States in 1871.

Generalate, Novitiate and Retreat House: 3431 Waverly Dr., Los Angeles, CA 90027. Tel: 213-664-1124. Sr. Rita Callanan, Supr. Gen.

Professed Sisters 17.

Properties staffed: High Schools and Grammar Schools.

Represented in the Archdiocese of Los Angeles.

[2940] (M.H.S.)—SISTERS OF THE MOST HOLY SACRAMENT (P)

Founded in France in 1851. First foundation in the United States in 1872. Pontifical Approbation 1935

Generalate: *Sisters of the Most Holy Sacrament,* 313 Corona Dr., P.O. Box 90037, Lafayette, LA 70509-0037. Tel: 337-981-8475. Sr. Judine Theriot, M.H.S., Major Supr.

Total number in community 34.

Legal Title: *St. Augustine Trust Fund,* Lafayette, LA; *Bethany Health Care Center,* Lafayette, LA.

Ministry in the field of Education; Homes for the Aged; Pastoral Care.

Represented in the Archdiocese of New Orleans and in the Dioceses of Baton Rouge, and Lafayette (LA).

[2950] (N.D.S.)—CONGREGATION OF NOTRE DAME DE SION (P)

Founded in France in 1850. First foundation in the United States in 1892.

Generalate: Rome, Italy. Sr. Mechthild Vahle, N.D.S., Supr. Gen.

Universal Total in Congregation 800.
Notre Dame de Sion: 3823 Locust St., Kansas City, MO 64109. Tel: 816-531-1374.
Represented in the Archdiocese of Chicago and in the Dioceses of Brooklyn and Kansas City-St. Joseph.

[2960] (N.D.)—NOTRE DAME SISTERS (P)

Founded in Czechoslovakia, Europe, in 1853. First foundation in the United States in 1910.
General Motherhouse: Hradec Kralove, Czech Republic. Mother Miriam Baumrukova, N.D., Supr. Gen.
U.S. Provincial Motherhouse: *Notre Dame Convent,* 3501 State St., Omaha, NE 68112-1709. Tel: 402-455-2994; Fax: 402-455-3974. Sr. Margaret Hickey, N.D., Prov.
Total number in community 61.
Sisters serve and staff: all levels of academic education; Hispanic Ministry; Pastoral Care; Housing for low income elderly; Social Work; Religious Education; Youth Ministry; Chemical Dependency Counseling; Health Care; TEC; Adult Education; Family Life-Diocesan Offices; Community Administration and Services.
Represented in the Archdioceses of Denver, Dubuque, and Omaha and in the Dioceses of Davenport, Kansas City-St. Joseph, Lincoln, and Pueblo.

[2970] (S.S.N.D.)—SCHOOL SISTERS OF NOTRE DAME (P)

Founded in Germany in 1833. First foundation in the United States in 1847.
General Motherhouse: Rome, Italy. Sr. Rosemary Howarth, Supr. Gen.
Milwaukee Province (1850); Milwaukee (1959); Mequon (1983); Milwaukee: *Milwaukee Province, Motherhouse,* 13105 Watertown Plank Rd., Elm Grove, WI 53122-2291. Tel: 262-782-9850; Fax: 262-782-5725. Sr. Marilyn Kesler, S.S.N.D., Leader.
Total number in community 510.
Legal Title: *School Sisters of Notre Dame Milwaukee Province, Inc.; School Sisters of Notre Dame at Milwaukee, Wisconsin, Inc. Charitable Trust.*
Various ministries to Women, Youth, the Poor, Sick and Elderly; all levels of Academic Education; D.R.E.'s; Pastoral Associates.
Properties owned: *Mount Mary College,* Milwaukee, WI; *Notre Dame of Elm Grove,* Elm Grove, WI; *Our Lady of Mt. Carmel Convent,* Mt. Calvary, WI.
Represented in the Archdioceses of Chicago, Detroit, Milwaukee, St. Paul-Minneapolis, Seattle and St. Louis and in the Dioceses of Davenport, Fairbanks, Fort Wayne-South Bend, Gary, Gallup, Grand Rapids, Green Bay, Jefferson, La Crosse, Lafayette (IN), Lexington, Madison, Marquette, New Ulm, Phoenix, Rockford, Saginaw, Shreveport, Springfield, Steubenville and Wheeling-Charleston. Also in Africa, Caroline-Marshall Islands, Central America and Guam.
Baltimore Province (1876): *School Sisters of Notre Dame,* 6401 N. Charles St., Baltimore, MD 21212-1099. Tel: 410-377-7774; Fax: 410-377-5363. Sr. Jane Burke, S.S.N.D., Prov. Leader.
Total number in community 345.
Legal Titles and Properties Owned: *School Sisters of Notre Dame in the City of Baltimore; Maria Health Care Center, Inc.; Villa Assumpta-Motherhouse of Baltimore Province; College of Notre Dame of Maryland; Notre Dame Preparatory School; Institute of Notre Dame,* Baltimore, MD.
Ministries to the Needy and Elderly; Teaching and Administering in the field of Academic Education at all levels; D.R.E.'s and Pastoral Associates.
Represented in the Archdioceses of Baltimore, Boston, Chicago, Los Angeles, Miami, Milwaukee, Newark, Philadelphia, St. Louis, and Washington and in the Dioceses of Arlington, Bridgeport, Camden, Charleston, Gary, Jackson, Laredo, Lexington, Palm Beach, Pittsburgh, Rockville Centre, St. Petersburg, Trenton, Tulsa, Venice and Wilmington. Also in Bolivia, Ghana, Kenya, Honduras, Rome, Vienna and Nigeria.
St. Louis Province (1895): *School Sisters of Notre Dame,* 320 E. Ripa Ave., St. Louis, MO 63125. Tel: 314-544-0455; Fax: 314-544-6754. Sr. Joanne Hanrahan, Prov. Supr.
Total number in community 593.
Legal Title: *The School Sisters of Notre Dame of St. Louis.*
Represented in the Archdioceses of Baltimore, Chicago, Denver, Detroit, Dubuque, Los Angeles, Milwaukee, Omaha, St. Louis, St. Paul-Minneapolis, San Antonio, and Washington and in the Dioceses of Albany, Austin, Belleville, Bismarck, Brownsville, Davenport, Evansville, Fresno, Jefferson City, Little Rock, Monterey, Oakland, Orange, Peoria, Phoenix, Rapid City, San Diego, Shreveport, Springfield-Cape Girardeau, Springfield n Illinois, Tucson and Venice. Also in Ghana, Kenya, Nigeria, Honduras, Puerto Rico, Italy, Japan, Nepal, Guam and Korea.
Mankato Province (1912): *School Sisters of Notre Dame,* 170 Good Counsel Dr., Mankato, MN 56001-3138. Tel: 507-389-4200; Fax: 507-345-6679. Sr. Catherine Bertrandl, Prov.; Sr. Irene Feltz, Community Archivist.
Total number in community 397.
Legal Title: *School Sisters of Notre Dame at Mankato, Minnesota, Inc.; School Sisters of Notre Dame at Mankato, Minnesota, Inc. - Charitable Trust; School Sisters of Notre Dame Cooperative Investment Fund.*
Represented in the Archdioceses of Chicago, Dubuque, Milwaukee, New Orleans, New York, San Antonio, St. Louis, St. Paul-Minneapolis, San Francisco, and Washington and in the Dioceses of Albany, Alexandria, Bismarck, Charlotte, Crookston, Duluth, Fargo, Forth Worth, La Crosse, New Ulm, Phoenix, Richmond, Sioux Falls, Superior, St. Cloud, and Winona. Also in Ghana, Guatemala, Kenya, Nigeria and Rome, Italy.
Northeastern Province (1957): *School Sisters of Notre Dame,* 345 Belden Hill Rd., Wilton, CT 06897. Tel: 203-762-1220; Fax: 203-762-9434. Sr. Mary Maher, Prov. Leader.
Total number in community 337.
Legal Holdings and Titles: *The Northeastern Province of the School Sisters of Notre Dame in the State of Connecticut; Motherhouse and Lourdes Health Care Center,* Wilton, CT; *Academy of the Holy Angels,* Demarest, NJ.
Represented in the Archdioceses of Baltimore, Boston, Hartford, Milwaukee, Newark, New York, and Washington and in the Dioceses of Albany, Bridgeport, Brooklyn, Grand Rapids, Manchester, Norwich, Paterson, Phoenix, Rochester, Rockville Centre, St. Petersburg, Springfield and Venice. Also in Chile, Switzerland, Ghana, Paraguay, Peru and Puerto Rico.
Dallas Province (1961): *Notre Dame of Dallas - School Sisters of Notre Dame,* P.O. Box 227275, Dallas, TX 75222. Tel: 214-330-9152; Fax: 214-330-9197. Sr. Addie Lorraine Walker, Prov.
Total number in community 154.
Legal Title: *School Sisters of Notre Dame of Dallas Charitable Trust.*
Represented in the Archdioceses of New Orleans and San Antonio and in the Dioceses of Alexandria, Austin, Baton Rouge, Brownsville, Dallas, El Paso, Fort Worth, Houma-Thibodaux, Jackson, Lafayette (LA), Little Rock, Phoenix, San Angelo and Victoria. Also in Guatemala, Honduras and West Africa.
Chicago Province: *School Sisters of Notre Dame,* 1431 Euclid Ave., Berwyn, IL 60402. Tel: 708-749-1380. Sr. Barbara Bowers, S.S.N.D., Prov. Leader.
Total number in the community 120.
Ministry in the field of Academic, Special and Religious Education; Day Care Centers; Foreign Mission work; Nurses; Pastoral Work; Apostolate of the Aging; Vicar for Women Religious.
Properties Owned: *Academy of Our Lady,* Chicago, IL.
Represented in the Archdioceses of Baltimore, Chicago, Los Angeles, Miami, Milwaukee, and Washington and in the Dioceses of Joliet, Peoria and Rockford. Also in Paraguay and Nigeria.

[2980] (C.N.D.)—SISTERS OF THE CONGREGATION DE NOTRE DAME (P)

Founded in Canada in 1653. First Foundation in United States in 1860. American Novitiate established at Ridgefield, Connecticut.
General Motherhouse: 4873 Westmount Ave., Montreal, Quebec, Canada.
Generalate: 2330 Sherbrooke St., W., Montreal, Quebec, Canada. Sr. Lorraine Caza, C.N.D., Congregational Leader.
U.S. Province (1946): *Blessed Sacrament Province,* 223 W. Mountain Rd., Ridgefield, CT 06877. Tel: 203-438-5282; Fax: 203-894-9686. Sr. Anne Leonard, C.N.D., Prov. Leader.
Total number in the U.S. Province 184.
Represented in the Archdioceses of Boston, Chicago, Hartford, Newark, New York, and Oklahoma City and in the Dioceses of Albany, Bridgeport, Brooklyn, Charlotte, Joliet, Pensacola-Tallahassee, Providence, Rapid City, Richmond, Scranton and Worcester.

[2990] (S.N.D.)—SISTERS OF NOTRE DAME (P)

Founded in Germany in 1850. First foundation in the United States in 1874.
Generalate: Rome, Italy. Sr. Mary Sujita Kallupurakkathu, S.N.D., Supr. Gen.
Universal Total in Congregation 2,492.
Cleveland Province (1874): *Notre Dame Educational Center - Provincial Center, Juniorate, & Novitiate,* 13000 Auburn Rd., Chardon, OH 44024-9331. Tel: 440-286-7101; Fax: 440-286-3377. Sr. Melannie Svoboda, Prov. Supr.; Sr. M. Patricia Teckman, Prov. Sec.
Total number in community 398.
Legal Titles: *The Corporation of the Sisters of Notre Dame of Cleveland, Ohio; The Sisters of Notre Dame Charitable Trust.*
Ministry in the field of Academic Education at all levels; Special Education for Exceptional Children; Foreign Mission Work; Religious Education; Pastoral Ministry; Hospital Chaplains; Counseling Ministries; Community Service; Diocesan and National Offices; Pastoral Associate and D.R.E.; Parish Ministry; Spiritual Life Ministries; Hispanic & Refugee Outreach; Sick and Elderly in Hospitals and Nursing Homes; Youth Ministry; Campus Ministry; Writing; Liturgy and Music.
Properties owned and sponsored: *Notre Dame Cathedral Latin School,* Chardon, OH; *Notre Dame Elementary School,* Chardon, OH; *Notre Dame Pre School,* Chardon, OH; *Regina High School,* Cleveland, OH; *Julie Billiart School,* Lyndhurst, OH.
Represented in the Archdioceses of Baltimore, Boston, Miami, and Washington and in the Dioceses of Arlington, Cleveland, Orlando, Raleigh, St. Petersburg, St. Augustine, Superior, Toledo, Venice and Youngstown. Also in Uganda and the Philippines.
Covington Province (1924): *Provincial House and Novitiate of the Sisters of Notre Dame,* 1601 Dixie Hwy., (St. Joseph Heights), Covington, KY 41011. Tel: 859-291-2040; Fax: 859-291-1774. Sr. Mary Shauna, S.N.D., Prov.
Total number in the community 150.
Legal Title: *Sisters of Notre Dame of Covington, KY, Inc.*
Ministry in the field of Education; Hospital and Health Care Services; Child Care.
Properties sponsored and owned: *St. Claire Medical Center,* Morehead, KY; *St. Charles Care Center and Village,* Covington, KY; *Notre Academy,* Covington, KY.
Represented in the Archdiocese of Cincinnati and in the Dioceses of Birmingham, Covington and Lexington. Also in Hoima, Uganda and East Africa.
Province of Toledo (1924): *Notre Dame Provincialate,* 3837 Secor Rd., Toledo, OH 43623. Tel: 419-474-5485. Sr. Anne Mary Molyet, S.N.D., Prov. Supr.
Total number in community 253.
Ministry in the field of Education; Specialized Education; Foreign Mission Work; Vocational School.
Properties owned and sponsored: *Notre Dame Academy; Ladyfield School; Maria Child Care; Mary Immaculate School; Notre Dame School of Music,* Toledo, OH; *Lial Elementary School; Convent & Renewal Center,* Whitehouse, OH; *Holy Trinity Mission,* Papua, New Guinea.
Represented in the Archdioceses of Detroit, Indianapolis, and Santa Fe and in the Dioceses of Charleston, Fort Wayne-South Bend, Grand Rapids, Joliet, Lafayette (IN), Orlando, St. Augustine and Toledo.
Province of Los Angeles (1924): *Notre Dame Provincialate,* 1776 Hendrix Ave., Thousand Oaks, CA 91360. Tel: 805-496-3243; Fax: 805-379-3616. Sr. Mary Kristin Battles, S.N.D. Prov. Supr.
Total number in Province 71.
Legal Titles: *Corporation of the Sisters of Notre Dame of Los Angeles; Notre Dame Academy High School; Notre Dame Academy Elementary School,* Los Angeles, CA; *Notre Dame Center; La Reina High School,* Thousand Oaks, CA; *Providence House,* Long Beach, CA.
Ministry in the field of Education and Parish and Social Ministry; Catechetics; Foreign Mission Work.
Represented in the Archdiocese of Los Angeles.

[3000] (S.N.D.deN.)—SISTERS OF NOTRE DAME DE NAMUR (P)

Founded in France in 1804. First foundation in the United States in 1840.
Generalate: *Suore di Nostra Signora di Namur,* Via Raffaello Sardiello 20, Rome, Italy. 00165, Tel: 011-39-06-6641-8704. Sr. Camilla Burns, S.N.D.deN., Gen. Moderator.
U.S. Notre Dame Congregational Center: *Generalate Offices,* 30 Jeffreys Neck Rd., Ipswich, MA 01938. Tel: 978-356-2159; Fax: 978-356-2118. Sr. Lorraine Connell, S.N.D.deN.
Boston Province (1973): *Sisters of Notre Dame de Namur,* 351 Broadway, Everett, MA 02149. Tel: 617-387-2500; Fax: 617-387-1303. Prov. Team: Sr. Theresa Carlow, S.N.D.deN.; Sr. Catherine Fleming, S.N.D.deN.; Sr. Patricia O'Malley, S.N.D.deN.
Total number in community 227.
Legal Title: *The Boston Province of the Sisters of Notre Dame de Namur, Inc.*
Ministry in the field of Academic Education at all levels; Adult Education Programs; Parish Ministries; Religious Education Programs; and Social Services.
Properties owned and sponsored: *Notre Dame Academy,* Worcester, MA, *Notre Dame Children's Class,* Wenham, MA; *Notre Dame Education Center,* South Boston, MA; *Mother St. Joseph House,* Boston, MA.
Represented in the Archdioceses of Boston, Hartford, Louisville, and Washington and in the Dioceses of Albany, Gallup, Manchester, Orlando, Springfield (MA) and Worcester.

Ipswich Province (1973): *Sisters of Notre Dame de Namur Provincialate,* 30 Jeffrey's Neck Rd., Ipswich, MA 01938. Tel: 978-356-4381; Fax: 978-356-9759. Prov. Admin. Team: Sr. Eileen Burns, S.N.D.deN.; Sr. Maryalyce Gilfeather, S.N.D.deN.; Sr. Anne Stevenson, S.N.D.deN.

Total number in community 201.

Legal Titles: *Notre Dame Training School, Inc.; The Sisters of Notre Dame de Namur Congregational Mission Office,* Ipswich, MA.

Ministry in all fields of Education; Pastoral Ministry; Health, Social and Community Services; Retreat Work.

Properties owned and sponsored: *Academy of Notre Dame,* Tyngsboro, MA; *Julie Country Day School,* Leominster, MA; *Notre Dame Academy,* Hingham, MA; *Notre Dame Long Term Health Care Facility,* Worcester, MA; *Notre Dame Education Center,* Lawrence, MA; *Cuvilly Arts and Earth Center,* Ipswich, MA; *Notre Dame du Lac,* Worcester, MA; *St. Julie Billiart Residential Care Center,* Ipswich, MA.

Represented in the Archdiocese of Boston and in the Dioceses of Manchester and Worcester.

Connecticut Province (1959): *The Connecticut Province of the Sisters of Notre Dame de Namur, Inc., Sisters of Notre Dame de Namur Province Center,* 468 Poquonock Ave., Windsor, CT 06095-2473. Tel: 860-688-1832. Prov. Admin. Team: Sr. Patricia Chappell, S.N.D.; Sr. Mary Beth Johnston, S.N.D.; Sr. Anne-Louise Nadeau, S.N.D.

Total number in community 134.

Sisters serve and staff: Colleges, High Schools, Grammar Schools.

Sisters Engaged in Specialized Educational Programs: Pastoral Ministry and Religious Education, Social Health and Community Services, Diocesan Offices.

Represented in the Archdioceses of Boston and Hartford and in the Dioceses of Bridgeport, Burlington, Norwich, Providence, Scranton, St. Augustine, Springfield (MA) and Worcester.

Baltimore Province (1934): *Sisters of Notre Dame de Namur, Maryland Province Center,* 1531 Greenspring Valley Rd., Stevenson, MD 21153. Tel: 410-486-5599. Sr. Marian Schaechtel, S.N.D.deN., Prov. Moderator, Leadership: Sr. Rosemary Donohue, S.N.D.deN.; Sr. Joan Kerrigan, S.N.D.deN.; Sr. Patricia Loome, S.N.D.deN.

Total in community 120.

Properties owned and sponsored: *Trinity School,* Ellicott City, MD; *Maryland Province Center,* Stevenson, MD; *Villa Julie Infirmary,* Stevenson, MD; *Maryvale Preparatory School,* Brooklandville, MD; *Notre Dame Academy,* Villanova, PA; *The Development Center, a joint activity of the Maryland, Chesapeake & Notre Dame Base Communities Provinces.*

Represented in the Archdioceses of Baltimore, Philadelphia and Washington and in the Dioceses of Brooklyn, Portland (ME), Rockville Centre and Wilmington.

Chesapeake Province (1990): *Sisters of Notre Dame de Namur Provincial Offices,* 305 Cable St., Baltimore, MD 21210-2511. Tel: 410-243-1993; Fax: 410-243-2279. Administrative Team: Sr. Mary Donohue, S.N.D.deN.; Sr. Edithann Kane, S.N.D.deN.

Total number in community 76.

Represented in the Archdioceses of Baltimore, Cincinnati, Miami, New York, Philadelphia and Washington and in the Dioceses of Brooklyn, Fort Wayne-South Bend, Metuchen, Raleigh, Richmond and Wheeling-Charleston. Also in Brazil, Kenya, Mexico, Peru, Dem. Republic of Congo and South Africa.

Ohio Province (1840): *Sisters of Notre Dame de Namur Provincial House,* 701 E. Columbia Ave., Cincinnati, OH 45215. Tel: 513-761-7636. Sr. Elizabeth Marie Bowyer, Prov.

Total number in community 216.

Legal Title: *St. Mary's Educational Institute at Cincinnati; Sisters of Notre Dame de Namur - Ohio Province; Sisters of Notre Dame de Namur, Ohio Province, Charitable Trust.*

Ministry in the field of Education at all levels; Pastoral Ministry; Administration and Services; Social Services; Communication; Health Care; Community Services.

Represented in the Archdioceses of Boston, Chicago, Cincinnati, Detroit, Indianapolis and Louisville and in the Dioceses of Austin, Buffalo, Columbus, Covington, Gallup, Joliet, Lafayette, Palm Beach, Phoenix, Saginaw, Sioux Falls and Tucson. Also in Brazil, Nicaragua, Nigeria, Rome and Peru.

California Province (1851): *Province Center - Sisters of Notre Dame de Namur,* 1520 Ralston Ave., Belmont, CA 94002. Provincial Team: Sr. Mary Laxague, S.N.D.deN.; Sr. Nancy O'Shea, S.N.D.deN.; Sr. Virginia Unger, S.N.D.deN.

Total number in community 145.

Legal Title: *Sisters of Notre Dame de Namur California Province.*

Ministries Include: Counselors; Convalescent Hospital Ministry; Diocesan Administrative Positions; Directors of Religious Education; Health Ministry; Missionary Work; Parish Ministry; Education at all levels; Religious Education for Adults; Retreat Work; Social Services.

Represented in the Archdioceses of Los Angeles, Portland OR, San Francisco, and Seattle and in the Dioceses of Burlington, Des Moines, Monterey, Oakland, Sacramento, San Jose and, Stockton.

Base Communities Province (1989): *Sisters of Notre Dame de Namur Base Communities Province Office,* 3037 Fourth St., N.E., Washington, DC 20017. Tel: 202-832-8770. Communications Network: Sr. Catherine Gorman, S.N.D.deN.; Sr. Mary Murphy, S.N.D.deN.; Sr. Marie Romejko, S.N.D.deN.

Total in Province 48.

Legal Title *Sisters of Notre Dame de Namur Base Communities, Inc.*

Ministry in Formal Education; Health Care; Social Services/Community Development; Pastoral Ministry.

Represented in the Archdioceses of Baltimore, Boston, Hartford, Philadelphia, and Washington and in the Dioceses of Brooklyn, Charleston, Charlotte, Harrisburg, Orlando, Richmond, Rockville Centre and Wilmington.

[3010] (O.S.B.S.)—OBLATE SISTERS OF THE BLESSED SACRAMENT (D)

Founded in 1935 by Rev. Sylvester Eisenman, O.S.B.

Motherhouse: *St. Sylvester's Convent,* P.O. Box 217, Marty, SD 57361. Tel: 605-384-3305. Sr. Patricia Mylott, O.S.B.S., Supr.

Kateri Convent: 624 Adams St., Rapid City, SD 57701. Tel: 605-343-6261. Sr. Madeleine LeCompte, O.S.B.S., Treas.

Total number in community 25.

Represented in the Dioceses of Rapid City and Sioux Falls.

[3020] (O.B.T.)—SISTERS OBLATES TO THE BLESSED TRINITY (D)

Founded in Italy in 1923. First foundation in the United States in 1987.

U.S. Generalate & Novitiate: *St. Aloysius Gonzaga Novitiate,* 306 Beekman Rd., P.O. Box 98, Hopewell Junction, NY 12533. Tel: 845-226-5671 Fax: 845-226-5671. E-mail: Jstab35097@aol.com. Mother Gloria Castro, Supr. Gen.

Total number in community 40.

Represented in the Archdioceses of New York and San Juan and in the Dioceses of Madison and Ponce. Also in Italy.

[3030] (O.SS.R.)—OBLATES OF THE MOST HOLY REDEEMER (P)

Founded in Madrid in 1864.

Motherhouse: *Ciempozuelos,* Madrid, Spain. Analita Albani. Mother Gen.

U.S. Foundation: *Our Lady of the Way Residence,* 60-80 Pond St., Jamaica Plain, MA 02130. Tel: 617-524-1640. Sr. Aurea Rendon, Supr.

Total number in community 3.

Represented in the Archdioceses of Boston and New York. Also in Puerto Rico.

[3035] (O.M.O.)—OBLATES OF THE MOTHER OF ORPHANS (P)

Founded in Italy on September 8, 1945.

General Motherhouse: via Amundsen 10, Milano, Italy. Sr. Lucilla Passoni, Gen. Supr.

Universal Total in Congregation 200.

U.S. Address: 20 E. 72nd St., New York, NY 10021. Sr. Maria Isabel Reina, O.M.O., Supr.

Total in community 3.

Represented in the Archdiocese of New York. Also in Cameroon, Colombia, El Salvador, Guatemala and Italy.

[3040] (O.S.P.)—OBLATE SISTERS OF PROVIDENCE (P)

Founded in the United States in 1829

General Motherhouse: *Our Lady of Mount Providence Convent,* 701 Gun Rd., Baltimore, MD 21227. Tel: 410-242-8500. Sr. Mary Annette Beecham, O.S.P., Supr. Gen.; Sr. Mary Ricardo Maddox, O.S.P., Asst. Supr. Gen.; Sr. Crescentia Proctor, O.S.P., Sec. Gen.; Sr. Sharon Young, O.S.P., Treas.

Professed Sisters 94.

Legal Title: *The Oblate Sisters of Providence of the City of Baltimore.*

Sisters serve as Pastoral Ministry-Associates; in the field of Education; Reading Centers; Day Care Centers; Teaching; Counseling; Hispanic & Migrant ministry.

Represented in the Archdioceses of Baltimore and Washington and in the Diocese of Buffalo. Also in Costa Rica.

[3050] (O.S.H.J.)—OBLATE SISTERS OF THE SACRED HEART OF JESUS (P)

Founded in 1894. First foundation in the United States in 1949.

General Motherhouse: Rome, Italy.

American Headquarters: *Villa Maria Teresa,* 50 Warner Rd., Hubbard, OH 44425. Tel: 330-759-9329; Fax: 330-759-7290. Sr. Teresina Rosa, O.S.H.J., Supr.

Total number in the community 20.

Represented in the Diocese of Youngstown.

[3060] (O.S.F.S.)—OBLATE SISTERS OF ST. FRANCIS DE SALES (P)

Founded in France in 1866. First foundation in the United States in 1951.

General Motherhouse: 10 rue des Terrasses, Troyes, France.

American Headquarters: *Villa Aviat Convent,* 399 Childs Rd., Childs, MD 21916. Tel: 410-398-3699. Sr. Anne Elizabeth, O.S.F.S., Supr.

Total number in the community 17.

Ministry in the field of Academic and Religious Education.

Represented in the Archdiocese of Philadelphia and in the Dioceses of Arlington and Wilmington.

[3070] (N.A.U.-O.L.C.)—NORTH AMERICAN UNION SISTERS OF OUR LADY OF CHARITY (P)

Founded in Caen, France in 1641, by St. John Eudes. First foundation in the United States in 1855; autonomous houses were federated in 1944 and in 1979 the Union was established.

General Motherhouse and Administrative Centre: 620 Roswell Rd., N.W.-P.O. Box 340, Carrollton, OH 44615-0340. Tel: 330-627-1641; Fax: 330-627-1935. E-mail: dkohio@bright.net Sr. Deana Kohlman, Supr. Gen.

Total Sisters Membership 102.

Legal Title: *North American Union of the Sisters of Our Lady of Charity, Inc.*

The primary work of the sisters is to devote themselves to the needs of women and girls in residential and non-residential settings; other ministries include: Nursing Homes; People with AIDS; Day Care Centers; Teaching Academic and Religious Education; Pastoral & Parish Ministries.

Represented in the Archdioceses of New York and San Antonio and in the Diocese of Buffalo, El Paso, Erie, Green Bay, Pittsburgh, Rochester, San Diego, Steubenville, Venice and Wheeling-Charleston. Also in Canada and Mexico.

San Diego

North American Union Sisters of Our Lady of Charity: 1930 Illion St., San Diego, CA 92110. Tel: 619-275-0764. Sr. Celia Robledo, Local Supr.

Fort Myers

North American Union Sisters of Our Lady of Charity: 2140 Cottage St., Fort Myers, FL 33901. Tel: 941-337-4550. Sr. Mary John Franey, Local Supr.

Buffalo

North American Union of the Sisters of Our Lady of Charity: 3800 Howard Rd., Hamburg, NY 14075. Tel: 716-648-4988; Fax: 716-648-3062. Sr. Rosemary Toth, Local Supr.

Legal Title: *Sisters of Our Lady of Charity of Refuge, Inc.*

El Paso

North American Union of Our Lady of Charity: 415 N. Glenwood Dr., El Paso, TX 79905. Tel: 915-722-0737; Fax: 915-779-2664. Sr. Yolanda Martinez, Local Supr. San Juan Day Care Centre, Inc., 5636 Frutas Ave., El Paso, TX 79905. Tel: 915-772-1681.

Legal Title: *North American Sisters of Our Lady of Charity, Inc.*

Erie

North American Union of the Sisters of Our Lady of Charity (1934): 4635 East Lake Rd., Erie, PA 16511. Tel: 814-899-1052; Fax: 814-899-1573. Sr. Severiana Morales, Local Supr.

Legal Titles: *Gannondale Residential Center for Girls,* Erie, PA; *North American Union Sisters of Our Lady of Charity, Inc.*

Green Bay

North American Union of the Sisters of Our Lady of Charity: 2560 Shawano Ave.; P.O. Box 10357, Green Bay, WI 54307. Tel: 920-434-8208; Fax: 920-662-0047. Sr. Patrick Dolan, Local Supr.

Legal Titles: *Sisters of Our Lady of Charity of the North American Union, Inc.; McClosky Program, Inc.,* Green Bay, WI.

Pittsburgh

North American Union of the Sisters of Our Lady of Charity: *Nativity Convent,* 4100 Vinceton St., Pittsburgh, PA 15214. Tel: 412-931-2299; Fax: 412-931-6044. Sr. Sheila Rooney, Local Supr.

Legal Titles: *North American Union Sisters of Our Lady of Charity, Inc.; Eudes Institute.*

Rochester

North American Union Sisters of Our Lady of Charity: 1280 Winton Rd. N., Rochester, NY 14609. Tel: 585-654-8600; Fax: 585-654-8601. Sr. Martha Teresa Gomez, Local Supr.

Legal Title: *Sisters of Our Lady of Charity of Refuge, Inc.*

San Antonio

North American Union Sisters of Our Lady of Charity (1897): 1900 Montana St., San Antonio, TX 78210. Tel: 210-475-9390; Fax: 210-475-9373. Sr. Agnes O'Mahony, Local Supr.

Legal Titles: *North American Union Sisters of Our Lady of Charity, Inc.; Our Lady of Victory School.*

Steubenville

North American Union Sisters of Our Lady of Charity: 620 Roswell Rd., N.W.; P.O. Box 158, Carrollton, OH 44615-0158. Tel: 330-627-7647; Fax: 330-627-4415. Sr. Carol Pregno, Local Supr.

Legal Title: *North American Union Sisters of Our Lady of Charity, Inc.*

Walden

North American Union of the Sisters of Our Lady of Charity: *St. Andrews Retreat House,* 257 St. Andrew's Rd., Walden, NY 12586. Tel: 845-778-5941; Fax: 845-778-5099 Sr. Martha Hernandez, Local Supr.

Legal Title: *North American Union Sisters of Our Lady of Charity, Inc.*

Wheeling

North American Union Sisters of Our Lady of Charity: 141 Edgington Ln., Wheeling, WV 26003. Tel: 304-242-7070; Fax: 304-242-8221. Sr. Carol Pregno, Local Supr.

Legal Title: *North American Union Sisters of Our Lady of Charity, Inc.*

[3071] (O.L.C.)—SISTERS OF OUR LADY OF CHARITY (P)

Mt. St. Michael Convent of Our Lady of Charity: 500 W. Davis St., Dallas, TX 75211. Tel: 214-331-1754; Fax: 214-333-1659. Sr. Therese Blanchette, Major Supr.

Total number in the community 11.

Legal Holding: *Mt. St. Michael Spiritual Life Center.*

[3072] (R.O.L.C.)—OUR LADY OF CHARITY OF REFUGE (P)

Monastery of Our Lady of Charity of Refuge: 1125 Malvern Ave., Hot Springs, AR 71901. Tel: 501-623-9651. Sr. Theresa Marie Lalancette, R.O.L.C., Supr.

Total number in the community 13.

[3080] (R.C.D.)—SISTERS OF OUR LADY OF CHRISTIAN DOCTRINE (P)

Founded in New York in 1910 for the work of religious education and social service.

Central Office: *Visitation House,* 629 North Midland Ave., Nyack, NY 10960. Tel: 845-727-1011. Sr. Agnes O'Connor, R.C.D., Pres.

Total number in the community 33.

Ministry in the field of Religious Education and Spirituality; Social Work, Nursing and Counseling.

Represented in the Archdiocese of New York.

[3090] (C.L.H.C.)—CONGREGATION OF OUR LADY, HELP OF THE CLERGY (D)

Maryvale Sisters

Founded in the United States in 1961.

Motherhouse: *Maryvale Motherhouse,* 2522 June Bug Rd., Vale, NC 28168. Tel: 704-276-2626. Mother Mary Louis, Supr.

Total number in the community 5.

Represented in the Diocese of Charlotte.

[3100] (R.S.R.)—CONGREGATION OF OUR LADY OF THE HOLY ROSARY (P)

Founded in Rimouski, P.Q., Canada, in 1874. First Foundation in the United States in 1899.

General Motherhouse: 300 Alle du Rosaire, Rimouski P. Q., Canada, G5L 3E3. Tel: 418-724-5940. Sr. Ida Cote, R.S.R., Supr. Gen.

U.S. Address: *Our Lady of the Holy Rosary,* 20 Thomas St., Portland, ME 04102. Tel: 207-774-3756; 772-3130 (Office). Sr. Carole Jean Lappa, R.S.R., Reg.

Total number in the region 8.

Our Lady of the Holy Rosary Regional House: 25 Portland Ave., Old Orchard Beach, ME 04064. Tel: 207-934-0592. Sr. Olla Laplante, R.S.R., Supr.

Ministry in the fields of Education; Diocesan Ministry; Retreat Ministry.

Represented in the Diocese of Portland (ME).

[3105] (S.O.L.T.)—OUR LADY OF THE MOST HOLY TRINITY CONVENT (D)

Regional House: P.O. Box 189, Skidmore, TX 78389. Tel: 361-287-3146. Sr. Mary Teresa Pacheco, S.O.L.T., Reg. Sister Servant.

Professed Sisters 70; Novices 12; Candidates 12.

Represented in the Archdiocese of Santa Fe and in the Dioceses of Corpus Christi, Fargo and Laredo.

[3110] (R.C.)—CONGREGATION OF OUR LADY OF THE RETREAT IN THE CENACLE (P)

Founded in France in 1826. First foundation in the United States in 1892.

Generalate: Piazza Madonna del Cenacolo, 15, Rome, Italy, 00136.

North American Province (2000): *Congregation of Our Lady of the Cenacle,* 513 Fullerton Pkwy., Chicago, IL 60614-5999. Tel: 773-528-6300; Fax: 773-549-0554. Sr. Mary Peters, R.C., Prov.

Total number in community 159.

Properties owned and sponsored: *Cenacle Sisters,* Hoschton, GA; *Cenacle of St. Regis of Flushing, Inc.,* Brooklyn, NY; *Cenacle Convent, Inc.,* Chicago, IL; *Cenacle Convent, Inc.,* Houston, TX; *Warrenville Cenacle Retreat House,* Warrenville, IL; *Religious of Our Lady of the Cenacle of New Brunswick, NJ,* Metuchen, NJ; *Convent of Our Lady of the Cenacle,* Metairie, LA; *The Cenacle Convent of Palm Beach Co., Inc.,* Palm Beach, FL; *Ronkonkoma Cenacle, Inc.,* Rockville Centre, NY; *Cenacle Sisters,* Gainesville, FL.

Represented in the Archdioceses of Atlanta, Chicago, Denver, New Orleans, New York, and St. Louis and in the Dioceses of Brooklyn, Fort Wayne-South Bend, Galveston-Houston, Joliet, Madison, Metuchen, Oakland, Palm Beach, Paterson, Rochester, Rockville Centre, St. Augustine, St. Petersburg, Santa Rosa and Wheeling-Charleston. Also in Canada.

[3120] (O.L.S.)—SISTERS OF OUR LADY OF SORROWS (P)

Founded in Italy in 1839. First foundation in the United States in 1947.

General Motherhouse: Viale Vaticano 90, Rome, Italy 00165. Mother Lina Rossi, O.L.S., Supr. Gen.

American Headquarters: *Sisters of Our Lady of Sorrows Convent,* 9894 Norris Ferry Rd., Shreveport, LA 71106. Fax: 318-797-7003. Sr. Seraphine Ricci, O.L.S., Supr.

Total number in community 31; Universal number 371.

Ministry in the field of Education; Work with people with mental retardation; Outreach to the poor; Pastoral Ministry; CCD & Adult Education.

Represented in the Dioceses of Alexandria and Shreveport.

[3130] (O.L.V.M.)—OUR LADY OF VICTORY MISSIONARY SISTERS (P)

Founded in the United States in 1922.

Motherhouse: *Victory Noll,* P.O. Box 109, Huntington, IN 46750-0109. Tel: 260-356-0628; Fax: 260-358-1504. E-mail: victorynoll@olvm.org. Sr. Jeanette Halbach, Pres.

Total number in the community 158.

Legal Holding: *Victory Noll Sisters Community Support Trust.*

Represented in the Archdioceses of Chicago, Cincinnati, Denver, Detroit, Dubuque, Kansas City in Kansas, Los Angeles, Louisville, Miami, Milwaukee, San Antonio, and Santa Fe and in the Dioceses of Austin, Belleville, Cheyenne, Cleveland, Fresno, Fort Wayne-South Bend, Phoenix, Salt Lake City, San Bernardino, San Diego, Sioux Falls, Toledo and Tucson. Also in Bolivia.

[3140] (C.S.A.C.)—SISTERS OF THE CATHOLIC APOSTOLATE (PALLOTTINE) (P)

Founded in Italy in 1835. First foundation in the United States in 1889.

General Motherhouse: Viale Kennedy No. 62, Grottaferrata, Rome, Italy. Mother M. Ivete Garlet, C.S.A.C., Supr. Gen.

Universal Total in Congregation 525.

Provincial Motherhouse in America: *St. Patrick's Villa, Harriman Heights,* P.O. Box 118, Harriman, NY 10926. Tel: 914-783-9007. Sr. Michele Ruggiero, C.S.A.C., Prov. Moderator.

Total number in the community 55.

Ministry in the field of Academic and Religious Education at Elementary and Secondary Levels; Pastoral Services.

Represented in the Archdioceses of Newark and New York and in the Diocese of Brooklyn.

[3150] (S.A.C.)—PALLOTTINE MISSIONARY SISTERS - QUEEN OF APOSTLES PROVINCE (P)

(Missionary Sisters of the Catholic Apostolate)

Founded in Rome, Italy, in 1838. First founded in the United States in 1912.

General Motherhouse: Rome, Italy. Sr. Stella Holitz, S.A.C., Supr. Gen.

American Provincialate: *Pallottine Renewal Center,* 15270 Old Halls Ferry Rd., Florissant, MO 63034. Tel: 314-837-7100; Fax: 314-837-1041. Sr. M. Elisabeth Heptner, S.A.C., Prov.; Sr. Marian Ruth Creamer, S.A.C., Community Archivist.

Total number in the community 686.

Sisters minister in the fields of Health Care; Child Day Care; Education; Retreat and Renewal Ministry; Social Services; Counseling; Parish and Pastoral Work.

Properties Owned: *Pallottine Renewal Center,* Florissant, MO; *Frascati Convent,* Londell, MO; *St. Mary's Hospital & Convent,* Huntington, WV; *Vincent Pallotti House,* Huntington, WV; *St. Joseph's Hospital & Convent,* Buckhannon, WV; *St. Vincent Pallotti Convent, High School & Child Care Center,* Laurel, MD.

Represented in the Archdioceses of St. Louis and Washington and in the Diocese of Wheeling-Charleston.

[3160] (P.V.M.I.)—PARISH VISITORS OF MARY IMMACULATE (P)

Founded in New York City in 1920 for family visitation and religious education. A contemplative-missionary community serving the Church by person-to person evangelization.

Motherhouse, Juniorate and Novitiate: *Marycrest,* P.O. Box 658, Monroe, NY 10950-0658. Tel: 845-783-2251. Sr. Mary Gemma Spoldi, Gen. Supr.; Sr. Ann Marie, Juniorate Dir.; Sr. Dolores Marie, Novice Dir.; Sr. Jean Marie, Postulant Dir.

Total number in community 62.

Ministry in evangelization, catechetics, & spiritual counseling; liaison for social services.

Represented in the Archdiocese of New York and in the Dioceses of Brooklyn, Scranton and Syracuse. Also in Nigeria.

[3170] (C.P.)—RELIGIOUS OF THE PASSION OF JESUS CHRIST (P)

(Passionist Nuns)

Founded in Italy in 1771, by St. Paul of the Cross. First foundation in the United States in 1910.

Our Lady of Sorrows Convent of the Passionist Nuns (Contemplative): 2715 Churchview Ave., Pittsburgh, PA 15227. Tel: 412-881-1155. Mother Joyce Foga, C.P., Supr.

Professsed 8; Novices 1.

The Religious of the Passion of Jesus Christ (Contemplative) (1926): *St. Gabriel's Monastery,* 631 Griffin Pond Rd., Clarks Summit, PA 18411. Tel: 570-586-2791; Fax: 570-586-8210. Sr. Mary Regina, C.P., Supr.

Professed Sisters 8.

Sisters serve and staff: Retreats and other Programs for Women and Men of all Faiths; Clergy and Religious; Ecumenical Groups; Business and Civic Groups.

Legal Holding: *St. Gabriel's Monastery and Retreat Center.*

Passionist Nuns (Cloistered Contemplative) (1946): *St. Joseph's Monastery,* 8564 Crisp Rd., Whitesville, KY 42378. Tel: 270-233-4571. Mother Catherine Marie, C.P., Supr.

Professed Nuns 16; Novices 1; Postulants 4.

Passionist Nuns (Contemplative) (1947): *Monastery of the Sacred Passion,* 1151 Donaldson Hwy., Erlanger, KY 41018. Tel: 859-371-8568. Sr. Margaret Mary, C.P., Supr.

Total number in community 9.

Legal Title: *Passionist Nuns of Covington, KY.*

Passionist Nuns (Cloistered) (1948): *Passionist Monastery,* 15700 Clayton Rd., Ellisville, MO 63011-2300. Tel: 636-527-6867. Mother Mary Veronica, C.P., Supr.

Total number in community 10.

[3180] (C.P.)—SISTERS OF THE CROSS AND PASSION (P)

(Passionist Sisters)

Founded in 1852. First foundation in the United States 1924.

Generalate: *Parkmount,* 458 Bury New Rd., Salford, England. M7 4LH Sr. Anne Cunningham, C.P., Congregational Leader.

Motherhouse-American Provincial Office: *Holy Family Convent,* One Wright Ln., North Kingstown, RI 02852. Tel: 401-294-3554. Sr. Rosemary Traynor, C.P., Prov. Leader.

Professed Sisters 43.

Sisters minister in Retreat Houses; Elementary and Secondary Education; Hospital Chaplaincy; Parish Ministry; Religious Education; Social Services.

Properties owned and operated: *Our Lady of Calvary Retreat,* Farmington, CT.

Represented in the Archdioceses of Hartford, New York and Washington and in the Dioceses of Memphis, Providence and Rockville Centre. Also in Jamaica, West Indies.

[3190] (A.P.)—NUNS OF THE PERPETUAL ADORATION OF THE BLESSED SACRAMENT (P)

Founded in Rome in 1807. First foundation in United States in 1925.

El Paso: *Expiatory Shrine of Christ the King and Monastery of Perpetual Adoration,* 145 N. Cotton Ave., El Paso, TX 79901. Tel: 915-533-5323. Mother Maria Guadalupe, A.P., Supr.

Sisters 17.

Represented in the Archdioceses of Anchorage and San Francisco and in the Diocese of El Paso and Sioux Falls.

San Francisco: *Monastery of Perpetual Adoration,* 771 Ashbury St., San Francisco, CA 94117. Tel: 415-566-2743. Mother Rosalba Maria, A.P., Supr.

Sisters 18.

Represented in the Archdiocese of San Francisco. Also in Africa, Chile, Mexico and Spain.

[3195] (A.P.G.)—SISTER OF PERPETUAL ADORATION OF GUADALUPE, INC. (P)

U.S. Foundation: 2403 W. Travis, San Antonio, TX 78207. Tel: 210-227-5546. Mother Luz del Carmen Sanchez, A.P.G., General Counsel.

Total number in community 8.

[3200] (Sch.P.)—SISTERS OF THE PIOUS SCHOOLS (Escolapias) (P)

Founded in Figueras, Spain in 1829. Universal Total in Congregation 844.

General Motherhouse: Via Crescenzio 77, Rome, Italy 00193. Mother Isolina Vasquez, Sch.P., Supr. Gen.

U.S. Headquarters (1954): 17601 Nordhoff St., Northridge, CA 91325. Tel: 818-885-6265; Fax: 818-718-6752. Sr. Guadalupe Gonzalez, Sch.P., Vice Prov.

Total number in community 20.

Ministry in Religious Education; Parish Schools.

Represented in the Archdiocese of Los Angeles.

[3210] (P.C.P.A.)—POOR CLARES OF PERPETUAL ADORATION (P)

Founded in France, 1854. First foundation in the United States at Cleveland, Ohio, 1921. Poor Clares of Perpetual Adoration, cloistered, contemplative, solemn vows. Object: Perpetual Adoration in spirit of Praise and Thanksgiving and Gospel living. Solemn Exposition day and night. Each monastery is autonomous.

Sancta Clara Monastery (1946): 4200 N. Market Ave., Canton, OH 44714. Tel: 330-492-1171; Fax: 330-492-2227. Sr. Marion Zeltmann, P.C.P.A., Abbess.

Total number in community 10.

Saint Joseph Adoration Monastery (1956): 2311 Stockham Ln., Portsmouth, OH, 45662-3049. Tel: 740-353-4713. Mother Dolores Marie, Abbess.

Total number in community 7.

Legal Holdings and Titles: *Poor Clares of Perpetual Adoration; St. Joseph Adoration Monastery.*

Adoration Monastery (1921): 4108 Euclid Ave., Cleveland, OH 44103. Tel: 216-361-0783. Mother Mary James, P.C.P.A., Abbess.

Total number in community 19.

Poor Clares of Perpetual Adoration (1954): *Our Lady of the Most Blessed Sacrament Monastery,* 3900 13th St., N.E., Washington, DC 20017. Tel: 202-526-6808; Fax: 202-526-0678. E-mail: claresdcpray4u@starpower.net Mother Margaret Mary, P.C.P.A., Abbess.

Total number in community is 11.

Our Lady of the Angels Monastery: *Shrine of the Most Blessed Sacrament,* 3222 County Rd. 548, Hanceville, AL 35077. Tel: 256-352-6267; Fax: 205-795-5702. Mother M. Angelica, P.C.P.A., Abbess & Pres.

Total number in community 41; Novices 6; Postulants 7.

Legal Titles and Holdings: *Our Lady of the Angels Monastery, Inc.*

Represented in the Diocese of Birmingham in Alabama.

[3220] (P.C.J.)—SISTERS OF THE POOR CHILD JESUS (P)

Founded on February 2, 1844 in Germany. First founded in the United States on July 2, 1924 at Parkersburg, West Virginia.

General Motherhouse: *Haus Loreto,* Simpelveld, Netherlands. Rev. Mother Clare Angela, P.C.J., Supr. Gen.

Universal number in Congregation 850.

American Region and Novitiate: *Our Lady of Bethlehem Convent,* 4567 Olentangy River Rd., Columbus, OH 43214. Tel: 614-451-3900; Fax: 614-451-4745. Sr. Frances Teresa Holzberger, P.C.J., Reg. Supr.

Total number in community 7.

Ministry in the field of Education.

Properties owned: *Kindergarten and a Day Care Center.*

Represented in the Dioceses of Columbus and Wheeling-Charleston.

[3230] (P.H.J.C.)—POOR HANDMAIDS OF JESUS CHRIST (P)

(The Ancilla Domini Sisters)

Founded in Germany in 1851. First foundation in the United States in 1868.

General Motherhouse: Dernbach, Westerwald, Germany. Sr. M. Hermana Brand, P.H.J.C., Supr. Gen.

American Province-Provincialate: *Convent Ancilla Domini,* 9601 Union Rd.; P.O. Box 1, Donaldson, IN 46513. Tel: 574-936-9936; Fax: 574-935-1785. Sr. Jolise May, P.H.J.C., Prov. Councilors: Sr. Mary Josef Shingler, P.H.J.C.; Sr. Shirley Bell, P.H.J.C.; Sr. Joetta Huelsmann, P.H.J.C.; Sr. Margaret Anne Henss, P.H.J.C., Treas.; Ms. Peg Van Nevel Dir. Devel.; Sr. M. Cecelia Bianchino, P.H.J.C., Archivist.

Professed Sisters 157.

Ministry in the field of Academic Education at all levels; Hospitals; Parish Ministries; Retreat Ministries; Child Care Institutions; and Retirement Homes.

Properties owned or sponsored: *Ancilla Domini College; Convent Ancilla Domini; Bethany Retreat House; St. Henry Convent; Sojourner Truth House; Maria Center; Catherine Kasper Life Center, Inc.; Lindenwood Retreat & Ministry Center; Earthworks, Inc.; Poor Handmaids of Jesus Christ Community Support Trust,* Donaldson, IN; *Ancilla Domini Convent,* Milwaukee, WI; *Ancilla Domini Hospitals; Self Insurance Trust; St. Catherine Convent,* East Chicago, IN; *Annunciation Convent,* Hoffman Estates, IL; *Poor Handmaids of Jesus Christ,* 1916 S. Clarence Ave., Berwyn, IL 60402; *Mary Katherine Convent,* Cairo, IL; *Marian Convent,* Fort Wayne, IN; *Beacon House,* Burlington, IA; *St. Mary Hospital; St. Mary Convent,* East St. Louis, IL; *Ancilla Systems, Inc.*

Represented in the Archdioceses of Chicago, Cincinnati and Milwaukee and in the Dioceses of Belleville, Fort Wayne-South Bend, Gary, Savannah, Springfield (IL) and Springfield-Cape Girardeau. Also in Africa, Brazil, Germany and Mexico.

[3240] (C.J.C.)—POOR SISTERS OF JESUS CRUCIFIED AND THE SORROWFUL MOTHER (D)

Founded in the United States in 1924.

General Motherhouse and Novitiate: *Our Lady of Sorrows Convent,* 261 Thatcher St., Brockton, MA 02302-3997. Sr. Mary Valliere, C.J.C., Gen. Supr.

Total number in community 40.

Ministry in Nursing Homes; Education Center; Elementary Schools; Assisted Living facilities; and Pastoral Ministry.

Properties owned: *St. Joseph Manor Health Care, Inc.; Mater Dei Adult Day Health Program; Our Lady of Sorrows Convent,* Brockton, MA; *St. Mary's Villa Nursing Home,* Elmhurst, PA; *St. Peter's Convent,* South Boston, MA.

Represented in the Archdiocese of Boston and in the Diocese of Scranton.

[3242] (C.S.N.)—THE CONGREGATION OF THE SISTERS OF NAZARETH (P)

Founded in England by Mother St. Basil.

Motherhouse: Hammersmith, London, W6 8DB, England. Sr. St. Hilary, Supr. Gen.

Regional Headquarters: *Nazareth House,* 3333 Manning Ave., Los Angeles, CA 90064. Tel: 310-839-2361. Sr. John Berchmans, Supr.

Professed Sisters 35.

Legal Title: *The Congregation of the Sisters of Nazareth Mother House U.S.A., Inc.*

Represented in the Archdioceses of Los Angeles and San Francisco and in the Dioceses of Fresno, Madison and San Diego. Also in American Samoa.

[3250] (P.S.S.J.)—POOR SISTERS OF ST. JOSEPH (P)

Founded in Buenos Aires, Argentina, 1880.

General Motherhouse: Leon Gallardo 734, Muniz, Buenos Aires, Argentina. Mother Agueda Magdalena Padros, Mother Gen.

U.S. Foundation: *Casa Belen,* 305 E. Fourth St., Bethlehem, PA, 18015. Tel: 610-867-4030.

U.S. Motherhouse: *St. Gabriel Convent,* 4319 Sano St., Alexandria, VA 22312. Tel: 703-354-0395.

Casa Nazareth: 532 Spruce St., Reading, PA 19602. Tel: 310-378-1947.

Total number in community 14.

Represented in the Dioceses of Allentown and Arlington.

[3260] (C.PP.S.)—SISTERS OF THE PRECIOUS BLOOD (DAYTON, OHIO) (P)

Founded in Switzerland in 1834. First foundation in the United States in 1844.

Generalate: 4000 Denlinger Rd., Dayton, OH 45426. Tel: 937-837-3302; Fax: 937-837-8825. Sr. Maryann Bremke, C.PP.S., Pres.; Sr. Nancy Raley, C.PP.S., Vice Pres. & Councilor; Sr. M. Elise Calmus, C.PP.S., Sec. & Councilor; Sr. Nadine Kaschalk, C.PP.S., Councilor; Sr. Benita Volk, C.PP.S., Councilor; Sr. Barbara Brown, C.PP.S., Treas.; Sr. Noreen Jutte, C.PP.S., Archivist.

Total Membership 275.

Ministry in Universities, High Schools, Elementary Schools; Diocesan Offices; Pastoral Ministry in Hospitals and Long-term Care Centers; Religious and Adult Education; Nursing Care; Homemaking Services in Homes for the Aged; Ethnic Minorities and Marginalized Peoples; Retreat and Music Ministry; Missionary and Volunteer Services.

Properties owned and sponsored: *Generalate,* Dayton, OH; *Salem Heights Convent,* Dayton, OH; *Maria Stein Center,* Maria Stein, OH; *San Luis Rey Academy, Inc.,* San Luis Rey, CA.

Represented in the Archdioceses of Cincinnati, Denver, Detroit, Philadelphia, and Washington and in the Dioceses of Cleveland, Columbus, Dallas, Gallup, Grand Rapids, Kalamazoo, Lafayette (IN), Lansing, Marquette, Phoenix, Saginaw, San Bernardino, San Diego, Toledo and Tucson. Also in Chile and Guatemala.

[3270] (C.PP.S.)—SISTERS OF THE MOST PRECIOUS BLOOD (O'FALLON, MO.) (P)

Founded in Switzerland in 1845. First foundation in the United States in 1870.

General Motherhouse: *St. Mary's Institute of O'Fallon,* 204 N. Main St., O'Fallon, MO 63366-2299. Tel: 636-240-3420; Fax: 636-272-5031. Sr. Susan Borgel, C.PP.S., Supr. Gen.; Gen. Councilors: Sr. Virginia Jaskiewicz; Sr. Ruth Kertz; Sr. Mary Whited; Sr. Nadine Flott, Treas. & Councilor; Sr. Charlene Grieshaber, Sec.; Sr. Mary Joan Dyer, Community Archivist.

Total number in community 240.

Ministry in the field of Education; Care of the Elderly; Pastoral and Parish Ministry; Ecclesiastical Art; Foreign Missions; Social Services; Prayer/Presence.

Properties owned: *St. Mary's Institute of O'Fallon,* O'Fallon, MO; *Charitable Trust, Sisters of the Most Precious Blood of O'Fallon, MO,* O'Fallon, MO; *Linda Vista Catholic School,* Chesterfield, MO; *St. Elizabeth Academy,* St. Louis, MO; *St. Elizabeth Adult Day Care Center,* St. Louis, MO; *Centers for Professional and Pastoral Services,* O'Fallon, MO.

Represented in the Archdioceses of Anchorage, Chicago, Philadelphia, St. Louis, and Washington and in the Dioceses of Des Moines, Jefferson City, Las Cruces, Springfield-Cape Girardeau, Springfield (IL) and Wheeling-Charleston.

[3310] (P.M.)—SISTERS OF THE PRESENTATION OF MARY (P)

Founded in France in 1796. First foundation in the United States in 1873.

General Motherhouse: *Presentazione di Maria,* Viale PIO XI,29 C.P. 104, Castelgandolfo, Italy 00040. Mother Angele Dion, Supr. Gen.

Inter-Provincial Novitiate: 180 Lowell Rd., Hudson, NH 03051. Tel: 603-880-8186. Sr. Suzette Tanguay, Dir.

Manchester Province: *Provincial Administration,* 495 Mammoth Rd., Manchester, NH 03104-5494. Tel: 603-669-1080. Sr. Suzanne Bourret, Prov. Supr.

Sisters 183.

Ministry in the field of Education at all levels; Pastoral Ministry; Youth Ministry; Ministry for Persons with Disabilities.

Properties owned: *Rivier College,* Nashua, NH; *Presentation of Mary Academy,* Hudson, NH; *Provincial House; St. Joseph Residence; St. Marie Residence,* Manchester, NH; *Our Lady of Hope House of Prayer,* New Ipswich, NH; *Bethany House,* Manchester, NH; *Trinity House; Presentation of Mary Novitiate,* Hudson, NH; *Emmanuel House,* Woonsocket, RI; *Emmaus Convent,* Manchester, NH; *Presentation of Mary Convent,* Nashua, NH.

Represented in the Dioceses of Fall River, Galveston-Houston, Manchester and Providence.

Methuen Province - Provincial Administration: *Sisters of the Presentation of Mary,* 209 Lawrence St., Methuen, MA 01844. Tel: 978-687-1369; 685-0980. Sr. Helene Bissonnette, P.M., Prov.

Total number in Province 136.

Ministry in High Schools; Elementary Schools; Montessori Kindergartens; Montessori Day Nurseries; Religious Instruction Centers; Spiritual Retreat Center.

Properties owned: *Montessori Kindergartens; Montessori Day Nurseries; Marie Joseph Spiritual Center,* Biddeford, ME; *Presentation of Mary Academy,* Methuen, MA.

Represented in the Archdiocese of Boston and in the Dioceses of Portland (ME), Springfield (MA) and Worcester.

[3320] (P.B.V.M.)—SISTERS OF THE PRESENTATION OF THE B.V.M. (P)

Founded in Ireland in 1775. First foundation in San Francisco CA in 1854.

Represented in the United States in the following Archdioceses and Dioceses:

Dubuque P

Mt. Loretto Convent, Motherhouse and Novitiate: 2360 Carter Rd., Dubuque, IA 52001-2997. Tel: 563-588-2008; Fax: 563-588-4463. Sr. Joy Peterson, P.B.V.M., Pres.

Total number in community 147.

Legal Title: *Sisters of the Presentation of the B.V.M.*, Dubuque, IA.

Ministry in the field of Religious and Academic Education; Hospital & Prison Chaplaincy; Elder Care; Parish & Campus Ministries; South American Bolivian Mission; Diocesan/Metropolitan Offices; Retreat & Spiritual Direction.

Represented in the Archdioceses of Chicago, Dubuque, St. Paul-Minneapolis and Washington and in the Dioceses of Birmingham, Brownsville, Covington, Davenport, Jackson, Knoxville, New Ulm, Orlando, Rapid City, Sioux City and Winona. Also in Bolivia.

New York (P)

Mt. St. Joseph Administration Center: *Sisters of the Presentation of the Blessed Virgin Mary,* 880 Jackson Ave., New Windsor, NY 12553. Tel: 845-564-0513; Fax: 845-567-0219. Sr. Catherine Cleary, P.B.V.M., Pres.; Sr. Luke Mulraney , P.B.V.M., Community Archivist.

Total number in community 164.

Ministry in the field of Academic Education at all levels; Pastoral Services; Health Care and Social Services.

Represented in the Archdioceses of Boston, Newark, New York and Washington and in the Dioceses of Brooklyn, Manchester, Metuchen, Norwich, Paterson, Providence, Rockville Centre, Trenton and Worcester. Also in Bolivia and Ghana.

Our Lady of the Presentation, Motherhouse and Novitiate: 419 Woodrow Rd., Staten Island, NY 10312. Tel: 718-356-2121. Sr. Catherine Quinn, Congregation Leader.

Professed Sisters 22.

Ministry in Elementary and High Schools; University; Campus Ministry; Pastoral Counseling; Adult Education; Healing & Parish Ministry.

Represented in the Archdioceses of New York, Newark and Philadelphia and in the Diocese of Sioux Falls.

San Francisco (P)

Presentation Convent-Motherhouse: 2340 Turk Blvd., San Francisco, CA 94118. Tel: 415-751-0406. Sr. Ann Therese Lynch, P.B.V.M., Pres.; Christine Catalano, Archivist.

Total number in community 117.

Legal Title: *Sisters of the Presentation of the Blessed Virgin Mary.*

Ministry in the field of Religious and Academic Education at all levels; Parish Ministry; Social and Health Ministry; College and University Teaching; Retreat Work; Church Related Administrative Positions; Missionary Work; Internal Ministry.

Represented in the Archdioceses of Los Angeles and San Francisco and in the Dioceses of Monterey Oakland, Orange, San Jose, and Santa Rosa.

Albany (P)

St. Colman's Presentation Convent, Motherhouse and Novitiate: *Sisters of the Presentation of the Blessed Virgin Mary PVBM,* Watervliet, NY 12189. Tel: 518-273-4911; Fax: 518-273-3312. Mother Mary Carmel, Supr.

Total number in community 42.

Ministry in the field of Academic Education; Day Care Center; Child Caring Institution; Resident School for Autistic & Emotionally Disturbed Children; Parish Ministry.

Represented in the Diocese of Albany.

Fargo (P)

Sacred Heart Convent, Motherhouse and Novitiate: *Sisters of Presentation of the Blessed Virgin Mary PBVM,* 1101 32nd Ave., S., Fargo, ND 58103. Tel: 701-237-4857. E-mail: presentationsrs@cableone.net. Sr. Paula Ringuette, Pres.; Sr. Mary Jo Hasey, Archivist.

Total number in community 57.

Sponsored Ministries: *Presentation Prayer Center,* Fargo, ND; *Presentation Center,* Fargo, ND; *Hughes, Inc.,* Fargo, ND; *The Presentation Sisters Foundation,* Fargo, ND.

Represented in the Archdiocese of Dubuque and in the Dioceses of Columbus, Fargo, Jackson, Knoxville, Rapid City and Springfield-Cape Girardeau. Also in Peru.

Sioux Falls (P)

Presentation Convent, Motherhouse and Novitiate: *Sisters of the Presentation of the Blessed Virgin Mary,* 1500 N. Second St., Aberdeen, SD 57401. Tel: 605-229-8419. Sr. Virginia McCall, Pres.; Sr. Lois Ann Sargent, Congregation Archivist.

Total number in community 122.

Ministry in the field of Academic Education; Hospitals; Homes for the Aged; Parish Pastoral Ministry; Missionary Ministry in Bolivia and Guatemala.

Represented in the Diocese of Sioux Falls.

Worcester (P)

Presentation Convent of the Presentation of the B.V.M.: 99 Church St., Leominster, MA 01453. Sr. Catherine Cleary, Pres.

Total number in community 164.

Sisters staff or sponsor: Elementary and High School Education; Spanish Apostolate; Pastoral Ministry; Social Services; Nursing.

Represented in the Archdioceses of Boston, Newark, New York and Washington and in the Dioceses of Brooklyn, Manchester, Metuchen, Norwich, Paterson, Providence, Rockville Centre, Trenton and Worcester. Also in Bolivia and Ghana.

[3330] (P.B.V.M.)—UNION OF SISTERS OF THE PRESENTATION OF THE BLESSED VIRGIN MARY (P)

The Congregation of the Presentation was founded in Cork, Ireland, 1775. By decree of the Sacred Congregation for Religious, the Union of Sisters of the Presentation was established in Ireland in 1976. First U.S.A. Province in 1989.

Generalate: Monasterevan Co. Kildare Ireland, Tel: 045-525-335. Sr. Wiona Engel, P.B.V.M., Supr. Gen.

Provincialate: 729 W. Wilshire Dr., Phoenix, AZ 85007. Tel: 602-271-9687. Sr. Joan O'Sullivan, P.B.V.M., Prov.; Sr. Katherine Fennell, P.B.V.M., Treas.

Novitiate: 10843 Gorman Ave., Los Angeles, CA 90059-1313. Tel: 714-527-4844. Sr. Gemma Pines, P.B.V.M., Dir.-Novices.

Perpetual Profession 79.

Sisters serve and staff: Elementary and Religious Education; Parish Ministry; Health & Hospital Services; Social Services.

Represented in the Archdioceses of Los Angeles, Mobile, New Orleans, San Antonio and San Francisco and in the Dioceses of Birmingham, Biloxi, Oakland, Orange, Phoenix, Sacramento, San Bernardino, Savannah and Tucson.

[3340] (S.P.)—SISTERS OF PROVIDENCE (D)

Founded in Kingston, Canada in 1861. First foundation in the United States in 1873. Became independent, diocesan foundation in 1892.

Providence Motherhouse: 5 Gamelin St., Holyoke, MA 01040-4081. Tel: 413-536-7511; Fax: 413-536-7917. E-mail: Sisters@sisofprov.org. Sr. Joan Mullen, S.P., Congregation Pres.

Professed Sisters 90.

Legal Holdings and Titles: *Sisters of Providence, Inc.,* Holyoke, MA, *Sisters of Providence Health System, Inc.,* Springfield, MA, *Hospitals: Mercy Hospital,* Springfield, MA; *Providence Hospital,* Holyoke, MA; *Sisters of Providence Care Centers, Inc. including: Beaven Kelly Home; St. Luke's Home, Inc.; Mt. St. Vincent Nursing Home,* Holyoke, MA; *Farren Care Center, Inc.,* Turners Falls, MA; *St. Joseph of the Pines Hospital, Inc.,* Southern Pines, NC; *Brightside for Children & Families, Inc.,* West Springfield, MA; *Family Services: Providence Ministries for the Needy, Inc.,* Holyoke, MA.; *Retreat House: Genesis Spiritual Life Center,* Westfield, MA; *Providence Place, Inc.,* Holyoke, MA.

Represented in the Dioceses of Raleigh, Springfield (MA) and Worcester.

[3350] (S.P.)—SISTERS OF PROVIDENCE (P)

Founded in Montreal in 1843. First foundation in the United States in 1856.

General Motherhouse and Novitiate: 12055 Grenet St., Montreal, Quebec, Canada, H4J 2J5. Sr. Kathryn Rutan, Supr. Gen.

Mother Joseph Province (2000): *Sisters of Providence,* 506 Second Ave. Ste. 1200, Seattle, WA 98104-2329. Tel: 206-464-3386; Fax: 206-464-3984. Web site: www.sistersofprovidence.net. Sr. Barbara Schamber, S.P., Prov. Supr.

Total number in community 990; Sisters in province 190.

Ministry in the field of Academic Education; Health Care Services; Hospitals & Skilled Nursing Facilities; Outpatient Health Care Services; Home, Health and Hospice; Retirement Homes; Children's Nursing Centers; Senior and Handicapped Housing Facilities; Shelters for Homeless Women with Children; Transitional Housing for Women; Assisted Living facilities; Health Plans; Health Care Clinics; Child and Family Services; Prison Ministry.

Properties, entities and divisions owned or operated: *Sisters of Providence - Mother Joseph Province; St. Joseph Residence,* Seattle, WA; *Mount St. Joseph,* Spokane, WA; *Providence-Pariseau; Providence Hospitality House,* Seattle, WA; *Sojourner Place,* Seattle, WA; *WomanSpirit Center,* Issaquah, WA; *Providence Alaska Medical Center,* Anchorage, AK; *Providence Extended Care Center,* Anchorage, AK; *Providence Health System Housing; Providence Horizon House,* Anchorage, AK; *Providence Home Health Care,* Anchorage, AK; *Providence Seward Medical Center,* Seward, AK; *Providence Kodiak Island Medical Center,* Kodiak, AK; *Providence Everett Medical Center,* Everett, WA; *Providence Health Care Center,* Everett, WA; *Providence Home Care and Hospice of Snohomish County,* Everett, WA; *Heritage House at the Market (leased),* Seattle, WA; *Hospice of Seattle,* Seattle, WA; *Providence Mount St. Vincent,* Seattle, WA; *Providence St. Peter Hospital,* Olympia, WA; *Providence Mother Joseph Care Center,* Olympia, WA; *Providence Marianwood,* Issaquah, WA; *Providence Centralia Hospital,* Centralia, WA; *Providence Sound HomeCare,* Olympia, WA; *Providence St. Francis Association dba St. Francis House,* Olympia, WA; *St. Luke Association dba-Providence Place,* Chehalis, WA; *Providence Blanchet Association dba Providence Blanchet House,* Centralia, WA; *Providence Rossi Association dba Providence Rossiouse,* Centralia, WA; *Providence Yakima Medical Center,* Yakima, WA; *Providence Hospital,* Toppenish, WA. *Sisters of Providence in Oregon—Oregon Regional Office; Providence St. Vincent Medical Center; Providence Portland Medical Center ; Providence Child Center,* Portland, OR; *Providence Milwaukie Hospital,* Milwaukie, OR; *Providence Newberg Hospital,* Newberg, OR; *Providence Seaside Hospital (leased),* Seaside, OR; *The Gamelin Association dba—Providence House,* Yakima, WA; *The Gamelin-Oregon Association dba—Emilie House,* Portland, OR; *The Gamelin-California Association—Providence House,* Oakland, CA; *Providence Medford Medical Center,* Medford, OR. *Sisters of Providence in California-Providence High School; Providence Saint Joseph Medical Center,* Burbank, CA. *Sisters of CA; Providence Services,* Spokane, WA; *The Providence Housing Association dba Vincent House,* Seattle, WA; *Providence Health System,* Seattle, WA.

Represented in the Archdioceses of Anchorage, Los Angeles, Portland (OR), and Seattle and in the Dioceses of Baker, Great Falls-Billings, Helena, Oakland, Spokane and Yakima.

Novitiate House: 1016 N. Superior, Spokane, WA 99202-1295. Tel: 509-487-7644; Fax: 509-489-0964. Sr. Elizabeth Cole, S.P., Novitiate Dir.

Vocation Office: 9 E. Ninth Ave., Spokane, WA 99202-1295 Tel: 509-474-2323.

Elisabeth Province (1987): *Our Lady of Province,* 47 W. Spring St., Winooski, VT 05404. Tel: 802-655-2395; Fax: 802-655-3888. Sr. Rita Bourassa, S.P., Supr.

Total number in community 28.

[3360] (S.P.)—SISTERS OF PROVIDENCE OF SAINT MARY-OF-THE-WOODS, INDIANA (P)

Founded in France in 1806. First foundation in the United States in 1840.

General Administration: Sisters of Providence- Owens Hall, St. Mary-of-the-Woods, IN 47876-1089. Tel: 812-535-4193. Web site: www.sistersofprovidence.org. Sr. Ann Margaret O'Hara, S.P., Gen. Supr.; Sr. Eileen Ann Kelley, S.P., Congregation Archivist; Sr. Rosemary Borntrager, S.P., Gen. Sec.

Total number Professed Sisters 513.

Legal Titles and Sponsored Institutions*: Mother Theodore Guerin High School,* River Grove, IL; *Saint Mary-of-the-Woods College,* Saint Mary-of-the-Woods, IN; *Woods Day Care/Preschool, Inc.,* St. Mary-of-the-Woods, IN; *Providence Self-Sufficiency Ministries, Inc.,* New Albany, IN; *Hispanic Education Center, Inc.,* Indianapolis, IN; Sisters of *Providence Community Support Trust (1969-Foundation to provide support for the aged and infirm members of the Congregation)* Indianapolis, IN; *Providence Health Care, Inc.,* St. Mary-of-the-Woods, IN.

Ministry in the fields of Education at all levels; Diocesan Offices; Parish and Pastoral Ministry; Health Care and Retirement Facilities; Congregation Administration; Social Services; Therapeutic/Rehabilitative/Mental Health Services.

Represented in the Archdioceses of Boston, Chicago, Cincinnati, Indianapolis, Louisville, Los Angeles, Oklahoma City, Omaha, Portland in Oregon, St. Paul-Minneapolis, San Francisco, and Washington and in the Dioceses of Belleville, Cleveland, Corpus Christi, Covington, Davenport, Evansville, Fort Wayne-South Bend, Galveston-Houston, Gary. Helena, Joliet, Lafayette (LA), Lafayette (IN), Lexington, Manchester, Orange, Owensboro, Peoria, Raleigh, Richmond, St. Petersburg, San Bernardino, Trenton, Venice and Worcester. Also in China and Taiwan.

Area of Taiwan: *Providence University,* 200 Chung Chi Rd., Shalu 433, Taichung County, Taiwan, Republic of China. Tel: 011-886-4-2631-1182. Sr. Rose Chiu, S.P., Area Rep.

Total number in community 8.

Ministry in the field of Education; Opportunity Center for Mentally Handicapped.
Represented in the Archdiocese of Taipei and in the Dioceses of Taichung and Tainan.

[3390] (R.A.)—RELIGIOUS OF THE ASSUMPTION (P)

Founded in France in 1839. Established in the United States of America in 1919.
Generalate: 17 rue de l'Assomption, 75016, Paris, France.
Universal total in Congregation 1,350.
Represented in the 31 countries through Europe, Africa, Asia, North America, Central America and South America.
North American Province: *Provincial House,* 227 N. Bowman Ave., Merion Station, PA 19066. Tel: 610-664-3074. Sr. Clare Teresa Tjader, R.A., Prov. Supr.
Total number in Province 25.
Ministry in Spiritual Formation; Counseling; Campus Ministry; Pastoral and Social Ministry; Education.
Represented in the Archdiocese of Philadelphia and in the Diocese of Worcester.

[3400] (R.S.C.)—RELIGIOUS SISTERS OF CHARITY (P)

Founded in Dublin, Ireland in 1815. Sisters in entire Congregation 546.
Motherhouse: *Caritas,* 15 Gilford Rd., Sandymount, Dublin 4, Ireland. Sr. Una O'Neill, Supr. Gen.
U.S. Headquarters & Novitiate (1953): *Regional Residence,* 10668 St. James' Dr., Culver City, CA 90230. Tel: 310-559-0176; Fax: 213-559-3530. Sr. Mary Christian, R.S.C., Reg. Leader.
Total in U.S. community 33.
Represented in the Archdiocese of Los Angeles.

[3410] (R.C.E.)—RELIGIOUS OF CHRISTIAN EDUCATION (P)

Founded in France in 1817. First foundation in the United States in 1905.
General Motherhouse: France.
Provincial Residence: 444 Centre St., Milton, MA 02186. Tel: 781-899-6292; Fax: 781-899-6293. Sr. Yvette Rivard, R.C.E., Pres.; Sr. Martha Brigham, R.C.E., Vice Pres.
Total number in community 22.
Legal Title: *Religious of Christian Education, Inc.*
Ministry in Religious Education Centers; Pastoral Associates; Teaching; Home Care.
Represented in the Archdiocese of Boston and in the Dioceses of Fall River and Springfield, MA.

[3430] (M.P.F.)—RELIGIOUS TEACHERS FILIPPINI (P)
(Maestre Pie Filippini)

Founded in Italy in 1692. First foundation in the United States in 1910.
General Motherhouse: *Villa Maria Regina,* Via Stazione Ottavia, 72, Rome, Italy. Sr. Mary DeBacco, M.P.F., Supr. Gen.
St. Lucy Filippini Province: *Villa Walsh,* Morristown, NJ 07960-4928. Tel: 973-538-2886. Sr. Ascenza Tizzano, Prov. Supr.; Sr. Clare Testa, Community Archivist.
Total number in community 257.
Ministry in the field of Religious and Academic Education in elementary and secondary schools; Child Care Centers; Parish Ministry; Pastoral Care; Foreign Mission Work; House of Prayer; Retreat House.
Properties owned and sponsored: *Villa Walsh,* Morristown, NJ; *Villa Victoria,* Trenton, NJ; *St. Joseph by The Sea,* South Mantoloking, NJ.
Represented in the Archdioceses of Newark, Philadelphia and Santa Fe, and in the Dioceses of Brooklyn, Cleveland, Camden, Metuchen, Paterson, Pittsburgh, Scranton and Trenton.
Queen of Apostles Province: *Religious Teachers Filippini M.P.F.,* 474 East Rd., Bristol, CT 06010. Tel: 860-584-2138. Sr. Frances Stavalo, M.P.F., Prov.; Sr. Josephine Riccio, M.P.F., Community Archivist.
Total number in community 30.
Ministry in the field of Education; Pastoral Ministry; Catechetical Centers; Youth Retreats; Foreign Mission Work.
Represented in the Archdiocese of Hartford and in the Dioceses of Bridgeport, Norwich, Orlando and Providence.

[3449] (C.V.I.)—RELIGIOUS OF THE INCARNATE WORD (P)

Founded in Lyon, France, in 1625. First foundation in United States in 1853, in Mexico 1894.
General Motherhouse: Mexico City, Industria #1-Col. Toriello Guerra, Deleg. Tlalpan, Mexico, D.F. 14050. Sr. Marta Patricia Ochoa, C.V.I., Gen. Supr.
U.S. Vice Provincial House: 153 Rainier Ct., Chula Vista, CA 91911. Tel: 619-420-0231. Sr. Camille Crabbe, C.V.I., Vice Prov.
Total number in Congregation 490.
Ministry in Parishes; Schools; Diocesan Offices and Missions.
Represented in the Diocese of San Diego. Also in Africa, Argentina, France, Guatemala, Mexico & Spain.

[3450] (R.J.M.)—RELIGIOUS OF JESUS AND MARY (P)

Founded at Lyons, France, 1818. First foundation in the U.S. in 1877.
Motherhouse: Via Nomentana 325, Rome Italy. Rev. Mother Aurora Trallero, R.J.M., Supr. Gen.
Universal number in Congregation 1,609.
United States Province Provincialate: 3706 Rhode Island Ave., Mount Rainier, MD 20712. Tel: 301-277-3794; Fax: 301-277-8656. Sr. Janet M. Stolba, R.J.M., Prov.; Sr. Yvette Beaulieu, R.J.M., Archivist.
Total in community 130.
Legal Title: *Religious of Jesus and Mary, Inc.*
Ministry in the field of Academic and Religious Education; Pastoral Ministry; Social Services; Volunteer Program.
Represented in the Archdioceses of Boston, Los Angeles, New York, and Washington and in the Dioceses of El Paso, Fall River, Manchester, Providence and San Diego. Also in Haiti.

[3460] (R.M.I.)—RELIGIOUS OF MARY IMMACULATE (P)

Founded in Madrid, Spain in 1876.
Mother House: Madrid, Spain.
Generalate: Rome, Italy.
U.S. Foundation (1954): *Villa Maria,* 719 Augusta St., San Antonio, TX 78215. Tel: 210-226-0025; Fax: 210-226-3305. Sr. Ada Mabel Mier, Local Supr.
Total number in community 13.
Headquarters: *Centro Maria,* 539 West 54th St., New York, NY 10019. Tel: 212-581-5273. Sr. Clara Echeverria, Local Supr.
Total number in community 6.
Represented in the Archdioceses of New York, San Antonio and Washington.

[3465] (R.S.H.M.)—RELIGIOUS OF THE SACRED HEART OF MARY (P)

Founded in France in 1849. First foundation in the United States in 1877.
Generalate: Via Adelaide Ristori 26, Curia Generalizia Rome, Italy 00197. Sr. Catherine Dolan, R.S.H.M., Gen. Supr.
Universal number in Congregation 1,030.
Eastern American Province (1907): 50 Wilson Park Dr., Tarrytown, NY 10591. Tel: 914 631-8872. Sr. Rosamond Blanchet, R.S.H.M., Prov.
Total number in community 205.
Ministries including Education; Pastoral Ministry; Retreat and Spiritual Direction; Health Care and Social Work.
Represented in the Archdioceses of Baltimore, New York and St. Louis and in the Dioceses of Arlington, Brooklyn, Norwich, Oakland, Palm Beach, Richmond, Rockville Centre, Trenton, Venice and Winona. Also in Africa and Europe.
Western American Province (1959): *Religious of the Sacred Heart of Mary R.S.H.M. Provincial Center,* 441 N. Garfield Ave., Montebello, CA 90640-2901. Tel: 323-887-8821; Fax: 323-887-8952. Sr. Patricia Connor, R.S.H.M., Prov.
Total number in Province 80.
Legal Titles or Holdings: *Religious of the Sacred Heart of Mary, Western American Province, a California corporation Marymount School, a California corporation.*
Ministry in the field of Academic Education at all levels; Diverse Pastoral Ministries; Prison Ministry; Justice and Peace Advocacies; Women Shelters; Youths at Risk.
Represented in the Archdioceses of Los Angeles, and San Francisco and in the Dioceses of Monterey, San Bernardino, San Diego and Stockton. Also in Mexico.

[3470] (S.R.C.M.)—SISTERS OF REPARATION OF THE CONGREGATION OF MARY, INC. (D)

Motherhouse and Novitiate: *St. Zita's Villa,* Monsey, NY 10952. Tel: 845-356-2011. Sr. Maureen Francis, S.R.C.M.
Total number in the community 10.
Represented in the Archdiocese of New York.

[3475] (S.R.)—SISTERS OF REPARATION OF THE SACRED WOUNDS OF JESUS (P)

Founded in 1959 in New York by Mother Mary Rose Therese, S.R. Established in the Diocese of San Diego in 1959. Motherhouse and Novitiate transferred to the Archdiocese of Portland in Oregon.
General Motherhouse and Novitiate: *Sacred Wounds of Jesus Convent,* 2120 S.E. 24th Ave., Portland, OR, 97214. Tel: 503-236-4207; Fax: 503-236-3400. Mother Mary of the Angels, S.R., Supr.
Sisters 3; Donne members 96.
Legal Title: *Sisters of Reparation of the Sacred Wounds of Jesus, Inc.,* Portland, OR.
Ministry in Health Care; Education; Pastoral Animation.
Represented in the Archdiocese of Portland in Oregon.

[3480] (C.R.)—SISTERS OF THE RESURRECTION (P)

Founded in Rome, Italy, in 1891. First foundation in the United States in 1900.
General Motherhouse: Via Marcantonio Colonna 52A, Rome, Italy. Rev. Mother Dolores Stepien, C.R., Supr. Gen.
Universal total in Congregation 586.
Western Province Provincialhouse and Novitiate: 7432 Talcott Ave., Chicago, IL 60631. Tel: 773-792-6363. Sr. Mary Barbara Sniegowski, C.R., Prov. Supr.
Total number in community 61.
Properties owned or sponsored: *Resurrection Day Care Center; Resurrection High School; Resurrection Health Care Corporation; Queen of Resurrection House of Prayer.*
Represented in the Archdioceses of Chicago, Milwaukee and Mobile.
Eastern Province Provincialhouse and Novitiate: *Sisters of the Resurrection,* 35 Boltwood Ave., Castleton-on-Hudson, NY 12033. Tel: 518-732-2226; Fax: 518-732-2898. E-mail: crsister@resurrectionsisters.org. Sr. Cecilia Mary Berdar, C.R., Prov. Supr.
Total number in community 59.
Legal Title: *Sisters of the Resurrection, New York, Inc.*
Ministry in Nursing Homes; Elementary Schools; Christian Doctrine Centers; High School for Girls; Preschools; Pastoral Associates.
Represented in the Archdiocese of New York and in the Dioceses of Albany and Trenton.

[3490] (O.S.S.)—RELIGIOUS OF THE ORDER OF THE BLESSED SACRAMENT AND OF OUR LADY (P)

Sacramentine Nuns Cloistered Contemplative
Founded in France in 1639. First foundation in the United States in 1912. The Sisters devote their lives to the perpetual adoration of Christ in the Eucharist.
Blessed Sacrament Monastery: 86 Dromore Rd., Scarsdale, NY 10583-1706. Tel: 914-722-1657. Sr. Mary Francis, O.S.S., Prioress.
Professed Sisters 11; Novices 1.
Monastery of Perpetual Adoration (1951): 2798 U.S. 31 N., P.O. Box 86, Conway, MI 49722-0086. Tel: 231-347-0447. Sr. Rosalie, O.S.S. Prioress.
Professed Sisters 2.
Represented in the Archdiocese of New York and in the Diocese of Gaylord.

[3499] (S.J.S.)—SISTERS SERVANTS OF THE BLESSED SACRAMENT (P)

Founded in Mexico in 1904. First foundation in the United States in 1926.
General Motherhouse: Juan Bernardino 650, Guadalajara, Jalisco, Mexico 45000. Sr. M. Concepcion Cervantez, S.J.S., Supr. Gen.
U.S. Vice Province: 215 Lomita St., El Segundo, CA 90245. Tel: 310-615-0766; Fax: 310-615-0571. Sr. Ana Rosa Aceves, S.J.S., Vice Prov.
Total number in the community 59.
Legal Title: *Sisters Servants of the Blessed Sacrament, Inc.*
Ministry in the field of Education.
Represented in the Archdiocese of Los Angeles and in the Dioceses of Fresno, Sacramento and San Diego.

[3500] (S.S.S.)—SERVANTS OF THE BLESSED SACRAMENT (P)

Founded in France in 1858; First foundation in the United States in 1947.
General Motherhouse: Via Aurelia, 145-Int. C-2, Rome, Italy 00165.
U.S. Address: *Blessed Sacrament Convent,* 101 Silver St., Waterville, ME 04901. Tel: 207-872-7072; Fax: 207-873-2317. Sr. Mary Catherine Perko, S.S.S., Prov.; Sr. Josephine Roney, S.S.S., Local Supr.
Total number in the community 14.
Represented in the Dioceses of Portland (ME) and Pueblo.

[3510] (S.S.C.K.)—CONGREGATION OF SISTER SERVANTS OF CHRIST THE KING (D)

Founded in the United States in 1936.
General Motherhouse: *Loretto Convent,* N. 8114 Calvary St., Mt. Calvary, WI 53057. Tel: 920-753-3211. Mother Mary Rose, Supr.
Professed Sisters 8.
Represented in the Archdiocese of Milwaukee and in the Diocese of Fargo.

[3520] (S.S.C.M.)—SERVANTS OF THE HOLY HEART OF MARY (P)

Founded in Paris, France in 1860. First foundation in the United States in 1889.

Generalate: 2029 rue Holy Cross, Montreal, Quebec, Canada H4E 2A4. Sr. Louise Payeur, S.S.C.M., Supr. Gen.

United States Region-Holy Family Province: *Provincialate,* 15 Elmwood Dr., Kankakee, IL 60901. Tel: 815-937-2380. Sr. Mary Ann Hettel, S.S.C.M., Prov. Supr.

Total number in region 50.

Legal Title: *Servants of the Holy Heart of Mary.*

Sponsor: *Provena Health.*

Ministry in Grammar Schools; Nursing Homes; Health Care; Education; Pastoral Ministry; Parishes; Ministry to the Aged; and Home Missions.

Represented in the Archdiocese of Chicago and in the Dioceses of Belleville, Joliet, Peoria and Rockford.

[3530] (S.Sp.S.)—MISSIONARY SISTERS SERVANTS OF THE HOLY SPIRIT (P)

Founded in Holland in 1889. First foundation in the United States in 1901.

General Motherhouse: *Convento dello Spirito Santo,* Via Cassia 645, Roma, Italy 00189. Sr. Agada Brand, S.Sp.S., Supr. Gen.

Universal Total in Congregation 3,529.

American Motherhouse (1901): *Convent of the Holy Spirit,* 319 Waukegan Rd. - P.O. Box 6026, Techny, IL 60082-6026. Tel: 847-441-0126; Fax: 847-441-5587. Sr. Margaret Anne Norris, S.Sp.S., Prov.

Total number in the community 104.

Legal Title: *Missionary Sisters Sponsorship, Inc.,* Techny, IL; *Arnold Janssen Foundation,* Techny, IL; *Helena Stollenwerk Foundation,* Techny, IL.

Ministry in Schools; Catechetical Work; Parish Ministry & Administration.

Represented in the Archdioceses of Chicago and New York and in the Dioceses of Burlington and Memphis.

[3540] (S.Sp.S.deA.P.)—SISTER-SERVANTS OF THE HOLY SPIRIT OF PERPETUAL ADORATION (P)

Cloistered Contemplative

Founded in Holland in 1896. First foundation in the United States in 1915.

Generalate: *Convent of the Most Holy Trinity,* Bad Driburg, Germany. Mother Mary Aurora, S.Sp.S.deA.P., Supr. Gen.

U.S. House of Formation: *Mount Grace Convent,* 1438 E. Warne Ave., St. Louis, MO. Tel: 314-381-5686. Sr. Mary Gemma, S.Sp.S.deA.P., Supr.

Professed Sisters 24; Postulants 2.

Convent of Divine Love: 2212 Green St., Philadelphia, PA 19130. Tel: 215-567-0123. Sr. Mary Catherine, S.Sp.S.deA.P., Supr.

Professed Sisters 25.

Convent of the Blessed Sacrament: 4105 Ocean Dr., Corpus Christi, TX 78411. Tel: 512-852-6212. Sr. Mary Margaret, S.Sp.S.deA.P., Supr.

Professed Sisters 10.

Adoration Convent of Christ the King Church: 1040 S. Cotner Blvd., Lincoln, NE 68510. Tel: 402-489-0765. Sr. Mary Caritas, S.Sp.S.deA.P., Supr.

Professed Sisters 67.

Represented in the Archdioceses of Philadelphia and St. Louis and the Diocese of Corpus Christi.

[3550] (S.C.I.M.)—SERVANTS OF THE IMMACULATE HEART OF MARY (P)

Good Shepherd Sisters of Quebec

Founded in Canada in 1850. First foundation in the United States in 1882.

Generalate: 2550, rue Marie-Fitzbach, Ste-Foy, Quebec, Canada. Sr. Helen Pelletier, S.C.I.M., Supr. Gen.

Universal total in Congregation 854.

Provincial House: *St. Joseph Province at Bay View,* 313 Seaside Ave., Saco, ME 04072. Tel: 207-283-3433; Fax: 207-282-7376. Sr. Lucille Gamache, S.C.I.M., Prov.

Total number in community 93.

Ministry in Grammar Schools; Adoption Agency; Group Home for Unmarried Mothers; C.C.D. Centers; Youth (Retreat Work); Apostolate to the Elderly & Homeless.

Represented in the Archdiocese of Boston and in the Diocese of Portland (ME).

[3560] (S.J.)—SERVANTS OF JESUS (D)

Founded in Detroit Michigan in 1974.

Headquarters: *Servants of Jesus,* 2600 Harvard Rd., Berkley, MI 48072. Tel: 248-548-6337.

Total number in community 21.

Ministries: Diocesan Offices; Parish Ministry; Religious Education; Catholic Schools; Legal Aid; Health Care.

Represented in the Archdiocese of Detroit and the Dioceses of Grand Rapids, Gaylord, Saginaw and Toledo.

[3570] (O.S.M.)—MANTELLATE SISTERS, SERVANTS OF MARY OF BLUE ISLAND (P)

Founded in Italy in 1861. First foundation in the United States in 1916.

Generalate and Novitiate: Rome, Italy.

U.S. Motherhouse & Novitiate: *Convent of Our Mother of Sorrows,* 13811 S. Western Ave., Blue Island, IL 60406. Tel: 708-385-2103. Sr. M. Eleanor Carella, O.S.M., Reg. Supr.

Professed Sisters 14.

Represented in the Archdiocese of Chicago.

[3572] (O.S.M.)—MANTELLATE SISTERS SERVANTS OF MARY OF PLAINFIELD (P)

Founded October 6, 1861 in Treppi, Italy. First founded in the United States 1916.

Universal number of Mantellate Sisters 700.

Mantellate Sisters Servants of Mary of Plainfield (1977): 16949 S. Drauden Rd., Plainfield, IL 60544-9219. Tel: 815-436-5796. Sr. Francis Gresser, O.S.M., Reg. Supr.

Sisters 9.

Ministry in the field of Academic Education; Parish Ministry; Retreats; Social Work; Nursing; Homes for the Aged; Foreign Missions.

Represented in the Archdiocese of Chicago and in the Diocese of Joliet.

[3580] (O.S.M.)—SERVANTS OF MARY (P)

Founded in Italy in the 13th Century. First foundation in the United States in 1893.

General Motherhouse: *St. Juliana's Convent,* 2a, Woodstock Rd. West, Begbroke, Oxen, England. 0X5 1RZ, Sr. M. Felicity McKeon, O.S.M., Prioress Gen.

American Province (1893): *Provincial Motherhouse, Convent of Our Lady of Sorrows,* 7400 Military Ave., Omaha, NE 68134-3398. Tel: 402-571-2547; Fax: 402-573-6055. Web site: http://osms.org. Sr. Jean Morrow, O.S.M., Prov.

Total number in community 105.

Ministry in the field of Religious and Academic Education at all levels; Parishes; Social Service Agencies; Diocesan Offices; Hospital Pastoral Care; Counseling Agencies; Peace and Justice Offices; Campus Ministry; Hospice; Health Care Services; Medical Research; Consulting; Spiritual Direction; Retreat Work; Missionary Work in Foreign Countries and in the United States.

Properties owned: *Marian High School,* Omaha, NE; *Our Lady of Sorrows Convent,* Omaha, NE.

Represented in the Archdioceses of Denver, Detroit, Omaha and Portland (OR) and in the Dioceses of Des Moines, Grand Island, Gaylord, Metuchen, Ogdensburg, St. Cloud, Sioux City and Tucson. Also in Jamaica, West Indies.

[3590] (O.S.M.)—SERVANTS OF MARY (SERVITE SISTERS) (D)

Founded in Italy in the 13th Century. First United States foundation in 1912.

General Motherhouse: *Servants of Mary,* 1000 College Ave. W., Ladysmith, WI 54848-2199. Tel: 715-532-3364; Fax: 715-532-6153. Sr. Theresa H. Sandok, O.S.M., Pres.

Total number in community 71.

Ministry in the field of Academic Education; Parish and Pastoral Ministry; Health Care; Social Services; Law; and Administration.

Represented in the Archdioceses of Boston, Chicago, Los Angeles, Milwaukee, St. Paul-Minneapolis and in the Dioceses of Joliet, La Crosse, Orlando, Superior, St. Petersburg, Tucson and Wheeling-Charleston.

[3595] (S.S.J.)—SERVANTS OF ST. JOSEPH (P)

Founded in Spain in 1874.

Motherhouse: Salamanca,. Spain.

General House: Rome, Italy. Mother Josefa Somoza, Supr. Gen.

U.S. Address (1957): 203 N. Spring St., Falls Church, VA 22046. Tel: 703-533-8441; 703-534-9549. Sr. Augustina Temprano, Supr.

Total number in community 8.

Represented in the Diocese of Arlington.

[3600] (S.M.)—SISTERS SERVANTS OF MARY (P)

(Ministers to the Sick)

Founded in Madrid, Spain by St. Maria Soledad Torres, August 15, 1851. First foundation in the United States in 1914.

Total Membership 1,950 Sisters.

General Motherhouse: via Antonio Musa 16, Rome, Italy. Mother Josefa Oyarzabal, S.M., Supr. Gen.

Provincial Motherhouse: 800 N. 18th St., Kansas City, KS 66102. Sr. Alfonsa Bellido, S.M., Prov. Supr.; Sr. Carmela Sanz, S.M., Locale Supr.; Sr. Silvia Enriguez, S.M., Community Archivist; Sr. Victoria P. Villarreal, S.M., Treas.

Total number in the province 251.

Represented in the Archdioceses of Kansas City in Kansas, Los Angeles, New Orleans and New York.

[3610] (S.S.M.I.)—SISTERS SERVANTS OF MARY IMMACULATE (P)

Founded in Zuzel, Ukraine on August 28, 1892. Approved by the Holy See, 1932. Arrived in the United States on August 15, 1935 at Stamford, Connecticut.

Generalate: Via Cassia Antica 104, Rome, Italy, 00191. Sr. Janice Soluk, S.S.M.I., Supr. Gen.

Sisters Servants of Mary Immaculate: *Sisters Servants Ln.,* 9 Emmanuel Dr., P.O. Box 9, Sloatsburg, NY 10974-0009. Tel: 845-753-2840. Sr. Michele Yakymovitch, S.S.M.I., Prov. Supr.

Total number in community 39.

Ministry in the field of Education; Parish and Pastoral ministry; Health Care; Administration; Retreat Ministry; Hospitality; Holy Dormition Pilgrimage.

Properties owned: *Immaculate Conception Provincialate & Novitiate; St. Joseph's Home (for the aged); Saint Mary's Villa Spiritual, Cultural and Educational Center,* Sloatsburg, NY.

Represented in the Ukrainian and Byzantine Rite Catholic Dioceses of the United States.

[3615] (E.I.N.)—SERVANTS OF THE IMMACULATE CHILD MARY (ESCLAVAS DE LA INMACULADA NINA) (P)

Founded in Mexico in 1901. First foundation in the United States in 1978.

Motherhouse: Mother Maria Reina Mula Casas, Dr. Espina #10, 28019, Madrid, Spain.

Provincial House: Matamoros #100, Tlalpan, D.F. Mexico, C.P. 14000. Mother Maria del Docorro Pech Moo, E.I.N.

U.S. Foundation: 5135 Dartmouth Ave., Los Angeles, CA 90032.

House of Formation: 350 Boyle Ave., Los Angeles, CA 90033. Sr. Dulce Ma. Villalba, E.I.N., Supr.

Total number of sisters in the U.S. 8.

Ministry in the field of religious education and adult formation in parishes.

Represented in the Archdiocese of Los Angeles.

[3620] (S.S.M.I.)—SISTERS SERVANTS OF MARY IMMACULATE (P)

First founded in Poland 1878.

General Motherhouse: Mariowka-Opoczynska, Poland. Mother Danuta Wrobel, Mother Gen.

Total number of sisters in the U.S. 8.

Universal Total in Congregation 1,100.

American Province (1935): 1220 Tugwell Dr., Catonsville, MD 21228. Tel: 410-747-1353. Sr. Bernadette Kozyra, S.S.M.I., Prov. Supr.; Sr. Marianna Danko, Community Archivist.

Total in the community 34.

Represented in the Archdioceses of Baltimore and Washington and in the Diocese of Cleveland.

[3630] (S.S.C.J.)—SERVANTS OF THE MOST SACRED HEART OF JESUS (P)

Founded in Poland in 1894.

General Motherhouse: Garncarska St., Cracow, Poland. Mother Szczesna Niemiec, Supr. Gen.

Sister Servants of the Most Sacred Heart of Jesus (1959): *Sacred Heart Province,* 866 Cambria St., Cresson, PA 16630-1713. Sr. Clare Marie, S.S.C.J., Prov. Supr.

Total number in U.S. Province 32.

Represented in the Archdiocese of Philadelphia and in the Dioceses of Altoona-Johnstown and Metuchen.

[3640] (S.M.G.)—POOR SERVANTS OF THE MOTHER OF GOD (P)

Founded in London, England in 1869. First foundation in the United States in 1947.

General Motherhouse: Maryfield, Roehampton, London S.W. 15, England. Sr. Rosarii O'Connor, S.M.G., Supr. Gen.

American Foundation: *Maryfield Nursing Home,* 1315 Greensboro Rd., High Point, NC 27260. Tel: 336-886-2444. Sr. Elizabeth Crehan, S.M.G., Supr.Gen; Sr. Teresa Twomey, S.M.G., Reg. Supr.

Total number in the community 19.

Ministry in Hospitals; Nursing Homes; Schools; Retreat House.

Represented in the Archdiocese of Philadelphia and in the Dioceses of Charlotte, Gallup, Metuchen and Richmond.

[3658] (S.S.H.J.)—SISTERS OF THE SACRED HEART OF JESUS (P)

Founded in Ragusa, Italy in 1889. First foundation in the United States in 1951.

Generalate House: *Instituto Sacro Cuore di Ragusa,* Via Cassia 1714, 00123 Rome, Italy.

Universal total in Congregation 620.
Motherhouse: *Instituto Sacro Cuore,* Via Suor Maria Schinina 2, 97100 Ragusa, Italy.
American Headquarters: *Sacred Heart Villa School & Convent,* 5269 Lewiston Rd., Lewiston, NY 14092. Tel: 716-284-8273.
Legal Titles: *Sacred Heart Villa School & Convent,* Lewiston, NY; *Saint Frances Cabrini Nursery and Convent,* North Haven, CT.
Ministry in the field of Religious and Academic Education at all levels; Hospitals; Homes for the Aged; Orphanages; Parish Ministry; Youth Ministry; Foreign Missions; Social Services.
Represented in the Archdiocese of Hartford and in the Diocese of Buffalo.

[3660] (S.S.H.J.P.)—SERVANTS OF THE SACRED HEART OF JESUS AND OF THE POOR (P)

Founded in Leon, Gto., Mexico in 1885. First foundation in U.S. in 1907.
Motherhouse: Apartado 92, Puebla, Pue, Mexico 72000. Tel: 01152-2222-42-18-69. Mother Magdalena Sofia Juarez, Gen. Supr.
U.S. Address: *Sacred Heart Children's Home Convent,* 3310 S. Zapata Hwy., Laredo, TX 78046. Tel: 956-723-3343. Fax: 956-723-3409. Mother Aurora Teresa Navarro, S.S.H.J.P., Major Supr.; Sr. Maria Teresa Grajeda, S.S.H.J.P., Admin.
Professed Sisters in U.S. 50.
Ministry in academic and religious education at all levels; Children's Home.
Represented in the Dioceses of Laredo and El Paso.

[3670] (S.S.C.J.)—SISTERS OF THE SACRED HEART OF JESUS OF SAINT JACUT (P)

Founded in France in 1816. First foundation in the United States in 1903.
Generalate: *Villa des Otages,* No. 8 85 rue Haxo, Paris, France 75020.
Motherhouse: St. Jacut les Pins, Brittany, France. 56220.
USA\Mexico Province (1916): *Provincialate Offices,* 11931 Radium St., San Antonio, TX 78216. Tel: 210-344-7203. Fax: 210-341-0721. Sr. Juana Villescas, S.S.C.J., Prov.
Total number in community 58.
Ministry in Education; Pastoral Work; Schools of Religion; Health Care; Mexico Missions.
Properties owned or sponsored: *Mount Sacred Heart School,* San Antonio, TX; *Casa Angelique, Mexico Casa San Antonio* ,San Antonio, TX.
Represented in the Archdioceses of San Antonio and Santa Fe and in the Dioceses of Brownsville, Jefferson City, and Galveston-Houston. Also in Mexico City.

[3680] (S.H.J.M.)—SISTERS OF THE SACRED HEARTS OF JESUS AND MARY (P)

Founded in France in 1866. First foundation in United States in 1953.
Motherhouse: Essex, England.
Regional House: 2150 Lake Shore Ave., Oakland, CA 94606. Tel: 510-832-2935; Fax: 510-625-9159. Sr. Lorna Walsh, S.H.J.M., Reg. Prov.
Universal Number 235; U.S. Community 14.
Ministry in Pastoral Care; Adult Education; Counseling.
Represented in the Dioceses of Oakland and Stockton.

[3690] (SS.CC.)—CONGREGATION OF THE SACRED HEARTS AND OF PERPETUAL ADORATION (P)

Founded in France in 1800 as a Congregation of men and women. Members are consecrated to the Hearts of Jesus and Mary. Special Ministries are Perpetual Adoration, the education of youth, especially the poor, parish work and foreign missions. First Catholic missionaries to Hawaii in 1827: Sisters started Catholic Schools for girls in Hawaii 1859. First foundation in the continental United States in 1908.
Generalate: Via Aurelia 145, Scala C-Int 10-14-00165, Rome, Italy. Mother Jeanne Cadiou, SS.CC., Supr. Gen.
Pacific Province: *Sisters of the Sacred Hearts,* 1120 Fifth Ave., Honolulu, HI 96816. Tel: 808-737-5822. Sr. Helene Wood, SS.CC., Prov.
Total number in community 41.
Legal Holdings and Titles: *Sisters of the Sacred Hearts Corporation; Regina Pacis Convent; Sacred Hearts Academy Corporation; Saint Anthony Retreat Center Corporation; Malia O Ka Malu Community,* Honolulu, HI.
East Coast Region: *Sisters of the Sacred Hearts of Jesus and Mary and of Perpetual Adoration,* 35 Huttleston Ave., Fairhaven, MA 02719-3154. Tel: 508-994-9341; Fax: 508-990-1967. Sr. Dolores Pavao, SS.CC., Supr.
Total number in community 4.
Represented in the Diocese of Fall River.

[3710] (C.S.A.)—CONGREGATION OF SISTERS OF SAINT AGNES (P)

Founded in the United States in 1858.
General Motherhouse: *St. Agnes Convent,* 320 County Rd., Fond du Lac, WI 54935-8958. Tel: 920-907-2300; Fax: 920-923-3194. Sr. Mary Christine Fellerhoff, C.S.A., Gen. Supr.; Sr. Julia Wiegerling, C.S.A., Gen. Vicar.; Councilors Sr. Patricia Hayes, C.S.A.; Sr. Joann Sambs.
Total number in Congregation 345.
Ministry in the field of Academic and Religious Education; Hospitals; Homes for Aged; Parish Ministry; Foreign Missions; Social Services; Healthcare.
Properties owned or sponsored: *Hazotte Ministries, Inc.; Marian College of Fond du Lac; Agnesian HealthCare of Fond du Lac, WI, Inc.; St. Francis Home,* Fond du Lac, WI; *Waupun Memorial Hospital,* Waupun, WI; *The Monroe Clinic,* Monroe, WI.
Represented in the Archdioceses of Chicago, Milwaukee, Mobile, New York, St. Paul-Minneapolis and in the Dioceses of Altoona-Johnstown, Columbus, Fort Wayne-South Bend, Gallup, Gary, Green Bay, Jackson, Joliet, Madison, Marquette, Memphis, Pal Beach, Phoenix, Raleigh, Salina, Superior, Toledo, Tucson, Venice and Wheeling-Charleston. Also in Honduras, Nicaragua.

[3718] (S.S.A.)—SISTERS OF ST. ANN (P)

Founded in Italy in 1834.
General Motherhouse: V.d. Aldobrandeschi, Rome, Italy. 100-00163, Franceschina Milanesio, S.S.A,Supr. Gen.
Universal Total in Congregation 1,500.
U.S. Delegation (1952): *Mount St. Ann,* P.O. Box 328, Ebensburg, PA 15931. Tel: 814-472-9354; Fax: 814-472-9354. Sr. Anna Maria Lorenzon, S.S.A., Delegate; Sr. Melany Pereira, S.S.A., Community Archivist.
Total number in Community 9.
Ministry in the field of Education; Retreat Ministry; Foreign Mission; Pastoral Ministry.
Represented in the Dioceses of Altoona-Johnstown and Corpus Christi.

[3720] (S.S.A.)—SISTERS OF SAINT ANNE (P)

Founded in Vaudreuil, Province of Quebec, Canada, 1850. First foundation in the United States in 1866.
Legal Title: *The Community of the Sisters of St. Anne.*
General Motherhouse: 1950 Provost St., Lachine, Quebec Canada. Sr. Mary Ellen King, S.S.A., Congregational Leader.
Saint Marie Province (1887): 720 Boston Post Rd. East, Marlboro, MA 01752. Tel: 508-485-3791; or 508-597-0200. Prov. Leaders: Sr. Yvette Dargy, S.S.A.; Sr. Paulette Gardner, S.S.A.
Total number in Province 152; In Community 806.
Ministry in the field of Academic and Religious Education at all levels; Center for Spiritual Renewal; Campus Ministry; Various Apostolates; Retreat Work; Pastoral Ministry; Ministry to the Aged, Shut-ins and the Poor; Hospital and Infirmary Nursing; Hospital Chaplaincies; Foreign Missions.
Properties owned: *Saint Anne Convent; Mary Martha House,* Marlboro, MA; *Emmanuel House,* Wayland, MA; *Esther House,* Worcester, MA; *Marie Esther Health Center Inc.,* Marlboro, MA.
Represented in the Archdioceses of Boston and Washington and in the Dioceses of Fall River, Manchester, Providence, Springfield (MA), Venice, Wheeling-Charleston and Worcester.

[3730] (O.S.B.M.)—SISTERS OF THE ORDER OF ST. BASIL THE GREAT (P)
(International Byzantine Rite)

Founded in Cappadocia in the 4th Century by St. Basil the Great and his sister St. Macrina. First foundation in the United States in 1911.
Basilian Generalate: Via San Alessio 26, Roma, Italy 00153. Sr. Alphonsa Danovich, Gen. Supr.
Philadelphia-Ukrainian Byzantine Rite: *Provincial and Motherhouse:* 710 Fox Chase Rd., Fox Chase Manor, PA 19046. Tel: 215-663-9153; Fax: 215-728-6129. Sr. Dorothy Ann Busowski, O.S.B.M., Prov.
Solemnly Professed Sisters 58.
Ministry in Education at all levels; Pastoral Ministry.
Represented in the Ukrainian Archdiocese of Philadelphia and the Ukrainian Dioceses of Chicago, Parma and Stamford.
Pittsburgh Ruthenian Byzantine Rite-Motherhouse and Novitiate: *Mount St. Macrina,* 500 W. Main St., P.O. Box 878, Uniontown, PA 15401. Tel: 724-438-8644. Sr. Ruth Plante, O.S.B.M., Prov.
Professed Sisters 85.
Legal Title: *Declaration of the Sisters of the Order of St. Basil the Great Endowment Trust; Declaration of Trust of the Sisters of the Order of St. Basil the Great Community Support Program; Mount St. Macrina Cemetery, Inc.,* Uniontown, PA.
Sister serve in Diocesan, Parish and Religious Education Ministry; Health Care; Pastoral Ministry.
Represented in the Byzantine Archdiocese of Pittsburgh and in the Dioceses of Parma, Passaic and Van Nuys.

[3735] (C.S.B.)—CONGREGATION OF ST. BRIGID (P)

Founded in Ireland in 1807.
U.S. Foundation (1953): *St. Brigid's Convent,* 5118 Loma Linda Dr., San Antonio, TX 78201. Tel: 210-733-0701. Sr. Mary Teresa Cullen, C.S.B., Reg. Coord.
Total number in community 16.
Ministry in Pastoral Ministry in Seminary, Detention and Hospitals; Academic Education at all levels; Ministry among immigrants and overseas; Music Ministry.
Properties owned: *Regional House; St. Brigid's Kindergarten,* San Antonio, TX.
Represented in the Archdioceses of Boston and San Antonio and in the Diocese of Wilmington.

[3740] (S.S.C.)—SISTERS OF ST. CASIMIR (P)

Founded by Mother Maria Kaupas in the United States in 1907.
General Motherhouse: 2601 W. Marquette Rd., Chicago, IL 60629. Tel: 773-776-1324; Fax: 773-776-8755. Sr. M. Immacula Wendt, S.S.C., Gen. Supr. Gen. Supr.; Sr. M. Elaine Kuizinas, S.S.C., Gen. Sec.; Sr. M. Christella, S.S.C., Archivist.
Total number in community 136.
Ministry in the field of Academic Education; Foreign Missions; Hospitals; Homes for the Aged; Pastoral Ministry.
Properties owned: *Maria High School; Holy Cross Hospital,* Chicago, IL; *Villa Joseph Marie High School,* Holland, PA.
Represented in the Archdioceses of Chicago, Philadelphia, and Washington and in the Diocese of Kalamazoo. Also in Argentina.

[3750] (S.S.Ch.)—SISTERS OF ST. CHRETIENNE (P)

Founded in France in 1807. First foundation in the United States in 1903.
General Motherhouse: *Metz (Moselle),* 57000, France.
Provincial House: 297 Arnold St., Wrentham, MA 02093-1798. Tel: 508-384-8066; Fax: 508-384-3170. Sr. Suzanne Beaudoin, S.S.Ch., Prov. Supr. Tel: 508-384-7841.
Total number in Province 61.
Legal Titles: *St. Chretienne Educational Institute, Inc.,* Marlboro, MA; *St. Chretienne Educational Institute Trust,* Wrentham, MA.
Properties owned: *Our Lady Preschool Learning Center,* Marlboro, MA; *St. Chretienne Retirement Residence,* Marlboro, MA.
Represented in the Archdiocese of Boston and in the Dioceses of Lexington, Manchester, Norwich, Portland (ME), Providence and St. Petersburg.

[3760] (P.C.C. or O.S.C.)—ORDER OF ST. CLARE (P)

Poor Clares-Poor Clares of the Primitive Observance

Founded in Assisi, Italy in 1212. First foundation in the United States in 1877.
Motherhouse: *Monastery of St. Clare, Franciscan Monastery of St. Clare,* 3626 N. 65th Ave., Omaha, NE 68104-3299. Tel: 402-558-4916; Fax: 402-558-5046. Assisi, Italy, is called the Motherhouse of the Order, but the Abbess of said Monastery has no jurisdiction over other Communities of Poor Clares. Some Monasteries, such as those at Omaha, Evansville, New Orleans, Memphis, Jamaica Plain, Greenville, Lowell and Spokane, are subject to a Father General and to the Provincial of the Franciscan Province in which the Monastery is located. Monasteries at Aptos, Cleveland, Kokomo. Los Altos Hills, Newport News, Rockford, Roswell and Santa Barbara are Colettines. Sr. Mary Clare Brown, O.S.C., Abbess.
Solemnly Professed Sisters 7; Simple Professed 1.
St. Clare's Monastery of the Blessed Sacrament O.S.C.: 720 Henry Clay Ave., New Orleans, LA 70118. Tel: 504-895-2019. Sr. Elizabeth Mortell, O.S.C., Abbess.
Cloistered.
Total number in community 9.
Franciscan Monastery of St. Clare O.S.C.: 6825 Nurrenbern Rd., Evansville, IN 47712-8518. Tel: 812-425-4396. Web site: http://poorclares.org/com Sr. Jean Marie DeLand, O.S.C., Abbess; Sr. Jeanne A. Maffet, O.S.C., Supr.; Sr. Mary Martha, O.S.C., Community Archivist.
Total number in community 14.
Monastery of St. Clare (1932): 1310 Dellwood Ave., Memphis, TN 38127. Tel: 901-357-6662. Sr. Mary Helen Kelley, O.S.C., Abbess.

Solemnly Professed Cloistered.
Total number in community 7.
The Franciscan Monastery of St. Clare: 920 Centre St., Jamaica Plain, MA 02130. Tel: 617-524-1760. Sr. Clare Frances McAvoy, O.S.C., Abbess.
Total number in community 20.
Monastery of St. Clare O.S.C.: 150 White Pine Rd., Columbus (Chesterfield Twnshp), NJ 08022. Tel: 609-324-2638; Fax: 609-324-2938. Sr. Claire Andre Gagliardi, O.S.C., Abbess.
Total number in community 15.
Franciscan Monastery of Saint Clare: 1271 Langhorne-Newtown Rd., Langhorne, PA 19047-1297. Tel: 215-968-5775; Fax: 215-968-6254. Sr. Evelyn L. Eynon, O.S.C., Abbess.
Total number in community 14.
Franciscan Monastery of St. Clare, Spokane, Washington: *Poor Clare Nuns,* 4419 N. Hawthorne St., Spokane, WA 99205. Tel: 509-327-4479. Solemn Vows, Papal Enclosure Franciscan Province of Santa Barbara. Mother Bentivoglio Federation of Poor Clares; Sr. Mary Rita Dolan, O.S.C., Abbess; Sr. Colleen Byrne, O.S.C., Community Archivist.
Professed Nuns 7.
Franciscan Poor Clare Nuns: *Monastery of St. Clare,* 86 Mayflower Ave., New Rochelle, NY 10801-1615. Tel: 914-632-5227; Fax: 914-632-5227. Sr. Mary Bernadette Quinn, O.S.C., Abbess, Solemn Vows, Papal Enclosure.
Total number in community 13.
St. Clare's Monastery: 421 S. Fourth St., Sauk Rapids, MN 56379. Tel: 320-251-3556. Mother Mary Peter, O.S.C., Abbess.
Total number in community 22.
St. Clare's Monastery of the Infant Jesus (1953): *Franciscan Poor Clare Nuns,* 8650 Russell Ave. S., Minneapolis, MN 55431-1998. Tel: 952-881-4766. Sr. Mary Catherine Martin, O.S.C., Abbess.
Total number in community 12.
Legal Title: *Franciscan Poor Clare Nuns.*
Monastery of Poor Clares(1877): *Order of St. Clare-Poor Clare Colettine Nuns P.C.C.,* 3501 Rocky River Dr., Cleveland, OH 44111-2998. Tel: 216-941-2820. Mother Mary Jude, P.C.C., Abbess. Poor Clare Nuns (Colettines), observing the Primitive Rule of St. Clare. Strictly cloistered, Solemn Vows, Perpetual Exposition of the Most Blessed Sacrament.
Total number in community 24.
Franciscan Monastery of St. Clare: *Order of St. Clare,* 1505 Miles Rd., Cincinnati, OH 45231-2427. Tel: 513-825-7177; Fax: 513-825-4071. Sr. Anne Marie Covely, O.S.C., Abbess.
Solemn vows; papal enclosure.
Total number in community 9.
Corpus Christi Monastery (Solemn Vows, Papal Enclosure): *Poor Clare Colettines P.C.C.,* 2111 S. Main St., Rockford, IL 61102. Tel: 815-963-7343. Mother Mary Regina, P.C.C., Abbess.
Cloistered.
Total number in community 25.
Annunciation Monastery: *Poor Clare Colettines P.C.C.,* 6200 E. Minooka Rd., Minooka, IL 60447-9458.
Monastery of Poor Clares-P.C.C. (1928): 215 E. Los Olivos St., Santa Barbara, CA 93105. Tel: 805-682-7670. Mother M. Clare of Jesus, Abbess.
Total number in community 15.
Monastery of St. Clare: 445 River Rd., Andover, MA 01810-4213. Tel: 978-683-7599; Fax: 978-683-6085. Sr. Therese Lacroix, O.S.C., Abbess.
Cloistered.
Total number in community 14.
Poor Clare Monastery of Our Lady of Guadalupe: 809 E. 19th St., Roswell NM 88201. Tel: 505-622-0868. Mother M. Francis, Abbess.
Cloistered.
Total number in community 29.
Legal Title: *Community of the Poor Clares of New Mexico, Inc.*
Immaculate Heart Monastery of Poor Clares: 28210 Natoma Rd., Los Altos Hills, CA 94022. Tel: 650-948-2947. Mother Maura, P.C.C., Abbess.
Total number in community 16.
Monastery of St. Clare: 1916 N. Pleasantburg Dr., Greenville, SC 29609-4080. Tel: 864-244-4514; Fax: 864-268-9379. Sr. Carolyn Forgette, O.S.C., Abbess.
Cloistered.
Total number in community 17.
Monastery of Poor Clares Colettine P.C.C.: 5500 Hollyfork Rd., Barhamsville, VA 23011. Tel: 757-596-5942. Solemn Vows. Mother Mary Colette, P.C.C., Abbess; Sr. Mary Agnes, P.C.C., Archivist.
Cloistered.
Total number in community 15.
Maria Regina Mater Monastery P.C.C.: *Poor Clare Nuns,* 1175 N., 300 W., Kokomo, IN 46901. Tel: 765-457-5743. Mother Miriam, Abbess.
Cloistered.
Total number in community 11.
Christ the King Monastery of St. Clare O.S.C.: 3900 Sherwood Blvd., Delray Beach, FL 33445. Tel: 561-498-3294. Sr. Mary Veronica Butler, O.S.C., Abbess.
Total number in community 11.
Monastery of St. Clare of the Immaculate Conception O.S.C.: *Poor Clares,* 200 Marycrest Dr., St. Louis, MO 63129. Tel: 314-846-2618. Mother Mary Leo Hoffmann, O.S.C., Abbess.
Total number in community 10.
Legal Title: *Nuns of the Order of St. Clare of St. Louis.*
Monastery of St. Clare (Solemn Vows, Papal Enclosure): 6029 Estero Blvd., Fort Myers Beach, FL 33931-4325. Tel: 239-463-5599; Fax: 239-463-4993. Sr. Mary Emmanuel Kilkenny, O.S.C., Abbess.
Cloistered Sisters 4.
Monastery of St. Clare: 9300 Hwy. 105, Brenham, TX 77833. Tel: 979-836-2444. Sr. Angela Chandler, O.S.C., Abbess.
Sisters in Community 5.
Poor Clares of Montana: 416 2nd. Ave. S.W., Great Falls, MT 59404-2904 Tel: 406-453-7891; Fax: 406-453-8689. Sr. Judith Ann Crosby.
St. Joseph Monastery of the Poor Clares Colettines P.C.C.: 1671 Pleasant Valley Rd., P.O. Box 160, Aptos, CA 95001-0160. Tel: 831-761-9659. Mother Mary Clare, Abbess.
(Reform of St. Colette) Daily Exposition of the Most Blessed Sacrament.
Total number in community 15; Juniors 1; Postulants 1.
Monastery of St. Clare, 107 North Depot St., Victoria, TX 77901-6826. Sr. Katherine Vallone, O.S.C., Supr.
St.Clare's Monastery, 4875 Shattuck Rd., Saginaw, MI 48603. Tel: 989-797-0593; E-mail: srsclare@saginaw.org. Sr. Dianne Doughty, O.S.C., Abbess.
Solemnly Professed 4.

[3765] (O.S.C.CAP.)—CAPUCHIN POOR CLARES (P)

Federation of Our Lady of the Angels in North America (1991): *Monastery of the Blessed Sacrament,* 4201 N.E. 18th St., Amarillo, TX 79107. Tel: 806-383-6771; Fax: 806-383-9877. Mother Catalina de Maria Banuelos, Pres.

[3770] (O.S.C.)—SISTERS OF ST. CLARE (P)

Generalate: 63 Harold's Cross Rd., Dublin 6W, Ireland. Sr. Patricia Rogers, O.S.C., Abbess Gen.
U.S. Foundation (California): *Santa Clara,* 1974 Cherrywood St., Vista, CA 92081. Tel: 760-945-0981. Sr. Madeline Fitzgerald, O.S.C., Contact Person; Sr. Patricia Rogers, O.S.C., Reg. Supr.-California; Sr. Maria Lucia Brady, O.S.C., Reg. Supr.-Florida.
Ministry in the field of Academic and Religious Education at all Levels; Pastoral & Social Ministry; Retreats; Ministry to the sick, poor and imprisoned.
Represented in the Dioceses of Orange, St. Petersburg, San Bernardino and San Diego. Also in Australia, El Salvador, England, Ireland and Wales.

[3780] (SS.C.M.)—SISTERS OF SAINTS CYRIL AND METHODIUS (P)

Founded in the United States in 1909.
General Motherhouse: *Villa Sacred Heart,* Danville, PA 17821-1698. Tel: 570-275-3581; Fax: 570-275-5997. Sr. Pamela Smith, Gen. Supr.
Total number in community 135.
Ministry in the field of Education; Parish Ministry and Religious Education; Retreat/Spiritual Direction; Hospital Chaplaincy; Prison Ministry; Deaf Apostolate; Homes for the Aged; Music Conservatory; Continuing Care Retirement Community.
Properties owned or sponsored: *St. Cyril Academy; Villa Sacred Heart; Sacred Heart Institute; Maria Hall; Maria Joseph Manor; The Meadows at Maria Joseph Manor,* Danville, PA; *Villa St. Cyril,* Highland Park, IL.
Represented in the Archdioceses of Chicago and Detroit and in the Dioceses of Allentown, Bridgeport, Charleston, Gary, Harrisburg, Joliet, Scranton, Syracuse and Wilmington.

[3790] (S.S.D.)—INSTITUTE OF THE SISTERS OF ST. DOROTHY (P)

Founded in Italy in 1834. First foundation in the United States in 1911.
General Motherhouse: Via del Gianicolo 4-a, Rome, Italy, 00165. Sr. Teresa Lopez, Gen. Coord.
Province of United States of America (1920): *Mt. St. Joseph,* 13 Monkeywrench Lane, Bristol, RI 02809. Tel: 401-253-7835. Sr. Dorothy Schwarz, S.S.D., Prov. Coord.
Universal number 1,259; Total number in the U.S. 43.
Ministry in the field of Education; Spiritual Life Centers; Hospital Chaplaincies; Social work with immigrants.
Properties owned or sponsored: *Villa Fatima,* Taunton, MA, *Mt. St. Joseph,* Bristol, RI, *Our Lady of Fatima High School,* Warren, RI, *St. Dorothy Academy,* Staten Island, NY.

[3810] (X.S.)—SOCIETY OF CATHOLIC MISSION SISTERS OF ST. FRANCIS XAVIER, INC. (D)
(Xavier Sisters)

Founded in the United States in 1946.
Convent: 37179 Moravian Dr., Clinton Township, MI 48036. Tel: 586-465-5082; Fax: 586-465-1990. Sr. Mary Agnes Malburg.
Total number in community 2.
Represented in the Archdiocese of Detroit.

[3820] (C.S.J.B.)—SISTERS OF ST. JOHN THE BAPTIST (P)

Founded in Italy in 1878. First foundation in the United States in 1906.
General Motherhouse: Rome, Italy. Mother John Marie White, C.S.JB., Supr. Gen.
U.S. Provincial House: 3308 Campbell Dr., Bronx, NY 10465-1358. Tel: 718-518-7820. Sr. John Agnes Barone, C.S.JB., Prov. Supr.
Total number in community 118.
Legal Titles and Holdings: *Mt. St. John Convent,* Purchase, NY; *St. John Villa Academy,* Staten Island, NY; *Providence Rest Nursing Home,* Bronx, NY; *St. Lucy School,* Newark, NJ; *Mt. St. John Convent,* Gladstone, NJ.
Ministry in the field of Education; Health Care for Aged Women & Men; Child Day Care.

[3830] (C.S.J. or S.S.J.)—SISTERS OF ST. JOSEPH

The Independent Motherhouses of the Sisters of St. Joseph are represented in the United States in the following Archdioceses and Dioceses:

[3830-01] BOSTON (D)

Motherhouse of the Congregation of the Sisters of St. Joseph of Boston-CSJ (1873): 637 Cambridge St., Brighton, MA 02135. Tel: 617-783-9090; Fax: 617-783-8246. Sr. Joan Duffy, C.S.J., Pres.; Sr. Therezon Sheerin, C.S.J., Community Archivist.
Total number in community 553.
Legal Holdings or Titles: *Motherhouse of the Sisters of Saint Joseph of Boston,* Brighton, MA; *Bethany Health Care Center, Inc.,* Framingham, MA; *Bethany Hill School, Inc.,* Framingham, MA; *Fontbonne Hall,* Framingham, MA; *Retreat Center,* Cohasset, MA; *The Merrimack Montessori School,* Haverhill, MA; *Walnut Park Montessori School,* Newton, MA; *Jackson School,* Newton, MA; *Fontbonne Academy,* Milton, MA; *Mount Saint Joseph Academy,* Brighton, MA; *Regis College,* Weston, MA; *Corporation for the Sponsored Ministries of the Sisters of St. Joseph of Boston,* Brighton, MA; *CSJ Ministries Connection, Inc.,* Brighton, MA; *The Literacy Connection,* Brighton, MA.

[3830-02] CHICAGO (D)

Sisters of St. Joseph of La Grange CSJ(1899): 1515 W. Ogden Ave., La Grange Park, IL 60526. Tel: 708-354-9200. Leadership Team: Sr. Marianne Race, C.S.J., Pres.; Sr. Kathleen Lucas, C.S.J.; Sr. Jean Anne McGrath, C.S.J.; Sr. Patricia Bergen, C.S.J.; Sr. Mary Schaefer, C.S.J.
Total number in community 96.
Legal Titles and Holdings: *Nazareth Academy, Sisters of St. Joseph of LaGrange Charitable Trust,* LaGrange Park, IL; *Christ in the Wilderness,* Stockton, IL.
Ministry in the field of Education; School Administration; Nursing; Pastoral Care in Hospitals; Nursing Homes; Work with the Elderly; Parish Ministry; Archdiocesan Administration; Spiritual Direction and Retreats.

[3830-03] ORANGE (P)

Sisters of St. Joseph of Orange -Motherhouse: 480 S. Batavia St., Orange, CA 92868. Tel: 714-633-8121; Fax: 714-744-3165. Sr. Katherine Gray, C.S.J., Gen. Supr.; Sr. Anne Hennessy, C.S.J., Community Archivist.
Total number in community 185.
Legal Holdings and Titles: *Sisters of St. Joseph of Orange; Sisters of St. Joseph Healthcare Foundation,* Orange, CA; *St. Joseph College,* Orange, CA; *Center for Spiritual Development,* Orange, CA; *St. Joseph Health System; St. Joseph Health System Foundation, Orange, CA; St. Jude Hospital, Inc. (dba St. Jude Medical Center); St. Jude Memorial Foundation,* Fullerton, CA; *St. Joseph Hospital Orange; St. Jude Hospital Yorba Linda, (dba St. Joseph Heritage Healthcare);* Yorba Linda, CA; *Mission Hospital Regional Medical Center,* Mission Viejo, CA; *Santa Rosa Memorial Hospital,* Santa Rosa, CA; *St. Joseph Hospital of Eureka,* Eureka, CA; *Redwood Memorial Hospital,* Fortuna, CA; *Redwood Memorial Foundation,* Fortuna, CA; *Queen of the Valley Hospital of Napa,* Napa, CA; *St. Mary of the Plains Hospital,* Lubbock, TX; *St. Mary Medical Center,* Apple Valley, CA.
Ministry in the field of Education; Health & Hospital Services; Pastoral and Social Services.

[3830-05] ROCKVILLE CENTRE (D)

St. Joseph's Convent - Congregation of the Sisters of Saint Joseph of Brentwood, NY CSJ: Brentwood, NY 11717. Tel: 516-273-4531. Sr. Jean Amore, Pres.; Sr. Edna McKeever, Community Archivist.
Total number in community 880.
Ministry in the field of Education; Health & Hospital Services.
Represented in the Dioceses of Brooklyn and Rockville Centre. Also in Puerto Rico, Dominican Republic and Brazil.

[3830-06] BUFFALO (P)

Generalate - Congregation of the Sisters of St. Joseph SSJ: 23 Agassiz Cir., Buffalo, NY 14214. Tel: 716-838-4400; Fax: 716-838-4102. E-mail: BUFFSSJ @ssjbuffalo.org. Sr. Elizabeth Savage, S.S.J., Pres.; Sr. Suzanne Rodriguez, S.S.J., Community Archivist.
Total number in community 127.
Ministry in the field of Education at all levels; School for Deaf; Youth Ministry; Justice Ministry; Pastoral Ministry; Hospital Chaplaincy; Prison Ministry; Spirituality Center.
Properties owned or sponsored: *Mt. St. Joseph Academy; Administrative Office; Sisters of St. Joseph Residence.*

[3830-08] CLEVELAND (D)

St. Joseph Convent - Sisters of St. Joseph CSJ: 3430 Rocky River Dr., Cleveland, OH 44111. Tel: 216-252-0440; Fax: 216-941-3430. Executive Team: Sr. Mary Brinkman; Sr. Pat Kozak; Sr. Mary Schrader; Sr. June Hansen, Community Archivist.
Total number in community 131.
Legal Holdings and Titles: *Saint Joseph Academy; Sisters of Saint Joseph Community Support Charitable Trust Fund.*
Ministry in the field of Academic and Religious Education at all levels; Parish and Pastoral Ministry; Deaf Apostolate; Parish Team Member; Justice Work; Health Care; Social Services; Bookstore and Radio; Social Concerns; Retreat Work.
Represented in the Archdioceses of Chicago and Washington and in the Dioceses of Cleveland, Columbus and Venice.

[3830-09] ERIE (D)

Sisters of St. Joseph SSJ: *Villa Maria,* 5031 W. Ridge Rd., Erie, PA 16506-1249. Tel: 814-836-4100; Fax: 814-836-4278. Sr. Ricarda Vincent, Pres.
Total number in the community 147.
Legal Title: *Sisters of St. Joseph of Northwestern Pa.*
Ministry in the field of Education at all levels; Social Ministries; Nursing Home; Health Care; Pastoral Work and other Diocesan Ministries.
Institutions sponsored: *Saint Vincent Health Center; St. Mary's Home of Erie; Villa Maria Elementary; Villa Maria Academy; Sisters of St. Joseph Neighborhood Network, Inc.*
Represented in the Archdioceses of Louisville, Miami and Washington and in the Dioceses of Arlington, Buffalo, Cleveland Memphis and Pittsburgh. Also in Labrador City.

[3830-10] LAFAYETTE-IN-INDIANA (D)

Sisters of St. Joseph of Tipton CSJ: 1440 W. Division Rd., Tipton, IN 46072. Tel: 765-675-6203; Fax: 765-675-7471. Sr. Martin McEntee, C.S.J., Pres.
Total number in community 39.
Ministry in Education; Health Care; Pastoral Ministry; Social Service; Evangelization.
Represented in the Archdioceses of Indianapolis and Louisville and in the Dioceses of Lafayette and Lansing.

[3830-11] KALAMAZOO (P)

Motherhouse and Novitiate - Sisters of St. Joseph of Nazareth SSJ: 3427 Gull Rd., Nazareth, MI 49074. Tel: 269-381-6290; Fax: 269-381-4909. Leadership Team: Sr. Janet Fleischhacker, Pres.; Sr. Christine Parks; Sr. Rita Ann Teichman; Sr. Theresa MacIntyre.
Total number in community 280.
Ministry in the field of Education; Social Services; Parish and Church-related Ministries; Foreign Missions.
Properties owned or sponsored: *Hospitals; Nursing Homes; Day Care Center for handicapped and senior citizens; Residence for Senior Citizens; Home Health Care Organizations; Ambulatory Care Services; Residential Treatment Center; Family Clinic; Gerontology Research Center; Outpatient Mental Health Clinic.*
Represented in the Archdioceses of Detroit, Los Angeles, New Orleans, and Santa Fe and in the Dioceses of Gaylord, Grand Rapids, Kalamazoo, Lafayette in Indiana, Lansing, Saginaw and St. Petersburg. Also in Peru and France.

[3830-12] OGDENSBURG (D)

Motherhouse of the Society of the Sisters of St. Joseph SSJ: 1425 Washington St., Watertown, NY 13601-4533. Tel: 315-782-3460. Sr. Annunciata Collins, Major Supr.; Sr. Mary Joseph Meichelbeck, Community Archivist.
Total number in community 62.
Ministry in the field of Education at all levels; Parish and Diocesan Administration.
Represented in the Diocese of Ogdensburg.

[3830-13] PITTSBURGH (P)

Sisters of St. Joseph CSJ-Motherhouse St. Joseph Convent: 1020 State St., Baden, PA 15005. Tel: 724-869-2151; Fax: 724-869-3336. Leadership Team: Sr. Marguerite Coyne; Sr. Diane Cauley; Sr. Rosanne Oberleitner; Sr. Helen Marie Shrift, Community Archivist.
Total number in community 270.
Ministry in the field of Religious and Academic Education; Health Care; Social Services; Spiritual Development; Prison Ministry; Missionaries; Diocesan Administrative Services.
Properties owned: *Motherhouse and 15 residences for sisters.*
Represented in the Archdioceses of Boston, Detroit, Hartford, New York, and Washington and in the Dioceses of Altoona-Johnstown, Arlington, Buffalo, Cheyenne, Erie, Fresno, Gallup, Greensburg, Harrisburg, Jackson, Memphis, Pittsburgh, Richmond, Sioux Falls and Wheeling-Charleston.

[3830-14] ROCHESTER (P)

Sisters of St. Joseph SSJ - Motherhouse: 150 French Rd., Rochester, NY 14618-3822. Tel: 585-641-8100; Fax: 585-586-1193. Sr. Janice Morgan, Congregational Pres.; Sr. Kathleen Urbanic, Archivist.
Total number in community 347.
Ministry in the field of Education at all levels; Homes for Aging; Health Care; Pastoral Ministry; School for Special Children and Adults; Homes for Emotionally Disturbed Children; Parish and Diocesan Evangelization; College Campus Ministry; Social Service; Justice and Peace Office; Drug Dependency Programs; Retreats & Spiritual Direction; AIDS Ministry; Prison Ministry.
Properties owned and sponsored: *Nazareth Schools; Nazareth Convent Motherhouse; St. Joseph Convent Infirmary.*
Sisters sponsor: Home Health Care; Food Kitchen; Spirituality Center; Domestic and Foreign Missions.
Represented in the Archdioceses of Mobile and St. Louis and in the Dioceses of Albany, Buffalo, Charlotte, Ogdensburg, Pensacola-Tallahassee, Rochester, and Venice. Also in Brazil and El Salvador.

[3830-15] SALINA (P)

General Administration Office (1884): *Nazareth Motherhouse - Sisters of St. Joseph of Concordia CSJ,* 215 Court St., P.O. Box 279, Concordia, KS 66901. Tel: 785-243-2149. Sr. Patricia McLennon, Pres.
Motherhouse: *Sisters of St. Joseph,* 1300 Washington St., Concordia, KS 66901. Tel: 785-243-2113.
Total sisters in community 202; Novices 5.
Ministry in Care for Elderly; Homeless; Education; Parish and Diocesan Evangelization; Social Services; Justice and Peace Offices; Marriage and Family Counseling; Youth Formation; Healthcare; College Campus Ministry; Drug Dependency Programs; Prisons; Consultants; Refugees; Continuous Prayer.
Properties owned: *Medaille Center,* Salina, KS; *Manna House of Prayer,* Concordia, KS; *Saint Joseph Foundation for Apostolic and Charitable Purposes, Inc.*
Represented in the Archdioceses of Atlanta, Boston, Denver, Kansas City in Kansas, New York, St. Paul-Minneapolis and in the Dioceses of Davenport, El Paso, Grand Island, Jefferson City, Kansas City, Las Cruces, Phoenix, Pueblo, Rockford, St. Cloud, Salina and Wichita.

[3830-16] SPRINGFIELD (MA) (D)

Motherhouse: *Mont Marie - Sisters of St. Joseph of Springfield SSJ,* 34 Lower Westfield Rd., Holyoke, MA 01040. Tel: 413-536-0853; Fax: 413-533-3275. Sr. Jane Morrissey, Pres.; Sr. Mary Lavelle, Archivist.
Total number in community 362.
Legal Holdings and Titles: *Mont Marie Child Care Center, Inc.; Mont Marie Health Care Center, Inc.; Mont Marie Conference Center,* Holyoke, MA.
Ministry in the field of Religious & Academic Education. Parish Ministry; Cross-Cultural; Diocesan Administration; Chaplaincy; Health Care, Social Services; Research and Study; Restorative Justice; AIDS Ministry; Creative Arts.
Properties owned or sponsored: *Fontbonne Hall; St. Francis Residence; Avila Hall; Maron Hall Residence,* Rutland, VT.
Represented in the Archdioceses of Hartford and Washington and in the Dioceses of Bridgeport, Burlington, Fall River, Lake Charles, Norwich, Providence, Springfield (MA) and Worcester.

[3830-17] WHEELING (D)

Motherhouse: *Mt. St. Joseph-Sisters of St. Joseph of Wheeling SSJ,* 137 Mount St. Joseph Rd., Wheeling, WV 26003. Tel: 304-232-8160. Sr. Marguerite O'Brien, Pres.; Sr. Mary Thomas Camilletti, Community Archivist.
Total number in community 90.
Ministry in the following areas: Parish Ministry; Pastoral Services; Elementary, Secondary, College Education; Health Care; Social Services; Spiritual Formation, Direction and Retreat Ministries; Diocesan; Administration and Service.
Properties owned and sponsored: *Sisters of St. Joseph of Wheeling Foundation, Inc.; A.B.L.E. Families, Inc.; Holy Family Child Care Center, Inc.; Sisters of St. Joseph House of Hospitality, Inc.; Sisters of St. Joseph Health System, Inc.; St. Joseph Health Initiative, Inc.; Sisters of St. Joseph Charitable Fund, Inc.; Sisters of St. Joseph Health and Wellness Foundation,* Wheeling, WV.
Represented in the Diocese of Wheeling-Charleston.

[3830-18] WICHITA (P)

Motherhouse: *Mt. St. Mary Convent - Sisters of St. Joseph of Wichita, CSJ,* 3700 E. Lincoln St., Wichita, KS 67218. Tel: 316-686-7171; Fax: 316-689-4056. Sr. Helene Lentz, Pres.; Sr. Romona Seidl, Archivist.
Total number in community 167.
Legal Holdings and Titles: *Properties owned and sponsored, CSJ "Dear Neighbor" Ministries, Inc.,* Wichita, KS; *St. Joseph Adoption Referral Services, Inc.,* Kansas City, KS; *The Sisters of St. Joseph of Wichita, Kansas; Co-Sponsor of: Via Christi Health System, Inc., (Parent organization) for: Via Christi Regional Medical Center, Inc.; St. Francis Campus; St. Joseph Campus; Via Christi Rehabilitation Hospital, Inc. - Lourdes Campus; GeorgeTown Village, Inc.,* Wichita, KS; *Cornerstone Assisted Living, Inc.,* Wichita, KS; *Mount Carmel Medical Center, Inc. Parent organization for: Mount Carmel Foundation,* Pittsburgh, KS; *St. Joseph Senior Community, Inc.,* Manhattan, KS; *Via Christi Oklahoma Regional Medical Center,* Ponca City, OK; *Westminster Village, Inc.,* Ponca City, OK; *Hayward Sisters Hospital, dba St. Rose Hospital, Parent organization for: St. Rose Medical Building, Inc.; St. Rose Hospital Foundation,* Hayward, CA.
Ministry in the fields of Religious and Academic Education; Adult Religious Correspondence Courses; Diocesan Program for the Handicapped; School of Special Education; Home for Aged; Pro-Life Ministry to Women; ESL Language School; G.E.D. Program; Home Hospice; Hospital and Clinical Care; Pastoral Ministry; Campus Ministry.
Represented in the Archdioceses of Kansas City in Kansas and Oklahoma City and in the Dioceses of Dodge City, Grand Island, Kansas City-St. Joseph, Oakland, Salina and Wichita. Also in Japan.

[3840] (C.S.J.)—SISTERS OF ST. JOSEPH OF CARONDELET (P)

Founded in France in 1650. First foundation in the United States in 1836.
Congregational Offices: 2311 S. Lindbergh Blvd., St. Louis, MO 63131. Tel: 314-966-4048; Fax: 314-966-5041. Congregational Leadership Team for the Provinces and Vice Province listed below: Sr. Joan Henehan, C.S.J.; Sr. Karen M. Kennelly, C.S.J.; Sr. Theresa Kvale, C.S.J.; Sr. Joan Lescinski, C.S.J.; Sr. Barbara A. Moore, C.S.J.
Province of St. Louis (1836): *St. Joseph's Provincial House,* 6400 Minnesota Ave., St. Louis, MO 63111. Tel: 314-481-8800; Fax: 314-481-2366; 351-3111. Province Leadership Team: Sr. MaryKay Hadican, C.S.J.; Sr. Mary Kay Liston, C.S.J.; Sr. Sandra Straub, C.S.J.
Total number in community 519.
Sponsored Institutions: Colleges 2; Academies 2; Hospitals 3; Institute for the Deaf 1; Long Term Care Facility 1.
Legal Title: *Sisters of St. Joseph of Carondelet, St. Louis Province.*
Ministries in the field of Academic Education; Pastoral Ministries; Diocesan Offices; Health Care; Child Care; Geriatric Care; Foreign Missions; Social Services; Community Services; Special Services; Fine Arts.
Represented in the Archdioceses of Atlanta, Boston, Chicago, Denver, Indianapolis, Kansas City in Kansas, Los Angeles, Miami, Mobile, St. Louis, St. Paul-Minneapolis, and Seattle and in the Dioceses of Brownsville, Charleston, Colorado Springs, El Paso, Evansville, Green Bay, Helena, Honolulu, Jackson, Kansas City-St. Joseph, Las Vegas, Marquette, Palm

Beach, Peoria, St. Petersburg, San Diego, San Jose, Savannah, Salt Lake City, Shreveport, Springfield-Cape Girardeau, Steubenville, Tucson and Venice.

Province of St. Paul (1851): *St. Joseph's Administration Center,* 1884 Randolph Ave., St. Paul, MN 55105. Tel: 651-690-7000; Fax: 651-690-7039. Province Leadership Team: Sr. Christine Ludwig, C.S.J.; Sr. Susan Oeffling, C.S.J.; Sr. Dolore Rochon, C.S.J.; Sr. Mary Kraft, C.S.J., Archivist.

Total number in community 378.

Legal Holdings or Titles: *St. Joseph of Carondelet - St. Paul Province Provincial House; The College of St. Catherine; Bethany Convent for Retired Sisters,* St. Paul, MN.

Ministry in the fields of Education; Health; Social Services; Spirituality.

Represented in the Archdioceses of St. Louis, St. Paul-Minneapolis, Seattle, and Washington and in the Dioceses of Brownsville, Charlotte, Duluth, El Paso, Fargo, Jackson, Jefferson City, New Ulm, St. Cloud and Superior.

Province of Albany (1858): *St. Joseph's Provincial House,* 385 Watervliet-Shaker Rd., Latham, NY 12110-4799. Tel: 518-783-3500. Leadership Team: Sr. Danielle Bonetti, C.S.J.; Sr. Laura Bufano, C.S.J.; Sr. Mary Catherine Ryan, C.S.J.; Sr. Christine Partisano, C.S.J.; Sr. Miriam Ukeritis, C.S.J.; Sr. Lauren VanDermark, C.S.J.; Sr. Anne L. Clark, C.S.J., Prov. Archivist.

Total number in community 507.

Novitiate: 369 Watervliet-Shaker Rd., Latham, NY 12110. Tel: 518-783-3536.

Ministry in the fields of Academic and Special Education at all levels; Hospital and Infirmary Services; Hospital Pastoral Ministries; Parish Ministry and Religious Education; Diocesan Offices; Youth Ministry; Counseling; Retreat and Spiritual Direction; Social and Community Services; Fine Arts.

Represented in the Archdioceses of Anchorage, Boston, Cincinnati, Detroit, Indianapolis, Los Angeles, New York, St. Louis, Seattle, San Francisco, and Washington and in the Dioceses of Albany, Birmingham, Brooklyn, Buffalo, Charleston, Erie, Harrisburg, Honolulu, Kansas City-St. Joseph, Ogdensburg, Palm Beach, Pensacola-Tallahassee, Pittsburgh, Rochester, Rockville Centre, Scranton, Shreveport, Spokane, Syracuse, Trenton, and Worcester. Also in Chile and Peru.

Province of Los Angeles (1878): *St. Mary's Provincialate and Carondelet Center,* 11999 Chalon Rd., Los Angeles, CA 90049-1524. Tel: 310-889-2100; Fax: 310-476-8735. Sr. Maureen O'Connor, C.S.J., Prov. Supr.; Sr. Patricia Rose Shanahan, C.S.J., Archivist.

Professed Sisters 418.

Legal Titles or Holdings: *Sisters of St. Joseph in California; Sisters of St. Joseph in Arizona; Sisters of St. Joseph Ministerial Services.*

Sisters serve in the fields of Education, Health Services; Social Services; Pastoral Ministry.

Represented in the Archdioceses of Boston, Los Angeles, St. Louis, San Francisco, and Seattle and in the Dioceses of Boise, Fresno, Honolulu, Little Rock, Monterey, Oakland, Orange, Phoenix, Sacramento, San Bernardino, San Diego, San Jose, Spokane, Stockton, Tucson and Yakima.

Hawaii Vice-Province (1956): *Sisters of St. Joseph of Carondelet, Carondelet Center,* 5311 Apo Dr., Honolulu, HI 96821-1829. Tel: 808-373-2096. Sr. Brenda Lau, C.S.J., Dir.

Professed Sisters 39.

Legal Title: *Sisters of St. Joseph of Carondelet-Hawaii Vice-Province.*

Ministries include: Elementary and Secondary Schools; Pastoral Associates; Prayer & Spirituality; Administering Diocesan Offices; Religious Education Directors; Campus Ministry; Counseling and social work to the physically impaired; Social Ministry.

Represented in the Diocese of Honolulu. Also in Chile & Japan.

[3850] (C.S.J.)—SISTERS OF ST. JOSEPH OF CHAMBERY (P)

Founded in France in 1650. First foundation in United States in 1885.

Generalate: Via Calandrelli 7, Rome, Italy. 00153, Sr. Lorraine Delaney, C.S.J., Supr. Gen.

Provincial House: *Convent of Mary Immaculate,* 27 Park Rd., West Hartford, CT 06119. Tel: 860-233-5126; 232-8252. Sr. Sally Hodgdon, C.S.J., Prov. Supr.

Total number in community 153.

Legal Title: *Sisters of St. Joseph Corporation.*

Ministry in the field of Academic and Religious Education at all levels; Social Services; Pastoral and Parish Ministries; Prisons; Law and Business; Child Day Care Center; Foreign Missions; Hospitals and Health Care.

Represented in the Archdioceses of Hartford, Miami, and Mobile and in the Dioceses of Bridgeport, El Paso, Fairbanks, Lexington, Monterey, Oakland, Norwich and Springfield (MA).

[3860] (S.J.C.)—SISTERS OF ST. JOSEPH OF CLUNY (P)

Founded in France in 1807.

Generalate: Paris, France. Sr. Morag Collins, Supr. Gen.

American Novitiate: *Mary Immaculate Queen Novitiate,* 20955 Halldale Ave., Torrance, CA 90501. Tel: 310-328-1807. Sr. Luke Parker, S.J.C., Local Coord.

Provincialate: 90 Brenton Rd., Newport, RI 02840-4392. Tel: 401-846-4757. Sr. Joan Vander Zyden, S.J.C., Prov. of U.S. & Canada.

Professed Sisters in U.S. & Canada 37.

Legal Title: *Sisters of St. Joseph of Cluny, Inc.*

Ministry in outreach ministry; pastoral work; retreats; healthcare; education.

Represented in the Archdiocese of Los Angeles and in the Dioceses of Little Rock and Providence. Also in Canada.

[3870] (C.S.J.)—SISTERS OF ST. JOSEPH OF LYONS, FRANCE (P)

Founded in France October 15, 1650. First foundation in United States in 1906 in Jackman, Maine.

General Motherhouse: Lyons, France. Sr. Janet Gagnon Supr. Gen.

Maine Province: *Sisters of St. Joseph,* 93 Halifax St., Winslow, ME 04901. Tel: 207-873-4512; Fax: 207-873-1976. Sr. Laurette Levasseur, Prov.

Total number in community 43.

Ministry in Catechesis; Holistic Care; Spirituality and Ecology; Pastoral Ministry; Education; Pastoral Care; Mental Illness, social work and canon law; Work with Migrants and Communities.

Properties owned and sponsored: *Mount St. Joseph Nursing Home,* Waterville, ME.

Represented in the Archdiocese of Los Angeles and in the Dioceses of El Paso, Laredo, Manchester and Portland (ME).

[3880] (C.S.J.)—SISTERS OF ST. JOSEPH OF MEDAILLE (P)

Founded in France in 1650. First foundation in the United States in 1855. Classified as an American Congregation November 30, 1977.

Central Office: *Congregation of the Sisters of Saint Joseph of Medaille,* 1821 Summit Rd., Suite 210, Cincinnati, OH 45237. Tel: 513-761-2888; Fax: 513-761-9957. Sr. Phyllis Manda, Pres.; Sr. Eleanor Bernstein, Vice Pres.; Sr. Anne Meridier, Gen. Councilor; Sr. Caroline Benken, Gen. Councilor.

Total number in community 152.

Legal Title: *Sisters of St. Joseph of Medaille, Ohio Corporation.*

Ministry in the field of Academic Education at all levels; Hospital and Clinic Care; Pastoral Ministry; Religious Education; Foreign Missions; Social Service; Centers for Christian Renewal; Services to Poor and Minorities; Community Service; Diocesan Offices; Activities Programs for Retired-Elderly; Chemical Dependency; Adult Mentally Retarded; Care for Retired Sisters.

Represented in the Archdioceses of Cincinnati, New Orleans, and St. Paul-Minneapolis and in the Dioceses of Baton Rouge, Columbus, Covington, Crookston, El Paso, Fargo, Green Bay and Houma-Thibodaux.

[3890] (C.S.J.P.)—SISTERS OF ST. JOSEPH OF PEACE (P)

Founded in England 1884. First United States foundation 1885.

Generalate: *Sisters of St. Joseph of Peace Generalate, Inc.,* 3043 Fourth St. N.E., Washington, DC 20017. Tel: 202-832-5333; Fax: 202-832-5327. Sr. Sheila Lemieux, C.S.J.P., Congregation Leader; Sr. Terry Donohue, C.S.J.P., Assistant Congregational Leader.

Total number in the community 293.

St. Joseph Province-Eastern Province (1885): Sr. Mary Rattigan, C.S.J.P., Prov.; Sr. Nora Molyneux, C.S.J.P., Vice Prov.

Total number in the Eastern Province 143.

Ministry in the field of Education; Health and Social Services.

Properties owned or sponsored: *St. Joseph's Home for the Blind; St. Ann's Home for The Aged; St. Mary's Residence; St. Joseph's Home; The Nurturing Place (York Street Child Development Center).*

Represented in the Archdioceses of Baltimore, Los Angeles, Newark, New York and Washington and in the Dioceses of Camden, Metuchen, Paterson, St. Petersburg and Trenton.

Our Lady Province (Western) (1909): *St. Mary's Provincialate,* 1663 Killarney Way, Box 248, Bellevue, WA 98009-0248. Tel: 425-451-1770; Fax: 425-462-9760. Sr. Andrea Nenzel, C.S.J.P., Prov. Leader.

Total number in community 87.

Corporate Titles: *Sisters of St. Joseph of Peace, Our Lady Province (Western); Sisters of St. Joseph of Peace Charitable Trust,* Bellevue, WA.

Ministry in the field of Education; Social Services; Religious Education; Parish Ministry, Retreat Ministry, Social and Minority Ministry.

Properties owned: *St. Mary's Residence and Novitiate,* Bellevue, WA; *Prospect House,* Seattle, WA; *St. Theres Residence,* Seattle, WA; *Grace House,* Seattle, WA; *Alicia Park House,* Seattle, WA; *Eugene Residence,* Eugene, OR.

Represented in the Archdioceses of Anchorage, Los Angeles, Portland (OR), San Francisco and Seattle and in the Dioceses of Great Falls-Billings, Juneau, San Diego, Spokane and Yakima. Also in Canada and El Salvador.

[3893] (S.S.J.)—SISTERS OF SAINT JOSEPH OF CHESTNUT HILL, PHILADELPHIA (P)

Founded in France in 1650. First foundation in Philadelphia in 1847.

Motherhouse (1847): *Mount St. Joseph Convent,* 9701 Germantown Ave., Philadelphia, PA 19118-2694. Tel: 215-248-7200; Fax: 215-248-7277. E-mail: msjc@ssjphila.org. Web site: www.ssjphila.org. Sr. Patricia Kelly, Supr. Gen.; Sr. Patricia Annas, Congregational.

Total number in Congregation 1,150.

Legal Holdings or Titles: *Saint Joseph Villa; Saint Joseph Guild; Bethlehem Retirement Village,* Flourtown, PA; *Academy Village,* McSherrystown, PA; *Saint Joseph Housing Corporation; Saint Mary by-the-Sea Convent,* Cape May Point, NJ; *Cecilian,* Philadelphia, PA; *Mount Saint Joseph Academy,* Flourtown, PA; *Norwood-Fontbonne Academy,* Philadelphia, PA; *Holy Family Academy,* Bayonne, NJ; *Chestnut Hill College,* Philadelphia, PA; *Saint Joseph Academy,* McSherrystown, PA; *The Convent of the Sisters of St. Joseph,* Chestnut Hill, PA.

Ministry in the field of Academic and Religious Education at all levels; Institutes for Dependent Children; Pastoral Ministry; Campus Ministry; Care of the Aged; Social Services; Prison Ministry; Health Care; Psychologists; Hospice Ministry; Hospital Chaplaincy; Spiritual Directors; Drug and Alcohol Counselors; Legal Services Ministry; Canon Law.

Represented in the Archdioceses of Baltimore, Newark, Philadelphia, San Antonio, San Juan, and Washington and in the Dioceses of Albany, Allentown, Arlington, Belleville, Camden, Charlotte, Harrisburg, Jackson, Lexington, Metuchen, Paterson, Raleigh, St. Petersburg, Savannah, Trenton and Wilmington. Also in Peru.

[3900] (S.S.J.)—SISTERS OF ST. JOSEPH OF ST. AUGUSTINE, FLORIDA (D)

Founded in France in 1650. First foundation in the United States in 1866. Classified as an American Congregation in 1899.

Motherhouse: *St. Joseph Convent,* 241 St. George St. P.O. Box 3506, St. Augustine, FL 32085. Tel: 904-824-1752. Website: www.ssjfl.com. Sr. Ann Kuhn, S.S.J.; General Supr. Sr. Thomas Joseph McGoldrick, S.S.J.; Community Archivist.

Total number in community 98.

Legal Title: *The Sisters of St. Joseph Continuing Community Support Trust Fund.*

Ministry in Hospital-Health Care Services; Social Services; Hospital Pastoral Care; Care of Aged; Academic and Religious Education at all levels; Parish Ministry; Diocesan Office Administration; Architectural Liturgical Design; Retreat Ministry; Ministry to the Handicapped.

Represented in the Archdiocese of Miami and in the Dioceses of Orlando, Palm Beach, Pensacola-Tallahassee, St. Augustine and St. Petersburg.

[3910] (S.J.S.M.)—SISTERS OF ST. JOSEPH OF ST. MARK (D)

Founded in France in 1845. First foundation in the United States in October, 1937.

Generalate: Colmar, France. Sr. Sophie Moog, Gen. Supr.

Universal Total number in Congregation 249.

General Motherhouse (Cleveland) (1939): 21800 Charden Rd., Euclid, OH 44117. Mother Mary Therese Trunk, Supr. Gen.

Youngstown Diocese: *Sisters of St. Joseph of St. Mark, Community Center,* 2300 Reno Dr., Louisville, OH 44641. Tel: 330-875-7967. Sr. Geralen Rybak, S.J.S.M., Supr.

Total number in U.S. 8.

Represented in the Dioceses of Cleveland and Youngstown.

[3920] (S.J.W.)—SISTERS OF ST. JOSEPH THE WORKER (D)

General Motherhouse: *St. William Convent,* 1 St. Joseph Ln., Walton, KY 41094. Mother Celeste Marie Downes, S.J.W., Supr. Gen.

Total number in the community 15.
Properties owned and operated: *Taylor Manor Nursing Home,* Versailles, KY; 16-acre property in Walton, KY: *Motherhouse Formation House*.
Represented in the Dioceses of Covington and Lexington.

[3930] (SSJ-TOSF)—SISTERS OF ST. JOSEPH OF THE THIRD ORDER OF ST. FRANCIS (P)

Founded in the United States in 1901.
Corporate Office: P.O. Box 305 - 1300 Maria Dr., Stevens Point, WI 54481-0305. Tel: 715-341-8457; Fax: 715-341-8830. Sr. Jeanne Conzemius, S.S.J.-T.O.S.F., Pres.; Sr. Katherine Wyszynski, S.S.J.-T.O.S.F., Vice Pres.; Sr. Mary Alice Jarosz, S.S.J.-T.O.S.F., Vice Pres.; Sr. Valerie Kulbacki, S.S.J.-T.O.S.F., Vice Pres.
Total number in the Congregation 414.
Sponsors: Learning Center; 2 High Schools; Health Care Facility; Continuing Care Retirement Community.
Ministries in the following areas: Academic Education at all levels; Pastoral Ministry; Health Care Services; Ministry abroad in South Africa, South America and Puerto Rico; 8th Day Center for Justice; Social Services.
Represented in the Archdioceses of Chicago, Detroit, Hartford, Los Angeles, Milwaukee, St. Paul-Minneapolis, and Washington and in the Dioceses of Arecibo, Cleveland, Fort Wayne-South Bend, Gary, Grand Island, Green Bay, Harrisburg, Joliet, Kalamazoo, Knoxville, La Crosse, Madison, Norwich, Oakland, Phoenix, Rockford, Superior, Toledo and Youngstown.

[3935] (S.S.L.)—THE CONGREGATION OF THE SISTERS OF ST. LOUIS, JUILLY-MONAGHAN (P)

Founded in France in 1842. First foundation in the United States in 1949.
General Motherhouse: *Louisville Monaghan,* Ireland. Sr. Uainin Clarke, S.S.L., Supr. Gen.
Regional House: *Louisville Convent,* 22300 Mulholland, Dr. Woodland Hills, CA 91364. Tel: 818-883-1678. Sr. Donna Hansen, S.S.L., Reg. Supr.
Finally Professed Sisters 68.
Legal Title: *Sisters of St. Louis, Juilly-Monaghan, Inc.*
Ministry in the field of Education; Pastoral and Social Ministries.
Represented in the Archdioceses of Chicago, Los Angeles and Washington and in the Dioceses of Orange, Raleigh, Salt Lake City, and San Diego.

[3950] (S.S.M.N.)—SISTERS OF SAINT MARY OF NAMUR (P)

Founded in Namur, Belgium, in 1819. First foundation in the United States in 1863.
General Motherhouse: Namur, Belgium. Sr. Judith Carroll, Gen. Supr.
Universal Total in Congregation 459.
Eastern Province: *Provincial House,* 241 Lafayette Ave., Buffalo, NY 14213-1453. Tel: 716-884-8221; Fax: 716-884-6598. Sr. Mary Veronica, S.S.M.N., Prov. Supr.
Total number in community 103.
Legal Holdings or Titles: *10 Residences.*
Ministry in the field of Religious and Academic Education; Pastoral Ministry; Community Organization; Social Services; Diocesan and Health related services; Refugee Assistance.
Represented in the Archdiocese of Boston and in the Dioceses of Buffalo, Charleston and Savannah. Also in Canada.
Western Province: *Provincial House - Our Lady of Victory Center,* 909 W. Shaw St., Fort Worth, TX 76110. Tel: 817-923-8393. Sr. Dorothy Powers, Prov. Supr.
Total number in community 54.
Ministry in the field of Religious and Academic Education; Diocesan Offices; Pastoral Ministry; Social Services; Health Care.
Properties owned or sponsored: *Our Lady of Victory Center,* Fort Worth, TX; *Our Lady of Victory Elementary School,* Fort Worth, TX; *Sisters of St. Mary of Namur,* Fort Worth, TX; *Notre Dame Convent; Mercy Convent,* Wichita Falls, TX.
Represented in the Dioceses of Dallas, Fort Worth, Galveston-Houston and Richmond.

[3960] (S.S.M.O.)—SISTERS OF ST. MARY OF OREGON (P)

Founded in Oregon in 1886.
General Motherhouse: *St. Mary of the Valley,* 4440 S.W. 148th Ave., Beaverton, OR 97007. Tel: 503-644-9181. Sr. Barbara Jean Laughlin, Supr. Gen.
Total number in Congregation 88.
Ministry in the field of Education; Nursing Homes; and Parish Services.
Properties owned or sponsored: *St. Mary of the Valley School & Convent; Valley Catholic School; Maryville Nursing Home; Little Flower Development Center,* Beaverton, OR.
Represented in the Archdioceses of Los Angeles, Portland (OR) and Seattle and in the Dioceses of Baker and Helena.

[3980] (S.P.C)—SISTERS OF SAINT PAUL DE CHARTRES (P)

Founded in France in 1696.
General House: 193 Via della Vignaccia, Rome, Italy. I-00163 Sr Myriam Kitcharoent, S.P.C., Supr. Gen.
Universal Total in Congregation 4,000.
U.S. Province: 1300 County Rd. 492, Marquette, MI 49855-9632. Tel: 906-226-3932; 226-2139. Sr. Gloria Schultz, S.P.C., Prov.
Total number in community 20.
Legal Holding: *Bishop Noa Home for Senior Citizens,* Escanaba, MI.
Ministry in the field of Academic and Religious Education; Hospital Chaplaincy; Pastoral Associates; Counseling; Ministry to the Aged & Impaired.
Represented in the Archdiocese of Washington and in the Diocese of Marquette.

[3990] (S.S.P.C.)—MISSIONARY SISTERS OF ST. PETER CLAVER (P)

Founded in 1894. First Foundation in the United States, 1914.
General House: 16 via dell' Olmata, Rome, Italy. Mother M. Elizabeth Adamiak, S.S.P.C., Supr. Gen.
Legal Title: *The Sodality of St. Peter Claver for the African Missions-Missionary Sisters of St. Peter Claver.*
American Headquarters: 667 Woods Mill Rd. S., P.O. Box 6067, Chesterfield, MO 63006-6067. Tel: 314-434-8084. Sr. M. Irene Brahmakulath, S.S.P.C., Supr.
Total number in community 16.
Represented in the Archdioceses of Chicago, St. Louis and St. Paul-Minneapolis.

[4010] (O.S.A.)—SISTERS OF ST. RITA (D)

General Motherhouse: F. Spee Str., Wurzburg, 87, Germany. Sr. M. Dolores Schneider, Gen. Supr.
Universal total in Congregation 190.
U.S. Address: *St. Monica's Convent,* 4014 Green Bay Rd., Racine, WI 53404. Tel: 262-639-1766. Sr. Hanika, Supr.
Represented in the Archdiocese of Milwaukee.

[4020] (S.T.J.)—SOCIETY OF ST. TERESA OF JESUS (P)
(Teresian Sisters)

Founded in Spain in 1876. First foundation in the United States in 1910.
Total Membership 1,703.
Generalate: Via Valcannuta, 134, Rome, Italy. 00166.
Provincial House: *St. Francis de Sales Province,* 18080 St. Joseph's Way, Covington, LA 70435-5623. Tel: 985-893-1470; Fax: 985-893-2476.
Formation House: 18158 St. Joseph's Way, Covington, LA 70435-5624. Tel: 985-893-1557 Sr. Martha L. Gonzalez, Community Archivist.
Total number in community 47.
Ministry in the field of Academic Education at all levels; Education in underdeveloped areas; Youth Ministry.
Properties owned: *St. Teresa's Convent,* San Antonio, TX; *Henry de Osso Convent,* San Antonio, TX; *Provincialate,* Covington, LA; *Blessed Mercedes Prat Convent,* New Orleans, LA.
Represented in the Archdioceses of Miami, New Orleans and San Antonio.

[4030] (S.S.T.V.)—CONGREGATION OF SISTERS OF ST. THOMAS OF VILLANOVA (P)

Founded in France in 1661. First foundation in the United States in 1948.
General Motherhouse: 52 Blvd. d'Argenson, Neuilly-sur-Seine, France.
Universal Total in Congregation 300.
Sisters of St. Thomas of Villanova Convent: Rocks Rd., Norwalk, CT 06851. Tel: 203-847-2885. Mother Edmond, Supr.
Total number in the community 4.
Properties owned: *Notre Dame Convalescent Home.*
Represented in the Diocese of Bridgeport.

[4040] (S.U.)—SOCIETY OF ST. URSULA (P)

Founded in Dole, France, in 1606. First foundation in the United States in 1901.
General Motherhouse: *St. Cyr-Loire,* France. Sr. Marie Bernard, Supr. Gen.
Provincialate: *American Regional Ctr.,* 50 Linwood Rd. Rhinebeck, NY 12572. Tel: 845-876-2557 & 876-2341. Sr Catherine Gormley, Prov.
Total number in the community 33.
Ministry in the field of Education; Parish Ministry; Social Work.
Represented in the Archdioceses of New York and Washington and in the Dioceses of Providence and Raleigh.

[4048] (F.C.J.)—SOCIETY OF THE SISTERS, FAITHFUL COMPANIONS OF JESUS (P)

Founded in France in 1820. First founded in United States 1895.
General Motherhouse: *Stella Maris Convent,* Northforeland, Broadstairs Kent, England.
American Province: *St. Philomena Convent,* 324 Cory's Ln., Portsmouth, RI 02871. Tel: 401-683-2222. Sr. Katherine Mary O'Flynn, F.C.J., Supr. Gen.; Sr. Marguerite Goddard, F.C.J., Novice Dir.
Sisters 24.

[4050] (S.D.S.H.)—SISTERS OF THE SOCIETY DEVOTED TO THE SACRED HEART (D)

Founded in Hungary in 1940.
Motherhouse (1956): 9814 Sylvia Ave., Northridge, CA 91324. Tel: 818-772-9961; Fax: 818-772-2742. Web site: www.sdsh.org. Sr. Lucia Tu, Supr. Gen.; Sr. Ida Peterfy, Foundress.
Novitiate House: 10480 Winnetka, Chatsworth, CA 91313. Tel: 818-831-9710; Fax: 818-831-0790. Web site: www.sdsh.org.
Total number in community 51.
Ministry in Parish Religious Education Centers; Catechist Formation Centers; Camp for year-round Retreats and summer Family Retreats Camps; Catechesis; Youth Leadership Programs; Day Retreat Center for Children and Adults; Catechesis in Parochial Schools and Catholic High Schools; "Sacred Heart Kids' Club" Video Catechesis; Hispanic, Chinese and Korean Catechetical Centers; Catechetical Programs on Military Bases; Catechetical Missions to Dioceses; Far East Mission in Taiwan; Mission in Hungary.
Properties owned: *Sacred Heart Motherhouse,* Northridge, CA; *Heart of Jesus Retreat Center,* Santa Ana, CA; *Sacred Heart Retreat Camp,* Big Bear Lake, CA; *Sacred Heart Novitiate,* Chatsworth, CA.
Represented in the Archdioceses of Los Angeles, and St. Louis and Dioceses of Orange and San Bernardino. Also in Taiwan and Hungary.

[4060] (S.H.C.J.)—SOCIETY OF THE HOLY CHILD JESUS (P)

Founded in England in 1846. First foundation in the United States in 1862.
Motherhouse: Via della Maglianella 379, Rome, Italy, 00166. Sr. Geraldine MacCarthy, S.H.C.J., Society leader.
American Province: *Provincial Offices,* 460 Shadeland Ave., Drexel Hill, PA 19026-2312. Tel: 610-626-1400. Sr. Marcia Sichol, Prov. Leader; Sr. Helena Mayer, Archivist, 1341 Montgomery Ave., Rosemont, PA 19010.
Total number in Province 217.
Ministry in a variety of Educational and Pastoral Work.
Properties owned or sponsored: *Connelly School of the Holy Child,* Potomac, MD; *Cornelia Connelly School,* Anaheim, CA; *Mayfield Junior School of the Holy Child Jesus; Mayfield Senior School of the Holy Child Jesus,* Pasadena, CA; *Oak Knoll School of the Holy Child,* Summit, NJ; *Old Westbury School of the Holy Child,* Old Westbury, NY; *Rosemont School of the Holy Child,* Rosemont, PA; *School of the Holy Child,* Drexel Hill, PA; *School of the Holy Child,* Rye, NY; *Providence Center,* Philadelphia, PA; *Cornelia Connelly Center for Education; Holy Child Middle School,* New York, NY.
Represented in the Archdioceses of Boston, Chicago, Los Angeles, Milwaukee, Newark, New Orleans, New York, Philadelphia, Portland (OR), St. Louis and Washington and in the Dioceses of Baker, Camden, Charlotte, Paterson, Rockville Centre, Sacramento, San Diego, Trenton and Venice.

[4070] (R.S.C.J.)—SOCIETY OF THE SACRED HEART (P)

Founded in France in 1800. First foundation in the United States in 1818.
Generalate: Via Tarquinio Vipera, 16, Rome, Italy. 00152, Sr. Clare Pratt, Supr. Gen.
United States Provincial House: 4389 W. Pine Blvd., St. Louis, MO 63108. Tel: 314-652-1500; Fax: 314-534-6800. E-mail: provincialhouse@rscj.org. Sr. Kathleen Hughes, Prov.; Sr. Frances Gimber, Prov. Archivist.
Total number in the Province 458.
Ministry in the field of Religious and Academic Education at all levels; Adult Education; Parish, Pastoral, Social and Health Care Ministries.
Province Corporations: *California Province of the Society of the Sacred Heart, Inc.; Society of the Sacred Heart, Chicago Province, Inc.; Religious of the Sacred Heart, Washington Province, Inc.; Religious of the Sacred Heart, New York Province, Inc.; Ladies of the Sacred Heart, MO; Religious of the Sacred Heart in Massachusetts, Inc. Network of Sacred Heart Schools, Inc.,* 860 Beacon St., Newton, MA 02459-1879. Tel: 617-244-9260.
Represented in the Archdioceses of Boston, Chicago, Detroit, Miami, New Orleans, New York, Omaha, St.

Louis, San Francisco, Seattle and Washington and in the Dioceses of Albany, Baton Rouge, Bridgeport, Galveston-Houston, Lafayette (LA), Metuchen, Richmond, San Bernardino, San Diego, Trenton and Venice.

[4080] (S.S.S.)—SISTERS OF SOCIAL SERVICE OF LOS ANGELES, INC. (P)

Founded in Hungary. Established in the United States at Los Angeles, California in 1926.

General Motherhouse: 2303 S. Figueroa Way, Los Angeles, CA 90007. Tel: 213-746-2117; Fax: 213-747-4499. Sr. Michele Walsh, Gen.

Total number in the community 100.

Legal Title: *Sisters of Social Service of Los Angeles; Sisters of Social Service Support Trust Fund.*

Social Service Work in Parishes and in Diocesan Agencies; Leadership Training of Youth and Adults; Summer Camps for Children and Families; Programs for the Elderly; Peace and Justice Work; Religious Education; Settlement Houses; Health Programs; Low Cost Legal Services; Family Counseling Services; International houses in Mexico, Philippines and Taiwan.

Represented in the Archdioceses of Boston, Los Angeles, Portland (OR), San Francisco and Seattle and in the Dioceses of Oakland, Sacramento and San Diego.

[4090] (S.S.S.)—SISTERS OF SOCIAL SERVICE (D)

Founded in Budapest, Hungary in 1923; Sr. Margaret Slachta, Foundress.

U.S. Residence: 296 Summit Ave., Buffalo, NY 14214. Tel: 716-834-0197. Sr. Agnes Pataki, S.S.S., District Moderator.

Total number in the United States 16.

Social Work in private and public agencies; Religious Education; Parish Ministry; Health Care; Ministry for Justice and Human Rights.

Represented in the Archdioceses of Miami and Washington and in the Dioceses of Buffalo and Ponce, PR.

[4100] (S.S.M.)—SISTERS OF THE SORROWFUL MOTHER (THIRD ORDER OF ST. FRANCIS) (P)

Founded in Italy in 1883. First foundation in the United States in 1889.

General Motherhouse: *Casa Generalizia della Suore dell'Addolorata,* Via Paolo III, Roma, Italy. 7-9, I-00165, Sr. Helen Malolepsy, S.S.M., General Superior.

U.S./Caribbean Province: *Our Lady of Sorrows Convent,* 17600 E. 51st St., Broken Arrow, OK 74012. Tel: 918-355-1148; Fax: 918-355-3534. Sr. Dorothy Ann M. Dirkx, S.S.M., Prov. Supr.

Total number in the U.S. community 153.

Legal Holding: *Sisters of the Sorrowful Mother - Marian Health System, Inc.; Sisters of the Sorrowful Mother - US / Caribbean Province, Inc.*

Ministry in the fields of Religious and Academic Education; Nursing Homes; Social Work; Hospitals and Hospital Administration.

Represented in the Archdioceses of Los Angeles and Milwaukee and in the Dioceses of Green Bay, Las Cruces, La Crosse, Paterson, Superior, Tulsa, Wichita and Winona. Also in Dominican Republic, Trinidad, Grenada and Castries.

[4110] (O.S.U.)—URSULINE NUNS (P)
(Roman Union)

Founded in Italy in 1535. First foundation in the United States New Orleans, Louisiana in 1727.

Generalate: Via Nomentana 236, Rome, Italy 00162. Mother Colette Lignon, O.S.U., Prioress Gen.

Eastern Province of the U.S. (1900): *Ursuline Provincialate-St. Mary's Hall,* 323 E. 198th St., Bronx, NY 10458. Tel: 718-365-7410; Fax: 718-733-4498. Sr. Dorothy Ann Kelly, O.S.U., Prov.

Total number in the Province 168.

Legal Title: *Ursuline Provincialate, Eastern Province of the United States, Inc.; Marian Residence Fund,* Bronx, NY; *OSU Charitable Trust,* Bronx, NY.

Ministry in the field of Academic Education at all levels; varied Pastoral and Social Services.

Represented in the Archdioceses of New York and Washington and the Dioceses of Bridgeport, Raleigh, Ogdensburg, Orlando and Wilmington.

Central Province of the U.S.: *Ursuline Provincialate,* 210 Glennon Heights Rd., Crystal City, MO 63019. Tel: 636-937-6206; Fax: 636-937-7627. Sr. Margaret Mary Moore, O.S.U., Prov. Prioress.

Total number in the community 158.

Ministry in the field of Religious and Academic Education.

Represented in the Archdioceses of Chicago, Cincinnati, New Orleans, St. Louis, St. Paul-Minneapolis, and San Antonio and in the Dioceses of Brownsville, Dallas, Galveston-Houston, Green Bay, Juneau, Laredo, Peoria, Springfield-Cape Girardeau and Springfield (IL). Also in Canada.

Western Province U.S. (1932): *Ursuline Provincialate,* 639 Angela Dr., Santa Rosa, CA 95403-1793. Tel: 707-545-6811; Fax: 707-579-8571. Sr. Margaret Johnson, O.S.U., Prov. Prioress.

Total number in the Province 43.

Ministry in the field of Elementary and Secondary Education; Work with the Eskimos, American Indians, & Hispanics; Parish Ministry; Catechetical Coordinators; Blind Apostolate; Spiritual Direction; Spiritual Growth Center; Counseling Services.

Represented in the Archdioceses of Anchorage, Los Angeles and San Francisco and in the Dioceses of Boise, Fairbanks, Great Falls-Billings, Juneau, San Jose and Santa Rosa.

Northeastern Province: *Ursuline Provincialate,* 45 Lowder St., Dedham, MA 02026-4200. Tel: 781-326-6219; Fax: 781-326-7296. Sr. Angela Krippendorf, O.S.U., Prov.

Total number in the community 39.

Ministry in the field of Education.

Represented in the Archdiocese of Boston and in the Diocese of Portland (ME).

[4120] (O.S.U.)—URSULINE NUNS, OF THE CONGREGATION OF PARIS (P)

Founded in Italy in 1535. First foundation in the United States in New Orleans, Louisiana in 1727.

Motherhouse (1845): *Ursulines of Brown County,* 20860 St. Rte. 251, St. Martin, OH 45118-9705. Tel: 513-875-2020 ext. 27; Fax: 513-875-2311. Web Site: www.ursulinesofbc.org. Sr. Nancy Vollman, O.S.U., Supr.

Total number in the community 36.

Legal Title: *St. Ursula Literary Institute; Ursulines of Brown County; Ursuline Academy of Cincinnati Chatfield College.*

Ministry in the field of Academic Education at all levels; Special Education; Adult Education; Catechetical Instruction; Administration; Retreats; Counseling; Organization Consultation; Social-Inner City & Rural; Hospital; Senior Services; Campus and Parish Ministry.

Represented in the Archdiocese of Cincinnati and in the Dioceses of Covington and Toledo.

[4120-01] Cincinnati (P)

Motherhouse: *Ursulines of Cincinnati, St. Ursula Convent,* 1339 E. McMillan St. (Walnut Hills), Cincinnati, OH 45206. Tel: 513-961-3410. Sr. Mary Jerome Buchert, O.S.U.

Total number in the community 20.

Legal Title: *Ursulines of Cincinnati.*

Ministry in the field of Academic Education at all levels; Adult Education; Pastoral Ministry; Communications; Hispanic Ministry; Social Services.

Represented in the Archdiocese of Cincinnati and in the Diocese of Covington.

[4120-02] Kansas City in Kansas (D)

Ursuline Convent of Our Lady of Lourdes: 901 E. Miami St., Paola, KS 66071. Tel: 913-557-2349. Sr. Kathleen Condry, O.S.U., Supr.

Total number in the community 30.

Legal Title: *Ursuline Sisters, Inc.; Ursuline Sisters Charitable Trust.*

Ministry in the field of Academic Education at all levels; Parish and Diocesan Services.

Represented in the Archdiocese of Kansas City in Kansas and in the Dioceses of Sacramento.

[4120-03] Louisville (P)

Ursuline Motherhouse of the Immaculate Conception: 3115 Lexington Rd., Louisville, KY 40206. Tel: 502-893-0125; Fax: 502-896-3913. Sr. Jean Anne Zappa, O.S.U., Pres.

Total number in the community 163.

Legal Title: *Ursuline Society and Academy of Education aka Ursuline Sisters.*

Ministry in the field of Academic Education; Child Care; Pastoral Ministry; Social Services; Health Care.

Properties owned and sponsored: *Sacred Heart Academy; Sacred Heart Model School; Ursuline Montessori; Ursuline Child Development Center; Ursuline School for the Performing Arts; Marian Home,* Louisville, KY.

Represented in the Archdioceses of Baltimore, Cincinnati, Indianapolis, Louisville, Philadelphia, and San Francisco and in the Dioceses of Charleston, Covington, Davenport, Evansville, Grand Island, Jackson, Lexington, Pittsburgh, and Wheeling-Charleston.

[4120-04] Cleveland (P)

Ursuline Motherhouse and Educational Center: 2600 Lander Rd., Cleveland, OH 44124. Fax: 440-449-3588. Sr. Virginia DeVinne, O.S.U., Supr. Gen.; Sr. Susan Mary Rathbun, O.S.U., Community Archivist.

Total number in the community 232.

Legal Title: *The Ursuline Academy of Cleveland; The Ursuline Sisters of Cleveland.*

Ministry in the field of Academic Education at all levels; Parish Ministry; Diocesan Offices; Seminary; Social Service Agency; Hospital and Health Care Ministry; Spiritual Direction and Retreat Ministry; Foreign Mission.

Properties sponsored: *Ursuline College; Beaumont High School; Ursuline Sophia Center.*

Represented in the Archdioceses of Indianapolis and San Antonio and in the Dioceses of Buffalo, Cleveland, Columbus, Kansas City-St. Joseph, Lexington, Manchester, Richmond, Pittsburgh and Youngstown.

[4120-05] Owensboro (P)

Mt. St. Joseph Ursuline Motherhouse: 8001 Cummings Rd., Maple Mount, KY 42356. Tel: 270-229-4103; Fax: 270-229-4127. Sr. Rose Marita O'Bryan, O.S.U., Congregational Leader.

Total number in community 176.

Legal Holdings and Titles: *St. Joseph's Female Ursuline Academy; Brescia University,* Owensboro, KY; *Mount Saint Joseph Conference and Retreat Center,* Maple Mount, KY.

Ministry in Colleges; High Schools; Elementary Schools; Parishes; Retreats and Spiritual Direction; Pastoral Care; Health Care; Social Services; Hispanic Outreach; Diocesan Offices.

Represented in the Archdioceses of Boston, Louisville, Santa Fe, and Washington and in the Dioceses of Gallup, Kansas City-St. Joseph, Lincoln, Memphis, Owensboro, Shreveport, and Springfield-Cape Girardeau. Also in Chile.

[4120-06] Toledo (P)

Ursuline Convent of the Sacred Heart Offices: 4045 Indian Rd., Toledo, OH 43606. Tel: 419-536-9587. Sr. Donna Frey, Gen. Supr.

Total number in the community 79; Associates 120.

Legal Title: *Ursuline Convent of the Sacred Heart.*

Ministry in the field of Administration; Religious and Academic Education; Health Care; Counseling Services; Pastoral Ministry; Pastoral Care; Retreat Work; Spiritual Direction; Education in Music; Home Health Care.

Properties owned or sponsored: *St. Ursula Academy,* Toledo, OH.

Represented in the Archdiocese of Washington and in the Dioceses of Fresno and Toledo. Also in Lima, Peru.

[4120-07] Youngstown (P)

Motherhouse: *Ursuline Motherhouse and Educational Center,* 4250 Shields Rd., Canfield, OH 44406. Tel: 330-792-7636. Sr. Regina Rogers, Gen. Supr.

Total number in the community 62.

Legal Title: *Ursuline Sisters of Youngstown.*

Ministry in the field of Religious and Academic Education at all levels; Parish Ministry; Social Services; Hospital Services; Single Parenting; AIDS Ministry; Preschool; Kindergarten; Nursing Home Service; Music.

Properties owned: *Ursuline Motherhouse; Ursuline Center; Ursuline Preschool & Kindergarten; Beatitude House.*

Represented in the Dioceses of Brownsville, Cleveland and Youngstown.

[4130] (O.S.U.)—URSULINE SISTERS OF THE CONGREGATION OF TILDONK, BELGIUM (P)
International Congregation

Founded in Italy in 1535 by St. Angela Merici (Ursulines). Congregation of Tildonk founded in Belgium in 1832. First foundation in the United States in Ozone Park, New York, in 1924.

Generalate: Brussels, Belgium. Sr. Judith O'Connor, O.S.U., Gen. Supr.

Ursuline Provincialate: 81-15 Utopia Pkwy., Jamaica, NY 11432. Tel: 718-591-0681. Sr. Catherine Talia, O.S.U., Prov. Supr.

Properties owned: *St. Ursula Center, (Convent & Retreat Center),* Blue Point, NY; *Ursuline Provincialate,* Jamaica, NY.

Total number in the Province 60.

Ministry in the field of Education in all its aspects; Retreat Work; Chaplaincies.

Represented in the Archdioceses of Hartford and New York and in the Dioceses of Bridgeport, Brooklyn, Burlington and Rockville Centre.

[4140] (O.S.U.)—URSULINE SISTERS OF BELLEVILLE (D)

Founded in Italy in 1535. First foundation in the United States in 1910. Newly established as Diocesan Community August 13, 1983.

Central House: 1026 N. Douglas Ave., Belleville, IL 62220-4198. Tel: 618-235-3444. Sr. Dorothy Helbling, O.S.U., Community Leader.

Total number in the community 10.

Ministry in the field of Religious and Academic Education; Retreat Work; Hospice; Pastoral Ministry.
Represented in the Dioceses of Belleville and Springfield (IL).

[4155] (M.T.G.)—ADORERS OF THE HOLY CROSS (P)

Founded in 1670 in Vietnam by Bishop Pierre Lambert de la Motte. First foundation in the U.S. 1976.
General Motherhouse: *Holy Cross Convent*, 7408 S.E., Alder, Portland, OR 97215. Tel: 503-254-3284. Sr. Agatha Thuy-Hang Tran, M.T.G., Supr.
Sisters 24; Novices 2; Candidates 4.
Represented in the Archdiocese of Portland, OR and in the Diocese of Arlington.

[4160] (V.S.C.)—VINCENTIAN SISTERS OF CHARITY (P)

First foundation in the United States in 1902.
General Motherhouse and Novitiate: *St. Vincent Hill*, 8200 McKnight Rd., Pittsburgh, PA 15237. Tel: 412-364-3000; Fax: 412-364-9055. Sr. Charlene Reebel, Major Supr.
Professed sisters 130.
Ministry in the field of Education at all levels; Health Care in Nursing Homes; Child Care Center; Catechetical Centers; Social Apostolates; Pastoral Ministries.
Properties owned or sponsored: *Vincentian Child Care Center; Vincentian High School; Vincentian Home, Inc.; Villa de Marillac Nursing Home; Regency Hall Nursing Home and Adult Day Care.*
Represented in the Archdiocese of Mobile and in Dioceses of Greensburg, Madison, Pittsburgh, Steubenville, Venice and Youngstown. Also in Canada.

[4170] (V.S.C.)— VINCENTIAN SISTERS OF CHARITY (D)

Founded in Bedford in 1928.
Motherhouse & Novitiate: *Villa San Bernardo*, 1160 Broadway, Bedford, OH 44146-4523. Tel: 440-232-4755; Fax: 440-232-7832. Sr. Christine Rody, Gen. Supr.; Sr. Regina Kusnir, Dir. Formation; Sr. Anita Maroun, Vocation Contact Person.
Professed 51.
Ministry in the field of Education at Elementary & College levels; Pastoral Ministry and Counseling; Social Services; Nursing; Care of the Elderly; Marian Shrine and Poustinia; Hospice; Poor in Appalachia; Facility for Elderly - Independent and Assisted Living; Light of Hearts Villa (Assisted Living Facility).
Represented in the Dioceses of Cleveland and Lexington.

[4180] (M.P.V.)—RELIGIOUS VENERINI SISTERS (P)

Founded in Italy in 1685. First foundation in the United States in 1909.
General Motherhouse: via Gioachino Belli 31, Rome, Italy. Rev. Mother Marcella Lorenzetti, Supr. Gen.
Universal total in Congregation 429.
Provincialhouse for the U.S.: 23 Edward St., Worcester, MA 01605. Sr. Mary Rose Zaccari, Prov.
Total number in community 30.
Legal Holdings: *Venerini Academy*, Worcester, MA.
Ministry in the field of Education; Health Care; Social Services; Parish and Diocesan Ministry; Foreign Missions.
Represented in the Dioceses of Albany, St. Petersburg and Worcester.

[4190] (V.H.M.)—VISITATION NUNS (P)

Founded in France in 1610. First foundation in the United States in Georgetown, Washington, DC in 1799.
First Federation of North America Major pontifical enclosure. Mother Margaret Mary McGuire, Federation Pres., residing at the Monastery of Visitation, Rockville, Virginia.
Listed in the Order of Foundation established.
Monastery of the Visitation (1833): 2300 Springhill Ave., Mobile, AL 36607-3202. Tel: 251-473-2321. Sr. Jane De Chantal Word, V.H.M., Supr.
Total number in the community 7.
Monastery of the Visitation: 14 Beach Rd.-P.O. Box 432, Tyringham, MA 01264. Tel: 413-243-3995; Fax: 413-243-3543. E-mail: vistyr@aol.com. Mother Mary Ruth Dolch, V.H.M., Supr.
Total number in the community 18.
Legal Title: *Visitation of Holy Mary.*
Monastery of the Visitation: 12221 Bienvenue Rd., Rockville, VA 23146. Tel: 804-749-4885. Mother Margaret Mary McGuire, V.H.M., Supr.
Professed Sisters 16; Temporary Professed 1.
Legal Title *Visitation of Holy Mary.*
Monastery of the Visitation: 5820 City Ave., Philadelphia, PA 19131-1295. Tel: 215-473-5888. Mother Frances de Sales Paganelli, V.H.M.,
Professed Sisters Cloistered 9.
Legal Title *Sisters of the Visitation of Philadelphia.*
Monastery of the Visitation (Contemplative): 1745 Parkside Blvd., Toledo, OH 43607-1599. Tel: 419-536-1343 Mother Sharon Elizabeth Gworek, V.H.M., Supr.
Professed Sisters 15; In formation 3.
Legal Title: *The Contemplative Order of the Visitation of Toledo Ohio.*
Monastery of the Visitation (Strictly Cloistered): 2055 Ridgedale Dr., Snellville, GA 30078. Tel: 770-972-1060. Mother Mary Jozefa Kowalewski, V.H.M., Supr.
Professed Sisters 12; Novices 1.
Legal Title: *Order of the Visitation.*
Second Federation of North America Monastery of the Visitation of Georgetown: 1500 35th St., N.W., Washington, DC 20007. Tel: 202-337-0[illegible]05; Fax: 202-965-3845. Mother Mary Philomena Tisinger, Supr.; Sr. Mada-anne Gell, Community Archivist.
Total number in the school community 4[illegible]2; Total number in religious community 24.
Legal Holdings and Titles: *Sisters of the Visitation of Georgetown; Georgetown Visitation Preparatory School.*
Monastery of the Visitation (1833): 3020 N. Ballas Rd., St. Louis, MO 63131. Tel: 314-432-5353. Sr. Anne Madeleine Godefroy, Supr.
Total number in the community 24.
Legal Holdings: *Visitation Academy of St. Louis County; Monastery of the Visitation,* St. Louis, MO.
Ministry in Education.
Monastery of the Visitation (1846): 200 E. Second St., Frederick, MD 21701. Tel: 301-62[illegible]-3322. Mother Marguerite Therese Leary, V.H.M., Supr.
Total number in the community 6.
Legal Holdings or Titles: *Monastery of the Visitation - Frederick, Maryland; Frederick Academy of the Visitation Cloistered Contemplative Order with Elementary School as Apostolate.*
Sisters of the Visitation of Holy Mary of Mount de Chantal, Inc. (1848): Wheeling, WV 26003. Tel: 304-2[illegible]2-1283. Sr. Mary Grace Flynn, V.H.M. Supr.
Total number in the community 23.
Legal Holdings or Titles: *Sisters of the Visitation of Holy Mary of Mount de Chantal, Inc.; Mount de Chantal Visitation Academy, Inc.*
Ministry in the field of Education.
Monastery of the Visitation (1855): 8902 Ridge Blvd., Brooklyn, NY 11209-5716. Tel: 718-745-5151; Fax: 718-745-3680. Mother Susan Marie Kasprzak, V.H.M., Supr.
Professed Sisters 19.
Legal Title: *Sisters of the Visitation of Brooklyn, NY.*
Villa de Chantal Monastery of the Visitation Mailing Address: 2936 36th St., Rock Island, IL 61201. Sr. Mary Veronica Haronik, V.H.M., Pres. Monastery located at 2000 16th Ave., Rock Island, IL 61201. Tel: 314-432-5353.
Legal Title: *Sisters of the Visitation.*
Ministry in Spiritual and Educational Center.
Monastery of the Visitation: 2455 Visitation Dr., Mendota Heights, MN 55120. Tel: 651-683-1700. Sr. Marie Therese Conaty, V.H.M., Supr.
Total number in the community 15.
Ministry in Prayer and Education.

[4200] (S.V.M.)—SISTERS OF THE VISITATION OF THE CONGREGATION OF THE IMMACULATE HEART OF MARY (D)

Founded in France in 1610. First foundation in the United States in 1799.
Visitation Convent: 2950 Kaufmann Ave., Dubuque, IA 52001-1631. Tel: 563-556-2440. Sr. Bernadine Curoe, Pres.
Total number in community 7.
Ministry in Elementary & Higher Education; Adult Education; Parish Ministry.
Represented in the Archdiocese of Dubuque and in the Diocese of Fort Wayne-South Bend.

[4210] (S.D.V.)—VOCATIONIST SISTERS (P)
(Sisters of the Divine Vocations)

Founded in Italy in 1921. First established in the United States in 1967.
General Motherhouse: *Corso Duca D'Aosta*, 22 Pianura, Naples, Italy. 80126, Sr. Giannina Di Francia, S.D.V., Mother Supr. Gen.
U.S. Foundation: *Perpetual Help Day Nursery*, 172 Broad St., Newark, NJ 07104. Tel: 973-484-3535. Sr. Romilda Borges, S.D.V., Supr.
Total number in community 6.
Ministry in Nursery Schools & Kindergartens; CCD Program and Parish Services.
Represented in the Archdiocese of Newark.
Sister Joanna Formation House: 88 Brooklake Rd., Florham Park, NJ 07932. Tel: 201-966-9762. Sr. Perpetua da Conceicao, Supr., Sr. Luisa Gargione, Delegate.
Total number in community 15.
Ministry in Nursery School; Formation House.
Represented in the Archdiocese of Newark and the Diocese of Paterson.

[4230] (X.M.M.)—XAVERIAN MISSIONARY SOCIETY OF MARY, INC. (P)

Founded in Italy in 1945. First established in the United States in 1954.
General Motherhouse: *Missionarie Saveriane Di Maria*, Via Omero 4, Parma, Italy. Sr. Giuseppina Caccia, X.M.M., Supr. Gen.
Total Membership 250.
U.S. Headquarters: *Xaverian Missionary Society of Mary*, 242 Salisbury St., Worcester, MA 01609. Tel: 508-757-0514. E-mail: xavsistersusa@aol.com. Sr. Stefanina Loi, X.M.M., Gen. Delegate.
Ministry to Hispanics; Elderly; Families; CCD Programs and Mission Education.
Represented in the Diocese of Worcester.

SPECIAL CARE FACILITIES

(For a complete listing, refer to the corresponding (Arch)Diocese.)

ALABAMA

Daphne

Archdiocese of Mobile

Mercy Medical
P.O. Box 1090, Daphne, AL 36526
Tel: 251-626-2694
E-mail: theresam@sa-mercymedical.org
Web site: www.mercymedical.com
A Corporation. Acute Rehabilitation Hospital, Hospice, Home Health, Long Term Care, Skilled Nursing Facility, Alzheimer's Care.

Marbury

Archdiocese of Mobile

Resurrection Catholic Nursing Home
165 County Rd. 20 E., P.O. Box 89, Marbury, AL 36051-0089.
Tel: 334-775-1139
Fax: 334-755-1461
Skilled Nursing Facility.

Montgomery

Archdiocese of Mobile

Father Walter Memorial Center for Handicapped Children
2815 Forbes Dr., Montgomery, AL 36199
Tel: 334-262-6421
Fax: 334-262-2265
A skilled nursing facility for the mentally and physically handicapped child. Operated by The Resurrection Catholic Missions.

Resurrection Early Childhood Center
2815 Forbes Dr., Montgomery, AL 36110.
Tel: 334-265-4615
Fax: 334-265-4568
Licensed by Alabama State Dept. of Human Resources for 45 Students, Ages two and a half to five years.

ALASKA

Anchorage

Archdiocese of Anchorage

Brother Francis Shelter
1021 E. Third Ave., Anchorage, AK 99501
Tel: 907-277-1731
Overnight shelter for homeless men and women.

Clare House
420 W. 54th Ave., Anchorage, AK 99518
Tel: 907-563-4545
Temporary shelter for homeless women and women with children.

* *Mary Conrad Center*
9100 Centennial Dr., Anchorage, AK 99504
Tel: 907-269-3201
Fax: 907-338-6789
E-mail: kgarber@provak.org
A long term care facility for the elderly, owned by Cook Inlet Housing Development Corporation and managed by Sisters of Providence in Washington.

ARIZONA

Avondale

Diocese of Phoenix

Vianney Villas Apartments
750 S. Fourth St., Avondale, AZ 85323
Tel: 623-932-2036
(Retirement)- HUD Rent Subsidized.

Kingman

Diocese of Phoenix

Kingman Heights Apartments
1020 Detroit Ave., Kingman, AZ 86401
Tel: 928-753-2425
Fax: 928-753-2425

Lake Havasu City

Diocese of Phoenix

Becket House Apartments (Retirement)
865 Cashmere Dr., Lake Havasu City, AZ 86403
Tel: 928-855-7178

Phoenix

Diocese of Phoenix

Sweetwater Gardens Apartments (Handicapped)
2035 E. Sweetwater, Phoenix, AZ 85022
Tel: 602-867-4549

Wickenburg

Diocese of Phoenix

Padua Hills Apartments
460 S. West Rd., Wickenburg, AZ 85390
Tel: 928-684-7034
(Retirement - HUD Rent Subsidized.

Williams

Diocese of Phoenix

St. Agnes Apartments (Retirement)
200 S. Ninth, Williams, AZ 86046
Tel: 928-635-2913

ARKANSAS

Jonesboro

Diocese of Little Rock

St. Bernard's Village, Inc.
1606 Heern Dr., Jonesboro, AR 72401
Tel: 870-932-8141
Fax: 870-932-5563
Web site: www.sbrmc.com
(Affiliated with Olivetan Benedictine Sisters, Inc., Jonesboro, AR)

Little Rock

Diocese of Little Rock

ABBA House, Missionaries of Charity
1014 S. Oak St., Little Rock, AR 72204
Tel: 501-663-3596 501-666-9718
Home for expectant mothers, homeless women & children.

CALIFORNIA

Chatsworth

Archdiocese of Los Angeles

Rancho San Antonio
21000 Plummer St., Chatsworth, CA 91311
Tel: 818-882-6400
Fax: 818-882-6404
Sponsored by Catholic Archdiocese of Los Angeles.

Culver City

Archdiocese of Los Angeles

Marycrest Manor, Convalescent Home
10664 St. James Dr., Culver City, CA 90230-5498
Tel: 310-838-2778
Fax: 310-838-9647
E-mail: marycrest@sbcglobal.net
Skilled Nursing Facility attended by priests from Loyola Marymount University and St. Augustine.

Fullerton

Diocese of Orange in California

Pro Sanctity Spirituality Center, Retreat House
205 S. Pine Dr., Fullerton, CA 92833
Tel: 714-956-1020
Fax: 714-525-8948
E-mail: psmcal@aol.com
Web site: prosanctitate.org
Capacity: 25 overnight, 32 day use.

Los Angeles

Archdiocese of Los Angeles

Convent of the Good Shepherd-Good Shepherd Shelter
2561 Venice Blvd., Los Angeles, CA 90019
Tel: 323-737-6111
Fax: 323-737-6113
E-mail: RGSLA1@aol.com
Shelter for battered women and their children.

Franciscan Health Center
2859 Glassell St., Los Angeles, CA 90026
Tel: 213-413-1050
A United Way Agency. Sponsored by Franciscan Sisters of the Sacred Heart. Community Clinic Offering Surgical, Medical, Obstetrician/Gynecology, Optometry, Ophthalmology, Pediatrics, and Dental patients. Payment based on ability to pay.

Knights of Malta Free Clinic, Inc.
2222 W. Ocean View #112, Los Angeles, CA 90057
Tel: 213-384-4323
Fax: 213-384-4097
E-mail: fremed112@aol.com
Primary Health Care for the frail elderly, the working poor and medically underserved children.

Little Flower Missionary House
2434 Gates St., Los Angeles, CA 90031-2824
Tel: 323-221-9248
Fax: 323-221-9831
E-mail: littleflowercenter@yahoo.com
Web site: www.littleflowercenter.org
Attended by Salesian priests. Child and Kindergarten Care Center.

Missionary Brothers of Charity
1345 Alvarado Ter., Los Angeles, CA 90006
Tel: 213-251-9707
Day center for homeless youth.

St. Anne's
155 N. Occidental Blvd., Los Angeles, CA 90026
Tel: 213-381-2931
Fax: 213-381-7804
E-mail: stannes@stannes.org
Web site: www.stannes.org
Residential care and community counseling programs for pregnant and parenting adolescents. St. Anne's also provides counseling to pregnant and parenting young women in their homes and pregnancy prevention (abstinence) classes in schools.

Mountain View

Diocese of San Jose in California

Villa Siena
1855 Miramonte Ave., Mountain View, CA 94040
Tel: 650-961-6484
Fax: 650-961-6254
E-mail: vsiena@pacbell.net Residential Care and Skilled Nursing Facility.

Newbury Park

Archdiocese of Los Angeles

Mary Health of the Sick Convalescent and Nursing Hospital
2929 Theresa Dr., Newbury Park, CA 91320.
Tel: 805-498-3644
Fax: 805-498-5112
E-mail: health@ftel.net
Skilled Nursing Facility.

Oakland

Diocese of Oakland

Bishop Begin Villa
3418 E. 18th St., Oakland, CA 94601
Tel: 510-536-0719
Fax: 510-536-3561
Retired Priests.

Mercy Retirement and Care Center
3431 Foothill Blvd., Oakland, CA 94601
Tel: 510-534-8540
Fax: 510-261-7551
(Affiliated with Elder Care Alliance).

Salinas

Diocese of Monterey in California

Villa Serra Corporation
1320 Padre Dr., Salinas, CA 93901
Tel: 831-754-5532
Fax: 831-754-5609
E-mail: villaserra2@emeritus.com
Sponsored by the Diocese of Monterey and Dominican Santa Cruz Hospital.

San Diego

Diocese of San Diego

Nazareth House Retirement Home
6333 Rancho Mission Rd., San Diego, CA 92108
Tel: 619-563-0480
Fax: 619-624-9215
E-mail: fmack@cts.com
Retired Priests Residential and Nursing.

San Fernando

Archdiocese of Los Angeles

Mother Gertrude Home for Senior Citizens
11320 Laurel Canyon Blvd., San Fernando, CA 91340
Tel: 818-898-1546
Fax: 818-365-3159
(Franciscan Missionary Sisters of the Immaculate Conception, Inc.)

San Francisco

Archdiocese of San Francisco

The Good Shepherd Gracenter
1310 Bacon St., San Francisco, CA 94134
Tel: 415-337-1938
Fax: 415-586-0355
E-mail: mmunday@aol.com
Web site: www.gsgracecenter.org
Residential treatment program for women recovering from drug and alcohol addiction.

Madonna Senior Center and Residence
350 Golden Gate Ave., San Francisco, CA 94102
Tel: 415-592-2864
Fax: 415-928-5867
E-mail: ckoger@stanthonysf.org
Web site: www.stanthonysf.org
Nonprofit social services and senior drop-in center residence for women over 60 on SSI.

Mercy Terrace Corporation Apartments
333 Baker St., San Francisco, CA 94117
Tel: 415-931-2325
Fax: 415-931-7206
E-mail: vagostino@mercyhousing.org
Web site: www.mercyhousing.org
The purpose of this corporation is to develop, construct, own, and operate housing for low and moderate income persons and families.

Mount St. Joseph-St. Elizabeth
(1976)
100 Masonic Ave., San Francisco, CA 94118
Tel: 415-567-8370
Fax: 415-351-5531
E-mail: jschindler@msjse.org
Web site: www.msjse.org
Successor Corporation to Mount St. Joseph Home for Girls and St. Elizabeth Infant Hospital.

San Jose

Diocese of San Jose in California

Giovanni Center, Inc.
85 S. Fifth St., San Jose, CA 95112
Tel: 408-288-7436
Fax: 408-288-7264
E-mail: alaujdm@aol.com
Web site: hometown.aol.com/alaujdm/myhomepage/business.html.
A California nonprofit charitable, public-benefit, housing project for low-income elderly. Sponsored by the Roman Catholic Bishop of San Jose, a Corporation Sole.

Jeanne d'Arc Manor
85 S. Fifth St., San Jose, CA 95112
Tel: 408-288-7421
Fax: 408-288-7264
E-mail: alaujdm@aol.com
Web site: members.aol.com/_ht_a/alaujdm/myhomepage/business.html
Housing project for low-income elderly and handicapped. Sponsored by the Roman Catholic Bishop of San Jose, A Corporation Sole.

Santa Barbara

Archdiocese of Los Angeles

St. Vincent Residence
4200 Calle Real, Santa Barbara, CA 93110-1454
Tel: 805-683-6381
Fax: 805-967-7508
E-mail: info@sv-sb.org
Web site: www.sv-sb.org
For single moms on welfare and/or very low income. We closed the Probation Program on Sept. 19, 2001.

Santa Cruz

Diocese of Monterey in California

Dominican Oaks Corporation
3400 Paul Sweet Rd., Santa Cruz, CA 95062
Tel: 831-462-6257
Fax: 831-462-6742
E-mail: droutley@chw.edu
Web site: www.dominicanoaks.com
Sponsored by the Dominican Santa Cruz Hospital.

Santa Monica

Archdiocese of Los Angeles

Saint John's Child Study Center, Saint John's Hospital & Health Center
1339 20th St., Santa Monica, CA 90404
Tel: 310-829-8921
Fax: 310-829-8455
Affiliated with Saint John's Hospital.

Saratoga

Diocese of San Jose in California

Our Lady of Fatima Villa
20400 Saratoga-Los Gatos Rd., Saratoga, CA 95070
Tel: 408-741-2950
Fax: 408-741-4930
E-mail: ourlady@earthlink.com
Web site: www.fatimavilla.org
Provides skilled nursing care for aged women and men and Special Alzheimer's Unit.

Sonoma

Diocese of Santa Rosa in California

Hanna Boys Center
P.O. Box 100, Sonoma, CA 95476
Tel: 707-996-6767
Fax: 707-996-4742
Web site: www.hannacenter.org
For underprivileged, emotionally disturbed and predelinquent boys, ages 9 to 18 years.

Sun Valley

Archdiocese of Los Angeles

Villa Scalabrini
10631 Vinedale St., Sun Valley, CA 91352
Tel: 818-768-6500
Fax: 818-768-0684
E-mail: villascalabrini.com Web site: www.villascalabrini.com
Retirement Center and Special Care Unit. Augustinian Recollect Sisters.

Sunland

Archdiocese of Los Angeles

** Tierra del Sol Foundation*
9919 Sunland Blvd., Sunland, CA 91040
Tel: 818-352-1419
Fax: 818-353-0777
E-mail: tierradelsol.org
Community Program/Supported Employment for Adults with Developmental Disabilities.

Van Nuys

Archdiocese of Los Angeles

Tierra Del Sol West
14547 Gilmore St., Van Nuys, CA 91411
Tel: 818-904-9164
Behavior Management Community Program for Adults with Developmental Disabilities.

COLORADO

Canon City

Diocese of Pueblo

Centura Health-Progressive Care Center
1338 Phay Ave., Canon City, CO 81212
E-mail: barbaracarochi@centura.org
Tel: 719-269-2000
Fax: 719-269-2016
An operating unit of Catholic Health Initiatives Mountain Region (an affiliate of Catholic Health Initiatives).

Denver

Archdiocese of Denver

Clare Gardens, Inc.
2626 Osceola St., Denver, CO 80212
Tel: 303-433-6268
Fax: 303-455-5359.
Web site: www.wfs-inc.org
Housing Ministry, low-income family units.

Damen Project c/o Sisters of St. Francis
2851 W. 52nd Ave., Denver, CO 80221-7636
Tel: 303-433-4280
Fax: 303-433-8225.
Web site: www.damenhouse.org
Shelter and Safehouse for Homeless Women and Children and Day Care Services.

Francis Heights, Inc.
2626 Osceola St., Denver, CO 80212
Tel: 303-433-6268
Fax: 303-455-5359.
Web site: www.wfs-inc.org
Housing Ministry and Senior Citizens.

** Gardens at St. Elizabeth*
2835 W. 32nd Ave., Denver, CO 80211
Tel: 303-964-2005
E-mail: jackieleech@centura.org
Web site: www.centura.org
An operating unit of Catholic Health Initiatives Mountain Region. (Men and Women).

Hospice of Peace
2420 W. 26th Ave., 200-D, Denver, CO 80211
Tel: 303-561-5100
Fax: 303-561-5050
E-mail: susietomes@centura.org
Home Hospice Care.

St. Raphael Catholic Center, Inc.
1300 S. Steele St., Denver, CO 80210
Tel: 303-715-2000
Fax: 303-715-2046
To acquire, develop, maintain, operate and dispose of real and personal property for the purpose of providing retirement, assisted living and long term care facilities for retired priests of the Archdiocese of Denver and other persons.

Special Religious Education-Pastoral Care of Developmentally Disabled Persons
3101 W. Hillside Pl., Denver, CO 80219
Tel: 303-934-1999
Fax: 303-935-7795
Religious education of approximately 400 mentally retarded children and adults. One 8 bed group.

Pueblo

Diocese of Pueblo

Villa Pueblo
1111 Bonforte Blvd., Pueblo, CO 81001
Tel: 719-545-5911
Fax: 719-544-1354
An operating unit of Catholic Health Initiatives Mountain Region (an affiliate of Catholic Health Initiatives).

CONNECTICUT

Bridgeport

Diocese of Bridgeport

Roncalli Apartments
430 Grant St., Bridgeport, CT 06610
Tel: 203-384-9984
Affiliate of the Roncalli Institute, Supervised Apartments for the Elderly & Handicapped.

Enfield

Archdiocese of Hartford

The Home for the Aged of the Little Sisters of the Poor
1365 Enfield St., Enfield, CT 06082-4900
Tel: 860-741-0791
Fax: 860-741-3982
E-mail: enmslsp@attglobal.net
Incorporated Operating as St. Joseph's Residence.

New Britain

Archdiocese of Hartford

Monsignor Bojnowski Manor, Inc.
50 Pulaski St., New Britain, CT 06053
Tel: 860-229-0336
Fax: 860-229-3252
E-mail: dblados@snet.net
Owned and operated by the Daughters of Mary of the Immaculate Conception.

New Haven

Archdiocese of Hartford

St. Francis Home for Children, Inc.
651 Prospect St., New Haven, CT 06511
Tel: 203-777-5513
Fax: 203-777-0644
E-mail: psalerno1@aol.com
Residential extended day treatment, group home, special education, and therapeutic preschool.

West Hartford

Archdiocese of Hartford

Saint Agnes Home, Inc.
104 Mayflower St., West Hartford, CT 06110
Tel: 860-521-7516
Fax: 860-521-6160
E-mail: safc@aol.com
Web site: www.stagnes.org
For adolescent single mothers and their infants.

McAuley Center, Inc.
275 Steele Rd., West Hartford, CT 06117
Tel: 860-920-6300
Fax: 860-232-4077
Continuing care retirement community Sisters of Mercy. 229 residential apartment units for individuals age 62 and over. Nursing care at St. Mary's Home included.

DELAWARE

Claymont

Diocese of Wilmington

Children's Home, Inc. - Adolescent Program
2901 Green St., Claymont, DE 19703
Tel: 302-798-0601
Fax: 302-798-0604
E-mail: fjones@ccwilm.org
Web site: www.cdow.org
Children (ages 12-18)

Hockessin

Diocese of Wilmington

Franciscan Health System / Care at Brackenville
100 St. Clare Dr., Hockessin, DE 19707
Tel: 302-234-5420
Fax: 302-234-5424
E-mail: jconnolly@che_east.org
Web site: www.stfrancishealthcare.org
A 104-bed skilled nursing facility.

Newark

Diocese of Wilmington

Marydale Retirement Village
135 Jeandell Dr., Newark, DE 19713
Tel: 302-368-2784
Fax: 302-731-0584
E-mail: rpierce384@aol.com
Apartments for Elderly.

Wilmington

Diocese of Wilmington

The Antonian
1701 W. 10th St., Wilmington, DE 19805
Tel: 302-421-3758
Fax: 302-421-3759
Congregate Housing for the Elderly.

St. Patrick's House, Inc.
115 E. 14th St., Wilmington, DE 19801
Tel: 302-654-6908
Affiliated with St. Patrick Parish. Congregate Independent Living Facility for the elderly.

FLORIDA

Clearwater

Diocese of St. Petersburg

St. Michael's Housing, Inc. dba Casa Miguel
2285 State Rd. #580, Clearwater, FL 33763
Tel: 727-797-8551
Independent Living.

Jacksonville

Diocese of St. Augustine

All Saints Nursing Home & Rehabilitation Center, Inc.
5888 Blanding Blvd., Jacksonville, FL 32244
Tel: 904-772-1220
Fax: 904-772-6334
E-mail: codonnell@allsaintsnursing.org
Web site: allsaintsnursing.org
Physical Therapy, Speech Therapy & Occupational Therapy Available.

St. Catherine Laboure Manor
1750 Stockton St., Jacksonville, FL 32204
Tel: 904-308-4700
Fax: 904-308-2987
E-mail: gart an@jaxhealth.com
Web site: www.stvincentshealth.com
Long term health care Skilled Nursing Facility.

Largo

Diocese of St. Petersburg

Bethlehem Centre, Inc.
10895 Hamlin Blvd., Largo, FL 34644
Tel: 727-596-9394
Fax: 727-596-6792
Senior Center offering programs in Fitness, Exercise, Social, Educational, Music, Art, Computers, and Religious Nature on Tuesday, Wednesday, and Friday. Hot luncheon is available on Tuesday and Friday.

Miami

Archdiocese of Miami

Camillus House, Inc.
P.O. Box 11829, Miami, FL 33101-1829
E-mail: savio@camillus.org
Web site: www.camillus.org
Provides services to the homeless: emergency services, substance abuse rehabilitation, transitional housing.

Orlando

Diocese of Orlando

Morning Star School
954 Leigh Ave., Orlando, FL 32804-2299
Tel: 407-295-3077
Fax: 407-522-1700
E-mail: mss954@aol.com
School for Exceptional Children.

Port Charlotte

Diocese of Venice

St. Charles Housing II, Inc. (dba Villa San Carlos II)
22250 Vick St., Port Charlotte, FL 33980
Tel: 941-624-4404
Fax: 941-624-5556
E-mail: villasancarlosii@comcast.net

St. Charles Housing I, Inc. (aka Villa San Carlos)
2550 Easy St., Port Charlotte, FL 33952
Tel: 941-624-2266 Fax: 941-624-2283
E-mail: villasancarlos@comcast.net

Sarasota

Diocese of Venice

St. Martha's Housing, Inc.
1576 Eighth St., Sarasota, FL 34236
Tel: 941-366-4448
Fax: 941-366-2544
E-mail: casasantamarta.csm@verizon.net
(Casa Santa Marta).

St. Martha's Housing II, Inc.
800 N. Lemon Ave., Sarasota, FL 34236
Tel: 941-365-7913
Fax: 941-365-8887
E-mail: casasantamarta.csm@verizon.net
(Casa Santa Marta II).

Venice

Diocese of Venice

St. Mark's Housing of Venice, Inc. (aka Villa San Marcos)
1030 Albee Farm Rd., Venice, FL 34292
Tel: 941-483-1960
Fax: 941-483-3934
E-mail: villamarcos@comcast.net

GEORGIA

Atlanta

Archdiocese of Atlanta

Our Lady of Perpetual Help Home
760 Pollard Blvd., S.W., Atlanta, GA 30315
Fax: 404-588-9568
Nursing Home for Free Care of Cancer Patients.

Saint Joseph's Mercy Care Services
424 Decatur St., Atlanta, GA 30312-1848
Tel: 404-880-3550
Fax: 404-880-3551
E-mail: aebberwein@sjha.org
Division of Saint Joseph's Health System. Operates Saint Joseph's Mercy Care Services (Atlanta, Georgia). Operates Mercy Senior Care (Rome, Georgia).

Village of St. Joseph Counseling Services Program
1961 N. Druid Hills Rd., Ste. 205-B, Atlanta, GA 30329
Tel: 404-321-2900
Fax: 404-321-2911
Web site: www.cssatlanta.com
A program of Catholic Social Services, Inc.

ILLINOIS

Bartlett

Archdiocese of Chicago

Bartlett Learning Center
801 W. Bartlett Rd., Bartlett, IL 60103
Tel: 630-289-4221
Fax: 630-289-4390
Operates Bartlett Learning Center Day School Program and the Cupertino Home, Warrenville, IL. Day School program serves developmentally delayed and multiple handicapped individuals ages 3 to 21 and accepts youth identified LD, BD, EMH, TMH.

Belleville

Diocese of Belleville

Charles and Bertha Hincke Residence for Priests and Sense Residence
2620 Lebanon Ave., Belleville, IL 62221
Tel: 618-234-5722
Fax: 618-234-5792
E-mail: hinckehome@aol.com
Owned by Diocese of Belleville.

Meredith Memorial Home
16 S. Illinois St., Belleville, IL 62220
Tel: 618-233-8780
E-mail: sueneuharth@aol.com
Web site: www.ccsil.org
Owned by the Diocese of Belleville.

Chicago

Archdiocese of Chicago

Catholic Home Care Home Services
721 N. LaSalle St., Chicago, IL 60610
Tel: 312-655-7415

Catholic Home Care
721 N. LaSalle St., Chicago, IL 60610
Home health agency, Medicare certified, JCAHO accredited, providing health care to individuals in their homes in Cook and Lake Counties.

Cortland Manor Retirement Home
1900 N. Karlov, Chicago, IL 60639
Tel: 773-235-3670
Catholic Charities Housing Development Corporation. Home health agency, private duty, JCAHO accredited.

House of the Good Shepherd
1114 W. Grace St., Chicago, IL 60613
Tel: 773-935-3434
Fax: 773-935-3523
Shelter for abused women with children.

* *L'Arche Chicago*
1049 S. Austin Blvd., Chicago, IL 60644
Tel: 773-287-8249
E-mail: larchechicago@hotmail.com
Web site: www.larchechicago.org
A Christian Community concerned with life sharing between persons with a developmental disability and persons who assist them.

Little Sisters of the Poor Center for the Aging
2325 N. Lakewood Ave., Chicago, IL 60614
Tel: 773-935-9600
Fax: 773-935-9614
Intermediate and skilled care facility.

Misericordia / Heart of Mercy Center
6300 N. Ridge, Chicago, IL 60660
Tel: 773-973-6300
Fax: 773-973-5214
Web site: www.misericordia.com
Children and adults with Developmental disabilities.

Resurrection Life Center
7370 W. Talcott Ave., Chicago, IL 60631
Tel: 773-594-7400
Fax: 773-594-7402
Web site: www.reshealth.org
Skilled intermediate and sheltered nursing care. A division of Resurrection Senior Services, Resurrection Health Care.

Resurrection Retirement Community
7262 W. Peterson Ave., Chicago, IL 60631
Tel: 773-792-7930
Fax: 773-792-8316
E-mail: kstadler@reshealthcare.org
Web site: www.reshealth.org
A division of Resurrection Senior Services, Resurrection Health Care.

St. Joseph's Carondelet Child Center
739 E. 35th St., Chicago, IL 60616
Tel: 773-624-7443
Fax: 773-624-7676
E-mail: jbmc@stjcc.org
Web site: www.stjcc.org
Treatment, rehabilitation and education of the dependent emotionally disturbed children and youth.

St. Mary of Providence
4200 N. Austin Ave., Chicago, IL 60634
Tel: 773-545-8300
Fax: 773-545-8035
E-mail: commsmop@aol.com
Developmental Training and residential care of developmentally disabled adults.

Clifton

Diocese of Joliet in Illinois

Merkle-Knipprath Countryside Home
1190 E. 2900 N. Rd., Clifton, IL 60927-7103
Tel: 815-694-2306
Apartment Community and Nursing Center.

Crete

Diocese of Joliet in Illinois

St. James Manor & Villas (Sub. of Franciscan Communities, Inc.)
1251 Richton Rd., Crete, IL 60417
Tel: 708-672-6700
Fax: 708-672-4939
E-mail: dstrutynski@franciscancommunities.com
Care of the Elderly. Sponsored by Franciscan Sisters of Chicago.

Des Plaines

Archdiocese of Chicago

Holy Family Nursing and Rehabilitation Center
2380 Dempster, Des Plaines, IL 60016
Tel: 847-296-3335
Fax: 847-296-2027
Web site: www.reshealth.org
Intermediate and skilled nursing facility. A division of Resurrection Senior Services, Resurrection Health Care.

Evanston

Archdiocese of Chicago

Saint Francis Nursing and Rehabilitation Center
500 Ashbury Ave., Evanston, IL 60202
Tel: 847-316-3320
Fax: 847-316-3337
Web site: www.reshealth.org
A division of Resurrection Senior Services, Resurrection Health Care Comprehensive nursing, rehabilitation and social services.

Franklin Park

Archdiocese of Chicago

Scalabrini Life Center
10500 W. Grand Ave., Franklin Park, IL 60131
Tel: 847-451-1520
Web site: www.reshealth.org
Comprehensive nursing, rehabilitation and social services.

Glenview

Archdiocese of Chicago

Maryhaven Nursing and Rehabilitation Center
1700 East Lake Ave., Glenview, IL 60025
Tel: 847-729-1300
Fax: 847-729-9620
Web site: www.reshealth.org
A division of Resurrection Senior Services, Resurrection Health Care. Home for Aged, Intermediate and Skilled Care Facilities, Medicare, Therapy.

Joliet

Diocese of Joliet in Illinois

Provena Villa Franciscan
210 N. Springfield Ave., Joliet, IL 60435
Tel: 815-725-3400
Fax: 815-725-2160
Extended, Intermediate, and Skilled Care, Respite Care.

Guardian Angel Home
1550 Plainfield Rd., Joliet, IL 60435
Tel: 815-729-0930
Fax: 815-744-6087
E-mail: sas726@aol.com
Web site: www.guardianangelhome.org
Sponsored by the Sisters of St. Francis of Mary Immaculate. Child and family welfare agency: therapeutic school, foster care, domestic violence shelter, child abuse prevention center, and counseling.

LaGrange Park

Archdiocese of Chicago

Bethlehem Woods Retirement Community
1571 Ogden Ave., LaGrange Park, IL 60526
Tel: 708-579-3663
Fax: 708-579-7159
Web site: www.reshealth.org
A division of Resurrection Senior Services, Resurrection Health Care.

Lake Zurich

Archdiocese of Chicago

Mt. St. Joseph Home
4955 North Hwy. 12, Lake Zurich, IL 60047
Tel: 847-438-5050
Fax: 847-438-6313
E-mail: msjlz@aol.com
Intermediate care for developmentally disabled women.

Lemont

Archdiocese of Chicago

Mother Theresa Home
1270 Franciscan Dr., Lemont, IL 60439
Tel: 630-243-3400
Fax: 630-257-5823
E-mail: rcoon@franciscancommunities.com
Continuing Care Retirement Community.

Lisle

Diocese of Joliet in Illinois

Villa St. Benedict
1920 Maple Ave., Lisle, IL 60532
Tel: 630-852-5360
Fax: 630-852-3196
E-mail: gtrembley@villastben.org
Web site: www.villastben.org
Retirement home.

Momence

Diocese of Joliet in Illinois

Good Shepherd Manor
P.O. Box 260, Momence, IL 60954
Tel: 815-472-6492
Fax: 815-472-2160
E-mail: gsmanor@prairieinet.net
Web site: www.goodshepherdmanor.org
Adult Male DD-MR.

Naperville

Diocese of Joliet in Illinois

St. John Vianney Villa
1464 Green Trails Dr., Naperville, IL 60540-8372
Tel: 630-983-0533
Fax: 630-983-6375
Retirement home for priests.

Niles

Archdiocese of Chicago

Saint Andrew Life Center
7000 N. Newark Ave., Niles, IL 60714-4497
Tel: 847-647-8332
Fax: 847-647-7073
Web site: www.reshealth.org
A division of Resurrection Senior Services, Resurrection Health Care.

Saint Benedict Nursing and Rehabilitation Center
6930 W. Touhy Ave., Niles, IL 60714
Tel: 847-647-0003
Fax: 847-647-1936
Web site: www.reshealth.org

Northlake

Archdiocese of Chicago

Casa San Carlo Retirement Community
420 N. Wolf Rd., Northlake, IL 60164
Tel: 708-562-4300
Fax: 708-562-5677
Web site: www.reshealth.org

Villa Scalabrini Nursing and Rehabilitation Center
480 N. Wolf Rd., Northlake, IL 60164-1667
Tel: 708-562-0040
Fax: 708-562-5180
Web site: www.reshealth.org

Oak Brook

Diocese of Joliet in Illinois

Cedarlake Village, Plainfield Campus, Inc.
1801 35th St., Oak Brook, IL 60523
Tel: 630-850-8232
Fax: 630-850-8233
E-mail: mayslakvlg@aol.com
Web site: www.mayslake.com
Senior Citizen Retirement Community.

Olympia Fields

Archdiocese of Chicago

Mercy Residence at Tolentine Center
20300 Governors Hwy., Olympia Fields, IL 60461
Tel: 708-748-9500
Fax: 708-481-2090
E-mail: mercyresidence@aol.com
Senior citizen housing.

Palos Park

Archdiocese of Chicago

St. Coletta's of Illinois
18350 Crossing Dr., Tinley Park, IL 60477
Tel: 708-342-5200
Fax: 708-342-3579
Sponsored by the Sisters of St. Francis of Assisi. Residential care, education, job training & job placement for developmentally disabled children and adults.

Park Ridge

Archdiocese of Chicago

Resurrection Nursing and Rehabilitation Center
1001 N. Greenwood, Park Ridge, IL 60068
Tel: 847-692-5600
Fax: 847-692-2305
Web site: www.reshealth.org
A division of Resurrection Senior Services, Resurrection Health Care.

Peoria Heights

Diocese of Peoria

Saint Clare Home
5533 N. Galena Rd., Peoria Heights, IL 61614
Tel: 309-682-5428
Skilled nursing facility.

Rockford

Diocese of Rockford

St. Anne Place
4444 Brendenwood Rd., Rockford, IL 61107
Tel: 815-399-6167
Fax: 815-399-6169
E-mail: eric@stanneplace.org
Web site: www.stanneplace.org
Owned by the Rockford Diocese, managed by Provena Senior Services.

Vianney Oaks
7712 E. McGregor Rd., Rockford, IL 61102
Tel: 815-399-4300
Fax: 815-399-5266
A retirement home for priests conducted by the Diocese of Rockford.

Skokie

Archdiocese of Chicago

* *Resurrection Home Health Services*
4930 W. Oakton St., Skokie, IL 60077
Tel: 877-742-7447
Fax: 847-568-8537
Web site: www.reshealth.org
Operated by Resurrection Health Care.

Springfield

Diocese of Springfield in Illinois

Brother James Court
2508 St. James Rd., Springfield, IL 62707
Tel: 217-544-4876
Fax: 217-747-5971
E-mail: bjcicfdd@aol.com
Web site: www.ffsc.net
Residence for Mentally Retarded Male Adults.

St. Joseph's Home
3306 S. Sixth St. Rd., Springfield, IL 62703
Tel: 217-529-5596
Fax: 217-529-8590
Residence for the Elderly & Nursing Home.

West Peoria

Diocese of Peoria

Guardian Angel Home
2900 W. Heading Ave., West Peoria, IL 61604
Tel: 309-636-7500
Fax: 309-673-3405
Web site: ccdop.org
Treatment for Abused and Neglected Youth.

INDIANA

Avilla

Diocese of Fort Wayne - South Bend

Provena LaVerna Terrace
517 N. Main St., Avilla, IN 46710
Tel: 260-897-2093
Fax: 260-897-2086
E-mail: sharonmckinley@provenahealth.com
Conducted by Franciscan Sisters Health Care Corp. whose sole member is Provena Health.

Delphi

Diocese of Lafayette in Indiana

St. Elizabeth Healthcare Center
701 Armory Rd., Delphi, IN 46923
Tel: 765-564-6380; 765-464-5689
Fax: 765-564-6384
E-mail: jgibson@franciscancommunities.com
Web site: www.franciscanservices.org
Owned by Franciscan Sisters of Chicago.

Evansville

Diocese of Evansville

Seton Residence
9200 New Harmony Rd., Evansville, IN 47720-8918
Tel: 812-963-7600
Fax: 812-963-7654
Home for the Senior Sisters of the Daughters of Charity of St. Vincent de Paul.

Fort Wayne

Diocese of Fort Wayne - South Bend

St. Anne Home of the Diocese of Fort Wayne - South Bend, Inc.
1900 Randallia Dr., Fort Wayne, IN 46805
Tel: 260-484-5555
Fax: 260-482-8929
E-mail: sah1900@aol.com
Web site: www.saintannehome.com
Purpose: Nursing Home, Independent Living Units and Assisted Living.

Saint Anne Home & Retirement Community
1900 Randallia Dr., Fort Wayne, IN 46805
Tel: 260-484-5555
Fax: 260-482-8929
E-mail: sah1900@aol.com
Web site: www.saintannehome.com
A Service of the Fort Wayne-South Bend Diocese, Inc.

Jasper

Diocese of Evansville

Providence Home, Nursing Home for the Needy
520 W. Ninth St., Jasper, IN 47546
Tel: 812-482-6603
Fax: 812-481-1778
Conducted by the Sons of Divine Providence.

San Pierre

Diocese of Gary

Trinity Continuing Care Services-Ind fka Holy Cross Care
7520 S. U.S. Hwy. 421, San Pierre, IN 46374-4275
Tel: 219-828-4111
Fax: 219-828-4275
E-mail: pegp@trinity-health.org
Comprehensive Nursing Care Home.

Terre Haute

Archdiocese of Indianapolis

Gibault
6301 S. U.S. Hwy. 41, P.O. Box 2316, Terre Haute, IN 47802-0316
Tel: 812-299-1156
Fax: 812-299-0019
E-mail: gibault@gibault.org
Web site: www.gibault.org
Residential treatment facility for males and females between the ages of 8 and 18, sponsored by the Knights of Columbus of Indiana.

IOWA

Cedar Rapids

Archdiocese of Dubuque

Hallmar-Mercy Medical Center
701 Tenth St. S.E., Cedar Rapids, IA 52403
Tel: 319-398-6241
Cedar Rapids Regional, owned and operated by Mercy Medical Center. Home for Aged.

Cresco

Archdiocese of Dubuque

Elder Hospitality of Iowa, Inc. Franciscan SKEMP Healthcare (Village Apartments)
301 First Ave., Cresco, IA 52136
Tel: 563-547-3325; 608-785-0940; 608-791-9749
Fax: 608-791-9780
Elderly housing for low income. HUD section 202.

Dubuque

Archdiocese of Dubuque

Villa Raphael
1155 Mt. Loretta Ave., Dubuque, IA 52003
Tel: 563-588-2049
E-mail: bqvilla@arch.pvt.k12.ia.us
Administered by the Archdiocese of Dubuque. Accommodations for 16 priests.

Dyersville

Archdiocese of Dubuque

Mercy Medical Center-Dubuque-Dyersville-Oakcrest Manor
1111 Third St., S.W., Dyersville, IA 52040
Tel: 563-875-7101
Fax: 563-875-2957
Web site: www.mercydubuque.com
(A Division of Mercy Health Services - Iowa).

Johnston

Diocese of Des Moines

Bishop Drumm Retirement Center
5837 Winwood Dr., Johnston, IA 50131-1651
Tel: 515-270-1100
Fax: 515-276-1714
Affiliate of Catholic Health Initiatives, Mercy Health Network & Mercy Medical Center-Des Moines.

KANSAS

Great Bend

Diocese of Dodge City

Cedar Park Place, Inc.
3910 Cedar Park Pl., Great Bend, KS 67530-3692
Tel: 620-793-8115
Fax: 620-792-1746
E-mail: cedarpark.@ckan.com
Low & middle income housing for elderly/handicapped.

Manhattan

Diocese of Salina

St. Joseph Village, Inc.
2800 Willow Grove, Manhattan, KS 66502
Tel: 785-539-7671
Fax: 785-539-9125
E-mail: dfrihart@via.christi.org
Web site: www.via-christi.org/stjosephvillage
Owned & operated by the Via Christi Health System of Wichita.

Mulvane

Diocese of Wichita

Villa Maria
116 S. Central, Mulvane, KS 67110
Tel: 316-777-1129
Fax: 316-777-4406
E-mail: chmathis@hotmail.com
Home for Aging Men and Women.

Olathe

Archdiocese of Kansas City in Kansas

Villa St. Francis, Inc.
16600 W. 126th St., Olathe, KS 66062
Tel: 913-829-5201
Fax: 913-829-5399
E-mail: villa_st_francis@msn.com
Skilled nursing care and independent boarding. Owned and operated by Villa St. Francis, Inc.

Wichita

Diocese of Wichita

Art of Learning Center
201 S. Millwood, Wichita, KS 67213
Tel: 316-265-6853
Speech, Language, Reading Therapy.

Catholic Care Center, Inc.
6700 E. 45th St. N., Wichita, KS 67226
Tel: 316-744-2020
Fax: 316-744-2182
Web site: www.catholiccarecenter.org
Operated by Catholic Diocese of Wichita & the Via Christ Health System.

KENTUCKY

Knottsville

Diocese of Owensboro

Bishop Soenneker Home
9545 Kentucky 144, Knottsville, KY 42366
Tel: 270-281-4881
Fax: 270-281-5804
Residential Care of the Handicapped.

Louisville

Archdiocese of Louisville

Boys' Haven
2301 Goldsmith Ln., Louisville, KY 40205
Tel: 502-458-1171
Fax: 502-451-2161
E-mail: vrickert@boyshaven.org
Web site: www.boyshaven.org
For dependent, neglected, or abused boys, 12-18 years of age.

Caritas Peace Center
2020 Newburg Rd., Louisville, KY 40205
Tel: 502-451-3330
Fax: 502-473-1797
E-mail: michaelahrens@chi-caritas.org
Web site: www.caritas.com
Hospital for Psychiatric Illness.

Sacred Heart Village, Inc. (Rudd-Taylor Memorial)
2120 Payne St., Louisville, KY 40206
Tel: 502-895-9425
Fax: 502-357-5549
Catholic Healthcare Partners, Cincinnati, OH.

LOUISIANA

Baton Rouge

Diocese of Baton Rouge

Department of Special Education
P.O. Box 2028, Baton Rouge, LA 70821-2028
Tel: 225-383-3066
Fax: 225-242-0344
E-mail: deptspecialed@csobr.org
Web site: www.csobr.org
Guardian Angels Center (7-14 yrs.) and Redemptorist Center (15-21 yrs.).

Chateau Louise
7555 Bishop Ott Dr., Baton Rouge, LA 70806
Tel: 225-926-5918
Housing for elderly and handicapped persons.

Ollie Steele Burden Manor
4250 Essen Ln., Baton Rouge, LA 70809-2196
Tel: 225-926-0091
Fax: 225-926-4937
Our Lady of the Lake Regional Medical Center, Our Lady of the Lake Pastoral Care.

Belle Chasse

Archdiocese of New Orleans

Padua Pediatric Residential Program
200 Beta St., Belle Chasse, LA 70037-1499
Tel: 504-392-0502
Fax: 504-392-5411
Residential Facility for Severely-Profound Retarded and Multi-handicapped Children.

Gretna

Archdiocese of New Orleans

St. Jude the Apostle
1430 Claire Ave., Gretna, LA 70053-7436
Tel: 504-361-8457
Fax: 504-367-6952

Ocean Avenue Community Home
361 Ocean Ave., Gretna, LA 70053-4726
Tel: 504-361-0674
Fax: 504-367-6952
Residential facility for developmentally disabled adults.

St. Rosalie
119 Kass St., Gretna, LA 70053-3828
Tel: 504-361-8320
Fax: 504-367-6952
Padua Adult Residential Program for Developmentally Disabled Adults.

Supervised Apartments
1430 Claire Ave., Gretna, LA 70053-7436
Tel: 504-367-1465
Fax: 504-367-6952
Supervised Apartments for Developmentally Disabled Adults.

Harvey

Archdiocese of New Orleans

St. Catherine of Siena Supervised Apartment
3021 Sienna Dr., Harvey, LA 70058-2180
Tel: 504-347-6069
Fax: 504-367-6952
Residential Program for Developmentally Disabled Adults.

Lafayette

Diocese of Lafayette

Village du Lac, Inc.
1404 Carmel Ave., Lafayette, LA 70501
Tel: 337-234-5106
Fax: 337-234-2630
Community housing for the handicapped and elderly with low income. Sponsored by the Diocese.

Mandeville

Archdiocese of New Orleans

Rouquette Lodge
4300 Hwy. 22, Mandeville, LA 70448-2824
Tel: 985-626-5217
Fax: 985-626-9226
St. Tammany Manor, Inc. Residence for Senior Citizens.

Marrero

Archdiocese of New Orleans

Hope Haven Center
(1925)
1101 Barataria Blvd., Marrero, LA 70072-3085
Tel: 504-347-5581
Fax: 504-340-2075
Residential Treatment Center and School.

Jefferson CARE Center
1108 Barataria Blvd., Marrero, LA 70072-3025
Tel: 504-347-0772
Fax: 504-371-8783
Temporary Residence for Homeless Families.

Wynhoven Apartments and Wynhoven II
4600-10th St., Marrero, LA 70072-3048
Tel: 504-347-8442
Fax: 504-340-6076
E-mail: jjones@christopherhomesinc.org
Private Nonprofit Residence for Senior Citizens Sponsored by the Archdiocese.

Metairie

Archdiocese of New Orleans

Ss. Mary & Elizabeth
720 N. Elm St., Metairie, LA 70003-6022
Tel: 504-738-6959 Fax: 504-738-8320
Residential facility for developmentally disabled adults.

Sisters of Mercy Ministries dba Mercy Family Center
110 Veterans Memorial Blvd., Ste. 425, Metairie, LA 70005
Tel: 504-838-8283
Fax: 504-838-9799
E-mail: sjc181@aol.com
Psychological and psychiatric evaluation and counseling.

Monroe

Diocese of Shreveport

Christus St. Joseph Home
2301 Sterlington Rd., P.O. Box 6057, Monroe, LA 71211-6057
Tel: 318-323-3426
Fax: 318-387-7157
Operated by Christus Health Monroe.

New Orleans

Archdiocese of New Orleans

Annunciation Inn
1220 Spain St., New Orleans, LA 70117-8369
Tel: 504-944-0512
Fax: 504-944-0514
Residence for Elderly.

Bishop Perry Middle School
(1941)
Dauphine St., New Orleans, LA 70116-1609
Tel: 504-943-3734
Fax: 504-943-1320
E-mail: bpms@bpms.org
Web site: www.bpms.org
(Boys).

Boys Hope Girls Hope
4128 Baudin St., New Orleans, LA 70119-6815
Tel: 504-486-6030
Fax: 504-484-6120
Web site: www.boyshopegirlshope.org
Group Homes for Boys and Girls.

CARE CENTER
4222 S. Broad St., New Orleans, LA 70125-3660
Tel: 504-822-3751
Fax: 504-822-3761
Temporary Residence for Homeless Women and their Children.

Chateau de Notre Dame
2832 Burdette St., New Orleans, LA 70125-2596
Tel: 504-866-2741
Fax: 504-866-6769
E-mail: jtieperman@archdiocese-no.org
Web site: cdnd.org
Residence and Nursing Home.

Christopher Inn Apts.
2110 Royal St., New Orleans, LA 70116-1693
Tel: 504-949-0312
Fax: 504-945-2634
Private Nonprofit Residence for Senior Citizens Sponsored by the Archdiocese.

* *Covenant House*
611 N. Rampart St., New Orleans, LA 70112-3540
Tel: 800-999-9999; 504-584-1111
Fax: 504-584-1171
E-mail: dlouque@covenanthouse.org
Web site: covenanthouseno.org
Home for Runaway, Abused & Homeless Youth.

Our Lady of Wisdom Health Care Center
5600 Gen. deGaulle Dr., New Orleans, LA 70131
Tel: 504-394-5991
Fax: 504-304-5421
E-mail: ourladyofwisdom@netscape.net
Web site: www.olwhealth.org
(Inter-Community Health Care, Inc.). Inter-community healthcare facility for Archdiocesan clergy and Religious Men: Order of Preachers, Society of Jesus, Society of Mary (Marists), Vincentian, Christian Brothers and Brothers of the Sacred Heart Religious Women: Sisters of St. Joseph of Meda.

Ozanam Inn
843 Camp St., New Orleans, LA 70130-3751
Tel: 504-523-1184
Fax: 504-523-1187
Shelter for Homeless Men.

Project Lazarus
P.O. Box 3906, New Orleans, LA 70177-3906
Tel: 504-949-3609
Fax: 504-944-7944
Residential Program for Persons with AIDS.

Villa St. Maurice
500 St. Maurice Ave., New Orleans, LA 70117-1568
Tel: 504-277-8477
Fax: 504-277-8493
E-mail: jmoore@christopherhomesinc.org
Residence for Senior Citizens & Handicapped.

Villa St. Maurice II (Villa Additions)
6101 Douglas St., New Orleans, LA 70117-2100
Tel: 504-277-8731
Fax: 504-277-8493
Residence for Senior Citizens & Handicapped.

Opelousas

Diocese of Lafayette

C'est La Vie Center of the Sisters Marianites of Holy Cross
960 E. Prudhomme St., Opelousas, LA 70570
Tel: 337-942-8154
Fax: 337-942-8279
E-mail: promptsuccor@bellsouth.net
Independent living for the elderly and handicapped.

Shreveport

Diocese of Shreveport

St. Catherine Community Center
331 E. 71st St., Shreveport, LA 71106-4305
Tel: 318-865-9817
Fax: 318-861-6177
E-mail: sccc@sport.rr.com
Web site: www.rc.net/shreveport/stcatherine.
Afterschool Enrichment, Summer Day Camp, Parenting, Arts, GED, Anger Management.

Slidell

Archdiocese of New Orleans

St. Peter the Fisherman
62269 Airport Rd., Slidell, LA 70460-5242
Tel: 985-641-4914
Fax: 985-641-7575
Residential Facility for Developmentally Disabled Adults.

MASSACHUSETTS

Boston

Archdiocese of Boston

Saint Anthony Residence
103 Arch St., Boston, MA 02110-1102
Tel: 617-542-6454
Fax: 617-542-6659
(For Retired Franciscan Friars.)

St. Helena House
89 Union Park St., Boston, MA 02118
Tel: 617-426-2922
Fax: 617-542-3460
Seniors, low income & disabled persons.

St. Joseph Nursing Care Center
321 Centre St., Boston, MA 02122
Tel: 617-825-6320
Fax: 617-825-7410
Member, Caritas Christi Healthcare System. 123 Bed Nursing Care Center. St. Joseph Nursing Care Center, Inc.

St. John of God Hospital
296 Allston St., Boston, MA 02135
Tel: 617-277-5750
Fax: 617-731-3094
A member of Caritas Christi, the Catholic Health Care System of the Archdiocese of Boston.

Regina Cleri, Inc.
60 William Cardinal O'Connell Way, Boston, MA 02114
Tel: 617-523-1861
Fax: 617-720-0585
E-mail: jtierney@reginacleri.org
Residence for Retired Archdiocesan Priests.

Cambridge

Archdiocese of Boston

* *Youville Hospital & Rehabilitation Center, Inc.*
1575 Cambridge Street, Cambridge, MA 02138-4398
Tel: 617-876-4344
Fax: 617-547-5501
Member of Youville Lifecare, Inc.

Fall River

Diocese of Fall River

Rose Hawthorne Lathrop Home
P.O. Box 2577, Fall River, MA 02724
Tel: 508-675-1311
Fax: 508-730-2447
(Servants of Relief for Incurable Cancer).

Lawrence

Archdiocese of Boston

M.I. Adult Day Health Center, Inc.
189 Maple St., Lawrence, MA 01841
Tel: 978-682 7575
Fax: 978-691-5374
E-mail: lori_barrett@mihs.com
Adult day health care for Senior Citizens also, bilingual/bicultural (Spanish) adult day health care.

M.I. Nursing-Restorative Center, Inc.
172 Lawrence St., Lawrence, MA 01841
Tel: 978-685-6321
Fax: 978-975-0050
E-mail: begrant@mihcs.com
Multi-level Skilled Nursing Facility. Member of Covenant Health System, Lexington, MA. Unit of: Mary Immaculate Health Care. Covenant Health Systems.

M.I. Residential Community, Inc.
189 Maple St., Lawrence, MA 01841
Tel: 978-682-7575
Fax: 978-691-5374
Assisted living for Elderly and Handicapped.

M.I. Residential Community II, Inc.
191 Maple St., Lawrence, MA 01841
Tel: 978-682-7575
Fax: 978-691-5374
Covenant Health Systems. Independent & assisted living for Elderly and Handicapped.

M.I. Residential Community III, Inc.
193 Maple St., Lawrence, MA 01841
Tel: 978-682-7575
Fax: 978-691-5374

Leominster

Diocese of Worcester

Presentation Health Care Center
99 Church St., Leominster, MA 01453-3147
Tel: 978-537-7856
Fax: 978-840-1564
Purpose: To operate and maintain a nursing home for aged and/or infirmed persons at Presentation Convent.

Waltham

Archdiocese of Boston

Maristhill Nursing & Rehabilitation Center
66 Newton St., Waltham, MA 02453- 6063
Tel: 781-893-0240
Fax: 781-894-6330
E-mail: jmurphy@maristhill.org
A member of Covenant Health Systems, offering skilled and rehabilitative nursing care.

West Springfield

Diocese of Springfield in Massachusetts

Brightside, Inc.
2112 Riverdale St., West Springfield, MA 01089
Tel: 413-827-4244; 413-788-7366
Fax: 413-747-0182; 413-827-4250
E-mail: brightside.intake@sphs.com
Web site: www.mercycares.com
Private, Nonprofit Agency.

Worcester

Diocese of Worcester

Vianney House
222 June St., Worcester, MA 01602
Tel: 508-791-0311.
Retired Priests' Home.

MARYLAND

Baltimore

Archdiocese of Baltimore

St. Elizabeth Rehabilitation and Nursing Center
3320 Benson Ave., Baltimore, MD 21227-1035
Tel: 410-644-7100
Fax: 410-646-6589
E-mail: info@catholiccharities-md.org
Web site: ww.catholiccharities-md.org
Sponsored by Associated Catholic Charities.

Dismas House West
105 S. Mount St., Baltimore, MD 21223-0435
Tel: 410-566-9400
Fax: 410-233-1622
Non-Sectarian-Use Diocesan Property Rehabilitation center under contract to the Maryland Division of Corrections to provide inmate services.

Good Shepherd Center
4100 Maple Ave., Baltimore, MD 21227
Tel: 410-247-2770
Fax: 410-247-3242
E-mail: info@goodshepherdcenter.org
Web site: www.goodshepherdcenter.org
Residential psychiatric treatment for adolescent girls with emotional and behavioral problems.

Beltsville

Archdiocese of Washington

Ammendale Normal Institute of Prince George's County-La Salle Hall
(1880)
6001 Ammendale Rd., Beltsville, MD 20705
Tel: 301-210-7443
Fax: 301-210-0614
E-mail: kevinerb20@hotmail.com
Residence for Retired and Convalescent Brothers.

Emmitsburg

Archdiocese of Baltimore

Villa St. Catherine, Inc.
331 S. Seton Ave., Emmitsburg, MD 21727
Tel: 301-447-7000
Fax: 301-447-7015
E-mail: info@stcatherinesnursingcenter.org
Web site: stcatherinesnursingcenter.org
Sponsored by Ascension Health.

Mitchellville

Archdiocese of Washington

Villa Rosa Nursing Home, Inc.
3800 Lottsford Vista Rd., Mitchellville, MD 20721-4026
Tel: 301-459-4700
Fax: 301-459-0754
Comprehensive Care Nursing Facility.

Rockville

Archdiocese of Washington

The Frost Center, Society of the Divine Savior
4915 Aspen Hill Rd., Rockville, MD 20853
Tel: 301-933-3451
Fax: 301-933-3330
E-mail: seanmcl@frostcenter.com
Web site: www.frostcenter.com
A School and Therapy Program for Emotionally Disturbed Students and Families. (Grades 1-12).

Timonium

Archdiocese of Baltimore

Francis X. Gallagher Services
2520 Pot Spring Rd., Timonium, MD 21093
Tel: 410-252-4005
Fax: 410-560-3495
E-mail: jhillman@cc-md.org
Web site: www.catholiccharities-md.org/programs/gallagher.
Residential, day habilitation and medical day programs for the developmentally disabled.

Stella Maris
2300 Dulaney Valley Rd., Timonium, MD 21093
Tel: 410-252-4500
Fax: 410-560-9675
E-mail: srabb@stellamarisinc.com
Web site: www.stellamarisinc.com
The management corporation for all programs of Stella Maris. Long-term care subacute care home health rehabilitative services hospice services hospice inpatient home/hospice care outreach ministries program independent living group home and counseling/bereavement services for adults and children. All applications for the facilities of the Center are processed directly through the Admissions Office at Stella Maris.

Villa Maria Treatment Center
2300 Dulaney Valley Rd., Timonium, MD 21093
Tel: 410-252-4700
Fax: 410-252-3040
E-mail: jhackbar@catholiccharities-md.org
Web site: www.catholiccharities-md.org
We operate a full continuum of 13 different mental health and special education programs for children and their families.

MAINE

Biddeford

Diocese of Portland (In Maine)

St. Andre Home, Inc.
Admin. Office, 283 Elm St., Biddeford, ME 04005-3093
Tel: 207-282-3351
E-mail: SaintAndre@aol.com
Web site: www.SaintAndreHome.com
Pregnant and Parenting Young Women, Adoption Services, Infant Foster Care Homes, Emergency Placement Public Information-Education Community Outreach Services Residences in Biddeford, Lewiston, Bangor.

Lewiston

Diocese of Portland (In Maine)

Maison Marcotte (Formerly: Marcotte Congregate Housing)
100 Campus Ave., Lewiston, ME 04240
Tel: 207-786-0062
Fax: 207-777-8570
E-mail: cmathieu@sochs.com

** St. Marguerite d'Youville Pavilion (Formerly: Marcotte Nursing Home)*
102 Campus Ave., Lewiston, ME 04240
Tel: 207-777-4200
Fax: 207-777-4255
E-mail: dfournier@sochs.com
Web site: www.stmarysme.com

Portland

Diocese of Portland (In Maine)

McAuley Residence, Inc.
91 State St., Portland, ME 04101
Tel: 207-773-5289
Fax: 207-773-2672
E-mail: mcauleyr@maine.rr.com
Transitional Housing and support services for women with or without children.

MICHIGAN

Alpena

Diocese of Gaylord

Huron House / Holy Cross Children's Services
4761 U.S. 23 N., Alpena, MI 49707
Tel: 989-356-3573
Fax: 989-356-4910
Residential and community-based treatment programs for troubled youth and families, with facilities located throughout the state of Michigan.

Battle Creek

Diocese of Kalamazoo

Mercy Pavilion Skilled Nursing Home and Senior Care Residence
80 N. 20 St., Battle Creek, MI 49015
Tel: 269-964-5400
Fax: 269-964-5559
Sub. of Battle Creek Health System.

Clinton Twp.

Archdiocese of Detroit

A Friend's House Adult Day Services
16931 19 Mile Rd., Ste. 140, Clinton Twp., MI 48038
Tel: 586-412-8494
Fax: 586-412-8084
Daytime care for older adults. Support services for care giving families. A service of Catholic Services of Macomb.

Dearborn Heights

Archdiocese of Detroit

Vista Maria
20651 W. Warren Ave., Dearborn Heights, MI 48127
Tel: 313-271-3050
Fax: 313-271-6250
Residential and community-based treatment programs for adolescent girls involved in The Juvenile Justice & Child Welfare Systems. Sponsored by the Sisters of the Good Shepherd.

Detroit

Archdiocese of Detroit

St. Catherine's House
1641 Webb Ave., Detroit, MI 48206
Tel: 313-868-4505
For elderly-ambulatory & younger disabled ambulatory women.

Don Bosco Hall, Inc.
2340 Calvert, Detroit, MI 48206
Tel: 313-869-2200
Fax: 313-869-8220
Residential treatment center for boys, ages 12-17, in need of care, guidance and therapy.

Holy Cross Children's Services
5555 Conner, Detroit, MI 48213
Tel: 313-579-4400
Fax: 313-267-1185
Residential and community based treatment programs for troubled youth and families with facilities located throughout the state of Michigan and one in the state of Ohio under the auspices of the Brothers of Holy Cross at Notre Dame.

St. Mary's Residence
2120 Orleans St., Detroit, MI 48207
Tel: 313-259-0459
A residence for women desiring home-like surroundings.

Farmington Hills

Archdiocese of Detroit

St. Vincent and Sarah Fisher Center
27400 W. Twelve Mile Rd., Farmington Hills, MI 48334
Tel: 248-626-7527
Fax: 248-626-0865
Pregnancy and Parenting For Teen Parents (Ages 16-19) Outreach Program. Licensed capacity for: Residential care 60 (ages 4-15), Specialized Foster Care 120 (ages 0-17).

Seton Nursery School and Infant-Toddler Child Care Center
29475 Inkster Rd., Farmington Hills, MI 48018
Tel: 810-626-6990
Center licensed for 80 children, 8 weeks-5.5 years.

Grand Blanc

Diocese of Lansing

Genesys Convalescent Center, Grand Blanc, Inc.
8481 Holly Rd., Grand Blanc, MI 48439-1899
Tel: 810-694-1711
Fax: 810-694-9717
E-mail: r.stevens@genesys.org
Web site: genesys.org
An affiliate of Genesys Health System. Nursing Home.

Lake Orion

Archdiocese of Detroit

Guest House for Women Religious
1840 W. Scripps Rd., Box 68, Lake Orion, MI 48360
Tel: 248-391-3100
Fax: 248-391-1553
Central Admissions Office, from U.S. & Canada call: 800-626-6910. A state licensed and JCAHO accredited endorsed residential treatment center for Catholic sisters and women in formation.

Livonia

Archdiocese of Detroit

Marycrest Manor
15475 Middlebelt Rd., Livonia, MI 48154
Tel: 734-427-9175
Fax: 734-427-5044
Ownership: Franciscan Sisters of St. Joseph.

Marywood Nursing Care Center
36975 W. Five Mile Rd., Livonia, MI 48154
Tel: 734-464-0600
Fax: 734-464-4846
Long-term care Facility.

Mount Clemens

Archdiocese of Detroit

St. Joseph Mercy Living Care Center
37700 Harper, Mount Clemens, MI 48043
Tel: 810-468-0827
A Division of Mercy Mt. Clemens Corp.

Otsego

Diocese of Kalamazoo

Otsego Senior Apts., Inc.
Baraga Manor, 301 Washington St., Otsego, MI 49078
Tel: 269-694-9711
Fax: 269-694-5857
Managed by Catholic Family Services, Diocese of Kalamazoo.

Saginaw

Diocese of Saginaw

St. Vincent Home-Boysville of Michigan, Inc.
925 N. River Rd., Saginaw, MI 48609
Tel: 989-781-2780
Fax: 989-781-5422
Residential and community based treatment programs for troubled youth and families with facilities located throughtout the state of Michigan, under the auspices of the Brothers of the Holy Cross at Notre Dame.

Southfield

Archdiocese of Detroit

St. Francis Family Services
17500 W. Eight Mile Rd., Southfield, MI 48075
Tel: 248-552-0750
Fax: 248-552-9019
Foster home respite & adoption services for infants through 17 years.

Sheltering Arms
18310 W. 12 Mile, Southfield, MI 48076
Tel: 248-557-7373
Fax: 248-559-1140
Adult day care for the elderly. A service of Catholic Social Services of Oakland County.

St. Clair Shores

Archdiocese of Detroit

Sisters of Bon Secours Nursing Care Center
26001 E. Jefferson, St. Clair Shores, MI 48081
Tel: 810-779-7000
A member of the Bon Secours of Michigan Healthcare Systems, Inc. operated by the Sisters of Bon Secours. The center provides short and long term nursing, residential care and rehabilitative services for older adults.

Waterford

Archdiocese of Detroit

Fox Manor, Inc.
2350 Watkins Lake Rd., Waterford, MI 48328
Tel: 248-674-9590
Fax: 248-674-1211
Residential facility for independent senior citizens of moderate or limited means.

Lourdes Nursing Home
2300 Watkins Lake Rd., Waterford, MI 48328
Tel: 248-674-2241
Fax: 248-674-1211
Dominican Sisters of Oxford, MI. Skilled & basic nursing facility for men and women rehabilitation and 24 hour nursing care.

MINNESOTA

Cold Spring

Diocese of St. Cloud

St. Anne's Home
103 10th Ave. N., Cold Spring, MN 56320
Tel: 320-685-7898
Fax: 320-685-8626
Contact Catholic Charities. Supervised Living Situation for Persons with Developmental Disabilities.

Bethany Home
13 Eighth Ave. S., Cold Spring, MN 56320
Tel: 320-685-7899
Fax: 320-685-9808
E-mail: jkrueger@gw.stcdio.org
Supervised Living Situation for Persons with Developmental Disabilities. Contact John Krueger at Catholic Charities.

John Paul Apartments
200 Eighth Ave. N., Cold Spring, MN 56320
Tel: 320-685-4429
Fax: 320-685-7044
E-mail: jpa@cloudnet.com
Pioneer Housing Development, Inc.

St. Luke's Home
411 Eighth Ave. N., Cold Spring, MN 56320
Tel: 320-685-7750
Adults with mild to moderate developmental disabilities. Contact Catholic Charities.

Mother Teresa Home
101 Tenth Ave., Cold Spring, MN 56320
Tel: 320-685-8626
Fax: 320-685-8626
Supervised Living Situation for Persons with Developmental Disabilities.

Duluth

Diocese of Duluth

Arrowhead Senior Living Community
503 E. 3rd St., Ste. 400, Duluth, MN 55805
Tel: 218-786-2370
Subsidiaries: St. Michael's Health and Rehab Center, Virginia, MN. Arrowhead Senior Living Community, Eveleth, MN.

Benedictine Health Center
935 Kenwood Ave., Duluth, MN 55811
Tel: 218-723-6408 Fax: 218-723-6449
(Sub. of Benedictine Health System) Rehabilitation services and respite care, Senior Housing and Assisted Living, post acute, Alzheimer Care.

Little Falls

Diocese of St. Cloud

Alverna Apartments
300 Eighth Ave., S.E., Little Falls, MN 56345
Tel: 320-632-1246
Fax: 320-632-1190
(An Affiliate of Catholic Health Initiatives.)

Minneapolis

Archdiocese of St. Paul and Minneapolis

St. Joseph's Home for Children
1121 E. 46th St., Minneapolis, MN 55407
Tel: 612-827-6241
Fax: 612-827-9321
Web site: www.ccspm.org
Intake Emergency Shelter Diagnostic and Assessment Serving 2400 Children Yearly Residential Treatment (services 24) Day Treatment (services 24).

Plainview

Diocese of Winona

Hillcrest Community Care Center
800 2nd Ave., N.W., Plainview, MN 55964
Tel: 507-534-3191
Fax: 507-534-2778
E-mail: bob.ferk@bhshealth.org
Benedictine Health System, sponsored by Sisters of St. Scholastica Monastery.

Green Prairie Place
810 2nd Ave., N.W., Plainview, MN 55964
Tel: 507-534-4204
Fax: 507-534-0139
E-mail: joann.klavetter@bhshealth.org

Rochester

Diocese of Winona

Madonna Meadows of Rochester
3035 Salem Meadows Dr., S.W., Rochester, MN 55902
Tel: 507-252-5400
Sponsored by: Benedictine Health System and Sisters of St. Scholastica Monastery.

Madonna Towers of Rochester, Inc.
4001 19th Ave., N.W., Rochester, MN 55901
Tel: 507-288-3911
Fax: 507-288-0393
E-mail: mark.cairns@bhshealth.org
Subsidiary of Benedictine Health System.

St. Cloud

Diocese of St. Cloud

St. Benedict's Senior Community
1810 Minnesota Blvd., S.E., St. Cloud, MN 56304
Tel: 320-252-0010
Fax: 320-654-2351
Care Center managed by St. Benedict's Senior Community. Corporate Division of the St. Cloud Hospital. Operated under the auspices of the local Catholic Church of St. Cloud.

St. Elizabeth Home
306 15th Ave. N., St. Cloud, MN 56303
Tel: 320-240-3350
E-mail: rhanish@gw.stcdio.org
Board and Lodging Home for Functionally Impaired Adults. Contact John Krueger at Catholic Charities.

Wabasha

Diocese of Winona

St. Elizabeth's Health Care Center
626 Shields Ave., Wabasha, MN 55981
Tel: 651-565-4581
Fax: 651-565-3414
Web site: www.ministryhealth.org
(Conducted in connection with St. Elizabeth's Hospital of Wabasha, Inc.)

Waite Park

Diocese of St. Cloud

St. Francis Home
P.O. Box 326, Waite Park, MN 56387
Tel: 320-251-7630
Fax: 320-240-8097
Supervised Living Situation for Persons with Developmental Disabilities.

West St. Paul

Archdiocese of St. Paul and Minneapolis

Guild Incorporated
1025 Dodd Rd., West St. Paul, MN 55118
Tel: 651-450-2220
Fax: 651-450-2221
E-mail: info@guildincorporated.org
Web site: www.guildincorporated.org
Programs formed by The Guild of Catholic Women. A variety of housing and support services for adults who have serious and persistant mental illness. Apartments and group living available.

Winona

Diocese of Winona

Saint Anne of Winona
1347 W. Broadway, Winona, MN 55987
Tel: 507-454-3621
Fax: 507-454-8626
Subsidiary of Benedictine Health Systems.

Winsted

Diocese of New Ulm

St. Mary's Care Center
551 4th St. N., P.O. Box 750, Winsted, MN 55395-0750
Tel: 320-485-2151
Fax: 320-485-4241
E-mail: dhschwartz@bhshealth.org
Web site: www.bhshealth.org
Subsidiary of the Benedictine Health System.

MISSOURI

Blue Springs

Diocese of Kansas City-St. Joseph

St. Mary's Manor
111 Mock Ave., Blue Springs, MO 64014
Tel: 816-228-5655
Fax: 816-228-8480
E-mail: pkelley@carondelet.com
Long term care facility with skilled nursing care and residential care.

Cameron

Diocese of Kansas City-St. Joseph

St. Patrick's Manor
514 Northland Dr., Cameron, MO 64429
Tel: 816-632-1684
Fax: 816-632-7624
E-mail: cpp61587@centurytel.net
A 31-unit apartment residence for the elderly and disabled.

Chesterfield

Archdiocese of St. Louis

St. Joseph Institute for the Deaf
1809 Clarkson Rd., Chesterfield, MO 63017-5065
Tel: 636-532-3211
Fax: 636-532-4560
E-mail: info@sjid.org
Web site: www.sjid.org
School for the Deaf. Auditory-oral day & residential school for hearing-impaired children from birth-8th grade. Early intervention therapy for children 0-5 pre- & elementary school offering intense speech & academic prog.

Eureka

Archdiocese of St. Louis

St. Joseph Hill Infirmary, Inc. dba St. Joseph Hill Infirmary
St. Joseph Rd., Eureka, MO 63025
Tel: 636-587-3661
Fax: 636-938-6398
A skilled nursing facility conducted by the Franciscan Missionary Brothers of the Sacred Heart of Jesus.

Price Memorial
Forby Rd., P.O. Box 476, Eureka, MO 63025
Tel: 636-587-3200
Fax: 636-938-5266
E-mail: pricesnf@mindspring.com
A skilled nursing facility conducted by the Franciscan Missionary Brothers of St. Joseph's Hill.

Florissant

Archdiocese of St. Louis

Marygrove
2705 Mullanphy Ln., Florissant, MO 63031
Tel: 314-837-1702
Fax: 314-830-6263
E-mail: hnegri@ccstl.org
Web site: www.marygroveonline.org
Owned and operated under the auspices of Catholic Charities. Residential treatment for emotionally disturbed males and females (ages 6-21). Special education, therapy and medical services. Overnight emergency care: and crisis nursery males and females (Birth-21).

Jefferson City

Diocese of Jefferson City

St. Joseph's Home
1306 W. Main St., Jefferson City, MO 65109
Tel: 573-635-0166
Fax: 573-635-1405
Conducted by the Carmelite Sisters of the Divine Heart of Jesus.

Villa Marie Skilled Nursing Facility
1030 Edmonds St., Jefferson City, MO 65109
Tel: 573-761-6700
Fax: 573-635-6685
Member of SSM Health Care.

Kansas City

Diocese of Kansas City-St. Joseph

Carondelet Manor
621 Carondelet Dr., Kansas City, MO 64114
Tel: 816-943-4777
Owned and operated by Carondelet Long Term Care Facilities, Inc. Sponsored by Sisters of St. Joseph of Carondelet.

Cathedral Square Towers
444 W. 12th St., Kansas City, MO 64105
Tel: 816-471-6555
Fax: 816-421-1279
E-mail: cath@swbell.net
Apartment residence for the elderly and handicapped.

Columbus Park Plaza
801 Pacific, Kansas City, MO 64106
Fax: 816-472-6105
E-mail: columbuspark1@swbell.net
Apartment residence for elderly and handicapped.

Marlborough Manor
1818 E. 79th St., Kansas City, MO 64132
Tel: 816-333-7761
Fax: 816-523-2388
E-mail: marlborough01@sbcglobal.net
Rental housing for low income (a 31-unit apartment residence for the elderly and disabled).

Tremont Place
6161 N. Chatham, Kansas City, MO 64151
Tel: 816-587-7707
Fax: 816-587-7637
E-mail: tremont1@swbell.net
A 50-unit apartment residence for the elderly and disabled. Must be sixty two or over.

Kansas City

Diocese of Kansas City-St. Joseph

Brighton Place
2429 Brighton, Kansas City, MO 64127
Tel: 816-561-4240
Fax: 816-561-3155
A 31-unit residence for the elderly and disabled.

Columbus Park Plaza
801 Pacific, Kansas City, MO 64106
Tel: 816-472-0887
Apartment residence for elderly and handicapped.

Kirkwood

Archdiocese of St. Louis

St. Agnes Home for the Elderly
10341 Manchester Rd., Kirkwood, MO 63122
Tel: 314-965-7616
Fax: 314-965-3179
Conducted for Elderly Ladies, Gentlemen and Couples by the Carmelite Sisters of the Divine Heart of Jesus.

Liberty

Diocese of Kansas City-St. Joseph

Immacolata Manor
2101 Hughes Rd., Liberty, MO 64068-9397
Tel: 816-781-4332
Fax: 816-781-8820
E-mail: imanor@sbcglobe.net
Operated by the Immacolata Board of Directors. Residential and day habilitation services for women with developmental disabilities.

Normandy

Archdiocese of St. Louis

Maria Droste Residence
7660 Natural Bridge Rd., Normandy, MO 63121
Tel: 314-383-5553
Fax: 314-382-5294.
Web site: goodshepherdsisters.org
For Women in Need.

St. Vincent Home for Children
7401 Florissant Rd., Normandy, MO 63121
Tel: 314-261-6011
Fax: 314-385-1467
E-mail: cblake@saintvincenthome.org
Web site: www.saintvincenthome.org
Chapel of the Sacred Heart.

Savannah

Diocese of Kansas City-St. Joseph

La Verna Village Apartments
1000-1005 Hall Ave., Savannah, MO 64485
Tel: 816-324-3179
Fax: 816-324-7264
E-mail: osf@ccp.com
Web site: www.sistersofstfrancis.org
Apartments for the elderly and handicapped.

Springfield

Diocese of Springfield-Cape Girardeau

St. John's Mercy Villa
1100 E. Montclair, Springfield, MO 65807
Tel: 417-820-8500
Fax: 417-820-8532
Skilled Care of Long Term Nursing Home, for the Aged and Chronically Ill.

St. Louis

Archdiocese of St. Louis

Boys Hope / Girls Hope of St. Louis, Inc.
755 S. New Ballas Rd., Ste. 120, St. Louis, MO 63141
Tel: 314-692-7477
Fax: 314-692-7810
E-mail: hopestlouis@bhgh.org
Web site: www.hopestlouis.org
Residential Care for Adolescent Boys and Girls, Troubled by Family Disruptions, who are Capable of College Preparatory High School Work. Ages 7-18.

Cardinal Ritter Institute
7601 Watson Rd., Saint Louis, MO 63119
Tel: 314-961-8000
Fax: 314-961-1934
E-mail: swesley@ccstl.org
Web site: www.ccstl.org
Catholic Charities network of agencies provides social services, in home services, residences, adult day care, employment and volunteer services for the elderly.

Cathedral Tower
325 N. Newstead Ave., St. Louis, MO 63108
Tel: 314-367-5500
Fax: 314-652-2139
E-mail: dfagin@ccstl.org
Web site: www.ccstl.org
Building which houses several agencies of Catholic Charities: Queen of Peace Center St. Elizabeth Hall Marian Hall Emergency Shelter, Dial Help and Peace for Kids, Inc.

Catholic Guidance Center
4472 Lindell Blvd., St. Louis, MO 63108
Tel: 314-533-3454
Fax: 314-533-0140
E-mail: special-education@att.net
Web site: www.special-education.org
Psycho-Educational Testing Facility and also Administrative Office for the Archdiocesan Department of Special Education, Serving Children with Developmental Disabilities, Mental Retardation, Learning Disabilities or Attention Deficit Disorder. Special Ungraded Day Classes, Schools, Preschool, PSR for Disabled children with Mental Retardation or Major Learning Disabilities (ages 5-16). Located in the Following Parish Schools: Epiphany of Our Lord (2 LD Classes) Sacred Heart (1 MR Classes) St. Christopher (5 LD Classes) Annunziata (6 LD Classes) St. John the Baptist (3 LD Classes) Our Lady of the Presentation (2 LD Classes) Ascension, Chesterfield (2 LD Classes).

Corporate Action for the Care of the Elderly, Inc.
335 S. Kirkwood Rd., St. Louis, MO 63122
Tel: 314-965-3700
Fax: 314-965-3710
Association Composed of Representatives of 14 Religious Communities. Grants offered to assist those who work with the elderly.

St. Elizabeth Adult Day Care Center
3401 Arsenal St., St. Louis, MO 63118
Tel: 314-772-5107
Fax: 314-772-3674
E-mail: sjamiller@juno.com
Web site: www.cpps-ofallon.org
Conducted by the Sisters of the Most Precious Blood to Provide Day Care for the Elderly and Handicapped.

Fusz Pavilion
3601 Lindell Blvd., St. Louis, MO 63108
Tel: 314-977-2591
Fax: 314-977-7910
A Retirement Home for Jesuits.

Marian Hall Agencies
1340 Partridge Ave., St. Louis, MO 63130
Tel: 314-726-3339
Fax: 314-726-3470
E-mail: sking@ccstl.org
Residential Care to Homeless, Neglected and Abused Adolescent Girls (ages 11-18) with Emotional and/or Behavioral Problems.

Marian Hall Emergency Shelter
1340 Partridge, St. Louis, MO 63130
Tel: 314-531-7233
Fax: 314-531-2993
E-mail: snewberry@ccstl.org
Emergency Shelter in a Residential Setting for Runaway, Homeless or Abused Adolescent Girls (ages 11-18), with Emotional and/or Behavioral Problems.

St. Martha's Hall
P.O. Box 4950, St. Louis, MO 63108
Tel: 314-533-1313
Fax: 314-533-2035
E-mail: stmarthas@igateway.net
Web site: www.saintmarthas.org
Provides Shelter, Advocacy and Support to Abused Women & their Children.

Mary, Queen and Mother Center
7601 Watson Rd., St. Louis, MO 63119
Tel: 314-961-8000
Fax: 314-961-1548
E-mail: rmantia@archstl.org
Web site: cardinalcarberry.org
Skilled Nursing Facility.

St. Mary's Special Services
1724 Redman Ave., St. Louis, MO 63138
Tel: 314-261-8533
Fax: 314-653-2591
Web site: www.special-education.org
Inclusionary early childhood education for children ages 3-6 years (capacity 20). Early Intervention therapies and child care for preschool children (ages 6 months-5 years) developmentally disabled in a normalized mainstream setting (capacity 80).

Mother of Good Counsel Home
6825 Natural Bridge Rd., (St. Louis Co.), St. Louis, MO 63121
Tel: 314-383-4765
Fax: 314-383-7256
E-mail: mogch@catholic.org
Web site: mogch.com
Skilled Nursing Facility for Men and Women.

Mother of Perpetual Help Residence
7609 Watson Rd., St. Louis, MO 63119
Tel: 314-918-2260
Fax: 314-961-3061
E-mail: swesley@ccstl.org
Web site: cardinalcarberry.org
A part of Cardinal Carberry Living Center.

Nazareth Living Center
2 Nazareth Ln., St. Louis, MO 63129
Fax: 314-487-8001
E-mail: lwesthoff@nlccsj.com
Web site: www.nazarethlivingcenter.com
Residential and Skilled Nursing Care Facility.

Our Lady of Life Apartments, Inc.
7655 Watson Rd., St. Louis, MO 63119
Tel: 314-968-9447
E-mail: twalther@archstl.org
A part of Cardinal Carberry Living Center.

St. Philippine Home
1015 Goodfellow Blvd., St. Louis, MO 63112
Tel: 314-454-1012
Fax: 314-367-7455
Transitional housing for drug affected homeless city women and their children.

Queen of Peace Center
325 N. Newstead Ave., St. Louis, MO 63108
Tel: 314-531-0511
Fax: 314-531-1458
E-mail: cneumann@ccstl.org
Web site: www.ccstl.org
Comprehensive substance abuse treatment and rehabilitation for women and their children, including in-patient/outpatient. Licensed by DMH and accredited by COA. Licensed day care, infant care, development center and licensed comprehensive psychiatric services, licensed by SMH, St. Louis City Health Department, Missouri Department of Health and accredited by COA. Transitional housing and therapeutic services for drug-affected, homeless city women and their children, accredited by COA. Housing subsidy for the disabled homeless.

Regina Cleri Residence
10 Archbishop May Dr., St. Louis, MO 63119
Tel: 314-968-2240
Fax: 314-968-1049

E-mail: reginacleri@earthlink.net
A Residence for Retired Diocesan Priests of the Archdiocese of St. Louis. Conducted by the Archdiocese of St. Louis.

Rosati Group Home, Inc.
4218 N. Grand Blvd., St. Louis, MO 63107
Fax: 314-535-4394
E-mail: nboland@stpatrickcenter.org
Web site: stpatrickcenter.org
Group Home and Stabilization Center for homeless mentally ill adults.

Rosati Stabilization Center
4224 N. Grand Ave., St. Louis, MO 63107
Tel: 314-534-6624
Fax: 314-535-4394
Managed by the St. Patrick Center. Residential Transitional Facility for Mentally Ill Homeless.

Special Religious Education Ministry
4472 Lindell Blvd., St. Louis, MO 63108
Tel: 314-533-3454, Ext. 231
E-mail: SpecRelEdu@aol.com
Web site: www.special-educationstl.org
Department of Special Education. Provides Catholic religious education for children with disabilities in public special programs, (ages 7-21) & for adults with disabilities living in institutions or in their own homes.

SSM Cardinal Glennon Children's Hospital
1465 S. Grand Blvd., St. Louis, MO 63104
Tel: 314-577-5600
Fax: 314-268-6468
E-mail: Doug_Ries@ssmhc.com
Web site: www.cardinalglennon.com
Member of SSM Health Care.

SSM Rehab
6420 Clayton Rd., Exec. Offices, St. Louis, MO 63117-1861
Tel: 314-768-5300
Fax: 314-768-5355
Web site: www.ssmrehab.com
Member of SSM Health Care. For rehabilitation of pediatrics, adolescents and adults.

Villa Maria Center
2647 Ohio Ave., St. Louis, MO 63118
Tel: 314-664-4715
Fax: 314-664-4970
E-mail: tcrumble@ccstl.org
Under the Auspices of Catholic Services for Children and Youth. Comprehensive Residential Program for Pregnant and Parenting Teenage Girls Provides Individual, Family and Group Counseling, Arranges Obstetrical and Pediatric Care, Provides Educational Services Including Academic and Personal Growth and Development, Training in Parenting and Living Skill.

MONTANA

Great Falls

Diocese of Great Falls - Billings

St. Thomas Child and Family Center
1710 Benefis Ct., Great Falls, MT 59405
Tel: 406-761-6538
Fax: 406-727-0670
E-mail: stcfc@mcn.net
Web site: stthomaskids.org
Child Care Center Family Life Education Prevention and Treatment of Child Abuse Education, Information, and Referral Service Summer Food Program for Low-Income Children Before- and After-School Care Programs.

NEBRASKA

Lincoln

Diocese of Lincoln

Bonacum House
3301 Sheridan Blvd., Lincoln, NE 68506
Tel: 402-483-0391
Residence for retired priests.

Madonna Rehabilitation Hospital
5401 South St., Lincoln, NE 68506
Tel: 402-489-7102
Fax: 402-483-9460
E-mail: feedback@madonna.org
Web site: www.madonna.org
Physical Medicine and Rehabilitation, Outpatient Services, Long-Term Care, Adult Day Care and Supportive Inpatient Hospice, Alzheimers Care.

Omaha

Archdiocese of Omaha

Mercy Villa
1845 S. 72nd St., Omaha, NE 68124
Tel: 402-391-6224
Fax: 402-391-1872
E-mail: jeannew@mercyoma.org
Retirement Home for the Sisters of Mercy of the Americas for the Omaha Region.

NEW HAMPSHIRE

Berlin

Diocese of Manchester

St. Vincent de Paul Healthcare Center
29 Providence Ave., Berlin, NH 03570-3199
Tel: 603-752-1820
Fax: 603-752-7149
E-mail: stvdp@ncia.net
New Hampshire Catholic Charities.

Dover

Diocese of Manchester

St. Ann Healthcare Center
195 Dover Point Rd., Dover, NH 03820-4693
Tel: 603-742-2612
Fax: 603-743-3055
E-mail: kjp@netway.com
New Hampshire Catholic Charities.

Jaffrey

Diocese of Manchester

Good Shepherd Healthcare Center
20 Plantation Dr., Jaffrey, NH 03452-1935
Tel: 603-532-8762
Fax: 603-532-6057

Laconia

Diocese of Manchester

St. Francis Healthcare Center
406 Court St., Laconia, NH 03246-3000
Tel: 603-524-0466
Fax: 603-527-0884
E-mail: fay444@aol.com

Manchester

Diocese of Manchester

St. Joseph Residence
495 Mammoth Rd., Manchester, NH 03104
Tel: 603-668-6011
Fax: 603-644-1276
E-mail: mjmakowski@presmarynh.org
New Hampshire Catholic Charities.

Mt. Carmel Healthcare Center
235 Myrtle St., Manchester, NH 03104-4399
Tel: 603-627-3811
Fax: 603-626-4696
E-mail: mtcadmin@metro2000.net
New Hampshire Catholic Charities.

St. Teresa Healthcare Center
519 Bridge St., Manchester, NH 03104-5396
Tel: 603-668-2373
Fax: 603-668-0059
E-mail: Linda@xtol.com
New Hampshire Catholic Charities.

Rochester

Diocese of Manchester

St. Charles Children's Home
19 Grant St., Rochester, NH 03867-3099
Tel: 603-332-4768
Fax: 603-332-3948
E-mail: stcharles@metrocast.net

Windham

Diocese of Manchester

Warde Health Center
21 Searles Rd., Windham, NH 03087-1297
Tel: 603-890-1290
Fax: 603-890-1293
E-mail: wardehealth@aol.com
Managed by New Hampshire Catholic Charities.

NEW JERSEY

Cedar Grove

Archdiocese of Newark

St. Vincent's Nursing Home
315 E. Lindsley Rd., Cedar Grove, NJ 07009
Tel: 973-754-4800
Fax: 973-812-4491
E-mail: kenny@sjhmc.org
(Div. of St. Joseph's Regional Medical Center)

Denville

Diocese of Paterson

St. Peter's Village
170 Diamond Spring Rd., Denville, NJ 07834
Tel: 973-627-0212
Fax: 973-627-3338
E-mail: srkatherine@nac.net
Staffed by School Sisters of Notre Dame.

Lawrenceville

Diocese of Trenton

Morris Hall / Saint Lawrence, Inc.
1 Bishops' Dr., Lawrenceville, NJ 08648-2050
Tel: 609-896-0006
Fax: 609-896-8037
E-mail: info@morrishall.org
Web site: www.morrishall.org
Morris Hall - St. Joseph's Nursing Center. Skilled Nursing Care Facility for the Chronically Ill.

Morris Hall-Saint Lawrence, Inc.
1 Bishops' Dr., Lawrenceville, NJ 08648-2050
Tel: 609-896-0006
Fax: 609-895-8037
E-mail: info@morrishall.org
Web site: www.morrishall.org
Morris Hall - St. Mary's Residence & Assisted Living.

Morris Hall / Saint Lawrence, Inc.
2381 Lawrenceville Rd., Lawrenceville, NJ 08648
Tel: 609-896-9500
Fax: 609-895-0242
E-mail: clb950@aol.com
Web site: www.slrc.org
St. Lawrence Rehabilitation Center.

North Plainfield

Diocese of Metuchen

Villa Maria Sanitarium
641 Somerset St., North Plainfield, NJ 07060-4909
Tel: 908-757-3050
Fax: 908-754-4939
Home for the aged.

Paterson

Diocese of Paterson

St. Joseph Rest Home for Aged Women
46 Preakness Ave., Paterson, NJ 07522
Tel: 973-956-1921
Fax: 973-956-1582
E-mail: dcpbchalouxi@aol.com
Conducted by Daughters of Charity of the Most Precious Blood.

Red Bank

Diocese of Trenton

Collier Group Home
180 Spring St., Red Bank, NJ 07701
Tel: 732-842-8337
Fax: 732-530-7096
E-mail: pauldesantis@earthlink.net
24 Hour Program-Therapy and Educational Services. Provided Under the Supervision of the Sisters of the Good Shepherd.

Saddle River

Archdiocese of Newark

Villa Marie Claire
12 W. Saddle River Rd., Saddle River, NJ 07458
Tel: 201-327-1325
Fax: 201-327-6647
E-mail: vcmoshea@aol.com
Residence for retired, independent men & women.

Totowa

Diocese of Paterson

St. Joseph's Home for the Elderly
140 Shepherd Ln., Totowa, NJ 07512
Tel: 973-942-0300
Fax: 973-942-7201
Conducted by Little Sisters of the Poor.

Mt. St. Joseph Children's Center
124 Shepherd Ln., Totowa, NJ 07512
Tel: 973-595-5720
Fax: 973-595-1930
Residential school for classified emotionally disturbed boys, 6-14, referred from public school districts. Under the direction of Catholic Family and Community Services.

Trenton

Diocese of Trenton

Cathedral Square Housing, Inc.
26 W. Hanover Pl., Trenton, NJ 08608
Tel: 609-392-1111
Fax: 609-683-7227
E-mail: cs@gershengroup.com
Senior Citizen Housing Project

Wickatunk

Diocese of Trenton

Collier Services Collier High School
160 Conover Rd., Wickatunk, NJ 07765
Tel: 732-946-4771
Fax: 732-946-3519
E-mail: info@collierservices.com
Web site: www.collierservices.com
Adolescent Boys and Girls.

NEW MEXICO

Albuquerque

Archdiocese of Santa Fe

Casa Angelica
5629 Isleta Blvd., S.W., Albuquerque, NM 87105
Tel: 505-877-5763
Fax: 505-873-2786
E-mail: lturner@casaangelica.org
Home for developmentally disabled children.

Good Shepherd Center, Inc.
218 Iron St., S.W., P.O. Box 749, Albuquerque, NM 87103
Tel: 505-243-2527
Fax: 505-247-2207
Direct Service Agency for the Homeless.

Good Shepherd Manor
10127 Guadalupe Tr., N.W., P.O. Box 10248, Albuquerque, NM 87184
Tel: 505-898-0177
Fax: 505-898-9756
Sponsored by Bro. Mathias Barrett, Inc. of New Mexico. Shelter Care Facility for aged adults.

Marie Amadea Shelter for Unwed Mothers
P.O. Box 708, Albuquerque, NM 87103
Tel: 505-242-1516
Fax: 505-243-0402
Home for unwed expectant women. (Alternative to Abortion)

Carlsbad

Diocese of Las Cruces

St. Mary's Health Care Center
2330 West Pierce, Carlsbad, NM 88220
Tel: 505-887-0516
Fax: 505-885-8239
(Sub. of St. Mary of the Plains Hospital)

Hobbs

Diocese of Las Cruces

St. Mary's Family Health Care Center
515 East Main, Hobbs, NM 88240
Tel: 505-393-1096
Fax: 505-393-3758

NEW YORK

Albany

Diocese of Albany

Saint Anne Institute
160 N. Main Ave., Albany, NY 12206
Tel: 518-437-6500
Fax: 518-437-6555
E-mail: rriccio@s-a-i.org
Web site: www.stanneinstitute.org
Residential and Community-based Preventive Service Center. Regents accredited and certified junior and senior H.S. for the emotionally handicapped and Preschool program for 3-4 year olds who are speech impaired and emotionally disturbed. Residential care and Day Treatment for young women ages 12-18. Family Services, Vocational Training, Sex Abuse Prevention and Juvenile Sex Offender Programs for male and female adolescents in crisis and their families.

Bishop Broderick Apartments Housing Development Fund Co., Inc.
50 Prescott St., Albany, NY 12205
Tel: 518-869-7441
Fax: 518-869-0443
E-mail: mrjbba@aol.com
Web site: www.depaulhousing.com
Senior Citizen and Handicapped Housing.

DePaul Housing Management Corp.
41 N. Main Ave., Albany, NY 12203
Web site: www.depaulhousing.com
Managing diocesan sponsored housing for persons who are elderly or mobility impaired.

Saint Catherine's Center for Children
40 N. Main Ave., Albany, NY 12203
Tel: 518-453-6700
Fax: 518-453-6712
Web site: www.st-cath.org
Residential and day treatment, group homes and foster family programs for children with special needs. Community based prevention programs Parent aides Parent Training Transitional Program for Homeless Families.

DePaul Housing Management Corp.
41 N. Main Ave., Albany, NY 12203
Tel: 518-459-0183
Fax: 518-459-0202
E-mail: Deborah.DammOBrien@rcda.org
Managing diocesan sponsored housing for persons who are elderly or mobility impaired.

Hospitality House Therapeutic Community Inc.
271 Central Ave., Albany, NY 12206
Tel: 518-434-6468
Fax: 518-434-6302
E-mail: lbecker@hospitalityhouse.info
A private, not-for-profit, residential treatment program for young people, 16 years or older, with a history of drug and/or substance abuse.

LaSalle School, Inc.
391 Western Ave., Albany, NY 12203
Fax: 518-242-4747
E-mail: information@lasalle-school.org
Web site: www.lasalle-school.org
Residential and day programs, independent living program, sexual victim/offender program, licensed substance abuse treatment program, and preventative services for boys (ages 12-18) and their families in New York State. Registered New York State Junior and Senior High School and certified School of Special Education.

Teresian House
(1974)
200 Washington Ave. Ext., Albany, NY 12203
Tel: 518-456-2000
Fax: 518-456-1142
E-mail: info@teresianhouse.com
Web site: www.teresianhouse.com
Corporate Title: Teresian House Nursing Home Co., Inc.

Villa Mary Immaculate
301 Hackett Blvd., Albany, NY 12208
Tel: 518-525-7600
Fax: 518-525-7673
E-mail: rcassano@stpetershealthcare.org
Web site: www.stpetershealthcare.org
S.N.F. and long term skilled care nursing home. Sponsored St. Peter's Health Care Services. Member of Catholic Health East.

St. Vincent Apartments Housing Development Fund Co., Inc.
475 Yates St., Albany, NY 12208
Tel: 518-482-8915
Fax: 518-489-0122
E-mail: ldcmrmsva@aol.com
Web site: www.depaulhousing.com
Senior Citizen and Handicapped Housing.

Altamont

Diocese of Albany

Bernard and Caroline Cobb Memorial School
100-300 Mt. Presentation Way, Altamont, NY 12009
Fax: 518-861-5228
E-mail: cobbschool@msn.com
Web site: www.timesunion/communities/cobbschool
12 month special education program for students 5-21 years.

Amsterdam

Diocese of Albany

Mt. Loretto Nursing Home
302 Swart Hill Rd., Amsterdam, NY 12010
Tel: 518-842-6790
Fax: 518-843-5993
E-mail: mtloretto@superior.net
Web site: MountLoretto.com
Health Care Facility, 24 Hour Skilled Nursing Care, Hospice, IV Therapy & Rehab. Conducted by the Sisters of the Holy Family of Nazareth and the Sisters of the Resurrection.

Barryville

Archdiocese of New York

New Hope Manor
35 Hillside Rd., Barryville, NY 12719
Tel: 845-557-8353
Fax: 845-557-6603
E-mail: newhopemnr@aol.com
Web site: www.newhopemanor.org
See listing in the Miscellaneous section for further details.

Bronx

Archdiocese of New York

Angela House, Inc.
3323 Steuben Ave., Bronx, NY 10467
Tel: 718-231-7592
Fax: 718-231-9487
A transitional residence for homeless women and their young children.

Convent of the Sisters Servants of Mary S.M.
3305 Country Club Rd., Bronx, NY 10465-1296
Tel: 718-829-0428
Fax: 718-829-2346
Mission: Private nursing in the homes.

Kolping-on-Concourse
2916 Grand Concourse, Bronx, NY 10458
Tel: 718-733-6119. (Catholic Kolping Society New York, Inc.)

Saint Dominic's Home - Prevention Program (ASTAAN)
2345 University Ave., Bronx, NY 10468
Tel: 718-584-4407
Fax: 718-584-4540
E-mail: annettet@stdominicshome.org
Web site: www.stdominicshome.org
Parent Aide Counseling Advocacy Information and Referral.

St. Joseph's School for the Deaf
1000 Hutchinson River Pkwy., Bronx, NY 10465
Tel: 718-828-9000; 718-828-1671
Fax: 718-792-6631
E-mail: PMartin@SJSDNY.org
(Birth to 14 years)

Brooklyn

Diocese of Brooklyn

**Bishop Francis J. Mugavero Center for Geriatric Care, Inc.*
155 Dean St., Brooklyn, NY 11217
Tel: 718-694-6700
Fax: 718-694-6710
Affiliated with Catholic Medical Centers.

Holy Family Home
1740 84th St., Brooklyn, NY 11214
Tel: 718-232-3666
Fax: 718-259-9180
E-mail: aschlossberg@sucmeny.org
Affiliated with Catholic Medical Center.

St. Jerome's Health Services Corp. dba Holy Family Home
1740 84th St., Brooklyn, NY 11214
Tel: 718-232-3666.

Buffalo

Diocese of Buffalo

St. Francis of Buffalo, Inc. (fka St. Francis Hospital)
34 Benwood Ave., Buffalo, NY 14214
Tel: 716-862-2500
Fax: 716-862-2505
E-mail: sperry@wnychs.org

The Franciscan Center, Inc.
1910 Seneca St., Buffalo, NY 14210-1842
Tel: 716-822-8017
Fax: 716-822-8537
Emergency and transitional shelters for adolescent males 16-20.

Nazareth Nursing Home
291 North St., Buffalo, NY 14201
Tel: 716-881-2323
Fax: 716-881-1578
E-mail: Dcrispel@chsbuffalo.org
Chapel attended by Oblate Fathers of Holy Angels Church.

Catskill

Diocese of Albany

St. Joseph's Villa Senior Living Services
38 Prospect Ave., Catskill, NY 12414
Tel: 518-943-5701
Fax: 518-943-5033
E-mail: carlasjv@mhcable.com
Web site: www.sjvadulthome.org
An Adult Care Facility for Men and Women, Adult Day Care Program, Respite.

Clifton Park

Diocese of Albany

Halfmoon Housing Development Fund Co., Inc. (dba Bishop Hubbard Senior Apartments)
54 Katherine Dr., Clifton Park, NY 12065
Tel: 518-383-2705
Fax: 518-383-6350
E-mail: jmsbhsa@aol.com
Web site: www.depaulhousing.com

Dunkirk

Diocese of Buffalo

St. Vincent's Home for the Aged
319 Washington Ave., Dunkirk, NY 14048
Tel: 716-366-2066
Fax: 716-366-0545
E-mail: dsmith@chsbuffalo.org
Catholic Charities of Buffalo, Inc.

Garrison

Archdiocese of New York

St. Christopher's Inn
P.O. Box 150, Garrison, NY 10524-0150
Tel: 914-424-3616
Fax: 914-424-3786
E-mail: bpalka@atonementfriars.org
Web site: atonementfriars.org
Temporary shelter for homeless men.

Glen Falls

Diocese of Albany

Wellsprings
93 Maple St., P.O. Box 406, Glens Falls, NY 12801
Tel: 518-745-8714
Fax: 518-792-3184
E-mail: info@wsprings.org
Web site: www.wsprings.org
A Program for Christian Members. Holistic Sabbatical/Renewal/Retreat Center.

Harrison

Archdiocese of New York

St. Vincent's Hospital and Medical Center Westchester Branch
275 North St., Harrison, NY 10528
Tel: 914-967-6500
Fax: 914-925-5157
Web site: www.svvmc.org
Psychiatric Hospital. Women Religious Program. Clergy Consultation Program. Services for pre/post-partum women. Inpatient and outpatient mental health and substance abuse services for adults, adolescents, children and their families. Sites in Harrison, Tuckahoe and Hawthorne. Services available in Spanish.

Jamaica

Diocese of Brooklyn

Msgr. James H. Fitzpatrick Pavilion for Skilled Nursing Care
152-11 89th Ave., Jamaica, NY 11432
Tel: 718-558-2800
Fax: 718-558-2476
St. Vincent's Catholic Medical Centers of NY.

Kenmore

Diocese of Buffalo

Kenmore Mercy Homes, Inc. (dba McAuley Residence)
Administrative Offices, 2950 Elmwood Ave., Kenmore, NY 14217
Tel: 716-447-6101
Fax: 716-447-6090
Sponsored by the Catholic Health System, Inc. Residential Health Care Facility.

Lackawanna

Diocese of Buffalo

Baker Victory Services
(formerly known as Baker Hall, Our Lady of Victory Infant Home, St. Joseph Orphanage and St. John's Protectory)
780 Ridge Rd., Lackawanna, NY 14218
Tel: 888-287-9986; 716-828-9500
Fax: 716-828-9526
E-mail: baker@buffnet.net
Web site: www.bakervictoryservices.org

Lake Placid

Diocese of Ogdensburg

Uihlein Mercy Center
420 Old Military Rd., Lake Placid, NY 12946
Tel: 518-523-2464
Fax: 518-523-1401
E-mail: mwilliams@muhc.org
Web site: muhc.org
Skilled Nursing Facility.

Millbrook

Archdiocese of New York

Cardinal Hayes Home for Children
St. Joseph Drive, P.O. Box CH, Millbrook, NY 12545
Tel: 845-677-6363
Fax: 845-677-6691
E-mail: fapers@cardinalhayeshome.org
Web site: www.cardinalhayeshome.org
Educational programs for multi-handicapped children. Residential care for developmentally disabled children and young adults.

Montrose

Archdiocese of New York

Kolping-on-Hudson
95 Montrose Point Rd., Montrose, NY 10548
Tel: 914-737-9547
(Catholic Kolping Society New York, Inc.

Nanuet

Archdiocese of New York

St. Agatha Home of the New York Foundling Hospital
135 Convent Rd., Nanuet, NY 10954
Tel: 914-623-3461
Ulster County Prevention. (Residential.) Refugee Assistance Program. Runaway Youth Program.

Nesconset

Diocese of Rockville Centre

Cleary Deaf Child Center, Inc.
301 Smithtown Blvd., Nesconset, NY 11767
Tel: 631-588-0530
Fax: 631-588-0016
E-mail: catherinef@clearyschool.org
Web site: www.clearyschool.org
Day School (Infants thru 21 years).

New York

Archdiocese of New York

St. Agnes' Residence
237 W. 74th St., New York, NY 10023
Tel: 212-874-1361
For students and working women.

Catholic Guardian Society
1011 First Ave., New York, NY 10022
Tel: 212-371-1000
Fax: 212-935-7820
E-mail: jfrei@catholicguard.org
Intermediate care facilities, individual residential alternatives and family support programs for mentally retarded, developmentally disabled adults. Group home program for boys and girls, ages 13-21 years agency operated boarding homes and adoption services for boys and girls ages 0-16 provides regular and therapeutic foster homes for boys and girls ages 0-21 and specialized foster homes for children with AIDS Child abuse and neglect prevention program Specialized group care programs for mother-child population and children with special needs.

Catholic Home Bureau
1011 First Ave., New York, NY 10022
Tel: 212-371-1000
Fax: 212-755-4110
E-mail: pgeorgini@chbureau.org ; 6269xx@dfa.state.ny.us.
Web site: www.catholichoicebureau.org

Centro Maria, Inc.
539 W. 54th St., New York, NY 10019
Tel: 212-581-5273
Fax: 212-307-5687
E-mail: cenmariany@mindspring.com
For young students and working women with children. Family day care program serves 352 yearly. Maternity Services Program provides free, confidential counseling, medical & shelter care to single married parents seeking help in planning for their unborn children. Toll-free hotline 1-800-592-HELP. Post Adoption Services for lower-income families.

Cor Mariae
c/o 1011 First Ave., Rm. 1130, New York, NY 10022
Tel: 212-371-1000, Ext. 2435.

Covenant House Under
21 460 W. 41st St., New York, NY 10036
Tel: 212-613-0300
Fax: 212-629-3756
E-mail: St.MarysRes72@aol.com
(Runaway and Homeless Youth.) For students and young working women.

The Dwelling Place
409 W. 40th St., New York, NY 10018
Tel: 212-564-7887
Fax: 212-695-3642
E-mail: thedwellingplace@juno.com
For homeless women.

Good Shepherd Services
305 7th Ave., 9th Fl., New York, NY 10001
Tel: 212-243-7070
Fax: 212-929-3412
E-mail: plomonaco@goodshepherds.org
Web site: www.goodshepherds.org
Provides foster care and adoption services (formerly McMahon Services for Children) and five residen-

tial programs for troubled adolescents, a training program for social service workers and a comprehensive range of neighborhood family services to individuals and youth from the South Brooklyn community. These services include educational support, employment, counseling, crisis intervention, literacy, and advocacy services.

Kateri Residence
150 Riverside Dr., New York, NY 10024-2201
Tel: 212-769-0744
Fax: 212-873-0658
E-mail: lbond@chcsnet.org
Web site: www.catholichealthcaresystem.org/kateri.
Skilled Nursing Care and/or Residential Health Care Facility for the Elderly.

Kolping Society of New York Men's Residence (Catholic Kolping Society New York, Inc.)
165 E. 88th St., New York, NY 10128
Tel: 212-369-6647
Fax: 212-987-5652
E-mail: residence@kolpingny.org
For young Catholic men.

New York Foundling Hospital for Pediatric, Medical and Rehabilitative Care, Inc.
590 Avenue of the Americas, New York, NY 10011
Tel: 646-459-3600
Fax: 646-459-3636
E-mail: patriciat@nyfoundling.org
Web site: www.nyfoundling.org
Sponsored by Sisters of Charity of St. Vincent de Paul of New York. (Children from Infancy to 21) Placement of dependent and neglected boys and girls ages birth-18 in foster and adoptive homes and agency-operated boarding homes. Three shelters serve 45 homeless women with 26 preschool Residence for formerly homeless senior women.

The Jeanne d'Arc Residence
253 W. 24th St., New York, NY 10011
Fax: 212-691-0257
E-mail: sramenke@yahoo.com
Women 18 to 40.

St. Joseph's Immigrant Home
425 W. 44th St., New York, NY 10036-4402
Tel: 212-246-5363.

The Leo House
332 W. 23rd St., New York, NY 10011
Tel: 212-929-1010
Fax: 212-366-6801
For the Clergy, Sisters & Laity.

St. Mary's Residence
225 E. 72nd St., New York, NY 10021
Tel: 212-249-6850
Fax: 212-249-4336

St. Rose's Home
71 Jackson St., New York, NY 10002
Tel: 212-677-8132
Fax: 212-982-3485
E-mail: maureendominican@verizon.net
Free home for incurable cancer patients.

Sacred Heart Residence
432 W. 20th St., New York, NY 10011
Tel: 212-929-5790
Fax: 212-924-0891
E-mail: sacredheartresidence@hotmail.com
Working or studying young ladies ages 19-29.

Terence Cardinal Cooke Health Care Center
1249 Fifth Ave., New York, NY 10029
Tel: 212-360-1000
Fax: 212-289-2739
E-mail: tcchcc@chcsnet.org
Web site: www.catholichealthcaresystem.org/tcc.
Skilled Nursing Facility AIDS Program. (See Special Hospitals Category for additional services offered from this Health Care Center.) Hospital for developmentally disabled.

North Greenbush

Diocese of Albany

S.J. Housing Development Fund Company, Inc.
50 Dana Ave., Wynantskill, NY 12198
Tel: 518-283-5690
Fax: 518-283-5893
Web site: www.depaulhousing.com
Nonprofit housing facility for elderly and handicapped persons of very low income.

Orchard Park

Diocese of Buffalo

W.N.Y. Catholic LongTerm Care, Inc. dba Father Baker Manor
6400 Powers Rd., Orchard Park, NY 14127
Tel: 716-667-0001
Fax: 716-667-0028
E-mail: bakermanor@aol.com
Nursing facility sponsored by the Catholic Health System, Inc.

Ossining

Archdiocese of New York

Dominican Sisters Family Health Services, Inc. (Central Services/Administration)
299 N. Highland Ave., Ossining, NY 10562
Tel: 914-941-1710
Fax: 914-941-0518
E-mail: VHanrahan@dsfhs.org
Web site: www.DominicanSistersFamilyHealthService.org; www.dsfhs.org
Community-based, certified, voluntary Home Health Agency and Long Term Home Health Care and AIDS Programs serving all of Westchester, Suffolk and the South Bronx.

Port Jefferson Station

Diocese of Rockville Centre

Maryhaven Center of Hope
Administrative Offices, 1010 Rte. 112, Port Jefferson Station, NY 11776
Tel: 631-474-4120
Fax: 631-474-4110
E-mail: LGrossman@maryhaven.org
Web site: www.maryhaven.org
Maryhaven provides services to approximately 2,000 mentally and physically challenged children and adults.

Rhinebeck

Archdiocese of New York

Astor Home for Children, The
6339 Mill St., P.O. Box 5005 , Rhinebeck, NY 12572-5005
Tel: 845-871-1000
Fax: 845-876-2020
E-mail: jmcguirk@astorservices.org
Residential Treatment Facility for severe emotionally disturbed-mentally ill boys and girls, ages 5-12.

Astor Learning Center, The
6339 Mill St., P.O. Box 5005, Rhinebeck, NY 12572-5005
Fax: 845-876-2020
E-mail: skeegan@astorservices.org
Web site: www.astorservices.org
The Astor Learning Center provides individualized special education for children with emotional disturbances in conjuction with the mental health services of the Residential Treatment programs. The ALC serves children between the ages of 5-11 at time of admission.

Rochester

Diocese of Rochester

St. Ann's Nursing Home Co., Inc.
1450 Portland Ave., Rochester, NY 14621
Tel: 585-697-6000
Fax: 585-342-9585
E-mail: info@stannscommunity.com
Web site: www.stannscommunity.com
(The Heritage)

Saranac Lake

Diocese of Ogdensburg

St. Joseph's Rehabilitation Center, Inc.
99 Glenwood Estates, P.O. Box 470, Saranac Lake, NY 12983
Tel: 518-891-3950; 518-891-4135
Fax: 518-891-3986
E-mail: stjoes@sjrcrehab.org
Web site: sjrcrehab.org
Alcoholism & Substance Abuse Rehab.

Slingerlands

Diocese of Albany

Marie-Rose Manor HDFCI, dba Marie Rose Manor
100 Marquis Dr., Slingerlands, NY 12159
Tel: 518-459-0204
Fax: 518-459-0527
E-mail: ldcmrmsva@aol.com
Web site: www.depaulhouseing.com
Senior Citizen and Handicapped Housing.

Spring Valley

Archdiocese of New York

Good Counsel / The Cardinal Cooke Residence
22 Linden Ave., Spring Valley, NY 10977
Tel: 800-723-8331; 845-356-0517
Fax: 845-356-4175
E-mail: cxbell@aol.com
Web site: goodcounselhomes.org
A program of Good Counsel in Hoboken, NJ, helping pregnant and single mothers with children. For information and intake referral, call 800-723-8331.

Staten Island

Archdiocese of New York

Pax Christi Hospice
355 Bard Ave., Staten Island, NY 10310
Tel: 718-876-1022
Fax: 718-876-1803
Hospice and Home Care Services for the terminally ill. Sisters of Charity Health Care System.

Syosset

Diocese of Rockville Centre

St. Mary's Children and Family Services
525 Convent Rd., Syosset, NY 11791-3864
Tel: 516-921-0808
Fax: 516-921-4542
E-mail: stmlg@cs.com
Web site: stmaryscfs.com
Residential treatment center, non-secure detention, group homes, supervised independent living apartments, foster boarding homes, diagnostic assessment prog., preventive svc. prog. in Nassau Co. and Queens. Residential treatment facility for mentally ill children. Abuse treatment & prevention program, hard to place (JD) program for males.

Syracuse

Diocese of Syracuse

L'Arche
1232 Teall Ave., Syracuse, NY 13206
Tel: 315-479-8088
Fax: 315-479-8118
E-mail: larchesyracuse@aol.com
Web site: www.larchesyracuse.com
Homes at 1701 James St., 1226 Butternut St., 1240-42 Teall Ave., Syracuse, 140 Highland Ave., Syracuse.

Loretto Rest, Inc.
750 E. Brighton Ave., Syracuse, NY 13205
Tel: 315-469-5061
Adult Home.

Tupper Lake

Diocese of Ogdensburg

Mercy Healthcare Center, Inc.
114 Wawbeek Ave., Tupper Lake, NY 12986
Tel: 518-359-3355
Fax: 518-359-9044
E-mail: boreilly@muhc.org
Web site: muhc.org
Skilled Nursing Facility.

Warwick

Archdiocese of New York

Villa Frances at the Knolls
22 Van Duzer Pl., Warwick, NY 10990
Tel: 914-987-5717
Fax: 914-986-1231
Franciscan Health Partner, Inc.

West Islip

Diocese of Rockville Centre

Our Lady of Consolation Nursing & Rehabilitative Care Center
111 Beach Dr., West Islip, NY 11795
Tel: 631-587-1600
Fax: 631-587-5960
Web site: www.olc.chsli.org
Member of Catholic Health Services of LI. Conducted in the tradition of the Sisters of St. Dominic.

Williamsville

Diocese of Buffalo

St. Francis of Williamsville
147 Reist St., Williamsville, NY 14221
Tel: 716-633-5400
Fax: 716-663-6404
E-mail: rzito@chsbuffalo.org
Skilled Nursing Facility.

NORTH CAROLINA

Belmont

Diocese of Charlotte

* *Holy Angels, Inc.*
6600 Wilkinson Blvd., P.O. Box 710, Belmont, NC 28012
Tel: 704-825-4161
Fax: 704-825-0553
E-mail: info@holyangelsnc.org
Web site: www.holyangelsnc.org
Residential and developmental programs and services for children and adults with mental retardation and physical disabilities.

NORTH DAKOTA

Bismarck

Diocese of Bismarck

Emmaus Place
1020 N. 26th St., Bismarck, ND 58501
Tel: 701-258-2618
Priests retirement home.

Dickinson

Diocese of Bismarck

St. Benedict's Health Center
851 Fourth Ave. E., Dickinson, ND 58601
Tel: 701-456-7242
Fax: 701-456-7250
E-mail: Jon.frantsvog@bhshealth.org
Web site: www.stbens.org
Operated by Benedictine Living Communities, Inc.

Ellendale

Diocese of Fargo

Prince of Peace Care Center
201 8th St. N., Ellendale, ND 58436
Tel: 701-349-3312
Fax: 701-349-3944

Fargo

Diocese of Fargo

Villa Nazareth dba Friendship, Inc.
801 Page Dr., Fargo, ND 58103
Tel: 701-235-8217
Fax: 701-235-7538
E-mail: jeffpederson@catholichealth.net
A community-based facility providing an array of residential, vocational, educational, social and clinical services for children and adults with mental retardation and other developmental disabilities.

Garrison

Diocese of Bismarck

Benedictine Living Center of Garrison fka Garrison Nursing Center
609 4th Ave., N.E., P.O. Box 219, Garrison, ND 58540
Tel: 701-463-2226
Fax: 701-463-2650
E-mail: scott.foss@bhshealth.org
Operated by Benedictine Health System Long Term Care, Inc.

La Moure

Diocese of Fargo

St. Rose Care Center
315 1st St., S.E., La Moure, ND 58458
Tel: 701-883-5363
Fax: 701-883-5711
E-mail: tony-hanson@bhshealth.org
Operated by Benedictine Living Communities, Inc.

Wahpeton

Diocese of Fargo

St. Catherine's Living Center
1307 N. Seventh St., Wahpeton, ND 58075
Tel: 701-642-6667
Fax: 701-642-2485

OHIO

Centerville

Archdiocese of Cincinnati

St. Leonard
8100 Clyo Rd., Centerville, OH 45458
Tel: 937-433-0480
Fax: 937-439-7165
E-mail: horvathe@stleonard.net
Web site: www.stleonard.net
A facility of the Franciscan Services Corporation, sponsored by the Sisters of St. Francis, Sylvania, OH. A residence for Senior Citizens.

Cincinnati

Archdiocese of Cincinnati

St. Aloysius Orphanage
4721 Reading Rd., Cincinnati, OH 45237
Tel: 513-242-7600
Fax: 513-242-2845
E-mail: pgoulet@staloysiuscincinnati.org
Web site: www.staloysiuscincinnati.org
Crisis group home girls/boys ages 5-17.

St. Joseph Orphanage
5400 Edalbert Dr., Cincinnati, OH 45239-7695
Tel: 513-741-3100
Fax: 513-741-5656
E-mail: sjo@one.net
Web site: www.stjosephorphanage.org
Archdiocesan Children's Residential Center.

Sisters of Charity Senior Care Corp., dba Bayley Place
990 Bayley Place Dr., Cincinnati, OH 45233
Tel: 513-347-5500
Fax: 513-347-5553
E-mail: bayleyplace@srcharitycinti.org
Web site: www.bayleyplace.org
Also includes Eldermount Adult Day Program and The Village at Bayley Place.

Cleveland

Diocese of Cleveland

St. Augustine Manor
7801 Detroit Ave., Cleveland, OH 44102
Tel: 216-634-7400
Fax: 216-634-7483
E-mail: pgareau@st-aug.org
Web site: www.staugustinemanor.org
Affiliated with Catholic Charities. Provider of rehabilitation services, subacute care, skilled nursing, assisted living and child day care.

Christ Child - DePaul Day Care Center
2320 E. 24th St., Cleveland, OH 44115
Tel: 216-687-0017
Fax: 216-687-0403
E-mail: depaul@dioceseofcleveland.org
Day Care program sponsored by Catholic Charities Services Corp. Funded by United Way & Catholic Charities.

Holy Family Home
6707 State Rd., Cleveland, OH 44134
Tel: 440-885-3100
Fax: 440-885-0644
E-mail: donations@holyfamilyhome.com
Web site: www.holyfamilyhome.com
Free nursing home for terminal cancer patients who are unable to pay. Administered by Dominican Sisters of the Third Order, Congregation of St. Rose of Lima.

Jennings Center for Older Adults
10204 Granger Rd., Cleveland, OH 44125
Tel: 216-581-2900
Fax: 216-581-1517; 216-581-4505
E-mail: martha.kutik@jenningscenter.org
Web site: jenningscenter.org
Continuum of Services Campus for older adults, including a skilled nursing facility independent, congregate and assisted living apartments, an adult day center, and intergenerational child day care center for 75 children. Under the sponsorship of the Sisters of the Holy Spirit.

Mount St. Joseph
21800 Chardon Rd., Cleveland, OH 44117
Tel: 216-531-7426
Fax: 216-531-4033
E-mail: mountstjoe@aol.com
Conducted by Sisters of St. Joseph of St. Mark - Mount St. Joseph.

Dayton

Archdiocese of Cincinnati

The Maria Joseph Living Care Center
4830 Salem Ave., Dayton, OH 45416
Tel: 937-278-2692
Fax: 937-278-9016
E-mail: mariajoseph@mariajoseph.org
Web site: www.mariajoseph.org
Skilled Nursing-Intermediate Nursing Independent Living, Alzheimer's Unit, Skilled Rehab.

Mercy Siena Springs
6215 N. Main St., Dayton, OH 45415
Tel: 937-279-6114
Fax: 937-279-6870
Apartments, Independent Living for the Elderly.

Mercy Siena Woods
6125 N. Main St., Dayton, OH 45415
Tel: 937-278-8211
Fax: 937-278-8046
E-mail: shayes@health-partners.org
Nursing Home, nonsectarian. A member of Catholic Healthcare Partners. Specialized Alzheimer's Center, Skilled Nursing Center. Assisted living and Independent Cottages. Sponsored by the Religious Sisters of Mercy. 58 years of ministry.

Green Springs

Diocese of Toledo

St. Francis Health Care Centre
401 N. Broadway St., Green Springs, OH 44836
Tel: 419-639-2626
Fax: 419-639-6225
E-mail: jsmith@sfhcc.org
Web site: www.sfhcc.org
Operated by Franciscan Sisters of Our Lady of Perpetual Help of Ohio Corp.

Hamilton

Archdiocese of Cincinnati

Mercy Franciscan Senior Health and Housing Services, Inc. dba Mercy Franciscan at Schroder
1302 Millville Ave., Hamilton, OH 45013
Tel: 513-867-1300
Fax: 513-867-1415
Web site: www.e-mercy.com
A Facility of the Mercy Health Partners. Sponsored by the Catholic Healthcare Partners. Special unit for Alzheimer Treatment.

Hubbard

Diocese of Youngstown

Villa Maria Teresa
50 Warner Rd., Hubbard, OH 44425
Tel: 330-759-9329; 330-875-4635
Fax: 330-759-7290
E-mail: jcoblate@aol.com
Web site: www.oblatesister.org
Retired Priests' Residence.

Louisville

Diocese of Youngstown

Emmaus House
1515 California Ave., Louisville, OH 44641
Tel: 330-875-4635
E-mail: rsacred@neo.rr.com

North Lima

Diocese of Youngstown

The Assumption Village
9800 Market St., North Lima, OH 44452
Tel: 330-549-0740
Fax: 330-549-701
Member: Catholic Healthcare Partners. Skilled Nursing Unit with Subacute Care Program. Special Care Unit for residents with Alzheimer's or Dementia Skilled Nursing Unit with Subacute Care Program Intermediate Care. Special Care Unit for residents with Alzheimer's or cognitive impairment.

Parma

Diocese of Cleveland

CCSC/Parmadale
6753 State Rd., Parma, OH 44134
Tel: 440-845-7700
Fax: 440-845-5910
E-mail: pdale@dioceseofcleveland.org
Web site: www.clevelandcatholiccharities.com
Specialized Residential Services Intensive Treatment Services Partial Hospitalization Community Flexible Clinical Response Specialized Foster Care Whole Family Treatment In-Home Services Outpatient Services Day Care Training and Consultation Services and Volunteer Program Adoption Services Head Start.

Richfield

Diocese of Cleveland

Regina Health Center
5232 Broadview Rd., Richfield, OH 44286-9608
Tel: 330-659-4161
Fax: 330-659-5113
E-mail: bflannery@reginahealthcenter.org
Sponsored by Sisters of Charity of St. Augustine.

Warren

Metropolitan Archeparchy of Pittsburgh, Byzantine

Infant of Prague Manor
169 Kenmore, N.E., Warren, OH 44483
Tel: 330-372-4700
Fax: 330-372-5965
E-mail: smm@netdotcomcom
Web site: www.stspeterandpaulbyz.org
Housing for the elderly.

Youngstown

Diocese of Youngstown

Beatitude House
287 Lora Ave., Youngstown, OH 44504
Tel: 330-744-3147
Fax: 330-744-3991
E-mail: beatitudehouse@juno.com
Web site: www.beatitudehouseonline.org
Transitional housing, job preparation, job training, counseling, education and case management for economically disadvantaged women.

OKLAHOMA

Oklahoma City

Archdiocese of Oklahoma City

Trinity Gardens Apartments
1501 N. Classen Blvd., Oklahoma City, OK 73106
Tel: 405-523-3000
58 low income apartments for senior citizens.

Villa Isenbart, Inc. c/o Catholic Charities
1501 Classen Blvd., Oklahoma City, OK 73106
E-mail: toconnor@catholiccharitiesok.org
40 Apartment Residences for Low-Income Elderly.

Bone and Joint Hospital
1111 North Dewey Ave., Oklahoma City, OK 73103
Tel: 405-272-9671
Fax: 405-552-9197
E-mail: cathy_mckinney@ssmhc.com
Web site: www.boneandjoint.com
A member of SSM Health Care.

Trinity Gardens Apartments
1501 N. Classen Blvd., Oklahoma City, OK 73106.
Fax: 405-523-3030
E-mail: toconnor@catholiccharitiesok.org
58 low income apartments for senior citizens.

Villa Isenbart, Inc. c/o Catholic Charities
1501 Classen Blvd., Oklahoma City, OK 73106
Tel: 405-523-3000
Fax: 405-523-3030
40 Apartment Residences for Low-Income Elderly.

Ponca City

Archdiocese of Oklahoma City

Westminster Village, Inc.
1601 Academy Rd., Ponca City, OK 74604
Tel: 580-762-0927
Fax: 580-762-0933
Continuum of Care for the Aged Via Christi Health System. Continuum of Care for the Aged.

Tulsa

Diocese of Tulsa

St. John Villas, Inc.
1923 S. Utica, Tulsa, OK 74104
Tel: 918-744-2180
Fax: 918-744-2716
Web site: www.stjohnhealthsystem.com/departments/seniorliving
Retirement Residence and Health Care Center for Intermediate Nursing Care.

OREGON

Beaverton

Archdiocese of Portland in Oregon

St. Mary's Home for Boys, Inc.
16535 S.W. Tualatin Valley Hwy., Beaverton, OR 97006
Tel: 503-649-5651
Fax: 503-649-7405
Residential & day treatment center for behaviorally & emotionally disturbed children.

Portland

Archdiocese of Portland in Oregon

St. Anthony Village (activity of St. Anthony Village Enterprise)
3560 S.E. 79th Ave., Portland, OR 97206
Tel: 503-775-4414
Fax: 503-771-9189
E-mail: mkellenbeck@villagesage.com
Web site: www.villagesage.com
Retirement village centered around Catholic parish. Independent and assisted living, Alzheimer's unit, activities director, gardens, interaction with neighbors.

* *Assumption Village (activity of St. Anthony Village Enterprise)*
9121 N. Burr, Portland, OR 97203
Tel: 503-283-5644
Fax: 503-283-5692
Retirement Village, Senior independent and assisted living, chapel with daily Mass multiple activities, gardens, intergenerational interaction with neighborhood and local social service agencies.

Mt. St. Joseph, Inc.
3060 S.E. Stark St., Portland, OR 97214-3099
Tel: 503-535-4700
Fax: 503-797-6702
Web site: www.mtstjoseph.org
Catholic Health Initiatives - Owner/Operator.

Pennsylvania

Diocese of Allentown

DeSales Service Works
2755 Station Ave., Center Valley, PA 18034
Tel: 610-282-1100, Ext. 2018
E-mail: lukefour18@hotmail.com
Web site: www.oblates.org
Membership are men and women at least 21 years of age, serving the urban poor in a selected placement for one year while living in a house community.

Ambler

Archdiocese of Philadelphia

St. Mary's Villa for Children and Families
701 Bethlehem Pk., P.O. Box 388, Ambler, PA 19002-0388
Tel: 215-643-7676
Fax: 215-542-9219
E-mail: fanning.rita@hfi-pgh.org
Web site: www.hfi.org
Provides services for dependent-neglected children with emotional problems 4-18 and their families.

Aston

Archdiocese of Philadelphia

Assisi House
600 Red Hill Rd., Aston, PA 19014
Tel: 215-459-8990
Fax: 610-558-5344
E-mail: JLAMANNA@osfPHILA.org
Home for retired Sisters of St. Francis of Philadelphia.

Audubon

Archdiocese of Philadelphia

St. Gabriel's Hall
Box 7280, Audubon, PA 19407-7280
Tel: 610-666-7970; 215-247-2776
Fax: 610-666-1479
E-mail: bromalloy@chs_adphila.org
Offers residential treatment for court-committed delinquent boys, ages 12-18.

Baden

Diocese of Pittsburgh

* *Villa St. Joseph of Baden, Inc.*
1030 State St., Baden, PA 15005
Tel: 724-869-6300
Fax: 724-869-6399
Purpose: to operate a 120 bed skilled/intermediate care licensed nursing home, striving to address not only medical needs, but to also maximize opportunities for physical activity, social interaction and Spiritual development - holistic care.

Bensalem

Archdiocese of Philadelphia

De La Salle Vocational Day Treatment Center
Box 344, Bensalem, PA 19020
Tel: 215-464-0344
Fax: 215-638-3767
A community based day treatment program for court-committed delinquent boys, ages 15-18.

St. Francis - St. Joseph Homes for Children
3400 Bristol Pike, Bensalem, PA 19020
Tel: 215-638-9310
Fax: 215-638-2498
E-mail: francisjoe2001@yahoo.com
Web site: sfsj.org
Provides residential treatment at 15 sites for boys, ages 9 to 21 also supervised living for boys 17 and older.

Bethlehem

Diocese of Allentown

Grace Mansion Assisted Living Residence of Holy Family Manor
1200 Spring St., Bethlehem, PA 18018
Tel: 610-865-6748
Fax: 610-997-8444
E-mail: kabruzzese@HRManor.com
Web site: www.hfmanor.com
Personal care/assisted living facility for 25 elderly.

Holy Family Manor
1200 Spring St., Bethlehem, PA 18018
Tel: 610-865-5595
Fax: 610-865-5866
E-mail: jpolaski@HFManor.com
Web site: www.hfmanor.com
Skilled and intermediate nursing care facility for the aged, chronically ill, or invalid.

Holy Family Apartments
330-338 13th Ave., Bethlehem, PA 18018
Tel: 610-866-4603
Fax: 610-866-1622
E-mail: hfabeth@nni.com
Catholic housing for the elderly.

Trexler Pavilion, Assisted Living Residence of Holy Family Manor
1220 Prospect Ave., Bethlehem, PA 18018
Tel: 610-868-7776

Fax: 610-865-7775
E-mail: kabruzzese@HFManor.com
Web site: www.hfmanor.com
Personal care/assisted living facility for 23 elderly.

Chester

Archdiocese of Philadelphia

Bernardine Center
2625 Ninth St., Chester, PA 19013
Tel: 610-497-3225
Fax: 610-497-3659
E-mail: bernardinecenter@hotmail.com
Web site: www.bernardinecenter.org
West Side Brunch, Emergency Food Cupboard, Supercupboard Program, Advocacy, Social Justice and Spirituality Education.

Danville

Diocese of Harrisburg

Holy Family Convent and Infirmary
One Montour St., Danville, PA 17821
Tel: 570-275-3141
Fax: 570-275-9511
Home for the Aged Sisters of Christian Charity.

Maria Hall
Maria Hall Dr., Danville, PA 17821
Tel: 570-275-1120
Fax: 570-275-1134
E-mail: sscmarhl@aol.com
Home for retired Sisters of SS. Cyril and Methodius.

Darby

Archdiocese of Philadelphia

St. Francis Country House
1412 Lansdowne Ave., Darby, PA 19023-1218
Tel: 610-461-6510
Fax: 610-461-3558
Opened June 30, 1913. Home for aged, infirm and convalescent priests of the Archdiocese of Philadelphia.

Little Flower Manor
1201 Springfield Rd., Darby, PA 19023
Tel: 610-534-6000
Fax: 610-534-6039
All Skilled Nursing Care.

Villa Saint Joseph
1436 Lansdowne Ave., Darby, PA 19023-1298
Tel: 610-586-8535
Fax: 610-586-2810
Home for aged, infirm and convalescent priests of the Archdiocese of Philadelphia.

Villa St. Teresa
1215 Springfield Rd., Darby, PA 19023
Tel: 610-583-0700
Fax: 610-583-5011
Residential.

Downingtown

Archdiocese of Philadelphia

Catholic Health Care Services-Villa Saint Martha
490 Manor Ave., Downingtown, PA 19335
Tel: 610-873-5300
Fax: 610-873-2855
E-mail: admissions.vsm@chs-adphila.org
Web site: www.vsm-phl.org
Independent Living, Assisted Living, Memory Support Assisted Living.

St. John Vianney Center
151 Woodbine Rd., Downingtown, PA 19335
Tel: 610-269-2600
Fax: 610-873-8028
Web site: sjvcenter.org
Center for Healing for Priests, Brothers, and Sisters.

Easton

Diocese of Allentown

Antonian Towers
2405 Hillside Ave., Easton, PA 18042
Tel: 610-258-2033
Fax: 610-258-6541
E-mail: antonian@nni.com
Catholic housing for the elderly.

Elverson

Archdiocese of Philadelphia

St. Mary of Providence Center
227 Isabella Rd., Elverson, PA 19520
Tel: 610-942-4166
Fax: 610-942-4259
E-mail: stmaryofprov@msn.com
Web site: stmaryofprov-pa.org
Residence for Senior Citizens. Center of Spirituality, Retreats and Days of Recollection.

Emsworth

Diocese of Pittsburgh

Holy Family Institute
8235 Ohio River Blvd., Emsworth, PA 15202
Tel: 412-766-4030
Fax: 412-766-5434
E-mail: schott.sandra@hfi-pgh.org
Web site: www.hfi-pgh.org
Holy Family Institute is committed to helping children, preserving families and strengthening communities by providing a network of services including in-home counseling, residential treatment, summer day camp, and out-patient mental health services. Holy Family provides special education and alternative education for grades K through 12. The Bellefonds Method serves K through 12 as well as the adult population. This method uses a technique of assessment and re-education for learning difficulties due to developmental disabilities, stroke, brain trauma or infection. Volunteer opportunities are also available at Holy Family Institute.

Greensburg

Diocese of Greensburg

Neumann House
2900 Seminary Dr., Greensburg, PA 15601
Tel: 724-834-7350
Fax: 724-834-7351
E-mail: jbertig@dioceseofgreensburg.org
Residence for retired Priests.

Holland

Archdiocese of Philadelphia

St. Joseph Home for the Aged
1182 Holland Rd., Holland, PA 18966
Tel: 215-357-5511
Fax: 215-357-1707
Personal Care and Licensed Nursing facility.

Huntingdon Valley

Archdiocese of Philadelphia

Redeemer Village - Redeemer Village II
1551 Huntingdon Pike, Huntingdon Valley, PA 19006
Tel: 215-947-8168
Web site: www.holyredeemer.com
Subsidiary of Holy Redeemer Health System. Low income housing for the elderly or handicapped, subsidized by HUD.

Levittown

Archdiocese of Philadelphia

Queen of the Universe Day Center
2477 Trenton Rd., Levittown, PA 19056
Tel: 215-945-6090
Fax: 215-945-7320
E-mail: qudcl@nni.com
Web site: www.qudaycenter.org
Mentally Retarded and Developmental Delay Students.

Merion Station

Archdiocese of Philadelphia

McAuley Convent
517 Montgomery Ave., Merion Station, PA 19066
Tel: 610-667-2775
Fax: 610-667-9650
Infirmary for Religious Sisters of Mercy.

New Brighton

Diocese of Pittsburgh

McGuire Memorial
2119 Mercer Rd., New Brighton, PA 15066-3437
Tel: 724-843-3400
Fax: 724-847-2004
E-mail: mcgm@mcguirememorial.org
Web site: www.mcguirememorial.org
Residential Facility- Intermediate Care for Developmentally Challenged.

Orwigsburg

Diocese of Allentown

Holy Family Adult Day Care at St. Francis Center
900 W. Market St., Orwigsburg, PA 17961
Tel: 570-366-2924
Fax: 570-366-2301
Day care for the elderly.

Holy Family Assisted Living Residence
900 W. Market St., Orwigsburg, PA 17961
Tel: 570-366-2912
Fax: 570-366-7781
Web site: www.hfmanor.com
Personal care/assisted living facility for 59 elderly of Holy Family Manor.

Philadelphia

Archdiocese of Philadelphia

St. Benedict Thrift Shop
437 W. Girard Ave., Philadelphia, PA 19122
Tel: 215-235-1848
A clothing and furniture thrift store operated by Franciscans.

Casa del Carmen
4400 N. Reese St., Philadelphia, PA 19140
Tel: 215-329-5660
Fax: 215-329-6722
Offers emergency crisis social services to the Spanish speaking community in Philadelphia and surrounding areas.

De La Salle-In-Towne Day Treatment Center
25 S. Van Pelt St., Philadelphia, PA 19103
Tel: 215-567-5500
Fax: 215-567-6922
E-mail: cguas@chs-adphila.org
A community based day treatment program for court-committed delinquent boys, ages 14-17.

Drueding Center / Project Rainbow
413 W. Master St., Philadelphia, PA 19122
Tel: 215-769-1931; 215-769-1830
Fax: 215-787-0999
E-mail: emarvel@holyredeemer.com
Web site: www.holyredeemer.com
Subsidiary of Holy Redeemer Health System. Provides transitional housing and support services for homeless women with children daycare is provided for the children.

St. Francis Inn
2441 Kensington Ave., Philadelphia, PA 19125
Tel: 215-423-5845
Fax: 215-423-2289
Hot meals for the poor.

St. Gabriel's System
Administrative Offices, 117 S. 17th St., Ste. 1701, Philadelphia, PA 19103
Tel: 215-665-8777
Fax: 215-665-8821
E-mail: br.dmalloy@chs-adphila.org
Administrative and Intake services for residential treatment Group Home care and Day Treatment for Court-committed delinquent boys, ages 12-17. (See St. Gabriel's Hall, De LaSalle in Towne, De LaSalle Vocational and De LaSalle Aftercare and Brother Rousseau Academy).

* *Holy Redeemer Home Health & Hospice Services*
12265 Townsend Rd., Ste. 400, Philadelphia, PA 19154
Tel: 215-671-9200
Fax: 215-671-1950
Web site: www.holyredeemer.com
Medicare certified home health agency serving patients in their own homes Medicare certified hospice program serving terminally ill patients and their families. *Holy Redeemer Support Services. Subsidiary of Holy Redeemer Health System, Inc. Sponsor: Sisters of the Holy Redeemer.

St. Ignatius Nursing Home
4401 Haverford Ave., Philadelphia, PA 19104
Tel: 215-349-8800
Fax: 215-222-3078
E-mail: smagatha@stignatiusnursinghome.org
Attended from St. Ignatius Church.

Immaculate Mary Home
2990 Holme Ave., Philadelphia, PA 19136-1829
Tel: 215-335-2100
Fax: 215-331-1016
E-mail: admin.imn@erols.com
Web site: IMH-PHL.org
Opened March 1976.

St. John's Hospice for Men
1221 Race St., Philadelphia, PA 19107
Tel: 215-563-7763
Fax: 215-563-0108
Web site: www.saintjohnshospice.org
Staffed by Catholic Social Services Archdiocese of Philadelphia.

St. Joseph Catholic Home for Children
5238 N. Broad St., Philadelphia, PA 19141
Tel: 215-324-2610
Fax: 215-457-8240
E-mail: knorris@chs-adphila.org
E-mail: srlouise@adphila .org
Provides Therapeutic Group Home Care Maternity Home Care Mother/Baby Residential Care. Mental Health services available on site for all residents.

Mercy Hospice
334 S. 13th St., Philadelphia, PA 19107
Tel: 215-545-5153
Fax: 215-545-1872
Provides temporary and extended shelter care, hot meals, clothing, casework and referral services to homeless and transient women and women with children.

Mount Nazareth
2755 Holme Ave., Philadelphia, PA 19152
Tel: 215-338-8992
Fax: 215-338-8752
Home for retired and infirm sisters.

Our Lady of Confidence Day School
314 N. Easton Rd., Willow Grove, PA 19090-2506
Tel: 215-276-2300
E-mail: APConf01@nni.com
Web site: www.ourladyofconfidence.com/
Mentally Handicapped.

Sacred Heart Free Home for Incurable Cancer
1315 W. Hunting Park Ave., Philadelphia, PA 19140
Tel: 215-329-3222
Fax: 215-329-4197
E-mail: sacredheartm@verizon.net
Opened April 27, 1930. Attended by Oblates of St. Francis de Sales.

St. Vincent's Home
7201 Milnor St., Philadelphia, PA 19135
Tel: 215-624-5600
Fax: 215-624-8355
E-mail: jlavoritano@chs-adphila.org
Provides Family Oriented residential care for children 6 mos.-16 years of age. Mother/baby/ for girls 12 to 21 years of age. Capacity - 12 mothers - 12 children. Residential program with 72 beds that provides comprehensive emergency shelter to over 300 boys and girls annually.

Women of Hope
251 N. Lawrence St., Philadelphia, PA 19106
Tel: 215-592-9116
Fax: 215-592-0650
Residential facility for chronically mentally ill homeless women.

Pittsburgh

Diocese of Pittsburgh

St. Anthony School Programs
2718 Custer Ave., Pittsburgh, PA 15227
Tel: 412-882-1333
Fax: 412-882-1668
E-mail: anthcoo@nauticomnet
Resource rooms for students with special needs in 7 elementary schools and 2 high schools.

The De Paul Institute
6202 Alder St., Pittsburgh, PA 15206
Tel: 412-924-1012
Fax: 412-924-1036
E-mail: vp@depaulinst.com
Web site: www.depaulinst.com
Auditory day school for children with hearing, speech and language impairments.

Marian Hall Home, Inc.
934 Forest Ave., Pittsburgh, PA 15202-1118
Tel: 412-761-1999
Fax: 412-761-2556
E-mail: marian@sgi.net
Purpose: to provide programs, facilities, and services, including, but not limited to, residential personal care, and long-term care homes for the elderly, ill, or disabled, including supportive services.

Mt. Alvernia Day Care & Learning Center
146 Hawthorne Rd., Pittsburgh, PA 15209
Tel: 412-821-4302
Fax: 412-821-3318
Web site: www.millvaleFranciscans.org
Provides infant, toddler, and preschool care as well as before- and after-school care for school age children.

St. Pius X Residence, Inc.
2681 Waddington Ave., Pittsburgh, PA 15226
Tel: 412-563-5040
Fax: 412-563-3776
(Affiliate of Pittsburgh Mercy Health System)

Vincentian Child Care, Inc.
8200 McKnight Rd., Pittsburgh, PA 15237
Tel: 412-366-8588
Fax: 412-366-7315
E-mail: sgeorgine@vincentiansrspgh.org
Web site: vincentiansrspgh.org/childcare/index.html
Purpose: to engage in educational activities operating a day care program to perform any lawful acts to effectuate purposes of this corporation and in this pursuit to apply funds or incomes exclusively for charitable, religious, scientific, literary, and educational purposes.

Vincentian de Marillac
5300 Stanton Ave., Pittsburgh, PA 15206
Tel: 412-361-2833
Fax: 412-361-2833
E-mail: atrzeciak@vcsdemarillac.org
Non-sectarian, skilled nursing home.

Pottsville

Diocese of Allentown

Queen of Peace Apartments
777 Water St., Pottsville, PA 17901
Tel: 570-628-4504
Fax: 570-628-4712
E-mail: qpeace@voicenet.com
Catholic housing for the elderly.

Reading

Diocese of Allentown

Queen of Angels Apartment
22 Rothermel St., Hyde Park , Reading, PA 19605
Tel: 610-921-3115
Fax: 610-921-8576
E-mail: qangels@voicenet.com

Rosemont

Archdiocese of Philadelphia

St. Edmond's Home for Children
320 S. Roberts Rd., Rosemont, PA 19010
Tel: 610-525-8800
Fax: 610-525-2693
Web site: cssmrserv.org
Licensed I.C.F./M.R. care for severely/profoundly impaired, physically handicapped boys and girls ages 2-21.

Saint Clair

Diocese of Allentown

Neumann Apartments
25 N. Nichols St., Saint Clair, PA 17970
Tel: 570-429-0699
Fax: 570-429-2368
Catholic housing for the elderly.

Springfield

Archdiocese of Philadelphia

Cardinal Krol Center
1799 S. Sproul Rd., Springfield, PA 19064
Tel: 610-543-3380
Fax: 610-544-1207
E-mail: fr.dweber@chs-adphila.org
Web site: www.cssmrserv.org
A residential facility for 131 mentally retarded male adults which provides an environment, both day and residential, that contributes to the individuals own growth and development by fulfilling their potential in the physical, mental, emotional, social, psychological, and spiritual areas of their lives.

Divine Providence Village
686 Old Marple Rd., Springfield, PA 19064
Tel: 610-328-7730
Fax: 610-544-1710
Care & specialized training for developmentally disabled females.

Don Guanella School
1797 S. Sproul Rd., Springfield, PA 19064-1195
Tel: 610-543-1418
Fax: 610-328-2136
E-mail: fr.dweber@chs-adphila.org
Web site: www.cssmrserv.org
Provides specialized care and residential treatment program for mentally retarded boys ages 6-21.

Upper Darby

Archdiocese of Philadelphia

St. Lucy Day School for Children with Visual Impairments
130 Hampden Rd., Upper Darby, PA 19082
Tel: 610-352-4555; 610-352-4550
Fax: 610-352-4582
E-mail: APLucy01@nni.com
Web site: www.stlucydayschool.org
Day school for children who are blind or visually impaired.

Ventnor

Archdiocese of Philadelphia

Villa St. Joseph by the Sea
114 S. Princeton Ave., Ventnor, PA 08406
Tel: 609-822-7184
Summer residence for aged, infirm, and convalescent priests of the Archdiocese of Philadelphia.

Warminster

Archdiocese of Philadelphia

Regina Coeli Residence for Priests
685 York Rd., Warminster, PA 18974
Tel: 215-441-4642
Home for retired priests of the Archdiocese of Philadelphia.

Wilkes-Barre

Diocese of Scranton

Little Flower Manor of the Diocese of Scranton
200 S. Meade St., Wilkes-Barre, PA 18702
Tel: 570-823-6131
Fax: 570-823-5171
E-mail: sjd@lfmstr.com
Conducted by the Carmelite Sisters for the Aged and Infirm.

Wynnewood

Archdiocese of Philadelphia

St. Katherine Day School
930 Bowman Ave., Wynnewood, PA 19096
Tel: 610-667-3958
Fax: 610-667-3625
E-mail: APKath01@nni.com
Children with Developmental Delay/Mental Retardation.

Yardley

Archdiocese of Philadelphia

D'Youville Manor
1750 Quarry Rd., Yardley, PA 19067
Tel: 215-579-1750
Fax: 215-579-3054
E-mail: dyouvillemanor@greynun.org
Web site: www.dyouvillemanor.org
Operated by Grey Nuns of the Sacred Heart. Assisted living retirement residence for the elderly.

PUERTO RICO

Bayamon

Archdiocese of San Juan, Puerto Rico

Hogar Del Nino
El Ave Maria BMS 239 P.O. Box 607061, Bayamon, PR 00960-7061
Tel: 787-797-2382; 787-279-3003
Fax: 787-799-1977
(For Abused Children)

Canovanas

Archdiocese of San Juan, Puerto Rico

Hogar Teresa Toda
P.O. Box 868, Canovanas, PR 00729
Tel: 787-886-2060
Fax: 787-886-2075
E-mail: htodapr@isla.net
Web site: www.teresatodapr.org
(For Girls)

Ponce

Diocese of Ponce, Puerto Rico

Residencia Santa Marta, Barrio Sabenetas
P.O. Box 242, Mercedita, Ponce, PR 00715
Tel: 787-840-7575
Fax: 787-840-1649
Home for Aged and Infirm.

Puerta De Tierra

Archdiocese of San Juan, Puerto Rico

Asylum For The Aged and Infirm
Stop 5, Puerta De Tierra, PR 00906-6571
Tel: 787-722-1331
Fax: 787-725-4308
(Hogar de la Providencia)

Rio Piedras

Archdiocese of San Juan, Puerto Rico

Centro N. Sra. de la Providencia
R.F.D. #2, Box 16T, Rio Piedras, PR 00928
Tel: 787-761-0273
Sisters of Notre Dame.

Centro Santa Luisa
Carretera 842, Camino Los Romeros km 1.9, Bo. Caimito, Rio Piedras, PR
Tel: 787-720-2764
Fax: 787-731-7795
E-mail: centrosantaluisa@yahoo.com
Web site: www.geocities.com/centrosantaluisa
(Day Care Center for the Elderly)

Hogar Carmelitano
Urb. San Martin, Rio Piedras, PR 00924
Tel: 787-769-6510; 787-769-3110
Fax: 787-768-1240
Julian Bengochea Final
(Elderly Retirement Hospice).

San Juan

Archdiocese of San Juan, Puerto Rico

Centro De Orientacion Vocacional Nuestra Senora del Consuelo Floral Park
20 C. Matienzo Citron, San Juan, PR 00919
Tel: 787-250-6323
Fax: 787-250-6323
E-mail: oblaheher@coqui.net
(Teenagers/Single Mothers)

Toa Alta

Archdiocese of San Juan, Puerto Rico

Hogar Santisima Trinidad
BMS 326 P.O. Box 607061, Bayamon, PR 00960-7061
Tel: 787-799-6208
Fax: 787-799-1977
(Drug Addiction Rehabilitation Home)

RHODE ISLAND

Cumberland

Diocese of Providence

Mount St. Rita Health Centre
15 Sumner Brown Rd., Cumberland, RI 02864
Tel: 401-333-6352
Fax: 401-333-1012
E-mail: mail@mountstrita.org
Web site: www.mountstrita.org
Licensed Nursing Home.

Newport

Diocese of Providence

St. Clare Home
309 Spring St., Newport, RI 02840
Tel: 401-849-3204
Fax: 401-849-5780
E-mail: mbdaigneault@stclarehome.com
Web site: stclarehome.com
Nursing Facility.

North Kingstown

Diocese of Providence

Scalabrini Villa
860 N. Quidnessett Rd., North Kingstown, RI 02852
Tel: 401-884-1802
Fax: 401-884-4727
E-mail: admin@scalabrinivilla.com
Web site: www.scalabrinivilla.com
Full Skilled Nursing Facility.

Providence

Diocese of Providence

Group Home for Adolescent Boys
1055 N. Main St., Providence, RI 02904
Tel: 401-351-7230
Fax: 401-421-0198
(Whitmarsh House)

St. Joseph Living Center
153 Dean St., Providence, RI 02903
Tel: 401-272-3335
Fax: 401-621-8604
Assisted and independent living and respite care facility, a division of St. Joseph Health Services of Rhode Island.

SOUTH DAKOTA

Sisseton

Diocese of Sioux Falls

Tekakwitha Nursing Center, Inc.
6 E. Chestnut, Sisseton, SD 57262
Tel: 698-698-7693
Fax: 605-698-3091
E-mail: tncceo@hotmail.com
Sub. of Benedictine Health System.
Owned and operated by: Benedictine Health System.

TENNESSEE

Memphis

Diocese of Memphis

St. Peter Villa
141 N. McLean, Memphis, TN 38104-2644
Tel: 901-276-2021
Fax: 901-725-3564
E-mail: kae@cathchar.org
Diocesan Nursing Home.

Signal Mountain

Diocese of Knoxville

Alexian Village Health Care Center
(1938)
100 James Blvd., Signal Mountain, TN 37377
Tel: 423-886-0338
Fax: 423-886-0470
E-mail: sfoote@abhses.com
Web site: www.alexianvillage.com
Licensed Skilled & Intermediate Care Nursing Home.

Alexian Village of Tennessee
100 James Blvd., Signal Mountain, TN 37377
Tel: 423-886-0100
Fax: 423-886-0470
E-mail: sfoote@abhses.com
Web site: www.alexianbrotherssoutheast.org
Life Care Residences and Nursing Home.

TEXAS

Arlington

Diocese of Fort Worth

Nuestro Hogar, Inc. Catholic Charities
709 Magnolia St., Arlington, TX 76012
Tel: 817-261-0608
E-mail: nuestrol@flash.net
Web site: www.ccdofw.org
65 unit apartment complex for the elderly and disabled.

Boerne

Archdiocese of San Antonio

Childrens' Inn
216 W. Highland Dr., Boerne, TX 78006
Tel: 830-249-9456
Fax: 830-249-3327
E-mail: childrensinn@netscape.net
Provides foster care for children with special needs in a holistic setting.

Brownsville

Diocese of Brownsville

Mother of Perpetual Help Nursing Home, Inc.
519 A East Madison St., Brownsville, TX 78520
Tel: 956-546-6745
Fax: 956-546-0711
E-mail: moph@sbcglobal.net
Owner: Sisters of the Holy Spirit and Mary Immaculate. Chapel attended from Immaculate Conception Cathedral.

Corpus Christi

Diocese of Corpus Christi

Villa Maria, Inc.
3146 Saratoga Blvd., Corpus Christi, TX 78415
Tel: 361-857-6171
Fax: 361-857-6173
Apartment complex for senior adults.

Crowley

Diocese of Fort Worth

St. Francis Village, Inc.
1 Chapel Plaza, Crowley, TX 76036
Tel: 817-292-5786
Fax: 817-294-2989
E-mail: deanamh@mindspring.com
Web site: www.saintfrancisvillage.com
Active Retirement village, on shores of Lake Benbrook near Fort Worth, for retirees and the elderly sponsored by Franciscan Tertiary Provinces Foundation & SFV, Inc. (Illinois).

Fort Worth

Diocese of Fort Worth

Catholic Charities, Inc.
2701 Burchill Rd. N., Fort Worth, TX 76105-3012
Tel: 817-534-0814
Fax: 817-535-8779
E-mail: webmaster@ccdofw.org
Web site: www.ccdofw.org
Provides direct financial and material assistance to families in financial crisis. An Independent Corporation Founded by the Diocese of Fort Worth.

Houston

Diocese of Galveston Houston

Casa de Esperanza, De Los Ninos, Inc.
Mailing Address: P.O. Box 66581, Houston, TX 77266
Tel: 713-529-0639
Fax: 713-529-9179
E-mail: casa@casahope.org
Web site: www.casahope.org
Homes for children in crisis situations, foster care, adoption.

Santa Maria Hostel
807 Paschall St., Houston, TX 77009
Tel: 713-228-0125
Fax: 713-222-0595
E-mail: cempey@hotmail.com
Web site: www.santamariahostel.org
Intensive residential treatment and outpatient services (substance abuse) for women ages 18 and above.

San Antonio

Archdiocese of San Antonio

Casa De Padres
8520 Cross Mountain Tr., P.O. Box 100, San Antonio, TX 78255
Tel: 830-698-0175
Fax: 830-698-0175
E-mail: jengberg@gvtc.com
Home for retired Priests of San Antonio.

St. Francis Nursing Home
630 W. Woodlawn, San Antonio, TX 78212
Tel: 210-736-3177
Fax: 210-783-2221
Home for the Aged and Convalescents.

Incarnate Word Retirement Community
4707 Broadway, San Antonio, TX 78209
E-mail: sftxnc@aol.com
Web site: www.IwRetire.org
For lay persons also.

Marianist Residence: Skilled Nursing
520 Fordham Ln., San Antonio, TX 78228-4821
Tel: 210-436-3771
Fax: 210-431-4240
E-mail: jaeckle@stmarytx.edu
Home for Infirm Marianist Brothers and Priests.

Oblate Madonna Residence
5722 Blanco Rd., San Antonio, TX 78216
Tel: 210-341-2350
Fax: 210-340-3732
E-mail: roblatemadonna@satx.rr.com
Home for retired Priests and Brothers.

Padua Place
80 Peter Baque Rd., San Antonio, TX 78209
Tel: 210-826-7721
Fax: 210-824-4554
E-mail: paduaplace@aol.com
Home for infirm and retired Priests and Brothers.

The South Texas Catholic Retirement Center, Inc.
11931 Radium Dr., San Antonio, TX 78216
Tel: 210-341-8884
Fax: 210-341-0271
Purpose: A collaborative effort of 16 Religious Congregations, men and women, to provide a facility for elderly religious and lay men and women who are economically disadvantaged.

Visitation House Ministries
945 W. Huisache, San Antonio, TX 78201
Tel: 210-735-6910
Fax: 210-738-8794
Web site: www.visitationhouseministries.org
A nonprofit corporation chartered under the laws of the State of Texas. Provides a transitional housing program for homeless women and children on a temporary basis.

Splendora

Diocese of Galveston Houston

Shalom Center, Inc.
13516 Morgan Dr., Splendora, TX 77372-3121
Tel: 281-399-0520
Fax: 281-399-3366
E-mail: sca@shalomcenterinc.org
Web site: www.shalomcenterinc.org
A residential treatment center for priests, brothers and sisters.

Stephenville

Diocese of Fort Worth

CASA Brendan & CASA II, Inc.
1300 Hyman, Stephenville, TX 76401
Tel: 254-965-6964
Fax: 254-968-3072
E-mail: casab@our-town.net
Web site: www.ccdofw.org
86 unit apartment complex for the elderly & handicapped.

Virginia

Lynchburg

Diocese of Richmond

McGurk House Apartments
2425 Tate Springs Rd., Lynchburg, VA 24501
Tel: 434-846-2425
Fax: 434-847-5046
E-mail: mcgurkhouse@lynchburg.net
Independent Living for adults 62 yrs. or older, or mobility impaired.

Norfolk

Diocese of Richmond

St. Mary's Home for Disabled Children
317 Chapel St., Norfolk, VA 23504
Tel: 757-622-2208
Fax: 757-627-5314
Long term care for multiply handicapped children birth to eleven years old.

Richmond

Diocese of Richmond

St. Joseph's Home for the Aged
1503 Michael Rd., Richmond, VA 23229
Tel: 804-288-6245
Fax: 804-288-8906
E-mail: msrichesp@earthlink.net
Attended by Rev. Donald F. Scales, O.S.B.

St. Joseph's Villa Housing Corp.
7700 Brook Rd., Richmond, VA 23227-1399
Tel: 804-553-3288
Fax: 804-553-3259
E-mail: sjvmail.net
Web site: www.stjosephsvilla.net
Apartments for adults with disabilities and the elderly.

Roanoke

Diocese of Richmond

DePaul Family Services, Inc.
5650 Hollins Rd., Roanoke, VA 24019
Tel: 540-265-8923
Fax: 540-265-7663
E-mail: info@DePaulFamilyServices.org
Web site: www.DePaulFamilyServices.org
Treatment Foster Care.

Sullivan House, Inc.
3333 Peter's Creek Rd., Roanoke, VA 24019
Tel: 540-563-4565
Fax: 540-362-2365
E-mail: jsink@csm.roacoxmail.com
7 units for very low income elderly.

Vermont

Burlington

Diocese of Burlington

St. Joseph's Home
243 N. Prospect St., Burlington, VT 05401
Tel: 802-864-0264
Fax: 802-864-5640
Managed by Vermont Catholic Charities.

Rutland

Diocese of Burlington

St. Joseph's Kervick Residence
131 Convent Ave., Rutland, VT 05701
Tel: 802-775-5133
Fax: 802-747-0617

Washington

Chehalis

Archdiocese of Seattle

Providence Place
350 S.E. Washington Ave., Chehalis, WA 98532
Tel: 360-740-8389
Fax: 360-740-6504
Sponsored by The Sisters of Providence.

Seattle

Archdiocese of Seattle

Providence Vincent House
1423 First Ave., Seattle, WA 98101
Tel: 206-682-9307
Fax: 206-682-0548

Spokane

Diocese of Spokane

St. Joseph Care Center
E. 17 Eighth Ave., Spokane, WA 99202
Tel: 509-474-5678
Fax: 509-455-4020
(A Nonprofit Corporation)

Tacoma

Archdiocese of Seattle

Franciscan Health System, Care Center at Tacoma
6220 S. Alaska, Tacoma, WA 98408
Tel: 253-473-2273
Fax: 253-475-2921
CHI-Catholic Health Initiatives.

Yakima

Diocese of Yakima

** The Gamelin Association-Providence House*
312 N. 4th St., Yakima, WA 98901-2459
Tel: 509-452-5017
Fax: 509-452-1947
E-mail: Dawn_Rodrigues@providence.org
Web site: www.providence.org/Long_Term_Care/Housing/e20ProvHouse.htm
Low income housing for elderly.

Wisconsin

Appleton

Diocese of Green Bay

Franciscan Care and Rehabilitation Center, Inc.
2915 N. Meade St., Appleton, WI 54911-1598
Tel: 920-831-8700
Fax: 920-731-3206
E-mail: nbassett@affinityhealth.org
Corporate Sponsors: Wheaton Franciscan Services, Inc. (Wheaton, IL) and Affinity Health System (Menasha, WI).

Baraboo

Diocese of Madison

St. Clare Meadows Care Center
1414 Jefferson St., Baraboo, WI 53913
Tel: 608-356-5764
Fax: 608-356-5441
Web site: www.stclare.com
Member of SSM Health Care.

Chippewa Falls

Diocese of La Crosse

Transitus House
1830 Wheaton St., Chippewa Falls, WI 54729
Tel: 715-723-1155
Fax: 715-723-1669
E-mail: transitu@discover-net.net
Web site: www.stjoeschipfalls.com
Transitional living facility for women recovering from chemical dependency.

Green Bay

Diocese of Green Bay

McClosky Program, Inc.
2560 Shawano Ave., P.O. Box 10357, Green Bay, WI 54313
Tel: 920-434-8208
Fax: 920-662-0047
A Community based residential facility for women 18 years old and over who are pregnant or in a crisis situation and in need of transitional supervision and guidance. Needs addressed are personal and family problems. Also, shelter offered during crisis or unemployment.

Greenfield

Archdiocese of Milwaukee

Clement Manor Health Center
3939 S. 92nd St., Greenfield, WI 53228
Tel: 414-321-1800
Fax: 414-546-7357
Web site: www.clementmanor.com
Corporate Title: Clement Manor, Inc.

Clement Manor Retirement Community
9339 W. Howard, Greenfield, WI 53228
Tel: 414-546-7374
Fax: 414-546-7357
Web site: www.clementmanor.com
Corporate Title: Clement Manor, Inc. Sponsored by the School Sisters of St. Francis.

Hillsboro

Diocese of La Crosse

St. Joseph's Nursing Home
400 Water St., P.O. Box 527, Hillsboro, WI 54634
Tel: 608-489-8000
Fax: 608-489-8187
E-mail: k.coblentz.stjoseph@mwt.net
Web site: stjhealthcare.org

Kenosha

Archdiocese of Milwaukee

St. Joseph's Home for the Aged
9244 29th Ave., Kenosha, WI 53143
Tel: 262-694-0080
Fax: 262-694-7325
E-mail: st.josephs1@wi.rr.com
Web site: www.stjosephs.com
St. Joseph's Villa, Independent living units. Corporate Title: Carmelite Sisters of the Divine Heart of Jesus.

La Crosse

Diocese of La Crosse

St. Joseph's Nursing Home
2902 East Ave. S., La Crosse, WI 54601
Tel: 608-788-9870
Fax: 608-788-7373
Operated by Catholic Residential Services, Inc., Diocese of La Crosse.

Madison

Diocese of Madison

St. Marys Care Center
1347 Fish Hatchery Rd., Madison, WI 53715
Tel: 608-257-0781
Fax: 608-257-9420
Member of SSM Health Care.

Merrill

Diocese of Superior

Bell Tower Residence, Inc.
1500 O'Day St., Merrill, WI 54452
Tel: 715-536-5575
Fax: 715-536-1765
E-mail: dives@belltowerresidence.org
Web site: www.belltowerresidence.org
Residence for the elderly.

Milwaukee

Archdiocese of Milwaukee

* *Milwaukee Catholic Home*
2462 N. Prospect Ave., Milwaukee, WI 53211-4462.
Fax: 414-224-1666
Corporate Title: Milwaukee Catholic Home, Inc.

Daystar, Inc.
P.O. Box 2130, Milwaukee, WI 53201-2130
Tel: 414-385-0334
Fax: 414-385-0336
E-mail: daystar@daystarinc.org
Transitional living program for formerly battered women without children, for up to two years.

Alexian Village of Milwaukee, Inc.
9301 N. 76th St., Milwaukee, WI 53223
Web site: www.alexianvillage.org
Continuing Care Retirement Community.

Milwaukee

Archdiocese of Milwaukee

Alexian Village of Milwaukee, Inc.
9301 N. 76th St., Milwaukee, WI 53223
Tel: 414-355-9300
Fax: 414-357-5106
E-mail: gmohn@abhses.com
Continuing Care Retirement Community.

Daystar, Inc.
P.O. Box 2130, Milwaukee, WI 53201-2130
Web site: www.daystarinc.org
Transitional living program for formerly battered women without children, for up to two years.

* *Milwaukee Catholic Home*
2462 N. Prospect Ave., Milwaukee, WI 53211-4462
Tel: 414-224-9700
E-mail: info@milwaukeecatholichome.org
Web site: milwaukeecatholichome.org
Corporate Title: Milwaukee Catholic Home, Inc.

Rosalie Manor Community & Family Services, Inc.
4803 W. Burleigh St., Milwaukee, WI 53210
Tel: 414-449-2868
Fax: 414-449-2870
E-mail: rosaliemanor@aeronet.
Web site: www.rosaliemanor.org
Sponsored by the Archdiocese of Milwaukee.

Sacred Heart Rehabilitation Institute, Inc.
2350 N. Lake Dr., Milwaukee, WI 53211
Tel: 414-298-6700
Fax: 414-298-6712
Ascension Health System.

The Terrace at St. Francis, Inc.
3200 S. 20th St., Milwaukee, WI 53215
Tel: 414-389-3200
Fax: 414-389-3300
Skilled Nursing Facility for Transitional & Extended Subacute Care.

Villa St. Francis, Inc.
1910 W. Ohio Ave., Milwaukee, WI 53215
Tel: 414-649-2888
Fax: 414-649-2880
Web site: www.villastfrancis.org
Independent & Assisted Living Facility.

Mount Calvary

Archdiocese of Milwaukee

Cristo Rey Ranch, Inc.
N8102 Calvary St., Mount Calvary, WI 53057
Tel: 920-753-3211; 920-753-2026
Fax: 920-753-3100
Provides weekend respite services to families caring for emotionally/behaviorally challenged children and adolescents. Program emphasis on pet therapy. Some day and evening programs thru County Social Services Department.

Neenah

Diocese of Green Bay

Assisi Homes of Neenah, Inc.
210 Byrd Ave., Neenah, WI 54956
Web site: www.wfs-inc.org
(An independent living community for Seniors.)

Villa St. Clare, Inc.
130 Byrd Ave., Neenah, WI 54946
Tel: 920-722-5100
Fax: 920-722-5171
Web site: www.wfs-inc.org
Special care facility, affordable housing with supportive accommodations in an independent setting for seniors 55+.

Niagara

Diocese of Green Bay

Maryhill Manor (SNF)
501 Madison Ave., Niagara, WI 54151
Tel: 715-251-3172
Fax: 715-251-1200
E-mail: maryhill@netnet.net
Sponsored by School Srs. of St. Francis, Milwaukee.

Oshkosh

Diocese of Green Bay

The Convent Project, Inc.
449 High Ave., Oshkosh, WI 54901
Tel: 920-233-1894
E-mail: bbalzerl@new.rr.com
For victims of domestic abuse.

Portage

Diocese of Madison

Divine Savior Nursing Home
2817 New Pinery Rd., P.O. Box 387, Portage, WI 53901
Tel: 608-742-4131
Fax: 608-742-3463
(See Divine Savior Hospital, Portage.)

Racine

Archdiocese of Milwaukee

St. Monica's Senior Citizens Home, Inc.
3920 N. Green Bay Rd., Racine, WI 53404
Tel: 262-639-5050
Fax: 262-639-5673
E-mail: srirene@clmail.com
Nonprofit Corp.

South Milwaukee

Archdiocese of Milwaukee

Franciscan Villa of South Milwaukee, Inc.
3601 S. Chicago Ave., South Milwaukee, WI 53172
Tel: 414-764-4100
Fax: 414-764-0706
E-mail: susangoelz@catholichealth.net
Web site: www.franciscanvilla.org
Catholic Health Initiatives

St. Francis

Archdiocese of Milwaukee

Canticle Court, Inc.
3201 S. Lake Dr., St. Francis, WI 53235
Tel: 414-744-9959
Fax: 414-744-7636
An Apartment building sponsored by the Sisters of St. Francis of Assisi funded by HUD for low income elderly persons who can live independently.

Juniper Court, Inc.
3209 S. Lake Dr., St. Francis, WI 53235-3702
Tel: 414-744-5878
Fax: 414-744-7636
E-mail: jcpres@seii.com
Sponsored by the Sisters of St. Francis of Assisi, St. Francis, WI. An apartment building with congregate meal site for persons of low to moderate income who can live independently.

Two Rivers

Diocese of Green Bay

Sisters Treatment Group Home
3904 Martin Ln., Two Rivers, WI 54241
Tel: 920-553-1524
Fax: 920-553-2442
For physically and mentally handicapped children.

Wausau

Diocese of La Crosse

Marywood Convalescent Center
1821 N. 4th Ave., Wausau, WI 54401
Tel: 715-675-9451
Fax: 715-675-9051
Operated by Catholic Residential Services, Inc.

Wauwatosa

Archdiocese of Milwaukee

St. Camillus Health Center, Inc.
10101 W. Wisconsin Ave., Wauwatosa, WI 53226
Tel: 414-258-1814
Fax: 414-259-4987
E-mail: rljohnson@stcam.com
Web site: www.stcam.com
Skilled Nursing Home.

San Camillo, Inc.
10200 W. Blue Mound Rd., Wauwatosa, WI 53226
Tel: 414-259-6300
Independent living facilities for older adults.

Woodruff

Diocese of Superior

Dr. Kate Newcomb Convalescent Center, Inc.
301 Elm St., P.O. Box 829, Woodruff, WI 54568
Tel: 715-356-8888
Fax: 715-356-8861
Sponsored by the Sisters of the Sorrowful Mother. Corporate Sponsor: Ministry Health Care, Inc. (Milwaukee, WI).

DIOCESAN & RELIGIOUS PRIESTS

eximious®

(eg-´zim-e-es), means...Distinguished, Unparalleled, Extraordinary.

Remarkable Paschal Candles

Extraordinary Paschal Candles, each made-to-order, mastercrafted with the finest beeswax formulation...individually benchworked and hand tooled to create splendid intricate inlays, rich onlays and classic sculptured engraving.

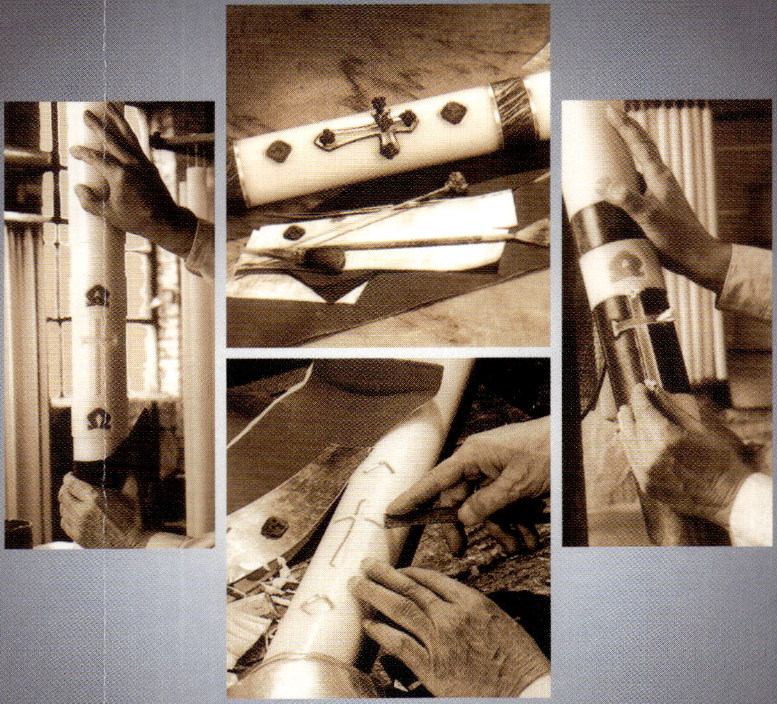

e x i m i o u s® Paschal Candle designs are unique and allow the candle decorators artistic talent to fingerprint each individual candle. No two candles are exactly alike and every candle is indeed, a work of art.

Contact Your Authorized Representative
For This Years Full Color
e x i m i o u s®
Paschal Candle Brochure.

An Alphabetical List of Diocesan and Religious Priests of the United States

REPORTED TO THE PUBLISHERS FOR THIS ISSUE
(Cardinals, Archbishops, Bishops, Archabbots and Abbots are listed in previous section)

ABBREVIATIONS

A.A.	Assumptionists
B.C.S.	Brothers of Christian Service
B.G.S.	Little Brothers of the Good Shepherd
B.S.O.	Basilian Salvatorian Fathers
C.F.A.	Alexian Brothers
C.F.C.	Congregation of Christian Brothers
C.F.M.M.	Brothers of Our Lady, Mother of Mercy
C.F.P.	Brothers of the Poor of St. Francis
C.F.R.	Franciscan Friars of the Renewal
C.F.X.	Brothers of St. Francis Xavier
C.I.C.M.	Missionhurst Congregation of the Immaculate Heart of Mary
C.J.	Josephite Fathers
C.J.M.	Congregation of Jesus and Mary
C.M.	Congregation of the Mission
C.M.C.	Congregation of Mother Coredemptrix
C.M.F.	Claretian Missionaries
C.M.I.	Carmelites of Mary Immaculate
C.M.L.M.	The Congregation of Maronite Lebanese Missionaries
C.M.M.	Congregation of Mananhill Missionaries, Marianhill Fathers & Brothers
C. M.Vd.	Mekhitarist Fathers
C.O.	Oratorians
C.P.	Congregation of the Passion
C.P.M.	Congregation of the Fathers of Mercy
C.PP.S.	Society of the Precious Blood
C.R.	Congregation of the Resurrection
C.R.	Theatine Fathers
C.R.I.C.	Canons Regular of the Immaculate Conception
C.R.L.	Canons Regular of the Lateran
C.R.M.	Adorno Fathers
C.R.S.	Somascan Fathers
C.R.S.P.	Clerics Regular of St. Paul
C.S.	Missionaries of St. Charles Scalabrinians
C.S.B.	Basilian Fathers
C.S.C.	Brothers of the Congregation of Holy Cross
C.S.C.	Priests of the Congregation of Holy Cross
C.S.J.	Congregation of St. Joseph
C.S.J.B.	Congregation of St. John the Baptist
C.S.P.	Paulist Fathers
C.S.P.X.	Brothers of Saint Pius X
C.S.S.	Stigmatine Fathers and Brothers.
C.S.Sp.	Congregation of the Holy Spirit
C.SS.R.	Redemptorist Fathers
C.S.V.	Clerics of St. Viator
D.L.P.	Diocesan Labor Priests
Er.Cam.	Camaldolese Hermits of the Congregation of Monte Corona
F.C.	Brothers of Charity
F.D.P.	Sons of Divine Providence
F.F.I.	Franciscan Friars of the Immaculate
F.F.S C.	Franciscan Brothers of the Holy Cross
F.I.C.	Brothers of Christian Instruction
F.J.	Congregation of St. John
F.M.M.	Brothers of Mercy
F.M.M.	Missionary Fraternity of Mary
F.M.S.	The Marist Brothers
F.M.S.I.	Sons of Mary Missionary Society
F.P.M.	Presentation Brothers
F.S.C.	Brothers of the Christian Schools
F.S.E.	Brothers of the Holy Eucharist
F.S.P.	Brothers of St. Patrick
F.S.R.	Brothers of the Congregation of Our Lady of the Holy Rosary
F.S.S.P.	Priestly Fraternity of St. Peter
G.H.M.	The Glenmary Home Missioners
H.J.D.	Los Hermanos de Juan Diego
H.M.C.	Hermits of Mount Carmel
I.C.	Institute of Charity
I.C.	Incarnational Consecration
I.H.M.	Brothers of the Immaculate Heart of Mary
I.M.C.	Consolata Missionaries
I.S.S.S.	Schoenstatt Institute of Secular Priests
L.B.S.F.	Little Brothers of Saint Francis
L.C.	Legionaries of Christ
M.Afr.	Missionaries of Africa
M.C.B.S.	Missionary Congregation of the Blessed Sacrament
M.C.C.J.	Comboni Missionaries of the Heart of Jesus (Verona)
M.Des.	Mercedarios Descalzos
M.E.P.	Paris Foreign Mission Society
M.G.	Guadalupe Missioners
M.H.M.	Mill Hill Missionaries
M.I.C.	Congregation of Marians of the Immaculate Conception
M.J.	Missionaries of St. Joseph (Mexico)
M.M.	Maryknoll
M.S.	The Missionaries of Our Lady of La Salette
M.S.A.	Missionaries of the Holy Apostles
M.S.C.	Missionaries of the Sacred Heart
M.S.F.	Congregation of the Missionaries of the Holy Family
M.S.P.	Missionaries of St. Paul
M.Sp.S.	Missionaries of the Holy Spirit
M.SS.CC.	Missionaries of the Sacred Hearts of Jesus and Mary
O.A.R.	Order of the Augustinian Recollects
O.Carm.	Carmelite Fathers and Brothers
O.Cart.	Order of Carthusians
O.C.D.	Discalced Carmelite Fathers
O.Cist.	Cistercian Fathers
O.C.S.O.	The Cistercian Order of the Strict Observance (Trappists)
O.de.M.	Order of Our Lady of Mercy
O.F.M.	Franciscan Friars
O.F.M-.Cap.	The Capuchin Friars
O.F.M-.Conv.	Conventual Franciscans
O.H.	Hospitaller Brothers of St. John of God
O.I.C.	Order of the Imitation of Christ
O.L P.	Brothers of Our Lady of Providence
O.M.	Minim Fathers
O.Mar.	Congregation of Maronite Monks
O.M.I.	Oblates of Mary Immaculate
O.M.V.	Oblates of the Virgin Mary
O.P.	Order of Preachers (Dominicans)
O.Praem.	Canons Regular of Premontre
O.R.C.	Operarios del Reina de Cristo
O.S.A.	The Augustinians
O.S.B.	Benedictine Monks
O.S.B-.Cam.	Camaldolese Hermits
O S.B.M.	Order of St. Basil the Great
O.S.C.	Canons Regular of the Order of the Holy Cross
O.S.Cam.	Camillian Fathers and Brothers
O.S.F.	Congregation of the Religious Brothers of the Third Order Regular of St. Francis
O.S.F.	Franciscan Brothers of Christ the King
O.S.F.	Franciscan Brothers of the Third Order Regular
O.S.F.	Franciscan Missionary Brothers of the Sacred Heart of Jesus
O.S.F.S.	Oblates of St. Francis de Sales
O.S.J.	Oblates of St. Joseph
O.S.M.	Servites
O.S-.P.P.E.	Pauline Fathers
O.Ss.S.	Brigittine Monks
O.SS.T.	Order of the Holy Trinity
P.I.M.E.	Pontifical Institute for Foreign Missions
R.C.J.	Rogationist Fathers
S.A.	Franciscan Friars of the Atonement
S.A.C.	Society of the Catholic Apostolate
S.C.	Brothers of the Sacred Heart
S.C.	Servants of Charity
S.Ch.	Society of Christ
Sch.P.	Piarist Fathers.
S.C.J.	Congregation of the Priests of the Sacred Heart
S.D.B.	Salesians of Don Bosco
S.D.S.	Society of the Divine Savior
S.D.V.	Vocationist Fathers
S.F.	Sons of the Holy Family
S.F.M.	Scarboro Foreign Missions
S.J.	Jesuit Fathers and Brothers
S.M.	Society of Mary (Marianists)
S.M.	Marist Fathers
S.M.A.	Society of African Missions
S.M.M.	Montfort Missionaries
S.M.P.	Society of Our Mother of Peace
S.O.Cist.	Cistercian Monks of the Strict Observance
S.O.L.T.	Society of Our Lady of the Most Holy Trinity
s.P.	Servants of the Paraclete
S.P.S.	St. Patrick Missionary Society
S.S.	Society of the Priests of Saint Sulpice
S.S.C.	Society of St. Columban
SS.CC.	Congregation of the Sacred Hearts of Jesus and Mary
S.S.E.	Society of Saint Edmund
S.S.J.	St. Joseph's Society of the Sacred Heart
S.S.P.	Pauline Fathers and Brothers
S.S.S.	Congregation of the Blessed Sacrament
S.S.T.	Missionary Society of St. Thomas the Apostle
S.T.	Missionary Servants of the Most Holy Trinity
S.V.D.	Society of the Divine Word
S.X.	Xaverian Missionary Fathers
T.O.R.	Third Order Regular of Saint Francis
V.C.	Vincentian Congregation (India)
V.D.C.	Verbum Dei Community

The letters in parentheses designate the diocese. See the "Diocesan Abbreviations". Letters in brackets designate categories in the Institution Section.

A

Aaron, Andrew '96 (BAL) Millersville, MD Our Lady of the Fields.

Aaron, James L. '54 (PIT) Pittsburgh, PA Most Holy Name of Jesus; Judges Retired.

Aaron, James (LEX) Associate Judges.

Aaron, Robert *o.m.i.* '72 (BEL)[H] Belleville, IL King's House Retreat and Renewal Center.

Aaron, Shawn *l.c.* '02 (LA)[Q] Pasadena, CA Legionaries of Christ.

Abad, Jose Antonio P. '82 (AGN) Tumon, GU Blessed Diego Luis de San Vitores Church.

Abadines, Allen '89 (MET) Martinsville, NJ Blessed Sacrament.

Abah, Joseph (WDC) Hyattsville, MD St. Jerome.

Abalon, Jose Amante '01 (NEW) Bloomfield, NJ Church of St. Thomas the Apostle.

Abalon, Jose M. (NEW) Secaucus, NJ Immaculate Conception.

Aban, Aristotle '83 (DAL) Bonham, TX St. Elizabeth; Bonham, TX Sam Rayburn Veterans Hospital; Dallas, TX St. Augustine Catholic Church.

Abano, Edgardo D. '85 (MET) Piscataway, NJ St. Frances Cabrini; Commission for the Filipino Apostolate.

Abara, Lawrence N. '78 (LAF) Chataignier LA Our Lady of Mount Carmel; Opelousas, LA St. Joseph.

Abarrategui, Leandro *o.f.m.* '54 (SJN) Carolina, PR Santa Clara de Asis.

Abarratelegui, Leanadro *o.f.m.* '68 (SJN).

Abas, Peter (ROC) Rochester, NY St. Anne.

Abata, Russell *c.ss.r.* '57 (NY)[EE] New York, NY Redemptorist Priests and Brothers, C.Ss.R..

Abaya, Francis '73 (NY) New York, NY St. Monica.

Abaya, Francisco (NY) Mount Sinai Medical Center.

Abbaticchio, Damian *o.s.b.* '45 (RIC) Virginia Beach, VA St. Gregory the Great.

Abbatiello, Robert *o.f.m.cap.* '90 (NOR) Middletown, CT St. Pius X.

Abbot, Kerry M. *o.f.m.conv.* (MO) Air Force Chaplains.

Abbott, Donald S. '73 (BO) South Boston, MA St. Augustine.

Abbott, Donald S. '73 (CHR) On Duty Outside the Diocese.

Abbott, Eugene J. '57 (STP) Retired.

Abbott, Kerry *o.f.m.conv.* '90 (MRY)[F] Arroyo Grande St. Joseph Cupertino Province, Provincial Center.
Abbott, Walter M. *s.j.* '56 (BO)[V] Weston, MA Campion Jesuit Community.
Abbott, William M. *s.j.* '72 (FgM).
Abdella, Peter *c.s.p.* '85 (OAK) Berkeley, CA Holy Spirit Parish/Newman Hall.
Abdoo, Louis *i.m.c.* '73 (SB) Riverside, CA St. Francis de Sales.
Abdulmasih, Youssef (OLD) North Hollywood, CA Sacred Heart Parish.
Abe, John Adam '84 (RIC) Staunton, VA St. Francis of Assisi.
Abel, Robert M. '73 (L) Payneville, KY St. Mary Magdalen of Pazzi; Payneville, KY St. Theresa.
Abelardo, Arnold M. *c.m.f.* '03 (LA) Los Angeles, CA Our Lady Queen of the Angels.
Abele, Alan Carl '73 (ANC) Retired.
Abele, Joseph P. '49 (GI) Retired.
Abell, Donald E. '76 (BEL) Eldorado, IL St. Mary; Elizabethtown, IL St. Joseph; Harrisburg, IL St. Mary.
Abell, Edward '67 (GAL)[A] Houston, TX St. Mary's Seminary.
Abella, Ray *o.s.f.s.* '93 (STO) Jamestown, CA Sierra Conservation Center.
Abels, Kevin P. '03 (BRK) Woodside, NY St. Sebastian.
Abercrombie, Jamie M. *c.s.b.* '73 (GAL) Angleton, TX Most Holy Trinity.
Abernathy, David *c.o.* (PIT)[Q] Pittsburgh, PA Carnegie–Mellon University; [Q] Pittsburgh, PA Chatham College; [Q] Pittsburgh, PA University of Pittsburgh.
Abernethy, David S. *c.o.* '94 (PIT)[N] Pittsburgh, PA Congregation of the Oratory of St. Philip Neri.
Abert, Richard P. *s.j.* '76 (MIL)[O] Milwaukee, WI Miguel Pro Jesuit Community; Minister to Priests.
Abgali, Anthony '95 (DET) Harper Hospital and Rehabilitation Center.
Abi–chedid, Elie '85 (SAM) Jacksonville, FL St. Maron Maronite.
Abi–Nader, Joseph '48 (SAM) Retired.
Abi–Sarkis, Elias '75 (OLL) Broken Arrow, OK St. Ephrem Mission.
Abiera, Fredric '03 (NY) Bronx, NY St. John's.
Ablahad, Najor '43 (EST) Retired.
Abler, Larry *o.f.m.* '66 (GB)[I] Appleton, WI St. Joseph Friary.
Abler, Lawrence E. *o.f.m.cap.* (GB) Appleton, WI St. Joseph.
Ablog, Frederico J.G. *s.s.s.* '90 (GAL) Houston, TX Corpus Christi; [K] Catholic Chaplain Corps, Texas Medical Center.
Abmayr, George J. *s.m.* '56 (CLV)[O] Cleveland, OH Marianist Community.
Aboh, Bede '88 (KNX)[D] Signal Mountain, TN Alexian Village of Tennessee.
Aboody, Charles '62 (NTN) Retired.
Aboody, Charles (NTN) Presbyteral Council.
Abosike, James (DEN) Northglenn, CO Immaculate Heart of Mary.
Abostino, Steven J. *s.j.* '93 (DET)[K] Detroit Jesuit Provincial Office–Detroit Province of the Society of Jesus.
Abraham, Benedict *s.a.c.* '65 (VEN) Sarasota, FL St. Martha.
Abraham, Chiu '90 (TR) Keansburg, NJ St. Ann.
Abraham, Johnson C. '88 (OAK) Newark, CA St. Edward's.
Abraham, Joseph '90 (RNO) Graduate Studies.
Abraham, Mathews '79 (CI) St. Francis Assisi.
Abraham, Mathews '79 (CI)[C] Tunnuk, Chuuk, FM Vicariate Residence.
Abraham, Philip *s.j.* '93 (MIL)[O] Milwaukee, WI Jesuit Community at Marquette University.
Abraham, Thomas J. '66 (LC) Hatley, WI St. Florian.
Abrahams, John J. '79 (BAL) Special Assignment.
Abrahim, Jirjis '67 (EST) Troy, MI St. Joseph Chaldean Parish.
Abrahim, Jirjis (EST) Eparchial College of Consultors.
Abramovic, Joseph M. *o.f.m.* '60 (STL) St. Louis, MO St. Joseph.
Abramowicz, Richard B. '86 (MET) Retired.
Abrams, John L. '51 (BRK)[V] Douglaston, NY Bishop Mugavero Residence Retired.
Abreau, Felix *c.s.sp.* (MO) Army National Guard Chaplains.
Abreu, John E. '74 (PRO) Warren, RI St. Thomas the Apostle.
Abruzzese, John A. '74 (BO) On Duty Outside the Archdiocese.
Absalon, Burt '01 (RCK) St. Charles, IL St. John Neumann.
Abts, John *o.f.m.* '90 (SAT) San Antonio, TX San Jose y San Miguel.
Abuan–Gaona, Antonio *m.s.* '84 (SB)[E] Moreno Valley, CA Missionaries of Our Lady of La Salette, MS.
Abucewicz, John A. '44 (BO) Senior Priests Retired.
Abugel, Alexander '80 (BRK) Flushing, NY Holy Family.
Aburto, Elias Juan Tello *o.s.b.* '01 (SFS)[F] Marvin, SD Blue Cloud Abbey.
Acaba, Jose A. '82 (ARE) Vega–Baja, PR Our Lady of Lourdes.
Acadinha, James M. '03 (BO) Woburn, MA St. Charles Borromeo.
Accardi, Joseph V. '90 (PH) Philadelphia, PA Maternity B.V.M..
Acciarito, Anthony '78 (BRK) On Leave/Unassigned.
Aceneaux, Jules M. '90 (LAF) Arnaudville, LA St. John Francis Regis; Arnaudville, LA St. Catherine.
Acerbi, Luigi *p.i.m.e.* '50 (PAT)[M] Wayne, NJ P.I.M.E. Missionaries Residence.
Acevedo, Anthony '73 (MIA)[G] Miami, FL Mercy Outpatient Services, Inc.; Special Assignment.
Acevedo, Bertulfo '55 (ARE) Utuado, PR Our Lady of Sorrows.
Acevedo, Edward '97 (MGZ) Las Marias, PR Immaculate Heart of Mary; Army National Guard Chaplains.
Acevedo, Jaime '99 (MIA) Pinecrest, FL St. Louis.
Acevedo, Joaquin *o.f.m.* '60 (ELP)[B] El Paso, TX St. Anthony's School of Theology.
Acevedo, Juan Burgos *o.p.* '89 (PCE) Yauco, PR Holy Rosary.
Acevedo, Luis H. '51 (ELP) Retired.
Achbach, Kevin Lee '03 (RC) Rapid City, SD Blessed Sacrament.
Achi, Stephen (NY) Kingston, NY Benedictine Hospital.
Acker, Karl H. '63 (MIL) Saukville, WI Immaculate Conception.
Acker, Thomas S. *s.j.* '63 (DET)[K] Detroit Jesuit Provincial Office–Detroit Province of the Society of Jesus.
Ackeret, Dennis '68 (MIL) Eagle, WI St. Theresa; Archdiocesan Consultors.
Ackerman, Donald K. '61 (EVN) Ireland, IN Annunciation of the Blessed Virgin Mary.
Ackerman, Donald (EVN) Deans.
Ackerman, J. Thomas '97 (BIR) Guntersville, AL St. William's; Members.
Ackerman, Phil '78 (FAR) Thompson, ND St. Jude.
Ackerman, Phil '78 (FAR) Grand Forks, ND Holy Family.
Ackerman, Ray '91 (OKL)[K] Ada, OK East Central State University.
Ackerman, Ray (OKL) Region III.
Ackerman, Raymond K. '91 (OKL) Ada, OK St. Joseph; Catholic Lawyers Guild.
Aclan, Alejandro '93 (LA) Pomona, CA St. Madeleine.
Acosta, Edgardo '83 (MGZ) Sabana Grande, PR Church of San Isidro.
Acosta, Edgardo (PCE)[B] The Pontifical Catholic University of Puerto Rico.
Acosta, Francisco '70 (BWN) Brownsville, TX Our Lady of Guadalupe.
Acosta, Giovanny '94 (BRK) Brooklyn, NY St. Rose of Lima.
Acosta, Jorge E. '02 (NEW) On Duty Outside the Archdiocese.
Acosta, Jorge '02 (PCE) Penuelas, PR St. Joseph.
Acosta, Jose '84 (OKL) Oklahoma City, OK Sacred Heart.
Acosta–Escobar, Bill John '02 (R) Cary, NC St. Michael the Archangel.
Acquaro, Philip A. *c.s.b.* '70 (PHX) Special Assignment.
Acquaro, Philip A. *c.s.b., j.c.l.* '70 (VNN) Gilbert, AZ St. Thomas the Apostle; [A] Phoenix, AZ Congregation of Saint Basil.
Acquaro, Philip *c.s.b.* (PHX) Adjutant Judicial Vicars.
Acquaro, Philip *c.s.b.* (VNN) Defender.
Acquaro, Philip *c.s.b.* (VNN) Commission for the Implementation of the Particular Law.
Acrea, John '62 (DM) On Special Assignment.
Acrea, John (DM) Vocations.
Acri, John A. '65 (HBG) Enola, PA Our Lady of Lourdes.
Acton, John A. '48 (LA) Glendora, CA St. Dorothy Retired.
Acton, Thomas M. '57 (LA) Gardena, CA Maria Regina Retired.
Adackapara, Matthew '60 (TR) Freehold, NJ St. Robert Bellarmine.
Adaickalam, Michael '85 (CHI) Maywood, IL St. Eulalia; [J] Melrose Park, IL Westlake Hospital.
Adaiuckalam, Michael *s.s.s.* (CHI)[J] Chicago, IL St. Anthony Hospital.
Adam, Charles A. '86 (DAV)[A] Davenport, IA St. Ambrose University Seminary; [B] Davenport, IA St. Ambrose University; [B] St. Ambrose University; Director of Clergy Formation.
Adam, Charles (DAV) Vocations.
Adam, John *s.j.* '61 (NY)[II] Bronx, NY Saint Jutta Foundation, Inc..
Adam, Nicholas '76 (DAV) Mount Pleasant, IA St. Alphonsus.
Adam, Nicholas (DAV) Diocesan Consultors.
Adam, Rich '88 (DAV) Riverside, IA St. Mary of the Assumption.
Adam, Richard A. '88 (SC) On Duty Outside the Diocese.
Adam, Richard A. '88 (DAV) Riverside, IA St. Joseph.
Adam, Richard '81 (DAV) Kalona, IA Holy Trinity.
Adama, Dominic A. '79 (GAL) Houston, TX Our Lady Star of the Sea.
Adama, Dominic V. '79 (GAL) Houston, TX Our Mother of Mercy.
Adamcik, Bryan F.J. '96 (NEW) Kearny, NJ St. Stephen's.
Adamczyk, Lawrence '03 (BAL) Baltimore, MD Cathedral of Mary Our Queen.
Adamec, Joseph *c.ss.r.* '52 (BO) Roxbury, MA Our Lady of Perpetual Help.
Adamiak, Leo '46 (SJP) Youngstown, OH Holy Trinity.
Adamiak, Leo (SJP) Vicar General.
Adamiak, Leo (SJP) Diocesan Administrative Council.
Adamiak, Leo (SJP) Clergy Examiners.
Adamiak, Leo (SJP) Presbyteral Council.
Adamiak, Leo (SJP) Diocesan Consultors.
Adamiak, Stephen (SJP) Retired.
Adamich, Albert R. '48 (CHI) Evergreen Park, IL Most Holy Redeemer Retired.
Adamik, Adrian '94 (SAT) Karnes City, TX St. Cornelius.
Adamko, Cyril A. '53 (Y) Retired.
Adamo, Joseph A. '73 (WOR) Worcester, MA Ascension; Deans.
Adamo, Robert B. '98 (BRK) Brooklyn, NY Our Lady of Guadalupe.
Adamo, Robert (BRK) Bishop Sullivan—.
Adams, Alvin J. '67 (PIT) Munhall, PA St. Rita; [C] Pittsburgh, PA Bishop Canevin High School.
Adams, Archie H. '55 (MAD) Absent on Sick Leave.
Adams, Daniel '80 (P) Wilsonville, OR St. Cyril.
Adams, David A. '88 (TR) Mount Holly, NJ Sacred Heart.
Adams, David C. '61 (KAL) Augusta, MI St. Ann; Diocesan Consultors; Finance Council; Presbyteral Council.
Adams, Dudley R. C. *s.j.* '92 (BO)[V] Weston, MA Campion Health Center, Inc..
Adams, Edmond F. '52 (SC) Retired.
Adams, George J. '50 (STU) Retired.
Adams, George (E) Retired.
Adams, Harry J. '68 (NO) Marrero, LA St. Joachim.
Adams, James P. '82 (ATL) Fayetteville, GA St. Gabriel.
Adams, Joel K. *s.j.* '95 (P)[L] Portland, OR Jesuit Provincial Office (Society of Jesus, Oregon Prov.).
Adams, John E. '69 (WDC) Special Ministries.
Adams, John '69 (RIC)[U] Washington, DC Community of Christ.
Adams, John *o.p.* '74 (SEA) Seattle, WA Blessed Sacrament.
Adams, Michael J. '59 (CHI) Chicago, IL St. Mary, Star of the Sea; Orland Park, IL St. Michael Retired.
Adams, Michael J. (CC) Presbyteral Council.
Adams, Michael T. '68 (MRY) Retired.
Adams, Michael '46 (CC) Retired.
Adams, Richard '65 (NY) New York, NY St. Agnes.
Adams, Robert '45 (OAK) Livermore, CA St. Michael.
Adams, Robert '45 (OAK) Retired.
Adams, Rodney T. '91 (OM) Omaha, NE St. Bridget; Omaha, NE St. Rose; Diaconate Program.
Adams, Scott '95 (OKL)[K] Goodwell, OK Oklahoma Panhandle State University.
Adams, Scott '95 (OKL) Guymon, OK St. Peter's.
Adams, Stephen '81 (DEN) Aurora, CO St. Pius X.
Adams, T. Edmund *o.s.b.* '89 (PRO)[P] Portsmouth, RI Abbey of St. Gregory the Great.
Adams, Terrance *t.o.r.* '67 (WH) Moundsville, WV St. Francis Xavier's.
Adams, Thomas J. '64 (OM) Omaha, NE St. Wenceslaus.
Adams, Walter C. '84 (NY)[E] New York, NY Cardinal Spellman High School.
Adams, William *c.ss.r.* '63 (LA)[Q] Whittier, CA Redemptorists of Whittier.
Adams, William *c.ss.r.* '63 (LA) Whittier, CA St. Mary of the Assumption.
Adams, William '78 (VEN) Fort Myers Beach, FL Ascension.
Adams, William (VEN) Co–Directors:.
Adamski, Donald '75 (LSC) Mesilla Park, NM Shrine and Parish of Our Lady of Guadalupe.
Adamski, Donald *o.f.m.conv.* (LSC) Members.
Adamski, Donald *o.f.m.conv.* (LSC) Presbyteral Council.
Adamski, John S. '71 (ATL) Atlanta, GA Our Lady of Lourdes.
Adamson, Fred '95 (PHX) Tempe, AZ Resurrection.
Adamson, Joseph J. '90 (CAM) Mantua, NJ Incarnation; Priests Personnel Board.
Adamson, Milton N. *c.s.c.* '66 (PHX) Phoenix, AZ St. Joseph's Hospital; [G] Phoenix, AZ Holy Cross Congregation/Casa Santa Cruz.
Adan, Aurelio '69 (CGS)[B] Aibonito, PR Casa Manresa.
Adan, Aurelio (CGS) Diocesan Consultors.
Adan, Aurelio (CGS) Priests Senate.
Addai, Augustine Asare '98 (RVC) Rockville Centre, NY St. Agnes Cathedral.
Addison, Nicholas '95 (NY) Cold Spring, NY Our Lady of Loretto.
Adducci, Anthony J. '76 (CHI)[J] Chicago, IL Saint Joseph Hospital.
Adekola, Patrick (NY) Spring Valley, NY St. Joseph.

Adelman, Norbert *c.pp.s.* '56 (ORL) Longwood, FL Church of the Nativity.
Adelmann, Edward *o.carm.* '75 (FgM).
Adelmann, Edward *o.carm.* '75 (JOL)[L] Prelate Nullius.
Adessa, Dominick J. '47 (RVC)[N] Amityville, NY Queen of the Rosary, Motherhouse.
Adessa, Dominick J. '47 (BRK) Retired.
Adhana, Gabre–Tinsaye '47 (GAL)[N] Houston, TX Pope John Paul XXIII Priests' Residence Retired.
Adhunga, Joseph O. *a.j.* '92 (ARL) Fairfax Station, VA St. Raymond of Penafort.
Adi, Astanto *c.m.* (PH) Philadelphia, PA St. Thomas Aquinas.
Adi, Cyprianus Kuntoro *s.j.* '93 (MIL)[O] Milwaukee, WI Arrupe House Jesuit Community.
Adibe, Anthony '91 (DM) Urbandale, IA St. Pius X.
Adiletta, David C. *o.p.* '98 (NEW) Jersey City, NJ Sacred Heart.
Adimakkeel, Joy Joseph '80 (MAR) Grand Marais, MI Holy Rosary Church.
Adiukwu, Richard '96 (LKC) Lake Charles, LA Immaculate Conception Cathedral.
Adolf, Gregory P. '91 (TUC) Sierra Vista, AZ St. Andrew.
Adonizio, Joseph J. '56 (SCR) Retired.
Adorno, Anibal '92 (DAL) Dallas, TX St. Monica.
Adragna, Joseph J. '65 (STL) St. Louis, MO St. George.
Adrian, Stephen J. '39 (NU) Retired.
Adrian, Stephen J. '68 (STP) St. Paul, MN St. Matthew; Presbyteral Council.
Adrians, Thomas M. '67 (PBL) Pueblo, CO Christ the King; Vicar General; Presbyteral Council–College of Consultors; Presbyteral Council; Clergy Assemblies; Clergy Conference of the Diocese of Pueblo.
Adrians, Tom (PBL) Personnel.
Adu, Martin K. '75 (MIA) Special Assignment.
Adu, Martin '75 (MIA) Miami, FL St. James.
Aduba, John I. '80 (LAN) Jackson, MI Queen of the Miraculous Medal.
Aduba, John '81 (LAN) Foote Hospital.
Aduri, Tom '03 (KCK) Overland Park, KS Holy Spirit.
Adversario, Efran F. (AGN) Air Force Chaplains.
Adversario, Efren '89 (AGN) On Duty Outside the Archdiocese.
Adzaku, Kofi (NO) New Orleans, LA Memorial Medical Center.
Aeila, Misael '98 (STO) Stockton, CA St. Mary of the Assumption Church (Pastor of).
Aelavanthara, Antony '68 (ALX) Powhatan, LA St. Francis of Assisi.
Aerts, John F. '02 (FAR) Fargo, ND Holy Spirit.
Affelt, Francis *o.f.m.* '52 (FTW)[J] Mishawaka, IN St. Francis Provincialate.
Affonso, Alexander '68 (SJ) Los Altos, CA St. Simon.
Afful, Robert Kodwo '94 (BRK) Flushing, NY St. Ann's.
Afulo, Joseph Oduor *s.j.* (MIL)[O] Milwaukee, WI Jesuit Community at Marquette University.
Afunugo, Emanuel (SAT) Defenders of the Bond.
Afunugo, Emmanuel *d.d.* '83 (AMA) On Duty Outside the Diocese.
Agaloos, Reinerio '89 (NEW) Rahway, NJ St. Mary's.
Agan, Jose '70 (NEW) Newark, NJ St. Michael Medical Center.
Aganbi, Isaac (NY) Mount Vernon, NY Mount Vernon Hospital.
Agapito, John *c.p.m.* '89 (WH)[F] Morgantown, WV Our Lady of Good Counsel Franciscan Friary.
Agar, Bartholomew A. *o.praem.* '58 (GB)[I] De Pere, WI St. Norbert Abbey.
Agbakwuru, Emmanuel C. '73 (PIT) Duquesne, PA St. Joseph.
Agbessi, Charles '96 (BAL)[S] Baltimore, MD Ferdinand Wheeler Jesuit Community.
Agbor, Emmanuel E. *m.s.p.* '95 (BR) Houston, TX St. Philip Neri.
Ageas, Cesar '83 (SAC) Sacramento, CA St. Joseph's.
Ager, Fay W. '79 (OG) Star Lake, NY St. Hubert.
Aggeler, Vince *c.ss.r.* '58 (FgM).
Agnew, Francis H. *c.m.* '60 (STL) Perryville, MO Our Lady of Victory; [O] Perryville, MO Congregation of the Mission.
Agnew, John '90 (CHI)[W] Chicago, IL Prelature of the Holy Cross and Opus Dei.
Agola, Daniel (BRK) Bayside, NY Sacred Heart of Jesus.
Agostinelli, Gianni *c.s.* '86 (BRK) Brooklyn, NY St. Joseph Patron of the Universal Church.
Agostini, Sixtus *m.c.c.j.* '71 (CHI)[N] La Grange Park, IL Comboni Missionaries.
Agostino, Emil *o.carm.* '68 (KCK) Garnett, KS St. Therese.
Agostino, Emil *o.carm.* '68 (KCK) Garnett, KS St. Boniface.
Agostino, Joseph V. *c.m.* '83 (BRK) Brooklyn, NY St. John the Baptist; [V] Brooklyn, NY St. John the Baptist Rectory.
Agostino, Joseph *c.m.* (BRK) Liturgical Commission.
Agostino, Steven J. *s.j.* '93 (STL)[O] St. Louis, MO Jesuit Community Corporation at St. Louis University – Jesuit Hall; [C] Saint Louis University.
Agresti, Frank P. '03 (PAT) Parsippany, NJ St. Peter the Apostle; Parsippany, NJ St. Peter the Apostle.
Agudelo, Gustavo '86 (CAM) Atlantic City, NJ Our Lady Star of the Sea.
Agudo, Moises '97 (SFR) San Francisco, CA St. Charles Borromeo.
Agudo, Teodoro *o.f.m.cap.* '54 (NO) New Orleans, LA St. Theresa of Avila.
Aguggia, Steven J. '93 (BRK) Brooklyn, NY Queen of All Saints; Vice–Chancellors; Bishop Valero—; Defenders of the Marriage Bond; Committee for Eastern Orthodox–Catholic Relations.
Agughara, Fide is '88 (BUR) Burlington, VT Fletcher Allen Health Care.
Aguilar, Arturo *s.s.c.* '84 (LA)[Q] Los Angeles, CA Columban Fathers, Procure House.
Aguilar, Benjamin *o.carm.* '94 (CHI)[D] Chicago, IL.
Aguilar, Benjamin *o.carm* '94 (CHI)[N] Chicago Carmelite Priory of St. Cyril.
Aguilar, David E. '96 (NEW) Orange, NJ Mt. Carmel.
Aguilar, Genaro P. *c.s.c.* '83 (FR)[A] North Easton, MA Stonehill College; [A] North Easton, MA Holy Cross Fathers Religious.
Aguilar, Richard '95 (AUS) Taylor, TX Our Lady of Guadalupe.
Aguilar, Rogelio Mur *o.carm.* '56 (MGZ) Anasco, PR St. Anthony Abbot.
Aguilar–Ramirez, Paulo *o.s.a.* '68 (LAR) Laredo, TX Holy Redeemer.
Aguilar Leal, Luis Roberto *o.p.* '92 (NO).
Aguilera, George '83 (LA)[P] Los Angeles, CA St. Aloysius Gonzaga.
Aguilera, Salvador '84 (ELP) On Duty Outside of Diocese; Navy Chaplains.
Aguirre, Emilson de J. (BO) Holy Rosary.
Aguirre, Ignacio *o.s.b.* '53 (CGS) Humacao, PR Maria Reina de la Paz.
Aguirre, Juan Carlos '99 (TUC) Tucson, AZ St. John the Evangelist.
Aguirre, Nery *o.f.m.* '74 (NY)[EE] St. Jude Friary.
Aguirre, Osmar R. '93 (YAK) Special Assignment.
Aguirre, Robert G. '73 (CHI) Mundelein, IL Santa Maria Del Popolo.
Aguirre–Garza, Jesus *o.f.m.* '96 (STL).
Agustin, Honesto '82 (RNO)[O] Reno, NV St. Therese Church of the Little Flower.
Agustin, Richard *m.m.* '85 (FgM).
Agyei, Paul K. (BRK) Brooklyn, NY St. Columba.
Ahanotu, Leonard '94 (TLS) Krebs, OK Holy Rosary.
Ahanotu, Leonard '94 (TLS) Krebs, OK St. Joseph's.
Ahearn, Donald J. '51 (CHI) Chicago, IL St Juliana Retired.
Ahearn, John E. *m.m.* '73 (FgM).
Ahearn, John S. *o.f.m.* '50 (PAT)[M] Butler, NJ St. Anthony Friary.
Ahearn, Richard F. '60 (BO) Senior Priests Retired.
Ahearn, Thomas A. *m.m.* '68 (NY)[EE] Maryknoll Maryknoll St. Teresa's Residence.
Ahern, Bernard '54 (ALB) Retired.
Ahern, Dennis P. *s.j.* '70 (CIN)[F] Cincinnati, OH St. Xavier High School; [M] Cincinnati, OH Jesuit Community at St. Xavier High School.
Ahern, John B. '54 (NY) New York, NY Our Lady of Loreto; [I] New York, NY Holy Name Centre for Homeless Men, Inc..
Ahern, John J. (CHI) AUXILIARY CHAPLAINS CONTRACT CHAPLAINS.
Ahern, John S. '54 (HRT) Norfolk, CT Immaculate Conception.
Ahern, John W. '67 (SY) Liverpool, NY Immaculate Heart of Mary.
Ahern, Thomas W. '48 (NOR) Old Lyme, CT Christ the King Retired.
Ahern, Thomas W. '94 (BRK) Brooklyn, NY St. Teresa of Avila.
Ahern, Thomas '54 (SJ) Retired.
Ahern, Thomas (SJ) Priests' Retirement Board.
Aherne, Greg *s.j.* '60 (SFR) San Francisco, CA Star of the Sea.
Aherne, James *m.s.* '73 (SPR) Holyoke, MA Immaculate Conception.
Aherne, John P. (MOB) Ex Officio Members.
Aherne, John '57 (MOB) Semmes, AL Holy Name of Jesus.
Aherne, John (MOB) Officers.
Aherne, John (MOB) Vicar General.
Aherne, John (MOB) Archdiocesan Consultors.
Aherne, John (MOB) Consultors.
Aherne, John (MOB) Co–Dirs..
Aherne, P. Vincent *c.m.* '52 (STL)[O] St. Louis Vincentian Residence.
Aherne, Patrick Vincent *c.m.* (SB) Hemet, CA Holy Spirit Parish.
Ahlbach, William J. '62 (SFR) San Mateo, CA St. Matthew.
Ahlemeyer, Richard J. '77 (BRK) Jamaica, NY St. Pius V.
Ahlemeyer, Richard (BRK) Jamaica, NY Presentation of the Blessed Virgin Mary.
Ahler, Richard H. *s.j.* '61 (MIL)[O] Milwaukee, WI Jesuit Community at Marquette University.
Ahles, Donald M. '71 (RCK) Freeport, IL St. Joseph.
Ahles, Jerome *o.f.m.* '44 (MRY)[F] San Miguel, CA Franciscan Friars, O.F.M..
Ahlin, Robert J. '71 (PIT) Pittsburgh, PA Holy Angels; Judicial Vicar.
Ahlstrom, Michael P. '69 (CHI) Brookfield, IL St. Barbara; Co–Vicars for the Diaconate Community.
Ahn, Dominic (NEW) Korean/Mary Most Humble Curia.
Ahn, John Byong Kwon '98 (CLV) Korean Catholic Apostolate; Cleveland, OH St. Andrew Kim.
Ahn, Peter *o.s.b.* '02 (PAT)[M] Newton, NJ St. Paul's Abbey.
Aho, Charles A. '70 (SY) Liverpool, NY Developmental Center; Special Assignment; [Q] Syracuse, NY Tommy Coyne Residence @ Dillon Hall.
Ahrens, Noel *o.carm.* '53 (NEW) Englewood, NJ St. Cecilia's.
Ahrens, William B. '51 (STL) Retired.
Ahrensfield, Michael E. '80 (ALN) Tower City, PA SS. Peter and Paul; Minersville, PA Immaculate Conception.
Ahumanda, Jose E. *c.s.c.* '83 (FTW)[I] Congregacion de Santa Cruz.
Aiardi, Reno *i.m.c.* '65 (SB) Special or Other Diocesan Assignment.
Aiardi, Reno *i.m.c.* (SB) Council Members.
Aiardi, Reno *i.m.c.* (SB) Mission Office of the Diocese of San Bernardino.
Aichele, Raymond P. '58 (CIN) Retired.
Aidoo, Hilary J. '84 (BRK) Flushing, NY Holy Family.
Aidoo, Thomas '85 (RVC) Stony Brook, NY Stony Brook University Hospital.
Aiello, Anthony '69 (DM) Des Moines, IA Holy Trinity.
Aiello, John D. '69 (MIL) Racine, WI St. Joseph; Defenders of the Bond Second Instance; Notaries.
Aiello, Louis F. '77 (SY) Syracuse, NY St. Charles.
Aigner, Edward M. '72 (WIL) Salisbury, MD St. Francis De Sales; Eastern Correctional Institution.
Aiken, Lloyd E. '70 (BAL) Glyndon, MD Sacred Heart.
Aiken, Richard J. '70 (MIL) Greendale, WI St. Alphonsus.
Aiken, Roy F. '46 (CHR) Retired.
Aime, Moise (RVC) Haitian–American Apostolate Ministry.
Aineto, Luis *s.d.b.* '61 (PMB) Belle Glade, FL St. Philip Benizi.
Ainikkal, Jose *c.m.i.* '85 (CAM) Blue Anchor, NJ Blessed John the Twenty–Third.
Aisa, Francisco (PCE) Playa de Ponce, PR Our Lady of Mt. Carmel.
Aita, Mark C. *s.j.* (BAL)[D] Baltimore, MD Loyola Blakefield; [S] Baltimore, MD Blessed Alberto Hurtado, S.J. Jesuit Community.
Aitcheson, William M. '88 (ARL) Woodstock, VA St. John Bosco.
Aitsebaomo, Martin *o.p.* (HBG) Hershey, PA St. Joan of Arc.
Ajamie, Albert '50 (IND) Retired.
Ajemian, David J. '01 (BO) Health Leave.
Ajiki, Pius T. '84 (WDC) Riverdale, MD Nigerian Catholic Community; Riverdale Park, MD St. Bernard.
Ajuria, Cruz *o.f.m.* '57 (SJN) San Juan, PR Resurreccion del Senor.
Akalonu, Cyril I. '81 (NY) Bronx, NY St. Raymond.
Akamike, Romanus A. (SAN) Eden, TX St. Charles.
Akers, Bert *s.j.* '61 (WDC) Washington, DC Holy Trinity.
Akiki, Joseph G. '87 (SAM) Olean, NY St. Joseph.
Akiona, Lane K. *ss.cc.* '81 (HON) Honolulu, HI St. Patrick; [G] Honolulu, HI St. Patrick's Monastery.
Akiona, Lane *ss.cc.* (HON) Tongan Ministry.
Akiona, Lane *ss.cc.* (HON) Knights of Columbus.
Akkin, Florentinus '93 (CI) Mortlock.
Akkin, Florentinus (CI) Defenders of the Bond.
Akordor, Edmund '80 (NO) New Orleans, LA Veterans Affairs Medical Center.
Akordor, Edmund (MO).
Akoury, Tanios K. '95 (SAM) Brockton, MA St. Theresa.
Akoury, Tanios (SAM) Approved Advocates.
Akpabio, Felix '78 (BRK) Cambria Heights, NY Sacred Heart.
Akpen, Thomas *c.s.sp.* (GB) Chilton, WI St. Martin.
Akpen, Thomas *c.s.sp.* (GB) Chilton, WI Holy Trinity.
Akpen, Thomas *c.s.sp.* (GB) Chilton, WI St. Elizabeth.
Akpen, Thomas *c.s.sp.* (GB) Chilton, WI St. Charles Borromeo.
Akpen, Thomas *c.s.sp.* (GB) Chilton, WI St. Augustine.
Akpen, Thomas *c.s.sp.* (GB) Chilton, WI St. Mary.
Akpoghiran, Peter C. '92 (ARL) Manassas, VA Sacred Heart.
Akpunonu, Peter Damian *s.s.l.* '66 (CHI).
Aksamit, Stanley J. '77 (SPR)[A] Turners Falls, MA Sacred Heart; Turners Falls, MA St. Mary's; Turners Falls, MA St. Anne.
Akso, Francisco *o.f.m.* '96 (SFR) San Francisco, CA St. Anthony of Padua.
Aku, Edmund (HRT)[I] Waterbury, CT St. Mary Hospital.
Akut, Basil (NY) Staten Island, NY Holy Child.

Akwue, Francis *c.s.sp.* '71 (MIA) Pompano Beach, FL St. Henry.
Al–Balaa, Pierre *m.l.m.* '95 (OLL)[J] Houston, TX The Congregation of Maronite Lebanese Missionaries.
Al–Shabi, Felix '98 (SPA) El Cajon, CA St. Peter Chaldean Cathedral.
Al–Shaikh, Emad Hanna (OLD) Saint Joseph's Mission; La Mesa, CA Our Mother of Perpetual Help Parish.
Alabart, Francis X. '40 (FRS) Retired.
Alade, Peter '92 (NY) Carmel, NY St. James the Apostle.
Alagia, Vincent P. *s.j.* '58 (CHL)[J] Mooresville, NC Jesuit Community; Charlotte, NC St. Peter.
Alaharasan, V. Antony '65 (NOR) North Stonington, CT St. Thomas More.
Alam, Alam '81 (NTN) Lawrence, MA St. Joseph.
Alamo, Emiliano '66 (PCE) Villalba, PR Our Lady of Mt. Carmel.
Alamo, Jose *c.s.sp.* '85 (ARE) Orocovis, PR Our Lady of Fatima.
Alanis, Francisco '03 (LA) Los Angeles, CA Immaculate Conception.
Alapide, Eduardo *o.p.* (NEW) Hackensack, NJ Church of St. Francis of Assisi.
Alappat, Joy '81 (NEW) New Milford, NJ Ascension; New Milford, NJ Syro–Malabar Catholic Mission of New Jersey Ascention Church.
Alappat, Joy '81 (WDC)[K] Washington, DC Georgetown University Hospital.
Alarcon, Carlos *o.m.i.* '90 (LA) San Fernando, CA Santa Rosa.
Alarcon, Felix '63 (RVC) Retired.
Alarcon–Martinez, Mauricio *t.o.r.* '01 (SAT) San Antonio, TX St. Leonard's.
Alarez, Milton *c.m.f.* '77 (CHI) Chicago, IL St. Paul.
Alaribe, Felix '98 (LR) Texarkana, AR St. Edward's; Ashdown, AR St. Elizabeth Ann Seton Church; Foreman, AR Sacred Heart Church.
Alava, Andres *o.a.r.* '63 (LSC)[C] Mesilla, NM Augustinian Recollect Fathers; Las Cruces, NM Santa Rosa de Lima.
Alava, Andres *o.a.r.* (LSC) Diocesan Consultors.
Alayon, Hermenegildo '79 (CGS) Humacao, PR Dulce Nombre de Jesus.
Alayon, Hermenegildo (CGS) Catechetical Vicar.
Alba, Jose M. '48 (NEW) Retired.
Albacete, Lorenzo '73 (WDC) On Duty Outside the Archdiocese.
Alba Infante, Saul '02 (BAK) Klamath Falls, OR Sacred Heart.
Albalaa, Pierre *m.l.m.* '95 (OLL) Thousand Oaks, CA Saints Peter and Paul Mission.
Albalaa, Pierre *m.l.m.* '95 (LA) Westlake Village, CA St. Jude.
Albaladejo, Juan A. '85 (MET) On Duty Outside the Diocese; [H] Raritan, NJ Clairvaux House.
Albamonti, Richard J. '76 (NOR) Westbrook, CT St. Mark.
Albano, Alwyn M. (MO) Army Chaplains.
Albano, Arturo L. '74 (SFR) San Mateo, CA St. Timothy.
Albano, George M. '44 (TR) Toms River, NJ St. Maximilian Kolbe Retired.
Albano, Peter J. *c.m.* '60 (PH).
Albano, Peter *c.m.* '68 (LA)[A] Camarillo, CA St. John's Seminary.
Albarano, Richard '68 (LA) Burbank, CA St. Francis Xavier.
Albee, Paul M. '84 (LA) Los Angeles, CA Cathedral of Our Lady of the Angels; Priest Secretary/Master of Ceremonies.
Albenesius, Paul '96 (OM) South Sioux City, NE St. Michael.
Alber, Michael '02 (GR) Fremont, MI St. Michael's.
Alber, Thomas L. '85 (JC) Jefferson City, MO Immaculate Conception.
Alberg, Leo W. '91 (LA) Santa Barbara, CA St. Raphael.
Albero, Steven J. *o.praem.* '92 (PH)[B] Paoli, PA Daylesford Abbey; [AA] Paoli, PA Daylesford Abbey.
Albers, Austin *o.f.m.* '64 (SFD)[L] Teutopolis, IL St. Francis Assisi Friary.
Albers, Austin *o.f.m.* '64 (SFD) Teutopolis, IL St. Francis of Assisi.
Albers, Austin *o.f.m.* '64 (SFD) Montrose, IL St. Rose of Lima.
Albers, Edwin O. *o.f.m.* '61 (SFD) Dieterich, IL St. Aloysius; Dieterich, IL Immaculate Conception; Dieterich, IL St. Joseph; [L] Teutopolis, IL St. Francis Assisi Friary.
Albers, George *c.pp.s.* '62 (CIN)[B] Carthagena, OH St. Charles.
Albers, James R. *o.s.b.* (KCK)[A] Atchison, KS Benedictine College; [H] Atchison, KS St. Benedict's Abbey.
Albers, Robert J. *s.a.c.* '48 (MIL)[O] Milwaukee, WI Pallotti House.
Albers, Thomas L. *c.pp.s.* '67 (JC) Sedalia, MO Sacred Heart; VII. Marshall.
Albers, Thomas *c.pp.s.* '67 (JC) Sedalia, MO St. Patrick.
Albert, Claude A. '64 (PRT) Springvale, ME Notre Dame.
Albert, Claude J. '64 (PRT) Sanford, ME Holy Family; Sanford, ME St. Ignatius Martyr; Clergy Benefit Plan–Clergy Pension Plan.
Albert, Claude (PRT) Diocesan Finance Council.
Albert, James R. '86 (PRT) Madawaska, ME St. Thomas Aquinas.
Albert, Patrick L. '92 (SCR) Forest City, PA Sacred Heart of Jesus; [D] Carbondale, PA Sacred Heart Junior/Senior High School.
Albert, Selvan *o.praem.* '91 (PH)[U] Darby, PA Mercy Fitzgerald Hospital.
Albert, Timothy J. '91 (PRT) Springvale, ME Notre Dame.
Albert, Xavier '63 (STL) Retired.
Alberth, Regis R. '80 (PIT) Allegheny County, PA Marian Manor, Inc..
Alberth, Regis '80 (PIT)[K] Pittsburgh, PA Marian Manor Corp..
Albertine, Richard P. *m.m.* '66 (FgM).
Alberto, Gerardo *m.sp.s.* (P) Hillsboro, OR St. Matthew.
Alberto Urguizo, Jose '98 (LA) Pomona, CA St. Joseph.
Alberts, Edward T. '75 (NSH) Brentwood, TN Holy Family; Presbyteral Council and College of Consultors; Liturgical Life.
Albertson, Clinton E. *s.j.* '49 (LA)[C] Los Angeles, CA Jesuit Community.
Albertson, Eric J. '86 (ARL) On Duty Outside the Diocese; Military Chaplains; Army Chaplains.
Albertson, Lawrence '65 (KCK) Bucyrus, KS Queen of the Holy Rosary.
Albietz, Henry F. '74 (CIN) Wapakoneta, OH St. Joseph.
Albino, Brian '79 (FR) Fall River, MA Santo Christo.
Albino, Brian (FR) Diocesan Department of Pastoral Care for the Sick.
Albino, Ramon E. '84 (MGZ) Aguadilla, PR La Milagrosa; [A] Aquadilla, PR Corpus Christi College.
Albosta, John T. '64 (SCR) Waymart, PA St. Mary's.
Albrecht, Craig L. '95 (SAG) Merrill, MI Sacred Heart; Merrill, MI St. Patrick.
Albrecht, James W. '58 (NY)[JJ] New York, NY Prelature of the Holy Cross and Opus Dei.
Albrecht, Louis H. (BAK) Army National Guard Chaplains.
Albrecht, Louis Henry '86 (BAK) La Grande, OR Our Lady of the Valley.
Albrecht, Walter H. '43 (SAC) Retired.
Albright, Brian V. *m.m.* '70 (NY).
Albright, R. Gerard *s.j.* '58 (DET)[K] Detroit, MI Jesuit Community at the University of Detroit Mercy.
Albright, Robert E. '72 (BAL) Special Assignment; [U] Baltimore, MD Archdiocesan Office–Newman Center; [U] Baltimore, MD Towson University; Campus Ministry (Newman Apostolate).
Alcantara, Miguel B. '65 (CHI) Other Assignments.
Alcarria, Antonio Munoz '64 (CGS) Caguas, PR San Pedro Apostol.
Alcazar, Emanuel '89 (ELP) El Paso, TX St. Paul the Apostle.
Alcazar, Emanuel (ELP) Presbyteral Council.
Alcazar, Victor H. '01 (RCK) Aurora, IL Holy Angels.
Alciati, Paul '77 (SY) Baldwinsville, NY St. Augustine.
Alco, James J. '90 (SCR) Wilkes–Barre, PA St. Joseph.
Alcocer, Jose '60 (ELP) El Paso, TX San Jose.
Alcott, Stephen Paul *o.p.* '01 (WDC)[B] Washington, DC Dominican House of Studies.
Alcott, Stephen *o.p.* '01 (CIN)[M] Cincinnati, OH St. Gertrude Priory.
Alcott, Stephen *o.p.* '01 (CIN) Cincinnati, OH St. Gertrude.
Alcuin, William *o.f.m.cap.* '52 (GB)[I] Appleton, WI St. Fidelis Friary.
Alcuino, Mike '88 (ELP) Alpine, TX Our Lady of Peace.
Aldana, Antonio '53 (NY) Bronx, NY Our Lady of Angels.
Aldasoro, Francisco '47 (SD) Retired.
Aldegunde, Jose R. '58 (BRK) Flushing, NY St. Michael.
Alder, Ronald '69 (DET) Retired.
Alderson, John *o.f.m.* '66 (BUF) Buffalo, NY SS. Rita & Patrick.
Aldin, Arthur (NY) Ossining, NY St. Ann.
Aldrich, Louis G. *s.j.* '86 (FgM).
Aldridge, William J. *o.p.* '46 (BR)[J] Ponchatoula, LA Rosaryville/Spirit Life Center.
Aldworth, Thomas *o.f.m.* (CHI) Chicago, IL St. Peter's.
Alecio–Rodriguez, Freddy (SJN) On Duty Outside the Archdiocese.
Aleksa, Thomas M. '75 (E) Tidioute, PA St. John.
Alenchery, Joseph '87 (RVC) Selden, NY St. Margaret of Scotland.
Alengadan, George *s.d.b.* '82 (OAK) Berkeley, CA St. Ambrose.
Aleria, Paul (NEW) Bloomfield, NJ Sacred Heart.
Alers, Juan '69 (LKC) Retired.
Alesandro, John A. '66 (RVC) Nassau County Police Department.
Alesandro, John A. '67 (RVC) Oyster Bay, NY St. Dominic's.
Alesandro, John A. (RVC) Judges for Interdiocesan Tribunal.
Alesandro, John A. (RVC) Vicar General.
Alesandro, John A. (RVC) Censors of Books.
Alesandro, John A. (RVC) Chaplains of the Nassau County Police Department.
Alesandro, John A. (RVC) Senate of Priests (Presbyteral Council/College of Consultors).
Alessandro, Michael J. '44 (NY)[Y] New York, NY Calvary Hospital Retired.
Alex, Boby Mannamplackal '94 (SHP) Monroe, LA St. Joseph.
Alexander, Alfred *s.s.s.* '68 (STO) Lodi, CA St. Anne Church (Pastor of).
Alexander, Andrew *s.j.* '79 (OM)[K] Omaha, NE Jesuit Community at Creighton University.
Alexander, Anthony F. '45 (CLV) Perry, OH St. Cyprian Retired.
Alexander, Dennis *o.m.i.* (SJN) Rio Piedras, PR Inmaculado Corazon de Maria.
Alexander, F. Leon '66 (WH) South Charleston, WV Blessed Sacrament; Vicars Forane.
Alexander, Fred *o.c.d.* '82 (MIL) Milwaukee, WI St. Florian.
Alexander, Fred '98 (CC)[G] Robstown, TX Society of Our Lady of the Most Holy Trinity.
Alexander, Jim *s.c.j.* '44 (MIL)[O] Franklin, WI Villa Maria.
Alexander, John D. *s.j.* '54 (NY)[EE] Loyola Hall, Jesuit Community; [II] New York, NY Brooklyn Prep Alumni Association.
Alexander, Jon *o.p.* '86 (Chicago Prov.)[P] Providence St. Thomas Aquinas Priory at Providence College.
Alexander, Marc R. '85 (HON) Honolulu, HI Sacred Heart; Honolulu, HI St. Pius X; Diocesan Theological Commission; Censor Liborum.
Alexander, Marc (HON) Presbyteral Council.
Alexander, Marc (HON) Diocesan Theologian.
Alexandrunas, Albert *o.f.m.cap.* '65 (WH)[M] Charleston, WV Capuchins–St. Anthony Friary.
Alexandrunas, Albert *o.f.m.cap.* '65 (WH) Belle, WV St. John.
Alfano, Michael A. '87 (BO) Groton, MA Sacred Heart–St. James.
Alfaro, Gustavo A. '02 (NEW) On Duty Outside the Archdiocese.
Alfaro, Jose N. '03 (MIA) Miami, FL St. John Neumann.
Alfaro, Juan '62 (SAT) San Antonio, TX St. Rose of Lima.
Alfonso, Jose de Jesus Sierra '87 (B) Blackfoot, ID St. Bernard's.
Alfonso, San Juan *c.p.* '60 (SAC)[I] Citrus Heights, CA Christ the King Retreat.
Algarin–Rosado, Rodney '01 (SJN) Canovanas, PR Sagrado Corazon de Jesus.
Alicea, Adrian '90 (BRK) Brooklyn, NY St. Barbara.
Alicea, John '94 (CGS) Comerio, PR Santo Cristo de la Salud.
Alicea, Luis Antonio '96 (CGS) Maunabo, PR San Isidro Labrador.
Alilonu, Augustine '00 (FAR) Grand Forks, ND St. Michael.
Alindogan, Peter J. (TR) Defender of the Bond; Promoters of Justice.
Alindogan, Peter James R. '89 (TR) Hamilton, NJ St. Raphael.
Alisauskas, Peter J. '43 (SCR) Retired.
Alkire, Thomas *o.carm.* '63 (JOL)[L] Darien Carmelite Provincial Office.
Alkire, Thomas *o.carm.* '63 (FgM).
Alkire, Timothy M. '85 (LFT) Lafayette, IN St. Boniface.
Allaire, Barry J. '61 (BUF)[D] Olean, NY Archbishop Walsh High School.
Allaire, Barry J. '72 (BUF) Hinsdale, NY St. Helen.
Allala, Patrick Nicanda '94 (CLV) Fairlawn, OH St. Hilary.
Allam, Joji Reddy '95 (SCR) Honesdale, PA St. John the Evangelist.
Allard, George L. '60 (PRO) West Warwick, RI Christ the King.
Allard, John C. '75 (PRO) Woonsocket, RI St. Agatha; Woonsocket, RI Precious Blood.
Allard, John E. *o.p.* '86 (PRO)[P] Providence St. Thomas Aquinas Priory at Providence College.
Allard, John E. *o.p.* '86 (BO)[X] Dover, MA St. Stephen Priory Spiritual Life Center.
Allard, Marcel M. '65 (MAN) Manchester, NH Our Lady of Perpetual Help.
Allbright, Brian V. '83 (P) Newport, OR Sacred Heart Parish.
Allega, Ernest '76 (WOR) South Barre, MA St. Thomas–A–Becket.
Allegra, John Christopher '70 (L) Springfield, KY Holy Trinity; [L] St. Catharine, KY Sansbury Care Center.
Allegretto, William M. *c.m.* '85 (BUF)[O] Niagara University, NY Vincentian Community at Niagara University; [C] Niagara University, NY Niagara University.
Allen, A. Christopher '81 (PMB) Stuart, FL St. Joseph.
Allen, Charles H. *s.j.* '73 (BGP)[B] Fairfield, CT Fairfield University; [P] Fairfield, CT The Fairfield Jesuit Community–Fairfield University.
Allen, Christopher (PMB) College of Consultors.

Allen, David E. '78 (BR) Baton Rouge, LA St. Jude the Apostle; Victim Assistance Coordinator.
Allen, David G. *s.j.* '79 (BAL)[S] Rezidence TJ.
Allen, David '95 (DEN) Denver, CO St. James.
Allen, Donald L. *m.m.* '69 (FgM).
Allen, Francis J. *s.m.m.* '51 (RVC)[M] Bay Shore, NY Montfort Missionaries.
Allen, Francis R. *s.j.* '56 (BGP)[P] Fairfield, CT The Fairfield Jesuit Community–Fairfield University.
Allen, Frederick J. *m.m.* '65 (NY).
Allen, James *o.m.i.* '68 (MIA)[EE] Miramar, FL St. Stephen.
Allen, Jeff *s.j.* (LA).
Allen, John A. '90 (CHL)[D] Special Assignment.
Allen, John (CHL)[D] Charlotte, NC Charlotte Catholic High School (Bishop Hafey Memorial); Vocations.
Allen, Joseph C. '50 (BIR) Athens, AL St. Paul's.
Allen, Joseph P. *o.p.* '67 (Y) Youngstown, OH St. Dominic.
Allen, Joseph P. '91 (CHI) Round Lake, IL St. Joseph.
Allen, Loren '94 (SR) Eureka, CA St. Bernard.
Allen, Loren (SR) Members of the Curia.
Allen, Loren (SR) Clergy Personnel Committee.
Allen, Loren (SR) Board of Consultors.
Allen, Loren (SR) Priests' Council.
Allen, Nathan (STP) St. Paul, MN Cathedral of St. Paul; Associate Judges.
Allen, Peter A. '71 (RVC) Cutchogue, NY Sacred Heart.
Allen, Philip J. '58 (WCH) Viola, KS St. John.
Allen, Philip T. '59 (OG) Au Sable Forks, NY Holy Name; Au Sable Forks, NY St. Matthew; Adjutant Judicial Vicars.
Allen, Richard F. '56 (CHL) Retired.
Allen, Richard J. '97 (E) Erie, PA St. Luke.
Allen, Richard L. '61 (GB) Neenah, WI St. Gabriel.
Allen, Shawn W. '99 (BO) Arlington, MA St. Agnes.
Allen, Terry E. '61 (ALX) Bordelonville, LA St. Peter; Bordelonville, LA St. Michael.
Allende, Santiago Rivera '83 (MGZ) Moca, PR Our Lady of Monserrate.
Allender, Raymond P. *s.j.* '75 (SJ).
Allender, Raymond *s.j.* (SJ)[D] Council of Religious.
Allender, Thomas G. *s.j.* '71 (SJ)[M] Los Gatos Sacred Heart Jesuit Center.
Aller, Domingo *o.s.a.* '61 (SJN) Bayamon, PR Ntra. Sra. de la Monserrate.
Aller, Domingo *o.s.a.* '61 (SJN)[C] Bayamon, PR Seminario Agustiniano Sto. Tomas De Villanueva.
Allessandro, Michael J. '44 (NY) Bronx, NY St. Anthony.
Alleyne, Edward D. '60 (CAM) Judges Retired.
Allgaier, Robert A. '98 (OM) Absent on Leave.
Allgaier, Sebastian *o.s.b.* '99 (KC)[J] Conception, MO Conception Abbey.
Allgaier, Sebastian *o.s.b.* '99 (KC)[A] Conception, MO Conception Seminary College.
Alliata, Peter R. '61 (WDC) Mount Rainier, MD St. James.
Alliata, Peter (WDC) Cursillo Movement.
Allie, Robert *o.m.i.* '51 (STP)[M] St. Paul, MN Oblate Residence.
Allie, Robert *o.m.i.* '51 (STP) St. Paul, MN St. Mary.
Allie, Stanley J. '58 (ALB) On Duty Outside the Diocese.
Alliegro, Michael J. '73 (MET) East Brunswick, NJ St. Bartholomew; Office of Worship.
Allin, R. Benedict *o.s.b.* '67 (STL) St. Louis, MO St. Anselm; [O] St. Louis, MO The Abbey of St. Mary and St. Louis.
Alling, James '92 (PHX) Kingman, AZ St. Mary's.
Allison, Bruce R. '61 (E) Erie, PA Our Lady of Mt. Carmel.
Allison, Bruce '61 (E).
Allison, Jeffrey '96 (AUS)[G] Austin, TX Congregation of Holy Cross – Southern Province.
Allison, Joseph C. '56 (CIN) Retired.
Allison, Michael P. '91 (E) Erie, PA Holy Rosary.
Allman, Mark '96 (ALB) Leave of Absence.
Allman, Matthew T. *c.ss.r.* '00 (FgM).
Allmaras, Alfred '59 (FAR) Retired.
Allt, John F. '73 (TUC) Tucson, AZ St. Joseph; Directors.
Alm, Robbie (HON) Board of Directors.
Almade, Frank D. '78 (PIT) Pittsburgh, PA St. John Vianney; [R] Pittsburgh, PA Christ Child Society of Pittsburgh.
Almagno, Romano *o.f.m.* '65 (NY)[EE] New York Franciscan Province of the Immaculate Conception.
Almazan, Humberto *m.s.a.* '66 (NOR)[F] Cromwell Society of the Missionaries of the Holy Apostles.
Almazan, Jose A. '63 (CC) Corpus Christi, TX Sacred Heart.
Almeida, George F. '65 (FR) Retired.
Almendra, Leoncio T. '60 (NOR) Retired.
Almendras, Joel J. '75 (MRY) Los Osos, CA St. Elizabeth Ann Seton.
Alminde, Joseph M. *s.j.* '62 (PH) Philadelphia, PA Old St. Joseph's.
Almonte, Alfred P. *c.s.* '61 (PRO) Providence, RI St. Bartholomew.
Almonte, Antonio '97 (NY) New York, NY Incarnation; Yonkers, NY St. Peter.
Alonso, Armando '90 (MIA) Higher Studies.
Alonso, Armando '90 (MIA) Miami, FL St. Timothy.
Alonso, Ignacio *c.m.* '60 (SJN) San Juan, PR Nuestra Senora del Pilar.
Alonso, Jose Luis *o.p.* '61 (PCE)[B] The Pontifical Catholic University of Puerto Rico.
Alonso, Oscar *sch.p.* '68 (MIA)[C] Fort Lauderdale, FL Cardinal Gibbons High School.
Alookaran, Charles '90 (NEW) Scotch Plains, NJ Immaculate Heart of Mary.
Alookaran, Charles (BIR) Birmingham, AL St. Paul's Cathedral.
Alookaran, Joy '80 (NEW) Scotch Plains, NJ St. Bartholomew.
Alookaran, Joy '80 (SYM) Scotch Plains, NJ Syro–Malabar Catholic Community of Scotch Plains, NJ.
Alphonso, John '68 (DAL).
Alphonso, John '68 (DAL)[G] Dallas, TX St. Paul Medical Center; Dallas, TX Mary Immaculate.
Alsola, Felix S. '86 (DET) Detroit, MI St. Joseph.
Alsola, Felix '86 (DET)[H] Southfield, MI Providence Hospital.
Alt, Clement *c.pp.s.* '51 (CIN)[B] Carthagena, OH St. Charles.
Alt, Kenneth G. *c.pp.s.* '78 (CIN) St. Peter, OH St. Peter; Fort Recovery, OH St. Anthony; St. Peter, OH St. Joseph.
Altarejos, Antonio *s.d.b.* '54 (MIA) Miami, FL St. Kieran.
Altavilla, Philip A. '92 (SCR) Taylor, PA Immaculate Conception; Procurator/Advocates; Deans; Presbyteral Council; Diocesan Commission on Ecumenism and Inter–Faith Matters; Diocesan Office of Ecumenism.
Altavista, Salvatore D. *m.s.* '64 (HRT)[M] Hartford, CT Missionaries of LaSalette.
Altenbaugh, Richard L. '60 (PT) Pensacola, FL St. John the Evangelist.
Altermatt, Gregory M. '76 (HRT) West Haven CT Our Lady of Victory; [I] New Haven, CT Hospital of St. Raphael.
Althoff, Arthur J. '55 (STL) Retired.
Altier, Robert J. '89 (STP) St. Paul, MN St. Agnes.
Altine, Richard L. '95 (KAL) Kalamazoo, MI St. Mary; Scouting Apostolate.
Altman, David *o.c.s.o.* '79 (SLC)[F] Huntsville, UT Abbey of Our Lady of the Holy Trinity of the Order of Cistercians.
Altman, Joseph W. '76 (CHI) Harvey, IL Ascension–St. Susanna; Markham, IL St. Gerard Majella.
Altmann, Robert T. '62 (LC) Archivist Retired
Altstock, Edward '59 (P) Retired.
Altuna, Javier *s.j.* '66 (LA) Inglewood, CA St. John Chrysostom.
Alumam, Rudolph '91 (OAK) Hayward, CA St. Bede.
Alva, Benedict *o.s.b.* '01 (JOL)[L] Lisle, IL St. Procopius Abbey.
Alvarado, Felix E. '90 (PCE)[B] The Pontifical Catholic University of Puerto Rico.
Alvarado, Felix Emilio '90 (PCE) Arroyo, PR Our Lady of Mt. Carmel.
Alvarado, John Paul '88 (MET) South Plainfield, NJ Sacred Heart.
Alvarado, John Paul (MET) Deans.
Alvarado, Roberto *c.m.f.* '39 (SAT) San Antonio, TX Immaculate Heart of Mary.
Alvarado, Roberto '89 (ELP) El Paso, TX St. Raphael.
Alvarado de Jesus, Jose R. '94 (PCE) Ponce, PR San Conrado.
Alvares, Augustine '50 (P) Retired.
Alvarez, Abel *o.s.a.* '58 (NY) Bronx, NY Lincoln Medical and Mental Health Center.
Alvarez, Abel *o.s.a.* '58 (NY) New York, NY Holy Rosary.
Alvarez, Antonio M. '93 (MET) New Brunswick, NJ Our Lady of Mt. Carmel.
Alvarez, Armando '72 (SJN) Santurce, PR Ntra. Sra. del Perpetuo Socorro.
Alvarez, Carlos A. '01 (PBL) Center, CO St. Francis Jerome; Del Norte, CO Holy Name of Mary; Monte Vista, CO St. Joseph; Catholic Charismatic Renewal Center.
Alvarez, Carlos (PBL) Presbyteral Council–College of Consultors.
Alvarez, Carlos (PBL) Presbyteral Council.
Alvarez, Eduardo *s.j.* '74 (MIA)[D] Miami, FL Belen Jesuit Preparatory School.
Alvarez, Eduardo *s.j.* '74 (MIA)[H] Miami FL Villa Javier.
Alvarez, Enrique '03 (SAC) Sacramento, CA St. Joseph's.
Alvarez, Fred *s.a.* '61 (NY)[EE] Garrison, NY Franciscan Friars of the Atonement.
Alvarez, Isaias *o.s.a.* '76 (SJN) Bayamon, PR Santa Rita de Casia.
Alvarez, Javier *o.f.m.* '89 (LA) San Jose, CA Our Lady of Guadalupe.
Alvarez, John J. '81 (STL)[P] Kirkwood, MO Prelature of the Holy Cross and Opus Dei.
Alvarez, Jose '03 (MIA) Miami, FL St. Brendan.
Alvarez, Manuel Francisco '02 (MIA) Key Biscayne, FL St. Agnes.
Alvarez, Miguel *sch.p.* '61 (PCE) Playa de Ponce, PR Our Lady of Mt. Carmel.
Alvarez, Milton *c.m.f.* '77 (ATL) Stone Mountain, GA Corpus Christi.
Alvarez, Nolasco Tamayo '98 (PRO) Providence, RI St. Edward.
Alvarez, Pablo D. *f.s.s.p.* '86 (PCE) On Duty Outside the Diocese.
Alvarez, Perfecto *o.s.a.* '52 (PCE)[B] The Pontifical Catholic University of Puerto Rico.
Alvarez, Pompilio '60 (NY) Bronx, NY St. Athanasius.
Alvarez, Porfirio '69 (LA) Oxnard, CA St. Anthony.
Alvarez, Ramon '81 (PCE)[G] Ponce, PR Prelature of the Holy Cross and Opus Dei.
Alvarez, Ramon '82 (DAL) Dallas, TX Cathedral–Santuario de Guadalupe.
Alvarez, Ramon '82 (DAL)[N] Dallas, TX Cathedral Restoration and Preservation Fund, Inc..
Alvarez, Ramon (DAL) Defensor Vinculi; Assistant Judicial Vicars; Diocesan Consultors; Presbyteral Council; Personnel Board; Cathedral Santuario de Guadalupe.
Alvarez–Garcia, Julio '75 (WDC) Retired.
Alvernaz, Dennis '71 (FRS) Retired.
Alvero, Joshua R. '99 (GAL)[K] Catholic Chaplain Corps, Texas Medical Center; Phoenix, AZ Most Holy Trinity.
Alvero, Sammy (CHI) Chicago, IL St. Timothy.
Alverson, Joe (CC)[D] Corpus Christi, TX.
Alves, Eugene L. '61 (BO) Gloucester, MA Our Lady of Good Voyage.
Alves, Francisco *s.j.* '95 (WDC)[M] Washington, DC The Jesuit Community at Georgetown University; Rockville, MD Shrine of St. Jude.
Alves, Joseph T. '53 (BO) Senior Priests Retired.
Alvey, J. Paul '53 (SC) Retired.
Alvey, Leonard J. '58 (OWN) Non–Parochial Assignments; [A] Owensboro, KY Brescia University.
Alvey, Leonard (OWN) Judges.
Alvey, Leonard (OWN) Committee for Education.
Alwell, Juniper *o.f.m.conv.* '56 (NY)[EE] Staten Island, NY St. Francis Friary.
Alzate, Alberto '77 (LAV) Las Vegas, NV St. Francis de Sales.
Alzugaray, Joseph '67 (SR) Napa, CA St. Apollinaris.
Amabile, Patsy C. '73 (CAM) Vineland, NJ Sacred Heart.
Amadeo, Michael A. '92 (DM) Elkhart, IA St. Mary/Holy Cross; On Special Assignment.
Amadeo, Michael (DM) Defenders of the Bond.
Amador, Alfonso *c.ss.r.* '58 (SJN) San Juan, PR San Agustin.
Amaechi, Jerome '94 (SY) North Syracuse, NY St. Rose of Lima.
Amah, Godwin '86 (LC) Ettrick, WI St. Bridget.
Amahi, Godwin '86 (LC) Ettrick, WI St. Kevin.
Amakiri, Paul C. '72 (CAM) Lakeland, NJ Camden County Hospital at Lakeland; Newfield, NJ St. Rose of Lima.
Amaldoss, G. '78 (NO) Crown Point, LA St. Pius X.
Amalfitano, Joseph A. '63 (PH) Marcus Hook, PA Immaculate Conception.
Amaliri, Paul O. '00 (TLS) Cushing, OK SS. Peter and Paul; Cushing, OK St. John.
Amalraj, Loyola '81 (NY) Croton–on–Hudson, NY Holy Name of Mary.
Aman, Gerald W. *s.j.* '73 (FgM).
Amandikwa, Anselm *c.m.f.* '93 (SPC)[I] Springfield, MO O'Reilly Catholic Student Center, Southwest MO State University, Drury College, Ozarks Technical Com.
Amann, John J. '66 (BRK) Brooklyn, NY Holy Family.
Amann, Steven J. '74 (MIL) New Berlin, WI St. Elizabeth Ann Seton.
Amann, William '54 (ROC) Rochester, NY St. Thomas More.
Amann, William '54 (ROC) Retired.
Amano, Antonio A. (MO) Army Chaplains.
Amantegui, Carmelo *s.j.* '53 (NY) Bronx, NY St. Jerome's.
Amantia, Damian Vincent *t.o.r.* '90 (VEN) Bradenton, FL Our Lady of the Angels.
Amanzeh, Augustine '74 (SAT) San Antonio, TX San Antonio State Hospital.
Amar, Joseph P. '74 (SAM)[B] University of Notre Dame Du Lac; On Duty Outside the Diocese.
Amar, Mubarak *f.s.s.p.* '91 (LIN)[A] Denton, NE Our Lady of Guadalupe Seminary; On Duty Outside the Diocese.
Amar, Zab '74 (E) Du Bois, PA St. Catherine.
Amaral, Angelo '91 (TR) Keansburg, NJ St. Ann.
Amaral, Stephen P. '78 (PRO) Coventry, RI Our Lady of Czenstochowa; Council Members.
Amarillas, Thomas R. *m.m.* '68 (FgM).
Amaro, Arlindo A. *c.s.sp.* '56 (PRO) Central Falls, RI Immaculate Heart of Mary.
Amato, Antonio '61 (PRT) Mechanic Falls, ME Our Lady of Ransom.
Amato, Benet *o.s.b.* '79 (IND)[K] St. Meinrad, IN St.

Meinrad Archabbey.
Amato, Frank *s.a.c.* '88 (NEW)[N] South Orange, NJ Pallottine Fathers & Brothers.
Amato, Frank *s.a.c.* '88 (BRK) Brooklyn, NY Our Lady of the Rosary of Pompeii.
Amato, Joseph S. (VEN) Judges.
Amato, Joseph '59 (ALB) Retired.
Amato, Joseph (VEN) Adjutant Judicial Vicars.
Amato, Nicholas P. '70 (BAL) Monkton, MD Our Lady of Grace.
Amato, Salvatore '69 (BRK) Rego Park, NY Resurrection–Ascension.
Amaya, Hernando Gomez '02 (SAC) Vallejo, CA St. Vincent Ferrer.
Amberger, Frank '96 (CIN) Russia, OH St. Remy.
Ambert, Jorge R. *s.j.* '66 (SJN) San Juan, PR San Ignacio de Loyola; [C] Rio Piedras, PR Jesuit Community.
Ambert, Jorge *s.j.* '66 (SJN)[D] San Juan, PR Renovacion Conyugal dba Fundacion Fernando Martinez.
Ambooken, Jose '75 (NY) Bronx, NY St. Margaret Mary.
Ambosta, Dawson '75 (NY) Bronxville, NY St. Joseph.
Ambrasas, Kazimieras *s.j.* '88 (CHI)[N] Chicago Lithuanian American Jesuits.
Ambre, John T. '75 (GRY) Gary, IN St. Mark.
Ambrogi, James J. '64 (PH) Malvern, PA St. Patrick.
Ambrose, Akalawu *c.s.sp.* '71 (SAT)[M] San Antonio, TX Holy Cross Community; [H] San Antonio, TX Christus Santa Rosa Health Care Corporation; San Antonio, TX Santa Rosa Hospital System.
Ambrose, Malcolm '72 (LA) Santa Clarita, CA Our Lady of Perpetual Help.
Ambrosio, Joseph F. (NEW) Ironbound Deanery 21; Members; Italian Apostolate.
Ambrosio, Joseph '74 (NEW) Newark, NJ Our Lady of Mt. Carmel.
Ambrosy, David J. '85 (DUB) Mount Vernon, IA St. John the Baptist; Springville, IA St. Isidore; Cedar Rapids, IA Immaculate Conception.
Amedee, Francis '48 (HT) Retired.
Ameling, Richard H. '66 (GRY) Merrillville, IN St. Andrew.
Amemiya, Hiroki *s.d.b.* '02 (OAK)[N] Berkeley Salesian Community.
Amen, Maurice E. *c.s.c.* '61 (FTW)[I] Notre Dame, IN Columba Hall.
Amen, Maurice *c.s.c.* '61 (FTW)[I] Notre Dame, IN Columba Hall.
Amendikwa, Anselm *c.m.f.* '93 (SPC)[E] Springfield, MO Claretians Missionaries' Residence–Villa Claret.
Amengual, Miguel '46 (LA) Retired.
Ament, Richard J. '66 (DUB) Cedar Rapids, IA St. Jude; College of Consultors.
Ament, Robert J. '52 (DUB) Retired.
Amerando, Gerald '84 (FRS) Fresno, CA St. Helen.
Amerando, Jerry '84 (FRS) Easton, CA St. Jude Mission; On Special Assignment.
Amershek, Charles M. '75 (ALT) Johnstown, PA St. Rochus.
Ames, Gregory '86 (DEN) Northglenn, CO Immaculate Heart of Mary.
Ames, John J. '82 (PH) Conshohocken, PA St. Matthew; [EE] Conshohocken, PA Tri–College Newman Cluster–Bryn Mawr, Haverford and Swarthmore Colleges.
Amesse, Michael J. *o.m.i.* '84 (NO) International Shrine of St. Jude; New Orleans, LA Our Lady of Guadalupe /International Shrine of St. Jude.
Amesse, Michael *o.m.i.* '84 (NO) New Orleans, LA Shrine of St. Jude Thaddeus.
Amey, Robert G. '69 (WDC) Silver Spring, MD St. Catherine Laboure; Advocates; Archdiocesan Council of Catholic Women.
Amezaga, Louis (LSC) Absent On Leave.
Amezcua, Mario M. *l.c.* (MO) Army Chaplains.
Amezcua, Pedro E. '86 (LA) Los Angeles, CA Immaculate Conception.
Amico, Alexander D. '73 (E) Coalport, PA St. Basil the Great.
Amico, Charles R. '52 (BUF) Retired.
Amico, Francis A. *c.s.b.* '75 (GAL)[Q] Sugar Land Basilian Mission Center.
Amico, Nicholas H. '51 (DET) Oak Park, MI Our Lady of Fatima.
Amico, Richard S. '60 (BUF) Niagara Falls, NY St. Joseph.
Amidon, Philip R. *s.j.* '74 (OM) Omaha, NE St. John; [K] Omaha, NE Jesuit Community at Creighton University.
Amiot, Ronald J. *s.j.* '78 (BO)[V] Weston, MA Campion Jesuit Community; [V] Weston, MA Campion Health Center, Inc..
Amiro, Raymond M. '43 (SFE) Retired.
Amissah, Kofi Ntsiful '79 (ALB) Albany, NY St. George; Albany, NY Sacred Heart of Jesus; Menands, NY St. Joan of Arc.
Ammering, Bruce F. '54 (ROC)[J] Rochester, NY Sisters St. Joseph Motherhouse.
Ammering, Bruce '54 (ROC) Retired.
Amn, Joseph (BRK) Legion of Mary.
Amo, Steven C. '92 (SPR) Agawam, MA All Saints.
Amodio, Francis *o.carm.* '83 (NY)[EE] Middletown, NY St. Albert's Priory.
Amora, Edito D. (Phil) Air National Guard Chaplains.
Amora, Eduardo '90 (NY) Staten Island, NY Holy Rosary.
Amora, Silvano '77 (TR) Toms River, NJ St. Justin.
Amoros, Juan Maria *o.carm.* '55 (MGZ) Anasco, PR St. Anthony Abbot.
Amos, John R. '73 (MOB) On Leave from the Archdiocese.
Amrhein, Peter T. '48 (MIL)[M] Wauwatosa, WI St. Camillus Health Center, Inc. Retired.
Amrhein, Quentin *c.p.* '53 (HRT)[M] West Hartford Holy Family Monastery/Retreat.
Amrhein, Raphael *c.p.* '62 (PMB)[J] North Palm Beach, FL Our Lady of Florida Spiritual Center.
Amrhein, Robert *o.f.m.conv.* '62 (SY) Syracuse, NY Assumption B.V.M..
Amsberry, John '97 (P) Portland, OR Church of St. Joseph the Worker.
Amundsen, Robert L. '69 (DEN) Lafayette, CO Immaculate Conception.
Amundsen, Robert (DEN) Presbyteral Council; Deaneries; Chairman of Deans.
Amy, Peter L. '64 (LA) Sylmar, CA St. Didacus.
Amyot, Andrew J. '64 (OG) Norfolk, NY Visitation of the B.V.M..
An, Dominic G. '86 (NEW) Demarest, NJ St. Joseph.
An, Joseph (NSH) Korean; Korean Catholic Community of St. Joseph.
Anable, Richard J. *s.j.* '45 (PAT)[I] Morristown, NJ Loyola House of Retreats.
Anadore, Charles E. '50 (BO) Senior Priests Retired.
Anaele, Ignatius I. '98 (CHI) Arlington Heights, IL Our Lady of the Wayside.
Anandappa, Mahendra *s.s.s.* '85 (FTW) Corpus Christi, TX Our Lady of the Rosary.
Anania, Alexis *o.f.m.* '58 (PIT) Pittsburgh, PA St. Pamphilus.
Anania, Alexis *o.f.m.* (PIT) Chaplains to Korean Catholic Community.
Anarcon, Angelito '81 (TR) Eatontown, NJ St. Dorothea.
Anastasia, Thomas '91 (SP) St. Petersburg, FL Holy Cross.
Anastasia, Thomas (SP) Presbyteral Council.
Anastasio, Thomas '58 (BRK) Brooklyn, NY St. Patrick.
Anaya, Sergio M. '92 (ATL) Buford, GA Prince of Peace.
Anchanickal, Thomas '96 (BIR) Demopolis, AL St. Leo.
Anchanickal, Thomas *m.s.f.s.* '96 (ATL)[K] Lawrenceville The Missionaries of St. Francis De Sales.
Ancharski, John J. '83 (TUC) Solomon, AZ Our Lady of Guadalupe; Safford, AZ Conservation Center; Fort Grant Rural Station, AZ Fort Grant Training Center; Solomon, AZ Our Lady of Guadalupe.
Ancheril, Jose '86 (BEL) Vienna, IL St. Francis de Sales.
Ancheril, Jose '86 (BEL) Metropolis, IL St. Rose of Lima.
Ancheril, Jose '86 (BEL) Vienna, IL St. Paul.
Ancona, Gaspar F. '63 (GR) Byron Center, MI St. Sebastian's.
Anctil, Leo '43 (SUP) Retired.
Anctil, Peter Claude *o.s.b.* '67 (BUR)[E] Weston, VT Priory of Benedictine Monks.
Andalikiewicz, Charles '58 (KCK) Kansas City, KS Sacred Heart.
Andalikiewicz, Charles '58 (KCK) Kansas City, KS St. John the Evangelist.
Andary, Edward J. '69 (PBL) Ignacio, CO St. Ignatius Parish.
Andary, John S. '51 (SAM) Retired.
Andary, Thomas M. '41 (MAR) Retired.
Andel, David '95 (SB) Riverside, CA St. Catherine of Alexandria.
Andel, David '95 (SB) Special or Other Diocesan Assignment.
Andel, David (SB) Judges; Elected Members.
Anderl, Henry *o.s.b.* '45 (SCL)[I] Collegeville, MN St. John's Abbey, of the Order of St. Benedict.
Anderl, Peter J. '01 (FAR) Fargo, ND SS. Anne & Joachim.
Anderlonis, Joseph J. *s.t.d.* '69 (PH) Philadelphia, PA St. George; Censores Librorum.
Anders, Arnold '50 (VIC) On Duty Outside the Diocese.
Anders, Arnold '88 (CC)[E] Corpus Christi, TX Mount Carmel Home.
Andersen, Emil (E) Retired.
Anderson, Alexander R. '75 (STL) Eureka, MO Sacred Heart.
Anderson, Andrew L. (SAM) Judges.
Anderson, Andrew L. (MIA) Judicial Vicar; Special Assignment.
Anderson, Andrew (MIA) Catholic Funeral Directors' Guild.
Anderson, Andrew (MIA) Catholic Lawyers' Guild.
Anderson, Andrew (MIA) Archdiocesan Council of Catholic Women.
Anderson, Anthony *s.o.l.t.* '91 (CC)[G] Robstown, TX Society of Our Lady of the Most Holy Trinity.
Anderson, Arthur C. '62 (RVC) Retired.
Anderson, Arthur T. '58 (CAM) Retired.
Anderson, B. Ernest '82 (B) Absent on Leave.
Anderson, Bertil J. '74 (PRO) Warwick, RI St. Rita.
Anderson, Daniel J. *o.f.m.* '76 (CIN)[M] Cincinnati, OH Pleasant Street Friary.
Anderson, David J. *s.j.* '97 (FBK) Toksook Bay, AK St. Peter the Fisherman; Tununak, AK St. Joseph; [E] St. Marys, AK Brother Joe Prince Jesuit Community.
Anderson, David '83 (STN) Ukiah, CA Ukrainian Catholic Mission.
Anderson, David *s.j.* '97 (FBK) Our Lady of Perpetual Help.
Anderson, Derek '03 (CC)[G] Robstown, TX Society of Our Lady of the Most Holy Trinity.
Anderson, Gabriel C. '89 (DUB) Walker, IA St. Mary; Walker, IA Sacred Heart; Deanery Representatives.
Anderson, George M. *s.j.* '73 (NY) New York, NY Nativity.
Anderson, Gregory M. *o.p.* '47 (P) Portland, OR Holy Rosary Parish & Dominican Priory.
Anderson, James B. '78 (GAL) Houston, TX St. Rose of Lima; Area Representatives.
Anderson, James W. *m.s.a.* (MO) AUXILIARY CHAPLAINS CONTRACT CHAPLAINS.
Anderson, James *m.s.a.* '77 (NOR)[F] Cromwell Society of the Missionaries of the Holy Apostles.
Anderson, Joe *o.s.b.* (LSC) Special Assignment.
Anderson, John C. '93 (SUP) Ladysmith, WI St. Mary of Czestowchowa; Ladysmith, WI Our Lady of Sorrows; Ladysmith, WI St. Anthony de Padua; St. Pius Priest Fund; Personnel Placement Board.
Anderson, John D. '62 (FAR) Retired.
Anderson, John E. '66 (LSC) Las Cruces, NM Holy Cross; Bishops Administrative Council; Vicar General; Director of Clergy Personnel; Defenders of the Bond; Diocesan Consultors; Presbyteral Council; Clergy Personnel Board; Finance Council; Holy Childhood Association; Propogation of the Faith.
Anderson, John F. '50 (CLV) Chesterland, OH St. Anselm Retired.
Anderson, John Flattery '59 (PEO) Retired.
Anderson, John '96 (ATL) Released from Archdiocesan Assignment.
Anderson, Jordan S. *o.praem.* '97 (ORG)[I] Silverado, CA Norbertine Fathers of Orange Inc..
Anderson, Joseph G. '63 (MIL) New Berlin, WI Holy Apostles.
Anderson, Joseph W. '62 (PEO) Creve Coeur, IL Sacre Coeur.
Anderson, Jude *o.s.b.* '94 (B) Absent on Leave.
Anderson, Ken (CC) Office of Worship.
Anderson, Kenneth A. '98 (COL) On Duty Outside the Diocese.
Anderson, Kenneth J. '87 (RCK) DeKalb, IL St. Mary.
Anderson, Kevin '83 (SCL)[L] St. Cloud, MN Newman Center, Inc..
Anderson, Kevin '83 (SCL) St. Cloud, MN Christ Church.
Anderson, Kevin (SCL) Campus Ministry.
Anderson, Kevin (SCL) Deans.
Anderson, Kevin (SCL) Presbyteral Council.
Anderson, Kevin (SCL) Diocesan Consultors.
Anderson, Knute *o.s.b.* '56 (SCL)[I] Collegeville, MN St. John's Abbey, of the Order of St. Benedict.
Anderson, Kurt J. *m.m.* '72 (FgM).
Anderson, Louis (GR) Retired.
Anderson, Luke *s.o.cist.* '54 (ALN)[K] New Ringgold, PA Cistercian Monastery.
Anderson, Marcel '57 (ALX) Retired.
Anderson, Michael F. '83 (STP) St. Paul, MN St. Bernard.
Anderson, Philip *o.s.b.* (TLS)[G] Hulbert, OK Our Lady of the Annunciation of Clear Creek Monastery.
Anderson, R. Bentley *s.j.* '96 (STL)[C] Saint Louis University; [O] St. Louis, MO Jesuit Community Corporation at St. Louis University – Jesuit Hall.
Anderson, Richard W. *s.j.* '66 (CIN)[P] Milford, OH Milford Spiritual Center.
Anderson, Robert Kevin *o.c.s.o.* '55 (WOR)[O] Spencer, MA St. Joseph's Abbey.
Anderson, Robert L. *s.j.* '50 (NO)[P] New Orleans, LA Ignatius Residence.
Anderson, Robert M. *o.s.m.* '65 (P)[N] Chicago, IL Order of Friar Servants of Mary (Servites) United States of America Province, Inc.; [N] Chicago Order of Friar Servants of Mary (Servites) United States of America Province, Inc..
Anderson, Robert S. *o.s.m.* '65 (P)[L] Portland, OR The Grotto, The National Sanctuary of Our Sorrowful Mother.
Anderson, Ronald '72 (DET) Milford, MI St. Mary, Our Lady of the Snows.
Anderson, Ronald *s.j.* '84 (BO)[V] Newton, MA The Jesuit Community at Boston College.
Anderson, Stephen A. '86 (E) Conneaut Lake, PA Our Lady Queen of the Americas.
Anderson, Steven D. '03 (LAN) Grand Blanc, MI Holy Family.
Anderson, Terry '84 (SFS) Aberdeen, SD Sacred Heart.
Anderson, Thomas S. *s.j.* '98 (MIL)[O] Pontifical Biblical Institute.

Anderson, William A. *v.f.* '63 (WH) Coalton, WV St. Patrick Church; Elkins, WV St. Brendan; Huttonsville, WV St. John Bosco; Diocesan Consultors; Vicars Forane; Liturgical Art and Architecture Commission.
Anderson, William C. '52 (TR) Retired.
Anderson, William R. '42 (BO) Senior Priests Retired.
Andert, Thomas *o.s.b.* '75 (SCL)[I] Collegeville, MN St. John's Abbey, of the Order of St. Benedict.
Andonian, Raphael *o.mech.* (ARM) Business Chancellor.
Andrade, Antonio L. '63 (BO) Health Leave.
Andrade, Bernardino '65 (OAK) Oakley, CA St. Anthony.
Andrade, David M. '86 (FR) Fall River, MA Holy Trinity; Procurator–Advocates; Auditors.
Andrade, Joseph Anthony '92 (STP) St. Paul, MN St. Thomas The Apostle.
Andrade, Sebastian '59 (ATL) Atlanta, GA St. Jude.
Andrae, Henry C. '78 (E) Stoneboro, PA St. Columbkille.
Andras, Emeric (ATH) "HIS– Press Service".
Andraschko, James F. '59 (SFS) Sioux Falls, SD Holy Spirit.
Andraschko, James '59 (SFS)[I] Sioux Falls, SD St. Mary/Holy Spirit School Endowment Trust.
Andre, Leonard J. '61 (MIL) Retired.
Andre, Ludwig '57 (SJ) Retired.
Andreano, Michael A. '00 (NEW) Nutley, NJ Holy Family.
Andreatta, Tullio '38 (SB) Retired.
Andree, Daniel *c.ss.r.* '80 (CHI) Chicago, IL St. Michael; [N] Chicago, IL The Redemptorist Fathers of Chicago.
Andree, John Paul *c.ss.r.* '68 (CHI) Chicago, IL St. Michael; [N] Chicago, IL The Redemptorist Fathers of Chicago; [X] Chicago, IL Co–Redemptorist Association Office.
Andrejek, Michael J. '98 (PEO) Moline, IL Sacred Heart; [B] Rock Island, IL Alleman High School.
Andres, Edmundo *c.m.f.* '57 (CHI) Chicago, IL Our Lady of Guadalupe.
Andres, James *o.f.m.cap.* '63 (DET) Clinton Twp., MI St. Ronald.
Andres, Joseph P. '48 (CIN) Retired.
Andres, Napoleon *m.s.* '85 (HON) Kalaheo, HI Holy Cross; Koloa, HI St. Raphael.
Andres, Tim *o.carm.* '86 (JOL)[L] Darien Carmelite Provincial Office.
Andreu, Ramon R. *s.j.* '55 (LA) Los Angeles, CA St. Kevin.
Andrews, Alexander *o.s.b.* '69 (SCL)[I] Collegeville, MN St. John's Abbey, of the Order of St. Benedict.
Andrews, Daniel R. '01 (OM) Omaha, NE Christ the King.
Andrews, Dennis M. *c.s.b.* '70 (GAL)[Q] Houston, TX Residence of the Basilian Fathers of the University of St. Thomas.
Andrews, Dennis (MIL) Thiensville, WI St. Cecilia.
Andrews, Edward A. *o.s.a.* '59 (CHI)[C] New Lenox, IL Providence Catholic High School; [L] New Lenox, IL Augustinian Friary.
Andrews, Eric P. *c.s.p.* '95 (KNX) Knoxville, TN John XXIII University Parish/Catholic Center; [H] Knoxville, TN UT–Knoxville, Newman Foundation, Inc.; University of Tennessee–Knoxville.
Andrews, John P. '62 (FR) Wellfleet, MA Our Lady of Lourdes.
Andrews, John S. '96 (OM) Omaha, NE St. Stephen the Martyr; Hartington, NE Holy Trinity.
Andrews, Mark W. *s.j.* '92 (CHI)[T] The Jesuit Retreat League of Chicago.
Andrews, Peter J. '88 (PRO) Tiverton, RI St. Christopher; Tiverton, RI St. Theresa; Worship.
Andrews, Robert F. *o.s.a.* '55 (PH)[AA] Villanova, PA St. Thomas Monastery.
Andrey, Roberto '83 (SFR) Belmont, CA Immaculate Heart of Mary.
Andrie, Donald A. *c.s.p.* '94 (STP) Minneapolis, MN St. Lawrence–Newman; [M] Minneapolis, MN Paulist Fathers; [U] Minneapolis, MN Newman Center at St. Lawrence.
Andrus, Albin A. '73 (PRT) Portland, ME Cathedral of the Immaculate Conception.
Andrus, Charles *s.s.j.* '76 (GAL) Houston, TX Our Mother of Mercy; Houston, TX Our Lady Star of the Sea.
Andrus, David L. *s.j.* '79 (NO)[P] Pohnpei, FM Jesuits of Pohnpei; [N] Berkeley, CA Jesuit Community at Jesuit School of Theology at Berkeley.
Andrus, Richard *s.v.d.* '83 (CHI) Chicago, IL St. Elizabeth.
Andrushkiw, Vladimir '36 (STF) Retired.
Andujar, J. Iriarte *o.p.* '86 (PRO)[P] Providence St. Thomas Aquinas Priory at Providence College.
Anemelu, Charles I. '97 (NEW) Berkeley Heights, NJ Runnells Specialized Hospital; Runnells Specialized Hospital.
Anemelu, Charles '97 (NEW) Berkeley Heights, NJ Church of the Little Flower.
Anewka, Paul '89 (SAT) San Antonio, TX Texas Center for Infectious Disease.
Angadiath, Joseph *c.m.i.* '69 (LKC) Lake Charles, LA St. Henry.
Angel, Ariel O. (BWN) Associate Judges.
Angel, Ariel Oliver '01 (BWN) San Juan, TX The Basilica of the National Shrine of Our Lady of San Juan del Valle; [J] San Juan, TX The Basilica of Our Lady of San Juan del Valle – National Shrine; Secretariat for the Diocesan Synod.
Angel, Jose Rene '99 (BWN)[A] Mission, TX The Saint Joseph and Saint Peter Seminary; Promoter of Justice; Defenders of the Bond.
Angeles, Joey F. (BR) Baton Rouge, LA St. George.
Angelicchio, Paul F. '77 (SY) Syracuse, NY Our Lady of Pompei; Syracuse, NY St. Peter.
Angelini, Joseph *o.f.m.conv.* '65 (ALB) Albany, NY Our Lady of Angels.
Angelini, Joseph *o.f.m.conv.* '65 (ALB) Albany, NY St. Casimir.
Angelini, Joseph '67 (MIA) Margate, FL St. Vincent Retired.
Angell, Charles *s.a.* '60 (NY)[EE] Garrison, NY St. Christopher's Inn.
Angell, Charles *s.a.* '60 (NY)[EE] Garrison, NY St. Christopher's Friary.
Angella, Ludovico '47 (NY) Middletown, NY St. Joseph.
Angelle, Robert G. '56 (LAF) Retired.
Angelle, Robert (LAF) Diocesan Consultors.
Angelo, Girard F. '55 (SCR) Retired.
Angelo, Thomas M. '85 (NOR) On Duty Outside the Diocese; Military Chaplains; Air Force Chaplains.
Angeloni, Michael '75 (WIL) Newark, DE Holy Family.
Angeloni, Owen *o.f.m.* '62 (ALB)[A] Catskill, NY St. Anthony Friary.
Angelov, Kiril '90 (STF) Rochester, NY St. Josaphat.
Angelov, Kiril (STF) Presbyteral Council.
Angelov, Kiril (STF) Administrative Council.
Angelov, Kiril (STF) Diocesan Consultors.
Angelovic, Michael '65 (SEA) Seahurst, WA St. Francis of Assisi.
Angelucci, Patrick *s.d.b.* '76 (NY)[EE] New Rochelle, NY Salesian Provincial House.
Anger, Raymond G. '57 (WOR) Retired.
Angert, James *t.o.r.* '71 (ARL) Herndon, VA St. Joseph.
Angi, Steve '85 (CIN) Cincinnati, OH Holy Family.
Angilella, Joseph T. *s.j.* '65 (SFR)[N] San Francisco, CA Jesuit Community at University of San Francisco.
Anginoli, Joseph T. '75 (PAT) Green Pond, NJ St. Simon the Apostle; Deans; Adjutant Judicial Vicar
Angkel, Julio '83 (CI) Holy Family Church.
Angkel, Julio '83 (CI)[C] Tunnuk, Chuuk, FM Vicariate Residence.
Angkel, Julio (CI) Vocations.
Anglada, Julio A. (ARE) Hatillo, PR Our Lady of Mt. Carmel.
Angle, Camillus *t.o.r.* '54 (ALT)[F] Newry, PA St. Bernardine Monastery.
Angles, Sebastian '44 (ORL) Retired.
Angles, Sebastian '44 (BRK) Retired.
Anglim, Ronald H. '65 (CHI) Antioch, IL St. Peter.
Anglim, Thomas G. '54 (VEN) Hartford, CT St. Luke; Fort Myers, FL St. Francis Xavier; [F] Fort Myers, FL Villa Francisco; [K] Fort Myers, FL St. Francis Xavier School Foundation; College of Consultors; Presbyteral Council; College of Consultors; Presbyteral Council.
Anglin, John *o.f.m.* '71 (NY)[EE] Hialeah, FL Comunidad de San Francisco.
Anglin, John *o.f.m.* '71 (MIA)[H] Hialeah, FL Franciscan Friars of the Holy Name Province.
Anglin, John *c.f.m.* '81 (BO)[V] Ministry of the Word.
Angotti, Joseph A. '91 (GRY) Military Chaplains; Army Chaplains.
Anguay, James *ss.cc.* '72 (HON)[G] Kaneohe, HI Sacred Hearts Center.
Anguiano, James M. '82 (LA) El Segundo, CA St. Anthony.
Angula, Michael '94 (SR)[G] Napa, CA Queen of the Valley Hospital of Napa.
Angulo, Raul '85 (MIA) Miami, FL Mother of Christ.
Anh, Anthony *s.j.* '90 (SPK)[L] Portland Jesuit Provincial Office (Society of Jesus, Oregon Prov.).
Anh, Tuan '00 (CIN) Leave of Absence.
Anholzer, Daniel *o.f.m.cap.* '80 (DET)[K] Detroit, MI Provincialate.
Anholzer, Daniel *o.f.m.cap.* '80 (FgM).
Aniban, Ives '66 (RNO)[B] Reno, NV St. Mary's Regional Medical Center.
Anich, Kenneth *s.v.d.* '73 (DUB)[B] Epworth, IA Divine Word College.
Anichini, Albert *m.c.c.j.* '62 (FgM).
Aniefuna, Clifford '85 (WDC)[L] Hyattsville, MD Sacred Heart Home Inc..
Aniello, Frederick M. (HRT) Commission for Priests' Retreats.
Anifer, Jeffrey '67 (DET) Melvindale, MI St. Mary Magdalen.
Animoottil, Thomas '89 (SYM) Los Angeles, CA St. Pius X (Knanaya Catholic) Mission of Los Angeles.
Aniszczyk, Leon S. '73 (MET) Bound Brook, NJ St. Mary of Czestochowa.
Ankenbrandt, Thomas F. *s.j.* '60 (DET)[P] Clarkston, MI Colombiere Center.
Ankenbrandt, Thomas W. '56 (TOL) Retired.
Anklan, Carlos *c.s.* '97 (MIA) O.L. Aparecida Roman Catholic Mission.
Anklan, Horecio Carlos *c.s.* '97 (NY) Hollywood, FL Our Lady Aparecida Mission.
Annese, Joseph P. '62 (LAV) Boulder City, NV St. Andrew's.
Annese, Joseph (LAV) Presbyteral Council for the Diocese of Las Vegas.
Annese, Joseph (LAV) Priests' Personnel Board.
Annie, Frederick P. '78 (WH) Wheeling, WV St. Joseph's Cathedral.
Annie, Frederick P. (BAL) Interdiocesan Judges.
Annie, Frederick P. (WH) Episcopal Vicar for Clergy.
An Ninh, Vincent Nguyen '71 (DET) Eastpointe, MI Our Lady of Grace Vietnamese Parish.
Annino, Sebastian V. '61 (CAM) Rosenhayn, NJ St. Mary's; [I] Newfield, NJ Mater Dei Nursing Home.
Annunziato, Michael *ss.cc.* '53 (BWN) Retired.
Anodee, Lazarus (BO) Dorchester, MA St. Margaret.
Anoia, John '57 (SPR) Retired.
Anoia, John '57 (SPR) New Port Richey, FL Our Lady Queen of Peace.
Anokwuru, Magnus (CHI) Chicago, IL St. Angela.
Anokwuru, Magnus (CHI)[J] Chicago, IL St. Anthony Hospital.
Anonuevo, Salvador '86 (RIC) Virginia Beach, VA St. Luke.
Anore, Joseph '97 (AGN) Dededo, GU Santa Barbara.
Anosike, Donatus *m.s.p.* (CHI) Chicago, IL Corpus Christi.
Anquilero, Roque '92 (HT) Morgan City, LA Sacred Heart of Jesus.
Ansaldi, Joseph C. '62 (NY)[F] New York, NY St. Joseph by the Sea, High School; [T] New York, NY Mission of the Immaculate Virgin.
Ansaloni, Edmund *o.f.m.* '49 (SP)[O] Clearwater Beach, FL St. Paul Friary.
Ansbro, Francis J. '51 (NY) Peekskill, NY Assumption.
Anschutz, Larry '82 (SFD) Mount Olive, IL Ascension.
Anschutz, Larry '82 (SFD) Mount Olive, IL Holy Trinity.
Anselment, Joseph E. (ALB) Priests Retirement Board.
Anselment, Joseph '61 (ALB) Queensbury, NY Our Lady of the Annunciation.
Anselment, Joseph (ALB) Deans.
Anselmi, Albert J. '71 (ALT) West Salisbury, PA St. Michael's.
Anslow, Thomas C. *c.m.* (LA)[Q] Los Angeles, CA Amat Residence II; Judges; Vicar for Canonical Services.
Anslow, Thomas *c.m.* (LA) Vicar for Canonical Services and Vice Chancellor; Canonical Services, Episcopal Vicar for.
Anson, Cesar R. '77 (TR) Brick Town, NJ Epiphany.
Anta, Antonio '55 (NEW) Retired.
Antal, Andras '68 (CLV) Cleveland, OH St. Elizabeth of Hungary.
Antall, Richard C. '80 (CLV) Casa Parroquial Inmaculada Concepcion.
Antao, John S. '60 (NEW) Elizabeth, NJ Our Lady of Fatima; Portugese Apostolate.
Antczak, John '63 (JOL) Bradley, IL St. Joseph.
Antczak, John '63 (JOL) Kankakee, IL Riverside Medical Center.
Antczak, Robert A. (NEW) Jersey City South Deanery 12.
Antczak, Robert '64 (NEW) Jersey City, NJ St. Paul's.
Antekeier, Charles R. '62 (GR) Retired.
Anthamatten, Joseph *c.pp.s.* '43 (CIN)[B] Carthagena, OH St. Charles.
Anthony, Angelo *c.pp.s.* '89 (CIN)[M] Dayton, OH Provincial Office of the Cincinnati Province of the Society of the Precious Blood.
Anthony, Hubert Hosanna (CC) Corpus Christi, TX St. Paul the Apostle.
Anthony, Joseph '80 (RNO) Virginia City, NV St. Mary in the Mountains.
Anthony, Julian '66 (PBR) Houston, TX St. John Chrysostom.
Anthony, Paul G. '61 (STL) Warson Woods, MO Ste. Genevieve Du Bois.
Anthony, Walter *c.s.p.* '56 (NY)[EE] Jamaica Estates Paulist Fathers Generalate.
Antillon, William R. '79 (RCK) Dundee, IL St. Catherine of Siena; Lena, IL St. Joseph.
Antinarelli, Ronald A. '74 (ROC) Rochester, NY Our Lady of Victory–St. Joseph.
Antiporek, James '81 (JOL) Warrenville, IL St. Irene.
Antl, Louis B. *o.f.m.* '48 (JOL) Joliet, IL St. John the Baptist; [L] Joliet, IL St. John the Baptist Friary.
Antl, Louis *o.f.m.* '48 (JOL)[K] Joliet, IL Our Lady of Angels Retirement Home.
Antoine, James *o.f.m.cap.* '67 (GF) Lodge Grass, MT Our Lady of Loretto.
Antolini, Vincenzo *o.m.v.* '58 (BO)[AA] Boston, MA St. Francis Chapel.
Antolini, Vincenzo *o.m.v.* '58 (BO)[V] Milton, MA Oblate Residence (St. Joseph House).
Anton, Bill (LUB) Director of Scouting.

Anton, Bill (LUB) Vocation Team Members.
Anton, Ronald J. *s.j.* '83 (BAL)[B] Timonium, MD Loyola Graduate Center –Timonium Campus; [S] Baltimore, MD Jesuit Community of Loyola College, Inc.; [N] Houston, TX Pope John Paul XXIII Priests' Residence Retired.
Anton, William J. '02 (LUB) Lubbock, TX St. John Neumann; Lubbock, TX St. Theresa's.
Anton, William '02 (LUB) Special Assignment.
Antonanzas, Jesus R. Diez '57 (PCE)[A] Ponce, PR Diocesan Seminary; Diocesan Consultors; Vocations.
Antonelli, Louis '49 (CHK) Rota, MP San Isidro Parish.
Antonelli, Louis (CHK) Presbyteral Council.
Antonelli, Robert *c.s.c.* '65 (P)[L] Portland, OR Holy Cross Fathers & Brothers, C.S.C. – University of Portland.
Antonelli, Robert *c.s.c.* '65 (P)[B] University of Portland.
Antonellis, Joseph A. '72 (BO) Revere, MA Immaculate Conception.
Antonicelli, Charles V. '93 (WDC) Washington, DC St. Joseph on Capitol Hill; Judges.
Antonik, Jan '03 (VEN) Punta Gorda, FL Sacred Heart.
Antonucci, Richard J. *o.praem.* '72 (PH)[AA] Paoli, PA Daylesford Abbey.
Antony, Irvdayam (NY) Bronxville, NY St. Joseph.
Antony, John Francis '91 (NY) Bronx, NY St. Barnabas.
Antony, John K. '96 (LR) North Little Rock, AR St. Anne; Little Rock, AR St. Edward; [L] Little Rock, AR The Guadalupe Prenatal Clinic; Vice Chancellors; Adjutant Judicial Vicars; Judges; Seminary Endowment Fund (The Msgr. James E. O'Connell Seminary Burse).
Antony, John (LR) Vocations.
Antony, Paul Peter '89 (CC) Sinton, TX Sacred Heart.
Antony, Satish Joseph '94 (CIN) Dayton, OH Our Lady of the Immaculate Conception.
Antos, Paul J. '54 (ALB) Watervliet, NY Immaculate Conception Retired.
Antoun, Elie '80 (SAM) Retired.
Antoun, Ziad *o.m.m.* '98 (OLL)[A] Ann Arbor, MI Maronite Order of Blessed Virgin Mary.
Antram, Cormac *o.f.m.* '54 (GLP) Houck, AZ St. John the Evangelist.
Antram, Cormac *o.f.m.* (GLP) Radio and Television.
Antry, Theodore J. *o.praem.* '62 (PH)[AA] Paoli, PA Daylesford Abbey.
Antunes, Ezio *s.d.v.* (PAT)[M] Florham Park, NJ Father Justin Vocationary.
Antunez, Bardo Fabian '03 (TUC) Tucson, AZ St. Ambrose.
Antunez, Roy L. *s.j.* '71 (P) Springfield, OR St. Alice.
Antus, Lawrence T. *o.m.i.* '58 (DUL) Cook, MN St. Mary's; Cook, MN Holy Cross.
Antus, Roland '62 (DUL) Longville, MN St. Edward's.
Antus, Roland '62 (DUL) Longville, MN St. Paul.
Antweiler, Donald J. '73 (JC) Monroe City, MO St. Stephen; Monroe City, MO Holy Rosary.
Antwi–Boasiako, Dominic '81 (VIC) Victoria, TX Our Lady of Victory Cathedral.
Anukam, Anselm A. '79 (AUS) Temple, TX St. Mary's.
Anuszewski, Albert M. *o.ss.t.* '91 (WDC)[M] Hyattsville, MD St. John de Matha Monastery, Order of Most Holy Trinity.
Anuszewski, Damian *o.ss.t.* '79 (WDC)[M] Hyattsville, MD St. John de Matha Monastery, Order of Most Holy Trinity.
Anuzis, Stanislovas '83 (LA) Los Angeles, CA St. Casimir.
Anyanike, Vitalis E. '02 (OM) Omaha, NE St. Pius X.
Anyanwa, Innocent (LAV) Hospital Apostolate.
Anyanwu, Celestine '83 (BRK) East Elmhurst, NY St. Gabriel.
Anyanwu, Christopher '80 (NEW) Newark, NJ Beth Israel Medical Center; Chaplains.
Anyanwy, Innocent '80 (LAV) Las Vegas, NV St. Anne.
Anyomi, Apollinaris '77 (BRK) Brooklyn, NY St. Matthew's.
Anziano, James J. '81 (PH) Absent on Sick Leave.
Anzoategui, Francisco J. '88 (BO) Lawrence, MA St. Patrick.
Apassa, Cyril '71 (RNO) Reno, NV St. Therese Church of the Little Flower.
Apel, John A. *s.j.* '69 (DEN)[D] Aurora, CO Regis Jesuit High School.
Apel, John *s.j.* '69 (DEN)[N] Centennial, CO Regis High Jesuit Community.
Apfelbeck, Keith B. '99 (LC) Special Assignment; Appointed Members.
Apfelbeck, Kurt J. '99 (LC) Cadott, WI St. Rose of Lima; Jim Falls, WI St. Anthony.
Apoldite, Dennis A. '78 (TR) Hopewell, NJ St. Alphonsus.
Apoldite, Dennis '78 (TR)[B] Trenton, NJ Notre Dame High School.
Apolinar, Moises '81 (LA) Los Angeles, CA Our Lady of Guadalupe.
Aponte, Jose R. *s.j.* (SJN)[H] San Juan, PR Comunidad Jesuita.
Aponte–Merced, Luis *o.f.m.* '03 (NO) New Orleans, LA St. Mary of the Angels.
Aponte Rivera, Eluid '86 (PCE) Coamo, PR St. Blase.
Apostol, Moises '78 (RCK) Mount Carroll, IL SS. John and Catherine.
Apostol, Moises '78 (RCK) Savanna, IL St. John the Baptist.
Apostoli, Andrew D. *c.f.r.* '67 (NY).
Apostoli, Andrew (NY)[EE] Yonkers, NY St. Leopold's Friary.
Apparcel, Greg *c.s.p.* '83 (LA)[CC] Pacific Palisades, CA Paulist Productions; Pacific Palisades, CA Corpus Christi.
Apparcel, Gregory *c.s.p.* '98 (LA) Los Angeles, CA St. Paul the Apostle.
Appel, Paul '03 (DAV) Davenport, IA St. Paul the Apostle.
Appelby, Gerald J. '59 (ROC) Retired.
Appelby, Gerald '59 (ROC) Avon, NY St. Agnes.
Appelt, Francis '52 (GRY)[I] Cedar Lake, IN Our Lady of Lourdes Friary.
Appiah, John '98 (KNX) Chattanooga, TN St. Stephen.
Appiah–Sekyere, Paul '88 (NY) White Plains, NY St. Bernard.
Appiasi, Samuel '83 (VIC) Blessing, TX St. Peter's.
Appiasi, Samuel (VIC) Procurator Advocate.
Appicci, Richard D. *o.s.a.* '60 (FgM).
Appicci, Richard D. *o.s.a.* '60 (PH)[AA] Villanova, PA Provincial Offices of the Order of St. Augustine, Province of St. Thomas of Villanova; [AA] Villanova, PA St. Thomas Monastery.
Applegate, Gary '81 (KCK) Kansas City, KS Cathedral of St. Peter the Apostle.
Applegate, Gary (KCK) Defenders of the Bond.
Applegate, Gary (KCK) Priests' Council.
Applegate, Gary (KCK) Archdiocesan Consultors.
Applewhite, Mark (RVC) Smithtown, NY St. Catherine of Siena Hospital.
Appleyard, George '68 (SJP) Austintown, OH St. Anne.
Appleyard, George (SJP) Diocesan Consultors.
Appleyard, George (SJP) Liturgical Commission.
Appleyard, George (SJP) Diocesan Ecumenical Office.
Appleyard, George (SJP) Catechetical Planning Committee.
Appleyard, George (SJP) Vicar for Religious.
Appleyard, George (SJP) Diocesan Resource Committee.
Appleyard, George (SJP) Presbyteral Council.
Appleyard, George (SJP) Permanent Diaconate Program.
Appleyard, Joseph A. *s.j.* '62 (BO)[V] Newton, MA The Jesuit Community at Boston College.
Appuhamy, Laus '77 (LKC) Lake Arthur, LA Our Lady of the Lake.
Appuhamy, Roger '85 (LKC) Lake Charles, LA St. Margaret.
Aprs, Joseph W. '02 (PRT) Bangor, ME Eastern Maine Medical Center.
Apura, Nilo '75 (TR) Toms River, NJ St. Maximilian Kolbe.
Apuzzo, Pasquale J. (RIC) Secretary to the Bishop Emeritus; Department of Communication & Administration; Office of Communication; Victim Assistance Coordinator.
Apuzzo, Pasquale '76 (RIC) On Special or Other Diocesan Assignment.
Apuzzo, Pasquale '76 (RIC) Office of Human Resources.
Apuzzo, Pasquale '76 (RIC) Moseley, VA St. Gabriel.
Aquino, Alexander '74 (SD) Lemon Grove, CA St. John of the Cross.
Aquino, Conrado *m.sp.s.* (LA) Oxnard, CA Our Lady of Guadalupe Parish.
Aquino, James J. '65 (WOR) Worcester, MA Our Lady of Loreto; Presbyteral Council.
Aquino, James (WOR) Co–Directors.
Aquino, Joe *m.s.* '69 (ORL) Orlando, FL Blessed Trinity.
Aquino, Oscar '64 (NY) New York, NY St. Francis de Sales.
Aquino, Oscar (NY) Judges.
Aquino, Peter M. '69 (NEW) Elizabeth, NJ SS. Peter and Paul's.
Aquirre, Mario '96 (KAL) Battle Creek, MI St. Joseph.
Aquwa, Jude '78 (NY) Croton Falls, NY St. Joseph.
Arabia, Peter K. *s.j.* '99 (RVC)[O] Manhasset, NY St. Ignatius Retreat House, Inisfada.
Aracich, Anthony *s.j.* '67 (NEW)[N] Jersey City, NJ Jesuit Community of St. Peter's Prep, Inc..
Arackal, Joseph J. *v.c.* '67 (SYM) Vermillion, MN St. John the Baptist; Vermillion, MN Syro–Malabar Catholics of Minnesota; Archdiocesan Consultors.
Arackal, Thomas A. *i.m.s.* '82 (LR) Eureka Springs, AR St. Elizabeth of Hungary.
Arackal, Thomas *i.m.s.* '82 (LR) Berryville, AR St. Anne.
Aragon, Ramon '50 (SFE) Retired.
Aragon, Ramon '50 (SFE) Albuquerque, NM Our Lady of Guadalupe.
Aragon, Salvador *o.f.m.* '55 (SFE) Tierra Amarilla, NM Santo Nino.
Aragon, Salvador *o.f.m.* '55 (SFE) Los Ojos, NM San Jose.
Arambasick, Dennis *o.f.m.* '85 (PRT) Manchester, NH Blessed Sacrament.
Aramburo, Eugenio '88 (MRY) Castroville, CA Our Lady of Refuge.
Aramburo, Eugenio (MRY) Administrative Committee Priests' Pension Plan; Presbyteral Council; Priestly Life and Ministry Board.
Aramburo, Eugenio (MRY) Advocates.
Aramburo, Eugenio (MRY) Administrative Committee Priests' Pension Plan; Presbyteral Council; Priestly Life and Ministry Board.
Aramburu, Jose A. *m.m.* '84 (FgM).
Arana, Francisco '64 (SJN) Bayamon, PR Nuestra Senora de Covadonga.
Arana, Francisco '64 (SJN)[E] San Juan, PR Centro Medico de P.R..
Aranda Ballestin, Benito '57 (PCE) Patillas, PR Inmaculado Corazon de Maria.
Arango, Andres *c.j.m.* '95 (SD)[L] San Diego, CA Newman Center – SDSU.
Arango, Fabio '66 (MIA) Hialeah, FL Santa Barbara.
Arango, Fabio '66 (MIA)[G] Miami, FL Mercy Outpatient Services, Inc..
Arango, Gilberto '75 (STO) Manteca, CA St. Anthony Church of Manteca (Pastor of).
Arango, Miguel '65 (SAT) Von Ormy, TX St. Peter the Fisherman.
Aranha, George '75 (SJ) Palo Alto, CA St. Thomas Aquinas.
Aranha, George '75 (SJ) Presentation High School.
Aranha, George '75 (SJ)[D] San Jose, CA Presentation High School.
Arano–Ponce, Gerardo '03 (KCK) Leawood, KS Church of the Nativity.
Araque, Alvaro U. '72 (STO) Stockton, CA St. Gertrude Church (Pastor of); Deans.
Arata, Miguel A. '95 (NEW) On Duty Outside the Archdiocese.
Araujo, Arturo *s.j.* '99 (SEA) Seattle, WA Christ the King; [A] Seattle, WA Seattle University.
Araujo, Manuel *c.m.* '54 (ARE) Manati, PR Sagrada Familia.
Araujo, Robert J. *s.j.* '93 (SPK)[B] Spokane, WA Gonzaga University.
Araujo, Robert J. *s.j.* '93 (BO)[V] Boston The Society of Jesus of New England–Provincial Offices.
Arauz, Eric '85 (SFR) Menlo Park, CA St. Anthony.
Aravindassery, Antony '75 (CHI) Chicago, IL St. Mary, Star of the Sea.
Aravindathu, Thadeus '18 (STP) South St. Paul, MN St. John Vianney.
Araya–Morales, Reynord '89 (ORL) Lakeland, FL St. Joseph's.
Arbanas, Harold P. '48 (GF) Retired.
Arbelaez, Ernesto *s.j.* '56 (COL)[M] Los Gatos Sacred Heart Jesuit Center.
Arbelaez, Ernesto *s.j.* '56 (STO) Hughson, CA St. Anthony Church of Hughson (Pastor of).
Arboleda, Jorge W. '93 (STO) Stockton, CA St. George Church (Pastor of).
Arboleda, Vidal '55 (ORL) Orlando, FL St. John Vianney Retired.
Arboleda, Vidal '55 (ORL) Retired.
Arcams, Flors B. '65 (SFR) San Francisco, CA Star of the Sea.
Arce, Aaron *o.p.* '80 (DAL)[A] Irving, TX Holy Trinity Seminary; [K] Irving, TX Dominican Priory of St. Albert the Great.
Arce, Carlos *o.f.m.* (R) Lumberton, NC St. Francis De Sales.
Arce, Juan Carlos '76 (ATL) Atlanta, GA Immaculate Heart of Mary.
Arce, Robert P. '64 (NY) Bronx, NY St. Margaret Mary.
Arceneaux, Chester '92 (LAF) Lafayette, LA Our Lady of Wisdom, University of Louisiana.
Arceneaux, Chester (LAF) Campus Ministry.
Arceneaux, Chester (LAF) Black Catholics.
Arceneaux, Chester (LAF)[L] Lafayette, LA Our Lady of Wisdom Catholic Student Center.
Arceneaux, Jules (LAF) Advocates.
Arceneaux, Jules (LAF) Diocesan Consultors.
Arceneaux, Louis A. *c.m.* '66 (LAF)[J] Grand Coteau, LA Jesuit Spirituality Center (St. Charles College).
Archambault, Donald '70 (DET) Detroit, MI St. Gerard; Detroit, MI Immaculate Heart of Mary.
Archambault, Henry N. '59 (NOR) Taftville, CT Sacred Heart; College of Consultors; Deans; Judicial Vicar.
Archambault, Henry (NOR) Diocesan Pastoral Council.
Archambault, Henry (NOR) Members.
Archambault, Henry (NOR) Lawyers, Guild of Catholic.
Archambault, James H. '67 (HRT) Retired.
Archambault, Richard L. '55 (NOR)[G] Putnam, CT Holy Spirit Provincial House; Project Northeast.
Archambault, Richard *m.afr.* '73 (FgM).
Archer, Arthur A. '80 (NOR) Niantic, CT St. Agnes.
Archer, Arthur (NOR) Members.
Archer, Richard *o.p.* '58 (NO) New Orleans, LA St. Anthony of Padua.
Archer, Scott '90 (PEO) Fairbury, IL St. John the Baptist.

Arcilesi, Leonard '89 (OWN) Owensboro, KY St. Martin.
Arcilia, M. David *o.d.c.* '93 (CHI) Mundelein, IL Santa Maria Del Popolo.
Arcilla, Remigio '85 (DAL) Dallas, TX All Saints.
Arciszewski, Gilbert '59 (MIL) Retired.
Arcoleo, Douglas R. '98 (RVC) Hicksville, NY St. Ignatius Loyola; Associate Vocation Directors.
Arcuri, Carmen J. '61 (COL) Columbus, OH St. Mary Magdalene.
Ardagh, Brian '95 (CHI) Palos Hills, IL Sacred Heart.
Ardinger, Scott '01 (ALN) Easton, PA St. Jane Frances de Chantal.
Ardis, John B. *c.s.p.* '90 (BO)[O] Boston, MA Paulist Center; [V] Boston, MA Paulist Fathers Residence; [AA] Boston, MA Chapel of the Holy Spirit.
Ardolf, Edward J. '64 (NU) Nicollet, MN St. Paul; New Ulm, MN St. Mary.
Ardolf, Paul C. '49 (STP) Norwood, MN Ascension.
Ardos, George A. '59 (TR) Titusville, NJ St. George; [M] Trenton, NJ St. Lawrence Rehabilitation Center.
Ardouin, Beaubrun '93 (NEW) East Orange, NJ Holy Spirit–Our Lady Help of Christians.
Arechiga, Dennis (SAT) Converse, TX St. Monica.
Arejola, Rodolfo '68 (AGN) Agana, GU Holy Family, Nino Perdido.
Arejola, Rudolfo (AGN) Nino Perdido Parish (Asan).
Arella, Gerard J. '28 (BRK) Retired.
Arella, Gerard '54 (BRK)[V] Douglaston, NY Bishop Mugavero Residence.
Arellano, Edgardo M. '74 (WIL)[L] Dover, DE Secular Institute of the Two Hearts.
Arellano, Mario *s.j.* '95 (LA) Los Angeles, CA St. Malachy.
Arenas, Joseph Victor '70 (NY) Staten Island, NY Blessed Sacrament.
Arends, Todd '02 (CR) Moorhead, MN St. Joseph's.
Arens, John F. '74 (BO)[E] Needham, MA St. Sebastian's School, Inc.; Army Reserve Chaplains.
Arens, Patrick O. (WIN) Madison Lake, MN All Saints; Immaculate Conception.
Arenz, James *s.j.* '65 (LA)[C] Los Angeles, CA Jesuit Community.
Areralo, Gilberto Rivera *m.sp.s.* '60 (LA) Huntington Park, CA St. Martha.
Ares, Francisco '83 (BRK)[A] Douglaston, NY Immaculate Conception Center.
Arevalo, Joseph '65 (RVC) Freeport, NY Our Holy Redeemer.
Arflack, Gregory A. '98 (OWN) Military Chaplains; Army Chaplains.
Argent, Robert W. '55 (STL) St. Louis, MO Resurrection of Our Lord.
Argentino, Ralph J. '68 (SP) Brandon, FL Church of the Nativity.
Argue, Patrick *ss.cc.* '62 (LA)[Q] Mission Hills, CA Congregation of the Sacred Hearts.
Argue, Patrick *ss.cc.* '62 (LA)[D] Mission Hills, CA Bishop Alemany High School.
Arguelles, Anthony (BLX) Presbyteral Council.
Arguelles, I. Anthony '74 (BLX) Biloxi, MS Cathedral of the Nativity of the Blessed Virgin Mary.
Arguinzoniz, Francisco '54 (PCE) On Duty Outside the Diocese.
Argy, William J. '40 (OG) Ogdensburg, NY St. Mary's Cathedral; Diocesan Consultors Retired.
Ariano, Joseph W. '51 (OM) Retired.
Arias, Ariel '85 (RNO) Fallon, NV St. Patrick.
Arias, Ariel (RNO) Diocesan Board of Consultors.
Arias, Ariel (RNO) Presbyteral Council.
Arias, Guillermo *s.j.* '72 (MIA)[H] Miami, FL Villa Javier.
Arias, Guillermo *s.j.* '72 (PMB)[A] Boynton Beach, FL St. Vincent de Paul Regional Seminary.
Arias, Hernan '85 (PAT) Passaic, NJ St. Anthony of Padua.
Arias, Hernan (PAT) Deans.
Arias, Hernan (PAT) Vocations Office.
Arias, Jesus J. '92 (MIA) Miami, FL St. Joachim.
Arias, Jose Antonio *o.a.r.* '60 (NEW) Los Angeles, CA Cristo Rey.
Arico, Carl '60 (NEW) Bayonne, NJ St. Vincent de Paul.
Aridas, Christopher '73 (RVC) Selden, NY St. Margaret of Scotland.
Arimond, Vincent '55 (DUL) Retired.
Arinze, Paul Ugo '99 (MAD) Dodgeville, WI St. Joseph.
Aristu, Camilo '62 (BAL) Glen Burnie, MD Holy Trinity.
Ariza, Campo E. (CGS) Diocesan Consultors; Priests Senate.
Ariza, Campo Emilio '75 (CGS) Caguas, PR Divino Nino.
Ariza, Vicente '75 (SJN)[G] Guaynabo, PR Opus Dei.
Arizpe, Samuel '87 (BWN) Edinburg, TX St. Joseph the Worker.
Arizpe, Samuel (BWN) Presbyteral Council.
Ariztí, Fernando *s.j.* '71 (LA)[BB] Los Angeles, CA Loyola Law School.
Arkestyn, John A. (RIC) Richmond, VA St. Bridget.
Arkins, Michael J. *s.s.s.* '73 (CLV) Highland Heights, OH St. Paschal Baylon.
Arkins, Michael *s.s.s.* '73 (CLV)[O] Cleveland, OH Blessed Sacrament Community.
Arko, Richard A. '90 (CLV) Barberton, OH Prince of Peace.
Arle, David '84 VEN) Fort Myers, FL St. Vincent de Paul.
Arledge, Joseph H. '97 (OKL) Altus, OK Prince of Peace.
Arledge, Thaddaeus R. *o.s.b.* '56 (SEA)[L] Lacey, WA St. Martin's Abbey.
Arlotta, Jack '82 (NY) Highland Falls, NY Sacred Heart of Jesus.
Armada, Leo *c.ss.r.* '90 (NY) New York, NY St. Cecilia.
Armano, Patrick S. '03 (BO) Needham, MA St. Joseph.
Armato, Robert J. '95 (BRK) Long Island City NY St. Joseph; Art and Architecture Commission.
Armato, Robert BRK) Bishop Valero—.
Armbrust, Leo F. '77 (PMB) Special Assignment; Secretary.
Armbruster, Julius *o.s.b.* '42 (SFS)[F] Marvin, SD Blue Cloud Abbey.
Armbruster, Timothy *c.pp.s.* '01 (KC) St. Joseph, MO St. Francis Xavier.
Armell, Francisco *o.carm.* '68 (SJN) San Juan, PR Santa Teresita Del Nino Jesus.
Armendariz, Antonio *m.sp.s.* '84 (LA) Huntington Park, CA St. Martha.
Armendariz, Antonio *m.sp.s.* '84 (P)[A] Mount Angel, OR Felix Rougier House of Studies.
Armengol, Jose *c.m.f.* '67 (SJN) Bayamon, PR San Jose.
Armenio, Peter V. '80 (CHI)[W] Chicago, IL Prelature of the Holy Cross and Opus Dei.
Armenta, Benito '87 (LA) Maywood, CA St. Rose of Lima.
Armey, Charles R. '80 (WOR) Southbridge, MA Sacred Heart.
Arminio, Alfonse M. '61 (NEW) Retired.
Arminio, Alfonse (NEW) AUXILIARY CHAPLAINS CONTRACT CHAPLAINS.
Arminio, Thomas G. '81 (NEW) Woodcliff Lake, NJ Our Lady Mother of the Church.
Arminio, Thomas '81 (NEW) Retired.
Arminio, Thomas (NEW) Ministry with Separated, Divorced and Widowed Catholics.
Armistead, John M. '71 (STO) Stockton, CA Cathedral of the Annunciation (Pastor of).
Armistead, John (STO) College of Consultors/ Presbyteral Council.
Armour, James E. '99 (NSH) Nashville, TN Cathedral of the Incarnation.
Armour, James (NSH) Presbyteral Council and College of Consultors.
Arms, Michael M. '68 (STP) Inver Grove Heights, MN St. Patrick.
Armshaw, Joseph *c.ss.r.* '52 (BLX)[E] Biloxi, MS St. John Neumann Residence.
Armshaw, Patrick J. '62 (RVC) Greenlawn, NY St. Francis of Assisi; [K] Bethpage, NY Central Council.
Armstrong, Christopher R. '80 (CIN) Cincinnati, OH St. Antoninus; Censors; Judges.
Armstrong, Daniel F. '78 (IND) Retired.
Armstrong, James L. '77 (PIT) Slippery Rock, PA St. Peter; [Q] Slippery Rock, PA Slippery Rock University, Newman Center (Slippery Rock).
Armstrong, John F. *s.j.* '78 (WDC)[M] Washington, DC Leonard Neale House.
Armstrong, Mark '03 (CIN) Minster, OH St. Augustine; Minster, OH St. Augustine.
Armstrong, Peter G. '54 (SFR) Retired.
Armstrong, Regis *o.f.m.cap.* '67 (WDC)[C] Catholic University of America, The.
Armstrong, Robert A. '62 (BAL) Baltimore, MD Cathedral of Mary Our Queen; Defenders of the Bond.
Armstrong, Robert (BAL) Consultors.
Armstrong, Robert (BAL) Consultors.
Armstrong, Rodney J. *s.s.j.* '91 (GAL) Baytown, TX Holy Family
Arnao, Thomas V. '82 (RVC) Adjutant Judicial Vicars.
Arnaud, Michael '75 (LAF) New Iberia, LA Nativity of Our Lady.
Arnaud, Michael (LAF) Clergy Personnel Advisory Board.
Arnberg, Todd '76 (SAG) St. Charles, MI Immaculate Conception.
Arneson, James E. '67 (IND) Retired.
Arnheiter, Burkard *o.s.b.* '37 (SCL)[I] Collegeville, MN St. John's Abbey, of the Order of St. Benedict.
Arnhols, Richard J. '73 (NEW) Bergenfield, NJ St. John the Evangelist; Vicar for Pastoral Life; Vicar for Pastoral Life.
Arnhols, Richard (NEW) Members.
Arnholt, Joseph M. '73 (PH) Ardmore, PA St. Colman.
Arnister, Edward J. '79 (TR) Trenton, NJ Holy Cross; Trenton, NJ St. Stanislaus; Vice Chancellors; Tribunal Judges.
Arnold, Andrew L. '59 (WH) Retired.
Arnold, Daniel K. '75 (E) Erie, PA St. Boniface.
Arnold, Edward C. '57 (NSH) Franklin, TN St. Philip.
Arnold, Erik J. '99 (BAL) Clarksville, MD St. Louis; Priest Personnel Board.
Arnold, J. Ralph '41 (BEL) Retired.
Arnold, John D. *s.j.* (STL)[F] St. Louis, MO De Smet Jesuit High School; [O] St. Louis, MO De Smet Jesuit High School Community.
Arnold, John P. '98 (TUC) Members.
Arnold, Robert P. '75 (SCR) Gouldsboro, PA St. Rita.
Arnold, Roger S. *s.v.d.* '61 (CHI)[N] Chicago, IL Divine Word Theologate.
Arnold, Wayne (MEM) Scouting.
Arnold, Wayne (MEM) Collierville, TN Incarnation.
Arnold, William L. '80 (COL) Dover, OH St. Joseph.
Arnold, William (COL) Diocesan Judges.
Arnoldt, David M. '68 (WIN) Military Chaplains; Army Chaplains.
Arnone, A. '80 (SJ) On Leave of Absence.
Arnone, Harry *c.m.* '98 (PH).
Arnone, John C. '99 (NO)[AA] New Orleans, LA Holy Name of Mary (Algiers).
Arnone, Leo '93 (ALT) Mount Union, PA St. Catherine's.
Arnott, John J. '74 (PIT) McMurray, PA St. Benedict the Abbot.
Arnoult, Paul '02 (SFR) San Mateo, CA St. Matthew.
Arnout, Eric R. '96 (ALN) Whitehall, PA St. Elizabeth.
Arnsparger, Roger '77 (CHL) Arden, NC St. Barnabas.
Arocho, Jose A. '91 (CGS) Ceiba, PR San Antonio de Padua; Master of Ceremonies.
Arocho, Marcelino '88 (MGZ) Mayaguez, PR Church of the Resurrection.
Arockiam, Arockiam *s.v.d.* '02 (LAF) St. Martinville, LA Notre Dame de Perpetuel Secours.
Arockiam, Emmanuel *s.j.* '87 (MIL)[O] Milwaukee, WI Jesuit Community at Marquette University.
Arockiam, Michael Arputham '78 (NY) Staten Island, NY St. Christopher.
Arockiasamy, Xavier '85 (ALB) Glens Falls, NY St. Mary.
Arogyasami, Joseph *i.m.s.* '89 (BR) Livonia, LA St. Frances Xavier Cabrini.
Arokiam, Ignatius (PAT).
Arokiasamy, Kulan–Daisamy '71 (DET)[J] Eastpointe, MI St. Veronica.
Arold, Richard J. '67 (NY) Retired.
Arong, Jose *o.m.i.* '66 (WDC)[M] Washington, DC Provincial Offices of the United States Province of the Missionary Oblates of Mary Immaculate.
Arong, Jose *o.m.i.* '66 (OAK)[N] Oakland, CA Oblate Residence.
Aronica, Paul *s.d.b.* '47 (NO)[D] Marrero, LA Archbishop Shaw High School.
Aronyu, Cuthbert '72 (OAK) Oakland, CA St. Benedict.
Arouje, Lonachan W. (STO) Newman Apostolate.
Arraiza, Fray Luis *o.f.m.cap.* '88 (DAL)[N] Dallas, TX Dallas Cursillo Center.
Arraiza, Luis Gerardo *o.f.m.cap.* '88 (DAL)[K] Dallas, TX Capuchin Franciscan Friars, Vice Province of Texas; Dallas, TX Our Lady of Lourdes.
Arrambide, Jaime C. *c.ss.r.* '73 (GAL) Houston, TX St. Raphael the Archangel.
Arrando, Angelo S. '71 (BGP) Danbury, CT St. Gregory.
Arrascue, Ricardo Coronado (DUB) Priests Assigned to Hispanic Ministry.
Arrazola, Rodrigo A. '01 (HBG) Chambersburg, PA Corpus Christi.
Arreola, Alberto *o.m.i* '02 (LAR) Eagle Pass, TX Sacred Heart.
Arriaga, Ernesto *c.s.b.* '01 (GAL)[Q] Sugar Land Basilian Mission Center.
Arriaga, Joaquin S. '97 (FRS) Fowler, CA St. Lucy.
Arriaga, Martin '74 (ELP) El Paso, TX Our Lady of Guadalupe.
Arribas, Santiago *c.m.* '66 (PCE) Ponce, PR San Vicente–Cantera.
Arrieta, David '62 (SJN) San Juan, PR Nuestra Senora de Lourdes.
Arririatu, Samuel (BRK) Far Rockaway, NY St. Mary Star of the Sea.
Arrizurieta, Candido *c.m.* '54 (NY) New York, NY Holy Agony.
Arrizurieta, Candido *c.m.* '54 (NY)[EE] New York, NY Vincentian Fathers.
Arroyave, Luis F. '88 (TYL) Mount Pleasant, TX St. Michael.
Arroyo, Brigido U. '61 (AGN) Tamuning, GU St. Anthony and St. Victor.
Arroyo, Brigido (AGN) Saint Anthony Parish.
Arroyo, Brigido (AGN) Archdiocesan Presbyteral Council.
Arroyo, Brigido (AGN) Catholic Daughters of the Americas.
Arroyo, Edward B. *s.j.* '75 (NO)[C] New Orleans, LA Loyola University New Orleans; [C] New Orleans, LA Loyola University New Orleans.
Arroyo, Joseph A. *s.j.* '62 (PH)[AA] Loyola Center and Manresa Hall.
Arroyo, Mario J. '77 (GAL) Houston, TX St. Cyril of Alexandria.
Arroyo, Miguel A. *o.c.d.* '99 (CGS) Caguas, PR San Jose.
Arroyo, Miguel *o.c.d.* (CGS) Priests Senate.
Arruda, Henry S. '67 (FR) Taunton, MA St. Anthony's; Diocesan Liaison with Portuguese Charismatic Groups.

Arsenault, Edward J. '91 (MAN) Manchester, NH St. Joseph Cathedral; [O] Manchester, NH CMC Healthcare System; Council of Priests; College of Consultors; Cabinet Secretary for Administration; Chancellor; Office of the Delegate for Ministerial Conduct; Personnel Officer; Legal Affairs Office.
Arsenault, James M. '89 (RIC) Blacksburg, VA St. Mary & Newman Community.
Arsenault, Joseph B. *m.m.* '59 (NY)[EE] Maryknoll Maryknoll Fathers and Brothers.
Arsenault, Raymond J. *s.m.* '51 (BO)[X] Framingham, MA The Marist House.
Arseneau, Vernon '72 (JOL) Momence, IL St. Patrick.
Arseneau, Vernon '72 (JOL) Hopkins Park, IL Sacred Heart.
Arseneault, David J. '81 (ALT)[H] Huntington, PA Juniata College; Huntingdon, PA Most Holy Trinity.
Arter, Ronald L. '61 (COL) Lancaster, OH St. Mark.
Arthasseril, Jerome S. '66 (NEW) East Orange, NJ Holy Name of Jesus.
Arthur, David J. *c.s.c.* '54 (FR)[A] North Easton, MA Holy Cross Fathers Religious.
Arthur, E. Eugene *s.j.* '66 (COS)[F] Sedalia, CO Sacred Heart Jesuit Community; [H] Sedalia, CO Sacred Heart Jesuit Retreat House.
Arthur, Francis '79 (FAR) Rugby, ND St. Therese, Little Flower.
Arthur, James K. '83 (LC) Bloomer, WI St. Paul.
Arthur, James '83 (LC) Bloomer, WI St. John the Baptist.
Arthur, John P. *s.j.* (SD) San Diego, CA East Mesa Detention Facility.
Artis, George *s.v.d.* '62 (BLX)[A] Bay St. Louis, MS St. Augustine's.
Artmann, Robert J. '64 (MIL) Kewaskum, WI St. Michael.
Arts, Paul–Louis '64 (SC) Sioux City, IA Cathedral of the Epiphany.
Arts, Paul–Louis (SC) Diocesan Consultors.
Arts, Paul–Louis (SC) St. Joseph Education Society.
Arts, Paul–Louis (SC) Judges.
Arts, Paul–Louis (SC) Building Commission.
Arturi, Bradley K. '62 (NY).
Artuso, Grazioso '64 (BGP)[JJ] Bridgeport, CT St. Raphael.
Artysiewicz, Chet *g.h.m.* '73 (LR) Warren, AR St. Luke Church.
Artysiewicz, Chet *g.h.m.* '73 (LR) Monticello, AR St. Mark.
Artzer, James *s.v.d.* '50 (TR)[M] Bordentown, NJ Society of the Divine Word.
Arul, John '70 (MRY) San Luis Obispo, CA San Luis Obispo.
Arulandu, Thaines '82 (FAR) Larimore, ND St. Stephen.
Arulappa, Devaraj '86 (TYL) Atlanta, TX St. Catherine of Siena Church.
Arulrajan, Peter '84 (NOR)[E] Windham, CT St. Joseph Living Center.
Arulsamy, Antony '89 (RVC) Mineola, NY Winthrop Hospital.
Arulsamy, Antony '89 (RVC) Mineola, NY Corpus Christi.
Arvay, Alfred S. '58 (NEW) On Duty Outside the Archdiocese.
Arzola Maisonet, Roberto *o.p.* '74 (PCE) Yauco, PR Holy Rosary.
Asare–Dankwah, John '94 (NO) New Orleans, LA St. Monica.
Ascencio, Joseph A. '82 (COL) On Duty Outside the Diocese.
Ascheman, Thomas *s.v.d.* '82 (FgM).
Aschenbrener, Thomas G. '03 (CHI) River Forest, IL St. Luke.
Aschenbrenner, George A. *s.j.* '65 (ALN)[C] Scranton, PA The University of Scranton.
Aschenbrenner, Ralph '61 (SAL) Belleville, KS St. George's.
Aschenbrenner, Ralph '61 (SAL) Belleville, KS St. Isidore's.
Aschenbrenner, Ralph '61 (SAL) Belleville, KS St. Edward's.
Aschenbrenner, Ralph (SAL) Procurator and Advocate.
Aschmann, Karl *c.ss.r.* '50 (CHR) Sumter, SC St. Anne's.
Ascolese, Robert J. '89 (MET) Washington, NJ St. Joseph.
Asemagema, Matthew '80 (TUC) Yuma, AZ Immaculate Conception.
Asencio, Enrique (CGS) Humacao, PR Maria Reina de la Paz.
Asencios–Pablo, Maximo *m.ss.a.* '68 (HRT) Waterbury, CT Immaculate Conception.
Asenjo, Jose Maria '65 (GAL) South Houston, TX Our Lady of Grace.
Asghedom, Tesfaldet *m.c.c.j.* '85 (LA)[CC] Covina, CA Comboni Mission Center.
Ashbaugh, William A. '93 (LAN) Howell, MI St. Joseph.
Ashbaugh, William '51 (LAN)[O] Lansing, MI Diocesan Service Committee.
Ashbaugh, William (LAN) Vicar for Charismatic Communities.
Ashbeck, David K. '68 (GB) Seymour, WI St. Sebastian; Bonduel, WI St. Lawrence.
Ashe, Brendan Michael '59 (CC) Vattman, TX Our Lady of Consolation.
Ashe, John F. '63 (NOR) Portland, CT St. Mary.
Ashe, Joseph C. '76 (NOR) Old Saybrook, CT St. John.
Ashe, Kevin P. '63 (NEW) Jersey City, NJ St. Anne's; Special Assignment in the Archdiocese; [S] Union City, NJ Park Performing Arts, Inc..
Ashe, Michael B. (CC) AUXILIARY CHAPLAINS CONTRACT CHAPLAINS.
Ashenbrenner, Robert D. *o.s.f.s.* '54 (PH)[AA] Philadelphia, PA Father Louis Brisson Residence.
Ashfeld, Bernard '82 (SFS) Retired.
Ashkar, Dominic F. '62 (SAM) Washington, DC Our Lady of Lebanon Church.
Ashkar, Dominic (SAM) AUXILIARY CHAPLAINS CONTRACT CHAPLAINS.
Ashley, Benedict M. *o.p.* '48 (STL)[O] St. Louis, MO St. Dominic Priory.
Ashman, Robert '86 (NY) Yonkers, NY St. Anthony.
Ashmore, Ronald M. '76 (IND) Terre Haute, IN St. Margaret Mary; Unassigned.
Ashton, John P. '55 (Y) Campbell, OH St. Lucy.
Ashurst, Peter '92 (OKL) Absent on Leave.
Asih, Paul *m.s.p.* '90 (BEA) Liberty, TX Our Mother of Mercy.
Asika, Raphael *m.s.p.* '92 (GAL) Houston, TX St. Peter the Apostle.
Asip, James W. '37 (BRK)[L] Brooklyn, NY Society of St. Vincent de Paul in Diocese of Brooklyn; [L] Brooklyn, NY District Council of Queens Retired.
Asir, Antony '82 (RVC) East Meadow, NY St. Raphael.
Asis, Alfonso '75 (AGN) Agana, GU Immaculate Heart of Mary.
Asma, Lawrance '83 (STL)[O] St. Louis Vincentian Residence.
Asma, Lawrence F. *c.m.* '83 (STL)[J] Bridgeton, MO SSM De Paul Health Center; [O] St. Louis, MO Vincentian Residence.
Asma, Lawrence *c.m.* '83 (STL) DePaul Health Center.
Asmar, Maroun '93 (SAM) Somerset, NJ St. Sharbel.
Aspinall, Campion W. *c.j.* '61 (LA) Santa Maria, CA St. Louis de Montfort Retired.
Aspiras, Jose '47 (SEA) Retired.
Assenga, Renatus J. '89 (GAL) Houston, TX St. Benedict the Abbot.
Assenga, Thomas (SCL) St. Cloud, MN St. Mary's Cathedral of St. Cloud.
Assenheimer, Roy C. *m.m.* '65 (FgM).
Assenmacher, Hugh *o.s.b.* '58 (LR)[A] Subiaco, AR Subiaco Monastery.
Assenyoh, Bernard Kwame *s.v.d.* '98 (NO) New Orleans, LA St. Paul the Apostle.
Ast, Nicholas K. *o.s.b.* '01 (OKL)[I] Shawnee St. Gregory's Abbey.
Astanto, Yulianus *c.m.* (PH) Indonesian Apostolate.
Astarita, Joseph J. '03 (NEW) Paramus, NJ Our Lady of the Visitation.
Astorino, Robert F. *m.m.* '70 (FgM).
Astudillo, Antonio P. '73 (LA) Long Beach, CA Holy Innocents.
Asturi, Bruno '76 (PBR) Upper St. Clair, PA St. Gregory Nazianzus.
Astuto, Lucian S. '57 (OM) Retired.
Asuncion, Leo Alban '79 (OAK) Mission San Jose, CA St. Joseph Mission Church.
Asuquo, Godwin '03 (RCK) Aurora, IL Holy Angels.
Atamian, Antranik '73 (ARM) Wynnewood, PA St. Mark's Armenian Catholic.
Atangana, Edouard '02 (BWN) Coordinator; Harlingen, TX St. Anthony.
Atangana, Edouard (BWN) Hospital Chaplains.
Atcher, Joseph R. *o.carm.* '76 (L) Louisville, KY Our Lady of Mount Carmel.
Atcher, Joseph *o.carm.* (L) College of Consultors.
Atcher, Joseph *o.carm.* (L) Ex Officio.
Atehortua, Jairo '95 (SP) New Port Richey, FL Our Lady Queen of Peace.
Aten, Robert L. '79 (STL) Special Assignment; [O] Centerville, MO Contemplative Heart of Mary Hermitage.
Atencio, Luis *i.v.e.* (BRK) Brooklyn, NY St. Michael's.
Aterado, Nestor (SFR) San Francisco, CA St. Charles Borromeo.
Athapilly, Andrews *c.m.i.* '64 (PH) Philadelphia, PA St. Katherine of Siena.
Atibagos, Jose '94 (TR) Red Bank, NJ St. James.
Atienza, Brian Joseph Cabrera '02 (SAC) Elk Grove, CA St. Joseph.
Atimnedi, Norbert Oloya *a.j.* '95 (CLV) Deaconess Hospital; St. Michael Hospital; Cleveland, OH Holy Name.
Atkin, Timothy *c.i.c.m.* '74 (FgM).
Atkins, Dan (IND) Council of Priests.
Atkins, Daniel '87 (IND) Bloomington, IN St. Paul Catholic Center.
Atkins, J. Daniel (IND)[O] Bloomington, IN Indiana University, Bloomington.
Atkins, James P. '75 (ATL) On Duty Outside the Archdiocese.
Atkins, James '72 (RVC) Mastic Beach, NY St. Jude.
Atkins, James '75 (PRM) Minneapolis, MN St. John the Baptist.
Atkins, James '81 (SFR) San Francisco, CA Cathedral of St. Mary (Assumption) Retired.
Atkins, James (PRM) Priest's Pension Board.
Atkinson, Anselm *o.s.b.* '82 (WOR)[O] Petersham, MA St. Mary's Monastery.
Atkinson, John V. '61 (MEM) Memphis, TN St. Michael's.
Atkinson, Sean '69 (JKS) Indianola, MS St. Benedict the Moor.
Atkinson, Sean '69 (JKS) Indianola, MS Immaculate Conception.
Atkinson, William E. *o.s.a.* '74 (PH)[D] Drexel Hill, PA Monsignor Bonner High School.
Ato, Lorenzo (NY) Bronx, NY St. Thomas Aquinas.
Atok, George *s.d.b.* '82 (NY)[GG] Stony Point, NY Marian Shrine.
Atok, George *s.d.b.* '82 (NY)[GG] Stony Point, NY Don Bosco Retreat Center and Marian Shrine.
Atonio, Falaniko '92 (SPP) Pago Pago, AS Christ the King; Pago Pago, AS Sts. Peter & Paul; Faculty Members.
Atoyebi, John B. '94 (CHI) Chicago, IL St. Clotilde.
Attak, Cyril '64 (PRM) Allen Park, MI St. Stephen.
Attanasio, Raymond V. '58 (MET) Retired.
Attanasio, Scott '95 (NEW) North Arlington, NJ Queen of Peace.
Attansey, Matthew '79 (FAR) Sanborn, ND St. Mary.
Attansey, Matthew '79 (FAR) Sanborn, ND Sacred Heart.
Attard, Joseph (BRK) Brooklyn, NY Most Precious Blood.
Attea, Antoine P. (BUF) Vicars; Chautauqua Catholic Community, Chautauqua Institution; Jamestown, NY St. James.
Atto, Dennis D. '02 (RCK) Rockford, IL Holy Family.
Attuanya, David *c.ss.p.* (BRK) Brooklyn, NY Holy Cross.
Atuah, Charles *m.s.p.* '90 (BEA) Raywood, TX Sacred Heart; Memoral Hermann Baptist Hospital.
Atuah, Charles *m.s.p.* (CHI) Chicago, IL Corpus Christi.
Atunzu, Kevin O. '79 (LR) Horseshoe Bend, AR St. Mary of the Mount.
Atunzu, Kevin '79 (LR) Cherokee Village, AR St. Michael's.
Atwell, Basil *o.s.b.* '02 (BIS) Dickinson, ND St. Wenceslaus; Lefor, ND St. Elizabeth; New England, ND St. Mary.
Atwell, Basil *o.s.b.* '02 (BIS)[A] Richardton, ND Assumption Abbey.
Atwell, Basil *o.s.b.* '02 (BIS) Dickinson, ND St. Wenceslaus; Lefor, ND St. Elizabeth; New England, ND St. Mary.
Atwill, William H. '44 (LA) Retired.
Atwine, Lucius *c.s.c.* '97 (FTW)[I] Kyarusozi Parish Community.
Atwood, Ray E. '94 (DUB) Riceville, IA St. Peter; Riceville, IA Immaculate Conception; Riceville, IA St. Stephen.
Atwood, Ronald E. '84 (OAK) Richmond, CA St. David of Wales.
Atwood, Ronald J. '69 (COL) Columbus, OH St. Joseph Cathedral.
Atwood, Wilbur J. *s.s.j.* '58 (NO)[P] New Orleans, LA The Josephite Faculty House of St. Augustine High School.
Au, Thomas Y. '79 (LIN) Roseland, NE Sacred Heart; Advocates; Diocesan Area CCD Directors.
Au, William A. '75 (BAL) Baltimore, MD SS. Philip and James; Priest Personnel Board.
Aubespin, Borgia *s.v.d.* '65 (GAL) Houston, TX St. Mary of the Purification.
Aubin, Jean Pierre '01 (BO) Somerville, MA St. Ann.
Aubin, Joseph G. '55 (OG) Retired.
Aubin, Joseph '55 (OG) Plattsburgh, NY St. Peter.
Aubin, Joseph '61 (LAN) Retired.
Aubin, Pierre *m.s.c.* '58 (OG) Cape Vincent, NY St. Vincent of Paul; Cape Vincent, NY Cape Vincent Correctional Facility.
Aubin, Pierre *m.s.c.* '58 (OG)[I] Cape Vincent, NY Mission Project Service.
Aubin, Pierre *m.s.c.* '58 (OG) Cape Vincent, NY St. Vincent de Paul.
Aubin, Pierre *m.s.c.* '58 (OG) Cape Vincent, NY All Saints.
Aubin, Pierre *m.s.c.* '58 (OG)[E] Watertown, NY Missionaries of the Sacred Heart.
Aubin, Pierre *m.s.c.* (OG) Diocesan Consultors.
Aubin, Ronald B. '81 (SP) Land O'Lakes, FL Our Lady of the Rosary.
Aubin, Ronald (SP) Judges.
Auble, Theodore J. '75 (ROC) Churchville, NY St. Vincent De Paul.
Aubrey, Robert J. '71 (DM) Dexter, IA City Chaplaincy Program; [J] Dexter, IA City Hospital Chaplaincy Service.
Aubry, Ronald J. '81 (COL) Millersburg, OH St. Peter.
Auby, John R. '94 (MAD) Janesville, WI St. William; Elected; Janesville.

Auchter, John A. '54 (ALN) Bethlehem, PA Notre Dame of Bethlehem; Lake Harmony, PA St. Peter the Fisherman.
Aucoin, Charles '47 (MOB) Retired.
Aucoin, Robert H. '70 (OG) Diocesan Director of Christian Formation; Diocesan Director of Christian Formation; Director of Deacon Formation and Director of Ordained Deacons; Alexandria Bay, NY St. Cyril of Alexandria; Alexandria Bay, NY St. Francis Xavier.
Auda, Lawrence '60 (SFD) Gillespie, IL St. Joseph.
Auda, Lawrence '60 (SFD) Gillespie, IL SS. Simon and Jude.
Auda, Lawrence (SFD) Litchfield Deanery.
Audet, Arthur J. '85 (HRT) Glastonbury, CT St. Dunstan; Marlborough, CT St. John Fisher.
Audet, Dennis J. '78 (MAN) Manchester, NH St. Joseph Cathedral; Council of Priests; Clergy Personnel Board; Department of Catholic Schools.
Audet, Phil '01 (LAV) Ely, NV Sacred Heart.
Audette, Albert D. '93 (BGP) Danbury, CT St. Peter.
Auer, Benedict L. *o.s.b.* '80 (SEA)[L] Lacey, WA St. Martin's Abbey.
Auer, John J. '57 (BAL) Retired.
Auer, John '79 (COS) Colorado Springs, CO Saint Paul.
Auer, John (COS) Diocesan Consultors.
Auer, John (COS) Metro–South Region (Colorado Springs).
Auer, Joseph E. '56 (CHI) Retired.
Auer, Peter *s.o.l.t.* '93 (CHY) Cheyenne, WY St. Mary's Cathedral.
Auer, Robert F. '51 (DUB) Retired.
Auerbach, Shay W. *s.j.* '99 (R) Raleigh, NC St. Raphael; [E] Raleigh Jesuit Community.
Aufdermauer, Joseph A. '68 (MIL) Milwaukee, WI St. Matthias.
Aufieri, Robert '74 (NY) New York, NY St. Michael; Office of Ecumenical and Interreligious Affairs; Pastoral Council, Archdiocesan; Coordinator for Special Ministries; Italian Apostolate, Office of the; New York, NY St. John the Evangelist.
Aufiero, Louis D. '65 (BRK)[V] Jamaica, NY Parsons Manor.
Auger, Gaston E. '32 (PRT) Retired.
Auger, George *c.s.v.* '61 (CHI)[N] Arlington Heights, IL Viatorian Province Center–Clerics of St. Viator.
Auger, Gerald E. '55 (MAN) Retired.
Auger, Raymond D. '56 (PRT) Retired.
August, Gothman L. '93 (CR) East Grand Forks, MN Sacred Heart.
Auguste, Jean–Miguel '91 (BRK) Brooklyn, NY Holy Innocents.
Augustin, Francois '90 (BRK) Brooklyn, NY St. Therese of Lisieux.
Augustine, Dom Daniel W. *c.r.n.j.* (LC)[M] La Crosse, WI Canons Regular of the New Jerusalem.
Augustine, Kenneth J. '77 (MIL) Franklin, WI St. James.
Augustine, Roger J. '59 (SC) Moville, IA Immaculate Conception; Vicars General; Diocesan Corporate Board; Presbyteral Council; Diocesan Consultors; Priests' Personnel Board.
Augustine, Roger (SC) Judges.
Augustine, Russell (BGP) Redding Ridge, CT St. Patrick.
Augustinowitz, Michael E. '75 (BUR) Elected Members; Canon 1742 Panel of Pastors; Hardwick, VT St. Norbert.
Augustyn, Andrew M. '47 (GI) Retired.
Augustyn, Boguslaw Adam *c.ss.r.* '93 (MET) Manville, NJ Sacred Heart of Jesus; Army Reserve Chaplains.
Augustyn, James M. '63 (BUF) Judges; Lackawanna, NY St. Michael the Archangel.
Augustyn, Richard H. '76 (BUF) Hospital Chaplains; Buffalo General Hospital; Buffalo, NY Immaculate Heart of Mary.
Auman, Robert '47 (SFE) Retired.
Aumannm, Jordan R. *o.p.* '45 (CHI)[N] St. Pius V Priory.
Aumen, Paul *c.pp.s.* '49 (CIN)[M] New Oxford, PA.
Au Quoc Thanh, Vincent de Paul M. *c.m.c.* (SPC)[E] Carthage, MO Congregation of the Mother Coredemptrix, United States Assumption Province; [E] Carthage, MO Congregation of the Mother Coredemptrix, United States Assumption Province.
Auquscik, Jerzy *o.f.m.conv.* '93 (BRK) Elmhurst, NY St. Adalbert.
Aureus, Antonio '77 (DAL) Sherman, TX St. Mary.
Aurilia, John C. *o.f.m.cap.* '66 (CHL) Hendersonville, NC Immaculate Conception.
Ausenbaugh, J. Andrew '95 (OWN) Absent on Leave.
Ausperk, Michael D. '89 (CLV) Stow, OH Holy Family.
Austgen, Robert J. *c.s.c.* '58 (FTW)[B] University of Notre Dame Du Lac; [F] Notre Dame, IN University Health Services; [I] Notre Dame, IN Holy Cross Community, Corby Hall, University of Notre Dame.
Austin, C. Gerard *o.p.* '59 (VEN)[B] Arcadia, FL Blessed Edmund Rice School for Pastoral Ministry.
Austin, David '03 (RCK) Dundee, IL St. Catherine of Siena.
Austin, John J. '97 (PRT) Bangor, ME St John's; Bangor, ME St. Joseph's Hospital.
Austin, John '97 (PRT)[H] Bangor, ME Pastoral Care Dept..
Austin, Jonathan '97 (DAL) Terrell, TX St. John; Terrell, TX State Hospital.
Austin, Michael '00 (BLX) Ocean Springs, MS St. Alphonsus; Mission Office.
Austin, Michael (BLX) Propagation of the Faith.
Austin, Michael (BLX) Interim Diocesan Liturgical Commission.
Austin, Michael (BLX) Pontifical Association of the Holy Childhood.
Austin, Michael (BLX) Mission Board.
Austin, Stephen E. '84 (TLS) Bartlesville, OK St. John's; Dewey OK Our Lady of Guadalupe.
Austin, Walter J. '81 (NO) Military Chaplains.
Auth, Clifford H. '99 (SY) Syracuse, NY Blessed Sacrament; Study Leave.
Auth, James E. '61 (TOL) Toledo, OH Regina Coeli; Judges.
Auth, William G. *o.s.f.s.* '69 (TOL)[J] Salt Lake City, UT.
Auther, John P. *s.j.* '90 (SD) San Diego, CA Our Lady of Guadalupe; San Diego, CA George F. Bailey Maximum Security Facility.
Auve, Perron J. '62 (YAK) On Duty Outside the Diocese.
Avallone, Paul P. *s.d.b.* '50 (PAT)[N] Haledon, NJ Institute of the Daughters of Mary Help of Christians.
Avallone, Paul *s.d.b.* (PAT) Paterson, NJ St. Anthony's.
Avau, Felix A. *c.i.c.m.* '54 (SAT)[M] San Antonio, TX Missionhurst Community Residence.
Avella, Alberto '30 (GLP) Milan, NM San Rafael.
Avella, Alberto '30 (GLP) Milan, NM San Mateo.
Avella, Alberto '30 (GLP) Grants, NM St. Teresa.
Avella, Alberto '30 (GLP) Milan, NM St. Vivian.
Avella, Alberto (GLP) Vicars Forane.
Avella, Alberto (GLP) Presbyteral Council.
Avella, Robert E. '75 (ARL) Arlington, VA Cathedral of St. Thomas More; Bishop's Delegate for Clergy; Defenders of the Bond; Permanent Diaconate; Clergy Personnel Board.
Avella, Steven M. (MIL) Special Assignment.
Avella, William '50 (RNO) Retired.
Avello, Vicente Salas *o.de.m.* '66 (PCE) Ponce, PR Santuario San Judas Tadeo.
Avendano, Alvaro '92 (ATL) Marietta, GA St. Joseph.
Avendano, Hilario '98 (PCE) Salinas, PR Our Lady of Monserrat.
Aveni, Paul J. '98 (BO) Chelmsford, MA St. John the Evangelist.
Avenido, Alberto '95 (LA) Woodland Hills, CA St. Bernardine of Siena.
Aver, John J. '57 (BAL) Severna Park, MD St. John the Evangelist.
Averbeck, Ronald J. '61 (CIN) Cincinnati, OH St. Stephen.
Avery, Edward V. '70 (PH) Philadelphia, PA St Jerome; [U] Philadelphia, PA Nazareth Hospital.
Avery, Raymond '44 (MET) Retired.
Avery, Raymond '44 (MET)[H] Somerset, NJ Maria Regina Residence.
Avia, Martin '57 (SFR)[K] San Rafael, CA Nazareth House Retired.
Avicolli, Maurice C. *o.praem.* '68 (PH) Paoli, PA St. Norbert; [AA] Paoli, PA Daylesford Abbey.
Avila, Bernardo Iniesta (TUC) Yuma, AZ Immaculate Conception.
Avila, Carlos Antonio Massieu '89 (MIA)[M] Coral Gables, FL House of the Divine Will, Inc. dba Casa de la Divina Voluntad.
Avila, Daniel C '87 (FRS) Hanford, CA St. Brigid.
Avila, Israel '91 (FRS) Pinedale, CA St. Agnes.
Avila, Martin C. '57 (SFR) Retired.
Avila, Rafael de '74 (SFR) Half Moon Bay, CA Our Lady of the Pillar.
Avila, Stephen J. '81 (FR) East Freetown, MA St. John Neumann; Office for Divine Worship; Television Apostolate.
Avila–Mora, Santiago *c.m.f.* '67 (CHR) Greer, SC Blessed Trinity.
Aviles, Joe '90 (SAT) San Antonio, TX St. Joseph.
Aviles, Mario A. *c.o.* '98 (BWN) Hidalgo, TX Sacred Heart; [C] Pharr, TX Oratory Academy.
Aviles, Mario Alberto *c.o.* '98 (BWN)[F] Pharr, TX Oratory of St. Philip Neri of Pontifical; [B] Pharr, TX Oratory Athenaeum for University Preparation.
Aviles, Victor Perez *o.p.* '67 (PCE) Yauco, PR Holy Rosary.
Avramenko, Alexander '96 (STN) St. Vladimir.
Avramenko, Alexander '96 (STN) San Francisco, CA Immaculate Conception.
Avula, Mariadasai J. '80 (TYL) Mount Vernon, TX Sacred Heart.
Awad, Assad '57 (SAM) Worcester, MA Our Lady of Mercy.
Awalt, William J. '47 (WDC) Potomac, MD Our Lady of Mercy Retired.
Award, Richard *c.p.* '81 (FgM).
Awoyemi, Valentine '82 (CAM) North Cape May, NJ St. John of God.
Axalan, Romeo J. (NEW) Hillside, NJ Christ the King.
Axe, Thomas R. '60 (CIN) Retired.
Axe, William J. *o.ss.t.* '74 (NO)[R] Crown Point, LA Ave Maria Retreat House; Ave Maria Retreat House.
Axe, William J. *o.ss.t.* '74 (BAL)[S] Philadelphia, PA St. John Neumann Nursing Home.
Axtmann, Mark '01 (SFS) Sioux Falls, SD Christ the King.
Ayala, Osvaldo *c.m.* '01 (FgM).
Ayamanathil, Mathew '59 (NEW) Retired.
Ayamanthil, Mathew '59 (NEW)[N] Caldwell, NJ The Rev. Msgr. James F. Kelley Residence for Retired Priests.
Ayang, John M. *s.o.l.t.* '98 (CC)[G] Robstown, TX Society of Our Lady of the Most Holy Trinity.
Ayang, John *s.o.l.t.* '98 (KCK) Easton, KS St. Lawrence.
Ayang, John *s.o.l.t.* '98 (KCK) Easton, KS St. Joseph of the Valley.
Ayathupadam, Joseph '61 (CHL) Denver, NC Holy Spirit.
Aydt, Raymond A. '46 (BIS) Grenora, ND St. Boniface.
Ayem, Alfred *s.v.d.* '83 (LAF) New Iberia, LA St. Edward.
Ayem, Alfred *s.v.d.* (TR) Asbury Park, NJ St. Peter Claver.
Ayers, J. Cameron *s.j.* '86 (SFR) San Francisco, CA St. Agnes.
Ayers, John J. '51 (SPR) Retired.
Ayers, William G. '99 (PH) Chester, PA Saint Katharine Drexel.
Aylward, Gerard J. *c.s.p.* '53 (CHR) Clemson, SC St. Andrew.
Aylward, James W. '64 (SFR) Absent on Leave.
Ayo, Nicholas *c.s.c.* '59 (FTW)[B] University of Notre Dame Du Lac.
Ayo, Nicholas *c.s.c.* '59 (FTW)[I] Notre Dame, IN Holy Cross Community, Corby Hall, University of Notre Dame.
Ayoob, John '65 (PIT) Moon Township, PA St. Margaret Mary.
Ayotte, David John (LA) Los Angeles, CA Ascension; Mission Office.
Ayoub, Fawaz '79 (SLC) Wendover, UT San Felipe.
Ayoub, S. Paul '53 (BUF) Cheektowaga, NY Mother of Divine Grace.
Ayres, William G. (PH) Office for Pastoral Care of Migrants and Refugees.
Ayuyu, Isaac M. '86 (CHK) Saipan, MP Cathedral of Our Lady of Mt. Carmel; Main Contact.
Ayuyu, Isaac (CHK) Presbyteral Council.
Azadian, Joseph G *s.j.* '52 (SJ)[M] Los Gatos, CA Sacred Heart Jesuit Center.
Azakath, Matthew (NY) Bronx, NY Montefiore Medical Center.
Azar, John '88 (NTN) Atlanta, GA St. John Chrysostom.
Azar, Peter F. '80 (SAM) Wilkes–Barre, PA St. Anthony/ St. George.
Azar, Peter Fahed (SAM) Presbyteral Council–Ex Officio Members; Protopresbyters.
Azcoiti, Vicente '56 (BWN) Mission, TX Our Lady of the Holy Rosary.
Azcoitia, Florentino *s.j.* '52 (MIA)[H] Miami, FL Villa Javier.
Azcoitia, Florentino *s.j.* (MIA) Encuentros Familiares (Spanish).
Azcona, Eric *o.f.m.cap.* '52 (DAL)[K] Dallas, TX Capuchin Franciscan Friars, Vice Province of Texas; Dallas, TX Our Lady of Perpetual Help; Dallas, TX Our Lady of San Juan De Los Lagos and St. Theresa.
Azcona, Samuel *o.f.m.* '73 (SJN) San Juan, PR Resurreccion del Senor.
Azcona–Weber, Jose L. '85 (DAL) Richardson, TX St. Paul the Apostle.
Azevedo, Ferdinand T. *s.j.* '70 (FgM).
Azhakath, Matthew '89 (NY) Bronx, NY St. Ann.
Azhikkakath, Martin (CHI) Northlake, IL St. John Vianney, Cure of Ars.
Aziz, George K. *s.j.* '57 (SJ) Ventura, CA San Buenaventura Mission; [M] Los Gatos Sacred Heart Jesuit Center.
Azizo, Toma B. (OLD) Vicar General.
Azizo, Tomas B. '54 (OLD) Southfield, MI Saint Toma's.
Aznar, Manuel *c.m.* '66 (SJN) San Juan, PR San Vicente de Paul.
Azoon, Philip '94 (NTN) Retired.
Azorji, Eugene '80 (DAL) Dallas, TX Baylor University Medical Center; Dallas, TX Cathedral–Santuario de Guadalupe.
Azpericueta, Lucas '79 (FRS) Arvin, CA St. Thomas.
Azpiazu, Jose *o.m.i.* '28 (SAT)[K] San Antonio, TX Oblate Madonna Residence.
Azrak, Albert *c.s.s.* '60 (NY) White Plains, NY Our Lady of Mt. Carmel.
Azzarone, Daniel M. '78 (PRO) Absent on Leave.
Azzarto, Anthony J. *s.j.* '69 (NEW)[C] Jersey City, NJ St. Peter's Preparatory School; [N] Jersey City, NJ Jesuit Community of St. Peter's Prep, Inc..

B

Baabuge, Martin Atanga '91 (TUC) Douglas, AZ St. Luke; Pirtleville, AZ St. Bernard's.
Baary, David (NY) Federal Correctional Institution.
Babcock, David J. *o.f.m.* '53 (FgM).
Babcock, James K. '81 (NTN) Placentia, CA Holy Cross.
Babcock, James (NTN) Presbyteral Council.
Babcock, Timothy F. '68 (DET) Monroe, MI St. Mary's; College of Consultors; Judges.
Babeu, Gill C. '87 (BGP) Stamford, CT St. Bridget.
Babich, Ronald J. '77 (DET) Fraser, MI Our Lady Queen of All Saints.
Babicz, Edmund A. '84 (MAN) Center Ossipee, NH St. Joseph; Sanbornville, NH St. Anthony; Carroll County House of Correction.
Babiczuk, Fred '86 (FR) Fall River, MA Parish of the Good Shepherd.
Babin, Albert *c.ss.r.* '52 (BLX)[E] Biloxi, MS St. John Neumann Residence.
Babin, Victor *s.s.c.* '75 (MIA) Hollywood, FL Nativity.
Babin, Victor *s.s.c.* '75 (MIA)[K] St. Columbans St. Columban's Foreign Mission Society.
Babineau, Alexis A. *a.a.* '45 (WOR)[O] Worcester, MA Assumptionists (Augustinians of the Assumption).
Babineau, William E. '68 (MAN) Franklin, NH St. Paul.
Babinski, Donald E. '81 (RVC) Elmont, NY St. Vincent de Paul.
Babiuch, Thomas '02 (ALB) Oneonta, NY St. Mary.
Babonas, Alphonse '62 (DET) Detroit, MI St. Anthony.
Babowitch, John F. '96 (PH) Priests' Personnel Board; Vocation Office for Diocesan Priesthood; Philadelphia, PA St. Lucy.
Babu, Gangolu Bob *s.a.c.* '92 (VEN) Sarasota, FL St. Martha.
Babu, Vaidhian '91 (PH) Philadelphia, PA Incarnation of Our Lord.
Babulu, Francois Gonda '90 (WH) Cameron, WV St. Martin; Proctor, WV St. Joseph's.
Bac, Isidore M. Dinh Thanh *c.m.c.* '83 (SPC)[E] Carthage, MO Congregation of the Mother Coredemptrix, United States Assumption Province.
Baca, Al (ORG) Ministry to Priests.
Baca, Joseph '01 (FRS) Merced, CA Our Lady of Mercy/St. Patrick's.
Bacatan, Sebastian F. '94 (NY) Scarsdale, NY St. Pius X.
Baccaro, Gaetano T. '85 (SY) Liverpool, NY St. John.
Baccellieri, Joseph '66 (P) Retired.
Bacchi, Lee F. '77 (JOL) Chebanse, IL SS. Mary and Joseph's; Clifton, IL St. Peter's.
Bacchi, Lee (JOL) Rural Life.
Bacchi, Robert A. '77 (CHI) La Grange, IL St. Francis Xavier.
Bacevice, Joseph A. '77 (CLV) Cleveland, OH St. George; Defenders of the Bond.
Bacevicius, John J. *o.f.m.* '62 (PRT)[I] Kennebunkport, ME St. Anthony's Friary.
Bach, Frank J. '56 (SPK) Retired.
Bach, Frank (SPK) Priests' Personnel Board.
Bach, Gregory J. '99 (COV) Falmouth, KY St. Francis Xavier; [B] Alexandria, KY Bishop Brossart High School.
Bach, Ignacio *o.c.d.* '50 (TUC) Tucson, AZ.
Bach, James Nguyen '94 (NO) Des Allemands, LA St. Gertrude.
Bach, John A. '71 (LFT)[D] Lafayette, IN St. Anthony Health Care; [F] Lafayette, IN Monastery of the Precious Blood.
Bach, Lester *o.f.m.cap.* '57 (GB)[L] Appleton, WI Monte Alverno Retreat Center.
Bachand, Brian G. '99 (BO) Holliston, MA St. Mary.
Bachelot, Alexis *ss.cc.* (HON) Former Prelates.
Bacher, Anthony A. *c.s.sp.* '46 (VEN)[G] Sarasota, FL Congregation of the Holy Ghost.
Bacher, Arthur A. '54 (CLV) Richfield, OH St. Victor.
Bacher, Arthur '54 (CLV) Retired.
Bacher, Robert E. '48 (CLV) Clinton, OH St. George.
Bachkay, John M. '83 (PIT) Pittsburgh, PA Incarnation of the Lord.
Bachman, Kevin J. *o.s.b.* '01 (PBL) Avondale, CO Sacred Heart; [F] Canon City, CO Holy Cross Abbey.
Bachman, Michael J. '84 (BGP) Bridgeport, CT St. Patrick Church.
Bachmeier, Bernard A. '68 (FAR) Retired.
Bachmeier, Brian M. (FAR) Deanery 4.
Bachmeier, Brian '97 (FAR) Walhalla, ND Our Lady of the Sacred Heart.
Bachmeier, Brian '97 (FAR) Walhalla, ND St. Joseph.
Bachmeier, Brian '97 (FAR) Walhalla, ND St. Boniface.
Bachmeier, Brian (FAR) Continuing Education of Priests.
Bachmeier, Brian (FAR) Diocesan College of Consultors.
Bachmeier, Mark V. '89 (P) Eugene, OR St. Mary.
Bachmeier, Mark (P) Personnel Board.
Bachner, James M. '96 (PIT) Aliquippa, PA St. Titus.
Bacia, Eliot *o.f.m.* '62 (MIL)[O] Provincial Offices.
Bacik, James J. '62 (TOL) Toledo, OH Corpus Christi, University of Toledo; [M] Toledo, OH University of Toledo Campus Ministry; [N] Toledo, OH U.T. Newman Foundation for Student Education and Development.
Bacik, Leonard M. '72 (CLV) Middleburg Heights, OH St. Bartholomew.
Bacino, Ben '75 (PBL) Pueblo, CO St. Leander.
Bacino, Ben (PBL) Personnel.
Backes, John J. '73 (NY) Garnerville, NY St. Gregory Barbarigo.
Backherms, Robert *s.m.* '56 (NY)[M] Dayton, OH Mercy Siena Gardens.
Backiel, Bernard *m.i.c.* '60 (SPR) Portland, ME St. Louis; [I] Eucharistic Apostles of The Divine Mercy.
Backmann, Albert P. (STP) Columbia Heights, MN Immaculate Conception.
Backous, Timothy *o.s.b.* '86 (SCL)[B] St. John's University; [I] Collegeville, MN St. John's Abbey, of the Order of St. Benedict.
Bacleon, Misael '83 (NY) Bronx, NY St. Ann.
Bacleon, Misael '84 (NY) New York, NY Immaculate Conception.
Bacovin, Ronald J. '66 (TR) Pennington, NJ St. James; Diocesan Council of Priests; Office of Priest Personnel.
Badaoui, Adib '52 (NTN) Retired.
Badawi, Alfred '91 (OLL) Oakbrook Terrace, IL Our Lady of Lebanon Church.
Badawi, Alfred (OLL) Presbyteral Council.
Baddick, Thomas D. '81 (ALN) Whitehall, PA Holy Trinity.
Badding, Joseph P. '69 (BUF) Gasport, NY St. Mary; Middleport, NY St. Stephen.
Badeaux, James '99 (PSC) Wilkes–Barre, PA St. John's.
Badeaux, James (PSC) Associate Editors:.
Badeaux, James (PSC) Retirement Plan Board.
Badeaux, Kevin *j.c.l.* '84 (BEA) Port Arthur, TX St. James.
Badeaux, Kevin (BEA) Diocesan College of Consultors and Presbyteral Council; Diocesan Judges.
Baden, Robert D. '77 (RC) Kadoka, SD Our Lady of Victory; Wall, SD St. Patrick's.
Badenes, Jose *s.j.* '93 (LA)[BB] Los Angeles, CA Loyola Marymount University.
Bader, Edward A. *c.s.b.* '63 (GAL)[Q] Houston, TX Residence of the Basilian Fathers of the University of St. Thomas.
Bader, Edward '82 (NY) Marlboro, NY St. Mary.
Bader, Paul A. '61 (CIN) Cincinnati, OH St. William.
Bader, Paul L. '58 (ALN) Coplay, PA St. Peter; [J] Bethlehem, PA Holy Family Villa Retired.
Badger, Arthur A. '53 (TOL) Retired.
Badgerow, Rock '79 (GR) Parnell, MI St. Patrick's.
Badgley, T. Augustine *p.v.* '87 (NY) Hawthorne, NY Holy Rosary.
Badia, Leonard F. '60 (BRK) Middle Village, NY St. Margaret.
Badilles, Jose '82 (LUB) Snyder, TX Our Lady of Guadalupe.
Badilles, Roy '82 (LUB) Snyder, TX St. Elizabeth's.
Badnerosky, Myron M. '56 (PSC) Levittown, PA Our Lady of Perpetual Help.
Bado, Walter *s.j.* '59 (LEX) Lexington, KY The Newman Center, Holy Spirit.
Bado, Walter *s.j.* '59 (LEX)[L] Lexington, KY The Newman Center Holy Spirit Parish University of Kentucky.
Badovsky, Thomas '73 (PEO) Peru, IL St. Valentine's.
Badurina, Gabriel *t.o.r.* '62 (PIT) Pittsburgh, PA St. Nicholas.
Badurina, Gabriel *t.o.r.* '62 (PIT)[N] Pittsburgh, PA Croatian Commissariate, T.O.R..
Badway, Gavin (PMB) Office of Vocations.
Bae, Benedict DoHa '97 (RVC) Great Neck, NY St. Aloysius.
Bae, Do Dong Andrew '91 (STP) St. Paul, MN St. Andrew Kim; Ministry to Koreans.
Baehr, David '64 (SY) Syracuse, NY St. Margaret.
Baek, Gus *s.d.b.* '95 (NEW)[N] Orange, NJ The Salesian Community.
Baek, John N.K. '91 (DET) Northville, MI St. Andrew Kim Korean Catholic Church.
Baenziger, Edward J. *c.s.b.* '76 (GAL)[Q] Houston, TX Residence of the Basilian Fathers of the University of St. Thomas.
Baer, Campion R. *o.f.m.cap.* '56 (CHI) Chicago, IL St. Kevin.
Baer, Campion *o.f.m.cap.* '56 (DET)[K] Detroit, MI Provincialate.
Baer, Robert W. *c.s.p.* '54 (NY)[EE] Jamaica Estates Paulist Fathers Generalate.
Baer, Timothy K. '96 (WDC) Cheverly, MD St. Ambrose.
Baer, William J. '96 (STP)[A] St. Paul, MN St. John Vianney Seminary; [C] St. Paul, MN University of St. Thomas.
Baerwald, Jeffrey P. *s.j.* '89 (BAL)[B] Timonium, MD Loyola Graduate Center –Timonium Campus; [S] Baltimore, MD Jesuit Community of Loyola College, Inc..
Baeten, David '62 (GB) Special Assignment.
Baeten, Lambert C. *o.praem.* '59 (GB)[I] Archdiocese of Iquitos, Peru.
Baez, Jose F. (MGZ) Diocesan Consultors.
Baeza, Manuel *m.c.c.j.* '96 (FgM).
Baez Camacho, Jose F. (PCE)[B] The Pontifical Catholic University of Puerto Rico.
Bafaro, Michael P. '53 (WOR) Worcester, MA Our Lady of Mt. Carmel and St. Ann.
Bafaro, Michael (WOR) Deans.
Baffour, Paul '94 (NY) Bronx, NY St. Brendan.
Baffuor–Awuah, Paul (NY) New York, NY Epiphany.
Bagabaldo, Clodorico V. (TR) Burlington, NJ St. Paul.
Bagan, Francis *o.m.i.* '52 (PT) Perry, FL Immaculate Conception.
Bagatin, Tarcisio *c.s.* '54 (PRO) Providence, RI Holy Ghost.
Bagdonis, Raymond *o.carm.* '94 (NY) Middletown, NY Our Lady of Mt. Carmel.
Bagert, Matthew '97 (DAL) Grand Prairie, TX Immaculate Conception.
Baggarly, John D. *s.j.* '60 (DET)[P] Clarkston, MI Colombiere Center.
Baggetta, Joseph J. '74 (BO) Boston, MA St. James the Greater; Roslindale, MA Judge John J. Connelly Youth Center; Mattapan, MA Metropolitan Youth Service Center; Navy Reserve Chaplains.
Baggio, Gianantonio *c.s.* '92 (SD) Imperial, CA St. Anthony of Padua.
Bagienski, Ronald A. '69 (BUF) Buffalo, NY Holy Apostles SS. Peter and Paul.
Baginskis, Boleslaus *m.i.c.* '42 (CHI) Chicago, IL Our Lady of Aglona.
Bagley, Gary J. '72 (BUF) Eggertsville, NY St. Benedict.
Bagley, Ronald M. *c.j.m.* '77 (BUF)[O] West Seneca, NY The Eudists, St. John Eudes Center; West Seneca, NY St. Bonaventure.
Bagnato, James D. *o.praem.* '79 (WIL)[J] Middletown, DE Immaculate Conception Priory of the Canons Regular of Premontre; [J] Middletown, DE Norbertine Fathers of Delaware, Inc..
Bahash, James '99 (SD) Calexico, CA Our Lady of Guadalupe.
Bahhuth, Albert '96 (LA) Burbank, CA St. Finbar.
Bahhuth, Albert (LA) Ministry to Recently Ordained Priests.
Bahleda, Aloysius J. '58 (GBG)[G] Greensburg, PA Neumann House Retired.
Bahlinger, Donald G. *s.j.* '59 (NO)[P] Chalatenango, El Salvador, CA Parroquia San Bartolome.
Bahlinger, Donald G. *s.j.* '59 (FgM).
Bahr, Joseph E. '60 (DOD) Garden City, KS St. Dominic; Ingalls, KS St. Stanislaus; Priests' Trust Fund; Diocesan School Council.
Baiardi, Sereno *o.f.m.* '66 (MIL)[X] Waterford, WI General Secretariat of the Franciscan Missions, Inc..
Baidoo, Joseph '85 (RVC) Mastic Beach, NY St. Jude.
Baidoo, Raphael *o.ss.t.* '77 (VIC) Goliad, TX Immaculate Conception.
Baier, Donald M. '70 (RVC) Malverne, NY Our Lady of Lourdes.
Baier, Donald '75 (VEN) Retired.
Baier, William J. '82 (STL) Elsberry, MO Sacred Heart.
Bailey, Casey *o.c.s.o.* '83 (P)[L] Lafayette, OR The Cistercian (Trappist) Abbey of Our Lady of Guadalupe.
Bailey, Declan *o.f.m.* '44 (PAT)[M] Ringwood, NJ Holy Name Friary, Inc..
Bailey, Doug (ORL)[A] Melbourne, FL Central Catholic High School.
Bailey, Douglas S. *s.d.s.* '77 (ORL)[F] Melbourne, FL Florida Institute of Technology Campus Ministry; Air Force Reserve Chaplains.
Bailey, Fred '83 (ORG) Aliso Viejo, CA Corpus Christi.
Bailey, Fred (ORG) Clergy Personnel Board.
Bailey, Harold '69 (PIT) Allegheny County, PA Mayview State Hospital.
Bailey, J. Lawrence '86 (SEA) Military Chaplains; Air Force Chaplains.
Bailey, J. Scott *c.ss.r.* '98 (BAL) Baltimore, MD Sacred Heart of Jesus.
Bailey, John L. '41 (WDC)[L] Washington, DC Cardinal O'Boyle Residence for Priests Retired.
Bailey, Justin J. *o.f.m.* '60 (BO)[AA] Boston, MA St. Anthony Shrine.
Bailey, Paul F. '58 (BO) Plymouth, MA St. Mary; Senior Priests Retired.
Bailey, Ricardo '03 (ATL) Marietta, GA St. Joseph; Marietta, GA St. Joseph.
Bailey, Richard L. *s.j.* '58 (STL)[O] St. Louis, MO De Smet Jesuit High School Community.
Bailey, Robert L. '93 (PRO) Greenville, RI St. Philip.
Baillargeon, Albert G. '47 (MAN) Dover, NH St. Mary Retired.
Baillargeon, Anatole *o.m.i.* '41 (BO)[Y] Tewksbury, MA Immaculate Heart of Mary Infirmary.
Bailleres, Anthony *l.c.* '81 (HRT)[B] Cheshire, CT Novitiate of the Legion of Christ.
Bailon, Abelardo '58 (LA) Huntington Park, CA St. Matthias.
Baily, Harold E. '69 (PIT)[Q] Robert Morris College, Moon Township Campus.
Baily, Harold '69 (PIT) McKees Rocks, PA St. John of God.

Baima, Thomas A. '80 (CHI) Skokie, IL St. Peter; [A] Mundelein Seminary.
Bain, Daniel '64 (RIC) Quinque, VA Shepherd of the Hills.
Bain, Daniel '64 (RIC) Elkton, VA Holy Infant.
Bain, J.F. Michael '62 (PHX) Retired.
Bain, John K. '70 (RNO) Army National Guard Chaplains.
Bain, John '70 (RNO) Absent on Sick Leave.
Bain, John (RNO) Priests' Personnel Board.
Bain, Ken '90 (SFS) Clark, SD St. Michael.
Bain, Richard A. '80 (SFR) Veterans' Hospital.
Bain, Richard C. '80 (SFR) Mill Valley, CA Our Lady of Mt. Carmel.
Bain, Thomas J. *s.j.* '56 (DET)[P] Clarkston, MI Colombiere Center.
Bain, Thomas J. *s.j.* '56 (CLV)[D] Cleveland, OH St. Ignatius High School.
Baird, James R. '93 (DEN) Sterling, CO St. Anthony; [Q] Sterling, CO Northeastern Junior College (Sterling).
Baird, James '93 (DEN) Iliff, CO St. Catherine of Siena.
Baird, James '93 (DEN) Peetz, CO Sacred Heart.
Baird, Joseph A. *o.s.f.s.* '68 (WIL)[J] Childs, MD Retirement and Assisted Care Facility.
Baird, Lawrence J. '69 (ORG) St. John Vianney; [O] Orange, CA Orange Catholic Foundation; Media Relations.
Baird, Lawrence (ORG) Development Office.
Baird, Lawrence (ORG) Diocesan Finance Council.
Baistra, Jorge '74 (SAT) Retired.
Bajek, Gerald '69 (NEW) Newark, NJ St. Casimir's.
Bajek, Mietek *o.m.i.* '81 (CR) Ogema, MN Most Holy Redeemer.
Bajkowski, Dennis W. '65 (CAM) Pennsville, NJ Queen of the Apostles.
Bajorek, James R. '80 (PH) Wallingford, PA St. John Chrysostom.
Bajorek, Joseph *s.d.b.* '45 (NEW)[N] Ramsey, NJ Don Bosco Prep Salesian Residence; [C] Ramsey, NJ Don Bosco Preparatory High School.
Bak, Bernard '88 (BAL) Retired.
Bak, Bernard (BAL) Advocates and Procurators.
Bak, Soo–Tae (CHL) Korean Catholic Cultural Center.
Bakatu, Sebastien '83 (STP) Hugo, MN St. John the Baptist.
Baker, Andrew R. '91 (ALN) On Duty Outside the Diocese.
Baker, Bartley '93 (NEW) Union, NJ St. Michael's.
Baker, Brad (JOL) Elmhurst, IL Immaculate Conception.
Baker, Bruce *o.carm.* '99 (JOL)[L] Darien Carmelite Provincial Office.
Baker, Donald C. '95 (NY) New York, NY St. Gregory; New York, NY St. Teresa.
Baker, Donald H. '66 (WOR) Gardner, MA Sacred Heart of Jesus.
Baker, Donald P. '80 (CHL) Absent On Leave.
Baker, George E. '81 (NY) New York, NY Our Lady of Victory.
Baker, Gerald H. '83 (OWN) Morganfield, KY St. Ann's.
Baker, Jack H. '93 (DET) Wayne, MI St. Mary; Inkster, MI Holy Family Parish; Inkster, MI SS. Kevin and Norbert.
Baker, James E. '63 (DOD) Garden City, KS St. Mary; Deans; Judicial Vicar; Synodal Judge; Diocesan Pastoral Council; Diocesan School Council; Scouting.
Baker, James H. *s.j.* '69 (STL)[C] Saint Louis University; [O] St. Louis, MO Jesuit Community Corporation at St. Louis University – Jesuit Hall.
Baker, Jay L. '92 (HT) Morgan City, LA Holy Cross; Coordinator; Clergy Personnel.
Baker, Jay (HT) Judges.
Baker, John C. '82 (PRO) Plantation, FL St. Gregory; On Duty Outside the Diocese.
Baker, John Sims '94 (NSH) McEwen, TN St. Patrick; Tennessee Ridge, TN St. Elizabeth Ann Seton; Defenders of the Bond.
Baker, Joseph M. '85 (TUC) Tucson, AZ Holy Family.
Baker, Joseph W. '51 (STL) St. Louis, MO St. Hedwig.
Baker, Joseph W. '69 (NY) New York, NY St. John the Martyr.
Baker, Justin J. '99 (BUR) Knights of Columbus; [H] Middlebury, VT Middlebury College; Middlebury, VT Assumption of the Blessed Virgin Mary.
Baker, Kenneth J. '84 (CHI) Chicago, IL Queen of All Saints Basilica.
Baker, Kenneth R. '62 (CIN) Dayton, OH St. Rita.
Baker, Kenneth *s.j.* '62 (PAT) Pequannock, NJ Our Lady of Fatima Chapel (Tridentine).
Baker, Nicholas '63 (LIN) Indianola, NE St. Catherine's.
Baker, Nicholas (LIN) Deaneries and Deans.
Baker, Nicholas (LIN) Diocesan Consultors.
Baker, Richard M. *m.m.* '71 (NY)[EE] Maryknoll Maryknoll Fathers and Brothers.
Baker, Richard '90 (NY).
Baker, Robert R. *c.s.c.* '70[A] (FgM).
Baker, Stephen *o.s.a.* '90 (PH)[D] Drexel Hill, PA Monsignor Bonner High School.
Baker, Thomas E. '89 (LA) Los Angeles, CA Our Lady of Guadalupe; Board of Directors:.
Baker, W. Pierre '78 (MAN) Farmington, NH St. Peter; Rochester, NH St. Mary.
Baker, William S. '55 (SY) Clayville, NY St. Patrick.
Baker, William T. '82 (ALN) Catasauqua, PA St. Andrew; Catasauqua, PA St. Lawrence.
Bakewell, Donald V. '66 (DUB) Dubuque, IA St. Joseph's.
Bakey, Christopher (CAM) Advocates; Vocations Apostolate; Charismatic Renewal; Vocation Advisory Board.
Bakh, Antoine '88 (OLL) Anaheim, CA St. John Maron.
Bakh, Antoine (OLL) Presbyteral Council.
Bakh, Antoine (OLL) College of Consultors.
Bakke, Lawrence M. '75 (MAD) University Hospitals.
Bakker, Richard T. *s.m.a.* '59 (BO) Malden, MA St. Joseph.
Bakle, John L. *s.m.* '67 (STL)[O] Columbus OH St. Agatha Rectory.
Bakle, John L. *s.m.* '67 (COL) Columbus, OH St. Agatha; Columbus, OH Saint Stephen the Martyr.
Bakos, Stephen '36 (Y) Retired.
Baky, Isidore '72 (MIA) Fort Lauderdale, FL St. Helen.
Baky, Isidore (MIA) Vietnamese.
Bakyil, Alphonsus (CC)[G] Robstown, TX Society of Our Lady of the Most Holy Trinity.
Bala, Paul '69 (SAG) Port Sanilac, MI St. Mary.
Balaban, Oryst '57 (SJP) Retired.
Balado, Armando '49 (MIA) Miami, FL St. Raymond.
Balagapo, Victorio '66 (SFR) Colma, CA Holy Angels.
Balagat, Arturo '75 (SB) Ontario, CA St. George.
Balagtas, Rodel G. '91 (LA) Los Angeles, CA Immaculate Heart of Mary.
Balas, Christopher *o.f.m.conv.* '57 (TR) Trenton, NJ Immaculate Conception.
Balas, David *o.cist.* '54 (DAL)[B] University of Dallas; [K] Irving, TX Cistercian Abbey of Our Lady of Dallas.
Balash, Michael D. '87 (Y) Mantua, OH St. Joseph's.
Balasko, George J. '67 (Y) East Liverpool, OH St. Ann.
Balazs, Richard *c.r.* '65 (CHI) Chicago, IL St. Stanislaus, Bishop and Martyr.
Balazy, Edwin W. '62 (DET) Dearborn Heights, MI St. John the Baptist.
Balbi, Abel Eduardo (SB) Indio, CA Our Lady of Perpetual Help; Riverside, CA Our Lady of Guadalupe Shrine
Balbi, Mario *s.d.b.* '47 (NEW)[N] Orange, NJ The Salesian Community.
Balcarski, Duane *c.s.c.* '71 (PHX)[K] Phoenix AZ Andre House of Arizona.
Balchunas, Henry A. '65 (HRT) Wolcott, CT St. Pius X.
Balcon, Anthony Dal *c.s.* (WDC)[L] Mitchellville, MD Villa Rosa Nursing Home, Inc..
Balczeniuk, Mark G. '83 (SCR) Wapwallopen, PA Our Lady Help of Christians.
Baldacchino, Peter '96 (NEW) On Duty Outside the Archdiocese.
Balderas, Jose L. (LAR) Presbyteral Council.
Balderas, Jose Luis '58 (LAR) Laredo, TX Christ the King; Priests Personnel Board.
Balderrama, George *s.c.j.* '73 (MIL)[O] Franklin, WI Villa Maria.
Baldonado, Angel *s.d.b.* '78 (CC).
Baldonado, Felipe *o.f.m.* '38 (LA)[Q] Santa Barbara, CA Franciscan Friary, Order of Friars Minor (Old Mission).
Baldonado, Luis *o.f.m.* '52 (PHX) Phoenix, AZ St. Mary's Basilica.
Baldonieri, Thomas F. '90 (CHI) Mt. Prospect, IL St. Raymond de Penafort.
Baldovin, John *s.j.* '75 (BO)[V] Cambridge, MA St. Edmunds House.
Balducelli, Roberto *o.s.f.s.* '36 (WIL) Wilmington, DE St. Anthony of Padua.
Balducelli, Roberto (WIL) Regina Coeli Society.
Balduf, Raymond J. *s.j.* '51 (NEW)[C] Jersey City, NJ St. Peter's Preparatory School; [N] Jersey City, NJ Jesuit Community of St. Peter's Prep, Inc..
Baldus, Leonard *o.m.i.* '42 (BEL)[F] Belleville, IL Shrine of Our Lady of the Snows.
Baldwin, Bradley *t.o.r.* '94 (ALT) Altoona, PA Our Lady of Mt. Carmel; Altoona, PA Altoona Hospital.
Baldwin, David E. '77 (CHI) Chicago, IL St. Benedict the African (East).
Baldwin, Edward J. '55 (DET) Presbyteral Council Retired.
Baldwin, John F. '59 (CHI) Retired.
Baldwin, Michael E. '83 (WCH) Andover, KS St. Vincent de Paul.
Baldwin, Paul C. '97 (DUB) Van Horne, IA St. Paul; Van Horne, IA St. Michael; Van Horne, IA Immaculate Conception; Van Horne, IA St. Patrick; Blairstown, IA St. John.
Baldyga, William L. '69 (HRT) Suffield, CT St. Joseph's.
Balen, Moacir *c.s.* (BO) Somerville, MA St. Anthony; Brazilian Community Centers.
Bales, Robert '57 (MIL) West Bend, WI Immaculate Conception.
Bales, Thomas E. '74 (RCK) Rockford, IL Holy Family; Diocesan Consultors.
Balestino, Francis P. '60 (ALT) Johnstown, PA Immaculate Conception.
Balestrieri, Edward '59 (BEL) Leave of Absence.
Baliege, Bonaventure *s.j.* (CHI)[J] Chicago, IL Resurrection Medical Center.
Balige, Bonaventura *s.j.* '99 (CHI)[C] Chicago, IL Jesuit Community at Loyola University Chicago.
Balili, Peter '89 (SB) Fontana, CA Kaiser Permanente Hospital.
Balili, Peter (SB) Rancho Cucamonga, CA Sacred Heart.
Balino, Cresencio '94 (NEW) North Bergen, NJ St. Brigid.
Balino, Cresencio '94 (NEW) Union City, NJ St. Rocco's.
Balinong, Alfredo *s.j.* '64 (NY) New York, NY Blessed Sacrament.
Balint, R. James '61 (DAL) Plano, TX Prince of Peace.
Balint, Stephen J. '65 (BGP) Norwalk, CT St. Ladislaus; Boy Scouts and Girl Scouts.
Balio, Paul '72 (SD) San Diego, CA St. Joseph Cathedral.
Balistreri, Anthony '93 (SJP) Arnold, PA St. Vladimir.
Balistreri, Anthony (SJP) Director of Youth Ministries.
Balistreri, Anthony (SJP) Presbyteral Council.
Balistreri, Anthony (SJP) Catechetical Planning Committee.
Balistreri, Anthony (SJP) League of Ukrainian Catholic Youth (LUCY).
Balistreri, Anthony (SJP) Diocesan Personnel Board.
Balizan, Daniel M. '89 (SFE) Albuquerque, NM St. Anne.
Balkan, Paschal *o.c.s.o.* '55 (ARL)[J] Berryville, VA Cistercian Abbey of Our Lady of the Holy Cross.
Balker, Joseph W. '44 (FRS) Retired.
Ball, Matthew J. '91 (RVC) Absent on Leave.
Ball, Raymond A. '87 (MAN)[C] Manchester, NH Trinity High School; Catholic Scouting Office.
Ball, Raymond '87 (MAN) Lancaster, NH All Saints.
Ball, Richard D. '77 (SC) Dow City, IA St. Boniface; Dow City, IA St. Marys.
Ball, Thomas J. '66 (BUR) Burlington, VT Cathedral of the Immaculate Conception.
Ball, Wayne L. (MO) Judges.
Ball, Wayne '89 (RIC) Highland Springs, VA St. John.
Ball, Wayne (RIC) Judges; International Airport.
Ballance, Harvey '57 (NEW) Retired.
Ballard, Kevin *s.j.* '85 (SJ) San Jose, CA Most Holy Trinity.
Ballard, Mark E. '02 (BO) Framingham, MA St. Bridget; Haverhill, MA All Saints.
Ballester, Buenaventura '43 (ARE) Arecibo, PR Church of Sagrado Corazon de Jesus Retired.
Ballester, Pedro J. '58 (PCE) Ponce, PR San Conrado.
Ballesteros, Enrique '89 (OAK) Oakland, CA St. Louis Bertrand.
Ballestrazzi, Libero *c.s.j.* '44 (CLV)[O] Avon, OH Congregation of St. Joseph.
Balleza, John A. '85 (SFR) San Francisco, CA St. Patrick.
Ballien, Paul '99 (DET) Novi, MI Holy Family.
Ballman, Luke '01 (ATL) Atlanta, GA Holy Spirit; Associate Vicars for Clergy.
Ballman, Thomas J. '43 (CIN) Retired.
Ballor, Milton *c.pp.s.* '55 (CIN)[B] Carthagena, OH St. Charles.
Ballou, Jeffrey A. '01 (SPR) Springfield, MA Holy Cross.
Balluff, John '88 (JOL) Piper City, IL St. Peter.
Balluff, John '88 (JOL) Gilman, IL Immaculate Conception.
Ballweber, Eugene L. (CHI) Retired.
Ballweg, John M. '56 (NEW) Union, NJ Holy Spirit Retired.
Ballweg, Lawrence F. '40 (RVC) Retired.
Balmeo, Simeon '65 (AGN) Agana, GU Our Lady of the Purification.
Balog, Robert A. '72 (RCK) McHenry, IL St. John the Baptist.
Balouck, Wally *o.f.m.cap.* (SAG)[G] Saginaw Queen of Angels Friary and Retreat House.
Balsas, Alvaro *s.j.* '01 (OAK)[N] Berkeley, CA Jesuit Community at Jesuit School of Theology at Berkeley.
Balser, Edward '56 (JKS) Madison, MS Holy Family Retired.
Balser, Robert *c.ss.r.* '49 (GR) Grand Rapids, MI St. Alphonsus; [I] Grand Rapids, MI The Society of the Redemptorists of the City of Grand Rapids.
Balskus, Charles '65 (CHI) Chicago, IL St. Christina.
Balta, Raymond A. '69 (PBR) Johnstown, PA St. Mary's; Protopresbyters.
Baltes, Gabriel *o.s.b.* '91 (JOL)[L] Lisle, IL St. Procopius Abbey.
Baltes, Gabriel *o.s.b.* (SUP) Office of Worship.
Baltes, Timothy '76 (SCL) St. Cloud, MN St. Paul.
Baltes, Timothy (SCL) Diocesan Corporate Board.
Balthazar, Ayala '43 (SJ) Retired.
Balthazar, Norman (SP) Calvary Catholic Cemetery and Miserere Guild.
Baltrusaitis, Gabriel *o.f.m.* '54 (PRT)[I] Kennebunkport, ME St. Anthony's Friary.
Baltz, Albert G. '70 (BUR) Elected Members; Brandon, VT St. Mary's.
Baltz, David *m.c.c.j.* '67 (FgM).

Baltz, John P. '43 (NSH) Retired.
Baluyot, Michael (BEA) Boy Scouts; Kountze, TX Holy Spirit Mission; Lumberton, TX Infant Jesus.
Balvo, Charles D. '76 (NY) On Duty Outside the Archdiocese.
Balwinski, Gerald E. '69 (SAG) Bay City, MI Our Lady of the Visitation.
Balys, Thomas I. *o.c.d.* '63 (GRY)[I] Munster, IN Discalced Carmelite Fathers Monastery.
Balzer, Raymond '49 (FTW) Retired.
Balzer, Raymond (FTW) Retired Clergy Committee.
Bambenek, Oliver *o.f.m.cap.* '65 (MIL)[B] Mount Calvary, WI St. Lawrence Seminary; [B] Mount Calvary, WI St. Felix Friary.
Bamber, William J. *c.m.* '55 (PH)[AA] Philadelphia Congregation of the Mission.
Bambera, Joseph C. '83 (SCR)[AA] Dickson City, PA Visitation of the Blessed Virgin Mary; Judges; Diocesan Consultors; Presbyteral Council.
Bamberg, Callistus *o.f.m.* '61 (ALB)[B] Siena College; [R] Albany, NY St. Francis Chapel.
Bambir, Vjekoslav *o.f.m.* '40 (CHI)[N] Chicago, IL St. Anthony's Friary.
Bambol, John *o.f.m.conv.* '41 (SPR)[H] Holyoke, MA Mont Marie Health Care Center, Inc..
Bambrick, John P. '91 (TR) Manalapan, NJ St. Thomas More.
Bambrick, John W. '70 (ALN) Pottsville, PA Mary Queen of Peace.
Banach, Henry S. '48 (WOR) Retired.
Banach, Michael '88 (WOR) On Special or Other Diocesan Assignment.
Banach, Michael '88 (WOR) On Duty Outside the Diocese.
Banal, Bernardo (CHK) Presbyteral Council; College of Consultors.
Bananiewicz, Joseph *o.s.f.s.* '57 (WIL)[J] Childs, MD Retirement and Assisted Care Facility.
Banarsi, Ed (AUS)[E] Austin, TX SETON Northwest Hospital.
Banas, James T. *c.s.c.* '57 (FTW)[I] Mathis House.
Banas, James T. *c.s.c.* '57 (FgM).
Banas, Leonard N. *c.s.c.* '57 (FTW)[B] University of Notre Dame Du Lac; [I] Notre Dame, IN Holy Cross Community, Corby Hall, University of Notre Dame.
Banazak, Gregory '85 (DET)[A] Orchard Lake, MI SS. Cyril and Methodius Seminary; Special Assignment.
Bancroft, Martin J. '01 (RVC) St. James, NY SS. Philip and James.
Banda, Charles '89 (SP) Dunedin, FL Our Lady of Lourdes.
Banden, Joseph W. '69 (STL) Florissant, MO Transfiguration.
Bandiera, Colombo F. '52 (WH) Morgantown, WV St. Francis De Sales Catholic Church Retired.
Bandivas, Gemnoli '91 (LA) Granada Hills, CA St. John Baptist de la Salle.
Bandres, Antonio *o.f.m.cap.* '75 (FWT) Fort Worth, TX Immaculate Heart of Mary.
Bandsuch, Mark R. *s.j.* (DET)[K] Detroit Jesuit Provincial Office–Detroit Province of the Society of Jesus.
Bandsuch, Mark *s.j.* '00 (LA)[C] Los Angeles, CA Jesuit Community.
Bandurski, Pawel *s.ch.* '92 (DET)[K] Sterling Heights, MI Society of Christ Provincial Home.
Bandurski, Pawel *s.ch.* (CHI) Chicago, IL Holy Trinity Mission.
Banet, Paul H. *s.s.j.* '55 (GAL) Galveston, TX Holy Rosary.
Banet, Stephen '77 (IND) Indianapolis, IN St. Jude.
Bang–Doan, Joseph '74 (GAL)[K] Catholic Chaplain Corps, Texas Medical Center.
Baniak, Walter '41 (ALB) Retired.
Banick, Thomas V. '63 (SCR) Wilkes–Barre, PA St. Mary's Church of the Immaculate Conception.
Banigan, Herbert '46 (DEN) Retired.
Bankemper, Stephen M. '03 (COV) Southgate, KY St. Therese of the Infant Jesus; [B] Newport, KY Newport Central Catholic High School.
Banken, Robert L. '68 (STL) St. Louis, MO St. Sebastian.
Banker, Richard A. '88 (STP) Prior Lake, MN St. Michael.
Banks, Charles D. *o.m.i.* '66 (WDC)[M] Washington, DC Provincial Offices of the United States Province of the Missionary Oblates of Mary Immaculate; [M] Washington, DC Oblate Community.
Banks, David A. '73 (SP) Homosassa, FL St. Thomas the Apostle.
Banks, Evan *o.f.m.* '50 (NEW) Fair Lawn, NJ St. Anne's.
Banks, Gary *s.t.* '76 (ARL)[J] Arlington, VA Missionary Servants of the Most Holy Trinity, S.T..
Banks, John P. *s.j.* '51 (BO)[V] Weston, MA Campion Health Center, Inc..
Banks, Michael *o.f.m.cap.* '84 (NY)[EE] New York, NY Development Office:.
Banks, Michael *o.f.m.cap.* '84 (FgM).
Banks, Peter *o.f.m.cap.* '73 (LA) Los Angeles, CA St. Lawrence of Brindisi.
Bannan, Martin '56 (BRK) Brooklyn, NY St. Patrick.
Bannan, Peter F. '67 (NY) Pelham, NY St. Catharine.
Bannantine, Thomas E. *s.j.* '65 (OM)[K] Omaha, NE Jesuit Community at Creighton University.
Banner, Russell '67 (CLV) Administrative Leave.
Bannin, Eugene T. *s.j.* '50 (NO)[P] New Orleans, LA Ignatius Residence.
Bannon, Anthony *l.c.* '75 (HRT)[V] Orange, CT Legion of Christ, Inc..
Bannon, Anthony *l.c.* '75 (NY)[II] Rye, NY Catholic Women@Work Inc..
Banos, Felix '58 (ORL) Lakeland, FL St. Joseph's Retired.
Bantz, William '60 (Y) Retired.
Banuelas, Arturo '76 (ELP) El Paso, TX St. Pius X.
Banuelas, Arturo (ELP) Tepeyac Institute.
Banuelas, Arturo (ELP) Laity, Office of the.
Banzin, Robert S. '64 (CHI) Riverside, IL St. Mary.
Bao, Tran Quoc *c.ss.r.* '90 (LA)[Q] Houston, TX.
Baptista, Diego '69 (SAC) Ione, CA Mule Creek State Prison.
Baptista, Diego '69 (SR) On Duty Outside the Diocese.
Baptista, Diogo '69 (SAC) Ione, CA.
Baptiste, Charles J. '96 (PIT) Ambridge, PA Good Samaritan.
Baptiste, Glen *c.r.* '91 (PT) Panama City, FL St. John the Evangelist.
Baraan, Geoffrey '97 (OAK) Antioch, CA St. Ignatius; Region 5.
Barachini, Nello A. *c.m.* '86 (BGP) Bridgeport, CT St. Ambrose; Bridgeport, CT Bridgeport Hospital.
Barachini, Nello (BGP) Shelton, CT St. Margaret Mary.
Barajas, Abel '96 (MIA) On Duty Outside the Archdiocese.
Barak, Christopher L. '87 (LIN) Palmyra, NE St. Leo's; Notaries; Commission for Sacred Liturgy and Sacred Music; Office of Religious Education (CCD); Evangelization Committee; Priests' Continuing Education Committee.
Baraki, Tesfamariam '75 (WDC) Washington, DC Kidane–Mehret Ge'ez Rite Catholic Church.
Baraki, Tesfamariam '75 (WDC) Washington, DC St. Gabriel.
Baraki, Tesfamariam '75 (WDC)[V] Washington, DC Ethiopian and Eritrean Catholic Mission, USA.
Baran, Blaise R. '82 (MET) Middlesex, NJ Our Lady of Mount Virgin.
Baran, Jody '89 (PSC) Leave of Absence.
Baran, John P. '84 (BGP) Fairfield, CT St. Anthony of Padua.
Baran, Joseph L. '47 (MIL) Retired.
Baran, Volodymyr '85 (PAT) Rockaway, NJ Sacred Heart.
Baran, Wolodomyr (PAT) Dover, NJ Dover General Hospital.
Baran, Wolodymyr (PAT).
Baran, Zbigniew *s.d.b.* '93 (OAK)[J] Bellflower, CA St. Dominic Savio.
Baranek, Raymond '76 (CLV) Absent on Leave.
Baraniak, James T. *o.praem.* '93 (GB)[A] De Pere, WI St. Norbert Abbey; [I] De Pere, WI St. Joseph Priory.
Baraniewicz, Joseph *o.s.f.s.* '57 (TOL)[J] Childs, MD Annecy Hall Retired.
Baranowski, Arthur R. '68 (DET) Marysville, MI St. Christopher.
Baranowski, David J. '73 (HRT) Hamden, CT St. Stephen's.
Baranowski, Stanley A. '55 (MIL) Retired.
Baranski, Andrew E. '92 (SY) Special Assignment; [Q] East Syracuse, NY Vianney House; Assistant Chancellor/Secretary to Bishop Moynihan; Management Team; Liturgy.
Baransky, Francis J. '79 (ALN) Jim Thorpe, PA St. Joseph.
Barasinski, John B. '81 (GRY) Beverly Shores, IN St. Ann.
Baratelli, David J. (NEW) Air Force Reserve Chaplains.
Barattini, John H. '44 (NO) Retired.
Barba, Hernando '81 (LA) Pico Rivera, CA St. Francis Xavier.
Barba, Rodrigo '55 (LAR) Hebbronville, TX Our Lady of Guadalupe.
Barbato, Robert *o.f.m. cap.* '87 (LA) Los Angeles, CA St. Lawrence of Brindisi.
Barbella, John '87 (MET) Bridgewater, NJ St. Bernard.
Barber, Bradley A. '94 (CC) Corpus Christi, TX St. Pius X.
Barber, Eugene J. *s.j.* '63 (BAL)[S] Resid. S. Pedro Claver.
Barber, Eugene J. *s.j.* '63 (FgM).
Barber, Hal '67 (SFS) Pierre, SD SS. Peter and Paul; Diocesan Consultors; Deans; Presbyteral Council.
Barber, Michael C. *s.j.* (SFR)[A] Navy Reserve Chaplains.
Barber, Michael D. *s.j.* '79 (STL)[C] Saint Louis University; [O] St. Louis, MO Leo Brown Jesuit Community.
Barber, Michael L. *s.j.* '75 (ALN)[A] Wernersville, PA Jesuit Center.
Barber, Stephen A. *s.j.* '98 (LA)[F] Los Angeles, CA Loyola High School of Los Angeles; California State Prison; [N] San Francisco, CA Jesuit Community at University of San Francisco.
Barbernitz, John P. '50 (BAL) Retired.
Barbero, Mario *i.m.c.* '65 (WDC)[V] Washington, DC Consolata Missionaries House of Studies.
Barbian, Leonard M. '65 (MIL) Waukesha, WI St. William.
Barbieto, Alex '86 (Philippines) Nutley, NJ Holy Family.
Barbone, Joseph F. '72 (NEW) Bayonne, NJ Our Lady of the Assumption.
Barbour, Claude–Marie (CHI).
Barbour, Hugh C. *o.praem.* '90 (ORG)[A] Silverado, CA St. Michael's Norbertine Postulancy, Novitiate and Juniorate; [I] Silverado, CA Norbertine Fathers of Orange Inc.; Ecumenical and Interreligious Affairs.
Barcellona, Thomas J. '95 (CAM)[O] Blackwood, NJ St. Pius X Retreat House; St. Pius X Retreat Center; Office of Youth Ministry; Office of Youth and Young Adult Activities.
Barcellona, Thomas (CAM) Catholic Family Health and Recreation Center.
Barch, Howard C. (PEO) Navy Reserve Chaplains.
Barcio, Robert G. '47 (E) Erie, PA St. Peter Cathedral; Diocesan Archivist and Historian Retired.
Barclay, Robert F. '75 (BRK) East Elmhurst, NY St. Gabriel.
Barclift, Richard L. '66 (PEO) Andalusia, IL St. Patrick's.
Barcome, Earl '52 (GB) Retired.
Barczak, Rene *o.f.m.* '64 (PH)[D] Philadelphia, PA Archbishop Ryan High School.
Barczak, Rene *o.f.m.* '64 (PH)[AA] Philadelphia, PA St. Pius X Friary.
Bardes, George F. '44 (NY) Retired.
Bardino, Jose I. '62 (MIA)[E] Coconut Grove, FL St. Hugh.
Barfknecht, David *o.s.b.* '89 (HON)[G] Waialua, HI Benedictine Monastery of Hawaii/Retreat Center.
Barga, Louis *c.pp.s.* '54 (CIN)[B] Carthagena, OH St. Charles.
Bargola, Cerino O. (MO) Navy Chaplains.
Baribeau, Donald G. *m.s.* '75 (R) Swansboro, NC St. Mildred.
Barica, Daniel *o.f.m.* '99 (LA) Los Angeles, CA St. Francis of Assisi.
Baril, Gerald M. *m.s.* '59 (ATL) Marietta, GA Church of St. Ann.
Barile, Ralph '82 (BRK) Middle Village, NY St. Margaret; Long Island City, NY St. Mary.
Barille, Nicholas *s.t.* '95 (ORG)[I] Santa Ana, CA Trinity Missionaries/Missionary Servants of the Most Holy Trinity.
Barille, Nicholas *s.t.* '95 (ORG) Santa Ana, CA All Adult and Juvenile Jail Facilities.
Baris, Bernard *m.s.* '69 (FR) Brewster, MA Our Lady of the Cape.
Barita, Joseph '87 (LA) Los Angeles, CA St. Eugene.
Barius, Placid *o.f.m.* '43 (PRT)[I] Kennebunkport, ME St. Anthony's Friary.
Barius, Placidas *o.f.m.* (LIT) Lithuanian Franciscan Province of St. Casimir.
Barkemeyer, John H. '90 (CHI) Chicago, IL St. Cajetan.
Barkenquest, Lehr *o.s.f.s.* '64 (LAN) Clarklake, MI St. Rita.
Barker, Brian '94 (BEL) Pinckneyville, IL St. Bruno.
Barker, Brian (BEL) Diocesan Consultors.
Barker, Jack D. (SB) Murrieta, CA St. Martha.
Barker, Jack (SB) On Sabbatical.
Barker, James '80 (BAL) Forest Hill, MD St. Ignatius; Priests' Council.
Barker, John A. '59 (L) Louisville, KY St. Barnabas.
Barker, Joseph '53 (ALB) Retired.
Barker, Joseph (ALB) Priests Retirement Board.
Barker, Richard E. '92 (GAL) Deer Park, TX St. Hyacinth.
Barker, Ronald A. '75 (BO) Stoneham, MA St. Patrick.
Barkett, James S. '91 (ARL) Lake Ridge, VA St. Elizabeth Ann Seton.
Barkey, Patrick '90 (PIT) Conway, PA Our Lady of Peace.
Barkin, Martin F. '77 (PIT) Penn Hills, PA St. Susanna; Judges.
Barley, Tom '91 (SAN) On Special or Other Diocesan Assignment; Wall, TX St. Ambrose.
Barley, Tom (SAN) Diocesan Consultors.
Barley, Tom (SAN) Director of Seminarians.
Barley, Tom (SAN) Judges.
Barley, Tom (SAN) Presbyteral Council.
Barlow, James P. *a.f.b.* '73 (SAT) Military Chaplains.
Barman, William '81 (ORG) Santa Ana, CA Our Lady of La Vang.
Barmann, Karl *o.s.b.* '65 (KC)[J] Conception, MO Conception Abbey.
Barmann, Karl *o.s.b.* '65 (KC) Kansas City, MO St. Gabriel Archangel.
Barmasse, Gerald R. *c.s.c.* '76 (FgM).
Barmasse, Gerald R. *c.s.c.* '76 (FTW)[I] Congregacion de Santa Cruz.
Barnard, Larry *o.f.m.* '66 (GLP) Laguna, NM St. Joseph.

Barnd, Donald *s.c.j.* '78 (MIL)[O] Franklin, WI Villa Maria.
Barnes, Bernard M. *o.s.m.* '48 (CHI)[N] Chicago Order of Friar Servants of Mary (Servites) United States of America Province, Inc..
Barnes, David J. (BO) Beverly, MA St. Mary Star of the Sea.
Barnes, Gavin *o.s.b.* '52 (IND)[K] St. Meinrad, IN St. Meinrad Archabbey.
Barnes, Gerard J. '62 (PH) Retired.
Barnes, James H. '69 (LA) Los Angeles, CA St. Joan of Arc.
Barnes, John E. '55 (LR)[H] Little Rock, AR St. John Manor Retired.
Barnes, John G. '52 (DUB) Retired.
Barnes, Joseph A. '57 (ALN)[J] Bethlehem, PA Holy Family Villa; Birdsboro, PA Immaculate Conception Retired.
Barnes, Robert W. '80 (NOR) Retired.
Barnes, Thomas C. '87 (COV) Covington, KY Holy Cross.
Barnett, Daniel '00 (SPK) Spokane, WA St. Patrick.
Barnett, Daniel (SPK) Spokane, WA St. Francis Xavier.
Barnett, Daniel (SPK) Diocesan Consultors/Presbyteral Council.
Barnett, Fred J. '52 (JC) Laurie, MO Shrine of St. Patrick.
Barnett, James Q. *o.p.* '65 (LFT) West Lafayette, IN St. Thomas Aquinas; [H] West Lafayette, IN St. Thomas Aquinas Parish and Foundation for Catholic Students Attending Purdue University.
Barnett, Larry *o.s.b.* '76 (SFS)[F] Marvin, SD Blue Cloud Abbey.
Barnett, Steven '70 (SFS) Clear Lake, SD St. Mary.
Barnett, Steven (SFS) Diocesan Consultors.
Barnett, Steven (SFS) Presbyteral Council.
Barnett, Steven (SFS) Deans.
Barnhardt, Bruno *o.s.b.cam.* '66 (MRY)[F] Big Sur, CA New Camaldoli Hermitage.
Barnhart, Victor A. (STL) Archdiocesan Deaf Ministry.
Barnhart, Victor '90 (STL) Normandy, MO St. Ann.
Barnhill, Robert K. (LIN) Commission for Sacred Liturgy and Sacred Music; Deaf Ministry; Scouting; Air National Guard Chaplains.
Barnhill, Robert '85 (LIN) Cambridge, NE St. John's.
Barnhill, Robert (LIN)[L] Lincoln, NE Camp Kateri.
Barnhill, Robert (LIN) Diocesan Area CCD Directors.
Barnufsky, Stephen *o.f.m.* '03 (TUC) Tucson, AZ Mission San Xavier del Bac.
Barnum, Martin '74 (CHI) On Duty Outside the Archdiocese.
Barnum, Martin '74 (MIL)[B] Hales Corners, WI Sacred Heart School of Theology.
Barnwell, Gerald P. '77 (FR) Dighton, MA St. Peter's.
Baron, John B. '73 (NEW) Lodi, NJ St. Francis de Sales; [Q] Newark, NJ Archdiocesan Campus Ministry; [Q] Teaneck, NJ Fairleigh Dickinson Univ.–Teaneck Campus; Campus Ministry.
Barona, German *m.s.c.* '86 (RCK)[G] Aurora Missionaries of the Sacred Heart Community.
Barona, Jaime '98 (ATL) Winder, GA St. Matthew.
Barone, Fernando *o.f.m.cap.* '40 (LA) Retired.
Barone, Michael J. '75 (TYL) Madisonville, TX St. Elizabeth Ann Seton.
Barone, Robert J. '67 (SCR) Scranton, PA St. Anthony of Padua; [O] Scranton, PA Immaculate Heart of Mary Center, Marywood.
Baroni, Barry J. '79 (ALT) Johnstown, PA St. Andrew's.
Baronti, David '73 (SPK) On Duty Outside the Diocese.
Baroody, Sami W. '94 (NTN) West Paterson, NJ St. Ann.
Baroody, Sami (NTN) Vocations Office.
Barousse, Raphael *o.s.b.* '55 (NO) Mandeville, LA St. Dymphna Catholic Center and Chapel.
Barousse, Raphael *o.s.b.* '55 (NO) Mandeville, LA Southeast Louisiana Hospital.
Barousse, Raphael *o.s.b.* '55 (NO)[P] St. Benedict, LA St. Joseph Abbey.
Barozzi, Al '65 (BRK) Ridgewood, NY Our Lady of the Miraculous Medal.
Barr, Brian P. (RVC) Associate Vocation Directors.
Barr, Brian '93 (RVC) Deer Park, NY SS. Cyril and Methodius.
Barr, Eric R. '84 (RCK) Durand, IL St. Mary; Special Assignment; Vicar for Clergy and Religious; Ministry to Priests Program; Priest Personnel.
Barr, Francis *o.s.a.* (BO) Lawrence, MA St. Mary Immaculate Conception.
Barr, Frederick L. (BO) Quincy, MA Star of the Sea.
Barr, Frederick *c.s.c.* '54 (P).
Barr, Frederick *c.s.c.* '54 (P)[L] Portland, OR Holy Cross Fathers & Brothers, C.S.C. – University of Portland.
Barr, Joseph F. '78 (BAL) Davidsonville, MD Holy Family; Priests' Council.
Barr, Liam M. '74 (LIN) Lincoln, NE St. Joseph; Office of Diocesan & Social Development.
Barr, Philip R. '48 (PH) Retired.
Barr, Pierre J. '51 (CHI) Chicago, IL Our Lady of Fatima Retired.
Barr, Stanley J. '57 (CAM) Retired.
Barragan, Juan Carlos '97 (AMA) Bovina, TX St. Ann's.
Barranco, Rogelio *s.d.b.* '61 (SJN) San Juan, PR Maria Auxiliadora.
Barrand, James '89 (VNN) On Leave.
Barranger, Joseph *o.p.* '87 (BO)[X] Dover, MA St. Stephen Priory Spiritual Life Center.
Barranger, Joseph *o.p.* (BO)[X] Dover, MA St. Stephen Priory Spiritual Life Center.
Barras, Greg '84 (BLX) Biloxi, MS Cathedral of the Nativity of the Blessed Virgin Mary.
Barras, Gregory '84 (JKS) Biloxi, MS Our Mother of Sorrows.
Barras, Michael J. '73 (LKC) Oberlin, LA St. Joan of Arc.
Barras, Randal Dale '02 (LAF) Lafayette, LA Cathedral of St. John the Evangelist.
Barras, Robert S. '80 (GAL) Katy, TX St. Edith Stein.
Barras, Robert (GAL) Western Vicariate.
Barre, Michael L. *s.s.* '70 (BAL).
Barreda, Giles M. *o.f.m.* '61 (TR)[A] Palenville, NY Sacred Heart.
Barrera, Albino F. *o.p.* '93 (PRO)[P] Providence St. Thomas Aquinas Priory at Providence College.
Barrera, Filiberto '98 (OAK) Richmond, CA St. Cornelius.
Barrera, Gustavo '79 (BWN) Brownsville, TX Mary, Mother of the Church.
Barrera, Gustavo (BWN) Presbyteral Council.
Barrera, Gustavo (BWN) Promoter of Justice.
Barrera, Gustavo (BWN) Defenders of the Bond.
Barrera, Luis '95 (ORL) Mount Dora, FL St. Patrick's; Sanford, FL All Souls.
Barrera Hernandez, Jose A. '92 (PCE) Ponce, PR Christ the King.
Barres, John O. '89 (WIL) Wilmington, DE St. Joseph on the Brandywine; Chancery Office; Associate Directors; College of Consultors; Priests' Council; Co Executive Officers.
Barres, John O. (BAL) Interdiocesan Judges
Barreto, Jose Alberto (CHI) Chicago, IL St. Genevieve.
Barrett, Daniel J. '46 (BO) Senior Priests Retired.
Barrett, David A. '97 (STP) St. Paul, MN Assumption.
Barrett, David S. '64 (GB) Keshena, WI St. Michael; Menominee Pastoral Program.
Barrett, David S. (GB) Gresham, WI St. Francis Solanus; Regional Vicars.
Barrett, David (STP) Presbyteral Council.
Barrett, Edward F. '61 (SCR) Scranton, PA Immaculate Conception.
Barrett, Edward J. '75 (CHI) Alsip, IL St. Terrence.
Barrett, Francis X. '55 (ALN) Retired.
Barrett, Gerard *o.m.i.* '64 (BWN) Port Isabel, TX Our Lady Star of the Sea.
Barrett, Gerard *o.m.i.* (BWN) Diocesan College of Consultors
Barrett, Gerard *o.m.i.* (BWN) Vicar for the Clergy.
Barrett, Gerard *o.m.i.* (BWN) Presbyteral Council.
Barrett, Harry C. '73 (NY) Crestwood, NY Church of the Annunciation; On Special or Other Archdiocesan Assignment.
Barrett, James L. '56 (KAL) Presbyteral Council Retired.
Barrett, James L. '82 (CHI) Evanston, IL St. Joan of Arc.
Barrett, James (KAL) Diocesan Consultors
Barrett, John J. '78 (RVC) Babylon, NY St. Joseph's.
Barrett, John W. '52 (WOR) Retired.
Barrett, John '59 (JOL) Elmhurst, IL Mary, Queen of Heaven.
Barrett, Kevin S. '92 (PCE) On Duty Outside the Diocese.
Barrett, Michael G. '76 (MIL) Grafton, WI St. Joseph.
Barrett, Michael G. *o.f.m.* '90 (IND) Indianapolis, IN Sacred Heart of Jesus.
Barrett, Michael J. *s.t.d.* '85 (GAL) Houston, TX Holy Cross Chapel.
Barrett, Michael '85 (GAL)[P] Houston, TX Opus Dei.
Barrett, Michael (MIL) Deans.
Barrett, Miles J. '82 (SC) On Duty Outside the Diocese; Navy Chaplains.
Barrett, Patrick H. '57 (MET) Carteret, NJ St. Elizabeth of Hungary.
Barrett, Thomas E. '93 (PMB) Fort Pierce, FL St. Mark; [B] Fort Pierce, FL John Carroll High School; Secretary.
Barrett, Thomas J. *c.ss.r.* '67 (TOL) Lima, OH St. Gerard.
Barrett, Thomas M. '71 (BEL) Lawrenceville, IL St. Francis Xavier.
Barrett, Thomas '71 (BEL) Lawrenceville, IL Immaculate Conception.
Barrett, Thomas '71 (BEL) Lawrenceville, IL St. Lawrence.
Barrett, Thomas '88 (ORL)[A] Orlando, FL Bishop Moore High School; Vocations.
Barrett, Thomas '88 (ORL) Special Assignment.
Barrett, Thomas '88 (ORL) Orlando, FL St. Charles Borromeo.
Barrett, Thomas '88 (ORL)[A] Orlando, FL Bishop Moore High School; Vocations.
Barrett, Thomas (ORL) Cemeteries.
Barrett, Walter C. '75 (RIC) McGuire VA Medical Center.
Barrett, Walter '75 (RIC) Richmond, VA Holy Rosary.
Barrett, William '59 (ROC) Retired.
Barrette, Donat A. '54 (PRO) Retired.
Barrette, Eugene *m.s.* '67 (ATL) Smyrna, GA St. Thomas the Apostle.
Barricks, Robert '94 (P) Portland, OR Holy Family.
Barricks, Robert (P) Area Vicars.
Barrientos, Gustavo '84 (OM) Schuyler, NE St. Augustine.
Barrientos, Gustavo '85 (OM) Schuyler, NE St. Mary.
Barringer, Robert J. *c.s.b.* '74 (GAL)[Q] Sugar Land Basilian Mission Center.
Barrios, Diego *c.m.f.* '42 (LA)[Q] Rancho Dominguez, CA Dominguez Seminary Inc..
Barrios, Eduardo *s.j.* '72 (MIA)[H] Miami, FL Villa Javier.
Barrios, Eduardo *s.j.* '72 (MIA)[D] Miami, FL Belen Jesuit Preparatory School.
Barron, Benito Rojas *m.s.p.* (SB) Riverside, CA St. John the Evangelist.
Barron, Cecil *c.m.f.* '42 (FRS) Retired.
Barron, Clemente *c.p.* '70 (SAT)[M] San Antonio, TX Casa Pasionista Guadalupe.
Barron, Dale F. *m.m.* '65 (FgM).
Barron, Daniel P. *o.m.v.* '96 (DEN) Denver, CO Holy Ghost.
Barron, Gerald *o.f.m.cap.* '66 (SFR)[B] Santa Ynez, CA San Lorenzo Seminary and Prayer Center.
Barron, John P. *s.j.* '82 (ALN)[A] Wernersville, PA Jesuit Center; [N] Wernersville, PA Jesuit Center for Spiritual Growth.
Barron, Robert E. '86 (CHI).
Barron, Stanley C. '74 (PAT)[A] Ogdensburg, NJ St. Thomas of Aquin; Mission Office.
Barron, Stanley (PAT) Presbyteral Council.
Barron, Stanley (PAT) Deans.
Barron, Stanley (PAT) College of Consultors.
Barron, Wayne *c.m.f.* '58 (CHI)[N] Oak Park, IL Claretian Fathers Headquarters of U.S.A. Eastern Province.
Barrons, Brian *m.m.* '84 (FgM).
Barrosa, Julian Michael A. *d.s.* '91 (GAL)[Q] Houston, TX Disciples of Hope (Texas).
Barrosa, Michael '91 (GAL)[K] Catholic Chaplain Corps, Texas Medical Center.
Barrosa, Michael '91 (GAL)[K] Houston, TX Chaplain Corps, Memorial Southwest Center Complex.
Barrow, John A. '80 (PMB) Stuart, FL St. Andrew; Propagation of the Faith/Mission Support; Holy Childhood Association.
Barrow, Joseph A. '96 (NEW) On Duty Outside the Archdiocese.
Barruetabena, Esteban '54 (ARE) Lares, PR St. Joseph.
Barruetabena, Felix *c.p.* '52 (SJN) Carolina, PR Santa Gema Galgani.
Barry, Bernard J. *s.j.* '01 (STL)[O] St. Louis, MO Jesuit Community Corporation at St. Louis University – Jesuit Hall.
Barry, David *s.j.* '78 (CHI)[D] Chicago, IL St. Ignatius Jesuit Community.
Barry, Donald M. *s.j.* '66 (BGP)[E] Fairfield, CT Fairfield College Preparatory School; [P] Fairfield, CT The Fairfield Jesuit Community–Fairfield University.
Barry, Edward '73 (NY) Dover Plains, NY St. Charles Borromeo.
Barry, Edward (NY) Bronx (Northeast); Canon 1742 Panel of Pastors.
Barry, Francis '75 (SAV) Retired.
Barry, Garrett J. '66 (BO) Quincy, MA St. Ann.
Barry, Gerard B. '50 (BO) Senior Priests Retired.
Barry, Gerard S. *s.j.* '63 (FgM).
Barry, Gerard S. *s.j.* '63 (BAL)[S] SJ House.
Barry, James D. '61 (NU) Retired.
Barry, James F. '67 (CAM) Egg Harbor City, NJ St. Nicholas; Defenders of the Bond.
Barry, James J. '69 (BO) Chelsea, MA Our Lady of Grace.
Barry, James *c.p.* '69 (CHI)[H] Niles, IL.
Barry, John F. '61 (LA) Manhattan Beach, CA American Martyrs.
Barry, John G. *c.ss.r.* '48 (ORL) New Smyrna Beach, FL Sacred Heart.
Barry, John M. '88 (WDC) Leonardtown, MD Our Lady's.
Barry, John (LA) Members.
Barry, John (LA) Deanery 19.
Barry, Lawrence E. *s.j.* '58 (STL)[N] St. Louis, MO Fusz Pavilion; [O] St. Louis, MO Jesuit Community Corporation at St. Louis University – Jesuit Hall.
Barry, Leo '51 (WOR) Retired.
Barry, Leo (WOR) Advocates.
Barry, Maurice J. '67 (HRT) Windsor, CT St. Gertrude's.
Barry, Michael W. *ss.cc.* '64 (LA)[Q] La Verne, CA Congregation of the Sacred Hearts of Jesus and Mary; [E] Upland, CA Congregation of the Sacred Hearts.

Barry, Patrick J. '54 (NY) Mt. Vernon, NY SS. Peter and Paul.
Barry, Paul '48 (WDC) Retired.
Barry, Peter J. *m.m.* '65 (FgM).
Barry, Raymond J. '65 (HRT) Branford, CT St. Therese.
Barry, Robert L. *o.p.* '73 (CHI)[N] St. Pius V Priory; Air National Guard Chaplains.
Barry, Ronald A. '52 (RVC) Retired.
Barry, Thomas J. '67 (HRT) Middlebury, CT St. John of the Cross.
Barry, Thomas M. '61 (WOR) Spencer, MA Mary, Queen of the Rosary.
Barry, William A *s.j.* '62 (BO)[V] Weston, MA Campion Jesuit Community.
Barry, William J. '44 (LA) Retired.
Barry, William (LA) Members.
Barsen, Herman J. '40 (LAF) Retired.
Barszcz, Jozef A. '88 (SUP) Mellen, WI St. George; Mellen, WI Most Precious Blood; Mellen, WI Holy Rosary; Mellen, WI St. Anne.
Barszcz, Jozef '88 (SUP) Mellen, WI St. Anthony.
Barszczewski, Francis A. '68 (PH) Clifton Heights, PA Sacred Heart; Censores Librorum.
Barta, Ardel H. '63 (DUB) Dubuque, IA St. Columbkille; Dubuque, IA St. Mary; Dubuque, IA St. Patrick.
Barta, James O. '55 (DUB) Holy Cross, IA Holy Trinity; [L] Dubuque, IA St. Joseph's Convent, Mount Carmel; On Special or Other Archdiocesan Assignment; Holy Cross, IA St. Joseph; Holy Cross, IA SS. Peter and Paul; Holy Cross, IA Holy Cross; Holy Cross, IA St. Francis of Assisi; Vicar General and Episcopal Vicar for Dubuque Region; Co–Directors; College of Consultors; Archdiocesan Pastoral Center; Continuing Formation of Clergy; Administrative Board; Ex Officio Members; Catholic Charities and St. Mary's Home Boards of Directors; Finance Council; Lay Formation Advisory Board; Pastoral Council; Ex Officio Members; Board of Directors/Priest Pension Plan Board of Trustees.
Barta, Wayne J. '60 (MIL) Campbellsport, WI St. Martin Retired.
Bartchak, Mark L. '81 (E) Judicial Vicar; Matrimonial Judges; Office of Conciliation & Arbitration.
Bartczyszyn, Steven *c.r.* '86 (CHI)[D] River Grove, IL Holy Cross High School; [N] Chicago, IL Archbishop Weber House.
Bartek, Valerian '82 (LIN) Ulysses, NE Immaculate Conception.
Bartek, William C. '61 (OM) Retired.
Bartel, Franklin '70 (PHX) Sun City, AZ St. Elizabeth Seton.
Bartel, Leo J. '58 (RCK) Morrison, IL St. Mary; Diocesan Consultors.
Bartel, Martin R. *o.s.b.* (GBG) Diocesan Pastoral Council.
Bartel, Martin *o.s.b.* '85 (GBG) New Derry, PA St. Martin.
Bartell, Ernest J. *c.s.c.* '61 (FTW)[B] University of Notre Dame Du Lac; [I] Notre Dame, IN Holy Cross Community, Corby Hall, University of Notre Dame.
Bartelme, James P. '82 (SUP) Lac du Flambeau, WI St. Anthony of Padua; Woodruff, WI St. Patrick; Lac du Flambeau, WI St. Mary; Woodruff, WI Our Lady Queen of the Universe.
Bartelt, Victor '50 (MIL)[M] Wauwatosa, WI St. Camillus Health Center, Inc..
Barter, Robert J. '61 (PRM) Detroit, MI St. Nicholas.
Barter, Robert (PRM) Priest's Pension Board.
Barter, Robert (PRM) Sacred Liturgy.
Barth, Charles P. '56 (CAM) Hammonton, NJ St. Anthony of Padua; Friends of the Sacred Heart.
Barth, J. Robert *s.j.* '61 (New York)[V] Newton, MA The Jesuit Community at Boston College.
Barth, John C. *m.m.* '91 (NY)[EE] Maryknoll Maryknoll Fathers and Brothers; (FgM).
Barth, Michael D. '94 (COV) Carrollton, KY St. John the Evangelist.
Barth, Michael K. *s.t.* '79 (CLV) Cleveland, OH St. Agnes – Our Lady of Fatima; [O] Cleveland, OH.
Barth, Raymond J. '85 (KAL) Bridgman, MI Our Lady Queen of Peace.
Barthel, Charles '82 (STL) St. Louis, MO St. Stephen, Protomartyr.
Bartko, Gerald L. *o.s.f.s.* '66 (BUF)[D] Niagara Falls, NY Niagara Catholic High School; Lockport, NY St. Patrick.
Bartko, Louis *o.f.m.* '91 (CIN)[C] Cincinnati, OH St. Anthony Shrine, Franciscan Candidacy.
Bartkus, Algimantas A. '65 (ALN) On Duty Outside the Diocese.
Bartkus, Algimantas (LIT) Pontifical Lithuanian College of St. Casimir.
Bartlet, James H. *s.m.* '69 (CIN)[D] Dayton, OH The University of Dayton.
Bartlett, H. James *s.m.* '69 (CIN) Dayton, OH Queen of Apostles; [M] Dayton, OH Marianist Community, Novitiate; [U] Galveston, TX The Bishop's Palace.
Bartley, David J. '70 (BO) Peabody, MA St. Thomas the Apostle.
Bartley, Denis *s.s.c.* '51 (OM)[K] St. Columbans, NE St. Columban's Foreign Mission Society.
Bartley, Vincent '69 (NY) Staten Island, NY St. Paul.
Bartman, Roch *o.f.m.conv.* '31 (MRY)[F] Arroyo Grande, CA St. Joseph Cupertino Friary Retired.
Bartnik, James T. '75 (BUF) Buffalo, NY St. Casimir.
Bartnikowski, Raymond '63 (CLV) Absent on Leave.
Bartnikowski, Raymond '63 (CLV) Administrative Leave.
Bartniski, Bill (GAL) Southern Vicariate.
Bartniski, William D. '67 (GAL) Galveston, TX St. Peter the Apostle; Area Representatives.
Bartok, Charles '47 (ORL) Retired.
Bartollotta, Victor W. '90 (ROC) On Duty Outside the Diocese.
Bartolo, Salvador *o.carm.* '52 (JOL)[L] Prelate Nullius.
Bartoloma, James L. '03 (CAM) Cherry Hill, NJ Queen of Heaven.
Bartolotta, Victor '90 (DAL)[C] Dallas, TX Bishop Lynch High School, Inc..
Barton, Deborah A. (SAC) Defenders of the Bond.
Barton, Michael *m.c.c.j.* '75 (FgM).
Barton, Raymond A. '66 (RIC) Virginia Beach, VA St. Nicholas; Delegate for Ecumenism & Ecumenical Affairs; Ecumenical Officer.
Bartos, Andrzej '83 (CHI) Chicago, IL St. Ladislaus.
Bartos, Francis J. '54 (PH) Retired.
Bartos, Kris '85 (MIA) Pembroke Pines, FL St. Boniface; Television and Radio Center.
Bartosic, Mark A. '94 (CHI) Cicero, IL St. Frances of Rome.
Bartosz, Andrzej '91 (CHI) Chicago, IL St. Thecla.
Bartoszek, Justin *c.p.* '64 (FgM).
Bartoszewicz, John (PT) Cantonment, FL St. Jude Thaddeus.
Bartoul, William '77 (SAM) On Duty Outside the Diocese; Air Force Chaplains.
Bartsch, Edward C. '49 (VIC) Flatonia, TX St. Mary's.
Bartsch, Ken *o.f.m.conv.* '75 (STP)[P] Prior Lake, MN Franciscan Retreats.
Bartylla, James R. '01 (MAD) Mount Horeb, WI St. Ignatius; Mount Horeb, WI St. Mary of Pine Bluff; Madison.
Barusefski, Ronald '89 (PSC) Hazleton, PA St. John the Baptist.
Barusefsky, Ronald '89 (PSC) Minersville, PA SS. Peter and Paul; Syncellus; Eparchial College of Consultors; Ex Officio Members.
Barwig, Regis N. '59 (GB)[I] Oshkosh, WI Community of Our Lady; Community of Our Lady.
Barwin, John G. '80 (E) Linesville, PA St. Philip.
Basa, Francis J. '71 (CLV) Akron, OH Christ the King.
Basarab, John G. '79 (PSC) Annandale, VA Epiphany of Our Lord; Syncellus; Eparchial College of Consultors; Ex Officio Members.
Baseford, Paul '57 (SB) Retired.
Basekela, Cletus '28 (STP) Burnsville, MN Mary, Mother of the Church.
Bash, Cletus '56 (OKL) Special Assignment Retired.
Bash, Cletus '56 (OKL)[E] Oklahoma City, OK Mercy Health Center.
Bashista, Brian G. '99 (ARL) Arlington, VA Our Lady of Lourdes; Notaries; Propagation of the Faith; Vocations, Office of.
Basil, Father *c.r.* (SB)[E] Newberry Springs, CA Holy Resurrection Community.
Basile, Gioacchino '95 (NEW) On Duty Outside the Archdiocese; Penuelas, PR Sacred Heart.
Basile, Gioacchino '95 (PCE) Penuelas, PR St. Joseph.
Basile, Gioacchino '95 (NEW) On Duty Outside the Archdiocese; Penuelas, PR Sacred Heart.
Basile, Nicholas F. '49 (NY) Bronx, NY Our Lady of Mt. Carmel Retired.
Basilious, Reynolds *o.c.d.* '97 (BRK) Brooklyn, NY St. Mary Mother of Jesus.
Basinow, Leonard '53 (SAM) Unassigned.
Basler, Howard B. '58 (BRK) Belle Harbor, NY St. Francis de Sales; [L] Brooklyn, NY Catholic Charities.
Basols, Jose A. *sch.p.* '68 (PCE)[C] Coto Laurel, PR Colegio Ponceno.
Basquel, Thomas *c.s.sp.* '76 (BRK) Woodside, NY Blessed Virgin Mary, Help of Christians.
Bass, Francis E. '48 (DAV)[M] Davenport, IA St. Vincent Center Retired.
Bass, Frank B. '03 (BR) Baton Rouge, LA St. Thomas More.
Bass, Michael E. '87 (LR) Benton, AR Our Lady of Fatima.
Bass, Ricardo E. '74 (DET) St. Clair Shores, MI St. Joan of Arc.
Bass, Ricardo E. (DET) College of Consultors; Presbyteral Council; Defenders of Bond.
Bassano, Michael '75 (SY) On Duty Outside the Diocese.
Bassano, Michael *m.m.* '75 (FgM).
Bassett, Frank (NY) Goshen, NY St. John the Evangelist.
Bassil, Pierre '98 (OLL) Dayton, OH Saint Ignatius Mission.
Bassil, Pierre '98 (OLL) Our Lady of Lebanon Maronite Mission.
Basso, Anthony *s.d.v.* '93 (PMB) Palm City, FL Holy Redeemer.
Basso, Richard '62 (SEA) Retired.
Bastia, Raymond B. '75 (PRO) Providence, RI St. Ann; Deans.
Bastian, James R. '95 (BUF) Williamsville, NY St. Gregory the Great; Hamburg, NY SS. Peter and Paul.
Bastian, Thomas '98 (RVC) Absent on Leave.
Bastidas, Alexis '82 (NY) New York, NY Blessed Sacrament.
Bastos, Luiz C. '85 (ORL) On Duty Outside the Diocese.
Bastress, Arthur W. '51 (BAL) Baltimore, MD St. Alphonsus, Shrine of.
Bastress, Arthur (BAL) Priests' Council.
Basulto–Pitol, Marco Antonio (TUC)[H] Douglas, AZ Cochise Community College; Casa Grande, AZ St. Anthony of Padua.
Basznianin, Richard '84 (TR) Forked River, NJ St. Pius X.
Batch, Thomas A. '76 (SAC) Retired.
Batcha, James '85 (PRM) Columbus, OH St. John Chrysostom.
Batcha, James (PRM) Office of Evangelization and Missionary Activity.
Batcha, James (PRM) Cantors' Institute.
Batcheldor, C. Joseph '57 (L) Bardstown, KY Basilica of St. Joseph Proto–Cathedral Retired.
Batcho, Robert '88 (STF) Auburn, NY SS. Peter and Paul.
Bateman, John B. (HBG) Lewistown, PA Sacred Heart of Jesus.
Bateman, John B. (HBG) Appointed.
Bateman, John '66 (HBG) Mifflintown, PA St. Jude.
Bateman, John (HBG) Consultors, College.
Bates, Donald J. *o.s.a.* '60 (CHI)[N] Matteson, IL Austin Friary.
Bates, James R. '63 (LFT) Noblesville, IN Our Lady of Grace Retired.
Bath, Winston L. '72 (ALB) Hudson, NY Church of St. Mary; Priests Retirement Board.
Bathke, Joseph *c.pp.s.* '78 (CHI)[A] Liberty, MO Society of the Precious Blood Provincial Offices.
Batista, George L. '83 (NEW) Retired.
Batour, Charbel *s.j.* '01 (N. East)[V] Newton, MA The Jesuit Community at Boston College.
Batson, John R. '57 (MEM) Retired.
Batt, Dacian *o.f.m.* '58 (PEO) Bloomington, IL St. Mary's.
Battafarano, Gregory *o.carm.* '67 (NEW) Bogota, NJ St. Joseph's.
Batterberry, Michael J. '70 (SEA)[B] Seattle, WA John F. Kennedy Memorial High School.
Battersby, Gerard W. '98 (DET) Detroit, MI St. Christopher; Presbyteral Council.
Battiato, Patrick (COS) On Leave of Absence.
Battiato, Ronald A. '61 (OM) Randolph, NE St. Frances de Chantal; Consultors; Ex Officio.
Battista, Leo J. (WOR) Northern Worcester County District Council.
Battista, Leo '48 (WOR) Retired.
Battisti, Lewis A. '62 (CAM) Margate, NJ Blessed Sacrament; Members.
Battle, Lawrence '49 (SB) Retired.
Battocletti, Richard L. '53 (STU) Martins Ferry, OH St. Mary Retired.
Battolini, Ottaviano *o.f.m.* '43 (FgM).
Batts, Peter M. *o.p.* '81 (NEW) Sacred Heart Priory.
Batts, Peter Martin *o.p.* '81 (NEW) Jersey City, NJ Sacred Heart.
Batule, Robert J. '85 (RVC) Amityville, NY St. Martin's; Associate Vocation Directors.
Batykefer, John J. '90 (PIT) Waynesburg, PA St. Ann; [Q] Waynesburg, PA Waynesburg College (Waynesburg).
Bau, Chau Xuan *c.ss.r.* '62 (LA)[Q] Houston, TX.
Bauer, Carl E. (WH) Retired.
Bauer, Charles A. '78 (MEM) Cordova, TN St. Francis of Assisi; Presbyteral Council and College of Consultors.
Bauer, Daniel *s.v.d.* '74 (FgM).
Bauer, Donald J. '48 (SY) Retired.
Bauer, Donald J. '01 (LC) Cashton, WI Sacred Heart of Jesus; Cashton, WI St. Augustine of Hippo; Cashton, WI Nativity of the Blessed Virgin Mary; Cashton, WI St. John the Baptist.
Bauer, Elmer *c.m.* '93 (PH).
Bauer, Elmer *c.m.* '93[AA] (FgM).
Bauer, Erwin J. '47 (DET) Columbus, MI St. Philip Neri Retired.
Bauer, Henry '48 (KC) Retired.
Bauer, Jacob F. '48 (GI) Retired.
Bauer, John F. '65 (E) Punxsutawney, PA SS. Cosmas and Damian.
Bauer, John J. *c.ss.r.* (MO) AUXILIARY CHAPLAINS CONTRACT CHAPLAINS.
Bauer, John M. '73 (PIT) Carmichaels, PA St. Hugh; Carmichael, PA Our Lady of Consolation.
Bauer, John M. '79 (STP) St. Paul, MN St. Gregory the Great (Highland Catholic Community); St. Paul, MN St. Leo (Highland Catholic Community); St. Paul,

MN St. Therese (Highland Catholic Community); [V] St. Paul, MN The Highland Catholic Community.
Bauer, Karl A. '67 (NY) Yonkers, NY St. Anthony.
Bauer, Lawrence T. *c.s.c.* '35 (FTW)[I] Notre Dame, IN Holy Cross House.
Bauer, Mark '86 (GR) Muskegon, MI St. Michael's.
Bauer, Mark '86 (GR) Muskegon Heights, MI Sacred Heart.
Bauer, Mark '86 (GR) Muskegon, MI St. Mary's.
Bauer, Mark '86 (GR) Muskegon, MI St. Jean Baptiste.
Bauer, Richard W. *m.m.* '85 (FgM).
Bauer, Rick '59 (SLC) On Duty Outside the Diocese.
Bauer, Robert A. '87 (DET) Carleton, MI St. Patrick.
Bauer, Robert '71 (PMB)[A] Boynton Beach, FL St. Vincent de Paul Regional Seminary.
Bauer, Roy R. '59 (SFD) Quincy, IL St. Peter.
Bauer, Scott A. '98 (LC) On Leave of Absence.
Bauer, Stephan *o.s.c.* '92 (STP)[M] Shoreview, MN Crosier Community of Shoreview.
Bauer, Stephen F. '77 (STL) St. Louis, MO St. Luke the Evangelist.
Bauer, Sylvester W. '42 (JC) Jefferson City, MO Algoa Correctional Center.
Bauer, Sylvester W. '42 (SPC) Retired.
Bauer, Sylvester W. (SPC) Rural Life Movement.
Bauer, Sylvester (SPC) Diocesan Peace and Justice Commission.
Bauer, William M. '73 (ALB) Greenville, NY St. John the Baptist.
Bauerle, Bernhard *o.carm.* '64 (JOL)[L] Darien, IL Carmelite Community.
Bauerle, Bernhard *o.carm.* '64 (JOL)[L] Darien, IL Carmelite Provincial Office.
Baugh, David G. '57 (CLV) Euclid, OH St. William; Wickliffe, OH Our Lady of Mount Carmel Retired.
Bauhoff, Richard C. '73 (RVC) Roslyn, NY St. Mary's; Judges for Interdiocesan Tribunal.
Bauhs, Eugene J. '48 (MAD) Retired.
Bauler, Gary P. '67 (LA) Simi Valley, CA St. Peter Claver.
Baum, Terrence A. *s.j.* '81 (CHI)[D] Wilmette, IL Loyola Academy.
Bauman, Dale '82 (FTW) Bluffton, IN St. Joseph.
Bauman, Dale (FTW) Advisory Board.
Bauman, John F. X. '69 (NEW) Jersey City, NJ St. Anne's; Newark, NJ St. Michael Medical Center.
Bauman, Rodger '82 (STP) White Bear Lake, MN St. Mary of the Lake.
Bauman, William A. '60 (KC) Kansas City, MO St. Thomas More.
Baumann, Anthony *o.f.m.* '44 (SFR) San Francisco, CA St. Anthony of Padua.
Baumann, Charles R. *s.j.* '80 (MIL)[O] Milwaukee, WI Jesuit Community at Marquette University.
Baumann, Hugh *o.s.b.* '41 (NO)[P] St. Benedict, LA St. Joseph Abbey.
Baumann, John A. *s.j.* '69 (OAK)[N] Oakland, CA Murray Residence Community; [S] Oakland, CA Pacific Institute for Community Organization.
Baumann, Lawrence L. '64 (PHX) Retired.
Baumann, Richard J. *s.j.* '75 (CHI)[N] Chicago, IL Miguel Pro Jesuit Community.
Baumann, Silas *o.f.m.cap.* '51 (GB)[I] Appleton, WI St. Fidelis Friary.
Baumann, Stephen A. '92 (ORL) Longwood, FL Annunciation.
Baumann, Theodore J. '67 (BEL) Freeburg, IL St. Joseph; Diocesan Consultors.
Baumann, Theodore J. '67 (BEL) Sparta, IL Our Lady of Lourdes.
Baumberger, Richard '89 (SFS) Yankton, SD Sacred Heart.
Baumert, Frank J. '78 (OM) Albion, NE St. Michael; Petersburg, NE St. John the Baptist; Rural Life Conference.
Baumgaertner, William L. '46 (STP)[C] St. Paul, MN University of St. Thomas Retired.
Baumgardner, Michael '95 (SD) San Diego, CA St. Didacus.
Baumgardner, Michael (SD) Vicars Forane.
Baumgartner, A. Thomas '58 (BAL) Baltimore, MD St. Ursula.
Baumgartner, Andrew *o.s.b.* '60 (B)[C] Jerome, ID Monastery of the Ascension.
Baumgartner, Bernard *c.ss.r.* '44 (BAL)[S] Annapolis, MD Saint Mary Rectory.
Baumgartner, Bernard *c.ss.r.* '44 (BAL) Annapolis, MD St. Mary.
Baumgartner, David '90 (CR) Finance Council; Deans; Ada, MN St. Joseph's.
Baumgartner, John H. '63 (MIL) West Allis, WI St. Aloysius.
Baumhart, Raymond C. *s.j.* '57 (CHI)[C] Chicago, IL Jesuit Community at Loyola University Chicago; Office of the Archbishop.
Baumiller, Robert C. *s.j.* '65 (CIN)[M] Cincinnati, OH Jesuit Community at Xavier University.
Baumstein, Paschal M. *o.s.b.* '79 (CHL)[J] Belmont, NC Belmont Abbey.
Baur, Joseph A. *o.f.m.* '52 (PHX) St. Guadalupe, AZ Our Lady of Guadalupe.
Baures, Steven H. '83 (LC) New Lisbon, WI Our Lady of the Lake; New Lisbon, WI St. Paul.
Bausch, Michael '79 (ROC) Pittsford, NY Church of the Transfiguration.
Bausch, William J. '55 (TR) Manasquan, NJ St. Denis Retired.
Bauschka, Joseph '55 (GB) Special Assignment.
Bauta, Krsysztof '85 (HON) Fort Worth, TX Federal Medical Center, Carswell.
Bauta, Krzysztof T. '86 (CC) On Duty Outside the Diocese.
Bautista, Gasper '75 (FRS) Mendota, CA Our Lady of Guadalupe.
Bautista, Jose A. '99 (LA) Norwalk, CA St. John of God.
Bautista, Jose '91 (ORL) Apopka, FL St. Francis of Assisi; Kissimmee, FL St. Catherine of Siena.
Bautista, Jose (ORL) Judges.
Bautista, Jose (ORL) Hispanic.
Bauwens, Thomas E. '87 (OM) Elgin, NE St. Boniface; Elgin, NE St. Bonaventure; Deans; Officers Deans.
Bava, David '73 (WDC) Washington, DC Holy Redeemer.
Bavaro, John D. *o.f.m.* '63 (BO)[O] Andover, MA Franciscan Center.
Bavaro, John *o.f.m.* '63 (MAN) Manchester, NH Blessed Sacrament; Manchester, NH St. Theresa.
Baver, John J. '91 (PIT) Monongahela, PA Transfiguration.
Baver, William F. '81 (ALN) Coplay, PA St. Peter; Cemeteries.
Bavero, Benvenute *o.f.m.* '44 (LA)[Q] Santa Barbara, CA Franciscan Friary, Order of Friars Minor (Old Mission).
Bavinger, R. Bruce *s.j.* '78 (WDC) Washington, DC St. Aloysius; [E] Washington, DC Gonzaga College High School.
Bawiec, Edward J. '54 (PEO) Retired.
Bawyn, Anthony E. (SEA) Judicial Vicar; Canonical Services.
Bawyn, Anthony '82 (SEA) Shoreline, WA St. Mark.
Bawyn, Anthony '82 (SEA) Special Assignment.
Bawyn, Anthony '82 (SEA) Seattle, WA St. Catherine.
Bawyn, Anthony (SEA) Judges.
Baxa, Henry R. '90 (SAL) Beloit, KS St. John the Baptist.
Baxa, Henry (SAL) Personnel Board.
Baxter, Gregory P. (OM) Chancellor; Finance Council; Building Commission; Catholic University, Friends of; Propagation of the Faith, Pontifical Assoc. of Holy Childhood and Catholic Students Mission Crusade; Archbishops Appointees; Consultor to Finance Office.
Baxter, Gregory '88 (OM) Omaha, NE St. Adalbert.
Baxter, Michael J. *c.s.c.* '85 (FTW)[B] University of Notre Dame Du Lac.
Baxter, Michael Shane '03 (BEA) Educational Leave of Absence.
Baxter, Michael *c.s.c.* '85 (FTW)[A] Notre Dame, IN Moreau Seminary.
Baxter, Stephen R. '81 (WCH) Fredonia, KS Sacred Heart; Neodesha, KS St. Ignatius; Judges.
Baxter, Thomas F. '76 (MAD) Madison, WI St. James; Building Commission.
Baxter, Thomas–Benedict *o.s.b.* '79 (CHI)[N] Chicago, IL Monastery of the Holy Cross.
Bay, Joseph N. '94 (COL) Columbus, OH St. Catharine; Judicial Vicar; Columbus, OH Columbus Vietnamese Catholic Community.
Bayard, Michael S. *s.j.* '98 (SEA)[A] Seattle WA Seattle University.
Bayard, Nicholas R. '46 (CHR) Charleston SC Church of the Nativity Retired.
Baybay, Felicito '74 (ORL) Orlando, FL Holy Family.
Bayer, Edward J. '56 (BAL) Retired.
Bayer, Ernest H. '01 (DEN) Craig, CO Saint Michael.
Bayer, Ernest '01 (DEN) Meeker, CO Holy Family.
Bayer, Ernest '01 (DEN) Rangely, CO St. Ignatius.
Bayer, Lawrence J. '58 (CLV) Parma, OH St. Bridget.
Bayer, Leonard '51 (SFE) Retired.
Bayer, Peter T. '71 (ROC)[E] Rochester, NY St. Ann's Home for the Aged; [E] Rochester, NY St. Ann's Nursing Home Co., Inc.; [E] Rochester NY Chapel Oaks:.
Bayer, Peter '71 (ROC) St. Ann's Home/Heritage.
Bayer, Peter '71 (ROC) Rochester, NY St. Margaret Mary.
Bayhi, M. Jeffery (NO) Closer Walk Ministries.
Bayhi, M. Jeffrey '79 (BR) Baton Rouge, LA St. Agnes; Serra Clubs; Vocations.
Bayhi, W. Peter *s.j.* '66 (LAF)[J] Convent LA Manresa House of Retreats.
Bayle, Stephen (BO)[C] Boston, MA Emmanuel College.
Bayne, David C. *s.j.* '52 (DET)[K] Detroit Jesuit Provincial Office–Detroit Province of the Society of Jesus.
Bayne, Joseph *o.f.m.conv.* '85 (BUF)[J] Buffalo, NY The Franciscan Center, Inc..
Bayne, Robert C. *m.m.* '63 (FgM).
Baysinger Leo *s.d.b.* '67 (LA)[F] Bellflower, CA St. John Bosco High School.
Baz, Louis '81 (OLL) Fairlawn, OH Our Lady of the Cedars of Mt. Lebanon.
Bazan, Joaquin '62 (WDC)[L] Washington, DC Jeanne Jugan Residence–St. Joseph's Villa Retired.
Bazan, Michael J. '84 (ARL) Warrenton, VA St. John the Evangelist.
Bazar, Ty '02 (VIC) El Campo, TX St. Philip the Apostle; Port Lavaca, TX Our Lady of the Gulf.
Bazina, Basile (BO) Rwandese.
Bazton, Jose M. Garcia *m.ss.cc.* '62 (SJN) Bayamon, PR San Juan Bautista de la Salle.
Bazyouros, Christopher '03 (LA) Hawthorne, CA St. Joseph.
Bazzel, Kevin M. (BIR) Defenders of the Bond.
Bazzel, Kevin '01 (BIR) Huntsville, AL Holy Spirit; [A] Huntsville, AL Catholic High School.
Bazzi, Michael J. '64 (SPA) El Cajon, CA St. Peter Chaldean Cathedral; Judicial Officer.
Bazzi, Michael J. '64 (SD) El Cajon, CA St. Peter Cathedral.
Bazzoli, Robert *o.s.f.s.* '88 (PH) Philadelphia, PA St. Joachim.
Beach, Francis W. '76 (PH) On Special or Other Archdiocesan Assignment; Regional Vicars; Priests' Personnel Board.
Beach, R. Paul '01 (L) Louisville, KY St. Margaret Mary.
Beach, Raymond *o.f.m.* '48 (PAT)[K] Totowa, NJ St. Joseph's Home for the Elderly.
Beachamp, Henry *c.ss.r.* '78 (CGS) Fajardo, PR Santiago Apostol.
Beachum, Edwin P. '84 (MOB) Mobile, AL St. Catherine of Siena.
Beacom, John F. '37 (OM) Retired.
Beacom, Vincent L. '44 (SC) Retired.
Beal, John P. '74 (E) On Duty Outside Diocese; Matrimonial Judges.
Beal, John P. '74 (WDC)[C] Catholic University of America, The.
Beale, Kenneth R. '92 (NEW) Military Chaplains; Air Force Chaplains.
Beale, Robert P. (BO) Dedham, MA Norfolk County House of Correction.
Bean, Charles S. '62 (CAM) Disabled Retired.
Bean, Donald A. '63 (BUR) Retired.
Bean, Earl Gray '03 (BIR)[A] Birmingham, AL John Carroll Catholic High School; Birmingham, AL St. Peter the Apostle.
Beans, Elmer '86 (FBK) Mountain Village, AK St. Lawrence.
Beard, Raymond '41 (BAK) Retired.
Beardsley, Frederick '60 (RIC) Retired.
Bearss, James M. '97 (GAY) Manistee, MI St. Mary of Mt. Carmel Shrine.
Beas, Shamaun '94 (GR) Portland, MI St. Patrick's.
Beat, Jerome A. '63 (WCH) Cursillo.
Beat, Jerome (WCH) Deans.
Beath, James D. '74 (CHI) Chicago, IL St. Dorothy.
Beaton, Kevin J. '87 (SAM) New Castle, PA St. John the Baptist.
Beaton, Kevin (SAM) Pro–Life Director.
Beattie, James T. '61 (WDC) Bethesda, MD St. Bartholomew.
Beattie, John A. *o.s.f.s.* '65 (VEN)[A] Fort Myers, FL Bishop Verot High School; [G] Fort Myers, FL Oblates of St. Francis de Sales.
Beattie, Joseph A. *o.s.f.s.* '65 (VEN)[A] Fort Myers, FL Bishop Verot High School; [G] Fort Myers, FL Oblates of St. Francis de Sales.
Beattie, Thomas '93 (SEA) Sequim, WA St. Joseph.
Beatty, James H. '74 (CLV) Avon Lake, OH Holy Spirit.
Beatty, Michael D. '64 (CIN) Cincinnati, OH St. Simon the Apostle; Judges.
Beaubein, David '93 (WDC) Waldorf, MD St. Peter.
Beauchamp, E. William *c.s.c.* '82 (FTW)[I] South Bend, IN Congregation of Holy Cross, Indiana Province, Provincial House.
Beauchamp, Henry *c.ss.r.* (CGS) Priests Senate.
Beauchamp, William *c.s.c.* '82 (P)[B] University of Portland.
Beauchamp, William *c.s.c.* '82 (P)[L] Portland, OR Holy Cross Fathers & Brothers, C.S.C. – University of Portland.
Beauchamp, William *c.s.c.* '82 (P)[B] University of Portland.
Beauchemin, Ronald A. *m.s.* '68 (GAL) Friendswood, TX Mary, Queen.
Beauclair, Stephen *o.s.b.* '67 (SCL) Richmond, MN SS. Peter and Paul's; [I] Collegeville, MN St. John's Abbey, of the Order of St. Benedict.
Beaudet, Christopher J. (STP) Graduate Studies.
Beaudet, Eugene J. '53 (OG) Retired.
Beaudin, William R. '82 (BUR) Ludlow, VT Annunciation of the Blessed Virgin Mary.
Beaudin, William *o.f.m.* '76 (ALB)[B] Loudonville, NY Siena College; [B] Siena College.
Beaudin, William *o.f.m.* '76 (ALB)[Q] Loudonville, NY Siena College.
Beaudoin, Andrew *s.s.s.* '54 (CLV)[O] Spring Hill, FL.
Beaudoin, Andrew *s.s.s.* '54 (SP) Spring Hill, FL St. Frances Xavier Cabrini.

Beaudry, David B. '82 (GB) Newton, WI St. Thomas the Apostle.
Beaulieu, Earl G. '60 (SHP) Retired.
Beaulieu, Kerry (ORG) Vicar for Priests.
Beaulieu, Kerry (ORG) Ministry to Priests.
Beaulieu, Kerry (ORG) Consultors.
Beaulieu, Kerry (ORG) Priests' Relief.
Beaulieu, Kerry (ORG) Council of Priests.
Beaulieu, Kerry (ORG) Liturgical Commission.
Beaulieu, Kerry (ORG) Building and Renovation Committee of the Liturgical Commission.
Beaulieu, Peter R. '83 (WOR)[K] Worcester, MA Saint Vincent Hospital, Inc..
Beaulieu, Raymond '42 (PRO) Retired.
Beaulieu, Richard C. '76 (BO) Winchester, MA St. Mary.
Beaulieu, Richard '71 (FR) Absent on Sick Leave.
Beaulieu, Robert J. (HEL) Clergy Senior Status and Security Trust Board.
Beaulieu, Robert '57 (HEL) Retired.
Beaulieu, Robert (HEL) Defenders of the Bond.
Beaumont, Gregory J. '96 (FRS) Lemoore, CA St. Peter; Ecumenical Affairs.
Beaumont, Joachim B. '59 (NY) New York, NY St. Benedict the Moor; New York, NY St. Emeric; New York, NY Sacred Heart of Jesus.
Beaumont, Richard '58 (FWT) Retired.
Beaupre, R. Bradley *c.s.c.* '68 (FR) South Easton, MA Holy Cross.
Beauregard, David N. *o.m.v.* '80 (BO)[B] Boston, MA Our Lady of Grace Seminary; [AA] Boston, MA St. Clement Archdiocesan Eucharistic Shrine.
Beauregard, James E. '70 (BUR)[D] Burlington, VT St. Joseph's Home Retired.
Beausoleil, Charles *o.m.i.* '56 (BO)[AA] Lowell, MA St. Joseph the Worker Residence.
Beausoleil, Charles *o.m.i.* '56 (BO)[V] Lowell, MA Andre Garin Retirement Residence.
Beausoleil, Gerald L. *m.m.* '52 (FgM).
Beauvais, David E. '62 (RCK) Rockford, IL St. James.
Beaven, Robert W. '68 (CHI) Grayslake, IL St. Gilbert.
Beaver, Nelson G. '76 (TOL) Norwalk, OH St. Mary, Mother of the Redeemer; Norwalk, OH St. Alphonsus Liguori.
Beaver, William A. *o.s.b.* '85 (GBG) Whitney, PA St. Cecilia; Youngstown, PA Sacred Heart.
Beavers, Carl A. '68 (CHY) Jackson, WY Our Lady of the Mountains.
Beavers, Carl (CHY) St. Joseph's Society for Priests (Clergy Mutual Benefit Society).
Bebak, Brian D. '86 (WCH) Colwich, KS Sacred Heart.
Bebel, Alfred J. '58 (SY) Syracuse, NY Our Lady of Solace; Syracuse, NY University Hospital; Special Assignment.
BeBlanc, Alvin J. '82 (HRT) Rocky Hill, CT St. Elizabeth Seton.
Becerra, Robert L. '89 (LSC) Santa Clara, NM Santa Clara.
Becerril, Julian *o.de.m.* '75 (BWN) Mission, TX San Martin de Porres.
Bechamps, Vincent *o.ss.t.* '66 (NO) New Orleans, LA University Hospital.
Bechard, Bernard J. *s.s.e.* '49 (BUR) Sheldon Springs, VT St. Anthony.
Bechard, Dean P. *s.j.* '91 (NY)[EE] Cardinal Spellman Hall, Jesuit Community.
Bechard, Gerard V. '80 (DET) Westland, MI SS. Simon and Jude.
Becher, Albert B. '84 (DAL) Dallas, TX St. Patrick.
Becherer, David '48 (MOB) Retired.
Becherer, David '48 (MOB) Dothan, AL St. Columba.
Becherer, James R. '54 (CLV) Retired.
Bechtel, James C. '71 (ALN) Lehighton, PA SS. Peter and Paul.
Bechtold, Paul I. *c.p.* '41 (CHI)[N] Chicago, IL Passionist Community–Immaculate Conception Monastery.
Beck, Albert '49 (GAL) Retired.
Beck, David J. '67 (TOL) Toledo, OH St. Jude.
Beck, Edward *c.p.* '85 (NY)[EE] Bronx, NY Passionist Residence.
Beck, Erwin G. *s.j.* '60 (NEW)[C] Jersey City, NJ St. Peter's Preparatory School; [N] Jersey City, NJ Jesuit Community of St. Peter's Prep, Inc..
Beck, Joseph C. '84 (PIT) Pittsburgh, PA St. Rosalia; Allegheny County, PA Forbes Nursing Center; Allegheny County, PA Kane Regional Center – Glen Hazel; Allegheny County, PA Woodhaven Convalescent Center; Allegheny County, PA Greater Pittsburgh Rehab Hospital; Allegheny County, PA Independent Court of Monroeville; Allegheny County, PA Manorcare Health Services North Hills.
Beck, R. Patrick (BEA) Air Force Chaplains.
Beck, Richard P. '55 (MIL) Retired.
Beck, Richard W. '74 (SCR) Pleasant Mount, PA St. James.
Beck, Richard *o.m.i.* '67 (GAL)[S] Dickinson, TX Christian Renewal Center.
Beck, Robert P. '76 (BEA) Military Chaplains.
Beck, Robert R. '66 (DUB)[L] Dubuque, IA Mt. St. Francis; [C] Loras College.
Becka, Robert R. *s.j.* '60 (FgM).
Becker, Anthony J. '47 (RCK) Retired.
Becker, Arthur '73 (ALB) Cohoes, NY Holy Trinity.
Becker, Arthur (ALB) Advocates.
Becker, Bruno *o.s.b.* '51 (P)[L] St. Benedict, OR Mt. Angel Abbey.
Becker, Daniel J. '96 (WOR) Warren, MA St. Paul's.
Becker, David R. '66 (ALT) Altoona, PA Veterans Medical Center; Altoona, PA Altoona Hospital Retired.
Becker, David R. (ALT).
Becker, Dennis E. '62 (NU) Retired.
Becker, Donald '67 (BUF) Retired.
Becker, Frederick J. '59 (NY) Bronx, NY St. Lucy; Our Lady of Mercy Medical Center; [X] Bronx, NY Florence D'Urso Pavilion.
Becker, John J. (GB) Waupaca, WI St. Mary Magdalene.
Becker, John R. *s.j.* '56 (PHX)[B] Phoenix, AZ Brophy College Preparatory.
Becker, John (GB) Elected Representatives.
Becker, Joseph P. *o.s.f.s.* '69 (ALN) Lehigh Valley Hospital at Cedar Crest; [B] Center Valley, PA DeSales University; [K] Center Valley, PA Oblates of St. Francis de Sales.
Becker, Michael '75 (ALT) Absent on Leave.
Becker, Michael '99 (STP) St. Michael, MN St. Michael.
Becker, Michael '99 (STP) Dayton, MN St. John the Baptist.
Becker, Nickolas '02 (SC) Sioux City, IA Blessed Sacrament.
Becker, Paul D. '73 (BIS) Bismarck, ND Corpus Christi.
Becker, Paul D. (BIS) Presbyteral Council; Diocesan Corporate Board; Diocesan Finance Council.
Becker, Richard F. '72 (PBL) Pueblo, CO Our Lady of Mt. Carmel; Pueblo, CO St. Joseph; Pueblo, CO St. Therese; Diocesan Council of Catholic Women.
Becker, Robert T. '64 (SFD) Springfield, IL St. Agnes.
Becker, Robert '79 (AUS) Austin, TX Sacred Heart.
Becker, Russell C. *o.f.m.* '72 (NY) New York, NY St. Stephen of Hungary; [II] New York, NY Franciscan Missionary Union, Province of the Most Holy Name.
Becker, Russell C. *o.f.m.* (FgM).
Becker, Thomas G. '80 (SCL) Glenwood, MN Sacred Heart.
Becker, Thomas '80 (SCL) St. Bartholomew's.
Becker, Thomas (SCL) Presbyteral Council.
Becker, Thomas (SCL) Diocesan Consultors.
Becker, Thomas (SCL) Deans.
Becker, Vincent J. '62 (BUF) Buffalo, NY St. Martin.
Becker, Vincent J. (BUF) Judges.
Becker, William M. '88 (WIN) Winona, MN St. Mary's; Censors of Books and Periodicals; Elected Deanery Representatives.
Beckermann, Julius *o.s.b.* '03 (SCL) Freeport, MN Immaculate Conception.
Beckermann, Julius *o.s.b.* '03 (SCL) Freeport, MN St. Rose of Lima.
Beckermann, Julius *o.s.b.* '03 (SCL) Freeport, MN Sacred Heart.
Beckfelt, John W. '74 (LC) River Falls, WI Nativity of the Blessed Virgin Mary.
Beckley, Clarence *s.s.c.* '66 (OM)[K] St. Columbans St. Columban's Foreign Mission Society.
Beckley, Clarence *s.s.c.* '66 (CHI) Chicago, IL St. Philomena.
Beckley, John F. *s.m.* '73 (WDC)[M] Tampa, FL.
Beckman, David M. '92 (DUB) Clarion, IA St. John; Eagle Grove, IA Sacred Heart; Belmond, IA St. Francis Xavier; Vocation Awareness; Medical–Moral Commission.
Beckman, Gary L. '95 (DAV) Charlotte, IA Assumption and St. Patrick's; Preston, IA Ss. Mary and Joseph.
Beckman, John J. *s.j.* '54 (CIN)[F] Cincinnati, OH St. Xavier High School.
Beckman, John *s.j.* '54 (CIN)[M] Cincinnati, OH Faber Jesuit Community.
Beckman, Joseph F. '54 (CIN)[B] Cincinnati, OH Mt. St. Mary's Seminary of the West Retired.
Beckman, Mark '90 (NSH) Franklin, TN St. Matthew.
Beckman, Mark (NSH) Clergy Personnel Board.
Beckman, Mark (NSH) Catholic Youth Office and Search Program.
Beckman, Martin A. '58 (STP) Retired.
Beckman, Richard J. '56 (OKL) Newkirk, OK St. Francis of Assisi.
Beckman, Robert E. *s.j.* '56 (CHI).
Beckman, Robert E. *s.j.* '56[N] (FgM).
Beckmann, Donald M. (RVC) Secretary for Pastoral Ministries; Ecumenical & Interreligious Affairs.
Beckmann, Donald '70 (RVC) Oyster Bay, NY St. Dominic's.
Becnel, Terry B. '64 (NO) Members of the Board; Executive Director; New Orleans, LA St. Mary Church.
Beczek, Mariusz *o.s.j.* '98 (SAC)[A] Loomis, CA Mount St. Joseph Novitiate and Seminary.
Bedard, Andre L. '57 (MAN) Manchester, NH Transfiguration; Nashua, NH Infant Jesus Retired.
Bedard, J. Raymond '53 (WOR) Retired.
Bedard, Paul *s.d.b.* '65 (NY)[GG] Stony Point, NY Marian Shrine.
Bedard, Paul *s.d.b.* '65 (NY)[GG] Stony Point, NY Don Bosco Retreat Center and Marian Shrine.
Bedenikovic, Stephen *o.f.m.* '85 (CHI) Chicago, IL Sacred Heart.
Bedessem, Henry W. '59 (GB) Retired.
Bednar, Gerald J. '83 (CLV)[A] Wickliffe, OH St. Mary Seminary and Graduate School of Theology.
Bednar, Martin *o.f.m.* '64 (MIA)[H] Hialeah, FL Franciscan Friars of the Holy Name Province.
Bednarik, John *o.f.m.cap.* '68 (PIT)[N] Pittsburgh, PA St. Augustine Friary.
Bednark, Walter '47 (SCL) Roscoe, MN St. Margaret's.
Bednark, Walter '47 (SCL) Retired.
Bednarski, Mitchell J. '44 (LAN) Retired.
Bednartz, August C. '52 (BRK) Farmingdale, NY St. Charles Retired.
Bednarz, Jan '72 (SLC) Taylorsville, UT St. Martin de Porres.
Bedodya, Omar A. '94 (ARE) Arecibo, PR Cathedral of San Felipe Apostol.
Bedoya, Carlos (ORL) Haines City, FL St. Ann.
Bedoya, Ferley de Jesus '01 (GAL) Houston, TX St. Francis de Sales.
Bedoya, Hugo '56 (BRK) Flushing, NY St. John Vianney.
Bedoya, Hugo (BRK) Vice Officiales–Associate Judicial Vicars.
Bedoya, Martin Educardo '03 (CHI) Streamwood, IL St. John the Evangelist.
Bedrossian, Armenaq '99 (ARM) Belmont, MA Holy Cross.
Beebe, Charles J. '70 (PEO) Roanoke, IL St. John; Roanoke, IL St. Joseph; Permanent Diaconate, Office of.
Beebe, David E. '61 (CAM) On Duty Outside the Diocese.
Beeching, Roy T. '74 (GRY) Hammond, IN St. Joseph; Priests' Personnel Board; Council of Catholic Women.
Beeda, Francis J. '61 (SCR) Hazleton, PA St. Joseph's.
Beegan, James *m.s.f.* '00 (BWN) Donna, TX St. Joseph.
Beek, Alois Van '73 (MIL) Neosho, WI St. Matthew.
Beekman, Carl E. '00 (RCK) Prophetstown, IL St. Catherine.
Beemster, John *s.v.d.* '40 (CHI)[B] Techny, IL Divine Word Residence.
Beemsterboer, Francis *s.v.d.* '51 (FgM).
Beerman, Andrew J. '96 (WIN) Luverne, MN St. Catherine's; Censors of Books and Periodicals; Pathways TEC (Teens Encounter Christ).
Beerman, Andrew J. (WIN) Vocations Advisory Council.
Beerntsen, Harold A. (GB) Oconto Falls, WI St. Anthony; Lena, WI St. Patrick.
Beerntsen, Harold '61 (GB) Retired.
Beers, Ervan *o.f.m.* '55 (FRS) Delano, CA Our Lady of Guadalupe.
Beers, John Michael '79 (ALN) On Duty Outside the Diocese; Air Force Reserve Chaplains.
Beers, William '85 (MAD)[E] Baraboo, WI St. Clare Hospital and Health Services.
Beeson, Lawrence A. '60 (DM) Atlantic, IA SS. Peter and Paul; Judges.
Beever, Carlton J. '74 (IND) Indianapolis, IN St. Philip Neri.
Beez, John E. *s.j.* '61 (DET)[P] Clarkston, MI Colombiere Center.
Beezer, Arnold R. *s.j.* '64 (SPK)[J] Spokane, WA Regis Community.
Befort, Daryl '95 (WCH) Wichita, KS St. Francis of Assisi.
Befort, Earl *o.f.m.cap.* '69 (SAL) Hays, KS Our Lady Help of Christians.
Befort, Earl *o.f.m.cap.* '69 (SAL) Catharine, KS St. Catherine's.
Befort, Earl *o.f.m.cap.* '69 (SAL)[D] Hays, KS St. John's of Hays; [E] Hays, KS St. Joseph's Friary; [E] Hays, KS St. Joseph's Friary; Hays, KS St. Joseph's.
Befort, Earl *o.f.m.cap.* '69 (SAL) Hays, KS St. Anthony's.
Befort, Earl *o.f.m.cap.* '69 (SAL)[B] Hays, KS Thomas More Prep–Marian Alumni Assoc..
Begay, Joseph N. *s.s.j.* '59 (WDC) Washington, DC St. Luke.
Begerimina, Pascal (BO) Boston, MA St. Cecilia.
Begg, Christopher T. '77 (WDC) Washington, DC St. Joseph on Capitol Hill; Special Ministries; [C] Catholic University of America, The.
Beggane, Thomas (LSC) Absent On Leave.
Beggans, Joseph A. '43 (NEW) Jersey City, NJ St. John the Baptist Retired.
Beggiani, Seely '61 (SAM)[C] Catholic University of America, The.
Beggiani, Seely '61 (SAM)[A] Washington, DC Our Lady of Lebanon Maronite Seminary.
Beggiani, Seely (SAM) Lebanon Commission.
Beggiani, Seely (SAM) Presbyteral Council–Ex Officio Members.
Beggin, Thomas M. '79 (GF) Retired.
Begin, Daniel L. '75 (CLV) Cleveland, OH St. Cecilia; Cleveland, OH Epiphany.
Begin, Raymond F. '52 (PRT) Associate Judges Retired.
Begin, Robert T. '64 (CLV) Cleveland, OH St. Colman; Avon, OH Our Lady of the Wayside.

Begley, James J. '82 (RIC) Mechanicsville, VA Church of the Redeemer.
Begley, John J. *s.j.* '62 (BO)[V] Boston The Society of Jesus of New England–Provincial Offices.
Begley, John J. *s.j.* '62 (SCR)[C] Scranton, PA The University of Scranton.
Begley, Paul '55 (OM) Retired.
Begley, Paul '55 (OM) Omaha, NE St. Bridget.
Begley, Thomas B. '60 (SPR) Retired.
Begley, Thomas M. '89 (STL) St. Louis, MO Christian Hospital Northeast–Northwest.
Begly, Mark S. '84 (ALT) Lakemont, Altoona, PA St. John the Evangelist.
Begnaud, Adam *o.s.b.* '96 (NO)[P] St. Benedict, LA St. Joseph Abbey; [A] St. Benedict, LA St. Joseph Seminary College.
Begolly, Michael J. '81 (GBG) Greensburg, PA Blessed Sacrament Cathedral.
Begue, Joseph E. *c.m.* '55 (STL)[O] St. Louis, MO Lazarist Residence; [U] St. Louis, MO The Vincentian Press Religious Supply.
Behan, George P. '56 (PRO) Warwick, RI St. William.
Behan, Harry P. '73 (NU) Tyler, MN St. Genevieve; Tyler, MN St. Dionysius; Board of Trustees for Pension Plan for Priests.
Behan, Hugh F. '64 (JC) Absent on Leave.
Behan, Laurence (RVC) Garden City, NY St. Joseph's.
Behan, Philip A. '70 (SB) Palm Springs, CA St. Theresa.
Behan, Thomas W. *o.s.a.* '58 (OAK) Los Angeles, CA Our Mother of Good Counsel.
Behen, John *c.pp.s.* '46 (CIN)[B] Carthagena, OH St. Charles.
Behl, Richard A. '66 (MET) Metuchen, NJ Cathedral of St. Francis; Office of the Missions; Commission for Pro–Life Action.
Behler, Donald A. '47 (CIN) Retired.
Behnen, Robert *o.f.m.* '60 (STL) St. Louis, MO St. Anthony of Padua; [O] St. Louis, MO Franciscan Friary of St. Anthony of Padua.
Behnke, John J. *c.s.p.* '76 (STP) Minneapolis, MN St. Lawrence–Newman; [M] Minneapolis, MN Paulist Fathers; [U] Minneapolis, MN Newman Center at St. Lawrence; Newman Centers.
Behnke, Robert C. '73 (CHI) Chicago, IL St. Barbara.
Behrend, Thomas J. (CLV) Lakewood, OH St. James.
Behringer, William *s.m.* '60 (CLV) Cleveland, OH St. Aloysius – St. Agatha.
Behrmann, Elmer H. '38 (STL) Retired.
Beichner, Paul E. *c.s.c.* '39 (FTW)[I] Notre Dame, IN Holy Cross House.
Beidelman, Patrick J. '98 (IND) Brookville, IN St. Michael.
Beidelman, Patrick '98 (IND) Cedar Grove, IN Holy Guardian Angels.
Beidelman, Patrick (IND) Priests' Personnel Board.
Beierwaltes, Charles *c.ss.r.* '67 (MIL)[R] Oconomowoc, WI The Redemptorist Retreat Center.
Beigel, Gerard '86 (DEN) Denver, CO St. Mary Magdalene.
Beighlie, James T. *c.m.* '79 (STL)[O] St. Louis, MO Vincentian Residence.
Beighlie, James '79 (STL)[O] St. Louis Vincentian Residence.
Beilman, J. Brian '86 (OM) Omaha, NE Assumption, B.V.M..
Beining, Paul R. *s.j.* '55 (SCR)[C] Scranton, PA The University of Scranton.
Beirne, Charles J. *s.j.* '69 (SY)[Q] Syracuse, NY Jesuits at LeMoyne, Inc..
Beirne, Gerald E. '62 (PRO) Greenville, RI St. Philip; Deans.
Beirne, M. Christen '69 (NEW) Mahwah, NJ Immaculate Conception.
Beirne, Robert M. '63 (PRO) On Duty Outside the Diocese.
Beischel, Richard L. *c.pp.s.* '56 (CIN).
Beischel, Thomas J. *c.pp.s.* '58 (CIN)[U] Dayton, OH Community Support Charitable Trust.
Beischel, Thomas *c.pp.s.* '58 (CIN)[M] Kettering, OH.
Beischel, Thomas *c.pp.s.* '58 (CIN) Dayton, OH St. Albert the Great.
Beisel, James D. '80 (PH)[V] Warminster, PA Regina Coeli Residence for Priests; Regional Vicars; Priests' Personnel Board.
Beitans, John '73 (IND) Indianapolis, IN St. Lawrence.
Beiter, Eugene J. '64 (LAN) Retired.
Beiter, Robert G. '64 (BUF) Brocton, NY St. Patrick.
Beiting, Ralph W. (LEX) Diocesan Consultors.
Beiting, Ralph '49 (LEX) Louisa, KY St. Jude.
Beitzinger, George J. '45 (MIL) Retired.
Bejan, Ciprian (BGP) Stamford, CT St. Mary.
Bejarano, Ramon '98 (STO) Turlock, CA Sacred Heart Church of Turlock (Pastor of).
Bejarano, Ramon (STO) Deans.
Bejenaru, Florin '97 (NY) Bronx, NY Holy Rosary.
Bejer, Domingo–James B. *s.s.j.* '79 (AGN) Agana, GU Dulce Nombre de Maria Cathedral – Basilica.
Bejgrowicz, Joseph S. '70 (NEW) Kenilworth, NJ St. Theresa's; College of Consultors.
Bek, Viktor '92 (PHU) Carteret, NJ St. Volodymyr's.
Bekavac, Ante (NY) New York, NY SS. Cyril and Methodius – St. Raphael.
Bekkedahl, Mark '85 (B)[B] Nampa, ID Mercy Medical Center.
Beksha, Francis W. '46 (BO) Senior Priests Retired.
Belair, Eugene '53 (SCL) Retired.
Belanger, Gerald R. '75 (MAN) Salem, NH St. Joseph; Council of Priests; Air National Guard Chaplains.
Belanger, Rene A. *s.s.s.* '50 (CLV)[O] New Bedford, MA.
Belanggoy, Plutarco *c.i.c.m.* '96 (BWN) Santa Rosa, TX St. Mary.
Belanggoy, Plutarco *c.i.c.m.* '98 (BWN) La Feria, TX St. Francis Xavier.
Belanich, Giordano '75 (NEW) Fairview, NJ St. John the Baptist; Secaucus, NJ Hudson County Juvenile Correctional Center; Secaucus, NJ Hudson County Juvenile Detention Center.
Belauskas, August J. '68 (CHI).
Belaustegui, Juan Luis '71 (SJN)[A] Sabana Seca, PR San Jose Obrero.
Belcher, Francis H. *s.j.* '61 (BO)[X] Gloucester, MA Eastern Point Retreat House.
Belczak, Edward A. '72 (DET) Troy, MI St. Thomas More.
Belczak, Thomas A. '80 (DET) Redford, MI St. Valentine; Presbyteral Council.
Belda, Leo W. '42 (MIL) Retired.
Belda, Leo '48 (MIL)[M] Wauwatosa, WI St. Camillus Health Center, Inc..
Belden, Corey '02 (STP) Stillwater, MN St. Mary; Stillwater, MN St. Michael.
Belen, Germain *o.f.m.conv.* '50 (LAN)[J] Mount St. Francis, IN Mount Saint Francis Friary and Retreat Center Retired.
Belfield, John '58 (STU) Retired.
Belford, William J. '74 (NY) LaGrangeville, NY Blessed Kateri Tekakwitha; Dutchess.
Belgarde, George H. *s.j.* '88 (NY)[EE] Hogansburg, NY St. Regis; [I] Hogansburg, NY St. Regis Mission.
Belger, Jeffry '03 (DAV) Clinton, IA Jesus Christ, Prince of Peace.
Belhumer, Roger E. '61 (PRO)[P] Providence St. John Vianney Residence.
Belhumeur, Paul *m.s.* '61 (BUR) Windsor, VT St. Francis of Assisi.
Belhumeur, Roger E. '61 (PRO) Retired.
Beligotti, Richard J. '68 (ROC) Rochester, NY St. Salome.
Beligotti, Robert '68 (ROC) Rochester, NY Our Lady of Mercy.
Belinda, Augustine *t.o.r.* '93 (ALT)[F] Loretto, PA Mount Assis. Friary.
Belinsky, Michael T. *c.s.c.* '89 (FTW)[I] Hyattsville, MD.
Belisch, Carl L. *c.s.b.* '65 (GAL)[F] Houston, TX St. Thomas High School; Elected Members.
Belisle, Peter Damian *o.s.b.cam.* '72 (MRY)[F] Big Sur, CA New Camaldoli Hermitage.
Belisle, Ronald '62 (SEA) Oak Harbor, WA St. Augustine.
Belitz, Justin *o.f.m.* '61 (IND) Indianapolis, IN Sacred Heart of Jesus.
Belitz, Ronald C. (GB) Green Bay, WI Annunciation of the Blessed Virgin Mary; Green Bay, WI Holy Martyrs of Gorcum; Denmark, WI Holy Trinity.
Belitz, Ronald (GB) Priests' Personnel Board.
Belizaire, Hilaire (BRK) South Ozone Park, NY St. Teresa of Avila.
Bell, Brian T. '70 (TUC) On Duty Outside the Diocese.
Bell, Brian '70 (PHX) Congress Junction, AZ Good Shepherd of the Desert; Wickenburg, AZ St. Anthony of Padua.
Bell, Carl F. '66 (LA) Encino, CA St. Cyril.
Bell, Edward H. '77 (PH) Philadelphia, PA St. Joan of Arc; Approved Advocates.
Bell, Edward M. '64 (WH) Parkersburg, WV St. Margaret Mary; Vicars Forane.
Bell, Gerald L. '73 (L) Lebanon, KY St. Augustine; Deans.
Bell, Gerard P. *s.j.* '57 (NY)[EE] Silver Spring, MD; [V] Silver Spring, MD Apostleship of Prayer.
Bell, John P. '75 (DAL) Plano, TX Our Lady of Angels; Judicial Vicar; Diocesan Consultors; Presbyteral Council; Media Division Head.
Bell, Joseph W. '74 (SPK) Spokane, WA St. Peter.
Bell, Joseph (SPK) Priests' Personnel Board.
Bell, Michael T. '61 (MRY) California Men's Colony West.
Bell, Richard A. *m.m.* '36 (SJ)[M] Los Altos, CA Maryknoll.
Bellafiore, L. Michael *s.j.* '03 (BO)[V] Boston The Society of Jesus of New England–Provincial Offices.
Bellamah, Timothy F. *o.p.* '98 (PRO)[P] Providence St. Thomas Aquinas Priory at Providence College.
Belland, David '87 (SCL) Special Assignment.
Bellantonio, Albert '69 (SCR) Tobyhanna, PA St. Ann.
Bellantonio, Albert '69 (SCR) East Stroudsburg, PA St. Matthew's
Bellefeuille, Albert A. '54 (MAN) Colebrook, NH St. Brendan.
Bellenoit, George C. '72 (FR) Mansfield, MA St. Mary's; Attleboro Deanery.
Belleque, Thomas '85 (SEA) Bellevue, WA St. Louise.
Beller, Frederic J. *o.s.b.* '43 (JOL)[L] Lisle, IL St. Procopius Abbey.
Bellesorte, Anthony R. *o.c.s.o.* '69 (SAC)[A] Vina, CA Abbey of New Clairvaux, Trappist Seminary; [I] Vina, CA Abbey of New Clairvaux, Trappist.
Belletty, Emile '78 (LA) Montebello, CA Our Lady of the Miraculous Medal.
Bellew, Francis P. '66 (NY) Wappingers Falls, NY St. Mary.
Bellew, Lawrence *c.p.* '53 (BRK)[V] Jamaica, NY Immaculate Conception Monastery.
Belley, Bernard *o.m.i.* '54 (BO)[V] Lowell, MA St. Eugene House (Residence).
Belli, Brian W. (ARL) Notaries.
Belli, Bryan W. '02 (ARL) Alexandria, VA Blessed Sacrament.
Bellinghausen, David *o.s.b.* '86 (LR)[A] Subiaco, AR Subiaco Monastery.
Bellino, Samuel P. *s.j.* (YAK) Director of Planned Giving; Diocesan Finance Council; [I] Yakima, WA Central Washington Catholic Foundation.
Bellisario, Andrew E. *c.m.* '84 (LA)[Q] Montebello, CA Vincentian Fathers and Brothers; [Q] Montebello, CA DePaul Evangelization Center; [W] Montebello, CA DePaul Evangelization Center; [N] Los Altos Hills, CA Daughters of Charity of St. Vincent de Paul, Seton Provincialate.
Bellittiere, David A. '89 (BUF) Dunkirk, NY Holy Trinity.
Belliveau, Gary J. '85 (MAN) Hudson, NH St. Kathryn.
Bello, David *o.p.* '81 (OAK)[N] Oakland Western Dominican Province.
Bello, David *o.p.* '81 (FgM).
Bello, Giles *o.f.m.* '55 (PAT)[M] Ringwood, NJ Holy Name Friary, Inc..
Bello, Jorge L. '03 (MIA) Hollywood, FL Little Flower.
Bellon, John E. *c.ss.r.* '41 (STL)[O] Liguori, MO St. Clement Health Care Center.
Bellopede, Louis P. '91 (PH) Philadelphia, PA St. Paul.
Bellow, Richard '70 (CHL) Charlotte, NC St. Gabriel.
Bellow, Richard (CHL) Diocesan Consultors.
Belluomini, Ralph '60 (FRS) Kern Medical Center, Bakersfield Memorial Hospital & San Joaquin Community Hospital.
Belmonte, John M. *s.j.* '96 (MIL)[E] Milwaukee, WI Marquette University High School; [O] Milwaukee, WI Jesuit Community at Marquette University.
Belogi, James '81 (ALB) Schenectady, NY St. Madeleine Sophie.
Belogi, James (ALB) Presbyteral Council; Diocesan Board of Consultors; Ecumenical and Interreligious Affairs of the Roman Catholic Diocese of Albany, Commission for.
Beloin, Robert L. '73 (HRT)[R] New Haven, CT Yale University–St. Thomas More Catholic Center and Chapel.
Belongea, David *o.f.m.cap.* '59 (GB)[I] Appleton, WI St. Fidelis Friary.
Belschner, Wayne L. '95 (BO) East Boston, MA Sacred Heart; Woburn, MA St. Charles Borromeo.
Belsole, Kurt J. *o.s.b.* '78 (GBG)[H] Latrobe, PA Saint Vincent Archabbey.
Belsole, Kurt *o.s.b.* '78 (GBG)[A] Latrobe, PA St. Vincent Seminary.
Belsome, Garland T. '90 (BR) Belle Rose, LA St. Jules; Paincourtville, LA St. Elizabeth; Defenders of the Bond; Board Members.
Belt, David D. '90 (OM) Norfolk, NE Sacred Heart.
Belt, Stephen M. *s.j.* (STL)[C] Saint Louis University.
Beltkowski, Andrew '90 (CHI) Hometown, IL Our Lady of Loretto.
Beltowski, Andrew (CHI)[J] Elk Grove Village, IL Alexian Brothers Medical Center.
Beltrami, Robert *o.f.m.* '62 (P) Rainier, OR Nativity B.V.M..
Beltran, Jacque B. (CHI).
Beltran, JoAndre '01 (CHI)[A] Evergreen Park, IL Queen of Martyrs.
Beltran, Justo '69 (BRK) Brooklyn, NY St. Vincent de Paul.
Beltran de Otalora, Esteban *ss.cc.* '56 (SJN) Guaynabo, PR Sagrados Corazones.
Beltzner, Lucian W. *o.carm.* '63 (NY) Tarrytown, NY Transfiguration.
Belzer, Paul J. '54 (BUF) Vicars; North Tonawanda, NY Good Shepherd.
Bempah, Richard Osei '92 (KCK) Lenexa, KS Holy Trinity.
Ben, Alvin Fong (IND) Greenwood, IN Our Lady of the Greenwood.
Benacchio, Onorio *c.s.* '50 (VEN) Immokalee, FL Our Lady of Guadalupe.
Benack, Henry I. '51 (RVC) Glen Cove, NY St. Patrick's Retired.
Benak, Wes E. *o.s.a.* '91 (CHI)[N] Chicago, IL St. Rita Monastery.
Benakovic, Benedict *o.f.m.conv.* '49 (GRY) Gary, IN St. Joseph The Worker.
Benas, Rolando T. '85 (SJ) Saratoga, CA Sacred Heart.

Benavente, James L.G. '94 (AGN) Agana, GU Dulce Nombre de Maria Cathedral – Basilica; Archdiocesan College of Consultors; Archdiocesan Finance Council; Archdiocesan Presbyteral Council; Advocate; Catholic Cemetery Office.
Benda, Frederick J. *s.j.* '72 (CIN)[M] Cincinnati, OH Jesuit Community at Xavier University.
Benda, Frederick J. *s.j.* '72 (DET)[K] Detroit Jesuit Provincial Office–Detroit Province of the Society of Jesus.
Benda, M. Eugene '60 (DAV) Tipton, IA St. Mary's.
Bendel, Eugene F. '57 (STL) O'Fallon, MO Assumption.
Benden, Stephen *c.ss.r.* '89 (MIL)[R] Oconomowoc, WI The Redemptorist Retreat Center.
Bender, Arthur C. *s.j.* '78 (NY)[F] New York, NY Regis High School; [EE] New York, NY St. Ignatius Loyola Residence.
Bender, James W. *c.pp.s.* '52 (CIN)[M] Parroquia Cristo Rey.
Bender, Lawrence A. *s.s.* '51 (WDC) Retired.
Bender, Lawrence A. *s.s.* '51 (BAL)[O] Baltimore, MD St. Charles Villa.
Bender, Philip M. '64 (ALT) State College, PA Good Shepherd.
Bender, Reginald G. *o.s.b.* '59 (GBG)[H] Latrobe, PA Saint Vincent Archabbey.
Bender, Thomas G. '56 (COL) Bremen, OH St. Mary.
Bender, Thomas J. '61 (ALN) Retired.
Bendernagel, Cajetan *c.p.* '52 (HRT)[M] West Hartford Holy Family Monastery/Retreat.
Bendik, John J. '67 (SCR) Pittston, PA St. John the Evangelist.
Bendorf, Richard *o.f.m.* '87 (STL)[O] St. Louis Franciscan Friary of St. Anthony of Padua; Army Chaplains.
Bendyk, Marion '82 (CLV) Garfield Heights, OH SS. Peter and Paul; Translators.
Bendzella, Sylvester J. '59 (ALT) Johnstown, PA St. Andrew's; Johnstown, PA Conemaugh Memorial Medical Center.
Bene, Philip J. '94 (STL) St. Louis, MO St. Stanislaus Kostka; Judges.
Benecki, Stanley '84 (COL) Columbus, OH St. Mary Magdalene.
Benecki, Stanley (COL) Deaf Apostolate.
Benedetti, Edmund *s.j.* '50 (CC) Corpus Christi, TX St. Patrick.
Benedict, Francis *o.s.b.* '76 (LA)[W] Valyermo, CA St. Andrew's Abbey Retreat Center (All Groups).
Benedict, Joseph '97 (SJ) San Jose, CA St. Francis of Assisi; Deacon Formation.
Benedicto, Benjamin '62 (ORG) Placentia, CA St. Joseph.
Benedik, Hilarion *o.s.b.m.* '48 (RVC)[M] Glen Cove, NY St. Josaphat's Monastery, Novitiate and Retreat House.
Benedik, Hilarion *o.s.b.m.* '48 (STF)[B] Glen Cove, NY Basilian Fathers Novitiate of the Order of St. Basil the Great.
Benefiel, Harry E. '60 (LAF) Retired.
Beneleit, Edward L. '74 (Y) Canton, OH St. Joseph.
Benestad, Thomas J. '70 (ALN) Allentown, PA St. Francis of Assisi.
Bengco, Jose '65 (CLV) Cleveland, OH Veterans Administration Hospitals, Brecksville V.A..
Bengford, Ronald J. '94 (PRO) Woonsocket, RI Sacred Heart.
Bengurria, Juan B. *c.p.* '57 (ARE) Lares, PR St. Joseph.
Benham, Michael '76 (MIL) Elkhorn, WI St. Patrick.
Benicewicz, Joseph *o.f.m.conv.* '88 (BUF)[O] Athol Springs, NY St. Francis of Assisi Friary; [D] Athol Springs, NY St. Francis High School.
Beninati, Francis H. *m.m.* '55 (FgM).
Benintede, Joseph (ALB) Priestly Life and Ministry Council.
Benintende, Joseph '70 (ALB) Ilion, NY Annunciation.
Benintende, Joseph (ALB) Deans.
Benischeck, Bernard J. '53 (PH) Philadelphia, PA St. Dominic Retired.
Benish, Bill (AUS)[L] San Marcos, TX H.L. Grant Catholic Student Center at Southwest Texas State University.
Benitez, Eduardo '66 (ORL) Retired.
Benitez, Gustavo '96 (SD) Escondido, CA St. Mary.
Benjamin, Jonh (SB) Retired.
Benjamin, Robert L. (SR) Ferndale, CA Church of the Assumption.
Benko, Robert *o.f.m.conv.* (R) Burlington, NC Blessed Sacrament.
Benko, Robert *o.f.m.conv.* (R)[E] Burlington, NC Conventual Franciscans.
Benkovic, Theodore *o.f.m.* '41 (CHI)[N] Chicago, IL St. Anthony's Friary.
Benkowski, Gregory '84 (OM) Omaha, NE Holy Ghost.
Benliro, Fernando C. '58 (OM) Retired.
Benn, Walter J. '77 (PH) Pottstown, PA St. Aloysius; Pottstown, PA Holy Trinity.
Bennerfield, Herbert '99 (LAF) Delcambre, LA Our Lady of the Lake; Delcambre, LA Saint Martin de Porres.
Bennett, Austin P. '49 (BRK)[N] Brooklyn, NY St. Vincent's Catholic Medical Center; [V] Brooklyn, NY Curial Residence; [W] Brooklyn, NY Monastery of the Sisters Adorers of the Precious Blood; Confraternity of the Precious Blood Retired.
Bennett, Christoper '90 (SJ) San Jose, CA Santa Teresa.
Bennett, Donald T. '67 (RVC) Hicksville, NY St. Ignatius Loyola.
Bennett, John F. '71 (RVC) Baldwin, NY St. Christopher; Co–Chaplains of the Nassau County Firemen's Association; Nassau County, Fire Chiefs, Council of; Senate of Priests (Presbyteral Council/College of Consultors).
Bennett, John (RVC) Rockville Centre Deanery; Priests' Personnel Policy Board.
Bennett, Joseph R. '66 (CHI) South Holland, IL Holy Ghost.
Bennett, Joseph T. *s.j.* '57 (BO)[E] Dorchester, MA Boston College High School & Jesuit Community.
Bennett, Melvin J. '69 (LFT) Crawfordsville, IN St. Bernard; Members.
Bennett, Melvin (LFT) Associate Judges.
Bennett, Michael X. '71 (HBG) On Duty Outside the Diocese.
Bennett, Noel I. '59 (MIA) In Res Retired.
Bennett, Norman S. *c.ss.r.* '71 (BRK) Brooklyn, NY Our Lady of Perpetual Help Basilica.
Bennett, Norman (BRK)[U] Chinese Apostolate–Brooklyn.
Bennett, Richard '72 (JOL) Naperville, IL Holy Spirit Catholic Community.
Bennett, Richard *c.ss.r.* (BO) Roxbury, MA Our Lady of Perpetual Help.
Bennett, Richard (JOL) Deans.
Bennett, Rolland *o.m.i.* '61 (PMB) Riviera Beach, FL St. Francis of Assisi.
Bennett, Thomas F. '68 (HRT) Washington Depot, CT Our Lady of Perpetual Help.
Bennett, Thomas M. '57 (COL) Columbus, OH Immaculate Conception; [C] Columbus, OH St. Charles Preparatory School.
Bennington, J. Clement '45 (PH) Retired.
Beno, Brian M. '76 (MIL) Special Assignment; Milwaukee, WI Congregation of the Blessed Trinity.
Beno, Joseph '57 (P) Retired.
Benoit, Adrian J. '65 (SPR) Granby, MA Immaculate Heart of Mary.
Benoit, Adrian (SPR) Building Commission.
Benoit, Bryan *s.c.j.* '93 (MIL)[O] Dittmer, MO.
Benoit, Charles J. *o.s.b.* '01 (NO)[P] St. Benedict, LA St. Joseph Abbey.
Benoit, Charles *o.s.b.* '01 (NO)[A] St. Benedict, LA St. Joseph Seminary College.
Benoit, Lloyd F. '90 (LAF) Kaplan, LA Our Lady of the Holy Rosary.
Benoit, Louis '79 (RIC) Clifton Forge, VA St. Joseph; Covington, VA Sacred Heart.
Benoit, Raymond P. '89 (BO) Dorchester, MA St. Margaret; Boston, MA Boston Medical Center.
Benoit, Ronald H. '55 (BUR) Richmond, VT Our Lady of the Holy Rosary.
Benoit, Vincent *o.p.* (SB) In. Res..
Benone, Jose (BO) East Boston, MA St. Mary, Star of the Sea.
Benonis, Richard R. '58 (PH) On Duty Outside the Archdiocese.
Benonis, Richard '52 (PH) Retired.
Benonis, William J. '52 (PH) Retired.
Benonis, William '52 (PH) Ambler, PA St. Joseph.
Bensman, Gerald E. '64 (CIN) Sidney, OH Holy Angels; Vicarri Foranei (Deans).
Bensman, John L. '56 (CIN) Chickasaw, OH Most Precious Blood; Chickasaw, OH St. Sebastian.
Benson, Gerard M. '42 (VEN)[G] Nokomis, FL Carmel at Mission Valley.
Benson, Gerard *o.carm.* (VEN) Divorced and Separated Ministry.
Benson, Joseph A. '84 (NO) New Orleans, LA Blessed Francis Xavier Seelos.
Benson, Richard B. *c.m.* (LA) Members.
Benson, Richard *c.m.* '78 (LA)[A] Camarillo, CA St. John's Seminary.
Bentivegna, Salvatore *o.s.j.* '63 (SCR)[B] Pittston, PA St. Joseph's Oblate Seminary.
Bentley, David '75 (ALB) Office of Administrative Advocate.
Benton, James '73 (LIN) Wallace, NE St. Mary's.
Bentz, John B. '66 (COL) Marysville, OH Our Lady of Lourdes; Columbus, OH.
Bentz, John Barry (COL) Vicariate 8: Marion.
Benusa, Jeffrey '03 (HEL) Anaconda, MT Anaconda Catholic Community.
Benwell, William (MET) College of Consultors.
Benwell, William (MET) Canonical Staff.
Benwell, William (MET) Vicars General.
Benwell, William (MET) Episcopal Council.
Benwell, William (MET) Moderator.
Benya, Edward G. *s.j.* '84 (FgM).
Benya, Edward G. *s.j.* '84 (NO).
Benz, David H. '75 (PH)[P] Lansdowne, PA St. Philomena.
Benz, Gary L. (BIS) Presbyteral Council.
Benz, Gary '99 (BIS) Flasher, ND St. Lawrence.
Benz, Gary '99 (BIS) Flasher, ND St. Theresa the Child Jesus.
Benz, Gary '99 (BIS) Flasher, ND St. Gertrude.
Benz, James J. '74 (STL) Richmond Heights, MO Little Flower, St. Teresa of the Infant Jesus.
Benz, Thomas G. *s.j.* (NY)[F] New York, NY Fordham Preparatory School; [EE] Jesuit Community, Kohlmann Hall.
Benzinger, Oscar L. *s.j.* '67 (MIL)[O] Aberdeen, SD Presentation Heights.
Benzmiller, James T. '99 (LC) Chippewa Falls, WI Notre Dame.
Benzoni, Martin R. *o.praem.* '81 (ORG)[I] Silverado, CA Norbertine Fathers of Orange Inc..
Benzoni, Martin *o.praem* '81 (ORG) Costa Mesa, CA St. John the Baptist.
Beof, Marlon *o.a.r.* '97 (NY)[B] Suffern, NY Tagaste Monastery.
Beran, Mark T. '02 (OM) Omaha, NE St. Cecilia's Cathedral.
Berard, Aram J. *s.j.* '66 (BO)[V] Boston The Society of Jesus of New England–Provincial Offices.
Berard, Aram *s.j.* '66 (ALN) Reading, PA St. Paul.
Berardi, Ferdinando D. '77 (NY) New Rochelle, NY Holy Family; [II] New York, NY Catholic Medical Mission Board, Inc..
Berardi, James J. '59 (CLV) Akron, OH Annunciation; Akron City Hospital.
Berardi, Thomas F. '76 (ALB) Cobleskill, NY St. Vincent de Paul; [B] Albany, NY Maria College; [Q] Cobleskill, NY State University of New York College of Agricultural & Technology at Cobleskill.
Berardi, Thomas (ALB) Advocates; Campus Ministry; Ministry to Priests.
Berardi, Thomas (ALB) Deans.
Berardi, Thomas (ALB) Advocates; Campus Ministry; Ministry to Priests.
Berbena, Christopher '80 (OAK) Walnut Creek, CA St. John Vianney.
Berberian, David V. (ALB) Bishop's Delegate for Marriage Dispensations.
Berberian, David '74 (ALB) Albany, NY St. Margaret Mary.
Berberian, David '74 (ALB) Special Assignment.
Berberian, David (ALB) Judges.
Berberian, David (ALB) Administrative Review Board (Due Process).
Berberich, Thomas E. '59 (HRT) Kent, CT Sacred Heart.
Berbig, Steven A. '87 (RVC) Huntington, NY St. Patrick's.
Berchmans, Britto '81 (CHI) Barrington, IL St. Anne.
Berchmanz, Anthony '67 (NEW) Military Chaplains.
Bercier, Barry *a.a.* '85 (WOR)[O] Worcester, MA Assumptionists of Assumption College.
Bercik, G. Michael *o.f.m.* '79 (BO) Marlborough, MA St. Ann.
Berding, Richard P. '84 (L) Louisville, KY St. Luke.
Berdis, Donald E. '63 (E) Farrell, PA Our Lady of Fatima.
Berdowicz, Wieslaw *s.ch.* (CHI) Chicago, IL Holy Trinity Mission.
Berdugo, Hernan '83 (SJN) Carolina, PR Inmaculada Concepcion.
Berean, Christopher H. '87 (NY) Phoenicia, NY St. Francis de Sales.
Bereda, Stanislaw J. '65 (GAY) Posen, MI St. Casimir.
Berendt, George *p.i.m.e.* '74 (DET)[K] Detroit, MI P.I.M.E. Motherhouse in Detroit.
Berendt, Peter *c.p.* '57 (GAL)[S] Houston, TX Holy Name Retreat Center.
Berendt, Peter *c.p.* '57 (GAL)[Q] Houston, TX Congregation of the Passion, Holy Name Retreat Center.
Berens, Cyprian *o.f.m.* '51 (CIN)[L] Cincinnati, OH Archbishop Leibold Home for the Aged.
Beres, Kevin J. (ARL) Springfield, VA St. Bernadette's; Notaries.
Beretta, J. Christian *o.s.f.s* '97 (VEN)[A] Fort Myers, FL Bishop Verot High School; [G] Fort Myers, FL Oblates of St. Francis de Sales; [K] Fort Myers, FL The Bishop Verot High School Foundation.
Bereza, Stepan '93 (STF) New Britain, CT St. Josaphat.
Berg, Blaise R. (SAC) Vice Chancellor and Secretary to the Bishop; Ecumenical & Interreligious Affairs.
Berg, Blaise (SAC) Sacramento, CA St. Joseph's.
Berg, Daniel J. (BIS) Crosby, ND St. Patrick.
Berg, Daniel (BIS) Priests' Benefit Association.
Berg, Donald M. '47 (LC) Edgar, WI St. John the Baptist Retired.
Berg, John *f.s.s.p.* '97 (SCR)[M] Indianapolis, IN Holy Rosary Church.
Berg, John *f.s.s.p.* '97 (SAC) Sacramento, CA St. Stephen the First Martyr Church.
Berg, John *f.s.s.p.* (SAC) "Ecclesia Dei" Community (Latin Mass).
Berg, Paul '48 (DET) Retired.
Berg, Peter M. '71 (OG) Long Lake, NY St. Henry; Newcomb, NY St. Therese.

Berg, Ralph B. *c.m.f.* '64 (LA) San Gabriel, CA San Gabriel.
Berg, Richard F. *c.s.c.* '63 (P)[O] Portland, OR Macdonald Center and Residence; [Q] Portland, OR St. Joseph the Worker Job Fund.
Berg, Richard V. '52 (STP) Retired.
Berg, Richard *c.s.c.* '63 (P)[L] Portland, OR Holy Cross Fathers & Brothers, C.S.C. – University of Portland.
Berg, Richard *c.s.c.* '63 (P).
Berg, Stephen '99 (FWT)[B] Henrietta, TX St. Joseph.
Berg, Stephen '99 (FWT) Henrietta, TX St. William.
Berg, Stephen '99 (FWT) Henrietta, TX St. Jerome.
Berg, Stephen '99 (FWT) Henrietta, TX St. Mary.
Berg, Theodore S. '61 (BUF) Retired.
Berg, Timothy '79 (SFE) On Duty Outside the Archdiocese.
Bergamo, John A. '65 (SCR) East Stroudsburg, PA St. Matthew's; [D] East Stroudsburg, PA Notre Dame Junior/Senior High School; Defenders of the Bond; Promoter of Justice; Auditors; Presbyteral Council.
Bergbower, Daniel J. '88 (SFD) Effingham, IL Sacred Heart; Air National Guard Chaplains.
Bergbower, Daniel (SFD) Commission for Buildings and Property.
Bergedick, Charles T. *s.m.* '57 (CIN) Dayton, OH Emmanuel; [M] Dayton, OH Marianist Community.
Bergen, William J. *s.j.* '55 (NY) New York, NY St. Ignatius Loyola; [EE] New York, NY St. Ignatius Loyola Residence.
Berger, Bernard M. '64 (GI) Burwell, NE Sacred Heart; Nenzel, NE St. Nicholas; Personnel Board.
Berger, John G. '67 (NU) St. Peter Regional Treatment Center; [F] St. Peter, MN St. Peter Regional Treatment Center; Vice–Chancellor; Judicial Vicar (Officialis); Priests' Council; Committee for Continuing Education of Clergy; College of Consultors.
Berger, John G. '67 (NU) Lafayette, MN St. Gregory the Great.
Berger, John G. '67 (NU) St. Peter Regional Treatment Center; [F] St. Peter, MN St. Peter Regional Treatment Center; Vice–Chancellor; Judicial Vicar (Officialis); Priests' Council; Committee for Continuing Education of Clergy; College of Consultors.
Berger, John G. '67 (NU) Lafayette, MN St. George.
Berger, John '98 (HON) Honolulu, HI Cathedral of Our Lady of Peace.
Berger, John (HON) Diocesan Liturgical Commission.
Berger, John (HON) Senior Priests' Committee.
Berger, Lawrence B. '66 (LC) La Crosse, WI Holy Trinity.
Berger, Robert F. '62 (HBG) Myerstown, PA Mary, Gate of Heaven.
Bergeron, Albert G. '62 (HT) Retired.
Bergeron, C. Paul '81 (LAF) Retired.
Bergeron, Marc H. '70 (FR) Fall River, MA St. Anne's; [H] Fall River, MA St. John Vianney House; Procurator–Advocates; Ecumenical Officer.
Bergeron, Michael '96 (HT) Schriever, LA St. Bridget.
Bergeron, Michael '96 (HT) Schriever, LA St. Lawrence; [E] Thibodaux, LA Marian Servants of the Word.
Bergeron, Robert E. '52 (BO) Senior Priests Retired.
Bergeur, John X. '45 (NEW) Retired.
Bergewisch, Fred F. *s.j.* '55 (CHI)[C] Chicago, IL Jesuit Community at Loyola University Chicago.
Berggreen, Robert H. '64 (BR) Baton Rouge, LA St. Agnes; Chancellor; College of Consultors; Diocesan Corporation (The Roman Catholic Church of the Diocese of Baton Rouge); Presbyteral Council.
Berghammer, Robert J. '49 (MIL) Retired.
Berghout, Paul A. '96 (ARL) On Leave of Absence.
Bergin, Clifford E. '53 (CHI) Retired.
Bergin, James *s.v.d.* '69 (CHI)[N] Techny, IL Divine Word Novitiate.
Bergin, James *s.v.d.* '69 (CHI)[B] Techny, IL Divine Word Residence.
Bergin, John J. *s.j.* '67 (STL)[O] St. Louis, MO De Smet Jesuit High School Community.
Bergin, John J. *s.v.d.* '67 (BO)[V] Duxbury, MA Society of the Divine Word.
Bergin, Paschal '57 (CC) On Duty Outside the Diocese.
Bergin, Paschal '57 (SAT) Runge, TX St. Anthony's.
Bergin, Robert D. '62 (HRT) Hartford, CT Cathedral of St. Joseph; Special and other Archdiocesan Assignment; [N] West Hartford, CT Mercyknoll, Incorporated; Catholic Deaf Apostolate.
Bergin, Thomas J. '62 (ORL) New Smyrna Beach, FL Our Lady Star of the Sea.
Bergin, Thomas J. (NY) Archdiocesan Consultors.
Bergin, Thomas '61 (NY) Bronx, NY St. Raymond.
Bergkamp, Roger *o.m.i.* '64 (DUL) International Falls, MN St. Thomas Aquinas.
Bergkamp, Roger *o.m.i.* '64 (DUL) Littlefork, MN St. Columban.
Bergman, Charles B. '58 (PIT)[N] Pittsburgh, PA St. John Vianney Manor.
Bergman, Richard '55 (DM) Retired.
Bergman, Richard (DM) Diocesan Consultors.
Bergman, Robert '71 (KCK) Shawnee, KS St. Joseph's.
Bergner, David J. *s.d.s.* '76 (WDC)[B] Silver Spring, MD Salvatorian Community; Navy Reserve Chaplains.
Bergner, David J. *s.d.s.* '76 (RIC)[K] Richmond, VA Commonwealth Catholic Charities; Commonwealth Catholic Charities.
Bergner, David J. *s.d.s.* '76 (WDC)[B] Silver Spring, MD Salvatorian Community; Navy Reserve Chaplains.
Bergner, David *s.d.s.* '76 (MIL)[O] Silver Spring, MD.
Bergquist, Patrick D. '90 (FBK) Fairbanks, AK St. Raphael's.
Bergquist, Patrick (FBK) Consultors.
Bergquist, Patrick (FBK) Presbyteral Council.
Bergs, David J '76 (LSC) Carrizozo, NM St. Rita.
Bergs, David (LSC) Presbyteral Council.
Bergs, David (LSC) Finance Council.
Bergs, David (LSC) Priestly Life and Ministry Committee.
Bergs, David (LSC) Defenders of the Bond.
Bergs, David (LSC) Priests Retirement Fund Committee.
Bergs, David (LSC) Clergy Personnel Board.
Bergs, David (LSC) Vicars.
Bergsbaken, Dennis L. (GB) Wrightstown, WI St. Paul; Regional Vicars.
Bergstadt, John P. (GB) Appleton, WI St. Bernard; Pastor Consultors.
Bergstadt, John (GB) Diocesan Consultors.
Berinti, Benjamin A. *c.pp.s.* '85 (ORL) Longwood, FL Church of the Nativity.
Beristain, Juan M. '71 (SJN) Levittown, PR Santisima Trinidad.
Berkery, Patrick J. '56 (HRT) Ansonia, CT St. Anthony's.
Berkey, William G. '02 (GBG) Lower Burrell, PA St. Margaret Mary; New Kensington, PA Mt. St. Peter.
Berkhout, Frans J. '87 (ALN) Whitehall, PA Holy Trinity; [C] Allentown, PA Allentown Central Catholic High School; Elected Members; Serra Club of Allentown.
Berko, Abraham A. '88 (NY) Amenia, NY Immaculate Conception.
Berland, Mark '74 (SAL) Park, KS Sacred Heart.
Berland, Mark '74 (SAL) Park, KS St. Agnes.
Berling, Alban *o.s.b.* '45 (IND)[K] St. Meinrad, IN St. Meinrad Archabbey.
Berlo, Benedict *c.p.* '57 (SCR)[M] Clarks Summit, PA St. Gabriel's Convent.
Bermudez, Alberto '86 (NO) Kenner, LA St. Jerome.
Bermudez, Jose A. '80 (SPR) Holyoke, MA Our Lady of Guadalupe.
Berna, Francis *o.f.m.* '80 (PH)[AA] Philadelphia, PA St. Pius X Friary.
Bernabe, Humberto '75 (LA) North Hills, CA Our Lady of Peace.
Bernacki, Edward *c.s.sp.* '45 (SB)[E] Hemet, CA Holy Ghost Fathers.
Bernacki, William J. *o.p.* '56 (CHI)[D] Oak Park, IL Fenwick High School; [N] River Forest, IL St. Thomas Aquinas Priory.
Bernadicou, Paul *s.j.* '81 (LA)[C] Los Angeles, CA Jesuit Community.
Bernadicou, Paul *s.j.* '81 (LA)[C] Los Angeles, CA Jesuit Community.
Bernal, Edward '87 (SAT) San Antonio, TX St. Benedict.
Bernans, Arvids '64 (COL) Retired.
Bernard, Andre '73 (SR) Retired.
Bernard, Donald *o.m.i.* '64 (LA) San Fernando, CA Santa Rosa.
Bernard, George C. *c.s.c.* '49 (P)[L] Portland, OR Holy Cross Fathers & Brothers, C.S.C. – University of Portland.
Bernard, Larry *o.f.m.* '66 (GLP) Pueblo of Acoma, NM San Esteban, Acoma Catholic Indian Mission.
Bernardi, Peter J. *s.j.* '87 (NO)[C] New Orleans, LA Loyola University New Orleans.
Bernardi, Peter J. *s.j.* '87 (DET)[K] Detroit Jesuit Provincial Office–Detroit Province of the Society of Jesus.
Bernardino, Eduardo '91 (SD) Escondido, CA Church of the Resurrection.
Bernardo, Emilio A. '42 (LA) Retired.
Bernardo, Joseph C. '03 (LIN) Nebraska City, NE St. Mary's; Lincoln, NE St. Mary; Advocates.
Bernardy, Patrick '60 (GB) Retired.
Bernas, Casimir *o.c.s.o.* '58 (SLC)[F] Huntsville, UT Abbey of Our Lady of the Holy Trinity of the Order of Cistercians.
Bernas, Eugene '66 (NEW) Newark, NJ Our Lady of Mt. Carmel.
Bernas, Thomas A. '94 (CHI) Chicago, IL St. Richard.
Bernasconi, Gino '50 (VIC) Retired.
Bernasconi, Gino '50 (VIC)[K] San Antonio, TX Padua Place.
Bernatonis, John F. '45 (BO) Senior Priests Retired.
Bernauer, Edmund G. '61 (NEW) Short Hills, NJ St. Rose of Lima; [D] Summit, NJ The Oratory Catholic Preparatory School; Berkeley Heights, NJ Church of the Little Flower Retired.
Bernauer, James W. *s.j.* '75 (New York)[V] Newton, MA The Jesuit Community at Boston College.
Bernauer, James '52 (CR) Diocesan Consultors; Priests' Council Retired.
Bernbrock, John *s.j.* '56 (PHX) Scottsdale, AZ Our Lady of Perpetual Help.
Berndt, Rudolph C. '76 (DAV) Veteran's Administration Hospital; [M] Iowa City, IA O'Keefe Hall; [J] Iowa City, IA Mercy Hospital.
Berndt, Wayne *o.f.m.cap.* '83 (FgM).
Bernelli, Matthew '64 (BGP) Bridgeport, CT St. Mary.
Bernelli, Matthew (BGP) Vicariate IV (East Bridgeport, Stratford, Trumbull, Monroe, Shelton).
Bernelli, Matthew (BGP) Presbyteral Council.
Berner, Albert J. '68 (NEW)[Q] Upper Montclair, NJ Montclair State University; West Essex Deanery 15.
Berner, Francis '70 (NO) On Medical Leave of Absence.
Berner, Michael '86 (DM) Earling, IA St. Joseph.
Berner, Michael '86 (DM) Defiance, IA St. Peter.
Bernhardt, Gary *o.f.m.* '99 (SUP) Bayfield, WI Holy Family.
Bernhardt, Gary *o.f.m.* '99 (SUP) Bayfield, WI St. Francis.
Bernhardt, Gary *o.f.m.* '99 (SUP) Bayfield, WI St. Joseph.
Bernhardt, Gary *o.f.m.* '99 (SUP) Washburn, WI St. Louis.
Bernhardt, Gary *o.f.m.* '99 (SUP) Washburn, WI St. Ann.
Bernier, Lawrence J. '63 (SPR) Retired.
Bernier, Michael F. '03 (SPR) Chicopee, MA St. Rose de Lima.
Bernier, Paul *s.s.s.* '64 (CLV).
Bernier, Paul (FR)[O] South Yarmouth, MA St. Pius Tenth.
Bernier, Philip J. *o.f.m.cap.* '01 (PIT) Rochester, PA St. Cecilia; [N] Rochester, PA St. Cecilia Friary.
Berning, James C. '91 (WIN) Madelia, MN St. Mary; St. James, MN St. James; Madelia, MN St. Katherine.
Berning, James *s.d.b.* '93 (NO) Washington, DC Nativity.
Bernotas, Robert J. '83 (LFT) Kentland, IN St. Joseph; Clergy Relief Association.
Bernott, Ernest J. '43 (GR) Muskegon, MI St. Mary's.
Berns, Eric R. '96 (LC) Cashton, WI Sacred Heart of Jesus; Cashton, WI St. Augustine of Hippo; Cashton, WI Nativity of the Blessed Virgin Mary; Cashton, WI St. John the Baptist.
Berny, Paul W. '72 (ATL) Marietta, GA St. Joseph; AACCW.
Berran, Donald M. '60 (BRK) South Ozone Park, NY Our Lady of Perpetual Help.
Berret, Anthony J. *s.j.* '71 (PH)[C] Jesuit Fathers; [AA] Philadelphia, PA St. Alphonsus House.
Berrigan, Daniel J. *s.j.* '52 (NY)[EE] New York, NY West Side Jesuit Community.
Berrio, Augusto *s.j.* '63 (SD) San Diego, CA Our Lady of Guadalupe.
Berrios, Adan Luis Marrero '97 (CGS)[C] Aibonito, PR Casa Salesiana de Retiros.
Berrios, Angel '65 (PCE) Santa Isabel, PR St. James.
Berrios, George E. '89 (TR) Long Branch, NJ St. John the Baptist.
Berrios, Israel '96 (CGS) Aibonito, PR Church of St. Joseph.
Berrios, Israel (CGS) Diocesan Consultors.
Berrios, Israel (CGS) Priests Senate.
Berrios, Raul Morales '88 (CGS) Cidra, PR Nuestra Senora del Carmen.
Berry, Bernard J. *s.j.* '00 (STL)[C] Saint Louis University.
Berry, Dennis *s.t.* '74 (MOB) Fort Mitchell, AL St. Joseph.
Berry, Dennis *s.t.* '74 (MOB)[K] Hurtsboro, AL John XXIII Center.
Berry, James A. '75 (HON) Kihei, HI St. Theresa.
Berry, James (HON) Clergy Personnel Board.
Berry, James (HON) Diocesan Planning and Building Commission.
Berry, James (HON) College of Consultors.
Berry, James (HON) Vicars Forane.
Berry, Thomas *c.p.* '42 (MET)[H] Greensboro, NC.
Berry, William F. '66 (WDC) College Park, MD Holy Redeemer.
Berryman, Harold L. '58 (GB) Appleton, WI St. Bernadette.
Berschied, Paul L. '86 (COV) Independence, KY St. Cecilia; Defenders of the Bond.
Bertasius, Anthony '37 (ELP) Retired.
Bertasius, Anthony (PAT) Retired.
Bertelli, Ameilio J. '59 (BO) Senior Priests Retired.
Bertels, George '55 (KCK) Topeka, KS Sacred Heart.
Bertels, George (KCK) Pro–Synodal Judges.
Bertels, George (KCK) Regional Pastoral Leaders.
Bertels, Henry J. *s.j.* '62 (NY)[B] Bronx, NY Ciszek Hall.
Bertha, Joseph '80 (PSC) Williamsville, NY St. Stephen's.
Bertha, Joseph (PSC) Evangelization.
Bertha, Joseph (PSC) Retirement Plan Board.
Berthelette, Ernest H. '74 (PRO) On Duty Outside the Diocese; Air Force Chaplains.
Berthiaume, Eugene F. '58 (WOR) Retired.
Berthiaume, Gary '68 (CLV) Administrative Leave.

Bertin, Gerard L. '89 (MAN) Keene, NH St. Margaret Mary; Cheshire County House of Corrections.
Bertini, Angelo '73 (AUS) Waco, TX St. Mary of the Assumption.
Bertino, Dominic V. '75 (GRY) Hobart, IN St. Bridget; Deans; Bishop's Council of Priests; Consultors; Priests' Personnel Board.
Bertke, Erwin J. '43 (CIN) Ex Officio Members; Consultors Retired.
Bertocchi, Luigi *o.s.b.* '70 (SCL)[I] Sant' Anselmo.
Bertogli, John '77 (DM) Council Bluffs, IA St. Patrick.
Bertolacci, Caesar *m.c.* '96 (DET)[T] Plymouth, MI Miles Christi.
Bertolotti, David '91 (BRK) Brooklyn, NY St. Malachy's.
Bertone, Thomas C. *c.s.c.* '81 (FR)[A] North Easton, MA Holy Cross Fathers Religious.
Bertoni, Albert *s.m.* '79 (RVC)[D] Uniondale, NY Kellenberg Memorial High School.
Bertoniere, Gabriel *o.c.s.o.* '58 (WOR)[A] Spencer, MA St. Joseph's Abbey School of Theology and Institute of Monastic Studies; [O] Spencer, MA St. Joseph's Abbey.
Bertrand, Aloysius J. '43 (PBL) Retired.
Bertrand, Armand J. '89 (SC) Cherokee, IA Immaculate Conception; Co–Directors:.
Bertrand, Conley '59 (LAF)[M] Lafayette, LA Come Lord Jesus! Inc..
Bertrand, Emmanuel *o.p.* '58 (COL) Zanesville, OH St. Thomas Aquinas.
Bertrand, Evarist *o.f.m.cap.* '63 (FgM).
Bertrand, Jerry (SC) Marcus, IA Holy Name.
Bertrand, Joseph *c.ss.r.* '55 (STV) Frederiksted, St. Croix, VI Church of St. Patrick.
Bertrand, Richard D. *s.j.* '79 (PRT) Portland, ME Sacred Heart/St. Dominic.
Bertrand, Richard D. *s.j.* '79 (BO)[V] Boston The Society of Jesus of New England–Provincial Offices.
Bertrand, Victor E. *c.s.v.* '62 (LR) Little Rock, AR John L. McClellan Memorial Hospital, VA Medical Center.
Bertrand, Victor E. '62 (CHI)[N] North Little Rock, AR.
Bertrand, Victor *c.s.v.* '62 (LR) North Little Rock, AR Fort Roots VA Medical Center.
Bertrand, Vincent E. '87 (SPC) Special Assignment; Adjutant Judicial Vicars.
Bertsche, Conrad J. '45 (BEL) Retired.
Berube, Paul W. '60 (BO) Newburyport, MA Immaculate Conception; Senior Priests Retired.
Berube, Richard N. *s.s.e.* '70 (BUR)[E] Colchester, VT Society of St. Edmund.
Besanceney, Paul H. *s.j.* '56 (FgM).
Beseau, Steven '95 (KCK) Prairie Village, KS St. Ann's.
Besendorfer, Ralph L. '59 (STA) Callahan, FL Our Lady of Consolation; Judicial Vicar.
Beshara, Ronald N. '71 (SAM) On Duty Outside the Diocese.
Beshara, Ronald '71 (SAM) Greenacres, FL Mary Mother of Light Maronite Mission.
Beshara, Ronald (PMB) Defenders of the Bond.
Beshara, Ronald (SAM) Office of Outreach.
Beshoner, Sebastian *o.s.b.* '55 (LR)[A] Subiaco, AR Subiaco Monastery.
Besinga, Dino J. (MO) Army Chaplains.
Besse, Joseph A. '45 (PRO) Retired.
Bessellieu, Mel '97 (FWT) Pilot Point, TX St. Thomas Aquinas.
Bessellieu, Mel (FWT) Presbyteral Council and Consultors.
Bessert, James W. '80 (SAG)[I] Midland, MI The James Cardinal Hickey Educational Endowment Fund for St. Brigid Catholic School.
Bessert, James '80 (SAG) Midland, MI St. Brigid.
Best, Richard '61 (JOL) Absent on Sick Leave.
Best, Russell W. '86 (BO) Roxbury, MA St. John–St. Hugh.
Bester, Robert '79 (ANC) Kodiak, AK St. Mary's of Kodiak and the Islands.
Bester, Robert '79 (CR) On Duty Outside the Diocese Retired.
Bestler, Joseph L. (GB) Luxemburg, WI St. Louis.
Bestler, Joseph '57 (GB) Retired.
Beston, William J. *c.s.c.* '48 (FTW)[I] Notre Dame, IN Holy Cross House.
Betancourt Ramirez, Jorge '03 (SJN) Awaiting Assignment.
Betancur, Nelson '75 (PAT) Paterson, NJ St. George.
Betancurt, Rigoberto '83 (SHP) Bossier City, LA Christ the King.
Betancurt, Rigoberto (SHP) Hispanic Ministry.
Bethancourt, Michael A. '60 (MRY) Special Assignment; Salinas, CA Madonna Del Sasso.
Betley, Michael E. (GB) Niagara, WI Sacred Heart; Florence, WI Immaculate Conception; Niagara, WI St. Anthony; Pembine, WI St. Margaret.
Betley, Michael (GB) Regional Vicars.
Betoni, John P. *o.s.a.* '62 (PH) Philadelphia, PA Our Lady of Consolation.
Betoni, John P. *o.s.a.* '62 (PH)[C] Villanova University; [AA] Villanova, PA St. Thomas Monastery.
Betrand, Conley '59 (LAF) Retired.
Betrozoff, Larry '73 (MRY) Tres Pinos, CA Retired.
Betschart, Joseph '99 (P) Ashland, OR Our Lady of the Mountain; [P] Ashland, OR Southern Oregon University (Ashland).
Bettencourt, Francisco Xavier '84 (SJ) San Jose, CA Five Wounds Portuguese National Church.
Bettendorf, James B. '59 (LAN) Flint, MI St. Leo the Great; [M] Flint, MI St. Leo the Great Church.
Betters, John D. '03 (CLV) Mentor, OH St. John Vianney.
Betti, Frederick G. *s.j.* '90 (BUF)[O] Buffalo, NY Canisius Jesuit Community.
Betti, Mark J. '96 (R) Roanoke Rapids, NC St. John the Baptist; Priests' Council.
Bettinger, Mark T. '93 (PBL) Delta, CO St. Michael; Ecclesiastical Notaries.
Bettley, Emil '83 (NY) Nyack, NY St. Ann.
Betts, David R. '98 (SCR) Dushore, PA St. Basil's.
Betts, John C. '68 (P) Albany, OR Our Lady of Perpetual Help.
Betz, James F. '71 (CAM) Egg Harbor City, NJ St. Nicholas; Advocates; Army Reserve Chaplains.
Betz, James S. '89 (WDC) Bowie, MD Ascension.
Betz, James (CAM) Vicars Forane, Presbyteral Council, Censor Librorum, Diocesan Historian.
Betz, Kenneth '65 (EVN) Haubstadt, IN St. James.
Betz, Robert '73 (MIL) South Milwaukee, WI Divine Mercy.
Betz, Thomas *o.f.m.cap.* '91 (PH) Philadelphia, PA; Chinese Apostolate.
Betzen, James G. *c.pp.s.* '81 (KC) Kansas City, MO Sacred Heart–Guadalupe.
Beunen, Emmanuel *o.f.m.* '70 (CLV)[O] Cleveland, OH St. Jude Friary.
Beunen, Emmanuel *o.f.m.* '70 (CLV) Cleveland House of Correction; Warrensville Heights, OH St. Jude.
Beuth, William J. *c.pp.s.* '59 (CIN).
Beuther, Richard J. '96 (BRK)[M] Brooklyn, NY SS. Peter and Paul's.
Beutner, Edward F. '65 (SUP) On Leave.
Beuzer, Vincent *s.j.* '58 (ANC)[G] Anchorage, AK Anchorage Jesuit Community.
Bevacqua, James '03 (LA) San Pedro, CA Holy Trinity.
Bevan, James J. '75 (LAV) Las Vegas, NV St. Joseph, Husband of Mary.
Bevan, James (LAV) Presbyteral Council for the Diocese of Las Vegas.
Bevan, James (LAV) Priests' Personnel Board.
Bevan, Norman E. *c.s.sp.* '63 (PIT) Priest Council.
Bevan, Norman E. *c.s.sp.* '63 (PH)[AA] Bensalem, PA Congregation of the Holy Ghost.
Bevan, Thomas R. '63 (BAL) Cumberland, MD St. Patrick.
Bevan, Thomas (BAL) Priests' Council.
Bevans, Stephen B. *s.v.d.* '71 (CHI)[B] Chicago, IL Edward McGuinn, S.V.D. Residence; [N] Chicago, IL Divine Word Theologate; [N] Chicago, IL Edward McGuinn House of Studies.
Bevard, Herbert A. '72 (PH) Philadelphia, PA St. Athanasius; College of Consultors; Council of Priests; Pastors Review Board.
Bevenour, Richard F. '57 (DAV) Retired.
Beveridge, John P. '72 (SFD) Collinsville, IL SS. Peter and Paul.
Bevilacqua, Jerome *o.s.a.* '65 (SD)[B] San Diego, CA Austin House.
Bevilacqua, Jerome *o.s.a.* '65 (SD)[H] San Diego, CA.
Bevington, William S. '51 (NSH) Hendersonville, TN Our Lady of the Lake; [L] Hendersonville, TN Legion of Mary; [L] Hendersonville, TN Priests Eucharistic League; Judges.
Bevins, John J. '58 (HRT) Waterbury, CT Immaculate Conception.
Beyer, Gregory *o.f.m.cap.* '62 (DEN)[E] Victoria, KS St. Fidelis Friary.
Beyer, Lawrence A. '96 (DAL) Plano, TX Prince of Peace Retired.
Beyer, Leroy O. '66 (WH) Retired.
Beyer, Richard J. '81 (DAV) On Duty Outside the Diocese.
Beyer, Richard '81 (AUS) Waco, TX V.A. Hospital.
Beyer, Richard '81 (AUS) Temple, TX V.A. Hospital.
Beyette, Paul V. '50 (OG) Retired.
Bez–Chabebe, Jorge '50 (MIA) Hialeah, FL San Lazaro.
Bezunartea, Herman O. '58 (FRS) Retired.
Bezuszka, Stanley J. *s.j.* '46 (BO)[V] Newton, MA The Jesuit Community at Boston College.
Bhia Wea, Raymundus *s.v.d.* '82 (ORG)[G] Fullerton, CA St. Jude Medical Center.
Biagi, Vincent L. *s.j.* '78 (NY)[F] New York, NY Regis High School; [EE] New York, NY St. Ignatius Loyola Residence.
Biain, Jose *o.f.m.* '48 (MIA)[H] Miami, FL Franciscan Fathers' Residence.
Biain, Jose *o.f.m.* (MIA) Judges.
Biala, Romeo B. (SEA) Navy Chaplains.
Bialecki, Michael *o.s.a.* (PH)[C] Radnor, PA Cabrini College.
Bialkowski, David W. '88 (BUF) Legion of Mary; Cheektowaga, NY St. John Gualbert.
Bialkowski, Henry A. '49 (NOR) Retired.
Bialkowski, Jacek '96 (SCR) Glen Lyon, PA Corpus Christi.
Bialoncik, Emmanuel *o.f.m.* '73 (BWN) Elsa, TX Sacred Heart.
Bialoncik, Emmanuel *o.f.m.* (BWN) Presbyteral Council.
Bialoncik, Emmanuel *o.f.m.* (BWN) Deans.
Biancalana, Angelo G. *m.c.c.j.* '58 (LA)[CC] Covina, CA Comboni Mission Center.
Bianchi, Paul '64 (DM) Portsmouth, IA St. Mary.
Bianchi, Paul (DM) Propagation of the Faith.
Bianchi, Raymond S. '52 (TR) Retired.
Bianco, Anthony M. *c.r.s.p.* '51 (ALN)[K] Bethlehem, PA The Barnabite Fathers Barnabite Spiritual Center.
Biase, Justin A. *o.f.m.conv.* '70 (SY) Syracuse, NY Assumption B.V.M.; Elected; [Q] Syracuse, NY Friary of Francis, Brother of Peace Conventual Franciscan Friars.
Biasiatto, Richard P. *o.f.m.* '64 (NEW) Elmwood Park, NJ St. Leo's.
Biasiol, Virgilio *o.f.m.* '42 (LA)[Q] Santa Barbara, CA Franciscan Friary, Order of Friars Minor (Old Mission).
Bibeault, Norbert P. *c.s.v.* '56 (LAV)[A] Las Vegas, NV Bishop Gorman High School; [D] Las Vegas, NV Clerics of St. Viator Retirement Home.
Biber, J. Morton '85 (RIC) Powhatan, VA St. John Neumann; [G] Powhatan, VA St. John Neumann Family Life Center.
Bich, Tran Ngoc *c.ss.r.* '52 (LA)[Q] Baldwin Park, CA Vietnamese Redemptorist Mission.
Bichl, William M. *s.j.* '67 (CLV)[B] University Heights, OH John Carroll University; [B] Cleveland, OH John Carroll University.
Bickel, Timothy C. '92 (MIL) Butler, WI St. Agnes.
Bickett, Tony '83 (OWN) St. Romuald.
Bickett, Tony (OWN) Diocesan Liturgical Committee.
Bico, Anthony '93 (NEW) Newark, NJ Essex County Juvenile Detention Center.
Bico, Anthony '93 (NEW) Newark, NJ Cura (Community United to Rehabilitate Addicts).
Bico, Anthony '93 (NEW) Newark, NJ Our Lady of Fatima.
Bico, Anthony (NEW) Members; Priestly Vocation Board; Chaplains; Newark, NJ Essex County Juvenile Detention Center.
Bicomong, Sergio '79 (TR) On Duty Outside the Diocese.
Bicomong, Sergio '79 (CAM) Vineland, NJ St. Francis of Assisi.
Bicomong, Sergio (CAM) Fairton, NJ Federal Correctional Institution.
Bicsey, John '55 (E) Retired.
Bicsko, Stephen C. *c.m.* '70 (BRK)[V] Queens Village, NY DePaul Residence.
Bicz, Marian '88 (RVC) Glen Cove, NY St. Patrick's.
Biczak, Arkad '63 (SFE) Albuquerque, NM St. John the Apostle.
Biczak, Arkad (SFE) Mission Office.
Bida, John A. (NY) Hyde Park, NY Regina Coeli; Auditors.
Bida, John (NY) Absent on Sick leave.
Bidawid, Kamal Warda '68 (SPA) Turlock, CA St. Thomas Assyrian–Chaldean Parish; Episcopal Vicar for Assyrian Affairs.
Biddle, Ward *c.p.* '51 (FgM).
Bidinger, Bruce M. *s.j.* '86 (PH)[G] Philadelphia, PA St. Joseph's Preparatory School; [AA] Philadelphia, PA Jesuit Community, Arrupe House.
Bidwill, Joseph E. *o.p.* '55 (STP) Minneapolis, MN St. Albert the Great.
Bie, Paul R. '83 (RVC) West Hempstead, NY St. Thomas, the Apostle.
Biebel, William E. '62 (E) Erie, PA St. Peter Cathedral; Deans; Lake Shore Visitor Advisory Board; Northern Vicariate.
Bieberle, Victor '51 (WCH) Retired.
Biedermann, Arnold '45 (LA) Ventura, CA Sacred Heart.
Biedermann, Arnold '45 (LA) Retired.
Biedermann, Arnold (LA) Defenders of the Bond.
Bieganowski, Ronald R. *s.j.* '72 (MIL)[O] Milwaukee, WI Jesuit Community at Marquette University.
Biegler, Steven '93 (RC) On Special Assignment.
Bielak, Andrew '97 (NY) Mahopac, NY St. John the Evangelist.
Bielanski, Joseph J. '80 (STU) Absent on Leave.
Bielawa, Thomas *s.d.s.* '72 (NSH) Joelton, TN St. Lawrence's.
Bielawa, Thomas *s.d.s.* (NSH) Presbyteral Council and College of Consultors.
Bielby, Donald J. *c.s.c.* '63 (FTW) South Bend, IN St. Patrick.
Bielek, Robert M. '74 (CLV) Cleveland, OH St. Leo the Great.
Bielen, Stephen A. '45 (MET) Hackettstown, NJ Assumption of the Blessed Virgin Mary; [H] Somerset, NJ Maria Regina Residence Retired.
Bielewicz, Harry R. '86 (PIT) Butler, PA St. Paul; Deans and Deaneries.

Bielonko, Joseph '59 (WOR) Dudley, MA St. Andrew Bobola.
Bielskas, Edward J. '41 (GR) Grand Rapids, MI St. John Vianney Retired.
Bieluch, Chester A. '48 (HRT) Retired.
Bien, Danilo C. '85 (AGN) Agana, GU San Juan Bautista.
Bien, Francis P. '58 (BRK)[V] Douglaston, NY Bishop Mugavero Residence.
Bienia, Michael A. '58 (GBG)[G] Greensburg, PA Neumann House Retired.
Bieniek, Stanley (LAR) Laredo, TX Sagrado Corazon de Jesus Mission.
Bien Quang Do, Joseph '64 (SD) El Cajon, CA Our Lady of Grace.
Bienvenu, Kenneth A. '60 (LAF) St. Martinville, LA St. Martin of Tours Retired.
Bienvenu, Paul G. '92 (LAF) Lafayette, LA St. Leo the Great.
Bier, Louis C. '76 (PH) Philadelphia, PA St. John the Baptist.
Biergans, Kent *o.f.m.conv.* '67 (L) Louisville, KY St. Anthony.
Biermann, John G. *s.a.c.* '69 (BAL) Baltimore, MD St. Jude Shrine.
Biernacki, Jacob S. '67 (SPC) Retired.
Biernat, Leon J. '92 (BUF) Vocations; Tonawanda, NY Blessed Sacrament.
Biersack, Thomas E. '81 (MIL) New Munster, WI St. Alphonsus.
Bierschenk, Stephen W. '76 (DAL) McKinney, TX St. Michael.
Biesiada, Louis W. (PAT) Retired.
Biesinger, Robert J. '56 (BUF)[O] Buffalo, NY Sheehan Residence for Priests Retired.
Bietz, Crispin *o.f.m.* '50 (SFE)[J] Santa Fe, NM Discalced Carmelite Monastery.
Biewend, Michael *c.j.* '80 (SAT) San Antonio, TX St. Luke; Air Force Chaplains.
Biffar, Cornelius *ss.cc.* '51 (FR).
Biffar, William *c.ss.r.* '47 (ALB)[L] Saratoga Springs, NY St. John Neumann Residence.
Bigelow, William R. '67 (BUF) Buffalo, NY Holy Family.
Biggane, Edward J. *s.m.a.* '58 (NEW)[N] Tenafly, NJ Society of African Missions, Provincialate, S.M.A. Fathers.
Biggers, Clarence J. *o.c.s.o.* '50 (ATL)[K] Conyers, GA The Monastery of the Holy Spirit.
Biglin, Martin J. '67 (NY) New Rochelle, NY Holy Name of Jesus.
Bignall, Douglas J. '93 (DET) Algonac, MI St. Catherine.
Bihr, Louis J. '68 (PAT) Methadone Maintenance Centers; Special Assignment.
Bihuniak, Michael J. '90 (MET) On Duty Outside the Diocese.
Bijura, Fortunatus '79 (PEO)[O] Champaign, IL St. John's Catholic Student Chapel and Newman Foundation, University of Illinois.
Bijura, Fortunatus '79 (Rulenge, Tanzania) Champaign, IL St. John's Catholic Chapel.
Bik, Michael *o.s.b.* '93 (SCL)[I] Collegeville, MN St. John's Abbey, of the Order of St. Benedict.
Bikoma, Edward J. '51 (EST) Chicago, IL St. Ephrem's Church; Chicago, IL Mart Mariam Parish.
Bilanych, John '40 (PHU) Retired.
Bilinsky, William M. '65 (STN).
Bilinsky, William '65 (NO) New Orleans, LA Memorial Medical Center.
Bill, J. Armand '56 (PRT) Retired.
Bill, Ronald C. '57 (SY) Ecumenical Commission; Fayetteville, NY Immaculate Conception; Army National Guard Chaplains Retired.
Bill, Ronald C. (SY) Elected.
Bill, Thomas *c.s.c.* '55 (P).
Bill, Thomas *c.s.c.* '55 (P)[L] Portland, OR Holy Cross Fathers & Brothers, C.S.C. – University of Portland.
Billac, Christopher A. *s.j.* '65 (GAL)[F] Houston, TX Strake, Jesuit College Preparatory Inc..
Biller, Andrew *s.v.d.* '61 (FgM).
Biller, Andrew *s.v.d.* '61 (STL) St. Louis, MO St. Thomas of Aquin.
Biller, Harold N. '70 (ALT) Johnstown, PA St. Patrick's.
Biller, Harold N. (ALT) Ecumenical Minister.
Billett, Robert *c.m.f.* '57 (LA)[Q] Rancho Dominguez, CA Dominguez Seminary Inc..
Billian, Michael R. '84 (TOL) Toledo, OH Historic Church of St. Patrick; Vicar General; Chancellor; Cabinet; Finance Council; Chancellor.
Billiard, Don *o.f.m.* '83 (SFE)[I] Albuquerque, NM Curia Juan Diego.
Billiard, Don *o.f.m.* '83 (SFE) Jemez Pueblo, NM San Diego Indian Missions.
Billicky, Louis S. '49 (BO) Senior Priests Retired.
Billing, Jerome D. '71 (STL) St. Louis, MO St. Michael; Defender of the Bond; Promoter of Justice.
Billinger, James J. '83 (WCH) Wichita, KS St. Elizabeth Ann Seton; Diocesan Building Commission.
Billinger, James (WCH) Deans.
Billman, George B. '72 (GAY)[D] Traverse City, MI Infant Jesus of Prague Monastery.
Billotte, Philip J. '66 (ROC) Corning, NY All Saints.
Billotti, Joseph E. *s.j.* '63 (CHK) Kristo Rai Parish; Vicar General; Finance Officer; Presbyteral Council; Commission on Justice and Development; Diocesan Publications Office; Electronic Media; Prison Chaplaincy; Police and Fire Departments Chaplaincy; College of Consultors.
Billotti, Joseph E. *s.j.* '63 (FgM).
Billy, Dennis *c.ss.r.* '80 (NY)[EE] Esopus, NY Redemptorist Priests and Brothers C.Ss.R. (Province of Baltimore).
Bilodeau, Leopold J. '73 (BUR) Shelburne, VT St. Catherine of Siena.
Bilodeau, Leopold J. (BUR) Army National Guard Chaplains.
Bilodeau, Roger P. '65 (MAN) Manchester, NH St. Anthony of Padua; Lincoln, NH St. Joseph; Council of Priests Retired.
Bilot, James L. '92 (DET) Special Assignment; Vocation Office.
Bilskie, Maurilius '43 (EVN) Retired.
Bilskie, Maurilius '43 (EVN) Evansville, IN Holy Rosary.
Bily, Edward '51 (SAT) New Braunfels, TX SS. Peter and Paul.
Bily, Edward (SAT) In Rural Area.
Bily, Edward (SAT) Archdiocesan Presbyteral Council.
Bily, John C. '58 (VIC) Weimar, TX St. Michael; Judges.
Bily, John (VIC) Presbyteral Council.
Bily, Lambert '63 (SAT) San Antonio, TX St. Clare.
Bilyk, Ivan (STF) Willimantic, CT Protection of B.V.M..
Bilyk, Stepan '01 (STF) Spring Valley, NY SS. Peter and Paul.
Binaghi, Maurizio *m.c.c.j.* '99 (CHI)[N] La Grange Park, IL Comboni Missionaries.
Binder, Mark J. '71 (SPC) Kimberling City, MO Our Lady of the Cove; Presbyteral Council.
Bindner, Charles J. '58 (L) Retired.
Binh, John Phan Cong '51 (SHP) Retired.
Binh, Peter Hoang Thai '96 (P) Portland, OR Our Lady of Lavang.
Biniek, Joseph P. '78 (ARL) Middleburg, VA St. Stephen the Martyr
Biniszkiewicz, Leonard E. '63 (BUF) Niagara Falls, NY St. Teresa of the Infant Jesus.
Binkowski, George '72 (STF) Fresh Meadows, NY Annunciation of the B.V.M..
Binkowski, George (STF) Judges.
Binkowski, George (STF) Diocesan Consultors.
Binkowski, George (STF) Educational Institutions.
Binkowski, George (STF) Presbyteral Council.
Binkowski, George (STF) Brooklyn.
Binsfeld, Douglas '98 (SFS) Henry, SD St. Henry.
Binsfeld, Douglas '98 (SFS) Florence, SD Blessed Sacrament.
Binsfeld, Steven '79 (SCL) St. Cloud, MN St. Mary's Cathedral of St. Cloud.
Binye, Gabriel (DUL) In Res.
Binzer, Joseph R. '94 (CIN) Cincinnati, OH St. Louis; [V] Cincinnati, OH Priests Eucharistic League; Archdiocesan Department Directors; Director; Chancellor; Adjutant Judicial Vicars; Victim Assistance Coordinator.
Bionda, Bonaventure *o.f.m.* '59 (ALB) Troy, NY St. Anthony of Padua (Shrine Church).
Biondi, Lawrence H. *s.j.* '70 (STL)[C] St. Louis, MO Saint Louis University; [O] St. Louis, MO Jesuit Community Corporation at St. Louis University – Jesuit Hall.
Biosca, Emilio *o.f.m.cap.* '94 (FgM).
Bir, Stanley *o.f.m.* '52 (CIN)[M] Cincinnati, OH St. Clement Friary.
Birarelli, Carl A. '58 (CIN) Retired.
Birch, Donald G. '67 (PH) Fallsington, PA St. Joseph the Worker.
Birch, Keith L. '71 (DUB) Tama, IA St. Patrick; Tama, IA St. Boniface.
Birch, Thomas J. '59 (ALN) Shillington, PA St. John Baptist de la Salle Retired.
Birchmeyer, Robert J. '73 (SY) Syracuse, NY St. Peter.
Bircumshaw, Colin F. '75 (SLC) Salt Lake City, UT St. Ann; College of Consultors; Finance Council; Liturgical Commission; Board of Directors; Priests' Personnel Board; Promoter of Justice; Vocation Office.
Bird, James F. '91 (E) Walston, PA St. Joseph; Walston, PA St. Adrian; Punxsutawney, PA SS. Cosmas and Damian; Walston, PA St. Anthony.
Bird, Stephen J. '76 (OKL) Okarche, OK Holy Trinity; Special Assignment; Region IX.
Bird, Stephen (OKL) Worship and Spiritual Life, Office of.
Bird, Steven '01 (PEO) Mendota, IL Holy Cross; Mendota, IL SS. Peter and Paul.
Birdsall, Anthony J. '60 (GB) Sturgeon Bay, WI Corpus Christi; Regional Vicars.
Birdsall, Hugh G. *s.d.s.* '62 (MIL)[O] Greendale, WI Salvatorian Community.
Birdsall, John M. '56 (RC) Retired.
Bireley, Robert L. *s.j.* '64 (CHI)[C] Chicago, IL Jesuit Community at Loyola University Chicago.
Biren, Timothy E. '99 (WIN) Mapleton MN St. Teresa's; [I] Mankato, MN St. Thomas More Newman Center, Minnesota State University.
Biren, Timothy E. (WIN) Emmaus House of Formation.
Biren, Timothy E. (WIN) Vocations Advisory Council.
Birge, George D. (BGP) Judges.
Biriruka, Ernest '81 (Ngozi) Miami, FL St. Kevin.
Birk, John G. '63 (SPK) Pasco, WA St. Patrick; CIVIL AIR PATROL.
Birk, John W. '70 (L) Louisville, KY Holy Name; Byzantine Rite Faithful.
Birk, John '63 (SPK) Special Ministry.
Birk, John '63 (SPK)[F] Pasco, WA Lourdes Medical Center.
Birkel, John B. '96 (LIN) Alma, NE St. Joseph's; Diocesan Area CCD Directors.
Birkel, Robert C. '49 (L) Retired.
Birkenfeld, Darryl '88 (AMA) Stratford, TX St. Joseph's; Absent on Leave.
Birket, Dwight J. '72 (WCH) Wichita, KS All Saints; Vicars General; Presbyteral Council/Diocesan Consultors; Deans; Diocesan Finance Committee; Presbyteral Council.
Birkhead, Henry G. '56 (PH) Retired.
Birkle, Walter A. '58 (NY) Bronx, NY Our Lady of Grace.
Birkmaier, James (GF) Clerical Benefit Association.
Birkmaier, Jim '68 (GF) Fort Benton, MT Immaculate Conception.
Birkmeyer, John R. *c.s.c.* '57 (AUS)[G] Austin, TX Congregation of Holy Cross – Southern Province Retired.
Birmingham, Kevin M. '97 (CHI) Orland Park, IL St. Francis of Assisi.
Birmingham, Robert F. '93 (HRT) On Duty Outside the Archdiocese Retired.
Birney, Timothy P. '98 (DET) Marine City, MI Holy Cross.
Biron, Robert G. '74 (MAN) New London, NH Our Lady of Fatima; Clergy Personnel Board; Ecumenical and Interreligious Affairs.
Biroschak, Robert V. (LA) Adjutant Judicial Vicar; Judges.
Birringer, Raphael *s.d.s.* '51 (MIL)[O] Milwaukee, WI.
Bisaillon, Rene *m.s.* '59 (HON) Kalaheo, HI Holy Cross; Koloa, HI St. Raphael.
Bisbee, Burnell B. *s.j.* '75 (OM)[K] Omaha, NE Jesuit Community at Creighton University.
Bischof, Donald R. '83 (PIT) Beaver Falls, PA Divine Mercy.
Bischof, Simon *o.s.b.* '55 (SCL)[I] Collegeville, MN St. John's Abbey, of the Order of St. Benedict.
Bischoff, Albert J. *s.j.* '56 (CIN) Cincinnati, OH St. Robert Bellarmine; [M] Cincinnati, OH Jesuit Community at Xavier University; [Q] Cincinnati, OH Xavier University Campus Ministry.
Bischoff, Francis J. (PAT) Retired.
Bisenius, Thomas R. '54 (DUB) Bernard, IA St. Patrick.
Bisgrove, Charles *s.c.j.* '90 (MIL)[O] Hales Corners, WI Priests of the Sacred Heart.
Bishara, Boctor '51 (LA)[J] Lynwood, CA St. Francis Medical Center.
Bisharat, George Said '92 (NTN) La Mesa, CA St. Jacob Mission.
Bishop, Clifton E. '98 (ALN)[O] Kutztown, PA Albright College (Reading); [O] Kutztown, PA Kutztown University (Kutztown).
Bishop, E. Louis *s.j.* '64 (PHX)[B] Phoenix, AZ Brophy College Preparatory.
Bishop, Marc J. (BO) Chelmsford, MA St. Mary; Navy Reserve Chaplains.
Bishop, Patrick A. '74 (ATL) Marietta, GA Church of the Transfiguration.
Bishop, Robert *c.m.f.* '71 (LA)[Q] Los Angeles, CA Claretian Retreat Center Community.
Bishop, Robert *c.m.f.* '71 (LA)[W] Los Angeles, CA Claretian Retreat Center (All Groups).
Bishop, Robert (OLL) Defender of the Bond.
Bishop, Robert (OLL) Promoter of Justice.
Bishop, Thomas G. '70 (Y) Canton, OH All Saints; Canton, OH St. Anthony.
Bishop, Thomas '75 (CHI) Glenview, IL Our Lady of Perpetual Help.
Bisignano, Joseph F. '81 (NY) Beacon, NY St. Joachim.
Bisignano, Joseph J. '81 (NY) Beacon, NY St. John Evangelist.
Bismonte, Honesto '54 (LA) On Administrative Leave.
Bisoffi, Joseph L. *o.s.cam.* '72 (MIL)[O] St. Francis, WI St. Camillus Provincialate; [O] Wauwatosa, WI St. Camillus Community House; [J] Milwaukee, WI St. Francis Hospital.
Bisson, Andrew R. '93 (PRT)[I] Kennebunkport, ME St. Anthony's Friary.
Bisson, Eddy N. '68 (MAN) Ashland, NH St. Agnes; Bristol, NH St. Timothy; Plymouth, NH St. Matthew.
Bisson, Joseph *s.v.d.* '63 (FgM).
Bissonette, James '88 (DUL) Proctor, MN St. Rose Catholic Church.
Bissonette, James '88 (DUL) Proctor, MN St. Philip Neri.
Bissonette, James (DUL) Corporate Board.
Bissonette, James (DUL) Judicial Vicar.

Bissot, Robert H. '57 (GAY) West Branch, MI St. Joseph.
Bistany, Joseph '37 (SAM) Retired.
Biszek, Robert J. '65 (ALN) Bethlehem, PA Holy Infancy.
Bitanga, Fred A. '64 (SFR) San Francisco, CA St. Patrick; Deans.
Bitangjol, Albert P. '56 (SFR) Retired.
Bitsko, Daniel J. '65 (PSC) Smithtown, NY Resurrection; Westbury, NY St. Andrew the Apostle.
Bittel, Patrick M. '82 (OWN) Fordsville, KY St. John the Baptist; Whitesville, KY St. Mary of the Woods.
Bitterman, John L. *s.s.* '69 (BAL)[S] Emmaus Spirituality Center.
Bittmenn, David J. '94 (SLC) Salt Lake City, UT St. Patrick's; Team.
Bittner, Gregory T. '85 (BIR) Birmingham, AL St. Stephen the Martyr; [H] Birmingham, AL St. Stephen the Martyr Catholic Church and Catholic Campus Center; Tribunal.
Bittner, Gregory '85 (BIR) Birmingham, AL Blessed Sacrament.
Bittner, Gregory (BIR) Members.
Bittner, Gregory (BIR) Members.
Bittner, Gregory (BIR) Diocesan College of Vicars.
Bittner, Gregory (BIR) Diocesan College of Consultors.
Bittner, Wayne W. '64 (MIL) Personal Leave.
Bitz, Al M. '69 (FAR) Jamestown, ND St. Margaret Alacoque; Jamestown, ND Sacred Heart; Jamestown, ND The Basilica of St. James.
Bitz, Al '69 (FAR) Jamestown, ND St. Michael; [J] Jamestown, ND Jamestown College.
Bitz, Al (FAR) Judges.
Biven, L. Russell (MOB) Group I.
Biven, Louis Russell '57 (MOB) Mobile, AL Our Savior.
Biven, Russell (MOB) Catholic University, Friends of.
Bixenman, Joseph E. (AMA)[I] Amarillo, TX Roman Catholic Diocese of Amarillo Deposit and Loan Fund.
Bixenman, Joseph '72 (AMA) Perryton, TX Immaculate Conception.
Bizaca, Mate '73 (LA) Los Angeles, CA St. Anthony.
Bizard, Hubert *f.s.s.p.* '98 (SCR)[M] Elmhurst Priestly Fraternity of St. Peter (F.S.S.P.), North American District Headquarters.
Bizzotto, Giovanni *c.s.* '86 (LA) Los Angeles, CA St. Peter.
Bjorum, James L. '76 (DET) St. Clair Shores, MI St. Germaine; Presbyteral Council; Judges.
Blacet, William J. '46 (KC) Kansas City, MO Our Lady of Good Counsel; Censor Librorum.
Blach, Brian (SJ) Priests' Retirement Board.
Blach, Leo M. '53 (DEN) Retired.
Black, Alvin A. *o.f.m.* '60 (PAT)[M] Butler, NJ St. Anthony Friary.
Black, Frank A. '80 (BRK) Brooklyn, NY St. Laurence.
Black, James P. '88 (COL) Chillicothe, OH St. Peter; Waverly, OH St. Mary, Queen of the Missions; Vicariate 13: Chillicothe.
Black, Michael G. '00 (RCK) Rockford, IL St. Patrick; DeKalb, IL Christ the Teacher, University Parish of Northern Illinois University; Vocations.
Black, Michael '00 (RCK)[L] DeKalb, IL Newman Foundation for Catholic Students of Northern Illinois University.
Blackall, John C. '51 (HRT) Retired.
Blackall, Randall L. '54 (HRT) Retired.
Blackburn, Clifford *o.m.i.* '47 (SAT)[K] San Antonio, TX Oblate Madonna Residence.
Blackburn, Michael *o.f.m.* '86 (LAV) Las Vegas, NV St. James the Apostle.
Blackowski, Theodore A. *o.f.m.* '45 (SP)[O] St. Petersburg St. Anthony Friary.
Blackwell, Edward A. '76 (MIA)[B] St. Thomas University.
Blackwell, Edward A. '76 (HBG) On Duty Outside the Diocese.
Blackwell, Edward (MIA) St. Thomas University.
Blackwell, Maurice J. '74 (BAL) Absent on Leave.
Blackwell, Michael J. '73 (WDC) Landover Hills, MD St. Mary's Catholic Church Retired.
Blackwood, Wallace E. '67 (BO) Essex, MA St. John the Baptist; Manchester by the Sea, MA Sacred Heart.
Bladt, Joel S. *s.t.* '61 (SAV) Bainbridge, GA St. Joseph's.
Blaes, Donald A. '56 (BEL) New Baden, IL St. George.
Blaes, James F. *c.s.c.* '55 (FTW)[I] Notre Dame, IN Holy Cross House.
Blaes, Paul '51 (KC) Retired.
Blaeser, Donald P. *o.f.m.* '70 (CHI)[N] Countryside, IL St. Gratian Friary, Franciscan Friars.
Blaettler, James R. *s.j.* '80 (SFR)[N] San Francisco, CA Jesuit Community at University of San Francisco.
Blaettler, James *s.j.* '80 (SFR) San Francisco, CA St. Ignatius.
Blain, Lionel A. '54 (PRO) Woonsocket, RI St. Joseph; Ecumenical Commission.
Blaine, James E. '77 (SLC) American Fork, UT St. Peter's; American Fork, UT Utah State Prison; Deans; Correctional Institution Ministry.
Blaine, Michael J. '91 (PH) Absent on Leave.
Blaine, Philip *o.f.m.conv.* '63 (NY)[EE] Staten Island, NY St. Francis Friary.
Blair, Guy *s.c.j.* '82 (SAT) San Antonio, TX San Francesco di Paola (Italian); [U] San Antonio, TX Deaf Ministries of San Antonio.
Blair, Guy *s.c.j.* (SAT) Ministry to Hearing Impaired.
Blair, Raymond O. '60 (MAN) Retired.
Blair, Raymond (PMB) Judges.
Blair, Stephen N. (MO) Air Force Reserve Chaplains.
Blais, Denis *c.p.m.* '93 (OWN)[F] Auburn, KY Fathers of Mercy.
Blais, George '90 (ORG) Costa Mesa, CA St. Joachim.
Blais, Melvin J. '42 (STP) Retired.
Blais, Robert L. '63 (PRO) On Duty Outside the Diocese.
Blais, Robert R. *o.p.* '68 (L) Louisville, KY St. Louis Bertrand.
Blais, Roland O. '44 (MAN) Retired.
Blake, Andrew P. '63 (RVC) Sag Harbor, NY St. Andrew's Retired.
Blake, Caryle *c.ss.r.* '62 (OAK)[N] Berkeley, CA Redemptorists (St. Clemens Maria House).
Blake, David D. *o.f.m.* '95 (BUF)[O] St. Bonaventure, NY St. Bonaventure Friary; [C] St. Bonaventure, NY Friar Community.
Blake, Jerry W. (DUB) Garner, IA St. Wenceslaus; Forest City, IA St. James; Garner, IA St. Boniface; Forest City, IA St. Patrick; Britt, IA St. Patrick; Forest City, IA St. Patrick; Deanery Representatives.
Blake, John Vincent *o.p.* '51 (MAD) Madison, WI Blessed Sacrament.
Blake, Lawrence R. '99 (STP) Chanhassen, MN St. Hubert.
Blake, Lawrence (STP) Office of Presbyteral Personnel Resources.
Blake, Peter M. '84 (STL) St. Louis, MO Assumption.
Blake, Peter (STL) Archdiocesan Consultors.
Blake, Philip C. *s.j.* '61 (PHX)[M] Los Gatos, CA Sacred Heart Jesuit Center.
Blake, Richard *s.j.* '69 (NY)[V] Newton, MA The Jesuit Community at Boston College.
Blake, Robert '77 (SR) Cloverdale, CA St. Peter's.
Blake, William B. '63 (SCR) Jessup, PA St. James.
Blakely, Leonard J. '80 (WIL) Chestertown, MD Sacred Heart.
Blakely, Paige A. '84 (ORL) DeBary, FL St. Ann's.
Blakely, Paige (ORL) Adjutant Judicial Vicar.
Blakely, Paige (ORL) Judges.
Blaker, John '96 (OAK) El Cerrito, CA St. John the Baptist.
Blaker, John (OAK) Episcopal Liturgies.
Blanch, Jose Maria *s.f.* '51 (SFE) Santa Cruz, NM Holy Cross.
Blanchard, David *o.carm.* '87 (WDC)[B] Washington, DC Whitefriars Hall; [L] Darien Carmelite Provincial Office.
Blanchard, Donald V. '69 (BR) Baton Rouge, LA Sacred Heart of Jesus.
Blanchard, Kirby '53 (DUL) Retired.
Blanchard, Peter R. *s.m.* '67 (NO)[P] New Orleans, LA Marist Fathers.
Blanchet, Leo '86 (MOB) Whistler, AL St. Bridget.
Blanchet, Leo (MOB) Holy Childhood Association.
Blanchet, Leo (MOB) Propagation of the Faith.
Blanchette, Brian D. '85 (PRT) Winthrop, ME St. Francis Xavier; Clergy Benefit Plan–Clergy Pension Plan.
Blanchette, Melvin C. *s.s.* '67 (SFR)[A] San Francisco, CA Vatican II Institute for Clergy Formation.
Blanchette, Oliver *a.a.* '44 (BO)[V] Austin House.
Blanchette, Oliver (WOR) Haitian Ministries Coalition of the Diocese of Worcester.
Blanchette, Roger E. *s.j.* '64 (SEA)[L] Seattle, WA Jesuit House, Seattle.
Blanchette, Roger *s.j.* '64 (SEA) Seattle, WA Our Lady of Mount Virgin.
Blanchfield, David W. '82 (BGP) Norwalk, CT St. Jerome; Presbyteral Council.
Blanchfield, John P. '50 (HRT) Plantsville, CT St. Aloysius.
Blanco, Adalberto (LA) Carpinteria, CA St. Joseph.
Blanco, Gonzalo *o.s.b.* '92 (BIS)[A] Richardton, ND Assumption Abbey.
Blanco, Gonzalo *o.s.b.* (FgM).
Blanco, Ignacio *c.m.f.* '51 (SAT) San Antonio, TX Immaculate Heart of Mary.
Blanco, Ildefonso *o.s.a.* '64 (MGZ) Aguada, PR St. Francis of Assisi.
Blanco, John P. *s.d.b.* '64 (NY) New York, NY Mary Help of Christians.
Blanco, John (NY) Port Chester, NY Corpus Christi.
Blanco, Joseph (DEN) Akron, CO St. Joseph.
Blanco, Telesforo R. *o.s.a.* '60 (BEA) Port Arthur, TX Our Lady of Guadalupe.
Blanco, Vincent '90 (ANC) Anchorage, AK Our Lady of Guadalupe.
Bland, Thomas A. (SAC) Co–Vicar for Clergy & Religious and Personnel Director for Priests.
Bland, Thomas '74 (SAC) Council of Priests; Sacramento, CA St. Philomene.
Bland, Thomas (SAC) Priests' Personnel Board, Diocesan.
Blanda, William C. '91 (LAF) Abbeville, LA St. Mary Magdalen.
Blandford, James T. '38 (LEX) Retired.
Blaney, Dennis J. '58 (GRY) Retired.
Blaney, Jim *o.m.i.* '65 (JUN) Skagway, AK St. Therese of the Child Jesus.
Blaney, Jim *o.m.i.* '65 (JUN) Haines, AK Sacred Heart.
Blaney, Robert M. '92 (BO) Dracut, MA St. Francis.
Blank, Severius '58 (FWT) Retired.
Blank, William H. '87 (NO) New Orleans, LA St. Julian Eymard; Franklinton, LA Holy Family.
Blankenship, John P. '63 (RIC) Retired.
Blankinship, Cal (B) Priest Personnel Commission.
Blankinship, Calvin '96 (B) Payette, ID Corpus Christi.
Blantz, James R. *c.s.c.* '59 (FTW)[I] Rolling Prairie, IN LeMans Academy; [R] Ventura, CA Sisters of the Holy Cross.
Blantz, Thomas E. *c.s.c.* '60 (FTW)[B] University of Notre Dame Du Lac; [I] Notre Dame, IN Holy Cross Community, Corby Hall, University of Notre Dame.
Blas, Wilson (DAL) Dallas, TX St. Augustine Catholic Church.
Blaschko, Harvey *o.p.* '81 (BR) Ponchatoula, LA St. Joseph.
Blasco, Ignacio '62 (MIA) Retired.
Blaser, John R. '64 (TOL) Toledo, OH Good Shepherd; Toledo, OH St. Louis; Toledo, OH St. Thomas Aquinas; To–Lu–Wo Deanery; Members.
Blasi, Augustine Di '45 (NY)[EE] Bronx, NY.
Blasich, Bernard '67 (MIL)[O] St. Francis, WI St. Camillus Provincialate.
Blasick, George W. *c.pp.s.* '60 (TOL)[J] Bellevue Mary Lay Center.
Blasick, George *c.pp.s.* '60 (TOL)[L] Bellevue, OH Sorrowful Mother Shrine.
Blasick, George *c.ss.r.* '01 (TOL) Lima, OH St. Gerard.
Blaska, John A. '53 (DET) Troy, MI St. Alan Retired.
Blasko, Joseph A. '99 (GAY) Mio, MI St. Mary; Vocations and Pastoral Care of Seminarians, Delegate for.
Blasko, Zvonko '82 (CLV) Cleveland, OH St. Paul.
Blastic, Michael *o.f.m. conv.* '75 (CHI)[N] St. Bonaventure, NY St. Bonaventure Friary.
Blastic, Michael *o.f.m.conv.* '75 (BUF)[O] St. Bonaventure, NY St. Bonaventure Friary; [C] St. Bonaventure, NY Friar Community.
Blaszczak, Gerald R. *s.j.* '79 (NY)[EE] Cardinal Spellman Hall, Jesuit Community.
Blaszczyk, Thaddeus J. '53 (DET) Retired.
Blattner, Joseph H. '58 (STL) On Duty Outside the Archdiocese.
Blattner, Joseph H. '58 (BUR) North Troy, VT St. Vincent de Paul.
Blau, Thomas J. '99 (RIC) Charlottesville, VA St. Thomas Aquinas.
Blaufuss, Tony '58 (KCK) Retired.
Blauvelt, Robert '59 (BRK) Rockaway Beach, NY St. Camillus.
Blay, Roberto Garcia '86 (PCE) Mercedita, PR Church of the Resurrection; Vicar General; Diocesan Consultors; Diocesan Board of Administration; Administrator.
Blazak, Camillus '51 (BIR) Retired.
Blazejewski, Richard J. '74 (BUF) Perry, NY St. Stanislaus Kostka.
Blazejewski, Richard W. '74 (BUF) Vicars; Catholic Alumni Club; Perry, NY St. Joseph.
Blazek, Camilius '51 (KNX)[D] Signal Mountain, TN Alexian Village of Tennessee.
Blazek, David J. '97 (DET) Harper Woods, MI Our Lady Queen of Peace; Archdiocesan Vicars.
Blazek, Eugene '76 (HON) On Duty Outside the Diocese; Air Force Chaplains.
Blazek, James F. '79 (CHI) Chicago, IL Immaculate Heart of Mary.
Blazek, John J. *c.s.c.* '67 (FTW)[I] Gates Mills, OH Gilmour Academy.
Blazek, John *c.s.c.* '58 (CLV)[D] Gates Mills, OH Gilmour Academy.
Blazek, John '98 (CHI) Chicago, IL St. Alphonsus.
Blazewicz, William J. '59 (LC) Retired.
Blazine, James A. '62 (BEL) Leave of Absence.
Blazovich, Victor M. (SPK) Colton, WA St. Gall; Colton, WA St. Boniface.
Bleaux, Floyd J. '73 (OG) Plattsburgh, NY Our Lady of Victory.
Bleboo, Lawrence T. (MO) Army Chaplains.
Blecha, Charles A. '40 (LC) Retired.
Blecha, Jordan R. *o.praem.* '39 (GB)[I] De Pere, WI St. Norbert Abbey.
Blee, Edward C. *s.m.* '55 (SFR)[N] San Francisco, CA Marist Center of the West.
Bleeke, Bob '71 (GB)[F] Manitowoc, WI Holy Family Memorial, Inc..
Bleich, Russell M. '60 (DUB) On Special or Other Archdiocesan Assignment; Episcopal Vicar for Cedar Rapids Region; College of Consultors; Ex Officio Members; Building Commission; Pastoral Council; Ex Officio Members.
Bleichner, Howard P. '67 (PIT) On Duty Outside the Diocese.

Bleiler, William James '66 (CAM) Cedarville, NJ St. Michael's; Leesburg, NJ New Jersey State Medium Security Prison.
Blenker, Ambrose J. '62 (LC) Plum City, WI St. John the Baptist; Elected Members.
Blenkle, Joseph A. '90 (NY) Valhalla, NY Holy Name of Jesus.
Blesnuk, Donald J. '85 (BUF) Absent on Leave.
Blessin, Thomas C. *s.j.* '63 (NEW)[B] Jersey City, NJ Jesuit Center; [N] Jersey City, NJ Jesuits of Saint Peter's College, Inc..
Blessing, Howard '76 (LAF) Lafayette, LA St. Patrick.
Blessing, Loren '81 (FRS) Fresno, CA St. Anthony of Padua.
Blessinger, James '64 (EVN) Evansville, IN Corpus Christi.
Blicharski, Michael *o.cist.* '93 (CHI)[N] Willow Springs, IL Cistercian Fathers, Our Lady Mother of the Church.
Blicharz, Dariusz '91 (BRK) Brooklyn, NY Our Lady of Czestochowa–St. Casimir.
Blick, Ned J. '92 (WCH) South Hutchinson, KS Our Lady of Guadalupe; [B] Hutchinson, KS Trinity High School.
Blickhan, Donald '74 (SFD) Bethalto, IL Our Lady Queen of Peace.
Blind, Thomas F. '81 (NEW) Summit, NJ St. Teresa's.
Bline, G. David '98 (CLV) Northfield, OH St. Barnabas.
Blinn, Richard J. *s.j.* '69 (SAC) Davis, CA St. James.
Bliss, Dennis (Y) Absent on Leave.
Bliss, Michael C. (PEO) Vicariates and Vicars.
Bliss, Michael '91 (PEO)[I] Peoria, IL Saint Francis' Medical Center.
Bliszcz, Michael '87 (SJP) Conyers, GA Mother of God.
Bliven, Edmond '50 (P) Retired.
Bliven, Robert J. *o.s.c.* '56 (PHX)[G] Phoenix, AZ Crosier Community of Phoenix (Canons Regular of the Order of the Holy Cross).
Blocher, James *c.s.b.* '75 (GAL) Rosenberg, TX Our Lady of Guadalupe.
Block, John G. '63 (PMB) Retired.
Blockley, Matthew (CHK) Presbyteral Council.
Blocklinger, James L. '66 (DUB)[H] Cedar Rapids, IA Mercy Medical Center–Cedar Rapids.
Blomberg, John '59 (STL) St. Louis, MO St. Aloysius Gonzaga.
Blondell, Robert H. '66 (DET) Ray Twp., MI St. Francis of Assisi; Macomb Township, MI St. Maximilian Kolbe.
Blonigen, Aloysius *c.m.m.* '65 (DET)[K] Vocation Office.
Blonski, Joachim '92 (GLP) Aztec, NM St. Joseph.
Blonski, Joachim '92 (GLP) Aztec, NM Holy Trinity.
Blood, Bernard M. *s.m.m.* '50 (RVC)[M] Bay Shore, NY Montfort Missionaries.
Blood, Francis X. '79 (STL) St. Louis, MO St. Cecilia.
Bloom, Phillip '71 (SEA) Seattle, WA Holy Family.
Blostic, Leonard *t.o.r.* '63 (ALT)[F] Newry, PA St. Bernardine Monastery.
Blotsky, Hugo L. *o.s.b.* '88 (BIS)[A] Richardton, ND Assumption Abbey.
Blotsky, Hugo L. *o.s.b.* '88 (CHY) Pine Bluffs, WY St. Paul's.
Blottman, William P. '65 (FR)[G] Fall River, MA Catholic Memorial Home Inc..
Blough, William G. '58 (PIT) Retired.
Blount, Anthony (CC)[G] Robstown, TX Society of Our Lady of the Most Holy Trinity.
Blount, James '99 (CC)[G] Robstown, TX Society of Our Lady of the Most Holy Trinity.
Blout, Daniel L. '86 (GBG) Greensburg, PA Our Lady of Grace; [C] Greensburg, PA Greensburg Central Catholic High School; [C] Connellsville, PA Geibel Catholic High School.
Blow, Thomas D. *o.f.m.* '87 (BUF)[O] St. Bonaventure, NY St. Bonaventure Friary; [C] St. Bonaventure University; [C] St. Bonaventure, NY Friar Community.
Blowers, Leslie F. *m.m.* '63 (CIN)[M] Cincinnati, OH The Catholic Foreign Mission Society of America, Inc..
Blowey, David *o.f.m.conv.* '87 (FgM).
Blowey, David *o.f.m.conv.* '87 (BAL).
Blubaugh, Homer D. '69 (COL)[S] Coshocton, OH Sacred Heart; Priests' Senate.
Bludnicki, Dennis G. '75 (BGP) Bridgeport, CT St. Ambrose.
Blue, Peter W. *o.s.b.* '70 (PAT)[M] Inkamana Abbey.
Blue, Peter W. *o.s.b.* '70 (FgM).
Blue Jacket, David '88 (DEN) Littleton, CO St. Mary.
Bluett, Anthony '69 (ORL) Lake Wales, FL Holy Spirit.
Bluett, Anthony (ORL) Deans.
Bluett, Anthony (ORL) Members.
Bluett, Anthony (ORL) Consultors.
Bluett, James K. '67 (PT) Military Chaplains; Army Chaplains.
Bluett, John J. '63 (ORL) Winter Springs, FL St. Stephen.
Blum, John '96 (SP) Spring Hill, FL St. Frances Xavier Cabrini.
Blum, John (SP) Presbyteral Council.
Blum, Stephen J. '76 (TOL) Lima, OH St. Charles Borromeo.
Blum, William G. *c.s.c.* '65 (FTW)[I] Notre Dame, IN.
Bluma, Dacian '49 (GRY)[I] Cedar Lake, IN Our Lady of Lourdes Friary.
Bluma, Dacian *o.f.m.* '49 (FTW)[J] Mishawaka, IN Our Lady of the Angels Convent.
Blume, Michael *s.v.d.* (FgM).
Blumenfeld, Donald F. '79 (NEW).
Blumenfeld, Donald (NEW)[B] School of Diplomacy and Intl. Rels..
Blumenfeld, Donald (NEW) Censors of Books.
Blumeyer, James A. *s.j.* '63 (KC)[J] Kansas City, MO Rockhurst Jesuit Community.
Blumeyer, James *s.j.* '63 (KC) Kansas City, MO St. Francis Xavier.
Blums, Burton *o.s.b.* '45 (SCL)[I] Collegeville, MN St. John's Abbey, of the Order of St. Benedict.
Blust, Christopher *f.s.s.p.* '01 (SCR)[M] Elmhurst Priestly Fraternity of St. Peter (F.S.S.P.), North American District Headquarters.
Blute, Robert H. '56 (BO) Senior Priests Retired.
Bly, Walter J. '64 (FTW) South Bend, IN Corpus Christi; [C] South Bend, IN Saint Joseph's High School.
Blyman, Robert Y. '70 (RVC) Hicksville, NY Our Lady of Mercy.
Blyskosz, Joseph '95 (FR) Special Assignment.
Boackle, Paul H. '89 (SAM) Retired.
Boadt, Lawrence E. *c.s.p.* '69 (NY) New York, NY Good Shepherd.
Boadt, Lawrence *c.s.p.* '69 (NEW)[N] Mahwah, NJ Paulist Fathers – Paulist Press.
Boadt, Lawrence *c.s.p.* '69 (NEW)[S] Mahwah, NJ Paulist Press.
Boarman, Leon J. *c.s.c.* '37 (AUS)[G] Austin, TX Congregation of Holy Cross – Southern Province Retired.
Boarman, Leon J. *c.s.c.* '37 (FTW)[I] Notre Dame, IN Holy Cross House.
Boateng–Mensah, Semanhyia '73 (PMB) Boca Raton, FL St. Joan of Arc.
Bobadilla, Tomas '81 (NY) Beacon, NY St. John Evangelist.
Bobal, Joseph K. '63 (E) Curwensville, PA St. Timothy.
Boban, Dujo *o.f.m.* '69 (SJ) San Jose, CA St. Mary of the Assumption.
Bobber, Raymar *o.f.m.* '57 (FWT)[I] Crowley, TX St. Maximilian Kolbe Friary; [L] Springfield, IL Our Lady of Angels Friary.
Bober, Charles S. '72 (PIT) Mars, PA St. Kilian; [R] Pittsburgh, PA Priests' Benefit Plan of the Diocese of Pittsburgh; Judges.
Bober, Francis J. '69 (WDC) Retired.
Bober, Marjan L. '63 (CAM) Retired.
Bober, Richard J. '57 (CLV) Euclid, OH St. Felicitas.
Bober, Richard R. (CLV) Translators.
Boberek, Aurelius *o.s.b.* '57 (IND)[K] St. Meinrad, IN St. Meinrad Archabbey.
Bobersky, Michael '35 (STN) Retired.
Bobis, Antonio '79 (AGN) Tamuning, GU St. Anthony and St. Victor.
Bobola, Adam *s.ch.* (CHI) Chicago, IL Five Holy Martyrs; Lombard, IL Divine Mercy Polish Mission.
Bobrek, Edwin *o.f.m.* '51 (NY)[EE] Encinitas, CA.
Boccaccio, Michael A. '71 (BGP) Norwalk, CT St. Philip; Judges.
Boccafola, Kenneth '63 (RVC) Priests Released from Diocesan Assignment.
Boccali, Ronald *p.i.m.e.* '60 (COL) Heath, OH St. Leonard.
Boccardi, Raymond C. '52 (PIT) Retired.
Boccio, Charles P. '61 (NY) Bronx, NY Veterans Administration Hospital.
Boccio, Charles P. '61 (BRK) Long Island City, NY Immaculate Conception.
Bochanski, Philip G. '99 (PH) Philadelphia, PA Resurrection of Our Lord.
Bochenek, Joseph G. '71 (BAL) Baltimore, MD St. Brigid.
Bochicchio Paul L. '71 (NEW) Garfield, NJ Our Lady of Mt. Virgin; Southwest Bergen Region Deanery 4; College of Consultors; Members; Elected Members; Staff.
Bochicchio, Paul (NEW) Our Lady of Fatima First Saturday Club.
Bochinski, Mark J. '58 (SCR) Avoca, PA SS. Peter and Paul.
Bochnak, Zenon A. '85 (GF) Special Assignment.
Bochnak, Zenon A. '85 (MET) On Duty Outside the Diocese; Air Force Chaplains.
Bocian, Ronald C. '72 (ALN) Shenandoah, PA St. Casimir; Shenandoah, PA St. Stanislaus.
Bocianowski, Thaddeus Nicholas '71 (BUF) Buffalo, NY St. Adalbert's Basilica.
Bock, Lawrence R. '62 (HRT) Newington, CT Holy Spirit; Auditors (Part–time Case Instructors).
Bockenfeld, Elgar *o.f.m.* '44 (STP) New Prague, MN St. John the Evangelist.
Bockenfeld, Elgar *o.f.m.* '44 (STP) New Prague, MN St. Benedict.
Bocklage, Richard F. *s.j.* '55 (DEN)[N] Denver, CO Xavier Jesuit Center.
Bockskopf, Richard J. '70 (STL) Maryland Heights, MO St. Blaise.
Bodah, Henry J. '78 (PRO) Providence, RI St. Joseph; [S] Providence, RI Brown University.
Bodde, Frederick A. '53 (DET) Marine City, MI Holy Cross Retired.
Bodden, Charles J. *o.s.a.* '78 (FgM).
Boddie, James R '78 (STA) Orange Park, FL St. Catherine's.
Boddie, James R. (STA) Defender of the Bond; Presbyteral Council; Scouts.
Boddie, John D. '88 (RIC) Mathews, VA Church of Francis de Sales; Topping, VA Church of the Visitation.
Bodenschatz, Ronald *t.o.r.* '49 (ALT)[F] Loretto, PA Mount Assisi Friary.
Bodensteiner, Peter C. '45 (DUB) Retired.
Bodnar, Edward W. *s.j.* '52 (WDC)[M] Washington, DC The Jesuit Community at Georgetown University.
Bodo, Murray L. *o.f.m.* '64 (CIN)[M] Cincinnati, OH Pleasant Street Friary.
Bodo, Murray *o.f.m.* '64 (CIN)[V] Cincinnati, OH Franciscans Network.
Bodziak, Charles F. '67 (ALT) Cassandra, PA St. Agnes; Wilmore, PA St. Bartholomew's.
Bodziony, Ralph A. '58 (CLV) Cleveland, OH St. John Cantius Retired.
Boeckman, Floyd B. *o.m.i.* '55 (BEL)[F] Belleville, IL Shrine of Our Lady of the Snows; [J] Belleville, IL Missionary Association of Mary Immaculate–Missionary Oblates of Mary Immaculate.
Boeckman, John R. '84 (E) Farrell, PA Holy Trinity; Farrell, PA St. Adalbert.
Boeckman, Scott A. '03 (OKL) Special Assignment; [C] Oklahoma City, OK Mount St. Mary High School; Oklahoma City, OK Sacred Heart.
Boedy, Thomas *s.j.* '70 (LA) Lakewood, CA St. Pancratius.
Boeff, Dismas '76 (CLV) SouthWest General Hospital.
Boeff, Dismas *o.s.b.* '76 (CLV) Brook Park, OH St. Peter the Apostle.
Boeff, Dismas *o.s.b.* '76 (CLV)[O] Cleveland, OH.
Boegel, Joseph L. *c.m.* '49 (PH)[AA] St. Catherine Infirmary.
Boeglin, John '78 (EVN) Jasper, IN Holy Family.
Boeglin, John (EVN) Rural Life Conference.
Boehm, Claude L. *c.s.c.* '35 (FTW)[I] Notre Dame, IN Holy Cross House.
Boehm, James A. '58 (STU) Retired.
Boehm, Michael P. '94 (STL)[U] St. Louis, MO Archdiocesan Stewardship Education Committee; Washington, MO St. Francis Borgia.
Boehm, Michael '75 (CHI) Waukegan, IL Holy Family.
Boehme, Arnold *o.c.d.* '68 (MIL)[O] Milwaukee Provincial Offices – Discalced Carmelites.
Boehme, Ferdinand '97 (LIN) Curtis, NE St. James.
Boehning, John A. '62 (NY) New York, NY St. Thomas More.
Boeke, Aloysius B. '41 (CIN)[B] Carthagena, OH St. Charles Retired.
Boeke, Anselm F. '43 (CIN) Piqua, OH St. Mary Retired.
Boekelman, Timothy J. '77 (SC) Fort Dodge, IA St. Joseph's; Lake City, IA St. Mary's; Lake City, IA St. Joseph's.
Boensch, Gregory A. '50 (CC) Retired.
Boenzi, Joseph *s.d.b.* '79 (OAK)[E] Richmond, CA Salesian High School.
Boes, Clair L. '65 (SC) Ashton, IA St. Mary's Catholic Church; Sibley, IA St. Andrew's.
Boes, Edward *s.a.* '98 (NY)[EE] Garrison, NY St. Francis of Assisi Novitiate.
Boes, Marvin '62 (SC) Retired.
Boes, Steven E. (OM) Deans; Deans.
Boes, Steven '85 (OM)[O] Winnebago, NE FEATHERS.
Boes, Steven '85 (OM) Walthill, NE St. Joseph.
Boes, Steven '85 (OM) Winnebago, NE St. Augustine's.
Boes, Steven '85 (OM)[O] Winnebago, NE St. Augustine's Indian Mission.
Boes, Steven '85 (OM) Macy, NE Our Lady of Fatima.
Boesel, James E. '54 (RVC) Hicksville, NY Our Lady of Mercy Retired.
Boeshans, Francis G. '48 (NO)[S] New Orleans, LA Stella Roman Foundation, Inc. Retired.
Boettcher, John '91 (SR) On Duty Outside the Diocese.
Boettner, David '94 (KNX) Lenoir City, TN St. Thomas the Apostle.
Boettner, David (KNX) Presbyteral Council.
Boettner, David (KNX) Diocesan Consultors.
Boever, Richard *c.ss.r.* '73 (STL)[B] St. Louis, MO St. John Neumann House.
Boff, Bernard J. '61 (TOL) Toledo, OH Queen of the Most Holy Rosary Cathedral; Mission of Accompaniment Pastoral Team Retired.
Bofto, Robert C. '63 (GF) Retired.
Bog–Merhi, Gebran '88 (SLC) Salt Lake City, UT Veterans Administration Hospital.
Bogan, Robert '58 (SY) Clinton, NY Church of the Annunciation.

Bogart, Kenneth C. *s.j.* '56 (FgM).
Bogda, Dennis M. '67 (PBR) Lyndora, PA St. John the Baptist; Consultors; Vocations; Revitalization and Renewal Commission.
Bogdan, Henry S. '48 (TR) Trenton, NJ Incarnation Retired.
Bogdan, Leonard A. '60 (KAL) Retired.
Bogdan, Palka *s.d.s.* '92 (NEW)[N] Verona, NJ The Salvatorian Fathers.
Bogert, James '67 (RVC) Priests Released from Diocesan Assignment Retired.
Bogetto, Clarence J. *c.m.* '45 (STL)[O] Perryville, MO Congregation of the Mission.
Boggs, Dennis R. '86 (ALT) Chancellor; Chancery; Johnstown, PA St. Benedict's.
Boghan, J. Patrick *m.s.a.* '77 (VEN) Marco Island, FL San Marco.
Boghossian, G. Scott '02 (PSC) Hazleton, PA St. John the Baptist.
Bognanno, Frank E. (DM) Des Moines, IA Christ the King.
Bogniak, Casimir '57 (E) Retired.
Boguslawski, Steven *o.p.* '87 (DET)[A] Detroit, MI Sacred Heart Major Seminary, Inc..
Bogusz, Dennis A. '79 (GBG) Connellsville, PA Holy Trinity; Connellsville, PA Highlands Hospital & Health Center; Mount Pleasant, PA Frick Community Health Center.
Bohan, Philip *o.f.m.cap.* '67 (RVC) East Patchogue, NY St. Joseph the Worker.
Bohdanowycz, Peter A. (DEN) Denver, CO Transfiguration of Our Lord; Denver, CO Transfiguration of Our Lord.
Bohlin, Thomas '97 (NY)[JJ] New York, NY Prelature of the Holy Cross and Opus Dei.
Bohn, John Joseph '97 (JKS) On Leave:.
Bohn, John (JKS) Personnel Board.
Bohn, John (JKS) Defenders of the Bond.
Bohner, Allan G. '98 (SR) Retired.
Bohnert, Edward A. '85 (SFR) South San Francisco, CA St. Veronica.
Bohnsack, David *m.c.c.j.* '94 (FgM).
Bohorquez, Carlos M. '99 (SFD) Decatur, IL Our Lady of Lourdes; Comite Diocesano de Ministerio Hispano – Diocesan Committee for Hispanic Ministry.
Bohorquez, Hernan D. '02 (BGP) Bridgeport, CT St. Augustine Cathedral; [C] Bridgeport, CT Kolbe-Cathedral High School.
Bohorquez, Jesus Alberto '01 (MIA) Miami, FL Epiphany.
Bohr, David A. '71 (SCR)[A] Dalton, PA Saint Pius X Seminary; Censor Librorum; Diocesan Commission on Ethics for Catholic Health Care Facilities; Permanent Diaconate Office; Pastoral Formation Institute; Renewal—Fatima Center.
Bohr, Gail G. *s.j.* '73 (OM)[K] Omaha, NE Jesuit Community at Creighton University.
Bohr, Luke *o.s.b.* '48 (RCK)[G] Aurora, IL Marmion Abbey.
Bohula, Edwin V. '55 (CHI) Retired.
Boiko, John '87 (AUS) Kyle, TX St. Anthony Marie De Claret.
Boileau, David A. '56 (NO) New Orleans, LA Mater Dolorosa; [C] New Orleans, LA Loyola University New Orleans.
Boisaubin, Robt. (STL) Manchester, MO St. Joseph.
Boisvert, Gilbert O. '71 (OG) Altona, NY Holy Angels; Altona, NY St. Louis.
Boisvert, Gregory *a.a.* '51 (BO)[V] Kingsport, TN; Kingsport, TN St. Dominic.
Boisvert, Gregory *a.a.* (KNX) Ongoing Formation of Deacons.
Boisvert, Keith W. '79 (BAL) Frederick, MD St. Katharine Drexel Roman Catholic Congregation, Inc..
Boisvert, Ralph '99 (PRT) Waterville, ME Parish of the Holy Spirit.
Boisvert, Robert G. '58 (MAN) Retired.
Boivin, Henry P. '57 (BO) Senior Priests Retired.
Boivin, John '76 (CHI) Chicago, IL Cathedral of the Holy Name.
Boivin, Louis R. '48 (FR) Retired.
Bojczuk, Thaddeus J. '73 (CHI) Summit, IL St. Joseph.
Boji, Manuel Y. '68 (EST) Southfield, MI Our Lady of Chaldeans Cathedral, Mother of God Chaldean Parish; Vicar General; Diocesan Corporation–The Chaldean Catholic Church of U.S.A..
Boji, Manuel (EST) Eparchial College of Consultors.
Bok, James M. *o.f.m.* '74 (CIN)[M] Cincinnati, OH St. Francis Seraph Friary; [M] Cincinnati, OH Pleasant Street Friary.
Bok, John *o.f.m.* '62 (GAL) Galveston, TX St. Patrick.
Bokenkotter, Thomas '50 (CIN) Cincinnati, OH Assumption of the Blessed Virgin Mary.
Bokinskie, Richard '79 (SAG) Marlette, MI St. Elizabeth.
Bokinskie, Richard '79 (SAG) Mayville, MI St. Joseph.
Bokinskie, Richard '79 (SAG) Deford, MI St. Michael.
Bokinskie, Richard (SAG) Vicars for Vicariates.
Bokinskie, Richard (SAG) Diocesan Consultors.
Bokinskie, Richard (SAG) Office of Church Ministries.
Bokinskie, Richard (SAG) Ministry to Priests.
Bokota, Marek '81 (NEW) Mahwah, NJ Immaculate Heart of Mary.
Boks, Lawrence E. '66 (GAY) Harrisville, MI St. Anne; Harrisville, MI St. Raphael.
Bolan, John E. *c.pp.s.* '53 (CLV) Cleveland, OH Veterans Administration Hospitals, Brecksville V.A..
Bolan, John *c.pp.s.* '52 (CIN)[M] Middleburg Heights, OH.
Boland, Eamonn '69 (DUL) Moose Lake, MN Holy Angels; Moose Lake, MN Moose Lake State Hospital.
Boland, Edward F. '44 (PRO)[P] Providence St. John Vianney Residence Retired.
Boland, Eugene M. '63 (PAT) Totowa, NJ St. James of the Marches.
Boland, Eugene (PAT) Deans.
Boland, Jeremiah M. (CHI) College of Consultors.
Boland, Jerimiah M. '81 (CHI) Chicago, IL Holy Family.
Boland, Jerimiah (CHI) Archbishop's Delegate for Extern and International Priests.
Boland, John P. '55 (PH) North Wales, PA St. Rose of Lima; Defenders of the Bond.
Boland, John V. '65 (PAT) McAfee, NJ St. Francis de Sales.
Boland, John '75 (GLP) Cuba, NM Immaculate Conception.
Boland, John (GLP) Defenders of the Bond.
Boland, Michael M. '86 (CHI)[G] Chicago, IL Mission of the Holy Cross; Administrative Council; Department Directors.
Boland, Thomas L. '65 (L) Louisville, KY St. Patrick; Archdiocesan Examiners.
Bolantete, Ramon '85 (ORL) Lakeland, FL St. Joseph's.
Bolcar, Andrew J. '65 (CAM) Westville, NJ St. Anne's.
Bolda, Eugeniusz *s.c.* '89 (PHX) Phoenix, AZ Our Lady of Czestochowa (Polish Pastoral Mission).
Bolderson, John D. '81 (STL) On Duty Outside the Archdiocese.
Bolderson, John '81 (KC) Kansas City, MO St. John Francis Regis.
Boldt, William J. '49 (NY) Staten Island, NY St. Teresa Retired.
Bolduc, Gerard *o.m.i.* '69 (DET)[A] The College of Liberal Arts; [A] The School of Theology.
Bolduc, John *s.m.* '70 (BRK) Brooklyn, NY St. Francis of Assisi–St. Blaise.
Bolduc, Marcel '39 (BO)[V] Lowell, MA Andre Garin Retirement Residence.
Bolduc, Richard *o.m.i.* '64 (BO)[Y] Tewksbury, MA Immaculate Heart of Mary Infirmary.
Boler, Martin *o.s.b.* '60 (ROC)[I] Pine City, NY Mount Saviour Monastery.
Bolerasky, Peter E. '55 (PEO) Streator, IL St. Stephen's Retired.
Boles, Joseph M. '65 (SCR)[N] Dunmore, PA Villa St. Joseph Retired.
Bolesta, Michael C. '89 (PH)[U] Meadowbrook, PA Holy Redeemer Hospital and Medical Center; [BB] Huntingdon Valley, PA Sisters of the Holy Redeemer Provincialate.
Boley, Robert *o.carm.* '75 (NEW) Englewood, NJ St. Cecilia's.
Boley, Robert *o.carm.* '75 (JOL) Darien, IL Our Lady of Mount Carmel.
Bolez, Edward C. '74 (ALN) Bethlehem, PA St. John Capistrano.
Bolger, Anthony '69 (HON) Leave of Absence Retired.
Bolger, John F. '50 (SP) St. Petersburg, FL Transfiguration Retired.
Bolger, Michael J. '92 (RCK) Shannon, IL St. Wendelin.
Bolger, Richard T. '66 (PH) Willow Grove, PA St. David.
Bolger, William '53 (SD) Retired.
Bolieau, Henry G. '72 (NOR) Absent on Leave.
Bolin, John F. *s.m.* (HON) Finance Committee.
Bolin, John *s.m.* '55 (HON)[G] Honolulu, HI Marianist Hall Community.
Bolin, John *s.m.* (HON) Diocesan Planning and Building Commission.
Bolin, John *s.m.* (HON) Presbyteral Council.
Bolin, John *s.m.* (HON) Board of Directors.
Boll, John E. '70 (SAC) Woodland, CA Holy Rosary; Vicars Forane.
Boll, John J. *o.p.* '82 (GAL)[Q] Houston, TX Dominican Friars, St. Mark Priory, Inc.; [T] Houston, TX Satellite Office.
Boll, John (SAC) Defenders of the Bond.
Bollea, Richard C. '62 (HRT) Waterbury, CT Waterbury Hospital; Beacon Falls, CT St. Michael's.
Boller, Kenneth J. *s.j.* '75 (NY) New York, NY St. Aloysius.
Boller, Robert J. '91 (STP) Retired.
Bolling, Joseph M. '91 (MOB) Mobile, AL St. Matthew.
Bollman, Richard W. *s.j.* '69 (CIN) Cincinnati, OH St. Robert Bellarmine; [D] Xavier University; [M] Cincinnati, OH Jesuit Community at Xavier University.
Bolman, Anthony P. '60 (SFE) Retired.
Bologna, Anthony F. '43 (DET) Retired.
Bolser, Robert T. *c.s.v.* '95 (CHI) Chicago, IL St. Victor.
Bolster, M. Thomas '82 (GR) Grand Rapids, MI St. James.
Bolte, Richard G. '83 (COV) Newport, KY Holy Spirit; [B] Newport, KY Newport Central Catholic High School; Deans.
Bolte, Thomas L. '80 (CIN) Cincinnati, OH St. Ignatius Loyola.
Bolton, Bill *s.d.b.* '86 (LA)[W] Rosemead, CA St. Joseph's Salesian Youth Renewal Center.
Bolton, Donald *c.ss.r.* '52 (ORL)[L] Saratoga Springs, NY St. John Neumann Residence.
Bolton, Norman B. '83 (SPR) Holyoke, MA Blessed Sacrament; [P] Springfield, MA Western New England College.
Bolton, Paul J. '62 (PRO) On Duty Outside the Diocese; Army Chaplains.
Bolton, Paul (ATL) Fort McPherson, GA Office of the Garrison Chaplain; Military Chaplains.
Boly, S.J., Craig '74 (SEA) Seattle, WA St. Joseph.
Bomar, Fred '60 (AUS) Austin, TX St. Peter the Apostle.
Bomar, Fred (AUS) Presbyteral Council.
Bomar, Fred (AUS) Consultors.
Bomba, Paul M. '77 (WOR) Military Chaplains; Army Chaplains.
Bombardier, Dennis P. '68 (SPR) Millers Falls, MA St. John's.
Bombardier, Paul A. '82 (SPR) Pittsfield, MA St. Francis; Pittsfield, MA St. Mary the Morning Star.
Bombera, Alex *t.o.r.* '46 (SFS) Plankinton, SD St. John.
Bomberger, Ray P. *s.s.j.* '71 (NO) New Orleans, LA Corpus Christi; New Orleans, LA Epiphany.
Bommarito, Vincent R. '77 (STL) St. Louis, MO St. Ambrose.
Bona, Joseph F. *s.j.* '72 (DEN)[N] Denver, CO Xavier Jesuit Center.
Bona, Richard '03 (CLV) Rocky River, OH St. Christopher.
Bonacci, Louis A. *s.j.* '73 (WH)[C] Scranton, PA The University of Scranton.
Bonacci, Paul '91 (ROC) Watkins Glen, NY St. Mary of the Lake.
Bonacci, Paul '91 (ROC) Watkins Glen, NY St. Benedict.
Bonacci, Thomas P. *c.p.* '72 (PIT)[N] Pittsburgh St. Paul of the Cross Monastery.
Bonacci, Tom *c.p.* '69 (PIT)[P] Pittsburgh, PA St. Paul of the Cross Retreat Center.
Bonacum, Thomas '79 (SB) Retired.
Bonadies, Kenneth P. '65 (HRT) Hamden, CT St. Ann's.
Bonadio, Joseph J. *s.s.* '64 (BAL) Baltimore, MD St. Francis of Assisi; [O] Baltimore, MD St. Charles Villa.
Bonafed, Joseph E. '92 (GBG) On Duty Outside the Diocese; Kensington, MD Holy Redeemer.
Bonanno, Raphael *o.f.m.* '62 (BO)[AA] Boston, MA St. Anthony Shrine.
Bonano, Salvatore *c.m.f.* '43 (LA)[Q] Rancho Dominguez, CA Dominguez Seminary Inc..
Bonarrigo, David C. *t.o.r.* '78 (ARL) Herndon, VA St. Joseph.
Bonavitacola, John M. '88 (PH) On Duty Outside the Archdiocese.
Bonavitacola, John '88 (PHX) Tempe, AZ Our Lady of Mt. Carmel.
Bonczewski, William D. '83 (OLL) Flint, MI Our Lady of Lebanon; [C] North Jackson, OH National Shrine of Our Lady of Lebanon.
Bonczweski, William (OLL) College of Consultors.
Bonczweski, William (OLL) Presbyteral Council.
Bond, Bob *g.h.m.* '60 (CIN)[M] Cincinnati Headquarters of Glenmary Home Missioners.
Bond, Daniel '84 (RIC) Hopewell, VA St. James Church.
Bond, Ernest W. '88 (COS) Bailey, CO St. Mary of the Rockies; Diocesan Consultors; Procurator–Advocates; Northern Region.
Bond, Robert E. *o.p.* '55 (PRO)[P] Providence St. Thomas Aquinas Priory at Providence College.
Bond, Thomas Aquinas *o.c.s.o.* '39 (ROC)[I] Piffard, NY Abbey of the Genesee.
Bond, William D. '99 (OM)[B] Columbus, NE Scotus Central Catholic High School.
Bonderenko, Thomas S. '80 (BAL) Absent on Leave.
Bondi, Paul '48 (ALB) St. Petersburg, FL Blessed Trinity Retired.
Bondi, Paul '48 (ALB) Retired.
Bondi, Richard A. '74 (SPR) South Hadley, MA St. Theresa of the Infant Jesus; [P] South Hadley, MA Mount Holyoke College.
Bondi, Steven '86 (JOL) Braidwood, IL Immaculate Conception.
Bondy, Alberto P. '86 (DET) Centerline, MI St. Clement.
Boneck, Norman D. '62 (LC) Edgar, WI St. John the Baptist.
Boned, Enrique '57 (MIA) Retired.
Bonelli, Theodore V. '61 (NEW) Retired.
Bonello, Joseph *o.f.m.* (FgM).
Bonello, Pablo *i.v.e.* '84 (SJ) San Jose, CA St. Leo the Great.
Bonetti, Henry *s.d.b.* '73 (FgM).
Boney, Vincent *c.p.* '57 (SCR)[M] Clarks Summit, PA St. Gabriel's Convent.
Bonfadini, Leo '74 (PBL) Absent on Leave.

Bonfiglio, David G. '51 (BO) Senior Priests Retired.
Bonfiglio, Gregory R. *s.j.* '94 (SAC)[D] Sacramento, CA Jesuit High School; [I] Carmichael, CA Jesuit High School Community of Sacramento.
Bongard, Joseph W. '86 (PH)[D] Pottstown, PA St. Pius X High School; Approved Advocates.
Bongard, Joseph '86 (PH) Collegeville, PA St. Eleanor.
Bonges, Charles *s.j.* '81 (BAL)[S] Baltimore, MD Jesuit Community of Loyola College, Inc..
Bonghanoy, Edgardo C. '80 (HON) Mountain View, HI St. Theresa.
Bonghanoy, Edgardo (HON) Filipino Ministry.
Bongila, Jean Pierre '91 (SFR) San Francisco, CA Cathedral of St. Mary (Assumption); Congolese Ministry.
Bongiorno, Angelo *s.d.b.* '43 (BO)[E] Boston, MA Savio Preparatory High School.
Bonham, Ray O. '94 (OM) Retired.
Bonian, Stephen J. *s.j.* '82 (BO)[V] Boston The Society of Jesus of New England–Provincial Offices.
Bonian, Steve *s.j.* '82 (OLL) St. Paul, MN Holy Family Church.
Bonifas, Roger D. '45 (TOL) Retired.
Bonifazi, Remo J. *c.s.sp.* '45 (FgM).
Bonikowski, Leon V. *o.s.f.s.* '65 (PH)[AA] Philadelphia, PA Father Louis Brisson Residence.
Bonikowski, Leon V. *o.s.f.s.* '65 (FgM).
Bonilla, Luis Angel (ALN) Reading, PA St. Peter.
Bonin, Harold A. '65 (CHI) Other Assignments.
Bonin, Richard G. '46 (NU) Retired.
Bonjean, Jerry *s.d.b.* '67 (OAK)[N] Berkeley Salesian Community.
Bonjean, Richard '76 (MRY) Retired.
Bonjean, Richard (MRY) St. Vincent De Paul.
Bonk, Carl A. *s.j.* '82 (DET)[K] Detroit, MI Jesuit Community at the University of Detroit Mercy; Detroit, MI SS. Peter and Paul Jesuit; Presbyteral Council.
Bonke, James R. '70 (IND) Indianapolis, IN SS. Peter and Paul Cathedral; Defenders of the Bond.
Bonke, James '70 (IND) Indianapolis, IN Christ The King.
Bonke, James (IND) Archdiocesan Review Board.
Bonn, Ferdinand C. '49 (JC) Retired.
Bonnar, David J. '88 (PIT) Pittsburgh, PA St. Bartholomew; Clergy Personnel Board.
Bonneau, Normand *o.m.i.* '76 (FgM).
Bonneau, Normand *o.m.i.* '76 (WDC)[M] Washington, DC Provincial Offices of the United States Province of the Missionary Oblates of Mary Immaculate.
Bonneau, Roger *o.carm.* '60 (JOL)[L] Darien, IL Carmelite Community.
Bonneau, Roger *o.carm.* '60 (JOL)[O] Darien, IL National Shrine of St. Therese.
Bonneau, Roger *o.carm.* '02 (JOL)[K] Darien, IL Carmelite Carefree Retirement Village.
Bonneau, Ronald E. *c.ss.r.* '71 (NY) Bronx, NY Immaculate Conception.
Bonnell, Robert A. '49 (CLV) Oberlin, OH Sacred Heart Retired.
Bonnell, Victor G. '60 (SLC) Layton, UT St. Rose of Lima; Ecumenical Commission; Board of Directors.
Bonner, Charles E. '65 (PH) Philadelphia, PA St. Cecilia.
Bonner, Dismas *o.f.m.* '58 (STL)[S] Dittmer, MO Il Ritiro–The Little Retreat.
Bonner, Michael J. *s.v.d.* '66 (CHI) Chicago, IL St. Bronislava; [B] Techny, IL Divine Word Residence.
Bonner, Patrick J. *o.s.b.* '59 (PAT)[M] Newton, NJ St. Paul's Abbey.
Bonner, William J. '67 (LA) Los Angeles, CA St. Malachy.
Bonner, William R. *c.ss.r.* '61 (NY)[EE] New York, NY Redemptorist Priests and Brothers, C.Ss.R..
Bonner, William (LA) College of Consultors.
Bonneville, Lionel E. '63 (SPR) Ludlow, MA St. John the Baptist; Northampton, MA Veterans Administration Hospital.
Bonnici, John S. '91 (NY)[D] New York, NY Family Life/Respect Life Office.
Bonnici, John '72 (NY) Bronx, NY St. Philip Neri.
Bonnici, William '67 (DET) Roseville, MI Sacred Heart.
Bonnot, Bernard R. '67 (Y) On Duty Outside the Diocese.
Bono, James P. '03 (PAT) Stirling, NJ St. Vincent de Paul.
Bonsignore, Dennis '81 (ROC) Monroe Community Hospital; Rochester, NY St. Anne.
Bonsignore, Dennis '81 (ROC) Strong Health System.
Bonsignore, Mark '95 (HRT)[I] Hartford, CT Saint Francis Hospital and Medical Center.
Bonsor, Jack '74 (SJ) San Jose, CA St. Martin of Tours.
Bonsu, Anthony (RVC) East Meadow, NY Nassau University Medical Center.
Bonvouloir, Philip E. *a.a.* '57 (PRO) Pawtucket, RI St. Leo the Great.
Bonzagni, John J. '80 (SPR) Lenox Dale, MA St. Vincent de Paul's; Adjutant Judicial Vicar.
Book, A. Joseph '63 (E) St. Francis Xavier.
Book, Theodore '76 (ATL) Kennesaw, GA St. Catherine of Siena.
Boone, Scott F. (DUB)[N] Ames, IA St. Thomas Aquinas Church and Catholic Student Center (Iowa State University); Ames, IA SS. Peter and Paul; Ames, IA St. Thomas Aquinas Church (and Catholic Student Center); Deanery Representatives.
Boone, Thomas A. '61 (CLV) Brook Park, OH Assumption of Mary.
Boosel, Brian D. *o.s.b.* '03 (GBG)[H] Latrobe, PA Saint Vincent Archabbey.
Booth, Earl J. '60 (LR)[H] Little Rock, AR St. John Manor Retired.
Booth, Edward '74 (STA) Switzerland, FL San Juan Del Rio.
Booth, John A. '82 (SY) Deposit, NY St. Joseph.
Booth, John '82 (SY) Binghamton, NY Binghamton Psychiatric Hospital.
Booth, John '82 (SY) Binghamton Psychiatric Hospital.
Booth, John '82 (SY) Windsor, NY Our Lady of Lourdes.
Booth, Mark–Thomas *o.f.m.conv.* '85 (ATL) Lithia Springs, GA St. John Vianney.
Booth, Raymond '57 (ROC) Pittsford, NY St. Louis.
Booth, Raymond '57 (ROC) Retired.
Booth, Stephen R. *m.m.* '86 (NY)[EE] Air Force Chaplains.
Boquet, Gregory M. *o.s.b.* '88 (NO)[A] St. Benedict, LA St. Joseph Seminary College; [P] St. Benedict, LA St. Joseph Abbey.
Boquet, Shenan J. '93 (HT) Galliano, LA St. Joseph.
Boras, Kurt D. '86 (CHI) Lansing, IL St. Ann.
Borawski, Gerald J. '72 (LFT) Frankfort, IN St. Mary; Associate Judges.
Borba, Joseph (SB) Finance Council Members.
Borbely, James A. *s.j.* '76 (ALN)[A] Wernersville, PA Jesuit Center; [A] Wernersville, PA Jesuit Center.
Borbridge, David C. *s.j.* '63 (FgM).
Borbridge, David *s.j.* '63 (MOB)[A] Mobile, AL Spring Hill College.
Borca, Dennis L. '81 (MAR) Munising, MI Sacred Heart of Jesus.
Borchardt, Edgar '96 (SPK) Pullman, WA Sacred Heart.
Borcherding, Martin '73 (LAF) Lafayette, LA Holy Cross.
Borcic, John J '76 (STL) Marthasville, MO St. Vincent de Paul.
Borcic, John J. (STL) Archdiocesan Council of Priests; Warren County Catholic Church Real Estate Corporation; [U] Marthasville, MO Warren County Catholic Church Real Estate Corporation.
Borcz, Casimir Adalbert *o.c.d.* '45 (GRY)[I] Munster, IN Discalced Carmelite Fathers Monastery.
Bord, William '99 (OM) Columbus, NE St. Isidore.
Borda, Peter Paul '42 (SD) Retired.
Bordeaux, Henry *o.c.d.* '62 (OKL) Oklahoma City, OK Our Lady of Mount Carmel and St. Therese Little Flower.
Bordeleau, Beau–Pierre G. '85 (BRK) Released from Diocesan Assignment.
Bordelon, H. Gerald *v.f.* '56 (ALX) College of Consultors; Priests Council; Rural Deans; Charismatic Movement; Cloutierville, LA St. John the Baptist.
Bordelon, Roland '50 (ALX) On Duty Outside the Diocese.
Borden, Wilfred F. *o.m.i.* '63 (LA)[C] Santa Paula, CA Thomas Aquinas College.
Bordenave, Ian (NO) New Orleans, LA St. Anthony of Padua.
Bordenkircher, Robert A. *o.p.* '54 (GAL)[Q] Houston, TX Dominican Friars, St. Mark Priory, Inc..
Borders, Larry D. (IND) Greensburg, IN Immaculate Conception; Napoleon, IN St. Maurice; Greensburg, IN St. Denis.
Bordignon, Narciso *c.r.s.* '67 (GAL) Houston, TX Assumption.
Bordonaro, Joseph C. '89 (PH) Primos, PA St. Eugene; [D] Springfield, PA Cardinal O'Hara High School.
Bordonaro, Richard D. '76 (BUF)[P] Williamsville, NY Sisters of St. Francis of the Third Order Regular, St. Mary of the Angels; Millard Fillmore Suburban Hospital.
Borek, Derek J. '99 (BO) Newburyport, MA Immaculate Conception
Borel, Albert W. '81 (LKC) Bell City, LA St. John Vianney.
Borel, Albert (LKC) Judges.
Boren, Edward *o.f.m.* '64 (JOL) Madisonville, TN St. Joseph the Worker; San Antonio, TX San Jose y San Miguel.
Borer, Gerald *sj* '59 (COS) Colorado Springs, CO Our Lady of the Pines–Black Forest.
Borer, Robert D. '76 (STU) Cambridge, OH St. Benedict; Lore City, OH SS. Peter and Paul.
Boretto, Christopher '87 (SY) Binghamton, NY Our Lady of Lourdes Memorial Hospital.
Boretto, Christopher '87 (SY) Binghamton, NY St. John the Evangelist.
Borg, Marcellinus *o.f.m.* '59 (ALB) Troy, NY St. Anthony of Padua (Shrine Church).
Borg, Ron *c.s.b.* '79 (DET) Detroit, MI St. Louis the King.
Borgea, Alfonso *o.f.m.conv.* '98 (LA) Hermosa Beach, CA Our Lady of Guadalupe.
Borgelt, Daniel E. '93 (TOL) Napoleon, OH St. Augustine.
Borgen–Reithel, Alfonso *o.f.m.conv.* '98 (LA) Torrance, CA Nativity.
Borger, Marvin G. '91 (TOL) Military Chaplains; Consultors; Judges; Navy Chaplains.
Borger, Theodore R. '83 (DAV) AUXILIARY CHAPLAINS CONTRACT CHAPLAINS Retired.
Borgerding, Terry J. '77 (STL) Lemay, MO St. Martin of Tours.
Borgers, Charles *o.m.i.* '41 (SAT)[K] San Antonio, TX Oblate Madonna Residence.
Borges, Charles *s.j.* '81 (BAL)[B] Timonium, MD Loyola Graduate Center –Timonium Campus.
Borges, Jose A. *s.j.* '69 (SJN)[D] Rio Piedras, PR Centro Universitario Catolico; [H] San Juan, PR Comunidad Jesuita.
Borges, Laurence J. '59 (BO) Framingham, MA St. Stephen.
Borges, Mario L. '82 (OAK) Castro Valley, CA Transfiguration.
Borgesen, Kenneth G. *o.ss.t.* '87 (TR) Asbury Park, NJ Our Lady of Mt. Carmel.
Borgia, Anthony A. '84 (TOL) Fort Jennings, OH St. Joseph; Ottoville, OH Immaculate Conception.
Borgmeyer, Dean G. '81 (WH) Star City, WV St. Mary's; Presbyteral Council.
Borgo, John V. *s.j.* '57 (BGP)[P] Fairfield, CT The Fairfield Jesuit Community–Fairfield University.
Borgognoni, Charles L. '48 (SY) Retired.
Borho, Charles D. '57 (P) St. Paul, OR St. Paul.
Borino, David J. '86 (HRT) East Haven, CT Our Lady of Pompeii; Waterbury, CT Our Lady of Mt. Carmel.
Borja, Charlito '03 (CHK) Saipan, MP Cathedral of Our Lady of Mt. Carmel; Presbyteral Council.
Borja, Jose A. (BO) Roxbury, MA St. Patrick.
Bork, Vincent P. '95 (ARL) Front Royal, VA St. John the Baptist.
Borkenhagen, Jason '01 (WCH)[B] Wichita, KS Kapaun Mt. Carmel Catholic High School.
Borkenhagen, Jason (WCH) Office of Worship.
Borkowski, Aloysius J. '39 (GBG) Retired.
Borkowski, Edward *s.v.d.* '44 (CHI)[B] Techny, IL Divine Word Residence.
Borkowski, Francis '77 (NY) Mahopac, NY St. John the Evangelist; Military Chaplains.
Borkowski, Mark '96 (DET) Detroit, MI St. Josaphat; Detroit, MI Sweetest Heart of Mary.
Borkowski, Raymond *o.f.m.conv.* '61 (NOR) Cromwell, CT St. John.
Borkowski, Thomas '81 (KC) Kansas City, MO St. Thomas More.
Borkowski, Tomasz J. '01 (WOR) Clinton, MA Our Lady of Jasna Gora.
Borlang, Stephen M. '86 (SAC) Vallejo, CA St. Vincent Ferrer.
Borlik, Dan Paul *c.m.* '76 (DAL)[K] Dallas, TX Congregation of the Mission, Southern Province.
Borlik, Dan Paul *c.m.* '76 (FgM).
Bormann, Charles P. '58 (PHX) Retired.
Bormann, Paul D. '85 (SC) Bancroft, IA St. John the Baptist's; Ledyard, IA Sacred Heart; Presbyteral Council.
Bornbach, Raymond H. '41 (LC) Retired.
Bornhauser, Emmanuel '98 (NEW) On Duty Outside the Archdiocese.
Borntrager, Conrad M. *o.s.m.* '60 (CHI) Chicago, IL Annunciata; [N] Chicago, IL Order of Friar Servants of Mary (Servites) United States of America Province, Inc.; [N] Chicago, IL Annunciata Priory.
Boroch, Andrzej '95 (SAG) Ruth, MI St. Anthony.
Boroch, Andrzej '95 (SAG) Ruth, MI St. Mary.
Borodach, John J. '57 (PBR) Donora, PA St. Michael; Consultors; Protopresbyters; Finance Council.
Borodach, Joseph '60 (PBR) Bradenville, PA St. Mary's.
Boronat, Francis *sch.p.* '54 (LA)[Q] Los Angeles, CA Piarist Fathers.
Boronat, Frank *sch.p.* '54 (LA) Los Angeles, CA St. Lucy.
Borosh, Carl A. '68 (STU) Retired.
Boroughs, Philip L. *s.j.* '78 (SEA)[M] Washington, DC The Jesuit Community at Georgetown University.
Boroughs, Philip L. *s.s.j.* (WDC)[C] Washington, DC Georgetown University.
Borowczyk, Martin R. '42 (CHI) Bartlett, IL St. Peter Damian Retired.
Borowiak, David J. '71 (BUF) Depew, NY St. James.
Borowiak, Kenneth A. '87 (LIN) Exeter, NE St. Stephen's; Office of Information and Media; Newspaper.
Borowik, John '66 (NEW) Retired.
Borowik, John '66 (NEW)[N] Rutherford, NJ St. John Vianney Residence for Priests.
Borowski, Charles E.J. '66 (WOR) Southbridge, MA St. Hedwig's.
Borowski, Paul J. *c.ss.r.* '87 (BRK)[C] Whitestone, NY St. Alphonsus Formation Residence.
Borre, Robert J. (MAD).
Borrelli, Anthony A. '54 (COL) Retired.
Borrelli, Anthony (COL) Diocesan Judges.

Borsari, John P. *c.r.s.* '94 (GAL) Houston, TX Assumption.
Borski, Charles J. *o.m.i.* '70 (GAL) Alvin, TX St. John the Baptist.
Borski, Chester L. '67 (GAL) Kingwood, TX St. Martha; [U] Houston, TX Martha's Kitchen Food Services; Appointees.
Borski, Jerome *o.s.b.* '92 (PAT)[M] Morristown, NJ St. Mary's Abbey.
Borsuk, Ronald W. '58 (PBR) Conemaugh, PA Holy Trinity.
Bortolazzo, Peter *c.s.* '39 (BO) Boston, MA Sacred Heart.
Bortolotti, Serafino '47 (SFE) Retired.
Boruszewski, Joseph A. '53 (BUF) Retired.
Boruta, Alexander *o.f.m.* '60 (GAY) Prescott, MI St. Stephen of Hungary.
Borzaga, Rinaldo '47 (BRK) Retired.
Borzaga, Rinaldo *f.s.c.a.* '47 (NY)[EE] New York, NY Brothers of the Christian Schools of Manhattan College, Inc..
Borzuchowski, John W. '68 (NY) Kingston, NY Immaculate Conception.
Borzych, Alexander J. '80 (GI) Military Chaplains; Navy Chaplains.
Bosack, Albert J. '43 (BUF)[O] Lackawanna, NY Bishop Head Residence Retired.
Bosch, Joseph J. '63 (P) Brookings, OR Star of the Sea; Sheridan, OR Good Shepherd.
Bosch, Stan *s.t.* '86 (LA) Compton, CA Sagrado Corazon, Sacred Heart.
Bosch, Stan *s.t.* '86 (LA) Compton, CA Our Lady of Victory.
Bosch, Stanley *s.t.* (LA) Board of Directors:.
Bosch, William J. *s.j.* '60 (SY)[Q] Syracuse, NY Jesuits at LeMoyne, Inc..
Boschert, Hubert J. *s.j.* (LC) Prairie du Chien, WI St. Gabriel.
Boschert, Joseph N. '60 (COV) California, KY Sts. Peter and Paul; Diocesan Consultors.
Boschetto, Dan *s.x.* '70 (PAT)[M] Wayne Xaverian Missionary Fathers.
Boschi, Marcelo *f.d.p.* '95 (BO)[T] East Boston, MA Don Orione Nursing Home.
Bosco, John M. '71 (LAN) Morrice, MI St. Mary.
Bosco, Mark G. *s.j.* '99 (SFR)[C] Chicago, IL Jesuit Community at Loyola University Chicago.
Boscoe, John L. *c.s.b.* '72 (GAL)[Q] Sugar Land Basilian Mission Center.
Boscutti, Darrio L. '86 (CHI) Hickory Hills, IL St. Patricia.
Bosken, Robert E. *s.j.* '56 (STL)[O] St. Louis, MO De Smet Jesuit High School Community.
Boslett, Donald E. '59 (ALT) Renovo, PA St. Joseph's.
Bosnich, David A. '95 (PBR) Braddock, PA SS. Peter and Paul; Duquesne, PA SS. Peter and Paul; Pittsburgh, PA Holy Spirit.
Bosse, Dennis (O.F.M)[T] Galveston, TX Galveston Newman Center.
Bossi, Paul R. '69 (BUF) Vicars; Buffalo, NY Blessed Sacrament.
Bossi, Stephen E. *c.s.p.* '85 (P) Portland, OR St. Philip Neri; [Q] Portland, OR Paulist Fathers Catholic Center for Evangelization.
Bossie, Robert W. *s.c.j.* '75 (CHI)[N] Chicago, IL SCJ Novitiate.
Bossman, David M. *o.f.m.* '65 (NY)[EE] South Orange, NJ Seton Hall University.
Bosso, Stephen C. '78 (PT)[A] Boynton Beach, FL St. Vincent de Paul Regional Seminary; On Duty Outside the Diocese.
Boster, Charles (SAL) Art and Architecture Commission.
Bostwick, John '69 (RIC) Unassigned.
Bostwick, John *o.praem.* '76 (GB)[B] St. Norbert College.
Bostwick, John *o.praem.* '76 (GB)[I] De Pere, WI St. Joseph Priory.
Boteju, Bernard *s.r.i.* '85 (TYL) Canton, TX St. Therese.
Boteju, Bernard (TYL) College of Consultors.
Boteju, Bernard (TYL) Priests' Personnel Board.
Boteju, Bernard (TYL) Priests' Pension Board.
Boteler, William M. *m.m.* '68 (LA)[Q] Monrovia, CA.
Botenhagen, Paul *o.f.m.* '82 (P) Portland, OR Ascension.
Botet, Manuel *c.m.* (BRK)[Z] Brooklyn, NY Centro Evangelization S. Vincente de Paul.
Botheroyd, Thomas (JOL) Lisle, IL St. Joan of Arc.
Botkin, Edward A. '73 (DAV) Delmar, IA St. Patrick's; Delmar, IA Immaculate Conception; Delmar, IA St. Anne; [B] St. Ambrose University.
Botsko, Jerome G. '82 (PBR) Brownsville, PA St. Nicholas; Elected Deanery Representatives.
Bottazzo, Alex '43 (LAN) Retired.
Botte, Gregory *o.f.m.* '68 (NY)[EE] St. Francis Friary.
Bottino, Dominic J. '78 (CAM) Pennsauken, NJ St. Stephen; Judicial Vicar; Judicial Vicar; Advocates.
Bottino, Edward J. '52 (BRK) Flushing, NY Mary's Nativity.
Botton, Pierre A. '56 (BGP) Retired.
Botz, Roger *o.s.b.* '60 (SCL)[I] Collegeville, MN St. John's Abbey, of the Order of St. Benedict.
Botz, Roger *o.s.b.* '60 (SCL)[G] St. Cloud, MN St. Cloud Hospital.
Botzum, William A. *c.s.c.* '43 (FTW)[I] Notre Dame, IN Holy Cross House.
Bou, Pedro L. *s.v.d.* '74 (TR) Trenton, NJ St. Mary Cathedral.
Bou–Merhi, Gebran '88 (SLC) Murray, UT St. Jude.
Bou–Merhi, Gebran '88 (OLL) Murray, UT Saint Jude Church.
Bouchard, Alfred '56 (MAN) Nashua, NH St. Aloysius.
Bouchard, Charles E. *o.p.* '79 (STL)[B] St. Louis, MO Aquinas Institute of Theology; [O] St. Louis, MO Dominican Community of St. Louis; [O] St. Louis, MO Dominican Community of St. Louis.
Bouchard, Denis *f.s.s.p.* (SCR)[M] Elmhurst Priestly Fraternity of St. Peter (F.S.S.P.), North American District Headquarters.
Bouchard, Lucien *o.m.i.* '55 (FgM).
Bouchard, Marcel H. '72 (FR) East Sandwich, MA Corpus Christi; Cape Cod Deanery.
Bouchard, Norman '88 (PBL) Absent on Leave.
Bouchard, Paul L. '72 (MAN) Promoter of Justice; Defenders of the Bond; Council of Priests; Manchester, NH Transfiguration.
Bouchard, Robert P. '84 (PRT) Brunswick, ME St. John the Baptist; South Portland, ME Men's Correctional Center; Thomaston, ME Maine State Prison; Warren, ME Super Maximum Facility & Minimum Facility.
Bouchard, Thomas '53 (DUL) Retired.
Bouchard, Thomas (VEN) Cape Coral, FL St. Andrew.
Boucher, Edward F. '60 (SAG) Retired.
Boucher, Gerard A. '53 (MAN) Meredith, NH St. Charles; Propagation of the Faith Retired.
Boucher, Gilmond C. *o.m.i.* (BO) Lowell, MA St. Marie; Lowell, MA Sacred Heart.
Boucher, Gilmond *o.m.i.* '58 (BO)[V] Lowell, MA Andre Garin Retirement Residence.
Boucher, Kevin '91 (FAR) Rugby, ND St. Therese, Little Flower.
Boucher, Kevin (FAR) Deanery 7.
Boucher, Kevin (FAR) Deanery 6.
Boucher, Maurice U. *s.s.e.* '48 (BUR)[I] Isle La Motte, VT St. Anne's Shrine; Alburg, VT St. Amadeus.
Boucher, Richard R. *m.s.* '60 (HRT)[M] Hartford, CT Missionaries of LaSalette.
Boucher, Roger R. '73 (WOR) Military Chaplains.
Boucher, Roger R. (WOR) Navy Chaplains.
Boucree, Thaddeus *s.v.d.* '52 (NO)[N] New Orleans, LA St. John Berchmans Manor.
Boudoin, Burt '82 (SD) Encinitas, CA St. John the Evangelist.
Boudreau, C. Paul '83 (NOR) On Duty Outside the Diocese.
Boudreau, George R. *o.p.* '83 (STL)[B] St. Louis, MO Aquinas Institute of Theology.
Boudreau, Paul '55 (SPR) Retired.
Boudreau, Thomas C. (BO) Abington, MA St. Bridget.
Boudreau, Thomas '56 (LA) Los Angeles, CA Divine Saviour.
Boudreaux, Claude P. *s.j.* '55 (NO)[F] New Orleans, LA Jesuit High School.
Boudreaux, John S. '73 (LAF) On Duty Outside the Diocese; Mobile, AL Corpus Christi.
Bouffard, James F. '70 (NEW) Haworth, NJ Sacred Heart.
Bouffard, James (NEW) Members.
Bouffard, Lionel A. *m.m.* '63 (NY)[EE] Maryknoll Maryknoll Fathers and Brothers.
Bouffier, Robert *s.m.* '74 (HON)[G] Honolulu, HI Chaminade Pohaku Marianist Community.
Boufford, Thomas F. '81 (GR) Lake Odessa, MI St. Edward's; Deans; College of Consultors.
Boufford, Thomas '81 (GR) Saranac, MI St. Anthony.
Boughton, Michael *s.j.* '79 (BGP)[P] Fairfield, CT The Fairfield Jesuit Community–Fairfield University.
Boughton, Michael *s.j.* '79 (BGP)[E] Fairfield, CT Fairfield College Preparatory School.
Bouhall, William G. '94 (CLV) Euclid, OH Holy Cross.
Boulanger, Andre '65 (PHX) Retired.
Boulanger, Gerard R. *m.s.* '73 (SPR) Westfield, MA Holy Trinity.
Boulanger, Raymond *s.m.* '51 (BO)[X] Framingham, MA The Marist House.
Boule, David (STL)[J] Bridgeton, MO SSM De Paul Health Center.
Boule, Roland B. '32 (FR) Retired.
Boulet, Marshall '71 (LKC) Elton, LA St. Paul.
Boulette, Michael J. '76 (SAT) Kerrville, TX Notre Dame.
Boulette, Michael (SAT) Archdiocesan Presbyteral Council.
Boulette, Michael (SAT) College of Consultors.
Boulette, Michael (SAT) In Rural Area.
Bouley, Allan *o.s.b.* '62 (SCL)[I] Collegeville, MN St. John's Abbey, of the Order of St. Benedict.
Boulos, Peter '93 (SAM) Atlanta, GA St. Joseph's Maronite Church.
Boulton, David G. *s.j.* '61 (BO)[V] Weston, MA Campion Health Center, Inc..
Boumans, Albert J. '52 (LAF) New Iberia, LA Nativity of Our Lady Retired.
Boumans, Albert '52 (LAF) Retired.
Bourcy, Robert Scott '82 (ROC) Macedon, NY St. Patrick.
Bourdeau, Leo *s.m.* '42 (BO)[X] Framingham, MA The Marist House.
Bourdon, Norman W. '73 (PRO) Cumberland, RI St. Joan of Arc.
Bourek, David F. '79 (LIN) Friend, NE St. Joseph's; Advocates; Rural Life Conference.
Bouressa, Donald J. '61 (PRO) Retired.
Bourg, Rodney P. '78 (NO) Slidell, LA St. Luke the Evangelist.
Bourgault, Ronald L. '63 (BO) Wayland, MA St. Zepherin.
Bourgea, Roger *s.m.* '59 (BRK) Brooklyn, NY St. Francis of Assisi–St. Blaise; Kings County Hospital Center.
Bourgeois, Bernard W. '95 (BUR) Waterbury, VT St. Andrew; State Hospital.
Bourgeois, Donald E. '85 (SY) Johnson City, NY Blessed Sacrament.
Bourgeois, Donald (SY) "The Catholic Sun".
Bourgeois, Francis L. '61 (LAF) Rayne, LA St. Leo IV.
Bourgeois, Frank '54 (HON) Ewa, HI Immaculate Conception.
Bourgeois, Henry *c.s.c.* '62 (FR)[H] North Dartmouth, MA Holy Cross Residence.
Bourgeois, Joseph '58 (NO) Terrytown, LA Christ the King.
Bourgeois, Lloyd '57 (SD) San Diego, CA San Rafael.
Bourgeois, Lloyd '57 (SD) Retired.
Bourgeois, Louis D. '59 (BO) Hamilton, MA St. Paul.
Bourgeois, Roger *s.s.s.* '57 (CLV) Highland Heights, OH St. Paschal Baylon.
Bourgeois, Roger *s.s.s.* '57 (CLV)[O] Cleveland, OH Blessed Sacrament Community.
Bourgeois, Roy L. *m.m.* '72 (NY).
Bourget, Laurence *o.c.s.o.* '42 (WOR)[O] Spencer, MA St. Joseph's Abbey.
Bourgoin, Raymond *o.m.i.* '66 (FgM).
Bourke, Charles E. '70 (BO) Winthrop, MA St. John the Evangelist.
Bourke, John F. '60 (CAM) Waterford, NJ St. Anthony.
Bourke, Martin '74 (SEA) Ocean Shores, WA St. Jerome.
Bourke, Martin '74 (SEA) Aberdeen, WA St. Mary.
Bourke, Martin '74 (SEA) Aberdeen, WA SS. Peter and Paul.
Bourke, Martin '74 (SEA) Hoquiam, WA Our Lady of Good Help.
Bourke, Myles M. '42 (NY) New York, NY Corpus Christi Retired.
Bourke, Myles '43 (NY)[EE] Bronx, NY.
Bourke, Nathaniel J. '59 (GF) Retired.
Bourke, Ulick *s.m.a.* '68 (BO)[V] Dedham, MA African Mission House.
Bourke, William D. *s.s.c.* '54 (FgM).
Bourque, Charles J. '62 (BO) Jamaica Plain, MA Our Lady of Lourdes; CENTRAL REGION.
Bourque, Joseph A. '55 (LKC) Retired.
Bourque, Real '54 (BEL)[F] Belleville, IL Missionary Oblates of Mary Immaculate – St. Henry's Oblate Residence.
Bourque, Thomas *t.o.r.* '82 (WDC)[M] Washington, DC St. Louis Friary.
Bourret, Philip L. *s.j.* '41 (SJ)[M] Los Gatos, CA Sacred Heart Jesuit Center.
Bourret, Philip L. *s.j.* '41 (FgM).
Bouska, Jeroma A. '56 (LA) Retired.
Bouska, Jerome A. (LA) Defenders of the Bond.
Bouska, Jerome '56 (LA) Los Angeles, CA St. Basil's Retired.
Bousquet, Roland '54 (FR) Retired.
Bouterie, Thomas '80 (HT) On Sabbatical.
Boutin, Emile R. '91 (BO) Stoughton, MA Immaculate Conception.
Bouton, Thomas F. '83 (BO) Health Leave.
Boutot, Michel R. *c.s.sp.* '93 (NO) New Orleans, LA Holy Ghost; Deans.
Boutros, Peter (NTN) Phoenix, AZ St. John of the Desert.
Boutros, Peter (NTN) Presbyteral Council.
Bouzigard, Michael A. *s.j.* '01 (NO).
Bova, Eugene R. '57 (BIS) Retired.
Bova Conti, Michael J. '71 (BO)[P] Sudbury, MA Our Lady of Fatima; WEST REGION.
Bovard, William R. '64 (PIT) Pittsburgh, PA St. John Neumann.
Bove, Ralph *c.s.* '78 (PRO) Johnston, RI St. Rocco.
Bovee, Brian '81 (RCK) Rockford, IL St. Mary Oratory, Institute of Christ the King Sovereign Priest.
Bovenzi, Angelo D. *c.s.b.* '67 (ROC)[I] Rochester, NY Basilian Residence.
Bovenzi, Robert *c.p.* '85 (CHI)[N] Chicago, IL Passionist Community–Immaculate Conception Monastery.
Bowden, John V. '62 (TR) Brick Town, NJ Epiphany; Cursillo.
Bowden, Lloyd '49 (JOL) Retired.
Bowe, John C. *c.r.* '68 (PBL) Pagosa Springs, CO Immaculate Heart of Mary.

Bowe, John F. '73 (PH) Sellersville, PA St. Agnes; Army National Guard Chaplains.
Bowen, Gerard J. '77 (BAL) Elkridge, MD St. Augustine.
Bowen, John W. *s.s.* '49 (BAL) Baltimore, MD St. Mark; [O] Baltimore, MD St. Charles Villa.
Bowen, Joseph D. '57 (PH) Abington, PA Our Lady Help of Christians.
Bowen, Robert *s.s.j.* '59 (NO)[P] New Orleans, LA The Josephite Faculty House of St. Augustine High School.
Bowens, Lorin M. '74 (MAD) Holy Family; Lime Ridge, WI St. Boniface; Council of Catholic Women.
Bower, Alan E. '89 (STA) Williston, FL Holy Family; Diocesan Consultors.
Bower, Alan (STA) Presbyteral Council.
Bower, Lawrence C. '88 (BAK) Retired.
Bower, Lawrence C. (BAK) Navy Reserve Chaplains.
Bowering, Gerhard H. *s.j.* '70 (BGP)[P] Fairfield, CT The Fairfield Jesuit Community–Fairfield University.
Bowers, Mark R. '98 (TOL) Health Leave.
Bowers, Philip T. (LFT) Clergy Relief Association.
Bowers, Phillip T. '64 (LFT) Fishers, IN Holy Spirit Church.
Bowers, Robert J. '87 (BO) Charlestown, MA St. Catherine of Siena.
Bowers, Ronald J. (STP) Adjutant Judicial Vicars.
Bowers, Ronald '64 (STP)[A] St. Paul, MN The Saint Paul Seminary.
Bowers, Ronald *j.c.d.* '64 (STP)[C] St. Paul, MN University of St. Thomas.
Bowes, Charles J. '71 (CIN) Cincinnati, OH Our Lady of the Rosary.
Bowes, David '46 (KNX) Retired.
Bowes, James J. *s.j.* '66 (NY).
Bowes, Vincent *o.c.d.* '61 (BO)[V] Boston, MA Carmelite Monastery.
Bowker, Jeffrey *l.c.* '94 (ATL)[K] Atlanta, GA Legionaries of Christ.
Bowlds, Kent '93 (JKS) Director of Vocations; Priests' Council; Jackson, MS St. Richard; Madison, MS Holy Family.
Bowler, James M. *s.j.* '74 (BGP)[B] Fairfield, CT Fairfield University.
Bowler, James S. *s.j.* '74 (BGP)[P] Fairfield, CT The Fairfield Jesuit Community–Fairfield University.
Bowler, Joseph D. *o.s.f.s.* '49 (WIL)[J] Childs, MD Retirement and Assisted Care Facility.
Bowler, Michael J. '57 (CHI) Retired.
Bowles, Richard (COS) Colorado Springs, CO Saint Paul Retired.
Bowles, William H. '91 (NU) Kandiyohi, MN St. Patrick; Lake Lillian, MN St. Thomas More; Regional Treatment Center.
Bowles, William '91 (NU)[F] Willmar, MN Willmar Regional Treatment Center.
Bowling, Theodore B. *s.j.* '53 (FgM).
Bowling, William M. '97 (L) Shelbyville, KY Annunciation of the Blessed Virgin Mary; Ex Officio.
Bowman, James C. '65 (RVC) Mineola, NY Corpus Christi.
Bowman, John '65 (SEA) Shoreline, WA St. Luke.
Bowman, R. Peter '55 (CHI) Retired.
Bowman, Ronald P. '82 (ALN) Reading, PA St. Catharine of Siena.
Bowski, Eugene '77 (GLP) On Duty Outside of Diocese.
Boxleitner, J. Jerome '56 (STP) Minnesota Correctional Facility; [H] Minneapolis, MN St. Joseph's Home for Children Retired.
Boyack, Kenneth G. *c.s.p.* '79 (WDC)[B] Washington, DC St. Paul's College; [V] Washington, DC Paulist National Catholic Evangelization Assoc..
Boyce, Edmund J. *o.s.b.* '62 (MIL)[O] Benet Lake, WI St. Benedict's Abbey.
Boyce, James *o.carm.* '77 (NEW) Leonia, NJ St. John the Evangelist's.
Boyd, C. Morris '78 (CHL) Jefferson, NC St. Francis of Assisi.
Boyd, Daniel A. *m.m.* '82 (FgM).
Boyd, Douglas A. '79 (PIT) Braddock, PA Good Shepherd; Allegheny County, PA UPMC Braddock.
Boyd, Ian (NEW)[B] School of Diplomacy and Intl. Rels..
Boyd, James A. '63 (BRK) Released from Diocesan Assignment.
Boyd, James '63 (SD) Port of San Diego.
Boyd, James (SD) Apostleship of the Sea.
Boyd, John D. *s.j.* '47 (NY)[EE] New York, NY Murray–Weigel Hall.
Boyd, Norman *s.a.* '65 (NY)[EE] Garrison, NY Franciscan Friars of the Atonement.
Boyd, Richard '79 (CR)[EE] Defenders of the Bond; Fosston, MN St. Mary's; Leave of Absence.
Boyd, Robert J. '02 (BGP) Norwalk, CT St. Thomas the Apostle.
Boyd, Theophane *o.c.s.o.* '55 (DEN)[N] Snowmass, CO St. Benedict's Monastery.
Boyer, Mark G. '76 (SPC) Mountain Grove, MO Sacred Heart; Special Assignment.
Boyer, Millard G. '75 (LAF) On Special Assignment.
Boyer, Thomas J. (OKL) Norman, OK Church of St. Mark the Evangelist; Personnel Committee
Boyer, Thomas (OKL) Consultors Archdiocesan.
Boyer, Wayne M. '87 (JC) Martinsburg, MO St. Joseph; Martinsburg, MO Resurrection; VIII. Mexico; Board of Trustees.
Boyhan, J. Patrick *m.s.a.* '77 (NOR)[F] Cromwell Society of the Missionaries of the Holy Apostles.
Boykins, Charles *s.v.d.* '65 (JKS) Vicksburg, MS St. Mary.
Boylan, Martin M. '80 (SCR) Honesdale, PA St. John the Evangelist; Deans.
Boyle, Daniel C. '78 (SPR) Adams, MA St. Stanislaus Kostka; Adams, MA Notre Dame des Sept Douleurs and St. Thomas Aquinas; Deans.
Boyle, Dennis P. '73 (PH) Military Chaplains; Navy Chaplains.
Boyle, Edward F. *s.j.* '69 (BO)[E] Dorchester, MA Boston College High School & Jesuit Community; Labor Guild.
Boyle, Eugene '46 (SJ) Retired.
Boyle, Francis V. '55 (NY) Staten Island, NY Blessed Sacrament.
Boyle, George J. '52 (PH) Havertown, PA Annunciation B.V.M. Retired.
Boyle, Gregory *s.j.* '84 (LA) Los Angeles, CA Dolores Mission.
Boyle, James E. '66 (ROC) Fairport, NY St John of Rochester.
Boyle, James E. *c.s.c.* '57 (SCR) Wilkes–Barre, PA St. Casimir's.
Boyle, James M. '56 (HRT) Retired.
Boyle, James '61 (SEA) Rainier School.
Boyle, John B. '76 (SCR) Pocono Pines, PA Our Lady of the Lake.
Boyle, John J. '56 (ALT) Retired.
Boyle, John L. *s.j.* '60 (SJ)[M] Los Gatos, CA Sacred Heart Jesuit Center.
Boyle, John P. '56 (DAV) Judges Retired.
Boyle, John T. '69 (CHI) Chicago, IL St. Felicitas.
Boyle, Leo A. '44 (KC) Retired.
Boyle, Leo A. '44 (CLV)[M] Cleveland, OH Sts. Mary and Joseph Home for the Aged.
Boyle, Michael J. *c.m.* '59 (PHX) Phoenix, AZ St. Vincent de Paul.
Boyle, Michael '95 (RVC) Absent on Leave.
Boyle, Patrick J. *s.j.* '63 (CHI)[A] AUXILIARY CHAPLAINS CONTRACT CHAPLAINS.
Boyle, Patrick J. (NY) Central Westchester; Retirement Plan for Priests.
Boyle, Patrick M. *o.s.m.* '56 (CHI)[N] Chicago Order of Friar Servants of Mary (Servites) United States of America Province, Inc..
Boyle, Patrick '65 (NY) Rye, NY Resurrection.
Boyle, Patrick *o.c.s.o.* '67 (SLC)[F] Huntsville, UT Abbey of Our Lady of the Holy Trinity of the Order of Cistercians.
Boyle, Patrick *o.f.m.* '80 (NY)[EE] New York, NY Franciscan Province of the Immaculate Conception.
Boyle, Raymond J. '56 (PEO) Seneca, IL St. Patrick's.
Boyle, Raymond (PEO) Vicariates and Vicars
Boyle, Richard M. *o.s.m.* '84 (ORG)[D] Anaheim, CA Servite High School, A California Corporation.
Boyle, Richard P. *s.j.* '75 (TUC)[E] Tucson, AZ Jesuit Community of the Vatican Observatory.
Boyle, Richard P. *s.j.* '75 (BO)[V] Boston The Society of Jesus of New England–Provincial Offices.
Boyle, Richard *o.s.m.* '84 (CHI)[N] Chicago Order of Friar Servants of Mary (Servites) United States of America Province, Inc.; Cottage Grove, OR Our Lady of Perpetual Help.
Boyle, Robert J. '51 (BO) Senior Priests Retired.
Boyle, Robert J. '63 (PIT) Finleyville, PA St. Francis of Assisi; Deans and Deaneries.
Boyle, Silvan *o.carm.* '48 (PHX)[G] Phoenix AZ Carmelite Community Retired.
Boyle, Stephen M. *o.praem.* '90 (ORG)[I] Silverado, CA Norbertine Fathers of Orange Inc..
Boyle, Stephen M. '95 (BO) Medford, MA St. James.
Boyle, Thomas S. '41 (CHI) Retired.
Boyle, Thomas '56 (PHX) Retired.
Boyle, Valentine *o.carm.* (PHX) Defenders of the Bond.
Boymer, Lloyd J. '43 (CLV) Brecksville, OH St. Basil the Great; Macedonia, OH Our Lady of Guadalupe Retired.
Boys, Samuel (FTW)[B] Donaldson, IN Ancilla Domini College.
Bozada, Mark S. '81 (STL) Catawissa, MO St. James.
Bozada, Mark (STL) Villa Ridge, MO St. Mary of Perpetual Help.
Bozek, Marek B '03 (SPC) Seneca, MO St. Mary.
Bozek, Marek B. '02 (SPC) Neosho, MO St. Canera.
Bozek, Robert '78 (WDC) Bethesda, MD Our Lady of Lourdes.
Bozel, Robert A. '48 (BAL)[O] St. Elizabeth Hall Retired.
Bozeman, Anthony M. '00 (PH) Philadelphia, PA Our Lady of Hope.
Boznar, Joseph P. '70 (CLV) Cleveland, OH St. Vitus; [Z] Cleveland, OH St. Vitus Development Corporation.
Bozung, James M. '61 (GR) Spring Lake, MI St. Mary's Retired.
Bozza, Nicholas G. (PAT) Netcong, NJ St. Michael's.
Bozza, Nicholas (PAT) Charismatic Renewal.
Bozzelli, Joseph V. '67 (WIL) Chester, MD St. Christopher.
Bozzelli, Richard J. '94 (BAL) Baltimore, MD Corpus Christi.
Bozzo, Kenneth J. '80 (FRS) Chowchilla, CA St. Columba.
Braak, Thomas E. '59 (DUB) Retired.
Braaten, James B. '89 (BIS) Dickinson, ND St. Wenceslaus; Diocesan Corporate Board; Diocesan Finance Council; Priests' Benefit Association.
Braathan, Scott *s.o.l.t.* (CC)[I] Corpus Christi, TX; [G] Robstown, TX Society of Our Lady of the Most Holy Trinity.
Braband, James *s.v.d.* '80 (CHI)[N] Techny, IL Society of the Divine Word, Provincial Headquarters–Chicago Prov..
Braband, James *s.v.d.* '80 (CHI)[B] Techny, IL Divine Word Residence.
Brabandt, James *o.f.m.* '95 (WDC)[M] Washington, DC Commissariat of the Holy Land, Franciscan Monastery – Mount St. Sepulchre.
Bracco, Theodore *o.f.m.* '66 (SFD)[L] Teutopolis, IL St. Francis Assisi Friary.
Bracht, Donald F. *s.m.* '43 (CIN)[M] Dayton, OH Mercy Siena Village.
Bracke, James *c.s.c.* '80 (CHI)[B] University of Notre Dame Du Lac; [I] Notre Dame, IN Holy Cross Community, Corby Hall, University of Notre Dame.
Bracken, Jerome *c.p.* '68 (BRK)[V] Jamaica, NY Immaculate Conception Monastery.
Bracken, John J. '67 (BRK)[Z] Brooklyn, NY Alive in Hope Foundation of the Diocese of Brooklyn; Episcopal Vicar for Temporalities; Development Office; Diocesan Budget Committee; Subcommittee for Agencies.
Bracken, Joseph A. *s.j.* '62 (CIN)[M] Cincinnati, OH Jesuit Community at Xavier University.
Bracken, W. Jerome *c.p.* '68 (NEW)[B] School of Diplomacy and Intl. Rels..
Bracken, Walter *s.v.d.* '71 (CHI)[B] Techny, IL Divine Word Residence.
Bracken, Walter *s.v.d.* '71 (CHI)[N] Techny, IL Divine Word Residence.
Brackenridge, David F. '52 (PH) Retired.
Bracket, Louis P. '47 (MAR) Retired.
Brackett, Anthony H. '59 (BUR) Retired.
Brackett, Christopher *l.c.* '93 (HRT)[B] Cheshire, CT Novitiate of the Legion of Christ.
Brackin, James D. *s.c.j.* '75 (MIL)[O] Hales Corners, WI Priests of the Sacred Heart; [B] Hales Corners, WI Sacred Heart School of Theology.
Brackley, J. Dean *s.j.* (FgM).
Bracq, Edward E. '50 (MAN) Retired.
Bradbury, Henry M. '59 (BRK)[V] Jamaica, NY Vincentian Residence.
Braddock, Joseph (JC) Finance.
Braddock, Stephen '98 (MIL)[O] St. Francis, WI St. Camillus Provincialate.
Braden, Leroy H. '53 (GAL)[N] Houston, TX Pope John Paul XXIII Priests' Residence Retired.
Braden, Michael L. *s.j.* '79 (BAL)[B] Timonium, MD Loyola Graduate Center –Timonium Campus; [S] Baltimore, MD Jesuit Community of Loyola College, Inc..
Braden, Patrick O. *c.s.b.* '52 (GAL)[Q] Houston, TX Residence of the Basilian Fathers of the University of St. Thomas.
Bradford, Richard S. '98 (BO) West Roxbury, MA St. Theresa of Avila; Special Chaplaincies.
Bradler, Robert C. '62 (ROC) Rochester, NY St. Thomas the Apostle; [M] Rochester, NY Holy Childhood Association; The Society for the Propagation of the Faith.
Bradley, Alfred E. *c.ss.r.* (BRK)[V] Brooklyn, NY Our Lady of Good Counsel Residence.
Bradley, Allan P. '72 (SUP) New Richmond, WI St. Patrick; New Richmond, WI Immaculate Conception.
Bradley, Allan W. '70 (COV) Retired.
Bradley, Bruce (DAL) Dallas, TX Mary Immaculate; Ordination & Accreditation Board.
Bradley, Daniel *m.s.* '94 (FR)[J] Attleboro, MA La Salette Center for Christian Living.
Bradley, Daniel *m.s.* '94 (FR)[H] Attleboro, MA La Salette Shrine.
Bradley, Dennis J. '77 (PIT) Pittsburgh, PA St. Aloysius.
Bradley, Ed (OWN) Board Members.
Bradley, Edward C. *s.j.* '79 (PH)[AA] Philadelphia, PA Thomas Jefferson Univ..
Bradley, Edward G. '66 (NEW)[C] Ex Officio Members; Ministry to Retired Priests.
Bradley, H. Cornell *s.j.* '69 (PH)[C] Jesuit Fathers; [AA] Loyola Center and Manresa Hall.
Bradley, Harold C. *s.j.* '61 (MIL)[O] Milwaukee, WI Jesuit Community at Marquette University.
Bradley, Hugh J. '89 (CAM) Somers Point, NJ St. Joseph's.

Bradley, J. Edward '75 (OWN) Henderson, KY Holy Name of Jesus; Deans; Priests' Council.
Bradley, J. Richard '81 (TLS) Owasso, OK St. Henry.
Bradley, James F. '43 (PH) Retired.
Bradley, James P. *s.j.* '58 (NO)[C] New Orleans, LA Loyola University New Orleans.
Bradley, James *s.j.* '58 (BAL)[D] Baltimore, MD Loyola Blakefield.
Bradley, James *s.d.s.* '61 (LA) Whittier, CA St. Bruno.
Bradley, James *o.s.f.s.* '61 (LAN)[B] Jackson, MI Lumen Christi Catholic High School.
Bradley, James '73 (BRK)[A] Douglaston, NY Immaculate Conception Center.
Bradley, John A. '65 (ORG) San Juan Capistrano, CA San Felipe de Jesus; Defenders of the Bond.
Bradley, John J. '63 (PH) Philadelphia, PA Sacred Heart of Jesus Retired.
Bradley, John J. '67 (ALB) Albany, NY Blessed Sacrament.
Bradley, John (ALB) Deans.
Bradley, John (ALB) Priests Placement Committee.
Bradley, Joseph '91 (SFR) Burlingame, CA St. Catherine of Siena.
Bradley, Joseph '93 (SFR)[D] San Mateo, CA Junipero Serra High School (Boys).
Bradley, Matthew '72 (BO)[X] Scituate, MA Foyer of Charity.
Bradley, Michael J. '78 (CHI) Chicago, IL St. Josaphat.
Bradley, Michael *o.m.i.* '66 (FgM).
Bradley, Michael (CHI) Judges.
Bradley, Paul F. '41 (TR) Retired.
Bradley, Paul F. *s.s.c.* '69 (ORG) Newport Beach, CA Our Lady Queen of Angels.
Bradley, Paul J. '71 (PIT) Pittsburgh, PA St. Paul Cathedral; Vicars General; General Secretary; Judges; Priest Council; College of Consultors; Diocesan Finance Council; Diocesan Pastoral Council; Clergy Personnel Board; Building Commission.
Bradley, Paul *s.s.c.* '69 (ORG)[K] St. Columbans St. Columban's Foreign Mission Society.
Bradley, Robert M. '57 (LA) Retired.
Bradley, Robert *s.j.* '55 (AUS) Austin, TX Sacred Heart.
Bradley, Robert '73 (CC) Retired.
Bradley, William J. '57 (NY) New Rochelle, NY Blessed Sacrament.
Bradower, Theodore J. *t.o.r.* '50 (FWT) Fort Worth, TX St. Andrew.
Bradshaw, Alexander H. '85 (ROC) Rochester, NY Our Mother of Sorrows.
Bradshaw, Jordan *o.p.* '92 (OAK) Antioch, CA Holy Rosary; [N] Oakland, CA Western Dominican Province.
Bradshaw, Paul F. '70 (FTW)[B] University of Notre Dame Du Lac.
Bradshaw, Terry L. '80 (L) Louisville, KY St. Athanasius.
Bradt, Kevin M. *s.j.* '79 (New York)[N] Berkeley, CA Jesuit Community at Jesuit School of Theology at Berkeley.
Bradtke, Thomas '62 (DEN) Carbondale, CO St. Vincent.
Brady, Charles '55 (SAC) Sacramento, CA Holy Spirit.
Brady, Coman V. '59 (BRK) Brooklyn, NY St. Vincent Ferrer.
Brady, Daniel J. '61 (CHI) Mt. Prospect, IL St. Cecilia.
Brady, Daniel O. '84 (RIC) Pocahontas, VA St. Elizabeth; Tazewell, VA St. Theresa.
Brady, Edmund P. '59 (BRK) Long Island City, NY St. Margaret Mary; Long Island City, NY Our Lady of Mount Carmel.
Brady, Edward E. '90 (PH) Philadelphia, PA St. Bartholomew.
Brady, Edward J. *s.j.* '59 (BAL)[S] Loyola House.
Brady, Edward J. *s.j.* '59 (FgM).
Brady, G. James *c.s.c.* '59 (P) Aumsville, OR St. Mary.
Brady, G. James *c.s.c.* '59 (FTW)[I] Aumsville, OR St. Mary.
Brady, Gerald '83 (SPR) Northfield, MA St. Patrick.
Brady, Gerald (SPR) The Catholic Charismatic Renewal of Springfield, Inc..
Brady, Gerald (SPR) Diocesan Charismatic Renewal.
Brady, Gerard J. '59 (SR) Napa, CA St. Thomas Aquinas.
Brady, Gerard (SR) Parish Priest Consultors.
Brady, James J. '53 (MIL) Retired.
Brady, James J. '57 (ALN)[J] Bethlehem, PA Holy Family Villa Retired.
Brady, James J. '72 (TR) Brick Town, NJ St. Dominic.
Brady, James R. '57 (ALN) Minersville, PA Immaculate Conception.
Brady, James '89 (CC)[G] Robstown, TX Society of Our Lady of the Most Holy Trinity.
Brady, James '89 (BAL)[O] St. Elizabeth Hall.
Brady, James *s.m.m.* '92 (BRK) Ozone Park, NY St. Mary Gate of Heaven.
Brady, James *s.m.m.* '92 (BRK)[V] Ozone Park, NY Montfort Missionaries Provincialate (Missionaries of the Company of Mary) – Formation Community.
Brady, Jeremiah A. *s.s.j.* '51 (MOB) Mobile, AL St. Joseph.
Brady, Jeremiah D. *s.s.j.* '51 (MOB) Mobile, AL Prince of Peace.
Brady, John A. *s.j.* '49 (LA)[F] Los Angeles, CA Loyola High School of Los Angeles.
Brady, John B. '55 (WDC) Avenue, MD Holy Angels; [V] Pomfret, MD Ministr–O–Media, Inc..
Brady, John F. *s.j.* '48 (DEN) Denver, CO St. Ignatius Loyola; [N] Denver, CO Loyola Parish – Jesuit Community.
Brady, John '55 (SFS) Retired.
Brady, John (WDC) Scouting.
Brady, Joseph '89 (SD) San Diego, CA St. Catherine Laboure.
Brady, Jude W. *o.s.b.* '80 (SAV)[B] Savannah, GA Benedictine Military School; [F] Savannah, GA The Benedictine Priory.
Brady, Jules M. *s.j.* '53 (STL)[N] St. Louis, MO Fusz Pavilion; [O] St. Louis, MO Jesuit Community Corporation at St. Louis University – Jesuit Hall.
Brady, Leo Patrick *c.p.* '44 (CHI)[N] Chicago, IL Passionist Community–Immaculate Conception Monastery.
Brady, Leo *c.p.* '44 (CHI)[N] Chicago, IL Daneo Hall.
Brady, Mel P. *o.f.m.* '50 (DET) Detroit, MI St. Aloysius.
Brady, Michael '01 (STO) Tracy, CA St. Bernard Church (Pastor of).
Brady, Patrick A. '61 (WIL) Retired.
Brady, Patrick J. '64 (CAM) Atlantic City, NJ Our Lady Star of the Sea.
Brady, Patrick J. '93 (PH) Graduate Studies.
Brady, Patrick *o.m.i.* '48 (NY)[GG] Newburgh, NY Our Lady of Hope Center.
Brady, Philip W. '43 (BGP) Retired.
Brady, Reginald '93 (DET) Absent on Leave.
Brady, Richard J. '59 (BO) Senior Priests Retired.
Brady, Roger J. '58 (BO) Senior Priests Retired.
Brady, Severin *o.f.m.* '66 (BO)[Y] Boston, MA Saint Anthony Residence.
Brady, Theodore E.A. *s.j.* '61 (BAL)[M] Baltimore, MD Mercy Health Services Inc.; [S] Baltimore, MD Ferdinand Wheeler Jesuit Community.
Brady, Thomas C. '54 (RCK) South Beloit, IL St. Peter; Vicars General; Diocesan Consultors; Cemeteries.
Brady, Thomas F. '59 (BRK) Brooklyn, NY Good Shepherd.
Brady, Timothy J. *o.de.m.* '03 (CLV) Cleveland, OH St. Rocco.
Brady, Vincent M. '95 (PSC) Leave of Absence.
Brady, William J. '80 (SFR) San Francisco, CA St. Emydius.
Brady, William (SFR) Archdiocesan Board of Education.
Braganza, Joe (NY) Port Chester, NY Our Lady of Mercy.
Braganza, Simon '92 (CHI) Chicago, IL St. Tarcissus.
Bragotti, Joseph *m.c.c.j.* '62 (FgM).
Bragotti, Joseph *m.c.c.j.* '62 (CIN)[M] Cincinnati, OH Comboni Missionaries (Verona Fathers)–Comboni Mission Center.
Brahill, John *o.s.b.* '82 (FgM).
Brahill, John *o.s.b.* '82 (RCK)[G] Aurora, IL Marmion Abbey.
Brahm, Harvey '51 (MIL) Retired.
Braida, Ernest E. '64 (DAV) Newton, IA Sacred Heart.
Braiden–Amissah, Anthony (BRK) Brooklyn, NY St. Catherine of Genoa.
Brainard, Ernest B. '45 (OAK) Oakland, CA St. Andrew–St. Joseph Retired.
Brainerd, Winthrop '87 (WDC) Washington, DC Epiphany.
Brajkovich, Thomas R. '61 (PEO) Retired.
Braley, James E. '75 (BO) Plymouth, MA Blessed Kateri Tekakwitha; Graduate Studies.
Brambilla, Charles A. '71 (STP) Lindstrom, MN St. Bridget of Sweden.
Brambilla, Sigmund *o.f.m.* '55 (NY)[EE] New York Franciscan Province of the Immaculate Conception.
Bramble, Donald *o.p.* '76 (ANC) Anchorage, AK Holy Family Cathedral.
Bramble, Donald *o.p.* (ANC) Diocesan Consultors.
Bramble, Donald *o.p.* (ANC) Vicar General.
Bramlage, Gregory D. '96 (IND) Sunman, IN St. Nicholas.
Bramlage, Gregory '96 (IND) Greensburg, IN St. Maurice.
Bramlage, Gregory '96 (IND) Oldenburg, IN St. John the Evangelist.
Bramlage, Gregory '96 (IND) Oldenburg, IN St. Anne.
Bramlage, James A. '64 (CIN) Cincinnati, OH St. Peter in Chains Cathedral; Judges.
Branch, Edward B. '74 (ATL)[N] Atlanta, GA The Catholic Center at Atlanta University Complex.
Branch, Edward B. '74 (L) On Duty Outside the Archdiocese.
Branch, Leslie '71 (WDC) Retired.
Brancolini, Luca *f.s.c.b.* '99 (FR) Attleboro, MA St. Joseph's.
Brancolini, Luca '99 (FR)[N] Attleboro, MA Priestly Fraternity of the Missionaries of St. Charles Borromeo.
Brand, Edmund H. *o.c.s.o.* '54 (ATL)[K] Conyers, GA The Monastery of the Holy Spirit.
Brand, Fred '67 (SFE) Retired.
Brande, Edward W. *s.j.* '63 (NEW)[B] Jersey City, NJ Jesuit Center; [N] Jersey City, NJ Jesuits of Saint Peter's College, Inc..
Brandenberger, Robert J. *c.m.* '52 (PH).
Brandenhoff, Peter B. '70 (WIN)[AA] On Duty Outside the Diocese.
Brandes, John F. '51 (STP) On Duty Outside the Archdiocese Retired.
Brando, Joseph J. '72 (KNX) Cleveland, TN St. Therese of Lisieux; Presbyteral Council; Diocesan Consultors; Army National Guard Chaplains.
Brandow, Stephen J. '96 (ALX) Scouting; Pineville, LA Veterans Administration Medical Center.
Brandow, Stephen J. (ALX).
Brandstrader, Frederick L. '68 (CHI) Wheeling, IL St. Joseph the Worker.
Brandt, Daniel J. '99 (CHI) Chicago, IL St. William.
Brandt, Joseph D. '83 (PH) Philadelphia, PA St. Anne.
Brandt, Lawrence E. '69 (E) Erie, PA St. Hedwig/St. Patrick.
Brandt, Paul C. '84 (PH) Lafayette Hill, PA St. Philip Neri; [D] Philadelphia, PA Roman Catholic High School for Boys.
Brankin, Anthony J. '75 (CHI) Chicago, IL St. Thomas More.
Brankin, Patrick M. '79 (TLS) Collinsville, OK St. Therese.
Brankin, Patrick M. '79 (CHI) On Duty Outside the Archdiocese.
Brankin, Patrick M. (TLS) Office of Permanent Diaconate.
Brankin, Patrick (TLS) Hispanic Ministry.
Brankin, Patrick (TLS) Diocesan Senators.
Brannan, Patrick T. *s.j.* '63 (PH)[AA] Philadelphia, PA Stella Maris Parish.
Brannan, Patrick T. *s.j.* '63 (SJ)[M] Los Gatos Sacred Heart Jesuit Center.
Brannen, Brett A. '91 (SAV) Macon, GA St. Peter Claver; College of Consultors; Council of Priests; Director of Vocations.
Brannon, Robert F. '58 (GBG)[G] Greensburg, PA Neumann House.
Branon, Philip J. '51 (BUR) South Hero, VT St. Rose of Lima.
Bransfield, Brian J. '94 (PH) Graduate Studies.
Bransfield, Christopher '98 (SJ) Los Gatos, CA St. Mary of the Immaculate Conception.
Bransfield, Michael J. '71 (PH) On Duty Outside the Archdiocese; [Q] Washington, DC Basilica of the National Shrine of the Immaculate Conception.
Bransfield, Michael (WDC)[C] Catholic University of America, The.
Bransfield, Sean P. '02 (PH) Chalfont, PA St. Jude.
Bransfield, Thomas A. '64 (BUR) Retired.
Branson, Bernard E. '59 (KC) Smithville, MO Church of the Good Shepherd.
Branson, Dale A. '97 (TUC) Hayden, AZ St. Joseph's; Council of Priests; Vicars Forane.
Branson, Keith *c.pp.s.* '00 (KC) Liberty, MO St. James.
Brant, David A. '65 (SEA) Seattle, WA St. James Cathedral Retired.
Brant, Paul W. *s.j.* '77 (R)[E] Raleigh Jesuit Community.
Brantman, Thomas E. '75 (RCK) Sterling, IL St. Mary; Tampico, IL St. Mary.
Brantome, Oscar '88 (MIA) Absent on Sick Leave.
Brantome, Oscar '88 (MIA) Miami Lakes, FL Our Lady of the Lakes.
Braquet, David J. '94 (ALX) Alexandria, LA Our Lady of Prompt Succor; Glenmora, LA St. Louis.
Braquet, Patrick X. '97 (ALX) Priests Council; Vocation Discernment Committee; Bunkie, LA St. Anthony of Padua.
Brasher, C. John '75 (SFE) Las Vegas, NM Our Lady of Sorrows Church; Associate Judges.
Brassard, Leo *a.a.* '69 (BO)[V] Haktari Songdang.
Brassard, Ronald E. '74 (PRO) Cranston, RI Immaculate Conception.
Brassil, James A. (RVC) Retired.
Brassil, Kevin J. '58 (PRO) Portsmouth, RI St. Barnabas.
Bratek, Martin *c.r.* '72 (PT) Panama City, FL St. John the Evangelist; Vicars Forane.
Bratek, Martin *c.r.* (PT) Schools, Diocesan Commission for.
Brath, John A. '68 (SPC) West Plains, MO St. Mary.
Bratko, Kenneth R. *c.r.* '64 (CHI) Schaumburg, IL St. Matthew.
Bratkowski, Allen J. '89 (MIL) Kenosha, WI Our Lady of the Holy Rosary.
Bratus, Walter N. '56 (GBG) Retired.
Braud, Dominic R. *o.s.b.* '61 (NO)[P] St. Benedict, LA St. Joseph Abbey.
Braud, Ronald '64 (NO) Metairie, LA St. Louis King of France.
Braud, William *o.f.m.* (LA)[O] Los Angeles, CA St. Anne's.
Brauer, Frank J. '86 (BAL) Edgewater, MD Our Lady of Perpetual Help.

Brauer, Mark S. '92 (DET)[T] Detroit, MI West Detroit Catholic Schools Alliance; Detroit, MI St. Christine; Detroit, MI St. Gemma Galgani.
Braukmann, Donald '86 (CR) Greenbush, MN Blessed Sacrament.
Brault, Bernard *s.m.m.* '68 (BRK) Ozone Park, NY St. Mary Gate of Heaven.
Brault, Laurence V. '77 (WOR) Upton, MA Holy Angels.
Brault, Y. David '77 (WDC) Clinton, MD St. Mary.
Braun, Brian *o.f.m.cap.* '60 (MIL)[O] Milwaukee, WI St. Conrad Friary; Milwaukee, WI St. Martin de Porres.
Braun, David J. '55 (MIL) Retired.
Braun, David L. '81 (BEL) Olney, IL St. Joseph; Newton, IL Holy Cross.
Braun, Donald B. '57 (MIL) Retired.
Braun, Edgar F. '40 (MIL) Retired.
Braun, Francis '54 (BUF) Buffalo, NY St. Mark.
Braun, Gary G. '77 (STL)[T] St. Louis, MO Washington University Newman Centers.
Braun, Gerard E. *s.j* '46 (NY)[EE] New York, NY Development Office of the New York Province; [EE] New York, NY St. Ignatius Loyola Residence.
Braun, Gerard (FAR) Deanery 8.
Braun, H. Gerard '85 (FAR) Valley City, ND St. Catherine.
Braun, John J. *m.afr.* '57 (SP)[O] St. Petersburg, FL Missionaries of Africa.
Braun, John S. '87 (SPC) Neosho, MO St. Canera; Seneca, MO St. Mary.
Braun, Michael C. '61 (LC) Retired.
Braun, Michael R. '67 (FRS) Bakersfield, CA Our Lady of Perpetual Help.
Braun, Michael (FRS) Defenders of the Bond.
Braun, Michael (FRS) Deposit and Loan Fund.
Braun, Michael (FRS) Finance Committee.
Braun, Robert *o.m.i.* '51 (BEL)[F] Belleville, IL Shrine of Our Lady of the Snows.
Braun, Virgil R. '60 (SCL) Eden Valley, MN The Church of the Assumption.
Braunreuther, Robert J. *s.j.* '65 (WDC).
Braunreuther, Robert J. *s.j.* '65 (BO)[V] Boston The Society of Jesus of New England–Provincial Offices.
Brausch, Anthony M. '02 (CIN) Cincinnati, OH Our Lady of Visitation; [E] Cincinnati, OH Elder High School.
Bravata, Kevin W. (MEM) Cordova, TN St. Francis of Assisi.
Bravo, Arnold '87 (LUB) Petersburg, TX Sacred Heart.
Bravo, Enrique *c.s.b.* '62 (GAL)[Q] Houston, TX Dillon House.
Bravo, Gregorio '58 (SJN) San Juan, PR Maria Madre de La Iglesia.
Bravo, Gregorio (SJN) Police Chaplains.
Bravo, Joseph '77 (SFR) Colma, CA Holy Angels.
Bray, Kevin '67 (FRS) Absent on Sick Leave.
Bray, Kevin '67 (LA) Retired.
Bray, Lorie (DAV)[I] Burlington, IA Act Day Treatment.
Brazaskas, Bob '66 (TUC) Pearce, AZ St. Jude Thaddeus.
Breaker, Donald J. '64 (CIN) On Special and Archdiocesan Assignment.
Bream, James '64 (SFS) Watertown, SD Immaculate Conception.
Breau, Paschal *s.a.* '79 (NY)[EE] Paul Wattson Friary.
Breault, Charles *o.m.i.* '59 (SAT)[M] San Antonio, TX.
Breault, William F. *s.j.* '62 (SAC)[I] Carmichael, CA Jesuit High School Community of Sacramento.
Breault, William *s.j.* (SAC) Archives.
Breaux, Allen '81 (LAF) Breaux Bridge, LA St. Bernard.
Breaux, O. Joseph '68 (LAF) Maurice, LA St. Alphonsus.
Breaux, Overton Joseph (LAF) Defenders of the Bond.
Brecheteau, Gabriel *c.p.* '48 (FgM).
Brecht, David L. *o.s.a.* '65 (FgM).
Brecht, David L. *o.s.a.* '65 (CHI)[N] Olympia Fields, IL The Augustinians–Provincialate; [N] Olympia Fields, IL Tolentine Monastery at Tolentine Center.
Breck, Steven H. (CLV) Strongsville, OH St. John Neumann.
Breckensiek, Marne *o.f.m.* '65 (PEO) Peoria, IL Sacred Heart.
Breczinski, Paul '98 (BAL) Bradshaw, MD St. Stephen.
Bredeck, Martin J. *s.j.* '64 (KC)[B] Kansas City, KS Rockhurst University Continuing Education Center/ National Seminars Group; [J] Kansas City, MO Rockhurst Jesuit Community.
Breedlove, Lawrence '56 (FWT) Fort Worth, TX Holy Name of Jesus.
Breen, Bernard J. '72 (L) Louisville, KY St. Margaret Mary; Vicars General; College of Consultors; Ex Officio; L.A.M.P..
Breen, Brendan *c.p.* '50 (BO) Brighton, MA St. Gabriel.
Breen, Brendan *c.p.* '50 (BO)[V] Boston, MA St. Gabriel Passionist Community.
Breen, Damian B. *o.s.b.* '98 (PAT)[M] Morristown St. Mary's Abbey.
Breen, Damian *o.s.b.* '98 (NEW) Linden, NJ St. Elizabeth's.
Breen, Edward J. '58 (BRK) Jackson Heights, NY Our Lady of Fatima.
Breen, Francis J. *m.m.* '70 (BO)[V] Walpole, MA Maryknoll Mission Promotion Department.
Breen, J.A. *o.p.* '63 (COL) Somerset, OH Holy Trinity.
Breen, J.A. *o.p.* '63 (COL) Somerset, OH St. Joseph's.
Breen, J.A. *o.p.* '63 (COL)[H] Somerset, OH St. Joseph's Rectory.
Breen, James J. '80 (BGP)[P] Stamford, CT The Catherine Dennis Keefe Queen of the Clergy Retired Priests' Residence.
Breen, John M. *m.m.* '51 (SJ)[M] Los Altos, CA Maryknoll.
Breen, Joseph P. '61 (NSH) Nashville, TN St. Edward.
Breen, Michael *s.s.c.* '47 (BO)[V] West Roxbury, MA St. John Chrystostom.
Breen, Philip M. '65 (NSH) Nashville, TN St. Ann; Vicar for Catholic Charities.
Breen, Phillip '65 (NSH)[L] Nashville, TN Ladies of Charity Welfare Agency, Inc..
Breen, Robert H. '57 (PH) Retired.
Brehob, Keith A. *s.j.* '96 (BAL)[B] Timonium, MD Loyola Graduate Center –Timonium Campus; [S] Baltimore, MD Jesuit Community of Loyola College, Inc..
Breidenbach, John '87 (EVN) Newburgh, IN St. John the Baptist.
Breidenbach, John (EVN) Diocesan Council of Priests.
Breier, Donald P. '69 (PIT) Pittsburgh, PA St. Anne; Deans and Deaneries; St. Paul Cathedral.
Breier, Henry J. (STL) Secretary to the Archbishop; Masters of Ceremonies to the Archbishop.
Breier, Henry '94 (STL) Special Assignment.
Breig, Gary R. '76 (STL) Military Chaplains; Air Force Chaplains.
Breighner, Joseph F. '71 (BAL) Baltimore, MD Cathedral of Mary Our Queen; Special Assignment.
Breit, Melvin '52 (MIL) Retired.
Breitbach, Richard C. '61 (MIL) Allenton, WI Resurrection.
Brelsford, William J. '70 (LA) Los Angeles, CA St. Timothy.
Brembos, George M. '56 (MET) Far Hills, NJ St. Elizabeth; [O] Peapack, NJ Msgr. George E. Everitt Academy; College of Consultors.
Bremer, Al '02 (OWN) Paducah, KY St. Francis de Sales.
Bremer, Al '02 (OWN) Paducah, KY Rosary Chapel.
Brenberger, Thomas R. *c.pp.s.* '66 (CIN)[U] Dayton, OH Community Support Charitable Trust.
Brenberger, Thomas *c.pp.s.* '66 (CIN) Rockford, OH St. Teresa.
Brenberger, Thomas *c.pp.s.* '66 (CIN) Celina, OH Immaculate Conception of the Blessed Virgin Mary.
Brenberger, Thomas *c.pp.s.* (CIN) Priest Councilors.
Brenda, William H. *o.p.* '49 (GAL) Houston, TX Holy Rosary.
Brendan, Ross (NY) Absent on Sick leave.
Brenes–Chavez, Fabio '85 (NEW) Elizabeth, NJ St. Patrick's; Elizabeth, NJ Immaculate Heart of Mary.
Brenk, Frederick E. *s.j.* '63 (MIL)[O] Pontifical Biblical Institute.
Brenkle, John J. '58 (SR) St. Helena, CA St. Helena; Members of the Curia; Adjutant Judicial Vicars; Diocesan Judges; Board of Consultors; Priests' Council; Finance Committee; Diocesan Building Committee; Review Board.
Brenkus, Pavol '01 (ATL) Decatur, GA St. Thomas More.
Brennan, Anthony V. *m.m.* '61 (FgM).
Brennan, Bernard '62 (SFR) On Special Assignment Retired.
Brennan, Brian C. '79 (NY) Mahopac, NY St. John the Evangelist; Army National Guard Chaplains.
Brennan, Cathal '52 (P) Retired.
Brennan, Charles M. *o.s.m.* '48 (CHI)[N] Chicago, IL Monastery of Our Lady of Sorrows.
Brennan, Dermot R. '56 (NY) Yorktown Heights, NY St. Patrick.
Brennan, Donald *o.s.a.* '53 (FWT) Gainesville, TX St. Mary.
Brennan, Edmund J. '82 (ALN) Unassigned.
Brennan, Eugene P. '70 (STL) Army National Guard Chaplains; St. Charles, MO St. Charles Borromeo.
Brennan, Eugene P. *m.s.* '80 (HRT).
Brennan, Francis C. *s.j.* '58 (STL)[O] St. Louis, MO Jesuit Community Corporation at St. Louis University – Jesuit Hall; [C] Saint Louis University.
Brennan, George J. '49 (BUF) Retired.
Brennan, George P. '68 (STL) Creve Coeur, MO St. Monica.
Brennan, George *m.s.* '75 (FR)[H] Attleboro, MA La Salette Shrine.
Brennan, George '87 (VEN) Sarasota, FL St. Patrick.
Brennan, Gerard M. '50 (BO) Senior Priests Retired.
Brennan, J. Gregory *o.f.m.* '79 (BUF)[O] St. Bonaventure, NY St. Bonaventure Friary; [C] St. Bonaventure, NY Friar Community; St. Bonaventure, NY St. Pacificus, Mission of St. Bonaventure University Friary.
Brennan, James F. '55 (BO) Senior Priests Retired.
Brennan, James H. *s.s.* '31 (BAL)[O] Baltimore, MD St. Charles Villa; Judges.
Brennan, James J. '89 (PH) Feasterville, PA Assumption B.V.M..
Brennan, James P. *c.ss.r.* '64 (WDC)[M] Washington, DC Holy Redeemer College.
Brennan, John A. '56 (TYL) Gun Barrel City, TX St. Jude.
Brennan, John D. '70 (PIT) Verona, PA St. Gerard Majella.
Brennan, John J. *s.j.* '46 (LA) Los Angeles, CA Blessed Sacrament.
Brennan, John J. '78 (SPR) Agawam, MA St. John the Evangelist.
Brennan, John P. *s.m.a.* '64 (LA)[A] Camarillo, CA St. John's Seminary; Members.
Brennan, John W. *o.s.f.s.* '73 (WIL)[J] Childs, MD Retirement and Assisted Care Facility.
Brennan, Joseph (Dennis) *o.s.b.* '74 (LA)[Q] Valyermo, CA St. Andrew's Abbey.
Brennan, Joseph F. '56 (LA) Veterans Affairs Medical Center Retired.
Brennan, Joseph F. *s.j.* '56 (BO)[V] Weston, MA Campion Health Center, Inc.; [X] Weston, MA Campion Renewal Center.
Brennan, Joseph F. '56 (SD) Retired.
Brennan, Joseph F. *s.j.* '56 (BO)[V] Weston, MA Campion Health Center, Inc.; [X] Weston, MA Campion Renewal Center.
Brennan, Joseph F. '56 (LA) Retired.
Brennan, Joseph F. '59 (LAF) Retired.
Brennan, Joseph P. '54 (ROC) Retired.
Brennan, Joseph T. *s.j.* '69 (CHI)[D] Chicago, IL St. Ignatius College Prep; [D] Chicago, IL St. Ignatius College Prep; [D] Chicago, IL St. Ignatius Jesuit Community.
Brennan, Joseph T. *o.s.f.s.* '98 (ARL)[D] Alexandria, VA Bishop Ireton High School; [J] Alexandria, VA Oblates of St. Francis de Sales Residence.
Brennan, Joseph V. '80 (LA) Norwalk, CA St. Linus.
Brennan, Joseph *o.s.c.* '45 (SCL)[I] Onamia, MN Crosier Monastery.
Brennan, Joseph *o.s.b.* '74 (LA) Retired.
Brennan, Joseph (LA) San Pedro Pastoral Region.
Brennan, Keith R. '84 (STA) Jacksonville, FL Blessed Trinity; Chancellor; Diocesan Consultors; Presbyteral Council; Building Commission; Special Assignment.
Brennan, Keith *s.d.s.* '70 (MIL)[O] Silver Spring, MD.
Brennan, Lawrence C. *s.t.d.* '76 (STL)[A] St. Louis, MO Kenrick School of Theology.
Brennan, Mark E. '76 (WDC) Gaithersburg, MD St. Martin; Advocates.
Brennan, Matthew '62 (BIR) Pell City, AL Our Lady of the Lake.
Brennan, Matthew (BIR) Diocesan College of Vicars.
Brennan, Michael J. '71 (BRK) Brooklyn, NY St. Cecilia; Brooklyn West.
Brennan, Michael *c.p.* '53 (MET)[H] Redding, CA Mercy Medical Center.
Brennan, Michael (BRK) Assignment Board.
Brennan, Michael (BRK) Presbyteral Council.
Brennan, Michael (BRK) Diocesan Consultors.
Brennan, P. Paul '59 (ROC) Willard, NY Drug Treatment Center; Romulus, NY Five Points Correctional Facility.
Brennan, Patrick A. *o.s.a.* '63 (ORG) Buena Park, CA St. Pius V.
Brennan, Patrick Ailbe *o.s.a.* (ORG) Society of St. Vincent de Paul of Orange County.
Brennan, Patrick J. '73 (CHI) Inverness, IL Holy Family.
Brennan, Patrick *c.p.* '73 (LA).
Brennan, Patrick *c.p.* '73 (LA)[Q] Sierra Madre, CA Passionist Residence.
Brennan, Patrick '77 (P) Portland, OR St. Rita.
Brennan, Patrick (P) Vicar for Clergy.
Brennan, Patrick (P) Clergy.
Brennan, Patrick (P) Judicial Vicar.
Brennan, Patrick (P) Clergy Personnel.
Brennan, Patrick (P) Board Members.
Brennan, Patrick (P) Personnel Board.
Brennan, Patrick *j.c.l.* (P) Judges.
Brennan, Paul P. '59 (ROC) Retired.
Brennan, Pierce A. *s.j.* '76 (RVC) Oceanside, NY St. Anthony.
Brennan, Pierce A. *s.j.* '76 (NY)[F] New York, NY Xavier High School.
Brennan, Ralph '57 (AUS) Retired.
Brennan, Raymond *c.ss.r.* '59 (FgM).
Brennan, Robert J. '49 (NY) Retired.
Brennan, Robert J. *c.s.c.* '68 (NO) New Orleans, LA Sacred Heart of Jesus.
Brennan, Robert J. '89 (RVC) Rockville Centre, NY St. Agnes Cathedral; Vicar General and Moderator of the Curia; Senate of Priests (Presbyteral Council/ College of Consultors); Priests' Personnel Assignment Board.
Brennan, Robert L. '64 (PH) Philadelphia, PA Resurrection of Our Lord.
Brennan, Robert M. '65 (NEW) Upper Montclair, NJ St. Cassian.

Brennan, Robert '49 (NY)[B] Beacon, NY St. Lawrence of Brindisi Friary.
Brennan, Robert (NY) Castle Point, NY Veterans Administration Medical Center.
Brennan, Ronan P. '50 (SAC) Sutter Creek, CA Immaculate Conception Retired.
Brennan, Ronan (SAC) Coordinator for Retired Priests.
Brennan, Ronan (SAC) Council of Priests.
Brennan, Seamus F. '72 (MET) Somerville, NJ Immaculate Conception; College of Consultors.
Brennan, Terrence M. *s.j.* '76 (MIL)[O] Milwaukee, WI Pere Marquette House Jesuit Community; [E] Milwaukee, WI Marquette University High School.
Brennan, Terrence P. '99 (SFE) San Juan Pueblo, NM St. John the Baptist.
Brennan, Thomas J. '74 (PH) Phoenixville, PA St. Mary of the Assumption.
Brennan, Thomas J. *s.j.* '96 (PH)[AA] Philadelphia, PA St. Alphonsus House.
Brennan, Thomas N. *s.j.* '63 (MIL)[O] Milwaukee, WI Arrupe House Jesuit Community.
Brennan, Thomas '66 (TR) Retired.
Brennan, Thomas '89 (LAN) Parr Hwy. Correctional Facility.
Brennan, Thomas '89 (LAN) Retired.
Brennan, Thomas *s.j.* '96 (PH)[C] Jesuit Fathers.
Brennan, Timothy J. *o.s.b.* '78 (PAT)[M] Morristown St. Mary's Abbey.
Brennan, Walter G. *s.j.* '60 (FgM).
Brennan, William J. '42 (SPK) Retired.
Brennan, William J. '49 (L) Louisville, KY St. Margaret Mary Retired.
Brennan, William J. *s.j.* '51 (MIL)[O] Milwaukee, WI Miguel Pro Jesuit Community; Milwaukee, WI St. Patrick.
Brennan, William P. '63 (CAM) Cherry Hill, NJ St. Pius X; Camden North Deanery; Members.
Brennell, John J. '78 (STL) Kirkwood, MO St. Peter.
Brennen, John E. (TOL) Sandusky, OH SS. Peter and Paul.
Brenner, Raymond '69 (EVN) Jasper, IN St. Joseph.
Brenner, Raymond (EVN) Personnel Board.
Brennick, Stephen F. '64 (BO) Permanent Disability.
Brennickmeyer, Edgar *s.j.* (SFR) Catholic Healthcare West/Bay Area Region.
Brenninkmeijer, Paul A. '67 (CHR) Awendaw, SC St. Benedict.
Brenny, Kenneth '63 (SCL) Retired.
Brenny, Kenneth (SCL) Diocesan Priests Pension Plan Trustees.
Brenon, Terence '91 (SAN) San Angelo, TX St. Mary's.
Brenon, Terry '91 (SAN) Carlsbad, TX St. Therese of the Child Jesus.
Brensinger, Richard C. '92 (ALN) Shenandoah, PA St. Mary Magdalen; Ringtown, PA St. Mary; Shenandoah, PA Annunciation.
Brentrup, Bruce *s.d.s.* '59 (MIL)[O] Richmond, VA.
Brenza, William J. '70 (HRT) Naugatuck, CT St. Francis of Assisi; Deans.
Breski, Martin *o.f.m.conv.* '69 (BGP) Bridgeport, CT St. Michael The Archangel.
Breslawski, William G. '79 (RVC) Lynbrook, NY Our Lady of Peace; Procurator & Advocates; Senate of Priests (Presbyteral Council/College of Consultors); Priests' Personnel Assignment Board.
Breslin, Cornelius J. (WIL) Easton, MD SS. Peter and Paul.
Breslin, J. Michael '65 (RIC) Cape Charles, VA St. Charles.
Breslin, John B. *s.j.* '73 (NY)[EE] Cardinal Spellman Hall, Jesuit Community.
Breslin, John E. '61 (PH) Regional Vicars; Drexel Hill, PA St. Andrew; Priests' Personnel Board.
Breslin, John S. '85 (CHI) Chicago, IL St. Ailbe.
Breslin, John *s.m.m.* '56 (BRK)[V] Ozone Park Montfort Missionaries Provincialate (Missionaries of the Company of Mary) – Formation Community.
Breslin, Lawrence K. '57 (CIN) Dayton, OH St. Charles Borromeo; Judges.
Breslin, Paul *o.f.m.* '88 (FgM).
Breslin, Peter W. *s.j.* '91 (CHI)[D] Wilmette, IL Loyola Academy.
Breslin, William E. '74 (DEN) Boulder, CO Sacred Heart of Jesus.
Bresnahan, James F. *s.j.* '59 (BO)[V] Newton, MA The Jesuit Community at Boston College.
Bresnahan, John E. *o.s.a.* '36 (PH)[AA] Villanova, PA St. Thomas Monastery.
Bresnahan, John J. *s.j.* '58 (BO)[X] Gloucester, MA Eastern Point Retreat House.
Bresnahan, John J. '60 (CHI) Schiller Park, IL St. Beatrice.
Bresnahan, Richard F. '58 (PEO) Retired.
Bresnahan, Thomas J. '60 (MAN) Salem, NH St. Joseph Retired.
Brethour, Gary G. '89 (LIN) McCook, NE St. Patrick.
Bretl, James J. *s.d.s.* '65 (NSH) McMinnville, TN St. Catherine; Smithville, TN St. Gregory.
Breton, Albert E. '54 (SPR) Blue Army.
Breton, Albert '54 (SPR) Retired.
Breton, Albert (SPR) Apostolate of the Suffering.
Breton, Louis M. *o.s.m.* '49 (CHI)[N] Chicago Order of Friar Servants of Mary (Servites) United States of America Province, Inc..
Breton, Louis M. *o.s.m.* '49 (P)[L] Portland, OR The Grotto, The National Sanctuary of Our Sorrowful Mother.
Breton, Ray '68 (OAK) Graduate Studies.
Breton, Raymond G. (OAK) Director & Judicial Vicar; Pastoral Leadership Placement Board (PLPB).
Breton, Raymond (OAK) Judicial Vicar.
Bretone, Richard '89 (BRK) Long Island City, NY Our Lady of Mount Carmel; [E] Campus Ministers and Ministry Centers.
Brett, Frank X. '59 (KNX) Retired.
Brett, Stephen *s.s.j.* '76 (MOB) Mobile, AL Most Pure Heart of Mary.
Bretton, Raymond G. (OAK) Adjutant Judicial Vicars and Canonical Consultant to the Bishop.
Bretton, Raymond (OAK) Judges.
Bretzke, James T. *s.j.* '81 (OAK)[N] Berkeley, CA Jesuit Community at Jesuit School of Theology at Berkeley; [N] San Francisco, CA Jesuit Community at University of San Francisco.
Breu, David L. '73 (NU) Ivanhoe, MN SS. Peter & Paul; Ivanhoe, MN St. John Cantius.
Breunig, Robert L. '51 (DEN) Retired.
Breunig, Rudy *s.t.* '65 (FgM).
Breuning, Walter '54 (PEO) Retired.
Brewczynski, Jacek '96 (DET) Sterling Heights, MI St. Michael.
Brewer, Dexter S. '89 (NSH) Decherd, TN Good Shepherd; Deans; Judicial Vicar; Judges; Univ. of South–Sewanee.
Brewer, Dexter (NSH) Clergy Benefit Foundation.
Brewer, Dexter (KNX) Marriage Tribunal.
Brewer, Gervase '43 (MAR) Retired.
Brewer, James P. '77 (PRT) Westbrook, ME St. Hyacinth.
Brewer, Mark Alan '03 (ROC) Canadaigua, NY St. Mary.
Brewer, Martin L. *s.j.* '54 (LA) Santa Barbara, CA Our Lady of Sorrows.
Brewer, Timothy M. '79 (WOR) Leominster, MA Our Lady of the Lake.
Brewerton, Peter H. '40 (HT) Retired.
Brey, Chris (SFD) Comite Diocesano de Ministerio Hispano – Diocesan Committee for Hispanic Ministry.
Brey, Christopher '97 (SFD) Casey, IL St. Charles Borromeo; Greenup, IL Christ the King; Marshall, IL St. Mary.
Brey, Lawrence S. '53 (MIL) Retired.
Breza, Paul J. '63 (WIN) Hokah, MN St. Peter's; Hokah, MN St. Patrick's.
Brezezinski, Hilary *o.f.m.* (BWN) Coordinator and Chaplain.
Brezik, Victor B. *c.s.b.* '40 (GAL)[Q] Houston, TX Residence of the Basilian Fathers of the University of St. Thomas.
Brezovec, John F. '66 (ALT) Johnstown, PA St. John Gualbert Cathedral.
Brian, Bertrand J. '50 (L) Retired.
Brice, Donald (WDC) Advocates.
Brice, Frederick J. '69 (MIA) Lighthouse Point, FL St. Paul the Apostle; Building Commission; Real Estate Board.
Brice, Frederick (MIA) The St. Vincent De Paul Society, Archdiocesan Council of Miami, Inc..
Brice, Steven J. '82 (LC) Wausau, WI St. Anne.
Briceland, Alan *s.j.* '63 (BRK) Elmhurst General Hospital.
Briceland, W. Alan *s.j.* '65 (NY)[EE] New York, NY West Side Jesuit Community.
Brichetto, James N. *s.j.* '63 (DET)[P] Clarkston, MI Colombiere Center.
Brick, Donald *o.c.d.* (MIL)[O] Holy Hill, WI Discalced Carmelite Monastery – Holy Hill National Shrine of Mary Help of Christians.
Brick, Maurice *o.f.m.* '45 (PAT)[M] Ringwood, NJ Holy Name Friary, Inc..
Brick, Paul T. *s.d.s.* '63 (SAV) Columbus, GA St. Benedict the Moor.
Bricker, Brian *o.p.* '89 (DEN) Denver, CO St. Dominic; [A] Denver, CO St. Dominic Priory.
Brickl, Joseph M. '37 (MAD) Retired.
Brickler, R. Richard '61 (ROC) Rochester, NY St. Boniface; Judges.
Brickman, Donald '81 (CLV) Administrative Leave.
Brickner, Charles W. '75 (RIC) Woodlawn, VA St. Joseph's.
Brickner, Ronald J. '92 (TOL)[B] Fremont, OH St. Joseph Central Catholic High School.
Bride, Harold L. *c.s.c.* '49 (FTW)[I] Jemez Springs, NM Servants of the Paraclete.
Bride, Thomas R. '67 (NOR) Quaker Hill, CT Our Lady of Perpetual Help; Vicar General; College of Consultors; Members; Notaries; Diocesan Finance Council; Board of Education; Vocations; Diocesan Vocation Review Committee.
Bride, Thomas (NOR) Diocesan Pastoral Council.
Bridge, George H. *c.ss.r.* '48 (ALB)[L] Saratoga Springs, NY St. John Neumann Residence.
Bridges, Clarence S. '88 (ALT) Johnstown, PA St. John Gualbert Cathedral.
Bridges, James P. '62 (SAN) Midland, TX St. Stephen's.
Bridgman, Mark D. '96 (OM) Columbus, NE St. Bonaventure.
Brieffies, John '56 (RIC) West Point, VA Our Lady of the Blessed Sacrament.
Brieffies, John *m.s.f.* '56 (RIC)[L] West Point, VA Missionaries of the Holy Family, General Mission Office—M.S.F., Inc..
Brien, Paul J. *m.m.* '60 (FgM).
Brien, Peter C. *m.m.* '60 (FgM).
Briendel, Charles (RIC) Danville, VA Sacred Heart.
Brienz, Edward R. '96 (Y) Leetonia, OH St. Patrick.
Bries, Marvin J. '73 (DUB)[F] Guttenberg, IA Guttenberg–North Buena Vista Consolidated School; Guttenberg, IA Immaculate Conception; Guttenberg, IA St. Mary; Deanery Representatives.
Briese, Dominic *o.p.* (LAV) Director.
Brietske, Richard C. '62 (TR) Willingboro, NJ Corpus Christi; Chancellor; Diocesan Finance Council; Building Commission.
Briffa, Philip '60 (DET) Warren, MI St. Cletus.
Briffa, Salvino '71 (DET) Westland, MI St. Bernardine.
Brigandi, Paul A. '54 (SY) Retired.
Brigandi, Paul '54 (SY) Syracuse, NY St. Peter Retired.
Brigandi, Stephen J. '97 (RVC) West Islip, NY Our Lady of Lourdes.
Briganti, Philip J. '73 (PAT) Military Chaplains; Army Chaplains.
Briggman, Michael J. '68 (ALN) Bally, PA Most Blessed Sacrament; [J] Bethlehem, PA Holy Family Villa; Elected Members Retired.
Briggs, Everett F. '33 (WH) Retired.
Briggs, Michael J. *m.m.* '76 (FgM).
Brigham, Kenneth M. '61 (CHI) Chicago, IL St. Angela; Chicago, IL St. Martin De Porres; Chicago, IL Our Lady Help of Christians; Deans.
Brighenti, Kenneth D. '88 (MET) Raritan, NJ St. Ann; Navy Reserve Chaplains.
Brignac, Horace L. '83 (NO) New Orleans, LA St. Raphael the Archangel.
Brillantes, Edgar B. '80 (HON) Honolulu, HI St. John the Baptist.
Brillantes, Edgar (HON) Presbyteral Council.
Brillantes, Edgar (HON) Filipino Ministry.
Brilliantes, Michael '83 (SFR) San Francisco General Hospital.
Brilliantes, Michael '83 (SFR) San Francisco, CA St. Peter.
Brimley, Wilfred A. *c.s.p.* '62 (NY)[EE] Jamaica Estates Paulist Fathers Generalate.
Brincat, George '57 (LA) Retired.
Brindamour, Albert H. '46 (PRO) Woonsocket, RI Precious Blood Retired.
Brindamour, Maurice L. '74 (PRO) Woonsocket, RI Our Lady, Queen of Martyrs.
Bringas, Daniel '76 (FRS) Wasco, CA Prison Facility.
Bringas, Salvador '67 (HON) Mililani Town, HI St. John Apostle and Evangelist.
Bringas, Salvador (HON) Filipino Ministry.
Brink, Joseph C. '63 (COV) Alexandria, KY St. Mary of the Assumption; Priests' Retirement Committee.
Brinker, Brian J. '88 (RVC)[M] Uniondale, NY St. Pius X Residence.
Brinker, Louis B. '50 (COV) Fort Thomas, KY St. Thomas Retired.
Brinker, Paul J. '36 (COV) Retired.
Brinker, William *c.s.c.* '46 (CHI)[D] Niles, IL Notre Dame High School Retired.
Brinkman, Barry '91 (SAL) Concordia, KS Our Lady of Perpetual Help.
Brinkman, Barry (SAL) Chancellor.
Brinkman, Barry (SAL) Associate Judges.
Brinkman, Barry (SAL) Diocesan Committee Regarding Alleged Cases of Child Sexual Abuse.
Brinkman, Barry (SAL) Priests' Continuing Formation Committee.
Brinkman, Barry (SAL) Council of Priests.
Brinkman, Barry (SAL) Personnel Board.
Brinkman, Charles J. '77 (PH) Absent on Leave.
Brinkman, James J. '81 (SUP) Somerset, WI Assumption of the Blessed Virgin Mary; Somerset, WI St. Anne; St. Pius Priest Fund.
Brinkman, John T. *m.m.* '71 (FgM).
Brinkman, Terence P. '73 (GAL) Crosby, TX Sacred Heart.
Brinkman, Terence (GAL) Censor Librorum.
Brinkmann, Charles J. *c.ss.r.* '56 (RIC)[N] Hampton, VA Holy Family Retreat.
Brinkmann, Frederick C. *c.ss.r.* '75 (NY).
Brinkmann, Gerard J. *c.ss.r.* '61 (PH)[II] Philadelphia, PA St. Boniface.
Brinkmann, Herman *c.ss.r.* '54 (PH) Philadelphia, PA St. Peter the Apostle.
Brinkmoeller, David E. '71 (CIN) Kettering, OH Ascension; Vicarri Foranei (Deans).
Brinn, Adrian '68 (SB) Palm Springs, CA Our Lady of Guadalupe.
Brinn, Adrian (SB) Pro–Synodal Judges.

Brinn, John J. '62 (NY) Poughkeepsie, NY St. Mary.
Brinsmade, John F. '81 (HRT) Manchester, CT Assumption.
Brint, George '57 (LA) Retired.
Briody, Hugh J. '63 (SUP) Retired.
Briody, Thomas '39 (SD) Retired.
Briones, Jose Maria '93 (TLS) Tulsa, OK St. Francis Xavier.
Brioni, Luigi *s.x.* (PAT)[M] Wayne Xaverian Missionary Fathers.
Brioschi, Thomas H. '86 (STP) Eagan, MN St. Thomas Becket; [G] St. Paul, MN Faithful Shepherd Catholic School.
Briseno, Pedro '81 (BWN) Harlingen, TX Immaculate Heart of Mary.
Briseno, Pedro '81 (BWN) Raymondville, TX St. Anthony.
Briseno, Pedro '81 (BWN)[J] Harlingen, TX KMBH–TV 60/KHID–FM 88.1/KMBH–FM 88.9.
Briseno, Pedro (BWN) Diocesan College of Consultors.
Briseno, Pedro (BWN) Ad Hoc Committee for Diocesan Insurance.
Briseno, Pedro (BWN) Diocesan Finance Council.
Briseno, Pedro (BWN) Procurators and Advocates.
Briseno, Pedro (BWN) Presbyteral Council.
Briseno, Pedro (BWN) Division for Communications.
Brislin, Thomas *c.p.* '68 (FgM).
Brisotti, William F. '68 (RVC) Wyandanch, NY Our Lady of the Miraculous Medal.
Brissette, Reginald R. '63 (PRT) Biddeford, ME St. Andre's.
Brisson, Robert A. '85 (NY)[JJ] New York, NY Prelature of the Holy Cross and Opus Dei.
Bristow, David '98 (FWT) Fort Worth, TX St. Mary of the Assumption.
Bristow, David (FWT) Deans.
Brito, Cristiano Aparecido *o.s.b.* '91 (GBG) Virginia Beach, VA St. Gregory the Great.
Brito, Larry R. (SFE) Wagon Mound, NM Santa Clara.
Brito, Larry (SFE) Roy, NM Holy Family–St. Joseph.
Britt, Jerome C. '82 (COV) Burlington, KY Immaculate Heart of Mary; Diocesan Consultors; Presbyteral Council; Catholic Scouting.
Britt, William J. '53 (STL) Retired.
Brittain, Gerald W. '62 (MIL) West Bend, WI Holy Angels; Deans.
Britto, Federico A. '82 (PH) Philadelphia, PA Saint Cyprian.
Britz, Francis '55 (SCL) Sauk Rapids, MN Annunciation.
Britz, Gerald F. '48 (DET) Retired.
Brixius, Hilary R. '68 (WIN) Worthington MN St. Mary's.
Brizio, Michele *i.m.c.* '73 (MET)[H] Somerset, NJ Consolata Society for Foreign Missions.
Brizzolara, Andrew *c.s.* '75 (HRT) New Haven, CT St. Michael's.
Broadhurst, T. Paul *c.s.b.* '60 (ROC)[I] Rochester, NY Basilian Residence.
Brobst, James P. *o.m.i.* '90 (CHI)[N] Chicago, IL The Oblate House of Theology.
Brobst, Richard A. '65 (Y) Boardman, OH St. Luke.
Brocato, John K. (ALX)[A] Alexandria, LA Holy Savior Menard Central; Alexandria, LA St. Frances Xavier Cabrini.
Brocato, Robert '95 (SJ) San Jose, CA Christ the King.
Broccolo, Gerard T. '65 (CHI) On Duty Outside the Archdiocese.
Brochu, Albert E. *a.a.* '43 (WOR)[O] Worcester, MA Assumptionists (Augustinians of the Assumption).
Brochu, Gerard H. '50 (BUR) Retired.
Brock, Bill '91 (DEN) Denver, CO St. James
Brock, David F. '56 (DET) Retired.
Brock, John '62 (JKS) Grenada, MS St. Peter.
Brockett, Norman L. '87 (HRT) Cheshire, CT Church of the Epiphany.
Brockhaus, Edward '64 (SD) Lemon Grove, CA St. John of the Cross; Presbyteral Council.
Brockhaus, Thomas *o.s.b.* '39 (P)[L] St. Benedict, OR Mt. Angel Abbey.
Brockhaus, Thomas *o.s.b.* (P) Judges.
Brockland, John A. (STL) Adjutant Judicial Vicars; Director of Advocate Services; Deaneries/Deans; Northeast.
Brockland, John '91 (STL) Hazelwood, MO St. Bartholomew.
Brockland, Robert J. *c.m.* '74 (STL)[O] Perryville, MO Congregation of the Mission.
Brockman, Blaise N. '77 (LA) Santa Clarita, CA Blessed Kateri Tekakwitha.
Brockman, David D. '90 (R) On Duty Outside the Diocese.
Brockman, Leon *o.c.s.o.* '55 (SPC)[E] Ava, MO Assumption Abbey (Trappist).
Brockman, Norbert C. *s.m.* '73 (SAT)[C] San Antonio, TX St. Mary's University of San Antonio, Texas.
Brockman, Norbert *s.m.* '73 (SAT)[M] San Antonio, TX Woodlawn Marianist Community.
Brockmyre, Philip J. '02 (SY) Syracuse NY Holy Family.
Brockson, Scott '96 (PH) Philadelphia, PA St Hugh of Cluny.
Broderick, C. Michael '87 (WOR) Whitinsville, MA St. Patrick's; Deans.
Broderick, James M. '60 (BO) Haverhill, MA Sacred Hearts; Senior Priests Retired.
Broderick, John F. *s.j.* '45 (BO)[V] Weston, MA Campion Health Center, Inc..
Broderick, John W. '89 (SY) Sherburne, NY St Malachy of Armagh.
Broderick, Kilian J. '67 (DAL)[N] Coppell, TX St. Catherine of Siena, Inc.; [N] Coppell, TX St Stephen, Inc.; Coppell TX St. Ann.
Broderick, Leo P. '56 (DET) Columbus, MI St. Philip Neri Retired
Broderick, Richard J. '70 (ALB) Special Assignment.
Broderick, Richard '70 (ALB) Albany County Jail.
Broderick, William '49 (SAC) Carmichael, CA Our Lady of the Assumption Retired.
Brodersen, Charles F. '48 (OM) Retired.
Brodersen, Steven W. '85 (SC) Sioux City, IA Immaculate Conception.
Brodeski, Aaron R. '98 (RCK) Vocations; Amboy, IL St. Patrick.
Brodeski, Aaron '98 (RCK) Special Assignment.
Brodeur, Dennis A. '77 (PRO) On Duty Outside the Diocese.
Brodeur, Henry *m.s.* '66 (FR) Brewster, MA Our Lady of the Cape.
Brodeur, Scott N. *s.j.* '90 (BO)[V] Boston The Society of Jesus of New England–Provincial Offices.
Brodeur, Ted (MAR) Apostleship of the Sea.
Brodeur, Theodore J. '66 (MAR) Sault Sainte Marie, MI Holy Name of Mary; Sault Sainte Marie, MI Sacred Heart.
Brodniak, Anthony B. *m.m.* '54 (FgM).
Brodnick, Edward J. '76 (COV) Crescent Springs, KY St. Joseph.
Brodnick, Joseph '69 (CLV) Administrative Leave.
Brody, Donald *o.f.m.cap.* '47 (GB)[I] Appleton, WI St. Fidelis Friary.
Brody, Philip (MAN) Woodsville, NH St. Joseph.
Brodzeller, Robert E. *s.j.* '63 (OM)[K] Omaha, NE Jesuit Community at Creighton University.
Broering, Joseph H. '53 (COV)[L] Fort Thomas, KY Carmel Manor Retired.
Broering, Raymond L. '53 (COV) Retired.
Brogan, Hugh T. '69 (WDC) Retired.
Brogan, John F. '75 (BRK)[Z] Brooklyn, NY Society of the Immaculate Conception of Brooklyn; Liturgical Commission.
Brogan, John '75 (BRK) Brooklyn, NY Our Lady of Monserrate–St. Ambrose.
Brogan, John (BRK) Propagation of the Faith.
Brogan, John (BRK) Holy Childhood, Pontifical Association.
Brogan, Leo '67 (PHX) Retired.
Brogan, Malachy *o.f.m.* '57 (FgM).
Brogan, Malachy *o.f.m.* '57 (CIN).
Brogus, Albert G. '45 (SCR) Retired.
Brohammer, Ronald '60 (MIA) Retired.
Broheimer, John P. '03 (OM)[M] Omaha, NE Mary Our Queen.
Brokman, James P. '97 (DUB) Cedar Rapids, IA Immaculate Conception; Lay Formation Advisory Board.
Bromenshenkel, Fintan *o.s.b.* '45 (SCL)[I] St. Augustine Monastery.
Bromenshenkel, Fintan *o.s.b.* '45 (FgM).
Bromenshenkel, Silvan *o.s.b.* '47 (SCL)[I] Collegeville, MN St. John's Abbey, of the Order of St. Benedict.
Bromley, Vincent M. '65 (SUP) Winter, WI Sacred Heart; Winter, WI St. Peter.
Bromschwig, Arthur F. '50 (STL) Florissant, MO Sacred Heart.
Bromwich, James S. '03 (L) Graduate Studies.
Bronder, Joseph P. *o.s.b.* '69 (GBG)[H] Latrobe, PA Saint Vincent Archabbey.
Broniak, Leonard *c.ss.r.* '79 (GAL) Houston, TX Holy Ghost; Deaf Apostolate.
Broniszewski, Leo *o.carm.* '56 (NY)[EE] Middletown, NY St. Albert's Priory.
Bronk, Philip *s.t.* '51 (SD) Little Flower Haven.
Bronk, Philip *s.t.* '51 (SD)[G] La Mesa, CA Little Flower Haven.
Bronkiewicz, Laurence R. '73 (BGP) Ridgefield, CT St. Mary.
Bronkiewicz Laurence R. '73 (BGP) Diocesan Censors; Diocesan Consultors; Presbyteral Council.
Brooker, Richard L. *m.m.* '55 (FgM).
Brooks, Armand L. '97 (FAR) Hope, ND St. Olaf; Hope, ND St. Agatha; Hope, ND St. James.
Brooks, Bryan V. (TLS) Priests' Personnel Committee.
Brooks, Bryan '93 (TLS) Muskogee, OK Saint Joseph Church.
Brooks, Charles R. '65 (GB) Appleton, WI St. Edward.
Brooks, Jeddie P. '77 (SPR) Monson, MA St. Patrick's; Procurators–Advocate; Deans; Brimfield, MA St. Christopher's.
Brooks, John E. *s.j.* '59 (WOR)[O] Worcester, MA Jesuits of Holy Cross College, Inc..
Brooks, Lawrence V. *s.j.* '74 (FgM).
Brooks, Michael *ss.cc.* '61 (SB) Upland, CA St. Joseph; [E] Upland, CA Congregation of the Sacred Hearts.
Brooks, Robert C. '61 (ARL) Leesburg, VA St. John the Apostle; Diocesan Judges.
Brooks, Robert E. '95 (SAC) Susanville, CA Sacred Heart.
Brooks, Thomas M. '78 (E) Erie, PA Our Lady of Peace.
Brooks, William C. '76 (AUS) Austin, TX St. Albert The Great.
Brooksbank, Kevin W. '01 (BAL) Baltimore, MD Immaculate Heart of Mary.
Broom, Edward *o.m.v.* '86 (LA) Hawaiian Gardens, CA St. Peter Chanel.
Brophy, Charles D. '39 (GR) Retired.
Brophy, Edward G. (BRK) Attorneys and Counselors at Canon Law.
Brophy, Edward '93 (BRK) Brooklyn, NY St. Edmund's.
Brophy, Edward (BRK) Presbyteral Council.
Brophy, Edward (BRK) Personnel Board (Clergy).
Brophy, John L. '69 (MIL) On Duty Outside the Archdiocese.
Brophy, Michael *s.j.* '69 (CIN)[M] Cincinnati, OH Jesuit Community at St. Xavier High School.
Brophy, Peter *o.f.m.* '85 (NY)[EE] New York, NY Saint Francis Monastery, Inc..
Brophy, Peter *o.f.m.* '85 (NY)[II] New York, NY St. Francis Monastery Breadline for the Poor, Inc..
Brophy, Peter *o.f.m.* '85 (NY) New York, NY St. Francis of Assisi.
Brophy, R. Michael *s.j.* '69 (CIN)[F] Cincinnati, OH St. Xavier High School.
Brosk, Steven J. '90 (NEW) Military Chaplains; Air Force Reserve Chaplains.
Broski, Mark *o.s.b.* (KCK) Catholic Scouts.
Brosmer, Thomas J. '69 (COL) Worthington, OH St. Michael.
Brosnahan, Bruce C. '01 (TLS) Fairfax, OK Sacred Heart.
Brosnahan, Bruce '01 (TLS) Fairfax, OK St. Joseph.
Brosnan, Dermot '57 (SAT) Retired.
Brosnan, John R. '37 (LA) Los Angeles, CA St. Ann Retired.
Brosnan, Liam P. '59 (SAT) San Antonio, TX St. Pius X.
Brosnan, Thomas F. '81 (BRK) Brooklyn, NY Blessed Sacrament.
Brossart, Scott (CC)[G] Robstown, TX Society of Our Lady of the Most Holy Trinity.
Brost, Frederick '56 (SUP) Stetsonville, WI Sacred Heart of Jesus.
Brothersen, Maynard J. '48 (DAV)[M] Davenport, IA St. Vincent Center Retired.
Brou, Francis R. *s.j.* '61 (LAF)[J] Grand Coteau, LA Jesuit Spirituality Center (St. Charles College).
Broudou, Joseph '96 (OM) Springfield, NE St. Joseph.
Brougher, Douglas C. '62 (NO) New Orleans, LA St. James Major; New Orleans, LA Touro Infirmary.
Brougher, Douglas (NO) Ministry to Sick Priests.
Brouillard, John '56 (P) Retired.
Brouillard, Louis A. (AGN) Retired.
Brouillette, Thomas S. (LIN) Diocesan Area CCD Directors.
Brouillette, Thomas '96 (LIN) North Platte, NE St. Elizabeth Ann Seton.
Brouke, Gabriel Vanden *ss.cc.* '48 (HON)[G] Honolulu, HI St. Patrick's Monastery.
Broussard, A. Rex '66 (LAF) Maurice, LA Our Lady of Perpetual Help; Advocates.
Broussard, Dennis A. '91 (MAN) Litchfield, NH St. Francis of Assisi.
Broussard, F. David '93 (LAF) Iota, LA St. Joseph.
Broussard, Henry J. '72 (LAF) Duson, LA St. Basil.
Broussard, Hubert C. '52 (HT) Retired.
Broussard, John S. *c.s.b.* '48 (GAL) Manvel, TX Sacred Heart of Jesus.
Broussard, Ken '03 (LAF) New Iberia, LA Our Lady of Perpetual Help.
Broussard, Oris '60 (LKC)[C] Lake Charles, LA Holy City Community.
Broussard, Oris '60 (LKC) Retired.
Broussard, Oris (LKC) Charismatic Renewal.
Broussard, Paul '02 (LAF) Cecilia, LA St. Joseph.
Broussard, Paul (LAF) Advocates.
Broussard, Richard Dale '00 (LAF) Pine Prairie, LA St. Peter.
Broussard, Ronald '88 (LAF) Duson, LA St. Benedict the Moor.
Broussard, Ronald (LAF) Vicars General.
Broussard, Ronald (LAF) Diocesan Consultors.
Broussard, Theodore '98 (LAF) Breaux Bridge, LA Our Lady of Mercy.
Broussard, Warren J. *s.j.* '88 (LAF)[J] Grand Coteau, LA Jesuit Spirituality Center (St. Charles College); Retreats.
Broussard, William L. '56 (GAL) On Duty Outside the Diocese.
Brouwers, Hans A.L. '78 (PH) Coatesville, PA Our Lady of the Rosary; Council of Priests.
Brovey, Steven L. '91 (CHR) Greer, SC Blessed Trinity; Taylors, SC Prince of Peace; Diocesan Curia; College of Consultors; Deans; Presbyteral Council; Building

& Renovation Commission; Divine Worship & Sacraments, Vicar for; Office of Prayer & Worship; Vocations Board.
Brown, Anthony M. '49 (HEL) Retired.
Brown, Arthur A. '57 (BO) Senior Priests Retired.
Brown, Benedict J. '74 (L) Military Chaplains; Navy Chaplains.
Brown, Bruce '63 (P) Retired.
Brown, Bruce '63 (P) Portland, OR Sacred Heart.
Brown, Charles D. '93 (GR) Holland, MI St. Francis de Sales.
Brown, Charles E. '71 (WDC) Burtonsville, MD Resurrection Parish.
Brown, Charles L. '67 (WIL) Bear, DE St. Elizabeth Ann Seton; Deans; Parish Priest Consultors.
Brown, Charles L. '73 (BRK) On Leave/Unassigned.
Brown, Charles '58 (SFE) Retired.
Brown, Charles *s.c.j.* '84 (MIL)[O] Milwaukee, WI SCJ Community.
Brown, Charles '87 (PSC) Retired.
Brown, Charles '89 (NY)[B] On Duty Outside the Archdiocese.
Brown, David A. *s.j.* '02 (NO)[P] Campion Hall.
Brown, David G. *o.s.b.* '75 (CHL)[J] Belmont, NC Belmont Abbey.
Brown, David M. *o.s.m.* '48 (CHI) Chicago, IL Assumption of the Blessed Virgin Mary; [N] Chicago, IL Assumption Priory.
Brown, Dennis '89 (RCK)[M] Aurora, IL Association of the Communications Congregation.
Brown, Dom Lawrence *o.s.b.* '84 (BUR)[F] Westfield, VT Monastery of the Immaculate Heart of Mary.
Brown, Duane *o.f.m.* '03 (MIL)[O] Burlington, WI St. Francis Friary.
Brown, Edward J. *m.s.* '81 (RVC)[P] Brookville, NY Interfaith Center.
Brown, Eugene M. '60 (NU) Marshall, MN Holy Redeemer; Priests' Council; College of Consultors.
Brown, Everett *s.m.m.* '61 (BRK)[V] Ozone Park Montfort Missionaries Provincialate (Missionaries of the Company of Mary) – Formation Community.
Brown, Francis E. '64 (BO) On Duty Outside the Archdiocese.
Brown, George *o.m.i.* '64 (BO)[V] Lowell, MA Missionary Oblates of Mary Immaculate.
Brown, Gerald L. *s.s.* '64 (SAT)[A] San Antonio, TX Assumption Seminary aka Assumption–St. John's Seminary; Assumption–St. John's Seminary.
Brown, Gerald *c.m.* '48 (STL)[O] St. Louis, MO Lazarist Residence.
Brown, Gerald *s.s.* '64 (SAT)[C] Oblate School of Theology.
Brown, Gerard J. '46 (TR) Leave of Absence.
Brown, Harold C. *c.pp.s.* '59 (TOL) Glandorf, OH St. John the Baptist.
Brown, Henry P. '51 (IND) Retired.
Brown, Henry '51 (IND)[I] Beech Grove, IN St. Paul Hermitage.
Brown, James E. '72 (TOL) Marblehead, OH St. Joseph; Spiritual Directors.
Brown, James T. '97 (NEW) Emerson, NJ Church of the Assumption.
Brown, James V. *o.a.r.* '46 (OM) Omaha, NE St. James.
Brown, Jerry W. '01 (OAK) Concord, CA St. Francis of Assisi.
Brown, John J. '83 (BRK) Brooklyn, NY Queen of All Saints; Defenders of the Marriage Bond; Office of Clergy Personnel; Assignment Board; Personnel Board (Clergy).
Brown, John T. *g.h.m.* '84 (TLS) Idabel, OK St. Francis De Sales.
Brown, Joseph A. *s.j.* '72 (MIL)[O] Carbondale, IL Southern Illinois University, Black American Studies Dept..
Brown, Joseph E. *s.j.* '56 (STL)[O] St. Louis, MO Jesuit Community Corporation at St. Louis University – Jesuit Hall.
Brown, Joseph Mary *f.j.* '97 (PEO)[M] Princeville, IL St. Joseph Priory and Novitiate.
Brown, Joseph *c.pp.s.* '98 (OAK) Alameda, CA St. Barnabas.
Brown, Justin *o.s.b.* '90 (NO)[P] St. Benedict, LA St. Joseph Abbey; [A] St. Benedict, LA St. Joseph Seminary College.
Brown, Justin *o.s.b.* (NO).
Brown, Keenan Wynn '02 (LAF)[A] Eunice, LA St. Anthony of Padua.
Brown, Kenneth '77 (STL) St. Louis, MO St. Margaret of Scotland.
Brown, Konstantin K. '88 (ROM) Unassigned.
Brown, Leonard J. *c.m.f.* '82 (CHI)[N] Oak Park, IL Claretian Fathers Headquarters of U.S.A. Eastern Province; [N] Oak Park, IL Claretian Missionaries Community Support Trust.
Brown, Lewis E. '67 (ROC) Military Chaplains; Navy Chaplains.
Brown, Lewis '67 (ROC) On Duty Outside the Diocese.
Brown, Lewis (MO) Presbyteral Council.
Brown, Matthew F. '63 (SY) Vestal, NY Our Lady of Sorrows; Vestal, NY Binghamton Nursing Homes.
Brown, Matthew J. *o.s.b.* '49 (OKL) Konawa, OK Sacred Heart; [I] Shawnee St. Gregory's Abbey.
Brown, Michael O. '74 (TOL) Toledo, OH Christ the King.
Brown, Michael R. '89 (ROC) Mount Morris, NY St. Patrick; Mount Morris, NY Holy Angels.
Brown, Michael '89 (ROC) Sonyea, NY Livingston Correctional Facility and Seneca Correctional Facility.
Brown, Michael *o.carm.* '93 (JOL)[L] Prelate Nullius.
Brown, Ned '99 (DAL)[K] Irving, TX Legionaries of Christ.
Brown, Nicholas *s.c.j.* '76 (SAT)[M] San Antonio, TX Hospital Ministry House.
Brown, Nicholas *s.c.j.* '76 (SAT) San Antonio, TX St. Luke's Baptist Hospital; University Hospital.
Brown, Patrick E. '78 (PAT) Stirling, NJ St. Vincent de Paul; Morris County Jail; Deans.
Brown, Patrick M. *o.f.m.* '59 (PAT)[M] Butler, NJ St. Anthony Friary.
Brown, Patrick *o.c.s.o.* '74 (WOR)[O] Spencer, MA St. Joseph's Abbey.
Brown, Phillip J. '89 (BAL).
Brown, Phillip '89 (BIS)[A] On Duty Outside the Diocese.
Brown, Richard H. *s.j.* '58 (SD) San Diego, CA Our Lady of Guadalupe.
Brown, Robert A. '42 (L) Retired.
Brown, Robert A. *o.s.f.s.* '67 (ARL) Reston, VA St. John Neumann.
Brown, Robert L. '69 (NOR) Uncasville, CT St. John; Chancellor; College of Consultors; Members; Notaries; Catholic Relief Services.
Brown, Robert P. (SC) Defenders of the Bond.
Brown, Robert W. '66 (ORL) Orlando, FL St. Joseph.
Brown, Robert '63 (SC) Carroll, IA Our Lady of Mt. Carmel.
Brown, Robert '63 (SC) Carroll, IA St. Francis of Assisi.
Brown, Robert (NOR) Diocesan Pastoral Council.
Brown, Roderick M. *o.p.* '79 (CHI)[N] St. Pius V Priory.
Brown, Shaun S. '94 (NTN) Military Chaplains; Navy Chaplains.
Brown, Stephan *s.v.d.* (IND) Indianapolis, IN St. Rita.
Brown, Steven P. '77 (SJ) Alviso, CA Our Lady, Star of the Sea.
Brown, Sylvester F. '56 (WIN) Retired.
Brown, Theophile W. *o.s.b.* '50 (RIC)[L] Richmond, VA Mary Mother of the Church Abbey.
Brown, Thomas E. '78 (E) Corry, PA St. Thomas The Apostle; Corry, PA St. Elizabeth.
Brown, Thomas J. '99 (GR) Baldwin, MI St. Ann's.
Brown, Thomas *o.m.i.* '55 (FgM).
Brown, Timothy B. *s.j.* '79 (FgM).
Brown, Timothy B. *s.j.* '86 (BAL)[S] Baltimore, MD Jesuit Fathers and Brothers Maryland Provincial Curia.
Brown, Timothy *s.j.* '86 (PH)[FF] Philadelphia, PA Apostleship of Prayer.
Brown, Timothy '87 (ROC) Rochester, NY St. Charles Borromeo.
Brown, Victor *o.p.* '63 (NO) New Orleans, LA St. Dominic.
Brown, W. Joseph '99 (IND) Unassigned.
Brown, W. P. '80 (PT) Panama City, FL Our Lady of the Rosary.
Brown, W.T. St. John '92 (CC) Retired.
Brown, Walter W. '94 (JKS) Woodville, MS St. Joseph.
Brown, Walter (JKS) Priests' Council.
Brown, Warren A. *o.m.i.* '82 (SAT)[M] San Antonio, TX De Mazenod House; Judges.
Brown, Warren *o.m.i.* '82 (SAT)[C] Oblate School of Theology.
Brown, William E. '88 (SFR) Daly City, CA Our Lady of Mercy.
Brown, William J. '55 (SY) Retired.
Brown, William M. *o.m.v.* '94 (BO)[B] Boston, MA Oblate Provincialate.
Brown, William P. '80 (PT) Panama City, FL Our Lady Queen of Peace Mission; Judges.
Brown–Claitty, Wanda (HRT)[S] New Britain, CT New Britain.
Browne, Denis P. *m.m.* '47 (FgM).
Browne, Dennis '79 (SJ) On Leave of Absence.
Browne, Francis *c.ss.r.* (ORL) New Smyrna Beach, FL Sacred Heart.
Browne, George '55 (DET) Marine City, MI Holy Cross; Presbyteral Council Retired.
Browne, Gerald '81 (MET) Carteret, NJ Sacred Heart.
Browne, J. Patrick '67 (SJ) San Jose, CA Cathedral Basilica of St. Joseph; College of Consultors; Deans.
Browne, John T. *o.s.b.* '56 (NEW)[N] Newark, NJ Newark Abbey.
Browne, Joseph P. *c.s.c.* '55 (P) Portland, OR St. Birgitta.
Browne, Joseph P. *c.s.c.* '55 (FTW)[I] Portland, OR.
Browne, Joseph P. *c.s.c.* '55 (P)[L] Portland, OR Holy Cross Fathers & Brothers, C.S.C. – University of Portland.
Browne, Joseph T. *s.j.* '43 (NY) New York, NY St. Ignatius Loyola.
Browne, Joseph T. *s.j.* '56 (NY)[EE] New York, NY St. Ignatius Loyola Residence.
Browne, Joseph *c.s.c.* (P) College of Consultors.
Browne, Joseph *c.s.c.* (P) Area Vicars.
Browne, Michael E. *s.j.* '71 (NEW)[C] Jersey City, NJ St. Peter's Preparatory School; [N] Jersey City, NJ Jesuit Community of St. Peter's Prep, Inc..
Browne, Robert M. '61 (BO) Stoneham, MA St. Patrick.
Browne, Ronald T. '91 (DET) Farmington, MI Our Lady of Sorrows; Promoter of Justice.
Browne, Stanley '81 (GB) Absent on Leave.
Browne, Vincent T. '54 (MAD) Retired.
Browne, William '98 (CHI) Oak Lawn, IL St. Linus.
Brownell, Patrick P. '94 (KNX) Crossville, TN St. Alphonsus.
Brownell, Patrick (KNX) Presbyteral Council.
Brownell, Robert A. '69 (RIC) Richmond, VA St. Peter.
Brownfield, Robert L. '92 (DAV)[M] Davenport, IA St. Vincent Center Retired.
Brownholtz, Andrew C. '01 (PH) Collegeville, PA St. Eleanor.
Brownholtz, George J. *o.s.f.s.* '69 (WIL)[J] Childs, MD Retirement and Assisted Care Facility.
Brownholtz, George J. *o.s.f.s.* '69 (FgM).
Browning, Thomas *s.s.c.* '90 (FgM).
Browning, William *c.p.* '49 (CHI)[N] Chicago, IL Passionist Community–Immaculate Conception Monastery.
Browning, William *c.p.* '49 (CHI)[N] Chicago, IL Daneo Hall.
Brownsey, Brian K. '96 (PEO) Peoria, IL St. Peter's; Vocations Office.
Brownsey, Brian (PEO) Cursillo Program.
Brownsey, Brian (PEO) TEC.
Brownstein, Donald P. '81 (COS) Parker, CO Ave Maria.
Brozat, Charles *s.a.* '57 (NY)[EE] Garrison Franciscan Friars of the Atonement, Minister General Office.
Brozena, Joseph M. '58 (SCR) Old Forge, PA St. Michael's.
Brozonowicz, Grzegorz P. '96 (NOR) Groton, CT St. Mary.
Brubaker, Claude E. '55 (VEN) Sarasota, FL St. Michael the Archangel.
Brubaker, Claude (VEN) Venice Diocesan Council of Catholic Women.
Brubaker, George J. '80 (WIL) Milford, DE St. John the Apostle; Milford, DE; Judicial Vicar; Court of First Instance Judges; Contact; Catholic Relief Services, Inc.; Air National Guard Chaplains.
Brubaker, W. Scott '82 (PHX) Mesa, AZ St. Bridget.
Bruce, Joseph J. *s.j.* '81 (BO) Roxbury, MA St. Mary of the Angels; [V] Boston The Society of Jesus of New England–Provincial Offices.
Bruce, Joseph *s.j.* '81 (BO)[V] Newton, MA The Jesuit Community at Boston College.
Bruce, Robert J. '64 (Y) Retired.
Bruce, Terry '67 (KC) Independence, MO St. Ann's.
Bruce, Terry '67 (KC) Sugar Creek, MO St. Cyril.
Bruch, James A. '65 (SC) Milford, IA St. Joseph's.
Bruch, Lynn '86 (SC) Fort Dodge, IA Holy Rosary; [G] Fort Dodge, IA Corpus Christi Parish Foundation of Fort Dodge.
Bruch, Lynn (SC) Fort Dodge, IA Catholic Cemetery Improvement Society.
Bruck, Donald '68 (DM) Shenandoah, IA St. Mary.
Bruck, Donald '68 (DM) Hamburg, IA St. Mary.
Bruck, Raymond E. '58 (GR) Howard City, MI Christ the King; Howard City, MI St. Francis de Sales Retired.
Brucker, G. Fredrick '76 (GR) On Special Assignment.
Brucker, George W. '56 (ALB) Schenectady, NY St. Paul the Apostle; Priests Placement Committee.
Bruckner, Ronald L. '65 (SFE) Albuquerque, NM Annunciation.
Bruckner, Ronald (SFE) Vicars Forane (Deans).
Brucksch, James L. '69 (GAY) Oscoda, MI Sacred Heart; Consultors, Diocesan Board of; Appointed Members; Elected Members.
Brucz, James M. *c.s.p.* '74 (KNX) Knoxville, TN Immaculate Conception.
Bruder, John W. *o.c.s.o.* '56 (BUR) Other Residence.
Brudzynski, Peter F. '50 (BO) Senior Priests; Venice, FL Epiphany Cathedral Retired.
Bruecken, Albert *o.s.b.* '77 (KC)[A] Conception, MO Conception Seminary College.
Bruecken, Albert *o.s.b.* '77 (KC)[J] Conception, MO Conception Abbey.
Bruemmer, Joseph A. '48 (CIN) Cincinnati, OH St. Thomas More Retired.
Bruemmer, Joseph J. *o.s.c.* '47 (PHX)[G] Phoenix, AZ Crosier Community of Phoenix (Canons Regular of the Order of the Holy Cross).
Bruening, Allen '51 (CLV) Administrative Leave.
Bruening, Bernard H. '59 (CIN) Retired.
Bruening, Joseph B. '53 (CIN) Retired.
Bruening, Robert '58 (CIN) Cincinnati, OH Corpus Christi.
Bruetsch, Joseph J. '70 (LFT) Retired.
Bruggeman, Donald R. '62 (DUB)[D] Gilbertville, IA Don Bosco High School; Jesup, IA St. Athanasius; Dunkerton, IA St. Francis.
Bruggeman, Gerald H. '49 (COS)[C] Colorado Springs, CO Penrose Hospital Retired.

Brugger, Craig F. '73 (PH) Absent on Leave.
Brugger, Robert L. '68 (E) Erie, PA St. Jude the Apostle; Finance Council.
Brum, Louis L. '74 (BWN) Alamo, TX Resurrection; Deans; Ad Hoc Committee for Diocesan Insurance; Building Committee.
Brum, Louis '74 (BWN).
Brum, Louis (BWN)[E] Episcopal Vicar for Religious.
Brumleve, Matthew '88 (KC) St. Joseph, MO St. Patrick's.
Brumleve, Matthew '88 (KC) Easton, MO St. Joseph's.
Brummel, Mark J. *c.m.f.* '60 (CHI)[N] Chicago, IL Claretian Missionaries, St. Jude League, Inc.; [N] Oak Park, IL Claretian Missionaries Community Support Trust.
Brummel, Mark *c.m.f.* '60 (CHI)[X] Chicago, IL Villa Guadalupe Senior Services Corporation.
Brummel, Thomas *c.m.f.* '59 (CHI) Chicago, IL Our Lady of Guadalupe.
Brummer, Lawrence *o.f.m.* '58 (SAT) San Antonio, TX San Francisco de la Espada.
Brummer, Lawrence *o.f.m.* (SAT) In Metropolitan Area.
Brummer, Lawrence *o.f.m.* (SAT) Archdiocesan Presbyteral Council.
Brundage, John '70 (MET) Somerset, NJ St. Matthias.
Brundage, Thomas T. '88 (MIL)[X] Milwaukee, WI Milwaukee Catholic Press Apostolate; Special Assignment; Milwaukee, WI SS. Peter and Paul; Judges for First Instance; Judges for Second Instance.
Brundage, Thomas *j.c.l.* '88 (MIL).
Brune, James '48 (EVN) Retired.
Brune, Meinrad *o.s.b.* '61 (IND)[K] St. Meinrad, IN St. Meinrad Archabbey.
Brunelle, J. Ernest *m.m.* '59 (SEA)[EE] Maryknoll Maryknoll Fathers and Brothers Retired.
Brunelle, Richard *a.a.* '63 (BO)[V] Austin House.
Brunet, Frederic J. '60 (HT) Chauvin, LA St. Joseph; Diocesan Finance Council.
Brunet, Frederick (HT) Finance Officer.
Brunet, Gerald *o.m.i.* '57 (ANC) Anchorage, AK St. Anthony.
Brunet, Gerald *o.m.i.* '57 (ANC) Glennallen, AK Holy Family.
Brunet, Gerald *o.m.i.* (ANC) Native Ministry.
Brunet, Jules A. '55 (BR) White Castle, LA Our Lady of Prompt Succor.
Brunetta, M. Juan–Diego *o.p.* '01 (HRT) New Haven, CT St. Mary's Priory; Defender of the Bond; Judges.
Brunetta, Mario Juan Diego *o.p.* '01 (WDC)[B] Washington, DC Dominican House of Studies.
Brunette, Bernard M. *o.praem.* '51 (GB)[I] De Pere, WI St. Norbert Abbey.
Brunette, Larry H. '99 (SFD) Granite City, IL Holy Family.
Bruney, J. Lawrence '84 (PIT) Sewickley, PA St. Mary; Defenders of the Bond.
Brungardt, Aloysius '71 (SAL) Junction City, KS St. Francis Xavier's.
Brungardt, John B. (WCH) Respect Life and Social Justice Office.
Brungardt, John Balthasar '98 (WCH) Arkansas City, KS Sacred Heart.
Brungs, Robert A. *s.j.* '64 (STL)[O] St. Louis, MO Jesuit Community Corporation at St. Louis University – Jesuit Hall; [U] St. Louis, MO Institute for Theological Encounter with Science & Technology (ITEST).
Bruni, John E. '76 (CAM) Gibbstown, NJ St. Michael's.
Brunick, Charles J. *c.s.p.* '70 (CHI) Chicago, IL Old St. Mary.
Bruning, Bill (KCK) Regional Pastoral Leaders.
Bruning, Bill (KCK) Priests' Council.
Bruning, David R. '78 (TOL) Fremont, OH St. Joseph.
Bruning, William '93 (KCK) St. Monica – St. Elizabeth.
Bruning, William '93 (KCK) Marysville, KS St. Gregory's.
Bruning, William '93 (KCK) Frankfort, KS Annunciation.
Brunkan, Walter L. '56 (DUB) Greene, IA St. Mary; Greene, IA St. Mary; Directors.
Brunner, Frank J. '55 (WH) Retired.
Brunner, James C. '54 (VIC) Victoria, TX St. Mary's; Vicars General; Diocesan Consultors; Presbyteral Council; Priests' Personnel Board; Diocesan Finance Board; Respect Life–Pro Life.
Brunner, John H. '62 (NU) Watkins, MN Church of St. Anthony; Board of Trustees for Pension Plan for Priests.
Brunnert, Edward J. *m.s.* '63 (LKC) Sulphur, LA Our Lady of Prompt Succor.
Brunnert, Jude *m.s.* '64 (LKC) Jennings, LA Immaculate Conception.
Brunnert, Theodore J. '54 (STL) Sullivan, MO St. Anthony.
Bruno, Anthony J. '68 (HRT) Enfield, CT St. Adalbert's; Wethersfield, CT Connecticut Department of Correction.
Bruno, John *r.c.j.* '74 (LA)[Q] Van Nuys, CA Rogationist Fathers.
Bruno, John *r.c.j.* '74 (LA) Van Nuys, CA St. Elisabeth.
Bruno, Robert A. *o.f.m.* (MO) Air Force Chaplains.
Brunovsky, Michael '93 (CLV)[O] Cleveland, OH.
Brunovsky, Michael *o.s.b.* '93 (CLV)[D] Cleveland, OH Benedictine High School.
Brunovsky, Stephen K. '92 (CLV) Medina, OH St. Francis Xavier.
Bruns, Wilbert H. *c.m.* '51 (STL)[O] St. Louis, MO Lazarist Residence.
Brunskill, Richard W. '83 (PEO) Chatsworth, IL SS. Peter and Paul.
Brunsman, Barry *o.f.m.* '56 (OAK)[P] Danville, CA San Damiano Retreat.
Brunton, Daniel B. '60 (SPR) Procurators–Advocate; [H] Lenox, MA Providence Care Center of Lenox Retired.
Bruntrup, Godehard *s.j.* '89 (NY)[EE] Cardinal Spellman Hall, Jesuit Community.
Brusato, Martin '89 (SAC) Absent on Leave.
Brusatti, Louis *c.m.* '75 (AUS)[G] Austin, TX Congregation of the Mission, C.M..
Brusatti, Louis *c.m.* (AUS)[A] St. Edward's University.
Bruse, James C. '84 (ARL) Kilmarnock, VA St. Francis de Sales.
Bruso, Robert D. '93 (WOR) Fitchburg, MA St Anthony of Padua; Hmong Ministry.
Brutus, Ferry '80 (MIA) North Miami, FL Holy Family.
Bryan, Francis E. '62 (IND)[B] Indianapolis, IN Marian College.
Bryan, Kevin J. '76 (L) Edmonton, KY Christ the Healer.
Bryan, Paul *c.ss.r.* '59 (HBG)[H] Ephrata St. Clement's Mission House.
Bryant, Curtis *s.j.* '67 (LA)[C] Los Angeles, CA Jesuit Community.
Bryant, F. Michael '69 (WDC) Washington, DC Holy Comforter—St. Cyprian; [V] Washington, DC District of Columbia Detention Facility.
Bryant, Michael M. '78 (SCR)[C] College Misericordia.
Bryant, Michael '69 (WDC)[V] Hyattsville, MD Prison Outreach Ministry.
Bryant, Michael '69 (WDC) Special Ministries.
Bryce, Edward M. '60 (PIT) Pittsburgh, PA St. Bede; Deans and Deaneries; Priest Council; College of Consultors.
Bryce, Vincent W. *o.p.* '57 (STL)[O] St. Louis, MO St. Dominic Priory.
Bryda, Ronald J. '66 (CLV) Litchfield, OH Our Lady Help of Christians Parish.
Bryerton, Robert R. '74 (TUC) Sierra Vista, AZ Our Lady of the Mountains.
Bryk, Daren (GAL) Houston, TX Queen of Peace.
Bryk, John J. '53 (CLV) Lakewood, OH St. Hedwig.
Bryl, Thaddeus J. '66 (MIL)[M] Racine, WI St. Monica's Senior Citizens Home, Inc. Retired.
Brylinski, Bruce C. *g.h.m.* '83 (COV) Vanceburg, KY Holy Redeemer; Grayson, KY Ss. John & Elizabeth; [M] Cincinnati Headquarters of Glenmary Home Missioners.
Brylka, Vincent R. '65 (OAK) Hayward, CA St. Clement.
Brynda, Gerald J. '57 (TUC) Retired.
Bryne, James A.P. *s.j.* '47 (PH) Philadelphia, PA Old St. Joseph's.
Brynes, John *o.s.a.* '55 (PH) Philadelphia, PA St. Nicholas of Tolentine.
Bryon, Paul J. '46 (R) Retired.
Bryon, Thomas C. '63 (STL) Kirkwood, MO St. Gerard Majella.
Bryson, John H. '50 (MAN) Retired.
Bryson, John *s.m.* '53 (DET)[E] Harper Woods, MI Notre Dame High School.
Brzek, Jon C. '83 (PIT) Military Chaplains; Navy Chaplains.
Brzezicki, Zbigniew '88 (STF) Manchester, NH Protection of B.V.M..
Brzezicki, Zbigniew (STF) Presbyteral Council.
Brzezinski, Hilary *o.f.m.* '76 (BWN) Elsa, TX Sacred Heart.
Brzezinski, Jerome A. '69 (DET)[S] Auburn Hills, MI St. John Fisher Chapel University Parish; Auburn Hills, MI St. John Fisher Chapel University Parish; Archdiocesan Vicars.
Brzezniak, Aurelian W. *o.f.m.conv.* '45 (BUF)[O] Athol Springs, NY St. Francis of Assisi Friary.
Brzezowski, Michael E. (YAK) Diocesan Commission for the Catechumenate.
Brzezowski, Michael (YAK) Prosser, WA Sacred Heart.
Brzoska, David (CHL) Mars Hill, NC St. Andrew the Apostle.
Brzostowski, Hilary *o.f.m.conv.* '69 (BGP) Danbury, CT Sacred Heart.
Brzozowski, Edward J. '44 (CHI) Retired.
Brzozowski, Simon *m.s.f.* (L)[J] Louisville, KY St. Joseph Home for the Aged.
Buby, Bertrand A. *s.m.* '64 (CIN)[D] Dayton, OH The University of Dayton; [M] Dayton, OH Marianist Community.
Bucaria, James A. '72 (SP) Masaryktown, FL St. Mary, Our Lady of Sorrows.
Bucaria, James (SP) Presbyteral Council.
Bucaria, James (SP) College of Consultors.
Bucaria, James (SP) Vicars Forane.
Bucaro, Michael '80 (SB) Chino, CA California Institute for Men.
Bucaro, Michael '80 (SB) Chino, CA Southern Conservation Center.
Buccafurni, Ferdinand '58 (PH) Philadelphia, PA Our Lady of Angels.
Buccafurni, Ferdinand '58 (PH) Philadelphia, PA St. Donato.
Buccellato, Sebastian *o.f.m.* '51 (NY)[EE] New York, NY Padua Friary.
Buccheri, Vincenzo *r.c.j.* '79 (LA)[Q] Van Nuys, CA Rogationist Fathers.
Bucchino, John *o.f.m.* '40 (NY) Manhattan, NY Lenox Hill Hospital.
Bucchino, John *o.f.m.* '73 (NY)[EE] Fall River, MA.
Bucci, Michael J. '62 (GBG) Retired.
Bucci, Richard A. '73 (PRO) West Warwick, RI Sacred Heart Church.
Bucciantini, Charles '72 (JKS) Leland, MS St. James.
Bucciantini, Charles (BLX) Association of Priests (Diocese of Biloxi and Jackson).
Bucciantini, Charles (JKS) Association of Priests.
Bucciantini, Charles (JKS) Approved Advocate and Auditors.
Bucciarelli, Michael R. '75 (TUC) San Manuel, AZ St. Bartholomew; All Vicars Forane.
Bucciarelli, Michael (TUC) Defenders of the Bond.
Bucciarelli, Michael (TUC) Diocesan Consultors.
Buccicone, Ananias *o.s.b.* '93 (ALT) Patton, PA Queen of Peace.
Bucciferro, Eugene '63 (JOL) Joliet, IL St. Patrick.
Bucciferro, William *s.d.b.* '82 (CHI) Chicago, IL St. John Bosco.
Bucek, Timothy P. '76 (GAL) Bellville, TX SS. Peter & Paul.
Buchanan, Caleb A. '97 (BRK) Cambria Heights, NY Sacred Heart.
Buchanan, Caleb Austin Pero '97 (BRK) Brooklyn, NY St. Ephrem's.
Buchanan, Caleb (BRK) Presbyteral Council.
Buchanan, David '93 (BIR) Jasper, AL St. Cecilia.
Buchanan, Donald '45 (SD) Retired.
Buchanan, LCDR Donald E. '65 (IND) Retired.
Buchanan, Robert E. '68 (SB) On Duty Outside the Diocese.
Buchanen, Caleb (BRK) Bishop Catanello—.
Buchek, Basil '68 (STN) Tucson, AZ St. Michael.
Bucher, Mel *o.f.m.* '61 (SD)[H] Oceanside, CA Mission San Luis Rey; [K] Oceanside, CA Mission San Luis Rey Retreat.
Bucher, Otto N. *o.f.m.cap.* '59 (MIL)[O] Milwaukee, WI St. Conrad Friary; [B] Hales Corners, WI Sacred Heart School of Theology.
Bucher, Philip A. '61 (SPC) Branson, MO Our Lady of the Lake; Vicars General; Promoter of Justice; Defenders of the Bond; Priests' Mutual Benefit Society; Diocesan Consultors; Appointed Members.
Bucher, Raymond J. *o.f.m.* '64 (OAK)[P] Danville, CA San Damiano Retreat.
Buchheit, Edward *c.p.* '63 (SCR)[M] Clarks Summit, PA St. Gabriel's Convent.
Buchheit, Jerome J. '51 (STL) Retired.
Buchheit, Richard A. '63 (STL) Archdiocesan Priests' Personnel Board; St. Louis, MO Visitation–St. Ann's Shrine.
Buchholz, Athanasius *o.s.b.* '54 (P)[L] St. Benedict, OR Mt. Angel Abbey.
Buchholz, Samuel James '02 (R) Elizabeth City, NC Holy Family.
Buchignani, Peter P. '65 (MEM) Cordova, TN St. Francis of Assisi; Vicar General and Moderator of the Curia; Presbyteral Council and College of Consultors; Adjutant Judicial Vicar.
Buchignani, Peter (MEM) Clergy Personnel Board.
Buchignani, Richard G. '62 (NSH) Lawrenceburg, TN Sacred Heart; Deans; Judges.
Buchlein, Neil R. '98 (WH) Hurricane, WV Catholic Church of the Ascension.
Buchleitner, Donald N. '70 (PIT) Pittsburgh, PA Holy Innocents.
Buchman, Joel R. '91 (LA)[J] Torrance, CA Little Company of Mary Hospital; [J] Torrance, CA Little Company of Mary Hospital Pavilion; [J] San Pedro, CA Little Company of Mary San Pedro Peninsula Hospital Pavillion; [J] Torrance, CA Little Company of Mary Sub–Acute Center–South Bay; On Duty Outside the Diocese.
Buchman, Joel '91 (LA)[J] San Pedro, CA Little Company of Mary San Pedro Hospital.
Buchmeier, Francis X. *s.j.* '73 (FgM).
Buchmeier, Robert P. '91 (WDC) Laurel, MD St. Nicholas.
Buchmiller, Ronald J. '69 (SD) Lakeside, CA Our Lady of Perpetual Help.
Buck, Daniel P. '71 (CHI) Other Assignments.
Buck, Frank '85 (ORL) Lakeland, FL St. John Neumann.
Buckalew, Jack '74 (SEA) Tracyton, WA Holy Trinity.
Bucki, John P. *s.j.* '79 (BUF)[O] Buffalo, NY Canisius Jesuit Community; [R] Buffalo, NY Campus Ministry Office; [C] Buffalo, NY Canisius College.

Buckius, Walter A. *s.j.* '52 (WH)[A] Wheeling, WV Wheeling Jesuit University.
Buckles, David J. (LFT) Vice Officialis; Presiding Judge.
Buckles, David '88 (LFT) Special Assignment.
Buckles, Luke D. *o.p.* '78 (OAK)[N] Oakland, CA Dominican Order (Western Province), St. Albert's Priory.
Buckley, Brendon *o.f.m.* (MAN)[N] Hanover, NH The Catholic Student Center at Dartmouth, Aquinas House, Aquinas at Dartmouth, Inc..
Buckley, Charles *o.s.b.* '70 (OKL)[I] Shawnee St. Gregory's Abbey.
Buckley, Cornelius M. *s.j.* '62 (LA)[J] Duarte, CA Santa Teresita Hospital.
Buckley, Francis J. *s.j.* '58 (SFR)[N] San Francisco, CA Jesuit Community at University of San Francisco.
Buckley, Gerald J. '57 (SY) Binghamton Psychiatric Hospital; Binghamton, NY Binghamton Psychiatric Hospital; [Q] Binghamton, NY McDevitt Residence for Retired Priests Retired.
Buckley, Gerald *o.p.* '57 (LA) Los Angeles, CA St. Dominic.
Buckley, Harold P. '53 (RVC) Retired.
Buckley, James B. *f.s.s.p.* '65 (LIN)[A] Denton, NE Our Lady of Guadalupe Seminary.
Buckley, James B. *f.s.s.p.* '65 (SCR)[M] Elmhurst Priestly Fraternity of St. Peter (F.S.S.P.), North American District Headquarters.
Buckley, James F. '59 (FR) Retired.
Buckley, James M. '90 (OM) Humphrey, NE St. Francis; [O] Humphrey, NE St. Francis Church of Humphrey Cemetery Endowment Trust Fund.
Buckley, James '82 (GLP) On Leave of Absence.
Buckley, John A. *s.s.c.* '68 (OM)[K] St. Columbans St. Columban's Foreign Mission Society.
Buckley, John A. *s.s.c.* '68 (FgM).
Buckley, John J. *c.m.* '57 (PH).
Buckley, John K. '47 (BO)[AA] Senior Priests Retired.
Buckley, John M. *s.j.* '56 (NEW)[B] Jersey City, NJ Jesuit Center; [N] Jersey City, NJ Jesuits of Saint Peter's College, Inc..
Buckley, Michael *o.c.d.* '47 (SR)[M] Oakville, CA Carmelite House of Prayer.
Buckley, Michael *s.j.* '62 (California)[V] Newton, MA The Jesuit Community at Boston College.
Buckley, Robert '57 (ALB) Retired.
Buckley, Thomas E. *s.j.* '70 (OAK)[N] Berkeley, CA Jesuit Community at Jesuit School of Theology at Berkeley.
Buckley, Thomas J. '61 (BO) Amesbury, MA Holy Family.
Buckley, Thomas J. *s.j.* '74 (WDC)[M] Washington, DC The Jesuit Community at Georgetown University.
Buckley, Thomas R. '76 (ALN) Limeport, PA St. Joseph.
Buckley, Thomas W. '55 (BO) Senior Priests Retired.
Buckley, Timothy J. '92 (PH) Fairless Hills, PA St. Frances Cabrini.
Buckman, Thomas J. '00 (OWN) Bardwell, KY St. Denis.
Buckner, Mark '02 (OWN) Owensboro, KY Blessed Mother; Bowling Green, KY Holy Spirit.
Bucko, Raymond A. *s.j.* '83 (NY)[K] Omaha, NE Jesuit Community at Creighton University.
Buckon, Neal J. '95 (CLV) Military Chaplains; Army Chaplains.
Bucon, Raymond H. '79 (DET) Military Chaplains; Livonia, MI St. Priscilla.
Bucon, Raymond H. (DET) Army Reserve Chaplains.
Bucther, Richard (BRK) Brooklyn, NY Epiphany.
Bucyznski, Edward '61 (DUL) Hill City, MN St. Paul.
Buczyna, Andrew L. '87 (JOL) Lockport, IL St. John Vianney; Joliet, IL Silver Cross Hospital.
Buczynski, Edward '61 (DUL) Hill City, MN St. John.
Buda, Jacek *o.p.* '95 (NY) New York, NY Notre Dame; [HH] New York, NY Columbia University.
Budde, John G. '77 (DET) Novi, MI Holy Family; Presbyteral Council.
Budde, Todd '01 (MIL) Milwaukee, WI St. Roman.
Budden, William A. '68 (RCK) Oregon, IL St. Mary Retired.
Buddendorff, Kenneth *s.j.* '61 (LAF)[J] Grand Coteau, LA Our Lady of the Oaks Retreat House.
Buddendorff, Kenneth *s.j.* (LAF) Retreats.
Budez, Jorge H. '02 (BUF) Tonawanda, NY St. Amelia.
Budka, Dennis G. '84 (MIL) Fond du Lac, WI Holy Family.
Budnar, Randy J. '88 (MAD) Darlington, WI Holy Rosary.
Budney, David F. '57 (CAM) Retired.
Budovic, Francis X. *s.j.* '49 (DET)[P] Clarkston, MI Colombiere Center.
Budwick, John J. '64 (NY) Newburgh, NY St. Patrick.
Budzikowski, Kenneth A. '80 (CHI) Chicago, IL St. Thecla.
Buebendorf, Victor J. '64 (NY) Staten Island, NY St. Mary.
Bueche, Charles C. *c.ss.r.* '53 (STL)[O] Liguori, MO Liguori Mission House/Redemptorists.
Bueche, William *c.ss.r.* '89 (CHI)[N] Chicago, IL The Redemptorists of Blessed Sacrament.
Bueche, William *c.ss.r.* (CHI) Chicago, IL Blessed Sacrament.
Buechele, Andrew C. *sch.p.* '69 (WDC)[B] Washington, DC Queen of Pious Schools House of Studies–Piarist Fathers; [M] Washington, DC Piarist Fathers.
Buehler, John A. '74 (SY) Utica, NY St. John; Eastern Area Vicars; Ex Officio; Priests' Personnel Committee.
Buehler, Paul *c.pp.s.* '44 (CIN)[B] Carthagena, OH St. Charles.
Buelt, Edward '82 (DEN) Foxfield, CO Our Lady of Loreto.
Buelt, Edward (DEN) College of Consultors.
Buencamino, Joey '92 (LA) Temple City, CA St. Luke the Evangelist.
Buening, Matthew '03 (BAL) Graduate Studies.
Buening, Robert B. '58 (CIN) Retired.
Bueno, Alberto *t.o.r.* (FWT) Hillsboro, TX Our Lady of Mercy; Clifton, TX Holy Angels; Morgan, TX Our Lady of Guadalupe.
Bueno, Jaime '88 (CHY) Jackson, WY Our Lady of the Mountains.
Buentello, Michael A. *c.s.b.* '95 (DET)[E] Redford, MI Catholic Central High School.
Buenzil, August H. '53 (MAD) Retired.
Buermann, Eric *o.s.b.* '45 (CGS)[C] Humacao, PR San Antonio Abad Abbey of the Order of St. Benedict.
Buersmeyer, David A. '80 (DET) Washington, MI SS. John and Paul; Presbyteral Council.
Buerster, James A. '79 (BEL) Belleville, IL Cathedral of St. Peter.
Buescher, David G. '71 (JC) Jefferson City, MO St. Joseph Cathedral.
Bueter, Paul R. (FTW) Hispanic Ministry Services; Milford.
Bueter, Paul '59 (FTW) Warsaw, IN Our Lady of Guadalupe.
Bueter, Paul (FTW) Cursillo.
Bueter, Paul (FTW) Warsaw.
Bueter, Robert J. *s.j.* '73 (CHI)[N] Chicago, IL Woodlawn Jesuit Community.
Buetow, Harold A. '44 (BRK)[V] Douglaston, NY Bishop Mugavero Residence Retired.
Buettner, George '52 (BAL) Retired.
Buettner, Matthew '03 (CHL) Charlotte, NC St. Gabriel.
Bueza, Ritche '03 (SJ) San Jose, CA Cathedral Basilica of St. Joseph.
Buffardi, Joseph G. '76 (PAT) Paterson, NJ St. Mary's.
Buffer, Thomas J. '91 (COL).
Buffer, Thomas '91 (COL).
Buffington, Jon '81 (EST)[J] Portland, OR Providence Portland Medical Center.
Buga, John '99 (ROM) Retired.
Bugarin, Fred '75 (ANC) Anchorage, AK St. Anthony.
Bugarin, Fred (ANC) Diocesan Consultors.
Bugarin, G. Michael '91 (DET)[T] Washington, DC Operations Office.
Bugarin, Michael '91 (DET) Special Assignment.
Bugay, Stephen R. '84 (GBG) New Salem, PA Madonna of Czestochowa; Republic, PA Holy Rosary.
Bugayong, Demetrio '70 (LA) Carson, CA St. Philomena.
Buggert, Donald W. *o.carm.* '66 (WDC)[B] Washington, DC Whitefriars Hall.
Bugler, Henry J. '75 (NO) Destrehan, LA St. Charles Borromeo; Deans; Vocation Office; Serra Club of New Orleans.
Bugliosi, Mario *o.s.f.s.* '43 (WIL) Wilmington, DE St. Anthony of Padua.
Bugliosi, Mario *o.s.f.s.* '43 (WIL)[H] Wilmington, DE The Antonian.
Bugman, John H. '52 (BUF) Lackawanna, NY Basilica of Our Lady of Victory Retired.
Bugner, Joseph *s.v.d.* '45 (CHI)[B] Techny, IL Divine Word Residence.
Bugno, Krzystof '85 (GRY) Bastrop, TX St. Mary's of the Assumption.
Bugno, Krzysztof *s.d.s.* '85 (AUS) Bastrop, TX Sacred Heart.
Buhl, Wilbert L. '60 (GB) Maplewood, WI St. Mary.
Buhler, Richard O. *s.j.* '70 (STL)[O] St. Louis, MO Office; [S] St. Louis, MO Retreat House.
Buhler, Richard O. *s.j.* (STL) Archdiocesan Council of Priests.
Buhman, Leo T. '48 (JC) Retired.
Buholzer, Robert E. '56 (MAD) Retired.
Buhr, Donald L. '66 (STL) Florissant, MO Our Lady of Fatima.
Buhr, Eugene '54 (LA) Hawthorne, CA St. Joseph.
Buhrfeind, William J. '38 (CHI) Oak Lawn, IL St. Gerald Retired.
Buhrman, Donald A. '86 (GI) Scottsbluff, NE St. Agnes; Personnel Board.
Bui, Dung Quang '02 (STA) Jacksonville Beach, FL St. Paul's.
Bui, Francis Q. (HT) College of Consultors.
Bui, Francis Quyet '90 (HT) Priests Council.
Bui, Francis Ty '75 (LA) North Hills, CA Our Lady of Peace.
Bui, Francis '90 (HT) Houma, LA St. Gregory Barbarigo.
Bui, Joseph T.P. '97 (GAL) Houston, TX Christ, The Incarnate Word.
Bui, Joseph '85 (OAK) Pastoral Center Special Ministries; De Land, FL St. Peter's.
Bui, Khue Si '01 (BEA) Beaumont, TX St. Jude Thaddeus.
Bui, Marion Joseph *o.c.d.* '95 (SAT)[M] San Antonio, TX Discalced Carmelites (Prov. of St. Therese).
Bui, Marion *o.c.d.* '95 (SAT) San Antonio, TX Basilica of The National Shrine of Our Lady of Mt. Carmel and St. Therese, Discalced Carmelite Fathe.
Bui, Minh C. '01 (ORG) Ecumenical and Interreligious Affairs.
Bui, Peter Tuan Quang *c.ss.r* (DAL)[K] Irving, TX St. John Neumann Formation House.
Bui, Peter *s.d.b.* '90 (LA)[C] Rosemead, CA Don Bosco Technical Institute.
Bui, Peter *s.d.b.* '90 (LA)[D] Rosemead, CA Don Bosco Technical Institute.
Bui, Tam A. '01 (WOR) Milford, MA St. Mary of the Assumption.
Bui, Tin Mahn '75 (SFE) Albuquerque, NM Our Lady of Lavang.
Bui, Vincent D. *s.s.* '95 (SFR).
Bui, Vincent '95 (LAN)[A] On Duty Outside the Diocese.
Bui–Trang–Nghiem, Joseph '73 (WDC)[L] Washington, DC Cardinal O'Boyle Residence for Priests.
Bui Anh Tuan, Athanasius M. *c.m.c.* '81 (SPC)[E] Carthage, MO Congregation of the Mother Coredemptrix, United States Assumption Province.
Buitrago, Alex '67 (DAL) Dallas, TX St. Elizabeth.
Buitrago, Luis '67 (DAL) Dallas, TX Parkland Health & Hospital System.
Buitrago, Tarsicio '64 (ARL) Falls Church, VA St. Anthony's.
Buitrago Franco, Justo P. '73 (STA) Crescent City, FL.
Buitron, Luis Segundo (CR) Dilworth, MN St. Elizabeth; Georgetown, MN St. John; Moorhead, MN St. Francis de Sales.
Bujnak, George A. '65 (PSC) McAdoo, PA St. Michael.
Bukala, Casimir R. *s.j.* '66 (CLV)[B] Cleveland, OH John Carroll University.
Bukaty, Lawrence J. '76 (ALN) Mahanoy City, PA Assumption B.V.M.; Mahanoy City, PA St. Casimir.
Bukauskas, Anthony '46 (STL) Retired.
Bukofsky, James W. '71 (BRK) Brooklyn, NY Our Lady of Good Counsel.
Bukoski, Joseph *ss.cc.* '79 (HON)[G] Kaneohe, HI Sacred Hearts Center.
Bulfer, Stephen C. '73 (FRS) Mariposa, CA St. Joseph.
Bulfer, Stephen (FRS) Personnel Committee.
Bulfer, Steve (FRS) Diocesan Consultors.
Bulfer, Steve (FRS) Priests' Council.
Bulfer, Steve (FRS) Vicars Forane.
Bulger, John '64 (SEA) Retired.
Bulinda, Ernest '88 (RIC) Norfolk, VA Basilica of St. Mary of the Immaculate Conception.
Bullene, Richard S. *c.s.c.* '83 (FTW)[B] University of Notre Dame Du Lac; [I] Notre Dame, IN Holy Cross Community, Corby Hall, University of Notre Dame.
Bullman, Rudy (HEL) Kalispell, MT Risen Christ.
Bullock, Gabriel G. *o.s.b.* '61 (PEO).
Bullock, Myron F. '53 (BO)[A] Gloucester, MA Sacred Heart.
Bullock, Robert W. '56 (BO) Sharon, MA Our Lady of Sorrows.
Bullock, Scott E. '91 (DUB)[A] Dubuque, IA Seminary of St. Pius X; Dubuque, IA St. Catherine; Dubuque, IA St. Donatus; Bellevue, IA St. Joseph; Judges; Newly Ordained Program; Seminarians; Priests' Council; Seminary Board.
Bultman, Robert '67 (EVN) Vincennes, IN St. Thomas The Apostle.
Bultman, Robert '67 (EVN) Vincennes, IN St. John the Baptist.
Bultman, Robert (EVN) St. Vincent De Paul Society.
Bultman, Robert (EVN) Deans.
Bulwith, Richard E. '67 (CHI) Chicago, IL St. Bonaventure; [G] Chicago, IL Catholic Charities of the Archdiocese of Chicago–Archdiocesan Offices; [G] Chicago, IL Cooke's Manor Transitional Housing For Men; Associate Administrators.
Bumbar, Philip '68 (SJP) Wheeling, WV Our Lady of Perpetual Help.
Bumbarger, Bruce *m.ss.cc.* '92 (BIR) Russellville, AL Good Shepherd Church.
Bump, James F. '78 (GBG) Masontown, PA All Saints.
Bumpus, Harold '63 (SP) Sun City Center, FL Prince of Peace.
Bunch, Timothy S. '79 (CIN) Hamilton, OH St. Peter in Chains; Vicarri Foranei (Deans).
Bunchek, Edward P. '65 (PIT) Absent on Sick Leave.
Bunda, Roland *s.m.* '78 (MRY)[I] Santa Cruz, CA Cabrillo College.
Bunda, Roland *s.m.* '78 (MRY)[I] Santa Cruz, CA University of California at Santa Cruz.
Bunda, Roland *s.m.* '78 (MRY)[F] Santa Cruz, CA Society of Mary, Marianists.

Bunda, Roland *s.m.* '78 (MRY)[I] California State University of Monterey Bay.
Bunda, Roland *s.m.* (MRY) Campus Ministry Department.
Bunda, Roland *s.m.* (MRY) Vocations Board.
Bundz, Michael '81 (STF) Utica, NY St. Volodymyr the Great.
Bundz, Michael '81 (STF) Utica, NY St. Michael.
Bundz, Michael (STF) Presbyteral Council.
Bunger, Kevin J. '83 (SY) Port Crane, NY St. Joseph.
Bungo, Samuel '77 (E) Frenchville, PA St. Mary of the Assumption.
Buni, Leon S. '75 (TR) Holmdel, NJ St. Benedict.
Bunik, Wasyl '93 (PHU) Chester, PA St. Nicholas.
Bunik, Wasyl '93 (PHU) Chester, PA Holy Ghost.
Bunn, James F. '64 (ALT) Fallentimber, PA St. Mary Magdalen's Retired.
Bunnell, Thomas J. *s.j.* '74 (YAK) Special Assignment.
Bunnell, Thomas *s.j.* '74 (SPK)[D] Pasco, WA Tri Cities Prep, A Catholic High School.
Bunny, Michael '65 (LA) Newbury Park, CA St. Julie Billiart.
Bunny, Michael (LA) Personnel Board of the Archdiocese.
Bunny, Michael (LA) Santa Barbara Pastoral Region.
Bunny, Michael (LA) Deanery 4.
Bunofsky, Walter *s.v.d.* '60 (DUB)[B] Epworth, IA Divine Word College.
Bunse, Gerald L. '83 (SFD) Edwardsville, IL St. Mary.
Bunse, Gerald (SFD) Presbyteral Council.
Bunse, Gerald (SFD) Diocesan Health Insurance Program Committee.
Bunse, Gerald (SFD) Board of Catholic Education.
Bunse, Gerald (SFD) Priests' Personnel Board.
Bunse, Gerald (SFD) Commission for the Care of Infirm and Retired Priests.
Bunsic, Albert *o.c.d.* '67 (LA) Alhambra, CA St. Therese.
Buonanno, Vito A. '81 (BRK) Elmhurst, NY Ascension.
Buonanno, Vito (BRK) Art and Architecture Commission.
Buonde, Randy J. (MAD) Deaneries.
Buongirno, Robert E. '02 (NOR) North Grosvenordale, CT St. Joseph.
Buono, Joseph *c.ss.r.* '43 (BRK) Brooklyn, NY Our Lady of Perpetual Help Basilica.
Buono, Joseph *c.ss.r.* '43 (ALB)[L] Saratoga Springs, NY St. John Neumann Residence.
Buote, Martin L. '60 (FR) New Bedford, MA St. Anne.
Bur, George W. *s.j.* '72 (PH)[AA] Loyola Center and Manresa Hall; [CC] Philadelphia, PA Urban House of Prayer; [C] Jesuit Fathers.
Bura, John '71 (PHU) Wilmington, DE St. Nicholas.
Bura, John (PHU) College of Archeparchial Counsultors.
Bura, John (PHU) Presbyteral Council.
Bura, John (PHU) Archeparchial Seminary Advisory and Admissions Board.
Bura, John (PHU) Censors.
Bura, John (PHU) Board Members.
Burak, Paul '72 (CHI) Chicago Ridge, IL Our Lady of the Ridge.
Burakowski, Wieslaw '92 (NSH) Clarksville, TN Immaculate Conception.
Buranosky, Dennis M. '72 (PIT) Bellevue, PA Assumption of the Blessed Virgin Mary on the Beautiful River.
Burasa, James *c.s.c.* '95 (FTW)[I] Bishop McCauley House.
Burba, Edward A. '75 (CLV) Akron, OH St. Mary; Presbyteral Conveners.
Burbach, Jude *o.s.b.* '53 (KCK)[H] Atchison, KS St. Benedict's Abbey.
Burbank, James *c.s.c.* '57 (BGP)[P] Stoneham, MA.
Burbank, Robert J. '64 (HRT) East Haven, CT St. Vincent de Paul's.
Burbank, William '62 (HRT) New Haven, CT St. Rose of Lima.
Burch, Edward '03 (R) Wilmington, NC Christ the King; Wilmington, NC St. Mark.
Burch, Francis F. *s.j.* '63 (PH)[C] Jesuit Fathers; [AA] Loyola Center and Manresa Hall.
Burch, Thaddeus J. *s.j.* '61 (MIL)[O] Milwaukee, WI Jesuit Community at Marquette University.
Burchell, Richard '75 (CLV) Barberton, OH St. Augustine.
Burchfield, Michael A. (FRS) Adjutant Judicial Vicar.
Burchfield, Michael '93 (FRS) On Special Assignment.
Burchfield, Michael '93 (FRS) Fresno, CA St. Paul; [G] Fresno, CA St. Paul Newman Center.
Burchianti, Leo R. '64 (PIT)[N] Pittsburgh, PA St. John Vianney Manor Retired.
Burchill, John P. *o.p.* '65 (PRO) Providence, RI St. Pius V; [P] Providence, RI St. Pius Priory.
Burckhart, William C. '53 (BO) Senior Priests; Members Retired.
Burden, George W. *s.s.j.* '91 (BR) Donaldsonville, LA St. Catherine of Siena.
Burden, Lewis E. '97 (SUP) Weyerhaeuser, WI St. Mary; Weyerhaeuser, WI St. Francis of Assisi; Weyerhaeuser, WI Assumption of the Blessed Virgin Mary; Weyerhaeuser, WI SS. Peter and Paul.
Burdess, James J. '88 (ALN) Weatherly, PA St. Nicholas.
Burdick, Thomas '84 (SB) Redlands, CA Sacred Heart.
Burdick, Thomas (SB) Finance Council Members.
Burdiek, Fabian F. *o.f.m.* '74 (STP) Maplewood, MN St. John's Hospital.
Bureau, German H. '53 (PRT) Retired.
Burek, Frank J. '71 (CHI) Oak Lawn, IL St. Louis De Montfort.
Burgaleta, Claudio *s.j.* '92 (RVC) Oceanside NY St. Anthony.
Burgard, David G. '94 (DET) Anchorville, MI Immaculate Conception; Archdiocesan Vicars.
Burgat, Boguslaw *s.ch.* '90 (CHI) Chicago, IL Five Holy Martyrs.
Burge, Robert '71 (CLV) Retired.
Burger, Edward K. *s.j.* '70 (KC)[B] Kansas City, KS Rockhurst University Continuing Education Center/ National Seminars Group; [J] Kansas City, MO Rockhurst Jesuit Community.
Burger, Frank J. '38 (KAL) Retired.
Burger, Frank '69 (KCK) Olathe, KS Prince of Peace.
Burger, Frank (KCK) Regional Pastoral Leaders.
Burger, Herman N. '73 (CAM) On Sick Leave Defenders of the Bond.
Burger, John *s.s.c.* '73 (OM)[K] St. Columbans, NE St. Columban's Foreign Mission Society.
Burger, Mark J. (CIN) Priest Councilors Vicarri Foranei (Deans); Consultors.
Burger, Mark '80 (CIN) West Chester, OH St. John.
Burger, Philip G. '83 (HBG) Hershey, PA St. Joan of Arc.
Burger, Philip (HBG)[J] Harrisburg, PA Hershey Medical Center.
Burger, Raymond '60 (KCK) Eudora, KS Holy Family.
Burger, Raymond (KCK) Vice–Chancellor.
Burger, Raymond (KCK) Defenders of the Bond.
Burger, Robert '48 (KCK) Retired.
Burger, Robert (KCK) Legion of Mary.
Burget, Joel *o.f.m.conv.* '61 (IND) Regional Hospital/ Union Hospital.
Burget, Joel *o.f.m.conv.* '66 (IND) Terre Haute, IN St. Benedict.
Burghardt, Walter J. *s.j.* '41 (WDC)[C] Catholic University of America, The.
Burghardt, Walter J. *s.j.* '41 (BAL)[S] Baltimore, MD Jesuit Fathers and Brothers Maryland Provincial Curia.
Burghoff, Theodore H. '55 (STL) Retired.
Burghoff, Theodore '55 (STL) Kirkwood, MO St. Peter.
Burgoon, Charles E. '64 (STL) St. Louis, MO St. Gabriel the Archangel.
Burgos, Adnel T. '89 (BRK) Richmond Hill, NY Our Lady of the Cenacle.
Burgos, Faustino '87 (SJN) San Juan, PR San Vicente de Paul.
Burgos, Jose Casco (ARE) Retired.
Burgoyne, Sidney C. '54 (PH) Ridley Park, PA St. Madeline; Council of Priests Retired.
Burian, Edward '65 (SFS) Wessington Springs, SD St. Joseph.
Burkard, Paul J.E. '69 (BUF) Finance Council; Orchard Park, NY Our Lady of the Sacred Heart.
Burkart, Donald R. '58 (GB) Crivitz, WI St. Mary.
Burkart, James '93 (GAL) Hempstead, TX St. Katherine Drexel.
Burkauskas, Peter M. '79 (PH) Philadelphia, PA St. Andrew; Philadelphia, PA St. Casimir.
Burke, Adrian *o.s.b.* '97 (IND)[K] Collegio Sant Anselmo.
Burke, Adrian *o.s.b.* '97 (IND)[A] St. Meinrad, IN St. Meinrad School of Theology.
Burke, Alfred M. *o.s.a.* '57 (CHI)[N] Olympia Fields, IL Tolentine Monastery at Tolentine Center.
Burke, Alfred M. *o.s.a.* '57 (FgM).
Burke, Amadeus *o.f.m.* '35 (PAT)[M] Ringwood, NJ Holy Name Friary, Inc..
Burke, Christopher R. '86 (PBR) Latrobe, PA St. Mary's.
Burke, Clement J. '61 (DUB) Minneapolis, MN Abbot–Northwestern Hospital.
Burke, Clement J. '61 (DUB) Retired.
Burke, David M. '42 (BO) Milton, MA St. Pius Tenth.
Burke, Donal *c.f.m.cap.* '75 (FRS) Community Hospital, Veterans' Hospital & University Medical Center.
Burke, Edmund M. '77 (NY) Kingston, NY St. Mary.
Burke, Edmund '77 (NY) Kingston, NY St. Peter.
Burke, Edward P. '73 (PH) Philadelphia, PA All Saints.
Burke, Edward T. *s.j.* '56 (SJ)[M] Los Gatos, CA Sacred Heart Jesuit Center.
Burke, Edward *o.f.m.* '62 (PAT)[M] Ringwood, NJ Holy Name Friary, Inc..
Burke, Edwin F. '62 (BGP) Norwalk, CT St. Ladislaus; Catholic Women, Council of.
Burke, Eugene A. *c.s.c.* '53 (PHX)[I] Notre Dame, IN Holy Cross House.
Burke, Francis J. *s.j.* '60 (MIL)[O] Milwaukee, WI Jesuit Community at Marquette University.
Burke, Geoffrey D. '79 (ALB) Latham, NY Our Lady of the Assumption; [M] Latham, NY Provincial House of the Sisters of St. Joseph of Carondelet (Albany Province).
Burke, Gilbert J. *o.s.b.* '62 (GBG) Latrobe, PA St. Vincent Basilica; [H] Latrobe, PA Saint Vincent Archabbey.
Burke, Gregory '51 (HEL) Retired.
Burke, Gregory '51 (HEL)[E] Butte, MT St. James Health System, Sisters of Charity of Leavenworth Health System.
Burke, Harry '63 (NY)[E] New York, NY Cardinal Hayes High School.
Burke, Henry J. '45 (CHR) Retired.
Burke, Herbert '92 (CHL) Forest City, NC Immaculate Conception.
Burke, J. David *c.s.c.* '65 (FTW)[I] Notre Dame, IN.
Burke, J. David *c.s.c.* '65 (FTW)[I] Notre Dame, IN.
Burke, James A. '56 (NEW) Retired.
Burke, James C. '64 (ROC) Auburn, NY Holy Family.
Burke, James E. '58 (NY) Pelham Manor, NY Our Lady of Perpetual Help.
Burke, James G. '77 (BO) Chestnut Hill, MA Infant Jesus–St. Lawrence; Defenders of the Bond; Archdiocesan Judges; Canonical Affairs Committee.
Burke, James J. *c.ss.r.* '56 (VEN) Wauchula, FL St. Michael.
Burke, James M. '64 (PMB) Secretary Retired.
Burke, James *o.p.* '49 (DAL)[K] Irving, TX Dominican Priory of St. Albert the Great.
Burke, James *c.s.sp.* '52 (SB)[E] Hemet, CA Holy Ghost Fathers.
Burke, James (PMB) Presbyteral Council.
Burke, James (PMB) Assessors.
Burke, James (PMB) College of Consultors.
Burke, James (PMB) Advocates.
Burke, John D. '56 (NY) Staten Island, NY St. Adalbert Retired.
Burke, John F. '55 (WOR) West Boylston, MA Our Lady of Good Counsel.
Burke, John R. '54 (E) Retired.
Burke, John R. '72 (L) Louisville, KY Christ the King; Louisville, KY St. William; Ex Officio.
Burke, John W. *o.p.* '60 (WDC)[B] Washington, DC Dominican House of Studies.
Burke, John '56 (NY) Retired.
Burke, Joseph F. *s.j.* '78 (BUF) Council of Priests; [O] Buffalo, NY Canisius Jesuit Community.
Burke, Kevin *s.j.* '86 (BO)[V] Cambridge, MA St. Edmunds House.
Burke, Mark J. *s.j.* '93 (BO)[V] Boston The Society of Jesus of New England–Provincial Offices.
Burke, Mark J. *s.j.* '93 (SPR) Williamstown, MA SS. Patrick and Raphael.
Burke, Michael A. '76 (PAT) Paterson, NJ St. Paul's.
Burke, Michael J. '62 (PH) Exton, PA SS. Philip and James.
Burke, Michael L. '74 (MAD) Madison, WI St. Maria Goretti; Appointed.
Burke, Michael M. *o.p.* '68 (R)[E] Raleigh, NC Dominican Priory.
Burke, Michael '50 (HRT) Waterbury, CT Immaculate Conception.
Burke, Michael '50 (CC) Retired.
Burke, Michael *s.c.j.* '63 (CHI)[N] Chicago, IL Priests of the Sacred Heart.
Burke, Michael (PAT) Catholic Family and Community Services.
Burke, Michael *s.t.m.* (PAT) Advocates.
Burke, Paul '96 (ATL)[B] Fairburn, GA Our Lady of Mercy Catholic High School.
Burke, Paul '96 (ATL) Archdiocesan Judges; Peachtree City, GA Holy Trinity Catholic.
Burke, Richard *c.p.* '76 (SCR)[M] Clarks Summit, PA St. Gabriel's Convent.
Burke, Robert M. *o.s.a.* '55 (PH)[AA] Villanova, PA St. Thomas Monastery.
Burke, Robert R. *s.j.* '64 (BO)[V] Weston, MA Campion Health Center, Inc..
Burke, Robert *s.s.c.* '49 (OM)[K] St. Columbans St. Columban's Foreign Mission Society Retired.
Burke, Ronald A. '54 (SFR) Retired.
Burke, Ronald '72 (HON) Retired.
Burke, Sean P. *m.m.* '78 (FgM).
Burke, Terry (AMA) Retired.
Burke, Thomas J. *o.ss.t.* '78 (BAL)[P] Baltimore, MD Trinitarian Counseling Services, Inc..
Burke, Thomas J. '01 (PIT)[S] Wexford, PA St. Alphonsus; Co Directors.
Burke, Vincent dePaul *o.s.f.s.* '57 (WIL)[J] Childs, MD Retirement and Assisted Care Facility.
Burke, Vincent '61 (STL) St. Louis, MO St. Nicholas.
Burke, Walter Dev '90 (SAC) Retired.
Burke, Walter E. '47 (DET) Retired.
Burke, Walter J. *o.praem.* '44 (WIL)[J] Middletown, DE Immaculate Conception Priory of the Canons Regular of Premontre.
Burke, William A. '65 (CHI) Oak Park, IL Ascension.
Burke, William A. '66 (CHI) Other Assignments.
Burke, William F. '43 (BRK)[V] Douglaston, NY Bishop Mugavero Residence.
Burke, William F. '43 (BRK) Retired.
Burke, William F. '59 (BAL) Baltimore, MD St. Francis of Assisi.

Burke, William F. '75 (MEM) Millington, TN St. William.
Burke, William F. (BAL) Campaign For Human Development, Archdiocese of Baltimore, Inc.; Priest Personnel Board.
Burke, William *s.j.* '51 (HEL)[E] Missoula, MT St. Patrick Hospital and Health Sciences Center, Sisters of Providence of Montana Corporation.
Burke, William *s.j.* '69 (HEL) Missoula, MT St. Francis Xavier.
Burke, William *s.d.b.* '93 (NY)[GG] Stony Point, NY Don Bosco Retreat Center and Marian Shrine.
Burke, William *s.d.b.* '93 (NY)[GG] Stony Point, NY Marian Shrine.
Burkemper, Robert W. '81 (STL) Florissant, MO St. Dismas.
Burkert, Gerald F. '61 (IND) Beech Grove, IN Holy Name.
Burkert, William C. '71 (MIL) Milwaukee, WI St. Roman.
Burkey, Blaine *o.f.m.cap.* '61 (STL)[O] St. Louis, MO St. Crispin's Friary.
Burkhalter, Ross C. '94 (OM) Hartington, NE Holy Family Church of Cedar County; Consultors; Deans; Deans; Ex Officio.
Burkhard, John *o.f.m.conv.* '67 (WDC)[B] Silver Spring, MD Austin Friars Hall, Order of St. Augustine.
Burkhardt, Alan T. '86 (LC) Stevens Point, WI St. Joseph; [L] Stevens Point, WI St. Joseph's Congregation, Stevens Point Endowment Trust.
Burkhardt, Godfrey F. *o.s.b.* '45 (GBG)[H] Latrobe, PA Saint Vincent Archabbey.
Burkhardt, Odilo *o.s.b.* '50 (SFS)[F] Marvin, SD Blue Cloud Abbey.
Burkhart, Roy *c.s.s.p.* '44 (FRS) Retired.
Burkle, Raymond A. '90 (DUB) Epworth, IA St. John's; Epworth, IA St. Patrick; Deanery Representatives.
Burkley, John T. '70 (CLV) Middlefield, OH St. Lucy; Parkman, OH St. Edward.
Burks, William P. '86 (L) Louisville, KY St. Polycarp.
Burkus, John '40 (ELP) Retired.
Burla, Frank J. '63 (NEW) Montclair, NJ Immaculate Conception.
Burlton, Francis H. '54 (BEA) Central Vicariate; Promoter of Justice; Defenders of Bond; Beaumont, TX Our Lady of the Assumption.
Burmester, Edwin J. '40 (STL) St. Louis, MO St. Gabriel the Archangel Retired.
Burn, William C. '56 (CHR) Retired.
Burnell, Robert J. '70 (CHI) Cicero, IL Our Lady of Charity.
Burnell, Thomas *s.j.* '74 (SPK) Pasco, WA.
Burnett, Eugene David *o.f.m.* '54 (ORG)[C] Santa Ana, CA Mater Dei High School.
Burnett, George P. '61 (HRT) Ansonia, CT Assumption.
Burnett, James E. '74 (DAV) On Duty Outside the Diocese.
Burnett, James '68 (JOL) Joliet, IL The Cathedral of St. Raymond.
Burnett, James (DAV).
Burnett, John '85 (SFD) Military Chaplains.
Burnett, Robert E. '55 (SCR) Retired.
Burnett, Timothy J. *o.s.b.* '80 (NO)[P] St. Benedict, LA St. Joseph Abbey; [A] St. Benedict, LA St. Joseph Seminary College.
Burnette, John C. (SFD) Navy Chaplains.
Burnette, Kurt '89 (VNN) Portland, OR St. Irene Byzantine Catholic Church.
Burnham, Martin J. '02 (BAL) Clarksville, MD St. Louis.
Burnia, Scott A. '88 (SD) Jamul, CA St. Pius X.
Burnie, James *c.s.sp.* (SLC) Kearns, UT St. Francis Xavier; St. George, UT St. George's.
Burniston, Blase *s.a.* '51 (NY) Retired.
Burns, A. Francis '63 (NY)[EE] Yonkers, NY Christ the King.
Burns, Basil David *o.s.b.* '01 (NO)[P] St. Benedict, LA St. Joseph Abbey.
Burns, Bernard J. '53 (SAC) Retired.
Burns, Charles E. '58 (GAL) Retired.
Burns, Charles F. *s.j.* '72 (STP) St. Paul, MN The Immaculate Heart of Mary; St. Paul, MN St. Luke.
Burns, Claude Thomas '02 (EVN) Jasper, IN St. Joseph.
Burns, Dennis J. '50 (BO) Marblehead, MA Our Lady, Star of the Sea.
Burns, Douglas C. *o.s.f.s.* '99 (ALN)[B] Center Valley, PA DeSales University; [K] Center Valley, PA Oblates of St. Francis de Sales.
Burns, Edward J. '54 (FR) Retired.
Burns, Edward J. '83 (PIT) On Duty Outside the Diocese.
Burns, Ernest '51 (HEL) Retired.
Burns, Eugene P. '55 (CHI) Retired.
Burns, G. Thomas '57 (NEW) Retired.
Burns, Gerald H. '69 (BR) Baton Rouge, LA St. Aloysius.
Burns, Hugh D. *o.p.* '82 (NEW) Sacred Heart Priory.
Burns, James P. '93 (STP) Graduate Studies; Defenders of the Bond.
Burns, John A. '48 (BRK) Brooklyn, NY Mary Queen of Heaven Retired.
Burns, John F. '48 (BO) Senior Priests Retired.
Burns, John M. *o. carm.* '82 (STP)[N] Lake Elmo, MN Carmel of Our Lady of Divine Providence; [M] Lake Elmo, MN Carmelite Hermitage of the Blessed Virgin Mary.
Burns, John P. '03 (FRS) Lone Pine, CA Santa Rosa.
Burns, John '65 (ALB) Morris, NY Holy Cross.
Burns, John '90 (PEO) East Moline, IL St. Mary's.
Burns, John (ALB) Deans.
Burns, Joseph C. *o.p.* '54 (L) Louisville, KY St. Louis Bertrand.
Burns, Joseph '55 (JOL) Steger, IL St. Liborius.
Burns, Laurence J. '64 (SC) Fort Dodge, IA St. Matthew's; Deans.
Burns, Lawrence E. '56 (MAN) Portsmouth, NH St. Catherine of Siena.
Burns, Lawrence E. '62 (BUF) Vicars; Blasdell, NY Our Mother of Good Counsel.
Burns, Malcolm J. '85 (RVC) Oyster Bay, NY St. Dominic's.
Burns, Michael J. '58 (SJ) Retired.
Burns, Michael J. '73 (TR) Bordentown, NJ St. Mary; Legion of Mary.
Burns, Norbert C. *s.m.* '53 (CIN)[D] Dayton, OH The University of Dayton; [M] Dayton, OH Marianist Community.
Burns, Patrick G. '92 (BRK) Brooklyn, NY St. Martin of Tours–Fourteen Holy Martyrs.
Burns, Patrick *s.j.* '63 (RC)[B] Pine Ridge, SD Jesuit Community of Holy Rosary Mission.
Burns, Patrick *s.j.* '63 (RC) Pine Ridge, SD Holy Rosary.
Burns, Paul D. *c.s.s.* '61 (SPR) Springfield, MA Our Lady of Mt. Carmel.
Burns, Peter *s.j.* '92 (LA) Los Angeles, CA St. Jerome.
Burns, Robert A. *o.p.* '61 (TUC) Tuscon, AZ St. Thomas More Chapel; [H] Tucson, AZ University of Arizona.
Burns, Robert I. *s.j.* '52 (LA)[C] Los Angeles, CA Jesuit Community.
Burns, Robert O. *s.j.* '57 (OM)[K] Omaha, NE Jesuit Community at Creighton University.
Burns, T. Lee '56 (PRT) Retired.
Burns, Thomas J. '54 (SFR) Retired.
Burns, Thomas J. *m.m.* '69 (FgM).
Burns, Thomas L. *s.c.j.* '65 (JKS) Booneville, MS St. Francis of Assisi; Corinth, MS St. James.
Burns, Tom *m.s.c.* '64 (SB) La Quinta, CA St. Francis of Assisi; Upland, CA St. Joseph.
Burns, Vincent M. *s.j.* '57 (BGP)[P] Fairfield, CT The Fairfield Jesuit Community–Fairfield University.
Burns, Vincent P. '67 (PH) Military Chaplains; Army Chaplains.
Burns, William L. '85 (HRT) Unassigned.
Burr, Jeremiah R. *m.m.* '67 (FgM).
Burr, Stephen '02 (DET) Rochester, MI St. Andrew.
Burr, Thomas E. '73 (RCK) McHenry, IL St. Mary.
Burrascano, Anthony P. *o.s.a.* '79 (FgM).
Burrascano, Anthony P. *o.s.a.* '79 (PH) Bryn Mawr, PA Our Mother of Good Counsel; [AA] Villanova, PA Provincial Offices of the Order of St. Augustine, Province of St. Thomas of Villanova.
Burrell, David B. *c.s.c.* '59 (FTW)[A] Notre Dame, IN Moreau Seminary; [B] University of Notre Dame Du Lac.
Burrill, Jeffrey D. '98 (LC) Durand, WI St. Mary's Assumption; Durand, WI Holy Rosary; Durand, WI Sacred Heart of Jesus; Deans; Office of Ecumenism; Elected Members.
Burrows, Michael *o.s.b.* '80 (RCK)[G] Aurora, IL Marmion Abbey.
Burshek, James J. *s.j.* '75 (STL)[O] St. Louis, MO Bellarmine House of Studies; [O] St. Louis, MO The Jesuits of the Missouri Province.
Burshnick, Francis J. *s.c.j.* '70 (JKS) Walls, MS Sacred Heart; [F] Nesbit, MS St. Michael Community House.
Burson, James *c.j.m.* '63 (SD) San Diego, CA Blessed Sacrament.
Burt, Donald X. *o.s.a.* '55 (PH)[AA] Villanova, PA St. Thomas Monastery.
Burt, William '85 (MIL)[O] St. Francis, WI St. Camillus Provincialate.
Burtchaell, James T. *c.s.c.* '60 (PHX)[G] Phoenix, AZ Holy Cross Congregation/Casa Santa Cruz.
Burton, C. Jeffries *s.j.* '67 (BAL)[S] Pomona, NJ Catholic Campus Ministry at Stockton; Pomona, NJ Assumption; [R] Pomona, NJ Assumption Rectory; [R] Pomona, NJ Catholic Campus Ministry Center at Stockton.
Burton, Charles '80 (KNX) Kingsport, TN St. Dominic.
Burton, Charles (KNX) Diaconate.
Burton, Jeffries *s.j.* (CAM) Stockton College of New Jersey – Pomona.
Burton, Jeffries *s.j.* (CAM) Atlantic Cape Community College – Mays Landing.
Burton, John H. '72 (CAM) Vineland, NJ St. Isidore; Cumberland Deanery; Liturgical Commission.
Burton, Richard T. '03 (BO) Holy Rosary.
Burton, Richard '63 (WDC) Washington, DC St. Anthony.
Burton, William *o.f.m.* '89 (SFD)[B] Quincy, IL Quincy University.
Burtschi, J. Richard *s.j.* '71 (STL)[O] St. Louis, MO Jesuit Community Corporation at St. Louis University – Jesuit Hall.
Burwinkel, Elmer J. '84 (IND) Retired.
Bury, Antoni (CHI) Chicago, IL St. Bruno.
Bury, Harold J. '55 (STP) On Duty Outside the Archdiocese Retired.
Buryadnyk, Mykola '02 (STN) Chicago, IL SS. Volodymyr and Olha.
Buryska, James F. '65 (WIN) On Special or Other Diocesan Assignment; [D] Rochester, MN Saint Mary's Hospital; Coordinator of Diocesan Health Ministry; Hospitals.
Burzawa, Janusz '86 (SP) St. Petersburg, FL The Mercy of God Polish Mission.
Burzynski, Michael H. '89 (BUF) Niagara Falls, NY St. Mary of the Cataract; Niagara Falls, NY Our Lady of the Rosary.
Bus, Anthony *c.r.* '84 (CHI) Chicago, IL St. Stanislaus Kostka.
Busch, Aloysius J. '52 (PAT)[P] Chester, NJ Nazareth Village Retired.
Busch, Arthur (WCH) Retired.
Busch, August '56 (EVN) Retired.
Busch, Joseph '80 (ALB) Watervliet, NY St. Brigid.
Busch, Joseph (ALB) Presbyteral Council.
Busch, Robert (AMA) Presbyteral Council; Priests' Pension Plan Retirement Committee; Dalhart, TX St. Anthony's; On Duty Outside the Diocese.
Busch, Vernon *o.f.m.cap.* '60 (BAL) Cumberland, MD SS. Peter and Paul.
Busch, Vernon *o.f.m.cap.* '60 (BAL)[S] Cumberland, MD SS. Peter and Paul Friary.
Busch, Vincent J. *s.s.c.* '74 (FgM).
Busco, J. John '40 (PH) Norristown, PA Holy Saviour.
Busco, John J. '40 (PH) Retired.
Buse, Harold J. '77 (OM) Omaha, NE St. Leo; St. Vincent de Paul Society; Deans.
Busemeyer, Louis E. *s.j.* '70 (CHI)[D] Chicago, IL St. Ignatius Jesuit Community.
Busemeyer, Louis *s.j.* '70 (RCK) Aurora, IL St. Rita of Cascia.
Bush, Bernard J. *s.j.* '65 (SJ)[L] Los Altos, CA Jesuit Retreat House.
Bush, Carson '03 (CHR) Columbia, SC St. Peter's.
Bush, Edward '57 (PEO) Retired.
Bush, Frederick '51 (ROC) Rochester, NY St. Mark.
Bush, Frederick '51 (ROC) Retired.
Bush, Joseph (ALB) Diocesan Board of Consultors.
Bush, Peter *t.o.r.* '45 (ARL)[J] White Post, VA Sacred Heart Friary.
Bush, Robert '69 (SAN) Abilene, TX Sacred Heart.
Bush, Scott '92 (HON) Keaukaha, Hilo, HI Malia Puka'O Kalani (Mary Gate of Heaven).
Bush, Scott '92 (HON) Hilo, HI St. Joseph.
Bush, Scott (HON) Presbyteral Council.
Bush, Scott (HON) College of Consultors.
Bush, Scott (HON) Vicars Forane.
Bush, Thomas M. '99 (LIN) Wahoo, NE St. Wenceslaus.
Bush, William C. '62 (LEX) Nicholasville, KY St. Luke; Diocesan Consultors.
Bush, William (LEX) Bluegrass West.
Bushee, Richard J. '88 (PRO) Retired.
Bushell, Ralph *c.pp.s.* '49 (KC)[N] Liberty, MO St. Gaspar Society.
Bushell, Ralph *c.pp.s.* '49 (KC)[J] Liberty, MO Precious Blood Center.
Busher, Robert J. '76 (DAV) Oskaloosa, IA St. Mary's; Judges.
Busher, Robert (DAV) Deans.
Bushmaker, Godfrey E. *o.praem.* '00 (ORG)[D] Silverado, CA St. Michael's Preparatory School; [I] Silverado, CA Norbertine Fathers of Orange Inc..
Bushy, Timothy F. '83 (CR) Red Lake Falls, MN St. Joseph's.
Bussen, Robert J. '71 (SLC) Park City, UT St. Mary of the Assumption.
Bussen, Robert J. (SLC) College of Consultors.
Bustamante, John Christopher '03 (DET) Allen Park, MI St. Frances Cabrini.
Busteed, Robert T. '69 (SCR) Williamsport, PA Immaculate Conception.
Bustos, Javier '01 (MIL) Graduate Studies.
Bustos, Martin A. *m.n.m.* '94 (ARE) Camuy, PR Our Lady of Asumption.
Butcavage, Leonard M. '72 (SCR) Hazleton, PA Holy Trinity.
Butch, Brian T. '93 (TR) Neptune, NJ Holy Innocents; Catholic Relief Services and Human Development.
Butera, George J. '68 (BO) Beverly, MA St. John the Evangelist.
Butkowski, Alto *o.s.b.* '41 (SCL)[I] Collegeville, MN St. John's Abbey, of the Order of St. Benedict.
Butler, Allan L. '67 (BO) Abington, MA St. Bridget.
Butler, Daniel J. '66 (PT) Niceville, FL Holy Name of Jesus.
Butler, Daniel (PT) Orders & Ministries, Commission for.
Butler, David A. *o.p.* '57 (NY) Manhattan, NY New York

Presbyterian Hospital; Washington, DC St. Dominic Church & Priory.
Butler, David Aloysius *o.p.* '57 (NY)[EE] New York, NY St. Catherine of Siena Priory.
Butler, Elmore J. '01 (SAV) Augusta, GA Church of the Most Holy Trinity.
Butler, Francis *s.s.j.* '96 (LAF) Church Point, LA Our Mother of Mercy.
Butler, James P. '86 (BO) Permanent Disability.
Butler, James '69 (R) Retired.
Butler, John J. '54 (L)[L] Louisville, KY Ursuline Motherhouse of the Immaculate Conception Retired.
Butler, John J. (HON).
Butler, John M. '72 (GBG) Connellsville, PA Holy Trinity; Connellsville, PA St. John the Evangelist.
Butler, John '60 (HON) On Duty Outside the Diocese.
Butler, John *s.j.* (BO)[V] Newton, MA The Jesuit Community at Boston College.
Butler, Leo J. '98 (NEW)[D] Paramus, NJ Paramus Catholic High School.
Butler, Michael A. '85 (R) Roanoke Rapids, NC St. John the Baptist; Absent on Leave.
Butler, Michael T. (STL) Office of Vocations; Air National Guard Chaplains.
Butler, Michael '84 (COS) Colorado Springs, CO St. Patrick's.
Butler, Norman H. *m.s.* '75 (HRT).
Butler, Patrick J. '82 (ALB)[M] Albany, NY Christ the King.
Butler, Patrick (ALB) Spiritual Director.
Butler, Paul F. '87 (RVC) Ronkonkoma, NY St. Joseph's.
Butler, Rene J. *m.s.* '73 (HRT)[M] Hartford Our Lady of Sorrows Rectory.
Butler, Rene *m.s.* '73 (STL)[O] Generalate, Missionari di N.S. de La Salette.
Butler, Richard J. '62 (BO) Stow, MA St. Isidore.
Butler, Robert J. '62 (BO) Pepperell, MA St. Joseph.
Butler, Robert R. *m.s.* '69 (HRT).
Butler, Thomas W. '82 (LAN)[M] Hillsdale, MI St. Anthony.
Butler, Thomas *o.carm.* '50 (TUC)[A] Tucson, AZ Salpointe Catholic High School.
Butler, Thomas *o.carm.* '50 (TUC)[E] Tucson, AZ Carmelite Priory.
Butler, Timothy A. '88 (BO) Military & VA Chaplains; Air Force Chaplains.
Butler, Victor *s.v.d.* '64 (TR)[M] Bordentown, NJ Society of the Divine Word.
Butler, William L. '61 (BO) Revere, MA St. Mary of the Assumption.
Butor, Walter *o.m.i.* '03 (SFS) Sisseton, SD St. Catherine; Sisseton, SD St. Peter.
Butori, Harry '52 (HEL) Retired.
Butori, Harry '52 (HEL) Butte, MT Butte Catholic Community North.
Butta, C. Gregory '91 (WDC) Washington, DC St. Francis Xavier.
Butters, Craig M. '83 (ORG) Rancho Santa Margarita, CA San Francisco Solano Church.
Butters, Joseph '65 (JOL) On Duty Outside the Diocese.
Butters, Joseph '65 (MRY) Arroyo Grande, CA St. Patrick.
Butters, Joseph (MRY) Presbyteral Council.
Buttinelli, Anthony '38 (NY) Retired.
Buttini, Mario *o.s.j.* '39 (SCR)[B] Pittston, PA St. Joseph's Oblate Seminary.
Buttino, James V. *m.m.* '47 (SJ)[M] Los Altos, CA Maryknoll.
Buttner, Michael J. '78 (CHL) Clemmons, NC Holy Family.
Buttner, Michael T. '75 (BAL) Retired.
Buttner, Michael (CHL) Diocesan Consultors.
Buttrick, Dean T. '63 (SUP) Superior, WI St. Anthony; Superior, WI St. Anthony; Northwest Deanery; Presbyteral Council & Diocesan Consultors.
Butts, James *s.d.v.* '01 (NEW) Newark, NJ St. Michael's.
Butz, Crispin C. *o.f.m.* (SFE) Associate Judges.
Butz, Joseph *c.ss.r.* '70 (FgM).
Butz, Robert J. '00 (MAD) Boscobel, WI Immaculate Conception; Boscobel, WI St. John Nepomucene.
Buu, Francis X. '74 (NY) New York, NY Immaculate Conception.
Buvala, Andrew G. *o.f.m.* (GAY) Native American Apostolate.
Buvala, Andrew *o.f.m.* '47 (GAY) Suttons Bay, MI Blessed Kateri Tekakwitha.
Buvala, Medard *o.f.m.* '43 (JOL)[L] Joliet, IL St. John the Baptist Friary.
Buvala, Medard *o.f.m.* '43 (JOL) Joliet, IL St. John the Baptist.
Buvens, Edward P. *s.j.* '69 (NO)[C] New Orleans, LA Loyola University New Orleans.
Buvens, Norman C. '64 (SHP) Retired.
Buxkemper, Roland '65 (LUB) Idalou, TX St. Philip Benizi; Priests' Retirement Board.
Buxkemper, Roland (LUB) Diocesan Building Commission.
Buxkemper, Roland (LUB) Promoter of Justice.
Buxman, Don (P) Personnel Board.
Buxman, Donald R. '70 (P) Milwaukie, OR Christ the King.
Buxman, Donald (P) College of Consultors.
Buyansky, Timothy *o.s.b.* '69 (CLV)[D] Cleveland, OH Benedictine High School.
Buyansky, Timothy *o.s.b.* '69 (CLV)[O] Cleveland, OH.
Buyung, Stefanus *o.carm.* '94 (WDC)[B] Washington, DC Whitefriars Hall.
Buzga, John P. '59 (E) Retired.
Buzzelli, Aaron N. *o.s.b.* '77 (GBG) Whitney, PA St. Cecilia; Youngstown, PA Sacred Heart.
Buzzerio, Joseph '77 (NEW) Paramus, NJ Bergen Regional Medical Center.
Buzzerio, Joseph '77 (NEW) Hackensack, NJ Bergen County Jail; Chaplains; Hackensack, NJ Bergen County Jail.
Bwanal, Peter N. *s.j.* '99 (MIL)[O] Milwaukee, WI Jesuit Community at Marquette University
Bwayo, Peter *a.j.* '89 (SP)[K] Tampa, FL St. Joseph's Hospital, Inc.
Byaruhanga, Frederick '89 (LA) Los Angeles, CA St. Joan of Arc.
Byeong–Hyeon, '98 (PIT) Pittsburgh, PA St. Pamphilus.
Byeong–Hyeon Woo, Matthew (PIT) Chaplains to Korean Catholic Community.
Byer, James M. '81 (CHL) Statesville, NC St. Philip the Apostle.
Byerley, E. Joseph '93 (CAM) Cherry Hill, NJ St. Pius X; [A] Haddonfield, NJ Paul VI High School.
Byerley, Joseph (CAM) Assistant Vocation Directors for Recruitment.
Byerley, Timothy E. '85 (CAM) Deptford, NJ St. John Vianney; Young Adult Ministry; [P] Glassboro, NJ Collegium Center for Faith and Culture.
Byers, Dohrman W. '74 (CIN) Georgetown, OH St. Mary; Georgetown, OH St. Michael; Georgetown, OH St. Elizabeth Parish.
Byers, John '95 (LAN) Lansing, MI Immaculate Heart of Mary.
Byers, John (LAN) Priest's Assignment Commission.
Byington, Edward J. '70 (FR) Somerset, MA St. Thomas More.
Bykowski, Norbert H. '56 (CHI) Retired.
Byrd, Charles A. '01 (ATL)[A] Latrobe, PA St. Vincent Seminary; On Duty Outside the Archdiocese.
Byrd, Freddie '88 (OWN) Owensboro, KY Blessed Mother.
Byrd, Freddie (OWN) Priest Personnel Committee.
Byrd, Freddie (OWN) Teens Encounter Christ.
Byrd, Howard W. *s.s.j.* '75 (NO) New Orleans, LA Blessed Sacrament.
Byrne, Albert F. '47 (STP) Sacerdotal Union of Daily Adoration Retired.
Byrne, Albert C. '79 (ALN) Allentown, PA Cathedral of St. Catharine of Siena; Vicars Forane; Board of Education.
Byrne, Basil *c.c.s.o.* '76 (WOR)[O] Spencer, MA St. Joseph's Abbey.
Byrne, Bernard P. *m.m.* '56 (SJ)[M] Los Altos, CA Maryknoll.
Byrne, David J. '78 (CHI) Palos Heights, IL Incarnation.
Byrne, David (WIN) On Special or Other Diocesan Assignment.
Byrne, Edward G. '64 (NY) Ossining, NY St. Ann.
Byrne, Edward *c.ss.r.* '44 (BRK) Brooklyn, NY Our Lady of Perpetual Help Basilica.
Byrne, Frederick *o.s.b.* '82 (GBG)[H] Latrobe, PA Saint Vincent Archabbey.
Byrne, George '69 (SD) Retired.
Byrne, Glenn '75 (BAL) Special Assignment.
Byrne, Harry J. '46 (NY) Retired.
Byrne, Harry M. *o.p.* '78 (STL)[B] St. Louis, MO Aquinas Institute of Theology; [O] St. Louis, MO Dominican Community of St. Louis.
Byrne, Henry L. '37 (STL) Retired.
Byrne, James D. '37 (CIN) St. Marys, OH Holy Rosary Retired.
Byrne, James P. *o.s.f.s.* '60 (R) Whiteville, NC Sacred Heart.
Byrne, Joel *o.f.m.* '51 (CIN)[M] Cincinnati, OH St. Clement Friary Retired.
Byrne, John F. *s.s.j.* '66 (BAL)[S] Baltimore, MD St. Joseph Society of the Sacred Heart House of Central Administration Retired.
Byrne, Joseph F. '69 (BO) Waltham, MA Our Lady, Comforter of the Afflicted; Unassigned.
Byrne, Joseph L. '54 (HEL) Townsend, MT Holy Cross; Holy Childhood Association; Propagation of the Faith.
Byrne, Laserian '48 (FRS) Retired.
Byrne, Laserian (FRS) Legion of Mary.
Byrne, Laurence *s.d.b.* '53 (OAK)[E] Richmond, CA Salesian High School Retired.
Byrne, Luke J. *s.j.* '65 (KC)[B] Kansas City, KS Rockhurst University Continuing Education Center/ National Seminars Group; [J] Kansas City, MO Rockhurst Jesuit Community.
Byrne, Mark '98 (CC)[G] Robstown, TX Society of Our Lady of the Most Holy Trinity.
Byrne, Patrick J. '55 (COL) Retired.
Byrne, Peter D. *s.j.* '75 (P)[L] Portland, OR Colombiere Community.
Byrne, Peter J. '84 (NY) Staten Island, NY Immaculate Conception; Staten Island, NY St. John the Baptist de La Salle.
Byrne, Peter *s.j.* '75 (P) Portland, OR St. Ignatius.
Byrne, Peter *f.s.s.p.* '03 (SCR)[M] Sacramento, CA.
Byrne, Raymond J. '57 (NY) Irvington–on–the–Hudson, NY Immaculate Conception.
Byrne, Robert H. '75 (SAG) Mount Pleasant, MI Sacred Heart.
Byrne, Robert P. '50 (LA) Retired.
Byrne, Robert (SAG) Diocesan Presbyteral Council.
Byrne, Thomas '58 (DET) Retired.
Byrne, Thomas *c.s.sp.* '64 (LR) Conway, AR St. Joseph's.
Byrne, William D. '88 (WIN)[D] Rochester, MN Saint Mary's Hospital.
Byrne, William D. '94 (WDC) Special Ministries; [S] College Park, MD University of Maryland Catholic Student Center.
Byrnes, Christopher *o.carm.* '51 (NY)[EE] Middletown, NY St. Albert's Priory.
Byrnes, Donald M. '55 (NO) Kenner, LA St. Jerome Retired.
Byrnes, Donald M. '55 (NO) Retired.
Byrnes, Francis J. '51 (BRK) Retired.
Byrnes, James J. '80 (STL) Florissant, MO North American Martyrs.
Byrnes, James T. '86 (NY)[E] Goshen, NY John S. Burke Catholic High School.
Byrnes, John D. '94 (ALT) Loretto, PA Basilica of St. Michael the Archangel.
Byrnes, John J. '66 (CAM) Merchantville, NJ St. Peter's.
Byrnes, John P. '45 (TR) Retired.
Byrnes, John W. '47 (BRK) Queens Village, NY SS. Joachim and Anne Retired.
Byrnes, John (ALT) Diocesan Shrines; Tribunal Office; Vocation Office.
Byrnes, Michael J. '96 (DET) Special Assignment; Graduate Studies.
Byrnes, Paul A. '62 (BAL) Frostburg, MD St. Michael; [V] Frostburg, MD St. Michael School Endowment Trust; Consultors; Consultors.
Byrnes, Paul '62 (BAL) Westernport, MD St. Peter.
Byrnes, Robert R. '67 (GBG) Greensburg, PA Westmoreland Hospital.
Byrnes, Thomas M. *c.m.* '50 (FgM).
Byrnes, Thomas '99 (NY) Warwick, NY St. Stephen.
Byrnes, Timothy '52 (LAN) Lansing, MI Holy Cross.
Byrns, Joseph P. '69 (BRK) On Leave/Unassigned.
Byrolly, Bruce '58 (WIL) Cambridge, MD St. Mary Refuge of Sinners.
Byron, J. Michael *s.t.d.* '89 (STP)[A] St. Paul, MN The Saint Paul Seminary.
Byron, Michael '89 (STP)[C] St. Paul, MN University of St. Thomas.
Byron, William J. *s.j.* '61 (WDC) Washington, DC Holy Trinity.
Byron, William '62 (YAK) Goldendale, WA Holy Trinity.
Byrth, Peter *o.carm.* '59 (NEW) Tenafly, NJ Our Lady of Mount Carmel.
Byun, Anselm *s.j.* (BO)[V] Newton, MA The Jesuit Community at Boston College.
Bzdyra, Stephen H. '79 (HRT) Union City, CT St. Hedwig; Union City, CT St. Stanislaus Kostka.

C

Caamano, Raphael '78 (BO)[U] Newton, MA Prelature of the Holy Cross and Opus Dei.
Cabafi, Csaba *s.j.* (ATH) Hungarian Priests' Association in Canada.
Cabala, Thomas S. '79 (CHI) South Holland, IL St. Jude the Apostle.
Caballero, Francisco '53 (TOL) Retired.
Caballero, Gilberto *c.m.* '03 (FgM).
Caballero, Lloyd C. '40 (BR) Retired.
Cabanas, Jamie '55 (BWN) Brownsville, TX St. Joseph.
Cabasino, Philip A. *c.ss.r.* '47 (BO) Roxbury, MA Our Lady of Perpetual Help; Bedford, MA Veterans Administration Hospital Bedford.
Cabazi, Ruta A. '65 (IND)[G] Beech Grove, IN St. Francis Hospital and Health Centers.
Cabell, Barry *c.s.c.* '89 (AUS) Copperas Cove, TX Holy Family.
Caberte, Constancio '63 (LA) Altadena, CA St. Elizabeth of Hungary.
Cabezas, Francisco Javier '79 (NEW) Bayonne, NJ Our Lady of the Assumption.
Cabezas, Richard (NEW) Short Hills, NJ St. Rose of Lima.
Caboboy, Juan '76 (ORG) Garden Grove, CA St. Columban.
Cabos, Aberlado (GAL) Houston, TX Prince of Peace.
Cabra, Artura *m.s.* '98 (R) Washington, NC Mother of Mercy.
Cabral, Clifford J. '79 (PRO) Pascoag, RI St. Joseph.
Cabral, Fernando '86 (PRO) Bristol, RI St. Elizabeth.
Cabral, Gerardo *m.g.* '82 (LA) Los Angeles, CA St. Paul.

Cabral, Jeffrey '02 (FR) Taunton, MA St. Anthony's.
Cabrera, Albert *c.p.* '65 (ALT)[J] Bedford, PA St. Mary's House of Greater Solitude.
Cabrera, Alberto '99 (MRY) Monterey, CA Cathedral of San Carlos Borromeo.
Cabrera, Alberto *c.p.* (BRK)[V] Jamaica, NY Immaculate Conception Monastery.
Cabrera, Sergio '73 (MIA) Miami, FL St. Raymond.
Cabrerizo, Juan L. *sch.p.* '77 (PCE)[C] Coto Laurel, PR Colegio Ponceno.
Cabrita, Paul *s.m.* '86 (ATL)[C] Atlanta, GA Marist School.
Cabulosan, Filomeno '75 (SAC) Vallejo, CA St. Vincent Ferrer.
Caccavale, Charles '81 (BRK) Released from Diocesan Assignment.
Caccavale, Charles (RVC) Censors of Books.
Caccavalle, Paschal *o.f.m.cap.* '45 (NEW) Hackensack, NJ Church of St. Francis of Assisi.
Caccavalle, Pius *o.f.m.cap.* '47 (NY)[EE] New York, NY Immaculate Conception Friary.
Cacciapuoti, Antonio '90 (LA) Los Angeles, CA Christ the King.
Cacciola, Thomas Francis '02 (NY)[EE] Bronx, NY Our Lady of the Angels Friary.
Caceres, Alonso '59 (ORG) Santa Ana, CA Our Lady of Guadalupe.
Caceres, Angel Diaz '76 (SJN)[A] Bayamon Central University.
Caceres, Blas *c.ss.r.* '88 (NY) New York, NY St. Cecilia.
Caceres, Carlos Humberto '81 (BRK) Brooklyn, NY St. Thomas Aquinas.
Caceres, Leonardo '03 (NEW) Elizabeth, NJ Our Lady of Most Holy Rosary/St. Michael.
Caceres, Marco A. '67 (MET) New Brunswick, NJ St. John the Baptist; Deans.
Cach, Mark '83 (P) Absent on Leave.
Cachat, Leo P. *s.j.* '66 (DET)[E] Detroit, MI University of Detroit Jesuit High School and Academy.
Cachola, Alvin *o.f.m.* '03 (LA) Los Angeles, CA St. Francis of Assisi.
Cadavid, Diego F. '02 (CHI) Chicago, IL St. Agnes of Bohemia.
Cadden, Donald R. *s.j.* '58 (SPK)[B] Spokane, WA Gonzaga University.
Cadden, Thomas J. '55 (COL)[G] Columbus, OH St. Rita Home.
Cadden, Thomas (COL) Diocesan Judges.
Caddy, James L. '64 (CLV) Gates Mills, OH St. Francis of Assisi.
Cadei, Adriano *p.i.m.e.* '56 (DET)[K] Detroit, MI P.I.M.E. Motherhouse in Detroit.
Cadera, James R. '57 (MRY) Retired.
Cadigan, Timothy J. *s.j.* '91 (SCR)[C] Scranton, PA The University of Scranton.
Cadorette, Curtis R. *m.m.* '77 (NY).
Cadran, Raymond *m.s.* '78 (LKC)[EE] Sulphur, LA Our Lady of Prompt Succor.
Cadusale, Jose '60 (BRK)[V] Jamaica, NY Parsons Manor.
Cadusale, Jose '60 (BRK) Queens Hospital Center—Pastoral Care Office.
Cadwallader, George B. '92 (PH) Philadelphia, PA Stella Maris.
Cady, Frank G. '81 (TUC) Rio Rico, AZ Nativity of Our Lord Jesus Christ; Charismatic Renewal Movement.
Cady, Frank '15 (TUC)[A] Nogales, AZ Lourdes Catholic School.
Caesar, Floyd '75 (ALN) Easton, PA St. Anthony of Padua.
Caesar, Floyd (ALN) Catholic Daughters of the Americas.
Caesar, Rodger J. *s.s.j.* '77 (BAL)[S] Baltimore, MD St. Joseph Society of the Sacred Heart House of Central Administration.
Cafareili, Francis *c.s.c.* '65 (SCR)[C] Holy Cross Community.
Cafarelli, Aquinas F. *o.s.b.* '65 (MAN)[K] Manchester, NH St. Anselm Abbey.
Caffe, John I. '62 (STL) O'Fallon, MO Immaculate Conception.
Caffery, James *m.s.* '60 (ATL) Smyrna, GA St. Thomas the Apostle.
Caffrey, Benet W. *o.s.b.* '58 (PAT)[M] Morristown, NJ St. Mary's Abbey.
Caffrey, Edward '57 (SPK) Retired.
Caffrey, Gerald *c.m.f.* '80 (PHX) Prescott, AZ United States Veterans Hospital (Prescott); Prescott, AZ Sacred Heart.
Caffrey, Joseph '63 (PT) On Leave of Absence.
Caffrey, William *s.v.d.* '59 (SB)[A] Riverside, CA Society of the Divine Word Missionaries; Council Members.
Caffrey, William *s.v.d.* (ORG)[G] Fullerton, CA St. Jude Medical Center.
Cafiero, John Paul *o.f.m.* '95 (CHI)[D] Chicago, IL Hales Franciscan High School, Inc..
Cafone, James M. '65 (NEW)[B] Seton Hall University; Members; Archdiocesan Theological Commission; Censors of Books.
Caforio, Stephen *o.f.m.* '49 (NY)[EE] Dobbs Ferry, NY St. Cabrini Nursing Home.
Caganap, Jason S. *c.r.m.* (NEW) Lodi, NJ St. Joseph's.
Caggianelli, Gregg '02 (VEN) Sarasota, FL Incarnation; Air Force Reserve Chaplains.
Caggiano, Frank J. (BRK) Censors of Books; Bishop Daily—.
Caggiano, Frank '87 (BRK) Permanent Diaconate Program; [A] Douglaston, NY Immaculate Conception Center.
Caggiano, Kyrin *o.carm.* '62 (L)[B] The Carmelite Community of The St. Francis DeSales Priory.
Cagney, John M. *o.praem.* '48 (PH)[AA] Paoli, PA Daylesford Abbey.
Cahalan, Patrick J. *s.j.* '65 (LA)[C] Los Angeles, CA Loyola Marymount University; [C] Los Angeles, CA Jesuit Community.
Cahalane, Thomas F. (TUC) Ecumenical Commission.
Cahalane, Thomas P. '63 (TUC) Tucson, AZ Our Mother of Sorrows.
Cahalane, Thomas (TUC) All Vicars Forane.
Cahalane, Thomas (TUC) Vicars Forane.
Cahalane, Thomas (TUC) Council of Priests.
Cahavet, Eugene *o.p.* '62 (NY) Bronx, NY St. Raymond.
Cahill, Brendan J. '90 (GAL)[A] Houston, TX St. Mary's Seminary.
Cahill, Brendan (GAL) Priests Personnel Committee.
Cahill, Clemente *c.ss.r.* '51 (CGS) Aguas Buenas, PR Church of Tres Santos Reyes.
Cahill, Clemente *c.ss.r.* (CGS) Legion of Mary.
Cahill, Daniel R. '43 (SFR) San Francisco, CA St. Paul Retired.
Cahill, Daniel '73 (TR) Keansburg, NJ St. Ann.
Cahill, Dennis H. '77 (DUB)[G] Mason City, IA Newman Catholic Child Care; Mason City, IA Holy Family.
Cahill, Edward B. '60 (PH) Springfield, PA Holy Cross.
Cahill, Frank '68 (MIA) Retired.
Cahill, J. Donald *s.m.* '61 (STL) St. Louis, MO Our Lady of the Pillar; [O] St. Louis, MO Marianist Community, Our Lady of the Pillar Parish.
Cahill, James '61 (CHL) Retired.
Cahill, John F. '51 (WOR)[N] Worcester, MA; Priests' Retirement Residence.
Cahill, John W. '63 (RCK) Freeport, IL St. Joseph; Diocesan Consultors.
Cahill, John W. '73 (COV) Covington, KY Cathedral, Basilica of the Assumption; Diocesan Consultors; Deans.
Cahill, John (WOR) Cemeteries.
Cahill, Joseph W. '76 (PRT) North Vassalboro, ME St. Bridget's; Oakland, ME St. Theresa.
Cahill, Richard M. '58 (BUF) Retired.
Cahill, Richard '39 (NY) New York, NY National Catholic Community Service.
Cahill, William C. '61 (SY) Rome, NY Transfiguration; Mohawk, NY Oneida Correctional Facility I.; Special Assignment.
Cahoon, John E. '89 (GAL) Houston, TX St. Cecilia.
Cahoon, John (GAL) Diocesan Judges.
Cahourt, Eugene *o.p.* '62 (WDC) Washington, DC St. Dominic Church & Priory.
Caiazzo, Gregory G. (RIC) Navy Chaplains.
Caiazzo, Nicholas '92 (NOR) On Duty Outside the Diocese.
Caiazzo, Nickolas '92 (NOR) Military Chaplains.
Caime, James M. *s.j.* '02 (NO)[C] New Orleans, LA Loyola University New Orleans.
Caimi, Luke A. '58 (WDC) Retired.
Cain, Dennis R. '79 (DUB) Farley, IA St. Joseph's; Epworth, IA St. Clement.
Cain, Frederick L. '70 (PIT) Bridgeville, PA Holy Child.
Cain, Harry J. *s.j.* '63 (BO)[V] Weston, MA Campion Jesuit Community.
Cain, J. C. *o.m.i.* '89 (AUS) Austin, TX Our Lady of Guadalupe.
Cain, James E. '50 (STO) Diamond Springs, CA; Cemeteries Retired.
Cain, James R. '56 (OM) Omaha Priests Retirement Plan and Trust, The Retired.
Cain, John F. '56 (SC) Sioux Rapids, IA St. Joseph Retired.
Cain, Joseph P. *o.s.c.* '44 (PHX)[G] Phoenix, AZ Crosier Community of Phoenix (Canons Regular of the Order of the Holy Cross).
Cain, Robert K.C. '95 (TLS) On Duty Outside the Diocese; Navy Chaplains.
Cain, Thomas *m.s.c.* '36 (ALN)[A] Center Valley, PA Sacred Heart Villa, Missionaries of the Sacred Heart.
Cain, William F. *s.j.* '69 (LA)[C] Los Angeles, CA Jesuit Community.
Caindec, Ferdinando '79 (NY) Nanuet, NY St. Anthony.
Caine, Martin J. '46 (BUF) Retired.
Cairns, John L. '63 (ALB) Clifton Park, NY St. Edward the Confessor.
Cairns, Stephen P. '68 (TOL) North Baltimore, OH Holy Family.
Cairone, A. Robert '64 (CAM) Audubon, NJ Church of the Holy Maternity.
Cal–Ortiz, Rodolfo '93 (GAL)[K] Catholic Chaplain Corps, Texas Medical Center; [Q] Houston, TX Disciples of Hope (Texas).
Calabrese, Charles L. '72 (STU)[N] Fort Worth, TX Texas Christian University Catholic Community; On Duty Outside the Diocese.
Calabrese, Peter M. *c.r.s.p.* (BUF)[B] Youngstown, NY St. Anthony M. Zaccaria Seminary; [B] Youngstown, NY The National Shrine Basilica of Our Lady of Fatima; Youngstown, NY Holy Family.
Calabrese, William M. '99 (E) Erie, PA Blessed Sacrament; [K] Erie, PA Saint Mary's Home at Asbury Ridge.
Calabria, Michael D. *o.f.m.* '03 (BUF)[O] St. Bonaventure, NY St. Bonaventure Friary; [C] St. Bonaventure, NY Friar Community.
Calabro, John E. '73 (PH) Philadelphia, PA Epiphany of Our Lord.
Calabro, Nicholas J. '66 (BGP) Greenwich, CT St. Roch.
Calais, Floyd J. '50 (LAF) Retired.
Calamari, Joseph *s.s.j.* '45 (BAL)[S] Baltimore, MD St. Joseph's Manor.
Calamari, Paul '80 (NO) On Duty Outside the Archdiocese.
Calasara, Mansuelo T. (MO) Army Chaplains.
Caldara, John N. '46 (ALB) Retired.
Caldarella, James J. '71 (WOR) Princeton, MA Prince of Peace.
Caldas, Constantino R. '51 (BGP) Bridgeport, CT Our Lady of Fatima; Portuguese–Speaking People, Apostolate for Retired.
Calder, Kenneth J. '60 (BRK) Brooklyn, NY Our Lady of Angels.
Calderon, Francisco *o.p.* '50 (MIA) Miami, FL St. Brendan.
Calderon, Juan L. *o.a.r.* (NEW) Hispanic Apostolate.
Calderon, Vicente '63 (ELP) El Paso, TX St. Raphael.
Calderon, Wilfredo *s.d.b.* '91 (SJN) San Juan, PR Maria Auxiliadora.
Calderone, Joseph D. *o.s.a.* '73 (PH)[AA] Villanova, PA St. Thomas of Villanova Friary; Navy Reserve Chaplains.
Calderone, Joseph *o.s.a.* '73 (PH)[C] Villanova University.
Calderwood, Vincent T. '44 (MET)[G] Somerset, NJ McCarrick Care Center Retired.
Caldognetto, Dominic *s.x.* '66 (MIL)[B] Franklin, WI Xaverian Missionary Fathers College Seminary.
Caldwell, Francis J. (RVC) Secretary for Ministerial Personnel; Priest Personnel; Priests' Personnel Assignment Board; Priests' Personnel Policy Board; Priests' Retirement Board.
Caldwell, Frank J. '81 (RVC) Rockville Centre, NY St. Agnes Cathedral.
Caldwell, Fred '95 (DAL) Ennis, TX St. John Nepomucene.
Caldwell, J. Ripley '54 (SJ)[M] Los Gatos, CA Sacred Heart Jesuit Center.
Caldwell, James A. '03 (TLS) Tulsa, OK Christ the King.
Caldwell, James V. '60 (SD) South Bay Detention Facility Retired.
Caldwell, John A. '70 (L) Pewee Valley, KY St. Aloysius.
Caldwell, Thomas *s.j.* '56 (MIL)[O] Milwaukee, WI Jesuit Community at Marquette University.
Caldwell, William '68 (KC) Excelsior Springs, MO St. Ann.
Calegari, Leonard J. '63 (SFR) Pacifica, CA St. Peter.
Calero, Luis F. *s.j.* '83 (SJ)[B] Santa Clara, CA Jesuit Community.
Calero, Nomar J. '91 (MGZ) Mayaguez, PR Cathedral of Our Lady of Purification; Communications Media.
Calgaro, John *o.f.m.conv.* '74 (FgM).
Calgaro, John *o.f.m.conv.* '74 (CHI)[N] Chicago Conventual Franciscans of St. Bonaventure Province.
Calhoun, Gerald '61 (OWN) Madisonville, KY Christ the King.
Calhoun, Gerald (OWN) Committee for Administration.
Calhoun, Gerald (OWN) Diocesan Pastoral Council.
Calhoun, Gerald (OWN) Priests' Council.
Calhoun, Gerald (OWN) Deans.
Calhoun, Gerald (OWN) Vicar General.
Calhoun, Lawrence E. *c.s.c.* '63 (FTW)[I] Sherman Oaks, CA.
Calhoun, Michael M. *o.s.b.* '89 (PEO).
Calhoun, Michael '02 (PEO).
Calhoun, Nathan '00 (ATL)[A] Lawrenceville, GA St. Lawrence.
Calhoun, Ronald G. (BO) Framingham, MA St. Jeremiah.
Calicchio, Isaac J. *o.f.m.* '56 (HRT) Meriden, CT St. Rose of Lima.
Calicott, John W. '74 (CHI) Chicago, IL Holy Angels.
Caligiuri, Angelo M. (BUF) Finance Council; Vicars; Cheektowaga, NY Infant of Prague.
Caligiuri, Anthony J. '49 (BUF)[O] Tonawanda, NY O'Hara Residence Retired.
Calik, Joseph *s.ch.* '60 (SEA) Seattle, WA St. Margaret of Scotland.
Calik, Jozef *s.ch.* (SEA) Polish Speaking, Ministry to.
Calimeri, Anthony F. '47 (ROC) Retired.
Calip, Ben F. '66 (RIC) Fincastle, VA Church of the Transfiguration.
Calis, Joseph A '99 (WDC) Silver Spring, MD St. John the Baptist; Sodality Union.

Calise, Joseph P. '80 (BRK)[B] Elmhurst, NY Cathedral Preparatory Seminary of the Immaculate Conception.
Caliwan, Marciano '72 (BRK) Brooklyn, NY St. Bernard's; Brooklyn, NY Resurrection.
Calkins, Arthur B. '70 (NO) On Duty Outside the Archdiocese.
Calkins, Howard W. '67 (NY) Mt. Vernon, NY Sacred Heart; [II] Bronx, NY Abraham House, Inc.; Westchester (South Shore).
Calkins, Martin J. *s.j.* '94 (DET)[K] Detroit Jesuit Provincial Office–Detroit Province of the Society of Jesus.
Calkins, Raymond J. '46 (SC) Retired.
Calkins, Ronald L. '78 (NO) Mandeville, LA Mary Queen of Peace; Deans; Serra Club of West St. Tammany.
Callaghan, Aloysius R. '71 (ALN) On Duty Outside the Diocese.
Callaghan, Aloysius R. (MO) Vicar General; Moderator of the Curia; Adjutant Judicial Vicar; Presbyteral Council.
Callaghan, George J. *o.s.a.* '56 (PH)[AA] Villanova, PA St. Thomas Monastery.
Callaghan, Michael J. *c.m.* '76 (BRK)[V] Jamaica, NY Vincentian Residence.
Callaghan, Michael J. '90 (BAL) Gambrills, MD Church of the Holy Apostles; Advocates and Procurators.
Callahan, Daniel P. *s.a.* '87 (OG)[D] Saranac Lake, NY St. Joseph's Rehabilitation Center, Inc.; [E] Saranac Lake, NY Atonement Friars.
Callahan, Daniel *s.a.* '87 (NY)[EE] Saranac Lake, NY St. Joseph's Rehabilitation Center, Inc..
Callahan, David P. '87 (BO) Littleton, MA St. Anne.
Callahan, Dennis D. '62 (MIL) Pell Lake, WI St. Mary.
Callahan, Edward M. '59 (SPR)[H] Springfield, MA St. Michael's Residence Retired.
Callahan, Francis J. '72 (SCR) Wilkes–Barre, PA St. Therese's.
Callahan, Francis X. '49 (HRT) Woodmont, CT St. Agnes.
Callahan, Francis X. '63 (BAL) Bel Air, MD St. Margaret.
Callahan, James A. '73 (PH) Philadelphia, PA Christ the King.
Callahan, James B. '98 (WOR) Athol, MA Our Lady Immaculate; Petersham, MA St. Peter.
Callahan, James F. *s.m.a.* '75 (WIN) St. Charles, MN Holy Redeemer; St. Charles, MN St. Charles Borromeo; St. Charles, MN St. Aloysius.
Callahan, James P. '74 (STL) St. Charles, MO St. Cletus; Deaneries/Deans.
Callahan, James P. (STL) St. Charles; Archdiocesan Council of Priests.
Callahan, Jerome *o.carm* '52 (JOL)[L] Darien Carmelite Provincial Office.
Callahan, John J. *s.j.* '70 (KC)[B] Kansas City, KS Rockhurst University Continuing Education Center/ National Seminars Group; [J] Kansas City, MO Rockhurst Jesuit Community.
Callahan, Joseph F. *c.s.c.* '70 (FR)[A] North Easton, MA Holy Cross Fathers Religious; [J] North Easton, MA Holy Cross Retreat House.
Callahan, Joseph H. '86 (CLV) Nuestra Senora de Guadalupe.
Callahan, Joseph W. '66 (PH) Retired.
Callahan, Kevin G. '84 (STL) Lemay, MO St. Martin of Tours; Special Assignment; Office of Priests' Personnel and Continuing Formation of Priests; Archdiocesan Priests' Personnel Board; St. Louis, MO Cure' of Ars.
Callahan, Kevin (STL) Archdiocesan Consultors.
Callahan, Michael G. *m.m.* '60 (LA) Monrovia, CA Annunciation; [Q] Monrovia, CA Retired.
Callahan, Nelson J. '53 (CLV)[EE] Bay Village, OH St. Raphael Retired.
Callahan, Richard B. *m.m.* '64 (NY)[EE] Maryknoll Maryknoll Fathers and Brothers; [EE] Maryknoll, NY M.M.A.F. Charitable Trust; [EE] Maryknoll, NY Maryknoll Fathers and Brothers Charitable Trust; [FF] Maryknoll, NY Maryknoll Sisters Charitable Trust.
Callahan, Richard J. '51 (CAM) Vineland, NJ St. Isidore; Liaison with Retired Priests Retired.
Callahan, Richard *m.m.* '64 (NY)[II] Maryknoll, NY The Asian Catholic News Fund.
Callahan, Ronan P. *c.p.* '51 (NOR)[A] Cromwell, CT Holy Apostles College and Seminary.
Callahan, Ronan *c.p.* '51 (HRT)[M] West Hartford, CT Holy Family Monastery/Retreat.
Callahan, Steven '87 (SD) San Diego, CA St. Brigid.
Callahan, Steven (SD) Judicial Vicar.
Callahan, Steven (SD) Finance Council.
Callahan, Steven (SD) Clergy Personnel Board.
Callahan, Steven (SD) College of Consultors.
Callahan, Steven (SD) Vicar General.
Callahan, Steven (SD) Presbyteral Council.
Callahan, Vincent '75 (CHI)[N] Chicago, IL St. Peter's Friary.
Callahan, William P. *o.f.m.conv.* '77 (MIL) Milwaukee, WI Basilica of St. Josaphat; Archdiocesan Consultors.
Callahan, Zachary '58 (RVC) Retired.
Callahan, Zachary (RVC) Merrick, NY Cure of Ars.
Callam, Daniel D. *c.s.b.* '64 (GAL)[Q] Houston, TX Residence of the Basilian Fathers of the University of St. Thomas.
Callam, Daniel *c.s.b.* '64 (GAL)[C] Houston, TX University of St. Thomas; [T] Houston, TX University of St. Thomas Campus Ministry.
Callan, John *sch.p.* '82 (MIA)[C] Fort Lauderdale, FL Cardinal Gibbons High School.
Callan, Patrick J. '61 (RVC) Point Lookout, NY Our Lady of the Miraculous Medal.
Callanan, Edward *s.j.* '58 (SAC)[D] Sacramento, CA Jesuit High School; [I] Carmichael, CA Jesuit High School Community of Sacramento.
Callari, William P. '79 (MAR) Vulcan, MI St. Barbara.
Calle, Diomedes '94 (SPR) Springfield, MA Blessed Sacrament; Springfield, MA All Souls.
Calle, Juan de la '54 (PMB) Retired.
Calle–Perez, Sergio '98 (ATL) Released from Archdiocesan Assignment.
Callea, Michael *m.i.c.* '02 (SPR)[I] Eucharistic Apostles of The Divine Mercy.
Calledo, James '94 (RVC) Seaford, NY St. James.
Calleja, Guido '53 (MOB) Magnolia Springs AL St. John the Baptist.
Callery, Peter J *s.j.* '72 (SP)[C] Tampa, FL Jesuit High School.
Callery, William '01 (FAR) Fessenden, ND St. Augustine; Fessenden, ND St. Joseph.
Calles, Robert B. '63 (ELP) El Paso, TX Most Holy Trinity.
Callipare, Joseph P. '85 (PT) Mary Esther, FL St. Peter.
Callipare, Joseph (PT) Auditors.
Callipare, Joseph (PT) Notaries.
Callis, Elbert '76 (MEM) Dyersburg, TN Holy Angels.
Calloway, Donald *m.i.c.* '03 (SPR)[I] Eucharistic Apostles of The Divine Mercy.
Caloca–Rivas, Rigoberto *o.f.m.* '82 (OAK).
Caloca–Rivas, Rigoberto *o.f.m.* '82 (OAK).
Caloca–Rivas, Rigoberto *o.f.m.* '82 (OAK)[N] Oakland, CA Franciscan Friars.
Calovini, Gerald D. (STU) College of Consultors.
Calovini, Gerald E. '73 (STU) Wintersville, OH Blessed Sacrament; Wintersville, OH Our Lady of Lourdes; [K] Steubenville, OH Campaign for Human Development; Defenders of the Bond; Deans; Pastoral Staff; Presbyteral Council; Diocesan Communications; Central Office of Catholic Charities; St. Vincent de Paul Society.
Calter, Arthur M. '56 (BO) Weymouth, MA Sacred Heart; Senior Priests Retired.
Caluda, Charles J. '62 (NO) Garyville, LA St. Hubert.
Calumbra, Faron '79 (HRT) Branford, CT St. Mary.
Calvert, Roland *o.s.f.s.* '65 (LAN)[J] Adrian, MI Congregation of the Most Holy Rosary.
Calvo, Angel Cuadrado *o.de.m.* '86 (PCE) Ponce, PR Santuario San Judas Tadeo.
Calvo, Gabriel '52 (WDC)[B] Washington, DC Diocesan Laborer Priests, House of Studies.
Calvo, Randolph R. (SFR) Board of Directors.
Calvo, Randolph R. (SFR) College of Consultors.
Calvo, Randolph '77 (SFR) Redwood City, CA Our Lady of Mount Carmel.
Calzada, Teodoro *c.m.* '55 (SJN) San Juan, PR Nuestra Senora del Pilar.
Camacho, Enrique '81 (YAK) Retired.
Camacho, Henry *o.p.* '60 (NEW) Sacred Heart Priory.
Camacho, Isaac *o.s.b.* '01 (SP)[O] St. Leo, FL St. Leo Abbey.
Camacho, Jesus '75 (B) Prison Ministry; Boise, ID St. Mary's.
Camacho, Jose Fco. Baez '87 (MGZ) Mayaguez, PR Ascension.
Camacho, Robert '79 (RCK) Aurora, IL Sacred Heart.
Camacho, Zoilo L.G. '54 (AGN) Dededo, GU Santa Barbara Retired.
Camacho, Zoilo (AGN) Associate Judges.
Camacho Torres, Orlando *c.ss.p.* '92 (SJN)[F] Dorado, PR Santuario del Espiritu Santo.
Camadella, Christian F. *o.f.m.* '56 (PAT) Paterson, NJ St. Bonaventure.
Camara, Michael M. '89 (FR) Fall River, MA Our Lady of Health; New Bedford, MA Our Lady of Mt. Carmel.
Camarda, Ronald A. '90 (STA) Jacksonville FL St. Patrick; Navy Reserve Chaplains.
Camayo, Ruben (NY) New York, NY Our Lady of Pompeii.
Cambra, Dan *m.i.c.* '86 (JOL) Darien, IL Our Lady of Peace.
Cambra, Daniel *m.i.c.* '86 (CHI)[N] Chicago, IL Congregation of Marian Fathers of the Immaculate Conception.
Cambra, Raymond '77 (FR) Fall River, MA Sacred Heart.
Cameli, Louis J. '70 (CHI) Chicago, IL St. Bonaventure; [T] Mundelein, IL Cardinal Stritch Retreat House; Cardinal Stritch Retreat House; Ongoing Formation for Priests.
Camera, Bede G. *o.s.b.* '88 (MAN)[K] Manchester, NH St. Anselm Abbey.
Cameron, Ben *c.p.m.* '97 (OWN)[F] Auburn, KY Fathers of Mercy.
Cameron, Hilary J. '64 (PRT) Berwick, ME Our Lady of Peace; Berwick, ME St. Michael.
Cameron, Kevin '84 (DM) Des Moines, IA Our Lady of the Americas.
Cameron, Peter J. *o.p.* '86 (NY).
Cameron, Peter John *o.p.* '86 (NY)[EE] New York, NY St. Vincent Ferrer Priory.
Cameron, Robert M. '59 (KC) Special Assignment; Cemetery (Catholic Cemeteries Associated, Diocese of Kansas City–St. Joseph, Inc.); Holy Childhood Association; Priests' Purgatorial Society; Propagation of the Faith.
Camilleri, Emanuel M. *o.p.* '37 (NO)[P] Home for the Clergy.
Camilleri, Emanuel *o.p.* '37 (FgM).
Camilleri, Joseph M. '74 (BR) Plaquemine, LA St. Joan of Arc.
Camilli, E. Michael *m.s.c.* '60 (ALN)[A] Center Valley, PA Sacred Heart Villa, Missionaries of the Sacred Heart; Secretariat for Catholic Life and Evangelization.
Camilo, Aristu (BAL) Laurel, MD Resurrection of Our Lord.
Camilo, Gabriel *m.j.* '87 (GAL) Houston, TX St. Stephen.
Camire, Bernard J. *s.s.s.* '66 (NY) New York, NY St. Jean Baptiste.
Camire, Bernard *s.s.s.* (NY) Manhattan, NY Lenox Hill Hospital.
Cammayo, Ruben '80 (NY) Bronx, NY Bronx–Lebanon Hospital Center.
Cammisa, James N. '49 (TR) Retired.
Camora, Tony '70 (AGN) Dededo, GU Santa Barbara.
Camorlinga, Angel *m.c.c.j.* (FgM).
Camp, Alfred L. '57 (JKS) Clarksdale, MS St. Elizabeth; Clarksdale, MS Immaculate Conception.
Camp, Steven '87 (RVC) Seaford, NY St. William, the Abbot.
Campagna, Robert M. *o.f.m.* '77 (NY)[EE] New York, NY Franciscan Province of the Immaculate Conception; [II] Mount Vernon, NY Franciscan Mission Associates; [II] Mount Vernon, NY St. Dymphna Devotion.
Campagnone, Nicholas '65 (ALB) Retired.
Campana, Pedro '56 (SJN) Bayamon, PR Santa Rosa de Lima.
Campana, Thomas J. '80 (CHI) Chicago, IL St. Pascal.
Campbell, Andrew S. *o.s.b.* '81 (GBG)[H] Latrobe, PA Saint Vincent Archabbey.
Campbell, Bernard J. *o.f.m.cap* '68 (MAN) Manchester, NH St. Anne.
Campbell, Bernard J. *c.s.p.* '68 (CHR) Clemson, SC St. Andrew; Presbyteral Council.
Campbell, Bernard '89 (STV) St. Croix, VI Church St. Ann Retired.
Campbell, Bernard *o.f.m.* (MAN) Catholic Medical Center.
Campbell, Bernard *o.f.m.cap.* (MAN) Council of Priests.
Campbell, Colm '60 (PH) East Lansdowne, PA St. Cyril of Alexandria; Irish Apostolate.
Campbell, Douglas '76 (WCH) Wichita, KS St. Jude.
Campbell, Douglas (WCH) Judges.
Campbell, Edward *o.s.b.* '56 (PMB)[F] West Palm Beach, FL Noreen McKeen Residence for Geriatric Care.
Campbell, Francis *o.m.i.* '42 (BO)[Y] Tewksbury, MA Immaculate Heart of Mary Infirmary.
Campbell, Francis '73 (P) Retired.
Campbell, Frank (P) College of Consultors.
Campbell, Gerard J. *s.j.* '51 (WDC) Washington, DC Holy Trinity; [M] Washington, DC The Jesuit Community at Georgetown University.
Campbell, Howard W. '88 (PIT) Aliquippa, PA Our Lady of Fatima.
Campbell, Hugh P. '61 (PH) West Chester, PA St. Maximilian Kolbe.
Campbell, J. Michael '71 (STU) Minerva, OH St. Francis Xavier; Presbyteral Council; College of Consultors; Priests Personnel Board; Vicar for Religious.
Campbell, James D. *o.p.* '62 (R)[E] Raleigh, NC Dominican Priory.
Campbell, James F. '57 (PEO)[N] Peoria, IL Immaculate Conception Convent Retired.
Campbell, James F. '64 (BUF) Finance Council; Buffalo, NY St. Joseph's Cathedral.
Campbell, Joe '99 (KNX) LaFollette, TN Our Lady of Perpetual Help.
Campbell, Joel A. *o.f.m.* '50 (BUF)[D] Buffalo, NY Bishop Timon–St. Jude High School.
Campbell, John D. *s.j.* '76 (MIL) Milwaukee, WI Gesu Parish.
Campbell, John G. (ORG) Judges.
Campbell, John J. *s.j.* '50 (DEN)[N] Denver, CO Xavier Jesuit Center.
Campbell, John Michael '71 (STU) Minerva, OH St. Gabriel the Archangel.
Campbell, John P. *c.s.p.* '69 (BO)[V] Boston, MA Paulist

Fathers Residence.
Campbell, John S. '66 (ALN) Easton, PA St. Bernard; Easton, PA St. Michael.
Campbell, John '55 (ORG) Retired.
Campbell, Joseph '60 (SPC) Caruthersville, MO Sacred Heart; On Duty Outside the Diocese.
Campbell, Joseph '99 (KNX) Helenwood, TN St. Jude Parish.
Campbell, Joseph '02 (KNX) Tazewell, TN Christ the King.
Campbell, Mark '71 (SD) San Diego, CA Immaculate Conception.
Campbell, Michael '93 (ATL) Buford, GA Prince of Peace.
Campbell, Norbert J. '60 (PIT) Wilmerding, PA St. Jude the Apostle.
Campbell, Paul B. *s.j.* '88 (SY)[Q] Syracuse, NY Jesuits at LeMoyne, Inc..
Campbell, Paul F. '65 (WOR) Dudley, MA St. Anthony's.
Campbell, Paul J. *o.s.f.s.* '82 (WIL) Middletown, DE St. Joseph.
Campbell, Peter E. *m.s.c.* '60 (RCK)[G] Aurora, IL Missionaries of the Sacred Heart Community.
Campbell, Ralph C. *s.j.* '59 (PH)[AA] Philadelphia, PA The St. John Neuman Nursing Home.
Campbell, Robert B. *s.j.* '57 (BO)[V] Weston, MA Campion Health Center, Inc..
Campbell, Robert *m.s.* '58 (MAN)[K] Enfield, NH Shrine of Our Lady of La Salette.
Campbell, Robert *m.s.* '58 (MAN)[M] Enfield, NH La Salette Shrine and Center of Enfield.
Campbell, Stephen *s.j.* '85 (MOB)[A] Mobile, AL Spring Hill College; [J] Mobile, AL Spring Hill College Campus Ministry.
Campbell, Theodore C. '72 (STP) Golden Valley, MN Good Shepherd.
Campbell, Thomas L. '48 (FR)[A] North Easton, MA Holy Cross Fathers Religious.
Campbell, Thomas P. '43 (BRK) Retired.
Campbell, Wayne '86 (OAK) San Leandro, CA St. Felicitas.
Campbell, William D. '58 (SCR) Carbondale, PA St. Rose of Lima.
Campbell, William G. '63 (FR) Marion, MA St. Rita's.
Campbell, William R. *s.j.* '98 (BO)[E] Dorchester, MA Boston College High School & Jesuit Community; [H] Boston, MA Nativity Preparatory School.
Campbell, William W. '52 (BO) Senior Priests Retired.
Campechano, Francisco '95 (STO) Tracy, CA St. Bernard Church (Pastor of).
Campechano, Francisco (STO) College of Consultors/ Presbyteral Council.
Campellone, Joseph G. *o.s.f.s.* '96 (PH)[D] Philadelphia, PA Father Judge High School for Boys; [AA] Philadelphia, PA Father Louis Brisson Residence.
Campi, Vincent L. '45 (WH) Retired.
Campion, John R. '48 (HBG) Doylesburg, PA Our Lady of Refuge; Doylesburg, PA Our Lady of Refuge Mission Retired.
Campion, Joseph J. '73 (ALN) Whitehall, PA St. John the Baptist.
Campion, Joseph J. *s.s.j.* '91 (NO) New Orleans, LA St. David.
Campion, Owen F. '66 (NSH) On Duty Outside the Diocese.
Campion, Thomas B. '52 (HRT) Wethersfield, CT Corpus Christi; Wethersfield, CT Sacred Heart.
Campion, Thomas F. '57 (MAD)[E] Monroe, WI The Monroe Clinic, Inc.; Apostolate to the Handicapped.
Campion, William T. '77 (ALN) Tamaqua, PA St. Jerome; Elected Members.
Campo, Lance J. '93 (NO).
Campo, Richard W. '85 (ALN)[J] Bethlehem, PA Holy Family Villa; Holy Family Villa for Priests.
Campoli, John F. '70 (TR) On Duty Outside the Diocese.
Campoli, Timothy J. '74 (SPR) Greenfield, MA Blessed Sacrament; Deans.
Camporese, Massimiliano '03 (KAL) Kalamazoo, MI St. Monica.
Campos, Miguel *sch.p.* '96 (LA)[Q] Los Angeles, CA Piarist Fathers.
Campuzano, J. Eduardo '46 (CAM) Retired.
Camuso, Robert '92 (SEA) Seattle, WA St. Anne.
Camuso, Robert '92 (SEA) Seattle, WA St. Margaret of Scotland.
Canaan, Timothy G. '93 (OG) Canton, NY St. Mary; Canton, NY St. Thomas More; Campus Ministry.
Canal, Manuel (MRY) Retired.
Canargo, Francisco Javier *o.f.m.* '87 (ELP)[B] El Paso, TX Roger Bacon College.
Canarro, John '01 (SY) Dewitt, NY Holy Cross.
Canary, John F. '69 (CHI)[A] Mundelein Seminary.
Canavan, Edward P. *o.s.f.s.* (FgM).
Canavan, Francis P. *s.j.* '50 (NY)[EE] Loyola Hall, Jesuit Community.
Canavan, Gerald D. '69 (PH) Eddystone, PA St. Rose of Lima.
Canavan, John D. '55 (DET) Retired.
Canavan, John '55 (LAN) Concord, MI St. Catherine Laboure Retired.
Canavan, Joseph T. '70 (BO) Cambridge, MA St. Mary of the Annunciation.
Canavan, Mark P. '71 (CHI) Mt. Prospect, IL St. Emily.
Canavan, Martin '68 (PHU) On Duty Outside the Diocese.
Canavera, Lawrence J. '67 (GB) Green Bay, WI St. Philip the Apostle.
Canazos, Gilberto *o.f.m.* (CHI)[D] Holy Spirit Friary.
Canceran, Danilo A. '89 (MET) Piscataway, NJ St. Frances Cabrini.
Cancro, Francis T. '81 (CHL) Asheville, NC St. Eugene.
Candalisa, Frank '02 (NO) Metairie, LA St. Ann Church and Shrine.
Candanedo, Wilmo A. *o.p.* '99 (SAT) San Antonio, TX St. Ann; [B] San Antonio, TX Dominican Priory of San Juan Macias and Novitiate.
Candelaria, Ernest *c.s.j.* '58 (LA) Lancaster, CA Blessed Junipero Serra.
Candreva, Arthur A. *i.v.dei* (BRK) Middle Village, NY Our Lady of Hope.
Candreva, Thomas D. '63 (RVC) East Rockaway, NY St. Raymond's; Judges for Interdiocesan Tribunal.
Candy, William '72 (STL)[J] St. Louis, MO St. Anthony's Medical Center.
Cane, Pere '93 (MIL)[X] Racine, WI Missionary Community of St. Paul the Apostle and Mary, Mother of the Church, Inc..
Cane–Gombau, Pere '93 (MIL) Special Assignment.
Canepa, Jorge A. *c.s.c.* '56 (FTW)[I] Congregacion de Santa Cruz.
Canez, Jorge '79 (PHX) Phoenix, AZ St. Edward Confessor.
Canez, Jorge '79 (PHX) Phoenix, AZ Holy Family.
Canfield, Francis E. *s.j.* '67 (TOL)[C] Toledo, OH St. John's Jesuit High School.
Caniff, James B. *c.m.* '60 (BO) Malden, MA Immaculate Conception.
Caniga, Branislav '96 (JOL) Joliet, IL SS. Cyril and Methodius.
Canino, Louis *o.f.m.* '69 (CHL)[J] Greensboro, NC Franciscan Friary.
Canino, Louis *o.f.m.* '69 (CHL)[Q] Greensboro, NC Franciscan Center.
Canizares, Dwight M. '81 (GAL) Baytown, TX St. Joseph.
Canjar, John A. '49 (DEN) Retired.
Cann, Hilarion V. '53 (WH) Retired.
Canna, Joseph '70 (LA) Irwindale, CA Our Lady of Guadalupe.
Cannan, Walter F. '68 (SY) Oriskany, NY St. Stephen, Protomartyr; Whitesboro, NY St. Anne.
Cannariato, Paul A. '83 (NEW) Bayonne, NJ St. Henry's.
Canniff, James B. '60 (BO) Senior Priests Retired.
Canning, John *o.carm.* '55 (NY) New York, NY Our Lady of the Scapular/St. Stephen.
Canning, Wilfred S. *c.s.b.* '55 (GAL)[Q] Houston, TX Dillon House Retired.
Cannizzo, Vito *c.s.s.* '43 (BO)[Y] Waltham, MA Stigmatine Fathers and Brothers.
Cannoles, Antonio *c.ss.r.* '69 (FgM).
Cannon, Hugh D. '66 (RVC) Islip Terrace, NY St. Peter the Apostle.
Cannon, John A. '48 (PH)[G] Holland, PA Villa Joseph Marie High School for Girls; [Y] Holland, PA St. Joseph Home for the Aged; [BB] Holland, PA Villa Joseph Marie Retired.
Cannon, Kenneth V. *s.x.* '97 (BO)[V] Holliston, MA Xaverian Missionaries.
Cannon, Kenneth *s.x.* '97 (FgM).
Cannon, Maro *c.f.a.* '85 (KNX)[C] Signal Mountain, TN Alexian Village Health Care Center.
Cannon, Maro *c.f.a.* '85 (KNX)[F] Signal Mountain, TN Alexian Brothers.
Cannon, Maro *c.f.a.* '85 (KNX)[D] Signal Mountain, TN Alexian Village of Tennessee.
Cannon, Richard E. '86 (BO) South Boston, MA St. Vincent de Paul; [AA] Boston, MA Our Lady of Good Voyage Chapel; Navy Reserve Chaplains.
Cannon, Robert R. '78 (VEN) Adjutant Judicial Vicars; Promoters of Justice; Judges; Associate Moderators; Military Chaplains; Air Force Reserve Chaplains.
Cannon, Robert R. (MO) Judges.
Cannuli, John *s.v.d.* '85 (CHI)[B] Techny, IL Divine Word Residence.
Cannuli, Richard G. *o.s.a.* '99 (PH)[C] Villanova University; [AA] Villanova, PA St. Thomas of Villanova Friary.
Canny, Michael '77 (SAC) Redding, CA Our Lady of Mercy.
Canny, Stephen J. '61 (SR) Cotati, CA St. Joseph; Promoter of Justice.
Canny, Stephen (SR) Parish Priest Consultors.
Cano, Emilio '37 (PCE) Retired.
Cano, Nicolas '97 (FgM).
Cano, Nicolas *o.s.b.* '97 (BIS)[A] Richardton, ND Assumption Abbey.
Canterbury, Keith '94 (SAC) Weaverville, CA St. Patrick.
Canterna, Charles J. '76 (BAL) Special Assignment.
Canterna, Charles '76 (BAL) Baltimore, MD St. Vincent de Paul.
Canterna, Chuck (BAL) Baltimore City Correctional Center, Baltimore Pre–Release Unit.
Cantillon, John Joseph '76 (OAK) Retired.
Cantley, Michael J. '55 (BRK) Douglaston, NY St. Anastasia.
Cantones, Joel P. '81 (NO) Edgard, LA St. John the Baptist.
Cantore, John *c.m.* '63 (SPC)[C] Cape Girardeau, MO Saint Francis Medical Center.
Cantu, Oscar '94 (GAL) Houston, TX Holy Name.
Cantu, Oscar '94 (GAL) On Duty Outside the Diocese.
Cantwell, Edward F. '58 (ALB) Hudson, NY Church of St. Mary; Hudson Correctional Facility; Special Assignment.
Cantwell, John '69 (SAC) Placerville, CA St. Patrick's.
Cantwell, Stephen F. *c.m.* '82 (PH) Brooklyn, NY St. John the Baptist; [V] Brooklyn, NY St. John the Baptist Rectory.
Cantwell, William J. *c.s.p.* '56 (NY)[EE] Jamaica Estates Paulist Fathers Generalate.
Cantwell, William J. *c.s.p.* '56 (PMB)[J] Vero Beach, FL Paulist Fathers Residence.
Canty, Richard J. '85 (SAV) Special Assignment Retired.
Canuel, Paul E. '66 (FR) Special Assignment; Diocesan Consultors.
Canzio, Celestino *o.f.m.* '73 (NY)[EE] St. Jane Frances de Chantal Friary.
Cao, Bill T. '01 (ORG) Brea, CA St. Angela Merici.
Cao, Duy '01 (CHI) Chicago, IL St. William.
Cao, Joseph Chuong Van *c.ss.r.* '01 (GAL) Houston, TX Holy Ghost.
Cao, Joseph T. '00 (DEN) Arvada, CO St. Joan of Arc.
Cao Phuong Ky, Joseph *s.s.* '59 (SPC)[E] Carthage, MO Congregation of the Mother Coredemptrix, United States Assumption Province.
Cao Tien Vu, John Eudes M. *c.m.c.* '01 (SPC)[E] Carthage, MO Congregation of the Mother Coredemptrix, United States Assumption Province.
Capacetti, Luis O. (SJN) Cursillos De Cristiandad.
Capacetti–Caraballo, Luis O. (SJN) Judicial Vicar; Diocesan Consultors.
Capacillo, Euben *o.a.r.* '75 (LA) Los Angeles, CA Cristo Rey.
Capalbo, Kenneth *o.f.m.* '74 (FgM).
Caparros, Angelo '94 (SAT) San Antonio, TX St. Rose of Lima.
Capato, Justin *o.s.b.* '80 (PAT) Cedar Knolls, NJ Notre Dame of Mt. Carmel.
Capato, Justin *o.s.b.* '80 (PAT)[M] Morristown St. Mary's Abbey.
Capdepon, Federico '83 (MIA) Miami Shores, FL St. Martha; Archdiocesan Vocations Review Board.
Capdeville, Henri *o.s.b.* '93 (TUC)[E] St. David, AZ Holy Trinity Monastery.
Capella, Joseph *s.a.c.* '90 (CAM)[C] Pennsauken, NJ Bishop Eustace Prep School.
Capelle, John J. *s.j.* '47 (NO)[P] New Orleans, LA Ignatius Residence.
Capellupo, Frank '75 (BRK) On Leave/Unassigned.
Capewell, Timothy J. '83 (TR) Princeton Jct., NJ Church of St. David the King.
Capik, William J. '54 (MET) Basking Ridge, NJ St. James.
Capitani, Anthony L. '46 (TR) Tribunal Judges Retired.
Capitani, Sylvan P. '64 (HBG) New Freedom, PA St. John the Baptist; Appointed.
Capitolo, Mario L. *s.j.* '59 (SJ).
Capitolo, Paul F. *s.j.* '69 (SFR)[E] San Francisco, CA St. Ignatius College Preparatory (Coed); [N] San Francisco, CA Jesuit Community at St. Ignatius College Preparatory.
Caplice, Richard J. *s.j.* '64 (NY) Cornwall–on–Hudson, NY St. Thomas of Canterbury.
Caplis, Robert J. '58 (CHI) Retired.
Capolarello, Salvatore '78 (BRK) On Leave/Unassigned.
Capone, Albert L. '80 (BO) Lowell, MA St. Michael.
Capone, Robert (ORG) Orange, CA Cathedral of the Holy Family.
Caponi, Francis J. *o.s.a.* '83 (PH)[C] Villanova, PA Villanova University.
Caponi, Francis J. *o.s.a.* '89 (WDC)[B] Washington, DC Augustinian College, Order of St. Augustine.
Caponi, Jerome '60 (VIC) Retired.
Caporali, Paul M. *s.d.b.* '54 (LA)[W] Rosemead, CA St. Joseph's Salesian Youth Renewal Center.
Caporiccio, Louis *c.p.m.* '97 (OWN)[F] Auburn, KY Fathers of Mercy.
Capoverdi, Giacomo '97 (PRO) Cranston, RI St. Mark.
Capozzelli, Emmanuel M. '49 (NEW)[N] Caldwell, NJ The Rev. Msgr. James F. Kelley Residence for Retired Priests Retired.
Cappel, Charles H. *m.m.* '44 (FgM).
Cappel, Joseph H. *m.m.* '35 (FgM).
Cappelletti, Edward *s.d.b.* '50 (NY)[EE] New Rochelle, NY Salesian Provincial House.
Cappelletti, Joseph '82 (CLV) Wickliffe, OH Our Lady of Mount Carmel.
Cappelli, Angelo J. '48 (STU) Retired.
Cappelloni, David P. '86 (SCR) Luzerne, PA Holy Family.

Cappelloni, Thomas A. '76 Hazleton, PA Our Lady of Grace.
Capperella, Thomas S. '01 (CAM) Haddonfield, NJ St. Vincent Pallotti; Advocates.
Cappleman, Gary *o.p.* '03 (ANC) Anchorage, AK Holy Family Cathedral.
Cappo, Louis C. '46 (MAR) Marquette, MI St. Peter Cathedral.
Cappucci, Chester J. *o.m.i.* '63 (BO)[Y] Tewksbury, MA Immaculate Heart of Mary Infirmary.
Cappuccino, Gregory J. '73 (RVC) Valley Stream, NY Blessed Sacrament.
Caprio, Albert A. *o.p.* '66 (HRT) New Haven, CT St. Mary's Priory.
Caprio, Robert J. *o.f.m.* '63 (BO)[V] Andover St. Francis Friary; [X] Andover, MA Franciscan Center – Retreat House.
Capriolo, Victor R. '71 (MIL) Fond du Lac, WI Holy Family.
Capua, Nicholas J. '56 (BRK) Whitestone, NY St. Luke.
Capuano, Vincent J. *s.j.* '98 (BAL)[S] Parroq. San Jose Obrero.
Capuano, Vincent J. *s.j.* '98 (FgM).
Capucci, Giovanni '03 (DEN) Westminster, CO Holy Trinity.
Capuci, John M. '90 (NO) On Duty Outside the Archdiocese; [R] Ponchatoula, LA Magnificat Center of the Holy Spirit.
Capuci, John M. (NO) Center of Jesus the Lord.
Caputo, Ralph J. '75 (BRK) Brooklyn, NY St. Bernard's.
Caputo, Salvatore '76 (OM)[K] St. Columbans, NE St. Columban's Foreign Mission Society.
Caraballo, Antonio '81 (ARE) Retired.
Carabello, Francis J. '68 (NO) Gretna, LA St. Joseph; Knights of Columbus.
Carao, Jorge '93 (AGN) Tamuning, GU St. Anthony and St. Victor.
Carathers, Patrick '81 (AMA) Amarillo, TX St. Hyacinth's.
Carbajales, Ignacio '60 (MIA) Retired.
Carberry, John '81 (SFD) Quincy, IL St. Boniface.
Carbine, Francis A. '62 (PH) Bensalem, PA St. Charles Borromeo.
Carbo, Eugene J. '62 (PH) Retired.
Carbo, Richard '75 (NY) New York, NY Guardian Angel.
Carbonaro, Dennis J. '81 (PH)[A] Permanent Diaconate Department.
Carbone, Anthony J. '93 (GBG) Slickville, PA St. Sylvester; Judges.
Carbone, Joseph M. *o.s.m.* '59 (CHI)[N] Chicago Order of Friar Servants of Mary (Servites) United States of America Province, Inc..
Carbone, Joseph M. *o.s.m.* '59 (DEN) Denver, CO Our Lady of Mt. Carmel.
Carbone, Roland J. *o.s.b.* '54 (JC) Kahoka, MO St. Michael the Archangel.
Carbone, Ronald J. *o.s.b.* '54 (JC) Canton, MO The Shrine of St. Patrick.
Carbone, Vito J. '62 (PH) Morrisville, PA St. John the Evangelist.
Carboneau, Dominique A. '99 (FTW) Yoder, IN St. Aloysius.
Carboneau, Dominique '99 (FTW)[C] Fort Wayne, IN Bishop Luers High School.
Carboneau, Dominique (FTW) Advisory Board.
Carbonneau, Robert *c.p.* '78 (NEW)[N] Passionist Archives.
Carbonneau, Robert *c.p.* '78 (BAL)[S] Baltimore, MD St. Joseph's Passionist Community.
Carboy, Daniel J. *c.ss.r.* '66 (CHR) Sumter, SC St. Anne's.
Carcar, Gerardo (CHI) Chicago, IL St. Ignatius; Instituto De Liderazgo Pastoral (Hispanic Programs for Lay Ministry and Permanent Diaconate).
Carcerano, Michael J. '76 (LA) Simi Valley, CA St. Rose of Lima.
Carcerano, Michael (LA) Judges.
Carchidi, Rudolph V. *c.s.c.* '55 (FR)[A] North Easton, MA Stonehill College; [A] North Easton, MA Holy Cross Fathers Religious.
Cardelli, Daniel E. '57 (OAK) Danville, CA St. Isidore's; [S] Oakland, CA Italian Catholic Federation; Bishop's Representative for Italian Speaking Faithful.
Cardelli, Daniel (OAK) Presbyteral Council.
Cardelli, Daniel (OAK) Consultors.
Carden, Robert F. '56 (PBL) Pueblo, CO St. Therese Retired.
Cardenas, David J. '61 (GAL) Houston, TX Resurrection.
Cardenas, Eugenio *m.sp.s.* '82 (LA)[A] Camarillo, CA St. John's Seminary.
Cardenas, Juan Raul (PMB) Palm Springs, FL St. Luke.
Cardenas, Manuel P. (ARE) Propagation of Faith; Holy Childhood.
Cardenas, Marco *c.m.f.* (CHI) Chicago, IL Our Lady of Fatima.
Cardenas, Marco *c.m.f.* (CHI)[J] Chicago, IL St. Anthony Hospital.
Cardenas–Ruiz, Prisciliano (SJN) Propagation of the Faith.
Cardenas–Ruiz, Prisciliano (SJN) Holy Childhood Association.
Cardenas–Suarez, Mario '94 (SAT) Charlotte, TX St. Rose of Lima.
Cardente, Edward S. '74 (PRO) Providence, RI St. Edward; North Providence, RI St. Anthony; Finance Council.
Cardenzana, Philip A. '65 (DAV) Colfax, IA Immaculate Conception.
Cardiel, Gabriel *o.f.m.* '99 (AMA) Bishop's Appointee; Amarillo, TX St. Laurence Cathedral.
Cardiff, John J. '45 (CHI) Oak Lawn, IL St. Linus Retired.
Cardinal, Maurice *m.s.* '50 (HON) Kapaau, HI Sacred Heart.
Cardinale, Kenneth R. '98 (WOR) Clinton, MA St. John the Evangelist.
Cardinale, Kenneth '98 (WOR)[C] Worcester, MA St. Peter–Marian Central Catholic Junior/Senior High School; St. John.
Cardinas, Edgar *o.d.c.* (CHI) Mundelein, IL Santa Maria Del Popolo.
Cardona, Carlos Garcia '92 (LKC) Kinder, LA St. Philip Neri.
Cardona, George '53 (MIA) Retired.
Cardona, George '53 (MIA) Hialeah, FL St. John the Apostle Retired.
Cardona, Jorge D. (CGS) Vocations.
Cardona, Jorge '93 (CGS)[F] Naranjito, PR Seminario Pablo VI – Propedeutico.
Cardona, Orlando *c.m.* (RVC) South Fork.
Cardona Matta, Jose Miguel '98 (SJN) Trujillo Alto, PR Exaltacion de la Santa Cruz.
Cardone, Joseph P. '87 (TOL) Special Assignment.
Cardone, Thomas A. *s.m.* '85 (RVC)[D] Uniondale, NY Kellenberg Memorial High School; [M] Mineola, NY Provincial Residence and Novitiate.
Cardone, Thomas *s.m.* (RVC) Senate of Priests (Presbyteral Council/College of Consultors).
Cardoni, Albert A. *s.j.* '60 (BO)[V] Weston, MA Campion Health Center, Inc..
Cardoso, Luis A. '58 (FR) Fall River, MA St. Michael.
Cardoso, Reinaldo M. '60 (PRO) West Warwick, RI St. Anthony.
Cardoza, Edward '57 (SB) Retired.
Cardoza, Timothy N. '83 (FRS) Tulare, CA St. Rita.
Cardy, William E. *o.f.m.* '72 (FgM).
Cardy, William *o.f.m.* '72 (STL)[O] St. Louis, MO Franciscan Friary of St. Anthony of Padua.
Carek, Peter P. 60 (MIL) Wauwatosa, WI St. Jude the Apostle.
Carew, Alphonso '96 (WDC) Memphis, TN Holy Spirit; Rockville, MD Shrine of St. Jude.
Carew, Lawrence F. '66 (BGP) Trumbull, CT Christ the King.
Carey, David '62 (BAL) Retired.
Carey, Dennis G. '98 (NOR) Middletown, CT St. John; Part Time; Priests' Retirement Plan Board.
Carey, Dennis (NOR) Priests Retirement Plan Board.
Carey, Dominic A. '98 (SCR)[M] Shohola, PA Society of Saint John.
Carey, Gerald P. '98 (PH) Philadelphia, PA Cathedral Basilica of SS. Peter and Paul.
Carey, J. Peter *s.j.* '64 (IND)[D] Indianapolis, IN.
Carey, James H. '66 (SY) Tully, NY St. Leo.
Carey, Joe *c.s.c.* '69 (FTW)[B] University of Notre Dame Du Lac.
Carey, John *o.f.m.cap.* (PIT) Clairton, PA St. Clare of Assisi.
Carey, Joseph H. *c.s.c.* '69 (FTW)[I] Notre Dame, IN Holy Cross Community, Corby Hall, University of Notre Dame.
Carey, Leo P. '51 (PAT)[P] Chester, NJ Nazareth Village Retired.
Carey, Paul J. '42 (PH) Retired.
Carey, Paul V. '71 (SY) St. Joseph.
Carey, Raymond '70 (P) Special Assignment.
Carey, Richard T. '65 (WOR) North Brookfield, MA St. Joseph's; Deans; Presbyteral Council.
Carey, Richard '55 (LA) Whittier, CA St. Gregory the Great.
Carey, Stephen A. '98 (NEW) Roseland, NJ Our Lady of the Blessed Sacrament.
Carey, Stephen '62 (CAM) Sea Isle City, NJ St. Joseph's.
Carey, William F. '67 (BGP) Military Chaplains; Army Chaplains.
Carey, William G. (BGP) New Canaan, CT St. Aloysius.
Carey, William H. '53 (SHP) Defenders of the Bond; Promoter of Justice; College of Consultors; Presbyteral Council; Health Ministry Retired.
Carey, William J. '43 (PRO) Retired.
Carfagna, Frank A. '67 (Y) Canton, OH St. Joseph; [Q] Youngstown, OH Catholic Cemeteries of the Diocese of Youngstown; Judges.
Cargill, Eugene '59 (GAL) League City, TX St. Mary.
Cargo, Thomas '78 (JOL) Addison, IL St. Joseph.
Carie, Giles *o.f.m.conv.* '61 (ELP) El Paso, TX Our Lady of Mt. Carmel.
Carie, Giles *o.f.m.conv.* (LSC) Judges.
Carie, Giles *o.f.m.conv.* (ELP) Judges.
Cariglio, Michael J. '70 (Y) Youngstown, OH Our Lady of Mt. Carmel.
Cariglio, Michael (Y) Department of Canonical Services.
Cariglio, Michael (Y) Judicial Vicar.
Cariglio, Michael (Y) College of Consultors.
Carignan, Armand *o.m.i.* '53 (FgM).
Carignan, Raymond P. *s.s.j.* '61 (BLX) Gulfport, MS St. Therese.
Carignan, Ronald *o.m.i.* '59 (FgM).
Carillo, Adrian Luevano '75 (SEA) Des Moines, WA St. Philomena; Poulsbo, WA St. Olaf.
Carillo, Victor M. '87 (SAT) LaVernia, TX St. Ann.
Carina, Chester H. '85 (MET) Matawan, NJ Most Holy Redeemer; Canonical Staff.
Carini, James P. '65 (NOR) Tolland, CT St. Matthew; Members.
Carini, James (NOR) District Moderators.
Carkenord, David '62 (FTW) Waterloo, IN St. Michael the Archangel.
Carkenord, David (FTW) Cemeteries.
Carkenord, David (FTW) Environment and Art.
Carkenord, David (FTW) Advisory Board.
Carkhuff, Thomas R. *o.s.c.* '76 (STP)[M] Shoreview, MN Crosier Provincial House Province of St. Odilia.
Carkhuff, Thomas *o.s.c.* '76 (FgM).
Carl, Scott M. (STP) St. Paul, MN St. Gregory the Great (Highland Catholic Community); St. Paul, MN St. Leo (Highland Catholic Community); St. Paul, MN St. Therese (Highland Catholic Community).
Carles, Alexander J. '88 (MET) Somerville, NJ Immaculate Conception.
Carley, Patrick F. '69 (SLC) West Jordan, UT St. Joseph the Worker.
Carlin, Bernard L. *c.ss.r.* '78 (CHI)[N] Chicago, IL Redemptorist Theology Residence.
Carlin, George '84 (CC)[G] Robstown, TX Society of Our Lady of the Most Holy Trinity.
Carlin, George *s.o.l.t.* '87 (SAT) Harper, TX St. Anthony's.
Carlin, Harry V. *s.j.* '48 (SFR)[E] San Francisco, CA St. Ignatius College Preparatory (Coed); [N] San Francisco, CA Jesuit Community at St. Ignatius College Preparatory.
Carlin, John T. '76 (CLV) Parma, OH St. Charles Borromeo.
Carlin, Warren *o.carm.* '58 (JOL)[L] Darien Carmelite Provincial Office.
Carlino, Richard A. '79 (ALB) Schenectady, NY Holy Cross; Schenectady, NY St. John the Evangelist.
Carlino, Richard '79 (ALB) Schenectady, NY St. Mary.
Carlo, Cyprian '73 (LA) Hacienda Heights, CA St. John Vianney.
Carlo, Edgar '97 (MGZ) Lajas, PR De la Merced Parish.
Carlo, Edgar (MGZ) Vocations.
Carlo, Joseph C. '63 (BUF) Tonawanda, NY St. Amelia Retired.
Carlo, Raymond J. '87 (CHR) Gaffney, SC Sacred Heart; Union, SC St. Augustine's; [H] Gaffney, SC Limestone College.
Carlone, Carmen A. '69 (CAM) Williamstown, NJ St. Mary's; Central Deanery.
Carlos, Joseph *o.f.m.* '75 (STL)[O] St. Louis Franciscan Friary of St. Anthony of Padua; Navy Chaplains.
Carlos, Juan Lopez '03 (AUS) Austin, TX San Jose.
Carlos, Miguel (LAN) Retired.
Carlsen, James F. (MOB) Daphne, AL Christ the King.
Carlsen, Jeffrey W. (BAL) Office of Pastoral Service for Senior and Retired Clergy.
Carlsen, Jeffrey '72 (BAL) Special Assignment.
Carlson, Curtis *o.f.m.cap.* '95 (COS)[I] Colorado Springs, CO Catholic Center at the Citadel.
Carlson, Edward A. '83 (CHI) Palatine, IL St. Thomas of Villanova.
Carlson, George F. '66 (BO) West Roxbury, MA Holy Name.
Carlson, Gerald J. '63 (GI) Retired.
Carlson, Gregory I. *s.j.* '74 (OM)[N] Berkeley, CA Jesuit Community at Jesuit School of Theology at Berkeley.
Carlson, James R. '73 (SAG) Bad Axe, MI Sacred Heart; Vicars for Vicariates.
Carlson, Kenneth F. '98 (CHI) Other Assignments; Army Chaplains.
Carlson, Richard D. '69 (NEW) Guttenberg, NJ St. John Nepomucene.
Carlson, Robert D. '63 (GAL) Galena Park, TX Our Lady of Fatima.
Carlson, Steven V. '96 (R) On Duty Outside the Diocese; Army Chaplains.
Carlton, Maurice T. '68 (MET) High Bridge, NJ St. Joseph.
Carman, Bernard P. *s.a.c.* '79 (WDC)[B] West Hyattsville, MD Pallottine Seminary at Green Hill.
Carman, Paul '00 (SY) Camillus, NY St. Joseph.
Carman, Paul (SY) Promoter of Justice.
Carmichael, Eugene J. *s.j.* '73 (CIN)[M] Cincinnati, OH Jesuit Community at Xavier University.
Carmichael, John F. '97 (BO) Swampscott, MA St. John the Evangelist.

Carmody, James F. '70 (WOR) Worcester, MA St. Andrew the Apostle; Army National Guard Chaplains.
Carmody, James '63 (RVC) Hicksville, NY St. Ignatius Loyola.
Carmody, Lawrence W. '90 (COS) Security, CO Holy Family.
Carmody, Michael J. '83 (GAL) Houston, TX St. Catherine of Siena.
Carmody, Stephen Francis *o.p.* '81 (NY) New York, NY St. Catherine of Siena.
Carmody, Stephen *o.p.* (NY) Manhattan, NY Memorial Sloan Kettering Cancer Center.
Carmody, W. Lawrence '90 (COS) Fountain, CO St. Joseph.
Carmola, Michael J. '64 (SY) Special Assignment; [S] Syracuse, NY Christ the King Retreat House; Laymen & Laywomen Retreat Movements.
Carmona, Edwardo '82 (SB)[E] Corona, CA Operarios Del Reino De Cristo, O.R.C..
Carmona, Henry (B) Judges.
Carmona, Henry (B) Priest Personnel Commission.
Carmona, Henry (B) Boise, ID Cathedral of St. John the Evangelist; Judicial Vicar.
Carmona, Hugo '85 (PRO) Providence, RI Our Lady of Mt. Carmel.
Carmona, Jose *m.n.m.* '90 (ARE) Camuy, PR Our Lady of the Miraculous Medal.
Carmone, Anthony F. '47 (PRO) Retired.
Carnago, William J. '88 (DET) Absent on Leave.
Carnes, Matthew E. *s.j.* '03 (SJ)[B] Santa Clara, CA Jesuit Community.
Carnevale, John *o.f.m.* '66 (PAT) Pompton Lakes, NJ Our Lady of the Assumption.
Carney, Aloysius S. '60 (NEW) Retired.
Carney, Angus N. *o.s.a.* '43 (PH)[AA] Villanova, PA St. Thomas Monastery.
Carney, Christopher '71 (BAL) Forest Hill, MD St. Ignatius.
Carney, Edward '63 (PEO) Retired.
Carney, James R. *s.j.* '56 (NY)[EE] New York, NY St. Ignatius Loyola Residence.
Carney, John F. '91 (SFE) Los Alamos, NM Immaculate Heart of Mary.
Carney, John J. *c.m.* '82 (FgM).
Carney, John '63 (BAL) Retired.
Carney, Joseph T. '68 (MIA) Miami Springs, FL Blessed Trinity.
Carney, Patrick J. '55 (NY) Hartsdale, NY Sacred Heart.
Carney, Patrick (NY) Canon 1742 Panel of Pastors.
Carney, Philita (CHI)[J] Blue Island, IL St. Francis Hospital and Health Center.
Carney, Richard F. '55 (KC) Administrative Committee Retired.
Carney, Robert E. '91 (TUC) Tucson, AZ St. Francis de Sales.
Carney, Robert V. *s.a.c.* '66 (MIL)[X] Milwaukee, WI Pallottine Fathers and Brothers, Inc., Disability Trust; [X] Milwaukee, WI Pallottine Fathers and Brothers, Inc., Educational and Apostolic Ministry Trust; [O] Milwaukee, WI Pallotti House; [D] Milwaukee, WI Pius XI High School.
Carnicelli, Xavier *o.f.m.* '57 (NY)[EE] New York Franciscan Province of the Immaculate Conception.
Caro, Luis A. *c.ss.r.* '75 (BRK) Brooklyn, NY Our Lady of Perpetual Help Basilica.
Caro, Robert V. *s.j.* '70 (LA)[C] Los Angeles, CA Loyola Marymount University; [C] Los Angeles, CA Jesuit Community.
Carola, Joseph A. *s.j.* '93 (NO)[P] Pontifical Gregorian Univ..
Carolan, Charles B. '55 (VIC) Flatonia, TX SS. Cyril and Methodius; Flatonia, TX Sacred Heart.
Carolan, Craig G. '91 (LAN) Adrian, MI St. Joseph.
Carolan, Emmet '62 (SAT) San Antonio, TX St. James the Apostle.
Carolan, Emmet (SAT) Judges.
Carolan, J. Lawrence '69 (SR) Sonoma, CA St. Leo.
Carolan, John J. '51 (CHI) Oak Park, IL St. Catherine of Siena–St. Lucy Retired.
Carolan, Thomas *o.f.m.* '58 (CLV)[O] Cleveland, OH St. Jude Friary.
Carolan, Thomas *o.f.m.* '58 (CLV) Warrensville Heights, OH St. Jude.
Carolin, Joeseph C. '66 (HBG) South Mountain, PA Restoration Center.
Caroluzza, Thomas J. (RIC) Regional Delegates.
Caro Morales, Jorge L. '89 (MGZ) Sabana Grande, PR Church of San Isidro.
Caron, Antonin R. '69 (PRT) Retired.
Caron, David *o.p.* '89 (MIA)[H] Miami, FL Dominican Fathers of Miami, Inc..
Caron, David *o.p.* '89 (MIA)[B] Miami, FL Barry University.
Caron, Eduardo *c.s.sp.* '57 (SJN)[F] Dorado, PR Santuario del Espiritu Santo.
Caron, Edward J. *c.s.sp.* (MO) CIVIL AIR PATROL.
Caron, Gerard J. '94 (PRO) Central Falls, RI The Holy Spirit Catholic Community.
Caron, Gerard *s.m.* '54 (BO)[V] Boston, MA Marist Fathers Lourdes Residence.
Caron, Gerard *s.m.* '54 (BO)[AA] Boston, MA Marist Fathers Residence.
Caron, Marc B. '89 (PRT) Portland, ME Cathedral of the Immaculate Conception; Special or Other Diocesan Assignment; Co–Chancellors; Guardian; Diocesan Consultors; Staff; Clergy Benefit Plan–Clergy Pension Plan; Ex Officio; College of Consultors; Ex Officio Members; Diocesan Office for Worship; Personnel Board.
Caron, Paul A. '83 (FR) Nantucket, MA St. Mary's, Our Lady of the Isle.
Caronan, John E. *o.praem.* '94 (ORG)[A] Silverado, CA St. Michael's Norbertine Postulancy, Novitiate and Juniorate; [I] Silverado, CA Norbertine Fathers of Orange Inc..
Caronan, John *o.praem.* (ORG)[O] Council of Priests.
Caronan, John *o.praem.* (ORG) Judges.
Carosella, Jerome A. '63 (VEN) Boca Grande, FL Our Lady of Mercy; College of Consultors; Presbyteral Council; The Florida Catholic of Venice, Inc.; Venice Catholic Communications, Inc.; Insurance Committee.
Carota, Peter (STO) College of Consultors/Presbyteral Council.
Carota, Peter (STO) Ripon, CA St. Patrick Church of Ripon (Pastor of).
Carotenuto, Anthony M. '68 (TR) Red Bank, NJ St. Anthony.
Carpena, Octavio R. '84 (MET) On Duty Outside the Diocese.
Carpender, John W. '53 (DUB) Retired.
Carpender, Thomas J. '48 (DUB) Retired.
Carpenter, Christopher '95 (PHX) Mesa, AZ Christ the King.
Carpenter, Edward C. '95 (ELP) San Elizario, TX San Elceario.
Carpenter, Todd *o.f.m.* '99 (CAM) Camden, NJ St. Anthony of Padua.
Carpenter, William *c.s.v.* '77 (SFD) Rochester, IL St. Jude.
Carpentier, Normand E. '71 (PRT) Windham, ME Our Lady of Perpetual Help; Clergy Benefit Plan–Clergy Pension Plan.
Carpine, Eric T. *o.f.m.* '75 (PRO)[N] Providence, RI St. Francis Chapel & City Ministry Center; [P] Providence, RI St. Francis Friary.
Carpinelli, Vincent G. '71 (CAM) Glassboro, NJ Our Lady of Lourdes.
Carr, Alton *c.ss.r.* '60 (SAT) San Antonio, TX St. Gerard Majella.
Carr, Andrew *c.ss.r.* '55 (BAL) Baltimore, MD St. Michael.
Carr, Andrew *c.ss.r.* '55 (BAL) Baltimore, MD St. Patrick.
Carr, Brandon '72 (BAL) Glen Burnie, MD Holy Trinity.
Carr, Cornelius J. *s.j.* '51 (STA) Jacksonville, FL Christ the King.
Carr, David W. '80 (WOR) Palm Springs, FL St. Luke; [B] West Palm Beach, FL Cardinal Newman High School; On Duty Outside the Diocese.
Carr, Ephrem *o.s.b.* '67 (IND) Indianapolis, IN St. John the Evangelist; [K] Collegio Sant' Anselmo.
Carr, Eugene R. '63 (SCR) Retired.
Carr, Gary M. '82 (SPC) Billings, MO St. Joseph; Monett, MO.
Carr, James A. '55 (CAM) Retired.
Carr, James P. *s.j.* '84 (SY)[A] Syracuse, NY Saint Andrew Hall.
Carr, James P. *s.j.* '92 (BO)[V] Boston, MA Arrupe House; [V] Boston The Society of Jesus of New England–Provincial Offices.
Carr, James V. '69 (RIC) Portsmouth, VA Church of the Resurrection.
Carr, John A. *c.s.p.* '40 (NY)[EE] Jamaica Estates Paulist Fathers Generalate.
Carr, John F. '47 (BO) Senior Priests Retired.
Carr, Mark V. '52 (BO) Senior Priests Retired.
Carr, Martin P. '74 (GB) Special Assignment.
Carr, Matthew '99 (ARL) On Duty Outside the Diocese.
Carr, Michael '68 (CHY) Casper, WY St. Anthony of Padua; [F] Casper, WY St. Anthony Tri–Parish School Foundation.
Carr, Michael '68 (CHY)[B] Casper, WY St. Anthony Manor.
Carr, Michael (CHY) College of Consultors.
Carr, Michael (CHY) Building Committee.
Carr, Michael (CHY) Vicar General.
Carr, Michael (CHY) Diaconate Board; Ex Officios, Voting.
Carr, Michael (CHY) Diocesan of Cheyenne, Board of Directors.
Carr, Michael (CHY) Judges.
Carr, Michael (CHY) Presbyteral Council.
Carr, Michael (CHY) Wyoming Catholic Ministries Foundation Board of Directors.
Carr, Michael (CHY) Board of Directors.
Carr, Michael (CHY) Vicars Forane.
Carr, Michael (CHY) Newspaper, Wyoming Catholic Register Board.
Carr, Raymond J. *s.m.* '63 (NO)[P] New Orleans, LA Marist Fathers.
Carr, Raymond J. *s.m.* '63 (WDC)[M] New Orleans, LA Malta Court Apartments.
Carr, Richard T. '01 (ARL) Woodbridge, VA Our Lady of Angels; Notaries.
Carr, Robert J (BO) Boston, MA Cathedral of the Holy Cross.
Carr, Walter F. '92 (AUS) Andice, TX Santa Rosa.
Carr, Walter (AUS) Serra Club – Austin.
Carr, William F. *s.j.* '56 (BGP)[P] Fairfield, CT The Fairfield Jesuit Community–Fairfield University.
Carr, William H. '69 (RIC) Williamsburg, VA St. Bede's.
Carr, William M. (WCH) Presbyteral Council/Diocesan Consultors; Presbyteral Council.
Carr, William (WCH) Retired.
Carranco, Juan *s.m.* '50 (SFR)[N] San Francisco, CA Marist Center of the West.
Carrano, Michael A. '70 (BRK) Brooklyn, NY Assumption of the Blessed Virgin Mary; Bishop Sullivan—.
Carranza, Claudio Cabrera '02 (MRY) Hollister, CA Sacred Heart/St. Benedict Catholic Community.
Carranza, Fernando '95 (NEW) Union City, NJ Sts. Joseph and Michael.
Carranza, Riz '80 (LA) Santa Maria, CA St. Mary of the Assumption.
Carrara, Christopher '94 (OG) Clayton, NY St. Mary of Clayton.
Carrara, Christopher '94 (OG) Clayton, NY St. John the Evangelist.
Carrara, Christopher (OG) Associate Vocations Directors.
Carraro, Francesco '97 (NEW) On Duty Outside the Archdiocese.
Carreiro, Walter A. '95 (BO) Hudson, MA St. Michael.
Carrella, Eugene J. '84 (NY) Staten Island, NY St. Adalbert.
Carreon, Albert (LA) Cursillo Movement.
Carreon, Noe (DEN) Aurora, CO Queen of Peace.
Carrero, Angel Dario *o.f.m.* '95 (SJN) Sabana Seca, PR San Jose Obrero; [A] Bayamon Central University.
Carrier, J. Victor '69 (SPR) Springfield, MA Holy Cross.
Carrier, Mark F. '99 (ARL) Dale City, VA Holy Family; Notaries.
Carrier, Michael J. '95 (WIL) Wilmington, DE Cathedral of St. Peter; Office of Worship; Catholic Scouting Program.
Carrier, Paul E. *s.j.* '77 (BGP)[B] Fairfield, CT Fairfield University; [W] Fairfield, CT Fairfield University.
Carrier, Paul E. *s.j.* '88 (BGP)[P] Fairfield, CT The Fairfield Jesuit Community–Fairfield University.
Carrieri, Leonard *m.ss.cc.* '36 (CAM)[M] Linwood, NJ Villa Pieta. Missionaries of the Sacred Hearts of Jesus & Mary.
Carriero, John P. *s.j.* '63 (ROC)[B] Rochester, NY McQuaid Jesuit High School.
Carrigan, Frederick (NY) New York, NY St. Rose of Lima.
Carrigan, John T. *o.p.* '38 (WDC) Washington, DC St. Dominic Church & Priory.
Carrigan, Thomas C. '60 (SAC) Retired.
Carrigg, George A. '57 (BO) Dorchester, MA St. Christopher.
Carrigg, William J. '56 (BO) Senior Priests Retired.
Carrilllo, Sergio '82 (MIA) Retired.
Carrillo, Arsenio S. '56 (TUC) Special Assignment; Vicar General; Diocesan Consultors; Council of Priests Retired.
Carrillo, Arsenio (TUC) Propagation of the Faith.
Carrillo, Arthur *c.p.* '70 (CHI)[N] Curia Generalizia Dei Passionisti.
Carrillo, Ron *s.f.* '74 (SFE) Santa Cruz, NM Holy Cross.
Carrillo, Ron *s.f.* (SFE) Presbyteral Council of the Archdiocese of Santa Fe.
Carrillo, Sergio '82 (MIA) Hialeah, FL St. John the Apostle Retired.
Carrillo–Adalpe, Jesus Benjamin '89 (LR) Fort Smith, AR Immaculate Conception.
Carrillo–Aldape, Jesus Benjamin '89 (LR) Hot Springs National Park, AR St. John the Baptist; Glenwood, AR Our Lady of Guadalupe Church; Leola, AR Blessed Juan Diego Church.
Carrilo, Arthur *c.p.* '70 (DET)[K] Detroit, MI St. Paul of the Cross Community, Congregation of the Passion.
Carrington, Richard J. '76 (NEW) West New York, NJ St. Joseph of the Palisades; County Dirs.; Navy Reserve Chaplains.
Carrion, Jose Antonio '77 (SJN) Toa Alta, PR San Esteban, Protomartir.
Carrion, Michael J. (BAL) Judges.
Carrion, Michael W. '77 (BAL) Baltimore, MD Immaculate Heart of Mary; [V] Baltimore, MD The Immaculate Heart of Mary School Endowment Trust.
Carrion, Patrick M. '82 (BAL) Special Assignment; Advocates and Procurators; Clergy Personnel, Division of; Office of Diaconate; Permanent Deacon Formation Program.
Carrion, Patrick M. (BAL) Clergy Personnel, Division of.
Carrion, Patrick '82 (BAL) Baltimore, MD St. Charles Borromeo.
Carrola, Rudolph T. '88 (SAT) Macdona, TX Our Lady

Queen of Heaven; Von Ormy, TX Sacred Heart.
Carroll, Aidan M. (LA) Valinda, CA St. Martha; [D] La Puente, CA Bishop Amat Memorial High School.
Carroll, Alban *s.a.* '55 (R) Apex, NC St. Andrew the Apostle.
Carroll, Brian '62 (JKS) Brandon, MS St. Paul; Priests' Council; Diocesan Consultors.
Carroll, Daniel *o.carm.* '60 (CHI)[D] Chicago, IL.
Carroll, Daniel *o.carm.* '60 (CHI)[N] Chicago, IL Carmelite Priory of St. Cyril Retired.
Carroll, Eamon *o.carm.* '46 (VEN)[G] Nokomis, FL Carmel at Mission Valley.
Carroll, Edmund F. *t.o.r.* '57 (PIT)[N] Pittsburgh, PA Third Order Regular of Saint Francis – Province of the Most Sacred Heart of Jesus.
Carroll, Edmund F. *t.o.r.* '57 (FgM).
Carroll, Edward E. '50 (MIL) Retired.
Carroll, Edward G. '67 (BO) Woburn, MA St. Barbara.
Carroll, Emmett H. *s.j.* '62 (SEA)[L] Seattle, WA Jesuit Community.
Carroll, Emmett J. *o.f.m.conv.* (TR) Tribunal Judges.
Carroll, Emmett *o.f.m.conv.* '54 (TR) Seaside Heights, NJ Our Lady of Perpetual Help.
Carroll, Francis P. *s.s.c.* '62 (FgM).
Carroll, Gilbert A. '41 (CHI) Chicago, IL St. Timothy Retired.
Carroll, J. Alfred *s.j.* '59 (SPK)[B] Spokane, WA Gonzaga University.
Carroll, James J. '45 (COL) Retired.
Carroll, James J. '56 (NEW) Fairview, NJ St. John the Baptist.
Carroll, James M. '68 (BO) MERRIMACK REGION; Georgetown, MA St. Mary.
Carroll, James '49 (JKS) Retired.
Carroll, James *o.f.m.* '79 (PSC)[A] Sybertsville, PA Holy Dormition Friary.
Carroll, James *o.f.m.* '79 (PSC) Mahanoy City, PA St. Mary's.
Carroll, John A. *s.s.j.* '66 (WDC) Washington, DC Incarnation.
Carroll, John J. *s.j.* '55 (FgM).
Carroll, John J. '66 (PAT) Kinnelon, NJ Our Lady of the Magnificat; Pro–Synodal Judges; Presbyteral Council.
Carroll, John P. '53 (BO) Boston, MA Beth Israel Deaconess Medical Center.
Carroll, John R. (BO) Woburn, MA St. Anthony.
Carroll, Joseph A. '74 (SD)[J] San Diego, CA St. Vincent de Paul Village; [J] Campo, CA Promiseland Ranch; [J] San Diego, CA S.V.D.P. Management Inc.; [M] San Diego, CA Catholic Committee on Scouting.
Carroll, Joseph P. *s.j.* '41 (SJ)[M] Los Gatos, CA Sacred Heart Jesuit Center.
Carroll, Joseph P. *s.j.* '42 (California)[N] Berkeley, CA Jesuit Community at Jesuit School of Theology at Berkeley.
Carroll, Joseph '55 (HON) Lihue, HI Immaculate Conception Retired.
Carroll, Lawrence J. '81 (BGP) Brookfield, CT St. Joseph; Fairfield, CT St. Pius X; Members of the Clergy Personnel Committee; Pastors' Vocation Advisory Board.
Carroll, Michael A. '85 (RVC) Baldwin, NY St. Christopher; Absent on Leave.
Carroll, Michael J. '61 (PH) Rydal, PA St. Hilary of Poitiers.
Carroll, Michael J. *c.m.* '77 (BRK)[D] St. John's University, Staten Island Campus; [D] St. John's University; [V] Jamaica, NY Vincentian Residence; Walnut, CA St. Lorenzo Ruiz.
Carroll, Michael '70 (GB) Absent on Leave.
Carroll, Michael '72 (SAC) Sacramento, CA Presentation of the Blessed Virgin Mary.
Carroll, Michael (SAC) Council of Priests.
Carroll, Norman P. '93 (WIL) Ridgely, MD St. Benedict.
Carroll, Owen '73 (OAK).
Carroll, Owen '73 (OAK)[A] Oakland, CA St. John The Theologian.
Carroll, Owen '73 (OAK)[B] St. Mary's College.
Carroll, Patrick A. '43 (OM) Retired.
Carroll, Patrick M. '71 (NY).
Carroll, Patrick '53 (NY) Retired.
Carroll, Patrick *c.s.sp.* '66 (STA)[E] Elkton, FL St. Ambrose.
Carroll, Ralph E. '58 (NO) Metairie, LA St. Clement of Rome.
Carroll, Richard L. '59 (NO) Retired.
Carroll, Robert B. '63 (PAT) Highland Lakes, NJ Our Lady of Fatima.
Carroll, Robert J. '75 (PH) Flourtown, PA St. Genevieve.
Carroll, Robert *o.carm.* '71 (CHI)[D] Mundelein, IL Carmel High School.
Carroll, Robert *o.carm.* '71 (CHI)[N] Mundelein, IL Carmelite Monastery.
Carroll, Roger '63 (STP) Retired.
Carroll, Sean O. *s.j.* (OAK) Oakland, CA St. Patrick's; [N] Berkeley, CA Jesuit Community at Jesuit School of Theology at Berkeley.
Carroll, Thomas J. *s.j.* '84 (BO)[V] Boston, MA Jesuit Urban Center & Immaculate Conception Community.
Carroll, Thomas R. *sch.p.* '70 (LEX)[B] Martin, KY The Piarist Schoo ; [G] Prestonsburg, KY Piarist Fathers.
Carroll, William R. '70 (BO) Marian Devotions.
Carroll, William '50 (B) Retired.
Carroll, William *s.j.* '69 (SJ)[M] Los Gatos, CA Sacred Heart Jesuit Center.
Carron, Malcolm *s.j.* '51 (DET)[P] Clarkston, MI Colombiere Center.
Carrozza, Andrew P. '90 (NY) Suffern, NY Sacred Heart.
Carrozzo, Anthony M. *o.f.m.* '66 (NY) New York, NY St. Stephen of Hungary.
Carruthers, Michael '91 (MIA) Hialeah, FL Immaculate Conception.
Carruthers, Michael '91 (MIA) Higher Studies.
Carruthers, Michael (MIA) Archdiocesan Vocations Review Board.
Carscallen, Edward C. '47 (TUC) Special Assignment; [J] Tucson, AZ Holy Hope Cemetery and Mausoleum; Clergy Health; Ministry to Priests Program Catholic Chaplain Retired.
Carson, John '64 (NY) Yonkers, NY St. Ann.
Carson, Michael '98 (SJ) Campbell, CA St. Lucy.
Carson, Robert E. *o.praem.* '46 (GB)[I] De Pere, WI St. Norbert Abbey.
Carson, Stanley B. '79 (ALT) Vicars General Altoona, PA Sacred Heart.
Cartagena, Antonio '85 (CGS) Caguas, PR San Juan Apostol y Evangelista.
Cartagena, Antonio (CGS) Diocesan Consultors.
Cartagena, Antonio (CGS) Priests Senate.
Cartagena, Antonio (CGS) Vicar General.
Cartaya, Pedro *s.j.* '67 (MIA)[H] Miami, FL Villa Javier.
Cartaya, Pedro *s.j.* '67 (MIA)[D] Miami, FL Belen Jesuit Preparatory School.
Carten, Thomas F. *c.s.c.* '79 (SCR)[C] Holy Cross Community.
Carter, Augustine W. *o.carm.* '51 (LA)[F] Encino, CA Crespi Carmelite High School; [Q] Los Angeles, CA Mount Carmel Priory, Carmelite Fathers and Brothers.
Carter, Francis T. '86 (HRT) West Hartford, CT St. Brigid's.
Carter, James A. '66 (CHR) Mount Pleasant, SC Christ Our King; Vicar General's Office; Diocesan Curia; College of Consultors; Finance Council; Presbyteral Council; Building & Renovation Commission; Investment Council; Parish Priest Consultors; Pastoral Council; Personnel Committee; Sites & Boundaries Committee.
Carter, James C. *s.j.* '58 (NO) New Orleans, LA Immaculate Conception.
Carter, John P. '70 (BAL) Williamsport, MD St. Augustine.
Carter, John T. '49 (E) Erie, PA St. George; Spiritual Apostolates.
Carter, Kevin E. '86 (NEW) Jersey City, NJ St. Nicholas; Our Lady of Fatima First Saturday Club.
Carter, Kevin E. (NEW) Jersey City North Region Deanery 10.
Carter, Martin J. *s.a.* '75 (BRK) Brooklyn NY Our Lady of Victory.
Carter, Raymond J. '49 (COL) Retired.
Carter, Robert E. *s.j.* '63 (NY)[EE] New York NY West Side Jesuit Community.
Carter, Stephen *o.f.m.cap.* '82 (WDC) Washington, DC Shrine of the Sacred Heart.
Carton, A. Richard '93 (PAT) Layton, NJ St. Thomas the Apostle; Montague, NJ St. James the Greater; Presbyteral Council.
Carton, Richard (PAT) College of Consultors
Carton, William J. '59 (TR) Sea Girt, NJ St. Mark.
Cartwright, Christopher M. *s.j.* '80 (HON) Honolulu, HI Newman Center–Holy Spirit Parish; [G] Honolulu, HI Jesuit Fathers House; Presbyteral Council.
Carty, John A. *s.j.* '59 (FgM).
Carty, John T '50 (PRO) Retired.
Caruana, Alfred E. *s.j.* '71 (NY)[EE] New York, NY Xavier Jesuit Community; [II] New York, NY Xavier Society for the Blind.
Carucci, David P. '95 (MOB) Mobile, AL Little Flower.
Carucci, David (MOB) Group III.
Carungay, Jovito '93 (BRK) Flushing, NY St. Ann's.
Carusi, Angelo N. '98 (PRO) Cranston, RI St. Mary; Catholic Scouting–Boy Scouts, Girl Scouts, Camp Fire.
Caruso, Carmen A. '66 (JOL) On Duty Outside the Diocese.
Caruso, Daniel '94 (SY) Binghamton, NY St. Mary of the Assumption.
Caruso, Michael *s.j.* '82 (LA)[C] Los Angeles CA Jesuit Community.
Caruso, Philip J. '78 (NY) Bronx, NY Our Lady of Grace; New Rochelle, NY St. Joseph.
Caruso, Robert J. (PHX) Defenders of the Bond.
Caruso, Robert '80 (PHX) Mesa, AZ All Saints.
Carvajal, Damian '53 (SJN) San Juan, PR Cristo Redentor.
Carvajal, Felipe N. '68 (PAT) Passaic, NJ St. Nicholas.
Carvajal, Raul H. '65 (MRY) Retired.
Carvalho, Antonio *c.s.* (BO) Everett, MA St. Anthony; Brazilian.
Carvalho, Gordian J. '85 (HON) Mililani Town, HI St. John Apostle and Evangelist.
Carvalho, Gordian (HON) Presbyteral Council.
Carvalho, Gordian (HON) Members.
Carvalho, Joaquim *o.s.b.* '82 (KCK)[H] Atchison, KS St. Benedict's Abbey.
Carven, John W. *c.m.* '60 (PH)[B] Philadelphia, PA St. Vincent's Seminary.
Carver, Dennis J. '94 (BLX)[AA] Pass Christian, MS St. Paul.
Carver, Dennis (BLX) Personnel Board.
Carver, Dennis (BLX) Vocations.
Carver, Dennis (BLX) Presbyteral Council.
Carvill, Michael *f.s.c.b.* '90 (FR) Attleboro, MA St. Joseph's.
Carvill, Michael '90 (FR)[N] Attleboro, MA Priestly Fraternity of the Missionaries of St. Charles Borromeo.
Carvill, Michael *f.s.c.b.* (FR) Attleboro.
Carville, John '63 (BR) Baton Rouge, LA Christ the King.
Carville, John *s.t.d.* '63 (BR)[K] Baton Rouge, LA Christ the King Parish and Catholic Student Center.
Carville, John (BR) Diocesan Corporation (The Roman Catholic Church of the Diocese of Baton Rouge).
Carville, John (BR) College of Consultors.
Carville, John (BR) Vicar General/Moderator of the Curia.
Carville, John (BR) Presbyteral Council.
Cary, Liam '92 (P) Medford, OR Sacred Heart of Jesus.
Cary, Robert M. *c.s.p.* '84 (KNX) Grand Rapids, MI Chapel of St. Paul–Catholic Information Center; Knoxville, TN John XXIII University Parish/Catholic Center; [H] Knoxville, TN UT–Knoxville, Newman Foundation, Inc..
Cary, William J. '58 (SUP) Retired.
Carzon, Thomas *o.m.v.* '96 (BO)[B] Boston, MA Our Lady of Grace Seminary.
Carzon, Thomas *o.m.v.* '96 (BO)[AA] Boston, MA St. Francis Chapel.
Cas, John J. (FgM).
Casabon, Luis '61 (MIA) Retired.
Casadia, James A. '01 (CAM) Sicklerville, NJ St. Charles Borromeo; Assistant Vocation Directors for Recruitment.
Casagram, Michael *o.c.s.o.* '82 (L)[K] Trappist, KY Abbey of Our Lady of Gethsemani, of the Order of Cistercians of the Strict Observance.
Casale, Charles B. '69 (FRS) Bishop, CA Our Lady of Perpetual Help.
Casale, Franklyn M. '67 (NEW) On Duty Outside the Archdiocese.
Casale, Franklyn M. '67 (MIA)[B] St. Thomas University.
Casaleggio, David E. (LAV) Air National Guard Chaplains.
Casaliggi, John R. '36 (GBG) Retired.
Casari, Michael T. '95 (WIL) Absent on Sick Leave.
Casarotto, Secondo *c.s.* '66 (BUF) Buffalo, NY St. Anthony of Padua.
Casavantes, Carlos S. *f.s.s.p.* '86 (SCR) Tyler, TX St. Joseph the Worker Church; [M] Tyler, TX St. Joseph the Worker Mission.
Casazza, David J. '43 (NEW) River Edge, NJ St. Peter the Apostle Retired.
Cascelli, George J. '55 (NY) New York, NY Epiphany.
Cascia, Philip J. '77 (HRT) Prospect, CT St. Anthony's.
Cascino, Marion *o.f.m.* '49 (NY)[EE] New York, NY Padua Friary.
Cascione, James *c.ss.r.* '83 (PH) Philadelphia, PA St. Boniface.
Casciotti, James A. *s.j.* '78 (BAL)[S] Curia SJ; Apostleship of Prayer.
Case, Francis E. *s.j.* '69 (P)[L] Portland Jesuit Provincial Office (Society of Jesus, Oregon Prov.).
Case, Francis J. '66 (SY) New Berlin, NY St. Theresa of the Infant Jesus.
Case, Lowell D. *s.s.j.* '80 (WDC) Washington, DC St. Augustine.
Case, Richard D. *s.j.* '75 (FBK)[C] Fairbanks, AK Jesuit Residence; Chancellor; Notaries; Diocesan Archivist; Finance Advisory Board; Personnel.
Casella, Thomas A. *c.m.* '71 (BUF)[O] Niagara University, NY Vincentian Community at Niagara University.
Casella, Thomas *c.m.* '71 (BUF)[C] Niagara University, NY Niagara University.
Casella, Thomas *c.m.* '71 (ALB)[M] Menands, NY De Paul Provincial House.
Casellas, R. Jaime *o.f.m.cap.* (SJN) San Juan–Santurce.
Casellas, Ramon Jaime *o.f.m.cap.* '85 (SJN) San Juan, PR San Francisco de Asis.
Casellas–Rivera, R. Jaime *o.f.m.cap.* (SJN) Diocesan Consultors.
Caserta, Angelo C. '45 (CIN) Piqua, OH Retired.
Caserta, Charles W. '54 (CIN) Retired.
Caserta, Thomas G. '79 (BRK)[B] Douglaston, NY

Cathedral Seminary Residence of the Immaculate Conception; Bishop Catanello—.
Caserta, Thomas (BRK) Ministerial Development Program.
Casey, Anthony C. '58 (BRK) Rockaway Beach, NY St. Rose of Lima.
Casey, Daniel '58 (SAC) Retired.
Casey, David J. *s.j.* '69 (NY)[EE] Loyola Hall, Jesuit Community.
Casey, Denis '57 (TLS) Retired.
Casey, Diarmuid *c.s.sp.* '69 (SJ) Mountain View, CA St. Athanasius.
Casey, Donald A. '65 (SB) Retired.
Casey, Edward J. '79 (PH) Norristown, PA St. Teresa of Avila.
Casey, Francis M. '64 (RVC)[M] Uniondale, NY St. Pius X Residence Retired.
Casey, George T. '37 (SCR) Retired.
Casey, James R. '00 (PH) Penndel, PA Our Lady of Grace.
Casey, John D. '55 (HRT) New Haven, CT St. Boniface's.
Casey, John F. '54 (BRK) Queens Village, NY Our Lady of Lourdes; Presbyteral Council.
Casey, John H. '57 (CAM) Retired.
Casey, John J. '84 (MET) North Plainfield, NJ St. Joseph; Deans.
Casey, John P. *m.m.* '56 (NY).
Casey, John V. '39 (PH)[AA] Villanova, PA St. Thomas Monastery.
Casey, John W. '45 (SCR) Retired.
Casey, John *s.a.c.* '67 (FWT) Weatherford, TX St. Stephen.
Casey, Joseph H. *s.j.* '49 (BO)[V] Weston, MA Campion Jesuit Community.
Casey, Joseph M. '66 (PAT) Morristown, NJ Assumption of the Blessed Virgin Mary; Morris Plains, NJ Greystone Park Psychiatric Hospital.
Casey, Kevin M. *c.p.* '56 (MET) Old Bridge, NJ St. Thomas the Apostle.
Casey, Kevin P. *s.j.* '72 (SD) Santee, CA Guardian Angels.
Casey, Kevin *c.p.* '67 (MET)[H] Old Bridge, NJ St. Thomas the Apostle.
Casey, Liam C. '62 (ALB) On Duty Outside the Diocese.
Casey, Liam C. '93 (HRT)[I] Hartford, CT Saint Francis Hospital and Medical Center.
Casey, M. Joseph *s.j.* '67 (DET)[P] Clarkston, MI Colombiere Center; [K] Detroit, MI Jesuit Provincial Office–Detroit Province of the Society of Jesus.
Casey, Marion G. '34 (NU) Divine Providence Hospital & Home; [B] Ivanhoe, MN Divine Providence Health Center Retired.
Casey, Martin J. *s.j.* '43 (WDC)[M] Washington, DC The Jesuit Community at Georgetown University.
Casey, Noah J. *o.s.b.* '76 (IND) Indianapolis, IN St. Bernadette; Indianapolis, IN St. John the Evangelist.
Casey, Noah *o.s.b.* '76 (IND)[K] Indianapolis, IN.
Casey, Patrick L. '65 (NU) Darwin, MN St. John; Litchfield, MN St. Gertrude; Finance Council.
Casey, Patrick M. *s.j.* '72 (FgM).
Casey, Patrick P. (DET) Archdiocesan Vicars.
Casey, Patrick T. *o.m.i.* '80 (CHI) Chicago, IL St. Malachy; Chicago, IL Precious Blood.
Casey, Patrick '97 (DET) Detroit, MI St. Dominic; Detroit, MI St. Patrick.
Casey, Paul E. *s.s.c.* '54 (OM)[K] St. Columbans, NE St. Columban's Foreign Mission Society Retired.
Casey, Peter J. '68 (BO) Milton, MA St. Agatha.
Casey, Richard L. '65 (BO) Emergency Response Group.
Casey, Robert E. '87 (BO) South Boston, MA St. Brigid; South Boston, MA Gate of Heaven.
Casey, Robert G. '94 (CHI) Chicago, IL Our Lady of Tepeyac.
Casey, Thomas J. *s.j.* '62 (KC)[B] Kansas City, KS Rockhurst University Continuing Education Center/National Seminars Group; [J] Kansas City, MO Rockhurst Jesuit Community.
Casey, Thomas Joseph *s.j.* '57 (STL)[O] St. Louis, MO Jesuit Community Corporation at St. Louis University – Jesuit Hall.
Casey, Thomas *o.s.a.* '69 (ALB) Troy, NY St. Augustine.
Casey, Walter E. '48 (BO) Senior Priests Retired.
Casey, William C. (KNX) Diocesan Consultors; Presbyteral Council.
Casey, William P. *c.p.m.* '91 (OWN)[F] Auburn, KY Fathers of Mercy.
Casey, William '69 (KNX) Retired.
Cash, Richard '89 (OWN) Sturgis, KY St. Ambrose; Marion, KY St. William; Sturgis, KY St. Francis Borgia.
Cashel, Richard '54 (SFS) Retired.
Cashen, Michael E. '91 (TLS) Coalgate, OK Blessed Sacrament Oratory; McAlester, OK St. John.
Cashin, James '65 (SAT) Comfort, TX Sacred Heart.
Cashman, Christopher T. '89 (BRK) Ridgewood, NY St. Aloysius.
Cashman, James H. *o.s.c.* '48 (SCL)[I] Onamia Crosier Monastery.
Cashman, James *o.s.c.* '48 (SCL) Foreston, MN St. Louis Bertrand.
Cashman, Jeremiah '55 (LC) Cornell, WI Holy Cross.
Cashman, John *c.p.* (MET)[H] Naples, FL.
Cashman, Joseph C. '60 (WIN) Absent on Leave.
Casillas, Rafael '72 (LA) Los Angeles, CA St. Joseph.
Casillas, Richard *s.v.d.* '97 (LA) Los Angeles, CA Our Lady of Lourdes.
Casimano, Santino '75 (NOR)[B] Uncasville, CT St. Bernard Academy.
Caskey, John U. '59 (L) Louisville, KY Most Blessed Sacrament.
Caskey, John '82 (SCL) Browerville, MN Christ the King; Browerville, MN St. Joseph; Browerville, MN St. Isidore.
Caskey, John (SCL) Diocesan Education Council.
Caskey, John (SCL) Diocesan Consultors.
Caskin, John J. *s.j.* '60 (BO) Dorchester, MA Carney Hospital; [V] Boston The Society of Jesus of New England–Provincial Offices; [V] Weston, MA Campion Jesuit Community.
Caslson, Curtis *o.f.m.cap* '95 (COS)[F] Colorado Springs, CO Padre Pio Friary.
Casper, Kenneth R. *o.f.m.cap.* '80 (MIL)[B] Mount Calvary, WI St. Felix Friary.
Casper, Paul *s.c.j.* '57 (MIL)[O] Franklin, WI Villa Maria.
Caspers, William A. '54 (CHY) Retired.
Cassar, Edward A. '69 (BRK) Brooklyn, NY St. Rosalia–Regina Pacis.
Cassar, Julian '77 (BAK) John Day, OR St. Elizabeth's.
Cassato, David L. '72 (BRK) Brooklyn, NY St. Athanasius; Presbyteral Council; Police Department.
Cassel, Harry A. *o.s.a.* '50 (PH) Bryn Mawr, PA Our Mother of Good Counsel Retired.
Cassella, John J. '58 (PIT) Pittsburgh, PA Madonna del Castello.
Cassem, Ned H. *s.j.* '70 (BO)[V] Weston, MA Campion Jesuit Community.
Casserly, Eugene D. '69 (PT) Pensacola, FL St. Mary.
Casserly, Eugene (PT) Defender of the Bond.
Cassese, Anthony '77 (CLV) Cleveland, OH St. Jerome.
Cassese, John–Marie *o.f.m.* '50 (NY)[EE] New York, NY Padua Friary.
Cassidy, Bernard F. *s.j.* '63 (HON)[G] Honolulu, HI Jesuit Fathers House.
Cassidy, Bernard *s.j.* (HON) Beginning Experience–Hawaii.
Cassidy, Charles C. (PAT) Retired.
Cassidy, Daniel J. *o.p.* '57 (PRO)[P] Providence St. Thomas Aquinas Priory at Providence College.
Cassidy, Daniel J. '78 (CHI) Chicago, IL St. Mark.
Cassidy, Felix F. *o.p.* '54 (SFR) San Francisco, CA St. Dominic; [N] San Francisco, CA St. Dominic Priory.
Cassidy, Francis P. '57 (CHI) Chicago, IL St. Nicholas of Tolentine Retired.
Cassidy, Francis '59 (LA) Monrovia, CA Immaculate Conception.
Cassidy, Frank P. '57 (CHI) Retired.
Cassidy, James G. *o.s.b.* '84 (MAN)[K] Manchester, NH St. Anselm Abbey.
Cassidy, James M. '61 (CLV) Ashland, OH St. Edward.
Cassidy, James P. '51 (NY)[II] New York, NY Catholic Foundation for the Dominican Republic.
Cassidy, James W. *o.s.a.* '90 (CHL) Monroe, NC Our Lady of Lourdes.
Cassidy, James '78 (STP) Metropolitan Medical Center.
Cassidy, James *o.s.a.* '90 (CHL) Charlotte, NC St. John Neumann.
Cassidy, James (NY) On Duty Outside the Archdiocese.
Cassidy, John M. '58 (CHI) Chicago, IL St. Daniel the Prophet Retired.
Cassidy, John T. '79 (PT) Pensacola, FL St. Thomas More; Priests' Pension Plan, Board for.
Cassidy, John V. '69 (LC) Retired.
Cassidy, John (PT) Finance, Diocesan Commission for.
Cassidy, John (PT) Clergy Concerns.
Cassidy, John (PT) Vicar for Priests.
Cassidy, Joseph L. '45 (NEW)[N] Rutherford, NJ St. John Vianney Residence for Priests Retired.
Cassidy, Kevin W. '60 (MAD) Retired.
Cassidy, Laurence L. *s.j.* '61 (NEW)[B] Jersey City, NJ Jesuit Center; [N] Jersey City, NJ Jesuits of Saint Peter's College, Inc..
Cassidy, Martin J. '57 (MIA) Lauderdale–by–the–Sea, FL Assumption.
Cassidy, Martin (MIA) Retired Priests' Committee.
Cassidy, Matthew J. *s.j.* (FgM).
Cassidy, Richard '67 (BUF) On Duty Outside the Archdiocese.
Cassidy, Robert T. '58 (STP)[A] Archdiocesan Consultors; Edina, MN Our Lady of Grace.
Cassidy, Robert '57 (STP) Retired.
Cassidy, Terry A '84 (PEO) Peoria, IL St. Ann.
Cassidy, Terry '84 (PEO) Peoria, IL St. Martin de Porres.
Cassidy, Theodore *s.m.* '68 (CAM)[P] Cape May Point, NJ Marianist Family Retreat Center.
Cassidy, Thomas J. '57 (ARL) Vienna, VA St. Mark.
Cassidy, Thomas J. '57 (ARL) Purcellville, VA St. Francis de Sales Retired.
Cassidy, Thomas *s.c.j.* '71 (MIL)[O] Milwaukee, WI SCJ Community.
Cassin, Andrew J. '54 (WDC) Retired.
Cassin, Andrew '54 (WDC) Waldorf, MD St. Peter; Staunton, VA St. Francis of Assisi.
Cassista, Fernand *m.s.* '65 (FR)[H] Attleboro, MA La Salette Shrine.
Cassista, Fernand *m.s.* '65 (FR)[J] Attleboro, MA La Salette Center for Christian Living.
Casstevens, Jennifer (BO)[EE] Cambridge, MA The Youville House, Inc..
Castaldi, Joseph '63 (NOR) New London, CT St. Joseph.
Castaldi, Joseph (NOR) Priests' Retirement Plan Board.
Castaldi, Joseph (NOR) Defenders of the Bond.
Castanda, Heibar (MRY) Advocates.
Castaneda, Brian '99 (LA) Los Angeles, CA Cathedral of Our Lady of the Angels.
Castaneda, Heibar '94 (MRY) Seaside, CA St. Francis Xavier.
Castaneda, Jesus Antonio *s.j.c.d.* (YAK) Cowiche, WA St. Juan Diego.
Castaneda, Jesus Antonio (YAK) Adjutant Judicial Vicars; Judges.
Castaneda, Mario (PMB) Wellington, FL St. Rita; Charismatic Renewal for Hispanics; Presbyteral Council.
Castaneda, Oscar '87 (MIA)[K] Miami, FL National Shrine of Our Lady of Charity.
Castaneda, Severiano '71 (LA) Los Angeles, CA San Francisco Church.
Castano, Jairo Motta '83 (CC) Kingsville, TX St. Joseph.
Castano, Rafael '88 (ATL) Cedartown, GA St. Bernadette's.
Casteel, Michael J. '84 (SPC) Marshfield, MO Holy Trinity.
Castejon, Antonio Garcia (SJN) Police Chaplains.
Castellani, John J. '48 (HRT) Retired.
Castellani, Paul J. '96 (PH) Philadelphia, PA St. Martin of Tours.
Castellano, Francis J. '60 (SCR) Williamsport, PA Mater Dolorosa.
Castellanos, Ricardo C. '70 (MIA) Pompano Beach, FL San Isidro; [M] Margate, FL Word & Life Catholic Ministry, Inc..
Castellanos Ruiz, Yesid Ricardo '82 (SJN) San Juan, PR Santa Luisa de Marillac.
Castellino, Albert *c.ss.r.* '61 (DEN) Denver, CO St. Joseph; [N] Denver, CO The Redemptorists of Denver, Colorado.
Castelow, Ralph T. '89 (WIL) Salisbury, MD St. Francis De Sales.
Castenada, Mario '95 (STO) On Duty Outside the Diocese.
Caster, Gary C. '92 (PEO)[O] Normal, IL St. Robert Bellarmine Newman Center, Illinois State Univ., Wesleyan Univ., Heartland Community & Eu.
Castillejo, Jorge '89 (SJN) Military Services.
Castillejo, Jorge (SJN)[A] Sacred Heart University.
Castillejo–Llusia, Jorge J. '89 (SJN) Carolina, PR Santo Cristo de la Agonia; Army National Guard Chaplains.
Castillo, Carlos C. *c.m.f.* '73 (LA)[Q] Los Angeles, CA Claretian Retreat Center Community; [W] Los Angeles, CA Claretian Retreat Center (All Groups).
Castillo, Domingo '91 (AMA) Absent on Leave.
Castillo, Francisco '67 (BWN) Mission, TX Our Lady of St. John of the Fields.
Castillo, Gustavo '01 (LA) Lomita, CA St. Margaret Mary Alacoque.
Castillo, Jose Luis (CHI) Chicago, IL Holy Innocents.
Castillo, Jose '80 (SD) San Ysidro, CA Our Lady of Mt. Carmel.
Castillo, Miguel '58 (NY) Haverstraw, NY St. Peter.
Castillo, Rene '89 (RIC) Wytheville, VA St. Mary's.
Castillo, Richard '83 (PT) On Leave of Absence.
Castillo, Rolando '94 (MIA) Miami, FL St. Timothy.
Castillo, Rolo B. '92 (RIC) Rocky Mount, VA Francis of Assisi.
Castillo, Romeo (NY) Staten Island, NY Holy Child.
Castillo–Castillo, Ricardo '03 (CHI) Rolling Meadows, IL St. Colette.
Castillo Aguillon, Pedro Alfonso '85 (AUS) Round Rock, TX St. William's.
Castle, Nathan G. *o.p.* '85 (PHX)[G] Tempe, AZ Dominicans (Dominican Community–Jordan House).
Castle, Nathan *o.p.* '76 (PHX)[I] Tempe, AZ Arizona State University.
Castle, Nathan *o.p.* (PHX) College of Consultors.
Castles, Patrick J. '69 (TR) Allentown, NJ St. John.
Castor, Timothy William '01 (RC) Rapid City, SD Cathedral of Our Lady of Perpetual Help.
Castori, Michael T. *s.j.* '98 (NY)[N] Berkeley, CA Jesuit Community at Jesuit School of Theology at Berkeley.
Castrillo, Jesus Saez *o.de.m.* '69 (CGS) Cayey, PR Nuestra Senora de la Merced.
Castrillo, Jesus *c.m.f.* '49 (LA) El Monte, CA Our Lady of Guadalupe.
Castro, Alberto (MGZ) Diocesan Board of Administration.

Castro, Antonio '84 (GAL) Navasota, TX Christ Our Light.
Castro, Dominic Joseph *o.f.m.conv.* '98 (MRY) Gonzales, CA St. Theodore; Soledad, CA Our Lady of Solitude.
Castro, Geronimo *m.s.* '99 (HON) Honolulu, HI St. Anthony; Waipahu, HI St. Joseph.
Castro, John *o.m.i.* '62 (SAN)[E] San Angelo, TX Christ the King Retreat Center.
Castro, Mario A. (BWN) Rio Hondo, TX St. Helen; Boy Scouts.
Castro, Mario (BWN) Procurators and Advocates.
Castro, Oscar M. *ss.cc.* '93 (GAL) Conroe, TX Sacred Heart.
Castro, Patrick *o.f.m.cap.* '88 (AGN)[F] Agana Heights, GU St. Fidelis Friary.
Castro, Patrick *o.f.m.cap.* '88 (AGN) Agana Heights, GU San Francisco d'Assisi.
Castro, Patrick *o.f.m.cap.* (AGN) Archdiocesan Presbyteral Council.
Castro, Robert '85 (SR) Napa, CA St. Apollinaris.
Castronovo, Edmund A. '76 (SY) Oneida, NY St. Joseph; Georgetown, NY Camp Georgetown; Camp Pharsalia.
Caswell, Thomas C. '66 (SPK) Cheney, WA St. Rose of Lima; [M] Cheney, WA Catholic Newman Center at Eastern Washington University.
Caswell, Thomas (SPK) Ecumenical Relations.
Catagnus, James N. '70 (PH) Philadelphia, PA St. Ambrose.
Catalana, Mark '91 (SJ) Special Assignment.
Catalana, Mark (SJ) Council of Priests.
Catalana, Mark (SJ) Vocation Office.
Catalana, Mark (SJ) Building Committee.
Catalana, Mark (SJ) Diocesan Clergy Personnel Board.
Catalano, James A. *s.j.* '95 (NEW)[B] Jersey City, NJ Jesuit Center; [N] Jersey City, NJ Jesuits of Saint Peter's College, Inc..
Catalano, James *o.s.j.* '63 (FRS) Bakersfield, CA Our Lady of Guadalupe.
Catallo, Sylvester *o.f.m.cap.* '54 (NY)[B] Beacon, NY St. Lawrence of Brindisi Friary.
Catanach, Richard '88 (LSC) Deming, NM St. Ann's.
Catanach, Richard (LSC) Defenders of the Bond.
Catanach, Richard (LSC) Clergy Personnel Board.
Catanach, Richard (LSC) Diocesan Consultors.
Catanach, Richard (LSC) Priestly Life and Ministry Committee.
Catania, Thomas M. '74 (BRK) Richmond Hill, NY Holy Child Jesus.
Catanise, Joseph R. '82 (ROC) Webster, NY St. Rita.
Cataudo, Anthony I. *o.p.* '60 (CAM)[M] Camden, NJ Dominican Sisters of the Perpetual Rosary Chaplain's Residence; [N] Camden, NJ Monastery of the Dominican Nuns of the Perpetual Rosary.
Catoir, John T. '60 (PAT) Passaic, NJ Assumption of the Blessed Virgin Mary; [P] Chester, NJ Nazareth Village; [P] Passaic, NJ St. Jude Media Ministries; Pro–Synodal Judges Retired.
Catucci, Thomas F. '82 (SY) Kirkwood, NY St. Mary.
Catullo, Pasquale R. '63 (PH) Retired.
Catuso, Orville J. *s.j.* '53 (MIL)[O] Wauwatosa, WI Jesuit Community at St. Camillus.
Caufield, Kenneth J. *s.j.* '67 (NY)[F] New York, NY Regis High School; [EE] New York, NY St. Ignatius Loyola Residence.
Caul, Robert F. '61 (PRO) Wakefield, RI St. Francis of Assisi; [R] Narragansett, RI Our Lady of Peace Spiritual Life Center.
Cauley, Thomas F. '81 (PMB) Port St. Lucie, FL Holy Family.
Caulfield, John F. *s.j.* '44 (BO)[V] Newton, MA The Jesuit Community at Boston College.
Caulfield, John J. '48 (PH) Philadelphia, PA Cathedral Basilica of SS. Peter and Paul Retired.
Caulfield, John P. '03 (WDC) Silver Spring, MD St. Bernadette.
Caulfield, John '59 (ORL) Lakeland, FL St. Joseph's.
Caulfield, Sean '49 (B) Retired.
Caulfield, Sean (B) Judges.
Cautela, Mauro J. '74 (PIT) Ellwood City, PA Holy Redeemer Parish; Deans and Deaneries.
Cauterucci, Francis J. '90 (PH) Glen Mills, PA St. Thomas the Apostle.
Cavagnaro, Camillus *o.f.m.* '46 (TUC) Tucson, AZ Mission San Xavier del Bac.
Cavagnaro, John A. '75 (CAM) Collings Lakes, NJ Our Lady of the Lakes.
Cavagnaro, Mark R. '70 (CAM) Marmora, NJ The Church of the Resurrection; Members.
Cavagnaro, Mark (CAM) Cape May County.
Cavagnuolo, Salvatore F. '67 (HRT) Yalesville, CT Our Lady of Fatima.
Cavalier, Robert C. '72 (NO) Abita Springs, LA St. Jane de Chantal.
Cavallaro, Galliano J. '42 (PRO)[P] Providence St. John Vianney Residence Retired.
Cavalli, Victor *o.p.* '48 (SAC) Benicia, CA St. Dominic.
Cavalluzzi, Kevin P. '93 (BRK) Brooklyn, NY St. Peter–St. Paul–Our Lady of Pilar.
Cavanagh, Brian '58 (LA) Covina, CA Sacred Heart.
Cavanagh, David J. '85 (BO)[U] Cambridge, MA Opus Dei, Prelature of the Holy Cross and Opus Dei.
Cavanagh, Gerald F. *s.j.* '64 (DET)[K] Detroit, MI Jesuit Community at the University of Detroit Mercy.
Cavanagh, James '80 (LA) On Sick Leave.
Cavanagh, Joseph A. *s.j.* '62 (CI)[C] Kolonia, Pohnpei, FM Jesuit House.
Cavanagh, Michael J. '59 (PBL) Retired.
Cavanaugh, Brian *t.o.r.* '82 (STU)[A] Steubenville, OH Franciscan University of Steubenville.
Cavanaugh, Brian *t.o.r.* '82 (STU)[F] Steubenville, OH Holy Spirit Friary.
Cavanaugh, Daniel J. '66 (PH) Ambler, PA St. Joseph.
Cavanaugh, Harry M. *c.pp.s.* '54 ((TOL)) New Riegel, OH St. Peter; New Riegel, OH St. Boniface; Maria Stein, OH Nativity of the Blessed Virgin Mary; Maria Stein, OH St. John the Baptist; Maria Stein, OH St. Rose.
Cavanaugh, Jack *s.c.j.* '79 (GAL) Houston, TX St. Matthew the Evangelist.
Cavanaugh, James K. '51 (Y) Retired.
Cavanaugh, John L. '51 (NY) Retired.
Cavanaugh, John L. '56 (CIN) Judges Retired.
Cavanaugh, John R. '55 (ROC)[I] East Rochester, NY Basilian Fathers of Fisher House.
Cavanaugh, John *c.ss.r.* '46 (ORL) New Smyrna Beach, FL Sacred Heart.
Cavanaugh, John '51 (NY)[EE] Bronx, NY.
Cavanaugh, John *m.ss.cc.* '72 (CAM)[M] Linwood, NJ Villa Pieta. Missionaries of the Sacred Hearts of Jesus & Mary.
Cavanaugh, John '90 (FAR) West Fargo, ND Blessed Sacrament.
Cavanaugh, Kevin P. '86 (HRT) Glastonbury, CT St. Paul's; South Glastonbury, CT St. Augustine; Deans; Army National Guard Chaplains.
Cavanaugh, Michael T. *o.s.f.s.* '76 (WIL)[J] Wilmington, DE Oblates of St. Francis De Sales.
Cavanaugh, Peter M. '66 (PRO) Misquamicut, RI St. Clare.
Cavanaugh, Thomas J. '03 (PH) Warminster, PA Nativity of Our Lord.
Cavazos–Gonzales, Gilberto *o.f.m.* '85 (CHI).
Caveglia, Patrick *o.s.b.* '94 (KC)[A] Conception, MO Conception Seminary College.
Caveglia, Patrick *o.s.b.* '94 (KC)[J] Conception, MO Conception Abbey.
Caveglia, Patrick *o.s.b.* '94 (KC)[N] Conception, MO The Pontifical Institute of Liturgy Foundation.
Cavell, Lawrence Arthur '89 (HT) Administrative Leave.
Cavellier, Richard '79 (DET) Clinton Twp., MI St. Valerie of Ravenna; Defenders of Bond.
Caverly, J. Bernard '65 (SP) St. Petersburg, FL St. Raphael; Ecumenical and Inter–Religious Affairs; Presbyteral Council.
Caverly, Patrick J. '61 (ORL) Longwood, FL Annunciation; Vicars General; Executive Committee; Consultors; Bishop's Executive Staff.
Caverte, Rolando A. '62 (SFR) South San Francisco, CA Mater Dolorosa.
Cavey, Donald J. '76 (RIC) Hampton, VA St. Rose of Lima; Hampton, VA VA Medical Center.
Caviedes, Victor '99 (VEN) LaBelle, FL Our Lady Queen of Heaven; Hispanic, Migrant and Spanish Speaking Apostolates/National Migration Week.
Caviglia, Caesar J. (LAV) Office of Peace and Social Justice.
Caviglia, Caesar '55 (LAV) Retired.
Caviglia, Caesar (LAV) Presbyteral Council for the Diocese of Las Vegas.
Cavoto, Joseph F. *s.a.* '80 (NY) Harrison, NY St. Vincent Hospital and Medical Center of New York.
Cawley, John F. *c.m.* (CHI)[N] Chicago DePaul Vincentian Residence.
Cawley, John P. *c.m.* '65 (DAL) Dallas, TX Holy Trinity.
Cawley, Martin *o.c.s.o.* '61 (P)[L] Lafayette, OR The Cistercian (Trappist) Abbey of Our Lady of Guadalupe.
Cawley, Patrick T. '70 (GAY) St. James, MI Holy Cross.
Cawley, Patrick '70 (GR) Retired.
Cawley, Thomas *c.m.* (KCK) Shawnee, KS St. Joseph's.
Cawley, William M. '73 (GF) On Duty Outside of the Diocese; York, PA St. Patrick; [A] York, PA York Catholic High School.
Cayer, John '96 (PT) On Leave of Absence.
Cayetano, Alvin *s.o.l.t.* '95 (PHX) Chandler, AZ St. Mary's.
Caylor, Dennis J. '75 (CIN) Springfield, OH St. Joseph; Springfield, OH St. Raphael; Judges.
Cazares, Felix A. '03 (BWN) Alamo, TX Resurrection.
Cazares, Salvador A. (TUC) Tucson, AZ St. Augustine's Cathedral.
Cazayoux, Clair M. *s.j.* '62 (NO) New Orleans, LA Holy Name of Jesus.
Cazenavette, John J. *s.j.* '53 (LAF)[J] Grand Coteau, LA Jesuit Spirituality Center (St. Charles College).
Cebula, Joseph '75 (ALB) Schenectady, NY Our Lady of the Assumption.
Cebula, Richard S. *o.s.b.* '41 (SEA)[L] Lacey, WA St. Martin's Abbey.
Cebula, Thomas '68 (Y) Massillon, OH St. Barbara.
Cebulka, Peter R. *c.o.* '93 (MET)[H] Somerset, NJ The Metuchen Oratory, Congregation of the Oratory of St. Philip Neri.
Cebulka, Peter *c.o.* '93 (MET)[N] New Brunswick, NJ Catholic Center at Rutgers University.
Cebulka, Peter *c.o.* (MET) Office of Vocations.
Cecere, Michael *c.m.f.* '43 (LA)[Q] Rancho Dominguez, CA Dominguez Seminary Inc..
Cecero, John J. *s.j.* '89 (NY)[EE] New York, NY Xavier Jesuit Community.
Cecil, Bruce *c.s.c.* '92 (SB)[E] Coachella, CA Congregation of the Holy Cross.
Cecil, Bruce *c.s.c.* '92 (SB) Coachella, CA Our Lady of Soledad.
Cecil, Ivo E. '54 (L) Lebanon Junction, KY St. Benedict; Shepherdsville, KY St. Aloysius Retired.
Cecil, Patrick G. '78 (CHI) Wadsworth, IL St. Patrick.
Cedolia, Robert J. '78 (PIT) Pittsburgh, PA Our Lady of Joy; Judges; Deans and Deaneries; Clergy Personnel Board.
Cedrone, Laurence C. '48 (BO) Senior Priests Retired.
Ceglarski, Roman '45 (NEW) Newark, NJ Holy Trinity – Epiphany.
Ceja, Miguel '90 (SB) Palm Springs, CA Our Lady of Solitude.
Cejudo, Serafin '56 (GAL) Galveston, TX Queen of Peace Mission.
Celano, Freddy '87 (CGS) Yabucoa, PR Santos Angeles Cutodios.
Celano, Joseph G. '87 (MET) Bridgewater, NJ St. Bernard; Office of Vocations.
Celano, Leo J. *o.praem.* '72 (ORG)[I] Silverado, CA Norbertine Fathers of Orange Inc..
Celeste, Charles R. '80 (ALB) Little Falls, NY Holy Family.
Celia, Jose *o.carm.* '67 (JOL) Lancaster, PA St. Leo the Great.
Celiano, Alfred V. '53 (NEW)[B] School of Diplomacy and Intl. Rels. Retired.
Celichowski, John *o.f.m.cap.* '93 (MIL) Milwaukee, WI St. Benedict the Moor.
Celino, Anthony '98 (ELP) El Paso, TX Santa Lucia; Diocesan Tribunal.
Celino, Juventino (ELP) Absent on Leave.
Celio, Victor F.A. '02 (GAL) Houston, TX Holy Rosary.
Celio, Victor *o.p.* '02 (DAL) Dallas, TX St. Jude Chapel and Information Center; [K] Irving, TX Dominican Priory of St. Albert the Great.
Cell, Robert *m.s.c.* '47 (ALN)[A] Center Valley, PA Sacred Heart Villa, Missionaries of the Sacred Heart.
Cella, John *o.f.m.* '78 (MIL)[X] Franklin, WI Franciscan Pilgrimage Programs, Inc.; [O] Provincial Offices; [B] Judges for Second Instance.
Cellini, Ronald R. '79 (PIT) Beaufort, SC St. Peter's; [H] Beaufort, SC University of South Carolina, Beaufort Extension; On Duty Outside the Diocese.
Cellini, Ronald R. (CHR) Evangelization, Catechesis & Christian Initiation.
Cellucci, Carl D. '53 (PH) Retired.
Celso, Thomas B. '79 (ROC) Unassigned.
Celuch, Martin '03 (Y) Struthers, OH St. Nicholas.
Cembor, Thomas M. '79 (NEW) Irvington, NJ St. Leo's.
Cencula, Leonard T. '63 (STU) Steubenville, OH St. Pius X.
Cendrowicz, Basil *o.s.p.* '00 (CHI) Harwood Heights–Norridge, IL St. Rosalie.
Cenefeldt, Harry E. '54 (TR)[M] Trenton, NJ Villa Vianney Retired.
Cenkner, William *o.p.* '58 (WDC)[C] Catholic University of America, The Retired.
Centala, Theodore *o.c.d.* '65 (BO)[V] Boston, MA Carmelite Monastery.
Centner, David *o.c.d.* '71 (MIL)[O] Holy Hill, WI Discalced Carmelite Monastery – Holy Hill National Shrine of Mary Help of Christians.
Centrella, Arthur J. '54 (PH) Springfield, PA Holy Cross Retired.
Centrella, Dismas J. *o.f.m.* (BO) Boston, MA St. Leonard of Port Maurice; Advocates.
Cenzon, Carlos G. *s.j.* '99 (WDC)[M] Washington, DC Leonard Neale House.
Cepeda, Arturo (SAT) Vocation Office; Pre–Seminary Program.
Cepeda, Jose Arturo '96 (SAT) Special Assignment.
Cepeda, Ray (AGN) Archdiocesan Presbyteral Council.
Cepeda, Ray (AGN) Archdiocesan College of Consultors.
Cepeda, Raymond F. '79 (AGN) Dededo, GU Santa Barbara; Associate Judges.
Ceperley, Eugene F. '55 (SC) Retired.
Cera, James B. '64 (MIL) Kansasville, WI St. Mary–Dover.
Cera, Raymond *c.pp.s.* '46 (CIN)[B] Carthagena, OH St. Charles.
Cerank, Gerald A. '72 (OG) Mooers Forks, NY St. Joseph; Mooers Forks, NY St. Ann.
Ceranowski, Albert B. '64 (TOL) Oregon, OH St. Ignatius; Bishop's Education Council.
Ceranowski, Gerald L. '67 (TOL) Toledo, OH St. Joan of Arc.

Cerbin, Walter A. *s.s.j.* '55 (GAL) Houston, TX Our Mother of Mercy; Houston, TX Our Lady Star of the Sea.
Cerbone, James *s.d.b.* '80 (NY)[HH] Bronx, NY Manhattan College.
Cerbone, James *s.d.b.* '80 (NY)[EE] New Rochelle, NY Salesian Provincial House.
Cerda, Victor Manuel Prado '01 (MRY) Watsonville, CA St. Patrick.
Ceresko, Anthony R. *o.s.f.s.* '70 (TOL)[J] Salt Lake City, UT.
Cerezo, Alberto F. '60 (YAK) Retired.
Cerezo, Alfonso '43 (SB) Retired.
Ceriello, Joseph A. '78 (BRK) Queens Village, NY Incarnation.
Cerkas, John W. '70 (GB) Laona, WI St. Leonard; Laona, WI St. Norbert; Laona, WI St. Hubert.
Cermak, Michael *o.mar.* '95 (SAM)[C] Petersham, MA Most Holy Trinity Monastery.
Cernauskas, Daniel '54 (MIA) Tamarac, FL St. Malachy.
Cerniglia, Francis J. '53 (CHI) Elk Grove Village, IL Queen of the Rosary Retired.
Cernoch, Gerard '64 (VIC) Bay City, TX Our Lady of Guadalupe.
Cerny, George F. '64 (CHI) Chicago, IL St. Bartholomew.
Cerpich, Richard J. '61 (MIL) Random Lake, WI Our Lady of the Lakes; Archdiocesan Consultors.
Cerratos, Ramon *s.x.* '99 (PAT)[M] Wayne Xaverian Missionary Fathers.
Cerrito, Albert J. '51 (PRO) Retired.
Cerrone, Michael J. '81 (SAV) Military Chaplains; Army Chaplains.
Cerullo, Fritz J. *o.s.a.* '71 (MAN) Dover, NH St. Mary.
Cerulo, Thomas N. *o.ss.t.* '78 (NY) Staten Island, NY Our Lady of Mt. Carmel–St. Benedicta.
Cervantes, Fidel (ELP) Retired.
Cervantes, Joey R. '91 (MET) Flemington, NJ St. Magdalen de Pazzi.
Cervantes, Leo (RIC) Retired.
Cervantes, Lucius F. *s.j.* '46 (STL)[N] St. Louis, MO Fusz Pavilion; [O] St. Louis, MO Jesuit Community Corporation at St. Louis University – Jesuit Hall.
Cervantes, Rhenne A. '92 (NO) Mandeville, LA Our Lady of the Lake.
Cervantes, Timothy '00 (GLP) Grants, NM St. Teresa.
Cervella, Albert T. '79 (ALN)[J] Bethlehem, PA Holy Family Villa Retired.
Cervenak, Andrew '78 (TR) Retired.
Cervera, Pascual '87 (NY)[A] Yonkers, NY St. John Neumann Residence and Hall.
Cervero, Joseph '89 (BGP) New Fairfield, CT St. Edward the Confessor.
Cervini, John '68 (RVC) Priests Released from Diocesan Assignment.
Cervinski, Paul L. '61 (BIS) Minot, ND St. Therese the Little Flower; AUXILIARY CHAPLAINS CONTRACT CHAPLAINS.
Cervoni, Stephen F. '67 (CAM) Woodstown, NJ St. Joseph's.
Cerwonka, Clarence J. '61 (SY) Binghamton, NY St. Mary of the Assumption Retired.
Cesa, Dean '98 (CHL) Tryon, NC St. John the Baptist.
Cesar, Floyd '75 (ALN)[I] Easton, PA Antonian Towers.
Cesaro, Nicholas J. '54 (HRT) Hartford, CT St. Augustine.
Cesarone, Jeffrey T. *o.praem.* '94 (WIL)[J] Middletown, DE Immaculate Conception Priory of the Canons Regular of Premontre.
Cessario, Romanus *o.p.* '71 (BO)[V] Dover, MA St. Stephen Priory.
Cessario, Romanus *o.p.* '71 (BO)[A] Brighton, MA St. John Seminary School of Theology.
Cesta, James M. '74 (SY) Oswego, NY St. Joseph; Oswego, NY Oswego County Jail.
Cestare, Gerald '95 (RVC) Rockville Centre, NY St. Agnes Cathedral; Associate Vocation Directors.
Cestaro, Joseph J. '46 (NEW) Newark, NJ St. Anthony's; [N] Rutherford, NJ St. John Vianney Residence for Priests Retired.
Cestaro, Joseph '62 (BRK) Whitestone, NY St. Luke.
Cevarrubias–Pina, Salomon '91 (YAK) Wapato, WA St. Peter Claver.
Cevasco, Darrell L. *c.ss.r.* '98 (CHL) Concord, NC St. James.
Ch'e, James '54 (AGN) Tamuning, GU St. Anthony and St. Victor.
Chaanine, Georges '96 (OLL) El Paso, TX St. Anthony of the Desert Mission.
Chaback, Michael J. '70 (ALN) Bethlehem, PA SS. Cyril and Methodius; Vicars Forane.
Chaback, Michael J. '70 (ALT)[J] Hollidaysburg, PA Conference of Slovak Clergy.
Chabak, Robert M. '72 (NEW) Bloomfield, NJ St. Valentine; North Essex Deanery 16.
Chabala, Brian J. '77 (DET) Farmington Hills, MI St. Fabian.
Chabot, Peter L. *m.m.* '65 (CIN)[M] Cincinnati, OH The Catholic Foreign Mission Society of America, Inc..
Chabot, Robert *s.s.s.* '66 (SP) Holiday, FL St. Vincent De Paul.
Chabot, Roger P. '65 (PRT) Farmington, ME St. Joseph's; [M] Farmington, ME University of Maine at Farmington; Pastoral Assocs.; Personnel Board.
Chacha, Lucas '90 (PMB) Palm Beach Gardens, FL St. Patrick.
Chachlowski, Marek '82 (NEW) Linden, NJ St. Theresa of the Child Jesus.
Chackalackel, Davis *m.s.f.s.* '80 (ATL)[K] Lawrenceville The Missionaries of St. Francis De Sales.
Chackaleckel, Davis *m.s.f.s.* '80 (NSH) Dover, TN St. Francis of Assisi.
Chacko, Abraham K. '88 (SYM) Yonkers, NY Knanaya Catholic Mission of Westchester and Bronx, NY; Yonkers, NY Knanaya Catholic Mission of Rockland, NY.
Chacko, Abraham '93 (NY) Yonkers, NY Christ the King.
Chacko, Anthony '96 (SJ) San Jose, CA Five Wounds Portuguese National Church; Detention Ministry for Juveniles.
Chacko, Joseph Ampatt *c.m.i.* '77 (SHP) Shreveport, LA St. John Berchmans Cathedral.
Chacko, Joseph C. '68 (MET) U.S. Veterans Medical Center.
Chacko, Joseph C. (MO).
Chacko, Joy T. '92 (TR) Delran, NJ Holy Name.
Chacko, Matthew *c.m.i.* '84 (BRK) Brooklyn, NY St. Edmund's.
Chacko, Sebastian '76 (HON) Waianae, HI Sacred Heart.
Chacko, Sebastian (HON) Samoan Ministry.
Chacon, Frank '89 (GLP) St. Johns, AZ St. John the Baptist.
Chacon, Frank '89 (GLP) Concho, AZ San Rafael.
Chacon, Frank (GLP) Diocesan Consultors.
Chacon, Frank (GLP) Presbyteral Council.
Chacon, Gilbert *s.j.* '73 (SD) San Diego, CA Our Lady of Guadalupe.
Chacon, Jorge '74 (NEW) Elizabeth, NJ Immaculate Conception.
Chacon, William '91 (BRK) East Elmhurst, NY St. Gabriel.
Chadwick, Brian D. '01 (GRY) Auditors; Bishop's Council of Priests; On Duty Outside the Diocese.
Chadwick, John '95 (NEW) Clark, NJ St. Agnes.
Chadwick, John (NEW) Archdiocesan Theological Commission.
Chadwick, Lawrence A. '75 (RVC) Dix Hills, NY St. Matthew.
Chadwick, Matthew C. *o.f.m.conv.* '88 (PH) Milmont Park, PA Our Lady of Peace.
Chaffman, Charles J. (LA) Judicial Vicar; Judges.
Chaffman, Charles '84 (LA) Los Angeles, CA Christ the King.
Chaisson, John C. '66 (BO) Peabody, MA St. Adelaide.
Chaker, Victor '03 (NOR) Coventry, CT St. Mary.
Chakian, Joy '78 (SYM) Roseville, MI St. Thomas Indian Catholic Mission, Detroit.
Chakian, Joy '78 (DET) Roseville, MI St. Angela.
Chakkalakal, Rafael Eugene '77 (GAL) Spring, TX St. James the Apostle.
Chalackal, R. David '88 (MET) Flemington, NJ St. Magdalen de Pazzi.
Chalangady, James J. *o.c.d.* '98 (ALN) Reading, PA St. Catharine of Siena.
Chalany, Robert '52 (WH) Retired.
Chalissery, Joy (BIR) Huntsville, AL Our Lady Queen of the Universe; [H] Talladega, AL Talladega College Catholic Campus Ministry.
Chalkey, Andrew G. *o.m.i.* '56 (BEL)[E] Belleville, IL Our Lady of the Snows Apartment Community Retirement Home; [F] Belleville, IL Missionary Oblates of Mary Immaculate – St. Henry's Oblate Residence.
Challancin, James P. (MAR) Executive Board.
Challancin, James '68 (MAR) Ishpeming, MI St. Joseph; Republic, MI St. Augustine.
Challinor, Michael '91 (NY) Yonkers, NY St. Denis.
Challman, Stephen G. '96 (NY) Staten Island, NY Holy Rosary.
Chalmers, H. Edward '79 (WOR) Fitchburg, MA St. Bernard's; Diocesan College of Consultors; Deans.
Chalupa, Fred (AUS) Presbyteral Council.
Chalupa, Fred (AUS) Chancery Office.
Chalupka, Anselm *o.s.p.p.e.* '95 (BUF) Buffalo, NY Corpus Christi.
Chalupka, Anzelm *o.s.p.p.e.* '95 (PH)[AA] Office.
Chamberlain, Charles M. *o.s.f.s.* '93 (ARL) Reston, VA St. John Neumann.
Chamberlain, Francis M. *s.j.* '68 (FgM).
Chamberlain, Henry T *s.j.* '61 (CHI)[N] Chicago Chicago Province of the Society of Jesus–Provincial Office.
Chamberlain, Michael J. (DEN) Deaneries; Judges.
Chamberlain, Robert F. '57 (GI) Retired.
Chamberlain, Robert J. '64 (DM) Des Moines, IA St. Joseph's.
Chamberlain, Tom '70 (AUS) Temple, TX Our Lady of Guadalupe.
Chamberland, Gary S. *c.s.c.* '98 (FTW)[I] Washington, DC St. Anthony Parish; Washington, DC St. Anthony.
Chamberlian, Michael (DEN) Julesburg, CO St. Anthony.
Chamberlin, Gregory D. *o.s.b.* '65 (EVN) Evansville, IN St. Benedict Cathedral; Evansville, IN Holy Trinity; [K] Evansville, IN.
Chamberlin, Gregory *o.s.b.* (EVN) Diocesan Council of Priests.
Chamberlin, Mark (CC) Deans; College of Consultors; Personnel Board – Priests; Presbyteral Council; Judges; Portland, TX Our Lady of Mount Carmel.
Chambers, Francis E. '78 (PH)[AA] Villanova, PA St. Thomas Monastery.
Chambers, Frank E. *o.s.a.* '78 (PH)[C] Villanova University.
Chambers, Henry G. '65 (BO) Millis, MA St. Thomas the Apostle.
Chambers, James E. *s.j.* '55 (CHI)[D] Chicago, IL St. Ignatius Jesuit Community.
Chambers, James *s.j.* (CHI) Chicago, IL John H. Stroger, Jr. Hospital of Cook County.
Chambers, Thomas E. *c.s.c.* '61 (NO)[I] South Bend, IN Congregation of Holy Cross, Indiana Province, Provincial House; New Orleans, LA Sacred Heart of Jesus; [S] Metairie, LA Willwoods Community; [I] New Orleans, LA Sacred Heart of Jesus.
Chamblain, Joseph M. *o.s.m.* '84 (CHI)[N] Chicago Order of Friar Servants of Mary (Servites) United States of America Province, Inc..
Chamblain, Joseph *o.s.m.* '84 (STL) St. Louis, MO Seven Holy Founders.
Champagne, Michael '94 (LAF)[M] Lafayette, LA Community of Jesus Crucified.
Champagne, Michael '94 (LAF) On Special Assignment.
Champagne, Rene *c.p.* '49 (DET)[K] Detroit, MI St. Paul of the Cross Community, Congregation of the Passion.
Champagne, Robert E. *s.m.* '51 (BO) Framingham, MA Metro West Medical Center; [X] Framingham, MA The Marist House.
Champanil, Jacob *s.d.b.* (PAT) Paterson, NJ St. Anthony's.
Champigny, Richard *o.carm.* '65 (NY) Tarrytown, NY Transfiguration.
Champigny, Roger G. '60 (PRO) Warwick, RI St. Catherine.
Champigny, Thomas R. '81 (SPR) Easthampton, MA Our Lady of Good Counsel.
Champion, James D. '76 (WOR) Blackstone, MA St. Paul's.
Champlin, Joseph M. '56 (SY) Syracuse, NY The Cathedral of the Immaculate Conception.
Champlin, Michael A. *o.p.* '66 (SUP)[H] Webster, WI Thomas More Center for Preaching and Prayer, Inc..
Champlin, William E. '93 (WOR) Worcester, MA Immaculate Conception.
Champoux, Thomas C. '67 (YAK) Richland, WA Christ the King; Defenders of the Bond; Diocesan Consultors; Diocesan Coordinator for Health Affairs; St. Vincent de Paul Society.
Chan, Albert *s.j.* '47 (SFR)[M] Los Gatos, CA Sacred Heart Jesuit Center.
Chan, Albert *s.j.* '47 (SFR)[S] San Francisco, CA The Ricci Institute for Chinese–Western Cultural History at the Center for the Pacific Rim.
Chan, Paul '50 (NY)[II] New York, NY Chinese Catholic Information Center.
Chan–A–Sue, Andrew '00 (MIA) Miami Springs, FL Blessed Trinity.
Chan–Kyu, Simeon Je '50 (JOL) Darien, IL Our Lady of Korean Martyrs Mission.
Chancler, Joseph *t.o.r.* '83 (SP) Tampa, FL St. Patrick.
Chandler, Anthony L. '89 (L) Louisville, KY St. Bartholomew; Defenders of the Bond.
Chandrankunnel, Mathew '64 (NEW) Englewood, NJ Englewood Hospital & Medical Center; Englewood Hospital & Medical Center.
Chandrankunnel, Mathew '64 (NEW) Dumont, NJ St. Mary's.
Chandy, Thomas *c.m.i.* '93 (ALX) Boyce, LA St. Margaret.
Chaney, Robert E. '88 (SAV) Savannah, GA Resurrection of Our Lord; Director of African American Ministry.
Chang, Andrew Se–Myung (R) Fayetteville, NC St. Andrew Kim Chapel.
Chang, Benedict '63 (SFR) San Francisco, CA Star of the Sea.
Chang, Cornelius P. *o.s.b.* '62 (GBG)[H] Latrobe Saint Vincent Archabbey.
Chang, Jeffrey G.L. *s.j.* '99 (BAL)[S] Fu Jen University Theologate.
Chang, Jeffrey G.L. *s.j.* '99 (FgM).
Chang, John O. (TR) Red Bank, NJ St. James.
Chang, Joseph *o.s.b.* '57 (JOL)[L] Lisle, IL St. Procopius Abbey.
Chant, William S. '88 (BUR) Retired.
Chao, Joseph '61 (NY) New York, NY St. James.
Chaparro, William Cesar '92 (ARE) Vega–Baja, PR Holy Rosary.

Chapdelaine, Gerard E. *s.j.* '66 (SEA)[C] Tacoma, WA Bellarmine Preparatory School.
Chapeau, Mary Paul *o.cart.* '45 (BUR)[E] Arlington, VT Carthusian Foundation in America, Inc., Charterhouse of the Transfiguration.
Chapel, Joseph R. '92 (NEW).
Chapell, Norbert A. '48 (CHI) Retired.
Chapin, Daniel L. '72 (OG)[B] Gouverneur, NY St. James; Gouverneur, NY Gouverneur Correctional Facility.
Chapin, John G. '68 (E) Clearfield, PA St. Francis.
Chapman, Lawrence J. '77 (MIL)[D] Burlington, WI Catholic Central High School; East Troy, WI St. Peter.
Chapman, Michael A. '82 (PH) Philadelphia, PA Ascension of Our Lord.
Chapman, Michael L. '69 (OKL) Weatherford, OK St. Eugene's; [K] Weatherford, OK Southwestern Oklahoma State University.
Chapman, Robert J. '67 (PH) Narberth, PA St. Margaret.
Chappell, James T. '67 (DUB) Dubuque, IA Sacred Heart.
Chappetto, Raymond F. '71 (BRK) Floral Park, NY Our Lady of the Snows; Parish Services Corp.; Peter Turner Insurance Co..
Charboneau, Damian M. *o.s.m.* '50 (CHI)[N] Chicago, IL Assumption Priory.
Charbonneau, Damian M. *o.s.m.* '50 (CHI) Chicago, IL Assumption of the Blessed Virgin Mary.
Charbonneau, Roger L. '71 (BUR) Elected Members; Defenders of the Bond; Canon 1742 Panel of Pastors; National Shrine of the Immaculate Conception, Washington; Colchester, VT Holy Cross.
Charbonneau, William R. '73 (HRT) On Duty Outside the Archdiocese; Air Force Chaplains.
Charbonnet, Clayton '03 (NO) Metairie, LA St. Edward the Confessor.
Charest, Roger M. *s.m.m.* '42 (RVC)[M] Bay Shore, NY Montfort Missionaries.
Charipar, Henry W. '68 (DUB) Cresco, IA Notre Dame; Cresco, IA St. Bridget.
Charland, George A. '60 (WOR) East Brookfield, MA St. John the Baptist.
Charland, Paul A. '71 (PRO) Foster, RI St. Paul the Apostle.
Charlebois, John J. '54 (GRY) Retired.
Charlebois, Robert L. '57 (GRY) Retired.
Charles, Jean Gabriel (BO) Dorchester, MA St. Matthew.
Charles, Robes C. '99 (MIA) Homestead, FL Sacred Heart.
Charlot, Lucien '61 (BRK) Kings County Hospital Center.
Charlton, Robert *ss.cc.* '88 (FR) Fairhaven, MA St. Joseph's.
Charlton, Terrence P. *s.j.* '76 (FgM).
Charm, Robert (OAK) Retired.
Charman, Eugene J. '71 (HRT) Cheshire, CT St. Thomas Becket.
Charnley, George (DET) Novi, MI St. James.
Charnoki, John J. '45 (PIT)[N] Pittsburgh, PA St. John Vianney Manor Retired.
Charnoki, William G. '65 (GBG) Indiana, PA St. Bernard; Deaneries; Judges; Bishop's Priests Council.
Charpentier, Alfred *o.m.i.* '71 (FgM).
Charters, Thomas S. *g.h.m.* '75 (OWN)[F] Hartford, KY Glenmary House.
Charthakuzhiyil, Mathew '97 (DET) Port Huron, MI St. Joseph Malankara Catholic Mission; Centerline, MI St. Clement.
Charvet, Louis *o.s.b.* '45 (P)[L] St. Benedict, OR Mt. Angel Abbey.
Chase, Charles E. '79 (OG) Retired.
Chase, Francis G. (BO) Duxbury, MA Holy Family.
Chase, Kenneth M. '84 (DET) South Lyon, MI St. Joseph.
Chase, Lee P. '93 (ROC) Rochester, NY St. Thomas More.
Chase, Martin L. *s.j.* '91 (DET)[K] Detroit Jesuit Provincial Office–Detroit Province of the Society of Jesus.
Chase, Martin *s.j.* '91 (NY)[EE] Cardinal Spellman Hall, Jesuit Community.
Chase, Maurice '53 (SD) Retired.
Chase, P. Geoffrey *o.s.b.* '59 (PRO)[P] Portsmouth, RI Abbey of St. Gregory the Great.
Chase, Raymond '78 (BAL)[L] Timonium, MD Villa Maria Treatment Center.
Chase, Raymond '78 (BAL) Baltimore, MD St. Charles Borromeo; Special Assignment.
Chase, Terrence R. '84 (GRY) Michigan City, IN Queen of All Saints.
Chassaniol, Warren F. '65 (HT) Grand Isle, LA Our Lady of the Isle.
Chasse, Joseph *s.m.* '52 (PRT) Van Buren, ME St. Joseph; Van Buren, ME St. Bruno – St. Remi.
Chasse, Lucien *s.m.* '43 (BO)[V] Boston, MA Marist Fathers of Our Lady of Victories (Boston Prov.).
Chateau, Paul F. '66 (DET) Oak Park, MI Our Lady of Fatima.
Chatigny, Donat W. *m.m.* '34 (NY).
Chau Do, Peter Quang '73 (NSH)[EE] Ashland City, TN St. Martha.
Chaupetta, Victor *m.s.* '70 (FR)[H] Attleboro, MA La Salette Shrine.
Chauvin, David M. '64 (BR) Vacherie, LA St. Philip.
Chavannes, Jacques E. '85 (PRO) Providence, RI St. Michael the Archangel.
Chavarin, Jose '79 (SFR) San Francisco, CA St. James.
Chavarin, Jose '79 (SFR) St. Thomas More Society.
Chavarin, Jose (SFR) Adjutant Judicial Vicar.
Chavarria, Horacio '66 (BWN) Harlingen, TX Our Lady of the Assumption.
Chavarria, Horacio (BWN) Presbyteral Council.
Chavarria, Jerome *c.ss.r.* '84 (ORL) Hapeville, GA St. John the Evangelist; [E] New Smyrna Beach, FL Redemptorist Fathers of the Vice Province of Richmond.
Chaverria, Juan '95 (KAL) Fennville, MI San Felipe de Jesus.
Chavez, Adolphus '56 (SB) Retired.
Chavez, Arturo '91 (SB) Retired.
Chavez, Carlos '84 (SFE) Clovis, NM Sacred Heart.
Chavez, Frank '76 (SAN) Odessa, TX Holy Redeemer.
Chavez, Gerald F. '73 (FRS) Corcoran, CA Our Lady of Lourdes.
Chavez, Gerry (FRS) Vicars Forane.
Chavez, Gerry (FRS) Personnel Committee.
Chavez, Gerry (FRS) Diocesan Consultors.
Chavez, Gerry (FRS) Priests' Council.
Chavez, Johnny Lee '76 (SFE) Albuquerque, NM Queen of Heaven.
Chavez, Johnny Lee (SFE) Army National Guard Chaplains.
Chavez, Jose *c.ss.r.* '84 (SAT)[M] San Antonio, TX Redemptorists of Texas–San Antonio #1.
Chavez, Jose '96 (MRY) Watsonville, CA St. Patrick.
Chavez, Jose '98 (GI) Kearney, NE St. James.
Chavez, Joseph (BRK) Flushing, NY St. Michael; Flushing, NY St. Michael.
Chavez, Luis Alfredo Garcia '02 (COS) Colorado Springs, CO Holy Apostles.
Chavez, Manuel Maya *o.s.m.* '58 (ORG)[I] Fullerton, CA St. Philip Benizi Priory.
Chavez, Manuel '96 (SR) Windsor, CA Our Lady of Guadalupe.
Chavez, Manuel (SR) Clergy Personnel Committee.
Chavez, Patrick J. '68 (SFE) El Rito, NM San Juan Nepomuceno.
Chavez, Phillip '93 (CC)[G] Robstown, TX Society of Our Lady of the Most Holy Trinity.
Chavez, Ricardo A. '63 (OAK) Pittsburg, CA St. Peter Martyr of Verona.
Chavez, Scott '97 (OAK) Fremont, CA Our Lady of Guadalupe.
Chavez, Vincent P. '91 (SFE) Las Vegas, NM Immaculate Conception.
Chavez, Vincent (SFE) LAS VEGAS: Newman Center.
Chavez, Walter Scott '97 (OAK) Castro Valley, CA Transfiguration.
Chavez–Vasquez, Raymundo (TYL) Nacogdoches, TX Our Lady of Guadalupe.
Cheah, Joseph M. *o.s.m.* '92 (CHI)[N] Chicago Order of Friar Servants of Mary (Servites) United States of America Province, Inc..
Cheatham, Louis W. '45 (GBG)[G] Greensburg, PA Neumann House Retired.
Checchia, Joseph *c.ss.r.* '63 (CGS) Fajardo, PR Santiago Apostol.
Checchio, James F. '92 (CAM) On Duty Outside the Diocese.
Check, Paul N. '97 (BGP) Stamford, CT St. John the Evangelist.
Checon, Amarilho *s.j.* (NY) Mt. Vernon, NY Our Lady of Victory.
Cheerakathil, Augustine *m.s.* '88 (HON) Honolulu, HI St. Anthony.
Cheerakathil, Augustine (HON) Oahu.
Cheeramkuzhy, Matthew '75 (NSH) Loretto, TN Sacred Heart; [K] Liberty, TN Carmel Center of Spirituality.
Cheeramkuzhy, Matthew *c.m.i.* '78 (NSH) Loretto, TN St. Joseph.
Cheeran, Kuriakose *c.m.i.* '84 (PH) Philadelphia, PA St. Anne.
Cheeran, Kuriakose *c.m.i.* (PH) Apostleship of the Sea.
Cheesman, Robert *c.ss.r.* '57 (BRK)[C] Whitestone, NY St. Alphonsus Formation Residence.
Cheetham, William J. '46 (PIT) Retired
Chelat, Sebastian '74 (CAM) Gibbsboro, NJ St. Andrew the Apostle.
Chelena, Thomas '68 (PRM) Absent on Leave.
Chelich, James A. '76 (GR) Grand Rapids, MI St. Thomas the Apostle.
Cheline, Paschal *o.s.b.* '64 (P)[L] St. Benedict, OR Mt. Angel Abbey.
Chellaian, Lawrence '92 (TYL) New Boston, TX St. Mary of the Cenacle; New Boston, TX Telford Unit, Texas Department of Corrections.
Chemazar, Blase *o.f.m.* '53 (CHI)[T] Lemont, IL St. Mary's Retreat House.
Chemazar, Blase *o.f.m.* '53 (CHI)[N] Lemont, IL The Slovene Franciscan Fathers, Order of Friars Minor, Commissariat of the Holy Cross.
Chembakassery, Vincent Lazar '80 (BIR) Scottsboro, AL St. Jude.
Chembakassery, Vincent '94 (BIR) Florence, AL St. Joseph's.
Chemino, Stephen Scott '93 (ALX) Priests Council; Ecumenical; Nachitoches, LA Immaculate Conception; Promoters of Justice; Administrator and Assessor.
Chen, Anthony K. '52 (CHI) Retired.
Chen, Peter '98 (DAL) Richardson, TX Mission of the Sacred Heart of Jesus.
Chen, Raphael '52 (AMA) Retired.
Chen, Vincent P. '57 (MET) Phillipsburg, NJ St. Philip & St. James; Phillipsburg, NJ Warren Hospital; Chinese Apostolate.
Cheney, Craig '03 (MAN) North Stratford, NH Sacred Heart.
Cheney, Craig '03 (MAN) Beecher Falls, VT St. Albert.
Cheney, Craig '03 (MAN) Groveton, NH St. Francis Xavier; Coos County House of Corrections.
Cheney, Craig (BUR) Beecher Falls, VT Assumption of the Blessed Virgin Mary.
Cheney, Edward K. *s.j.* '42 (BO)[V] Weston, MA Campion Health Center, Inc..
Cheney, James W. '95 (FAR) Cooperstown, ND Sacred Heart; Navy Reserve Chaplains.
Cheney, James '95 (FAR) Cooperstown, ND St. George.
Cheney, Jesse C. '43 (LR)[H] Little Rock, AR St. John Manor Retired.
Cheng, Joseph *s.d.b.* '59 (LA) Los Angeles, CA St. Bridget's Chinese Catholic Center.
Cheng, Joseph *s.d.b.* '59 (LA)[Q] Los Angeles, CA Dominic Savio Salesian Residence.
Cheng, Joseph '03 (NEW) Hackensack, NJ Holy Trinity.
Cheng, Thomas (BRK) Vice Officiales–Associate Judicial Vicars.
Chenot, Paul *c.p.* '51 (BRK)[V] Jamaica, NY Immaculate Conception Monastery.
Chenot, Paul *c.p.* '51 (BRK) Creedmoor Psychiatric Center.
Cheny, James '95 (FAR) Cooperstown, ND St. Lawrence.
Cheon, Houng Sik '01 (FRS) Kerman, CA St. Patrick.
Chepaitis, Peter S. *o.f.m.* '72 (NY)[EE] Middleburgh, NY Bethany Ministries.
Chepanis, Anthony J. '48 (PMB) Highland Beach, FL St. Lucy Retired.
Cheplic, Peter '72 (NEW) Bayonne, NJ St. Henry's.
Chepponis, James J. '85 (PIT) Pittsburgh, PA St. John Capistran; Music, Office for.
Cheramie, Lonnie James (HT) Thibodaux, LA St. Joseph Co–Cathedral.
Cheri, Fernand *o.f.m.* (BEL)[F] East St. Louis, IL St. Benedict the Black Friary.
Cherian, Thomas Kottayil '68 (DAL) Garland, TX St. Mary Malankara.
Chermeil, Tony '91 (VEN) Naples, FL St. Peter the Apostle.
Chermeil, Tony (VEN) Ministry to Haitian People in Collier County.
Chern, James N. '99 (NEW) West Orange, NJ Our Lady of Lourdes.
Cherolikal, John '74 (LUB) Anson, TX St. Michael's; Vicars Forane.
Cherry, Athanasius C. *o.s.b.* '68 (GBG)[H] Latrobe, PA Saint Vincent Archabbey.
Cherry, Richard W. *s.j.* '69 (FgM).
Cherubini, Perry A. '85 (CAM) Bellmawr, NJ Annunciation; Margate, NJ Blessed Sacrament.
Cherukarakunnel, Alexander J. '63 (HRT) North Haven, CT St. Therese.
Cherup, Michael A. (PT) Youth Ministry, Office of.
Cherup, Michael '81 (PT) Fort Walton Beach, FL St. Mary.
Cherup, Michael (PT) Clergy Concerns.
Cherup, Michael (PT) College of Consultors.
Cherup, Michael (PT) Administrative Council.
Cheruparambil, Francis '82 (TR) Keyport, NJ Holy Family.
Chervenak, Gregory *o.f.m.cap.* (WH)[M] Wheeling, WV Capuchin Hermitage of St. Joseph.
Chervenak, Stephen M. '60 (PIT) White Oak, PA St. Angela; Deans and Deaneries.
Chesebrough, Charles S. '67 (IND) Bloomington, IN St. Charles Borromeo; Deaneries and Deans; French Lick, IN Our Lady of the Springs; Paoli, IN Our Lord Jesus Christ the King.
Chesney, Michael *s.j.* '91 (DAL)[D] Dallas, TX Jesuit College Preparatory School.
Chethipuzha, Varghese I. '69 (NY) New City, NY St. Augustine.
Chetock, James J. '93 (WH) Vienna, WV St. Michael's.
Chetwynde, Clyde H. '80 (BO) Townsend, MA St. John.
Chevalier, Martin '83 (DM) Leave of Absence.
Chevalier, Thomas H. '80 (ALB) Albany, NY St. Margaret Mary.

Chevalier, Thomas (ALB) Diocesan Board of Consultors.
Chevalier, Thomas (ALB) Presbyteral Council.
Chevedden, James N. *s.j.* '78 (SJ)[M] Los Gatos, CA Sacred Heart Jesuit Center.
Cheveney, Anthony *s.s.p.* '58 (DET)[K] Dearborn, MI Society of St. Paul.
Chew, Randolph G. '71 (PRO) Cranston, RI St. Paul; Deans; College of Consultors.
Chewning, Seraphim John '93 (PBR) Retired.
Chia, Luis P. '59 (GAL) Houston, TX St. Rose of Lima.
Chiang, John B. '53 (NY) Retired.
Chiang, Joseph '59 (NEW)[N] Rutherford, NJ St. John Vianney Residence for Priests Retired.
Chiang, Joseph (NEW) Chinese Apostolate.
Chiara, Peter A. '48 (RVC) East Islip, NY St. Mary's Retired.
Chiaramonte, Anthony J. (ALB) Office.
Chiaramonte, Anthony '65 (ALB) Special Assignment.
Chiaravalle, Dominic M. '65 (PH) Philadelphia, PA Epiphany of Our Lord.
Chiarilli, Patrick S. '61 (CAM) Retired.
Chichetto, James W. *c.s.c.* '68 (FR)[A] North Easton, MA Stonehill College; [A] North Easton, MA Holy Cross Fathers Religious.
Chidiac, Bakhos '91 (OLL) Wheeling, WV Our Lady of Lebanon.
Chidili, Bartholomew *o.s.a.* '80 (BRK) Brooklyn, NY Holy Family.
Chidozie, Marcus '93 (DAL) Garland, TX St. Michael the Archangel.
Chieffo, Ralph J. '75 (PH) Media, PA St. Mary Magdalen; Diocesan Priests' Compensation and Benefits Committee.
Chiesa, Robert E. (FgM).
Chiew, Charles '90 (NY) Bronx, NY St. Raymond.
Chiezey, Daniel *o.p.* '76 (SEA) Mount Vernon, WA Immaculate Conception.
Chiezey, Daniel *o.p.* '76 (SEA) Sedro Woolley, WA Immaculate Heart of Mary.
Chiezey, Daniel *o.p.* '76 (SEA) LaConner, WA Sacred Heart; Burlington, WA St. Charles.
Chiffriller, Edward J. *s.s.j.* '74 (BAL)[S] Baltimore, MD St. Joseph Society of the Sacred Heart House of Central Administration; [V] Baltimore, MD St. Joseph Manor Foundation, Inc.; [V] Baltimore, MD The Josephite Retirement and Disability Benefits Trusts.
Chiffriller, Edward J. *s.s.j.* (BAL)[V] Baltimore, MD St. Josephite Seminarian Education Trust.
Chihak, John P. '36 (DUB) Retired.
Chikawe, Hugh '71 (SP) Indian Rocks Beach, FL St. Jerome.
Chikezie, Emmanuel '92 (FTW) Fort Wayne, IN St. Henry; Fort Wayne, IN Sacred Heart.
Chilagorom, Desmond '79 (BAK) Condon, OR St. Francis; Condon, OR St. John's.
Child, John F. '59 (DET) Dearborn, MI Sacred Heart Retired.
Childs, G. Anthony (ALB) Albany, NY Blessed Sacrament.
Chilen, Michael D. '69 (CC) Military Chaplains.
Chilen, Michael D. (CC) Army Chaplains.
Chiles, Richard P. *o.praem.* '87 (JKS) Jackson, MS St. Mary; Jackson, MS Christ the King; [F] Jackson, MS Priory of St. Moses the Black; [I] Jackson, MS Jackson State University Newman Center.
Chilinda, Charles *s.j.* '01 (LA)[C] Los Angeles, CA Jesuit Community.
Chillog, Thomas A. '84 (STU) St. Clairsville, OH St. Mary's; [J] St. Clairsville, OH Ohio University – Eastern; Episcopal Vicar for Pastoral Planning & Personnel; Auditors; Defenders of the Bond; Pastoral Staff; Presbyteral Council; College of Consultors; Priests Personnel Board; Health Panel of the Clergy; Vicar for Priests.
Chilmark, Richard '60 (NEW) Livingston, NJ St. Barnabas Medical Center; Chaplains.
Chilson, Elbert '78 (DEN) Aurora, CO St. Therese.
Chilson, Richard *c.s.p.* '72 (STP) Minneapolis, MN St. Lawrence–Newman.
Chilson, Richard *c.s.p.* '72 (STP)[M] Minneapolis, MN Paulist Fathers.
Chimera, Angelo M. '69 (BUF) Buffalo, NY The Nativity of the Blessed Virgin.
Chimiak, Karl A. '80 (WDC) Newburg, MD Holy Ghost; Air Force Reserve Chaplains.
Chin, Bertram *c.p.* '91 (FgM).
Chin, Donald J. *o.f.m.* '67 (FgM).
Chin–SuSin, Columbano '98 (PHX) Scottsdale, AZ Korean Catholic Community.
Chinchar, Gerald T. *s.m.* '82 (CIN)[D] Dayton, OH The University of Dayton; [M] Dayton, OH Marianist Community; [Q] Dayton, OH University of Dayton Campus Ministry.
Chinchilla, Ricardo *c.j.m.* '93 (SD)[L] San Diego, CA Newman Center – SDSU.
Ching, Herbert '47 (HON) Retired.
Chinh, Michael Do Quang *c.m.c.* (BO)[E] Carthage, MO Congregation of the Mother Coredemptrix, United States Assumption Province.
Chinh, Peter '50 (ORG) Retired.
Chinnabathini, Gnana Prakash '95 (CC) Refugio, TX Our Lady of Refuge.
Chinnappa, Ambrose (TYL) Daingerfield, TX Our Lady of Fatima.
Chinnici, Joseph P. *o.f.m.* '72 (OAK)[A] Berkeley, CA Franciscan School of Theology; [N] Berkeley, CA Franciscan Friars.
Chiodini, Jasper J. '42 (STL) Retired.
Chiodo, Frank E. '76 (OM) Omaha, NE St. Thomas More.
Chiodo, Frank '76 (DM) On Duty Outside the Diocese.
Chiodo, Peter *c.pp.s.* '60 (CIN)[M] Ludlow Falls, OH.
Chiola, Richard L. '72 (SFD) Ashland, IL St. Augustine.
Chioso, James *s.d.b.* '49 (NY)[GG] Stony Point, NY Marian Shrine.
Chiosso, James *s.d.b.* '49 (NY)[GG] Stony Point, NY Don Bosco Retreat Center and Marian Shrine.
Chirapurathel, J. Felix '72 (TYL) Mineola, TX St. Peter the Apostle.
Chirayath, Chummar *o.s.j.* '78 (FRS) Bakersfield, CA Our Lady of Guadalupe.
Chirayath, Joseph Vadake '75 (TLS) Henryetta, OK St. Michael.
Chirayath, Koshy George '80 (NY) New York, NY Our Saviour.
Chircop, Manuel J. *c.s.b.* '72 (DET) Detroit, MI Ste. Anne.
Chirdon, Howard *c.p.* '50 (ALT)[J] Bedford, PA St. Mary's House of Greater Solitude.
Chiriaco, William J. '86 (PH) Jenkintown, PA Immaculate Conception; [D] Wyncote, PA Bishop McDevitt High School.
Chirichiello, Richard *o.s.b.* '95 (WH) Nitro, WV Holy Trinity.
Chirichiello, Richard *o.s.b.* '95 (WH) Nitro, WV Christ the King.
Chirico, Peter *s.s.* '56 (SEA) Retired.
Chirovsky, John '90 (SJP) Miami, FL Assumption of B.V.M..
Chisholm, Gregory C. *s.j.* '93 (LA)[V] Boston The Society of Jesus of New England–Provincial Offices; Los Angeles, CA Holy Name of Jesus.
Chisholm, Thomas *o.s.b.* '89 (JOL)[L] Lisle, IL St. Procopius Abbey.
Chiusano, Louis *o.f.m.cap.* '57 (FgM).
Chizmar, John G. '75 (ALN) Jim Thorpe, PA Immaculate Conception; Vicars Forane.
Chladek, Melchior *o.cist.* '55 (DAL)[K] Irving, TX Cistercian Abbey of Our Lady of Dallas.
Chlebo, John C. '80 (CLV) Rocky River, OH St. Christopher.
Chleborad, Gerald F. (CHY) Judges; Building Committee; Ecumenism Commission; Liturgical Commission.
Chleborad, Gerald '60 (CHY) Saratoga, WY St. Ann's.
Chlopecki, Robert J. '74 (BEL) Leave of Absence.
Chludzinski, Andrzej *o.f.m.cap.* (CHI) Chicago, IL St. Priscilla.
Chmiel, Bronislaus '69 (CHI) Chicago, IL St. Pancratius.
Chmiel, Gerald J. '70 (TOL) Fremont, OH St. Ann; Building Commission.
Chmielewski, Francis J. '73 (BUF) Buffalo, NY St. Bernard.
Chmielewski, Philip J. *s.j.* '81 (CHI)[N] Chicago Chicago Province of the Society of Jesus–Provincial Office; [C] Los Angeles, CA Jesuit Community.
Chmil, John J. '95 (SCR) Scranton, PA St. Lucy's.
Chmura, Gary D. '78 (CLV) Cleveland, OH Our Lady of Peace.
Chmura, Gary '78 (CLV) Northfield, OH Northcoast Behavioral Healthcare System South.
Chmura, Gary '78 (CLV) Northcoast Behavioral Healthcare System North Campus.
Chmura, Julian '64 (DET) Detroit, MI St. Andrew.
Chmura, Stanislaus '70 (RIC) Retired.
Chmurski, Marek (FR) West Harwich, MA Holy Trinity.
Cho, Jung–Rae '91 (NO) Metairie, LA Hanmaum Korean Catholic Chapel.
Cho, MinHyun '99 (NEW) Hohokus, NJ St. Luke's.
Cho, Paul P. '66 (RIC) Richmond, VA St. Kim Taegon.
Choate, Lawrence M. *o.s.m.* '78 (CHI)[N] Chicago, IL Monastery of Our Lady of Sorrows.
Choby, David R. '74 (NSH) Gallatin, TN St. John Vianney; Deans; Judges; Diocesan Finance Board.
Choc, Pedro *o.s.b.* '90 (SFS)[F] Marvin, SD Blue Cloud Abbey.
Chocarro, Antonio (CGS) Retired.
Chochol, Ronald '64 (STL) St. Louis, MO St. Stephen, Protomartyr.
Chodacki, Jeremy *o.f.m.conv.* '29 (SPR) Chicopee, MA St. Stanislaus Basilica.
Chodacki, Jeremy *o.f.m.conv.* '29 (BAL)[S] Holyoke, MA Sisters of Providence Infirmary Retired.
Chodakowski, Ireneusz *m.i.c.* '78 (PRT) Portland, ME St. Louis.
Chodakowski, Ireneusz *m.i.c.* '78 (PRT).
Choi, Mark '94 (LA)[I] Paramount, CA Catholic Korean Community of St. Raphael.
Choi, Youngmin *s.j.* '00 (SFR) Los Angeles, CA St. Agnes.
Choiniere, John Marie *o.mar.* '95 (SAM)[C] Petersham, MA Most Holy Trinity Monastery.
Chojnacki, Anthony (MIL)[O] Burlington, WI Queen of Peace Friary.
Chojnacki, Gerald J. *s.j.* '73 (NY)[EE] New York, NY Jesuit Provincial's Office.
Chojnacki, Gerald J. *s.j.* '73 (FgM).
Cholette, John B. '36 (NY) Retired.
Choma, James A. '86 (NEW) Clark, NJ St. Agnes.
Chomko, Stephen '46 (PHU) Berwick, PA SS. Cyril and Methodius.
Chomko, Stephen '46 (STF) Retired.
Chomko, Stephen (PHU) Protopresbyters (Deans).
Chong, Young–Ku (MO) AUXILIARY CHAPLAINS CONTRACT CHAPLAINS.
Chonko, Michael J. '43 (Y) Retired.
Chontos, Joseph '82 (KCK) Special Assignment.
Choo, Paul '03 (CLV) Brecksville, OH St. Basil the Great.
Choo, Thomas *ss.cc.* '69 (HON) Honolulu, HI St. Augustine.
Choo, Thomas *ss.cc.* (HON) Holy Name Society, Diocesan Union of the.
Choong, Norbert '84 (AMA) Retired.
Choorackunnel, John V. *c.m.i.* '64 (TLS)[E] Tulsa, OK Saint Francis Hospital.
Chooshukunnel, Kurian Stephen *o.s.h.* '94 (GAL) Houston, TX Prince of Peace.
Choozhukunnel, Kurian Stephen *o.s.h.* '94 (GAL)[Q] Spring, TX The Society of the Oblates of Sacred Heart.
Choppesky, John C. *s.j.* '44 (STL)[N] St. Louis, MO Fusz Pavilion; [O] St. Louis, MO Jesuit Community Corporation at St. Louis University – Jesuit Hall.
Choquet, Alexei H. '83 (CHL) Absent On Leave.
Choquette, David P. '98 (NOR) Norwich, CT St. Patrick Cathedral; Gales Ferry, CT Our Lady of Lourdes.
Choquette, David (NOR) Liturgical Commission.
Chorey, Robert '02 (RNO) Carson City, NV St. Teresa of Avila.
Chorikavunkal, Joseph Augustine '75 (LUB) Muleshoe, TX Immaculate Conception; Presbyteral Council.
Chornyak, Joseph I. '53 (PBR) Retired.
Chorpenning, Joseph F. *o.s.f.s.* '79 (PH)[C] Jesuit Fathers; [AA] Wyndmoor, PA Villa de Sales Oblate Residence; [AA] Wyndmoor, PA Oblates of St. Francis de Sales (O.S.F.S.).
Chortos, Donald '66 (PIT) Bridgeville, PA St. Barbara.
Chortos, George F. '66 (PIT) Pittsburgh, PA Our Lady of Loreto; Allegheny County, PA Allegheny County Jail.
Chotin, Joseph L. '64 (NO) Mandeville, LA Our Lady of the Lake.
Chouinard, Lionel G. '65 (PRT) Lisbon Falls, ME Holy Trinity; Clergy Benefit Plan–Clergy Pension Plan.
Chouinard, Marcel G. '56 (PRT) Retired.
Chouinard, Marcel '56 (PRT)[G] Waterville, ME Mt. St. Joseph Holistic Care Community.
Choutapalli, Joseph '74 (SAN) San Angelo, TX St. Margaret; Eldorado, TX Our Lady of Guadalupe.
Chovanec, Paul R. '72 (GAL) Houston, TX St. Christopher.
Chovanec, Paul (GAL) Central Vicariate.
Chow, Louis Y. '89 (HRT) Medical Leave.
Chow, Luke L. '54 (PH) Philadelphia, PA St. Philip Neri Retired.
Chow, Stephen *s.j.* '94 (BO)[V] Cambridge, MA Faber House.
Chow, Stephen *s.j.* '94 (BO)[V] Cambridge, MA Faber House.
Chowning, Daniel *o.c.d.* '88 (CHI)[N] Chicago, IL Discalced Carmelite Friars; Edith Stein House of Studies.
Chowning, Michael *o.f.m.* '68 (LEX)[K] Hazard, KY Father Farrell Spiritual Life Center.
Chowning, Michael *o.f.m.* '68 (LEX) Jackson, KY Holy Cross.
Chowning, Michael *o.f.m.* '68 (LEX) Hazard, KY Mother of Good Counsel.
Chowning, Michael *o.f.m.* (LEX) Mountain East.
Chowning, Michael *o.f.m.* (LEX) Diocesan Consultors.
Chretien, Richard L. '67 (FR) Fall River, MA Notre Dame de Lourdes; Fall River, MA Our Lady of the Immaculate Conception.
Christ, John P. *o.s.c.* '65 (DET)[K] Riverview, MI Crosier Community of Riverview; Royal Oak, MI St. Dennis.
Christ, Raymond J. *o.s.f.s.* '51 (PH)[AA] Wyndmoor, PA Villa de Sales Oblate Residence.
Christancho, Jorge H. '78 (ATL) Released from Archdiocesan Assignment.
Christensen, Brian Patrick '99 (RC) Rapid City, SD St. Therese the Little Flower.
Christensen, Brian (RC) Vocation Program.
Christensen, Christian *i.sch.* '71 (CC)[I] Corpus Christi, TX Secular Institute of the Schoenstatt Fathers aka Schoenstatt Fathers.
Christensen, Christian *c.c.* '71 (MIL).
Christensen, Donald L. '59 (SAG)[S] Saginaw, MI St. Andrew.
Christensen, Lawrence P. *c.m.* '84 (DEN) Fort Collins, CO St. Elizabeth Ann Seton.

Christensen, Michael R. '79 (LIN) Lincoln, NE St. Peter.
Christensen, Peter '85 (STP) St. Paul, MN The Nativity of Our Lord.
Christian, George G. *o.p.* '55 (L) Louisville, KY St. Louis Bertrand.
Christian, John S. '84 (TR) Leave of Absence.
Christian, Lawrence '83 (SAT)[A] San Antonio, TX Assumption Seminary aka Assumption–St. John's Seminary; Priests Personnel Board.
Christian, Robert *o.p.* '76 (OAK)[N] Oakland Western Dominican Province.
Christiana, Michael S. *s.j.* (IND)[D] Indianapolis, IN.
Christiansen, Andrew J. *s.j.* '72 (NY)[EE] New York, NY "America;" Residence and publication office of the America Press.
Christie, Frank M. *o.s.m.* '56 (CHI)[N] Chicago Order of Friar Servants of Mary (Servites) United States of America Province, Inc..
Christman, Bernard E. '59 (OG) Lyon Mountain, NY St. Bernard; Lyon Mountain, NY Lyon Mountain Correctional Facility; Judges.
Christman, Ralph *m.m.* '56 (HON)[G] Honolulu, HI Maryknoll Fathers House (M.M.).
Christman, Robert '79 (MIA) Absent on Leave.
Christofferson, Kevin '97 (HEL) Frenchtown, MT St. John the Baptist.
Christopher, Charles A. *c.s.b.* '60 (GAL)[Q] Houston, TX Dillon House.
Christopher, Mark '57 (PMB) Fort Pierce, FL St. Anastasia.
Christopher, Mark '57 (PMB) Retired.
Christopher, Mark '62 (ORL) Sanford, FL All Souls.
Christopher, Patrick J. (STL).
Christopher, Patrick '91 (STL) Hazelwood, MO St. Martin de Porres.
Christudasl, Velanmarukudiyil *o.s.b.* '86 (TR) Brick, NJ Visitation.
Christy, Jacob '90 (SYM) Jenkintown, PA St. Thomas Catholic Mission; Jenkintown, PA Immaculate Conception.
Christy, Jacob (PH) Indian Apostolate, Syro Malabar Rite.
Christy, Timothy '92 (MET) Flemington, NJ St. Magdalen de Pazzi.
Christy, William H. *c.s.sp.* '92 (FgM).
Chriszt, Dennis *c.pp.s.* '82 (CIN)[M] Chicago, IL.
Chrobak, Lyle *o.f.m.* '62 (FgM).
Chrobak, Lyle *o.f.m.* '62 (GB).
Chrobot, Leonard F. '64 (FTW)[I] South Bend, IN St. Hedwig.
Chrobot, Leonard '64 (FTW) South Bend, IN St. Patrick.
Chruma, Francis '57 (AUS)[G] Jonestown, TX Hermitage.
Chrusciel, Bogumil '68 (NEW) Newark, NJ St. Stanislaus.
Chrysostom, Francis X. '60 (LA)[J] Inglewood, CA Daniel Freeman Memorial Hospital.
Chryst, Robert D. '68 (SY) Syracuse, NY St. Anthony of Padua; Special Assignment; Spanish Apostolate.
Chrzan, John P. '03 (CHI) Arlington Heights, IL St. James.
Chu, Bernard M.C. *s.j.* '60 (OAK)[S] Berkeley, CA Inter–Friendship House Association, Friendship Center.
Chu, Joseph Ly Quy '02 (DM) Des Moines, IA St. Ambrose Cathedral.
Chu, Peter Ngoc Thanh (GAL) Retired.
Chu, Peter '55 (GAL)[N] Houston, TX Pope John Paul XXIII Priests' Residence Retired.
Chu, Peter *s.j.* '68 (LA)[Q] Los Angeles, CA Columbiere House.
Chu, Quang '91 (ORG) Garden Grove, CA St. Columban.
Chua, Freddie T. '98 (LA) Rancho Palos Verdes, CA St. John Fisher.
Chua, Freddie (LA) Personnel Board of the Archdiocese.
Chubirko, Michael *s.d.b.* '60 (PSC) Elizabeth, NJ SS. Peter and Paul.
Chudy, Carl *s.x.* '86 (PAT)[M] Wayne Xaverian Missionary Fathers.
Chudy, Carl *s.x.* '86 (FgM).
Chueca, Ubaldo A. *s.d.b.* '66 (LA) San Francisco, CA Corpus Christi.
Chukwu, Christopher '80 (MAN) Dartmouth–Hitchcock Medical Center.
Chukwu, Christopher *c.s.sp.* '93 (ARE) Sabana Hoyos, PR Inmaculado Corazon de Maria; [M] New Braunfels, TX Congregation of the Holy Ghost.
Chukwu, Donatus '93 (CHI) Chicago, IL St. Gregory.
Chukwu, Donatus (CHI)[J] Chicago, IL St. Anthony Hospital.
Chukwu, Robert M. (MO).
Chukwu, Robert '78 (CLV) Cleveland, OH Veterans Administration Hospitals, Brecksville V.A..
Chukwu, Robert *c.l.v.* '78 (SAT) San Antonio, TX Audie Murphy VA Hospital.
Chukwuleta, Daniel '91 (FTW) Fort Wayne, IN St. Joseph Medical Center.
Chun, Francis '63 (P)[M] Beaverton, OR St. Mary of the Valley Convent Retired.
Chun, Glen *s.j.* '98 (CIN)[M] Cincinnati, OH Jesuit Community at Xavier University.
Chung, Alex '88 (LA) Los Angeles, CA St. Gregory Nazianzen.
Chung, Alex (LA) Personnel Board of the Archdiocese.
Chung, Anthony '71 (SFR) Retired.
Chung, Brian Gabriel (LA) Redondo Beach, CA St. Lawrence Martyr.
Chung, Francis *s.j.* '93 (AUS) Austin, TX St Andrew Kim Taegon Korean Catholic Church.
Chuong, Joseph Doan Huy '77 (GAL)[Q] New Caney, TX Congregation of the Mother Coredemptrix.
Chuong, Matthias *c.m.c.* (STP) Ministry to Vietnamese.
Chura, Andrew '58 (PBR) Toronto, OH St. Joseph.
Chura, Andrew (PBR) Elected Deanery Representatives.
Church, James F. (SAC) Priests' Diocesan Aid Society.
Church, James '58 (SAC) Sacramento, CA St. Charles Borromeo.
Church, James (SAC) Council of Priests.
Church, James (SAC) Propagation of the Faith.
Church, James (SAC) College of Consultors.
Church, Timothy A. '95 (DAL)[N] Allen, TX St. Jude Parish Building Trust; Allen, TX St. Jude.
Church, Wenceslaus '59 (CHI)[N] Chicago, IL St. Peter's Friary.
Churchwell, Stephen T. '76 (ATL)[N] Dahlonega, GA; Clergy Retirement.
Churchwell, Stephen T. '76 (ATL) Dahlonega, GA St. Luke Catholic; Judges.
Chwalek, John '48 (SPR) Retired.
Chwalek, Kazimierz *m.i.c.* '87 (SPR)[I] Eucharistic Apostles of The Divine Mercy.
Chwalek, Kazimierz *m.i.c.* '87 (SPR)[I] Provincial Office.
Chwalinski, Stanley R. '67 (BUF) Attica, NY St. Vincent de Paul.
Chwaliszewski, Roman *o.f.m.conv.* '60 (FR New Bedford, MA Our Lady of Perpetual Help.
Chwieroth, Edward J. '50 (PH) Retired.
Chycinski, Gregory A. '71 (MIL) Milwaukee, WI Our Lady of Sorrows.
Chylewski, Anthony '52 (SD) Retired.
Chylko, Gerard *c.ss.r.* '79 (BAL) Baltimore, MD Our Lady of Fatima.
Chylko, Gerard *c.ss.r.* '79 (BAL) Baltimore, MD Our Lady of Fatima.
Ciaiola, Joseph A. '47 (E) Farrell, PA Our Lady of Fatima Retired.
Cialone, Donald F. '75 (NEW) Westfield, NJ Holy Trinity.
Ciambelli, Blase A. '64 (WOR) On Special or Other Diocesan Assignment.
Ciampaglio, Joseph A. (PAT) Diocesan Council of Catholic Women.
Ciampaglio Joseph M. (PAT) Retired.
Ciancimino David S. *s.j.* '88 (NY)[F] New York, NY Xavier High School.
Ciandella, Roch *o.f.m.* '72 (NY)[GG] Wappingers Falls, NY Mt. Alvernia Retreat House.
Ciani, Francis P. '39 (ALB) Retired.
Ciano, Ken '95 (IND) Seelyville, IN Holy Rosary.
Ciappi, Angel (SJN) Legion of Mary.
Ciappi–Azcorra, Angel '98 (SJN) San Juan, PR Francisca Javiera Cabrini.
Ciaramitaro, James *o.f.m.conv.* '88 (CHI)[N] Libertyville, IL Marytown, Our Lady of Fatima Friary.
Ciaramitaro, Victor P. '72 (MEM) Paris, TN Holy Cross; Presbyteral Council and College of Consultors.
Ciaramitaro, Victor (MEM) Dean of the Jackson Deanery.
Ciardiello, Bruno *o.f.m.* '45 (BRK) Brooklyn, NY Our Lady of Peace.
Ciarvalo, Ronald '54 (NY) Retired.
Ciavaglia, Julio M. *c.r.s.p.* '66 (BUF)[B Youngstown, NY St. Anthony M. Zaccaria Seminary; [B] Youngstown, NY The National Shrine Basilica of Our Lady of Fatima.
Ciba, Thomas J. '74 (NEW) Nutley, NJ Our Lady of Mount Carmel.
Cibulskis Pete *m.i.c.* '53 (MIL) Kenosha, WI St. Peter.
Ciccarino Christopher (NEW)[B] School of Diplomacy and Intl. Rels..
Ciccolini, Samuel R. '69 (CLV) Akron, OH Immaculate Conception; [U] Akron, OH Interval Brotherhood Home Alcohol–Drug Rehabilitation Center.
Ciccone, Joseph A. *c.s.p.* '89 (BO)[C] Boston, MA Paulist Center; [V] Boston, MA Paulist Fathers Residence; [AA] Boston, MA Chapel of the Holy Spirit.
Ciccone, Mark K. *s.j.* '85 (California)[M] Berkeley, CA Jesuit Community at Jesuit School of Theology at Berkeley.
Ciccone, Mark *s.j.* '01 (SFR) San Francisco, CA Our Lady of Fatima Byzantine Catholic Church.
Ciccone, Michael A. *o.p.* '75 (PRO) Providence, RI St. Pius V; [P] Providence, RI St. Pius Priory; Council Members.
Ciccone, Nicholas C. '84 (BO).
Ciccone, Nicholas C. (BO)[EE] Dorchester, MA St. Margaret; CENTRAL REGION.
Cicerale, Charles W. '75 (MET) Raritan, NJ St. Joseph; Woodbridge, NJ St. James; Office of Ministry to Priests.
Ciceri, Cesare *c.s.* (BO) Framingham, MA St. Tarcisius.
Cichon, Michael W. '85 (NY) Staten Island, NY St. Joseph, St. Thomas.
Cicinato, Michael '76 (MRY) San Luis Obispo, CA Nativity of Our Lady; Permanent Diaconate Advisory Board.
Cicola, Alfred C. '67 (PIT) Canonsburg, PA St. Patrick.
Cid, Robert J. '74 (NEW) West New York, NJ St. Joseph of the Palisades.
Ciemiega, Ernest D. '58 (CHI) Chicago, IL St. Bruno Retired.
Cieniewicz, Donald W. '83 (ALN) Hamburg, PA St. Mary.
Cienik, Kenneth *s.a.* '77 (WDC)[B] Washington, DC Atonement Seminary–Franciscan Friars of the Atonement; Navy Reserve Chaplains.
Cieri, Domenic L. '81 (BAL) Severn, MD St. Bernadette.
Ciesielski, Marek *s.ch.* '96 (DET) Sterling Heights, MI Our Lady of Czestochowa.
Ciesla, Fred *c.r.* '94 (CHI)[D] Chicago, IL Gordon Tech High School.
Ciesla, Marek *s.ch.* '82 (TOL) Toledo, OH St. Adalbert.
Ciesla, Walter M. '81 (GRY) Michigan City, IN St. Stanislaus Kostka; Blue Army.
Cieslak, William M. *o.f.m.cap.* '73 (OAK)[A] Berkeley, CA Franciscan School of Theology; [N] Berkeley, CA Franciscan Friars.
Cieslik, Adam *o.f.m.conv.* (BO) South Boston, MA Our Lady of Czestochowa.
Cieslik, R. Dale '82 (L) Louisville, KY St. Leonard; Archivist; Clergy Personnel Commission.
Cieslikowski, Thomas J. '88 (HRT) New Britain, CT St. Jerome's.
Cieslinski, Robert '43 (P) Retired.
Ciesniewski, Richard P. '57 (DET) Retired.
Ciferni, Andrew D. *o.praem.* '66 (PH)[AA] Paoli, PA Daylesford Abbey.
Ciferni, Andrew *o.praem* (CHI)[N] Chicago, IL Premonstratensian Fathers and Brothers (Norbertines).
Cigan, John J. *j.c.b.* '74 (PSC) Binghamton, NY Holy Spirit.
Cihak, John '98 (P)[A] St. Benedict, OR Mount Angel Seminary.
Cilia, Francis V. '79 (SJ) Special Assignment; [P] Santa Clara, CA Roman Catholic Seminary Corporation of San Jose; Vicar General and Moderator of the Curia; Bishop's Executive Committee; College of Consultors; Council of Priests; Defenders of the Bond; Building Committee; Priests' Retirement Board.
Cilia, Jose *o.carm.* '68 (JOL) Joliet, IL Mount Carmel.
Ciliberti, Francis J. *o.praem.* '44 (WIL)[J] Middletown, DE Immaculate Conception Priory of the Canons Regular of Premontre.
Cilino, Angelo R. '77 (PH) Warminster, PA Nativity of Our Lord.
Cilinski, John T. '48 (ARL) Arlington, VA St. Agnes Retired.
Cilinski, Julius J. '45 (ARL) Retired.
Cilinski, Robert C. '79 (ARL) Manassas, VA All Saints; Deans; Diocesan Consultors.
Cilwick, Theodore T. '43 (CHR) Retired.
Cima, Jose '58 (SB) Retired.
Cima, Thomas E. '67 (CHI) Calumet City, IL St. Victor; Deans.
Cimarrusti, Francis A. '64 (CHI) Chicago, IL St. Matthias; [G] Chicago, IL Catholic Charities of the Archdiocese of Chicago–Archdiocesan Offices; Associate Administrators.
Cimbala, Edward G. '88 (PSC) Hillsborough Township, NJ St. Mary's; Elected Members; Vocations; Priesthood & Diaconate Formation Programs.
Cimerman, Krizolog *o.f.m.* '73 (NY) New York, NY St. Cyril.
Cimino, Michael '86 (SFE) Albuquerque, NM Our Lady of the Assumption.
Cimperman, Victor J. '43 (CLV) Akron, OH Christ the King Retired.
Cimpl, Charles L. '78 (SFS) Sioux Falls, SD St. Therese.
Cimpl, Charles (SFS) Tribunal Judges.
Cincinnati, Anthony '87 (WH) Follansbee, WV St. Anthony.
Cinco, Joel *c.s.* (LA) Sun Valley, CA Our Lady of the Holy Rosary.
Cincoski, Edward E. *s.j.* '50 (DET)[P] Clarkston, MI Colombiere Center.
Cincotta, Anthony '74 (SY) On Duty Outside the Diocese.
Cindric, John R. '74 (GBG)[G] Greensburg, PA Neumann House.
Cine, Syriaque *s.m.m.* (RVC) Westbury, NY St. Brigid.
Cinesi, Joseph '80 (MIA) Absent on Leave.
Cingle, Martin A. '73 (ALT) Johnstown, PA St. Francis of Assisi.

Cini, J. Thomas '68 (WIL) Vicar General for Administration and Moderator of the Curia; Diocesan Planning; Diocesan Real Estate Committee; Catholic Ministry to the Elderly; College of Consultors; Diocesan Building Committee; Public Affairs Advisory Committee; Catholic Diocese of Wilmington, Inc.; Catholic Ministry to the Elderly, Inc.; Catholic Press of Wilmington, Inc.; Catholic Youth Organization, Inc.; Delawareans United for Education; Maryland Catholic Conference; Wilmington, DE St. Ann.
Cini, Robert *m.s.s.p.* '53 (DET) Detroit, MI Our Lady of Mt. Carmel.
Cink, James J. (MOB) Victim Assistance Coordinator.
Cink, James '85 (MOB) Mobile, AL St. Vincent de Paul.
Cinque, Stephen J. '81 (NEW) Maywood, NJ Our Lady Queen of Peace.
Cinquegrani, David *c.p.* '96 (HRT)[C] West Hartford, CT Saint Joseph College.
Cinquegrani, David *c.p.* '96 (HRT)[M] West Hartford Holy Family Monastery/Retreat.
Cinquegrani, David *c.p.* '96 (HRT)[Q] West Hartford, CT Holy Family Passionist Retreat Center.
Cinquegrani, R. Bruce '79 (MEM) Bartlett, TN St. Ann; Secretary; Spiritual Advisors.
Cinson, Victor '74 (STU) Lowell, OH St. Henry.
Cinson, Victor '74 (STU) Lowell, OH Our Lady of Mercy.
Cinson, Victor (STU) Presbyteral Council.
Cinson, Victor (STU) College of Consultors.
Cinson, Victor (STU) Priests Personnel Board.
Cintron, Angel L. '91 (CGS) Las Piedras, PR San Juan Bautista.
Cintron, Segismundo '89 (PCE)[B] The Pontifical Catholic University of Puerto Rico.
Cintron, Segismundo '89 (PCE) Yauco, PR St. Martin de Porres.
Cintula, Francis M. '65 (CHL) Retired.
Cio, Robert '74 (NEW) Irvington, NJ St. Paul the Apostle.
Cioch, Gregory (DEN) Estes Park, CO Our Lady of the Mountains.
Cioffi, Alfred '85 (MIA) Higher Studies.
Cioffi, Paul L. *s.j.* '59 (WDC)[M] Washington, DC The Jesuit Community at Georgetown University; [V] Washington, DC Institute for Pastoral Renewal, Inc..
Cioffi, Phillip F. '81 (CHI) Forest Park, IL St. Bernardine.
Cioffi, Ronald J. '69 (TR) Keyport, NJ St. Joseph.
Cioffi, Ronald (TR) Office of Social Concerns.
Ciomek, Christopher '98 (CHI) Palatine, IL St. Theresa.
Cionca, Calin (NEW) Hohokus, NJ St. Luke's.
Cioppa, Philip '83 (ALB) Leave of Absence.
Cioppa, Philip '83 (ALB)[C] Glens Falls, NY St. Mary–St. Alphonsus Regional Catholic School.
Cioppi, Martin T. '81 (PH) Philadelphia, PA Our Lady of Lourdes; [EE] Philadelphia, PA Newman Apostolate for Archdiocese of Philadelphia; Office for Catechetical Formation.
Ciordia, Pedro M. '61 (LA) Retired.
Ciorra, Anthony J. '73 (PAT)[B] Morristown, NJ College of Saint Elizabeth; [P] Morristown, NJ College of St. Elizabeth, Center for Theological and Spiritual Development.
Ciosek, Scott A. (FR) Fall River, MA St. Michael; Bristol Community College; [M] Fall River, MA Bristol Community College Newman Center.
Ciotola, Romano '65 (COL) Columbus, OH Our Lady of Victory.
Ciotoli, Vincent J. '76 (ALB) Ravena, NY St. Patrick.
Ciotoli, Vincent (ALB) Cursillo in Christianity.
Cipar, Daniel '61 (Y) East Palestine, OH Our Lady of Lourdes.
Cipolla, Richard G. '84 (BGP) Stamford, CT St. Mary.
Cippel, John A. '60 (SP) Spring Hill, FL St. Frances Xavier Cabrini.
Ciprian, Carl A. '76 (CLV) Barberton, OH Holy Trinity.
Cipriano, Joseph F. '59 (SCR) Old Forge, PA St. Mary's.
Cipriano, Robert P. '87 (SFR) Fairfax, CA St. Rita.
Ciranni, Salvatore *r.c.j.* '55 (FRS) Sanger, CA St. Mary Retired.
Cirba, Richard J. '89 (SCR) Swoyersville, PA Holy Trinity.
Ciriaco, Dominic G. '99 (WDC) On Duty Outside the Archdiocese.
Cirignani, Anthony *o.f.m.* '83 (MIL)[B] Milwaukee, WI St. Anthony.
Cirilli, Matthew R. '64 (PIT) Absent on Sick Leave.
Cirillo, Nicholas A. '95 (BGP) Shelton, CT St. Lawrence.
Cirino, Andre *o.f.m.* (NY)[EE] Mount Vernon, NY St. Bernardine of Siena Friary.
Ciriza, Jesus M. *m.ss.cc.* '59 (SJN) Bayamon, PR San Juan Bautista de la Salle.
Ciryak, Michael A. *o.f.m.* '98 (FR) Fall River, MA Holy Name; [B] Fall River, MA Bishop Connolly High School.
Cis, James '38 (FTW) Retired.
Ciscar, Tomas *o.carm.* '78 (SJN) San Juan, PR Santa Teresita Del Nino Jesus.
Cisco, Bede *o.s.b.* '78 (IND)[K] Indianapolis, IN.
Cisco, Bede *o.s.b.* '78 (IND) Indianapolis, IN St. Michael the Archangel.
Cisco, Bede *o.s.b.* '78 (IND)[A] St. Meinrad, IN St. Meinrad School of Theology.
Cisco, Bede *o.s.b.* (IND) Council of Priests.
Cisco, Bede (IND) Deacon Formation.
Cisco, Mariano '82 (BRK) Brooklyn, NY St. Joseph Patron of the Universal Church.
Cisek, Herman W. *m.m.* '65 (FgM).
Cisetti, Joseph I. '91 (KC) Pleasant Hill, MO St. Bridget.
Cisetti, Joseph (KC) Vocations.
Cisewski, John '71 (NO) New Orleans, LA St. Leo the Great.
Ciski, Michael *t.o.r.* (FWT) Arlington, TX St. Maria Goretti.
Cislo, Robert '65 (DET) Taylor, MI St. Paschal.
Cisneros, Daniel '03 (SAT) San Antonio, TX Holy Spirit.
Cisneros, Octavio '71 (BRK)[B] Douglaston, NY Cathedral Seminary Residence of the Immaculate Conception.
Cisneros, Octavio '71 (NY)[II] New York, NY Felix Varela Foundation, Inc., The.
Cisneros, Ramon '99 (ORG) Garden Grove, CA St. Callistus.
Cistone, Joseph R. '75 (PH) On Special or Other Archdiocesan Assignment; Vicars General; Office of the Vicar for Administration; Priests' Personnel Board; College of Consultors; Council of Managers for Development; Council of Priests; Administrative Board.
Citero, Samuel *o.carm.* '84 (NEW) Cresskill, NJ St. Therese of Lisieux.
Citro, Anthony M. '94 (GAY) Roscommon, MI St. Michael; Vicars (by region).
Ciuba, Edward J. '59 (NEW) North Caldwell, NJ Notre Dame; College of Consultors.
Ciuba, Edward (NEW) Censors of Books.
Ciullo, Salvator L. '84 (ARL) Retired.
Ciupek, James D. '97 (BUF) Hamburg, NY SS. Peter and Paul.
Ciurej, Richard S. '54 (OM) Retired.
Ciurpita, John '89 (PHU) Cherry Hill, NJ St. Michael's.
Ciurpita, John (PHU) College of Archeparchial Counsultors.
Ciurpita, John (PHU) Ecumenical Relations.
Ciurpita, John (PHU) Presbyteral Council.
Ciurpita, John (PHU) Protopresbyters (Deans).
Civiello, John D. '68 (PRT) Portland, ME Cathedral of the Immaculate Conception Retired.
Civille, John R. '66 (CIN) Middletown, OH Holy Family; Priest Councilors; Consultors.
Cizewski, Albert '71 (SFS) Armour, SD St. Paul the Apostle.
Cizik, Ladis '87 (PIT) Allegheny County, PA Manorcare Health Services Monroeville.
Cizik, Ladis '87 (PIT) St. Margaret Seneca Place.
Cizik, Ladis '87 (PIT) Sunrise Assisted Living.
Cizik, Ladis '87 (PIT) Allegheny County, PA Presbyterian Seniorcare Westminister Place; Seneca Hills Retirement Village.
Cizik, Ladis '87 (PIT) Seneca Manor Assisted Living.
Cizik, Ladis '87 (PIT) Allegheny County, PA Presbyterian Seniorcare Westminister Place; Seneca Hills Retirement Village.
Cizik, Ladis '87 (PIT) Hamilton Hills Personal Care; Allegheny County, PA Ladies of the Grand Army Republic (LGAR); On Duty Outside the Diocese.
Cizur, Ignacio *o.f.m.cap.* '72 (DAL)[K] Dallas, TX Capuchin Franciscan Friars, Vice Province of Texas; Dallas, TX Our Lady of Lourdes.
Cizur Gaston, Juan *o.f.m.cap.* '67 (DAL)[K] Dallas, TX Capuchin Franciscan Friars, Vice Province of Texas.
Claerr, Francis *c.m.m.* '48 (DET)[K] Vocation Office.
Clagett, Carl P. '55 (COL) Retired.
Clair, John J. '82 (CHI) Other Assignments.
Clancy, Bede *o.f.m.* '44 (CIN)[M] Cincinnati, OH St. Clement Friary Retired.
Clancy, Douglas P. '71 (HRT) Manchester, CT St. James; Archbishop's Annual Appeal.
Clancy, Frank *s.c.j.* '74 (BWN) Harlingen, TX Valley Baptist Medical Center.
Clancy, Frank *s.c.j.* '74 (BWN)[F] Harlingen, TX Priests of the Sacred Heart.
Clancy, Frank *s.c.j.* (BWN) Valley Baptist Medical Center.
Clancy, Raphael '74 (AUS) Killeen, TX St. Joseph.
Clancy, Rian *c.p.* '53 (CHI)[N] Chicago, IL Passionist Community–Immaculate Conception Monastery.
Clancy, Rian *c.p.* '53 (CHI)[J] Elk Grove Village, IL Alexian Brothers Medical Center.
Clancy, Richard F. (BO) South Boston, MA St. Brigid; Randolph, MA St. Bernadette.
Clancy, Richard J. (BO) Campus Ministry.
Clancy, Robert E. '74 (CLV) Akron, OH Sacred Heart of Jesus; Akron General Hospital.
Clancy, Thomas C. '45 (BRK) Brooklyn, NY St. Brendan's Retired.
Clancy, Timothy R. *s.j.* '89 (SPK)[B] Spokane, WA Gonzaga University.
Clanton, Bruce *s.d.s.* '78 (MIL)[O] Racine, WI.
Clapham, Bruce R. '95 (CHY) Newcastle, WY Corpus Christi.
Clapp, Kenneth '90 (MIL) Personal Leave.
Clarahan, Michael '58 (CHI)[N] Chicago, IL St. Peter's Friary.
Clark, Anthony P. *s.v.d.* '85 (MEM) Memphis, TN St. Joseph's.
Clark, Anthony '79 (LSC) Lordsburg, NM St. Joseph.
Clark, Anthony *s.v.d.* '85 (MEM)[I] Memphis, TN Society of the Divine Word (Chicago Province); Office of Multicultural & African American Catholic Ministries; Office of Hispanic Ministry.
Clark, Dana '01 (SAL) Colby, KS Sacred Heart.
Clark, Dana (SAL) Vocation Ministry Committee.
Clark, David '84 (P) On Duty Outside the Archdiocese.
Clark, Dennis R. '66 (SD) Rancho Santa Fe, CA Church of the Nativity.
Clark, Douglas K. '76 (SAV) Savannah, GA Cathedral of St. John the Baptist; Censor Librorum; Finance Council; College of Consultors; Council of Priests; Newspaper.
Clark, Eugene V. '51 (NY) New York, NY Cathedral of St. Patrick; [II] New York, NY Friends of American Art in Religion, Inc.; [II] New York, NY Patrons of the Arts in the Vatican Museums.
Clark, Howard T. '57 (WIL) Retired.
Clark, J. Michael '95 (OWN) Utica, KY St. Anthony; Judges.
Clark, James B. '95 (BO) Rockland, MA Holy Family.
Clark, James E. '96 (ALB) Wynantskill, NY St. Jude the Apostle; Catholic Deaf Ministry.
Clark, James P. '52 (NY) Bronx, NY St. Francis of Assisi Retired.
Clark, James W. '84 (GBG) Uniontown, PA Uniontown Hospital; New Salem, PA Madonna of Czestochowa.
Clark, John F. *c.m.* '70 (STL)[A] St. Louis, MO Kenrick School of Theology; [O] St. Louis, MO Lazarist Residence; [Q] St. Louis, MO Provincial Offices.
Clark, John J. '53 (CAM) Retired.
Clark, John R. '96 (WDC) Rockville, MD St. Patrick.
Clark, John W. *s.j.* '59 (LA)[Q] Los Angeles, CA Columbiere House.
Clark, John *s.j.* (LA) Cardinal Manning House of Prayer for Priests.
Clark, Joseph J. '96 (ARL) Clifton, VA St. Andrew the Apostle.
Clark, Joseph L. '76 (RIC) Retired.
Clark, Keith *o.f.m.cap.* '65 (MIL)[O] Mount Calvary, WI St. Lawrence Friary; [B] Mount Calvary, WI St. Lawrence Seminary.
Clark, Laurence E. '54 (LA) Retired.
Clark, Matthew R. *o.s.b.* '87 (NO)[J] St. Benedict, LA Abbey Youth Camp, Inc.; [P] St. Benedict, LA St. Joseph Abbey; [A] St. Benedict, LA St. Joseph Seminary College.
Clark, Patrick S. '61 (SEA) Seattle, WA St. Patrick.
Clark, Paul M. '03 (HBG) Hershey, PA St. Joan of Arc; Hershey, PA St. Joan of Arc.
Clark, Peter A. *s.j.* '92 (PH)[C] Jesuit Fathers; [AA] Loyola Center and Manresa Hall.
Clark, Peter '02 (LAN) Fenton, MI St. John.
Clark, Ray '91 (OWN) Sebree, KY St. Michael; Owensboro, KY St. Peter of Alcantara.
Clark, Richard D. '63 (ALT) Johnstown, PA Visitation of the B.V.M..
Clark, Richard D. '92 (MRY) Tres Pinos, CA Immaculate Conception.
Clark, Robert J. '99 (CHI) Orland Park, IL St. Michael.
Clark, Robert J. *o.s.b.* (MO) Navy Reserve Chaplains.
Clark, Robert *s.s.c.* '65 (OM)[K] St. Columbans St. Columban's Foreign Mission Society.
Clark, Robert *s.s.c.* '65 (SB) Fontana, CA St. Mary.
Clark, Steven E. '90 (NY) Peekskill, NY Assumption.
Clark, Thomas F. *s.j.* '81 (BO) Roxbury, MA St. Francis de Sales–St. Philip; [V] Boston, MA Loyola House; [V] Boston The Society of Jesus of New England–Provincial Offices.
Clark, Thomas R. '62 (L) Liberty, KY St. Bernard; Ex Officio.
Clark, Timothy *o.c.s.o.* '80 (P)[L] Lafayette, OR The Cistercian (Trappist) Abbey of Our Lady of Guadalupe.
Clark, Timothy '80 (SEA) Redmond, WA St. Jude.
Clark, Vernon F. '80 (CHY) Cody, WY St. Anthony.
Clark, Vernon (CHY) College of Consultors.
Clark, Vernon (CHY) Catholic Family and Respect Life Ministries Board.
Clark, Vernon (CHY) Presbyteral Council.
Clark, Vernon (CHY) Episcopal Vicar for Priests.
Clark, William A. *s.j.* '93 (WOR)[O] Worcester, MA Jesuits of Holy Cross College, Inc..
Clark, William *o.m.i.* '55 (GAL)[F] Belleville, IL Missionary Oblates of Mary Immaculate – St. Henry's Oblate Residence.
Clarke, Arthur A. *s.j.* '47 (NY)[EE] New York, NY St. Ignatius Loyola Residence.
Clarke, Brian J.W. '02 (SCR) Blossburg, PA St. Mary's.
Clarke, David M. *s.j.* '64 (DEN)[B] Denver, CO Regis University; [N] Denver, CO Regis Jesuit Community (The Jesuits at Regis University).
Clarke, James A. '70 (Y) North Canton, OH St. Paul; College of Consultors; Catholic Women, Diocesan Council of.

Clarke, James T. '38 (SCR)[N] Dunmore, PA Villa St. Joseph Retired.
Clarke, James '81 (LA)[A] Camarillo, CA St. John's Seminary.
Clarke, James (LA) Spirituality Commission.
Clarke, John A. '59 (CAM) Turnersville, NJ SS. Peter and Paul.
Clarke, John '45 (DM) Retired.
Clarke, Kevin T. *s.j.* '93 (P)[L] Portland, OR Colombiere Community.
Clarke, Mark *c.m.f.* '03 (LA) San Gabriel, CA San Gabriel; [Q] San Gabriel, CA Claretian Missionaries (Missionary Sons of the Immaculate Heart of Mary).
Clarke, Peter '63 (CHR) Retired.
Clarke, Peter (CHR) Parish Priest Consultors.
Clarke, Peter (CHR) College of Consultors.
Clarke, Peter (CHR) Presbyteral Council.
Clarke, Thomas E. *s.j.* '50 (NY)[FF] Highland Mills, NY Religious of Jesus and Mary; [GG] Highland Mills, NY Bethany Retreat House.
Clarke, W. Norris *s.j.* '45 (NY)[EE] Loyola Hall, Jesuit Community.
Clarkin, Herbert J. '59 (HRT) Retired.
Clarkin, Herbert '45 (HRT)[K] West Hartford, CT Saint Mary Home.
Clarkson, Theodore J. *s.j.* '44 (SY)[Q] Syracuse, NY Jesuits at LeMoyne, Inc..
Claro, Carlos L. *c.s.v.* '98 (CHI)[N] Arlington Heights Viatorian Province Center–Clerics of St. Viator.
Claro, Mario R. '67 (WH) Franklin, WV St. Elizabeth Ann Seton; Moorefield, WV Epiphany of the Lord; Petersburg, WV St. Mary's.
Claros, Victor H. '92 (RCK) Freeport, IL St. Joseph; Freeport, IL St. Mary; Freeport, IL St. Thomas Aquinas.
Clary, Brian M. '97 (BO) Brookline, MA St. Mary of the Assumption; Priests Recovery Program.
Clary, Michael '77 (KC) Lee's Summit, MO Our Lady of the Presentation.
Clary, Michael (KC) Presbyteral Council.
Class, Michael D. *s.j.* '90 (MIL)[O] Milwaukee, WI Jesuit Community at Marquette University.
Class, Michael J. *s.j.* '90 (CHI)[N] Chicago, IL Chicago Province of the Society of Jesus–Provincial Office.
Classen, Joseph F. '03 (STL) Chesterfield, MO Incarnate Word.
Classik, Bede *o.s.b* '67 (SEA)[L] Lacey, WA St. Martin's Abbey.
Clauder, J. Gibbs '73 (MAD) Leave of Absence.
Claudio, Antonio C. '75 (SFR) South San Francisco, CA St. Augustine.
Clausen, Kenneth J. '53 (GF) Retired.
Clausen, William J. '62 (RCK) Maple Park, IL St. Mary; Deans.
Clavenna, Charles G. '56 (STL) Retired.
Clavero, Jose M. *sch.p.* '64 (NY) New York, NY Annunciation; [EE] New York, NY Calasanzian Fathers (Piarists).
Clavey, William J. '98 (CHI) Berwyn, IL St. Mary of Celle.
Clavin, M. Oliver '70 (SPC) Kelso, MO St. Augustine.
Clavin, Nicholas P. '73 (SD) San Diego, CA St. Vincent de Paul.
Clay, Christopher R. '98 (SCR) Unassigned or Leave of Absence.
Clay, David J. *s.s.c.* (FgM).
Clay, John C. '51 (STP) St. Paul, MN St. Stanislaus.
Clay, Michael G. '80 (R) Special Assignment; [I] Chapel Hill, NC Vocations Office; Vocations.
Clayton, C. Murray '56 (SHP) Shreveport, LA Sacred Heart of Jesus.
Clayton, Daniel '68 (DAL) Dallas, TX Methodist Dallas Medical Center; Dallas, TX Methodist Charlton Medical Center.
Cleary, Christopher *c.p.* '86 (RVC)[O] Shelter Island Heights, NY St. Gabriel's Spiritual Center for Youth.
Cleary, Dennis W. *m.m.* '77 (NY)[EE] Maryknoll Maryknoll Fathers and Brothers.
Cleary, Donald M. '71 (OM) Fullerton, NE St. Peter; Fullerton, NE St. Peter.
Cleary, Donald R. '68 (KC) Retired.
Cleary, Edward L. *o.p.* '57 (Chicago Prov.)[P] Providence St. Thomas Aquinas Priory at Providence College.
Cleary, Edward M. '56 (SFR) Retired.
Cleary, Edward '41 (SFR)[K] San Rafael, CA Nazareth House Retired.
Cleary, Francis X. *s.j.* '63 (STL)[N] St. Louis, MO Fusz Pavilion; [O] St. Louis, MO Jesuit Community Corporation at St. Louis University – Jesuit Hall.
Cleary, Gerard M. (BLX) Deans.
Cleary, Gerard '61 (BLX) Pascagoula, MS Our Lady of Victories.
Cleary, Gerard (BLX) Presbyteral Council.
Cleary, Herbert J. *s.j.* '68 (BO)[T] South Boston, MA Marian Manor; [V] Boston, MA Loyola House.
Cleary, Hugh W. *c.s.c.* '73 (BGP).
Cleary, James L. *o.f.m.cap.* '70 (LA)[P] Los Angeles, CA St. Lawrence of Brindisi.
Cleary, James *t.o.r.* '41 (ARL)[J] White Post, VA Sacred Heart Friary.
Cleary, James *o.f.m.* '70 (LA)[J] Lynwood, CA St. Francis Medical Center.
Cleary, Kevin '48 (FRS) Retired.
Cleary, Paul '74 (SAT) San Antonio, TX St. Dominic.
Cleary, Paul (SAT) Defenders of the Bond.
Cleary, Philip C. '79 (CHI) Missionary Work.
Cleary, Richard E. *o.s.f.s.* '59 (WIL)[J] Childs, MD Retirement and Assisted Care Facility.
Cleary, Richard T. *s.j.* '66 (BO)[V] Boston The Society of Jesus of New England–Provincial Offices [V] Newton, MA The Jesuit Community at Boston College.
Cleary, Richard *o.s.b.* '55 (LR)[I] Jonesboro, AR Holy Angels Convent–Motherhouse.
Cleary, Richard *s.j.* (SPR)[P] Amherst, MA University of Massachusetts.
Cleary, William D. '55 (IND) Retired.
Cleary, William M. *o.s.a.* '61 (WDC)[B] Silver Spring, MD Austin Friars Hall, Order of St. Augustine.
Cleary, William M. *c.ss.r.* '62 (FgM).
Cleary, William '61 (WDC)[D] Washington DC Archbishop Carroll High School.
Cleary, William *c.ss.r.* '62 (DEN).
Cleaton, C. Thomas '75 (CLV)[N] Avon, OH St. Mary of the Immaculate Conception.
Cleator, Gerard B. *o.p.* '65 (CHI)[N] Chicago Dominicans (Provincial Office).
Clegg, Thomas '90 (IND) Jeffersonville, IN Sacred Heart.
Clegg, Thomas (IND) Priests' Personnel Board.
Clegg, Timothy '71 (LFT) On Duty Outside the Diocese.
Clemens, Bailey T. '98 (PEO) DePue, IL St. Mary's.
Clemens, John W. '72 (CHI) Chicago, IL St. Benedict; [X] Chicago, IL The Aquin Guild; Priests Placement Board.
Clemens, Neal C. '01 (OAK) Martinez, CA St. Catherine of Siena.
Clement, Frederick *m.ss.cc.* '94 (CAM)[M] Linwood, NJ Villa Pieta. Missionaries of the Sacred Hearts of Jesus & Mary; Philadelphia, PA Cathedral Basilica of SS. Peter and Paul.
Clement, Richard '85 (ALN) Reading, PA St. Joseph.
Clement, Thomas '95 (SFS) Ipswich, SD Our Lady of Perpetual Help.
Clement, Thomas '95 (SFS) Ipswich, SD Holy Cross.
Clemente, Joseph J. '81 (SY) East Syracuse, NY St. Matthew.
Clemente, Maximo '99 (WIL) Dover, DE Holy Cross.
Clemente, Michael '55 (ALB) Retired.
Clemente, Vincent L. '76 (VEN) Sarasota, FL St. Martha.
Clemente, Vincent (VEN) Legion of Mary.
Clementich LeRoy E. *c.s.c.* '57 (FTW)[I] Anchorage, AK Archdiocese of Anchorage.
Clements, Charles '62 (MIA) Special Assignment.
Clements, Charles '62 (MIA) Miami, FL Christ the King.
Clements, Daniel A. '54 (NSH) Retired.
Clements, George H. '57 (CHI) On Duty Outside the Archdiocese.
Clements, Robert '90 (PHX) Chandler, AZ St. Mary's.
Clements, Thomas P. '55 (CHL) Retired.
Clemo, Ronald M. *s.j.* '67 (SJ).
Clemons, Delma (OWN)[D] Priests' Council.
Clennon, Raymond *o.carm.* '67 (CHI) Darnee, IL St. Paul the Apostle.
Clerical, Luke U. *m.s.f.s.* '88 (TYL) Chandler, TX St. Boniface.
Clerkin, Robert J. '80 (RVC) Glen Head NY St. Paul the Apostle; Priests' Retirement Board
Clerkin, Thomas J. *c.s.p.* '85 (LA) Los Angeles, CA St. Paul the Apostle.
Clermont, John *o.f.m.cap.* '53 (NY) New York, NY St. John the Baptist.
Clermont, John *o.f.m.cap.* '53 (FgM).
Cletus, Sales T. (Ranjan) *i.m.s.* '84 (TYL) Temple, TX St. Mary's.
Cleu, Paul E. '74 (OAK) Fremont, CA St. James The Apostle.
Cleveland S. Gregory *o.m.v.* '95 (BO)[E] Boston, MA Our Lady of Grace Seminary.
Cleves, Simeon *o.f.m.* '55 (CIN)[M] Cincinnati, OH St. Francis Seraph Friary.
Cleves, William F. '78 (COV) Florence, KY St. Paul.
Click, Patrick R. '71 (LFT) Fishers, IN Holy Spirit Church.
Clifford, Donald G. '61 (BO) Senior Priests Retired.
Clifford, Donald G. *s.j.* '62 (PH)[C] Jesuit Fathers; [AA] Loyola Center and Manresa Hall.
Clifford, Donald P. '61 (BO) Marshfield, MA Our Lady of the Assumption.
Clifford, Francis M. '54 (MAN) Retired.
Clifford, James J. '45 (WOR)[N] Worcester, MA Retired.
Clifford, James *o.s.a.* '72 (P)[L] Myrtle Creek, OR Augustinian Community.
Clifford, James *o.s.a.* '72 (P) Central Point, OR Shepherd of the Valley.
Clifford, Jerome *s.c.j.* '61 (MIL)[O] St. Louis, MO.
Clifford, John *s.s.c.* '53 (SD)[K] St. Columbans St. Columban's Foreign Mission Society.
Clifford, Joseph G. '89 (VEN) Fort Myers, FL St. Columbkille.
Clifford, Leo *o.f.m.* '46 (BO)[Y] Boston, MA Saint Anthony Residence.
Clifford, Marc *o.s.f.s.* (FWT)[N] Denton, TX University of North Texas and Texas Woman's University.
Clifford, Michael J. '60 (GB) Retired.
Clifford, Paul J. *s.j.* '56 (DET)[P] Clarkston, MI Colombiere Center.
Clifford, Paul T. (BO) Dracut, MA St. Marguerite D'Youville.
Clifford, Peter C. '76 (ROC) Newark, NY St. Michael.
Clifford, Richard J. *s.j.* '66 (BO)[V] Cambridge, MA.
Clifford, Richard L. *m.m.* '53 (FgM).
Clifford, Thomas A. *o.p.* '60 (GAL)[Q] Houston, TX Dominican Friars, St. Mark Priory, Inc..
Clifford, Thomas F. *s.j.* '81 (PH)[G] Philadelphia, PA St. Joseph's Preparatory School; [AA] Philadelphia, PA Jesuit Community, Arrupe House.
Clift, James C. '57 (OAK)[M] Oakland, CA Bishop Begin Villa Retired.
Clifton, James F. '88 (OM)[K] Omaha, NE Jesuit Community at Creighton University.
Clinch, Kevin D. '83 (TUC)[H] Casa Grande, AZ Central Arizona College, Holy Family Newman Center.
Clinch, Kevin O. '83 (TUC) Casa Grande, AZ St. Anthony of Padua.
Clines, Paul J. '44 (CLV) Barberton, OH St. Augustine Retired.
Clinton, Donald J. '90 (MAN) Suncook, NH St. John the Baptist.
Clinton, Kevin I. (STP) Mendota, MN St. Peter; [G] St. Paul, MN Faithful Shepherd Catholic School.
Clisch, Norman A. '65 (MAR) Caspian, MI St. Cecilia; Iron River, MI St. Agnes; Consultors.
Clody, Albert W. '65 (BUF) Consultors, College of; Council of Priests; Buffalo, NY All Saints.
Clogan, Paul M. '99 (AUS) Llano, TX St. Joseph's; Special or Other Diocesan Assignment.
Clogan, Pual '99 (AUS) Llano, TX Holy Trinity.
Cloherty, Francis J. '62 (BO) Brockton, MA St. Patrick.
Cloherty, Francis V. (BO) SOUTH REGION.
Cloherty, Thomas '74 (DAL) Dallas, TX All Saints.
Clonerty, John J. '60 (SFR) Mill Valley, CA Our Lady of Mt. Carmel.
Cloney, Michael '68 (SR) Ukiah, CA St. Mary of the Angels.
Cloney, Robert D. *s.j.* '60 (NY)[EE] Cardinal Spellman Hall, Jesuit Community.
Cloonan, Dennis '03 (CHY) Rock Springs, WY Holy Spirit Catholic Community.
Cloonan, Paul F. '44 (ROC) Retired.
Clooney, David '64 (PHU) Northampton, PA St. John the Baptist.
Clooney, Francis X. *s.j.* '78 (New York)[V] Newton, MA The Jesuit Community at Boston College.
Cloquell, Bernardo *t.o.r.* '48 (NEW) Newark, NJ Immaculate Heart of Mary.
Cloquet, Victor '50 (SEA) Retired.
Clore, Victor '65 (DET) Detroit, MI Christ the King.
Close, Frederick J. '01 (WDC) Clinton, MD St. Mary.
Close, James J. '63 (CHI)[H] Chicago, IL Mission of Our Lady of Mercy–Mercy Home for Boys and Girls; Mercy Home for Boys and Girls.
Close, James (CHI)[G] Chicago, IL Mercy Home for Boys & Girls.
Close, John A. '69 (PH) Philadelphia, PA Cathedral Basilica of SS. Peter and Paul; Philadelphia, PA Chapel of Our Lady of the Miraculous Medal (La Milagrosa).
Close, John '82 (ALB) New Lebanon, NY Immaculate Conception.
Cloud, Charles W. '89 (TUC) Florence, AZ Assumption of the Blessed Virgin Mary.
Cloud, Charles (TUC) Advocates and Auditors.
Clough, Wulfstan F. *o.s.b.* '96 (GBG)[H] Latrobe, PA Saint Vincent Archabbey.
Clougherty, Paul L. '60 (BO) Senior Priests Retired.
Cloutier, Rolamd C. '66 (NOR) Putnam, CT St. Mary.
Cloutier, Roland C. (NOR) Deans; Continuing Education and Formation Commission.
Cloutier, Roland '66 (NOR)[J] Portland, CT Affirmation Counseling Center.
Cloutier, Roland (NOR) Presbyteral Council.
Cloutier, Ronald F. '72 (GAL) Houston, TX All Saints; Harris County Jail; Correctional Ministries (Jail Chaplains).
Cloutier, Ronald F.. '72 (GAL) Houston, TX Federal Correctional Center.
Cloutier, Timothy D. '83 (STP) Associate Judges.
Cloutier, Timothy (STP) Waverly, MN St. Mary.
Clovis, Stephen M. '89 (P) Eugene, OR St. Paul; Navy Reserve Chaplains.
Clovis, Stephen (P) Area Vicars.
Clubb, Ronald E. *s.t.p.* '86 (HON) Retired.
Clune, Malachi *o.p.* '60 (SJN) Catano, PR Nuestra Senora del Carmen.
Clyne, James B. '47 (LA) Retired.
Clyne, Vincent F. '45 (NY) Staten Island, NY St. Ann Retired.
Cnircop, Manual *c.s.b.* (DET)[T] Detroit, MI Gabriel Richard Historical Society.

Coady, Frank '76 (SAL) Salina, KS St. Elizabeth Ann Seton.
Coady, Frank (SAL) College of Consultors.
Coady, Frank (SAL) Priests' Continuing Formation Committee.
Coady, Frank (SAL) Diocesan Committee Regarding Alleged Cases of Child Sexual Abuse.
Coady, Frank (SAL) Office of Liturgy.
Coady, Frank (SAL) Council of Priests.
Coady, Frank (SAL) Art and Architecture Commission.
Coady, Frank (SAL) Director of Religious Studies/ School of Pastoral Leadership.
Coady, John '59 (GF) Retired.
Coakley, John P. *s.j.* '70 (CHI)[D] Chicago, IL St. Ignatius Jesuit Community; [J] Maywood, IL Foster G. McGaw Hospital of Loyola University of Chicago.
Coakley, Paul S. '83 (WCH)[H] Wichita, KS Spiritual Life Center; Ongoing Formation of the Clergy Committee; Retreats.
Coakley, Richard J. *s.j.* '37 (BO)[V] Weston, MA Campion Health Center, Inc..
Coan, Gregory S. '03 (WDC) Graduate Studies.
Coates, John T. '45 (PH) Retired.
Coates, Roderick J.D. *s.s.j.* '89 (GAL) Washington, DC St. Luke.
Cobardo, Donato '99 (NEW) Jersey City, NJ Our Lady of Mercy.
Cobb, Gerald T. *s.j.* '81 (SEA)[A] Seattle, WA Seattle University.
Cobb, Richard E. *s.j.* '62 (SJ).
Cobel, Lawrence F. '73 (BUF)[D] Lackawanna, NY St. Barbara.
Cobenas, Pedro '92 (LA) Winnetka, CA St. Joseph the Worker.
Coble, Scott W. *s.j.* '79 (SPK)[B] Spokane, WA Gonzaga University.
Cobos, Abelardo '03 (GAL) Houston, TX Prince of Peace.
Coburn, Vincent P. '41 (NEW) Bloomfield, NJ Church of St. Thomas the Apostle; Short Hills, NJ St. Rose of Lima Retired.
Coby, Thomas W. '73 (RVC) Riverhead, NY St. John the Evangelist.
Cocca, Stephen M. '96 (WDC) Absent On Leave.
Cocca, Stephen '96 (HEL) Three Forks, MT Holy Family.
Coccarelli, August '63 (Y) Retired.
Cochran, George L. *o.p.* '62 (PRO)[P] Providence St. Thomas Aquinas Priory at Providence College.
Cochran, Paul M. *s.j.* '94 (FBK)[E] St. Marys, AK Native Ministry Training Program.
Cochran, Paul W. '88 (LFT) Alexandria, IN St. Mary; Diocesan Consultors; Members.
Cochran, Paul *s.j.* '94 (FBK) Chefornak, AK St. Catherine.
Cochran, Paul *s.j.* '94 (FBK)[E] St. Marys, AK Brother Joe Prince Jesuit Community.
Cochran, Paul *s.j.* '94 (FBK) Newtok, AK Holy Family.
Cochran, Paul *s.j.* (FBK) Presbyteral Council.
Cochran, Paul *s.j.* (FBK) Consultors.
Cochran, Ronald '01 (SD) San Diego, CA St. Michael.
Cocio, Carlos '83 (TUC) Administrative Leave of Absence.
Cockayne, John E. '85 (HRT) Thomaston, CT St. Thomas.
Coco, Francis J. *s.j.* '51 (LAF)[J] Grand Coteau, LA Our Lady of the Oaks Retreat House.
Cocucci, Joseph M.P.R. '96 (WIL) Vocation Office.
Coda, Joseph F. '63 (NEW)[N] Rutherford, NJ St. John Vianney Residence for Priests Retired.
Codd, Kevin '79 (SPK) On Duty Outside the Diocese.
Coddaire, Louis '52 (SR)[K] Arcata, CA Newman Community, Humboldt State University.
Code, Sean K. '93 (ALT) Lock Haven, PA St. Agnes.
Codega, John C. '99 (PRO) Salve Regina University; [B] Newport, RI Salve Regina University.
Cody, Aelred *o.s.b.* '57 (IND)[K] St. Meinrad, IN St. Meinrad Archabbey.
Cody, Daniel '62 (STA) Jacksonville, FL St. Joseph's.
Cody, Daniel (STA) Family Life, Diocesan Center for.
Cody, Henry P. '58 (HRT) West Hartford, CT St. Timothy's; Auditors (Part–time Case Instructors).
Cody, John K. '73 (COL) Columbus, OH Holy Family; Adjutant Judicial Vicars; Presiding Judges of First Instance.
Cody, John *c.ss.r.* (STU)[F] Steubenville, OH Holy Spirit Friary.
Cody, Kevin W. '93 (MAN) Military Chaplains; Air Force Chaplains.
Cody, Michael *s.s.c.* '73 (CHI)[K] St. Columbans St. Columban's Foreign Mission Society.
Cody, Nicholas A. '54 (STP) Retired.
Cody, Thomas '68 (STA) Absent on Sick Leave.
Coelho, Adilso *c.o.* '01 (CHR)[E] Rock Hill, SC Oratory of St. Philip Neri, Congregation of the Oratory of Pontifical Rite.
Coelho, Adilso *c.o.* '01 (CHR) Rock Hill, SC St. Anne's.
Coelho, Blaise (CHI) Tinley Park, IL St. George.
Coelho, Gabriel '98 (FTW) Fort Wayne, IN St. Charles Borromeo.
Coelho–Harguindeguy, John '67 (FRS) Fresno, CA St. Anthony of Padua.
Coello, Demetrio *s.d.b.* '60 (ARE) Orocovis, PR San Juan Bautista.
Coen, Alphonsus *c.p.* '74 (SCR)[M] Clarks Summit, PA St. Gabriel's Convent.
Coen, Charles P. '68 (NY)[H] Red Hook, NY St. Christopher.
Coen, Mark '90 (DUL) Silver Bay, MN St. Mary.
Coen, Mark '90 (DUL) Two Harbors, MN Holy Spirit.
Coenen, Thomas '77 (DM) Clarinda, IA St. Clare.
Coenen, Thomas '77 (DM) Clarinda, IA Sacred Heart.
Coenen, Thomas '77 (DM) Clarinda, IA St. Joseph.
Coens, Frank *o.f.m.* '73 (NSH)[H] Nashville, TN Franciscan Friars.
Coens, Frank *o.f.m.* '73 (NSH) Nashville, TN St. Vincent de Paul.
Coerber, Joseph H. '66 (MIL) New Holstein, WI St. Mary; Fond du Lac, WI St. John the Baptist.
Coerver, Richard V. '76 (STL) Washington, MO St. Gertrude.
Coerver, Robert F. *c.m.* '41 (STL)[O] St. Louis, MO Lazarist Residence.
Coerver, Robert M. (DAL) Censor Librorum; Priestly Life and Ministry Office.
Coffey, Andrew V. '47 (SAC) Davis, CA St. James; Charismatic Renewal Retired.
Coffey, Brian *m.h.m.* (NY) Suffern, NY Good Samaritan Hospital.
Coffey, Charles *c.s.sp.* '50 (SB)[E] Hemet, CA Holy Ghost Fathers.
Coffey, David '58 (MIL)[O] Milwaukee, WI Jesuit Community at Marquette University.
Coffey, Edward N. '37 (CHI) Retired.
Coffey, James Brian *m.h.m.* '72 (NY)[EE] Hartsdale, NY Mill Hill Fathers Residence.
Coffey, James F. '31 (RVC) Bay Shore, NY St. Patrick's Retired.
Coffey, James H. '45 (BO) Senior Priests Retired.
Coffey, Joseph L. '96 (PH) Military Chaplains; Navy Chaplains.
Coffey, Michael J. '91 (CAM) Stratford, NJ St. Luke.
Coffey, Peter *s.d.s.* '68 (NSH) Cookeville, TN St. Thomas Aquinas.
Coffey, Thomas A. '48 (TR)[M] Trenton, NJ Villa Vianney Retired.
Coffield, John V. '41 (ORG) San Juan Capistrano, CA San Felipe de Jesus Retired.
Cogan, Patrick *s.a.* '77 (NY)[EE] Paul Wattson Friary.
Cogan, William B. *s.j.* '55 (NY)[EE] New York, NY Murray–Weigel Hall.
Coghill, Elstan *o.f.m.* '48 (GAY)[L] Springfield, IL Our Lady of Angels Friary.
Coghlan, Brian '63 (ORG) Seal Beach, CA Holy Family.
Coghlan, John A. '44 (STO) Diamond Springs, CA Retired.
Coghlan, John '74 (MOB) Citronelle, AL St. Thomas.
Cogo, Joseph A. *c.s.* '58 (NY) New York, NY Our Lady of Pompeii.
Cohan, Dennis J. '74 (NEW) Glen Rock, NJ St. Catharine.
Cohea, Victor H. '80 (NO) New Orleans, LA St. Francis De Sales.
Cohelo, Gabriel *o.f.m.cap.* (DET) Harper Hospital and Rehabilitation Center.
Coholan, John F. *m.m.* '46 (FgM).
Coindreau, James M. *l.c.* (MO) Army Chaplains.
Coine, Robert E. '76 (WIL) Easton, MD SS. Peter and Paul.
Coira, Mark J. '94 (BO) Medway, MA St. Joseph.
Coiro, Gregory *o.f.m.cap.* '02 (LA)[F] La Canada Flintridge, CA St. Francis High School.
Cokman, Christopher '93 (BRK) Brooklyn, NY Our Lady of Monserrate–St. Ambrose.
Cokonougher, Brian K. '99 (DET) Detroit, MI St. Jude; Presbyteral Council.
Cokus, Joseph J. '58 (LA) Sierra Madre, CA St. Rita.
Colacicco, Frank L. '79 (SAN) Danville, CA St. Isidore's Retired.
Colacicco, Gerardo J. '82 (NY) Hopewell Junction, NY St. Columba.
Colacicco, Gerardo (NY) Canon 1742 Panel of Pastors.
Colacino, John A. *c.pp.s.* '80 (ROC)[I] Rochester, NY Missionaries of the Precious Blood.
Colagreco, Michael A. '77 (PH) Lenni, PA St. Francis de Sales.
Colaicovo, Arthur S. '92 (PAT) Convent Station, NJ St. Thomas More; Netcong, NJ St. Michael's.
Colaj, Rene Otzoy *o.s.b.* '82 (RCK)[G] Aurora, IL Marmion Abbey.
Colamaria, Francis A. '01 (BRK) Ozone Park, NY Nativity of the Blessed Virgin Mary.
Colamarino, Dennis J. (PIT) Defenders of the Bond.
Colamarino, Dennis '73 (PIT) Duquesne, PA Christ the Light of the World.
Colamarino, Dennis '73 (PIT) Duquesne, PA St. Joseph.
Colankin, Dimitrij '76 (AUS) Caldwell, TX Holy Rosary.
Colankin, Dimitrij '76 (AUS) Caldwell, TX St. Mary's.
Colankin, Dimitrij (AUS) Deans.
Colapietro, Peter M. '76 (NY) New York, NY Holy Cross; New York Sanitation Department.
Colaresi, Robert E. *o.carm.* '67 (JOL)[L] Darien, IL Carmelite Community; [N] Darien, IL Carmelite Spiritual Center; [O] Darien, IL Society of the Little Flower.
Colasito, Basil C. '59 (RVC) Great Neck, NY St. Aloysius.
Colasurdo, Peter H. (STA) Associate Judges.
Colasurdo, Peter '77 (STA) Retired.
Colautti, Federico '92 (DEN)[A] Denver, CO Redemptoris Mater House of Formation.
Colautti, John *o.s.b.* '55 (DET)[K] Detroit, MI St. Sylvester Monastery.
Colavechio, Francis D. '50 (LR) Jacksonville, AR St. Jude the Apostle.
Colavechio, Xavier G. *o.praem.* '55 (GB)[A] De Pere, WI St. Norbert Abbey; [L] De Pere, WI Norbertine Center for Spirituality.
Colavechio, Xavier *o.praem.* (JKS) Defenders of the Bond.
Colberg, James P. '55 (LA) Santa Maria, CA St. Mary of the Assumption Retired.
Colbert, Richard A. *c.pp.s.* (JC) Senators.
Colbert, Richard K. *s.m.* '64 (WDC)[M] St. Petersburg Beach, FL.
Colbert, Richard *c.pp.s.* '69 (JC) Warsaw, MO St. Ann.
Colborn, Francis R. (LA) Deanery 10; Members.
Colborn, Francis '64 (LA) Pasadena, CA St. Andrew.
Colchin, Stephen '84 (FTW) Monroeville, IN St. Rose of Lima; Council of Priests.
Colchin, Stephen E. '84 (FTW) New Haven, IN St. Louis.
Coldwell, Michael P. (SAT) Defenders of the Bond.
Cole, Barry '82 (PEO)[P] Urbana, IL Opus Dei.
Cole, Basil Burr *o.p.* '66 (WDC)[B] Washington, DC Dominican House of Studies.
Cole, Edwin J. '64 (JC) Columbia, MO Sacred Heart; Columbia, MO Columbia Catholic Hospital Ministry; Columbia, MO Veterans' Administration Medical Center; Appointed Members; Board of Trustees.
Cole, James J. '71 (BGP)[Q] Monroe, CT Provincial House, Immaculate Heart of Mary Province, Sisters of the Holy Family of Nazareth, C.S.F.N.
Cole, Raymond L. '72 (MET) Hillsborough, NJ St. Joseph; Pastoral Life; Deans; Episcopal Council.
Cole, Robert F. '72 (MAN) Dover, NH St. Joseph.
Cole, Robert J. '72 (CLV) Olmsted Falls, OH St. Mary of the Falls.
Cole, Vincent P. *m.m.* '71 (FgM).
Colella, David L. *o.ss.t.* '57 (DAL) Dallas, TX Santa Clara; Assistant Judicial Vicars.
Colella, David *o.ss.t.* '57 (BAL)[S] Dallas, TX.
Colello, Michael A. '01 (PRO) East Greenwich, RI Our Lady of Mercy.
Coleman, Brian P. (GB) Green Bay, WI St. Patrick; Adjutant Judicial Vicars; Judges in Second Instance.
Coleman, C. Michael '67 (KC) Special Assignment; Judicial Vicar; Archivist.
Coleman, Christopher L. '94 (BRK) Brooklyn, NY St. Ann–St. George.
Coleman, Donald E. '74 (SD) Carlsbad, CA St. Elizabeth Seton.
Coleman, Edward W. '70 (ALN) Brockton, PA St. Bartholomew; Brockton, PA St. Bertha.
Coleman, Gerald D. *s.s.* '68 (SFR)[A] Censores Librorum.
Coleman, Gerald J. '78 (TLS)[E] Tulsa, OK St. John Medical Center, Inc..
Coleman, James G. '77 (HRT) Waterbury, CT SS. Peter and Paul; Administrative Leave of Absence; Episcopal Vicars; College of Consultors.
Coleman, James Montini '99 (MOB) Mobile, AL St. Ignatius.
Coleman, James '73 (P) Salem, OR St. Joseph.
Coleman, James '76 (COL) Columbus, OH St. Timothy.
Coleman, James '85 ((P)) (FgM).
Coleman, John Kenneth (SFR).
Coleman, John P. '50 (KC) Retired.
Coleman, John R. '88 (PHX) Tempe, AZ Our Lady of Mt. Carmel.
Coleman, John '50 (SJ) Gilroy, CA St. Mary.
Coleman, John '50 (SJ) Retired.
Coleman, John *s.j.* '67 (LA)[C] Los Angeles, CA Jesuit Community.
Coleman, John '71 (SFR) On Duty Outside the Archdiocese.
Coleman, John *o.carm.* '78 (LA)[F] Encino, CA Crespi Carmelite High School.
Coleman, Joseph K. '81 (BO) Brighton, MA St. John of God Hospital; [Q] Boston, MA St. John of God Hospital.
Coleman, Michael A. '81 (JC) Moberly, MO St. Pius X; Moberly, MO Moberly Correctional Center; II. Columbia; Teens Encounter Christ (TEC).
Coleman, Michael *ss.cc.* '58 (FR).
Coleman, Paul *i.v.e.* '03 (SJ)[H] Santa Clara, CA Our Lady of Peace.
Coleman, R. Ed '86 (P) Molalla, OR St. James.
Coleman, Robert F. '78 (NEW)[B] School of Theology; [B] College Seminary; [B] School of Diplomacy and Intl. Rels.; Promoter of Justice.
Coleman, Robert J. '87 (JOL) Beaverville, IL St. Mary; Beaverville, IL St. Martin.

Coleman, Robert P. '78 (CHI) Other Assignments.
Coleman, William J. *m.m.* '39 (NY).
Coless, Gabriel M. *o.s.b.* '57 (PAT)[M] Morristown, NJ St. Mary's Abbey.
Coletta, Ralph V. '61 (CLV) Akron, OH St. John the Baptist.
Coletta, Thomas J. '63 (PAT) Paterson, NJ Our Lady of Victories; Deans.
Coletti, Arnold F. '62 (BO) Lexington, MA Sacred Heart.
Coley, James E. '47 (TR) Retired.
Coley, James '47 (TR)[M] Trenton, NJ St. Lawrence Rehabilitation Center.
Colfer, Robert *o.m.i.* '40 (PMB) Riviera Beach, FL St. Francis of Assisi.
Colgan, Arthur J. *c.s.c.* '73 (BGP)[P] Bridgeport, CT Provincial Offices of the Priests and Brothers of Holy Cross, Eastern Province.
Colgan, John '48 (SP) Retired.
Colgan, Marvin '40 (PEO) Retired.
Colgan, Richard J. *s.j.* '55 (PH)[AA] Loyola Center and Manresa Hall.
Colgan, Richard *c.s.p.* '78 (BO)[O] Boston, MA Paulist Center; Portland, OR St. Philip Neri; [Q] Portland, OR Paulist Fathers Catholic Center for Evangelization.
Colgan, Thomas A. '75 (SPK)[N] Spokane, WA Kateri Northwest Ministry Institute.
Colgan, Thomas J. '49 (RVC) Northport, NY St. Philip Neri Retired.
Colgan, Tobias *o.s.b.* '82 (EVN)[G] Ferdinand, IN Sisters of St. Benedict of Ferdinand, IN, Inc., Monastery Immaculate Conception.
Colgan, Tobias *o.s.b.* '82 (IND)[K] St. Meinrad, IN St. Meinrad Archabbey.
Colhour, David *c.p.* '94 (FgM).
Colhour, David *c.p.* '94 (CHI)[N] Passionist Theologate Community.
Colibraro, Daniel '56 (CHY) Retired.
Colibraro, Philip '57 (CHY) Retired.
Colicchio, Damian '62 (NEW)[B] Rutherford, NJ.
Colicchio, Damian '62 (NEW)[O] Lodi, NJ Immaculate Conception Convent.
Colicchio, Ralph M. '67 (HRT) Hamden, CT Our Lady of Mt. Carmel.
Colina, Jose '89 (SP) Tampa, FL St. Paul.
Coll, Eduardo *i.v.e.* '88 (PH) Philadelphia, PA St. Veronica.
Coll, Jerome B. *s.j.* '59 (PH)[C] Jesuit Fathers; [AA] Loyola Center and Manresa Hall.
Coll, John J. *s.j.* '56 (WH)[A] Wheeling, WV Wheeling Jesuit University.
Coll, Robert J. '59 (ALN) Retired.
Collard, Bruce W. '80 (MAN) Nashua, NH St. Christopher; [L] Manchester, NH St. George Manor.
Colleoni, Xavier *m.c.c.j.* '52 (LA) Los Angeles, CA St. Cecilia.
Coller, Jerome *o.s.b.* '59 (SCL)[I] Collegeville, MN St. John's Abbey, of the Order of St. Benedict.
Colleran, James A. '63 (CHI) Chicago, IL St. Mary of the Lake.
Collet, John '67 (DAL)[B] University of Dallas.
Collette, Richard '52 (WOR) Retired.
Colletti, Peter '84 (CLV) Independence, OH St. Michael.
Colletti, Richard M. '78 (WIN) Mankato, MN St. John the Baptist's.
Colletti, Richard M. (WIN) Auditors.
Collier, Joseph Mel '58 (SD) San Diego, CA St. Agnes.
Colligan, James P. *m.m.* '55 (LA)[Q] Los Angeles, CA.
Colligan, Joseph F. '50 (RVC)[EE] Centerport, NY Our Lady Queen of Martyrs Retired.
Colling, Paul J. '87 (GI) Lexington, NE St. Ann's; Justice and Peace Office; Priests' Advisory Board (Presbyteral Council); Cursillo.
Collini, Celsus O. '47 (BRK) Flushing, NY Queen of Peace Retired.
Collins, Austin I. *c.s.c.* '82 (FTW)[B] University of Notre Dame Du Lac; [I] Notre Dame, IN Holy Cross Community, Corby Hall, University of Notre Dame.
Collins, Carl '91 (HT) Golden Meadow, LA Our Lady of Prompt Succor.
Collins, Charles E. '72 (BO) Cambridge, MA St. John the Evangelist.
Collins, Charlie I. '82 (WIN) Byron, MN Christ the King; Byron, MN Holy Family; Propagation of the Faith.
Collins, Charlie I. (WIN) Auditors.
Collins, Corwin *o.s.b.* '57 (SCL)[I] Collegeville, MN St. John's Abbey, of the Order of St. Benedict.
Collins, Corwin *o.s.b.* '57 (SCL) Albany, MN Seven Dolors.
Collins, Daniel J. '58 (CHI) Chicago, IL St. Mary of the Lake Retired.
Collins, David J. *s.j.* '98 (CHI)[C] Chicago, IL Jesuit Community at Loyola University Chicago.
Collins, Denis E. *s.j.* '69 (SFR)[N] San Francisco, CA Jesuit Community at University of San Francisco.
Collins, Edward A. '68 (PAT) Pequannock, NJ Holy Spirit; RCIA Commission.
Collins, Edwin J. '54 (RVC) Malverne, NY Our Lady of Lourdes Retired.
Collins, Frederick J. '55 (BO) Senior Priests Retired.
Collins, James J. '64 (PH)[C] Philadelphia PA Holy Family University.
Collins, James M. *s.j.* '58 (BO)[V] Newton MA The Jesuit Community at Boston College; [V] Cohasset, MA Bellarmine House.
Collins, James M. '95 (CHL) Newton, NC St Joseph.
Collins, James R. '68 (CIN) Cincinnati, OH St. James of the Valley.
Collins, James R. '81 (PRO) Cranston, RI St Matthew.
Collins, James (BRK) Retired.
Collins, John E. *c.s.p.* '74 (NY) New York, NY St. Paul the Apostle.
Collins, John M. '79 (CHI) Chicago, IL St. Joachim.
Collins, John P. '72 (PH) Milmont Park, PA Our Lady of Peace.
Collins, John *c.s.s.r.* '87 (PH)[C] Gwynedd Valley, PA Gwynedd–Mercy College.
Collins, John '98 (LA) Pasadena, CA St. Philip the Apostle.
Collins, John (CHI) Presbyteral Council.
Collins, Kevin A. *o.m.i.* '82 (GAL) Houston, TX Immaculate Conception.
Collins, Lawrence E. '77 (CHI) Cicero, IL Our Lady of the Mount.
Collins, Leonard J. *c.s.c.* '69 (FgM).
Collins, Leonard J. *c.s.c.* '69 (AUS)[G] Austin, TX Congregation of Holy Cross – Southern Province.
Collins, Michael J. *o.s.b.* '37 (PAT)[M] Morristown, NJ St. Mary's Abbey.
Collins, Michael J. '67 (BR) Baton Rouge, LA Most Blessed Sacrament.
Collins, Michael T. *o.praem.* '78 (WIL)[AA] Paoli, PA Daylesford Abbey; [B] Claymont, DE Archmere Academy.
Collins, Michael '43 (ORG) Seal Beach, CA St. Anne's.
Collins, Michael '43 (ORG) Retired.
Collins, Neil J. '58 (NEW) Retired.
Collins, Patrick W. '64 (PEO) On Duty Outside the Diocese.
Collins, Raymond F. '59 (PRO) On Duty Outside the Diocese.
Collins, Raymond F. '59 (WDC)[C] Catholic University of America The.
Collins, Raymond F. *c.ss.r.* '70 (HBG) Ephrata, PA Mother of Perpetual Help.
Collins, Raymond G. *o.s.f.s.* '59 (WIL)[J] Childs, MD Retirement and Assisted Care Facility.
Collins, Raymond *c.ss.r.* '70 (HBG)[H] Ephrata, PA St. Clement's Mission House.
Collins, Raymond *c.ss.r.* (HBG) Presbyteral Council.
Collins, Robert C. *s.j.* '67 (NY)[EE] New York, NY "America;" Residence and publication office of the America Press; [II] New York, NY America Press, Inc..
Collins, Robert '81 (AUS) Retired.
Collins, Robert '88 (BRK) On Leave/Unassigned.
Collins, Russell J. '37 (BO) Senior Priests Retired.
Collins, Seamus *o.p.* '58 (SP) Hudson, FL St. Michael.
Collins, Shannon *c.p.m.* (OWN)[F] Auburn, KY Fathers of Mercy.
Collins, Stephen L. '83 (E) Retired.
Collins, T. Byron *s.j.* '52 (WDC)[M] Washington, DC The Jesuit Community at Georgetown University.
Collins, Terrence '71 (R) Hampstead, NC St. Jude the Apostle.
Collins, Terrence (R) Priests' Council.
Collins, Terrence (R) Deans.
Collins, Thomas E. '92 (NY)[E] White Plains, NY Archbishop Stepinac High School; Air National Guard Chaplains.
Collins, Thomas R. '72 (RIC) Richlands, VA St. Mary.
Collins, Thomas S. '92 (PT) Santa Rosa Beach, FL Christ the King Mission; Santa Rosa Beach, FL St. Rita.
Collins, Timothy '54 (BAK) Retired.
Collins, Timothy '58 (NY) New York, NY Our Lady of the Rosary.
Collins, Timothy '58 (NY) Retired.
Collins, Vincent '72 (ARL)[J] Berryville, VA Cistercian Abbey of Our Lady of the Holy Cross.
Collins, William A. '61 (BAL) Randallstown, MD Holy Family; Special Assignment; Adjutant Judicial Vicar.
Collins, William B. '74 (PAT) Hamburg, NJ St. Jude the Apostle.
Collins, William F. '65 (CAM) Retired.
Collins, William J. '60 (NY) Livingston Manor, NY St. Aloysius.
Collins, William P. '56 (RCK) Retired.
Collins, William *c.ss.r.* '49 (TR)[Q] Long Branch, NJ San Alfonso Retreat House.
Collins, William *m.s.c.*. '67 (SAT) San Antonio, TX Immaculate Conception.
Collins, Wm. Emmett *c.ss.r.* '52 (STL)[B] St. Louis, MO St. John Neumann House.
Collison, Craig A. '78 (SC) Sioux City, IA Sacred Heart; Carroll, IA St. Mary's.
Collogan, Robert '82 (JOL) Oswego, IL St. Anne.
Collopy, John C. '56 (BAL) Hydes, MD St. John the Evangelist; [O] Saint John Hall–Long Crandon Retired.
Collucci, Bennett *o.f.m.cap.* '57 (SAL)[E] Hays, KS St. Joseph's Friary.
Collucci, Bennett *o.f.m.cap.* '57 (SAL)[E] Hays, KS St. Joseph's Friary.
Collucci, Bennett '57 (SAL) Hays, KS St. Joseph's.
Collum, Patrick '92 (NO) New Orleans, LA Our Lady of Good Counsel.
Colnaghi, Andrew '79 (OAK)[S] Berkeley, CA Incarnation Monastery, Camaldolese Benedictines.
Colnaghi, Andrew *o.s.b.cam.* '79 (MRY)[F] Berkeley, CA Incarnation Monastery.
Colohan, Edward A. '61 (BGP) Trumbull, CT St. Stephen.
Colom, Marti (MIL)[X] Racine, WI Missionary Community of St. Paul the Apostle and Mary, Mother of the Church, Inc.; On Duty Outside the Archdiocese.
Colomb, Jackson '90 (CHI) Mundelein, IL Santa Maria Del Popolo.
Colombo, Ronald A. '72 (GB) Denmark, WI St. James; Denmark, WI All Saints; Kellnersville, WI St. Joseph; Denmark, WI Holy Trinity.
Colominas, Octavio Guillermo '02 (MIA) Southwest Ranches, FL St. Mark.
Colon, Alberto Diaz (ARE) Defenders of the Bond.
Colon, Angel '95 (CGS) Gurabo, PR San Jose.
Colon, Hector *c.ss.r.* '76 (CGS) San Lorenzo, PR Nuestra Senora de la Mercedes.
Colon, Jose E. '63 (PCE) On Duty Outside the Diocese.
Colon, Jose '61 (PCE) Retired.
Colon, Jose '01 (ARE) Graduate Studies.
Colon, Ricardo (ARE) Utuado, PR San Miquel.
Colon, Vincent A. '50 (STP) Retired.
Colon Marrero, Miguel Angel '02 (SJN) Toa Alta, PR San Fernando Rey; Toa Baja, PR San Pedro Apostol.
Colopy, James L. '86 (COL) Columbus, OH St. Dominic.
Colopy, James '86 (COL) OSU Hospital East.
Colosimo, Eugene J. '43 (SJ)[M] Los Gatos, CA Sacred Heart Jesuit Center.
Colosimo, Felix R. '65 (SY) New Hartford, NY Our Lady of the Rosary.
Colozzi, Charles J. '02 (CAM) Sewell, NJ Holy Family; Advocates.
Colpitts, Albert B. '73 (PRT) York, ME St. Christopher–by–the–Sea.
Colter, Dennis J. '66 (DUB) Waterloo, IA Queen of Peace; Personnel Advisory Board.
Colton, Bernard '50 (PHX) Retired.
Colton, Bradford '45 (HRT) Wethersfield, CT Corpus Christi.
Colton, Bradford '45 (HRT) Retired.
Colton, Gary '68 (HON) Honolulu, HI Co–Cathedral of St. Theresa of the Child Jesus.
Colton, Gary (HON) Diocesan Planning and Building Commission.
Colton, Gary (HON) Presbyteral Council.
Colucci, Gregory (PAT) Retired.
Colucci, Gregory (PAT) Paterson, NJ St. Joseph's.
Colvin, Andrew '02 (BAK) Hermiston, OR Our Lady of Angels.
Colwell, Michael P. (AMA) Ex Officio; Vicar General; Chancellor; Ex Officio; College of Consultors; Vocation Development Team; Promoter of Justice; [I] Amarillo, TX Project Solidarity; [I] Amarillo, TX Marriage Encounter.
Comandini, Glenn J. '86 (MET) Hopelawn, NJ Our Lady of the Most Holy Rosary; Office for Multicultural Ministries; College of Consultors; Theological Commission.
Comboy, Richard *s.j.* '69 (STL)[O] St. Louis, MO Jesuit Community Corporation at St. Louis University – Jesuit Hall.
Combs, Gordon *o.f.m.cap.* '64 (HON) Aiea, HI St. Elizabeth.
Combs, Gordon *o.f.m.cap.* (HON) Secular Franciscan Order.
Combs, Ronald P. '03 (CIN) Kettering, OH Ascension.
Comeau, Ronald R. '71 (LFT) On Duty Outside the Diocese.
Comellas, Wilfredo T. '03 (SCR) Tobyhanna, PA St. Ann.
Comelo, Gabriel (DET) Detroit, MI Detroit Receiving Hospital; Detroit, MI Hutzel Hospital.
Comer, John P. '64 (STL) Crestwood, MO St. Elizabeth of Hungary.
Comer, Michael E. '80 (COV) Bellevue, KY Divine Mercy; Dayton, KY St. Bernard; [B] Newport, KY Newport Central Catholic High School.
Comerford, Christopher J. '96 (SFD) Nokomis, IL St. Louis; Nokomis, IL St. Barbara.
Comerford, John J. *o.carm.* '77 (JOL)[L] Joliet, IL St. Elias Carmelites.
Comerford, Patrick '69 (LA)[L] Santa Monica, CA Saint John's Child Study Center, Saint John's Hospital & Health Center.
Comerford, Patrick '69 (LA)[J] Santa Monica, CA Saint John's Health Center; Hospital Chaplains.
Comesanas, Raul E.L. '77 (NEW) Newark, NJ St. Thomas Aquinas.
Comeskey, Edwin T. '55 (SY) Retired.
Comeskey, John H. '56 (SY) Utica, NY St. Elizabeth Hospital; [M] Utica, NY St. Elizabeth Hospital Retired.
Comesky, Clement *o.f.m.* '55 (NY).

Comesky, Clement *o.f.m.* '55[EE] (FgM).
Comiskey, James '50 (LUB) Retired.
Comiskey, John P. '60 (NY)[E] New York, NY Monsignor Farrell High School.
Commane, William J. '51 (BO) Senior Priests Retired.
Commons, Patrick M. '51 (IND) Retired.
Commons, Thomas *s.v.d.* '47 (CHI)[B] Techny, IL Divine Word Residence.
Commyn, James E. '86 (DET) Richmond, MI St. Augustine.
Como, Denis R. *s.j.* '66 (FgM).
Compaired, Fernando '63 (MIA) Miami, FL Mother of Our Redeemer.
Compentente, Virgilio '67 (NY) Yonkers, NY Immaculate Conception.
Complo, Daniel C. '54 (DET) Retired.
Compos, Pedro '02 (CHI) Chicago, IL Our Lady of Tepeyac.
Comstock, Douglas G. '67 (OG) Sackets Harbor, NY St. Andrew.
Comstock, Eliot *o.f.m.conv.* '69 (IND)[J] Mount St. Francis, IN Mount Saint Francis Friary and Retreat Center.
Comtois, Norman *o.m.i.* '73 (BO)[V] Lowell, MA Missionary Oblates of Mary Immaculate.
Conaboy, Conan *c.p.* '47 (SCR)[M] Clarks Summit, PA St. Gabriel's Convent.
Conahan, John J. '62 (PH) Jenkintown, PA Immaculate Conception.
Conan, Constantine J. *c.ss.p.* '48 (PIT)[P] Bethel Park, PA Holy Spirit Animation Center.
Conard, James A. *m.m.* '56 (FgM).
Conard, Ray J. '55 (GB) Retired.
Conaty, Charles '88 (CAM) Hammonton, NJ St. Martin de Porres; Assistant Vocation Directors for Recruitment.
Conboy, Joseph T. '53 (SCR) Retired.
Conboy, Michael F. '62 (ROC) East Rochester, NY St. Jerome; Priests' Personnel Board.
Conboy, Michael (ROC) Department of Priest Personnel.
Conboy, Richard L. *s.t.l.* '60 (PIT) Allegheny County, PA Kane Regional Center – Scott.
Conboy, Richard '60 (PIT)[O] Coraopolis, PA Our Lady of the Sacred Heart Convent.
Concagh, Thomas V. *c.m.* '52 (BRK)[V] Jamaica, NY Vincentian Residence.
Concagh, Thomas *c.m.* '52 (NY)[HH] Staten Island, NY St. John's University.
Concannon, Stephen F. '64 (PRT) Brunswick, ME St. Charles; [M] Brunswick, ME Newman Center.
Concannon, Stephen (PRT) Pastoral Assocs..
Concepcion, Francisco '65 (ARE) Vega–Alta, PR Immaculate Conception of Blessed Virgin Mary.
Concepcion, Francisco (ARE) Diocesan Consultors.
Concepcion, Francisco (ARE) Priest's Senate (Consejo Presbiteral).
Concepcion, Mervin '03 (SAC) Elk Grove, CA Good Shepherd Catholic Church.
Concepcion, Pablo '93 (MGZ)[D] Mayaguez, PR Opus Dei (Prelature of the Holy Cross and Opus Dei).
Concha, Alfonso J. '76 (PH) Military Chaplains; Navy Chaplains.
Concha, Antonio *s.j.* '63 (ELP) El Paso, TX Sacred Heart.
Concha, Augusto '72 (ARE) Barceloneta, PR Church of Our Lady of Mt. Carmel.
Concha, Augusto '72 (PH) On Duty Outside the Archdiocese.
Concordia, Don Stefano *o.s.b.* '95 (HRT)[N] Bethlehem, CT Abbey of Regina Laudis.
Concordia, George Lawrence *o.p.* '58 (NY)[EE] New York, NY St. Catherine of Siena Priory; [II] New York, NY Dominican Shrine of St. Jude, Inc.; [EE] New York, NY St. Vincent Ferrer Priory.
Conde, Jose Maria *s.f.* '68 (SFE)[B] Silver Spring, MD Holy Family Seminary.
Conde, Norberto '89 (GAL) Houston, TX Our Lady of Sorrows.
Conde, Thomas P. '87 (CHI).
Conde–Ocampo, Ramon *o.m.* '59 (SJN)[A] San Juan, PR Ntra. Sra. de Fatima.
Condon, Daniel J. (ROC) Chancellor; Chancellor and Director of the Department of Legal Services; College of Consultors; Board of Directors; Vicar for Religious.
Condon, Daniel '81 (ROC) Rochester, NY St. Thomas More.
Condon, Daniel (ROC) Newly Ordained Priests.
Condon, Denis '78 (CHI) Schaumburg, IL St. Marcelline.
Condon, Edwin A. '61 (BO) Graduate Studies.
Condon, Edwin D. '61 (BO) Westwood, MA St. Denis.
Condon, Gerald A. '56 (DUB) Retired Priests' Representatives; Directors Retired.
Condon, Gerald W. '55 (BAK) Heppner, OR St. Patrick's; Heppner, OR St. William.
Condon, Liam '63 (ALB) Salem, NY Holy Cross.
Condon, Liam '63 (ALB) Cambridge, NY St. Patrick.
Condon, Michael J. '41 (LA) Retired.
Condon, Robert M. '56 (SC)[A] Sioux City, IA Briar Cliff University Retired.
Condon, Sean '57 (ORG) Fountain Valley, CA Holy Spirit.
Condon, T. Mark (PAT) Special Assignment; Vice Chancellor; Secretary to the Bishop; Defenders of the Bond.
Condon, Thomas M. *o.p.* '88 (MEM) Special Assignment.
Condon, Thomas *o.p.* '88 (NO)[P] Metairie, LA St. Martin de Porres Shrine.
Condon, William F. '54 (RIC) Retired.
Condon, William G. *c.s.c.* '61 (FR)[H] North Dartmouth, MA St. Joseph's Hall; Navy Reserve Chaplains.
Condren, William '73 (PT) Retired.
Condron, Patrick A. '76 (WH) Wheeling, WV St. Alphonsus; Promoter Justitiae.
Condron, Robert F. '69 (HRT) Ansonia, CT Assumption.
Condry, John T. *s.j.* '49 (LAF)[J] Grand Coteau, LA Our Lady of the Oaks Retreat House.
Conen, Paul F. '57 (DET)[P] Clarkston, MI Colombiere Center.
Conesa, Diego '57 (STA) Retired.
Confer, Bernard T. *o.p.* '73 (HRT) New Haven, CT St. Mary's Priory.
Confer, Thomas B. *o.p.* '73 (HRT).
Confroy, Thomas J. *o.s.b.* '58 (PAT)[M] Morristown, NJ St. Mary's Abbey.
Cong, Joseph Chu *o.c.s.o.* '48 (WOR)[O] Spencer, MA St. Joseph's Abbey.
Congdon, John '87 (FRS) On Special Assignment.
Congdon, John (FRS) Fresno, CA St. Therese.
Congdon, Lois (CC).
Congdon, Robert J. '87 (BO)[A] Brighton, MA St. John Seminary School of Theology; [C] Brighton, MA St. John Seminary College.
Congro, Basil P. '78 (CHR) Spartanburg, SC Jesus Our Risen Savior; Absent On Leave; Pilgrimages, Diocesan Coordinator for.
Conheeney, Thomas P. '55 (NEW) Bayonne, NJ St. Mary Star of the Sea.
Coning, Jeffrey '97 (COL) Dublin, OH St. Brigid of Kildare.
Conkle, Francis J. *s.t.* '78 (SJN) Loiza, PR Santiago Apostol, El Mayor.
Conlan, F. Allan '54 (SCR) Elmhurst, PA St. Eulalia.
Conlan, Timothy *o.p.* '67 (OAK)[N] Oakland Western Dominican Province.
Conlan, Timothy *o.p.* '67 (FgM).
Conlan, Walter *s.j.* '76 (BAH)[V] Newton, MA The Jesuit Community at Boston College.
Conley, Brian J. *s.j.* '01 (BO)[V] Boston The Society of Jesus of New England–Provincial Offices; [M] Washington, DC The Jesuit Community at Georgetown University.
Conley, Charles '74 (MIL) Elm Grove, WI St. Mary.
Conley, James '85 (WCH) On Duty Outside the Diocese.
Conley, John E. *c.s.c.* '79 (FTW)[B] University of Notre Dame Du Lac; [I] Notre Dame, IN Holy Cross Community, Corby Hall, University of Notre Dame.
Conley, John J. *s.j.* '83 (NY)[EE] Loyola Hall, Jesuit Community.
Conley, John *c.p.* '76 (L) Louisville, KY St. Agnes; [K] Louisville, KY Sacred Heart Retreat.
Conley, John *c.p.* (L) Ex Officio.
Conley, Lawrence J. '67 (PRT) Gorham, ME St. Anne.
Conley, Lawrence '67 (PRT)[M] Gorham Campus.
Conley, Lawrence (PRT) Maine Diocesan Council of Catholic Women.
Conley, Lawrence (PRT) Pastoral Assocs..
Conley, Martin P. '57 (OM) Retired.
Conley, Peter V. '64 (BO) Norfolk, MA St. Jude; SOUTH REGION.
Conley, Raymond J. '36 (DM) Retired.
Conley, Rory T. '89 (WDC) Leonardtown, MD St. Aloysius; Special Ministries.
Conley, Roy H. '61 (PIT) Pittsburgh, PA St. Elizabeth.
Conley, Seraphin *t.o.r.* '61 (ORL)[E] New Smyrna Beach, FL Villa Madonna.
Conley, Thomas P. '47 (CHI) Retired.
Conlin, Bernard J. '40 (WOR) Retired.
Conlin, Dan '90 (STP) St. Paul, MN St. Columba.
Conlin, Daniel C. (STP) Special Assignment; Judicial Vicar.
Conlin, Edwin J. '42 (NY) New York, NY Immaculate Conception.
Conlin, Edwin '42 (NY) Retired.
Conlin, John A. *s.j.* '54 (WDC) Washington, DC St. Aloysius; [E] Washington, DC Gonzaga College High School.
Conlon, Anthony J. '62 (WH) Retired.
Conlon, Arthur F. '46 (TR) Retired.
Conlon, Christopher W. *s.m.* '66 (CIN)[D] Dayton, OH The University of Dayton; [M] Dayton, OH Marianist Community; [Q] Dayton, OH University of Dayton Campus Ministry.
Conlon, Colm '59 (ORG) Irvine, CA St. John Neumann.
Conlon, Colm (ORG) Council of Priests.
Conlon, James '64 (OAK)[B] Holy Names College.
Conlon, James '02 (LAN) Ann Arbor, MI St. Francis of Assisi.
Conlon, Matthew T. *o.f.m.* '45 (ALB) Mount McGregor Correctional Facility; [B] Siena College.
Conlon, Philip J. '55 (MAD) Retired.
Conlon, Richard '90 (BRK) Jackson Heights, NY Blessed Sacrament.
Conlon, Timothy *o.s.c.* '79 (PHX) Special Assignment.
Conlon, Timothy *o.s.c.* '79 (PHX)[G] Phoenix, AZ Crosier Community of Phoenix (Canons Regular of the Order of the Holy Cross).
Conlon, Timothy *o.s.c.* (PHX) Office of Hispanic Ministry.
Conmy, John J. *o.s.f.s.* '36 (WIL)[J] Childs, MD Retirement and Assisted Care Facility.
Conn, James J. *s.j.* (BAL) Canonical Adviser, Office of.
Conn, James *s.j.* (BAL) Promoter of Justice.
Conn., James J. *s.j.* '74 (BAL)[S] Pont. Univ. Greg..
Connaghan, Daniel H. '90 (HRT) Milford, CT Christ the Redeemer.
Connall, Darrin '92 (SPK)[A] Spokane, WA Bishop White Seminary.
Connall, Darrin (SPK) Vocation Director.
Connall, Darrin (SPK) Priests' Personnel Board.
Connall, Darrin (SPK) Bishop White Seminary.
Connaughton, James '50 (MIA) Retired.
Connaughton, James '50 (MIA) Deerfield Beach, FL St. Ambrose.
Connaughton, Lawrence M. '70 (NY) New York, NY St. Joseph.
Connaughton, Lawrence (NY) Canon 1742 Panel of Pastors.
Conneally, J. Philip *s.j.* '44 (LA)[F] Los Angeles, CA Loyola High School of Los Angeles.
Connealy, Gerald A. '87 (OM) Pierce, NE St. Joseph; [G] Norfolk, NE Faith Regional Health Services.
Conneely, Sean *s.s.c.* '69 (CHI)[N] Chicago, IL Columban Fathers Mission Center.
Connell, Andrew F. '51 (BO) South Boston, MA St. Vincent de Paul; [AA] Boston, MA St. Thomas More Chapel; [EE] Boston, MA Propagation of the Faith and Holy Childhood Association & Society of St. Peter the Apostle; Pontifical Society of St. Peter the Apostle.
Connell, James C. (MIL) Vice Chancellor; Vice Chancellor.
Connell, James E. '87 (MIL)[X] Milwaukee, WI St. Thomas More Lawyers Society; Special Assignment; Sheboygan, WI St. Clement; Sheboygan, WI Holy Name; Judges for Second Instance.
Connell, John Andrew '80 (PAT) Randolph, NJ Resurrection.
Connell, John F. '62 (WOR) Northbridge, MA St. Peter.
Connell, John K. '66 (BO) Senior Priests Retired.
Connell, John M. '85 (LR) Little Rock, AR St. Theresa's.
Connell, Kevin G. *s.j.* '95 (P)[L] Portland, OR Colombiere Community.
Connell, Kevin *s.j.* '95 (P)[F] Portland, OR St. Andrew Nativity School.
Connell, Loren *o.f.m.* '76 (CIN)[M] Cincinnati, OH St. John the Baptist Friary; [M] Cincinnati, OH St. Francis Seraph Friary.
Connell, Mark '55 (NY)[HH] Newburg, NY Mt. St. Mary College.
Connell, Mark '86 (NY)[C] Newburgh, NY Mt. St. Mary College.
Connell, Mark (NY) On Duty Outside the Archdiocese.
Connell, Martin T. *s.j.* '94 (DET)[K] Detroit Jesuit Provincial Office–Detroit Province of the Society of Jesus.
Connell, Patrick J. '92 (DET) Berkley, MI Our Lady of La Salette.
Connell, Stephen J. '62 (WIL) Wilmington, DE St. Joseph on the Brandywine.
Connell, William J. '76 (Y) Poland, OH Holy Family.
Connell, William R. '75 (MAD) Oregon, WI Holy Mother of Consolation.
Connellan, Thomas J. *c.s.p.* '56 (PMB)[J] Vero Beach, FL Paulist Fathers Residence.
Connellan, Thomas J. *c.s.p.* '56 (NY)[EE] Jamaica Estates Paulist Fathers Generalate.
Connelley, Brennan *o.f.m.* '56 (NY) Bronx, NY Holy Cross.
Connelly, Christian T. '96 (ARL) On Duty Outside the Diocese; Military Chaplains; Army Chaplains.
Connelly, Christopher D. '93 (SPR) Springfield, MA Sacred Heart; Vice–Chancellors; Secretary to the Bishop; Diocesan Director of Ceremonies; Presbyteral Council.
Connelly, Donald F. '58 (WIN) Plainview, MN St. Joachim's.
Connelly, Donald F. (WIN) Auditors.
Connelly, Edward C. '65 (BAL) Crofton, MD St. Elizabeth Ann Seton.
Connelly, James F. '55 (PH) Philadelphia, PA Stella Maris.
Connelly, James N. '49 (BUF)[O] Tonawanda, NY O'Hara Residence Retired.
Connelly, James *c.s.c.* '64 (P)[B] University of Portland.
Connelly, James *c.s.c.* '64 (P)[L] Portland, OR Holy Cross Fathers & Brothers, C.S.C. – University of Portland.
Connelly, John J. '50 (BO) Newton Center, MA Sacred Heart.

Connelly, Laurence D. (GAL) Retired.
Connelly, Mark J. *s.j.* '87 (BAL)[S] Baltimore Jesuit Fathers and Brothers Maryland Provincial Curia.
Connelly, Michael J. '60 (BRK) Rockaway Point, NY St. Thomas More–St. Edmund.
Connelly, Norbert T. (STU) Presbyteral Council.
Connelly, Norbert '56 (STU) Retired.
Connelly, Paul J. '50 (DM) Retired.
Connelly, Peter *o.s.b.* '87 (WOR)[O] Still River, MA Benedictine Monks, St. Benedict Abbey.
Connelly, William P. '45 (RIC) Retired.
Connelly, Xavier *o.s.b.* '89 (WOR)[O] Still River, MA Benedictine Monks, St. Benedict Abbey.
Conner, Glenn T. '52 (PIT)[N] Pittsburgh, PA St. John Vianney Manor Retired.
Conner, Herbert K. *s.j.* '61 (CHR) Simpsonville, SC St. Mary Magdalene.
Conner, James *o.c.s.o.* '57 (L)[K] Trappist, KY Abbey of Our Lady of Gethsemani, of the Order of Cistercians of the Strict Observance.
Conner, Michael P. '85 (GAY) Onekama, MI St. Joseph; Vicars (by region).
Conner, Paul M. *o.p.* '67 (Oakland Prov.)[P] Providence St. Thomas Aquinas Priory at Providence College.
Conner, Robert J. '49 (PH) Morrisville, PA St. John the Evangelist Retired.
Conner, Steven '94 (NEW) Fort Lee, NJ Holy Trinity.
Conners, Quinn *o.carm.* '71 (WDC)[B] Washington, DC Whitefriars Hall.
Connerton, Barry R.L. '70 (PRO) Providence, RI St. Augustine.
Connery, J. Thomas '63 (ALB) Glenville, NY Immaculate Conception; Priests Retirement Board.
Connery, Sean P. *o.s.f.s.* '69 (WIL) Elsmere, DE Veteran's Hospital; [B] Wilmington, DE Salesianum School.
Connery, Thomas '83 (ORL) De Land, FL St. Peter's; [F] De Land, FL Stetson University Catholic Campus Ministry.
Connery, Thomas (ALB) Deans; Ministry to Priests.
Conniff, John J. '49 (BUF)[S] Buffalo, NY Office; [H] Buffalo, NY Society of St. Vincent de Paul Retired.
Connole, Marlin '68 (SEA) Seattle, WA St. Bridget.
Connolly, Andrew P. (RVC) Patchogue, NY St. Francis de Sales.
Connolly, Andrew (RVC) Brookhaven.
Connolly, Brian W. '55 (PIT) On Duty Outside the Diocese.
Connolly, Charles B. *s.j.* '74 (BO)[V] Boston, MA Loyola House.
Connolly, Clement J. '64 (LA) South Pasadena, CA Holy Family.
Connolly, Edward B. '66 (ALN) Pottsville, PA St. Francis de Sales; Pottsville, PA St. Joseph.
Connolly, Edward J. '49 (SB) Riverside, CA Sacred Heart.
Connolly, Fidelis *c.p.* '50 (WOR)[O] Shrewsbury, MA Calvary Retreat Center, Passionist Fathers of Shrewsbury, Inc..
Connolly, Francis T. '59 (CHL) Retired.
Connolly, Gerard M. *t.o.r.* '69 (ALT)[F] Newry, PA St. Bernardine Monastery; [F] Hollidaysburg, PA Province Econome's Office.
Connolly, James H. '48 (BO) Senior Priests Retired.
Connolly, James M.T. '78 (ALN) Military Chaplains; Navy Chaplains.
Connolly, James P. '54 (NY) New York, NY St. John the Evangelist; Holy Name Society Archdiocesan Union of New York.
Connolly, Jerry '69 (GF) Forsyth, MT Immaculate Conception.
Connolly, Jerry (GF) Personnel Board.
Connolly, Jerry (GF) '63 Continuing Formation of Clergy.
Connolly, John G. '63 (BO) Wrentham, MA St. Mary.
Connolly, John J. '94 (BO) Graduate Studies; Secretaries to the Archbishop and Masters of Ceremonies.
Connolly, John P. *o.s.f.s.* '57 (WIL)[J] Childs, MD Retirement and Assisted Care Facility.
Connolly, John T. '78 (PAT) Paterson, NJ St. Stephen's; Advocates.
Connolly, John *s.d.b.* '81 (NEW) Bloomfield, NJ Church of St. Thomas the Apostle.
Connolly, John *s.d.b.* (NEW) Assoc. Superintendents.
Connolly, Joseph F. *t.o.r.* '68 (VEN) Sarasota, FL Our Lady Queen of Martyrs.
Connolly, Joseph M. *c.s.s.* '57 (BO)[Y] Waltham, MA Stigmatine Fathers and Brothers.
Connolly, Joseph *s.v.d.* '60 (BO)[V] Duxbury, MA Society of the Divine Word.
Connolly, Joseph *t.o.r.* (VEN) Presbyteral Council.
Connolly, K. Scott '95 (SEA) Longview, WA St. Rose de Viterbo.
Connolly, Kevin '85 (WIN) Fairmont, MN Holy Family.
Connolly, Kevin '85 (WIN) Fairmont, MN St. John Vianney.
Connolly, Kevin (WIN) Auditors–in–Training.
Connolly, Larkin '47 (PMB) Palm Springs, FL St. Luke.
Connolly, Larkin '47 (PMB) Retired.
Connolly, Leo L. '81 (COL)[C] Zanesville, OH Bishop Rosecrans High School; Priests' Senate; Priests' Senate.
Connolly, Leo '81 (COL) Zanesville, OH St. Nicholas.
Connolly, Leo (COL) Diocesan Judges.
Connolly, Leon L. '37 (DUB) Retired.
Connolly, Leon L. '58 (DUB) On Special or Other Archdiocesan Assignment.
Connolly, Leon L. (DUB) Vicar for Hispanic Ministry; Priests Assigned to Hispanic Ministry; Ex Officio Members.
Connolly, Luke '52 (CHI)[N] Chicago, IL Passionist Community–Immaculate Conception Monastery.
Connolly, Luke *c.p.* '52 (CHI)[N] Chicago, IL Passionist Missions, Inc..
Connolly, Luke *c.p.* '52 (FgM).
Connolly, Mark '57 (BGP) Greenwich, CT St. Michael the Archangel.
Connolly, Mark '57 (BGP)[X] Greenwich, CT Clemons Productions, Inc..
Connolly, Mark (BGP) Communications.
Connolly, Matthew J. '53 (ORL) Special Assignment; Judicial Vicar.
Connolly, Matthew (ORL) Judges.
Connolly, Maurice V. '62 (BO) Senior Priests Retired.
Connolly, Michael J. *s.j.* '68 (BO)[V] Boston The Society of Jesus of New England–Provincial Offices; [B] Spokane, WA Gonzaga University.
Connolly, Michael '78 (NY)[EE] Yonkers, NY St. Clare Friary.
Connolly, Neil A. '58 (NY) New York, NY St. Mary.
Connolly, Patrick F. *o.p.* '52 (WDC) Washington, DC St. Dominic Church & Priory.
Connolly, Patrick *s.j.* '66 (Wisconsin)[Q] Los Angeles, CA Columbiere House.
Connolly, Paul E. '83 (DAV) Keokuk, IA All Saints.
Connolly, Paul '83 (DAV) Montrose, IA St. Joseph's.
Connolly, Paul (DAV) Diocesan Consultors
Connolly, Peter *c.ss.r.* '77 (DEN)[N] Denver, CO.
Connolly, Peter (DEN)[S] Denver, CO Redemptorist Society of Iowa; [S] Denver, CO Redemptorist Fathers.
Connolly, Peter (DEN)[S] Denver, CO Redemptorist Fathers (Idaho).
Connolly, Robert P. '79 (PIT) Cecil, PA St. Mary.
Connolly, Thomas '52 (SFS) Retired.
Connolly, Thomas *s.j.* '63 (B) DeSmet, ID Sacred Heart.
Connolly, Thomas (SPK) Dayton, WA St. Mark.
Connolly, Thomas (SPK) Pomeroy, WA Holy Rosary.
Connolly, Thomas (SPK) Dayton, WA St. Joseph.
Connolly, Vincent F. *s.j.* '70 (BO)[V] Boston, MA Loyola House.
Connolly, William *s.j.* '46 (BO)[V] Newton, MA The Jesuit Community at Boston College.
Connor, Adrian J. *o.praem.* '95 (ORG)[I] Silverado, CA Norbertine Fathers of Orange Inc..
Connor, Bernard *c.m.f.* '50 (LA)[W] Los Angeles, CA Claretian Retreat Center (All Groups).
Connor, Brian P. '89 (LIN) David City, NE St. Francis; [C] David City, NE Aquinas/St. Mary's Schools; [L] David City, NE Aquinas High School Endowment Fund.
Connor, Brian (LIN) Presbyteral Council.
Connor, Charles P. '90 (SCR) Carbondale, PA St. Rose of Lima; Diocesan Historian.
Connor, Gerald T. '54 (ROC) Rochester NY St. Theodore Retired.
Connor, J Patrick '61 (NSH) Columbia, TN St. Catherine; Vicars General.
Connor, Jack *c.p.* '84 (SCR)[M] Clarks Summit, PA St. Gabriel's Convent.
Connor, James E. '60 (PRT)[J] Saco, ME Bay View Community.
Connor, James L. '59 (BAL)[S] Baltimore, MD Jesuit Community of Loyola College, Inc..
Connor, James L. *s.j.* '59 (BAL)[B] Timonium, MD Loyola Graduate Center –Timonium Campus.
Connor, James '78 (HEL) Helena, MT St. Mary.
Connor, John F. (NEW) Full–time Staff
Connor, John S. *c.s.c.* '70 (SB) Coachella, CA Our Lady of Soledad; [E] Coachella, CA Congregation of the Holy Cross.
Connor, Kevin T. '87 (MAN) Hanover, NH St. Denis.
Connor, Martin J. (BO) League of Catholic Women.
Connor, Martin P. '64 (BO)[A] Brighton, MA St. John Seminary School of Theology; [EE] Boston, MA League of Catholic Women of the Archdiocese of Boston.
Connor, Patrick L. '83 (ROC) Elmira, NY Sts. Peter and Paul of Eastside Catholic Parish.
Connor, Patrick *s.v.d.* '57 (TR)[M] Bordentown, NJ Society of the Divine Word.
Connor, Patrick (ROC) Board of Directors; Elmira, NY St. Mary.
Connor, Sean M. '01 (BO) South Boston, MA St. Brigid.
Connor, Stephen J. '89 (NY)[EE] Jamaica Estates, NY Paulist Fathers Generalate.
Connor Stephen J. *c.s.p.* '89 (NY) New York, NY St. Paul the Apostle.
Connor Vincent '71 (SB) Corona, CA St. Matthew.
Connor, William J. '46 (COL) Retired
Connor, William *m.s.c.* '57 (OG)[E] Watertown, NY Missionaries of the Sacred Heart.
Connors, Albert *c.m.f.* '73 (LA)[Q] Rancho Dominguez, CA Dominguez Seminary Inc..
Connors, Brocard *o.carm.* '57 (NY)[EE] Office of Lay Carmelites.
Connors, Canice *o.f.m.conv.* '61 (ALB)[A] Rensselaer, NY Conventual Franciscan Friars.
Connors, Canice *o.f.m.conv.* '61 (ALB)[L] Rensselaer, NY Provincialate, Immaculate Conception Friary – Order of Friars Minor Conventual.
Connors, Canice *o.f.m.conv.* '61 (FgM).
Connors, Cletus *o.s.b.* '72 (SCL) Cold Spring, MN St. Boniface.
Connors, Cletus *o.s.b.* '72 (SCL)[I] Collegeville, MN St. John's Abbey, of the Order of St. Benedict.
Connors, Cletus *o.s.b.* (SCL) Deans.
Connors, Cletus *o.s.b.* (SCL) Presbyteral Council.
Connors, Edmund P. '66 (NY) Katonah, NY St. Mary of the Assumption; [E] New York, NY Moore Catholic High School.
Connors, Edward M. '46 (NY) Scarsdale, NY Immaculate Heart of Mary Retired.
Connors, Francis E. '73 (BUR)[E] Fairfax, VT St. Luke.
Connors, J. M. *o.p.* '51 (FgM).
Connors, John E. '01 (SPR) Springfield, MA Holy Name.
Connors, John P. '99 (CAM) Merchantville, NJ St. Peter's.
Connors, John (SPR) Presbyteral Council.
Connors, Joseph *s.v.d.* '52 (CHI)[B] Techny, IL Divine Word Residence.
Connors, Michael E. *c.s.c.* '84 (FTW)[I] Notre Dame, IN Holy Cross Community, Corby Hall, University of Notre Dame.
Connors, Michael *c.s.c.* '84 (FTW)[B] University of Notre Dame Du Lac.
Connors, Paul *s.v.d.* '63 (TR)[M] Bordentown, NJ Society of the Divine Word.
Connors, Richard P. '79 (PH) Willow Grove, PA St. David.
Connors, Robert A. '55 (NEW) Retired.
Connors, Robert A. '55 (TR) Bradley Beach, NJ Ascension.
Connors, Robert L. '71 (BO) Archdiocesan College of Consultors; Secretary for Ministerial Personnel; Ministerial Personnel; Members; Priestly Renewal Advisory Board; Ex Officio.
Connors, Terrence '75 (MAD) Madison, WI St. Thomas Aquinas.
Conole, Robert W. '91 (BO) Braintree, MA St. Francis of Assisi.
Conoscenti, Frederick M. '65 (BUF) On Duty Outside the Diocese.
Conover, James A. '78 (TR) Keyport, NJ St. Joseph.
Conover, Sylvan J. *o.f.m.cap.* '49 (NY)[EE] Yonkers, NY St. Clare Friary.
Conrad, Anthony J. '49 (DAV)[L] Davenport, IA Kahl Home for the Aged and Infirm Retired.
Conrad, Brian P. '76 (HBG) Lancaster, PA St. Philip the Apostle.
Conrad, John '63 (GB) Absent on Leave.
Conrad, Simon R. *o.f.m.cap.* '46 (STL) St. Louis, MO St. Patrick; [O] St. Louis, MO St. Patrick Friary.
Conroy, Donald B. '64 (GBG) On Duty Outside the Diocese; [V] Washington, DC National Institute for the Family, Inc..
Conroy, Francis M. '64 (BO) Wayland, MA St. Ann; Unassigned.
Conroy, Francis X. '72 (BEA) Commission for Continuing Education of Clergy & Religious; Beaumont, TX St. Pius X.
Conroy, J. Peter *s.j.* '71 (NY)[EE] Cornwall, NY Jogues Retreat.
Conroy, James A. '53 (CLV) Retired.
Conroy, James P. '53 (DAV) Retired.
Conroy, James R. *s.j.* '78 (WDC)[E] Washington, DC Gonzaga College High School.
Conroy, James R. *s.j.* '78 (BAL)[W] Baltimore, MD Ignatian Lay Volunteer Corps.
Conroy, John Jerome *o.p.* '49 (NY)[EE] New York, NY St. Catherine of Siena Priory.
Conroy, Kevin M. '82 (CLV) Loudonville, OH St. Peter; Ministers.
Conroy, Kevin (CLV)[X] Ashland.
Conroy, Patrick J. *s.j.* '83 (Oregon)[M] Washington, DC The Jesuit Community at Georgetown University.
Conroy, Philip M. '64 (BO) Groveland, MA St. Patrick.
Conroy, Philip '64 (BO)[P] Brighton, MA St. Elizabeth's Hospital of Boston.
Conroy, Phillip M. (BO) Boston, MA St. Elizabeth's Medical Center.
Conroy, Thomas J. '48 (STP)[C] St. Paul, MN University of St. Thomas Retired.
Conry, Austin '65 (MOB) Butler, AL St. John The Evangelist.
Conry, James A. '53 (CLV) Parma, OH St. Charles Borromeo; Wadsworth, OH Sacred Heart of Jesus.
Conry, Roy *o.carm.* '56 (TUC)[E] Tucson, AZ Carmelite Priory.
Conry, Roy *o.carm.* '56 (TUC)[A] Tucson, AZ Salpointe Catholic High School.
Consalvi, Mark *ss.cc.* '43 (HON) Honolulu, HI Blessed Sacrament.

Consalvi, Mark *ss.cc.* (HON) Honolulu Institute No. 84.
Consani, Robert E. '59 (KAL) Kalamazoo, MI St. Monica Retired.
Consani, Robert E. '63 (KAL) Retired.
Conserva, Stephen *o.m.i.* '74 (MIA) Miramar, FL St. Stephen.
Considine, James '02 (MET) Warren, NJ Our Lady of the Mount.
Considine, Matthew J. *s.m.m.* '77 (BRK) Ozone Park, NY St. Mary Gate of Heaven; [V] Ozone Park, NY Montfort Missionaries Provincialate (Missionaries of the Company of Mary) – Formation Community.
Considine, William J. *s.m.m.* '73 (BRK)[V] Ozone Park Montfort Missionaries Provincialate (Missionaries of the Company of Mary) – Formation Community.
Consiglio, Cyprian *o.s.b.cam.* '98 (MRY)[F] Big Sur New Camaldoli Hermitage; Santa Cruz, CA Holy Cross.
Consla, Federico *c.ss.r.* '70 (CGS) Aguas Buenas, PR Church of Tres Santos Reyes.
Constance, Jogues *o.f.m.cap.* '53 (DET)[P] Washington, MI Capuchin Retreat.
Constance, Samuel C. '55 (TR)[M] Trenton, NJ Villa Vianney; Tribunal Judges Retired.
Constant, Van '93 (HT) Houma, LA Cathedral of St. Francis De Sales.
Constant, Van '93 (HT) Terrebonne Parish General Hospital.
Constantin, Rodrigue '03 (OLL) St. Paul, MN Holy Family Church.
Constantine, Bennett P. (LAN) Defenders of the Bond.
Constantine, Bennett '58 (LAN) Eaton Rapids, MI St. Peter.
Constantine, Cyprian G. *o.s.b.* '77 (GBG)[H] Latrobe, PA Saint Vincent Archabbey.
Contadino, Eugene *s.m.* '70 (CIN)[D] Dayton, OH The University of Dayton; [D] Dayton, OH The University of Dayton; [M] Dayton, OH Marianist Community.
Contant, Robert '46 (FTW) Retired.
Contant, Robert '46 (FTW)[B] Carthagena, OH St. Charles.
Contardi, Michael *o.de.m.* '60 (CLV) Cleveland, OH St. Rocco.
Conte, James W. '48 (NY) Retired.
Conte, John P. '58 (ALN) Reading, PA Holy Rosary.
Conte, John P. '64 (HRT) Madison, CT St. Margaret; Episcopal Vicars.
Conterno, Austin *s.d.b.* '48 (SFR) San Francisco, CA SS. Peter and Paul.
Conti, Cornelius *o.f.m.* '62 (SP)[O] St. Petersburg, FL St. Anthony Friary.
Conti, John P. '46 (NY) Retired.
Conti, Vincent G. *s.j.* '01 (WDC) Washington, DC Holy Trinity; [C] Scranton, PA The University of Scranton.
Continillo, Rocco A. '56 (CAM)[E] Carneys Point, NJ Corpus Christi; Southwest Deanery.
Contons, Albert J. '48 (BO) Senior Priests Retired.
Contons, Albert (LIT) Lithuanian R. Catholic Priests' League of America.
Contran, Sergio *m.c.c.j.* '50 (CIN)[M] Cincinnati, OH Comboni Missionaries (Verona Fathers)–Comboni Mission Center; [N] Montclair, NJ Comboni Missionaries of the Heart of Jesus (Verona Fathers).
Contreras, David '93 (AMA) Pampa, TX Sacred Heart; Pampa, TX St. Vincent de Paul.
Contreras, Eloy Trujillo '89 (SB)[E] Corona, CA Operarios Del Reino De Cristo, O.R.C..
Contreras, Rigoberto '89 (FWT) Denton, TX Immaculate Conception.
Contreras, Wilfredo '03 (MIA) Miami, FL St. John Bosco.
Conva, Mathias T. (NEW) Union North Deanery 23.
Conva, Matthias T. '62 (NEW) Union, NJ St. Michael's.
Converse, Brian J. '91 (NOR) Lebanon, CT St. Francis of Assisi.
Converse, Brian J. (NOR) Army National Guard Chaplains.
Convertino, David *o.f.m.* '77 (BO)[AA] Boston, MA St. Anthony Shrine.
Convery, James S. '02 (MET) Somerville, NJ Immaculate Conception.
Convery, Paul C. *c.o.* '84 (PH) Philadelphia, PA St. Francis Xavier; [AA] Philadelphia, PA The Philadelphia Congregation of The Oratory of St. Philip Neri.
Convery, Thomas L. *s.s.c.* '40 (PRO)[P] Bristol, RI St. Columban's Retirement House.
Convey, Edwin H. *s.j.* '53 (BAL)[S] Baltimore, MD Jesuit Community of Loyola College, Inc..
Conway, David '52 (WDC) Washington, DC St. Mary, Mother of God.
Conway, Dennis *m.c.c.j.* '68 (CIN)[M] Cincinnati, OH Comboni Missionaries (Verona Fathers)–Comboni Mission Center.
Conway, Dennis *m.c.c.j.* '68 (FgM).
Conway, Gerald W. '56 (WIN) Elected Senior Member Retired.
Conway, James P. '60 (PH)[AA] Villanova, PA St. Thomas Monastery.
Conway, James '65 (SAT) Castroville, TX St. Louis.
Conway, Jeffrey '73 (NY) Staten Island, NY Our Lady Star of the Sea.
Conway, John E. *m.m.* '73 (FgM).
Conway, John L. '56 (GBG) Irwin, PA Immaculate Conception; Deaneries; College of Consultors; Bishop's Priests Council.
Conway, John R. '69 (SFE) Albuquerque, NM St. Jude Thaddeus; Associate Judges.
Conway, John T. '77 (PH) Regional Vicars; Priests' Personnel Board; Philadelphia, PA Saint Cyprian.
Conway, John T. '03 (ATL) Washington, GA St. Joseph's.
Conway, John (SFE) Finance Council.
Conway, Laurence '59 (MIA) Retired.
Conway, Malachy '95 (SAC) Absent on Leave.
Conway, Michael J. *o.ss.t.* '73 (NY) New York, NY St. Brigid.
Conway, Michael *s.d.b.* '92 (NO)[D] Marrero, LA Archbishop Shaw High School.
Conway, Michael (PAT) Retired.
Conway, Neil '63 (CLV) Retired.
Conway, Pierre H. *o.p.* '41 (WDC)[B] Washington, DC Dominican House of Studies.
Conway, Richard C. '63 (BO) Brockton, MA St. Margaret; Brockton, MA St. Patrick.
Conway, Richard J. '45 (BAK) Retired.
Conway, Richard T. '63 (BO) Andover, MA St. Robert Bellarmine.
Conway, Robert *c.pp.s.* '53 (CIN)[M] Ypsilanti, MI.
Conway, Thomas A. *c.pp.s.* '57 (KC)[J] Liberty, MO Precious Blood Center.
Conway, Thomas D. '60 (BO) Reading, MA St. Athanasius.
Conway, Thomas '86 (BLX) Hattiesburg, MS St. Thomas Aquinas.
Conway, Thomas '86 (BLX) University of Southern Mississippi.
Conway, Thomas (BLX) Defenders of the Bond.
Conway, Thomas (BLX) Campus Ministry.
Conway, Thomas (BLX) Presbyteral Council.
Conway, Thomas (BLX) Association of Priests (Diocese of Biloxi and Jackson).
Conway, Thomas (JKS) Association of Priests.
Conway, Thomas (BLX) Deans.
Conway, Tommy '72 (BLX)[G] Hattiesburg, MS University of Southern Mississippi.
Conway, William '77 (JOL) West Chicago, IL St. Mary.
Conwell, Joseph *s.j.* '50 (SPK)[D] Spokane, WA Gonzaga Preparatory School.
Conwill, Giles '73 (SD) On Duty Outside the Diocese.
Conyard, James R. *s.j.* '62 (P)[L] Portland, OR Colombiere Community.
Conyers, Richard *c.s.c.* '69 (CHI)[D] Niles, IL Notre Dame High School.
Conziemus, Jay (STP) Defenders of the Bond.
Coogan, Roch A. *o.f.m.* '54 (SP)[O] Belleair Bluffs, FL St. James Friary; Air Force Reserve Chaplains.
Coogan, Thomas M. (RVC) Senate of Priests (Presbyteral Council/College of Consultors).
Coogan, Thomas '97 (RVC) Wantagh, NY St. Frances de Chantal.
Coogan, Thomas (RVC) Vocations.
Cook, A. '90 (ALX) Nachitoches, LA Holy Cross.
Cook, Adrian L. '72 (MOB) Brewton, AL St. Maurice.
Cook, Damien J. '99 (OM) Fremont, NE St. Patrick; Age Groups.
Cook, Daniel A. '90 (ALX)[I] Natchitoches, LA Northwestern State University.
Cook, Daniel '90 (GR) On Duty Outside the Diocese.
Cook, Douglas '94 (ORG)[H] Yorba Linda, CA Polish Center.
Cook, Douglas '94 (ORG) Special Assignment.
Cook, Douglas (ORG) Council of Priests.
Cook, Douglas (ORG) Judges.
Cook, Douglas (ORG) Judicial Vicar.
Cook, Douglas (ORG) Consultors.
Cook, Edward J. '67 (MIL) Milwaukee, WI Congregation of the Great Spirit.
Cook, Emil *o.f.m.conv.* '66 (FgM).
Cook, John B. '49 (TR) Retired.
Cook, John Joseph *f.i.* '02 (SY)[U] Maine, NY Mount St. Francis Hermitage, Inc..
Cook, John N. '56 (GI) Retired.
Cook, John P. '45 (HRT) Retired.
Cook, Joseph T. '86 (CHI) Matteson, IL St. Lawrence O'Toole.
Cook, Kevin A. '01 (FR) New Bedford, MA Our Lady of Mt. Carmel.
Cook, Louis G. '58 (WIN) Retired.
Cook, Michael J. '73 (WIL) Newark, DE St. John the Baptist–Holy Angels.
Cook, Michael L. *s.j.* '66 (SPK)[B] Spokane, WA Gonzaga University.
Cook, Millard S. '92 (NY) New York, NY Our Lady of Lourdes; Bronx, NY St. Gabriel.
Cook, Millard *o.s.b.* '92 (GBG)[H] Latrobe Saint Vincent Archabbey.
Cook, Paul G. '59 (BAL) Cockeysville, MD St. Joseph; [V] Cockeysville, MD St. Joseph, Texas; Consultors; League of the Little Flower; Consultors; [V] Cockeysville, MD St. Joseph, Texas.
Cook, Philip C. *o.s.a.* '97 (TLS)[B] Tulsa, OK Cascia Hall Preparatory School.
Cook, Rob '03 (B) Nampa, ID St. Paul's.
Cook, Robert J. (LC) Viroqua, WI Annunciation of the Blessed Virgin Mary.
Cook, Robert W. (CHY) Casper, WY Our Lady of Fatima.
Cook, Robert (CHY) Presbyteral Council.
Cook, Robert (CHY) College of Consultors.
Cook, Stephen M. '97 (KC) Holden, MO St. Patrick's.
Cook, Stephen (KC) Vocations.
Cook, Thomas E. '97 (WIN) Easton, MN Our Lady of Mount Carmel; Easton, MN St. John the Baptist; Vocations; Appointed Members; Vocations Advisory Council.
Cook, Thomas R. *o.s.a.* '57 (MIA)[H] Miami, FL Casa San Lorenzo.
Cook, Thomas '88 (LA) Santa Maria, CA St. Mary of the Assumption.
Cook, Timothy R. '83 (STL) St. Louis, MO Visitation–St. Ann's Shrine; St. Louis, MO Sts. Teresa and Bridget.
Cook, William G. '88 (NEW) East Orange, NJ Holy Name of Jesus.
Cooke, Colman M. '65 (SP) Clearwater, FL St. Michael The Archangel.
Cooke, John F. '59 (CAM) Pitman, NJ Our Lady Queen of Peace.
Cooke, Vincent M. *s.j.* '67 (BUF)[O] Buffalo, NY Canisius Jesuit Community; [C] Buffalo, NY Canisius College.
Cookson, Edmund L. *m.m.* '65 (FgM).
Cool, Brian '93 (ROC)[L] Rochester, NY Catholic Newman Community at the University of Rochester.
Cool, Thomas L. '01 (SFS) Pierre, SD SS. Peter and Paul.
Cooley, Fred *s.j.* '54 (FgM).
Cooley, John E. '48 (LA) Retired.
Cooley, Stephen V. *o.carm.* '67 (GAL) Houston, TX St. Michael.
Coolong, Raymond E. *s.m.* '71 (BO)[X] Framingham, MA The Marist House.
Coombs, James R. *s.s.e.* '52 (BUR) Putney, VT Our Lady of Mercy Retired.
Coomes, J. Eugene *s.j.* '48 (STL)[O] St. Louis, MO Jesuit Community Corporation at St. Louis University – Jesuit Hall.
Coon, David N. '93 (SPC) Scott City, MO St. Joseph.
Coon, J.C. '01 (BEA) Beaumont, TX St. Anne; Port Arthur, TX St. James.
Coonan, James J. '65 (PH) Retired.
Coonan, Robert J. '65 (SPR) Hatfield, MA St. Joseph's; Hatfield, MA Holy Trinity; Deans.
Cooney, Albert *s.m.a.* '55 (FgM).
Cooney, Camillus *o.s.b.* '56 (LR)[A] Subiaco, AR Subiaco Monastery.
Cooney, David *s.d.s.* '67 (PHX) Phoenix, AZ St. Mark.
Cooney, Dennis J. '74 (VEN) Lehigh Acres, FL St. Raphael.
Cooney, Dennis (VEN) Associate Moderators.
Cooney, Francis C. *m.s.* '69 (HRT) Hartford, CT Our Lady of Sorrows; [M] Hartford, CT Our Lady of Sorrows Rectory.
Cooney, Gerald '50 (FWT) Retired.
Cooney, John M. '62 (HRT) Watertown, CT St. John the Evangelist; Cursillo Movement, Archdiocesan Director of.
Cooney, Michael N. '75 (DET) Mount Clemens, MI St. Peter; Archdiocesan Vicars.
Cooney, Patrick *o.s.b.* '91 (IND)[A] St. Meinrad, IN St. Meinrad School of Theology.
Cooney, Patrick *o.s.b.* '91 (IND)[K] St. Meinrad, IN St. Meinrad Archabbey; Air National Guard Chaplains.
Cooney, Robert F. *c.s.v.* '57 (LAV)[D] Las Vegas, NV Clerics of St. Viator Retirement Home.
Cooney, Roger P. '70 (COV) Melbourne, KY St. Philip.
Cooney, Romaeus *o.carm.* '58 (ALB) Troy, NY St. Joseph.
Cooney, Romaeus *o.carm.* '58 (ALB) Troy, NY Holy Trinity.
Cooney, Sean K. '59 (ORL) Winter Park, FL Saints Peter and Paul.
Cooney, Stephen A. '76 (LIN) Holdrege, NE All Saints; Deaneries and Deans.
Cooney, Theophane *c.p.* '52 (BRK)[V] Jamaica, NY Immaculate Conception Monastery.
Cooney, Theophane *c.p.* '52 (BRK) Jamaica, NY Immaculate Conception.
Cooney, Xavier *s.v.d.* '83 (WH) Summersville, WV St. John The Evangelist.
Cooper, Brian G. *c.s.v.* (CHI)[N] Arlington Heights Viatorian Province Center–Clerics of St. Viator.
Cooper, David E. '70 (MIL) Milwaukee, WI St. Matthias.
Cooper, Donald A. '53 (NEW) Retired.
Cooper, Donald J. '63 (E) Houtzdale, PA Christ the King.
Cooper, Donald L. '63 (E) Ramey, PA Holy Trinity.
Cooper, Harold V. '49 (SC) Retired.
Cooper, James W. '80 (LIN) Bruno, NE St. Anthony; Advocates.
Cooper, Jeffrey A. *c.s.c.* '94 (COS)[F] Cascade, CO Holy

Cross Novitiate.
Cooper, John A. '80 (LIN) Tecumseh, NE St. Andrew's; Diocesan Area CCD Directors.
Cooper, Joseph M. '95 (MAN) Manchester, NH St. Joseph Cathedral; Masters of Ceremonies; Office for Worship.
Cooper, Leo '43 (KCK) Special Assignment.
Cooper, Leo (KCK) Archdiocesan Archivist.
Cooper, Mark A. *o.s.b.* '76 (MAN)[K] Manchester, NH St. Anselm Abbey.
Cooper, Michael W. *s.j.* '73 (SP)[N] Chicago Chicago Province of the Society of Jesus–Provincial Office.
Cooper, Michael *s.j.* '73 (SP)[A] St. Leo, FL Saint Leo University, Institutional Research.
Cooper, Patrick E. '91 (CHR) Mauldin, SC St. Elizabeth Ann Seton.
Cooper, Ronald C. '83 (CIN) Fayetteville, OH St. Angela Merici.
Cooper, Warren L. '71 (NO) Marrero, LA Immaculate Conception.
Coopmans, Joseph R. *o.praem.* (GB) Denmark, WI St. Isidore the Farmer.
Coover, Thomas '78 (SAM) On Duty Outside the Diocese.
Coover, Thomas '02 (MAN) Somersworth, NH St. Mary.
Coover, Thomas '02 (MAN) Somersworth, NH Holy Trinity.
Copeland, Leonard R. *o.c.d.* '67 (MIL) Milwaukee, WI St. Florian.
Copeland, Robert F. '99 (LAN) Flint, MI St. Mary; Flushing, MI St. Robert.
Copenhaver, John L. '88 (LIN) Lincoln, NE Nebraska Penal Complex; Apostolate to the Elderly.
Copp, Rodney J. '73 (BO) Waltham, MA St. Charles Borromeo; Archdiocesan Judges; Canonical Affairs Committee.
Coppenrath, Leonard A. (BO) Spiritual Directors..
Coppenrath, Leonard '53 (BO) Senior Priests Retired.
Coppinger, Edmund '59 (WIL) Georgetown, DE St. Michael the Archangel Retired.
Coppola, Anthony '02 (SP) Largo, FL St. Patrick.
Coppola, Anthony (SP) Scouting Office, Boys.
Coppola, Paul R. '51 (BUF) Retired.
Coppola, Vincent J. *c.s.c.* '01 (BUR) Bennington, VT Sacred Heart St. Francis de Sales.
Cops, Augustine *o.f.m.cap.* '86 (DET) Detroit, MI St. Charles Borromeo.
Cops, Peter *s.s.s.* '52 (CLV)[O] La Crosse, WI Holy Cross Diocesan Center.
Cops, Peter (LC)[H] La Crosse, WI Holy Cross (Seminary) Diocesan Center.
Copsey, Robert A. '78 (SAC) Marysville, CA St. Joseph.
Corali, Serafino A. '47 (RVC)[M] Uniondale, NY St. Pius X Residence Retired.
Corapi, John '91 (CC)[G] Robstown, TX Society of Our Lady of the Most Holy Trinity.
Corbaton, P. Jose Alcocer *m.ss.cc.* '64 (SJN) Trujillo Alto, PR San Bartolome.
Corbett, Eugene J. *s.j.* '62 (SJ).
Corbett, Eugene *s.j.* '62 (SJ)[D] Santa Clara Valley Medical Center.
Corbett, John B. '56 (PIT)[N] Pittsburgh, PA St. John Vianney Manor.
Corbett, John Dominic *o.p.* '80 (WDC)[B] Washington, DC Dominican House of Studies.
Corbett, Michael E. '54 (PBL) Retired.
Corbett, Ricard (NEW) Priestly Vocation Board.
Corbett, Richard R. (NEW) CYO Youth and Young Adult Ministries.
Corbett, Robert '51 (STL) Manchester, MO Christ, Prince of Peace.
Corbett, W. Joseph '95 (ATL) Alpharetta, GA St. Brigid.
Corbin, Don '70 (TOL)[G] Oregon, OH St. Charles Mercy Hospital.
Corbino, Thomas A. '72 (JOL) Frankfort, IL St. Anthony.
Corbley, Timothy L. '93 (STP) Special Assignment.
Corbo, Alfred P. '56 (CHI) Franklin Park, IL St. Gertrude.
Corces, Pedro M. (MIA) Vocations.
Corces, Pedro '88 (MIA) Miami, FL Prince of Peace.
Corces, Pedro (MIA) Television and Radio Center.
Corces, Pedro (MIA) Archdiocesan Vocations Review Board.
Corcione, Michael *o.f.m.* '01 (NY)[EE] St. Peter Friary.
Corciulo, Cosimo '56 (SB) Norco, CA California Rehabilitation Center.
Corcoran, Anthony J. *s.j.* (NO)[P] P/Box "Inigo".
Corcoran, Brian M. '72 (SD) El Cajon, CA Holy Trinity; Presbyteral Council.
Corcoran, Clifton J. '54 (AMA)[C] Panhandle, TX St. Joseph's Home for Retired Priests Retired.
Corcoran, D. Stanley '90 (DAL)[M] Commerce, TX East Texas State University; Campbell, TX St. Joseph.
Corcoran, Frank '54 (JKS) Retired.
Corcoran, John J. '55 (RVC) Center Moriches, NY St. John the Evangelist.
Corcoran, John J. *m.m.* '63 (FgM).
Corcoran, John W. '53 (BO) Senior Priests Retired.
Corcoran, Kevin '88 (SY) Canastota, NY St. Agatha.
Corcoran, Lawrence E. *s.j.* '63 (BO)[V] Weston, MA Campion Jesuit Community; [X] Weston, MA Campion Renewal Center.
Corcoran, Lawrence J. '43 (COL) Columbus, OH Holy Cross Retired.
Corcoran, Michael P. *s.j.* '88 (NY)[EE] Jesuit Community, Kohlmann Hall.
Corcoran, Seamus *t.o.r.* (ORL)[E] New Smyrna Beach, FL Villa Madonna.
Corcoran, Shawn D. (COL) Columbus, OH St. Cecilia.
Corcoran, Shawn '00 (COL) Corrections Reception Center.
Corcoran, Shawn (COL) Diocesan Consultors.
Corcoran, Shawn (COL) Priests' Senate.
Corcoran, T. Kevin '99 (PAT) Hawthorne, NJ St. Anthony's.
Corcoran, Thomas B. '98 (BO) Dorchester, MA St. Ann.
Corcoran, William T. '81 (CHI) Oak Lawn, IL St. Linus.
Corcuera, Manuel '70 (CHK) Saipan, MP San Vicente Parish; Chancellor.
Corcuera, Manuel (CHK) Presbyteral Council.
Corcuera, Manuel (CHK) College of Consultors; Legion of Mary.
Corcuera, Manuel (CHK) Commission on Family Life.
Corcuera, Manuel (CHK) Cursillo Movement.
Corcuera, Manuel (CHK) Diocesan Pastoral Council.
Cordano, Virgil *o.f.m.* '45 (LA)[Q] Santa Barbara, CA Franciscan Friary, Order of Friars Minor (Old Mission).
Cordaro, Frank '85 (DM) Leave of Absence.
Cordeiro, Anthony *o.p.* '67 (OAK)[N] Oakland, CA Dominican Order, Siena House.
Corder, Stephen J. *s.j.* '01 (OAK)[N] Berkeley, CA Jesuit Community at Jesuit School of Theology at Berkeley; [N] San Francisco, CA Jesuit Community at University of San Francisco.
Cordero, Carlos *o.s.a.* '99 (SJN) Bayamon, PR San Agustin; [E] San Juan, PR Centro Medico de P.R..
Cordero, Faustino '71 (BRK) Brooklyn, NY St. Rocco's.
Cordero, Faustino (BRK) Presbyteral Council.
Cordero, Jovito (AGN) Tamuning, GU St. Anthony and St. Victor.
Cordero, Martin '99 (LSC) Las Cruces, NM Holy Cross.
Cordero, Mert '74 (NEW) Ridgewood, NJ Our Lady of Mount Carmel.
Cordero, Mert '74 (NEW) Ridgewood, NJ Valley Hospital.
Cordero, Mert '74 (NEW) Chaplains.
Cordery, Robert J. '80 (MO) Unassigned.
Cordery, Robert J. (BOS) Air Force Reserve Chaplains.
Cordes, Christopher L. '95 (JC) Jonesburg, MO St. Patrick; Montgomery City, MO Immaculate Conception; Appointed Members; Ministry to Priests.
Cordes, John '03 (KCK) Frankfort, KS Annunciation; St. Monica – St. Elizabeth.
Cordes, John '03 (KCK) Marysville, KS St. Gregory's.
Cordier, Michael L. '02 (CIN) Cincinnati, OH Guardian Angels.
Cordisco, Philip *o.ss.t.* '60 (TR) Trenton, NJ St. James.
Cordoba, Guillermo '00 (ATL) Duluth, GA St. Benedict.
Cordori, Joseph B. (PIT) Pittsburgh, PA St. Thomas More.
Cordova, Hugo *o.f.m.* '91 (ELP) El Paso, TX Our Lady of Guadalupe.
Coreas, Edwin A. '92 (GAL) Houston, TX Our Lady of St. John.
Corel, Joseph S. '02 (JC) Jefferson City, MO St. Joseph Cathedral; Bonnots Mill, MO St. Louis; Loose Creek, MO Immaculate Conception; Jefferson City, MO Jefferson City Correctional Center; Ministry to Priests.
Coric, Christopher *o.f.m.conv.* '71 (BUF) Veterans Hospital; Lackawanna, NY Our Lady of Bistrica.
Coriden, James A. '57 (GRY) On Duty Outside the Diocese.
Corigliano, Anthony M. *c.s.s.* '55 (SPR) Springfield, MA Our Lady of Mt. Carmel.
Corkery, Daniel '55 (ALX) Simmesport, LA Christ the King.
Corkery, Raymond *o.carm.* '59 (JOL) Joliet, IL Mount Carmel.
Corl, Ronald *c.p.* '66 (SAC)[K] Citrus Heights, CA Christ the King Passionist Retreat Center.
Corl, Ronald *c.p.* '66 (SAC)[I] Citrus Heights, CA Christ the King Retreat.
Corl, Ronald *c.p.* '66 (GAL)[S] Houston, TX Holy Name Retreat Center.
Corley, Joseph '75 (PH) Darby, PA Blessed Virgin Mary.
Corley, Malachy *o.c.s.o.* '55 (ATL)[K] Conyers, GA The Monastery of the Holy Spirit.
Corley, Theodosius *o.f.m.cap.* '74 (NY) Yonkers, NY Sacred Heart.
Corley, Thomas '85 (JOL)[K] Naperville, IL St. John Vianney Villa.
Corley, Thomas '85 (JOL) Retired.
Cormack, James B. *c.m.* '76 (STL) St. Louis, MO St. Catherine Laboure.
Cormack, James *c.m.* (STL) Society of St. Vincent de Paul, Council of St. Louis.
Cormack, Michael J. '54 (SAC) Roseville, CA St. Rose of Lima Retired.
Cormier, Gregory P. '83 (LAF) Baldwin, LA Sacred Heart; Franklin, LA St. Peter the Apostle.
Cormier, Leo G. '57 (BO) Senior Priests Retired.
Cormier, Michael Robert (SP) St. Petersburg, FL St. Paul.
Cormier, Robert J. '82 (NEW) Newark, NJ Cura (Community United to Rehabilitate Addicts); Chaplains; Chaplains.
Cormier, Robert '82 (NEW) Newark, NJ Northern State Prison.
Cormier, Roger C. '61 (BO) Senior Priests Retired.
Cormier, William N. '71 (WOR) East Douglas, MA St. Denis.
Cornea, Sergiu '96 (ROM) Aurora, IL Ss. Peter and Paul Mission.
Corneille, Cecil C. '95 (STV) St. Croix, VI Church of St. Joseph; Army National Guard Chaplains.
Corneille, Cecil (STV) Vocations.
Corneille, Cecil (STV) Diocesan Consultors.
Cornejo, Quirino H. '91 (SAN) San Angelo, TX St. Joseph.
Cornejo, Quirino (SAN) Presbyteral Council.
Cornejo, Vincent C. '56 (MET) Woodbridge, NJ Our Lady of Mount Carmel.
Cornelius, Leonard *o.f.m.* '69 (MAR)[E] Iron Mountain, MI Monastery of the Holy Cross.
Cornelius, William R. '58 (STU) Presbyteral Council; College of Consultors Retired.
Cornell, R. Paul (BO) Lowell, MA St. Patrick.
Cornell, Robert J. *o.praem.* '44 (GB)[B] St. Norbert College; [I] De Pere, WI St. Joseph Priory.
Cornelli, Laurenti Magesa '74 (ALB) Glenville, NY Immaculate Conception.
Cornelli, Leo *o.s.b.* '35 (DET)[K] Detroit, MI St. Sylvester Monastery.
Cornelli, Neil '37 (LAN) Retired.
Cornelli, Neil '37 (STA) Fernandina Beach, FL St. Michael's.
Cornely, Francis J. '48 (PH) Retired.
Cornely, Joe *s.t.* '60 (LA) Compton, CA Our Lady of Victory.
Cornely, Joseph *s.t.* '67 (LA) Compton, CA Sagrado Corazon, Sacred Heart.
Cornett, David *s.v.d.* '87 (WH) Webster Springs, WV St. Anne's.
Corniel, Rafael G. (NY) Canonical Consultants.
Cornish, Daryl G. *s.j.* '82 (STL)[N] St. Louis, MO Fusz Pavilion; [O] St. Louis, MO Jesuit Community Corporation at St. Louis University – Jesuit Hall.
Cornish, Ron '68 (KCK) Olathe, KS Prince of Peace.
Cornwell, Malcolm *c.p.* '69 (WOR)[O] Shrewsbury, MA Calvary Retreat Center, Passionist Fathers of Shrewsbury, Inc..
Corominas, John *c.m.f.* '49 (LA)[Q] Rancho Dominguez, CA Dominguez Seminary Inc..
Corona, Andrew J. '93 (GRY) Merrillville, IN St. Joan of Arc.
Corona, John '71 (RNO) Retired.
Corona, John '71 (RNO) Reno, NV Our Lady of the Snows.
Corona, Michael J. '68 (MET) Phillipsburg, NJ St. Philip & St. James; Episcopal Vicars; Catholic Scouting Movement; Diocesan Home School Association; Episcopal Council.
Corona, Michael (MET) Department of Education.
Coronado, Genero '51 (LA) Retired.
Coronado, Ricardo '90 (DUB) Cedar Rapids, IA St. Matthew.
Coronado, Victorino '95 (CAM) Atlantic City, NJ St. Monica's.
Coroztieta, Jose Madoz '53 (SJN) Retired.
Corpora, Joseph V. *c.s.c.* '84 (P) Portland, OR Holy Redeemer.
Corr, John F. '51 (PAT)[C] Madison, NJ Bayley–Ellard High School Retired.
Corr, John Raymond *o.p.* '56 (TYL)[C] Lufkin, TX Monastery of the Infant Jesus.
Corradi, Frank '85 (LC) Eau Claire, WI St. Olaf.
Corradin, Albert *c.s.* '47 (LA) Sun Valley, CA Our Lady of the Holy Rosary.
Corrado, Dennis M. *c.o.* '70 (BRK) Brooklyn, NY The Oratory Church of St. Boniface; [V] Brooklyn, NY Oratory of Saint Philip Neri, Congregation Pontifical Rite.
Corral, Jose '79 (TOL) On Duty Outside the Diocese.
Corral, Jose '79 (SFR) San Francisco, CA St. Finn Barr; [S] San Francisco, CA Charismatic Movement.
Corral, Roberto *o.p.* '88 (OAK) Berkeley, CA St. Mary Magdalen; [N] Oakland, CA Western Dominican Province.
Corral, Roberto *o.p.* '88 (FgM).
Corrales, Alirio '91 (LAR) Laredo, TX Santa Margarita de Escocia.
Corrales, Miguel A. '64 (SJN) Carolina, PR Cristo Rey.
Corrales, Orlando '89 (NY) Bronx, NY Our Saviour.
Corrales, Orlando *m.x.y.* '89 (NY)[EE] Bronx, NY Yarumal Mission Society, Inc..
Corrales–Diaz, Roger '02 (CHI) Lake Zurich, IL St. Francis de Sales.
Correa, Gino *o.f.m.* '76 (SFE) Albuquerque, NM Holy Family; [I] Albuquerque, NM Curia Juan Diego.
Correa, Lawrence *s.v.d.* '80 (NEW) Jersey City, NJ St. John the Baptist.

Correa, Peter (SFR) Menlo Park, CA The Church of the Nativity.
Corredato, John *c.s.v.* '68 (SFD) Edwardsville, IL St. Boniface.
Correia, Edward E. '68 (FR) New Bedford, MA St. James; New Bedford Deanery.
Correio, Bruce '85 (LA) Santa Barbara, CA St. Raphael.
Correz, Steven (ORG) Dana Point, CA St. Edward.
Corriere, Basil *e.c.* '87 (STU)[F] Bloomingdale, OH Holy Family Hermitage.
Corrigan, Allen F. '82 (CLV) Richfield, OH St. Victor; Defenders of the Bond.
Corrigan, Bernard J. '47 (NY) Warwick, NY St. Stephen Retired.
Corrigan, Edward J. *s.m.* '43 (CLV)[M] Cleveland, OH Sts. Mary and Joseph Home for the Aged.
Corrigan, F. J. '38 (SFD) Retired.
Corrigan, Gregory M. '86 (WIL) Wilmington, DE Corpus Christi; [A] Wilmington, DE St. Mark's High School.
Corrigan, Gregory (WIL) KAIROS Ministries, Inc..
Corrigan, Hugh J. '63 (NY) Yonkers, NY Immaculate Conception.
Corrigan, Hugh (NY) Westchester (Yonkers).
Corrigan, J. David *s.j.* '65 (STL)[O] St. Louis, MO Hallahan House; [C] Saint Louis University.
Corrigan, James V. *o.s.a.* '66 (CHI)[N] Olympia Fields, IL Tolentine Monastery at Tolentine Center; Sharp Memorial Hospital.
Corrigan, Kevin *c.s.sp.* '60 (SJ) Millbrae, CA St. Dunstan.
Corrigan, Michael T. '75 (GAL) Florence, SC St. Ann; [H] Florence, SC Francis Marion University; On Duty Outside the Diocese.
Corrigan, Peter H. '69 (CLV)[D] Cleveland, OH St. Ignatius High School.
Corrigan, Roy *o.f.m.* '55 (FgM).
Corriveau, Kip '95 (ROC) Absent on Leave.
Corriveau, Raymond *o.p.* '55 (PRT)[I] Lewiston, ME SS. Peter and Paul House.
Corriveau, Raymond *o.p.* '55 (PRT)[G] Lewiston, ME St. Marguerite d'Youville Pavilion.
Corriveau, Real *o.m.i.* '61 (FgM).
Corry, Francis J. '74 (NY) Bronx, NY St. Frances of Rome.
Corry, James J. *c.s.sp.* '57 (STA) Jacksonville, FL St. Paul's.
Corso, Charles W. *c.s.c.* '75 (FTW)[I] Fremont, CA.
Cortes, Antonio '96 (MRY) Vocations Board; Greenfield, CA Holy Trinity.
Cortes, Ariel '96 (BUF) Jamestown, NY St. James.
Cortes, Jesse '63 (LAV) Las Vegas, NV Our Lady of Las Vegas.
Cortes, Jesse (LAV) Hospital Apostolate.
Cortes, Raul '62 (LA) Reseda, CA St. Catherine of Siena.
Cortes, Victor '96 (DAL)[J] Irving, TX Opus Dei.
Cortese, Francis X. *o.praem.* '62 (PH)[AA] Paoli, PA Daylesford Abbey.
Cortese, Patrick S. '48 (SCR) Retired.
Cortese, Richard '82 (MEM) Memphis, TN St. Louis.
Cortese, Richard (MEM) Comunidad Hispana Catolica de Memphis.
Cortesi, David J. '63 (CHI) Chicago, IL St. Ferdinand.
Cortez, Augusto *c.m.* (RVC) South Fork.
Cortez, Fernando '77 (OAK) Alameda, CA St. Albert.
Cortez, Fernando (OAK) Consultors.
Cortez, Jose '73 (TYL) Rusk, TX Jerry H. Hodge Unit and Sky view Unit, Texas Department of Corrections.
Cortez, Jose '73 (TYL) New Summerfield, TX Our Lady of Guadalupe.
Cortez, Jose (TYL) Advocates.
Cortez, Ramiro *o.m.i.* '70 (SAT) Del Rio, TX St. Joseph's.
Cortez, Ruben Dario *s.x.* '95 (PAT) Paterson, NJ Cathedral of St. John the Baptist.
Cortney, Edward P. '63 (GI) Chadron, NE St. Patrick's.
Coruna, Roberto '77 (MET) Bloomsbury, NJ Church of the Annunciation; Sayreville, NJ Our Lady of Victories.
Coryer, Francis J. '82 (OG) Redford, NY Church of the Assumption; Charismatic Renewal.
Corzo, Wilson O. '98 (FTW) Elkhart, IN St. Vincent de Paul.
Corzo, Wilson (FTW) Elkhart.
Cos, Rafael '82 (MIA) Miami, FL St. Catherine of Siena.
Cosby, R. Roy '54 (ARL) Annandale, VA Holy Spirit; Vicar General; Defenders of the Bond; Diocesan Consultors Retired.
Coschignano, Joseph C. '69 (RVC) Center Moriches, NY St. John the Evangelist.
Cosentino, Jack A. '70 (FAR) Retired.
Cosentino, Jack '70 (FAR) Venice, FL Epiphany Cathedral.
Cosgrove, Edward C. *c.ss.r.* '55 (BLX)[E] Biloxi, MS St. John Neumann Residence.
Cosgrove, Francis J. '65 (JKS) Madison, MS St. Francis of Assisi; Office of Vicar General.
Cosgrove, Francis (JKS) Diocesan Consultors.
Cosgrove, J. Kelly '43 (ORL) Retired.
Cosgrove, Jerome P. '63 (SC) Armstrong, IA St. Mary's; Estherville, IA St. Patrick's.
Cosgrove, Jerome (SC) Judges.
Cosgrove, Joseph J. '92 (BAL) Hancock, MD St. Peter's.
Cosgrove, Joseph '60 (LA) Moorpark, CA Holy Cross.
Cosgrove, Thomas H. *c.ss.r.* '45 (STL)[O] Liguori, MO Liguori Mission House/Redemptorists; [O] Liguori, MO St. Clement Health Care Center.
Cosgrove, William B. '74 (NY) Hopewell Junction, NY St. Denis; [II] Scarsdale, NY Catholic Charismatic Renewal Office; Charismatic Renewal Office.
Cosgrove, William J. (ROC).
Cosgrove, William P. '99 (BIS) Fort Yates, ND St. Peter – Catholic Indian Mission; Fort Yates, ND St. Philomena.
Cosgrove, William '55 (ROC) Retired.
Cosgrove, William '55 (ROC) Canandaigua, NY Veteran's Hospital.
Cosio, Fernando '00 (TUC) Nogales, AZ San Felipe de Jesus.
Coskery, J. (PRT) Former Bishops.
Coskren, Thomas M. *o.p.* '54 (PRO)[P] Providence St. Thomas Aquinas Priory at Providence College.
Coslowsky, Marion '42 (SB) Retired.
Cosmic, John J. '90 (OG) Retired.
Coss, John *f.m.s.i.* '56 (BO).
Cossavella, Anthony J. '81 (PH)[B] Philadelphia, PA St. Monica.
Cossette, Raymond '55 (DUL) Retired.
Costa, Anthony J. '90 (PH)[A] Wynnewood, PA Theological Seminary of St. Charles Borromeo, Overbrook.
Costa, Caetano F. '64 (RVC) Deer Park, NY SS. Cyril and Methodius.
Costa, Carl A. *m.m.* '71 (FgM).
Costa, David A. '85 (FR) North Attleboro, MA Sacred Heart; St. Vincent De Paul Society.
Costa, Eugene E. '76 (SFD) Sherman, IL Holy Family; Sherman, IL St. John Vianney; Chancellor; Corporate Board Members; Office for Chancellor/Planning Coordinator; Consultants.
Costa, Eugene (SFD) Presbyteral Council.
Costa, Gabriel B. '79 (NEW)[B] School of Diplomacy and Intl. Rels..
Costa, Gene A. *o.de.m.* '74 (PH)[AA] Philadelphia, PA Monastery of Our Lady of Mercy.
Costa, Lucas Torrell deAlmeida *o.s.b.* '67 (GBG)[H] Latrobe Saint Vincent Archabbey.
Costa, Mario C. '53 (RVC) Retired.
Costa, Thomas C. '78 (RVC) Glen Cove, NY St. Patrick's; Procurator & Advocates; Senate of Priests (Presbyteral Council/College of Consultors).
Costantino, Anthony J. '44 (SAT)[K] San Antonio, TX Padua Place Retired.
Costantino, Joseph S. *s.j.* '87 (RVC)[O] Manhasset, NY St. Ignatius Retreat House, Inisfada.
Costanza, Jared J. '99 (PRO) Riverside, RI St. Brendan.
Costanzo, John J. '64 (PBL) Presbyteral Council–College of Consultors; Presbyteral Council Retired.
Costello, Andrew *c.ss.r.* '65 (BAL) Annapolis, MD St. Mary.
Costello, Andrew *c.ss.r.* '65 (BAL)[S] Annapolis, MD Saint Mary Rectory.
Costello, Aquinas *o.p.* '68 (P) Portland, OR Holy Rosary Parish & Dominican Priory.
Costello, Bernard B. '63 (PIT) Charleroi, PA Mary Mother of the Church.
Costello, Brian L. (SFR) Novato, CA St. Anthony of Padua.
Costello, Charles P. *s.j.* '60 (BAL)[S] Baltimore, MD Jesuit Fathers and Brothers Maryland Provincial Curia; [W] Baltimore, MD Ignatian Lay Volunteer Corps.
Costello, Coleman '67 (BRK) Bayside, NY Sacred Heart of Jesus.
Costello, Daniel F. '98 (CHI) Chicago, IL St. John Fisher.
Costello, Edward *o.f.m.conv.* '61 (TR) Point Pleasant Beach, NJ St. Peter's.
Costello, Francis M. '45 (NY) Retired.
Costello, Frank B. *s.j.* '52 (SPK)[B] Spokane, WA Gonzaga University.
Costello, James J. *s.j.* '66 (STL) St. Louis, MO St. Francis Xavier.
Costello, James P. '60 (CLV) Parma, OH Holy Family.
Costello, James. J. '66 (STL)[O] St. Louis, MO Jesuit Community Corporation at St. Louis University – Jesuit Hall.
Costello, John F. *s.j.* '83 (CHI)[N] Chicago, IL Clark Street Jesuit Residence; Bradenton, FL St. Joseph; Presbyteral Council.
Costello, John J. '89 (BRK) Brooklyn, NY Immaculate Heart of Mary.
Costello, John M. '72 (STL) Washington, MO St. Francis Borgia; Franklin County Catholic Church Real Estate Corporation; [U] Washington, MO Franklin County Catholic Church Real Estate Corporation.
Costello, John M. *s.j.* '84 (ROC)[B] Rochester, NY McQuaid Jesuit High School.
Costello, Mark Joseph *o.f.m.cap.* '91 (CHI)[N] Chicago, IL St. Clare Friary.
Costello, Raymond *m.s.c.* '45 (ALN)[A] Center Valley, PA Sacred Heart Villa, Missionaries of the Sacred Heart.
Costello, Richard D. *s.j.* '53 (BGP)[P] Fairfield, CT The Fairfield Jesuit Community–Fairfield University.
Costello, Robert B. '53 (BO) Senior Priests Retired.
Costello, Robert T. *s.j.* '63 (FgM).
Costello, Ted '85 (SP) Clearwater, FL St. Michael The Archangel.
Costello, Timon W. '58 (MIL)[O] Milwaukee, WI St. Conrad Friary.
Costello, Vincent F. '76 (CHI) Arlington Heights, IL Our Lady of the Wayside.
Costello, William E. (RVC) Senate of Priests (Presbyteral Council/College of Consultors).
Costello, William F. '52 (RVC) Franklin Square, NY St. Catherine of Sienna; Garden City, NY St. Anne Retired.
Costello, William J. '64 (CHI) Chicago, IL St. Eugene.
Costello, William M. '74 (FR) East Falmouth, MA St. Anthony's.
Coster, Henry C. *s.j.* '59 (SCR)[C] Scranton, PA The University of Scranton.
Costigan, George (PAT) Retired.
Costigan, James P. *c.p.m.* '02 (OWN)[F] Auburn, KY Fathers of Mercy.
Costigan, P. James '68 (SAV) Tybee Island, GA St. Michael.
Costigan, Richard F. *s.j.* '64 (CHI)[C] Chicago, IL Jesuit Community at Loyola University Chicago.
Costigan, Richard J. '50 (TUC) Retired.
Cotant, Charles *c.ss.r.* '41 (FgM).
Cote, Aaron J. *o.p* '86 (PRO) Providence, RI St. Pius V; Washington, DC St. Dominic Church & Priory; [P] Providence, RI St. Pius Priory.
Cote, David P. '68 (PRT) Military Chaplains; Air Force Chaplains.
Cote, Duaine M. '62 (FAR) Edgeley, ND Transfiguration; [J] Fargo, ND Cursillo Movement.
Cote, Duaine '62 (FAR) Edgeley, ND Holy Spirit.
Cote, E. Joseph '69 (BAL) Baltimore, MD St. Pius X; [T] Baltimore, MD The School Sisters of Notre Dame in the City of Baltimore (Baltimore Prov.); Advocates and Procurators.
Cote, Gerald M. '56 (TUC) Retired.
Cote, Joseph (BAL) Special Assignment.
Cote, Norman J. '58 (OG) Retired.
Cote, Normand C. '58 (OG) Rouses Point, NY St. Joseph; Plattsburgh, NY St. John the Baptist.
Cote, Paul E. '71 (PRT) Saco, ME Notre Dame de Lourdes.
Cote, Richard G. *o.m.i.* '60 (WDC)[M] Washington, DC Provincial Offices of the United States Province of the Missionary Oblates of Mary Immaculate.
Cote, Richard G. *o.m.i.* '60 (FgM).
Cotone, Michael *o.s.c.* '74 (STP)[M] Shoreview, MN Crosier Provincial House Province of St. Odilia.
Cotta, Myron J. (FRS) Vicar General and Moderator of the Curia; Finance Committee; Deposit and Loan Fund; Holy Childhood, Pontifical Association; Personnel Committee; Priests' Council; Propagation of the Faith and St. Peter Society; Vicar for Clergy; Continuing Formation of Priests; Victim Assistance Coordinator.
Cotta, Myron '87 (FRS) On Special Assignment.
Cotta, Myron (FRS) Diocesan Consultors.
Cotter, David *o.s.b.* '79 (SCL)[I] Collegeville, MN St. John's Abbey, of the Order of St. Benedict.
Cotter, Eugene J. '56 (NEW)[B] School of Diplomacy and Intl. Rels..
Cotter, George C. *m.m.* '60 (FgM).
Cotter, John F. '80 (SAG) Mount Pleasant, MI St. Joseph the Worker.
Cotter, Lawrence E. '52 (OG) Colton, NY St. Patrick; Waddington, NY St. John the Baptist; Defenders of the Bond; Diocesan Archivist; Censor Librorum Retired.
Cotter, Patrick J. '57 (LA) Retired.
Cotter, Pius *o.f.m.cap.* '88 (GB) Brussels, WI St. Francis–St. Mary Parish.
Cotter, Raymond C. '86 (GAY) Frankfort, MI St. Ann.
Cotter, Robert L. '47 (OG) Lowville, NY St. Mary; Judges Retired.
Cotter, Vince (OAK) Deans.
Cotter, Vincent '83 (OAK) Alameda, CA St. Philip Neri.
Cotter, Vincent (OAK) Consultors.
Cotter, Vincent (OAK) Presbyteral Council.
Cotton, Charles E. '73 (COL) Columbus, OH St. Elizabeth; Priests' Senate.
Cottone, Paul P. '49 (SCR)[N] Dunmore, PA Villa St. Joseph Retired.
Cottrell, James '68 (SP) Retired.
Cotugno, Joseph '64 (ALB) Albany, NY St. James.
Cotugno, Joseph '64 (ALB) Special Assignment.
Cotugno, Joseph '64 (ALB) Capital District Psychiatric Center.
Cotugno, Joseph (ALB) Initial & Ongoing Formation Cluster.
Coucelo, Andres '68 (MIA) Retired.
Coughlan, Michael J. '52 (SD) Retired.
Coughlan, Robert '90 (SFE) Retired.
Coughlin, Bernard J. *s.j.* '55 (Missouri)[B] Spokane, WA

Gonzaga University.
Coughlin, Conall R. *o.s.b.* '58 (PAT)[M] Morristown St. Mary's Abbey.
Coughlin, Daniel C. *c.s.c.* '50 (FTW)[I] Notre Dame, IN Holy Cross House.
Coughlin, Daniel P. '60 (CHI) On Duty Outside the Archdiocese.
Coughlin, Edward J. *s.j.* '74 (NY) New York, NY St. Francis Xavier; [EE] New York, NY Xavier Jesuit Community.
Coughlin, Howard L. '53 (CHR) Mauldin, SC St. Elizabeth Ann Seton Retired.
Coughlin, James *s.j.* '98 (NY)[F] New York, NY Xavier High School.
Coughlin, John C. *o.f.m.* '02 (CAM) Camden, NJ St. Anthony of Padua.
Coughlin, John J. *o.f.m.* (FTW)[B] University of Notre Dame Du Lac.
Coughlin, John *o.f.m.* '83 (NY) New York, NY St. Stephen of Hungary.
Coughlin, Joseph F. '44 (BUF) West Seneca, NY Queen of Heaven Retired.
Coughlin, Kenneth F. '90 (LAN) Pinckney, MI St. Mary.
Coughlin, Leo '56 (LAV) Overton, NV St. John the Evangelist.
Coughlin, Paul E. '66 (PRT) South Portland, ME Church of the Holy Cross; South Portland, ME St. John the Evangelist; [M] South Portland, ME Southern Maine Technical College.
Coughlin, Paul F. '91 (BO) Charlestown, MA St. Mary.
Coughlin, Roger J. '51 (CHI)[G] Chicago, IL Catholic Charities of the Archdiocese of Chicago–Archdiocesan Offices; Associate Administrators; Maternity Fund Retired.
Coughlin, Thomas *h.n.l.* '77 (SFR) San Francisco, CA St. Benedict Parish at St. Francis Xavier Church.
Coughlin, Thomas '77 (HON) On Duty Outside the Diocese.
Coughlin, Thomas '77 (SFR).
Coughlin, William D. '66 (BO)[S] Wakefield, MA Most Blessed Sacrament.
Coughlin, William *c.s.b.* '56 (LSC) Las Cruces, NM Cathedral of Immaculate Heart of Mary.
Couhig, Michael D. *c.s.c.* '80 (FTW) South Bend, IN St. Joseph.
Coulter, Gary '99 (LIN) Graduate Studies.
Coulter, Larry '02 (GI) Greeley, NE Sacred Heart.
Coulter, Lawrence W. '86 (GI) Farwell, NE St. Anthony of Padua; Priests' Pension and Welfare Board.
Coulthard, Gregory *s.d.s.* '67 (GB) St. Nazianz, WI St. Gregory.
Coulthard, Gregory *s.d.s.* '67 (GB) Kiel, WI Holy Trinity; Air Force Reserve Chaplains.
Coulthardt, Gregory *s.d.s.* '67 (GB)[I] New Holstein, WI Salvatorian Public Relations.
Counce, Paul D. '79 (BR) Special Assignment; Vice-Chancellor; Judicial Vicar; Presbyteral Council.
Counce, Paul '79 (NO).
Countie, Charles *o.carm.* '78 (JOL)[A] Joliet, IL Mount Carmel.
Courier, Rick L. '85 (MAR) Escanaba, MI St. Thomas the Apostle; St. Joseph Association.
Courneyer, Alfred '85 (SPR) On Duty Outside the Diocese.
Cournoyer, Michael '98 (ALB) Cohoes, NY St. Joseph.
Cournoyer, Michael '98 (ALB) Seton Health.
Cournoyer, Michael '98 (ALB) Samaritan Hospital.
Courteau, Allen *o.m.i.* '76 (FgM).
Courtemanche, Normand L. '65 (PRO) Pawtucket, RI Our Lady of Consolation.
Courtney, Edward '55 (HEL) Butte, MT St. John the Evangelist.
Courtney, Joseph B. *c.s.b.* (GAL)[Q] Houston, TX Dillon House Retired.
Courtney, Patrick E. '87 (LFT) Unassigned.
Courtney, Scott (LIN) Hastings, NE St. Michael's.
Courtney, Thomas M. '51 (SPR)[H] Springfield, MA St. Michael's Residence Retired.
Courtney, William '99 (PBL) Pueblo, CO Shrine of St. Therese.
Courtright, Lawrence P. '61 (TLS) Retired.
Courtright, Raymond P. '92 (FAR) Grand Forks, ND St. Thomas Aquinas (University of North Dakota); [I] Grand Forks, ND St. Thomas Aquinas Newman Center, UND.
Courville, J. Douglas '76 (LAF) Lafayette, LA St. Jules; Judicial Vicar.
Courville, Robert '63 (LAF) Mamou, LA St. Ann.
Courville, Robert (LAF) Advocates.
Coury, Paul *c.ss.r.* '72 (DEN)[N] Denver, CO.
Coury, Philip *c.m.* '71 (PBL) Aguilar, CO St. Anthony.
Cousens, Dennis '77 (L) Louisville, KY St. Martin.
Cousineau, Robert H. *s.j.* '60 (CHY) Guernsey, WY St. Anthony's.
Cousins, John P. *o.f.m.cap.* '76 (DEN) Colorado Springs, CO St. Mary's Cathedral; [F] Colorado Springs, CO Solanus Casey Friary.
Coutinha, Paul '82 (FTW) Sarasota, FL St. Martha.
Coutinho, Absalom (PAT) Absent on Leave.
Couto, Robert '96 (MAN) Londonderry, NH St. Jude.
Couto, Robert (MAN) Liaisons.
Couture, Bernard G. '50 (BUR) Retired.
Couture, Fern *s.p.* '70 (AMA) Dimmitt, TX Immaculate Conception.
Couture, Fernand '43 (STA) Retired.
Couture, Paul E. *s.s.e.* '56 (BUR)[E] Colchester, VT Society of St. Edmund.
Couture, Roger *o.m.i.* '55 (NOR)[F] Willimantic, CT Missionary Oblates of Mary Immaculate; [I] Willimantic, CT Immaculata Retreat House.
Couture, Roland '53 (BO)[V] Lowell, MA Andre Garin Retirement Residence.
Couturier, Albert '88 (GAY) St. Helen, MI St. Helen.
Couturier, David *o.f.m.cap.* '79 (NY)[EE] New York, NY Development Office:.
Couturier, George M. '81 (HRT) Newington, CT St. Mary; Special and other Archdiocesan Assignment.
Covarrubias, Raul R. '83 (B) Mountain Home, ID Our Lady of Good Counsel; AUXILIARY CHAPLAINS CONTRACT CHAPLAINS.
Covarrubias–Pina, Salomon (YAK) Defenders of the Bond.
Covas, Peter 57 (SB) Retired.
Coveney, James B. '64 (ALT) Altoona, PA St. Mark's.
Coveny, Richard C. '56 (BUF) Colden, NY Our Lady of the Sacred Heart.
Cover, Phillip B. '70 (LFT) On Duty Outside the Diocese.
Covert, Kevin A. '90 (KAL) Portage, MI St. Catherine of Siena.
Covington, Charles L. (AUS) Ecumenism.
Covington, Larry '85 (AUS) Austin, TX St. Louis.
Covington, Larry '85 (AUS) Austin, TX School for the Blind.
Cowan, Steven '99 (RIC) Military Chaplains; Navy Chaplains
Cowan, Vincent '43 (MRY) Retired.
Coward, Robert *c.p.* '68 (CHI)[N] Curia Generalizia Dei Passionisti.
Cowart, Conrad '96 (STA) Gainesville, FL St. Patrick's; Special Assignment; AUXILIARY CHAPLAINS CONTRACT CHAPLAINS.
Cowden, David A. '82 (OKL) Okeene, OK St. Anthony's.
Cowell, Raymond '56 (FgM).
Cowell, Raymond '57 (CHI) Retired.
Cower, D. Craig '54 (RC)[D] Rapid City, SD Priest Retirement and Aid Association/Pension Plan Board; Vicar for Retired Priests Retired.
Cowhig, Edward D. '45 (BO) Beverly, MA St. Alphonsus; Senior Priests Retired.
Cowie, Donald *s.m.* '61 (SAT)[M] San Antonio, TX Central Catholic Marianist Community.
Cowie, Donald *s.m.* '61 (SAT)[F] San Antonio, TX Central Catholic High School.
Cowles, James '86 (RIC) Colonial Heights, VA St. Ann.
Cox, Alan B. '76 (B) On Duty Outside the Diocese.
Cox, Bernard '91 (IND) Bedford, IN St. Vincent de Paul.
Cox, Bernard '91 (IND) Mitchell, IN St. Mary/Assumption.
Cox, Brian '68 (BAL) Absent on Leave.
Cox, Christopher *c.s.c.* '97 (FTW) South Bend, IN St. Casimir
Cox, Christopher *c.s.c.* '99 (FTW) South Bend; South Bend, IN St. Adalbert.
Cox, Craig A. '78 (LA) Encino, CA Our Lady of Grace; Clergy, Vicar for; Vicar for Clergy; College of Consultors; Members.
Cox, David D. '81 (JC) Rolla, MO St. Patrick; X. Rolla; Senators; Ministry to Priests.
Cox, Francis '50 (WCH) Retired.
Cox, Gregory A. '76 (LA) Los Angeles, CA St. Anastasia; [Y] Los Angeles, CA Catholic Charities of Los Angeles, Inc.; [Y] Los Angeles, CA Central Administrative Offices; Executive Director.
Cox, James '51 (NY) Retired.
Cox, James '98 (PH) King of Prussia PA Mother of Divine Providence.
Cox, James '98 (PH)[D] Norristown, PA 0.Kennedy–Kenrick Catholic High School.
Cox, Jesse DePorres (DET) Presbyteral Council.
Cox, John F. '36 (PRO) Warwick, RI St. Peter; Censors of Books Retired.
Cox, John *o.m.i.* '87 (BO)[AA] Lowell, MA St. Joseph the Worker Residence.
Cox, Joseph C. '46 (MAD) Retired.
Cox, Joseph *o.s.b.* '91 (IND)[K] St. Meinrad, IN St. Meinrad Archabbey.
Cox, Paul '54 (ALB) Retired.
Cox, Paul (ALB) Priests Retirement Board.
Cox, William E. '42 (MIL) Retired.
Cox, William J. '56 (PH) Retired.
Coxen, Gervis J. *m.m.* '37 (NY).
Coy, Richard D. '00 (MEM)[EE] Memphis, TN St. Therese of the Infant Jesus.
Coy, William J. *m.m.* '55 (NY)[EE] Maryknoll Maryknoll Fathers and Brothers.
Coyle, Alcuin *o.f.m.* '54 (NY) New York, NY St. Francis of Assisi.
Coyle, Arthur M. (BO) Secretary for Pastoral Services; Members; Pastoral Services.
Coyle, Dan '89 (FRS) Bakersfield, CA Sacred Heart.
Coyle, Edward J. '80 (ALN) Bally, PA Most Blessed Sacrament; Office of Worship; Army National Guard Chaplains.
Coyle, Eugene P. '54 (BRK)[V] Douglaston, NY Bishop Mugavero Residence Retired.
Coyle, Patrick J. *s.m.* '45 (SFR)[N] San Francisco, CA Marist Center of the West.
Coyle, Patrick '60 (DUL) Retired.
Coyle, Robert '91 (RVC) Priests Released from Diocesan Assignment; Navy Chaplains.
Coyle, Thomas J. '70 (MAD) Jefferson, WI St. John the Baptist; Jefferson, WI St. Lawrence.
Coyne, Christopher J. *s.l.d.* '86 (BO)[A] Brighton, MA St. John Seminary School of Theology; Public Relations.
Coyne, Christopher J. (BO) Secretary for Public Relations.
Coyne, Edwin J. '62 (BGP) Retired.
Coyne, Emmett A.. '66 (MAN) On Duty Outside the Diocese.
Coyne, George R. '59 (STU) Tiltonsville, OH St. Joseph; Tiltonsville, OH St. Lucy's; Presbyteral Council; College of Consultors; Priests Personnel Board; Priests' Retirement Board.
Coyne, George V. *s.j.* '65 (TUC)[E] Tucson, AZ Jesuit Community of the Vatican Observatory.
Coyne, Gregory '89 (WDC)[T] Washington, DC Tenley Study Center.
Coyne, James '75 (SEA) Covington, WA St. John the Baptist.
Coyne, John J. *o.s.f.s.* '71 (FgM).
Coyne, Liam '98 (ATL) Cumming, GA Good Shepherd.
Coyne, Michael J. '55 (CAM) Retired.
Coyne, Robert F. *m.m.* '83 (FgM).
Coyne, Robert R. '76 (PIT) Bairdford, PA St. Victor.
Coyne, Ronald D. '73 (BO) Weymouth, MA St. Albert the Great.
Coyte, Thomas '74 (DEN) Denver, CO Holy Cross.
Cozzens, Andrew '97 (STP)[C] St. Paul, MN University of St. Thomas.
Cozzens, Andrew '97 (STP)[A] St. Paul, MN The Saint Paul Seminary; Graduate Studies.
Cozzens, Donald '65 (CLV) Released from Diocesan Assignment.
Cozzini, Robert P. '60 (NEW)[N] Caldwell, NJ The Rev. Msgr. James F. Kelley Residence for Retired Priests Retired.
Cozzubbo, Gregory P. *c.m.* '84 (PH) Philadelphia, PA Immaculate Conception; Philadelphia, PA Philadelphia Prison System.
Crabb, John T. *s.j.* '79 (BO) Methuen, MA Holy Family Hospital, Inc.; [X] Gloucester, MA Eastern Point Retreat House.
Crable, John M. '53 (OG) Retired.
Crafts, George '65 (PRO)[O] Providence, RI Prelature of the Holy Cross and Opus Dei.
Crager, Richard *s.d.b.* '85 (BO)[N] Boston, MA Orient Heights Unit.
Craig, Bruce *s.d.b.* '74 (MIA) Miami, FL St. Kieran.
Craig, Christopher A. '93 (IND) Aurora, IN St. Mary of the Immaculate Conception.
Craig, Dale *s.o.l.t.* '97 (FAR) Belcourt, ND St. Anthony.
Craig, Dale *s.o.l.t.* '97 (FAR) Belcourt, ND St. Ann.
Craig, Dale *s.o.l.t.* '97 (FAR) Belcourt, ND St. Ann; St. John, ND St. John the Baptist.
Craig, Dale '97 (CC)[G] Robstown, TX Society of Our Lady of the Most Holy Trinity.
Craig, Dale *s.o.l.t.* '97 (FAR) Belcourt, ND Immaculate Heart of Mary.
Craig, Dale *s.o.l.t.* '97 (FAR) Belcourt, ND St. Ann; St. John, ND St. John the Baptist.
Craig, Dale *s.o.l.t.* '97 (FAR) Belcourt, ND St. Louis King of France.
Craig, Donald R. '74 (CHI) Chicago, IL St. Mary of Perpetual Help.
Craig, John V. *s.j.* '77 (STL)[O] St. Louis, MO De Smet Jesuit High School Community.
Craig, Lawrence J. '73 (CHI) Chicago, IL Assumption; Kolbe House; [X] Chicago, IL Kolbe House; Prison Ministry/Kolbe House.
Craig, Lawrence *ss.cc.* '41 (FR).
Craig, Paul *o.f.m.cap.* '66[H] (FgM).
Craig, Richard J. '61 (BO) Senior Priests Retired.
Craig, Robert G. '64 (E) Retired.
Craig, Robert N. *o.f.m.cap.* '67 (PIT) Allegheny County, PA Department of Veterans Affairs Medical Center Oakland.
Craig, Robert *o.f.m.cap.* '67 (PIT)[N] Pittsburgh, PA St. Augustine Friary; Allegheny County, PA VA Pittsburgh Health Care System–H.J. Heinz and University Drive Divisions.
Craig, Rod L. '77 (FRS) Dinuba, CA St. Catherine.
Craig, Samuel L. '76 (WDC) Bowie, MD Ascension.
Craig, Thomas '82 (FWT) Arlington, TX St. Vincent de Paul.
Craig, Thomas (FWT) Mission Council.
Craig, Willliam R. *o.praem.* '55 (PH)[AA] Paoli, PA Daylesford Abbey.
Cramblitt, Richard E. '72 (BAL) Baltimore, MD Shrine of the Sacred Heart; Consultors; Advocates and Procurators; Consultors.

Cramer, David W. '91 (SCR) Dalton, PA Our Lady of the Abingtons.
Cramer, Donald W. '01 (HBG) Camp Hill, PA Good Shepherd.
Cramer, Harry N. '84 (WH) Bridgeport, WV All Saints.
Cramer, Joseph '77 (KCK) Osawatomie, KS Our Lady of Lourdes.
Cramer, Joseph '77 (KCK) Osawatomie, KS St. Philip Neri.
Cramer, Joseph '77 (KCK) Osawatomie, KS Sacred Heart Shrine to St. Philippine Duchesne.
Cramer, Terry A. '99 (ARL) Fairfax, VA St. Leo's; Notaries.
Cramer, William N. '77 (PAT)[J] Paterson, NJ St. Joseph's Hospital and Medical Center; Unassigned.
Crandall, Thomas '81 (PT) On Leave of Absence; AUXILIARY CHAPLAINS CONTRACT CHAPLAINS.
Crandall, William W. (ALB) Holy Name Societies.
Crandall, William '48 (ALB) Retired.
Crane, Thomas E. '57 (BUF) Censors—Board of Diocesan Censors of Books and Vigilance for the Faith; North Tonawanda, NY St. Joseph.
Crane, William H. *m.s.* '41 (HRT)[M] Hartford, CT Missionaries of LaSalette.
Crangle, Thomas A. *o.f.m.cap.* '89 (NEW) Hoboken, NJ St. Ann's; [N] Union City, NJ Capuchin Friars – Province of the Sacred Stigmata of St. Francis; [N] Union City, NJ Capuchin Friars – Province of the Sacred Stigmata of St. Francis.
Cranor, Bernard *o.s.b.* '62 (SFE)[I] Abiquiu, NM Monastery of Christ in the Desert.
Crasta, Rudolf '89 (LUB) Lamesa, TX St. Margaret Mary.
Crasta, Shabas '95 (DEN) Denver, CO Church of the Risen Christ.
Craven, Thomas P. '56 (PH) Retired.
Crawford, Brian *o.s.j.* '92 (SAC) Santa Cruz, CA St. Vincent De Paul; Santa Cruz, CA.
Crawford, Brian *o.s.j.* '92 (MRY)[F] Shrine of St. Joseph.
Crawford, C. Slade '65 (PT) Perry, FL Immaculate Conception; [E] Tallahassee, FL Casa Calderon, Inc.; Seminarian Candidate Review Board; Seminarians, Office of; Vocations, Office of.
Crawford, John G. '63 (CLV) South Euclid, OH St. Gregory the Great Retired.
Crawford, Larry P. '66 (IND) Indianapolis, IN St. Gabriel the Archangel.
Crawford, Richard E. '75 (PEO) Retired.
Crawford, Robert F. *m.m.* '61 (FgM).
Crawford, Slade (PT) Orders & Ministries, Commission for.
Cray, David *s.s.e.* (BUR) Charlotte, VT Our Lady of Mount Carmel; Hinesburg, VT St. Jude the Apostle.
Craycroft, Bernard L. '57 (L) Ex Officio Retired.
Craycroft, George P. '58 (L) Retired.
Creagan, Daniel A. *s.j.* '58 (GAL) Spring, TX St. Ignatius of Loyola.
Creagan, Michael '97 (STP) Robbinsdale, MN Sacred Heart.
Creagan, Robert F. '88 (KAL) Paw Paw, MI St. Mary; Archivist; Diocesan Pilgrimages; Knights of Columbus; Vocations; Gobles, MI St. Jude.
Creager, Robert '54 (PEO) Retired.
Creagh, Kevin G. *c.m.* '96 (BRK)[V] Jamaica, NY Vincentian Residence.
Creagh, Richard C. '76 (CHI) Chicago, IL Holy Rosary.
Crean, Hugh F. '62 (SPR) Westfield, MA Our Lady of the Blessed Sacrament; Bishop's Commission for Clergy; Diocesan Consultors; Deans; Presbyteral Council.
Creane, Anthony J. '56 (SPR) Westfield, MA Our Lady of the Blessed Sacrament.
Creane, Anthony '56 (SPR) Retired.
Creary, J. Edwin '73 (MEM) Germantown, TN Our Lady Of Perpetual Help; Presbyteral Council and College of Consultors.
Creason, Richard H. '67 (STL) St. Louis, MO Most Holy Trinity.
Creaven, John J. *c.ss.r.* '49 (HBG)[H] Ephrata, PA St. Clement's Mission House.
Creed, Peter '67 (RIC) Fort Monroe, VA St. Mary Star of the Sea.
Creed, Peter '67 (SY) On Duty Outside the Diocese.
Creed, William E. *s.j.* '71 (CHI)[C] Chicago, IL Jesuit Community at Loyola University Chicago.
Creeden, Brendan D. *o.s.b.* '78 (CHI)[N] Chicago, IL Monastery of the Holy Cross.
Creedon, Gerard '68 (ARL) Arlington, VA St. Charles Borromeo.
Creedon, James J. *m.s.a.* '79 (NOR)[F] Cromwell Society of the Missionaries of the Holy Apostles.
Creedon, James *o.s.a.* '79 (CAM) Camden, NJ St. Joseph's Pro–Cathedral.
Creedon, Joseph D. '68 (PRO) Kingston, RI Christ the King; [S] Kingston, RI.
Creegan, Kevin '01 (PEO) Raritan, IL Church of St. Patrick.
Creegan, Kevin '01 (PEO) Monmouth, IL Immaculate Conception.
Creel, Jesse '57 (R) Retired.
Cregan, Francis A. *o.a.r.* '95 (NY)[X] Suffern, NY Good Samaritan Hospital of Suffern.
Cregan, Francis *o.a.r.* '95 (LA)[N] West Orange, NJ Augustinian Recollects.
Cregan, James F. '63 (PT) Lanark Village, FL Sacred Heart of Jesus.
Cregan, John C. '87 (ARL) Alexandria, VA Blessed Sacrament; Deans; Diocesan Judges.
Cregan, John J. '61 (CLV) Cleveland, OH Our Lady of Angels.
Cregan, Mark T. *c.s.c.* '83 (FR)[A] North Easton, MA Stonehill College; [A] North Easton, MA Holy Cross Fathers Religious.
Cregan, Robert G. *s.j.* '67 (NY)[EE] Jesuit Community, Kohlmann Hall.
Crehan, Joseph L. *s.s.c.* '54 (BO)[V] Everett, MA Immaculate Conception.
Crehan, Joseph *s.s.c.* '54 (PRO)[P] Bristol, RI St. Columban's Retirement House.
Crehan, Lawrence F. '74 (PH) Croydon, PA St. Thomas Aquinas.
Crehan, Mathias J. *o.f.m.* (MO) Phoenix.
Crehan, Matthias *o.f.m.* '75 (CIN)[M] Washington, DC The Catholic University of America.
Creider, Philip B. '77 (OKL) Military Chaplains; Navy Chaplains.
Creighton, Bernard R. *o.f.m.* '67 (PAT)[M] Butler, NJ St. Anthony Friary.
Creighton, Edward '47 (SD) Retired.
Creighton, Henry *ss.cc.* '49 (FR)[H] Fairhaven, MA Damien Residence.
Creighton, James J. *s.j.* '60 (CHI)[D] Chicago, IL St. Ignatius Jesuit Community; [J] Maywood, IL Foster G. McGaw Hospital of Loyola University of Chicago.
Creighton, Matthew E. *s.j.* '57 (CHI)[C] Chicago, IL Jesuit Community at Loyola University Chicago.
Crellana, Samuel '68 (LA) Los Angeles, CA Presentation of the Mary.
Cremaldi, Angelo '60 (LAF) Opelousas, LA Our Lady Queen of Angels.
Cremin, Michael *s.a.c.* '83 (DET)[K] Wyandotte, MI Pallottine Missionary Center (Irish Province).
Cremins, John J. '69 (BRK) Forest Hills, NY Our Lady of Mercy.
Cremonie, Louis D. '72 (HRT) Manchester, CT St. James.
Crepaz, Ilario '56 (NEW) Union City, NJ St. Anthony of Padua.
Crescenzi, Rocco *f.d.p.* '43 (BO)[T] East Boston, MA Don Orione Nursing Home.
Creson, Michael '87 (KNX) Soddy Daisy, TN Holy Spirit Catholic Church; [H] Chattanooga, TN Newman Foundation of Chattanooga, Inc..
Creson, Michael (KNX) University of Tennessee–Chattanooga; Ministries of the Chattanooga Deanery.
Creson, Michael (KNX) Presbyteral Council.
Creson, Michael (KNX) Deans of the Diocese.
Crespi, Herman *i.m.c.* '63 (MET)[H] Somerset, NJ Consolata Society for Foreign Missions.
Crespin, George E. '62 (OAK) Berkeley, CA St. Joseph The Worker.
Crespo, Charles '01 (STV) St. John, VI Our Lady of Mt. Carmel Parish.
Crespo, Charles (STV) Diocesan Newspaper.
Cressman, Richard *s.d.b.* '80 (COL)[H] Columbus, OH Salesian Residence.
Creus, John Therese (PEO)[M] Peoria, IL Congregation of St. John; [O] Peoria, IL Newman Foundation at Bradley University & Illinois Central College.
Crevcoure, Stuart '01 (TLS) Sapulpa, OK Sacred Heart; [I] Tulsa, OK St. Philip Neri Newman Center at The University of Tulsa.
Crevcoure, Stuart (TLS) Campus Ministry.
Crewe, Ronald O. '63 (MIL)[V] Milwaukee, WI Milwaukee Archdiocesan Council of Catholic Women; Racine, WI Sacred Heart Congregation.
Crews, Clyde F. '73 (L).
Crews, John S. '71 (SR)[H] Sonoma, CA Hanna Boys Center.
Crews, John (SR) Diocesan Judges.
Cribben, Andrew G. *o.praem.* '94 (GB)[A] De Pere, WI St. Norbert Abbey; [I] De Pere, WI St. Norbert Abbey.
Cribben, Philip J. '62 (PH) Newtown Square, PA St. Anastasia.
Cribbin, Austin J. '56 (BAK) Retired.
Cricchio, Santo *o.f.m.conv.* (MO) Navy Reserve Chaplains.
Crider, Robert E. '53 (KC) Plattsburg, MO St. Ann's.
Crifasi, Peter D. '49 (BR) Retired.
Crilly, James *c.s.v.* '56 (LAV)[D] Las Vegas, NV Clerics of St. Viator Retirement Home.
Crilly, Marc *o.s.b.* '93 (WOR)[O] Still River, MA Benedictine Monks, St. Benedict Abbey.
Crilly, Patrick *o.s.a.* (SB) Norco, CA St. Mel.
Crimmins, Michael C. '70 (NY) New York, NY St. Joseph; [II] New York, NY Committee for Mission Responsibility Society, Inc..
Crimmins, Michael (NY) Propagation of the Faith, Society for the.
Crimmins, Michael (NY) Holy Childhood Pontifical Association.
Crino, Patrick M. (TUC) Council of Priests; Vicars Forane; All Vicars Forane.
Crino, Patrick '88 (TUC) Yuma, AZ St. Francis of Assisi.
Criqui, J. Kenneth (KC) Diocesan Consultors.
Criqui, Kenneth '63 (KC) Carrollton, MO St. Mary's.
Criscitelli, Anthony M. *t.o.r.* (STP) Minneapolis, MN St. Bridget.
Criscuolo, Salvatore A. '78 (WDC) Washington, DC St. Patrick; Special Ministries.
Crisman, James H. '01 (DEN) Aurora, CO St. Michael the Archangel.
Crisologo, Aurelio '59 (SD) Retired.
Crisostomo, Abraham *o.f.m.conv.* '96 (CHI)[N] Chicago Conventual Franciscans of St. Bonaventure Province.
Crisostomo, Abraham *o.f.m.conv.* '96 (FgM).
Crisostomo, Michael '96 (AGN) Merizo, GU San Dionisio.
Crisostomo, Michael '96 (AGN) Merizo, GU San Dimas and Our Lady of the Rosary.
Crisp, Michael L. '97 (SUP) Iron River, WI St. Peter; Iron River, WI St. Florian; Ashland, WI SS. Peter and Paul; Presbyteral Council & Diocesan Consultors.
Crisp, Robert R. '75 (DAL)[N] Dallas, TX Commission on Ecumenism; Rowlett, TX Sacred Heart.
Crispo, John R. '50 (BO) Burlington, MA St. Margaret.
Crispo, Roderick A. *o.f.m.* '55 (BRK) Brooklyn, NY Our Lady of Peace.
Cristina, Mark Mary *m.v.f.a.* '03 (BIR)[E] Birmingham, AL Franciscan Missionaries of the Eternal Word, A Public Association of the Christian Faithful.
Cristler, Richard '00 (TLS) Broken Arrow, OK St. Benedict.
Cristobal, Adrian F. '89 (AGN) Barrigada, GU San Vicente Ferrer.
Cristobal, Adrian L.F. (AGN) Chancellor; Archdiocesan College of Consultors; Archdiocesan Presbyteral Council; Office of Vocations; Catholic Charities Appeal.
Cristobal, Adrian (AGN) San Vicente Ferrer Parish.
Cristobal, Daniel *o.f.m.cap.* '59 (AGN) Talofofo, GU San Miguel.
Cristobal, Daniel *o.f.m.cap.* '59 (AGN)[H] Agana, GU Secular Franciscans.
Cristobal, Daniel *o.f.m.cap.* '59 (AGN)[F] Agana Heights, GU St. Fidelis Friary.
Cristobal, Daniel *o.f.m.cap.* (AGN) Secular Franciscans (Third Order).
Critchlow, Donald E. '82 (CC) Retired.
Crivello, Peter A. '93 (MRY) Aptos, CA Resurrection; Vicar General.
Crivello, Peter A. (MRY) Catholic Charities Board; Finance Council; Presbyteral Council; St. Francis Central Coast Catholic High School, Inc.; Evangelization Board.
Crivello, Peter (MRY) Special Assignment; Deans.
Crivello, Peter (MRY) Diocesan Consultors.
Crivello, Peter (MRY) Special Assignment; Deans.
Crivello, Peter (MRY) Priest's Personnel Board.
Crivello, Peter (MRY) Diocesan Consultors.
Crkva, Odilo *o.s.b.* '53 (JOL)[A] Lisle, IL Benedictine University.
Crkva, Odilo *o.s.b.* '53 (JOL)[L] Lisle, IL St. Procopius Abbey.
Croak, David P. '66 (DEN) Arvada, CO Shrine of St. Anne.
Croak, Thomas *c.m.* '65 (CHI)[N] Chicago, IL Vincentian Community, Congregation of the Mission, Midwest Province.
Croal, Thomas '58 (ORG) Retired.
Croce, Albert A. *c.s.c.* '50 (FR)[H] North Dartmouth, MA St. Joseph's Hall.
Crochet, Barry F. '93 (LAF) Morgan City, LA St. Bernadette.
Crocker, John R. *s.j.* '61 (Rome)[N] Chicago Chicago Province of the Society of Jesus–Provincial Office.
Croft, George *o.m.i.* '44 (BO) Tewksbury, MA St. William.
Crofut, Robert J. '72 (BGP) Norwalk, CT St. Thomas the Apostle.
Croghan, James P. *s.j.* '85 (CI)[B] Chuuk, FM Xavier High School.
Croghan, John P. '75 (SY) Clinton, NY St. Mary; [T] Clinton, NY Hamilton College Newman Center; Priests' Personnel Committee.
Croglio, James C. '80 (BUF) Clergy Personnel Board; Ecumenism; Council of Priests; [D] Buffalo, NY St. Joseph's Collegiate Institute; [H] Diocesan Counseling Center for Clergy and Religious.
Crohan, Robert F. *m.m.* '62 (FgM).
Croisetiere, David N. '77 (SD) San Diego, CA Our Lady of Refuge.
Croisetiere, David (SD) Diocesan Judges.
Crombie, Francis H. '68 (SPR) Springfield, MA St. Patrick's.
Cron, Steven D. '78 (GR) Grand Rapids, MI Catherdral of St. Andrew.
Cron, Walter '59 (NEW)[O] Englewood Cliffs, NJ St. Michael Villa.
Cronauer, David '73 (ALT) Retired.

Cronauer, Patrick T. *o.s.b.* '84 (GBG)[H] Latrobe, PA Saint Vincent Archabbey.
Crone, Patrick H. '71 (CIN) Cincinnati, OH St. Saviour.
Crone, Terence '02 (ATL) Woodstock, GA St. Michael the Archangel.
Cronin, Brian '74 (ALB) Schenectady, NY St. Paul the Apostle Retired.
Cronin, Daniel C. '55 (NOR) Columbia, CT St. Columba.
Cronin, Daniel F. '46 (BO) Westford, MA St. Catherine of Alexandria; Senior Priests Retired.
Cronin, Daniel V. '53 (PMB) Palm Springs, FL St. Luke Retired.
Cronin, Edward J. '80 (CHI) Palos Heights, IL St. Alexander.
Cronin, Frank C. '58 (STU) Shadyside, OH St. John Vianney; Shadyside, OH St. Mary's.
Cronin, Harry C. *c.s.c.* '62 (FTW)[I] Berkeley, CA Holy Cross Center.
Cronin, Harry *c.s.c.* '62 (OAK)[N] Berkeley, CA Holy Cross Fathers–Holy Cross Center.
Cronin, James D. '76 (JUN) Retired.
Cronin, James J. '45 (BAL) Baltimore, MD St. Isaac Jogues; Baltimore, MD St. Joseph Retired.
Cronin, James J. '62 (HRT) Milford, CT St. Mary; Pro–Life Activities.
Cronin, James *o.s.b.* '54 (ROC)[I] Pine City, NY Mount Saviour Monastery.
Cronin, John F. '47 (BRK)[V] Douglaston, NY Bishop Mugavero Residence Retired.
Cronin, Joseph R. '98 (HRT) West Haven, CT Our Lady of Victory; West Haven, CT St. John Vianney.
Cronin, Kevin *o.f.m.* '74 (NEW)[N] Hohokus, NJ St. Anthony of Padua.
Cronin, Michael J. '73 (CHI) Lemont, IL St. Patrick.
Cronin, Michael J. '95 (WIN) Rollingstone, MN St. Mary's; Rollingstone, MN Holy Trinity; Winona, MN Catholic Cemeteries of Winona; Chancellor; Diocesan Board of Administration; Deposit and Loan Board; Defenders of the Bond; Chancellor; Archives; Cemeteries; Misconduct Issues.
Cronin, Michael J. (WIN) Continuing Education for Clergy.
Cronin, Patrick '67 (SAT) San Antonio, TX Prince of Peace.
Cronin, Paul T. '56 (BUF)[O] Buffalo, NY Sheehan Residence for Priests Retired.
Cronin, Peadar *ss.cc.* '72 (LA)[Q] La Verne, CA Congregation of the Sacred Hearts of Jesus and Mary.
Cronin, Peadar *ss.cc.* '72 (LA)[D] La Verne, CA Damien High School.
Cronin, Peter *s.s.c.* '54 (BUF)[M] Silver Creek, NY St. Columbans on the Lake, Home for the Aged; [P] Silver Creek, NY Missionary Sisters of St. Columban, St. Columban's on the Lake.
Cronin, Richard J. *o.s.b.* '66 (PAT)[M] Morristown, NJ St. Mary's Abbey.
Cronin, Richard '60 (JC) Retired.
Cronin, Robert J. *s.o.l.t.* '83 (FAR) Belcourt, ND St. Ann; Belcourt, ND St. Ann.
Cronin, Robert W. '52 (NOR) Censor of Books Retired.
Cronin, Robert (NOR) Members.
Cronin, Sean '73 (LA) Northridge, CA Our Lady of Lourdes.
Cronin, Sylvester J. (MET) Office of Stewardship.
Cronin, Sylvester '88 (MET) Monmouth Junction, NJ St. Cecilia.
Cronin, Thomas J. *s.j.* '53 (BR)[J] Convent, LA Manresa House of Retreats.
Cronin, Thomas '69 (RNO) Fernley, NV St. Robert Bellarmine.
Cronin, Thomas '69 (KC) On Duty Outside the Diocese.
Cronin, Timothy P. '85 (STL)[A] St. Louis, MO Cardinal Glennon College; Cardinal Glennon College.
Cronin, W. Vincent '43 (HRT) Retired.
Cronin, William F. *o.s.cam.* (WOR)[S] Whitinsville, MA St. Camillus Institute, Inc..
Cronin, William '76 (MIL)[O] Wauwatosa, WI St. Camillus Community House.
Cronkleton, Thomas E. '86 (CHY) Cheyenne, WY Holy Trinity; College of Consultors; Presbyteral Council; Ex Officios, Non–Voting; Judicial Vicar; Judges; St. Joseph's Society for Priests (Clergy Mutual Benefit Society).
Cronkleton, Thomas (CHY) Liturgical Commission.
Cronogue, Michael P. *s.s.e.* '77 (BUR)[E] Colchester, VT Society of St. Edmund.
Crook, David G. '81 (BEL) Retired.
Crooker, Robert W. *c.s.b.* '53 (GAL)[Q] Houston, TX Residence of the Basilian Fathers of the University of St. Thomas.
Crookston, James F. '71 (ALT) Altoona, PA St. Rose of Lima.
Crookston, Michael J. '80 (GBG) Indiana, PA St. Thomas More University Parish.
Crosara, Lawrence *s.x.* '58 (MIL)[B] Franklin, WI Xaverian Missionary Fathers College Seminary.
Crosby, Charles E. '56 (MAN) Retired.
Crosby, Dan *o.f.m.cap.* '64 (LC)[H] Marathon City, WI St. Anthony Retreat Center.
Crosby, Dan *o.f.m.cap.* '64 (LC)[G] Marathon City, WI St. Anthony Retreat Center.
Crosby, Donald F. *s.j.* '68 (California)[N] Berkeley, CA Jesuit Community at Jesuit School of Theology at Berkeley.
Crosby, Michael *o.f.m.* '64 (STL)[S] Dittmer, MO Il Ritiro–The Little Retreat.
Crosby, Michael *o.f.m.cap.* '66 (MIL) Milwaukee, WI St. Benedict the Moor.
Crosby, Neil A. '81 (CLV) Cuyahoga Falls, OH St. Eugene.
Crosby, Theodore A. (OG) Watertown, NY Holy Family.
Crosby, Vincent R. *o.s.b.* '72 (GBG)[H] Latrobe Saint Vincent Archabbey.
Crosier, Raymond '75 (AMA) Bishop's Appointee; Amarillo, TX St. Joseph's.
Cross, Michael L. '62 (MRY) Felton, CA St. John's; Administrative Committee Priests' Pension Plan.
Cross, Peter '50 (DAV) Retired.
Cross, Robert A. '52 (CHI) Retired.
Cross, William D. '85 (STU) Graduate Studies; Auditors; Defenders of the Bond; Pastoral Staff; College of Consultors.
Cross, William H. '74 (CIN) Cincinnati, OH St. John Vianney.
Crosse, Charles '53 (SEA) Retired.
Crossen, Jason '00 (DAV) Muscatine, IA SS. Mary and Mathias of Muscatine.
Crosser, Raymond G. '56 (ALT) Retired.
Crossin, John W. *o.s.f.s.* '76 (ARL)[B] Washington, DC Deshairs Community–Oblates of St. Francis de Sales Residence.
Crossman, James '46 (DUL) Duluth, MN Cathedral of Our Lady of the Rosary.
Crossmeyer Robert *c.p.* '88 (BIR) Birmingham, AL Holy Family.
Crossmeyer Robert *c.p.* '88 (BIR)[I] Birmingham, AL Congregation of the Passion: Holy Family Community, Inc..
Crossmyer, Robert *c.p.* (BIR) Diocesan College of Vicars.
Crosthwait Joseph H. '41 (GAL) Retired.
Crosthwait Joseph '53 (GAL)[A] Houston, TX St. Mary's Seminary.
Croston, John J. *c.s.c.* '62 (FTW)[K] Notre Dame, IN Holy Cross Mission House.
Croteau, Francois A. '42 (HRT) Retired.
Croteau, Roger H. '67 (MAN) Derry, NH Holy Cross; Advocates.
Crotly, Christopher *c.p.m.* '01 (OWN)[F] Auburn, KY Fathers of Mercy.
Crotty, Columban *ss.cc.* '58 (FR).
Crotty, Columban *ss.cc.* '58 (FR)[H] Fairhaven, MA National Center of the Enthronement.
Crotty, Desmond G. '72 (NO) New Orleans, LA St. Francis of Assisi; Deans; Air Force Reserve Chaplains.
Crotty, John C. *s.s.j.* '55 (BAL)[S] Baltimore, MD St. Joseph's Manor.
Crotty, John M. '47 (NY) Retired.
Crotty, Matthew M. '44 (BAK) Vicar General; Judge; Council of Priests and Diocesan Consultors; Building Committee; Church Property, Administration of; Special Assignment.
Crotty, Thomas M. *o.s.m.* '60 (CHI)[N] Chicago Order of Friar Servants of Mary (Servites) United States of America Province, Inc.; [I] Anaheim, CA Servite Fathers and Brothers; [I] Anaheim, CA Seven Holy Founders Priory.
Crotty, Vincent *c.ss.r.* '49 (RVC) Bethpage, NY St. Martin of Tours.
Crouse, William S. '59 (ALT) Retired.
Crowe, Francis R. *o.p.* '47 (CHI)[N] River Forest, IL St. Thomas Aquinas Priory.
Crowe, George W. '65 (PH) Philadelphia, PA Stella Maris; Absent on Sick Leave.
Crowe, Hugh '58 (LA) Los Angeles, CA St. Ann.
Crowe, Martin *c.ss.r.* '40 (BRK) Brooklyn, NY Our Lady of Perpetual Help Basilica.
Crowe, Raymond *o.m.i.* '54 (MIA) Miami, FL Christ the King.
Crowley, Alan N. *o.carm.* '41 (BO)[O] Peabody, MA Catholic Information Center; [AA] Peabody, MA St. Theresa Carmelite Chapel.
Crowley, Cale J. *s.s.* '69 (BAL)[S] St. Augustine's Major Seminary.
Crowley, Charles G. *s.j.* '51 (BO)[V] Boston, MA Loyola House.
Crowley, Daniel J. (BO) Wellesley, MA St. James the Great.
Crowley, Daniel (BO) South Weymouth, MA South Shore Hospital.
Crowley, Dennis J. '89 (PAT) Morristown, NJ Assumption of the Blessed Virgin Mary.
Crowley, Edmund G. '70 (MAN) Hooksett, NH Holy Rosary; Air National Guard Chaplains.
Crowley, Francis J. '53 (BO) Military & VA Chaplains; Providence, RI Veterans Administration Hospital.
Crowley, Francis *c.m.* '57 (KC)[J] Kansas City, MO Vincentian Parish Mission Center.
Crowley, James M. '86 (CHR) Camden, SC Our Lady of Perpetual Help.
Crowley, John A. '61 (PMB) Vero Beach, FL St. John of the Cross.
Crowley, John C. '03 (PH) Maple Glen, PA St. Alphonsus.
Crowley, Patrick J. *ss.cc.* '72 (OAK) Alameda, CA St. Joseph Basilica.
Crowley, Paul G. *s.j.* '92 (SJ)[B] Santa Clara, CA Jesuit Community.
Crowley, R. Kevin '68 (MET) Retired.
Crowley, Richard P. '62 (BO) Middleborough, MA Sacred Heart.
Crowley, Stephen L. '55 (HRT) Retired.
Crowley, Thomas F. '76 (WDC) Greenbelt, MD St. Hugh.
Crowley, Thomas J. '51 (BUF)[O] Buffalo, NY Sheehan Residence for Priests Retired.
Crowley, Thomas '87 (DM) Leave of Absence.
Crowley, William F. *c.s.sp.* (PIT)[B] Pittsburgh, PA Duquesne University of the Holy Spirit.
Crowley, William '74 (B) Grangeville, ID SS. Peter and Paul.
Crowley, William (B) College of Consultors.
Crowley, William (B) Judges.
Crowley, William (B) Adjutant Judicial Vicars.
Crozzoletto, Provvido *m.c.c.j.* '70 (CHI)[N] La Grange Park, IL Comboni Missionaries.
Crucet, Jose '88 (PMB) West Palm Beach, FL St. Juliana.
Crum, Thomas J. '75 (Y) Rootstown, OH St. Peter of the Fields.
Crum, William '76 (NEW) Paramus, NJ Annunciation.
Crumbley, Charles W. '67 (Y) Warren, OH St. James.
Crumbley, Charles (Y) College of Consultors.
Crumley, William *c.s.c.* '64 (LAF) Charenton, LA Immaculate Conception.
Crumlish, Richard C. '45 (BUF) Retired.
Crummy, Michael E. '86 (MET) Milford, NJ St. Edward the Confessor.
Crunican, James '63 (P) Retired.
Cruz, Alexander '91 (NEW) Linden, NJ St. Elizabeth's.
Cruz, David R. (LUB) Priests Personnel Board.
Cruz, David '86 (LUB) Lubbock, TX Our Lady of Grace.
Cruz, Dennys Walter *c.p.* '00 (MGZ) San Sebastian, PR San Sebastian Martir.
Cruz, Domingo '73 (HT) Thibodaux, LA St. Lawrence the Martyr.
Cruz, Edwin *o.s.a.* '95 (SJN) Bayamon, PR Nuestra Sra. de los Dolores.
Cruz, Faustino *s.m.* '88 (OAK).
Cruz, Fausto *c.m.f.* '02 (SJN)[A] Bayamon, PR San Jose.
Cruz, Francisco '69 (CHR) Greenville, SC St. Mary's.
Cruz, Gilbert J. '81 (SJN) Retired.
Cruz, Gilbert '81 (LA) San Pedro, CA Mary, Star of the Sea.
Cruz, Gustavo '74 (LAV) Las Vegas, NV Prince of Peace.
Cruz, Gustavo (LAV) Presbyteral Council for the Diocese of Las Vegas.
Cruz, Hector J. *s.m.* '77 (MRY)[F] Santa Cruz, CA Society of Mary, Marists.
Cruz, Hector *s.m.* '77 (MRY) Santa Cruz, CA Star of the Sea.
Cruz, Jesse (LUB) Priests' Retirement Board.
Cruz, Jesse (LUB) Morton, TX St. Ann.
Cruz, Jesse (LUB) Diocesan Pastoral Liturgy Commission.
Cruz, Luciano '86 (PAT) Paterson, NJ St. Therese.
Cruz, Luis Antonio Rivera '83 (CGS) San Lorenzo, PR Sagrado Corazon de Jesus y 12 Apostoles.
Cruz, Manuel '80 (NEW) Newark, NJ Office of Health Care Personnel; Newark, NJ St. Michael Medical Center.
Cruz, Manuel '93 (NEW)[G] Newark, NJ Saint Michael's Medical Center, a Division of Cathedral Health Services, Inc.; Office of Hospital Ministry; Chaplains.
Cruz, Martin de la '01 (BWN) Brownsville, TX Holy Family.
Cruz, Remberto '49 (SJN) Retired.
Cruz, Robert Joel '96 (HT) Lockport, LA Holy Savior.
Cruz, Robert (HT) Priests Council.
Cruz, Robert (HT) College of Consultors.
Cruz, Victor Rual de la (CHI) Northlake, IL St. John Vianney, Cure of Ars.
Cruz Davila, Carlos D. '80 (SJN) On Duty Outside the Archdiocese.
Cruz Velazquez, Johnny *o.ss.t.* '91 (SJN) Guaynabo, PR Santa Rosa de Lima.
Cryan, James F. *o.s.f.s.* '65 (TOL)[J] Toledo, OH Provincial Residence.
Cryan, John J. '81 (NEW) Jersey City, NJ Our Lady of Mercy; Members; Elected Members; Archdiocesan Judges.
Cryan, John '81 (NEW) Jersey City, NJ Church of Our Lady of Sorrows; Staff.
Cryans, Andrew W. '75 (MAN) Milford, NH St. Patrick.
Crynes, J. Peter '67 (SCR) Shavertown, PA St. Therese.
Csaszar, James C. '99 (COL)[C] Zanesville, OH Bishop Rosecrans High School.
Csaszar, James '99 (COL) Kenton, OH Immaculate Conception.

Cser, Ladislas *s.j.* '45 (NY)[EE] New York, NY Murray–Weigel Hall.
Cser, Ladislaus *s.j.* '45 (RVC) Retired.
Cserhati, Ferenc (ATH) Delegate of the Bishop in Europe.
Cserhati, Ferenc (ATH) Newspapers & Magazines.
Csete, Ivan L. '81 (NY) Forestburgh, NY St. Thomas Aquinas.
Csizmar, Richard A. '68 (BUF) Finance Council; Vicars; Albion, NY St. Mary Assumption; Albion, NY St. Joseph.
Csorba, Dominic L. *o.f.m.* '35 (NY)[II] New York, NY Hungarian Catholic League of America, Inc..
Csorba, Dominic *o.f.m.* '62 (NY) New York, NY St. Stephen of Hungary.
Cuadrado, Hector F. *c.m.f.* '91 (SJN) Bayamon, PR San Jose.
Cuadros, Jesus '66 (BRK) Brooklyn, NY St. Thomas Aquinas.
Cubelo, Felix '73 (SAN) Big Spring, TX Sacred Heart.
Cubelo, Felix '73 (SAN) Big Spring, TX St. Thomas.
Cuccaro, John J. '79 (PBR) Pittsburgh, PA St. John Chrysostom.
Cuccia, Callons '03 (NO) River Ridge, LA St. Matthew the Apostle; Harahan, LA St. Rita.
Cuccia, Salvatore H. *o.praem.* '66 (GB) De Pere, WI St. Norbert College; [I] De Pere, WI St. Norbert Abbey.
Cuddigan, John *s.j.* '62 (SD) San Diego, CA St. Therese.
Cuddihy, William '56 (SD) Retired.
Cuddy, John '53 (SAV) Macon, GA St. Joseph.
Cuddy, William F. '79 (BO) Military & VA Chaplains; Navy Chaplains.
Cudemo, Nicholas V. '63 (PH) Retired.
Cudnik, Chester C. '48 (CLV) Cleveland, OH St. Barbara Retired.
Cuenca, Fernando Augusto *o.m.v.* '02 (SFD) Alton, IL St. Mary's.
Cuenin, Walter H. '70 (BO) Newton, MA Our Lady Help of Christians; Pilgrimages.
Cuesta, Benedicto '51 (SFE) Retired.
Cuevas, Diego O. '03 (MAD) Waunakee, WI St. John the Baptist.
Cuevas, Fernando *c.s.* '02 (SJ) San Jose, CA Holy Cross.
Cuevas, Jose Luis *m.c.c.j.* '74 (CIN)[Q] Azusa, CA Casa Comboni Mission Seminary.
Cuevas, Randy M. '82 (BR) Donaldsonville, LA Ascension of Our Lord Jesus Christ; Air Force Reserve Chaplains.
Cuevas, Wilson '81 (ELP) El Paso, TX Corpus Christi.
Cuff, John P. *m.m.* '69 (FgM).
Culhane, Alberic *o.s.b.* '57 (SCL)[I] Collegeville, MN St. John's Abbey, of the Order of St. Benedict.
Culhane, Eugene K. *s.j.* '45 (NY)[EE] New York, NY Murray–Weigel Hall.
Culhane, Thomas '47 (KCK) Retired.
Culhane, Thomas '47 (KCK)[G] Olathe, KS Villa St. Francis, Inc..
Culkin, Francis J. '44 (SY) Rome, NY St. Mary of the Assumption Retired.
Culkin, Harry M. '42 (BRK)[V] Douglaston, NY Bishop Mugavero Residence Retired.
Culkin, Michael '78 (WDC) On Duty Outside the Archdiocese.
Culkin, Michael (HBG) Lancaster General Hospital and Lancaster Community Hospital.
Cull, Lawrence W. '69 (NEW) Ramsey, NJ St. Paul.
Cull, Paul J. '45 (CHI) Retired.
Cullen, Bernard J. *o.c.s.o.* '48 (DUB)[K] Peosta, IA New Melleray Abbey, Order of Cistercians of the Strict Observance.
Cullen, Christopher M. *s.j.* '94 (NY)[EE] Cardinal Spellman Hall, Jesuit Community.
Cullen, Daniel *s.m.a.* '47 (NEW)[N] Tenafly, NJ Society of African Missions, Provincialate, S.M.A. Fathers.
Cullen, Donald '71 (KCK) Roeland Park, KS St. Agnes.
Cullen, George H. '48 (CHI) Retired.
Cullen, J. Peter (BGP) Vicars General; Moderator of the Curia; Presbyteral Council; Finance Council; Pastors' Vocation Advisory Board; Diocesan Consultors.
Cullen, John F. '41 (PH) Retired.
Cullen, John J. '99 (BUF) Portageville, NY Assumption B.V.M.; Portageville, NY St. Mary.
Cullen, Kevin L. *s.j.* '86 (DEN)[N] Denver, CO Loyola Parish – Jesuit Community.
Cullen, Kevin *s.j.* '86 (STP)[B] St. Paul, MN Jesuit Novitiate.
Cullen, Patrick P. '68 (BIR) Birmingham, AL St. Mark the Evangelist.
Cullen, Patrick *s.p.s.* '52 (NEW)[N] Cliffside Park, NJ St. Patrick's Missionary Society; [N] Cliffside Park, NJ St. Patrick's Missionary Society.
Cullen, Patrick (BIR) Apostolate with Mentally Retarded Persons.
Cullen, Paul M. *o.s.m.* '65 (CHI) Chicago, IL Annunciata; [N] Chicago, IL Annunciata Priory.
Cullen, Robert B. *s.j.* '58 (ALN)[A] Wernersville, PA Jesuit Center.
Cullen, Thomas F. '53 (CLV) Westlake, OH St. Ladislas Retired.
Cullen, Thomas J. '52 (MOB) Retired.
Cullen, William J. *s.j.* '65 (BO)[P] Fairfield, CT The Fairfield Jesuit Community–Fairfield University; [V] Boston The Society of Jesus of New England–Provincial Offices.
Cullen, William '48 (JOL) Retired.
Cullen, William '83 (JKS)[J] Jackson, MS Parroquia De San Miguel Del Arcangel.
Culleton, James P. '46 (PEO) Retired.
Culley, Brian *c.m.f.* '84 (FRS) Fresno, CA St. Anthony Claret.
Culley, Thomas D. *s.j.* '65 (NO)[P] New Orleans, LA Ignatius Residence.
Culligan, Kevin *o.c.d.* (CHI)[N] Chicago, IL Discalced Carmelite Friars; Edith Stein House of Studies.
Culligan, Martin J. *c.m.* '57 (STL)[O] St. Louis, MO Lazarist Residence.
Culligan, Michael A. '59 (SR) Petaluma, CA St. James.
Cullinan, John F. '46 (PHX) Phoenix, AZ St. Joan of Arc Retired.
Cullinane, Brian *o.f.m.* '71 (NEW) Wood Ridge, NJ Our Lady of the Assumption.
Cullinane, Briant *o.f.m.conv.* '57 (ALB)[A] Rensselaer, NY Conventual Franciscan Friars; [L] Rensselaer, NY Provincialate, Immaculate Conception Friary – Order of Friars Minor Conventual.
Cullinane, Jeremiah J. '59 (WH) On Duty Outside the Diocese.
Cullinane, John '56 (BRK) Breezy Point, NY St. Genevieve.
Cullings, David Ronald '67 (P) Eugene, OR St. Peter.
Culloty, John P. '72 (BO) Norwood, MA St. Timothy.
Culnane, William R. '60 (SCR) Wilkes-Barre, PA St. Dominic.
Culotta, Joachim N. *o.p.* '64 (STL)[O] St. Louis, MO St. Dominic Priory.
Culotta, Joachim *o.p.* (DET) Judges.
Culotta, Joseph '83 (BIR) Decatur, AL Annunciation of the Lord.
Culotta, Joseph (BIR) Diocesan College of Consultors.
Culotta, Joseph (BIR) Members.
Culotta, Salvador J. '53 (BEA) Retired.
Culotta, Thomas C. '61 (HRT) East Berlin, CT Sacred Heart.
Culver, Garry '64 (DM) Retired.
Culver, James A. '55 (SY) Rome, NY St. Peter Retired.
Culver, Richard J. '85 (OAK) Bay Point, CA Our Lady Queen of the World.
Culver, T. Joseph '63 (GAL) La Marque, TX Our Lady Queen of Peace; Diocesan Judges; Southern Vicariate; Appointees; College of Consultors; Building Commission.
Cumberland, Matthew T. '92 (JUN) Los Angeles, CA St. Sebastian.
Cummings, Brian J. *s.s.e.* '96 (BUR)[E] Colchester, VT Society of St. Edmund.
Cummings, Carl F. '75 (BAL) Baltimore, MD St. Agnes.
Cummings, Carl (BAL) Priest Personnel Board.
Cummings, Charles J. '68 (SCR) Williamsport, PA Ascension; Deans.
Cummings, Charles J. *o.c.s.o.* '71 (SLC)[A] Huntsville, UT Abbey of Our Lady of the Holy Trinity; [F] Huntsville, UT Abbey of Our Lady of the Holy Trinity of the Order of Cistercians.
Cummings, Gabriel '84 (SAV) St. Marys, GA Our Lady Star of the Sea.
Cummings, George '43 (SP) Retired.
Cummings, George '43 (SP) Citrus Springs, FL St. Elizabeth Ann Seton.
Cummings, John J. '88 (LFT) Lake Village, IN St. Augusta; Associate Judges.
Cummings, Jose Emilio *c.m.* '72 (SJN) San Juan, PR Catedral de San Juan Bautista; [D] San Juan, PR Santa Ana Chapel.
Cummings, Juniper *o.f.m.conv.* '50 (FgM).
Cummings, Leo B. *m.s.* '66 (ATL) Marietta, GA Church of St. Ann.
Cummings, Leo P. '64 (SCR)[I] Carbondale, PA Marian Community Hospital.
Cummings, Marilyn (SP)[K] Tampa, FL St. Joseph's Hospital, Inc..
Cummings, Maurice H. *o.carm* (DOD) Ashland, KS St. Joseph; Coldwater, KS Holy Spirit Station.
Cummings, Patrick J. '78 (GAL) Houston, TX Annunciation.
Cummings, Patrick '78 (GAL)[K] Catholic Chaplain Corps, Texas Medical Center.
Cummings, Paul J. '55 (LAN) Ovid, MI Holy Family.
Cummings, Thomas W. *s.j.* '69 (STL)[O] St. Louis, MO St. Louis University High School Jesuit Community.
Cummins, Anthony O. '65 (SAT) Boerne, TX St. Peter the Apostle.
Cummins, Anthony (SAT) Priests Personnel Board.
Cummins, Charles E. '68 (SLC) Ogden, UT St. Joseph's.
Cummins, Charles T. '68 (SLC) Ogden, UT St. Florence Catholic Community; [H] Ogden, UT Weber State University, Newman Center.
Cummins, Joseph V. *c.m.* '72 (PH)[B] Philadelphia, PA DePaul Novitiate.
Cummins, Michael E. '95 (KNX) Athens, TN St. Mary.
Cummins, Michael J. *c.m.* '77 (BRK)[V] Queens Village, NY DePaul Residence.
Cummins, Michael (KNX) Deaf Ministry.
Cummins, Michael (KNX) Youth Ministry.
Cummins, Robert L. '82 (RIC) Chesapeake, VA St. Therese of Lisieux.
Cummins, Timothy '45 (FRS) Retired.
Cuneo, J. James '67 (BGP) Stratford, CT Holy Name of Jesus; Judges; Catholic Lawyers.
Cuneo, James J. '63 (DEN) AUXILIARY CHAPLAINS CONTRACT CHAPLAINS Retired.
Cung, Ephrem M. Vu Khiem *c.m.c.* '81 (SPC)[E] Carthage, MO Congregation of the Mother Coredemptrix, United States Assumption Province.
Cunha, Egionor '92 (NEW) Military Chaplains; Navy Chaplains.
Cunnane, Jarlath '77 (LA) Los Angeles, CA St. Thomas the Apostle.
Cunnane, Jarlath (LA) Deanery 15.
Cunnane, Jarlath (LA) Members.
Cunnane, Michael A. '61 (SD) Santee, CA Guardian Angels.
Cunneen, Sean R. (NEW) Regional Bishops and Regional Vicars; Members.
Cunneen, Sean '67 (NEW) New Providence, NJ Our Lady of Peace.
Cunneen, Sean (NEW) College of Consultors.
Cunney, Henry M. (BO) Danvers, MA St. Richard.
Cunniff, Charles *c.s.p.* '83 (GR) Grand Rapids, MI Chapel of St. Paul–Catholic Information Center.
Cunniff, Declan J. *o.s.b.* '68 (NEW)[N] Newark, NJ Newark Abbey.
Cunniff, Hubert F. *s.j.* '38 (BO)[V] Weston, MA Campion Health Center, Inc..
Cunniff, Vincent '53 (P) Retired.
Cunniffe, James A. *s.c.j.* '57 (JKS) Hernando, MS Holy Spirit; [F] Nesbit, MS St. Michael Community House.
Cunnigham, James K. '95 (BRK) Far Rockaway, NY St. Mary Star of the Sea.
Cunningham, Ambrose '50 (PEO) Rock Island, IL Sacred Heart.
Cunningham, Christopher '90 (LA) Covina, CA St. Louise de Marillac.
Cunningham, Donald M. *s.j.* '64 (STL)[O] St. Louis, MO Office; [S] St. Louis, MO Retreat House.
Cunningham, Douglas '87 (SY) Norwich, NY Church of the Holy Apostles, St. Paul Roman Catholic Community of Norwich, NY.
Cunningham, Edward *o.m.i.* '58 (WIN) Minnesota City, MN St. Paul's.
Cunningham, James B. '87 (BUF) Buffalo, NY St. Agnes.
Cunningham, James K. (BRK) Presbyteral Council.
Cunningham, James *c.s.s.* '50 (BO)[Y] Waltham, MA Stigmatine Fathers and Brothers.
Cunningham, James (BRK) Bishop Sullivan—.
Cunningham, John E. '51 (DM) Retired.
Cunningham, John F. *o.p.* '53 (PRO)[P] Providence St. Thomas Aquinas Priory at Providence College.
Cunningham, John F. '56 (LA) Retired.
Cunningham, John H. '65 (ALX) Retired.
Cunningham, John J. '56 (CHI) Chicago, IL St. Priscilla.
Cunningham, John P. '79 (BAL) Baltimore, MD St. Thomas More.
Cunningham, John Vianney *t.o.r.* '70 (ORL).
Cunningham, John '74 (PHX)[D] Higley, AZ St. Mary Magdalene.
Cunningham, Joseph C. '71 (PH) Wayne, PA St. Isaac Jogues.
Cunningham, Joseph L. '56 (MIL) Retired.
Cunningham, Joseph L. '63 (BRK) Bellerose, NY St. Gregory the Great.
Cunningham, Kieran P. *o.s.b.* '62 (SEA)[L] Lacey, WA St. Martin's Abbey.
Cunningham, Leonard A. *o.c.s.o.* '50 (CHR)[E] Moncks Corner, SC Mepkin Abbey.
Cunningham, Lloyd *s.v.d.* '81 (CHI)[N] Chicago, IL House of Religious Men: Divine Word Theologate.
Cunningham, Lloyd *s.v.d.* '81 (CHI)[N] Chicago, IL Divine Word Theologate.
Cunningham, Lloyd *s.v.d.* '81 (CHI).
Cunningham, Mark '99 (ALB)[B] Herkimer, NY St. Francis de Sales.
Cunningham, Mark (ALB) Members.
Cunningham, Michael '86 (OAK) Concord, CA Queen of All Saints.
Cunningham, Nicholas J. '79 (TOL) Shelby, OH Sacred Heart of Jesus; Shelby, OH Most Pure Heart of Mary.
Cunningham, Peter J. '56 (MOB) Mobile, AL St. Mary; Archdiocesan Consultors; Group I.
Cunningham, Peter (MOB) Officers.
Cunningham, Peter (MOB) Consultors.
Cunningham, Philip *c.s.p.* '56 (SFR) San Francisco, CA Old St. Mary's Cathedral Retired.
Cunningham, Richard G. '57 (BO)[A] Brighton, MA St. John Seminary School of Theology; Promoter of Justice; Archdiocesan Judges.
Cunningham, Robert J. (BUF) The Diocese of Buffalo, N.Y.; Finance Council; Vicars General; Chancellor; Defenders of the Bond; Consultors, College of; Council of Priests; Buffalo, NY St. Louis.
Cunningham, Vincent P. *s.m.m.* '60 (RVC) West Islip,

NY Good Samaritan Hospital Medical Center; [M] Bay Shore, NY Montfort Missionaries.
Cuny, W. Timothy *o.s.a.* '70 (DET) Grosse Pointe Park, MI St. Clare of Montefalco.
Cuomo, Rocco A. '64 (TR) Freehold, NJ St. Rose of Lima.
Cupp, Edwin '69 (WH) Absent on Sick Leave.
Cupple, Gerard J. '85 (DET) Lincoln Park, MI St. Henry.
Curalli, Joseph *c.ss.r.* '78 (KC)[J] Kansas City, MO Redemptorists Fathers of Kansas City, Missouri.
Curalli, Joseph *c.ss.r.* '78 (KC) Kansas City, MO Our Lady of Perpetual Help.
Curbelo, Luis A. (ARE) Arecibo, PR Our Lady of Guadalupe.
Curci, Richard G. '72 (GBG) Arnold, PA All Saints; New Kensington, PA Mt. St. Peter.
Curcio, Ralph V. '61 (NY) Port Chester, NY Our Lady of Mercy.
Curesky, Mark L. *o.f.m.conv.* '75 (BAL)[S] Ellicott City, MD Friary of St. Joseph Cupertino.
Curley, Augustine J. *o.s.b.* '88 (NEW)[N] Newark, NJ Newark Abbey.
Curley, Joseph K. '62 (RVC) Centereach, NY Assumption of the Blessed Virgin Mary.
Curley, Martin W. '56 (RVC) Retired.
Curley, Patrick '70 (JKS) Vicksburg, MS St. Michael; Personnel Board.
Curley, Terence P. '72 (BO) Nahant, MA St. Thomas Aquinas.
Curley, Thomas J. '70 (NY) Chester, NY St. Columba.
Curnutte, William G. '82 (SLC) Retired.
Curran, Anthony T. '67 (ATL) Atlanta, GA St. Anthony of Padua.
Curran, Anthony '72 (ALB) Schenectady, NY St. Mary.
Curran, Anthony '72 (ALB) Schenectady, NY Holy Cross.
Curran, Anthony '72 (ALB) Schenectady, NY St. John the Evangelist.
Curran, Brendan A. *o.p.* '01 (CHI) Chicago, IL St. Pius V.
Curran, Brendan *o.p.* '01 (CHI)[N] Chicago, IL Dominican Community.
Curran, Charles E. '58 (ROC) On Duty Outside the Diocese.
Curran, Francis D. '50 (CLV) Willoughby, OH Immaculate Conception.
Curran, Francis L. '38 (MAN) Retired.
Curran, Francis T. (GI) Grand Island, NE Blessed Sacrament.
Curran, Gerald X. '48 (Y) Retired.
Curran, Hugh D. '54 (NY) Pelham Manor, NY Our Lady of Perpetual Help.
Curran, Hugh J. '51 (GAL)[Q] Houston, TX Dillon House.
Curran, James P. '63 (RIC) Gloucester, NJ St. Mary's.
Curran, James P. (CAM) Priests Personnel Board; Parent–Teachers Association.
Curran, James *s.d.b.* '51 (NO) Harvey, LA St. Rosalie.
Curran, James *c.m.f.* '83 (ATL) Stone Mountain, GA Corpus Christi.
Curran, James '00 (RIC) Yorktown, VA St. Joan of Arc.
Curran, John F. *s.j.* (CI)[C] Kolonia, Pohnpei, FM Jesuit House; Vicar General; Diocesan Consultors; Finance Committee; Pohnpei–Kosrae; Notaries.
Curran, John W. *o.f.m. conv.* '71 (L) Louisville, KY St. Rita.
Curran, John '54 (WCH) Retired.
Curran, John *o.f.m.conv.* '71 (L) Louisville, KY St. Anthony.
Curran, Joseph F. *s.j.* '56 (PH)[AA] Loyola Center and Manresa Hall.
Curran, Joseph L. '76 (BO) Watertown, MA Sacred Heart.
Curran, Michael J. '81 (BRK) Brooklyn, NY St. Catharine of Alexandria.
Curran, Oliver '76 (GLP) Pinetop, AZ St. Mary of the Angels.
Curran, Patrick J. '55 (SLC) On Duty Outside the Diocese.
Curran, Patrick J. '55 (SLC) West Hartford, CT St. Thomas the Apostle Church.
Curran, Patrick '01 (STO) Turlock, CA Sacred Heart Church of Turlock (Pastor of).
Curran, Paul E. '59 (BO) Whitman, MA Holy Ghost; Senior Priests Retired.
Curran, Paul F. '57 (PH) Huntingdon Valley, PA St. Albert the Great.
Curran, Peter *o.m.i.* '71 (FgM).
Curran, Richard G. '76 (BO) Hanover, MA St. Mary of the Sacred Heart.
Curran, Robert F. *s.j.* '74 (SJ)[M] Los Gatos Sacred Heart Jesuit Center.
Curran, Thomas B. *o.s.f.s.* '84 (WIL)[B] Wilmington, DE Salesianum School.
Curran, Vincent J. '98 (HRT) Hamden, CT St. Rita's.
Curran, William J. '69 (CHI) Berwyn, IL St. Leonard.
Curran, William *m.afr.* '66 (FgM).
Currans, Clem W. '74 (SC) Boone, IA Sacred Heart.
Currans, Clement W. (SC) Presbyteral Council.
Current, Maurice H. '80 (LIN) Beaver Crossing, NE Sacred Heart; Adjutant Judicial Vicars; Commission for Sacred Liturgy and Sacred Music; Diocesan Area CCD Directors; Ecumenical Affairs, Commission for; Priests' Continuing Education Committee.
Currie, Charles L. *s.j.* '63 (WDC)[M] Washington, DC Leonard Neale House.
Currie, Donald '79 (SAT) On Leave.
Currie, John A. '97 (BO) Norwood, MA St. Catherine of Siena.
Currie, Joseph A. *s.j.* '68 (NY)[EE] Cardinal Spellman Hall, Jesuit Community.
Currie, Joseph *s.j.* '68 (NY)[HH] Bronx, NY Fordham University at Rosehill.
Currie, Robert F. *s.j.* '71 (BAL).
Currie, Robert F. *s.j.* '71[S] (FgM).
Currie, William J. *s.j.* '67 (BAL)[S] SJ House.
Currin, John M. '98 (DET) Absent on Leave; Detroit, MI St. Luke.
Curry, Frederic F. '49 (TUC) Tucson, AZ St. Joseph Retired.
Curry, James J. *s.j.* '74 (NY)[F] New York, NY Loyola School; [EE] New York, NY St. Ignatius Loyola Residence.
Curry, Joseph M. '86 (MET) New Brunswick, NJ St. Peter Apostle.
Curry, Robert S. *s.j.* '64 (PH)[AA] Loyola Center and Manresa Hall.
Curry, Stephen M. *o.s.a.* '96 (PH)[G] Malvern, PA Malvern Preparatory School for Boys; [AA] Malvern, PA Augustinian Friars (O.S.A.).
Curry, Terence M. *s.j.* '94 (NY)[EE] Cardinal Spellman Hall, Jesuit Community.
Curry, Terence W. *s.j.* '77 (WOR)[O] Worcester, MA Jesuits of Holy Cross College, Inc..
Curry, Thomas P. '51 (BRK)[S] Queens Village, NY Queen of Peace Residence Retired.
Curry, Thomas P. *o.s.b.* '03 (GBG) Latrobe, PA St. Vincent Basilica; [H] Latrobe, PA Saint Vincent Archabbey.
Curso, Manuel '72 (SFR) Colma, CA Holy Angels.
Curtin, Cornelius L. *s.j.* '56 (DET)[P] Clarkston, MI Colombiere Center.
Curtin, Eugene P. '56 (BO) Lexington, MA St. Brigid.
Curtin, James E. '52 (DET) Retired.
Curtin, James F. '51 (BO) Senior Priests Retired.
Curtin, Jim '69 (JOL) Lockport, IL St. Dennis.
Curtin, Paul *c.ss.r.* '67 (TUC)[E] Cortaro, AZ Redemptorist Society of Arizona.
Curtin, Paul *c.ss.r.* '67 (TUC)[G] Cortaro, AZ Redemptorist Society of Arizona.
Curtin, Timothy *s.j.* '52 (BGP)[R] Bridgeport, CT The Society of Our Lady of the Way.
Curtin, Vincent *s.j.* '68 (WDC) Washington, DC Holy Trinity.
Curtis, Howard *o.c.s.o.* '57 (P)[L] Lafayette, OR The Cistercian (Trappist) Abbey of Our Lady of Guadalupe.
Curtis, John C. '84 (LEX) Berea, KY St. Clare; Berea, KY Our Lady of Mt. Vernon; [L] Berea KY St. Clare Church–Berea College; HIV/AIDS Ministry.
Curtis, Joseph C. '69 (CHI) Indian Creek, IL St. Mary of Vernon.
Curtis, Robert J. '36 (TOL) Retired.
Curtis, Robert P. *c.s.p.* '71 (NY)[EE] Jamaica Estates Paulist Fathers Generalate.
Curtiss, Donald A. (ROC)[L] Aurora, NY Wells College, c/o St. Patrick Church; Defenders of the Bond.
Curtiss, Donald J. '71 (ROC) Aurora, NY Good Shepherd Catholic Community; Judges.
Curtsinger, George '52 (FWT) Retired.
Curzydio, Miecislaus I. (ROC) Canandaigua, NY Veteran's Hospital.
Cusack, Andrew T. '60 (BGP) On Duty Outside the Diocese.
Cusack, Andrew T. '60 (NEW)[B] Seton Hall University; [B] School of Diplomacy and Intl. Rels..
Cusack, Francis V. '54 (MOB) Mobile, AL Our Lady of Lourdes; Archdiocesan Consultors.
Cusack, Francis W. *c.p.* '58 (L)[K] Louisville, KY Sacred Heart Retreat.
Cusack, Frank (MOB) Group I.
Cusack, John J. *c.m.* '45 (PH).
Cusack, John J. '71 (PAT)[AA] Military Chaplains; Air Force Chaplains.
Cusack, John J. '71 (B) Mountain Home Air Force Base, ID St. Mary's.
Cusack, Paul *c.p.* '59 (MET).
Cusack, Thomas *s.s.c.* '62 (LA)[Q] Los Angeles, CA Columban Fathers, Procure House; [K] St. Columbans St. Columban's Foreign Mission Society.
Cusack, Thomas *s.s.c.* (LA) Members.
Cusatis Girard J. '63 (PH) Drexel Hill, PA St. Andrew.
Cusato, Michael F. *o.f.m.* '81 (BUF)[O] St. Bonaventure, NY St. Bonaventure Friary; [C] St. Bonaventure University; [C] St. Bonaventure, NY Friar Community.
Cuschieri, Albert '61 (DAL) Forney, TX St. Martin.
Cush, John P. '98 (BRK) Howard Beach, NY St. Helen.
Cush, John (BRK) Censors of Books.
Cushing, Alan '57 (SFE) Retired.
Cushing, Charles B. '54 (BRK) Retired.
Cushing, Robert A. '78 (SAV) Special Assignment; Augusta, GA St. Teresa of Avila.
Cushing, Vincent de Paul *o.f.m.* '63 (WDC)[M] Silver Spring, MD Gemelli House.
Cushing, Walter F. '56 (ROC) Rochester, NY St. Cecilia.
Cushing, Walter '56 (ROC) Retired.
Cusick, Eugene G. '64 (PH) Holland, PA St. Bede the Venerable.
Cusick, John C. '70 (CHI) Chicago, IL St. Patrick; Young Adult Ministry/Singles; Archdiocesan Council of Catholic Men.
Cusick, Kevin M. '92 (WDC) Military Chaplains; Navy Chaplains.
Cusick, Thomas H. '64 (DET) Belleville, MI St. Anthony; Archdiocesan Vicars.
Cusick, Timothy J. *s.s.* (SFR).
Cusick, Timothy S. (STA)[A] On Duty Outside the Diocese.
Cusimano, Gabriel *o.s.b.* '76 (SFE)[I] Abiquiu, NM Monastery of Christ in the Desert.
Cusimano, Salvatore J. '49 (BUF)[O] Tonawanda, NY O'Hara Residence Retired.
Cusma, Joseph S. '53 (NY) Retired.
Custer, Edward O. *m.m.* '72 (FgM).
Custer, John S. '83 (PSC) On Duty Outside Diocese.
Custer, John S. '83 (PBR)[A] Pittsburgh, PA Byzantine Catholic Seminary of SS. Cyril and Methodius.
Custer, Michael H. *o.s.b.* '41 (MAN)[K] Manchester, NH St. Anselm Abbey.
Custodio, Rinaldo B. '62 (STP) Savage, MN St. John the Baptist.
Cutajar, Alfred D. *s.j.* '69 (PH)[AA] Loyola Center and Manresa Hall.
Cutcher, Anthony E. '99 (CIN) Fort Loramie, OH SS. Peter and Paul.
Cutie, Alberto '95 (MIA) Pompano Beach, FL San Isidro.
Cutie, Alberto (MIA) Radio Peace – WAXY, 790 AM.
Cutie, Alberto (MIA) Radio Ke Poze – WLQY, 1320 AM.
Cutie, Alberto (MIA) Radio Paz – WACC, 830 AM.
Cutrone, Dominick F. '55 (BRK) Brooklyn, NY Our Lady of Grace Retired.
Cvitkovic, Vincent *o.f.m.* '69 (CHI)[N] Chicago, IL St. Anthony's Friary.
Cwiekowski, Bruce '75 (P)[G] Portland, OR Catholic Charities Social Service Division of Portland.
Cwiekowski, Frederick J. *s.s.* '62 (SFR) On Duty Outside the Archdiocese.
Cwik, Thomas G. *s.j.* '00 (STL)[O] St. Louis, MO The Jesuits of the Missouri Province; [O] St. Louis, MO Bellarmine House of Studies.
Cwynar, Paul D. '87 (PIT) Oakmont, PA St. Irenaeus.
Cyenas, Joel (STP) Coon Rapids, MN Church of the Epiphany.
Cyktor, Ronald L. (GBG) Belle Vernon, PA St. Sebastian.
Cyktor, Ronald. L. (GBG) Monessen, PA The Epiphany of Our Lord.
Cylwicki, Albert W. *c.s.b.* '60 (ROC)[I] Rochester, NY Basilian Residence.
Cymbor, John A. '50 (STU) Flushing, OH St. Paul's.
Cymerman, Alexander B. *o.f.m.conv.* '65 (SPR) Holyoke, MA Mater Dolorosa.
Cyprys, Ronald '69 (DET) Dearborn Heights, MI Our Lady of Grace.
Cyr, Joel R. '71 (PRT) Brewer, ME St. Joseph's; Brewer, ME St. Teresa's.
Cyr, John '02 (PEO) Aledo, IL St. Catherine's Church; Matherville, IL St. Anthony's Church.
Cyr, L. Chanel '53 (PRT) Limestone, ME St. Louis Retired.
Cyr, L. Philip '69 (PRT) St. Agatha, ME St. Luce's; Madawaska, ME St. Agatha's; St. Agatha, ME St. Joseph.
Cyr, Lawrence S. *c.pp.s.* '44 (SAN) Coleman, TX Sacred Heart.
Cyr, Myles *o.m.i.* '54 (PRT) Lincoln, ME St. Mary.
Cyr, Richard E. '60 (DET) Sterling Heights, MI St. Matthias.
Cyr, Roger '59 (PRT) Lincoln, ME St. Mary.
Cyr, Terrence *o.carm.* '75 (NEW) Bogota, NJ St. Joseph's.
Cyr, William F. '71 (SPR) Springfield, MA St. Catherine of Siena.
Cyscon, Peter J. '73 (CHI) Berwyn, IL St. Odilo.
Cyscon, Philip E. '84 (CHI) Chicago, IL Our Lady of Victory.
Cyvas, Matthew '41 (ALB) Retired.
Cyz, Edward T. '54 (SUP) Retired.
Czachor, Christopher '51 (PSC) Absent on Sick Leave.
Czachor, Richard E. '77 (SCR) Tannersville, PA Our Lady of Victory.
Czahur, John P. '77 (TR) Riverton, NJ Sacred Heart.
Czaicki, Franciszek *o.c.d.* '97 (GRY)[I] Munster, IN Discalced Carmelite Fathers Monastery.
Czaja, Blaise *c.p.* '64 (CHI)[N] Jnan Nilaya–Passionist Community.
Czaja, Joseph S. '46 (Y) Retired.
Czajka, Norman M. '61 (CHI) Chicago, IL St. Camillus Retired.
Czajkowski, Andrew A. '74 (LAN) Davison, MI St. John

the Evangelist; Priest's Assignment Commission.
Czajkowski, Richard S. *m.m.* '60 (WDC)[B] Washington, DC Maryknoll Fathers and Brothers.
Czapiewski, Stanislaus *s.j.* '40 (DET)[P] Clarkston, MI Colombiere Center; Hamtramck, MI St. Ladislaus.
Czapinski, Richard J. '58 (PIT) Retired.
Czapla, Bruce C. *o.f.m.* '89 (HRT) Winsted, CT St. Joseph's.
Czapla, Donald J. '03 (DUB) Cedar Rapids, IA St. Jude.
Czarcinski, Edward A. '88 (MET) Milltown, NJ Our Lady of Lourdes.
Czarkowski, Joseph R. '74 (E) St. Joseph.
Czarnecki, Anthony S. (WOR) Defenders of the Bond.
Czarnecki, Anthony '66 (WOR) Webster, MA St. Joseph's Basilica; Polish Ministry.
Czarnecki, Edward R. '66 (BUF) Defenders of the Bond; Blasdell, NY Our Mother of Good Counsel.
Czarnecki, Stanislaw *s.j.* '97 (CHI)[N] Chicago, IL Sacred Heart Mission House.
Czarnota, Paul '03 (DET) Northville, MI Our Lady of Victory.
Czartorynski, David F. '84 (ALN) Military Chaplains; Air Force Chaplains.
Czaster, Herman *o.f.m.conv.* '65 (HRT) Kensington, CT St. Paul's.
Czaus, Joseph C. '89 (ALN) Unassigned.
Czech, Edward M. '73 (CLV) Military Chaplains; Army Chaplains.
Czechowicz, Bernard J. '54 (BUF) Retired.
Czeck, Thomas *o.f.m.conv.* '98 (LA) Hermosa Beach, CA Our Lady of Guadalupe.
Czekala, Henry *c.m.* '44 (HRT) Ansonia, CT St. Joseph's.
Czekala, Henry *c.m.* '44 (HRT)[M] Manchester DePaul Provincial Residence.
Czelusniak, Donald '78 (ALB) Gloversville, NY St. Mary of Mt. Carmel.
Czelusniak, Donald (ALB) Deans.
Czemerda, Edward M. '87 (PIT) Pittsburgh, PA St. Albert the Great.
Czerkies, Joseph '62 (PAT) Passaic, NJ St. Joseph's.
Czerwinski, James *o.f.m.* '77 (ALB)[B] Siena College.
Czerwinski, James *o.f.m.* '77 (ALB)[R] Albany, NY St. Francis Chapel.
Czerwionka, Francis *c.s.v.* '59 (JOL) Kankakee, IL St. Patrick.
Czerwonka, Paul G. '03 (LC)[A] La Crosse, WI Holy Cross Seminary House of Formation; La Crosse, WI St. James the Less.
Czok, Robert W. '66 (BRK) Brooklyn, NY St. Anthony of Padua–St. Alphonsus.
Czyzynski, John *s.c.j.* '63 (CHI)[N] Chicago, IL SCJ Novitiate.

D

D'Abele, Peter *s.m.m.* '75 (BRK)[V] Ozone Park Montfort Missionaries Provincialate (Missionaries of the Company of Mary) – Formation Community.
D'Aco, Joseph '99 (FAR) Wales, ND St. Clotilde.
D'Aco, Joseph '99 (FAR) Wales, ND St. Michael's.
D'Aco, Joseph '99 (FAR) Wales, ND St. Joseph.
D'Aco, Joseph '99 (FAR) Wales, ND Our Lady of Mount Carmel.
D'Addezio, Louis A. '61 (PH) Philadelphia, PA Cathedral Basilica of SS. Peter and Paul; Ecclesiastical Exchange Program.
D'Agostino, Angelo *s.j.* '66 (BAL)[S] Loyola House.
D'Agostino, Carl L. '59 (CLV) Independence, OH St. Michael.
D'Agostino, Joseph '41 (ALB) Retired.
D'Agostino, Rodolfo *r.c.j.* '64 (LA) Van Nuys, CA St. Elisabeth.
D'Agostino, Rodolfo *r.c.j.* '64 (LA)[Q] Van Nuys, CA Rogationist Fathers.
D'Albro, Thomas G. '71 (BRK) Released from Diocesan Assignment.
D'Albro, Thomas '71 (NY) Poughkeepsie, NY St. Martin de Porres.
D'Alessandro, Benedict J. *o.f.m.* (NY) Manhattan, NY Terence Cardinal Cooke Health Care Center; [EE] Mount Vernon, NY St. Bernardine of Siena Friary.
D'Alonzo, Alfred F. *c.s.c.* '53 (FTW)[A] Notre Dame, IN Moreau Seminary; [B] University of Notre Dame Du Lac.
D'Amato, James J. '49 (BRK) Retired.
D'Ambrosi, Girolamo *s.a.c.* '39 (NY) New York, NY Our Lady of Mt. Carmel.
D'Ambrosi, Girolamo *s.a.c.* '39 (NY)[EE] New York, NY Pallottine Fathers.
D'Ambrosia, Peter J. *s.m.* '85 (PRO) Cranston, RI St. Matthew; Providence, RI Rhode Island Hospital.
D'Amico, Carducci S. '64 (BGP) Bridgeport, CT St. Raphael.
D'Amico, Carmen A. '82 (PIT) Pittsburgh, PA St. Benedict the Moor; [Q] Pittsburgh, PA Robert Morris College, Downtown Pittsburgh Campus; Priest Council.
D'Amico, Frank A. '87 (STL) Silex, MO St. Alphonsus; Lincoln County Catholic Church Real Estate Corporation; [U] Silex, MO Lincoln County Church Real Estate Corporation.
D'Amico, Joseph A. (NEW) Elected Members; Part–time Staff.
D'Amico, Joseph '95 (NEW) Hoboken, NJ SS. Peter and Paul's; Priestly Vocation Board.
D'Amico, Michael H. '64 (CAM) Atlantic City, NJ St. Michael's.
D'Anca, Achille '45 (BRK) Retired.
D'Andrea, Edward R. '73 (RVC)[A] Huntington, NY Diocesan Seminary of the Immaculate Conception; Priests' Personnel Policy Board.
D'Andrea, Stephen D. '97 (NEW) Wallington, NJ Most Sacred Heart of Jesus.
D'Angelico, Anthony J. '74 (PH) Southampton, PA Our Lady of Good Counsel.
D'Angelo, Anthony *s.d.b.* '67 (BIR) Birmingham, AL Holy Rosary (Gate City).
D'Angelo, Donald S. '68 (SFR) San Francisco, CA Holy Name of Jesus; Deans.
D'Angelo, Joseph J. *m.a.c.* '68 (RVC) Rockville Centre, NY Campus Parish of Long Island; Nassau County Police Department; [P] Rockville Centre, NY The Campus Parish of Long Island; [P] Hempstead, NY Chaplains' Office; Campus Ministry.
D'Angelo, Joseph (RVC) Chaplains of the Nassau County Police Department.
D'Angelo, Rocco '56 (SP) Retired.
D'Angelo, Thomas P. '84 (NY) Elmsford, NY Our Lady of Mt. Carmel.
d'Anjou, Henry G. '48 (NY) Retired.
d'Anjou, John R. *s.j.* '72 (BO)[E] Dorchester, MA Boston College High School & Jesuit Community; [V] Boston The Society of Jesus of New England–Provincial Offices.
d' Anjou, John R.. *s.j.* '72 (NOR) Norwich, CT SS. Peter and Paul.
D'Anjou, Larry (OAK) Priestly and Religious & Director for Seminarians.
D'Anjou, Lawrence (OAK) Presbyteral Council.
D'Antonio, Anthony '39 (NY) Bronx, NY Our Lady of Mt. Carmel.
D'Antonio, Anthony '39 (NY) Retired.
D'Antonio, John '73 (SP) Tampa, FL St. Mark the Evangelist.
D'Antonio, Ronald M. '77 (BRK) College Point, NY St. Fidelis.
d'Auby, Phillip *s.m.* '61 (SFR)[N] San Francisco, CA Marist Center of the West.
D'Auriol, Vincent '60 (NY) Retired.
D'Aurizio, Joseph F. '56 (ROC) Hilton, NY St. Leo Retired.
D'Aurora, Joseph '73 (RIC) On Special or Other Diocesan Assignment; [E] Richmond, VA St. Mary's Hospital; Navy Reserve Chaplains.
D'Aversa, Robert *t.o.r.* '76 (ORL).
D'Cruz, Ferreolus '59 (ALX)[D] Tallulah, LA St. Edward.
D'Cruz, Michael *o.f.m.* '57 (NY)[EE] St. Charles Borromeo Friary.
D'Cruz, Sylvester '85 (MIA) Miami, FL St. Richard.
D'Elia, Michael A. '54 (BGP) Bridgeport, CT Bridgeport Health Care.
D'Emma, Gregory J. '70 (NEW) Military Chaplains; Army Chaplains.
D'Eon, Earl '89 (PHX) Sun City, AZ St. Clement of Rome.
d'Escoto, Miguel F. *m.m.* '61 (NY)[EE] (FgM).
D'heedene, Walter O. *c.i.c.m.* '67 (SAT) San Antonio, TX Sacred Heart.
D'heedene, Walter *c.i.c.m.* (SAT) In Metropolitan Area.
D'heedene, Walter *c.i.c.m.* (SAT) Archdiocesan Presbyteral Council.
D'Incecco, Alfred '75 (NY)[E] New York, NY Cardinal Hayes High School.
D'Lima, Erroll *s.j.* (BO)[V] Newton, MA The Jesuit Community at Boston College.
D'Mello, John C. '73 (PMB) West Palm Beach, FL Holy Name of Jesus.
D'Onofrio, Ernest *o.f.m.* '43 (NY).
D'Onofrio, Ernest *o.f.m.* '43 (NY)[GG] Poughkeepsie, NY Dutchess County Jail.
D'Ostilio, Silvio *c.s.sp.* '54 (SB)[E] Hemet, CA Holy Ghost Fathers.
D'Ostilio, Silvio *c.s.sp.* '54 (SB)[E] Hemet, CA Holy Spirit.
D'Oultremont, Thibaus (OAK) French Speaking Community.
D'Silva, Aloysius '61 (CHL) Retired.
D'Silva, Joseph R. (MO) Army Chaplains.
D'Silva, Percival L. '64 (WDC) Washington, DC Blessed Sacrament, Shrine of the Most.
D'Souza, Claude '65 (RVC) Palm Springs, FL St. Luke.
D'Souza, Claude '65 (RVC) Priests Released from Diocesan Assignment.
D' Souza, Gerard *o.c.s.o.* '01 (ROC)[I] Piffard, NY Abbey of the Genesee.
D'Souza, Gilbert P. '73 (BGP) Norwalk, CT St. Joseph.
D'Souza, Joseph *o.c.d.* '99 (NY) New York, NY Our Lady of Victory.
D'Souza, Keith *s.j.* '95 (MIL)[O] Milwaukee, WI Jesuit Community at Marquette University.
D'Souza, Matthew F. (MO) Navy Chaplains.
D'Souza, Maurice *c.s.c.* (FTW)[A] Notre Dame, IN Moreau Seminary.
D'Souza, Peter (LUB) Presbyteral Council.
D'Souza, Robert '73 (FTW) Fort Wayne, IN Parkview Memorial Hospital.
D'Souza, Robert '73 (FTW) Fort Wayne, IN St. Jude.
D'Souza, Robert (FTW) Council of Priests.
D'Souza, William '76 (GF) Special Assignment.
D'Souza, William '76 (GF) Ashland, MT St. Labre's.
Dabaen, Hisham '72 (LA) Lakewood, CA St. Pancratius.
Dabaen, Hisham (SB) Arab–American Ministry.
Dabash, G. Adrian *o.p.* '71 (PRO)[P] Providence St. Thomas Aquinas Priory at Providence College.
Dabbene, Bernard *s.d.b.* '66 (SFR)[N] San Francisco, CA Salesian Provincial Residence.
Dabney, Philip *c.ss.r.* '78 (BRK)[C] Whitestone, NY St. Alphonsus Formation Residence.
Dabria, Jerry J. '55 (NO) Retired.
Dabrowski, George J. *c.m.* '58 (HRT)[M] Manchester DePaul Provincial Residence.
Dabrowski, James O. '84 (CAM) Bellmawr, NJ Annunciation.
Dabrowski, Klemens *s.ch.* '82 (WDC)[V] Silver Spring, MD Friends of John Paul II Foundation.
Dabrowski, Klemens *s.chr.* '87 (WDC) Silver Spring, MD Our Lady Queen of Poland and Saint Maximilian Kolbe.
Dabruzzi, James S. '53 (SUP) Retired.
Dacey, Donald '53 (DET) Retired.
Dachauer, Andrew C. *s.j.* '64 (STO) Mammoth Lakes, CA St. Joseph Church of Mammoth Lakes.
Dachille, Arnold V. '59 (DET) Dearborn, MI St. Clement.
Da Corte, Allan *o.f.m.* '77 (WDC)[V] Silver Spring, MD National Association for Treasurers of Religious Institutes.
Da Costa, Darrell '97 (BRK) Woodside, NY St. Teresa.
DaCosta, Eriberto '81 (SC) Storm Lake, IA St. Mary's.
DaCosta, Lee '73 (BWN) Weslaco, TX St. Joan of Arc.
da Cunha, Domingos M. '71 (PRO) Cumberland, RI Our Lady of Fatima.
da Cunha, Edgar *s.d.v.* (NEW) Regional Bishops and Regional Vicars.
Dada, Jacek '93 (CHI) Chicago, IL St. Daniel the Prophet.
DaDamio, Paul A. (ALN) Emmaus, PA St. Ann.
Dadey, Neil R. '81 (ALT) Bellefonte, PA St. John the Evangelist's; Spring Mills, PA Blessed Kateri Tekakwitha.
Dadson, Eric '90 (RVC) Port Jefferson, NY St. Charles Hospital, Port Jefferson, New York.
Dadson, Eric '90 (RVC) Port Jefferson, NY Infant Jesus.
Daechen, Mario *o.s.b.m.* '88 (STF) New York, NY St. George.
Dae Choi, Mateo Hong *s.j.* '95 (CIN)[V] Cincinnati, OH St. Andrew Kim Korean Catholic Community.
Dagelen, Anthony L. *s.j.* '65 (MIL)[O] Wauwatosa, WI Jesuit Community at St. Camillus.
Dagher, George *b.s.o.* '43 (NTN) Retired.
Dagit, Rick A. '86 (DUB)[F] Gilbertville, IA Immaculate Conception–St. Joseph School.
Dagit, Rick D. '86 (DUB) Gilbertville, IA St. Joseph; Gilbertville, IA Immaculate Conception.
Dagle, Harold F. '59 (ALN) Allentown, PA Immaculate Conception.
Dagle, Thomas W. '02 (WH) Elkins, WV St. Brendan; Coalton, WV St. Patrick Church; Huttonsville, WV St. John Bosco.
Dagnoli, Albert *ss.cc.* '68 (FR)[H] Fairhaven, MA Sacred Hearts Provincial House.
Dahl, Henry J. '96 (FR) Provincetown, MA St. Peter the Apostle; [M] Fall River, MA Diocesan Education Center; Auditors.
Dahl, Philip *o.cart.* '65 (BUR)[E] Arlington, VT Carthusian Foundation in America, Inc., Charterhouse of the Transfiguration.
Dahlberg, Daniel J. '67 (SUP) Superior, WI Cathedral of Christ the King; Vicar General; Ex Officio Members:; Presbyteral Council & Diocesan Consultors.
Dahlby, Charles G. '77 (SFD) Kincaid, IL St. Rita; Kincaid, IL St. Mary.
Dahlheimer, Cosmas *o.s.b.* '36 (SCL)[I] Collegeville, MN St. John's Abbey, of the Order of St. Benedict.
Dahlheimer, Ronald W. '59 (STP) Kilkenny, MN St. Canice.
Dahlinger, James H. *s.j.* '91 (SY)[Q] Syracuse, NY Jesuits at LeMoyne, Inc..
Dahlke, Robert W. *s.j.* '65 (NY)[EE] New York, NY Murray–Weigel Hall.
Dahlquist, Thomas S. (YAK) Retired.
Dahm, Charles W. *o.p.* '64 (CHI) Chicago, IL St. Pius V; [N] Chicago, IL Dominican Community.
Dahm, Paul J. '62 (RVC) West Islip, NY Good Samaritan Hospital Medical Center Retired.
Dahms, Paul G. '58 (RC) Deadwood, SD St. Ambrose.
Dahms, Paul (RC) Catholic Relief Service.
Dahms, Paul (RC) Campaign for Human Development.
Dahms, Paul (RC) Holy Childhood Pontifical Association.

Dahms, Paul (RC) Propagation of the Faith.
Daiber, Sean J. '67 (CAM) On Duty Outside the Diocese.
Daigle, Chris '78 (TLS) Wilburton, OK Sacred Heart.
Daigle, David A. '03 (BGP) Greenwich, CT St. Mary.
Daigle, Donald R. J. '68 (PRT) Whitefield, ME St. Denis.
Daigle, Donald R.J. '68 (PRT) Augusta, ME Augusta Mental Health Institute.
Daigle, Eugene *c.ss.r.* '72 (ORL) New Smyrna Beach, FL Sacred Heart.
Daigle, Gregory J. '93 (BR) Lakeland, LA Immaculate Conception.
Daigle, H.C. Paul '46 (HT) Retired.
Daigle, Karl J. '97 (SHP) Minden, LA St. Paul; College of Consultors; Presbyteral Council.
Daigle, Karl (SHP) Advocates.
Daigle, Robert E. '63 (GAL) Retired.
Daigle, Roland *o.f.m.cap.* '84 (FgM).
Daigle, Steven '89 (DUL) Bigfork, MN Our Lady of the Snows.
Daigle, Steven '89 (DUL) Squaw Lake, MN St. Catherine.
Dailey, Gary M. '85 (SPR) Lee, MA St. Mary's; Bishop's Commission for Clergy.
Dailey, Gary (SPR) Priests Committee.
Dailey, John '64 (Y) On Duty Outside the Diocese.
Dailey, Joseph E. '77 (DET) Lake Orion, MI Christ the Redeemer.
Dailey, Thomas F. *o.s.f.s.* '87 (ALN)[B] Center Valley, PA DeSales University; [K] Center Valley, PA Oblates of St. Francis de Sales.
Dailey, William R. *c.s.c.* '01 (FTW)[I] New York, NY Holy Trinity Parish.
Dailey, William R. *c.s.c.* '01 (NY) New York, NY Holy Trinity.
Dailey, William '59 (RVC)[J] West Islip, NY Our Lady of Consolation Nursing & Rehabilitative Care Center Retired.
Dailey, William (RVC) West Islip, NY Consolation Nursing Home.
Daily, John A. '56 (BO) Senior Priests Retired.
Daily, Leo J. '44 (HRT) Yalesville, CT Our Lady of Fatima Retired.
Daily, Vincent E. '58 (BO) Graduate Studies; Senior Priests Retired.
Daily, Vincent E. *s.t.d.* '90 (BO)[A] Brighton, MA St. John Seminary School of Theology.
Dair, Richard J. '80 (ARL) Retired.
Daka, Lawrence *s.j.* (Zim)[V] Newton, MA The Jesuit Community at Boston College.
Dakes, John T. '87 (WDC) Hyattsville, MD St. Mark; Advocates.
Dakin, Kenneth M. '88 (SAT) Uvalde, TX Sacred Heart.
Dalbelo, Americo *c.ss.r.* (WOR) Brazilian Ministry; Brazilian Pastoral Ministry.
Dalbon, Luis '47 (CGS)[C] Aibonito, PR Casa Salesiana de Retiros.
Dale, Douglas '88 (ORG) Huntington Beach, CA St. Bonaventure.
Daleiden, Francis *o.s.b.* '57 (RCK)[G] Aurora, IL Marmion Abbey.
Daleo, Joseph P. '71 (BEA) Orange, TX St. Mary.
Dalessandro, Dennis G. '83 (HBG) Berwick, PA St. Joseph's; Deans.
Daley, Brian *s.j.* '70 (FTW)[B] University of Notre Dame Du Lac; [M] Granger, IN Jesuit Community.
Daley, Daniel P. '70 (GLP) Bloomfield, NM St. Rose of Lima; Bloomfield, NM St. Mary.
Daley, Daniel (GLP) Ecumenical Affairs in New Mexico, New Mexico Council of Churches.
Daley, Ernest J. '55 (E) Erie, PA St. Jude the Apostle.
Daley, Francis E. '63 (BO) Arlington, MA St. James the Apostle.
Daley, Frederick D. '74 (SY) Utica, NY St. Francis de Sales; Utica, NY Mohawk Valley Psychiatric Center.
Daley, Jacques de Paul *o.s.b.* '71 (GBG) Greensburg, PA Westmoreland Hospital; [H] Latrobe, PA Saint Vincent Archabbey.
Daley, James D. '54 (ALB) Delmar, NY St. Thomas the Apostle Retired.
Daley, James M. '42 (BUF) Retired.
Daley, John A. '56 (BO) Arlington, MA St. Agnes.
Daley, John J. '46 (SY) Fulton, NY Holy Family–St. Michael's Retired.
Daley, Joseph A. '68 (CHY) Retired.
Daley, Neil '55 (ANC) Retired.
Daley, Owen W. *s.j.* '60 (NY)[EE] New York, NY West Side Jesuit Community.
Daley, Raymond *o.p.* '52 (NY)[FF] Sparkill, NY Dominican Convent of Our Lady of the Rosary.
Daley, Thomas J. '38 (WOR)[N] Worcester, MA Vianney House Retired.
Daley, William F. *m.m.* '56 (FgM).
Dall, Norbert P. '45 (LC) Retired.
Dallas, Benjamin '02 (SAV) Augusta, GA St. Mary on the Hill.
Dallen, James '69 (SAL) On Duty Outside the Diocese.
Dallmeier, Michael *o.f.m.* '63 (RNO) Dayton, NV St. Ann.
Dally, Peter F. '85 (TLS) Retired.
Dalpiaz, Alex *c.s.* (ORL) Winter Garden, FL Resurrection.
Dalpiaz, Gino *c.s.* (CHI) Italian Catholic Apostolate.
Dalpiaz, Gino *c.s.* (CHI) Melrose Park, IL St. Charles Borromeo.
Dalpiaz, Gino *c.s.* (CHI) College of Consultors.
Dalseth, Gerald '64 (SCL) Pierz, MN St. Michael's.
Dalseth, Gerald '64 (SCL) Pierz, MN St. Joseph's.
Dalseth, Gerald (SCL) Directors.
Dalseth, Gerald (SCL) Diocesan Ecumenical Commission.
Dalton, Brendan '69 (MIA) Hollywood, FL St. Bernadette.
Dalton, Donald T. '60 (STL) Special Assignment.
Dalton, George R. '84 (PIT) Pittsburgh, PA St. Bernard.
Dalton, J. Paul '78 (SEA) Sammamish, WA Mary, Queen of Peace.
Dalton, James '68 (SEA) Lynnwood, WA St. Thomas More.
Dalton, James *o.s.f.s.* '72 (WIL)[B] Wilmington, DE Salesianum School.
Dalton, John A. '55 (L) Retired.
Dalton, John Bryan '70 (MIA) Deerfield Beach, FL St. Ambrose.
Dalton, John C. '48 (CLV) Cleveland, OH Holy Name.
Dalton, John W. '58 (DUB) Retired.
Dalton, John '48 (CLV) Retired.
Dalton, John (AMA) Amarillo, TX St. Francis.
Dalton, Michel *o.f.m.cap.* '78 (HON) Aiea, HI St. Elizabeth.
Dalton, Michel *o.f.m.cap.* (HON) College of Consultors.
Dalton, Michel *o.f.m.cap.* (HON) Bishop's Administrative Advisory Council.
Dalton, Michel *o.f.m.cap.* (HON) Consulting Pastors.
Dalton, Michel *o.f.m.cap.* (HON) Vicars Forane.
Dalton, Michel *o.f.m.cap.* (HON) Presbyteral Council.
Dalton, Peadar '70 (MOB) On Leave from the Archdiocese.
Dalton, Robert '62 (NSH)[L] Nashville, TN Glenmary Office of Pastoral Coordinators.
Dalton, Robert '62 (NSH)[H] Nashville, TN Glenmary Home Missioners.
Dalton, Robert *g.h.m.* '62 (LEX) Grayson, KY Ss. John & Elizabeth.
Dalton, William P. '56 (NY) Mt. Kisco, NY St. Francis of Assisi Retired.
Dalupang, Arturo O. '95 (CHR) Florence, SC St. Anthony's All Souls Memorial.
Daly, Albert *o.carm.* '33 (NY) Franklin D. Roosevelt Hospital.
Daly, Albert *o.carm.* '33 (NY)[EE] Middletown, NY St. Albert's Priory.
Daly, Anthony C. *s.j.* '72 (STL)[C] Saint Louis University; [O] St. Louis, MO Jesuit Community Corporation at St. Louis University – Jesuit Hall.
Daly, Bartholomew *m.h.m.* '62 (NY) New York, NY Our Lady of Peace.
Daly, Bartholomew *m.h.m.* (NY) Vicars for Religious.
Daly, Charles W. '51 (HRT) Hartford, CT St. Luke Retired.
Daly, Christopher H. '60 (NY) White Plains, NY St. John the Evangelist.
Daly, Claude R. (NO)[P] New Orleans, LA Ignatius Residence.
Daly, Claude *s.j.* '43 (FgM).
Daly, Denis E. *s.j.* '64 (STL)[C] Saint Louis University; [O] St. Louis, MO Jesuit Community Corporation at St. Louis University – Jesuit Hall.
Daly, Desmond '66 (SP) Tampa, FL Christ the King.
Daly, Desmond (SP) Presbyteral Council.
Daly, Desmond (SP) College of Consultors.
Daly, Desmond (SP) Priests Personnel Board.
Daly, Desmond (SP) Vicars Forane.
Daly, Ernst *l.c.* (DET)[T] Clarkston, MI The Legion of Christ, Inc..
Daly, Francis J. *s.j.* '72 (CIN)[F] Cincinnati, OH St. Xavier High School; [M] Cincinnati OH Jesuit Community at St. Xavier High School.
Daly, George '47 (OAK) Retired.
Daly, J. Daniel *s.j.* '92 (DEN)[N] Denver, CO Regis Jesuit Community (The Jesuits at Regis University).
Daly, James F. *c.s.sp.* '63 (MIA) Fort Lauderdale, FL St. John the Baptist.
Daly, James J. '44 (BO) Senior Priests Retired.
Daly, James P. '39 (PH) Retired.
Daly, Jerome R. '87 (ARL) Annandale, VA St. Michael's.
Daly, John J. '46 (PH) Retired.
Daly, John J. '58 (HRT) North Haven, CT St. Barnabas.
Daly, John K. '36 (NY) White Plains, NY Our Lady of Sorrows
Daly, John P. *s.j.* '56 (LA)[C] Los Angeles, CA Jesuit Community.
Daly, John R. *s.j.* '63 (DEN)[N] Denver, CO Xavier Jesuit Center.
Daly, John V. *s.j.* '66 (FgM).
Daly, John '36 (NY) Retired.
Daly, John '59 (LA) Los Angeles, CA Holy Trinity.
Daly, John '59 (LA) Retired.
Daly, Joseph F. '42 (BRK) Retired.
Daly, Joseph V. *c.m.* '60 (BRK)[D] St. John's University, Staten Island Campus; [D] St. John's University; [V] Jamaica, NY St. Vincent's House.
Daly, Kevin *o.f.m.* '80 (TR) Brant Beach, NJ St. Francis of Assisi.
Daly, Leo J. *s.j.* '61 (NEW)[B] Jersey City, NJ Jesuit Center; [N] Jersey City, NJ Jesuits of Saint Peter's College, Inc..
Daly, Manus P. '65 (JC) Absent on Leave.
Daly, Peter J. '86 (WDC) Prince Frederick, MD St. John Vianney.
Daly, Richard L. '58 (BEL) Retired.
Daly, Robert J. *s.j.* '63 (BO)[V] Newton, MA The Jesuit Community at Boston College.
Daly, Robert L. '41 (MET) Retired.
Daly, Shawn T. '95 (HRT) Meriden, CT St. Joseph; Meriden, CT St. Mary; Deans.
Daly, Simeon *o.s.b.* '48 (IND)[K] St. Meinrad, IN St. Meinrad Archabbey.
Daly, Thomas A. '87 (SFR) San Francisco Police Department; Serra Club of San Francisco (Downtown); On Special Assignment; [D] Kentfield, CA Marin Catholic College Preparatory (Coed); [D] Kentfield, CA Marin Catholic College Preparatory (Coed).
Daly, Thomas A. (SFR)[P] College of Consultors; Council of Priests; Office of Vocations.
Daly, Thomas J. '52 (BO) Senior Priests; Livingston, NJ St. Philomena; West Orange, NJ St. Joseph's Retired.
Daly, Timothy P. '96 (ORL) Ormond Beach, FL Prince of Peace; [F] Daytona Beach, FL Office of the Chaplain.
Daly, Vincent M. '71 (BRK) Long Island City, NY Queen of Angels.
Dam, LoXuan *m.m.* '00 (FgM).
Damazio, Pedro J. (BO) Lowell, MA St. Anthony; Lowell, MA Sacred Heart.
Damazio, Pedro (BO) Brazilian Community Centers.
Dambrauskas, Stephen '48 (SP) Retired.
Dambrauskas, Stephen (SP) Defenders of the Bond.
Dambrauskas, Stephen (SP) Promoter of Justice.
Damhorst, Joseph *s.j.* '68 (STL) Colorado Springs, CO Our Lady of the Pines–Black Forest; [O] St. Louis, MO The Jesuits of the Missouri Province.
Damian, Lawrence P. '71 (BUF) Council of Priests; Warsaw, NY St. Michael.
Damian, Rinaldo (WOR).
Damian, Ronald '77 (WOR) On Duty Outside the Diocese.
Damico, Rodney M. '92 (COL) Marion, OH St. Mary.
Damien, Paul E. '97 (SAM) Miami, FL Maronite Mission of Tampa.
Damien, Paul '97 (SP) Tampa, FL St. Mary.
Damis, Frank J. '84 (NY) Kingston, NY St. Joseph.
Dammay, Dante U. '77 (STO) Modesto, CA St. Joseph Church of Modesto (Pastor of).
Dammeir, James L. '79 (MIL) Milwaukee, WI Prince of Peace/Principe de Paz; Deans.
Damron, Robert '83 (LEX) Salyersville, KY St. Luke.
Damron, Robert '83 (LEX) Prestonsburg, KY St. Martha.
Damroth, William J. '93 (NY) Crestwood, NY Church of the Annunciation.
Danaher, Mortimer '53 (STA) Retired.
Danaher, Philip '83 (JOL) Downers Grove, IL Good Samaritan Hospital.
Danaher, Philip '83 (JOL) Woodridge, IL Christ The Servant Parish.
Danaher, T. Leo '55 (STA) Retired.
Danber, Bernard R. *o.s.a.* '86 (CHI)[N] Chicago, IL St. Rita Monastery.
Danber, Bernard *o.s.a.* '86 (CHI)[D] Chicago, IL St. Rita of Cascia High School.
Dance, Kevin *c.p.* '65 (BRK)[V] Jamaica, NY Immaculate Conception Monastery.
Danczyk, Mark J. '92 (MIL) Caledonia, WI St. Louis.
Dandelet, James D. '54 (WIN) Retired.
Dandry, Anthony M. '89 (MET) On Duty Outside the Diocese Retired.
Dandurand, Douglas E. '82 (STP) On Duty Outside the Diocese; [A] St. Paul, MN The Saint Paul Seminary; [C] St. Paul, MN University of St. Thomas; Eden Prairie, MN Pax Christi.
Dandurand, Michael G. '97 (TOL) Perrysburg, OH St. Rose.
Dane, James E. '83 (MOB) Bay Minette, AL St. Agatha Church.
Dane, John '91 (LEX) Retired.
Danek, Michael E. *c.r.* '86 (CHI) Chicago, IL St. Stephen, King of Hungary; Chicago, IL St. Wenceslaus.
Danek, Michael *c.r.* (CHI) Deans.
Danel, Joseph B. *s.j.* '52 (FgM).
Danel, Joseph B. *s.j.* '52 (P)[L] Portland Jesuit Provincial Office (Society of Jesus, Oregon Prov.).
Danella, Francis W. *o.s.f.s.* '73 (WDC) Vienna, VA Our Lady of Good Counsel; [C] Catholic University of America, The.
Dang, Chin Van '83 (RIC) Military Chaplains; Navy Chaplains.
Dang, Hai Duc '99 (GAL) The Woodlands, TX Sts. Simon and Jude.

Dang, Hoa Francis *c.ss.r.* (TUC) Tucson, AZ Our Lady of La Vang.
Dang, Joseph Oahn *s.v.d.* '95 (MET) Woodbridge, NJ St. James.
Dang, Joseph Oanh *s.v.d.* (MET) Vietnamese Apostolate.
Dang, Thomas Thien *o.s.b.* '93 (P)[L] St. Benedict, OR Mt. Angel Abbey.
Dang, Vincent '95 (SCR) Wilkes–Barre, PA St. Mary's Church of the Immaculate Conception.
Dang Ha, Thuy '84 (SLC) Salt Lake City, UT Our Lady of Perpetual Help.
Dang Minh Tan, Bernadine M. *c.m.c.* '02 (SPC)[E] Carthage, MO Congregation of the Mother Coredemptrix, United States Assumption Province.
Danhauer, Richard T. '57 (OWN) Princeton, KY St. Paul.
Daniel, John '92 (SFE) Socorro, NM San Miguel.
Daniel, John (SFE) Vicars Forane (Deans).
Daniele, Anthony J. '56 (BO) Senior Priests Retired.
Daniels, Jerrell Michael '01 (JKS) On Leave:.
Daniels, Joel *o.f.m.cap.* '67 (NY)[EE] New York, NY Development Office:.
Daniels, John W. '36 (GRY) Retired.
Daniels, Joseph E. '90 (PRT) Bridgton, ME St. Joseph.
Daniels, Larry *o.c.d.* '65 (MIL)[O] Holy Hill, WI Discalced Carmelite Monastery – Holy Hill National Shrine of Mary Help of Christians.
Daniels, Leo Francis *c.o.* '65 (BWN) Pharr, TX St. Jude Thaddeus; [F] Pharr, TX Oratory of St. Philip Neri of Pontifical.
Daniels, Paul A. '57 (MIL) Retired.
Danielsen, Thomas *c.ss.r.* '64 (STL)[O] Liguori, MO Liguori Mission House/Redemptorists.
Danielson, Charles R. '92 (BUR)[H] Castleton, VT Castleton State College; Castleton, VT St. John the Baptist; Orwell, VT St. Paul.
Danielson, Daniel E. '63 (OAK) Pleasanton, CA The Catholic Community of Pleasanton; Presbyteral Council.
Danielson, Daniel (OAK) Deans.
Danielson, Daniel (OAK) Consultors.
Danielson, Harold *s.d.b.* '66 (LAR) San Francisco, CA SS. Peter and Paul.
Danik, Daniel A. '48 (NEW) Bloomfield, NJ Sacred Heart; Union–Westfield; Serra Clubs Retired.
Danik, Daniel (NEW) Archdiocesan Council of Catholic Women (N.C.C.W.).
Daniszewski, Alfred '45 (MAN) Manchester, NH St. Hedwig.
Daniszewski, John D. '43 (E) Retired.
Danko, Michael S. '52 (LIN) Retired.
Dankowski, Dariusz *s.j.* '01 (CHI)[C] Chicago, IL Jesuit Community at Loyola University Chicago.
Danks, Arthur J. '43 (GB) Retired.
Danks, Arthur (GB) Judges in Second Instance.
Danna, Anthony '67 (BRK) Ridgewood, NY Our Lady of the Miraculous Medal.
Danneker, David L. '82 (HBG) Elizabethtown, PA St. Peter; [J] Elizabethtown, PA Elizabethtown College.
Danneker, Edward A.J. '64 (ATL) Retired.
Dannenfelser, Lambert R. *o.f.m.* '40 (CIN)[P] Cincinnati, OH Friarhurst Retreat Center Retired.
Danner, Brian J. '95 (SC) Madrid, IA St. Malachy's; Madrid, IA St. John of God.
Danner, Brian J. '95 (SC) Ogden, IA St. John's.
Danner, Brian (SC) Liturgy Commission.
Danner, James L. '74 (MEM) Military Chaplains; Navy Chaplains.
Danner, Michael A. '65 (GR) On Special Assignment.
Danner, Michael '64 (GR) Grand Rapids, MI St. Jude.
Danner, Michael (GR) Director of Seminarians.
Danos, Dean F. '80 (HT) Larose, LA Our Lady of the Rosary.
Danos, Dean (HT) Priests Council.
Danos, Dean (HT) College of Consultors.
Danos, Dean (HT) South Lafourche Deanery.
Danowski, Alexander J. '59 (PBL) Retired.
Dansak, Thomas E. '73 (PIT) Military Chaplains; Navy Chaplains.
Dant, J. Nicholas '77 (IND) Indianapolis, IN Our Lady of Lourdes; Indianapolis, IN St. Bernadette.
Dante, Neal F. '64 (CAM) Westville Grove, NJ Most Holy Redeemer.
Danter, Albert F. '43 (STL) St. Louis, MO St. Andrew Retired.
Dantinne, Gary J. '68 (GB) Suamico, WI St. Pius; Suamico, WI St. Benedict.
Danylo, Bohdan '96 (STF)[A] Stamford, CT Ukrainian Catholic Seminary Inc. St. Basil College.
Danylo, Bohdan (STF) Vocations.
Danylo, Bohdan (STF) Presbyteral Council.
Danyluk, Richard J. *ss.cc.* '75 (OAK) Alameda, CA St. Joseph Basilica.
Danzi, Rocco C. *s.j.* (BRK) Brooklyn, NY St. Ignatius.
Dao, Ha Nam Thanh (CHI) Chicago, IL St. Margaret Mary.
Dao, Ngo Van *c.ss.r.* '86 (LA)[Q] Long Beach, CA.
Dao, Nhuong V. '75 (LA) Retired.
Dao, Paul '94 (NY) New York, NY St. Joseph.
Dao, Thanh X. '03 (SEA) Renton, WA St. Anthony.
Daoust, Joseph P. *s.j.* '69 (DET)[K] Detroit Jesuit Provincial Office–Detroit Province of the Society of Jesus.
Daoust, Joseph P. *s.j.* '69 (OAK)[A] Berkeley, CA The Jesuit School of Theology at Berkeley.
Daoust, Joseph P. *s.j.* '69 (DET)[N] Berkeley, CA Jesuit Community at Jesuit School of Theology at Berkeley.
Dao Vu, Joseph *s.v.d.* '88 (MEM) Memphis, TN Sacred Heart.
daPonte, Robert '64 (HON) Retired.
Daprile, James M. '76 (Y) Youngstown, OH St. Brendan.
Darbouze, Gerard '55 (MIA) Miami, FL Notre Dame d'Haiti.
Darbouze, Gerard (MIA) Haitians.
Darbouze, Joseph '58 (NY) New York, NY St. Gregory.
Darbouze, Rollin J. '69 (BRK) Brooklyn, NY Holy Innocents.
Darby, Thomas J. '47 (NY) New York, NY Our Lady of Victory Retired.
Darcy, Brendan *s.m.a.* '67 (NEW)[N] Tenafly, NJ Society of African Missions, Provincialate, S.M.A. Fathers.
Darcy, David M. '94 (SPR) Ludlow, MA St. Mary.
Darcy, James F. '66 (BO) Medford, MA St. James.
Darcy, John J. '79 (PRO) Providence, RI Cathedral of SS. Peter and Paul; Providence, RI St. Maron; [U] Providence, RI Miscellaneous Listings for the Diocese of Providence; Chancellor; Officers; Council Members; Finance Council; Judges.
Darcy, Michael J. *c.o.* (PIT)[N] Pittsburgh, PA Congregation of the Oratory of St. Philip Neri.
Darcy, Michael P. (WIL) Dover, DE Holy Cross; [A] Magnolia, DE St. Thomas More Academy.
Darcy, Michael *c.o.* '03 (PIT)[Q] Pittsburgh, PA Carnegie–Mellon University.
Darcy, Michael *c.o.* (PIT)[Q] Pittsburgh, PA University of Pittsburgh.
Darcy, Michael (WIL) Catholic Scouting Program.
Dardis, Hugh A. '49 (NY) Retired.
Dare, Glenn O. '74 (SAC) Portola, CA Holy Family.
Dargan, Peter S. '61 (HRT) Orange, CT Holy Infant; Deans.
Dargis, Andre *a.a.* '67 (WOR) Gardner, MA Our Lady of the Holy Rosary.
Daries, Joseph *c.m.f.* '56 (LA)[Q] Rancho Dominguez, CA Dominguez Seminary Inc..
Darilek, Dennis '73 (SAT) San Antonio, TX Our Lady of Good Counsel.
Darin, David M. '91 (BEL) Carlyle, IL St. Felicitas; Centralia, IL St. Mary; Carlyle, IL St. Teresa of Avila; Sandoval, IL St. Lawrence; Diocesan Deans.
Darkowski, Leon S. '43 (PIT) Retired.
Darling, Franklin '58 (SPR) Retired.
Darling, George E. '84 (GR) Grandville, MI St. Pius X.
Darling, William G. '73 (ROC) Army Reserve Chaplains.
Darnall, Thomas W. '52 (OKL) Retired.
Darnell, Lawrence T. *o.m.v.* '82 (LA) Hawaiian Gardens, CA St. Peter Chanel.
Darnieder, Donald A. '55 (MIL) Retired.
Darow, Robert G. '63 (CHI) Chicago, IL St. Hilary.
Da Roza, George *s.s.c.* '85 (OM)[K] St. Columbans St. Columban's Foreign Mission Society.
Darragh, John J. '68 (HEL) Hamilton, MT St. Francis; Presbyteral Council.
Darragh, John (HEL) Clergy Senior Status and Security Trust Board.
Dascenzo, Joseph J. '58 (PIT) Baden, PA St. John the Baptist.
Daschbach, Edwin G. *s.v.d.* '66 (WH) Glenville, WV Good Shepherd.
Dash, Alan J. '67 (R) Retired.
Dash, George J. *o.f.m.cap.* '92 (NY) Fishkill Correctional Facility; Anna M. Kross Center; [EE] New York, NY Development Office:.
da Silva, A. Paul (MET) Legion of Mary.
da Silva, Antonio F. '88 (NEW) Newark, NJ Our Lady of Fatima.
da Silva, Antonio *s.d.v.* '83 (NEW) Newark, NJ St. Michael's.
DaSilva, Colbert *s.d.b.* (NY) Mamaroneck, NY St. Vito.
Da Silva, Gilberto *c.m.v.* '97 (ARE) Sabana Hoyos, PR Nuestra Senora de Fatima.
Da Silva, Jose Carlos (BRK)[U] Brazilian Apostolate; Long Island City, NY St. Rita.
da Silva, Joseph '72 (B) Boise, ID Risen Christ Catholic Community; College of Consultors; Deans; Ecumenical Commission.
daSilva, Joseph (B) Priest Personnel Commission.
daSilva, Paul '98 (MET) Piscataway, NJ Our Lady of Fatima.
da Silva, Sergio (BGP) Bridgeport, CT St. Charles.
Das Neves, Antonio C. '61 (SB) Sun City, CA St. Vincent Ferrer.
Dass, Joseph '90 (LA) Ventura, CA Our Lady of the Assumption.
Dasseville, Armand *o.f.m.cap.* '49 (NY) New York, NY St. John the Baptist Retired.
Dathil, Joseph Valliyamtha (DUL) Virginia, MN Sacred Heart.
Datko, James *o.m.i.* (DUL) Duluth, MN Holy Family.
Dattilo, Anthony A. '90 (STL) Apple Creek, MO St. Joseph; Perryville, MO St. Maurus.
Dattilo, Anthony M. '84 (CIN) Cincinnati, OH St. Catharine.
Datty, Edward J. *s.a.* '49 (NY) Staten Island, NY Bayley Seton Hospital.
Datzman, Harold L. *o.s.b.* '65 (PEO) Ladd, IL St. Benedict's.
Daues, Mark J. *s.j.* '94 (KC)[D] Kansas City, MO Rockhurst High School; [J] Kansas City, MO Rockhurst Jesuit Community.
Daugherty, Daniel L. '94 (TYL) Whitehouse, TX Prince of Peace.
Daugherty, Patrick *c.p.* '02 (R) Greenville, NC St. Peter's.
Daugherty, Scott '83 (FRS) Porterville, CA St. Anne.
Dauich, George '62 (SLC) Retired.
Daum, John J. '45 (Y) Canton, OH St. Joan of Arc Retired.
Dauphinais, Louis Marie *o.mar.* '70 (SAM)[C] Petersham, MA Most Holy Trinity Monastery.
Dauses, Jeffrey S. '90 (BAL) Hunt Valley, MD Catholic Community of St. Francis Xavier.
Dauses, Jeffrey (BAL) Priest Personnel Board.
Dauss, Francis '48 (SP) Retired.
Dautremont, Charles R. '60 (GR) Grand Rapids, MI St. Dominic; Ecumenical Commission.
Davadilla, Joel '88 (FRS) Tehachapi, CA St. Malachy.
Davalos, Carlos '78 (SAT) Pleasanton, TX St. Andrew.
Davalos, Carlos (SAT) In Rural Area.
Davalos, Carlos (SAT) Archdiocesan Presbyteral Council.
Davanzo, Joseph V. '97 (RVC) Kings Park, NY St. Joseph's.
Dave, Kyle V. '01 (NO) Violet, LA Our Lady of Lourdes.
Davenport, Bernard '74 (WOR) Webster, MA St. Louis.
Davenport, Christopher M. '61 (PRO) West Warwick, RI SS. Peter and Paul.
Davenport, Clement A. '48 (SFR) San Mateo, CA St. Matthew Retired.
Davenport, Thomas J. '42 (SFD) Retired.
Davern, Raymond J. '58 (KCK) Kansas City, KS Christ the King.
Davern, Raymond (KCK) Archdiocesan Consultors.
Davern, Robert B. '51 (SY)[Q] Syracuse, NY Tommy Coyne Residence @ Dillon Hall.
Davern, Robert '51 (SY) Retired.
Davern, Timothy R. '78 (PHX) Tempe, AZ Tongan Catholic Community; Tempe, AZ Resurrection; Special Assignment; Judicial Vicar; Censor Librorum.
Davern, Timothy (PHX) College of Consultors.
Davey, Edward M. '53 (PAT)[P] Chester, NJ Nazareth Village Retired.
Davey, Philip D. *o.s.b.* '75 (PEO).
Davey, Philip *o.s.b.* '65 (PEO).
Davey, Robert W. (SAG)[C] Judges; Advocate.
Davey, Robert '62 (SAG) Retired.
David, Christopher J. '97 (DAV) Keokuk, IA All Saints; Montrose, IA St. Joseph's.
David, Craig '96 (ATL) On Duty Outside the Archdiocese.
David, George '71 (ROM) Roebling, NJ St. Mary.
David, George '71 (ROM) Trenton, NJ St. Basil.
David, George *v.g.* (ROM) Protosyncellus.
David, George *v.g.* (ROM) Board of Consultors.
David, John M. (RIC) Richmond, VA Church of the Vietnamese Martyrs.
David, Joseph '93 (SAM) Uniontown, PA St. George.
Davidowich, Glenn M. '89 (PSC) Mont Clare, PA St. Michael.
Davidowich, Glenn (PSC) Associate Editors:.
Davidson, Carl J. '64 (NO) Retired.
Davidson, John '64 (EVN) Evansville, IN St. Anthony.
Davidson, John (EVN) Personnel Board.
Davies, Daniel *o.p.* '58 (NY) Pleasantville, NY Holy Innocents.
Davies, Julian A. *o.f.m.* '60 (ALB)[B] Siena College.
Davies, Robert F. (DUB) Maquoketa, IA Sacred Heart; Deanery Representatives.
Davignon, Charles P. '56 (BUR) Woodstock, VT Our Lady of the Snows.
Davignon, Philip A. '62 (FR) Osterville, MA Our Lady of the Assumption.
Davila, Andres (ARE) On Duty Outside the Diocese.
Davila, Johnny '84 (SAT) On Leave.
Davila, Justo V. *s.d.b.* '70 (MRY) Watsonville, CA Our Lady Help of Christians.
Davila, Justo *s.d.b.* '70 (MRY)[F] Watsonville, CA Saint Francis Salesian Community.
Davila, Rafael R. *m.m.* '58 (GAL)[Q] Houston, TX St. Mary Seminary.
Davila, Raphael *m.m.* '58 (GAL)[A] Houston, TX St. Mary's Seminary.
Davin, Neil W. *c.p.* '52 (MET) Edison, NJ St. Matthew; [H] Edison, NJ St. Mathew's Rectory; Canonical Staff.
Davin, Neil *c.p.* '52 (BRK)[V] Jamaica, NY Immaculate Conception Monastery.
Davin, William *c.p.* '56 (PIT)[N] Pittsburgh, PA St. Paul of the Cross Monastery.

Davino, Louis *o.f.m.* '72 (CHI)[N] Chicago, IL St. Joseph Interprovincial Post–Novitiate Formation House.
Davino, Michael J. '86 (CHR) Absent On Leave.
Davis, Alexander *o.f.m.cap.* '64 (NY)[B] Beacon, NY St. Lawrence of Brindisi Friary.
Davis, Augustine *o.s.b.* '59 (IND)[K] St. Meinrad, IN St. Meinrad Archabbey.
Davis, Charles J. '62 (CAM) On Duty Outside the Diocese Retired.
Davis, Christopher *o.s.b.* '58 (PRO)[P] Portsmouth, RI Abbey of St. Gregory the Great.
Davis, Christopher '98 (CHL) Reidsville, NC Holy Infant.
Davis, Clement T. '70 (IND) Columbus, IN St. Bartholomew.
Davis, Clyde F. *m.m.* '63 (SJ)[M] Los Altos, CA Maryknoll.
Davis, Cyprian *o.s.b.* '56 (IND)[K] St. Meinrad, IN St. Meinrad Archabbey.
Davis, Cyprian *o.s.b.* '56 (IND)[A] St. Meinrad, IN St. Meinrad School of Theology.
Davis, D.G. "Skip" '98 (E) Ridgway, PA St Leo the Great.
Davis, Daniel C. *o.p.* '94 (LFT)[H] West Lafayette, IN St. Thomas Aquinas Parish and Foundation for Catholic Students Attending Purdue University; Aquinas Educational Foundation, Inc.; Newman Apostolate, Purdue University.
Davis, Daniel C. *o.p.* '94 (LFT) West Lafayette, IN St. Thomas Aquinas.
Davis, David '99 (LIN) Morse Bluff, NE St. George.
Davis, Edward J. '49 (NOR) Retired.
Davis, Edward V. *m.m.* '61 (FgM).
Davis, Ernest P. '02 (KC) Special Assignment.
Davis, F. Hampton '90 (NO).
Davis, Francis R. '45 (ROC) Retired.
Davis, Gary G. '75 (L)[A] Louisville, KY St. Michael.
Davis, Hampton '90 (LAF) On Duty Outside the Diocese.
Davis, Henry J. *s.s.j.* '93 (NO) New Orleans, LA St. Joan of Arc.
Davis, James J. *o.p.* '53 (PRO)[P] Providence St. Thomas Aquinas Priory at Providence College.
Davis, John E. '69 (FAR) On Duty Outside the Diocese.
Davis, John E. '69 ((FAR)) (FgM).
Davis, John P. '63 (PRT) Retired.
Davis, Joseph P. '72 (PAT) Succasunna, NJ St. Therese.
Davis, Kenneth *o.f.m.conv.* '86 (IND)[A] St Meinrad, IN St. Meinrad School of Theology.
Davis, Kenneth *o.f.m.conv.* '86 (IND)[J] Mount St. Francis, IN Mount Saint Francis Friary and Retreat Center.
Davis, L. Donald *s.j.* '64 (SPK)[J] Spokane, WA Regis Community.
Davis, Mark E. '96 (TOL) Maumee, OH St. Joseph.
Davis, Michael J. '87 (PH) Collingdale, PA St. Joseph.
Davis, Michael '90 (MIA)[C] Miami, FL Archbishop Coleman Carroll High School.
Davis, Michael '90 (MIA) Miami, FL Our Lady of Lourdes.
Davis, Noel '62 (LAR) Laredo, TX Santo Nino.
Davis, Noel (LAR) Priests Personnel Board.
Davis, Noel (LAR) Presbyteral Council.
Davis, Raphael J. *o.praem.* '99 (ORG)[I] Silverado, CA Norbertine Fathers of Orange Inc..
Davis, Richard L. *t.o.r.* '80 (ALT)[F] Loretto, PA St. Bonaventure Friary.
Davis, Richard P. '63 (LR) Bigelow, AR St. Elizabeth's; Bigelow, AR St. Boniface's; Bigelow, AR St. Francis of Assisi Church.
Davis, Robert '97 (FRS) Orange Cove, CA St. Isidore the Farmer.
Davis, Steven E. '77 (SFR) Pacifica, CA Good Shepherd Retired.
Davis, Terrence '69 (SJ) Retired.
Davis, Thomas A. '68 (LAR) Laredo, TX St. Patrick; Presbyteral Council; College of Consultors.
Davis, Thomas R. '83 (R) Jacksonville, NC Shrine of the Infant of Prague, Church of the Holy Spirit.
Davis, Wilbur (ORG) Consultors.
Davis, Wilbur (ORG) Council of Priests.
Davis, Wilbur (ORG) Vocations Office.
Davis, William C. *o.m.i.* '57 (GAL) Houston, TX Immaculate Heart of Mary; [L] Houston, TX Holy Family Clinic.
Davis, William F. '56 (MEM) Retired.
Davis, William F. *o.s.f.s.* '61 (WDC).
Davis, William W. *o.s.f.s.* '82 (PH)[AA] Philadelphia, PA Father Louis Brisson Residence.
Davis, William *ss.cc.* '44 (FR)[H] Fairhaven, MA Damien Residence.
Davison, Ben '92 (SD) Brawley, CA Sacred Heart.
Davison, Don *c.p.p.s.* (IND) Bloomington, IN St. Charles Borromeo.
Davison, Donald *c.pp.s.* '80 (CIN)[M] Bloomington, IN.
Davison, Timothy L. '85 (TLS) Tulsa, OK SS. Peter and Paul; Diocesan Senators.
Davitti, Michael *s.x.* '70 (CHI) Chicago, IL St. Therese Catholic Chinese Church.
DaVola, F. Robert '67 (BWN) Mission, TX St. Paul; Defenders of the Bond.
Davoren, Steve V. '96 (LA) Manhattan Beach, CA American Martyrs.
Daw, Timothy M. '91 (CLV) Cleveland, OH Annunciation; Rocky River, OH St. Christopher.
Dawber, Stephen F. *s.j.* '69 (BO)[E] Dorchester, MA Boston College High School & Jesuit Community; [V] Boston, MA Jesuit Urban Center & Immaculate Conception Community.
Dawis, Ralph '54 (NY) Staten Island, NY St Vincent's Medical Center of Richmond.
Daws, Dominic '55 (B) Retired.
Dawson, George *c.ss.r.* '50 (LA)[Q] Whittier, CA Redemptorists of Whittier.
Dawson, George *c.ss.r.* '50 (LA) Whittier, CA St. Mary of the Assumption.
Dawson, Ivan *c.ss.r.* '94 (WCH) Wichita, KS St. Joseph.
Dawson, Ivan *c.ss.r.* '94 (WCH)[F] Wichita, KS Redemptorist Mission House.
Dawson, James D. '54 (LIN) Lincoln, NE St. Michael; Priests' Continuing Education Committee
Dawson, James (LIN) Evangelization Committee.
Dawson, Joseph I. '62 (L) Retired.
Dawson, Richard '81 (PT) Bonifay, FL Blessed Trinity.
Dawson, Richard '81 (PT) De Funiak Springs, FL St. Margaret.
Dawson, Wayne '98 (P) Salem, OR St. Joseph.
Dawson, William A. *s.j.* '58 (BAL)[S] Baltimore, MD Jesuit Fathers and Brothers Maryland Provincial Curia.
Dawson, William F. '54 (DAV)[B] St. Ambrose University.
Dawson, William *s.j.* '58 (BAL) Baltimore, MD St. Mark.
Day, Charles J. '81 (CHR) Retired.
Day, Dennis C. '76 (B) Sandpoint, ID St. Joseph's.
Day, Dennis (B) Priest Personnel Commission.
Day, James E. *o.ss.t.* '72 (PH) Bristol, PA St. Ann.
Day, James Richard '96 (NO) New Orleans, LA St. Rita.
Day, Jeffrey '99 (DET) Dearborn Heights, MI St. Sebastian.
Day, Jerome J. *o.s.b.* '95 (MAN) Manchester, NH St. Raphael; [K] Manchester, NH St. Anselm Abbey.
Day, John D. '39 (BO) Senior Priests Retired.
Day, John P. *c.p.* '72 (CHI)[N] Maryland Heights, MO St. Blaise Parish.
Day, John Patrick *c.p.* '72 (STL) Maryland Heights, MO St. Blaise.
Day, Lenox C. *s.j.* '63 (SJ)[M] Los Gatos, CA Sacred Heart Jesuit Center.
Day, Martin *o.f.m.conv.* '91 (WDC)[B] Washington, DC St. Bonaventure Friary.
Day, Wilfred E. '67 (IND) New Albany, IN Holy Family.
Day, William F. '86 (GLP) Overgaard, AZ Our Lady of Assumption; Ecumenical Affairs in Arizona, Arizona Ecumenical Council.
Daya, John *o.f.m.cap.* '78 (PIT) Pittsburgh, PA Our Lady of the Angels.
Daz, Rudolph A. '54 (SLC) Bountiful, UT St. Olaf.
Daz, Rudolph (SLC) Deans.
Daza, Wilmer de Jesus '99 (DAL)[N] Dallas, TX Nuestra Senora del Pilar Land & Development Trust; Dallas, TX Nuestra Senora del Pilar.
Ddungu, Josephat '95 (ORG) Anaheim, CA St. Anthony Claret.
Deaconson, James '85 (AUS)[L] Waco, TX St. Peter Catholic Student Center at Baylor University.
DeAdder, James W. '55 (BO) Senior Priests; Judge Auditor Retired.
De Agostini, Claudio *c.s.j.* '58 (LA) San Pedro, CA St. Peter.
DeAguiar, Luiz Antonio '85 (BRK) Jamaica, NY St. Pius V.
DeAguilar, Arturo '97 (CHL) Absent On Leave.
DeAmato, Norbert *o.f.m.* '48 (BO) Cambridge, MA St. Francis of Assisi.
Dean, Frederic D. '65 (PRO)[P] Providence St. John Vianney Residence Retired.
Dean, Gregory (CC) Finance Council.
Dean, James N. '91 (MOB) Montgomery, AL Our Lady, Queen of Mercy; [J] Montgomery, AL Huntington College Newman Center; Air Force Reserve Chaplains.
Dean, John T. '72 (SPR) Westfield, MA St. Peter and St. Casimir; [P] Westfield, MA Westfield State College.
Dean, Joseph *g.h.m.* '45 (CIN)[M] Cincinnati Headquarters of Glenmary Home Missioners.
Dean, Joseph *s.c.j.* '84 (MIL)[X] Franklin WI Congregation of the Priests of the Sacred Heart Support and Maintenance Trust; [O] Hales Corners, WI Priests of the Sacred Heart.
Dean, Joseph *s.c.j.* '84 (GB)[L] Baileys Harbor, WI St. Joseph Retreat Center.
Dean, Joseph (TYL) Retired.
Dean, Mark *o.m.i.* '83 (SAT)[B] San Antonio, TX George Sexton House of Studies.
Dean, Maximilian *f.i.* (SY)[U] Maine, NY Mount St. Francis Hermitage, Inc..
Dean, Walter R. *o.s.f.s.* '49 (WIL)[J] Wilmington Oblates of St. Francis De Sales.
Dean, William E. '76 (PH) Philadelphia, PA Sacred Heart of Jesus.
Deane, Declan '72 (OAK) Moraga, CA St. Monica.
Deane, Declan (OAK) Presbyteral Council.
Deane, Gregory S. '54 (CC) Port Aransas, TX St. Joseph.
Deane, J. Peter *s.j.* '66 (DET)[K] Detroit Jesuit Provincial Office–Detroit Province of the Society of Jesus.
Deane, Joseph '59 (AUS) Buda, TX Santa Cruz.
DeAngelis, Antonio *c.s.* '81 (SJ) San Jose, CA Holy Cross.
De Angelis, Mark J. '88 (BO) Absent on Leave.
De Angelis, Sante *o.f.m.* '62 (MIL)[X] Waterford, WI General Secretariat of the Franciscan Missions, Inc..
DeAngelo, Jude T. *o.f.m.conv.* '84 (CHL) Winston–Salem, NC Our Lady of Mercy; [L] Winston–Salem, NC Salem College and N.C. School of the Arts.
DeAntoniis, Paul J. *o.praem.* '63 (PH)[AA] Paoli, PA Daylesford Abbey.
DeAntonio, Michael R. '71 (CHR) Spartanburg, SC St. Paul the Apostle.
Dear, John *s.j.* '93 (NY) Cimarron, NM Immaculate Conception Church; Springer, NM St. Joseph.
Deardorff, Joseph F. *c.pp.s.* '82 (CIN)[M] Nuestra Senora de la Luz.
Dearhammer, John W. '91 (CHI) Chicago, IL St. Gall.
de Armas, Alexio Jose *o.c.d.* '58 (PCE) Ponce, PR San Jose.
Deary, John F. *o.s.a.* '66 (VEN) Cape Coral, FL Saint Katharine Drexel.
Deary, John *o.s.a.* (VEN) Cursillo Movement.
Deas, George T. '51 (BRK)[V] Douglaston, NY Bishop Mugavero Residence Retired.
Dease, Dennis J. '69 (STP)[C] St. Paul, MN University of St. Thomas; Censores Librorum.
Deasio, August J. '75 (STU) Formation Council Retired.
Deasy, Jeremiah *v.f.* '67 (BIR) Tuscaloosa, AL Holy Spirit; [I] Tuscaloosa, AL The Harrison Family Endowment Trust for the Benefit of Holy Spirit School.
Deasy, Jeremiah (BIR) Members.
Deasy, Jeremiah (BIR) Diocesan College of Vicars.
Deasy, Ken '87 (LA) Los Angeles, CA St. Agatha.
Deasy, Kenneth (LA) Board of Directors:.
Deasy, Timothy '58 (MOB) Daphne, AL Christ the King.
Deasy, Timothy (MOB) Ex Officio Members.
Deasy, Timothy (MOB) Regional Episcopal Vicars.
Deasy, Wayman P. *m.m.* '59 (NY)[EE] Maryknoll Maryknoll Fathers and Brothers; [EE] Maryknoll, NY Maryknoll Fathers and Brothers Charitable Trust.
Deatrick, John D. '66 (L) Louisville, KY St. Martha.
Deaver, Stephen F. '59 (GI) Mitchell, NE St. Theresa's; Council of Catholic Women, Diocesan.
de Azevedo, Antonio Carvalho '62 (BGP) Danbury, CT Immaculate Heart of Mary.
Debaenst, Emmanuel '34 (SFE) Retired.
Debany, Edgar J. *s.j.* '84 (BAL).
DeBellis, John A. '85 (NY)[S] Staten Island, NY Our Lady, Queen of Peace.
De Bellis, John A. '85 (NY) Yonkers, NY St. Ann.
DeBellis, Peter '97 (ROC) Auburn, NY St. Francis of Assisi.
DeBenedictis, Salvatore *o.f.m.* '44 (ALB)[A] Catskill, NY St. Anthony Friary.
Debes, Donald *o.f.m.cap.* '70 (FgM).
DeBiase, William *o.f.m.* '66 (PH)[AA] Philadelphia, PA Order of Friars Minor of the Province of the Most Holy Name.
Debicki, John P. '64 (CHI) Chicago, IL St. Mary of the Angels; [W] Chicago, IL Midtown Center.
DeBisschop, James P. '88 (PEO) Rapids City, IL St. John the Baptist.
Debitetto, Ronald E. '63 (WOR) Retired.
DeBlanc, Irving A. '38 (LKC) Lake Charles, LA Our Lady Queen of Heaven; [E] Lake Charles, LA Our Lady Queen of Heaven Manor Retired.
DeBlanc, Irving (LKC) Diocesan Consultors.
DeBlanc, Jefferson J. '77 (LAF) Opelousas, LA Our Lady of Mercy.
DeBlanc, Jefferson (LAF) Advocates.
De Blas, Alonso *o.f.m.* '64 (PHX) Phoenix, AZ St. Mary's Basilica.
DeBlase, Dominic *s.d.b.* '61 (FgM).
DeBlasio, Dominck A. '40 (PIT) Retired.
DeBlasio, Ernie '88 (MEM) Memphis, TN Church of the Resurrection.
Debo, Peter '89 (PIT) Pittsburgh, PA Word of God.
Debo, William D. '95 (JC) Hermann, MO St. George; Rhineland, MO Church of the Risen Savior.
DeBock, William A. '49 (MAD)[G] Madison, WI Bishop O'Connor Catholic Pastoral Center Retired.
DeBoe, Stanley W. *o.ss.t.* '83 (BAL) Hanover, MD St. Lawrence.
De Boisse, Arnaud Mortemard *f.s.s.p.* '01 (PAT) Pequannock, NJ Our Lady of Fatima Chapel (Tridentine).
de Boisse, Arnaud *f.s.s.p.* '01 (SCR)[M] Littleton, CO Our Lady of Mount Carmel Community.
Debold, Walter A. '42 (NEW)[B] School of Diplomacy and Intl. Rels. Retired.
DeBona, Guerric *o.s.b.* '86 (IND)[A] St. Meinrad, IN St.

Meinrad School of Theology.
DeBona, Guerrie *o.s.b.* '86 (IND)[K] St. Meinrad, IN St. Meinrad Archabbey.
De Brito Alves, Joseph '67 (BGP) Bridgeport, CT Our Lady of Fatima.
de Bruijn, Johan *o.cart.* '91 (BUR)[E] Arlington, VT Carthusian Foundation in America, Inc., Charterhouse of the Transfiguration.
DeBruycker, James R. '82 (STP) Minneapolis, MN St. Leonard of Port Maurice; Minneapolis, MN Hennepin County Medical Center.
Debski, Joseph E. '64 (MIL) Burlington, WI Immaculate Conception.
Decaen, Ramon E. '00 (LIN) Hastings, NE St. Cecilia's; Advocates.
Decal, Wilfredo '77 (HT) Houma, LA Annunziata.
de Cardenas, Javier Garcia '85 (NY)[JJ] New York, NY Prelature of the Holy Cross and Opus Dei.
DeCarlo, Philip J. '55 (PIT) Retired.
DeCarlo, Thomas M. '69 (DM)[E] Johnston, IA Bishop Drumm Retirement Center.
De Carlo Mena, Francisco '50 (SJN) Retired.
DeCarolis, Joseph R. '59 (HRT) Prospect, CT St. Anthony's.
DeCarolis, Vito C. '54 (HRT) Retired.
De Celles, John C. '96 (ARL) Annandale, VA St. Michael's.
Decewicz, Michael W. '78 (PIT) Monroeville, PA St. Bernadette; [Q] Monroeville, PA Community College of Allegheny County – Boyce Campus.
Dechant, Leo *c.s.j.* '80 (CLV)[O] Avon, OH Congregation of St. Joseph.
Dechant, Paul '90 (VEN) Fort Myers, FL St. Cecilia.
Dechering, Anton '62 (SP) St. Petersburg, FL Blessed Trinity.
Dechering, Anton (SP) College of Consultors.
Dechering, Anton (SP) Scouting Office, Girls.
Dechering, Anton (SP) Vicars Forane.
Dechering, Anton (SP) Presbyteral Council.
DeChico, Philip '74 (HBG) Gettysburg, PA St. Joseph.
DeChico, Philip '74 (HBG)[J] Gettysburg, PA Gettysburg College.
DeCicco, Pascal A. *o.s.a.* '52 (PH) Philadelphia, PA St. Augustine.
Deck, Alcuin *o.s.b.* '39 (RCK)[G] Aurora, IL Marmion Abbey.
Deck, Allan F. *s.j.* '76 (ORG)[H] Orange, CA Loyola Institute for Spirituality.
Deck, Allan *s.j.* '76 (ORG)[I] Garden Grove, CA Manresa Jesuit Residence.
Deck, Allan *s.j.* (ORG) Ecumenical and Interreligious Affairs.
Deck, Marion *t.o.r.* '69 (ARL)[J] White Post, VA Sacred Heart Friary.
Decker, Douglas A. (OG) Advocates; Air National Guard Chaplains.
Decker, Douglas '78 (OG) Adams, NY St. Cecilia.
Decker, James D. '85 (MAN) Military Chaplains; Air Force Chaplains.
Decker, Jonathan *s.j. m.j.* '76 (OLL) Portland, OR Saint Sharbel.
Decker, Lawrence J. '84 (ALB) Amsterdam, NY St. Joseph–St. Michael–Our Lady of Mount Carmel.
Decker, Maurice C. '50 (DET) Retired.
Decker, Neil F. *s.j.* '58 (BO)[V] Newton, MA The Jesuit Community at Boston College.
Decker, Raymond G. '58 (SFR) Retired.
Decker, Robert L. '83 (OG) Harrisville, NY St. Francis Solanus; Star Lake, NY St. Hubert; Campus Ministry.
Deckman, Peter '64 (ROC) Rochester, NY St. Michael.
Deckman, Peter '64 (ROC) Rochester, NY Our Lady of Perpetual Help.
DeClippel, Ludo *c.j.* '68 (LA) Santa Barbara, CA Holy Cross.
DeCneudt, Ferdinand '39 (DET) Retired.
De Cola, Vincent P. *s.j.* '88 (NY) New York, NY Nativity.
DeCola, Vincent *s.j.* '01 (NY)[II] New York, NY Nativity Mission Center, Inc..
DeConciliis, Anthony J. *c.s.c.* '67 (BGP)[P] Loretto, PA St. Francis University.
De Conciliis, Anthony J. *c.s.c.* (ALT)[A] Loretto, PA St. Francis University.
De Condorpusa, Alphonse '95 (NEW) Kearny, NJ St. Cecilia's.
DeCosta, George '64 (HON) Retired.
DeCosta, Joseph F. '90 (NOR) Gales Ferry, CT Our Lady of Lourdes.
DeCosta, Joseph (NOR) District Moderators.
DeCoste, D. Wade '03 (ALX) Alexandria, LA St. Francis Xavier Cathedral.
Decoteau, Joseph A. *m.s.* '40 (HRT)[M] Hartford, CT Missionaries of LaSalette.
Decoteau, Vernon P. (SPR) Vicars for the Clergy; Presbyteral Council.
Decoteau, Vernon '75 (SPR) Belchertown, MA St. Francis of Assisi.
DeCraemer, Willy *s.j.* '57 (BAL)[S] Philadelphia, PA Chancellor Park.
DeCrans, Joseph J. (CR) CIVIL AIR PATROL.
DeCrans, Joseph '84 (CR) Callaway, MN Assumption; Frazee, MN Sacred Heart; Detroit Lakes, MN St. Mary of the Lakes.
de Cristobal, Fernando '65 (GRY) East Chicago, IN St. Patrick.
Dedal, Gregorio '92 (HON) Pahoa, HI Sacred Heart; Filipino Ministry.
Dede, John F. '47 (IND) Retired.
Dede, John (IND) Archdiocesan Judges.
Dede, Paul M. '64 (IND) Spencer, IN St. Jude the Apostle.
de Dios, Alfredo *o.a.r.* '60 (ORG) Santa Ana, CA Our Lady of the Pillar.
de Dios, Francisco Mendez '60 (ARL) Arlington, VA St. Charles Borromeo.
DeDomenico, Dominic *o.p.* '66 (OAK)[S] Oakland, CA Dominican Community Support Charitable Trust; [N] Oakland, CA Western Dominican Province.
De Dominici, Lorenzo '46 (LA) San Pedro, CA Mary, Star of the Sea Retired.
DeDominici, Lorenzo '46 (LA) Retired.
de Duenas, Jesus *l.d.* '97 (PCE) Ponce, PR Church Santisimo Sacramento.
Dee, Dacian '56 (SP) Indian Rocks Beach, FL St. Jerome.
Dee, Dacian (SP) College of Consultors.
Dee, Dacian (SP) Judges.
Dee, Dacian (SP) Judicial Vicar.
Dee, Dacian (SP) Presbyteral Council.
Deegan, James D. *o.m.i.* '70 (STP) St. Paul, MN St. Casimir.
Deegan, John E. *o.s.a.* '61 (PH)[C] Villanova, PA Villanova University; [AA] Villanova, PA St. John Stone Friary.
Deegan, Ronan J. *t.o.r.* '58 (WH) Moundsville, WV St. Francis Xavier's.
Deehan, Robert J. '83 (BO) Plymouth, MA St. Bonaventure.
Deehr, Anselm *s.t.* '90 (LA) Veterans Affairs Medical Center.
Deeke, Von C. '03 (BEL) Mount Vernon, IL St. Mary; Radom, IL St. Michael; Scheller, IL St. Barbara.
Deeker, Geoffrey J. *c.s.s.* '60 (SPR) Pittsfield, MA Our Lady of Mt. Carmel.
Deeley, Kevin J. '74 (BO) Military & VA Chaplains; Navy Chaplains.
Deeley, Robert P. '73 (BO) Quincy, MA St. Ann; SOUTH REGION; Archdiocesan Judges; Canonical Affairs Committee.
Deely, John *o.m.i.* '70 (FgM).
Deely, Thomas (Martin) *c.ss.r.* '65 (NY) Bronx, NY Immaculate Conception.
Deeney, Charles J. *o.m.i.* '71 (ORL) Longwood, FL Annunciation.
Deeney, John J. *s.j.* '52 (BAL)[S] St. Xavier's High School.
Deering, Mark '53 (AUS) Retired.
Deering, Mark (AUS) Consultors.
Deering, Michael J. '02 (BIR) Birmingham, AL Our Lady of Sorrows.
Deering, Michael '02 (BIR)[A] Birmingham, AL John Carroll Catholic High School.
Deering, William '56 (EVN) Retired.
Deering, William '56 (EVN) Fort Branch, IN St. Bernard.
Deery, James T. *o.s.a.* '51 (PH)[AA] Villanova, PA St. Thomas Monastery.
Deery, Lawrence *o.m.i.* '41 (BO)[Y] Tewksbury, MA Immaculate Heart of Mary Infirmary.
Deeves, John F. *s.j.* '58 (DAL)[D] Dallas, TX Jesuit College Preparatory School; Procurator–Advocates.
Deevy, Edward '62 (ALX) Absent on Leave.
Defayette, Jeffrey M. '88 (WDC) Lanham, MD St. Matthias Apostle.
DeFazio, Crescenzio '57 (BIR) Retired.
DeFazio, Vincent '92 (SFE) Retired.
DeFelice, Jonathan P. *o.s.b.* '74 (MAN)[B] Manchester, NH Saint Anselm College; [K] Manchester, NH St. Anselm Abbey.
Deffenbaugh, J. (PT) Saufley Field Federal Prison Camp.
Deffenbaugh, Joseph T. '79 (Y) On Duty Outside the Diocese.
Deffenbaugh, Terry A. *o.s.a.* '75 (CHI)[N] Matteson, IL Austin Friary.
Define, William G. *s.j.* '57 (BO)[V] Weston, MA Campion Health Center, Inc..
Define, William *f.s.s.p.* '02 (LR)[L] North Little Rock, AR Priestly Fraternity of St. Peter.
Define, William *f.s.s.p.* '02 (SCR)[M] Corpus Christi, TX.
Defler, Herman J. *m.s.f.* '38 (BWN) Donna, TX St. Joseph; Associate Judges.
De Folco, Joseph A. '85 (SEA) Snohomish, WA St. Michael.
DeFolco, Joseph (SEA) Presbyteral Council; Deans.
DeForge, Michael W. '79 (BUR) Members Ex Officio; Vocations and Seminarians; Vicar for Ministries; Diocesan Administrative Board; Diocesan Consultors; Vicar for Ministries; House of Discernment; [H] Burlington, VT University of Vermont–The Catholic Center at UVM; [H] Northfield, VT Norwich Newman Apostolate.
DeFrancisco, Joseph '75 (BEA) On Duty Outside the Diocese.
De Francisco, Joseph '75 (BEA)[B] St. Ambrose University.
De Franco, Anthony '38 (ALB) Retired.
DeFranco, Anthony '38 (ALB) Schenectady, NY St. Anthony.
DeFranco, Anthony '38 (ALB) Schenectady, NY St. John the Evangelist.
DeFrange, Jonathan M. *o.s.b.* '78 (NO) Folsom, LA St. John the Baptist; [P] St. Benedict, LA St. Joseph Abbey.
de Fromage, Olivier *s.j.* (WDC)[E] Washington, DC Gonzaga College High School.
DeFronzo, Anthony R. '81 (PSC) Special or Other Diocesan Assignment.
DeGaal, Emery '00 (CHI).
DeGaetano, Louis J. '79 (BRK)[A] Belle Harbor, NY St. Francis de Sales.
Degagne, Richard E. '82 (FR) Taunton, MA Our Lady of the Immaculate Conception.
De Gante, Adelberto (DEN) Yuma, CO St. John.
Degaris, Herbert P. '91 (NY) Blauvelt, NY St. Catharine.
Degen, Jerome A. '59 (SC) Presbyteral Council Retired.
Degenhardt, Gervase *o.f.m.cap.* '58 (PIT)[O] Pittsburgh, PA St. Francis Convent.
DeGeorge, Salvatore *o.m.i.* '65 (SAT)[M] San Antonio, TX Missionary Oblates of Mary Immaculate.
DeGeorge, Salvatore *o.m.i.* '65 (SAT)[M] San Antonio, TX Oblate Vocation Office.
DeGeorge, Salvatore *o.m.i.* '65 (WDC)[M] Washington, DC Provincial Offices of the United States Province of the Missionary Oblates of Mary Immaculate.
DeGeorge, Salvatore *o.m.i.* '65 (SAT)[M] San Antonio, TX Oblate Benson Residence (Southwest Area).
DeGerolami, Michael '74 (SAT) San Antonio, TX St. Philip of Jesus.
Degeyter, Edward '70 (LAF) Jeanerette, LA St. John the Evangelist.
DeGiovine, Christopher '77 (ALB) Albany, NY St. John–St. Ann.
DeGiovine, Christopher '77 (ALB)[B] Albany, NY The College of Saint Rose.
DeGiovine, Christopher '77 (ALB) Special Assignment.
DeGiovine, Christopher (ALB) Ongoing Formation and Continuing Education for Priests.
Deglaire, Pierre L. *c.s.sp.* '70 (SB) Hemet, CA Our Lady of the Valley; [E] Hemet, CA Our Lady of the Valley.
Degnan, Daniel A. *s.j.* '66 (NEW)[C] Jersey City, NJ St. Peter's Preparatory School; [N] Jersey City, NJ Jesuit Community of St. Peter's Prep, Inc..
Degnan, Henry B. '48 (PH) Norristown, PA St. Paul; Priests' Personnel Board Retired.
Degnan, James F. '55 (BO) Hopkinton, MA St. John the Evangelist.
de Gonzaga Furtado, Luiz (PH) Portuguese and Brazilian Apostolates.
Degraff, Jean Marie '01 (STV) Charlotte Amalie, VI Cathedral of Sts. Peter and Paul.
DeGrand, Robert L. '80 (SFD) Sigel, IL St. Mary of the Assumption; Sigel, IL St. Michael the Archangel.
DeGrand, Robert (SFD) Priests' Personnel Board.
DeGrandis, Robert *s.s.j.* '59 (WDC)[B] Washington, DC St. Joseph's Seminary.
DeGrood, Donald E. '97 (STP)[C] St. Paul, MN University of St. Thomas.
DeGroot, Francis J. '93 (MAR) Menominee, MI Resurrection; Advocates.
DeGroot, Ignatius *o.f.m.* '64 (FgM).
De Groot, Kenneth J. *o.praem.* '61 (GB) Green Bay, WI St. Willebrord.
DeGuzman, Dennis U. '91 (OM) Dodge, NE St. Wenceslaus; Dodge, NE Sacred Heart; Deans.
De Guzman, Dennis (OM) Army Reserve Chaplains.
DeGuzman, Francis *o.mar.* '95 (SAM)[C] Petersham, MA Most Holy Trinity Monastery.
De Heredia, Agnel '80 (SFR) South San Francisco, CA All Souls.
de Herrera, Christopher '97 (PCE) Villalba, PR Our Lady of Mt. Carmel.
Dehler, William A. *s.j.* '44 (DET)[P] Hamtramck, MI St. Ladislaus.
Dehne, Carl A. *s.j.* '70 (STL)[O] St. Louis, MO Jesuit Community Corporation at St. Louis University – Jesuit Hall.
Dehner, Eugene *o.s.b.* '40 (KCK)[H] Atchison, KS St. Benedict's Abbey.
Dehner, Philip R. *o.c.s.o.* '53 (ATL)[K] Conyers, GA The Monastery of the Holy Spirit.
DeHondt, Ronald (DET) St. Clair Shores, MI St. Margaret of Scotland.
Deibel, David L. '83 (SR)[M] Napa, CA Provincialate Community.
Deibel, David L. (SAC) Judicial Vicar; Canonical Affairs; Due Process.
Deibel, David (SAC) Vicar for Canonical Affairs.
Deibel, David (STO) Judges.
Deichert, Joseph '84 (BIS) On Duty Outside the Diocese; Air Force Chaplains.

Deig, Robert A. '50 (EVN) Evansville, IN St. John the Evangelist.
Deikel, Jeff J. '76 (LA) Panorama City, CA St. Genevieve.
Deiloreto, Anthony '54 (B) Pocatello, ID Holy Spirit Catholic Community Retired.
Deimeke, L. Edward '75 (ALB) Colonie, NY St. Clare; Special Assignment; Administrative Advocate for Priests; Priests Placement Committee; Priestly Life and Ministry Council; Members; Priests Retirement Board.
Deimel, George *c.ss.r.* '37 (ALB)[L] Saratoga Springs, NY St. John Neumann Residence.
Deis, Dennis *o.m.i.* '65 (SFS) Rosholt, SD St. John the Baptist.
Deis, Michael S. *o.m.i.* '47 (BEL)[F] Belleville, IL Missionary Oblates of Mary Immaculate – St. Henry's Oblate Residence.
Deisch, Raymond J. '62 (RC) Gregory, SD St. Joseph.
Deisch, Raymond (RC) Deaneries.
Deister, Charles C. '63 (STL)[Q] St. Louis, MO School Sisters of Notre Dame.
Deitch, Richard S. '86 (SFR) Sausalito, CA St. Mary Star of the Sea; Young Ladies' Institute.
Deitchman, Carl *o.s.b.* '84 (IND) Tell City, IN St. Paul.
Deitchman, Carl *o.s.b.* '84 (IND)[K] Tell City, IN.
Deitchman, Carl *o.s.b.* (IND) Deaneries and Deans.
Deitelhoff, Bernard H. '57 (MAD) Retired.
Deiters, James E. '91 (BEL) O'Fallon, IL St. Clare.
Deiters, James R. (BEL) Formation of Priests.
Deitz, Christopher L. '85 (MRY)[F] Arroyo Grande, CA St. Joseph Cupertino Province, Provincial Center.
Deitzer, Gerald E. *c.m.* '55 (PH)[AA] Philadelphia Congregation of the Mission.
DeJardin, Joseph R. *s.j.* '61 (P).
DeJesus, Alejandro *o.s.b.* '84 (SAT)[D] San Antonio, TX St. Vincent de Paul.
De Jesus, Dwight '85 (ALX) Winnsboro, LA St. Mary.
de Jesus, Hector Bruno '85 (CGS)[F] Caguas, PR Movimiento Juan XXIII.
de Jesus, Herminio '69 (PCE) Juana Diaz, PR Nuestra Senora de Lourdes; [B] The Pontifical Catholic University of Puerto Rico; Parish Priests Consultors.
De Jesus, Herminio (PCE) Diocesan Consultors.
De Jesus, Herminio (PCE) Committee for Community Planning.
De Jesus, Herminio (PCE) Episcopal Vicar for Diocesan Administration.
De Jesus, Herminio (PCE) Chancellor.
de Jong, Jan *s.c.j.* '64 (MIL)[O] Franklin, WI St. Francis Residence; [O] Hales Corners, WI Priests of the Sacred Heart.
DeJulio, David '90 (SP)[B] Tampa, FL St. Mark the Evangelist.
DeJulio, Robert J. '72 (NY) Brewster, NY St. Lawrence O'Toole.
Dekat, Carl '53 (KCK) Topeka, KS St. Joseph's.
Dekat, Earl '66 (KCK) St. Bede's; Seneca, KS SS. Peter and Paul's.
Deken, John C. '72 (STL) New Haven, MO St. Paul; New Haven, MO Assumption.
Deket, Earl (KCK) St. Patrick's.
Dekrem, Bruno '92 (RVC) Williston Park, NY St. Aidan's Church.
de la Calle, Juan '54 (PMB) Indiantown, FL Holy Cross.
De La Cruz, Jenaro *o.c.d.* '66 (OKL) Oklahoma City, OK Our Lady of Mount Carmel and St. Therese Little Flower.
de la Cruz, Juan '57 (ATL) Marietta, GA Holy Family.
de la Cruz, Perlito '03 (SAC) Rancho Cordova, CA St. John Vianney.
DelaCruz, Rafael *s.d.b.* '90 (OAK)[N] Berkeley Salesian Community.
DeLa Cruz, Vicente '90 (HT) Bourg, LA St. Ann.
DeLa Cruz, Vicente (HT) Judges.
DeLa Cruz, Vicente (HT) Judicial Vicar.
deLadurantaye, Paul F. '88 (ARL) Arlington, VA Cathedral of St. Thomas More; Diocesan Judges; Catholic Education, Office of Catechetics; Liturgy, Office of Sacred.
Delaere, Paul *c.i.c.m.* '43 (FgM).
De La Garza, Joseph '51 (SAT) Retired.
Delahanty, Patrick D. '69 (L) Eminence, KY St. John Chrysostom.
Delahunty, Richard A. '65 (ORG) Laguna Woods, CA St. Nicholas.
Delahunty, Richard (ORG) Ministry to Priests.
Delahunty, Thomas P. '55 (SAC) Retired.
Delahunty, Thomas '54 (SEA) Retired.
de Laire, Georges F. '97 (MAN) Pittsfield, NH Our Lady of Lourdes.
DeLand, Robert J. '73 (SAG) Saginaw, MI SS. Peter and Paul.
Deland, Robert J. (SAG) Defenders of the Bond.
DeLand, Robert (SAG) Judicial Vicar.
Delaney, Brian '75 (LA) Montebello, CA Our Lady of the Miraculous Medal.
Delaney, Charles A. *c.s.c.* '49 (FTW)[I] Congregacion de Santa Cruz.
Delaney, Charles A. *c.s.c.* '49 (FgM).
Delaney, Dennis M. (STL) Moderator of the Curia; Vicar for Pastoral Planning; Archdiocesan Pastoral Council.
Delaney, Dennis '76 (STL) St. Louis, MO St. John the Apostle and Evangelist.
Delaney, Dennis (STL) Archdiocesan Consultors.
Delaney, Donald *s.d.b.* '76 (NEW) Elizabeth NJ St. Anthony's.
Delaney, Francis H. '52 (BO) Peabody, MA St. Adelaide; Senior Priests Retired.
Delaney, Howard L. '40 (PBL) Retired.
Delaney, James P. *o.m.i.* '36 (SAT)[K] San Antonio, TX Oblate Madonna Residence.
Delaney, James *c.s.sp.* '54 (NEW) Jersey City, NJ St. Aloysius.
Delaney, James *c.s.sp.* '54 (BRK)[V] Long Island City, NY Holy Ghost Fathers of Ireland.
Delaney, James *c.s.sp.* '54 (BRK)[Z] Long Island City, NY World Compassion Link.
Delaney, John H. '81 (FTW) Goshen, IN St. John the Evangelist.
Delaney, John J. '62 (NY) New York, NY Immaculate Conception; Judges.
Delaney, John W. '64 (MIA) Fort Lauderdale, FL St. Helen Retired.
Delaney, John W. (BO) North Andover, MA St. Michael.
DeLaney, John (FTW) Advisory Board.
Delaney, Larry '90 (CR) East Grand Forks, MN Sacred Heart; Members; Priests Retirement Board of Trustees.
Delaney, Larry (LAN) Priestly Life and Ministry.
Delaney, Lawrence '67 (LAN)[L] De Witt, MI St. Francis Retreat Center.
Delaney, Matthew S. '51 (LA) Retired.
Delaney, Michael J. '85 (SCR) Hazleton, PA St. Gabriel's.
DeLaney, Michael M. *c.s.c.* '87 (CHI)[D] Niles, IL Notre Dame High School.
Delaney, Michael V. *s.j.* '85 (DEN) Fort Collins, CO St. Joseph.
Delaney, Richard F. '62 (RVC)[M] Uniondale, NY St. Pius X Residence.
Delaney, Richard '62 (RVC) Retired.
Delaney, T. Timothy '79 (SCR) Retired.
Delaney, Thomas P. *s.j.* '61 (LA) Santa Barbara, CA Our Lady of Sorrows.
Delaney, Thomas '57 (JKS) Greenwood, MS Immaculate Heart of Mary.
Delaney, Thomas *o.m.i.* '60 (FgM).
Delaney, Thomas (JKS) Priests' Council.
Delaney, Thomas (JKS) Approved Advocate and Auditors.
Delaney, William B. '42 (NY) White Plains, NY St. John the Evangelist Retired.
Delaney, William I. '61 (RVC) Retired.
Delaney, William J. '54 (NY) New York, NY Holy Innocents.
Delaney, William J. *c.pp.s.* '99 (LA) Los Angeles, CA St. Aloysius Gonzaga.
Delaney, William K. *s.j.* '85 (LA)[Q] Los Angeles, CA Columbiere House.
Delaney, William '44 (CHY) Retired.
Delaney, William '44 (CHY) Cheyenne, WY Holy Trinity Retired.
Delaney, William '61 (RVC) Freeport, NY Our Holy Redeemer.
Delaney, William *s.j.* '85 (LA)[CC] Burbank, CA SCRC (Southern California Renewal Communities).
Delange, Maurice '71 (COV) Leave of Absence.
Delano, Kenneth J. '60 (FR) Retired.
De La Pena, Jose Manuel (NEW) East Boston, MA Our Lady of the Assumption; On Duty Outside the Archdiocese
DeLaPena, Richard (NY) Castle Point, NY Veterans Administration Medical Center.
De La Pena, Rick '82 (NY) Kingston, NY St. Joseph.
De la Pena, Udarico (MO).
De La Pinera, Fernando '51 (NO) Retired.
de la Puebla, Tomas *c.m.* '58 (ARE) Manati, PR La Candelaria.
De Lara, Miguel Diaz '95 (TLS) Tulsa, OK SS. Peter and Paul.
Delargy, Torlach C. '66 (SFR).
De La Riva, John *o.f.m.cap.* '99 (SFR)[R] Burlingame, CA Our Lady of Angels.
Delarm, Curtis R. '89 (HBG) Harrisburg, PA St. Catherine Laboure.
De La Rosa, Jose Luis '84 (SAT) San Antonio, TX St. Vincent de Paul; Air National Guard Chaplains.
De La Rosa, Vincent '55 (SAT) On Leave.
de la Rosa Peguero, Frank '78 (SJN) Carolina, PR San Francisco de Asis.
Delarue, Louis '75 (BEA) Nederland, TX St. Charles Borromeo.
de La Torre, Alejandro '89 (SAT) San Antonio, TX St. Joseph.
de la Torre, Bartholomew *o.p.* '67 (SAC) Benicia, CA St. Dominic.
De La Torre, Gerardo '87 (TUC) San Luis, AZ St. Jude Thaddeus.
de la Torre, Jorge Luis *m.s.c.* '97 (FRS) Earlimart, CA St. Jude Thaddeus; Tipton, CA St. John The Evangelist.
Delauney, Herbert C. '75 (LAF) Absent on Sick Leave.
De Laura, Felice J. '63 (BRK) Woodhaven, NY St. Thomas Apostle.
Delay, Donald R. '83 (BO) Walpole, MA St. Mary.
DeLazzer, Dorino '59 (DEN) Boulder, CO Sacred Heart of Mary.
Delbel, James A. '81 (OG) Willsboro, NY St. Joseph; Willsboro, NY St. Philip of Jesus; Mineville, NY.
del Burgo, Lucio *o.c.d.* '73 (MIA)[M] Miami, FL Discalced Carmelite Friars of Miami, Inc..
del Cerro, Helios *c.m.* '61 (LA) Los Angeles, CA Our Lady of the Rosary of Talpa.
Delclos, John A. '71 (BAL) Baltimore, MD St. Bernardine.
Del Conte, Eugene A. *o.s.a.* '55 (MIL)[O] Racine, WI Augustinian Novitiate.
DelConte, Eugene *o.s.a.* '55 (MIL) Racine, WI St. Rita.
DelDuca, John A. '68 (CAM) Hammonton, NJ St. Martin de Porres; Members.
DeLeers, Stephen V. '84 (MIL) On Leave.
DeLeers, Vincent J. *o.praem.* '46 (SFE)[I] Albuquerque, NM Santa Maria de la Vid Priory.
DeLeeuw, John '44 (LAF) Retired.
Delehanty, Thomas F. '41 (SPR) Retired.
de Leis, Sean *c.s.sp.* '81 (PMB) Fort Pierce, FL St. Mark.
DeLellis, Francis V. '49 (PRO) Retired.
Delelse, Salvatore '66 (CAM) Retired.
Delendick, John '77 (BRK) Brooklyn, NY St. Michael's.
Delendick, John (BRK) Fire Department.
Delendick, John (BRK) Diocesan Real Estate Board.
DeLeo, Roy James '69 (NEW) Elizabeth, NJ St. Genevieve's.
DeLeon, Benedict '80 (SAC) Oroville, CA St. Thomas the Apostle.
DeLeon, Benedict (SAC) Council of Priests.
DeLeon, Benedict (SAC) Vicars Forane.
deLeon, Cezar '88 (OAK) Pinole, CA St. Joseph's.
DeLeon, Eddie *c.m.f.* '91 (SPC)[I] Springfield, MO O'Reilly Catholic Student Center, Southwest MO State University, Drury College, Ozarks Technical Com.
DeLeon, Eddie *c.m.f.* '91 (SPC)[E] Springfield, MO Claretians Missionaries' Residence–Villa Claret.
DeLeon, Eddie *c.m.f.* (SPC) Campus Ministries.
DeLeon, Edward *o.m.i.* '80 (SAT)[M] San Antonio, TX Joseph Gerard House.
DeLeon, Edward *o.m.i.* '80 (SAT)[M] San Antonio, TX.
DeLeon, Edward *o.m.i.* '80 (SAT)[U] San Antonio, TX Oblate Missions.
de Leon, Jose A. '81 (CGS) Barranquitas, PR San Andres Apostol.
DeLeon, Juancho G. '94 (NEW) Bloomfield, NJ St. Valentine.
DeLeon, Marco Tulio '01 (PMB) Port St. Lucie, FL St. Lucie.
De Leon, Michael '86 (LAR) Laredo, TX Divine Mercy.
DeLeon, Michael (LAR) Charismatic Renewal.
de Leon, Robert E. *c.s.c.* '85 (ALB) Albany Medical Center Hospital.
deLeon, Robert E. *c.s.c.* '85 (ALB)[L] Valatie, NY St. Joseph Center.
De Leonardis, Gerard *o.f.m.cap.* '49 (NY)[B] Beacon, NY St. Lawrence of Brindisi Friary.
Delgado, Alfonso *ss.cc.* '95 (GAL) Houston, TX St. Ambrose.
Delgado, Alvaro H. '02 (STO) Modesto, CA Our Lady of Fatima Church (Pastor of).
Delgado, Enrique '96 (MIA) Key Largo, FL St. Justin Martyr.
Delgado, Jose D. *c.s.b.* '01 (GAL)[Q] Sugar Land Basilian Mission Center.
Delgado, Joseph '95 (SJ) On Leave of Absence.
Delgado, Julio *c.ss.r.* (WDC)[M] Washington, DC Holy Redeemer College.
Delgado, Lenin (NY) New York, NY Most Holy Redeemer.
Delgado, Leslie N. '55 (LA) Los Angeles, CA Our Lady of Guadalupe Sanctuary.
Delgado, Manuel Rodriguez *c.ss.r.* '71 (SJN) San Juan, PR San Agustin.
Delgado, Rodolfo '82 (SAC) Gridley, CA Sacred Heart.
Delgado, Rodolfo (SAC) Pro–Synodal Judges.
Delgado, Rodolfo (SAC) Council of Priests.
Del Giudice, Carl '81 (CHL) Brevard, NC Sacred Heart.
Delich, David L. *o.p.* '63 (STL)[O] St. Louis, MO St. Dominic Priory.
De Lillio, Richard R. *o.s.f.s.* '66 (WIL)[J] Wilmington, DE Oblates of St. Francis De Sales.
de Lima, Jose Alfonso '91 (FR) South Yarmouth, MA St. Pius Tenth.
Deliman, Edward M. '73 (PH) West Chester, PA St. Agnes.
Delis, Robert *s.d.b.* '79 (SFR)[N] Oceanside, CA; Navy Chaplains.
Delisi, Anthony *o.c.s.o.* '54 (ATL)[K] Conyers, GA The Monastery of the Holy Spirit.
Delisle, Eric T. '03 (MAN) Keene, NH St. Bernard; Keene, NH St. Anthony.

DeLisle, Henri A. *o.m.i.* '58 (NOR)[K] Colebrook, NH Shrine of Our Lady of Grace.
Dell, Robert S. *c.o.* '90 (CHR)[E] Rock Hill, SC Oratory of St. Philip Neri, Congregation of the Oratory of Pontifical Rite.
Dell, Robert *c.o.* '90 (SEA)[L] Seattle, WA Seattle Oratory.
Dell'Anno, Anthony V. '69 (BRK) Brooklyn, NY St. Bernadette.
DellaBadia, Leonard *c.s.s.* '35 (NY) White Plains, NY Our Lady of Mt. Carmel.
Della Neve, Louis '52 (BUF) Retired.
De Llano, Domingo '68 (CC) Retired.
della Picca, Angelo A. '45 (CIN)[D] Cincinnati, OH College of Mount St. Joseph.
della Picca, Paul B. '59 (ALN) Bethlehem, PA Our Lady of Pompeii.
DellaPietra, Douglas '96 (ROC) Henrietta, NY Church of the Good Shepherd.
Delli Carpini, John J. '76 (PH) Absent on Leave.
Dello Russo, John F. *o.s.a.* '87 (NY) Bronx, NY St. Nicholas of Tolentine.
Dellos, Richard E. '68 (SY) Utica, NY St. George; Utica, NY St. Joseph and St. Patrick.
Dell'Oro, Italo *c.r.s.* '82 (GAL) Houston, TX Christ the King.
Del Monaco, Marian *o.s.b.* '66 (P)[L] St. Benedict, OR Mt. Angel Abbey.
Delmonte, Albert '64 (ROC) Rochester, NY Holy Ghost.
Delmore, Eugene P. *s.j.* '69 (FBK) Bethel, AK Immaculate Conception; [E] St. Marys, AK Brother Joe Prince Jesuit Community.
DeLong, Allen *s.m.* '77 (HON)[G] Honolulu, HI Center Marianist Community.
DeLong, James Allen *s.m.* '77 (HON)[C] Honolulu, HI Saint Louis School.
Delonnay, Lawrence '75 (DET) Waterford, MI Our Lady of the Lakes.
DeLora, John P. '94 (NY) Staten Island, NY Holy Rosary.
DeLora, John (NY) Staten Island University Hospital North.
DeLorenzo, John R. '76 (SY) Syracuse, NY St. John the Baptist.
DeLorme, R. Daniel '57 (SY) Homer, NY St. Margaret.
Delos, Bernard M. '45 (ALB) Retired.
de los Reyes, Joel '75 (AGN) Barrigada, GU San Vicente Ferrer.
delos Reyes, Joel (AGN) Cursillo in Christianity.
de los Reyes, Joselito '91 (CLV) Cleveland, OH Holy Rosary.
De Los Rios, Enrique (LA) Los Angeles, CA St. Alphonsus.
De los Santos, Ernesto '93 (FWT) Fort Worth, TX All Saints.
De Los Santos, Jorge (DEN) Centro San Juan Diego.
de Loza, Jose '87 (YAK) Mattawa, WA Our Lady of the Desert; Diocesan Consultors.
Del Prete, Frank G. '77 (NEW) Hoboken, NJ SS. Peter and Paul's; Judicial Vicar Archdiocesan Metropolitan Tribunal; Archdiocesan Incardination Board; Judicial Vicar.
del Riego, Rutilio J. *d.l.p.* '65 (SB) Riverside, CA Our Lady of Perpetual Help.
del Toro, Alfredo *m.c.c.j.* '86 (CHI) Chicago, IL St. Michael the Archangel.
Del Toro, Alfredo *m.c.c.j.* '86 (CHI)[N] La Grange Park, IL Comboni Missionaries.
Del Toro, Jose L. *t.o.r.* (MO) Air Force Chaplains.
DeLuca, Albert J. '57 (NY) Retired.
De Luca, Albert '57 (NY) New York, NY Sacred Hearts of Jesus and Mary.
DeLuca, Albert (NY) Judges.
De Luca, Albert (NY) Defender of the Bond.
DeLuca, Anthony '53 (PIT) Retired.
DeLuca, David *m.s.c.* '66 (Y)[A] Center Valley, PA Sacred Heart Villa, Missionaries of the Sacred Heart.
DeLuca, Paul F. '81 (CIN) Dayton, OH St. Helen.
DeLuca, Stephen J. '65 (BGP) Greenwich, CT St. Agnes.
DeLucca, Daniel N. (PH).
DeLucia, Gerald M. '78 (Y)[A] Lowellville, OH Our Lady of the Holy Rosary.
DeLucia, Gerald (Y) College of Consultors.
DeLucia, Vincent G. *o.p.* '94 (PRO)[P] Providence St. Thomas Aquinas Priory at Providence College.
Deluney, Gerald C. '69 (SB) Corona, CA Corpus Christi Church.
Del Valle, Thomas '79 (NY) New York, NY Holy Cross.
Del Valle, Tomas '79 (SJN) On Duty Outside the Archdiocese.
Delvard, Quesnel *s.d.b.* '03 (WDC) Washington, DC Nativity.
Del Vecchio, Joseph *s.s.j.* '72 (BAL) Baltimore, MD St. Pius V.
Del Vecchio, Joseph *s.s.j.* '72 (BAL) Baltimore, MD St. Peter Claver.
DelVecchio, Michael E. '54 (BUF) Retired.
Delzell, David G. '50 (TR) Retired.
Delzingaro, Richard M. *c.r.s.p., m.a.* '96 (ALN)[K] Bethlehem, PA The Barnabite Fathers Barnabite Spiritual Center.
de M. Pereira, Luciano J. '54 (FR) Somerset, MA St. John of God Retired.
DeMaio, Joseph *o.carm.* '65 (ROC)[B] Rochester, NY McQuaid Jesuit High School.
DeMaio, Joseph *o.carm.* '65 (ROC)[I] Rochester, NY Whitefriars Priory.
DeMan, Thomas *o.p.* '62 (P)[N] McKenzie Bridge, OR St. Benedict Lodge Dominican Retreat & Conference Center.
DeManuele, James *c.p.* '78 (L)[K] Louisville, KY Sacred Heart Retreat.
Demarais, Garvin J. '81 (OG) Altona, NY Altona Correctional Facility; Malone, NY Franklin Correctional Facility; Malone, NY Upstate Correctional Facility; Advocates.
DeMarco, Peter A. '60 (BGP) Trumbull, CT St. Catherine of Siena; Deaf, Apostolate for.
DeMaria, Lawrence A. '51 (NO) Retired.
DeMarinis, John H. '62 (Y) Youngstown, OH St. Anthony's.
DeMarinis, John (Y) College of Consultors.
DeMartini, Rodney (SR) AIDS Ministry Outreach.
DeMartinis, Michael G. '97 (E) Erie, PA Blessed Sacrament.
De Martinis, O. Robert '86 (ALB) Schenectady, NY Immaculate Conception.
DeMartino, Robert J. '92 (ARL) Washington, VA St. Peter.
Demasi, Michael A. '43 (BUR) Retired.
DeMattia, John '68 (PAT) Whippany, NJ Our Lady of Mercy.
DeMayo, John B. '61 (PH) Pocono Pines, PA Our Lady of the Lake Retired.
deMayo, Martin P. '03 (BGP) Stratford, CT St. Mark.
Demeck, Norman *c.p.* '52 (MET)[H] Lakewood, NJ Georgian Institution.
Demeck, Norman *c.p.* '52 (TR)[A] Lakewood, NJ Georgian Court College.
DeMeersman, Clement *c.i.c.m.* '52 (FgM).
Demek, Martin H. '75 (BAL) Baltimore, MD St. William of York.
Demers, Bertrand '48 (KNX)[B] Knoxville, TN St. Mary's Health System, Inc..
Demers, Donald (FR)[H] Fairhaven, MA Sacred Hearts Provincial House.
Demers, Francis L. *o.m.i.* (MAN) Diocesan Judges.
Demers, Francis *o.m.i.* '55 (BO)[Y] Tewksbury, MA Immaculate Heart of Mary Infirmary.
Demers, Normand J. '58 (PRO) Absent on Leave.
Demers, Paul R. *s.c.* '81 (MAN)[B] Nashua, NH Rivier College.
Demers, Raymond A. '55 (MAN) Retired.
Demers, Richard D. '83 (OG) Absent on Sick Leave.
Demers, Richard '83 (OG) Massena, NY St. Mary.
Demers, Thomas *o.p.* '39 (PRT)[I] Lewiston SS. Peter and Paul House.
Demers, Wilfred G. '59 (MAN) Retired.
Demers, Wilfred '55 (MAN) Manchester, NH St. Marie.
Demets, Laurent *f.s.s.p.* '00 (ATL) Mableton, GA St. Francis De Sales; [M] Vienna, OH.
DeMeulemeester, Patrick '95 (PEO) Rock Island, IL St. Mary; Rock Island, IL St. Joseph's.
DeMeulenaere, Martin *o.s.b.* '73 (KC) Kansas City, MO Cathedral of Immaculate Conception.
DeMeulenaere, Martin *o.s.b.* '73 (KC)[J] Kansas City, MO.
Demkiv, Ivan '92 (PHU) Press, The Way; Philadelphia, PA St. Nicholas.
Demko, Dennis *c.ss.r.* '80 (PH) Philadelphia, PA St. Peter the Apostle.
Demko, James J. '82 (PSC) Beaver Meadows, PA SS. Peter and Paul.
Demkovich, John J. '65 (PAT) Passaic, NJ Assumption of the Blessed Virgin Mary; Pro–Synodal Judges; Mission Office; Legion of Mary.
Demkovich, Michael T. *o.p.* '81 (SFE) Albuquerque, NM St. Thomas Aquinas University Parish; [M] Albuquerque, NM Dominican Ecclesial Institute; Ecumenical Commission and Inter–Religious Affairs.
Deml, Francis S. '57 (DEN) Retired.
Demmer, Donald '73 (DET) Garden City, MI St. Dunstan.
Demo, John M. '88 (OG) Burke, NY St. George; Chateaugay, NY St. Patrick.
DeMolen, Richard '98 (RNO) Zephyr Cove, NV Our Lady of Tahoe.
DeMolen, Richard (RNO) Respect Life Core Committee.
de Morchoven, Werner Papeians *o.s.b.* '38 (LA)[Q] Valyermo, CA St. Andrew's Abbey.
DeMott, Lester T. *c.m.* '44 (PH).
De Mott, Stephen T. *m.m.* '76[AA] (FgM).
Dempsey, Dennis '80 (STP) St. Paul, MN St. James.
Dempsey, Dennis '80 (STP) St. Paul, MN St. Francis De Sales.
Dempsey, Edward M. '67 (NOR) Absent on Leave.
Dempsey, James '56 (BEA) Retired.
Dempsey, John G. '64 (STL) Florissant, MO St. Ferdinand; Archdiocesan Consultors.
Dempsey, Michael J. '58 (BRK) Forest Hills, NY Our Lady, Queen of Martyrs; Pastoral Communications, Office of.
Dempsey, Nicholas '71 (SD) San Diego, CA St. William of York.
Dempsey, Patrick '97 (WDC) Washington, DC St. Patrick.
Dempsey, Robert J. '80 (CHI) Northfield, IL St. Philip the Apostle.
Dempsey, Sean *s.j.* (LA)[C] Los Angeles, CA Jesuit Community.
Dempsey, Terrence E. *s.j.* '85 (STL)[C] Saint Louis University; [O] St. Louis, MO Jesuit Community Corporation at St. Louis University – Jesuit Hall.
Dempsey, Thomas J. '61 (RCK) Crystal Lake, IL St. Elizabeth Ann Seton.
Dempsey, Thomas J. '62 (STL) Ballwin, MO Holy Infant.
Dempski, Daniel G. *o.s.b.* '79 (MAN)[K] Manchester, NH St. Anselm Abbey.
Demse, Thomas P. '76 (MIL) Hartland, WI St. Charles.
Demski, Arthur A. '54 (BRK) Retired.
Demski, Ronald G. '69 (TYL) Gladewater, TX St. Theresa of the Infant Jesus.
DeMuro, S. Patrick '85 (HRT) Retired.
DeMuro, Salvatore (HRT) CIVIL AIR PATROL.
Demuth, George R. '46 (SCR) Retired.
Demuth, Paul E. '68 (GB) Green Bay, WI Resurrection.
Demuth, Paul (GB) Priests' Personnel Board.
Demyanets, Vitaliy '98 (PHU) Carteret, NJ St. Mary's.
De Nard, Silvio *s.c.* '79 (PH)[B] Springfield, PA Don Guanella House of Formation.
DeNardi, Charles A. '36 (OWN) Retired.
Denburger, John J. *o.c.s.o.* '63 (ROC)[I] Piffard, NY Abbey of the Genesee.
Dendinger, Robert L. '75 (TOL) New Washington, OH St. Bernard; New Washington, OH Mother of Sorrows.
Dendinger, William J. '65 (OM) Omaha, NE St. Stephen the Martyr; Consultors; Ex Officio.
Dendinger, William (OM) Age Groups.
Dene, Charles J. '58 (ALN) Shenandoah, PA St. Mary Magdalen; FCI–Schuylkill, Federal Correctional Institute.
Dene, Joseph '62 (WH) Retired.
Deneault, Normand J. '45 (PRO)[P] Providence St. John Vianney Residence Retired.
Denemark, Emil J. *s.j.* '81 (FgM).
Denemark, Emil J. *s.j.* (MO) Army Reserve Chaplains.
Denesha, J. Everett '50 (OG) Raymondville, NY St. Raymond.
DeNguyen, Thomas '98 (ORG) Anaheim, CA St. Boniface.
Denha, Suleiman '59 (EST) Oak Park, MI Mar Addai Chaldean Parish.
Denha, Suleiman (EST) Eparchial College of Consultors.
Den Hallegado, Salvador '03 (CHI) Mundelein, IL St. Mary of the Annunciation.
Denig, Philip P. '85 (DEN) On Duty Outside the Archdiocese; Army Chaplains.
Denig, Stephen J. *c.m.* '75 (BUF)[O] Niagara University, NY Vincentian Community at Niagara University; [C] Niagara University, NY Niagara University.
Deniger, Joseph L. *c.s.sp.* '58 (SB) Hemet, CA Our Lady of the Valley; [E] Hemet, CA Our Lady of the Valley.
DeNinno, Dale E. '78 (PIT) Pittsburgh, PA Immaculate Conception–St. Joseph.
DeNinno, Louis L. '76 (PIT) Pittsburgh, PA Holy Wisdom; Defenders of the Bond.
Denison, Frederick J. '73 (IND) Depauw, IN St. Bernard; Depauw, IN St. Joseph.
Denk, Kurt M. *s.j.* (BAL)[B] Timonium, MD Loyola Graduate Center –Timonium Campus; [S] Baltimore, MD Jesuit Community of Loyola College, Inc..
Denman, Donald '42 (P) Retired.
Denn, James J. *c.s.c.* '61 (FTW)[I] New Orleans, LA Sacred Heart of Jesus Parish.
Denn, James *c.s.c.* '61 (NO) New Orleans, LA Sacred Heart of Jesus.
Dennehy, John D. '81 (NEW)[B] School of Diplomacy and Intl. Rels..
Dennehy, Mark M. *o.s.m.* '46 (CHI)[N] Chicago Order of Friar Servants of Mary (Servites) United States of America Province, Inc..
Dennehy, Martin J. '51 (BGP) Retired.
Dennemann, Thomas J. '73 (CIN) Cincinnati, OH St. Ann.
Dennerlein, Arno A. '69 (JOL) Lombard, IL Sacred Heart.
Dennerlein, John L. '74 (JOL) Shorewood, IL Holy Family.
Denning, John F. *c.s.c.* '87 (FR)[A] North Easton, MA Stonehill College; [A] North Easton, MA Holy Cross Fathers Religious.
Denning, Joseph B. '60 (DAV) Camanche, IA Church of the Visitation; Judges.
Dennis, George *s.j.* '54 (LA)[C] Los Angeles, CA Jesuit Community.
Dennis, John J. *o.s.f.s.* '45 (PH)[AA] Philadelphia, PA Father Louis Brisson Residence.
Dennis, John M. *s.j.* '86 (BAL)[D] Baltimore, MD

Loyola Blakefield.
Dennis, Patrick '78 (B) Absent on Leave.
Dennis, Peter K. *ss.cc.* '62 (LA)[Q] La Verne, CA Congregation of the Sacred Hearts of Jesus and Mary.
Dennis, Sam *o.s.b.* '57 (SFE)[I] Pecos, NM Our Lady of Guadalupe Abbey.
Dennis, Samuel *o.s.b.* '57 (SFE)[K] Pecos, NM Our Lady of Guadalupe Olivetan Benedictine Abbey.
Dennis, Thomas J. '92 (SFD) Graduate Studies.
Dennis, Thomas (SFD) Chicago, IL St. Clement.
Dennison, Arthur '73 (MIA) Coral Gables, FL Little Flower.
Denniston, John '79 (RVC) Huntington, NY St. Patrick's.
Denny, Charles J. '69 (TOL) Martin, OH Our Lady of Mt. Carmel; Oregon, OH St. Charles Mercy Hospital; [G] Oregon, OH St. Charles Mercy Hospital.
Denny, David '80 (PBL)[I] Crestone, CO Spiritual Life Institute of America, Inc..
Denny, John T. *o.s.a.* '90 (PH)[C] Villanova University; [AA] Villanova, PA Fray de Leon Community.
Denny, Joseph P. '67 (PH) Philadelphia, PA St. Bartholomew.
Denny, Thomas F. *s.j.* '68 (NY)[EE] New York, NY St. Ignatius Loyola Residence.
Deno, Lawrence M. '59 (OG) Cadyville, NY St. James Church.
DeNoble, Augustine *o.s.b.* '55 (P)[L] St. Benedict, OR Mt. Angel Abbey.
Denomme, George E. '48 (WOR) Leominster, MA St. Cecilia's.
Dente, Thomas A. '93 (NEW) Hillsdale, NJ St. John the Baptist; Worship Office.
Denti, Carl J. '42 (SY) Retired.
Dentici, Thomas '53 (DEN) Retired.
Dentinger, Roy E. '50 (L) Retired.
Dentinger, Vincent Paul '54 (L) Retired.
Denys, Charles *c.i.c.m.* '44 (ARL)[J] Arlington, VA Missionhurst, C.I.C.M.–Central House and Provincialate.
Denzel, F. William *o.m.i.* '55 (BO)[Y] Tewksbury, MA Immaculate Heart of Mary Infirmary.
Denzer, Joseph W. '68 (BRK) On Leave/Unassigned; [A] Douglaston, NY Immaculate Conception Center.
Denzer, Thomas F. *s.j.* '61 (STL)[N] St. Louis, MO Fusz Pavilion; [O] St. Louis, MO Jesuit Community Corporation at St. Louis University – Jesuit Hall.
De Oca, Jose Monte '96 (NEW) Jersey City, NJ St. Aloysius.
de Oliveira, Pedro *o.f.m.conv.* (ATL) Jonesboro, GA St. Philip Benizi.
deOtero, Roberto '77 (HON) Leave of Absence.
DePalma, Michael '03 (SFE) Rio Rancho, NM St. Thomas Aquinas.
DePaoli, Edward M. '70 (PH) Absent on Leave.
De Pascale, Daniel '61 (ALB) Retired.
DePasquale, Dominic '61 (SB) Retired.
DePasquale, Leonard *i.m.c.* '71 (MET)[H] Somerset, NJ Consolata Society for Foreign Missions.
DePasquale, Leonard *i.m.c.* '71 (MET)[O] Somerset, NJ Mission International, Inc..
Depatie, Donald L. '78 (PRO) Cumberland, RI St. Aidan.
De Paula, Cristobal '02 (MIA) Coral Springs, FL St. Andrew.
Depcik, Michael *o.s.f.s.* (LAN) Ministry with Persons with Disabilities/Deaf Ministry/Catholic Inquiry for the Blind.
Depeaux, Bernard F. '50 (BUR) Promoter of Justice Retired.
De Peaux, Rowland C. *o.praem.* '51 (GB)[I] De Pere, WI St. Joseph Priory.
DePenning, Bruce '01 (COS)[C] Colorado Springs, CO Penrose Community Hospital.
de Peralta, Miquel Grave '96 (SAV)[E] Augusta, GA St. Joseph Hospital, Augusta, GA, Inc..
DePew, Daniel R. '85 (GR) Alpine, MI Holy Trinity.
DePietro, Arthur J. '63 (BO) Senior Priests Retired.
Depinet, Robert L. *m.m.* '61 (FgM).
DePinto, Basil '58 (OAK) Piedmont, CA Corpus Christi.
DePinto, Basil '58 (OAK) Highland Hospital.
DePinto, Basil '58 (OAK) Retired.
Depman, Francis J. '81 (PH) West Grove, PA Assumption B.V.M..
Deponai, Joseph J. '83 (NY) Military Chaplains; Army Chaplains.
DePorres–Cox, Jesse *o.p.* '87 (DET) Special Assignment.
de Porres Walsh, Martin *o.p.* '69 (LA) Los Angeles, CA St. Dominic.
DePorter, Arnold W. '63 (WDC) Suitland, MD St. Bernardine.
DePra, Italo '51 (P) Retired.
DePriest, Ellis L. *s.m.* '53 (NO) New Orleans, LA Byzantine Catholic Mission; [P] New Orleans, LA Marist Fathers.
De Priest, Ellis *s.m.* '53 (PBR) New Orleans, LA St. Nicholas of Myra Mission.
DeProfio, Louis A. '56 (BGP) Diocesan Consultors; Parochial Examiners; Retired Priests.
DeProspero, Nicholas '70 (PSC) Pottstown, PA St. John the Baptist; Retirement Plan Board.
Deptula, Stanley L. '96 (PEO) Wenona, IL St. Mary's; Vicariates and Vicars; Associate Directors.
Deptula, Stanley '96 (PEO) Wenona, IL St. John the Baptist's; Minonk, IL St. Patrick's.
de Ramos, Fidel A. '64 (WDC) Silver Spring, MD St. Michael.
de Ranitz, Richard *o.p.* '70 (CHI)[N] Chicago Dominicans (Provincial Office).
Derasmo, John M. '81 (RVC) Farmingville, NY Church of the Resurrection.
Derasmo, John (RVC) Procurator & Advocates.
Derbes, Louis J. *c.m.* '51 (STL)[O] Perryville, MO Congregation of the Mission.
Derbish, Michael *o.f.m.* '62 (SJP) Aliquippa, PA Ss. Peter and Paul.
Derbyshire, Joseph V. '46 (NEW) Retired.
Derbyshire, Joseph '46 (NEW)[N] Rutherford, NJ St. John Vianney Residence for Priests.
Derbyshire, Joseph (NEW) Serra Clubs.
DeRea, Philip *m.s.c.* '68 (ALN)[K] Reading, PA Missionaries of the Sacred Heart.
DeRea, Philip *m.s.c.* '68 (WDC)[V] Washington, DC Missionary Vehicle Association, Inc..
Deresienski, Stanley *s.s.e.* '78 (BUR) Elected Members; Brattleboro, VT St. Michael.
Derfus, Kenneth J. '56 (MIL) Retired.
Dericks, John H. '41 (PAT) Retired.
Derise, Mark '97 (LAF) Evangeline, LA St. Joseph.
DeRiso, John *c.s.c.* '02 (PHX) Goodyear, AZ Saint John Vianney.
DeRitis, Gilbert J. *m.m.* '54 (SJ)[M] Los Altos, CA Maryknoll.
Derivan, Thomas B. '72 (NY) Bronx, NY St. Helena.
Derivaux, Don '55 (JKS) Mound Bayou, MS St. Gabriel.
Derivaux, Don '55 (JKS) Shelby, MS St. Mary.
Derivaux, Don (JKS) Approved Advocate and Auditors.
Derivaux, Donald F. '55 (JKS) Shaw, MS St. Francis of Assisi Retired.
DeRivera, Sonny *s.v.d.* '81 (CHI)[B] Techny, IL Divine Word Residence.
Dermody, Michael '62 (SAC) Retired.
Dermody, Thomas '62 (SAC) Retired.
Dermond, John K. '68 (TR) Trenton, NJ St. Mary Cathedral; Trenton, NJ St. Francis of Assisium; [T] Trenton, NJ The Haitian Community Center; Assistant Chancellors; Judicial Vicar; The Haitian Apostolate.
Dermott, William R. '82 (ALN) Navy Chaplains.
Dernbach, Arthur '53 (P) Retired.
Dernek, Daniel R. '62 (WIN) Winona, MN St. Stanislaus.
Dernek, Richard J. '70 (WIN) Blooming Prairie, MN St. Columbanus; Blooming Prairie, MN Sacred Heart.
DeRoche, Wilfred L. '65 (OG) Retired.
De Rosa, Arnold P. '63 (NEW)[B] School of Diplomacy and Intl. Rels. Retired.
deRosa, Francis M. '97 (ARL) Alexandria, VA St. Louis.
DeRose, Martin '88 (ALB) Special Assignment.
DeRose, Martin '88 (ALB) Greenfield Center, NY St. Joseph.
DeRosia, Volney J. '03 (MAN) Exeter, NH St. Michael.
Derosier, Edmond M. '73 (BO) Shirley, MA St. Anthony.
De Rouchey, Gary K. '02 (SFS) Army Reserve Chaplains.
DeRouen, Keith J. '83 (LAF) Lafayette, LA Cathedral of St. John the Evangelist.
DeRouen, Keith (LAF) Worship.
DeRouen, Robert R. *s.j.* '54 (DEN)[N] Denver, CO Xavier Jesuit Center.
Derrane, Mark G. '95 (BO) Lynnfield, MA Our Lady of the Assumption; Army National Guard Chaplains.
Derrenbacher, James W. '45 (NY) Saugerties, NY St. John the Evangelist Retired.
Derrera, A. Ferdinand *s.j.* '61 (GAL)[F] Houston, TX Strake, Jesuit College Preparatory Inc..
Derrig, Joseph M. '63 (PH) Broomall, PA St. Pius X.
Derry, Daniel '53 (SJ) Gilroy, CA St. Mary.
Derry, Daniel (SJ) Building Committee.
Derwinski, Victor A. '44 (LIN) Retired.
Dery, Henry R. '48 (HRT)[A] Bloomfield CT St. Thomas Seminary Retired.
Derylo, Walter W. '68 (GAY) Special Assignment.
Derzack, Thomas A. '76 (ALN) Lansford, PA St. Ann; Lansford, PA St. Michael; Lansford, PA SS. Peter and Paul.
DeSa, Walter *o.s.f.s.* (FgM).
DeSalvia, Michele *c.s.* (CHI) Melrose Park, IL St. Charles Borromeo.
DeSalvo, Donald D. '69 (RCK) Somonauk, IL St. John the Baptist.
DeSalvo, Raphael *o.s.b.* '45 (LR).
DeSalvo, Raphael *o.s.b.* '45 (LR)[K] New Blaine, AR St. Scholastica's
DeSalvo, William '88 (JOL) Westmont, IL Holy Trinity.
Desam, Thomas Augustine '94 (SCR) Dunmore, PA St. Mary of Mount Carmel.
DeSanctis, Albert '80 (SAL) Tipton, KS St. Boniface's.
DeSanctis, Albert (SAL) Board of Trustees.
DeSanctis, Peter A. '79 (BRK) Bayside, NY Our Lady of the Blessed Sacrament; Army Reserve Chaplains.
DeSandre, John G. '64 (TR) Deal, NJ St. Mary of the Assumption.
De Santi, Bruno *c.s.j.* '51 (LA) San Pedro, CA St. Peter.
DeSantis, Joseph A. '75 (ALN) Reading, PA Sacred Heart; College of Consultors.
DeSantis, Linus *o.f.m.conv.* '71 (ATL) Lithia Springs, GA St. John Vianney; Lithia Springs, GA St. John Vianney.
DeSantis, Linus *o.f.m.conv.* '71 (ATL)[N] Kennesaw, GA Kennesaw State University.
De Santis, Linus *o.f.m.conv.* '71 (ATL)[N] Kennesaw, GA.
DeSanto, John '54 (NY) On Duty Outside the Archdiocese.
DeSanto, Joseph A. '54 (NY) Larchmont, NY St. Augustine.
Desaulniers, Richard P. '70 (PRO) Manville, RI St. James; Council Members.
Desautels, Alfred R. *s.j.* '50 (WOR)[O] Worcester, MA Jesuits of Holy Cross College, Inc..
Desch, Paul *o.f.m.* '56 (CIN)[P] Cincinnati, OH Friarhurst Retreat Center.
Deschamps, Wilfred H. (MAN) Council of Priests; College of Consultors.
Deschamps, Wilfred '90 (MAN) Jaffrey, NH St. Patrick.
de Serpa, Roberto '46 (PRO) Retired.
Deshaies, Richard A. *s.j.* '92 (BO) Bridgeport, CT St. Ambrose; [P] Fairfield, CT The Fairfield Jesuit Community–Fairfield University; [V] Boston The Society of Jesus of New England–Provincial Offices.
Desharnais, Gary L. (YAK) Grandview, WA Blessed Sacrament; Mabton, WA Immaculate Conception.
Deshotel, Douglas '78 (DAL)[A] Irving, TX Holy Trinity Seminary.
Deshotel, J. Douglas (DAL) Presbyteral Council.
Deshotels, James M. *s.j.* '93 (NO)[C] New Orleans, LA Loyola University New Orleans; [O] New Orleans, LA Daughters of Charity Neighborhood Health Partnership.
DeSiano, Francis P. *c.s.p.* '72 (CHI) Chicago, IL Old St. Mary.
Desiderio, Frank *c.s.p.* '82 (LA) Pacific Palisades, CA Corpus Christi.
Desiderio, Frank *c.s.p.* '82 (LA)[CC] Pacific Palisades, CA Paulist Productions.
Desiderio, Frank *c.s.p.* '82 (LA) Los Angeles, CA St. Paul the Apostle.
Desilets, Viateur '46 (LAF) Retired.
deSilva, Helio '91 (TR) Long Branch, NJ St. John the Baptist.
DeSilva, L. Praxid '69 (NY) Briarcliff Manor, NY St. Theresa.
de Silva, Lionel A. *c.s.p.* '59 (NY) New York, NY Good Shepherd.
De Simonc, David A. '87 (NY) Port Jervis, NY Most Sacred Heart.
DeSimone, Russell J. *o.s.a.* '51 (PH)[AA] Villanova, PA St. Thomas Monastery.
DesJardins, Dominic '38 (SFR) Redwood City, CA Our Lady of Mount Carmel Retired.
Desjardins, George A. '59 (MAN) Retired.
Desjardins, James M. *s.j.* '77 (BAL).
Desjardins, Raymond S. '42 (MAN) Retired.
Deskevich, Andrew J. '97 (PBR)[S] Erie, PA SS. Peter and Paul.
Deskevich, Andrew (PBR) Revitalization and Renewal Commission.
Deslate, Jamie Noel '94 (BAL) Baltimore, MD St. Agnes.
DeSloover, A. Robert '74 (TOL) Miller City, OH St. Nicholas; Miller City, OH Holy Family.
Desmarais, Gerard R. '75 (MAN) Absent on Leave.
Desmarais, Paul E. '79 (PRO) Pawtucket, RI Sacred Heart of Jesus.
Desmarais, Rene L. '63 (DET) Port Huron, MI St. Joseph; [S] Port Huron, MI John Courtney Murray Newman Center.
Desmond, Barry '59 (MOB) Retired.
Desmond, David A. '02 (SFS) Sioux Falls, SD St. Joseph Cathedral; [C] Sioux Falls, SD O'Gorman High School; Army Reserve Chaplains.
Desmond, Donald J. '64 (RVC) East Hampton, NY Most Holy Trinity; Peconic Deanery.
Desmond, Hubert E. '58 (BO) Senior Priests Retired.
Desmond, Joseph E. '47 (MAN) Hudson, NH St. John the Evangelist Retired.
Desmond, Joseph L. '74 (MET) On Duty Outside the Diocese.
Desmond, Joseph '74 (NSH) Springfield, TN Our Lady of Lourdes.
Desmond, Joseph (NSH) Presbyteral Council and College of Consultors.
Desmond, Michael Finbar '40 (MOB)[E] Mobile, AL Little Sisters of the Poor, Home For the Aged, Inc..
Desmond, Michael J. '71 (NEW) Kearny, NJ St. Stephen's.
Desmond, Nicholas R. '84 (CHI) Chicago, IL St. Aloysius.
DeSocio, John A. (ROC) Navy Reserve Chaplains.
De Socio, John '78 (ROC) On Duty Outside the Diocese.
Desormeaux, Roland *c.s.* '82 (PMB) Our Lady of

Perpetual Help Mission.
DesOrmeaux, Scott '91 (LKC) De Quincy, LA Our Lady of La Salette.
DesOrmeaux, Scott '91 (LKC) Lake Charles Memorial Hospital.
DeSouza, Carl '66 (RIC) Farmville, VA St. Theresa.
de Souza, Owen '70 (LA) Carson, CA St. Philomena.
Desrochers, Timothy H. '64 (MAR)[F] Garden, MI Marygrove Retreat Center; Cursillo; Retreats.
DesRosiers, Denis A. '69 (OAK) Walnut Creek, CA St. Stephen.
DesRosiers, N. Wilfrid *s.s.j.* '55 (BAL)[S] Baltimore, MD St. Joseph Society of the Sacred Heart House of Central Administration Retired.
Desrosiers, Paul H. '75 (NO) Retired.
DesRosiers, Philip J. '66 (BO) Permanent Disability.
DesRosiers, Ronald *s.m.* '63 (DET)[K] Livonia, MI Marist Fathers & Brothers Community.
DesRuisseaux, Charles E. '60 (MAN) Manchester, NH St. Anthony of Padua.
Desruisseaux, G. Frantz '78 (BGP) Norwalk, CT St. Joseph; Episcopal Vicar for Haitians; Promoter of Justice.
Desso, Leo '79 (ANC) Palmer, AK St. Michael.
DeStefano, Richard A. '62 (BEA) Diocesan College of Consultors and Presbyteral Council; Building Commission, Diocesan; [H] Beaumont, TX The Catholic Foundation of the Diocese of Beaumont, Inc; Groves, TX St. Peter the Apostle Retired.
DeStephano, Mark T. *s.j.* '88 (NEW)[B] Jersey City, NJ Jesuit Center; [N] Jersey City, NJ Jesuits of Saint Peter's College, Inc..
DeSutter, Mark A. '82 (PEO) Morton, IL Blessed Sacrament.
DeSutter, Mark (PEO) Clergymen's Aid, Inc..
Detemple, Michael *o.p.* '81 (CIN) Cincinnati, OH St. Gertrude.
Detemple, Michael *o.p.* '81 (CIN)[M] Cincinnati, OH St. Gertrude Priory.
Determan, Joseph *o.p.* '51 (SAT) San Antonio, TX Methodist Hospital; [B] San Antonio, TX Dominican Priory of San Juan Macias and Novitiate.
Deters, Frederick J. *s.j.* '67 (IND)[D] Indianapolis, IN; [G] Beech Grove, IN St. Francis Hospital and Health Centers.
Deters, Gregory J. '87 (DET) Temperance, MI St. Anthony.
Detig, Joseph *s.v.d.* '62 (BLX)[A] Bay St. Louis, MS St. Augustine's.
Detisch, John J. '88 (E) Erie, PA Sacred Heart.
Detisch, Scott P. '87 (E) On Duty Outside Diocese.
Detisch, Scott '87 (BUF).
De Tomasi, Gerardo *m.c.c.j.* '63 (HON)[A] Lahaina, HI Maria Lanakila; Hispanic Ministry–Maui.
De Tommaso, Louis D. *o.f.m.* '54 (NY)[EE] New York, NY Franciscan Province of the Immaculate Conception; [EE] New York, NY Padua Friary.
DeTore, Richard H. *c.m.f.* '64 (PHX) Prescott, AZ Sacred Heart.
Detscher, Alan F. '71 (BGP) Riverside, CT St. Catherine of Siena.
Dettenwanger, Dennis '64 (CIN) Hamilton, OH St. Joseph.
Dettenwanger, Dennis '64 (CIN) Hamilton, OH St. Ann.
Dettling, William *o.p.* '59 (COL).
Dettmer, Alfred J. '56 (GRY) Retired.
Dettmer, David J. '80 (BRK)[A] Brooklyn, NY St. Bernadette; [G] Brooklyn, NY Xaverian.
Deutsch, Bernard F. '51 (STL) Retired.
Deutsch, Daniel J. '94 (RCK) Batavia, IL Holy Cross; Bishop's Secretary for Retired Priests; Diocesan Consultors; Clergy Relief Society, Priests' Retirement Committee.
Deutsch, George E. '57 (TR) Retired.
Deutsch, Marvin F. *m.m.* '57 (NY).
Deutsch, Paul *s.j.* '90 (NO)[P] New Orleans, LA Jesuit Provincial Office.
Deutsch, Paul *s.j.* '90 (NO)[F] New Orleans, LA Jesuit High School.
Deutsch, Timothy '94 (DUL) Youth Conservation Camp.
Deutsch, Timothy '94 (DUL) St. Isidore; Willow River, MN St. Mary's.
Deutschmann, Edward J. '52 (STL) Retired.
Deutschmann, Edward '52 (STL) St. Louis, MO Mary, Mother of the Church Retired.
Devadhason, Masilamony '94 (SD) Spring Valley, CA Santa Sophia.
Devane, John F. *s.j.* '52 (BO)[V] Weston, MA Campion Health Center, Inc..
Devaney, Michael J. *o.m.i.* '57 (COL) West Jefferson, OH SS. Simon and Jude; [H] West Jefferson, OH SS. Simon and Jude.
Devany, John *c.p.* '45 (DET)[K] Detroit, MI St. Paul of the Cross Community, Congregation of the Passion.
Devaraj, Peter '81 (RVC) Ronkonkoma, NY St. Joseph's.
Devassy, Joy Mankulam '82 (NY) New Rochelle, NY Holy Name of Jesus.
Deveau, Adhemar S. *o.m.i.* (BO) Lowell, MA Saint Jeanne d'Arc.
Deveau, Adhemar *o.m.i.* '52 (BO)[V] Lowell, MA Andre Garin Retirement Residence.
Deveau, Daniel R. '75 (MAN) Groveton, NH St. Francis Xavier; North Stratford, NH Sacred Heart.
Deveau, Daniel R. (BUR) Beecher Falls, VT Assumption of the Blessed Virgin Mary.
Deveau, Daniel '75 (MAN) Beecher Falls, VT St. Albert.
DeVeer, Richard S. (BO) Chelsea, MA St. Rose of Lima; Archdiocesan College of Consultors.
Develis, Mark *o.c.d.* '99 (MIL)[O] Holy Hill, WI Discalced Carmelite Monastery – Holy Hill National Shrine of Mary Help of Christians; Hubertus, WI St. Mary of the Hill.
Dever, Daniel J. '52 (HON)[I] Kaneohe, HI Augustine Educational Foundation Retired.
Dever, Daniel (HON) Ecumenical Commission.
Dever, Daniel (HON) Senior Priests' Committee.
Dever, Dennis A. '60 (BO) Medford, MA St. Clement.
Dever, James T. *o.s.f.s.* '73 (PH) Philadelphia, PA Our Mother of Consolation.
Dever, William '65 (MIA) Fort Lauderdale, FL St. Helen.
DeVera, Percival '91 (BRK) Ridgewood, NY St. Aloysius.
DeVera, Purcival (BRK) Wyckoff Heights Hospital.
Devereaux, Martin C. '54 (PMB) Retired.
Devereaux, Thomas W. '68 (SR) Healdsburg, CA St. John the Baptist; Ecumenical and Interreligious Affairs.
Devereux, James A. *s.j.* '58 (R)[M] Washington, DC The Jesuit Community at Georgetown University.
Devereux, Peter '99 (ATL)[K] Atlanta, GA Legionaries of Christ.
Devereux, Raymond P. '68 (CHI) Chicago, IL All Saints–St. Anthony.
Devereux, Thomas W. *o.s.b.* '59 (GBG)[H] Latrobe, PA Saint Vincent Archabbey.
deVerteuil, Jack '89 (FBK) Nenana, AK St. Theresa.
de Verteuil, Jack '89 (FBK) Healy, AK Holy Mary of Guadalupe.
Devery, Thomas P. '77 (NY) Staten Island, NY Holy Child.
de Vianney Guerra, Jesus *o.p.* '57 (NO)[P] Parroquia de Santiago Apostol.
DeVille, George T. '57 (PIT) Muse, PA Holy Rosary.
DeVille, William H. '62 (COL) Columbus, OH Our Lady of the Miraculous Medal; Priests' Senate.
Devine, Charles '65 (SB) Retired.
Devine, Charles '65 (SB) Idyllwild, CA Queen of Angels.
Devine, Daniel P. '65 (PH) Feasterville, PA Assumption B.V.M..
Devine, Donald G. *s.j.* '65 (PAT)[EE] New York, NY St. Ignatius Loyola Residence; [I] Morristown, NJ Loyola House of Retreats.
Devine, J. Donald *s.s.c.* '54 (OM)[K] St. Columbans, NE St. Columban's Foreign Mission Society.
Devine, J. Frank *s.j.* '54 (BO)[V] Weston, MA Campion Health Center, Inc..
Devine, James T. '60 (BRK) Jamaica, NY Our Lady of the Skies Chapel; Rockaway Beach, NY St. Rose of Lima.
Devine, Joseph A. '49 (HRT) Waterbury, CT Our Lady of Loreto; Priests Retirement Plan for Secular Priests of the Archdiocese of Hartford.
Devine, Joseph T. '80 (HRT) Hartford, CT St. Lawrence O'Toole; Deans.
Devine, Kevin A. *c.s.p.* '56 (NY) New York, NY Good Shepherd.
Devine, Michael F. '57 (SP) Clearwater, FL St. Brendan.
Devine, Patrick A. '69 (HBG) Bloomsburg, PA St. Columba; Consultors, College; Appointed.
Devine, Paul '63 (OAK) Apostleship of the Sea Retired.
Devine, Richard J. *c.m.* '55 (BRK)[V] Queens Village, NY DePaul Residence.
Devine, Stephen M. '64 (FRS) Hanford, CA Immaculate Heart of Mary.
Devine, Terry '85 (OWN) Waverly, KY Sacred Heart.
Devine, Terry '85 (OWN) Uniontown, KY St. Agnes.
Devine, Terry '85 (OWN) Waverly, KY St. Peter.
Devine, Thomas J. *o.a.r.* '68 (LSC) Anthony, NM St. Anthony's.
Devine, Thomas *o.a.r.* (LSC) Vicars.
Devine, Thomas *o.a.r.* (LSC) Presbyteral Council.
Devine, William B. '58 (SC) Retired.
Devine, William J. '73 (BO) Military & VA Chaplains.
Devine, William J. (CHI) Retired.
Devine, William P. '52 (DUB) Retired.
Deviney, Raymond L. '59 (SCR) Blakeslee, PA Christ the King.
Devino, Terrence P. '87 (BGP)[B] Fairfield, CT Fairfield University.
Devino, Terrence P. *s.j.* '02 (BGP)[P] Fairfield, CT The Fairfield Jesuit Community–Fairfield University.
Deviny, Edward *c.p.* '66 (R) Tarboro, NC St. Catherine.
De Vita, James C. '57 (RVC) Retired.
Devito, Darius *o.f.m.cap.* '57 (NY)[EE] Yonkers, NY St. Clare Friary.
DeVliegher, Joseph *c.s.c.* '68 (AUS) Bertram, TX Holy Cross.
DeVliegher, Joseph *c.s.c.* '68 (AUS) Burnet, TX Our Mother of Sorrows.
Devlin, Charles V. '55 (PH) College of Consultors; Council of Priests; Philadelphia, PA St. Joan of Arc Retired.
Devlin, David J. *o.s.f.s.* '77 (ALN) Robesonia, PA St. Francis de Sales.
Devlin, Francis X. *o.s.a.* '73 (PH)[D] Drexel Hill, PA Monsignor Bonner High School.
Devlin, James E. '72 (BRK) Brooklyn, NY Our Lady of Angels.
Devlin, Joseph D. *s.j.* '66 (BO)[V] Boston, MA Loyola House.
Devlin, Joseph M. '36 (NY) Bronx, NY St. Frances de Chantal Retired.
Devlin, Joseph P. '91 (PH) Philadelphia, PA St. Barnabas.
Devlin, Joseph '36 (NY) Bronx, NY St. Theresa of the Infant Jesus.
Devlin, Kevin '54 (OKL) Retired.
Devlin, Mark '79 (TR) Tuckerton, NJ St. Theresa.
Devlin, Michael H. '68 (SPR) Chicopee, MA Assumption; [H] Holyoke, MA Providence Place, Inc..
Devlin, Philip T. *c.s.c.* '56 (FTW).
Devlin, Philip T. *c.s.c.*[I] (FgM).
Devlin, Raymond A. *s.j.* '55 (SJ)[M] Los Gatos, CA Sacred Heart Jesuit Center.
Devlin, Vianney M. *o.f.m.* '55 (NY) New York, NY St. Stephen of Hungary.
Devoe, Richard M. *m.m.* '56 (FgM).
Devold, Cyprian '84 (NO) New Orleans, LA St. Leo the Great.
DeVolder, Philip '80 (FTW) Decatur, IN St. Mary.
Devolder, Philip (FTW) Pro–Synodal Judges.
Devorak, James W. '72 (NU) Area Pastoral Leaders:; Montevideo, MN St. Joseph.
Devorak, James '72 (NU) Granite Falls, MN St. Andrew.
DeVore, C. John *m.s.f.s.* '86 (ATL)[K] Lawrenceville, GA The Missionaries of St. Francis De Sales.
Devore, Daniel B. '79 (STA) Jacksonville, FL St. Matthew's.
DeVore, David G. '88 (CIN) On Special and Archdiocesan Assignment.
Devot, Paul D. *s.j.* '72 (SJ)[M] Los Gatos, CA Sacred Heart Jesuit Center; [M] Los Gatos, CA Sacred Heart Jesuit Center.
DeVries, Thomas D. '89 (MIL) Mequon, WI St. James.
DeVries, William J. '90 (MEM) Covington, TN St. Alphonsus.
Devron, Christopher J. *s.j.* '01 (NY)[F] New York, NY Regis High School.
Dewaele, Joseph *c.i.c.m.* '49 (ARL)[J] Arlington, VA Missionhurst, C.I.C.M.–Central House and Provincialate.
DeWalt, Homer C. '50 (E)[I] Canton, OH House of Loreto Retired.
Dewan, Wilfred *c.s.p.* '53 (NY)[EE] Jamaica Estates Paulist Fathers Generalate.
Dewan, Wilfred *c.s.p.* '53 (BRK) Flushing, NY St. Andrew Avellino.
Dewan, William G. '86 (JOL) Bradley, IL St. Joseph.
Dewane, Daniel '71 (GB) Retired.
Dewane, Frank J. '88 (GB) On Duty Outside the Diocese.
Dewane, John B. '62 (GB) Special Assignment; [N] Green Bay, WI Sacred Heart Seminary, Inc.; Vicars General; Vicar for Administration; Diocesan Consultors; Diocesan Pastoral Council; Ex Officios; Bishop's Finance Council; Support Services.
deWasseige, Eric *o.p.* '65 (CHI)[N] Chicago Dominicans (Provincial Office).
deWater, Joseph M. '67 (NO) On Duty Outside the Archdiocese.
Dewes, John W. '65 (CHI) Barrington, IL St. Anne.
Dewit, Phil (GB)[F] Oshkosh, WI Mercy Medical Center.
DeWitt, David D. '84 (PIT) Chicora, PA Mater Dolorosa; Chicora, PA St. Joseph; Judges.
DeWolf, Paul *c.i.c.m.* '50 (ARL)[J] Arlington, VA Missionhurst, C.I.C.M.–Central House and Provincialate.
Dewson, John H. '47 (WIL) Retired.
Deye, Walter C. *s.j.* '66 (CIN)[F] Cincinnati, OH St. Xavier High School.
Deye, Walter C. *s.j.* '75 (CIN)[M] Cincinnati, OH Jesuit Community at St. Xavier High School.
Deyo, Paul *ss.cc.* '61 (FR)[H] Fairhaven, MA Damien Residence.
De Young, Thomas J. '83 (GR) Grand Rapids, MI Basilica of St. Adalbert; Deans.
Deziel, William *o.s.c.* '97 (STP)[M] Anoka, MN Crosier Community of Anoka.
Deziel, William *o.s.c.* '97 (STP) Anoka, MN St. Stephen.
Deziel, William *o.s.c.* (STP) Presbyteral Council.
Dhanwar, Walter *i.m.s.* '91 (AUS) Burlington, TX St. Ann's.
Dharamaraj, Anthony *m.s.f.s.* '92 (ATL)[K] Lawrenceville The Missionaries of St. Francis De Sales.
Dharmaraj, Anthony *m.s.f.s.* '92 (ALX) Priests Council; Cottonport, LA St. Mary Assumption.
Dhein, William A. '02 (LC) Eau Claire, WI Sacred

Heart of Jesus–St. Patrick; [C] Eau Claire, WI Regis Middle School; [C] Eau Claire, WI Regis High School; Elected Members; Navy Reserve Chaplains.
Dhondt, Edward F. '69 (LFT) Anderson, IN St. Ambrose; Associate Judges.
Diab, Thomas P. '71 (SAN) Military Chaplains; Air Force Chaplains.
Diacetis, Anthony C. '69 (ALB) Ballston Lake, NY Our Lady of Grace; Army National Guard Chaplains.
Diachek, Robert M. (PAT) Special Assignment; [P] Madison, NJ Priests Residence; Office of Health Care Ministry; Office of the Permanent Diaconate.
Diachek, Robert (PAT) Vicar for Deacons.
Diadia, Chester '58 (RVC) Floral Park, NY St. Hedwig's.
Diamond, David E. '83 (PH)[A] Wynnewood, PA Theological Seminary of St. Charles Borromeo, Overbrook.
Diamond, Matthew J. '71 (BRK) Flushing, NY St. Andrew Avellino Retired.
Dianda, Carl F. '59 (WDC) Washington, DC St. Francis de Sales; Ladies of Charity.
Dias, D. Francis '71 (NY) Sloatsburg, NY St. Joan of Arc.
Dias, John F. *c.s.c.* '63 (FR)[H] North Dartmouth, MA St. Joseph's Hall.
Dias, John *c.s.c.* (FR) Diocesan Department of Pastoral Care for the Sick.
Dias da Costa, Josias *o.s.b.* '86 (KCK)[H] Atchison, KS St. Benedict's Abbey.
Diaz, Alberto '85 (ARE) Arecibo, PR Nuestra Senora del Carmen.
Diaz, Alberto (SJN) Clergy Social Security (Prevision Social del Clero).
Diaz, Alvaro '45 (SJN) Retired.
Diaz, Alvaro '73 (CAM) Pleasantville, NJ St. Peter's.
Diaz, Alvero (CAM) Spanish Cursillo.
Diaz, Angel R. '85 (ARE) Lares, PR St. Judas Tadeos.
Diaz, Angel '76 (ARE) Vega Baja, PR N.S. de la Providencia.
Diaz, Angel *o.p.* '99 (SJN) Bayamon, PR Santo Domingo de Guzman.
Diaz, Claudio (CHI) Chicago, IL Saint Ita.
Diaz, Erno (NY) New York, NY St. Malachy's.
Diaz, Francisco G. '77 (MIA) Miami, FL Prince of Peace.
Diaz, Francisco '87 (FRS) Fresno, CA St. John Cathedral.
Diaz, German Perez '97 (KAL) Hartford, MI Immaculate Conception.
Diaz, Gilbert M. '94 (KNX) Dayton, TN St. Bridget.
Diaz, Gonzalo '52 (SJN)[G] Guaynabo, PR Opus Dei.
Diaz, Gonzalo '63 (MGZ) On Special Assignment.
Diaz, Gonzalo (MGZ) For Diocesan Administration.
Diaz, Gonzalo (PCE) Mayaguez:.
Diaz, Gonzalo (MGZ) Diocesan Consultors.
Diaz, Gonzalo (MGZ) Chancellor.
Diaz, Gonzalo (MGZ) Vicar General.
Diaz, Gonzalo (MGZ) Cursillos de Cristiandad.
Diaz, Guillermo *c.s.* '93 (LA) Los Angeles, CA St. Peter.
Diaz, Heberto M. '89 (BWN) Brownsville, TX Christ the King; Deans; Office of the Chancellor; Moderator of the Curia, Lower Valley; Presbyteral Council; Diocesan College of Consultors; Parish Priests' Consultors & Priest Personnel Board.
Diaz, Hector (SJN)[E] San Juan, PR Centro Medico de P.R..
Diaz, Hernando '71 (SLC) Ogden, UT St. Joseph's; [C] Ogden, UT St. Joseph Regional School; College of Consultors.
Diaz, Jaime A. *o.p.* (BR) Hammond, LA Holy Ghost.
Diaz, Jaime (SAT) Poteet, TX St. Philip Benizi.
Diaz, Javier '98 (TR) Trenton, NJ St. Mary Cathedral.
Diaz, Jesus '54 (ARE) Retired.
Diaz, Jesus (ARE) Vega–Alta, PR Santa Ana Retired.
Diaz, Jose Juan Cardona '01 (MGZ) Hormigueros, PR Shrine of Our Lady of Monserrate.
Diaz, Jose Luis Garcia *o.de.m.* '63 (SJN) San Juan, PR Nuestra Senora de la Merced.
Diaz, Jose Matias '89 (NEW)[A] Kearny, NJ Redemptoris Mater.
Diaz, Joseph '94 (HON) Honokaa, HI Our Lady of Lourdes; Filipino Ministry.
Diaz, Juan Carlos '94 (LA) Huntington Park, CA St. Matthias.
Diaz, Kevin Hunt '84 (PHX) Mayer, AZ St. Joseph.
Diaz, Manuel A. *c.m.f.* '95 (LA) San Gabriel, CA San Gabriel; [Q] San Gabriel, CA Claretian Missionaries (Missionary Sons of the Immaculate Heart of Mary).
Diaz, Martin *o.p.* '78 (SB)[E] Riverside, CA St. Vincent Ferrer House.
Diaz, Melvin (PCE)[B] The Pontifical Catholic University of Puerto Rico.
Diaz, Michael '73 (SD) Military Chaplains; Navy Chaplains.
Diaz, Oscar '94 (SR) Napa, CA St. John the Baptist.
Diaz, Oscar (SR) Hispanic Ministry – South.
Diaz, Oscar (SR) Priests' Council.
Diaz, Raul '97 (FRS) Parlier, CA Our Lady of Sorrows.
Diaz, Robert '79 (BWN) Retired.
Diaz, Thomas K. '81 (SFR)[A] On Duty Outside the Diocese.
Diaz, Thomas (SR) Vocations.
Diaz–Munoz, Javier A. '90 (TR) Trenton, NJ St. Joseph.
Diaz–Munoz, Javier (TR) The Hispanic Apostolate.
Diaz–Munoz, Javier (TR) The Portuguese Apostolate.
Diaz–Torre, Emilio *l.c.* '93 (NY)[II] Thornwood, NY Catholic Net Inc..
Diaz–Torre, Emilio *l.c.* '93 (HRT)[V] Orange, CT Racebrook, Inc..
Diaz Aponte, Melvin '02 (PCE)[A] Ponce, PR Diocesan Seminary.
Diaz De Leon, Juan Ramon '72 (SR) Special Assignment.
Diaz Perez, Angel A. *o.p.* '96 (SJN)[E] Bayamon, PR Hospital Matilde Brenes.
Diaz Vilar, J. Juan *s.j.* '69 (NEW)[N] Jersey City, NJ Jesuits of Saint Peter's College, Inc..
DiBacco, John V. '67 (WH) Martinsburg, WV St. Joseph's; Vicars Forane.
DiBardino, Anthony '76 (CAM) Mullica Hill NJ Holy Name of Jesus.
Dibb, William C. *s.j.* '60 (SPK)[J] Spokane, WA Regis Community.
Dibble, Michael B. '60 (NY) New York, NY St. Peter.
Dibble, Michael '60 (NY) Retired.
DiBlasi, Augustine J. '45 (NY) Retired.
DiBuo, Roger F. '89 (WIL)[E] Bear, DE St. Elizabeth Ann Seton.
Di Cerbo, Almerico F. '46 (ALB) Retired.
DiCerbo, Almerico F. (ALB) Promoter of Justice.
Dicharry, Harold E. *c.m.* '42 (NO) New Orleans, LA St. Stephen Retired.
Dicharry, Harold *c.m.* (NO) Ladies of Charity of the Archdiocese
DiCicco, Mario *o.f.m.* '59 (CHI)[B] Quincy, IL Quincy University.
Dick, Firmus '54 (EVN) Retired.
Dick, Gregory M. *o.praem.* '96 (ORG)[A] Silverado, CA St. Michael's Norbertine Postulancy, Novitiate and Juniorate; [I] Silverado, CA Norbertine Fathers of Orange Inc.
Dick, John '96 (DAL) Denison, TX St. Patrick.
Dickes, Jerome H. '48 (OM) Retired.
Dickie, John A. '56 (SD) San Diego, CA St. Mary Magdalene; College of Consultors.
Dickie, John (SD) Presbyteral Council.
Dickinson, Stephen '58 (FAR) Retired.
Dickinson, William R. '89 (CLV) Brecksville, OH St. Basil the Great.
Dickinson, William '89 (CLV) Cleveland, OH St. Catherine.
Dickman, John W. '48 (L) Retired.
Dickman, Richard C. '93 (LC) On Leave of Absence.
Dickmann, Louis H. '59 (COV) Retired.
Dickrell, Cyril *s.d.s.* '53 (MIL)[O] Chilton, WI.
Dicks, Leon *o.f.m.conv.* '57 (ALB) Fonda, NY St. Cecilia.
Dicks, Thomas '87 (NY) Goshen, NY St. John the Evangelist.
Dicks, Tom (NY)[R] Bronx, NY District Council of the Bronx.
Dickson, Henry E. *s.s.j.* '60 (MOB) Prichard, AL St. James Major; Religious.
Dickson, Norman J. *s.j.* '67 (DET)[K] Detroit, MI Jesuit Community at the University of Detroit Mercy; Detroit, MI Gesu.
Dicristina, Frank T. '86 (SB) Phelan, CA Blessed Junipero Serra Church; Wrightwood, CA Our Lady of the Snows.
Didam, John '44 (NY) Kingston, NY Kingston City Hospital.
Didier, Jacques R. *m.e.p.* '53 (SFR)[N] San Francisco, CA Paris Foreign Mission Society Residence.
Didier–Marie, *f.j.* '94 (PEO)[M] Princeville, IL St. Joseph Priory and Novitiate.
Didone, Matthew *c.s.* '67 (PMB) Delray Beach, FL Our Lady Queen of Peace.
Diebel, Thomas '79 (LUB) Retired.
Dieckhaus, Joseph C. '74 (PH)[BB] Philadelphia, PA Sister Servants of the Holy Spirit of Perpetual Adoration (S.Sp.S.A.P.); Assistant Judicial Vicars; Council of Priests.
Dieckhaus, Joseph C. (MO) Judges.
Dieckman, Vincent *o.f.m.* '38 (CIN)[M] Cincinnati, OH Archbishop Leibold Home for the Aged.
Dieckmann, Michael '74 (STL) Fenton, MO St. Paul.
Dieckmann, Michael (STL) Archdiocesan Consultors.
Diederich, Donald F. '58 (RVC) Retired.
Diederich, Everett A. *s.j.* '52 (STL)[O] St Louis, MO Jesuit Community Corporation at St. Louis University – Jesuit Hall.
Diederichs, Carl E. '02 (MIL) Milwaukee, WI Cathedral of St. John the Evangelist.
Diedrick, Charles T. '78 (CLV) Northfield, OH St. Barnabas College of Consultors; Associate Judges.
Diegel, Ronald L. (TYL) Deans; Presbyteral Council.
Diegel, Ronald (TYL) Priests' Personnel Board.
Diegel, Ronald (TYL) Paris, TX Our Lady of Victory; College of Consultors.
Diegel, Ronald (TYL) Priests' Pension Board.
Diegelman, Robert W. '93 (R) Laurinburg, NC St. Mary.
Diehl, Dennis P. '74 (BAL) Fulton, MD St. Francis of Assisi.
Diehl, Michael C. '55 (TUC) Retired.
Diehl, Thomas J. *s.j.* '50 (CIN)[P] Milford, OH Milford Spiritual Center.
Diekemper, Barnabas '65 (SFD)[M] Springfield, IL St. Francis Convent.
Dieker, James P. (DOD) Ulysses, KS St. Bernadette; Ulysses, KS Mary Queen of Peace.
Diekhans, Joseph '65 (GF) Chester, MT St. Mary's; Chester, MT Our Lady of Ransom.
Diekhans, Joseph (GF) Priests' Council.
Diekhans, Joseph (GF) Clerical Benefit Association.
Diekhans, Joseph (GF) Diocesan Consultors.
Diekhoff, Bernard *c.pp.s.* '47 (CIN)[B] Carthagena, OH St. Charles.
Diele, Joseph D. (BRK) South Ozone Park, NY St. Clement Pope.
Dielinikaitis, Juan A. '03 (LIT) Brooklyn, NY Shrine of Our Lady of Mount Carmel; Brooklyn, NY Annunciation of the Blessed Virgin Mary.
Diels, Gaston *ss.cc.* '47 (HON)[G] Honolulu, HI St. Patrick's Monastery.
Diem, John Tran Dinh *c.m.c.* '96 (SB)[E] Corona, CA Congregation of the Mother Co–Redemptrix.
Diem, Joseph '85 (BO) Hopkinton, MA St. John the Evangelist.
Diemand, James E. '68 (SPR) Retired.
Diemer, Joseph *o.s.b.cam.* '49 (MRY)[F] Big Sur, CA New Camaldoli Hermitage.
Diemer, Michael J. *m.j.* '96 (PCE) Ponce, PR Santa Maria.
Dienert, Robert T. '62 (LR) North Little Rock, AR Immaculate Heart of Mary.
Diere, Emiliano Auwen (DET) Henry Ford Hospital.
Dieringer, James J. '58 (P) Retired.
Dierkes, Richard '81 (KC) St. Joseph, MO St. Joseph's Co–Cathedral.
Diermeier, Joseph '78 (LC) Marathon City, WI Nativity of the Blessed Virgin Mary.
Diermeier, Joseph (LC) Deans.
Diers, Darrel (GB)[F] Appleton, WI St. Elizabeth Hospital.
Diesbourg, Raymond *m.s.c.* '74 (FgM).
Diesbourg, Raymond *m.s.c.* '74 (RCK)[G] Aurora, IL Missionaries of the Sacred Heart Community.
Dieter, Thomas M. '83 (JOL) On Duty Outside the Diocese.
Dieter, Xavier L. *o.c.s.o.* '58 (DUB)[K] Peosta, IA New Melleray Abbey, Order of Cistercians of the Strict Observance; Religious Priests Representative.
Dietlein, Damian *o.s.b.* '57 (IND)[A] St. Meinrad, IN St. Meinrad School of Theology.
Dietlein, Damian *o.s.b.* '57 (IND)[A] Richardton, ND Assumption Abbey.
Dietlein, Raymond *o.s.b.* '54 (BIS)[A] Richardton, ND Assumption Abbey.
Dietrich, Christopher *o.f.m.cap.* '59 (NY) Yonkers, NY Sacred Heart.
Dietrich, Douglas D. (LIN) Permanent Deacon Continuing Education Committee.
Dietrich, Douglas '96 (LIN) Wilber, NE St. Wenceslaus.
Dietrich, John J. '93 (HRT) On Duty Outside the Archdiocese.
Dietrich, John '93 (BAL).
Dietrich, Robert J. *s.j.* '43 (CLV)[D] Cleveland, OH St. Ignatius High School.
Dietrich, Severin *o.f.m.conv.* '53 (MET)[I] North Plainfield, NJ Servants of the Holy Child Jesus Regional House.
Dietrich, Severin *o.f.m.conv.* '53 (MET)[G] North Plainfield, NJ Villa Maria Sanitarium.
Dietsch, William '71 (EVN) New Harmony, IN Holy Angels.
Dietsch, William '71 (EVN) Poseyville, IN St. Francis Xavier.
Dietz, Conrad R. '57 (RVC)[B] Douglaston, NY Cathedral Seminary Residence of the Immaculate Conception; Oceanside, NY St. Anthony.
Dietz, Donald *o.m.i.* '57 (CHI) Volo, IL St. Peter.
Dietz, Francis '40 (DET) Retired.
Dietz, Joseph S. '87 (NY) Sleepy Hollow, NY The Magdalene.
Dietz, Joseph (NY) Westchester County Jail.
Dietz, Norbert J. '49 (STL) University City, MO Our Lady of Lourdes Retired.
Dietz, Xavier Ortiz '77 (SAT) On Leave.
Dietzel, Elmer J. '51 (MAD) Retired.
Dietzel, Elmer '51 (MAD)[G] Madison, WI Bishop O'Connor Catholic Pastoral Center.
Dietzen, John J. '54 (PEO) Retired.
Dietzen, Vincent E. '53 (PEO) Bloomington, IL St. Patrick's Retired.
Dietzenbach, John A. '80 (BAL) Libertytown, MD St. Peter.
Dietzenbach, John (BAL) Priests' Council; Consultors; Consultors.
Dietzler, William J. '69 (MIL)[J] Racine, WI All Saints Medical Center, Inc.; Special Assignment.

Diez, Antonio Oscar '68 (DAL) Greenville, TX St. William.
Diez, Antonio '59 (SP) Riverview, FL Resurrection.
Diez, Antonio (SP) Spanish Speaking Spiritual Monitor.
Diez, Oscar '68 (DAL) Absent on Leave.
Diez, Toribio Pascual *o.s.b.* '40 (MGZ) Mayaguez, PR Sacred Heart.
Diez Antonanzas, Jesus R. '57 (PCE)[B] The Pontifical Catholic University of Puerto Rico.
DiFede, Thomas V. *o.p.* '59 (COL) Zanesville, OH St. Thomas Aquinas.
DiFederico, Gabriel '78 (MEM) Memphis, TN Holy Rosary.
DiFederico, Gabriel (MEM) Auditor.
Diffenbacher, Brian (ROC) St. James Mercy Hospital.
Diffley, Francis A. *m.m.* '64 (NY)[EE] Maryknoll Maryknoll Fathers and Brothers.
DiFilippo, John V. *o.s.f.s.* '45 (PH)[AA] Philadelphia, PA Father Louis Brisson Residence.
DiFiore, John *s.d.b.* '97 (BO)[E] Boston, MA Savio Preparatory High School.
DiFiore, Jonn (PMB) Belle Glade, FL St. Philip Benizi.
DiFolco, Thomas P. '83 (CIN) Cincinnati, OH St. Agnes; Cincinnati, OH St. Martin De Porres; Priestly Formation.
DiFruscio, John A. '69 (BO) Permanent Disability.
Digal, Danilo C. '78 (NO) Chalmette, LA Our Lady of Prompt Succor; Filipino Catholic Ministry.
DiGeronimo, Michael A. '76 (WOR) Leicester, MA St. Joseph's; Leicester, MA St. Pius X; Advocates; Deans; Presbyteral Council.
DiGiacobbe, Albert C. '66 (PH) Philadelphia, PA St. Helena.
DiGiacomo, James J. *s.j.* '56 (NY)[EE] New York, NY "America;" Residence and publication office of the America Press.
DiGiovanni, Alfonso '96 (NEW) On Duty Outside the Archdiocese.
Di Giovanni, Stephen M. '77 (BGP) Stamford, CT St. John the Evangelist.
DiGiralamo, Gerald *s.a.* '81 (NY).
DiGirolamo, Dante '48 (NEW) Retired.
DiGirolamo, Paul A. '83 (PH)[EE] Philadelphia, PA St. Joan of Arc; Assistant Judicial Vicars.
DiGiulio, Richard S. (BUF) Charismatic Renewal Program; Advocates; Buffalo, NY St. Francis of Assisi.
Dignan, Eamon '59 (WDC) Waldorf, MD Our Lady Help of Christians.
Dignan, Thomas L. '57 (BIS) Retired.
DiGregorio, Joseph L. '66 (PH) Military Chaplains; Army Chaplains.
Di Gregorio, Michael F. *o.s.a.* '73 (PH) Philadelphia, PA St. Rita of Cascia.
DiGuglielmo, Anthony J. '03 (PH) Glenside, PA St. Luke the Evangelist.
Dihn, Joseph Maria Huy Quang *c.s.sp.* (SB) Hemet, CA Our Lady of the Valley.
DiIanni, Albert *s.m.* '60 (BO)[V] Boston, MA Marist Fathers of Our Lady of Victories (Boston Prov.).
DiIenno, Nicholas O. *o.s.f.s.* '43 (WIL)[J] Childs, MD Retirement and Assisted Care Facility.
DiIorio, Michael C. '77 (PH) Philadelphia, PA Our Lady of Consolation.
Dikete, Fidele '01 (SAT) San Antonio, TX Our Lady of Good Counsel.
Dilanni, Albert *s.m.* (BO) Boston, MA Our Lady of Victories.
Di Lella, Alexander A. *o.f.m.* '55 (WDC)[C] Catholic University of America, The.
DiLella, Alexander *o.f.m.* '55 (NY)[EE] Washington, DC Catholic University, Curley Hall.
DiLella, Christopher C. '79 (PAT) Madison, NJ St. Vincent Martyr.
Dilella, Christopher (PAT) Apostleship of Prayer.
Dilella, Christopher (PAT) Priests Eucharistic League.
Di Lella, Mario *o.f.m.* '53 (ATL)[N] Atlanta, GA Georgia Institute of Technology.
DiLeo, Anthony '64 (SB) Retired.
Dileo, Richard *s.c.j.* '81 (GAL) Houston, TX Our Lady of Guadalupe.
DiLeonardi, Rocco *o.carm.* '56 (JOL)[L] Joliet, IL St. Elias Carmelites Retired.
Dilettuso, Joseph A. '72 (BLX) V.A. Center.
Dilettuso, Joseph '72 (BLX) Special Assignment.
Dilettuso, Joseph '72 (BLX) V.A. Hospital.
Dilg, Donald W. *c.s.c.* '75[I] Notre Dame, IN Holy Cross Mission House.
Dilgen, William M. *s.m.m.* '47 (RVC)[M] Bay Shore, NY Montfort Missionaries.
Dilger, Basil *o.s.b.* '61 (SFS)[F] Marvin, SD Blue Cloud Abbey.
Dilger, Basil *o.s.b.* '61 (FgM).
Dilger, Donald '59 (EVN) Retired.
Diliberto, Peter J. '43 (LA)[Q] Montebello, CA DePaul Evangelization Center; [W] Montebello, CA DePaul Evangelization Center Retired.
Dilion, Joseph A. '46 (HRT) Retired.
Dilipiy, Basilio '94 (CI)[F] Yigo, GU St. Ignatius of Loyola House of Studies; Immaculate Heart of Mary Cathedral.
Dilipy, Basilio '94 (CI)[C] Tunnuk, Chuuk, FM Vicariate Residence.
Dill, Edwin *s.t.* '59 (WDC)[M] Adelphi, MD Missionary Servants of the Most Holy Trinity.
Dilla, Francis E. (CHI) Retired.
Dillabough, Daniel J. (SD) College of Consultors.
Dillabough, Daniel '74 (SD)[B] San Diego, CA University of San Diego.
Dillabough, Daniel (SD) Defenders of the Bond.
Dillabough, Daniel (SD) Promoter of Justice.
Dillane, Maurice '63 (SAT) On Duty Outside the Archdiocese.
Dillard, Steven C. *s.j.* '86 (P)[B] Bronx, NY Ciszek Hall.
Dillard, William '98 (P) On Duty Outside the Archdiocese.
Dillard, William '98 (SD) San Diego, CA St. John the Evangelist.
Dillenburg, James E. (GB) Green Bay, WI St. Elizabeth Ann Seton; Oconto Falls, WI St. Anthony; Lena, WI St. Patrick.
Dillenburg, James (GB) Diocesan Consultors.
Dilley, Gary D. '72 (CHR) On Duty Outside the Diocese.
Dillinger, Joseph A. (SC) Lidderdale, IA Holy Family.
Dillingham, Charles C. '73 (WIL) Wilmington, DE St. Elizabeth; Parish Priest Consultors.
Dillingham, Charles (BAL) Defenders of the Bond.
Dillman, Alan M. '59 (ATL) AUXILIARY CHAPLAINS CONTRACT CHAPLAINS Retired.
Dillon, Arthur J. '45 (CHI) Retired.
Dillon, Charles P. *s.s.* '39 (BAL)[O] Baltimore, MD St. Charles Villa.
Dillon, Ciarian *o.m.i.* '54 (OAK) Crockett, CA St. Rose of Lima.
Dillon, David *o.carm.* '65 (JOL) Glendale Heights, IL St. Matthew.
Dillon, Dennis T. *s.j.* '69 (DET)[K] Detroit, MI Jesuit Provincial Office–Detroit Province of the Society of Jesus.
Dillon, Dennis T. *s.j.* '69 (COL) Columbus, OH Community of Holy Rosary and St. John.
Dillon, Desmond P. '41 (YAK) Kennewick, WA St. Joseph's; Diocesan Pastoral Council Retired.
Dillon, Edward J. '60 (ROC) Lyons, NY St. Michael Retired.
Dillon, Edward J. '67 (ATL) Atlanta, GA Holy Spirit; [O] Atlanta, GA Catholic Foundation of North Georgia, Inc.; Archdiocesan Judges; Catholic Foundation of North Georgia.
Dillon, Edward J. (PAT) Unassigned.
Dillon, Geoffrey R. *s.j.* '83 (NOR)[N] San Francisco, CA Jesuit Community at University of San Francisco.
Dillon, Gerald F. *c.s.b.* '62 (GAL)[Q] Houston, TX Dillon House.
Dillon, James P. '73 (BRK) Military Chaplains.
Dillon, Jeffry T. '81 (BRK) Springfield Gardens, NY Christ the King.
Dillon, Jerome V. '77 (OM) Military Chaplains; Navy Chaplains.
Dillon, John D. '59 (ROC) Retired.
Dillon, John J. '98 (WDC) Bethesda, MD Little Flower.
Dillon, John T. *s.j.* '63 (CHI)[T] Barrington, IL Bellarmine Hall.
Dillon, Kevin J. '03 (RVC) Westbury, NY St. Brigid.
Dillon, Kevin M. (HRT) West Hartford, CT St. Peter Claver.
Dillon, Michael J. '61 (SAC) Rocklin, CA SS. Peter and Paul.
Dillon, Richard J. '61 (NY) On Duty Outside the Archdiocese.
Dillon, Robert W. '97 (NY) Staten Island, NY St. Charles.
Dillon, Thomas J. '59 (GI) Retired.
Dillon, William *s.a.* '69 (NY)[EE] Garrison Franciscan Friars of the Atonement, Minister General Office.
DiLorenzo, Thomas A. '79 (BO) Winthrop, MA Holy Rosary.
DiLoreto, Anthony '54 (B) Retired.
Dilworth, Kevin *s.j.* '84 (PHX)[B] Phoenix, AZ Brophy College Preparatory.
DiMaggio, Joseph '55 (ALB) Retired.
Dimapilis, Jose Rizal *o.p.* '67 (NOR) Middletown, CT Connecticut Valley Hospital.
DiMarco, Abel A. '56 (PCE)[B] The Pontifical Catholic University of Puerto Rico.
Di Marco, Abel (PCE) Sacred Music Commission.
DiMaria, Peter '93 (PH)[Y] Elverson, PA St. Mary of Providence Center.
DiMaria, Peter '93 (PH)[D] Downingtown, PA Bishop Shanahan High School; On Special or Other Archdiocesan Assignment.
Di Marzio, Vito *r.c.j.* '75 (FRS) Sanger, CA St. Mary.
DiMarzio, Vito *r.c.j.* '75 (FRS) Sanger, CA St. Katherine.
DiMarzio, Vito *r.c.j.* (FRS) Priests' Council.
DiMascola, Charles J. '81 (SPR) Turners Falls, MA Our Lady of Czestochowa.
DiMattei, Robert A. '91 (BAL) Curtis Bay, MD St. Athanasius.
DiMatteo, John *o.ss.t.* '36 (PH) Bristol, PA St. Ann.
DiMauro, John C. *o.f.m.* '56 (BO)[V] Andover St. Francis Friary; [X] Andover, MA Franciscan Center – Retreat House.
DiMauro, Joseph A. *o.s.f.s.* '73 (ALN)[K] Center Valley, PA Oblates of St. Francis de Sales.
DiMauro, Joseph F. *o.s.f.s.* '73 (ALN)[B] Center Valley, PA DeSales University.
DiMauro, Joseph V. '67 (CAM) Blackwood, NJ St. Agnes; Members.
Dimauro, Joseph *s.a.* '78 (NY)[EE] Garrison, NY Franciscan Friars of the Atonement.
Dimengo, Michael '77 (CLV) Absent on Leave.
Dimic, Milan '85 (BGP) Newtown, CT St. Rose of Lima.
Dimic, Milan '85 (BGP) Fairfield, CT Holy Cross.
Dimke, John '60 (GF) Retired.
Dimke, Richard *s.j.* '63 (LA) Venice, CA St. Mark.
Dimler, G. Richard *s.j.* '63 (NY)[EE] Loyola Hall, Jesuit Community.
Dimock, Giles Richard *o.p.* '66 (WDC)[B] Washington, DC Dominican House of Studies.
Di Modugno, Diego '74 (PCE)[B] The Pontifical Catholic University of Puerto Rico.
Dinan, Denis M. '92 (NY) Port Jervis, NY Immaculate Conception.
Dinan, John '58 (WCH) Retired.
Dinardo, Daniel A. '66 (CAM) Wildwood Crest, NJ Assumption B.V.M..
DiNardo, Hector *c.r.m.* '56 (NEW) Lodi, NJ St. Joseph's.
DiNardo, Lawrence A. *m.ch.a.* '74 (PIT) Pittsburgh, PA Holy Wisdom; Director, Department of Canon and Civil Law Services; Judges; Priest Council; Canon and Civil Law Services, Dept. for; Canonical Services, Office for; Health Care Liaison, Office of the; Ministerial Assessment, Office for.
DiNardo, Mark A. '58 (CLV) Cleveland, OH St. Patrick; Apostleship of the Sea Chaplain for the Diocese of Cleveland (Port Chaplain).
DiNardo, Mark (CLV) Presbyteral Conveners.
DiNardo, Salvatore M. *o.p.* '31 (SJ) Villa Siena.
DiNardo, Salvatore M. *d.c.* '54 (SJ)[K] Mountain View, CA Villa Siena.
Dincher, Carl L. *s.j.* '57 (BAL)[S] Jesu Bhavan.
Dinda, John J. '62 (PH) Spring City, PA St. Joseph.
Dindorf, Meinrad *o.s.b.* '58 (SCL)[I] Collegeville, MN St. John's Abbey, of the Order of St. Benedict.
Dindorf, Meinrad *o.s.b.* '58 (SCL)[H] St. Cloud, MN St. Benedict's Senior Community.
Dindorf, Meinrad *o.s.b.* (SCL) Personnel Committee.
Dineen, Michael P. '49 (MIL) Retired.
Dineen, William *c.pp.s.* '66 (KC)[J] Liberty, MO Precious Blood Society Provincial Office.
Dineen, William '66 (KC)[N] Liberty, MO St. Gaspar Society.
Dineen, William *c.pp.s.* '66 (KC)[J] Liberty, MO Precious Blood Center.
Dinelli, William J. '61 (SAC) Walnut Grove, CA St. Anthony.
Dinello, John E. '85 (PIT) Pitcairn, PA St. Michael; West Penn Allegheny Health System–Forbes Regional; Army Reserve Chaplains.
Dineros, Santiago A. '55 (RVC) Retired.
Dinga, William '75 (RIC) Retired.
Dinges, Anthony '57 (RIC) Blackstone, VA Immaculate Heart of Mary.
Dinges, Anthony '57 (RIC) Crewe, VA St. John the Baptist.
Dinges, Anthony '57 (RIC) Retired.
Dinh, Dominic Hai *c.ss.r.* '95 (DAL) Garland, TX Mother of Perpetual Help.
Dinh, Hao '93 (SJ) San Jose, CA Holy Family; On Sabbatical.
Dinh, Hao (SJ) Building Committee.
Dinh, Joseph Maria Huy Q. *c.s.sp.* '00 (SB)[E] Hemet, CA Our Lady of the Valley.
Dinh, Joseph Thien *s.c.j.* '02 (GAL) Houston, TX Our Lady of Guadalupe.
Dinh, Joseph Truc *s.d.b.* '99 (ORG) Santa Ana, CA St. Barbara's.
Dinh, Joseph Long (CHL) Asheville, NC Basilica of St. Lawrence.
Dinh, Michael Van '02 (OAK) Martinez, CA St. Catherine of Siena.
Dinh, Peter '00 (DEN) Denver, CO Assumption.
Dinh, Quang Duc *s.v.d.* '92 (CHI)[N] Chicago, IL House of Religious Men: Divine Word Theologate.
Dinh, Thomas Tranh *i.c.m.* '65 (BR)[H] Baton Rouge, LA Incarnatio Consecratio Mission.
Dinh, Tran Thuc '61 (OAK) San Leandro, CA St. Felicitas Retired.
Dinh, Tri M. *s.j.* (LA)[C] Los Angeles, CA Jesuit Community; [BB] Los Angeles, CA Loyola Marymount University; [BB] Los Angeles, CA Loyola Law School.
Dinh, Van (OAK) Air Force Reserve Chaplains.
Dinh, Victor '03 (FRS) Bakersfield, CA St. Francis.
Dinh–Van–Thiep, Philip '83 (GB) Wautoma, WI St. Joseph.
Dinh–Van–Thiep, Philip (GB) Regional Vicars.
Dinh Tuan Ngan, Joseph '54 (SPC)[E] Carthage, MO Congregation of the Mother Coredemptrix, United States Assumption Province.
Dinh Viet Luan, Felix M. *c.m.c.* '89 (SPC)[E] Carthage, MO Congregation of the Mother Coredemptrix, United States Assumption Province.
Dinh Vuong Can, Anselm M. *c.m.c.* '77 (SPC)[E]

Carthage, MO Congregation of the Mother Coredemptrix, United States Assumption Province.
Dinicco, Henry P. (GBG) Legion of Mary.
Dininni, Nicholas J. '93 (PH) Malvern, PA St. Patrick.
Dinio, Miguel *o.p.* '64 (SAN) San Angelo, TX St. Joseph.
Diniz, Pedro D. '71 (BGP) Danbury, CT St. Peter.
Dinkel, Emil *c.pp.s.* '52 (TOL)[J] Bellevue Mary Lay Center.
Dinkel, Emil *c.pp.s.* '52 (TOL)[L] Bellevue, OH Sorrowful Mother Shrine.
Dinkel, Harvey P. *o.f.m.cap.* '61 (DEN)[N] Denver, CO St. Francis of Assisi Friary.
Dinkins, Jack M. '63 (GAL) Katy, TX Epiphany of the Lord.
Dinneen, John A. *s.j.* '60 (NY)[C] Jersey City, NJ St. Peter's Preparatory School; [N] Jersey City, NJ Jesuit Community of St. Peter's Prep, Inc..
Dinnico, Henry P. '58 (GBG) Retired.
Dino, Gerald N. *o.e.s.l.* '65 (PSC) Linden, NJ St. George's; Protosyncellus–Vicar General; Eparchial Finance Council; Eparchial College of Consultors; Ex Officio Members; Cemeteries Commission; Retirement Plan Board.
DiNoia, Joseph Augustine *o.p.* '70 (WDC)[B] Washington, DC Dominican House of Studies.
DiNola, Leonard J. '58 (NY) Buchanan, NY St. Christopher.
Dinovo, Anthony A. '01 (COL) Columbus, OH St. Andrew.
Dinovo, Anthony (COL) Priests' Senate.
Dinsdale, Samuel '03 (SLC) Midvale, UT St. Therese of the Child Jesus.
Diogo, Louis M. '46 (PRO) East Providence, RI St. Francis Xavier Retired.
Diokno, Rolando V. '70 (GAL) Houston, TX Notre Dame.
Diomartich, Felix S. '37 (LA) Los Angeles, CA St. Anthony Retired.
Dion, Maurice B. '44 (SAL) Retired.
Dion, Richard H. '99 (MAN) Nashua, NH St. Aloysius; Council of Priests; Hispanic Apostolate.
Dionne, Adrian L. *o.p.* '49 (WDC) Washington, DC St. Dominic Church & Priory.
Dionne, Earl J. '58 (MIL) Retired.
Dionne, Francis '81 (SP) Retired.
Dionne, J. Joseph *c.ss.r.* '80 (PCE) Guayama, PR St. Anthony of Padua.
Dionne, Leo *o.m.i.* '59 (MIA) Opa Locka, FL St. Monica.
Dionne, Nelson *s.c.* '96 (PRO)[P] Burrillville, RI Brothers of the Sacred Heart Provincial House.
Dionne, Rene *m.afr. (spain)* '61 (FgM).
DiOrio, John R. '99 (PH) Morton, PA Our Lady of Perpetual Help.
DiOrio, Ralph A. '57 (WOR) On Special or Other Diocesan Assignment.
Diorio, Ralph A. (WOR) Apostolate Office of Divine Mercy and Healing.
Di Pasquale, Donald J. '62 (NEW) Cliffside Park, NJ Epiphany.
DiPasquale, Donald (NEW) Southeast Bergen Region Deanery 6.
Di Pasquale, Ralph *o.f.m.* '56 (NY)[EE] New York, NY.
DiPeri, Joseph B. '56 (NEW) Retired.
DiPerri, James M. '88 (BO)[A] Weston, MA Blessed John XXIII National Seminary; Canonical Affairs Committee.
Diphe, Juan M. '76 (HEL) Military Chaplains; Air Force Chaplains.
DiPietro, Leroy A. '70 (PIT) Brentwood, PA St. Sylvester.
DiPietro, Rodric J. '76 (COL) Hilliard, OH St. Brendan.
Dipre, Gilio L. '55 (E)[B] Erie, PA Gannon University Retired.
Direen, John '01 (OAK) Oakland, CA St. Andrew–St. Joseph.
DiRenzo, Michael J. '70 (LA) Fort MacArthur Annex; On Duty Outside the Diocese.
Dirig, Walter F. *c.m.* '39 (PH)[AA] St. Catherine Infirmary.
Dirkx, Dennis A. '72 (MIL) Milwaukee, WI All Saints; Deans.
Dirscherl, Denis A. *s.j.* '67 (BAL)[N] Chicago Chicago Province of the Society of Jesus–Provincial Office.
DiRuscio, Romano *s.c.* '51 (PH)[N] Rosemont, PA St. Edmond's Home for Children.
Di Russo, Anthony '63 (MAN) Greenville, NH Sacred Heart.
Di Russo, Anthony '63 (MAN) Greenville, NH Sacred Heart.
DiSalvatore, Remo *o.f.m.cap.* '97 (SP) Tampa, FL Most Holy Redeemer.
Disch, John H. '39 (LAF) New Iberia, LA St. Peter Retired.
Dischler, Raymond J. '73 (MAD) Poynette, WI St. Thomas; Poynette, WI St. Joseph; Deaneries.
DiSciacca, Joseph V. '73 (HRT) Meriden, CT Our Lady of Mount Carmel; Meriden, CT St. Laurent.
DiSenso, Gerald '53 (NY) Retired.
Diskin, Francis X. *c.s.p.* '46 (NY) New York, NY St. Paul the Apostle; [EE] Jamaica Estates Paulist Fathers Generalate.
Diskin, John J. *s.j.* '63 (BO)[V] Weston, MA Campion Health Center, Inc..
Diskin, Michael L. '77 (PHX) Special Assignment; Assistant Chancellor; College of Consultors; Advocates; Catholic Cemeteries; Ecumenical and Interreligious Affairs; Priests' Assurance Association.
DiSpigno, Francis J. *o.f.m.* '96 (NY) New York NY Holy Name of Jesus; [EE] New York, NY The Franciscan Vocation Ministry of Holy Name Province.
DiSpigno, Gennaro J. '81 (RVC) Bellport, NY Mary Immaculate.
Dissek, Jerome M. '69 (BUF) Cuba, NY Our Lady of the Angels; Cuba, NY St. Mary.
DiStefano, John '52 (BEA) Retired.
DiStefano, Joseph '84 (ORG) Absent on Sick Leave.
DiStefano, Salvatore '03 (NEW) Lyndhurst, NJ Sacred Heart.
Distefano, Simeon C. *o.f.m.* '63 (NY) New York, NY St. Anthony of Padua.
Dister, John E. *s.j.* '62 (DET)[K] Detroit, MI Jesuit Provincial Office–Detroit Province of the Society of Jesus.
Distor, Leo *s.s.c.* '96 (CHI)[K] St. Columbans St. Columban's Foreign Mission Society.
DiTaddeo, Alessandro '54 (LAR) Laredo, TX Blessed Sacrament Retired.
Ditch, Robert G. '56 (STL) Retired.
Ditenhafer, John A. '61 (STL) University City, MO Christ the King.
Ditillo, James J. *s.j.* '74 (WH)[A] Wheeling, WV Wheeling Jesuit University.
DiTomasi, Francisco *o.s.m.* '53 (ELP) El Paso, TX St. Ignatius of Loyola.
Ditta, Angelo *c.* '86 (RVC)[M] Uniondale, NY St. Pius X Residence.
Dittberner, Jerome M. *s.t.d.* '64 (STP)[A] St. Paul, MN The Saint Paul Seminary; [C] St. Paul, MN University of St. Thomas.
Dittmeier, Charles R. '70 (L) On Duty Outside the Archdiocese
Dittmeier, Charles R. '70 (FgM).
Ditto, Anthony W. '90 (GBG) Brady's Bend, PA St. Patrick; Brady's Bend, PA St. Mary, Our Lady of the Snows.
Dittoe, John T. '45 (COL) Diocesan Judges Retired.
Ditton, Edmund Augustine *o.p.* '84 (NY)[EE] New York St. Vincent Ferrer Priory.
Ditty, James '39 (RIC) Retired.
DiTullio, Peter S. *s.c.* '68 (PRO) East Providence, RI Sacred Heart.
Diulio, Al *s.j.* '74 (LA) Los Angeles, CA St. Brendan.
DiUlio, Albert J. *s.j.* '74 (LA) Los Angeles, CA St. Brendan; Schools, Department of Catholic; Members:.
Diurczak, Eugene '68 (NEW) Linden, NJ Holy Family.
Divan, Anthony L. '65 (PEO) Retired.
Divine, Finbarr '70 (LA) San Gabriel, CA St. Anthony.
Diviney, Andrew *s.j.* '61 (LA) Northridge, CA Our Lady of Lourdes.
Divis, Daniel O. '79 (CLV) Lorain, OH St. Mary.
Divis, M. James '76 (LIN)[A] Seward, NE St. Gregory the Great Seminary; Censores Librorum; Commission on Alcohol and Drug Abuse; Commission for Sacred Liturgy and Sacred Music; Ecumenical Affairs, Commission for; Evangelization Committee.
DiVito, John *c.s.* (CHI) Melrose Park, IL Our Lady of Mount Carmel.
Divizia, John *s.d.b.* '35 (NY)[GG] Stony Point, NY Marian Shrine.
Divizia, John *s.d.b.* '35 (NY)[GG] Stony Point, NY Don Bosco Retreat Center and Marian Shrine.
Dixey, Edward J. *o.s.a.* '57 (ALB) Mechanicville, NY Assumption–St. Paul.
Dixon, David C. '57 (PIT) Allegheny County, PA Vincentian Regency Home; [K] Allison Park, PA Vincentian Regency; [N] Pittsburgh, PA St. John Vianney Manor Retired.
Dixon, Francis F. *o.carm.* '76 (NY) Middletown, NY Our Lady of Mt. Carmel.
Dixon, J. Isidore '64 (WDC) Upper Marlboro, MD Church of the Most Holy Rosary.
Dixon, James M. *s.j.* '73 (GRY)[I] East Chicago, IN Roque Gonzalez Residence–Jesuit Fathers; [N] Hammond, IN Heartland Center; Peace and Social Justice, Office of; Rural Life Conference.
Dixon, James R. '70 (NO) Military Chaplains; Chancellor; Presbyteral Council.
Dixon, James *s.j.* (GRY) Indiana Catholic Conference.
Dixon, James *s.j.* (GRY) Heartland Center.
Dixon, Jerome A. '57 (PIT) Allegheny County, PA Little Sisters of the Poor (James P. Wall Home for the Aged) Retired.
Dixon, Jerome A. (PIT) Retired Priests, Office for.
Dixon, Jerome '57 (PIT)[K] Pittsburgh, PA Little Sisters of the Poor Home for the Aged.
Dlabal, Norbert '61 (SAL) Sharon Springs, KS Holy Ghost.
Dlabal, Norbert '72 (SAL) Goodland, KS Our Lady of Perpetual Help.
Dlabal, Norbert (SAL) Catholic Charities Board.
Dlabal, Norbert (SAL) Diocesan Pastoral Council.
Dlugos, Raymond F. *o.s.a.* '83 (PH)[C] Villanova, PA Villanova University.
DMoch, Paul '76 (NY) Washingtonville, NY St. Mary.
Do, Bien Quang (SD) Vietnamese.
Do, Dominic Dinh '80 (SJ) San Jose, CA St. Maria Goretti.
Do, Joseph Chung Van *o.p.* '95 (GAL) Houston, TX Our Lady of Lavang Church.
Do, Joseph Luc Van *o.p.* '74 (GAL) Houston, TX Our Lady of Lourdes.
Do, Peter Quan '02 (L) Elizabethtown, KY St. James; White Mills, KY St. Ignatius.
Do, Vien Van '90 (PEO) Moline, IL Sacred Heart.
Doaling, Patrick (MRY)[K] Watsonville, CA Magnificat the Monterey Bay Chapter.
Doan, John Baptist Minh Binh *o.p.* '03 (ARL) Arlington, VA Holy Martyrs of Vietnam.
Doan Quang Bau, Mark M. *c.m.c.* (SPC)[E] Carthage, MO Congregation of the Mother Coredemptrix, United States Assumption Province.
Do Ba Cong, James '61 (SPC)[E] Carthage, MO Congregation of the Mother Coredemptrix, United States Assumption Province.
Dobbin, Edmund J. *o.s.a.* '62 (PH)[C] Villanova, PA Villanova University; [AA] Villanova, PA St. Thomas Monastery.
Dobbin, Jay D. '64 (GF) On Duty Outside of the Diocese.
Dobbins, Michael J. '99 (ARL) Falls Church, VA St. Philip; Notaries.
Dobbins, Robert R. *s.j.* '67 (NY)[EE] Loyola Hall, Jesuit Community.
Dober, Edward J. '76 (LA) Paramount, CA Our Lady of the Rosary.
Dobes, George E. '68 (CHI) Military Chaplains; Judges.
Dobihal, Robert F. '50 (STP) Retired.
Do Binh Dinh, Luke M. *c.m.c.* '77 (SB)[E] Corona, CA Congregation of the Mother Co–Redemptrix.
Dobkowski, Paulin J. '54 (BEL) Retired.
Dobnikar, Ivan *o.s.b.* '49 (JOL)[L] Lisle, IL St. Procopius Abbey.
Dobo, Leo '46 (ORL) Lake Wales, FL Holy Spirit Retired.
Dobo, Leo '46 (ORL) Retired.
Dobosiewicz, Leon W. '46 (Y) Retired.
Dobosiewiez, Leon (ORL) Lake Wales, FL Holy Spirit.
Dobosz, Eugene '85 (ROC) Elmira, NY St. Casimir.
Dobosz, Eugene '85 (ROC) Elmira Heights, NY St. Charles Borromeo.
Dobosz, George '95 (CC) Alice, TX St. Peter Mission.
Dobranski, John '89 (BAL) Ellicott City, MD Resurrection.
Dobrosky, John M. '83 (TR) Leave of Absence.
Dobrowolski, Thomas R. '68 (FTW) Mishawaka, IN St. Michael Ukrainian Catholic Church.
Dobrowolski, Thomas '88 (STN) Mishawaka, IN St. Michael.
Dobrowski, Peter P. '71 (PHX) Bullhead City, AZ St. Margaret Mary.
Dobrowski, Peter (PHX) Defenders of the Bond.
Dobry, Jerome *o.s.b.* '44 (JOL)[L] Lisle, IL St. Procopius Abbey.
Dobrzenski, Francis G. '77 (MAR) Escanaba, MI St. Joseph & St. Patrick.
Dobrzynski, Martin J. '84 (GRY) Schererville, IN St. Michael; Worship and Spirituality, Office of.
Dobson, Christopher *t.o.r.* '78 (ARL) Herndon, VA St. Joseph.
Dobson, Gregory J. '83 (BUF) Vicars; Olean, NY St. Mary of the Angels.
Do Cao Tung, Francis Xavier M. *c.m.c.* '88 (SPC)[E] Carthage, MO Congregation of the Mother Coredemptrix, United States Assumption Province.
Do Cao Tung, Francis Xavier M. *c.m.c.* '88 (SPC)[A] Carthage, MO Congregation of the Mother Co–Redemptrix.
Dockendorf, Ronald '82 (SCL) Greenwald, MN St. Andrew's.
Dockendorf, Ronald '82 (SCL) Greenwald, MN St. John's.
Dockendorf, Ronald (SCL) Pastoral Council.
Dockendorf, Ronald (SCL) Presbyteral Council.
Dockendorf, Ronald (SCL) Deans.
Dockerill, Walter '60 (PMB) Retired.
Doctor, John L. *o.f.m.* '76 (FgM).
Doda, Eugene J. '77 (MIL) Menomonee Falls, WI St. James.
Dodd, Michael A. (TLS) Tulsa, OK Holy Family Cathedral; Defender of the Bond; Promoter of Justice.
Dodd, Michael *s.s.c.* '61 (WDC)[K] St. Columbans St. Columban's Foreign Mission Society.
Dodd, Michael *o.c.d.* (CHI)[N] Chicago, IL Discalced Carmelite Friars; Edith Stein House of Studies.
Dodds, Michael J. *o.p.* '77 (OAK) Berkeley, CA St. Mary Magdalen.
Dodds, Michael *o.p.* '77 (OAK)[N] Oakland, CA Western Dominican Province.
Dodds, Perry W. '54 (B) Retired.
Dodo, Andrew (SPR) Springfield, MA Our Lady of Hope.
Doerfler, John F. (GB) Casco, WI Holy Trinity; Judges

in First Instance.
Doerfler, John (GB) Presbyteral Council; Appointed Representatives.
Doerfler, John (GB) Assistant Chancellor.
Doerfler, Marvin G. '59 (SAT) Canyon Lake, TX St. Thomas the Apostle.
Doerger, Berard *o.f.m.* '61 (GLP) St. Michaels, AZ St. Michael.
Doerger, Stanley D. '58 (CIN) Cincinnati, OH St. Bernard.
Doerhoff, Dennis E. '76 (STL) St. Louis, MO St. Mary Magdalen; Deaneries/Deans.
Doerhoff, Dennis (STL) South.
Doering, Christopher E. '98 (CHI) Tinley Park, IL St. George.
Doerner, David L. *s.a.* '60 (LA) Los Angeles, CA Maryknoll Japanese Catholic Center; [Q] Los Angeles, CA Atonement Friars.
Doerr, Brian '98 (LFT) Special Assignment.
Doerr, Brian (LFT) Vocation Director.
Doerr, Richard J. '93 (LFT) Carmel, IN Our Lady of Mount Carmel.
Doerre, Edmund J. '63 (LC) Chippewa Falls, WI Holy Ghost; Chippewa Falls, WI St. Bridget.
Doersching, Lawrence *s.m.* '73 (FWT)[B] Fort Worth, TX Nolan Catholic High School.
Doffing, Gordon M. '60 (STP) Retired.
Dogali, Michael F. '92 (BGP) Bridgeport, CT St. Augustine Cathedral; Danbury, CT St. Joseph.
Dohar, William J. *c.s.c.* '80 (FTW)[I] San Francisco, CA.
Doheny, Richard '48 (SAC) Fair Oaks, CA St. Mel.
Doheny, Thomas R. '58 (MAD) Retired.
Doherty, Charles '58 (CC) Retired.
Doherty, D. G. *o.p.* '57 (FgM).
Doherty, Daniel C. *s.j.* '76 (BAL)[S] Baltimore Jesuit Fathers and Brothers Maryland Provincial Curia.
Doherty, Daniel J. *s.s.* '94 (BAL)[S] Washington, DC Catholic University of America; On Duty Outside the Diocese.
Doherty, Declan M. *o.s.m.* '60 (CHI)[N] Chicago Order of Friar Servants of Mary (Servites) United States of America Province, Inc..
Doherty, Donald J. *m.m.* '62 (NY).
Doherty, Edward C. *m.ss.a.* '68 (BGP)[L] Bridgeport, CT Roncalli Apartments.
Doherty, Edward C. *m.s.a.* '69 (NOR)[F] Cromwell, CT Society of the Missionaries of the Holy Apostles.
Doherty, Edward *o.s.a.* '57 (MIA)[H] Miami, FL Casa San Lorenzo.
Doherty, Francis E. '41 (MAD) Retired.
Doherty, Glennon C. '78 (STL) St. Louis, MO Our Lady of Providence; [A] St. Louis, MO Kenrick School of Theology.
Doherty, Henry F. '56 (BO) Hanover, MA St. Mary of the Sacred Heart.
Doherty, James J. *c.s.c.* '78 (PRT) Saco, ME Most Holy Trinity.
Doherty, John B. '39 (LA) Retired.
Doherty, John E. *c.ss.r.* '38 (BO) Boston, MA Dana Farber Cancer Institute.
Doherty, John R. '64 (NEW) Bayonne, NJ St. Andrew's.
Doherty, John T. '45 (NY) Bronx, NY St. Gabriel Retired.
Doherty, Louis *c.p.* '57 (CHI)[N] Pierce City, MO.
Doherty, Louis *c.p.* '57 (CHI)[N] Chicago, IL Passionist Community–Immaculate Conception Monastery.
Doherty, Michael *o.f.m.* '76 (LA)[W] Malibu, CA Serra Retreat.
Doherty, Neil '69 (MIA) Margate, FL St. Vincent.
Doherty, Patrick A. '56 (ORG) Newport Beach, CA Our Lady of Mount Carmel.
Doherty, Patrick D. *s.j.* '65 (SJ)[M] Los Gatos, CA Sacred Heart Jesuit Center.
Doherty, Patrick G. '45 (FRS) Retired.
Doherty, Patrick J. '59 (MAD) Absent on Sick Leave.
Doherty, Patrick '55 (BWN) San Juan, TX The Basilica of the National Shrine of Our Lady of San Juan del Valle.
Doherty, Patrick '55 (BWN)[J] San Juan, TX The Basilica of Our Lady of San Juan del Valle – National Shrine.
Doherty, Paul J. '95 (WOR) Uxbridge, MA St. Mary's.
Doherty, Raymond J. *s.s.e.* '58 (BUR)[E] Colchester, VT Society of St. Edmund; Burlington, VT St. Joseph's.
Doherty, Robert G. *s.j.* '60 (BO)[V] Weston, MA Campion Jesuit Community; [X] Weston, MA Campion Renewal Center.
Doherty, Robert J. '70 (BO) Medford, MA Sacred Heart.
Doherty, Terrance *s.m.a.* '70 (NEW)[N] Tenafly, NJ Society of African Missions, Provincialate, S.M.A. Fathers.
Doherty, Timothy L. '76 (RCK) Byron, IL St. Mary; Ethicist for Health Care Issues, Diocesan.
Doherty, William J. '55 (SPR) Holyoke, MA Immaculate Conception.
Dohle, Benedict *o.s.b.* '54 (OM)[K] Elkhorn, NE Mount Michael Abbey.
Dohman, William '73 (B) Retired.
Dohman, William (SAC) Legion of Mary.
Dohner, Stephen J. '76 (CLV) Cleveland Heights, OH St. Louis; Marriage and Family Office.
Dohogne, David J. '92 (SPC) Advance, MO St. Joseph; Dexter, MO Sacred Heart; Region IX; Diocesan Pastoral Council.
Doiron, David E. '69 (WOR) Worcester, MA St. Paul's Cathedral; On Special or Other Diocesan Assignment.
Dokupil, Edward J. '64 (AUS) Bastrop, TX Ascension.
Dokupil, Edward (AUS) Deans.
Dolan, Bernard M. '66 (BGP) Trumbull, CT Christ the King.
Dolan, Charles F.X. *s.j.* '46 (NEW)[C] Jersey City, NJ St. Peter's Preparatory School; [EE] New York, NY Murray–Weigel Hall.
Dolan, Charles *c.s.s.* '58 (BO)[V] Waltham, MA Stigmatine Fathers & Brothers Provincial House.
Dolan, Daniel D. *m.m.* '54 (NY)[EE] Maryknoll Maryknoll Fathers and Brothers.
Dolan, Edward *s.s.c.* '58 (OM)[K] St. Columbans, NE St. Columban's Foreign Mission Society.
Dolan, Gerald M. *o.f.m.* '56 (CAM) Cape May, NJ Our Lady Star of the Sea.
Dolan, Hugh '57 (PT) Retired.
Dolan, James J. '49 (RVC)[M] Uniondale, NY St. Pius X Residence Retired.
Dolan, James L. *o.p.* '60 (FgM).
Dolan, James Linus *o.p.* '60 (NO)[P] Provincia Dominicana de San Juan Bautista del Peru.
Dolan, James R. *s.j.* '70 (ROC)[B] Rochester, NY McQuaid Jesuit High School.
Dolan, James W. '75 (PIT) Butler, PA St. Michael the Archangel.
Dolan, Jarlath '74 (LA) Camarillo, CA Blessed Junipero Serra.
Dolan, Jarlath (LA) Judges.
Dolan, Jason R. '03 (PBR) McKees Rocks, PA Holy Ghost.
Dolan, John '89 (SD) Chula Vista, CA St. Rose of Lima; Presbyteral Council.
Dolan, Joseph K. '60 (BRK) Brooklyn, NY St. Bernadette.
Dolan, Joseph M. '92 (WOR) Auburn, MA St. Joseph's.
Dolan, Joseph V. *s.j.* '52 (NY)[EE] Loyola Hall, Jesuit Community.
Dolan, Joseph (BRK) Retired.
Dolan, Laurence P. *o.f.m.* '65 (PHX)[H] Scottsdale, AZ Franciscan Renewal Center, Inc. (Casa de Paz Y Bien).
Dolan, Lawrence F. *c.ss.r.* '42 (BRK)[V] Brooklyn, NY Our Lady of Good Counsel Residence.
Dolan, Leo A. '52 (STP) Retired.
Dolan, Leo M. '60 (SAT) San Antonio, TX St. Helena.
Dolan, Louis F. *c.s.sp.* '44 (PIT)[P] Bethel Park, PA Holy Spirit Animation Center.
Dolan, Mark A. '76 (STL) St. Louis, MO St. Jerome.
Dolan, Michael F. '99 (WDC) Lexington Park, MD Immaculate Heart of Mary.
Dolan, Michael J. '96 (HRT) Newington, CT St. Mary; [R] Hartford, CT University of Hartford Newman Center.
Dolan, Neal '64 (SD) Poway, CA St. Michael.
Dolan, Patrick G. '71 (JC) Jefferson City, MO Immaculate Conception; Ministry to Priests.
Dolan, Patrick J. '78 (L) Radcliff, KY St. Christopher; Defenders of the Bond; Army National Guard Chaplains.
Dolan, Patrick '95 (DEN) Denver, CO St. Rose of Lima; Deaneries.
Dolan, Paul A. '84 (RVC) Mineola, NY Corpus Christi.
Dolan, Paul F. '45 (BAL) Taneytown, MD St. Joseph Retired.
Dolan, Peter C. '54 (PMB) Retired.
Dolan, Raymond '56 (B) On Duty Outside the Diocese.
Dolan, Robert *s.j.* '76 (LA) Los Angeles, CA Dolores Mission.
Dolan, Thomas D. '51 (BRK) Ozone Park, NY St. Elizabeth's Retired.
Dolan, Thomas P. '45 (RCK) Harmon, IL St. Flannen; Harmon, IL St. Patrick; Harmon, IL St. Mary Retired.
Dolan, Timothy '83 (STP) Minneapolis, MN Annunciation.
Dolan, Walter *o.f.m.* '61 (CLV)[O] Brooklyn, OH Padua Franciscan Friary.
Dolan, William S. *s.j.* '82 (SY)[Q] Syracuse, NY Jesuits at LeMoyne, Inc..
Dolbec, Jacques D. *s.o.l.t.* (MO) Army Reserve Chaplains.
Dolbec, Jacques '95 (CC)[G] Robstown, TX Society of Our Lady of the Most Holy Trinity.
Dolciamore, John V. '52 (CHI) Retired.
Dolciamore, John V. (VEN)[A] Judicial Vicar; Judges; Vicar for Marriage Matters.
Dolehide, John R. *o.p.* '47 (CHI) Oak Lawn, IL St. Catherine of Alexandria; [N] Chicago Dominicans (Provincial Office).
Dolezal, Richard R. '76 (MIL) On Duty Outside the Archdiocese; Sharon, WI St. Catherine.
Dolezal, Thomas '70 (KCK) Lenexa, KS Holy Trinity.
Dolinic, Louis S. '66 (BUF) Depew, NY Our Lady of the Blessed Sacrament.
Dolinski, Pawel *s.d.s.* '97 (BRK) Brooklyn, NY Our Lady of Consolation.
Doll, Donald A. *s.j.* '68 (OM)[K] Omaha, NE Jesuit Community at Creighton University.
Doll, William P. '50 (PBL) Holly, CO St. Frances of Rome.
Dollar, Robert J. '60 (BEL) Retired.
Dollard, John J. '45 (OAK) Retired.
Dollard, Mark E. '91 (MAN) Henniker, NH St. Theresa.
Dollen, Bernard '53 (ROC) Retired.
Dollinger, John M. '57 (E) Retired.
Dolsina, Stanley '46 (DUL) Retired.
Dolski, V. Anthony '59 (GB) De Pere, WI St. Francis Xavier.
Dolter, Dennis R. *s.o.l.t.* '02 (SFE) La Joya, NM Our Lady of Sorrows.
Dolter, Dennis (CC)[G] Robstown, TX Society of Our Lady of the Most Holy Trinity.
Domagas, Reynaldo (NY) Manhattan, NY Beth Israel Medical Center.
Domandich, Anthony '58 (SEA) Retired.
Domas, John '50 (SB) Retired.
Domaszewicz, Chester '78 (VEN) LaBelle, FL Our Lady Queen of Heaven.
Dombroski, Dean W. '64 (GB) Luxemburg, WI St. Thomas the Apostle; New Franken, WI St. Kilian.
Dombroski, Dean (GB) Priests' Personnel Board.
Dombrow, William A. '70 (PH) Philadelphia, PA Resurrection of Our Lord.
Dombrowski, Francis J. *o.f.m.cap.* '59 (MIL)[R] Milwaukee, WI The Dwelling Place.
Dombrowski, John *o.f.m.* '84 (JOL) Joliet, IL St. John the Baptist; [L] Joliet, IL St. John the Baptist Friary.
Dombrowski, Robert J. '60 (FTW) Retired.
Dombrowski, Ronald J. '72 (SAG) Saginaw, MI St. Josaphat.
Dombrowski, Stanley J. *o.s.f.s.* '83 (VEN) Fort Myers, FL St. Cecilia.
Dombrowski, Steven G. '89 (CHI) Arlington Heights, IL St. Edna; Lake Villa, IL Prince of Peace.
Dombrowski, Timothy '73 (LAN)[H] Ann Arbor, MI St. Joseph Mercy Hospital.
Dome, Thomas J. *c.r.i.c.* '98 (LA) Santa Paula, CA St. Sebastian; [B] Santa Paula, CA Dom Grea House (House of Formation) Canons Regular of the Immaculate Conception, (C.R.I.C.); [Q] Santa Paula, CA Canons Regular of the Immaculate Conception.
Domec, Charles C. '56 (GAL) The Woodlands, TX Sts. Simon and Jude; Building Commission.
Domek, Kasimierz '73 (SP) Brandon, FL Church of the Nativity.
Domek, Kazimierz (SP) Cursillo, Spanish.
Domfeh–Boateng, Joseph '95 (NY) Nyack, NY St. Ann.
Domhoff, Ronald J. '72 (L) Louisville, KY Our Lady of Lourdes.
Domin, Edward R. '88 (ALN) Catasauqua, PA Annunciation B.V.M. – St. Mary's.
Domin, John M. '50 (P)[K] Beaverton, OR Maryville Nursing Home Retired.
Domin, John (P) Liturgical Commission.
Domingo, Alberto *c.m.f.* '79 (LA)[Q] Rancho Dominguez, CA Dominguez Seminary Inc..
Domingo, Santiago '65 (LAR) Laredo, TX St. Jude.
Domingos, Jaques '47 (OAK) Retired.
Domingos, Virgilio *s.j.* '02 (OAK)[N] Berkeley, CA Jesuit Community at Jesuit School of Theology at Berkeley.
Domingue, Kenneth '91 (LAF) Basile, LA St. Augustine.
Dominguez, Jesus '02 (RCK) Sterling, IL St. Mary.
Dominguez, Julio Fernandez *o.m.* '48 (SJN) San Juan, PR Ntra. Sra. de Fatima.
Dominguez, Julio '03 (CHL) Salisbury, NC Sacred Heart.
Dominguez, Patricio G. *o.m.i.* '60 (LAR) Laredo, TX San Francisco Javier Independent Mission.
Dominguez, Patricio *o.m.i.* (LAR) Cursillo Movement.
Dominguez, Ramon (FR) New Bedford.
Dominguez, Ramon (FR) New Bedford, MA St. Hedwig.
Dominguez, Ramon (FR) New Bedford, MA Nuestra Senora de Guadalupe.
Dominiak, Gerald J. '59 (MIL) Brookfield, WI St. John Vianney.
Dominiak, Thomas M. '61 (GAY) Onaway, MI St. Monica; Onaway, MI St. Paul.
Dominic, Francis J. '52 (MAD) Retired.
Dominic, Sunny (SC)[C] Carroll, IA St. Anthony Regional Hospital.
Dominicis, Severino *s.a.c.* '39 (NY) New York, NY Our Lady of Mt. Carmel.
Dominicis, Severino *s.a.c.* '39 (NY)[EE] New York, NY Pallottine Fathers.
Dominik, Kevin J. (PIT) On Duty Outside the Diocese; Judges.
Dominik, Kevin '88 (GBG)[A] Latrobe, PA St. Vincent Seminary.
Dominik, Stanley J. '58 (GRY) East Chicago, IN Holy Trinity; Whiting, IN Immaculate Conception; Whiting, IN St. Adalbert; Vicar General; Deans; Bishop's Council of Priests; Consultors; Priests' Personnel Board; Cemeteries.
Dominik, Stanley '58 (GRY) Whiting, IN Sacred Heart.

Domininc, Sunny '94 (SC) Carroll, IA Holy Spirit.
Dominique, Todd M. '94 (TOL) Sandusky, OH St. Mary.
Domme, Edward C. '79 (SFE) Albuquerque, NM Our Lady of the Assumption.
Domme, Edward (SFE) Exec. Board Members.
Dommer, Ian *o.s.b.* '79 (SCL)[I] Collegeville, MN St. John's Abbey, of the Order of St. Benedict.
Dompke, Ramon *c.ss.r.* '64 (CHI) Chicago, IL Our Lady of Lourdes.
Dompke, Ramon *c.ss.r.* '64 (CHI)[N] Chicago, IL The Redemptorists of Blessed Sacrament.
Domurat, Thomas S. '79 (BO) Lowell, MA St. Margaret.
Don, Sextus '79 (FTW) Wabash, IN St. Bernard.
Dona, Thomas M. '65 (DEN) Retired.
Donadio, Vincent J. '73 (TR) Leave of Absence.
Donaghey, Bernard '29 (SB) Patton State Hospital.
Donaghey, John *s.v.d.* '54 (CHI)[B] Techny, IL Divine Word Residence.
Donaghey, Patrick H.M. '85 (ATL) Lilburn, GA St. Stephen the Martyr.
Donaghy, Thomas J. '79 (BAL) Wallingford, PA St. John Chrysostom Retired.
Donahoe, Patrick *t.o.r.* '74 (ALT)[A] Loretto, PA St. Francis University; [F] Loretto, PA Mount Assisi Friary.
Donahoe, Thomas (SC) Retired.
Donahue, Aidan N. '86 (HRT) Bloomfield, CT Sacred Heart; Ecumenical Affairs, Commission for; Office of Continuing Formation of Priests.
Donahue, Aidan '86 (HRT)[C] West Hartford, CT Saint Joseph College.
Donahue, Anthony *o.f.m.cap.* '51 (SP)[O] Seminole, FL Capuchin Franciscan Residence.
Donahue, Bernard F. *o.s.f.s.* '58 (ALN)[B] Center Valley, PA DeSales University; [K] Center Valley, PA Oblates of St. Francis de Sales.
Donahue, Brian G. '83 (FAR) Special Assignment; Moderator of the Curia; Vicars General; Vicar for Clergy; Diocesan College of Consultors; Corporate Board; Diocesan Finance Council.
Donahue, Cecil J. *o.s.b.* '54 (MAN)[K] Manchester, NH St. Anselm Abbey.
Donahue, Denis M. '90 (ARL) Alexandria, VA St. Rita's.
Donahue, Edward J. '80 (ALN) Unassigned.
Donahue, Eugene L. *s.j.* '70 (MIL)[O] Milwaukee, WI Miguel Pro Jesuit Community; [O] Milwaukee, WI Jesuit Provincial Office, Wisconsin Province.
Donahue, John G. '60 (STP) Retired.
Donahue, John J. *s.j.* '64 (BAL).
Donahue, John J. *c.s.c.* '70 (NY)[A] Manhattan, NY St. Clare's Hospital & Health Center.
Donahue, John R. *s.j.* '64 (BAL)[B] Timonium, MD Loyola Graduate Center –Timonium Campus; [S] Baltimore, MD Jesuit Community of Loyola College, Inc..
Donahue, Joseph P. '45 (HRT) Retired.
Donahue, L. Scott '82 (CHI) Chicago, IL St. Robert Bellarmine; [H] Chicago, IL Mission of Our Lady of Mercy–Mercy Home for Boys and Girls.
Donahue, Martin P. '61 (WOR) Worcester, MA St. Christopher; Deans.
Donahue, Michael E. *s.j.* '80 (NY)[EE] New York, NY.
Donahue, Richard T. '68 (BO) On Duty Outside the Archdiocese.
Donahue, Scott (CHI) Mercy Home for Boys and Girls; [G] Chicago, IL Mercy Home for Boys & Girls.
Donahue, Stephen D. '86 (IND) North Vernon, IN St. Mary/Nativity of the Blessed Virgin Mary.
Donahue, Timothy C. (SAV) Macon, GA Holy Spirit; Council of Priests.
Donahue, William P. '70 (GBG) Latrobe, PA St. Rose.
Donahue, William P. '86 (SR) Unassigned.
Donahue, William *c.s.c.* '49 (ORL)[E] Cocoa Beach, FL Congregation of Holy Cross, Eastern Province.
Donahugh, Donald E. '62 (RCK)[C] Port Arthur, TX CHRISTUS Health Southeast Texas.
Donahugh, Donald E. '62 (RCK) Active Outside the Diocese.
Donajkowski, Charles G. '91 (GAY) Rogers City, MI St. Ignatius; Vicars (by region); Procurators–Advocates.
Donald, Michael L. '72 (STL) Crystal City, MO Sacred Heart.
Donaldson, Richard *o.f.m.cap.* '57 (SP)[O] Seminole, FL Capuchin Franciscan Residence.
Donaldson, Thomas J. '68 (LC) Ellsworth, WI St. Francis of Assisi; Personnel Council.
Donaldson, Thomas *c.ss.r.* '79 (GR) Grand Rapids, MI St. Alphonsus; [I] Grand Rapids, MI The Society of the Redemptorists of the City of Grand Rapids.
Donarski, Richard *o.c.s.o.* '57 (ATL)[K] Conyers, GA The Monastery of the Holy Spirit.
Donat, Robert J. '66 (SB) Montclair, CA Our Lady of Lourdes.
Donatelli, Gene M. *s.j.* '82 (CHI)[C] Chicago, IL Jesuit Community at Loyola University Chicago.
Donatelli, Gino *s.j.* '82 (CHI)[J] Maywood, IL Foster G. McGaw Hospital of Loyola University of Chicago.
Donatelli, Philip J. '67 (PIT) McMurray, PA St. Benedict the Abbot.
Donato, John *c.s.c.* '91 (P)[B] University of Portland.
Donato, John *c.s.c* '91 (P)[L] Portland, OR Holy Cross Fathers & Brothers, C.S.C. – University of Portland.
Donato, John *c.s.c.* '91 (P)[P] Portland, OR University of Portland.
Donato, Thomas A. '65 (NEW)[A] Elected Members; [B] School of Diplomacy and Intl. Rels..
Don Bosco, Dasam F. '85 (CAM) Cherry Hill, NJ St. Thomas More.
Dondanville, Joseph '95 (PEO) Champaign, IL St. Joseph's; Tolono, IL St. Patrick's; [B] Champaign, IL High School of St. Thomas More.
Donders, Sjef *m.afr.* '57 (WDC)[M] Washington, DC Missionaries of Africa.
Dondi, Edward K. (OAK)[K] Hayward, CA St. Rose Hospital.
Dondzila, Henry J. '56 (GR) Retired.
Donegan, Augustine *t.o.r.* '46 (STU)[F] Steubenville, OH Holy Spirit Friary.
Donegan, Augustine *t.o.r.* '46 (STU)[A] Steubenville, OH Franciscan University of Steubenville.
Donegan, William *ss.cc.* '65 (FR).
Donehue, Ambrose A. *o.f.m.* '51 (PRO)[N] Providence, RI St. Francis Chapel & City Ministry Center.
Donehue, Ambrose *o.f.m.* '51 (PRO)[P] Providence, RI St. Francis Friary.
Donellan, Thomas J. '56 (BAL) Hunt Valley, MD Catholic Community of St. Francis Xavier.
Donellen, Thomas J. '56 (BAL) Retired.
Doner, Roy '81 (SAC) Colusa, CA Our Lady of Lourdes.
Dong, Quang Minh '91 (OAK) Pinole, CA St Joseph's; Presbyteral Council.
Dong, Quang (OAK) Consultors.
Dongo, Bruno '01 (CAM) Cherry Hill, NJ Queen of Heaven.
Donini, Leone '95 (NEW) On Duty Outside the Archdiocese.
Donio, Frank S. *s.a.c.* '94 (BAL) Baltimore, MD St. Jude Shrine.
Donio, Thomas S. '95 (CAM) Cherry Hill, NJ St. Thomas More.
Donish, Peter M. '70 (PSC) Hazleton, PA St. Mary's.
Donlan, Paul A. '62 (OAK)[X] Los Angeles, CA Prelature of the Holy Cross and Opus Dei; [R] Berkeley, CA Opus Dei.
Donlan, Robert R. '67 (SP) Brooksville, FL St. Anthony.
Donlan, Robert (SP) Incardination Commission.
Donlon, Aidan *s.a.c.* '55 (FWT) Wichita Falls, TX State Hospital.
Donlon, Aidan *s.a.c.* '55 (FWT)[G] Wichita Falls, TX United Regional Health Care System.
Donlon, Aidan *s.a.c.* (FWT) Wichita Falls–United Regional Health Care System–Chaplain.
Donlon, James I. '75 (ALB) Lake George, NY Sacred Heart; Special Assignment; Vicar Judicial; Judges; Bishop's Delegate for Marriage Dispensations; Presbyteral Council; Diocesan Board of Consultors.
Donlon, James I. (COS) Associate Judges.
Donlon, James W. '65 (PH) Conshohocken, PA St. Matthew.
Donlon, James '75 (ALB)[M] Albany, NY Religious of the Sacred Heart.
Donnar, Jeffrey '78 (SAG) Rosebush, MI St. Henry.
Donnay, Dave *o.s.c.* '01 (STP) Shoreview, MN St. Odilia.
Donnay, David *o.s.c.* '01 (STP)[M] Shoreview, MN Crosier Community of Shoreview.
Donnay, Raymond '50 (SCL) Retired.
Donnell, Hugh F. *c.m.* (FgM).
Donnellan, Francis A. *s.s.e.* '45 (MOB)[G] Selma, AL Edmundite Fathers.
Donnelly, Brendan '52 (ORL) Retired.
Donnelly, Eamonn *s.v.d.* '70 (LA) Los Angeles, CA Our Lady of Lourdes.
Donnelly, Edward J. '54 (RVC) Hicksville, NY Holy Family.
Donnelly, Eugene F. '48 (BRK) Jackson Heights, NY Our Lady of Fatima Retired.
Donnelly, John P. *s.j.* '65 (MIL)[O] Milwaukee, WI Jesuit Community at Marquette University.
Donnelly, John '58 (SPK) Retired.
Donnelly, Joseph T. '71 (HRT) Southbury, CT Sacred Heart.
Donnelly, Joseph–Benedict *o.c.s.o.* '43 (P)[L] Lafayette, OR The Cistercian (Trappist) Abbey of Our Lady of Guadalupe.
Donnelly, Lawrence E. '49 (LA) Retired.
Donnelly, Michael *s.s.c.* '63 (OM)[K] St. Columbans St. Columban's Foreign Mission Society.
Donnelly, Michael *s.s.c.* '63 (PRO)[P] Bristol, RI St. Columban's Retirement House.
Donnelly, P. Martin '64 (TOL) Toledo, OH St. Martin de Porres; Toledo, OH St. Mary of the Assumption.
Donnelly, Paul J. '58 (BIR) Retired.
Donnelly, Richard A. '62 (PRO) Cranston, RI St. Mark.
Donnelly, Robert *m.m.* '59 (HON)[G] Honolulu, HI Maryknoll Fathers House (M.M.).
Donnelly, Robert '91 (ALB) Retired.
Donnelly, Sean J. '82 (CLV) Brunswick, OH St. Ambrose.
Donnelly, Sean '54 (SPK) Retired.
Donnelly, Stephen H. (RVC) Sound Beach, NY St. Louis de Montfort.
Donnelly, Thomas *m.m.* '57 (HON) Kamuela, HI Church of the Annunciation; [G] Kamuela, HI.
Donnelly, Thomas '61 (RNO) Reno, NV St. Rose of Lima.
Donnelly, Timothy *o.s.b.* '65 (LR)[A] Subiaco, AR Subiaco Monastery.
Donnelly, William F. *s.j.* '63 (SJ)[B] Santa Clara, CA Jesuit Community.
Donnelly, William J. *m.m.* '65 (FgM).
Donnelly, William J. *o.s.a.* '67 (PH)[AA] Villanova, PA St. John Stone Friary.
Donnelly, William P. '64 (PH) Upper Darby, PA St. Alice.
Donnelly, William '64 (ROC) Rochester, NY St. Mary.
Donnelly, William '64 (ROC)[I] Rochester, NY Becket Hall.
Donnelly, William '64 (ROC)[L] Rochester, NY Eastman School of Music Catholic Students Organization.
Donnelly, William '71 (JOL) Hinsdale, IL St. Isaac Jogues.
Donnelly, William (ROC) Office of Vocations.
Donner, Jeffrey '78 (SAG) Mount Pleasant, MI St. Mary University Parish.
Donner, Jeffrey (SAG) Vicars for Vicariates.
Dono, Abram E. *s.t.* '64 (TUC) Tucson, AZ Blessed Kateri Tekakwitha; [I] South Tucson, AZ Blessed Kateri Tekakwitha Parish Center.
Donofrio, Michael J. '76 (PH) Absent on Leave.
Donoghue, Henry A. '64 (WOR) Worcester, MA St. George.
Donoghue, Henry Thomas *o.p.* '57 (WDC)[B] Washington, DC Dominican House of Studies.
Donoghue, John F. '54 (B) Retired.
Donoghue, Pat (P) Board Members.
Donoghue, Patrick F. *m.m.* '50 (FgM).
Donoghue, Patrick '82 (P) Sublimity, OR St. Boniface.
Donoghue, Paul *s.m.* '68 (STL)[O] St. Louis Provincialate of the Society of Mary, Province of the United States.
Donoher, Edward W. *c.s.b.* '49 (DET)[E] Redford, MI Catholic Central High School.
Donohoe, Edward '50 (STO) Diamond Springs, CA Retired.
Donohoe, Patrick K. '82 (CC) Beeville, TX St. Joseph.
Donohoe, Peter '50 (SFD) Retired.
Donohoe, Philip M. '53 (OKL) El Reno, OK Sacred Heart; Defenders of the Bond.
Donohoe, Richard E. '84 (BIR) Birmingham, AL St. Paul's Cathedral; Moderator of the Curia; Members; Diocesan College of Consultors; Diocesan College of Vicars; Diocesan Finance Council; Army National Guard Chaplains.
Donohoe, Richard (BIR) Judges.
Donohoe, Robert W. '50 (CLV) Peninsula, OH Mother of Sorrows.
Donohoe, Stephen S. '92 (BO) Natick, MA St. Patrick; Navy Reserve Chaplains.
Donohoe, Thomas E. '62 (RVC) Long Beach, NY St. Mary of the Isle.
Donohoe, Thomas P. '52 (BO) Carlisle, MA St. Irene.
Donohoe, William *c.pp.s.* '48 (CIN)[B] Carthagena, OH St. Charles.
Donohoo, Daniel B. '86 (IND) Indianapolis, IN St. Matthew.
Donohoo, Daniel (IND) Archdiocesan Judges.
Donohoo, Daniel (IND) Council of Priests.
Donohoo, Lawrence J. *o.p.* '85 (WDC)[B] Washington, DC Dominican House of Studies.
Donohue, Edward J. *o.f.m.* '56 (NEW) East Rutherford, NJ St. Joseph's.
Donohue, James T. *c.s.c.* '61 (BGP)[P] Bridgeport, CT Provincial Offices of the Priests and Brothers of Holy Cross, Eastern Province.
Donohue, James *c.r.* '83 (BAL)[B] Emmitsburg, MD Mount Saint Mary's College.
Donohue, John F. *o.carm.* '48 (JOL)[L] Darien Carmelite Provincial Office.
Donohue, John J. '48 (CHI) Retired.
Donohue, John J. *s.j.* '59 (FgM).
Donohue, John J. '73 (NEW) Bloomfield, NJ St. Valentine.
Donohue, John W. *s.j.* '50 (NY)[EE] New York, NY "America;" Residence and publication office of the America Press.
Donohue, John '73 (NEW) Belleville, NJ Clara Maass Medical Center; Chaplains.
Donohue, Michael T. '75 (NOR) East Lyme, CT St. Matthias; Deans; Building Commission; Campaign for Human Development; Navy Reserve Chaplains.
Donohue, Patrick W. '75 (NEW) Hackensack, NJ Holy Trinity; South Central Bergen Deanery 5.
Donohue, Paul *m.c.c.j.* '75 (CIN)[M] Cincinnati, OH Comboni Missionaries (Verona Fathers)–Comboni Mission Center; [V] Cincinnati, OH The Comboni Missionaries Auxiliary, Inc..
Donohue, Peter M. *o.s.a.* '79 (PH)[C] Villanova University; [AA] Villanova, PA Fray de Leon Community.
Donohue, Peter *c.s.c.* '56 (ORL)[E] Cocoa Beach, FL Congregation of Holy Cross, Eastern Province.
Donohue, Peter *c.s.c.* '56 (ORL) Retired.

Donohue, Raymond A.J. '85 (BUF) Mayville, NY St. Isaac Jogues; Mayville, NY St. Mary.
Donohue, Robert W. '50 (CLV) Retired.
Donohue, Steven *s.p.s.* '59 (SJ)[M] Saratoga, CA St. Patrick's Missionary Society.
Donohue, Thomas E. '41 (L) Louisville, KY St. Clement Retired.
Donohue, Timothy C. *o.carm.* '51 (NY)[EE] Scarborough, NY Carmelite Fathers, NY Prov. of St. Elias.
Donoso, Fermin J. *c.s.c.* '67 (FTW)[I] Congregacion de Santa Cruz.
Donovan, Brian G. *o.p.* '64 (GAL)[Q] Houston, TX Dominican Friars, St. Mark Priory, Inc..
Donovan, Charles A. *c.s.p.* '40 (NY)[EE] Jamaica Estates Paulist Fathers Generalate; San Francisco, CA Old St. Mary's Cathedral Retired.
Donovan, Charles *c.ss.r.* '72 (ATL) Hapeville, GA St. John the Evangelist.
Donovan, Daniel E. *c.m.* '42 (PH).
Donovan, David I. *s.j.* '68 (BO)[V] Watertown, MA The Society of Jesus of New England–Provincial Offices.
Donovan, Dennis *s.d.b.* '83 (COL)[H] Columbus, OH Salesian Residence.
Donovan, Donald F. *m.m.* '55 (FgM).
Donovan, Edward R. *c.s.p.* '59 (NY)[EE] Jamaica Estates Paulist Fathers Generalate.
Donovan, Edward '54 (NY) Retired.
Donovan, Edward *c.s.p.* '59 (LA) Los Angeles, CA St. Paul the Apostle.
Donovan, J. Michael '65 (SY) Marcellus, NY St. Francis Xavier.
Donovan, J. Paul '58 (TLS) Owasso, OK St. Henry; Diocesan Senators Retired.
Donovan, James J. '87 (CHI) Hometown, IL Our Lady of Loretto.
Donovan, James W. *c.s.p.* '68 (WDC)[B] Washington, DC St. Paul's College.
Donovan, James *o.m.i.* '51 (BEL)[F] Belleville, IL Missionary Oblates of Mary Immaculate – St. Henry's Oblate Residence.
Donovan, James *o.p.* '55 (PRT)[I] Lewiston, ME SS. Peter and Paul House.
Donovan, John L. '53 (BO) Senior Priests Retired.
Donovan, John P. '86 (SY) Special Assignment; Judges; Priests' Personnel Committee; Vocation Promotion.
Donovan, John T. '44 (MIL) Retired.
Donovan, Joseph F. '53 (BO) Senior Priests Retired.
Donovan, Joseph J. '51 (NEW) Bergenfield, NJ St. John the Evangelist Retired.
Donovan, Joseph J. *m.m.* '79 (FgM).
Donovan, Kevin G. '88 (HRT) Milford, CT St. Mary.
Donovan, Michael A. '62 (DET) Roseville, MI St. Donald.
Donovan, Michael B. *o.s.f.s.* '67 (WIL)[J] Childs, MD Retirement and Assisted Care Facility.
Donovan, Michael *o.de.m.* (BUF)[O] LeRoy, NY Order of the BVM of Mercy/Mercedarian Friars; [O] LeRoy, NY St. Raymond Nonnatus Novitiate.
Donovan, Patrick J. *o.s.m.* '55 (ORG) New Britain, CT St. Francis of Assisi; [R] New Britain, CT Central Connecticut State University Newman House; Fullerton, CA St. Juliana Falconieri; [M] Fullerton, CA California State University Fullerton, Newman Center.
Donovan, Patrick J. *m.m.* '57 (SJ)[M] Los Altos, CA Maryknoll.
Donovan, Patrick M. *o.s.m.* '55 (CHI)[N] Chicago Order of Friar Servants of Mary (Servites) United States of America Province, Inc.; [I] Fullerton, CA St. Juliana Falconieri Priory.
Donovan, Paul A. *s.j.* '56 (BAL)[S] Poway, CA.
Donovan, Richard R. '58 (RVC) Malverne, NY Our Lady of Lourdes.
Donovan, Robert C. '70 (FR) Pocasset, MA St. John the Evangelist.
Donovan, Robert '53 (ROC) Retired.
Donovan, Thomas A. '50 (GAL)[N] Houston, TX Pope John Paul XXIII Priests' Residence Retired.
Donovan, Thomas F. '57 (BRK) Bayside, NY Sacred Heart of Jesus; Lawyers.
Donovan, Victor *c.p.* '36 (HRT)[M] West Hartford Holy Family Monastery/Retreat.
Donovan, Walter J. '44 (ATL) Atlanta, GA Sacred Heart of Jesus Retired.
Donovan, William G. '94 (PH) Graduate Studies.
Donovan, William L. '43 (SCR)[N] Dunmore, PA Villa St. Joseph; Presbyteral Council Retired.
Donovan, William '50 (SY) Retired.
Donovan, William '79 (RVC) Absent on Leave.
Donovon, Michael (CLV) Lutheran Medical Center.
Donton, Joseph P. '91 (PEO) Washington, IL St. Patrick's.
Doocey, Michael F. '52 (BO) Senior Priests Retired.
Doody, Cyril J. '57 (BRK) Brooklyn, NY St. Mark's Retired.
Doody, Michael J. *s.j.* '78 (BO)[V] Boston The Society of Jesus of New England–Provincial Offices; [C] Saint Louis University; [O] St. Louis, MO Jesuit Community Corporation at St. Louis University – Jesuit Hall.
Doody, Patrick *c.s.sp.* '68 (BRK)[V] Long Island City, NY Holy Ghost Fathers of Ireland.
Doody, Patrick *c.s.sp.* '68 (BRK)[Z] Long Island City, NY World Compassion Link.
Doody, Peter J. '71 (PAT) Clifton, NJ St. Philip the Apostle; Presbyteral Council; College of Consultors.
Doody, Timothy F. '42 (GRY) Retired.
Doogan, James A. *s.j.* '98 (SAC)[D] Sacramento, CA Jesuit High School; [I] Carmichael, CA Jesuit High School Community of Sacramento.
Doogan, Joseph H. '48 (SEA) Seattle, WA Our Lady of Fatima; Adjunct Judicial Vicar; Judges; Special Assignment Retired.
Dooher, John A. (BO) Dedham, MA St. Mary.
Doolan, Ailbe *o.c.d.* '53 (SJ)[M] San Jose, CA Carmelite Monastery, Novitiate.
Doolan, John M. *s.j.* '63 (NY)[EE] New York, NY Murray–Weigel Hall.
Doolan, Vincent P. '80 (BO) Quincy, MA St. Joseph.
Dooley, Bernard J. *s.j.* '55 (BAL)[S] Juno Beach, FL.
Dooley, Bernard *s.j.* (PMB) Palm Beach Gardens, FL St. Patrick.
Dooley, Daniel M. '61 (PH) Philadelphia, PA St. Matthew.
Dooley, Harry J. *c.s.p.* '58 (NY)[EE] Jamaica Estates Paulist Fathers Generalate.
Dooley, Joseph P. '56 (ALN) Retired.
Dooley, Joseph W. '44 (IND) Retired.
Dooley, Kevin F. '84 (MAD) Mazomanie, WI St. Barnabas; Mazomanie, WI St. John the Baptist.
Dooley, Michael D. *s.j.* '85 (LAF)[A] Grand Coteau, LA St. Charles College.
Dooley, Peter C. '76 (RVC) Bellmore, NY St. Barnabas the Apostle.
Dooley, Thomas V. '91 (DM) Leon, IA St. Brendan; Maloy, IA Immaculate Conception.
Dooley, William E. *s.j.* '46 (MIL)[O] Wauwatosa, WI Jesuit Community at St. Camillus.
Dooling, Patrick '82 (MRY) Capitola, CA St. Joseph.
Dooling, Patrick (MRY) Presbyteral Council.
Dooling, Patrick (MRY) Defenders of the Bond.
Dooner, William B. '70 (PH) Penndel, PA Our Lady of Grace.
Dopierala, Rafael '94 (CC) Corpus Christi, TX Saint John the Baptist.
Do Quang Chou, Peter (NSH) Vietnamese Ministry.
Dora, Peter A. '72 (ATL) Madison, GA St. James; Defenders of the Bond.
Dora, Peter P. '67 (BGP) Stratford, CT Holy Name of Jesus; Presbyteral Council.
Dora, Peter P. '67 (BGP) Trumbull, CT St. Theresa.
Dorado, Jaime (PMB) Cursillo Movement for Hispanics.
Dorais, Gerald A. '55 (WOR) Fitchburg, MA St. Francis of Assisi.
Doran, Austin C. '78 (LA) Encino, CA Our Lady of Grace.
Doran, Brian '71 (LA) West Hollywood, CA St. Ambrose.
Doran, Brian '71 (LA) On Sick Leave.
Doran, Edward E. *o.s.a.* '61 (PH) Philadelphia, PA St. Rita of Cascia.
Doran, Edward P. '84 (BRK) Hollis, NY St. Gerard Majella.
Doran, James B. *o.m.v., p.v.* '86 (DEN) Denver, CO Holy Ghost.
Doran, James *o.s.b.* (WOR)[O] Still River, MA Benedictine Monks, St. Benedict Abbey.
Doran, John E. '66 (WOR) Leominster, MA St. Leo's.
Doran, John E. '72 (NEW) South Orange, NJ Our Lady of Sorrows; College of Consultors; Members.
Doran, Joseph '66 (NY) Chester, NY St. Columba.
Doran, Joseph *s.d.b.* '66 (NY)[EE] New Rochelle, NY Salesian Provincial House.
Doran, Thomas M. '47 (SY) Utica, NY Blessed Sacrament Retired.
Doran, William J. *s.j.* '55 (OM)[C] Omaha, NE Creighton Preparatory School.
Dorcey, Joseph P. *c.ss.r.* '79 (CHI)[N] Chicago, IL Redemptorist Theology Residence.
Dorcey, Joseph *c.ss.r.* '79 (DEN).
Dorcy, Roger P. '80 (PBL)[N] Pueblo, CO Sacred Heart Cathedral; Presbyteral Council.
Dorcy, Roger (PBL) Presbyteral Council–College of Consultors.
Dore, Bernard M. '82 (PRO) Misquamicut, RI St. Clare.
Dore, James M. *o.s.m.* '59 (CHI) Chicago, IL Annunciata; [N] Chicago, IL Annunciata Priory; [N] Chicago, IL Order of Friar Servants of Mary (Servites) United States of America Province, Inc..
Dore, Robert '89 (JKS) Chatawa, MS St. Teresa.
Dore, Thomas M. '61 (CHI) Oak Park, IL St. Giles.
Dore, Timothy *o.f.m.conv.* '92 (SPR) Chicopee, MA St. Stanislaus Basilica.
Dorenbusch, Thomas A. '57 (CIN) Retired.
Dorff, Francis W. *o.praem.* '60 (SFE)[I] Albuquerque, NM Santa Maria de la Vid Priory.
Dorgan, Gerard L. '58 (BO) Danvers, MA St. Mary of the Annunciation.
Dorgan, John J. '65 (RIC) Norfolk, VA Basilica of St. Mary of the Immaculate Conception.
Dorhauer, C. Robert '63 (STL) St. Louis, MO St. Richard.
Dorian, Brendan '58 (YAK) Retired.
Dorich, John M. '61 (VNN) Retired.
Dorin, Bob *s.j.* '67 (SPK)[F] Spokane, WA Sacred Heart Medical Center.
Dorin, Robert R. *s.j.* '67 (BO)[V] Boston The Society of Jesus of New England–Provincial Offices; [B] Spokane, WA Gonzaga University.
Doriot, Thomas E. '49 (FTW) Retired.
Doris, Andrew T. '47 (SAV) Augusta, GA Church of the Most Holy Trinity Retired.
Doris, John A. '75 (SCR) Dunmore, PA St. Mary of Mount Carmel; Diocesan Finance Council; Deans.
Dorley, Paul D. '49 (TOL) Retired.
Dormer, David J. '77 (SCR) Military Chaplains; Army Chaplains.
Dormido, Arecio '83 (NY) Downstate Correctional Facility.
Dormido, Arecio (NY) Beacon Correctional Facility.
Dorn, George *c.ss.r.* '50 (ORL)[E] New Smyrna Beach, FL St. Alphonsus Villa–Redemptorist Fathers and Brothers.
Dorn, Jerry *g.h.m.* '78 (CIN)[M] Cincinnati Headquarters of Glenmary Home Missioners.
Dorn, Jim Van *o.f.m.conv.* '67 (IND)[J] Mount St. Francis, IN Mount Saint Francis Friary and Retreat Center.
Dorn, John *o.ss.t.* '81 (BAL) Hanover, MD St. Lawrence.
Dorn, John *o.ss.t.* '81 (BAL)[S] Hanover, MD St. Lawrence Rectory.
Dorn, Louis E. '72 (JC) Louisiana, MO St. Joseph; IV. Jefferson City; Senators; Liturgical Commission; Residents Encounter Christ.
Dorn, Rupert *o.f.m.cap* '51 (MAD)[K] Madison, WI San Damiano Friary.
Dorn, Thomas E. '03 (CIN) Coldwater, OH Holy Trinity.
Dornak, Melvin '92 (AUS) Waco, TX St. Louis.
Dornbos, William '68 (HEL) Special Assignments.
Dorner, Joseph E. (GB) Marinette, WI Holy Family.
Dorner, Joseph (GB) Society of St. Vincent de Paul.
Dorney, Dennis C. '67 (TLS) Tulsa, OK Church of St. Mary; [J] Tulsa, OK Priest Retirement Trust of the Roman Catholic Diocese of Tulsa; Vicar General; Diocesan Senators; Ex Officio; Diocesan Consultors; Priests' Personnel Committee; Seminary Board.
Dorney, James J. '58 (NY) Staten Island, NY St. Peter; Staten Island.
Dorney, James J. (NY) AUXILIARY CHAPLAINS CONTRACT CHAPLAINS.
Dorney, James (NY)[G] Staten Island, NY Seton Foundation for Learning, Inc..
Dorniak, Joseph *o.f.m.conv.* '79 (BUF) Athol Springs, NY St. Francis of Assisi.
Doro, Michael J. '72 (MAD) Janesville, WI St. John Vianney.
Doroin, Elias E. '64 (GAL)[K] Catholic Chaplain Corps, Texas Medical Center.
Dorpe, Ray Van *c.m.* '82 (STL)[O] St. Louis, MO Lazarist Residence.
Dorr, James *c.m.* '58 (BRK)[V] Jamaica, NY Vincentian Residence.
Dorr, Richard J. '55 (DET) Retired.
Dorrill, James F. '60 (MOB) Retired.
Dorrler, Michael E. *s.j.* '83 (CHI)[N] Chicago, IL Clark Street Jesuit Residence.
Dorrmann, William J. '55 (CIN) Harrison, OH St. John the Baptist Retired.
Dorsch, Henry L. '68 (SPR) Southwick, MA Our Lady of the Lake; [P] Pittsfield, MA Berkshire Community College.
Dorsch, Larry W. '75 (WH) Wheeling, WV St. Joseph's Cathedral.
Dorsel, John F. '61 (R) Retired.
Dorsey, Dan *g.h.m.* '78 (CIN)[M] Fairfield, OH.
Dorsey, Garrett D. '59 (PIT) Allison Park, PA St. Ursula.
Dorsey, Joseph A. *c.s.c.* '57 (FTW)[I] Congregacion de Santa Cruz.
Dorsey, Patrick J. *s.j.* '96 (MIL)[O] Milwaukee, WI Jesuit Community at Marquette University.
Dorson, James E. '77 (RIC) Lynchburg, VA St. Thomas More.
Dorsonville, Mario E. '85 (WDC) Bethesda, MD Our Lady of Lourdes.
Dorta, Juan M. *s.j.* '55 (MIA)[H] Miami, FL Villa Javier.
Dorta, Juan Manuel *s.j.* '55 (MIA)[D] Miami, FL Belen Jesuit Preparatory School; [H] Belen Jesuit Alumni Association.
Dorton, John '70 (DM) On Sabbatical.
Dorton, John (DM) Advocates.
Dorula, Douglas E. '02 (GBG) Indiana, PA St. Bernard.
Dorwart, William D. *c.s.c.* '80 (FTW)[I] Notre Dame, IN.
Dory, Michael '76 (GB) Military Chaplains; Navy Chaplains.
Dosch, Leander *o.c.s.o.* '50 (SLC)[F] Huntsville, UT Abbey of Our Lady of the Holy Trinity of the Order of Cistercians.
Doscher, Joseph *s.c.j.* '73 (SP)[O] Pinellas Park, FL Priests of the Sacred Heart Retired.

Dosen, Anthony *c.m.* (CHI)[N] Chicago DePaul Vincentian Residence.
Dosh, Mark B. '58 (STP) Excelsior, MN St. John the Baptist; Censores Librorum.
Dosiak, Mykhalo (STF) Chancery Secretary.
Dosiak, Mykhaylo (STF) Brooklyn, NY St. Nicholas; Staten Island, NY Holy Trinity.
Doskey, Clinton J. '54 (NO) New Orleans, LA St. Pius X; Adjutant Judicial Vicar; Archdiocesan Consultors.
Dos Reis, Antonio (OAK) Co Directors.
Dos Reis, Jose Q. '64 (PRO) Cranston, RI.
dos Reis, Jose Q. '64 (PRO)[C] Warwick, RI Bishop Hendricken High School.
dos Remedios, Francis *o.s.b.* '82 (BIS)[A] Richardton, ND Assumption Abbey Retired.
Dos Santos, Jose A.F. '53 (FR) Retired.
Dos Santos, Tarcisio *s.d.b.* '89 (NY) Port Chester, NY Our Lady of the Rosary.
Dostie, Benoit *m.s.c.* '40 (OG)[E] Watertown, NY Missionaries of the Sacred Heart.
Dotson, Paul J. '68 (LA) Redondo Beach, CA St. Lawrence Martyr.
Doty, Craig A. '97 (LIN) Aurora, NE St. Mary's; Judges.
Doucet, David A. '69 (BO) Somerville, MA St. Benedict.
Doudican, James '48 (CHY) Cheyenne, WY Holy Trinity Retired.
Doudican, James '48 (CHY) Retired.
Dougher, James P. '03 (SCR) Scranton, PA St. Patrick's; [D] Scranton, PA Bishop Hannan High School.
Dougherty, C. Peter (LAN) Retired.
Dougherty, Charles '63 (SJ) Saratoga, CA Church of the Ascension.
Dougherty, Charles *c.p.* '68 (RVC) Shelter Island Heights, NY Our Lady of the Isle.
Dougherty, Damien R. *o.f.m.* '75 (STL)[A] St. Louis, MO Kenrick School of Theology; [S] Dittmer, MO Il Ritiro–The Little Retreat.
Dougherty, Daniel J. '70 (PH) Drexel Hill, PA St. Dorothy.
Dougherty, David *c.pp.s.* '49 (CIN)[B] Carthagena, OH St. Charles.
Dougherty, Denis *o.s.b.* '56 (SPC) Springfield, MO St. Joseph's.
Dougherty, Denis *o.s.b.* (SPC) Presbyteral Council.
Dougherty, Edward C.A. *s.j.* '72 (BAL)[S] Jesuit House of Studies.
Dougherty, Edward J. '53 (TR) Retired.
Dougherty, Edward J. *s.j.* '70 (NO).
Dougherty, Edward M. *m.m.* '79[P] (FgM).
Dougherty, Edward '53 (TR)[M] Trenton, NJ Villa Vianney.
Dougherty, Eugene J. '53 (PIT)[N] Pittsburgh, PA St. John Vianney Manor Retired.
Dougherty, Francis D. *o.s.f.s.* '38 (FgM).
Dougherty, Henry E. '41 (PH) Retired.
Dougherty, Hugh J. '69 (PH) Pottstown, PA St. Thomas More.
Dougherty, James J. *s.j.* '59 (STL)[O] St. Louis, MO St. Louis University High School Jesuit Community.
Dougherty, James R. '68 (BEL) Trenton, IL St. Mary.
Dougherty, James '67 (JOL) Glen Ellyn, IL St. Petronille.
Dougherty, John J. *c.s.c.* '94 (PHX) Phoenix, AZ St. Gregory.
Dougherty, Paul V. '80 (PH)[A] Wynnewood, PA Theological Seminary of St. Charles Borromeo, Overbrook.
Dougherty, Stephen J. '73 (PH) Narberth, PA St. Margaret.
Dougherty, Steve '03 (CC)[G] Robstown, TX Society of Our Lady of the Most Holy Trinity.
Dougherty, Terrence *o.c.d.* '63 (BO)[V] Boston, MA Carmelite Monastery.
Dougherty, Terrence *o.c.d.* (WOR) Worcester, MA Our Lady of the Angels.
Dougherty, William J. *o.s.f.s.* '59 (WIL) Elsmere, DE Veteran's Hospital; [J] Wilmington, DE DeSales House.
Dougherty, William J. *c.s.p.* '63 (AUS) Horseshoe Bay, TX St. Paul the Apostle.
Dougherty, William J. '69 (PH) Absent on Leave.
Dougherty, William N. *o.s.f.s.* '65 (ARL) Reston, VA St. John Neumann.
Dougherty, William *c.pp.s.* '46 (CIN)[B] Carthagena, OH St. Charles.
Doughty, Edward F '95 (BO) Randolph, MA St. Bernadette; Weymouth, MA St. Jerome.
Doughty, Rees W. '94 (NY) Bronx, NY St. Barnabas.
Douglas, David M. '65 (LFT) West Lafayette, IN Blessed Sacrament.
Douglas, Gordon '68 (SEA)[B] Seattle, WA Bishop Blanchet High School.
Douglas, Jack *c.p.* '81 (BRK)[V] Jamaica, NY Immaculate Conception Monastery.
Douglas, Louis '58 (ALB) Retired.
Douglas, Louis '58 (ALB) Leave of Absence.
Douglas, Marian *o.f.m.* '57 (ALN)[K] Easton, PA St. Francis Friary.
Douglas, Norman K. '74 (CLV) Akron, OH St. Bernard.
Douglass, Vincent '66 (RIC)[N] Hampton, VA Holy Family Retreat.
Douglass, Vincent *c.ss.r.* '84 (ORL)[E] New Smyrna Beach, FL Redemptorist Fathers of the Vice Province of Richmond.
Doussan, Douglas A. '60 (NO) New Orleans LA St. Gabriel the Archangel; Continuing Formation for Priests; Priest Personnel Office.
Dove, Thomas J. *c.s.p.* '61 (SFR) San Francisco, CA Old St. Mary's Cathedral Retired.
Dove, Thomas J. '61 (NY)[EE] Jamaica Estates Paulist Fathers Generalate.
Dover, Edward '85 (LA) Gardena, CA St. Anthony of Padua.
Dover, Edward (LA) Ministry to Recently Ordained Priests.
Dovick, Robert E. '53 (CHI) Retired.
Dovzhuk, Mykola (STN) Detroit, MI St. Vladimir's.
Dowalgo, Mitchell G. *c.s.b.* '88 (LSC) Las Cruces, NM St. Albert the Great Newman Parish; [C] Las Cruces, NM Basilian Fathers.
Dowalgo, Mitchell *c.s.b.* (LSC) Campus Ministry.
Dowd, Barry G. '84 (BUR) On Duty Outside the Diocese.
Dowd, Barry '82 (ORL) Orlando, FL Mary Queen of the Universe Shrine.
Dowd, Brian P. '91 (BRK) Flushing, NY St. John Vianney.
Dowd, James '56 (P) Retired.
Dowd, John M *o.s.m.* '69 (CHI) Chicago, IL Assumption of the Blessed Virgin Mary; [N] Chicago, IL Assumption Priory.
Dowd, John *c.ss.r.* '61 (CHI)[N] Chicago IL The Redemptorist Fathers of Chicago.
Dowd, John *c.ss.r.* '61 (CHI) Chicago, IL St. Michael.
Dowd, Robert A. *c.s.c* '94 (FTW)[B] University of Notre Dame Du Lac; [I] Notre Dame, IN Holy Cross Community, Corby Hall, University of Notre Dame.
Dowd, Thomas M. '54 (GI) Retired.
Dowdel, Lawrence '91 (LA) Covina, CA St. Louise de Marillac.
Dowdell, Aaron M. *o.ss.t.* '74 (NY)[S] Baltimore, MD; New York, NY St. Brigid; [S] Baltimore, MD Holy Trinity Monastery.
Dowdell, Joseph M. '63 (BUF) Lakewood, NY Sacred Heart.
Dowdell, Thomas '71 (OKL) Perry, OK St. Rose of Lima.
Dowdle, David P. '62 (CHI).
Dowdle, David (CHI)[A] Diaconate Formation Program.
Dowdy, James H. '69 (BAL) Absent on Leave.
Dowell, Aaron M. *o.ss.t.* (BAL)[P] Baltimore, MD Franciscan Center.
Dowell, William J. '45 (DET) Retired.
Dower, Douglas '87 (RVC) West Islip, NY Good Samaritan Hospital Medical Center.
Dowgiert, Andrew '88 (MIA) Miami, FL Good Shepherd.
Dowling, Edward T. *s.j.* '69 (NY)[EE] Loyola Hall, Jesuit Community.
Dowling, Finbarr *o.s.b.* '68 (STL) Marthasville, MO St. Ignatius.
Dowling, John C. '51 (NEW) Retired.
Dowling, John J. *o.s.a.* '68 (FgM).
Dowling, John R. '83 (KNX) Knoxville, TN St. John Neumann.
Dowling, John *s.s.s.* (CLV)[O] Cleveland, OH Blessed Sacrament Community.
Dowling, Joseph Kevin '80 (NSH) Centerville, TN Christ the Redeemer; Hohenwald, TN Holy Trinity; Hohenwald, TN St. Cecilia.
Dowling, Kevin '80 (NSH)[L] Nashville, TN Diocesan Council of Catholic Women.
Dowling, Lawrence R. '91 (CHI) Chicago, IL St. Denis; Deans; College of Consultors.
Dowling, P. Finbarr *o.s.b.* '68 (STL)[O] St. Louis, MO The Abbey of St. Mary and St. Louis.
Dowling, Patrick '82 (JC) Chamois, MO Most Pure Heart of Mary.
Dowling, Patrick '82 (JC) Chamois, MO Assumption.
Dowling, Patrick '82 (JC) Jefferson City, MO Central Missouri Correctional Center.
Dowling, Patrick '82 (JC) Fulton, MO Diagnostic and Reception Center.
Dowling, Philip J. '56 (PH) Philadelphia, PA St. Patrick.
Dowling, Raymond '61 (GB) Retired.
Dowling, Timothy '93 (PAT) Succasunna, NJ St. Therese.
Dowling, William P. '52 (SAV) Retired.
Downes, Stephen N. '66 (LA) Palmdale, CA St. Mary.
Downes, Thomas J. '51 (CHI) Retired.
Downey, Alvin T. *o.s.b.* '70 (GBG)[H] Latrobe, PA Saint Vincent Archabbey.
Downey, David C. '03 (PMB) Jupiter, FL St. Peter.
Downey, Donald '81 (CC) On Special Assignment.
Downey, James *o.s.b.* '46 (KCK)[H] Atchison, KS St. Benedict's Abbey.
Downey, Joseph F. *s.j.* '48 (DET)[K] Temperance, MI; [P] Hamtramck, MI St. Ladislaus.
Downey, Joseph J. '43 (BO) Senior Priests; [T] Somerville, MA Jeanne Jugan Residence Retired.
Downey, Kevin *o.f.m.* (PAT) Pompton Lakes, NJ Our Lady of the Assumption.
Downey, Michael '72 (SAC) Fairfield, CA Holy Spirit.
Downey, Richard E. *m.m.* '44 (NY).
Downie, Arley T. '88 (GLP) Retired.
Downing, Brendan W. '79 (BRK)[EE] Far Rockaway, NY St. Gertrude.
Downing, Charles E. (PRO) Deans.
Downing, Charles H. '65 (PRO) West Warwick, RI St. Joseph.
Downing, Joseph C. '62 (CAM) Bellmawr, NJ Mary, Mother of the Church.
Downs, Bruce '94 (PHX) Phoenix, AZ Corpus Christi.
Downs, Gregory Todd '91 (LAF) On Duty Outside the Diocese.
Downs, Gregory '91 (ALX) Nachitoches, LA St. Anthony.
Downs, James A. '70 (PIT) Hillsville, PA Christ the King; Lawrence County, PA Lawrence County Jail.
Downs, James *m.s.a.* '01 (NOR)[F] Cromwell Society of the Missionaries of the Holy Apostles.
Downs, John L. '55 (OG) Massena, NY St. Joseph.
Downs, L. James '66 (WDC) Rockville, MD St. Mary.
Downs, Richard J. '45 (ALB) Retired.
Downs, Richard (ALB) Society of St. Vincent de Paul.
Downs, Robert '51 (ROC) Retired.
Downs, Walter *m.s.c.* '43 (ALN)[A] Center Valley, PA Sacred Heart Villa, Missionaries of the Sacred Heart.
Dowsey, Gary '82 (SP) Brandon, FL Church of the Nativity.
Doyen, Mitchell S. '91 (STL) Normandy, MO Ascension–St. Paul.
Doyle, Alan T. *m.m.* '64 (FgM).
Doyle, Brendan P. '63 (JC) Holts Summit, MO St. Andrew.
Doyle, Brendan '63 (JC)[A] Jefferson City, MO Helias High School.
Doyle, Brendan '63 (JC) Jefferson City, MO Immaculate Conception.
Doyle, Brendan '89 (ATL) Lawrenceville, GA St. Marguerite D'Youville.
Doyle, Brendan (JC) Judicial Vicar.
Doyle, Brendan (JC) Vice–Chancellors.
Doyle, Charles E. '53 (GRY) Retired.
Doyle, Daniel E. *o.s.a.* '86 (PH)[B] Villanova, PA St. Augustine Friary; [C] Villanova University.
Doyle, Daniel *s.m.* (MIA) Catholic Charismatic Services—Archdiocese of Miami.
Doyle, Dennis J. '65 (STL) St. Charles, MO Sts. Joachim and Ann.
Doyle, Dennis M. '92 (STL) Judges; St. Louis, MO St. Ambrose.
Doyle, Donald L. *c.m.* '41 (PH)[AA] St. Catherine Infirmary.
Doyle, Donald (ALB) Retired.
Doyle, Edward A. '64 (JC) Senators.
Doyle, Eugene '76 (SCL) Sauk Rapids, MN Sacred Heart.
Doyle, Francis J. *o.s.a.* '70 (CHL) Maggie Valley, NC St. Margaret.
Doyle, James F. '59 (NY) Bronxville, NY St. Joseph.
Doyle, James J. *c.s.c.* '50 (FR)[H] North Dartmouth, MA Holy Cross Residence.
Doyle, James Michael '57 (SFS) Retired.
Doyle, James P. '57 (CHI) Retired.
Doyle, James '49 (ROC) Retired.
Doyle, James '61 (LKC) Lake Charles, LA St. Theodore's.
Doyle, James (NY) Canon 1742 Panel of Pastors.
Doyle, James (LKC) Defenders of the Bond.
Doyle, Jerald A. '69 (BGP) Stratford, CT Our Lady of Grace; Judicial Vicar; Diocesan Consultors; Presbyteral Council.
Doyle, John A. *c.m.* '41 (PH)[AA] St. Catherine Infirmary.
Doyle, John J. '58 (JOL) Crest Hill, IL St. Ambrose; Crest Hill, IL St. Anne.
Doyle, John J. '70 (CHI) Flossmoor, IL Infant Jesus of Prague.
Doyle, John L. '52 (BO) Senior Priests Retired.
Doyle, John T. *o.s.f.s.* '52 (VEN) Fort Myers, FL St. Cecilia Retired.
Doyle, John '52 (DUL) Virginia, MN Sacred Heart.
Doyle, John '52 (DUL) Virginia, MN Sacred Heart.
Doyle, Joseph C. '72 (NEW) Ridgefield Park, NJ St. Francis of Assisi.
Doyle, Joseph M. *s.s.j.* '68 (NO)[F] New Orleans, LA St. Augustine High School; [H] New Orleans, LA St. Augustine High School; [S] New Orleans, LA Pierre Toussaint Foundation of New Orleans, Inc..
Doyle, Joseph *s.s.j.* '68 (NO)[P] New Orleans, LA The Josephite Faculty House of St. Augustine High School.
Doyle, Joseph *s.j.* '70 (SP)[C] Tampa, FL Jesuit High School.
Doyle, Joseph (NEW) Priestly Vocation Board.
Doyle, Kenneth (ALB) Public Information.
Doyle, Kenneth (ALB) Chancellors.
Doyle, Kenneth (ALB) Presbyteral Council.
Doyle, Kennth '66 (ALB) Albany, NY St. Catherine of Siena.
Doyle, Lawrence J. '45 (BO) Senior Priests Retired.
Doyle, Lawrence Michael *o.s.m.* '65 (CHI)[N] Chicago

Order of Friar Servants of Mary (Servites) United States of America Province, Inc..
Doyle, Mark A. '58 (LC) Retired.
Doyle, Mathias *o.f.m.* '62 (BO)[AA] Boston, MA St. Anthony Shrine.
Doyle, Michael J. '85 (BO) Canton, MA St. John the Evangelist; Navy Reserve Chaplains.
Doyle, Michael J. (CAM) Apostleship of the Sea.
Doyle, Michael M. '89 (NU) Appleton, MN St. John; Prairie Correctional Facility; [F] Appleton, MN Prairie Correctional Facility; Building Committee.
Doyle, Michael '59 (CAM) Camden, NJ Sacred Heart.
Doyle, Michael *o.s.m.* '65 (STL) St. Louis, MO Seven Holy Founders.
Doyle, Michael '94 (TYL) Lufkin, TX St. Andrew.
Doyle, Michael (CAM) Camden City Deanery.
Doyle, Oliver '78 (GF) Special Assignment.
Doyle, Oliver '78 (GF) Great Falls, MT St. Ann's Cathedral.
Doyle, Patrick A. '75 (IND) Indianapolis, IN St. Joan of Arc.
Doyle, Patrick '75 (IND) Indianapolis, IN St. Andrew the Apostle.
Doyle, Patrick (IND) Priests' Personnel Board.
Doyle, Patrick (IND) Deaneries and Deans.
Doyle, Paul F. *c.s.c.* '77 (FTW)[B] University of Notre Dame Du Lac; [I] Notre Dame, IN Holy Cross Community, Corby Hall, University of Notre Dame.
Doyle, Philip R. '48 (NY) Retired.
Doyle, Robert M. '49 (BO) Senior Priests Retired.
Doyle, Seamus '56 (MIA) Miami Shores, FL St. Rose of Lima.
Doyle, Seamus (MIA) Retired Priests' Committee.
Doyle, Seamus (MIA) Deans and Deaneries.
Doyle, Stephen *o.f.m.* '62 (BO)[AA] Boston, MA St. Anthony Shrine.
Doyle, Thomas D. '82 (BUF) Ecumenism; Clarence, NY Our Lady of Peace.
Doyle, Thomas F. '66 (PH) Royersford, PA Sacred Heart.
Doyle, Thomas J. *s.m.* '52 (STL)[O] Port Washington, NY.
Doyle, Thomas M. *s.j.* '97 (MIL)[O] Milwaukee, WI Pere Marquette House Jesuit Community; [E] Milwaukee, WI Marquette University High School.
Doyle, Thomas P. *o.p.* '71 (CHI)[N] Chicago Dominicans (Provincial Office).
Doyle, Thomas P. *c.s.c.* '98 (FTW)[I] South Bend, IN Congregation of Holy Cross, Indiana Province, Provincial House; [I] Newton, MA Our Lady Help of Christians Parish.
Doyle, Thomas V. (BRK) Presbyteral Council; Subcommittee for Assisted Schools and Parishes; Art and Architecture Commission.
Doyle, Thomas *s.s.* '51 (NSH) Retired.
Doyle, Thomas '54 (LA) Retired.
Doyle, Thomas *s.s.* '60 (BAL)[S] Brentwood, TN Retired.
Doyle, Thomas '62 (DAV) Mechanicsville, IA St. Mary's.
Doyle, Thomas '84 (BRK) Brooklyn, NY St. Mary, Star of the Sea.
Doyle, Thomas *c.s.c.* (BO) Newton, MA Our Lady Help of Christians.
Doyle, Vincent J. '65 (NEW) Union, NJ Holy Spirit; Defenders of the Bond.
Doyle, Walter H. '43 (STO) Diamond Springs, CA Retired.
Doyle, William F. *s.j.* '53 (BO)[V] Boston, MA Loyola House.
Doyne, David A. '56 (PH) Lansdale, PA St. Stanislaus.
Drab, John P. '46 (RVC) Retired.
Drabek, Howard E. '91 (GAL) Richmond, TX Sacred Heart; Air Force Reserve Chaplains.
Drabik, Richard *m.i.c.* '60 (SPR)[I] Eucharistic Apostles of The Divine Mercy.
Drabiska, Frank J. '76 (PIT) Pittsburgh, PA Word of God.
Drag, Roderick *o.f.m.* '49 (PH)[AA] Philadelphia, PA St. Pius X Friary.
Dragga, Thomas M. '83 (CLV)[A] Wickliffe, OH Borromeo Seminary; [A] Wickliffe, OH St. Mary Seminary and Graduate School of Theology.
Dragga, Thomas (CLV) Associate Directors:.
Drago, Julio Mirables '72 (MIL) Lake Geneva, WI St. Francis de Sales.
Dragon, Joseph W. '78 (PH) West Chester, PA SS. Peter and Paul.
Draim, David *o.s.b.* '73 (SP)[O] St. Leo St. Leo Abbey.
Draim, David *o.s.b.* '73 (CHL) Hamlet, NC St. James.
Drake, Roy A. *s.j.* '63 (NY)[EE] New York, NY Murray–Weigel Hall.
Drake, Sebastian *o.f.m.* '45 (OAK)[P] Danville, CA San Damiano Retreat.
Drake, Timothy '71 (RIC) Norton, VA St. Anthony.
Drapankal, Abraham '83 (NY) Stony Point, NY Immaculate Conception.
Drapeau, Benoit J. *c.j.m.* '59 (BUF)[O] West Seneca, NY The Eudists, St. John Eudes Center; West Seneca, NY St. Bonaventure.
Draper, Andrew *t.o.r.* '88 (CHL) Mocksville, NC St. Francis of Assisi.
Drass, Damian P. *t.o.r.* '60 (WH) Philippi, WV St. Elizabeth Parish and Newman Center; [P] Philippi, WV Alderson–Broaddus College Newman Center.
Drator, Kent (DEN)[A] Denver, CO St. John Vianney Theological Seminary.
Draugialis, Josef '63 (LA) Los Nietos, CA Our Lady of Perpetual Help.
Draves–Arpaia, Cornelius '79 (PHX) On Leave.
Dreasen, John R. (RVC) East Northport, NY St. Anthony of Padua; Procurator & Advocates.
Dreese, John J. '59 (COL) Retired.
Dreese, John (COL) Diocesan Judges.
Dreffein, Larry *o.f.m.* '76 (JOL)[K] Oak Brook, IL Cedarlake Village, Plainfield Campus, Inc..
Dreffein, Larry *o.f.m.* '76 (JOL)[O] Oak Brook, IL Mayslake East Wing, Inc..
Dreger, Francis X. '51 (PH) Retired.
Dreher, Ernest O. '48 (MIL) Retired.
Dreher, Jacob J. '43 (DOD) Retired.
Dreher, John D. '64 (PRO) Pawtucket, RI Sacred Heart of Jesus Retired.
Dreici, Patrick *c.ss.r.* '44 (FRS) Retired.
Dreier, Bruce A. '78 (SFR) San Francisco, CA Church of the Epiphany; Deans.
Dreiling, Augustine *o.s.b.* '58 (KC) Conception Junction, MO St. Columba.
Dreiling, Gerald G. *c.pp.s.* '58 (CIN).
Dreiling, Raymond C. '75 (FRS)[M] Clovis, CA Our Lady of Perpetual Help.
Dreisbach, Charles U. (BAK) Priestly Life and Ministry.
Dreisbach, Charles V. '59 (BAK) Southern; Diocesan Financial Board; Health and Retirement Board; Klamath Falls, OR Sacred Heart.
Dreisbach, Charles V. (BAK) Council of Priests and Diocesan Consultors.
Drennan, Jimmy D. '96 (SAT) San Antonio, TX St. Paul.
Drennan, Jimmy (SAT) Priests Personnel Board.
Drennan, Lawrence J. '61 (BO) Bridgewater, MA St. Thomas Aquinas.
Drennan, William A. '55 (STL) St. Louis, MO St. Raphael The Archangel.
Drenzek, Peter C. '69 (MIL) Wauwatosa, WI St. Bernard.
Dresen, Arthur G. '44 (COS) Retired.
Dressel, Willard J. *s.j.* '54 (MIL)[O] Milwaukee, WI Arrupe House Jesuit Community.
Dressel, Willard J. *s.j.* '54 (OM)[C] Omaha, NE Creighton Preparatory School.
Dressell, Stephen G. *m.s.* '47 (HRT)[M] Hartford, CT Missionaries of LaSalette.
Dressler, Paul *o.f.m.cap.* '99 (PH) Philadelphia, PA.
Dressler, Philip J. '61 (CHI) Chicago, IL St. Juliana.
Dressler, Robert A. '59 (ALN) Fountain Hill, PA St. Ursula; Marriage Encounter; McAdoo, PA Immaculate Conception Retired.
Dressman, James J. *s.j.* '61 (NOR) Storrs, CT St. Thomas Aquinas; [K] Storrs, CT University of Connecticut.
Dressman, James *s.j.* (NOR) Chaplains.
Dressman, Richard E. '72 (CIN) Cincinnati, OH St. Jude the Apostle; [V] Cincinnati, OH Catholic Charismatic Renewal Liaison.
Dressman, Robert C. *s.j.* '53 (CHI)[T] The Jesuit Retreat League of Chicago.
Dreves, Mark '95 (LEX) Corbin, KY Sacred Heart; Williamsburg, KY St. Boniface; Williamsburg, KY Our Lady of Perpetual Help.
Dreves, Mark '95 (LEX) Special Assignment.
Dreves, Mark (LEX) Vocations.
Drew, Andrew *o.f.m.cap.* '61 (NY) New York, NY St. John the Baptist Retired.
Drew, George *c.ss.r.* '50 (ALB)[L] Saratoga Springs, NY St. John Neumann Residence.
Drew, James F. '74 (HON) On Duty Outside the Diocese.
Drew, James '74 (RVC) Setauket, NY St. James.
Drew, John J. *m.m.* '42 (NY).
Drewniak, Stanley '78 (JOL)[EE] Joliet, IL St. Mary Nativity.
Drewniak, Stanley (CHI) Judges.
Drexel, John *o.m.i.* '62 (FgM).
Drexler, Harold J. '55 (DUB) Dubuque, IA Sacred Heart Retired.
Drez, Alvaro (YAK) Grandview, WA Blessed Sacrament; Mabton, WA Immaculate Conception.
Drieci, Pascal '44 (DEN)[N] Fresno, CA Nazareth House.
Driesch, Albert *t.o.r.* '46 (WH) Moundsville, WV St. Francis Xavier's.
Driesch, David A. '82 (PIT) Pittsburgh, PA St. Bernard.
Drilling, Peter J. '67 (BUF)[A] Lackawanna, NY St. Anthony.
Drinan, Robert F. *s.j.* '53 (BO)[V] Boston The Society of Jesus of New England–Provincial Offices; [M] Washington, DC The Jesuit Community at Georgetown University.
Drinane, Gerald A. *s.j.* '62 (FgM).
Drinkwater, Warren *c.ss.r.* '62 (BLX)[E] Biloxi, MS St. John Neumann Residence.
Driscoll, Arthur J. '52 (BO) Senior Priests Retired.
Driscoll, Brian J. '96 (JC) Absent on Leave.
Driscoll, Daniel '76 (HEL) Libby, MT St. Joseph.
Driscoll, Donald D. *s.j.* '65 (OM)[K] Omaha, NE Jesuit Community at Creighton University.
Driscoll, Donald T. (NY) Rockland Psychiatric Center.
Driscoll, Eugene J. '70 (LUB) Lubbock, TX Holy Spirit; Defender of the Bond; Defender of the Bond–Appeal; Presbyteral Council.
Driscoll, James A. *o.p.* '54 (PRO)[B] Providence, RI Providence College; [P] Providence St. Thomas Aquinas Priory at Providence College.
Driscoll, James E. '55 (OAK) Danville, CA St. Isidore's Retired.
Driscoll, Jeremy *o.s.b.* '81 (P)[L] St. Benedict, OR Mt. Angel Abbey.
Driscoll, John M. *o.s.a.* '51 (PH)[AA] Villanova, PA St. Thomas Monastery.
Driscoll, John P. '47 (FR) Retired.
Driscoll, John P. *s.j.* '52 (NO)[P] New Orleans, LA Ignatius Residence.
Driscoll, John '54 (JOL) Romeoville, IL St. Andrew the Apostle.
Driscoll, John '54 (JOL) Retired.
Driscoll, Joseph J. '79 (BO)[X] Milwaukee, WI National Association of Catholic Chaplains.
Driscoll, Joseph J. '79 (BO) On Duty Outside the Archdiocese.
Driscoll, Maurice F. '42 (BEL) Mobile, AL Retired.
Driscoll, Michael A. '68 (MET) Retired.
Driscoll, Michael *o.carm.* '67 (PMB) Boca Raton, FL St. Jude.
Driscoll, Michael '76 (FTW)[B] University of Notre Dame Du Lac.
Driscoll, Michael '77 (HEL) On Duty Outside the Diocese.
Driscoll, Michael (FTW) Liturgical Commission.
Driscoll, Michael *o.carm.* (PMB) Office for Liturgy.
Driscoll, Nicholas J. '57 (BO) Permanent Disability.
Driscoll, Paul G. '64 (RVC) Seaford, NY St. James.
Driscoll, Richard A. '55 (BO) Senior Priests Retired.
Driscoll, Richard *s.d.s.* '65 (MIL).
Driscoll, Samuel *o.f.m.cap.* '59[O] (FgM).
Driscoll, Thomas J. '61 (BGP) Easton, CT Notre Dame of Easton; Vicars General; Judges; Diocesan Censors; Diocesan Consultors; Presbyteral Council; Finance Council; Pastors' Vocation Advisory Board.
Driscoll, Timothy Paul '99 (FR) New Bedford, MA Our Lady of the Immaculate Conception.
Driscoll, William D. '55 (NEW) Retired.
Driscoll, William J. *o.mar.* '63 (SAM)[C] Petersham, MA Most Holy Trinity Monastery.
Driscoll, William J. '65 (E) Retired.
Drobach, William *s.a.* '88 (NY)[EE] Garrison, NY St. Christopher's Friary.
Drobach, William *s.a.* '88 (NY)[EE] Garrison, NY St. Christopher's Inn.
Drobin, Paul J. '66 (SY)[T] Utica, NY SUNY Institute of Technology at Newman Center; [T] Utica, NY Utica College Newman Center; Elected.
Drobinski, Joseph J. '75 (WIL) Wilmington, DE St. Matthew.
Droessler, Joseph '95 (ORG) Anaheim, CA St. Justin Martyr.
Droessler, Wayne J. '69 (DUB) Prairieburg, IA St. Joseph; Central City, IA St. Stephen; Coggon, IA St. John the Evangelist.
Drogon, Greg (PAT) Absent on Leave; Straight and Narrow, Inc..
Drohan, Joseph W. '56 (ATL) Retired.
Droll, Larry J. '73 (SAN) Wall, TX St. Ambrose; Vicar General; Defensores Vinculi; Diocesan Consultors; Catholic Relief Services; Priests' Pension Plan; Midland, TX St. Ann's.
Droll, Louis J. '68 (SAN) Retired.
Droll, Louis '68 (AUS) Retired.
Drongowski, Stanley A. *o.p.* '79 (MIL)[O] Kenosha, WI Order of Preachers, Province of St. Albert the Great.
Droski, Norman (GR) Retired.
Drotar, Kent (DEN) Our Lady of the New Advent Theological Institute.
Drouin, Marc B. '90 (MAN) Exeter, NH St. Michael; Charismatic Renewal & Cursillo Movement.
Drouncheck, Anthony M. '89 (ALN) Lake Harmony, PA St. Peter the Fisherman.
Drown, Maurice (ALB) Ecumenical and Interreligious Affairs of the Roman Catholic Diocese of Albany, Commission for.
Drozd, Henry J. '62 (DAL) Retired.
Drozd, Marian '91 (MET) Bound Brook, NJ St. Mary of Czestochowa.
Drozdzal, John S. '74 (SY) Utica, NY St. Joseph and St. Patrick.
Drozdzik, Roch T. '96 (R) Edenton, NC St. Anne; Deans; Priests' Council; Edenton, NC St. Anne.
Droze, D. Anthony '85 (CHR) Columbia, SC Our Lady of the Hills; Presbyteral Council; Marian Programs; Personnel Committee.
Drucker, James N. '78 (PSC) On Duty Outside Diocese; Lebanon, PA Veterans Administration Hospital.
Druding, John C. '76 (ATL) Lilburn, GA St. John

Neumann; Judges.
Druggan, Dennis *o.f.m.cap.* '84 (MIL)[O] Mount Calvary, WI St. Lawrence Friary; [B] Mount Calvary, WI St. Lawrence Seminary.
Drum, John *c.ss.r.* '54 (ALB)[L] Saratoga Springs, NY St. John Neumann Residence.
Drummond, Alexander R. '94 (ARL) Advocates; Great Falls, VA St. Catherine of Siena.
Drummond, Elsyn J. '54 (NOR) Retired.
Drummy, John A. '71 (SUP) Amery, WI St. Joseph; Southwest Deanery; Pastoral Consultors; Presbyteral Council & Diocesan Consultors.
Drupieski, Stanley R. *o.s.f.s.* '64 (WIL)[B] Wilmington, DE Salesianum School; Court of First Instance Judges.
Drury, Dennis G. '82 (GB) Casco, WI St. Peter–St. Hubert; Elected Representatives.
Drury, George *s.j.* '52 (BO)[V] Newton, MA The Jesuit Community at Boston College.
Drury, Michael J. '74 (PAT) Long Valley, NJ St. Luke.
Drury, Michael P. *c.o.* '84 (MRY)[F] Monterey, CA Oratorian Community–Congregation of the Oratory of Pontifical Right; AUXILIARY CHAPLAINS CONTRACT CHAPLAINS.
Drury, Robert '79 (OWN) Hardin, KY St. Henry; Calvert City, KY St. Pius Tenth.
Drutowski, Robert J. '79 (MIL) Mukwonago, WI St. James.
Drybka, Krzysztof *o.s.p.* (NY) Yonkers, NY St. Casimir.
Drywal, Justin *o.s.b.* '98 (CLV) Broadview Heights, OH Assumption.
Drzaic, Frank *s.v.d.* '62 (MEM)[I] Memphis, TN Society of the Divine Word (Chicago Province).
Drzaic, Frank *s.v.d.* '62 (MEM) Memphis, TN Sacred Heart.
Drzal, Stanislaw '68 (ATL) Lawrenceville, GA St. Marguerite D'Youville.
Duaime, Jeffrey T. *c.s.sp.* '86 (PH)[G] Bensalem, PA Holy Ghost Preparatory School; [AA] Bensalem, PA Congregation of the Holy Ghost.
Duane, Robert J. '53 (NY) Ardsley, NY Our Lady of Perpetual Help Retired.
Duane, Thomas J. '71 (PH) Roslyn, PA St. John of the Cross.
Duarte, J. Scott '78 (RIC) Ladysmith, VA St. Mary of the Annunciation; Adjutant Judicial Vicars.
Duarte, Scott (RIC) Delegate for the Causes of Saints.
Dubay, Thomas E. *s.m.* '50 (WDC)[M] Washington, DC Marist Center.
Dube, Joseph *s.j.* '99 (PHX) Phoenix, AZ St. Francis Xavier.
Dube, Marcel *o.carm.* '54 (VEN) Rotonda West, FL St. Francis of Assisi.
Dube, Stephen D. '78 (WH) Weirton, WV St. Joseph the Worker; Diocesan Consultors; Vicars Forane; Scouting.
Dubell, James H. '65 (TR) Cemeteries; Medford, NJ St. Mary of the Lakes.
Dubert, James W. '98 (DUB) Eldora, IA St. Mary; Iowa Falls, IA St. Mark.
Dubi, Leonard A. '68 (CHI) Hazel Crest, IL St. Anne.
Dubitsky, Roman '65 (PHU) Perth Amboy, NJ Assumption of B.V.M..
Dubitsky, Roman '65 (PHU) Perth Amboy, NJ St. Stephen's.
Dubitsky, Roman (PHU) College of Archeparchial Counsultors.
Dubitsky, Roman (PHU) Presbyteral Council.
Dubitsky, Roman (PHU) Board Members.
Dubitsky, Roman (PHU) Archeparchial Corporation.
Dublinski, Steve (SPK) Vicars General.
Dublinski, Steve (SPK) Diocesan Liturgical Commission.
Dublinski, Steven L. '85 (SPK) Rosalia, WA St. Catherine of Alexandria; Rosalia, WA Holy Rosary; St. John, WA Our Lady of Perpetual Help; Rosalia, WA Sacred Heart.
Dublinski, Steven (SPK) Moderator of the Curia.
Dublinski, Steven (SPK) Members.
Dublinski, Steven (SPK) Diocesan Pastoral Council.
Dubois, Andrew '95 (PRT) Lewiston, ME Holy Family.
Dubois, Andrew (PRT) Personnel Board.
Dubois, Charles J. '64 (LKC) Lake Charles, LA St. Theodore's.
DuBois, David '80 (GAL) Pattison, TX Sacred Heart.
DuBois, Francis J. '70 (ALB) Latham, NY St. Ambrose.
Dubois, Raymond *s.s.s.* '49 (CLV)[O] Richfield, OH Regina Health Center.
Dubois, Raymond *s.s.s.* '49 (CLV)[O] Richfield, OH Regina Health Center.
DuBois, William '48 (SP) Retired.
Dubovici, Mihai '94 (STF)[A] Stamford, CT Ukrainian Catholic Seminary Inc. St. Basil College.
Dubovici, Mihai (STF) Administrative Council.
Dubovici, Mihai (STF) Notary Publics.
Dubovici, Mihai (STF) Ecumenical Commission.
Dubovici, Mihai (STF) Vice Econome.
Dubovsky, Peter *s.j.* '89 (BO)[V] Cambridge, MA.
Dubowski, George (MIL)[O] Burlington, WI Queen of Peace Friary.
Dubriske, Edward J. *s.s.e.* '64 (FgM).
Dubriske, Edward J. *s.s.e.* '64 (BUR)[E] Colchester, VT Society of St. Edmund.
Dubrouillet, James N. '97 (CHR) Anderson, SC St. Joseph's.
Du Buisson, William *o.m.i.* '55 (SAN) Sonora, TX St. Ann's.
Du Buisson, William *o.m.i.* (SAN) Judicial Vicar; Presbyteral Council.
Dubuisson, William *o.m.i.* (SAN) Judges.
Du Buisson, William *o.m.i.* (SAN) Judicial Vicar; Presbyteral Council.
Du Buisson, William *o.m.i.* (SAN) Diocesan Consultors.
Duc, Dominic Tran Minh '90 (PH) Pottstown, PA St. Aloysius.
Duca, Michael (DAL)[A] Irving, TX Holy Trinity Seminary; Assistant Judicial Vicars; Assistant Judicial Vicars; Diocesan Consultors; Presbyteral Council; Seminary.
Ducaji, John '54 (JOL) Wheaton, IL St. Mark.
Ducate, Richard G. '67 (KC) Retired.
Ducci, Alex '61 (STA) Retired.
Ducette, John I. '62 (BUF) Apostleship of the Sea; Tonawanda, NY St. Timothy.
Duch, Robert G. '64 (PIT) Aspinwall, PA St. Scholastica.
Duchaine, R. Mark '78 (SC) Mapleton, IA St. Mary's; Episcopal Vicar for Canonical Affairs; Judicial Vicar; Judges.
DuCharme, Paul '55 (GB) Retired.
Duchez, Daniel B. *o.s.* (LC) Chippewa Falls, WI St. Charles Borromeo; [D] Chippewa Falls, WI St. Joseph's Hospital.
Duchnowicz, Artur F. '01 (GAY) Cadillac, MI St. Ann; Lake City, MI St. Stephen; Lake City, MI St. Theresa.
Duchschere, Paul C. (FAR) Deanery 2.
Duchschere, Paul '90 (FAR)[I] Fargo, ND St. Paul's Catholic Chapel.
Duchschere, Paul '90 (FAR) Fargo, ND St. Paul Newman Center, N.D.S.U..
Duc Minh, Joseph '61 (LA) On Duty Outside the Archdiocese.
Duc Odilon, Yoo Yong *s.v.d.* '01 (STL) St. Louis, MO St. Nicholas.
Ducre, Ken (ELP) Presbyteral Council.
Ducre, Kennon Y. '83 (ELP) El Paso, TX All Saints.
Duda, Robert '84 (JOL) Villa Park, IL St. John the Apostle.
Dudak, George A. (PAT) Retired.
Dudak, George '56 (PAT) Randolph, NJ Resurrection.
Dudash, Derrick F. '74 (GRY) Hebron, IN St. Helen; Bishop's Council of Priests.
Duddy, Patrick A. '39 (PH) Retired.
Dudek, Berard *o.f.m.conv.* '54 (ROC) Auburn, NY St. Hyacinth.
Dudek, Ladislaus J. '66 (ALN) Allentown, PA SS. Peter and Paul.
Dudek, Stanislaw '62 (BUF) Perrysburg, NY St. Joan of Arc; Perrysburg, NY St. John Fisher.
Dudek, Stephen S. '84 (GR) Grand Rapids, MI Holy Name of Jesus; Grand Rapids, MI St. Joseph The Worker; On Special Assignment.
Dudink, Edward *s.v.d.* '46 (BO)[V] Duxbury, MA Society of the Divine Word.
Dudkiewicz, Stanley '52 (SY) Syracuse, NY Sacred Heart Basilica.
Dudley, James *m.s.c.* '56 (SAT)[M] San Antonio, TX Missionaries of the Sacred Heart.
Dudziak, Paul M. '69 (WDC) Owings, MD Jesus the Good Shepherd.
Dudziak, Paul (WDC) Deans.
Dudzik, Darius Z. '95 (NOR)[A] Orchard Lake, MI SS. Cyril and Methodius Seminary.
Dudzik, Dariusz '95 (NOR) On Duty Outside the Diocese.
Dudzinski, Andrew '96 (FAR) Lisbon, ND St. Vincent.
Dudzinski, Andrew '96 (FAR) Lisbon, ND St. Aloysius.
Dudzinski, Brian A. '97 (LFT) Carmel, IN St. Elizabeth Ann Seton.
Dudzinski, Paul L. '86 (ARL) Clifton, VA St. Clare of Assisi.
Dudzinski, Theodore '97 (LFT) Kokomo, IN St. Patrick.
Due, J. Michael (COV) Episcopal Vicar for Pastoral Services; Diocesan Consultors.
Duell, James S. '82 (CIN) Bradford, OH Immaculate Conception; Covington, OH St. Teresa; Priest Councilors.
Duellman, Virgil S. '60 (WIN) Retired.
Duenas, Jaime H. '50 (NY) Bronx, NY Nativity of Our Blessed Lady Retired.
Dueppen, David '99 (MIA) Key West, FL St. Mary, Star of the Sea.
Duerr, Gregory *o.s.b.* '64 (P)[L] St. Benedict, OR Mt. Angel Abbey.
Duesdieker, Robert W. '80 (JC) Boonville, MO SS. Peter and Paul; Fayette, MO St. Joseph; [E] Fayette, MO Central Methodist College; Defenders of the Bond.
Duesman, Jerome P. '68 (DAL) Irving, TX Holy Family of Nazareth; Building Commission.
Duesman, Leon '65 (DAL) Frisco, TX St. Francis of Assisi; Presbyteral Council.
Duesterhaus, Michael R. '91 (ARL) Stafford, VA St. William of York; Navy Reserve Chaplains.
Duet, Wayne J. '75 (LAF) Erath, LA Our Lady of Lourdes.
Dueweke, Donald G. '66 (SAG) Croswell, MI St. Patrick.
Dueweke, Robert F. *o.s.a.* '79 (CHI) Chicago, IL St. Rita of Cascia.
Dufault, Wilfred J. *a.a.* '34 (WOR)[B] Worcester, MA Assumption College; [O] Worcester, MA Assumptionists (Augustinians of the Assumption).
Duff, Gerard M. *o.s.a.* '59 (PH)[AA] Villanova, PA St. Thomas Monastery.
Duff, John J. '77 (NY) Pawling, NY St. John the Evangelist.
Duff, Paul J. *c.s.c.* '55 (FR)[A] North Easton, MA Holy Cross Fathers Religious.
Duff, William '63 (LAV) Retired.
Duffe, Stephen J. '96 (NEW) Washington Township, NJ Our Lady of Good Counsel.
Duffell, John P. '69 (NY) New York, NY Ascension.
Duffey, Harry *s.s.j.* '03 (BEA) Beaumont, TX Our Mother of Mercy.
Duffey, Joseph A. '52 (PH) Bryn Mawr, PA Our Mother of Good Counsel Retired.
Duffey, Thomas J. '49 (DET) Detroit, MI St. Patrick Retired.
Duffey, William R. *s.j.* '51 (MIL)[O] Milwaukee, WI.
Dufficy, Edward C. '50 (CHI) Oak Park, IL St. Edmund Retired.
Duffin, Stephen '91 (ORG) Inactive Leave.
Duffin, Stephen (ORG) Council of Priests.
Duffley, Stephen (MAN) Charismatic Renewal & Cursillo Movement.
Duffner, Paul A. *o.p.* '40 (P) Portland, OR Holy Rosary Parish & Dominican Priory.
Duffner, Paul *o.p.* '40 (OAK)[N] Oakland, CA Western Dominican Province.
Duffner, Ralph J. '56 (SPC) Chaffee, MO St. Ambrose; Priests' Mutual Benefit Society Retired.
Dufford, Robert *s.j.* '73 (GB)[L] Oshkosh, WI Jesuit Retreat House.
Duffy, David J. *o.s.a.* '57 (PH)[G] Malvern, PA Malvern Preparatory School for Boys; [AA] Malvern, PA Augustinian Friars (O.S.A.).
Duffy, Donald J. '43 (CHI) Retired.
Duffy, Donald '59 (NO) Lafitte, LA St. Anthony Retired.
Duffy, Edwin J. '61 (HON) Retired.
Duffy, Emmanuel *o.f.m.* '30 (PAT)[M] Butler, NJ St. Anthony Friary.
Duffy, Eugene J. '50 (LA) Retired.
Duffy, Francis C. *o.p.* '60 (PRO)[P] Providence St. Thomas Aquinas Priory at Providence College.
Duffy, Francis J. '70 (PAT) Morristown, NJ St. Margaret's; Deacon Internship Program.
Duffy, Francis R. *c.s.sp.* '41 (VEN)[G] Sarasota, FL Congregation of the Holy Ghost.
Duffy, Francis X. '49 (NY) Retired.
Duffy, G. Ralph '65 (WDC) Rockville, MD Shrine of St. Jude Retired.
Duffy, George A. *s.j.* '55 (BO)[E] Dorchester, MA Boston College High School & Jesuit Community.
Duffy, George '63 (MIA) Retired.
Duffy, Hugh E. *o.s.f.s.* '60 (WIL)[J] Childs, MD Retirement and Assisted Care Facility.
Duffy, Hugh '66 (PMB) Okeechobee, FL Sacred Heart.
Duffy, James D. *s.m.* '79 (ATL) Atlanta, GA Our Lady of the Assumption; Advocates.
Duffy, James H. '56 (MIL) Special Assignment.
Duffy, James '55 (JOL) Retired.
Duffy, John F. *c.s.p.* '75 (NY)[EE] Jamaica Estates, NY Paulist Fathers Generalate.
Duffy, Joseph P. *s.j.* '57 (BO)[V] Newton, MA The Jesuit Community at Boston College.
Duffy, Jude *o.f.m.cap.* '58 (NEW)[N] Union City, NJ Capuchin Friars – Province of the Sacred Stigmata of St. Francis.
Duffy, Jude *o.f.m.cap.* '58 (CHL) Charlotte, NC Our Lady of Consolation.
Duffy, Michael A. *o.f.m.* '71 (PH)[S] Philadelphia, PA St. Francis Inn; [AA] Philadelphia, PA Order of Friars Minor of the Province of the Most Holy Name.
Duffy, Michael M. '76 (RIC) Tappahannock, VA St. Timothy; Judges.
Duffy, Patrick D. '74 (CIN) Cincinnati, OH St. Peter in Chains Cathedral; Cincinnati, OH St. Joseph.
Duffy, Patrick S. '81 (SFE) Anton Chico, NM San Jose.
Duffy, Paul J. *m.m.* '79 (FgM).
Duffy, Raymond '68 (FRS) Yosemite National Park, CA Our Lady of the Snows.
Duffy, Regis A. *o.f.m.* '61 (BUF)[O] St. Bonaventure, NY St. Bonaventure Friary; [C] St. Bonaventure, NY Friar Community.
Duffy, Richard *o.f.m.* '58 (FgM).
Duffy, Robert E. '48 (NEW) Retired.
Duffy, Stephen F. '65 (NEW) Retired.
Duffy, Stephen V. *s.j.* '43 (NY)[EE] New York, NY Murray–Weigel Hall.
Duffy, Stephen '57 (NO) Unassigned.
Duffy, Stephen '57 (NO)[C] New Orleans, LA Loyola University New Orleans.
Duffy, Thomas J. '66 (PH) Blue Bell, PA St. Helena.
Duffy, Thomas M. '53 (WDC) Washington, DC Blessed

Sacrament, Shrine of the Most; Archdiocesan College of Consultors.
Duffy, Thomas R. '58 (CHR) Murrells Inlet, SC St. Michael; Diocesan Curia; Defenders of the Bond; College of Consultors; Deans; Presbyteral Council; Parish Priest Consultors.
Duffy, Vincent *s.d.b.* '43 (NY)[EE] New Rochelle, NY Salesian Provincial House; Paterson, NJ St. Anthony's.
Dufner, Andrew J. *s.j.* '67 (P)[N] Pacific City, OR Nestucca Sanctuary.
Dufner, Dan (YAK) Diocesan Finance Council.
Dufner, Daniel G. '96 (YAK) Chelan, WA St. Anne's; Chelan, WA St. Francis de Sales.
Dufner, Thomas W. '83 (STP) St. Louis Park, MN Holy Family.
Dufour, Clement E. '58 (FR) Retired.
Dufour, David W. '94 (NO) Metairie, LA Our Lady of Divine Providence.
Dufour, George J. '70 (BO) Salem, MA St. Anne.
Dufour, Louis C. '58 (BO) Senior Priests Retired.
DuFour, Rene *o.m.i.* '54 (BEL)[F] Belleville, IL Missionary Oblates of Mary Immaculate – St. Henry's Oblate Residence.
Dufresne, Oliver J. '45 (STP) Retired.
Dufresne, Vincent J. '83 (BR) Denham Springs, LA Immaculate Conception; Promoter of Justice; Defenders of the Bond.
Dugal, James H. *c.pp.s.* '56 (CIN) Montezuma, OH Our Lady of Guadalupe.
Dugal, James *c.pp.s.* '56 (CIN)[M] Montezuma, OH.
Dugal, William '76 (JOL) Absent on Sick Leave.
Dugan, J. Thomas '70 (E) Fairview, PA Holy Cross.
Dugan, James L. *s.j.* '73 (NY)[EE] Pontifical Bible Institute.
Dugan, James M. '89 (ALT) Meyersdale, PA SS. Philip and James.
Dugan, John L. *c.s.b.* '90 (ROC) Rochester, NY St. Ambrose; [I] Rochester, NY Basilian Residence.
Dugan, Paul J. *s.j.* '56 (BUF)[O] Buffalo, NY Canisius Jesuit Community.
Dugan, T. Michael (DAL) Dallas, TX St. Elizabeth; Worship Office.
Dugan, Thomas F. (PH)[V] Downingtown, PA St. John Vianney Center.
Dugan, Thomas P. *c.s.b.* '60 (GAL)[Q] Sugar Land Basilian Mission Center.
Dugan, William M. '49 (SPK) Retired.
Dugandzic, Nicholas *o.p.* '65 (CHI)[N] Chicago, IL Croatian Dominican Fathers.
Dugandzic, Nicholas *o.p.* '65 (CHI) Chicago, IL Blessed Alojzije Cardinal Stepanic Mission.
Dugas, Jerome A. '62 (BR) Retired.
Dugas, Laurence A. *m.m.* '54 (FgM).
Dugas, Scott '77 (HT) Houma, LA Cathedral of St. Francis De Sales.
Dugas, Willard '77 (LAF) Retired.
Duggan, Brendan *c.s.sp.* (BRK) Bellerose, NY St. Gregory the Great.
Duggan, Charles T. '44 (BO) Senior Priests Retired.
Duggan, Eugene F. '46 (SFR) Sausalito, CA St. Mary Star of the Sea Retired.
Duggan, J. Edward '50 (CHI) Chicago, IL St. Bartholomew Retired.
Duggan, John H. *s.j.* '57 (SCR)[S] Campion Hall; [C] Scranton, PA The University of Scranton.
Duggan, John M. '43 (BUF) Retired.
Duggan, Joseph P. '64 (VEN) Retired.
Duggan, Karl '99 (ATL) Griffin, GA Sacred Heart.
Duggan, Kevin F.X. '98 (SEA) Kirkland, WA St. John Mary Vianney.
Duggan, Kevin P. '87 (MET) South River, NJ Corpus Christi.
Duggan, Kevin *s.m.* (MRY) Campus Ministry Department.
Duggan, Michael A. *m.m.* '59 (NY)[EE] Maryknoll Maryknoll Fathers and Brothers.
Duggan, Nicholas '62 (SAC) Sacramento, CA St. Paul Retired.
Duggan, Oliver '71 (SEA) Seattle, WA Assumption.
Duggan, Oliver (SEA) Presbyteral Council.
Duggan, Oliver (SEA) Deans.
Duggan, Paul E. '48 (SFR) Retired.
Duggan, Paul O'Donnell '70 (PAT) Clifton, NJ SS. Cyril and Methodius.
Duggan, Peter '55 (SEA) Seattle, WA St. Peter.
Duggan, Robert D. '69 (WDC) Gaithersburg, MD St. Rose of Lima.
Duggan, Sean B. *o.s.b.* '88 (NO)[P] St. Benedict, LA St. Joseph Abbey.
Duggan, Thomas '47 (JC) Brookfield, MO Immaculate Conception.
Duggan, Thomas *c.ss.r.* '53 (STL)[O] Liguori, MO Liguori Mission House/Redemptorists.
Duggan, William E. '53 (SFR) Judges; Diocesan Judges Retired.
Duggan, William '53 (SFR) On Duty Outside the Archdiocese.
Duggins, Dominic R. *g.h.m.* '74 (CIN)[M] Fairfield, OH; [U] Fairfield, OH Glenmary Home Missioners Charitable Trust.
Dugue, Nerva '93 (NEW) Roselle, NJ Church of St. Joseph the Carpenter.
Duhaime, James H. '61 (PRO) Retired.
Duhaime, John N. '58 (WH) Retired.
Duhe, Thomas P. '78 (BR) Greenwell Springs, LA St. Alphonsus Liguori.
Duhon, Chris '01 (LAF) Lafayette, LA St. Edmond.
Duignan, Andrew '58 (CAM) Ocean City, NJ St. Augustine's.
Dukart, George A. '59 (BIS) Menoken, ND St. Hildegard; Pro–Synodal Judges.
Dukart, Norman J. '67 (BIS) Retired.
Duke, Charles J. '47 (NO) Retired.
Duke, Jerome J. '68 (CLV) Lakewood, OH SS. Cyril and Methodius; Associate Judges.
Dukehart, Claude H. *s.s.* '43 (BAL)[O] Baltimore, MD St. Charles Villa.
Dukeley, Boris '98 (SJP) Brooksville, FL St. Andrew.
Duker, Russell A. *s.e.o.d.* '70 (PBR) Braddock, PA SS. Peter and Paul; Pittsburgh, PA Holy Spirit; Protosyncellus; Consultors; Priests' Pension Board; Duquesne, PA SS. Peter and Paul.
Dukowski, James *o.m.i.* '67 (BO)[V] Lowell, MA Contemplative Mission Center.
Dulaney, William R. '73 (BRK) Flushing, NY St. Mel.
Dulanto, Angel *o.s.a.* '51 (NY) New York, NY Holy Rosary.
Dulek, Lawrence V. '73 (MIL) On Leave.
Dullahan, Robert J. '57 (ALN)[A] Wernersville, PA Jesuit Center.
Dullea, Charles W. *s.j.* '47 (SJ)[M] Los Gatos, CA Sacred Heart Jesuit Center.
Dullea, Denis '61 (ATL) Retired.
Dullea, Jack F. *s.j.* '59 (LA)[D] Los Angeles, CA Verbum Dei High School.
Dulock, Vincent J. *c.s.b.* '69 (GAL) Angleton, TX Most Holy Trinity.
Dulock, Vincent *c.s.b.* (GAL) Southern Vicariate.
Dulzer, Kenan '48 (FWT)[I] Crowley, TX St. Maximilian Kolbe Friary.
Dumag, Peter '92 (HON) Kihei, HI St. Theresa.
Dumag, Peter (HON) Filipino Ministry.
Dumais, George J. *s.j.* '71 (HEL) Missoula, MT St. Francis Xavier; Special Assignments.
Duman, Charles J. '53 (SFS) Salem, SD St. Mary Retired.
Dumas, Emile E. *m.m.* '67 (FgM).
Dumas, Salvador '74 (CHK) Tinian, MP San Jose.
Dumas, Salvador (CHK) Presbyteral Council.
Dumas, Salvador (CHK) College of Consultors.
Dumas, Terrence J. '88 (LAN) Ann Arbor, MI St. Patrick.
Dumias, George *s.j.* '71 (HEL)[E] Missoula, MT St. Patrick Hospital and Health Sciences Center, Sisters of Providence of Montana Corporation.
Duminiak, John J. '60 (ALN) Beaver Meadows, PA St. Mary.
Duminuco, Vincent J. *s.j.* '64 (NY)[EE] New York, NY Jesuit Community at Fordham University.
Dumm, Demetrius R. *o.s.b.* '47 (GBG)[H] Latrobe, PA Saint Vincent Archabbey.
Dumm, Wilfred M. *o.s.b.* '45 (SAV)[B] Savannah, GA Benedictine Military School; [F] Savannah, GA The Benedictine Priory.
Dummer, Anthony B. *o.m.i.* '80 (JUN) Juneau, AK St. Paul The Apostle; Diocesan Consultors.
Dummer, Donald *o.m.i.* '64 (STP)[M] St. Paul, MN Oblate Residence.
Dummer, Leo *o.m.i.* '59 (FgM).
Dumont, C. Peter '71 (MAN) Auburn, NH St. Peter; Council of Priests; College of Consultors.
Dumont, C. Peter (MAN) Clergy Personnel Board.
Dumont, Gerald '80 (BRK) Brooklyn, NY St. Catherine of Genoa.
Dumouchel, Raymond E. '56 (CHR) Retired.
Dumoulin, Marcel L. '61 (PRT) Fairfield, ME Immaculate Heart of Mary.
Dumphrey, Joseph C. *o.s.f.s.* '64 (BUF) Lockport, NY St. John the Baptist.
Dumphy, Charles J. '55 (WOR) Worcester, MA Blessed Sacrament.
Dumpson, Roland J. '83 (NY) Retired.
Dunan, Said '95 (TYL) Teague, TX St. Mary.
Dunavan, Thomas B. '98 (LIN) Rulo, NE Immaculate Conception; [C] Falls City, NE Sacred Heart School.
Dunbar, Francis '55 (ALB) Retired.
Duncan, Andrew D. '93 (CHY) Riverton, WY St. Margaret's.
Duncan, Andrew (CHY) Education Office Board.
Duncan, Andrew (CHY) College of Consultors.
Duncan, Andrew (CHY) Cursillo Board.
Duncan, Drew (CHY) Presbyteral Council.
Duncan, Drew (CHY) Youth Ministry Board.
Duncan, Edward J. '41 (PEO)[O] Champaign, IL St. John's Catholic Student Chapel and Newman Foundation, University of Illinois Retired.
Duncan, John C. '60 (LFT) Carmel, IN Our Lady of Mount Carmel; [I] Carmel, IN Our Lady of Mount Carmel Parochial School; Associate Judges.
Duncan, Joseph P. '89 (PH) Philadelphia, PA St. Stanislaus; Assocs. to the Vicar Admin..
Duncan, William H. '90 (GR) On Special Assignment; Moderator of the Curia; Vicar General; College of Consultors; Moderator of the Curia.
Duncanson, Richard F. '71 (SD) Solana Beach, CA St. James.
Duncanson, Richard (SD) Censores Librorum.
Duncklee, Lawrence T. (RVC) Procurator & Advocates.
Duncklee, Lawrence '80 (RVC) Brentwood, NY St. Luke; West Babylon, NY Our Lady of Grace.
Dundon, Robert W. *s.j.* '69 (OM) Omaha, NE St. Benedict the Moor; [K] Omaha, NE Jesuit Community at Creighton University.
Dunfee, Dirk J. *s.j.* '97 (KC)[J] Kansas City, MO Rockhurst Jesuit Community.
Dunfee, James M. '84 (STU) Mingo Junction, OH St. Agnes; Judges.
Dung Bui, Joseph (ORL) Vietnamese.
Dunghe, Adelmo P. *s.j.* '95 (NY)[EE] Regis College.
Dunham, Larry C. *o.f.m.* '74 (SFE)[I] Albuquerque, NM Curia Juan Diego; AUXILIARY CHAPLAINS CONTRACT CHAPLAINS.
Dunham, Larry *o.f.m.* (SFE) Finance Council.
Dunham, Larry *o.f.m.* (SFE) College of Consultors.
Dunklee, Lawrence G. '78 (LC) Special Assignment; [H] La Crosse, WI Holy Cross (Seminary) Diocesan Center; Catholic Women, Council of; Hospitals and Health Affairs; Ex Officio; Ex Officio Members.
Dunkley, George '70 (WOR) On Duty Outside the Diocese.
Dunkley, George '70 (SD) San Marcos, CA St. Mark.
Dunlap, James E. (CHI)[J] Evanston, IL Saint Francis Hospital.
Dunlap, William M. '74 (TR) Brick, NJ Visitation.
Dunleavy, Francis J. '40 (MIA) Retired.
Dunleavy, Francis '40 (MIA) Miami Beach, FL St. Patrick Retired.
Dunleavy, Thomas J. '75 (PH) Philadelphia, PA St. Anselm.
Dunleavy, Thomas J. *m.m.* '75 (FgM).
Dunmyer, Ray (BIR) Priests' Council.
Dunmyer, Raymond A. '76 (BIR) Birmingham, AL Our Lady of the Valley.
Dunmyer, Raymond (BIR) Diocesan College of Consultors.
Dunn, Bob '85 (CC) Corpus Christi, TX Most Precious Blood.
Dunn, Charles J. *s.j.* '55 (WOR)[O] Worcester, MA Jesuits of Holy Cross College, Inc..
Dunn, Christopher J. *o.f.m.* '82 (FgM).
Dunn, Didacus Joseph *o.f.m.cap.* '56 (STL)[O] St. Louis, MO St. Crispin's Friary.
Dunn, Didacus '56 (STL) St. Louis, MO St. Matthias.
Dunn, Donald F. '61 (COS) Colorado Springs, CO St. Mary's Cathedral; Vicar General; Diocesan Consultors; Metro–Central Region (Colorado Springs).
Dunn, Donald (COS) Vocations Office.
Dunn, Edmond J. '72 (DAV) Oxford, IA St. Peter's; Oxford, IA St. Mary's; [B] St. Ambrose University.
Dunn, Edward C. '43 (TOL) Tiffin, OH St. Joseph Retired.
Dunn, Edward T. *s.j.* '56 (BUF)[O] Buffalo, NY Canisius Jesuit Community.
Dunn, Gerald R. '57 (MAN) Retired.
Dunn, Harold *m.s.a.* '78 (NOR)[F] Cromwell Society of the Missionaries of the Holy Apostles.
Dunn, Harold (WH) Williamson, WV Sacred Heart.
Dunn, Jerome *o.f.m.cap.* '68 (CLV)[M] Parma, OH Franciscan Communities – Mount Alverna Home.
Dunn, John '54 (DET) Retired.
Dunn, Laurence J. '68 (CHI) Deerfield, IL Holy Cross.
Dunn, Lawrence E. (DET) Retired.
Dunn, Lawrence *m.i.c.* '87 (WDC)[B] Washington, DC Marian Fathers Scholasticate.
Dunn, Mark (TYL) Diocesan Christian Initiation Team.
Dunn, Michael L. '94 (BGP) Bethel, CT St. Mary.
Dunn, Michael '03 (TR) Princeton, NJ St. Paul.
Dunn, Richard B. '80 (SY) Military Chaplains; Air Force Chaplains.
Dunn, Richard C. '45 (TOL) Retired.
Dunn, Richard F. '58 (BRK) Woodside, NY Corpus Christi.
Dunn, Robert M. '92 (NY) Ossining, NY St. Augustine.
Dunn, Stephen *c.p.* '64 (MET)[H] St. Gabriel's Monastery.
Dunn, Stephen '71 (SD)[B] University of San Diego.
Dunn, Stephen '71 (SD) Unassigned.
Dunn, Steven '98 (MIL) Graduate Studies; Milwaukee, WI St. Gregory The Great.
Dunn, William A. '65 (COL) Logan, OH St. John; Parochial Examiners.
Dunn, William J. '51 (OAK) San Lorenzo, CA St. John the Baptist Retired.
Dunne, Andrew J. *o.s.f.s.* '59 (LAN) Michigan Center, MI Our Lady of Fatima.
Dunne, Dermot J. '00 (OM) Omaha, NE St. Wenceslaus; Norfolk, NE Sacred Heart; Age Groups.
Dunne, Edward *c.ss.r.* '49 (BRK)[L] Saratoga Springs, NY St. John Neumann Residence; Brooklyn, NY Our Lady of Perpetual Help Basilica.
Dunne, George W. *s.s.s.* '82 (ORL) Winter Springs, FL St. Stephen.

Dunne, Gerald M. *o.s.f.s.* '77 (SUP)[D] Philadelphia, PA Father Judge High School for Boys; [AA] Philadelphia, PA Father Louis Brisson Residence.
Dunne, James M. '61 (BRK) Rockaway Beach, NY St. Camillus.
Dunne, John S. *c.s.c.* '54 (FTW)[B] University of Notre Dame Du Lac; [I] Notre Dame, IN Holy Cross Community, Corby Hall, University of Notre Dame.
Dunne, John *c.s.c.* '54 (OAK)[N] Berkeley, CA Holy Cross Fathers–Holy Cross Center.
Dunne, Joseph A. '42 (NY)[EE] Bronx, NY Retired.
Dunne, Mark '02 (TYL) Longview, TX St. Anthony; Presbyteral Council.
Dunne, P. Gerard *s.s.c.* '69 (LA)[K] St. Columbans St. Columban's Foreign Mission Society.
Dunne, Patrick J. '70 (NY) White Plains, NY Our Lady of Sorrows; White Plains, NY Burke Rehabilitation Center.
Dunne, Peter F. '44 (OM) Legion of Mary Retired.
Dunne, Peter J. '54 (PH) Retired.
Dunne, Raymond A. *s.j.* '50 (CHI) Prospect Heights, IL St. Alphonsus Liguori.
Dunne, Thomas A. *s.d.b.* (BO) Youth Ministry.
Dunnigan, Daniel D. *s.j.* '63 (DET)[P] Bloomfield Hills, MI Manresa Jesuit Retreat House.
Dunning, James P. '63 (ORG) Mission Viejo, CA St. Kilian.
Dunnivan, John '53 (KCK) Retired.
Dunphy, James R. *m.s.* '57 (STL)[O] La Salette Communications Center.
Dunphy, Richard W. *s.j.* '73 (COS)[F] Sedalia, CO Sacred Heart Jesuit Community; [H] Sedalia, CO Sacred Heart Jesuit Retreat House.
Dunphy, Robert J. '65 (CAM) Mount Ephraim, NJ Sacred Heart.
Dunphy, Thomas R. '58 (CLV) Valley City, OH St. Martin of Tours.
Dunson, Donald '82 (CLV)[A] Wickliffe, OH St. Mary Seminary and Graduate School of Theology.
Dunson, Donald '82 (CLV)[A] Wickliffe, OH Borromeo Seminary.
Duoba, Jonas *m.i.c.* '46 (CHI)[N] Chicago, IL Congregation of Marian Fathers of the Immaculate Conception.
Duong, Cu Minh '87 (MOB) Mobile, AL St. Monica; Vicar for Vietnamese Affairs.
Duong, Duc '01 (CHL) Charlotte, NC St. Matthew.
Duong, Duc (BEA) Beaumont, TX St. Joseph.
Duong, Paul '74 (SJ) Saratoga, CA Church of the Ascension.
Duong, Tien '01 (CHL) Charlotte, NC St. Gabriel.
Duplessis, Donald *o.s.m.* '61 (CHI)[N] Chicago, IL Monastery of Our Lady of Sorrows.
Duplessis, Omer *o.m.i.* '43 (FgM).
DuPont, Arthur J. '54 (HRT) Plantsville, CT Mary Our Queen.
Dupont, Guy B. *o.p* '68 (WDC) Washington, DC St. Dominic Church & Priory.
Dupre, Matthew C. '98 (BR) Brusly, LA St. John the Baptist; Presbyteral Council.
Dupre, Stephane *f.s.s.p.* '03 (SAC) Sacramento, CA St. Stephen the First Martyr Church; [M] Indianapolis, IN Holy Rosary Church.
Du Preez, Frank V. '86 (ATL) Mount Rainier, MD St. James.
Duprey, Dennis J. '70 (OG) Malone, NY St. Helen; Malone, NY Notre Dame; Malone, NY St. John Bosco; Malone, NY St. Joseph's; Advocates; Deans; Bishop's Delegates for Religious.
Dupuis, George H. '50 (BUR) Catholic Women, Vermont Council of; Arlington, VT St. Margaret Mary.
Dupuis, George H. (BUR) CIVIL AIR PATROL.
Dupuis, Laurent *o.m.i.* '36 (SAT)[K] San Antonio, TX Oblate Madonna Residence.
Dupuis, Philip '51 (LAN) Retired.
Dupuis, Ronald S. *s.c.* '77 (PRO)[P] Burrillville, RI Brothers of the Sacred Heart Provincial House; [P] Burrillville, RI Brothers of the Sacred Heart Provincial House.
Dupuis, Wayne G. *c.s.v.* '70 (LAV) Las Vegas, NV St. Viator.
Duque, Luis A. (BO) Everett, MA St. Anthony.
DuQuesnay, Damian *o.s.b.* '46 (SP)[O] St. Leo, FL St. Leo Abbey.
Duquet, Heribert *m.e.p.* '39 (SFR)[K] San Francisco, CA Home for the Aged of the Little Sisters of the Poor; [N] San Francisco, CA Paris Foreign Mission Society Residence.
Duquette, Don Bosco *o.f.m.cap.* '64 (PRT) Portland, ME St. Joseph's; [M] Portland, ME.
Duquette, Lucien G. '56 (BUR) Retired.
Duquette, Roy H. '58 (SPR) Florence, MA Annunciation.
Dura, Eduardo '77 (SFR) San Francisco, CA St. Anne.
Dura, Eduardo '77 (SFR).
Duraczynski, Jerome A. '42 (SFS) Retired.
Duran, Ernesto '42 (BRK) Retired.
Duran, George '52 (LA) Retired.
Duran, Jorge '75 (SAT)[P] On Leave.
Duran, Said (TYL) Teague, TX Boyd Unit, Texas Department of Correction.
Durand, Donald '58 (P) Retired.
Durant, Thomas M. '76 (SY) Utica, NY St. Peter.
Durante, Charles '94 (RNO) Reno, NV Our Lady of Wisdom.
Durante, Charles '94 (RNO)[F] Reno, NV University of Nevada, Newman Community.
Durante, Charles (RNO) Advocates.
Durante, Charles (RNO) Seminary Board.
Durante, Charles (RNO) Priests' Personnel Board.
Durante, Charles (RNO) Vocations Awareness Board.
Durbin, Clarence R. *c.s.c.* '45 (FTW)[B] University of Notre Dame Du Lac; [I] Notre Dame, IN Holy Cross Community, Corby Hall, University of Notre Dame.
Durbin, Clement B. '54 (COL) Retired.
Durbin, John G. '79 (R) Chapel Hill, NC St. Thomas More.
Durchholz, Jack J. (EVN) Diocesan Council of Priests.
Durchholz, Jack '95 (EVN) Evansville, IN St. Boniface.
Durette, Mathias D. *o.s.b.* '93 (MAN)[K] Manchester, NH St. Anselm Abbey.
Durette, Robert *o.m.i.* '60 (FgM).
Durham, Neil *s.d.s.* '82 (MIL)[M] Milwaukee, WI St. Anne's Salvatorian Campus.
Durig, D. Kent '93 (WH) Weirton, WV Sacred Heart of Mary.
Duris, Lawrence M. '69 (CHI) Chicago, IL Our Lady of Peace; Chicago, IL St. Philip Neri.
Duritsa, George M. '53 (Y) Retired.
Durkee, David R. '80 (CLV) Uniontown, OH Queen of Heaven.
Durken, Daniel *o.s.b.* '56 (SCL)[I] Collegeville, MN St. John's Abbey of the Order of St. Benedict.
Durkin, Charles J. '55 (SFR) Retired.
Durkin, Daniel '73 (FTW) Avilla, IN St. Mary of the Assumption.
Durkin, Edward J. *s.j.* '75 (BUF) Buffalo, NY St. Ann.
Durkin, Eugene F. '49 (CHI) Chicago, IL Cathedral of the Holy Name Retired.
Durkin, James J. '68 (CAM) Stratford, NJ St. Luke; Ladies of Charity.
Durkin, John F. '99 (ATL) Lithonia, GA Christ Our Hope.
Durkin, John L. '67 (NY) Amenia, NY Immaculate Conception.
Durkin, John E. '42 (DAV) Retired.
Durkin, John (NY) Taconic, D.D.S.O..
Durkin, Joseph T. *s.j.* '33 (WDC)[M] Washington, DC The Jesuit Community at Georgetown University.
Durkin, Patrick J. *c.s.v.* (MO).
Durney, Charles W. '63 (PH) Retired.
Durso, Michael H. *s.j.* '66 (STL)[O] St. Louis, MO De Smet Jesuit High School Community.
Duscher, Romuald *o.s.b.cam.* '76 (MRY)[F] Big Sur, CA New Camaldoli Hermitage.
Duschl, Frederick J. '65 (TOL) Blakeslee, OH St. Joseph; Blakeslee, OH Sacred Heart; Will–Ful–L Deanery.
Dusecina, Regis '73 (PBR) Greensburg, PA St. Nicholas of Myra.
Dushack, Douglas L. '72 (MAD) Middleton, WI St. Bernard; Personnel Board.
Dusheck, Leo *s.v.d.* '61 (TR)[M] Bordentown, NJ Society of the Divine Word.
Duston, Allen *o.p.* '78 (OAK)[N] Oakland Western Dominican Province.
Duston, Thomas L. '92 (MAN) Londonderry, NH St. Mark the Evangelist; Deaf Ministry.
Dusza, Donald W. '83 (ALT) Clearville, PA Seven Dolors B.V.M.; Bedford, PA St. Thomas.
Dutchoff, C. Robert '56 (MAD) Absent on Sick Leave.
Dutel, Gilbert J. '70 (LAF) Scott, LA Sts. Peter and Paul.
Dutkiewicz, Eugene M. *s.j.* '61 (NO)[P] Jesuit Health Trust.
Dutkiewicz, Eugene M. *s.j.* '61 (MIL)[X] Milwaukee, WI The Jesuit Partnership; [O] Wauwatosa, WI Jesuit Community at St. Camillus; [O] Milwaukee, WI Jesuit Provincial Office, Wisconsin Province.
Dutkiewicz, Thomas A. *o.f.m.cap.* '56 (PIT)[N] Pittsburgh, PA St. Francis Friary; [N] Pittsburgh, PA St. Augustine Friary.
Dutra, Luis C. '55 (LAF)[H] Lafayette, LA De La Salle Christian Brothers Retired.
Dutram, Charles J. '58 (WOR) Retired.
DuVall, Justin *o.s.b.* '78 (IND)[K] St. Meinrad, IN St. Meinrad Archabbey.
Duvall, Justin *o.s.b.* '78 (IND)[A] St. Meinrad, IN St. Meinrad School of Theology.
Duvelius, Dennis M. *f.s.s.p.* '96 (IND) Indianapolis, IN SS. Peter and Paul Cathedral; Indianapolis, IN Holy Rosary; [M] Shawnee, KS.
Duvelsdorf, Peter L. '58 (RVC)[M] Uniondale, NY St. Pius X Residence Retired.
DuWell, Ralph I. (ORL) Deltona, FL Our Lady of the Lakes.
Dux, James M. '48 (PH) Retired.
Dux, John H. '73 (STA) On Duty Outside the Diocese.
Duyka, Stephen J. '97 (TYL) Nacogdoches, TX Nacogdoches, St. Mary's Chapel, Stephen F. Austin State University; [D] Nacogdoches, TX Stephen F. Austin University Catholic Student Center; Advocates; Young Adult/Campus Ministries; Diocesan Pastoral Team – DPT; Diocesan Liturgical Commission.
Duyshart, Edwin C. '84 (LA) Altadena, CA St. Elizabeth of Hungary.
Duzinski, Paul A. *o.f.m.conv.* '81 (CLV)[M] Cleveland, OH Sts. Mary and Joseph Home for the Aged.
Duzinski, Paul *o.f.m.conv.* '81 (BAL)[S] Cleveland, OH Sts. Mary and Joseph Home Retired.
Dvorak, Donald *o.p.* '63 (NO) New Orleans, LA St. Dominic.
Dvorak, Franklin A. '70 (OM) Omaha, NE St. Wenceslaus.
Dvorak, Gerald (STP) Hopkins, MN St. Joseph's.
Dvorscak, James '76 (JOL) Mokena, IL St. Mary Church.
Dwomik, Peter '99 (HRT) Forestville, CT St. Matthew.
Dwomoh, Charles '86 (VIC) Palacios, TX St. Anthony's.
Dwomoh, Charles (VIC) Presbyteral Council.
Dwomoh, Charles (VIC) Procurator Advocate.
Dworak, Joseph J. '65 (ALB)[H] Amsterdam, NY St. Mary's Hospital.
Dworak, Joseph '65 (ALB) Fort Edward, NY St. Joseph.
Dworak, Joseph (ALB) Priests Retirement Board.
Dworak, Walter W. '72 (PIT) Pittsburgh, PA St. Philip.
Dwulit, Andrij Taras '90 (STN) Houston, TX Protection of the Mother of God.
Dwyer, Arthur J. *m.m.* '49 (NY)[EE] Maryknoll, NY Maryknoll Fathers and Brothers Charitable Trust; [M] Los Altos, CA Maryknoll.
Dwyer, Daniel P. *o.f.m.* '88 (ALB)[B] Siena College.
Dwyer, David P. *c.s.p.* (DEN) Boulder, CO St. Thomas Aquinas University Parish; [Q] Boulder, CO University of Colorado (Boulder).
Dwyer, Dennis E. '66 (COS) Elizabeth, CO Our Lady of the Visitation Quasi–Parish.
Dwyer, Dermot '62 (SAC) Retired.
Dwyer, Donald M. '79 (NY) Bronx, NY Our Lady of the Assumption; Bronx (East); Bronx, NY St. Barnabas.
Dwyer, Eugene F. *s.j.* '59 (CHI)[C] Chicago, IL Jesuit Community at Loyola University Chicago.
Dwyer, J. Dermot (SAC) Opus Sanctorum Angelorum.
Dwyer, J. Floyd '48 (LC)[H] La Crosse, WI Holy Cross (Seminary) Diocesan Center; Building Commission Retired.
Dwyer, James *s.s.c.* '58 (PRO)[P] Bristol, RI St. Columban's Retirement House.
Dwyer, John A. '74 (WOR) Fitchburg, MA Sacred Heart of Jesus.
Dwyer, John F. '56 (NY) Tappan, NY Our Lady of the Sacred Heart.
Dwyer, Kevin F. *o.s.a.* '62 (BO)[C] North Andover, MA Merrimack College; [C] Villanova, PA Villanova University; [C] Our Mother of Good Counsel Monastery.
Dwyer, Michael F. '38 (NY) Retired.
Dwyer, Morris L. '38 (OG) Plattsburgh, NY St. Peter Retired.
Dwyer, Robert D. '62 (SY) Bainbridge, NY St. John the Evangelist.
Dwyer, Thomas P. *o.s.a.* '53 (FgM).
Dwyer, Timothy *s.m.* '68 (STL)[O] St. Louis, MO Provincialate of the Society of Mary, Province of the United States.
Dwyer, Timothy *s.m.* '68 (STL)[O] St. Louis, MO Maryland Avenue Marianist Community.
Dwyer, William M. '38 (SY) Retired.
Dy, Angel '69 (DOD) Dodge City, KS The Cathedral of Our Lady of Guadalupe.
Dybas, Richard W. '59 (ALB) Cohoes, NY St. Michael.
Dybdal, Gerald '68 (OAK) Retired.
Dyck, Peter (PEO)[I] Urbana, IL Provena Covenant Medical Center.
Dye, David M. '92 (ATL) Dunwoody, GA All Saints Catholic.
Dye, Robert M. '91 (TLS) Muskogee, OK Saint Joseph Church; Special Assignment; Hispanic Ministry.
Dyer, Edward J. '41 (WOR) Retired.
Dyer, Francis X. *o.p.* '69 (CHI)[N] Chicago Dominicans (Provincial Office); [M] Aurora, IL The J. Chevalier Charitable Trust.
Dyer, Gene J. '85 (CHI) Des Plaines, IL St. Mary.
Dyer, George J. '53 (CHI) Wadsworth, IL St. Patrick; [X] Mundelein, IL Civitas Dei Foundation Retired.
Dyer, George *o.p.* '61 (FgM).
Dyer, James W. '97 (STL) Farmington, MO St. Joseph.
Dyer, John J. '56 (WOR) Retired.
Dyer, Joseph '74 (JKS) Canton, MS Sacred Heart; Canton, MS Holy Child Jesus.
Dyer, Raymond E. '46 (PRO)[P] Providence St. John Vianney Residence Retired.
Dyer, Thomas P. '69 (Y) Canton, OH St. Joan of Arc; [C] Louisville, OH St. Thomas Aquinas High School; [P] Louisville, OH St. Thomas Aquinas High School Endowment Fund.
Dyer, Timothy J. '74 (LA) Los Angeles, CA Nativity; Los Angeles, CA St. Columbkille; Deanery 16.
Dyer, Timothy (LA) Members.
Dyer, Timothy (LA) Our Lady of the Angels Region.
Dyer, William *m.afr.* '70 (FgM).
Dygula, Rafal *s.ch.* '96 (CHI) Chicago, IL Holy Trinity Mission.

Dykas, Benjamin '71 (ALT) Retired.
Dyke, Neil Van '98 (CHI) Stickney, IL St. Pius X.
Dylag, Michael R. '65 (GBG) On Duty Outside the Diocese.
Dylag, Michael R. '65 (DET) Special Assignment.
Dymcwski, Thomas *o.ss.t.* '85 (BAL)[S] Victoria, TX.
Dymowski, Tom *o.ss.t.* '85 (VIC) Victoria, TX Our Lady of Sorrows.
Dymski, Daniel J. '60 (E) Erie, PA Sacred Heart.
Dymski, J. Daniel '60 (E) Cambridge Springs Correction Institution; Pleasant Ridge Manor West.
Dynek, Wieslaw A. (MO) Army Chaplains.
Dynetius, Thomas (LFT)[F] Kokomo, IN Maria Regina Mater Monastery.
Dyrcz, Michael S. '73 (CLV) Cleveland, OH St. Barbara.
Dyrwal, Justin *o.s.b.* '98 (CLV)[O] Cleveland, OH.
Dysinger, Luke *o.s.b.* '78 (LA)[A] Camarillo, CA St. John's Seminary.
Dysinger, Luke *o.s.b.* '86 (LA)[Q] Valyermo, CA St. Andrew's Abbey.
Dysinger, Luke *o.s.b.* (LA) Members.
Dytkowski, Louis M. '60 (BGP) Sherman, CT Holy Trinity.
Dzankic, Zvonko *o.p.* (CHI)[N] Chicago, IL Croatian Dominican Fathers.
Dzermejko, David F. '74 (PIT) Charleroi, PA Mary Mother of the Church.
Dziadek, Vladimir '82 (SP) Gulfport, FL Most Holy Name of Jesus.
Dziadosz, Edward T. '55 (PH) Retired.
Dziak, Theodore A. *s.j.* '83 (FgM).
Dziedzic, Gerald H. '74 (HRT) Terryville, CT Immaculate Conception; St. Casimir; Army Reserve Chaplains.
Dzieglewicz, John T. *s.j.* '83 (NY)[EE] Cardinal Spellman Hall, Jesuit Community.
Dziekan, Wayne H. '94 (GAY) Suttons Bay, MI St. Gertrude; Suttons Bay, MI St. Michael the Archangel; Migrant Apostolate.
Dzielak, Thomas L. '63 (RCK) Rock Falls, IL St. Andrew; Deans; Council of Catholic Women, Diocesan.
Dzien, Joseph Duc '83 (NO) Luling, LA St. Anthony of Padua.
Dzieszko, Thaddeus '88 (CHI) Chicago, IL St. Constance.
Dzieszko, Thaddeus '88 (CHI)[U] Chicago, IL Catholic League for Religious Assistance to Poland.
Dzikowski, Piotr *s.ch.* '87 (SEA) Tacoma, WA SS. Peter & Paul.
Dzikowski, Piotr *s.ch.* (SEA) Polish Speaking, Ministry to.
Dziob, Michael W. '42 (PRO)[P] Providence St. John Vianney Residence Retired.
Dziordz, Walter *m.i.c.* '84 (SPR)[I] Provincial Office.
Dziordz, Walter *m.i.c.* '84 (SPR)[I] Eucharistic Apostles of The Divine Mercy.
Dziorek, Anthony *c.r.* '75 (CHI) Chicago, IL St. Stanislaus, Bishop and Martyr.

E

Eagan, Joseph *s.j.* '53 (SFR) Larkspur, CA St. Patrick Retired.
Eagan, William J. *s.j.* '02 (BGP)[P] Fairfield, CT The Fairfield Jesuit Community–Fairfield University.
Eagan, William J. *s.j.* (BGP)[E] Fairfield, CT Fairfield College Preparatory School.
Eagle, Raohael *tor* (FWT) Fort Worth, TX St. Bartholomew.
Eagleson, Donald W. '86 (SR)[K] San Rafael, CA Nazareth House Retired.
Earl, John '94 (RCK) Rockford, IL St. Patrick.
Earl, Marcellus R. *o.c.s.o.* '63 (ROC)[I] Piffard, NY Abbey of the Genesee.
Earley, Daniel J. *o.s.f.s.* '48 (TOL)[C] Toledo, OH St. Francis de Sales High School; [J] Toledo, OH Retired.
Earley, Jerome *o.c.d.* '95 (DAL)[I] Dallas, TX Mount Carmel Center.
Earley, Kiernan *c.p.* '57 (HRT)[M] West Hartford Holy Family Monastery/Retreat.
Earley, Philip B. '74 (BO) Wilmington, MA St. Thomas of Villanova.
Earls, John Patrick *o.s.b.* '65 (SCL)[I] Collegeville, MN St. John's Abbey, of the Order of St. Benedict.
Early, Francis J. '85 (WDC) Bushwood, MD Sacred Heart; Deans.
Early, Thomas C. '51 (ALX) Retired.
Early, William F. '68 (BRK) On Leave/Unassigned.
Earner, Thomas '62 (SP) Retired.
East, Raymond G. '81 (WDC) Washington, DC St. Francis Xavier; Archdiocesan College of Consultors.
East, Raymond (WDC) Executive Directors.
East, Raymond (WDC) Executive Director.
East, Raymond (WDC) Contact.
Easterling, William T. '82 (LA) Valinda, CA St. Martha.
Eastman, Patrick W. '84 (TLS) Retired.
Easton, Frederick C. '66 (IND) Indianapolis, IN St. Gabriel the Archangel.
Easton, Frederick (IND) Archdiocesan Pastoral Council.
Easton, Frederick (IND) Vicariate Judicial Metropolitan Tribunal.
Easton, William M. '70 (DET) Royal Oak, MI National Shrine of the Little Flower.
Eaton, John *o.f.m.* '78 (SUP) Bayfield, WI St. Francis.
Eaton, John *o.f.m.* '78 (SUP) Bayfield, WI Holy Family.
Eaton, John *o.f.m.* '78 (SUP) Washburn, WI St. Ann.
Eaton, John *o.f.m.* '78 (SUP) Bayfield, WI St. Joseph.
Eaton, John *o.f.m.* '78 (SUP) Washburn, WI St. Louis.
Eaton, John *o.f.m.* (SUP) Presbyteral Council & Diocesan Consultors.
Ebach, Aloys *c.pp.s.* '74 (KC)[J] Liberty, MO Precious Blood Center.
Ebach, Aloys *c.pp.s.* '74 (KC)[A] Liberty, MO Society of the Precious Blood Provincial Offices; [J] Liberty, MO Precious Blood Society Provincial Office.
Ebacher, Jerome *o.c.s.o.* '49 (P)[L] Lafayette, OR The Cistercian (Trappist) Abbey of Our Lady of Guadalupe.
Ebarb, Walter E. '62 (SHP) San Antonio, TX St. Patrick; On Duty Outside the Diocese.
Ebben, Bertrand E. *o.p.* '59 (MEM) Memphis, TN St. Peter's; [I] Memphis, TN Order Of Preachers (Southern Dominican Prov.).
Ebben, Bertrand *o.p.* '59 (MEM)[I] Memphis, TN The Dominican Friars of Memphis, Inc..
Ebbesmier, John '78 (PHX) Glendale, AZ Our Lady of Perpetual Help.
Ebejer, Lino P. '91 (WH) Thomas, WV St. Thomas Aquinas.
Ebel, Stephen P. '70 (DAV) Long Grove, IA St. Ann's.
Ebenhoeh, John O. *o.s.f.s.* '64 (TOL)[C] Toledo, OH St. Francis de Sales High School; [J] Toledo, OH.
Eberle, Richard *o.s.f.s.* '82 (LAN) Hudson, MI Sacred Heart.
Eberly, Herbert *c.p.* '58 (FgM).
Ebert, Mark S. '76 (STL) St. Louis, MO St. Simon the Apostle.
Ebey, Carl F. *c.s.c.* '72 (FTW)[B] University of Notre Dame Du Lac; [I] Notre Dame, IN Holy Cross Community, Corby Hall, University of Notre Dame.
Eble, James E. *m.m.* '88 (FgM).
Eblen, James '64 (SEA) Puyallup, WA Holy Disciples; Special Assignment.
Eblen, James (SEA) Theological Resources.
Eblen, James (SEA) Judges.
Ebner, Frank '47 (SCL) Retired.
Ebrom, Robert L. '71 (CHI) Elk Grove Village, IL Queen of the Rosary.
Ebron, Jose Erlito '93 (NEW) Kenilworth, NJ St. Theresa's.
Eburn, Brian '68 (STA) Fernandina Beach, FL St. Michael's; Holy Childhood Association, The.
Eburn, Brian (STA) Propagation of the Faith.
Ebuziem, Cajetan (CHI) Chicago, IL Corpus Christi.
Eccleston, John '55 (SCL) Retired.
Echert, John P. '87 (STP)[C] St. Paul, MN University of St. Thomas; Air National Guard Chaplains.
Echert, John '87 (STP)[A] St. Paul, MN The Saint Paul Seminary; Military Chaplains.
Echevarria, Pedro Faustino '84 (PCE) Jayuya, PR Our Lady of Monserrate.
Echevarria, Rafael (ORG) Santa Ana, CA Immaculate Heart of Mary.
Echevarria, Wilfredo *o.ss.t.* '81 (ARE) Isabela, PR St. Anthony.
Echeverria, Miguel *o.a.r.* '61 (LSC) Chaparral, NM St. Thomas More.
Echevia, Les Suberi '61 (RCK) Virgil, IL SS. Peter and Paul.
Echle, Harry A. '42 (WDC) Washington, DC Our Lady of Victory Retired.
Eck, Gregory J. *s.j.* '99 (WDC)[E] North Bethesda, MD Georgetown Preparatory School.
Eck, Ivan C. '51 (WCH) Mount Hope, KS St. Rose; Mount Hope, KS St. Joseph; Mt. Hope, KS St. Louis; Deans.
Eck, John E. *c.s.v.* '63 (CHI) Chicago, IL St. Victor.
Eck, Reinhard C. '50 (WCH) Andale, KS St. Joseph.
Eckard, John A. (BAL) Baltimore, MD St. Joseph; Advocates and Procurators.
Eckart, Frank E. '69 (TOL) Toledo, OH Holy Rosary.
Eckart, Frank K. '69 (TOL) Toledo, OH Sacred Heart of Jesus; Toledo, OH St. Stephen; Building Commission.
Eckart, Placidus *o.s.b.* '49 (LR)[E] Fort Smith, AR St. Edward Mercy Medical Center.
Eckberg, Joseph A. '00 (WCH) Hutchinson, KS Holy Cross; [L] Wichita, KS Serra Club of Reno County.
Eckelkamp, David *o.f.m.* '53 (SFD)[M] Springfield, IL St. Francis Convent; [L] Springfield, IL Our Lady of Angels Friary.
Eckenrod, Edward L. '78 (ALT) Altoona, PA Our Lady of Lourdes; Altoona, PA Altoona Hospital.
Ecker, John A. '58 (YAK) Yakima, WA St. Paul Cathedral; Vicar General; Diocesan Consultors; Ecumenical Liaison; Diocesan Finance Council; Clergy Personnel Board; Presbyteral Council Executive Committee; Vocations; Lay Advisory Board.
Ecker, Robert J. '51 (BRK) Retired.
Eckermann, Charles H. '56 (SY) Syracuse, NY Blessed Sacrament; Elected Retired.
Eckert, Carl E. '54 (LFT) Retired.
Eckert, John C. '72 (PH) Morrisville, PA Holy Trinity.
Eckert, Sidney J. '66 (DET) Livonia, MI St. Maurice.
Eckert, Tom *c.s.c.* '02 (FTW)[B] University of Notre Dame Du Lac.
Eckert, William F. '64 (CAM) Retired.
Eckhoff, Evan *o.f.m.* '57 (KNX)[F] Knoxville, TN Franciscan Friars.
Eckinger, Ambrose *o.p.* '81 (COL) Columbus, OH St. Patrick.
Eckley, Michael P. '91 (OM) Hooper, NE St. Rose of Lima; Age Groups.
Eckman, Mark A. '85 (PIT) Brentwood, PA St. Sylvester; Diocesan Pastoral Council.
Eckrich, James P. '53 (WIL) Retired.
Eckroth, Leonard A. '58 (BIS) Hague, ND St. Mary; Strasburg, ND Sts. Peter and Paul; Defensor Vinculi.
Eckroth, Richard *o.s.b.* '52 (SCL)[I] Collegeville, MN St. John's Abbey, of the Order of St. Benedict.
Eckstein, Francis J. '58 (IND) Retired.
Eco, Roy V. '80 (OAK)[K] Hayward, CA St. Rose Hospital.
Edakkulathoor, Jos Shepherd *c.m.i.* '89 (NSH)[K] Liberty, TN Carmel Center of Spirituality.
Edamattan, Thomas '66 (RVC) Huntington, NY St. Patrick's.
Edamattan, Thomas '66 (RVC) Huntington, NY Huntington Hospital.
Edapaddy, Thomas *c.m.i.* '64 (LAF) St. Martinville, LA St. Elizabeth.
Edara, Inna *s.v.d.* (BAL)[S] Baltimore, MD Society of Mary (Marianists).
Edassery, Matthew '74 (TYL) Jacksonville, TX Our Lady of Sorrows.
Edathinatt, Job *c.m.i.* '94 (SHP) Monroe, LA Our Lady of Fatima.
Edathinatt, Job *c.m.i.* '94 (SHP)[G] Monroe, LA Catholic Campus Ministry at the University of Louisiana at Monroe.
Edayadiyil, Jose '73 (SCL) Isanti, MN St. Elizabeth Ann Seton.
Eddy, Corbin '68 (BAL).
Eddy, William A. '75 (CHI)[A] Chicago Heights, IL St. Kieran.
Edelen, Luke A. *o.s.b.* '80 (NEW)[N] Newark, NJ Newark Abbey; Archdiocesan Commission for Christain Unity; [Q] Jersey City, NJ New Jersey City University, Gilligan Student Center.
Edelen, Richard D. '75 (LEX) Beattyville, KY Queen of All Saints.
Edelen, Richard '75 (LEX) Stanton, KY Our Lady of the Mountains.
Edelen, Richard '75 (LEX) Ravenna, KY St. Elizabeth of Hungary.
Edelen, Tom '01 (TYL) Trinity, TX Most Holy Trinity.
Eden, Timothy E. *s.m.* '77 (HON)[A] Honolulu, HI Chaminade University of Honolulu; [I] Honolulu, HI Our Lady the Mystical Rose Chapel.
Eden, Timothy *s.m.* '77 (HON)[G] Honolulu, HI Center Marianist Community.
Eden, Timothy *s.m.* (HON) Hawaii Catholic Conference.
Eden, Timothy *s.m.* (HON) Members.
Edens, William L. *c.s.p.* '81 (CHR) Clemson, SC St. Andrew; [H] Clemson, SC Clemson University, Southern Wesleyan University.
Eder, Donald '54 (LAN) Retired.
Eder, Donald '60 (LFT) Oxford, IN St. Patrick.
Ederer, John A. (SAG) Association of Saginaw Priests.
Ederer, John '77 (SAG) Vassar, MI St. Frances Xavier Cabrini.
Edgerly, Leo J. '84 (OAK) Piedmont, CA Corpus Christi.
Edgerly, Leo (OAK) Cursillo Movement.
Edison, Pamintuan *m.s.* '02 (SB)[E] Moreno Valley, CA Missionaries of Our Lady of La Salette, MS.
Ediza, Manuel '79 (SD) San Diego, CA Children's Hospital.
Ediza, Manuel '79 (SD) San Diego, CA St. John the Evangelist.
Ediza, Manuel '79 (SD) Sharp Memorial Hospital.
Ediza, Manuel (SD) Filipino.
Edlefsen, Frederick H. '01 (ARL) Falls Church, VA St. James; Notaries.
Edmiston, James *o.f.m.* '98 (STL)[O] Franciscan Friars.
Edmiston, James *o.f.m.* '98 (FgM).
Edmunds, Garrett *o.f.m.* '82 (SD) Oceanside, CA Mission San Luis Rey; [H] Oceanside, CA Mission San Luis Rey.
Edmunds, John *s.t.* '76 (NEW) Jersey City, NJ Christ, the King.
Edogwo, Linus V. '86 (NEW) Newark, NJ St. Mary's.
Edomobi, Eustace '75 (NEW) Newark, NJ St. Antoninus.
Edomobi, Eustace '75 (NEW) Newark, NJ University of Medicine & Dentistry (UMDNJ); UMDNJ University Hospital.
Edrich, Paul J. '54 (CIN) Retired.
Eduarte, Edmund P. '93 (GAL) Houston, TX Sacred Heart Co–Cathedral.
Edward, Yew '02 (TLS) Special Assignment.

Edwards, Brice '70 (WOR)[O] Shrewsbury, MA Calvary Retreat Center, Passionist Fathers of Shrewsbury, Inc..
Edwards, Byron H. '87 (SPC) Retired.
Edwards, Charles A. '86 (SFD)[D] Quincy, IL Quincy Notre Dame High School.
Edwards, Charles '86 (SFD) Springfield, IL Little Flower.
Edwards, Cyril D. '84 (SCR) Scranton, PA Holy Rosary; Presbyteral Council.
Edwards, Dale '83 (FWT) Retired.
Edwards, David A. '02 (BEA) Nederland, TX St. Charles Borromeo.
Edwards, Edward M. '83 (CHI)[I] Watchung, NJ Mount St. Mary.
Edwards, Guy F. '85 (OG) Dannemora, NY Clinton Correctional Facility.
Edwards, Guy '85 (OG) Dannemora, NY St. Joseph.
Edwards, J. Daniel '94 (LAF) Church Point, LA St. Edward.
Edwards, James F. '61 (ORL) Retired.
Edwards, James T. '76 (STL) Crestwood, MO St. Elizabeth of Hungary.
Edwards, John F. '55 (HRT) Wethersfield, CT Incarnation; Deans.
Edwards, John H. *s.j.* '54 (NO)[P] New Orleans, LA Ignatius Residence.
Edwards, Michael W. '79 (PMB) Vero Beach, FL St. Helen; Assessors; College of Consultors.
Edwards, Paul '83 (MIA) Weston, FL St. Katharine Drexel.
Edwards, Philip *o.s.b.* '67 (LA)[W] Valyermo, CA St. Andrew's Abbey Retreat Center (All Groups).
Edwards, Philip *o.s.b.* '67 (LA)[Q] Valyermo, CA St. Andrew's Abbey.
Edwards, R. Dale (FWT) AUXILIARY CHAPLAINS CONTRACT CHAPLAINS.
Edwards, Robert '81 (Y) Lisbon, OH St. George.
Edwards, Robert (Y) Charismatic Prayer Group.
Edwards, Roy D. '46 (LAF) Retired.
Edwards, Tom J. '90 (OAK) Oakland, CA Sacred Heart.
Edyk, Eugene '61 (DET) Clinton Twp., MI St. Paul of Tarsus.
Eelman, William C. '53 (TR) Retired.
Eftink, Edward M. '66 (SPC) Jackson, MO Immaculate Conception; Advocate; Priests' Mutual Benefit Society.
Eftink, Glenn A. '93 (SPC) Campbell, MO St. Teresa; Campbell, MO St. Ann; Diocesan Development Fund.
Egan, Anthony *o.f.m.cap.* '65 (PRT) Portland, ME St. Joseph's.
Egan, Arthur B. '57 (CLV) Avon, OH St. Mary of the Immaculate Conception Retired.
Egan, Brennan *o.f.m.* (FR)[H] Onset, MA St. Joseph Friary–Franciscan Friars.
Egan, Brennan *o.f.m.* (NY) Castle Point, NY Veterans Administration Medical Center.
Egan, Brian '50 (BIR) On Special or Other Diocesan Assignment.
Egan, Brian *v.a.* '50 (BIR) Birmingham, AL Our Lady of Sorrows.
Egan, Brian '50 (BIR)[I] Birmingham, AL Catholic Housing of Birmingham, Inc..
Egan, Brian (BIR) Diocesan Finance Council.
Egan, Brian (BIR) Annual Catholic Charities Appeal, Campaign for Human Development.
Egan, Brian (BIR) Defenders of the Bond.
Egan, Brian (BIR) Members.
Egan, Brian (BIR) Diocesan College of Consultors.
Egan, Brian (BIR) Diocesan College of Vicars.
Egan, Edward F. '41 (PRO)[P] Providence St. John Vianney Residence Retired.
Egan, Eugene E. '54 (WIN) Retired.
Egan, Gerard P. '65 (CHI) Other Assignments.
Egan, Harvey D. *s.j.* '69 (BO)[V] Newton, MA The Jesuit Community at Boston College.
Egan, Harvey F. '41 (STP) Retired.
Egan, James A. *s.j.* '65 (FgM).
Egan, James A. *s.j.* '65 (MIL)[O] Xavier House.
Egan, John Martin *o.p.* '56 (WDC)[B] Washington, DC Dominican House of Studies.
Egan, Kerry (DUB)[H] Cedar Rapids, IA Mercy Medical Center–Cedar Rapids.
Egan, Patrick '66 (LAN)[O] Ann Arbor, MI Catholic Men's Movement.
Egan, Philip '82 (KC) Kansas City, MO St. Monica.
Egan, Philip (KC) Deans.
Egan, Richmond J. *s.m.* '67 (ATL)[C] Atlanta, GA Marist School.
Egan, Robert J. *s.j.* '62 (SEA)[L] Seattle, WA Jesuit House, Seattle.
Egan, Robert J. *s.j.* '73 (SPK)[B] Spokane, WA Gonzaga University.
Egan, Robert M. *c.s.v.* '78 (CHI) Chicago, IL St. Victor.
Egan, Robert '54 (ROC) Retired.
Egan, Thomas F. '75 (WOR) Leominster, MA Holy Family of Nazareth.
Egan, Thomas R. *m.m.* '74 (FgM).
Egbeji, Jude '89 (NY) Sleepy Hollow, NY St. Teresa of Avila.
Egbers, James B. '96 (COV) Fort Thomas, KY St. Catherine of Siena.
Egege, Christian Paul '72 (SAC) Citrus Heights, CA Holy Family.
Egert, Clifford A. '38 (DAV)[L] Davenport, IA Kahl Home for the Aged and Infirm Retired.
Eggerling, Milton '54 (OAK)[V] Boston, MA The Society of St. James the Apostle, Inc..
Eggerling, Milton '54 (OAK) Retired.
Eggerling, Milton '54 (FgM).
Eggerling, Milton '54 (BO)[AA] Boston, MA St. Stephen.
Eggert, Francis X. '58 (SFE) Albuquerque, NM Our Lady of Fatima.
Eggert, Francis (SFE) College of Consultors.
Egging, Martin L. '93 (GI) Chappell, NE St. Joseph's; Diocesan Consultors; Priests' Advisory Board (Presbyteral Council).
Eggleston, Earl E. '96 (SD) San Diego, CA Mission Basilica San Diego De Alcala; [A] San Diego, CA St. Francis De Sales Center.
Eggleston, Earl (SD) Assistant to Bishop Robert H. Brom.
Eggleston, Earl (SD) Presbyteral Council.
Egierd, Henry A. '80 (MET) Retired.
Egitto, Phil (ORL) Members.
Egitto, Philip J. '88 (ORL) Daytona Beach, FL Our Lady of Lourdes.
Egli, Max '71 (OAK)[N] Berkeley Salesian Community.
Egloff, Adolph '40 (EVN) Retired.
Eglsaer, Harry S. *s.j.* '51 (OM)[K] Omaha, NE Jesuit Community at Creighton University.
Ego, Anthony M. '85 (PEO) Milan, IL St. Ambrose.
Eguiguren, Jose Martin '67 (CGS) Caguas, PR Santisimo Sacramento.
Eguino, Desiderio *o.p.* '78 (MIA)[H] Miami, FL Dominican Fathers of Miami, Inc..
Eguino, Desiderio *o.p.* '78 (MIA) Miami, FL St. Dominic.
Egurrola, Vicente '46 (SJN) San Juan, PR Santos Pedro y Pablo los Apostoles.
Egurrola, Vicente '46 (SJN) Retired.
Ehalt, William L. '99 (IND) Cambridge City, IN St. Elizabeth of Hungary; Knightstown, IN St. Rose; New Castle, IN St. Anne.
Ehalt, William (IND) Council of Priests.
Ehiemere, Michael '81 (CHY) Greybull, WY Sacred Heart.
Ehmke, Lyle *o.s.c.* '70 (STP)[M] St. Mary's International School.
Ehr, Donald J. *s.v.d.* '55 (CHI) Chicago, IL St. Anselm.
Ehreman, Terry *c.s.c.* '00 (P)[L] Portland, OR Holy Cross Fathers & Brothers, C.S.C. – University of Portland.
Ehrens, Richard J. '58 (CHI) Harwood Heights–Norridge, IL St. Rosalie; [M] Wheeling, IL Addolorata Villa Retired.
Ehrhardt, Joseph B. *o.f.m.* '67 (FgM).
Ehrhart, Charles M. '60 (RVC) Priests Released from Diocesan Assignment; Army Chaplains.
Ehrich, John D. (PHX) Phoenix, AZ St. Thomas the Apostle; Advocates.
Ehrman, Dale *o.s.c.* '90 (STP)[M] Shoreview, MN Crosier Provincial House Province of St. Odilia.
Ehwald, Joseph A. '62 (COL) Reynoldsburg, OH St. Pius X.
Eichenberger, Thomas '76 (MIL) Cedarburg, WI St. Francis Borgia.
Eichenseer, Donald W. '61 (BEL) Albers, IL St. Bernard.
Eichenseer, Donald W. '61 (BEL) Damiansville, IL St. Damian.
Eichenseer, Donald W. '61 (BEL) Defensores Vinculi; Diocesan Finance Council.
Eichhoff, Paul E. '70 (TLS) Claremore, OK St. Cecilia; Diocesan Senators.
Eichhoff, Paul (TLS) Diocesan Consultors.
Eichhorst, Franklin *o.f.m.cap* (LSC) Priestly Life and Ministry Committee.
Eichner, Philip K. *s.m.* '66 (RVC)[D] Uniondale, NY Kellenberg Memorial High School; [M] Mineola, NY Provincial Residence and Novitiate.
Eichor, Edward C. '59 (STL)[A] St. Louis, MO Kenrick School of Theology.
Eichorn, Harry B. *c.s.c.* '57 (FR)[A] North Easton, MA Stonehill College; [A] North Easton, MA Holy Cross Fathers Religious.
Eichorn, Harry B. *c.s.c.* '57 (FTW)[I] North Easton, MA Stonehill College.
Eickhoff, Jeffrey '95 (LIN)[A] Seward, NE St. Gregory the Great Seminary.
Eickhoff, Jeffrey (LIN) Pro Life.
Eickhoff, Matthew F. (LIN) Engaged Encounter; PREP.
Eickhoff, Matthew '89 (LIN) Brainard, NE Holy Trinity; Evangelization Committee.
Eickhoff, Matthew (LIN) Family Life Office.
Eickhoff, Matthew (LIN) Evangelization Office.
Eickhoff, Matthew (LIN) Commission for Sacred Liturgy and Sacred Music.
Eickhoff, Matthew (LIN) Natural Family Planning.
Eickhoff, Matthew (LIN) Marriage Encounter.
Eickholt, Henry C. '44 (SAG) Retired.
Eid, Frederick M. '47 (NEW) Hoboken, NJ Our Lady of Grace Retired.
Eidenschenk, John *o.s.b.* '41 (SCL)[I] Collegeville, MN St. John's Abbey, of the Order of St. Benedict.
Eifler, John G. '61 (L) Louisville, KY St. Frances of Rome.
Eigo, Francis A. *o.s.a.* '64 (PH)[C] Villanova University; [AA] Villanova, PA St. Thomas Monastery.
Eikens, Leroy F. '62 (WIN) Retired.
Eikmeier, Bernard J. '51 (HON) Retired.
Eilerman, Craig R. '87 (COL) Columbus, OH St. Cecilia.
Eilerman, William *c.pp.s.* '51 (CIN)[J] Bellevue Mary Lay Center; [L] Bellevue, OH Sorrowful Mother Shrine.
Eimer, Frank J. '58 (L) Retired.
Eis, Charles R. '66 (SPK) Retired.
Eisel, Howard P. *s.s.c.* '54 (DUL) Crosby, MN St. Joseph's.
Eisel, Howard *s.s.c.* '54 (DUL) Crosby, MN St. Joseph; [K] St. Columbans St. Columban's Foreign Mission Society.
Eisele, Francis X. '54 (RVC) East Rockaway, NY St. Raymond's.
Eisele, James F. '88 (LAN) Flint, MI St. Agnes.
Eisele, Paul '68 (SC) Algona, IA St. Cecelia.
Eisemann, Frederick F. '53 (ROC) Retired.
Eisler, Rudolph '63 (NY) Pearl River, NY St. Margaret; West Harrison, NY St. Anthony.
Eisweirth, Thomas '74 (Y) Salem, OH St. Paul.
Eivers, Michael '55 (MIA) Pembroke Pines, FL St. Edward.
Ejeh, Ameh Ambrose (PIT) Pittsburgh, PA All Saints.
Ejimabo, Nichodemus (AUS) Blanco, TX St. Ferdinand's.
Ejimadu, Festus '93 (DET) Romulus, MI St. Aloysius.
Ejimofor, Frances *c.s.sp.* '90 (CLV) Akron, OH St. Bernard.
Ejrofor, Pius '86 (NEW) Newark, NJ Blessed Sacrament/ St. Charles Borromeo.
Ekanem, Anthony *m.s.p.* '89 (GAL) Barrett Station, TX St. Martin de Porres.
Ekdahl, Kenneth W. '91 (TR) Keyport, NJ Jesus the Lord.
Eke, Casimir *c.s.sp.* '74 (CHI) Chicago, IL St. Felicitas.
Eke, Casimir *c.s.sp.* '74 (CHI) Chicago, IL St. Felicitas.
Eke, Raphael E. '01 (SAT) San Antonio, TX Our Lady of Sorrows.
Ekechukwu, Alexander *c.s.sp.* '73 (MIA) Miami, FL St. Agatha.
Ekechukwu, Alexander *c.s.sp.* (MIA) African Apostolate.
Ekechukwu, Alexander (MIA) FIU–University Park.
Ekenachi, Donatus '83 (LA) Downey, CA St. Raymond.
Ekka, Louis T. (LAN) Jackson, MI Queen of the Miraculous Medal.
Ekpo, Joseph '86 (CHI)[D] Oak Park, IL Fenwick High School.
Ekpo, Joseph '86 (CHI) Bellwood, IL St. Simeon.
Eksterowicz, Francis C. '85 (BUR) Richford, VT All Saints.
Ekweariri, Joseph E. '77 (AUS)[G] Austin, TX Mackay St. Barbara.
Ekwugha, Francis Xavier '82 (MAD) Hazel Green, WI St. Joseph; Dickeyville, WI Holy Ghost; Kieler, WI Immaculate Conception.
El–Bacha, Assaad *m.l.m.* '92 (OLL)[A] Houston, TX The Congregation of Maronite Lebanese Missionaries.
El–Bacha, Assaad *m.l.m.* '92 (OLL) Lewisville, TX Our Lady of Lebanon Mission.
El–Far, George '82 (LA) Pomona, CA St. Joseph.
El–Feghali, Antonio *o.m.m.* '01 (OLL)[A] Ann Arbor, MI Maronite Order of Blessed Virgin Mary.
El–Ghazal, Antoine '00 (OLL) Cincinnati, OH St. Anthony of Padua.
El–Hayek, Nehmatallah '62 (SAM) Retired.
El–Khalli, Georges '81 (SAM) Williamsville, NY St. John Maron.
El–Khalli, Georges (SAM) Religious Education.
El–Thom, Gregory *b.c.o.* '93 (NTN) Warren, MI Our Lady of Redemption.
El–Thom, Gregory (NTN) Presbyteral Council.
Elam, Ray *o.s.a.* '70 (SD) Buena Park, CA St. Pius V.
Elambassery, Xavier '66 (SJP) Latrobe, PA Assumption of B.V.M..
Elambassery, Xavier (SJP) Catechetical Planning Committee.
Elambassery, Xavier (SJP) Presbyteral Council.
Elamparayil, Joseph *o.c.d.* (WDC) Hyattsville, MD St. Jerome.
Elanjileth, John M. '45 (ROM) McKeesport, PA St. Mary.
Elanjileth, John M. '50 (ROM) Allegheny County, PA McKeesport UPMC.
Elanjimannil, Sebastian C. *s.j.* '83 (LA) Los Angeles, CA Blessed Sacrament.
Elanjimattathil, Michael *c.m.i.* (SAL) Manhattan, KS Seven Dolors.
Elano, Elvis '92 (BRK) Long Island City, NY Immaculate Conception.
Elbert, William '73 (MIA) North Miami Beach, FL St. Lawrence.

Elbert, William (MIA) Spiritual Moderators.
Elbert, William (MIA) Archdiocesan Fund–Raising & Assessments Committee; The St. Vincent De Paul Society, Archdiocesan Council of Miami, Inc..
Elder, John W. *s.j.* '65 (BGP)[B] Fairfield, CT Fairfield University; [P] Fairfield, CT The Fairfield Jesuit Community–Fairfield University.
Elder, Leonard F. *s.c.j.* '96 (GAL) Houston, TX Christ the Redeemer.
Elder, William S. '81 (NY) Vice Judicial Vicars.
Eldred, Richard '99 (IND) Mooresville, IN St. Thomas More.
Eldredge, Richard *t.o.r.* '78 (FWT) Seymour, TX Sacred Heart.
Eldredge, Richard *t.o.r.* '78 (FWT) Seymour, TX St. Mary.
Eldredge, Richard *t.o.r.* (FWT) Presbyteral Council and Consultors.
Eldridge, Francis *s.a.* '02 (LA) Los Angeles, CA St. Odilia.
Eldringhoff, John P. '68 (KC) Retired.
Elejalde, Manuel *c.p.* '49 (SJN) San Juan, PR Nuestra Senora de la Piedad.
Eles, Joseph '65 (PSC) Retired.
Elewaut, Thomas J. *c.j.* '86 (LA)[D] Santa Barbara, CA Bishop Garcia Diego High School; Santa Barbara, CA Holy Cross.
Elford, Ricardo *c.ss.r.* '64 (DEN)[N] Tucson, AZ.
Elghazal, Antoine (OLL) Cincinnati, OH Maronite Catholic Community of Louisville.
Eli, Jude *o.p.* '76 (OAK)[N] Oakland, CA Western Dominican Province.
Elia, Faouzi Y. '77 (OLL) Peoria, IL St. Sharbel.
Elia, Victor *c.m.* '57 (NY)[EE] New York, NY Vincentian Fathers.
Elia, Victor *c.m.* '57 (NY) New York, NY Holy Agony.
Elias, Mario '93 (SD) National City, CA St. Mary.
Elias, Woodrow '43 (DM) Retired.
Elias–Haddix, Ralph *o.c.d.* '98 (MIL) Milwaukee, WI St. Florian.
Elis, Patrick H. '69 (BUF) Vicars; Cassadaga, NY St. John the Evangelist; Cassadaga, NY Immaculate Conception.
Elis, Tomas A. '70 (LA) Santa Monica, CA St. Clement.
Elizardo, Pedro (Pete) T. '01 (CC) Corpus Christi, TX Corpus Christi Cathedral.
Elizardo, Pete '01 (CC) Office of Youth And Young Adult Ministry; [I] Corpus Christi, TX Search Retreats; [I] Corpus Christi, TX FirePower Retreats.
Elizondo, Ernesto (AUS) San Marcos, TX St. John the Evangelist.
Elizondo, Eusebio *m.sp.s.* '84 (SEA) Mill Creek, WA St. Elizabeth Ann Seton.
Elizondo, Ruben *o.m.i.* '62 (FgM).
Elizondo, Virgil '63 (SAT) San Antonio, TX St. Rose of Lima.
Elizondo, Virgilio P. (FTW)[B] University of Notre Dame Du Lac.
Elkin, Frederic F. '77 (SY) On Sabbatical.
Elko, Joseph M. '70 (HRT) New Haven, CT Saint Martin de Porres.
Eller, Hugh *o.f.m.* '53 (PRO)[N] Providence, RI St. Francis Chapel & City Ministry Center.
Eller, Hugh *o.f.m.* '53 (PRO)[P] Providence, RI St. Francis Friary.
Ellerman, Thomas E. *s.m.* '01 (OAK)[N] Berkeley, CA Marist Fathers and Brothers.
Ellias, John J. '64 (ALT) Retired.
Elliot, Thomas (BGP)[Q] Wilton, CT Lourdes Health Care Center, Inc..
Elliott, Edward C. '44 (MEM) Germantown, TN Our Lady Of Perpetual Help Retired.
Elliott, James K. (SEA) Chinese, Ministry to.
Elliott, James '99 (SEA) Mercer Island, WA St. Monica.
Elliott, Joseph W. '71 (OG) Morrisonville, NY St. Alexander; Morrisonville, NY St. Joseph.
Elliott, Joseph *c.ss.r.* '49 (LA) Whittier, CA St. Mary of the Assumption.
Elliott, Joseph *c.ss.r.* '49 (LA)[Q] Whittier, CA Redemptorists of Whittier.
Elliott, Patrick H. (SLC) Salt Lake City, UT Cathedral of the Madeleine; Monroe, UT St. Elizabeth's; Correctional Institution Ministry.
Elliott, Peter J. (WDC)[V] Silver Spring, MD Catholics Committed to Support the Pope.
Elliott, Roger *c.p.* '58 (SCR)[M] Clarks Summit, PA St. Gabriel's Convent.
Elliott, Roger *c.p.* '58 (SCR) Scranton, PA St. Ann's Basilica Parish.
Elliott, Ronald J. '03 (KC) Higginsville, MO St. Mary's; Richmond, MO Immaculate Conception.
Elliott, Thomas A. '99 (LR) Van Buren, AR St. Michael's; Winslow, AR Our Lady of the Ozarks Shrine.
Elliott, Thomas F. *c.s.c.* '67 (FTW)[I] Wilton, CT School Sisters of Notre Dame.
Elliott, Thomas *c.s.c.* '63 (BGP)[Q] Wilton, CT School Sisters of Notre Dame Motherhouse (Northeastern Province).
Elliott, Timothy P. '82 (STL) Wentzville, MO St. Joseph.
Elliott, Trumie C. '88 (L) Springfield, KY St. Dominic.
Elliott, W. Gregg (TLS) Miami, OK Sacred Heart.
Elliott, William J. *s.j.* '61 (WDC)[E] North Bethesda, MD Georgetown Preparatory School.
Elliott, William '60 (SD) Retired.
Ellis, Alfred J. *o.s.a.* '63 (BO) Andover, MA St. Augustine.
Ellis, John H.R. '91 (VEN) Holmes Beach, FL St. Bernard.
Ellis, Kail C. *o.s.a.* '67 (PH)[C] Villanova University; [AA] Villanova, PA St. John Stone Friary.
Ellis, Matthew '88 (DET) Absent on Leave.
Ellorin, Raymund '91 (HON) Lanai City, HI Sacred Hearts.
Ellorin, Raymund (HON) Filipino Ministry.
Ellos, William J. *s.j.* '68 (MIL)[O] San Antonio, TX.
Ellspermann, Camillus *o.s.b.* '50 (IND)[K] Casper, WY.
Elmer, Charles '53 (AUS) On Duty Outside the Diocese; [A] Houston, TX St. Mary's Seminary.
Elmer, Gregory *o.s.b.* '76 (LA)[Q] Valyermo, CA St. Andrew's Abbey.
Elmer, Richard J. *c.s.b.* '57 (DET)[E] Redford, MI Catholic Central High School.
Elmer, Timothy S. '73 (SY) East Syracuse, NY St. Matthew; Management Team; Elected; Judicial Vicar.
Elorriaga, Javier *o.ss.t.* '68 (SJN) Bayamon, PR Ascension Del Senor.
Elosi, Felix *m.s.p.* '86 (GAL) Houston, TX St. Anne de Beaupre.
Elsasser, Thomas G. '88 (CLV) Mentor, OH St. Mary of the Assumption.
Elsbernd, James H. '90 (CIN) On Special and Archdiocesan Assignment.
Elsen, Vincent *o.f.m* '47 (FWT)[I] Crowley, TX St. Maximilian Kolbe Friary.
Elsen, Vincent *o.f.m.* '47 (FWT) Fort Worth, TX St. Mary of the Assumption.
Elsen, Vincent *o.f.m.* (FWT) Hospital Chaplaincy.
Elser, William '86 (LR) Fort Smith, AR St. Boniface.
Elshoff, Matthew *o.f.m.cap.* '82 (LA)[F] La Canada Flintridge, CA St. Francis High School.
Elskamp, Fred J. (JC) Personnel Board; Diaconate Office; Priests' Eucharistic League.
Elskamp, Frederick J. '62 (JC) Jefferson City, MO St. Joseph Cathedral.
Elsner, Martin L. *s.j.* '62 (SAT) San Antonio, TX Our Lady of Guadalupe.
Elston, Joseph '85 (SCR) Avoca, PA St. Mary's.
Elukunnel, Joseph Dominic *s.a.c.* '80 (MIL)[O] Milwaukee, WI Pallotti House.
Elworthy, Joseph J. *c.ss.r* '39 (STL)[O] Liguori, MO St. Clement Health Care Center.
Ely, Peter B. *s.j.* '69 (SEA)[A] Seattle, WA Seattle University.
Elzi, Joseph *c.m.* (CHL)[O] Charlotte, NC Our Lady of Guadalupe Hispanic Center.
Emanuel, John '92 (TUC) Willcox, AZ Federal Prison Camp.
Emanuel, John '92 (TUC) Fort Grant Rural Station, AZ Fort Grant Training Center.
Emanuel, John '92 (TUC) Willcox, AZ Sacred Heart.
Emanuel, Steven D. '93 (OM)[B] Elgin, NE Pope John XXIII Central Catholic High School at Elgin.
Emanuel, Steven '93 (OM) Neligh, NE St. Francis.
Emanuel, Steven '93 (OM) Tilden, NE Our Lady of Mt. Carmel.
Emechete, Innocent '72 (SAC) Vacaville, CA California Medical Facility; Navy Reserve Chaplains.
Emeh, Martins '02 (RCK) Rockford, IL St. Peter Cathedral.
Emerick, Hydo *c.m.* '50 (MET)[H] Princeton, NJ Vincentian Residence.
Emerick, Stephen J. '58 (CIN)[L] Cincinnati, OH Mercy Franciscan Senior Health and Housing Services Inc..
Emerling, James R. '53 (HRT) Retired.
Emerson, George F. '56 (BO) Norwood, MA St. Timothy; Senior Priests; Selected Retired.
Emerson, Richard A. '78 (GRY) Michigan City, IN Notre Dame.
Emerson, Robert F. '55 (JOL)[K] Naperville, IL St. John Vianney Villa Retired.
Emery, Robert E. '87 (NEW) Weehawken, NJ St. Lawrence's; Vice Chancellor; Archdiocesan Judges; Vice Chancellors.
Emery, Robert (NEW) Ministry with Separated, Divorced and Widowed Catholics.
Emezie, Charles '83 (SFS)[D] Aberdeen, SD Avera St. Luke's.
Emezie, Charles '83 (SFS)[D] Aberdeen, SD Avera St. Luke's.
Emge, John P. '50 (EVN) Retired.
Emmanuel, Joseph '81 (NY) Tuckahoe, NY Immaculate Conception.
Emmanuel, Joseph '81 (NY) Tuckahoe, NY Assumption.
Emmanuel, Mbondo *c.i.c.m.* (OAK) Alameda, CA St. Barnabas.
Emmanuel, Vethamuther (NY) New Rochelle, NY Sound Shore Medical Center.
Emmareddy, Lawrence '97 (SCR) Wilkes–Barre, PA St. Nicholas.
Emmons, Rayford E. '74 (PH) Philadelphia, PA Incarnation of Our Lord.
Emoile, Jose *s.j.* '89 (BAL)[B] Timonium, MD Loyola Graduate Center –Timonium Campus.
Emon, Neil *o.s.c.* '67 (PHX)[G] Phoenix, AZ Crosier Community of Phoenix (Canons Regular of the Order of the Holy Cross).
Emperur, James L. *s.j.* '65 (SAT) San Antonio, TX Cathedral of San Fernando.
Emrich, Jack '98 (IND) Community Hospital North; Unassigned.
Emrich, Jack '98 (IND) Winona Medical Center.
Emrich, Jack '98 (IND) Community Hospital North; Unassigned.
Emrisek, Gene *o.f.m.cap.* '68 (COS)[I] Colorado Springs, CO Catholic Center at the Citadel; [F] Colorado Springs, CO Padre Pio Friary.
Emuwen, Victor (NY) New York, NY St. Joseph of the Holy Family.
Encinares, Cesar '77 (SB) Colton, CA San Salvador; Filipino Ministry.
Encinares, Cesar '77 (SB) Colton, CA Our Lady of the Immaculate Conception.
Enciso, Jesus (RIC) Norfolk, VA St. Pius X.
Endebrock, Donald M. '51 (MET) Carteret, NJ St. Joseph Retired.
Endejan, John '57 (MIL) Retired.
Enderle, Gilbert A. *c.ss.r.* '62 (SAT) San Antonio, TX Our Lady Of Perpetual Help; [M] San Antonio, TX Redemptorists of Texas–San Antonio #1.
Enderlin, Joseph J. '46 (LR) Retired.
Enderlin, R. E. '69 (PEO) Monmouth, IL Immaculate Conception; Raritan, IL Church of St. Patrick.
Enderlin, Ronald '69 (PEO) Alexis, IL St. Theresa's.
Enders, Robert F. '39 (MIL) Retired.
Endres, Gilbert J. '52 (STP) Retired.
Endres, James F. '82 (PH) Warminster, PA Nativity of Our Lord; [D] Warminster, PA Archbishop Wood Catholic High School.
Endres, John C. *s.j.* '76 (OAK)[N] Berkeley, CA Jesuit Community at Jesuit School of Theology at Berkeley.
Endres, William '69 (ROC) Highland Hospital.
Endres, William '69 (ROC) Strong Health System.
Endres, William '69 (ROC) Scottsville, NY St. Mary of the Assumption.
Endress, James R. '60 (EVN) Special Assignment.
Endress, James (EVN) Defenders of the Bond.
Endress, James (EVN) Personnel Board.
Endress, James (EVN) Diocesan Consultors.
Enette, Rawlin B. *s.s.j.* '59 (GAL) Houston, TX St. Peter Claver.
Eng, Clarence A. (FgM).
Engbarth, David R. '76 (RCK) Aurora, IL St. Nicholas.
Engbers, Thomas '67 (MIA) Retired.
Engel, Paul *o.f.m.cap.* '64 (NY)[EE] New York, NY Development Office:.
Engel, Ronald '77 (MIL) Milwaukee, WI St. Veronica.
Engelbrecht, Henry H. '68 (NO) New Orleans, LA St. Henry; Army National Guard Chaplains.
Engelbrecht, Scott (PEO) Peoria Heights, IL St. Thomas.
Engelhardt, Charles F. *o.s.f.s.* '77 (PH) Philadelphia, PA Mater Dolorosa.
Engelhardt, Herbert G. '40 (BUF) Retired.
Engelhart, Henry R. '63 (BEL) Fairfield, IL St. Edward; Mount Carmel, IL St. Sebastian.
Engels, Francis '62 (PEO) Retired.
Engels, Richard J. '60 (WIN) Retired.
Engen, Bruce '89 (DUL) Pine River, MN Our Lady of Lourdes.
Engh, Michael E. *s.j.* '81 (LA)[C] Los Angeles, CA Jesuit Community.
England, Barry C. '68 (FTW) Mishawaka, IN St. Bavo.
Engle, Richard F. '56 (COL) Priests' Senate Retired.
Engler, Ernest J. '51 (DUB) Mount Vernon, IA St. John the Baptist Retired.
Engler, Simon Mary *t.o.r.* '49 (ALT)[F] Loretto, PA Mount Assisi Friary.
Englert, Anthony A. '87 (CHI)[S] Chicago, IL Kolping Center; Other Assignments.
Englert, Michael *o.f.m.conv.* '89 (HRT) Kensington, CT St. Paul's.
Englert, Wilfred '86 (EVN) Celestine, IN St. Peter Celestine.
Englert, Wilfred '86 (EVN) Dubois, IN St. Raphael.
English, James M. *s.j.* '66 (BAL)[S] Baltimore, MD Jesuit Fathers and Brothers Maryland Provincial Curia.
English, Joseph R. *m.m.* '44 (NY).
English, Joseph *o.f.m.cap.* '90 (AGN)[F] Agana Heights, GU St. Fidelis Friary.
English, Joseph *o.f.m.cap.* (AGN) Archdiocesan Presbyteral Council.
English, Paul F. *c.s.b.* '85 (GAL) Houston, TX St. Anne.
English, Robert K. '88 (OM) Crofton, NE St. Joseph; Crofton, NE St. Rose of Lima.
English, Tobias P. '63 (LA) Pasadena, CA St. Andrew Retired.
English, William J. '60 (BO) Quincy, MA Most Blessed Sacrament.
English, William J. '69 (WDC) Silver Spring, MD St. John the Evangelist; Archdiocesan College of Consultors.
Engo, David *f.p.o.* '97 (FR) Special Assignment; [H] Fall

River, MA Priests' Hostel.
Enke, Paul P. '72 (COL) Granville, OH St. Edward the Confessor; Parochial Examiners.
Enlow, Leo J. '75 (SFD) Effingham, IL St. Anthony of Padua; Effingham Deanery.
Enlow, Leo *v.f.* '75 (SFD) Shumway, IL Annunciation.
Enman, Frederick *s.j.* '88 (BO)[V] Newton, MA The Jesuit Community at Boston College.
Enneking, Marvin '91 (SCL) St. Cloud, MN St. John Cantius.
Enneking, Marvin (SCL) Presbyteral Council.
Enneking, Marvin (SCL) Diocesan Corporate Board.
Enneking, Marvin (SCL) Diocesan Consultors.
Enneking, Marvin (SCL) Diocesan Finance Council.
Enneking, Marvin (SCL) Directors.
Enneking, Marvin (SCL) Personnel Committee.
Enneking, Marvin (SCL) Vicar General.
Enneking, Marvin (SCL) Judges.
Enneking, Marvin (SCL) Diocesan Priests Pension Plan Trustees.
Enneking, Thomas *o.s.c.* '84 (CHI)[N] Chicago, IL Crosier Community of Chicago.
Enneking, Tom *o.s.c.* '74 (STP)[M] Shoreview, MN Crosier Community of Shoreview.
Ennis, Timothy *o.carm.* '02 (NY)[EE] Middletown, NY Brandsma Priory.
Ennis, William '64 (ORL) Orlando, FL Holy Family.
Enojo, Jesus P. '67 (NY) New York, NY St. James.
Enrico, Philip J. '02 (MAN) Hampton, NH Our Lady of the Miraculous Medal.
Enright, Columba James *t.o.r.* '56 (ORL).
Enright, Edward J. *o.s.a.* '73 (PH)[C] Villanova University.
Enright, James C. '69 (BUF) On Duty Outside the Diocese.
Enright, James C. '69 (ROC) Auburn, NY St. Mary; Auburn, NY Auburn Correctional Facility.
Enright, John P. '53 (CHI) Retired.
Enright, Michael P. '84 (CHI) Chicago, IL Immaculate Conception of the Blessed Virgin Mary; Deans.
Enright, Thomas M. '66 (CHI) Wauconda, IL Transfiguration.
Enright, Vincent L. '47 (E) Retired.
Enriguez, Juan '03 (LA) Lynwood, CA St. Philip Neri.
Enriquez, Alex '85 (TR) Red Bank, NJ St. James.
Enriquez, Rean F. (MO) Navy Chaplains.
Ensey, Eric S. '95 (SCR)[M] Shohola, PA Society of Saint John; Unassigned or Leave of Absence.
Enslow, Batholomew *s.s.j.* '49 (BLX) Pass Christian, MS Our Mother of Mercy.
Ensman, Raymond E. '66 (TOL) Port Clinton, OH Immaculate Conception; Fremont Deanery; Members.
Enverga, Edgardo *c.r.m.* '86 (CHR) Goose Creek, SC Immaculate Conception.
Enyan–Boadu, Peter '84 (ROC) Brockport, NY Nativity of the Blessed Virgin Mary.
Enzler, John J. '73 (WDC) Potomac, MD Our Lady of Mercy; Archdiocesan College of Consultors.
Enzler, John (WDC) Secretary for Development.
Enzman, David '83 (CLV) Absent on Leave.
Enzweiler, Donald A. '87 (COV) Cold Spring, KY St. Joseph; Diocesan Tribunal; Judges.
Eppenbrock, Donald J. '60 (SAG) Lexington, MI St. Denis; Diocesan Council of Catholic Women.
Epperely, Wayne F. *c.s.sp.* '83 (SLC) Kearns, UT St. Francis Xavier.
Epperson, Frank '01 (SR) Sonoma, CA St. Francis Solano.
Epperson, Frank (SR) Priests' Council.
Eppler, Jeff '03 (CC)[B] Robstown, TX St. Anthony School; [G] Robstown, TX Society of Our Lady of the Most Holy Trinity.
Equihua Gonzalez, Jose Manuel (OM) Omaha, NE St. Agnes; Omaha, NE Our Lady of Guadalupe.
Eraly, Mathew '75 (SYM) Staten Island, NY Kerala Catholic Association, Staten Island, NY.
Eraly, Mathew '75 (NY) Staten Island, NY St. Ann.
Eraly, Mathew (MO).
Erb, Francis J. '54 (ROC) Retired.
Erb, Vincent I. '50 (CHL) Retired.
Erbacher, Joseph '72 (EVN) Jasper, IN Precious Blood.
Erbacher, Joseph (EVN) Defenders of the Bond.
Erbacher, William J. '87 (ARL) On Leave of Absence.
Erbe, Edward J. '51 (MAD)[G] Madison, WI Bishop O'Connor Catholic Pastoral Center Retired.
Ercolano, Anthony S. '73 (BRK) Bayside, NY American Martyrs; [G] Middle Village, NY Christ the King Regional High School.
Erdei, Joseph J. *o.s.b.m.* '58 (PSC)[A] Matawan, NJ Basilian Fathers of Mariapoch.
Erdeljac, Frank G. '83 (PIT) New Castle, PA St. Vincent de Paul; Lawrence County, PA Jameson Memorial Hospital; [O] Villa Maria, PA Sisters of the Humility of Mary.
Erdle, Thomas M. '55 (ROC) Rochester, NY St. Mark.
Erdlen, Harry J. *o.s.a.* '57 (BO) Andover, MA St. Augustine.
Erestain, Alfonso E. (MO) Navy Chaplains.
Erhart, Charles M. '60 (RVC) Military Chaplains.
Erhart, Henry J. *s.j.* '55 (ALN)[A] Wernersville, PA Jesuit Center.
Erickson, David '97 (PEO) Westville, IL St. Mary's.
Erickson, John R. *o.s.b.* '50 (GBG)[H] Latrobe, PA Saint Vincent Archabbey.
Erickson, Philip L. '95 (L) Brandenburg, KY St. John the Apostle.
Erickson, Philip Lee (L) Adjutant Judicial Vicar.
Erickson, Richard M. '85 (BO) Military & VA Chaplains; Air Force Chaplains.
Erickson, Robert E. *c.s.v.* '67 (CHI)[N] Arlington Heights, IL Viatorian Province Center–Clerics of St. Viator.
Erickson, Robert L. *s.j.* '74 (GF) Hays, MT St. Paul's Indian Mission.
Erickson, Robert '58 (SB) Retired.
Erickson, Robert (SB) Pro–Synodal Judges.
Erickson, Ryan G. '00 (SUP) Ladysmith, WI St. Mary of Czestochowa; Ladysmith, WI Our Lady of Sorrows; Ladysmith, WI St. Anthony de Padua.
Erickson, Scott Matthew *o.p.* '90 (NY)[EE] New York, NY St. Vincent Ferrer Priory; [EE] New York, NY St. Catherine of Siena Priory.
Erickson, Scott Matthew *o.p.* '90 (FgM).
Erlander, Michael '68 (STP) St. Joseph's Hospital; Presbyteral Council; [I] St. Paul, MN HealthEast St. Joseph's Hospital.
Ermatinger, Cliff *l.c.* '97 (DAL)[D] Irving, TX The Highlands School; [E] Irving, TX The Highland School; [K] Irving, TX Legionaries of Christ.
Ermer, James R. '78 (FAR) Fargo, ND St. Anthony of Padua; [B] Fargo, ND Fargo Catholic Schools Network.
Ermer, James (FAR) Diocesan College of Consultors.
Ermis, Norman '83 (SAT) San Antonio, TX St. Margaret Mary.
Ernest, Bryan D. '82 (GI) Alliance, NE Holy Rosary; Personnel Board; Vocations.
Ernest, Joseph (CHI) Haitian Catholic Apostolate.
Ernest, Stephen *s.v.d.* '67 (OAK) Oakland, CA St. Bernard's.
Ernest, Stephen *s.v.d.* '67 (OAK).
Ernest, Stephen *s.t.* '86 (PAT)[M] Stirling, NJ Holy Spirit Missionary Cenacle.
Erno, Shaun A. (MAR) Leave of Absence.
Ernst, Albert C. '53 (NO) Retired.
Ernst, Anthony '98 (EVN) Fort Branch, IN Holy Cross; Fort Branch, IN St. Bernard.
Ernst, Anthony '98 (EVN) Haubstadt, IN SS. Peter and Paul.
Ernst, Anthony (EVN) Diocesan Council of Priests.
Ernst, Francis P. *s.j.* '57 (BAL)[S] Baltimore, MD Jesuit Fathers and Brothers Maryland Provincial Curia.
Ernst, Jeff *c.f.m.cap.* '96 (STL)[N] Allison Park, PA St. Conrad Friary.
Ernst, Norbert A. '72 (STL) House Springs, MO Our Lady, Queen of Peace; Archdiocesan Priests' Personnel Board.
Ernst, William W. '64 (IND) New Albany, IN St. Mary.
Ernster, James M. '55 (MIL) Retired.
Ernster, Milo L. '55 (WIN) Retired.
Ernstmann Mark C. '51 (SPC) Forsyth, MO Our Lady of the Ozarks; Censor Of Books; Priests' Purgatorial Society.
Erondu, Isaac Emeka '93 (BWN) San Benito, TX Our Lady, Queen of the Universe.
Erpelding, Edward '66 (FTW) Fort Wayne, IN St. Joseph.
Erpelding, Michael J. '89 (SC) Graduate Studies.
Erpen, B.A. '47 (AMA)[I] Amarillo, TX Monsignor B.A. Erpen Trust Fund Retired.
Erps, James *s.j.* '80 (BO)[BB] Chestnut Hill, MA.
Erps, James *s.j.* '80 (California)[V] Newton, MA The Jesuit Community at Boston College.
Errecalde, Javier *o.de.m.* '54 (SJN) San Juan, PR Nuestra Senora de la Merced.
Erro, Sabino *o.f.m.* '54 (DAL)[K] Dallas, TX Capuchin Franciscan Friars, Vice Province of Texas; Dallas, TX Our Lady of Perpetual Help.
Erstad, William '56 (SB) Retired.
Ertle, Thomas J. *o.p.* '56 (PRO)[P] Providence St. Thomas Aquinas Priory at Providence College.
Ertzbischoff, Edmond L. '76 (LAN) Ypsilanti, MI St. John.
Ervin, Mark W. '90 (WDC) Valley Lee, MD St. George.
Ervin, Thomas '74 (SFR) Absent on Leave.
Erving, James *o.m.i.* '67 (BO)[V] Lowell, MA Oblate Vocation Office, Northeast Area.
Erving, James *o.m.i.* (BO)[V] Lowell, MA Contemplative Mission Center.
Erwin, Michael J. '98 (MIL) Twin Lakes, WI St. John.
Erwin, Patrick O. '68 (PAT) On Duty Outside the Diocese.
Erwin, Patrick O. '91 (MGZ) Mayaguez, PR Church De El Buen Pastor.
Escala, Rafael '57 (MIA) Retired.
Escalante, Agustin (LAR) Laredo, TX St. John Neumann.
Escalante, Augustin '88 (SFR) On Duty Outside the Archdiocese.
Escalante, Peter '78 (SD) Spring Valley, CA Santa Sophia.
Escalante, Ronald S. '95 (ARL) Spotsylvania, VA St. Matthew; [M] Fredericksburg, VA Mary–Washington College; Advocates.
Escalante, William '93 (LA) Santa Maria, CA St. John Neumann.
Escalera, Enriqez Lopez '93 (LSC) Las Cruces, NM St. Genevieve.
Esch, Eugene *o.s.b.* '54 (B) Glenns Ferry, ID Our Lady of Limerick Station.
Esch, Eugene *o.s.b.* '54 (B)[C] Jerome, ID Monastery of the Ascension.
Eschbach, Victor J. '72 (PH) Parkesburg, PA Our Lady of Consolation.
Eschweiler, Edward R. '48 (MIL) Retired.
Escobar, Adolfo Martinez '03 (TUC) Tucson, AZ St. John the Evangelist.
Escobar, Alonso '69 (NY) Bronx, NY St. Margaret Mary.
Escobar, Augustin '87 (ORG) Costa Mesa, CA St. Joachim.
Escobar, Joseph A. '88 (PRO) Providence, RI Our Lady of the Rosary; Council Members.
Escobedo, Armando '64 (BWN) Retired.
Escobedo, Gilberto (ORG) Lake Forest, CA Santiago de Compostela.
Escobedo, Gilberto (ORG) Council of Priests.
Escobedo, Gilberto (ORG) Ecumenical and Interreligious Affairs.
Escobedo, Jaime '93 (SD) El Centro, CA Our Lady of Guadalupe.
Escobedo, Jaime (SD) Vicars Forane.
Escribano, Peter E. '88 (MET) On Duty Outside the Diocese.
Escurel, Armando *s.v.d.* '79 (SD) San Marcos, CA St. Mark.
Escutin, Ciriaco E. '80 (LA) Retired.
Esenther, Keith J. *s.j.* '71 (CHI)[C] Chicago, IL Jesuit Community at Loyola University Chicago.
Esguerra, Bernadino '87 (TR) Lakewood, NJ St. Mary of the Lake.
Eshikena, Dominic *o.p.* (WDC) Washington, DC Children's Medical Center.
Eshikena, Dominic *o.p.* (WDC)[V] West Hyattsville, MD Dominican Province of Nigeria.
Eshikena, Dominic *o.p.* (WDC) Washington, DC Washington Hospital Center.
Eskind, Jace '87 (LKC) Lake Charles, LA Immaculate Conception Cathedral.
Eskind, Jace (LKC) Office For Worship.
Eskind, Jace (LKC) Diocesan Consultors.
Eskind, Jace (LKC) Diocesan Board of Administration; Vicar Judicial; Judges; Episcopal Vicars.
Esmilla, Efren V. '93 (PH)[A] Wynnewood, PA Theological Seminary of St. Charles Borromeo, Overbrook.
Esmond, William '55 (ALB) Retired.
Espejel, Rene J. *c.s.b.* '87 (GAL)[Q] Sugar Land Basilian Mission Center.
Espelage, Arthur *o.f.m.* '71 (CIN)[M] Washington, DC The Catholic University of America.
Espelage, Thomas '70 (CIN) Cincinnati, OH St. John the Evangelist.
Espeleta, Bonifacio '84 (CHK) Rota, MP San Francisco de Borja Parish.
Esper, Abraham L. '85 (SY) Whitesboro, NY St. Paul.
Esper, Jerome *c.s.c.* '61 (CHI)[D] Niles, IL Notre Dame High School.
Esper, John C. '83 (DET)[T] St. Clair Shores, MI St. Lucy.
Esper, Joseph M. '82 (DET) Lakeport, MI St. Edward's on the Lake; Archdiocesan Vicars.
Esper, Thomas '51 (DET) Retired.
Espinel, Luis *o.p.* '59 (SJN)[A] Bayamon Central University.
Espinel, Marcos '61 (SJN) Bayamon, PR Invencion de la Santa Cruz.
Espino, Jose '83 (MIA) On Duty Outside the Archdiocese.
Espinosa, Anthony '96 (OM) Omaha, NE St. Joseph.
Espinosa, Anthony '96 (OM) Omaha, NE Immaculate Conception, B.V.M..
Espinosa, David F. '98 (BRK) Brooklyn, NY St. Finbar's.
Espinosa, David (BRK) Liturgical Commission.
Espinosa, David (BRK) Bishop Valero—.
Espinosa, David (BRK) Attorneys and Counselors at Canon Law.
Espinosa, Donald *a.a.* '71 (WOR)[O] Worcester, MA Assumptionists of Assumption College.
Espinoza, Luis '98 (PAT) Paterson, NJ Cathedral of St. John the Baptist.
Espinoza, Pedro '02 (MRY) Salinas, CA Sacred Heart.
Espinoza, Walter '99 (MRY) San Luis Obispo, CA San Luis Obispo.
Espinoza, Walter (MRY) Finance Council.
Esplana, Ramilo '93 (PAT) Passaic, NJ St. Anthony of Padua.
Esposito, Alberto '01 (STA) Gainesville, FL Queen of Peace.
Esposito, Anthony '56 (Y) Retired.
Esposito, Augustine M. *o.s.a.* '79 (PH)[D] Drexel Hill, PA Monsignor Bonner High School.
Esposito, Charles '99 (GBG) Murrysville, PA Mother of Sorrows.

Esposito, Ernest T. '67 (BGP) Fairfield, CT Assumption; [H] Bridgeport, CT Family Life Ministry; Episcopal Vicar for Religious; Office for Clergy Personnel; Office for the Continuing Education of Clergy; Office of the Permanent Diaconate; Catholic Women, Council of.
Esposito, Joseph J. '28 (BRK) Retired.
Esposito, Lawrence J. '76 (WOR) Auburn, MA St. Joseph's; Evangelization, Office of.
Esposito, Luigi '64 (BAL) Baltimore, MD Our Lady of Pompei.
Esposito, Mario *o.carm.* '77 (ALB)[M] Germantown, NY Postulation Office.
Esposito, Ralph J. '67 (LR) Retired.
Esposito, Samuel J. '78 (PIT) Ambridge, PA Good Samaritan.
Esposito, Stanislao '03 (WIL) Wilmington, DE St. Mary Magdalen.
Esposito, William C. '58 (SY) Retired.
Espuelas, Gil '78 (SD) El Centro, CA Our Lady of Guadalupe.
Esquerro, Miguel (SJN) San Juan, PR Catedral de San Juan Bautista.
Esquivel, John '68 (FRS) Fresno, CA St. John Cathedral.
Esquivel, John (FRS) Priests' Council.
Esquivel, John (FRS) Advocates.
Ess, Thomas '66 (CHI)[N] Chicago, IL St. Peter's Friary.
Esseff, John A. '53 (SCR)[A] Dalton, PA Saint Pius X Seminary Retired.
Esselman, Thomas E. *c.m.* '80 (STL)[B] St. Louis, MO Aquinas Institute of Theology; [O] St. Louis, MO Vincentian Residence; [V] Cambridge, MA Faber House; [O] St. Louis, MO Vincentian Residence.
Essen, Peter Von *o.f.m.cap.* '56 (FgM).
Esser, James *o.f.m.* '67 (GB) Krakow, WI St. Casimir.
Esser, Paul M. '57 (MIL) Racine, WI St. Paul the Apostle.
Essex, Donald S. '73 (WDC) Bethesda, MD St. Jane Frances de Chantal; Archdiocesan College of Consultors.
Essig, Edward J. '94 (ALN) Bethlehem, PA Notre Dame of Bethlehem.
Essig, Herbert '74 (JOL) Lombard, IL St. Pius X.
Essling, Harold W. *c.s.c.* '78 (AUS) Austin, TX St. Ignatius Martyr; [G] Austin, TX Steiner Lodge.
Essman, Charles P. '56 (COL) Retired.
Essman, Ronald (DET) Clinton Twp., MI St. Paul of Tarsus.
Esswein, Michael J. '98 (STL) Ellisville, MO St. Clare of Assisi.
Estabrook, Joseph W. (HON) Military Chaplains.
Estabrook, Joseph '69 (ALB) Military Chaplains; Navy Chaplains.
Estada, Julio '59 (MIA)[G] Miami, FL Mercy Outpatient Services, Inc..
Esteban, Antonio '85 (LA) South El Monte, CA Epiphany.
Estensoro, Jose '60 (ARE) Hatillo, PR Perpetual Help.
Estepa, Isaias '94 (CC) Corpus Christi, TX Holy Family.
Estephan, Andre S. *m.l.m.* '90 (OLL)[A] Houston, TX The Congregation of Maronite Lebanese Missionaries.
Estephan, Andre *m.l.m.* '90 (OLL) Houston, TX Our Lady of the Cedars Maronite Mission.
Esters, Guillermo (PCE)[H] Coto Laurel, PR Diocesan Fathers of Schoenstatt–Santuary of Schoenstatt.
Estes, Dan '99 (CC)[G] Robstown, TX Society of Our Lady of the Most Holy Trinity.
Estes, Daniel *s.o.l.t.* '99 (FAR) Belcourt, ND St. Ann.
Esteves, Jose *o.dem.* '58 (PCE)[D] Ponce, PR Residencia Santa Marta.
Estevez, Felipe '70 (MIA)[A] Boynton Beach, FL St. Vincent de Paul Regional Seminary.
Estibalez, Inocencio '52 (SP) Retired.
Estilette, Grady J. '63 (LAF) Retired.
Estok, Edward T. '85 (CLV) Cleveland, OH Cathedral of St. John the Evangelist; [Y] Cleveland, OH St. John Cathedral Endowment Trust; Assistant Chancellors; Secretary to Bishop Pilla; Procurators; Continuing Education and Formation of Ministers.
Estok, Edward (CLV) Translators.
Estrada, Enrique J. '93 (MIA) Miami Beach, FL St. Joseph; Archdiocesan Vocations Review Board.
Estrada, Francisco Javier Maciel (CHI) Chicago, IL St. George.
Estrada, Ignacio *s.v.d.* '03 (LA) Los Angeles, CA St. John, The Evangelist.
Estrada, Manuel '86 (SFR) San Rafael, CA St. Raphael.
Estrada, Sabino '72 (BRK) Woodside, NY St. Sebastian.
Estram, John R. '86 (STP) North St. Paul, MN St. Peter.
Estrem, John '86 (STP) St. Paul, MN Cathedral of St. Paul; Building Commission; St. Paul, MN Cathedral of St. Paul.
Esty, Gregory L. '75 (STP) St. Paul Park, MN St. Thomas Aquinas.
Ethapemi, Felix '88 (SJ) Campbell, CA St. Lucy.
Ethen, Jeff '88 (SCL) Parkers Prairie, MN Sacred Heart.
Ethen, Jeff '88 (SCL) Parkers Prairie, MN Church of St. William.
Ethen, Jeffrey D. '88 (SCL) Carlos, MN St. Nicholas; Navy Reserve Chaplains.
Etheredge, F. William '83 (RCK)[B] Aurora, IL Aurora Central Catholic High School.
Ethier, Raymond '85 (ALB) Elizaville, NY Holy Cross.
Ethier, Raymond '85 (ALB) Philmont, NY Sacred Heart.
Ethier, Robert D. '45 (PRO) Retired.
Etienne, Bernard '93 (EVN) Oakland City, IN Blessed Sacrament.
Etienne, Bernard '93 (EVN) Princeton, IN St. Joseph.
Etienne, Bernard '93 (EVN) Special Assignment.
Etienne, Bernard (EVN) Vocation Office.
Etienne, Paul D. '92 (IND) New Albany, IN Our Lady of Perpetual Help; Archdiocesan Review Board.
Etienne, Paul (IND) Board of Consultors.
Ettampola, Patrick '90 (Sri Lanka) New York, NY Our Saviour.
Ettel, Dale *o.s.c.* '82 (DET)[K] Riverview, MI Crosier Community of Riverview; Riverview, MI St. Cyprian.
Ettensohn, John Mark *o.m.i.* '89 (STP)[P] Buffalo, MN Christ the King Retreat Center.
Etter, Kenneth J. (STL) St. Louis, MO St. Joan of Arc.
Ettlinger, Gerard H. *s.j.* '66 (NY)[EE] Whitestone, NY.
Ettner, Wilhelm J. '93 (ARL) McLean, VA St. John's.
Ettolil, Sebastian *m.c.b.s.* '68 (MAR) Calumet, MI St. Paul the Apostle.
Ettolil, Sebastian *m.c.b.s.* '68 (MAR) Mohawk, MI Our Lady of Peace.
Ettolil, Thomas '67 (MAR) White Pine, MI St. Jude.
Etuale, Etuale '77 (HON) On Duty Outside the Diocese.
Etuale, Kolio '03 (SPP) Pago Pago, AS Church of the Holy Cross; Faculty Members.
Etuale, Viane '90 (SPP) Pago Pago, AS St. Paul.
Etuale, Viane (SPP) Vicar General of Diocese; Diocesan Pastoral Council; Fatuoaiga Multipurpose Cultural and Pastoral Center.
Etuale, Viane (SPP) Faculty Members.
Etuale, Viane (SPP) Vicar General of Diocese; Diocesan Pastoral Council; Fatuoaiga Multipurpose Cultural and Pastoral Center.
Etuale, Viane (SPP) Director of Vocations.
Etuale, Viane (SPP) Diocesan Consultors.
Etzel, Peter J. *s.j.* '94 (MIL) Milwaukee, WI Gesu Parish.
Etzel, Peter *s.j.* (STP) Newman Centers.
Etzel, Raymond A. '50 (TOL) Retired.
Euglielmo, Alan (NEW) Newark, NJ Coordinator for Health Care Apostolate Continuing Education.
Euk, Vincent '86 (NY) New York, NY Our Lady of the Rosary.
Euk, Vincent (NY) Manhattan, NY New York University Medical Center.
Euker, John T. '74 (GBG) Perryopolis, PA St. John the Baptist.
Euresti, Jesse '65 (AUS) Luling, TX St. John the Evangelist.
Eustace, Alexander F. *o.f.m.* '50 (FgM).
Euteneuer, Thomas J. '88 (PMB) On Duty Outside the Diocese.
Euteneur, Thomas J. '88 (ARL)[N] Front Royal, VA Human Life International.
Euvard, Scott A. '94 (BO) Lowell, MA St. Louis de France; Graduate Studies.
Evan, Jesus *s.x.* (PAT)[M] Wayne Xaverian Missionary Fathers.
Evancho, George '64 (PBR) East Pittsburgh, PA St. Mary's.
Evancho, George '64 (PBR) East Pittsburgh, PA St. John's.
Evancho, Robert '79 (PSC) St. Petersburg, FL St. Therese.
Evancho, Robert (PSC) Syncellus.
Evangelisto, Louis Anthony '54 (HRT) New Haven, CT St. Donato's; [R] Hamden, CT Catholic Community at Quinnipiac University.
Evanick, Michael '60 (PRM) Merrillville, IN St. Michael.
Evanick, Michael (PRM) Eparchial Consultors.
Evanish, Robin '83 (PIT) Moon Township, PA St. Margaret Mary.
Evanko, Joseph J. '91 (SCR) Conyngham, PA St. John Bosco; On Duty Outside the Diocese; [D] Hazleton, PA Bishop Hafey Junior/Senior High School.
Evanofski, Bernard P. '86 (VEN) On Duty Outside the Diocese.
Evans, Edward '80 (WDC) Retired.
Evans, G. William '78 (TR) Eatontown, NJ St. Dorothea.
Evans, George J. *o.c.s.o.* '61 (SAT)[K] Conyers The Monastery of the Holy Spirit Retired.
Evans, George *s.s.s.* '57 (CLV)[O] Richfield, OH Regina Health Center.
Evans, George *s.s.s.* '57 (CLV)[O] Richfield, OH Regina Health Center.
Evans, James L. '94 (AUS) Dripping Springs, TX St. Martin de Porres; Air National Guard Chaplains.
Evans, John '80 (FAR) Fargo, ND Prairie St. John's.
Evans, John '80 (FAR) Special Assignment.
Evans, John '80 (FAR)[D] Fargo, ND Prairie St. John's.
Evans, Ken '86 (NEW) Roselle Park, NJ The Assumption.
Evans, Larry '01 (NEW) Upper Saddle River, NJ Church of the Presentation.
Evans, Larry (NEW) Staff.
Evans, Michael A. *s.j.* '83 (FgM).
Evans, Michael A. *s.j.* '83 (DET)[K] Loyola House.
Evans, Michael J. '92 (LA) Arcadia, CA Holy Angels.
Evans, Paul J. '42 (DUB) Retired.
Evans, Richard A. '82 (CLV) Parma, OH St. Columbkille.
Evans, Robert C. '73 (PRO) On Duty Outside the Diocese.
Evans, Robert T. '03 (STL) Richmond Heights, MO Immacolata.
Evans, Timothy '94 (MOB) Coden, AL St. Michael the Archangel.
Evans, Timothy '94 (MOB) Bayou LaBatre, AL St. Margaret.
Evans, Timothy (MOB) Catholic Youth Ministry.
Evans, Wilfred F. '68 (SY) Syracuse, NY Veterans Administration Hospital; Special Assignment.
Evans, William Morris '81 (CHL) Cashiers, NC St. Jude; Highlands, NC Our Lady of the Mountains.
Evard, Paul A. '61 (IND) Retired.
Evardoni, Luis '99 (GAL)[K] Catholic Chaplain Corps, Texas Medical Center.
Evardoni, Luis Paolo Agostino V. *d.s.* '99 (GAL)[Q] Houston, TX Disciples of Hope (Texas).
Evenson, Dennis D. '67 (STP) Northfield, MN Annunciation of the B.V.M..
Evenson, Robert L. '91 (SEA) Issaquah, WA St. Joseph.
Everding, Richard F. '66 (STL) On Medical Leave.
Everett, Willis E. '90 (COL) Military Services; Navy Chaplains.
Everitt, Edward E. *o.p.* '68 (MEM) Memphis, TN St. Peter's; [I] Memphis, TN Order Of Preachers (Southern Dominican Prov.); [I] Memphis, TN The Dominican Friars of Memphis, Inc..
Everling, Robert M. '47 (SCR)[N] Dunmore, PA Villa St. Joseph Retired.
Evers, Gerard A. '40 (CIN) Cincinnati, OH St. Matthias Retired.
Evers, Leonard M. '68 (GB) Cecil, WI St. Martin; Shawano, WI Sacred Heart.
Evers, Paul C. '54 (WIN) Currie, MN Immaculate Heart of Mary; Currie, MN St. Gabriel's; Currie, MN St. Anthony's.
Evers, Paul H. '80 (HON) On Duty Outside the Diocese; Navy Chaplains.
Evers, Robert B. '60 (GRY) Retired.
Eversole, Paul M. '95 (ARL) Stafford, VA St. William of York; Defenders of the Bond.
Everson, Joseph M. *m.m.* '99 (FgM).
Everts, Donald E. (GB) Bear Creek, WI St. Mary; Clintonville, WI St. Rose.
Evrard, Donald J. '56 (IND) Retired.
Ewen, Sharbel *o.s.b.* '88 (SD)[H] Oceanside, CA Prince of Peace Abbey, Benet Hill.
Ewers, Paul *m.c.c.j.* '65 (NEW)[N] Montclair, NJ Comboni Missionaries of the Heart of Jesus (Verona Fathers).
Ewert, Michael *o.f.m.* '59 (SFD)[L] Springfield, IL Our Lady of Angels Friary.
Ewherido, Anthony '86 (RVC) Stony Brook, NY Stony Brook University Hospital.
Ewing, Mathias *o.carm.* '54 (LA)[F] Encino, CA Crespi Carmelite High School.
Ewing, Matt J. *o.carm.* '54 (LA)[Q] Los Angeles, CA Mount Carmel Priory, Carmelite Fathers and Brothers.
Ewing, Richard A. '46 (MET) Retired.
Extejt, John I. *o.s.f.s.* '85 (TOL)[C] Toledo, OH St. Francis de Sales High School; [J] Toledo, OH.
Extejt, Thomas J. '73 (TOL) Toledo, OH St. Charles Borromeo; Toledo Central; CCMT (Central City Ministries of Toledo).
Eybel, John W. *m.m.* '70 (FgM).
Eyerman, Matthew S. '95 (CHI) Chicago, IL St. Columbanus.
Eyerman, Matthew (CHI) The Tuite House at St. Columbanus Church.
Eyman, Bryan R. '85 (PRM) Mentor–on–the–Lake, OH St. Michael; Mentor–on–the–Lake, OH St. Andrew the Apostle.
Eyman, Bryan (PRM) Presbyteral Council.
Eyman, Bryan (PRM) Ohio.
Eyman, Bryan (PRM) Building Commission.
Eyrrick, John (NY) MID Hudson Psychiatric Center.
Ezaki, Bernard J. '88 (ALN) Bethlehem, PA Notre Dame of Bethlehem; [C] Bethlehem, PA Bethlehem Catholic High School.
Ezama, Natale (CHI) Chicago, IL Our Lady of Peace.
Eze, Cyprian '88 (LAF) Lafayette, LA Our Lady of Fatima.
Ezeh, Gabriel I. '94 (BWN) Roma, TX Sacred Heart.
Ezeh, Raphael *m.s.p.* '96 (NO) New Orleans, LA Our Lady of Lourdes.
Ezeibeke, Samuel '79 (FAR) Michigan, ND St. Lawrence O'Toole.
Ezeibekwe, Samuel '79 (FAR) Michigan, ND St. Catherine.

Ezeibekwe, Samuel '79 (FAR) Michigan, ND SS. Peter & Paul.
Ezenwata, Aloysius '94 (NEW) Jersey City, NJ St. Nicholas.
Ezenwata, Aloysius '94 (NEW) Jersey City, NJ Christ Hospital; Christ Hospital.
Ezeoke, Alphonsus '90 (NEW) Hackensack, NJ Hackensack University Medical Center; Chaplains.
Ezeonyido, John Paul '03 (ATL) Atlanta, GA Holy Cross.
Ezharath, Joseph '66 (WH) Sistersville, WV Holy Rosary.
Ezharath, Joseph '66 (WH) Paden City, WV Mater Dolorosa.
Ezop, Dwight M. '97 (LAN) De Witt, MI St. Jude.
Ezop, Dwight (LAN) College of Consultors.
Ezop, Dwight (LAN) Faith Magazine.

F

Faber, Emmet N. '55 (LC) Retired.
Faber, William '36 (FTW) Retired.
Fabian, Cyril *o.p.* '56 (WIN) Winona, MN Cathedral of the Sacred Heart.
Fabian, Jack '68 (DET)[T] Detroit, MI Clergy Health Plan; [T] Paradise, MI Companions of Christ the Lamb.
Fabian, John C. *o.p.* '59 (CHI)[N] Chicago Dominicans (Provincial Office).
Fabian, John L. '48 (SCR)[N] Dunmore, PA Villa St. Joseph Retired.
Fabian, John '68 (DET) Special Assignment.
Fabiano, Philip *o.f.m.cap.* '64 (MIA) Miami, FL St. Thomas the Apostle; East Patchogue, NY St. Joseph the Worker.
Fabing, Robert J. *s.j.* '74 (SJ)[L] Los Altos, CA Jesuit Retreat House; [P] Los Altos, CA Jesuit Institute for Family Life.
Fabish, Rapael A. *o.p.* '53 (CHI)[N] St. Pius V Priory.
Fabj, Frank T. '84 (GAL) Galveston, TX Sacred Heart; [D] Galveston, TX O'Connell Catholic High School.
Fabre, Richard '73 (LAF) Lydia, LA St. Nicholas.
Fabre, Shelton J. '89 (BR) Grosse Tete, LA St. Joseph; Maringouin, LA Immaculate Heart of Mary; Defenders of the Bond; College of Consultors; Black Catholics; Board Members; Presbyteral Council.
Facci, John *s.a.c.* '71 (ALB) Cohoes, NY St. Rita–Sacred Heart.
Fackler, Neil E. '98 (CHI) Park Ridge, IL St. Paul of the Cross.
Facura, Joseph '68 (RIC) Virginia Beach, VA St. Matthew.
Facura, Joseph (RIC) Defenders of the Bond.
Fadallan, Elbert A. (LUB) Air Force Chaplains.
Fadden, Joseph A. '54 (SCR) Scranton, PA St. Clare Retired.
Fador, Francis R. '96 (HRT) Cornwall Bridge, CT St. Bridget; Sharon, CT St. Bernard's.
Fadrowski, Stanislaus '39 (SCL) Retired.
Fadrowski, William J. '87 (NEW) North Arlington, NJ Queen of Peace; Priest Personnel Policy Board.
Faeh, Linus *o.f.m.cap.* (FgM).
Faesser, Arthur A. '76 (GI) North Platte, NE Holy Spirit.
Fafinski, Donald S. '66 (BUF) Retired.
Fagan, Arthur J. '67 (CHI) Elk Grove Village, IL Queen of the Rosary.
Fagan, Edward J. *o.a.r.* '63 (NY) Bronx, NY St. John's.
Fagan, Emmet '55 (RVC)[L] Brooklyn, NY Ecclesial Consultants, Inc..
Fagan, George V. '69 (COS) Limon, CO Our Lady of Victory; Diocesan Consultors; Defenders of the Bond; Eastern Region.
Fagan, George V. (PBL) Defensores Vinculi.
Fagan, John T. '52 (RVC)[P] Brooklyn, NY Little Flower Children's Services; [G] Wading River, NY Little Flower Children's Services of New York Retired.
Fagan, Joseph K. (BO)[A] Weston, MA Blessed John XXIII National Seminary.
Fagan, Joseph P. '37 (NEW) Berkeley Heights, NJ Church of the Little Flower Retired.
Fagan, Paul E. *m.m.* '60 (FgM).
Fagan, Paul R. *c.p.* '86 (NY)[EE] Riverdale, NY Passionist Spiritual Center; [GG] Bronx, NY Cardinal Spellman Retreat House.
Fagan, Robert '58 (ALN) Easton, PA St. Jane Frances de Chantal.
Fagin, Gerald M. *s.j.* '69 (NO)[C] New Orleans, LA Loyola University New Orleans.
Fagone, Benedict *o.f.m.conv.* '67 (SPR) Chicopee, MA St. Anthony's.
Fagot, Hacker J. *s.j.* '57 (BR)[J] Convent, LA Manresa House of Retreats.
Faherty, William B. *s.j.* '44 (STL)[O] St. Louis, MO Jesuit Community Corporation at St. Louis University – Jesuit Hall; [O] St. Louis, MO The Jesuits of the Missouri Province.
Fahey, Charles J. '58 (SY)[L] Brooklyn, NY Ecclesial Consultants, Inc.; [EE] Loyola Hall, Jesuit Community; Syracuse, NY St. Lucy; On Duty Outside the Diocese.
Fahey, Edward J. '86 (WIL) Ocean City, MD St. Luke and St. Andrew.
Fahey, Gerard '51 (SR) Santa Rosa, CA Star of the Valley.
Fahey, Gerard (SR) Cemeteries.
Fahey, James L. '59 (BO) Beverly, MA St. Margaret.
Fahey, James W. '70 (FR) South Attleboro, MA St. Theresa of the Child Jesus.
Fahey, John H. '61 (WH) Washington, WV St. Monica's; Ravenswood, WV St. Matthew.
Fahey, John M. '54 (TUC) Woonsocket, RI Precious Blood Retired.
Fahey, John F. '84 (LA) Retired.
Fahey, John '84 (LA) Santa Barbara, CA St. Raphael.
Fahey, John *c.ss.r.* '96 (DOD)[F] Liberal, KS Liberal Redemptorist Hispanic House Ministry, Inc..
Fahey, Michael A. *s.j.* '64 (MIL)[X] Milwaukee, WI Theological Studies, Inc.; [O] Milwaukee, WI Arrupe House Jesuit Community.
Fahey, Michael A. *s.j.* '64 (BO)[V] Boston The Society of Jesus of New England–Provincial Offices.
Fahey, Robert *s.m.* '53 (WDC)[M] Tampa, FL Retired.
Fahey, Thomas C. *o.f.m.* '47 (CHY)[J] Huntington, IN Victory Noll—Motherhouse of Our Lady of Victory Missionary Sisters Retired.
Fahey–Guerra, John *c.ss.r.* (DOD) Office of Hispanic Ministry.
Fahnestock, John *m.s.c.* '70 (SB) Hesperia, CA Holy Family.
Fahrbach, Paul A. '84 (TOL) Custar, OH St. Louis; Deshler, OH Immaculate Conception.
Fahy, Francis J. '61 (BRK) Brooklyn, NY Resurrection.
Fahy, Joseph *c.p.* '56 (ATL) Atlanta, GA St. Paul of the Cross; Lawrenceville, GA St. Lawrence; [H] Lawrenceville, GA.
Fahy, Thomas *o.s.b.* '57 (WDC)[M] Washington, DC St. Anselm's Abbey.
Faiella, William W. *c.s.c.* '79 (FTW)[I] Berkeley, CA Holy Cross Center.
Fain, John '03 (LAN) Lansing, MI St. Gerard.
Faiola, Samuel J. (BUF) Censors—Board of Diocesan Censors of Books and Vigilance for the Faith Retired.
Faiola, Thomas *o.f.m. cap.* '85 (NY) Manchester, NH St. Augustin.
Fairbanks, Gregory J. '90 (PH) Graduate Studies; Philadelphia, PA St. John the Baptist.
Fairbanks, Patrick A. *s.j.* (CHI)[D] Chicago, IL St. Ignatius Jesuit Community.
Fairbanks, Patrick *s.j.* (CHI)[D] Chicago, IL St. Ignatius College Prep.
Fairchild, Edward '59 (COL) Retired.
Fairfield, Jeffry *o.carm.* '46 (JOL)[L] Darien Carmelite Provincial Office.
Fairman, Timothy J. '88 (CHI) Ingleside, IL St. Bede.
Faistl, Clement F. '37 (COL) Retired.
Faith, Rudolph '41 (DUL) Retired.
Faix, William R. *o.s.a.* '63 (WDC)[B] Silver Spring, MD Austin Friars Hall, Order of St. Augustine.
Fajella, Francis *m.s.a.* '82 (NOR)[F] Cromwell Society of the Missionaries of the Holy Apostles.
Fala, John G. '65 (PH) Philadelphia, PA St. Bernard Retired.
Falabella, J. Robert (CHR) Simpsonville, SC St. Mary Magdalene.
Falardeau, Ernest R. *s.s.s.* '56 (NY) New York, NY St. Jean Baptiste.
Falardeau, Norman R. *s.s.s.* (SFE) Associate Judges.
Falardeau, Normand R. *s.s.s.* '52 (SFE) Albuquerque, NM St. Charles Borromeo.
Falbo, Samuel '60 (SFE) Retired.
Falco, Frank M. *o.s.m.* '67 (CHI)[N] Berwyn, IL St. Bonfilius Priory.
Falco, Ronald G. '81 (WOR) Leominster, MA St. Anna's.
Falcone, Emilio '57 (RCK) Retired.
Falcone, Mark D. *o.praem* (GB)[I] De Pere, WI St. Norbert Abbey.
Falcone, Sabastian '51 (ROC) Retired.
Faletoi, Konelio '92 (HON) Ewa Beach, HI Our Lady of Perpetual Help; Clergy Personnel Board; Presbyteral Council.
Faley, Roland *t.o.r.* '56 (RVC) Syosset, NY St. Edward Confessor.
Faliskie, Edmund J. *c.ss.r.* '91 (FgM).
Falk, Gerald R. '59 (GB) Appleton, WI St. Thomas More.
Falk, Robert *s.d.b.* '63 (FgM).
Falkenhan, Pierre M. '80 (PIT) Glenshaw, PA St. Bonaventure.
Falkenthal, Thomas W. '75 (CHI) Military Chaplains; Navy Chaplains.
Falla, Gustavo A. (BGP) Presbyteral Council; Stamford, CT Saint Benedict – Our Lady of Montserrat.
Faller, Henry E. '47 (KC) Retired.
Falletta, Frank J. '66 (ROC) Rochester, NY St. Lawrence.
Falletta, Joseph '72 (ALB) Copake Falls, NY St. Bridget; Special Assignment.
Fallgren, Matthew '01 (RC) Belle Fourche, SD St. Paul; Spearfish, SD St. Joseph.
Fallon, Daniel R. '76 (CHI) Chicago, IL Our Lady, Mother of the Church.
Fallon, David F. '70 (CLV) Cleveland, OH Sagrada Familia; [W] Cleveland, OH Hispanic Parishes: Iglesia La Sagrada Familia.
Fallon, James J. '62 (SY) Johnson City, NY St. James Retired.
Fallon, James L. '43 (PAT) Morris Plains, NJ St. Virgilius; [C] Madison, NJ Bayley–Ellard High School Retired.
Fallon, James P. *s.s.j.* '68 (LAF) Breaux Bridge, LA St. Francis of Assisi.
Fallon, John C. '71 (ATL) Prison Apostolate.
Fallon, John C.K. '71 (ATL) Atlanta, GA Holy Spirit.
Fallon, John F. '58 (BO) Senior Priests Retired.
Fallon, John J. '46 (BO) Senior Priests Retired.
Fallon, John P. *o.s.f.s.* '60 (STO)[A] Stockton, CA St. Mary's High School; College of Consultors/ Presbyteral Council; Diocesan Finance Council.
Fallon, John P. '95 (FAR) Enderlin, ND St. Patrick.
Fallon, John '55 (OG)[Q] Syracuse, NY Tommy Coyne Residence @ Dillon Hall.
Fallon, John '69 (BIR) Birmingham (Hoover), AL Prince of Peace; Members; Diocesan College of Consultors.
Fallon, John '95 (FAR) Enderlin, ND St. Henry (of Alice); Enderlin, ND St. Mary, Our Lady of the Scapular.
Fallon, Joseph '96 (NY) Tuckahoe, NY Immaculate Conception; Tuckahoe, NY Assumption.
Fallon, Marc F. *c.s.c.* '91 (FR)[H] North Dartmouth, MA Holy Cross Residence.
Fallon, Marc *c.s.c.* (FR) North Dartmouth, MA.
Fallon, Vince *ss.cc.* '91 (RNO) Reno, NV Our Lady of the Snows.
Fallon, William J. '64 (CAM) On Sick Leave; Disabled.
Fallone, Thomas H. '02 (PAT) Sparta, NJ Blessed Kateri Tekakwitha.
Falls, Thomas B. '32 (PH) Retired.
Falotico, Ronald S. '69 (CAM) Pleasantville, NJ St. Peter's; Office of Ethnic Ministries.
Falsey, James E. '72 (SAG) AuGres, MI St. Mark.
Falter, John F. *c.pp.s.* '61 (CIN)[M] Parroguia Sangre de Cristo.
Faluszczak, James G. '96 (E) Clarion, PA Immaculate Conception.
Faluszczak, James '96 (E)[P] Clarion, PA Clarion University of Pennsylvania.
Falvella, Richard J. '41 (BUR) Retired.
Falvey, Edmund F. '61 (WOR) Retired.
Falvey, Jeremiah A. *c.s.sp.* '55 (PIT)[P] Bethel Park, PA Holy Spirit Animation Center.
Falvey, Sinon '45 (ORG) Retired.
Falzon, Angelo *o.f.m.* '84 (FgM).
Falzon, Raymond *o.f.m.* '83 (NY)[EE] St. Francis Friary.
Fama, Lawrence J. '92 (NEW) Westfield, NJ St. Helen; Members.
Fambrini, Robert A. *s.j.* '79 (LA)[Q] Culver City, CA.
Famiglietti, Rocco *o.f.m.* '47 (FgM).
Famiyeh, Emmanuel '90 (LC) Richland Center, WI St. Mary (Assumption of B.V.M.); Deans.
Fanale, James *c.s.v.* '69 (JOL) St. Anne, IL St. Anne.
Fane, Kevin R. *o.p.* '69 (CHI) River Forest, IL St. Vincent Ferrer.
Fanelli, Charles V. '71 (CHI) Northlake, IL St. John Vianney, Cure of Ars; [X] Northlake, IL Italian Catholic Federation.
Fanelli, James G. '56 (HRT) East Hartford, CT St. Christopher.
Faneye, Benedict *o.p.* '94 (PIT) West Mifflin, PA St. Agnes.
Fangman, Frederick '63 (DUB)[H] Oelwein, IA Mercy Hospital of Franciscan Sisters.
Fangman, James E. '63 (SC) Retired.
Fangman, Paul J. '49 (OM) Retired.
Fangman, Robert M. '54 (SC) Retired.
Fangman, Thomas M. '92 (OM) Omaha, NE Sacred Heart; [F] Omaha, NE Christian Urban Education Service Foundation; [O] Omaha, NE Christian Urban Education Service.
Fangmann, Frederick C. '63 (DUB) Monona, IA St. Mary; Monona, IA St. Patrick; Oelwein, IA Sacred Heart; Monona, IA St. Bridget's; Deans.
Fangmeyer, Lee J. '89 (WDC) Derwood, MD St. Francis of Assisi.
Fanio Fernandez, Epi *o.ss.t.* '59 (SJN) Bayamon, PR Ascension Del Senor.
Fanning, John E. '68 (NY) New York, NY Our Lady of Victory.
Fanning, Leo M. '54 (PAT) Retired.
Fanning, Patrick F. *ss.cc.* '83 (FR).
Fannon, Noel (BLX)[H] Kiln, MS St. Matthew the Apostle.
Fannon, Thomas J. '41 (BAL) Pasadena, MD St. Jane Frances de Chantal; [O] St. Elizabeth Hall Retired.
Fanotti, Richard *c.s.* '75 (LA) Sun Valley, CA Our Lady of the Holy Rosary.
Fanrak, James M. '71 (LR) Mountain Home, AR St. Peter the Fisherman; Mountain View, AR St. Mary Church.
Fanta, Thomas G. '88 (CLV) Shaker Heights, OH St. Dominic.
Fanta, Thomas '88 (CLV)[Y] Shaker Heights, OH St. Dominic Endowment Fund.

Fanti, Joseph '90 (SCR)[L] Scranton, PA Home for Aged of the Little Sisters of the Poor, Holy Family Residence.
Fanucci, Santino J. '58 (SCR) Peckville, PA Sacred Heart of Jesus; Deans.
Faour, George '91 (NEW) Orange, NJ St. John's.
Farace, Frederick A. '55 (HBG) Retired.
Faraci, Douglas F. '69 (BUF) Retired.
Faraci, Francis '59 (LAN) Otisville, MI St. Francis Xavier Retired.
Faraj, John *b.s.o.* '78 (NTN) Brooklyn, NY Church of the Virgin Mary; Methuen, MA Basilian Salvatorian Order; Protopresbyters; College of Eparchial Consultors; Presbyteral Council; Priest's Sickness & Disability, and Retirement Plans; Canonical Consultants.
Faraj, John (NTN) Judges.
Farana, Mario P. '71 (SFR) San Francisco, CA St. Paul; Deans.
Farano, Michael A. '68 (ALB) Special Assignment; Propagation of the Faith–Pontifical Society; Ministry to Priests; Loudonville, NY St. Pius X.
Farao, John *o.f.m.conv.* '76 (SB)[E] Riverside, CA Conventual Franciscans, OFM Conv..
Farao, John *o.f.m.conv.* '88 (SB) Riverside, CA Queen of Angels.
Farao, John *o.f.m.conv.* (SB) Appointed Members; Vicars Forane.
Faraone, Emmanuel *o.f.m.* '41 (NY)[EE] New York, NY Padua Friary.
Faraone, Joseph J. '72 (NY) Carmel, NY St. James the Apostle.
Farbolin, Alberic R. *o.c.s.o.* '02 (DUB)[K] Peosta, IA New Melleray Abbey, Order of Cistercians of the Strict Observance.
Fardellone, Emil (MIA) Chaplains—Dade County – Serra Club.
Fardelone, Emil *s.d.b.* '44 (MIA) Miami, FL St. Kieran.
Fares, Lawrence '50 (DET) Retired.
Faretra, Albert M. '86 (BO) Belmont, MA St. Joseph.
Farfaglia, James '87 (CC) Corpus Christi, TX Our Lady of Perpetual Help.
Farfan, Marco '64 (CHI) Chicago, IL St. Gall.
Farge, William J. *s.j.* '78 (NO)[P] Arrupe International Residence.
Faria, Carl M.D. '88 (MRY) On Leave.
Farias, Joseph A. *s.d.b.* '64 (LA) Los Angeles, CA St. Mary.
Farias, Joseph G. '75 (PAT)[O] Madison, NJ Drew University Catholic Campus Ministry; [O] Madison, NJ Catholic Campus Ministry; AUXILIARY CHAPLAINS CONTRACT CHAPLAINS.
Farias, Joseph *s.d.b.* '64 (LA)[Q] Los Angeles, CA Dominic Savio Salesian Residence.
Faricy, Robert L. *s.j.* '62 (MIL)[O] Milwaukee, WI Jesuit Community at Marquette University.
Farina, Carlo A. *s.j.* '64 (SJ).
Farina, Michael Di Teccia (WDC)[D] Paul VI Institute for the Arts.
Farina, Michael diTeccia '54 (WDC) Washington, DC St. Patrick; [V] Washington, DC Paul VI Institute for the Arts.
Farina, Michael F. '54 (WDC) Retired.
Faris, John D. '76 (NY)[II] New York, NY Catholic Near East Welfare Association (CNEWA); [II] New York, NY CNEWA UNITED STATES.
Faris, John D. '76 (SAM) On Duty Outside the Diocese.
Faris, John D. (NTN) Canonical Consultants.
Farke, Rodney '72 (SFS) Yankton, SD St. Benedict; [I] Yankton, SD The House of Mary Shrine, Inc..
Farke, Rodney (SFS) Tribunal Judges; Diocesan Consultors; Deans; Presbyteral Council; Cursillo.
Farland, George A. '68 (SPR) Springfield, MA Sacred Heart; Bishop's Commission for Clergy; Diocesan Consultors; Deans; Co–Vicars For Clergy; Clergy Counseling Service.
Farland, George (SPR) Vicars for the Clergy; Presbyteral Council.
Farland, Norman '66 (ORL) Wahneta, FL Our Lady of Guadalupe.
Farland, Roch *o.f.m.* '54 (DET) Southfield, MI St. Michael Retired.
Farleo, Brennan Joseph *o.f.m.conv.* '86 (TR) Seaside Park, NJ St. Catharine of Siena.
Farley, Bernard C. '68 (PH)[X] Philadelphia, PA St. John Neumann Nursing Home.
Farley, Daniel H. '98 (LC) Amherst, WI St. Maximilian Maria Kolbe; Army National Guard Chaplains.
Farley, James V. '65 (PRO) Ashaway, RI Our Lady of Victory; Bradford, RI St. Vincent de Paul.
Farley, John B. '93 (PBL) Pueblo, CO Historic Southside Catholic Community; [J] Pueblo, CO Historic Southside Catholic Community.
Farley, John J. '62 (NY) Bronx, NY St. Margaret of Cortona.
Farley, John *s.v.d.* '60 (CHI)[B] Techny, IL Divine Word Residence.
Farley, John (PBL) Personnel.
Farley, John (NY) Canon 1742 Panel of Pastors.
Farley, Leo O. '54 (NEW)[N] Caldwell, NJ The Rev. Msgr. James F. Kelley Residence for Retired Priests Retired.
Farley, Leslie A. '93 (LR) Jacksonville, AR St. Jude the Apostle.
Farley, Thomas B. '79 (P) Portland, OR St. Clare.
Farley, Thomas F. '02 (PRT) Lewiston, ME St. Patrick's.
Farmer, Bruce L. '81 (TOL) Toledo, OH Sisters of Notre Dame; [K] Toledo, OH Notre Dame Provincialate.
Farmer, J. Kevin '93 (BAL) Baltimore, MD Cathedral of Mary Our Queen; Special Assignment; Vocation Office.
Farmer, James '79 (BAL) Baltimore, MD St. Thomas Aquinas.
Farmer, James (BAL) Priests' Council.
Farmer, Michael L. '95 (MOB) Mobile, AL Cathedral of the Immaculate Conception; Chancellor; Apostleship of Prayer; Catholic Housing of Mobile, Inc.; Cemeteries; Censor Librorum; Ecumenical Commission; Liturgical Commission; Co–Dirs.; Officers; Ex Officio Members; [K] Mobile, AL Apostleship of Prayer.
Farmer, Regis M. '73 (PIT) Wildwood, PA St. Catherine of Sweden.
Farmer, Ricard R. *o.p.* '55 (CHI)[N] Chicago Dominicans (Provincial Office).
Farmer, Richard *o.p.* '55 (WDC) Washington, DC St. Dominic Church & Priory.
Farmer, Terrence '03 (PRM) Brunswick, OH St. Emilian; Cleveland, OH St. Mary; Young Adults.
Farnan, Donald P. '87 (KC) Blue Springs, MO St. John La Lande.
Farnan, James B. (PIT) Graduate Studies.
Farnik, John *c.ss.r.* '62 (SAT) San Antonio, TX St. Gerard Majella.
Farnum, David *c.s.p.* '99 (CHI) Chicago, IL Old St. Mary.
Faroh, Paul *o.f.m.conv.* '85 (FTW) LaGrange, IN St. Joseph.
Farrand, John L. *s.j.* '53 (NY)[EE] New York, NY Murray–Weigel Hall.
Farrar, Charles '97 (DET) Absent on Leave.
Farre, Raymond P. '41 (TR) Retired.
Farrell, Anthony G. '64 (DAV).
Farrell, Bernard '65 (BLX) Ocean Springs, MS St. Elizabeth Ann Seton; Catholic Housing Board; Personnel Board; Presbyteral Council.
Farrell, Charles A. *o.p.* '54 (CIN)[M] Cincinnati, OH St. Gertrude Priory.
Farrell, Charles *o.p.* '54 (CIN) Cincinnati, OH St. Gertrude.
Farrell, Daniel J. '78 (YAK) Coulee City, WA St. Patrick's.
Farrell, Dennis J. '73 (BRK) Brooklyn, NY Holy Name.
Farrell, Dennis (BRK) Holy Name Society.
Farrell, Edward '56 (DET) Retired.
Farrell, Emmet L. '65 (SD) On Duty Outside the Diocese; National City, CA St. Anthony of Padua.
Farrell, Francis '55 (BLX) Biloxi, MS Our Lady of Fatima; Building and Real Estate Committee Retired.
Farrell, Gerald J. *m.m.* '57 (FgM).
Farrell, James E. *s.j.* '32 (CLV)[D] Cleveland, OH St. Ignatius High School.
Farrell, James *s.j.* '46 (CLV)[T] Cleveland, OH Jesuit Retreat House.
Farrell, James *c.ss.r.* '56 (OAK)[N] Berkeley, CA Redemptorists (St. Clemens Maria House).
Farrell, James '75 (IND) Indianapolis, IN St. Barnabas; Priests' Personnel Board.
Farrell, John E. '62 (BO) Lynnfield, MA Our Lady of the Assumption; NORTH REGION.
Farrell, John F. '47 (PRO) Retired.
Farrell, John J. *o.s.a.* '59 (PH)[C] Villanova University; [AA] Villanova, PA St. Thomas Monastery.
Farrell, Joseph A. *m.m.* '59 (NY).
Farrell, Joseph J. '74 (TR)[EE] New Egypt, NJ The Church of the Assumption.
Farrell, Joseph L. *o.s.a.* '91 (BO)[BB] North Andover, MA Merrimack College Campus Ministry Center.
Farrell, Joseph L. '95 (PH) Schwenksville, PA St. Mary.
Farrell, Kevin R. '65 (JOL) Wood Dale, IL Holy Ghost.
Farrell, Kurt (WIN) Austin, MN St. Edward's; Hispanic Ministry.
Farrell, Lawrence M. '01 (KAL) Kalamazoo, MI St. Monica.
Farrell, Lawrence *o.p.* '71 (SB)[E] Riverside, CA St. Vincent Ferrer House.
Farrell, Lawrence (KAL) Finance Council; Holy Childhood Association; Missions.
Farrell, Michael A. '70 (ORL) Merritt Island, FL Divine Mercy.
Farrell, Michael J. *s.s.j.* '60 (FWT) Fort Worth, TX Our Mother of Mercy.
Farrell, Patrick J. *o.c.d.* '62 (MIL)[O] Holy Hill, WI Discalced Carmelite Monastery – Holy Hill National Shrine of Mary Help of Christians.
Farrell, Patrick '60 (JKS) Vicksburg, MS St. Paul; Priests' Council.
Farrell, Patrick (BLX) Trustees.
Farrell, Patrick (JKS) Diocesan Judges; Diocesan Consultors; Trustees.
Farrell, Paul *c.ss.r.* '52 (STL)[O] Liguori, MO Liguori Mission House/Redemptorists.
Farrell, Philip N. '93 (PIT) New Castle, PA St. Camillus.
Farrell, Philip '93 (PIT)[Q] New Castle, PA Westminster College.
Farrell, Richard T. '84 (ROC) Elmira, NY St. Mary; Pine City, NY Southport Correctional Facility.
Farrell, Richard *c.m.* '52 (SPC)[E] Springfield, MO Claretians Missionaries' Residence–Villa Claret.
Farrell, Richard *c.m.f.* '52 (SPC) Springfield, MO Sacred Heart.
Farrell, Richard '84 (ROC) Elmira, NY Elmira Correctional Facility, Center and Camp Monterey.
Farrell, Richard (ALB) Presbyteral Council.
Farrell, Robert J. '80 (CIN) Cincinnati, OH St. Bartholomew.
Farrell, Robert *s.j.* '64 (BO)[V] Newton, MA The Jesuit Community at Boston College.
Farrell, Ronald J. (CHR) Georgetown, SC St. Mary's; Georgetown, SC St. Cyprian; Vocations Board.
Farrell, Seamus J. '67 (OAK) Hayward, CA St. Bede; Deans.
Farrell, Thomas F. '43 (HRT) Windsor Locks, CT St. Robert Bellarmine.
Farrell, Thomas '82 (LEX) Lexington, KY The Newman Center, Holy Spirit; [L] Lexington, KY The Newman Center Holy Spirit Parish University of Kentucky.
Farrell, Thomas (GB) Green Bay, WI SS. Peter and Paul.
Farrell, Timothy W. (GLP) Vocations.
Farrell, Timothy '89 (GLP) Farmington, NM Sacred Heart; Presbyteral Council.
Farrell, Tom (GB) Priests' Personnel Board.
Farrell, Walter L. *s.j.* '47 (DET)[B] Berkley, MI Loyola House; [K] Detroit, MI Jesuit Provincial Office–Detroit Province of the Society of Jesus.
Farrell, William '78 (CHL) Absent On Leave.
Farrelly, John P. (ATL) Released from Archdiocesan Assignment.
Farrelly, John *o.s.b.* '55 (WDC)[M] Washington, DC St. Anselm's Abbey.
Farrelly, Matthew *c.s.sp.* '42 (NY) New York, NY St. Agnes.
Farrelly, Terence J. '50 (ORL) Rockledge, FL St. Mary's Retired.
Farren, John A. *o.p.* '64 (BO) St. John Seminary; [A] Brighton, MA St. John Seminary School of Theology.
Farris, Semaan '54 (ORL) Retired.
Farris, William *o.f.m.* '77 (CIN)[E] Cincinnati, OH Roger Bacon High School; [M] Cincinnati, OH St. Clement Friary; [U] Cincinnati, OH Roger Bacon High School Endowment.
Farrow, Raphael G. '85 (FRS) Visalia, CA St. Thomas the Apostle; Visalia, CA Holy Family.
Farrugia, David J. *o.p.* '60 (SAC) Benicia, CA St. Dominic.
Farrugia, Edwin W. '60 (SFR) San Francisco, CA St. Elizabeth.
Farrugia, William '63 (BRK) Long Island City, NY St. Joseph.
Farry, John A. '65 (CHI) Chicago, IL St. Andrew.
Farry, John J. '67 (PH) Philadelphia, PA St. Leo.
Farsaci, Francis A. *o.s.a.* '64 (PH)[AA] Villanova, PA St. Thomas Monastery.
Farsaci, Francis *o.s.a.* '64 (PH) Abington, PA Our Lady Help of Christians.
Fary, Francis Solanus *o.f.m.cap.* '67 (FgM).
Fasano, Eric R. '02 (RVC) Seaford, NY St. William, the Abbot.
Fasano, Jerome W. '77 (ARL) Clifton, VA St. Andrew the Apostle.
Faschan, Matthew '46 (BR) Retired.
Fasching, Jeffery A. (WCH) Council Grove, KS St. Rose; Council Grove, KS St. Anthony of Padua.
Fasching, Jeffrey A. '97 (WCH) Wichita, KS St. Elizabeth Ann Seton.
Fasciglione, Max S. '74 (CAM) Delair, NJ St. Veronica's.
Fasline, Anthony '62 (Y) Retired.
Faso, Charles '67 (CHI)[N] Chicago, IL St. Peter's Friary.
Fassbinder, Richard W. '53 (CHI) Retired.
Fassero, Jonathan *o.s.b.* '78 (IND)[A] St. Meinrad, IN St. Meinrad School of Theology; [K] St. Meinrad, IN St. Meinrad Archabbey.
Fassett, Edward S. *s.j.* '88 (SFR)[D] Sacramento, CA Jesuit High School; [I] Carmichael, CA Jesuit High School Community of Sacramento.
Fata, Joseph A. '68 (Y) Boardman, OH St. Luke.
Fater, Douglas '70 (SAT) San Antonio, TX Holy Trinity; Priests Personnel Board.
Fath, Howard *m.s.c.* '61 (RCK)[G] Aurora, IL Missionaries of the Sacred Heart Community.
Fath, Robert *c.m.f.* '79 (CHI)[N] Oak Park, IL Claretian Fathers Headquarters of U.S.A. Eastern Province.
Fatooh, Charles G. '85 (MRY) Seaside, CA St. Francis Xavier; On Leave; Former Prelates of the Diocese of Monterey.
Fatora, Joachim R. *o.s.b.* '54 (GBG) Latrobe, PA Forty Martyrs; [H] Latrobe, PA Saint Vincent Archabbey.
Faucher, Eugene J. '51 (CHI) Arlington Heights, IL St. Edna Retired.

Faucher, W. Thomas '71 (B) Boise, ID St. Mary's; Judges.
Faugno, Valerian *o.f.m.* '58 (ALB)[A] Catskill, NY St. Anthony Friary.
Faul, Charles '80 (RIC) Virginia Beach, VA Church of the Ascension; Virginia Beach, VA Church of the Holy Apostles.
Faulhaber, Gregory M. '79 (BUF) Defenders of the Bond; Council of Priests.
Faulkner, Matthew *o.carm.* '89 (NY)[EE] Tappan, NY St. Eliseus Priory; [EE] Middletown, NY Carmelite Friars (North American Province of St. Elias).
Faulstich, Paul J. *s.j.* '68 (CHI)[D] Wilmette, IL Loyola Academy; [N] Chicago, IL Chicago Province of the Society of Jesus–Provincial Office.
Fauser, Arthur W. '50 (DET) Retired.
Fauser, Steven W. '03 (HBG) Hanover, PA St. Joseph.
Faust, Gary J. '78 (STL) Jefferson Barracks, MO St. Bernadette.
Faust, Louis J. '74 (WDC) Brandywine, MD St. Michael.
Faustina, John M. '47 (PHX) Retired.
Faustner, William J. '76 (COL) Newcomerstown, OH St. Francis de Sales.
Fausz, Kevin P. *c.m.* '91 (STL) Perryville, MO St. Vincent De Paul; Perryville, MO St. Rose of Lima; [U] Perryville, MO St. Vincent De Paul Educational Foundation; Perry County Catholic Church Real Estate Corporation; [U] Perryville, MO Perry County Catholic Church Real Estate Corporation.
Favara, Joseph F. '41 (SAG) Retired.
Favret, J. Raymond '48 (CIN) West Chester, OH St. John; Judges.
Favret, James '48 (CIN)[L] Cincinnati, OH St. Margaret Hall.
Favret, Raymond J. '48 (CIN) Retired.
Fawcett, Brian '97 (RC) Lemmon, SD Blessed Sacrament; Lemmon, SD St. Mary's; [D] Rapid City, SD Priest Retirement and Aid Association/Pension Plan Board; Deaneries.
Fawcett, Henry F. '64 (SD) San Diego, CA Our Lady of Mt. Carmel.
Fawls, Daniel J. '97 (BUF) Depew, NY St. Barnabas; Lackawanna, NY Basilica of Our Lady of Victory.
Fay, David E. '64 (CIN) Cincinnati, OH St. Gabriel; Cincinnati, OH St. Matthias; Judges.
Fay, Gregory J. (STA) Building Commission.
Fay, Gregory '76 (STA) Jacksonville, FL Holy Family.
Fay, M. Jude (BGP) Presbyteral Council.
Fay, Michael Jude '78 (BGP) Darien, CT St. John.
Fay, William J. '64 (PIT) On Duty Outside the Diocese.
Fay, William P. '74 (BO) On Duty Outside the Archdiocese.
Fayad, Samuel *c.s.s.* '48 (BO)[Y] Waltham, MA Stigmatine Fathers and Brothers.
Faylona, Joey '03 (SAN) San Angelo, TX St. Mary's; Carlsbad, TX St. Therese of the Child Jesus.
Fayos, Javier *l.c.* '97 (PRO)[E] South Kingstown, RI Immaculate Conception Academy.
Fazio, Cosimo '48 (NY) Retired.
Fazio, Paul *o.f.m.conv.* '74 (OAK) San Pablo, CA St. Paul.
Fazzalaro, Francis J. '45 (MIA) Retired.
Fears, Ernest A. (VEN) Presbyteral Council.
Fears, Ernest '99 (VEN) Bonita Springs, FL St. Leo.
Fecher, Vincent '50 (SAT)[G] San Antonio, TX St. Anthony's School; [K] San Antonio, TX Casa De Padres Retired.
Fechner, Eric A. '92 (STL) Archdiocesan Council of Priests.
Fechner, Erich A. '92 (STL) Warrenton, MO Holy Rosary.
Fecht, Geoffrey *o.s.b.* '88 (SCL) St. Cloud, MN St. Augustine; [I] Collegeville, MN St. John's Abbey, of the Order of St. Benedict.
Fecko, Leonard F. '89 (CIN) Cincinnati, OH St. John Vianney; Cincinnati, OH St. Margaret of Cortona.
Fecteau, Raymond L. '72 (WDC) Darnestown, MD Our Lady of the Visitation.
Fedak, Dennis Z. '98 (PH) Philadelphia, PA St. Cecilia.
Fedak, Paul C. '98 (FR) Wareham, MA St. Patrick's.
Fedders, William '68 (LEX) Special Assignment.
Fedell, Anthony R. *o.f.m.* '66 (NEW) Fair Lawn, NJ St. Anne's.
Federico, Cesidio J. '62 (WH) Clarksburg, WV Immaculate Conception.
Federico, Ralph P. '52 (BUF) Retired.
Federline, Thomas A. '85 (GBG) Freeport, PA St. Mary.
Feders, Joseph *o.s.b.* '99 (SCL)[I] Collegeville, MN St. John's Abbey, of the Order of St. Benedict; Wayzata, MN Holy Name.
Fedewa, Matthew (LAN) Department of Formation and Lay Ministry; Joseph H. Albers Trust Fund for Diocesan Vocations.
Fedewa, Sylvester L. '54 (LAN) Cursillo Retired.
Fedor, Gregory F. '83 (Y) Orwell, OH St. Mary; Rock Creek, OH Sacred Heart.
Fedor, Lawrence M. *o.s.b.* '76 (TUC)[E] St. David, AZ Holy Trinity Monastery.
Fedor, Lawrence '65 (CHY) Thermopolis, WY St. Francis.
Fedor, Mark Q. '72 (CLV) Cleveland, OH St. Mel; Adjutant Judicial Vicars; Defender of the Bond; Promoters of Justice.
Fedor, Robert P. (E) Erie County Prison.
Fedora, Joseph *m.m.* '84 (FgM).
Fedorowich, Michael '55 (PHU) Shamokin, PA Transfiguration of Our Lord.
Fee, James M. *o.m.i.* '71 (LA) Pacoima, CA Mary Immaculate
Fee, John M. *ss.cc.* '56 (DET) Harper Woods, MI Our Lady Queen of Peace.
Fee, Pat '61 (ORG) Retired.
Feehan, Kenneth *s.v.d.* '59 (BO)[V] Boston, MA Divine Word Missionaries.
Feehan, Stephen S. '62 (NEW) Berkeley Heights, NJ Church of the Little Flower; Union Northwest Deanery 22
Feehily, John W. '73 (OKL) Moore, OK St. Andrew's; Defenders of the Bond.
Feela, Paul F. *m.a.* '78 (STP) St. Louis Park MN Most Holy Trinity; [C] St. Paul, MN University of St. Thomas.
Feeley, Sylvester E. *c.ss.r.* '48 (BRK) Brooklyn, NY Our Lady of Perpetual Help Basilica.
Feeley, Thomas M. '55 (FR)[A] North Easton, MA Holy Cross Fathers Religious.
Feeley, Thomas *c.s.c.* '55 (FR)[N] North Easton, MA Holy Cross Family Ministries.
Feely, James '58 (GB) Diocesan Consultors Retired.
Feely, Thomas H. *s.j.* '75 (NY)[B] Bronx, NY Ciszek Hall.
Feenan, J. Francis '53 (PAT) Retired.
Feeney, John J. '54 (PRT) Retired.
Feeney, John J. '55 (LA) Retired.
Feeney, John P. '52 (GB) Retired.
Feeney, John *s.m.a.* '49 (NEW)[N] Tenafly, NJ Society of African Missions, Provincialate, S.M.A. Fathers Retired.
Feeney, Joseph J. *s.j.* '65 (PH)[C] Jesuit Fathers; [AA] Philadelphia, PA St. Alphonsus House.
Feeney, Kevin J. '77 (CHI)[A] Mundelein Seminary.
Feeney, Kevin (LA) Archives.
Feeney, Leo J. '66 (DAV) LeClaire, IA Our Lady of the River; Defenders of the Bond.
Feeney, Martin E. *s.j.* '72 (NY).
Feeney, Robert E. '56 (GBG)[G] Greensburg, PA Neumann House.
Feeney, Robert E. '56 (BIS) Retired.
Feeney, Robert T. '86 (PH) Philadelphia, PA St. Clement.
Feeney, Thomas M. '48 (PH) Retired.
Feeney, Thomas P. (CC) Office of the Bishop; Tribunal; Judges; Canonical Affairs; Judicial Vicar
Feeney, William P. '72 (PIT) Washington, PA Immaculate Conception; Judges; Clergy Personnel Board.
Feeny, Michael *o.f.m.* '48 (PAT)[M] Ringwood, NJ Holy Name Friary, Inc..
Feeser, William '77 (SAC) Sacramento, CA Immaculate Conception; Sacramento, CA University of California, Davis Medical Center.
Fegan, Joseph Peter *o.p.* '01 (WDC)[B] Washington, DC Dominican House of Studies; [P] Providence St. Thomas Aquinas Priory at Providence College.
Fegan, William P. '75 (CHI) Cicero, IL Mary, Queen of Heaven.
Fehn, Jerome W. '78 (STP) Edina, MN Our Lady of Grace; Military Chaplains; Defenders of the Bond; Army National Guard Chaplains.
Fehrenbach, Charles '35 (ALB)[L] Saratoga Springs, NY St. John Neumann Residence.
Fehrenbach, James *o.f.m.* '71 (CIN).
Fehrenbacher, Henry '48 (SCL).
Fehring, Fabian *o.f.m.cap.* '53 (GF)[M] Hardin, MT St. Joseph's.
Feicht, Donald L. '70 (Y) Alliance, OH St. Joseph.
Feierfeil, Gerald F. (SC) Presbyteral Council; Episcopal Representative for Hospitals and Health Care.
Feierfeil, Gerald '67 (SC) Sioux City, IA Nativity of Our Lord Jesus Christ; Board of Education.
Feigh, Conan E. *o.s.b.* '57 (GBG)[H] Latrobe, PA Saint Vincent Archabbey.
Feil, Carl M. *o.s.m.* '61 (CHI)[N] Chicago Order of Friar Servants of Mary (Servites) United States of America Province Inc..
Feild, Martin E. (BAL) Advocates and Procurators; Priest Personnel Board.
Feild, Martin Eugene '59 (BAL) Taneytown, MD St. Joseph.
Feiss, Hugh *o.s.b.* '66 (B)[C] Jerome, ID Monastery of the Ascension.
Feit, Matthias '56 (PHX) Sun City, AZ St. Clement of Rome Retired.
Fekete, George J. '65 (GR) Lowell, MI St. Mary's; On Special Assignment.
Feketie, Michael J. '57 (NEW) Rahway, NJ St. Mary's.
Felago, John F. *m.m.* '68 (FgM).
Felczak, Leonard J. '44 (CHI) Retired.
Feld, Norbert F. *s.s.c.* '49 (PRO)[P] Bristol, RI St. Columban's Retirement House.
Feldcamp, William J. '65 (SCR) Scranton, PA St. Clare.
Feldhaus, Eugene A. '46 (BRK) Hollis, NY St. Gerard Majella; Ex Officio Members Retired.
Feldkamp, Angelo J. *o.praem.* '68 (GB)[I] De Pere, WI St. Norbert Abbey.
Feldmeier, Peter E. '87 (STP)[C] St. Paul, MN University of St. Thomas.
Feldmeier, Russell J. *m.m.* '80 (FgM).
Felice, John M. *o.f.m.* '68 (NY) New York, NY St. Francis of Assisi; [EE] New York, NY Franciscan Friars, Order of Friars Minor, Holy Name Province; [II] New York, NY Shrine of St. Jude, Inc.; [II] New York, NY Foundation of the Order of Friars Minor of the Province of the Most Holy Name.
Felices, Fernando B. (SJN) Graduate Studies.
Felion, Jerome '47 (CR) Retired.
Feliotas, Godofrcoo '83 (BRK) Brooklyn, NY St. Athanasius.
Felipe, Marvin P. *s.d.b.* '92 (SFR) San Francisco, CA Corpus Christi.
Felix, Paul G. '90 (GAL) Dickinson, TX Shrine of the True Cross.
Felix, William P. '81 (LC) Chippewa Falls, WI St. Charles Borromeo; Bloomer, WI St. John the Baptist; Chippewa Falls, WI St. Peter; [M] Chippewa Falls, WI Institute of St. Joseph; Deans.
Feliz, Manuel '92 (NY) New York, NY Our Lady Queen of Martyrs.
Feliz, Normando (VEN) Office of the Bishop; Continuing Education of Clergy.
Felker, Joseph '73 (SB) Riverside, CA St. Thomas the Apostle.
Fell, John N. '88 (MET) Bernardsville, NJ Our Lady of Perpetual Help; [K] Bernardsville, NJ Sacred Heart Chapel.
Fell, Timothy J. '99 (BAL) Ellicott City, MD Resurrection.
Fellenz, Ralph *o.f.m.cap.* '68 (FgM).
Feller, Donald J. '46 (GB) Retired.
Feller, Donald (GB) Priests Eucharistic League.
Feller, Richard J. '53 (CHI) Retired.
Fellin, Joseph *c.s.s.* '45 (BO)[Y] Waltham, MA Stigmatine Fathers and Brothers.
Fellrath, Frank W. '89 (MET) Old Bridge, NJ St. Ambrose.
Felt, James W. *s.j.* '56 (SJ)[B] Santa Clara, CA Jesuit Community.
Felt, Richard '69 (PHX) Scottsdale, AZ St. Bernadette.
Felter, Francis J. *m.m.* '69 (FgM).
Feltman, Philip S. '66 (TOL) Sandusky, OH St. Mary.
Feltman, Thomas '01 (FAR) Grand Forks, ND St. Michael.
Felton, Daniel J. '81 (GB) Oshkosh, WI St. Raphael the Archangel.
Feltz, John G. (BUR) Army National Guard Chaplains; Defenders of the Bond; Milton, VT St. Ann.
Feltz, Joseph E. '79 (PIT) Monongahela, PA St. Anthony.
Feltz, Joseph Michael '02 (IND) Richmond, IN Holy Family; Richmond, IN St. Andrew; Richmond, IN St. Mary; [C] Richmond, IN Seton Catholic High School.
Feltz, Thomas F. '85 (LA) Bellflower, CA St. Bernard.
Feminelli, John '87 (CC) Retired.
Fenech, Francis X. '50 (PMB) Lake Worth, FL Sacred Heart Retired.
Fenelon, David '70 (DM) Retired.
Fenger, Guy '77 (MIA) Absent on Leave.
Fenili, J. Robert *c.ss.r.* '62 (CHI)[N] Chicago, IL Redemptorist Theology Residence.
Fenlon, John P. '70 (SY) Cortland, NY St. Mary; Pastoral Examiners.
Fenlon, Thomas B. '61 (NY) Bronx, NY St. Augustine.
Fenlon, Thomas J. '42 (HEL) Retired.
Fennell, Joseph G. *s.j.* '45 (BO)[V] Weston, MA Campion Health Center, Inc..
Fennell, Patrick A. *o.s.b.* '89 (PEO).
Fenner, Eric *o.f.m.conv.* '46 (TR)[A] Seaside Park, NJ St. Catharine of Siena.
Fennessey, Keith (NY) Absent on Sick leave.
Fennessy, James J. '68 (ATL) Atlanta, GA St. Jude.
Fennessy, James '02 (ROC) Geneva, NY St. Francis de Sales; Geneva, NY St. Stephen.
Fennessy, Joseph H. '56 (HBG) Retired.
Fennessy, Peter J. *s.j.* '70 (DET)[P] Bloomfield Hills, MI Manresa Jesuit Retreat House.
Fenske, Donald J. '58 (CHI) Calumet City, IL Our Lady of Knock Retired.
Fenstermaker, James *c.s.c.* '84 (FR)[A] North Easton, MA Holy Cross Fathers Religious.
Fenton, Cornelius *c.pp.s.* '49 (CIN)[B] Carthagena, OH St. Charles.
Fenton, Jerry F. (STP) St. Paul, MN Blessed Sacrament.
Fenton, Joseph D. *s.m.* '72 (ORG) Cypress, CA St. Irenaeus.
Fenton, Lawrence E. '63 (GI) Retired.
Fenton, Norman H. *o.p.* '62 (WDC)[B] Washington, DC Dominican House of Studies.
Fenzl, Rod *o.praem.* '55 (SFE)[I] Albuquerque, NM Santa Maria de la Vid Priory.
Fenzl, Roderick R. *o.praem.* '55 (GB)[I] De Pere, WI St. Norbert Abbey.
Ferangco, Nicanor '84 (DOD) Kinsley, KS St. Nicholas;

Diocesan School Council.
Ference, Damian J. '03 (CLV) Hudson, OH St. Mary.
Ferens, Boniface D. '64 (BUF) Retired.
Ferens, Joseph F. '53 (DET) Retired.
Feret, Francis S. '62 (PH) Philadelphia, PA St. Adalbert; Polish Apostolate.
Fergeus, Kieran *o.p.* (PAT)[O] Madison, NJ Drew University Catholic Campus Ministry; [O] Madison, NJ Catholic Campus Ministry.
Ferguson, Gary M. '71 (TOL) Archbold, OH St. Peter; Archbold, OH St. John the Evangelist.
Ferguson, James A. (ALX) Defender of the Bond; Plaucheville, LA Mater Dolorosa; Promoters of Justice.
Ferguson, James J. *c.s.c.* '61 (FTW) South Bend, IN Holy Cross; South Bend, IN St. Stanislaus.
Ferguson, John *s.j.* '54 (SLC) Ogden, UT St. Mary's.
Ferguson, Paul Anthony '02 (EVN) Evansville, IN Holy Redeemer.
Ferguson, Robert *f.s.s.p.* '02 (SCR)[M] Rapid City, SD; Tulsa, OK Parish of Saint Peter.
Ferguson, Ronald J. *s.j.* '65 (CHI).
Ferguson, Thomas P. '94 (ARL) Springfield, VA St. Bernadette's; Defenders of the Bond; Ecumenical and Interreligious Affairs Commission; Presbyteral Council.
Ferland, Martin *o.mar.* '95 (SAM)[C] Petersham, MA Most Holy Trinity Monastery.
Ferland, Thomas J. '87 (PRO) Bristol, RI St. Elizabeth.
Ferlita, Ernest *s.j.* '62 (NO)[C] New Orleans, LA Loyola University New Orleans.
Ferme, Brian '80 (WDC)[C] Washington, DC Catholic University of America, The.
Fermeglia, Charles '88 (BRK) On Leave/Unassigned.
Fernan, Matthew F. '89 (NY) Scarsdale, NY Immaculate Heart of Mary.
Fernandes, Babasino '75 (FTW) Ligonier, IN Blessed Sacrament; Ligonier, IN St. Patrick.
Fernandes, Cyril '87 (FTW) Fort Wayne, IN St. Patrick.
Fernandes, David A. '97 (PH) Philadelphia, PA St. Anselm.
Fernandes, Earl K. '02 (CIN) Sidney, OH Holy Angels.
Fernandes, John '77 (OAK) Oakland, CA St. Cyril; Oakland, CA St. Lawrence O'Toole.
Fernandes, Jose Manuel '59 (NEW) Elizabeth, NJ Our Lady of Fatima.
Fernandes, Lourdino '59 (FTW) South Bend, IN St. John the Baptist.
Fernandes, Mauro de Souza *o.s.b.* '84 (GBG)[H] Latrobe Saint Vincent Archabbey.
Fernandes, Patrick O. '83 (BUF) Buffalo General Hospital.
Fernandes, Peter *s.f.x.* '99 (P) Beaverton, OR St. Cecilia.
Fernandes, Rogue '69 (LA) Azusa, CA St. Frances of Rome.
Fernandes, Stephen A. '76 (FR) New Bedford, MA Our Lady of Fatima; Pro–Life Apostolate; Air Force Reserve Chaplains.
Fernandes, Sydney '79 (HON) Kahuku, HI St. Roch; Kaneohe, HI Our Lady of Mt. Carmel.
Fernandes De Araujo, Herondi '76 (PAT)[M] Wayne, NJ Xaverian Missionary Fathers.
Fernandez, Cesar A. '95 (LA) La Puente, CA St. Louis of France.
Fernandez, Daniel '96 (ARE)[A] Arecibo, PR Seminario de Jesus Maestro; Priest's Senate (Consejo Presbiteral); Seminario Jesus Maestro College Seminary; Pastoral Vocational Program; Retreat House, Centro Diocesano Mons. Mendez; Vocations.
Fernandez, Daniel (SJN) San Juan Bautista Regional Seminary.
Fernandez, Daniel (ARE) Diocesan Consultors.
Fernandez, Eduardo C. *s.j.* '92 (NO)[N] Berkeley, CA Jesuit Community at Jesuit School of Theology at Berkeley.
Fernandez, Eduardo *s.j.* (OAK).
Fernandez, Edward P. '70 (DAL) Retired.
Fernandez, Elias *o.ss.t.* '69 (ARE)[A] Isabela, PR St. Anthony; Diocesan Consultors; Priest's Senate (Consejo Presbiteral).
Fernandez, Emmanuel '79 (LAF) Berwick, LA St. Stephen.
Fernandez, Felipe *o.s.a.* '71 (SJN) Bayamon, PR San Agustin.
Fernandez, Fidel '74 (CGS) Cayey, PR Nuestra Senora de la Merced.
Fernandez, Francis X. *o.f.m.cap.* (FWT) Cursillo.
Fernandez, Francis *o.f.m.cap.* '58 (FWT) Fort Worth, TX Our Lady of Guadalupe.
Fernandez, Frank '79 (PHX) Phoenix, AZ St. Joseph.
Fernandez, Gerardo '91 (SD) San Diego, CA Holy Family.
Fernandez, Jorge I. *m.x.y.* '88 (NY)[EE] Bronx, NY Yarumal Mission Society, Inc.; Bronx, NY Our Saviour.
Fernandez, Jose A. '60 (BGP) Retired.
Fernandez, Jose Luis *o.ss.t.* '69 (PCE) Ponce, PR La Santisima Trinidad.
Fernandez, Jose Maria '59 (GAL) Houston, TX St. Frances Cabrini.
Fernandez, Jose *o.p.* '53 (PCE) Yauco, PR Holy Rosary.
Fernandez, Jose '70 (NEW) Orange, NJ St. John's.
Fernandez, Julio (MGZ) Censor Librorum; Religious Consultor; Religious Coordinator.
Fernandez, Luis J. '71 (NO) On Duty Outside the Archdiocese.
Fernandez, Manuel A. '62 (ORL) Eustis, FL St. Mary of the Lakes.
Fernandez, Manuel (ORL) Deans; Members; Consultors.
Fernandez, Marcellus '68 (B) Emmett, ID Sacred Heart.
Fernandez, Miguel A. '50 (MIA) Retired.
Fernandez, Nelson '56 (MIA) Retired.
Fernandez, Nobincio *ss.cc.* '65 (HON)[G] Kaneohe, HI Sacred Hearts Center.
Fernandez, Rafael *o.f.m.* '87 (FgM).
Fernandez, Rodolfo '98 (HT) Houma, LA Annunziata.
Fernandez, Romualdo *c.m.f.* '53 (SJN) Bayamon, PR Santa Maria.
Fernandez, Salvador *l.c.* '84 (LA)[Q] Pasadena, CA Legionaries of Christ.
Fernandez, Serapio '50 (ARE) Arecibo, PR Church of Christ the King.
Fernandez, Vicente '82 (SJN) Guaynabo, PR Maria Madre de la Misericordia.
Fernandez–Bueno, Alirio '96 (AUS) Austin, TX St. Louis.
Fernandez–Marino, Vicente (SJN) Cursillos De Cristiandad.
Fernandez–Mendez, Jose R. '59 (SJN) Retired.
Fernando, A. Thomas '66 (KAL) Kalamazoo, MI St. Augustine Cathedral.
Fernando, Augustine '64 (RVC) Farmingdale, NY St. Kilian.
Fernando, Bernard '65 (NEW) Montclair, NJ Mountainside Hospital; Nutley, NJ St. Mary's; Chaplains.
Fernando, Cresus '82 (NY) Nyack, NY St. Ann.
Fernando, Damian '70 (LA) Tujunga, CA Our Lady of Lourdes.
Fernando, Gamini E. '71 (NY) Poughkeepsie, NY Holy Trinity; Green Haven Correctional Facility.
Fernando, Joachim '62 (BRK) Rosedale, NY St. Pius X.
Fernando, Lionel '87 (TYL) Grand Saline, TX St. Celestine; Emory, TX St. John the Evangelist Church.
Fernando, Peter '64 (BAK) Enterprise, OR St. Katherine's.
Fernando, Polycarp '78 (FTW) Bremen, IN St. Dominic.
Fernando, Roger Marcus '76 (LA) West Covina, CA St. Christopher.
Fernando, Sebastian M. '70 (NEW) Glen Rock, NJ St. Catharine.
Fernando, Sebastian '70 (NEW) Paramus, NJ Bergen Regional Medical Center; Chaplains.
Fernando, Shelton '78 (FRS) Visalia, CA St. Mary.
Fernando, Simon '60 (RVC) Commack, NY Christ the King.
Fernando, Sriyananda (RVC) Lynbrook, NY Our Lady of Peace.
Fernando, Stan '78 (CHI)[J] Elk Grove Village, IL Alexian Brothers Medical Center.
Fernando, Susil '87 (LKC) Vinton, LA St. Joseph; Priest's Senate.
Fernando, Venantius M. '61 (NEW) Hillside, NJ Christ the King.
Fernando, Venantius (NEW) Archdiocesan Incardination Board; Adjunct Clergy Personnel; Ex Officio Members.
Fernando, Walter '73 (LA) Pasadena, CA Assumption of the Blessed Virgin Mary.
Fernz, John (BO) Wrentham, MA Wrentham State School.
Ferone, John M. *s.j.* '83 (CIN)[M] Cincinnati, OH Faber Jesuit Community.
Ferraioli, Frank B. '61 (PAT) Parsippany, NJ St. Christopher.
Ferraioli, Joseph *o.m.i.* '77 (NO) International Shrine of St. Jude.
Ferrante, Frank J. *c.m.f.* '70 (LA)[Q] Los Angeles, CA Prov. Headquarters of the Western Prov. of the USA; [Q] Los Angeles, CA Claretian Retreat Center Community; [W] Los Angeles, CA Claretian Retreat Center (All Groups).
Ferrante, Frank *c.m.f.* (LA) Coordinators:.
Ferrara, Alberto A. *c.s.b.* (GAL)[Q] Sugar Land Basilian Mission Center.
Ferrara, Bede *o.f.m.* '50 (BO)[V] Lynn, MA Franciscan Community (Province of Immaculate Conception).
Ferrara, Charles F. *s.j.* '90 (STL) Wildwood, MO St. Alban Roe.
Ferrara, John *o.m.v.* '82 (BO).
Ferrara, Joseph R. '77 (CAM)[B] Egg Harbor Township, NJ St. Katharine Drexel; Priests Personnel Board.
Ferrarese, Fernando '77 (BRK) Brooklyn, NY St. Therese of Lisieux; [L] Brooklyn, NY Italian Board of Guardians; Brooklyn East; Assignment Board; Liturgical Commission.
Ferrari, Steven A. '80 (BRK) Ozone Park, NY St. Elizabeth's.
Ferraro, Joseph A. '90 (NEW) Newark, NJ St. Anthony's.
Ferraro, Joseph '67 (OAK) Retired.
Ferraro, Michael M. '68 (BO) Lynn, MA St. Mary.
Ferraro, Pat '92 (Y) Streetsboro, OH St. Joan of Arc.
Ferraro, Ronald A. '60 (HRT) Waterbury, CT Our Lady of Lourdes; Waterbury, CT St. Lucy's.
Ferraro, Vincent J. '70 (BUF)[K] Kenmore, NY Kenmore Mercy Hospital; Kenmore, NY St. Andrew.
Ferrazoli, Henry R. '61 (NEW) Retired.
Ferrazzi, Charles J. '02 (BO) Stoughton, MA Immaculate Conception.
Ferrecchia, Leonard J. *c.s.s.* '55 (BO) Milford, MA Sacred Heart.
Ferreira, Alfonse *o.f.m.* '72 (BO)[V] Lynn, MA Franciscan Community (Province of Immaculate Conception); [V] Lynn, MA "The Listening Place" (Counseling Center).
Ferreira, Jose S. '56 (BO) Cambridge, MA St. Anthony.
Ferreira, Joseph A. '59 (OAK)[M] Oakland, CA Bishop Begin Villa Retired.
Ferreira, Manuel P. '60 (FR) Retired.
Ferrer, Charles M. '64 (CHI) Chicago, IL St. Mary of the Angels; [W] Chicago, IL Midtown Center.
Ferrer, Chris (AUS) Moderator of the Curia.
Ferrer, Christopher *m.f.* (AUS) Marlin, TX Sacred Heart; Marlin, TX St. Joseph's; Adjutant Judicial Vicar; Diocesan Judges.
Ferrer, Gonzalo *t.o.r.* '81 (AUS) Austin, TX San Francisco; AUXILIARY CHAPLAINS CONTRACT CHAPLAINS.
Ferrer, Joaquin *s.v.d.* '87 (CHI)[B] Techny, IL Divine Word Residence.
Ferrer, Jorge *s.j.* '77 (SJN)[H] San Juan, PR Comunidad Jesuita.
Ferrer, Peter C. '61 (LA) Retired.
Ferrer Martinez, Miguel '67 (SJN) On Duty Outside the Archdiocese.
Ferrero, Anthony T. (SB) Adjutant Judicial Vicar; Judges.
Ferrero, Anthony '81 (SB) Perris, CA St. James; Special or Other Diocesan Assignment; Vicars Forane; College of Consultors; Appointed Members.
Ferrero, Bartholomew '60 (DET) Retired.
Ferrett, Walter L. '66 (SCR) Scranton, PA Sacred Hearts of Jesus and Mary.
Ferretti, Sam (CAM) Cape May, NJ United States Coast Guard, Command Chaplain's Office; Navy Chaplains.
Ferretti, Samuel J. '74 (SCR) Military Chaplains.
Ferri, Gregory '98 (BAL) Pasadena, MD St. Jane Frances de Chantal.
Ferrick, Michael P. '99 (E) Erie, PA St. Jude the Apostle.
Ferrick, Raymond J. '77 (PRO) Barrington, RI Holy Angels.
Ferrie, Francis '65 (NO) New Orleans, LA Incarnate Word; New Orleans, LA St. Theresa of the Child Jesus.
Ferrier, Francis V. *s.j.* '61 (BR) Baton Rouge, LA Sacred Heart of Jesus; Special Assignment.
Ferrier, Ronald J. '68 (PH)[BB] Philadelphia, PA Provincial House of the Sisters of the Holy Family of Nazareth.
Ferrigan, Robert E. '61 (CHI) Winnetka, IL Sacred Heart.
Ferring, Robert L. '50 (DUB) Holy Childhood, Pontifical Association; Propagation of the Faith Retired.
Ferris, Carl A. '55 (GI) Retired.
Ferris, James *c.ss.r.* '35 (ALB)[L] Saratoga Springs, NY St. John Neumann Residence.
Ferris, Norman J. '53 (SAM) Appointed Members Retired.
Ferris, Robert '01 (CHL) Greensboro, NC St. Benedict.
Ferris, Thomas B. '63 (PIT) Pittsburgh, PA St. Cyril of Alexandria; Deans and Deaneries.
Ferris, Timothy F. '03 (TOL) Tiffin, OH St. Mary.
Ferrito, Joseph L. (PAT) Retired.
Ferro, Ralph '71 (RVC) New Hyde Park, NY Holy Spirit; East Meadow, NY Nassau County Correctional Center; Chaplains.
Ferruzzi, William A. *s.d.b.* '76 (COL)[E] Tampa, FL Mary Help of Christians School.
Ferry, James T. *m.m.* '56 (FgM).
Ferry, James '84 (FR) Fall River, MA Espirito Santo.
Ferry, John T. '84 (NY) New York, NY Cathedral of St. Patrick.
Feser, Victor *o.s.b.* '64 (BIS)[A] Richardton, ND Assumption Abbey; [B] Bismarck, ND University of Mary.
Fesniak, Mark '03 (PHU) Press, The Way.
Fessio, Joseph D. *s.j.* '72 (SJ)[M] Los Gatos Sacred Heart Jesuit Center.
Fest, Donald M. *s.s.j.* '76 (WDC) Washington, DC Our Lady of Perpetual Help.
Festle, Robert H. '55 (CHI)[X] Wilmette, IL Musica Pacis Retired.
Fesuh, Tesfay Woldemarian '88 (WDC) Washington, DC St. Anthony.
Fetcho, John E. '64 (SY) Syracuse, NY Our Lady of Peace.
Fete, Kevin L. '85 (Y) North Canton, OH St. Therese Little Flower.
Fetscher, James F. '68 (MIA) Pinecrest, FL St. Louis.

Fetscher, James (MIA) Deans and Deaneries.
Fetters, Donald G. *c.s.c.* '76 (FTW)[I] Congregacion de Santa Cruz.
Feucht, Urban C. '55 (SEA)[L] Lacey, WA St. Martin's Abbey.
Feucht, Urban *o.s.b.* '55 (SEA)[G] Tacoma, WA St. Joseph Medical Center.
Feudjio, Jerome '90 (STV) Charlotte Amalie, VI Cathedral of Sts. Peter and Paul; Chancellor; Diocesan Consultors; Catholic Television Network (CTN); Prison Ministry; Carenage, VI Chapel of St. Anne.
Feusahrens, Frederick J. '72 (RIC) Richmond, VA St. Paul.
Feusahrens, Frederick J. (MO) Judges.
Feusahrens, Frederick J. (BAL) Interdiocesan Judges.
Fey, Albert J. *c.pp.s.* '46 (KCK) Baileyville, KS Sacred Heart.
Fey, Christian *o.f.m.cap.* '45 (SAL).
Fey, Joseph H. *c.s.c.* '51 (FTW)[I] Notre Dame, IN Holy Cross House.
Fey, Thomas J. '70 (ALX) Military Chaplains.
Fey, Thomas J. (LUB) Air Force Chaplains.
Fey, William *o.f.m.cap.* '68 (FgM).
Fiala, John M. '84 (CC)[G] Robstown, TX Society of Our Lady of the Most Holy Trinity.
Fiala, Timothy R. '96 (CHI) Graduate Studies.
Fiala, Vit *o.f.m.* '98 (Y)[J] Youngstown, OH Mt. Alverna Friary.
Fialkowski, Edward R. '78 (CHI) Niles, IL St. Isaac Jogues; College of Consultors; Presbyteral Council.
Fialkowski, Thomas M. '66 (E) Veterans Administration Hospital; Board of Members.
Fiano, Guy *o.carm.* '83 (PMB)[B] Boca Raton, FL Pope John Paul II High School; [J] Boca Raton, FL St. Elias Priory–Order of Carmelites, NY.
Fice, Joseph J. *s.j.* '72 (SJ)[L] Los Altos, CA Jesuit Retreat House.
Ficenec, Leonard C. '57 (OM) Retired.
Fichteman, William L. '81 (L) Louisville, KY Cathedral of the Assumption; Archdiocesan Examiners.
Fichter, Stephen J. (NEW) Saddle River Borough, NJ St. Gabriel the Archangel.
Fichtner, Joseph A. *o.s.c.* '43 (PHX)[G] Phoenix, AZ Crosier Community of Phoenix (Canons Regular of the Order of the Holy Cross).
Fichtner, Robert C. '55 (BO) Senior Priests; Archdiocesan College of Consultors Retired.
Fick, David J. '88 (ALN) Reading, PA Sacred Heart; Reading Hospital and Medical Center.
Fickel, William F. *s.s.s.* '81 (CLV) Houston, TX Corpus Christi.
Fickes, Daniel R. '91 (CLV) Litchfield, OH Our Lady Help of Christians Parish; Presbyteral Conveners.
Ficorilli, Chad R. *o.s.b.* '79 (ALT) Hastings, PA St. Bernard.
Fictum, Robert A. '78 (MIL) Ripon, WI St. Patrick; Ripon, WI St. Wenceslaus.
Fidalgo, Federico '63 (CC) Retired.
Fider, William P. '66 (DUL) Duluth, MN St. Michael's.
Fider, William (DUL) Priests' Pension Board.
Fiebelkorn, Daniel F. '97 (BUF) Council of Priests; Grand Island, NY St. Stephen.
Fiedler, Donald J. '59 (DOD) Retired.
Fiedler, Ernest J. '52 (KC) Kansas City, MO Cathedral of Immaculate Conception; Kansas City, MO Old St. Patrick's.
Fiedler, Kenneth J. '71 (MAD) Madison, WI Our Lady, Queen of Peace; Deaneries; Saint Joseph.
Fiedorczyk, Henry P. '42 (HRT) New Britain, CT Sacred Heart of Jesus Retired.
Fiedorowicz, Joseph '75 (OAK) Brentwood, CA Immaculate Heart of Mary.
Fiedurek, Jan *s.chr.* '89 (MIA) Houston, TX Our Lady of Czestochowa.
Field, Eugene J. '94 (NEW) Ridgefield Park, NJ St. Francis of Assisi; Boy Scouts of America/Catholic Committee on Scouting.
Field, James A. '90 (BO) Melrose, MA Incarnation of Our Lord and Savior Jesus Christ.
Field, Michael J. '82 (CAM) Swedesboro, NJ St. Joseph's.
Field, Raymund *c.s.v.* '48 (SJ) Saratoga, CA Church of the Ascension.
Field, Tom *g.h.m.* '78 (CIN)[M] Cincinnati Headquarters of Glenmary Home Missioners.
Fields, Dominic *o.p.* '91 (WDC)[B] Washington, DC Dominican House of Studies.
Fields, John '86 (PHU) Warrington, PA Presentation of Our Lord; Warrington, PA St. Anne's; [D] Philadelphia, PA Ascension Manor, Inc.; College of Archeparchial Counsultors; Presbyteral Council; Archeparchial Corporation; Archeparchial Council for Economic Affairs; Apostolate.
Fields, Robert H. '82 (JC) Jefferson City, MO St. Peter; Russellville, MO St. Michael.
Fields, Robert '82 (JC)[B] Jefferson City, MO St. Mary's Health Center.
Fields, Stephen M. *s.j.* '86 (WDC)[M] Washington, DC The Jesuit Community at Georgetown University.
Fields, William '91 (MOB) On Leave from the Archdiocese.
Fier, Brian J. STP) Presbyteral Council.
Fierro, David G. '76 (ELP) El Paso, TX St. Matthew; Defenders of the Bond.
Fierro, David ELP) Finance Council.
Fierros, Rick '78 (FRS) Delano, CA St. Mary's of the Miraculous Medal.
Fifagrowicz, Joseph G. '62 (BUF) Lyndonville, NY St. Joseph; Medina, NY Sacred Heart.
Figaredo, Tarsicio Gotay *o.carm.* '73 (SJN) San Juan, PR Santa Teresita Del Nino Jesus; Subcommission for Popular Piety.
Figel, Terence J. *o.m.i.* '64 (PMB) West Palm Beach, FL St. John Fisher.
Figge, Urban '57 (BEL)[F] Belleville, IL Missionary Oblates of Mary Immaculate – St. Henry's Oblate Residence.
Figler, Michael B. '98 (TR) Hamilton, NJ St. Raphael.
Figlia, Sidney *s.d.b.* '68 (NO) Harvey, LA St. John Bosco.
Figliola, Nicholas J. '64 (RVC) Coram, NY St. Frances Cabrini.
Figliozzi, Richard M. '79 (RVC) Freeport, NY Our Holy Redeemer.
Figueiredo, Anthony J. '94 (NEW).
Figueiredo, Anthony (NEW)[B] School of Diplomacy and Intl. Rels..
Figueredo, Sergio *s.j.* '60 (MIA) Miami, FL Gesu.
Figuereido, Anthony (NEW) Censors of Books.
Figueroa, Alberto *o.f.m.cap.* '90 (SJN) San Juan, PR San Francisco de Asis.
Figueroa, Domingo *c.r.l.* '96 (ARE) Corozal, PR La Milagrosa.
Figueroa, Edward *o.m.i.* '60 (FgM).
Figueroa, Henecimo '99 (BWN) Edinburg, TX Immaculate Conception; San Isidro, TX St. Isidore; Presbyteral Council; Rio Grande City; [A] Mission, TX The Saint Joseph and Saint Peter Seminary.
Figueroa, Jose I. (DAL) Dallas, TX Cathedral–Santuario de Guadalupe.
Figueroa, Marco Antonio *o.f.m.* '93 (OAK) Oakland, CA St. Elizabeth's; Oakland, CA Mary Help of Christians Church; [F] Oakland, CA Franciscan Friars; Deans.
Figueroa, Oscar '00 (SAC) On Duty Outside the Diocese.
Figueroa, Ruben C. *o.f.m.* (TYL) Hispanic Ministry Advisory Council.
Figueroa, Ruben '70 (TYL) Tyler, TX Our Lady of Guadalupe; Priests' Personnel Board.
Figueroa Esquer, Francisco J. '01 (OAK) Hayward, CA St. Clement.
Figueroa Sanchez, Angel '86 (SJN) Bayamon, PR Santa Teresa de Jesus.
Figuerola, Adrian '71 (IND)[I] Indianapolis, IN St. Augustine Home, Little Sisters of the Poor.
Figurelli, Nicholas G. '82 (NEW)[D] Summit, NJ The Oratory Catholic Preparatory School.
Filacchione, Marc A. '80 (NY) New York, NY St. Michael; New York Fire Department.
Filardi, Edward J. (WDC) Secretary To The Archbishop; Pastoral Center Special Ministries.
Filary, Richard M. '82 (SAG) Midland, MI Assumption Blessed Virgin Mary; Vicars for Vicariates; Judges.
Filho, Felix I. (BO) Brazilian Community Centers; Stoughton, MA Immaculate Conception.
Filiatreau, Hilary *o.s.b.* '49 (LR) Altus, AR St. Mary.
Filice, Francis '79 (SFR) San Francisco, CA St. Thomas the Apostle Retired.
Filice, Peter F. *s.j.* '71 (SJ)[B] Santa Clara, CA Jesuit Community.
Filice, Peter *s.j.* (SJ) Council of Religious.
Filice, Richard W. '76 (CC) Robstown, TX St. Anthony.
Filipkowski, Peter '86 (PAT) Newton, NJ St. Joseph's.
Filippelli, John L.M. *s.s.j.* '57 (WDC)[B] Washington, DC St. Joseph's Seminary.
Filippello, Michael A. (PH) Springfield, PA St. Francis of Assisi.
Filippini, Renato *s.x.* '97 (PAT)[M] Wayne Xaverian Missionary Fathers.
Filips, Mark D. '89 (OM) O'Neill, NE St Patrick.
Filipski, Raymond R. '75 (NEW) Bergenfield, NJ St. John the Evangelist.
Fillion, Normand A. *o.m.i.* '50 (MAN) Lowell, MA Saint Jeanne d'Arc; Manchester, NH St. Antnony of Padua.
Fillion, Stephen '79 (SAG) Cass City, MI St. Pancratius.
Fillion, Steve (SAG) Vicars for Vicariates.
Fillman, G. Allan '77 (TOL) Paulding, OH St. Joseph; Payne, OH St. John the Baptist; Defiance Deanery.
Filmanski, Francis E. '53 (RVC) Floral Park, NY St. Hedwig's.
Filmyer, Bernard G. *s.j.* '52 (BAL)[S] San Diego, CA.
Filut, David C. '68 (MIL) New Berlin, WI Holy Apostles.
Fimbel, Duane G. '57 (BUF) North Tonawanda, NY DeGraff Memorial Hospital; North Tonawanda, NY St. Albert the Great.
Fimiani, Louis F. '60 (NEW) Roseland, NJ Our Lady of the Blessed Sacrament.
Fin, Robert G. '43 (E)[B] Erie, PA Gannon University Retired.
Finamore, Robert A. '70 (WDC) Oxon Hill, MD St. Ignatius.
Finan, James '59 (WDC)[L] Washington, DC Cardinal O'Boyle Residence for Priests.
Finch, G. William '89 (WDC) Rockville, MD St. Raphael.
Finch, Joseph E. '58 (OM) Retired.
Finch, Joseph E. '58 (ALB)[M] Germantown, NY St. Teresa's Motherhouse.
Fincutter, John F. *s.v.d.* '50 (MIL)[O] East Troy, WI Divine Word Missionaries.
Fincutter, Patrick *s.v.d.* '55 (MIL)[O] East Troy, WI Divine Word Missionaries.
Finder, James '91 (JC) Bourbon, MO St. Francis; Cuba, MO Holy Cross; Bourbon, MO St. Michael.
Finder, L. James (JC) Personnel Board.
Findlan, Joseph G. '38 (PIT)[N] Pittsburgh, PA St. John Vianney Manor Retired.
Findlay, David '62 (E) Meadville, PA Crawford County Care Center.
Findlay, David '67 (E) Meadville, PA St. Brigid.
Finegan, Gerard '67 (VEN) Sarasota, FL Incarnation; College of Consultors; Vicar for Priests.
Finegan, Lawrence J. '70 (SFR) San Francisco, CA Cathedral of St. Mary (Assumption).
Finelli, Jay A. '92 (PRO) Tiverton, RI Holy Ghost.
Finelli, Victor F. '89 (ALN) Allentown, PA St. Paul; Promoter of Justice; Judges.
Fineo, Richard '02 (FAR) Fargo, ND Nativity.
Fineran, A. Gerard *s.j.* '50 (NO).
Finerty, Bernard *o.f.m.cap.* '61 (BAL)[P] Cumberland, MD SS. Peter and Paul; [S] Cumberland, MD SS. Peter and Paul Friary.
Finerty, D. Bryan '59 (PRO) Woonsocket, RI St. Charles.
Finerty, Raymond *o.p.* '71 (LA) Los Angeles, CA St. Dominic.
Fink, Charles R. '76 (RVC) Hewlett, NY St. Joseph's.
Fink, Daniel *o.f.m.conv.* (NOR) Stafford Springs, CT St. Edward.
Fink, Frederick T. '61 (NU) Spicer, MN St. Anthony (Mission); Spicer, MN Our Lady of the Lakes.
Fink, John L. '67 (IND) Bradford, IN St. Michael.
Fink, John '71 (MIA) Special Assignment.
Fink, Joseph '83 (STP) Shakopee, MN St. Mary.
Fink, Karel '91 (AUS) Smithville, TX St. Paul the Apostle.
Fink, Peter *s.j.* '69 (BO)[V] Cambridge, MA.
Fink, Philip *o.f.m.cap.* '77 (PIT) Rochester, PA St. Cecilia; Beaver County, PA Villa St. Joseph; [N] Rochester, PA St. Cecilia Friary; [O] Baden, PA Sisters of St. Joseph–St. Joseph Convent.
Finken, Basil *o.s.b.* '40 (KCK)[H] Atchison, KS St. Benedict's Abbey.
Finlan, Robert T. '94 (ALN) Reading, PA Holy Guardian Angels; [C] Reading, PA Holy Name High School; Reading Serra.
Finlay, Joseph F. '57 (STA) Palatka, FL St. Monica's.
Finley, James F. '63 (BRK) Released from Diocesan Assignment; Navy Chaplains.
Finley, Jeffrey *c.pp.s.* '90 (OAK) Newark, CA St. Edward's; Washington Hospital.
Finley, John Thomas '75 (LAF) On Special Assignment.
Finley, Thomas M. *c.m.* '54 (PH).
Finley, Thomas '75 (LAF)[AA] Lafayette, LA Our Lady of Wisdom, University of Louisiana.
Finn, Daniel J. '72 (BO) Dorchester, MA St. Mark; Irish; Dorchester, MA St. Peter.
Finn, David '03 (RCK) St. Charles, IL St. Patrick.
Finn, Dominick F. *o.s.f.s.* '56 (PH) Norristown, PA St. Francis of Assisi; Norristown, PA Norristown State Hospital.
Finn, Edward S. '52 (SCR) On Special or Other Diocesan Assignment.
Finn, Firman *o.f.m.conv.* '55 (ALB)[L] Rensselaer, NY Provincialate, Immaculate Conception Friary – Order of Friars Minor Conventual.
Finn, Firmin *o.f.m.conv.* '55 (ALB)[A] Rensselaer, NY Conventual Franciscan Friars; [J] Latham, NY Our Lady of Hope Residence.
Finn, Francis J. '39 (NEW) Retired.
Finn, Gregory T. *o.s.j.* '89 (SCR)[B] Pittston, PA St. Joseph's Oblate Seminary; [M] Pittston, PA Eastern Province of the Oblates of St. Joseph.
Finn, James F. *o.f.m.* '02 (SFD) Quincy, IL St. Francis Solanus; [L] Quincy, IL St. Francis Solanus Friary.
Finn, John A. *o.s.f.s.* '62 (WIL)[J] Wilmington, DE DeSales House.
Finn, John P. '81 (NO) Luling, LA Holy Family.
Finn, John *o.s.f.s.* '62 (WIL) Wilmington, DE St. Francis Hospital; [I] Wilmington, DE St. Francis Hospital, Inc..
Finn, Joseph P. '98 (LIN) Lincoln, NE St. Mary.
Finn, Michael E. '77 (SCR) Moscow, PA St. Catherine of Siena.
Finn, Peter G. '65 (NY)[A] Yonkers, NY St. Joseph's Seminary; [I] New York, NY The Ladies of Charity of the Catholic Charities of the Archdiocese of New York.
Finn, Peter (NY) Archdiocesan Consultors.
Finn, Raymond C. *o.p.* '70 (NO)[P] Metairie, LA Southern Dominican Foundation; [S] Metairie, LA

Southern Dominican Foundation; Metropolitan Tribunal.
Finn, Robert E. *s.j.* '91 (CHI)[N] Chicago, IL Woodlawn Jesuit Community.
Finn, Robert W. '79 (STL) Webster Groves, MO Holy Redeemer.
Finn, Robert *s.j.* (CHI) Chicago, IL John H. Stroger, Jr. Hospital of Cook County.
Finn, Seamus P. *o.m.i.* '76 (WDC)[M] Washington, DC Provincial Offices of the United States Province of the Missionary Oblates of Mary Immaculate; [M] Washington, DC Oblate Community.
Finn, William P. *c.m.* '48 (PH)[AA] St. Catherine Infirmary.
Finnane, Daniel P. '63 (MAD) Waunakee, WI St. Mary of the Lake.
Finnegan, Charles *o.f.m.* '58 (PH)[AA] Philadelphia, PA Order of Friars Minor of the Province of the Most Holy Name.
Finnegan, Gerald F. *s.j.* '67 (BO)[V] Boston The Society of Jesus of New England–Provincial Offices; [C] Jesuit Fathers; [AA] Loyola Center and Manresa Hall.
Finnegan, J. Kevin '96 (STP) Faribault, MN Divine Mercy Catholic Church.
Finnegan, James P. *o.s.f.s.* '58 (ALN) Bethlehem, PA Assumption B.V.M.; [B] Center Valley, PA DeSales University; [K] Center Valley, PA Oblates of St. Francis de Sales.
Finnegan, John P. '54 (CHI) Retired.
Finnegan, John T. '60 (BO) Senior Priests Retired.
Finnegan, Joseph '65 (HEL) Retired.
Finnegan, Michael J. '74 (SP) Clearwater, FL St. Catherine of Siena.
Finnegan, Robert K. *o.praem.* '52 (GB)[I] De Pere, WI St. Norbert Abbey; [N] De Pere, WI Canons Regular of Magnovarad, Ltd.; [N] De Pere, WI Norbertine Generalate, Inc.; Bishop's Finance Council.
Finnegan, Roscoe L. '47 (SCL) Retired.
Finnegan, Thomas J. '51 (BO) Senior Priests Retired.
Finnegan, William J. '57 (CHI) Flossmoor, IL Infant Jesus of Prague Retired.
Finnell, Eugene '56 (PEO) Retired.
Finnell, John H. '78 (WH) Camden, WV St. Boniface.
Finnell, Terrell M. '92 (KC) Lexington, MO Immaculate Conception.
Finnell, Terrell (KC) Presbyteral Council; Deans.
Finnerty, D. Joseph '63 (BRK) Flushing, NY St. Kevin.
Finnerty, James J. '55 (NEW) Newark, NJ St. John's; Minister for Priests.
Finnerty, Joseph G. '61 (NOR) Norwich, CT St. Mary; [J] Uncasville, CT Emmaus–Diocesan Spiritual Life Center.
Finnerty, Joseph L. '57 (SD) Poway, CA St. Michael.
Finnerty, Joseph '57 (SD) Retired.
Finnerty, Vincent *c.m.* '79 (CHL)[O] Charlotte, NC Our Lady of Guadalupe Hispanic Center.
Finnerty, William '55 (KCK) Retired.
Finnestad, Jerald L.C. '80 (FAR) Grand Forks, ND St. Mary.
Finney, Donald T. *m.i.c.* '94 (PMB) Jupiter, FL St. Peter.
Finnigan, Francis *c.p.* '68 (MET)[H] South River Passionist Provincial Office.
Finnigan, Francis *c.p.* '68 (PMB)[J] North Palm Beach, FL Our Lady of Florida Spiritual Center.
Finnigan, John B. '61 (MAN) Newmarket, NH St. Mary.
Finnigan, John C. '59 (Y) Canton, OH St. Peter.
Finnigan, John (Y) College of Consultors.
Finno, James '72 (CHI) Tinley Park, IL St. Stephen, Deacon and Martyr.
Finsterbach, Thomas P. *s.j.* '76 (SJ)[M] Los Gatos, CA Sacred Heart Jesuit Center.
Finucan, J. Thomas '55 (LC) Retired.
Finucan, James P. '47 (LC)[H] La Crosse, WI Holy Cross (Seminary) Diocesan Center Retired.
Finucane, Gerard J. '99 (KNX) Clinton, TN St. Therese; Norris, TN St. Joseph.
Finucane, Joseph F. '59 (E) Erie, PA St. Mark the Evangelist Retired.
Finucane, Robert '54 (B) Genesee, ID St. Mary Station Retired.
Fior, Ubaldo M. *c.r.s.p.* '51 (BUF)[B] Youngstown, NY St. Anthony M. Zaccaria Seminary.
Fiore, Arthur B. '75 (WIL) New Castle, DE St. Peter; Deans.
Fiore, Benjamin *s.j.* '74 (BUF)[O] Buffalo, NY Canisius Jesuit Community.
Fiore, James '72 (PMB) Delray Beach, FL Emmanuel.
Fiore, John J. *c.s.b.* '57 (GRY)[B] Merrillville, IN Andrean High School; [I] Merrillville, IN Basilian Fathers Residence.
Fiore, Joseph A. '70 (BUF) Darien Center, NY Our Lady of Good Counsel; Attica, NY Sacred Heart of Jesus.
Fiore, Peter A. *o.f.m.* '55 (ALB)[B] Siena College.
Fiorelli, Lewis S. *o.s.f.s.* '70 (WDC)[B] Washington, DC Deshairs Community–Oblates of St. Francis de Sales Residence.
Fiorelli, Lewis *o.s.f.s.* (WDC) St. Francis de Sales Association.
Fiorillo, Antimo '43 (NY) Bronx, NY Santa Maria.
Fiorino, Alfred L. *s.j.* '60 (NY)[EE] Cornwall, NY Jogues Retreat.
Fiorino, Dominic J. '61 (NEW)[N] Caldwell, NJ The Rev. Msgr. James F. Kelley Residence for Retired Priests Retired.
Firestone, Thomas M. '78 (LAN) Ann Arbor, MI St. Mary Student Parish; [M] Ann Arbor, MI St. Mary Student Parish; [O] Ann Arbor, MI Alma Redemptoris Mater.
Firestone, Thomas (LAN) Regional Vicars; Campus Ministries.
Firko, Frank A. *s.t.l.* '77 (PBR) Hermitage, PA St. Michael; Elected Deanery Representatives.
Firpo, John A. '77 (ROC) Rochester, NY St. Helen.
Fisch, Gerald M. '57 (SC) Retired.
Fischer, Andrew C. '82 (PIT) Sharpsburg, PA St. John Cantius; Sharpsburg, PA St. Mary; Sharpsburg, PA Madonna of Jerusalem; Deans and Deaneries.
Fischer, Barry J. *c.pp.s.* '73 (CIN)[M] Dayton Provincial Office of the Cincinnati Province of the Society of the Precious Blood.
Fischer, Brian J. '79 (CHI) Chicago, IL St. Gregory.
Fischer, Brian R. '03 (STL) Ellisville, MO St. Clare of Assisi.
Fischer, Charles H. '71 (KAL) Battle Creek, MI St. Philip; Advocates.
Fischer, Charles M. '90 (FAR) Special Assignment.
Fischer, Don L. '67 (DAL) Richardson, TX St. Joseph; Presbyteral Council.
Fischer, Eugene '65 (SD) Retired.
Fischer, G. William *o.s.f.s.* '69 (E) Special or Diocesan Assignment.
Fischer, Henry J. '71 (BEL) Bartelso, IL St. Cecilia.
Fischer, Hilary *m.s.c.* '57 (RCK)[G] (FgM).
Fischer, James A. *c.m.* '43 (STL)[O] Perryville, MO Congregation of the Mission.
Fischer, James J. *s.j.* '55 (ROC)[B] Rochester, NY McQuaid Jesuit High School.
Fischer, James *c.m.* '43 (LR) Fayetteville, AR St. Thomas Aquinas University Parish; [J] Fayetteville, AR University of Arkansas, St. Thomas Aquinas University Parish.
Fischer, John M. '63 (E) Albion, PA St. Lawrence.
Fischer, John P. '76 (CIN) Ripley, OH St. George; Ripley, OH St. Michael; Priest Councilors; Consultors; Judges.
Fischer, John '86 (SFS) Yankton, SD Sacred Heart.
Fischer, Jonathan *o.s.b.* '61 (SCL)[I] Collegeville, MN St. John's Abbey, of the Order of St. Benedict; [I] St. Paul, MN HealthEast St. Joseph's Hospital.
Fischer, Kenneth J. '71 (CHI) River Forest, IL St. Luke.
Fischer, Louis A. '63 (SLC) Retired.
Fischer, Mark *f.s.s.p.* '95 (ATL) Pequannock, NJ Our Lady of Fatima Chapel (Tridentine); [M] Littleton, CO Our Lady of Mount Carmel Community.
Fischer, Norman A. (LEX) Winchester, KY St. Joseph.
Fischer, Norman '00 (LEX) Mt. Sterling, KY St. Patrick; Bluegrass East.
Fischer, Philip C. *s.j.* '61 (STL)[O] St. Louis, MO Jesuit Community Corporation at St. Louis University – Jesuit Hall.
Fischer, Richard O. '76 (BAK) Air Force Reserve Chaplains; Council of Priests and Diocesan Consultors; Priestly Life and Ministry; Vocations; Chiloquin, OR Our Lady of Mt. Carmel; Klamath Falls, OR St. Pius X; Merrill, OR St. Augustine.
Fischer, William J. *o.praem.* '78 (PH)[AA] Paoli, PA Daylesford Abbey.
Fischer, William '69 (E).
Fischler, James *c.i.c.m.* '76 (SAT)[C] Del Rio, TX Sacred Heart; In Rural Area; Archdiocesan Presbyteral Council.
Fisette, Kevin R. '81 (PRO) Providence, RI Holy Name of Jesus.
Fish, Alfred H. '77 (OG) St. Regis Falls, NY Church of the Holy Cross; St. Regis Falls, NY St. Ann.
Fish, Eugene J. '97 (FAR) Grafton, ND Retired.
Fish, Michael *c.ss.r.* '78 (MRY)[F] Big Sur, CA New Camaldoli Hermitage.
Fishel, Gregory *s.d.b.* '89 (SP)[B] St. Petersburg, FL St. Petersburg Catholic High School.
Fisher, A. J. '56 (BAK) Retired.
Fisher, Albert '81 (BIR) On Duty Outside the Diocese.
Fisher, Andrew J. '98 (ARL) On Duty Outside the Diocese; [Q] Washington, DC Basilica of the National Shrine of the Immaculate Conception.
Fisher, Bernard *s.v.d.* '45 (MIL)[O] East Troy, WI Divine Word Missionaries.
Fisher, Charles '74 (RIC) Richmond, VA Our Lady of Lourdes.
Fisher, Clarence L. '61 (HON) Wahiawa, HI Our Lady of Sorrows; Ecumenical Commission; Oahu.
Fisher, Clarence (HON) Clergy Personnel Board.
Fisher, D. Theodore *s.j.* '53 (LA)[C] Los Angeles, CA Jesuit Community.
Fisher, David E. '86 (LAN) Owosso, MI St. Joseph.
Fisher, David S.J. '53 (LA) Retired.
Fisher, David '84 (OLL) Special Assignment.
Fisher, Donald C. '61 (PIT) Pittsburgh, PA St. Regis.
Fisher, Edward K. '92 (MEM) Camden, TN St. Mary Church.
Fisher, Edward T. '49 (BUF) North Tonawanda, NY St. Albert the Great.
Fisher, Harold *o.m.i.* '00 (PMB) San Fernando, CA Santa Rosa.
Fisher, Harry '64 (FWT) Retired.
Fisher, John J. *o.s.f.s.* '88 (WIL)[B] Wilmington, DE Salesianum School.
Fisher, Kyle *c.ss.r.* '63 (DEN) Denver, CO St. Joseph; [N] Denver, CO The Redemptorists of Denver, Colorado.
Fisher, Martin J. '86 (ALB) Round Lake, NY Corpus Christi.
Fisher, Martin '51 (GF) Retired.
Fisher, Michael W. '90 (WDC) Gaithersburg, MD St. John Neumann.
Fisher, Paul R. *o.pream* '95 (HBG) Cornwall, PA Sacred Heart of Jesus.
Fisher, Paul (HBG) Pastoral Council, Diocesan.
Fisher, Raymond A. '71 (TOL)[H] Green Springs, OH St. Francis Health Care Centre.
Fisher, Robert D. '80 (DEN) Denver, CO Our Lady of Lourdes.
Fisher, Robert J. '92 (DET) Utica, MI St. Lawrence.
Fisher, Robert *s.v.d.* '65 (LR) Little Rock, AR St. Bartholomew's; Presbyteral Council.
Fisher, Rouville '02 (STA) Jacksonville, FL Christ the King.
Fisher, Terry (FTW) South Bend, IN St. Anthony de Padua; Consultors; School Board, Diocesan.
Fisher, Virginia E. (BIR).
Fisher, William F. *o.s.f.s.* '61 (DET) Monroe, MI St. Anne; Monroe, MI St. Joseph's.
Fisher, William '93 (KCK) Baldwin, KS Annunciation; Edgerton, KS Assumption of the Blessed Virgin Mary.
Fishwick, Joseph '75 (MIA) Special Assignment; [G] Miami, FL Mercy Outpatient Services, Inc..
Fiske, Jack Jason *c.ss.r.* '80 (ROC)[K] Canandaigua, NY Notre Dame Retreat House.
Fister, Anselm *o.s.b.* '82 (Oregon)[H] Oceanside, CA Prince of Peace Abbey, Benet Hill.
Fister, Stephen J. '82 (P)[N] Gold Hill, OR St. Rita's Retreat Center.
Fitch, David *s.j.* '54 (SJ)[M] Los Gatos, CA Sacred Heart Jesuit Center.
Fitch, John '02 (VEN) Naples, FL St. William.
Fitterer, L. Paul *s.j.* '63 (SEA)[L] Seattle, WA Jesuit Community.
Fittin, Edward Seton *o.s.b.* '93 (PAT)[M] Morristown, NJ St. Mary's Abbey.
Fitts, Robert L. *s.j.* '69 (SPK) Wellpinit, WA St. Philip Benizi; Inchelium, WA St. Michael's Mission; Wellpinit, WA Sacred Heart; Wellpinit, WA Our Lady of Lourdes; [D] Spokane, WA Gonzaga Preparatory School; [J] Spokane, WA Regis Community; Spokane, WA St. Aloysius.
Fitz, James *s.m.* '74 (STL)[O] St. Louis, MO Provincialate of the Society of Mary, Province of the United States.
Fitz–Henry, Edward '85 (MRY) San Juan Bautista, CA San Juan Bautista.
Fitz–Patrick, David M. '79 (WDC) Military Chaplains; Air Force Chaplains.
Fitzgerald, Brennan *o.f.m.* '61 (NY) New York, NY St. Francis of Assisi.
Fitzgerald, Christopher *i.c.* '58 (SP) Seffner, FL St. Francis of Assisi.
Fitzgerald, David E. *s.a.* '65 (R) Apex, NC St. Andrew the Apostle.
Fitzgerald, David *s.a.* '65 (NY).
Fitzgerald, David *s.p.* '78 (SB)[EE] Rialto, CA St. Catherine of Siena.
Fitzgerald, Donald J. '55 (BUF) Retired.
Fitzgerald, Durkin *c.ss.r.* '49 (GR) Grand Rapids, MI St. Alphonsus; [I] Grand Rapids, MI The Society of the Redemptorists of the City of Grand Rapids.
Fitzgerald, Edmund H. '57 (PRO) Retired.
Fitzgerald, Edmund J. '68 (FR) Westport, MA St. John the Baptist; Diocesan Consultors; Fall River Deanery; Diocesan Health Facilities.
Fitzgerald, Edward P. '40 (CHI) Retired.
Fitzgerald, Edward T. '59 (SPR) Ware, MA All Saints.
Fitzgerald, Edward W. '95 (CHR) Hanahan, SC Divine Redeemer.
Fitzgerald, Edward (CHR) Defenders of the Bond.
Fitzgerald, Garrett J. *s.j.* '55 (NY)[EE] Cardinal Spellman Hall, Jesuit Community.
Fitzgerald, Garrett J. '75 (MET) On Duty Outside the Diocese; Trenton, NJ Holy Angels.
Fitzgerald, George R. *c.s.p.* '65 (DEN) Vail, CO St. Patrick's; [EE] Jamaica Estates Paulist Fathers Generalate.
Fitzgerald, Howard E. '78 (DM) Altoona, IA SS. John and Paul.
Fitzgerald, Howard (DM) Advocates.
Fitzgerald, J. Terrence (SLC) Vicar General and Moderator of the Curia; College of Consultors; Finance Council; Board of Directors; Priests' Personnel Board; Defenders of the Bond.

Fitzgerald, J. Thomas '68 (MAD) Clinton, WI St. Stephen.
Fitzgerald, James E. '67 (BUF)[O] Milwaukee, WI Jesuit Community at Marquette University; Silver Creek, NY Our Lady of Mt. Carmel.
Fitzgerald, John B. '55 (LA) Retired.
Fitzgerald, John E. '57 (PH) Philadelphia, PA Resurrection of Our Lord.
Fitzgerald, John G. '62 (LA) Lompoc, CA Our Lady Queen of Angels; Deanery 1.
Fitzgerald, John J. *o.s.a.* '41 (PH)[AA] Villanova, PA St. Thomas Monastery.
Fitzgerald, John J. '58 (RVC) Setauket, NY St. James Retired.
Fitzgerald, John L. '67 (BAL) Special Assignment.
Fitzgerald, John P. (PIT) Pittsburgh International Airport; Air National Guard Chaplains.
Fitzgerald, John '63 (STO) Twain Harte, CA All Saints Church (Pastor of); Deans.
Fitzgerald, John '74 (PIT) McKees Rocks, PA Holy Trinity.
Fitzgerald, Joseph M. '58 (BGP) Shelton, CT St. Lawrence.
Fitzgerald, Joseph *o.carm.* '86 (LA)[F] Encino, CA Crespi Carmelite High School.
Fitzgerald, Kevin T. *s.j.* '88 (WDC)[M] Washington, DC The Jesuit Community at Georgetown University.
Fitzgerald, Matthew '68 (PMB) Retired.
Fitzgerald, Michael J. '80 (PH) Philadelphia, PA Annunciation B.V.M.; Archdiocesan Judges; Promoters of Justice; Office for Legal Services.
Fitzgerald, P. Timothy '75 (DM) On Special Assignment; Office of Adult Faith Formation.
Fitzgerald, Patrick (RVC) Bellport, NY Mary Immaculate.
Fitzgerald, Paul J. *s.j.* '92 (SJ)[B] Santa Clara, CA Jesuit Community.
Fitzgerald, R. Martin '89 (R) On Duty Outside the Diocese.
Fitzgerald, Raymond *s.j.* '91 (DAL)[D] Dallas, TX Jesuit College Preparatory School.
Fitzgerald, Richard M. (R) Air Force Chaplains.
Fitzgerald, Richard W. (BO) Wellesley, MA St. Paul; Clergy Personnel; Ex Officio; Members.
Fitzgerald, Robert H. *s.j.* '66 (OM)[K] Omaha, NE Jesuit Community at Creighton University.
Fitzgerald, Thomas J. '42 (CHI) Chicago, IL St. Thomas Apostle Retired.
Fitzgerald, Thomas J. *s.s.s.* '64 (SAT) San Antonio, TX St. Joseph.
Fitzgerald, Thomas J. '75 (PAT) Clifton, NJ St. Clare's.
Fitzgerald, Thomas P. '66 (STP) Centerville, MN St. Genevieve.
Fitzgerald, Thomas R. *s.j.* '52 (WDC)[M] Washington, DC The Jesuit Community at Georgetown University.
Fitzgerald, Tim (SC) Liturgy Commission.
Fitzgerald, Timothy J. '90 (SC) Royal, IA St. Louis.
Fitzgerald, Timothy *c.p.* '56 (PIT)[N] Pittsburgh, PA St. Paul of the Cross Monastery; [N] Pittsburgh St. Paul of the Cross Monastery.
Fitzgerald, Timothy (SC) Building Commission.
Fitzgerald, Vincent *o.m.i.* '50 (BEL)[F] Belleville, IL Missionary Oblates of Mary Immaculate – St. Henry's Oblate Residence.
Fitzgerald, William F. '50 (TR)[M] Trenton, NJ Villa Vianney; Diocesan Consultors Retired.
Fitzgerald, William F. '58 (OM) Retired.
Fitzgerald, William M. *o.praem.* '79 (COV) Initiation; Worship Commission; Office of Worship, Evangelization & Initiation; Fort Thomas, KY St. Thomas.
Fitzgerald, William *c.ss.r.* '43 (FgM).
Fitzgerald, William *c.ss.r.* '43 (DEN).
Fitzgerald, William '57 (LAN) Retired.
Fitzgibbon, Edmond J. '59 (STL)[N] St. Louis, MO St. Michael.
Fitzgibbons, John A. '68 (PH) Absent on Sick Leave.
Fitzgibbons, John P. *s.j.* '85 (STP)[B] St. Paul, MN Jesuit Novitiate.
Fitzgibbons, Peter L. '84 (CHL) Military Chaplains; Army Reserve Chaplains.
Fitzhenry, John Stephen *o.p.* '58 (BO)[V] Dover, MA St. Stephen Priory.
Fitzhenry, Stephen *o.p.* '58 (BO)[X] Dover, MA St. Stephen Priory Spiritual Life Center; [X] Dover, MA St. Stephen Priory Spiritual Life Center.
Fitzmaurice, Francis J. '48 (PH) Retired.
Fitzmaurice, James T. '84 (ALB) Johnstown, NY Holy Trinity.
Fitzmaurice, James *o.f.m.* '84 (BO)[V] Ministry of the Word.
Fitzmaurice, James (ALB) Members.
Fitzmaurice, Terence *o.s.b.* '63 (JOL)[L] Lisle, IL St. Procopius Abbey.
Fitzmaurice, V. Paul '73 (GBG) Harrison City, PA St. Barbara.
Fitzmyer, Joseph A. *s.j.* '51 (WDC)[C] Catholic University of America, The; [M] Washington, DC The Jesuit Community at Georgetown University.
Fitzpatrick, Bede *o.f.m.* '55 (FgM).
Fitzpatrick, Daniel J. *s.j.* '55 (NY)[EE] Loyola Hall, Jesuit Community; [II] Bronx, NY Metro New York Life Communities, Inc..
Fitzpatrick, Donnelly J. '63 (PEO) Atkinson, IL St. Anthony's; Sheffield, IL St. Patrick's; Vicariates and Vicars.
Fitzpatrick, Edmund J. '47 (CHI) Retired.
Fitzpatrick, Edward C. '68 (RVC) Uniondale, NY St. Martha.
Fitzpatrick, Edward J. '70 (DAV)[H] Iowa City, IA Newman Catholic Student Center; [M] Iowa City, IA O'Keefe Hall; Judges; Deans.
Fitzpatrick, Edward T. *o.s.f.s.* '74 (WIL)[J] Wilmington, DE Oblates of St. Francis De Sales.
Fitzpatrick, Edward '58 (ALB) Retired.
FitzPatrick, Emmett J. '58 (PHX) Sun Lakes, AZ St. Steven.
Fitzpatrick, Franklin E. '47 (BRK) Retired.
Fitzpatrick, Gerald J. *s.j.* '71 (CAM)[O] Blackwood, NJ St. Pius X Retreat House.
Fitzpatrick, J. Vincent '92 (FAR) Geneseo, ND St. Martin of Tours; Lidgerwood, ND St. Boniface.
Fitzpatrick, James F. (BRK) Vocations, Office of.
Fitzpatrick, James J. '84 (PH) Pontifical Society for the Propagation of the Faith; Morrisville, PA St. John the Evangelist.
Fitzpatrick, James M. '71 (SAG) Standish, MI Resurrection of the Lord.
Fitzpatrick, James M. '84 (FR) North Attleboro, MA St. Mary's.
Fitzpatrick, James '95 (BRK) East Elmhurst, NY St. Gabriel; [X] Douglaston, NY Immaculate Conception Center, St. Paul's Center.
Fitzpatrick, James (PH) Pontifical Society of St. Peter Apostle.
Fitzpatrick, James (PH) Pontifical Missionary Union.
Fitzpatrick, James (PH) Pontifical Missionary Society of the Holy Childhood (Holy Childhood Assoc.).
Fitzpatrick, John E. '70 (PAT) Oak Ridge, NJ St. Thomas, the Apostle.
Fitzpatrick, John J. '60 (SAV) College of Consultors Retired.
Fitzpatrick John P. '52 (STP) Retired.
Fitzpatrick John P. (BO) Sudbury, MA St. Anselm.
Fitzpatrick John *c.s.sp.* '63 (SJ) Mountain View, CA St. Athanasius.
Fitzpatrick, Joseph F. *s.j.* '65 (NY)[EE] New York, NY Murray–Weigel Hall.
Fitzpatrick, Mallick J. *s.j.* '60 (NY)[F] New York, NY Fordham Preparatory School; [EE] Jesuit Community, Kohlmann Hall.
Fitzpatrick, Michael J. *s.j.* '77 (BAK) Pendleton, OR St. Andrew's Indian Mission.
Fitzpatrick, Michael J. '83 (PH) Honey Brook, PA St. Peter; Council of Priests; Philadelphia Archdiocesan Holy Name Union.
Fitzpatrick, Michael Joseph '03 (FR) Mansfield, MA St. Mary's.
Fitzpatrick, Patrick G. '62 (TR) Keyport, NJ Holy Family.
Fitzpatrick, Paul E. *s.m.* '77 (BO)[A] Weston, MA Blessed John XXIII National Seminary.
Fitzpatrick, Paul K. '98 (LA) Redondo Beach, CA St. James.
Fitzpatrick, R. Michael *s.t.l.* '71 (OM) Omaha, NE St. Stanislaus; Promoter of Justice; Defenders of the Bond; Consultors; Finance Council; Cemeteries; Ex Officio.
Fitzpatrick, R. Michael '71 (OM) Special Assignment.
Fitzpatrick, Robert J. '54 (CHI) Ingleside, IL St. Bede Retired.
Fitzpatrick, Robert J. '73 (STP) Little Canada, MN St. John the Evangelist.
Fitzpatrick, Robert M. (OM) Air Force Reserve Chaplains.
Fitzpatrick, Robert *o.m.i.* '71 (FgM).
Fitzpatrick, Thomas J. *o.s.f.s.* '61 (CHL) Thomasville, NC Our Lady of the Highways.
Fitzpatrick, Thomas J. *s.j.* '68 (FgM).
Fitzpatrick, Thomas P. '61 (SY) Syracuse, NY Our Lady of Lourdes.
Fitzpatrick, Vincent *s.t.* '44 (PAT)[M] Stirling, NJ Holy Spirit Missionary Cenacle.
Fitzsimmons, Donald J. *c.s.v.* '60 (CHI)[N] Arlington Heights, IL Viatorian Province Center–Clerics of St. Viator.
Fitzsimmons, Eugene J. '60 (CAM) Haddonfield, NJ St. Vincent Pallotti; Presiding Judge for Court of Second Instance Cases; Judges; Commission on Ecumenical and Interreligious Affairs.
Fitzsimmons, Francis *m.s.* '68 (LKC) Sulphur, LA St. Theresa.
Fitzsimmons, Gerald J. *s.m.m.* '75 (BRK)[V] Ozone Park, NY Montfort Missionaries Provincialate (Missionaries of the Company of Mary) – Formation Community.
Fitzsimmons, Gerald *s.s.m.* '75 (HRT)[V] Litchfield, CT Lourdes Shrine Guild, Inc..
Fitzsimmons, J. Thomas '62 (CIN) Eaton, OH Visitation of the Blessed Virgin Mary; Eaton, OH St. John the Evangelist.
Fitzsimmons, Philip *o.p.* (NY) Manhattan, NY New York Presbyterian Hospital.
Fitzsimmons, Ricahrd '56 (PEO) Retired.
Fitzsimmons, Robert Philip *o.p.* '55 (NY) New York, NY St. Catherine of Siena; [EE] New York, NY St. Catherine of Siena Priory.
Fitzsimmons, Thomas (CAM) Vocation Advisory Board; Diocesan Finance Council.
Fitzsimons, Patrick '01 (LEX) Lexington, KY Cathedral of Christ the King.
Fitzsommons, Thomas B. '62 (CAM) Wildwood, NJ St. Ann's.
Fitzwilliam, Ivan '48 (SB) Retired.
Fives, Carl J. '42 (SCR)[B] Emmitsburg, MD Mount Saint Mary's College; On Duty Outside the Diocese.
Fix, Donald P. '80 (PIT) Military Chaplains; Navy Chaplains.
Fix, Joseph J. '68 (GR) Evart, MI Sacred Heart; Evart, MI St. Agnes.
Fix, Robert H. '53 (CHR) Retired.
Flach, Carl J. '58 (P) Oregon City, OR St. Philip Benizi; Judges.
Flach, Carl (P) Area Vicars; Adjutant Judicial Vicar.
Flach, James A. '86 (SFD) Marine, IL St. Gertrude; Marine, IL St. Elizabeth; Marine, IL St. James.
Flach, Thomas D. '71 (BEL) Waterloo, IL SS. Peter and Paul; Defensores Vinculi.
Flacherty, Malachy C. *o.f.m.cap.* '42 (RVC)[J] Huntington, NY St. Joseph's Guest Home for the Aged, Inc..
Flack, Robert S. *s.j.* '74 (STL)[C] Saint Louis University; [O] St. Louis, MO Jesuit Community Corporation at St. Louis University – Jesuit Hall.
Fladung, Charles J. '92 (DAV) Richland, IA St. Joseph's; Richland, IA St. Frances Xavier Cabrini.
Flagg, Wayne N. '88 (VIC) New Ulm, TX SS. Peter and Paul; Alleyton, TX St. Roch.
Flagg, Wayne (VIC) Presbyteral Council; Ecumenical Commission.
Flagor, David A. '91 (DOD) On Leave of Absence.
Flahavan, Edward J. '57 (STP) Retired.
Flaherty, Charles B. *s.s.c.* '50 (BO)[V] West Roxbury, MA St. John Chrystostom.
Flaherty, Daniel J. '54 (DEN) Retired.
Flaherty, Daniel L. *s.j.* '60 (CHI)[N] Chicago, IL Chicago Province of the Society of Jesus–Provincial Office; [N] Evanston, IL Canisius House.
Flaherty, Daniel '54 (DEN) Louisville, CO St. Louis Retired.
Flaherty, Edward F. *s.j.* '65 (DEN)[N] Denver, CO Xavier Jesuit Center.
Flaherty, Francis T. '62 (WDC) Retired.
Flaherty, Frederick R. *m.s.* '57 (HRT)[M] Hartford, CT Missionaries of LaSalette.
Flaherty, J. Francis '55 (CAM) Retired.
Flaherty, J. Francis '57 (CAM) Pennsauken, NJ St. Stephen; Members.
Flaherty, Jack R. (DUB) Deanery Representatives.
Flaherty, James J. '80 (PT) Pensacola, FL Holy Spirit; Judicial Vicar; Judges; Administrative Council; Permanent Diaconate Formation Board.
Flaherty, James P. *s.j.* '92 (MIL)[O] Milwaukee, WI Jesuit Community at Marquette University.
Flaherty, Jay M. '85 (KNX) Pigeon Forge, TN Holy Cross.
Flaherty, John J. *o.s.a.* '55 (CHI)[N] Olympia Fields, IL Tolentine Monastery at Tolentine Center.
Flaherty, John R. '90 (DUB)[O] Webster City, IA St. Thomas Aquinas Foundation; Webster City, IA St. Thomas Aquinas; Webster City, IA St. Mary.
Flaherty, Kenneth *t.o.r.* '57 (ALT)[F] Loretto, PA Mount Assisi Friary.
Flaherty, Kevin H. *s.j.* '83 (CHI).
Flaherty, Leon *c.pp.s.* '61 (CIN)[M] Superior, WI.
Flaherty, Leon *c.p.p.s.* '61 (SUP) Superior, WI Cathedral of Christ the King.
Flaherty, Malachy *o.c.s.o.* '60 (SLC)[F] Huntsville, UT Abbey of Our Lady of the Holy Trinity of the Order of Cistercians.
Flaherty, Michael T. '73 (CIN) Cincinnati, OH St. Veronica; Judges.
Flaherty, Richard C. *o.f.m.* '82 (BUF)[O] St. Bonaventure, NY St. Bonaventure Friary.
Flaherty, William J. '52 (CHI) Winnetka, IL SS. Faith, Hope and Charity Retired.
Flahive, James J. '48 (SPR)[H] Springfield, MA St. Michael's Residence.
Flajole, John *o.f.m.* '64 (GAL) Galveston, TX St. Patrick.
Flamm, Paul M. *c.s.sp.* '99 (FgM).
Flammia, Paul G. '96 (BO) Health Leave; Wilmington, MA St. Thomas of Villanova.
Flanagan, Bernard A. '82 (ALN) Allentown, PA Our Lady Help of Christians; [I] Pottsville, PA Queen of Peace Apartments.
Flanagan, Brian '98 (PMB) Palm Beach Gardens, FL St. Patrick; Office of Ecumenical and Interfaith Activities.
Flanagan, Brian (PAT) Clifton, NJ St. Paul.
Flanagan, Bruce G. '78 (BO) Danvers, MA St. Richard.
Flanagan, Christopher '99 (R) Absent on Leave.
Flanagan, Damian '91 (MIA) Coral Springs, FL St. Andrew.

Flanagan, David J. '87 (MAD) Cuba City, WI St. Rose of Lima; Gratiot, WI St. Joseph; Gratiot, WI St. John.
Flanagan, Edward R. '88 (MET) Monroe Township, NJ Nativity of Our Lord.
Flanagan, Edward *o.f.m.* '64 (SP)[O] Belleair Bluffs, FL St. James Friary.
Flanagan, Francis B. '32 (BUR) Retired.
Flanagan, Hubert *s.a.c.* (DET)[K] Wyandotte, MI Pallottine Missionary Center (Irish Province).
Flanagan, James D. '71 (NY) Bronx, NY Holy Family.
Flanagan, James E. *c.s.s.* '50 (BO)[Y] Waltham, MA Stigmatine Fathers and Brothers.
Flanagan, James W. '61 (DUB) On Duty Outside the Archdiocese.
Flanagan, James *s.o.l.t.* '52 (CC)[G] Robstown, TX Society of Our Lady of the Most Holy Trinity.
Flanagan, John B. '97 (PH) Priests' Personnel Board; Philadelphia, PA Immaculate Heart of Mary.
Flanagan, John J. '74 (SAT) San Antonio, TX St. Jerome.
Flanagan, John '59 (SY) Utica, NY Sacred Heart.
Flanagan, Joseph F. X. *s.j.* '59 (BO)[V] Newton, MA The Jesuit Community at Boston College.
Flanagan, Lawrence W. *s.j.* '52 (OM)[K] Omaha, NE Jesuit Community at Creighton University.
Flanagan, Michael J. *m.s.* '60 (ORL) Orlando, FL Blessed Trinity.
Flanagan, Michael T. '65 (JC) Columbia, MO Our Lady of Lourdes; Episcopal Vicars; Diocesan Consultors; Personnel Board; Ex Officio Members; Finance Committee; Board of Trustees.
Flanagan, P. Kevin '59 (PAT) Chester, NJ St. Lawrence the Martyr.
Flanagan, Patrick J. '56 (SAT) Retired.
Flanagan, Patrick S. '92 (BRK)[V] Jamaica, NY Vincentian Residence.
Flanagan, Patrick *c.m.* '92 (CHI)[N] Chicago DePaul Vincentian Residence.
Flanagan, Sean B. '59 (LA) Long Beach, CA St. Bartholomew; Los Angeles, CA L.A. City Fire Dept..
Flanagan, Thomas J. '49 (BRK) Retired.
Flanagan, Thomas J. '74 (SC) On Duty Outside the Diocese.
Flanagan, William F. '64 (JC) Monroe City, MO Retired.
Flanagan, William J. '46 (SFR) Belmont, CA St. Mark Retired.
Flanery, Joseph–Mary *o.c.d.* '55 (MIL)[O] Holy Hill, WI Discalced Carmelite Monastery – Holy Hill National Shrine of Mary Help of Christians.
Flanigan, Edward J. *m.m.* '56 (NY).
Flanigan, Gerald A. '51 (DET) Retired.
Flanigan, James F. *c.s.c.* '62 (FTW)[B] University of Notre Dame Du Lac.
Flanigan, James *c.s.c.* '62 (FTW)[A] Notre Dame, IN Moreau Seminary; Environment and Art.
Flanigan, Thomas P. '69 (PH) Lansdale, PA Corpus Christi.
Flannery, John *o.p.* '60 (SD) Clergy Counseling and Spiritual Direction.
Flannery, Joseph D. '53 (SCR)[N] Dunmore, PA Villa St. Joseph Retired.
Flannery, Kevin L. *s.j.* '87 (DET)[K] Pontificia Universita Gregoriana.
Flannery, Michael '64 (JKS) Jackson, MS St. Peter Cathedral.
Flannery, Michael '97 (ALB) Delhi, NY St. Peter; Walton, NY St. John the Baptist.
Flannery, Michael (JKS) Office of Vicar General; Chancellor; Continuing Formation Committee; Defenders of the Bond; Diocesan Consultors; Personnel Board; Priests' Council.
Flannery, Patrick R. '97 (NEW) Belleville, NJ St. Peter's.
Flannery, Robert B. '73 (BEL) Carbondale, IL St. Francis Xavier; Diocesan Deans; Ecumenical and Interreligious Affairs.
Flannigan, John G. *s.j.* '43 (STL)[N] St. Louis, MO Fusz Pavilion; [O] St. Louis, MO Jesuit Community Corporation at St. Louis University – Jesuit Hall.
Flannigan, Patrick *o.f.m.* '90 (WDC)[M] Washington, DC Commissariat of the Holy Land, Franciscan Monastery – Mount St. Sepulchre.
Flaska, John A. '68 (SFE) Retired.
Flaska, Mickey (DEN) Longmont, CO St. John the Baptist.
Flater, Gerald *o.m.i.* '57 (BO)[Y] Tewksbury, MA Immaculate Heart of Mary Infirmary.
Flatley, Brian M. '66 (BO) Arlington, MA St. Agnes; Selected.
Flavin, James A. '87 (BO) Brockton, MA St. Edith Stein.
Flavin, James Joseph *o.m.i.* '63 (MIA) Miami, FL Christ the King.
Flavin, John E. '61 (CHI) Glenview, IL Our Lady of Perpetual Help.
Flax, Myron *o.f.m.* '64 (COS)[I] Colorado Springs, CO Catholic Center at the Citadel; [F] Colorado Springs, CO Padre Pio Friary.
Fleck, David '75 (EVN) Mt. Vernon, IN St. Philip's; Diocesan Consultors; Diocesan Council of Priests.
Fleck, John W. '59 (TOL) Delphos, OH St. John Baptist; Delphos, OH St. Patrick.
Fleck, Kenneth J. '76 (CHI) Tinley Park, IL St. George.
Fleck, Richard A. *o.p.* '55 (BO)[V] Dover, MA St. Stephen Priory.
Fleckenstein, John '02 (KAL) Battle Creek, MI St. Philip.
Flecky, Michael J. *s.j.* '77 (OM)[K] Omaha, NE Jesuit Community at Creighton University.
Flegge, William '60 (SLC) Salt Lake City, UT Our Lady of Lourdes; Ministry to Priests Team.
Fleischhacker, John J. *o.s.c.* '61 (DUL) McGregor, MN Holy Family; [I] Onamia Crosier Monastery.
Fleischhacker, John *o.s.c.* '61 (DUL) McGregor, MN Our Lady of Fatima.
Fleischman, Richard J. '68 (MIL) Fredonia, WI Holy Rosary.
Fleischmann, George R. '56 (MIL) Retired.
Fleiter, Robert V. '61 (STL) Herculaneum, MO Church of the Assumption of B.V.M..
Flek, Ladislaus J. (PAT) Retired.
Fleming, Alfred J. *m.m.* '60 (FgM).
Fleming, Austin H. '73 (BO) Concord, MA Our Lady Help of Christians.
Fleming, Brendan '52 (P) Retired.
Fleming, David J. *o.f.m.* '43 (BO)[Y] Boston, MA Saint Anthony Residence.
Fleming, David L. *s.j.* '65 (STL)[C] Saint Louis University; [O] St. Louis, MO Jesuit Community Corporation at St. Louis University – Jesuit Hall; [O] St. Louis, MO The Jesuits of the Missouri Province; [U] St. Louis, MO Review for Religious; [O] St. Louis, MO The Jesuits of the Missouri Province.
Fleming, David '90 (DM) Stuart, IA All Saints.
Fleming, Edward J. '44 (NEW)[B] School of Diplomacy and Intl. Rels. Retired.
Fleming, Francis J. '39 (STP) Retired.
Fleming, George '94 (ALB) Chestertown, NY St. John the Baptist; Hague, NY Blessed Sacrament; North Creek, NY St. James; Presbyteral Council; Diocesan Board of Consultors.
Fleming, James *s.j.* '95 (BO)[V] Newton, MA The Jesuit Community at Boston College.
Fleming, Jeffrey M. '92 (HEL) Dillon, MT St. Rose of Lima; Associate Judges.
Fleming, Jeffrey M. '93 (HEL)[H] Dillon, MT University of Montana – Western.
Fleming, John F. '49 (NY) Retired.
Fleming, John M. '61 (CAM) Hammonton, NJ St. Anthony of Padua.
Fleming, John R. '42 (NU) Retired.
Fleming, John W. '96 (MAN) Salem, NH Mary, Queen of Peace.
Fleming, Joseph H. '43 (ALT) Retired.
Fleming, Joseph W. '74 (ALT) Dysart, PA St. Augustine.
Fleming, Martin M.P. '52 (STP) Retired.
Fleming, Patrick V. '48 (ALT) Retired.
Fleming, Raymond H. '82 (ROC) Rochester, NY Emmanuel Church of the Deaf of the Diocese of Rochester; Rochester, NY Roman Catholic Community of the 19th Ward.
Fleming, T. J. (SAG) Vicars for Vicariates.
Fleming, Terence K. '67 (SP) On Duty Outside the Diocese; [K] St. Petersburg, FL St. Anthony's Hospital, Inc.; [K] Tampa, FL St. Joseph's Hospital, Inc..
Fleming, Terrance L. '73 (LA) Los Angeles, CA Cathedral of Our Lady of the Angels; Los Angeles, CA St. Brendan; Judges.
Fleming, Terrance (LA) Propagation of the Faith.
Fleming, Thomas B. '76 (WOR) Bolton, MA St. Francis Xavier; [M] Worcester, MA Compassion House.
Fleming, Thomas F. *s.j.* '42 (BO)[V] Newton, MA The Jesuit Community at Boston College.
Fleming, Thomas J. '59 (BO) Senior Priests; Lynn, MA Sacred Heart Retired.
Fleming, Thomas J. '85 (SAG) Argyle, MI St. Joseph; Ubly, MI St. Columbkille; Ubly, MI St. John the Evangelist.
Fleming, Thomas '55 (JOL)[K] Naperville, IL St. John Vianney Villa Retired.
Fleming, Vincent A. '44 (SR) Retired.
Flemming, Neil '58 (VEN) Retired.
Flens, Daniel A. '89 (CHI) Chicago, IL Cardinal's Residence; Office of the Archbishop.
Flesey, John W. '69 (NEW)[B] School of Diplomacy and Intl. Rels.; Continuing Formation of Priests; Ex Officio Members.
Fletcher, Luke Mary *c.f.r.* '03 (NY)[EE] New York, NY St. Joseph's Friary; [EE] Yonkers, NY St. Leopold's Friary.
Fletcher, Patrick '85 (PCE) On Duty Outside the Diocese; Air Force Chaplains.
Fleury, Joseph M. *s.m.* '84 (WDC)[M] Fort Knox, NY; Army Chaplains.
Flickinger, Don D. '64 (FRS) On Duty Outside the Diocese; San Jose, CA St. Frances Cabrini.
Flickinger, Robert E. '75 (KAL) Advocates; Diocesan Consultors; Presbyteral Council; Mendon, MI St. Edward.
Flilau, John P. '90 (CI)[C] Manresa Jesuit House.
Flinn, George B. '66 (ALT) Vicars General; Priests' Personnel Board; Johnstown, PA St. John Gualbert Cathedral.
Flint, Edward A. *s.j.* '69 (COL) Toledo, OH Gesu.
Flint, James *o.s.b.* '83 (JOL)[A] Lisle, IL Benedictine University; [L] Lisle, IL St. Procopius Abbey.
Flint, Kenneth '42 (NOR) Priests Retirement Plan Board; Priests' Retirement Plan Board Retired.
Flis, Stanislaw '69 (DET)[A] Orchard Lake, MI SS. Cyril and Methodius Seminary.
Flisk, Louden Hans '01 (FAR) Sykeston, ND St. Patrick; Sykeston, ND Holy Family; Sykeston, ND St. Elizabeth.
Fliss, James W. '75 (BUF) Farnham, NY St. Anthony's; Brant, NY Our Lady of Mt. Carmel.
Fliss, Paul '92 (MIL) Special Assignment; Office for Multi–Cultural Concerns.
Fliss, Richard L. '66 (LC) On Duty Outside the Diocese.
Floch, W. Roy '77 (SPK) Wilbur, WA St. Joseph; Wilbur, WA Sacred Heart.
Flock, Robert H. '82 (LC) Foreign Missions.
Floersh, Philip M. *c.m.* '62 (STL)[O] St. Louis Vincentian Residence.
Flood, Augustine A. '64 (GBG)[H] Latrobe, PA Saint Vincent Archabbey.
Flood, Charles J. *o.ss.t.* '90 (BAL)[S] Baltimore, MD The Trinitarians at Holy Rosary.
Flood, David *o.f.m.* '58 (BUF)[O] St. Bonaventure, NY St. Bonaventure Friary; [C] St. Bonaventure, NY Friar Community.
Flood, Eric *f.s.s.p.* '00 (SCR)[M] Omaha, NE St. Patrick Church.
Flood, Eric *f.s.s.p.* (OM)[E] Maple Hill, KS St. John Vianney Preparatory School.
Flood, Francis *o.s.b.* '93 (NEW)[N] Newark, NJ Newark Abbey.
Flood, J. Michael '68 (PH) Glenside, PA St. Luke the Evangelist; [EE] Glenside, PA Arcadia University.
Flood, James F. '62 (CLV)[M] Fairlawn, OH St. Edward Home; [M] Fairlawn, OH St. Edward Home.
Flood, James J. '58 (PH) Philadelphia, PA St. Timothy.
Flood, Matthew C. *s.j.* '61 (NY)[F] New York, NY Fordham Preparatory School; [EE] Jesuit Community, Kohlmann Hall.
Flood, Maurice *o.c.s.o.* '91 (SR)[N] Whitethorn, CA Our Lady of the Redwoods Abbey.
Flood, Maurice *o.c.s.o.* '91 (ARL)[J] Berryville, VA Cistercian Abbey of Our Lady of the Holy Cross.
Flood, Patrick (FRS).
Flood, Paul '90 (ATL) Woodstock, GA St. Michael the Archangel.
Flood, Peter J. '69 (TR) Retired.
Flood, William J. (BRK) Sanitation Department.
Flood, William '57 (BRK) Howard Beach, NY Our Lady of Grace.
Flor, Carlos '97 (NEW) Union City, NJ St. Anthony of Padua.
Flora, Carmel *o.f.m.cap.* '53 (DET) (FgM); [K] St. Lawrence Community.
Florczyk, Franciszek '81 (CHI) Lemont, IL SS. Cyril and Methodius.
Florczyk, Walker '62 (SY) Retired.
Florek, Frederick J. '64 (SD) San Diego, CA St. Therese.
Florek, Richard *o.f.m.conv.* '72 (BAL) Baltimore, MD St. Clement Mary Hofbauer.
Florek, Thomas W. *s.j.* '86 (DET)[N] Chicago Chicago Province of the Society of Jesus–Provincial Office; [T] Detroit, MI Midwest Cultural Institute of Leadership (ICLM).
Flores, Arthur '92 (SAT) San Antonio, TX San Juan De Los Lagos.
Flores, Benjamin '93 (ELP) El Paso, TX San Antonio; Pecos, TX Santa Rosa Church.
Flores, Cirilo (ORG) Clergy Personnel Board.
Flores, Daniel E. *s.t.d.* '88 (CC) On Special Assignment.
Flores, Daniel '88 (CC)[A] Houston, TX St. Mary's Seminary.
Flores, Efrain '91 (ORG) Anaheim, CA St. Justin Martyr.
Flores, Francisco '00 (B) Idaho Falls, ID Holy Rosary; Priest Retirement Committee; Knights of Columbus; Idaho Falls, ID Christ the King.
Flores, Gabriel '85 (SFR) San Francisco, CA Mission Dolores Basilica.
Flores, Gerardo *v.d.m.f.* '95 (SFR)[N] Daly City, CA Verbum Dei Missionary Fraternity.
Flores, Guillermo *m.sp.s.* '03 (LA) Huntington Park, CA St. Martha.
Flores, Jesus (ROC) Office of Interdiocesan Hispanic Migrant Ministry.
Flores, Jose A. '73 (CGS) Yabucoa, PR Santos Angeles Cutodios.
Flores, Jose G. (BO) Marlborough, MA Immaculate Conception; Brazilian Community Centers.
Flores, Juan M. '98 (YAK) Diocesan Commission for the Catechumenate; Presbyteral Council Executive Committee.
Flores, Juan Manuel '98 (YAK) Yakima, WA St. Paul Cathedral; Porterville, CA St. Anne.
Flores, Juan (YAK) Diocesan Commission on Public Worship.

Flores, Lee '85 (GAL) Sweeny, TX Our Lady of Perpetual Help.
Flores, Miguel *o.s.m.* (ELP) El Paso, TX St. Ignatius of Loyola.
Flores, Ramiro '95 (OAK) Oakland, CA St. Anthony's; Presbyteral Council.
Flores, Richard '84 (FWT) Fort Worth, TX St. Rita.
Flores, Virgilio '66 (LSC) Mesilla, NM St. Albino.
Flores–Ruiz, Benjamin (ELP) Presbyteral Council.
Floreth, Michael *c.s.c.* '02 (PHX) Phoenix, AZ St. Gregory.
Florez, Andrew '93 (NY) Rosendale, NY St. Peter.
Florez, Carlos '03 (MIL)[X] Kenosha, WI St. Mark Latin American Center.
Florez, Luis '59 (STA) Jacksonville, FL Assumption; Hispanic Ministry.
Florez Ardila, Carlos A. '03 (MIL) Kenosha, WI St. Mark.
Flori, David J. '86 (DAL) Richardson, TX St. Paul the Apostle; Finance Council.
Florida, Sotico H. '87 (LC) Custer, WI Immaculate Conception.
Floridi, Nicholas (PHX) Phoenix, AZ St. Theresa; Advocates.
Florido, Raphael A. '45 (BRK) Retired.
Florido, Robert A. '79 (CHI) Chicago, IL Transfiguration of Our Lord.
Florido, Robert '79 (CHI)[J] Chicago, IL Saint Elizabeth's Hospital.
Florio, Philip A. *s.j.* '01 (SCR)[C] Scranton, PA The University of Scranton.
Flott, Philip M. '02 (GI) Grand Island, NE Cathedral of the Nativity of the Blessed Virgin Mary.
Flover, Antonio Herrera (CC) Instructor.
Flower, Thomas A. '65 (HRT) Tariffville, CT St. Bernard's.
Flowers, Thomas A. '77 (WIL) Smyrna, DE St. Polycarp; Delaware Home & Hospital for the Chronically Ill; Catholic Charismatic Renewal.
Fluet, Gregoire J. '82 (NOR) Moodus, CT St. Bridget; Part Time; Archivist.
Fluetsch, John P. '91 (FRS) Wasco, CA St. John the Evangelist.
Fluetsch, John (FRS) Scouting.
Flum, Martin E. '01 (WDC) Hollywood, MD St. John.
Flusche, Ernest A. '54 (OKL) Enid, OK St. Francis Xavier Retired.
Flusche, Vincent '90 (LR) Atkins, AR Assumption B.V.M..
Flusk, Joseph F. '53 (NEW) Retired.
Flynn, Arthur C. '52 (BO) Reading, MA St. Agnes.
Flynn, Brian L. '03 (BO) South Boston, MA Gate of Heaven.
Flynn, Brian V. *o.f.m.* '60 (SPK) Spokane, WA St. Francis of Assisi.
Flynn, Charles '69 (DUL) Duluth, MN St. James.
Flynn, D. Michael *s.j.* '73 (NY) Staten Island, NY St. Mary of the Assumption.
Flynn, Daniel V. '48 (NY) Harrison, NY St. Gregory the Great.
Flynn, Edmund *o.c.s.o.* '70 (ARL)[J] Berryville, VA Cistercian Abbey of Our Lady of the Holy Cross.
Flynn, Edward R. '54 (SD) Retired.
Flynn, Francis J. '50 (BRK) Retired.
Flynn, Francis J. '69 (OG) Constable, NY The Catholic Community of Constable, Westville and Trout River; Constable, NY St. Bridget's Oratory.
Flynn, Francis J. *m.m.* '76 (FgM).
Flynn, Francis '67 (PMB) Retired.
Flynn, George '56 ((BO)) (FgM).
Flynn, J. Francis *m.m.* '52 (NY).
Flynn, J. Joseph *o.f.m.cap.* (NY)[C] New Rochelle, NY The College of New Rochelle.
Flynn, James B. '64 (WOR) Southborough, MA St. Matthew; [C] Worcester, MA Holy Name Central Catholic Junior/Senior High School.
Flynn, James E. '55 (L) Retired.
Flynn, James E. *s.j.* '73 (PHX)[B] Phoenix, AZ Brophy College Preparatory.
Flynn, James F. '67 (CHI) Chicago, IL Holy Name of Mary.
Flynn, James P. '47 (NY) Patterson, NY Sacred Heart Retired.
Flynn, James R. *o.s.a.* '72 (PH) Philadelphia, PA St. Rita of Cascia; [C] Villanova, PA Villanova University; [G] Malvern, PA Malvern Preparatory School for Boys; [AA] Villanova, PA Provincial Offices of the Order of St. Augustine, Province of St. Thomas of Villanova; [AA] Malvern, PA Augustinian Friars (O.S.A.).
Flynn, John C. '55 (NY) Bronx, NY St. Martin of Tours.
Flynn, John H. '55 (BO) Senior Priests Retired.
Flynn, John Joseph *o.f.m.cap.* (NY)[HH] New Rochelle, NY College of New Rochelle.
Flynn, John L. *s.j.* '64 (SJ).
Flynn, John (TYL)[D] Judges; Advocates.
Flynn, Joseph A. '47 (HRT) Retired.
Flynn, Joseph P. *c.s.p.* '44 (NY) New York, NY St. Paul the Apostle; [EE] Jamaica Estates Paulist Fathers Generalate.
Flynn, Joseph *o.f.m.cap.* '66 (NY)[EE] New York, NY Development Office:.
Flynn, Lawrence W. *m.m.* '87 (NY)[EE] Maryknoll Maryknoll Fathers and Brothers.
Flynn, Mark F. '72 (HRT) Farmington, CT St. Patrick's.
Flynn, Matthew *o.c.s.o.* '58 (WOR)[O] Spencer, MA St. Joseph's Abbey.
Flynn, Michael E. '77 (CHI) Berwyn, IL St. Leonard.
Flynn, Michael F. (BGP)[K] Danbury, CT The Pope John Paul II Center for Health Care, Inc..
Flynn, Michael J. '94 (PT) Destin, FL Church of the Resurrection.
Flynn, Michael J. *s.m.* '01 (BO)[X] Framingham, MA The Marist House.
Flynn, Michael *o.carm.* '60 (CHI) Chicago, IL Nativity of Our Lord.
Flynn, Michael '71 (RVC) Copiague, NY Our Lady of the Assumption.
Flynn, Michael '91 (BGP) Danbury, CT St. Peter.
Flynn, Michael *s.m.* '01 (DET)[D] Pontiac, MI Notre Dame Preparatory High School and Marist Academy.
Flynn, Patrick *c.ss.r.* '69 (BAL) Annapolis, MD St. Mary; [S] Annapolis, MD Saint Mary Rectory.
Flynn, Patrick *c.ss.r.* (HBG) Lancaster, PA St. Anthony of Padua.
Flynn, Sean P. '75 (TR) Toms River, NJ St. Joseph.
Flynn, Stephen F.X. '58 (ALN) Retired.
Flynn, Stephen '58 (ALN)[J] Bethlehem, PA Holy Family Villa.
Flynn, Thomas A. '49 (SCR)[N] Dunmore, PA Villa St. Joseph Retired.
Flynn, Thomas A. '60 (CLV) North Olmsted, OH St. Clarence Retired.
Flynn, Thomas J. *c.s.sp.* '53 (SHP) Retired.
Flynn, Thomas M. '58 (CAM) Longport, NJ Epiphany.
Flynn, Thomas P. '60 (DET) Retired.
Flynn, Thomas '61 (HEL) On Duty Outside the Diocese.
Flynn, William J. *s.s.* '59 (SCR) Olyphant, PA Corpus Christi; Deans.
Flynn, William J. '64 (NOR) Taftville, CT Sacred Heart; Judges; Full Time.
Fobare, Scott D. '87 (OG) Old Forge, NY St. Anthony of Padua; Old Forge, NY St. Bartholomew; Old Forge, NY St. William; Deans.
Fodor, Nicholas Vitez *sch.p.* '49 (BUF)[O] Lackawanna, NY Piarist Fathers Residence; Lackawanna, NY Assumption.
Foeckler, Christopher *m.j.* (CHI)[X] Chicago, IL Men's Formation Center.
Foelker, James *o.m.i.* '55 (CC) Kingsville, TX St. Martin.
Foeller, Charles J. '50 (COL) Cardington, OH Sacred Hearts; Legion of Mary.
Foerch, Benjamin J. *o.f.m.* '65 (NY) New York, NY St. Francis of Assisi.
Foerstier, Vincent *o.p.* '57 (PHX) Los Angeles, CA St. Dominic.
Fogal, Joseph B. (WIN) Austin, MN St. Augustine's; Austin, MN St. Edward's; Elected At–Large Representatives; Priest Assignments Committee; Diocesan Pastoral Council.
Fogarty, Austin '83 (ATL) Newnan, GA St. George's.
Fogarty, Daniel '49 (NY) Retired.
Fogarty, George V. '46 (BRK) Flushing, NY St. Kevin; [V] Douglaston, NY Bishop Mugavero Residence Retired.
Fogarty, Gerald P. *s.j.* '70 (WDC)[M] Washington, DC The Jesuit Community at Georgetown University.
Fogarty, Gerald *o.m.i.* '59 (GAL)[S] Dickinson, TX Christian Renewal Center.
Fogarty, James '54 (SLC) Retired.
Fogarty, John C. *o.carm.* '50 (VEN)[G] Nokomis, FL Carmel at Mission Valley.
Fogarty, Joseph A. *o.p.* '59 (CHI)[N] St. Pius V Priory.
Fogarty, Noel '57 (MIA) Plantation, FL St. Gregory.
Fogarty, Noel (MIA) Pension.
Fogarty, Noel (MIA) Deans and Deaneries.
Fogarty, Paul '67 (ATL) Decatur, GA St. Thomas More; Deans.
Fogarty, Thomas *s.s.p.* '57 (Y)[A] Canfield, OH Society of St. Paul.
Fogle, Bruce '83 (OWN) Providence, KY Holy Cross; Dawson Springs, KY Resurrection; Earlington, KY Immaculate Conception.
Foglio, John '61 (LAN) Retired.
Fohlin, Paul *o.c.d.* '72 (MIL)[O] Holy Hill, WI Discalced Carmelite Monastery – Holy Hill National Shrine of Mary Help of Christians.
Fohn, Kurt '01 (CHL) Statesville, NC St. Philip the Apostle.
Foisy, Leonard R. '57 (MAN) Manchester, NH Transfiguration Retired.
Foken, Herman J. '43 (TLS) Retired.
Folbrecht, Robert A. '75 (LA) L.A. County Fire Dept..
Folbrecht, Robert '75 (LA) Whittier, CA St Gregory the Great.
Folchetti, John T. '74 (BRK) Released from Diocesan Assignment.
Folda, John T. '89 (LIN)[A] Seward, NE St Gregory the Great Seminary; Notaries; Vicars For Religious; Censores Librorum; Members; Diocesan Health Ministries, Inc.; Diocesan Housing Ministries, Inc.; Priests' Continuing Education Committee.
Folda, John (LIN) Presbyteral Council; Catholic Physicians Guild.
Foley, Augustine E. *o.s.b.* '89 (NO)[A] St. Benedict, LA St. Joseph Seminary College.
Foley, Bernard P. *c.s.c.* '56 (FTW)[I] Notre Dame, IN Holy Cross House.
Foley, Brendan P. '55 (HT) Retired.
Foley, Brendan (HT) Judges.
Foley, Daniel R. '60 (SPR) Holyoke, MA St. Jerome's; Vicars for the Clergy; Judges; Presbyteral Council.
Foley, Daniel (SPR) Diocesan Consultors.
Foley, David M. '72 (MEM) Retired.
Foley, Dennis *c.ss.r.* '61 (TR)[Q] Long Branch, NJ San Alfonso Retreat House.
Foley, Edward *o.f.m.cap.* '75 (CHI).
Foley, Edwin '47 (BAL)[B] Baltimore, MD Our Lady of Fatima.
Foley, Francis P. '84 (PH) Military Chaplains; Navy Chaplains.
Foley, Francis P. (SD) Presbyteral Council.
Foley, George '58 (FWT) Albany, TX Jesus of Nazareth; Breckenridge, TX Sacred Heart.
Foley, Gerald J. '55 (BO) Senior Priests Retired.
Foley, Gerald J. '59 (GB) Manitowoc, WI Holy Innocents.
Foley, Gerald K. '61 (CR) HealthEast, Inc.; On Duty Outside the Diocese.
Foley, Gerard M. '56 (ALX) Priests Council; Retirement Board; Tioga, LA Immaculate Heart of Mary; College of Consultors.
Foley, James D. '60 (BO) Salem, MA St. Joseph; [P] St. Benedict, LA St. Joseph Abbey.
Foley, James J. '66 (PH) West Chester, PA SS. Peter and Paul.
Foley, James P. '84 (SFR) San Francisco, CA St. James.
Foley, John B. *s.j.* '72 (STL)[C] Saint Louis University; [O] St. Louis, MO Jesuit Community Corporation at St. Louis University – Jesuit Hall.
Foley, John F. *s.j.* '58 (BO)[V] Weston, MA Campion Health Center, Inc..
Foley, John J. *c.s.p.* '67 (PAT)[A] Oak Ridge, NJ Paulist Novitiate; [I] Oak Ridge, NJ Mount Paul Retreat Center; Advocates.
Foley, John J. '74 (WOR) Worcester, MA Christ the King; Clergy Benefit Plan.
Foley, John J. *s.j.* (CHI)[D] Wilmette, IL Loyola Academy.
Foley, John K. '59 (LA) Montrose, CA Holy Redeemer.
Foley, John P. *s.j.* '67 (CHI) Chicago, IL St. Procopius; [D] Chicago, IL Cristo Rey Jesuit High School, Inc.; [N] Chicago, IL Miguel Pro Jesuit Community.
Foley, John T. '58 (BO) Senior Priests Retired.
Foley, John (WOR) Diocesan Building Commission Members.
Foley, Joseph P. *c.m.* '68 (BRK)[V] Queens Village, NY DePaul Residence.
Foley, Joseph *s.m.a.* '67 (NEW)[N] Tenafly, NJ Society of African Missions, Provincialate, S.M.A. Fathers Retired.
Foley, Marc *o.c.d.* '81 (WDC)[B] Washington, DC Discalced Carmelite Friars.
Foley, Matthew E. '89 (CHI) Chicago, IL St. Agnes of Bohemia.
Foley, Matthew F. '56 (BRK) Brooklyn, NY Epiphany.
Foley, Michael G. '70 (WOR) Milford, MA St. Mary of the Assumption.
Foley, Michael G. '86 (CHI) Evergreen Park, IL Most Holy Redeemer.
Foley, Michael '70 (PT) Tallahassee, FL Good Shepherd.
Foley, Noel (JKS).
Foley, Odoric *o.f.m.conv.* (SY)[Q] Syracuse, NY Friary of Francis, Brother of Peace Conventual Franciscan Friars.
Foley, Patrick '72 (PT) Pensacola, FL St. Anthony of Padua; Pensacola, FL St. Joseph; Vicars Forane.
Foley, Patrick '73 (SD) Unassigned.
Foley, Peter J. '67 (PH) Linwood, PA Holy Saviour.
Foley, Richard L. *o.s.a.* '60 (BO) Andover, MA St. Augustine.
Foley, Thomas C. '57 (BO) Braintree, MA St. Clare; Senior Priests; Braintree, MA St. Clare Retired.
Foley, Thomas F. *m.m.* '48 (NY).
Foley, Thomas F. '77 (SFR)[EE] San Francisco, CA Old St. Mary's Cathedral.
Foley, Thomas S. '86 (BO) Winchester, MA Immaculate Conception.
Foley, Timothy M. '65 (STL) St. Louis, MO Our Lady of Sorrows; Florissant, MO St. Thomas the Apostle.
Foley, Walter W. '76 (ATL) Retired.
Foley, William A. *s.m.* '48 (ORL) Retired.
Foley, William B. *s.j.* '77 (BO)[V] Boston The Society of Jesus of New England–Provincial Offices; [O] St. Louis, MO Jesuit Community Corporation at St. Louis University – Jesuit Hall.
Foley, William E. '79 (WDC) Bowie, MD St. Edward.
Foley, William Gerard '03 (TYL) Texarkana, TX Sacred Heart.
Foley, William J. '67 (NY) New City, NY St. Augustine.

Foley, William P. '74 (BAL) Baltimore, MD Annunciation; Priests' Council.
Foley, William (BAL) Advocates and Procurators.
Folger, Benedict *ss.cc.* '57 (FR)[H] Artesia, NM Our Lady of Grace Rectory.
Folger, Benedict *ss.cc.* '58 (WDC) Seat Pleasant, MD St. Margaret.
Folger, Benedict *ss.cc.* (LSC) Artesia, NM Our Lady of Grace.
Folger, Roland H. '67 (CHI) Antioch, IL St. Peter.
Folinio, Frank *o.f.m.* (CHI)[D] Holy Spirit Friary.
Follen, George R. *s.j.* '49 (DET)[P] Hamtramck, MI St. Ladislaus.
Folliard, John P. '50 (LA) Retired.
Folliard, John '50 (LA) Long Beach, CA St. Cornelius.
Follmann, Roland F. *o.s.a.* '60 (JOL)[C] New Lenox, IL Providence Catholic High School; [L] New Lenox, IL Augustinian Friary.
Follmar, A. Joseph '59 (LC) Greenwood, WI St. Mary Help of Christians; Greenwood, WI Holy Family.
Folmer, John (SAC) Defenders of the Bond.
Folorunso, Stephen Olutade '00 (RCK) Rockford, IL Holy Family; Cary, IL SS. Peter & Paul.
Folsey, William David *o.p.* '60 (PRO)[P] Providence St. Thomas Aquinas Priory at Providence College.
Folsom, Cassian *o.s.b.* '84 (IND)[K] Monastero San Benedetto.
Folsom, Paul '65 (SCL) Battle Lake, MN Our Lady of the Lake; Underwood, MN Church of Saint James at Maine.
Folsom, William P. '91 (MOB) Retired.
Foltyn, Emilian '64 (AUS) Dime Box, TX St. Joseph's; Dime Box, TX Holy Family.
Foltz, Michael H. '89 (CR) Finance Council; Moorhead, MN St. Joseph's.
Folzenlogen, John N. *s.j.* '65 (GAL)[F] Houston, TX Strake, Jesuit College Preparatory Inc..
Folzenlogen, Joseph D. *s.j.* '71 (IND)[M] Cincinnati, OH Claver Jesuit Community.
Folzenlogen, Joseph *s.j.* (CIN) Priest Councilors.
Fonck, Benet *o.f.m.* '72 (SFD)[L] Springfield, IL Our Lady of Angels Friary.
Fondevilla, Perfecto '62 (SJN) San Juan, PR San Francisco de Monte Alvernia.
Fones, Michael S. *o.p.* '92 (TUC) Tuscon, AZ St. Thomas More Chapel; [H] Tucson, AZ University of Arizona.
Fones, Michael *o.p.* '92 (OAK)[N] Oakland, CA Western Dominican Province.
Fones, Michael *o.p.* '92 (P)[P] Eugene, OR University of Oregon (Eugene).
Fonseca, Erwin A. *c.s.c.* '91 (FTW)[I] Congregacion de Santa Cruz.
Fonseca, Harvey '92 (FRS) Livingston, CA St. Jude Thaddeus; Priests' Council.
Fonseca, Rolando (ELP) El Paso, TX St. Pius X.
Fonseka, Matthew '69 (NEW) Saddle Brook, NJ St. Philip the Apostle.
Fontaine, David O. *o.carm.* (STO) Davis, CA St. James.
Fontaine, John–Paul '52 (WOR) Retired.
Fontana, Alphonso R. '99 (HRT) Vocations; West Hartford, CT St. Brigid's.
Fontana, Charles S. '69 (DET) Trenton, MI St. Timothy.
Fontana, Glenn J. '92 (PEO) Pekin, IL St. Joseph's.
Fontana, John M. *o.s.m.* '78 (CHI)[N] Chicago Order of Friar Servants of Mary (Servites) United States of America Province, Inc.; [N] Chicago, IL Order of Friar Servants of Mary (Servites) United States of America Province, Inc..
Fontana, John *o.s.m.* '78 (STL) St. Louis, MO Seven Holy Founders.
Fontanella, Paul C. '02 (SCR)[D] Kingston, PA Bishop O'Reilly High School; Wilkes–Barre, PA St. Patrick's.
Fontanez, Rafael '57 (SJN) Guaynabo, PR San Jose; Knights of Columbus.
Fontanini, Chris '97 (DM) Panora, IA St. Cecilia.
Fontanini, Christ '97 (DM) Guthrie Center, IA St. Mary.
Fontanini, Christopher '97 (DM) Audubon, IA Holy Trinity; [J] Panora, IA St. Thomas More Center.
Fonte, Martin M. *f.f.i.* '94 (FR)[H] New Bedford, MA Marian Friary of Our Lady, Queen of the Seraphic Order.
Fontenot, Anthony '01 (LKC) Iowa, LA St. Raphael; Priest's Senate; Scouting.
Fontenot, Bryan *o.p.* '81 (NO)[P] New Orleans Dominican Friars, Southern Dominican Province of St. Martin de Porres.
Fontenot, James *o.p.* '81 (GAL)[Q] Houston, TX Dominican Friars, St. Mark Priory, Inc..
Fonti, Joseph G. '92 (BRK) Brooklyn, NY Annunciation of the Blessed Virgin Mary; Brooklyn, NY Shrine of Our Lady of Mount Carmel; Presbyteral Council.
Foote, Job *o.s.b.* (ALT) Navy Reserve Chaplains; Nicktown, PA St. Nicholas.
Foppiano, Steven Eugene '02 (SAC) Paradise, CA St. Thomas More.
Foradori, V. David '86 (E) Titusville, PA St. Titus.
Foran, Peter '22 (LA) Long Beach, CA St. Cyprian.
Forand, Clarence W. '45 (SPR) Retired.
Forbes, Eric *o.f.m.cap.* '90 (AGN)[F] Agana Heights, GU St. Fidelis Friary; Archdiocesan College of Consultors; Archdiocesan Presbyteral Council.
Forbes, Eugene A. '41 (SAG) Judges Retired.
Forbes, John J. '91 (R) Sanford, NC St. Stephen The First Martyr.
Forbes, Richard L. '67 (CAM) North Cape May, NJ St. John of God.
Forbes, Wayne A. '61 (P) Portland, OR St. John Fisher.
Forbes, Wayne (P) Area Vicars; Personnel Board.
Forbi, Kizito S. *s.j.* '92 (NY)[EE] Loyola Hall, Jesuit Community.
Forbidussi, John E. '94 (PIT) Pittsburgh, PA St. Athanasius.
Forcano, Benito *sch.p.* '66 (SJN) San Juan, PR Santisimo Salvador.
Forcelle, Joseph '80 (SFS) Vermillion, SD St. Patrick; [H] Vermillion, SD University of South Dakota; Newman Apostolate.
Forcier, Richard–Jacob *o.f.m.conv.* '86 (NOR) Stafford Springs, CT St. Edward.
Forcier, Robert H. '03 (PRO) Cranston, RI St. Paul.
Ford, Christopher M. '87 (HRT) Branford, CT St. Mary.
Ford, Harold L. '49 (LA) Long Beach, CA St. Joseph Retired.
Ford, J. Joseph '67 (PRT) Wells, ME St. Mary; Deans; Clergy Benefit Plan–Clergy Pension Plan; Diocesan Council of Priests.
Ford, James M. '66 (LA) Santa Barbara, CA San Roque.
Ford, John E. *s.t.* '74 (BLX) Pass Christian, MS The Catholic Church in DeLisle; College of Consultors; Insurance Committee.
Ford, John T. *c.s.c.* '59 (FTW)[I] Washington, DC Catholic University.
Ford, John T. *c.s.c.* '59 (FTW)[C] Catholic University of America, The.
Ford, John *s.t.* (BLX) Presbyteral Council.
Ford, Lawrence *o.f.m.* '96 (WDC)[B] Silver Spring, MD Holy Name College.
Ford, Mark *c.m.* '92 (NO) New Orleans, LA St. John the Baptist; New Orleans, LA St. Joseph.
Ford, Matthew M. *o.s.m.* '48 (CHI)[N] Chicago, IL Monastery of Our Lady of Sorrows.
Ford, Michael F. *s.j.* '75 (WOR)[O] Worcester, MA Jesuits of Holy Cross College, Inc.; [R] Holy Cross College.
Ford, Nevin *o.f.m.* '54 (LA)[Q] Santa Barbara, CA Franciscan Friary, Order of Friars Minor (Old Mission); [Q] Santa Barbara, CA St. Anthony's Seminary.
Ford, Patrick J. *s.j.* '74 (P)[L] Portland, OR Jesuit Provincial Office (Society of Jesus, Oregon Prov.); [L] Portland, OR Colombiere Community.
Ford, Richard J. '60 (ALN) Allentown, PA St. Stephen of Hungary; Ecumenical and Interreligious Affairs Office; American Catholic Overseas Aid Fund.
Ford, Robert '44 (NY) Retired.
Ford, William A. '82 (STO) Diamond Springs, CA Retired.
Fording, John D. '42 (PIT)[N] Pittsburgh, PA St. John Vianney Manor Retired.
Forest, Gerald *m.s.* '49 (FR)[H] Attleboro, MA La Salette Shrine.
Forester, Raymond L. (WIL) Rehoboth Beach, DE St. Edmond; Deans.
Forgach, Carl J. '60 (Y) Retired.
Forget, Timothy W. '02 (OM) Omaha, NE Holy Cross.
Forgit, Ambrose *ss.cc.* '55 (FR)[G] Fairhaven, MA Our Lady's Haven of Fairhaven Inc.; [H] Fairhaven, MA Sacred Hearts Provincial House.
Forgit, Ambrose *ss.cc.* (WDC)[B] Cheverly, MD Damien House.
Forintos, Bradley '91 (DET) Armada, MI St. Mary Mystical Rose.
Forish, Andrew '42 (DET) Retired.
Foriska, John M. '70 (GBG) Jeannette, PA Ascension.
Foriska, John '70 (GBG) Penn, PA St. Boniface.
Forkin, Gerald *o.m.i.* '52 (BO)[Y] Tewksbury, MA Immaculate Heart of Mary Infirmary.
Forlani, Joseph *m.c.c.j.* '58 (LA)[CC] Covina, CA Comboni Mission Center.
Forlano, Philip M. '03 (PH) West Chester, PA St. Agnes.
Forliti, John E. '62 (STP) Minneapolis, MN St. Olaf.
Forman, Bruce H. '74 (STL) St. Louis, MO Sts. Peter and Paul.
Forman, Patrick J. '89 (BUR) Catholic Daughters of The Americas; St. Johnsbury, VT St. John the Evangelist.
Formolo, Frank '03 (DAL)[K] Irving, TX Legionaries of Christ.
Formusa, Salvatore '35 (JOL) Retired.
Fornal, Andrzej J. *o.p.* '94 (NY) New York, NY Notre Dame; [HH] New York, NY Columbia University.
Fornasari, Archimede *m.c.c.j.* '50 (CHI) Blue Island, IL St. Donatus.
Forner, Craig '75 (SFR)[B] San Francisco, CA St. Kevin.
Forni, John V. '77 (ROC) Rochester, NY St. John the Evangelist.
Forno, R. Adam '87 (ALB) Rensselaer, NY St. John the Evangelist; Rensselaer, NY St. Joseph.
Forrest, Thomas *c.ss.r.* '54 (WDC)[M] Washington, DC Holy Redeemer College.
Forrester, Donal F. *c.s.p.* '34 (NY) New York, NY St. Paul the Apostle.
Forrey, William C. '90 (HBG) Harrisburg, PA St. Margaret Mary Alacoque; [J] Harrisburg, PA Catholic Campus Ministry; Secretary for Parish and Special Ministries; Campus Ministry; Prison Ministry; Special Ministries, Department for.
Forsen, James '79 (LA) Graduate Studies; Los Angeles, CA St. Columbkille.
Forsman, David '01 (DUL) Hoyt Lakes, MN Queen of Peace; Aurora, MN Holy Rosary.
Forsmann, Len (SPK) Members.
Forsmann, Leonard '76 (SPK) Clarkston, WA Holy Family.
Forson, Cletus M.K. '92 (BRK) Endicott, NY St. Anthony of Padua.
Forst, Aloysius A. '49 (STL) Retired.
Forst, Charles J. '49 (STL) Retired.
Forst, Robert M. '51 (ALN) Allentown, PA Our Lady Help of Christians Retired.
Forst, William '54 (JC) Retired.
Forster, Francis P. *o.s.b.* '64 (CHL)[J] Belmont, NC Belmont Abbey.
Forster, William J. '54 (BO) Senior Priests Retired.
Forsyth, Kevin J. '86 (HRT) Naugatuck, CT St. Vincent Ferrer.
Forte, Anthony J. *s.j.* '83 (BO)[V] Boston The Society of Jesus of New England–Provincial Offices.
Forte, Anthony '91 (NEW) Newark, NJ St. Lucy's.
Forte, John *o.p.* (SD)[L] San Diego, CA University of California at San Diego (Campus Ministry).
Fortenberry, Jerome D. *c.m.* '55 (BEL) Cairo, IL St. Patrick.
Fortener, Kenneth R. '69 (L) Louisville, KY St. Mary; Associate Judges.
Fortier, Joel '69 (JOL) Naperville, IL St. Thomas the Apostle; Deans.
Fortier, Joseph C. *s.j.* '90 (STL)[O] St. Louis, MO Jesuit Community Corporation at St. Louis University – Jesuit Hall.
Fortier, Joseph C. *s.j.* '90 (SEA)[B] Spokane, WA Gonzaga University; [A] Seattle, WA Seattle University.
Fortier, Theodore L. *a.a.* '53 (BO) Quincy, MA Quincy Hospital.
Fortin, John R. *o.s.b.* '76 (MAN)[K] Manchester, NH St. Anselm Abbey; Council of Priests.
Fortin, Philip (PT) Tallahassee, FL Good Shepherd; Tallahassee.
Fortin, Richard A. '62 (WOR) Millbury, MA Assumption.
Fortin, Robert *a.a.* '58 (BO)[V] Ratisbonne Pontifical Institute.
Fortin, Roger L. (PRO) AIDS Ministry.
Fortin, Roger M. '65 (PRO) St. Antonie Residence.
Fortman, Anthony T. *c.pp.s.* '01 (CLV) Cleveland, OH Our Lady of Good Counsel.
Fortner, Douglas F. '70 (COV) Covington, KY St. John.
Fortner, Mark *s.c.j.* (GB)[L] Baileys Harbor, WI St. Joseph Retreat Center.
Fortney, Kenneth E. '79 (HEL) Plains, MT St. James; Thompson Falls, MT St. William.
Fortuna, Joseph J. '80 (CLV) Cleveland, OH Ascension.
Fortuna, Stanley *c.f.r.* '90 (NY)[EE] Bronx, NY Our Lady of the Angels Friary.
Fortunato, Anthony M. *o.de.m.* '67 (SP) St. Petersburg, FL Transfiguration.
Fortunato, Anthony *o.de.m.* '67 (SP)[O] St. Petersburg, FL St. Peter Nolasco Residence.
Fortunato, Vincent *o.f.m.cap.* '80 (NEW)[N] Union City, NJ Capuchin Friars – Province of the Sacred Stigmata of St. Francis; [N] Union City, NJ Capuchin Friars – Province of the Sacred Stigmata of St. Francis.
Fortunio, Carlo *o.p.* '85 (NEW) West New York, NJ St. Mary Help of Christians; North Hudson Deanery 8.
Foschiatto, Edi *s.x.* '81 (PAT)[M] Wayne Xaverian Missionary Fathers.
Foshage, Nathanael *o.s.b.* '68 (OM)[K] Elkhorn, NE Mount Michael Abbey.
Foshage, Nathanael *o.s.b.* '68 (PBL) Ouray, CO St. Daniel the Prophet; Ouray, CO St. Patrick; Telluride, CO St. Patrick; Presbyteral Council–College of Consultors; Presbyteral Council; Personnel.
Foshage, Ronald B. *m.s.* (BEA) Northern Vicariate.
Foshage, Ronald *m.s.* '75 (BEA) Jasper, TX St. Michael; Jasper, TX Our Lady of La Salette Mission; Jasper, TX St. Raymond Mission.
Fosnot, James M. (RIC) Jonesville, VA Church of the Holy Spirit.
Fosnot, James '94 (RIC) Big Stone Gap, VA Sacred Heart.
Fossati, Sergio *p.i.m.e.* '89 (LAN) Ypsilanti, MI Holy Trinity Student Parish.
Fosselman, Albert M. (RNO) Judges.
Fosselman, Albert '60 (RNO) Retired.
Fosselman, John A. '42 (LA) Downey, CA Rancho Los Amigos Medical Center Retired.
Fossier, Emile '43 (HT) Retired.
Foster, Clyde K. '75 (CLV) Maple Heights, OH St. Wenceslas.
Foster, Edward '51 (DUL) Retired.

Foster, James A. '72 (ALX) Priests Council; Colfax, LA St. Joseph.
Foster, James J. '80 (STL) St. Louis, MO Corpus Christi.
Foster, James K. *c.s.c.* '95 (FTW)[B] University of Notre Dame Du Lac; [I] Notre Dame, IN Holy Cross Community, Corby Hall, University of Notre Dame.
Foster, John F. *s.j.* '68 (SEA)[A] Seattle, WA Seattle University.
Foster, John J. '51 (PH) Retired.
Foster, John J.M. '91 (STO) Stockton, CA Cathedral of the Annunciation (Pastor of); Judicial Vicar; Diocesan Building Committee; Office for Worship; Catholic Committee on Scouting.
Foster, John Mary *f.j.* '87 (SAT) Special Assignment.
Foster, Jonathan D. *o.f.m.* '60 (JOL)[N] Westmont, IL Mayslake Ministries, Inc..
Foster, Michael S. '80 (BO) Cambridge, MA St. Peter; Presbyteral Council; Appointed; Judicial Vicar; Archdiocesan Judges; Canonical Affairs Committee.
Foster, Patrick '56 (EVN) Retired.
Foster, Raymond *o.carm.* '73 (JOL)[L] Joliet, IL St. Elias Carmelites.
Foster, Reginald *o.c.d.* '66 (MIL)[O] Milwaukee Provincial Offices – Discalced Carmelites.
Foster, Thomas J. (DUL) Army National Guard Chaplains.
Foster, Thomas W. *s.j.* '72 (SJ)[M] Los Gatos, CA Sacred Heart Jesuit Center.
Fostner, Jay M. *o.praem.* '88 (GB)[B] St. Norbert College; [I] De Pere, WI St. Joseph Priory.
Fosu, Peter H. '86 (MAR) Brimley, MI St. Francis Xavier; Brimley, MI Blessed Kateri Tekakwitha.
Foudy, John T. '40 (SFR) San Francisco, CA St. Cecilia Retired.
Foudy, Thomas F. '67 (MIA) Pompano Beach, FL St. Coleman.
Fountain, Dennis '81 (LSC) Hobbs, NM St. Helena.
Fountain, Dennis *o.f.m.conv.* (LSC) Diocesan Consultors.
Fountain, Michael *o.f.m.cap.* '73 (MIL).
Fountain, Robert J. '55 (BO)[X] Medford, MA St. Joseph.
Fournier, Denis *o.s.b.* '60 (BIS)[A] Richardton, ND Assumption Abbey; [B] Bismarck, ND University of Mary.
Fournier, Raymond A. *s.m.* '49 (BUR) Chester, VT St. Joseph.
Fournier, Raymond J. *o.c.s.o.* '81 (ROC)[I] Piffard, NY Abbey of the Genesee.
Fournier, W. Donald '53 (SPR) Retired.
Fournier, William '73 (DUL) Duluth, MN St. Joseph's; Duluth, MN St. Lawrence's.
Foutts, Patrick D. *o.praem.* '93 (ORG)[I] Silverado, CA Norbertine Fathers of Orange Inc..
Fowerbaugh, F. Raymond '55 (GRY) Retired.
Fowler, Eugene A. '48 (NY) Retired.
Fowler, J. Richard (HRT) Bristol, CT Bristol Hospital.
Fowler, John W. '53 (DAL) Retired.
Fowler, Joseph M. '61 (L) Louisville, KY St. Cecilia; Louisville, KY Our Lady.
Fowler, Joseph (PT) Vice Chancellor & Notary; Pensacola, FL Cathedral of the Sacred Heart.
Fowler, Richard A. '88 (BUR) Retired.
Fox, Daniel A. '82 (LA) South Pasadena, CA Holy Family.
Fox, Daniel *o.f.m.cap.* '75 (DET)[T] St. Clair Shores, MI Catholic Kolping Society of America, Detroit Branch, Inc.; [K] Detroit St. Bonaventure Friary.
Fox, Donal R. *o.s.b.* '66 (NEW) Linden, NJ St. Elizabeth's; [M] Morristown St. Mary's Abbey.
Fox, Francis E. '58 (PH) Philadelphia, PA Maternity B.V.M..
Fox, Gabriel '74 (GAY) Retired.
Fox, George W. '61 (MAD) Retired.
Fox, James E. '74 (DEN) Aurora, CO St. Michael the Archangel; Deaneries.
Fox, James R. '90 (DEN) Westminster, CO St. Mark; Deaneries.
Fox, John J. '60 (BUF) Retired.
Fox, Joseph F. '43 (SCR) Retired.
Fox, Leo '56 (SFS) Retired.
Fox, Leonard '55 (SFS) Retired.
Fox, Martin E. '03 (CIN) Dayton, OH St. Albert the Great.
Fox, Martin F. '65 (GB) Seymour, WI St. John.
Fox, Melvin E. '63 (GR) Ionia, MI SS. Peter and Paul.
Fox, Patrick '52 (SD) Retired.
Fox, Richard E. '92 (SCR) Nanticoke, PA Holy Trinity; Presbyteral Council.
Fox, Richard *o.c.s.o.* '59 (SPC)[E] Ava, MO Assumption Abbey (Trappist).
Fox, Richard '85 (SFS) Colman, SD St. Peter; Flandreau, SD SS. Simon and Jude.
Fox, Robert J. '59 (GF) Defenders of the Bond; Clerical Benefit Association Retired.
Fox, Robert '01 (CHY) Evanston, WY St. Mary Magdalen; Board of Trustees.
Fox, Sean P. '53 (SEA) Mountlake Terrace, WA St. Pius X.
Fox, Sean (SEA) Priests' Health Plan; Priests' Pension Plan.
Fox, Thomas E. '59 (BRK) Brooklyn, NY Holy Family.
Fox, Thomas E '60 (LFT) Remington, IN Sacred Heart; Deans; Members.
Fox, Thomas *m.m.* '56 (NY).
Fox, Thomas *o.f.m.* '62 (IND)[EE] Indianapolis, IN St. Patrick.
Fox, Thomas (LFT) Clergy Relief Association.
Fox, Tom *o.f.m.* '62 (IND) Indianapolis, IN Sacred Heart of Jesus.
Foxen, David *m.s.c.* '67 (RCK) (FgM).
Foye, Harold J. *c.s.p.* '46 (NY)[EE] Jamaica Estates Paulist Fathers Generalate.
Foye, Thomas M. '55 (NEW) Bayonne, NJ St. Andrew's Retired.
Foynes, Aiden '33 (SP)[F] Clearwater, FL Little Nazareth Early Childhood Center.
Foynes, Aiden '61 (SP) Clearwater, FL St. Cecelia; Incardination Commission.
Foyo, Alexis *o.s.b.* '83 (SD)[H] Oceanside, CA Prince of Peace Abbey Benet Hill.
Fraats, Ralph '60 (ROC) Auburn, NY St. Francis of Assisi.
Fracaro, Mark '67 (JOL) Minooka, IL St. Mary.
Frade, Paulo '97 (NEW) Harrison, NJ Holy Cross.
Fraenzle, Wilfred J. '64 (LEX) Lexington, KY St. Elizabeth Ann Seton.
Fraenzle, Wilfred '64 (LEX) Ravenna, KY St. Elizabeth of Hungary; Stanton, KY Our Lady of the Mountains.
Fraga, Bento R. *v.f.* '56 (FR) Taunton, MA St. Paul's; Taunton Deanery.
Fragomeni, Richard '75 (ALB) On Duty Outside the Diocese.
Fragomeni, Richard '75 (CHI).
Fraher, Joseph P. '50 (CHY) Retired.
Fraher, Kevin *c.ss.r.* '73 (CHI)[N] Glenview, IL The Redemptorists of Glenview, Illinois.
Fraher, Leonard W. '56 (SUP) Retired.
Fraile, Mariano *o.c.d.* '47 (PCE) Ponce, PR San Jose.
Fraile, Tomas *c.r.* '63 (DEN) Denver, CO St. Cajetan.
Frain, Brian *s.j.* '02 (NY)[GG] Staten Island, NY Mount Manresa Jesuit Retreat House.
Frambes, John *o.f.m.* '79 (CHL)[J] Greensboro, NC Franciscan Friary; [L] Greensboro, NC University of North Carolina–Greensboro, Greensboro College & Guilford College; Campus Ministry – UNC–Greensboro [Q] Greensboro, NC Franciscan Center.
Francavilla, Joseph F. '68 (NTN) McLean, VA Holy Transfiguration.
Francavilla, Joseph (NTN) Priest's Sickness & Disability, and Retirement Plans.
France–Kelly Kenneth A. *o.p.* '81 (WDC) Washington, DC St. Dominic Church & Priory; [V] Washington, DC Rosary Shrine of St. Jude.
Franceschini, Mark M. *o.s.m.* '59 (CHI)[N] Chicago Order of Friar Servants of Mary (Servites) United States of America Province, Inc..
Franceschini, Philip J. '66 (NY) Staten Island, NY Our Lady of Pity.
Francesco, Richard G. '87 (NEW) West Orange, NJ St. Joseph's; Remarriage Ministry.
Franceshini, Mark '59 (DEN) Denver, CO Our Lady of Mt. Carmel.
Franci, J. (FgM).
Francik, Gerard C. '87 (BAL) Baltimore, MD Cathedral of Mary Our Queen; [W] Baltimore, MD Serra Club Vocation Office.
Francik, Gerard '87 (BAL) Special Assignment; Vocation Office.
Francis, Bernard C. '69 (NO) Hahnville, LA Our Lady of the Holy Rosary.
Francis, Daniel *c.ss.r.* '91 (NY) Bronx, NY Immaculate Conception.
Francis, Eugene G. '52 (GAL) Houston, TX St. John Neumann.
Francis, Isaac O. '97 (GAL) Houston, TX St. Thomas More.
Francis, John '90 (BRK) Woodside, NY St. Sebastian.
Francis, Joseph A. *o.p.* '78 (NY) New York, NY St. Monica.
Francis, Paul R. (BO) Senior Priests Retired.
Francis, Rashid Peter *o.f.m.* '80 (NY) New York, NY St. Anthony of Padua.
Francis, Sunny *s.v.d.* '88 (CHI)[B] Techny, IL Divine Word Residence.
Francis, William C. '58 (BO) Dorchester, MA Holy Family.
Francisco, Manuel *s.j.* '97 (BO)[V] Cambridge, MA.
Francisko, Gary '82 (PRM) Absent on Leave.
Franck, James *c.pp.s.* '64 (LA) Los Angeles, CA St. Agnes.
Franck, John L. *a.a.* '77 (BO)[V] Boston, MA Assumptionist Center.
Franck, John *c.pp.s.* '67 (LA) Los Angeles, CA St. Agnes.
Franco, David *o.s.f.s.* '76 (LAN) Ypsilanti, MI Transfiguration Catholic Church.
Franco, Hilary '55 (NY) Ossining, NY St. Augustine.
Franco, Juan *m.s.c.* '03 (FRS) Avenal, CA St. Joseph; Los Angeles, CA San Miguel.
Franco, Robert J. '82 (CLV) Sheffield, OH St. Teresa of Avila.
Franco, Robert M. '73 (PIT) Pittsburgh, PA St. Catherine of Siena; Defenders of the Bond; Deans and Deaneries.
Franco, Robert (CLV) Catholic Renewal Ministries.
Franco, Rodolfo '99 (BWN) San Benito, TX St. Theresa; Presbyteral Council; Diocesan College of Consultors; Parish Priests' Consultors & Priest Personnel Board.
Franco, Ronald *c.s.p.* '95 (NY) New York, NY St. Paul the Apostle.
Franco, Victor *l.c.* '81 (MAN)[A] Center Harbor, NH Immaculate Conception Apostolic School.
Francois, Ducasse *i.v. dei.* '88 (PMB) Fort Pierce, FL St. Anastasia; Fort Pierce, FL Notre Dame Mission.
Franczek, J. August '48 (GAY) Hale, MI St. Pius X; Vicars (by region).
Franey, John A. '63 (PH) West Chester, PA St. Agnes.
Frank, Chrysostom '85 (DEN) Denver, CO St. Elizabeth of Hungary.
Frank, Edward R. '57 (SAV) Augusta, GA St. Mary on the Hill Retired.
Frank, Gerald W. '70 (BWN) La Joya, TX Our Lady, Queen of Angels.
Frank, Joseph A. '49 (NEW)[N] Caldwell, NJ The Rev. Msgr. James F. Kelley Residence for Retired Priests Retired.
Frank, Paul *o.m.i.* '50 (MIA) Fort Lauderdale, FL St. John the Baptist.
Frank, Richard C. *m.m.* '53 (FgM).
Frank, Richard W. '72 (JC) Bowling Green, MO St. Clement; Bowling Green, MO Northeast Correctional Center.
Frank, Thomas *s.s.j.* '77 (WDC)[B] Washington, DC St. Joseph's Seminary.
Frank, Thomas (AUS) Presbyteral Council.
Frank, Tom '70 (AUS) Austin, TX San Jose.
Franken, William F. '88 (BAL) Hydes, MD St. John the Evangelist.
Frankenberger, William J. *c.s.b.* '73 (GAL)[Q] Sugar Land Basilian Mission Center.
Frankhauser, William E. *s.j.* '66 (BUF) Cattaraugus, NY St. Mary; Cattaraugus, NY St. Mary.
Franklin, Claude W. '97 (SAM) Liturgy; Graduate Studies.
Franklin, David W. '85 (BGP) Greenwich, CT Greenwich Hospital; Stamford, CT Stamford Hospital; Ridgefield, CT St. Elizabeth Seton.
Franklin, George '86 (STV) Charlotte Amalie, VI Cathedral of Sts. Peter and Paul.
Franklin, Mark E. '02 (SHP) Bossier City, LA St. Jude.
Franklin, Mark (SHP) Scouting.
Franklin, Osvaldo (NY) Yonkers, NY Our Lady of Fatima.
Frankman, Gregory '81 (SFS) Kranzburg, SD Holy Rosary.
Franko, George M. '50 (Y) Retired.
Franko, John *o.m.i.* '67 (GAL) Alvin, TX St. John the Baptist.
Frankovich, Francis A. '68 (GAL) Houston, TX Queen of Peace; [Q] Houston, TX Companions of the Cross (Texas); [U] Houston, TX Catholic Charismatic Center.
Frankovich, Frank '68 (SB) On Duty Outside the Diocese.
Frankovich, Lawrence *o.f.m.* '66 (MIL) West Allis, WI St. Augustine.
Franks, Becket '86 (JOL)[M] Lisle, IL Benedictine Sisters of the Sacred Heart, Sacred Heart Monastery.
Franks, Donald E. '79 (COL) Lancaster, OH St. Mary; [L] Lancaster, OH St. Mary of the Assumption Foundation.
Franks, Gabriel '57 (VIC) On Special or Other Diocesan Assignment.
Franks, T. Becket *o.s.b.* '86 (JOL)[L] Lisle, IL St. Procopius Abbey.
Fransco, Peter J. '58 (SC) Retired.
Fransiscus, Thomas J. *c.ss.r.* '65 (RNO) Reno, NV St. Michael's.
Fransiscus, Thomas *c.ss.r.* (RNO) Judicial Vicar/ Officialis.
Fransiscus, Tom *c.ss.r.* (LAV) Promoter of Justice; Diocesan Advocate.
Fransiscus, Tom *c.ss.r.* (RNO) Curia; Diocesan Board of Consultors; Presbyteral Council.
Frantz, Henry L. *c.pp.s.* '54 (ORL) Longwood, FL Church of the Nativity.
Franz, Louis *c.m.* (GLP) Presbyteral Council; Diocesan Consultors.
Franz, Paul R. '66 (BO) Health Leave.
Franz, S. Michael '69 (CLV) Cleveland, OH St. Stephen.
Franzen, Robert B. '53 (SFD) Chatham, IL St. Joseph.
Franzinell, Benjamin '50 (LAV) Retired.
Franzman, Thomas R. '70 (CHI) Other Assignments.
Frapaul, Sam *o.f.m.cap.* '78 (PAT) Passaic, NJ Our Lady Of Mt. Carmel.
Frappier, George L. '56 (PRO) Minister for Senior Priests Retired.
Frascadore, Henry C. '59 (HRT) Southington, CT St. Dominic.
Frascati, Marino *o.de.m.* '51 (CLV) Cleveland, OH Our

Lady of Mount Carmel; [O] Cleveland, OH Mercedarians.
Fraser, Bernard (DET) Taylor, MI St. Cyril of Jerusalem.
Fraser, Christopher J. '01 (PHX) Chandler, AZ St. Andrew the Apostle.
Fraser, Daniel J. '99 (TOL) Toledo, OH St. Agnes.
Fraser, Donald D. '74 (B) McCall, ID Our Lady of the Lake.
Fraser, Gerald C. '72 (BO) Permanent Disability.
Fraser, Gerald D. '38 (CHI) Retired.
Fraser, James F. '65 (BRK) Whitestone, NY Holy Trinity.
Fraser, John '96 (NY) New York, NY Cathedral of St. Patrick.
Fraser, Michael B. '75 (NO) Marrero, LA The Visitation of Our Lady.
Fratic, Joseph P. '64 (BO) Arlington, MA St. Jerome.
Fratt, Gregory Perkins '98 (HT) Amelia, LA St. Andrew.
Fratt, Gregory (HT) Catholic Daughters of the Americas.
Fratts, Ralph J. '60 (ROC) Retired.
Fratus, James F. '81 (BO) Dorchester, MA St. Brendan; Juvenile Court Chaplain.
Fratus, Thomas '52 (CHI)[N] Chicago, IL St. Peter's Friary.
Frausto, Jorge '86 (ELP)[B] El Paso, TX St. Anthony's School of Theology.
Frawley, Gerard *s.c.a.* '68 (DET) Allenton, MI St. John the Evangelist; Capac, MI St. Nicholas.
Frawley, John P. '44 (CHI) Chicago, IL St. Thomas More Retired.
Frawley, Patrick J. '78 (BRK) Jackson Heights, NY Our Lady of Fatima.
Frazer, Edward J. *s.s.* '61 (WDC)[C] Catholic University of America, The.
Frazer, J. Francis '75 (PIT) Bethel Park, PA St. Valentine.
Frazer, Joseph '84 (AUS) Franklin, TX St. Francis of Assisi.
Frazier, Lawrence K. '71 (BAL) Buckeystown, MD St. Joseph–on–Carrollton Manor.
Frazier, Richard W. '96 (COV) Cynthiana, KY St. Edward.
Frazier, William B. *m.m.* '56 (NY)[EE] Maryknoll Maryknoll Fathers and Brothers.
Frazzita, Barry '59 (BRK) Jackson Heights, NY St. Joan of Arc.
Frechette, Christopher *s.j.* '99 (BO)[V] Cambridge, MA Faber House; [V] Cambridge, MA Faber House.
Frechette, Leo L. '55 (MAN) Retired.
Frechette, Paul G. '78 (NTN) Worcester, MA Our Lady of Perpetual Help.
Frechette, Paul *s.m.* '76 (FgM).
Frechette, Paul (NTN) Continuing Education of Clergy Office.
Frechette, Richard *c.p.* '79 (FgM).
Frechette, Thomas A. '86 (FR) Hyannis, MA St. Francis Xavier's; Family Ministry.
Frecker, A. Anthony '72 (COL) Canal Winchester, OH Pope John XXIII; Diocesan Consultors; Diocesan Judges.
Fredeman, Felix *o.s.b.* '57 (LR)[A] Subiaco, AR Subiaco Monastery.
Frederici, David C. '01 (FR) Centerville, MA Our Lady of Victory.
Frederick, Curt J. '75 (MIL) Brookfield, WI St. Dominic; Judges for Second Instance.
Frederick, Joseph B. '56 (MIL) Retired.
Frederick, Lawrence A. '66 (LR)[B] Little Rock, AR Catholic High School.
Frederick, Robert (ATL) Alpharetta, GA St. Brigid.
Fredericks, James L. '77 (SFR) On Duty Outside the Archdiocese.
Fredericks, James '77 (LA)[C] Los Angeles, CA Jesuit Community.
Fredericks, Michael '87 (SB) Air Force Reserve Chaplains.
Fredette, Joseph *a.a.* '60 (BO)[V] Boston, MA Assumptionist Center.
Free, Daniel *c.p.* '52 (HRT)[M] West Hartford Holy Family Monastery/Retreat.
Free, Henry *c.p.* '58 (FgM).
Freed, Eric '90 (SJ) St. Francis High School; [D] Mountain View, CA St. Francis High School; [C] Belmont, CA Notre Dame de Namur University.
Freed, Eric '90 (SR) On Duty Outside the Diocese.
Freed, Robert '83 (WCH) Retired.
Freed, Robert '83 (ALN) Bally, PA Most Blessed Sacrament.
Freeh, Vincent *m.s.c.* (Y) Catholic Alumni Club of Youngstown, Inc..
Freel, Francis *c.ss.r.* '46 (ALB)[L] Saratoga Springs, NY St. John Neumann Residence.
Freeman, George J. '65 (STP) New Prague, MN St. Wenceslaus.
Freeman, James A. '65 (TUC) Tucson, AZ St. Joseph; [D] Tucson, AZ St. Joseph Hospital.
Freeman, James '65 (DM) On Duty Outside the Diocese.
Freeman, John A. '73 (PH) Newtown, PA St. Andrew.
Freeman, Roland P. '67 (DEN)[G] Denver, CO Special Religious Education–Pastoral Care of Developmentally Disabled Persons.
Freemesser, Paul J. '59 (ROC) Auburn, NY St. Alphonsus Retired.
Freeswick, William J. '69 (PAT)[K] Denville, NJ St. Francis Residential Community.
Freeswick, William (PAT).
Freeze, Donald J. *s.j.* '63 (PH)[AA] Loyola Center and Manresa Hall.
Frego, Max '63 (SAG) Retired.
Freidel, John J. '86 (SPC)[I] Cape Girardeau, MO Southeast Missouri State University, Newman Center.
Freidl, Thomas A. '92 (CR) On Duty Outside the Diocese.
Freidl, Thomas (CR) AUXILIARY CHAPLAINS CONTRACT CHAPLAINS.
Freiermuth, Harry '59 (MRY) Retired.
Freire, Gerardo *s.j.* '56 (MIA)[H] Miami, FL Villa Javier.
Freitag, Patrick W. '96 (SEA) Bremerton, WA Our Lady, Star of the Sea.
Freitag, Patrick (SEA) Presbyteral Council; Deans.
Freitas, Daniel L. '49 (FR) Retired.
Freitas, Daniel '47 (ORL) Retired.
Freitas, Fernando P. '48 (PRO) Retired.
Freitas, Patrick (HON) Ewa Beach, HI Our Lady of Perpetual Help; Ana Malia Institute No. 208.
Fremgen, Edward '92 (LA) Retired.
Fremont–Smith, Peter *s.o.l.t.* (MO) Navy Chaplains.
French, D. James *s.j.* '74 (NY)[EE] New York, NY "America;" Residence and publication office of the America Press; [EE] New York, NY Jesuit Provincial's Office.
French, Donald J. '76 (HRT) Hamden, CT Blessed Sacrament.
French, James R. '78 (STL) Park Hills, MO Immaculate Conception.
French, John F. '54 (ALB) Retired.
French, Michael D. *s.j.* '85 (BAL)[S] Baltimore, MD Jesuit Fathers and Brothers Maryland Provincial Curia.
French, Raymond D. *c.s.sp.* '91 (PIT)[B] Pittsburgh, PA Duquesne University of the Holy Spirit; [Q] Pittsburgh, PA Duquesne University.
French, Robert E. '63 (RIC) Hampton, VA Immaculate Conception.
French, Thomas A. '49 (SAT)[K] San Antonio, TX Incarnate Word Retirement Community; [N] San Antonio, TX Incarnate Word Retirement Community.
French, Thomas *s.m.* '97 (SFR)[N] San Francisco, CA Marianist Community; [D] San Francisco, CA Archbishop Riordan High School (Boys).
French, Thomas (SAT) Vicars for Religious.
French, Walter V. '65 (NEW) Retired.
Frenier, Steven G. *o.f.m.conv.* '82 (BUF) Athol Springs, NY St. Francis of Assisi.
Frenoy, Fortune C. *s.m.* '54 (WDC)[M] Sun City Center, FL Retired.
Freret, Warren Joseph '88 (GAL) Retired.
Frerichs, Glenn K. (WIN) Janesville, MN St. Ann's; St. Joseph's.
Frerker, Jack W. '63 (BEL) Retired.
Frerkes, James J. '62 (MRY) Paso Robles, CA Santa Margarita de Cortona.
Fresno, Leonidas *o.s.a.* '64 (SAT) San Antonio, TX St. Jude.
Freson, Kenan *o.f.m.* '67 (CIN)[C] Cincinnati, OH St. Anthony Shrine, Franciscan Candidacy; [M] Cincinnati, OH St. Francis Seraph Friary; [U] Cincinnati, OH Community Support Charitable Trust; [U] Cincinnati, OH Friars Club Foundation, Inc..
Freuh, Robert '63 (BRK) Brooklyn, NY St. Augustine.
Freund, John B. *c.m.* '65 (BRK)[V] Jamaica, NY St. Vincent's House.
Freund, Melchior *o.s.b.* '57 (SCL)[I] Collegeville, MN St. John's Abbey, of the Order of St. Benedict.
Frey, Andrew F. '48 (BR) Retired.
Frey, Francis '58 (SAN) Odessa, TX St. Mary's.
Frey, Jerome V. '50 (LAF) On Special Assignment; [M] Lafayette, LA Community of Jesus Crucified.
Frey, John T. '70 (CAM) Haddon Heights, NJ St. Rose's; Episcopal Vicar for Priestly Life & Development; Vicariate for Priestly Life and Development; Advanced Studies for Priests; Amicus; English Cursillo; Vocation Advisory Board.
Frey, John (CAM) Members.
Freyer, Tim (ORG) Ministry to Priests.
Freyer, Timothy '89 (ORG) Anaheim, CA St. Boniface.
Freymuth, Mike '79 (STL) St. Louis, MO St. Elizabeth, Mother of John the Baptist.
Freyne, Bernard '60 (SJ) Retired.
Frias, Martin '03 (PBL) Center, CO St. Francis Jerome; Del Norte, CO Holy Name of Mary; Monte Vista, CO St. Joseph.
Frias, Santiago C. '59 (RIC) Norfolk, VA Holy Trinity; Apostleship of the Sea; Apostleship of the Sea.
Friberc, Daniel '62 (STP) Retired.
Friday, Robert M. '61 (PIT) On Duty Outside the Diocese; [C] Catholic University of America, The.
Fride, Edward O. '86 (LAN) Ann Arbor, MI Christ the King.
Fridrich, Sylvester W. '51 (CLV) Gates Mills, OH St. Francis of Assisi Retired.
Friebel, Richard *c.pp.s.* (CIN) Priest Councilors.
Friebel, Rick *c.pp.s.* '78 (CIN) Dayton, OH Holy Trinity.
Fried, Francis L. '68 (STP) Roseville, MN Corpus Christi.
Fried, John F. '70 (TUC) Yuma, AZ St. John Neumann.
Friedel, J. (SPC) Region VII (A).
Friedel, James *o.s.a.* '65 (CHI)[N] Olympia Fields, IL Tolentine Monastery at Tolentine Center.
Friedel, John (J) F. (SPC) Diocesan Consultors.
Friedel, John (J.) F. (SPC) Campus Ministries.
Friedel, Robert E. '57 (CLV) Twinsburg, OH SS. Cosmas and Damian Retired.
Friedell, John C. '54 (DUB) Retired.
Friedell, Ronald G.. '66 (DUB)[I] Dubuque, IA Holy Family Hall Infirmary; Dubuque, IA St. Columbkille.
Friederick, John J. '65 (DUB) CIVIL AIR PATROL; Edgewood, IA St. Patrick; Edgewood, IA St. Mark.
Friedl, Erwin J. '71 (CHI) Melrose Park, IL Sacred Heart.
Friedl, Francis P. '43 (DUB) Retired.
Friedl, Thomas '92 (RNO) Fallon, NV Fallon Naval Air Station Base Chapel.
Friedman, Cecil H. '50 (SC) Retired.
Friedman, Daniel J. '72 (BEL) Aviston, IL St. Francis of Assisi.
Friedman, Robert '89 (Y) Hubbard, OH St. Patrick.
Friedrich, Aloys *c.pp.s.* '36 (CIN).
Friedrich, James '89 (SFS)[D] Sioux Falls, SD Avera McKennan; Defender of the Matrimonial Bond.
Friedrich, Jim '89 (SFS) Sioux Falls, SD St. Mary.
Friedrich, Lawrence '47 (SFS) Retired.
Friedrich, Ralph '43 (Y) Retired.
Friedrichs, Richard M. '70 (PRO)[R] Narragansett, RI Our Lady of Peace Spiritual Life Center.
Friedrichsen, Timothy A. '84 (SC) On Duty Outside the Diocese.
Friedrichsen, Timothy '84 (WDC)[C] Catholic University of America, The.
Friel, Edward M. '89 (CAM) Cherry Hill, NJ St. Peter Celestine.
Friel, James E. '52 (PBL) Pueblo, CO St. Anne.
Friel, Lee G. *o.f.m.cap.* '56 (FgM).
Friel, Lee *o.f.m.cap.* '56 (AGN)[F] Agana Heights, GU St. Fidelis Friary.
Friel, Mark M. '63 (BUF)[O] Buffalo, NY Sheehan Residence for Priests Retired.
Friend, R. Scott (LR) Cursillo Movement; Presbyteral Council.
Friend, Scott '87 (LR) Springdale, AR St. Raphael's.
Frient, Lawrence '84 (Y) Niles, OH Our Lady of Mt. Carmel.
Fries, Richard R. *m.m.* '76 (NY)[EE] Maryknoll Maryknoll Fathers and Brothers.
Frigault, Edward F. '49 (NOR) Willimantic, CT St. Joseph Retired.
Frigo, Martin A. *o.praem.* '49 (WIL)[J] Middletown, DE Immaculate Conception Priory of the Canons Regular of Premontre.
Frigo, William M. *o.f.m.cap.* '63 (CHI).
Frigo, William *o.f.m.cap.* '63 (CHI)[N] Chicago, IL St. Clare Friary.
Frilot, Eugene P. '55 (LA) Glendale, CA Church of the Incarnation Retired.
Frink, John A. '87 (ALN) Ashland, PA St. Joseph; Ashland, PA St. Mauritius.
Frinsko, Donald S. *t.o.r.* (STU)[F] Steubenville, OH Holy Spirit Friary.
Frisbie, Kenneth J. '48 (HRT)[A] Bloomfield, CT St. Thomas Seminary Retired.
Frisch, Kenneth J. '78 (MAD) Highland, WI SS. Anthony and Philip; Montfort, WI St. Thomas.
Frisch, Michael F. *o.praem.* '97 (GB)[I] De Pere, WI St. Norbert Abbey.
Frisch, Ralph *s.t.* '59 (WDC)[M] University Park, MD Holy Trinity Missionary Cenacle.
Frische, Emile *m.h.m.* (NY) New York, NY Holy Family; Coordinator for Special Ministries.
Friske, Joseph P. '62 (SAG) On Duty Outside the Diocese Retired.
Frisoli, John B. *o.f.m.* '48 (ALB).
Frison, Ted '72 (P) Salem, OR Hillcrest Youth Correctional Facility; Woodburn, OR MacLaren Youth Correctional Facility.
Frister, Jerome '57 (JUN) Retired.
Fritsch, Albert *s.j.* '67 (LEX) Frankfort, KY Good Shepherd.
Fritsch, Michael C. '85 (IND) Bloomington, IN St. John the Apostle.
Fritschen, Thomas *f.s.s.p.* '00 (SCR)[M] Maple Hill, KS.
Fritschen, Thomas *f.s.s.p.* (COS) Colorado Springs, CO Immaculate Conception.
Fritz, Germain L. *o.s.b.* '61 (PAT)[M] Morristown, NJ St. Mary's Abbey.
Fritz, Henry H. *o.s.b.* '52 (PEO) Peru, IL St. Joseph's; Peru, IL St. Mary's.
Fritz, John C. (RCK)[A] Secretary to the Bishop & Diocesan Master of Ceremonies.

Fritz, John (RCK) Special Assignment.
Fritz, Norbert '42 (P) Retired.
Fritz, Peter *o.f.m.* '50 (FWT)[I] Crowley, TX St. Maximilian Kolbe Friary.
Fritz, Richard A. '75 (KAL) Bronson, MI St. Mary's.
Fritz, Robert J. '75 (CAM) Paulsboro, NJ St. John's.
Fritzen, James C. '69 (SY) Syracuse, NY St. Mary–St. Agnes; Catholic Cemeteries.
Frizelle, John D. '51 (AUS) Granger, TX SS. Cyril and Methodius Retired.
Frizzell, Lawrence E. '62 (NEW)[B] School of Diplomacy and Intl. Rels..
Frizzell, Lawrence (NEW) Archdiocesan Theological Commission.
Froehle, Charles L. '63 (STP) Minneapolis, MN Our Lady of Lourdes; Presbyteral Council; Censores Librorum.
Froehlich, Canice *o.f.m.cap.* '47 (STL)[O] St. Louis, MO St. Patrick Friary.
Froehlich, James *o.f.m.cap.* '82 (HBG) York, PA St. Joseph.
Froehlich, Mark J. '69 (STU) Bridgeport, OH St. Joseph; Judges.
Froelich, Canice *o.f.m.cap.* '47 (STL) St. Louis, MO St. Patrick.
Froeschl, Martin H. '49 (KC) Retired.
Frohlich, Attila '01 (EVN) Evansville, IN Holy Rosary.
Froidurot, Michael '78 (SD) Poway, CA St. Gabriel.
Fromageot, Robert *f.s.s.p.* '01 (PAT) Mableton, GA St. Francis De Sales.
Fromageot, Robert *f.s.s.p.* '01 (SCR)[M] Vienna, OH.
Fromholzer, Francis J. '58 (ALN) Retired.
Fronckewicz, Stephen *o.s.b.* '57 (NOR)[E] Willimantic, CT Holy Family Home and Shelter, Inc..
Fronckowiak, Dennis F. '77 (BUF) North Tonawanda, NY Our Lady of Czestochowa.
Fronczak, Dennis A. '75 (BUF) Defenders of the Bond; Holland, NY St. Joseph.
Fronk, Christopher S. *s.j.* '97 (BAL)[S] Baltimore Jesuit Fathers and Brothers Maryland Provincial Curia; Navy Chaplains.
Fronske, Edward *o.f.m.* '67 (GLP) Whiteriver, AZ St. Francis; Presbyteral Council; Diocesan Consultors.
Fronterio, Anthony R. (MAN) Office of Priestly Life and Ministry.
Frontiero, Anthony R. '91 (MAN) Manchester, NH St. Pius X; Clergy Personnel Board.
Frost, Arthur *c.ss.r.* '41 (LA) Whittier, CA St. Mary of the Assumption; [Q] Whittier, CA Redemptorists of Whittier.
Frost, James (BRK) Retired.
Frost, John M. '87 (DM) Avoca, IA St. Mary, Mediatrix of All Graces; Avoca, IA St. Patrick.
Frost, Stephen A. '77 (FRS) Oildale, CA Christ the King; Judicial Vicar.
Frost, Stephen (RNO) Judges.
Frost, Stephen (FRS) Personnel Committee; Priests' Council.
Frost, Thomas *o.f.m.* '60 (TUC) Topawa, AZ San Solano Missions – Tohono O'odham Indian Reservation.
Frozena, Kenneth R. '60 (GB) Hilbert, WI St. Mary; Sherwood, WI St. John–Sacred Heart; Stockbridge, WI St. Mary.
Frueh, Robert '63 (BRK) Kingsboro Psychiatric Center.
Fruge, Donald J. '72 (GAL) On Duty Outside the Diocese.
Frugoli, Francis A. *s.j.* '45 (SJ)[M] Los Gatos, CA Sacred Heart Jesuit Center.
Frundt, Oscar H. '56 (WIL) Retired.
Fruth, Paul '74 (DUL) Aitkin, MN St. James; Garrison, MN Our Lady of Fatima; Aitkin, MN Holy Family; Deans; Council of Catholic Women.
Fry, James Q. '79 (ORG) Military Chaplains; Navy Chaplains.
Fry, Richard C. '58 (SJ) Retired.
Fry, Richard '58 (SJ) Santa Clara, CA St. Clare.
Fry, Timothy *o.s.b.* '41 (KCK)[H] Atchison, KS St. Benedict's Abbey.
Fryar, Thomas S. (DEN) Littleton, CO St. Mary; Vicar for Clergy and Seminarians; Presbyteral Council; Priests' Continuing Education Committee; College of Consultors; Secretary of Deans; Defenders of the Bond.
Fryda, William *m.m.* '88 (FgM).
Frydrych, Jerzy *s.ch.* '85 (GAL) San Francisco, CA Nativity; Polish, Croatian, Slovenian Mission.
Fryer, Patrick L. '61 (WH) Weirton, WV St. Paul's.
Fu, Joseph '60 (NEW) Retired.
Fuccile, Dominic G. '66 (NEW) Montclair, NJ St. Peter Claver.
Fucheck, Robert '66 (ORL) Lady Lake, FL St. Timothy.
Fuchs, Moritz A. '55 (SY) Retired.
Fuchs, Moritz (SY) Pastoral Examiners.
Fuchs, Sylvester '49 (GAL) Retired.
Fuchs, Sylvester '49 (AUS) Retired.
Fucinaro, Thomas J. '89 (LIN) On Duty Outside the Diocese.
Fuemmeler, James R. '58 (JC) Retired.
Fuenmayor, Jose Maria (DEN)[A] Denver, CO Redemptoris Mater House of Formation.
Fuente, Alberto *o.a.r.* '94 (NEW) Union City NJ Holy Family.
Fuentes, Ruben *o.f.m.* '64 (SD) Lemon Grove, CA St. John of the Cross.
Fuentes, Theo *c.m.f.* '51 (LA)[Q] Los Angeles, CA Claretian Retreat Center Community; [W] Los Angeles, CA Claretian Retreat Center (All Groups).
Fuentes Rodriguez, Josi '45 (SJN) Retired.
Fuentez, Trincad (ELP) St. Peter.
Fuentez, Trini (ELP) Defenders of the Bond; Priests' Personnel Advisory Committee.
Fuentez, Trindad '78 (ELP) El Paso, TX Queen of Peace.
Fugini, Francis *o.f.m.cap.* '54 (PIT)[N] Pittsburgh, PA St. Augustine Friary; (FgM).
Fugolo, Joseph *c.s.* '67 (NY)[II] New York, NY Friends of RADIO MARIA, Inc.; [II] New York, NY American Committee on Italian Immigration, Inc.; [II] New York, NY Trust for the Center for Migration Studies in New York.
Fugolo, Joseph *c.s.* '67 (BRK)[V] Jamaica, NY Saint Charles House of Studies.
Fugolo, Joseph *c.s.* '67 (NY)[EE] Staten Island, NY Scalabrinian Missionaries; [II] New York, NY Scalabrini Pastoral Center.
Fuhrman, Robert J. '81 (NEW) Saddle River Borough, NJ St. Gabriel the Archangel; [II] New York, NY Catholic Medical Mission Board, Inc.; Propagation of the Faith; Apostleship of Prayer; Propagation of the Faith; Society of St. Peter the Apostle Missionary Union of Priests/Religious.
Fuhrmann, Bruno *o.s.b.* '54 (LR) Booneville, AR Church of Our Lady of the Assumption; [A] Subiaco, AR Subiaco Monastery; (FgM).
Fuhrmann, Nicholas *o.s.b.* '54 (LR)[A] Subiaco, AR Subiaco Monastery.
Fuino, Crispin *o.f.m.conv.* '48 (TR) Point Pleasant Beach, NJ St. Peter's.
Fuino, Michael A. (NEW) Hispanic Curia of Essex and Union Retired.
Fuino, Michael '42 (NEW)[N] Rutherford, NJ St. John Vianney Residence for Priests.
Fujihara, Fidelis *s.a.* '65 (NY)[EE] Garrison Franciscan Friars of the Atonement, Minister General Office.
Fukes, Gary M. '88 (SY) Military Chaplains; Army Chaplains.
Fukes, James '98 (SY) Binghamton, NY SS. Cyril and Method.
Fulcher, John M. '56 (COL) Retired.
Fulco, William J. *s.j.* '66 (LA)[C] Los Angeles CA Jesuit Community
Fuld, Charles L. '86 (SD) San Diego, CA Ascension Retired.
Fuld, Charles (SD) Presbyteral Council.
Fulgenzi, Mario '68 (RIC) Virginia Beach, VA St. Gregory the Great.
Fullam, Dominick '94 (BLX) Moss Point, MS St. Joseph; Pastoral Services.
Fullam, Vincent F. '65 (BRK) Rego Park, NY Resurrection–Ascension; Legion of Mary.
Fullen, John N. '95 (BAL) Retired.
Fuller, Gerard *o.m.i.* '55 (SPC).
Fuller, Jon D. *s.j.* '90 (BO)[V] Boston, MA Jesuit Urban Center & Immaculate Conception Community.
Fuller, Leigh A. *s.j.* '66 (BAL)[S] Huntington, WV St. Mary's Hospital.
Fuller, Mark L. '79 (STL) Kirkwood, MO St. Joseph Hospital; [J] Kirkwood, MO SSM St. Joseph Hospital of Kirkwood.
Fuller, Mark '79 (STL) Webster Groves, MO Annunciation.
Fuller, Michael J. '97 (CHI).
Fuller, Michael J.K. '97 (RCK)[A] Special Assignment.
Fuller, Neil D. *s.v.d.* '69 (SB) Frontera, CA California Institute for Women.
Fuller, Orland R. (MO) Army Chaplains.
Fuller, Robert D. '56 (TUC) Tucson, AZ St. Frances Cabrini; Council of Priests; Vicars Forane; Directors.
Fuller, Timothy '93 (OKL) Elk City, OK St. Matthew's; Master of Ceremonies; Air National Guard Chaplains.
Fullerton, Daniel J. '91 (SCR)[M] Shohola, PA Society of Saint John.
Fullmer, Hugh '72 (JOL) Aurora, IL Our Lady of Mercy.
Fullum, John J. '67 (BRK) East Glendale, NY Sacred Heart.
Fulmer, Jeffrey M. '97 (CIN) Dayton, OH St. Anthony of Padua.
Fulton, David I. '67 (MET) Baptistown, NJ Our Lady of Victories; Diocesan Judges.
Fulton, David L. '02 (OM) Omaha, NE St. Leo.
Fulton, Eugene J. (NY) Spiritual Development, Office of.
Fulton, Eugene '67 (PSC) On Duty Outside Diocese.
Fulton, Eugene '67 (NY)[GG] Larchmont, NY Trinity Retreat.
Fulton, Kenneth S. '50 (TLS) Retired.
Fulton, Malachy *o.s.b.* '43 (IND)[K] St. Meinrad, IN St. Meinrad Archabbey.
Fulton, Robert W. '62 (MOB) Gulf Shores, AL Our Lady of the Gulf.
Fulton, Terry '94 (SAC) Chico, CA St. John the Baptist.
Funaro, Carmine *o.f.m.cap.* (ROC)[I] Interlaken, NY St. Fidelis Friary.
Funaro, Joseph A. '65 (BRK) Forest Hills, NY Our Lady, Queen of Martyrs; [L] Brooklyn, NY Catholic Charities.
Funes, Jose G. *s.j.* '95 (TUC)[E] Tucson, AZ Jesuit Community of the Vatican Observatory.
Funesti, Peter K. '88 (NEW) Bloomfield, NJ Church of St. Thomas the Apostle; Engaged Encounter.
Funk, C. Alan '91 (LFT) Union City, IN St. Mary.
Funk, David R. '74 (COL) Columbus, OH St. Agatha; Vicariate 2: Northwest; Diocesan Judges.
Funk, Peter C. '64 (PH) On Duty Outside the Archdiocese.
Funk, Peter C. '64 (BEA)[F] Beaumont, TX Holy Family Retreat Center.
Funk, Virgil C. '63 (RIC) Retired.
Funk, Wayne G. '62 (BAL) Frederick, MD St. John the Evangelist.
Funk, Wiatt A. '68 (NSH) Murfreesboro, TN St. Rose of Lima; Presbyteral Council and College of Consultors; MTSU–Murfreesboro.
Funk, Wyatt (NSH) Clergy Benefit Foundation.
Funke, Gerald J. '80 (B) Nampa, ID St. Paul's; St. Vincent de Paul Society.
Funke, Gerald (B) Adjutant Judicial Vicars; Judges; College of Consultors.
Funke, Richard P. '60 (DUB) On Duty Outside the Archdiocese; Defenders of the Bond; Ecclesiastical Attorneys; Finance Council.
Funke, Ronald R. *s.j.* '68 (SEA)[A] Seattle, WA Seattle University.
Funtila, Aloysius '83 (CHI) Waukegan, IL St. Anastasia.
Furey, J. Barry '71 (BGP) Darien, CT St. Thomas More; Members of the Clergy Personnel Committee.
Furey, John *c.ss.r.* '60 (BO) Roxbury, MA Our Lady of Perpetual Help.
Furey, Matthew J. '99 (NY) Staten Island, NY St. Clare.
Furey, Thomas J. '73 (PH) King of Prussia, PA Mother of Divine Providence.
Furfaro, Virgil '83 (SFE) Bernalillo, NM Our Lady of Sorrows.
Furlan, Gerard *s.x.* '58 (BO)[V] Holliston, MA Xaverian Missionaries.
Furlan, Juan Esteban '97 (SJ) San Jose, CA St. Leo the Great.
Furlan, Michael J. '75 (CHI) Oak Lawn, IL St. Germaine.
Furlan, William '48 (SCL) Retired.
Furlong, Aidan M. *a.a.* '53 (WOR) Fiskdale, MA St. Anne's and St. Patrick's.
Furlong, J. Daryl '66 (MAD) Janesville, WI St. Patrick.
Furlong, Thomas D. '60 (OM) Retired.
Furman, Henry P. '02 (BUR) Barre, VT St. Monica.
Furman, Walter L. *s.j.* '50 (MOB)[P] New Orleans, LA Ignatius Residence.
Furmanski, Leonard A. '59 (PH)[U] Philadelphia, PA Nazareth Hospital.
Furnari, Casper J. '68 (BRK) Brooklyn, NY St. Mary Mother of Jesus.
Furrell, Reynold '98 (ORG) San Clemente, CA Our Lady of Fatima.
Furrevig, Edward G. '67 (NEW) Union, NJ Holy Spirit.
Furtado, Al *c.s.sp.* '64 (SFR) Belmont, CA St. Mark.
Furtado, Jose '97 (SP) Tampa, FL Blessed Sacrament.
Furtado, Luis '94 (PH) Philadelphia, PA St. Martin of Tours.
Fusare, Francis *c.p.m.* '96 (OWN)[F] Auburn, KY Fathers of Mercy.
Fusco, Albin *o.f.m.* '61 (ALB)[A] Catskill, NY St. Anthony Friary.
Fusco, Blaise J. *o.f.m.cap.* '41 (PIT)[N] Allison Park, PA St. Conrad Friary.
Fusco, Christopher J. '97 (OG) Heuvelton, NY St. Raphael's; Lisbon, NY SS. Philip and James; Vice Chancellors; Auditor; Cemeteries.
Fusco, Frederick *o.f.m.* '42 (ALB)[A] Catskill, NY St. Anthony Friary.
Fusco, Thomas M. '85 (RVC) Syosset, NY St. Edward Confessor.
Fuselier, Karl '94 (LKC) Lake Charles, LA Immaculate Heart of Mary; Diocesan Consultors.
Fushek, Dale J. '78 (PHX) Mesa, AZ St. Timothy; Special Assignment.
Fushek, Dale (PHX) Vicar General; College of Consultors.
Fuss, Edward F. *s.m.* '89 (BR) Convent, LA St. Michael the Archangel; Gramercy, LA Most Sacred Heart of Jesus; Paulina, LA St. Joseph.
Fussner, Donald T. '60 (NY) New York, NY St. Peter.
Futie, Richard F. '82 (BGP) Stamford, CT St. Mary; Defenders of the Bond; Pastors' Vocation Advisory Board.
Futo, Yoshio Ignatius *s.j.* '81 (STL)[C] Saint Louis University; [O] St. Louis, MO Jesuit Community Corporation at St. Louis University – Jesuit Hall.
Futrell, John C. *s.j.* '58 (DEN)[N] Denver, CO Xavier Jesuit Center.

Futter, Volker *o.s.b.* '69 (OM)[K] Schuyler, NE Benedictine Mission House.
Fye, Lawrence C. '59 (Y) Youngstown, OH Cathedral of St. Columba; Youngstown, OH St. Casimir; Judges.
Fynn, Isaac A. '79 (TUC) Tucson, AZ St. Joseph; Tucson, AZ St. Joseph's Hospital; [D] Tucson, AZ St. Joseph Hospital.

G

Gaa, David *o.f.m.* '98 (TUC) (FgM).
Gaalaas, Patrick J. '72 (TLS) Broken Arrow, OK St. Benedict; Vice Chancellor; Diocesan Consultors; Ecumenism.
Gabba, Herbert T. *m.m.* '68 (CHI)[N] Chicago, IL Maryknoll Fathers & Brothers.
Gabel, Martin M. '68 (JOL) Bensenville, IL St. Charles Borromeo.
Gabela, Jose Luis Diez *o.s.a.* '72 (MGZ) Aguada, PR St. Francis of Assisi.
Gaber, Francis '51 (DUL) Retired.
Gaberle, Jiri '89 (MIL) Special Assignment.
Gabet, George G. *f.s.s.p.* '97 (SCR)[M] Elmhurst, PA Priestly Fraternity of St. Peter (F.S.S.P.), North American District Headquarters.
Gabin, John D. '75 (PH) Philadelphia, PA St. Dominic.
Gaborit, Mauricio *s.j.* '78 (FgM).
Gaboury, Victor *s.s.c.* '57 (OM)[K] St. Columbans St. Columban's Foreign Mission Society; [P] Bristol, RI St. Columban's Retirement House Retired.
Gabriel, Eduardo *o.p.* '92 (NO) New Orleans, LA St. Dominic.
Gabriel, John D. '87 (NEW) Fairfield, NJ St. Thomas More; Staff.
Gabriel, John *m.s.* '91 (FR)[H] Attleboro, MA La Salette Shrine.
Gabriel, John '98 (ALX)[B] Alexandria, LA Christus Health Central Louisiana; Alexandria, LA St. Frances Xavier Cabrini.
Gabriel, Michael A. '84 (CHI) Lansing, IL St. Ann.
Gabriel, Vicente S. '40 (LA) Retired.
Gabriele, John J. '68 (RVC) Absent on Leave.
Gabrielli, Theodore E. *s.j.* '96 (FgM).
Gabrielli, Theodore (SJ)[P] Los Gatos, CA California Jesuit Missions.
Gabrus, Alois '72 (STL)[O] St. Louis, MO Franciscan Friary of St. Anthony of Padua.
Gabuzda, Richard J. '81 (OM)[O] Omaha, NE Institute for Priestly Formation, Creighton University; On Duty Outside the Diocese.
Gadarowski, Bronislaw A. '43 (NOR) Retired.
Gaddy, James '65 (LKC) Jennings, LA Our Lady Help of Christians; Diocesan Board of Administration; Episcopal Vicars; Diocesan Consultors.
Gaddy, Kenneth *c.ss.r.* (STV) Frederiksted, St. Croix, VI Church of St. Patrick; [B] COR (Christ in Others Retreat); Diocesan Consultors; Youth Coordinator; Permanent Diaconate.
Gadenz, Pablo (TR) On Duty Outside the Diocese.
Gadient, Peter J. '45 (LIN) Dwight, NE Assumption; Building Commission; Diocesan Council of Catholic Women; Legion of Mary Retired.
Gadziala, Timothy A. (ATL) Archdiocesan Judges.
Gaebelein, Claude J. '46 (CLV)[M] Cleveland, OH Sts. Mary and Joseph Home for the Aged Retired.
Gaeke, Thomas M. '75 (CIN) Medical Leave of Absence.
Gaelens, Albert R. *c.s.b.* '60 (GAL)[F] Houston, TX St. Thomas High School.
Gaesser, Ronald E. '61 (ROC) Auburn, NY Holy Family Retired.
Gaeta, Bernard N. '73 (Y) East Liverpool, OH St. Aloysius; Wellsville, OH Immaculate Conception; Advocates.
Gaeta, David R. '80 (SLC) On Duty Outside the Diocese.
Gaeta, David (SLC) AUXILIARY CHAPLAINS CONTRACT CHAPLAINS.
Gaeta, Francis X. '63 (RVC) Deer Park, NY SS. Cyril and Methodius; Babylon Deanery.
Gaetano, Francis M. *s.a.c.* '48 (NEW) Fairview, NJ.
Gaetano, Lew (Y) Walsh University; [B] North Canton, OH Walsh University.
Gaetano, Lewis F. '73 (STU) On Duty Outside the Diocese.
Gaffey, Eugene F. '69 (PRT) Eastport, ME St. Joseph.
Gaffey, James P. '60 (SR) Santa Rosa, CA Cathedral of St. Eugene; Diocesan Judges; Finance Committee.
Gaffey, Kevin P. '57 (SFR)[M] Menlo Park, CA Vallombrosa Center.
Gaffey, Kevin '57 (SFR) Retired.
Gaffigan, Charles A. '62 (ALB) Corinth, NY Immaculate Conception; Lake Luzerne, NY Holy Infancy.
Gaffigan, William J. '64 (ALB) Canajoharie, NY St. Peter's and Paul's.
Gaffney, David F. (PRO) Barrington, RI St. Luke.
Gaffney, Edward M. *o.p.* '02 (HBG)[I] Lancaster, PA Dominican Nuns of the Perpetual Rosary, Incorporated.
Gaffney, Francis P. (CAM) Judges.
Gaffney, Francis '64 (CAM) Cherry Hill, NJ St. Mary's.
Gaffney, J. Michael '73 (OG) Lake Placid, NY St. Agnes; Deans.
Gaffney, J. Patrick *s.m.m.* '54 (RVC)[M] Bay Shore, NY Montfort Missionaries.
Gaffney, James F. '85 (ALN) Unassigned.
Gaffney, James J. '50 (CAM) Glassboro, NJ Our Lady of Lourdes Retired.
Gaffney, John H. *o.s.a.* '45 (TLS)[B] Tulsa, OK Cascia Hall Preparatory School.
Gaffney, Michael *o.f.m.cap.* (DET)[K] Detroit, MI St. Mary's Friary.
Gaffney, Patrick *c.s.c.* '74 (FTW)[B] University of Notre Dame Du Lac; [I] Notre Dame, IN Holy Cross Community, Corby Hall, University of Notre Dame.
Gaffney, Thomas F. '58 (HRT) New Britain, CT St. Joseph's; New Britain, CT St. Peter's; Deans.
Gaffney, Thomas J. '50 (NY) Staten Island, NY St. Charles Retired.
Gaffney, William *c.ss.r.* '60 (NY) Bronx, NY Immaculate Conception.
Gagala, John '58 (DET)[H] Southfield, MI Providence Hospital; Southfield, MI St. Beatrice; Judges.
Gagan, Charles R. *s.j.* '68 (SFR) San Francisco, CA St. Ignatius; [N] San Francisco, CA Jesuit Community at University of San Francisco.
Gagan, Philip R. '79 (STA) Special Assignment.
Gage, George D. '79 (ROM) Boardman, OH St. Mary; Boardman, OH St. John the Baptist.
Gage, George (ROM) Board of Consultors; Diocesan Collections Coordinator.
Gage, Gregory A. '67 (P) Retired.
Gage, Philip S. *s.m.* '69 (WDC)[M] Washington, DC Marist Center.
Gaggawala, Paul O. *a.j.* '80 (ALN)[P] Shenandoah, PA Apostles of Jesus; [P] Northampton, PA Apostles of Jesus.
Gaglia, Fred '78 (SB).
Gagliano, Philip J. '76 (NY) Ardsley, NY Our Lady of Perpetual Help.
Gagliardi, Richard '62 (OAK) Pinole, CA St. Joseph's Retired.
Gagliardo, Anthony F. '61 (BUF) AUXILIARY CHAPLAINS CONTRACT CHAPLAINS Retired.
Gaglione, John R. '76 (BUF) Air Force Reserve Chaplains; Kenmore, NY St. Paul.
Gagnard, Louis '52 (ALX) Retired.
Gagne, Donald *s.m.* '59 (PRT) Lewiston, ME Central Maine Medical Center; [H] Lewiston, ME St. Mary's Regional Medical Center.
Gagne, Marc R. '85 (MAN) Nashua, NH Immaculate Conception.
Gagne, Rene E. '51 (PRO)[P] Providence St. John Vianney Residence Retired.
Gagne, Roger C. '75 (PRO) Warwick, RI St. Peter.
Gagne, Ron *m.s.* '71 (ORL) Orlando, FL Blessed Trinity.
Gagne, Ronald '66 (DUL) Nashwauk, MN St. Mary's; Nashwauk, MN St. Cecilia's; Nashwauk, MN St. Kevin; Deans.
Gagne, Walter *s.a.* '71 (NY)[EE] Garrison, NY Franciscan Friars of the Atonement.
Gagnepain, John F. *c.m.* '62 (STL)[O] Perryville, MO Congregation of the Mission; Ecumenism; Diocesan Director of Continuing Formation of Clergy.
Gagnier, John F. '78 (ROC) Shortsville, NY St. Dominic.
Gagnon, Adelard J. '53 (BO) Senior Priests Retired.
Gagnon, Andre J. '57 (MAN)[J] Laconia, NH St. Francis Healthcare Center.
Gagnon, Daniel *o.m.i.* '87 (FgM).
Gagnon, Donald *s.m.* '59 (PRT) St. Mary's Regional Medical Center.
Gagnon, George '55 (ALB).
Gagnon, Henry W. '64 (BO) Senior Priests; Bedford, MA St. Michael Retired.
Gagnon, Herve *o.m.i.* '45 (BO)[V] Lowell, MA St. Eugene House (Residence).
Gagnon, Joseph A. '61 (DET) Melvindale, MI St. Conrad.
Gagnon, Leo G. '72 (MAN) Richmond, VA St. Patrick Retired.
Gagnon, Mariano *o.f.m.* '58 (FgM).
Gagnon, Michael *o.f.m.* '57 (SD)[H] Oceanside, CA Mission San Luis Rey.
Gagnon, Michel *o.f.m.* '57 (SD)[K] Oceanside, CA Mission San Luis Rey Retreat.
Gagnon, Raymond E. '72 (MAN) Nashua, NH Infant Jesus.
Gagnon, Richard *s.d.s.* '65 (NSH) Smyrna, TN St. Luke; Hispanic Ministry.
Gagnon, Roland *o.m.i.* '51 (FgM).
Gagnon, Ronald P. '56 (TUC) Retired.
Gago, Jose *o.m.i.* '56 (OAK)[N] Oakland, CA Oblate Residence.
Gahagan, William H. '70 (KNX) Johnson City, TN St. Mary; [H] Johnson City, TN ETSU–Catholic Center; [I] Knoxville, TN Diocesan Council of Catholic Women; Deans of the Diocese; Presbyteral Council; Diocesan Consultors; East Tennessee State University; Ministries of the Five Rivers Deanery.
Gahan, James L. '68 (STL) St. Charles, MO Sts. Joachim and Ann; [E] St. Charles, MO Duchesne High School.
Gaiardo, Martin J. '70 (SCR) Retired.
Gaines, G. Timothy '87 (DEN) Louisville, CO St. Louis.
Gaines, Michael T. '87 (E) Erie, PA St. Peter Cathedral; Western Vicariate; Administrative Cabinet; College of Consultors; Priest Personnel Board; Staff; Clergy Personnel.
Gaitan, Ramon *o.a.r.* '60 (ORG) Santa Ana, CA Our Lady of Guadalupe; [I] Santa Ana, CA Augustinian Recollects.
Gaiter, Chester E. *s.j.* '76 (STL)[N] St. Louis, MO Fusz Pavilion; [O] St. Louis, MO Jesuit Community Corporation at St. Louis University – Jesuit Hall.
Gajda, Peter J. (CC) Deans.
Gajda, Piotr J. (CC) College of Consultors; Personnel Board – Priests; Presbyteral Council; Three Rivers, TX Sacred Heart.
Gajdos, T. George '70 (MIL) Wauwatosa, WI Christ King; Archdiocesan Consultors.
Gajdzinski, Norman A. '63 (CLV) Garfield Heights, OH St. Therese.
Gajewski, Andrzej '87 (MET) Spotswood, NJ Immaculate Conception.
Gajewski, Chester A. '50 (SCR)[N] Dunmore, PA Villa St. Joseph Retired.
Galambos, L. Stephen *o.f.m.* '96 (MET) New Brunswick, NJ St. Ladislaus.
Galan, Jose M. '65 (PCE) Mercedita, PR Church of the Sacred Heart.
Galang, Jose '78 (SJ) Santa Clara, CA St. Justin; On Sabbatical.
Galant, Andrzej *s.ch.* '81 (MIL) Milwaukee, WI SS. Cyril and Methodius; Milwaukee, WI St. Maximilian Kolbe.
Galarza, Edison *o.c.c.s.s.* '99 (STP) Minneapolis, MN SS. Cyril & Methodius.
Galas, Daniel D. '57 (OM) Retired.
Galasso, Michael S. '71 (HRT) Hartford, CT St. Peter.
Galaz, Jesse C. '81 (LA) Los Angeles, CA St. Alphonsus; Deanery 9.
Galaz, Jesse (LA) Members.
Galdon, Peter P. '68 (NEW) Bayonne, NJ St. Vincent de Paul.
Galea, John M. '62 (STU) Steubenville, OH Our Lady of Perpetual Help Mission Retired.
Galea, Michael A. '80 (BR) Donaldsonville, LA St. Francis of Assisi.
Galeano, John '02 (NEW) Jersey City, NJ Our Lady of Mt. Carmel.
Galek, Adams S. '71 (CHI) Niles, IL St. John Brebeuf.
Galek, Peter '83 (CHI) Hillside, IL St. Domitilla.
Galens, Jeffrey R. '90 (NY) Rhinebeck, NY The Good Shepherd.
Gales, Oscar '70 (DAL) Ferris, TX Corpus Christi.
Galetto, Paul W. '82 (CAM)[C] Richland, NJ St. Augustine Preparatory School.
Galiardi, Roman *o.s.b.* '57 (JOL)[L] Lisle, IL St. Procopius Abbey.
Galic, Bernard J. '70 (FTW) South Bend, IN Holy Family.
Galic, Bernard (FTW) Budget Committee; Council of Priests; Vocations.
Galic, Joseph N. *o.f.m.* '66 (ALN) Bethlehem, PA St. Joseph.
Galier, Victor A. (ATL) Tyrone, GA St. Matthew's; Advocates.
Galinac, Robert *o.f.m.* '69 (STL) St. Louis, MO St. Joseph.
Galinada, Michael *s.m.* '78 (ORG) Santa Ana, CA St. Anne's.
Galipeau, Roland J. '64 (SPR) Holyoke, MA Holy Cross; Deans.
Galivan, James F. '81 (CHI) Other Assignments.
Gall, Jacob M. '62 (FTW) Kendallville, IN Immaculate Conception.
Gall, Sylvester '38 (SCL) Retired.
Gall, Thomas S. '92 (OM) Butte, NE SS. Peter and Paul; Lynch, NE Assumption B.V.M.; Spencer, NE St. Mary.
Gallagher, Andrew J. '46 (RVC) Point Lookout, NY Our Lady of the Miraculous Medal Retired.
Gallagher, Brian T. '60 (YAK) Retired.
Gallagher, Brian *s.s.c.* '52 (PRO)[P] Bristol, RI St. Columban's Retirement House.
Gallagher, Cathal '74 (SFS)[K] St. Columbans St. Columban's Foreign Mission Society; De Smet, SD St. Thomas Aquinas.
Gallagher, Charles A. *s.j.* '58 (NEW)[B] Jersey City, NJ Jesuit Center; [N] Jersey City, NJ Jesuits of Saint Peter's College, Inc..
Gallagher, Charles G. '44 (CHI) Retired.
Gallagher, Charles '44 (CHI) La Grange, IL St. Cletus.
Gallagher, Charles (NEW) Pastoral & Matrimonial Renewal Center.
Gallagher, Cornelius F. '42 (STU) Retired.
Gallagher, Cyrus *o.f.m.cap.* '65 (DEN) Denver, CO Annunciation; [N] Denver, CO Fraternidad San Antonio.
Gallagher, Daniel B. '99 (GAY) Faith Formation of Children and Youth, Secretariat for.
Gallagher, Daniel J. '51 (PH) Retired.
Gallagher, Daniel N. (JKS).
Gallagher, Daniel '65 (JKS) Jackson, MS St. Peter

Cathedral; University of Mississippi Medical Center; Veterans Administration Hospital; Defenders of the Bond; Cursillo Movement.
Gallagher, David F. *c.s.s.* '59 (BO)[Y] Waltham, MA Stigmatine Fathers and Brothers.
Gallagher, Dennis J. *o.s.a.* '65 (PH)[C] Villanova University; [AA] Villanova, PA St. Thomas Monastery.
Gallagher, Dennis *a.a.* '78 (WOR)[B] Worcester, MA Assumption College; [O] Worcester, MA Assumptionists of Assumption College.
Gallagher, E. Henry *o.p.* '36 (BO)[V] Dover, MA St. Stephen Priory.
Gallagher, Edward L. '53 (BO) Senior Priests Retired.
Gallagher, Edward *s.a.* '71 (NY)[EE] Garrison Franciscan Friars of the Atonement, Minister General Office.
Gallagher, Eugene P. '38 (NY) Retired.
Gallagher, F. Anthony '61 (TOL) Grand Rapids, OH St. Patrick; Consultors.
Gallagher, Francis J. *s.j.* '55 (SJ)[M] Los Gatos, CA Sacred Heart Jesuit Center.
Gallagher, Francis J. '73 (PH) Absent on Leave.
Gallagher, Francis L. '48 (BO) Senior Priests Retired.
Gallagher, Francis M. '64 (PEO) Philadelphia, PA St. Helena.
Gallagher, Greg *o.m.i.* '92 (STP) St. Paul, MN St. Casimir.
Gallagher, J. Gerald '57 (CAM) Woodbury, NJ St. Patrick's.
Gallagher, J. Peter '92 (IND)[C] Indianapolis, IN Father Thomas Scecina Memorial High School.
Gallagher, Jack *o.s.cam.* '81 (WOR)[L] Whitinsville, MA.
Gallagher, James E. '87 (RIC) Harrisonburg, VA Blessed Sacrament.
Gallagher, James R. '65 (CHI)[J] Evergreen Park, IL Little Company of Mary Hospital and Health Care Centers.
Gallagher, John A. '55 (NY) Yonkers, NY St. Paul the Apostle.
Gallagher, John E. '59 (BO) Senior Priests Retired.
Gallagher, John J. *o.s.a.* '45 (PH)[AA] Villanova, PA St. Thomas Monastery.
Gallagher, John J. *o.s.cam.* '81 (WOR)[L] Whitinsville, MA St. Camillus Hospice, Inc..
Gallagher, John M. '71 (GB) Gillett, WI St. John; Suring, WI St. Michael; Regional Vicars.
Gallagher, John M. *o.f.m.cap.* '78 (MAN) Manchester, NH St. Anne; Manchester, NH St. Augustin; Defenders of the Bond; Hispanic Apostolate.
Gallagher, John P. '51 (SCR) Retired.
Gallagher, John P. '57 (PH) Huntingdon Valley, PA St. Albert the Great Retired.
Gallagher, John P. '68 (PIT) Cranberry Township, PA St. Ferdinand; Priest Council.
Gallagher, John P. '80 (DAV) Muscatine, IA SS. Mary and Mathias of Muscatine; Air Force Reserve Chaplains.
Gallagher, John P. *c.ss.r.* '95 (FgM).
Gallagher, John R. '55 (DUB) Retired.
Gallagher, John R. *v.g.* '93 (WH) Wheeling, WV St. Joseph's Cathedral; [O] Wheeling, WV John S. Thoner Family Charitable Trust; [R] Wheeling, WV Retirement Trust Agreement of the Infirm Priests' Association of the Diocese of Wheeling–Charleston; Wheeling, WV Mount Calvary; Vicar General; Chancellor; Diocesan Consultors; Finance Officer; Catholic University, Friends of; Cemeteries; Finance Office; Home and Foreign Missions, Society for the Propagation of the Faith; Infirm Priests Association; Vocations, Office of; West Virginia State Catholic Conference; Victim Assistance Coordinator.
Gallagher, John *o.s.cam.* '81 (WOR)[O] Whitinsville, MA St. Camillus Community.
Gallagher, John '92 (PMB) Palm Beach Gardens, FL Cathedral of St. Ignatius Loyola.
Gallagher, Joseph J. '55 (BAL) Retired.
Gallagher, Joseph J. '63 (PH) Philadelphia, PA St. Richard.
Gallagher, Joseph P. '73 (PH) Absent on Leave.
Gallagher, Joseph T. '42 (PRO) Retired.
Gallagher, Joseph W. *c.s.p.* '61 (GR) Grand Rapids, MI Chapel of St. Paul–Catholic Information Center.
Gallagher, Kevin E. *s.j.* '61 (CHI).
Gallagher, Kevin J. '02 (PH)[N] Havertown, PA St. Denis.
Gallagher, Kevin P. '83 (ALN) St. Clair, PA St. Boniface; St. Clair, PA St. Mary; St. Clair, PA SS. Peter and Paul.
Gallagher, Maurice O. '50 (PBL) Retired.
Gallagher, Michael J. '66 (SD) San Pedro, CA Mary, Star of the Sea; [CC] San Pedro, CA Apostleship of the Sea, Catholic Maritime Ministry; El Cajon, CA Our Lady of Grace.
Gallagher, Michael J. '69 (WIL) On Duty Outside the Diocese.
Gallagher, Michael S. *s.j.* '84 (NO)[P] Luwisha House.
Gallagher, Otmar *o.f.m.cap.* '48 (VEN)[N] Pittsburgh, PA St. Augustine Friary.
Gallagher, Padraig *c.ss.r.* '82 (CHI) Chicago, IL St. Teresa.
Gallagher, Patrick J. '70 (MOB) Dothan, AL St. Columba; [J] Dothan, AL George C. Wallace Jr. Community College Newman Center.
Gallagher, Patrick *o.f.m.conv.* '65 (ALB) Fonda, NY St. Cecilia; Tribes Hill, NY Sacred Heart.
Gallagher, Patrick (LA) Apostleship of the Sea.
Gallagher, Patrick (MOB) Regional Episcopal Vicars; Ex Officio Members.
Gallagher, Paul V. '63 (RIC) Retired.
Gallagher, Peter '92 (IND) Indianapolis, IN St. Simon the Apostle.
Gallagher, Philip P. '78 (LAN) Flint, MI St. Michael; Flint, MI Sacred Heart.
Gallagher, Raymond '90 (SAN) Retired.
Gallagher, Richard J. '49 (STL) St. Louis, MO St. Joan of Arc; Archdiocesan Building and Boundary Commission.
Gallagher, Richard '36 (SEA) Retired.
Gallagher, Richard '44 (TR) Leave of Absence.
Gallagher, Robert A. '77 (STU) On Duty Outside the Diocese; Air Force Chaplains.
Gallagher, Robert J. '73 (LA) North Hollywood, CA St. Charles Borromeo.
Gallagher, Robert (LA) San Fernando Pastoral Region.
Gallagher, Roger P. '54 (WDC)[L] Washington, DC Cardinal O'Boyle Residence for Priests Retired.
Gallagher, Simeon *o.f.m.cap.* '71 (STL) St. Louis, MO St. Patrick; [O] St. Louis, MO St. Patrick Friary.
Gallagher, Simon P. *o.s.b.* '73 (PAT)[M] Morristown, NJ St. Mary's Abbey; [M] Morristown St. Mary's Abbey.
Gallagher, Thomas B. '56 (OAK)[M] Oakland, CA Bishop Begin Villa Retired.
Gallagher, Thomas G. '68 (RVC) North Merrick, NY Sacred Heart.
Gallagher, Thomas J. '61 (CLV) Retired.
Gallagher, Thomas J. *s.j.* '70 (BO)[V] Boston, MA Loyola House.
Gallagher, Thomas M. *o.f.m.* '82 (WIL) Wilmington, DE St. Paul's.
Gallagher, Thomas N. *s.j.* '61 (FBK)[C] Fairbanks, AK Jesuit Residence.
Gallagher, Thomas P. *o.s.f.s.* '67 (PH)[D] Philadelphia, PA Father Judge High School for Boys; [AA] Philadelphia, PA Father Louis Brisson Residence.
Gallagher, Thomas V. '45 (NY) Retired.
Gallagher, Timothy M. *o.m.v.* '79 (BO)[B] Boston, MA Our Lady of Grace Seminary.
Gallagher, William E. '46 (SEA) Retired.
Gallagher, William G. '53 (RVC) Worcester, MA St. Paul's Cathedral Retired.
Gallagher, William J. '47 (WOR) Retired.
Gallagher, William J. '69 (BUF) Orchard Park, NY St. John Vianney.
Gallagher, William M. '53 (PRO) Retired.
Gallahue, John J. *m.m.* '62 (FgM).
Gallant, Jon–Paul '78 (FR) Chatham, MA Holy Redeemer.
Gallant, Rodrigue J. '47 (MAN) Retired.
Gallardo, David '84 (LA) Pico Rivera, CA St. Mariana de Paredes.
Gallardo, Joseph J. *o.a.r.* '94 (LA) Montebello, CA St. Benedict.
Gallarelli, George A. *s.j.* '62 (BGP)[E] Fairfield, CT Fairfield College Preparatory School; [P] Fairfield, CT The Fairfield Jesuit Community–Fairfield University.
Gallaro, George D. '72 (NTN) Warren, MI Our Lady of Redemption; Canonical Consultants.
Gallas, James R. *s.j.* '52 (LA) Los Angeles, CA Blessed Sacrament.
Gallatin, Joseph G. '97 (STP) Delano, MN St. Mary of Czestochowa; St. Bonifacius, MN St. Boniface.
Gallatin, Paul H. '58 (OKL) Oklahoma City, OK St. Charles Borromeo.
Gallego, Jose M. *o.m.* '57 (SJN) San Juan, PR Ntra. Sra. de Fatima.
Gallegos, Albert M. *o.s.m.* '64 (CHI)[N] Chicago Order of Friar Servants of Mary (Servites) United States of America Province, Inc..
Gallegos, Albert *o.s.m.* '64 (SFE) Peralta, NM Our Lady of Guadalupe.
Gallegos, David M. *o.s.m.* '66 (CHI)[N] Chicago Order of Friar Servants of Mary (Servites) United States of America Province, Inc..
Gallegos, Joseph *c.r.* '69 (PBL) Durango, CO Sacred Heart.
Gallegos, Stephen *c.m.* '88 (FgM).
Gallela, Prasad '89 (SAN) Miles, TX St. Thomas; Rowena, TX St. Boniface; Rowena, TX St. Joseph's.
Gallemore, Tim (FRS) Priests' Council.
Gallemore, Timothy A. '92 (FRS) Firebaugh, CA St. Joseph.
Gallemore, Timothy (FRS) Office of Liturgy, Worship and Evangelization.
Gallen, Charles V. '47 (PH) Retired.
Gallen, F. Thomas '47 (COL) Diocesan Judges Retired.
Gallen, Francis H. '47 (PH) Retired.
Gallen, Gerard *s.j.* '03 (BO)[V] Newton, MA The Jesuit Community at Boston College.
Gallen, John J. *s.j.* '63 (NY)[EE] New York, NY "America;" Residence and publication office of the America Press.
Gallen, John '69 (HT) Thibodaux, LA Christ The Redeemer.
Gallenbach, Thomas E. '58 (LAV) Las Vegas, NV St. Joseph, Husband of Mary.
Gallenbach, Thomas '58 (SFD) On Duty Outside the Diocese.
Gallenstein, Joseph A. '90 (COV) Leave of Absence.
Gallerini, Philip G. '62 (SPR) Retired.
Galles, Francis A. '52 (WIN) Retired.
Galli, Clarence F. '53 (SFE) Corrales, NM San Ysidro.
Galli, Clarence '53 (SFE) Retired.
Gallia, Andrew R. '62 (SCR) Jessup, PA St. Mary's Assumption.
Galligan, Charles H. '87 (PRO) Pawtucket, RI St. Edward.
Galligan, Eymard P. *s.s.e.* (WOR) Retired.
Galligan, James L. *o.s.a.* '50 (PH) Philadelphia, PA St. Rita of Cascia.
Galligan, Richard R. *s.j.* '70 (NY)[EE] New York, NY Jesuit Provincial's Office; [EE] New York, NY St. Ignatius Loyola Residence.
Gallina, Leo J. '65 (E) Bradford, PA St. Bernard.
Gallinger, Carl J. '89 (CHY) Laramie, WY St. Paul's Newman Center; [E] Laramie, WY University of Wyoming.
Gallinger, Carl (CHY) College of Consultors; Presbyteral Council; Defenders of the Bond; Youth Ministry Board.
Gallipoli, Mario *c.p.* '61 (BRK)[V] Jamaica, NY Immaculate Conception Monastery.
Gallivan, David M. '66 (BUF) Hispanic Apostolate; Buffalo, NY Holy Cross; Buffalo, NY Immaculate Conception.
Gallo, David (NY)[HH] Riverdale, NY College of Mt. St. Vincent.
Gallo, Dennis G. *c.m.f.* '85 (LA) Los Angeles, CA Our Lady Queen of the Angels; [Q] Los Angeles, CA Prov. Headquarters of the Western Prov. of the USA; [Q] San Gabriel, CA Claretian Missionaries (Missionary Sons of the Immaculate Heart of Mary).
Gallo, Dennis *c.m.f.* (LA) Members.
Gallo, Gerardo '85 (NEW) Hoboken, NJ Our Lady of Grace; Hoboken, NJ St. Joseph's.
Gallo, Regis *o.f.m.* '62 (NY)[GG] Wappingers Falls, NY Mt. Alvernia Retreat House.
Gallo, Vincent '60 (BRK) Glendale, NY St. Pancras.
Gallogly, Francis *o.s.a.* '65 (PH)[B] Villanova, PA St. Augustine Friary.
Gallus, David *o.s.c.* '66 (SCL) Onamia, MN St. Therese, Little Flower Indian Mission; [I] Onamia, MN Crosier Monastery.
Galluzzo, James '90 (P) Absent on Leave.
Galo, Ricarte *m.s.p.* '01 (SPP) Pago Pago, AS Cathedral of the Holy Family.
Galonek, David B. '56 (WOR) West Brookfield, MA Sacred Heart of Jesus.
Galos, Artemio '85 (DET) Warren, MI St. Sylvester.
Galovich, George '71 (STL) Potosi, MO St. James.
Galuszka, Thaddeus *m.s.* '51 (MIL)[O] Twin Lakes, WI La Salette Missionaries Shrine.
Galvan, Alfred '65 (LSC) Ruidoso, NM St. Eleanor.
Galvan, John *s.j.* '99 (LA)[F] Los Angeles, CA Loyola High School of Los Angeles.
Galvan, Michael '77 (OAK) San Leandro, CA Assumption of the Blessed Virgin Mary.
Galvez, Elias *o.f.m.* '56 (FgM).
Galvez, Manuel *o.f.m.conv.* '99 (RNO) Reno, NV St. Thomas Aquinas Cathedral.
Galvez–Orellano, Jose Antonio *o.f.m.conv.* '96 (R) Pinehurst, NC Sacred Heart.
Galvin, Aloysius C. *s.j.* '57 (WDC)[E] North Bethesda, MD Georgetown Preparatory School.
Galvin, Edward J. *s.m.a.* '62 (VEN) Fort Myers, FL St. Peter Claver Mission.
Galvin, Edward *s.m.a.* '62 (NEW)[N] Tenafly, NJ Society of African Missions, Provincialate, S.M.A. Fathers Retired.
Galvin, Garret *o.f.m.* '00 (WDC)[M] Silver Spring, MD Gemelli House.
Galvin, Gregory P. (NOR) Faith Formation, Office for.
Galvin, Gregory '94 (NOR)[B] Middletown, CT Xavier High School; [F] Middletown, CT Congregation of the Brothers of St. Francis Xavier.
Galvin, James G. '94 (SAT) San Antonio, TX San Juan Capistrano.
Galvin, James M. '51 (LA)[Q] Santa Barbara, CA St. Mary's Center; [W] Santa Barbara, CA St. Mary's Seminary Center.
Galvin, James *c.m.* (LA) Chaplain.
Galvin, John P. '68 (BO) On Duty Outside the Archdiocese; [C] Catholic University of America, The.
Galvin, John *s.m.* '63 (FgM).
Galvin, Richard *o.s.b.* '48 (P).
Galvin, Thomas J. '82 (PIT) Pittsburgh, PA Risen Lord.
Galvin, William J. *m.m.* (FgM).
Galvis, Alirio Araque (CGS) Comerio, PR Santo Cristo de la Salud.

Galyo, John M. '54 (PH) Collegeville, PA St. Eleanor Retired.
Gamache, Barry J. '81 (PRO) Bristol, RI St. Mary; [S] Bristol, RI Roger Williams University.
Gamache, Roland L. '67 (WOR) Winchendon, MA Immaculate Heart of Mary; Advocates.
Gamallo, Edito '75 (NEW) Newark, NJ St. Anthony's.
Gamarra Cortijo, Manuel '44 (SJN) Rio Piedras, PR Santismo Sacramento; Grupo Reina De La Paz.
Gamba, John J. '42 (COL) Retired.
Gamba, Jose '86 (NEW) Jersey City, NJ St. Paul's.
Gambaro, Giampiero *o.f.m.cap.* '90 (NY)[EE] White Plains, NY Capuchin Friars International, Inc.; [EE] White Plains, NY St. Francis of Assisi Foundation, c/o Capuchin Franciscans.
Gambatese, Angelus *o.f.m.* '59 (NY) New York, NY St. Stephen of Hungary; [II] New York, NY Shrine of St. Jude, Inc..
Gamber, Matthew *s.j.* '94 (SPK)[A] Spokane, WA Bishop White Seminary.
Gamber, Matthew *s.j.* '95 (SPK)[B] Spokane, WA Gonzaga University.
Gamber, William K. '64 (STP) Special Assignment Retired.
Gambet, Daniel G. *o.s.f.s.* '57 (ALN)[B] Center Valley, PA DeSales University; [K] Center Valley, PA Oblates of St. Francis de Sales.
Gambino, Anthony J. '69 (MET)[H] Somerset, NJ Maria Regina Residence Retired.
Gamble, Anthony *c.pp.s.* '42 (CIN)[B] Carthagena, OH St. Charles.
Gamboa, Arthur *o.f.m.conv.* (RNO) Reno, NV St. Thomas Aquinas Cathedral.
Gamboa, Damian *o.f.m.* '64 (SFR).
Gambon, John A. '49 (STL) Retired.
Gambro, John M. *o.p.* '57 (CHI)[N] River Forest, IL St. Thomas Aquinas Priory.
Gamel, Robert E. '90 (FRS) Ridgecrest, CA St. Ann.
Gameros, Ignacio L. '81 (TUC) On Medical Leave.
Gamez, Francisco J. '03 (SFR) San Mateo, CA St. Matthew.
Gamm, David B. '72 (COV) Edgewood, KY St. Pius X.
Gamm, Joseph *c.m.f.* '45 (LA)[Q] Rancho Dominguez, CA Dominguez Seminary Inc..
Gammad, Engelberto '84 (LA) Los Angeles, CA St. Teresa of Avila.
Gamrot, Jaroslaw *m.i.c.* '91 (WDC) Lanham, MD St. Matthias Apostle.
Gana, Stanley M. '70 (PH) Absent on Leave.
Ganahl, James '56 (SB) Retired.
Gancarz, Eugeniusz '71 (SP) Tampa, FL Incarnation.
Gancayco, Richard K. '92 (WDC) On Duty Outside the Archdiocese.
Gancila, Joseph A. '01 (BRK) East Glendale, NY Sacred Heart.
Gandara, Jose Roberto *c.ss.r.* '92 (PCE) Bo. Puente Jobos, PR SS. Peter and Paul.
Gandolfi, Louis *c.s.* '63 (CHI) Melrose Park, IL Our Lady of Mount Carmel.
Gandolfi, Luigi *c.s.* '63 (CHI)[N] Chicago, IL Scalabrini House of Theology.
Gandrau, James '58 (SEA) Retired.
Gang, Dennis *t.o.r.* '76 (STU)[F] Steubenville, OH Holy Spirit Friary.
Gang, Dennis *t.o.r.* '79 (STU)[A] Steubenville, OH Franciscan University of Steubenville.
Gangarapu, Balaswamy (ANC) Anchorage, AK St. Elizabeth Ann Seton.
Ganiel, Joseph F. '83 (CAM) Salem, NJ St. Mary's.
Ganley, Charles '52 (SAG) Retired.
Ganley, Thomas P. '85 (MET)[G] Somerset, NJ McCarrick Care Center; [H] Somerset, NJ Maria Regina Residence.
Ganly, John C. *m.m.* '59 (STL)[O] St. Louis, MO Maryknoll House.
Gann, Sean '94 (RVC) Commack, NY Christ the King.
Gannon, Bernard J. '71 (CAM) Egg Harbor City, NJ St. Nicholas.
Gannon, Brian P. '73 (BGP) Shelton, CT St. Margaret Mary.
Gannon, Daniel J. *s.j.* '68 (CHY) St. Stephens, WY St. Stephen's; [C] St. Stephens, WY St. Stephens Mission – Jesuit Community.
Gannon, Dismas *o.c.s.o.* '50 (P)[L] Lafayette, OR The Cistercian (Trappist) Abbey of Our Lady of Guadalupe.
Gannon, Donald C. *s.j.* '76 (NY) New York, NY Nativity.
Gannon, George J. '02 (BAL) Severna Park, MD St. John the Evangelist.
Gannon, Gerard M. '56 (SCR) Archbald, PA St. Thomas Aquinas.
Gannon, Joseph T. '75 (STP) Retired.
Gannon, Josephjude C. '03 (BRK) Long Island City, NY Our Lady of Mount Carmel.
Gannon, Michael F. '65 (NY)[S] Nanuet, NY St. Agatha Home of the New York Foundling Hospital.
Gannon, Patrick J. '60 (LA) La Mirada, CA St. Paul of the Cross.
Gannon, Patrick '76 (NO) Gretna, LA St. Anthony.
Gannon, Robert I. '60 (NY) Staten Island, NY Our Lady, Queen of Peace; [E] New York, NY Moore Catholic High School.
Gannon, Roger *c.p.* '47 (BO) Brighton, MA St. Gabriel; [V] Boston, MA St. Gabriel Passionist Community.
Gannon, Thomas M. *s.j.* '67 (GRY)[I] East Chicago, IN Roque Gonzalez Residence–Jesuit Fathers; [N] Hammond, IN Heartland Center; Catholic Campaign for Human Development; Global Solidarity Partnership Program; Heartland Center; Peace and Social Justice, Office of.
Gannon, William Robert *o.p.* '53 (NY) Manhattan, NY Memorial Sloan Kettering Cancer Center; [EE] New York, NY St. Vincent Ferrer Priory.
Ganshert, Daniel T. '74 (MAD) Lancaster, WI St. Clement; Diocesan Consultors; Appointed.
Ganss, Karl P. '68 (RCK) DeKalb, IL St. Mary; Elburn, IL St. Gall.
Ganssle, Joseph *o.f.m.* '58 (NY)[EE] Denver, CO.
Gantert, Richard M. '75 (MEM) Memphis, TN St. Paul The Apostle; Presbyteral Council and College of Consultors.
Gantley, Mark J. '91 (SY) Las Vegas, NV St. Elizabeth Ann Seton.
Ganuza, Felix *sch.p.* '20 (NY)[EE] New York, NY Calasanzian Fathers (Piarists).
Ganuza, Felix *sch.p.* '76 (NY) New York, NY Annunciation.
Gaquit, Teodulo '70 (HON) Honolulu, HI St. Anthony; Hospital Ministry.
Garabedian, Thomas '03 (NY) Awaiting Assignment.
Garabedian, Thomas '03 (ARM) Brooklyn, NY St. Ann's Cathedral.
Garaizabal, Miguel *s.j.* '72 (OAK)[N] Berkeley, CA Jesuit Community at Jesuit School of Theology at Berkeley.
Garamendi, Martin *o.m.* '52 (SJN) San Juan, PR Ntra. Sra. de Fatima.
Garand, J. Douglas '01 (TOL) Fostoria, OH St. Wendelin.
Garanzini, Michael J. *s.j.* '80 (CHI)[C] Chicago, IL President's Office.
Garanzini, Michael *s.j.* '80 (CHI)[C] Chicago, IL Jesuit Community at Loyola University Chicago.
Garatea, Juan Maria '59 (B) Burley, ID St. Theresa.
Garavaglia, Henry J. '64 (STL)[N] St. Louis, MO Nazareth Living Center.
Garavel, Andrew J. *s.j.* '92 (BGP)[P] Fairfield, CT The Fairfield Jesuit Community–Fairfield University.
Garaventa, Louis T. *s.j.* '76 (BUF)[O] Buffalo, NY Canisius Jesuit Community.
Garayoa, Jose Luis *o.a.r.* (ELP) El Paso, TX Saint Therese of the Little Flower Parish.
Garbaciak, Dariusz *s.v.d.* '96 (CHI)[B] Techny, IL Divine Word Residence; [N] Techny, IL Society of the Divine Word, Provincial Headquarters–Chicago Prov.; [N] Blessed Arnold Charitable Trust; [N] Techny, IL DWTCRE Charitable Trust; [N] S.V.D. Funds, Inc..
Garbacik, Louis S. '54 (SCR) Hazleton, PA St. Stanislaus.
Garbacz, Kazimierz *s.v.d.* '69 (CHI)[B] Techny, IL Divine Word Residence.
Garbarino, Joseph J. '83 (PAT) Montville, NJ St. Pius X.
Garber, Stephen A. *s.j.* '54 (PH)[AA] Loyola Center and Manresa Hall.
Garbin, Raymond '63 (JOL) Elmhurst, IL Immaculate Conception.
Garbo, Francis Mark Maria '90 (SFR) Novato, CA Our Lady of Loretto.
Garceau, James G. *c.r.i.c.* '84 (LA)[Q] Santa Paula, CA Canons Regular of the Immaculate Conception; [D] Silverado, CA St. Michael's Preparatory School.
Garced, Wilberto Reyes '34 (NY)[II] New York, NY Lumen Dei.
Garces, Francis *o.f.m.cap.* '66 (FWT) Fort Worth, TX Our Lady of Guadalupe.
Garces, Gilberto G. '91 (ARE) Vega–Alta, PR Santa Ana.
Garces, Gilberto (ARE) Priest's Senate (Consejo Presbiteral).
Garcia, Abraham R. *m.g.* '80 (LA)[Q] Los Angeles, CA Guadalupe Missioners Procure.
Garcia, Adalberto *o.r.c.* '90 (SB) Chino, CA St. Margaret Mary.
Garcia, Albert *ss.cc.* '69 (HON)[G] Kaneohe, HI Sacred Hearts Center.
Garcia, Alfredo *ss.cc.* '63 (FR).
Garcia, Antonio '81 (SJN)[H] Carolina, PR Ntra. Sra. Del Carmen.
Garcia, Avelino R. '68 (SP) On Duty Outside the Diocese.
Garcia, Avelino R. (BO) Brockton, MA Veterans Administration Hospital Brockton–West Roxbury.
Garcia, Camilo (STO) Riverbank, CA St. Frances of Rome Church (Pastor of).
Garcia, Daniel E. '88 (AUS) Austin, TX St. Vincent de Paul.
Garcia, Daniel (AUS) Presbyteral Council; Associates.
Garcia, David '75 (SAT) San Antonio, TX Cathedral of San Fernando; [S] San Antonio, TX Historical Centre Foundation; College of Consultors; Archdiocesan Presbyteral Council.
Garcia, Dennis '02 (SFE) Albuquerque, NM San Jose; Albuquerque, NM St. Francis Xavier; Exec. Board Members:; Vocations.
Garcia, Edgar *o.m.i.* '85 (LA) Pacoima, CA Mary Immaculate.
Garcia, Eduardo C. '84 (LA) Baldwin Park, CA St. John the Baptist.
Garcia, Eduardo '90 (CC) Retired.
Garcia, Efren '02 (SAC) Anderson, CA Sacred Heart.
Garcia, Eliseo *o.s.a.* '59 (SJN) Bayamon, PR Santa Rita de Casia.
Garcia, Emilio '57 (ORL) Retired.
Garcia, Esau '87 (ORL) Orlando, FL Holy Cross.
Garcia, Francisco Javier *c.m.* '94 (LA) Los Angeles, CA Our Lady of the Rosary of Talpa.
Garcia, Francisco Juan *s.d.b.* '63 (SJN) Catano, PR San Francisco de Sales.
Garcia, Francisco *o.f.m.cap.* '78 (PCE) Ponce, PR Santa Teresita; [E] Ponce, PR Fraternidad Santa Teresita, Frailes Capuchinos; [H] Ponce, PR Albergue La Providencia, Inc..
Garcia, George '73 (MIA) Coconut Grove, FL St. Hugh.
Garcia, Gerardo M. *o.s.a.* (CHI) Chicago, IL St. Rita of Cascia.
Garcia, Gerardo *c.s.* '91 (CHI)[N] Chicago, IL Scalabrini House of Theology.
Garcia, Gildardo (MO) Air Force Chaplains.
Garcia, Guillermo C. *c.j.* '75 (LA) El Monte, CA Nativity.
Garcia, Guillermo *c.s.* '88 (GAL) Houston, TX St. Leo the Great.
Garcia, Higinio '99 (SD) San Diego, CA Our Lady of Angels.
Garcia, Isidor *c.m.f.* '54 (LA)[Q] Rancho Dominguez, CA Dominguez Seminary Inc..
Garcia, James L. '70 (SFR) Menlo Park, CA St. Anthony.
Garcia, Jesus A. '94 (SJN) Carolina, PR Ntra. Sra. Reina de la Paz.
Garcia, Jorge Eugenia '86 (B) Aberdeen, ID Presentation of the Lord.
Garcia, Jose Isidore *o.m.i.* '64 (GAL) Houston, TX Blessed Sacrament.
Garcia, Jose Luis (BWN) Pharr, TX St. Margaret Mary.
Garcia, Jose Ma. *ss.cc.* '63 (SJN) Guaynabo, PR Sagrados Corazones.
Garcia, Jose Ricardo *o.p.* '73 (FgM).
Garcia, Jose '52 (MIA) Miami, FL St. Kevin.
Garcia, Juan A. '94 (LA) San Gabriel, CA St. Anthony.
Garcia, Juan F. '67 (SPR) Springfield, MA All Souls; Springfield, MA Blessed Sacrament.
Garcia, Juan L. '70 (WDC)[B] Washington, DC Diocesan Laborer Priests, House of Studies.
Garcia, Juan L. *d.l.p.* '70 (SB) Riverside, CA Our Lady of Perpetual Help.
Garcia, Juan *d.l.p.* '70 (SB)[A] Riverside, CA Blessed Junipero Serra House of Formation; [E] Riverside, CA Diocesan Labor Priests, DLP.
Garcia, Juan '96 (SHP) Unassigned.
Garcia, Juan *c.r.i.c.* (SPR) Procurators–Advocate.
Garcia, Juan (SB) Blessed Junipero Serra House of Formation.
Garcia, Lorenzo '97 (SAV) Hazlehurst, GA Good Shepherd; Council of Priests.
Garcia, Luis J. (BWN) Office for the Church in Latin America.
Garcia, Luis Javier (BWN) Judicial Department (Diocesan Tribunal); Presiding Judges; Office for Propagation of the Faith.
Garcia, Luis '50 (LA) Lynwood, CA St. Emydius.
Garcia, Luis '97 (MIA) Hialeah, FL St. Cecilia.
Garcia, Manuel '75 (SJN) Dorado, PR Ntra. Sra. de La Salud; [E] San Juan, PR Centro Medico de P.R..
Garcia, Marcelino *s.j.* '70 (MIA)[D] Miami, FL Belen Jesuit Preparatory School; [H] Miami, FL Villa Javier.
Garcia, Marcial '95 (VEN) Clewiston, FL St. Margaret.
Garcia, Mario *o.f.m.cap.* '88 (DAL)[K] Dallas, TX Capuchin Franciscan Friars, Vice Province of Texas; Dallas, TX Our Lady of Lourdes.
Garcia, Michael A. *o.p.* '81 (CHI)[N] St. Pius V Priory.
Garcia, Miguel A. *c.ss.r.* '71 (PCE) Guayama, PR St. Anthony of Padua.
Garcia, Millan '62 (SFE) Prison Ministry; Air Force Reserve Chaplains.
Garcia, Nelson *s.j.* '67 (MIA)[D] Miami, FL Belen Jesuit Preparatory School; [H] Miami, FL Villa Javier.
Garcia, Otto L. '73 (BRK) Brooklyn, NY The Cathedral–Basilica of St. James; Vicar General and Moderator of the Curia; Presbyteral Council; Diocesan Consultors.
Garcia, Patrick '89 (CHK) Saipan, MP San Jude Parish; Commission on Ministerial Development; Confraternity of Christian Mothers.
Garcia, Pedro '64 (MIA) Naranja, FL St. Ann Mission; Rural Life Ministry.
Garcia, Pedro '01 (AUS) Washington, TX Blessed Virgin Mary.
Garcia, Pedro (GR) Retired.
Garcia, Rafael *o.f.m.* '90 (AMA) Dumas, TX SS. Peter and Paul.

Garcia, Rafael *s.j.* '93 (ELP) El Paso, TX Sacred Heart; St. Paul; Diocesan Building Committee; Priests' Personnel Advisory Committee.
Garcia, Ramon V. '55 (SAT)[K] San Antonio, TX Padua Place.
Garcia, Raul Valencia '03 (TUC) Tucson, AZ St. Monica.
Garcia, Raymond '55 (SAT) Retired.
Garcia, Raymundo '74 (TYL) Athens, TX St. Edward Church.
Garcia, Reynaldo A. *s.j.* '76 (DET)[P] Hamtramck, MI St. Ladislaus.
Garcia, Reynaldo *s.j.* '76 (GAY) Suttons Bay, MI St. Wenceslaus; Migrant Apostolate.
Garcia, Ricardo '92 (BWN) Pharr, TX St. Anne, Mother of Mary; Judicial Department (Diocesan Tribunal); Presiding Judges.
Garcia, Roberto '86 (PCE)[B] The Pontifical Catholic University of Puerto Rico.
Garcia, Rodolfo '98 (DAL) Plano, TX St. Mark the Evangelist.
Garcia, Rolando G. '86 (MIA) Miami, FL St. Agatha.
Garcia, Rolando (MIA) FIU–University Park.
Garcia, Samuel (LSC) Absent On Leave.
Garcia, Sergio '86 (FRS) Las Vegas, NV Prince of Peace.
Garcia, Sergio *c.r.i.c.* '94 (LA)[Q] Santa Paula, CA Canons Regular of the Immaculate Conception.
Garcia, Severiano *c.m.f.* '50 (SJN) Bayamon, PR San Jose.
Garcia–Cardova, Carlos (LKC) Hispanic Ministry.
Garcia–Espino, Alfonso (ORG) Santa Ana, CA Immaculate Heart of Mary.
Garcia–Inostroza, Sergio '94 (LA) Pomona, CA Sacred Heart.
Garcia–Martinez, Antonio *o.m.* '67 (SJN) San Juan, PR Ntra. Sra. de Fatima.
Garcia–Miro, Sergio '78 (MIA) Retired.
Garcia–Pena, Carlos '66 (DOD) Garden City, KS St. Mary.
Garcia–Ramirez, Pedro '01 (AUS) Somerville, TX St. Ann's.
Garcia–Tunon, Guillermo *s.j.* (MIA)[D] Miami, FL Belen Jesuit Preparatory School; [H] Miami, FL Villa Javier.
Garcia Almodovar, Angel L. '03 (ALN) Reading, PA St. Peter.
Garcia Padron, Victor Julio '89 (SJN) On Duty Outside the Archdiocese.
Garcia Rodriguez, Jesus '94 (SJN)[E] Carolina, PR Hospital Regional.
Gardin, Vernon E. '71 (STL)[H] St. Louis, MO Catholic Guidance Center; [H] St. Louis, MO St. Mary's Special Services; Vicars General.
Gardiner, Christopher B. '68 (MAR) Bark River, MI St. Elizabeth Ann Seton; Consultors.
Gardiner, James K. '69 (GAY) Kalkaska, MI St. Aloysius; Kalkaska, MI St. Mary of the Woods; Traverse City, MI St. Francis of Assisi; Vicars (by region).
Gardiner, James *s.a.* '69 (NY)[EE] Garrison, NY Franciscan Friars of the Atonement.
Gardiner, Richard E. '67 (WDC) Solomons, MD Our Lady Star of the Sea.
Gardner, Clarence W. '42 (ROC) Retired.
Gardner, Clement G. (ALT) Juniata Deanery.
Gardner, Clement '67 (ALT) Hollidaysburg, PA St. Michael's.
Gardner, Daniel L. '78 (KCK) Emporia, KS Sacred Heart; Emporia, KS St. Catherine.
Gardner, G. Duff (DAL) Diocesan Consultors.
Gardner, Glenn D. '70 (DAL) Plano, TX St. Mark the Evangelist; Vicar General; Assistant Judicial Vicars; Presbyteral Council; Censor Librorum; Pastoral Concerns Board; Personnel Board.
Gardner, Jerome J. '79 (CIN) Cincinnati, OH St. Margaret Mary.
Gardner, Maurice '52 (KCK) Retired.
Gardner, Royal J. '51 (SPR) Pittsfield, MA St. Teresa Retired.
Gardner, William M. '92 (PEO) Odell, IL Sacred Heart; Odell, IL St. Paul's.
Gardner, William P. '62 (TR) Toms River, NJ St. Joseph.
Gardner, William (PEO) Illinois State Penitentiary.
Gardocki, Patrick M. *o.f.m.* (MO) Navy Chaplains.
Gardocki, Thomas F. '65 (WIL) Retired.
Gardon, Emmanuel *c.p.* '50 (PMB)[J] North Palm Beach, FL Our Lady of Florida Spiritual Center.
Gardzalla, Leo M. '45 (SCR) Retired.
Gareau, Timothy W. '88 (CLV) Bay Village, OH St. Raphael.
Gargani, Francis *c.ss.r.* '71 (NY) Bronx, NY Immaculate Conception.
Gargantiel, Isidro T. '68 (GR) Scottville, MI St. Jerome.
Gargatiel, Isidro '68 (GR) Custer, MI St. Mary's.
Gargotta, Anthony '01 (PIT) Natrona Heights, PA Our Lady of the Most Blessed Sacrament.
Gariboldi, Ronald J. '61 (BO) Rockport, MA St. Joachim.
Gariepy, Andre M. '58 (WOR) Gardner, MA Holy Spirit.
Gariepy, Robert E. '63 (WOR) Retired.
Gariepy, Thomas P. *c.s.c.* '74 (FR)[A] North Easton, MA Stonehill College; [A] North Easton, MA Holy Cross Fathers Religious.
Gariolo, Joseph M. *c.r.s.p.* '50 (BUF)[B] Youngstown, NY St. Anthony M. Zaccaria Seminary.
Garisto, James A. '77 (NY) Poughkeepsie, NY St. Peter.
Garisto, James '77 (NY) Staten Island, NY Our Lady, Queen of Peace.
Garkowski, John G. '66 (BRK) South Ozone Park, NY Our Lady of Perpetual Help.
Garland, Reynolds *o.f.m.* '61 (HT) Houma, LA Our Lady of the Most Holy Rosary; Houma, LA St. Lucy.
Garland, Robert P. '53 (PIT) Retired.
Garland, William T. *o.s.a.* '62 (PH)[C] Villanova, PA Villanova University; [C] Our Mother of Good Counsel Monastery.
Garlick, Thomas B. '84 (WOR) Sterling, MA St. Richard of Chichester.
Garneau, James F. '84 (R) On Duty Outside the Diocese.
Garner, Andy '01 (OWN)[B] Owensboro, KY Owensboro Catholic High School; Non–Parochial Assignments.
Garner, Glenn D. (DAL) Finance Council.
Garner, Joel P. *o.praem.* '65 (SFE) Albuquerque, NM Our Lady of Most Holy Rosary; [I] Albuquerque, NM Santa Maria de la Vid Priory; [M] Albuquerque, NM Norbertine Community of New Mexico, Inc..
Garner, Kirby D. '77 (AUS) Bryan, TX St. Anthony's.
Garner, Kirby (AUS) Presbyteral Council; Consultors; Defenders of the Bond.
Garofalo, Kenneth *o.f.m.* '55 (BO) East Boston, MA Our Lady of Mt. Carmel.
Garoffolo, Vincent '41 (NEW) Retired.
Garoin, Vernon E. '71 (STL) St. Louis, MO Cathedral Basilica of Saint Louis.
Garone, Thomas *o.f.m.* '73 (NY)[GG] Wappingers Falls, NY Mt. Alvernia Retreat House.
Garrahy, Michael '51 (WCH) Retired.
Garralda, Angel *sch.p.* '63 (PCE)[C] Coto Laurel, PR Colegio Ponceno.
Garramone, Dominic M. *o.s.b.* '92 (PEO).
Garret, Sean '64 (SAT)[A] On Duty Outside the Archdiocese.
Garrett, Mark A. *o.s.a.* '70 (WDC)[B] Washington, DC Augustinian College, Order of St. Augustine.
Garrett, Scott '03 (ANC) Eagle River, AK St. Andrew.
Garrett, Thomas P. *o.s.a.* '39 (SD)[H] San Diego, CA Augustinian Community.
Garrido, Alejandro '92 (CHI) Chicago, IL Notre Dame; Casa Jesus; Chicago, IL St. Adalbert.
Garrido, Mariano '96 (AGN) Barrigada, GU San Vicente Ferrer.
Garrigan, Gerard *o.s.b.* '89 (STL) St. Louis, MO St. Anselm; [O] St. Louis, MO The Abbey of St. Mary and St. Louis.
Garringer, Grant S. *s.j.* '97 (MIL)[O] Milwaukee, WI Jesuit Community at Marquette University.
Garritty, Bernard R. *m.m.* '47 (NY).
Garritty, Stephen M. *s.j.* '70 (R)[E] Raleigh Jesuit Community.
Garrity, Charles *o.c.d.* '66 (SEA) Stanwood, WA St. Cecilia.
Garrity, Francis D. '56 (BO) Senior Priests Retired.
Garrity, G. Patrick '76 (KNX) Morristown, TN St. Patrick; Presbyteral Council.
Garrity, Paul V. '73 (BO) Lynn, MA St. Mary; NORTH REGION
Garrity, Robert M. '81 (RCK) Huntley, IL St. Mary.
Garrity, Sean *c.s.b.* '88 (LSC) Truth or Consequences, NM Our Lady of Perpetual Help; Presbyteral Council.
Garrity, Stephen M. *s.j.* '70 (R) Durham, NC Holy Cross; [H] Durham, NC North Carolina Central University.
Garrity, Thomas F. *m.m.* '46 (NY).
Garrote, Sancho G. '76 (NY)[EE] Bronx Municipal Hospital Center, Abraham Jacobi Hospital, Nathan B. VanEtten Hospital.
Garrow, Mark *m.i.c.* '84 (SPR).
Garry, Gerald *s.v.d.* '59 (CHI)[B] Techny, IL Divine Word Residence.
Garry, Peter J. '68 (RVC) Northport, NY St. Philip Neri.
Garry, Ron '83 (RC) Philip, SD Sacred Heart.
Garst, Charles C. *o.s.f.s.* '83 (WIL) Wilmington, DE St. Anthony of Padua.
Gartland, Daniel B. '82 (LFT) Lafayette, IN St. Lawrence; Deans; Diocesan Consultors; Presbyteral Council; Members.
Gartland, Daniel (LFT) Greater Lafayette Catholic School Board.
Gartland, James G. *s.j.* '93 (CHI)[N] Chicago, IL Miguel Pro Jesuit Community.
Gartland, R. Vincent '81 (TR) Lawrenceville, NJ St. Ann.
Gartner, Charles A. '58 (RVC) Hicksville NY Our Lady of Mercy Retired.
Gartner, Joseph *g.h.m.* '40 (CIN)[M] Cincinnati Headquarters of Glenmary Home Missioners.
Garvey, Francis J. *m.m.* '43 (SJ)[M] Los Altos, CA Maryknoll.
Garvey, Francis J. '59 (NU) Grove City, MN Church of Our Lady; College of Consultors; Committee on Parishes; Members; Priests' Council; Vocations Team; Vicar for Retired Priests.
Garvey, James W. '76 (PIT) Pittsburgh, PA Epiphany.
Garvey, John M. *m.s.* '53 (HRT).
Garvey, John '58 (SFS) Retired.
Garvey, Michael '71 (Y)[M] Military Chaplains; Navy Chaplains.
Garvey, Roderick J. *c.ss.r.* '49 (LSC) Jal, NM St. Cecilia.
Garvey, Thomas J. '57 (STP) Presbyteral Council Retired.
Garvin, Joseph P. '73 (PH) Philadelphia, PA St. Christopher.
Garvin, Thomas R. *s.j.* '58 (SPK)[J] Spokane, WA Regis Community.
Garvy, John '83 (ORL) Retired.
Gary, Paul Q. '84 (CHL) Charlotte, NC St. Patrick Cathedral.
Gary, Paul (CHL) Diocesan Consultors.
Garza, Amador '85 (BWN) Rio Grande City, TX Immaculate Conception.
Garza, Jesus Aguirre *o.f.m.* '96 (FgM).
Garza, Juan P. '02 (WCH) Wichita, KS Cathedral of the Immaculate Conception.
Garza, Raul '86 (NO)[P] New Orleans, LA Vincentian Fathers.
Garza, Roberto '96 (MIA) Pompano Beach, FL San Isidro; [M] Margate, FL Word & Life Catholic Ministry, Inc.; [M] Pompano Beach, FL Ministerio Catolico Verbo y Vida, Inc.; Catholic Charities of the Archdiocese of Miami, Inc..
Garzarelli, Santo R. '61 (PH) Retired.
Garzarelli, Santo '61 (PH) Philadelphia, PA Our Lady of Calvary Retired.
Garzon, Fabio H. *s.d.b.* '86 (RCK) Carpentersville, IL St. Monica.
Garzon–Blanco, Armando '95 (TUC) Administrative Leave of Absence.
Gaske, Bartholomew *o.f.m.conv.* '40 (SY) Syracuse, NY Assumption B.V.M..
Gaskin, Matthew L. *o.f.m.* '50 (PAT)[M] Butler, NJ St. Anthony Friary.
Gasnick, Roy *o.f.m.* '60 (SP)[O] St. Petersburg, FL St. Anthony Friary.
Gaspar, Joseph *m.s.c.* '41 (ALN)[A] Center Valley, PA Sacred Heart Villa, Missionaries of the Sacred Heart.
Gaspar, Mark S. '98 (PH) Collingdale, PA St. Joseph.
Gasparik, Francis *o.f.m.cap.* '86 (NY) New York, NY St. John the Baptist; (FgM).
Gasparin, Giampietro *c.s.j.* '79 (LA)[Q] Los Angeles, CA Congregation of St. Joseph Casa Nazareth.
Gasparin, Giampietro *c.s.j.* '79 (CLV)[C] Lorain, OH Lorain Catholic High School; [O] Avon, OH Congregation of St. Joseph; [T] Avon, OH St. Leonard Youth Retreat Center.
Gasparini, Louis *m.c.c.j.* (CHI) Blue Island, IL St. Donatus.
Gasparini, Luigi *m.c.c.j.* '66 (CHI)[CC] Covina, CA Comboni Mission Center.
Gaspeny, Peter J. '83 (SAG) Midland, MI Blessed Sacrament.
Gass, Michael W. '77 (DEN) Lakewood, CO St. Jude.
Gass, Robert J. '53 (OM)[L] Omaha, NE Sisters of the Annunciation of the Archdiocese of Omaha Retired.
Gassert, Adelbert J. '48 (CLV) Brook Park, OH Assumption of Mary; Independence, OH St. Michael Retired.
Gastalver, Alfredo '76 (SJN)[G] Guaynabo, PR Opus Dei.
Gaston, James T. '70 (GBG) Lower Burrell, PA St. Margaret Mary; Deaneries; Bishop's Priests Council.
Gaston, Juan Cruz *o.f.m.cap.* '67 (DAL) Dallas, TX Our Lady of Perpetual Help.
Gately, R. Troy '89 (GAL) Houston, TX Sacred Heart Co–Cathedral; On Special or Other Diocesan Assignment; Vice Chancellor.
Gately, Robert E. '52 (COL) Retired.
Gathenya, John '86 (ROC) Naples, NY Our Lady of the Lakes Catholic Community; Penn Yan, NY St. Michael; Penn Yan, NY St. Theresa.
Gatlin, Bernard '68 (LA) Fillmore, CA St. Francis of Assisi.
Gatlin, Jeffrey D. (L) Louisville, KY Holy Spirit.
Gatlin, Larry B. '67 (OKL) Bison, OK St. Joseph's.
Gatman, Ronald P. *o.s.b.* '79 (SAV)[B] Savannah, GA Benedictine Military School; [F] Savannah, GA The Benedictine Priory.
Gatschet, Fred '93 (SAL)[H] Hays, KS Comeau Catholic Campus Center at Fort Hays State University; Vocation Ministry Committee.
Gattari, Valentine A. '54 (DET) Retired.
Gatti, Daniel J. *s.j.* '72 (NY)[F] New York, NY Xavier High School.
Gatto, Joseph C. '83 (BUF)[A] Lockport, NY St. John the Baptist.
Gatto, Reynold J. *s.j.* '68 (SAC)[M] Los Gatos, CA Sacred Heart Jesuit Center.
Gatto, Vincent S. '55 (WDC) Garrett Park, MD Holy Cross.
Gatzak, John P. '75 (HRT) Hartford, CT Cathedral of St. Joseph; Special and other Archdiocesan Assignment; Office of Radio and Television.
Gau, David H. *s.j.* '62 (CHY) Lander, WY Holy Rosary;

St. Stephens, WY St. Stephen's.
Gau, Guy *o.s.b.* '62 (SFS)[F] Marvin, SD Blue Cloud Abbey.
Gauchat, Eric *o.f.m.cap.* '92 (CLV)[O] Cleveland, OH St. Paul Friary.
Gauchet, Eric *o.f.m.cap.* '92 (CLV) Cleveland, OH Conversion of St. Paul.
Gauci, Albert *o.f.m.* '71 (FgM).
Gauci, John *c.ss.r.* '59 (BRK) Brooklyn, NY Our Lady of Perpetual Help Basilica.
Gaudet, Joseph A. '57 (BO) Senior Priests Retired.
Gaudio, Dean A. '03 (TR) Toms River, NJ St. Joseph.
Gaudio, Robert '74 (ROC) Palmyra, NY St. Gregory; Palmyra, NY St. Anne.
Gaudreau, Bernard E. (BUR) Office of Ministerial Formation and Permanent Diaconate; Members Ex Officio; Diocesan Consultors; Stowe, VT Blessed Sacrament.
Gaudreau, James E. '69 (BO) Lynn, MA St. Joseph.
Gaudreau, Walter *s.m.* '64 (PRT) Brunswick, ME St. John the Baptist; Diocesan Council of Priests.
Gaudreault, Lucien *s.v.d.* '88 (MIL)[O] East Troy, WI Divine Word Missionaries.
Gaughan, Joseph '94 (FTW) Fort Wayne, IN St. Vincent de Paul.
Gaughan, Patrick E. '68 (STU) Athens, OH St. Paul's.
Gaughan, Patrick (STU) Deans; Priests Personnel Board.
Gaughan, Paul '52 (RIC) Virginia Beach, VA St. John the Apostle Church Retired.
Gaughan, Thomas E. *c.s.c.* '87 (FTW)[B] University of Notre Dame Du Lac; [I] Notre Dame, IN Holy Cross Community, Corby Hall, University of Notre Dame.
Gaughran, John '53 (PEO) Retired.
Gaugler, Robert *c.ss.r.* '39 (ALB)[L] Saratoga Springs, NY St. John Neumann Residence.
Gaugler, Robert *c.ss.r.* '39 (SJN) San Juan, PR San Agustin.
Gaul, Richard G. '68 (DUB) Garnavillo, IA St. Joseph.
Gaul, Thomas J. '73 (R) Hope Mills, NC Good Shepherd.
Gaulin, Frederick J. *c.m.* '50 (PH).
Gaulin, Roger M. '65 (NOR)[AA] Absent on Leave.
Gaumond, Normand R. '73 (WOR) Harvard, MA St. Theresa's.
Gaumond, Paul J. '74 (NOR) Essex, CT Our Lady of Sorrows.
Gaunt, James J. *c.s.b.* '64 (GAL) Manvel, TX Sacred Heart of Jesus.
Gaunt, Thomas P. *s.j.* '81 (WDC)[M] Washington, DC Leonard Neale House; [V] Washington, DC Jesuit Conference, Inc..
Gaunt, Thomas *s.j.* '81 (FgM).
Gaus, Arnold L. '59 (ALT) Ebensburg, PA Holy Name.
Gauthier, Donald F. '75 (MAN) Goffstown, NH St. Lawrence.
Gauthier, Ernest '62 (KC) Retired.
Gauthier, John C. '65 (PHX) Retired.
Gauthier, Lawrence T. '55 (MAR) Catholic Relief Services; Holy Childhood Association; Propagation of the Faith Retired.
Gauthreaux, L. Earl '56 (NO) New Orleans, LA St. Maria Goretti; Judges; Deans.
Gautreau, Henry W. '79 (BR) Catholic Charismatic Renewal Retired.
Gautreaux, Francis *c.ss.r.* '50 (FgM).
Gauvin, Leo *o.m.i.* '51 (SAT)[K] San Antonio, TX Oblate Madonna Residence.
Gauvin, Maurice O. '86 (FR) New Bedford, MA St. John the Baptist.
Gauxreau, Michael M. '03 (FR)[H] New Bedford, MA Marian Friary of Our Lady, Queen of the Seraphic Order.
Gavaler, Campion P. *o.s.b.* '59 (GBG)[H] Latrobe, PA Saint Vincent Archabbey.
Gavamukulya, Albert (CHI) Chicago, IL St. Philip Neri.
Gavigan, P. Patrick '53 (CHL) Retired.
Gavigan, Peter '62 (NY) Bronx, NY Our Lady of Victory.
Gavigan, Thomas J. *c.ss.r.* '60 (PH) Philadelphia, PA St. Peter the Apostle.
Gavin, Carney E. '65 (BO) Brighton, MA St. Columbkille.
Gavin, Emmett J. *o.carm.* (MO) Judges.
Gavin, Emmett *o.carm.* '87 (WDC)[B] Washington, DC Whitefriars Hall.
Gavin, Harold E. '51 (WIN) Retired.
Gavin, James *o.f.m.cap.* '65 (NY) New York, NY St. John the Baptist.
Gavin, John F. *s.j.* '02 (BO)[V] Boston The Society of Jesus of New England–Provincial Offices.
Gavin, John T. *o.s.f.s.* '60 (CAM) Atco, NJ Assumption.
Gavin, John *o.s.a.* '48 (STL) St. Louis, MO Immaculate Conception–St. Henry.
Gavin, Kenneth J. *s.j.* '75 (NY)[V] Washington, DC Jesuit Refugee Service; [M] Washington, DC Leonard Neale House.
Gavin, Patrick *o.carm.* '94 (LA) North Hollywood, CA St. Jane Frances de Chantal.
Gavin, Robert A. *o.f.m.* '59 (NY) New York, NY St. Francis of Assisi.
Gavin, Thomas M. *s.j.* '75 (BAL)[S] Casa Ejercicios.
Gavin, William F. *s.j.* '62 (PH) Philadelphia, PA Old St. Joseph's.
Gavit, James F. '54 (SAG) Bay City, MI St. Maria Goretti; Vicars General; Vicar for Canonical Affairs; Defenders of the Bond; Promoter of Justice.
Gavit, Steven M. '97 (SAG) Palms, MI St. Patrick.
Gavit, Steven W. '97 (SAG) Ruth, MI SS. Peter and Paul.
Gavitt, J. Duane '84 (SCR) Tunkhannock, PA Nativity of Blessed Virgin Mary.
Gavotto, Robert *o.s.a.* '64 (LA)[F] Ojai, CA Villanova Preparatory School.
Gawienawski, John '01 (SPR) Florence, MA Annunciation.
Gawlik, Gilbert *s.v.d.* '54 (CHI)[B] Techny, IL Divine Word Residence.
Gawlowski, Michael '02 (DET) Clinton Twp, MI St. Claude; Clinton Twp., MI St. Thecla.
Gawlowski, Paul *o.f.m.conv.* '99 (SFR) San Francisco, CA St. Paul of the Shipwreck.
Gawronski, Gerald '01 (LAN) Burton, MI Holy Redeemer.
Gawronski, Marc A. '91 (DET) Rockwood, MI St. Mary.
Gawronski, Raymond T. *s.j.* '86 (MIL)[O] Milwaukee, WI Jesuit Community at Marquette University.
Gawrylewski, Patrick *o.f.m.* (GB) Seymour, WI St. Stanislaus; Pulaski, WI Assumption of the Blessed Virgin Mary; Appointed Representatives.
Gay, James A. '59 (BGP) Military Chaplains; Navy Chaplains.
Gay, James '59 (TUC) Yuma, AZ MCAS Chapel.
Gay, John Curry '56 (HRT) Waterbury, CT Immaculate Conception.
Gayam, Francis '78 (NY) Bronx, NY St. Francis Xavier.
Gayarre, Domingo *s.s.s.* '52 (CGS) Caguas, PR Santisimo Sacramento.
Gayarre, Eugenio '61 (ARE) Corozal, PR Holy Family.
Gaydos, Anthony M. *o.s.m.* '48 (CHI)[N] Chicago Order of Friar Servants of Mary (Servites) United States of America Province, Inc.; Ironton, MO Ste. Marie Du Lac.
Gaydosik, David L. '87 (STU) Woodsfield, OH St. Joseph's; Woodsfield, OH St. John the Baptist; Woodsfield, OH St. John Bosco Mission.
Gaydosik, David '87 (STU) Woodsfield, OH St. Sylvester.
Gaynor, James E. *c.pp.s.* '67 (CIN)[M] San Francisco de Borja.
Gayso, Edward V. '50 (IND) Retired.
Gaytan, Alfredo *s.o.l.t.* '82 (CC)[G] Robstown, TX Society of Our Lady of the Most Holy Trinity.
Gaytan, Jose Alfredo *s.o.l.t.* '85 (LAR) Laredo, TX St. Frances Cabrini.
Gaytan, Rodolfo '02 (CHI) Chicago, IL St. Tarcissus.
Gayton, John J. '86 (WIL) Claymont, DE Holy Rosary.
Gayton, John J. *m.i.c.* (MO) Navy Reserve Chaplains.
Gaza, J. Patrick '68 (GRY) Gary, IN SS. Monica–St. Luke.
Gbur, Andrzej *o.c.d.* '98 (GRY)[I] Munster, IN Discalced Carmelite Fathers Monastery.
Geaney, James *o.carm.* '59 (JOL)[L] Prelate Nullius; (FgM).
Geaney, John J. *c.s.p.* '64 (MEM) Memphis, TN St. Augustine.
Geaney, John S. *c.s.p.* '64 (MEM) Memphis, TN St. Patrick's.
Geany, Nash P. (NY) Stewart Field.
Gearhart, Edwin F. '73 (CIN) Cincinnati, OH St. Leo the Great; Judicial Vicar.
Gearhart, Lawrence M. '03 (CIN) Cincinnati, OH Our Lady of Lourdes.
Gearheard, William '94 (LAF) Carencro, LA Our Lady of the Assumption.
Gearing, Barry T. (CLV) Chesterland, OH St. Anselm.
Gearing, Edward P. '44 (GBG) Retired.
Gearwar, David C. '03 (OG) Malone, NY St. Helen; Malone, NY Notre Dame; Malone, NY St. John Bosco; Malone, NY St. Joseph's.
Geary, Brian A. '98 (RCK) Rockford, IL St. Patrick.
Geary, Edward P. '64 (BO) Beverly, MA St. Mary Star of the Sea.
Geary, John C. *s.j.* '47 (SJ)[M] Los Gatos, CA Sacred Heart Jesuit Center.
Geary, Patrick G. '56 (DUB) Directors Retired.
Geaves, Gerald (NEW) Part–time Staff.
Gebbia, Gregory *o.f.m.* '86 (PAT) Little Falls, NJ Our Lady of the Holy Angels.
Gebelein, Gary M. '74 (STL) St. Louis, MO St. Francis of Assisi.
Gebhard, Robert L. '87 (BUF) Vicars; Buffalo, NY St. James.
Gebhardt, Paul L. '91 (CIN) Cincinnati, OH St. Vivian.
Geddes, Thomas C. (E) Retired.
Gedeon, Thomas W. *s.j.* '56 (CLV)[T] Cleveland, OH Jesuit Retreat House.
Geders, Joseph C. *c.m.* '84 (CHI)[N] Chicago, IL Vincentian Community, Congregation of the Mission, Midwest Province; [O] Earth City, MO Congregation of the Mission Midwest Province (Vincentians).
Geditz, Roger '69 (SFS) Retired.
Gedvainis, Vytautas '89 (NOR)[G] Putnam, CT Immaculate Conception Convent, Spiritual Renewal Center and Novitiate.
Gedvila, Izidorius '48 (GF) Retired.
Gee, Daniel N. '95 (ARL) Miami, FL San Francisco de Asis, Banica; Miami, FL San Jose, Pedro Santana; On Duty Outside the Diocese.
Gee, John F. '53 (WOR) Auburn, MA North American Martyrs.
Geelan, Thomas E. '62 (SC) Graettinger, IA Immaculate Conception; Directors:.
Geenen, Roy J. '68 (GB) Menasha, WI St. Patrick; Regional Vicars.
Geers, Frank *o.f.m.* '58 (CIN)[C] Cincinnati, OH St. Anthony Shrine, Franciscan Candidacy.
Geers, Harold *o.f.m.* '60 (CIN)[M] (FgM).
Geevarughese, Charuvilayil Jacob '72 (WDC) Landover Hills, MD St. Mary's Catholic Church; Landover Hills, MD Syro–Malankara Mission.
Gefell, Gerard J. '41 (OG) Retired.
Geffrard, Yves '01 (PMB) Boca Raton, FL Our Lady of Lourdes; Office for Haitian Ministry.
Gegotek, Tadeusz '91 (BEL) Military Chaplains; Navy Chaplains.
Gehant, Rembert *o.s.b.* '44 (IND)[K] St. Meinrad, IN St. Meinrad Archabbey.
Gehl, James C. '74 (LA) Winnetka, CA St. Joseph the Worker.
Gehl, James C. (LA) Deanery 5.
Gehl, James E. '69 (SY) Cicero, NY Sacred Heart.
Gehl, James (LA) Ministry to Recently Ordained Priests; San Fernando Pastoral Region.
Gehl, Walter N. '44 (MIL) Retired.
Gehlen, Elzear *s.v.d.* '44 (CHI) Mt. Prospect, IL St. Cecilia; [B] Techny, IL Divine Word Residence.
Gehling, Kenneth B. '62 (DUB)[H] Mason City, IA Mercy Medical Center–North Iowa; Mason City, IA Holy Family; Deans.
Gehring, Robert P. '66 (GRY) Gary, IN Cathedral of Holy Angels; Gary, IN Holy Rosary; Bishop's Council of Priests.
Gehringer, Andrew N. (ALN) Allentown, PA Sacred Heart of Jesus.
Geib, David *o.p.* '67 (SB) Riverside, CA St. Andrew; [E] Riverside, CA St. Vincent Ferrer House; [H] Riverside, CA St. Andrews Newman Center; Education Committee.
Geib, Harry F. *s.j.* '92 (PH)[AA] Loyola Center and Manresa Hall.
Geigel, Francis '38 (GB) Retired.
Geiger, Angelo Mary '91 (NOR)[F] Griswold, CT Marian Friary of Our Lady of Guadalupe.
Geiger, Bernard *o.f.m.conv.* '59 (CHI)[N] Bloomingdale, OH Apostolate for Family Consecration.
Geiger, Damon *o.ss.t.* '71 (BAL)[S] Victoria, TX Trinity House.
Geiger, Damon *o.ss.t.* '71 (VIC)[F] Victoria, TX Trinity House.
Geiger, James A. '50 (COL) Sugar Grove, OH St. Joseph.
Geiger, James H. *c.ss.r.* '60 (CHL) Concord, NC St. James.
Geiger, James (COL) Diocesan Judges.
Geiger, Michael A. '02 (TOL)[B] Toledo, OH Central Catholic High School; Toledo, OH Historic Church of St. Patrick.
Geiger, William G. *c.ss.r.* '54 (HBG) Ephrata, PA Mother of Perpetual Help.
Geiger, William *c.ss.r.* '54 (HBG)[H] Ephrata, PA St. Clement's Mission House.
Geinzer, Eugene M. *s.j.* '74 (BAL)[B] Jesuit Community of Loyola College, Inc.; [S] Baltimore, MD Jesuit Community of Loyola College, Inc..
Geinzer, John A. '67 (PIT) Military Chaplains; Navy Chaplains.
Geinzer, Patrick *c.p.* '95 (R)[V] Jamaica, NY Immaculate Conception Monastery.
Geis, John F. '64 (IND) Floyds Knobs, IN St. Mary–of–the–Knobs.
Geis, John (IND) Priests' Personnel Board; Associates.
Geiser, Allen '90 (GB) Greenleaf, WI St. Patrick.
Geiser, Xavier *o.f.m.* '55 (FgM).
Geisinger, Robert J. *s.j.* '91 (CHI)[N] Chicago Chicago Province of the Society of Jesus–Provincial Office.
Geisser, Raymond E. '60 (PH)[AA] Villanova, PA St. Thomas Monastery.
Geissler, Lloyd F. '42 (LC) Retired.
Geissler, Robert '47 (NY) Retired.
Geissler, Robert '47 (NY) Retired.
Geiszel, John I. *s.j.* '57 (LA)[F] Los Angeles, CA Loyola High School of Los Angeles.
Geizner, Patrick *c.p.* '95 (BRK) Jamaica, NY Immaculate Conception.
Gelati, Dario '53 (PIT) Retired.
Gelencser, Paul L. *o.praem.* '41 (ORG)[I] Silverado, CA Norbertine Fathers of Orange Inc..
Geleney, Joseph F. '01 (AUS) Austin, TX St. Thomas More.
Gelfenbein, Gary (ALB) Deans.
Gelfenbien, Gary Paul '71 (ALB) Chatham, NY St. James.
Gelido, Manuel T. (WH)[P] Athens, WV Concord College Newman Center.

Gelido, Manuel '79 (WH) Princeton, WV Sacred Heart.
Gelin, Henry C. *s.j.* '51 (DET)[P] Hamtramck, MI St. Ladislaus.
Gelineau, Edward J. '42 (BUR)[D] Burlington, VT St. Joseph's Home Retired.
Gelineau, Raymond H. '69 (WOR) On Duty Outside the Diocese.
Gellel, Lawrence *s.j.* '54 (BRK) Rego Park, NY Our Lady of the Angelus.
Geller, Charles H. '73 (BEL) Special Assignment.
Gelpi, Donald L. *s.j.* '64 (OAK)[N] Berkeley, CA Jesuit Community at Jesuit School of Theology at Berkeley.
Gelsomino, Peter (NY) Port Chester, NY Sacred Heart of Jesus.
Gelson, James N. *s.j.* '60 (BAL)[S] Highland Beach, FL.
Gelthaus, Harry J. '85 (L) Louisville, KY St. Clement; Ex Officio.
Gelthaus, Lawrence J. '88 (L) Albany, KY Emmanuel Catholic.
Gelvez, Raul O. '98 (BRK) Corona, NY Our Lady of Sorrows.
Gelvez Tarazona, Jairo '93 (SJN) Toa Baja, PR San Pedro Apostol.
Gembala, Joseph J. '87 (DET) Sterling Heights, MI St. Malachy.
Gemme, Stephen M. '02 (WOR) Northboro, MA St. Bernadette.
Gemperline, Joachim *c.p.* '53 (L)[K] Louisville, KY Sacred Heart Retreat.
Gemskie, Charles A. '77 (JOL) Carol Stream, IL Corpus Christi.
Gemza, Richard J. '95 (BGP) Greenwich, CT St. Mary.
Genabia, Joel '03 (SAC) Vallejo, CA St. Basil.
Gendernalik, Leonard J. *sch.p.* '71 (MA)[M] Washington, DC Piarist Fathers.
Gendernalik, Leonard *sch.p.* '71 (WDC)[B] Washington, DC Queen of Pious Schools House of Studies–Piarist Fathers.
Gendreau, Claude R. '93 (PRT) Fort Kent, ME St. Louis; St. Francis, ME St. Charles; Clergy Benefit Plan–Clergy Pension Plan.
Gendreau, Claude (PRT) Pastoral Assocs..
Gendreau, Michael P. '90 (PRT) Augusta, ME St. Mary's; Augusta, ME St. Andrew's.
Gendreau, Richard R. '69 (FR) Swansea, MA St. Louis de France.
Gendron, Charles A. *m.s.* '44 (HRT)[M] Hartford, CT Missionaries of LaSalette.
Gendron, Michael E. '95 (MAN) Charlestown, NH St. Catherine; North Walpole, NH St. Peter; Advocates.
Genello, Patrick J. '83 (SCR) Hazleton, PA Holy Rosary.
Genereux, Wayn *o.de.m.* '97 (BUF)[O] LeRoy, NY Order of the BVM of Mercy/Mercedarian Friars.
Generose, Anthony J. '99 (SCR) Mocanaqua, PA St. Mary, Our Lady of Perpetual Help.
Genest, Gilles *m.s.* '62 (MAN) Lebanon, NH Sacred Heart; Council of Priests.
Genevive, Frank *o.f.m.* '83 (NY)[GG] Wappingers Falls, NY Mt. Alvernia Retreat House.
Geng, Dennis *o.c.d.* '89 (MIL)[O] Milwaukee Provincial Offices – Discalced Carmelites.
Gengaro, Nicholas S. '81 (NEW)[B] School of Diplomacy and Intl. Rels.; Members.
Gengras, Joseph C. '49 (HRT)[A] Bloomfield, CT St. Thomas Seminary Retired.
Geniesse, Joseph F. *c.s.c.* '57 (AUS) Austin, TX St. John Neumann.
Genilo, Eric *s.j.* '97 (BO)[V] Cambridge, MA; Filipino.
Genito, Joseph A. *o.s.a.* '75 (WDC)[B] Washington, DC Augustinian College, Order of St. Augustine.
Gennardo, Vincent *c.s.* '64 (CHI) Chicago, IL Santa Maria Addolorata.
Genovard, Juan J. *m.ss.cc.* (SJN) Movimiento "Por Un Mundo Mejor".
Genovese, Anthony M. *o.s.a.* '73 (PH) Rosemont, PA St. Thomas of Villanova Parish.
Genovese, Seamus D. '75 (OAK) Oakland, CA Our Lady of Lourdes.
Genovese, Seamus (OAK) Deans.
Genovesi, Vincent J. *s.j.* '69 (PH)[C] Jesuit Fathers; [AA] Loyola Center and Manresa Hall.
Genska, Depaul A. *o.f.m.* '58 (NY)[EE] Chicago, IL Catholic Theological Union.
Gensler, Harry J. *s.j.* '74 (CLV)[B] Cleveland, OH John Carroll University.
Gentile, Carl J. '60 (PIT) Pittsburgh, PA St. John Fisher.
Gentile, Domenic *f.s.s.p.* '02 (SCR)[M] Elmhurst Priestly Fraternity of St. Peter (F.S.S.P.), North American District Headquarters.
Gentile, Emile A. *t.o.r.* '64 (ORL) Mount Dora, FL St. Patrick's; Special Assignment.
Gentile, Emile *t.o.r.* (ORL) Executive Committee; Bishop's Executive Staff; Vicar for Clergy; Permanent Diaconate; Priests' Personnel.
Gentile, Robert A. '03 (SPR) West Springfield, MA St. Thomas the Apostle.
Gentile, Thomas E. '73 (L) Louisville, KY St. Helen.
Gentili, Joseph P. '87 (PH)[A] Wynnewood PA Theological Seminary of St. Charles Borromeo, Overbrook; Department of Continuing Formation for Diocesan Priests; Moderator of Priests Conferences.
Gentleman, Gerard (RVC) Levittown, NY St Bernard; [C] Hicksville, NY Holy Trinity; Associate Vocation Directors.
Gentleman, John W. '87 (BO) Amesbury, MA Holy Family.
Genua, Ronald L. '65 (HRT) Ansonia, CT Holy Rosary.
Genuardi, Gasper A. '68 (PH) Conshohocken, PA SS. Cosmas and Damian; Council of Priests; Pastors Review Board.
Genuario, William A. '56 (BGP) Riverside, CT St. Catherine of Siena; Judges.
Genzlinger, Walter L. '49 (NEW) Jersey City, NJ Our Lady of Mt. Carmel Retired.
Geo, Patrick '93 (RVC) Roslyn, NY St. Francis Hospital.
Geogan, Philip J. '79 (NOR) Stonington, CT St. Mary.
Geoghegan, Arthur T. '41 (MIA) Pompano Beach, FL St. Henry Retired.
Geoghegan, James *o.c.d.* '60 (P)[Q] Mt. Angel, OR Carmelite House of Studies.
Geoghegan, John F. '45 (STL) Retired.
Geong, Hee-Wan (OAK)[N] Oakland, CA Murray Residence Community.
George, Alexander C. '65 (LA) Retired.
George, Dale J. '58 (SC) Retired.
George, David M. '76 (SAM) Waterbury, CT Our Lady of Lebanon; Elected Members.
George, Francis M. '87 (LAN) Howell, MI St. John The Baptist.
George, Gary *c.ss.r.* '92 (OLL) Youngstown, OH St. Maron; Office of Youth Ministries.
George, George C. (AUS) Air Force Chaplains.
George, J. Clark '56 (ALT) Retired.
George, Jilson '00 (RVC) Smithtown, NY St. Patrick.
George, Jose '77 (TYL) Crockett, TX St. Francis of the Tejas; Lovelady, TX Eastham Unit, Texas Department of Corrections.
George, Joseph '62 (LA) Retired.
George, Lloyd *s.j.* '73 (BAL)[D] Baltimore, MD Loyola Blakefield.
George, Mark *s.j.* '98 (CLV) University Heights, OH Gesu.
George, Patrick *t.o.r.* '55 (SP) St. Petersburg, FL St. Mary Our Lady of Grace.
George, Patrick '98 (PIT) Pittsburgh, PA Epiphany.
George, Richard '95 (PMB)[B] West Palm Beach, FL Cardinal Newman High School.
George, Rick (PMB) Charismatic Renewal for Hispanics.
George, Robert J. '76 (PIT)[O] Pittsburgh, PA Convent of Mercy.
George, Robert J. '95 (ALN) Bethlehem, PA Sacred Heart of Jesus; [C] Easton, PA Notre Dame High School.
George, Saji M. '92 (RVC) Hempstead, NY St. John Chrysostom Malankara Mission.
George, Saji '92 (RVC) Valley Stream, NY Holy Name of Mary.
George, Sojan '00 (FWT) Fort Worth, TX St. John the Apostle.
George, Thomas '96 (SCR) Conyngham, PA St. John Bosco.
George, Wallis W. *c.ss.r.* '50 (STL)[O] Liguori, MO St. Clement Health Care Center.
George, William F. *o.s.b.* '75 (CHL)[J] Belmont, NC Belmont Abbey.
George, William L. '73 (WDC)[E] North Bethesda, MD Georgetown Preparatory School.
Georgia, John J. '75 (HRT) Bristol, CT St. Gregory's; Deans.
Gephart, John B. '46 (L)[K] Louisville, KY Bishop David Apartments Retired.
Geracci, John R. *c.s.c.* '92 (SCR)[C] Holy Cross Community.
Geraci, Anthony J. '74 (CIN) Dayton, OH Our Lady of the Immaculate Conception.
Geraghty, Martin T. '64 (BRK) Belle Harbor, NY St. Francis de Sales.
Gerardi, Joseph A. (DET) St. Clair Shores, MI St. Joan of Arc.
Gerathy, Kenneth A. '54 (NY) Staten Island, NY St. Christopher.
Gerber, Francis J. '84 (DEN) Granby, CO St. Anne.
Gerber, Martin '76 (WDC) Chireno, TX Our Lady of Lourdes; Moral, TX Immaculate Conception.
Gerbus, Bernard *o.f.m.* '38 (CIN).
Gerdelmann, Clemens J. '85 (PH) Southampton, PA Our Lady of Good Counsel.
Gerdes, Harry J. '62 (CIN) Retired.
Gerend, Lawrence '76 (GB) Retired.
Gerg, Joseph U. *o.s.b.* '65 (GBG)[H] Latrobe, PA Saint Vincent Archabbey.
Gergel, Stephen J. '62 (ALT) Navy Chaplains; Military Chaplains.
Gergen, Michael *s.d.b.* '79 (LA)[C] Rosemead, CA Don Bosco Technical Institute; [D] Rosemead, CA Don Bosco Technical Institute.
Gerhard, J. Peter *o.p.* '53 (L) Louisville KY St. Louis Bertrand.
Gerhard, John J. *s.j.* '49 (NY)[EE] Staten Island, NY.
Gerhardt, Bernard C. '53 (WDC) Washington, DC St. Matthew Cathedral; Pastoral Center Special Ministries; Delegate to Ordinary; Judges; Archdiocesan College of Consultors.
Gericke, Timothy '65 (MAD)[F] Janesville, WI St. Elizabeth Home.
Gering, Ken *o.f.m.conv.* '58 (L) Louisville, KY St. Anthony.
Gerken, Theodore '57 (ALB) Germantown, NY Resurrection; Columbia County Jail.
Gerl, Robert '79 (LAN) On Duty Outside the Diocese.
Gerlach, Dominic B. *c.pp.s.* '50 (LFT)[A] Rensselaer, IN Saint Joseph's College.
Gerlach, John *o.p.* '63 (MAD)[H] Sinsinawa, WI Dominican Motherhouse.
Gerlach, Matthew J. '96 (TLS) Tulsa, OK St. Catherine; Office of Divine Worship; Propagation of Faith.
Gerlach, Michael J. '82 (PH) Linwood, PA Holy Saviour.
Gerlich, Robert S. *s.j.* '73 (NO)[C] New Orleans, LA Loyola University New Orleans.
Gerlock, Stanley J. '60 (SY) Chenango Forks, NY St. Rita; Broome County Jail.
Gerloff, Charles W. '45 (ARL) Retired.
Germain, Jean M. '47 (SHP) Retired.
Germain, Levelt '02 (NY) Bronx, NY Holy Rosary.
Germaine, Kenneth *s.d.b.* (BIR) Birmingham, AL Holy Rosary (Gate City).
German, Ambrose *o.f.m.* '53 (STL)[O] Hermann, MO Frene Valley Geriatric Center Retired.
German, Michael J. '68 (NEW) River Edge, NJ St. Peter the Apostle.
Germann, Daniel V. *s.j.* '63 (SJ)[M] Los Gatos, CA Sacred Heart Jesuit Center.
Germann, Lauren '78 (SCL) Sartell, MN St. Francis Xavier.
Germovnik, Francis *c.m.* '41 (STL)[O] Perryville, MO Congregation of the Mission.
Geroge, Benny '88 (LA) Burbank, CA St. Francis Xavier.
Gerosa, Julian *c.r.s.* '78 (GAL) Houston, TX Christ the King.
Gerres, Daniel W. '66 (WIL) Wilmington, DE St. Thomas; Gander Hill Correctional Center; Deans.
Gerrety, James P. '57 (COV) Retired.
Gerritts, John R. '91 (SUP) Rhinelander, WI St. John; Rhinelander, WI Immaculate Conception; Rhinelander, WI St. Joseph's; Presbyteral Council & Diocesan Consultors.
Gerrity, Raymond J. '45 (CHI) Retired.
Gersbach, Karl A. *o.s.a.* '61 (PH)[AA] Villanova, PA St. Thomas Monastery.
Gerth, John '93 (SP) Largo, FL St. Matthew; Incardination Commission.
Gerth, Kenneth *m.c.c.j.* '64 (SP)[K] Tampa, FL St. Joseph's Hospital, Inc..
Gerth, Kenneth *m.c.c.j.* '65 (CIN)[M] Cincinnati, OH Comboni Missionaries (Verona Fathers)–Comboni Mission Center.
Gerum, Jerome G. '50 (LC) Retired.
Gerut, William F. *s.j.* '67 (OM)[K] Omaha, NE Jesuit Community at Creighton University.
Gerut, William F. *s.j.* '67 (LC) Prairie du Chien, WI St. John Nepomucene.
Gervacio, Adrian R. '67 (LA) On Duty Outside the Diocese; Naval Air Station; Naval Construction Battalion Center.
Gervacio, Adrian R. (HON) Navy Chaplains.
Gervais, Bernard P. *o.s.b.* '44 (PBL)[F] Canon City, CO Holy Cross Abbey.
Gervasio, Thomas N. '82 (TR) Trenton, NJ St. Anthony.
Ges, Glenn (FgM).
Gese, David '78 (SEA) Elma, WA St. Joseph.
Gessler, James *s.m.a.* '63 (NEW)[N] Tenafly, NJ Society of African Missions, Provincialate, S.M.A. Fathers.
Gesy, Lawrence J. '75 (BAL) Retired.
Gesy, Lawrence '75 (BAL) Brunswick, MD St. Francis of Assisi.
Getchel, Richard '76 (GB) Green Bay, WI St. Agnes.
Getchel, Richard (GB) Adjutant Judicial Vicars; Judges in Second Instance.
Getigan, Bernardito '85 (SAN) Garden City, TX St. Lawrence.
Getsinger, Ronald A. '68 (WH) New Cumberland, WV Immaculate Conception.
Getsy, John *o.f.m.cap.* '66 (PIT) Cabot, PA St. Joseph.
Gettig, Diego *c.pp.s.* '71 (CIN)[M] Dayton, OH.
Gettinger, Robert J. '64 (STL) St. Louis, MO St. Augustine.
Getty, Roy G. '39 (PIT) Retired.
Getz, Joseph *o.s.a.* '51 (ALB) Mechanicville, NY Assumption–St. Paul.
Getz, Robert L. (LSC) Episcopal Vicar for Clergy and Personnel; Diocesan Consultors; Clergy Personnel Board; Priestly Life and Ministry Committee; Priests Retirement Fund Committee.
Getz, Robert '61 (LSC) Roswell, NM Assumption of the Blessed Virgin Mary; Vicars; Presbyteral Council.
Geurtz, Gary '81 (FWT) Keller, TX St. Elizabeth Ann Seton.
Geyer, Kenneth A. *o.s.b.* '53 (CHL)[J] Belmont, NC Belmont Abbey.
Geyer, Raymond J. *o.s.b.* '49 (CHL)[J] Belmont, NC

Belmont Abbey.
Geyman, Donald R. '96 (GAY) East Tawas, MI Holy Family.
Geysen, Clement *ss.cc.* '49 (HON)[G] Honolulu, HI St. Patrick's Monastery.
Ghaby, Jean '92 (NTN) Brooklyn, NY Church of the Virgin Mary.
Ghanoum, Gabriel *b.s.o.* '93 (NTN) Miami, FL St. Jude; Miami, FL St. Nicholas; Continuing Education of Clergy Office; Order of St. Nicholas.
Ghansah, John *s.j.* '96 (NY)[V] Cambridge, MA Faber House.
Ghazal, Edmond J. *b.c.o.* '58 (NTN) Plymouth, MI St. Michael.
Ghazarian, David '87 (ARM) Tujunga, CA Mekhitarist School.
Ghezzi, Giancarlo *p.i.m.e.* '84 (PAT)[M] Wayne, NJ P.I.M.E. Missionaries Residence.
Ghezzi, Richard G. '86 (SCR) Friendsville, PA St. Joseph's.
Ghietti, Mario *s.d.b.* '62 (MGZ) San Antonio, PR San Jose Obrero.
Ghiloni, Mark V. '83 (COL) Columbus, OH Saint Anthony.
Ghio, John J. '80 (STL) St. Charles, MO St. Peter.
Ghiorso, David '81 (SFR) Redwood City, CA Our Lady of Mount Carmel.
Ghisalberti, Giacomo G. '51 (R) Retired.
Ghozairan, Poulos '75 (SPA) Scottsdale, AZ Mar Auraha Chaldean Catholic Parish.
Ghys, Philip *o.s.b.* '53 (RIC)[O] Williamsburg, VA Little Sisters of St. Francis, United States and Canada Regional Center.
Ghyselinck, Mark R. *c.s.c.* '88 (FTW)[I] Notre Dame, IN Holy Cross College.
Ghyselinck, Mark *c.s.c.* '88 (FTW)[A] Notre Dame, IN Moreau Seminary.
Giachino, Valeriano *s.s.p.* '57 (LA)[Q] Los Angeles, CA Society of St. Paul.
Giacomini, Antonio *o.f.m.cap.* '39 (R) Retired.
Giacomini, Salvatore *s.d.b.* '51 (SFR) San Francisco, CA SS. Peter and Paul.
Giacosa, Charley '62 (NSH) Nashville, TN St. Henry; Clergy Benefit Foundation.
Giammona, John J. '59 (GR) Retired.
Giampietro, Anthony E. *c.s.b.* '93 (GAL)[Q] Houston, TX Residence of the Basilian Fathers of the University of St. Thomas.
Giandurco, Joseph R. '87 (NY)[A] Yonkers, NY St. Joseph's Seminary.
Gianelli, Gene E. '70 (HRT) Woodbridge, CT Church of the Assumption; Auditors (Part–time Case Instructors).
Giangiacomo, Toselle *c.s.s.p.* '48 (ARE) Orocovis, PR Our Lady of Fatima.
Giannamore, Anthony J. '56 (CIN)[V] Centerville, OH St. Leonard Faith Community.
Giannamore, Anthony J. '56 (STU) Retired.
Giannamore, Anthony '56 (CIN)[L] Centerville, OH St. Leonard.
Giannamore, Peter A. '95 (WH).
Gianni, Vincent J. '70 (BO) Peabody, MA St. Adelaide.
Giannini, Stephen W. '93 (IND) Indianapolis, IN St. Luke.
Giannini, Stephen (IND) Priests' Personnel Board; Archdiocesan Judges.
Giannitelli, Michael C. '91 (NOR) Colchester, CT St. Andrew.
Giannone, Ronald *o.f.m.cap.* '90 (WIL) Wilmington, DE Sacred Heart; [G] Wilmington, DE Ministry of Caring, Inc.; [J] Wilmington, DE St. Felix Friary; [K] Wilmington, DE Monastery of St. Veronica Giuliani.
Gianola, William '62 (CHY) Retired.
Gianzmann, Edward J. *o.s.b.* '79 (CHI)[N] Chicago, IL Monastery of the Holy Cross.
Giaquinto, Albert C. '48 (NOR) Retired.
Giaquinto, Albert C. *s.s.* '48 (WDC)[C] Catholic University of America, The.
Giardina, Robert J. '76 (PRO) Providence, RI St. Charles Borromeo.
Giardino, Andrew *o.f.m.* '62 (HRT) Hartford, CT St. Patrick–St. Anthony.
Giardino, Louis '75 (BIR) Absent on Leave; Diocesan College of Consultors; Judges.
Gibas, Robert G. '62 (Y) Navarre, OH St. Clement; Judges.
Gibbeaut, Wayne *o.f.m.* '83 (SFE) Pena Blanca, NM Nuestra Senora De Guadalupe.
Gibbons, Christopher W. *m.m.* '45 (NY).
Gibbons, Donald Patrick '91 (SFD)[EE] Jerseyville, IL St. Francis Xavier.
Gibbons, Edward '97 (VEN) Graduate Studies.
Gibbons, James M. '52 (BO) Senior Priests Retired.
Gibbons, James *o.m.i.* '69 (FgM).
Gibbons, John J. '58 (NEW) Bayonne, NJ St. Michael's Retired.
Gibbons, John M. '89 (ALN) Reading, PA St. Margaret; College of Consultors.
Gibbons, John '56 (DEN).
Gibbons, John '60 (TR) Retired.
Gibbons, John *o.f.m.* '01 (FgM).
Gibbons, John *o.f.m.* (LSC) Mescalero, NM St. Joseph.
Gibbons, Peter D. '89 (NY) Bronx, NY St. Francis Xavier.
Gibbons, Robert C. '81 (SP) St. Petersburg, FL St. Paul; Chancellor; Judges; Ex Officio; Incardination Commission; Diocesan Finance Council; College of Consultors.
Gibbons, Robert (SP) Presbyteral Council.
Gibbons, Thomas F. *m.m.* '48 (NY).
Gibbs, Phillip G. '94 (DUB)[EE] On Special or Other Archdiocesan Assignment; [A] Dubuque, IA Seminary of St. Pius X; Vocation Awareness; Family Life Advisory Board.
Gibeault, Gerard *m.s.a.* '58 (NOR)[A] Cromwell, CT Holy Apostles College and Seminary.
Gibino, Joseph R. (BRK) Liturgical Commission.
Gibino, Joseph '81 (BRK) Brooklyn, NY Immaculate Heart of Mary.
Giblin, Lawrence E. '44 (SY)[Q] Binghamton, NY McDevitt Residence for Retired Priests Retired.
Giblin, Richard J. '66 (SY) Vestal, NY St. Vincent de Paul.
Giblin, William M. '59 (NEW) Edgewater, NJ Holy Rosary Retired.
Gibney, Laurence '54 (NY) Retired.
Gibney, Robert G. '54 (NEW) Ridgewood, NJ Our Lady of Mount Carmel; [N] Caldwell, NJ The Rev. Msgr. James F. Kelley Residence for Retired Priests.
Gibowski, Boguslaw T. '69 (PRO) Woonsocket, RI St. Stanislaus.
Gibson, Beryl '96 (SAL) St. Francis, KS St. Joseph's; St. Francis, KS St. Francis.
Gibson, Bruno *o.p.* '60 (OAK) Berkeley, CA St. Mary Magdalen.
Gibson, Christopher '75 (SAC)[I] Citrus Heights, CA Christ the King Retreat.
Gibson, Christopher *c.p.* '75 (FgM).
Gibson, Jack *s.d.b.* '70 (LA)[Q] Los Angeles, CA Dominic Savio Salesian Residence.
Gibson, James *c.r.* '79 (CHI)[N] Via San Sebastianello 11.
Gibson, John L. '88 (GRY)[I] Munster, IN Discalced Carmelite Fathers Monastery.
Gibson, John W. '45 (PIT) Retired.
Gibson, Lawrence J. '55 (LA) Retired.
Gibson, Robert J. '58 (SCR) Unassigned or Leave of Absence.
Gibson, Stephen C. *c.s.c.* '70 (FTW)[K] Notre Dame, IN Holy Cross Mission House; [L] Notre Dame, IN Our Lady of Fatima Retreat Center.
Gibson, Stephen G. '81 (GRY) East Chicago, IN St. Mary.
Gicewicz, Edward *c.m.* '38 (HRT)[M] Manchester DePaul Provincial Residence.
Gicherhein, Simon '86 (BGP)[J] Bridgeport, CT St. Vincent's Medical Center.
Gick, Francois *s.j.* '80 (BO)[V] Boston The Society of Jesus of New England–Provincial Offices.
Gidaro, Joseph C. *o.ss.t.* '87 (NY) New York, NY St. Brigid.
Gidaro, Joseph C. *o.ss.t.* '87 (BAL)[S] Jersey City, NJ.
Gideon, Peter M. '76 (COL) New Boston, OH St. Monica; Wheelersburg, OH St. Peter; Vicariate 14: Scioto County.
Gideon, Stephen '97 (NSH) Dickson, TN St. Christopher.
Giebel, Alfred W. '72 (ANC) Anchorage, AK St. Benedict; Diocesan Consultors.
Giedgaudas, Francis *o.f.m.* '47 (BRK)[V] Brooklyn, NY St. Casimir's Monastery, Printing Plant and Cultural Center.
Giel, John C. '78 (ORL) Leesburg, FL St. Paul's.
Giel, John (ORL) Judges.
Gielow, Richard *c.m.* '70 (KC)[J] Kansas City, MO Vincentian Parish Mission Center.
Gier, Gregory A. '67 (TLS) Tulsa, OK Holy Family Cathedral; Diocesan Senators.
Gier, Thomas '62 (CC)[G] Robstown, TX Society of Our Lady of the Most Holy Trinity.
Gierut, Casimir '49 (SFD) Retired.
Gies, Norman J. '49 (BAL) Retired.
Gies, William '53 (ALN)[A] Center Valley, PA Sacred Heart Villa, Missionaries of the Sacred Heart.
Giese, Samuel C. '85 (WDC) On Duty Outside the Archdiocese; Army National Guard Chaplains.
Giesen, Cal '47 (FWT)[I] Crowley, TX St. Maximilian Kolbe Friary.
Giesige, Randy P. '98 (TOL) Delphos, OH St. John the Evangelist.
Giesing, Anthony '55 (SD) Retired.
Giesler, Michael '79 (STL)[P] Kirkwood, MO Prelature of the Holy Cross and Opus Dei.
Gietl, Joseph A. '73 (GAL) Spring, TX St. Edward.
Gietzen, Albin J. '56 (GAY) Retired.
Gigantiello, Jamie J. '95 (BRK) Brooklyn, NY Mary Queen of Heaven.
Giganto, Jose A. *o.s.a.* '65 (SAT) San Antonio, TX St. Jude.
Giggi, J. Robert '53 (BO) Natick, MA St. Linus.
Giglio, Michael E. '94 (ORL) Lakeland, FL St. Anthony's.
Gigliotti, James *t.o.r.* '80 (FWT) Arlington, TX St. Maria Goretti.
Gigliotti, Vincent J. '76 (GBG) Brownsville, PA St. Peter; Brownsville, PA St. Mary.
Gignac, Francis T. *s.j.* '67 (WDC)[C] Catholic University of America, The.
Gignac, Francis T. *s.j.* '67 (DET)[M] Washington, DC The Jesuit Community at Georgetown University; [K] Temperance, MI.
Gikonyo, David Kamau *i.m.c.* '97 (WDC)[H] Somerset, NJ Consolata Society for Foreign Missions; [V] Washington, DC Consolata Missionaries House of Studies.
Gil, Fernando '89 (ORL) Defenders of the Bond; Orlando, FL St. Isaac Jogues.
Gilb, Eugene A. '57 (LA) Rancho Palos Verdes, CA St. John Fisher Retired.
Gilbert, Dennis '71 (MRY) Cambria, CA Santa Rosa.
Gilbert, Donald J. '68 (MAN) Windham, NH St. Matthew; Defenders of the Bond; Diocesan Review Board.
Gilbert, John Mary '03 (LC)[M] Chippewa Falls, WI Institute of St. Joseph.
Gilbert, Joseph T. '79 (SCR) Wilkes–Barre, PA Sacred Heart–St. John.
Gilbert, Maurice L. '66 (WOR) Southbridge, MA Notre Dame.
Gilbert, Patrick N. '01 (MAN) Berlin, NH Good Shepherd; Council of Priests.
Gilbert, Paul T. '01 (MAN) Merrimack, NH Our Lady of Mercy.
Gilbert, Paul '01 (MAN) Elliott Hospital.
Gilbert, Philip F. *c.pp.s.* '60 (LFT)[A] Rensselaer, IN Saint Joseph's College.
Gilbert, Robert J. '98 (CHI) Harvey, IL Ascension–St. Susanna.
Gilbert, Valmont R. '57 (PRT) Retired.
Gilbertson, C. Lee '86 (SPR) Springfield, MA St. Paul.
Gilbo, Roberto M. *c.s.c.* '67 (FTW)[I] Congregacion de Santa Cruz.
Gilborges, Anthony *o.s.f.s.* '89 (CHL) High Point, NC Immaculate Heart of Mary.
Gilchrist, Francis J. '45 (ALB) Ministry to Priests Retired.
Gilchrist, Frank '45 (ALB) Fort Edward, NY St. Joseph; Advocates.
Gilchrist, John J. '57 (NEW) Harrison, NJ Holy Cross; College of Consultors.
Gilchrist, John (NEW) Archdiocesan Commission for Interreligious Affairs.
Gilday, Robert J. '75 (IND) Adjunct Vice Vicars Judicial; Indianapolis, IN St. Therese of the Infant Jesus (Little Flower).
Gilday, Robert (IND) Council of Priests.
Gildea, Arthur P. *c.ss.r.* '67 (ALB)[L] Saratoga Springs, NY St. John Neumann Residence.
Gildea, Charles *c.ss.r.* '53 (ALB)[L] Saratoga Springs, NY St. John Neumann Residence.
Gildea, John J. '66 (BRK) Brooklyn, NY Sacred Heart.
Gildner, Leo H. '53 (PEO) Retired.
Gile, Honesto DeGuzman '87 (SFR) San Rafael, CA St. Raphael.
Gile, Joseph M. (WCH) On Duty Outside the Diocese.
Giles, Charles *o.m.i.* '38 (BEL)[F] Belleville, IL Missionary Oblates of Mary Immaculate – St. Henry's Oblate Residence.
Giles, Gabriel *o.f.m.cap* '35 (PIT)[N] Allison Park, PA St. Conrad Friary.
Giles, John H. '87 (LKC) Lake Charles, LA Our Lady Queen of Heaven.
Giles, John (LKC) Diocesan Consultors.
Gilfether, Francis *s.m.a.* '60 (NEW)[N] Tenafly, NJ Society of African Missions, Provincialate, S.M.A. Fathers.
Gilfillan, James M. '47 (SD) La Jolla, CA Mary, Star of the Sea Retired.
Gilg, James E. '66 (OM) Omaha, NE St. Mary Magdalene; [B] Omaha, NE V.J. & Angela Skutt Catholic High School of Omaha; Deans; Officers; Deans.
Gilgun, Bernard E. '54 (WOR) Retired.
Gilhooley, James '55 (NY) Retired.
Gilhooley, John P. '57 (BRK) Military Chaplains Retired.
Giliberti, Francis A. '70 (PH) Media, PA Nativity of the Blessed Virgin Mary.
Giljum, Stephen P. '03 (STL) St. Louis, MO St. Clement.
Gill, David H. *s.j.* '67 (BO) Roxbury, MA St. Mary of the Angels; [V] Newton, MA The Jesuit Community at Boston College; [V] Boston The Society of Jesus of New England–Provincial Offices.
Gill, Dennis G. '83 (PH) On Duty Outside the Archdiocese.
Gill, Desmond '46 (SP) Inverness, FL Our Lady of Fatima; Sun City Center, FL Prince of Peace.
Gill, Edward B. '41 (OM) Retired.
Gill, James J. *s.j.* '57 (CHI).
Gill, Joseph C. *s.j.* '59 (MIL)[O] Wauwatosa, WI Jesuit Community at St. Camillus.

Gill, Michael J. '66 (NOR) Plainfield, CT St. John the Apostle.
Gill, Nicholas *c.p.* '40 (HRT)[M] West Hartford Holy Family Monastery/Retreat.
Gill, Paul '66 (SB) Retired.
Gill, Richard '56 (BUF) Retired.
Gill, Richard *l.c.* '91 (WDC)[M] Potomac, MD Legionaries of Christ; [V] Bethesda, MD Alpha Omega, Inc. The Legion of Christ Inc..
Gill, William J. '55 (RVC) Hampton Bays, NY St. Rosalie's.
Gillece, Eugene J. '51 (GAL) Retired.
Gilleece, Thomas E. '67 (NY) New York, NY; Chancellor.
Gilleece, Thomas (NY) Archdiocesan Consultors.
Gillelan, Robert M. '89 (HBG) York, PA Immaculate Conception of the Blessed Virgin Mary; Deans; Presbyteral Council.
Gillelan, Robert (HBG) Consultors, College.
Gillen, C. H. '85 (BAK) Retired.
Gillen, George D. '71 (NEW) Roselle, NJ Church of St. Joseph the Carpenter.
Gillen, James G. '52 (WDC) Retired.
Gillen, John J. '45 (NY) Bronx, NY St. Benedict Retired.
Gillen, Kevin *s.o.l.t.* (CC)[G] Robstown, TX Society of Our Lady of the Most Holy Trinity.
Gillen, Peter D. '78 (BRK) Rockaway Beach, NY St. Rose of Lima.
Gillen, Peter (BRK) Presbyteral Council; Diocesan Consultors.
Giller, Roderic *o.s.b.* '62 (KCK) Seneca, KS SS. Peter and Paul's; [H] Atchison, KS St. Benedict's Abbey.
Gilles, Brian *c.s.s.r.* '03 (DOD) Liberal, KS St. Anthony; [F] Liberal, KS Liberal Redemptorist Hispanic House Ministry, Inc...
Gilles, Richard W. (LC) Special Assignment; [A] La Crosse, WI Holy Cross Seminary House of Formation; [J] La Crosse, WI Catholic Charities of the Diocese of La Crosse, Inc.; Vicar General; Moderator of the Curia; Ecclesiastical Notaries; Promoter of Justice; Diocesan Judges; Building Commission; Pastoral Council; Ex Officio Members; Consultors; Ex Officio.
Gilles, Thomas C. '67 (CLV) Chardon, OH St. Mary.
Gillespie, Barnabas *o.s.b.* '80 (IND) Tell City, IN St. Michael; Tell City, IN St. Pius; [K] Tell City, IN; Tell City, IN St. Paul.
Gillespie, C. Kevin *s.j.* '86 (BAL)[B] Timonium, MD Loyola Graduate Center –Timonium Campus.
Gillespie, Edward F. '57 (RCK) Retired.
Gillespie, Francis P. *s.j.* '64 (R) Raleigh, NC St. Raphael.
Gillespie, Francis P. *s.j.* '72 (R)[E] Raleigh Jesuit Community.
Gillespie, Francis T. '59 (ALN)[J] Bethlehem, PA Holy Family Villa Retired.
Gillespie, Jerome F. '82 (BO) Methuen, MA St. Monica.
Gillespie, John D. '72 (STA) Gainesville, FL St. Augustine.
Gillespie, John E. '53 (PH) Absent on Leave.
Gillespie, John L. '95 (R) Wilmington, NC St. Mary.
Gillespie, John (STA) Directors.
Gillespie, Joseph P. *o.p.* '70 (STP) Minneapolis, MN The Basilica of St. Mary Co–Cathedral; Minneapolis, MN St. Albert the Great.
Gillespie, Joseph '50 (PHX) Retired.
Gillespie, Kevin *s.j.* (BAL)[S] Baltimore, MD Ferdinand Wheeler Jesuit Community.
Gillespie, Paul G. *o.s.f.s.* '56 (TOL)[C] Toledo, OH St. Francis de Sales High School; [J] Toledo, OH Retired.
Gillespie, Robert B. '43 (GR) Retired.
Gillespie, Thomas E. '72 (MAD) Marshall, WI St. Mary's of the Nativity; Waterloo, WI St. Joseph.
Gillespie, Thomas M. '68 (BO) North Reading, MA St. Theresa.
Gillespie, Thomas '61 (SB) Retired.
Gillespie, Thomas *o.s.b.* '64 (SCL)[I] Collegeville, MN St. John's Abbey, of the Order of St. Benedict.
Gillespie, Victor *o.s.b.* '56 (LR) Subiaco, AR St. Benedict.
Gillette, James R. *c.p.* '71 (NY)[EE] Pelham Manor, NY St. Vincent's Residence; [II] Pelham, NY Passionist Communications, Inc..
Gillette, Peter '91 (SEA) Vancouver, WA St. Joseph.
Gillgannon, Francis G. '54 (JC) Judges Retired.
Gillgannon, Michael '58 (KC) Mission Duty.
Gillick, Lawrence D. *s.j.* '72 (OM)[K] Omaha, NE Jesuit Community at Creighton University.
Gilligan, Adrian *o.s.a.* '68 (PH) Bryn Mawr, PA Our Mother of Good Counsel.
Gilligan, James M. *m.m.* '55 (FgM).
Gilligan, Michael J. '69 (CHI) Other Assignments.
Gillin, Thomas P. '74 (PH)[G] Bryn Mawr, PA Country Day School of the Sacred Heart.
Gillis, David C. '79 (ALN) Shillington, PA St. John Baptist de la Salle.
Gillis, Edward F. '46 (BO) Senior Priests Retired.
Gillis, James B. *c.s.c.* '56 (FTW)[I] Notre Dame, IN Holy Cross House.
Gillis, Ralph J. '59 (GB) Crandon, WI St. Joseph; Wabeno, WI St. Ambrose.
Gillis, Roger E. *s.j.* '78 (SEA)[A] Seattle, WA Seattle University.
Gillis, Ronald S. '67 (WDC)[T] Washington, DC.
Gillium, William *o.f.m.cap.* (PIT) Beaver County, PA McGuire Memorial Home.
Gillon, James A. *s.j.* '74 (FgM).
Gillooly, Patrick J. '53 (WH) Retired.
Gills, Thomas '86 (BAL) Military Chaplains; Air Force Chaplains.
Gillum, William *o.f.m.cap.* '76 (PIT) Rochester, PA St. Cecilia; [N] Rochester, PA St. Cecilia Friary.
Gilman, Leonard *o.carm.* '98 (NEW)[P] Mahwah, NJ Carmel Retreat.
Gilmartin, Daniel J. '46 (BO) Senior Priests Retired.
Gilmartin, Daniel J. '47 (BO) Bellingham, MA St. Blaise.
Gilmartin, John D. '72 (RVC) Garden City, NY St. Anne; Belmont Deanery.
Gilmartin, John E. '56 (BGP) Stratford, CT Our Lady of Peace; Parochial Examiners.
Gilmartin, Paul P. *s.j.* '62 (BO)[V] Weston, MA Campion Health Center, Inc..
Gilmore, Alan *o.c.s.o.* '70 (L)[K] Trappist, KY Abbey of Our Lady of Gethsemani, of the Order of Cistercians of the Strict Observance.
Gilmore, Lawrence *s.d.b.* '84 (FgM).
Gilmore, Raymond V. '62 (HEL) Bonner, MT St. Ann; Associate Judges.
Gilmore, Vincent M. *o.praem.* '90 (ORG)[I] Silverado, CA Norbertine Fathers of Orange Inc..
Gilmore, Vincent *o.praem* '90 (ORG) Costa Mesa, CA St. John the Baptist.
Gilmour, James W. *c.ss.r.* '72 (BAL) Baltimore, MD St. Patrick.
Gilmour, James–Santiago W. *c.ss.r.* '72 (BAL) Baltimore, MD St. Michael.
Gilmour, Robert G. *c.s.c.* '68 (AUS)[G] Austin, TX Congregation of Holy Cross – Southern Province.
Gilroy, Gregory *o.f.m.conv.* '88 (RNO) Reno, NV St. Thomas Aquinas Cathedral.
Gilroy, Robert G. *s.j.* '97 (BO)[X] Gloucester, MA Eastern Point Retreat House.
Gilsdorf, Daniel '60 (GB) Absent on Leave.
Gilsdorf, Gordon J. '49 (GB) Special Assignment.
Gilsdorf, Richard '56 (GB) Retired.
Gilsenan, John P. '56 (WCH) Wichita, KS Blessed Sacrament; Vicar for Priests; Presbyteral Council/ Diocesan Consultors; Parish Priest Consultors; Promoter of Justice; Defenders of the Bond; Deans; Presbyteral Council.
Gilson, Michael *s.j.* '02 (PHX)[B] Phoenix AZ Brophy College Preparatory.
Gilvey, John A. *o.s.f.s.* '79 (WIL)[J] Wilmington Oblates of St. Francis De Sales.
Gilvey, John *o.s.f.s.* '79 (NY) Bronx, NY St. Augustine.
Gimeno, Fabian G. '60 (ORL) St. Cloud, FL St. Thomas Aquinas.
Gimpl, Carl '55 (P)[P] Western Oregon State College (Monmouth).
Gimpl, Carl (P) Judges.
Gin, Regis B. (FgM).
Ginart, Arthur J. '66 (NO) New Orleans, LA St. Nicholas of Myra.
Ginel, Robert J. '78 (NY) Monticello, NY St. Peter; Carmel, NY Putnam Hospital Center.
Gingras, Dennis C. '90 (HRT) Waterbury, CT St. Anne; Waterbury, CT SS. Peter and Paul.
Gingras, Jerome R. '78 (ALB) East Greenbush, NY St. Mary.
Gini, John E. *o.f.m.* '63 (MRY) Jolon, CA San Antonio Mission.
Ginn, Roman *o.c.s.o.* '53 (L)[K] Trappist, KY Abbey of Our Lady of Gethsemani, of the Order of Cistercians of the Strict Observance.
Ginpl, Carl '55 (P) Independence, OR St. Patrick.
Gins, Paul M. *o.s.m.* '75 (CHI)[N] Chicago, IL Order of Friar Servants of Mary (Servites) United States of America Province, Inc.; [N] Chicago Order of Friar Servants of Mary (Servites) United States of America Province, Inc..
Gins, Paul M. *o.s.m.* '75 (ORG)[I] Anaheim, CA Servite Fathers and Brothers; [I] Anaheim, CA Seven Holy Founders Priory.
Ginsterblum, John M. *s.j.* '53 (OM)[K] Omaha, NE Jesuit Community at Creighton University.
Ginter, Michael W. (JOL) Judges.
Ginter, Michael '79 (JOL) Peotone, IL St. Paul the Apostle.
Ginter, Michael (JOL) Adjutant Judicial Vicar.
Ginther, Lawrence P. '46 (WIN) Retired
Ginther, Richard M. '83 (IND) Indianapolis, IN SS. Peter and Paul Cathedral.
Ginther, Richard (IND) Council of Priests; Archdiocesan Cathedral.
Gintoli, Blase M. '69 (BGP) Fairfield, CT Assumption.
Ginty, Thomas M. '85 (HRT) Special and other Archdiocesan Assignment; Chancellor; Secretary to the Archbishop; College of Consultors; Office for Divine Worship.
Gion, Chad O. '02 (BIS) Center, ND St. Martin; New Salem ND St. Pius V.
Gion, Chad (BIS) Presbyteral Council.
Gionet, Urbain J. '51 (WOR) Retired.
Gioppato, Alfonso *o.m.i.* '64 (LAR) Eagle Pass, TX St. Joseph.
Giorda, Adolph *o.f.m.* '46 (NY)[EE] New York, NY Padua Friary.
Giordani, Mark J. '69 (PAT) Paterson, NJ Cathedral of St. John the Baptist; Paterson, NJ St. Agnes; Passaic County Jail; [P] Paterson, NJ The Association of the Marian Apostolate of Mercy, Inc.; Army Reserve Chaplains.
Giordano, John C. '67 (MET) North Plainfield, NJ St. Luke; [H] Somerset, NJ Maria Regina Residence.
Giordano, Joseph *c.i.c.m.* '72 (ARL)[J] Arlington, VA Missionhurst, C.I.C.M.–Central House and Provincialate.
Giorgi, Daniel (BAL)[S] Baltimore, MD The Trinitarians at Holy Rosary.
Giorno, Stephen *s.t.* '86 (CHI).
Giovanoni, Peter M. '01 (WDC)[A] Olney, MD St. Peter.
Giovenco, Robert (RIC) Richmond, VA St. Bridget.
Gipson, Robert W. '62 (LA) La Crescenta, CA St. James the Less.
Gira, Steve *c.r.* (BEL) Columbia, IL Immaculate Conception of the B.V.M..
Giraldo, Jesus Antonio '97 (KNX) Cleveland, TN St. Therese of Lisieux.
Girard, Armand '45 (SAL) Retired.
Girard, Charles A. *s.m.* '66 (ATL)[C] Atlanta, GA Marist School.
Girard, Stephen P. '74 (BAL) Retired.
Girardeau, Robert A. '93 (SAV) Columbus, GA Our Lady of Lourdes.
Girardeau, Robert (SAV) Council of Priests.
Girardin, Peter T. '60 (BO) Senior Priests Retired.
Girnius, Charles F. *m.m.* '44 (NY)[EE] Maryknoll Maryknoll Fathers and Brothers.
Giroir, Frank J. '81 (NO) Harahan, LA St. Rita; Deans; Parish Sites & Boundaries Committee.
Girolami, Dante L. *o.s.a.* '41 (PH)[AA] Villanova, PA St. Thomas Monastery.
Girone, Joseph D. '83 (NEW) Belleville, NJ St. Peter's.
Girone, Joseph F. *o.s.a.* '81 (PH)[B] Villanova, PA St. Augustine Friary.
Girone, Joseph *o.s.a.* (WIL) Associate Directors.
Girotti, John W. (GB) Green Bay, WI Nativity of Our Lord.
Girotti, John (GB) Appointed Representatives.
Girouard, Robert J. '59 (PRT) Retired.
Giroux, Garry B. '76 (OG) Potsdam, NY St. Mary; Potsdam, NY St. Francis of Assisi Campus Parish (Newman Center); Advocates; Campus Ministry.
Giroux, Harry E. '76 (OG) West Chazy, NY St. Joseph; Young Adult Ministry.
Giroux, Joseph W. (OG) Lowville, NY St. Mary; Lowville, NY St. Hedwig; Lowville, NY St. Peter; Associate Vocations Directors.
Giroux, Peter *f.p.o.* '98 (FR)[H] New Bedford, MA Franciscans of Primitive Observance.
Giroux, Raymond A. '63 (BUR) Advocates Retired.
Giroux, Regis J. '70 (SPR) Sabbatical.
Giroux, Richard M. '69 (MAN) Tilton, NH St. Mary of the Assumption.
Giroux, William P. '80 (BUR) Essex Junction, VT St. Pius X.
Girres, Edward M. '79 (SC) Fort Dodge, IA Sacred Heart; Priests' Personnel Board; [G] Fort Dodge, IA Sacred Heart Parish Foundation of Fort Dodge; [G] Fort Dodge, IA Holy Rosary Parish Foundation of Fort Dodge.
Girzone, Joseph '55 (ALB) Retired.
Gismondi, Carl *f.s.s.p.* '03 (SCR) Scranton, PA St. Michael's; [M] Elmhurst, PA Priestly Fraternity of St. Peter (F.S.S.P.), North American District Headquarters.
Gits, Douglas J. '53 (WIN) Retired.
Gitter, Paul R. '93 (LC) Eau Claire, WI Sacred Heart of Jesus–St. Patrick; Fall Creek, WI St. Raymond of Penafort; Deans.
Gittins, Anthony *c.s.sp.* '67 (CHI).
Gittins, Gordon '68 (DM)[B] Absent on Sick Leave.
Gitzen, Patrick *o.m.i.* '75 (FgM).
Giudice, Anthony *o.f.m.cap.* '54 (NY)[B] Beacon, NY St. Lawrence of Brindisi Friary.
Giudice, Francis J. '56 (PRO) Providence, RI Cathedral of SS. Peter and Paul.
Giuffre, Frank A. '97 (PH) King of Prussia, PA Mother of Divine Providence; Graduate Studies.
Giuliani, John B. '60 (BGP)[O] West Redding, CT The Benedictine Grange.
Giuliani, John P. *c.o.* '80 (CHR) Fort Mill, SC St. Philip Neri; [E] Rock Hill, SC Oratory of St. Philip Neri, Congregation of the Oratory of Pontifical Rite.
Giuliano, Anthony J. '84 (NY) Hawthorne, NY Holy Rosary.
Giuliano, Steven B. '80 (WIL) Middletown, DE St. Joseph.
Giulietti, Julio *s.j.* '72 (BO)[V] Newton, MA The Jesuit Community at Boston College.
Giunta, Jose G. *i.v.e.* '91 (FR) New Bedford, MA St. Kilian.

Giunta, Jose *i.v.e.* '91 (FR)[N] New Bedford, MA The Institute of the Incarnate Word, Inc..
Giunta, S. C. '54 (JOL) Manhattan, IL St. Patrick.
Giuntini, Robert J. '76 (RVC)[J] Huntington, NY St. Joseph's Guest Home for the Aged, Inc..
Giusani, Augustine H. '47 (HRT) New Britain, CT St. Ann Retired.
Giusta, Frank J. '63 (ATL) Atlanta, GA Sacred Heart of Jesus.
Givey, David W. '71 (PH) Absent on Leave.
Gizler, John B. '02 (PIT) Canonsburg, PA St. Patrick; Graduate Studies Retired.
Gjergji, Nue '73 (DET) Beverly Hills, MI Our Lady of Albanians.
Glab, Joseph *c.r.* '75 (CHI)[D] Chicago, IL Gordon Tech High School.
Glab, Stephen *c.r.* '82 (CHI)[N] Woodstock, IL Resurrection Center Retreat House.
Glabinski, Janusz (LAR) Laredo, TX St. Joseph.
Glabinski, Jozef '89 (LAR) Laredo, TX St. Joseph.
Glackin, Thomas J. '68 (VEN) Naples, FL St. John the Evangelist.
Glade, Albert G. *o.p.* '72 (STL)[B] St. Louis, MO Aquinas Institute of Theology; [O] St. Louis, MO St. Dominic Priory.
Gladstone, James J. *s.j.* '66 (MIL)[O] Milwaukee, WI Jesuit Community at Marquette University.
Glahn, Carl '52 (OWN) Retired.
Glancy, Christopher *c.s.v.* '93 (CHI)[N] Colegio San Viator.
Glancy, Joseph '59 (SFS) Dimock, SD SS. Peter and Paul.
Glandorf, Ken (DUB)[H] Cedar Rapids, IA Mercy Medical Center–Cedar Rapids.
Glapiak, Edward '61 (WIL) Special or Other Diocesan Assignment.
Glaros, Matthew J. '99 (CLV) Keesler Airforce Base; Military Chaplains; Air Force Chaplains.
Glaser, Kenneth J. (DUB) Waterloo, IA Queen of Peace; Priest Representatives; Adult Members.
Glaser, Lawrence A. *o.c.s.o.* '58 (SAC)[A] Vina, CA Abbey of New Clairvaux, Trappist Seminary; [I] Vina, CA Abbey of New Clairvaux, Trappist.
Glasgow, Dennis T. *s.j.* '84 (DET)[K] Temperance, MI.
Glasgow, Dennis T. *s.j.* '84 (LAN) Ann Arbor, MI St. Mary Student Parish.
Glasgow, Mark W. '62 (PIT) Homestead, PA St. Maximilian Kolbe; Military Chaplains; Allegheny County, PA VA Pittsburgh Health Care System–H.J. Heinz and University Drive Divisions.
Glasgow, Robert K. '85 (MAN) Military Chaplains.
Glasgow, Robert K. (WIL) Army Chaplains.
Glasgow, T. Gaspard '69 (NO) New Orleans, LA St. Brigid.
Glass, Gerald J. '56 (PHX) Retired.
Glass, Robert H. *c.s.b.* '74 (OAK)[C] Oakland, CA Bishop O'Dowd High School.
Glass, Rolland T. '43 (MIL) Retired.
Glass, Senan *o.f.m.cap.* '57 (PH) Philadelphia, PA St. John the Evangelist.
Glassmire, David Richard (BUF) Navy Reserve Chaplains.
Glastetter, Donald A. '65 (STL) Wentzville, MO St. Patrick.
Glastetter, Michael *o.f.m.conv.* '99 (MIL) Milwaukee, WI Basilica of St. Josaphat.
Glatts, Joseph M. '66 (PH) Drexel Hill, PA St. Andrew.
Glaub, Eugene *o.m.i.* '55 (BEL)[F] Belleville, IL Shrine of Our Lady of the Snows.
Glaves, John J. '56 (LIN)[E] Lincoln, NE Bonacum House Retired.
Glavin, Leonard *o.f.m.cap.* '54 (NY) New York, NY St. John the Baptist Retired.
Glavin, Patrick *o.f.m.cap.* '59 (PRT) Portland, ME St. Joseph's; Portland, ME Maine Medical Center.
Glavina, Charles '54 (NY) Dobbs Ferry, NY Our Lady of Pompeii.
Gleason, Carl *s.d.s.* '56 (FgM).
Gleason, Jack A. '95 (TLS) Tulsa, OK Church of the Madalene.
Gleason, Jack (TLS) Diocesan Senators; Diocesan Consultors; Seminary Board; Vocations.
Gleason, James '50 (STL)[O] Liguori, MO Liguori Mission House/Redemptorists.
Gleason, Joseph F. '87 (PH)[A] Wynnewood, PA Theological Seminary of St. Charles Borromeo, Overbrook.
Gleason, Laurence '96 (PH) Horsham, PA St. Catherine of Siena.
Gleason, Paul D. '47 (PRT) Retired.
Gleason, Richard J. '67 (LA) Culver City, CA St. Augustine.
Gleba, Peter W. '53 (SY) Syracuse, NY Sacred Heart Basilica; Syracuse, NY St. Stephen.
Gleba, William P. '58 (SY) Retired.
Glebe, Edward *c.ss.r.* '57 (GAL) Houston, TX Holy Ghost.
Gleeson, Edward D. '69 (CHI) Lemont, IL St. James at Sag Bridge.
Gleeson, Martin J. *o.p.* '98 (NO) New Orleans, LA St. Dominic; [P] New Orleans, LA Dominican Friars, Southern Dominican Province of St. Martin de Porres; [P] Metairie, LA Southern Dominican Foundation; [S] Metairie, LA Southern Dominican Foundation; (FgM).
Gleeson, Michael '75 (LA) San Gabriel, CA St. Anthony.
Gleeson, Stephen J. '63 (BGP) Trumbull, CT St. Stephen; Nurses, Council of Catholic.
Gleeson, Thomas F. *s.j.* '68 (PH)[AA] Loyola Center and Manresa Hall; [AA] Loyola Center and Manresa Hall.
Gleeson, William T. '66 (PBL) Alamosa, CO Sacred Heart; Deans.
Gleissner, Leopold *o.f.m.cap.* (GB) Kaukauna, WI St. Mary of the Annunciation.
Gleixner, Joseph *m.s.c.* '65 (Y) Canton, OH St. Paul.
Glenn, Michael '90 (DEN)[A] Denver, CO St. John Vianney Theological Seminary; Our Lady of the New Advent Theological Institute.
Glenn, Nicholas '98 (STN)[A] Eagle Harbor, MI Skete of Holy Transfiguration Monastery.
Glennon, Bertin *s.t.* '71 (KNX) Chattanooga, TN SS. Peter and Paul.
Glennon, James G. *o.s.a.* '52 (MIA) Dania, FL Church of the Resurrection.
Glennon, Thomas G. *s.s.c.* '79 (CHI)[N] Chicago, IL Columban Fathers Mission Center.
Glepko, Robert J. '76 (CLV) Lorain, OH Nativity of the Blessed Virgin Mary.
Gliatta, Ronald *o.f.m.* '77 (HRT) Waterbury, CT St. Michael.
Glimm, Francis X. '35 (RVC)[J] Huntington, NY St. Joseph's Guest Home for the Aged, Inc.; Censors of Books Retired.
Glinkowski, Raphael K. *o.s.p.p.e.* '62 (GBG) Kittanning, PA Armstrong County Hospital; [H] Kittanning, PA Pauline Fathers Monastery.
Glisson, Nicholas J. '79 (STA) On Duty Outside the Diocese.
Glisson, Nicholas '79 (OAK) Pleasanton, CA The Catholic Community of Pleasanton.
Glockner, Dave *g.h.m.* '66 (WH) Logan, WV St. Francis of Assisi; Man, WV St. Edmund; Chapmanville, WV St. Barbara.
Glockner, Michael W. *c.s.c.* '70 (FTW)[I] South Bend, IN St. Paul's Retirement Community.
Glogowski, John J. '62 (ROC) Hilton, NY St. Leo.
Glogowski, John '71 (SFR) Redwood City, CA St. Matthias.
Gloninger, Hugh M. '56 (PIT)[N] Pittsburgh, PA St. John Vianney Manor Retired.
Glorie, John W. '60 (MIA) Retired.
Glorioso, Charles '95 (SHP) Shreveport, LA St. Pius X; College of Consultors; Presbyteral Council; Continuing Education for the Clergy.
Gloss, John C. '03 (MET) Metuchen, NJ Cathedral of St. Francis.
Glosser, William F. '84 (ALN) Mahanoy City, PA St. Canicus; Mahanoy City, PA St. Fidelis.
Gloudeman, Francis M. *o.praem.* '91 (ORG)[I] Silverado, CA Norbertine Fathers of Orange Inc..
Gloudeman, Robert J. '64 (MIL) Milwaukee, WI Froedtert Memorial Lutheran Hospital; Special Assignment.
Glover, George R. *o.s.b.* '88 (RCK) Aurora, IL St. Peter.
Glover, George *o.s.b.* '88 (RCK)[G] Aurora, IL Marmion Abbey.
Glover, Jason '02 (E) Hermitage, PA Church of Notre Dame.
Glovik, Karl L. '61 (DUB) Cedar Rapids, IA Immaculate Conception; Cedar Rapids, IA St. Wenceslaus; Directors.
Gluc, Vincent *o.f.m.conv.* '79 (ATL) Jonesboro, GA St. Philip Benizi.
Glueckert, Leopold *o.carm.* '68 (JOL)[L] Joliet, IL St. Elias Carmelites.
Glynn, Canon Thomas '64 (STN) Chicago, IL St. Joseph.
Glynn, Edward *s.j.* '67 (CLV)[B] University Heights, OH John Carroll University; [B] Cleveland, OH John Carroll University.
Glynn, Francis J. '37 (NY) Staten Island, NY Holy Family; [EE] Bronx, NY Retired.
Glynn, Francis M. '70 (BO) Lowell, MA St. Anthony.
Glynn, Gerard N. '41 (STL) Retired.
Glynn, Joseph *c.s.sp.* '76 (SFR) Millbrae, CA St. Dunstan.
Glynn, Martin G. '78 (PAT) Franklin, NJ Immaculate Conception.
Glynn, Michael '46 (JKS) Jackson, MS St. Richard Retired.
Glynn, Robert *s.j.* '91 (SAC) Sacramento, CA St. Ignatius of Loyola.
Glynn, Seamus A. '58 (ORG) Anaheim, CA San Antonio.
Glynn, Thomas J. '54 (LA) San Pedro, CA Holy Trinity.
Glynn, Thomas (STN) South–West.
Glynn, William F. '47 (BO) Duxbury, MA Holy Family.
Gmerek, Ronald E. '71 (E) Erie, PA St. Paul; On Leave of Absence.
Gnall, Joseph *o.s.b.* (MO) AUXILIARY CHAPLAINS CONTRACT CHAPLAINS.
Gnall, Julian M. *o.s.b.* '55 (PBR) Retired.
Gnarackatt, Joseph '67 (TR) Brick Town, NJ St. Dominic.
Gnidzinski, Marek '85 (BUF) Batavia, NY St. Joseph.
Gniewyk, Eugene '90 (NEW) Fairfield, NJ St. Thomas More.
Gnirk, Lloyd A. '78 (OM) Omaha, NE St. Pius X.
Gobbo, Paolo *s.x.* '94 (PAT) (FgM).
Gober, Christopher (CHL) Spruce Pine, NC St. Lucien.
Gobitas, Gerald E. (ALN) Orefield, PA St. Joseph The Worker; Chancellor; Secretary to the Bishop; Secretariat for Clergy; Priest Personnel Office; College of Consultors; Ex Officio Members.
Goblirsch, Robert P. '60 (NU) Ortonville, MN St. James; Ortonville, MN St. John; Ortonville, MN St. Joseph.
Goda, Paul J. *s.j.* '66 (SJ)[B] Santa Clara, CA Jesuit Community.
Godecker, Jeffery H. '69 (IND) Indianapolis, IN Immaculate Heart of Mary.
Godenciuc, Iura '94 (STF) New Haven, CT St. Michael.
Godenciuc, Vasile '81 (STF) Elmira Heights, NY St. Nicholas.
Godfrey, Donal *s.j.* '92 (SFR)[C] Chicago, IL Jesuit Community at Loyola University Chicago.
Godfrey, Joseph J. *s.j.* '69 (PH)[C] Jesuit Fathers.
Godfrey, Timothy S. *s.j.* '85 (Missouri)[N] Berkeley, CA Jesuit Community at Jesuit School of Theology at Berkeley.
Godfrey, Timothy S. *s.j.* '85 (OAK) Oakland, CA St. Patrick's.
Godic, Frank G. '73 (CLV) Cleveland, OH Immaculate Conception.
Godic, Frank (CLV) Pastoral Care Services.
Godin, Normand J. '73 (PRO) Providence, RI St. Agnes; Minister for Priests; Clergy Benefit Fund.
Godinez, Rodolfo '91 (STA) Jacksonville, FL San Jose.
Godleski, David A. *s.j.* '98 (CHI)[C] Chicago, IL Jesuit Community at Loyola University Chicago; [N] Chicago, IL Chicago Province of the Society of Jesus–Provincial Office.
Godlewski, Andrew (CHI) Chicago, IL St. Turibius.
Godley, James '40 (CHY) Retired.
Godley, Patrick '53 (SEA) Retired.
Goebel, Joseph A. '50 (CLV) Cleveland, OH St. Jerome; Cleveland, OH Euclid Hospital Retired.
Goebel, Robert A. *s.j.* '63 (SRA)[C] Tacoma, WA Bellarmine Preparatory School.
Goebel, Robert W. '74 (CIN) Cincinnati, OH St. Therese, The Little Flower.
Goeckner, Jeffrey '95 (SFD) Robinson, IL Our Lady of Lourdes; Robinson, IL St. Elizabeth; Presbyteral Council.
Goedde, Bernard C. '72 (BEL) Millstadt, IL St. James; Office of Youth Ministry.
Goedert, Robert A. *o.p.* '51 (CHI)[N] St. Pius V Priory.
Goedert, William O. '55 (CHI) Oak Lawn, IL St. Germaine Retired.
Goehring, Raymond J. (LAN) Judicial Vicar.
Goehring, Raymond '64 (LAN) Lansing, MI Resurrection; Bellevue, MI St. Ann.
Goeke, James F. *s.j.* '88 (STL)[C] Saint Louis University.
Goekler, Thomas F. *m.m.* '67 (FgM).
Goellen, Richard M. '63 (FAR) Military Chaplains; Army Chaplains; AUXILIARY CHAPLAINS CONTRACT CHAPLAINS.
Goellner, Glennon J. '50 (STL) Retired.
Goergen, David *m.afr.* '69 (FgM).
Goergen, Donald J. *o.p.* '75 (CHI)[N] Chicago Dominicans (Provincial Office).
Goergen, Donald J. *o.p.* '75 (MIL)[O] Kenosha, WI Order of Preachers, Province of St. Albert the Great.
Goergen, Michael A. '62 (CHI) Chicago, IL St. Robert Bellarmine.
Goering, Joseph P. (FAR) Special Assignment; [J] Fargo, ND Catholic Chaplains Association; Chancellor and Secretary to the Bishop; Archivist; Notaries; Corporate Board; Diocesan Finance Council; Office of Worship and Sacraments; Holy Childhood Association; Propagation of the Faith.
Goerner, Basil S. '93 (MAR) Retired.
Goerner, James E. '93 (PH) Philadelphia, PA St. Matthew.
Goertz, Alois J. '48 (SAT)[K] San Antonio, TX Casa De Padres Retired.
Goertz, Bernard C. '52 (AUS) Austin, TX Santa Barbara; Special Assignments.
Goertz, Howard '77 (AUS) Kyle, TX St. Anthony Marie De Claret.
Goertz, Victor '52 (AUS) Special Assignments; Presbyteral Council.
Goeser, Peter J. *o.s.b.* (MO) CIVIL AIR PATROL.
Goethals, Gregory M. *s.j.* '88 (SFR)[E] San Francisco, CA St. Ignatius College Preparatory (Coed); [N] San Francisco, CA Jesuit Community at St. Ignatius College Preparatory.
Goettemoeller, Leonard *c.pp.s.* '49 (KC)[J] Liberty, MO Precious Blood Center.
Goetz, Donald R. '68 (L) Louisville, KY St. Brigid; Louisville, KY St. James; Defenders of the Bond.
Goetz, Donatus *o.f.m.cap.* '45 (NY)[EE] Yonkers, NY St. Clare Friary.

Goetz, Gerald E. *s.j.* '73 (STP)[P] Lake Elmo, MN Jesuit Retreat House.
Goetz, J. Raymond '81 (OWN)[I] Murray, KY Murray State University Newman House.
Goetz, Joseph W. '60 (CIN) Priest Councilors; Consultors Retired.
Goetz, Maris *o.f.m.cap.* '64 (SAL)[E] Victoria, KS St. Fidelis Friary.
Goetz, Martin G. '92 (DAV) Keota, IA Holy Trinity.
Goetz, Ray '81 (OWN) Murray, KY St. Leo; Deans; Priests' Council.
Goff, William P. *c.m.* '66 (BAL)[S] Emmitsburg, MD Vincentian House.
Goff, William *c.m.* '66 (BAL) Emmitsburg, MD St. Joseph.
Goggin, Cornelius J. '56 (MAN) Retired.
Goggin, John T. '64 (NU) On Duty Outside the Diocese.
Goggins, James K. '94 (DEN) Wheat Ridge, CO SS. Peter and Paul.
Goguen, Francis T. '66 (WOR) Leominster, MA St. Cecilia's; Diocesan College of Consultors; Deans.
Gohm, Robert S. '75 (SAG) Bay City, MI Holy Trinity; Delegate to Senior Priests.
Gohm, Robert (SAG) Office of Church Ministries.
Gohmann, Myron *c.p.* '48 (CHI)[N] Chicago, IL Passionist Community–Immaculate Conception Monastery; [N] Chicago, IL Daneo Hall.
Goicoechea, Greg *o.f.m.* '45 (FWT) Fort Worth, TX Immaculate Heart of Mary.
Goin, James A. '92 (OKL) Oklahoma City, OK St. Charles Borromeo.
Gojuk, Peter P. *o.v.m.* '81 (BO)[B] Boston, MA Our Lady of Grace Seminary.
Golas, Eugene S. '55 (GR) Retired.
Golas, John S. '81 (HRT) Unionville, CT St. Mary's; Deans.
Golas, Robert W. '03 (WDC) Graduate Studies.
Golasinski, Donald J. '62 (BEA) Groves, TX Immaculate Conception.
Golasinski, Donald (BEA) Southern Vicariate; Catholic Women, Council of.
Golasinski, James L. '58 (GAL) Houston, TX Annunciation.
Goldasich, Mark '81 (KCK) Tonganoxie, KS Sacred Heart; Newspaper "The Leaven".
Goldbach, Edmund *o.f.m.conv.* '65 (GR) Elyria, OH St. Mary.
Goldbach, Peter D. *c.m.* '44 (BRK)[V] Jamaica, NY Vincentian Residence.
Goldberg, James M. '76 (GBG) Delmont, PA St. John Baptist de La Salle; Export, PA St. Mary.
Golden, Edward '61 (ROC) Rochester, NY St. Anthony of Padua; Rochester, NY Holy Apostles; Rochester, NY Holy Family.
Golden, Francis P. *s.j.* '71 (NY)[EE] New York, NY Xavier Jesuit Community.
Golden, George E. '76 (WDC) Forestville, MD Mt. Calvary; Advocates.
Golden, James '48 (DUL) Retired.
Golden, Patrick '96 (RIC) Christiansburg, VA St. Jude.
Golden, Paul L. *c.m.* '65 (DEN)[N] Denver, CO Congregation of the Mission Midwest Province: De Paul House.
Golden, Thomas P. *m.m.* '51 (NY)[EE] Maryknoll Maryknoll Fathers and Brothers.
Golden, Thomas '63 (GB) Special Assignment.
Goldian, Edward R. *s.j.* '69 (STL) Imperial, MO St. Joseph.
Golding, Edward '88 (ALB) Summit, NY St. Anna; Worcester, NY St. Joseph.
Goldrick, Timothy J. '72 (FR) Assonet, MA St. Bernard's.
Gole, Joseph *s.t.d.* '43 (MIL)[O] Hales Corners, WI Priests of the Sacred Heart; [B] Hales Corners, WI Sacred Heart School of Theology.
Golemba, Roman '75 (STF) Fall River, MA St. John–the–Baptist; Woonsocket, RI St. Michael; Presbyteral Council.
Golias, Andrew J. '70 (PH) Norristown, PA St. Teresa of Avila.
Golik, Stanislaus '39 (OM) Retired.
Golini, Ronald '68 (NTN) Leave of Absence.
Golino, Arthur A. '80 (NY) Staten Island, NY St. Sylvester.
Golish, Robert *m.m.* '53 (NY).
Golka, James R. '01 (GI)[EE] Scottsbluff, NE Our Lady of Guadalupe; Continuing Education for the Clergy; Personnel Board.
Gollatz, Ronald J. '72 (CHI) Lake Zurich, IL St. Francis de Sales.
Gollinge, Donald '58 (NY) Retired.
Gollob, Timothy A. '58 (DAL) Judges; Dallas, TX Holy Cross.
Gollob, Timothy '58 (DAL) Dallas, TX Veterans Administration Hospital; Dallas, TX St. Anthony; Consultors of Pastors; Presbyteral Council.
Golobich, John '48 (DUL) Retired.
Golombek, Robert K. '65 (BUF) Tonawanda, NY Blessed Sacrament.
Goloran, Mauricio O. '84 (LA) Valinda, CA St. Martha.
Golyzniak, Grzegorz '98 (SY) Rome, NY St. John the Baptist.
Goman, Ralph J. '64 (STP) Hopkins, MN St. John the Evangelist.
Gomes, Agnelo *s.f.x.* '94 (P) Portland, OR St. Charles.
Gomes, Christopher *o.f.m.* '88 (FR) New Bedford, MA St. Anthony of Padua's.
Gomes, Herman *ss.cc.* '78 (HON) Kaneohe, HI St. Ann.
Gomes, Ignatius *s.f.x.* '70 (LR)[E] Little Rock, AR St. Vincent Infirmary Medical Center.
Gomes, John A. '69 (FR) Taunton, MA Annunciation of the Lord.
Gomes, Martin *ss.cc.* '69 (FR).
Gomes, Robert '66 (SP)[H] On Duty Outside the Diocese; Clearwater, FL St. Cecelia.
Gomes, Ronald A. '87 (BO) Permanent Disability.
Gomes, Stanley '95 (NEW)[A] South Orange, NJ Seton Hall University College Seminary; [B] School of Diplomacy and Intl. Rels..
Gomes, William J. '69 (RVC) Elmont, NY St. Boniface; Senate of Priests (Presbyteral Council/College of Consultors).
Gomes–Kelly, John R. '62 (SD) Unassigned.
Gomez, Antonio '51 (SJN) San Juan, PR Cristo Rey.
Gomez, Carlos '03 (PHX) Mesa, AZ St. Timothy.
Gomez, Cesar '98 (WIL) Georgetown, DE St. Michael the Archangel.
Gomez, Daniel '85 (MET) Bernardsville, NJ Our Lady of Perpetual Help.
Gomez, Edmund '93 (SB) Colton, CA Our Lady of the Immaculate Conception; Peace and Justice Committee.
Gomez, Edmundo '69 (NY) Bronx, NY St. Helena.
Gomez, Emerito *o.f.m.* '82 (FRS) Delano, CA Our Lady of Guadalupe.
Gomez, Enrique '77 (CGS) Aibonito, PR Church of St. Joseph.
Gomez, Eusebio *o.c.d.* '70 (MIA)[M] Miami, FL Discalced Carmelite Friars of Miami, Inc..
Gomez, Fernando *s.j.* (SJN)[D] Rio Piedras, PR Centro Universitario Catolico.
Gomez, Francisco *s.t.* '83 (LA) Los Angeles, CA Our Lady of Victory.
Gomez, Frank '61 (BWN) Retired.
Gomez, Gustavo '02 (YAK) East Wenatchee, WA Holy Apostles; [F] East Wenatchee, WA Holy Apostles Parish Conference.
Gomez, Henry '58 (LA) Bell Gardens, CA St. Gertrude.
Gomez, Henry (LA) Deanery 17; Personnel Board of the Archdiocese.
Gomez, Humberto '88 (SAC) Sacramento, CA California State Youth Authority Center; Sacramento, CA California Youth Authority; Co Directors.
Gomez, Jorge '90 (FRS) Planada, CA Sacred Heart.
Gomez, Jose A. '58 (ELP) El Paso, TX Holy Family.
Gomez, Jose H. (DEN) Moderator of the Curia.
Gomez, Jose Leonardo '99 (CHI) Chicago, IL Our Lady of Grace.
Gomez, Jose Luis *s.d.b.* '61 (SJN) San Juan, PR Maria Auxiliadora.
Gomez, Jose R. '95 (PCE) Mercedita, PR Church of the Resurrection.
Gomez, Jose '95 (AMA) Amarillo, TX St. Mary's; Borger, TX St. John the Evangelist; Silverton, TX Our Lady of Loreto.
Gomez, Jose (ELP) Movimiento Familiar Cristiano.
Gomez, Leo '63 (GLP) Farmington, NM St. Mary's.
Gomez, Leo (GLP) Vicar General; Presbyteral Council; Diocesan Consultors.
Gomez, Lorenzo *l.c.* '73 (DET)[T] Bloomfield Hills, MI Opdyke, Inc.; [T] Bloomfield Hills, MI Logos, Inc. (Michigan); [T] Oxford, MI Queen of the Family Retreat Center.
Gomez, Lorenzo *s.d.v.* '98 (NEW) Newark, NJ St. Michael's.
Gomez, Miguel '81 (MIA) Hialeah, FL Santa Barbara.
Gomez, Orlando De Jesus '86 (CGS) Caguas, PR El Salvador.
Gomez, Orlando Perez *o.s.b.* '01 (RCK)[G] Aurora, IL Marmion Abbey.
Gomez, Ramon J. '85 (OAK) Union City, CA St. Anne; Deans; Presbyteral Council.
Gomez, Raul *s.d.s.* '87 (MIL)[O] St. Francis, WI St. Joseph's Salvatorian Community (Novitiate); [B] Hales Corners, WI Sacred Heart School of Theology.
Gomez, Rene J. '63 (SFR) San Bruno, CA St. Bruno.
Gomez, Salvador *l.c.* '85 (SAC) Sacramento, CA Our Lady of Guadalupe Shrine.
Gomez, Steve *s.d.b.* '01 (LA)[Q] Los Angeles, CA Dominic Savio Salesian Residence.
Gomez, Tony '98 (LA) Baldwin Park, CA St. John the Baptist.
Gomez, Walter '80 (ARE) On Duty Outside the Diocese; Guaynabo, PR San Jose; Air National Guard Chaplains.
Gomez–Serna, Otoniel J. '90 (PRO) Central Falls, RI The Holy Spirit Catholic Community.
Gomez–Torres, Fredi '02 (PEO) Kewanee, IL St. Francis of Assisi; Kewanee, IL St. Mary's Catholic Church.
Gomez del Valle, Jorge *m.sp.s.* '73 (SEA) Mill Creek, WA St. Elizabeth Ann Seton.
Gomide, Tomaz '71 (RVC) Mineola, NY Corpus Christi.
Gomolski, Joseph T. '81 (VEN) Marco Island, FL San Marco.
Gomolski, Joseph T. '81 (WIL) Absent on Sick Leave.
Gomulka, Eugene T. '74 (ALT) Military Chaplains.
Gomulka, Eugene T. (HON) Military Chaplains; Navy Chaplains.
Gonchar, John Joseph *o.f.m.* '57 (CIN)[M] Sts. Philip and James Friary; (FgM).
Gonda, Andrew '46 (GI) Building Committee Retired.
Gonda, Gerard *o.s.b.* '80 (CLV)[D] Cleveland, OH Benedictine High School; [O] Cleveland, OH.
Gondek, Albert J. *o.s.f.s.* '66 (CHL) Lexington, NC Our Lady of the Rosary.
Gondek, Joseph A. '37 (MAR) Retired.
Gonderinger, Gerald E. '74 (OM) West Point, NE Assumption B.V.M.; Special Assignment; Deans.
Gonet, Charles F. '58 (SPR)[H] Springfield, MA St. Michael's Residence Retired.
Goni, Joachim *o.a.r.* '40 (ORG) Santa Ana, CA Our Lady of the Pillar.
Goni, Paul *o.a.r.* '51 (ORG) Santa Ana, CA Our Lady of Guadalupe.
Gonia, Raymond L. '90 (SUP) Military Chaplains.
Gonnelly, Theophane *o.s.b.* '47 (SFS)[F] Marvin, SD Blue Cloud Abbey.
Gonsalves, Lino '86 (NY) Yonkers, NY St. John the Baptist.
Gonsalves, Valerian *o.s.b.* '90 (TLS) Durant, OK St. William.
Gonser, Richard A. '62 (CLV) North Ridgeville, OH St. Julie Billiart.
Gonyo, Lance M. '93 (ROC) Sodus, NY Epiphany.
Gonyo, Lance (ROC) Conciliation Board.
Gonzales, Flavio V. '77 (CHI) Des Plaines, IL St. Mary.
Gonzales, Gabriel '84 (LA) North Hollywood, CA St. Charles Borromeo; Vicar for Clergy; Clergy, Vicar for.
Gonzales, George (SB) Blythe, CA St. Joan of Arc; Pastoral Practices Committee.
Gonzales, Gilberto Cavazos *o.f.m.* '85 (CHI)[N] Chicago, IL St. Joseph Interprovincial Post–Novitiate Formation House.
Gonzales, Loren M. *o.s.m.* '89 (CHI)[N] Chicago Order of Friar Servants of Mary (Servites) United States of America Province, Inc..
Gonzales, Loren '89 (PHX) Cashion, AZ St. William.
Gonzales, Loreto '78 (LA) Artesia, CA Holy Family; [CC] Los Angeles, CA Filipino Pastoral Ministry.
Gonzales, Richard '98 (CC) Beeville, TX Our Lady of Victory.
Gonzales, Robert A. '78 (TUC)[A] On Duty Outside the Diocese.
Gonzales, Ronald D. '03 (SFE)[A] Albuquerque, NM Immaculate Conception.
Gonzalez, Angel '52 (FRS) Reedley, CA St. Anthony.
Gonzalez, Anthony '92 (LA) Los Angeles, CA St. Frances Xavier Cabrini.
Gonzalez, Antonio '50 (FRS) Retired.
Gonzalez, Antonio '62 (LUB) Retired.
Gonzalez, Aquilino D. *o.s.a.* '72 (FgM).
Gonzalez, Arnold J. *c.m.f.* '58 (LA)[Q] San Gabriel, CA Claretian Missionaries (Missionary Sons of the Immaculate Heart of Mary).
Gonzalez, Arnold *c.m.f.* '58 (LA) San Gabriel, CA San Gabriel.
Gonzalez, Arturo *o.s.m.* (ELP) El Paso, TX Our Lady of Sorrows.
Gonzalez, Bernardo *o.f.m.* (AMA) Dumas, TX SS. Peter and Paul.
Gonzalez, Charles G. *s.j.* '67 (CAM) Camden, NJ Holy Name.
Gonzalez, Charles S. *s.j.* '67 (CAM) Camden, NJ Camden County Jail.
Gonzalez, Cruz Gil '48 (SJN) Retired.
Gonzalez, Daniel I. '92 (TYL) On Duty Outside the Diocese.
Gonzalez, Eduardo *s.d.b.* '81 (DAL) Dallas, TX St. Edward; Presbyteral Council.
Gonzalez, Eliseo *o.a.r.* '03 (LA)[Q] Oxnard, CA St. Augustine Priory O.A.R..
Gonzalez, Emilio '88 (SEA) Lynden, WA St. Joseph.
Gonzalez, Fernando '95 (BWN) Weslaco, TX San Martin de Porres.
Gonzalez, Flavio V. '77 (CHI) Des Plaines, IL St. Stephen Protomartyr.
Gonzalez, George G. '67 (SAT) Military Chaplains; Army Chaplains.
Gonzalez, George '87 (BWN) Harlingen, TX Immaculate Heart of Mary; [D] Brownsville, TX Jail Ministry; Chaplains.
Gonzalez, George (SB) Pro–Synodal Judges.
Gonzalez, Gonzalo *o.s.a.* '49 (SJN) Bayamon, PR Santa Rita de Casia; [E] Bayamon, PR Hospital Regional.
Gonzalez, Hilario Rivera (CGS) Culebra, PR Nuestra Senora del Carmen.
Gonzalez, Hugo '89 (PHX) Peoria, AZ St. Charles Borromeo.
Gonzalez, Ivan '01 (RVC) Mastic Beach, NY St. Jude.
Gonzalez, Jaime Martinez *o.r.c.* '83 (PCE) Adjuntas, PR St. Joachim.

Gonzalez, Jaime *c.m.* (CHL)[O] Charlotte, NC Our Lady of Guadalupe Hispanic Center.
Gonzalez, Jamie '90 (TR) Mount Holly, NJ Christ the Redeemer.
Gonzalez, Jesus *c.m.v.* '87 (ARE) Sabana Hoyos, PR Nuestra Senora de Fatima.
Gonzalez, John Alex '03 (R) Chapel Hill, NC St. Thomas More.
Gonzalez, Jorge L. *s.d.b.* '89 (SJN) Catano, PR San Francisco de Sales.
Gonzalez, Jose G. '54 (SP) St. Petersburg, FL St. Raphael.
Gonzalez, Jose R. *o.f.m.cap.* (PCE)[E] Ponce, PR Fraternidad Santa Teresita, Frailes Capuchinos.
Gonzalez, Jose '69 (SR) Santa Rosa, CA Resurrection; Renovacion Carismatica Catolica.
Gonzalez, Jose '91 (VEN) Lake Placid, FL Communidad Catolica Hispana Santiago Apostol (Santiago Mission); [I] Lake Placid, FL Campo San Jose; Hispanic, Migrant and Spanish Speaking Apostolates/National Migration Week; Sebring, FL St. Catherine.
Gonzalez, Jose (VEN) Juventud Hispana (Hispanic Youth Ministry).
Gonzalez, Juan Jose *m.sp.s.* '00 (P) Hillsboro, OR St. Matthew; [A] Mount Angel, OR Felix Rougier House of Studies.
Gonzalez, Juan *c.pp.s.* '76 (GRY) East Chicago, IN Our Lady of Guadalupe; Cursillos in Christianity.
Gonzalez, Juan *s.m.* '82 (DET)[E] Harper Woods, MI Notre Dame High School.
Gonzalez, Julio Angel (MGZ) Army National Guard Chaplains.
Gonzalez, Julio *s.f.* (SFE) Chimayo, NM Holy Family.
Gonzalez, Lazaro *o.f.m.* '68 (ELP) Presidio, TX Santa Teresa de Jesus.
Gonzalez, Lorenzo '01 (VEN) Bonita Springs, FL St. Leo.
Gonzalez, Lorenzo '03 (RCK) Belvidere, IL St. James.
Gonzalez, Luis Francisco *o.f.m.cap.* '98 (SJN) San Juan, PR San Antonio; [E] San Juan, PR Centro Medico de P.R..
Gonzalez, Luis O. '00 (NEW) Newark, NJ Cathedral Basilica of the Sacred Heart.
Gonzalez, Luis P. '94 (NEW) On Duty Outside the Archdiocese; Takoma Park, MD Our Lady of Sorrows.
Gonzalez, Luis P. '94 (WDC)[M] Takoma Park, MD Redemptoris Mater Archdiocesan Missionary Seminary.
Gonzalez, Luis P. '94 (NEW) On Duty Outside the Archdiocese; Takoma Park, MD Our Lady of Sorrows.
Gonzalez, Luis *o.f.m.cap.* '93 (SJN)[E] Rio Piedras, PR Hospital San Francisco.
Gonzalez, Marcos J. '94 (LA) Pasadena, CA St. Andrew.
Gonzalez, Marcos (LA) Members.
Gonzalez, Mario '55 (VEN) Retired.
Gonzalez, Mario *o.s.a.* '58 (SJN) Bayamon, PR Ntra. Sra. de la Monserrate.
Gonzalez, Masseo *o.f.m.conv.* '96 (OAK) San Pablo, CA St. Paul.
Gonzalez, Miguel '98 (ORL) Orlando, FL St. John Vianney; Executive Committee; Members.
Gonzalez, Octavio '01 (NEW) Irvington, NJ St. Leo's.
Gonzalez, Orestes '86 (MIA)[L] Miami, FL Prelature of the Holy Cross and Opus Dei.
Gonzalez, Rafael J. *c.r.l.* (ARE) Corozal, PR Christ the King.
Gonzalez, Ricardo '57 (NEW) Orange, NJ St. John's Retired.
Gonzalez, Rodolfo '88 (TR) Trenton, NJ St. Mary Cathedral.
Gonzalez, Romualdo *sch.p.* '71 (LA) Los Angeles, CA Our Lady Help of Christians (Maria Auxiliadora).
Gonzalez, Rudolph F. '87 (NY) Spring Valley, NY St. Joseph.
Gonzalez, Salvador '01 (FRS) Kingsburg, CA Holy Family.
Gonzalez, Silvino *o.dem.* '41 (PCE) Ponce, PR La Merced.
Gonzalez, Teodulo P. *s.j.* '87 (BAL)[B] Timonium, MD Loyola Graduate Center –Timonium Campus.
Gonzalez, Tomas '01 (SJN) San Juan, PR San Lucas.
Gonzalez–Abreu, Hector '79 (MIA) Miami, FL St. Vincent De Paul.
Gonzalez–Florez, Jose Duvan '96 (ATL) Office of Hispanic Apostolate; Associate Vicars for Clergy.
Gonzalez–Gayton, Jose Enrique '03 (CHL) Hickory, NC St. Aloysius.
Gonzalez–Gonzalez, Tomas (SJN) Cursillos De Cristiandad.
Gonzalez–Martinez, Edward '98 (SAT) San Antonio, TX St. Gabriel.
Gonzalez–Montenegro, Julian *o.f.m.cap.* '84 (SFR)[B] San Francisco, CA Capuchin House of Studies; [N] Burlingame, CA Capuchin Provincial House.
Gonzalez–Ovalle, Jesus A. '95 (CAM) Bridgeton, NJ Immaculate Conception.
Gonzalez Chao, Luis '58 (SJN) Retired.
Gonzalez Pola, Antonio '63 (SJN)[A] Bayamon Central University.
Good, Clarence P. '46 (STL) Retired.
Goode, Francis *o.p.* '80 (SFR) San Francisco, CA St. Dominic.
Goode, Francis *o.p.* '87 (OAK)[N] Oakland, CA Western Dominican Province.
Goode, Francis *o.p.* '87 (SFR)[N] San Francisco, CA St. Dominic Priory.
Goode, James E. *o.f.m.* '72 (NY)[EE] New York, NY St. Clare Friary.
Goode, Joseph J. '73 (PAT) Kinnelon, NJ Our Lady of the Magnificat; Catholic Deaf Society.
Goode, Lawrence C. '64 (SFR) East Palo Alto, CA St. Francis of Assisi; [S] Palo Alto, CA Legion of Mary.
Goode, William F. '60 (WDC) Indian Head, MD St. Mary Star of the Sea.
Goodill, Robert D. '38 (E) Erie, PA St. Luke Retired.
Goodly, Timothy '93 (LKC) Lake Charles, LA St. Henry; Director of Seminarians; Seminary Advisory Board; Vocation Director.
Goodman, Fidelis C. *m.m.* '49 (NY).
Goodman, Julian '66 (RIC) Retired.
Goodman, Leo M. '91 (HBG)[EE] Lancaster, PA Assumption of the Blessed Virgin Mary.
Goodman, Norman '60 (PEO) Retired.
Goodrow, David C. (BO) Franklin, MA St. Mary.
Goodrow, Robert A. '62 (DET) Retired.
Goodrum, James R. '57 (LFT) Monticello, IN Our Lady of the Lakes; Associate Judges.
Goodson, Todd Michael '02 (IND) Columbus, IN St. Bartholomew.
Goodwin, Calvin R. *f.s.s.p.* '79 (LIN)[A] Denton, NE Our Lady of Guadalupe Seminary.
Goodwin, Calvin R. *f.s.s.p.* '79 (SCR)[M] Elmhurst Priestly Fraternity of St. Peter (F.S.S.P.), North American District Headquarters.
Goodwin, James P. *s.j.* '43 (SPK)[J] Spokane, WA Regis Community.
Goodwin, James S. '97 (FAR) Hankinson, ND St. Philip.
Goodwin, James (FAR) Defensor Vinculi.
Goodwin, Owen F. *ss.cc.* '54 (PRO)[P] Narragansett, RI Christian Brothers' Center.
Goodwin, Owen F. *ss.cc.* '54 (FR)[H] Fairhaven, MA Damien Residence.
Goodwin, Patrick '69 (OAK) Oakland, CA St. Theresa of the Infant Jesus (The Little Flower); Vicar of Temporalities; Diocesan Finance Committee.
Goodwin, Raymond F. (WOR) North Grafton, MA St. Mary's.
Goodwin, Robert T. '57 (MAN) Retired.
Goodwin, Thomas L. '85 (CC) Corpus Christi, TX St. Joseph.
Goodyear, Robert *s.t.* '75 (JKS) Magee, MS St. Stephen; Boswell Retardation Center; Approved Advocate and Auditors.
Gooley, Lawrence L. *s.j.* '65 (B) Priest River, ID St. Catherine's.
Gooley, Lawrence P. *s.j.* '65 (SPK)[J] Spokane, WA Regis Community.
Goolsby, Gregory D. (ATL) Judges.
Goolsby, Gregory '93 (ATL) Duluth, GA Catholic Church Of St. Monica.
Goossens, Hippolyte L. *c.j.* '56 (LA) Camarillo, CA Camarillo State Hospital–Development Center.
Gootee, Jason E. (ALX) Campus Ministry; Seminarians; Vocations Recruitment; [I] Alexandria, LA Louisiana State University at Alexandria.
Gopaul, Antonius P. '97 (BRK) Brooklyn, NY St. Saviour.
Goraieb, Charles '91 (PHX) Buckeye, AZ Saint Henry.
Gorak, Stanley C. '38 (GI) Retired.
Gorak, Stanley (GI) Building Committee.
Gorak, Wladyslaw '82 (NEW) Garfield, NJ St. Stanislaus Kostka.
Gorczyca, Andrzej '74 (BRK) Brooklyn, NY Our Lady of Czestochowa–St. Casimir.
Gordinier, William J. '58 (ROC) Defenders of the Bond Retired.
Gordon, Charles B. *c.s.c.* '87 (FTW)[A] Notre Dame, IN Old College; [I] Notre Dame, IN Holy Cross Community, Corby Hall, University of Notre Dame.
Gordon, Charles *s.t.* '67 (FgM).
Gordon, Charles *c.s.c.* '87 (FTW)[B] University of Notre Dame Du Lac.
Gordon, Gerald R. *s.j.* '60 (SPK)[B] Spokane, WA Gonzaga University; [F] Spokane, WA Sacred Heart Medical Center.
Gordon, Gerald *t.o.r.* '69 (ORL) Bradenton, FL Sacred Heart.
Gordon, Greg (LAV) Presbyteral Council for the Diocese of Las Vegas; Priests' Personnel Board.
Gordon, Gregory W. '88 (LAV) Henderson, NV St. Francis of Assisi.
Gordon, James E. '81 (RIC) Chesapeake, VA St. Stephen, Martyr.
Gordon, James *i.c.* '69 (SP) Seminole, FL Blessed Sacrament.
Gordon, John B. '85 (MET) Perth Amboy, NJ La Asuncion; Commission for Hispanic Ministry.
Gordon, John F. (NEW) On Duty Outside the Archdiocese.
Gordon, John '85 (MET)[A] South Amboy, NJ Cardinal McCarrick High School.
Gordon, John '88 (PAT)[P] Paterson, NJ The Association of the Marian Apostolate of Mercy, Inc..
Gordon, John '88 (NEW)[F] Steubenville, OH Holy Spirit Friary.
Gordon, John *o.m.i.* '01 (MIA) Miami, FL Christ the King.
Gordon, Kevin M. '83 (SUP) Presbyteral Council & Diocesan Consultors; Personnel Placement Board.
Gordon, Kevin (SUP) Diocesan Coordinator of Health Affairs.
Gordon, L. William '65 (OG) Chazy, NY Sacred Heart.
Gordon, Robert J. '73 (PAT) Presbyteral Council; College of Consultors; Environment & Architecture Commission; Long Valley, NJ St. Mark the Evangelist.
Gore, Robert D. '65 (BEL)[E] Belleville, IL Meredith Memorial Home; [G] Belleville, IL Poor Clare Monastery of Our Lady of Mercy.
Gore, William R. *o.s.f.s.* '69 (WIL)[J] Wilmington, DE DeSales House; [J] Wilmington Oblates of St. Francis De Sales.
Gorena, Pedro *o.ss.t.* '66 (SJN) Bayamon, PR Ascension Del Senor; Bayamon, PR Espiritu Santo; [F] Toa Alta, PR Hogar Santisima Trinidad; [F] Bayamon, PR Hogar Del Nino "El Ave Maria".
Gorges, Bernard X. '95 (WCH) Winfield, KS St. Mary; Winfield, KS Holy Name.
Gorges, Bernard (WCH) Rural Life Ministry.
Gorges, Peter '68 (JUN) Diocesan Consultors Retired.
Gorgis, Noel '89 (LA) North Hollywood, CA St. Paul Assyrian–Chaldean.
Gorgis, Noel '89 (SPA) North Hollywood, CA St. Paul Assyrian–Chaldean Catholic Parish.
Gorham, Francis X. *o.m.i.* '58 (BO)[Y] Tewksbury, MA Immaculate Heart of Mary Infirmary.
Gori, Peter G. *o.s.a.* (BO) Court Advocate; Canonical Affairs Committee.
Gorka, Thaddeus '88 (PH) Philadelphia, PA St. Adalbert.
Gorman, Charles '54 (GF) Columbus, MT St. Mary's.
Gorman, Cyril *o.s.b.* '90 (SCL)[I] Collegeville, MN St. John's Abbey, of the Order of St. Benedict.
Gorman, Edmund M. *o.p.* '92 (NY) New York, NY St. Catherine of Siena; [II] New York, NY Dominican Shrine of St. Jude, Inc..
Gorman, Francis A. *o.f.m.* '39 (SP)[O] St. Petersburg St. Anthony Friary.
Gorman, Francis P. '59 (NY) North Tarrytown, NY Holy Cross; Sleepy Hollow, NY St. Teresa of Avila.
Gorman, George F. '36 (PRO) Retired.
Gorman, James P. '73 (PH) Graduate Studies.
Gorman, James T. '57 (NY) Retired.
Gorman, James '81 (STP) Burnsville, MN Church of the Risen Savior.
Gorman, John J. '45 (RVC) Babylon, NY St. Joseph's Retired.
Gorman, John '58 (SB) Retired.
Gorman, John *s.d.s.* '69 (MIL)[O] Milwaukee Salvatorian Provincial Residence.
Gorman, Joseph F. '55 (HRT) Waterbury, CT St. Leo the Great; Deans.
Gorman, Kevin D. *o.s.b.* '51 (PEO) Arlington, IL St. Patrick's; Cherry, IL Holy Trinity.
Gorman, Leo J. *c.p.* '57 (ORL)[EE] Pelham Manor, NY St. Vincent's Residence; [II] Pelham, NY Passionist Communications, Inc.; Orlando, FL Mary Queen of the Universe Shrine.
Gorman, Michael J. '80 (LC) La Crosse, WI St. Joseph the Workman Cathedral.
Gorman, Michael J. (LC) Diocesan Judges.
Gorman, Michael J. (LC) College of Consultors; St. Joseph's Priest Fund, Inc., (Benevolent Society).
Gorman, Patrick J. '59 (LA) Los Angeles, CA St. Bernadette.
Gorman, Patrick '59 (LA) Retired.
Gorman, Richard F. '82 (NY)[E] New York, NY Cardinal Spellman High School; [I] New York, NY The Catholic Charities of the Archdiocese of New York.
Gorman, Robert G. '80 (MET) Perth Amboy, NJ Holy Spirit.
Gorman, Rody I. '55 (LA) Huntington Park, CA St. Matthias Retired.
Gorman, Thomas J. '59 (TOL) Delphos, OH St. John the Evangelist.
Gorman, William N. '76 (MOB) Dauphin Island, AL St. Edmund–by–the–Sea.
Gorman, William '73 (ALB) Margaretville, NY Sacred Heart; Special Assignment.
Gorman, William (MOB) Group II.
Gormley, Charles E. '51 (PH) Bala Cynwyd, PA St. Matthias Retired.
Gormley, Eugene *l.c.* '83 (DAL)[D] Irving, TX The Highlands School; [E] Irving, TX The Highland School; [K] Irving, TX Legionaries of Christ.
Gormley, Gerard '85 (SR) Santa Rosa, CA St. Rose of Lima.
Gormley, James J. *s.j.* '54 (PH)[AA] Loyola Center and Manresa Hall.
Gormley, James W. '54 (PH) Stowe, PA St. Gabriel of the Sorrowful Mother.

Gormley, Kevin '64 (JC) Marshall, MO St. Peter; Marshall, MO Marshall State School–Hospital; Ministry to Priests; Board of Trustees.
Gormley, Michael *s.a.c.* '41 (DET) Oakwood Hospital.
Gormley, Raymond P. '92 (CAM) Blackwood, NJ St. Agnes.
Gormley, Raymond (CAM) Cumberland County.
Gormley, William J. *c.m.* '49 (PH).
Gorney, Joseph *c.ss.r.* '51 (ORL)[E] New Smyrna Beach, FL St. Alphonsus Villa–Redemptorist Fathers and Brothers.
Gorny, Ed *g.h.m.* '68 (CIN)[M] Cincinnati Headquarters of Glenmary Home Missioners.
Gorospe, Paterno '66 (NEW) Teaneck, NJ Holy Name Hospital; [G] School of Nursing; Chaplains.
Gorowski, Roman *c.m.* '72 (BRK)[M] Manchester, CT DePaul Provincial Residence.
Gorr, Benjamin '79 (VEN) Retired.
Gorsic, Gregor '97 (JOL) Kankakee, IL St. Teresa.
Gorski, Barnabas *o.f.m.* '60 (GB)[I] (FgM).
Gorski, Donald '59 ((CHR)) (FgM).
Gorski, Eugene F. *c.s.c.* '60 (FTW)[B] University of Notre Dame Du Lac; [I] Notre Dame, IN Holy Cross Community, Corby Hall, University of Notre Dame.
Gorski, J. Donald '59 (CHR) On Duty Outside the Diocese.
Gorski, John F. *m.m.* '63 (FgM).
Gorski, John J. '64 (CLV) Avon, OH Holy Trinity Retired.
Gorski, Lawrence E. '75 (CHI) Chicago, IL Our Lady of Grace.
Gorski, Robert E. (MAN) Council of Priests; College of Consultors.
Gorski, Robert '80 (MAN) Manchester, NH St. Catherine.
Gorski, Terrence *o.f.m.* '75 (BWN) Grulla, TX Holy Family.
Gorton, Timothy J. '82 (PRO) Warwick, RI St. Francis of Assisi.
Gosche, Joseph E. '55 (SPC) Retired.
Gosciniak, Dariusz '92 (HRT) East Haven, CT St. Vincent de Paul's.
Gosma, Robert D. '59 (MIL) Genesee Depot, WI St. Paul.
Gosnell, David H. '65 (GRY) Valparaiso, IN St. Elizabeth Seton; Bishop's Council of Priests.
Gosnell, Stephen D. '78 (BAL) Annapolis, MD St. Andrew by the Bay; [V] Annapolis, MD St. Andrew by the Bay Endowment Trust.
Goss, Francis G. '47 (BO) Brockton, MA Our Lady of Lourdes; Senior Priests Retired.
Goss, Joseph U. *o.p.* '55 (BR) Donaldsonville, LA Ascension of Our Lord Jesus Christ.
Gosselin, Andre *s.m.* '64 (PRT) Van Buren, ME St. Joseph; Van Buren, ME St. Bruno – St. Remi.
Gosselin, Fernand L. *m.m.* '70 (FgM).
Gosselin, G. Gerard '85 (PRT) Special or Other Diocesan Assignment.
Gosselin, Homer P. '69 (SPR) Ludlow, MA St. John the Baptist.
Gosselin, Larry *o.f.m.* (LSC) Presbyteral Council.
Gosselin, Lawrence '76 (NTN) Military Chaplains; Air Force Chaplains.
Gosselin, Richard R. '58 (BO) Ayer, MA St. Mary.
Gosselin, Robert H. '56 (BO) Senior Priests Retired.
Gossman, John A. '71 (DUB) Marion, IA St. Joseph; [D] Cedar Rapids, IA Xavier High School; Stewardship and Development Committee.
Goth, Dennis J. '84 (LFT) Muncie, IN St. Lawrence.
Gothe, Marcus '59 (P) Retired.
Gothie, George J. '67 (PAT) Hopatcong, NJ St. Jude's.
Gothing, Donald B. '65 (WOR) On Special or Other Diocesan Assignment; Holy Trinity.
Gothman, August (CR) Priests' Personnel Board.
Gotimer, James E. '53 (BRK) Elmhurst, NY St. Bartholomew's Retired.
Gott, Camillus *o.f.m.* '60 (STP)[P] Prior Lake, MN Franciscan Retreats.
Gottemoeller, Mark '76 (IND) Martinsville, IN St. Martin of Tours.
Gottemoller, Bartholomew *o.c.s.o.* '42 (SLC)[F] Huntsville, UT Abbey of Our Lady of the Holy Trinity of the Order of Cistercians.
Gottschalk, Dave *o.f.m.cap.* '69 (SAL)[E] Victoria, KS St. Fidelis Friary.
Gottschalk, David *o.f.m.cap.* '69 (SAL) Victoria, KS St. Fidelis; Victoria, KS St. Boniface.
Gottschalk, Matthew *o.f.m.cap.* '53 (MIL)[X] Whitefish Bay, WI Association of Ladies of Charity of Milwaukee, Wisconsin; [X] Milwaukee, WI House of Peace.
Gotwalt, Joseph F. '65 (HBG) Hanover, PA St. Joseph; Deans.
Goudreau, Joseph L. '63 (PRT) Military Chaplains; Army Chaplains.
Goudreau, Paul '60 (SP) Hudson, FL St. Michael.
Goudreau, William G. *s.j.* '52 (FgM).
Gouger, John *c.ss.r.* '65 (FgM).
Gouin, Joseph O. '65 (MAR) Kingsford, MI American Martyrs.
Goul, Richard G. '68 (DUB) Monona, IA St. Bridget's.
Gould, Clayton '81 (LR) West Memphis, AR St. Michael's; West Memphis, AR Sacred Heart Church; West Memphis, AR St. Mary of the Lake Church
Gould, James G. *s.j.* '74 (MI) Cathedral of the Assumption; Outer Island Parish; Vocations.
Gould, James C. *s.j.* (MI) Majuro, MH.
Gould, James R. '81 (ARL) Fairfax Station, VA St. Raymond of Penafort.
Gould, Lawrence *s.a.c.* (MO).
Gould, Louis J. '62 (WOR)[K] Worcester, MA Saint Vincent Hospital, Inc..
Gould, Michael A. *m.m.* '54 (FgM).
Gould, William R. '65 (B) Post Falls, ID St. George's.
Gould, William (B) College of Consultors.
Goulding, Laurence *g.h.m.* '62 (SAV) Waynesboro, GA Sacred Heart.
Gouldrick, John W. *c.m.* '69 (PH).
Gouldrick, John W. *c.m.* (PRT)[AA] Lewiston, ME Holy Family; Vicars for Priests; Ex Officio; Vicars for Priests.
Goulet, Raymond O. '57 (BO) Senior Priests Retired.
Goulet, Wayne F. '74 (PHX) Special Assignment.
Gourchin, Vincent '55 (SLC) Retired.
Goupil, Ronald R. '00 (MAN) North Conway, NH Our Lady of the Mountains; Absent on Sick Leave.
Gousse, Paul M. '99 (MAN) Concord, NH Immaculate Heart of Mary.
Gouthro, Arthur *s.a.* '69 (BO)[O] Brockton, MA Chapel of Our Savior–Catholic Pastoral and Information Center; [V] Brockton, MA Chapel of Our Savior; [AA] Brockton, MA Chapel of Our Saviour.
Govern, William H. '34 (RVC) Retired.
Governale, Russell *o.f.m.conv.* '88 (BRK) Brooklyn, NY Most Holy Trinity; Presbyteral Council.
Govindu, Balaswamy (SFR) San Francisco, CA St. Brendan; Laguna Honda Home.
Gowen, Daniel F. '89 (TR) Highlands, NJ Our Lady of Perpetual Help.
Gower, James M. '53 (PRT) Retired.
Gower, Peter J. '84 (PRO) Warren, RI St. Jean Baptiste; Warren, RI St. Mary of the Bay.
Gowing, Thomas '69 (SR) Garberville, CA Our Lady of the Redwoods; Scotia, CA St. Patrick.
Goyeneche, Venancio *c.m.* '57 (NY) New York, NY Holy Agony; [EE] New York, NY Vincentian Fathers.
Goyette, Giles R. *o.mar.* '82 (SAM)[C] Petersham, MA Most Holy Trinity Monastery.
Gozaloff, Paul J. '56 (WDC) Mechanicsville, MD Immaculate Conception.
Graap, Augustine *o.carm.* '66 (NY) Mid–Orange Correctional Facility; Otisville Correctional Facility.
Grab, Michael J. '77 (HBG) Lancaster, PA Sacred Heart of Jesus.
Grabarz, Casimir F. *c.s.c.* '39 (FTW)[I] Notre Dame, IN Holy Cross House.
Grabert, Colman *o.s.b.* '65 (IND)[K] St. Meinrad, IN St. Meinrad Archabbey.
Grabish, John J. '72 (ALN) Allentown, PA Our Lady of Mt. Carmel; Allentown, PA Sacred Heart of Jesus.
Grabner, Donald *o.s.b.* '54 (KC)[A] Conception, MO Conception Seminary College; [J] Kansas City, MO.
Grabner, Kenneth E. *c.s.c.* '60 (FTW)[I] Notre Dame, IN Holy Cross College.
Grabner, Kenneth *c.s.c.* '60 (FTW)[I] Notre Dame, IN Holy Cross Village.
Grabner, Robert J. '00 (STP) St. Paul, MN St. Vincent de Paul.
Grabner, Robert '99 (STP) Ministry to Hmong.
Grabnickas, Antana '85 (PRT)[I] Kennebunkport, ME St. Anthony's Friary.
Grabowski, Eugene '89 (R) Wrightsville Beach, NC St. Therese.
Grabowski, Walter P. '81 (BUF) Eden, NY Immaculate Conception.
Grabowsky, Myron '67 (PHU) Bristol, PA St. Mary's; Pro–Life and Family Ministry.
Grabrian, Dennis '70 (COS) On Duty Outside Diocese.
Grabrian, John '70 (DEN) Lakewood, CO Christ on the Mountain Parish.
Grabys, Joseph '49 (ALB) Retired.
Grace, Edward D. '67 (CHI) Skokie, IL St. Peter; Deans.
Grace, Edward G. *o.s.a.* '41 (CHI)[N] Olympia Fields, IL Tolentine Monastery at Tolentine Center.
Grace, Floyd A. (NY) Bronx, NY St. Frances de Chantal.
Grace, Gerald *s.s.e.* '55 (VEN)[G] Englewood, FL Society of St. Edmund Residence.
Grace, Gerald '65 (PMB) Highland Beach, FL St. Lucy; College of Consultors; Presbyteral Council.
Grace, Hugh R. '64 (NY) Saugerties, NY St. Mary of the Snow.
Grace, James N. '59 (CHI) Retired.
Grace, James P. '61 (BRK) Flushing NY St. Andrew Avellino.
Grace, John A. '79 (RIC) Harrisonburg, VA Blessed Sacrament.
Grace, John J. '48 (SAC) South Lake Tahoe, CA St. Theresa Retired.
Grace, John J. (CHI) Chicago, IL St. Tarcissus Retired.
Grace, John M. '88 (MAN) Manchester, NH St. Marie; Manchester, NH Sacred Heart of Jesus.
Grace, John *o.s.a.* '62 (ORG) Buena Park, CA St. Pius V.
Grace, Joseph W. '53 (LFT) U.S. Veteran's Hospital.
Grace, Joseph W. (FTW).
Grace, Peter *c.p.* '78 (BRK)[V] Jamaica, NY Immaculate Conception Monastery.
Grace, Robert S. '55 (WDC) Retired.
Gracey, John '93 (FRS) California City, CA Our Lady of Lourdes.
Gracz, Henry C. '65 (ATL) Atlanta, GA Shrine of the Immaculate Conception.
Graczyk, Carl *o.f.m.* '73 (PH)[D] Philadelphia, PA Archbishop Ryan High School; [AA] Philadelphia, PA St. Pius X Friary.
Graczyk, Glen '81 (MIL) Personal Leave.
Graczyk, Randolph *o.f.m.cap.* '68 (DET) Pryor, MT St. Charles Borromeo Mission; [K] Detroit, MI Provincialate.
Grad, Malcolm S. '58 (CIN) On Special and Archdiocesan Assignment; Office of the Archbishop; Vice Chancellor; Pastoral Council Secretariat.
Graden, John *o.s.f.s.* '76 (BUF)[T] Stella Niagara, NY DeSales Resources and Ministries.
Gradilone, Thomas '25 (BRK) Retired.
Grady, Bernard C. '68 (DUB) Marshalltown, IA St. Mary; Priests Assigned to Hispanic Ministry; Stewardship and Development Committee.
Grady, Brian D. (RCK) Rockford, IL Holy Family.
Grady, Donald F. *s.j.* '44 (BO)[V] Weston, MA Campion Health Center, Inc..
Grady, Francis J. *s.s.c.* '63 (CHI) Forest Park, IL St. Bernardine.
Grady, James P. '77 (STL) St. Louis, MO Holy Innocents.
Grady, John P. *m.m.* '55 (NY).
Grady, L. Augustine *s.j.* '46 (NY)[EE] Loyola Hall, Jesuit Community.
Grady, Michael '94 (MIA) Hollywood, FL Nativity.
Grady, Peter W. '53 (FAR) Retired.
Graef, Franz '57 (SHP) Shreveport, LA Holy Trinity.
Graef, Franz (SHP) Judges; College of Consultors; Presbyteral Council; Censor of Books; Church Vocations Board.
Graehler, Kenneth '63 (EVN) Retired.
Graf, Gary M. '84 (CHI) Waukegan, IL Holy Family.
Graf, Henry C. '49 (PH) Retired.
Graf, Herbert *o.f.m.conv.* '59 (SAV) Carey, OH Our Lady of Consolation, Basilica–National Shrine.
Graf, James W. '72 (L) Raywick, KY St. Vincent de Paul; Ex Officio; Raywick, KY St. Francis Xavier Church.
Graf, John W. '74 (PH) West Grove, PA Assumption B.V.M..
Graf, Paul '82 (LFT)[C] Lafayette, IN St. Elizabeth Medical Center.
Graf, William E. '60 (ROC) Fairport, NY Church of the Resurrection; Censores Librorum; Staff; Clergy Relief Society.
Graf, William (ROC) Ministry to Priests.
Graff, Francis C. '65 (PIT) New Castle, PA St. Camillus; Lawrence County, PA Almira Home; Lawrence County, PA Belvedere Residence, Inc.; Lawrence County, PA Golden Hill Nursing, Inc.; Lawrence County, PA Haven Convalescent Home; Lawrence County, PA Highland Hall Care Center; Lawrence County, PA Hillview Manor; Lawrence County, PA Indian Creek Nursing Home; Lawrence County, PA Jack Rees Nursing and Rehabilitation Center; Lawrence County, PA Overlook Nursing Home; Lawrence County, PA Castle Manor; Lawrence County, PA Cedar Manor; Lawrence County, PA Majors Manor; Lawrence County, PA Shenango United Presbyterian Home; Lawrence County, PA Silver Oak Nursing.
Graff, J. Austin '36 (CHI) Chicago, IL St. Thomas More Retired.
Graff, Joseph P. '76 (GAY) Harbor Springs, MI Holy Childhood of Jesus.
Graff, Robert L. '52 (TUC) Retired.
Graff, Timothy G. '85 (NEW) Lodi, NJ St. Francis de Sales.
Graffis, Joseph T. '71 (L) Louisville, KY St. Edward.
Graffius, Peregrine M. *o.s.m.* '59 (CHI)[I] Anaheim, CA Servite Fathers and Brothers; [I] Anaheim, CA Seven Holy Founders Priory; [N] Chicago Order of Friar Servants of Mary (Servites) United States of America Province, Inc..
Grafsky, George J. '71 (STP) Le Sueur, MN St. Anne; Montgomery, MN Holy Redeemer; Shieldsville, MN St. Patrick; Archdiocesan Consultors.
Graham, D. Clifford *o.m.v.* '81 (BO).
Graham, Edgar B. *s.j.* '54 (BAL)[B] Baltimore, MD Immaculate Heart of Mary; [B] Timonium, MD Loyola Graduate Center –Timonium Campus; [B] Jesuit Community of Loyola College, Inc..
Graham, Edgar *s.j.* '54 (BAL)[S] Baltimore, MD Jesuit Community of Loyola College, Inc..
Graham, George Nelson (LC) Rudolph, WI St. Philip; Wisconsin Rapids, WI St. Lawrence.
Graham, George P. '52 (RVC) Levittown, NY St. Bernard; Censors of Books; Judges for Interdiocesan Tribunal; Priests' Retirement Board; Catholic Lawyer's Guild Retired.

Graham, Gilbert J. *o.p.* '49 (CHI)[N] St. Pius V Priory.
Graham, J. David '91 (MEM) Lexington, TN St. Andrew.
Graham, James G. '66 (PIT) Pittsburgh, PA St. Lawrence O'Toole.
Graham, James J. '73 (PH) North Wales, PA St. Rose of Lima; Judicial Vicar.
Graham, James K. '93 (NTN) San Jose, CA St. Elias; San Jose, CA St. John Vianney.
Graham, James P. *c.m.* '37 (STL)[O] Earth City, MO Vincentian Foreign Mission Society; [O] Perryville, MO Congregation of the Mission.
Graham, James (NTN) Associates:.
Graham, Jerry S. *s.j.* '66 (P) Missoula, MT St. Francis Xavier.
Graham, John K. *c.ss.r.* '53 (NY) New York, NY St. Cecilia.
Graham, John K. '74 (NY)[E] New York, NY Cardinal Hayes High School.
Graham, John *c.ss.r.* '53 (ALB)[L] Saratoga Springs, NY St. John Neumann Residence.
Graham, Joseph B. '63 (PH) Philadelphia, PA St. Jerome.
Graham, Michael J. *s.j.* '88 (CIN)[D] Cincinnati, OH Xavier University; [M] Cincinnati, OH Jesuit Community at Xavier University.
Graham, Neil '59 (NY) White Plains, NY St. John the Evangelist.
Graham, Raymond *s.m.m.* '47 (RVC)[M] Eastport, NY Shrine of Our Lady of the Island.
Graham, Robert *s.m.* '50 (BO)[W] Framingham, MA Fontbonne Hall; [X] Framingham, MA The Marist House.
Graham, Thomas A. '62 (BRK) Rosedale, NY St. Pius X; Home School Association.
Graham, Thomas D. '48 (PH) Retired.
Graham, Walter F. *c.m.* '49 (BRK)[V] Jamaica, NY Vincentian Residence.
Graham, William C. '76 (DUL) On Duty Outside the Diocese.
Graham, William P. '65 (CAM) Lindenwold, NJ St. Lawrence's; Camden South Deanery.
Graham, William *o.f.m.cap.* '72 (WDC)[B] Washington, DC St. Francis Friary–Capuchin College.
Graia, Paul (CC)[G] Robstown, TX Society of Our Lady of the Most Holy Trinity.
Grajeda, Miguel A. '97 (MRY) Salinas, CA Christ the King.
Grajeda, Miguel (MRY) Presbyteral Council.
Grajek, Lawrence '57 (SB) Retired.
Gralapp, Robert W. '64 (SC) Manilla, IA Sacred Heart; Ecumenical Commission.
Gralinski, Thomas J. '41 (HBG) Lancaster, PA Assumption of the Blessed Virgin Mary.
Gramaje, Art *c.m.f.* '94 (LA)[Q] Los Angeles, CA Prov. Headquarters of the Western Prov. of the USA.
Gramajo, Rodolfo '92 (SR) Napa, CA St. John the Baptist.
Gramata, Raymond '70 (E) Sheffield, PA St. Anthony; Warren State Hospital; [G] Erie, PA Saint Vincent Health Center.
Grambow, Arnold J. '69 (MAR) Gladstone, MI All Saints.
Gramigna, Francis J. '64 (CAM) Barrington, NJ St. Francis de Sales.
Grams, Douglas L. '87 (NU) New Ulm, MN St. Mary; Vicar General; Associate Judges; College of Consultors; Committee on Parishes; Corporate Board; Priests' Council; Priest Personnel; Priest Personnel Board; Bishop's Delegate in Matters Pertaining to Sexual Misconduct; Board of Trustees for Pension Plan for Priests; On Special or Other Diocesan Assignment.
Gramza, Ronald J. (MIL) Deans.
Gramza, Ronald '73 (MIL) South Milwaukee, WI Divine Mercy.
Gran, Thomas '50 (PBR) Retired.
Granadino, David F. '81 (LA) Azusa, CA St. Frances of Rome.
Granadino, David '81 (LA) On Administrative Leave.
Granados, Carlos E. '88 (ARE) Arecibo, PR Church of Santa Cecilia; Director of Youth; Pastoral Vocational Program.
Granados, Carlos Santiago '84 (SAV) Lakeland, GA Queen of Peace.
Granata, Joseph P. '75 (RVC) Central Islip, NY St. John of God; Port Washington, NY Our Lady of Fatima.
Granato, Anthony F. '56 (NEW) East Newark, NJ St. Anthony's.
Granato, Joseph J. '55 (NEW) Newark, NJ St. Lucy's.
Granato, Marius *o.c.s.o.* '64 (WOR)[O] Spencer, MA St. Joseph's Abbey.
Grancini, Steven M. *c.r.s.p.* '57 (SD) San Diego, CA Our Lady of the Rosary.
Grande, Bernadine *c.p.* '45 (BO)[V] Boston, MA St. Gabriel Passionist Community.
Grande, Bernardine *c.p.* (BO) Brighton, MA St. Gabriel.
Grande, Kenneth J. (BRK) Brooklyn, NY St. Nicholas.
Grandi, Nelson '80 (MIA) Silver Spring, MD Our Lady of Fatima Parish; Silver Spring, MD St. Bernadette.
Grandstrand, Charles P. (NEW) Northeast Bergen Region Deanery 2.
Graner, Thomas M. '94 (FAR) Rolette, ND Sacred Heart; Judges.
Graner, Thomas '94 (FAR) Rolette, ND Holy Rosary; Willow City, ND Notre Dame des Victoires; Rural Life.
Graney, William F. '71 (WIL) Claymont, DE Holy Rosary; Wilmington, DE Wilmington Hospital.
Granfield, David *o.s.b.* '52 (WDC)[M] Washington, DC St. Anselm's Abbey.
Granfield, Patrick *o.s.b.* '57 (WDC)[C] Catholic University of America, The; [M] Washington, DC St. Anselm's Abbey.
Grange, John '66 (NY) Bronx, NY St. Jerome's.
Granich, Bernard '44 (STL)[N] Kirkwood, MO St. Agnes Home for the Elderly.
Granillo, Paul C. (SB) Administrative Assistant to the Bishop, Priest Secretary & Director of Catholic Communications.
Granillo, Paul (SB) Riverside, CA St. Catherine of Alexandria; Special or Other Diocesan Assignment; [I] San Bernardino, CA Caritas Telecommunications; Appointed Members; Diocesan Curia; College of Consultors; The Ministry of Communications; Caritas Telecommunications; Moreno Valley, CA St. Patrick.
Granito, Mark E. '98 (SFE) Abiquiu, NM St. Thomas Apostle; Tijeras, NM Holy Child.
Grankauskas, Paul M. '00 (ARL) Fairfax, VA St. Mary of Sorrows; Notaries.
Grankowski, Zbigniew '83 (DET) Detroit, MI St. Cunegunda; Dearborn, MI St. Barbara.
Granstrand, Charles P. '66 (NEW) Park Ridge, NJ Our Lady of Mercy.
Grant, Frederick A. '62 (BO) Senior Priests Retired.
Grant, James A. '66 (PH) Warrington, PA St. Joseph.
Grant, James '56 (SPK) Retired.
Grant, James (PHU) Defender of the Bond.
Grant, Jeffery A. '82 (SFD) Decatur, IL St. Patrick; Decatur, IL St. James.
Grant, Matthew '30 (BRK) Retired.
Grant, Robert J. '93 (HRT) Windsor, CT St. Gabriel's; Enfield, CT Carl Robinson Correctional Institution; Enfield, CT Willard–Cybulski Correction Institute.
Grant, Robert L. '80 (DAV)[B] Davenport, IA St. Ambrose University; [B] St. Ambrose University.
Grant, Robert '84 (DM) On Duty Outside the Diocese.
Grant, Robert '93 (HRT) Suffield, CT Walker RSMU.
Grant, W. Douglas '80 (PRO) North Providence, RI Mary, Mother of Mankind.
Grant, William D. (LIN) Commission for Sacred Liturgy and Sacred Music; Diocesan Area CCD Directors; Diocesan Director of Liturgy; Evangelization Committee.
Grant, William David '86 (LIN) Fairbury, NE St. Michael's.
Grant, Zachary *o.f.m.cap.* (BO)[V] Boston, MA St. Benedict the Moor Friary.
Grantz, Leon *c.p.* (CHI)[M] Park Ridge, IL Resurrection Nursing and Rehabilitation Center; [N] Chicago, IL Passionist Community–Immaculate Conception Monastery.
Granville, William A. '43 (BO) Stoughton, MA New England Sinai Hospital; Senior Priests Retired.
Granzotto, Peter *s.d.b.* '57 (NY) Port Chester, NY Corpus Christi.
Grappoli, Frank B. *s.x.* '63 (PAT)[M] Wayne, NJ Xaverian Missionary Fathers; (FgM).
Graselli, Renato (NEW) Members.
Grasha, Donald F. '84 (LA) Temple City, CA St. Luke the Evangelist.
Grasher, Al '86 (SPK) Deer Park, WA St. Mary's Presentation.
Grasing, John '88 (WIL) Newark, DE Holy Family.
Grass, Aloysius P. *c.m.* '51 (PH)[AA] St. Catherine Infirmary.
Grass, Don C. '61 (GRY) Crown Point, IN St. Mary.
Grass, Kenneth E. *c.m.* '56 (STL)[O] Perryville, MO Congregation of the Mission.
Grasselli, Renato '94 (NEW)[A] Kearny, NJ Redemptoris Mater; College of Consultors; Priestly Vocation Board.
Grassi, Dominic J. '73 (CHI) Chicago, IL St. Josaphat.
Grassi, Timothy J. '00 (WH) Charleston, WV Sacred Heart Co–Cathedral.
Grassl, Joseph A. '50 (LC) Mosinee, WI St. Francis Xavier; Mosinee, WI St. John the Baptist.
Grasso, Aldo *o.s.j.* '44 (MRY)[F] Shrine of St. Joseph.
Grasso, Anthony R. *c.s.c.* '78 (SCR)[C] Kings College; [C] Holy Cross Community.
Grasso, Antonio *c.s.* (LA) Sun Valley, CA Our Lady of the Holy Rosary.
Grasso, Joseph A. *c.pp.s.* '90 (ROC)[C] Rochester, NY Siena Catholic Academy; [I] Rochester, NY Missionaries of the Precious Blood.
Grasso, Philip A. '43 (MAD) Retired.
Grasso, Richard E. '63 (ORL) Retired.
Grasso, Richard '63 (PAT) On Duty Outside the Diocese.
Grathwohl, John M. '55 (KAL) Portage, MI St. Catherine of Siena Retired.
Gratkowski, Eugene W. '67 (CHI) Chicago, IL St. John Berchmans.
Grattaroti, Robert A. '62 (WOR) Charlton City, MA St. Joseph's; Cursillo.
Gratto, Stephen H. '73 (OG) Brasher Falls, NY St. Patrick; Brasher Falls, NY St. Lawrence.
Grauel, Frank B. '84 (L) Louisville, KY Holy Spirit Retired.
Grauls, Paul *s.d.b.* '62 (NY) New York, NY St. Thomas the Apostle.
Grave de Peralta, Miguel '97 (NTN) Augusta, GA St. Ignatios of Antioch.
Gravel, Claude J. *o.ss.t.* '81 (PH) Bristol, PA St. Ann.
Gravel, Claude *o.ss.t.* '81 (BAL)[S] Bristol, PA.
Graven, John P. '57 (FAR) On Duty Outside the Diocese; Anaheim, CA Retired.
Graven, Thomas J. '68 (STU) Maynard, OH St. Joseph; Maynard, OH St. Stanislaus.
Graves, Clarence Edwin '92 (LR) Wynne, AR St. Peter's; Deans.
Graves, Edwin '92 (LR) Forrest City, AR St. Francis of Assisi; Wynne, AR St. Mary Church.
Graves, W. Robert *c.s.sp.* '50 (VEN)[G] Sarasota, FL Congregation of the Holy Ghost.
Grawe, Michael *o.f.m.* '70 (FgM).
Gray, Brian M. '86 (BGP) New Fairfield, CT St. Edward the Confessor; Danbury, CT Danbury Hospital.
Gray, Daniel J. '76 (PRO) Portsmouth, RI St. Anthony.
Gray, Edward J. *c.ss.r.* '58 (CHL) Concord, NC St. James.
Gray, Francis Jerome '49 (CHI)[N] Chicago, IL St. Peter's Friary.
Gray, Howard J. *s.j.* '61 (CLV)[B] Cleveland, OH John Carroll University.
Gray, Howard *s.j.* '61 (CLV)[B] University Heights, OH John Carroll University.
Gray, Hugh *s.j.* '55 (SJ)[M] Los Gatos, CA Sacred Heart Jesuit Center.
Gray, Jack (PT) Priests' Pension Plan, Board for.
Gray, James C. '88 (STL) St. Louis, MO St. Boniface; Barnes – Jewish Hospital.
Gray, Jason A. '97 (PEO) Peoria, IL St. Peter's; Divine Worship, Office of.
Gray, Jason (PEO) Vice Chancellors.
Gray, John F. '86 (PT) Pensacola, FL St. Anne's.
Gray, John W. '58 (PRO) Retired.
Gray, John (PT) Ecumenical & Interreligious Affairs, Office of.
Gray, Jude J. *o.s.b.* '68 (MAN)[K] Manchester, NH St. Anselm Abbey.
Gray, Kevin J. '84 (HRT) Waterbury, CT Sacred Heart–Sagrado Corazon; Waterbury, CT St. Anne; [T] Waterbury, CT Spanish–Speaking Center.
Gray, Paul '85 (DAL) Dallas, TX All Saints; Prison Ministry.
Gray, Philip A. '60 (SCR) Scranton, PA St. Francis; Deans; Diocesan Building Commission.
Gray, Robert B. '57 (L) Louisville, KY St. Elizabeth of Hungary; Louisville, KY St. Therese Retired.
Gray, Robert '88 (SJ) On Leave of Absence.
Gray, Ronald *o.carm.* '43 (NEW).
Gray, Tim *s.c.j.* (GAL) Central Vicariate.
Gray, Timothy J. *s.c.j.* '78 (GAL) Houston, TX Our Lady of Guadalupe.
Gray Marks, Teodoro '49 (SJN) Retired.
Graziadio, Domenick T. '66 (RVC) Plainview, NY St. Pius X; Judges for Interdiocesan Tribunal.
Graziani, Joseph A. '45 (HRT) Retired.
Graziano, Damien (JOL) Propagation of the Faith.
Graziano, Gerard J. '61 (NEW) Hackensack, NJ Immaculate Conception.
Graziano, J. Damien '67 (JOL) Oakbrook Terrace, IL Ascension of Our Lord.
Graziano, Peter N. '63 (FR) Attleboro Falls, MA St. Mark's.
Grazulis, Antanas *s.j.* (LIT) Lithuanian Jesuit Province.
Grbes, Jozo *o.f.m.* '93 (CHI) Chicago, IL St. Jerome.
Greaney, Thomas M. *o.s.m.* '70 (CHI)[N] Chicago, IL Monastery of Our Lady of Sorrows.
Greany, Brendan P. *c.ss.r.* '63 (HBG) Ephrata, PA Mother of Perpetual Help.
Greany, Brendan *c.ss.r.* '63 (HBG)[H] Ephrata, PA St. Clement's Mission House.
Greatorex, Robert W. '57 (LC)[I] Stevens Point, WI St. Joseph Congregational Home Retired.
Greaves, Gerald (NEW) Members.
Greaves, John G. '58 (PRO) Retired.
Greb, Michael *o.f.m.cap.* '89 (PIT)[M] Wheeling, WV Capuchin Hermitage of St. Joseph.
Grebasch, Richard L. '58 (MIL) Retired.
Grecco, Robert J. '93 (PIT) Pittsburgh, PA St. Paul Cathedral; Bishop's Office; Bishop, Office of the Diocesan.
Grech, Garvin *o.carm.* (CHI)[N] Chicago, IL Brandsma House.
Grech, Joseph '52 (MRY) Retired.
Greco, Anthony F. '79 (WIL) Secretary, MD Our Lady of Good Counsel.
Greco, Raymond '63 (PHX) Sun City, AZ St. Elizabeth Seton.

Greco, Raymond *o.s.b.* '63 (MRY)[F] San Luis Obispo, CA Men's Residence Retired.
Greco, Robert *o.carm.* '55 (NY) Middletown, NY Our Lady of Mt. Carmel.
Greeley, Andrew M. '54 (CHI) Retired.
Greeley, Joseph F. '74 (LA) Lakewood, CA St. Pancratius.
Green, Austin E. *o.p.* '53 (DAL)[K] Irving, TX Dominican Priory of St. Albert the Great; Ministries to People with Disabilities.
Green, Bernard *s.d.s.* '73 (GLP) Cibecue, AZ St. Catherine.
Green, Charles C. '95 (WDC) Washington, DC St. Augustine.
Green, David E. '88 (PRO) Carolina, RI St. Mary.
Green, Gerard L. '56 (BUF) Council of Priests Retired.
Green, Gregory A. *c.s.c.* '62 (FTW)[B] University of Notre Dame Du Lac; [I] Notre Dame, IN Holy Cross Community, Corby Hall, University of Notre Dame.
Green, James P. '76 (PH) On Duty Outside the Archdiocese.
Green, Michael R. *o.s.b.* '70 (DET)[B] Oxford, MI St. Benedict Monastery.
Green, Romuald *o.f.m.* '55 (WDC)[M] Silver Spring, MD Gemelli House.
Green, Ron (MRY) Vocations Board; Permanent Diaconate Advisory Board.
Green, Ronald L. *m.m.* '85 (NY)[EE] Maryknoll Maryknoll Fathers and Brothers.
Green, Ronald L. '96 (MRY) King City, CA St. John the Baptist.
Green, Ronald (NY) Manhattan, NY Terence Cardinal Cooke Health Care Center.
Green, Thomas J. '63 (BGP) On Duty Outside the Diocese; [C] Catholic University of America, The.
Green, Thomas P. *s.j.* '61 (NY) New York, NY St. Aloysius.
Green, William H. '63 (SUP) Cable, WI St. Ann; Hayward, WI St. Joseph's; Pastoral Consultors; St. Pius Priest Fund.
Greenburg, Alcuin E. '55 (GAL)[N] Houston, TX Pope John Paul XXIII Priests' Residence.
Greene, Daniel '58 (ORL) Orlando, FL Mary Queen of the Universe Shrine Retired.
Greene, Francis J. *o.s.f.s.* '48 (WIL)[J] Childs, MD Retirement and Assisted Care Facility.
Greene, Gordon L. '94 (KAL) Albion, MI St. John the Evangelist.
Greene, J. Gerard *m.m.* '43 (NY).
Greene, John C. '85 (GAY)[EE] Absent on Leave.
Greene, John L. '76 (SFR) San Francisco, CA St. Monica; San Francisco Fire Department.
Greene, Michael *c.p.* '82 (BRK)[V] Jamaica NY Immaculate Conception Monastery; [X] Jamaica, NY Bishop Molloy Retreat House for Laymen; Released from Diocesan Assignment.
Greene, Padraig '76 (OAK) Pleasanton, CA The Catholic Community of Pleasanton.
Greene, Richard *v.e.* '65 (LAF) Patterson, LA St. Joseph; South Region.
Greene, Robert W. *m.m.* '37 (NY).
Greene, Thomas S. '55 (SPR)[H] Springfield, MA St. Michael's Residence Retired.
Greene, William L. '50 (BR) Judges Retired.
Greenfield, James J. *o.s.f.s.* '90 (WDC)[S] Washington, DC George Washington Univ. Newman Center.
Greenhalgh, Donald C. '84 (ARL) Fairfax, VA St. Mary of Sorrows; Deans.
Greenlaw, Martin '68 (SFR) Retired.
Greenleaf, Daniel P. '95 (PRT) Special or Other Diocesan Assignment.
Greenough, Patrick *o.f.m.conv.* '88 (CHI)[N] Libertyville, IL Marytown, Our Lady of Fatima Friary; [Q] Libertyville, IL Marytown, U.S. National Center of the Militia of the Immaculata Movement.
Greenwald, Alfred E. '58 (GAL) Retired.
Greenwald, Alfred (TUC)[D] Tucson, AZ St. Mary's Hospital.
Greenway, George G. '87 (SPR) Retired.
Greenwell, Charles C. '82 (SAN) San Angelo, TX Holy Angels.
Greenwell, Charles (SAN) Defensores Vinculi; Priests' Pension Plan.
Greenwell, Joseph M. *c.ss.r* '48 (STL)[O] Liguori, MO St. Clement Health Care Center.
Greenwell, Michael *o.carm.* '79 (JOL)[L] Darien Carmelite Provincial Office.
Greenwell, Michael *o.carm.* '79 (SFR) Kaiser Hospital San Francisco; St. Mary's Medical Center.
Greenwood, Kevin L. '90 (STU) Absent on Leave.
Greer, G. Michael '81 (COV) Erlanger, KY St. Barbara.
Greer, Jack '02 (SJ) Cupertino, CA St. Joseph of Cupertino.
Greer, Michael '75 (MIA) Miami, FL Good Shepherd; Spiritual Moderators; Worship & Spiritual Life Commission.
Grega, Bernard F. '62 (ALT) Colver, PA Holy Family.
Gregoire, Paul L. (MAN) Dover, NH St. Charles; Clergy Personnel Board.
Gregoire, Wilfrid G. '56 (PRO) Westerly RI Immaculate Conception; Council Members.
Gregor, Robert M. *c.p.m.* (OWN)[F] Auburn, KY Fathers of Mercy.
Gregorek, Joseph C. '65 (E)[B] Erie, PA Gannon University; Deans.
Gregorek, Stan M. '66 (PIT) Natrona Heights, PA Our Lady of the Most Blessed Sacrament; [H] Wildwood, PA Cursillo Movement–Diocese of Pittsburgh.
Gregori, Anthony F. '53 (GF) Retired.
Gregori, Emidio O. '58 (BGP) Retired.
Gregori Costa, Vicente *rr.t.c.* '72 (SJN)[F] Santurce, PR Casa Manuel Fernandez Juncos.
Gregorie, Jocelyn *c.s.sp.* '86 (PIT)[B] Pittsburgh, PA Duquesne University of the Holy Spirit.
Gregorio, Robert J. '68 (CAM) Blue Anchor NJ Blessed John the Twenty–Third; Members.
Gregoris, Nicholas L. '97 (SCR) On Duty Outside the Diocese.
Gregoris, Nicholas '97 (SCR) Omaha, NE St. Anthony.
Gregory, James T. '99 (HRT) Torrington, CT St. Francis of Assisi; Torrington, CT Sacred Heart Torrington, CT St. Mary's; Torrington, CT St. Peter's.
Gregory, Kenneth '73 (ALB) Berlin, NY Sacred Heart; Grafton, NY St. John Francis Regis; Albany Medical Center Hospital; Special Assignment; [C] Watervliet, NY St. Colman's Home; [M] Watervliet, NY St. Colman's Convent.
Gregory, Peter A. '73 (SPR) Pittsfield, MA St. Charles.
Gregory, Robert S. '69 (KC) Kansas City, MO St. Elizabeth's.
Grehl, Paul F. *o.s.f.s.* '60 (LAN) Southern Michigan Prison; [B] Jackson, MI Lumen Christi Catholic High School; College of Consultors; Cooper Street Correctional Facility.
Grehl, Paul F. *o.s.f.s.* '79 (LAN) Manitou Beach, MI St. Mary on the Lake.
Greig, Harry D. '76 (LKC) Big Lake, LA St. Mary of the Lake; Defenders of the Bond.
Greig, Kenneth R. '67 (BEA) Diocesan Judges; Groves, TX St. Peter the Apostle.
Grein, Blaine *o.f.m.* (GLP) Ministry Formation Program.
Grein, Blane *o.f.m.* '62 (GLP) Chinle, AZ Our Lady of Fatima; [A] Chinle, AZ Native American Lay Ministry and Diaconate Program.
Greiner, James A. '63 (OKL) Mustang, OK Church of the Holy Spirit.
Greiner, James (OKL) Rural Life.
Greiner, Kenneth A. '53 (ALT) Retired.
Greiner, Lawrence '37 (SAG) Retired.
Greiner, Lawrence (SB) Retired.
Greiner, Robert '93 (BAK) Prineville, OR St. Joseph's.
Greisen, Thomas A. '82 (OM) Elkhorn, NE St. Patrick; Office for Lay Ministry Formation.
Greiten, Gregory J. '92 (MIL) Menomonee Falls, WI St. Mary.
Greiwe, Edward *o.s.c.* '64 (SCL)[I] Onamia, MN Crosier Monastery.
Grek, Richard *c.r.* '67 (CHI)[N] Woodstock, IL Resurrection Center Retreat House; [A] Woodstock, IL Resurrection Center Retreat House.
Greka, David E. '62 (GAY) Alpena, MI St. Bernard.
Greka, David '62 (AMA) On Duty Outside the Diocese.
Grelak, Andrew T. '71 (BO) Chelsea, MA St. Stanislaus.
Grell, Lonas K. '96 (LIN) Dwight, NE Assumption.
Grellinger, R. Michael '62 (MIL) Pewaukee, WI Queen of Apostles.
Grembla, Joseph P. '57 (CHI) Chicago, IL St. Francis Borgia Retired.
Grembocki, Joseph L. '71 (ALN) Slatington, PA Assumption B.V.M..
Gremillion, Rickey J. '98 (ALX) Deville, LA St. John the Baptist.
Gremmels, John '91 (FWT) Keller, TX St. Elizabeth Ann Seton; Mission Council.
Grenache, Claude *a.a.* '66 (BO)[V] Boston, MA Assumptionist Center; [BB] Waltham, MA Bentley College Spiritual Life Center.
Grendler, Albert O. '59 (SC) Spirit Lake, IA St. Mary's.
Grenham, John P. '80 (NO) Metairie, LA St. Benilde.
Grennan, James '44 (SAL) Retired.
Grennan, Larry (SAL) Personnel Board.
Grennan, Lawrence E. '66 (SAL) Manhattan, KS Seven Dolors.
Grennon, John *o.c.d.* '97 (BO)[V] Boston, MA Carmelite Monastery.
Grenon, Paul R. '78 (PRO) Coventry, RI SS. John and Paul.
Gres–Gayer, Jacques '69 (WDC)[C] Catholic University of America, The.
Greschel, Mark '01 (CHI) Chicago, IL St. Clement.
Greskiewicz, Joseph A. '69 (SCR) Plains, PA SS. Peter and Paul; Diocesan Building Commission.
Greskowiak, Neri *o.f.m.* '63 (PEO) Metamora, IL St. Mary of Lourdes.
Greskowiak, Stephen '89 (VNN) On Leave.
Gresock, Thomas G. '85 (BUF) Absent on Leave.
Gretchko, A. Edward '72 (Y) Massillon OH Saint Mary.
Gretchko, A. Edward '72 (PBR) Massillon, OH St. Nicholas.
Gretz, James R. '94 (PIT) Pittsburgh, PA St. Anne.
Grevatch, William N. '64 (LC) Wausau, WI St. Michael; College of Consultors; Consultors; Ex Officio Members.
Greving, Dan '97 (SC) Wesley, IA Sacred Heart.
Greving, Daniel M. '97 (SC) Wesley, IA St. Benedict's; Wesley, IA St. Joseph's.
Grewe, Michael W. (OM) Omaha, NE St. James; Vicar General; Consultors; Finance Council; Ex Officio.
Grey, Michael T. *c.s.sp.* '79 (GAL)[Q] Houston, TX Residence of the Basilian Fathers of the University of St. Thomas; [T] Houston, TX Rice University/Texas Medical Center Schools; Catholic Student Center.
Greytak, William '56 (HEL) Boulder, MT St. Catherine; Boulder River School and Hospital.
Grib, Philip J. *s.j.* '72 (CHI) Chicago, IL St. Eugene; [D] Chicago, IL St. Ignatius Jesuit Community.
Grib, Robert *s.j.* (CHI) Chicago, IL St. Juliana.
Gribbin, Robert C. '47 (HBG) Abbottstown, PA Immaculate Heart of Mary.
Gribble, G. Michael '81 (COL) Columbus, OH St. Joseph Cathedral; Priests' Senate; Diocesan Judges; Priests Continuing Education.
Gribble, Richard E. *c.s.c.* '89 (FR)[A] North Easton, MA Holy Cross Fathers Religious.
Gribble, Richard E. *c.s.c.* '89 (FTW)[I] North Easton, MA Stonehill College.
Gribble, Richard *c.s.c.* '89 (FR)[A] North Easton, MA Stonehill College.
Gribbon, John J. '50 (BRK) Douglaston, NY St. Anastasia.
Gribbon, Joseph *c.ss.r.* '56 (ORL)[E] New Smyrna Beach, FL St. Alphonsus Villa–Redemptorist Fathers and Brothers.
Gribbon, Joseph *c.ss.r.* '56 (ALB) AUXILIARY CHAPLAINS CONTRACT CHAPLAINS.
Gribbon, Michael C. '81 (BRK) Cambria Heights, NY Sacred Heart.
Gribik, John '89 (SJP) Jeannette, PA St. Demetrius.
Grice, Edward M. '80 (NO) Military Chaplains; Army Reserve Chaplains.
Grieco, Frank M. '01 (RVC) Deer Park, NY SS. Cyril and Methodius.
Grieco, Michael S. '83 (LA) Los Angeles, CA St. Martin of Tours.
Grieco, Nicholas V. '59 (BGP) Weston, CT St. Francis of Assisi; Diocesan Consultors; Presbyteral Council; Vicariate II (Norwalk, New Canaan, Wilton, Weston, Westport).
Grieman, Gerald G. '79 (STP) Retired.
Griener, George E. *s.j.* '73 (New Orleans)[N] Berkeley, CA Jesuit Community at Jesuit School of Theology at Berkeley.
Griener, George E. *s.j.* '73 (OAK).
Grier, Matthew *m.h.m.* '69 (NY)[EE] Hartsdale, NY Mill Hill Fathers Residence.
Gries, Andrew *o.c.s.o.* '59 (ARL)[J] Berryville, VA Cistercian Abbey of Our Lady of the Holy Cross.
Gries, Eugene *o.praem.* '68 (SFE) Albuquerque, NM Our Lady of Most Holy Rosary; [I] Albuquerque, NM Santa Maria de la Vid Priory.
Griesbach, John '76 (FRS) Advocates; Retreat Master; On Special Assignment.
Griesedieck, Edmund O. '65 (STL)[A] St. Louis, MO Kenrick School of Theology.
Griesemer, Edward *s.c.j.* '57 (MIL)[V] Wauwatosa, WI Milwaukee Archdiocesan Holy Name Union; [O] Franklin, WI Villa Maria.
Griffen, Robert '03 (RIC) Richmond, VA Our Lady of Lourdes.
Griffey, Brendan '74 (JC) Milan, MO St. Mary.
Griffin, Barry *s.d.s.* '64 (NSH) McMinnville, TN St. Catherine.
Griffin, Charles R. '56 (COL) Chillicothe, OH St. Peter; Chillicothe, OH Chillicothe Correctional Institution; Chillicothe, OH Ross Correctional Institution Retired.
Griffin, Charles T. '58 (BUF)[O] Tonawanda, NY O'Hara Residence Retired.
Griffin, David G. '66 (BUF) Niagara Falls, NY St. Leo.
Griffin, David R. *o.s.b.* '76 (ALT)[H] University Park, PA Penn State University; [I] University Park, PA Penn State Catholic Community.
Griffin, Devin *o.carm.* '75 (JOL).
Griffin, Edward V. *o.s.a.* '49 (PH) Philadelphia, PA St. Rita of Cascia.
Griffin, George J. (BAL) Interdiocesan Judges.
Griffin, James *c.m.f.* '48 (LA)[Q] Rancho Dominguez, CA Dominguez Seminary Inc..
Griffin, James '49 (NY) Retired.
Griffin, James '82 (RIC) Virginia Beach, VA St. Mark.
Griffin, John C. '77 (MRY) Carmel, CA San Carlos Borromeo Basilica; Deans; Diocesan Consultors; Advocates; Diocesan Consultors; Presbyteral Council; Priest's Personnel Board.
Griffin, John '72 (SR) Rohnert Park, CA St. Elizabeth Seton.
Griffin, John (MRY) Contact Persons.
Griffin, Joseph J. *o.s.f.s.* '56 (PH)[AA] Philadelphia, PA Father Louis Brisson Residence.
Griffin, Joseph M. '82 (SAG) Chesaning, MI Our Lady of Perpetual Help.
Griffin, Joseph '82 (SAG) Oakley, MI St. Michael.

Griffin, Joseph (SAG) Vicars for Vicariates.
Griffin, Michael J. '49 (MAN) Hampton, NH Our Lady of the Miraculous Medal Retired.
Griffin, Michael *o.c.d.* '50 (MIL)[O] Holy Hill, WI Discalced Carmelite Monastery – Holy Hill National Shrine of Mary Help of Christians.
Griffin, Michael '90 (SFS) Sioux Falls, SD Christ the King; Bishop's Bulletin.
Griffin, Noel '64 (LA) On Sick Leave.
Griffin, Patrick E. '67 (STP) Minneapolis, MN St. Stephen.
Griffin, Patrick J. '45 (COL) Retired.
Griffin, Patrick J. *c.m.* '79 (RVC)[A] Huntington, NY Diocesan Seminary of the Immaculate Conception; [M] Oyster Bay, NY Vincentian Community.
Griffin, Paul D. '95 (BGP) Leave of Absence.
Griffin, Robert E. *s.j.* '61 (SJ)[D] Mesa, ID Marymount Hermitage, Inc., Hermit Sisters of Mary.
Griffin, Robert F. '49 (MAN) Retired.
Griffin, Thomas A. *s.j.* '58 (MIA) Miami, FL Gesu.
Griffin, Thomas *o.s.a.* (CHI)[J] Chicago, IL Holy Cross Hospital; Navy Reserve Chaplains.
Griffith, Daniel F. '02 (STP) Lakeville, MN All Saints; Presbyteral Council.
Griffith, Darragh '97 (ATL) Toccoa, GA St. Mary's.
Griffith, Edwin '64 (LSC) Retired.
Griffith, Gavin *o.f.m.* '65 (MRY)[H] San Juan Bautista, CA St. Francis Retreat Center.
Griffith, Sidney H. *s.t.d.* '65 (WDC)[C] Catholic University of America, The; [M] Riverdale, MD Holy Spirit Missionary Cenacle.
Griffith, Sydney '61 (BAL) Glen Burnie, MD Holy Trinity.
Griffith, Thomas *s.v.d.* '69 (BO)[V] Duxbury, MA Society of the Divine Word.
Griffiths, James '56 (SJP) Retired.
Griffiths, John M. '76 (CHI) Chicago, IL Queen of Angels.
Griffiths, John (CHI) Judges.
Griffiths, Thomas *c.p.* '57 (BRK)[V] Jamaica, NY Immaculate Conception Monastery.
Grifone, Fabian *o.f.m.* '54 (NY) New York, NY Most Precious Blood.
Grigus, John *o.f.m.conv.* (CHI)[N] Libertyville, IL Marytown, Our Lady of Fatima Friary.
Grigus, Paschal *o.f.m.* '53 (MIL)[O] Burlington, WI Queen of Peace Friary.
Grile, Harry A. *c.ss.r.* '68 (STL)[O] Liguori, MO Liguori Mission House/Redemptorists; [U] Liguori, MO Redemptorist Fathers dba Liguori Publications.
Grile, Patrick *c.ss.r.* '71 (STP) Brooklyn Center, MN St. Alphonsus.
Grill, Philip L. '43 (LA) Retired.
Grilliot, Thomas J. '76 (CIN) Piqua, OH St. Mary.
Grimaldi, Joseph A. '62 (HON)[I] Kaneohe, HI Augustine Educational Foundation; Vicars General; Vice–Chancellor; Judicial Vicar; Judges; Commission Members; Administrative Council; Bishop's Administrative Advisory Council; Clergy Personnel Board; College of Consultors; Finance Committee; Presbyteral Council; Senior Priests' Committee; Board of Trustees; Board of Directors; Reparation of the Immaculate Heart of Mary Association.
Grimaldi, Joseph R. '83 (BRK) Brooklyn, NY St. Mark's; Presbyteral Council.
Grimaldi, Joseph (BRK) Vice Officiales–Associate Judicial Vicars.
Grimalia, Vincent J. '68 (SCR) Plymouth, PA Nativity of the Blessed Virgin Mary; Diocesan Consultors; Deans; Presbyteral Council; Diocesan Board of Education.
Grimes, Donald J. *c.s.c.* '73 (SCR)[C] Kings College; [C] Holy Cross Community.
Grimes, Edwin T. *o.s.a.* '36 (PH)[AA] Villanova, PA St. Thomas Monastery.
Grimes, John C. (MET) Metuchen, NJ Cathedral of St. Francis.
Grimes, John J. (BO) Dover, MA Most Precious Blood.
Grimes, Jordan K. *c.p.* '49 (ORL)[E] Orlando, FL Bethany House of Beutel.
Grimes, Kenneth F. '57 (COL) Columbus, OH Our Lady of Peace.
Grimes, Mark E. '64 (BGP) Georgetown, CT Sacred Heart.
Grimes, Price D. '88 (OKL) Absent on Sick Leave.
Grimes, Raymond P. '55 (PBL) Las Animas, CO St. Mary.
Grimes, Robert R. *s.j.* '84 (NY)[C] Bronx, NY Fordham University; [EE] Cardinal Spellman Hall, Jesuit Community.
Grimm, John S. '02 (WIL) St. Thomas More Society; Hockessin, DE St. Mary of the Assumption.
Grimm, Robert B. *s.j.* '76 (P)[L] Portland Jesuit Provincial Office (Society of Jesus, Oregon Prov.).
Grimme, D. Timothy '77 (ALT) Liturgical Commission; Altoona, PA St. Therese of the Child Jesus.
Grimmer, James A. '54 (BUF)[O] Lackawanna, NY Bishop Head Residence Retired.
Grimmond, Christopher J. '87 (OM) Absent on Leave.
Griner, William S. '61 (L) Louisville, KY Epiphany; Clergy Personnel Commission; Continuing Education for Clergy–Ministry to Priests.
Grinis, Bruno B. '40 (CHI) Chicago, IL SS. Peter and Paul Retired.
Grinko, Francis Xavier *o.f.m.cap.* '81 (STL)[O] St. Louis, MO St. Crispin's Friary.
Grinnell, Horace H. '74 (ARL) Falls Church, VA St. Anthony's; Diocesan Judges.
Grinnen, John *t.o.r.* '72 (ARL)[J] White Post, VA Sacred Heart Friary.
Grinsell, John *s.d.b.* '71 (SP)[B] St. Petersburg, FL St. Petersburg Catholic High School.
Grippe, Louis A. '69 (SCR) Swoyersville, PA Holy Name/St. Mary's.
Grippo, Robert F. '72 (NY) Bronx, NY St. Theresa of the Infant Jesus.
Gripshover, Ronald J. '96 (ARL) Alexandria, VA St. Louis; Advocates.
Grise, J. Clifford '45 (BGP) Retired.
Grispino, Frank *s.m.* '56 (DET)[K] Livonia, MI Marist Fathers & Brothers Community.
Grissom, Joel *s.m.* (BO) Lawrence, MA Sacred Heart.
Griswold, Edward J. '73 (TR) Colts Neck, NJ St. Mary; Diocesan Consultors; Office of Continuing Formation for Priests.
Grix, Robert *o.f.m.cap.* (NY)[EE] New York, NY Immaculate Conception Friary.
Grizzelle–Reid, Paul *s.c.j.* '72 (MIL)[O] Hales Corners, WI Priests of the Sacred Heart.
Groarke, Francis P. '73 (PH)[B] Philadelphia, PA St. Edmond; Diocesan Priests' Compensation and Benefits Committee.
Grob, Jeffrey S. '92 (CHI) Winnetka, IL SS. Faith, Hope and Charity.
Grob, Jeffrey (CHI) Associate Vicars.
Grochowski, Bernard J. '63 (WOR) Retired.
Grodecki, Henry *c.m.* '75 (COS) Salida, CO St. Joseph.
Groden, Michael F. '65 (BO) Boston, MA St. Cecilia; Unassigned.
Grodnicki, Robert *o.s.a.* '88 (CHI) Chicago, IL St. Mary of the Lake.
Groenewold, Thomas W. '87 (RVC) Franklin Square, NY St. Catherine of Sienna; Priests' Personnel Assignment Board.
Groeschel, Benedict J. *c.f.r.* '59 (NEW)[K] Hoboken, NJ Good Counsel, Inc. (St. Francis Home); [K] Hoboken, NJ Good Counsel, Inc..
Groeschel, Benedict J. *c.f.r.* '59 (NY)[EE] Bronx, NY Franciscan Friars of the Renewal; [GG] Larchmont, NY Trinity Retreat; [GG] Larchmont, NY St. Francis Retreat, Inc..
Groeschel, Benedict J. *c.f.r.* '59 (NEW)[K] Hoboken, NJ Good Counsel, Inc. (St. Francis Home); [K] Hoboken, NJ Good Counsel, Inc..
Groeschel, Benedict J. *c.f.r.* '59 (NY)[EE] Bronx, NY Franciscan Friars of the Renewal; [GG] Larchmont, NY Trinity Retreat; [GG] Larchmont, NY St. Francis Retreat, Inc..
Groeschel, Benedict J. *c.f.r.* '59 (BRK)[P] Brooklyn, NY St. Francis Home for Boys.
Grogan, Brendan '61 (MIA) Absent on Leave.
Grogan, Gerald P. '60 (VEN) Avon Park, FL Our Lady of Grace.
Grogan, J. Clyde '68 (BEL) East St. Louis, IL St. John Francis Regis; Campaign for Human Development.
Grogan, James Clyde '68 (BEL) East St. Louis, IL St. Patrick.
Grogan, James M. '95 (STP) Cottage Grove, MN St. Rita.
Grogan, Richard P. *s.j.* '73 (NY)[EE] New York, NY Murray–Weigel Hall.
Grogan, Todd '90 (CIN) Englewood, OH St. Paul's.
Grogan, Vincent B. *o.f.m.* '63 (NY) New York, NY St. Francis of Assisi; Judges.
Grogan, William E. '83 (PH) Philadelphia, PA St. Agatha–St. James.
Grogan, William E. (PH)[EE] Philadelphia, PA Drexel University.
Grogan, William P. '76 (CHI) Chicago, IL St. Ignatius.
Groh, Chris '79 (JOL) Joliet, IL Holy Cross; Presbyteral Council.
Groh, Christopher '79 (JOL) Joliet, IL St. Mary Nativity.
Grohe, Eugene J. *c.ss.r.* '42 (NY) Esopus, NY Sacred Heart.
Grohe, Eugene J. *c.ss.r.* '50 (NY)[EE] Esopus, NY Redemptorist Priests and Brothers C.Ss.R. (Province of Baltimore).
Groher, Robert C. '66 (GB) Special Assignment.
Grollig, Francis X. *s.j.* '53 (DET)[P] Hamtramck, MI St. Ladislaus.
Grollmes, Eugene E. *s.j.* '64 (STL)[O] St. Louis, MO Jesuit Community Corporation at St. Louis University – Jesuit Hall.
Gromadzki, Michael '01 (MET) Fords, NJ Our Lady of Peace.
Gromadzki, Stanely G. '89 (MET) South River, NJ St. Mary of Ostrabrama.
Gromadzki, Stanley G. (MET) Deans.
Gron, Ryszard '88 (CHI) Berwyn, IL St. Odilo.
Groncki, Richard F. (NEW) Worship Office.
Groncki, Richard '66 (NEW) Newark, NJ Cathedral Basilica of the Sacred Heart.
Grondin, Charles R. '03 (PRO) Cranston, RI St. Matthew.
Groner, Eric *s.v.d.* '96 (JKS) Greenville, MS Sacred Heart; Continuing Formation Committee; Priests' Council.
Groner, John W. '71 (JC) St. Robert, MO St. Jude; St. Robert, MO St. Robert Bellarmine; Senators.
Gronert, Stephen F. '86 (WCH) Marion, KS Holy Family.
Gronifilo, Alejandro '74 (TR) Brick Town, NJ St. Dominic.
Groody, Daniel *c.s.c.* '93 (FTW)[B] University of Notre Dame Du Lac; [I] Notre Dame, IN Holy Cross Community, Corby Hall, University of Notre Dame.
Groover, Henry B. *o.p.* '92 (NO) New Orleans, LA St. Anthony of Padua; [P] New Orleans, LA Dominican Friars, Southern Dominican Province of St. Martin de Porres.
Gros, Edwin L. *s.j.* '80 (NO)[C] New Orleans, LA Loyola University New Orleans.
Grosch, Robert D. '74 (GF) Havre, MT St. Jude Thaddeus; [K] Havre, MT St. Jude's Education Trust; Judicial Vicar.
Grosch, Robert (GF) Diocesan Consultors; Priests' Council.
Grosch, Robert (HEL) Promoter of Justice.
Groschen, Ronald *m.s.* '63 (GAL) Friendswood, TX Mary, Queen.
Groshek, Richard J. '62 (LAN) Flint, MI St. Pius X.
Groshek, Richard (LAN) Vicar General; Regional Vicars.
Grosko, Joseph R. '59 (PIT) West Mifflin, PA St. Agnes; West Mifflin, PA Holy Trinity.
Gross, Barry R. '75 (LFT)[E] Wheaton, MD Good Counsel High School.
Gross, Barry '75 (LFT) On Duty Outside the Diocese.
Gross, Donald L. '59 (LFT) Fowler, IN Sacred Heart of Jesus; Defenders of the Bond; Ministry to Priests' Program.
Gross, Donald '59 (LFT) Ambia, IN St. Mary.
Gross, Francis J. *o.s.f.s.* (FgM).
Gross, Francis *o.s.f.s.* '52 (BUF) Niagara Falls, NY St. Mary of the Cataract.
Gross, Gary L. '83 (LIN) Army Chaplains.
Gross, Gary '83 (LIN) On Duty Outside the Diocese.
Gross, Gerard *o.c.s.o.* '78 (ATL)[K] Conyers, GA The Monastery of the Holy Spirit.
Gross, James '99 (FAR)[B] Fargo, ND Shanley High School and Sullivan Middle School.
Gross, Joseph J. *o.ss.t* '70 (BAL)[S] Baltimore, MD Holy Trinity Monastery.
Gross, Kenneth '71 (DM) Red Oak, IA St. Patrick; Red Oak, IA St. Mary; Diocesan Consultors.
Gross, Lawrence A. '66 (ROC) Honeoye Falls, NY St. Paul of the Cross.
Gross, Lawrence C. '52 (HBG) Lancaster, PA St. Philip the Apostle.
Gross, Lawrence F. '66 (ROC) Lima, NY St. Rose.
Gross, Lee W. '87 (ARL) On Duty Outside the Diocese.
Gross, Matthew *o.f.m.cap.* '61 (COS)[I] Colorado Springs, CO Catholic Center at the Citadel; [F] Colorado Springs, CO Solanus Casey Friary.
Gross, Ralph C. (MIL) Milwaukee, WI St. Margaret Mary; Deans; Archdiocesan Consultors.
Gross, Richard C. '62 (NU) Retired.
Gross, Richard J. '63 (FAR) Special Assignment; Grand Forks, ND Retired.
Gross, Richard K. *s.j.* '76 (BO)[V] Boston The Society of Jesus of New England–Provincial Offices.
Gross, Richard *s.j.* (NSH) Campus Ministries; Vanderbilt.
Gross, Stephen F. '66 (LC) Wausau, WI Church of the Resurrection.
Gross, Thomas L. '75 (HON) Kailua, HI St. John Vianney; Vicars General; Administrative Council; Bishop's Administrative Advisory Council; Clergy Personnel Board; College of Consultors; Members.
Gross, Thomas (HON) Presbyteral Council.
Gross, Val '63 (FAR) Fargo, ND SS. Anne & Joachim.
Grossenburg, Tony '99 (RC) McLaughlin, SD St. Bonaventure's; McLaughlin, SD St. Bernard; McLaughlin, SD Standing Rock Reservation.
Grosser, Elmer J. '46 (COV) Southgate, KY St. Therese of the Infant Jesus Retired.
Grossi, Anthony J. *o.s.b.* '99 (GBG)[H] Latrobe, PA Saint Vincent Archabbey.
Grosskopf, Albert A. *s.j.* '83 (SFR) San Francisco, CA St. Ignatius; [N] San Francisco, CA Jesuit Community at University of San Francisco.
Grosso, James D. '79 (BGP) Presbyteral Council.
Grosso, Lucius *o.f.m.* '44 (PHX)[Q] Santa Barbara, CA Franciscan Friary, Order of Friars Minor (Old Mission).
Grote, Alan W. '82 (GBG) Latrobe, PA Holy Family.
Groth, Ronald '69 (LKC) Lake Charles, LA Our Lady Queen of Heaven; Diocesan Consultors.
Grothjan, James K. *c.pp.s.* (MO) AUXILIARY CHAPLAINS CONTRACT CHAPLAINS.
Grothjan, James *c.pp.s.* '51 (CIN).
Grotovsky, Ed '94 (JOL) Manteno, IL St. Joseph.

Groucutt, George L. '46 (E) Retired.

Grous, Albin J. '87 (PH) On Duty Outside the Archdiocese.

Grove, Stanley *m.s.a.* (NOR)[F] Cromwell, CT Society of the Missionaries of the Holy Apostles.

Grovenburg, Gregg H. *s.j.* '88 (STL)[N] St. Louis, MO Fusz Pavilion; [O] St. Louis, MO Jesuit Community Corporation at St. Louis University – Jesuit Hall.

Grovenburg, Gregg H. *s.j.* '88 (BGP)[W] Fairfield, CT Fairfield University.

Grover, David A. '83 (CAM) Mullica Hill, NJ Holy Name of Jesus; Men's Ministry.

Grover, Peter *o.m.v.* '90 (BO) Boston, MA Beth Israel Deaconess Medical Center; [B] Boston, MA Our Lady of Grace Seminary; [AA] Boston, MA St. Clement Archdiocesan Eucharistic Shrine.

Groves, Edmund '49 (PHX) Retired.

Grozio, Stephen M. *c.m.* '78 (PH) Philadelphia, PA St. Vincent de Paul; [B] Philadelphia, PA St. Vincent's Seminary; [AA] Philadelphia Congregation of the Mission.

Grubb, James E. '55 (DAV) Retired.

Grubba, Dale W. '66 (MAD) Neshkoro, WI St. James; Princeton, WI St. John the Baptist; Elected; Deaneries.

Gruben, John A. *o.a.r.* '74 (NEW)[N] West Orange, NJ Augustinian Recollects.

Gruber, Aloys Conrad '67 (STO) Oakdale, CA St. Mary of the Annunciation Church (Pastor of).

Gruber, Anthony P. '70 (NOR) Absent on Leave.

Gruber, Eric J. '91 (ALN) Minersville, PA Our Lady of Mount Carmel; Minersville, PA St. Vincent de Paul.

Gruber, Kevin W. '80 (RVC) Bohemia, NY St. John Nepomucene.

Gruber, Mark F.X. *o.s.b.* '83 (GBG)[H] Latrobe, PA Saint Vincent Archabbey.

Grubisch, Donald W. '53 (WIN) Dakota, MN Holy Cross; La Crescent, MN The Crucifixion; Deposit and Loan Board.

Gruchot, Stanley J. '45 (CHI) Retired.

Gruchot, Stanley '45 (CHI)[M] Niles, IL Saint Andrew Life Center.

Gruden, William J. '79 (SAG) Munger, MI St. Norbert; Reese, MI St. Elizabeth.

Grudowski, Robert J. '61 (PH) Conshohocken, PA St. Mary; West Conshohocken, PA St. Gertrude.

Gruenbauer, Hans H. '76 (CIN) Amelia, OH St. Bernadette's.

Gruenes, Bernard '98 (SCL) St. Cloud, MN St. Michael; Diocesan Consultors; Directors; Diocesan Priests Pension Plan Trustees.

Gruhn, Raymond C. '66 (BRK) Brooklyn, NY St. Sylvester; Presbyteral Council.

Grumm, Thomas J. '75 (PH) Absent on Leave.

Grummer, James E. *s.j.* '82 (MIL)[O] Milwaukee, WI Arrupe House Jesuit Community; [O] Milwaukee, WI Jesuit Provincial Office, Wisconsin Province; (FgM).

Grumsey, Dennis *o.f.m.conv.* '86 (HBG) Shamokin, PA Mother Cabrini.

Grundhaus, Roger L. '66 (CR) Vicar General; Moderator of the Curia; Information Officer; Diocesan Consultors; Finance Council; Fertile, MN St. Joseph; Mentor, MN St. Lawrence; [E] Crookston, MN; Holy Childhood Association; Priests' Council; Priests' Personnel Board; Propagation of the Faith; Diocesan Sexual Misconduct Review Board.

Grundman, David '97 (SCL) Kimball, MN Church of Saint Anne; St. Cloud, MN St. Wendelin's.

Grundowski, Francis M. '71 (ALN) Retired.

Grunewald, Bernard *er.o.l.s* '77 (OLL)[D] Philippi, WV Our Lady of Solitude Maronite Hermitage, Inc..

Grunloh, Donatus *o.f.m.* '49 (SHP) West Monroe, LA St. Paschal.

Grunow, Stephen E. '97 (CHI) Lake Forest, IL St. Mary.

Grupczynski, Gerald *s.ch.* '88 (CHI) Chicago, IL Five Holy Martyrs.

Gruss, Robert (DAV) Pella, IA St. Mary's.

Gruver, David '85 (ORG) Lake Forest, CA Santiago de Compostela.

Grybowski, Robert *o.f.m.conv.* '53 (HBG) Shamokin, PA Mother Cabrini.

Gryga, Theodore '64 (SY) Military Chaplains.

Grzechowiak, Francis *c.r.* '46 (CHI) Chicago, IL St. Stanislaus, Bishop and Martyr Retired.

Grzela, Marek B. '92 (CHI) Burbank, IL St. Albert the Great.

Grzelak, Thaddeus A. '69 (BRK) Brooklyn, NY St. Charles Borromeo.

Grzeskowiak, Edward S. '36 (STP) Retired.

Grzybowski, Joseph *o.f.m.conv.* '49 (BAL)[S] Baltimore, MD Immaculate Heart of Mary Friary.

Grzymski, Donald *o.f.m.conv.* '80 (BAL)[S] Ellicott City, MD Order of Friars Minor Conventual.

Gschwend, James P. *s.j.* '65 (CHI)[N] Chicago, IL Clark Street Jesuit Residence.

Gschwind, Fred H. '52 (LFT)[F] Tipton, IN St. Joseph Center: Sisters of St. Joseph; Associate Judges; Rural Life Program.

Guadagnoli, Michael (DAL) Waxahachie, TX St. Joseph; Procurator–Advocates.

Guagliardo, Salvatore J. '59 (RCK) Retired.

Guajardo, Hilario '89 (AUS) China Spring, TX St. Philip; Hamilton, TX St. Thomas; McGregor, TX St. Eugene; McGregor, TX Our Lady of San Juan.

Gualtieri, Raymond A. '64 (PIT) Retired.

Guarcello, Russell V. '43 (BO) Senior Priests Retired.

Guardiola, Louis *c.p.m.* '01 (OWN)[F] Auburn, KY Fathers of Mercy.

Guarin, Angelo Michael M. *f.f.i.* '99 (FR)[H] New Bedford, MA Marian Friary of Our Lady, Queen of the Seraphic Order.

Guarino, Charles A. '67 (RVC) Bellmore, NY St. Barnabas the Apostle; Adjutant Judicial Vicars; Promoter of Justice.

Guarino, Mario *f.d.p.* '81 (BO)[T] East Boston, MA Don Orione Nursing Home; [AA] Boston, MA Madonna Queen Shrine.

Guarino, R. Michael '68 (BO) Revere, MA St. Anthony of Padua; Revere, MA St. Mary of the Assumption.

Guarino, Thomas G. '77 (NEW)[B] School of Diplomacy and Intl. Rels.; Archdiocesan Theological Commission; Censors of Books.

Guarnieri, Lee '77 (RIC) Gloucester, VA St. Therese, the Little Flower.

Guarnieri, Richard '71 (NY) Bronx, NY St. Clare of Assisi.

Guarnizo, John '03 (STA) Green Cove Springs, FL Sacred Heart.

Guarracino, Ralph J. '54 (BRK) Retired.

Guarracino, Ralph '54 (BRK) Middle Village, NY St. John's.

Guasp–Santos, Walter '01 (CAM) Pennsauken, NJ St. Cecilia's; Assistant Vocation Directors for Recruitment.

Guastella, Luke *o.f.m.cap.* '41 (PAT) Passaic, NJ St. Mary Hospital.

GuasTella, Luke *o.f.m.cap.* '55 (NY)[B] Beacon, NY St. Lawrence of Brindisi Friary.

Guastella, Richard J. '72 (NY) Staten Island, NY Holy Rosary.

Guastella, Richard (NY) Canon 1742 Panel of Pastors.

Guay, Robert F. (PIT) Judges; Deans and Deaneries.

Guay, Robert '73 (PIT) Conway, PA Our Lady of Peace.

Guba, Michael '65 (NEW) Garfield, NJ Church of Our Lady of Sorrows.

Gubbels, Wayne '71 (DM) Audubon, IA St. Patrick; Carlisle, IA St. Elizabeth Seton; Audubon, IA Holy Trinity.

Gubbins, John '70 (MIA) Military Chaplains.

Gubbins, William B. '55 (CHI) Orland Hills, IL St. Elizabeth Seton Retired.

Gubernat, Michael E. '77 (NEW) Fairview, NJ St. John the Baptist.

Gubser, John H. '62 (Y) Niles, OH St. Stephen.

Gubser, Paul '67 (Y) Retired.

Guckert, William T. '66 (SY) Brewerton, NY St. Agnes.

Guckin, Matthew W. '99 (PH)[D] Downingtown, PA Bishop Shanahan High School; Diocesan Priests' Compensation and Benefits Committee; Malvern, PA St. Patrick.

Gude, Thomas A. '66 (WDC) Forestville, MD Mt. Calvary.

Gudelis, Rimantas (CHI) Chicago, IL Nativity of the Blessed Virgin Mary.

Gudewicz, John L. '70 (PIT) McKeesport, PA St. Martin de Porres.

Guenter, Frank '66 (GAL) Houston, TX St. Gregory the Great.

Guenther, Daniel C. (SC) Emmetsburg, IA Holy Family; Deans; Continuing Education for Priests.

Guenther, Donald E. '62 (NEW) Wyckoff, NJ St. Elizabeth; Priestly Vocation Board.

Guenther, George J. *s.j.* '45 (MIL)[O] Wauwatosa, WI Jesuit Community at St. Camillus.

Guenther, Thomas A. '64 (CAM) Ocean City, NJ Our Lady of Good Counsel; Bishop's Representative to Labor Unions.

Guentner, Francis J. *s.j.* '47 (STL)[O] St. Louis, MO Jesuit Community Corporation at St. Louis University – Jesuit Hall.

Guentner, Hugh *o.s.m.* '91 (CHI)[N] Chicago Order of Friar Servants of Mary (Servites) United States of America Province, Inc..

Guerin, Louis T. '87 (PMB)[M] Diocese of Palm Beach Health Plan Trust.

Guerin, Louis '87 (PMB) Wellington, FL St.Therese de Lisieux.

Guerin, Peter J. *o.s.b.* '63 (MAN)[K] Manchester, NH St. Anselm Abbey.

Guerin, William A. *o.s.f.s.* '57 (PH)[AA] Wyndmoor, PA Villa de Sales Oblate Residence.

Guerra, Araldo (NY) New York, NY Incarnation.

Guerra, Jesus *o.p.* '57 (FgM).

Guerra, Juan Gabriel *l.c.* '91 (DET)[T] Bloomfield Hills, MI Logos, Inc. (Michigan).

Guerra, Richard *o.m.i.* '78 (LAR) Eagle Pass, TX Sacred Heart; College of Consultors.

Guerra, Robert '00 (VIC) Hallettsville, TX Sacred Heart; Hallettsville, TX St. John the Baptist.

Guerra–Mayaudon, Gerardo *o.p.* '69 (AUS)[G] Austin, TX Dominican Friars of Austin.

Guerreiro, Clarence L. *ss.cc.* '70 (HON) Kaneohe, HI St. Ann; [G] Kaneohe, HI Congregation of the Sacred Hearts of Jesus and Mary (Hawaii Province SS.CC.).

Guerreiro, Clyde *ss.cc.* '76 (HON)[G] Kaneohe, HI Sacred Hearts Center.

Guerrero, Abel '00 (ATL) Norcross, GA Saint Patrick's.

Guerrero, Andres '57 (PCE) Coamo, PR San Antonio de Padua; Diocesan Consultors; Parish Priests Consultors.

Guerrero, Cristobal Jose Amate *o.s.b.* '96 (MGZ) Mayaguez, PR Sacred Heart.

Guerrero, Felix Leon *o.f.m.cap.* '86 (AGN)[F] Agana Heights, GU St. Fidelis Friary.

Guerrero, Felixberto Leon *o.f.m.cap.* (AGN) Notary; Confraternity of Christian Mothers.

Guerrero, Jaime '02 (LUB) Denver City, TX St. William.

Guerrero, Jose Ma. (ARE) On Duty Outside the Diocese.

Guerrero, Juan Manuel '81 (OKL) Ardmore, OK St. Mary.

Guerrero, Lawrence M. '83 (STO) Newman, CA St. Joachim Church of Newman (Pastor of).

Guerrero, Toribio C. '96 (LAR) Asherton, TX Immaculate Conception; Presbyteral Council; Vocation Office.

Guerrette, William J. '55 (BO) Senior Priests Retired.

Guerrini, Ademir *c.s.* '87 (NY) Mt. Vernon, NY Our Lady of Victory.

Guerrini, Roderic '63 (LA) Retired.

Guerrs, Juan Gabriel *l.c.* (DET)[T] Clarkston, MI The Legion of Christ, Inc..

Guertin, Donald F. *c.s.c.* '64 (FTW) South Bend, IN Holy Cross; South Bend, IN St. Stanislaus.

Guesnier, Rene *o.s.b.* '61 (DOD) St. John, KS St. John the Apostle; Seward, KS St. Francis Xavier.

Guest, Richard M. '94 (ARL) Ashburn, VA St. Theresa.

Guevara, Alfonso M. '77 (BWN) McAllen, TX St. Joseph the Worker.

Guevara, Alfonso (BWN) Parish Priests' Consultors & Priest Personnel Board.

Guevara, Jose M. (LAR) Presbyteral Council; College of Consultors.

Guevara, Jose Maria '68 (LAR) Crystal City, TX Sacred Heart.

Guevara, Miguel H. '67 (GI) Retired.

Guevin, Benedict M. *o.s.b.* '85 (MAN)[K] Manchester, NH St. Anselm Abbey.

Guffey, David L. *c.s.c.* '91 (COS)[F] Cascade, CO Holy Cross Novitiate.

Guglielmelli, Michael V. '70 (NEW) Hoboken, NJ St. Francis.

Guglielmi, Donald A. *s.t.d.* (BGP) Stratford, CT St. Mark; Presbyteral Council.

Guglielmo, Alan F. '68 (NEW) Bloomfield, NJ St. Valentine; Office of Hospital Ministry; Chaplains; Newark, NJ Office of Health Care Personnel.

Guglielmone, Robert E. '78 (RVC) Wantagh, NY St. Frances de Chantal; Seaford Deanery; Priests' Retirement Board.

Gugliotta, Francis *s.x.* '52 (PAT)[M] Wayne Xaverian Missionary Fathers; (FgM).

Gugliotta, Kevin A. '96 (NEW) Short Hills, NJ St. Rose of Lima; Boy Scouts of America/Catholic Committee on Scouting.

Guiao, Raymond P. *s.j.* '82 (CLV)[D] Cleveland, OH St. Ignatius High School.

Guichard, Alvaro '69 (MIA) Miami Beach, FL St. Francis de Sales.

Guico, Manuel R. (LAV) Military Chaplains.

Guico, Maual R. (SJF) Air Force Chaplains.

Guida, Amedeo '85 (SY) Syracuse, NY The Cathedral of the Immaculate Conception.

Guidera, John F. *s.j.* '56 (BAL).

Guido, Frank *c.j.* (LA)[B] Santa Maria, CA St. Joseph Seminary (Josephite Fathers' Novitiate).

Guido, Joseph J. *o.p.* '81 (PRO)[P] Providence St. Thomas Aquinas Priory at Providence College.

Guido, Paul R. *o.f.m.* '66 (HRT) New Britain, CT St. Francis of Assisi.

Guido, Thomas J. '87 (PT) Port St. Joe, FL St. Joseph.

Guido, Thomas (PT) Orders & Ministries, Commission for.

Guido, William F. '44 (NY) Retired.

Guidon, Patrick *o.m.i.* '50 (SAT)[K] San Antonio, TX Oblate Madonna Residence.

Guidry, Dale '82 (AMA) Absent on Leave.

Guidry, Joseph *s.v.d.* '57 (BLX)[A] Bay St. Louis, MS St. Augustine's Retreat Center; [A] Bay St. Louis, MS St. Augustine's.

Guidry, Michael '71 (LAF) New Iberia, LA Our Lady of Perpetual Help; Seminarians; Knights of Columbus.

Guidry, Mitchell '97 (LAF) Advocates; Diocesan Consultors.

Guidry, Raymond *s.v.d.* '57 (BLX)[A] Bay St. Louis, MS St. Augustine's.

Guijarro de Corzo, Mario A. '78 (SJN) Guaynabo, PR San Pedro Martir de Verona.

Guijarro del Corzo, Mario A. (SJN) Guaynabo–Puerto Nuevo.

Guilbeau, Aubrey V. '82 (LKC) Lake Charles, LA Immaculate Conception Cathedral; Diocesan Board

of Administration; Vicar General; Episcopal Vicars; Diocesan Consultors.
Guilbeau, Aubrey '82 (LKC) Diocesan Consultors; Deaf Apostolate.
Guilbeau, Jeremy '02 (LAF) On Duty Outside the Diocese.
Guilbert, Norman J. '97 (BGP) Stamford, CT St. Leo.
Guiliano, Carmen *s.a.* '61 (NY)[EE] Saranac Lake, NY St. Joseph's Rehabilitation Center, Inc..
Guiliano, Carmen *s.a.* '61 (OG)[E] Saranac Lake, NY Atonement Friars.
Guilka, Robert (WDC) Washington, DC Holy Name.
Guillame, Lemier (ORL) Haitian.
Guillemette, Marc F. '90 (MAN) Auburn, NH St. Peter; Council of Priests; Masters of Ceremonies; Cabinet Secretary for Pastoral Services; Directors; Office of the Permanent Diaconate.
Guillemette, Marc F. (MAN) Men of St. Joseph.
Guillemette, Robert G. '01 (MAN) Pelham, NH St. Patrick.
Guillen, Fernando '90 (NEW) Elizabeth, NJ Blessed Sacrament; Members.
Guillen, Jorge '69 (LA) South Gate, CA St. Helen.
Guillen, Juan '74 (TUC) Administrative Leave of Absence.
Guillen, Oswaldo *s.d.b.* '02 (WDC) Chicago, IL St. John Bosco.
Guillen, Patricio '57 (SB) Retired.
Guillen, Randy '96 (NEW) West New York, NJ St. Joseph of the Palisades.
Guillet, Bernard *a.a.* '44 (WOR)[O] Worcester, MA Assumptionists (Augustinians of the Assumption).
Guillot, Leo '56 (BR) Albany, LA St. Margaret Queen of Scotland.
Guillot, Raymond Joseph (NO) Pointe a la Hache, LA St. Thomas.
Guilmain, Roland O. *a.a.* '53 (WOR)[O] Worcester, MA Assumptionists (Augustinians of the Assumption); [R] Worcester, MA Assumption College.
Guilmette, Emile *s.m.* '57 (BO)[X] Framingham, MA The Marist House.
Guilmette, Leo *o.m.i.* '63 (FgM).
Guiltnane, Justin *s.c.j.* '53 (MIL)[O] Hales Corners, WI Priests of the Sacred Heart.
Guimon, Michael M. *o.s.m.* '70 (CHI)[N] Berwyn, IL St. Bonfilius Priory; [N] Chicago Order of Friar Servants of Mary (Servites) United States of America Province, Inc..
Guimond, John C. *o.f.m.cap.* '82 (FTW) Huntington, IN SS. Peter and Paul Retired.
Guinan, Frank '66 (PMB) Delray Beach, FL St. Vincent Ferrer.
Guinan, Michael D. *o.f.m.* '63 (OAK).
Guinan, Michael '53 (GF) Retired.
Guindon, William G. *s.j.* '50 (BO)[V] Weston, MA Campion Health Center, Inc..
Guiney, John *s.m.a.* '61 (NEW)[N] Tenafly, NJ Society of African Missions, Provincialate, S.M.A. Fathers Retired.
Guiney, John *s.m.a.* '61 (JOL) Retired.
Guischard, John A. '68 (BUR)[D] Rutland, VT St. Joseph's Kervick Residence Retired.
Guise, Cyril *o.c.d.* '59 (MIL)[O] Holy Hill, WI Discalced Carmelite Monastery – Holy Hill National Shrine of Mary Help of Christians.
Guiterrez, Jose '76 (CC).
Guitron, Steven '94 (LA)[D] Pacoima, CA Guardian Angel.
Guixa, Jaime '82 (SJN)[G] Guaynabo, PR Opus Dei.
Gula, Richard *s.s.* '73 (OAK).
Gulash, George M. '92 (ALT)[A] Fallentimber, PA St. Thomas Aquinas; Fallentimber, PA St. Joan of Arc.
Gulczynski, John T. '36 (DAL) Retired.
Gulig, Robert F. (GB) Kellnersville, WI St. Joseph.
Gulig, Robert '61 (GB) Special Assignment.
Gulino, Stephen '97 (NOR) Uncasville, CT St. John.
Guljas, Andrew *c.s.c.* '68 (FTW)[K] Notre Dame, IN Holy Cross Mission House.
Gulley, Anthony D. '56 (ALB) Special Assignment; [B] Albany, NY The College of Saint Rose; Catholic Office for Motion Pictures.
Gulley, Anthony '56 (ALB) Amsterdam, NY St. Mary.
Gulley, James '81 (ALB) Amsterdam, NY St. Mary; Deans.
Gullickson, Thomas E. '76 (SFS) On Duty Outside the Diocese.
Gullo, Joseph A. '86 (BUF) Council of Priests; Falconer, NY Our Lady of Loreto; Frewsburg, NY Our Lady of Victory; Jamestown, NY St. John.
Gully, Bernard L. '62 (SAN) Andrews, TX Our Lady of Lourdes.
Gully, Bernard (SAN) Presbyteral Council; Cursillos de Cristiandad; Deans.
Gumapo, Polycarp (SAC) Priests' Personnel Board, Diocesan.
Gumapo, Polycarpo '70 (SAC) Lincoln, CA St. Joseph; College of Consultors.
Gumataotao, Agustin *o.f.m.cap.* '82 (AGN) Agana Heights, GU Our Lady of Mount Carmel; Agana, GU Our Lady of Guadalupe; [F] Agana Heights, GU St. Fidelis Friary; [F] Agat, GU Capuchin Fraternity; Archdiocesan Presbyteral Council.
Gumbert, Kenneth R. *o.p.* '85 (Oakland Prov.)[P] Providence St. Thomas Aquinas Priory at Providence College; Fall River, MA Notre Dame de Lourdes; [N] Oakland, CA Western Dominican Province.
Gummersheimer, Gary P. '79 (BEL) Murphysboro, IL St. Andrew.
Gumprecht, Thomas *s.a.* '68 (NY) Yonkers, NY Our Lady of the Rosary.
Gunderman, Richard J. *s.a.c.* '50 (MIL)[O] Milwaukee, WI St. Vincent Community; [X] Milwaukee, WI Pallottine Fathers and Brothers, Inc., Disability Trust; [X] Milwaukee, WI Pallottine Fathers and Brothers, Inc., Educational and Apostolic Ministry Trust; [D] Milwaukee, WI Pius XI High School.
Gunderson, Gerald T. '76 (CHI) Riverside, IL St. Mary.
Gundlapalli, Bobu '92 (LA) Ventura, CA Our Lady of the Assumption.
Gundrum, Alfredo *o.f.m.cap.* '67 (CHI) Chicago, IL St. Kevin.
Gunia, Edward S. '49 (CHI) Retired.
Gunn, Andrew '97 (AUS) Pflugerville, TX St. Patrick.
Gunn, Francis *o.f.m.* '81 (NEW) East Rutherford, NJ St. Joseph's.
Gunn, James L. '77 (MAD) Waunakee, WI St. John the Baptist; Diocesan Consultors; Elected.
Gunning, Eugene L. '55 (SCR) Scranton, PA St. John the Evangelist.
Gunning, Joseph *s.v.d.* '47 (TR)[B] Techny, IL Divine Word Residence.
Gunnoud, James B. '59 (HRT) Cheshire, CT St. Bridget's; College of Consultors.
Gunther, William '60 (MIA) Retired.
Gunti, Charles *o.f.m.* '68 (SAT) San Antonio, TX San Jose y San Miguel.
Gunti, Frederick W. '64 (LR) On Duty Outside the Diocese; [A] Mobile, AL Spring Hill College.
Guntzelman, Louis J. '57 (CIN) Retired.
Guppenberger, August '61 (CIN).
Gural, Marion A. '56 (BRK) Retired.
Gurath, Guy '64 (MIL)[M] Newburg, WI Holy Trinity.
Gurdak, Joseph *o.f.m.cap.* '70 (NY) New York, NY Our Lady of Sorrows.
Gurgul, Walter *m.i.c.* '60 (SPR)[I] Eucharistic Apostles of The Divine Mercy.
Gurka, Gerald J. '80 (SCR) Plymouth, PA St. Anthony of Padua.
Gurkis, Albin *m.i.c.* '43 (NOR)[C] Thompson, CT Marianapolis Preparatory School; [F] Thompson, CT Marian Fathers.
Gurnell, Anthony '64 (SAC) Retired.
Gurnell, Anthony '64 (MRY) Cayucos, CA St. Joseph.
Gurnick, Michael K. '98 (CLV) Wickliffe, OH Our Lady of Mount Carmel.
Gurovich, Daniel '74 (PHU) Bethlehem, PA St. Josaphat's; College of Archeparchial Counsultors; Presbyteral Council; Adjunct Judicial Vicar; Synodal Judge; Archeparchial Council for Economic Affairs; Priests Beneficial Fund.
Gurrieri, John A. '67 (BRK) Brooklyn, NY St. John Cantius.
Gurski, John K. '64 (NEW) Garfield, NJ Church of Our Lady of Sorrows.
Gurtler, Gary *s.j.* '79 (New York)[V] Newton, MA The Jesuit Community at Boston College.
Gurtner, Mark Allen '96 (FTW) Fort Wayne, IN St. Vincent de Paul.
Gurtner, Mark (FTW) Consultors.
Gurtubay, Ramon *c.p.* (SJN)[C] Dorado, PR Estudiantado Pasionista.
Gurzynski, James C. '63 (AMA) Defender of the Bond Retired.
Gusiora, Alphonsus '83 (PCE) On Duty Outside the Diocese.
Gusmer, Charles W. *v.e.* '66 (NEW) Cedar Grove, NJ St. Catherine of Siena; Worship Office.
Gusmer, Charles (NEW) Censors of Books; Staff.
Gussoni, Lino '44 (NY) Retired.
Gustafson, Christopher M. '95 (CHI) Lake Forest, IL St. Mary.
Guste, Placid *s.m.p.* '61 (SPC)[E] Marionville, MO The Society of Our Mother of Peace, Sons of Our Mother of Peace.
Guste, Placid *s.m.p.* '61 (STL)[O] High Ridge, MO Society of Our Mother of Peace; [S] High Ridge, MO Society of Our Mother of Peace Mary the Font Solitude.
Guste, Robert I. '50 (NO) Kenner, LA Our Lady of Perpetual Help; Ministry of Evangelization & Spiritual Renewal; Jesus Caritas Fraternity of Priests; Living Waters Program (Radio Ministry).
Gustin, Clem *o.s.c.* '55 (DUL) Hibbing, MN Blessed Sacrament.
Gustin, Clement N. *o.s.c.* '55 (SCL)[I] Onamia Crosier Monastery.
Gustin, Theodore F. '57 (BIS) Retired.
Gutauskas, Vaclovas *s.j.* '45 (CHI)[N] Chicago Lithuanian American Jesuits.
Gutekunst, John P. '80 (PH) Philadelphia, PA St. Christopher.
Gutgsell, Michael F. '74 (OM) Fort Calhoun, NE St. John the Baptist; Moderator of the Curia; Associate Judicial Vicar; Finance Council; Censor Librorum; Archbishop's Appointees.
Gutgsell, Stephen F. '84 (OM)[O] Omaha, NE Womens' Care Center of the Heartland (Holy Family House).
Gutgsell, Stephen J. '84 (OM) Omaha, NE St. Patrick.
Guth, Edward L. *s.j.* '60 (BUF) Buffalo, NY St. Michael.
Guthneck, Peter E. '71 (GF) Box Elder, MT St. Margaret Mary; Vicar for Ministry to Native Americans.
Guthridge, Timothy J. *c.pp.s.* '97 (JC) Sedalia, MO St. Patrick; Sedalia, MO Sacred Heart.
Guthrie, Alfred '30 (BRK) Retired.
Guthrie, Alfred '55 (BRK)[V] Douglaston, NY Bishop Mugavero Residence.
Guthrie, John G. '90 (BIS) Williston, ND St. Joseph; Continuing Education for Clergy.
Guthrie, Paul *o.f.m.* '53 (PHU) Sayre, PA Ascension of Our Lord.
Guthrie, Raymond '84 (RCK)[B] Freeport, IL Aquin Central Catholic Junior–Senior High School; Freeport, IL St. Mary; [E] Freeport, IL St. Vincent's Community Living Facility and Supported Living Arrangement; [F] Freeport, IL Provena St. Joseph Adult Day Care Services; [F] Freeport, IL Provena St. Joseph Center.
Guthrie, Raymond '84 (PEO) On Duty Outside the Diocese.
Guthrie, Raymond '84 (RCK)[B] Freeport, IL Aquin Central Catholic Junior–Senior High School; Freeport, IL St. Mary; [E] Freeport, IL St. Vincent's Community Living Facility and Supported Living Arrangement; [F] Freeport, IL Provena St. Joseph Adult Day Care Services; [F] Freeport, IL Provena St. Joseph Center.
Gutierrez, Alfonso '85 (SAV) Tifton, GA Our Divine Saviour.
Gutierrez, Alvin P. (PIT) Chaplains to Latino Catholic Community.
Gutierrez, Alvin '61 (PIT) Pittsburgh, PA Word of God.
Gutierrez, Celestino '64 (VEN) Sarasota, FL St. Martha; Hispanic, Migrant and Spanish Speaking Apostolates/National Migration Week.
Gutierrez, Fernando '66 (SD) San Diego, CA Metropolitan Correction Center.
Gutierrez, Francisco '01 (YAK) Wenatchee, WA St. Joseph's.
Gutierrez, Franco '65 (SJN) San Juan, PR Nuestra Senora de la Altagracia.
Gutierrez, Fulgencio (BRK) Far Rockaway, NY St. Mary Star of the Sea.
Gutierrez, Gilberto '73 (PAT) Passaic, NJ Our Lady of Fatima.
Gutierrez, Gustavo '99 (MIA) Pompano Beach, FL San Isidro.
Gutierrez, Jeronimo '81 (SJ) San Jose, CA Sacred Heart of Jesus.
Gutierrez, Jose Gregorio '97 (NY) Bronx, NY St. Rita of Cascia Shrine Church.
Gutierrez, Jose '73 (STP) Retired.
Gutierrez, Luis '98 (JOL) Bolingbrook, IL St. Dominic.
Gutierrez, Michael D. '93 (LA) Santa Monica, CA St. Anne.
Gutierrez, Oscar '96 (SAC) Vacaville, CA St. Mary.
Gutierrez, Raphael '89 (TUC) Somerton, AZ Immaculate Heart of Mary.
Gutierrez Fernandez, Javier *o.dem.* '71 (PCE) Ponce, PR La Merced.
Gutirerrez, Jose '76 (CC) On Special Assignment.
Gutmann, David '83 (P) Portland, OR Holy Cross.
Gutmann, Don '91 (P) Reedsport, OR St. John the Apostle.
Gutmann, Donald K. '91 (P) Florence, OR St. Mary, Our Lady of the Dunes.
Gutowski, Edmund *c.m.* '60 (BRK) Brooklyn, NY St. Stanislaus Kostka.
Gutowski, Matthew J. '88 (STL)[A] St. Louis, MO Kenrick School of Theology.
Gutt, Antony (NY) Larchmont, NY St. Augustine.
Guttendorf, James R. '65 (RIC) Retired.
Gutting, James G. '75 (E) Erie, PA Holy Rosary.
Gutting, John C. '54 (LA) Retired.
Guvvala, Balaswamy (KCK) St. John Vianney; St. Stanislaus.
Guyder, Thomas F. '40 (SY) Retired.
Guyer, James B. *s.j.* '72 (DEN)[N] Denver, CO Regis Jesuit Community (The Jesuits at Regis University).
Guyon, Guy E. *o.praem.* '40 (GB)[I] De Pere, WI St. Norbert Abbey.
Guz, Edmund F. '55 (CHI) Burnham, IL Mother of God.
Guz, Leonard J. '55 (JOL) Downers Grove, IL Divine Savior.
Guzik, Michael A. *s.j.* '03 (RVC) Oceanside, NY St. Anthony.
Guzikowski, Gerard F. (GAY) Holy Childhood Pontifical Association; Propagation of the Faith.
Guzikowski, Gerard '43 (GAY) Manistee, MI Guardian Angels.
Guzinski, Joseph D. *c.p.* '51 (BRK)[V] Jamaica, NY Immaculate Conception Monastery.
Guzman, Alfonso D. *o.f.m.* '71 (NY)[EE] San Juan, PR

Arzobispado de San Juan.
Guzman, Alfonso D. *o.f.m.* '71 Sabana Seca, PR San Jose Obrero; Secretary to the Archbishop; Vicar for Religious; (FgM).
Guzman, Armando '86 (SEA) Everett, WA St. Mary Magdalen.
Guzman, Baudilio *s.j.* (SJN) Renovacion Conyugal (Fundacion Fernando Martinez Calle, Inc.).
Guzman, David *m.x.y.* '88 (NY)[EE] Bronx, NY Yarumal Mission Society, Inc..
Guzman, Gonzalo *o.f.m.* (GLP) Gallup, NM St. Francis of Assisi.
Guzman, Jesus *o.s.a.* '60 (NY) Bronx, NY St. Nicholas of Tolentine.
Guzman, Julian *s.d.s.* '68 (WDC)[B] Silver Spring, MD Salvatorian Community.
Guzman, Mariano *o.f.m.* '57 (FgM).
Guzman, Salvador (DAL) Dallas, TX Cathedral–Santuario de Guadalupe.
Guzman, Walter F. '02 (HBG) Harrisburg, PA Holy Name of Jesus.
Gwarek, Leslaw M. *s.a.c.* '76 (BUF)[O] North Tonawanda, NY Society of the Catholic Apostolate.
Gwiazda, Francis A. '69 (PH) Philadelphia, PA St. Laurentius.
Gwinner, David E. '83 (COL) Zaleski, OH St. Sylvester.
Gwozdz, John P. '86 (HRT) Enfield, CT St. Martha's.
Gwozdz, Thomas L. *s.b.d.* '75 (NO)[A] St. Benedict, LA St. Joseph Seminary College.
Gwozdz, Thomas *o.f.m.conv.* '53 (BAL)[S] Danbury, CT Pope John Paul II Center Retired.
Gwozdz, Thomas *o.f.m.conv.* '53 (BGP) Danbury, CT Sacred Heart.
Gwudz, John S. '72 (NOR) On Duty Outside the Diocese; Military Chaplains; Navy Chaplains.
Gyabbah, Andrew (NY) Brewster, NY St. Lawrence O'Toole.
Gyamfi–Appiah, Aaron *c.ss.p.* (NY) Bronx, NY Christ the King.
Gyhra, Lawrence J. '66 (LIN) Hastings, NE St. Cecilia's; Deaneries and Deans.
Gyhra, Lawrence (LIN) Presbyteral Council.
Gyhra, Richard A. '99 (LIN) Lincoln, NE St. Peter; Advocates.
Gyim–Austin, Joseph K. '81 (LC) Wausau, WI Holy Name of Jesus.
Gyure, William '91 (NEW) Nutley, NJ Our Lady of Mount Carmel; Montclair, NJ Mountainside Hospital; Chaplains.

H

Ha, Abraham '02 (ALN) Sinking Spring, PA St. Ignatius Loyola.
Ha, Dominic Vinh Van '93 (CHI) Chicago, IL St. Henry.
Ha, Joseph Hieu Minh '00 (ATL) Riverdale, GA Our Lady of Vietnam.
Ha, Peter '74 (LA) North Hollywood, CA St. Charles Borromeo.
Ha, Thomas Do Thanh '63 (ORG) Absent on Sick Leave Retired.
Ha, Thomas (ORG) Judges.
Haag, Theodore *o.f.m.* '79 (CLV)[D] Parma, OH Padua Franciscan High School; [O] Brooklyn, OH Padua Franciscan Friary.
Haake, Chris G. '97 (PEO) Kewanee, IL St. Francis of Assisi; Kewanee, IL St. Mary's Catholic Church.
Haaland, Byron *s.c.j.* '77 (GB)[L] Baileys Harbor, WI St. Joseph Retreat Center.
Haar, George B. '51 (STL) Retired.
Haas, Dietrich A. '67 (MIL)[S] Waukesha, WI Schoenstatt Fathers.
Haas, Joseph H. '59 (MIL) Port Washington, WI St. Peter of Alcantara.
Haas, Lawrence W. '63 (FAR) Carrington, ND Sacred Heart.
Haas, Ralph L. '55 (BEL) Retired.
Haas, Robert L. '62 (TOL) New London, OH Our Lady of Lourdes; Wakeman, OH St. Mary.
Haas, Roger *o.f.m.conv.* '69 (PAT) Clifton, NJ St. John Kanty.
Haas, Theodore A. '44 (COS) Colorado Springs, CO St. Mary's Cathedral.
Haas, Theodore '44 (COS) Retired.
Haase, Albert *o.f.m.* '83 (STL)[O] (FgM).
Haase, Howard G. '83 (MIL) Union Grove, WI St. Robert Bellarmine.
Haasl, Edgar '58 (LC) Milladore, WI St. Kilian.
Haasl, Edgar '58 (OAK) Retired.
Habahag, Jimmy '82 (PMB) West Palm Beach, FL Mary Immaculate.
Habach, Yousif '75 (LA) North Hollywood, CA Sacred Heart Syriac Catholic Parish.
Habash, Yousif (OLD) North Hollywood, CA Sacred Heart Parish.
Habe, Robert W. '62 (PIT) Russellton, PA Transfiguration.
Habenight, James F. *m.m.* (MO) AUXILIARY CHAPLAINS CONTRACT CHAPLAINS.
Haber, Edward A. '58 (NEW) Elizabeth, NJ Trinitas Hospital; Chaplains Retired.
Haber, Edward '58 (NEW) Elizabeth, NJ St. Mary of the Assumption.
Haber, Thomas N. '01 (BGP) Danbury, CT St. Peter.
Haberak, Jerome A. (PRO) Army Chaplains.
Haberek, Jerome A. '77 (PRO) On Duty Outside the Diocese.
Haberek, Jerome A. (MO) Presbyteral Council.
Haberkorn, Timothy A. '92 (KCK) St. Mary's; Olpe, KS St. Joseph's.
Haberman, C. Robert '75 (PBL) On Duty Outside the Diocese.
Haberman, Clayton J. '50 (WIN) Auditors Retired.
Haberman, Robert (SFR)[C] San Rafael, CA Dominican University of California.
Habetz, Thomas E. '01 (LAF) Abbeville, LA St. Mary Magdalen; Mermentau, LA St. John the Evangelist.
Habiger, James D. '51 (WIN) Retired.
Habiger, James D. (STP) Archdiocesan Council of Catholic Women.
Habiger, James '51 (STP)[C] St. Paul, MN University of St. Thomas.
Habiger, Matthew *o.s.b.* '68 (KCK)[H] Atchison, KS St. Benedict's Abbey.
Habing, Paul '80 (SFD) On Duty Outside the Diocese.
Habison, Gerhart '76 (LA) Torrance, CA Nativity.
Hablewitz, James A. '67 (GB) Green Bay, WI Nativity of Our Lord; Pastor Consultors.
Haby, Gerald *s.m.* '69 (SAT)[F] San Antonio, TX Central Catholic High School; [M] San Antonio, TX Central Catholic Marianist Community.
Hacala, Joseph R. *s.j.* '75 (WH)[A] Wheeling, WV Wheeling Jesuit University.
Hache, Yvon '88 (ORL) Kissimmee, FL St. Catherine of Siena.
Hachey, Paul J. *s.m.* (ATL) Special or Other (Arch)Diocesan Assignment; [C] Atlanta, GA Marist School; Judicial Vicar.
Hack, Michael A. '70 (CHI) Flossmoor, IL Infant Jesus of Prague; Judges.
Hack, Michael A. (KAL) Defenders of the Bond.
Hack, Thomas '55 (GR) Remus, MI St. Michael's Retired.
Hackel, Daniel H. '02 (LC) Marshfield, WI St. John the Baptist.
Hackel, Robert E. *s.m.* '65 (GAL)[Q] Pinehurst, TX Marianist Community.
Hackenmueller, Jerome B. '69 (STP) St. Paul, MN St. Patrick.
Hacker, Jack *c.ss.r.* '59 (STL)[B] St. Louis, MO St. John Neumann House.
Hacker, Louis *o.s.b.* (MO) AUXILIARY CHAPLAINS CONTRACT CHAPLAINS.
Hackett, Denis *o.f.m.conv.* '74 (R) Burlington, NC Blessed Sacrament; [E] Burlington, NC Conventual Franciscans.
Hackett, James F. '68 (L) Louisville, KY St. Raphael the Archangel.
Hackman, Marvin R. '71 (CIN) Springfield, OH St. Joseph; Springfield, OH St. Raphael; [K] Springfield, OH Mercy Health Systems – Western Ohio; [Q] Springfield, OH Mercy Medical Center.
Hadad, Gerard A. '69 (DET) Retired.
Hadberg, Dennis C. '72 (E) Erie, PA St. James.
Haddad, Edmond G. '46 (WOR)[N] Worcester, MA Vianney House Retired.
Haddad, James J. '58 (BO) Senior Priests Retired.
Haddad, Norman '61 (RIC) Charlottesville, VA St. Thomas Aquinas.
Haddad, Wayne M. '97 (MET) On Duty Outside the Diocese; Navy Chaplains.
Hadden, Thomas P. '58 (R) Diocesan Judges; Ex Officio; African–American Ancestry Ministry Retired.
Hadel, Richard E. *s.j.* '65 (STL)[F] St. Louis, MO St. Louis University High School, George H. Backer Memorial; [O] St. Louis, MO St. Louis University High School Jesuit Community.
Hadgkiss, Joseph '93 (CC)[G] Robstown, TX Society of Our Lady of the Most Holy Trinity.
Hadnagy, John Raphael *o.f.m.conv.* '90 (IND) Sellersburg, IN St. Joseph; [J] Mount St. Francis, IN Mount Saint Francis Friary and Retreat Center.
Hadusek, Paul J. '69 (NU) Cottonwood, MN St. Mary; Cottonwood, MN St. Clotilde.
Hadyka, Richard J. '67 (CAM) Wildwood Crest, NJ Assumption B.V.M..
Hae, Peter Lee (WIL) Korean Catholics; Korean Catholic Community, Inc..
Haefeli, Joaquin '51 (LA) Retired.
Haefling, Maurice *o.s.b.* '94 (KCK)[H] Atchison, KS St. Benedict's Abbey.
Haefner, Douglas J. '83 (MET) Somerset, NJ St. Matthias.
Haeglin, William '76 (KCK) Administrative Leave.
Haemmerle, Gerald R. '67 (CIN)[A] Cincinnati, OH The Athenaeum of Ohio; [B] Cincinnati, OH Mt. St. Mary's Seminary of the West; [B] Cincinnati, OH Mt. St. Mary's Seminary of the West; Judges.
Haesaert, William F. *c.s.v.* '80 (LAV) Las Vegas, NV St. Viator.
Haesaert, William *c.s.v.* (LAV) Presbyteral Council for the Diocese of Las Vegas.
Hafeman, Harry G. '76 (GB) Leopolis, WI St. Mary.
Hafemann, George T. M. '99 (NY) Croton Falls, NY St. Joseph.
Haffey, Thomas P. '69 (HEL) Butte, MT St. Ann; Associate Judges; Personnel Board; Continuing Formation of the Clergy.
Haffey, Thomas (HEL) Diocesan Consultors; Presbyteral Council; Vicariates.
Hafner, Gerard '62 (ROC) Retired.
Hagan, Aelred *o.c.s.o.* '89 (CHR)[E] Moncks Corner, SC Mepkin Abbey.
Hagan, Charles H. '70 (PH) Doylestown, PA Our Lady of Mount Carmel.
Hagan, David I. *o.s.f.s.* '66 (PH)[AA] Philadelphia, PA Inner City House.
Hagan, Harry *o.s.b.* '86 (IND)[A] St. Meinrad, IN St. Meinrad School of Theology; [K] St. Meinrad, IN St. Meinrad Archabbey.
Hagan, James '69 (SFR) On Duty Outside the Archdiocese.
Hagan, Martin *s.j.* '50 (STL)[F] St. Louis, MO St. Louis University High School, George H. Backer Memorial; [O] St. Louis, MO Jesuit Community Corporation at St. Louis University – Jesuit Hall.
Hagan, Paul '82 (LFT) Unassigned.
Hagan, Robert A. *s.j.* '72 (PBL) Trinidad, CO Most Holy Trinity, Trinidad Area Catholic Community (Trinidad Cluster); [F] Trinidad, CO Business Address:.
Hagan, Robert '83 (SEA) Vancouver, WA St. Joseph.
Hagan, Robert *o.s.a.* '03 (PH)[C] Villanova University; [AA] Villanova, PA Fray de Leon Community.
Hagarman, Vincent A. *s.j.* '54 (CLV)[D] Cuyahoga Falls, OH Walsh Jesuit High School; [T] Akron, OH Loyola of the Lakes Jesuit Retreat House, Inc..
Hage, Simon *b.s.o.* '39 (NTN) Retired.
Hagearty, Charles B. '59 (HRT) Unassigned.
Hagedorn, Robert L. '44 (CIN) Censors Retired.
Hagedorn, Thomas J. '71 (CLV) Cleveland, OH St. Patrick.
Hagee, Robert J. *s.j.* '61 (CIN)[M] Cincinnati, OH Faber Jesuit Community.
Hagemann, John *o.s.b.* '75 (OM)[C] Elkhorn, NE Mount Michael High School; [K] Elkhorn, NE Mount Michael Abbey.
Hagen, Gerald A. '91 (SUP) Phillips, WI St. Paul the Apostle; Phillips, WI Our Lady of the North; Phillips, WI St. John the Baptist.
Hagen, John J. *o.s.a.* '57 (PH)[C] Villanova University; [AA] Villanova, PA St. Thomas Monastery.
Hagen, Joseph B. *o.f.m.* '46 (SUP) Bayfield, WI Holy Family; Washburn, WI St. Ann; Bayfield, WI St. Joseph; Bayfield, WI St. Francis; Washburn, WI St. Louis.
Hagenbach, George G. '54 (PH) Retired.
Hagendorf, Thomas A. *o.praem.* '63 (GB) Green Bay, WI Holy Cross; [I] De Pere, WI St. Norbert Abbey.
Hager, Raymond '97 (STL) Ste. Genevieve, MO Ste. Genevieve.
Hager, Van Allen *i.m.c.* '73 (MET)[H] Somerset, NJ Consolata Society for Foreign Missions.
Hagerman, James W. '86 (MET) Parlin, NJ St. Bernadette.
Hagerty, John B. '55 (E) Hermitage, PA Church of Notre Dame.
Haggar, Joseph S. (NTN) Defender of the Bond and Promoter of Justice; Protopresbyters; College of Eparchial Consultors; Presbyteral Council; Diocese of Newton for the Melkites in the USA, Inc., a Massachusetts Corporation; Priest's Sickness & Disability, and Retirement Plans.
Haggar, Joseph (NTN) Liturgical Commission.
Haggerty, Colman *c.p.* '46 (BRK)[V] Jamaica, NY Immaculate Conception Monastery.
Haggerty, Donald F. '89 (NY)[A] Yonkers, NY St. Joseph's Seminary.
Haggerty, Donald (NY) Censors Librorum.
Haggerty, Edward '57 (CIN) Dayton, OH Holy Family.
Haggerty, Edward *g.h.m.* '57 (CIN)[M] Cincinnati Headquarters of Glenmary Home Missioners.
Haggerty, Thomas J. '79 (RVC) East Meadow, NY St. Raphael.
Haggerty, Thomas M. '64 (BRK) Brooklyn, NY St. John the Evangelist.
Haggerty, Thomas (RVC) Procurator & Advocates.
Haggins, Martin *o.f.m.cap.* '65 (BAK) Board of Education; Bend, OR St. Francis of Assisi.
Hagileiram, John S. *s.j.* '85 (CI) St. Ignatius; Diocesan Consultors; Yap.
Haglof, Anthony *o.c.d.* '71 (BO)[V] Boston, MA Carmelite Monastery.
Hagman, William J. '55 (OWN) Retired.
Hagstrom, Thomas '93 (SFD) Brussels, IL St. Barbara; Hardin, IL St. Agnes; Brussels, IL St. Mary; Hardin, IL St. Norbert; Hardin, IL St. Anselm; Brussels, IL St. Joseph; Hardin, IL St. Michael; Priests' Personnel Board.
Hahley, Boniface *o.f.m.* '50 (CAM)[M] Margate, NJ Franciscan Friary.
Hahn, Bernardine '43 (STL)[O] St. Louis, MO Franciscan Friary of St. Anthony of Padua.
Hahn, Dominic D. '80 (SEA) Shelton, WA St. Edward.
Hahn, Francis *o.m.i.* '72 (FgM).

Hahn, Gerald T. '79 (NEW) Westwood, NJ St. Andrew's.
Hahn, James C. *o.p.* '64 (CHI)[N] St. Pius V Priory.
Hahn, James David '61 (SCL) Cambridge, MN Christ the King.
Hahn, Jerry '79 (NEW) Northvale, NJ St. Anthony's.
Hahn, Peter I. '02 (HBG) Columbia, PA St. Peter.
Hahn, Raymond W. '74 (E) Erie, PA St. Boniface.
Hahn, Scott R. '03 (WDC)[C] Silver Spring, MD St. John the Evangelist.
Hai, Dinh Minh *c.ss.r.* '96 (LA)[Q] Irving, TX.
Hai, Nguyen Tat *c.ss.r.* '97 (LA)[Q] Long Beach, CA.
Hai–Nguyen, Joseph '67 (RIC) Norfolk, VA Our Lady of Lavang.
Hai Duong, Ignatius M. *c.m.c.* '89 (FWT) Fort Worth, TX Our Lady of Fatima.
Haig, Frank R. *s.j.* '60 (BAL)[B] Timonium, MD Loyola Graduate Center –Timonium Campus; [S] Baltimore, MD Jesuit Community of Loyola College, Inc..
Haig, Scott *s.s.s.* '98 (CLV) Highland Heights, OH St. Paschal Baylon; Houston, TX Corpus Christi.
Hain, Raymond B. '48 (LIN)[E] Lincoln, NE Bonacum House; Building Commission Retired.
Hain, Raymond (LIN) Presbyteral Council.
Haines, Jeffrey R. (MIL) West Bend, WI St. Frances Cabrini; Archdiocesan Consultors; Archdiocesan Council of Priests.
Haines, Kevin J. '87 (LFT) Westfield, IN St. Maria Goretti.
Haiss, Maurice *s.t.* '56 (WDC)[M] Adelphi, MD Missionary Servants of the Most Holy Trinity.
Hajduch, Joseph *c.pp.s.* '47 (CIN)[B] Carthagena, OH St. Charles.
Hajduk, Edward J. '53 (NEW) Bayonne, NJ St. Henry's.
Hajkowski, Stanislaw *s.ch.* '82 (DET)[K] Sterling Heights, MI Society of Christ Provincial Home.
Hakala, Thomas *o.carm.* '78 (JOL)[L] Darien Carmelite Provincial Office.
Hake, James E. '60 (SAL) Salina, KS Cathedral of the Sacred Heart; Lincoln, KS St. Joseph's; Lincoln, KS St. Mary's; Lincoln, KS St. Patrick's; Vicar General; Defender of the Bond; College of Consultors; Council of Priests; Personnel Board; Art and Architecture Commission; Due Process Board; Holy Childhood, Pontifical Association; Propagation of the Faith; Diocesan Committee Regarding Alleged Cases of Child Sexual Abuse.
Hake, James (SAL) Vocation Ministry Committee; Ex Officio.
Halabura, Stephen J. '61 (ALN) Barnesville, PA St. Richard of Chichester.
Haladej, Peter '02 (Y) Girard, OH St. Rose.
Haladus, Jerome Joachim *o.p.* '64 (NY)[EE] New York St. Vincent Ferrer Priory.
Haladus, Victorian *o.f.m.* '61 (SFD)[L] Springfield, IL Our Lady of Angels Friary.
Halaiko, David J. '67 (CLV) Akron, OH Nativity Of the Lord Jesus.
Halbert, John K. *m.m.* '59 (NY).
Halbing, William J. '82 (NEW)[EE] Newark, NJ St. Antoninus.
Halbing, William '82 (NEW) Newark, NJ St. Ann.
Halborg, John E. '80 (NY) New York, NY St. Thomas More; [II] New York, NY St. Ansgar Scandinavian Catholic League.
Haldane, Richard S. '92 (B) Lewiston, ID St. James.
Hale, Robert *o.s.b.cam.* '66 (OAK)[S] Berkeley, CA Incarnation Monastery, Camaldolese Benedictines.
Hale, Robert *o.s.b.cam.* '66 (MRY)[F] Berkeley, CA Incarnation Monastery.
Haley, James A. *c.s.p.* '68 (KNX) Knoxville, TN Immaculate Conception; Knoxville, TN Calvary; Presbyteral Council; Cemeteries.
Haley, James R. '87 (ARL) On Leave of Absence.
Haley, Joseph V. *c.m.* '54 (SJ)[Q] Montebello, CA DePaul Evangelization Center; [W] Montebello, CA DePaul Evangelization Center.
Haley, Thomas '78 (STL) St. Louis, MO St. George.
Haley, William J. '52 (BO) Holliston, MA St. Mary.
Halfacre, Philip D. (PEO) Diocesan Education Commission; Presbyteral Council.
Halfacre, Philip '91 (PEO) Ottawa (Naplate), IL St. Mary's; Ottawa, IL St. Patrick's; Diocesan College of Consultors.
Halfmann, Curtis T. '59 (LUB) Retired.
Halfpenny, Patrick F. '75 (DET)[A] Detroit, MI Sacred Heart Major Seminary, Inc.; Special Assignment.
Halka, Frantisek A. '98 (ALT) Military Chaplains.
Halka, Frantisek (ALT) Army Chaplains.
Halkovic, Thomas M. *c.s.c.* '71 (FR)[A] North Easton, MA Stonehill College; [A] North Easton, MA Holy Cross Fathers Religious.
Hall, Adrian B. '64 (NO) Slidell, LA Our Lady of Lourdes.
Hall, Alan *o.m.v.* '88 (BO)[V] Milton, MA Oblate Residence (St. Joseph House); [AA] Boston, MA St. Francis Chapel.
Hall, Charles D. '79 (GR) Portland, MI St. Patrick's.
Hall, Daniel R. *c.s.v.* '88 (CHI)[D] Arlington Heights, IL St. Viator High School.
Hall, Douglas C. '79 (OM) Military Chaplains; Air Force Chaplains.
Hall, Eric *o.f.m.cap.* '96 (NY)[EE] New York, NY Immaculate Conception Friary.
Hall, Henry '48 (MRY) Retired.
Hall, Howard B. '62 (BR) Morganza, LA St. Ann.
Hall, Howard *o.f.m.* '53 (LA) Santa Barbara, CA Old Mission Santa Barbara; [Q] Santa Barbara, CA Franciscan Friary, Order of Friars Minor (Old Mission).
Hall, James W. '70 (ELP) El Paso, TX St. Thomas Aquinas; Judges.
Hall, James *m.s.c.* '01 (RCK)[G] Aurora, IL Missionaries of the Sacred Heart Community.
Hall, Jerome M. *s.j.* '77 (WDC)[C] Catholic University of America, The.
Hall, Jerome M. *s.j.* (BAL)[D] Baltimore, MD Loyola Blakefield.
Hall, John F. '55 (DET) Retired.
Hall, John M. '80 (IND) Seymour, IN Our Lady of Providence; Seymour, IN St. Ambrose.
Hall, John R. '80 (CHI) Niles, IL Our Lady of Ransom.
Hall, John '82 (PHX) On Leave.
Hall, Joseph S. '85 (L)[J] Louisville, KY Nazareth Home; [M] Louisville, KY Sacred Heart Village, Inc..
Hall, Martin J. '52 (RVC) Levittown, NY St. Bernard Retired.
Hall, Michael *o.s.b.* '65 (WDC)[M] Washington, DC St. Anselm's Abbey.
Hall, Ralph T. *o.p.* '55 (PRO)[P] Providence St. Thomas Aquinas Priory at Providence College.
Hall, Richard *o.m.i.* '93 (LAR) Austin, TX Our Lady of Guadalupe.
Hall, Robert C. '79 (ALT) Conemaugh, PA Sacred Heart; Conemaugh, PA Assumption of B.V.M..
Hall, Robert Eric '01 (WH) Wheeling, WV St. Michael's.
Hall, Robert '85 (HEL) Bozeman, MT Resurrection; [H] Bozeman, MT Montana State University.
Hall, Rodney '91 (SAC) Retired.
Hall, Sidney Peter '57 (SAC) West Sacramento, CA Holy Cross.
Hall, Sidney '57 (SAC) Retired.
Hall, Thomas P. *c.s.p.* '77 (NY)[EE] Jamaica Estates Paulist Fathers Generalate; Navy Chaplains.
Hall, Walter J. '49 (ALN) Pottsville, PA St. Kieran.
Hall, Warren R. '89 (NEW)[B] St. Thomas University; On Duty Outside the Archdiocese.
Hall, Warren (MIA) St. Thomas University.
Halladay, Paul A. (MOB) Mobile, AL St. Ignatius.
Halladay, Paul (MOB) Group IV.
Hallahan, Kenneth P. '75 (CAM) Camden, NJ St. Joan of Arc; Campaign for Human Development.
Hallahan, Timothy J. '57 (SPR) Retired.
Hallahan, William *o.m.i.* (OAK)[H] Soquel, CA St. Clare's Retreat House; Oakland, CA Sacred Heart.
Hallee, Roger *o.m.i.* (FgM).
Hallemann, John L. '55 (STL) Oakville, MO Queen of All Saints.
Haller, Joseph A. *s.j.* '55 (WDC)[M] Washington, DC The Jesuit Community at Georgetown University.
Halleran, Thomas *s.v.d.* '44 (CHI)[B] Techny, IL Divine Word Residence.
Halleron, James E. '97 (TOL)[B] Tiffin, OH Calvert High School.
Hallett, Garth L. *s.j.* '59 (STL)[C] Philosophy and Letters, College of; [C] Saint Louis University; [O] St. Louis, MO Jesuit Community Corporation at St. Louis University – Jesuit Hall.
Halligan, Damian O. *s.j.* '67 (RVC)[O] Manhasset, NY St. Ignatius Retreat House, Inisfada.
Halligan, James J. '51 (NY) New York, NY St. Peter.
Halligan, James '51 (NY) Retired.
Halligan, Raymond Ferrer *o.p.* '60 (NY)[EE] New York, NY St. Vincent Ferrer Priory; [II] New York, NY St. Jude Dominican Missions.
Hallin, Albert W. '61 (PEO) Champaign, IL Holy Cross; Vicariates and Vicars; Clergymen's Aid, Inc.; Commission for Ecumenism.
Hallinan, Edward J. '83 (PH) Philadelphia, PA St. Martin De Porres.
Hallinan, Mark C. *s.j.* '95 (NY) New York, NY St. Ignatius Loyola; [EE] New York, NY Jesuit Provincial's Office; [EE] New York, NY St. Ignatius Loyola Residence.
Hallisey, James T. (B) AUXILIARY CHAPLAINS CONTRACT CHAPLAINS.
Hallissey, James T. '40 (B) Retired.
Hallissey, LaSalle *o.p.* '79 (OAK) Antioch, CA Holy Rosary; Portland, OR Holy Rosary Parish & Dominican Priory.
Hallisy, Peter *c.p.* '51 (HRT)[M] West Hartford Holy Family Monastery/Retreat.
Halliwell, Raymond *m.s.a.* '93 (NOR)[A] Cromwell, CT Holy Apostles College and Seminary; [F] Cromwell, CT Society of the Missionaries of the Holy Apostles.
Halliwell, Robert J. '57 (NEW) Northvale, NJ St. Anthony's Retired.
Hallock, Addison *m.s.a.* '74 (NOR)[A] Cromwell, CT Holy Apostles College and Seminary; [F] Cromwell, CT Society of the Missionaries of the Holy Apostles.
Halloran, Emmett J. '50 (ROC) Canadaigua, NY St. Mary Retired.
Halloran, James '43 (COS) Retired.
Halloran, John C. '62 (PRO) Narragansett, RI St. Thomas More; Deans; College of Consultors.
Halloran, John J. '48 (LA) Retired.
Halloran, John M. '87 (PH) Philadelphia, PA Incarnation of Our Lord.
Halloran, John '48 (HON) Retired.
Halloran, John '48 (SJ) Milpitas, CA St. Elizabeth.
Halloran, Joseph H. '47 (COS) Retired.
Halloran, Joseph '53 (ALB) Troy, NY St. Paul the Apostle.
Halloran, Paul F. '53 (WIN) Retired.
Halloran, Walter H. *s.j.* '54 (MIL)[O] Wauwatosa, WI Jesuit Community at St. Camillus.
Hallsten, Thomas *o.s.b.* '90 (SCL)[I] Collegeville, MN St. John's Abbey, of the Order of St. Benedict.
Halovatch, Paul J. '70 (HRT) Medical Leave.
Halphen, Jude '94 (LAF) New Iberia, LA St. Peter.
Halpin, Joseph A. '79 (TR) Retired.
Halpin, Joseph W. *m.m.* '52 (FgM).
Halpine, James F. '52 (TLS) Tulsa, OK Holy Family Cathedral.
Halsema, Doug (PT) Independent Review Board; Pensacola.
Halsema, Douglas (PT) Pensacola, FL St. Paul.
Halstead, James R. *o.s.a.* '76 (CHI) Evanston, IL St. Nicholas.
Halter, Robert *c.ss.r.* '70 (CHI) Chicago, IL St. Michael.
Haltere, Robert *c.ss.r.* '70 (CHI)[N] Chicago, IL The Redemptorist Fathers of Chicago.
Halton, Thomas P. '50 (WDC)[C] Catholic University of America, The Retired.
Halus, Robert E. '82 (PBR) Perryopolis, PA St. Nicholas.
Haluska, Charles A. '51 (COL) Retired.
Halvey, William *s.v.d.* '76 (MIL)[O] East Troy, WI Divine Word Missionaries.
Halvey, William *s.v.d.* (CHY) In Residence.
Ham, George E. '67 (MAN) Wolfeboro, NH St. Cecilia; Wolfeboro, NH St. Katharine Drexel.
Ham, Jerome '68 (PEO) Streator, IL St. Anthony of Padua; Streator, IL St. Casimir; Diocesan College of Consultors.
Hamaday, Ronald A. *o.s.a.* '78 (CAM)[C] Richland, NJ St. Augustine Preparatory School; Navy Reserve Chaplains.
Hamak, William '92 (SFS) Webster, SD Christ the King.
Hambrough, Patrick K. '85 (STL) St. Louis, MO St. Mark.
Hambrough, Patrick K. (STL) Archdiocesan Consultors; Archdiocesan Council of Priests.
Hamburger, Donald C. '46 (CHR) Retired.
Hamel, J. Thomas *s.j.* '58 (WOR)[O] Worcester, MA Jesuits of Holy Cross College, Inc..
Hamel, James A. '92 (NEW) Military Chaplains; Air Force Chaplains.
Hamel, Philip N. '85 (FR) South Dartmouth, MA St. Mary's.
Hamel, Robert F. '83 (STP) Retired.
Hamernick, Joseph M. *s.j.* '62 (BAL)[S] Baltimore, MD Jesuit Fathers and Brothers Maryland Provincial Curia.
Hamernik, Peter P. (WOR) Retired.
Hamill, Francis J. *s.j.* '61 (NY).
Hamill, Gregory J. '94 (PH) Downingtown, PA St. Joseph.
Hamill, William A. *o.s.a.* '68 (TLS)[B] Tulsa, OK Cascia Hall Preparatory School.
Hamilton, Daniel E. '72 (ARL) On Leave of Absence; Defenders of the Bond.
Hamilton, Daniel S. '58 (RVC) Lindenhurst, NY Our Lady of Perpetual Help.
Hamilton, Donald Joseph *o.c.s.o.* '46 (SPC)[E] Ava, MO Assumption Abbey (Trappist).
Hamilton, Edward A. '59 (ORL) Retired.
Hamilton, James J. '53 (PRO) Retired.
Hamilton, James '58 (CC) Judges Retired.
Hamilton, John W. '70 (BUR) Deans; South Burlington, VT St. John Vianney.
Hamilton, Ken *s.v.d.* '82 (OAK) Oakland, CA St. Lawrence O'Toole.
Hamilton, Lamont R. '79 (NY) Larchmont, NY SS. John and Paul.
Hamilton, Mark M. '94 (L) On Duty Outside the Archdiocese.
Hamilton, Philip A. '44 (DUB) Retired.
Hamilton, Stephen V. '99 (OKL) Guymon, OK St. Peter's.
Hamilton, Terence J. '73 (CIN) Cincinnati, OH St. Vincent Ferrer.
Hamilton, Thomas M. *s.m.* '88 (SFR) San Bruno, CA St. Robert; AUXILIARY CHAPLAINS CONTRACT CHAPLAINS.
Hamilton, Thomas *o.f.m.conv.* '76 (SB) Riverside, CA Queen of Angels; [E] Riverside, CA Conventual Franciscans, OFM Conv..
Hamilton, William J. *s.j.* '63 (MAN) Elliott Hospital; Manchester, NH St. Anthony of Padua; Veterans Administration Medical Center.
Hamilton, William J. *s.j.* '63 (BO)[E] Dorchester, MA

Boston College High School & Jesuit Community; [V] Boston The Society of Jesus of New England–Provincial Offices.
Hamilton, William J. *s.j.* '63 (MAN) Elliott Hospital; Manchester, NH St. Anthony of Padua; Veterans Administration Medical Center.
Hamilton, William J. *s.j.* '63 (BO)[E] Dorchester, MA Boston College High School & Jesuit Community; [V] Boston The Society of Jesus of New England–Provincial Offices.
Hamilton, William J. *s.j.* '63 (MAN) Elliott Hospital; Manchester, NH St. Anthony of Padua; Veterans Administration Medical Center.
Hamilton, William J. *k.h.s.* '80 (SPR) Easthampton, MA Immaculate Conception.
Hamilton, William J. (SPR) Diocesan Commission for the Liturgy; Commission on Church Music.
Hamlet, Ralph '62 (RIC) Retired.
Hamlett, Christopher M. '82 (E) Erie, PA St. Andrew; [B] Erie, PA Gannon University.
Hamm, David A. *s.t.* '75 (JKS) Philadelphia, MS Holy Rosary.
Hamm, M. Dennis *s.j.* '70 (OM)[K] Omaha, NE Jesuit Community at Creighton University.
Hamm, Robert E. *s.j.* '68 (BAL).
Hamm, Thomas F. (STU)[S] Wintersville, OH Blessed Sacrament; Wintersville, OH Our Lady of Lourdes.
Hammeke, Gerald A. (DOD) Priests' Trust Fund.
Hammel, Gerald *s.m.* '78 (SAT) Helotes, TX Our Lady of Guadalupe.
Hammelman, William *o.s.b.* '71 (P) Silverton, OR St. Paul; [L] St. Benedict, OR Mt. Angel Abbey.
Hammer, Edmond '42 (NY) Retired.
Hammer, James *o.f.m.cap.* '65 (NOR) Middletown, CT St. Pius X.
Hammer, Jefferson '60 (NY) Manhattan, NY St. Vincent Hospital.
Hammer, Michael J. '69 (MIL) Special Assignment.
Hammer, William D. '80 (L) Louisville, KY Cathedral of the Assumption; Clergy Personnel Commission; Office of Ecumenical and Interreligious Relations.
Hammerl, Leo E. '44 (BUF)[O] Tonawanda, NY O'Hara Residence Retired.
Hammerschmitt, Clemens '73 (PMB) Lake Worth, FL St. Matthew; [H] West Palm Beach, FL Palm Beach District Council.
Hammerschmitt, Clemens '77 (PMB)[M] Diocesan Council of Catholic Women.
Hammerstein, Harold *o.s.b.* '48 (IND)[K] Evansville, IN.
Hammett, Peter E. *o.s.b.* '72 (NO)[P] St. Benedict, LA St. Joseph Abbey; Franklinton, LA Holy Family.
Hammo, Gerard E. (FgM).
Hammond, Charles '76 (SAG) Alma, MI St. Mary; St. Louis, MI St. Joseph.
Hammond, H. Martin '73 (BAL) Baltimore, MD St. Isaac Jogues.
Hammond, John *o.s.b.* '50 (BUR)[E] Weston, VT Priory of Benedictine Monks.
Hammond, Joseph Mary *c.h.s.* '89 (KNX) Greeneville, TN Notre Dame.
Hammond, Joseph '89 (KNX) Morristown, TN St. Patrick.
Hammond, Mark J. '89 (COL) Columbus, OH St. Mary; Parochial Examiners; Vicariate 6: South; Presiding Judges of First Instance; Health Affairs Department (Hospitals).
Hammond, Robert '52 (FTW)[G] Fort Wayne, IN Saint Anne Home & Retirement Community; [G] Fort Wayne, IN St. Anne Home of the Diocese of Fort Wayne – South Bend, Inc..
Hamon, Victor '93 (TYL) Tyler, TX Cathedral of the Immaculate Conception.
Hampe, Ray '54 (STL)[J] St. Charles, MO SSM St. Joseph Health Center.
Hampe, Raymond A. '54 (STL) St. Charles, MO St. Peter.
Hampe, Raymond H. '54 (STL) St. Charles, MO St. Joseph Health Center.
Hamperzonian, Jerry '70 (PSC) On Duty Outside Diocese.
Hamperzonian, Jerry '70 (SD) San Diego, CA Blessed Sacrament; La Jolla, CA Veterans Administration Hospital.
Hampsch, John *c.m.f.* '52 (LA)[Q] Los Angeles, CA Claretian Retreat Center Community.
Hampton, James '88 (MIA) Retired.
Hamrogue, John *c.ss.r.* '63 (BRK) Brooklyn, NY Our Lady of Perpetual Help Basilica.
Han, Deog–Su (NEW) Saddle Brook, NJ Korean Martyrs.
Han, Mariusz *s.j.* '01 (CHI)[N] Chicago, IL Sacred Heart Mission House.
Hanauska, Joseph F. '40 (MIL) Retired.
Hanbury, Kevin M. '72 (NEW)[B] School of Diplomacy and Intl. Rels..
Hanbury, Kevin (NEW) Members.
Hanchon, Donald F. '74 (DET) Detroit, MI Holy Redeemer.
Hancock, George H. '47 (OWN) Grand Rivers, KY St. Anthony of Padua.
Hand, Dennis M. '75 (GRY) On Duty Outside the Diocese.
Hand, John D. '98 (PH) Ridley Park, PA St. Madeline.
Hand, Kenneth J. '72 (BRK) Released from Diocesan Assignment; Bayside, NY Sacred Heart of Jesus.
Hand, Kevin '52 (AMA)[I] Amarillo, TX Monsignor B.A. Erpen Trust Fund; White Deer, TX Sacred Heart Retired.
Hand, Raymond *o.f.m.cap.* '62 (NY)[EE] Yonkers, NY St. Clare Friary.
Hand, Robert T. '97 (SAV) Savannah, GA St. Peter the Apostle Church.
Hand, Thomas G. *s.j.* '51 (SJ)[M] Los Gatos Sacred Heart Jesuit Center.
Handal, Ephrem '03 (NTN) McLean, VA Holy Transfiguration.
Handges, William E. '64 (ALN) Bethlehem, PA Notre Dame of Bethlehem.
Handrahan, John B. *s.j.* '58 (BO)[V] Boston The Society of Jesus of New England–Provincial Offices.
Handrahan, John *s.j.* '58 (MIA) Lauderdale–by–the–Sea, FL Assumption.
Handwerker, Valentine N. '74 (MEM) Memphis, TN Cathedral of the Immaculate Conception; Office of Ecumenism; Presbyteral Council and College of Consultors.
Handwerker, Valentine '74 (MEM)[C] Memphis, TN Immaculate Conception High School.
Hane, Howerd S. '67 (BO) Senior Priests Retired.
Hanefeldt, Joseph G. '84 (OM) Omaha, NE St. Elizabeth Ann.
Hanel, Charles T. '83 (MIL) Hubertus, WI St. Gabriel.
Hanes, Sebastian *o.s.p.p.e.* '81 (PH)[AA] Office.
Haney, John R. '61 (PIT) Pittsburgh, PA St. Gabriel of the Sorrowful Virgin; Priest Council College of Consultors; Clergy Personnel Board.
Haney, Michael *o.f.m.* '74 (SHP) West Monroe, LA St. Paschal; Diocesan Liturgy Commission.
Haney, T. Ronald (HBG) Secretary for Communications; The "Catholic Witness"; Public Relations, Department for.
Haney, Thomas R. '58 (HBG) New Cumberland, PA St. Theresa of the Infant Jesus.
Hanh, Joseph Phan Trong '70 (KC) Kansas City, MO Church of the Holy Martyrs.
Hanhauser, Martin *o.f.m.* '42 (BO)[Y] Boston, MA Saint Anthony Residence.
Hanic, John D. '83 (CHL) North Wilkesboro, NC St. John Baptist de LaSalle.
Hanic, Johnathan '02 (CHL) Winston–Salem, NC St. Leo's.
Hanifin, Michael '87 (ORG) Yorba Linda, CA Santa Clara de Asis.
Hankee, Robert Jason '02 (IND) Brownsburg, IN St. Malachy
Hankiewicz, Edward A. '79 (GR) Grand Rapids, MI Sacred Heart of Jesus.
Hankiewicz, Edward A. (KAL) Judges.
Hankiewicz, Edward '79 (GR) On Special Assignment.
Hankinson, Aloysius *t.o.r.* '50 (ALT)[F] Hollidaysburg, PA St. Joseph Friary.
Hankomoone, Cornelius *s.s.* '96 (BAL)[S] Emmaus Spirituality Center.
Hanks, Sebastian *o.s.p.p.e.* '81 (BUF) Buffalo, NY Corpus Christi.
Hankus, David J. '84 (JOL) Bolingbrook, IL St. Francis of Assisi.
Hanley, Andrew W. '40 (SD) Retired.
Hanley, Dennis P. '81 (HRT) Military Chaplains; Air Force Chaplains.
Hanley, Foster *o.carm.* '63 (TUC)[A] Tucson, AZ Salpointe Catholic High School; [F] Tucson, AZ Carmelite Priory.
Hanley, Francis *c.s.sp.* '59 (PIT)[B] Pittsburgh, PA Duquesne University of the Holy Spirit.
Hanley, Gerald T. '73 (RNO) Carson City, NV St. Teresa of Avila.
Hanley, James P. '51 (COL) Retired.
Hanley, James R. *s.j.* '58 (SJ)[L] Los Altos, CA Jesuit Retreat House.
Hanley, John A. *o.s.f.s.* '86 (ALN)[B] Center Valley, PA DeSales University; [B] Center Valley, PA DeSales University; [K] Center Valley, PA Oblates of St. Francis de Sales; [O] Center Valley, PA DeSales University (Center Valley).
Hanley, John F. *o.m.i.* (BO) MERRIMACK REGION.
Hanley, John P. '94 (PAT) Paterson, NJ St. Casimir's; Paterson, NJ St. Gerard Majella; Auditors.
Hanley, John W. *o.m.i.* (BO) Tewksbury, MA St. William.
Hanley, John '56 (PHX) Tempe, AZ Holy Spirit.
Hanley, Joseph F. '68 (CHR) Charleston, SC Blessed Sacrament.
Hanley, Joseph F. (CHR) Deans.
Hanley, Joseph F. (CHR) College of Consultors; Presbyteral Council.
Hanley, Joseph (CHR) Diocesan Curia.
Hanley, Lawrence F. '52 (CHI) Retired.
Hanley, Thomas E. '65 (WIL) Absent on Sick Leave; Parish Priest Consultors; Cursillo Movement.
Hanley, William '45 (SPK) Retired.
Hanley, William '69 (ORL) Melbourne, FL Our Lady of Lourdes.
Hanlon, Andrew J. '68 (PH) Brookhaven, PA Our Lady of Charity.
Hanlon, Berard J. *o.f.m.* '63 (FgM).
Hanlon, Capistran *o.f.m.* '60 (ALB)[B] Siena College.
Hanlon, Edward J. '86 (WOR) Worcester, MA Sacred Heart.
Hanlon, Francis J. *o.s.f.s.* '76 (WIL)[J] Wilmington, DE Oblates of St. Francis De Sales; [J] Wilmington, DE DeSales House.
Hanlon, Robert M. *s.j.* '64 (BO)[V] Boston The Society of Jesus of New England–Provincial Offices.
Hanlon, Robert P. *o.s.f.s.* '57 (WIL)[J] Childs, MD Retirement and Assisted Care Facility.
Hanly, Joseph M. *c.s.p.* '53 (NY)[EE] Jamaica Estates Paulist Fathers Generalate.
Hanly, Joseph M. *c.s.p.* '53 (SFR) San Francisco, CA Old St. Mary's Cathedral Retired.
Hanly, Michael A. '67 (NEW) Verona, NJ Our Lady of the Lake.
Hann, Michael *c.i.c.m.* '73 (ARL)[J] Arlington, VA Missionhurst, C.I.C.M.–Central House and Provincialate.
Hanna, Austin B. '36 (ROC) Retired.
Hanna, Don Michael '64 (RIC) Retired.
Hanna, George *s.d.b.* '66 (NEW) Orange, NJ Our Lady of the Valley.
Hanna, George *s.d.b.* '66 (NY)[II] New York, NY Don Bosco Harlem Association, Inc..
Hanna, Jack H. *c.s.b.* '74 (GAL)[F] Houston, TX St. Thomas High School.
Hannafey, Francis T. *s.j.* '93 (BGP)[B] Fairfield, CT Fairfield University; [P] Fairfield, CT The Fairfield Jesuit Community–Fairfield University.
Hannafin, Steven J. '01 (RVC) Wantagh, NY St. Frances de Chantal.
Hannah, Raymond *s.v.d.* '58 (BLX)[A] Bay St. Louis, MS St. Augustine's.
Hannan, Gabriel *s.t.* '55 (WDC)[M] Adelphi, MD Missionary Servants of the Most Holy Trinity.
Hannan, James E. *o.s.a.* '44 (SD)[H] San Diego, CA Augustinian Community.
Hannan, John P. (BAL) Interdiocesan Judges.
Hannan, John '55 (SAC) Sacramento, CA St. Philomene.
Hannan, W. Patrick *c.s.c.* '89 (CHI)[D] Niles, IL Notre Dame High School.
Hannappel, Joseph A. '84 (GI) Spalding, NE St. Michael's; Priests' Advisory Board (Presbyteral Council).
Hanneke, Richard E. '76 (STL) Ellisville, MO St. Clare of Assisi.
Hanneman, Dennis A. '72 (OM) Omaha, NE St. Vincent de Paul.
Hannes, David A. '83 (PRM) Flushing, MI St. Michael.
Hannes, David (PRM) Presbyteral Council; Eparchial Consultors; Vicar Judicialis.
Hannick, Anthony S. '58 (YAK) Walnut Creek, CA St. Anne Retired.
Hannigan, John T. '76 (CHI) Morrisonville, IL St. Maurice; Raymond, IL St Raymond; Navy Chaplains; Military Chaplains.
Hannigan, Thomas J. '49 (MAN) Manchester, NH St. Catherine; Council of Priests; Clergy Personnel Board.
Hannon, James J. '45 (BLX) Promoter of Justice; Defenders of the Bond; Pro–Synodal Judges Retired.
Hannon, James J. '57 (RVC) Brentwood, NY St. Anne's.
Hannon, James '81 (BRK) On Leave/Unassigned.
Hannon, James '88 (BAL) Emmitsburg, MD St. Anthony Shrine; Emmitsburg, MD Our Lady of Mount Carmel; Advocates and Procurators.
Hannon, John M. '60 (BO) Hanson, MA St. Joseph the Worker.
Hannon, John P. '76 (HRT) Retired.
Hannon, Joseph F. *s.d.b.* (MO) Army Chaplains.
Hannon, Ken *o.m.i.* '72 (SAT)[C] Oblate School of Theology; [M] San Antonio, TX De Mazenod House.
Hannon, Kevin '75 (SY) Manlius, NY St. Ann.
Hannon, Michael '47 (ORL) Retired.
Hannon, Richard T. '93 (GAY) Elmira, MI St. Thomas Aquinas.
Hannon, Robert E. '54 (HON) Leave of Absence Retired.
Hannon, Robert '54 (HON) Honolulu, HI Cathedral of Our Lady of Peace.
Hannon, Timothy G. '62 (MIA) Fort Lauderdale, FL St. Anthony.
Hanowsky, Andrew '88 (SJP) Parma, OH St. Josaphat Cathedral.
Hanrahan, Denis G. '59 (OKL) Guthrie, OK St. Mary's.
Hanrahan, Edward J. *s.j.* '61 (BO)[V] Newton, MA The Jesuit Community at Boston College.
Hanrahan, John A. '66 (RCK) Polo, IL St. Mary's.
Hanrahan, John W. '55 (L) Retired.
Hanrahan, William P. '69 (NEW) Military Chaplains; Air Force Chaplains.
Hanratty, Brendan *o.c.s.o.* '58 (SLC)[F] Huntsville, UT Abbey of Our Lady of the Holy Trinity of the Order of Cistercians.

Hansen, Howard *o.f.m.conv.* '57 (STP)[P] Prior Lake, MN Franciscan Retreats.
Hansen, Lawrence H. '68 (PH)[U] Darby, PA Mercy Fitzgerald Hospital; [U] Langhorne, PA St. Mary Medical Center.
Hansen, Lawrence H. '68 (NU) On Duty Outside the Diocese.
Hansen, Michael '67 (NEW) Emerson, NJ Church of the Assumption.
Hansen, Thomas J. *s.j.* '96 (OM)[K] Omaha, NE Jesuit Community at Creighton University.
Hanser, F. Patrick *c.m.* '70 (DAL).
Hanser, Patrick F. '70 (DAL)[G] Dallas, TX St. Paul Medical Center; Dallas, TX Zale/Lipshy University Hospital.
Hansmann, Joseph D. '62 (BEL) Hecker, IL St. Augustine of Canterbury; Waterloo, IL St. Michael.
Hanson, Christopher *o.s.b.* '96 (STL)[F] Creve Coeur, MO St. Louis Priory School; [O] St. Louis, MO The Abbey of St. Mary and St. Louis.
Hanson, Donald M. '71 (RVC) Carle Place, NY Church of Our Lady of Hope.
Hanson, Donald (RVC) Hicksville Deanery.
Hanson, James E. '61 (STL) Ste. Genevieve, MO St. Joseph.
Hanson, Kirby C. '70 (SFR) Retired.
Hanson, Richard N. '75 (CHL) Charlotte, NC St. Vincent de Paul.
Hanson, William A. '72 (RVC) Port Jefferson Station, NY St. Gerard Majella.
Hanudel, Francis A. *o.f.m.* '72 (DET) Troy, MI St. Anastasia.
Hanus, Thomas J. '66 (AUS) Cameron, TX St. Monica's.
Hanwell, John J. *s.j.* '91 (BO)[E] Dorchester, MA Boston College High School & Jesuit Community.
Hapanowicz, Arthur R. '56 (SY) Utica, NY Holy Trinity; Utica, NY Holy Trinity.
Ha Pham, Louis *c.m.c.* '94 (ROC) Rochester, NY St. Anthony of Padua.
Hapka, Jerome A. *s.a.c.* '55 (MIL)[O] Milwaukee, WI Pallotti House.
Harahan, Robert E. '74 (NEW) Summit, NJ St. Teresa's.
Harak, G. Simon *s.j.* '79 (BO)[V] Boston The Society of Jesus of New England–Provincial Offices.
Harak, G. Simon *s.j.* '79 (NY)[EE] New York, NY West Side Jesuit Community.
Haran, Ignatius '59 (SAC) Folsom, CA St. John the Baptist.
Haran, James E. '44 (BUF) Retired.
Harbaugh, James M. *s.j.* '76 (SEA)[L] Seattle, WA Jesuit Community.
Harbaugh, James *s.j.* '76 (SEA) Seattle, WA St. Therese.
Harbaugh, Paul E. '74 (BEL) Leave of Absence.
Harbert, Bruce '78 (WDC) Washington, DC St. Mary, Mother of God.
Harbison, William J. *c.ss.r.* '66 (PH) Philadelphia, PA St. Peter the Apostle.
Harbour, Gerald G. '73 (PRO) Providence, RI Rhode Island Hospital.
Harbour, Linn S. '86 (MOB) On Leave from the Archdiocese; Air Force Chaplains.
Harcarik, Bernard M. '63 (PIT) Pittsburgh, PA Prince of Peace.
Hardebeck, Donald E. '45 (LFT) Retired.
Harder, Kenneth J. '96 (TLS) Stillwater, OK St. Francis Xavier; Stillwater, OK St. John University Parish and Catholic Student Center; Judges; Campus Ministry.
Harder, Kenneth '96 (TLS)[I] Stillwater, OK St. John's University Parish and Catholic Student Center.
Harder, William (NY) On Leave of Absence.
Hardesty, Ernest L. '75 (LR) Russellville, AR St. John's; [J] Russellville, AR St. Leo the Great University Parish; Russellville, AR St. Leo the Great University Parish.
Hardesty, Ernest '75 (LR)[J] Russellville, AR Arkansas Tech University, St. Leo the Great University Parish.
Hardesty, Ernest (LR) Deans.
Hardiman, Michael J. '78 (BRK) Woodside, NY St. Sebastian; [U] Irish Apostolate; [V] Douglaston, NY Institutional Services Residence; Diocesan Institute of Languages.
Hardiman, Michael (BRK) Institutional Services.
Hardin, Boniface *o.s.b.* '59 (IND)[K] Indianapolis, IN.
Hardin, John *o.f.m.* '82 (OAK)[N] Berkeley, CA Franciscan Friars.
Hardin, John *o.f.m.* '86 (SFR)[S] San Francisco, CA St. Anthony Foundation.
Harding, Ignatius *o.f.m.* '65 (FgM).
Harding, Nicholas J. '99 (GAL) Houston, TX St. Charles Borromeo; Area Representatives.
Harding, Pius X *o.s.b.* '93 (P)[L] St. Benedict, OR Mt. Angel Abbey.
Hardman, John E. *s.s.j.* '44 (BAL)[S] Baltimore, MD St. Joseph's Manor.
Hardon, John *s.j.* '47 (WDC)[V] Kensington, MD Inter Mirifica.
Hardt, Gervase Degenhardt *o.f.m.cap.* '58 (PIT)[N] Pittsburgh, PA St. Augustine Friary.
Hare, Robert '70 (NSH)[H] Nashville, TN Glenmary Home Missioners; [L] Nashville, TN Glenmary Berson Office.
Haremza, Shawn T. '00 (WIN) Lewiston, MN St. Anthony's; Lewiston, MN St. Rose of Lima; Mankato, MN St. John the Baptist's; Lewiston, MN Immaculate Conception.
Haren, Donald J. *m.m.* '47 (SJ)[M] Los Altos, CA Maryknoll.
Haren, Thomas A. '73 (CLV) Cleveland, OH St. Jerome.
Haren, Thomas (CLV) Presbyteral Council; Holy Name Societies, Cleveland Diocesan Union.
Harer, Eric K. '84 (SY) Oswego, NY St. Paul; Oswego, NY St. Peter & St. Paul.
Harfmann, John G. *s.s.j.* '62 (BAL)[S] Baltimore, MD St. Joseph Society of the Sacred Heart House of Central Administration.
Hargaden, Kevin J. '99 (ATL) Atlanta, GA Cathedral of Christ the King; [B] Roswell, GA Blessed Trinity Catholic High School.
Harger, Bruce E. '01 (NEW) Summit, NJ St. Teresa's.
Hargesheimer, Thomas J. '68 (WIN) Owatonna, MN St. Joseph's; Elected At–Large Representatives; Council of Catholic Women.
Harguindeguy, John (FRS) Personnel Committee.
Harhager, John H. *s.m.* '79 (WDC)[M] Washington, DC Marist Center.
Harkabus, Donald W. *o.s.a.* '58 (CHI)[N] Olympia Fields, IL Tolentine Monastery at Tolentine Center.
Harkin, William C. *o.s.a.* (CHL) Maggie Valley, NC St. Margaret.
Harkins, Conrad *o.f.m.* '61 (STU)[A] Steubenville, OH Franciscan University of Steubenville; [F] Steubenville, OH Holy Spirit Friary.
Harkins, John M. '65 (PH) Philadelphia, PA St. Ambrose.
Harkins, Kenneth *o.p.* '67 (WDC)[B] Washington, DC Dominican House of Studies.
Harkins, Michael J. '79 (BO) Cambridge, MA Blessed Sacrament.
Harkins, Thaddeus '55 (JKS) Port Gibson, MS St. Joseph.
Harlow, Denis '58 (BLX) Biloxi, MS Sacred Heart; Biloxi Regional Hospital, Gulf Coast Community Hospital.
Harlow, Lance W. '93 (BUR) Elected Members; Charismatic Renewal; Bethel, VT St. Anthony.
Harlow, Sean R. *o.carm.* '69 (NY) New York, NY Our Lady of the Scapular/St. Stephen.
Harman, Charles W. '54 (LA) Retired.
Harman, Paul F. *s.j.* '68 (BO)[V] Boston, MA Arrupe House; [V] Newton, MA The Jesuit Community at Boston College.
Harman, Peter C. '99 (SFD) Springfield, IL St. Agnes.
Harman, Peter (SFD) Commission for the Liturgy; Presbyteral Council.
Harmening, Adrian W. *o.s.b.* '55 (RIC) Richmond, VA St. Joseph; [L] Richmond, VA Mary Mother of the Church Abbey.
Harmeyer, Gary (RIC) Virginia Beach, VA St. Luke.
Harmless, William J. *s.j.* '87 (OM)[K] Omaha, NE Jesuit Community at Creighton University.
Harmon, Alban *c.p.* '58 (BAL)[S] Baltimore, MD St. Joseph's Passionist Community; Defenders of the Bond.
Harmon, Alban *c.p.* (R) Defenders of the Bond.
Harmon, Barry J. '90 (SFD) Newton, IL St. Thomas the Apostle; Ste. Marie, IL St. Mary; Presbyteral Council.
Harmon, John '93 (DM) Logan, IA St. Anne.
Harmon, Philip Gregory '76 (STN) Waianae, HI St. Sophia Byzantine Missions.
Harms, William C. '65 (NEW) Westfield, NJ St. Helen.
Harms, William (NEW) Members; Staff.
Harnan, James *m.s.c.* '64 (AUS) Lampasas, TX St. Mary's; Lampasas, TX Good Shepherd; Deans.
Harness, H. Robert '82 (DAV) DeWitt, IA St. Joseph's; Grand Mound, IA Church of St. Philip and James; Deans.
Harnett, Brendan G. '73 (PRT) Biddeford, ME St. Mary's.
Harnett, Edward F. '58 (CHI) Wilmette, IL St. Francis Xavier Retired.
Harnett, Timothy '56 (SD) Encinitas, CA St. John the Evangelist.
Harney, Kenneth '89 (NO) Metairie, LA St. Christopher the Martyr.
Harney, Thomas C. '62 (GF) Laurel, MT St. Anthony's.
Harney, Thomas (GF) Personnel Board; Clerical Benefit Association.
Harnischfeger, William '93 (PHX) Sun City, AZ St. Elizabeth Seton.
Harold, Thomas J. '91 (RVC) Valley Stream, NY Holy Name of Mary.
Harpe, David L. (GR) Free Soil, MI St. John Cantius; Irons, MI St. Bernard's.
Harpel, John *s.v.d.* '44 (DUB)[H] New Hampton, IA Mercy Medical Center–New Hampton.
Harper, Henry *s.s.j.* '50 (BAL) Baltimore, MD St. Peter Claver.
Harper, John H. '87 (GB) De Pere, WI St. Mary.
Harper, John '47 (R) Retired.
Harr, Gerald J. '62 (GI) Gering, NE Christ the King.
Harr, Richard *o.m.i.* (BO)[Y] Tewksbury, MA Immaculate Heart of Mary Infirmary.
Harren, Robert C. '66 (SCL) St. Stephen, MN St. Stephen's; Censores Librorum.
Harren, Robert (SCL) Judges; Diocesan Priests Pension Plan Trustees.
Harrer, Frederic J. '45 (RVC) Hicksville, NY St. Ignatius Loyola; [M] Uniondale, NY St. Pius X Residence Retired.
Harrer, Michael (MIL)[X] Greendale, WI COURAGE Association.
Harrer, Ronald *o.m.i.* '70 (STP)[M] St. Paul, MN Oblate Residence.
Harrigan, Maurice D. '96 (LA) Glendale, CA Holy Family.
Harrigan, Philip K. *s.j.* '56 (BO)[V] Weston, MA Campion Health Center, Inc..
Harriman, Michael D. '68 (SFR) San Francisco, CA St. Cecilia; College of Consultors.
Harrington, Ashley *o.carm.* '67 (NEW) Tenafly, NJ Our Lady of Mount Carmel.
Harrington, Brian J. '67 (FR) North Dartmouth, MA St. Julie Billiart.
Harrington, Daniel J. *s.j.* '71 (BO)[V] Cambridge, MA.
Harrington, Donald J. *c.m.* '73 (BRK)[D] Staten Island, NY St. John's University, Staten Island Campus; [D] Jamaica, NY St. John's University; [V] Jamaica, NY St. Vincent's House.
Harrington, Donald J. *c.m.* '73 (NY)[C] Staten Island, NY St. John's University Staten Island Campus.
Harrington, Donald J. *c.m.* '73 (BRK)[D] Staten Island, NY St. John's University, Staten Island Campus; [D] Jamaica, NY St. John's University; [V] Jamaica, NY St. Vincent's House.
Harrington, Ignatius '82 (NTN) Dublin, OH Holy Resurrection; Dublin, OH Holy Trinity; Continuing Education of Clergy Office; Vocations Office.
Harrington, James J. '53 (BO) Senior Priests Retired.
Harrington, Jay *o.p.* '85 (PH).
Harrington, Jeremy *o.f.m.* '59 (CIN)[M] Cincinnati, OH St. Francis Seraph Friary; [U] Cincinnati, OH Community Support Charitable Trust.
Harrington, John D. '56 (BO)[E] Reading, MA Austin Preparatory School.
Harrington, John F. '35 (SPR) Promoter of Justice; Diocesan Consultors; Presbyteral Council; Holy Childhood Association; Propagation of the Faith Retired.
Harrington, John P. '66 (BRK) Long Island City, NY St. Rita.
Harrington, John S. *s.j.* '48 (SPK)[J] Spokane, WA Regis Community.
Harrington, John '45 (NY) Pearl River, NY St. Margaret Retired.
Harrington, Joseph D. '56 (HEL)[B] Helena, MT Carroll College; Liaison to Senior Status Priests Retired.
Harrington, Joseph (HEL) Clergy Senior Status and Security Trust Board; Friends of The Catholic University.
Harrington, Kevin '75 (FR) New Bedford, MA St. Francis of Assisi.
Harrington, Kieran E. '01 (BRK) Brooklyn, NY St. Thomas Aquinas.
Harrington, Mark E. '79 (SC) On Duty Outside the Diocese.
Harrington, Mark '79 (PHX) Sun City, AZ Church of St. Joachim & St. Anne.
Harrington, Michael C. (BO) Wellesley, MA St. Paul.
Harrington, Richard L. '66 (BO) Randolph, MA St. Mary.
Harrington, Robert J. (NEW) Elizabeth, NJ St. Mary of the Assumption; Archdiocesan Judges.
Harrington, Russell J. '79 (LAF) Church Point, LA Assumption of the Blessed Virgin Mary; Chancellor.
Harrington, Russell (LAF) Vicar for Priests; Diocesan Consultors.
Harrington, Thomas J. '64 (FR) New Bedford, MA Holy Name of the Sacred Heart of Jesus; Defenders of the Bond; Catholic Charities Appeal.
Harris, Alfred J. '94 (WDC) Washington, DC Our Lady Queen of Peace.
Harris, Andrew *o.m.i.* '53 (P) Sweet Home, OR St. Helen.
Harris, Anton T. *s.j.* '75 (SEA)[A] Seattle, WA Seattle University.
Harris, Daniel E. *c.m.* '74 (STL)[O] St. Louis Vincentian Residence.
Harris, Daniel E. *c.m.* '74 (LA)[A] Camarillo, CA St. John's Seminary.
Harris, David T. '47 (MAR) Retired.
Harris, Edward D. *s.j.* '45 (STL)[N] St. Louis, MO Fusz Pavilion; [O] St. Louis, MO Jesuit Community Corporation at St. Louis University – Jesuit Hall.
Harris, Edwin B. *s.j.* '75 (SJ)[C] Saint Louis University.
Harris, George G. *c.s.v.* '63 (CHI).
Harris, Gerald P. '79 (SUP) River Falls, WI St. Bridget; Pastoral Consultors; Personnel Placement Board.
Harris, Glenn H. (PEO) Chillicothe, IL St. Edward's.
Harris, Jack D. *v.f.* '74 (LR) Pine Bluff, AR St. Joseph's; Pine Bluff, AR St. Peter's; [B] Pine Bluff, AR St.

Joseph Catholic Senior High School.
Harris, Jack D. (LR) Diocesan Consultors.
Harris, Jack D. (LR) Deans.
Harris, Julian P. '91 (PMB) Boynton Beach, FL St. Thomas More; Secretary.
Harris, Martin P. '55 (WDC) Hollywood, MD St. John.
Harris, Michael B. '89 (SCR) Scranton, PA St. Paul's; Presbyteral Council.
Harris, Raymon L. '94 (BAL).
Harris, Raymond L. '94 (BAL)[A] Special Assignment; [B] Emmitsburg, MD Mount Saint Mary's College; Priests' Council.
Harris, Richard D. '93 (CHR) Greenwood, SC Our Lady of Lourdes; [H] Greenwood, SC Lander University; Building & Renovation Commission; Pastoral Council; Vocations.
Harris, Richard '93 (CHR) Abbeville, SC Sacred Heart; [H] Due West, SC Erskine College.
Harris, Robert M. '59 (BRK)[P] Brooklyn, NY St. Vincent's Services, Inc..
Harris, Robert '96 (DM) Missouri Valley, IA St. Patrick.
Harris, Steven J. '80 (PH) Yeadon, PA St. Louis; Archdiocesan Judges.
Harris, Wallace A. '72 (NY) New York, NY St. Charles Borromeo; New York, NY St. Peter; New York, NY Resurrection; [R] New York, NY District Council of Manhattan; Priests Council of the Archdiocese of New York.
Harris, Wallace (NY) Manhattan (Central Harlem).
Harris, Whitney G. '80 (LKC) On Duty Outside the Diocese.
Harris, William R. '78 (SEA) Anacortes, WA St. Mary.
Harris, Xavier J. *o.f.m.* '48 (OAK)[C] Belmont, CA Notre Dame de Namur University.
Harrison, Arthur '56 (SJ) Retired.
Harrison, Brian W. *o.s.* '85 (PCE)[H] Ponce, PR Oblates of Wisdom; [B] The Pontifical Catholic University of Puerto Rico.
Harrison, Brian *o.s.* (PCE) Censores Librorum.
Harrison, Craig F. '87 (FRS) Bakersfield, CA St. Francis.
Harrison, Cyprian *o.c.s.o.* '57 (SPC)[A] Ava, MO Assumption Novitiate (Trappists); [E] Ava, MO Assumption Abbey (Trappist).
Harrison, Eugene R. *c.ss.r.* '01 (GR) Grand Rapids, MI St. Alphonsus; [I] Grand Rapids, MI The Society of the Redemptorists of the City of Grand Rapids.
Harrison, George E. '68 (FR) Seekonk, MA Our Lady of Mt. Carmel; [M] Fall River, MA Diocesan Education Center.
Harrison, James '55 (ATL) Kennesaw, GA St. Catherine of Siena.
Harrison, Jeffrey D. *s.j.* '82 (STL) St. Louis, MO St. Matthew, Apostle.
Harrison, Jeffrey D. *s.j.* '87 (STL)[F] St. Louis, MO St. Louis University High School, George H. Backer Memorial; [O] St. Louis, MO St. Matthew Jesuit Community.
Harrison, John *c.ss.r.* '67 (WIL) Seaford, DE Our Lady of Lourdes.
Harrison, Michael *s.s.c.* '48 (PRO)[P] Bristol, RI St. Columban's Retirement House.
Harrison, Patrick C. '91 (OM) Omaha, NE St. Joan of Arc; Judicial Vicar; Archbishop's Appointees.
Harrison, Robert '64 (NY)[E] New York, NY Cardinal Hayes High School.
Harrison, Timothy A. '91 (BO) Gloucester, MA St. Ann.
Harrison, Timothy '75 (ALB) Leave of Absence.
Harrison, William S. '72 (PH) Cheltenham, PA St. Joseph; Cheltenham, PA Presentation of Blessed Virgin Mary.
Harrity, Dennis '60 (DET) Grosse Pointe, MI Our Lady Star of the Sea.
Harrity, Patrick V. *c.m.* '68 (STL)[O] Perryville, MO Congregation of the Mission.
Harrity, Patrick *c.m.* '68 (EVN)[G] Evansville, IN Daughters of Charity of St. Vincent de Paul of Indiana, Inc..
Harrold, James *s.m.a.* '42 (NEW)[N] Tenafly, NJ Society of African Missions, Provincialate, S.M.A. Fathers Retired.
Harrold, John J. '92 (GBG) Donegal, PA St. Raymond of the Mountains.
Harrold, Michael (VIC) Victoria, TX Our Lady of Victory Cathedral; Diocesan Consultors; Victoria Deanery; Presbyteral Council; Judges; Priests' Personnel Board.
Harry, Alwyn C. *s.j.* '54 (BO)[V] Weston, MA Campion Health Center, Inc..
Harry, William *o.carm.* '83 (JOL)[L] Darien Carmelite Provincial Office.
Harshaw, Albert E. '73 (CAM) Woodbine, NJ St. Casimir's; Scouting.
Hart, Addison H. '99 (RCK) DeKalb, IL Christ the Teacher, University Parish of Northern Illinois University; [L] DeKalb, IL Newman Foundation for Catholic Students of Northern Illinois University; Ecumenism, Office of; Special Assignment.
Hart, Brian '63 (SEA) Unassigned.
Hart, Charles *o.f.m.* '79 (DET)[K] Detroit St. Bonaventure Friary.
Hart, Edward J. '55 (BUR)[D] Burlington, VT St. Joseph's Home Retired.
Hart, Gregory G. '84 (LR) Harrison, AR Mary, Mother of God; Deans; Yellville, AR St. Andrew Church.
Hart, James '65 (KC) Retired.
Hart, James '96 (FWT) Fort Worth, TX St. Peter The Apostle.
Hart, John E. '81 (PAT) Rockaway, NJ St. Cecilia's; Rockaway, NJ Sacred Heart.
Hart, John E. (PAT) Chancellor; Pro–Synodal Judges; Presbyteral Council; College of Consultors; Finance Council.
Hart, John '60 (SLC) Kanab, UT St. Christopher's.
Hart, Joseph A. '73 (ROC) Rochester, NY Our Lady Queen of Peace.
Hart, Joseph A. (ROC) Vicars General; Moderator of the Pastoral Center; Censores Librorum.
Hart, Joseph L. *s.s.e.* '55 (VEN)[G] Englewood, FL Society of St. Edmund Residence.
Hart, Joseph (ROC) Board of Directors.
Hart, Kevin T. '74 (WDC) Washington, DC St. Ann; Defenders of the Bond.
Hart, Kevin (WDC) Archdiocesan College of Consultors; Priests Retirement Board.
Hart, Paul S. '89 (NO) New Orleans, LA St. Andrew the Apostle.
Hart, Philip W. *c.s.p.* '73 (NY).
Hart, Richard *o.f.m.cap.* '55 (MIL)[O] Milwaukee, WI St. Conrad Friary.
Hart, Richard '01 (SAV) Dublin, GA Immaculate Conception; Council of Priests.
Hart, Robert A. '75 (GR) North Muskegon, MI Prince of Peace.
Hart, Robert H. (STP) Oakdale, MN Transfiguration; Presbyteral Council.
Hart, Robert P. *s.j.* '62 (MIL)[O] Wauwatosa, WI Jesuit Community at St. Camillus; [M] Wauwatosa, WI St. Camillus Health Center, Inc..
Hart, Rolland A. '64 (OG) Indian Lake, NY St. Mary's.
Hart, Ronald '71 (JOL) Bonfield, IL Sacred Heart; Herscher, IL St. Margaret Mary; Kankakee, IL St. James The Apostle.
Hart, Thomas B. '44 (PRO) Retired.
Hart, Thomas J. '74 (SC) Fonda, IA Our Lady of Good Counsel; Fonda, IA St. Columbkille's.
Hart, Thomas M. *o.s.b.* '88 (GBG)[H] Latrobe, PA Saint Vincent Archabbey.
Hart, William H. '58 (CAM) Priests Personnel Board Retired.
Hart, William '58 (GLP) Retired.
Harte, F. Joseph '61 (ORL) Orlando, FL Mary Queen of the Universe Shrine.
Harte, Paul D. '76 (CAM) Franklinville, NJ Nativity; Members
Harten, Dennis *o.s.a.* '75 (VEN) Naples, FL St. Elizabeth Seton.
Hartenbach, William *c.m.* '64 (STL) Ministry to Priests Office; [O] St. Louis, MO Vincentian Residence.
Harter, Benedict W. '46 (SPC)[C] Joplin, MO St. John's Regional Medical Center; Mercy Lifecare Systems, Inc.; Priests' Purgatorial Society Retired.
Harter, Leon A. *m.m.* '39 (NY).
Hartford, A. Dixon (ELP) Retired.
Hartgen, Dennis T. '73 (ALN)[EE] Reading, PA Holy Guardian Angels; [I] Reading, PA Queen of Angels Apartment; Vicars Forane.
Hartgen, William E. *s.s.* '76 (BAL)[S] Washington, DC Retired.
Harth, Charles F. '36 (BRK)[S] Queens Village, NY Queen of Peace Residence Retired.
Harth, John M. '87 (SPC) Oran, MO Guardian Angel; Region VII (B); Priests' Mutual Benefit Society.
Hartigan, Dennis P. '80 (TOL) Bluffton, OH St. Mary; Lima, OH St. John the Evangelist; [B] Lima, OH Central Catholic High School.
Hartin, Patrick '71 (SPK) Spokane, WA St. Paschal.
Hartlage, Albert J. '56 (L) Fairfield, KY St. Michael Retired.
Hartlage, William C. '41 (L)[K] Louisville, KY Bishop David Apartments Retired.
Hartle, Thomas R. *o.f.m.* '79 (PAT) Butler, NJ St. Anthony.
Hartlein, Jerome D. '58 (BEL) Mascoutah, IL Holy Childhood of Jesus; Diocesan Consultors; Building Commission, Chancery Office; Clergymen's Aid Society.
Hartley, Christopher (NY) On Duty Outside the Archdiocese.
Hartley, Gregory C. *s.j.* '86 (BAL)[B] Timonium, MD Loyola Graduate Center –Timonium Campus; [S] Baltimore, MD Jesuit Community of Loyola College, Inc..
Hartley, Paul M. '81 (JC) Shelbina, MO St. Patrick; Macon, MO Immaculate Conception; Shelbina, MO St. Mary.
Hartling, Charles W. '79 (NEW) Rutherford, NJ St. Mary's.
Hartlove, Walter J. *o.s.f.s.* '48 (FgM).
Hartman, Augustine *o.p.* '66 (SEA) Seattle, WA Blessed Sacrament.
Hartman, Glenn '76 (CAM) Sicklerville, NJ St. John Neumann.
Hartman, Joseph F. *o.s.a.* '47 (DET) Grosse Pointe Park, MI St. Clare of Montefalco.
Hartman, Raymond S. '68 (COV) Covington, KY Mother of God; [B] Covington, KY Covington Latin School.
Hartman, Thomas J. '71 (RVC)[C] Hicksville, NY Holy Trinity; Television (Telecare/TV 29).
Hartman, Thomas (RVC) Chaplains of the Nassau County Police Department; Nassau County Police Department.
Hartmann, Edward J. '76 (FBK) Fairbanks, AK Sacred Heart Cathedral; On Duty Outside the Archdiocese.
Hartmann, Edward (FBK) Presbyteral Council; Consultors.
HartmanN, John F. '53 (BRK) Retired.
Hartmann, Joseph A. '78 (DEN) Loveland, CO St. John the Evangelist; Deaneries.
Hartmann, Paul B.R. (MIL)[X] Milwaukee, WI St. Thomas More Lawyers Society; Special Assignment; Judicial Vicar; Judges for First Instance; Judges for Second Instance; Office for Marital Reconciliation–Separation; Archdiocesan Court of Equity.
Hartmann, Richard A. '73 (DET) Flat Rock, MI St. Roch; Presbyteral Council.
Hartmann, Robert J. '85 (WCH) Wichita, KS St. Francis of Assisi.
Hartmayer, Gregory J. *o.f.m.conv.* '79 (ATL) Jonesboro, GA St. Philip Benizi.
Hartnett, Daniel F. *s.j.* '74 (CHI)[C] Chicago, IL Jesuit Community at Loyola University Chicago.
Hartnett, George F. '74 (SY) Solvay, NY St. Cecilia.
Hartnett, James L. *s.m.* '55 (ATL)[C] Atlanta, GA Marist School Retired.
Hartnett, James '72 (ORG) Westminster, CA Blessed Sacrament; Judges.
Hartnett, Richard G. *s.j.* '43 (NO)[P] New Orleans, LA Ignatius Residence.
Hartnett, Robert L. '79 (BAL) Baltimore, MD Our Lady of Mount Carmel.
Hartnett, Robert (BAL) Advocates and Procurators.
Hartnett, Walter J. '45 (PH) Retired.
Hartrich, Kurt *o.f.m.* '66 (CHI)[X] Chicago, IL S.F.V., Inc..
Hartrich, Kurt *o.f.m.* '66 (SFD) Quincy, IL St. Francis Solanus; [L] Quincy, IL St. Francis Solanus Friary; Presbyteral Council.
Hartsfield, John '01 (BIR) Chancellor; Altoona, AL Corpus Christi.
Hartshorn, Christopher '94 (DM) Winterset, IA St. Joseph.
Hartshorn, Christopher (DM) Judicial Vicar; Judges.
Hartwell, James '02 (BUF) Cheektowaga, NY Infant of Prague.
Hartz, Gerald A. '59 (SC) Retired.
Hartzer, John '54 (IND) Lawrenceburg, IN St. Lawrence.
Hartzler, Joseph *s.m.* (SFR)[N] San Francisco, CA Marianist Community.
Harvey, Arthur S. *c.s.c.* '51 (FTW)[I] Notre Dame, IN Holy Cross House.
Harvey, Charles K. '52 (WCH) Retired.
Harvey, David W. '68 (LAN) Fenton, MI St. John.
Harvey, David (LAN) Worship Office.
Harvey, Fred R. (BIS) Mohall, ND St. Jerome.
Harvey, James P. *o.s.f.s.* '60 (WIL).
Harvey, James P. '96 (KNX) Greeneville, TN Notre Dame.
Harvey, Jeffrey H. *c.m.* '93 (STO) Phoenix, AZ St. Vincent de Paul.
Harvey, John A. '66 (PIT) McDonald, PA St. Alphonsus.
Harvey, John A. (PIT) Deans and Deaneries.
Harvey, John D. *o.f.m.cap.* '72 (BAL) Baltimore, MD St. Jerome; Baltimore, MD St. Martin; Baltimore, MD St. Peter the Apostle.
Harvey, John F. *o.s.f.s.* '44 (NY)[B] Center Valley, PA DeSales University; [K] Center Valley, PA Oblates of St. Francis de Sales; New York, NY St. Vincent de Paul; [II] New York, NY Courage.
Harvey, John L. '86 (CHI) Chicago, IL St. Mary of the Assumption.
Harvey, John *o.f.m.cap.* '72 (BAL)[S] Baltimore, MD St. Ambrose Friary.
Harvey, L. Warren '88 (LR) North Little Rock, AR St. Augustine; North Little Rock, AR St. Mary; North Little Rock, AR St. Patrick's.
Harvey, Lee *c.p.* (CHI)[N] Chicago, IL Passionist Community–CTU.
Harvey, Michael K. '99 (BO) Randolph, MA St. Mary.
Harvey, Michael L. *o.f.m.* '89 (ORG) Huntington Beach, CA SS. Simon and Jude; [I] Huntington Beach, CA Franciscan Friars.
Harvey, Peter J. *o.s.f.s.* '60 (PH)[AA] Philadelphia, PA Father Louis Brisson Residence; (FgM).
Harvey, Richard R. '51 (PRT) Retired.
Harvey, Warren (LR) Diocesan Council for Black Catholics.
Harvey, Wilfred *o.m.i.* '63 (BO)[V] Lowell, MA Missionary Oblates of Mary Immaculate.
Harwas, Roman '98 (SJP) McKees Rocks, PA St. John the Baptist.
Haryasz, Francis S. '58 (STA) Retired.

Hascall, John S. *o.f.m.cap.* '67 (MAR) Sault Sainte Marie, MI Holy Family Mission; Sault Sainte Marie, MI St. Isaac Jogues Mission; Sault Sainte Marie, MI St. Isaac Jogues.
Haschka, David J. *s.j.* '75 (WDC)[M] Washington, DC Leonard Neale House.
Haschka, Jonathan *s.j.* '75 (MIL)[O] St. Francis Xavier; (FgM).
Hascinger, Philip S. '72 (LFT) Grissom, IN Grissom Air Force Base, St. Michael's Chapel.
Hascorro, Miguel *sch.p* '98 (LA) Los Angeles, CA Our Lady Help of Christians (Maria Auxiliadora).
Haselbauer, Joseph *s.c.j.* '55 (MIL)[O] Franklin, WI Villa Maria.
Haselhorst, Vincent '57 (BEL) Retired.
Hasenberg, Aloysius J. '49 (MAR) Watersmeet, MI Immaculate Conception Retired.
Hasenkamp, Robert '63 (KCK) Meriden, KS St. Aloysius; Perry, KS St. Theresa's.
Hasiebar, Joseph S. '73 (PH) Coatesville, PA Veterans Administration Medical Center.
Hasieber, Joseph S. '73 (ALX) On Duty Outside the Diocese.
Haskamp, Gregory '93 (KC) St. Joseph, MO Our Lady of Guadalupe.
Haske, Henry B. *s.j.* '57 (WDC)[A] Wernersville, PA Jesuit Center; [E] Washington, DC Gonzaga College High School.
Haskin, Jay C. '67 (BUR) Colchester, VT Our Lady of Grace.
Haskins, Robert J. *s.j.* '54 (NY)[EE] New York, NY Murray–Weigel Hall.
Haslach, Stephen *c.p.* '54 (NY)[EE] Pelham Manor, NY St. Vincent's Residence; [II] Pelham, NY Passionist Communications, Inc..
Haslinger, Philip '72 (LFT) Logansport, IN All Saints.
Haspedis, George '56 (SPK) Retired.
Hasse, James A. *s.j.* '69 (CIN)[M] Cincinnati, OH Claver Jesuit Community.
Hassett, James F. '75 (BUF) Olcott, NY St. Charles Borromeo; Barker, NY St. Patrick.
Hassey, Athanase '50 (NTN) Retired.
Hasso, Bede J. *o.s.b.* '57 (GBG)[H] Latrobe, PA Saint Vincent Archabbey.
Hast, James *o.f.m.cap.* '77 (SAG) Sanford, MI St. Agnes.
Hastings, Joel '99 (DUL) Eveleth, MN Resurrection.
Hastings, Joel (DUL) Department of Liturgy.
Hastings, Timothy (SAG)[E] Saginaw, MI St. Mary's Medical Center of Saginaw, Inc..
Hastings, William J. '73 (CHI) Chicago, IL St. William; Deans.
Hastrich, George M. '50 (MAD) Retired.
Hastrich, George M. '50 (RCK).
Hastrich, George M. '50 (MAD)[I] Madison, WI Saint Martin House.
Hatcher, John *s.j.* '74 (RC) Rapid City, SD St. Isaac Jogues; St. Francis, SD Rosebud Reservation; [B] Howes, SD Kino Jesuit Community.
Hatcher, William C. '71 (NEW) Bloomfield, NJ Church of St. Thomas the Apostle; Commission for the Men's Apostolate.
Hater, Robert J. '59 (CIN) Cincinnati, OH St. Clare Retired.
Hatfield, Placid W. *o.s.b.* '58 (PEO).
Hathaway, Christopher *f.s.s.p.* '01 (SCR)[M] Pequannock, NJ Our Lady of Fatima Chapel.
Hathaway, Edward C. '91 (ARL) McLean, VA St. John's; Notaries.
Hatrick, Brian M. '79 (BUF) North Evans, NY St. Vincent.
Hattie, Eugene F. *s.j.* '53 (FgM).
Hatton, Ronald '95 (PSC) Williamsburg, VA Ascension of Our Lord.
Hattrick, Edward V. *o.s.a.* (FgM).
Hattrup, Theobald *o.f.m.* '56 (CIN)[M] Cincinnati, OH Archbishop Leibold Home for the Aged.
Hauber, Douglas L. '89 (JOL) Itasca, IL St. Peter the Apostle.
Hauck, Herbert C. '64 (STL) Kirkwood, MO St. Gerard Majella.
Hauer, Joseph L. '81 (DUB) Dubuque, IA Church of the Resurrection; Judges.
Hauer, Maurus *o.f.m.conv.* '45 (LSC) Carlsbad, NM St. Edward.
Haugan, Daniel C. '03 (STP) Minnetonka, MN Immaculate Heart of Mary.
Haugen, John S. '84 (DUB) On Special or Other Archdiocesan Assignment; [C] Dubuque, IA Loras College; Campus Ministry; Permanent Diaconate Formation Board.
Haugh, John '61 (DAL) Retired.
Haughey, John C. *s.j.* '61 (CHI)[C] Chicago, IL Jesuit Community at Loyola University Chicago.
Haughney, William J. '47 (MET)[H] Somerset, NJ Maria Regina Residence Retired.
Haupt, Lloyd '54 (SCL) Retired.
Haus, Robert A. *s.j.* '55 (BUF)[O] Buffalo, NY Canisius Jesuit Community.
Hausen, C. William '65 (PIT) Pittsburgh, PA Sacred Heart.
Hauser, Albert J. '81 (OG) Morristown, NY St. Peter; Morristown, NY St. John the Evangelist; Advocates; Department of Worship; Apostleship of Prayer; Priests' Eucharistic League.
Hauser, Albert *o.s.b.* '60 (KCK) Axtell, KS St. Michael's; Beattie, KS St. Malachy's; Summerfield, KS Holy Family; [H] Atchison, KS St. Benedict's Abbey.
Hauser, Gerald B. '45 (MIL) Retired.
Hauser, Nathanael *o.s.b.* '83 (SCL)[I] Collegeville, MN St. John's Abbey, of the Order of St. Benedict.
Hauser, Richard J. *s.j.* '68 (OM)[K] Omaha, NE Jesuit Community at Creighton University.
Hausfeld, Bruce *o.f.m.* '62 (LSC) Alamogordo, NM Immaculate Conception.
Hausfeld, Bryant *o.f.m.* '65 (LSC) Alamogordo, NM Immaculate Conception; Presbyteral Council.
Hausladen, Robert '00 (IND) Indianapolis, IN St. Monica; Brazil, IN Annunciation of the Blessed Virgin Mary.
Hausmann, Leo '92 (RC) Colome, SD St. Isidore; Diocesan Consultors.
Hausmann, Leo '92 (RC) Winner, SD Immaculate Conception.
Haut, Vincent J. '68 (STA) Jacksonville, FL Resurrection; Vicar General and Moderator of Curia; Presbyteral Council; Building Commission; Finance Committee; Insurance Committee, Diocesan; Investment Committee.
Haut, Vincent (STA) Diocesan Consultors.
Hautz, Roland *g.h.m.* '53 (RIC) Gate City, VA St. Bernard.
Hauver, James '97 (NY) Yorktown Heights, NY St. Patrick.
Hauver, James '97 (DUL) On Duty Outside the Diocese.
Havel, Elias *o.mar.* '95 (SAM)[C] Petersham, MA Most Holy Trinity Monastery.
Havel, Gregory G. '90 (WIN) Stewartville, MN St. Bridget's; Stewartville, MN St. Bernard's.
Havener, J. Riley *o.s.a.* '55 (ALB) Waterford, NY St. Mary of the Assumption.
Havens, James A. (MOB) Officers; Group II.
Havens, James '79 (MOB) Grove Hill, AL Sacred Heart.
Haviland, William T. '62 (HBG) Sunbury, PA St. Monica.
Havron, Daniel *o.f.m.* '77 (DET) Special Assignment; Evangelization.
Hawes, Cletus J. '52 (DUB)[E] Calmar, IA Christian Family School & Religion; Ossian, IA St. Francis de Sales; Festina, IA Our Lady of Seven Dolors.
Hawes, Donald J. '53 (DUB)[F] Calmar, IA Calmar–Festina–Spillville (CFS) Catholic Elementary School; Ossian, IA St. Francis de Sales; Spillville, IA St. Wenceslaus; Calmar, IA St. Aloysius.
Hawes, Roger '01 (VIC) Yoakum, TX St. Joseph.
Hawk, Patrick *c.ss.r.* '69 (TUC)[G] Tucson, AZ Redemptorist Society of Arizona.
Hawk, Vincent J. '02 (CLV) North Olmsted, OH St. Brendan.
Hawken, Michael '94 (KCK) Burlington, KS St. Francis Xavier's; Emerald, KS St. Patrick's; St. Joseph's; St. Teresa's.
Hawker, James '63 (CHL) Charlotte, NC St. Luke; Education.
Hawkes–Teeples, Steven B. *s.j.* '93 (FgM).
Hawkins, Allan R.G. '94 (FWT) Arlington, TX Church of St. Mary the Virgin.
Hawkins, Charles '78 (PMB) Boca Raton, FL Ascension.
Hawkins, Donald A. *s.j.* '76 (NO) New Orleans, LA Holy Name of Jesus.
Hawkins, Douglas W. *c.s.c.* '57 (BUR) Bennington, VT Sacred Heart St. Francis de Sales Retired.
Hawkins, John G. *o.s.c.* '66 (DET)[K] Riverview, MI Crosier Community of Riverview; Riverview, MI St. Cyprian; Taylor, MI St. Alfred.
Hawkins, Robert F. '75 (PRO) Warwick, RI St. Kevin; Officers; College of Consultors; Council Members.
Hawkins, Thomas '70 (KC) Weston, MO Holy Trinity.
Hawley, Benjamin *s.j.* (IND)[D] Indianapolis, IN Brebeuf Jesuit Preparatory School, Inc.; [D] Indianapolis, IN.
Hawley, Gerard L. '92 (SCR) Hawley, PA St. John Neumann.
Hawthorne, Patrick J. '82 (WOR) Worcester, MA St. Margaret Mary.
Hawver, Carl *o.f.m.* '74 (ALN)[K] Easton, PA St. Francis Friary.
Hay, Francis J. '42 (WCH) Retired.
Hay, Theodore H. *s.t.l.* '55 (MOB) Retired.
Hay, W. Michael '92 (CIN) Hamilton, OH Queen of Peace.
Hayatsu, Richard K. '65 (SEA) Seahurst, WA St. Francis of Assisi.
Hayburn, Edmund L. '45 (OAK)[M] Oakland, CA Bishop Begin Villa Retired.
Haycock, Anthony J. '72 (SEA) Seattle, WA St. Mary; [K] Seattle, WA Catholic Seamen's Club.
Haycock, Donald J. *c.s.c.* '58 (ROC) Rochester, NY St. Lawrence.
Hayda, Pavlo '92 (STN) Chicago, IL St. Joseph; Presbyteral Council.
Hayde, Ronald E. '81 (RVC) Rockville Centre, NY St. Agnes Cathedral; Ocean Beach, NY Our Lady of the Magnificat.
Hayde, Ronald (RVC) Worship.
Hayden, Carl T. '45 (GI) Retired.
Hayden, Donald *o.ss.t.* '81 (VIC) Yorktown, TX Holy Cross.
Hayden, Donald *o.ss.t.* '84 (VIC) Shiner, TX SS. Cyril and Methodius.
Hayden, Hilary *o.s.b.* '56 (WDC)[M] Washington, DC St. Anselm's Abbey.
Hayden, James P. '91 (GAY) Kingsley, MI St. Mary; Traverse City, MI Immaculate Conception; Consultors, Diocesan Board of; Elected Members; Elected Members; Procurators–Advocates.
Hayden, Johnrose '95 (LUB) Retired.
Hayden, Joseph F. '63 (L) On Duty Outside the Archdiocese.
Hayden, Joseph J. *s.j.* '70 (WH)[A] Wheeling, WV Wheeling Jesuit University.
Hayden, Joseph M. '48 (CAM) Retired.
Hayden, Joseph M. '48 (ORL) Lakeland, FL St. Anthony's Retired.
Hayden, Joseph Mark '48 (ORL) Retired.
Hayden, Joseph *s.j.* '70 (WH) Benwood, WV St. John's; McMechen, WV St. James.
Hayden, Michael M. *o.c.s.o.* '54 (ROC)[I] Piffard Abbey of the Genesee.
Hayden, Michael T. '85 (SUP) Medford, WI Our Lady of the Holy Rosary; Presbyteral Council & Diocesan Consultors.
Hayden, Patrick T. '90 (STL) On Duty Outside the Archdiocese.
Hayden, Robert L. '70 (RVC) Williston Park, NY St. Aidan's Church.
Hayden, Terence '77 (NO) Norco, LA Sacred Heart of Jesus.
Hayden, Thomas E. *s.m.a.* '58 (NEW)[N] Tenafly, NJ Society of African Missions, Provincialate, S.M.A. Fathers.
Hayden, William Vander (MO) Presbyteral Council.
Haydinger, Christian J. (BAL) Interdiocesan Judges.
Haydinger, Christian '76 (RIC) Chesapeake, VA Prince of Peace.
Haydock, Kenneth '80 (SEA) Edmonds, WA Holy Rosary.
Hayduk, Michael '77 (PRM) Parma, OH Saint John the Baptist, Cathedral; Syncellus for Doctrine and Worship; Presbyteral Council; Eparchial Pastoral Council; Sacred Liturgy; Cantors' Institute; Seminary Education Formation Board; Priest's Pension Board; Pre–Cana Office.
Hayek, Herbert *o.p.* '71 (COS) Castle Rock, CO St. Francis of Assisi.
Hayek, Sami '59 (SAM)[A] Easton, PA Our Lady of Lebanon.
Hayek, Stanley J. '59 (DUB) Building Commission; Directors Retired.
Hayer, James '89 (PSC) Wilkes–Barre, PA St. Mary's; Wyoming Valley Protopresbyterate; Communications and Telecommunications; Eparchial Newspaper; Elected Members.
Hayes, Brian C. '92 (SD) Borrego Springs, CA St. Richard.
Hayes, Brian (SD) Diocesan Judges; Presbyteral Council.
Hayes, Charles V. *o.f.m.* '46 (PAT)[M] Butler, NJ St. Anthony Friary.
Hayes, Denis A. '37 (PAT) Retired.
Hayes, Dennis J. '76 (SY) Marietta, NY Corpus Christi.
Hayes, Dennis J. '86 (NO) Arabi, LA St. Louise De Marillac.
Hayes, Donald J. *s.j.* '56 (CLV)[T] The Jesuit Retreat League of Chicago.
Hayes, Edward J. '57 (SY) Chadwicks, NY St. Anthony of Padua.
Hayes, Edward '58 (KCK) Retired.
Hayes, Eugene J. *o.praem.* '77 (ORG).
Hayes, Finbarr *o.p.* '59 (OAK)[N] Oakland, CA Dominican Order (Western Province), St. Albert's Priory.
Hayes, Gary '90 (OWN) Cloverport, KY St. Rose; Cloverport, KY Holy Guardian Angels.
Hayes, Gerard C. '60 (HT) Houma, LA St. Anthony.
Hayes, Giles P. *o.s.b.* '65 (PAT)[M] Morristown, NJ St. Mary's Abbey.
Hayes, J. Wayne '59 (FRS) Los Banos, CA St. Joseph; Finance Committee; Deposit and Loan Fund; Italian Catholic Federation; Personnel Committee; Vicar for Insurance and Retirement Affairs.
Hayes, James A. *m.s.c.* '50 (CC) Agua Dulce, TX St. Frances of Rome.
Hayes, James A. *s.s.j.* '55 (BAL)[S] Baltimore, MD St. Joseph Society of the Sacred Heart House of Central Administration Retired.
Hayes, James A. *s.s.j.* '55 (WDC)[B] Washington, DC St. Joseph's Seminary.
Hayes, James L. '38 (DET) Retired.
Hayes, James M. *s.j.* '85 (BO)[V] Watertown, MA The Society of Jesus of New England–Provincial Offices.
Hayes, James '66 (ALB) New York State Department of Corrections; Special Assignment.
Hayes, James *s.s.s.* '77 (NY) New York, NY St. Andrew.

Hayes, James *s.j.* '85 (BO)[V] Newton, MA The Jesuit Community at Boston College.
Hayes, John H. '87 (ROC) Livonia, NY St. Matthew Catholic Church Society.
Hayes, John J. '60 (CLV) Cleveland, OH Immaculate Conception.
Hayes, John '60 (CLV) Retired.
Hayes, Lawrence J. *o.f.m.* '89 (WDC) Silver Spring, MD St. Camillus.
Hayes, Leo J. '61 (BEL) Ava, IL St. Elizabeth; Ava, IL St. Ann; Ava, IL St. Joseph; Menard, IL Menard Correctional Center.
Hayes, Martin E. '84 (OWN) Leitchfield, KY St. Elizabeth of Hungary; Leitchfield, KY St. Paul.
Hayes, Martin *s.s.s.* (CLV)[O] Richfield, OH Regina Health Center.
Hayes, Marty (OWN) Committee for Administration.
Hayes, Maurice *o.f.m.conv.* '69 (L) Louisville, KY St. Paul.
Hayes, Patrick '71 (BLX) Gautier, MS St. Mary; Interim Diocesan Liturgical Commission; Personnel Board; Presbyteral Council.
Hayes, Paul J. '48 (NEW) New Providence, NJ Our Lady of Peace Retired.
Hayes, Robert '71 (SJ) Cupertino, CA St. Joseph of Cupertino.
Hayes, Robert (SJ) Defenders of the Bond; Ongoing Formation of Clergy Committee.
Hayes, Sam '83 (CHY) Worland, WY St. Mary Magdalen.
Hayes, Samuel (CHY) Vicars Forane; Defenders of the Bond.
Hayes, Stephen Dominic *o.p.* '88 (L) Springfield, KY St. Rose.
Hayes, Terrence M. '72 (STP) Minneapolis, MN Our Lady of Victory; Presbyteral Council.
Hayes, Thomas J. '73 (ALB) Waterford, NY St. Mary.
Hayes, Thomas P. '67 (STO) Lodi, CA St. Anne Church (Pastor of); Deans.
Hayes, Thomas *o.p.* '59 (OAK)[N] Oakland, CA Western Dominican Province.
Hayes, Thomas *o.m.i.* '64 (OAK) Oakland, CA Sacred Heart.
Hayes, Timothy M. '85 (COL) Newark, OH Church of the Blessed Sacrament; Diocesan Judges.
Hayes, William E. *s.j.* '58 (P).
Hayes, William J. '42 (HRT) Retired.
Hayes, Xavier *c.p.* '59 (BRK)[V] Jamaica, NY Immaculate Conception Monastery.
Hayes, Zachary *o.f.m.* '59 (CHI)[N] Chicago, IL St. Joseph Interprovincial Post–Novitiate Formation House.
Hayman, Robert W. '66 (PRO) Providence, RI St. Sebastian.
Hayn, Carl H. *s.j.* '47 (SJ)[B] Santa Clara, CA Jesuit Community.
Haynes, Mark J. '85 (PH) Broomall, PA St. Pius X.
Haynes, Stephen *c.ss.r.* '88 (BAL) Baltimore, MD Our Lady of Fatima.
Hayon, Anthony *s.v.d.* '99 (SB) San Bernardino, CA St. Anthony.
Hays, Henry Bryan *o.s.b.* '62 (SCL)[I] Collegeville, MN St. John's Abbey, of the Order of St. Benedict.
Hays, John '93 (SP) Zephyrhills, FL St. Joseph.
Hays, Joseph C. '51 (BEL) Retired.
Hays, Kevin W. '77 (CHI) Missionary Work.
Hays, Kevin '77 ((CHI)) (FgM).
Hays, Ray *c.m.* '93 (DAL) Dallas, TX Holy Trinity.
Hays, Tim (SPK) Members.
Hays, Timothy '96 (SPK) Walla Walla, WA Assumption of the Blessed Virgin Mary.
Hayward, William *m.i.c.* '89 (MIL) Kenosha, WI St. Peter.
Hazard, Michael D. '72 (KAL) Kalamazoo, MI St. Joseph; Advocates.
Hazebrouck, Maurice L. '45 (PRO) Retired.
Hazel, Robert '66 (STP) New Hope, MN St. Joseph.
Hazel, Terrence J. '75 (Y) Canfield, OH St. Michael.
Hazel, Terrence (Y) Defenders of the Bond; Physically and Developmentally; Deaf and Hearing Impaired.
Hazelton, James '61 (HEL) Santo Tomas La Union; On Duty Outside the Diocese.
Hazeur, Darren S. *s.s.j.* (NO) New Orleans, LA Epiphany.
Hazeur, Darren *s.s.j.* (NO) New Orleans, LA Corpus Christi.
Hazewski, Eugene J. '59 (NEW) Emerson, NJ Church of the Assumption.
Hazler, George F. '67 (SJ)[P] Los Altos, CA Voluntas Dei Institute.
Hazuka, Jeremy L. '97 (LIN) Bellwood, NE St. Peter's; Apostleship of Prayer; Legion of Mary.
Hazzard, William M. '63 (WIL) Wilmington, DE St. Matthew.
Hazzouri, Alex J. '57 (SCR)[N] Dunmore, PA Villa St. Joseph Retired.
Hdubowicz, Vincent B. '89 (MIL) Sick Leave.
Head, Bernard '53 (IND) St. Mary–of–the–Woods, IN St. Mary; West Terre Haute, IN St. Leonard of Port Maurice; Archdiocesan Judges.
Headley, Donald J. '58 (CHI) Chicago, IL St. Mary of the Woods Retired.
Headley, William '64 (BAL) Glen Burnie, MD Holy Trinity.
Heagerty, John J. '54 (SY) Retired.
Heagle, John L. '65 (LC) On Duty Outside the Diocese.
Healey, Andrew *ss.cc.* '59 (FR)[H] Fairhaven, MA Sacred Hearts Provincial House.
Healey, Augustine *o.c.d.* '49 (FWT)[H] Crowley, TX St. Francis Village, Inc..
Healey, Bernard A. '95 (PRO) Albion, RI St. Ambrose; Government Liaison; Newspaper.
Healey, Charles J. *s.j.* '65 (BO)[A] Weston, MA Blessed John XXIII National Seminary; [V] Newton, MA The Jesuit Community at Boston College.
Healey, Edward F. '43 (COL) Retired.
Healey, Edward J. '87 (FR) Fall River, MA Cathedral of St. Mary of the Assumption; Diocesan Consultors; Diocesan Department of Pastoral Care for the Sick.
Healey, Fergus *o.f.m.* '54 (BO)[AA] Boston, MA St. Anthony Shrine.
Healey, John E. '70 (MAN) Nashua, NH St. Patrick.
Healey, Kenneth *s.m.* '70 (BO)[E] Reading, MA Austin Preparatory School.
Healey, Patrick D. '51 (SCR) Scranton, PA St. Mary of the Assumption; Legion of Mary Retired.
Healey, Stephen M. '85 (BO) Unassigned.
Healey, Timothy A. *s.j.* '61 (NY) Manhattan, NY Goldwater Memorial Hospital; [EE] New York, NY St. Ignatius Loyola Residence.
Healey, William B. '55 (SCR) Hawley, PA Blessed Virgin Mary, Queen of Peace.
Healy, Clement *o.f.m.* '45 (PAT)[M] Ringwood, NJ Holy Name Friary, Inc..
Healy, Daniel H. '01 (MET)[M] Phillipsburg, NJ The Anawim Community.
Healy, Daniel (ROC)[M] Corning, NY Anawim Community Center.
Healy, Gabriel *ss.cc.* '57 (FR)[H] Fairhaven, MA Sacred Hearts Provincial House; [H] Fairhaven, MA Damien Residence.
Healy, George Christopher '02 (MIA) Hialeah, FL St. John the Apostle.
Healy, George *c.s.sp.* (SB) Hemet, CA Our Lady of the Valley; [E] Hemet, CA Holy Ghost Fathers; [E] Hemet, CA Our Lady of the Valley.
Healy, Gerard M. '61 (MAD) Stoughton, WI St. Ann; Personnel Board.
Healy, J. Cletus *s.j.* '51 (MIL)[O] Wauwatosa, WI Jesuit Community at St. Camillus.
Healy, Jack *o.carm.* '70 (ROC)[B] Rochester, NY McQuaid Jesuit High School; [I] Rochester, NY Whitefriars Priory.
Healy, James E. '72 (KC) Independence, MO St. Mark.
Healy, James F. '66 (NY) Mamaroneck, NY St. Vito.
Healy, James J. *s.s.* '46 (BAL)[O] Baltimore, MD St. Charles Villa.
Healy, John J. (SAC) Hospitals, Diocesan Liaison for Catholic.
Healy, John '41 (SR) Retired.
Healy, John (SAC) AIDS, Ministry to.
Healy, Joseph '98 (SFR) Belmont, CA Immaculate Heart of Mary.
Healy, Kieran J. *o.p.* '61 (OAK)[N] Oakland Western Dominican Province; (FgM).
Healy, Michael J. '70 (SFR) San Francisco, CA St. Philip the Apostle; San Francisco Police Department.
Healy, Neil '66 (SFR) Ross, CA St. Anselm.
Healy, Patrick F. *o.m.i.* '47 (BO)[Y] Tewksbury, MA Immaculate Heart of Mary Infirmary.
Healy, Patrick S. *s.s.j.* '76 (BEA) Beaumont, TX Our Mother of Mercy.
Healy, Peter C. '53 (LA) Burbank, CA St. Robert Bellarmine Retired.
Healy, Robert *g.h.m.* '46 (CIN)[M] Cincinnati Headquarters of Glenmary Home Missioners.
Healy, Robert *g.h.m.* '46 (SAV) Vidalia, GA Sacred Heart Retired.
Healy, Terence P. '62 (ALB) West Winfield, NY St. Joseph.
Healy, Terence '62 (ALB) Richfield Springs, NY St. Joseph.
Healy, Thomas F. *s.j.* '65 (HEL) Missoula, MT St. Francis Xavier; Diocesan Consultors; Presbyteral Council.
Healy, Thomas I. '52 (CHI) Chicago, IL Our Lady of Mount Carmel Retired.
Healy, Thomas J. '66 (BRK) Corona, NY Our Lady of Sorrows.
Healy, Thomas '67 (SAV) On Duty Outside the Diocese.
Healy, William P. '66 (PHX) On Leave.
Healy, William *o.c.d.* '46 (MIL) Milwaukee, WI St. Florian.
Heaney, John F. '57 (PRO) Retired.
Heaney, John J. *s.j.* '52 (DAL) Dallas, TX St. Rita.
Heaney, John P. '53 (SFR) Retired.
Heaney, Joseph P. '53 (PRO) Woonsocket, RI St. Agatha Retired.
Heanue, William *c.ss.r.* '47 (ALB)[L] Saratoga Springs, NY St. John Neumann Residence.
Hearn, Philip A. '66 (SY) Rome, NY St. Mary of the Assumption; Rome, NY St. Peter; Eastern Area Vicars; Board of Diocesan Consultors; Ex Officio.
Hearty, Joseph *f.s.s.p.* '03 (LR)[L] North Little Rock, AR Priestly Fraternity of St. Peter; [M] Corpus Christi, TX.
Heath, Caroline '02 (MAD).
Heath, Christopher '88 (ORG)[E] Orange, CA La Purisima.
Heath, Thomas R. *o.p.* (FgM).
Heavey, Edward J. *s.j.* '60 (NEW)[B] Jersey City, NJ Jesuit Center; [N] Jersey City, NJ Jesuits of Saint Peter's College, Inc..
Hebcen, W. Scott '99 (CHI).
Hebda, Bernard A. '89 (PIT)[A] On Duty Outside the Diocese.
Hebda, Martin J. '67 (CHI)[J] Chicago, IL Mercy Hospital and Medical Center.
Hebda, Michael J. '96 (SAC) Red Bluff, CA Sacred Heart.
Hebda, Michael (SAC) Vicars Forane; College of Consultors; Council of Priests.
Heberle, Frederick L. '56 (SPR) Retired.
Heberlein, Kenneth '71 (GAL) Deer Park, TX St. Hyacinth.
Heberlein, Louis J. '51 (E) Retired.
Hebert, Adrien T. *c.s.sp.* '58 (FgM).
Hebert, Daniel J. (ANC) Diocesan Consultors.
Hebert, Donald J. '68 (SY) Army National Guard Chaplains.
Hebert, Earl '52 (SPR) Retired.
Hebert, Francis '60 (B) Retired.
Hebert, Gerard A. '81 (FR) Westport, MA St. George's; Defenders of the Bond.
Hebert, J. Gaston (LR) Vicars General; Diocesan Consultors.
Hebert, J. Marc *c.s.c.* '50 (FR)[H] North Dartmouth, MA Holy Cross Residence.
Hebert, John M. '51 (LIN) Retired.
Hebert, Joseph E. *m.afr.* '63 (SP)[O] St. Petersburg, FL Missionaries of Africa.
Hebert, Lloyd P. '57 (LAF) Retired.
Hebert, Marvin A. '51 (GAL) Retired.
Hebert, Oliver J. *t.o.r.* '71 (PBR) Northern Cambria, PA St. John the Baptist; Patton, PA SS. Peter and Paul.
Hebert, Paul L. '59 (NOR) Pomfret, CT Most Holy Trinity.
Hebert, Ray P. '52 (NO) Archdiocesan Consultors Retired.
Hebert, Roland G. '47 (WOR) Retired.
Hebert, Ronald '65 (SD) San Diego, CA Sacred Heart.
Hebert, T. J. '49 (LAF) Retired.
Hebl, John H. '61 (MAD) Palmyra, WI St. Mary; Sullivan, WI St. Mary Help of Christians.
Hechenberger, Gerald R. '96 (BEL) Cahokia, IL Holy Family; Dupo, IL Sacred Heart of Jesus.
Heck, Quintin T. (MIL) Menomonee Falls, WI St. Mary.
Heck, Quintin '00 (FAR) On Duty Outside the Diocese.
Heck, Roger C. '51 (MIL) Retired.
Heck, Theodore *o.s.b.* '29 (IND)[K] St. Meinrad, IN St. Meinrad Archabbey.
Heck, Thomas A. '76 (VEN) Cape Coral, FL St. Andrew.
Heckel, Guerric Frederick A. '66 (CHR)[E] Moncks Corner, SC Mepkin Abbey.
Hecker, Lawrence A. '58 (NO) Retired.
Hedderman, John J. '60 (SLC) Judges Retired.
Hederman, James J. *s.j.* '99 (BGP)[E] Fairfield, CT Fairfield College Preparatory School; [P] Fairfield, CT The Fairfield Jesuit Community–Fairfield University.
Hederman, Kevin F. '75 (STL) On Duty Outside the Archdiocese.
Hedges, John P. '87 (DET) Wyandotte, MI St. Stanislaus Kostka; Mount Clemens General Hospital.
Hedges, L. John '43 (ROC) Retired.
Hedrick, John H. '70 (MAD) Briggsville, WI St. Mary Help of Christians; Pardeeville, WI St. Andrew; Portage, WI St. Mary; Portage, WI St. Mary of the Immaculate Conception; Diocesan Consultors; Elected.
Hedrick, Kenneth J. '73 (NO) Metairie, LA St. Angela Merici.
Heeg, Lawrence '57 (GRY) Retired.
Heekin, John M. '63 (PAT) Retired.
Heelan, Patrick A. *s.j.* '58 (WDC)[M] Washington, DC The Jesuit Community at Georgetown University.
Heemrood, Jan *o.m.i.* '45 (SAT)[C] Oblate School of Theology; [M] San Antonio, TX De Mazenod House.
Heenan, Michael F. '55 (RVC) Retired.
Heenan, Patrick F. '55 (MEM) Memphis, TN St. James.
Heerdink, Eugene (EVN) Spanish Speaking Ministry.
Heery, Stephen *o.carm.* '42 (LA) Retired.
Heery, William *o.carm.* '42 (LA)[F] Encino, CA Crespi Carmelite High School.
Heese, Henry '61 (CC) Odem, TX Sacred Heart.
Heet, Donald J. *o.s.f.s.* '76 (WDC)[B] Washington, DC Deshairs Community–Oblates of St. Francis de Sales Residence; [C] Catholic University of America, The.
Hefferan, John E. '56 (CHI) Retired.
Hefferman, Henry *s.j.* (WDC) Bethesda, MD National Institutes of Health, Clinical Center.
Heffern, Colman *o.s.b.* '76 (SFE)[I] Pecos, NM Our Lady of Guadalupe Abbey; [K] Pecos, NM Our Lady of Guadalupe Olivetan Benedictine Abbey.
Heffern, Colman *o.s.b.* '76 (LSC)[F] San Patricio, NM

Benedictine Center.
Heffernan, Henry G. *s.j.* '62 (WDC)[E] Washington, DC Gonzaga College High School.
Heffernan, James F. '50 (BRK) Released from Diocesan Assignment Retired.
Heffernan, John J. *o.f.m.* '89 (R) Wilmington, DE St. Paul's.
Heffernan, Joseph A. '65 (FRS) Retired.
Heffernan, Raymond '57 (SEA) Friday Harbor, WA St. Francis Retired.
Heffernan, Robert G. '63 (HRT) East Haven, CT St. Clare; Branford, CT St. Elizabeth.
Heffernan, Thomas A. '61 (BRK) Released from Diocesan Assignment.
Heffernan, Thomas '61 (NY)[X] Poughkeepsie, NY St. Francis Hospital; [X] Poughkeepsie, NY St. Francis Hospital.
Heffernan, William P. (FgM).
Heffernon, Thomas A. (NY) Poughkeepsie, NY St. Francis Hospital.
Heffner, Carroll '61 (NO) New Orleans, LA Our Lady of Good Counsel.
Heffner, George *s.v.d.* '57 (LAF) Eunice, LA St. Lawrence.
Heffron, William M. '53 (MIL) Retired.
Heffron, William *ss.cc.* '68 (FR)[H] Fairhaven, MA Damien Residence.
Hefner, Helmut A. '69 (LA)[A] Camarillo, CA St. John's Seminary; Promoters of Justice; Defenders of the Bond.
Hefner, Helmut (LA) Members.
Heft, James L. *s.m.* '73 (CIN)[D] Dayton, OH The University of Dayton; [D] Dayton, OH The University of Dayton; [M] Dayton, OH Marianist Community.
Hegarty, Daniel P. '63 (BO) Allston, MA St. Anthony.
Hegarty, Frederick J. *m.m.* '53 (FgM).
Hegarty, John C. *c.s.sp.* '53 (NO) Port Sulphur, LA St. Jude.
Hegarty, Michael P. '95 (CAM) Haddon Heights, NJ St. Rose's; Advocates.
Hegarty, William *s.v.d.* '67 (CHI)[B] Techny, IL Divine Word Residence.
Hegedus, Gaspar '65 (SAV) Savannah, GA St. James.
Hegenbarth, Robert S. '56 (LC) West Salem, WI St. Mary; West Salem, WI St. Leo the Great.
Hegener, Wilbert *o.f.m.* '36 (SFD)[L] Springfield, IL Our Lady of Angels Friary.
Hegumen, Abbot Nicholas '81 (SB)[E] Newberry Springs, CA Holy Resurrection Community.
Hegyi, Martin A. *s.j.* '63 (NY)[EE] Cardinal Spellman Hall, Jesuit Community.
Heher, Michael '78 (ORG) Garden Grove, CA St. Columban.
Heher, Michael (ORG) Clergy Personnel Board; Council of Priests; Consultors.
Hehir, J. Bryan '66 (BO) Secretary for Social Services; Social Services; Catholic Social Services, Inc.; Catholic Charitable Bureau of the Archdiocese of Boston, Inc..
Hehir, J. Bryan '66 (ARL) Alexandria, VA St. Mary's.
Hehir, J. Bryan '66 (BO) Secretary for Social Services; Social Services; Catholic Social Services, Inc.; Catholic Charitable Bureau of the Archdiocese of Boston, Inc..
Hehman, Lawrence W. '65 (LEX) Lexington, KY Pax Christi Catholic Church.
Hehman, Lawrence '65 (LEX) Mt. Sterling, KY St. Patrick; Priests' Personnel.
Hehn, Robert E. '63 (DEN) Rifle, CO St. Mary's.
Heiar, Donald J. (MAD) Building Commission.
Heiar, Donn Joseph '00 (MAD) Brodhead, WI St. Patrick; Brodhead, WI St. Rose; Evansville, WI St. Paul; Footville, WI St. Augustine.
Heiar, James *s.v.d.* '70 (DUB)[B] Epworth, IA Divine Word College.
Heid, Clement J. *o.s.b.* '44 (GBG)[H] Latrobe, PA Saint Vincent Archabbey.
Heid, Richard J. '47 (SCL) Brandon, MN Church of St. Ann Retired.
Heidecke, Albert '93 (JOL) Westmont, IL Holy Trinity.
Heidelberger, Ronald '46 (DET) Retired.
Heidenreich, Robert A. '69 (CHI) Chicago, IL St. Benedict.
Heidenreich, Robert J. (CHI) Deans.
Heidenrich, Peter J. '77 (CHI) Chicago, IL St. Walter.
Heidjen, Warren *osb* '60 (COS) Colorado Springs, CO St. Joseph's Retired.
Heidlage, Benno *o.f.m.* '48 (IND) Oldenburg, IN Holy Family.
Heidt, Charles A. '59 (BIS) Retired.
Heier, Thomas *c.m.m.* '58 (DET)[K] Vocation Office.
Heier, Vergil *c.m.m.* '63 (DET)[K] Vocation Office.
Heier, Vincent A. '77 (STL) University City, MO All Saints; Office for Ecumenical & Interreligious Affairs.
Heigl, John J. *m.afr.* '59 (BUF) Silver Springs, NY St. Mary.
Heikkala, Gregory R. '91 (MAR) Baraga, MI The Most Holy Name of Jesus–Blessed Kateri Tekakwitha; L'Anse, MI Sacred Heart; Baraga, MI The Most Holy Name of Jesus–Blessed Kateri Tekakwitha.
Heikkala, Gregory '91 (MAR)[B] L'Anse, MI Sacred Heart School Endowment Fund.
Heil, Jack '74 (STL) St. Louis, MO Our Lady of Sorrows.
Heil, John P. '74 (STL)[A] St. Louis, MO Kenrick School of Theology.
Heille, Gregory J. *o.p.* '75 (STL)[B] St. Louis, MO Aquinas Institute of Theology; [O] St. Louis, MO St. Dominic Priory.
Heilman, Richard M. '88 (MAD) Montello, WI St. John the Baptist; Montello, WI Good Shepherd.
Heim, Edward L. '71 (STL) Augusta, MO Immaculate Conception.
Heim, Gerald B. *c.ss.r.* '51 (STL)[O] Liguori, MO St. Clement Health Care Center.
Heim, Howard J. *s.j.* '53 (PH)[AA] Loyola Center and Manresa Hall; [BB] Philadelphia, PA Monastery of the Visitation Nuns.
Heim, John S. '51 (PH) Retired.
Heim, Joseph A. *m.m.* '61 (NY)[EE] Maryknoll Maryknoll Fathers and Brothers.
Heim, Michael J. '82 (PH) Philadelphia, PA St. Dominic.
Heiman, Harold *o.s.b.* '39 (LR) St. Anthony; [A] Subiaco, AR Subiaco Monastery.
Heiman, Lawrence F. *c.pp.s.* '43 (LFT)[A] Rensselaer, IN Saint Joseph's College.
Heimer, Michael G. '71 (GRY) Walkerton, IN St. Anthony; Walkerton, IN St. John Kanty.
Heimerman, Francis D. '44 (DUB) Retired.
Heimos, Robert L. '67 (STL) Washington, MO Our Lady of Lourdes.
Heimsoth, Larry '99 (AUS) Temple, TX St. Luke's.
Hein, Gary (MAD).
Hein, John '63 (RVC)[E] Floral Park, NY Our Lady of Victory.
Heina, Steve (SAL) Council of Priests.
Heina, Steven '82 (SAL) Salina, KS St. Mary's.
Heindl, Arthur W. '40 (MAD) Retired.
Heindl, Elmer W. '36 (ROC) Rochester, NY St. Charles Borromeo Retired.
Heine, Michael *o.f.m.conv.* '90 (BAL)[C] Baltimore, MD Archbishop Curley High School; [S] Baltimore, MD Immaculate Heart of Mary Friary.
Heine, Simeon *s.a.* '48 (NY) Retired.
Heinecke, Gary L. *c.ss.r.* '73 (STL)[O] Liguori, MO St. Clement Health Care Center.
Heineman, Donald P. '47 (DUB) Retired.
Heinen, Francis A. '59 (NEW) New Providence, NJ Our Lady of Peace.
Heinen, Gerard (NEW) Teaneck, NJ St. Anastasia's.
Heinen, Virgil O. '60 (SUP) Retired.
Heines, Timothy '94 (DAL) Duncanville, TX Holy Spirit.
Heiney, Lawrence W. '75 (CHL) Albemarle, NC Our Lady of the Annunciation.
Heinl, David A. '57 (CIN) St. Marys, OH Holy Rosary.
Heinlein, Anthony J. '65 (RVC) Massapequa Park, NY Our Lady of Lourdes.
Heinlein, John T. '61 (RVC) Sayville, NY St. Lawrence the Martyr.
Heinrich, Harold D. '56 (HRT) Retired.
Heinsch, James *o.f.m.* (GB)[I] Pulaski, WI Friary.
Heintz, Daniel '54 (SY) North Syracuse, NY St. Rose of Lima Retired.
Heintz, Michael '93 (FTW) South Bend, IN St. Matthew Cathedral.
Heintz, Michael (FTW) Consultors; Censor Librorum; Inter City Catholic League.
Heintz, Robert L. '49 (SFD) Retired.
Heintzelman, Edward F. '84 (CAM) Clayton, NJ St. Catherine's.
Heintzelman, Gerard '59 (HBG)[G] Napa, CA Queen of the Valley Hospital of Napa.
Heinz, David C. '77 (PEO) Bartonville, IL St. Anthony.
Heinz, John *o.f.m.conv.* '93 (SFR) San Francisco, CA St. Paul of the Shipwreck.
Heinz, Martin G. '94 (RCK) Aurora, IL Holy Angels.
Heinz, Robert P. '80 (CHI) Prospect Heights, IL St. Alphonsus Liguori.
Heinz, Vernon R. *s.j.* '73 (COS)[F] Sedalia, CO Sacred Heart Jesuit Community; [H] Sedalia, CO Sacred Heart Jesuit Retreat House.
Heinz, Walter E. '62 (STU) Pomeroy, OH Sacred Heart.
Heinze, Arthur G. '68 (MIL) Hales Corners, WI St. Mary.
Heinzel, Thomas R. '75 (HON) Kula, HI Our Lady Queen of the Angels.
Heinzen, George *c.pp.s.* '40 (KC)[J] Liberty, MO Precious Blood Center.
Heis, Clarence G. '82 (CIN) Mechanicsburg, OH St. Michael's; Mechanicsburg, OH Immaculate Conception.
Heise, Bert *o.f.m.* '57 (HT) Houma, LA Our Lady of the Most Holy Rosary.
Heise, Bert *o.f.m.* '57 (CIN) Houma, LA St. Lucy.
Heise, George C. (RIC) Fincastle, VA Church of the Transfiguration; New Castle, VA Saint John the Evangelist Mission.
Heiser, Basil *o.f.m.conv.* '32 (IND)[K] Curia Generalizia.
Heiser, W. Charles *s.j.* '53 (STL)[C] Saint Louis University; [O] St. Louis, MO Jesuit Community Corporation at St. Louis University – Jesuit Hall.
Heisig, Kazimierz '78 (HRT) Hartford, CT SS. Cyril and Methodius.
Heisler, John F. '99 (ARL) Springfield, VA St. Bernadette's; Notaries.
Heithoff, James H. '77 (GI) Personnel Board; Ord, NE Our Lady of Perpetual Help.
Heiting, R. Paul '87 (WIN)[A] Winona, MN Immaculate Heart of Mary Seminary; Judicial Officers; Second Instance Court Judges.
Heitkamp, Samuel (SAT) San Antonio, TX St. Joan of Arc; In Metropolitan Area; Archdiocesan Presbyteral Council.
Heitz, Louis S. '57 (LFT) Winchester, IN St. Joseph.
Heitz, Warren *o.s.b.* '66 (IND)[K] St. Meinrad, IN St. Meinrad Archabbey.
Heitzman, Clarence J. '56 (COV) Southgate, KY St. Therese of the Infant Jesus.
Heizman, Leo J. '69 (SY) Syracuse, NY Transfiguration.
Heizman, Les (SY) Syracuse, NY Crouse Irving Memorial Hospital.
Hejdak, Andrew '84 (CC) Benavides, TX St. Rose of Lima.
Hejna, Lewis E. '81 (SPC) Springfield, MO Immaculate Conception; Presbyteral Council.
Helbing, Brendan *o.s.b.* '65 (OKL)[I] Shawnee St. Gregory's Abbey.
Held, Aloys *o.f.m.* '43 (CIN)[M] Cincinnati, OH Archbishop Leibold Home for the Aged.
Heles, Frederic G. '44 (DUB) Retired.
Helfrey, Donald C. '68 (KC) Retired.
Helfrey, Donald (KC) Diocesan Consultors.
Helfrich, Emil *o.m.i.* '49 (BEL)[F] Belleville, IL Missionary Oblates of Mary Immaculate – St. Henry's Oblate Residence.
Helfrich, George J. '54 (CHI) Retired.
Helfrich, Jeremiah P. *s.j.* '68 (LA)[F] Los Angeles, CA Loyola High School of Los Angeles.
Helfrich, P. Frederick '71 (ROC) Webster, NY Holy Spirit.
Helfrich, P. Jerry *s.j.* '68 (LA) Whittier, CA Fred C. Nelles Correctional Facility.
Helfrich, Paul D. *b.h.* (BO)[BB] Boston, MA The Catholic Center at Boston University.
Helfrich, Peter G. '76 (OG) Absent on Sick Leave.
Helfrich, Thomas J. *o.s.f.s.* '78 (LAN) Adrian, MI St. Mary of Good Counsel.
Heller, Christopher J. '79 (RVC) Port Jefferson Station, NY St. Gerard Majella; North Brookhaven Deanery.
Heller, James '68 (SAG) Bay City, MI St. Mary; Vicars for Vicariates.
Hellman, David E. '73 (LFT) Fishers, IN St. Louis de Montfort.
Hellmann, Andreas '00 (GB)[N] Green Bay, WI Latin Mass Apostolate.
Hellmann, Donald F. '53 (COV) Florence, KY St. Paul; Williamstown, KY St. William; Diocesan Consultors; Priest Personnel Retired.
Hellstrom, Christopher (DEN) Spirituality Year.
Hellwig, Lee W. '86 (HRT) Military Chaplains; Navy Chaplains.
Hellwig, Lee (HON) Military Chaplains.
Helman, Bradford N. '68 (Y) Canton, OH St. Michael the Archangel.
Helmich, George F. *c.s.p.* '57 (NY)[EE] Jamaica Estates Paulist Fathers Generalate.
Helmich, George F. *c.s.p.* '57 (PMB)[J] Vero Beach, FL Paulist Fathers Residence.
Helmick, Raymond G. *s.j.* '63 (BO) West Roxbury, MA St. Theresa of Avila; [V] Newton, MA The Jesuit Community at Boston College.
Helmick, William M. '62 (BO) West Roxbury, MA St. Theresa of Avila; Members.
Helmin, Virgil A. '75 (SCL) St. Cloud, MN Holy Spirit.
Helmin, Virgil (SCL) Judicial Vicar; Notaries.
Helmin, Virgil (CR) Defenders of the Bond.
Helmin, Virgil (SCL) Judicial Vicar; Notaries.
Helminski, Gregory *c.r.* (CHI) Chicago, IL St. Wenceslaus.
Helms, Michael L. '90 (DOD) Deerfield, KS Christ the King; Lakin, KS St. Anthony; Syracuse, KS St. Raphael; Presbyteral Council.
Helms, Walter (DAV) Iowa City, IA St. Thomas More.
Helmueller, John J. '01 (SFS) Orient, SD St. Liborius.
Helmueller, Lawrence C. *s.j.* '42 (MIL)[O] Wauwatosa, WI Jesuit Community at St. Camillus.
Helwangi, Fadi *m.l.m.* '98 (OLL) San Antonio, TX St. George Maronite; [A] Houston, TX The Congregation of Maronite Lebanese Missionaries.
Helwig, Alan R. '58 (WDC) Bethesda, MD St. Jane Frances de Chantal.
Helwig, Paul C. '74 (HBG) Camp Hill, PA Good Shepherd; Consultors, College; Deans; Appointed.
Heman, Richard J. '67 (STL) Arnold, MO Immaculate Conception.
Hemann, Dave (SC) Liturgy Commission.
Hemann, David '85 (SC) Holstein, IA Our Lady of Good

Counsel; Ida Grove, IA Sacred Heart.
Hemann, Everett '71 (DUB)[N] Ames, IA St. Thomas Aquinas Church and Catholic Student Center (Iowa State University); Ames, IA SS. Peter and Paul; Ames, IA St. Thomas Aquinas Church (and Catholic Student Center); Deans; Worship Commission.
Hemann, John W. '60 (DUB) Nashua, IA St. Michael; Nashua, IA Immaculate Conception; Elma, IA Immaculate Conception; Nashua, IA St. Boniface; Elma, IA Our Lady of Lourdes; Elma, IA St. Bernard; Deans.
Hemann, Maurice *o.m.i.* '50 (FgM).
Hemann, Melvin D. '59 (DUB) Retired.
Hemauer, Gil *o.f.m.cap.* '64 (GF) Miles City, MT Sacred Heart.
Hemauer, Gilbert *o.f.m.cap.* (GF) Vicars Forane.
Hemberger, Kent A. '88 (WCH) Wichita, KS St. Anne; Diocesan Building Commission.
Hemberger, Kent (WCH) Ongoing Formation of the Clergy Committee.
Hemberger, Robert E. '70 (WCH)[G] Wichita, KS Mt. St. Mary Convent, Motherhouse and Novitiate of the Sisters of St. Joseph.
Hemberger, Robert E. (WCH) Vicars General; Moderator of the Diocesan Curia; Director of Diocesan Planning; Chancellor; Presbyteral Council/Diocesan Consultors; Ongoing Formation of the Clergy Committee; Diocesan Building Commission; Diocesan Finance Committee; Diocesan Liaison for Health Affairs; Presbyteral Council.
Hemberger, Robert E. (WCH) Judges.
Hembrow, William '60 (SFD) Jerseyville, IL St. Mary; Jerseyville, IL Holy Ghost.
Hemler, Edward B. '64 (BAL) Fallston, MD St. Mark.
Hemler, Thomas J. '56 (HBG) Waynesboro, PA St. Andrew.
Hemm, Thomas *c.pp.s.* '78 (TOL) Ottawa, OH SS. Peter and Paul.
Hemm, Thomas *c.pp.s.* '78 (CIN)[M] Ottawa, OH.
Hemmelgarn, Larry J. *c.pp.s.* '84 (CIN)[M] Dayton, OH Provincial Office of the Cincinnati Province of the Society of the Precious Blood.
Hemmer, Joseph *o.f.m.* '54 (FBK) Kaltag, AK St. Teresas; Ruby, AK St. Peter–in–Chains; (FgM).
Hemmerle, R. Joseph '67 (L) Loretto, KY Holy Cross; St. Francis, KY St. Francis of Assisi.
Hemmerling, Henry L. '66 (MET) Retired.
Hemmersbach, Alfred F. '45 (LC)[H] La Crosse, WI Holy Cross (Seminary) Diocesan Center Retired.
Hemming, Philip M. '67 (P) Banks, OR St. Francis of Assisi.
Hemp, Lawrence A. '67 (LUB) Slaton, TX Our Lady of Guadalupe.
Hemp, Lawrence (LUB) Priests' Retirement Board.
Hemrick, Eugene F. '63 (JOL) On Duty Outside the Diocese.
Hemrick, Eugene '63 (JOL) Washington, DC St. Joseph on Capitol Hill.
Hemsing, John D. '88 (MIL) Wind Lake, WI St. Clare; Deans.
Henao, Luis '74 (BAL) Slidell, LA St. Margaret Mary.
Henault, James A. *m.s.* '80 (ATL) Snellville, GA St. Oliver Plunkett.
Henault, John *o.m.i.* '63 (FgM).
Henchal, Michael J. '73 (PRT) Cape Elizabeth, ME St. Bartholomew; Vicar General; Promoter of Justice; Associate Judges; Diocesan Consultors.
Henchal, Michael J. (PRT) Personnel Board; Officio Members.
Henchal, Michael J. (PRT) Ex Officio; College of Consultors.
Hencheu, Joseph C. *c.s.s.* (BO)[A] Weston, MA Blessed John XXIII National Seminary.
Henchey, Joseph *c.s.s.* '56 (BO)[V] Waltham, MA Stigmatine House.
Hencier, John Gregory *c.m.f.* '72 (LA) San Gabriel, CA San Gabriel; [Q] San Gabriel, CA Claretian Missionaries (Missionary Sons of the Immaculate Heart of Mary).
Hendel, Lawrence '77 (SJ) San Jose, CA St. John Vianney; Military Chaplains; College of Consultors.
Hendel, Thomas W. '45 (BRK) Retired.
Henden, Brian *o.carm.* '93 (TUC)[A] Tucson, AZ Salpointe Catholic High School; [E] Tucson, AZ Carmelite Priory.
Henderson, Christopher '94 (SAM) Unassigned.
Henderson, Christopher *c.p.m.* '98 (RCK)[H] Rockford, IL The Poor Clares of Rockford.
Henderson, Christopher *c.p.m.* '98 (OWN)[F] Auburn, KY Fathers of Mercy.
Henderson, Donald '70 (PEO) Champaign, IL Holy Cross.
Henderson, James B. *o.c.s.o.* '60 (DUB)[K] Peosta, IA New Melleray Abbey, Order of Cistercians of the Strict Observance.
Henderson, John A. '87 (JC) Perry, MO St. William; Boonville, MO.
Henderson, John *o.f.m.conv.* (P)[P] Corvallis, OR Trinity Court (Student Housing); Area Vicars.
Henderson, Robert J. '65 (COV) Cold Spring, KY St. Joseph.
Hendren, Lucien '63 (SFE) Retired.
Hendrick, Frank J. '54 (ARL) Retired.
Hendrick, Matthew D. '85 (R) Wilmington, NC Christ the King; Wilmington, NC St. Mark.
Hendricks, Clare '63 (GRY) On Duty Outside the Diocese.
Hendricks, Donald W. '55 (NY) Buchanan, NY St. Christopher.
Hendricks, Edward S. '77 (BAL) Special Assignment; [U] Frostburg, MD Frostburg State University.
Hendricks, James P. '60 (L) Retired.
Hendricks, Joseph M. '72 (COL) Dublin, OH St. Brigid of Kildare; [L] Columbus, OH Diocesan Retirement Community Corp.; [G] Columbus, OH The Villas at St. Therese Independent Living, Inc.; [G] Columbus, OH The Villas at St. Therese Assisted Living, Inc..
Hendricks, Theodore J. '65 (GB) Black Creek, WI St. Mary; Bonduel, WI St. Lawrence.
Hendrickson, Frederick '56 (L) Retired.
Hendrickson, Michael D. '01 (SJ) Military Chaplains.
Hendrickson, Michael (SJ) Ongoing Formation of Clergy Committee.
Hendriks, Joseph *ss.cc.* '48 (HON) Kalawao, HI St. Francis; [F] Kalaupapa, HI Kalaupapa Care Home.
Hendriks, Randall C. '02 (GAL) Houston, TX Queen of Peace.
Hendry, Owen J. (NEW) Livingston, NJ St. Philomena.
Hendry, Simon J. *s.j.* '77 (NO)[C] New Orleans, LA Loyola University New Orleans.
Heneghan, James A. '83 (CHI) Chicago, IL St. Bonaventure.
Heneghan, Jarlath '55 (SEA) Retired.
Heneghan, John F. '55 (YAK) Retired.
Heneghan, John F. (YAK) Judges.
Heneghan, Martin '71 (NY).
Henehan, Patrick '98 (PEO)[JJ] Downs, IL St. Mary's; [B] Bloomington, IL Central Catholic High School.
Henehan, Thomas P. *m.m.* '65 (NY) (FgM).
Henery, Ronald *o.p.* '58 (NO) New Orleans, LA St. Anthony of Padua; New Orleans, LA Delgado College; [EE] New York St. Vincent Ferrer Priory.
Heney, David '78 (LA) Thousand Oaks, CA St. Paschal Baylon.
Heney, Fred *s.j.* '58 (LA)[C] Los Angeles, CA Jesuit Community.
Hengel, Warren '92 (FRS) Fresno, CA Our Lady of Mt. Carmel.
Henger, Alcuin *o.m.i.* '55 (DUL) Sandstone, MN Sacred Heart; Sandstone, MN St. Joseph; Sandstone, MN St. Luke.
Hengle, John R. '68 (CLV) Tallmadge, OH Our Lady of Victory; College of Consultors; Presbyteral Conveners; Associate Judges.
Heninger, Michael B. (ATL) Military Chaplains; Army Chaplains.
Henk, Jan '83 (CHI) Argo, IL St. Blase.
Henke, Donald E. '93 (STL) Special Assignment; Air National Guard Chaplains.
Henke, James '66 (SAT) San Antonio, TX St. Francis of Assisi; Judges; Office of Worship.
Henkels, Edmund *o.s.b.* '59 (WDC)[M] Washington, DC St. Anselm's Abbey.
Henkes, Donald E. '66 (MEM) Mount Pleasant, MI Sacred Heart.
Henkle, Charles *o.f.m.conv.* '97 (CLV) Lorain, OH St. Anthony of Padua.
Henley, Earl Joseph *m.s.c.* '69 (SB) San Jacinto, CA St. Joseph.
Henley, Earl *m.s.c.* '69 (SB) Council Members; Native American Ministry; Special or Other Diocesan Assignment.
Henley, Fred M. *s.j.* '88 (DET)[K] Temperance, MI; [P] Hamtramck, MI St. Ladislaus.
Henley, Fred *s.j.* '58 (TUC) Tucson, AZ St. John the Evangelist.
Henn, Joseph *s.d.s.* '78 (MIL).
Henn, William *o.f.m.cap.* '78 (PIT)[N] Pittsburgh, PA St. Augustine Friary.
Henne, Paul G. '56 (PIT) Retired.
Henne, Paul '56 (PIT)[O] Coraopolis, PA Our Lady of the Sacred Heart Convent.
Hennelly, Michael F. '91 (PH) Philadelphia, PA Immaculate Conception; Graduate Studies.
Henner, Joseph *o.s.c* '67 (STP)[M] Shoreview, MN Crosier Provincial House Province of St. Odilia.
Hennessey, Daniel F. '02 (BO) South Boston, MA St. Brigid.
Hennessey, John E. '67 (CHI) Libertyville, IL St. Joseph.
Hennessey, Joseph M. '88 (BO) Kingston, MA St. Joseph; Archdiocesan Judges.
Hennessey, Lawrence R. '71 (CHI).
Hennessey, Robert F. (BO)[A] East Boston, MA Most Holy Redeemer; Selected.
Hennessey, William J. '61 (MIA)[B] St. Thomas University; [M] Miami Shores, FL Archdiocese of Miami Millennium Appeal, Inc.; [M] Miami Shores, FL Archdiocese of Miami, Inc.; Vicars General; Moderator of the Curia; Consultors; Incardination Committee; Consultants; Executive Director; Catholic Charities of the Archdiocese of Miami, Inc.; Archdiocesan Fund–Raising & Assessments Committee; Finance Council.
Hennessy, Augustine Paul *c.p.* (SPR)[H] Holyoke, MA Mont Marie Health Care Center, Inc..
Hennessy, Brian P. '99 (PH) Philadelphia, PA St. Josaphat; Graduate Studies.
Hennessy, Douglas J. '63 (PEO) Danville, IL St. Paul's.
Hennessy, Douglas (PEO) Clergymen's Aid, Inc..
Hennessy, James W. '61 (WIN) Retired.
Hennessy, John J. *s.j.* '69 (RC) Martin, SD Our Lady of the Sacred Heart.
Hennessy, John P. *o.s.a.* '44 (NY).
Hennessy, John '78 (FWT) Burleson, TX St. Ann.
Hennessy, Joseph I. '63 (PHX) Chandler, AZ St. Andrew the Apostle.
Hennessy, Patrick D. '71 (NY) Bronx, NY St. Brendan.
Hennessy, Thomas C. *s.j.* '47 (NY)[EE] Loyola Hall, Jesuit Community.
Hennessy, Thomas J. '97 (ATL) Norcross, GA Saint Patrick's.
Henning, James *o.f.m.conv.* '82 (DET) Detroit, MI Our Lady Queen of Angels.
Henning, Michael L. '74 (STL) St. Peters, MO All Saints; [U] St. Louis, MO Archdiocesan Stewardship Education Committee.
Henning, Phillip D. '93 (SAT) San Antonio, TX Divine Providence.
Henning, Richard G. '92 (RVC)[A] Huntington, NY Diocesan Seminary of the Immaculate Conception.
Henninger, George '85 (IND) Indiana University Hospital/Riley Hospital for Children.
Henninger, George '85 (VIC) On Duty Outside the Diocese.
Hennington, Bruce M. '68 (MAD) Columbus, WI St. Jerome; Doylestown, WI St. Patrick.
Henrich, Steven *o.s.c.* '74 (STP)[M] Shoreview, MN Crosier Community of Shoreview.
Henrick, John C. '62 (NSH) Antioch, TN St. Ignatius of Antioch; Defenders of the Bond; Presbyteral Council and College of Consultors.
Henricksen, Francis C. '55 (DAV) Promoter of Justice; Vicar for Religious Retired.
Henriot, Peter J. *s.j.* '70 (FgM).
Henriques, Eduardo *s.j.* '99 (BO)[V] Newton, MA The Jesuit Community at Boston College.
Henriquez, Genaro '99 (BWN) McAllen, TX Our Lady of Perpetual Help.
Henriquez, Mauricio '92 (WDC) Washington, DC St. Gabriel.
Henritzy, Curtis E. *o.p.* '93 (PRO)[P] Providence St. Thomas Aquinas Priory at Providence College.
Henry, Charles W. *o.s.b.* '53 (NEW)[N] St. Maur Priory.
Henry, Donald H. '71 (VEN) Sarasota, FL St. Thomas More.
Henry, Earl J. *o.s.b.* '64 (GBG)[H] Latrobe, PA Saint Vincent Archabbey.
Henry, Earl *o.s.b.* (GBG) Diocesan Pastoral Council; Special Appointment.
Henry, James R. (MRY) Presbyteral Council.
Henry, James T. '64 (PH) Southampton, PA Our Lady of Good Counsel.
Henry, James *s.v.d.* '59 (LA)[D] Lakewood, CA Saint Joseph High School.
Henry, James '71 (MRY) Nipomo, CA St. Joseph.
Henry, James (MRY) Deans; Diocesan Consultors; Diocesan Consultors; Priest's Personnel Board; Episcopal Vicar; Special Assignment.
Henry, John F. *s.j.* '55 (BAL)[S] Resid. S. Pedro Claver.
Henry, John P. '52 (RVC) Cutchogue, NY Sacred Heart; Tarpon Springs, FL St. Ignatius Retired.
Henry, Joseph P. '58 (PRO) Retired.
Henry, Joseph *s.j.* '60 (ALN)[A] Wernersville, PA Jesuit Center.
Henry, Joseph *s.j.* '60 (PIT) Pittsburgh, PA Most Holy Name of Jesus.
Henry, Leo G. '55 (PIT)[N] Pittsburgh, PA St. John Vianney Manor Retired.
Henry, Patrick J. '92 (SAC) Alturas, CA Sacred Heart.
Henry, Patrick J. (CHI) Oak Lawn, IL St. Catherine of Alexandria.
Henry, Patrick '81 (CLV) Euclid, OH St. Christine.
Henry, Paul J. '68 (ORL) Orlando, FL St. John Vianney; Deans; Members.
Henry, Paul '70 (BAL) Special Assignment.
Henry, Paul (ORL) Bishop's Executive Staff; Campus Ministry.
Henry, Perry F. *c.m.* '83 (NO) New Orleans, LA St. Joseph; New Orleans, LA St. Stephen.
Henry, Perry *c.m.* '83 (NO) New Orleans, LA St. John the Baptist; [P] New Orleans, LA Vincentian Fathers.
Henry, Peter '68 (ORL) On Duty Outside the Diocese.
Henry, Robert P. '79 (NY) Nyack, NY St. Ann.
Henry, Terence *t.o.r.* '75 (STU)[F] Steubenville, OH Holy Spirit Friary.
Henry, Terence *t.o.r.* '76 (STU)[A] Steubenville, OH Franciscan University of Steubenville.
Henry, Thomas '44 (RIC) Retired.
Henry, William F. '84 (JKS) McComb, MS St. Alphonsus.
Henry, William (JKS) Charismatic Renewal.

Henseler, J. Thomas '63 (PEO) On Duty Outside the Diocese.
Henseler, Michael *s.d.s.* '77 (MIL)[O] Richmond, VA.
Henseler, Phillip (CHI) Mt. Prospect, IL St. Raymond de Penafort.
Henseler, Thomas '63 (SFD) Mount Sterling, IL Holy Family.
Hensell, Eugene *o.s.b.* '69 (IND)[A] St. Meinrad, IN St. Meinrad School of Theology; [K] St. Meinrad, IN St. Meinrad Archabbey.
Henson, Jerome '77 (ORG) Administrative Leave.
Henson, Joel '93 (LA)[A] Camarillo, CA St. John's Seminary College of the Archdiocese of Los Angeles.
Hensy, Patrick E. *c.s.p.* '78 (LA) Los Angeles, CA St. Paul the Apostle.
Hensy, Patrick *c.s.p.* '78 (LA)[BB] Los Angeles, CA University of California, Los Angeles, University Catholic Center.
Hentschel, Cletus B. '51 (BEL) Retired.
Hentz, Otto H. *s.j.* '68 (WDC)[M] Washington, DC The Jesuit Community at Georgetown University.
Hentzner, John T. '45 (MIL) Retired.
Henverson, Roy '85 (BGP) Norwalk, CT St. Matthew.
Henz, Kenneth W. '51 (CIN) Retired.
Heon, Charles *o.m.i.* '64 (FgM).
Heon, Paul J. *m.afr.* '41 (SP)[O] St. Petersburg, FL Missionaries of Africa.
Hepburn, Timothy M. '93 (ATL)[N] Atlanta, GA Emory University, Agnes Scott College; [O] Roswell, GA Blessed Trinity High School.
Hephner, John (GB).
Hepnar, Bede '57 (GB)[I] Green Bay, WI St. Mary of the Angels Friary.
Hepner, Ernest C. '61 (CLV) Bedford Heights, OH Holy Trinity.
Hepner, Ernest '61 (CLV) Retired.
Heppe, Patrick E. '77 (MIL) Fond du Lac, WI Holy Family; Deans.
Heppen, Michael J. *c.s.c.* '63 (DET) Royal Oak, MI National Shrine of the Little Flower; Beverly Hills, MI Our Lady Queen of Martyrs.
Heppen, Michael J. *c.s.c.* '63 (FTW)[I] Beverly Hills, MI.
Heppen, Michael J. *c.s.c.* '63 (DET) Royal Oak, MI National Shrine of the Little Flower; Beverly Hills, MI Our Lady Queen of Martyrs.
Heppner, Sylvester *o.f.m.* '69 (GAL) Galveston, TX St. Patrick.
Hept, Wilfred A. *o.f.m.* '44 (BO)[Y] Boston, MA Saint Anthony Residence.
Herald, Robert '89 (AUS) Gatesville, TX Our Lady of Lourdes.
Heras, Michael '84 (CC) Corpus Christi, TX Our Lady of Perpetual Help.
Heraty, John T. '67 (RCK) Sandwich, IL St. Paul.
Herb, Robert (SFR) San Francisco, CA St. Paul of the Shipwreck.
Herba, Stanislaw '64 (SLC) Salt Lake City, UT St. Ambrose.
Herbe, Donnan *o.f.m.* '45 (SFE) Pena Blanca, NM Nuestra Senora De Guadalupe.
Herbein, John J. '74 (E) Franklin, PA St. Patrick.
Herbek, Adrian F. '59 (LIN) David City, NE St. Mary's; Deaneries and Deans; Building Commission; Members.
Herbek, Adrian (LIN) Diocesan Consultors.
Herber, Alvin *c.pp.s.* '50 (KCK) Overland Park, KS Church of the Ascension.
Herber, John *c.pp.s.* '68 (CIN)[B] Carthagena, OH St. Charles.
Herber, Stanley J. '64 (IND) Connersville, IN St. Gabriel; Knightstown, IN St. Rose; New Castle, IN St. Anne; Deaneries and Deans.
Herberger, Roy T. '68 (BUF) Sheehan Memorial Emergency Hospital; Buffalo, NY SS. Columba & Brigid.
Herbers, Simon *c.p.* '50 (GAL)[Q] Houston, TX Congregation of the Passion, Holy Name Retreat Center.
Herbert, Daniel J. '79 (ANC) Anchorage, AK Holy Cross.
Herbert, Eugene '81 (LA) Monrovia, CA Annunciation.
Herbert, G. Paul '86 (WDC) Poolesville, MD Our Lady of the Presentation; Pastoral Center Special Ministries; Judges; Air Force Reserve Chaplains.
Herbert, G. Paul (MO) Judges.
Herbert, John J. '83 (BUR) Rutland, VT St. Peter.
Herbert, Leo P. '67 (ATL) Lookout Mountain, GA Our Lady of the Mount.
Herbst, Justin J. '58 (TR)[J] Lawrenceville, NJ Morris Hall/Saint Lawrence, Inc.; [L] Lawrenceville, NJ Morris Hall–Saint Lawrence, Inc.; [O] Lawrenceville, NJ Our Lady of the Rosary Chapel; [T] Lawrenceville, NJ Morris Hall Home for the Aged.
Herbst, Robert M. *o.f.m.conv.* '91 (SB) Riverside, CA Our Lady of Guadalupe.
Herbst, Robert M. *o.f.m.conv.* (SFR) Judges.
Herbst, Robert M. *o.f.m.* (MO) Judges.
Herbster, Kenneth J. '63 (NEW) Hoboken, NJ Our Lady of Grace; Hoboken, NJ St. Joseph's; Central Hudson Region Deanery 9; College of Consultors; Presbyteral Council.
Hercek, Joseph R. '72 (MRY) Atascadero, CA St. William's.
Hercik, Terry A. '80 (GBG) Connellsville, PA Immaculate Conception.
Herda, Jerome G. '90 (MIL) Special Assignment; Secretary to Archbishop.
Herdegen, Anthony '46 (FRS) Retired.
Heredia, Juan Victor '91 (BWN)[A] Mission, TX The Saint Joseph and Saint Peter Seminary; Office for Vocations; Office for Seminarians.
Heredia, Leonardo *o.f.m.* (LAR) Presbyteral Council.
Hereford, Thomas D. '56 (JC) On Duty Outside the Diocese.
Hereley, Peter J. *o.p.* '63 (CHI) River Forest, IL St. Vincent Ferrer; [N] River Forest St. Thomas Aquinas Priory; [U] River Forest, IL American Friends of the Ecole Biblique.
Hereshko, David M. '00 (HBG) Carlisle, PA St. Patrick; [J] Carlisle, PA Dickinson School of Law.
Herff, Jerome R. *c.m.* (GLP) Diocesan Review Board for Sexual Abuse & Misconduct by Clergy, Religious and Other Church Personnel.
Herff, Jerome *c.m.* '67 (GLP) Kayenta, AZ Our Lady of Guadalupe.
Herff, Jerry *c.m.* (GLP) Defenders of the Bond.
Hergenrother, John C. (CHI) Judges.
Hergenrother, John '66 (CHI) Chicago, IL St. Ladislaus.
Herhenrerder, Peter V. '59 (SCR) Retired.
Heria, Fernando (MIA) Judges; Miami, FL St. Brendan; [C] Miami, FL St. Brendan High School.
Herian, Kenneth J. *s.j.* '55 (MIL) Milwaukee, WI Gesu Parish.
Heric, William '81 (SEA) Duvall, WA Holy Innocents.
Herkowski, Arthur M. '54 (MIL) Retired.
Herkowski, Arthur M. '54 (RNO) Retired.
Herle, Clifford *o.f.m.* '55 (MRY)[F] San Miguel, CA Novitiate House for the Franciscan Friars, O.F.M.; [F] San Miguel, CA Franciscan Friars, O.F.M..
Herlihy, Daniel J. (MET) South Bound Brook, NJ Our Lady of Mercy; Episcopal Vicars; Episcopal Council.
Herlihy, Jude M. *o.s.m.* '56 (ORG) Fullerton, CA St. Juliana Falconieri; [I] Fullerton, CA St. Juliana Falconieri Priory.
Herlihy, Jude M. *o.s.m.* '56 (CHI)[N] Chicago Order of Friar Servants of Mary (Servites) United States of America Province, Inc..
Herlihy, Jude *o.s.m.* '56 (ORG)[I] Fullerton, CA Servite Fathers and Brothers.
Herlocker, Brian L. '03 (PEO) Champaign, IL St. John's Catholic Chapel; [O] Champaign, IL St. John's Catholic Student Chapel and Newman Foundation, University of Illinois.
Herlong, T. L. (LKC) Advocates.
Herlong, Theophilus L. '58 (LKC) Retired.
Herman, Charles A. '97 (FTW) Auburn, IN Immaculate Conception.
Herman, Gerald *o.f.m.conv.* '57 (SAT)[M] San Antonio, TX San Damiano Friary.
Herman, Gerard *o.f.m.conv.* '57 (SAT)[B] San Antonio, TX San Damiano Friary, Prenovitiate House of Formation.
Herman, Jerome A. '43 (DET) Retired.
Herman, John A. *c.s.c.* '94 (PHX) Goodyear, AZ Saint John Vianney.
Herman, John A. *c.s.c.* '95 (FTW)[K] Goodyear, AZ St. John Vianney School Development Fund.
Herman, Michael T. '89 (CHI) Chicago, IL St. Sylvester.
Herman, Robert D. '60 (WIN) Medford, MN Christ the King Retired.
Herman, William J. (DET) Utica, MI St. Lawrence.
Hermann, Carlton P. '35 (SFS) Retired.
Hermann, Robert (STL)[U] St. Louis, MO Archdiocesan Planned Giving & Endowment Council.
Hermanns, Harold T. '54 (NEW)[N] Rutherford, NJ St. John Vianney Residence for Priests Retired.
Hermanns, Mel *o.f.m.cap.* '64 (CHI) Chicago, IL Our Lady Gate of Heaven.
Hermes, Alphonsus B. *o.praem.* '01 (ORG)[D] Silverado, CA St. Michael's Preparatory School; [I] Silverado, CA Norbertine Fathers of Orange Inc..
Hermes, Daniel J. '69 (RCK) Crystal Lake, IL St. Thomas the Apostle; Diocesan Consultors.
Hermes, Eustace '41 (VIC) Defenders of the Bond Retired.
Hermes, Michael '91 (KCK) Kansas City, KS SS. Cyril and Methodius; Kansas City, KS St. Joseph and St. Benedict; Regional Pastoral Leaders.
Hermes, Richard T. *s.j.* '98 (NO)[F] New Orleans, LA Jesuit High School.
Hermes, Roger J. '53 (STP) Retired.
Hermes, Thomas W. '82 (KC) Clinton, MO Holy Rosary.
Hermley, Robert J. *o.s.f.s.* '55 (WIL)[J] Childs, MD Retirement and Assisted Care Facility.
Hermoso, Joseph '57 (ELP) El Paso, TX St. Joseph's.
Hermoso, Seth '67 (GAL) Houston, TX St. Augustine; Ethnic Vicars.
Hern, Thomas G. *c.m.* '77 (FgM).
Hernanco, Henry L. '67 (LA) Federal Correctional Institution.
Hernandez, Alfred Ricardo '66 (SAT) Military Chaplains.
Hernandez, Alfred '82 (LA) Torrance, CA Nativity.
Hernandez, Alfredo '92 (PMB) West Palm Beach, FL St. Juliana; Presbyteral Council; Secretary.
Hernandez, Angelo '93 (PH) Philadelphia, PA St. William.
Hernandez, Anthony '95 (BRK) Brooklyn, NY SS. Peter and Paul's.
Hernandez, Anthony '00 (VNN) Los Gatos, CA St. Basil the Great; Sacramento, CA St. Philip the Apostle; Director of Religious Education.
Hernandez, Anthony (BRK) Vice Officiales–Associate Judicial Vicars.
Hernandez, Anthony (BRK) Bishop Valero—.
Hernandez, Antonio *c.ss.r.* '67 (CGS) Aguas Buenas, PR Church of Tres Santos Reyes.
Hernandez, Antonio '92 (SAT) On Leave.
Hernandez, Apolinar '90 (SR) On Leave.
Hernandez, Ariel '03 (CAM) Vineland, NJ Immaculate Heart of Mary.
Hernandez, Bernardo *c.m.* '63 (PCE) Ponce, PR San Vicente–Cantera.
Hernandez, Edwin R. '83 (CGS) Caguas, PR San Pablo Apostol.
Hernandez, Eliseo *o.r.c.* '82 (SB) San Bernardino, CA Our Lady of Guadalupe; [E] Corona, CA Operarios Del Reino De Cristo, O.R.C..
Hernandez, Elmon *s.d.b.* '97 (ARE) Orocovis, PR San Juan Bautista.
Hernandez, Enrico '96 (SJ) Archbishop Mitty High School; [C] San Jose, CA Archbishop Mitty High School; Building Committee; Diocesan Clergy Personnel Board; Ongoing Formation of Clergy Committee.
Hernandez, Esteban *m.s.f.* '87 (BWN) Brownsville, TX St. Luke.
Hernandez, Federico *o.f.m.* '79 (AMA) Amarillo, TX St. Laurence Cathedral.
Hernandez, Felix Nunez '99 (CGS) Juncos, PR Inmaculada Concepcion.
Hernandez, Fernando A. '90 (NY) Bronx, NY Christ the King.
Hernandez, Fernando *t.o.r.* (AUS) Waco, TX St. Francis on the Brazos.
Hernandez, Fidel *o.a.r.* '97 (LA)[Q] Oxnard, CA St. Augustine Priory O.A.R..
Hernandez, Francis G. *s.j.* '63 (SAC)[D] Sacramento, CA Jesuit High School; [I] Carmichael, CA Jesuit High School Community of Sacramento.
Hernandez, Francisco J. '90 (LAR) Zapata, TX Our Lady of Lourdes.
Hernandez, Francisco J. '90 (YAK) On Duty Outside the Diocese.
Hernandez, Francisco J. '94 (MIA) Key West, FL St. Mary, Star of the Sea; Local Chaplain:.
Hernandez, Francisco '95 (OM) Omaha, NE St. Ann; Caguas, PR Nuestra Senora del Perpetuo Socorro.
Hernandez, Francisco '01 (SAC) Maxwell, CA Sacred Heart.
Hernandez, George '97 (BRK) Brooklyn, NY St. Brigid; Bishop Daily—.
Hernandez, Gonzalo Diaz '63 (MGZ) Hormigueros, PR Shrine of Our Lady of Monserrate; Diocesan Board of Administration; Parish Priests Consultors.
Hernandez, Jaime B. '03 (WDC) Rockville, MD Shrine of St. Jude.
Hernandez, Javier '74 (CGS) Caguas, PR Cathedral Dulce Nombre de Jesus.
Hernandez, Javier '79 (CGS) Caguas, PR Maria Madre de la Iglesia.
Hernandez, Javier (CGS) Government Regional Hospital; Hospitals; Hospital Hima.
Hernandez, Jesus (OAK) Brentwood, CA Immaculate Heart of Mary.
Hernandez, Jimmy '83 (ARE) Retired.
Hernandez, Jorge *o.f.m.* '98 (SD) Oceanside, CA Mission San Luis Rey; [H] Oceanside, CA Mission San Luis Rey.
Hernandez, Jose A. '60 (SFE) Tome, NM Immaculate Conception.
Hernandez, Jose G. (SJN) Graduate Studies.
Hernandez, Jose Luis (SPK) Brewster, WA Sacred Heart; Twisp, WA St. Genevieve.
Hernandez, Jose *m.s.p.* '98 (LA) Los Angeles, CA Santa Isabel.
Hernandez, Joseph '69 (LA) Fillmore, CA St. Francis of Assisi; Santa Barbara Pastoral Region.
Hernandez, Juan Ramon *c.ss.r.* '80 (CGS) San Lorenzo, PR Nuestra Senora de la Mercedes.
Hernandez, Lawrence C. *o.ss.t.* '78 (BAL).
Hernandez, Luis E. *o.s.a.* '74 (GAL)[S] Baytown, TX Our Lady of Guadalupe.
Hernandez, Luis E. (DAL) Dallas, TX Santa Clara.
Hernandez, Manuel '96 (CC) Corpus Christi, TX Our Lady of Guadalupe.
Hernandez, Martin A. '81 (BR) Prairieville, LA St. John the Evangelist; On Leave.
Hernandez, Miguel A. '02 (ORG) Garden Grove, CA St. Columban.
Hernandez, Oscar '86 (SAT) San Antonio, TX St. Timothy's.

Hernandez, Pablo E. *s.j.* (STL)[N] St. Louis, MO Fusz Pavilion; [O] St. Louis, MO Jesuit Community Corporation at St. Louis University – Jesuit Hall.
Hernandez, Pedro '89 (ARE) Caonillas–Utuado, PR Nuestra Senora del Monte Carmelo.
Hernandez, Rafael '93 (BWN) Brownsville, TX Church of the Good Shepherd.
Hernandez, Ramon '73 (SP) Dade City, FL St. Rita; Hispanic Apostolate.
Hernandez, Refugio (SD) El Centro Juvenile Hall; Imperial County Jail.
Hernandez, Rene J. '95 (MGZ) Mayaguez, PR Cathedral of Our Lady of Purification.
Hernandez, Reynaldo '98 (OAK) Concord, CA St. Francis of Assisi; Concord, CA Queen of All Saints.
Hernandez, Ricardo '00 (RCK) Algonquin, IL St. Margaret Mary.
Hernandez, Stephen '82 (LA) Retired.
Hernandez, Victor M. *s.j.* '76 (MIA)[D] Miami, FL Belen Jesuit Preparatory School; [H] Miami, FL Villa Javier.
Hernandez, Victor *s.j.* (MIA) Comunidad de Vida Cristiana (CVX) Regina Mundi.
Hernandez–Correa, David *s.j.* (BO)[V] Newton, MA The Jesuit Community at Boston College.
Hernandez–Gomez, Francisco '01 (SAC) Colusa, CA Our Lady of Lourdes; Priests' Personnel Board, Diocesan.
Hernandez–Toboada, Jesus Antonio *s.s.p.* '95 (LA)[Q] Los Angeles, CA Society of St. Paul.
Hernandez Baeza, Martin Eduardo '90 (LA) Los Angeles, CA Mother of Sorrows.
Hernandez Herrera, Julian de Jesus (CHI) Franklin Park, IL St. Gertrude.
Hernandez Morales, Ricardo '98 (SJN) Toa Baja, PR Espiritu Santo.
Hernandez Relat, Edwin '01 (SJN) San Juan, PR San Luis Rey.
Hernandez Velez, Daniel Enrique '03 (MGZ) Moca, PR Our Lady of Monserrate.
Hernando, Henry L. (LA) Bell Gardens, CA St. Gertrude; [CC] San Pedro, CA Apostleship of the Sea, Catholic Maritime Ministry; Navy Reserve Chaplains.
Hernando, Henry (LA) Apostleship of the Sea.
Hernando, Jose L. '62 (MIA) Key Biscayne, FL St. Agnes; Deans and Deaneries.
Hernando, Jose Luis (MIA) Pax Catholic Communications.
Herne, Robert G. '47 (CHI) Palos Hills, IL Sacred Heart Retired.
Hernick, Jan *o.f.m.conv.* (BO) Boston, MA New England Medical Center.
Herold, Anthony '79 (DAV) Clinton, IA Jesus Christ, Prince of Peace.
Heron, J. Thomas '78 (PH) Norwood, PA St. Gabriel.
Herpin, Wayne D. *s.j.* '74 (NO)[P] New Orleans, LA Ignatius Residence; Alamogordo, NM St. Jude.
Herr, Charles W. '48 (NEW) Retired.
Herr, Charles W.A. '48 (NEW)[N] Rutherford, NJ St. John Vianney Residence for Priests.
Herr, Kenneth '68 (EVN) Special Assignment; [A] Evansville, IN Reitz Memorial High School.
Herrador, Blas P. '52 (GAL) Houston, TX Resurrection.
Herradura, Rainee *m.f.* '91 (LA) Santa Clarita, CA Our Lady of Perpetual Help.
Herrera, Anthony W. '91 (OAK) Danville, CA St. Isidore's.
Herrera, David '89 (SAN) Fort Stockton, TX St. Joseph's; Fort Stockton, TX St. Agnes; Sanderson, TX St. James.
Herrera, Ed (LSC) Presbyteral Council; Clergy Personnel Board.
Herrera, Edward '91 (LSC) Sunland Park, NM St. Martin de Porres.
Herrera, Emigdio '77 (LA) Lynwood, CA St. Emydius.
Herrera, Enrique '96 (MRY) Priestly Life and Ministry Board; Salinas, CA St. Mary of the Nativity.
Herrera, Francisco '67 (ELP) Presbyteral Council Retired.
Herrera, Hernando '98 (FR) Absent on Leave.
Herrera, Jorge '03 (RNO) Gardnerville, NV St. Gall.
Herrera, Jose F. (BRK) Woodside, NY Corpus Christi.
Herrera, Jose G. '89 (STV) Army Chaplains.
Herrera, Jose '89 (STV) On Duty Outside the Diocese.
Herrera, Jose *o.s.b.* '02 (GAL)[Q] Sugar Land Basilian Mission Center.
Herrera, Jose (KCK) St. Ignatius Chapel.
Herrera, Jose (OM) Omaha, NE St. Peter.
Herrera, Lawrence P. *s.j.* '81 (CHI)[N] Chicago, IL Woodlawn Jesuit Community.
Herrera, Pedro E. *c.s.v.* '80 (CHI)[N] Arlington Heights Viatorian Province Center–Clerics of St. Viator.
Herreras, Jose Maria *s.j.* '57 (MIA) Miami, FL Corpus Christi.
Herrero, Jose M. '52 (PCE) Mercedita, PR Church of the Resurrection; [B] The Pontifical Catholic University of Puerto Rico.
Herrero, Nicolas '59 (FRS) Retired.
Herres, Joseph W. '72 (LA) Los Angeles, CA San Antonio de Padua.
Herring, James B. *o.praem.* '02 (GB)[I] De Pere, WI St. Norbert Abbey.
Herrlich, Neale *s.j.* '52 (SLC) Ogden, UT St. Mary's.
Herrmann, Austin *c.pp.s.* '48 (DOD) Kinsley, KS St. Nicholas.
Herrmann, Francis R. *s.j.* '74 (NY)[V] Newton, MA The Jesuit Community at Boston College.
Herrmann, Gilbert P. (DOD) Presbyteral Council.
Herrmann, Jim *o.s.c.* '70 (STP)[M] St. Mary's International School.
Herrmann, Richard J. '44 (LC) Retired.
Herrmann, Robert W. '58 (PIT) McKees Rocks, PA Holy Trinity.
Herron, Bernard J. '54 (PH) Retired.
Herron, Dennis M. '73 (BRK) Woodside, NY St. Teresa.
Herron, Francis X. '55 (PH) Retired.
Herron, Jack B. '74 (MAJ) Military Chaplains.
Herron, Jack (HON) Military Chaplains.
Herron, John B. (FAR) Army Chaplains.
Herron, Joseph P. '62 (CAM)[G] Camden, NJ The Frank J. and Rosina W. Suttill Catholic Foundation; Diocesan Finance Council; Wildwood Crest, NJ Assumption B.V.M. Retired.
Herron, Thomas J. '73 (PH) Upper Darby, PA St. Laurence.
Hersey, Bryan '98 (SEA) Des Moines, WA St. Philomena.
Hertel, James R. (PAT) Retired.
Hertel, John *o.carm.* '53 (JOL)[L] Darien Carmelite Provincial Office; (FgM).
Hertel, Joseph M. *o.f.m.* '66 (PAT)[P] Paterson, NJ St. Anthony's Guild.
Hertel, Joseph M. *o.f.m.* '66 (NY) New York, NY St. Francis of Assisi.
Herttna, Matthew M. '45 (Y)[P] Massillon, OH National Shrine of St. Dymphna Retired.
Hertweck, Robert W. *s.m.* '64 (HON)[G] Honolulu, HI Marianist Hall Community.
Hertzfeld, Adam L. '02 (TOL) Findlay, OH St. Michael the Archangel.
Heruday, Joseph C. '43 (CLV) Maple Heights, OH St. Wenceslas Retired.
Hervey, Paul '95 (SP) Palm Harbor, FL St. Luke the Evangelist; Knights of Columbus.
Herzing, Joseph '99 (SCL) Holdingford, MN St. Hedwig's; Holdingford, MN St. Mary's; Holdingford, MN Our Lacy of Mt. Carmel; Holdingford, MN Immaculate Conception; Holdingford, MN St. Columbkille's; Diocesan Planning Council.
Herzog, John M. '56 (DUB) Retired.
Herzog, Lawrence A. '80 (STL) St. Louis MO St. Roch.
Herzog, Mark J. '79 (TOL) Fremont, OH Sacred Heart.
Herzog, Ronald P. '68 (BLX) Laurel, MS Immaculate Conception; Waynesboro, MS St. Bernadette; Defenders of the Bond; Liturgy, Office of; Army National Guard Chaplains.
Herzog, Ronald (BLX) College of Consultors; Interim Diocesan Liturgical Commission; Presbyteral Council.
Herzstein, Joseph M. *c.ss.p.* (FgM).
Hesburgh, Theodore M. *c.s.c.* '43 (FTW)[B] University of Notre Dame Du Lac; [I] Notre Dame, IN Holy Cross Community, Corby Hall, University of Notre Dame.
Heskamp, Charles *s.v.d.* '58 (BLX)[A] Bay St. Louis, MS St. Augustine's.
Hesketh, John E. *o.s.b.* '94 (PAT)[M] Morristown, NJ St. Mary's Abbey.
Heskin, Thomas M. *o.s.m.* '55 (CHI)[J] Maywood, IL Foster G. McGaw Hospital of Loyola University of Chicago; [N] Berwyn, IL St. Bonfilius Priory.
Hesko, Daniel C. '84 (TR) Middletown NJ St. Catherine.
Heslin, James J. '54 (STA) Jacksonville FL Holy Spirit.
Heslin, Philip J. (SUP) On Special or Other Diocesan Assignment; Moderator of the Curia; Ex Officio Members:; Presbyteral Council & Diocesan Consultors.
Heslin, Sean '67 (ORL) Cocoa Beach, FL Church of Our Saviour.
Hess, George A. *s.j.* '50 (BAL)[S] Loyola Bhavan.
Hess, James W. '53 (MIL) Retired.
Hess, James *o.carm.* '76 (PMB)[B] Boca Raton, FL Pope John Paul II High School; [J] Boca Raton, FL St. Elias Priory–Order of Carmelites, NY; Secretary.
Hess, Joseph R. (PH) Yardley, PA St. Ignatius of Antioch.
Hess, Larry J. (ALN) Charismatic Renewal; Catholic Men of Good News (CMOGN); Bangor, PA Our Lady of Good Counsel.
Hess, Michael N. '71 (DM) West Des Moines, IA Sacred Heart.
Hess, Michael (DM) Priests' Pension Fund Society.
Hess, Norbert F. *c.s.c.* '56 (FTW)[I] Notre Dame, IN Holy Cross House.
Hess, Richard J. '60 (DUB) Cedar Rapids, IA Immaculate Conception Retired.
Hess, Stephen *s.j.* '95 (BO)[V] Newton, MA The Jesuit Community at Boston College.
Hesse, Anthony R. '01 (NU) Canby, MN St. Peter; St. Leo, MN St. Leo; Members.
Hesse, Paul '91 (CC) Bishop's Office; Seminary Formation & Vocations; [I] Corpus Christi, TX FirePower Retreats.
Hesse, Peter *o.f.m.cap.* '43 (LC)[H] Marathon City, WI St. Anthony Retreat Center.
Hesse, Robert T. *c.s.c.* '58 (FTW)[I] Holy Cross Bugembe.
Hesse, Thomas '63 (KCK) Holton, KS St. Dominic's; Holton, KS St. Francis Xavier Retired.
Hessel, Gerald (MIL)[H] Milwaukee, WI All Saints Catholic East School System, Inc.; Milwaukee, WI Our Lady of Divine Providence.
Hesseling, Jason E. '00 (MAD) Briggsville, WI St. Mary Help of Christians; Pardeeville, WI St. Andrew; Portage, WI St. Mary; Portage, WI St. Mary of the Immaculate Conception; Elected.
Hessian, Patrick J. '53 (STP) Retired.
Hessian, Roger J. '61 (STP) Cannon Falls, MN St. Pius V.
Hession, Anthony '99 (FAR) Munich, ND St. Mary; Munich, ND Assumption of the Blessed Virgin Mary.
Hession, Edward I. '41 (FTW) Fort Wayne, IN St. Charles Borromeo Retired.
Hession, James J. '59 (BO) Senior Priests Retired.
Hession, Mark R. '84 (CHI)[U] Chicago, IL National Organization for Continuing Education of Roman Catholic Clergy, Inc..
Hession, Mark R. (FR) Centerville, MA Our Lady of Victory; Judges; Continuing Education of the Clergy; Diocesan Council of Catholic Nurses.
Hessling, Ambrose B. *o.s.b.* '57 (PEO).
Hester, John '59 (SJ)[A] Palo Alto, CA St. Thomas Aquinas; Stanford Medical Center.
Heter, Bernard P. '74 (NY) Cornwall–on–Hudson, NY St. Thomas of Canterbury.
Hetteberg, Marcan *o.f.m.* '54 (CIN)[M] Cincinnati, OH St. Clement Friary.
Hetzler, Leo A. *c.s.b.* '55 (ROC)[I] Rochester, NY Basilian Residence.
Heuberger, Joseph '70 (P) Salem, OR St. Vincent de Paul; Building Commission.
Heuberger, Mark '80 (VEN) Cape Coral, FL St. Andrew.
Heumann, Carl J. *s.j.* '92 (DEN)[D] Aurora, CO Regis Jesuit High School; [N] Centennial, CO Regis High Jesuit Community.
Heuring, Alvan P. '44 (DUB) Retired.
Heuschkel, Robert R. '50 (Y) Youngstown, OH St. Dominic.
Heusel, Daniel (STU) Toronto, OH St. Francis of Assisi; Toronto, OH St. Joseph's; Notary; Vocations.
Heusel, Daniel (STU) Auditors.
Heusel, Daniel (STU) Toronto, OH St. Francis of Assisi; Toronto, OH St. Joseph's; Notary; Vocations.
Heuser, Frederick A. '55 (MIL) Kenosha, WI St. James.
Heuser, James *s.d.b.* '84 (NY) New York, NY Mary Help of Christians; [EE] New Rochelle, NY Salesian Provincial House; (FgM).
Heusser, John F. (PAT) Retired.
Hever, John J. '52 (BO) Medfield, MA Medfield State Hospital.
Hever, Thomas '62 (PHX) Scottsdale, AZ Our Lady of Perpetual Help.
Hevern, Vincent W. *s.j.* '76 (SY)[Q] Syracuse, NY Jesuits at LeMoyne, Inc..
Hevia, Todd O. '67 (PT) On Leave of Absence.
Hewe, Manuel A. '97 (HON) Pahala, HI Sacred Heart; Pahala, HI Holy Rosary.
Hewe, Manuel (HON) Filipino Ministry.
Hewes, James E. '74 (ROC) Clyde, NY St. John the Evangelist.
Hewes, Robert S. '78 (RVC) Seaford, NY St. James; Air Force Reserve Chaplains.
Hewes, Russell L. '01 (OKL) Woodward, OK St. Peter's.
Hewett, Alfred J. '56 (CAM) Retired.
Hewitt, Anthony '99 (VEN) Graduate Studies.
Hewitt, Bernard P. '47 (CAM) Retired.
Hewitt, Kenneth R. (PAT) Retired.
Hewson, William J. '40 (BR) Retired.
Heyburn, Theodore *c.ss.r.* '60 (BAL) Annapolis, MD St. Mary; [S] Annapolis, MD Saint Mary Rectory.
Heyd, James '89 (CHI) Evanston, IL St. Athanasius.
Heyd, Joseph J. *o.s.b.* '56 (PEO) Peru, IL St. Joseph's.
Heying, John (RC)[A] Faith, SD St. Joseph.
Heyman, George P. '81 (ROC) Wolcott, NY St. Thomas the Apostle; Wolcott, NY St. Mary Magdalene.
Heyman, Jerome M. *o.s.a.* '61 (KAL) Allegan, MI Blessed Sacrament.
Heymen, Richard '56 (GB) Retired.
Heymer, Edward Odell '45 (MEM) Memphis, TN Holy Rosary Retired.
Heyndricks, Eugene P. '81 (NEW) Retired.
Hezel, Francis X. *s.j.* '69 (CI)[A] Pohnpei, FM Micronesian Seminar; [C] Kolonia, Pohnpei, FM Jesuit House.
Hezel, Kenneth *s.j.* (AGN) Archdiocesan College of Consultors; Archdiocesan Presbyteral Council.
Hgi, Francis (WDC) Washington, DC Shrine of the Sacred Heart.
Hibner, Cyprian *o.carm.* '61 (PHX) Glendale, AZ St. Raphael.
Hibner, Jerome H. '64 (BEL) Retired.
Hicarte, Mateo '53 (LA) Los Angeles, CA Immaculate

Heart of Mary.
Hickel, John J. '55 (STL) St. Paul, MO St. Paul.
Hickens, William F. *c.s.c.* '46 (FTW)[I] Notre Dame, IN Holy Cross House.
Hickey, Christopher J. '94 (BO) Dorchester, MA St. William.
Hickey, Daniel J. '59 (BO) Malden, MA Sacred Hearts.
Hickey, Dennis W. *c.s.p.* '76 (NY) New York, NY St. Paul the Apostle; AUXILIARY CHAPLAINS CONTRACT CHAPLAINS.
Hickey, George W. '73 (PRT) Hallowell, ME Sacred Heart.
Hickey, Gregory J. '79 (PH)[C] Immaculata, PA Immaculata University.
Hickey, James C. *s.m.a.* '46 (NEW)[N] Tenafly, NJ Society of African Missions, Provincialate, S.M.A. Fathers Retired.
Hickey, James F. '68 (BO) Rockland, MA Holy Family.
Hickey, Jerome J. *o.c.s.o.* '59 (ATL)[K] Conyers, GA The Monastery of the Holy Spirit.
Hickey, John W. (NY).
Hickey, John '96 (AMA) Nazareth, TX Holy Family; Panhandle, TX St. Theresa.
Hickey, Kieran *o.f.m.cap.* (GB) Kaukauna, WI St. Mary of the Annunciation.
Hickey, Meldon *o.e.m.* '51 (GLP) Fort Defiance, AZ Our Lady of Blessed Sacrament; St. Michaels, AZ St. Michael; Vicars Forane; Presbyteral Council; Cursillos.
Hickey, Michael '62 (VEN) Retired.
Hickey, Peter D. *s.j.* '76 (BO)[E] Dorchester, MA Boston College High School & Jesuit Community.
Hickey, Regis *o.s.b.* '50 (KCK)[H] Atchison, KS St. Benedict's Abbey.
Hickey, Robert P. '65 (NY) Ellenville, NY St. Mary and St. Andrew.
Hickey, Thomas E. '70 (CHI) Chicago, IL St. Clement.
Hickey, Thomas F. *c.ss.r.* '54 (BRK) Brooklyn, NY Our Lady of Perpetual Help Basilica.
Hickey, Timothy *c.s.sp.* (PIT)[Q] Pittsburgh, PA Duquesne University.
Hickey, William M. '86 (ATL) Cumming, GA St. Brendan.
Hickey, William T. '47 (BRK) Rego Park, NY Our Lady of the Angelus Retired.
Hickie, J. Noel '67 (BAK)[J] Eugene, OR Sacred Heart Medical Center; On Duty Outside the Diocese.
Hickin, Michael '97 (FAR) Graduate Studies.
Hickl, Robert *o.m.i.* '79 (FgM).
Hickman, Stephen J. '82 (RIC) Waynesboro, VA St. John the Evangelist.
Hicks, Alfred J. *s.j.* '66 (BO)[H] Boston, MA Nativity Preparatory School.
Hicks, Francis J. (LA) San Pedro, CA Holy Trinity.
Hicks, Ronald A. '94 (CHI).
Hicks, Steven '82 (SAN)[A] Military Chaplains.
Hidaka, Ronald E. *s.j.* '74 (FgM).
Hiebl, Charles J. '62 (LC) Athens, WI St. Anthony de Padua; Edgar, WI Holy Family; Athens, WI St. Thomas.
Hien, Joachim L. (SPK) Vietnamese Apostolate.
Hien, Joachim '74 (SPK) Spokane, WA St. Anthony.
Hien, Joseph '64 (NY) New York, NY St. Columba.
Higdon, C. Paul '46 (DET)[H] Port Huron, MI Mercy Hospital of Port Huron Retired.
Higdon, Francis B. *m.m.* '67 (FgM).
Higginbotham, Matthew P. '94 (LAF) New Iberia, LA Our Lady of Prompt Succor.
Higginbotham, Robert '75 (BLX) Military Chaplains; Air Force Chaplains.
Higgins, Brian J. '99 (ATL) Roswell, GA St. Peter Chanel; Special or Other (Arch)Diocesan Assignment; Office of Vocations.
Higgins, Charles J. '88 (BO) Allston, MA St. Anthony; West Roxbury, MA St. Theresa of Avila; Brookline, MA St. Mary of the Assumption.
Higgins, Damian '02 (STN) Waianae, HI St. Sophia Byzantine Missions.
Higgins, Donald *c.s.s.* '64 (SPR) Springfield, MA Our Lady of Mt. Carmel.
Higgins, E. E. (PEO) Vicariates and Vicars.
Higgins, E. Edward '57 (PEO) Elkhart, IL St. Patrick; Lincoln, IL Holy Family.
Higgins, Edward F. '54 (GBG) Retired.
Higgins, Edward J. '76 (PSC) Philadelphia, PA Holy Ghost; Elected Members.
Higgins, Francis C. '68 (SAV) Savannah, GA Sacred Heart of Jesus.
Higgins, Francis E. '64 (SC) On Duty Outside the Diocese.
Higgins, George G. '40 (CHI)[C] Catholic University of America, The Retired.
Higgins, Grant J. '56 (BUF) Retired.
Higgins, James P. *s.j.* '85 (BUF)[O] Buffalo, NY Canisius Jesuit Community.
Higgins, Jerome *o.f.m.cap.* '54 (MIL).
Higgins, John F. *m.s.* '72 (HRT).
Higgins, John J. '52 (WDC) Retired.
Higgins, John J. *s.j.* '66 (BGP)[B] Fairfield, CT Fairfield University; [P] Fairfield, CT The Fairfield Jesuit Community–Fairfield University.
Higgins, John J. '96 (NY) Garnerville, NY St. Gregory Barbarigo.
Higgins, John '81 (LA) Downey, CA St. Raymond.
Higgins, John '01 (BEL) Belleville, IL Cathedral of St. Peter.
Higgins, Joseph P. '58 (MAD) Diocesan Consultors Retired.
Higgins, Laurence E. '53 (SP) Tampa, FL St. Lawrence.
Higgins, Leonard H. '82 (TLS) Pawhuska, OK Immaculate Conception.
Higgins, Michael *c.p.* '70 (FgM).
Higgins, Michael *c.p.* '70 (CHI)[N] Chicago, IL Passionist Provincial Office; [N] Chicago, IL Passionist Community–Immaculate Conception Monastery.
Higgins, Patrick '54 (CC) Cursillo Movement (English); [I] Corpus Christi, TX Cursillo Movement Eastern Vicariate; Corpus Christi, TX Holy Cross.
Higgins, Peter '56 (VIC) Retired.
Higgins, Phillip '73 (RIC) Retired.
Higgins, Raymond (DM) Des Moines, IA St. Anthony's.
Higgins, Richard B. '68 (SAC) Military Chaplains; Army Chaplains.
Higgins, Robert J. *s.j.* '50 (BO)[V] Weston, MA Campion Health Center, Inc..
Higgins, Thomas C. *m.m.* '50 (NY).
Higgins, Thomas M. '85 (PH)[EE] Philadelphia, PA Visitation B.V.M..
Higgins, Thomas P. *s.j.* '64 (LA)[C] Los Angeles, CA Jesuit Community; [BB] Los Angeles, CA Loyola Marymount University; [BB] Los Angeles, CA Loyola Law School.
Higgins, Vincent *l.c.* '01 (HRT)[V] Orange, CT Legion of Christ, Inc..
Higgs, Donald X. '88 (WH) Morgantown, WV St. John University Parish, Newman Hall.
Highberger, Donald E. *s.j.* '81 (DEN)[N] Denver, CO Regis Jesuit Community (The Jesuits at Regis University).
Highberger, George '61 (PHX) Chandler, AZ St. Mary's; Queen Creek, AZ Our Lady of Guadalupe.
Highfill, H. Brian '74 (LAV) North Las Vegas, NV St. Christopher; On Duty Outside the Archdiocese.
Hight, Michael '82 (RC) Retired.
Hightower, Oliver Lee '61 (SEA) Lakewood, WA St. John Bosco.
Higley, Gregory L. '81 (JC) California, MO Annunciation; Vicar General; Moderator of the Curia; Adjutant Judicial Vicar; Diocesan Consultors; Personnel Board; Ex Officio Members; Diocesan Excellence in Education Fund, Inc.; Finance Committee; Board of Trustees.
Higuera, Federico '82 (BEL) Cobden, IL St. Joseph.
Higuera, Francisco P. (YAK) East Wenatchee, WA Holy Apostles; [F] East Wenatchee, WA Holy Apostles Parish Conference.
Hiland, George '58 (PEO) Retired.
Hiland, Gerard P. '85 (CIN) Owensville, OH St. Louis; Owensville, OH St. Philomena.
Hilbert, J. Robert *s.j.* '56 (CHY) St. Stephens, WY St. Stephen's; [C] St. Stephens, WY St. Stephens Mission – Jesuit Community.
Hilbert, John J. '60 (E)[P] Erie, PA Mercyhurst College, North East; Cursillo Movement.
Hilbert, Joseph C. '52 (HBG) Lancaster, PA St. Joseph.
Hilbert, Michael P. *s.j.* '83 (NY)[EE] Pontificia Universita Gregoriana.
Hildebrand, Thomas M. '75 (TLS) Tulsa, OK St. Pius X.
Hildebrandt, Henry F. '87 (DOD) Jetmore, KS St. Anthony; Jetmore, KS St. Lawrence; Spearville, KS St. John the Baptist.
Hildebrandt, Henry (DOD) Technical Services.
Hilden, Michael J. *o.s.a.* '73 (FgM).
Hilderbrand, Michael '76 (IND) Jeffersonville, IN Sacred Heart; [C] Clarksville, IN Our Lady of Providence Junior & Senior High School; Floyds Knobs, IN St. Mary.
Hilferty, John G. '78 (ALN)[G] Allentown, PA Sacred Heart Hospital.
Hilferty, Thomas J. '52 (PH) Philadelphia, PA St. Madeleine Sophie Retired.
Hilfiker, Robert G. '87 (NY) New Windsor, NY St. Joseph.
Hilgartner, Richard '95 (BAL) Graduate Studies.
Hilgeman, Edward J. '52 (STL) Retired.
Hilgeman, Edward (STL) Spiritual Directors.
Hilgeman, James L. *m.m.* '65 (FgM).
Hilgendorf, Patrick '97 (DAV) Burlington, IA SS. John & Paul.
Hilgert, John E. *c.p.* '75 (L)[K] Louisville, KY Sacred Heart Retreat.
Hilgert, John *c.p.* '75 (L) Louisville, KY St. Agnes.
Hilinski, Joseph J. (CLV) Diocesan Interfaith Commission.
Hilinski, Joseph T. '76 (CLV) Cleveland, OH Our Lady of Mercy.
Hilinski, Joseph (CLV) Procurators.
Hilkert, Robert C. '42 (CLV) Brunswick, OH St. Ambrose.
Hill, Allan J. '83 (HRT) Harwinton, CT Immaculate Heart of Mary.
Hill, Benet *o.s.b.* '85 (WDC)[M] Washington, DC St. Anselm's Abbey; Doylestown, PA Our Lady of Mount Carmel.
Hill, Charles E. (LA) College of Consultors.
Hill, Charles '64 (LA) Los Angeles, CA St. Basil's.
Hill, Donald M. '94 (L) Louisville, KY St. Albert the Great.
Hill, Donald '67 (BIS) On Duty Outside the Diocese.
Hill, Edward T. '60 (BAL) Retired.
Hill, Eric '00 (ATL) Buford, GA Prince of Peace.
Hill, Frederick '67 (RVC) Smithtown, NY St. Patrick; Smithtown, NY St. Catherine of Siena Hospital.
Hill, George H. '68 (WOR) On Duty Outside the Diocese.
Hill, George H. '68 (NY) Bronx, NY St. Raymond.
Hill, Michael *o.f.m.* '77 (SAT) San Antonio, TX San Jose y San Miguel; [C] San Antonio, TX Oblate School of Theology.
Hill, Patrick (LA) Canonical Services Coordinator; Canonical Staff; Judges.
Hill, Philip W. '71 (NY) Military Chaplains; Army Chaplains.
Hill, R. Cary '66 (WDC) Pastoral Center Special Ministries; Continuing Education for Clergy.
Hill, Robert Cary '66 (WDC) Washington, DC St. Stephen Martyr.
Hill, Robert '57 (Y) Retired.
Hill, Scott F. *o.m.i.* '79 (MRY) Special Assignment.
Hill, Thomas F. *o.f.m.cap.* '66 (STP) Rosemount, MN St. Joseph.
Hill, Timothy '59 (BIR) Retired.
Hill, W. Paul '64 (WDC) Bowie, MD St. Pius X.
Hill, William J. *o.p.* '50 (WDC)[B] Washington, DC Dominican House of Studies.
Hillen, Daniel (HEL) Retired.
Hillenbrand, John T. '70 (CHI) Chicago, IL St. Peter Canisius.
Hillenbrand, Thomas *o.s.b.* (SFS) Presbyteral Council.
Hiller, Everett J. '54 (RCK) Retired.
Hilley, Stephen J. '79 (MIA) Miami, FL St. Richard.
Hilliard, Richard '79 (SJ) On Leave of Absence.
Hilliard, William J. '62 (HRT) Enfield, CT Holy Family; Enfield, CT Willard–Cybulski Correction Institute.
Hilliard, William '62 (HRT) Enfield, CT Enfield Correctional Institute; Suffield, CT Walker RSMU.
Hilliard, William (NOR) Chaplains.
Hillier, David A. '76 (TR) Leave of Absence; Lancaster, PA St. John Neumann.
Hillier, John G. '88 (WOR) Brookfield, MA St. Mary's.
Hillier, John '88 (NOR)[A] Cromwell, CT Holy Apostles College and Seminary.
Hillman, H. Eugene *c.s.sp.* '50 (VEN)[G] Sarasota, FL Congregation of the Holy Ghost.
Hills, Richard L. '32 (CHI) Retired.
Hillyard, Matthew J. *o.s.f.s.* '91 (ARL)[D] Alexandria, VA Bishop Ireton High School; [J] Alexandria, VA Oblates of St. Francis de Sales Residence.
Hilmer, Garth L. (GAY) Acme, MI Christ the King.
Hilmer, Robert E. '86 (DUB) Retired.
Hils, Damian J. '95 (FAR) Minto, ND St. Stanislaus.
Hils, Damian '95 (FAR) Grafton, ND St. Luke.
Hilton, Francis G. *s.j.* '92 (BAL)[S] Baltimore, MD Jesuit Community of Loyola College, Inc..
Hilton, Hank *s.j.* '92 (BAL)[B] Timonium, MD Loyola Graduate Center –Timonium Campus.
Hilton, John L. '82 (DEN) Westminster, CO Holy Trinity.
Hiltz, John T. '59 (TOL) Retired.
Hiltz, John T. '59 (ORG) Yorba Linda, CA St. Martin Retired.
Himes, Kenneth R. *o.f.m.* '76 (WDC)[M] Silver Spring, MD Gemelli House.
Himes, Michael J. '72 (BRK) Released from Diocesan Assignment.
Himes, Robert P. '58 (YAK) Grand Coulee, WA St. Henry's; Coulee City, WA St. Patrick's.
Himmelsbach, James R. '77 (STP) Waconia, MN St. Joseph; Military Chaplains.
Himsworth, Raymond J. '62 (PH) Elkins Park, PA St. James; [EE] Elkins Park, PA Moss Rehab Einstein at Elkins Park.
Hinacay, Floro A. '87 (SAN) Menard, TX Sacred Heart.
Hinacay, Floro '87 (SAN) Junction, TX St. Theresa of the Child Jesus.
Hinch, Lawrence E. '59 (BRK) Richmond Hill, NY Holy Child Jesus.
Hinde, Peter *o.carm.* '52 (JOL)[L] Darien Carmelite Provincial Office.
Hindel, Richard *o.s.b.* '47 (IND) Floyds Knobs, IN St. John the Baptist; [K] Floyds Knobs, IN.
Hindelang, Joseph C. *s.m.* '78 (DET)[D] Pontiac, MI Notre Dame Preparatory High School and Marist Academy.
Hinder, Paul *o.f.m.cap.* '67 (NY)[EE] White Plains, NY St. Francis of Assisi Foundation, c/o Capuchin Franciscans.
Hindman, John '75 (SB) Corona, CA St. Mary Magdalene.
Hinds, Edward J. '74 (PAT) Chatham, NJ St. Patrick's; Defenders of the Bond; Liturgical Commission.
Hinds, William H. '87 (COV) Maysville, KY St. Patrick; [B] Maysville, KY St. Patrick High School; [T] Fort

Mitchell, KY Mission Share.
Hinds, William H. (COV) Deans.
Hindsley, Leonard *o.p.* '84 (FR) Fall River, MA Notre Dame de Lourdes.
Hines, Bede *t.o.r.* '47 (ALT)[F] Loretto, PA Mount Assisi Friary.
Hines, Hugh *o.f.m.* '60 (NY) New York, NY Holy Name of Jesus.
Hines, J. William '72 (WDC) Landover Hills, MD St. Mary's Catholic Church; Deans.
Hines, William F. '47 (SCR) Retired.
Hinkley, Michael F.X. '91 (HRT) Waterbury, CT Blessed Sacrament.
Hinnebusch, John Frederick *o.p.* '50 (WDC)[B] Washington, DC Dominican House of Studies.
Hinnen, James W. '71 (MAD) Mineral Point, WI Congregation of St. Mary–St. Paul; Judges.
Hinni, Thomas R. *c.m.* '63 (PBL) Pueblo, CO St. Francis Xavier; Deans.
Hinojal, Ricardo *o.a.r.* '62 (LSC)[C] Mesilla, NM Augustinian Recollect Fathers.
Hinojal, Ricardo *o.a.r.* '68 (LSC) Las Cruces, NM Our Lady of Health.
Hinojal, Ricardo *o.a.r.* (LSC) Priestly Life and Ministry Committee.
Hinojos–Ortega, Jaime '02 (DET) Detroit, MI Holy Redeemer.
Hinojosa, Damian *c.s.b.* '87 (GAL) Missouri City, TX Holy Family.
Hinojosa, P. Nolasco '96 (LAR) Laredo, TX Holy Family; Encinal, TX Immaculate Heart of Mary; Presbyteral Council; College of Consultors; Finance Council.
Hinrichsen, Carl D. '55 (NEW) Park Ridge, NJ Our Lady of Mercy Retired.
Hinrichsen, Carl (NEW) Serra Clubs.
Hinsvark, John '66 (FBK) Kotzebue, AK St. Francis Xavier; Nome, AK St. Joseph; Teller, AK St. Ann; Presbyteral Council; Consultors; Vocation Director.
Hinton, Frederick M. '70 (BUF) Pavilion, NY St. Mary.
Hinton, John T. '73 (NO) New Orleans, LA Mater Dolorosa.
Hintz, David R. '86 (LIN) Lincoln, NE St. Patrick's; [L] Lincoln, NE Calvary Cemetery and Mausoleum; Cemeteries.
Hintz, David (LIN) Diocesan Consultors.
Hippee, Michael E. '73 (MAD) Madison, WI St. Bernard; Judicial Vicar; Judges; Building Commission.
Hipskind, J. Timothy *s.j.* '00 (CIN)[M] Cincinnati, OH Claver Jesuit Community.
Hipsley, Milton A. '70 (BAL) Cumberland, MD St. Mary.
Hipwell, Patrick J. '77 (STP) Minnetonka, MN Immaculate Heart of Mary; Presbyteral Council.
Hiramatsu, Joseph *s.a.* '82 (NY)[EE] Garrison Franciscan Friars of the Atonement, Minister General Office.
Hire, Richard '70 (FTW) Mishawaka, IN Queen of Peace.
Hirniak, Mark '98 (STF) Glen Spey, NY St. Volodymyr.
Hirsch, Clinton F. '45 (EVN) Defenders of the Bond Retired.
Hirsch, Harold L. '53 (MET) Spotswood, NJ Immaculate Conception.
Hirsch, Joseph W. '86 (LC) Special Assignment; [H] La Crosse, WI Holy Cross (Seminary) Diocesan Center; Elected Members; Boy Scouts; Ex Officio.
Hirsch, Robert M. '47 (DUB) Monona, IA St. Mary Retired.
Hirt, Al *o.f.m.* '77 (CIN) Cincinnati, OH Holy Name.
Hirt, Alan *o.f.m.* '77 (CIN) Cincinnati, OH St. Monica–St. George Parish Newman Center; [Q] Cincinnati, OH University of Cincinnati Newman Center; [V] Cincinnati, OH Concerned Catholics for Gay/Lesbian Inclusion – Within Archdiocese of Cincinnati.
Hirte, Mateo '53 (LA) Retired.
Hirten, Timothy '93 (BRK) Brooklyn, NY St. Rosalia–Regina Pacis; Air Force Reserve Chaplains.
Hirtz, Daniel J. '73 (SPC) Salem, MO Sacred Heart; South Central Correctional Center; Region V.
Hislop, Edward '73 (HEL) Missoula, MT Pope John XXIII; Presbyteral Council.
Hissey, L. Pierre '66 (PHX) Phoenix, AZ St. Jerome.
Hissrich, John E. '86 (PIT) Pittsburgh, PA Guardian Angels.
Hitch, David '68 (DAV) St. Joseph's; Parnell, IA St. Joseph's.
Hitchcock, James '46 (NSH) Retired.
Hitchcock, Martin B. '51 (BGP) Retired.
Hitchens, Robert '94 (PHU)[F] Fox Chase Manor, PA Provincial Motherhouse of the Sisters of St. Basil the Great; Press, The Way; Office of Vocations; Archeparchial Seminary Advisory and Admissions Board.
Hitchko, Daniel D. '64 (SCR) Exeter, PA St. Cecilia.
Hite, Gregory R. '81 (TOL)[B] Toledo, OH Central Catholic High School; Judges.
Hite, Jordan *t.o.r.* '70 (SFS) Dante, SD Assumption B.V.M.; Wagner, SD St. John the Baptist; Tribunal Judges.
Hite, Richard B. *m.s.a.* '70 (WH)[F] Old Fields, WV Holy Spirit Hermitage.
Hite, Richard *m.s.a.* '70 (NOR)[F] Cromwell Society of the Missionaries of the Holy Apostles.
Hitpas, Joseph H. *o.m.i.* '65 (WDC)[M] Washington, DC Provincial Offices of the United States Province of the Missionary Oblates of Mary Immaculate.
Hitpas, Joseph H. *o.m.i.* '65 (STP)[M] St. Paul, MN Oblate Residence; [V] St. Paul, MN Missionary Oblates of Mary Immaculate.
Hitpas, William J. '67 (BEL) O'Fallon, IL St. Nicholas; Diocesan Consultors.
Hitt, Tobin E '96 (SFE) Portales, NM St. Helen.
Hitt, Tobin '96 (SFE)[L] Portales, NM University Catholic Center – St. Thomas More Chapel; PORTALES: St. Thomas Moore Newman Center.
Hitti, Michael '38 (SAM) Retired.
Hitti, Michael '38 (OLL) Retired.
Hladik, Dusan (CHI) Cicero, IL Our Lady of the Mount; Czech Catholic Mission.
Hladky, Sylvester '36 (PBR) Warren, OH SS. Peter and Paul's.
Hladni, Mirko '71 (CLV) Cleveland, OH St. Paul.
Hladni, Mirko (CLV) Associate Judicial Vicars.
Hlavacek, John F. '55 (LR)[H] Little Rock, AR St. John Manor Retired.
Hlavaty, Kirby '99 (VIC) Vocations Committee; Cuero, TX Our Lady of Guadalupe; Cuero, TX St. Michael.
Hlebs, Milan '51 (SJ) Retired.
Hlond, Waclaw *c.m.* '55 (HRT) New Haven, CT St. Stanislaus.
Hlopko, John J. '36 (SCR) Retired.
Hlubik, Joseph G. '92 (TR) Moorestown, NJ Our Lady of Good Counsel.
Hlubik, Joseph G. '93 (ALT) On Duty Outside the Diocese.
Hmircik, Donald A. '56 (MIL) Retired.
Hnatyshyn, Robert '64 (SJP) McKeesport, PA St. John the Baptist; Diocesan Consultors.
Ho, Antonius *c.s.j.b.* '95 (BRK) Elmhurst, NY Our Lady of China Chapel; [U] Chinese Apostolate–Queens; [V] Astoria, NY Congregation of St. John the Baptist of China.
Ho, Joseph Thanh (BEA) Western Vicariate; Diocesan Judges; Winnie, TX St. Louis.
Ho, Matthias '55 (ORG) Stanton, CA St. Polycarp Retired.
Ho, Nicholas (SAC) Sacramento, CA Cathedral of the Blessed Sacrament.
Ho, Viet–Peter (ORG) Garden Grove, CA St. Callistus.
Hoa, Trinh Duc *c.ss.r.* '93 (LA)[Q] Baldwin Park, CA Vietnamese Redemptorist Mission.
Hoag, Michael R. *s.j.* '71 (NEW)[C] Jersey City, NJ St. Peter's Preparatory School; [N] Jersey City, NJ Jesuit Community of St. Peter's Prep, Inc.
Hoag, Timothy '95 (RC) Belle Fourche, SD St. Paul; Spearfish, SD St. Joseph.
Hoagland, James N. '57 (WCH) Lyons, KS St. Paul Retired.
Hoagland, Victor *c.p.* '59 (NEW)[N] "Compassion" Magazine.
Hoak, Jack W. *o.f.m.* '75 (HRT) New Milford, CT St. Francis Xavier.
Hoan, Basil P. '21 (TYL) Hemphill, TX St. Pius I.
Hoan, Joseph Nguyen '73 (FRS) Fresno, CA St. Helen.
Hoan, Michael '72 (ORG) Special Assignment; [H] Santa Ana, CA Vietnamese Catholic Center; Council of Priests; Consultors; Ministry to Priests.
Hoang, Dat '03 (GAL) Houston, TX Holy Name.
Hoang, Doan *s.j.* '97 (LA) Apostleship of Prayer; [Q] Los Angeles, CA Columbiere House.
Hoang, Dominic Hung '90 (OKL) Oklahoma City, OK St. Andrew Dung–Lac.
Hoang, John Minh Toan '68 (GAL) Houston, TX Vietnamese Martyrs.
Hoang, Joseph Vien *s.d.b.* '83 (NO)[D] Marrero, LA Archbishop Shaw High School.
Hoang, Joseph Viet '94 (SD) Oceanside, CA St. Mary, Star of the Sea.
Hoang, Joseph '99 (P) Portland, OR St. Pius X.
Hoang, Khanh '94 (SD) Kapolei, HI St. Jude.
Hoang, Luat '98 (SJ) Sunnyvale, CA St. Martin.
Hoang, Peter Thien Van *o.p.* '72 (GAL) Houston, TX Our Lady of Lourdes.
Hoang, Phuong '89 (SEA) Auburn, WA Holy Family.
Hoang, Son Linh '03 (PMB) Stuart, FL St. Joseph.
Hoang, Thuan V. '97 (SFR) San Francisco, CA St. Philip the Apostle; Defenders of the Bond.
Hoang, Trung D. '95 (HON) Kailua, HI St. Anthony.
Hoar, Leo James '66 (SPR) Northampton, MA St. Mary of the Assumption; [P] American International College; Springfield College; Springfield Tech. Comm. College.
Hoar, Richard J. *s.j.* '56 (BUF) Buffalo, NY St. Michael.
Hoar, Thomas F.X. *s.s.e.* '78 (NOR)[A] Enders Island, CT St. Edmund's Novitiate; [I] Mystic, CT St. Edmund's Retreat; [F] Mystic, CT Society of St. Edmund.
Hoare, Richard '69 (BRK) South Ozone Park, NY St. Teresa of Avila.
Hoat, Rochus Vu Dinh '60 (BAL) Baltimore, MD St. Mary of the Assumption.
Hoban, Paul T. *o.carm.* '41 (NEW) Cresskill, NJ St. Therese of Lisieux.
Hoban, Robert L. '79 (CLV) Parma, OH St. Francis de Sales.
Hoban, Thomas E. '60 (ALN) Emmaus, PA St. Ann.
Hobbes, Thomas F. '56 (SY) Endwell, NY Christ the King; Elected.
Hobbs, James V. '57 (BAL) Baltimore, MD Basilica of the National Shrine of the Assumption of the Blessed Virgin Mary.
Hober, Henry P. '02 (DUB) Holy Cross, IA Holy Trinity.
Hober, Ray *s.v.d.* '60 (PIT)[N] Pittsburgh, PA Society of The Divine Word.
Hobert, James M. (TUC) Vicar for Priests.
Hobert, James '85 (TUC) Tucson, AZ St. Ambrose; Tucson, AZ St. Monica; Advocates and Auditors; Members.
Hobson, J. Mark '86 (CLV) Solon, OH Resurrection of Our Lord.
Hobson, Michael A. (BO) Middleton, MA St. Agnes.
Hobt, Phillip '92 (DM)[C] Council Bluffs, IA Saint Albert Catholic Schools.
Hoch, George B. *s.j.* '44 (NY).
Hochheim, William A. '60 (STA) Retired.
Hochreiter, Robert S. '68 (SCR) Military Chaplains; Air Force Chaplains.
Hochstatter, Theodore '80 (PEO) On Duty Outside the Diocese.
Hock, G. Harry *s.j.* '64 (RIC) Richmond, VA Sacred Heart.
Hocking, Harold J. *s.j.* '52 (ALN)[A] Wernersville, PA Jesuit Center.
Hockman, Richard C. *c.s.c.* '80 (SCR)[C] Kings College; [C] Holy Cross Community.
Hoctor, Thomas D. '57 (ROC) Retired.
Hodapp, Timothy L. '85 (WIN) Absent on Leave.
Hodde, William '52 (FTW)[G] Fort Wayne, IN Saint Anne Home & Retirement Community; [G] Fort Wayne, IN St. Anne Home of the Diocese of Fort Wayne – South Bend, Inc.; Retired Clergy Committee Retired.
Hoderny, Thomas S. '79 (E) Du Bois, PA St. Michael.
Hodes, Bertrand *o.f.m.conv.* '39 (FgM).
Hodge, William A. '74 (CAM) Atlantic City, NJ St. Nicholas of Tolentine; Vocation Advisory Board; Marian Commission; Legion of Mary; Members.
Hodges, Leo '86 (ORL) Palm Bay, FL Our Lady of Grace; Black Community.
Hodges, Robert S. *o.praem.* '74 (ORG)[I] Silverado, CA Norbertine Fathers of Orange Inc..
Hodgson, William M. '79 (SPC) Carthage, MO St. Ann; Secretariat for Cursillo.
Hodnett, John J. *c.m.* '59 (PH).
Hoeberechts, Dwight *o.m.i.* '97 (BUF)[AA] Buffalo, NY Holy Angels.
Hoebing, Philibert *o.f.m.* '50 (SFD)[B] Quincy, IL Quincy University.
Hoeck, Andreas '92 (DEN) Denver, CO Cathedral of the Immaculate Conception.
Hoedebeck, Paul '43 (LR)[A] Subiaco, AR Subiaco Monastery.
Hoedl, John D. (FAR) Navy Chaplains.
Hoeffner, Robert J. '73 (ORL) Palm Bay, FL St. Joseph; Deans.
Hoeffner, Robert (ORL) Members; Consultors.
Hoefgen, Francis *o.s.b.* '79 (SCL)[I] Collegeville, MN St. John's Abbey, of the Order of St. Benedict.
Hoefler, David J. '02 (SFD) Springfield, IL Blessed Sacrament.
Hoefler, Robert A. '85 (DM) Des Moines, IA St. Theresa of the Child Jesus; Harlan, IA St. Michael.
Hoefler, Robert (DM) Diocesan Consultors.
Hoegerl, Carl W. *c.ss.r.* '50 (BRK)[V] Brooklyn, NY Our Lady of Good Counsel Residence.
Hoelle, Philip C. *s.m.* '42 (CIN)[M] Dayton, OH Mercy Siena Gardens.
Hoelscher, James '58 (SAT) Pleasanton, TX St. Luke–Loire.
Hoelsken, Mark A. *s.j.* '91 (FBK)[E] St. Marys, AK Brother Joe Prince Jesuit Community; Superior Regular; Presbyteral Council; Consultors; Office of Native Permanent Diaconate.
Hoene, Robert E. *s.j.* '53 (MIL)[O] Wauwatosa, WI Jesuit Community at St. Camillus.
Hoenig, Gerald A. '52 (DAV) Montrose, IA St. Joseph's Retired.
Hoening, Gerald '52 (DAV) Retired.
Hoeper, Robert J. *s.m.* '51 (CIN)[M] Dayton, OH Mercy Siena Gardens.
Hoeppner, Michael J. (WIN) Winona, MN Cathedral of the Sacred Heart; Vicar General and Moderator of the Curia; Finance Council; Diocesan Board of Administration; Deposit and Loan Board; Vicar General; Pastoral Planning; Ex Officio; Priest Assignments Committee; Diocesan Pastoral Council; Bishop's Council; Charismatic Renewal; Misconduct Issues; Associate Judges; Second Instance Court Judges.
Hoerburger, Henry R. '43 (LC) Elk Mound, WI St. Joseph; Elected Members.
Hoernig, Alphonse X. *c.m.* '56 (STL)[O] Perryville, MO Congregation of the Mission.
Hoerning, Richard P. '73 (RVC) Rocky Point, NY St. Anthony of Padua.

Hoeser, Jerome G. '63 (LC) Eau Galle, WI St. Henry.
Hoesing, Kenneth F. '97 (LIN) Davey, NE St. Mary's.
Hoesing, Kenneth (LIN) Presbyteral Council.
Hoesing, Paul C. '02 (OM) Omaha, NE St. Bernard; [B] Omaha, NE Roncalli Catholic High School of Omaha.
Hoesli, Fred *o.p.* '64 (GR) Holland, MI St. Francis de Sales Retired.
Hoevel, Robert J. '42 (FTW) Retired.
Hoevel, Robert (FTW) Retired Clergy Committee.
Hoewischer, Harry E. *s.j.* '57 (DEN)[N] Denver, CO Xavier Jesuit Center.
Hoey, James F. '65 (WOR) Spencer, MA Mary, Queen of the Rosary.
Hofer, Kenneth Andrew *o.p.* '02 (FgM).
Hoff, Alphonse A. *o.f.m.* '44 (CIN)[M] Cincinnati, OH St. Clement Friary Retired.
Hoff, James E. *s.j.* '65 (CIN)[M] Cincinnati, OH Jesuit Community at Xavier University.
Hoff, Wilfrid *o.p.* '47 (SFE) Albuquerque, NM St. Thomas Aquinas University Parish.
Hoffbauer, James A. '00 (CIN) Kettering, OH Ascension; Piqua, OH St. Boniface.
Hoffenkamp, Robert A. '89 (JOL) Morris, IL Immaculate Conception of the Blessed Virgin Mary.
Hoffer, Charles J. '46 (COV) Retired.
Hoffman, Andrew '79 (SC)[B] Le Mars, IA Gehlen Catholic School.
Hoffman, David (GB) Manitowoc, WI Sacred Heart; Regional Vicars.
Hoffman, Dennis L. '90 (DAV) Houghton, IA St. John's; Houghton, IA St. James.
Hoffman, Dennis '70 (DUL) Crosslake, MN Immaculate Heart.
Hoffman, Edward L. '61 (PIT) Allegheny County, PA West Penn Allegheny Health System–West Penn Hospital; Allegheny County, PA Collins Nursing Center; Allegheny County, PA Heartland Health Care Center; Allegheny County, PA Shadyside Nursing and Rehabilitation Center.
Hoffman, Emmett G. '53 (GF) Retired.
Hoffman, Francis T. (BGP) Presbyteral Council.
Hoffman, Frank '92 (CHI)[W] Chicago, IL Prelature of the Holy Cross and Opus Dei.
Hoffman, Gerald J. '73 (PH) Doylestown, PA Our Lady of Mount Carmel.
Hoffman, Henry J. '03 (BGP) Fairfield, CT Holy Family.
Hoffman, James A. *o.f.m.* '67 (CHI)[N] Countryside, IL St. Gratian Friary, Franciscan Friars.
Hoffman, James A. '67 (SUP) Woodruff, WI St. John Vianney; Woodruff, WI St. Patrick; Woodruff, WI Our Lady Queen of the Universe; East Deanery.
Hoffman, John R. '75 (CHI) Chicago, IL St. Teresa.
Hoffman, Joseph M. '79 (BRK) Elmhurst, NY St. Bartholomew's.
Hoffman, Joseph (BRK) Fire Department.
Hoffman, Mark A. '90 (E) Meadville, PA St. Mary; [P] Meadville, PA Allegheny College.
Hoffman, Matthias H. '40 (CHI) Retired.
Hoffman, Michael *s.d.s.* '82 (MIL)[O] Milwaukee, WI.
Hoffman, Patrick '68 (AMA)[C] Panhandle, TX St. Joseph's Home for Retired Priests.
Hoffman, Raniero *o.s.b.cam.* '75 (MRY)[F] Big Sur, CA New Camaldoli Hermitage; [H] Big Sur, CA New Camaldoli Hermitage.
Hoffman, Richard L. '50 (EVN) Retired.
Hoffman, Robert B. '69 (RCK) St. Charles, IL St. John Neumann; Deans.
Hoffman, Robert M. *c.s.c.* '47 (FTW)[K] Notre Dame, IN Holy Cross Mission House; [I] Notre Dame, IN Holy Cross House.
Hoffman, Robert '56 (PEO) Retired.
Hoffman, Thomas A. *s.j.* '56 (OM)[K] Omaha, NE Jesuit Community at Creighton University.
Hoffman, Thomas W. *s.j.* '76 (NO) New Orleans, LA St. Thomas the Apostle; New Orleans, LA Delgado College; New Orleans, LA Southern University in New Orleans; New Orleans, LA University of New Orleans; New Orleans, LA Louisiana State University Medical Center.
Hoffman, Thomas '80 (CHI) Bartlett, IL St. Peter Damian.
Hoffman, William A. (GB) Appleton, WI St. Therese.
Hoffman, William G. '61 (ATL) Dalton, GA St. Joseph's.
Hoffman, William G. (ATL) Deans.
Hoffman, William '61 (ATL)[N] Dalton, GA.
Hoffmann, Andrew W. '74 (SC) Le Mars, IA St. Joseph's.
Hoffmann, Charles G. '63 (GB) Antigo, WI St. John; Marion, WI St. Mary; Marion, WI Holy Family–St. William; Tigerton, WI St. Anthony.
Hoffmann, Christopher '87 (ORL) Clermont, FL Blessed Sacrament; Air Force Reserve Chaplains.
Hoffmann, Edward M. (DEN) Denver, CO Church of the Risen Christ; College of Consultors; Deaneries.
Hoffmann, Edward (PIT) Pittsburgh, PA St. Charles Lwanga Parish.
Hoffmann, Emmett G. '53 (GF)[K] Ashland, MT St. Labre Indian School Educational Association.
Hoffmann, Francis T. '90 (BGP) Shelton, CT St. Joseph.
Hoffmann, Frank T. (BGP) Pastors' Vocation Advisory Board.
Hoffmann, Frank '71 (RNO) On Duty Outside the Diocese.
Hoffmann, Frank '71 (SD) Scripps Mercy Hospital; [F] San Diego, CA Scripps Mercy Hospital.
Hoffmann, Lawrence R. '71 (DM) Defenders of the Bond.
Hoffmann, Lawrence '71 (DM) Des Moines, IA St. Theresa of the Child Jesus.
Hoffmann, Philip '64 (GB) Absent on Leave.
Hoffmaster, Harry '70 (DET) Retired.
Hofmann, Raymond *c.r.* '56 (L)[K] Louisville, KY Villa Pacis, Resurrectionist Retirement Home.
Hofmann, Stephen *o.s.b.* '41 (P)[L] St. Benedict, OR Mt. Angel Abbey.
Hofmann, Thomas X. (CHR) Canonical Consultant; Office of Tribunal.
Hofschulte, Charles *c.j.* '71 (LA) Santa Maria, CA St. Louis de Montfort.
Hofstetter, Robert J. '54 (KNX) Chattanooga, TN St. Jude; [I] Knoxville, TN Diocesan Council of Catholic Women; Diocesan Consultors; Censor Librorum.
Hogan, Daniel M. '53 (STL) O'Fallon, MO St. Barnabas.
Hogan, David J. '55 (SC) Retired.
Hogan, Dennis J. '73 (PAT) Lincoln Park, NJ St. Joseph's; Deans.
Hogan, Francis T. '46 (BUF) Retired.
Hogan, Francis X. *c.m.f.* '49 (LA)[Q] Rancho Dominguez, CA Dominguez Seminary Inc..
Hogan, Gary *c.r.* '86 (CHI) Chicago, IL St. Hedwig.
Hogan, George G. (BO) North Andover, MA St. Michael.
Hogan, George '73 (VEN) Sarasota, FL St. Martha.
Hogan, J. Vincent (WCH) Retired.
Hogan, James J. '61 (HEL) Missoula, MT Christ the King; [H] Missoula, MT University of Montana.
Hogan, John A. '57 (GRY) Retired.
Hogan, John F. '88 (SY) Rome, NY St. John the Baptist.
Hogan, John J. *o.m.i.* '65 (BO) Lowell, MA Immaculate Conception; Lowell, MA Saints Memorial Medical Center.
Hogan, John P. *o.f.m.* '75 (PRO)[N] Providence, RI St. Francis Chapel & City Ministry Center; [P] Providence, RI St. Francis Friary.
Hogan, John *s.s.c.* '62 (ORG) Special Assignment; [H] Westminster, CA Korean Catholic Ministry; [I] Westminster, CA Columban Fathers.
Hogan, John *o.f.m.* (BO) Court Experts for Languages.
Hogan, Joseph F. '88 (MET) Retired.
Hogan, Joseph T. '88 (PEO) Spring Valley, IL St. Anthony's.
Hogan, LeRoy '57 (GB) Retired.
Hogan, Michael C. '51 (ROC) Fairport, NY St. John of Rochester Retired.
Hogan, Michael '65 (ALB) Schenectady, NY Sacred Heart–St. Columba; Schenectady, NY St. John the Baptist; Schenectady, NY St. Joseph.
Hogan, Peter E. *s.s.j.* '46 (BAL)[S] Baltimore, MD St. Joseph Society of the Sacred Heart House of Central Administration.
Hogan, Phil D. *o.f.m.* '62 (CHI)[D] Chicago, IL Hales Franciscan High School, Inc..
Hogan, Ralph R. '52 (PRO) Retired.
Hogan, Richard '86 (DET) Absent on Leave.
Hogan, Richard (STP) On Duty Outside the Archdiocese.
Hogan, Robert E. *s.m.* '83 (SAT) San Antonio, TX St. Mary Magdalen; [M] San Antonio, TX Casa San Juan Marianist Community; [U] San Antonio, TX Brothers of the Beloved Disciplel.
Hogan, Robert E. *s.m.* '83 (STL)[O] San Antonio, TX Casa San Juan.
Hogan, Robert G. '59 (DUB) Clear Lake, IA St. Patrick; Finance Council; Directors; Ex Officio.
Hogan, Sean M. *c.s.sp.* '67 (PIT)[B] Pittsburgh, PA Duquesne University of the Holy Spirit; [B] School of Health Sciences.
Hogan, Terence (MIA) Miami, FL St. Mary's Cathedral; Archdiocesan Fund–Raising & Assessments Committee; Executive Director; Celebration and Rite Committee.
Hogan, Thomas J. *s.j.* '65 (STL)[O] St. Louis, MO Hallahan House.
Hogan, Thomas *s.m.* '46 (LA)[F] Marianist Community.
Hogan, Timothy A. '66 (L) Louisville, KY St. Boniface.
Hogan, Timothy D. '82 (DET) Navy Chaplains; Military Chaplains.
Hogan, Timothy J. '82 (SC) Sioux City, IA St. Michael; Diocesan Consultors.
Hogan, Verne F. '57 (COV) Flemingsburg, KY St. Charles; May's Lick, KY St. Rose of Lima.
Hogan, William A. '66 (GF) Billings, MT St. Thomas the Apostle.
Hogan, William D. *s.s.j.* '51 (LKC) Welsh, LA St. Joseph.
Hogan, William E. '38 (L) Retired.
Hogan, William T. *s.j.* '54 (NY).
Hogan, William *c.ss.r.* '48 (STL)[O] Liguori, MO Liguori Mission House/Redemptorists.
Hogan, William (GF) Vicars Forane.
Hogarty, Paul '48 (PT) Retired.
Hoge, James *o.s.b.* '43 (SP) Lecanto, FL St. Scholastica; [O] St. Leo St. Leo Abbey.
Hogen, James Vanden '64 (GB) Little Chute, WI St. John Nepomucene.
Hogenkamp, Leon J. *s.j.* '70 (ROC)[B] Rochester, NY McQuaid Jesuit High School.
Hohenbrink, Michael G. '74 (TOL) Findlay, OH St. Michael the Archangel; Tiffin Deanery.
Hohenstein, Robert J. '68 (ALB) Schenectady, NY Our Lady of Mt. Carmel.
Hohenstein, Robert (ALB) Catholic Women's Service League; Priestly Life and Ministry Council.
Hohenwarter, Norman C. '96 (HBG) Mount Carmel, PA Divine Redeemer.
Hohl, Alan *o.c.s.o.* '63 (SLC)[A] Huntsville, UT Abbey of Our Lady of the Holy Trinity; [F] Huntsville, UT Abbey of Our Lady of the Holy Trinity of the Order of Cistercians.
Hohlmayer, Louis R. '53 (CIN) Retired.
Hohlmayer, Louis (CIN) St. Vincent de Paul Society.
Hohman, Andrew *o.f.m.cap.* '54 (CLV) Cleveland, OH Conversion of St. Paul; [O] Cleveland, OH St. Paul Friary.
Hohman, George R. *s.j.* '58 (WH)[A] Wheeling, WV Wheeling Jesuit University.
Hoi, Joseph '84 (JC) Belle, MO St. Alexander; Owensville, MO Immaculate Conception.
Hoisington, Thomas M. '95 (WCH) Conway Springs, KS St. Joseph.
Hokanson, Richard P. '74 (CHL) On Sabbatical.
Hoke, John R. '75 (HBG) York, PA St. Rose of Lima; On Duty Outside the Diocese; Navy Chaplains.
Holahan, Thomas J. *c.s.p.* '77 (DEN) Boulder, CO St. Thomas Aquinas University Parish; [Q] Boulder, CO University of Colorado (Boulder).
Holbrook, Harold M. '57 (BGP) On Duty Outside the Diocese.
Holbrook, Harold '57 (FgM).
Holbrook, John G. *s.j.* '52 (MIL)[O] Wauwatosa, WI Jesuit Community at St. Camillus.
Holbrook, William M. '70 (LFT) On Duty Outside the Diocese.
Holbrook, William M. '70 (CHI) Chicago, IL St. Ferdinand Retired.
Holbus, Brian '81 (MIL) Delavan, WI St. Andrew.
Holcomb, Joseph T. '80 (BRK) Brooklyn, NY St. Finbar's.
Hold, William '77 (SAC) Retired.
Holden, James T. '62 (MOB)[E] Montgomery, AL City of St. Jude, Inc., The; [K] Montgomery, AL The City of St. Jude, Inc..
Holden, James '62 (MOB) St. Jude, AL St. Jude.
Holden, Robert A. '62 (TOL) Wauseon, OH St. Caspar.
Holder, Thomas '95 (KC) Kansas City, MO Holy Cross; Deans.
Holdereid, Kurt *o.carm.* '59 (VEN)[G] Venice, FL Carmel in Venice.
Holdren, John C. '71 (RCK) Absent on Leave.
Holguin, Joseph '75 (LA) Sherman Oaks, CA St. Francis de Sales; Hospital Chaplains.
Holian, John P. '63 (NEW) Summit, NJ Overlook Hospital; Overlook Hospital.
Holick, Robert *m.h.m.* '69 (NY) Bronx Municipal Hospital Center, Abraham Jacobi Hospital, Nathan B. VanEtten Hospital.
Holicky, Gregory '72 (GRY)[E] Hammond, IN St. Margaret Mercy Healthcare Centers – North Campus.
Holihan, Daniel M. '57 (CHI) Other Assignments.
Holihan, John W. '49 (NY) Retired.
Holinga, Thomas P. '74 (SFD) Springfield, IL St. Joseph; Commission for the Care of Infirm and Retired Priests.
Holl, James E. '48 (STP) Retired.
Holl, Kermit *o.s.c.* '90 (STP)[M] Shoreview, MN Crosier Community of Shoreview; [M] Anoka, MN Crosier Community of Anoka.
Holland, Cajetan *c.s.c.* '79 (ORL)[E] Cocoa Beach, FL Congregation of Holy Cross, Eastern Province Retired.
Holland, Daniel F. '65 (ROC) Rochester, NY St. Pius Tenth.
Holland, Edward '97 (CLV) Parma, OH Holy Family.
Holland, Francis M. '52 (BUR) Elected Members; Propagation of the Faith; Diocesan Consultors; Holy Childhood Association; Burlington, VT St. Mark's.
Holland, George G. '55 (WOR) Retired.
Holland, George T. '48 (PBL) Retired.
Holland, James P. '98 (PIT) Allegheny County, PA West Penn Allegheny Health System–West Penn Hospital.
Holland, Jeremiah *ss.cc.* '67 (OAK) Alameda, CA St. Joseph Basilica.
Holland, Jerome *c.ss.r.* '56 (NY) New York, NY Most Holy Redeemer.
Holland, Kilian '56 (SD) Retired.
Holland, Paul D. *s.j.* '80 (NOR) Storrs, CT St. Thomas Aquinas; [K] Storrs, CT University of Connecticut; Chaplains.
Holland, Stan *t.o.r.* '96 (STU)[A] Steubenville, OH Franciscan University of Steubenville.
Holland, Stanley *t.o.r.* '96 (STU)[F] Steubenville, OH Holy Spirit Friary.
Hollas, Eric *o.s.b.* '75 (SCL)[I] Collegeville, MN St.

John's Abbey, of the Order of St. Benedict.
Holleman, John L. '81 (MOB) Andalusia, AL Christ the King.
Hollenbach, David *s.j.* '71 (Maryland)[V] Newton, MA The Jesuit Community at Boston College.
Hollenbach, Frank A. '49 (MAR) Retired.
Holler, Martin J. '66 (STU) Athens, OH Christ the King University Parish; [J] Athens, OH Christ the King University Parish – Ohio University; Campus Ministry.
Holleran, J. Warren '52 (SFR).
Holleran, Michael (NY)[A] Bronx, NY St. Lucy.
Holleran, Warren (SFR) Censores Librorum.
Holley, Martin D. '87 (PT) Pensacola, FL Little Flower.
Hollfelder, Eugene F. '68 (MAD) Middleton, WI St. Peter's.
Hollis, Keith *o.s.a.* '02 (PH) Rosemont, PA St. Thomas of Villanova Parish.
Hollis, Mark L. '72 (CLV) Medina, OH St. Francis Xavier.
Holloran, Michael J. '82 (CIN) Dayton, OH St. Adalbert; Dayton, OH Holy Cross; Dayton, OH Our Lady of the Rosary; Dayton, OH St. Stephen.
Holloway, Alvin J. *s.j.* '56 (NO)[C] New Orleans, LA Loyola University New Orleans.
Holloway, David L. '82 (KC) On Duty Outside the Diocese.
Holloway, Gerald '98 (BIR) Tuscaloosa, AL St. Francis of Assisi University Parish; [H] Tuscaloosa, AL Diocesan Campus Ministry Office; Campus Ministry; [H] Tuscaloosa, AL University of Alabama in Tuscaloosa.
Holloway, James P. '70 (WDC) Riverdale Park, MD St. Bernard.
Holloway, Thomas '99 (PEO) Champaign, IL St. John's Catholic Chapel; [O] Champaign, IL St. John's Catholic Student Chapel and Newman Foundation, University of Illinois.
Holly, Dennis *g.h.m.* '64 (OWN) Lafayette, TN Holy Family; Scottsville, KY Christ the King.
Holly, John *o.f.m.cap* '80 (CHI)[N] Chicago, IL St. Clare Friary.
Holly, Michael *o.m.i.* (OAK)[N] Oakland, CA Oblate Residence.
Holly, Walter *o.f.m.* '51 (TUC) Tucson, AZ Mission San Xavier del Bac.
Hollywood, Patrick J. *o.m.i.* '60 (BO) Lowell, MA Immaculate Conception.
Holm, Greg *s.x.* '87 (PAT) (FgM).
Holmer, James J. '76 (TOL) Vermilion, OH St. Mary.
Holmes, Albert '93 (SCL) Verndale, MN St. Hubert's; Bluffton, MN St. John the Baptist; Bluffton, MN The Church of the Assumption of Our Lady of Menahga; Verndale, MN St. Frederick's; Wadena, MN St. Ann's.
Holmes, Caedmon '96 (PRO)[P] Portsmouth, RI Abbey of St. Gregory the Great.
Holmes, Emmett P. *s.j.* '59 (CLV)[D] Cuyahoga Falls, OH Walsh Jesuit High School.
Holmes, Kay (CC).
Holmes, Kevin D. '84 (MAD)[D] Sauk City, WI St. Aloysius.
Holmes, Paul A. '81 (NEW)[B] School of Diplomacy and Intl. Rels..
Holmes, Paul (NEW) Archdiocesan Theological Commission.
Holmes, Raymond M. '65 (NEW) Hasbrouck Heights, NJ Corpus Christi.
Holmes, Richard J. '44 (NEW) Glen Rock, NJ St. Catharine; Hohokus, NJ St. Luke's Retired.
Holmes, Stephen '00 (ARL) Manassas, VA All Saints; Notaries.
Holmes, Thomas '91 (ALB) Middleburgh, NY St. Catherine; Schoharie, NY St. Joseph.
Holmgren, Raymond O. '53 (RCK) Retired.
Holohan, Patrick *c.s.sp.* '56 (BRK)[V] Long Island City, NY Holy Ghost Fathers of Ireland.
Holoman, Thomas L. '55 (LIN) Denton, NE U.S. Veterans' Hospital; Pro Life Retired.
Holoubek, K. William '97 (LIN) Harvard, NE St. Joseph's; Sutton, NE St. Mary's; Holy Childhood, Pontifical Association; Missionary Union of the Clergy; Propagation of the Faith.
Holoubek, Roger '69 (MIA) Dania Beach, FL St. Maurice.
Holpp, Lawrence V. '62 (PIT) Bobtown, PA St. Ignatius of Antioch.
Holquin, Arthur A. (ORG) Judges.
Holquin, Arthur '74 (ORG) San Juan Capistrano, CA Mission Basilica; Council of Priests; Consultors; Liturgical Commission; Building and Renovation Committee of the Liturgical Commission.
Holroyd, Patrick '74 (ARL) Vienna, VA St. Mark; Diocesan Judges.
Holscher, Frans *c.i.c.m.* '56 (FgM).
Holt, Paul S. (MO) Presbyteral Council.
Holt, Paul '72 (DM) Des Moines, IA United States Veterans Hospital.
Holt, Paul–Stephen '72 (WDC) On Duty Outside the Archdiocese.
Holt, William A. *o.p.* '76 (HRT) New Haven, CT St. Mary's Priory; [M] New Haven, CT St. Mary Priory.
Holtel, Melvin *o.f.m.* '60 (CIN)[M] Cincinnati, OH St. John the Baptist Friary.
Holterhoff, Edward G. '70 (PAT) On Duty Outside the Diocese.
Holterhoff, Edward J. '70 (MRY) Morro Bay, CA St. Timothy.
Holtey, Gary '84 (SD) San Diego, CA St. Charles Borromeo; San Diego, CA San Diego Airport; Presbyteral Council.
Holtgrewe, Donald E. *o.f.m.* '63 (CIN) Cincinnati, OH St. Clement; [M] Cincinnati, OH St. Clement Friary.
Holthaus, Paul '70 (BAL) Baltimore, MD St. Ursula.
Holtman, Elmer E. '64 (AUS) Austin, TX St. Thomas More.
Holtman, Elmer (AUS) Presbyteral Council.
Holtman, W. Jeffrey *s.f.o.* '85 (SFD) Maryville, IL Mother of Perpetual Help.
Holtmann, Christopher F. (STL) Chesterfield, MO Ascension.
Holtschneider, Dennis H. *c.m.* '89 (BUF)[C] Niagara University, NY Vincentian Community at Niagara University; [C] Niagara University, NY Niagara University.
Holtz, Albert T. *o.s.b.* '69 (NEW)[N] Newark, NJ Newark Abbey.
Holtz, Raymond C. '58 (COV) Retired.
Holtz, Robert '03 (TR) Jackson, NJ St. Aloysius Gonzaga.
Holtz, Vernon A. *o.s.b.* '62 (GBG)[H] Latrobe, PA Saint Vincent Archabbey.
Holtzinger, William (P) Forest Grove, OR St. Anthony; [P] Pacific University (Forest Grove).
Holtzman, Jerome '57 (SFS) Retired.
Holubowicz, Vincent '44 (MIL)[M] Wauwatosa, WI St. Camillus Health Center, Inc..
Holup, James '59 (JOL) Ashkum, IL Assumption of the Blessed Virgin Mary.
Holup, Joseph M. '60 (MET)[H] Somerset, NJ Maria Regina Residence Retired.
Holup, Joseph (MET) Diocesan Holy Name Society.
Holwell, Harry '89 (P) Cave Junction, OR St. Patrick.
Holzer, Claudio *c.s.* (CHI) Melrose Park, IL St. Charles Borromeo; Deans.
Holzhauser, J. Joseph '82 (SFS) Huron SD Holy Trinity.
Holzhauser, John J. (SFS) Army National Guard Chaplains.
Holzmann, Michael F. '88 (RVC) Medford, NY St. Sylvester.
Homa, Joseph '56 (PSC) Retired.
Homa, Richard M. '73 (CHI) Palos Hills, IL Sacred Heart; Members.
Homa, Thomas D. '57 (PH) Bensalem, PA Our Lady of Fatima.
Homan, Daniel J. *o.s.b.* '69 (DET)[B] Oxford, MI St. Benedict Monastery.
Homann, Frederick A. *s.j.* '62 (PH)[AA] Loyola Center and Manresa Hall.
Hombach, Leo J. *s.j.* '61 (LA)[M] Los Gatos CA Sacred Heart Jesuit Center.
Homes, Dennis '72 (BAK) Retired.
Homes, Ronald G. '93 (LIN) Prague, NE St. John's.
Homick, Cajetan P. *o.s.b.* '03 (GBG)[H] Latrobe Saint Vincent Archabbey.
Homick, Joseph '91 (STN)[A] Redwood Valley, CA Holy Transfiguration Monastery.
Hommel, George W. '66 (NY) Woodstock, NY St. John.
Hommes, Ray '72 (ORG)[G] Fullerton, CA St. Jude Medical Center.
Hommrich, Thomas A. '64 (L) Louisville, KY St. Elizabeth Ann Seton; Louisville, KY St. Mary; Associate Judges.
Homolak, William J. '59 (GBG)[G] Greensburg, PA Neumann House.
Homsey, Sam *c.pp.s.* '36 (SAN) Sweetwater, TX Holy Family; Sweetwater, TX Immaculate Heart of Mary.
Honan, Eugene D. '67 (SPR) Northampton, MA St. Mary of the Assumption.
Honer, Paul '79 (PT) Pensacola, FL St. Thomas More.
Honeygosky Stephen R. *o.s.b.* '75 (ALT)[H] University Park, PA Penn State University; [I] University Park, PA Penn State Catholic Community.
Honhart, Mark '80 (SFE) Belen, NM Our Lady of Belen; On Duty Outside the Diocese.
Honma, Kenji *ss.cc.* '89 (FR).
Honner, Paschal D. *o.s.b.* '56 (JOL)[L] Lisle, IL St. Procopius Abbey.
Honold, Thomas G. '87 (MIA) Sunny Isles Beach, FL St. Mary Magdalen.
Honor, Michael P. (MO) Army Chaplains.
Honore, Lionel P. *s.j.* '68 (WOR)[O] Worcester, MA Jesuits of Holy Cross College, Inc..
Hont, Leon *o.s.b.* '80 (GBG) Jeannette PA Sacred Heart.
Hood, Carl J. '86 (MEM) Bolivar, TN St. Mary; Selmer, TN St. Jude.
Hood, Mervin J. '54 (SC) Presbyteral Council; Diocesan Consultors Retired.
Hoog, Eric R. *c.ss.r.* (MO) Navy Chaplains.
Hook, Stephen '03 (BAL) Baltimore, MD Holy Cross; Baltimore, MD St. Mary, Star of the Sea; Baltimore, MD Our Lady of Good Counsel.
Hool, Fernando *o.s.b.* '98 (SFE)[I] Abiquiu, NM Monastery of Christ in the Desert.
Hoolahan, Michael J. *c.p.* '61 (CHI) Chicago, IL Immaculate Conception; [N] Chicago, IL Passionist Community–Immaculate Conception Monastery.
Hoolahan, Michael (CHI)[N] Chicago, IL Province Finance Office.
Hoolan, Andrew (CHI) Chicago, IL St. Ignatius.
Hooper, J. Leon *s.j.* '75 (WDC)[M] Washington, DC Woodstock Jesuit Community; [V] Washington, DC Woodstock Theological Center.
Hooper, Robert K. '70 (PAT) Clifton, NJ St. Paul; Passaic, NJ Passaic General Hospital.
Hoorman, Albert F.H. '67 (PHX) Phoenix, AZ Corpus Christi.
Hoormann, Harry H. *s.j.* '58 (STL)[O] St. Louis, MO Jesuit Community Corporation at St. Louis University – Jesuit Hall.
Hoover, Brett *c.s.p.* '97 (NY) New York, NY St. Paul the Apostle.
Hoover, Conrad '89 (CHL) Charlotte, NC St. Ann.
Hoover, Gary *o.s.b.* '83 (CLV)[D] Cleveland, OH Benedictine High School; [O] Cleveland, OH.
Hoover, James '60 (SAL) South Beloit, IL; Hanover, KS Sacred Heart; Hanover, KS St. John the Baptist; Washington, KS SS. Peter and Paul; Washington, KS St. Augustine's; College of Consultors; Council of Priests.
Hoover, John P. '76 (CHL) Special Assignment.
Hoover, Matthew N. '95 (COL) Gahanna, OH St. Matthew; Vocations Office.
Hopcus, Daniel R. '64 (IND)[L] St. Mary–of–the–Woods, IN Sisters of Providence General Administration.
Hopcus, Daniel R. (ORG) Judges.
Hopcus, Daniel '64 (ORG) On Duty Outside the Diocese.
Hope, Abbott J. '54 (CAM) Retired.
Hope, Donald E. '76 (SLC) East Carbon, UT Good Shepherd; Price, UT Notre Dame de Lourdes; [H] Price, UT College of Eastern Utah, Newman Club; Board of Directors.
Hopefl, Gregory J. '76 (SUP) Stone Lake, WI St. Ignatius; Stone Lake, WI St. Francis of Solanus; Stone Lake, WI St. Philip; Personnel Placement Board; Holy Childhood Association; Propagation of the Faith.
Hopka, John '79 (DAL) Dallas, TX St. Monica.
Hopkins, John P. '78 (WIL) Newark, DE St. Margaret of Scotland; College of Consultors; Priests' Council; Priests' Continuing Formation Committee.
Hopkins, Michael *c.ss.r.* '63 (PH) Philadelphia, PA St. Peter the Apostle.
Hopkins, Peter *l.c.* '91 (NY)[II] Thornwood, NY Legion of Christ, Incorporated.
Hopkins, Richard J. '44 (GF) Billings, MT St. Patrick's Co–Cathedral Retired.
Hopkins, Robert F. '48 (BAL) Retired.
Hopkins, William J. '90 (FWT) Graford, TX St. Francis of Assisi; Mineral Wells, TX Our Lady of Lourdes.
Hopkins, William (FWT) Deans; Presbyteral Council and Consultors.
Hopmeir, Ronald J. '91 (STL) De Soto, MO St. Rose of Lima.
Hopp, Raymond (BAK) Council of Priests and Diocesan Consultors; Priestly Life and Ministry; Lakeview, OR St. Patrick's.
Hoppe, Arthur '47 (SCL) Retired.
Hoppe, Leslie J. *o.f.m.* '71 (CHI)[B] Chicago, IL The Catholic Theological Union at Chicago; [N] Chicago, IL Holy Name Friary.
Hoppe, Ronald C. (ALX) Vicar General; Moderator of the Curia; College of Consultors; Finance Council; Priests Council; Permanent Deacons; [K] Alexandria, LA Catholic Charitable Endowment of Alexandria; Glenmora, LA St. Louis.
Hoppe, Sean *o.s.b.* '82 (IND) Leopold, IN St. Augustine; Tell City, IN St. Mark; [K] Leopold, IN.
Hoppe, William M. '78 (BRK) Woodhaven, NY St. Thomas Apostle.
Hoppe, William (BRK) Diocesan Consultors.
Hoppenjans, Terence E. '55 (LEX) Paintsville, KY St. Michael Catholic Church.
Hoppenjans, Terence (LEX) Diocesan Consultors; Big Sandy/Licking.
Hopping, John Paul '85 (ORG) Anaheim, CA St. Anthony Claret.
Hoppough, Gregory J. *c.s.s.* '74 (BO)[A] Weston, MA Blessed John XXIII National Seminary; [V] Waltham, MA Stigmatine Fathers & Brothers Provincial House; [Y] Waltham, MA Stigmatine Fathers and Brothers.
Hopwood, Robert *c.ss.r.* '52 (FgM).
Hora, Robert J. '83 (BUF) Buffalo, NY Holy Name of Jesus.
Horak, Donald E. '63 (STU) Athens, OH Christ the King University Parish; Athens, OH St. Paul's; [J] Athens, OH Christ the King University Parish – Ohio University Retired.
Horak, Mark F. *s.j.* '94 (CHL) Philadelphia, PA Old St. Joseph's.

Horan, Brendan R. *s.j.* '93 (BAL)[S] Campion Hall.
Horan, Denis F. '48 (MAN) Retired.
Horan, George '72 (LA) Los Angeles, CA Sacred Heart; Los Angeles, CA Office of Detention Ministry; Los Angeles, CA L.A. Men's Central Jail; Co Directors.
Horan, Gerald M. *o.s.m.* '82 (CHI)[N] Chicago Order of Friar Servants of Mary (Servites) United States of America Province, Inc.; [I] Buena Park, CA Order of Friar Servants of Mary (Servites) U.S.A. Province.
Horan, Gerald M. *o.s.m.* (ORG)[D] Anaheim, CA Servite High School, A California Corporation; Council of Priests.
Horan, Gerald *o.s.m.* (ORG) Consultors.
Horan, James P. *s.d.b.* '82 (NO)[D] Marrero, LA Archbishop Shaw High School.
Horan, John C. '51 (MAN) Hudson, NH St. John the Evangelist.
Horan, John '46 (SEA) Retired.
Horan, Michael '80 (SAT) San Antonio, TX St. Luke.
Horan, Terence J. (SFR) St. Anne's Home.
Horan, Terrence '68 (SFR)[K] San Francisco, CA Home for the Aged of the Little Sisters of the Poor.
Horan, Thomas A. '62 (ALN) Gordon, PA Our Lady of Good Counsel Retired.
Horan, Thomas *o.m.i.* '94 (SAT)[O] San Antonio, TX Oblate Renewal Center.
Horan, Timothy E. '79 (ROC) Rochester, NY St. Margaret Mary.
Horanzy, Joseph M. '59 (SCR) Wilkes–Barre, PA St. Stanislaus Kostka.
Horath, George B. '63 (MAD) Fennimore, WI St. Mary; Fennimore, WI St. Lawrence O'Toole.
Horath, James R. '73 (SUP) Merrill, WI St. Francis Xavier.
Horath, William G. '75 (SUP) Three Lakes, WI St. Kunegunda; Three Lakes, WI St. Theresa; Defender of the Bond.
Horejsi, Jeffrey P. '91 (NU) Madison, MN St. Michael; Members; Liturgical Guidelines Committee; Committee for Continuing Education of Clergy.
Horgan, D. Brian '98 (PMB) Port St. Lucie, FL St. Lucie.
Horgan, John E. '72 (WOR) Millbury, MA St. Brigid.
Horgan, Joseph E. '53 (PRO) Retired.
Horgan, Paul L. *s.j.* '68 (CI)[B] Pohnpei, FM PATS (Pohnpei Agriculture and Trade School).
Horgan, Sean *m.s.c.* '67 (AUS)[G] Blanco, TX Missionaries of the Sacred Heart, M.S.C..
Horgan, Timothy J. '55 (NEW) Retired.
Horgan–Kung, John V. '40 (BGP)[P] Stamford, CT The Catherine Dennis Keefe Queen of the Clergy Retired Priests' Residence Retired.
Horgas, Robert '91 (E) Brandy Camp, PA Holy Cross; Falls Creek, PA St. Bernard.
Horihan, Robert (WIN) Rochester, MN Resurrection.
Horkan, Edward R. '03 (ARL) Annandale, VA Holy Spirit; Notaries.
Horkan, Vincent J. '41 (DET) Dearborn, MI St. Clement Retired.
Horley, Ray J. '58 (CLV)[M] Cleveland, OH Sts. Mary and Joseph Home for the Aged.
Horley, Ray '58 (CLV) Retired.
Horn, Augustine S. *o.s.b.* '45 (OKL)[I] Shawnee St. Gregory's Abbey.
Horn, Bryan '01 (ATL) Marietta, GA Church of the Transfiguration.
Horn, Francis G. *o.s.a.* (WDC) Judges.
Horn, Francis J. *o.s.a.* '75 (WDC)[B] Washington, DC Augustinian College, Order of St. Augustine.
Horn, John P. *s.j.* '85 (OM)[K] Omaha, NE Jesuit Community at Creighton University.
Horn, Joseph K. *o.praem.* '81 (ORG)[I] Silverado, CA Norbertine Fathers of Orange Inc..
Horn, Joseph R. '97 (DET) Memphis, MI All Saints.
Horn, Stephen R. '73 (GAL) Houston, TX St. Luke the Evangelist.
Hornacek, Joseph F. '66 (MIL) Special Assignment; Vicars General; Archdiocesan Consultors; Vicar for Clergy.
Hornat, Stephen W. *s.s.e.* '76 (BUR) Misconduct Review Board; Burlington, VT St. Joseph's.
Horner, Timothy *o.s.b.* '53 (STL)[O] St. Louis, MO The Abbey of St. Mary and St. Louis.
Hornicak, John Joseph '03 (JOL) Downers Grove, IL St. Joseph.
Horning, Roy (LAN) Priest's Assignment Commission.
Hornstein, Eugene *o.s.b.* '46 (BIS)[A] Richardton, ND Assumption Abbey.
Hornung, Eugene H. '03 (SUP) Cumberland, WI St. Anthony Abbot; Cumberland, WI Sacred Heart of Jesus Church; Cumberland, WI St. Ann.
Horrigan, Alfred F. '40 (L) Retired.
Horrigan, Kevin D. '53 (STL).
Horrigan, Kevin P. '70 (BO) Wilmington, MA St. Dorothy.
Horrigan, Leo R. '59 (DEN) Denver, CO Notre Dame.
Horrigan, Philip (CHI) Divine Worship, Office for.
Horrigan, Sean P. '98 (GAL) Houston, TX St. John Vianney.
Horrigan, Sean (GAL) Priests Personnel Committee.
Hortiguela, Fernando *o.f.m.* '75 (SJN) Carolina, PR Santa Clara de Asis.
Horton, John C. '66 (PEO) Mahomet, IL Our Lady of the Lake.
Horton, W. Peter '79 (PIT)[B] Pittsburgh, PA La Roche College; [Q] Pittsburgh, PA Office for Campus Ministry; Campus Ministry, Office for.
Horvat, Francis '58 (KCK) Kansas City, KS St. John the Baptist.
Horvat, Matt J. '65 (KCK) Kansas City, KS St. Mary–St. Anthony.
Horvath, Gerlac A. *o.praem.* '46 (ORG)[I] Silverado, CA Norbertine Fathers of Orange Inc..
Horvath, Joseph K. *o.de.m.* '02 (CLV) Cleveland, OH Our Lady of Mount Carmel; [O] Cleveland, OH Mercedarians.
Horvath, Pius L. *o.s.b.* '53 (SFR)[N] Portola Valley, CA Woodside Priory.
Horvath, Stephen G. '40 (TR) Retired.
Horvath, Stephen '50 (Y) Retired.
Horzen, Bernard A. *o.s.b.* '53 (PEO) Dalzell, IL St. Thomas More.
Hosak, Peter J. '83 (PSC)[C] Bethlehem, PA Bethlehem Catholic High School; Bethlehem, PA SS. Peter and Paul; South Pennsylvania Protopresbyterate.
Hose, Samuel '91 (AUS) Round Rock, TX St. John Vianney; Deans.
Hosey, Keith P. '56 (LFT)[G] Hartford City, IN John XXIII Center.
Hosie, James J. *s.j.* '65 (BO)[E] Dorchester, MA Boston College High School & Jesuit Community.
Hosie, Stanley W. *s.m.* '46 (WDC)[M] Santa Monica, CA.
Hosinski, Thomas *c.s.c.* '73 (P)[B] University of Portland; [L] Portland, OR Holy Cross Fathers & Brothers, C.S.C. – University of Portland.
Hosko, George H. *c.s.b.* '68 (GAL)[Q] Houston, TX Residence of the Basilian Fathers of the University of St. Thomas.
Hosler, Gregory '01 (PSC) Passaic, NJ St. Michael Cathedral; Dunellen, NJ St. Nicholas.
Hospodar, Robert J. '78 (PSC) New York, NY St. Mary's; Syncellus; Chancellor; Eparchial College of Consultors; Ex Officio Members; Defender of the Bond; Promoter of Justice; Respect Life; Eparchial Historian; Retirement Plan Board.
Host, Dick '74 (GR) Grand Rapids, MI St. Mary's.
Hostetter, Larry '87 (OWN) Non–Parochial Assignments; [A] Owensboro, KY Brescia University; Consultors; Priests' Council.
Hostettler, Paul A. '50 (KNX) Copperhill, TN St. Catherine Laboure Retired.
Hosty, Thomas J. '35 (CHI) Retired.
Hotovy, Dennis W. '57 (LIN) Wymore, NE St. Mary's.
Hottinger, Paul '75 (JOL) Downers Grove, IL St. Joseph.
Hottinger, Theodore J. *s.j.* '63 (WIN) Mankato, MN SS. Peter and Paul's; Southern Minnesota Retrouvaille.
Hottle, Maximilian *o.f.m.* (TUC) Topawa, AZ San Solano Missions – Tohono O'odham Indian Reservation; Council of Priests; Vicar for Native Americans; Vicars Forane; All Vicars Forane.
Hottovy, Jamie '99 (LIN) Lincoln, NE St. John the Apostle; Building Commission.
Hotz, Ernest *c.p.* '45 (BRK)[V] Jamaica, NY Immaculate Conception Monastery.
Hotz, Robert V. *s.j.* '86 (OM)[C] Omaha, NE Creighton Preparatory School.
Hotze, John V. '93 (WCH) Newton, KS St. Mary; Presbyteral Council/Diocesan Consultors; Judicial Vicar; Judges; Presbyteral Council.
Hotze, Leo *s.v.d.* '43 (CHI)[B] Techny, IL Divine Word Residence.
Houck, Gregory *o.carm.* '92 (GAL)[Q] Houston, TX Carmelite Priory.
Houck, Peter '46 (ANC) Retired.
Houde, Daniel *o.ss.t.* '87 (NY) Staten Island, NY Our Lady of Mt. Carmel–St. Benedicta.
Houde, Paul C. '96 (BUR)[H] Morrisville, VT Johnson State College (Johnson); Morrisville, VT Holy Cross.
Houdek, Francis J. *s.j.* '65 (DET)[K] Temperance, MI.
Houdek, Francis J. *s.j.* '65 (OAK) Lafayette, CA St. Perpetua.
Hougan, Andrew C. '01 (RCK)[A] Elgin, IL St. Thomas More.
Hough, Roger W. '64 (SAL) Osborne, KS St. Aloysius.
Hough, Roger (SAL) Board of Trustees.
Houghton, Francis J. '51 (NEW) Retired.
Houghton, Francis (NEW) Part–time Staff.
Houghton, Timothy '91 (RVC) Absent on Leave.
Houlahan, Richard A. *o.m.i.* '58 (SAT)[K] San Antonio, TX Oblate Madonna Residence; [T] San Antonio, TX Oblate Lourdes Grotto Shrine of the Southwest, Tepeyac de San Antonio; [U] San Antonio, TX Oblate Missions.
Houle, Andre L. *o.m.i.* '52 (PRT) Howland, ME St. Leo.
Houle, Angelus M. *c.f.r.* '02 (NY)[EE] Bronx, NY Franciscan Friars of the Renewal.
Houle, Carroll B. *m.m.* '62 (NY)[EE] Maryknoll Maryknoll Fathers and Brothers.
Houle, Michael R. '79 (STA)[A] Jacksonville, FL Bishop Kenny High School; Special Assignment.
Houle, Roger A. '77 (PRO) North Scituate, RI St. Joseph.
Houle, Thomas *o.f.m.cap.* '78 (NY) New York, NY St. John the Baptist; Correctional Institution for Men.
Houle, Wilfred Andre '74 (BUR) Elected Members; Rutland, VT St. Peter.
Houlihan, John J. '64 (GF) Billings, MT St. Patrick's Co–Cathedral; Continuing Formation of Clergy.
Houlihan, Michael K. '79 (LIN) Hastings, NE St. Michael's; Advocates.
Houlihan, Ralph D. *s.j.* '65 (STL)[F] St. Louis, MO St. Louis University High School, George H. Backer Memorial; [O] St. Louis, MO St. Louis University High School Jesuit Community.
Houran, J. William '52 (SFD) Retired.
Hourigan, Michael '66 (MIA) Sunrise, FL St. Bernard.
Hourihan, John P. '49 (NEW) Retired.
Hourihan, Raymond B. '87 (CHL) Retired.
Hourihane, Francis '51 (RVC) Retired.
House, Christopher A. '02 (SFD) Collinsville, IL SS. Peter and Paul; Presbyteral Council.
House, Richard M. '92 (YAK) Military Chaplains; Navy Chaplains.
Householder, Paul C. '73 (PIT) McKees Rocks, PA St. John of God.
Houseknecht, Eric '95 (CHL) Shelby, NC St. Mary's.
Houser, Samuel E. '76 (HBG) Steelton, PA Prince of Peace; Appointed.
Houser, Samuel (HBG) Consultors, College.
Housey, Walter *c.m.* '56 (LA)[Q] Santa Barbara, CA St. Mary's Center; [W] Santa Barbara, CA St. Mary's Seminary Center.
Houston, James A. '68 (WOR) Northboro, MA St. Rose of Lima.
Houston, Michael *c.ss.r.* '98 (STV) Christiansted, VI Church of the Holy Cross; [B] St. Croix, VI Hispanic Ministry; [B] St. Croix, VI Legion of Mary; Hispanic Ministry.
Hovanec, Craig M. '03 (CLV) Bay Village, OH St. Raphael.
Hovley, Vincent E. *s.j.* '69 (COS)[F] Sedalia, CO Sacred Heart Jesuit Community; [H] Sedalia, CO Sacred Heart Jesuit Retreat House.
Howaniec, Henry *o.f.m.* '56 (GB).
Howard, Anthony '37 (L) Retired.
Howard, C. Donald *s.a.* '72 (ARL)[I] Herndon, VA Christ the Redeemer.
Howard, Clarence J. '61 (L) New Haven, KY St. Catherine.
Howard, Dennis '90 (LAN)[K] Flushing, MI Mt. Zion Pastoral Center.
Howard, Donald E. *c.s.p.* '58 (NY)[EE] Jamaica Estates Paulist Fathers Generalate.
Howard, Donald *c.s.p.* (BO) Malden, MA St. Peter.
Howard, Edward F. *s.j.* '66 (BO)[V] Boston The Society of Jesus of New England–Provincial Offices.
Howard, Evan *o.f.m.* '55 (PHX) Sacramento, CA St. Francis of Assisi.
Howard, James J. '52 (PH) Retired.
Howard, John W. *s.j.* '68 (BO)[V] Newton, MA The Jesuit Community at Boston College.
Howard, John *c.j.m.* '67 (SD) Solana Beach, CA St. James.
Howard, Joseph C. '89 (ARL) Stafford, VA St. William of York.
Howard, Joseph R. *f.s.s.p.* '02 (SCR)[M] Elmhurst, PA Priestly Fraternity of St. Peter (F.S.S.P.), North American District Headquarters; Scranton, PA St. Michael's.
Howard, Joseph '89 (SHP) On Duty Outside the Diocese.
Howard, Kenneth J. *s.s.* '87 (GAL) Houston, TX St. Francis Xavier.
Howard, Philip R. *c.s.sp.* '79 (GAL) Houston, TX St. Joseph.
Howard, Randy '01 (OWN) Leitchfield, KY St. Joseph's; Sunfish, KY St. John the Evangelist; Consultors; Priests' Council.
Howard, Robert '62 (LA) Montebello, CA Our Lady of the Miraculous Medal.
Howard, Theodore J. '65 (RVC) Shoreham, NY St. Mark.
Howard, Timothy J. *s.j.* '63 (MIL)[O] Tucson, AZ.
Howard, Vincent '47 (LAN) Gus Harrison Regional Facility.
Howarth, Joseph A. (MO) Vice Chancellors; Judicial Vicar; Presbyteral Council.
Howarth, Joseph E. '80 (PH) Philadelphia, PA St. Timothy; Approved Advocates.
Howe, Christopher *o.s.a.* (CHI) Chicago, IL St. Rita of Cascia.
Howe, J. Norbert '56 (TOL) Retired.
Howe, Robert J. '94 (SAG) Shepherd, MI St. Vincent De Paul.
Howe, Timothy A. *s.j.* '98 (CHI) Chicago, IL St. Procopius; [N] Chicago, IL Miguel Pro Jesuit Community.
Howell, Charles (LEX) Williamsburg, KY St. Boniface; London, KY St. William; Mountain West; Priests' Retirement Board; Williamsburg, KY Our Lady of Perpetual Help.

Howell, David W. '65 (BGP) Norwalk, CT St. Joseph.
Howell, David '78 (LAN) Brighton, MI; Regional Vicars.
Howell, F. Scott *s.j.* '77 (BAL)[S] SJ House.
Howell, Michael J. '69 (KAL)[G] Nazareth, MI Sisters of St. Joseph.
Howell, Michael '74 (CC) Presbyteral Council; Judges; Corpus Christi, TX Corpus Christi Cathedral.
Howell, Patrick J. *s.j.* '72 (SEA)[A] Seattle, WA Seattle University.
Howell, Stephen H. '74 (SFR) Belmont, CA Immaculate Heart of Mary; [E] Belmont, CA Notre Dame High School (Girls).
Hower, William J. '64 (MAD) Edgerton, WI St. Joseph.
Howley, Edward J. (BGP)[P] Stamford, CT The Catherine Dennis Keefe Queen of the Clergy Retired Priests' Residence.
Howley, Vincent dePaul '97 (NY) Carmel, NY St. James the Apostle; Monroe, NY Sacred Heart Church.
Howren, John T. (ATL) Covington, GA St. Augustine Church; Deans.
Hoy, Daniel J. '48 (PH) Strafford, PA Our Lady of the Assumption Retired.
Hoye, Daniel F. '72 (FR) Attleboro, MA St. John the Evangelist; Promoter Justitiae; Defenders of the Bond.
Hoyer, Michael '80 (MIA) Fort Lauderdale, FL Our Lady Queen of Martyrs; Presbyteral Council; Retired Priests' Committee.
Hoying, David A. *c.pp.s.* '83 (CIN) St. Henry, OH St. Aloysius; St. Henry, OH St. Francis.
Hoying, John J. *c.pp.s.* '62 (LFT) Winamac, IN St. Peter.
Hoying, Leo A. '56 (CIN) Retired.
Hoying, Mark *c.pp.s.* '85 (COL) Children's Hospital.
Hoying, Mark *c.pp.s.* '85 (CIN)[M] Columbus, OH St. James the Less Church.
Hoying, Vincent *c.pp.s.* '58 (TOL)[G] Lima, OH St. Rita's Medical Center.
Hoying, William *c.pp.s.* '61 (CIN)[M] Wapakoneta, OH.
Hoyle, Thomas *o.f.m.* '78 (NY) George Vierno Center.
Hoynes, Richard '88 (LA) Compton, CA St. Albert the Great.
Hoyos, Jose Eugenio '84 (ARL) Dale City, VA Holy Family.
Hrebic, Alban *o.s.b.* '52 (JOL)[L] Lisle, IL St. Procopius Abbey; (FgM).
Hreha, James D. '87 (WIL) Lewes, DE St. Jude The Apostle; Catholic Scouting Program.
Hren, Joseph I. *o.p.* '47 (CHI)[D] Oak Park, IL Fenwick High School; [N] River Forest, IL St. Thomas Aquinas Priory.
Hrezo, Paul (STU) Marietta, OH St. Mary's; Propagation of the Faith.
Hribsek, Aloysius J. '49 (BGP) Retired.
Hribsek, Aloysius '49 (BGP) Holmes Beach, FL St. Bernard.
Hricko, Michael A. '73 (BAL) Philadelphia, PA Old St. Joseph's.
Hrisko, Zachary *o.s.b.* '57 (JOL)[L] Lisle, IL St. Procopius Abbey.
Hritsko, William A. '97 (COL) Westerville, OH St. Paul the Apostle.
Hritz, Paul J. '53 (CLV) Cleveland, OH Community of St. Malachi; Cleveland, OH St. Malachi Retired.
Hritzko, John '89 (STN) San Diego, CA Our Lady of Perpetual Help; Munster, IN St. Josaphat; La Mesa, CA Our Lady of Perpetual Help.
Hronsky, Peter '71 (STF) Hartford, CT St. Michael.
Hrubiak, Dennis M. '70 (PRM) Parma, OH Holy Spirit; Fairview Park, OH St. Mary Magdalene.
Hrubiak, Dennis (PRM) Chancellor; Presbyteral Council; Eparchial Consultors; Cantors' Institute; Office of Vocations; Seminary Education Formation Board.
Hruby, Paul '82 (LA) Glendale, CA Church of the Incarnation; Ministry to Recently Ordained Priests.
Hruska, Eugene P. '58 (GF) Fort Shaw, MT St. Ann.
Hruska, Timothy W. '96 (MAR) Engadine, MI Our Lady of Lourdes.
Hrydziuszko, Michael '95 (DET) Macomb, MI St. Isidore.
Hrynkiw, Wasyl '91 (STF) Johnson City, NY Sacred Heart Ukrainian Catholic Church.
Hrynuck, Stephen '38 (PHU) Olyphant, PA SS. Cyril and Methodius.
Hsu, Peter '57 (BEL) Retired.
Hu, Paul *s.o.l.t.* '94 (CC)[I] Corpus Christi, TX; [G] Robstown, TX Society of Our Lady of the Most Holy Trinity.
Huan, Joseph Van Tran '73 (RIC) Military Chaplains.
Huang, James '95 (PIT) Los Angeles, CA St. Camillus De Lellis; [N] Pittsburgh, PA Society of The Divine Word.
Huar, Ralph '81 (STP) Long Lake, MN St. George.
Huard, Jeffrey H. (STP) Campus Ministry.
Huard, Jeffrey '94 (STP)[C] St. Paul, MN University of St. Thomas; [S] St. Paul, MN The Companions of Christ.
Huard, Leo *o.carm.* '65 (JOL)[L] Darien Carmelite Provincial Office.
Hubba, David C. '74 (NEW) Nutley, NJ St. Mary's.
Hubbard, J. Randall '90 (L) Louisville, KY St. Stephen, Martyr.
Hubbard, Lawrence E. '68 (STP) Special Assignment; [V] Minneapolis, MN Sagrado Corazon de Jesus.
Hubbert, Joseph G. *c.m.* '77 (BUF)[O] Niagara University, NY Vincentian Community at Niagara University; [C] Niagara University, NY Niagara University.
Hubble, Karl D. '39 (DET) Retired.
Hubbs, Timothy L. '84 (CAM) On Duty Outside the Diocese; Army Chaplains.
Huber, Clarence '69 (LUB) Retired.
Huber, Daniel R. '50 (PBL) Montrose, CO St. Mary.
Huber, David '86 (RCK) McHenry, IL St. Mary.
Huber, George L. '48 (MIL) Retired.
Huber, Henry P. '02 (DUB) Holy Cross, IA St. Joseph; Holy Cross, IA Holy Cross; Dubuque, IA Holy Ghost; Holy Cross, IA St. Francis of Assisi; Vocation Awareness.
Huber, Henry '82 (DUB) Holy Cross, IA SS. Peter and Paul.
Huber, J. William '59 (PBL) Pueblo, CO St. Pius X.
Huber, John *c.s.b.* '92 (OAK)[C] Oakland, CA Bishop O'Dowd High School.
Huber, Kevin R. '91 (GRY) Merrillville, IN St. Andrew; Priests' Personnel Board; Vocations.
Huber, Larry T. (STL) St. Charles, MO St. Joseph; Archdiocesan Council of Priests.
Huber, Leo R. '67 (STP)[C] St. Paul, MN University of St. Thomas Retired.
Huber, Mark D. '94 (LIN) Lincoln, NE Cathedral of the Risen Christ; Chancellor; Judges; Presbyteral Council; Building Commission; Catholic Relief Services; Liturgical Ministries; Permanent Deacon Continuing Education Committee; Priests' Continuing Education Committee Victim Assistance Coordinator.
Huber, Matthew P. (HEL) Associate Judges.
Huber, Matthew '87 (HEL) Missoula, MT Holy Family; Diocesan Consultors; Presbyteral Council; Vicariates; Personnel Board; Board of Directors.
Huber, Paul A. *s.j.* '45 (CIN) Cincinnati, OH St. Francis Xavier; [V] Cincinnati, OH Apostleship of Prayer.
Huber, Richard *m.s.c.* '59 (OG)[E] Watertown, NY Missionaries of the Sacred Heart.
Huber, Robert L. '56 (L) Louisville, KY St. Athanasius Retired.
Huber, Vincent J. '64 (STU) Toronto, OH St. Francis of Assisi; Toronto, OH St. Joseph's; Judges; Vicar for Retired Priests.
Hubert, Raymond P. '58 (PMB) Delray Beach, FL Emmanuel Retired.
Hubert, Raymond (PMB) Presbyteral Council.
Hubertus, Albert '50 (SAT)[K] San Antonio, TX Casa De Padres Retired.
Hubertus, Albert (SAT) Judges.
Hubertus, Gerald (SAT) Seguin, TX St. James; In Rural Area; Archdiocesan Presbyteral Council.
Huberty, Mark A. '96 (STP) Maple Lake, MN St. Timothy.
Huberty, Ronald V. '90 (NU) Fairfax, MN St. Andrew; Fairfax, MN Sacred Heart; Gibbon, MN St. Willibrord; Winthrop, MN St. Francis de Sales; Members.
Huck, Joseph '69 (MIA) Retired.
Hudak, Cyril '53 (MIA) Retired.
Hudak, Francis J. '55 (HBG) Mount Carmel, PA Our Lady of Mount Carmel.
Hudak, Mark J. *o.f.m.* '93 (CIN)[E] Cincinnati, OH Roger Bacon High School; [M] Cincinnati, OH Pleasant Street Friary.
Hudak, Ralph '77 (CLV) Cleveland, OH Immaculate Heart of Mary; Cleveland Diocesan Council, NCCW.
Hudak, Richard E. '68 (CLV) South Euclid, OH St. Margaret Mary.
Hudak, Thomas R. '73 (SCR) Unassigned or Leave of Absence; Army Reserve Chaplains.
Hudanish, Jeffrey A. '93 (BGP) Leave of Absence.
Hudepohl, Howard *o.f.m.* '54 (CIN)[L] Cincinnati, OH Mercy Franciscan Senior Health and Housing Services, Inc; [M] Cincinnati, OH St. Clement Friary.
Hudert, John P. *m.m.* '62 (NY)[EE] Maryknoll Maryknoll St. Teresa's Residence.
Hudgin, Christopher J. *o.s.f.s.* '81 (ALN)[B] Center Valley, PA DeSales University.
Hudgins, David William '01 (LAN) East Lansing, MI St. Thomas Aquinas.
Hudgins, James C. '98 (ARL) Manassas, VA All Saints.
Hudock, Paul '98 (WH) Charleston, WV Sacred Heart Co–Cathedral; Morgantown, WV St. John University Parish, Newman Hall.
Hudson, Donald (OAK) Canonical Consultant to the Bishop Retired.
Hudson, Frank X. '74 (CAM) On Leave of Absence.
Hudson, Gerald F. *s.j.* '81 (SFR)[E] San Francisco, CA St. Ignatius College Preparatory (Coed); [N] San Francisco, CA Jesuit Community at St. Ignatius College Preparatory.
Hudson, Richard '96 (AUS) Belton, TX Christ the King.
Hudzan, Volodymyr (STN) Chicago, IL St. Nicholas Ukrainian Catholic Cathedral.
Hudziak, Jerome M. '64 (MIL) Wauwatosa, WI St. Joseph Congregation; Deans; Archdiocesan Consultors.
Huebner, Donald C. '54 (CIN)[N] Dayton, OH Sisters of the Precious Blood, Salem Heights Convent Retired.
Huebner, Terrance J. '74 (MIL) Lake Geneva, WI St. Francis de Sales.
Huebsch, Joseph R. '50 (FAR) Retired.
Huegelmeyer, Charles T. *m.m.* '51 (NY)[EE] Maryknoll Maryknoll Fathers and Brothers; [EE] Maryknoll, NY Maryknoll Fathers and Brothers Charitable Trust.
Huehlefeld, Matthew '96 (VIC) Bloomington, TX St. Patrick; Procurator Advocate; Vocations Committee; Director of Seminarians.
Hueller, Francis *s.a.c.* '48 (MIL)[O] Milwaukee, WI St. Vincent Community.
Huelsing, Justin H. *o.m.i.* '54 (BEL)[F] Belleville, IL Missionary Oblates of Mary Immaculate – St. Henry's Oblate Residence.
Huerga, Alvaro *o.p.* '50 (PCE)[B] The Pontifical Catholic University of Puerto Rico.
Huerta, Enrique *s.v.d.* '86 (LA) Wilmington, CA Holy Family.
Huertas, Alvaro '81 (MIA) Miami, FL St. Thomas the Apostle.
Huertas–Colon, Ivan L. '93 (SJN)[C] Rio Piedras, PR Seminario Mayor Regional San Juan Bautista; San Juan Bautista Regional Seminary; Vocations Promoter.
Huertas–Colon, Ivan Luis (SJN) Vicar for Vocations.
Huesca, Omar A. '81 (MIA) Miami, FL St. Robert Bellarmine.
Huesing, Paul D. *c.s.p.* '82 (DEN) Boulder, CO St. Thomas Aquinas University Parish; [Q] Boulder, CO University of Colorado (Boulder).
Huesman, E. Gerard '41 (BAL) Baltimore, MD Ascension Retired.
Huete, Francis W. *s.j.* '82 (LAF)[A] Grand Coteau, LA St. Charles College.
Huffman, David L. '72 (STU) Little Hocking, OH St. Ambrose; [K] Little Hocking, OH Boy Scouts.
Huffstetter, Stephen *s.c.j.* '89 (RC) Lower Brule, SD St. Mary's; Lower Brule, SD Lower Brule Reservation; [B] Lower Brule, SD SCJ Community House; Fort Thompson, SD St. Joseph; Lower Brule, SD Immaculate Conception.
Hug, James E. *s.j.* '72 (WDC)[M] Washington, DC Leonard Neale House; [V] Washington, DC Center of Concern.
Huggins, Michael '89 (L) Louisville, KY St. Martin de Porres.
Huggins, Scott '01 (JOL) Addison, IL St. Philip The Apostle.
Huggins, William A. '67 (SPC) Leopold, MO St. John.
Hughes, Albert C. '57 (BO) Framingham, MA St. George; Senior Priests Retired.
Hughes, Brian C. (SC) Vocations.
Hughes, Brian '81 (SC) Sioux City, IA Sacred Heart; Building Commission.
Hughes, Charles J. '74 (BO) Beverly, MA St. Mary Star of the Sea.
Hughes, Charles *g.h.m.* '54 (CIN)[M] Cincinnati Headquarters of Glenmary Home Missioners.
Hughes, Charles *g.h.m.* '54 (SAV) Sylvania, GA Our Lady of the Assumption.
Hughes, Christopher '98 (SFS) Mellette, SD All Saints.
Hughes, Dennis E. '75 (SP) Port Richey, FL St. James the Apostle.
Hughes, Derek '86 (MRY) Paso Robles, CA St. Rose.
Hughes, Edward R. '58 (RCK) West Brooklyn, IL Our Lady of Perpetual Help; West Brooklyn, IL St. Mary.
Hughes, Eugene E. *s.m.* '57 (WDC)[M] Atlanta, GA Retired.
Hughes, F. Rodger '64 (WH) Chester, WV Sacred Heart.
Hughes, Francis J. '80 (BRK) Brooklyn, NY Our Lady of Miracles.
Hughes, Gerald T. *s.j.* '85 (MOB)[A] Mobile, AL Spring Hill College.
Hughes, James A. '80 (BRK) Brooklyn, NY St. Ann–St. George; Brooklyn, NY St. Michael Archangel and St. Edward.
Hughes, James F. '52 (PH) Retired.
Hughes, John C. '49 (LA) Camarillo, CA St. Mary Magdalen Retired.
Hughes, John J. '54 (ARL) Retired.
Hughes, John Jay '54 (STL) University City, MO Christ the King.
Hughes, John *m.s.* '53 (WOR) Fitchburg, MA St. Joseph's.
Hughes, John (BEA) Director of Seminarians; Beaumont, TX St. Jude Thaddeus.
Hughes, Joseph B. '67 (BAL) Retired.
Hughes, Joseph W. '70 (TR) Rumson, NJ Holy Cross.
Hughes, Kenneth J. *s.j.* '66 (BO)[V] Cambridge, MA Faber House; [V] Cambridge, MA Faber House.
Hughes, Lawrence J. '64 (MAN) Retired.
Hughes, Mark '82 (WDC) Washington, DC St. Gabriel.
Hughes, Michael J. *o.s.a.* '75 (ORL) Casselberry, FL St. Augustine.
Hughes, Patrick M. '56 (LA) Retired.
Hughes, Paul *o.m.i.* '73 (FgM).
Hughes, Pete '81 (OWN) Owensboro, KY Precious Blood.

Hughes, Peter *c.s.sp.* '61 (FAR) Fargo, ND St. Mary Cathedral.
Hughes, Peter '81 (OWN) Calhoun, KY St. Sebastian.
Hughes, Raymond E. '02 (TR) Howell, NJ St. Veronica.
Hughes, Richard A. '52 (WDC) Upper Marlboro, MD Saint Mary of the Assumption.
Hughes, Robert E. *s.m.* '59 (CIN)[M] Dayton, OH Marianist Community.
Hughes, Robert E. '90 (CAM) Vicar for Pastoral Life; Secretariate for Catholic Schools; Church Architectural Commission; Sewell, NJ Holy Family; Members.
Hughes, Robert W. '68 (MAD) Lake Mills, WI St. Mary Magdalene; Lake Mills, WI St. Francis Xavier.
Hughes, Robert '54 (PEO) Retired.
Hughes, Ronald J. '82 (SCR) Towanda, PA SS. Peter and Paul; Deans.
Hughes, Royce (GAL) Retired.
Hughes, Tony '93 (LAV) Henderson, NV St. Peter the Apostle.
Hughes, William C. '47 (STO) Diamond Springs, CA Retired.
Hughson, D. Thomas *s.j.* '71 (MIL)[O] Milwaukee, WI Arrupe House Jesuit Community.
Hughson, Robert S. '79 (BUF) Council of Priests; Niagara Falls, NY Prince of Peace.
Hugli, Richard *o.s.b.* '95 (SP)[O] St. Leo St. Leo Abbey.
Hugo, William *o.f.m.cap.* '80 (DET)[K] Detroit, MI Provincialate; [K] Detroit, MI St. Mary's Friary.
Huguley, Vernon '93 (BIR) Birmingham, AL Our Lady Queen of the Universe; Members.
Huhmann, John F. '50 (KC) Retired.
Huhn, Thomas *m.s.* '69 (MAN) Enfield, NH St. Helena.
Huitrado, Juan '80 (CHI) Graduate Studies.
Hulko, Joseph D. '64 (ALN) Retired.
Hull, Francis M. *s.s.j.* '57 (ARL) Alexandria, VA St. Joseph's.
Hull, Michael F. '93 (NY)[A] Yonkers, NY St. Joseph's Seminary; [A] Yonkers, NY St. John Neumann Residence and Hall; Censors Librorum.
Hullinger, Jon '99 (KCK) Holton, KS St. Dominic's; Holton, KS St. Francis Xavier; Nortonville, KS St. Joseph's; Regional Pastoral Leaders; Nortonville, KS St. Mary's Immaculate Conception.
Hullings, Clifford '61 (SPK) Retired.
Hulscher, Alfred J. *o.s.b.* '60 (SEA)[L] Lacey, WA St. Martin's Abbey.
Hulshof, David F. '82 (SPC) Springfield, MO Cathedral of St. Agnes; Aurora, MO Holy Trinity; Aurora, MO Sacred Heart; Special Assignment; Advocate; Vocations–Seminarians; Diocesan Lay Endowment Board; Diocesan Council Of Catholic Women (DCCW).
Hulshof, Jan *s.m.* '66 (FgM).
Hultberg, William J. *o.s.f.s.* '62 (WIL)[J] Wilmington Oblates of St. Francis De Sales.
Hultquist, Thomas H. '76 (WOR) Barre, MA St. Joseph's.
Humbert, Robert G. *s.j.* '53 (DET)[P] Hamtramck, MI St. Ladislaus.
Humbrecht, T. Allen '72 (KNX) Knoxville, TN Cathedral of the Sacred Heart of Jesus; Deans of the Diocese; Presbyteral Council; Diocesan Consultors; Ecumenism; Ministries of the Smoky Mtn. Deanery.
Hume, Kenneth '63 (P) Retired.
Humenay, Robert L. (E) Air National Guard Chaplains.
Huminski, Gregory J. '80 (BGP) Norwalk, CT St. Mary.
Humitz, Robert S. '60 (DET) Clarkston, MI St. Daniel; College of Consultors; Presbyteral Council.
Hummel, Donald K. '78 (NEW) Scotch Plains, NJ St. Bartholomew; Archdiocesan Girl Scouts.
Hummel, Donald (NEW) Boy Scouts of America/ Catholic Committee on Scouting.
Hummel, Kenneth J. '98 (PEO)[O] Macomb, IL St. Francis of Assisi Newman Center.
Hummell, John F. '65 (PH) Oxford, PA Sacred Heart; [EE] Oxford, PA Lincoln University.
Hummer, Lawrence L. '73 (COL) Chillicothe, OH St. Mary.
Humphrey, Arthur Frank '75 (NEW) Little Ferry, NJ St. Margaret of Cortona.
Humphrey, Stephen J. '67 (BEL) Germantown, IL St. Boniface.
Humphrys, Richard '57 (SB) Bloomington, CA St. Charles Borromeo.
Hund, Francis '82 (KCK) Shawnee, KS Good Shepherd.
Hund, Joseph *o.f.m.* '89 (FgM).
Hund, William *c.s.c.* '60 (P)[B] University of Portland; [L] Portland, OR Holy Cross Fathers & Brothers, C.S.C. – University of Portland.
Hundt, George F. '81 (PAT) Hawthorne, NJ St. Anthony's; Defenders of the Bond; Clergy Personnel Office.
Hundt, Robert P. '61 (LC) La Crosse, WI Blessed Sacrament; Judicial Vicar; Diocesan Judges.
Hundt, Robert P. (DEN) Judges.
Huneger, Richard J. '73 (P) Portland, OR St. Rose of Lima.
Huneger, Richard (P) Diaconate Office.
Hung, Joseph Pham '70 (SFR) San Mateo, CA St. Gregory.
Hung, Peter (CHI) Indochinese Catholic Center.
Hung, Pham Quoc *c.ss.r.* '94 (LA)[Q] Baldwin Park, CA Vietnamese Redemptorist Mission.
Hung, Trinh Peter '65 (CHI) Chicago, IL St. Thomas of Canterbury.
Hunke, Norman F. '73 (OM) Omaha, NE St. Cecilia's Cathedral; Consultors; Officers; Ex Officio.
Hunkeler, Edward J. '44 (OM) Retired.
Hunkler, Jerome '83 (FAR) Steele, ND Our Lady of the Lake; Steele, ND St. Francis de Sales; Steele, ND St. Paul.
Hunko, Gerard A. '91 (GAY) Lake Leelanau, MI St. Mary.
Hunstiger, Thomas P. '63 (STP)[V] St. Paul, MN The Highland Catholic Community.
Hunt, Brendan *o.m.i.* '42 (BO).
Hunt, Dennis M. (LIN) Diocesan Area CCD Directors.
Hunt, Dennis '81 (LIN) Lawrence, NE Sacred Heart; Diocesan Consultors.
Hunt, Douglas *c.r.* '94 (DEN) Fort Collins, CO Holy Family.
Hunt, George *s.j.* '67 (NY)[EE] Cardinal Spellman Hall, Jesuit Community.
Hunt, James M. '83 (GI) Ainsworth, NE St. Pius X; Procurator; Advocates.
Hunt, John M. '69 (OG) De Kalb Junction, NY St. Henry; De Kalb Junction, NY Sacred Heart.
Hunt, John W. '68 (PRO) Cumberland, RI St. Joseph.
Hunt, Kevin *o.c.s.o.* '79 (WOR)[O] Spencer, MA St. Joseph's Abbey.
Hunt, Lawrence J. *s.j.* '57 (CHL) Winston–Salem, NC St. Benedict the Moor; [J] Mooresville, NC Jesuit Community.
Hunt, Luke (PT) Gulf Breeze, FL St. Ann; Vicar General; Building & Renovation, Diocesan Commission for; Finance, Diocesan Commission for; Knights of Columbus; Permanent Diaconate Formation Board; Priests' Pension Plan, Board for; Real Estate, Diocesan Commission for.
Hunt, Mark J. '85 (PH) Fallsington, PA St. Joseph the Worker.
Hunt, Mark '01 (NSH) Franklin, TN St. Matthew; [B] Nashville, TN Father Ryan High School.
Hunt, Michael J. *c.s.p.* '67 (NEW)[S] Mahwah, NJ Paulist Press; New York, NY St. Paul the Apostle.
Hunt, Patrick J. '39 (PRO) Retired.
Hunt, Richard D. *s.j.* '71 (BUF)[B] Rochester, NY McQuaid Jesuit High School; [O] Buffalo, NY Canisius Jesuit Community.
Hunt, Robert *c.pp.s.* '54 (CIN)[M] Orlando, FL.
Hunter, Alan '77 (SFD) Taylorville, IL St. Mary.
Hunter, Alcuin M. *o.f.m.conv.* '67 (LSC) Carlsbad, NM St. Edward.
Hunter, Eric '72 (SP) Tampa, FL Incarnation.
Hunter, John J. '86 (NY) Poughkeepsie, NY St. Mary Retired.
Hunter, William R. '86 (LA) Retired.
Hunthausen, John F. '52 (HEL)[B] Helena, MT Carroll College Retired.
Hunthausen, John M. '70 (STL)[O] St. Louis, MO Jesuit Community Corporation at St. Louis University – Jesuit Hall; [A] St. Louis, MO Kenrick School of Theology.
Hunthausen, John (HEL) Clergy Senior Status and Security Trust Board.
Huntimer, Donald W. *c.s.v.* '59 (CHI)[N] Tucson, AZ.
Huntstiger, Thomas '65 (STP) Retired.
Huntzinger, Ralph J. '50 (COL) Retired.
Huon, Phan Phat *c.ss.r.* '53 (LA)[Q] Long Beach, CA.
Huot, Leopold J. '45 (PRT) Retired.
Huppenbauer, Walter E. '57 (CHI) Retired.
Hurbanczuk, Adam (STL) St. Louis, MO St. Stanislaus Kostka.
Hurd, R. Scott (WDC) Special Ministries; Pastoral Center Special Ministries; Hearts Aflame Program.
Hurd, Steven F. *s.j.* '80 (CHI)[D] Wilmette, IL Loyola Academy; [P] Milford, OH Milford Spiritual Center.
Hurd, Timothy C. '92 (SHP) Zwolle, LA St. Joseph; College of Consultors; Presbyteral Council.
Hurkes, Charles *o.m.i.* '58 (WDC)[M] Washington, DC Provincial Offices of the United States Province of the Missionary Oblates of Mary Immaculate; [M] Washington, DC Oblate Community.
Hurlbert, James F. '90 (CHI) Chicago, IL St. Alphonsus.
Hurley, Brendan *s.j.* '93 (BAL)[S] Baltimore, MD Blessed Alberto Hurtado, S.J. Jesuit Community.
Hurley, Brian '02 (DET) Dearborn, MI Divine Child.
Hurley, Cornelius P. *s.j.* '59 (NY)[EE] New York, NY Murray–Weigel Hall.
Hurley, Daniel A. *o.f.m.* '45 (BUF)[Q] West Clarksville, NY Mount Irenaeus, Franciscan Mountain Retreat & Holy Peace Friary; [R] St. Bonaventure, NY St. Bonaventure University; [C] West Clarksville, NY Holy Peace Friary.
Hurley, Daniel J. '59 (RVC) Massapequa, NY St. Rose of Lima.
Hurley, Edward '70 (DM) West Des Moines, IA St. Francis of Assisi; Vicar for Finance; Priests' Pension Fund Society.
Hurley, Francis J. *c.s.c.* '53 (FR)[A] North Easton, MA Stonehill College; [A] North Easton, MA Holy Cross Fathers Religious.
Hurley, George '55 (JOL) Retired.
Hurley, Gerard '76 (JKS) Columbus, MS Annunciation; [I] Columbus, MS Mississippi University for Women Student Center.
Hurley, James P. *m.s.* '48 (HRT)[M] Hartford, CT Missionaries of LaSalette.
Hurley, John E. *c.s.p.* '77 (WDC)[B] Washington, DC St. Paul's College.
Hurley, John J. '56 (CHI) Retired.
Hurley, John J. *o.s.f.s.* '68 (WIL) Arlington Heights, IL St. Edna; [J] Wilmington, DE DeSales House.
Hurley, John J. *o.s.f.s.* '68 (FgM).
Hurley, John J. '82 (WDC) Washington, DC St. Matthew Cathedral.
Hurley, John W. '74 (CHI) Cicero, IL Mary, Queen of Heaven.
Hurley, Joseph T. *c.ss.r.* '54 (CHI)[N] Glenview, IL The Redemptorists of Glenview, Illinois.
Hurley, Leonard F. '58 (WDC) Special Ministries; Hospital & Nursing Home Ministries; [L] Washington, DC Cardinal O'Boyle Residence for Priests; [V] Washington, DC Carroll Manor Nursing & Rehabilitation Center; Catholic Hospital Chaplains.
Hurley, Leonard J. (WDC) Cardinal O'Boyle Residence for Priests.
Hurley, Michael F. '43 (PHX) Retired.
Hurley, Patrick J. *s.j.* '57 (SPK)[J] Spokane, WA Regis Community.
Hurley, Patrick M. *o.s.b.* '76 (PAT)[I] Morristown, NJ St. Mary's Abbey Retreat Center; [M] Morristown, NJ St. Mary's Abbey.
Hurley, Paul K. '95 (BO) Military & VA Chaplains; Army Chaplains.
Hurley, Steven P. '03 (WIL) New Castle, DE Our Lady of Fatima.
Hurley, Thomas J. '93 (CHI) Chicago, IL St. Patrick.
Hurst, Maynard E. '79 (BR) Baton Rouge, LA St. Louis, King of France.
Hurst, Paul F. '77 (CIN) Springfield, OH St. Bernard.
Hurst, Thomas R. *s.s.* '73 (ALB) On Duty Outside the Diocese.
Hurst, Thomas R. *s.s.* '73 (WDC)[C] Washington, DC Catholic University of America, The.
Hurtado–Badillo, Domingo '83 (CHI) Other Assignments; [J] Hoffman Estates, IL St. Alexius Medical Center.
Hurtuk, Joseph C. *s.m.* '74 (WDC)[B] Washington, DC Marist College, The Scholasticate.
Husain, Nicolas '85 (LC)[D] Spiritual Services Dept..
Huse, Charles *o.a.r.* '61 (NEW)[N] West Orange, NJ Augustinian Recollects.
Huse, Ralph G. *s.j.* '75 (STL)[O] St. Louis, MO Bellarmine House of Studies.
Huse, Robert *o.a.r.* '58 (LA)[Q] Oxnard, CA St. Augustine Priory O.A.R..
Hushen, Mark A. *o.s.f.s.* '91 (WIL)[J] Wilmington Oblates of St. Francis De Sales.
Huske, Leonard G. '56 (CHI) Retired.
Hussey, Daniel C. '85 (GLP) Winslow, AZ St. Joseph's; Winslow, AZ Madre de Dios; Navy Reserve Chaplains.
Hussey, Dennis R. '45 (HRT) Retired.
Hussey, Edmund M. '58 (CIN) Retired.
Hussey, Gerald W. '78 (PRO) Little Compton, RI St. Catherine of Siena; Tiverton, RI St. Madeleine Sophie.
Hussey, Michael J. *o.m.i.* '60 (CHR) Ridgeland, SC St. Anthony's.
Hussey, Patrick *s.j.* '68 (TOL)[C] Toledo, OH St. John's Jesuit High School.
Hussey, Robert M. *s.j.* (WDC)[M] Washington, DC The Jesuit Community at Georgetown University.
Hussli, Edward J. '67 (MIL) Retired.
Hussmann, John R. (DUB) Legion of Mary Retired.
Husted, Richard *o.f.m.* '65 (BUF) Allegany, NY St. John the Baptist; Allegany, NY St. Bonaventure.
Hustedde, Edwin H. '56 (BEL) Valmeyer, IL Immaculate Conception; Valmeyer, IL Seven Dolors of the B.V.M..
Huston, Richard '95 (SD) San Diego, CA Good Shepherd.
Huszti, Michael J. '76 (PRM) Cleveland, OH Holy Ghost; Cleveland, OH St. Nicholas; Vicar Adjutant; Cantors' Institute.
Hut, Clemens '36 (EVN) Retired.
Hutcherson, Bartholomew *o.p.* '97 (OAK)[N] Oakland, CA Western Dominican Province.
Hutchins, James '67 (PH) Broomall, PA St. Pius X.
Hutchins, Michael *s.v.d.* '75 (DUB)[B] Epworth, IA Divine Word College.
Hutchinson, Ronald D. '94 (GR) Jenison, MI Holy Redeemer.
Hutchison, William J. *s.j.* '66 (STL) St. Louis, MO St. Matthew, Apostle.
Hutchison, William *s.j.* '66 (STL)[O] St. Louis, MO St. Matthew Jesuit Community.
Huth, James P. *o.praem.* '88 (SFE) St. Joseph Medical Center; [I] Albuquerque, NM Santa Maria de la Vid Priory.
Hutmacher, Robert '79 (CHI)[N] Chicago, IL St. Peter's Friary.

Hutsko, Basil J. '79 (PRM) Sterling Heights, MI St. Basil.
Hutsko, Basil (PRM) Presbyteral Council; Eparchial Pastoral Council; Eparchial Consultors; Associates; Office of Youth Ministry; Priest's Pension Board.
Hutsko, Joseph (VNN) Fontana, CA St. Nicholas; Eparchial Consultors – Presbyteral Council; Liturgy & Music Commission.
Hutsko, Michael '84 (PHU) Minersville, PA Nativity of B.V.M.; Minersville, PA St. Nicholas; College of Archeparchial Counsultors; Presbyteral Council; Archeparchial Corporation; Archeparchial Council for Economic Affairs; Protopresbyters (Deans); Board Members; Archeparchial Seminary Advisory and Admissions Board.
Hutter, Eugene '88 (PSC) Leave of Absence.
Hutter, John S. '92 (PH) Philadelphia, PA Our Lady of Calvary.
Hutton, Leon '80 (LA)[A] Camarillo, CA St. John's Seminary.
Huvane, James H. *m.m.* '70 (CLV)[O] Cleveland, OH Maryknoll Fathers.
Huyett, Gerald T. *s.j.* '73 (NY)[EE] New York, NY West Side Jesuit Community.
Huynh, Joseph Dinh C. '67 (PH) Philadelphia, PA St. Thomas Aquinas.
Huynh, Loi (SJ) Council of Priests.
Huynh, Mark Nguyen Thanh *c.m.c.* '77 (LIN) Lincoln, NE Immaculate Heart of Mary.
Huynh, Peter Loi '02 (SJ) Milpitas, CA St. John the Baptist.
Huynh, Viet Tan '93 (PT) Panama City, FL SS. Peter & Paul Mission.
Huynh, Viet '93 (PT) Panama City, FL St. Dominic.
Huy Quyen, Nguyen '73 (JOL) Glen Ellyn, IL Queenship of Mary; Glen Ellyn, IL St. Petronille.
Hvozdovic, Andrew S. '87 (SCR) Jersey Shore, PA St. Luke's; Pilgrimages.
Hwang, Bernard *o.s.b.* (P) Retired.
Hwang, In–Kyun (DEN) Aurora, CO St. Lawrence Korean Catholic Church.
Hy, Hilary Tran–Khac '57 (WDC) Silver Spring, MD Our Lady of Vietnam Retired.
Hyatt, Donald *c.s.b.* '68 (LSC) Truth or Consequences, NM Our Lady of Perpetual Help.
Hyatt, Martin A. *b.s.o.* '84 (NTN) Methuen, MA Seminary of St. Basil the Great; Methuen, MA Basilian Salvatorian Order.
Hyatt, Robert A. '63 (RVC) Amityville, NY South Oaks Psychiatric Hospital Retired.
Hybner, Joseph '63 (VIC) Ganado, TX Assumption of the B.V.M.; Vocations Committee.
Hyclak, Walter J. '69 (CLV)[T] Cleveland, OH St. Joseph Christian Life Center; St. Joseph Christian Life Center.
Hyde, Gregory J. *s.j.* '98 (DET)[K] Canisius College.
Hyde, Robert L. *o.praem.* '43 (GB)[I] De Pere, WI St. Norbert Abbey.
Hyde, Robert P. '88 (SY) Whitney Point, NY St. Patrick; Judges.
Hying, Donald '89 (MIL) Milwaukee, WI Our Lady of Good Hope.
Hykavy, Roman *o.s.b.m.* '94 (STN) Warren, MI St. Josaphat.
Hyl, Robert J. '63 (BGP) Stamford, CT Holy Spirit.
Hyland, Edward F. '67 (HRT) Retired.
Hyland, James M. '81 (CHI) Chicago, IL Our Lady of Good Counsel; Chicago, IL SS. Peter and Paul.
Hyland, John M. '68 (DAV) Burlington, IA SS. John & Paul; Vicar General and Moderator of the Curia; Diocesan Consultors; Deans; Diocesan Corporate Board; Pastoral Services.
Hyland, Sean '84 (MIA) Pompano Beach, FL St. Gabriel.
Hyland, Terrance W. *o.s.a.* '71 (CHL)[N] Maggie Valley, NC Living Waters Catholic Reflection Center.
Hyland, Thomas J. '63 (CLV) North Ridgeville, OH St. Peter Retired.
Hyman, David L. *o.f.m.* '60 (CHR) Anderson, SC St. Mary of the Angels.
Hyman, Robert A. '61 (TUC) Retired.
Hyndman, Ernest R. '96 (MOB) Mobile, AL Holy Family.
Hyndman, Ernest (MOB) Group IV.
Hynes, Aidan '81 (PMB) Hobe Sound, FL St. Christopher.
Hynes, Christopher J. '92 (NEW)[B] School of Diplomacy and Intl. Rels..
Hynes, Gerald *c.p.* '51 (MET)[H] Baltimore, MD St. Ursula Rectory.
Hynes, Gerald *c.p.* '51 (BAL) Baltimore, MD St. Ursula.
Hynes, James B. '94 (NY) Poughkeepsie, NY St. Martin de Porres.
Hynes, James F. *o.f.m.* '80 (HRT) Hartford, CT St. Patrick–St. Anthony.
Hynes, James P. '49 (PRO) Retired.
Hynes, James '73 (SAT) San Antonio, TX Our Lady of the Angels.
Hynes, John F. '55 (DAV) Retired.
Hynes, John M. '65 (WIL) Wilmington, DE St. Catherine of Siena.
Hynes, Joseph P. '55 (PRO) Retired.
Hynes, Richard P. '72 (CHI) Western Springs, IL St. John of the Cross; Deans.
Hynes, Thomas J. *c.m.* '59 (BIR) Alexander City, AL St. John the Apostle.
Hynes, William '49 (SR) Sebastopol, CA St. Sebastian.
Hynous, David M. *o.p.* '59 (CHI)[N] River Forest, IL St. Thomas Acuinas Priory; Judges.
Hypolite, Douglas *s.j.* (SP)[C] Tampa, FL Jesuit High School.

I

Iacona, Frank *c.m.f.* '02 (ATL) Perth Amboy, NJ Our Lady of Fatima.
Iaconis, Anthony '97 (RVC) Bellmore, NY St. Barnabas the Apostle.
Iacovacci, Nicholas J. '51 (PRO) Warwick, RI St. Peter Retired.
Iacovone, Angelo *c.p.* '46 (BRK)[V] Jamaica, NY Immaculate Conception Monastery.
Iaia, Paul J. '56 (BAL) Buckeystown, MD St. Joseph–on–Carrollton Manor.
Iaia, Paul P. '56 (BAL) Retired.
Iannone, Raphael *o.f.m.cap.* '64 (BRK)[V] Brooklyn, NY St. Michael's Friary.
Ianotti, Pascal '61 (ALB) Retired.
Iantosca, August J. '77 (BRK) Forest Hills, NY Our Lady of Mercy; Creedmoor Psychiatric Center.
Ianucci, Thomas '94 (RIC) Navy Chaplains.
Iaquinta, Patsy J. (WH) Catholic Charismatic Renewal.
Iaquinta, Patsy '70 (WH) Bluefield, WV Sacred Heart.
Iaquinto, Richard *o.s.b.* '68 (BUR)[E] Weston, VT Priory of Benedictine Monks.
Iaquinto, Robert '81 (NEW) Retired.
Iasiello, Louis V. *o.f.m.* '78 (NY)[EE] Washington, DC Deputy Chief of Chaplains; Navy Chaplains.
Iasiello, Louis (MO) Presbyteral Council.
Iaucci, Thomas '94 (RIC) Military Chaplains.
Ibach, Michael J. (YAK) Yakima, WA Holy Family; Judicial Vicar; Judges.
Ibach, William *s.j.* '59 (BO)[V] Cambridge, MA.
Ibanez, Armando P. *o.p.* '93 (LA) Los Angeles, CA St. Bernard.
Ibanez, Armando *o.p.* '93 (NO)[P] New Orleans Dominican Friars, Southern Dominican Province of St. Martin de Porres.
Ibanez, Armando *o.p.* '93 (LA)[R] Los Angeles, CA Monastery of the Angels (Contemplative).
Ibanez, Rodolfo '51 (BR) Retired.
Ibarra, Brando (PAT) Spanish Cursillos.
Ibarra, Cesar *m.s.p.* (LA) Los Angeles, CA Our Lady of Solitude.
Ibarra, J. Brando '99 (PAT) Morristown, NJ St. Margaret's.
Ibarra, Manuel '98 (LSC) Hobbs, NM St. Helena; Presbyteral Council; Clergy Personnel Board.
Ibarra, Martin *o.f.m.* (OAK).
Ibasco, Philip (NY)[S] Bronx, NY St. Philip Neri.
Ibe, Sanctus K. '00 (MAD) Hollandale, WI Immaculate Conception; Hollandale, WI St. Patrick; Hollandale, WI Holy Redeemer.
Ibeh, Eliseus *m.s.p.* '86 (NO) New Orleans, LA St. Matthias.
Ibekwe, James O. (HRT) Hartford, CT St. Augustine.
Iber, Francis '80 (TUC) Yuma, AZ St. Francis of Assisi.
Iber, Simeon T. (DET) Port Huron, MI St. Joseph; [S] Port Huron, MI John Courtney Murray Newman Center.
Idler, Peter M. '97 (CAM) Bridgeton, NJ Immaculate Conception; Members.
Idler, Peter (CAM) Assistant Vocation Directors for Recruitment.
Idranyi, Edmund M. '54 (VNN) San Luis Obispo, CA Saint Anne.
Idyu, Matthias *c.s.sp.* '92 (PIT)[B] Pittsburgh, PA Duquesne University of the Holy Spirit; [Q] Pittsburgh, PA Duquesne University.
Idzik, George '74 (NEW) Jersey City, NJ St. Ann's.
Iffert, Wilbert J. '52 (BEL) Retired.
Ifkovits, Edward M. *s.j.* '86 (WDC) Washington, DC St. Aloysius.
Igelsias, Etelvino *o.a.r.* '60 (LA) Oxnard, CA Mary Star of the Sea.
Iglesias, Clement '58 (BEA) Retired.
Iglesias, Fernando '56 (LA).
Iglesias, Jose Estevez *o.dem.* '58 (PCE) Ponce, PR La Merced.
Iglesias, Luis Fernando '53 (CC) Retired.
Ignacio, Alex C. '74 (FRS) Lindsay, CA Sacred Heart.
Ignacio, Roberto '74 (TR) Toms River, NJ St. Joseph.
Ignaszak, Michael A. '84 (MIL)[H] Milwaukee, WI Holy Wisdom Academy; Milwaukee, WI St. Helen.
Ignaszek, Gabriel *o.f.m.conv.* '49 (CHI)[K] Libertyville, IL Marytown, Our Lady of Fatima Friary.
Ignatovich, Doreen (SCR) Liturgical Commission.
Igo, James P. '54 (OG) Retired.
Igoe, Martin S. '62 (BGP) Greenwich, CT Sacred Heart; Catholic Women, Council of.
Igrobay, Manuel '89 (CHK) Saipan, MP San Antonio Parish; Presbyteral Council; College of Consultors; Hospital Chaplaincy (Saipan); El Shaddai Movement; Legion of Mary at San Antonio Parish.
Igwilo, Peter '90 (NEW) Hackensack, NJ Hackensack University Medical Center; Chaplains.
Igwinwanne, Fidelis '90 (PHX) Lake Havasu City, AZ Our Lady of the Lake.
Iheaka, Emmanuel '90 (BIR) Pittsfield, ME St. Agnes.
Iheanaho, Kenneth '90 (TLS) Tahlequah, OK St. Brigid; [I] Tahlequah, OK Northeastern State University Catholic Student Organization.
Ihenacho, David '87 (BRK) Brooklyn, NY St. Mary, Star of the Sea.
Iheonunekwu, Alexander N. '77 (NY) Bronx, NY St. Mary Star of the Sea.
Ihewulezi, Cajetan *o.p.* (STL) St. Louis, MO St. Cecilia.
Ihnatowicz, Janusz '62 (GAL)[Q] Houston, TX Residence of the Basilian Fathers of the University of St. Thomas.
Ihrie, Bernard R. '55 (WDC) Camp Springs, MD St. Philip the Apostle Retired.
Ijeoma, John Vianney '88 (LKC) Jennings, LA Our Lady of Perpetual Help.
Ijeoma, John Vianney '89 (LKC) Phelps Correctional Center.
Ijeoma, John (LKC) Priest's Senate.
Ijere, Ignatius (GRY)[E] Dyer, IN St. Margaret Mercy Healthcare Centers, South Campus.
Ikataere, John *m.s.c.* '72 (CI) Sacred Heart.
Ike, Roberto (JC) Jefferson City, MO St. Francis Xavier.
Ikeocha, Ikechukuu "I.K." (LA) Diamond Bar, CA St. Denis.
Ilano, Jovencio '96 (RIC) Retired.
Ilgen, Timothy W. '03 (SEA) Chehalis, WA St. Joseph; Centralia, WA St. Mary; Pe Ell, WA St. Joseph; Toledo, WA St. Francis Xavier; Winlock, WA Sacred Heart; Frances, WA Holy Family.
Ililau, John Paul '90 (CI) St. John Baptist; St. Thomas Apostle; Palau.
Illig, A. Mark '85 (BUF) Ecumenism; [R] Snyder, NY; Bowmansville, NY Sacred Heart.
Illikattil, Mathew K. '71 (KAL) Three Rivers, MI Immaculate Conception.
Illo, Joseph '91 (STO) Modesto, CA St. Joseph Church of Modesto (Pastor of); Personnel Board; Deans.
Illy, Lawrence (RIC) Virginia Beach, VA St. Luke.
Ilnicki, Teodosij *o.s.b.m.* '88 (STF) New York, NY St. George.
Ilnicki, Teodosius *o.s.b.m.* (STF) Judges.
Ilnicki, Theodosius *o.s.b.m.* (STF) Ecumenical Commission.
Ilokaba, Damien (SPR)[F] Springfield, MA CHE – The Mercy Hospital, Inc.; Springfield, MA St. Joseph.
Im, Andrew Young–Min (MET) Korean Apostolate.
Imamshah, Harold '90 (ALX)[G] Pineville, LA Maryhill Renewal Center.
Imbelli, Robert '65 (NY) Bronx, NY St. Theresa of the Infant Jesus.
Imbelli, Robert '66 (NY) On Duty Outside the Archdiocese.
Imberi, Anthony '62 (SFS) Garretson, SD St. Joseph the Workman.
Imbroll, Gregory E. *o.f.m.* '57 (NY)[EE] St. Charles Borromeo Friary.
Imfeld, Thomas J. '59 (LEX) Retired.
Imgrund, Norman P. '64 (ALT) Everett, PA St. John the Evangelist.
Imhoff, James *s.m.* '51 (SJ)[M] Cupertino, CA Villa Saint Joseph.
Iminga, Wilfredo *m.s.* '92 (SB) Waipahu, HI St. Joseph.
Immel, William A. '53 (DET) Retired.
Imming, David B. '65 (OKL) Retired.
Imming, Donald '60 (SFS) Vermillion, SD St. Agnes.
Imokhai, Charles '68 (NY) New Rochelle, NY Blessed Sacrament.
Imperial, Francisco '59 (NY) Bronx, NY Our Lady of Solace.
Inametti, Vincent *m.s.p.* '86 (HON) Fort Worth, TX Federal Medical Center, Carswell.
Incardona, Victor S. *m.i.c.* '02 (JOL) Plano, IL St. Mary.
Ince, Michael W. '64 (STP) Elysian, MN St. Andrew, Waterville, MN; Waterville, MN Holy Trinity.
Ince, Owen F. (NEW) East Boston, MA Our Lady of the Assumption; On Duty Outside the Archdiocese.
India, Stephen J. *c.m.* '49 (ALB)[L] Albany, NY Vincentian Fathers Residence.
Ines, Paul *s.d.b.* '96 (SCR) Hazleton, PA St. Gabriel's.
Infanger, Frank '02 (JOL) Bloomingdale, IL St. Isidore.
Infante, Richard A. '92 (PIT) Pittsburgh, PA Nativity.
Infuhr, Frank J. '49 (LA) Retired.
Ingalls, Fred D. '74 (BUF) Judges; Strykersville, NY St. Cecilia; Varysburg, NY St. Joseph.
Ingelmo, Manuel '99 (WDC) Takoma Park, MD Our Lady of Sorrows; [M] Takoma Park, MD Redemptoris Mater Archdiocesan Missionary Seminary.
Ingels, Gregory G. '74 (SFR) Absent on Leave.
Ingemie, Dominic '67 (ALB) Albany, NY St. James; Priestly Life and Ministry Council; Members.
Ingham, G. Nicholas *o.p.* '81 (PRO)[P] Providence St. Thomas Aquinas Priory at Providence College.
Ingham, Jeffrey A. '75 (R) Southern Pines, NC St. Anthony of Padua; Deans; Priests' Council.
Inghilterra, Vincent J. '72 (TR) Military Chaplains;

Army Chaplains.
Inglot, Mark '81 (LAN) East Lansing, MI St. John the Evangelist, Student Parish.
Ingold, Michael (GB) Green Bay, WI St. Joseph.
Ingram, Walter Mike '02 (SAV) Columbus, GA St. Anne.
Inhenacho, David (BRK)[E] Campus Ministers and Ministry Centers.
Inigo, Juan Javier *c.m.* (SJN)[I] San Juan, PR Servicios Pastorales Paules.
Injacka Pappu, Arun John '92 (BR) Baton Rouge, LA St. Aloysius.
Inman, Robert D. '03 (YAK) Yakima, WA Holy Family.
Innes, Ben R. *o.f.m.* '84 (SD)[H] Oceanside, CA Mission San Luis Rey; [K] Oceanside, CA Mission San Luis Rey Retreat.
Innocenti, Mark '99 (SCL) Little Falls, MN Holy Family; Little Falls, MN Our Lady of Lourdes; Deans; Presbyteral Council; Advocates; Personnel Committee.
Innocenzi, James G. '76 (TR) Trenton, NJ St. Michael; Assistant Chancellors; Associate Judicial Vicar.
Inserra, John J. '03 (BGP) Newtown, CT St. Rose of Lima.
Intranuovo, Ralph *s.c.j.* '83 (GAL) Houston, TX Christ the Redeemer; AUXILIARY CHAPLAINS CONTRACT CHAPLAINS.
Introini, Elso C. (PAT) Retired.
Introvigne, Raymond D. '64 (NOR) Coventry, CT St. Mary; Co–Directors.
Inverso, Leon '85 (TR) Trenton, NJ Incarnation.
Inwang, Ausustine '90 (BAL) Baltimore, MD St. Veronica.
Inweregbu, Jude '87 (DET)[H] Livonia, MI St. Mary Hospital.
Inyanwach, Edward S. '94 (SFR) San Francisco, CA Holy Name of Jesus.
Inzina, J. Robert (SHP) Priests' Retirement Board.
Inzina, Joseph Robert '60 (SHP) Bastrop, LA St. Joseph.
Iodice, Ciro *o.f.m.* '72 (NY)[EE] Cottonwood, AZ.
Iorio, Peter '93 (KNX) Knoxville, TN Cathedral of the Sacred Heart of Jesus; Priestly Life and Ministry; Vocations.
Iott, Martin J. *o.p.* '70 (R)[E] Raleigh, NC Dominican Priory.
Iovino, Paul '61 (PAT) Totowa, NJ St. James of the Marches; Auditors.
Ipasu, Gabriel '03 (ORL) Ocala, FL Blessed Trinity.
Ipolito, Pascal D. '70 (BUF) West Seneca, NY St. Catherine of Siena.
Ippolito, Robert F. *m.s.* '73 (HRT)[M] Honolulu, HI; Air Force Chaplains.
Ippolito, Robert (HON) Military Chaplains.
Irace, Dominic P. '75 (ARL) Annandale, VA St. Ambrose.
Ireland, David R. '83 (CLV) Eastlake, OH St. Justin Martyr.
Ireland, Donald '63 (MIA) Retired.
Irish, Robert '92 (LAN) On Duty Outside the Diocese.
Irizarry, Alan M. (ARE) Army Chaplains.
Irizarry, Elvin A. '97 (ARE) Vega–Alta, PR Immaculate Conception of Blessed Virgin Mary; Prison Services.
Irizarry, Rafael (ARE) Retired.
Irizzary, Jose Fernando *o.f.m.cap.* '01 (SJN) San Juan, PR San Francisco de Asis.
Iroh, Anthony '94 (BRK) Brooklyn, NY St. Catherine of Genoa.
Ironomo, Donatus (SPR)[F] Springfield, MA CHE – The Mercy Hospital, Inc..
Ironuma, Donatus (SPR) Springfield, MA St. Joseph.
Iroz, Anthony *o.a.r.* '36 (LA) Los Angeles, CA Cristo Rey.
Irrgang, Kenneth E. '68 (NU) Retired.
Irudayanathan, Arokiasamy '83 (NEW)[G] Newark, NJ St. James Hospital; Newark, NJ St. James Hospital; St. James Hospital.
Irvin, Charles '67 (LAN) Promoter of Justice Retired.
Irving, Alfred E. '71 (PRT) Presque Isle, ME St. Joseph; Presque Isle, ME Nativity of B.V.M..
Irving, Peter '83 (LA) Wilmington, CA SS. Peter and Paul's.
Irwin, James W. *c.s.c.* '65 (FTW)[I] Calle Esmeralda.
Irwin, Joseph F. '62 (NY) Mamaroneck, NY Holy Trinity.
Irwin, Kevin W. '71 (NY) On Duty Outside the Archdiocese.
Irwin, Kevin W. '89 (NY)[C] Catholic University of America, The.
Irwin, Michael D. (MOB) Priests' Eucharistic League.
Irwin, Michael Dennis '01 (MOB) Mobile, AL St. Pius X.
Irwin, Michael T. *f.s.s.p.* '64 (SCR)[M] Elmhurst Priestly Fraternity of St. Peter (F.S.S.P.), North American District Headquarters.
Irwin, Patrick F. '59 (MAN) Retired.
Irwin, Patrick '69 (SP) Valrico, FL St. Stephen.
Irwin, Robert C. '95 (BAK) Baker, OR Cathedral of St. Francis De Sales.
Irwin, Robert '78 (SD) El Cajon, CA St. Louise de Marillac; On Duty Outside the Diocese; Diocesan Judges.
Isaac, Dominic (PH) Pakistani Outreach.
Isacsson, Alfred *o.carm.* '58 (NY) Middletown, NY Our Lady of Mt. Carmel.
Ischay, Matthew A. '75 (CLV) Cleveland, OH Blessed Sacrament.
Ischler, Paul *o.m.i.* '39 (STP)[M] St. Paul, MN Oblate Residence.
Isek, Frederick *m.s.p.* '97 (BR) Napoleonville, LA St. Benedict the Moor.
Isenbarger, Donald '55 (FTW) Retired.
Isern, Fernando '93 (MIA) Miami, FL Our Lady of Lourdes.
Iseszczuk, Cyril *o.s.b.m.* '89 (RVC)[M] Glen Cove, NY St. Josaphat's Monastery, Novitiate and Retreat House.
Ishmael, Keith E. '03 (ALX) Marksville, LA St. Joseph's.
Isho, Emanuel (EST) Eparchial College of Consultors.
Isla, Elias (NY) New York, NY St. Jude.
Isopo, Dominic '80 (ALB) Schenectady, NY St. Luke; Priestly Life and Ministry Council.
Issac, Dominic *j.c.d.* '87 (PH) Philadelphia, PA St. William.
Issac, Jose '75 (RNO) Winnemucca, NV St. Paul.
Issinq, Daniel *c.s.c.* '83 (OAK)[N] Berkeley, CA Holy Cross Fathers–Holy Cross Center.
Iten, Werner *o.f.m.conv.* '74 (FgM).
Itodo, Pius '90 (LA) Los Angeles, CA St. Gerard Majella.
Ittiyappara, Mathew '67 (SR) Yountville, CA St. Joan of Arc.
Ittykunju, Michael '74 (BRK) Floral Park, NY Our Lady of the Snows; [U] Knanaya Indian Apostolate.
Iturbe, Rene *s.m.* '74 (SFR) San Francisco, CA Notre Dame des Victoires.
Itzaina, John T. *s.d.b.* '63 (MRY) Watsonville, CA; Watsonville, CA Our Lady Help of Christians.
Itzaina, John *s.d.b.* '74 (MRY)[F] Watsonville, CA Saint Francis Salesian Community.
Itzaina, John *s.d.b.* '74 (LA)[CC] Bellflower, CA St. John Bosco High School Alumni.
Ivan, Nicholas '56 (PRM) Livonia, MI Sacred Heart.
Ivans, Joseph *o.c.d.* '53 (GRY)[I] Munster, IN Discalced Carmelite Fathers Monastery.
Ivers, Leslie J. '79 (NY) Bronx, NY St. Frances de Chantal; Prison Apostolate.
Ivers, Leslie (NY) Canon 1742 Panel of Pastors; Archdiocesan Consultors.
Ivers, Victor J. '45 (CHI) Libertyville, IL St. Joseph Retired.
Ivey, David J. '86 (LA) Brenham, TX St. Mary of the Immaculate Conception; Vandenberg Air Force Base.
Ivory, Thomas P. (NEW) Censors of Books.
Ivory, Thomas '64 (NEW) Upper Saddle River, NJ Church of the Presentation.
Iwan, Janusz '76 (DET) Lapeer, MI Immaculate Conception of the Blessed Virgin Mary.
Iwaniec, Wieslaw '86 (SAT) Stockdale, TX St. Mary.
Iwanowski, Thomas B. '75 (NEW) Jersey City, NJ Our Lady of Czestochowa; Worship Office.
Iwasiw, Nestor '93 (PHU) Washington, DC Ukrainian Catholic National Shrine of the Holy Family; Archeparchial Seminary Advisory and Admissions Board.
Iweh, Emmanuel '84 (SEA) Bellevue, WA St. Madeleine Sophie.
Iwu, Ifeanyi Ethelbert '90 (SAV) Augusta, GA St. Mary on the Hill.
Iwuc, Anthony D. '53 (PRO) Central Falls, RI St. Joseph; Council Members; College of Consultors.
Iwuchukwu, Pius A. '77 (LR) Crossett, AR Holy Cross; Crossett, AR Holy Spirit Church.
Iwuchukwu, Pius (LR) Judges.
Iwuji, Matthew C. '74 (GRY) On Duty Outside the Diocese; Judges.
Iwuji, Matthew C. '74 (AUS) Austin, TX Seton/ Brackenridge Hospital.
Iwuji, Matthew (AUS) Judicial Vicar.
Iwuji, Okeychuwu '97 (DET) Detroit, MI Cathedral, Church of the Most Blessed Sacrament.
Iwuoha, Anastasius (JUN) Juneau, AK Cathedral of the Nativity of The Blessed Virgin Mary; Port Chaplains.
Izac, Andre C. '64 (R) Buxton, NC Our Lady of the Seas; On Duty Outside the Archdiocese.
Izczuk, Cyril *o.s.b.m.* '89 (STF)[B] Glen Cove, NY Basilian Fathers Novitiate of the Order of St. Basil the Great.
Izer, Wesley (VNN) Anchorage, AK Saint Nicholas of Myra; Eparchial Consultors – Presbyteral Council; Building Commission; Eparchial Finance Commission.
Izquierdo, William *l.c.* '58 (WDC)[M] Potomac, MD Legionaries of Christ.
Izral, John '56 (BLX) Retired.
Izuchi, Baaju *c.s.sp.* '73 (PBL) Florence, CO St. Benedict; [D] Canon City, CO Centura Health–St. Thomas More Hospital.
Izyk, Andrew (CHI) Bishop Abramowicz House.
Izzo, Archimandrite Januarius *o.f.m., m.a., j.c.d.* (VNN) Denver, CO Holy Protection of the Mother of God.
Izzo, Brian A. '98 (PH) Norristown, PA Holy Saviour.
Izzo, D. Dominic *o.p.* '94 (FgM).
Izzo, David Dominic *o.p.* '94 (NY)[EE] New York, NY St. Vincent Ferrer Priory; [II] New York, NY St. Thomas Aquinas Foundation.
Izzo, John *s.j.* '80 (California)[V] Newton, MA The Jesuit Community at Boston College.

J

Jablonski, Edward J. '96 (PH) Downingtown, PA St. Joseph; [Y] Downingtown, PA Catholic Health Care Services–Villa Saint Martha; [X] Downingtown, PA St. Martha Manor.
Jablonski, Joseph *m.s.c.* '76 (RCK)[G] Aurora, IL Missionaries of the Sacred Heart Community.
Jablonski, William W. '63 (RVC) East Rockaway, NY St. Raymond's; Five Towns Deanery.
Jabo, Scott W. '90 (E)[C] Erie, PA Cathedral Preparatory School.
Jabusch, Willard F. '56 (CHI)[X] Wilmette, IL Musica Pacis Retired.
Jach, Edward M. *s.m.* '64 (CIN) Cincinnati, OH St. Francis de Sales; [M] Cincinnati, OH De Sales Crossings Marianist Community; Priest Councilors.
Jacinto, Martin Borbon '01 (NEW) Jersey City, NJ Our Lady of Mercy.
Jack, Cuthbert A. *o.s.b.* '90 (GBG)[H] Latrobe, PA Saint Vincent Archabbey; Homer City, PA Holy Protection of Mary, The Mother of God.
Jack, Duane C. '67 (PEO) Colona, IL St. Patrick's.
Jack, J. Robert '92 (CIN)[B] Cincinnati, OH Mt. St. Mary's Seminary of the West.
Jackels, Michael O. '81 (LIN) On Duty Outside the Diocese.
Jackiewicz, Frederick W. '71 (TR) Leave of Absence.
Jacklin, Richard '84 (JOL) Kankakee, IL Shapiro Development Center.
Jackner, Joseph *s.m.* (STL)[O] St. Louis, MO Marianist Community.
Jackovic, George V. '46 (PIT) Retired.
Jackson, Charles A. '60 (COL).
Jackson, David *s.c.j.* '66 (BWN)[A] Lyford, TX Prince of Peace.
Jackson, James A. *m.m.* '48 (NY).
Jackson, James J. '72 (SUP)[EE] Park Falls, WI Immaculate Conception; Park Falls, WI St. Francis of Assisi; Park Falls, WI St. Anthony; South Central Deanery.
Jackson, James M. '75 (WIL) Delaware State Correctional Center.
Jackson, James W. '60 (STP)[J] St. Paul, MN Our Lady of Good Counsel Home.
Jackson, James W. *f.s.s.p.* '85 (LIN)[A] Denton, NE Our Lady of Guadalupe Seminary.
Jackson, James *f.s.s.p.* '85 (SCR)[M] Elmhurst Priestly Fraternity of St. Peter (F.S.S.P.), North American District Headquarters.
Jackson, Joseph M. '74 (CHI) Chicago, IL St. Ignatius.
Jackson, Lawrence J. '60 (DET)[A] Sterling Heights, MI St. Michael.
Jackson, Pio *o.f.m.* '91 (NSH) Nashville, TN St. Vincent de Paul; [H] Nashville, TN Franciscan Friars.
Jackson, Raymond A. *c.s.b.* '58 (VIC) Wharton, TX Our Lady of Mt. Carmel.
Jackson, Robert H. '84 (CLV) Akron, OH St. Sebastian; [D] Akron, OH St. Vincent–St. Mary High School; Air National Guard Chaplains.
Jackson, Robert '54 (RCK) Retired.
Jackson, William J. *c.s.sp.* '58 (PIT)[P] Bethel Park, PA Holy Spirit Animation Center.
Jacob, Abraham Mutholath (SYM) Vicar General (Syncellus); Chicago, IL Our Lady of Victory.
Jacob, Abraham '80 (CHI) Los Angeles, CA St. Jerome; [J] Chicago, IL Our Lady of the Resurrection Medical Center.
Jacob, Anthony J. *o.s.b.* '65 (JOL)[C] Lisle, IL Benet Academy; [L] Lisle, IL St. Procopius Abbey.
Jacob, Jerome '92 (CHI) Arlington Heights, IL St. Edna.
Jacob, Joseph E. (LFT) Rochester, IN St. Ann; Rochester, IN St. Joseph; Members.
Jacob, Leonaldo M. '88 (RCK) Crystal Lake, IL St. Elizabeth Ann Seton.
Jacob, William *c.ss.r.* '46 (NY) New York, NY St. Cecilia.
Jacobberger, Joseph '65 (P) Portland, OR Cathedral of the Immaculate Conception; College of Consultors; Area Vicars; Judges.
Jacobi, Joseph A. '91 (OKL) Oklahoma City, OK St. Eugene's; Consultors Archdiocesan; Council of Priests Archdiocesan; AUXILIARY CHAPLAINS CONTRACT CHAPLAINS.
Jacobs, Charles E. '86 (HRT) Hartford, CT Holy Trinity.
Jacobs, David E. '75 (LR) Pocahontas, AR St. John the Baptist; Pocahontas, AR St. Paul the Apostle.
Jacobs, Eugene S. '46 (WH) Retired.
Jacobs, Gilbert H. *o.praem.* (GB)[A] De Pere, WI St. Norbert Abbey; [I] De Pere, WI St. Norbert Abbey.
Jacobs, Harry W. '73 (WDC) Retired.
Jacobs, James T. '43 (GB) Retired.
Jacobs, Richard A. (PAT) Retired.
Jacobs, Richard '75 (ALB) Catskill, NY St. Patrick.
Jacobs, Richard *o.s.a.* '76 (PH)[C] Villanova University.
Jacobs, Timothy *ss.cc.* '35 (HON)[G] Honolulu, HI St. Patrick's Monastery.
Jacobs, William J. '03 (KAL) Benton Harbor, MI Ss.

John & Bernard.
Jacobsen, James E. *s.j.* '59 (P)[L] Portland, OR Colombiere Community.
Jacobson, Cliff (CHY) Youth Ministry Board; Diaconate Board.
Jacobson, Clifford '96 (CHY) Douglas, WY St. James.
Jacobson, Gary '65 (P) Retired.
Jacobson, James *s.j.* '59 (P) Salem, OR Oregon State Penitentiary; Salem, OR Santiam Correctional Institution; Salem, OR Mill Creek Correctional Facility.
Jacquel, John B. '83 (E) Edinboro, PA Our Lady of the Lake; Presbyteral Council.
Jacquemin, George P. (CIN) Priest Councilors.
Jacquemin, George (CIN) Cincinnati, OH St. Clare; Vicarri Foranei (Deans).
Jacques, Alfred '60 (PRT) Mexico, ME St. Theresa; Rumford, ME St. Athanasius–St. John; Deans.
Jacques, Donald W. '53 (PRT) Retired.
Jacques, E. J. *s.j.* '66 (MOB) Mobile, AL St. Joseph.
Jacques, Eugene F. '80 (NO) Gretna, LA St. Cletus.
Jacques, Kenneth *o.s.b.* '67 (P)[L] St. Benedict, OR Mt. Angel Abbey.
Jacques, Michael P. *s.s.e.* '82 (NO) New Orleans, LA St. Peter Claver; Deans.
Jacques, Roger N. '78 (BO) Waltham, MA St. Joseph.
Jacunski, Robert D. '56 (NEW)[N] Caldwell, NJ The Rev. Msgr. James F. Kelley Residence for Retired Priests Retired.
Jadaa, John *b.s.o.* '46 (NTN) Retired.
Jadin, Samuel D. *o.praem.* '55 (GB)[J] Manitowoc, WI Holy Family Convent of Franciscan Sisters of Christian Charity.
Jadulco, Jeremias T. '94 (HT) Thibodaux, LA St. Joseph Co–Cathedral.
Jadwisiak, Edmund '79 (PRM) Retired.
Jaeb, Maurus P. *o.s.b.* '95 (OKL) Shawnee, OK St. Benedict; [I] Shawnee St. Gregory's Abbey.
Jaeger, David–Marie A. *o.f.m.* (SAT) Judges.
Jaeger, James P. '86 (ROC) Hornell, NY St. Ann; Hornell, NY St. Ignatius Loyola; Canisteo, NY St. Mary; Air Force Reserve Chaplains.
Jaeger, Louis M. '73 (DUB)[F] Marshalltown, IA Marshalltown Area Consolidated Catholic School; Marshalltown, IA St. Henry; Marshalltown, IA Immaculate Conception; Seminary Board.
Jaeger, Robert E. '90 (COS) Monument, CO St. Peter; Vicar for Clergy; Diocesan Consultors.
Jaenicke, Alfred J. '54 (HRT) Waterbury, CT Sacred Heart–Sagrado Corazon Retired.
Jaffe, Joel D. '03 (ARL) Alexandria, VA Blessed Sacrament.
Jagdfeld, Lawrence *o.f.m.* '75 (JOL) Joliet, IL St. John the Baptist; [L] Joliet, IL St. John the Baptist Friary.
Jagela, Walter M. '94 (WH) Wellsburg, WV St. John The Evangelist.
Jagodensky, Joe *s.d.s.* '80 (MIL)[M] Milwaukee, WI Alexian Village of Milwaukee, Inc..
Jagodzinski, Charles *o.f.m.conv.* '68 (BUF)[O] Athol Springs, NY St. Francis of Assisi Friary; [D] Athol Springs, NY St. Francis High School.
Jagodzinski, John J. '62 (PH) Wayne, PA St. Katharine of Siena.
Jagodzinski, Stanislaw *s.d.b.* '87 (OAK)[N] Berkeley Salesian Community.
Jagoe, Bede R. *o.p.* '60 (CHI)[N] Chicago Dominicans (Provincial Office); [N] River Forest, IL St. Thomas Aquinas Priory.
Jagoe, Bede *o.p.* '60 (FgM).
Jahner, Anton P. *s.j.* '67 (SPK)[J] Spokane, WA Regis Community.
Jairo, John (BIR) Anniston, AL Sacred Heart of Jesus.
Jakel, Pat G. '85 (SFD) Granite City, IL St. Elizabeth; Presbyteral Council.
Jakobiak, Arthur '56 (SFE) St. Vincent's Hospital.
Jakopac, George I. (BAL) Frederick, MD St. John the Evangelist.
Jakows, Ronald M. '90 (PH) Philadelphia, PA Holy Cross; [D] Philadelphia, PA Roman Catholic High School for Boys.
Jaksina, Edward S. '55 (HRT) Seymour, CT Good Shepherd.
Jakub, John T. '02 (TR) Barnegat, NJ St. Mary.
Jakubauskas, Richard A. '99 (WOR) Worcester, MA St. Casimir's.
Jakubco, Bernard *m.s.c.* '64 (OG) Evans Mills, NY St. Mary; Antwerp, NY St. Michael; [E] Watertown, NY Missionaries of the Sacred Heart.
Jakubek, Eugene J. *s.j.* '54 (OM)[K] Omaha, NE Jesuit Community at Creighton University.
Jakubik, Richard '93 (CHI) Wilmette, IL St. Francis Xavier.
Jakubowski, Allen F. '75 (LC) Stevens Point, WI St. Stanislaus; Personnel Council.
Jakubowski, Joseph J. '40 (KC) Retired.
Jakubowski, Kenneth J. '91 (CLV) Middleburg Heights, OH St. Bartholomew; Cleveland, OH Cathedral of St. John the Evangelist; [Y] Cleveland, OH St. John Cathedral Endowment Trust.
Jalbert, Edward *c.j.* '87 (LA)[B] Santa Maria, CA St. Joseph Seminary (Josephite Fathers' Novitiate); [D] Santa Maria, CA St. Joseph High School.
Jalbert, Jason Y. '03 (MAN) Gonic, NH St. Leo; Rochester, NH Holy Rosary.
Jalbert, Robert A. *m.m.* '79 (NY)[EE] Maryknoll Maryknoll Fathers and Brothers.
Jallas, Robert J. '84 (SFD) Quincy, IL All Saints; Quincy, IL St. Anthony of Padua; Quincy, IL St. Joseph; Quincy Deanery; Pittsfield, IL Holy Redeemer; Pittsfield, IL St. Mary.
Jamail, Michael A. (BEA) Vicar General and Moderator of the Curia; Diocesan College of Consultors and Presbyteral Council; Defenders of Bond; Psychologists for the Tribunal; Diaconate Formation; Beaumont, TX St. Anne.
Jambon, Jeffrey *l.c.* '01 (SAC) Sacramento, CA Our Lady of Guadalupe Shrine.
James, David J. '91 (SY) Pompey, NY Immaculate Conception.
James, David L. '96 (ALN) Allentown, PA Cathedral of St. Catharine of Siena; Advocates.
James, James (CHI) Chicago, IL St. James.
James, Joseph W. '57 (LUB)[B] Slaton, TX Our Lady of Mercy Retreat Center Retired.
James, Melvin P. *s.v.d.* '75 (LA) Los Angeles, CA St. John, The Evangelist.
James, Peter Paul *o.f.m.* '51 (CIN)[M] Cincinnati, OH St. Francis Seraph Friary Retired.
James, Thomas *s.v.d.* '69 (LAF) Lafayette, LA Immaculate Heart of Mary; Central Region.
James, Thomas *s.v.d.* '02 (BLX)[E] Bay St. Louis, MS Southern Province of St. Augustine – Provincial Residence.
James, V. Warwick '80 (SJ) Santa Clara, CA St. Lawrence the Martyr; College of Consultors; Deans.
James, William R. '54 (MOB) Robertsdale, AL St. Patrick; Montgomery–Dothan Deaneries.
Jameson, W. Ronald '68 (WDC) Washington, DC St. Matthew Cathedral; Archdiocesan College of Consultors; Deans; Archdiocesan Sacred Arts Committee.
Jamieson, Andrew '88 (TR) Tabernacle, NJ Holy Eucharist.
Jamison, Dale *o.f.m.* '74 (SFE) Espanola, NM Franciscan Tewa Missions.
Jammes, Jean Marie '43 (LAF) St. Martinville, LA St. Martin of Tours Retired.
Jamnicky, John A. '72 (CHI) On Duty Outside the Archdiocese; [I] Port Arthur, TX Apostleship of the Sea of the United States of America (AOSUSA).
Jamros, Daniel P. *s.j.* '76 (BO)[V] Boston The Society of Jesus of New England–Provincial Offices.
Jamros, Daniel P. *s.j.* '76 (BUF)[O] Buffalo, NY Canisius Jesuit Community.
Jamroz, Sigmund S. *m.m.* '66 (FgM).
Jamroz, Waclaw *s.d.s.* '92 (CHI) Chicago, IL St. Symphorosa and Seven Sons.
Jana, Humberto *c.pp.s.* '89 (ORL) Orlando, FL St. Andrew; Apopka, FL St. Francis of Assisi.
Janacek, Balthasar J. '50 (SAT) San Antonio, TX Old Spanish Missions.
Janacek, Balthasar (SAT) College of Consultors; In Metropolitan Area; Archdiocesan Presbyteral Council; Priests Personnel Board.
Janacek, Balty '50 (SAT) Retired.
Janaczek, Joseph J. '71 (BUF) Dunkirk, NY St. Hedwig.
Janaites, Stanley '55 (BAL) Special Assignment.
Janak, Gary W. *j.c.l.* '88 (VIC) Vice–Chancellor; Judges; Victim Assistance Coordinator; El Campo, TX St. Philip the Apostle.
Janas, Camillus W. *o.f.m.* (GB) Manitowoc, WI St. Boniface; Manitowoc, WI St. Andrew.
Janas, Camillus *o.f.m.* (GB) Elected Representatives.
Jancarz, Janusz '83 (VEN) Parrish, FL St. Frances Xavier Cabrini; Presbyteral Council.
Janda, James A. '72 (SLC) Sandy, UT Blessed Sacrament.
Jandaczek, Peter *m.s.* '99 (ATL) Snellville, GA St. Oliver Plunkett.
Janderna, Ronald L. '94 (MET) Blairstown, NJ St. Jude.
Janecek, James E. (CC) Army National Guard Chaplains.
Janeck, Thomas More *o.f.m.cap.* '46 (DEN)[N] Denver, CO St. Francis of Assisi Friary; [O] Denver, CO Monastery of Our Lady of Light (Capuchin Poor Clares).
Janeczek, Vladimir '59 (GRY) Hammond, IN St. Casimir.
Janelli, Anthony '64 (FRS) Cursillo Movement; Vocations; On Special Assignment.
Janes, David '75 (P) Yamhill, OR St. John.
Janes, David '83 (SFS) Bristol, SD St. Anthony; Groton, SD St. Elizabeth Ann Seton.
Janes, David (SFS) Diocesan Consultors; Deans; Presbyteral Council.
Janeske, John A. '52 (LR) Stuttgart, AR SS. Cyril and Methodius; Stuttgart, AR Holy Rosary; [L] Stuttgart, AR Holy Rosary Catholic School "Vision 2000" Educational Trust Fund.
Janette, Paul '63 (MIL) Retired.
Janezic, Larry *o.f.m.* '78 (CHI)[X] Chicago, IL Franciscan Outreach Association.
Janezic, Lawrence *o.f.m.* '78 (CHI)[N] Chicago, IL St. Peter's Friary.
Jang, Antonius Hyo Kang (RIC) Hampton, VA Catholic Community of the Korean Martyrs.
Jang, Theodore '88 (LA) Los Angeles, CA Holy Trinity.
Janicki, Carl F. '94 (PH) Flourtown, PA St. Genevieve; [D] Philadelphia, PA Cardinal Dougherty High School.
Janicki, Laurian *o.f.m.* '64 (JOL) Wayne, IL Resurrection.
Janiga, Bruce G. '83 (NEW).
Janiga, Joseph '45 (DET) Retired.
Janik, Anthony F. *o.f.m.* '70 (GRY)[I] Cedar Lake, IN Our Lady of Lourdes Friary.
Janik, Bruno '66 (CHI) Burbank, IL St. Albert the Great.
Janik, Leszek T. '92 (NOR) Versailles, CT St. Joseph; Members; Adjutant Judicial Vicar.
Janish, James '69 (SAT) Spring Branch, TX St. Joseph.
Janish, James (SAT) Judges.
Janiszeski, Joseph J. *t.o.r.* '78 (PIT) Pittsburgh, PA St. Matthew.
Janiunas, Albin F. '48 (BO) Senior Priests Retired.
Jankaitis, Ronald V. '79 (ALN) St. Clair, PA St. Casimir; [C] Pottsville, PA Nativity B.V.M. High School; [I] St. Clair, PA Neumann Apartments; Appointed Members.
Janko, Jack *s.d.b.* '78 (BO)[E] Boston, MA Savio Preparatory High School; [N] Boston, MA Orient Heights Unit.
Jankowiak, Patrick '92 (SAG) Gladwin, MI Sacred Heart.
Jankowski, James *o.f.m.conv.* '99 (RCK) Rockford, IL St. Anthony of Padua.
Jankowski, Marcellus A. '57 (KC) Special Assignment Retired.
Jankowski, Richard '92 (SP) Lecanto, FL St. Scholastica; Presbyteral Council.
Jankowski, Stan *o.f.m.* (CHI) Archdiocesan Council of Catholic Women (ACCW).
Jankowski, Stanislaw *c.r.* '94 (CHI) Chicago, IL St. Hyacinth Basilica.
Jankowski, Valentine M. *o.f.m.conv.* '61 (LSC) Carlsbad, NM San Jose.
Jankowski, Valentine *o.f.m.conv.* '61 (LSC) Loving, NM Our Lady of Grace; Vicars; Diocesan Consultors; Presbyteral Council; Priestly Life and Ministry Committee.
Jann, Francis J. '47 (BUF) Rushford, NY St. Mark Retired.
Janning, Timothy J. '82 (CIN) Military Chaplains; Navy Chaplains.
Janoch, Edward J. (CLV) Lyndhurst, OH St. Clare.
Janocha, Carl William '91 (OKL) Clinton, OK St. Mary's.
Janoski, Steven A. '88 (SFD) Troy, IL St. Jerome.
Janoski, Wesley *c.r.* '93 (LC) Stevens Point, WI St. Mary.
Janovec, James J. '64 (GI) Paxton, NE Sacred Heart; Wood River, NE St. Mary's.
Janowiak, Paul A. *s.j.* '84 (SEA)[A] Seattle, WA Seattle University.
Janowicz, Barney J. '57 (SAG) Retired.
Janowicz, Richard (STN) Springfield, OR Nativity of the Mother of God; Diocesan Consultors; Presbyteral Council; Personnel Board; South–West.
Janowski, Lawrence *o.f.m.* '73 (CHI)[N] Chicago, IL Holy Name Friary.
Janowski, Michael S. '03 (GAY) Kingsley, MI St. Mary; Traverse City, MI Immaculate Conception.
Janowski, Rock J. '64 (LA) Retired.
Janowski, Stanley *o.f.m.* '66 (CHI)[O] Chicago, IL Mother of Good Counsel Provincialate.
Janowski, Wesley '93 (LC) Stevens Point, WI St. Casimir.
Jansch, Ronald *o.f.m.cap.* '50 (MIL)[O] Mount Calvary, WI St. Lawrence Friary.
Jansen, Anthony G. *s.m.* '43 (STL)[O] Marianist Community.
Jansen, James H. '55 (BEL) Retired.
Jansen, Raymond L. '99 (LIN) Graduate Studies.
Jansen, William J. *m.c.c.j.* '66 (CIN)[V] Cincinnati, OH Hispanic Ministries at St. Charles, Archdiocese of Cincinnati.
Jansen, William *m.c.c.j.* '66 (CIN)[M] Cincinnati, OH Comboni Missionaries (Verona Fathers)–Comboni Mission Center; Archdiocesan Office of Hispanic Ministry.
Janski, Jerome J. '50 (STP) Retired.
Janson, Chris *s.m.* '73 (SAT)[C] San Antonio, TX St. Mary's University of San Antonio, Texas; [M] San Antonio, TX Casa Maria Marianist Community.
Janson, Eugene '76 (VIC)[K] San Antonio, TX Padua Place.
Janson, Leo F. '45 (GF) Retired.
Janssen, Henry *o.m.i.* '43 (BWN) McAllen, TX Sacred Heart.
Janssen, James M. '48 (DAV)[M] Davenport, IA St. Vincent Center Retired.
Janton, Anthony W. '77 (PH) Philadelphia, PA St. Martin of Tours.
Januszkiewicz, Henry '62 (WDC) Retired.

Janze, John E. '75 (ORG) Irvine, CA St. Thomas More.
Jaques, Domingos '47 (OAK) Retired.
Jaramillo, Anselmo (Bud) *c.r.* (DEN)[A] Denver, CO St. Andrew's Theatine Religious House.
Jaramillo, Fabio E. '81 (NY) Bronx, NY Sacred Heart.
Jaramillo, Jose G. *m.g.* '80 (SB) Special or Other Diocesan Assignment.
Jaramillo, Leonardo '92 (NEW) Elizabeth, NJ Blessed Sacrament.
Jaramillo, Luis '60 (SFE) Retired.
Jaramillo, Oscar '90 (B) Caldwell, ID Our Lady of the Valley; College of Consultors; Deans.
Jaramillo, Peter '81 (AMA) Army National Guard Chaplains; On Duty Outside the Diocese.
Jaramillo, Peter '81 (KCK) Olathe, KS St. Paul's; [J] Kansas City, KS Society of St. Augustine – Public Association of the Faithful.
Jaramillo, Roberto '93 (SAC) Sacramento, CA Immaculate Conception.
Jaranilla, Roberto '96 (LA) Alhambra, CA All Souls; Downey, CA St. Raymond.
Jarboe, J. Bruce '86 (BAL) Glen Burnie, MD Holy Trinity.
Jarboe, Raymond (BAK) Eastern.
Jarboe, W. Raymond (BAK) Board of Education; Campus Ministry Apostolate; Ontario, OR Blessed Sacrament.
Jardiniano, Rolly P. '84 (LA) Artesia, CA Holy Family.
Jarecki, Michael S. '44 (OG) Retired.
Jarecki, Raynold *o.f.m.* '55 (GB).
Jarema, William '83 (COS)[I] Colorado Springs, CO Divine Redeemer; [I] Colorado Springs, CO Society of Missionaries of Mercy; Seminarian Formation.
Jarka, Thomas H. '59 (CAM) Retired.
Jarman, Glenn M. *c.p.m.* (MO) Air Force Chaplains.
Jarmoluk, Joseph F. '84 (RCK) Geneva, IL St. Peter.
Jaros, Joseph P. '56 (TOL) Judges Retired.
Jarosch, Eugene H. *s.a.c.* '51 (MIL)[O] Milwaukee, WI St. Vincent Community.
Jarosewic, Daniel '71 (CHI) Chicago, IL St. Mary, Star of the Sea.
Jarosz, Peter '89 (JOL) Lombard, IL Christ the King.
Jarosz, Stanley '65 (MET) Helmetta, NJ Holy Trinity.
Jaroszeski, Paul A. '76 (STP) St. Paul, MN St. Cecilia.
Jaroszeski, Paul (STP) Personnel Director; Commission on Pastoral Health Care; Office of Presbyteral Personnel Resources.
Jarreau, Niel J. '56 (ATL)[M] Atlanta, GA Ignatius House.
Jarrell, Stephen '73 (IND) Greencastle, IN St. Paul the Apostle; Council of Priests; Indiana State Farm; [O] Greencastle, IN DePauw University.
Jarret, Peter A. *c.s.c.* '92 (FTW)[B] University of Notre Dame Du Lac; [B] University of Notre Dame Du Lac; [I] South Bend, IN Congregation of Holy Cross, Indiana Province, Provincial House; [I] Notre Dame, IN Holy Cross Community, Corby Hall, University of Notre Dame.
Jarumbo, James J. (MIL) Sheboygan, WI St. Dominic; Judges for Second Instance.
Jarvis, Edward A. *s.j.* '54 (WH)[A] Wheeling, WV Wheeling Jesuit University.
Jarzombek, Casimir '60 (VIC) Bay City, TX Holy Cross.
Jarzombek, Dennis '79 (SAT) On Leave.
Jasany, Robert J. '79 (CLV) Cleveland, OH St. John Nepomucene.
Jascura, Patricuo *s.j.* (BO)[V] Cambridge, MA Faber House.
Jasinski, Andrew '98 (FAR) Wishek, ND St. David; Wishek, ND St. Patrick; Wishek, ND St. Andrew.
Jasinski, Anthony J. '49 (BUF)[O] Lackawanna, NY Bishop Head Residence Retired.
Jasinski, Raymond J. '54 (CHI)[M] Justice, IL Rosary Hill Home Retired.
Jaskot, Robert '98 (BAL) Baltimore, MD Cathedral of Mary Our Queen.
Jaskowiak, Wojciech '03 (NEW) Elizabeth, NJ Immaculate Heart of Mary.
Jaskulski, Bronislaus *o.f.m.* '46 (GRY)[I] Cedar Lake, IN Our Lady of Lourdes Friary.
Jaskulski, George *o.f.m.* '55 (Pulaski, WI)[O] Garfield Heights, OH Marymount Convent.
Jaskulski, George *o.f.m.* '55 (CLV)[P] Cleveland, OH Marymount Congregational Home.
Jaskulski, Nathan *o.f.m.* '61 (GB) Green Bay, WI St. Mary of the Angels; [I] Green Bay, WI St. Mary of the Angels Friary.
Jasper, Frank *o.f.m.* '73 (IND) Indianapolis, IN Sacred Heart of Jesus.
Jasper, John (BAK) Nyssa, OR St. Bridget of Kildare.
Jasper, Louis H. '51 (COV) Retired.
Jasper, Louis '51 (VEN) Bonita Springs, FL St. Leo.
Jaspers, J. Dennis '66 (CIN) Cincinnati, OH All Saints.
Jaspers, Louis *c.i.c.m.* '52 (SAT) San Antonio, TX St. Gabriel.
Jasso, Stephen *t.o.r.* '65 (FWT) Fort Worth, TX All Saints.
Jastrab, David J. '75 (PIT) Wildwood, PA St. Catherine of Sweden.
Jastrzebski, Edmund *c.r.* '74 (CHI) Chicago, IL St. Stanislaus Kostka.
Jaszczuk, Radoslaw *c.ss.r.* '91 (MET) Manville, NJ Sacred Heart of Jesus; Somerville, NJ Somerset Medical Center.
Jaszek, Stanislaw (FBK) St. Michael, AK St. Michael; St. Bernard; Unalakleet, AK Church of the Holy Angels.
Jaume, John *c.r.* '66 (NY) Plattekill, NY Our Lady of Fatima.
Jautz, Martin L. '44 (MIL) Retired.
Java, Miguel '73 (LA) Gardena, CA Maria Regina.
Javier, Nazareno '98 (BRK) On Leave/Unassigned.
Javier, Senen *c.ss.r.* (NY) New York, NY St. Cecilia.
Javier Lopez, Francisco *sch.p.* '67 (SJN) San Juan, PR Santisimo Salvador.
Javier Munoz, Francisco '96 (SJN) Trujillo Alto, PR Bienventurada Virgen Maria de Lourdes.
Javor, Egon J. *o.s.b.* '41 (SFR) Knights of Malta; [N] Portola Valley, CA Woodside Priory.
Jawidzik, Edward M. '81 (TR) Freehold, NJ St. Robert Bellarmine.
Jaworowski, Anthony E. '44 (PH) Swedesburg, PA Sacred Heart Retired.
Jaworowski, Leon E. '43 (PH) Retired.
Jayachandra, Hermanagild '68 (DEN) Boulder, CO St. Martin de Porres.
Jayaraj, M. Jones '83 (TYL) Center, TX St. Therese.
Jayarara, Vincent (TLS) Stillwater, OK St. Francis Xavier; Stillwater, OK St. John University Parish and Catholic Student Center.
Jayaselanraj, Lucas (TYL) Bradshaw State Facility, Texas Department of Corrections.
Jayasuria, Jerome '61 (DAL) Retired.
Jayatilake, Benedict '62 (FTW) Fort Wayne, IN Cathedral of the Immaculate Conception.
Jazdzewski, Brian J. '99 (LC) Chippewa Falls, WI Notre Dame; [C] Chippewa Falls, WI McDonell Central Catholic High School; Jim Falls, WI Sacred Heart.
Jazmin, Romeo '85 (RIC) Portsmouth, VA Holy Angels.
Jazmines, Vicente F. '79 (OG) Peru, NY St. Augustine.
Jazowski, John F. '48 (BGP)[P] New Milford, CT Retired.
Jazwiecki, John *s.m.* '64 (SP) Tampa, FL Our Lady of Perpetual Help Retired.
Je, Gabriel Byong–Young *s.j.* '94 (ATL)[O] Doraville, GA Korean Martyrs Pastoral Center.
Jeager, James '86 (ROC) Canisteo, NY St. Joachim.
Jean, Agapit H. '95 (MAN) Merrimack, NH St. John Neumann.
Jean, Anthonio '99 (VEN) Fort Myers, FL St. Francis Xavier.
Jean, Antonio (VEN) Ministry to Haitian People in Lee County.
Jean, Franky '93 (MIA) Fort Lauderdale, FL Divine Mercy Mission; Haitians.
Jean, Lesly '83 (MIA)[A] Miami, FL St. John Vianney College Seminary.
Jean, Thony R. (ATL) Atlanta, GA Sacred Heart of Jesus.
Jean–Louis, Arlin *o.m.i.* '91 (HRT) Hartford, CT St. Justin.
Jean–Louis, Isaie '88 (BRK) Brooklyn, NY St. Matthew's.
Jean–Mary, Reginald '01 (MIA) Miami, FL Notre Dame d'Haiti.
Jeanfreau, James J. '92 (NO) On Duty Outside the Archdiocese.
Jean Paul, Souvenir '97 (BRK) Brooklyn, NY St. Francis of Assisi–St. Blaise.
Jebadu, Alex '95 (WH) Franklin, WV St. Elizabeth Ann Seton; Moorefield, WV Epiphany of the Lord.
Jecewiz, Jerome T. '75 (BRK) Brooklyn, NY Holy Spirit.
Jedrychowski, Janusz '95 (STF) Rochester, NY Epiphany of Our Lord.
Jedrzejewski, Richard '74 (BUF) Buffalo, NY Assumption; Buffalo, NY St. Elizabeth of Hungary.
Jedynak, Jerzy *c.r.* '69 (CHI) Chicago, IL St. Hyacinth Basilica.
Jeffers, Robert A. '54 (NY) Bronx, NY St. Margaret Mary; Bronx, NY Bronx–Lebanon Hospital Center.
Jeffers, Vincent W. '31 (NY) Retired.
Jeffrey, Donald *m.s.* '64 (MAN)[K] Enfield, NH Shrine of Our Lady of La Salette; [M] Enfield, NH La Salette Shrine and Center of Enfield.
Jeffrey, George A. '65 (SCR) Wilkes–Barre, PA St. Therese's.
Jeffrey, James C. '59 (FAR) Retired.
Jeffries, Brian E. '73 (HRT) Seymour, CT St. Augustine's.
Jelinek, Anthony J. (CHI)[N] Libertyville, IL Marytown, Our Lady of Fatima Friary; AUXILIARY CHAPLAINS CONTRACT CHAPLAINS.
Jemejcic, Timothy L. (SB) Rialto, CA St. Thomas More.
Jendrek, Michael '87 (BAL) Ellicott City, MD St. Paul.
Jendrysik, Mark '85 (JOL) Bolingbrook, IL St. Dominic; Cursillo Movement.
Jenemann, Albert H. *s.j.* '60 (PH)[C] Jesuit Fathers; [AA] Loyola Center and Manresa Hall.
Jenik, John J. '70 (NY) Bronx, NY Our Lady of Refuge.
Jenkins, J. Michael '79 (SFD) Pittsfield, IL Holy Redeemer; Pittsfield, IL St. Mary; Priests' Personnel Board.
Jenkins, John I. *c.s.c.* '83 (FTW)[B] University of Notre Dame Du Lac; [B] University of Notre Dame Du Lac; [I] South Bend, IN Congregation of Holy Cross, Indiana Province, Provincial House; [I] Notre Dame, IN Holy Cross Community, Corby Hall, University of Notre Dame.
Jenkins, John M. '60 (CLV) Akron, OH St. Paul.
Jenkins, Joseph A. '86 (WDC) Forestville, MD Church of the Holy Spirit.
Jenkins, Kenneth '80 (SB) Yucaipa, CA St. Frances Xavier Cabrini; Elected Members.
Jenkins, Ron '89 (AUS) On Duty Outside the Diocese.
Jenkins, Ronny E. (AUS) Defenders of the Bond.
Jenkins, Ronny E. (DAL) Defensor Vinculi.
Jenkins, Wayne '72 (L) Louisville, KY St. Barnabas.
Jenkins, Wayne *s.c.j.* '77 (MIL)[O] Hales Corners, WI Priests of the Sacred Heart.
Jenkinson, William R. '57 (PRO) Barrington, RI St. Luke.
Jenko, Aloysius '35 (NY)[EE] Bronx, NY Retired.
Jenks, Francis C. '70 (CHI) Lemont, IL St. Alphonsus.
Jenne, Walter H. '70 (CLV) Brecksville, OH St. Basil the Great.
Jenner, James *o.p.* '51 (SEA) Seattle, WA Blessed Sacrament.
Jennett, Michael '74 (LA) Ventura, CA Our Lady of the Assumption; College of Consultors.
Jenniges, Leonard J. '48 (STP) Retired.
Jennings, Bernard J. '41 (LA) Altadena, CA St. Elizabeth of Hungary Retired.
Jennings, Earl *t.o.r.* '59 (BAL)[J] White Post, VA Sacred Heart Friary.
Jennings, Francis *c.ss.r.* '48 (ORL)[E] New Smyrna Beach, FL St. Alphonsus Villa–Redemptorist Fathers and Brothers Retired.
Jennings, Henry J. '62 (BO) Somerville, MA St. Joseph.
Jennings, John A. '50 (SEA)[M] Seattle, WA St. Joseph's Residence Retired.
Jennings, John J. '49 (BO) Senior Priests Retired.
Jennings, Joseph '43 (MOB) Retired.
Jennings, Michael T. '69 (KNX) Rogersville, TN St. Henry.
Jennings, Mike '69 (KNX) Sneedville, TN St. James the Apostle.
Jennings, Paul F. '74 (WIL) Chester, MD St. Christopher.
Jennings, Thomas J. '69 (WIN)[A] Winona, MN Immaculate Heart of Mary Seminary; Diocesan Consultors; Appointed Members.
Jennings, Tommie '88 (SD) Military Chaplains; Navy Chaplains.
Jennings, William E. '40 (WIL) Retired.
Jenniskens, Thomas J. *s.j.* '56 (LAF)[J] Grand Coteau, LA Jesuit Spirituality Center (St. Charles College).
Jennrich, Michael J. *o.f.m.* '87 (SUP) Ashland, WI Our Lady of the Lake Catholic Community.
Jensen, Daniel P. *m.m.* '62 (SJ)[M] Los Altos, CA Maryknoll.
Jensen, Jen P. '01 (COS) Colorado Springs, CO St. Francis of Assisi.
Jensen, John A. *m.m.* '44 (FgM).
Jensen, Joseph *o.s.b.* '54 (WDC)[C] Catholic University of America, The; [M] Washington, DC St. Anselm's Abbey; [V] Washington, DC Catholic Biblical Association.
Jensen, Larry '88 (SAM) Danbury, CT St. Anthony.
Jensen–Rieser, Jon '79 (VNN)[A] Santa Ysabel, CA Good Shepherd Monastery.
Jenson, Glen T. '95 (STP) New Market, MN St. Nicholas.
Jeong, Marco *o.f.m.* (LA) Gardena, CA Maria Regina.
Jeong–Bay–Pak, Benedict '92 (SFR) San Francisco, CA St. Michael Church.
Jerabeck, Joseph F. '48 (COL) Retired.
Jerek, John M. '88 (Y) Kent, OH Immaculate Heart of Mary; [O] Kent, OH Kent State University Newman Center.
Jerek, John (Y) Office of Campus Ministry; Immaculate Heart of Mary University Parish (Kent State Newman Center).
Jerge, Lawrence A. *c.s.c.* '68 (FR) Mashpee, MA Christ The King.
Jerome, Harry J. '61 (BEL) Du Quoin, IL Sacred Heart of Jesus.
Jerome, Louis '88 (NY) Staten Island, NY Sacred Heart.
Jerome, Marc–Arthur (RVC) Central Islip, NY St. John of God.
Jerome, Ru Ken–Bae '92 (BIR) Birmingham, AL Korean Catholic Community, St. Luke Hwang.
Jerse, William M. '80 (CLV) Euclid, OH St. Paul; Adjutant Judicial Vicars.
Jervis, Paul W. '83 (BRK) Corona, NY St. Paul the Apostle.
Jeselnick, Stephen E. '77 (E) On Duty Outside Diocese; Air National Guard Chaplains.
Jesiolowski, Sylvester E. '41 (PEO) Retired.
Jesionowski, Richard A. '68 (BUF) Cheektowaga, NY Our Lady Help of Christians.

Jeske, Richard M. *o.f.m.* '59 (SFD) Quincy, IL Illinois Veterans' Home; [B] Quincy, IL Quincy University.
Jette, Donald J. *s.s.s.* '53 (CLV) Highland Heights, OH St. Paschal Baylon; [O] Cleveland, OH Blessed Sacrament Community.
Jette, Mark R. '72 (HRT) West Haven, CT St. Lawrence's.
Jeung, Louis Young Han '80 (OAK) Oakland, CA St. Lawrence O'Toole.
Jewdrek, Michael J. (BAL)[V] Ellicott City, MD The St. Paul's Parish Endowment Trust.
Jewison, Harry P. '54 (WIN) Retired.
Jewitt, Bernard C. '59 (TLS) Tulsa, OK St. Bernard of Clairvaux; Diocesan Senators.
Jeyabalan, Fedelis *s.j.* '77 (Andhra)[N] Berkeley, CA Jesuit Community at Jesuit School of Theology at Berkeley.
Jezak, Thomas M. '66 (ALX) Marksville, LA St. Genevieve.
Jicha, John J. '95 (BAL) Iamsville, MD St. Ignatius Loyola.
Jicha, John (BAL) Priest Personnel Board.
Jillisky, William F. '56 (ALB) Cohoes, NY St. Bernard.
Jimeinez, Benjamin P. *s.j.* '77 (CLV)[D] Cleveland, OH St. Ignatius High School.
Jimenez, Adrian '87 (ARE) Camuy, PR St. Joseph.
Jimenez, Alvaro '84 (TYL) Palestine, TX Sacred Heart.
Jimenez, Amiro '90 (BRK) Brooklyn, NY Our Lady of Guadalupe.
Jimenez, Armando '46 (WDC)[L] Washington, DC Cardinal O'Boyle Residence for Priests Retired.
Jimenez, Benjamin P. *s.j.* '01 (CLV) Cleveland, OH St. Augustine.
Jimenez, Carlos '67 (SJN) Rio Piedras, PR Asuncion de La Virgen.
Jimenez, David J. '95 (YAK) Special Assignment.
Jimenez, Edgar '84 (FRS) Tranquillity, CA St. Paul.
Jimenez, Eduardo '82 (MIA) Miami, FL Good Shepherd.
Jimenez, Emilio B. '99 (CC) Alice, TX St. Joseph.
Jimenez, Emilio (CC) College of Consultors; Presbyteral Council; Chancellor.
Jimenez, Emilo (CC) Office of the Bishop.
Jimenez, Felix *sch.p.* '26 (NY)[EE] New York, NY Calasanzian Fathers (Piarists).
Jimenez, Felix *sch.p.* '70 (NY) New York, NY Annunciation.
Jimenez, Francisco '88 (ARE) Retired.
Jimenez, Fredy '93 (PRO) Providence, RI Our Lady of Mt. Carmel.
Jimenez, John T. '98 (SFR) San Francisco, CA Visitacion, Church of the.
Jimenez, Jose Luis '59 (ORG) Santa Ana, CA Our Lady of the Pillar.
Jimenez, Jose Vicente '97 (RCK) South Beloit, IL St. Peter.
Jimenez, Rafael '74 (DET) Detroit, MI St. Stephen–Mary Mother of the Church.
Jimenez, Ryan '03 (CHK) Presbyteral Council; Kristo Rai Parish.
Jimenez, Victorino (ARE) Retired.
Jimenez–Londono, Fredy '93 (PRO) West Warwick, RI St. Joseph.
Jiminez, Juan Bosco *s.d.b.* '90 (CHI) Chicago, IL St. John Bosco.
Jindra, Frank E. '84 (OM) Duncan, NE St. Stanislaus; Silver Creek, NE St. Lawrence.
Jirak, John F. '02 (WCH) Wichita, KS Blessed Sacrament.
Jiron, Keith (KC) Vocations.
Jissera, W. Edward (DAV) Enfield, CT St. Martha's.
Joachim, Thomas *f.j.* '95 (LAR)[D] Laredo, TX St. John Priory, F.J.; [F] Laredo, TX Holy Spirit Retreat and Conference Center.
Joaquin, M. Joseph '81 (BGP) Georgetown, CT Sacred Heart.
Jobst, Frank *o.m.i.* '72 (FgM).
Jocco, Joseph P. *o.s.f.s.* '84 (WIL)[J] Childs, MD Retirement and Assisted Care Facility.
Jocelyn, Yves '62 (MIA) Miramar, FL St. Bartholomew.
Jocson, Edgardo P. '01 (NEW) Jersey City, NJ Parish of the Resurrection; Cranford, NJ St. Michael's.
Jocson, Salvador '57 (SFR).
Jocys, Leonard '51 (GAY) Retired.
Joda, Robert J. *s.j.* '58 (MIL)[O] Milwaukee, WI Jesuit Community at Marquette University.
Joensen, William M. '89 (DUB)[A] Dubuque, IA Seminary of St. Pius X; [C] Loras College; Medical–Moral Commission.
Joerger, Jacob J. *o.p.* '48 (CHI)[N] St. Pius V Priory.
Joerger, Robert *c.p.* '77 (NY)[EE] Bronx, NY Passionist Residence.
Joffe, William I. '57 (RCK) On Disability Leave.
Johanek, John '43 (GB) Retired.
Johansen, Robert '01 (KAL) St. Joseph, MI St. Joseph.
John, Andre (FgM).
John, Reginald '60 (NY) Manhattan Detention Center.
John, Richard *o.s.c.* '46 (STP) Anoka, MN St. Stephen; [M] Anoka, MN Crosier Community of Anoka.
John, Tomy '95 (SP) Hudson, FL St. Michael.
Johns, Thomas W. '78 (CLV) Mentor, OH St. John Vianney.
Johnson, Andrew *o.c.s.o.* '91 (WOR)[O] Spencer, MA St. Joseph's Abbey.
Johnson, Arte *s.a.* (NY)[II] Barryville, NY New Hope Manor.
Johnson, Arthur D. *o.s.a.* '63 (NY) Charlotte, NC St. John Neumann.
Johnson, Arthur M. *s.a.* '77 (NY)[EE] Garrison, NY Franciscan Friars of the Atonement, Minister General Office.
Johnson, Bede L. *c.j.* '39 (LA)[B] Santa Maria, CA St. Joseph Seminary (Josephite Fathers' Novitiate).
Johnson, Bernard M. *o.praem.* '81 (ORG)[I Silverado, CA Norbertine Fathers of Orange Inc..
Johnson, Brian A. '97 (OWN) Clarkson, KY St. Augustine; Clarkson, KY St. Anthony's; Clarkson, KY St. Benedict.
Johnson, Brian *c.ss.r.* '86 (LA) Whittier, CA St. Mary of the Assumption; [Q] Whittier, CA Redemptorists of Whittier.
Johnson, Brian (OWN) Committee for Education.
Johnson, C. Lincoln (FTW)[B] University of Notre Dame Du Lac.
Johnson, Carl D. '78 (NY) Monroe, NY Sacred Heart Church.
Johnson, Carl '77 (LEX) Special Assignment.
Johnson, Charles B. '60 (HRT) Manchester, CT St. James.
Johnson, Charles W. *o.praem.* (MO) Navy Chaplains.
Johnson, Christopher *o.p.* '60 (NY)[EE] New York, NY St. Vincent Ferrer Priory; [EE] New York, NY St. Catherine of Siena Priory.
Johnson, Daniel E. '51 (HRT) Wallingford, CT Resurrection; Diocesan Labor Institute Retired.
Johnson, Daniel '54 (ORG) Huntington Beach, CA St. Mary's by the Sea.
Johnson, Dave '89 (OWN) Fancy Farm, KY St. Jerome.
Johnson, David W. *s.j.* '69 (WDC)[C] Catholic University of America, The Retired.
Johnson, Donald '55 (NY) Manhattan, NY Columbia Presbyterian Medical Center.
Johnson, Edward A. '55 (PRO) Retired.
Johnson, Edward J. '58 (LA) Los Angeles, CA St. Gregory Nazianzen.
Johnson, Edwin *s.m.* '86 (LA)[F] Marianist Community.
Johnson, Eric Matthew '02 (IND) Indianapolis, IN St. Pius X; [C] Indianapolis, IN Bishop Chatard High School.
Johnson, Francis P. '60 (HRT) West Hartford, CT St. Helena.
Johnson, Gary *o.f.m.conv.* (SPR) Chicopee, MA St. Stanislaus Basilica.
Johnson, Gregory '47 (BLX) Retired.
Johnson, H. Thomas '78 (DET) Shelby Twp., MI St. Kieran.
Johnson, Henry J. '57 (LA) Retired.
Johnson, Henry '76 (STO) Diamond Springs, CA Retired.
Johnson, Howard J. '54 (MIL) Retired.
Johnson, Howard '60 (JKS)[B] Washington, DC St. Joseph's Seminary Retired.
Johnson, J. Raymond *s.j.* '65 (NY)[EE] Loyola Hall, Jesuit Community; [EE] New York, NY Jesuit Provincial's Office; [N] Berkeley, CA Jesuit Community at Jesuit School of Theology at Berkeley.
Johnson, James B. '80 (SP) Inverness, FL Our Lady of Fatima; [S] Floral City, FL Our Lady of Good Counsel Camp; Air Force Reserve Chaplains.
Johnson, James '42 (NEW)[N] Rutherford, NJ St. John Vianney Residence for Priests Retired.
Johnson, James *s.p.* '68 (Y) Massillon, OH Saint Mary.
Johnson, James (SP) Our Lady of Good Counsel Camp.
Johnson, James (SEA) Seattle, WA Our Lady of Fatima; Presbyteral Council.
Johnson, Jeff G. '92 (MAR) Marquette, MI Marquette General Hospital.
Johnson, Jerome A. '86 (MET) Iselin, NJ St. Cecelia; Commission for Ecumenical and Interreligious Affairs.
Johnson, John G. '74 (COL) Columbus, OH St. Peter; Defenders of the Bond.
Johnson, John J. '66 (STL) St. Louis, MO St. James the Greater
Johnson, John R. '72 (SAG) Bay City, MI St. James.
Johnson, Joseph R. '98 (STP) Graduate Studies; Censores Librorum.
Johnson, Kevin '87 (PT) Tallahassee, FL St. Louis; Respect Life Committee.
Johnson, Lawrence C. *o.praem.* '94 (ORG)[I] Silverado, CA Norbertine Fathers of Orange Inc.
Johnson, Lawrence M. '83 (BAL) Special Assignment; [O] Timonium, MD Stella Maris; Priests' Council; [M] Baltimore, MD Mercy Health Services Inc..
Johnson, Lawrence P. '76 (DUL) On Duty Outside the Diocese; Navy Chaplains.
Johnson, Lawrence R. '75 (STP) Chaska, MN Guardian Angels Presbyteral Council.
Johnson, Leo Bede *c.j.* '39 (LA) Retired
Johnson, Lyle '76 (LIN) Lincoln, NE St. John the Apostle.
Johnson, Malcolm D. *c.s.c.* '59 (FTW)[I] Congregacion de Santa Cruz.
Johnson, Marcus '02 (LKC) Lake Charles, LA St. Margaret.
Johnson, Maxwell E. '78 (FTW)[B] University of Notre Dame Du Lac.
Johnson, Michael *o.f.m.* '02 (WDC) Silver Spring, MD St. Camillus.
Johnson, Oliver F. '62 (AUS) Austin, TX St. Catherine of Siena.
Johnson, Patrick A. *c.s.p.* '74 (AUS) Austin, TX St. Austin; Austin, TX State School.
Johnson, Patrick D. *c.s.p.* (MO) Navy Reserve Chaplains.
Johnson, Paul T. '63 (GR) Twin Lake, MI St. Mary of the Woods.
Johnson, Peter '91 (CHY) Lovell, WY St. Joseph's; Powell, WY St. Barbara; [E] Powell, WY NorthWest College; Ecumenism Commission; Rural Life Ministry.
Johnson, Philip L. (FWT) Diocesan Finance Council; Catholic Foundation of North Texas.
Johnson, Philip '64 (FWT) Bedford, TX St. Michael.
Johnson, Richard E. '60 (DAL) Dallas, TX St. Patrick; Consultors of Pastors; Presbyteral Council.
Johnson, Richard G. '47 (BO) Senior Priests Retired.
Johnson, Richard *c.p.* '51 (CHI)[N] Boca Raton, FL.
Johnson, Robert E. '76 (STP) Bloomington, MN Nativity of the Blessed Virgin Mary.
Johnson, Robert K. '90 (WOR) Worcester, MA St. Paul's Cathedral.
Johnson, Robert '51 (DAL) Retired.
Johnson, Robert (WOR) Diocesan Building Commission Members; Office for Worship.
Johnson, Stephen D. '72 (WOR) Athol, MA Our Lady Immaculate; Athol, MA St. Francis; Petersham, MA St. Peter.
Johnson, Terrence M. '94 (CHI) La Grange, IL St. Francis Xavier.
Johnson, Thomas (DET) Archdiocesan Vicars.
Johnson, Tim A. '93 (SC) Remsen, IA St. Mary's.
Johnson, Timothy K. '71 (OAK) Oakland, CA St. Leo's.
Johnson, Timothy *o.carm.* '83 (PMB) Boca Raton, FL St. Jude; Presbyteral Council.
Johnson, Timothy '01 (FAR) Oriska, ND St. Bernard.
Johnson, W. Robert '51 (FWT)[H] Crowley, TX St. Francis Village, Inc. Retired.
Johnson, Walter W. '53 (SJ)[M] Los Altos, CA Maryknoll.
Johnson, William J. '50 (CLV) Retired.
Johnson, William T. *s.j.* '91 (MIL)[O] Milwaukee, WI Miguel Pro Jesuit Community; [G] Milwaukee, WI Nativity Jesuit Middle School, Inc..
Johnson, William '83 (OAK) Pittsburg, CA St. Peter Martyr of Verona; Concord, CA Mount Diablo Hospital, Director of Pastoral Care; Kaiser–Permanente Medical Center; Martinez, CA Contra Costa Regional Medical Center and VA Administrative Skilled Nursing Center.
Johnston, Donald '55 (NY) New York, NY Our Lady Queen of Martyrs.
Johnston, German Bartolome Vasquez *o.s.b.* '93 (TUC) Sierra Vista, AZ St. Andrew.
Johnston, J. Vann '90 (KNX) Knoxville, TN Cathedral of the Sacred Heart of Jesus; Moderator of the Curia; Chancellor; Presbyteral Council; Archives; Cemeteries; Chancellor; Moderator of the Curia; Propagation of the Faith.
Johnston, John F. '64 (BRK) Released from Diocesan Assignment.
Johnston, Kenneth J. '68 (CAM) Runnemede, NJ St. Teresa of the Infant Jesus.
Johnston, Kenneth (CAM) Continuing Education & Spiritual Formation of Priests (CESF); Vocation Advisory Board.
Johnston, Michael O. '70 (NSH) Nashville, TN St. Henry.
Johnston, Michael P. '91 (P) Portland, OR St. Thomas More.
Johnston, Michael (P) Personnel Board; Judges.
Johnston, Paul '03 (CC)[G] Robstown, TX Society of Our Lady of the Most Holy Trinity.
Johnston, Richard A. *s.c.j.* '58 (GAL) Wallis, TX Guardian Angel.
Johnston, Robert F. '71 (SAT) Retired.
Johnston, Thomas J. *o.p.* '96 (CHI)[N] St. Pius V Priory.
Joji, Kunduru *s.j.* (KCK) Horton, KS St. Leo's; Purcell, KS St. Mary's.
Jolley, Edward W. '38 (BRK)[V] Douglaston, NY Bishop Mugavero Residence Retired.
Joly, Henry L. '58 (ALT) Retired.
Joly, Michael D. '94 (PAT) Clifton, NJ Sacred Heart.
Joly, Philip '01 (VEN) Bradenton, FL SS. Peter and Paul the Apostles.
Jonas, Larry *s.j.* '59 (MIL) Milwaukee, WI Gesu Parish.
Joncas, Jan Michael '69 (STP)[C] St. Paul, MN University of St. Thomas.
Jonczyk, Dariusz G. '97 (PRO) West Warwick, RI SS. John and James Parish.
Jones, Augustine *o.s.b.* '53 (RCK)[G] Aurora, IL Marmion Abbey.

Jones, C. Gregory *c.s.v.* (COL)[B] Columbus, OH Ohio Dominican University.
Jones, Carleton Parker *o.p.* '87 (NY)[EE] New York, NY St. Vincent Ferrer Priory.
Jones, Charles F. '63 (KC) Retired.
Jones, Charles '45 (DEN) Retired.
Jones, Clarence Edward *c.o.* '94 (CHR)[E] Rock Hill, SC Oratory of St. Philip Neri, Congregation of the Oratory of Pontifical Rite.
Jones, Clarence Edward *c.o.* '94 (SEA)[L] Seattle, WA Seattle Oratory.
Jones, Clarence *c.o.* '94 (SEA) Federal Way, WA St. Vincent De Paul.
Jones, Daniel J. '97 (DET) Graduate Studies.
Jones, David A. '89 (CHI) Chicago, IL St. Ambrose; [A] Chicago, IL Archbishop Quigley Preparatory Seminary; Deans; Members; Archbishop Quigley Preparatory Seminary.
Jones, David J. *m.m.* '62 (NY)[EE] Maryknoll Maryknoll Fathers and Brothers.
Jones, Donald R. '86 (PIT) Retired.
Jones, Dunstan *o.f.m.cap.* '61 (FgM).
Jones, Edward T. '03 (PT) Tallahassee, FL Blessed Sacrament.
Jones, Frank W. '67 (GAL) Magnolia, TX St. Matthias the Apostle.
Jones, Herbert J. *o.carm.* '60 (BO)[O] Peabody, MA Catholic Information Center; [AA] Peabody, MA St. Theresa Carmelite Chapel.
Jones, Herbert *o.f.m.* '77 (SAT) San Antonio, TX San Jose y San Miguel; [B] San Antonio, TX Franciscan Formation Program in San Jose Friary (Casa Juan Diego).
Jones, J. Overton '64 (CAM) Retired.
Jones, James R. '51 (R) New Bern, NC St. Paul.
Jones, James W. '69 (COL) Columbus, OH Christ the King Retired.
Jones, James W. *o.f.m.cap.* '77 (NY)[EE] White Plains St. Conrad Friary; Army Chaplains.
Jones, James '57 (R) Retired.
Jones, James *o.f.m.* '76 (SP)[O] St. Petersburg St. Anthony Friary.
Jones, Jim *o.f.m.* '76 (SP)[K] St. Petersburg, FL St. Anthony's Hospital, Inc..
Jones, John B. '48 (GAL) Retired.
Jones, John E. '59 (L) Retired.
Jones, John L. '45 (ALB) Albany, NY St. Teresa of Avila Retired.
Jones, Joseph *c.p.* '65 (MET)[H] South River Passionist Provincial Office; (FgM).
Jones, Kenneth '69 (NEW) Plainfield, NJ St. Mary.
Jones, Kevin C. '90 (MET) On Duty Outside the Diocese.
Jones, Mark R. '92 (MIL) West Bend, WI Immaculate Conception; Kewaskum, WI Holy Trinity.
Jones, Martin '94 (NOR) Middletown, CT St. Francis; St. Francis of Assisi Church – Spanish Apostolate.
Jones, Michael K. '92 (BGP) Graduate Studies.
Jones, Michael P. *o.f.m.* '01 (HRT) Hartford, CT St. Patrick–St. Anthony.
Jones, Michael T. '85 (WDC)[E] Wheaton, MD Good Counsel High School; Washington, DC St. Benedict the Moor; Air Force Reserve Chaplains.
Jones, Neil G. *m.s.* '72 (ATL) Canton, GA Our Lady of LaSalette.
Jones, Ralph '03 (CC)[G] Robstown, TX Society of Our Lady of the Most Holy Trinity.
Jones, Ralph *s.o.l.t.* (FAR) Belcourt, ND St. Ann.
Jones, Raymond N. '59 (DEN) Denver, CO Mother of God; Vicars General; College of Consultors.
Jones, Raymond *s.v.d.* '67 (LAF) Opelousas, LA Holy Ghost; Port Barre, LA St. Mary; On Special Assignment.
Jones, Richard S. '88 (PIT) Coraopolis, PA St. Malachy.
Jones, Richard T. *s.j.* '46 (RC) St. Francis, SD Rosebud Reservation.
Jones, Rick L. '90 (SPC) Leave of Absence.
Jones, Robert J. *c.m.* '69 (LA) Los Angeles, CA St. Camillus De Lellis; Los Angeles, CA Norris Cancer and USC University Hospital; [Q] Montebello, CA DePaul Evangelization Center; [W] Montebello, CA DePaul Evangelization Center.
Jones, Robert M. '68 (BO)[X] Duxbury, MA Miramar Retreat Center.
Jones, Robert S. '60 (SY) Special Assignment.
Jones, Robert W. '92 (RCK) Dixon, IL St. Patrick.
Jones, Robert *s.v.d.* '68 (BO)[V] Duxbury, MA Society of the Divine Word.
Jones, Thomas J. *c.s.c.* '72 (FTW) South Bend, IN Christ the King.
Jones, Thomas *o.f.m.* '59 (NY) Narrowsburg, NY St. Francis Xavier.
Jones, Tom *c.s.p.* '82 (LA) Los Angeles, CA St. Paul the Apostle.
Jones, Tony '89 (OWN) Mayfield, KY St. Joseph.
Jones, W. Thomas *s.m.* '47 (WDC)[M] Sublimity, OR Marian Estates Retired.
Jones, W. Paul (JC) Hermitage, MO St. Bernadette; Senators.
Jones, William E. '60 (ALN) Retired.
Jones, William H. '47 (DEN) Retired.
Jones, William P. '69 (ALN)[J] Bethlehem, PA Holy Family Villa Retired.
Jones, William R. '67 (SY) Syracuse, NY Our Lady of Solace; Priests' Personnel Committee; Syracuse, NY St. Therese the Little Flower of Jesus.
Jong, Lyndon (JC) Mexico, MO St. Brendan.
Jong–A–Kiem, Paschal '02 (OM) Omaha, NE St. Bernadette.
Jonientz, Bernard '63 (SEA) Retired.
Jordan, Brian *o.f.m.* '85 (NY) New York, NY St. Francis of Assisi.
Jordan, Collins P. '85 (RC) Retired.
Jordan, Daniel J. '99 (BUR) Auditors; Defenders of the Bond; Notaries; Burlington, VT St. Mark's.
Jordan, Edward '62 (AUS) Austin, TX St. John Neumann; Presbyteral Council.
Jordan, Francis G. '60 (DOD) Ingalls, KS St. Stanislaus Retired.
Jordan, Francis W. '50 (MIL) Retired.
Jordan, Harold F. '49 (STA) St. Augustine, FL Cathedral – Basilica of St. Augustine; Charismatic Renewal Retired.
Jordan, Harold '54 (STA)[K] St. Augustine, FL Nombre de Dios House of Prayer.
Jordan, Harry J. '61 (CAM)[M] Cherry Hill, NJ Sacred Heart Residences; Members; Sacred Heart Residences; [M] Cherry Hill, NJ Neumann House; [M] Cherry Hill, NJ Vianney Villa Retired.
Jordan, Jesus *m.ss.c.* '94 (SJN) Bayamon, PR Santiago Apostol.
Jordan, John J. '69 (SCR) On Duty Outside the Diocese.
Jordan, John M. '83 (PIT) Midland, PA St. Blaise.
Jordan, Joseph A. *o.s.a.* '58 (PH)[AA] Villanova, PA St. Thomas Monastery.
Jordan, Lawrence *s.m.* '34 (SAT)[K] San Antonio, TX Marianist Residence: Skilled Nursing.
Jordan, Maryon *o.s.b.* '79 (LC)[H] La Crosse, WI Holy Cross (Seminary) Diocesan Center.
Jordan, Michael *s.o.l.t.* '83 (CC)[G] Robstown, TX Society of Our Lady of the Most Holy Trinity.
Jordan, Michael *s.o.l.t.* (SFE) Mora, NM St. Gertrude.
Jordan, Milton E. (PH) Huntingtown, MD Jesus the Divine Word Parish.
Jordan, Phelim *s.v.d.* '81 (WDC) Washington, DC Providence Hospital; [K] Washington, DC Providence Hospital; [M] Washington, DC Divine Word College; [M] Washington, DC Divine Word College.
Jordan, Regis *o.c.d.* '64 (WDC)[B] Washington, DC Discalced Carmelite Friars; [V] Washington, DC Spiritual Life.
Jordan, Salvador *s.j.* '77 (WDC) Port Tobacco, MD St. Ignatius.
Jordan, Thomas *o.carm.* '70 (JOL)[L] Darien Carmelite Provincial Office; (FgM).
Jorden, James A. '83 (PT) Retired.
Joseph, Benedict *o.p.* '49 (COL)[I] Columbus, OH Mohun Health Care Center.
Joseph, Dominic '93 (SJ) San Jose, CA St. Frances Cabrini.
Joseph, Dominic '93 (SYM) San Jose, CA Knanaya Catholic Community of Northern California.
Joseph, Eappen '77 (LKC) Jennings, LA St. Lawrence.
Joseph, Francis A. *o.c.d.* '79 (STO) Modesto, CA St. Joseph Church of Modesto (Pastor of).
Joseph, George Kallarackal *m.c.b.s.* '81 (MAR) Ewen, MI Sacred Heart; Watersmeet, MI Immaculate Conception; Watersmeet, MI Lac Vieux Desert Reservation.
Joseph, George '94 (NEW) Belleville, NJ Clara Maass Medical Center; Chaplains.
Joseph, George '99 (AUS) Pflugerville, TX St. Elizabeth.
Joseph, Jacob *c.m.i.* '83 (NY) Irvington–on–the–Hudson, NY Immaculate Conception.
Joseph, Jean Ronald (VEN) Ministry to Haitian People in Manatee and Sarasota Counties.
Joseph, Mathew '81 (MEM) Memphis, TN St. Louis.
Joseph, Milam J. '64 (DAL)[B] University of Dallas; Irving, TX Church of the Incarnation.
Joseph, Pierre–Louis '86 (MIA) Miami, FL St. Mary's Cathedral.
Joseph, Ronald J. '93 (VEN) Bradenton, FL St. Joseph.
Joseph, Saju Puthenpurackal '71 (WH) West Union, WV St. Patrick's; Salem, WV Sacred Heart.
Joseph, Saju '94 (SJ) San Jose, CA St. Julie Billiart.
Joseph, Simon '76 (BRK) Brooklyn, NY Sacred Hearts of Jesus and Mary and St. Stephen.
Joseph, Varkey V. *s.a.c.* '79 (LC) Elmwood, WI Sacred Heart; Spring Valley, WI Sacred Heart of Jesus.
Joseph, Vincent Elhanikatt '84 (WH) Hinton, WV Sacred Heart; Hinton, WV St. Patrick.
Joseph, William T. '66 (PH) Retired.
Joseph, William '62 (PT) Retired.
Joslin, James R. '74 (ALB) Special Assignment.
Joslyn, James W. '73 (CHI) Military Chaplains; Navy Chaplains.
Josoma, Stephen S. (BO) Dedham, MA St. Susanna.
Joson, Rolando (CHK) Presbyteral Council.
Jost, Al *o.f.m* '80 (IND) Indianapolis, IN Sacred Heart of Jesus; Indianapolis, IN St. Patrick.
Jost, C. Thomas *s.j.* '68 (DEN) Denver, CO St. Ignatius Loyola; [N] Denver, CO Loyola Parish – Jesuit Community.
Jost, Edward F. '96 (BUF) West Seneca, NY Fourteen Holy Helpers.
Josten, Paul '87 (SFS) Platte, SD St. Peter the Apostle.
Jovanovic, Robert P. '61 (STL) Oakville, MO Queen of All Saints.
Jowdy, Albert W. '84 (ATL) Lawrenceville, GA St. Lawrence; Judges.
Joy, James B. '61 (WDC) Retired.
Joy, Laurence '60 (LA) Foreign Mission.
Joy, William F. (BO) Campaign for Human Development.
Joy, William P. (BO) Mattapan, MA St. Angela Merici; Hyde Park, MA St. Joseph; Dorchester, MA St. Matthew; Social Justice.
Joyce, Brian T. '63 (OAK) Pleasant Hill, CA Christ the King.
Joyce, Brian (OAK) Deans.
Joyce, Daniel R.J. *s.j.* '01 (WH)[A] Wheeling, WV Wheeling Jesuit University.
Joyce, David J. '68 (SPR) Springfield, MA Our Lady of Hope; Bishop's Commission for Clergy; Diocesan Consultors; Presbyteral Council; Co–Vicars For Clergy.
Joyce, David (SPR) Vicars for the Clergy.
Joyce, Donald J. *o.m.i.* '58 (SAT)[C] Oblate School of Theology.
Joyce, Edmund P. *c.s.c.* '49 (FTW)[I] Notre Dame, IN Holy Cross House.
Joyce, Edward *c.pp.s.* '56 (CIN)[M] Laguna Niguel, CA.
Joyce, Edwin '58 (JOL) Absent on Sick Leave.
Joyce, George V. '43 (WDC) Retired.
Joyce, Gerald P. '61 (CHI) Westchester, IL Divine Infant.
Joyce, James F. *s.j.* '75 (BUF) Buffalo, NY St. Ann.
Joyce, James K. '72 (SPR) Pittsfield, MA Sacred Heart.
Joyce, James M. (SFS) Worldwide Marriage Encounter.
Joyce, James '48 (SFS) Retired.
Joyce, James (SPR) Priests Committee.
Joyce, John J. '89 (BEL) Evansville, IL St. Boniface; Walsh, IL St. Pius.
Joyce, John M. '54 (ORG) Retired.
Joyce, John Paul '01 (OM) Omaha, NE St. Philip Neri.
Joyce, Kevin P. (SJ) Deans.
Joyce, Kevin '80 (SJ) San Jose, CA St. Maria Goretti; Presentation Center.
Joyce, Michael S. *o.f.m.* '67 (PRO)[N] Providence, RI St. Francis Chapel & City Ministry Center; [P] Providence, RI St. Francis Friary.
Joyce, Michael '63 (OAK) Retired.
Joyce, Michael *o.f.m.cap.* '84 (BAL)[S] Baltimore, MD St. Ambrose Friary.
Joyce, Michael *o.f.m.cap.* '84 (CLV)[O] Cleveland, OH St. Paul Friary.
Joyce, Michael *c.m.* (STL) Archdiocesan Council of Priests.
Joyce, Peter M. '92 (CAM)[M] Blackwood, NJ Bishop's Residence; Vice Chancellor; Adjutant Judicial Vicars; Priests Personnel Board; [V] Camden, NJ Padre Pio Shrine, Buena Borough, N.J., Inc.; [V] Camden, NJ Diocese of Camden Historic Preservation Corporation.
Joyce, Peter '83 (WOR) Southbridge, MA St. Mary's; St. Mary.
Joyce, Randal *c.p.* '50 (DET)[K] Detroit, MI St. Paul of the Cross Community, Congregation of the Passion.
Joyce, Raymond (WCH)[D] Wichita, KS Via Christi Regional Medical Center, Inc..
Joyce, Thomas J. '91 (NY) White Plains, NY St. John the Evangelist.
Joyce, Thomas *c.p.* '69 (BRK) Jamaica, NY Immaculate Conception; [V] Jamaica, NY Immaculate Conception Monastery.
Joyce, Thomas *c.m.f.* (CHI) Chicago, IL Holy Cross/ Immaculate Heart of Mary.
Joyce, Timothy J. '59 (BO)[V] Hingham, MA Glastonbury Abbey.
Joyce, William F. '60 (BO) Readville, MA St. Anne.
Joynes, Joseph P. '64 (CAM) Magnolia, NJ St. Gregory's.
Jozefiak, Gregory '92 (PEO) Oglesby, IL Holy Family.
Jozefiak, Matthew W. *c.pp.s.* '87 (CIN) Burkettsville, OH St. Bernard; Fort Recovery, OH St. Wendelin; Fort Recovery, OH St. Paul.
Jozwiak, Lawrence '87 (GAL) On Special or Other Diocesan Assignment.
Jozwiak, Lawrence (GAL) Tribunal Judicial.
Jozwiak, Richard E. (SAG).
Jozwiak, Richard M. '48 (CHI) Retired.
Jozwiak, Richard '59 (SAG) Retired.
Jozwiak, Ronald J. '79 (DET) Troy, MI St. Elizabeth Ann Seton; Judges.
Juan, Dennis R. '98 (ATL) Douglasville, GA St. Theresa.
Juan, Marcial '66 (LA) Panorama City, CA St. Genevieve.
Juan, Vincent '03 (SAC) Roseville, CA St. Clare.
Juantorena, Raphael (BR) Hispanic Apostolate.
Juarez, Hernan (BAL) Baltimore, MD St. Patrick.
Juarez, Jaime Molina *m.n.m.* '88 (ATL) Smyrna, GA St. Thomas the Apostle.

Juarez, Lawrence '75 (CIN) Cincinnati, OH Old St. Mary.
Juarez, Lucio '91 (LA) Gardena, CA St. Anthony of Padua.
Juarez, Rene *o.f.m.* '69 (SJ) San Jose, CA Our Lady of Guadalupe.
Juarez, Robert '80 (LA) Vocations.
Juarez, Rudolph T. '80 (DAV) Davenport, IA St. Mary's; Judges; Vicar for Hispanics.
Juarez, Rudolph (DAV) Diocesan Consultors.
Juarez, Thomas *s.d.b.* '66 (LAR) Laredo, TX San Luis Rey.
Juchcinski, Clarence J. '48 (CHI) Harvey, IL St. John the Baptist Retired.
Juchniewicz, Leon '80 (SAC) Vallejo, CA St. Basil; [M] Marysville, CA Grand Council, Catholic Ladies Relief Society of the Diocese of Sacramento; Vicars Forane.
Juchnowski, Francis B. '56 (BUF) Holy Name Society; Buffalo, NY St. Bernard Retired.
Judd, Stephen P. *m.m.* '78 (FgM).
Judd, Timothy '56 (LUB) Retired.
Jude, Robert J. '49 (STP) Retired.
Jude, Walter F. '45 (GR) Retired.
Judge, Anthony *c.ss.r.* '79 (DOD)[F] Liberal, KS Liberal Redemptorist Hispanic House Ministry, Inc..
Judge, James G. '72 (BUF) North Collins, NY Holy Spirit.
Judge, John G. '69 (NEW) Upper Montclair, NJ St. Cassian.
Judge, Philip G. *s.j.* '93 (ROC)[B] Rochester, NY McQuaid Jesuit High School.
Judge, Robert K. *s.j.* '65 (BAL) Martinsburg, WV St. Joseph's.
Judge, Russell R. '78 (JC) Vandalia, MO Sacred Heart; Vandalia, MO Women's Eastern Missouri Reception, Diagnostic and Correctional Center.
Judge, Timothy M. '79 (PH)[U] Meadowbrook, PA Holy Redeemer Hospital and Medical Center; [BB] Huntingdon Valley, PA Sisters of the Holy Redeemer Provincialate; Navy Reserve Chaplains.
Judge, Tony *c.ss.r.* (DOD) Office of Hispanic Ministry; Coordinators, Spanish.
Judie, John T. '87 (L) Louisville, KY Mother of Good Counsel.
Judy, Albert P. *o.p.* '62 (CHI) River Forest, IL St. Vincent Ferrer.
Judy, Edward *o.f.m.cap.* '68 (DEN).
Judy, Myron *o.carm.* '63 (JOL)[L] Darien Carmelite Provincial Office.
Juelfs, Daniel '73 (RC) New Underwood, SD St. John the Evangelist.
Juelfs, Daniel (RC) Officialis; Diocesan Consultors.
Juelfs, Daniel (RC) Vicar General.
Juenker, Paul R. '45 (BUF) Clergy Personnel Board; [O] Tonawanda, NY O'Hara Residence Retired.
Juergens, William H. *o.s.f.s.* '57 (WIL)[J] Wilmington, DE DeSales House.
Juettner, Mark R. '79 (STP) Crystal, MN St. Raphael.
Jugan, Joseph J. (PBR) Protopresbyters.
Jugan, Joseph '58 (PBR) Canonsburg, PA St. Michael.
Jugenheimer, James R. '87 (PH) Cato, WI Immaculate Conception; Whitelaw, WI St. Michael; On Duty Outside the Archdiocese.
Jugenheimer, James (GB) Appointed Representatives.
Juhas, John S. '75 (CLV) Brooklyn, OH St. Thomas More.
Juhasz, Ladislaus F. *s.j.* '54 (BUF)[O] Buffalo, NY Canisius Jesuit Community.
Juhl, Dennis D. '73 (DUB) Waterloo, IA Blessed Sacrament; Waterloo, IA St. Mary of Mt. Carmel; Waterloo, IA Sacred Heart; Waterloo, IA Immaculate Conception; Deans; Church Design/Renovation Commission; Lay Formation Advisory Board.
Juknialis, Joseph J. '69 (MIL)[A] St. Francis, WI Saint Francis Seminary; [A] Milwaukee, WI College Formation Program; Milwaukee, WI SS. Peter and Paul; College Program.
Juleen, Stuart '77 (SAT) San Antonio, TX St. John, The Evangelist; Priests Personnel Board.
Julian, Mario F. *o.f.m.* '81 (HRT) New Milford, CT St. Francis Xavier.
Julien, Jean Ridly '96 (BGP)[X] Stamford, CT Haitian American Catholic Center of Greater Stamford; Haitian American Catholic Center of Greater Stamford.
Julien, Roland M. '65 (STA) Gainesville, FL St. Patrick's; [K] Gainesville, FL Spirit Radio of North Florida, Inc.; Presbyteral Council; Deans.
Julius, James A. '65 (STL) Retired.
Julius, Joseph W. '45 (NSH) Townsend, TN St. Francis of Assisi Retired.
Julius, Joseph W. '45 (KNX) Townsend, TN St. Francis of Assisi.
Junak, Jacek *c.r.* '95 (CHI) Chicago, IL St. Hyacinth Basilica.
Jung, Dennet *o.f.m.* '63 (CIN)[I] Cedar Lake, IN San Damiano Friary.
Jung, Dominic *c.pp.s.* '95 (BUF) Tonawanda, NY St. Andrew Kim.
Jung, Dominic *c.pp.s.* '95 (ROC) Rochester, NY St. Anne.
Jung, Eugene *m.s.c.* '50 (ALN)[K] Reading, PA Missionaries of the Sacred Heart.
Jung, Jay *c.m.* '77 (COS) Leadville, CO Catholic Community of Leadville, Annunciation (1879) & St. Joseph (1899); Diocesan Consultors; Western Region.
Jung, Jerome L. '93 (CHI)[R] San Francisco, CA Prelature of the Holy Cross and Opus Dei.
Jung, Joseph B. '56 (PH) Retired.
Jung, Michael *o.s.b.* '63 (BR) Baton Rouge, LA Sacred Heart of Jesus; Baton Rouge, LA Baton Rouge General Medical Center.
Jung, Michael *o.s.b.* '63 (NO)[P] St. Benedict, LA St. Joseph Abbey.
Jung, Paul Young Hoon (ALB) Korean Catholic Apostolate.
Jung, Tae Woo '95 (PIT) Pittsburgh, PA St. John Vianney.
Jung–Nam, Lee "Luke" (ORL) Korean.
Jung–Nam, Luke (ORL) Orlando, FL St. Ignatius Kim Korean Mission.
Junge, Heiko '96 (P) Bandon, OR Holy Trinity; Area Vicars.
Jungmann, William '03 (DEN) Denver, CO Notre Dame.
Jungwirth, Alphonse *c.pp.s.* '43 (CIN)[B] Carthagena, OH St. Charles.
Junio, Jover *m.s.* '86 (HON) Waipahu, HI St. Joseph; Filipino Ministry; Filipino Catholic Clubs, Diocesan Congress of.
Junius, Richard *o.m.i.* '56 (FgM).
Jupin, Alan D. '62 (ALB) Leave of Absence.
Juracek, Joseph *o.f.m.* '83 (NY) New York, NY St. Francis of Assisi.
Juran, Michael P. '76 (BUF) Fillmore, NY St. Patrick; Belfast, NY St. Patrick.
Juras, Callistus *o.f.m.conv.* '54 (BAL)[S] Timonium, MD Stella Maris Retired.
Jurcak, Lawrence (CLV) Cleveland, OH Cathedral of St. John the Evangelist; Presbyteral Council; Adjutant Judicial Vicars; Clergy Personnel Board; Senior Priests.
Jurek, Daniel J. '73 (BEL) Mount Vernon, IL St. Mary; Radom, IL St. Michael.
Jurek, Daniel '73 (BEL) Scheller, IL St. Barbara.
Jurewicz, Francis Z. '59 (PIT) Richeyville, PA St. Agnes.
Jurgelonis, Joseph J. '73 (WOR) Ashburnham, MA St. Denis; Ashburnham, MA St. Anne.
Jurgensmeier, Charles L. *s.j.* '88 (OM) Papillion, NE St. Columbkille; [K] Omaha, NE Jesuit Community at Creighton University.
Juric, Ante *o.f.m.* '72 (SJ) San Jose, CA St. Mary of the Assumption.
Jurich, James P. *s.j.* '67 (NY)[EE] New York, NY Murray–Weigel Hall.
Jurisich, Melvin A. *o.f.m.* '70 (OAK)[N] Berkeley, CA Franciscan Friars; [N] Oakland, CA Franciscan Friars Provincial Office, Province of St. Barbara.
Jurkiewicz Benedict '83 (STA)[J] Bunnell, FL Discalced Carmelite Fathers of Florida.
Jurkowski, Joseph V. '58 (CAM) Atlantic City, NJ St. Nicholas of Tolentine.
Jurkus, Alan F. '70 (MIL) Whitefish Bay, WI St. Monica.
Jurzyk, Marek '91 (CHI) Chicago, IL St. Ferdinand.
Jusino Flores, Luis (PCE) Adjuntas, PR St. Joachim.
Jusseaume, John E. '46 (BO) Senior Priests Retired.
Just, Feliz *s.j.* '91 (LA)[C] Los Angeles, CA Jesuit Community.
Just, Marcos *c.ss.r.* (NEW) Newark, NJ St. James.
Justen, Bernard *s.d.b.* '48 (SP)[E] Tampa, FL Mary Help of Christians School.
Justi, Marvin L. *o.f.m.cap.* '58 (PIT).
Justi, Marvin (PIT) Va Medical Center Butler.
Justice, William J. '68 (SFR) San Francisco, CA Mission Dolores Basilica.
Justiniano, Benny (SB) Alta Loma, CA St. Peter & St. Paul.
Juszczak, Walter *c.ss.r.* '88 (CHI) Cicero, IL St. Mary of Czestochowa.
Jutt, Anthony J. '51 (SPR) Housatonic, MA Corpus Christi; Housatonic, MA All Saints.
Jutte, Edgar *c.pp.s.* '62 (CIN)[M] Iglesia Del Sagrado Corazon de Jesus.
Jutton, David J. '66 (SY) Retired.
Juya, Filemon '81 (CHR) Batesburg–Leesville, SC St. John of the Cross; Vicar for Hispanic Ministry.
Juya, Filemon '81 (CHR) Special Assignment.
Juza, Philip J. '95 (SUP) Gilman, WI SS. Peter and Paul; Gilman, WI St. Michael; Gilman, WI St. Stanislaus; Gilman, WI St. John the Apostle; Catholic Women, Council of.
Juzix, Richard *o.f.m.* '74 (FRS) Santa Barbara, CA Old Mission Santa Barbara.
Juzix, Richard '75 (FRS)[Q] Santa Barbara, CA Franciscan Friary, Order of Friars Minor (Old Mission).

K

Kaack, John H. *s.j.* '74 (NO)[P] New Orleans, LA Ignatius Residence.
Kabali, Joseph '86 (NEW) Newark, NJ St. Patrick's Pro–Cathedral.
Kabarega, Gerard (ROC) Horseheads, NY St. Mary Our Mother.
Kabari, Joseph (CHI) Evanston, IL St. Nicholas.
Kabat, Daniel *o.f.m.cap.* '60 (LA) Solvang, CA Old Mission Santa Ines.
Kabat, Robert J. '79 (GB) Greenleaf, WI St. Mary; Wrightstown, WI St. Paul; Judicial Vicar; Judges in First Instance; Judges in Second Instance; Conciliation and Arbitration Board.
Kaberia, Joseph '83 (STL) St. Louis, MO St. Pius the Fifth.
Kaberia, Silvio '83 (RIC) Clarksville, VA St. Catherine of Siena; South Hill, VA Good Shepherd.
Kabipi, Narcis '98 (OAK) Castro Valley, CA Transfiguration.
Kabot, Damian *s.v.d.* '02 (OAK) Oakland, CA St. Bernard's.
Kabuk, Clement '84 (STP) Forest Lake, MN St. Peter.
Kacena, Edward T. (LFT) Clergy Relief Association.
Kacena, T. Edward '97 (LFT) Muncie, IN St. Mary.
Kacergius, Edward S. '82 (ALB)[Q] Troy, NY University Parish of Christ Sun of Justice.
Kacerguis, Edward S. '82 (ALB) Special Assignment.
Kacerguis, Edward '82 (ALB)[Q] Troy, NY Rensselaer Polytechnic Institute.
Kachel, C. Leon '57 (PRO)[K] Providence, RI St. Joseph Health Services of Rhode Island – St. Joseph Hospital for Specialty Care.
Kachel, Steven J. '95 (LC) Tomah, WI St. Mary (Immaculate Conception); Warrens, WI St. Andrew; Deans; St. Joseph's Priest Fund, Inc., (Benevolent Society).
Kachmar, Walter '43 (SJP) Retired.
Kachuba, John S. '74 (PRM) Euclid, OH St. Stephen.
Kachuba, John (PRM) Protosyncellus; Presbyteral Council; Eparchial Pastoral Council; Eparchial Finance Officer; Eparchial Consultors; Office of Religious Education; Seminary Education Formation Board; Priest's Pension Board.
Kachur, Oleh '03 (SJP) On Assignment Outside the Diocese.
Kachurka, Edward M. '89 (BRK) Brooklyn, NY St. Mark's.
KacirkMontague, Raymond J. *s.m.* '59 (STL)[O] Dearborn Heights, MI.
Kacprowicz, Joseph A. '36 (E) Retired.
Kacprzak, Stanley '85 (ROC) Webster, NY St. Paul.
Kaczkowski, Conrad J. *s.m.* '68 (SAT)[C] San Antonio, TX St. Mary's University of San Antonio, Texas; [M] San Antonio, TX Chaminade Community House.
Kaczmarczyk, Pawel '03 (DET) Clawson, MI Guardian Angels.
Kaczmarek, James A. '69 (MAR) Iron Mountain, MI Immaculate Conception of the Blessed Virgin Mary; Deans.
Kaczmarek, Peter '69 (RVC) Bayville, NY St. Gertrude's.
Kaczmarek, Thaddeus J. '71 (GBG) North Huntingdon, PA St. Agnes; Finance Council.
Kaczorowski, Edward J. '58 (WIL) Wilmington, DE St. Stanislaus Kostka.
Kaczorowski, James T. '73 (CHI) Chicago, IL Our Lady of Lourdes; Vicar for Priests.
Kaczorowski, James (CHI) Commission on the Mission and Life of the Diocesan Priest.
Kaczowka, Julian *s.ch.* (CHI) Chicago, IL Five Holy Martyrs.
Kaczynski, Krzysztof '93 (MET) Clinton, NJ Immaculate Conception.
Kadavil, Antony (MAR)[G] Marquette, MI Catholic Campus Ministry–Northern Michigan University.
Kadavil, Mathew Antony '67 (MAR) Negaunee, MI St. Paul.
Kaddo, Joseph F. '72 (SAM) Fall River, MA St. Anthony of the Desert; [D] Brooklyn, NY Bishop's Residence.
Kadera, Thomas '87 (CHY) Gillette, WY St. Matthew's; Defenders of the Bond; Air Force Reserve Chaplains.
Kadlec, Jared '97 (FAR) Judges; Graduate Studies.
Kadlec, Josef *s.j.* '77 (WDC)[M] Washington, DC The Jesuit Community at Georgetown University.
Kaduppil, Roy Joseph (SYM) Chancellor & Secretary to Bishop; Eparchial Consultors.
Kadylo, Wasyl '03 (STF) Syracuse, NY St. John the Baptist.
Kadzielawski, Edwin J. *c.s.c.* '49 (AUS) Austin, TX Nuestra Senora De Dolores; [G] Austin, TX Steiner Lodge.
Kaeding, Robert F. '73 (TR) Wayside, NJ St. Anselm.
Kaelin, Walter *c.p.* '42 (FgM).
Kaelin, Walter *c.p.* '42 (CHI)[N] Chicago, IL Passionist Missions of India.
Kaelin, Walter *c.p.* '42 (L)[K] Louisville, KY Sacred Heart Retreat.
Kafara, Andrew '85 (SAT) Pearsall, TX Immaculate Heart of Mary.
Kagan, David D. '75 (RCK) Special Assignment; Vicars General; Moderator of the Curia; Judicial Vicar; Diocesan Consultors.
Kagoo, Edwin '80 (AUS) Rockdale, TX St. Joseph's.
Kahan, Paul *s.v.d.* '99 (BEA) Cleveland, TX St. Mary.
Kahle, George G. *c.s.c.* '53 (FTW)[I] Notre Dame, IN

Holy Cross House.
Kahlhamer, Bernard '59 (SCL) Foley, MN St. Lawrence's; Sauk Rapids, MN St. Patrick.
Kahlich, Daniel P. '66 (VIC) Columbus, TX St. Anthony's; Defenders of the Bond.
Kahlich, Daniel P. (SAT) Air Force Reserve Chaplains.
Kahrs, Lee J. (GB) De Pere, WI St. Mary; Defenders of the Bond.
Kahumburu, Joseph '83 (NY) Mamaroneck, NY Holy Trinity.
Kaicher, Bud '80 (SD) Rainbow Work Camp.
Kaicher, Edward '80 (SD) Fallbrook, CA St. Peter.
Kaichiramattathil, Stephen *s.a.c.* '96 (MIL)[O] Milwaukee, WI Pallotti House.
Kail, Michael '74 (OLL) Warren, MI St. Rafka Maronite Mission; Warren, MI St. Sharbel.
Kaim, Phillip '03 (RCK) Rockford, IL St. Peter Cathedral; Air Force Reserve Chaplains.
Kaim, Phillip '03 (RCK) Active Outside the Diocese.
Kaimann, Gerald J. '70 (JC) Marceline, MO St. Bonaventure; Ministry to Priests.
Kain, Peter V. '65 (BRK) Brooklyn, NY St. Ephrem's; Presbyteral Council.
Kairouz, Elie G. '01 (SAM) Troy, NY St. Ann.
Kaiser, Joseph W. '55 (RCK) Richmond, IL St. Joseph.
Kaiser, Lawrence B. '73 (DEN) Fort Morgan, CO St. Helena.
Kaiser, Lawrence H. '64 (DET) Dearborn, MI Sacred Heart.
Kaiser, Ralph L. '54 (KC) Buckner, MO Church of the Santa Fe.
Kaiser, Roman F. '58 (LC) Loyal, WI St. Anthony of Padua.
Kaiser, Thomas J. '49 (SLC) Salt Lake City, UT St. Vincent de Paul; Decker Lake Youth Detention Center Retired.
Kaiss, Paul '02 (WDC)[T] Washington, DC Tenley Study Center.
Kaithackal, Sebastian D. *c.m.i.* '81 (MET) Woodbridge, NJ St. James; Perth Amboy, NJ Raritan Bay Medical Center.
Kaithamatton, Sebastian *c.m.i.* '80 (STA) Palm Coast, FL St. Elizabeth Ann Seton.
Kaitharan, Varghese '86 (LA) Camarillo, CA Blessed Junipero Serra.
Kakalec, Joseph M. *s.j.* '67 (PH)[C] Scranton, PA The University of Scranton.
Kakaniyil, Chacko D. '73 (MAR) Wakefield, MI Immaculate Conception of the Blessed Virgin Mary.
Kakareka, Joseph R. '72 (SCR)[I] Wilkes–Barre, PA Mercy Hospital; Stillwater, PA St. Martha's.
Kakascik, Edward '55 (STU) Marietta, OH St. Mary's; [J] Marietta, OH Marietta College.
Kakaty, Edward G. '72 (NTN) Waterford, CT St. Ann; Ecumenical & Interreligious Commission.
Kakaty, Edward (NTN) National Association of Melkite Women; Liturgical Commission; Vocations Office.
Kalabat, Frank Y. '95 (EST) West Bloomfield, MI St. Thomas Chaldean Catholic Parish.
Kalabat, Frank (EST) Eparchial College of Consultors; Diocesan Corporation–The Chaldean Catholic Church of U.S.A.
Kalafsky, Andrew J. '43 (ROC) Addison, NY St. Stanislaus Retired.
Kalaj, Frederick '01 (DET) White Lake, MI St. Patrick.
Kalamaja, Theodore M. *s.j.* '67 (NO) New Orleans, LA Orleans Parish Correctional Center; [C] New Orleans, LA Loyola University New Orleans.
Kalappura, George *c.m.i.* '60 (BEA) Orange, TX St. Francis of Assisi.
Kalarickal, Lukose *m.s.f.s.* '88 (ATL)[K] Lawrenceville The Missionaries of St. Francis De Sales.
Kalarickal, Thomas *c.m.i.* '55 (NY) White Plains, NY St. John the Evangelist.
Kalariparampil, Joseph '53 (MIA) Fort Lauderdale, FL St. Helen.
Kalas, Ronald N. '59 (CHI) Park Ridge, IL Mary, Seat of Wisdom; Deans Retired.
Kalata, Dominik P. '65 (ALN) Frackville, PA St. Ann; Frackville, PA Annunciation B.V.M..
Kalathiveettil, Francis X. '91 (BIS) Garrison, ND St. Nicholas.
Kalb, Howard E. *s.j.* '54 (OM)[K] Omaha, NE Jesuit Community at Creighton University.
Kalbicki, Timothy *o.f.m.conv.* '86 (BAL).
Kalchik, Paul J. '99 (CHI)[A] In res.; [A] Chicago, IL Archbishop Quigley Preparatory Seminary.
Kalck, Michael V. '74 (CHI) Midlothian, IL St. Christopher.
Kaleikoa, Charles '81 (HON) Leave of Absence.
Kalema, Josephat Kato *o.c.s.o.* '85 (NEW) Newark, NJ St. Rocco's.
Kalema, Mark '88 (CHI) Chicago, IL Immaculate Conception of the Blessed Virgin Mary; [A] Chicago, IL Archbishop Quigley Preparatory Seminary.
Kaler, Adolph K. *o.m.i.* '57 (CC) Sarita, TX Our Lady of Guadalupe.
Kalert, David A. *o.m.i.* '64 (STP)[V] St. Paul, MN Oblate Media and Communication Corporation.
Kalert, David A. *o.m.i.* '64 (WDC)[M] Washington, DC Provincial Offices of the United States Province of the Missionary Oblates of Mary Immaculate; [M] Washington, DC Oblate Community.
Kalert, David *o.m.i.* '64 (FgM).
Kaley, Richard *o.f.m.conv.* '75 (IND) Terre Haute, IN St. Joseph University Parish.
Kalich, Patrick J. '94 (GRY) Crown Point, IN St. Mary.
Kalicky, John E. *c.pp.s.* '61 (GRY) Whiting, IN St. John the Baptist.
Kalil, Gordon '94 (SR) Napa, CA St. John the Baptist; Clergy Personnel Committee.
Kalin, Leonard I. '56 (LIN) Retired.
Kalin, William A. '59 (BAK) Milton Freewater, OR St. Francis of Assisi.
Kalin, William A. '59 (LIN) On Duty Outside the Diocese.
Kalina, Isaac *o.s.b.* '89 (LA)[Q] Valyermo, CA St. Andrew's Abbey.
Kalinowski, Dariusz '99 (FR) Mansfield, MA St. Mary's.
Kalinowski, Loren M. '75 (SAG) Saginaw, MI St. John Vianney.
Kalinowski, Loren (SAG) Diocesan Consultors.
Kalinowski, Ryszard *s.v.d.* '74 (JKS) Jackson, MS Holy Ghost; [I] Jackson, MS Tougaloo College Newman Center.
Kalinowski, Stainslaus J. '45 (SCR) Retired.
Kalinski, Eugene E. '60 (GB)[I] Oshkosh, WI Community of Our Lady.
Kalist, Pancrose '88 (NY) Staten Island, NY St. Ann.
Kalista, Timothy D. '03 (CLV) Parma, OH St. Charles Borromeo.
Kalita, Thomas M. '74 (WDC) Olney, MD St. Peter.
Kalita, Thomas (WDC) Deans.
Kaliyadan, William *m.s.* '94 (FR) Brewster, MA Our Lady of the Cape.
Kalkman, Richard '56 (SCL) Retired.
Kall, Anthony *o.f.m.conv.* '71 (ALB) Albany, NY St. Casimir; Albany, NY Our Lady of Angels; Members.
Kallabat, Stephen H. (EST) Eparchial Tribunal.
Kallabat, Stephen '66 (EST) Oak Park, MI Mar Addai Chaldean Parish; Eparchial College of Consultors.
Kalladan, Joseph K. '69 (GAL) New Waverly, TX St. Joseph.
Kallaher, Timothy S. '72 (CIN) Cincinnati, OH St. John the Baptist; Judges.
Kallampally, George *c.m.f.* '80 (SYM) Baltimore, MD Indian Catholic Society of Baltimore.
Kallampally, George *c.m.f.* '80 (BAL) Baltimore, MD St. Benedict; [M] Baltimore, MD St. Agnes HealthCare, Inc..
Kallarackal, Moses *c.m.i.* (AMA) Amarillo, TX Our Lady of Guadalupe; White Deer, TX Sacred Heart; [A] Amarillo, TX Holy Cross Catholic Academy.
Kallarackal, Sebastian *c.m.i.* '77 (SHP) Monroe, LA Our Lady of Fatima; [G] Monroe, LA Catholic Campus Ministry at the University of Louisiana at Monroe.
Kallock, Michael J. *c.s.p.* '73 (NY)[EE] Jamaica Estates, NY Paulist Fathers Generalate.
Kallookalam, Joseph *c.m.i.* '71 (TYL) Malakoff, TX Mary Queen of Heaven.
Kallukalam, Joseph '72 (CC) Edroy, TX Our Lady of Guadalupe Mission.
Kallumady, Thomas '73 (NY) New York, NY Most Holy Crucifix; New York, NY St. Patrick Old Cathedral.
Kallumkalkudy, George *c.m.i.* '76 (STP) Little Canada, MN St. John the Evangelist.
Kalonga, Simon '84 (DEN) Denver, CO Cure D'Ars.
Kalousieh, George '81 (ARM) Little Falls, NJ Sacred Heart.
Kalscheuer, Henry N. '59 (MAD) Retired.
Kalscheuer, Roger '80 (OM) Omaha, NE St. Frances Cabrini.
Kalscheur, Gregory *s.j.* '01 (MD)[V] Newton, MA The Jesuit Community at Boston College.
Kaltenbach, Victor J. '62 (SFD) Greenville, IL St. Lawrence.
Kaltreider, Carl E. '79 (CHL) On Duty Outside the Diocese; Holly Hill, SC St. Ann; Summerton, SC St. Mary's.
Kalungi, John *a.j.* '89 (NY) Bronx, NY St. Angela Merici.
Kamanda, Joseph '85 (WDC)[B] Washington, DC St. Joseph's Seminary.
Kamas, John *s.s.s.* '75 (CLV) New York, NY St. Andrew; [O] Gretna, LA.
Kamau, Peter James Mwaura '03 (CHY) Cheyenne, WY St. Mary's Cathedral.
Kamber, Kenneth L. '53 (L) Vicar for Retired Clergy Retired.
Kambitsch, Larry '69 (MRY) Salinas, CA Madonna Del Sasso; Diocesan Consultors; Diocesan Consultors; Presbyteral Council; Priest's Personnel Board.
Kamenski, Thomas *o.f.m.* '82 (LAF) On Special Assignment; [F] Lafayette, LA Our Lady of Lourdes Regional Medical Center, Inc..
Kamide, Paul T. '63 (ORL) Port Orange, FL Epiphany.
Kamienski, Luciano *s.d.b.* '66 (LA) Inglewood, CA St. John Chrysostom.
Kamiensky, Joseph J. *s.j.* '77 (BUF)[O] Buffalo, NY Canisius Jesuit Community.
Kamilwa, Dominic '91 (TUC) Nogales, AZ Sacred Heart.
Kaminski, Dariusz '91 (PAT) Passaic, NJ St. Joseph's.
Kaminski, Edward J. *c.s.c.* '75 (PHX) Tempe, AZ Holy Spirit.
Kaminski, Edward J. *c.s.c.* '75 (FTW)[I] Tempe, AZ.
Kaminski, Frank T. *s.j.* '76 (WDC)[P] Faulkner, MD Loyola Retreat House.
Kaminski, Joseph M. '51 (GF) Retired.
Kaminski, Kevin A. '78 (MET) Raritan, NJ St. Joseph.
Kaminski, Ladislaus J. '54 (HRT) Retired.
Kaminski, Louis T. '77 (SCR) Great Bend, PA St. Lawrence's.
Kaminski, Mark P. '01 (SY) Cortland, NY St. Anthony.
Kaminski, Stephen J. '91 (CLV) Medina, OH St. Francis Xavier; North Ridgeville, OH St. Peter.
Kaminski, Thomas J. '66 (CHI) Chicago, IL St. Helena.
Kaminsky, Joseph T. '61 (HRT) North Branford, CT St. Augustine.
Kamla, Jerome J. '42 (LC) Retired.
Kammer, Alfred C. *s.j.* '76 (NO)[C] New Orleans, LA Loyola University New Orleans; [P] New Orleans, LA Jesuit Provincial Office.
Kammerer, James '97 (SAT) On Leave.
Kammerer, Raymond '64 (CIN) Waynesville, OH St. Augustine.
Kammerer, Richard F. '80 (RVC) Babylon, NY St. Joseph's.
Kamp, Francis J. *s.v.d.* '47 (CHI)[B] Techny, IL Divine Word Residence; [X] Techny, IL DWTCRE Charitable Trust.
Kampine, Robert J. (ATL) Auditors; Defenders of the Bond.
Kampschneider, Daniel J. '79 (OM) Omaha, NE St. Philip Neri.
Kampschneider, Daniel (OM) Deans.
Kamtitsch, Larry (MRY) Deans.
Kamugisha, Joseph '69 (SJ) San Jose State University Catholic Campus; [O] San Jose, CA The Newman Community/Catholic Campus Ministry.
Kanai, Charles '94 (CIN) Dayton, OH Holy Family.
Kanar, Richard '94 (PSC) Annandale, VA Epiphany of Our Lord.
Kanat, Joseph Kurian '58 (LAF) Lafayette, LA Cathedral of St. John the Evangelist; On Special Assignment.
Kanda, Francis P. *c.s.sp.* '53 (PRO)[P] Bethel Park, PA Holy Spirit Animation Center.
Kanda, John R. *c.s.sp.* '42 (PIT)[P] Bethel Park, PA Holy Spirit Animation Center.
Kandathikudy, Jos '71 (SYM) Bronx, NY St. Thomas Syro–Malabar Catholic Church; Eparchial Consultors.
Kandathil, Thomas (TYL)[A] Tyler, TX Trinity Mother Frances Health System.
Kandathiparampil, Joseph '63 (WIL) Wilmington, DE St. John the Beloved.
Kandel, Timothy '81 (ORL) On Duty Outside the Diocese.
Kandrac, Antone *o.f.m.conv.* '57 (ALB) Nassau, NY St. Mary; [L] Rensselaer, NY Franciscan Mission House.
Kandt, Gregory '90 (RIC) Charlottesville, VA Church of the Incarnation.
Kandyuk, Valeriy (STN) Sacramento, CA St. Andrew the Apostle.
Kane, Aloysius T. '38 (PH) Retired.
Kane, Brian (LIN) Lincoln, NE St. Thomas Aquinas; [I] Lincoln, NE University of Nebraska, Newman Club; Vocations.
Kane, Cornelius T. *o.p.* '52 (WDC) Washington, DC St. Dominic Church & Priory.
Kane, Edward J. *c.ss.r.* '47 (KC) Kansas City, MO Our Lady of Perpetual Help.
Kane, Edward R. '78 (BRK) Brooklyn, NY Holy Family; Army Reserve Chaplains.
Kane, Eugene '54 (PEO) Retired.
Kane, Farrell J. *o.carm.* '65 (CHI) Gurnee, IL St. Paul the Apostle.
Kane, Farrell *o.carm.* (CHI) Deans.
Kane, George J. '51 (CHI) Retired.
Kane, Herbert T. *s.j.* '52 (NY)[EE] New York, NY Murray–Weigel Hall.
Kane, Ignatius B. *o.s.b.* '61 (BIR)[E] Cullman, AL St. Bernard Abbey.
Kane, James D. '58 (SY)[Q] Binghamton, NY McDevitt Residence for Retired Priests Retired.
Kane, James E. '51 (DEN) Retired.
Kane, James J. '71 (ALB) Schenectady, NY St. Helen; Special Assignment.
Kane, James (ALB) Ecumenical and Interreligious Affairs of the Roman Catholic Diocese of Albany, Commission for.
Kane, John E. *c.m.* '70 (MOB) Opelika, AL St. Mary of the Mission.
Kane, John '69 (SP) Retired.
Kane, Joseph F. '46 (SY)[Q] Syracuse, NY Tommy Coyne Residence @ Dillon Hall Retired.
Kane, Joseph M. '70 (BO) Permanent Disability.
Kane, Joseph P. *s.j.* '68 (NY) George M. Motchan Detention Center; Rose M. Singer Center; [EE] New York, NY Murray–Weigel Hall; [EE] Bronx, NY.

Kane, Joseph T. '62 (PH) Warrington, PA St. Robert Bellarmine.
Kane, Joseph '67 (EVN) Evansville, IN Good Shepherd.
Kane, Michael N. '80 (PSC) Coconut Creek, FL Our Lady of the Sign.
Kane, Michael (PSC) Elected Members.
Kane, Paul '96 (MIA) Pompano Beach, FL St. Elizabeth of Hungary Catholic Church.
Kane, Philip M. '88 (JC) Glasgow, MO St. Mary; Slater, MO St. Joseph; Diocesan Consultors; Senators.
Kane, Terence '68 (ATL) Hartwell, GA Sacred Heart of Jesus.
Kane, Thomas A. '52 (WDC) Rockville, MD St. Patrick; Archdiocesan College of Consultors; Holy Name Society.
Kane, Thomas A. *c.s.p.* '75 (NY)[EE] Jamaica Estates Paulist Fathers Generalate.
Kane, Thomas A. *c.s.p.* '75 (BO)[V] Boston, MA Paulist Fathers Residence.
Kane, Thomas C. *o.p.* '52 (WDC)[C] Catholic University of America, The Retired.
Kane, Thomas S. '67 (RVC) Holbrook, NY Good Shepherd.
Kane, Timothy '82 (DET) Detroit, MI St. Rita.
Kane, Walter J. *s.j.* '68 (BO)[V] Boston, MA Loyola House.
Kane, William J. *s.j.* '48 (STL)[N] St. Louis, MO Fusz Pavilion; [O] St. Louis, MO Jesuit Community Corporation at St. Louis University – Jesuit Hall.
Kane, William J. '60 (WDC) Bethesda, MD Little Flower; Archdiocesan College of Consultors.
Kanfush, Philip M. *o.s.b.* (GBG)[H] Latrobe, PA Saint Vincent Archabbey.
Kang, Chul–Hyun '99 (COS) Colorado Springs, CO St. Andrew Kim Quasi Parish.
Kang, Paul '91 (NY) On Duty Outside the Archdiocese.
Kangley, Bernard *o.carm.* '44 (LA)[Q] Los Angeles, CA Mount Carmel Priory, Carmelite Fathers and Brothers.
Kania, Witold '92 (GAL) Houston, TX St. Vincent de Paul.
Kanicki, Philip A. '85 (RIC) Military Chaplains; Navy Chaplains.
Kanka, Robert '56 (ROC) Hornell, NY St. Ann Retired.
Kanna, Jayanna '93 (SP) Zephyrhills, FL St. Joseph.
Kannampuzha, Joe (TYL) Sulphur Springs, TX St. James.
Kanonik, Stephen F. '82 (CHI) Chicago, IL St. Ladislaus.
Kantanka, Michael '95 (KCK) Topeka, KS Most Pure Heart of Mary.
Kantor, Adolph A. '43 (SY) Retired.
Kantor, Robert Joseph '98 (VEN) Bradenton, FL SS. Peter and Paul the Apostles; Navy Reserve Chaplains.
Kantor, Robert (VEN) Presbyteral Council; Vocations/Seminarian Formation.
Kantz, Robert J. '01 (CAM) Penns Grove, NJ St. James; Statistics and Technology; Advocates.
Kanzic, Gerald B. '92 (PAT) Absent on Leave.
Kao, Paulus '59 (LSC) Bayard, NM Our Lady of Fatima.
Kapa, Benedict E. '00 (WH) Parkersburg, WV St. Margaret Mary; White Sulphur Springs, WV St. Charles Borromeo.
Kapfer, Lee *s.j.* '53 (SEA) Seattle, WA St. Joseph.
Kapinus, Augustine '58 (TR) Seaside Heights, NJ Our Lady of Perpetual Help.
Kapitan, John *o.f.m.* '95 (PRM) Dayton, OH St. Barbara; Indianapolis, IN St. Athanasius Church; Presbyteral Council.
Kapitz, Donald '73 (SFE) Retired.
Kaplan, Jan F. '67 (CHI) Wauconda, IL Transfiguration.
Kappalumakkel, Mathew '89 (HRT) Unassigned.
Kappas, Joseph B. *s.j.* '77 (CLV) Mooresville, NC St. Therese.
Kappe, John H. '71 (GAL) Hitchcock, TX Our Lady of Lourdes.
Kappes, Christiaan Wesley '02 (IND) Batesville, IN St. Louis.
Kappes, Joseph B. *s.j.* '77 (DET)[J] Mooresville, NC Jesuit Community; [K] Temperance, MI.
Kappler, Stephan (OAK) On Leave of Absence.
Kapral, Richard J. '70 (SY) Waterville, NY St. Bernard.
Kapron, Alan '94 (PSC) On Duty Outside Diocese.
Kapron, Alan '94 (PRM) Akron, OH St. Michael the Archangel; Barberton, OH St. Nicholas.
Kapushion, Marvin J. '56 (PBL) Rye, CO St. Aloysius; Judicial Experts; Presbyteral Council.
Kapushion, Marvin (PBL) Presbyteral Council–College of Consultors Retired.
Kapusnak, Joseph '66 (PBR) Leisenring, PA St. Stephen; Revitalization and Renewal Commission.
Karachira, Thomas '90 (WH) Harrisville, WV Christ Our Hope; St. Marys, WV St. John.
Karal, John W. '53 (DUB) Retired.
Karalus, Peter J. '97 (BUF) Collins Center, NY St. Frances Cabrini; North Collins, NY St. Martin.
Karam, Peter '88 (SEA) Seattle, WA St. Matthew.
Karam, Peter '88 (OLL) Seattle, WA St. Joseph Maronite Mission.
Karamitis, Dennis R. *s.j.* '75 (CHI) Chicago, IL St. Adalbert.
Karani, Stephen '93 (ROC) Wayland, NY Holy Family Catholic Community.
Karas, Stephen '65 (Y) Retired.
Karasek, Edward '87 (AUS) West, TX Assumption; Associates
Karaszewski, Piotr *s.a.c.* '98 (BRK) Brooklyn, NY St. Frances de Chantal.
Karava, Norbert *o.f.m.cap.* '80 (PAT)[M] Oak Ridge–Milton, NJ St. Stanislaus B. M. Friary; Navy Chaplains.
Karban, Roger R. '64 (BEL) Renault, IL Our Lady of Good Counsel.
Karcher, Jerome T. '83 (ORG) Huntington Beach, CA St. Vincent de Paul.
Karcher, Jerome (ORG) Council of Priests.
Karcsinski, George M. '63 (BGP) Bridgeport CT Blessed Sacrament.
Karcsinski, Joseph J. '79 (BGP) Monroe, CT St. Jude.
Karcz, Lawrence *o.f.m.* (GB)[I] Pulaski, WI Friary.
Karczewski, Julian A. '74 (CAM) Elmer, NJ St. Ann's; Westville Grove, NJ Most Holy Redeemer; Members.
Kardian, Richard S. *m.m.* '56 (CLV)[O] Cleveland, OH Maryknoll Fathers.
Kardong, Terrence *o.s.b.* '63 (BIS)[A] Richardton, ND Assumption Abbey.
Kardos, Blase B. *o.f.m.conv.* '43 (NY) Staten Island, NY Seaview Hospital and Home; [EE] Staten Island, NY St. Francis Friary.
Kardzis, Christopher '84 (TOL) On Duty Outside the Diocese; Mission of Accompaniment Pastoral Team.
Karegeye, Jean–Pierre *s.j.* '99 (OAK)[N] Berkeley, CA Jesuit Community at Jesuit School of Theology at Berkeley.
Karekatt, Raphael *m.s.f.s.* '86 (ATL)[K] Lawrenceville The Missionaries of St. Francis De Sales.
Karels, Agdus S. (STP) Retired.
Karels, Ambrose G. '59 (KC) Retired.
Karempelis, Daniel *m.s.a.* '87 (NOR) Middletown, CT St. Sebastian; [F] Cromwell, CT Society of the Missionaries of the Holy Apostles.
Karenbauer, Richard P. '70 (GBG) New Kensington, PA St. Mary of Czestochowa.
Karepin, James M. *o.p.* '90 (CHI)[N] Chicago Dominicans (Provincial Office).
Karepin, James *o.p.* '90 (PHU) West Easton, PA Holy Ghost; West Easton, PA St. Nicholas.
Kareta, Gregory *o.f.m. conv.* '56 (MRY)[F] Arroyo Grande, CA St. Joseph Cupertino Friary Retired.
Karg, Andrew H. '64 (E) Greenville, PA St. Michael; [P] Thiel College.
Karg, William C. '57 (E) Oil City, PA St. Stephen.
Karg, William D. '64 (CLV) Akron, OH St. Sebastian.
Kari, Arnold '77 (RC) Sturgis, SD St. Francis of Assisi.
Kariamadam, Jose *c.m.i.* '74 (NSH)[K] Liberty, TN Carmel Center of Spirituality.
Karickal, Kurian *m.s.f.s.* '92 (ATL)[K] Lawrenceville, GA The Missionaries of St. Francis De Sales.
Karieakatt, Paul *o.s.b.* '77 (LUB) Post, TX Holy Cross.
Kariekatt, Paul *o.s.b.* '54 (PAT)[M] Clifton, NJ Holy Face of Jesus Monastery.
Karikattil, Jose '77 (SAC) Carmichael, CA Our Lady of the Assumption.
Karikunnel Joseph (NY) Staten Island, NY St. Clare.
Karimadam, Jose *c.m.i.* '74 (NSH) Pulaski, TN Immaculate Conception.
Karimi, Samuel '93 (BRK) Brooklyn, NY Our Lady of Peace.
Karl, Charles E. '57 (PEO) Retired.
Karl, Edward B. '57 (BGP) Bethel, CT St. Mary.
Karl, Kevin '69 (OWN) Absent on Leave.
Karl, Ralph J. *o.m.i.* '57 (COL) West Jefferson, OH SS. Simon and Jude; [H] West Jefferson, OH SS. Simon and Jude Retired.
Karl, Robert J. '57 (PBR) Portage, PA SS. Peter and Paul; Portage, PA St. Michael's; Revitalization and Renewal Commission.
Karle, William J. '72 (SCR) Sayre, PA Church of the Epiphany.
Karlen, Donald H. '64 (SY) Boonville, NY St. Joseph; Forestport, NY St. Patrick; Board of Diocesan Consultors.
Karls, Victor *c.ss.r.* '70 (STL)[O] Liguori, MO Liguori Mission House/Redemptorists.
Karmanocky, Bernard *o.f.m.* '73 (ALT) Johnstown, PA St. Therese of the Child Jesus.
Karnik, George W. '58 (DUB) Retired.
Karnish, Robert A. (GI) Personnel Board; Priests' Advisory Board (Presbyteral Council).
Karnish, Robert '66 (GI) Kimball, NE St. Joseph's.
Karns, David W. '74 (ALN) Frackville, PA St. Joseph; Frackville, PA Our Lady of Siluva.
Karoblis, Andrew K. '54 (LC) Wisconsin Rapids, WI SS. Peter and Paul.
Karoor, Isaac '69 (BAL) Ellicott City, MD Our Lady of Perpetual Help.
Karott, Abraham *m.c.b.s.* '95 (SYM) West Hempstead, NY St. Mary Syro–Malabar Catholic Church.
Karottekunnel, Paul P. *m.s.t.* '97 (MAR) Newberry, MI St. Gregory.
Karp, Joseph A. '67 (ORG) Absent on Sick Leave.
Karpiey, Daniel J. '59 (HRT) Wallingford, CT SS. Peter and Paul.
Karpil, Luke '56 (BRK) Veterans Administration Medical Center.
Karpowicz, Jan *s.chr.* '94 (SJ) San Jose, CA St. Brother Albert Chmielowski Polish Catholic Pastoral Mission; [P] San Jose, CA Society of Christ for Polonia.
Karpyn, Gregory R. '87 (ALN) Girardville, PA St. Joseph; Gordon, PA Our Lady of Good Counsel.
Karr, Raymond E. '59 (ALT) Retired.
Karrer, Walter C. *c.ss.r.* '47 (WCH) Wichita, KS St. Joseph; [F] Wichita, KS Redemptorist Mission House.
Karris, Robert *o.f.m.* '65 (CHI)[N] Chicago, IL St. Peter's Friary.
Karris, Robert *o.f.m.* '65 (BUF)[O] St. Bonaventure, NY St. Bonaventure Friary; [C] St. Bonaventure, NY Friar Community.
Karssen, John H. *c.m.* '46 (DEN)[N] Denver, CO Congregation of the Mission Midwest Province: De Paul House.
Kartje, John F. '02 (CHI) Chicago, IL St. Benedict.
Karuhn, Robert J. (GB) Appleton, WI Sacred Heart.
Karumanchi, John V. '91 (CC) Corpus Christi, TX Our Lady of the Rosary; Corpus Christi, TX Sacred Heart.
Karuthi, Cyrus *i.m.c.* '98 (WDC)[V] Washington, DC Consolata Missionaries House of Studies.
Karvelis, Bryan J. '56 (BRK) Brooklyn, NY Transfiguration.
Karvelis, Francis V. '49 (HRT) Retired.
Karwacki, Bart *o.f.m.conv.* '75 (BAL)[S] Ellicott City, MD Friary of St. Joseph Cupertino.
Karwacki, Francis J. '83 (HBG) Coal Township, PA Our Lady of Hope; Trevorton, PA St. Patrick.
Karwacki, Francis (HBG) Charismatic Movement.
Karwin, John J. *s.j.* '67 (WH)[A] Wheeling, WV Wheeling Jesuit University.
Karwin, John J. *s.j.* '67 (BO)[V] Boston The Society of Jesus of New England–Provincial Offices.
Karwowski, Edmund K. '87 (HRT) Plainville, CT Our Lady of Mercy.
Karwowski, Ephrem *o.f.m.cap.* '88 (RVC) Middletown, CT St. Pius X; Middletown, CT St. Sebastian Retired.
Karzeniowski, Marion (RIC) Chesapeake, VA St. Mary.
Kasanziki, Pascal *s.x.* '94 (CHI)[N] Chicago, IL Xaverian Missionaries (S.X.).
Kasarda, John '61 (PBR) Newton Falls, OH St. Michael.
Kasayan, Ihor (SJP) Parma, OH St. Andrew.
Kaschenbach, Arthur J. '51 (SCR) Mount Pocono, PA St. Mary of the Mount.
Kasekende, Anthanasius '97 (FWT) Fort Worth, TX St. Patrick Cathedral.
Kasela, Adam J. '01 (SAV) Savannah, GA St. James.
Kaseta, Peter *o.f.m.cap.* '67 (PRT) Portland, ME St. Joseph's; [J] Portland, ME Motherhouse of the Sisters of Mercy of the Americas; [M] Portland, ME.
Kash, Robert J. '52 (CHI) Retired.
Kashangaki, David *c.s.c.* '99 (FTW)[B] University of Notre Dame Du Lac; [I] Notre Dame, IN Corby Hall; [I] Notre Dame, IN Holy Cross Community, Corby Hall, University of Notre Dame.
Kashmer, George B. '58 (GRY) Retired.
Kasinski, James J. '66 (BUF) Niagara Falls, NY Sacred Heart.
Kasiyan, Andriv '02 (STF) Lackawanna, NY Our Lady of Perpetual Help.
Kaska, E. William '69 (DAV)[M] Iowa City, IA O'Keefe Hall.
Kaskie, Brian '92 (JKS) Jackson, MS St. Peter Cathedral; [I] Jackson, MS University of Mississippi Medical Center – Newman Center; Propagation of the Faith; Approved Advocate and Auditors; Priests' Council; [I] Jackson, MS Belhaven College Newman Center; [I] Jackson, MS Millsaps College Newman Center.
Kaskperczuk, Marek (CHI) Chicago, IL St. Constance.
Kaslyn, Robert J. *c.p.* '85 (WDC)[C] Catholic University of America, The.
Kaslyn, Robert J. *s.j.* '85 (WDC)[E] Washington, DC Gonzaga College High School.
Kasparek, John A. '69 (PMB) Palm Beach Gardens, FL Cathedral of St. Ignatius Loyola.
Kasparek, John (PMB) Presbyteral Council.
Kasper, Eugene J. '59 (NEW) Retired.
Kasper, John *o.s.f.s.* '79 (OAK) Lafayette, CA St. Perpetua; Deans.
Kasper, Larry '97 (TUC) Bisbee, AZ St. Patrick.
Kasperek, David D. '63 (GB) Green Bay, WI SS. Edward and Isidore.
Kasprick, Roger *o.s.b.* '59 (SCL)[I] Collegeville, MN St. John's Abbey, of the Order of St. Benedict.
Kasprzak, John F. '75 (BUF) Woodlawn, NY Our Lady of Grace.
Kasprzak, Roman A. *m.m.* '51 (NY).
Kasprzyk, James H. '65 (BUF)[EE] Tonawanda, NY St. Francis of Assisi; Depew, NY St. Barnabas Retired.
Kasprzyk, Leon J. '61 (MET) Lambertville, NJ St. John the Evangelist.
Kasputis, Thomas R. '76 (CHI) Chicago, IL St. Rene Goupil.
Kass, Dainis '98 (CHI) Chicago, IL Our Lady of Aglona.

Kass, Thomas G. *c.s.v.* '77 (CHI)[N] Goffstown, NH.
Kassian, Jeffery '96 (KAL) Kalamazoo, MI St. Augustine Cathedral.
Kassian, Jeffrey A. (KAL) Judges.
Kassian, Jeffrey (LAN) Tribunal Judges.
Kassis, Daniel F. '81 (GLP) On Leave of Absence.
Kassis, Daniel F. '81 (SR) Eureka, CA St. Bernard.
Kassis, Paskal (OLD) Paroisse Saint Ephrem.
Kasteel, Ben '64 (LUB) Lubbock, TX Cathedral Christ the King; Presbyteral Council; Priests Personnel Board; Diocesan Building Commission; Diocesan Pastoral Liturgy Commission.
Kasten, Edward F. '54 (MIL) Retired.
Kastenholz, John P. *o.praem.* '65 (GB)[B] St. Norbert College; [I] De Pere, WI St. Norbert Abbey; [N] De Pere, WI NORBERT & CO..
Kastenholz, Nicholas E. '02 (STL) St. Louis, MO St. Francis of Assisi.
Kaster, Alfred D. '60 (DUL) On Duty Outside the Diocese.
Kastigar, James J. '82 (CHI) Cicero, IL St. Anthony.
Kastigar, John J. '52 (CHI) Retired.
Kastner, Edwin H. '51 (BEL) Retired.
Kastner, James A. '59 (OKL) Retired.
Kastner, Juan Patron '73 (SJN)[A] Carolina, PR Epifania Del Senor.
Kasulo, Boniface '96 (SEA) Everett, WA Immaculate Conception; Everett, WA Our Lady of Perpetual Help.
Kasun, Stanley L. '94 (OM) Madison, NE St. Leonard; Absent on Leave; [K] Schuyler, NE Benedictine Mission House.
Kasza, John '93 (DET) Special Assignment.
Kaszczak, Ivan '85 (STF) Syracuse, NY St. John the Baptist; Syracuse; Presbyteral Council; Air Force Reserve Chaplains.
Kasznel, Richard C. '65 (STL) St. Mary, MO Immaculate Conception.
Katanga, Wenceslaus '03 (FAR) Fargo, ND St. Anthony of Padua.
Katcher, Gene '93 (DET) Yale, MI Sacred Heart.
Katende, Fulgentius *c.s.c.* '91 (FTW)[I] Bishop McCauley House.
Kathol, Quentin *o.s.b.* '63 (KC)[A] Conception, MO Conception Seminary College; [J] Kansas City, MO.
Kato, Kei *s.d.b.* '95 (OAK)[N] Berkeley Salesian Community.
Katompa, Zephyrin '98 (NEW) On Duty Outside the Archdiocese.
Katorski, Robert '63 (MIL) West Allis, WI St. Rita.
Katoski, Eugene *o.f.m.* '45 (SFD)[L] Springfield, IL Our Lady of Angels Friary.
Katren, Scott E. '92 (E) Erie, PA Sacred Heart; Priest Personnel Board; Bishop's Delegate for Dispensations; Matrimonial Judges; Adjutant Judicial Vicar.
Katricak, Kenneth J. *o.s.b.* '83 (CLV)[E] Cleveland, OH Incarnate Word Academy; [O] Parma Heights, OH; [P] Cleveland, OH Sisters of the Incarnate Word and Blessed Sacrament.
Katsouros, Stephen N. *s.j.* '98 (NY)[F] New York, NY Loyola School; [EE] New York, NY St. Ignatius Loyola Residence.
Kattackal, Joseph Varkey (CHI)[J] Chicago, IL St. Anthony Hospital.
Kattady, Augustine '71 (TUC) Superior, AZ St. Francis of Assisi Parish.
Katz, Jerome A. '71 (SY) Camillus, NY St. Joseph.
Katz, Roger L. '89 (DUB) Retired.
Katzenberger, Scott *c.ss.r.* '99 (NO) New Orleans, LA St. Alphonsus.
Katziner, Stephen F. '74 (PH) Bensalem, PA Saint Ephrem.
Kauchak, Justin R. *o.p.* '66 (BR) Ponchatoula, LA St. Joseph.
Kaucheck, Kenneth R. '76 (DET) Troy, MI St. Anastasia; Archdiocesan Vicars; Judges.
Kauffman, James F. (BAL) Defenders of the Bond.
Kauffman, John (DEN) Frisco, CO St. Mary.
Kauffman, Niles J. *o.f.m.cap.* '58 (MIL)[O] Milwaukee, WI St. Conrad Friary; [A] St. Francis, WI Saint Francis Seminary.
Kauffman, William B. '90 (WIL) Wilmington, DE Corpus Christi; Elsmere, DE Veteran's Hospital; Apostleship of the Sea.
Kauffmann, James '76 (RIC) Richmond, VA St. Benedict; Nocturnal Adoration Society.
Kaufman, Harry J. '02 (BO) Weymouth, MA Sacred Heart.
Kaufman, Kent R. '93 (TOL) Upper Sandusky, OH St. Mary; Upper Sandusky, OH St. Joseph; Upper Sandusky, OH St. Peter.
Kaufman, Philip *o.s.b.* '45 (SCL)[I] Collegeville, MN St. John's Abbey, of the Order of St. Benedict.
Kaufman, William C. '74 (PH) Philadelphia, PA Resurrection of Our Lord.
Kaukus, Edwin J. '57 (BUF) Retired.
Kaul, John L. (DET) Navy Chaplains.
Kaul, John '75 (DET) Military Chaplains.
Kaunas, Bronius *o.s.j.* '42 (MRY)[F] Shrine of St. Joseph.
Kaut, Bernd '72 (WDC) McLean, VA Nativity of the Blessed Virgin (German Mission); [V] McLean, VA Physical Location.
Kauta, John B. '67 (NY) Bedford, NY St. Patrick.
Kauth, Matthew (CHL) Franklin, NC St. Francis of Assisi.
Kautzman, Jerome G. '59 (BIS) Priests' Benefit Association Retired.
Kauzlarich, John '55 (CHI) Retired.
Kavanagh, Aelred *o.s.b.* '94 (NO)[A] St. Benedict, LA St. Joseph Seminary College; [P] St. Benedict, LA St. Joseph Abbey.
Kavanagh, Aidan *o.s.b.* '57 (IND)[K] Hamden, CT.
Kavanagh, Donald A. '72 (BRK) Brooklyn, NY SS. Simon and Jude.
Kavanagh, Edward J. '48 (SAC) Sacramento, CA St. Rose; [F] Sacramento, CA St. Patrick Children's Home, Inc.; Diocesan Council of Catholic Women.
Kavanagh, Francis X. *o.c.s.o.* '38 (ATL)[K] Conyers, GA The Monastery of the Holy Spirit.
Kavanagh, Henry *c.p.* '75 (BRK)[V] Jamaica, NY Immaculate Conception Monastery.
Kavanagh, James F. '64 (LA) Redondo Beach, CA St. James.
Kavanagh, Kevin J. '83 (COL) Delaware, OH St. Mary.
Kavanagh, Kevin (COL) Diocesan Judges.
Kavanagh, Richard T. '36 (IND) Retired.
Kavanaugh, John F. *s.j.* '71 (STL)[O] St. Louis, MO Jesuit Community Corporation at St. Louis University – Jesuit Hall.
Kavanaugh, John J. '57 (WIL) Wilmington, DE St. John the Beloved; College of Consultors; Parish Priest Consultors.
Kavanaugh, John J. *s.j.* '71 (STL)[C] Saint Louis University.
Kavanaugh, John P. '48 (SFR) Knights of Malta Retired.
Kavanaugh, Kieran *o.c.d.* '55 (WDC)[B] Washington, DC Discalced Carmelite Friars; [V] Washington, DC Institute of Carmelite Studies and ICS Publications.
Kavanaugh, Michael J. '85 (SAV) Port Wentworth, GA Our Lady of Lourdes; Ecumenism and Interreligious Affairs.
Kavanaugh, Richard '36 (IND)[I] Beech Grove, IN St. Paul Hermitage.
Kavanaugh, Thomas *c.m.* '41 (SAT) San Antonio, TX St. Matthew's.
Kavcak, John P. *m.s.c.* '73 (ALN) Nazareth, PA Holy Family.
Kaveney, Thomas J. '47 (CHI) Berwyn, IL St. Odilo Retired.
Kaverenge, Fausto '82 (SEA) Seattle, WA St. Edward; Seattle, WA St. George; Seattle, WA St. Paul.
Kavin, Edward F. '56 (NEW)[N] Rutherford, NJ St. John Vianney Residence for Priests; St. John Vianney Priests' Residence Retired.
Kavookjian, Perry '87 (FRS) Fresno, CA St. Paul; [G] Fresno, CA St. Paul Newman Center; Newman Apostolate; Ecclesiastical Notaries.
Kavumkal, Sebastian *m.s.t.* '79 (MAR) DeTour, MI Sacred Heart; Goetzville, MI St. Stanislaus Kostka.
Kawa, Edward *s.d.s.* '64 (GRY)[I] Merrillville, IN Salvatorian Fathers (Society of the Divine Savior).
Kawa, Robert J. '69 (STU) Beverly, OH St. Bernard; [K] Beverly, OH Marriage Encounter.
Kawa, Robert (STU) Deans.
Kawalec, Zachary M. '02 (CLV) Gates Mills, OH St. Francis of Assisi.
Kawamata, Louis *ss.cc.* '74 (FR).
Kawamura, Peter *o.s.b.* '88 (SCL)[I] St. Augustine Monastery.
Kawcznski, Ronald L. (FAR) Navy Chaplains.
Kawczynski, Ronald '90 (LT) Military Chaplains.
Kawecki, Andrew M. '80 (GBG) Clymer, PA Church of the Resurrection; Diocesan Pastoral Council.
Kawka, Frederick J. '64 (SAG) Frankenmuth, MI Blessed Trinity; Diocesan Consultors.
Kay, Joseph *m.afr.* '48 (SP)[O] St. Petersburg, FL Missionaries of Africa.
Kay, Kieran *o.f.m.conv.* '55 (TOL) Carey, OH Our Lady of Consolation, Basilica–National Shrine.
Kayajan, Daniel R. *c.s.c.* (BO) Brockton, MA St. Patrick.
Kayalaparambil, Jacob '03 (BIS) Williston, ND St. Joseph.
Kayanga, John Mary (CHI) Chicago, IL Our Lady of Peace.
Kayatta, Francis P. '80 (PRO) Providence, RI St. Thomas; Judges; Air Force Reserve Chaplains.
Kayita, Ignatius '87 (PIT) McKeesport, PA St. Martin de Porres.
Kaylor, Lee '81 (SFR) Absent on Leave.
Kaylor, Robert W. '62 (Y)[C] Canton, OH Central Catholic High.
Kaylor, Robert W. '70 (Y) Brewster, OH St. Therese.
Kayser, DeWayne '98 (SFS) Britton, SD St. John de Britto.
Kayser, Leonard '59 (SFS) Mickelson Center for the Neurosciences Retired.
Kayser, Robert '52 (RVC) Dix Hills, NY St. Matthew.
Kaywell, Jerome P. (VEN) Presbyteral Council.
Kaywell, Jerry (VEN) Naples, FL St. John the Evangelist.
Kaza, Charles A. '72 (E) Brockway, PA St. Tobias; Eastern Vicariate; Administrative Cabinet; College of Consultors; Finance Council.
Kazadi, Andre B. *c.i.c.m.* '03 (BWN) La Feria, TX St. Francis Xavier; Santa Rosa, TX St. Mary.
Kazanecki, Thaddeus J. '77 (BRK) Flushing, NY Mary's Nativity; Graduate Studies.
Kazanecki, Thaddeus (BRK) Liturgical Commission.
Kazanjian, Stephen C.A. '02 (PH) Downingtown, PA St. Joseph.
Kazarnowicz, Anthony S. (WOR) Army Chaplains.
Kazarnowski, Anthony S. '75 (TUC) Fort Huchuca, AZ Fort Huchuca Army Post.
Kazer, Michael '80 (DET) Warren, MI St. Anne's.
Kazhunadiyil, Abraham '82 (MAR) Ontonagon, MI Holy Family; Ontonagon, MI St. Mary.
Kazhuvidayil, Joseph '83 (NY) Spring Valley, NY St. Joseph.
Kazista, Francis G. '66 (WDC) Silver Spring, MD St. John the Baptist.
Kazista, Francis (WDC) Deans.
Kazmekcziak, Eugene '51 (FTW) Retired.
Kazmierczak, Carl M. '55 (MIL) Milwaukee, WI St. John Kanty.
Kaznowski, Valentine J. '41 (DET) Retired.
Kcira, Anton '67 (DET) Rochester Hills, MI St. Paul Albanian Catholic Community.
Keahi, Christopher *ss.cc.* '65 (HON) Waialua, HI St. Michael.
Kealey, Edward J. '89 (RVC) Medford, NY St. Sylvester.
Kealy, Francis de Paul *o.f.m.* '50 (NY) New York, NY St. Stephen of Hungary.
Kealy, Hubert J. '64 (GAL) Pasadena, TX St. Pius the Fifth.
Kealy, Robert L. '72 (CHI) Other Assignments.
Kealy, Sean *c.s.sp.* '65 (PIT)[B] Pittsburgh, PA Duquesne University of the Holy Spirit.
Kean, James F. '97 (DET) Taylor, MI St. Alfred; Archdiocesan Vicars.
Kean, james F. (DET) Army Reserve Chaplains.
Kean, Joseph H. '64 (ALN) Retired.
Keane, Alfred V. *m.m.* '58 (NY).
Keane, Aquinas *o.c.s.o.* '73 (WOR)[O] Spencer, MA St. Joseph's Abbey.
Keane, Brendan '50 (SFD) Retired.
Keane, Denis J. '63 (GF) Red Lodge, MT St. Agnes.
Keane, Dennis P. '71 (NY) New York, NY Our Lady of Good Counsel; Crestwood, NY Church of the Annunciation; Inter–Parish Financing, Commission for.
Keane, Edward M. '39 (BRK) Flushing, NY Holy Family Retired.
Keane, Eugene '55 (NY) Highland, NY St. Augustine.
Keane, James P. '45 (SFR) Retired.
Keane, James T. '55 (LFT) Muncie, IN St. Mary.
Keane, John F. '65 (BO) Health Leave.
Keane, John J. *s.a.* '62 (WDC)[B] Washington, DC Atonement Seminary–Franciscan Friars of the Atonement.
Keane, John J. '62 (HRT) New Haven, CT St. John the Baptist; McKeesport, PA St. Pius V.
Keane, John *s.a.* '62 (NY)[EE] Garrison, NY Franciscan Friars of the Atonement, Minister General Office.
Keane, Joseph P. '49 (BRK) Retired.
Keane, Michael J. '57 (SFR) San Rafael, CA St. Isabella; Deans.
Keane, Michael '90 (NY) Croton–on–Hudson, NY Holy Name of Mary.
Keane, Patrick J. *o.s.a.* '52 (LA) Ojai, CA St. Thomas Aquinas Retired.
Keane, Patrick '03 (R) Fayetteville, NC St. Patrick.
Keane, Philip S. *s.s.* '67 (BAL).
Keane, Philip S. *s.s.* '67 (SY)[A] On Duty Outside the Diocese; In Res:.
Keane, Robert E. '78 (STP) Retired.
Keane, Robert L. *s.j.* '78 (BO)[V] Boston The Society of Jesus of New England–Provincial Offices; Navy Chaplains.
Keane, Thomas F. '56 (BO) Senior Priests Retired.
Keane, Thomas S. *m.m.* '56 (NY).
Keane, Vincent A. '58 (BRK)[B] Douglaston, NY Cathedral Seminary Residence of the Immaculate Conception.
Keane, Vincent (BRK) Apostleship of Prayer.
Keaney, Francis *s.s.c.* '65 (PRO)[P] Bristol, RI St. Columban's Retirement House.
Keaney, James P. '54 (R) Retired.
Kearney, A. Damian *o.s.b.* '56 (PRO)[P] Portsmouth, RI Abbey of St. Gregory the Great.
Kearney, Brendan *s.j.* '68 (LA) Redondo Beach, CA St. James.
Kearney, Christopher '68 (OAK)[N] Saint Conrad Friary.
Kearney, Daniel S. '87 (NY) New York, NY Our Lady Queen of Martyrs.
Kearney, Edward J. '51 (NEW) Jersey City, NJ St. Patrick's Retired.
Kearney, John T. '83 (NY) Lake Katrine, NY St. Catherine Laboure.
Kearney, Joseph A. '67 (SCR) Wilkes–Barre, PA Blessed

Sacrament; Wilkes–Barre, PA Geisinger Wyoming Valley Hospital.
Kearney, Joseph V. '46 (LA) Retired.
Kearney, Lawrence T. *o.p.* '50 (CHI)[N] St. Pius V Priory.
Kearney, Michael J. '82 (BO) Quincy, MA St. Elizabeth Ann Seton.
Kearney, Myles J. '71 (BR) On Leave.
Kearney, Patrick J. '53 (SD) Retired.
Kearney, Thomas L. *o.p.* (MO) AUXILIARY CHAPLAINS CONTRACT CHAPLAINS.
Kearney, Timothy E. '96 (BO) Roslindale, MA Sacred Heart.
Kearney, William '83 (SP).
Kearns, Adam '54 (TR)[M] Trenton, NJ Villa Vianney Retired.
Kearns, Daniel J. '86 (PH) Philadelphia, PA St. Raymond of Penafort.
Kearns, Daniel P. *c.m.* '69 (STL) St. Louis Vincentian Community.
Kearns, David *o.carm.* '61 (NY) Bronx, NY St. Simon Stock.
Kearns, Dominic *s.m.a.* (BO) Dorchester, MA St. Gregory.
Kearns, Edward A. '63 (MET) Retired.
Kearns, Edward T. '77 (PH) East Lansdowne, PA St. Cyril of Alexandria.
Kearns, Harold M. '61 (HRT) Thomaston, CT St. Thomas.
Kearns, John P. (BO) Belmont, MA St. Luke.
Kearns, Joseph J. '48 (SAG) Retired.
Kearns, Owen *l.c.* '83 (HRT).
Kearns, Robert M. *s.s.j.* '63 (BAL)[B] Los Angeles, CA St. Brigid's.
Kearns, Thomas '60 (KCK) Paola, KS Holy Trinity.
Keating, Bernard A. '47 (BAK) Retired.
Keating, Carroll *s.j.* '61 (SAC) Fair Oaks, CA St. Mel.
Keating, David '54 (SFS) Retired.
Keating, Earl *c.p.* '58 (SCR)[M] Clarks Summit, PA St. Gabriel's Convent.
Keating, Edward C. *o.f.m.* '58 (SP) Tampa, FL St. Lawrence.
Keating, Edward J. '94 (HBG) Selinsgrove, PA St. Pius X; Selinsgrove, PA Selinsgrove Center; [J] Selinsgrove, PA Susquehanna University Catholic Campus Ministry.
Keating, George M. '54 (NEW) Kenilworth, NJ St. Theresa's; Union, NJ Union Hospital; [S] Union, NJ The Association of St. Philomena's Helpers to the Suffering & Poor; Union Hospital Retired.
Keating, George (NEW) Association of St. Philomena's Helpers to the Suffering and the Poor.
Keating, James D. *o.p.* '56 (WDC) Washington, DC St. Dominic Church & Priory.
Keating, James P. '51 (CHI) Chicago, IL St. Francis de Sales Retired.
Keating, James R. *o.s.a.* '84 (ORL) Philadelphia, PA St. Nicholas of Tolentine.
Keating, James V. '43 (NY) Kingston, NY St. Joseph Retired.
Keating, James W. '34 (CHI) Retired.
Keating, John R. *s.j.* '61 (NY)[EE] Loyola Hall, Jesuit Community.
Keating, Joseph H. '77 (HRT) Retired.
Keating, Joseph R. '57 (LC) Retired.
Keating, Michael J. '02 (STP) New Brighton, MN St. John the Baptist.
Keating, Michael P. '97 (OM) Omaha, NE St. Wenceslaus.
Keating, Pius F. *s.a.* '46 (NY)[EE] Garrison Franciscan Friars of the Atonement, Minister General Office.
Keating, Thomas F. '66 (SY) Maine, NY Most Holy Rosary.
Keating, Thomas *o.c.s.o.* '49 (DEN)[N] Snowmass, CO St. Benedict's Monastery.
Keating, Thomas (SY) Pastoral Examiners.
Keating, Timothy G. *s.m.* '85 (WDC)[M] College Park, MD.
Keating, Timothy *c.ss.r.* '66 (TR)[Q] Long Branch, NJ San Alfonso Retreat House.
Keaveney, George J. *c.ss.r.* (NY)[EE] Esopus, NY Redemptorist Priests and Brothers C.Ss.R. (Province of Baltimore).
Keaveney, John J. '59 (NY) Washingtonville, NY St. Mary.
Kebung, Konrad '84 (WDC)[M] Washington, DC Divine Word College.
Keck, Barnabas *o.f.m.cap.* '51 (NY) New Paltz, NY St. Joseph; [EE] New Paltz, NY St. Joseph Friary.
Keck, Edward '73 (COL) Bolivar, OH Holy Trinity.
Keck, Robert J. *s.j.* '60 (NY)[EE] New York, NY West Side Jesuit Community.
Kedjierski, Walter F. '02 (RVC) Franklin Square, NY St. Catherine of Sienna.
Kedzierski, Casimir '60 (PIT) Glassport, PA Queen of the Rosary.
Kee, James S. '95 (MOB) Mobile, AL Cathedral of the Immaculate Conception; Judicial Vicar.
Keebler, William C. '91 (PEO) Penfield, IL St. Lawrence's.
Keech, William J. *o.s.f.s.* '57 (WIL)[J] Wilmington, DE DeSales House.
Keefe, Bernard A. '63 (BGP) Stamford, CT St. Maurice.
Keefe, Charles R. '76 (MIL)[M] Milwaukee, WI Milwaukee Catholic Home; Special Assignment.
Keefe, Danel T. '54 (OG) Plattsburgh, NY St. Mary of the Lake.
Keefe, Daniel G. '83 (HRT) Hamden, CT St. Joan of Arc.
Keefe, Daniel T. (OG) Judges; Deans; Priest Personnel Board.
Keefe, Francis J. '58 (PRO)[P] Providence St. John Vianney Residence Retired.
Keefe, Gerald E. '47 (STP) Hopkins, MN St. Joseph's Retired.
Keefe, Jeffrey *o.f.m.conv.* '52 (SY) Syracuse, NY Assumption B.V.M..
Keefe, John J. (LIN) Apostolate to the Spanish Speaking.
Keefe, John P. *c.s.c.* '59 (PHX)[G] Phoenix AZ Holy Cross Congregation/Casa Santa Cruz.
Keefe, John '68 (LIN) Lincoln, NE Christo Rey.
Keefe, Joseph L. '71 (WIN) Rochester, MN Pax Christi; Diocesan Consultors; Appointed Members.
Keefe, Thomas H. *m.m.* '55 (NY)[EE] Maryknoll Maryknoll Fathers and Brothers; [EE] Maryknoll, NY Maryknoll Fathers and Brothers Charitable Trust.
Keefer, Hugh *o.s.b.* '67 (KCK)[H] Atchison, KS St. Benedict's Abbey.
Keefer, John E. *o.p.* '56 (SAT) San Antonio, TX St. Ann; [B] San Antonio, TX Dominican Priory of San Juan Macias and Novitiate.
Keeffe, Anthony J. '63 (SY) Retired.
Keegan, Fintan *s.s.c.* '33 (PRO)[P] Bristol, RI St. Columban's Retirement House.
Keegan, James M. *s.j.* '71 (BO)[V] Watertown, MA The Society of Jesus of New England–Provincial Offices; [X] Gloucester, MA Eastern Point Retreat House.
Keegan, John E. *m.m.* '60 (NY).
Keegan, John W. *s.j.* '69 (BO)[C] Portland, ME Cheverus High School; [C] Portland, ME Cheverus High School.
Keegan, John *s.j.* (PRT)[I] Portland, ME St. Ignatius Residence.
Keegan, Marvin P. *m.m.* '65 (NY)[EE] Maryknoll Maryknoll Fathers and Brothers.
Keegan, Terence *o.p.* '68 (PRO)[B] Providence, RI Providence College; [P] Providence St Thomas Aquinas Priory at Providence College.
Keegan, William F. *c.s.c.* '56 (FTW)[I] Notre Dame, IN Holy Cross House.
Keegstra, Garrett *o.f.m.cap.* '86 (MAD)[K] Madison, WI San Damiano Friary.
Keehan, Daniel J. '54 (NY) Retired.
Keehan, John J. '67 (CHI) Chicago, IL St. Ann.
Keehan, Terence M. '86 (CHI) Chicago, IL St. Matthias; Chicago, IL Transfiguration of Our Lord.
Keehner, John E. (Y) Judges.
Keehner, John '93 (Y) Youngstown, OH Cathedral of St. Columba; Youngstown State University.
Keel, Edwin L. *s.m.* '70 (NO)[P] New Orleans, LA Marist Fathers.
Keelen, Kevin T. '91 (TR) Bayville, NJ St. Barnabas.
Keeley, Patrick J. *c.m.* '58 (SPC)[O] St. Louis, MO Lazarist Residence.
Keeling, Paul M. *c.r.s.p.* '75 (BUF)[B] Youngstown, NY St. Anthony M. Zaccaria Seminary; [B] Youngstown, NY The National Shrine Basilica of Our Lady of Fatima.
Keena, James R. *c.ss.r.* '57 (OM) Omaha, NE Holy Name; [K] Omaha, NE The Redemptorists of Nebraska.
Keena, James *c.ss.r.* (OM) Religious Orders.
Keenan, Alexander J. '76 (BO) Cambridge, MA Immaculate Conception.
Keenan, Basil *o.s.b.* '67 (OKL) Seminole, OK Immaculate Conception; [I] Shawnee St. Gregory's Abbey.
Keenan, Charles J. '42 (LIN)[E] Lincoln, NE Bonacum House Retired.
Keenan, Christopher B. *o.f.m.* '71 (NY) New York, NY All Saints; EE] New York, NY All Saints Friary.
Keenan, Desmond R. '49 (R) Retired.
Keenan, Eugene '71 (TR) Leave of Absence.
Keenan, Francis X. *c.p.* '61 (CHI)[N] Chicago, IL Passionist Community–Immaculate Conception Monastery.
Keenan, James F. *s.j.* '69 (NEW)[C] Jersey City, NJ St. Peter's Preparatory School; [N] Jersey City, NJ Jesuit Community of St. Peter's Prep, Inc.
Keenan, James R. '99 (RCK) Fulton, IL Immaculate Conception Albany, IL St. Patrick.
Keenan, James *s.j.* '69 (NY)[V] Newton, MA The Jesuit Community at Boston College.
Keenan, James *s.j.* '82 (BO)[V] Cambridge, MA.
Keenan, John C. '51 (ORG) Retired.
Keenan, John J. '43 (SD) Retired.
Keenan, John J. *s.j.* '55 (ALN)[A] Wernersville, PA Jesuit Center.
Keenan, John *s.s.s.* '69 (CHI)[U] Chicago, IL Trinity House; [N Chicago, IL The Blessed Sacrament House of Studies.
Keenan, Joseph F. '84 (PIT) Monroeville, PA St. Bernadette.
Keenan, Joseph *s.t.* '79 (PAT)[M] Stirling, NJ Holy Spirit Missionary Cenacle.
Keenan, Patrick J. '69 (NY) Cortlandt Manor, NY St. Columbanus; Navy Reserve Chaplains.
Keenan, Paul A. '77 (NY) New York, NY Our Lady of Peace.
Keenan, Paul (NY) Communications Office (Bureau of Information for the Media).
Keenan, Roberto (R) Havelock, NC Annunciation.
Keenan, Terence '65 (FR) South Dartmouth, MA St. Mary's.
Keenan, Thomas E. '55 (MAN) Retired.
Keenan, Thomas L. '63 (PRO) Rumford, RI St. Margaret.
Keenan, William R. *o.f.m.* '56 (FgM).
Keene, David A. (BO) Somerville, MA St. Ann.
Keene, James H. *s.j.* '73 (LA)[C] Los Angeles, CA Jesuit Community.
Keene, Kenneth R. '95 (PIT) New Castle, PA St. Vincent de Paul.
Keene, Mark A. '84 (COV) Fort Wright, KY St. Agnes.
Keene, Warren '81 (STA) Jacksonville, FL Immaculate Conception.
Keener, Michael '92 (MIA) Absent on Leave.
Keener, Robert J. '95 (CHI) Hazel Crest, IL St. Anne.
Keeney, Charles P. '78 (BRK) Long Island City, NY St. Francis of Assisi; [G] Astoria, NY St. John Preparatory School.
Keeney, Charles '77 (NY) Bayview Correctional Facility; Anna M. Kross Center.
Keeney, Edward *ss.cc.* '61 (FR).
Keeney, Timothy E. '96 (RIC)[H] Bristol, VA St. Anne.
Keenoy, John A. '87 (STL) Pacific, MO St. Bridget Church.
Keernan, Joseph *o.f.m.* '69 (PAT)[M] Ringwood, NJ Holy Name Friary, Inc..
Keese, John H. (LA) Deanery 7; Personnel Board of the Archdiocese.
Keese, John '74 (LA) North Hills, CA Our Lady of Peace.
Keesler, Robert L. '36 (WDC) Laurel, MD St. Mary Retired.
Keferl, Francis J. '73 (CIN) Vandalia, OH St. Christopher.
Keffer, Joseph D. *o.s.a.* '47 (ALB) Troy, NY St. Augustine.
Keffer, Robert F. '68 (WDC) Burtonsville, MD Resurrection Parish.
Keffer, Robert *o.cist.* '97 (LC)[H] Sparta, WI Our Lady of Spring Bank, Cistercian Abbey.
Keffer, Thomas '77 (SR) Retired.
Keffler, Leopold *o.f.m.conv.* '63 (IND)[B] Indianapolis, IN Marian College; [P] Indianapolis, IN Mount Saint Francis Sanctuary, Inc..
Kegel, William M. *s.j.* '42 (OAK) Walnut Creek, CA St. Anne; [N] Berkeley, CA Jesuit Community at Jesuit School of Theology at Berkeley.
Kegley, Jeffrey '96 (TR) Howell, NJ St. Veronica.
Kehew, Donal R. '63 (PRO) Block Island, RI St. Andrew.
Kehoe, Daniel J. '39 (PH) Sharon Hill, PA Holy Spirit Retired.
Kehoe, James P. '70 (CHI) Chicago, IL Nativity of Our Lord; Navy Reserve Chaplains.
Kehoe, Joseph F. '66 (SY) Durhamville, NY St. Francis; Durhamville, NY St. Therese of the Infant Jesus.
Kehoe, Mark '99 (MET) Phillipsburg, NJ St. Philip & St. James.
Kehoe, Richard *c.m.* '57 (MET)[H] Princeton, NJ Vincentian Residence.
Kehoe, Thomas F. '75 (WDC) Retired.
Kehres, Franklin P. '68 (TOL) Norwalk, OH St. Paul; Sandusky Deanery.
Kehres, John C. *s.j.* '50 (DET)[P] Hamtramck, MI St. Ladislaus.
Keifer, John J. (LFT) Newman Foundation, Ball State, Inc..
Keigher, Bernard '74 (TR) Lakehurst, NJ St. John.
Keil, Joseph V. (BO) Milton, MA St. Agatha.
Keine, Joachim *o.f.m.conv.* (IND) Veterans' Administration Hospital.
Keiser, Jerome F. '71 (STP) Lake St. Croix Beach, MN St. Francis Of Assisi.
Keiser, Ray W. '70 (BIR) Bessemer, AL St. Aloysius Church; [I] Bessemer, AL St. Aloysius Educational Foundation; Bessemer, AL St. Francis of Assisi.
Keiter, James E. '01 (OM) Norfolk, NE Sacred Heart.
Keitz, Bernard Lawrence *o.p.* '54 (NY) New York, NY St. Vincent Ferrer; [EE] New York, NY St. Vincent Ferrer Priory.
Kejbo, Sabri A. '68 (SPA) El Cajon, CA St. Michael Chaldean Catholic Church; Vicar General; Victim Assistance Coordinator.
Kekeisen, William '58 (SFD) Retired.
Keladu, Joseph '95 (WDC)[M] Washington, DC Divine Word College.
Kelash, David '94 (PHX) El Mirage, AZ Santa Teresita.
Kelbel, Joseph A. '80 (BAK) Dufur, OR St. Alphonsus; The Dalles, OR St. Peter's; Wasco, OR St. Mary's.
Kelchak, Joseph M. '50 (GRY)[E] Hobart, IN St. Mary Medical Center.

Kelchak, Joseph M. '50 (SUP) Retired.
Keleher, J. Patrick '68 (BUF)[R] Amherst, NY State University of New York at Buffalo (North Campus) Newman Center.
Keliher, Michael P. *c.s.v.* '76 (LAV) Henderson, NV St. Thomas More.
Kelleher, Cornelius '56 (DUL) Beroun, MN St. Joseph's; Hinckley, MN St. Patrick's; Deans.
Kelleher, James R. *s.o.l.t.* '96 (CC)[G] Robstown, TX Society of Our Lady of the Most Holy Trinity.
Kelleher, John P. *o.s.b.* '89 (BO)[V] Hingham, MA Glastonbury Abbey.
Kelleher, Joseph '53 (CHL) Retired.
Kelleher, Lawrence A. '93 (GAY) Ossineke, MI St. Gabriel; Ossineke, MI St. Catherine.
Kelleher, Mark A. '96 (WIL) Newark, DE St. John the Baptist–Holy Angels; Air Force Reserve Chaplains.
Kelleher, Michael '65 (BLX) Pascagoula, MS Sacred Heart.
Kelleher, Robert N. '59 (BO) Emergency Response Group.
Kelleher, Timothy J. '71 (BO) Walpole, MA Blessed Sacrament.
Kelleher, Walter T. *m.m.* '56 (NY).
Kelleher, William A. '91 (NY)[EE] Bronxville, NY St. Joseph Retired.
Kellen, Elmer W. '50 (WIN)[D] Wabasha, MN Saint Elizabeth's Medical Center; [F] Wabasha, MN St. Elizabeth's Nursing Home Retired.
Keller, Brendan '60 (MOB) Retired.
Keller, Brian '73 (BRK) On Leave/Unassigned.
Keller, Daniel E. '82 (OM) Special Assignment.
Keller, David S. '98 (HBG) Middletown, PA Seven Sorrows of the Blessed Virgin Mary.
Keller, Gerald J. '65 (CLV) Berea, OH St. Adalbert.
Keller, Harvey M. '45 (TOL) Retired.
Keller, Herbert B. *s.j.* '81 (SCR)[C] Scranton, PA The University of Scranton; [E] Scranton, PA Scranton Preparatory School.
Keller, J. Rod '54 (ORG) Retired.
Keller, John D. *o.s.a.* '55 (SD)[C] San Diego, CA St. Augustine High School.
Keller, John D. *o.s.a.* '64 (SD)[H] San Diego, CA Augustinian Community.
Keller, John R. '54 (ORG) Judges; Huntington Beach, CA St. Bonaventure Retired.
Keller, John T. '74 (GAL) Houston, TX Prince of Peace; Area Representatives.
Keller, Ken '69 (AMA) Dimmitt, TX Immaculate Conception.
Keller, Lawrence E. '47 (STP) Retired.
Keller, Mathew '02 (GLP) Grants, NM St. Teresa.
Keller, Matthew '02 (GLP) Milan, NM St. Vivian; Milan, NM San Mateo; Milan, NM San Rafael; Priests' Retirement Fund.
Keller, Neil J. '55 (CIN) Retired.
Keller, Paul (STP) Woodbury, MN Saint Ambrose of Woodbury.
Keller, Robert J. '74 (DET) Air National Guard Chaplains; Harper Woods, MI St. Peter the Apostle.
Keller, Robert J. *o.p.* '83 (SFE) Albuquerque, NM St. Thomas Aquinas University Parish; [L] Albuquerque, NM St. Thomas Aquinas (Newman Center) University Parish; ALBQ: Aquinas Newman Center.
Keller, Robert L. '67 (CIN) Cincinnati, OH Resurrection of Our Lord.
Keller, Rod (ORG) Ministry to Priests.
Keller, Theodore A. '46 (LEX) Lexington, KY St. Peter Retired.
Keller, Theodore '46 (LEX) Retired.
Keller, Thomas G. '97 (STL) St. Louis, MO Cathedral Basilica of Saint Louis; Archdiocesan Master of Ceremonies.
Keller, Thomas W. '58 (LR) Fairfield Bay, AR St. Francis Assisi; Clinton, AR St. Jude Church.
Keller, Thomas *m.s.c.* '55 (ORG) Placentia, CA St. Joseph; Defenders of the Bond.
Keller, Thomas (STL) Archdiocesan Commission for Sacred Liturgy.
Keller, V. Robb '84 (B) Buhl, ID Immaculate Conception.
Kellerman, Leonard P. *s.m.* '46 (NO)[P] New Orleans, LA Marist Fathers.
Kellerman, Leonard P. *s.m.* '46 (WDC)[M] New Orleans, LA Mary Joseph Residence Retired.
Kellerman, Raymond C. '73 (CIN) Cincinnati, OH Holy Trinity Church; Judges.
Kellett, William K. *s.j.* '65 (STL)[O] St. Louis, MO Hallahan House.
Kelley, Aloysius P. *s.j.* '62 (BGP)[B] Fairfield, CT Fairfield University; [E] Fairfield, CT Fairfield College Preparatory School; [P] Fairfield, CT The Fairfield Jesuit Community–Fairfield University.
Kelley, Charles F. *s.j.* '84 (BO)[V] Boston The Society of Jesus of New England–Provincial Offices.
Kelley, Clark T. *o.s.f.s.* '64 (STO)[A] Stockton, CA St. Mary's High School.
Kelley, Daniel '95 (FWT) Presbyteral Council and Consultors; Fort Worth, TX St. George.
Kelley, David F. '88 (WIL) Bethany Beach, DE St. Ann.
Kelley, David *o.s.a.* '73 (ALB) Waterford, NY St. Mary of the Assumption.
Kelley, Donald *s.s.c.* '62 (OM)[K] St. Columbans St. Columban's Foreign Mission Society.
Kelley, Edward J. '66 (MAN) Portsmouth, NH Immaculate Conception.
Kelley, Edward J. '68 (PRO) On Duty Outside the Diocese; Army Chaplains.
Kelley, Francis H. '68 (BO) Roslindale, MA Sacred Heart.
Kelley, John E. '61 (WOR) Baldwinville, MA St. Vincent De Paul.
Kelley, John '91 (AUS) Uhland, TX St. Michael's.
Kelley, John '91 (AUS) Martindale, TX Immaculate Heart of Mary.
Kelley, Joseph '87 (PH) Philadelphia, PA St. Monica.
Kelley, Laurence E. '60 (BO) Health Leave.
Kelley, Michael A. '00 (PRO) Westerly, RI Immaculate Conception.
Kelley, Michael J. '75 (WDC) Washington, DC St. Martin of Tours.
Kelley, Michael '85 (IND) Unassigned.
Kelley, Omer C. '49 (GB)[F] Antigo, WI Langlade Memorial Hospital Retired.
Kelley, Paul G. '49 (BO) Winchester, MA St. Mary; Senior Priests Retired.
Kelley, Richard J. '72 (MAN) Nashua, NH St. Christopher.
Kelley, Robert E. '79 (WOR)[N] Worcester, MA.
Kelley, Thomas J. '51 (PH) Philadelphia, PA St. Matthew Retired.
Kelley, Thomas L. '88 (MAD) Cross Plains, WI St. Francis Xavier; Deaneries.
Kelley, Thomas P. '70 (BO) Emergency Response Group.
Kelley, Thomas W. *o.s.f.s.* (MO) AUXILIARY CHAPLAINS CONTRACT CHAPLAINS.
Kelley, Thomas '67 (SAN) Midland, TX Our Lady of San Juan de Los Lagos.
Kelley, William H. *c.s.c.* '70 (FR) Taunton, MA St. Mary's.
Kelley, William J. '54 (MAN) Peterborough, NH St. Peter.
Kelley, William J. *s.j.* '85 (CHL) Camden, NJ Holy Name.
Kelley, William J. *s.v.d.* (MO) AUXILIARY CHAPLAINS CONTRACT CHAPLAINS.
Kellick, John W. '52 (GAL) Retired.
Kelligar, William L. '53 (OM) Retired.
Kelliher, Alexander *s.a.* '77 (NY) Retired.
Kelliher, Michael M. *s.j.* '67 (SEA)[A] Seattle, WA Seattle University.
Kellner, Winfried '63 (ROC) Rochester, NY Our Mother of Sorrows; Rochester, NY Unity Health System; Rochester, NY Park Ridge Hospital/Unity Health System.
Kellogg, Michael '02 (SCL) St. Cloud, MN Holy Spirit.
Kelly, Albert P. '72 (MOB) Millbrook, AL St. Elizabeth Ann Seton.
Kelly, Andrew E. '70 (DAV)[J] Iowa City, IA Mercy Hospital.
Kelly, Anthony *s.a.c.* '59 (NY) New York, NY Our Lady of Mt. Carmel.
Kelly, Anthony *s.c.j.* '73 (BWN) Raymondville, TX Our Lady of Guadalupe; Lyford, TX Prince of Peace.
Kelly, Arnold '51 (BO)[T] Lowell, MA D'Youville Manor Senior Care, Inc..
Kelly, Augustine G. *o.s.b.* '88 (MAN)[K] Manchester, NH St. Anselm Abbey.
Kelly, Bernard A. *c.s.sp.* '62 (CHI) Chicago, IL St. Mary Magdalene.
Kelly, Bernard R. '61 (FR) Retired.
Kelly, Bernard T. '41 (LC) Retired.
Kelly, Bernard *c.h.s.* '73 (NY)[EE] Glenham, NY Apostolic Society of the Crusade of the Holy Spirit.
Kelly, Brian F. '77 (SCR) Military Chaplains; Navy Chaplains.
Kelly, C. Richard '70 (DET) Canton, MI St. Thomas a Becket.
Kelly, Charles A. (BAL) Interdiocesan Judges.
Kelly, Charles F. '48 (CHI)[X] Chicago, IL St. Daniel the Prophet Retired.
Kelly, Charles F. '64 (MET) Old Bridge, NJ St. Ambrose.
Kelly, Charles S. '69 (NY) Chappaqua, NY St. John and St. Mary.
Kelly, Charles *s.c.j.* '71 (GAL) Raymondville, TX Our Lady of Guadalupe.
Kelly, Charles '99 (SAC) Winters, CA St. Anthony.
Kelly, Columba *o.s.b.* '58 (IND)[A] St. Meinrad, IN St. Meinrad School of Theology; [K] St. Meinrad, IN St. Meinrad Archabbey.
Kelly, Cornelius *o.f.m.* '62 (PAT)[M] Ringwood, NJ Holy Name Friary, Inc..
Kelly, Daniel A. '67 (PAT) Wayne, NJ Immaculate Heart of Mary.
Kelly, Daniel J. '56 (LC) Retired.
Kelly, Daniel '72 (RIC) Amherst, VA St. Francis of Assisi; Lovingston, VA St. Mary.
Kelly, David A. *c.pp.s.* '82 (CHI)[X] Chicago, IL Kolbe House; [M] Chicago, IL.
Kelly, David C. *m.m.* '57 (FgM).
Kelly, David F. '66 (WOR) On Duty Outside the Diocese.
Kelly, David *c.pp.s.* (CHI)[X] Chicago, IL Precious Blood Ministry of Reconciliation.
Kelly, Donald '63 (ALB) Green Island, NY St. Joseph.
Kelly, E. Francis '67 (SCR) Wilkes–Barre, PA Holy Saviour; Deans.
Kelly, Edward C. '90 (PH) Philadelphia, PA St. Matthew.
Kelly, Edward J. '68 (PH) Philadelphia, PA Our Lady Help of Christians.
Kelly, Edward M. '68 (MIA) Coral Springs, FL St. Elizabeth Ann Seton.
Kelly, Edward '65 (MEM) On Duty Outside the Diocese.
Kelly, Eugene L. *o.s.f.s.* '65 (PH)[D] Philadelphia, PA Father Judge High School for Boys; [AA] Philadelphia, PA Father Louis Brisson Residence.
Kelly, Evangelist *o.f.m.cap.* '49 (LA)[B] Santa Ynez, CA San Lorenzo Seminary and Prayer Center; [B] Santa Ynez, CA San Lorenzo Seminary and Prayer Center.
Kelly, Francis D. '63 (BO)[A] Weston, MA Blessed John XXIII National Seminary; Blessed John XXIII National Seminary.
Kelly, Francis D. '80 (WOR) On Duty Outside the Diocese.
Kelly, Francis E. '55 (PH) Retired.
Kelly, Francis Joseph *f.p.o.* '98 (FR)[H] New Bedford, MA Franciscans of Primitive Observance.
Kelly, Francis X. *o.f.m.* '88 (PH)[AA] Philadelphia, PA St. Pius X Friary.
Kelly, Francis '57 (LA) Veterans Administration Wadsworth Hospital Center.
Kelly, Francis *o.f.m.* '89 (PH)[D] Philadelphia, PA Archbishop Ryan High School.
Kelly, Frank F. '77 (GF) Retired.
Kelly, George A. '42 (NY) New York, NY St. John the Evangelist Retired.
Kelly, George F. *c.ss.r.* '59 (MET) U.S. Veterans Medical Center.
Kelly, George F. *c.ss.r.* (MO).
Kelly, George *c.ss.r.* '59 (NEW) East Orange, NJ Holy Spirit–Our Lady Help of Christians; East Orange, NJ Veterans Administration Hospital; Veterans Administration Hospital.
Kelly, George *c.ss.r.* '59 (ORL)[E] New Smyrna Beach, FL Redemptorist Fathers of the Vice Province of Richmond.
Kelly, Gerald E. *m.m.* '67 (GAL)[Q] Houston, TX Maryknoll Fathers and Brothers.
Kelly, Gerard D. '49 (PIT)[N] Pittsburgh, PA St. John Vianney Manor Retired.
Kelly, Gerard P. *c.m.* '82 (CHI)[G] Chicago, IL Catholic Charities of the Archdiocese of Chicago–Archdiocesan Offices; [N] Chicago, IL Vincentian Community, Congregation of the Mission, Midwest Province.
Kelly, Gerard (CHI) Associate Administrators.
Kelly, Gregory '82 (DAL) McKinney, TX St. Gabriel the Archangel; Procurator–Advocates; Presbyteral Council.
Kelly, J. Patrick *o.f.m.* '71 (NY)[EE] Elmwood Park, NJ FrancisCare, Elmwood Park Plaza.
Kelly, James A. '82 (SFR)[R] San Francisco, CA Prelature of the Holy Cross and Opus Dei.
Kelly, James E. *c.s.c.* '58 (FTW)[I] Holy Cross Bugembe.
Kelly, James G. '62 (BUF) Peace and Justice (Diocesan Commission); Buffalo, NY St. Margaret.
Kelly, James J. '50 (PH) Plymouth Meeting, PA Epiphany of Our Lord Retired.
Kelly, James J. '60 (BRK) Brooklyn, NY St. Brigid.
Kelly, James J. '83 (LA) Arcadia, CA Holy Angels.
Kelly, James J. *s.j.* '03 (CHL) Charlotte, NC St. Peter; [J] Mooresville, NC Jesuit Community.
Kelly, James Joseph '50 (PH) Retired.
Kelly, James M. *c.m.* '53 (BRK)[S] Bayside, NY Ozanam Hall of Queens Nursing Home, Inc.; [V] Jamaica, NY Vincentian Residence.
Kelly, James P. '62 (RVC) Rockville Centre, NY St. Agnes Cathedral.
Kelly, James P. *o.s.f.s.* '63 (PH)[AA] Philadelphia, PA Father Louis Brisson Residence.
Kelly, James T. '92 (BO) Haverhill, MA Sacred Hearts.
Kelly, James '44 (DOD) Retired.
Kelly, James *g.h.m.* '48 (CIN)[M] Cincinnati Headquarters of Glenmary Home Missioners.
Kelly, James *o.s.b.* '58 (ROC)[I] Pine City, NY Mount Saviour Monastery.
Kelly, James '60 (PHX) Camp Verde, AZ St. Frances Cabrini.
Kelly, James *o.f.m.* '78 (SFD)[L] Springfield, IL Our Lady of Angels Friary.
Kelly, Joel *o.s.b.* '66 (SCL) Minnesota State Reformatory for Men; [I] Collegeville, MN St. John's Abbey, of the Order of St. Benedict.
Kelly, John D. '86 (ARL) Fairfax, VA St. Leo's.
Kelly, John E. '73 (BO) Stoughton, MA St. James.
Kelly, John E. '87 (BUF) Boy Scouts; East Eden, NY St. Mary.
Kelly, John Edward (SAT) On Duty Outside the Archdiocese.
Kelly, John F. '84 (PT) Gulf Breeze, FL St. Sylvester.

Kelly, John J. *o.s.a.* '42 (MIA)[H] Miami, FL Casa San Lorenzo.
Kelly, John J. '64 (BLX) Lakeshore, MS St. Ann.
Kelly, John J. '87 (PH) Philadelphia, PA St. Bridget.
Kelly, John J. (PH) Archbishop's Delegate to Charismatic Prayer Groups.
Kelly, John L. '54 (BAL) Glen Burnie, MD Church of the Good Shepherd; [V] Glen Burnie, MD The Church of the Good Shepherd Parish Endowment Trust.
Kelly, John P. '45 (BO) Somerville, MA St. Joseph; Senior Priests Retired.
Kelly, John R. '68 (R) Fayetteville, NC St. Patrick; Priests' Council.
Kelly, John T. '61 (ALB) Memorial Hospital; Special Assignment.
Kelly, John T. *s.j.* '74 (BAL)[S] Kolleg St. Georgen.
Kelly, John W. '44 (LIN)[E] Lincoln, NE Bonacum House Retired.
Kelly, John W. *c.ss.r.* '51 (HBG)[H] Ephrata St. Clement's Mission House.
Kelly, John *o.s.f.s.* '71 (CHL) High Point, NC Immaculate Heart of Mary.
Kelly, John *s.a.c.* '72 (DET)[K] Wyandotte, MI Pallottine Missionary Center (Irish Province).
Kelly, Joseph A. *s.j.* '63 (NY) New York, NY St. Malachy's.
Kelly, Joseph J. '78 (NY) Bronx, NY St. Anthony.
Kelly, Joseph L. *s.s.sp.* '50 (PIT)[P] Bethel Park, PA Holy Spirit Animation Center.
Kelly, Joseph P. '66 (SCR) Scranton, PA Nativity of Our Lord; [Q] Tunkhannock, PA Camp St. Andrew.
Kelly, Justin J. *s.j.* '66 (DET)[E] Detroit, MI Loyola High School; Detroit, MI St. Francis de Sales.
Kelly, Kenneth W. '79 (KCK) Mission, KS St. Pius X.
Kelly, Kevin J. '02 (PH) Lansdale, PA Corpus Christi.
Kelly, Lawrence D. *s.j.* '46 (MIL)[O] Wauwatosa, WI Jesuit Community at St. Camillus.
Kelly, Martin C. '48 (PHX) Retired.
Kelly, Martin T. '89 (MAN) Nashua, NH St. Patrick.
Kelly, Martin '47 (NEW) Jersey City, NJ St. Aloysius Retired.
Kelly, Matthew H. '42 (LA) Retired.
Kelly, Maurus *o.f.m.* '56 (LA)[Q] Santa Barbara, CA Franciscan Friary, Order of Friars Minor (Old Mission).
Kelly, Michael C. '95 (ARL) Winchester, VA Sacred Heart of Jesus.
Kelly, Michael D. '71 (MOB) Foley, AL St. Margaret Queen of Scotland; Absent on Sick Leave; [E] Mobile, AL Little Sisters of the Poor, Home For the Aged, Inc..
Kelly, Michael D. '76 (SFS) Hartford, SD St. George; Office of Worship.
Kelly, Michael E. '66 (NEW)[C] West Orange, NJ Seton Hall Preparatory School; Liaison to the Irish Community.
Kelly, Michael J. '82 (PH) Hilltown, PA Our Lady of the Sacred Heart.
Kelly, Michael M. '81 (SR) Sonoma, CA St. Francis Solano.
Kelly, Michael M. (SR) Advocates.
Kelly, Michael M. (SR) Parish Priest Consultors.
Kelly, Michael M. (SR) Clergy Personnel Committee.
Kelly, Michael T. *s.j.* '77 (NY)[EE] New York, NY Xavier Jesuit Community.
Kelly, Michael *ss.cc.* '63 (FR)[H] Santa Fe, NM.
Kelly, Neil '91 (NY) Bronx, NY St. Lucy.
Kelly, Patrick J. '48 (BO) Woburn, MA St. Charles Borromeo; Senior Priests Retired.
Kelly, Patrick M. *s.j.* '99 (LA)[F] Los Angeles, CA Loyola High School of Los Angeles.
Kelly, Patrick M. *s.j.* '99 (DET)[K] Temperance, MI.
Kelly, Paul J. '74 (OG) Speculator, NY St. James Major; Speculator, NY St. Ann's.
Kelly, Paul J. '83 (SC) Sioux City, IA Cathedral of the Epiphany.
Kelly, Paul J. (SC) Priests' Personnel Board.
Kelly, Paul M. '47 (LA) Retired.
Kelly, Paul *s.c.j.* '77 (MIL)[O] Milwaukee, WI SCJ Community.
Kelly, Philip J. '93 (NY) New York, NY St. Joseph of the Holy Family.
Kelly, Randy J. '94 (SAG) New Lothrop, MI St. Michael.
Kelly, Raymond J. '61 (BRK) Brooklyn, NY St. Malachy's; [L] Brooklyn, NY District Council of Kings.
Kelly, Raymond M. '49 (PRO) Retired.
Kelly, Richard J. '88 (NEW) Jersey City, NJ St. Aloysius.
Kelly, Richard *o.f.m.* '92 (WDC)[M] Silver Spring, MD Gemelli House.
Kelly, Robert D. (PRM) Lakewood, OH St. Gregory the Theologian.
Kelly, Robert G. *s.j.* '57 (NY)[EE] Loyola Hall, Jesuit Community.
Kelly, Robert J. *s.j.* '52 (FgM).
Kelly, Robert J. '53 (CHR) Folly Beach, SC Our Lady of Good Counsel; [A] Charleston, SC Bishop England High School; Judges; College of Consultors; Presbyteral Council; Bishop's Missionary Support Committee; Holy Childhood Association; Parish Priest Consultors; Propagation of the Faith; Personnel Committee.
Kelly, Robert J. (ALT) Holy Childhood Association; Society for the Propagation of the Faith; Philipsburg, PA SS. Peter and Paul.
Kelly, Robert L. '77 (SY) Utica, NY Blessed Sacrament.
Kelly, Robert M. *o.p.* (GR)[F] Grand Rapids, MI Motherhouse of the Dominican Sisters.
Kelly, Robert *s.v.d.* (CHI)[B] Techny, IL Divine Word Residence.
Kelly, Robert (PRM) Notary; Presbyteral Council; Eparchial Finance Council; Priest's Pension Board.
Kelly, Stephen M. *s.j.* '90 (OAK)[N] Oakland, CA Murray Residence Community.
Kelly, Thomas D. '77 (DEN) On Duty Outside the Archdiocese; Air Force Reserve Chaplains.
Kelly, Thomas E.J. *s.j.* '79 (STL)[C] Saint Louis University; [O] St. Louis, MO Leo Brown Jesuit Community.
Kelly, Thomas F. '41 (BRK) Brooklyn, NY Our Lady of Angels.
Kelly, Thomas F. '47 (Y) Retired.
Kelly, Thomas F. '56 (PEO) Retired.
Kelly, Thomas J. '68 (ALB) Ballston Spa, NY St. Mary; Troy, NY St. Patrick.
Kelly, Thomas M. '90 (BIR) Gadsden, AL St. James.
Kelly, Thomas P. (BO) Carver, MA Our Lady of Lourdes.
Kelly, Thomas R. '67 (NY) Bronx, NY St. Gabriel.
Kelly, Thomas *o.f.m.* '62 (NEW) Wood Ridge, NJ Our Lady of the Assumption.
Kelly, Thomas '86 (HRT) Lakeville, CT St. Mary's.
Kelly, Timothy J. '99 (TYL) On Duty Outside the Diocese.
Kelly, Timothy *o.s.b.* '61 (SCL)[I] Collegeville, MN St. John's Abbey, of the Order of St. Benedict.
Kelly, Tony *s.a.c.* '55 (NY)[EE] New York, NY Pallottine Fathers.
Kelly, Vincent J. *c.ss.r.* '39 (BO)[L] Saratoga Springs, NY St. John Neumann Residence.
Kelly, Vincent J. '57 (SY) Oriskany Falls, NY St. Joseph.
Kelly, Vincent T. '56 (MIA) Fort Lauderdale, FL St. John the Baptist; [C] Fort Lauderdale, FL St. Thomas Aquinas High School; Consultors; Incardination Committee; Executive Director; Department of Schools; Retired Priests' Committee; Archbishop Hurley Scholarship Fund.
Kelly, Vincent '56 (MIA)[M] Miami Shores, FL Catholic Community Foundation, Inc..
Kelly, William A. '59 (STA) Jacksonville Beach, FL St. Paul's; Diocesan Consultors; Presbyteral Council; Deans.
Kelly, William E. '40 (NY)[EE] Bronx, NY Retired.
Kelly, William J. '48 (CHI) Retired.
Kelly, William J. *s.j.* '54 (MIL)[O] Milwaukee, WI Jesuit Community at Marquette University.
Kelly, William M. '47 (SY) Rome, NY St. Paul.
Kelly, William M. '76 (NSH) Manchester, TN St. Mark.
Kelly, William M. *s.d.s.* '79 (BIR) Tullahoma, TN St. Paul the Apostle.
Kelly, William T. '78 (GAL) Danbury, TX St Anthony de Padua.
Kelly, William T. '78 (CIN) On Duty Outside the Archdiocese.
Kelly, William T. '88 (BO)[A] Brighton, MA St. John Seminary School of Theology.
Kelmartin, John J. '49 (BAL) Retired.
Kelpsas, Anthony *m.i.c.* '53 (JOL) Darien, IL Our Lady of Peace.
Kelpsas, Jaunius '94 (CHI) Chicago, IL Immaculate Conception.
Kelso, Francis E. '61 (MAN) Retired.
Keltos, Adam *o.f.m.conv.* (SY)[Q] Syracuse, NY Friary of Francis, Brother of Peace Conventual Franciscan Friars.
Kelty, Edward J. *o.s.* '89 (PCE) On Duty Outside the Diocese; AUXILIARY CHAPLAINS CONTRACT CHAPLAINS.
Kelty, Leo '50 (TR) Retired.
Kelty, Matthew *o.c.s.o.* '46 (L)[K] Trappist KY Abbey of Our Lady of Gethsemani, of the Order of Cistercians of the Strict Observance.
Kemayou, Louis '92 (STV) St. Croix, VI Church St. Ann.
Kemberling, Andrew *o.s.b.* (DEN) Centennial, CO St. Thomas More.
Kemeter, Robert '72 (PSC) Somerset, NJ SS. Peter and Paul; Retirement Plan Board.
Kemme, Allen '91 (SFD) Arcola, IL St. John the Baptist; Tuscola, IL Forty Martyrs; Comite Diocesano de Ministerio Hispano – Diocesan Committee for Hispanic Ministry; Presbyteral Council.
Kemme, Carl A. *v.g.* '86 (SFD) Petersburg, IL St. Peter; Lay Employees' Pension Plan Administrative Committee; Diocesan Health Insurance Program Committee; Comite Diocesano de Ministerio Hispano – Diocesan Committee for Hispanic Ministry; Ex Officios.
Kemme, Carl (SFD) Vicars General; Corporate Board Members; Board of Catholic Education; Commission for Buildings and Property; Black Catholic Advisory Board; Ex Officio; Moderator of the Curia; Consultants; Consultants; Presbyteral Council.
Kemme, Joseph A. '64 (ALN)[A] Wernersville, PA Jesuit Center.
Kemmer, Victor A. '43 (MIL) Retired.
Kemmery, Robert J. '54 (MAN) Retired.
Kemner, Gregory *o.f.m.* '55 (FgM).
Kemner, Kieran *o.f.m.* '53 (CHI)[N] Countryside, IL St. Gratian Friary, Franciscan Friars.
Kemo, Kurt H. '83 (STU) Toronto, OH St. Francis of Assisi; Toronto, OH St. Joseph's; [K] Steubenville, OH RCIA; Vicar General; Moderator of the Curia; Diocesan Finance Office; Diocesan/Parish Share Campaign; Judicial Vicar; Child Protection Review Board; Pastoral Staff; Presbyteral Council; Priests Personnel Board; Continuing Education of Priests; Diocesan Finance Council; Vocations; Woman's Club.
Kemp, Dennis '73 (SEA) Mercer Island, WA St. Monica.
Kemp, Patrick W. '55 (WDC) Retired.
Kemp, Raymond B. '67 (WDC) Special Ministries; [V] Washington, DC Woodstock Theological Center.
Kemp, Thomas L. '52 (BUF) East Bethany, NY Immaculate Conception.
Kempa, Stanley (BO) Lowell, MA Holy Trinity.
Kempczynski, John '51 (BUF) Tonawanda, NY St. Timothy Retired.
Kempen, Gerald B. *o.praem.* '51 (GB)[I] De Pere, WI St. Norbert Abbey.
Kemper, Jeffrey M. '79 (CIN)[B] Cincinnati, OH Mt. St. Mary's Seminary of the West; [B] Cincinnati, OH Mt. St. Mary's Seminary of the West.
Kemper, John C. *s.s.* '83 (HBG) On Duty Outside the Diocese.
Kemper, John *s.s.* '83 (SAT)[C] Oblate School of Theology.
Kempf, Joseph G. '80 (STL) O'Fallon, MO Assumption.
Kempf, William G. '84 (STL) Normandy, MO St. Ann.
Kempf, William '84 (STL)[T] St. Louis, MO University of Missouri, St. Louis, Catholic Newman Center.
Kempfer, James '69 (JOL) Absent on Leave.
Kempfirl, Fred '65 (NY) Milton, NY St. James.
Kemphues, Carl *o.f.m.* '56 (CIN)[M] Franciscan Renewal Center; (FgM).
Kempinger, Stephen *c.s.c.* '01 (FTW) South Bend, IN Christ the King.
Kempkes, Lambert *c.m.m.* '50 (DET)[K] Vocation Office.
Kempski, Leonard J. '66 (WIL) Perryville, MD Church of the Good Shepherd; Liaison for Non–Christian Religions.
Kenaston, Perry (JUN) Yakutat, AK St. Ann; Diocesan Consultors; Finance Council; Commission for Social Justice; Hoonah, AK Sacred Heart.
Kencik, Marian M. '62 (KAL) Niles, MI St. Mary.
Kendall, Jeffrey A. '97 (CHR) Charleston, SC Sacred Heart; Charleston, SC Christ the Divine Teacher; [H] Charleston, SC The Citadel; Campus Ministry; Vocations Board.
Kendall, Michael *s.d.s.* '61 (MIL)[O] Tucson, AZ.
Kendall, Philip E. *c.s.v.* (KCK) Pro–Synodal Judges.
Kendall, Philip *c.s.v.* '62 (KCK) Kansas City, KS Cathedral of St. Peter the Apostle; [I] Kansas City, KS; Judicial Vicar.
Kendall, R. Daniel *s.j.* '70 (SFR)[N] San Francisco, CA Jesuit Community at University of San Francisco.
Kendzierski, James *o.f.m.* '81 (MIL) Sturtevant, WI St. Sebastian.
Kendzierski, Norbert V. '64 (DET) Farmington Hills, MI St. Colman.
Kenealy, Thomas L. *s.j.* '58 (CHI)[N] Evanston, IL Canisius House.
Kenefick, Paul F. '56 (HRT) Hartford, CT St. Lawrence O'Toole.
Kenehan, David A. *o.s.f.s.* (MO) Army Chaplains.
Kenkel, Benedict J. '53 (DM) Retired.
Kenkel, Leonard A. '60 (DM) Creston, IA Holy Spirit.
Kenlon, Knute *o.f.m.cap.* '58 (BRK)[V] Brooklyn, NY St. Michael's Friary Retired.
Kenna, Daniel T. *o.f.m.* '73 (R) Raleigh, NC St. Francis of Assisi.
Kenna, Donald J. '64 (BRK) Brooklyn, NY All Saints.
Kenna, Joseph J. '67 (YAK) On Duty Outside the Diocese.
Kenna, Joseph R. '99 (ARL) Fredericksburg, VA St. Mary; Notaries.
Kenna, Richard A. *s.j.* '57 (BAL)[S] Loyola Hall.
Kenna, Thomas J. '63 (NEW) Lyndhurst, NJ Our Lady of Mount Carmel; Saddle Brook, NJ St. Philip the Apostle.
Kenna, Thomas (NEW) Part–time Staff.
Kennard, George V. *s.j.* '50 (STL)[O] St. Louis, MO Jesuit Community Corporation at St. Louis University – Jesuit Hall.
Kenneally, John A. '69 (SAV) St. Simons Island, GA St. Williams; Vicars General; Finance Council.
Kenneally, William F. '53 (BO) Milton, MA St. Agatha; Senior Priests Retired.
Kenneally, William G. '61 (CHI) Chicago, IL St. Gertrude.

Kennealy, Thomas P. *s.j.* '62 (CIN)[D] Xavier University; [M] Cincinnati, OH Jesuit Community at Xavier University.
Kennebeck, Brian A. (STL) St. Charles, MO St. Joseph.
Kennedy, Alan '52 (P) Retired.
Kennedy, Alex '90 (TLS) Grove, OK St. Elizabeth; Langley, OK St. Frances of Rome; Vinita, OK Holy Ghost.
Kennedy, Andrew '63 (BIR) Birmingham, AL Our Lady of Lourdes.
Kennedy, Arthur L. '66 (BO) On Duty Outside the Archdiocese.
Kennedy, Arthur L. '67 (BO)[C] St. Paul, MN University of St. Thomas.
Kennedy, Brian *c.ss.r.* '75 (RNO) Carlin, NV Sacred Heart; Elko, NV St. Joseph's; Eureka, NV St. Brendan's.
Kennedy, Charles J. '66 (PH) Norristown, PA St. Patrick.
Kennedy, Christopher J. '44 (LA) Long Beach, CA St. Barnabas Retired.
Kennedy, David G. '55 (BUR) Retired.
Kennedy, David W. '53 (GAL) Conroe, TX Sacred Heart; Northern Vicariate.
Kennedy, David William '97 (OWN) Oak Grove, KY St. Michael the Archangel.
Kennedy, David '97 (OWN) Hawesville, KY Immaculate Conception; Lewisport, KY St. Columba.
Kennedy, David (GAL) Defenders of the Bond.
Kennedy, Edward F.X. *s.j.* '52 (NY)[EE] Loyola Hall, Jesuit Community.
Kennedy, Edward J. '59 (CAM) Retired.
Kennedy, Edward J. '68 (PH)[X] Darby, PA St. Francis Country House.
Kennedy, Edward J. '93 (GRY) Cedar Lake, IN Holy Name; Bishop's Council of Priests; Cursillos in Christianity; Priestly Life.
Kennedy, Edward '68 (PH) Darby, PA Blessed Virgin Mary.
Kennedy, Ernest E. '56 (CHR) North Charleston, SC St. John's; Special Assignment.
Kennedy, Francis B. '39 (CIN) Retired.
Kennedy, Francis M. '64 (SPR) Chicopee, MA Nativity of the Blessed Virgin Mary; Chicopee, MA St. Mary's.
Kennedy, Gary L. '68 (PBL) St. Mary Corwin Medical Center.
Kennedy, Gary '68 (PBL)[D] Pueblo, CO Centura Health–St. Mary–Corwin Medical Center.
Kennedy, Glenn C. '99 (RVC) Absent on Leave.
Kennedy, Hugh A. *s.j.* '48 (BAL)[S] Baltimore, MD Jesuit Fathers and Brothers Maryland Provincial Curia.
Kennedy, J. Nevin '58 (MET)[H] Somerset, NJ Maria Regina Residence Retired.
Kennedy, James M. '54 (SY) North Syracuse, NY St. Rose of Lima.
Kennedy, James (SY) Pastoral Examiners.
Kennedy, John D. '93 (SHP) Absent on Sick Leave.
Kennedy, John F. '63 (NEW) Scotch Plains, NJ Immaculate Heart of Mary.
Kennedy, John J. '49 (STL) Retired.
Kennedy, John V. *c.m.* '49 (PH).
Kennedy, John '56 (SFD) Retired.
Kennedy, John '90 (CAM)[AA] Marmora, NJ The Church of the Resurrection.
Kennedy, Joseph J. '48 (PH) Media, PA Nativity of the Blessed Virgin Mary Retired.
Kennedy, Joseph M. *s.j.* '55 (BAL)[B] Timonium, MD Loyola Graduate Center –Timonium Campus.
Kennedy, Joseph M. *s.j.* (BAL)[S] Baltimore, MD Jesuit Community of Loyola College, Inc..
Kennedy, Joseph P. '73 (WDC) Silver Spring, MD St. Andrew Apostle.
Kennedy, Kevin J. '95 (WDC) Potomac, MD Our Lady of Mercy.
Kennedy, Kevin '99 (SFR) Redwood City, CA St. Pius.
Kennedy, Laurence W. '57 (SY) Syracuse, NY St. Brigid and St. Joseph.
Kennedy, Leo R. *m.m* '59 (NY)[EE] Maryknoll Maryknoll Fathers and Brothers.
Kennedy, Leo *o.f.m.conv.* '90 (TOL) Carey, OH Our Lady of Consolation, Basilica–National Shrine.
Kennedy, Louis J.P. '57 (CHR) Anderson, SC St. Joseph's.
Kennedy, Malcolm M. '61 (NY)[JJ] New Rochelle, NY.
Kennedy, Michael E. *s.j.* '77 (LA) Los Angeles, CA Dolores Mission.
Kennedy, Michael J. *c.m.* '51 (BAL) Emmitsburg, MD St. Joseph; [S] Emmitsburg, MD Vincentian House.
Kennedy, Michael J. '67 (STP) Oak Grove, MN St. Patrick.
Kennedy, Oliver *s.s.c.* '47 (OM)[K] St. Columbans, NE St. Columban's Foreign Mission Society.
Kennedy, Paddy '59 (SP)[F] Lutz, FL St. Timothy Catholic Early Childhood Learning Center.
Kennedy, Patrick J. R. '70 (NO) Retired.
Kennedy, Patrick J.R. '30 (NO) Gretna, LA St. Anthony Retired.
Kennedy, Patrick '53 (DEN) Denver, CO Our Lady of Grace.
Kennedy, Patrick '59 (SP) Lutz, FL St. Timothy.
Kennedy, Patrick '77 (STP) Coon Rapids, MN Church of the Epiphany.
Kennedy, Paul M. '77 (PH) Rydal, PA St. Hilary of Poitiers; [D] Philadelphia, PA Cardinal Dougherty High School.
Kennedy, Richard C. '73 (ORG) Santa Ana, CA St. Barbara's.
Kennedy, Richard *m.s.c.* '67 (RCK).
Kennedy, Richard *m.s.c.* '67[G] (FgM).
Kennedy, Robert E. *s.j.* '65 (NEW)[B] Jersey City, NJ Jesuit Center; [N] Jersey City, NJ Jesuits of Saint Peter's College, Inc..
Kennedy, Robert J. '74 (ROC) Rochester, NY Blessed Sacrament.
Kennedy, Robert R. '66 (BO) East Boston, MA St. Mary, Star of the Sea.
Kennedy, Robert T. '59 (NY) On Duty Outside the Archdiocese; [C] Catholic University of America, The.
Kennedy, Russell F. (NOR) Part Time; Advisory Council.
Kennedy, Russell (NOR) Norwich, CT St. Mary; St. Mary Church – Spanish Apostolate; Chaplains.
Kennedy, Santhiagu John '92 (MIL) Milwaukee, WI St. Catherine.
Kennedy, Stanley T. *m.s.* '70 (HRT)[M] Hartford, CT Missionaries of LaSalette.
Kennedy, T. Frank *s.j.* '76 (BO)[V] Newton, MA The Jesuit Community at Boston College.
Kennedy, Thaddeus J. *o.c.s.o.* '58 (DUB)[K] Peosta, IA New Melleray Abbey, Order of Cistercians of the Strict Observance.
Kennedy, Thomas R. *c.m.* '64 (PH).
Kennedy, Victor P. '77 (NEW)[AA] Jersey City, NJ St. Anne's; Members; Boy Scouts of America/Catholic Committee on Scouting.
Kennedy, William J. *s.j.* '65 (BO)[V] Boston The Society of Jesus of New England–Provincial Offices.
Kennedy, William J. *s.j.* '65 (BGP) Greenwich, CT St. Michael the Archangel; [P] Fairfield, CT The Fairfield Jesuit Community–Fairfield University.
Kennedy, William J. '69 (NY) Retired.
Kennedy, William M. '71 (BO) Military & VA Chaplains; Navy Chaplains.
Kennedy, William M. '71 (CIN) Cincinnati, OH Assumption.
Kennedy, William '69 (NY)[EE] Bronx, NY.
Kennedy, William (NY) New York, NY St. Agnes Retired.
Kennehan, John P. '62 (SPC) St. John's Regional Health Center; St. Francis de Sales Association.
Kennehan, John P. '62 (OG) Brownville, NY Immaculate Conception of the B.V.M.; On Duty Outside the Diocese; Springfield, MO Cathedral of St. Agnes.
Kennelley, James J. '70 (E) Immaculate Heart.
Kennelly, Daniel '77 (BGP)[J] Bridgeport, CT St. Vincent's Medical Center.
Kennelly, Michael F. *s.j.* '46 (SP)[P] New Orleans, LA Ignatius Residence.
Kennelly, Stephen '69 (SAN) Miles, TX St. Thomas.
Kenney, Albert A. '94 (PRO)[A] Providence, RI Seminary of Our Lady of Providence; [E] Providence, RI La Salle Academy; Seminary of Our Lady of Providence; Vocations.
Kenney, Brian A. '02 (L) Bardstown, KY Basilica of St. Joseph Proto–Cathedral.
Kenney, C. Doug (BAL) Advocates and Procurators.
Kenney, Daniel J. *s.j.* '63 (MIL)[O] Milwaukee, WI Jesuit Community at Marquette University.
Kenney, Douglas '99 (BAL) Frostburg, MD St. Michael; Grantsville, MD St. Ann; Mount Savage, MD St. Patrick.
Kenney, Francis J. *s.m.* '49 (CIN)[M] Dayton, OH Marianist Community.
Kenney, Francis P. '87 (WIL) Elkton, MD Immaculate Conception.
Kenney, Gerard J. '97 (LUB) Plainview, TX Sacred Heart; Director of Vocations.
Kenney, Gerard (LUB) Vicars Forane; Diocesan Council of Catholic Women.
Kenney, Henry *s.j.* '52 (LEX) Special Assignment; Lexington, KY St. Peter.
Kenney, Jeremiah F. '72 (BAL) Towson, MD Church of the Immaculate Conception; Special Assignment; [W] Baltimore, MD Holy Name Society (Union); Vice Chancellor; Judicial Vicar; Cardinal's Delegate for Canonical Affairs; St. Vincent de Paul Society.
Kenney, John B. '57 (BUR) Retired.
Kenney, Joseph *m.s.a.* '79 (NOR)[F] Cromwell Society of the Missionaries of the Holy Apostles.
Kenney, Kevin T. '94 (STP) Minneapolis, MN Our Lady of Peace.
Kenney, Mark G. *s.m.* '79 (WDC)[B] Washington, DC Marist College, The Scholasticate.
Kenney, Paul C. *s.j.* '72 (BO)[V] Cambridge, MA Faber House; [V] Weston, MA Campion Jesuit Community.
Kenney, Paul *s.j.* (BO)[BB] Weston, MA Regis College Office of Campus Ministry.
Kenney, Peter J. *s.s.j.* '46 (BAL)[S] Baltimore, MD St. Joseph Society of the Sacred Heart House of Central Administration.
Kenney, Philip J. '39 (MAN) Retired.
Kenney, Robert D. *o.s.f.s.* '52 (WIL)[B] Wilmington, DE Salesianum School.
Kenney, Sean W. '91 (MET) Basking Ridge, NJ St. James.
Kenney, Timothy M. *s.m.* '82 (SFR)[N] San Francisco, CA Marianist Community.
Kenney, Timothy *s.m.* '82 (STL)[O] St. Louis, MO Provincialate of the Society of Mary, Province of the United States; [O] St. Louis, MO Maryland Avenue Marianist Community.
Kenney, W. Henry *s.j.* '52 (CHI) Lexington, KY Veterans' Administration Hospital.
Kenney, William J. *c.s.p.* '51 (NY)[EE] Jamaica Estates Paulist Fathers Generalate.
Kenney, William J. '56 (STP) Minneapolis, MN Our Lady of Mount Carmel Retired.
Kenney, Wilton Henry *s.j.* (MO).
Kenning, Herman H. '43 (CIN)[N] Cincinnati, OH St. Clare Convent, Franciscan Sisters of the Poor; Defenders of the Bond Retired.
Kennington, John *c.ss.r.* '59 (NY).
Kenny, Albert N. '54 (BRK) Retired.
Kenny, Donald '66 (JOL) Retired.
Kenny, Eugene '53 (DOD) Retired.
Kenny, Gregory D. *c.m.f.* '59 (ATL)[II] Stone Mountain, GA Corpus Christi; [N] Stone Mountain, GA.
Kenny, James E. '49 (OM) Retired.
Kenny, James T. '45 (SLC) Retired.
Kenny, John F. *o.s.f.s.* '69 (WIL)[J] Childs, MD Retirement and Assisted Care Facility.
Kenny, John R. '51 (OAK)[M] Oakland, CA Bishop Begin Villa.
Kenny, John '51 (OAK) Retired.
Kenny, John *c.s.p.* '58 (GR) Grand Rapids, MI Chapel of St. Paul–Catholic Information Center.
Kenny, Joseph H. *o.p.* '50 (FgM).
Kenny, Joseph P. *o.p.* '63 (CHI)[N] Chicago Dominicans (Provincial Office).
Kenny, Kevin *o.f.m.conv.* '66 (ALB) Fonda, NY St. Cecilia; [N] Fonda, NY Blessed Kateri Guest House.
Kenny, Michael '73 (SAT) On Leave.
Kenny, Michael '03 (LA) Oxnard, CA Mary Star of the Sea.
Kenny, P. Edward '74 (BAL) Baltimore, MD Blessed Sacrament Church; Baltimore, MD St. Mary of the Assumption.
Kenny, Peter *s.s.c.* '58 (LA)[Q] Los Angeles, CA Columban Fathers, Procure House.
Kenny, Pierce *c.ss.r.* '69 (BRK) Brooklyn, NY Our Lady of Perpetual Help Basilica.
Kenny, Raymond G. '63 (SJ) San Jose, CA St. Martin of Tours.
Kenny, Robert J. '03 (SEA) Olympia, WA St. Michael.
Kenny, Simon *o.carm.* '64 (VEN)[G] Venice, FL Carmel in Venice.
Kenny, Thomas A. '46 (NEW) Retired.
Kenny, Thomas C. *o.s.a.* '56 (BO)[C] Our Mother of Good Counsel Monastery.
Kenny, Thomas '65 (ATL) Atlanta, GA Cathedral of Christ the King.
Kenny, Walter F. '54 (NY) Larchmont, NY St. Augustine.
Kenny, Walter F. (NY) Judicial Vicar.
Kenny, Walter F. (ALB) Inter Diocesan Tribunal for the Province of NY.
Kenny, William J.M. '71 (LAV) Las Vegas, NV Christ the King.
Kenny, William (LAV) Presbyteral Council for the Diocese of Las Vegas.
Kenshol, Joseph W. '73 (GR) Sand Lake, MI Mary Queen of Apostles; Deans.
Kenshol, Joseph (GR) Presbyteral Council.
Kent, Daniel '63 (MIA)[B] St. Thomas University Retired.
Kent, James *o.f.m.conv.* '91 (IND)[K] Pleasure Ridge Park, KY St. Paul Friary.
Kent, James *o.f.m.conv.* '91 (L)[K] Louisville, KY St. Francis of Assisi Friary.
Kent, Thomas J. *s.j.* '47 (SY)[Q] Syracuse, NY Jesuits at LeMoyne, Inc..
Keogh, James *s.j.* '52 (CHL) Mooresville, NC St. Therese; [J] Mooresville, NC Jesuit Community.
Keogh, Simeon *o.f.m.cap.* '49 (MIL)[B] Mount Calvary, WI St. Felix Friary.
Keogh, Thomas '45 (SR) Retired.
Keogh, William '78 (JC) On Duty Outside the Diocese.
Keohan, Edward M. '59 (BO) Salem, MA North Shore Medical Center.
Keohane, Daniel T. '78 (SFR) San Mateo, CA St. Bartholomew.
Keohane, Donal '68 (SAV) On Duty Outside the Diocese.
Keohane, Donal '68 (LA) Los Angeles, CA St. Martin of Tours.
Keolker, Richard F. '63 (YAK) On Duty Outside the Diocese.
Keon, James J. *c.s.b.* '52 (GAL)[Q] Houston, TX Residence of the Basilian Fathers of the University of St. Thomas.
Keough, Joseph F. '96 (HRT) Madison, CT St. Margaret.

Keppel, Timothy F. *c.r.* '77 (SB) Crest Park, CA Our Lady of the Lake; Running Springs, CA St. Anne in the Mountains.
Keppeler, Richard J. '54 (BUF) Retired.
Keppens, Gustaaf M. *s.j.* '61 (WDC)[K] Washington, DC Georgetown University Hospital; [M] Washington, DC The Jesuit Community at Georgetown University.
Kepple, Robert '74 (LR) Retired.
Keppler, Daniel J. '58 (DUB) Retired.
Keppler, John F. '60 (BRK) Bayside, NY American Martyrs.
Kerbawy, Kevin '76 (SAG) Bay City, MI Holy Trinity.
Kerber, John V. '58 (STL) Festus, MO Our Lady.
Kerber, Joseph P. '88 (SFD) New Berlin, IL Visitation B.V.M.; New Berlin, IL Sacred Heart of Jesus; New Berlin, IL Sacred Heart of Mary.
Kerber, Justin *c.p.* '72 (R) Greenville, NC St. Peter's; Deans; Priests' Council.
Kerby, Robert L. '70 (NTN) South Bend, IN St. John of Damascus.
Kerdiejus, John B. *s.j.* '58 (BO)[X] Gloucester, MA Eastern Point Retreat House.
Kerestes, Michael '89 (PSC) Beltsville, MD St. Gregory of Nyssa; Retirement Plan Board.
Kerestus, Thomas J. '69 (ALN)[J] Bethlehem, PA Holy Family Villa Retired.
Kereszty, Rochus *o.cist.* '60 (DAL)[K] Irving, TX Cistercian Abbey of Our Lady of Dallas.
Kerin, Joseph A. '57 (CHL) Retired.
Kerin, Michael *g.h.m.* '88 (BIR) Winfield, AL Holy Spirit.
Kerkemeyer, Carl '02 (TLS) Tulsa, OK St. Thomas More.
Kerketta, George '81 (BWN) Mercedes, TX Our Lady of Mercy.
Kerkof, Loren *o.f.m.* '60 (P) Portland, OR Ascension.
Kern, Crosby W. '65 (NO) New Orleans, LA St. Louis Cathedral; New Orleans, LA St. Mary Church; Archdiocesan Consultors; Newspaper; Old Ursuline Convent.
Kern, John R. '68 (MIL) Racine, WI St. Richard of Chichester; Deans.
Kern, Joseph R. '57 (IND) Retired.
Kern, Joseph '57 (IND) Deaneries and Deans; Terre Haute, IN St. Margaret Mary.
Kern, Martin F. '94 (ALN) Allentown, PA St. Francis of Assisi; Cursillo Movement.
Kern, Walter O. '58 (BUF) Retired.
Kernan, Eugene J. '49 (CAM) Retired.
Kernan, H. Michael (PIT) Retired Priests, Residences for.
Kernan, James *o.m.i.* '59 (SD) Calipatria, CA St. Patrick.
Kernan, Michael H. '54 (PIT) Retired.
Kernan, William A. '93 (SD) Valley Center, CA St. Stephen.
Kerner, Terrence D. '72 (DET) Northville, MI Our Lady of Victory.
Kerner, Timothy J. *c.ss.r.* '81 (BR)[F] Baton Rouge, LA Our Lady of the Lake Regional Medical Center.
Kerns, John '85 (P) Portland, OR St. Juan Diego.
Kerns, Paul R. '71 (PRT) Bradley, ME St. Ann; Old Town, ME St. Ann Church, Indian Island.
Kerper, Michael '85 (MAN) Portsmouth, NH St. James; Rockingham County House of Corrections; Advocates.
Kerr, Charles L. *s.j.* '50 (MIL)[O] Wauwatosa, WI Jesuit Community at St. Camillus.
Kerr, Cherubin *o.s.a.* '44 (CAM)[C] Richland, NJ St. Augustine Preparatory School.
Kerr, John W. '98 (LR) De Queen, AR St. Barbara's; Nashville, AR St. Martin Church.
Kerr, Robert '95 (KC) Hamilton, MO Sacred Heart; Gallatin, MO Mary Immaculate; Deans.
Kerr, Seamus '60 (YAK) Ephrata, WA St. Rose of Lima; Presbyteral Council Executive Committee.
Kerr, William A. '66 (PIT)[B] Pittsburgh, PA La Roche College; On Duty Outside the Diocese.
Kerrigan, Bernard A. '48 (WIN)[F] Wabasha, MN St. Elizabeth's Health Care Center Retired.
Kerrigan, James P. '70 (WOR) Rutland, MA St. Patrick's; Advocates.
Kerrigan, Joseph J. '90 (MET) East Brunswick, NJ St. Bartholomew.
Kerrigan, Joseph (MET) Catholic Relief Services.
Kerrigan, Michael F. '64 (DEN) Idaho Springs, CO St. Paul.
Kerrigan, Michael P. *c.s.p.* '87 (NY).
Kerrigan, Neal *o.f.m.cap.* '52 (NY).
Kerschen, Leo A. '62 (WCH)[EE] Eureka, KS Sacred Heart; Eureka, KS St. John; Eureka, KS St. Teresa of Avila.
Kerschen, Leon J. '62 (WCH) Iola, KS St. John; Yates Center, KS St. Joseph.
Kerscher, Charles J. '79 (ATL) Conyers, GA St. Pius X Catholic Retired.
Kerscher, Francis '55 (GB) Retired.
Kersgieter, Paul J. '45 (STL) Retired.
Kerst, Patrick '90 (SPK) Walla Walla, WA St. Francis of Assisi; Walla Walla, WA St. Patrick; Priests' Personnel Board.
Kersten, Edward J. *o.s.a.* '56 (CHI) Chicago, IL St. Rita of Cascia.
Kersten, Jay J. '98 (LAN) On Duty Outside the Diocese; Navy Chaplains.
Kersten, John *s.v.d.* '40 (BLX)[A] Bay St. Louis, MS St. Augustine's.
Kersten, Kevin *s.j.* '72 (Wisconsin)[V] Newton, MA The Jesuit Community at Boston College.
Kertz, Leo *o.m.i.* '63 (FgM).
Kertz, Raymond N. '67 (MAD) Cottage Grove, WI St. Patrick; Deaneries.
Kerwan, Francis T. '43 (HRT) Enfield, CT Holy Family.
Kerwin, Eugene H. '52 (OM) Retired.
Kerze, William F. '69 (LA) Malibu, CA Our Lady of Malibu.
Kesicki, Michael T. '88 (E)[A] Erie, PA St. Mark's Seminary; [B] Erie, PA Gannon University; [M] Erie, PA Holy Family Monastery; The Bishop's Theological Advisory Committee; St. Mark Seminary
Kesicki, Timothy P. (CLV) Presbyteral Council.
Kesicki, Timothy *s.j.* (CLV)[D] Cleveland, OH St. Ignatius High School.
Kessing, Bernadine C. *o.f.m.* '60 (NEW) Fair Lawn, NJ St. Anne's.
Kessing, Bernardine *o.f.m.* '60 (BO)[Y] Boston, MA Saint Anthony Residence.
Kessinger, David R. *o.s.b.* '58 (CHL)[J] Belmont, NC Belmont Abbey.
Kessler, Edward L. '48 (COL) Retired.
Kessler, Matt *c.ss.r.* '72 (STL)[O] Liguori, MO Liguori Mission House/Redemptorists.
Kessler, Thomas '75 (EVN) Loogootee, IN St. John; Loogootee IN St. Martin's; Loogootee, IN St. Joseph's; St. Mary's.
Kessler, Thomas '84 (CHL) Winston–Salem, NC St. Leo's.
Kessler, W. Thomas (COL) Diocesan Judges.
Kessler, William Thomas (COL)[A] Censor of Books.
Kessler, William '99 (SFD) Effingham, IL St. Anthony of Padua.
Kester, Kevin A. '81 (LA) La Canada Flintridge, CA St. Bede the Venerable.
Kester, William J. '70 (STL) St. Louis, MO St. Matthias.
Kestermeier, Charles T. *s.j.* '75 (OM)[K] Omaha, NE Jesuit Community at Creighton University.
Kestler, Theodore E. *s.j.* '75 (FBK) St. Marys, AK Church of the Nativity; [E] St. Marys, AK Native Ministry Training Program; [E] St. Marys, AK Brother Joe Prince Jesuit Community.
Ketcham, Gregory K. '94 (PEO) Peoria, IL St. Philomena's; Nauvoo, IL SS. Peter and Paul's.
Kettelberger, John *c.m.* '78 (PH) Philadelphia, PA St. Vincent de Paul.
Ketteler, Ronald M. '61 (COV) Crescent Springs, KY St. Joseph; Continuing Education of Priests; Ecumenism.
Kettenring, Michael J. '01 (NO) New Orleans, LA St. Andrew the Apostle.
Kettle, Laurence *o.f.m.* (MO) AUXILIARY CHAPLAINS CONTRACT CHAPLAINS.
Kettron, W. Michael '57 (LFT) Cicero, IN Sacred Heart.
Keulman, Kenneth P. '69 (SJ) On Leave of Absence.
Keulman, Kenneth P. '69 (NO)[C] New Orleans, LA Loyola University New Orleans.
Keusal, Eugene '61 (CHI) Makawao, HI St. Joseph Retired.
Keusenkothen, Stephen *c.m.f.* '03 (CHI)[N] Kingston, Jamaica, WI.
Keveney, William '56 (DET) Retired.
Keville, Joseph F. '96 (BO) Health Leave.
Kew, Larry J. '66 (GRY) Hammond, IN St. Catherine of Siena.
Key, Oren W. *s.j.* '53 (FWT) Vernon, TX St. Joseph; Vernon, TX St. Mary; Vernon, TX Holy Family.
Key, William W. '75 (MIL)[V] Racine, WI Cursillos in Christianity; Beaver Dam, WI St. Katharine Drexel.
Keyes, Patrick A. *c.ss.r.* '89 (DOD) Liberal, KS St. Anthony; [F] Liberal, KS Liberal Redemptorist Hispanic House Ministry, Inc..
Keyes, Paul T. '63 (BO) North Andover, MA St. Michael.
Keyes, Raphael P. '64 (JC) Camdenton, MO St. Anthony; Appointed Members.
Keyes, Thomas E. '73 (BO) Revere, MA Our Lady of Lourdes
Keyickal, Thomas (PT) Cantonment, FL St. Jude Thaddeus.
Keymont, Walter F. '80 (BO) Dorchester, MA St. Ann.
Keyrouze, Joseph '50 (ALB) Retired.
Keys, Gordon L. *s.j.* '55 (SPK)[J] Spokane, WA Regis Community.
Keys, Thomas J. '70 (SR) Santa Rosa, CA Star of the Valley.
Kezmarsky, Kenneth E. '86 (PIT) Washington County, PA Bradley Center South; Washington County, PA West Penn Allegheny Health System–Canonsburg Hospital; Washington County, PA Beverly South Hills; Washington County, PA Canon House; Washington County, PA Charles House Home for the Aged; Washington County, PA Greenery Nursing Home; Washington County, PA Horizon Senior Care; Washington County, PA Pine Lawn Home; Washington County, PA Rest Haven Personal Care Home I; Washington County, PA Rest Haven Personal Care Home II; Washington County, PA Rest Haven Personal Care Home V.
Khachan, Bernard C. '60 (OLL) Cleveland, OH St. Maron.
Khai Vu, Joseph '96 (NEW) Newark, NJ St. Patrick's Pro–Cathedral; Kearny, NJ West Hudson Hospital.
Khalil, Naim *b.s.o.* '93 (NTN) Miami, FL St. Jude; Miami, FL St. Nicholas.
Kham, Peter Nguyen '80 (WDC) Washington, DC St. Mary, Mother of God.
Khanh, San Hoag '94 (COS) On Duty Outside Diocese.
Kharuk, Wasyl '92 (PHU) Baltimore, MD St. Michael's.
Khiet, Nquyen '96 (TLS) Special Assignment.
Khoi, Jim N. *c.m.c.* '91 (STP) Minneapolis, MN St. Joseph Hien.
Khonde, Charles Phukuta *c.i.c.m.* '99 (R) Wendell, NC St. Eugene.
Khoueiry, Joseph '00 (SAM) Dover, NH St. George.
Khoury, Ghattas '90 (OLL) Detroit, MI St. Maron.
Khoury, James T. '75 (SAM) Lawrence, MA St. Anthony.
Ki–Kuk, John Youn '74 (STL) University City, MO St. Andrew Kim.
Kibby, Patrick J. '84 (NSH) Nashville, TN Cathedral of the Incarnation.
Kiberu, John Baptist (CHI) Chicago, IL SS. Peter and Paul.
Kibler, Gary R. '71 (BUF) Lockport, NY St. Mary.
Kibuka, Matthias W. '58 (BUF) Retired.
Kichak, Joseph A. '43 (MAR) Retired.
Kickham, Robert T. (BO) Secretaries to the Archbishop and Masters of Ceremonies.
Kiczuk, Casimir *c.m.* '34 (HRT)[M] Manchester DePaul Provincial Residence.
Kidd, Michael C. '54 (WDC) Mitchellville, MD Holy Family.
Kidd, Wayne R. '73 (LC) Hillsboro, WI St. Aloysius; Wonewoc, WI St. Jerome.
Kidd, William J. *s.j.* '63 (MIL)[O] Milwaukee, WI Jesuit Community at Marquette University.
Kidder, James C. '67 (SAC) El Dorado Hills, CA Holy Trinity; Defenders of the Bond.
Kiddy, Curtis '92 (MIA) Absent on Leave.
Kidner, M. Paul *o.s.b.* '58 (STL)[F] Creve Coeur, MO St. Louis Priory School; [O] St. Louis, MO The Abbey of St. Mary and St. Louis.
Kidney, Liam J. '68 (LA) Pacific Palisades, CA Corpus Christi.
Kidney, Timothy '71 (SJ) Sunnyvale, CA St. Cyprian.
Kidwell, William *s.j.* '55 (MIA) Miami, FL Gesu.
Kiedinger, Daniel J. '91 (LC) Mauston, WI St. Patrick.
Kiefer, David (GB) Priests' Personnel Board.
Kiefer, John D. '70 (LFT) Muncie, IN St. Francis of Assisi; [H] Muncie, IN St. Francis of Assisi University Church.
Kiefer, R. David '62 (GB) Mattoon, WI Holy Family; Neopit, WI St. Anthony; Phlox, WI St. Joseph.
Kiefer, Robert '91 (SJ) San Jose, CA St. Frances Cabrini; Priests' Retirement Board.
Kiefer, Thomas A. '46 (LA) Retired.
Kiefer, Thomas P. '81 (SPC) Cape Girardeau, MO Cathedral of St. Mary; Vice Chancellor; Adjutant Judicial Vicars; Associate Director of Vocations/Seminarians; Diocesan Consultors.
Kiefer, Thomas '46 (LA) North Hollywood, CA St. Charles Borromeo.
Kiefer, William J. '58 (SB) Trona, CA St. Madeleine Sophie Barat Retired.
Kieferle, Norbert '66 (AMA) Retired.
Kieffer, Charles G. '80 (PHX) Phoenix, AZ St. Theresa; Defenders of the Bond.
Kieffer, Charles (PHX) College of Consultors.
Kieffer, John L. *s.j.* '68 (LEX) Monticello, KY St. Peter; [J] Mount Vernon, KY Appalachia Science in the Public Interest.
Kieffer, John L. *s.j.* '68 (DET)[K] Temperance, MI.
Kieffer, Kenneth *o.f.m.* '55 (STL)[O] Oceanside, CA.
Kieffer, Lawrence J. '50 (MAD) Retired.
Kieffer, Merlin '60 (SAL) Clay Center, KS SS. Peter and Paul.
Kieffer, Robert '69 (SCL) Fergus Falls, MN Our Lady of Victory; Deans; Presbyteral Council; Diocesan Planning Council.
Kieffer, Thomas A. *c.o.* '65 (MRY)[F] Monterey, CA Oratorian Community–Congregation of the Oratory of Pontifical Right.
Kieffer, Thomas A. *orat.* '65 (MRY)[K] Monterey, CA Newman Institute for Historical and Religious Studies.
Kieffer, Thomas *c.o.* (MO) AUXILIARY CHAPLAINS CONTRACT CHAPLAINS.
Kiel, William J. '93 (GBG) Uniontown, PA St. John The Evangelist.
Kielb, John T. '75 (TR) Monmouth Beach, NJ Church of the Precious Blood.
Kielbasa, Richard '59 (SC) Retired.

Kieliszewski, Jan M. '73 (MIL) Burlington, WI St. Charles.
Kielkowski, Andrzej *s.d.s.* '81 (BRK) Jamaica, NY St. Joseph.
Kielkowski, Andrzej *s.d.s.* '81 (NEW)[N] Verona, NJ The Salvatorian Fathers.
Kieltyka, Robert '58 (MOB) St. Jude, AL St. Jude Retired.
Kiely, Benedict '94 (BUR) Office of Continuing Education for Clergy; Enosburg Falls, VT St. John the Baptist.
Kiely, Brian R. '78 (BO) Natick, MA St. Patrick.
Kiely, Cornelius '67 (BAK) On Duty Outside the Diocese; (FgM).
Kiely, Thomas P. '88 (NY) Cortlandt Manor, NY Holy Spirit.
Kiely, Thomas R. '03 (CAM) Lindenwold, NJ St. Lawrence's.
Kiem, Anthony '46 (PT) Retired.
Kiemen, Mathias *o.f.m* '43 (SFD)[L] Springfield, IL Our Lady of Angels Friary.
Kiene, Joseph *o.f.m.conv.* (MO).
Kienzle, Jerome C. '72 (MIL) Navy Chaplains; Military Chaplains.
Kiepura, Kenneth '69 (CHI) Libertyville, IL St. Joseph.
Kieran, Edward '59 (AMA) Retired.
Kieran, John C. '67 (ATL) Conyers, GA St. Pius X Catholic.
Kieran, Richard A. '65 (ATL) On Sick Leave.
Kierce, J. Joseph '45 (BO) Senior Priests Retired.
Kiernan, Donald R. '49 (ATL) Special or Other (Arch-)Diocesan Assignment; [O] Doraville, GA Korean Martyrs Pastoral Center.
Kiernan, James F. *c.m.* '70 (NY)[C] Staten Island, NY St. John's University Staten Island Campus.
Kiernan, James F. *c.m.* '70 (BRK)[D] St. John's University.
Kiernan, James O. *c.m.* '70 (PH)[B] Philadelphia, PA St. Vincent's Seminary; [FF] Philadelphia, PA The Central Association of the Miraculous Medal.
Kiernan, James W. '62 (DM) Des Moines, IA St. Ambrose Cathedral.
Kiernan, James *c.m.* '70 (PH) Philadelphia, PA St. Francis of Assisi.
Kiernan, John G. '55 (PBL) Retired.
Kiernan, Michael F. '49 (SAC) North Highlands, CA St. Lawrence; [M] Sacramento, CA Catholic Social Service of Sacramento; Vicar for Social Services.
Kiernan, Michael (SAC) Catholic Charities of Sacramento, Inc.; Priests' Personnel Board, Diocesan.
Kiernan, R. Donald '49 (ATL) Dunwoody, GA All Saints Catholic; Vicars General; Judges; Consultors.
Kiernan, Robert J. *o.s.b.* '60 (BUR)[E] Weston, VT Priory of Benedictine Monks.
Kiernan, Thomas '48 (SY) Retired.
Kierney, Bede *o.s.b.* '83 (WOR)[O] Petersham, MA St. Mary's Monastery.
Kies, Emil '44 (P) Retired.
Kiesel, James P. '95 (BAL) Baltimore, MD St. Dominic.
Kiesel, Leo C. '63 (EVN)[I] Loogootee, IN American–Innsbruck Alumni Association.
Kieselbach, Joseph '61 (CR) Barnesville, MN Assumption.
Kiesling, John *s.a.* '68 (NY).
Kieton, Dennis J. '85 (PRO)[EE] Cumberland, RI Our Lady of Fatima.
Kieu, Hoc Thai *o.c.s.o.* (OAK) Oakland, CA St. Mary, Immaculate Conception–St. Francis de Sales.
Kiff, Herbert J. '95 (NO) St. Bernard, LA San Pedro Pescador; St. Bernard, LA St. Bernard.
Kifolo, Patrick J. *o.s.f.s.* (ARL)[J] Alexandria, VA Oblates of St. Francis de Sales Residence.
Kiggins, Roy '64 (ROC) Geneva, NY St. Francis de Sales; Geneva, NY St. Stephen.
Kiggins, Roy '67 (ROC)[L] Geneva, NY Hobart and William Smith College.
Kightlinger, Jon '03 (BAL) Hagerstown, MD St. Ann.
Kigozi, Denis S. '91 (COL) Diocesan Judges.
Kigozi, Denis '91 (COL) Columbus, OH St. Thomas the Apostle.
Kihm, Frederick C. '93 (STU) Marietta, OH St. John the Baptist.
Kihm, Peter J. '81 (NY) Poughkeepsie, NY St. John the Baptist; Poughkeepsie, NY Our Lady of Mt. Carmel.
Kihneman, Louis F. '77 (CC) Finance Council; Presbyteral Council; Rockport, TX Sacred Heart.
Kijauskas, Gediminas *s.j.* '60 (CLV) Cleveland, OH Our Lady of Perpetual Help.
Kikeram, Joseph '99 (NEW) Newark, NJ Our Lady of Mt. Carmel.
Kilbride, Eugene M. '59 (HRT) West Hartford, CT St. Helena.
Kilbridge, Robert *o.p.* '47 (CHI) River Forest, IL St. Vincent Ferrer.
Kilburg, Jack *m.s.f.* '79 (SAT) Seguin, TX Our Lady of Guadalupe.
Kilburn, Clay *c.m.* (GLP) Presbyteral Council.
Kilburn, Clayton F. *c.m.* '79 (GLP) Keams Canyon, AZ St. Joseph's Indian Mission.
Kilburn, Clayton *c.m.* (GLP) Vicars Forane.
Kilcarr, Stephen M. '56 (NEW).
Kilcline, Francis I. '81 (LFT)[C] Peru, IN St. Charles Borromeo; Deans; Members.
Kilcourse, George A. '76 (L).
Kilcoyne, John '45 (CLV) Retired.
Kilcoyne, Patrick '75 (SJ) Retired.
Kilcoyne, Terence T. '76 (WOR)[A] Westminster, MA St. Edward the Confessor.
Kilcoyne, Terrence T. (WOR) Advocates.
Kileo, Albert '92 (SLC) Roosevelt, UT St. Helen's.
Kiley, Brian R. (BO) Designated.
Kiley, Francis *o.f.m.conv.* '54 (CHI)[N] St. Louis, MO.
Kiley, J. Cletus '74 (CHI) On Duty Outside the Archdiocese.
Kiley, John A. '66 (PRO) Pawtucket, RI St. Leo the Great; Deans.
Kiley, John G. '70 (BO) Ipswich, MA Our Lady of Hope.
Kiley, Philip *s.j.* '71 (BO)[V] Newton, MA The Jesuit Community at Boston College.
Kiley, Phillip C. '78 (CHI) Chicago, IL St. Francis de Sales; Chicago, IL St. George.
Kiley, Raymond P. '96 (BO) Quincy, MA St. John the Baptist.
Kilgallen, John J. *s.j.* '65 (CHI)[C] Chicago, IL Jesuit Community at Loyola University Chicago.
Kilgallon, John J. '69 (PH) Roslyn, PA St. John of the Cross.
Kilian, Bill '53 (SAL) Damar, KS St. Joseph's Retired.
Kilian, Waldemar Aleksander '87 (CHI) Chicago, IL St. Bruno; Navy Reserve Chaplains.
Kilian, William T. '53 (SAL) Retired.
Kilianski, Edward *s.j.c.* '83 (SR) Special Assignment.
Kilianski, Edward *s.c.j.* '83 (MIL)[O] Hales Corners, WI Priests of the Sacred Heart; [O] Occidental, CA.
Kilidjian, Vincent *m.s.a.* '68 (NOR)[F] Cromwell Society of the Missionaries of the Holy Apostles.
Kilisara, Thomas '85 (NO) Slidell, LA St. Margaret Mary; Slidell, LA Greenbriar Nursing & Convalescent Home; Slidell, LA Guest House of Slidell Nursing Home; Slidell, LA Trinity Neurologic Rehabilitation Center at Slidell.
Kill, Robert J. '71 (TOL) Cloverdale, OH St. Barbara; Cloverdale, OH St. John the Baptist; Cloverdale, OH St. Joseph.
Killackey, Cypprian *o.c.d.* '52 (TUC)[E] Tucson, AZ Discalced Carmelite Friars of St. Margaret Mary's.
Killackey, Cyprian *o.c.d.* '52 (TUC) Tucson, AZ St. Margaret Mary.
Killackey, Edward R. *m.m.* '57 (NY).
Killackey, Thomas B. *m.m.* '56 (HON)[EE] Mililani Town, HI St. John Apostle and Evangelist; [G] Mililani, HI.
Killeen, Bernard D. '49 (HRT) Orange, CT Holy Infant Retired.
Killeen, Bernard (HRT) Auditors (Part–time Case Instructors).
Killeen, John C. '59 (CAM) Cherry Hill, NJ St. Mary's.
Killeen, John P. '57 (CC) Retired.
Killeen, Joseph P. '62 (DET) Retired.
Killeen, Michael F. '59 (LA) Rowland Heights, CA St. Elizabeth Ann Seton.
Killeen, Thomas *o.m.i.* '58 (ANC) Cordova, AK St. Joseph.
Killeen, William E. '75 (CHI) Midlothian, IL St. Christopher.
Killeen, William J. '59 (HRT) Derby, CT St. Jude.
Killey, Steven S. '98 (SAG) Pinconning, MI St. Michael.
Killian, Wayne E. '84 (ALN)[O] Bethlehem, PA Lehigh University (Bethlehem); [O] Bethlehem, PA Moravian College (Bethlehem).
Killilea, Patrick *ss.cc.* '69 (FR) Fairhaven, MA St. Mary's.
Killion, Dennis W. *o.s.f.s.* '80 (PH)[D] Philadelphia, PA Father Judge High School for Boys; [AA] Philadelphia, PA Father Louis Brisson Residence.
Killop, John '62 (SAG) Rapson, MI St. Joseph.
Killoren, John J. *s.j.* '45 (STL)[O] St. Louis, MO Jesuit Community Corporation at St. Louis University – Jesuit Hall; [N] St. Louis, MO Fusz Pavilion.
Kilmartin, John *f.d.p.* '86 (BO) East Boston, MA St. Joseph–St. Lazarus; Shirley, MA MCI–Shirley; Legion of Mary.
Kilmurray, Fintan J. '77 (BLX) Wiggins, MS St. Francis Xavier; Army National Guard Chaplains.
Kilpatrick, Andrew W. '96 (SCR) Unassigned or Leave of Absence.
Kilpatrick, John J. '61 (SCR) Wilkes–Barre, PA St. Patrick's; Diocesan Consultors; Presbyteral Council; Priests' Retirement Advisory Board.
Kilpatrick, Vincent J. '50 (SY) Warners, NY Our Lady of Good Counsel.
Kilpatrick, Vincent '50 (SY) Retired.
Kilroy, Brendan K. *s.p.s.* '62 (NEW)[C] Ramsey, NJ Don Bosco Preparatory High School; [N] Cliffside Park, NJ St. Patrick's Missionary Society.
Kilroy, C. A. *o.p.* '61 (STP) Minneapolis, MN St. Albert the Great.
Kilroy, Paul E. '70 (BO) Newton, MA St. Bernard.
Kilroy, Robert F. *o.m.i.* '40 (BO)[Y] Tewksbury, MA Immaculate Heart of Mary Infirmary.
Kilty, Cornelius F. *o.s.f.s.* '61 (PH) Philadelphia, PA Mater Dolorosa.
Kilumanga, Raphael '71 (SP) Land O'Lakes, FL Our Lady of the Rosary.
Kilzer, James *o.s.b.* '98 (BIS)[A] Richardton, ND Assumption Abbey.
Kim, Alapaki '82 (HON) Nanakuli, HI St. Rita; Presbyteral Council.
Kim, Alex K. '40 (ORG)[H] Anaheim, CA St. Thomas Korean Catholic Center.
Kim, Alex '91 (ORG) Special Assignment.
Kim, Alexander (NY)[C] Mt. Kisco, NY Legion of Christ College, Inc..
Kim, Alfonso *m.m.* '97 (NY)[EE] Maryknoll Maryknoll Fathers and Brothers.
Kim, Andrew M. '98 (BRK) Bayside, NY St. Robert Bellarmine.
Kim, Augustine Doo Wan '82 (SAT) Boerne, TX Korean Martyrs Catholic Church.
Kim, Benedict *s.v.d.* '01 (MEM) Germantown, TN Our Lady Of Perpetual Help; [I] Memphis, TN Society of the Divine Word (Chicago Province); Korean Catholic Ministry.
Kim, Bosco Kuin *o.s.b.* '71 (PAT)[M] Newton, NJ St. Paul's Abbey.
Kim, Carlos C. '91 (BO) Franklin, MA St. Mary.
Kim, Chrysostom *o.s.b.* '60 (SCL)[I] Collegeville, MN St. John's Abbey, of the Order of St. Benedict.
Kim, Francis *o.f.m.* '96 (NY) New York, NY St. Francis of Assisi; [II] New York, NY Franciscan Missionary Charities, Inc..
Kim, Jae Hwa (NEW) Mountainside, NJ Our Lady of Lourdes.
Kim, Jerome *s.s.t.* '92 (MET) Woodbridge, NJ St. James.
Kim, Joseph S. (LAN).
Kim, Joseph Sy '90 (LAN) Burton, MI Blessed Sacrament; [N] Blessed Sacrament Educational Trust Fund.
Kim, Joseph Y. '74 (BAL) Baltimore, MD Holy Korean Martyrs.
Kim, Josephus Y. '97 (JOL) Itasca, IL St. Andrew Kim.
Kim, Jungsoo '03 (NEW) Cliffside Park, NJ Epiphany.
Kim, Luis '61 (NEW) Orange, NJ St. Andrew Kim.
Kim, Mary Joseph *o.cart* '92 (BUR)[E] Arlington, VT Carthusian Foundation in America, Inc., Charterhouse of the Transfiguration.
Kim, Nam J. *s.s.* '90 (BAL)[S] College Saint Paul.
Kim, Paul *c.p.* (DET)[K] Detroit, MI St. Paul of the Cross Community, Congregation of the Passion.
Kim, Robert '77 (CHI) Des Plaines, IL St. Paul Chong Hasang.
Kim, Roy '94 (ORG) Los Alamitos, CA St. Hedwig; [H] Orange, CA St. Vincent de Paul Society; Ministry to Priests; Ecumenical and Interreligious Affairs.
Kim, Samuel *o.s.b.* '95 (PAT)[M] Newton, NJ St. Paul's Abbey.
Kim, Stephano Insoo (SEA) Koreans, Ministry to.
Kim, Sung Heum (John) '91 (CAM) Northfield, NJ St. Bernadette.
Kim, Tu–Jin Paul *c.p.* (DET)[P] Detroit, MI St. Paul of the Cross Retreat Center.
Kim, Yong–Jae (NEW) Demarest, NJ St. Joseph.
Kim (Wonju), Thaddaues Yong Song '88 (ARL) Fairfax, VA St Paul Chung.
Kim–Dae–Shik, Alexander *s.d.b.* '96 (OAK)[N] Berkeley Salesian Community.
Kimble, Percy *s.m.* '69 (MRY)[F] Santa Cruz, CA Society of Mary, Marists.
Kimbrough, Conrad '78 (CHL) Retired.
Kime, David W. '97 (GRY) La Porte, IN St. Joseph.
Kimecz, Aloysius *o.cist.* '53 (DAL)[K] Irving, TX Cistercian Abbey of Our Lady of Dallas.
Kimes, John Paul (OLL) Special Assignment.
Kimla, James '76 (MIL) Milwaukee, WI St. Rafael the Archangel.
Kimm, Gregory C. '87 (SJ) San Jose, CA St. Thomas of Canterbury.
Kimminau, Bernard '94 (LIN) Dawson, NE St. Mary's; Diocesan Area CCD Directors.
Kimminau, Irenaeus *o.f.m.* '49 (SFD)[B] Quincy, IL Quincy University.
Kimmons, Steven E. *s.j.* '94 (CHI)[C] Chicago, IL Jesuit Community at Loyola University Chicago.
Kimpel, Edward J. *o.praem.* '49 (PH)[AA] Paoli, PA Daylesford Abbey.
Kim Thien, Joseph Tran '81 (PH) Upper Darby, PA St. Alice.
Kin, Bohdan '77 (PHU) Absent on Leave.
Kinane, Gerard P. '73 (NO) Slidell, LA St. Luke the Evangelist.
Kinane, Joseph J. '52 (CHI) Retired.
Kinast, Robert L. '68 (ATL) On Duty Outside the Archdiocese.
Kincl, Robert L. (AUS) Diocesan Judges; Army Chaplains.
Kincl, Robert L. (MO) Judges.
Kindall, John J. *s.j.* '57 (P)[A] Portland, OR Jesuit Novitiate of St. Francis Xavier.
Kinderman, Dennis *c.pp.s.* '67 (CHI)[X] Chicago, IL Precious Blood Ministry of Reconciliation; [M] Chicago, IL.

Kindon, W. Frederick '74 (PH) Philadelphia, PA St. Bernard.
Kinerk, Edward *s.j.* '72 (KC)[B] Kansas City, MO Rockhurst University; [B] Kansas City, KS Rockhurst University Continuing Education Center/ National Seminars Group; [J] Kansas City, MO Rockhurst Jesuit Community.
Kines, G. Jerome *o.s.a.* '62 (CHI)[N] Matteson, IL Austin Friary.
King, Andrew R. '96 (NY)[A] Yonkers, NY St. Joseph's Seminary.
King, Arthur J. *o.m.i.* '59 (BO)[Y] Tewksbury, MA Immaculate Heart of Mary Infirmary.
King, Brian Madison '97 (LKC)[B] Lake Charles, LA CHRISTUS Health Southwestern Louisiana.
King, Brian (PMB) Episcopal Secretary.
King, Bruce *i.c.* '85 (PEO) Elmwood, IL St. Patrick's; Farmington, IL St. Matthew's.
King, Charles '56 (FWT) Denton, TX Immaculate Conception; Deans; Ecumenism, Office of.
King, Donald E. '74 (Y) Warren, OH Blessed Sacrament.
King, Donald J. '37 (PRO) Retired.
King, Edward L. '55 (BO) Haverhill, MA St. James; Senior Priests Retired.
King, Francis *o.c.s.o.* '58 (P)[L] Lafayette, OR The Cistercian (Trappist) Abbey of Our Lady of Guadalupe.
King, George L. '53 (B) Kamiah, ID St. Catherine's of Siena; Orofino, ID St. Theresa's.
King, George (B) Judges.
King, Gerald J. *t.o.r.* '71 (FgM).
King, Gregory C. '76 (LA) North Hollywood, CA St. Patrick.
King, Howard J. '63 (E) West Middlesex, PA Good Shepherd.
King, Hugh *o.f.m.* '44 (PAT)[M] Ringwood, NJ Holy Name Friary, Inc..
King, James B. *c.s.c.* '88 (FTW)[A] Notre Dame, IN.
King, James E. '71 (PH) Philadelphia, PA Veterans Administration Medical Center.
King, James E. '71 (PBL) Canon City, CO St. Michael; Finance Advisory Council.
King, James E. (NTN) Brooklyn, NY SS. Peter and Paul's Retired.
King, James E. (NEW) CIVIL AIR PATROL.
King, James E. (NTN) Brooklyn, NY SS. Peter and Paul's Retired.
King, James J. *s.j.* '63 (CLV)[D] Cuyahoga Falls, OH Walsh Jesuit High School.
King, James P. '46 (BRK)[V] Douglaston, NY Bishop Mugavero Residence Retired.
King, James W. '91 (BRK) Brooklyn, NY St. Vincent de Paul.
King, James *c.s.c.* '88 (FTW)[B] University of Notre Dame Du Lac.
King, James (BRK) Bishop Catanello—; Presbyteral Council.
King, Jeffrey '87 (GLP) Vanderwagen, NM St. Patrick; Gallup, NM Good Shepherd Catholic Mission; Ramah, NM San Lorenzo.
King, Jeramy *o.s.b.* '76 (IND)[K] St. Meinrad, IN St. Meinrad Archabbey.
King, Jim B. *c.s.c.* '88 (FTW)[I] Notre Dame, IN Holy Cross Community, Corby Hall, University of Notre Dame.
King, John D. '88 (CLV) Casa Parroquial San Pedro Teotepeque.
King, John F. *c.m.* '42 (PH)[AA] St. Catherine Infirmary.
King, John J. *s.j.* '53 (NY)[GG] Staten Island, NY Mount Manresa Jesuit Retreat House.
King, John R. *m.m.* '53 (NY)[EE] Maryknoll Maryknoll Fathers and Brothers.
King, John '48 (PEO) Retired.
King, John *o.m.i.* '54 (NY)[GG] Newburgh, NY Our Lady of Hope Center.
King, John *o.m.i.* '54 (BO)[V] Lowell, MA Missionary Oblates of Mary Immaculate.
King, Kenneth A. '57 (TLS) Retired.
King, Larry '89 (GR) Grand Rapids, MI St. John Vianney.
King, Leo *ss.cc.* '45 (FR)[H] Fairhaven, MA Damien Residence.
King, Martin '96 (P) On Duty Outside the Archdiocese; Air Force Chaplains.
King, Michael J. '77 (WDC) Oxon Hill, MD St. Columba; Defenders of the Bond.
King, Nicholas '66 (ORL) Rockledge, FL St. Mary's; Executive Committee; Members; Real Estate Committee.
King, Norman '88 (RNO) Sparks, NV Immaculate Conception; Diocesan Board of Consultors; Presbyteral Council.
King, Philip J. '49 (BO) Senior Priests Retired.
King, Stephen *o.f.m.conv.* '96 (BUF)[O] Athol Springs, NY St. Francis of Assisi Friary; [D] Athol Springs, NY St. Francis High School.
King, Thomas F. '64 (LA) Los Angeles, CA St. Anastasia.
King, Thomas J. '60 (ALN) Bethlehem, PA Sacred Heart of Jesus.
King, Thomas M. *s.j.* '64 (WDC)[M] Washington, DC The Jesuit Community at Georgetown University.
King, Thomas M. '73 (CIN) Cincinnati, OH Guardian Angels.
King, Thomas P. *c.s.c.* '69 (FTW)[B] University of Notre Dame Du Lac; [I] Notre Dame, IN Holy Cross Community Corby Hall, University of Notre Dame.
King, Thomas *c.s.c.* '69 (FTW) South Bend, IN Sacred Heart.
King, Thomas *o.f.m.* '93 (FgM).
King, William F. *s.j.* '57 (DET)[K] Temperance, MI.
King, William F. *s.j.* '57 (CIN)[M] Cincinnati, OH Jesuit Community at Xavier University.
King, William J. '83 (HBG) Camp Hill, PA Good Shepherd; Youth Protection Program.
King, William J. (HBG) Secretary for Canonical Services; Judicial Vicar; Judicial Vicar.
King, William M. *s.j.* '60 (SFE) Albuquerque, NM Immaculate Conception.
Kingery, Michael G. '99 (ATL) Calhoun, GA St. Clements; Girl and Boy Scouts.
Kingery, Patrick '93 (ATL) Atlanta, GA Holy Cross.
Kingery, Victor *o.f.m.* '49 (SFD)[L] Springfield, IL Our Lady of Angels Friary.
Kingori, James *i.m.c.* '87 (BUF)[O] Williamsville, NY Consolata Fathers.
Kingsbury, John G. *c.ss.r.* '80 (NY)[GG] Esopus, NY Mount St. Alphonsus Redemptorist Retreat Center.
Kingsbury, John G. *c.ss.r.* '80 (ROC)[K] Canandaigua, NY Notre Dame Retreat House.
Kingsley, Richard '83 (TUC) Tuscon, AZ Corpus Christi.
Kingsley, Thomas '03 (CHR) Mount Pleasant, SC Christ Our King.
Kiniry, Joseph R. '50 (ALT) Retired.
Kiniry, Lawrence R. '65 (GBG) Coral, PA St. Francis; Lucernemines, PA St. Louis; College of Consultors; Bishop's Priests Council.
Kinkead, James A. '55 (BR) Retired.
Kinkel, Robert J. '70 (DEN) Arvada, CO Spirit of Christ Parish.
Kinkel, Robert (DEN) College of Consultors.
Kinkopf, John J. '57 (CLV) Chagrin Falls, OH St. Joan of Arc; Kirtland, OH Divine Word Retired.
Kinn, James W. '57 (CHI) Mundelein, IL Santa Maria Del Popolo Retired.
Kinnaman, Leroy G. '73 (LFT) Tipton, IN St. John the Baptist.
Kinnane, James F. '63 (HRT) Special and other Archdiocesan Assignment; Judges; Office for Religious; Adjutant Judicial Vicar; Army Reserve Chaplains.
Kinney, Donald *o.c.d.* '88 (P)[Q] Mt. Angel, OR Carmelite House of Studies; [L] Mount Angel, OR Discalced Carmelite Friars (OCD).
Kinney, Francis L. *c.pp.s.* '47 (STU) Ironton, OH St. Mary.
Kinney, George R. '63 (STP) Hamel, MN St. Thomas the Apostle.
Kinney, James J. '98 (SUP) Solon Springs, WI St. Anthony of Padua; Solon Springs, WI St. Mary; Solon Springs, WI St. Pius X.
Kinney, John M. '76 (LFT) Military Chaplains; Air Force Chaplains.
Kinney, Leo '92 (FAR) Anamoose, ND St. Francis Xavier; Drake, ND St. Margaret Mary; Anamoose, ND Sacred Heart.
Kinney, M. Eugene '84 (MIL)[V] Horicon, WI Legion of Mary; Horicon, WI Sacred Heart.
Kinney, Thomas E. (NO) Judges; Air National Guard Chaplains.
Kinney, Thomas '77 (NO) Metairie, LA St. Francis Xavier Retired.
Kinney, William G. '96 (CHR) Yonges Island, SC St. Mary.
Kinney, William J. *m.s.* '42 (HRT)[M] Hartford, CT Missionaries of LaSalette.
Kinsella, Arthur L. *o.p.* '46 (CHI)[O] St. Louis, MO St. Dominic Priory; [N] St. Pius V Priory.
Kinsella, Charles R. '65 (BO) Permanent Disability.
Kinsky, Richard C. *c.s.b* '59 (ROC)[I] Rochester, NY Basilian Residence.
Kinter, John P. '67 (WDC) Washington, DC St. Thomas More; Hospital & Nursing Home Ministries.
Kintiba, George *s.v.d.* '96 (TR) St. Louis, MO St. Nicholas.
Kinuthia, Joachim Mahugu '95 (SY) Syracuse, NY St. Margaret.
Kinzer, Gary '70 (ORG) Absent on Sick Leave.
Kinzer, Victor '49 (SCL) Retired.
Kinzler, Dale H. '74 (FAR)[J] Fargo, ND Marriage Encounter; Healthcare Director.
Kinzler, Dale '74 (FAR) Fargo, ND Nativity.
Kipfer, David '88 (PEO) Ottawa, IL St. Columba.
Kirby, Daniel J. '94 (DM) Council Bluffs, IA Holy Family; Council Bluffs, IA Our Lady, Queen of Apostles.
Kirby, Daniel '94 (DM) Carter Lake, IA Our Lady of Carter Lake.
Kirby, Donald J. *s.j.* '72 (SY)[Q] Syracuse, NY Jesuits at LeMoyne, Inc..
Kirby, Edward A. '61 (PT) Retired.
Kirby, Gerald S. '84 (NOR) On Duty Outside the Diocese.
Kirby, Jim '96 (DM)[C] West Des Moines, IA Dowling Catholic High School.
Kirby, Louis M. *o.s.b.* '48 (PBL) Westcliffe, CO Our Lady of the Assumption; [F] Canon City, CO Holy Cross Abbey.
Kirby, Martin F. '67 (BRK)[B] Douglaston, NY Cathedral Seminary Residence of the Immaculate Conception; [A] Douglaston, NY Immaculate Conception Center.
Kirby, Robert F. '59 (FR) Retired.
Kirby, Thomas M. '57 (PIT)[O] Elizabeth, PA Divine Redeemer Motherhouse.
Kirchgessner, Christopher A. *o.s.b.* '80 (CHL)[J] Belmont, NC Belmont Abbey.
Kirchhoefer, Thomas A. (STL) Military Chaplains; Army Chaplains.
Kirchmeyer, Robert W. '52 (BO) Beverly, MA St. Alphonsus.
Kirchner, Donnell *c.ss.r.* '66 (FgM).
Kirchner, James A. '63 (NEW) On Duty Outside the Archdiocese.
Kirchner, James '63 (FRS) Frazier Park, CA Our Lady of the Snows.
Kirchner, Paul *o.carm.* '40 (JOL)[L] Darien Carmelite Provincial Office.
Kirchner, Peter '93 (SCL) Motley, MN St. Michael's; Staples, MN Sacred Heart; Personnel Committee.
Kirianthan, Jose '87 (STP) Hastings, MN St. Elizabeth Ann Seton.
Kirila, Michael '87 (ROM) Detroit, MI St. John the Baptist; Board of Consultors; Pro–Life Commission.
Kirk, Albert E. '68 (MEM) Memphis, TN Holy Spirit.
Kirk, Allan F. *s.j.* '65 (CHI)[C] Chicago, IL Jesuit Community at Loyola University Chicago.
Kirk, Daniel *o.s.b.* '49 (WDC)[M] Washington, DC St. Anselm's Abbey.
Kirk, David R. '83 (TOL) Military Chaplains; Army Chaplains.
Kirk, David '64 (NTN) Leave of Absence.
Kirk, James T. '86 (WIL) Wilmington, DE Church of the Holy Child.
Kirk, John L. '70 (NSH) Franklin, TN St. Philip.
Kirk, John (NSH) Catholic Charismatic Renewal.
Kirk, Thomas '69 (MEM) Savannah, TN St. Mary's.
Kirk, William J. *o.s.b.* '46 (PEO).
Kirk, William S. '72 (PH)[A] Secane, PA Our Lady of Fatima.
Kirke, Eugene K. '62 (BO) Society of St. James the Apostle; (FgM).
Kirkendoll, Tom *g.h.m.* '87 (OWN)[F] Hartford, KY Glenmary House.
Kirkhoff, Gerald J. '69 (IND) Indianapolis, IN St. Pius X.
Kirkhoff, Gerald (IND) Associates.
Kirkilas, Michael '36 (CHI) Retired.
Kirkness, Michael D. '77 (GF) On Duty Outside of the Diocese.
Kirkness, Michael D. '77 (LA) Lompoc, CA Lompoc Federal Correctional Institution; Lompoc, CA US Penitentiary.
Kirley, Victor '65 (BAL) Cumberland, MD SS. Peter and Paul.
Kirlin, Bernard G. '71 (MIA) Coral Gables, FL St. Augustine.
Kirlin, Bernard (MIA) Deans and Deaneries; University of Miami.
Kirrane, James A. '46 (BRK) Retired.
Kirsch, Gerard D. *o.s.b.* '70 (SEA)[L] Lacey, WA St. Martin's Abbey.
Kirsch, Gregory A. '81 (E) St. Agnes; Defender of the Bond.
Kirsch, Gregory G. '88 (STL) Richmond Heights, MO Little Flower, St. Teresa of the Infant Jesus.
Kirsch, Gregory '88 (STL)[J] St. Louis, MO SSM St. Mary's Health Center.
Kirsch, Myron M. *o.s.b.* '73 (GBG)[H] Latrobe, PA Saint Vincent Archabbey.
Kirsch, Patrick V. '81 (SB) Alta Loma, CA St. Peter & St. Paul.
Kirsch, Patrick (SB) Parish Status and Pastoral Relations Committee.
Kirschner, Anthony *c.m.m.* '37 (DET)[K] Vocation Office Retired.
Kirtland, Robert B. '55 (TOL) Retired.
Kirtz, Raymond R. *o.m.i.* '58 (STP)[P] Buffalo, MN Christ the King Retreat Center.
Kirwan, Christopher J. '92 (BO) Graduate Studies; [A] Brighton, MA St. John Seminary School of Theology; [C] Brighton, MA St. John Seminary College.
Kirwan, Thomas '69 (DET) Absent on Sick Leave.
Kirwen, Michael C. *m.m.* '63 (FgM).
Kirwin, Arthur R. *o.p.* '84 (MEM) Memphis, TN St. Peter's; [I] Memphis, TN Order Of Preachers (Southern Dominican Prov.).
Kirwin, Arthur (MEM) Memphis.
Kirwin, George *o.m.i.* '58 (BUF) Buffalo, NY Holy Angels.

Kirwin, John D. (ALB) Priestly Life and Ministry Council.
Kirwin, John '66 (ALB) Albany, NY St. John–St. Ann.
Kirwin, Michael J. '76 (SCR) Old Forge, PA St. Lawrence O'Toole.
Kirwin, Peter *o.f.m.* '81 (SD) Oceanside, CA Mission San Luis Rey; [H] Oceanside, CA Mission San Luis Rey.
Kirwin, Robert J. '45 (RVC) Williston Park, NY St. Aidan's Church Retired.
Kis–Horvath, Pascal *o.cist.* '57 (DAL)[K] Irving, TX Cistercian Abbey of Our Lady of Dallas.
Kiselica, John '83 (DET).
Kiser, Karl *s.j.* '97 (DET)[E] Detroit, MI University of Detroit Jesuit High School and Academy.
Kish, Carl '62 (Y) Cortland, OH St. Robert Bellarmine Parish.
Kish, Jerome '98 (JOL) Naperville, IL Sts. Peter and Paul.
Kish, Les (B) College of Consultors; Deans.
Kish, Leslie P. '97 (B) Lewiston, ID Our Lady of Lourdes.
Kish, Matthew J. '43 (GRY) Retired.
Kish, Michael A. '65 (MIA) Pinecrest, FL St. Louis.
Kish, Michael (MIA) Miami Dade CC–South; Police Chaplains.
Kishe, Venace Max (SPR) Pittsfield, MA St. Joseph's.
Kiss, Barnabas G. *o.f.m.* '78 (DET) Detroit, MI Holy Cross.
Kiss, Barnabas G. *o.f.m.* (ATH) Middle East Division:.
Kiss, Gabriel *s.j.* '55 (NY) Yonkers, NY St. Margaret of Hungary.
Kissane, James M. (RVC) East Northport, NY St. Anthony of Padua; Senate of Priests (Presbyteral Council/College of Consultors).
Kissane, James (RVC) Chaplains of the Suffolk County Police Department.
Kissane, Maurice J. '64 (CHI) Brookfield, IL St. Barbara.
Kissane, Michael *o.carm.* '86 (NY) Bronx, NY St. Simon Stock; [EE] Middletown, NY Carmelite Friars (North American Province of St. Elias).
Kissel, Anthony '73 (SP)[A] St. Leo, FL Saint Leo University, Institutional Research.
Kissel, Anthony '73 (EVN) On Duty Outside the Diocese.
Kissel, Francis J. *s.m.* '71 (ATL)[C] Atlanta, GA Marist School.
Kissel, Ignatius M. *o.s.m.* '65 (CHI)[N] Chicago Order of Friar Servants of Mary (Servites) United States of America Province, Inc.; Fullerton, CA St. Philip Benizi; [I] Fullerton, CA St. Philip Benizi Priory.
Kissell, Terrence '78 (DEN) Commerce City, CO Our Lady Mother of the Church.
Kissell, Wilbur T. '51 (MOB) Montgomery, AL St. Andrew; [J] Montgomery, AL Alabama State University Newman Center.
Kissell, Wilbur '51 (MOB) Montgomery, AL St. John the Baptist.
Kissinger, Rodney T. *s.j.* '53 (NO)[P] New Orleans, LA Ignatius Residence.
Kissling, John M. '53 (DUB) Retired.
Kist, Harold W. '74 (CIN) Russells Point, OH St. Mary of the Woods.
Kisting, Thomas '73 (DUL) Absent on Sick Leave.
Kistler, Leonard A. *c.pp.s.* '61 (TOL)[B] Carthagena, OH St. Charles.
Kistner, Hilarion *o.f.m.* '55 (CIN)[M] Cincinnati, OH St. Francis Seraph Friary.
Kisuka–Kilumbu, Claudes '94 (WDC) Silver Spring, MD St. Michael.
Kita, August *s.d.b.* '60 (NY)[GG] Stony Point, NY Don Bosco Retreat Center and Marian Shrine; [GG] Stony Point, NY Marian Shrine.
Kita, John M. '98 (SCR) Unassigned or Leave of Absence.
Kitchin, George '70 (BLX) Gulfport, MS St. James; Personnel Board; Charismatic Renewal.
Kitenge, Denis '87 (SP) Dunedin, FL Our Lady of Lourdes.
Kitko, Joseph F. '55 (BAL) Laurel, MD Resurrection of Our Lord Retired.
Kitt, Liam J. '43 (CLV) Elyria Township, OH St. Vincent de Paul.
Kitt, William J. '43 (CLV) Retired.
Kitten, Marvin C. *s.j.* '65 (NO)[C] New Orleans, LA Loyola University New Orleans.
Kittock, Francis R. '55 (STP) Retired.
Kitz, Raphael *o.c.d.* '59 (LR)[A] Little Rock, AR Marylake – Carmelite Novitiate.
Kitzke, Timothy L. '89 (MIL) Milwaukee, WI Three Holy Women.
Kivel, Joseph G. '61 (STP) Minneapolis, MN St. Anthony of Padua.
Kiwera, Thaddeus Simon '96 (CC)[G] Robstown, TX Society of Our Lady of the Most Holy Trinity.
Kiwus, John *c.ss.r.* (NY)[EE] Esopus, NY Redemptorist Priests and Brothers C.Ss.R. (Province of Baltimore).
Kiyingi, David '64 (BUR) St. Albans, VT Holy Angels.
Kizis, Kenneth G. '59 (SCR) Retired.
Kizito, John Fisher '02 (FAR) Jamestown, ND The Basilica of St. James.
Klaas, Gregory '67 (SR)[H] Sonoma, CA Hanna Boys Center.
Klaers, Marvin J. '50 (STP) Hampton, MN St. Mary Retired.
Klag, Michael A. '03 (WCH) Wichita, KS Church of the Magdalen.
Klaiber, Jeffrey L. *s.j.* '74 (CHI).
Klajbor, Richard J. '79 (CHI)[N] Chicago, IL Holy Innocents.
Klak, Jan Piotr '79 (SAT)[C] Oblate School of Theology.
Klak, Jan '79 (SAT) San Antonio, TX St. Anthony Mary Claret.
Klamet, Francis X. '78 (CLV) Greenfield, OH St. Benignus; Released from Diocesan Assignment.
Klamut, Charles '99 (PEO) Peoria, IL St. Peter's; [B] Peoria, IL Notre Dame High School.
Klanichka, Volodymyr '01 (PHU) Nanticoke, PA St. Nicholas; Nanticoke, PA Transfiguration of Our Lord.
Klapperich, Giles R. *o.p.* '53 (DEN) Denver, CO St. Dominic; [A] Denver, CO St. Dominic Priory.
Klapps, William J. '58 (WIL) Wilmington, DE St. Matthew Retired.
Klarer, Michael E. '79 (MAD) Monroe, WI St. Victor; Navy Reserve Chaplains.
Klasek, Stephen A. '83 (NSH) Nashville, TN Holy Rosary; Diocesan Finance Board; Clergy Personnel Board; Diocesan Planning.
Klasinski, George '51 (KCK) Retired.
Klasinski, Stanley J. '77 (CLV) Lyndhurst, OH St. Clare.
Klass, Raymond E. '50 (MAD) Retired.
Klassen, John *o.s.b.* '77 (SCL)[A] Collegeville, MN St. John's School of Theology and Seminary; [B] Collegeville, MN St. John's University; [B] St. John's University; [I] Collegeville, MN St. John's Abbey, of the Order of St. Benedict.
Klassen, Roger *o.s.b.* '66 (SCL) Freeport, MN Sacred Heart; Freeport, MN Immaculate Conception; Freeport, MN St. Rose of Lima; [I] Collegeville, MN St. John's Abbey, of the Order of St. Benedict; Advocates.
Klatka, Joseph S. '67 (MAN) Littleton, NH St. Rose of Lima.
Klauck, Michael '94 (BIR) On Duty Outside the Diocese.
Klauck, Peter N. (GB) Pastor Consultors.
Klauck, Peter '55 (GB) Diocesan Consultors; Appointed Representatives Retired.
Klauck, Stanley B. '46 (MIL) Retired.
Klauer, Gary *o.f.m.conv.* '75 (LA) Hermosa Beach, CA Our Lady of Guadalupe.
Klaus, John Mark *t.o.r.* '99 (ALT)[A] Loretto, PA St. Francis University; [F] Loretto, PA Mount Assisi Friary; [H] Loretto, PA St. Francis College (Loretto).
Klaus, Joseph J. '54 (R) Retired.
Kleas, Milam '51 (GAL) Houston, TX St. Maximilian Kolbe.
Kleba, Gerald J. '67 (STL) St. Louis, MO St. Cronan.
Kleber, Cecil *o.f.m.* '50 (SFE)[J] Rio Rancho, NM Felician Sisters.
Klecha, Joseph A. *m.m.* '69 (SJ)[M] Los Altos, CA Maryknoll.
Kleczewski, Kieran '78 (PHX) Avondale, AZ St. Thomas Aquinas; College of Consultors.
Kledzik, Jim '03 (FRS) Madera, CA St. Joachim.
Klee, Joseph C. '01 (COL) Worthington, OH St. Michael.
Klee, Robert A. '49 (COL) Retired.
Klees, Raymond F. '73 (CHI) La Grange, IL St. Cletus.
Kleffman, James '60 (DM) Council Bluffs, IA Retired.
Kleiber, Kenneth R. '68 (CHI) Other Assignments.
Klein, Bernard C. '49 (STP) Retired.
Klein, Charles R. '59 (BAL) Retired.
Klein, Charles (BAL) Harbor Hospital.
Klein, David F. *s.j.* '71 (SAC)[D] Sacramento, CA Jesuit High School; [I] Carmichael, CA Jesuit High School Community of Sacramento.
Klein, David J. '90 (CAM) Haddonfield, NJ Christ the King; Adjutant Judicial Vicars; Health Care Ministry; Judges.
Klein, David O. *c.s.b.* (MO).
Klein, David *c.s.b.* '70 (SFE) Veterans Administration Medical Center.
Klein, Dennis (BRK) Brooklyn, NY St. Martin of Tours–Fourteen Holy Martyrs.
Klein, Donald L. '65 (DUB)[F] Cedar Rapids, IA Regis Middle School; Mount Vernon, IA St. John the Baptist; Springville, IA St. Isidore; Cedar Rapids, IA St. Pius X; Belle Plaine, IA St. Joseph; Anamosa, IA St. Patrick; Belle Plaine, IA St. Michael; Deans.
Klein, Douglas M. '96 (SC) Rock Valley, IA St. Mary's.
Klein, Douglas (SC) Presbyteral Council.
Klein, Eugene M. '74 (WIN) Winona, MN Cathedral of the Sacred Heart; [I] Winona, MN St. Thomas Aquinas Newman Center; Dakota, MN Holy Cross.
Klein, Frank W. '45 (WIN) Retired.
Klein, George W. '54 (CIN) Trenton, OH Holy Name.
Klein, George W. '59 (CHI) Wilmette, IL St. Francis Xavier.
Klein, Gregory L. *o.carm.* '75 (BUF)[C] Niagara University, NY Niagara University.
Klein, Gregory *o.carm.* '75 (JOL)[L] Darien Carmelite Provincial Office.
Klein, J. Leo *s.j.* '64 (CIN)[D] Xavier University; [M] Cincinnati, OH Jesuit Community at Xavier University.
Klein, James J. '02 (COS) Parker, CO Ave Maria.
Klein, James T. (CLV) Euclid, OH St. William.
Klein, John J. '70 (PAT) Paterson, NJ St. George.
Klein, John Oliver '02 (JOL) Elmhurst, IL Visitation.
Klein, John P. '78 (LAN) Lansing, MI St. Gerard.
Klein, John (LAN) Regional Vicars.
Klein, Larry '84 (BWN) Brownsville, TX Our Lady of Good Counsel.
Klein, Louis S. '81 (BUF)[K] Buffalo, NY Sisters of Charity Hospital of Buffalo, NY.
Klein, Martin L. '91 (RVC) Glen Cove, NY St. Patrick's.
Klein, Pascal L. '87 (DOD) Hoisington, KS St. John the Evangelist; Hoisington, KS Holy Family.
Klein, Peter J. '74 (WIN) Owatonna, MN Holy Trinity; Owatonna, MN Sacred Heart.
Klein, Pius *o.s.b.* '74 (EVN) Huntingburg, IN Visitation of the Blessed Virgin Mary.
Klein, Pius *o.s.b.* '74 (IND)[K] Huntingburg, IN St. Mary Rectory.
Klein, Stanley H. '44 (BUF) Retired.
Klein, Terrance W. '84 (COL) On Duty Outside the Diocese.
Klein, Terrence W. '84 (COL) Brooklyn, NY St. Augustine.
Klein, Theodore J. '69 (NOR) Diocesan Commission for Ecumenical and Interreligious Affairs Retired.
Kleiner, James *p.v.* '67 (DEN)[H] Denver, CO St. Joseph Hospital.
Kleiner, Robert *m.c.c.j.* '71 (LA) Los Angeles, CA St. Cecilia.
Kleinfehn, Walter J. '60 (DUB) Retired.
Kleinheinz, Joseph L. '54 (SUP) Retired.
Kleinhenz, John H. *s.j.* '37 (CLV)[D] Cleveland, OH St. Ignatius High School.
Kleinmann, Dennis W. '93 (ARL) Alexandria, VA St. Mary's.
Kleinschmidt, John '02 (FAR) Grand Forks, ND Holy Family.
Kleinschmidt, Sylvester '50 (SCL) Retired.
Kleinstuber, Joseph J. '64 (WDC) Bryantown, MD St. Mary.
Kleinwachter, John '77 (CR) Deans; Oklee, MN St. Francis Xavier's.
Kleinweber, Dennis J. '78 (CLV) East Cleveland, OH St. Philomena; Presbyteral Conveners.
Kleinworth, Robert (ELP) Absent on Leave.
Kleissler, Thomas A. '57 (NEW) Special Assignment in the Archdiocese; [S] Plainfield, NJ RENEW International.
Klejnowski, Arcadius '54 (TR) Trenton, NJ St. Hedwig.
Klem, Daniel N. '83 (RIC) Norfolk, VA Sacred Heart.
Klem, Robert J. *c.s.b.* '56 (GAL)[Q] Sugar Land, TX Basilian Mission Center.
Klemash, Dennis *o.f.m.cap.* '90 (BAL)[S] Baltimore, MD St. Ambrose Friary.
Klemme, Dennis C. '57 (MIL)[P] Pewaukee, WI Carmel of the Mother of God; Judges for Second Instance Retired.
Klemme, Dennis C. (VEN) Judges.
Klemme, Robert '91 (LFT) Lafayette, IN St. Mary Cathedral.
Klemmer, Marvin J. '66 (BIS) Bismarck, ND Ascension; Pro–Synodal Judges; Vicar for Presbyters; Ecumenism; Priests' Personnel Board.
Klepac, Kenneth J. '58 (MOB) Mobile, AL St. Joan of Arc; Associate Judges.
Klepacki, Michael S. '78 (CHL) Military Chaplains; Navy Chaplains.
Klepec, George '71 (JOL) Joliet, IL St. Paul the Apostle.
Kleppner, Joseph J. '71 (PIT) Aliquippa, PA St. Frances Cabrini; College of Consultors; Theological Commission; Priest Council.
Klettner, Frederick J. '65 (DET) Farmington Hills, MI St. Clare of Assisi.
Kletzel, Thomas P. '83 (PH) Philadelphia, PA Our Lady of the Rosary; Philadelphia, PA Our Lady of Victory.
Klevence, John P. '85 (WIL) Ocean City, MD St. Mary, Star of the Sea; Mission Office.
Klikunas, Bruce M. *o.s.m.* '72 (CHI)[N] Chicago Order of Friar Servants of Mary (Servites) United States of America Province, Inc..
Klim, Vincent (PAT) Retired.
Klima, James A. '76 (COL) Diocesan Consultors.
Klima, James '76 (COL) Pickerington, OH Seton Parish.
Klimanskis, Adolfo '53 (NOR) On Duty Outside the Diocese.
Klimanskis, Adolph '53 (NOR) Providence, RI St. Casimir.
Klimas, George H. '51 (SAG) Retired.
Klimchuk, Walter '66 (STN) On Duty Outside the Diocese.
Klimczyk, John '81 (FTW) New Carlisle, IN St. Stanislaus Kostka.
Klimczyk, Leon F. *s.j.* '79 (STP) Minneapolis, MN St. Olaf.

Klimek, Edmund J. '53 (LC) Eau Claire, WI Newman Community; [D] Eau Claire, WI Sacred Heart Hospital; [K] Eau Claire, WI Newman Parish; Hospitals and Health Affairs.
Klimek, Jan (CR) Detroit Lakes, MN Holy Rosary; Hawley, MN St. Andrew; Lake Park, MN St. Francis Xavier's.
Klimowicz, Sigmund M. *o.f.m.cap.* '45 (PAT)[M] Oak Ridge–Milton, NJ St. Stanislaus B. M. Friary.
Kline, Charles '62 (LFT) Attica, IN St. Francis Xavier.
Kline, Charles '62 (LFT) Covington, IN St. Joseph.
Kline, Charles (LFT) Members.
Kline, Donald J. (PHX) Notaries.
Kline, Donald '95 (PHX) Special Assignment.
Kline, Donald '95 (PHX) Phoenix, AZ SS. Simon and Jude Cathedral.
Kline, Donald (PHX) Vocations.
Kline, Edwin J. *c.s.b.* '56 (DET)[E] Redford, MI Catholic Central High School.
Kline, John J. '47 (CLV) Lorain, OH St. Mary Retired.
Kline, Omer U. *o.s.b.* '49 (GBG)[H] Latrobe, PA Saint Vincent Archabbey.
Kline, Robert W. '48 (CLV) Mentor, OH St. John Vianney; [A] Wickliffe, OH Borromeo Seminary Retired.
Kline, Roy F. '51 (ALT) Altoona, PA Cathedral of the Blessed Sacrament.
Kline, Roy '50 (ALT) Retired.
Klingeisen, Richard H. '72 (GB) Manitowoc, WI St. Boniface; [F] Manitowoc, WI Holy Family Memorial, Inc..
Klingeisen, Richard '72 (GB)[F] Manitowoc, WI Holy Family Memorial, Inc..
Klingeisen, Richard (GB) Diocesan Health Services.
Klingele, Brian '02 (KCK)[B] Kansas City, KS Bishop Ward High School.
Klingele, Brian '02 (KCK) Kansas City, KS Cathedral of St. Peter the Apostle.
Klinger, Charles F. '83 (COL) Diocesan Judges.
Klinger, Charles '83 (COL) Westerville, OH St. Paul the Apostle.
Klinger, Donald P. (KAL) Diocesan Council of Catholic Women (D.C.C.W.).
Klinger, Nevin J. '82 (ALN) Birdsboro, PA Immaculate Conception; Judges.
Klinger, Nevin (SAM) Approved Advocates.
Klingler, Donald P. '61 (KAL) Otsego, MI St. Margaret.
Klingler, John *s.c.j.* '67 (MIL)[O] Hales Corners, WI Priests of the Sacred Heart; [O] Milwaukee, WI SCJ Community.
Klingler, Ronald M. '65 (Y) Canton, OH St. John the Baptist.
Klingler, Ronald (Y) College of Consultors.
Klink, Anthony G. '58 (MIL) Retired.
Klink, Delbert D. '60 (MAD) Retired.
Klink, Eugene A. '63 (LC) Eau Claire, WI Immaculate Conception; Consultors; Ex Officio Members.
Klink, Kenneth J. '66 (MAD) Belleville, WI St. Mary of Lourdes; Belleville, WI St. James; Elected.
Klink, Peter J. *s.j.* '81 (RC) Pine Ridge, SD Holy Rosary; [B] Pine Ridge, SD Jesuit Community of Holy Rosary Mission.
Klinzing, Thomas J. (PMB) Judicial Vicar; Judges; College of Consultors; Presbyteral Council; Secretary.
Klish, Richard (STP) Eagan, MN St. John Neumann; Associate Judges.
Klismet, Kurt J. *o.ss.t.* '02 (BAL)[S] Baltimore, MD Holy Trinity Monastery.
Klister, Roy '69 (GB)[A] Mundelein, IL The Liturgical Institute; Diocesan Consultors; On Duty Outside the Diocese.
Klizek, Duane R. '82 (BUF) Niagara Falls, NY Our Lady of Mount Carmel.
Kloak, David G. '78 (CHI) Military Chaplains; Navy Chaplains.
Klobuka, John *s.m.* '78 (SAT)[M] San Antonio, TX Woodlawn Marianist Community.
Klockeman, John A. '00 (STP).
Klockman, John (STP)[A] Presbyteral Council.
Kloda, Marshall J. '89 (PH) Philadelphia, PA St. Martin of Tours.
Klode, Steven '00 (CIN) West Chester, OH St. John.
Kloepfer, John S. '53 (RIC) Retired.
Kloepfer, John S. '53 (JOL) Retired.
Kloppenborg, Thomas *c.m.* '91 (STL)[O] St. Louis, MO Lazarist Residence.
Klores, Stanley P. '82 (NO) New Orleans, LA St. Patrick.
Klores, Stanley '82 (NO).
Klos, Joseph (BUF)[A] Judges; Buffalo, NY St. Stephen.
Klos, Michael E. (LC) Coon Valley, WI St. Mary.
Klos, Walter '40 (BUF) Retired.
Kloskowski, Stanley E. '58 (CAM) Retired.
Kloss, Anthony *o.s.b.* '91 (WOR)[O] Still River, MA Benedictine Monks, St. Benedict Abbey.
Kloster, George M. '68 (CHL) Murphy, NC St. William.
Kloton, Michael J. '87 (SCR) Tobyhanna, PA St. Ann; Holy Childhood Association; Propagation of the Faith.
Klotter, Frederick W. '96 (L) Graduate Studies.
Kluba, Zbigniew '73 (PAT) Morristown, NJ Morristown Memorial Hospital.
Kluba, Zbigniew '73 (PAT) Convent Station, NJ St. Thomas More.
Klucinec, Benedict *m.s.a.* '87 (NOR)[F] Cromwell, CT Society of the Missionaries of the Holy Apostles.
Kluckman, J. Anthony *s.c.j.* '73 (RC) Eagle Butte, SD All Saints; Eagle Butte, SD Cheyenne River Reservation; [B] Eagle Butte, SD Sacred Heart Community House.
Kluczynski, Campion '59 (MIL)[O] Burlington, WI Queen of Peace Friary.
Klug, Jerome G. '49 (CHI) Retired.
Klug, Richard L. '51 (CIN) Cincinnati, OH Annunciation of the Blessed Virgin Mary; Censors; Judges.
Kluge, Stephen *o.f.m.* '01 (TR) Brant Beach, NJ St. Francis of Assisi.
Klump, Gregory S. '98 (STL) O'Fallon, MO Immaculate Conception.
Klunk, Timothy '79 (BAL) Baltimore, MD Our Lady of Victory.
Kluthe, Paul E. *s.s.j.* '56 (BAL)[S] Baltimore, MD St. Joseph's Manor.
Klybus, George '01 (NEW) River Edge, NJ St. Peter the Apostle.
Kmech, John '61 (STN) Retired.
Kmiec, Roman *c.m.* '86 (HRT) Brooklyn, NY SS. Cyril and Methodius.
Knab, George *o.m.i.* '67 (MIA) Chicago, IL Precious Blood.
Knapek, John A. *s.j.* '57 (CLV)[B] Cleveland, OH John Carroll University.
Knapik, Andrew G. '57 (ALT) Retired.
Knapik, Andrew '78 (CLV) Cleveland, OH Immaculate Heart of Mary.
Knapp, Charles (TUC) Defenders of the Bond.
Knapp, Gerard J. *c.ss.r.* '75 (BRK)[V] Brooklyn, NY Our Lady of Good Counsel Residence.
Knapp, James G. *s.j.* '81 (STL)[F] St. Louis, MO St. Louis University High School, George H. Backer Memorial; [M] Washington, DC The Jesuit Community at Georgetown University.
Knapp, John M. '86 (NY) Bronx, NY Our Lady of Solace.
Knapp, John '86 (NY) Bronx, NY St. Dominic.
Knapp, Joseph G. *s.j.* '81 (ARL) Fairfax Station, VA St. Raymond of Penafort.
Knapp, Kenneth R. *a.c.s.w.* '63 (EVN) Evansville, IN Christ the King; Special Assignment; Vicar General; Diocesan Consultors; Diocesan Council of Priests; Deans; Ex Officio.
Knapp, Kenneth (EVN) Personnel Board.
Knapp, Richard S. (SFR) Promoter of Justice.
Knapp, Richard '55 (SFR) Novato, CA Our Lady of Loretto Retired.
Knapp, Richard '55 (SFR) Retired.
Knapp, Richard '55 (SFR)[S] San Rafael, CA Sisters of the Third Order of St. Dominic Support Charitable Trust Fund.
Knapp, Roger A. '85 (DET) Gibraltar, MI St. Victor.
Knapp, William L. '48 (SFR) San Rafael, CA St. Isabella Retired.
Knappik, Richard *c.ss.r.* '58 (ALB)[L] Saratoga Springs, NY St. John Neumann Residence.
Knauer, Paul F. '64 (PAT) Sparta, NJ Our Lady of the Lake.
Knauf, Edwin L. '33 (LC) Retired.
Knauf, Randall *o.f.m.cap.* '91 (DET)[P] Washington, MI Capuchin Retreat.
Knaup, Alan J. '77 (STL) St. Louis, MO St. Margaret Mary Alacoque Retired.
Knaup, Daniel '98 (STP) Special Assignment.
Kneafsey, Cornelius T. '58 (BRK) Richmond Hill, NY Our Lady of the Cenacle.
Kneal, Ellsworth '44 (STP) Retired.
Kneal, Ellsworth '44 (STP)[C] St. Paul, MN University of St. Thomas.
Kneemiller, William C. '99 (DAV) Army Reserve Chaplains.
Kneemiller, William (DAV) State University of Iowa Hospital; Military Chaplains.
Kneifl, Rodney V. '85 (OM) Platte Center, NE St. Joseph.
Kneifl, Rodney '85 (OM) Platte Center, NE St. Michael.
Kneip, Paschal *o.s.b.* '51 (RIC) Chincoteague, VA St. Andrew.
Kneipp, August J. '41 (CIN) Retired.
Knepper, Daniel J. '70 (DUB) Dubuque, IA St. Anthony; Deanery Representatives.
Knepper, Timothy P. *c.pp.s.* '03 (TOL) Ottawa, OH SS. Peter and Paul.
Knerr, Joseph '80 (ORG) Yorba Linda, CA St. Martin.
Knestout, Barry '89 (WDC) Pastoral Center Special Ministries; Secretary To The Archbishop.
Knestout, Mark D. '98 (WDC) Derwood, MD St. Francis of Assisi.
Kniepp, August J. '41 (CIN)[L] Cincinnati, OH Archbishop Leibold Home for the Aged.
Knies, G. Jerome *o.s.a.* '62 (CHI)[N] Olympia Fields, IL The Augustinians–Provincialate.
Knight, David B. '61 (MEM) Retired.
Knight, James D. '01 (OKL) Woodward, OK St. Peter's.
Knight, James (OKL) Region VI.
Knight, Jeffrey N. '88 (STL) Villa Ridge, MO St. John the Baptist; Deaneries/Deans; Washington.
Knipe, Michael J. '88 (TLS) Tulsa, OK Resurrection; Judicial Vicar; Judges.
Knipe, William T. *m.m.* '58 (NY)[EE] Maryknoll Maryknoll Fathers and Brothers.
Knippel, Kenneth P. '76 (MIL) Fox Point, WI St. Eugene; Deans.
Knippenberg, Robert E. (VIC) Shiner, TX SS. Cyril and Methodius.
Knipper, Daniel J. '67 (DUB) Lansing, IA St. Mary; [E] Lansing, IA Lansing School of Religion; Lansing, IA St. Joseph's; Lansing, IA Immaculate Conception.
Knittel, Kilian '60 (CHI) Chicago, IL St. Columba.
Knoblach, Thomas '87 (SCL) Henning, MN Church of St. Edward of Henning.
Knoblach, Thomas '87 (SCL) Bertha, MN St. Joseph's.
Knoblach, Thomas (SCL) Catholic Women, Council of.
Knoblach, Thomas (SCL) Health Ministry.
Knoebel, Thomas L. '69 (MIL)[B] Hales Corners, WI Sacred Heart School of Theology; Special Assignment.
Knoernschild, John *o.carm.* '70 (CHI)[N] Chicago Carmelite Priory of St. Cyril.
Knoernschild, John *o.carm.* '70 (LA)[F] Encino, CA Crespi Carmelite High School.
Knoernschild, John *o.carm.* '70 (CHI)[N] Chicago, IL Carmelite Priory of St. Cyril.
Knoernschild, John *o.carm.* '70 (CHI)[D] Chicago, IL.
Knoll, Charles *o.f.m.cap.* '54 (WDC)[B] Washington, DC St. Francis Friary–Capuchin College.
Knoll, Jerome E. *c.s.c.* '60 (FTW)[B] University of Notre Dame Du Lac; [I] Notre Dame, IN Holy Cross Community, Corby Hall, University of Notre Dame.
Knoll, Lester *o.f.m.cap.* '64 (PIT) Herman, PA St. Mary of the Assumption.
Knoll, Urban H. '69 (STL) Retired.
Knop, Andrew *o.m.i.* '89 (STP)[M] St. Paul, MN Oblate Residence.
Knopik, Andrew J. '83 (BEL) Belleville, IL St. Augustine of Canterbury.
Knopp, Benjamin *o.f.m.conv.* '55 (L) Louisville, KY St. Paul.
Knopp, John '78 (ELP) Absent on Leave.
Knotek, Michael P. '96 (CHI) Chicago, IL St. John de la Salle.
Knoth, Bernard P. *s.j.* '77 (NO)[C] New Orleans, LA Loyola University New Orleans.
Knott, William P. '59 (RCK) Retired.
Knox, James '51 (PRT) Lyman, ME St. Philip Retired.
Knox, James (PRT) Clergy Benefit Plan–Clergy Pension Plan.
Knox, Sean Vincent '01 (PT) Gulf Breeze, FL St. Ann.
Knox, Stephen J. '89 (RCK)[L] DeKalb, IL Newman Foundation for Catholic Students of Northern Illinois University; Diocesan Consultors; Newman–Campus Ministry; DeKalb, IL Christ the Teacher, University Parish of Northern Illinois University.
Knudsen, Ronald '72 (SEA) Mountlake Terrace, WA St. Pius X.
Knueven, Gerald E. '68 (TOL) Toledo, OH Good Shepherd; Toledo, OH St. Anthony; Toledo, OH St. Stanislaus.
Knueven, Harold L. '58 (IND) Greensburg, IN St. Mary Retired.
Knuffman, Donald '65 (SFD) Quincy, IL St. Dominic.
Knuffman, Donald (SFD) Presbyteral Council.
Knuge, Richard K. *s.m.* '56 (CIN)[M] Dayton, OH Marianist Community.
Knurek, Dennis A. '77 (BGP) Retired.
Knusel, Frank '73 (P) Absent on Leave.
Kobak, Cantius J. *o.f.m.* '57 (MIL)[M] Milwaukee, WI St. Ann Rest Home.
Kobak, David *o.f.m.* '03 (DET) Southfield, MI St. Michael.
Kobasuk, Maxim *o.s.b.m.* '77 (STF) Hempstead, NY St. Vladimir.
Kobayashi, Augustine *ss.cc.* '64 (FR).
Kobbeman, Gerald P. '66 (RCK)[H] Rockford, IL St. Rita; Pro Synodal Judges.
Kobe, Robert S. '79 (ELP) El Paso, TX Christ The Savior; Judges.
Kobel, Stanley *o.f.m.cap.* '96 (CHL) Charlotte, NC St. Thomas Aquinas.
Kobia, Vincent F. '80 (MIL) Milwaukee, WI Our Lady of Guadalupe Parish; Milwaukee, WI St. Vincent de Paul.
Kobler, John F. *c.p.* '54 (CHI)[N] Chicago, IL Passionist Community–Immaculate Conception Monastery.
Kobos, Martin *o.f.m.conv.* '76 (FgM).
Kobos, Martin *o.f.m.conv.* '76 (BAL)[S] Ellicott City, MD Order of Friars Minor Conventual.
Kobti, Labib '75 (SFR) San Francisco, CA St. Thomas More.
Kobti, Labib '75 (SFR)[Q] San Francisco, CA Newman Center, San Francisco State University.
Kobti, Labib (SFR) Arab–American Catholic Ministry.
Kobus, Boguslaw '92 (PAT) Clifton, NJ St. Andrew the Apostle.
Kobus, Damian M. *o.s.m.* '49 (CHI)[N] Chicago Order of

Friar Servants of Mary (Servites) United States of America Province, Inc..
Kobus, Damian M. *o.s.m.* '49 (P)[L] Portland, OR The Grotto, The National Sanctuary of Our Sorrowful Mother.
Kobus, John '77 (CHI)[J] Chicago, IL Saint Elizabeth's Hospital.
Kobus, John '77 (CHI)[J] Chicago, IL Saint Mary of Nazareth Hospital Center.
Kobuszewski, Thomas P. '64 (SY) Syracuse, NY Transfiguration.
Kobza, John *m.i.c.* '54 (WDC)[M] Brookeville, MD Marian Monastery–Brookeville.
Koch, Andrew *o.s.b.* '97 (WOR)[O] Still River, MA Benedictine Monks, St. Benedict Abbey.
Koch, Charles J. '63 (EVN) Special Assignment; Judges; Censors Of Books.
Koch, David J. '69 (GB) Neenah, WI St. Margaret Mary.
Koch, Donald J. '60 (STL) On Duty Outside the Archdiocese.
Koch, Edward H. '01 (RVC) West Babylon, NY Our Lady of Grace.
Koch, Eugene R. '59 (DM) Granger, IA Assumption of the Blessed Virgin Mary; Advocates.
Koch, Eugene '69 (NEW) On Duty Outside the Archdiocese.
Koch, George J. *s.j.* '59 (SJ)[M] Los Gatos, CA Sacred Heart Jesuit Center.
Koch, Ivor '84 (FWT) Wichita Falls, TX Sacred Heart.
Koch, Ivor (FWT) Catholic Women, Council of.
Koch, Joseph A. *c.v.* (MO) Navy Chaplains.
Koch, Kevin A. '85 (CHY) Torrington, WY St. Rose.
Koch, Kevin (CHY) St. Joseph's Society for Priests (Clergy Mutual Benefit Society).
Koch, Kevin (CHY) Vicars Forane.
Koch, Kevin (CHY) Newspaper, Wyoming Catholic Register Board.
Koch, Michael R. '53 (GB)[J] Oshkosh, WI SSM Franciscan Courts Retired.
Koch, Patrick H. *s.j.* '57 (DAL) Dallas, TX St. Rita.
Koch, Paul M. '61 (FgM).
Koch, Paul M. '61 (DM) On Duty Outside the Diocese.
Koch, Terrence E. *s.j.* '60 (SJ)[M] Los Gatos, CA Sacred Heart Jesuit Center.
Kochan, Frederick A. '55 (WIL) Retired.
Kocherry, Varghese *c.ss.r.* '62 (RVC) Hicksville, NY Holy Family.
Kochery, Peter '70 (TR) Howell, NJ St. Veronica.
Kochon, Michael A. '81 (MET) On Duty Outside the Diocese.
Kochu, Paul '74 (SP) Tampa, FL St. Peter Claver.
Kochuparampil, Jose *c.m.f.* '87 (ATL) Stone Mountain, GA Corpus Christi.
Kochupurkal, Sebastian '76 (HRT) Plainville, CT Our Lady of Mercy.
Kochuvelikkakam, George *c.m.i.* (SAL) Oberlin, KS Sacred Heart.
Kochuvelikkakam, George *c.m.i.* (SAL) Selden, KS Immaculate Conception.
Kochuvelikkakam, George *c.m.i.* (SAL) Selden, KS Sacred Heart.
Kocik, Francis W. '76 (CAM) On Duty Outside the Diocese.
Kocik, Thomas '97 (FR) On Duty Outside the Diocese.
Kocik, Thomas (OM)[B] Omaha, NE Daniel J. Gross Catholic High School of Omaha.
Kociolek, Charles J. *c.s.c.* '79 (SCR)[C] Holy Cross Community.
Kociolek, Charles *c.s.c.* '79 (SCR)[M] Wilkes–Barre, PA Moreau House.
Kociolek, Henry *s.ch.* '88 (P) Portland, OR St. Stanislaus.
Kocour, Robert F. '43 (WCH) Retired.
Kocurek, Antonin (BRK)[U] Czech/Slovak.
Kodakassery, Thomas *o.s.b.* (FTW) Fort Wayne, IN St. Elizabeth Ann Seton.
Koebel, Joseph A. '54 (VIC) Nada, TX Nativity of the Blessed Virgin Mary; El Campo, TX St. John Nepomucene.
Koehl, Keith '97 (AUS) College Station, TX St. Mary's.
Koehl, Keith '97 (AUS)[L] College Station, TX St. Mary's Catholic Center.
Koehler, John '65 (SEA) Retired.
Koehler, Jon C. '74 (BR) Baton Rouge, LA St. Pius X.
Koehler, Kenneth '72 (DEN) Denver, CO Most Precious Blood.
Koehler, Ralph *o.s.b.* '62 (KCK) Hiawatha, KS St. Ann's.
Koehler, Steven C. '82 (DET) Madison Heights, MI St. Vincent Ferrer; Archdiocesan Vicars.
Koehne, David '49 (GB) Retired.
Koehr, Louis '87 (BEL) Albers, IL Retired.
Koelker, Harry H. '68 (DUB) Mason City, IA St. Joseph.
Koelsch, John '56 (B)[F] Twin Falls, ID College of Southern Idaho.
Koelsch, John '56 (B) Twin Falls, ID St. Edward The Confessor.
Koelsch, John (B) Priest Retirement Committee.
Koelsch, John (B) College of Consultors.
Koelsch, John (B) Deans.
Koen, Stephen A. '58 (BO) Senior Priests Retired.
Koenig, Bernard '56 (HEL) Retired.
Koenig, John H. '42 (NEW) Union, NJ Holy Spirit; [N] Caldwell, NJ The Rev. Msgr. James F. Kelley Residence for Retired Priests Retired.
Koenig, Paul *o.f.m.cap.* '93 (MIL) Milwaukee, WI St. Francis of Assisi.
Koenig, Paul *o.c.d.* '93 (SEA) Stanwood, WA St. Cecilia.
Koenig, William E. '83 (RVC) Seaford, NY St. William, the Abbot; Priests' Personnel Assignment Board; Catholic Youth Organization of Nassau and Suffolk.
Koenigsfeld, James F. '68 (PBL) Pueblo, CO Our Lady of Mt. Carmel; Pueblo, CO St. Joseph; Durango, CO St. Columba; Deans.
Koenigsfeld, James (PBL) Personnel.
Koenigsknecht, William J. '68 (LAN) Lansing, MI Resurrection.
Koeninger, Francis F. '79 (STL) Hawk Point, MO St. Mary.
Koeplin, John P. *s.j.* '91 (SFR)[N] San Francisco, CA Jesuit Community at University of San Francisco.
Koerber, George M. '60 (TOL) Retired.
Koerner, Frederick C. '59 (NEW)[N] Rutherford, NJ St. John Vianney Residence for Priests Retired.
Koers, Eugene '62 (FTW) Retired.
Koesel, Douglas H. '78 (CLV) Cleveland, OH St. Mark.
Koester, Timothy J. '83 (BUF) Military Chaplains.
Koester, Timothy J. (BUF) Navy Chaplains.
Koesterer, David W. *s.j.* '64 (STL)[O] St. Louis, MO Office; [S] St. Louis, MO Retreat House.
Koetter, Paul D. '77 (IND) Indianapolis, IN St. Monica.
Koetter, Paul (IND) Archdiocesan Pastoral Council.
Koetter, Paul (IND) Board of Consultors.
Koetter, Paul (IND) Council of Priests.
Koeune, August '84 (CHY) Casper, WY Saint Patrick's.
Koeune, August (CHY) Advocates.
Koeune, George '95 (CHI) Chicago, IL Queen of All Saints Basilica.
Kofski, James W. *m.m.* '91 (WDC)[B] Washington, DC Office of Justice and Peace.
Koharchik, George D. '74 (ALT) Shade Gap, PA St. Mary's; Huntingdon, PA State Correctional Institution.
Kohler, Edward '77 (HEL) Browning, MT Church of the Little Flower.
Kohler, Girard J. *c.s.sp.* '63 (PIT)[N] Bethel Park, PA Holy Spirit Fathers and Brothers Provincialate; [P] Bethel Park, PA Holy Spirit Animation Center.
Kohler, Lawrence A. *m.s.* '61 (LKC) Sulphur, LA Our Lady of LaSalette.
Kohler, Russell E. '73 (DET)[Q] Detroit, MI Pope John XXIII Hospitality House; [Q] Onsted, MI St. Patrick's Retreat; Special Assignment; Detroit, MI Most Holy Trinity.
Kohler, Thomas M. '68 (PH) Absent on Leave.
Kohler, William (Guillo) *c.ss.r.* '83 (TUC) Tucson, AZ St. Joseph; Tucson, AZ Tucson Medical Center.
Kohler, William E. (MIL) Special Assignment; Associate Vicar for Clergy.
Kohler, William F. '55 (PIT) Retired.
Kohlerman, Charles W. *c.s.c.* '63 (FTW)[I] Notre Dame, IN Holy Cross House.
Kohli, Charles F. '61 (RVC) Stony Brook, NY L.I. State Veterans' Home Retired.
Kohlmann, Vernon *s.d.v.* (NEW)[M] Florham Park, NJ Father Justin Vocationary.
Kohls, Eugene C. '57 (STA) Vicar for Senior Priests Retired.
Kohmescher, Matthew F. *s.m.* '48 (CIN)[D] Dayton, OH The University of Dayton; [M] Dayton, OH Marianist Community.
Kohner, David W. '90 (STP)[A] St. Paul, MN The Saint Paul Seminary; [C] St. Paul, MN University of St. Thomas.
Kohrman, Glenn '92 (FTW) Culver, IN St. Mary of the Lake.
Kohrman, Glenn (FTW) Fort Wayne.
Kohrman, Glenn (FTW) Council of Priests.
Kohuch, Robert Andrew '66 (PIT) Elrama, PA St. Isaac Jogues; Allegheny County, PA Jefferson Hospital.
Kohut, Joseph J. '62 (BGP) Darien, CT St. John Retired.
Koilparampil, Augustine '64 (OAK) Livermore, CA St. Michael.
Koilparampil, Augustine '64 (OAK) Veterans Administration Hospital.
Koitharayil, Stephen C. '95 (STL)[O] St. Louis, MO Jesuit Community Corporation at St. Louis University – Jesuit Hall; [C] Saint Louis University.
Kokeram, Sudash J. '99 (NEW) Military Chaplains; Army Chaplains.
Kokjohn, Joseph E. '54 (DAV)[B] St. Ambrose University Retired.
Kokocinski, Bernard A. '82 (TOL) Awaiting Assignment.
Kolakowski, Marcel *o.f.m.* '49 (PH) Philadelphia, PA St. John Cantius.
Kolakowski, Robert B. '02 (BUR) Diocesan Coordinator of the Vietnamese Ministry; [H] Burlington, VT University of Vermont–The Catholic Center at UVM.
Kolanko, John R. '40 (MIL) Retired.
Kolanko, John R. '40 (MIL) Milwaukee, WI Our Lady of Good Hope.
Kolano, Stanislaw '80 (MET) South River, NJ St. Mary of Ostrabrama.
Kolar, Bogdan *s.d.b.* '79 (OAK)[N] Berkeley Salesian Community.
Kolarec, William T. *s.j.* '69 (OM)[K] Omaha, NE Jesuit Community at Creighton University.
Kolasa, Stanley *ss.cc.* '95 (FR) New Bedford, MA Our Lady of the Assumption.
Kolb, James '76 (P) Portland, OR St. Elizabeth of Hungary.
Kolb, James *c.s.p.* '76 (NY)[EE] Jamaica Estates Paulist Fathers Generalate.
Kolb, Jim *c.s.p.* '76 (P) Portland, OR Oregon Health Sciences University.
Kolb, Joseph C. '53 (OKL) Council of Catholic Women, Archdiocesan Retired.
Kolb, Joseph E. *s.j.* '63 (WH)[A] Wheeling, WV Wheeling Jesuit University.
Kolb, Michael R. *s.j.* '82 (MIL)[O] Milwaukee, WI Pere Marquette House Jesuit Community; [E] Milwaukee, WI Marquette University High School.
Kolberg, Lawrence R. '68 (ORG) Absent on Sick Leave.
Kolcun, Stephen J. '46 (PBR) Retired.
Kolczaski, Richard '55 (PEO) Retired.
Kolda, Donald *s.j.* '55 (ORG) Laguna Niguel, CA St. Timothy.
Kole, Eugene *o.f.m.conv.* '75 (BAL)[S] Ellicott City, MD Friary of St. Joseph Cupertino.
Kolencherry, Francise '79 (NY) New York, NY Sacred Hearts of Jesus and Mary.
Kolenkiewicz, Louis J. '93 (PH) Yardley, PA St. Ignatius of Antioch.
Kolenski, Robert D. '62 (LAN) Owosso, MI St. Paul.
Kolesar, John C. '64 (STU) Adena, OH St. Casimir's; Adena, OH St. Adalbert; Deans; Diocesan Director of Cemeteries.
Kolf, Gerald '95 (GAL)[P] Houston, TX Opus Dei.
Kolibas, Kenneth R. '94 (MET) Parlin, NJ St. Bernadette.
Kolinovsky, Sebastian *c.p.* '51 (NEW)[N] Union City, NJ Congregation of the Passion (Passionists)–St. Michael's Residence.
Kolinovsky, Sebastian *c.p.* (FgM).
Kolla, Edward R. '01 (CAM) Mays Landing, NJ St. Vincent de Paul; Advocates.
Kollar, Anton *o.carm.* '51 (JOL)[L] Darien Carmelite Provincial Office.
Kollar, Anton *o.carm.* (SD) Christ Child Society.
Kollar, Rene M. *o.s.b.* '74 (GBG)[H] Latrobe, PA Saint Vincent Archabbey.
Kollasch, Louis '58 (SC) Retired.
Kollasch, Merle F. '64 (SC) Pocahontas, IA Church of the Resurrection.
Kollasch, Merle '64 (SC) Pocahontas, IA St. Margaret's.
Kollath, Robert '97 (GB)[M] Oshkosh, WI University of Wisconsin Newman Center.
Kollath, Robert '97 (GB) Oshkosh, WI St. Peter.
Koller, Gerold *c.pp.s.* '49 (CIN)[B] Carthagena, OH St. Charles.
Koller, Thomas *o.c.d.* '90 (SB)[E] Redlands, CA Discalced Carmelites, OCD.
Kolling, James '65 (LA) Retired.
Kollithanath, Philip '84 (CHL) High Point, NC Christ the King.
Kollman, Paul V. *c.s.c.* '91 (FTW)[A] Notre Dame, IN Moreau Seminary.
Kollross, Dennis D. '81 (SFD) Decatur, IL St. James; Decatur, IL St. Thomas the Apostle; [N] Decatur, IL Millikin University Newman Catholic Community; Commission for the Care of Infirm and Retired Priests.
Kolmaga, Bogdan *o.s.p.* '92 (NY) New York, NY St. Stanislaus.
Kolmaga, Jan *o.s.p.p.e.* '82 (PH)[AA] Office.
Kolo, Vincent F. '95 (PIT) Pittsburgh, PA Holy Wisdom.
Kolodziej, John A. *o.s.f.s.* '99 (WIL)[B] Wilmington, DE Salesianum School.
Kolodziej, Maynard *o.f.m.* (GB)[I] Pulaski, WI Friary.
Kolodziej, Michael *o.f.m.conv.* '70 (BAL)[S] Ellicott City, MD Order of Friars Minor Conventual.
Kolodziej, Michael *o.f.m.conv.* '70 (FgM).
Kolodziej, Ryszard '96 (R) Castle Hayne, NC St. Stanislaus Kostka.
Kolodziejczyk, Sebastian J. '99 (LC) Foreign Missions.
Kolodziejski, Karl *o.f.m.conv.* '78 (ALT) Davidsville, PA St. Anne; Hooversville, PA Holy Family.
Kolp, James '50 (Y) Retired.
Kolson, Lawrence F. '74 (BAL) Bradshaw, MD St. Stephen.
Kolton, Stanislaus J. '46 (CAM) Retired.
Koltuniak, Michael P. '39 (DET) Retired.
Koltzenburg, Otto '81 (SEA) Shoreline, WA St. Mark.
Koltzenburg, Otto '81 (SPK) On Duty Outside the Diocese.
Kolumber, Denis *m.s.* '67 (ATL) Canton, GA Our Lady of LaSalette.
Kolzow, Andrew K. *o.p.* '58 (SAT) San Antonio, TX St. Ann.
Kolzow, Andrew K. *o.p.* '58 (SAT)[B] San Antonio, TX

Dominican Priory of San Juan Macias and Novitiate.
Koma, Joseph W. *c.s.c.* '61 (KAL) Niles, MI St. Mark.
Koma, Joseph W. *c.s.c.* '61 (FTW)[I] Niles, MI.
Komakec, Michael L. '94 (PIT) Pittsburgh, PA St. Benedict the Moor.
Komakech, William (PIT) Chicora, PA Mater Dolorosa.
Komar, John E. '64 (NEW) Englewood, NJ Englewood Hospital & Medical Center.
Komar, Michael A. '36 (NEW) Linden, NJ Holy Family Retired.
Komaska, James R. '54 (STL) Retired.
Komatz, David M. *o.praem.* '75 (GB)[A] De Pere, WI St. Norbert Abbey; [B] St. Norbert College; [I] De Pere, WI St. Norbert Abbey; [N] De Pere, WI NORBERT & CO..
Kombo, Honore (BO) Congolese.
Kombo, Livingstone '01 (CHI) Oak Park, IL St. Giles.
Komechak, Michael E. *o.s.b.* '59 (JOL)[A] Lisle, IL Benedictine University; [L] Lisle, IL St. Procopius Abbey.
Kommer, Jason '43 (STL)[O] St. Louis, MO Franciscan Friary of St. Anthony of Padua Retired.
Kommer, Venard *o.f.m.* '46 (JOL)[L] Joliet, IL St. John the Baptist Friary.
Kommer, Venard *o.f.m.* '46 (JOL) Clarendon Hills, IL Notre Dame.
Kommers, Thomas M. '80 (STP) Red Wing, MN St. Joseph.
Komonchak, Joseph A. '64 (NY) On Duty Outside the Archdiocese; [C] Catholic University of America, The.
Komorowski, Louis A. *o.s.f.s.* '56 (LAN) Adrian, MI St. Mary of Good Counsel.
Komosinski, Martin M. '51 (TR) Retired.
Konath, Jacob '95 (BIS) Glenburn, ND St. Philomena.
Koncik, Michael *c.ss.r.* '82 (STA) Jacksonville, FL Holy Rosary.
Konda, Bernard A. '67 (TUC) Apache Junction, AZ St. George.
Kondeja, Stanley '62 (RVC) Southampton, NY Our Lady of Poland.
Konderla, David (AUS) Vocations.
Kondik, Curtis L. (CLV) Fairview Park, OH St. Angela Merici.
Kondzielski, Thaddeus T. '67 (E) Edinboro, PA St. Philip.
Kondziolka, Ronald L. '76 (CHI) Chicago, IL Holy Rosary; [J] Chicago Heights.
Konen, Lyle *c.ss.r.* '61 (SEA)[L] Seattle, WA The Redemptionist Society of Washington.
Konen, Lyle *c.ss.r.* '61 (SEA) Twin Rivers Correction Center.
Konen, Lyle *c.ss.r* '61 (SEA) Seattle, WA Sacred Heart of Jesus.
Konen, Lyle *c.ss.r.* '61 (SEA) Monroe Washington State Reformatory.
Konerman, Gregory J. '93 (CIN) Urbana, OH Sacred Heart; Urbana, OH St. Mary.
Konicek, John *s.j.* '93 (NO)[V] Newton, MA The Jesuit Community at Boston College.
Konicki, William C. '78 (WOR) Hopedale, MA Sacred Heart of Jesus.
Konieczka, Edward J. '63 (SAG) Bay City, MI St. Hyacinth.
Konieczny, Anthony M. *o.f.m.conv.* '43 (BUF)[O] Athol Springs, NY St. Francis of Assisi Friary.
Koninkx, William '46 (HT) Retired.
Koninkx, William (HT) Judges.
Konkel, Eugene J. *s.s.* '57 (SFR).
Konkel, Eugene J. *s.s.* '57 (MIL)[A] On Duty Outside the Archdiocese.
Konkel, Joseph D. *o.p.* '70 (GAL) Houston, TX Holy Rosary.
Konkel, Joseph J. *o.p.* '70 (NO)[P] New Orleans, LA Dominican Friars, Southern Dominican Province of St. Martin de Porres; [P] Metairie, LA Southern Dominican Foundation; [S] Metairie, LA Southern Dominican Foundation.
Konkel, Robert *o.f.m.* (MIL) Milwaukee, WI St. Anthony.
Konkel, Thomas '96 (STP) Lino Lakes, MN St. Joseph.
Konkler, Paul Jerome *o.c.s.o.* '68 (SAC)[A] Vina, CA Abbey of New Clairvaux, Trappist Seminary; [I] Vina, CA Abbey of New Clairvaux, Trappist.
Kono, Mario '91 (VEN) Fort Myers, FL St. Francis Xavier.
Konold, Lon *o.m.i.* '77 (NOR)[I] Willimantic, CT Immaculata Retreat House.
Konold, Lon *o.m.i.* '77 (NOR)[F] Willimantic, CT Missionary Oblates of Mary Immaculate.
Konopa, Brian D. '98 (LC)[C] Marshfield, WI Columbus High School; [C] Marshfield, WI Holy Family Middle School; Kendall, WI St. Patrick; Kendall, WI St. Joseph; Kendall, WI St. John the Baptist.
Konopa, Robert *o.f.m.* '91 (SAG) Saginaw, MI St. Thomas Aquinas.
Konopacky, Joseph R. '82 (LC) On Leave of Absence.
Konopelski, Louis *s.d.b.* '02 (NEW)[C] Ramsey, NJ Don Bosco Preparatory High School.
Konopelski, Louis *s.d.b.* '02 (NEW)[N] Ramsey, NJ Don Bosco Prep Salesian Residence.
Konopka, Edward F. '45 (DET) Retired.
Konopka, Edward M. '60 (NOR) Higganum, CT St. Peter; Council of Catholic Women.
Konopka, Edward (NOR) Members.
Konopka, Thomas E. '90 (ALB) Troy, NY St. Michael the Archangel; Van Rensselaer Manor; Special Assignment.
Konopka, Thomas (ALB) Formation for Priesthood/ Vocation Awareness.
Konopka, Thomas (ALB) Vocations and Vocation Awareness Program.
Konowalek, Zenon '89 (CC) Refugio, TX St. James the Apostle.
Konrad, Erwin '89 (JC) Retired.
Konrad, Joseph C. (BRK) Physicians.
Konrad, Joseph G. '43 (BRK) Ridgewood, NY St. Matthias Retired.
Kontendick, Steven J. '85 (MAD) Beloit, WI St. Jude.
Konz, Gregory N.P. *s.j.* '90 (MIL)[O] Milwaukee, WI Arrupe House Jesuit Community.
Konzen, Joel M. *s.m.* '79 (ATL)[C] Atlanta, GA Marist School.
Koo, Matthew '88 (SJ) San Jose, CA St. Leo the Great.
Koo, Matthew '88 (SJ) Santa Clara, CA Chinese Catholic Community.
Koo, Matthew (SJ) Chinese Catholic Community.
Koo, Paul Bon Young '92 (PH) Newtown Square, PA St. Anastasia Korean Apostolate.
Koob, Edward H. '45 (PH) Retired.
Kookoothe, Neil P. '95 (CLV) North Olmsted, OH St. Clarence.
Koons, Thomas P. '97 (ALN) Allentown, PA St. Thomas More; [L] Coopersburg, PA Carmelite Monastery; Judges; Vicar for Religious.
Koopman, Dennis *o.f.m.* '70 (CHI)[N] Countryside, IL St. Gratian Friary, Franciscan Friars.
Koopman, Joseph M. '01 (CLV) Parma, OH St. Charles Borromeo.
Koopmann, Robert *o.s.b.* '81 (SCL)[I] Collegeville, MN St. John's Abbey, of the Order of St. Benedict.
Koos, Gerald J. '66 (E) Erie, PA St. Ann; Erie, PA Hamot Medical Center.
Kopacek, Jerry F. (DUB) Liaisons; Directors; Seminary Board.
Kopacek, Jerry (DUB)[D] Waterloo, IA Columbus High School dba Cedar Valley Catholic Schools; Waterloo, IA St. Edward; Advisory Committee of Persons with Disabilities; [F] Waterloo, IA Cedar Valley Catholic Schools Office.
Kopacz, Joseph R. '77 (SCR) Scranton, PA Sacred Hearts of Jesus and Mary; Diocesan Consultors; Ex Officio; Vicar for Priests; Priests' Purgatorial Society; Priests' Retirement Advisory Board.
Kopacz, K. S. '95 (FAR) Oriska, ND Holy Trinity.
Kopacz, Kazimierz (FAR) Graduate Studies.
Kopacz, Mark W. '92 (WIL) Wilmington, DE Cathedral of St. Peter.
Kopacz, Matthew S. (BUF) Council of Priests; Buffalo, NY St. Casimir.
Kopacz, Stephen A. '72 (NEW) Livingston, NJ St. Philomena.
Kopaczynski, Germain *o.f.m.conv.* '74 (BO)[EE] Boston, MA National Catholic Bioethics Center.
Kopaczynski, Germain *o.f.m.conv.* '74 (BO) South Boston, MA Our Lady of Czestochowa.
Kopchik, Martin *m.s.f.s.* '86 (ATL)[K] Lawrenceville, GA The Missionaries of St. Francis De Sales.
Kopczynski, Sean *c.p.m.* (OWN)[F] Auburn, KY Fathers of Mercy.
Kopec, Christopher A. '93 (WIL) Military Chaplains.
Kopec, Edward S. '92 (PEO) Spring Valley, IL SS. Peter and Paul's.
Kopec, Jerome E. '79 (BUF) Niagara Falls, NY St. John de La Salle.
Kopec, Krzysztof A. (WIL) Army Chaplains.
Kopec, Rajmind (HON) Military Chaplains.
Kopec, Rajmund '92 (NEW) Military Chaplains; Army Chaplains.
Kopecky, Joseph A. '45 (PIT) Retired.
Kopel, Jerome '77 (SFS) Brandon, SD Risen Savior.
Koper, Francis B. '71 (WIL) On Duty Outside the Diocese.
Koper, Ryszard '78 (BRK) Maspeth, NY Holy Cross.
Kopezewski, Linus *o.f.m.* '65 (MIL)[O] Burlington, WI St. Francis Friary.
Kopfensteiner, Thomas R. '81 (STL) On Duty Outside the Archdiocese.
Kopff, Herbert C. '38 (BEL) Retired.
Kopinski, Richard P. (RVC) Judges for Interdiocesan Tribunal; Oyster Bay Deanery.
Kopinski, Richard '64 (RVC) Glen Head, NY St. Hyacinth.
Koplik, William J. '62 (NEW) Ridgefield, NJ St. Matthew's Retired.
Koplinka, Stephen '79 (PRM) Brunswick, OH St. Emilian.
Koplinka, Steven '79 (PRM) Cleveland, OH St. Mary.
Koplinka, Steven (PRM) Presbyteral Council.
Koplinka, Steven (PRM) Seminary Education Formation Board.
Koplinka, Steven (PRM) Eparchial Pastoral Council.
Koplinka, Steven (PRM) Syncellus for Clergy and Religious.
Koplinka, Steven (PRM) Sacred Liturgy.
Kopp, Anthony Mary J. *o.praem.* '93 (ORG)[I] Silverado, CA Norbertine Fathers of Orange Inc..
Kopp, Anthony *o.praem.* '93 (ORG)[H] Silverado, CA St. Michael's Summer Camp.
Kopp, Richard M. '69 (SY) Baldwinsville, NY St. Mary; Western Area Vicars; Board of Diocesan Consultors; Ex Officio.
Kopp, Thomas A. (BO) Halifax, MA Our Lady of the Lake.
Koppert, Elias *o.f.m.* '41 (SFD)[L] Springfield, IL Our Lady of Angels Friary.
Koppes, Albert P. *o.carm.* '59 (LA)[C] Los Angeles, CA Loyola Marymount University; [C] Los Angeles, CA Jesuit Community.
Koppes, Albert P. *o.carm.* '59 (JOL)[L] Darien Carmelite Provincial Office.
Koprowski, Mitchell J. '41 (GI) Retired.
Kopystynski, Andraej Rafal *c.m.* '88 (BRK) Brooklyn, NY St. Stanislaus Kostka.
Korba, Frank '66 (PRM) Munster, IN Saint Nicholas.
Korba, Frank (PRM) Midwest.
Korba, Frank (PRM) Associates.
Korba, Frank (PRM) Catechetical Board.
Korban, Janusz '97 (RC) Fairfax, SD St. Anthony's.
Korban, Janusz '97 (RC) Bonesteel, SD Immaculate Conception.
Korbelak, John J. '74 (NEW) North Bergen, NJ Our Lady of Fatima.
Korcsmar, John S. *c.s.c.* '74 (AUS) Austin, TX Nuestra Senora De Dolores; [G] Austin, TX Congregation of Holy Cross – Southern Province.
Korcsmar, John *c.s.c.* (AUS) Kyle, TX Blessed Juan Diego; Deans.
Korcsmar, John *c.s.c.* (AUS) Presbyteral Council.
Korcz, Krzystof '85 (WOR) Worcester, MA Our Lady of Czestochowa.
Korczagin, Nicolau (STF) Brooklyn, NY Holy Ghost.
Korda, Edward L. '49 (CAM) Magnolia, NJ St. Gregory's Retired.
Korda, J. James '79 (Y) Austintown, OH St. Joseph.
Kordas, Edward J. '68 (CLV) Hudson, OH St. Mary; Associate Judges.
Kordsmeier, John '49 (LR) Retired.
Kordsmeier, John '49 (LR)[H] Little Rock, AR St. John Manor.
Kordsmeier, John (LR) Defenders of the Bond.
Korecki, Maximilian *o.f.m.conv.* '62 (IND)[J] Mount St. Francis, IN Mount Saint Francis Friary and Retreat Center.
Korenek, Greg (VIC) Defenders of the Bond.
Korenek, Greg (VIC) Presbyteral Council.
Korenek, Gregory E. '93 (VIC) Victoria, TX Holy Family of Joseph, Mary & Jesus.
Koressel, James '69 (EVN) All Saints.
Koressel, James '69 (EVN) Montgomery, IN St. Peter.
Koressel, James (EVN) Deans.
Koressel, James (EVN) Diocesan Council of Priests.
Korf, Joseph '74 (SCL) Elk River, MN The Church of St. Andrew.
Korf, Joseph (SCL) Diocesan Finance Council.
Korf, Joseph (SCL) Advocates.
Kormeyer, Thomas E. '90 (OG) Lake Clear, NY St. John in the Wilderness.
Kornacki, Matthew J. '73 (PH)[A] Absent on Leave.
Kornacki, Thomas J. *o.f.m.* '88 (FgM).
Kornath, Edwin M. '84 (MIL) Waterford, WI St. Thomas Aquinas.
Kornmeyer, Thomas E. '90 (OG) Bloomingdale, NY St. Paul; Saranac Lake, NY St. Bernard; Campus Ministry; Pro–Life Office.
Korogi, Dale J. '83 (STP) Minneapolis, MN Christ the King; North Memorial Hospital.
Korte, Edward F. '62 (BIS) Washburn, ND St. Edwin; Underwood, ND St. Bonaventure.
Korte, Owen W. '81 (OM) Fremont, NE St. Patrick; Age Groups.
Korte, William L. '83 (JC) Salisbury, MO St. Joseph; Fulton, MO Missouri School for the Deaf; Senators; Legion of Mary.
Kortendick, Steven J. (MAD) Elected.
Korth, David M. '92 (OM) Duncan, NE St. Stanislaus; Silver Creek, NE St. Lawrence; Walthill, NE St. Joseph; Macy, NE Our Lady of Fatima; Winnebago, NE St. Augustine's; Age Groups.
Korycki, Walter R. '49 (RVC) Retired.
Korzinek, Richard *o.s.cam.* '53 (MIL)[O] Wauwatosa, WI St. Camillus Community House.
Kos, Donald *o.f.m.conv.* '61 (BAL)[S] Convento S. Antonio, 56.
Kos, Stanislaw '96 (RCK) Hanover, IL St. John the Evangelist.
Kosak, Michael F. '70 (STV) St. Croix, VI Church St. Ann; School of Evangelization; [B] Catholic Charismatic Renewal; [B] Lumen 2000/Caribbean Region; [B] Kingshill, St. Croix, VI Disciples of the Holy Spirit, Inc..
Kosak, Michael (STV) Diocesan Consultors.
Kosak, Michael (STV) Charismatic Movement.

Kosak, Michael (STV) Caribbean Catholic Network (CCN).
Kosak, Michael (STV) Communications Coordinator.
Kosaka, Paulo R. *o.f.m.cap* '84 (HON) Pearl City, HI Our Lady of Good Counsel.
Kosanke, Charles '85 (DET)[T] Clawson, MI American Friends of the Vatican Library; Clawson, MI Guardian Angels.
Kosatka, Leonard *c.p.* '42 (FgM).
Kosch, Leo D. '93 (LIN) Bellwood, NE Presentation; [C] David City, NE Aquinas/St. Mary's Schools; Diocesan Area CCD Directors.
Kosch, Leo (LIN) Commission for Sacred Liturgy and Sacred Music.
Kosciesza, Bogumil '94 (WDC) Silver Spring, MD St. Catherine Laboure.
Kosco, Arnold J. '60 (DET) West Bloomfield, MI Prince of Peace.
Kosco, William (PHX) Gilbert, AZ St. Anne.
Kose, Robert *o.f.m.cap* (MIL) Milwaukee, WI St. Anthony; Milwaukee, WI St. Francis of Assisi.
Kosem, Frank P. '70 (CLV) Elyria, OH St. Jude.
Koser, Albert C. '59 (PIT) Boyers, PA St. Alphonsus.
Koser, Rudolph J. '74 (GBG) Clymer, PA Church of the Resurrection.
Koshko, Dennis '75 (HON) Kailua, HI St. Anthony.
Kosicki, Bohdan W. '50 (DET) Retired.
Kosicki, George *c.s.b.* '54 (ROC)[I] Paradise, MI c/o Companions of Christ the Lamb.
Kosinski, Pawel *s.j.* '92 (CHI)[N] Chicago, IL Jan Beyzym Society, Inc..
Kosinski, Pawel *s.j.* '92 (CHI)[N] Chicago, IL Sacred Heart Mission House.
Kosinski, Stephen D. '81 (GRY) Hammond, IN All Saints.
Kosisko, Richard J. '85 (GBG) North Huntingdon, PA St. Elizabeth Ann Seton; Judges; Bishop's Priests Council.
Kosler, Timothy '71 (VIC) Schulenburg, TX St. John The Baptist.
Kosler, Timothy '71 (VIC) Schulenburg, TX Nativity of the Blessed Virgin Mary.
Kosler, Timothy '71 (VIC) Schulenburg, TX St. Rose of Lima.
Kosler, Timothy (VIC) Defenders of the Bond.
Kosler, Timothy (VIC) Presbyteral Council.
Kosler, Timothy (VIC) Diocesan Consultors.
Kosler, Timothy (VIC) Schulenburg Deanery.
Kosler, Timothy (VIC) Priests' Personnel Board.
Kosmicki, Raymond '68 (GI) St. Paul, NE SS. Peter and Paul.
Kosmoski, David B. *o.m.v.* '81 (MET) Avenel, NJ St. Andrew.
Kosmowski, Gary J. '90 (MAN) Laconia, NH St. Joseph.
Kosnac, Benjamin '93 (DET) Sterling Heights, MI SS. Cyril and Methodius.
Kosowicz, Wojciech '65 (LAR) Laredo, TX St. Peter The Apostle.
Kosowicz, Wojciech (LAR) Presbyteral Council.
Kosse, Gerald C. '76 (WIN) Adrian, MN St. Adrian; Lismore, MN St. Anthony's; Adrian, MN Our Lady of Good Counsel; Deans; Advocates; Bishop's Council; Commission on Sacred Liturgy.
Kosse, Gerald C. (WIN) Auditors.
Kosse, Theodore C. '71 (CIN) West Union, OH St. Mary Queen of Heaven; West Union, OH Holy Trinity; Vicarri Foranei (Deans).
Kostek, John S. '72 (NY) Staten Island, NY Holy Child.
Kostelnick, Albert T. '54 (PH) Retired.
Kostelnik, Kevin J. '82 (LA) Los Angeles, CA Cathedral of Our Lady of the Angels.
Kostelnik, Kevin (LA) Master of Ceremonies for Stational Liturgies.
Kostelz, Richard F. '52 (JOL) Cabery, IL St. Joseph.
Koster, Dale F. '54 (SC) Retired.
Koster, John *s.v.d.* '44 (CHI)[B] Techny, IL Divine Word Residence.
Koster, Ken '76 (SFS) Tea, SD St. Christina.
Koster, Ken (SFS) Tribunal Judges.
Koster, Kenneth J. '76 (SFS) Tea, SD St. Nicholas; Veteran's Hospital.
Kosterman, Richard A. '93 (GAY) Copemish, MI St. Raphael.
Kostic, Andrew (PAT).
Kostiuk, Nick '80 (PHU) Retired.
Kostka, Leonard J. *c.pp.s.* '40 (LFT) Rensselaer, IN St. Augustine; [A] Rensselaer, IN Saint Joseph's College Retired.
Kostrzomb, Stanley '77 (NEW) Newark, NJ St. Casimir's.
Kosty, Robert J. '74 (WDC) Port Tobacco, MD St. Ignatius Loyola; Port Tobacco, MD St. Catherine of Alexandria.
Kostyk, Jaroslaw (STF) Directors:.
Kostyk, Marian '90 (STF) Little Falls, NY St. Nicholas.
Kostyk, Marian '90 (STF) Amsterdam, NY St. Nicholas.
Kostyk, Yaroslaw (STF) Campbell Hall, NY St. Andrew's.
Koszarek, Paul P. '54 (GB) Retired.
Koszarek, Paul (GB) Diocesan Consultors.
Koszarek, Paul (GB) Appointed Representatives.
Koszarek, Robert J. '74 (SUP) Eagle River, WI St. Peter the Fisherman; Land O'Lakes, WI St. Albert; Land O'Lakes, WI St. Mary; Presbyteral Council & Diocesan Consultors.
Koszarek, Thaddeus J. '39 (GB)[H] Green Bay, WI The McCormick Memorial Home for the Aged; McCormick Memorial Home for the Aged Retired.
Koszyk, Seweryn J. *s.a.c* '59 (BUF) Niagara Falls, NY St. George.
Kot, Krystian '94 (NOR) Putnam, CT St. Mary.
Kot, Luke C. *o.c.s.o.* '48 (ATL)[K] Conyers, GA The Monastery of the Holy Spirit.
Kotara, James A. (SAT) Defenders of the Bond.
Kotara, James '76 (SAT) San Antonio, TX Holy Family.
Kotecki, Ronald E. '72 (MIL) Milwaukee, WI St. Stanislaus; Milwaukee, WI St. Hyacinth.
Koterski, Joseph W. *s.j.* '92 (NY)[EE] Cardinal Spellman Hall, Jesuit Community.
Koth, Arthur R. '57 (MAD) Retired.
Kothapalli, Samuel '77 (SFD) Springfield, IL Cathedral of the Immaculate Conception.
Kotlanger, Michael J. '78 (SFR)[N] San Francisco, CA Jesuit Community at St. Ignatius College Preparatory.
Kotlanger, Michael J. *s.j.* '78 (SFR)[E] San Francisco, CA St. Ignatius College Preparatory (Coed).
Kotlarczyk, Mark E. '88 (SB) Victorville, CA Holy Innocents; Elected Members.
Kotlarz, Robert J. '69 (DET) Detroit, MI Our Lady of Good Counsel; Detroit, MI St. Raymond.
Kotlinski, Bede *o.s.b.* '84 (CLV)[D] Cleveland, OH Benedictine High School.
Kotlinski, Bede *o.s.b.* '84 (CLV)[O] Cleveland, OH.
Kotlinski, Bede *o.s.b.* (CLV) Translators.
Kotnis, Gregory M. '56 (PHX) Retired.
Kottackal, Paul '54 (SYM) Chatsworth, CA Bl. Alphonsa Syro–Malabar Catholic Mission of Los Angeles.
Kottackal, Paul '74 (LA) Chatsworth, CA St. John Eudes.
Kottar, Michael T. '94 (MET) On Duty Outside the Diocese.
Kottar, Michael '94 (CHL) Andrews, NC Holy Redeemer.
Kottaram, Mathew '78 (RVC) Setauket, NY St. James.
Kottaramallaseril, Vaidhian (PH) Indian Apostolate, Syro Malankara Rite.
Kottas, Charles '70 (DM) Council Bluffs, IA St. Peter.
Kottayarikil, Cyriac *m.c.b.s.* '67 (MAR) Rudyard, MI St. Joseph.
Kottayil, Joseph '79 (MIA) Miramar, FL Blessed John XXIII Church.
Kottenstette, William P. '73 (JC) Kirksville, MO Mary Immaculate; Memphis, MO St. John; [E] Kirksville, MO Catholic Newman Center, Truman State University.
Kouba, Charles J. '51 (CHI) Chicago, IL St. Simon the Apostle Retired.
Kouba, John *s.d.s.* '52 (MIL)[O] Sacramento, CA.
Koury, James '92 (NTN) Leave of Absence.
Koury, Joseph A. '50 (JKS) Retired.
Koury, Joseph J. '77 (PRT) Orono, ME St. Mary's; Orono, ME Our Lady of Wisdom Personal Campus Parish; [M] Orono, ME University of Maine; Associate Judges; Diocesan Council of Priests; Newman Apostolate.
Koury, Joseph (NTN) Judges.
Koury, Joseph *s.j.* (COS) Associate Judges.
Koutnik, Jerome P. '99 (RCK) Rockford, IL St. Edward.
Kovacevich, Steven '87 (CHI)[J] Blue Island, IL St. Francis Hospital and Health Center.
Kovach, John '65 (PRM) Parma, OH Holy Spirit; Fairview Park, OH St. Mary Magdalene.
Kovach, John '65 (VNN) On Special Assignment.
Kovach, William J. '55 (ALT) Retired.
Kovacic, Anthony '47 (CHL) Retired.
Kovacic, Anthony (CHL) Propagation of the Faith.
Kovacik, Jozef '98 (ALT) Johnstown, PA St. Benedict's.
Kovacs, Matthew *o.cist.* '57 (DAL)[K] Irving, TX Cistercian Abbey of Our Lady of Dallas.
Kovalcin, John A. '81 (STL) Military Chaplains; Air Force Chaplains.
Kovalik, George J. '47 (STP) Minneapolis, MN All Saints.
Kovalyshin, Severyn '00 (SJP) North Port, FL Entrance of B.V.M. into the Temple.
Kovanis, Joel '94 (SP) Tarpon Springs, FL St. Ignatius.
Kovarik, James *o.s.cam.* '66 (MIL) Wood, WI Veterans Administration Medical Center.
Kovarik, James '90 (MIL)[O] St. Francis, WI St. Camillus Provincialate.
Kovarik, James *o.s.cam.* (MIL) CIVIL AIR PATROL.
Kovarik, Peter '91 (RC) Custer, SD St. John the Baptist.
Kovarik, Peter '91 (RC) Hot Springs, SD St. Anthony's.
Kovarik, Peter (RC) Deaneries.
Kowal, William D. '79 (R) Retired.
Kowalczyk, Adolph M. '88 (BUF) Buffalo, NY St. Agatha.
Kowalczyk, Joseph W. *m.m.* '61 (SJ)[M] Los Altos, CA Maryknoll.
Kowalczyk, Miroslaw *f.d.p.* (BO) East Boston, MA St. Joseph–St. Lazarus.
Kowalczyk, Sigismund C. '56 (DET) Retired.
Kowalczyk, Thomas M. '67 (SAG) Linwood, MI St. Anne.
Kowalczyk, Thomas (SAG) Vicars for Vicariates.
Kowalewski, Francis P. '59 (BUF) Darien Center, NY Our Lady of Good Counsel Retired.
Kowalewski, John A. *o.s.f.s.* '77 (WIL)[B] Wilmington, DE Salesianum School.
Kowalik, Jacek '79 (VEN) Military Chaplains; Air Force Reserve Chaplains.
Kowalske, Kevin J. '95 (MIL) Lomira, WI St. Mary; St. Theresa, WI St. Theresa.
Kowalski, Al '51 (NEW) Kenilworth, NJ St. Theresa's Retired.
Kowalski, Aleksy '84 (CAM)[I] Cherry Hill, NJ St. Mary's Catholic Home; [P] Berlin, NJ Mater Ecclesiae Chapel.
Kowalski, Alfred J. '51 (NEW) Retired.
Kowalski, Eric '93 (CHL) Mt. Airy, NC Holy Angels.
Kowalski, George '56 (DET) Retired.
Kowalski, James C. '68 (GR) Ada, MI St. Robert.
Kowalski, James (GR) Deans.
Kowalski, Janusz '89 (LC) Rothschild, WI St. Therese of the Child Jesus.
Kowalski, Kasimierz A. '91 (NY) New York, NY St. Agnes.
Kowalski, Lawrence T. '69 (OKL) Enid, OK St. Gregory the Great.
Kowalski, Leo S. '39 (MIL) Retired.
Kowalski, Matthew '87 (SFS)[F] Marvin, SD Blue Cloud Abbey.
Kowalski, Ralph E. '42 (DET) Retired.
Kowalski, Ronald C. '81 (SUP) Rib Lake, WI Assumption of the Blessed Virgin Mary; Rib Lake, WI St. John the Baptist; Rib Lake, WI St. Theresa; Rib Lake, WI Our Lady of Perpetual Help.
Kowalski, Ronald '81 (MIL) On Duty Outside the Archdiocese.
Kowalski, Stanislaw *s.ch.* '87 (DET) Sterling Heights, MI Our Lady of Czestochowa.
Kowalski, Wladyslaw J. '51 (SUP) Mosinee, WI St. John the Baptist Retired.
Kowalski, Wojciech *s.d.s.* '69 (NEW)[N] Verona, NJ The Salvatorian Fathers.
Kowalski, Wojciech *s.d.s.* (NEW) Elizabeth, NJ St. Hedwig's.
Kowalsky, Myron *o.f.m.cap.* '58 (MIL) Milwaukee, WI St. Francis of Assisi.
Kowatch, Thomas P. '85 (CLV) Lakewood, OH St. James; Cleveland, OH Lakewood Hospital.
Kownacki, Francis J. *s.j.* '60 (SCR)[C] Scranton, PA The University of Scranton.
Kownacki, Raymond F. '60 (BEL) Leave of Absence.
Kownacki, Robert '63 (SAT) On Duty Outside the Archdiocese.
Koyickal, Joseph *s.a.c.* '80 (MIL) Milwaukee, WI St. Vincent Pallotti.
Koys, Thomas R. '85 (CHI) Chicago, IL Immaculate Conception.
Kozachesan, Roman *o.f.m.cap.* '61 (BAL)[S] Baltimore, MD St. Ambrose Friary.
Kozak, David J. '83 (ALN) Bethlehem, PA Holy Infancy; Defenders of the Bond.
Kozak, Remigius A. '54 (BLX) Retired.
Kozak, Richard J. '67 (CHI) Homewood, IL St. Joseph.
Kozanecki, Charles *o.f.m.conv.* '53 (MRY) Pismo Beach, CA St. Paul the Apostle.
Kozanko, Andrzej J. '00 (FR) New Bedford, MA Holy Name of the Sacred Heart of Jesus.
Kozar, John E. '71 (PIT) On Duty Outside the Diocese.
Kozar, John E. '71 (NY) New York, NY St. Patrick Old Cathedral.
Kozar, John (NY) Propagation of the Faith, National Office.
Kozar, Joseph F. *s.m.* '77 (CIN)[D] Dayton, OH The University of Dayton; [M] Dayton, OH Marianist Community.
Kozar, Joseph *s.m.* '77 (CIN) Troy, OH St. Patrick.
Kozel, Robert F. '61 (ALN) Allentown, PA St. John the Baptist.
Kozen, Bert S. (SCR) Army National Guard Chaplains; Military Chaplains.
Koziczuk, Andrzej A. '79 (SAC) Quincy, CA St. John.
Koziczuk, Andrzej (SAC) Vicars Forane.
Koziel, Piotr A. '97 (CC) Kingsville, TX St. Thomas Aquinas, University Catholic Center; Kingsville, TX St. Gertrude.
Kozien, Casimir J. '50 (CHI) Chicago, IL St. Bartholomew Retired.
Kozikowski, Thad '75 (GF) Glasgow, MT St. Raphael's.
Kozikowski, Thad (GF) Personnel Board.
Kozina, Vladimir '45 (OAK) Retired.
Kozlak, Stanley '74 (STP) Retired.
Kozlowski, Edward A. '38 (NY) Bronx, NY Veterans Administration Hospital.
Kozlowski, Joseph F. '73 (BUF) Holley, NY St. Mary; Holley, NY St. Mark.
Kozlowski, Joseph P. '49 (RVC) Glen Head, NY St. Hyacinth Retired.

Kozlowski, Theodore J. (GR) College of Consultors.
Kozlowski, Theodore '58 (GR) Grand Rapids, MI Our Lady of Sorrows.
Kozlowski, Theodore (GR) Deans.
Kozminski, Andrzej *s.a.c.* '88 (BUF) East Aurora, NY Immaculate Conception.
Kozminski, Max M. '60 (BUF) Retired.
Kozoil, Micah E. '76 (GBG) Uniontown, PA Nativity of the Blessed Virgin Mary.
Kozon, John A. '32 (NOR) Retired.
Kozub, Tomasz '93 (CC) Corpus Christi, TX Collegiate Parish of St. Thomas More.
Kozyra, Oscar Z. *o.de.m.* '73 (SP) St. Petersburg, FL Transfiguration.
Kozyra, Oscar *o.de.m.* '73 (SP)[O] St. Petersburg, FL St. Peter Nolasco Residence.
Krach, Joseph W. '57 (BAL) Retired.
Kraeger, David *t.o.r.* '68 (FWT) Windthorst, TX St. Mary.
Kraeger, David *t.o.r.* '68 (FWT) St. Boniface.
Kraemer, Bartholomew *o.s.b.* '64 (DET)[K] Detroit, MI St. Sylvester Monastery.
Kraemer, Edwin '55 (SCL) Retired.
Kraemer, Edwin (SCL) Directors.
Kraemer, John A. '57 (RCK) Retired.
Kraeszig, Charles J. '52 (IND) Retired.
Krafchak, John S. '56 (SCR) Nanticoke, PA St. Mary of Czestochowa.
Krafft, Joseph M. '02 (NO) Metairie, LA St. Clement of Rome.
Krafinski, Thomas S. *c.m.* '68 (BRK) Brooklyn, NY St. John the Baptist; [V] Brooklyn, NY St. John the Baptist Rectory.
Kraft, Philip '62 (SFD) Special or Other Diocesan Assignment.
Kraft, Thomas *o.p.* '84 (FgM).
Kraft, Thomas *o.p.* '86 (OAK)[N] Oakland Western Dominican Province.
Kraft, Thomas *o.p.* '86 (FgM).
Kraft, William '86 (STO) Sonora, CA St. Patrick Church of Sonora (Pastor of).
Krah, James B. '71 (PIT) Darlington, PA St. Rose of Lima.
Krahel, David H. '86 (BGP) Stamford, CT Our Lady Star of the Sea; Catholic Ministry for the Elderly.
Krahenbuhl, Gary L. '84 (MAD) Beloit, WI Our Lady of the Assumption; Elected; Beloit.
Krahman, Phil '72 (STL) St. Louis, MO St. Richard.
Krahman, Philip G. '72 (STL) St. Louis, MO St. John's Mercy Medical Center; [J] Creve Coeur, MO St. John's Mercy Medical Center.
Kraig, Robert J. '72 (CLV) Strongsville, OH St. John Neumann.
Krajci, Anthony *s.v.d.* '45 (CHI)[B] Techny, IL Divine Word Residence.
Krajcovic, Bernard '56 (STU) Retired.
Krajewski, Joseph A. '73 (MET) New Brunswick, NJ St. Joseph.
Krajewski, Paul A. (PAT) Retired.
Krajewski, Robert L. '98 (SUP) On Leave.
Krajicek, Robert P. '53 (OM) Retired.
Krajnak, Josef (NY) Yonkers, NY Yonkers General Hospital.
Krajnik, Paul '50 (CLV) Lorain, OH SS. Cyril and Methodius.
Kraker, Joseph H. '64 (CLV) Akron, OH St. Vincent.
Kraljic, John R. '69 (NY)[E] New York, NY Cardinal Spellman High School.
Krall, Jack '63 (P) Retired.
Krall, Kenneth R. *s.j.* '71 (SPK)[B] Spokane, WA Gonzaga University.
Kralovich, Louis W. '60 (TR) Toms River, NJ St. Luke; Tribunal Judges.
Kram, Thomas J. '49 (PIT) Retired.
Kramarz, Andreas *l.c.* '03 (HRT).
Kramberg, Donald F. '74 (OG)[B] Tupper Lake, NY Holy Name of Jesus; Tupper Lake, NY St. Alphonsus.
Kramer, Anthony *o.mar.* '95 (SAM)[C] Petersham, MA Most Holy Trinity Monastery.
Kramer, Carl '52 (SAL) Retired.
Kramer, Daniel J. *c.m.* '47 (PH).
Kramer, Gary J. '93 (PH)[AA] Warminster, PA Nativity of Our Lord.
Kramer, George C. '53 (BO) Senior Priests Retired.
Kramer, George (JC) Ministry Formation.
Kramer, James F. '68 (CLV) Copley, OH Guardian Angels.
Kramer, James G. '48 (MAD)[G] Madison, WI Bishop O'Connor Catholic Pastoral Center Retired.
Kramer, Lawrence A. '60 (FTW) Columbia City, IN St. Paul of the Cross; [C] Fort Wayne, IN Bishop Luers High School.
Kramer, Lawrence (FTW) Council of Priests.
Kramer, Lawrence (FTW) Pro–Synodal Judges.
Kramer, Lawrence (FTW) Bluffton.
Kramer, Noel R. *o.f.m.conv.* '58 (LSC) Carlsbad, NM St. Edward.
Kramer, Noel *o.f.m.conv.* (LSC) Defenders of the Bond.
Kramer, Peter '79 (BIS) Retired.
Kramer, Richard R. '66 (RCK) Oregon, IL St. Mary.
Kramer, Robert L. *c.s.c.* '64 (PHX)[G] Phoenix, AZ Holy Cross Congregation/Casa Santa Cruz.
Kramer, Scott T. *c.pp.s.* '90 (CIN)[U] Dayton, OH Community Support Charitable Trust.
Kramer, Scott *c.pp.s.* '90 (TOL) Kalida, OH St. Isidore.
Kramer, Scott *c.pp.s.* '90 (TOL) Kalida, OH St. Michael.
Kramer, Thomas E. '58 (BIS) Bismarck, ND Cathedral of the Holy Spirit; Vicar General; Pro–Synodal Judges; Presbyteral Council; Diocesan Corporate Board; Diocesan Finance Council.
Kramer, Thomas J. '77 (DET) Dearborn Heights, MI St. Mel; Archdiocesan Vicars.
Kramer, William J. '73 (CIN) Beavercreek, OH St. Luke.
Kramer, William *c.pp.s.* '44 (CIN)[B] Carthagena, OH St. Charles.
Kramis, Joseph '57 (SEA) Retired.
Kramlich, Lloyd P. *s.d.s.* '58 (PHX) Mesa, AZ Queen of Peace.
Kramper, James P. *s.j.* '44 (MIL)[O] Wauwatosa, WI Jesuit Community at St. Camillus.
Kramper, James V. '73 (OM) Tekamah, NE St. Patrick; Decatur, NE Holy Family.
Krank, Michael T. '52 (BIS) Pro–Synodal Judges; Priests' Benefit Association Retired.
Krantz, Ernest *c.pp.s.* '76 (GRY)[A] Whiting, IN Calumet College of St. Joseph.
Krantz, Robert V. '78 (SFS) Parkston, SD Sacred Heart.
Krantz, Robert (SFS) Diocesan Consultors.
Krantz, Robert (SFS) Deans.
Krantz, Robert (SFS) Presbyteral Council.
Kranyc, Andrew G. '87 (WH) Huntington, WV Sacred Heart; Huntington, WV St. Peter Claver.
Kranz, Stephen *o.s.b.* '55 (BIS)[A] Richardton, ND Assumption Abbey.
Kranz, Stephen *o.s.b.* '55 (BIS) Mandaree, ND St. Anthony.
Kranz, Stephen *o.s.b.* '55 (BIS) New Town, ND St. Anthony.
Krapfl, Daniel A. '58 (DUB)[E] Cascade, IA Aquin Religious Education Center; Bernard IA Sacred Heart.
Krapfl, Daniel J. '58 (DUB) Cascade, IA St. Matthias.
Krapfl, Gary '72 (DUB) Decorah, IA St. Benedict; Deans; Human Resources Advisory Committee.
Krasauskas, Rapolas (NOR)[G] Putnam, CT Matulaitis Nursing Home Inc..
Krasen, John W. '60 (CLV) Lakewood, OH St. Luke.
Krasevac, Edward *o.p.* '77 (OAK) Antioch, CA Holy Rosary; [N] Oakland, CA Western Dominican Province.
Krasevac, Edward *o.p.* '77 (OAK).
Krasman, James *o.f.m.* '86 (GAY)[A] Whittemore, MI St. James.
Krastel, Francis W. '54 (WDC)[S] St. Mary's City, MD St. Mary's College Campus Ministry.
Krastel, Joseph F. *c.ss.r.* '64 (FgM).
Krasulski, Andrew '98 (SJP) St. Petersburg, FL Epiphany of Our Lord.
Kraszewski, Thomas J. '97 (Y) North Canton, OH St. Paul.
Kratje, John F. '02 (CHI) Chicago, IL St. Benedict.
Kratz, Conrad J. *o.praem.* '73 (GB) De Pere, WI Our Lady of Lourdes; [I] De Pere, WI St. Joseph Priory.
Kraus, Charles A. '58 (BRK) Brooklyn, NY St. Charles Borromeo.
Kraus, Conrad L. '67 (E) Emlenton, PA St. Michael.
Kraus, Conrad (E) Administrative Cabinet.
Kraus, Conrad (E) Co Directors; Office of Worship and Worship Outreach.
Kraus, David H. '67 (DOD) Dighton, KS St. Theresa; Scott City, KS St. Joseph.
Kraus, David H. (DOD) Promoter of Justice; Defender of the Bond.
Kraus, David *o.m.i.* '57 (BEL)[H] Belleville, IL King's House Retreat and Renewal Center.
Kraus, Donald W. '54 (PIT) Retired.
Kraus, Joseph D. '01 (MET) Sayreville, NJ Our Lady of Victories.
Kraus, Leonard E. *s.j.* '72 (STL) St. Louis, MO St. Francis Xavier; [O] St. Louis, MO Jesuit Community Corporation at St. Louis University – Jesuit Hall.
Kraus, Philip D. *s.j.* '75 (STL)[N] St. Louis, MO Fusz Pavilion; [O] St. Louis, MO Jesuit Community Corporation at St. Louis University – Jesuit Hall.
Kraus, Robert J. '42 (STL) Retired.
Kraus, Stephen '75 (ROC) Sonyea, NY Groveland Correctional Facility.
Kraus, Stephen '75 (ROC) Wayland, NY Holy Family Catholic Community.
Kraus, Theodore W. *s.j.* '63 (OAK) Orinda, CA Santa Maria.
Kraus, William *o.f.m.cap.* '73 (FgM).
Krause, Bruce J. *c.m.* '82 (BIR) Alexander City, AL St. John the Apostle.
Krause, Edward C. *c.s.c.* '66 (FTW)[I] Erie, PA Gannon University.
Krause, Edward C. *c.s.c.* '70 (E) Erie PA Immaculate Conception; [B] Erie, PA Gannon University; Black Apostolate.
Krause Edward *c.s.c.* (E) Lake Shore Visitor Advisory Board.
Krause, Edward (E) The Bishop's Theological Advisory Committee.
Krause, Joseph A. '68 (TUC) Payson, AZ Saint Philip the Apostle.
Krause, Joseph (TUC) Judge.
Krauser, Karl *c.ss.r.* '85 (NY) New York, NY St. Cecilia.
Krauth, Lothar '73 (GF) Great Falls, MT Our Lady of Lourdes.
Krautsack, Blaise P. *o.praem.* '74 (WIL)[B] Claymont, DE Archmere Academy.
Krautsack, Blaise R. *o.praem.* '74 (PH)[AA] Paoli, PA Daylesford Abbey.
Krawchuk, Thaddeus *c.ss.r.* '60 (PHU) Plymouth, PA St. Vladimir's.
Krawchuk, Thaddeus '60 (PHU) Plymouth, PA SS. Peter and Paul.
Krawczenko, Artur '03 (SY) Binghamton, NY St. John the Evangelist.
Krawinkel, Robert M. '58 (STL) St. Louis, MO Church of the Annunziata.
Krawontka, Stephen A. '77 (SCR) Hazleton, PA St. Joseph's.
Kraynak, Nicholas '59 (PSC) Old Forge, PA St. Nicholas.
Kraynak, William B. '81 (Y) Louisville, OH Sacred Heart of Mary; [I] Louisville, OH Emmaus House.
Krebs, Bruce D. '78 (BIS) Bismarck, ND St. Mary; Pro–Synodal Judges.
Krebs, Donald H. '55 (CR) Retired.
Krebs, Donald '55 (MIL).
Krebs, Gerard H. '63 (E)[B] Erie, PA St. Joseph.
Krebs, Henry L. '60 (E) Clearfield, PA St. Francis.
Krebs, John F. '57 (CHI) Retired.
Krebs, Paul F. '57 (COV) Retired.
Krebs, Peter *s.t.* '69 (PAT)[M] Stirling, NJ Holy Spirit Missionary Cenacle.
Krebs, Peter *s.t.* '69 (PAT)[M] Stirling, NJ Shrine of St. Joseph.
Kreckel, Robert G. '54 (ROC) Penfield, NY St. Joseph Retired.
Kredel, Thomas E. '72 (PIT) Pittsburgh, PA St. Louise de Marillac.
Kreder, Mark A. '03 (TR) New Monmouth, NJ St. Mary.
Kreder, Michael J. '85 (NEW) Rutherford, NJ St. Mary's; Staff.
Kreft, Henry S. '45 (DET) Retired.
Kreher, Albert E. '65 (BEL) Prairie du Rocher, IL St. Joseph.
Kreidler, Thomas W. '77 (CIN) Loveland, OH St. Margaret of York.
Kreikemeier, Leo A. '43 (OM) Retired.
Kreilein, Philip '74 (EVN) Evansville, IN Resurrection.
Kreimer, Richard '79 (CIN).
Kreimes, Paul '72 (DET)[M] Special Assignment.
Kreis, Mark *s.s.p.* '87 (RCK) Crystal Lake, IL St. Thomas the Apostle.
Kreiser, Thomas L. '94 (NY) Hopewell Junction, NY St. Columba.
Kreitinger, Todd (MOB) Auburn, AL St. Michael.
Kreitinger, Todd (MOB)[J] Auburn, AL Auburn University Newman Center.
Krejci, Albert L. '41 (OM) Omaha, NE St. Bernadette Retired.
Krekelberg, Richard '73 (LA) Long Beach, CA St. Anthony.
Krekelberg, William '70 (ORG) Irvine, CA St. Thomas More.
Krekelberg, William (ORG) Archivist.
Kremeier, James '55 (GI) Retired.
Kremen, Timothy M. *o.s.m.* '61 (CHI)[N] Chicago Order of Friar Servants of Mary (Servites) United States of America Province, Inc..
Kremer, Barry *o.carm.* '46 (VEN)[L] Darien Carmelite Provincial Office.
Kremer, John R. '59 (DUB) Delhi, IA St. John; Hopkinton, IA St. Luke.
Kremer, Leroy '68 (SCL) Braham, MN St. Peter & Paul.
Kremer, Leroy '68 (SCL) Princeton, MN St. Edward's.
Kremer, Philip *o.s.b.* '57 (RCK)[G] Aurora, IL Marmion Abbey.
Kremmell, William T. '66 (BO)[BB] Framingham, MA Framingham State College Campus Ministry; Merrimac, MA Nativity.
Kremp, Bruno *o.f.m.* '65 (CIN)[M] Cincinnati, OH St. John the Baptist Friary.
Kremp, Bruno *o.f.m.* '65 (CIN)[M] Cincinnati, OH St. Francis Seraph Friary.
Krempa, Adam J. '90 (BUR)[H] Poultney, VT Green Mountain College; Middletown Springs, VT St. Anne; Poultney, VT St. Raphael.
Krempa, Stanley J. '70 (ARL) Winchester, VA Sacred Heart of Jesus.
Krempel, Matthew *o.f.m.* '74 (CIN)[M] Franciscanos.
Krenik, Michael J. '84 (STP) White Bear Lake, MN St. Pius X.
Krenik, Robert L. '84 (RIC) Lebanon, VA Good Shepherd; St. Paul, VA St. Therese.
Krenik, Thomas '77 (STP) Richfield, MN St. Richard.
Krenzke, John '57 (DEN) Denver, CO Christ the King Retired.

Krenzke, John '57 (COS) Retired.
Krepp, Theodore '82 (PSC) Kingston, PA St. Mary's.
Krepp, Theodore (PSC) Elected Members.
Kresinski, Daniel J. '70 (E) Eldred, PA St. Raphael; Shinglehouse, PA St. Theresa.
Kress, Dennis '99 (KNX) Elizabethton, TN St. Elizabeth.
Kress, Robert '58 (EVN) On Duty Outside the Diocese.
Kret, John A. *o.s.a.* '61 (CHI)[N] Matteson, IL Austin Friary.
Kretowicz, Antoni J. '87 (CHI) Waukegan, IL Immaculate Conception B.V.M.; Aurora, IL Our Lady of Good Counsel.
Krettek, Daniel F. (DM) Judges.
Krettek, Daniel '78 (DM) St. Mary's, IA Assumption of the Blessed Virgin Mary; [H] Des Moines, IA Emmaus House; St. Marys, IA St. Patrick; St. Marys, IA Immaculate Conception.
Krettek, Daniel (DM) Charismatic Renewal Liaison.
Krettek, G. Thomas *s.j.* '82 (MIL)[O] Milwaukee, WI Jesuit Community at Marquette University.
Kretz, Edward J. '56 (GBG)[G] Greensburg, PA Neumann House.
Kretz, James C. '91 (PEO) Toluca, IL Sacred Heart; Toluca, IL St. Ann's.
Kreul, Ronald G. *o.p.* '78 (MAD) Madison, WI Blessed Sacrament.
Kreul, Ronald *o.p.* '78 (MAD)[B] Madison, WI Edgewood College.
Kreutzer, Dan '98 (OWN) LaCenter, KY St. Mary.
Kreutzer, Dan (OWN) Priest Personnel Committee.
Krewer, Edward M. '43 (PEO) Retired.
Kribs, Charles R. '51 (BEL) Retired.
Kribs, Don R. '61 (LA) Los Angeles, CA Martin Luther King, Jr., Drew Medical Center Retired.
Kricek, Henry C. '80 (CHI) Chicago, IL St. Edward.
Kricek, Henry '80 (CHI).
Krick, Howard K. '58 (PH) Retired.
Krick, Howard (PHI)[A] AUXILIARY CHAPLAINS CONTRACT CHAPLAINS.
Krieg, Charles F. *c.m.* '63 (MET)[H] Princeton, NJ Vincentian Residence.
Krieg, Gerard C. '53 (ROC) Pittsford, NY St. Louis; Judges.
Krieg, Gerard '53 (ROC) Retired.
Krieg, Jerome L. '38 (DET) Retired.
Krieg, Peter *o.f.m.* '43 (OAK)[N] Oakland, CA Franciscan Friars.
Krieg, Peter *o.f.m.* '43 (OAK) Oakland, CA St. Elizabeth's.
Krieg, Thomas J. '92 (LC)[K] Menomonie, WI The Ministry to the University of Wisconsin–Stout; Menomonie, WI St. Joseph.
Kriegel, Henry A. '70 (E) On Leave of Absence.
Krieger, Wilfred L. '46 (STL) Retired.
Kriegshauser, J. Laurence *o.s.b.* '69 (STL)[F] Creve Coeur, MO St. Louis Priory School; [O] St. Louis, MO The Abbey of St. Mary and St. Louis.
Kriegsmann, William A. '44 (RCK) Pro Synodal Judges Retired.
Krier, John P. '69 (GF) On Duty Outside of the Diocese; Medical Lake, WA St. Anne.
Krijnen, Joseph G. '46 (PHX) Tempe, AZ Resurrection Retired.
Krile, George F. '41 (FAR) Retired.
Krile, Stephen L. '83 (COL) Circleville, OH St. Joseph's.
Kriley, Victor *o.f.m.cap* '65 (BAL)[S] Cumberland, MD SS. Peter and Paul Friary.
Kriley, Victor *o.f.m.cap.* '69 (BAL)[M] Cumberland, MD Sacred Heart Hospital of the Western Maryland Health System.
Krill, Jude Michael *o.f.m.conv.* '83 (PH)[C] Aston, PA Neumann College.
Krill, Jude Michael *o.f.m.conv.* '83 (TR) Riverside, NJ St. Casimir.
Kringe, Charles J. '64 (SCR) Unassigned or Leave of Absence.
Krings, James A. '71 (STL)[J] Kirkwood, MO SSM St. Joseph Hospital of Kirkwood.
Krings, James (STL) Manchester, MO St. Joseph.
Krinzner, William R. '79 (CLV)[C] Parma Heights, OH Holy Name High School.
Krisak, Anthony F. *s.s.* '75 (TR) On Duty Outside the Diocese; [V] Washington, DC Paulist National Catholic Evangelization Assoc..
Krisanda, Stephen J. *m.s.* '60 (ORL) Orlando, FL Good Shepherd.
Krische, Francis '57 (KCK) Topeka, KS Most Pure Heart of Mary.
Krische, Francis (KCK) Archdiocesan Consultors.
Krische, James J. '91 (BRK) Brooklyn, NY St. Peter Claver; Army Reserve Chaplains.
Krische, Vincent E. '64 (KCK)[K] Lawrence, KS St. Lawrence Catholic Campus Center at the University of Kansas and Residence.
Krisciunevicius, Victor '49 (DET) Retired.
Kriski, Francis (KC) Kansas City, MO Our Lady of Sorrows.
Kriski, Frank *c.ss.r.* '63 (KC)[J] Kansas City, MO Redemptorists Fathers of Kansas City, Missouri.
Kriski, Frank *c.ss.r.* '63 (KC) Kansas City, MO Our Lady of Perpetual Help.
Krisman, Ronald '73 (LUB) On Duty Outside the Diocese.
Krisman, Ronald (ORL) Judges.
Kriss, Aaron '91 (PIT) Pittsburgh, PA St. John the Baptist.
Kriss, David J. '79 (PIT) Donora, PA Our Lady of the Valley.
Kriss, Zigford J. '58 (HRT) West Hartford, CT St. Helena; Special and other Archdiocesan Assignment; Office of Catholic Schools.
Kristancic, Dennis J. '83 (CLV) Euclid, OH St. Felicitas.
Kristofak, Terence *c.p.* '69 (FgM).
Kristofak, Terence *c.p.* '69 (MET)[H] South River, NJ Passionist Provincial Office.
Kristy, Mark *o.c.d.* '85 (SR)[M] Oakville, CA Carmelite House of Prayer.
Krivak, John A. '82 (ALN)[O] Allentown, PA The Newman Center; [O] Allentown, PA Cedar Crest College (Allentown); [O] Allentown, PA Muhlenberg College (Allentown); Campus Ministry Office.
Krivanek, George E. *s.j.* '59 (SJ)[M] Los Gatos, CA Sacred Heart Jesuit Center.
Kriz, Dennis *o.s.m.* '99 (CHI) Chicago, IL Annunciata; [N] Chicago, IL Annunciata Priory.
Kriz, Mark G. *s.j.* '95 (BUF)[O] Buffalo, NY Canisius Jesuit Community.
Krlis, William F. (BRK) Diocesan Building Commission; Consultants.
Krlis, William '68 (BRK) Corona, NY St. Leo.
Krock, Gearoge E. *c.m.* '43 (PH)[AA] St. Catherine Infirmary.
Kroeger, Gerald C. *o.p.* '58 (CHI) Summit, IL St. Joseph; [N] Chicago Dominicans (Provincial Office).
Kroeger, James H. *m.m.* '75 (FgM).
Kroeger, John '72 (CIN) Cincinnati, OH St. Vivian.
Kroeger, Timothy D. '90 (LFT) Fishers, IN St. Louis de Montfort.
Kroger, Daniel *o.f.m.* '73 (CIN).
Kroger, John H. '55 (COV)[M] Bellevue, KY Divine Mercy; Bellevue, KY Retired.
Krogman, David '81 (SFS) Sioux Falls, SD St. Mary.
Krogman, David (SFS) Diocesan Consultors.
Krogman, David (SFS) Presbyteral Council.
Krogman, David (SFS) Deans.
Krogman, Philip J. '60 (MAD) Green Lake, WI Our Lady of the Lake.
Krogol, Jude *o.s.b.* '65 (SP)[O] St. Leo, FL St. Leo Abbey.
Krol, Boleslaus '61 (DET) Detroit, MI St. Bartholomew; Detroit, MI St. Louis the King.
Krol, Miroslaw K. '99 (NEW) Linden, NJ St. Theresa of the Child Jesus.
Krolczyk, David B. '72 (CHI) Sauk Village, IL St. James.
Krolikowski, Walter P. *s.j.* '57 (CHI)[C] Chicago, IL Jesuit Community at Loyola University Chicago.
Kroll, Anthony '61 (SCL)[H] Breckenridge, MN St. Francis Home.
Kroll, Anthony '61 (SCL) Kent, MN St. Thomas.
Kroll, Anthony '61 (SCL)[G] Breckenridge, MN St. Francis Medical Center.
Kroll, Larry (KAL) Wayland, MI SS. Cyril and Methodius.
Kroll, Lawrence W. '86 (KAL) Wayland, MI St. Therese; St. Vincent DePaul Society.
Kroll, Robert J. *s.j.* '99 (MIL)[O] Milwaukee, WI Pere Marquette House Jesuit Community; [E] Milwaukee, WI Marquette University High School.
Kroll, Robert '72 (GB)[I] Green Bay, WI St. Mary of the Angels Friary.
Kroll, Robert '72 (GB)[I] Warner Robins, GA.
Kroll, Robert *o.f.m.* (GB)[C] Marinette, WI Marinette Catholic Central High School.
Kroll, Robert (GB) Educational Leadership/School Program Development.
Kromenaker, Joseph '47 (SFD) On Duty Outside the Diocese.
Kromenaker, Joseph (CHI) Chicago, IL St. Ferdinand.
Kronewitter, Frank '62 (FTW)[G] Fort Wayne, IN Saint Anne Home & Retirement Community.
Kronkowski, Leonard J. '55 (GRY) Retired.
Kropac, Robert J. '82 (CLV) Cleveland, OH St. Henry.
Kropf, Richard '58 (LAN) On Duty Outside the Diocese.
Kropf, Richard '58 (GAY)[H] Johannesburg, MI Stella Maris Hermitage.
Kropiwnicki, Henry '58 (FR) Retired.
Kros, Donald M. '59 (OM) Retired.
Krosfield, George '70 (ALX) Moreauville, LA Sacred Heart.
Krosnicki, Thomas A. *s.v.d.* '66 (FgM).
Krosnicki, Thomas A. *s.v.d.* '66 (CHI)[B] Techny, IL Divine Word Residence; [N] Techny, IL Society of the Divine Word, Provincial Headquarters–Chicago Prov.; [N] S.V.D. Funds, Inc..
Krotec, Ivan '70 (STN) Chicago, IL SS. Volodymyr and Olha.
Krotec, Ivan (STN) Chicago.
Krotkiewicz, Luke '83 (DET) Bi–County Osteopathic.
Krouse, Dennis '68 (SD)[B] University of San Diego.
Krouse, Dennis (SD) Censores Librorum.
Krozser, John J. '56 (NEW) Retired.
Kruc, James '89 (RIC) Retired.
Krudwig, William C. '61 (SPC) El Dorado Springs, MO St. Elizabeth.
Krueger, Robert W. '56 (P) Portland, OR St. Andrew.
Krueger, Robert (P) Area Vicars.
Krug, Clement M. *c.ss.r.* (NEW) Brazilian Apostolate.
Krug, Clement *c.ss.r.* (NEW) Newark, NJ St. James.
Krugel, Stephen A. '88 (HRT) Milford, CT Christ the Redeemer; Cheshire, CT Cheshire Correctional Institution.
Kruger, Brent A. '97 (FTW) South Bend, IN St. Joseph.
Kruis, Ron '52 (PBL)[E] Pueblo, CO Villa Pueblo.
Krul, Valentine C. '77 (SY) New York Mills, NY St. Mary.
Krulak, Michael '84 (PSC) Pittston, PA St. Michael.
Krull, Michael G. '86 (MET) Sayreville, NJ Our Lady of Victories; College of Consultors.
Krumm, John E. '76 (CIN) Dayton, OH Holy Family; Dayton, OH St. Mary's.
Krummert, Gary W. '02 (PIT) Cranberry Township, PA St. Ferdinand.
Krupa, Stephen T. *s.j.* '86 (CLV)[B] Cleveland, OH John Carroll University.
Krupa, Thomas J. '71 (ALB) Castleton–on–Hudson, NY Sacred Heart.
Krupa, Thomas (ALB) Presbyteral Council.
Krupa, Thomas (ALB) Diocesan Board of Consultors.
Krupa, Thomas (ALB) Members.
Krupa, Thomas (ALB) Advocates; Deans.
Krupich, Thomas '88 (FAR) Fairmount, ND St. Anthony; [G] Wahpeton, ND Carmel of Mary.
Krupinski, Wieslaw *s.j.* '82 (CHI)[N] Chicago, IL Sacred Heart Mission House.
Krupka, Michael '77 (SJP) Johnstown, PA St. John the Baptist.
Krupka, Michael (SJP) Presbyteral Council.
Krupnik, Marion I. '54 (HRT) Retired.
Krupp, Albert A. '65 (CLV) Elyria, OH St. Agnes.
Krupp, Joseph J. '98 (LAN) East Lansing, MI St. Thomas Aquinas.
Kruse, Clement '41 (SAL) Retired.
Kruse, David B. '94 (BAL) Military Chaplains; Air Force Chaplains.
Kruse, James E. '96 (PEO) Mendota, IL Holy Cross; Mendota, IL SS. Peter and Paul; Vicariates and Vicars; Associate Directors.
Kruse, Jay L. '91 (OM) Verdigre, NE St. Wenceslaus; Niobrara, NE St. William; Deans; Deans.
Kruse, Phillip F. '81 (DUB) Dubuque, IA St. Columbkille.
Kruse, Robert J. *c.s.c.* '58 (FR)[A] North Easton, MA Stonehill College; [A] North Easton, MA Holy Cross Fathers Religious.
Krusinski, Andrew J. '45 (SCR) Williamsport, PA Holy Rosary.
Kruszynski, Joseph *o.f.m.conv.* '68 (CHI)[N] Chicago, IL Conventual Franciscans of St. Bonaventure Province; [N] Chicago, IL Sacred Heart Friary.
Kruszynski, Joseph *o.f.m.conv.* (CHI) Office for Evangelization.
Krutcik, Stanley F. '80 (WOR) Manchaug, MA St. Anne's.
Krutewicz, Jan (CHI) Zion–Beach Park, IL Our Lady of Humility.
Krutzik, Norman '57 (GB) Retired.
Kruzel, Len '83 (CHI) Oak Lawn, IL St. Linus.
Krylowicz, Mark J. '91 (SLC) Copperton, Bingham Canyon, UT Immaculate Conception.
Krylowicz, Mark J. '91 (CHI) On Duty Outside the Archdiocese.
Krymski, Christopher M. *o.s.m.* '83 (CHI)[N] Chicago, IL Order of Friar Servants of Mary (Servites) United States of America Province, Inc.; [N] Chicago, IL Monastery of Our Lady of Sorrows.
Krynski, Leo J. '52 (SUP) Retired.
Krysa, Czeslaw M. '80 (BUF) Arcade, NY St. Mary's; Arcade, NY SS. Peter and Paul.
Kryston, Edward L. '74 (PIT)[N] Pittsburgh, PA St. John Vianney Manor.
Krystosek, Robert H. '56 (GI) Retired.
Kryszkiewicz, Pawel '93 (CAM) Vineland, NJ Sacred Heart.
Kryvokulsky, Oleh (STN) Eparchial Office of Religious Education & Catechesis.
Krzanowski, Lukasz *m.s.* '91 (SPR) Westfield, MA Holy Trinity.
Krzewinski, Charles *o.m.i.* '52 (FgM).
Krzysiak, Casimir J. '50 (SY) Utica, NY St. Stanislaus.
Krzyston, Stanley '85 (TR) Yardville, NJ St. Vincent de Paul.
Krzywda, Jorge (LAR) Laredo, TX San Carlos Mission; Laredo, TX Santa Terisita Mission.
Krzywda, Leonard *c.r.* '65 (SB) Fontana, CA Church of the Resurrection.
Krzywda, Leonard *c.r.* '65 (SB)[E] Fontana, CA Congregation of the Resurrection, CR.
Krzywicki, Lance P. '83 (PT) Military Chaplains.

Krzyzaniak, Timothy D. '91 (LAN) Manchester, MI St. Mary.
Krzyzanowski, Casimir *m.i.c.* '56 (SPR).
Krzyzopolski, Al '50 (SFS) Retired.
Krzyzopolski, Al (SFS)[I] Tribunal Judges.
Kselman, John J. *s.s.* '67 (TR) On Duty Outside the Diocese.
Kselman, John J. *s.s.* '67 (BO)[V] Cambridge, MA.
Kselman, John J. *s.s.* '67 (BAL)[S] Cambridge, MA.
Ku, Michael Tong–uk *s.j.* '01 (OAK)[N] Berkeley, CA Jesuit Community at Jesuit School of Theology at Berkeley.
Kuan, Joseph S. (MO) Air Force Chaplains.
Kub, Francis Q. '65 (CHI) Chicago, IL St. Simon the Apostle.
Kuba, William M. '62 (E) East Brady, PA St. Eusebius.
Kubacki, William J. '78 (TOL) Toledo, OH St. Patrick of Heatherdowns.
Kubajak, James '77 (PRM) Northwood, OH St. Michael the Archangel.
Kubajak, James (PRM) Great Lakes.
Kubajak, James (PRM) Promoter of Justice.
Kubajak, James (PRM) Defender of the Bond.
Kubala, Daniel I. '76 (MIA) Miami, FL St. Thomas the Apostle.
Kubat, Alphonse M. '42 (STP) Retired.
Kubat, Christopher '99 (LIN) Lincoln, NE St. Mary; Catholic Social Services; Lincoln, NE St. Thomas Aquinas; [I] Lincoln, NE University of Nebraska, Newman Club; [K] Lincoln, NE Catholic Social Services.
Kubat, Christopher (GI) Charities.
Kubeck, John C. '65 (MIL)[N] Brookfield, WI Prelature of the Holy Cross and Opus Dei..
Kubiak, Joseph *o.f.m.cap.* '78 (PAT)[M] Oak Ridge–Milton, NJ St. Stanislaus B. M. Friary.
Kubiak, Lukasz *o.p.* '01 (NY) New York, NY Notre Dame.
Kubicki, James M. *s.j.* '83 (MIL)[X] Milwaukee, WI Apostle of Prayer; [O] Milwaukee, WI Jesuit Community at Marquette University.
Kubik, John M. '49 (DET) Retired.
Kubik, Thomas *c.r.* '72 (CHI)[D] Chicago, IL Gordon Tech High School.
Kubina, Eugene *t.o.r.* '53 (ALT) Johnstown, PA St. Clare of Assisi.
Kubinski, Scott M. '84 (ROC)[L] Ithaca, NY The Catholic Community of Ithaca College.
Kubinski, Scott '84 (ROC) Lansing, NY All Saints.
Kubinyi, Julius '51 (PBR) Retired.
Kubisa, Jan '82 (GAL) Texas City, TX St. Mary.
Kubishyn, Ivan (SJP) Apopka, FL St. Mary's.
Kuca, Stanislaus (CHI) Chicago, IL Holy Innocents.
Kucaj, Wolodymr '98 (STF) Yonkers, NY St. Michael.
Kucan, Jerome *o.f.m.* '51 (CHI)[N] Chicago, IL St. Anthony's Friary.
Kucera, David G. '98 (DUB) Manly, IA Sacred Heart; Manly, IA St. Michael.
Kucera, Edward C '73 (GAL) Plantersville, TX St. Mary.
Kucera, Edward J. *o.s.b.* '53 (JOL)[L] Lisle, IL St. Procopius Abbey; AUXILIARY CHAPLAINS CONTRACT CHAPLAINS.
Kuchar, Matthew *o.s.b.* (MO) AUXILIARY CHAPLAINS CONTRACT CHAPLAINS.
Kuchar, Michael W. '80 (LAN) On Duty Outside the Diocese.
Kucharczyk, Dennis H. '80 (SAG) Caro, MI Sacred Heart; Navy Reserve Chaplains.
Kucharczyk, John J. '99 (BAL) Absent on Leave.
Kucharski, Steven M. '77 (MAN) Absent on Leave.
Kucharski, Zbigniew (LC) Camp Douglas, WI St. James.
Kuchera, Michael J. *s.j.* '87 (BAL)[S] Pont. Ist Orientale.
Kuchinsky, William J. '97 (WH) Romney, WV Our Lady of Grace.
Kucingis, John A. '37 (LA) Los Angeles, CA St. Casimir Retired.
Kucyk, Herman W. '57 (DET) Dearborn, MI Divine Child.
Kuczaik, Stanislaw *s.ch.* (DET) Hamtramck, MI St. Florian.
Kuczborski, Joseph M. (PMB) Air Force Reserve Chaplains.
Kuczmanski, Gregory M. '75 (BWN) Edcouch, TX St. Theresa of the Infant Jesus.
Kuczynski, Edward P. '77 (PH) Pottstown, PA St. Peter.
Kuczynski, James H. *m.s.* '73 (HRT)[M] Hartford, CT Missionaries of LaSalette; [V] Hartford, CT Religious Trust of the Missionaries of Our Lady of LaSalette.
Kuczynski, John *c.m.* '44 (HRT) Derby, CT St. Michael.
Kuczynski, Kazimierz '76 (NEW) Bayonne, NJ Mt. Carmel.
Kuder, Donald E. *c.s.b.* '63 (GAL)[K] Catholic Chaplain Corps, Texas Medical Center; [Q] Houston, TX Dillon House.
Kuder, Stephen R. *s.j.* '73 (SPK)[B] Spokane, WA Gonzaga University.
Kudilil, Jim '63 (FRS) Rosamond, CA St. Mary.
Kudleychuk, Bohdan '97 (PHU) Mount Carmel, PA Assumption of B.V.M..
Kudleychuk, Bohdan '97 (PHU) Mount Carmel, PA SS. Peter and Paul.
Kudlo, Frank '88 (MIA) Absent on Leave.
Kueber, Michael I. (P) Gresham, OR St. Anne.
Kuebler, A.M. Seamus '75 (WDC) On Duty Outside the Archdiocese
Kuehler, Norbert '55 (AMA) Borger, TX St. John the Evangelist.
Kuehnemund, H. Thomas '93 (DET) Waterford, MI St. Benedict.
Kuehner, Joseph '79 (SB) San Bernardino, CA Our Lady of the Rosary Cathedral.
Kuehner, Ralph J. '50 (WDC) Derwood, MD St. Francis of Assisi.
Kuenzig, Aloysius A. '43 (PIT) Retired.
Kuenzig, Peter A. '46 (PIT) Retired.
Kuffel, Thomas '89 (LIN) Valparaiso, NE Sts. Mary and Joseph's.
Kuffner, Patrick J. '02 (MET) East Brunswick, NJ St. Bartholomew.
Kugler, Michael '89 (GLP) On Leave of Absence.
Kuhlmann, John L. '68 (BUF) Bemus Point, NY Our Lady of Lourdes.
Kuhlmann, Steven F. *o.p.* '92 (LFT) West Lafayette, IN St. Thomas Aquinas.
Kuhlmann, Steven *o.p.* '93 (LFT)[H] West Lafayette, IN St. Thomas Aquinas Parish and Foundation for Catholic Students Attending Purdue University.
Kuhn, Christopher A. *c.s.c.* '77 (CHI)[D] Niles, IL Notre Dame High School.
Kuhn, Christopher J. '97 (RCK) Elizabeth, IL St. Mary; Hanover, IL St. John the Evangelist.
Kuhn, Dennis R. '82 (CHL) Absent On Leave.
Kuhn, George J. '64 (NY) Yonkers, NY St. Joseph.
Kuhn, James G. '71 (MAD) Beloit, WI St. Thomas the Apostle.
Kuhn, James J. *m.m.* '51 (NY).
Kuhn, John G. '58 (WDC)[EE] Special Ministries.
Kuhn, John H. '43 (BIS)[G] Bismarck, ND Emmaus Place Retired.
Kuhn, Michael F. '97 (FR)[B] Attleboro, MA Bishop Feehan High School; [N] Fall River, MA Youth Apostles.
Kuhn, Richard W. '53 (DUB)[F] Farley, IA Seton Catholic Elementary School; Peosta, IA Holy Family; Peosta, IA St. John the Baptist.
Kuhn, Richard *s.m.* '58 (R)[E] North Topsail Beach, NC Marianist Community.
Kuhn, Thomas W. '57 (TOL) Retired.
Kuhns, Clement *c.pp.s.* '48 (CIN)[B] Carthagena, OH St. Charles.
Kuhns, Howard *c.s.c.* '46 (PHX)[G] Phoenix, AZ Holy Cross Congregation/Casa Santa Cruz.
Kuhns, James '61 (SPK) Spokane, WA Our Lady of Fatima; Members.
Kuhr, William M. (GB) Algoma, WI St. Mary; Kewaunee, WI Holy Rosary.
Kuizon, Antonio '77 (NEW) Scotch Plains, NJ St. Bartholomew.
Kujawinski, Matthew J. '03 (E) Erie, PA Our Lady of Peace.
Kujovsky, Thomas J. '57 (HBG) Elizabethtown, PA St. Peter; Catholic History and Archives, Office of; Advocates Retired.
Kujur, Innocent '92 (LAN) St. Johns, MI St. Joseph.
Kukla, Gerald F. '67 (SAG) Harbor Beach, MI Our Lady of Lake Huron.
Kukla, Jerry (SAG) Diocesan Consultors.
Kuklich, Stepan '96 (STF) Kenmore, NY St. John the Baptist.
Kukucka, Joseph G. '65 (PBL) AUXILIARY CHAPLAINS CONTRACT CHAPLAINS Retired.
Kukulka, Janusz '85 (DET)[A] Orchard Lake, MI SS. Cyril and Methodius Seminary.
Kukulski, Stanislaus C. '55 (DET) Detroit, MI Northville State Hospital Retired.
Kukura, Joseph W. '67 (NEW) On Duty Outside the Archdiocese.
Kula, Francis J. *m.s.* (HRT) Rocky Hill, CT Veterans' Home and Hospital.
Kula, Joseph '55 (BIR) Retired.
Kulak, Joseph F. '66 (RCK) Elgin, IL St. Laurence.
Kulan, Michael *o.f.m.* '70 (MIL)[O] Burlington, WI St. Francis Friary.
Kulandai, Chinnappan '84 (LAN) East Lansing, MI St. Thomas Aquinas.
Kulandai, Peter S. '69 (CHR) Charleston, SC St. Patricks; Charleston, SC Our Lady of Mercy.
Kulandairajan, S. '78 (NY) Shrub Oak, NY Saint Elizabeth Ann Seton.
Kulas, John *o.s.b.* '57 (SCL)[I] Collegeville, MN St. John's Abbey, of the Order of St. Benedict.
Kulas, Robert A. '54 (WIN) Retired.
Kulas, William J. '74 (WIN) Rushford, MN St. Joseph's; Priests Pension Board; Rushford, MN St. Mary's.
Kulas, William J. (WIN) Second Instance Court Judges.
Kulas, William (WIN) Associate Judges.
Kulathinal, Jose *c.m.i.* '92 (STA) Orange Park, FL St. Catherine's.
Kulavich, John J. '83 (SCR) Mayfield, PA Sacred Heart of Jesus.
Kulbicki, Timothy *o.f.m.conv.* '86 (BAL) Baltimore, MD St. Casimir.
Kulbicki, Timothy *o.f.m.conv.* '86 (BAL)[W] Baltimore, MD Catholic Community at Relay.
Kulbicki, Timothy *o.f.m.conv.* '86 (BAL).
Kulbis, Augustine M. *o.s.m.* '58 (CHI)[N] Chicago, IL Monastery of Our Lady of Sorrows.
Kulczynski, A. Jason '89 (PH) Lansdowne, PA St. Philomena.
Kulczynski, Jason '89 (PH)[D] Drexel Hill, PA Archbishop Prendergast High School.
Kulesa, Daniel J. '62 (Y) McDonald, OH Our Lady of Perpetual Help; Judges.
Kulhawik, Frank '40 (CR) Retired.
Kulick, Larry J. '92 (GBG) New Kensington, PA St. Joseph; College of Consultors; Special Appointment; Bishop's Priests Council; Office for Ministry Development.
Kulig, Anthony J. '61 (NEW) Bayonne, NJ Mt. Carmel; Bayonne Deanery 13.
Kulig, Christopher J. *o.carm.* '00 (GAL) Houston, TX St. Bernadette Soubirous; [B] Washington, DC Whitefriars Hall.
Kuligowski, Peter J. '97 (ALT) Clarence, PA St. Michael's; Clarence, PA St. Mary's.
Kulik, Alexander T. '54 (SCR) Wilkes–Barre, PA Maternity of the Blessed Virgin Mary.
Kulik, Francis J. '69 (SCR) Unassigned or Leave of Absence.
Kulinski, Kenneth E. '72 (OKL) Del City, OK St. Paul, Apostle.
Kull, John J. *o.f.m.* '66 (PAT)[M] Butler, NJ St. Anthony Friary.
Kull, Martin R. '76 (BRK) Brooklyn, NY St. Anselm's.
Kulleck, Donald R. '52 (SD) Chula Vista, CA St. Pius X.
Kulleck, Donald '54 (SD) Retired.
Kulleck, Thomas G. (BWN) Office of the Chancellor.
Kulleck, Thomas (BWN) Associate Judges.
Kulleck, Tom '74 (BWN) Brownsville, TX Mary, Mother of the Church.
Kuller, Thomas J. *s.j.* '79 (ALN)[A] Wernersville, PA Jesuit Center.
Kullmann, Charles R. '78 (SFR) San Francisco, CA Old St. Mary's Cathedral.
Kulma, Ryszard '02 (GAL) Kingwood, TX St. Martha.
Kulovits, Fred A. '59 (LC) Retired.
Kulwiec, Richard *o.m.i.* '81 (NY)[GG] Newburgh, NY Our Lady of Hope Center.
Kulwiec, Richard *o.m.i.* '81 (BO) Lowell, MA Notre Dame de Lourdes; [V] Lowell, MA Andre Garin Retirement Residence.
Kumai, Felix '86 (NY) Spring Valley, NY St. Joseph.
Kuman, Henry *m.s.* '84 (STL)[O] Generalate, Missionari di N.S. de La Salette.
Kumbalaprampil, Xavier '66 (SAV) Retired.
Kumblanthanath, Thomas *m.s.t.* '94 (SP) Tarpon Springs, FL St. Ignatius.
Kumblumkal, Jose *c.m.i.* '90 (TYL) Winnsboro, TX Clyde Johnston Unit, Texas Department of Corrections; Winnsboro, TX St. Ann Church.
Kummer, John R. '72 (CIN) Germantown, OH St. Augustine.
Kummer, William '75 (FTW) Plymouth, IN St. Michael.
Kummer, William (FTW) Council of Priests.
Kummer, William (FTW) Liturgical Commission.
Kummer, William (FTW) Permanent Diaconate.
Kummerer, Timothy M. '83 (TOL) Defiance, OH St. Mary.
Kumordji, Gabriel E. *s.v.d.* '85 (LA) Montrose, CA Holy Redeemer.
Kumplam, Chacko K. '80 (HRT) West Haven, CT St. Lawrence's; [I] New Haven, CT Hospital of St. Raphael.
Kumse, John M. '79 (CLV) Cleveland, OH St. Mary; [Z] Cleveland, OH Cleveland Slovenian Community Center.
Kumse, John (CLV) Presbyteral Conveners.
Kuna, Lech '74 (HRT) New Britain, CT Holy Cross.
Kunco, Edward J. '69 (PIT) Pittsburgh, PA Immaculate Conception–St. Joseph.
Kunda, Brendan J. '65 (SUP) Retired.
Kunert, Kenneth M. *s.j.* '57 (DET)[P] Bloomfield Hills, MI Manresa Jesuit Retreat House; [P] Hamtramck, MI St. Ladislaus.
Kunes, James F. *s.m.* '60 (STL)[O] St. Louis, MO.
Kung'u, Steven '91 (ROC)[I] Rochester, NY Basilian Residence.
Kung'u, Steven '91 (ROC) North Chili, NY St. Christopher.
Kunigonis, Mark S. '00 (PH) Philadelphia, PA St. Timothy.
Kunisch, Robert *c.pp.s.* '56 (TOL)[L] Bellevue, OH Sorrowful Mother Shrine.
Kunisch, Robert *c.pp.s.* '56 (TOL)[J] Bellevue Mary Lay Center.
Kunisch, William '02 (HON) Lahaina, HI Maria Lanakila.
Kunisch, William (HON) Ecumenical Commission.
Kunkel, A. Henry '70 (BAL) Pylesville, MD St. Mary.

Kunkel, Albert A. '57 (CLV)[M] Akron, OH Francesca Residence.
Kunkel, Albert '57 (CLV)[P] Akron, OH Provincial Motherhouse and Novitiate of the Daughters of Divine Charity.
Kunkel, Charles *o.s.c.* '67 (SCL) Milaca, MN St. Mary's; [I] Onamia, MN Crosier Monastery.
Kunkel, George C. '77 (CIN) Cincinnati, OH St. Martin of Tours.
Kunkel, James E. '73 (PIT) Turtle Creek, PA St. Colman; Judges.
Kunkel, Ronald T. (CHI) Chicago, IL Cathedral of the Holy Name.
Kunkel, Steven A. '01 (PHX) Phoenix, AZ St. Jerome.
Kunkle, Albert A. '57 (CLV) Retired.
Kunnakkattuthara, Zacharias S. '75 (TYL) Palestine, TX Sacred Heart; Frankston, TX St. Charles Borromeo; Palestine, TX Beto I Unit and Louie C. Powledge Unit, Texas Department of Corrections; Tennessee Colony, TX Coffield Unit, Texas Department of Corrections; Tennessee Colony, TX Gurney Unit; Tennessee Colony, TX Michael Unit; College of Consultors; Deans; Priests' Pension Board; Priests' Personnel Board.
Kunnalakat, Peter (CHI)[J] Melrose Park, IL Westlake Hospital.
Kunnalakatt, Peter '85 (CHI) Melrose Park, IL Sacred Heart.
Kunnath, George *m.c.b.s.* '74 (CC) Taft, TX Holy Family.
Kunnath, Matthew '60 (NEW) Nutley, NJ St. Mary's.
Kunnath, Sebastian '73 (NEW) Paramus, NJ Our Lady of the Visitation.
Kunnath, Sebastian '73 (SYM) Paramus, NJ Syro–Malabar Catholic Community of Dumont.
Kunnath, Sebastian (NEW) Chaplain to the India Catholic Association (Syro–Malabar Rite).
Kunnath, Thomas '85 (TR) Browns Mills, NJ St. Ann.
Kunnel, Lawrence '60 (TR) Neptune, NJ Holy Innocents.
Kunnel, Thomas *t.o.r.* '88 (STP) Coon Rapids, MN Church of the Epiphany.
Kunnumpuram, Paul *m.s.f.s.* '76 (ALX) Vidalia, LA Our Lady of Lourdes.
Kunnumpuram, Paul *m.s.f.s.* '76 (ATL)[K] Lawrenceville The Missionaries of St. Francis De Sales.
Kunst, Richard '98 (DUL) Duluth, MN St. Benedict's.
Kunst, Richard (DUL) Assistant Directors.
Kuntz, Donald B. '41 (DET) Retired.
Kuntz, Ildephonse *ss.cc.* '46 (HON)[G] Honolulu, HI St. Patrick's Monastery.
Kuntz, Ken (DAV) Diocesan Consultors.
Kuntz, Kenneth E. '77 (DAV) Iowa City, IA St. Mary.
Kunz, David C. '80 (LC) La Crosse, WI Mary, Mother of the Church; Personnel Council.
Kunz, Francis P. '49 (WIN) Retired.
Kunz, James H. '73 (WIN) On Special or Other Diocesan Assignment; [D] Rochester, MN Saint Mary's Hospital.
Kunz, John M. '76 (WIN) Waseca, MN Sacred Heart; Deans; Bishop's Council.
Kunze, Robert W. '74 (CAM) Gibbsboro, NJ St. Andrew the Apostle.
Kunze, Robert W. '74 (NEW) On Duty Outside the Archdiocese.
Kunzman, Richard T. '63 (CAM) On Duty Outside the Diocese.
Kuolt, Benedict J. '47 (NY) White Plains, NY St. Bernard; White Plains, NY White Plains Hospital Retired.
Kuper, Raymond L '64 (EVN) Evansville, IN Holy Rosary.
Kuper, Raymond L. (EVN) Judges.
Kupisz, Julian '74 (FAR) Esmond, ND St. Boniface.
Kupisz, Julian '74 (FAR) Esmond, ND St. William.
Kupka, Marek S. '01 (PRO) North Kingstown, RI St. Francis De Sales.
Kupke, Raymond J. '73 (PAT) Florham Park, NJ Holy Family; Archivist.
Kuppayil, George J. *m.s.t.* '91 (MAR) Channing, MI St. Rose.
Kuppayil, George J. (MAR) Deans.
Kuppe, Paul *o.f.m.cap.* '70 (FgM).
Kuppe, Paul *o.f.m.cap.* '70 (PIT)[N] Pittsburgh, PA St. Augustine Friary.
Kurapati, Victor '94 (OKL) Duncan, OK Assumption.
Kuras, Alexander A. '69 (DET) Westland, MI Church of the Divine Savior.
Kuras, Hippolite *o.f.m.conv.* '35 (CHI)[N] Chicago, IL Conventual Franciscans of St. Bonaventure Province.
Kurash, Stanley J. '71 (SCR) Old Forge, PA St. Mary's.
Kurdziel, Dennis M. '75 (ALT) Altoona, PA Our Lady of Lourdes.
Kurea, Pius '80 (FRS) Retired.
Kurek, Gerard *c.ss.r.* '51 (BAL) Baltimore, MD Sacred Heart of Jesus.
Kurera, Pius '80 (FRS)[C] Fresno, CA Nazareth House.
Kurgan, Charles *o.carm.* '65 (LA)[L] Darien Carmelite Provincial Office.
Kuriappilly, Johnson '90 (BIS) Tioga, ND St. Thomas.
Kurilec, Robert '68 (SB) On Duty Outside the Diocese.
Kurimay, Michael D. *s.j.* '73 (MIL)[O] Milwaukee, WI Jesuit Community at Marquette University.
Kurimay, Michael D. *s.j.* '73 (STL)[O] St. Louis, MO St. Louis University High School Jesuit Community.
Kurimsky, Frank M. '86 (PIT) Monaca, PA St. John the Baptist.
Kuris, Silvester (PH) Philadelphia, PA St. Francis de Sales.
Kurkiewicz, Raymond J. '42 (MIL) Retired.
Kurnath, Joseph G.M. '91 (HRT) Medical Leave.
Kurovsky, Andrew '85 (SCR) Williamsport, PA St. Ann's.
Kurovsky, Andrew (SCR) Presbyteral Council.
Kurowski, Canon Andrzej *s.a.c.* '76 (BRK) Brooklyn, NY St. Frances de Chantal.
Kurowski, Clement *o.f.m.* '53 (PH) Philadelphia, PA St. Monica.
Kurpel, Yaroslav '93 (PHU) Philadelphia, PA Christ the King.
Kurps, Jack *s.c.j.* '77 (JKS)[J] Walls, MS Sacred Heart Southern Missions, Inc..
Kurps, Jack *s.c.j.* '77 (JKS)[J] Walls, MS Sacred Heart Southern Missions Housing Corporation.
Kurt, Allan J. '55 (DUB) Retired.
Kurt, David L. '77 (PEO) Bushnell, IL St. Bernard; Bushnell, IL St. Augustine.
Kurt, David '77 (PEO) Rushville, IL St. Rose.
Kurt, Edgar J. '41 (DUB) Archives Retired.
Kurtenbach, Harold R. '60 (GI) Continuing Education for the Clergy Retired.
Kurtenbach, Harold (GI) Charismatic Renewal.
Kurth, Dave '92 (OM)[O] Winnebago, NE St. Augustine's Indian Mission.
Kurth, Earl J. *s.j.* '49 (MIL)[O] Wauwatosa, WI Jesuit Community at St. Camillus.
Kurtyka, Edward J. '71 (PAT) Paterson, NJ St. Paul's; Judicial Vicar.
Kurtz, James *o.f.m.cap.* '87 (BAL) Cresaptown, MD St. Ambrose.
Kurtz, James *o.f.m.cap.* '87 (BAL) Cumberland, MD SS. Peter and Paul.
Kurtz, James *o.f.m.cap.* '87 (BAL)[S] Cumberland, MD SS. Peter and Paul Friary.
Kurtz, R. James *s.j.* '77 (DET)[K] Temperance, MI.
Kurtzke, John *c.s.c.* '85 (P)[B] University of Portland.
Kurtzke, John *c.s.c.* '85 (P)[L] Portland, OR Holy Cross Fathers & Brothers, C.S.C. – University of Portland.
Kurucz, Frank A. '98 (CHI) Palos Heights, IL St. Alexander.
Kurutz, Gregory *o.f.m.* '54 (GAY) Lewiston, MI St. Francis of Assisi.
Kurutz, Joseph V. '59 (PIT) Pittsburgh, PA St. Raphael.
Kuruvila, Prince (CC) Presbyteral Council; Orange Grove, TX St. John of the Cross.
Kuruvilla, George *c.m.i.* '75 (STA) Lake City, FL Epiphany.
Kurwicki, Robert A. '85 (JC) Westphalia, MO St. Anthony of Padua; Westphalia, MO St. Joseph; Secretary to the Bishop; Vice–Chancellors; To The Bishop; Personnel Board; Cemeteries; Historical Archivist; Ministry to Priests; Priestly and Religious Vocations Committee.
Kurylo, Michael '34 (STN) Retired.
Kurylowicz, Martin '79 (GR) On Duty Outside the Diocese.
Kuryvial, George *o.m.i.* '58 (BEL)[F] Belleville, IL Missionary Oblates of Mary Immaculate – St. Henry's Oblate Residence.
Kurz, Andrew J. '02 (LIN) Plattsmouth, NE Church of the Holy Spirit.
Kurz, Andrew (LIN) Advocates.
Kurz, Michael '75 (RCK) Rockford, IL St. Rita.
Kurz, Michael '75 (RCK) Special Assignment.
Kurz, Michael (RCK) Adjutant Judicial Vicar.
Kurz, William S. *s.j.* '70 (MIL)[O] Milwaukee, WI Jesuit Community at Marquette University.
Kurzaj, Franciszek '76 (SAT) San Antonio, TX Holy Name.
Kurzak, John F. '75 (SC) On Duty Outside the Diocese; Air Force Chaplains.
Kurzawa, Ronald '64 (DET) Livonia, MI St. Aidan.
Kurzawinski, Zygmunt '03 (WDC) Kensington, MD Holy Redeemer.
Kurzyna, Andrew E. '74 (NY) Verplanck, NY St. Patrick.
Kurzynski, James R. '03 (LC) Durand, WI St. Mary's Assumption; Durand, WI Holy Rosary; Durand, WI Sacred Heart of Jesus.
Kus, Robert J. '98 (R) Wake Forest, NC St. Catherine of Siena.
Kus, Sebastian *o.f.m.* '57 (NEW)[O] Lodi, NJ Immaculate Conception Convent.
Kuse, Michael '67 (SFD) Quincy, IL St. Mary.
Kuse, Michael (SFD) Presbyteral Council.
Kusi, David (CHI) Chicago, IL Holy Angels.
Kusi, Gordon P. '95 (BRK) Brooklyn, NY Our Lady of Miracles.
Kusi, Gordon '95 (BRK) Brooklyn Development Center.
Kusi, Gordon '95 (BRK) Bernard Fineson Development Center.
Kusibab, Justin *o.f.m.conv.* '87 (CHI)[N] Chicago, IL Conventual Franciscans of St. Bonaventure Province.
Kusmirek, Mark '77 (TYL) Rusk, TX Sacred Heart; Rusk, TX Jerry H. Hodge Unit and Sky view Unit, Texas Department of Corrections.
Kusnad, Rony *s.j.* '99 (BAL)[B] Timonium, MD Loyola Graduate Center –Timonium Campus.
Kusnadi, Rony '99 (BAL) Bradshaw, MD St. Stephen.
Kuss, Allen R. '84 (BIS) On Duty Outside the Diocese; Navy Chaplains.
Kusunoki, Peter *ss.cc.* '79 (FR).
Kusy, George '86 (CLV)[H] Cleveland, OH St. Stanislaus.
Kutch, Joseph P. '88 (SCR) White Mills, PA St. Joseph's.
Kutch, Peter P. *o.f.m.cap.* '66 (MIL) Mount Calvary, WI Holy Cross; St. Cloud, WI St. Cloud; St. Cloud, WI St. Joseph.
Kutil, Dale '73 (RC) Fort Pierre, SD St. John; [D] Rapid City, SD Priest Retirement and Aid Association/Pension Plan Board.
Kutiuk, Casimir '57 (GB) Retired.
Kutner, Raymond W. '64 (BRK) Jackson Heights, NY Blessed Sacrament; Subcommittee for Parishes; Diocesan Real Estate Board.
Kutsch, Eugene C. (DUB) Board of Directors/Priest Pension Plan Board of Trustees Retired.
Kuttiyanickal, Thomas *s.a.c.* '77 (MIL)[O] Milwaukee, WI Pallotti House.
Kutulas, Nicholas *s.m.* '55 (SFR)[N] San Francisco, CA Marist Center of the West.
Kutys, Daniel J. '80 (PH) On Duty Outside the Archdiocese.
Kutz, Lawrence A. '65 (WDC)[T] Washington, DC Prelature of the Holy Cross and Opus Dei.
Kutzner, Roger '90 (JOL) Steger, IL St. Liborius.
Kuveikis, Rufin *o.f.m.cap.* '48 (BGP) Norwalk, CT Norwalk Hospital.
Kuveikis, Rufin *o.f.m.cap.* '48 (BGP) Stamford, CT Sacred Heart.
Kuykendall, Andrew (WCH) Presbyteral Council.
Kuykendall, Andrew (WCH) Presbyteral Council/Diocesan Consultors.
Kuykendall, Andy '78 (WCH) Haysville, KS St. Cecilia.
Kuykendall, Henry '86 (EVN) Evansville, IN Nativity.
Kuykendall, Henry '86 (EVN) Evansville, IN Holy Spirit.
Kuykendall, Henry (EVN) Deaf Ministry.
Kuykendall, Thomas S. (YAK) Diocesan Commission on Public Worship; Clergy Personnel Board.
Kuykendall, Thomas '94 (YAK) Wenatchee, WA St. Joseph's.
Kuykendall, Thomas (YAK) Presbyteral Council Executive Committee.
Kuzara, George J. *c.pp.s.* '98 (PHU) Frackville, PA St. Michael's.
Kuzara, George *c.pp.s.* '78 (TOL)[M] Frackville, PA.
Kuzdal, Anthony P. '56 (NOR) Retired.
Kuzhippallil, George (PAT) Retired.
Kuzia, Anthony F. *c.m.* '75 (PRT) Lewiston, ME Holy Family; Vicars for Priests; Ex Officio; Vicars for Priests.
Kuzia, Anthony F. *c.m.* '76 (HRT)[M] Manchester DePaul Provincial Residence.
Kuziemski, Ignatius H. '60 (MET) Great Meadows, NJ SS. Peter and Paul.
Kuzilla, John A. '55 (E) Kersey, PA St. Boniface.
Kuzinskas, John A. '52 (CHI) Vicar for Senior Priests Retired.
Kuziol, John *o.f.m.conv.* '88 (WDC)[B] Washington, DC St. Bonaventure Friary.
Kuzma, Boleslaw '73 (COS) Security, CO Holy Family.
Kuzma, Mykhailo '81 (STN) Palatine, IL Immaculate Conception.
Kuzma, Mykhailo (STN) Personnel Board.
Kuzma, Mykhailo (STN) Diocesan Consultors.
Kuzma, Mykhailo (STN) Presbyteral Council.
Kuzma, Mykhailo (STN) Chicago.
Kuzma, Mykhailo (STN) Chancellor.
Kuzmann, Robert J. '85 (SP) Clearwater, FL Light of Christ; On Duty Outside the Diocese.
Kuzmeski, Charles H. '75 (SPR) Ware, MA St. Mary's.
Kuzmich, John M. '65 (FTW) Fort Wayne, IN St. Vincent de Paul.
Kuzniewski, Anthony J. *s.j.* '79 (WOR)[O] Worcester, MA Jesuits of Holy Cross College, Inc..
Kvedas, Leonard J. '61 (HRT) Beacon Falls, CT St. Michael's; Deans.
Kvedas, Leonard (HRT) Auditors (Part–time Case Instructors).
Kwak, Thaddeus '59 (FTW) South Bend, IN Our Lady of Hungary.
Kwakman, Hans *m.s.c.* '63 (PH) Boothwyn, PA St. John Fisher.
Kwapisz, Gregory *o.f.m.conv.* '60 (BAL)[S] Baltimore, MD St. Joseph Nursing Home.
Kwapisz, Gregory *o.f.m.* (BAL)[O] Baltimore, MD St. Joseph's Nursing Home.
Kwatera, Michael *o.s.b.* '77 (SCL)[I] Collegeville, MN St. John's Abbey, of the Order of St. Benedict.

Kwebuza, Silverino *a.j.* (ALX) Marksville, LA Holy Ghost.
Kweder, Joseph J. '85 (ALN) Cumbola, PA St. Anthony of Padua; New Philadelphia, PA Holy Family; New Philadelphia, PA Sacred Heart.
Kwiatkowski, Constantine '47 (BUF) Retired.
Kwiatkowski, Michael '78 (SPK) Colbert, WA St. Joseph.
Kwiatkowski, Michael (SPK) Director of Deacon Formation.
Kwiatkowski, Paul M. '64 (TOL) Toledo, OH Immaculate Conception; Toledo, OH St. James.
Kwiatkowski, Richard P. '72 (NEW) Bloomfield, NJ Sacred Heart.
Kwiatkowski, Robert M. '83 (HRT) Woodbury, CT St. Teresa's; Deans.
Kwiatkowski, Sylvester (SAC) Sacramento, CA Sacred Heart of Jesus.
Kwiecien, Jan '80 (MET) Manville, NJ Sacred Heart of Jesus.
Kwiecien, John S. '76 (BUF) Springville, NY St. Aloysius.
Kwiecien, Michael *o.carm.* '80 (PHX) Phoenix, AZ St. Agnes.
Kwiecien, Michael *o.carm.* '80 (PHX)[J] Phoenix, AZ Kino Institute of Theology.
Kwiecien, Wojciech '79 (CHI) Chicago, IL St. James.
Kwoka, Edward '78 (TR) Lakewood, NJ St. Mary of the Lake.
Kwolek, Joseph '45 (BUF)[O] Buffalo, NY Sheehan Residence for Priests Retired.
Kwon, Peter Il Seong (SB) Korean Ministry.
Kyabuta, Jean Baptiste '88 (NSH) Clarksville, TN Immaculate Conception.
Kyazze, Richard *c.s.c.* '03 (FTW).
Kyeah, Barnabas (LC)[I] Marathon City, WI Sacred Heart; Mosinee, WI St. Patrick.
Kyebasuuta, John '98 (LA) Glendale, CA Holy Family.
Kyere, William (NY) Millbrook, NY St. Joseph.
Kyfes, Robert J. '77 (CHI) Chicago, IL St. John Fisher.
Kyle, Eric *o.f.m.* '52 (NY)[AA] Staten Island, NY Carmel Richmond Healthcare and Rehabilitation Center.
Kyne, John J. '50 (SAC) Dixon, CA St. Peter.
Kyomya, Romanus '86 (WDC) Washington, DC St. Francis de Sales.
Kyrie, James *o.f.m.* '57 (FRS) Delano, CA St. Mary's of the Miraculous Medal Retired.
Kyte, Michael G. *o.p.* '87 (DEN) Denver, CO St. Dominic; [A] Denver, CO St. Dominic Priory.
Kythe, Jay K. '02 (STP) Faribault, MN Divine Mercy Catholic Church.

L

L'Arche, Jeffrey '75 (ALB)[P] Altamont, NY La Salette Shrine.
L'Heureux, Ernest L. '62 (PRT) Retired.
L'Heureux, William D. '91 (OM) Omaha, NE St. Adalbert; Omaha, NE Our Lady of Lourdes.
Laba, Gerald *c.p.* '73 (MET)[H] South River Passionist Provincial Office.
Laba, Gerald *c.p.* '73 (FgM).
Labadie, Michael William '02 (MOB) Montgomery, AL Church of the Holy Spirit.
LaBaff, Arthur J. '66 (OG) Watertown, NY St. Patrick; Deans; Diocesan Consultors.
LaBaff, Arthur '66 (OG)[I] Watertown, NY Watertown Catholic Education Council.
LaBaire, Steven M. '87 (WOR) Westborough, MA St. Luke the Evangelist.
Labak, Joseph L. '77 (CLV) Wadsworth, OH Sacred Heart of Jesus.
Labaky, Mansour (OLL)[F] St. Louis, MO Our Lady of Smiles Orphanage.
LaBarbera, Robert '70 (OAK) San Leandro, CA St. Alphonsus Liguori.
Labarda, Nathaniel C. '93 (HRT) Litchfield, CT St. Anthony's.
LaBarge, Charles F. '46 (DUB) Retired.
LaBarge, Chris (WIL) Parish Priest Consultors.
LaBarge, Christopher '85 (WIL) Marydel, MD Immaculate Conception.
LaBarge, Christopher (WIL) Deans.
Labarre, Renald D. '60 (PRT) Biddeford, ME St. Joseph's; Diocesan Board of Education.
Labat, Dennis C. '74 (NU) Springfield, MN St. Raphael; On Special or Other Diocesan Assignment; Riverbend TEC (Adult/Teens Encounter Christ); Liturgical Guidelines Committee; Priest Personnel Board; Pastoral Administrators.
LaBau, Anthony F. *s.j.* '46 (NY)[EE] New York, NY Development Office of the New York Province; [EE] New York, NY St. Ignatius Loyola Residence.
LaBauve, J. Joel '70 (BR) Gonzales, LA St. Mark.
LaBauve, John N. *s.v.d.* '51 (GAL) Galveston, TX St. Mary's Cathedral Basilica.
Labbe, Clifton *s.v.d.* '69 (BEA) Livingston, TX St. Martin de Porres Mission; Livingston, TX St. Joseph.
Labbe, Clifton *s.v.d.* '69 (FgM).
Labbe, Donavan J. '97 (LAF) New Iberia, LA St. Marcellus.
Labbe, Emil J *c.pp.s.* (CIN) Judges.
Labbe, Emil *c.pp.s.* '68 (CIN)[B] Carthagena, OH St. Charles.
Labbe, Jason M. '01 (BR) Prairieville, LA St. John the Evangelist.
Labbe, Joseph '75 (CLV) Administrative Leave.
Labbe, Wilfred P. '99 (PRT) Eagle Lake, ME St. Mary's; Wallagrass, ME St. Joseph's.
Labedis, Anthony *o.f.m.conv.* '60 (CHI)[N] Chicago, IL Conventual Franciscans of St. Bonaventure Province.
Labedis, Anthony *o.f.m.conv.* '60 (FgM).
Labella, Robert '54 (CLV) Akron, OH St. Anthony of Padua.
LaBelle, Jeffrey T. *s.j.* '88 (SFR)[N] San Francisco, CA Jesuit Community at University of San Francisco.
La Belle, Joseph T. *o.m.i.* '92 (SAT)[B] San Antonio, TX George Sexton House of Studies; [C] Oblate School of Theology.
LaBelle, Patrick *o.p.* '65 (SJ) Stanford, CA Catholic Community at Stanford.
LaBelle, Patrick *o.p.* '65 (OAK)[N] Oakland, CA Western Dominican Province.
Labinski, Jacek '83 (TR) Burlington, NJ All Saints.
Labinsky, Paul '81 (PHU) Cherry Hill, NJ SS. Peter and Paul.
Labita, Francis J. '49 (BRK)[V] Douglaston, NY Bishop Mugavero Residence Retired.
Labo, Timothy P. (ORL) Apopka, FL St. Francis of Assisi; Navy Reserve Chaplains; AUXILIARY CHAPLAINS CONTRACT CHAPLAINS.
Laboe, Timothy A. '99 (DET)[T] Pontiac, MI Mt. Hope Catholic Cemetery Association; Pontiac, MI St. Joseph; Pontiac, MI St. Michael; Pontiac, MI St. Vincent de Paul.
Labonee, Adelard *s.d.b.* (PAT) Paterson, NJ St. Anthony's.
Labonte, Adelard *s.d.b.* (PAT) Paterson, NJ St. Anthony's.
Labonte, Richard H. '70 (WOR) Retired.
LaBonte, Roger A. *m.afr.* '62 (FgM).
Labonte, Roger '94 (LA) Redondo Beach, CA St. James.
Laboon, Joseph D. '57 (PIT) Retired.
Labosky, James '79 (R) Absent on Leave.
LaBove, Keith (LAF) Advocates.
LaBove, Keith (LAF) Hospitals.
LaBove, M. Keith '81 (LAF) Milton, LA St. Joseph.
LaBran, Joseph J. *s.j.* '47 (BO)[V] Weston, MA Campion Health Center, Inc..
LaBran, Joseph J. *s.j.* '47 (WOR)[R] Holy Cross College.
Labranche, Raymond '94 (NEW)[A] Kearny, NJ Redemptoris Mater.
LaBrec, Paul '03 (PRT) Lewiston, ME Holy Cross.
LaBrecque, Frederick '67 (CHR) Conway, SC St. James.
LaBrecque, Frederick (CHR) Personnel Committee.
Labrie, Jean Paul '82 (PRT) Caribou, ME Holy Rosary; Fort Fairfield, ME St. Denis; Limestone, ME St. Louis.
Labrie, Jean–Paul (PRT) Personnel Board.
LaBrie, Joseph *s.j.* '97 (LA)[C] Los Angeles, CA Jesuit Community.
Labrie, Ray J. '03 (MAN) Salem, NH St. Joseph.
LaBrie, Robert G. '64 (BO) Canton, MA St. John the Evangelist; Norwood, MA Caritas Norwood Hospital.
LaBuda, David E. *m.m.* '71 (FgM).
LaBurt, Brian *g.h.m.* '86 (SAV) Claxton, GA St. Christopher.
Labute, Marvin W. *c.s.b.* '66 (DET)[E] Redford, MI Catholic Central High School.
LaCanne, Stephen J. '76 (STP)[I] St. Paul, MN HealthEast St. Joseph's Hospital.
La Canne, Steve '76 (STP) St. Joseph's Hospital.
LaCasse, Andre Joseph *o.p.* '92 (COL) Columbus, OH St. Patrick.
Lacasse, Eugene *o.c.s.o.* '54 (WOR)[O] Spencer, MA St. Joseph's Abbey.
Lacasse, J.A. Roger '53 (PRO) Woonsocket, RI All Saints Catholic Community.
La Casse, James *s.j.* '74 (FRS) On Special Assignment.
LaCasse, John P. '74 (DET) Ida, MI St. Joseph.
Lacasse, Roger '53 (PRO) Retired.
Lacasse, Roland *s.m.* (BO) Lawrence, MA Sacred Heart.
LaCaze, Carson J. (SHP) Ecumenism and Interreligious Affairs.
LaCaze, J. Carson '57 (SHP) Shreveport, LA Our Lady of the Holy Rosary; Priests' Retirement Board.
Lacerna, Rodolfo '68 (ELP) Kermit, TX St. Thomas & St. Joseph.
Lacey, Francis A. *p.a.* '51 (SFR) Tiburon, CA St. Hilary Retired.
Lacey, Joseph P. *s.j.* '71 (BAL) Woodstock, MD St. Alphonsus Rodriguez.
Lacey, Joseph *s.j.* (BAL) Priests' Council.
Lacey, Mark W. (ATL) Released from Archdiocesan Assignment.
Lacey, Michael (OAK) San Lorenzo, CA St. John the Baptist.
Lacey, Thomas *c.ss.r.* '55 (TOL) Lima, OH St. Gerard.
LaChance, Charles P. '84 (CHI) Other Assignments.
LaChance, Marcel '56 (NOR) Retired.
LaChance, Matthew G. '03 (TLS) Graduate Studies.
Lachance, Pierre E. *o.p.* '42 (FR)[I] Lewiston, ME SS. Peter and Paul House.
LaChance, Roger '67 (B) Coeur D'Alene, ID St. Pius X.
LaChance, Roger '67 (B)[F] Coeur D'Alene, ID North Idaho College.
LaChance, Roger (B) College of Consultors.
LaChance, Roger (B) Deans.
LaChance, Roger (B) Catholic Scouts.
Lachapelle, Alphonsus *s.o.cist.* '82 (ALN)[K] New Ringgold, PA Cistercian Monastery.
La charite, Roger J. *s.s.e.* '55 (MOB)[K] Selma, AL Edmundite Guild.
LaCharite, Roger J. *s.s.e.* '55 (MOB)[G] Selma, AL Edmundite Fathers.
Lache Avila, Jose Rodolfo '81 (CHR) Joanna, SC St. Boniface; Newberry, SC St. Mark.
Lachendro, Vincent *o.f.m.conv.* '63 (FgM).
Lachendro, Vincent *o.f.m.conv.* '63 (BAL).
Lachowicz, Francis B. '60 (PIT)[S] McKeesport, PA St. Mary Czestochowa.
Lachowitzer, Charles V. '90 (STP) Eagan, MN St. John Neumann; [G] St. Paul, MN Faithful Shepherd Catholic School.
Lachowski, Joseph *c.m.* '54 (BRK) Brooklyn, NY St. Stanislaus Kostka.
Lachowsky, Clement *c.ss.sp.* '47 (SB)[E] Hemet, CA Our Lady of the Valley; Hemet, CA Our Lady of the Valley Retired.
Lacienski, Michael *o.f.m.* '43 (GB).
Lack, Chris (CIN)[I] Cincinnati, OH St. Dominic.
Lackenmier, James *c.s.c.* '64 (BGP)[P] Bridgeport, CT Provincial Offices of the Priests and Brothers of Holy Cross, Eastern Province.
Lackie, Dan *o.f.m.* '96 (SFR)[S] San Francisco, CA St. Anthony Foundation.
Lackie, Dan *o.f.m.* (OAK)[A] Berkeley, CA Brother Giles Franciscan Formation Community.
Lackie, Daniel *o.f.m.* '96 (OAK)[N] Berkeley, CA Franciscan Friars.
Lackner, Bede *o.cist.* '52 (DAL)[K] Irving, TX Cistercian Abbey of Our Lady of Dallas.
Lackner, Francis J. X. '44 (PIT)[N] Pittsburgh, PA St. John Vianney Manor Retired.
Lackner, Joseph *s.m.* '72 (STL)[O] St. Louis, MO Provincialate of the Society of Mary, Province of the United States.
Lackner, Paul M. '42 (PIT) Retired.
Lacomara, Aelred *c.p.* '57 (FgM).
LaCombe, C. Terrence (GB) Denmark, WI St. Therese de Lisieux.
Lacombe, Robert E. '91 (PRO) Warwick, RI St. Timothy; Eleanor Slater Hospital.
LaCoste, James P. *m.m.* '56 (FgM).
La Count, Daniel '89 (SFD) Absent on Leave.
Lacovic, Lawrence L. '69 (ALT) Northern Cambria, PA Prince of Peace.
Lacre, Cormac '03 (SAC) Folsom, CA St. John the Baptist.
Lacroix, Daniel W. '88 (FR) Acushnet, MA St. Francis Xavier's; Auditors.
Lacroix, Maurice R. '53 (MAN) Veterans Administration Medical Center; [L] Manchester, NH Monastery of the Precious Blood Retired.
LaCroix, Robert A. '95 (DET) Dearborn Heights, MI St. Linus.
LaCroix, Wilfred L. *s.j.* '69 (KC)[B] Kansas City, KS Rockhurst University Continuing Education Center/ National Seminars Group; [J] Kansas City, MO Rockhurst Jesuit Community.
LaCrosse, James *s.m.* '67 (WH) Wheeling, WV St. Vincent de Paul's.
LaCrosse, James *s.m.* (WH) Diocesan Consultors.
Lacruz, Cecilio *sch.p.* '59 (SJN) Playa de Ponce, PR Our Lady of Mt. Carmel.
Lacson, Anthony Luis '86 (TR) Jersey Shore Medical Center.
Lacson, Luis '86 (TR) Spring Lake, NJ St. Catharine.
Lacy, Aidan '93 (PMB) West Palm Beach, FL Holy Name of Jesus.
Laczko, T. Ansgar '60 (WDC) Washington, DC Assumption.
Ladamus, Robert G. '70 (HRT) Retired.
Ladd, John O. '79 (GAY) Prudenville, MI Our Lady of the Lake.
Ladewski, Roman *c.s.c.* '40 (FTW)[K] Notre Dame, IN Holy Cross Mission House.
Ladish, Robert W. '53 (HRT) Retired.
Ladkau, William D. '84 (CHR) Columbia, SC Good Shepherd.
Ladniak, Lawrence J. (CHI) Navy Reserve Chaplains.
Ladra, Jose '82 (NO) Terrytown, LA Christ the King.
Ladzinski, Casimir H. (TR) Burlington County and Ocean County.
Ladzinski, Casmir H. '62 (TR) Belmar, NJ St. Rose.
Laenen, Hendrik *o.m.i.* '52 (SAN) Alvin, TX St. John the Baptist.
Laenen, Joseph C. *o.praem.* '51 (PH)[U] Darby, PA Mercy Fitzgerald Hospital; [AA] Paoli, PA Daylesford Abbey.
LaFache, Anthony '68 (SY) Utica, NY St. Anthony of Padua.

LaFavia, Louis M. *c.pp.s.* '47 (WDC)[C] Catholic University of America, The Retired.
La Femina, Anthony A. '61 (VEN) On Special Assignment.
LaFerrara, John (NEW) County Dirs..
Laferrara, Robert G. (NEW) Central Bergen Region Deanery 3.
Laferrera, John J. '73 (NEW) Caldwell, NJ St. Aloysius.
Laferrera, Robert G. '88 (NEW) Dumont, NJ St. Mary's; Archdiocesan Liturgical Commission.
Laferty, Charles P. *o.s.a.* '53 (PH)[C] Villanova University; [AA] Villanova, PA St. Thomas Monastery.
Lafey, Kevin *o.carm.* '72 (FgM).
Lafey, Kevin *o.carm.* '72 (JOL)[L] Prelate Nullius.
Lafferty, Charles L. '55 (BAL)[O] Saint John Hall–Long Crandon Retired.
Lafferty, David M. '85 (OKL) Oklahoma City, OK Corpus Christi.
Lafferty, James K. '54 (SC) Censor Librorum Retired.
Lafferty, John J. '53 (ALT) Retired.
Lafferty, Owen J. '66 (NY) New York, NY St. Joseph.
Laffey, Matthew T. *o.s.b.* (E) St. Marys, PA Queen of the World.
LaFlamme, Julien J. '58 (BUR) Retired.
LaFlamme, Paul C. '98 (SPR) Lee, MA St. Mary's; Absent on Leave.
LaFleur, Gerard A. '53 (SPR) Chicopee, MA Assumption; Diocesan Consultors; Deans.
Lafleur, Gerard (SPR) Presbyteral Council.
LaFleur, Paul J. '85 (LAF) Washington, LA St. Peter.
La Fleur, Reginald '79 (ARL) Alexandria, VA Queen of Apostles.
Lafond, Donald E. '62 (MAN) Catholic Medical Center Retired.
LaFontaine, Paul A. '72 (STP) Minneapolis, MN St. Charles Borromeo; Presbyteral Council.
LaFontant, Roland P. (MO).
LaFontant, Roland '69 (NY) U.S.V.A. Medical Center.
Laforet, Albert '02 (AUS) Austin, TX St. Mary's Cathedral.
LaForge, Paul *s.v.d.* '58 (DUB)[B] Epworth, IA Divine Word College.
LaFosse, William D. *m.s.* '68 (HRT)[M] Hartford, CT Missionaries of LaSalette.
Laframboise, Ross '03 (FAR) West Fargo, ND Holy Cross.
La France, Val *o.p.* '58 (NEW) Sacred Heart Priory.
La Fratta, William '63 (RIC) Retired.
Lafrenz, James '54 (ELP) Retired.
Lafrenz, James '54 (LSC) Retired.
Lagace, Raymond R. *o.f.m.* (PRT) Togus, ME Dept. of Veteran Affairs.
Lagan, Hugh '54 (SP) Retired.
Laganson, Noe '85 (LAV) Las Vegas, NV Our Lady of Las Vegas; Hospital Apostolate.
Lagasse, C. Brian '93 (PRO) North Providence, RI St. Anthony.
Lagasse, Ronald (OAK) Retired.
Lager, John *o.f.m.cap.* '79 (DEN)[N] Denver, CO St. Francis of Assisi Friary.
Lagges, Patrick R. (TUC) Promoter of Justice – Penal Cases.
Lagges, Patrick R. (CHI) College of Consultors; Canonical Services; Judicial Vicar; Judges.
Lagges, Patrick '77 (CHI) Chicago, IL Cathedral of the Holy Name.
Lagges, Patrick (CHI) Presbyteral Council.
Laghezza, Pasquale V. *ss.cc.* (NY) Manhattan, NY U.S.V.A. Medical Center.
Lagiovane, John '92 (NY)[E] New York, NY Monsignor Farrell High School.
Lago, Danilo *s.x.* '77 (PAT)[M] Wayne Xaverian Missionary Fathers.
Lago, Danilo *s.x.* '77 (FgM).
Lago, William J. '99 (TR) Belmar, NJ St. Rose.
Lagoa, Raul M. '79 (FR) Somerset, MA St. John of God.
Lagodinski, Dale '72 (FAR)[I] Wahpeton, ND State College of Science Newman Student Parish.
Lagodinski, Dale '72 (FAR) Wahpeton, ND St. John's.
Lagodinski, Dale (FAR) Deanery 1.
La Goe, John P. '61 (GR) Retired.
Lagomarsino, John *s.s.c.* '70 (SAC) Carmichael, CA St. John the Evangelist.
Lagomarsino, Vincent J. *s.j.* '56 (WH)[A] Wheeling, WV Wheeling Jesuit University.
Lagor, Joseph J. '54 (BUR) Retired.
Lagueux, Maurice '61 (MAN)[J] Manchester, NH Mt. Carmel Healthcare Center.
Laguna, Enrique *o.carm.* '90 (FgM).
Laguna, Jorge (DAL) Dallas, TX St. Edward.
Laguna–Vargas, Enrique *o.carm.* '90 (JOL)[L] Prelate Nullius.
Lagututta, Nunzio J. '78 (SJ) On Leave of Absence.
Lah, Peter *s.j.* '95 (CHI)[C] Chicago, IL Jesuit Community at Loyola University Chicago.
Lahart, Daniel K. *s.j.* '94 (GAL)[F] Houston, TX Strake, Jesuit College Preparatory Inc..
LaHart, Richard T. '52 (PH) Diocesan Priests' Compensation and Benefits Committee Retired.
LaHart, Richard '52 (PH) West Chester, PA SS. Simon and Jude.
Lahens, Albert '95 (MIA) Miami, FL St. John Neumann.
Lahey, John F. *c.s.c.* '70 (FTW)[I] Notre Dame, IN Holy Cross House.
Lahey, John '67 (SAL) Retired.
Lahey, Maurice '50 (FRS) Retired.
Lahey, Piers M. '82 (SFR) Pacifica, CA Good Shepherd.
LaHood, Thomas G. (WDC) Olney, MD St. Peter.
Lahoud, Joseph F. '59 (SAM) Jamaica Plain, MA Our Lady of the Cedars of Lebanon.
Lahoud, Joseph (SAM) Protopresbyters.
Lahoud, Joseph (SAM) Presbyteral Council–Ex Officio Members.
Lahrs, Carey T. *s.d.s.* '72 (MIL) Milwaukee, WI Mother of Good Counsel.
Lai, Doan Van '73 (SD) San Diego, CA Holy Spirit.
Laible, Jeffrey G. '88 (PEO) Rantoul, IL St. Malachy's; Thomasboro, IL St. Elizabeth's; Air National Guard Chaplains.
Laing, Vincent Thu (SAL) New Almelo, KS St. Joseph's; Norton, KS St. Francis of Assisi.
Laini, Valerian '69 (CHI) Libertyville, IL St. Joseph.
Lair, Gerard P. *o.s.b.* '60 (PAT) Flanders, NJ St. Elizabeth Ann Seton; [M] Morristown, NJ St. Mary's Abbey.
Laird, Kenneth W. '75 (BR) Zachary, LA St. John the Baptist.
Laird, Martin S. *o.s.a.* '90 (PH)[AA] Villanova, PA St. Thomas Monastery.
Laird, Martin *o.s.a.* '81 (PH)[C] Villanova University.
Laird, Peter A. '97 (STP) Graduate Studies.
Laird, Peter '97 (STP)[A] St. Paul, MN The Saint Paul Seminary.
Laird, Peter '97 (STP)[C] St. Paul, MN University of St. Thomas.
Laird, William F. (ROC) Censores Librorum.
Laird, William '75 (ROC) Seneca Falls, NY St. Patrick.
Laiton, Rafael '92 (NY) Middletown, NY St. Joseph.
Lajack, Edward F. '68 (CLV) Barberton, OH SS. Cyril and Methodius.
Lajack, Jerome M. '66 (CLV) Cleveland, OH St. Wendelin.
Lajiness, Todd (DET)[A] Detroit, MI Sacred Heart Major Seminary, Inc.; [A] The College of Liberal Arts; Special Assignment.
Lajo, Saturino *o.m.i.* '63 (SAT)[T] San Antonio, TX Oblate Lourdes Grotto Shrine of the Southwest, Tepeyac de San Antonio.
Lajo, Saturnino *o.m.i.* '63 (SAT)[U] San Antonio, TX Oblate Missions.
Lajoie, Marcel *s.m.* '56 (BO)[AA] Boston, MA Marist Fathers Residence.
Lajoie, Marcel *s.m.* '56 (BO)[V] Boston, MA Marist Fathers Lourdes Residence.
Lajoie, Roland *s.m.* '74 (BO)[V] Boston, MA Marist Fathers of Our Lady of Victories (Boston Prov.).
Lakers, John J. *o.f.m.* '58 (SFD)[B] Quincy, IL Quincy University.
Lal, Joseph '95 (SD) Chula Vista, CA St. Rose of Lima.
Laliberte, George G. '56 (HRT) Retired.
Laliberte, Robert L. '73 (FAR) Special Assignment; [A] Fargo, ND Cardinal Muench Seminary; Liaison with Charismatic Movement.
Laliberte, Robert (FAR) Diocesan College of Consultors.
Laliberte, Robert (FAR) Permanent Diaconate.
Laliberte, Robert (FAR) Censor Librorum.
Laliberte, William F. '43 (BUR) Retired.
Lalic, Paul '58 (BGP)[V] Stamford, CT Villa Maria Retreat.
Lalli, Tony *s.x.* '66 (BO)[V] Holliston, MA Xaverian Missionaries.
Lally, Brendan G. *s.j.* '77 (BAL)[S] North American College.
Lally, Campion *o.f.m.* '53 (FgM).
Lally, Dennis M. '65 (GB) New London, WI St. Patrick; Judges in First Instance; Judges in Second Instance.
Lally, Martin '78 (DEN) Aurora, CO Queen of Peace.
Lally, Owen *c.p.* '59 (BRK)[V] Jamaica, NY Immaculate Conception Monastery.
Lally, Owen *c.p.* '59 (NY)[II] Jamaica, NY The Fellowship of the Beloved Disciple.
LaLonde, Emile G. '41 (OG) Retired.
Lalonde, Venant *o.f.m.* '54 (NY)[EE] New York, NY St. Agnes Rectory.
Lalor, Thomas '66 (JKS) Cleveland, MS Our Lady of Victories.
Lalor, Thomas '66 (JKS)[I] Cleveland, MS Delta State University Newman Center.
Lalor, Thomas '66 (JKS) Rosedale, MS Sacred Heart.
Lalor, Thomas (JKS) Continuing Formation Committee.
Lam, Anthony Phan (OAK) Defenders of the Bond.
Lam, John *s.d.b.* '71 (SFR) San Francisco, CA SS. Peter and Paul.
Lama, Michael '61 (SB) Adelanto, CA Christ the Good Shepherd.
Lama, Michael (SB) Appointed Members.
Lama, Michael (SB) Vicars Forane.
Lamanna, Alfred '49 (ALB) Retired.
Lamanna, Thomas J. *s.j.* '97 (P)[A] Portland, OR Jesuit Novitiate of St. Francis Xavier.
LaMante, Joseph (WIN) Auditors.
Lamantia, A. Robert '48 (TOL) Retired.
LaMar, Joseph P. *m.m.* '83 (NY)[EE] Maryknoll Maryknoll Fathers and Brothers; [EE] Maryknoll Maryknoll Fathers and Brothers.
Lamar, Rodolfo (SJN) Subcommission for Sacred Art.
LaMarre, Theodore E. '45 (SAG) Retired.
LaMartina, Liborio J. *s.j.* '67 (BAL)[S] Baltimore, MD Jesuit Fathers and Brothers Maryland Provincial Curia.
Lamas, Rodolfo '80 (SJN) Caguas, PR Divino Nino Jesus.
Lamaute, Serges *s.d.b.* '50 (CHI) Chicago, IL St. John Bosco.
Lamb, Bruce '89 (SR) Willits, CA St. Anthony.
Lamb, Bruce (SR) Vocations.
Lamb, Louis J. '61 (OKL) Retired.
Lamb, Matthew L. '62 (MIL) On Duty Outside the Archdiocese.
Lamb, Patrick H. '83 (ALN) Northampton, PA Our Lady of Hungary; [C] Bangor, PA Pius X High School; Forks of the Delaware Serra.
Lamb, Paul T. '96 (FR) Hyannis, MA St. Francis Xavier's.
Lamb, Thomas J. '71 (PRO)[R] San Antonio, TX Opus Dei Prelature of the Holy Cross and Opus Dei.
Lamb, Weston J. *o.ss.t.* '81 (BAL)[S] Hagerstown, MD.
Lambeck, Robert W. *s.j.* '49 (MIL)[O] Milwaukee, WI Jesuit Community at Marquette University.
Lambelho, Jose Fernando (LA) Cursillo Movement.
Lamberson, Bryan (L) Catholic Deaf Office.
Lambert, Andre John *o.f.m.conv.* '54 (FgM).
Lambert, Andre *o.f.m.conv.* '57 (ALB)[L] Rensselaer, NY Provincialate, Immaculate Conception Friary – Order of Friars Minor Conventual.
Lambert, Cornelius F. '83 (CAM) Retired.
Lambert, Curtis '74 (CHI) Chicago, IL Our Lady of Lourdes.
Lambert, James J. '80 (PT) Mexico Beach, FL Our Lady of Guadalupe.
Lambert, James L. *s.j.* '66 (NO)[P] New Orleans, LA Jesuit Provincial Office.
Lambert, James L. *s.j.* '66 (SAT) San Antonio, TX Our Lady of Guadalupe.
Lambert, John C. '84 (SCR) East Stroudsburg, PA St. John; Priests' Retirement Advisory Board.
Lambert, Leo M. '45 (MIL)[M] Wauwatosa, WI St. Camillus Health Center, Inc. Retired.
Lambert, Louis J. *s.j.* '66 (SFE) Albuquerque, NM Immaculate Conception.
Lambert, Peter S. '79 (DUL) Military Chaplains; Air Force Chaplains.
Lambert, Peter '72 (MIA) Fort Lauderdale, FL St. Clement.
Lambert, Richard D. '80 (CR) Commission on Building and Planning; Mahnomen, MN St. Michael's.
Lambert, Richard I. '75 (PBR) Youngstown, OH Assumption of the Blessed Virgin; Consultors; Protopresbyters; Pro–Synodal Judges.
Lambert, Rick (CR) Priests' Personnel Board.
Lambert, Rollins E. '49 (CHI) Retired.
Lambert, Theodore '76 (STO) Stockton, CA O.H. Close School.
Lambert, Theodore (MO) Army Reserve Chaplains.
Lambert, Theodore (STO) Modesto, CA St. Joseph Church of Modesto (Pastor of).
Lambert, Timothy J. '92 (MET) South River, NJ Corpus Christi.
Lamberty, Darrell '79 (SFS) Ramona, SD St. William of Vercelli.
Lamberty, Darrell '79 (SFS) Ramona, SD St. John the Evangelist.
Lamberty, Philip J. *o.p.* '59 (STL) Special Assignment.
Lambertz, Wilfred *o.s.b.* '58 (SFS) Milbank, SD St. Lawrence.
Lambertz, Wilfrid *o.s.b.* '58 (SFS)[F] Marvin, SD Blue Cloud Abbey.
Lambeth, K. Michael '94 (TR) Trenton, NJ Sacred Heart; Diocesan Council of Priests; Office of Vocations.
Lambour, Stephen *c.s.c.* '55 (ORL)[E] Cocoa Beach, FL Congregation of Holy Cross, Eastern Province.
Lambour, Stephen *c.s.c.* '55 (ORL) Retired.
Lambro, Edward (PAT) Secretariat for Catholic Charities; Special Assignment.
Lamela, Juan *c.m.* '62 (PCE) Ponce, PR La Milagrosa.
Lamendola, Salvatore R. '90 (GBG)[A] On Duty Outside the Diocese; AUXILIARY CHAPLAINS CONTRACT CHAPLAINS.
LaMere, Cletus *s.d.s.* (GB) Kiel, WI SS. Peter and Paul.
Lamica, Alan J. '78 (OG) Malone, NY Barehill Correctional Facility; Advocates.
Lamitie, James F. '53 (OG) Retired.
Lamitie, Robert O. '57 (OG) Ray Brook, NY Federal Correctional Institution; CIVIL AIR PATROL Retired.
Lamkin, Donald '01 (EVN) On Leave of Absence.
Lamm, Timothy J. *o.s.b.* '54 (SEA)[L] Lacey, WA St. Martin's Abbey.
Lamm, William F. *s.j.* '57 (BAL)[S] Baltimore, MD

Jesuit Fathers and Brothers Maryland Provincial Curia.
Lammeier, Francis G. '55 (CIN) Judges Retired.
Lammers, Donald W. '66 (JC) Jefferson City, MO St. Peter; Personnel Board.
Lammers, Ralph A. '63 (OM) Ralston, NE St. Gerald Retired.
Lammert, Edward H. *o.f.m.* '58 (LEX) Cumberland, KY St. Stephen; Harlan, KY Holy Trinity; Cumberland, KY Church of the Resurrection.
LaMoine, Gary '81 (CR) Boy Scouts; Deans; Argyle, MN St. Rose; Warren, MN SS. Peter and Paul; Priests Retirement Board of Trustees.
Lamonde, Joseph R. '74 (PIT) Military Chaplains; Navy Chaplains.
Lamont, Andre *o.f.m.conv.* '57 (ALB)[A] Rensselaer, NY Conventual Franciscan Friars.
LaMontagne, Bernard L. '63 (PRO) On Duty Outside the Diocese.
Lamore, Victor E. '80 (OG) Gabriels, NY Gabriel's Correctional Facility; Ray Brook, NY Adirondack Correctional Facility.
LaMorte, Joseph P. '81 (NY) Poughkeepsie, NY Holy Trinity; Air National Guard Chaplains.
LaMorte, Richard (NY)[HH] Poughkeepsie, NY Marist College.
Lamothe, C. Romero '48 (WOR) Retired.
Lamothe, Daniel O. '62 (MAN) Keene, NH St. Bernard; Keene, NH St. Anthony.
Lamothe, Donat R. *a.a.* '62 (WOR)[O] Worcester, MA Assumptionists of Assumption College.
LaMothe, Philip R. '55 (BUR) Bradford, VT Our Lady of Perpetual Help.
Lamoureux, Richard *a.a.* '71 (BO)[V] Padri Assunzionisti.
Lamoureux, Roger E. *o.m.i.* '83 (BO) Lowell, MA St. Marie; Lowell, MA Sacred Heart; [V] Lowell, MA Andre Garin Retirement Residence.
Lamoureux, Roger J. *o.m.i.* '59 (NOR) Willimantic, CT St. Mary; Defenders of the Bond.
Lamoureux, Roger '62 (SR) Santa Rosa, CA Holy Spirit.
Lamp, Edward '82 (SP) On Duty Outside the Diocese.
Lampe, Irvin F. '43 (WCH) Retired.
Lampe, Stephen J. '82 (MIL)[A] St. Francis, WI Saint Francis Seminary; Special Assignment; Sheboygan, WI St. Peter Claver.
Lampert, Robert E. '65 (STL) On Duty Outside the Archdiocese.
Lampert, Vincent P. '91 (IND) Indianapolis, IN St. Therese of the Infant Jesus (Little Flower); Greenwood, IN SS. Francis and Clare of Assisi.
Lampert, Vincent (IND) Council of Priests.
Lamping, Thomas E. '84 (CHI) Chicago, IL Queen of Angels.
Lamprea, Gefford C. (SPC) Poplar Bluff, MO Sacred Heart.
Lamprich, Mark '90 (CHL) Huntersville, NC St. Mark.
Lampron, Alfred J. '75 (PAT) Pequannock, NJ Holy Spirit.
Lampron, Maurice W. '63 (MAN) Rochester, NH St. Mary Retired.
Lamy, Raymond J. '81 (MAN) Absent on Leave.
Lamy, Robert E. *c.m.* '51 (NO)[P] New Orleans, LA Vincentian Fathers.
Lan, Augustine Pham Van (CLV) Vietnamese–American Apostolate.
Lanahan, Daniel *o.f.m.* '62 (NEW)[N] Hohokus, NJ St. Anthony of Padua; East Rutherford, NJ St. Joseph's; [N] Hohokus, NJ St. Anthony of Padua.
Lancaster, Leo '54 (WOR) Shrewsbury, MA St. Mary's.
Lancaster, Robert '99 (SFE) Albuquerque, NM St. Anne.
Lancelloti, Vincent '68 (NY) Retired.
Landa, Florencio *c.p.* '63 (SJN) San Juan, PR Nuestra Senora de la Piedad.
Landa, Salvador '94 (ORG) Fullerton, CA St. Mary's.
Landauer, Joseph '78 (PIT)[W] Chicago, IL Northview University Center.
Lander, Mark C. (SB) La Quinta, CA St. Francis of Assisi.
Landewe, Robert A. '59 (SPC) Mount Vernon, MO St. Susanne.
Landeza, Jayson '87 (OAK) Oakland, CA St. Columba's.
Landeza, Jayson (OAK) Presbyteral Council.
Landeza, Jayson (OAK) Consultors.
Landgraff, Thomas A. *o.s.f.s.* '64 (TOL) Toledo, OH St. Pius X.
Landgraff, Thomas J. *o.s.f.s.* (TOL) Consultors.
Landherr, Clayton '91 (DUB) Waterloo, IA Sacred Heart; Deanery Representatives; Worship Commission.
Landi, L. Joseph '90 (SFR)[S] San Francisco, CA Charismatic Movement.
Landi, Lodovico Joseph '90 (SFR) San Francisco, CA St. Cecilia.
Landini, Lawrence C. *o.f.m.* '61 (COL).
Lando, Camillo *c.s.* '66 (BO)[A] Everett, MA St. Anthony.
Landrau Roman, Jose Antonio '90 (SJN) On Duty Outside the Archdiocese.
Landreau, Edward J. '57 (LA) Retired.
Landreville, Norbert B. '58 (MAR) Retired.
Landry, Charles R. '83 (BR) St. Francisville, LA Our Lady of Mount Carmel; Angola, LA Louisiana State Penitentiary; Presbyteral Council.
Landry, Francis *c.p.* '76 (CHI)[N] Chicago, IL Passionist Community–CTU.
Landry, Gary *c.m.* '73 (LA)[A] Camarillo, CA St. John's Seminary College of the Archdiocese of Los Angeles; [Q] Montebello, CA DePaul Evangelization Center; [W] Montebello, CA DePaul Evangelization Center.
Landry, George *s.m.a.* '54 (NEW)[N] Tenafly, NJ Society of African Missions, Provincialate, S.M.A. Fathers Retired.
Landry, Leroy *o.m.i.* '61 (NOR)[F] Willimantic, CT Missionary Oblates of Mary Immaculate.
Landry, Leroy *o.m.i.* '61 (NOR)[I] Willimantic, CT Immaculate Retreat House.
Landry, Maurice A. *s.m.m.* '41 (RVC)[M] Bay Shore, NY Montfort Missionaries.
Landry, Oneil Anthony '47 (LAF) Retired.
Landry, Philip G. '88 (NO) Metairie, LA St. Edward the Confessor.
Landry, Ralph James '62 (LAF) Retired.
Landry, Roger J. '99 (FR) Hyannis, MA St. Francis Xavier's.
Landry, Thomas '83 (WOR) Worcester, MA Blessed Sacrament.
Landry, Thomas '83 (WOR) Memorial Hospital.
Landsberger, Nicholas '61 (SCL) Little Falls, MN Holy Family.
Landsberger, Nicholas '61 (SCL) Little Falls, MN St. Mary.
Landsberger, Nicholas (SCL) Defensor Vinculi.
Landsberger, Robert '57 (SCL) Judges Retired.
Landwerlen, Paul E. '54 (IND) Shelbyville, IN St. Vincent de Paul; Greensburg, IN Immaculate Conception; Greensburg, IN St. Denis.
Landwermeyer, Bart '56 (FWT) Retired.
Landwermeyer, Francis M. *s.j.* '66 (SAT) San Antonio, TX St. Cecilia; [U] San Antonio, TX The Southside Consortium of Catholic Schools, Inc..
Landy, Joseph V. *s.j.* '54 (NY)[EE] New York, NY Murray–Weigel Hall.
Lane, Brian '89 (RC)[D] Rapid City, SD Priest Retirement and Aid Association/Pension Plan Board.
Lane, Brian '89 (RC) Rapid City, SD St. Therese the Little Flower.
Lane, Brian (RC) Diocesan Finance Council.
Lane, Brian (RC) Continuing Education of Clergy.
Lane, Brian (RC) Director of Ongoing Formation.
Lane, Brian (RC) Diocesan Consultors.
Lane, Edmund C. *s.s.p.* '64 (NY)[B] New York, NY Society of St. Paul.
Lane, Frank P. '67 (COL) Columbus, OH St. Margaret of Cortona; Diocesan Judges.
Lane, George A. *s.j.* '67 (CHI)[N] Chicago, IL Woodlawn Jesuit Community; [X] Chicago, IL Loyola Press.
Lane, James H. '62 (BO) South Boston, MA St. Monica; Senior Priests Retired.
Lane, John Thomas *s.s.s.* '92 (GAL) Albuquerque, NM St. Charles Borromeo.
Lane, Mark J. *c.o.* '83 (BRK) Brooklyn, NY The Oratory Church of St. Boniface; [V] Brooklyn, NY Oratory of Saint Philip Neri, Congregation Pontifical Rite.
Lane, Mark E. (BAL) Interdiocesan Judges.
Lane, Mark '74 (RIC) On Special or Other Diocesan Assignment.
Lane, Michael '74 (JOL) Elmhurst, IL Visitation.
Lane, Robert C. '69 (STL) St. Peters, MO All Saints.
Lane, Thomas V. '64 (YAK) Moxee, WA Holy Rosary.
Lane, Timothy R. *c.j.* '95 (LA)[B] Santa Maria, CA St. Joseph Seminary (Josephite Fathers' Novitiate); [D] Santa Maria, CA St. Joseph High School; AUXILIARY CHAPLAINS CONTRACT CHAPLAINS.
Lane, William '50 (SEA) Retired.
Lanergan, James F. '61 (BO) Rochester, MA St. Rose of Lima; Bridgewater, MA Bridgewater State Hospital & Treatment Center.
Lanese, John R. '73 (ALB) Clifton Park, NY St. Edward the Confessor.
Lanese, Pasquale *o.m.i.* '53 (BWN) Brownsville, TX Immaculate Conception Cathedral.
Lang, B. Benedict *o.s.b.* '53 (PRO)[P] Portsmouth, RI Abbey of St. Gregory the Great.
Lang, Brian E. '98 (SY) Binghamton, NY St. Catherine of Siena.
Lang, Charles E. '65 (DUB) Retired.
Lang, Charles F. '75 (CIN) Fairborn, OH Mary Help of Christians
Lang, Frederick *c.pp.s.* '54 (CIN)[M] Colorado Springs, CO.
Lang, Henry A. '46 (BRK) Bayside, NY St. Robert Bellarmine Retired.
Lang, Hugh J. '56 (PIT) Munhall, PA St. Therese of Lisieux.
Lang, James P. '75 (SY) Syracuse, NY St. James; Board of Diocesan Consultors; Management Team; Ex Officio; Vicar for Parishes; Boy Scouts/Girl Scouts; Priests' Personnel Committee.
Lang, James Paul '75 (Y) Windham, OH St. Michael's; Army National Guard Chaplains.
Lang, James Paul '75 (SY) Special Assignment.
Lang, James Paul '75 (Y) Windham, OH St. Michael's; Army National Guard Chaplains.
Lang, Joseph R. *m.m.* '52 (NY).
Lang, Joseph R. *m.m.* '52 (PMB)[EE] Boca Raton, FL Ascension.
Lang, Joseph (CLV) Administrative Leave.
Lang, Jovian *o.f.m* '46 (FWT)[I] Crowley, TX St. Maximilian Kolbe Friary.
Lang, Julius '42 (FAR) Retired.
Lang, Leonard P. '75 (TR) Lincroft, NJ St. Leo the Great.
Lang, Michael P. '92 (TR) Lakewood, NJ St. Mary of the Lake.
Lang, Raymond '43 (SCL) Retired.
Langan, James J. '57 (SCR) Retired.
Langan, John P. *s.j.* '72 (DET)[K] Temperance, MI.
Langan, John P. *s.j.* '72 (DET)[M] Washington, DC The Jesuit Community at Georgetown University.
Langan, Thomas F. '59 (HBG) Abbottstown, PA Immaculate Heart of Mary; Presbyteral Council.
Langan, Thomas (HBG) Consultors, College.
Langan, Vincent F. '60 (SCR) South Waverly, PA St. John the Evangelist.
Langan, William J.P. '77 (SCR) Nanticoke, PA St. Francis of Assisi; Nanticoke, PA St. Joseph's; Navy Reserve Chaplains.
Langdon, Robert H. '56 (NEW)[N] Rutherford, NJ St. John Vianney Residence for Priests Retired.
Lange, Donald F. '70 (MAD) Ridgeway, WI Immaculate Conception; Ridgeway, WI St. Bridget.
Lange, George O. '57 (WOR) Westborough, MA St. Luke the Evangelist.
Lange, John J. *m.m.* '58 (FgM).
Lange, John W. *s.j.* '61 (SCR)[C] Scranton, PA The University of Scranton.
Lange, Maurice *o.m.i.* '90 (SFD)[A] Godfrey, IL Immaculate Heart of Mary Novitiate.
Lange, Milton R. '52 (LR) Retired.
Lange, Raymond L. '50 (WOR) Retired.
Lange, Robert A. '86 (ARL) Woodbridge, VA Our Lady of Angels.
Lange, Steven J. '02 (RCK) Crystal Lake, IL St. Thomas the Apostle; Spring Grove, IL St. Peter.
Lange, Timothy J. '61 (OM) Stanton, NE St. Peter; [G] Norfolk, NE Faith Regional Health Services.
Lange, William S. '92 (PH) Newtown, PA St. Andrew.
Langelier, Gerald J. '61 (BRK) Forest Hills, NY Our Lady of Mercy.
Langell, Michael '68 (NSH)[L] Nashville, TN Glenmary Department of Pastoral Services.
Langenbrunner, Norman W. (CIN) Judges.
Langenbrunner, Norman '70 (CIN) Fairfield, OH Sacred Heart of Jesus.
Langenderfer, Carl J. *o.f.m.* '71 (CIN) Cincinnati, OH St. Clement; [M] Cincinnati, OH St. Clement Friary; Priest Councilors.
Langenkamp, August *s.v.d.* '57 (JKS) Tupelo, MS St. James.
Langer, Thomas E. '56 (LC)[I] Eau Claire, WI St. Bede Monastery Retired.
Langford, Terry L. '96 (L) Louisville, KY Our Mother of Sorrows.
Langhals, Henry *c.pp.s.* '37 (CIN)[B] Carthagena, OH St. Charles.
Langhans, Victor E. '84 (HEL) Kalispell, MT St. Matthew.
Langheim, Albert *o.f.m.* '55 (GAY) Indian River, MI Cross in the Woods Catholic Shrine.
Langhorst, Randall L. '92 (LIN) Weston, NE St. John Nepomucene.
Langille, Justin '80 (SD) Unassigned.
Langley, Barry J. *o.f.m.* '94 (WIL) Franciscan Pastoral Team:; Wilmington, DE St. Paul's; [O] Wilmington, DE The Franciscan Center.
Langley, Barry *o.f.m.* (WIL) College of Consultors.
Langley, Terence *s.c.j.* '79 (MIL)[X] Franklin, WI Congregation of the Priests of the Sacred Heart Support and Maintenance Trust; [O] Milwaukee, WI SCJ Community.
Langlois, Charles '97 (LAF) New Iberia, LA St. Peter.
Langlois, Charles (LAF) Diocesan Consultors.
Langlois, Charles (LAF) Ecumenism.
Langlois, Frederick M. '91 (HRT) New Milford, CT Our Lady of the Lakes; [V] New Milford, CT Our Lady of the Lakes Corporation.
Langlois, John A. *o.p.* '91 (PRO)[P] Providence St. Thomas Aquinas Priory at Providence College.
Langlois, William A. '74 (GR) Grand Haven, MI St. Patrick's.
Langone, Robert *s.a.* '89 (NY)[EE] Garrison, NY Franciscan Friars of the Atonement.
Langsch, Gerold M. '72 (MIL)[S] Waukesha, WI Schoenstatt Fathers.
Langsdorf, Karl '72 (CHI)[N] Chicago, IL St. Patrick's Missionary Society.
Langsfeld, Paul J. '77 (WDC) On Duty Outside the Archdiocese.
Langsfeld, Paul J. (COL).
Langston, Micheas *o.s.b.* '65 (IND)[K] Columbia, SC The Hollows; AUXILIARY CHAPLAINS CONTRACT

CHAPLAINS.
Langton, Bernard F. *o.p.* '69 (PRO)[P] Providence St. Thomas Aquinas Priory at Providence College.
Langweld, John *o.f.m.cap.* '46 (NY)[B] Beacon, NY St. Lawrence of Brindisi Friary.
LaNier, Michael L. '83 (LA) On Sick Leave.
Lanigan, Leo *c.ss.r.* '44 (ORL)[E] New Smyrna Beach, FL St. Alphonsus Villa–Redemptorist Fathers and Brothers.
Lanigan, Patrick J. '51 (SAC) Retired.
Lankford, Michael G. '92 (TR) West Long Branch, NJ St. Jerome.
Lankford, Michael '92 (TR)[S] West Long Branch, NJ Catholic Center at Monmouth University.
Lannan, Paul A. '66 (LA) Los Angeles, CA St. Paul the Apostle.
Lanning, Michael J. '78 (CLV) Parma, OH St. Columbkille.
Lannon, Timothy R. *s.j.* '86 (PH)[AA] Loyola Center and Manresa Hall; [C] Jesuit Fathers.
LaNoue, Bertrand *o.s.b.* '52 (KCK) St. Patrick's.
LaNoue, Bertrand *o.s.b.* '52 (KCK) Atchison, KS St. Joseph's; [H] Atchison, KS St. Benedict's Abbey.
Lanphear, William *o.s.f.s.* '63 (LAN)[H] Ann Arbor, MI St. Joseph Mercy Hospital.
Lansang, Ferdinand *o.carm.* '96 (LA) Chicago, IL St. Thomas Apostle.
Lantry, Jerome *o.c.d.* '46 (LA) Alhambra, CA St. Therese.
Lantry, Stephen C. *s.j.* '81 (P)[L] Portland, OR Jesuit Provincial Office (Society of Jesus, Oregon Prov.); Tacoma, WA St. Leo the Great.
Lantry, Stephen *s.j.* '81 (SPK)[B] Spokane, WA Gonzaga University.
Lantsberger, James *o.m.i.* '57 (SR) Imola, CA Napa State Hospital.
Lantsberger, John '76 (SFS) Watertown, SD Holy Name.
Lantsberger, John (SFS) Tribunal Judges.
Lantz, David S. '78 (SFD) Springfield, IL Christ The King; [C] Springfield, IL Springfield College in Illinois.
Lantz, David (SFD) Office for Ministry Formation.
Lanuevo, Victor '75 (HON) On Duty Outside the Diocese; Army Chaplains.
Lanz, Mathias F. '94 (FAR) Leeds, ND St. Vincent de Paul.
Lanz, Mathias '94 (FAR) Leeds, ND St. James.
Lanz, Mathias '94 (FAR) Leeds, ND St. Mary.
Lanza, Daniel A. *m.m.* '59 (NY).
Lanza, Steven M. '81 (CHI)[EE] Tinley Park, IL Saint Julie Billiart.
Lanzaderad, Francisco H. '82 (NY) Staten Island, NY St. Patrick.
Lanzalaco, Joseph M. *c.s.b.* '87 (ROC)[I] Rochester, NY Basilian Residence.
Lanzalaco, Joseph *c.s.b.* '87 (ROC)[L] Rochester, NY St. John Fisher College.
Lanzrath, Curt C. *o.f.m.* '54 (AUS)[G] Brenham, TX Order of Friars Minor; [H] Brenham, TX Monastery of St. Clare.
Lanzrath, John P. '88 (WCH)[H] Wichita, KS Spiritual Life Center.
Lao, Jonathan D. '75 (WDC) Washington, DC St. Gabriel.
Lap, Gilbert D. '03 (RVC) Bellmore, NY St. Barnabas the Apostle.
LaPalme, Paul M. '97 (WOR) Gilbertville, MA St. Aloysius.
La Pan, Kenneth *t.o.r.* '52 (ALT)[F] Newry, PA St. Bernardine Monastery.
LaPastina, Cyprian P. '97 (BGP) Danbury, CT St. Joseph.
LaPata, Richard C. *o.p.* '59 (CHI)[D] Oak Park, IL Fenwick High School; [N] River Forest, IL St. Thomas Aquinas Priory.
La Patka, Gerald '56 (DUL) Retired.
La Paz, Gabriel '78 (NY) New York, NY Incarnation.
Lape, Lydell T. '90 (OM) Columbus, NE St. Anthony.
Lape, Steven W. '99 (ROC) Auburn, NY St. Mary.
Lapensky, John G. '77 (STP) Veseli, MN Most Holy Trinity.
LaPenta, Charles A. *o.s.f.s.* '54 (TOL)[J] Salt Lake City, UT Retired.
Lapera, John M. '84 (SCR) Scranton, PA St. Joseph's; Diocesan Building Commission.
Laperle, Theodore R. '54 (WOR) Fitchburg, MA St. Bernard's Retired.
LaPierre, Yves '61 (PMB) West Palm Beach, FL St. Ann.
Lapinski, Daniel A. '79 (BUF)[G] Cheektowaga, NY Mary Queen of Angels School; Buffalo, NY Queen of Martyrs.
LaPlante, David W. '78 (OM)[G] Omaha, NE Archbishop Bergan Mercy Medical Center; Hospitals.
LaPlante, Eugene *a.a.* '58 (BO)[V] Boston, MA Assumptionist Center.
Laplante, Jean–Paul '50 (BUR) Retired.
LaPlante, Joseph A. '54 (WIN)[A] Winona, MN Immaculate Heart of Mary Seminary Retired.
Laplante, Laurent R. '57 (PRT) Kennebunk, ME St. Martha's.
LaPlante, Philip *s.m.* '48 (BO) Boston, MA Our Lady of Victories.
La Plante, Philip *s.m.* '48 (BO)[AA] Boston, MA Our Lady of Good Voyage Chapel.
Laplante, Philip *s.m.* '48 (BO)[V] Boston, MA Marist Fathers of Our Lady of Victories (Boston Prov.).
LaPlante, Philip *s.m.* (BO) Seaport of Boston.
LaPlante, Robert J. '95 (CR) Roseau, MN Sacred Heart.
LaPlante, Roland M. '62 (HRT) South Meriden, CT Holy Angels.
Lapointe, J. Donald R. (SPR) Psychotherapeutic Counselor.
Lapointe, J. Donald R. '67 (SPR) Haydenville, MA St. Mary's; Leeds, MA St. Catherine's; Our Lady of Providence Children's Center, West Springfield.
LaPointe, John G. '72 (PRO) Johnston, RI St. Robert Bellarmine.
LaPointe, Laurence A.M. '70 (NOR)[K] Willimantic, CT Campus Ministry; [K] New London, CT Connecticut College.
LaPointe, Laurence A.M. (NOR) College of Consultors; Members; Deans; Campus Ministry; New London; Chaplains; Censor of Books.
Lapomarda, Vincent A. *s.j.* '64 (WOR)[O] Worcester, MA Jesuits of Holy Cross College, Inc..
LaPore, Arthur '76 (JOL) Joliet, IL St. Anthony.
La Porta, Gerald '57 (BAL) Retired.
LaPorta, Gerald (BAL) Lonaconing, MD St. Mary of the Annunciation.
Laporta, Ross A. '51 (BAL) Baltimore, MD St. Mark.
La Porta, Ross A. '51 (BAL) Retired.
LaPorte, Gerard B. *c.ss.r.* '83 (NO) New Orleans, LA St. Alphonsus.
Laporte, Jean–Marc *s.j.* '67 (FgM).
Laporte, Paul J. '65 (PRO) Coventry, RI St. Vincent de Paul.
Lappe, Derek (SEA) Camas, WA St. Thomas Aquinas.
Laptuta, Demetrius *c.ss.r.* '45 (STF) Niagara Falls, NY Protection of B.V.M..
LaPuebla, Enrique *m.s.* '21 (SB) Lucerne Valley, CA St. Paul.
LaPuebla, Enrique *m.s.* '80 (SB) Morena Valley, CA Riverside County Regional Medical Center.
Lara, Gustavo '59 (LA) Los Angeles, CA Norris Cancer and USC University Hospital.
Lara, Jaime C. '57 (SP) Retired.
Lara, James C. '57 (SP) Brandon, FL Church of the Nativity.
Lara, Rafael *sch.p.* '99 (LA) Los Angeles, CA Santa Teresita.
Lara, Santiago G. '72 (LA)[Q] Los Angeles, CA Guadalupe Missioners Procure.
LaRaia, Joseph P. '46 (BO) Senior Priests Retired.
Laraneta, Jesus (SJN)[E] San Juan, PR Centro Medico de P.R..
Larche, James M. (OG) Army Reserve Chaplains.
Lardner, Gerald V. *s.s.* '67 (BAL)[S] Emmaus Spirituality Center.
Laredo, Leopoldo *sch.p.* '40 (SJN) San Juan, PR Santisimo Salvador.
Larena, Ismael '47 (PCE) Santa Isabel, PR St. James.
Large, John J. '75 (PH) Norwood, PA St. Gabriel.
Largente, Laurent '59 (SJ) Retired.
Lariviere, Robert D. '78 (PRT) Lewiston, ME SS. Peter and Paul; Diocesan Council of Priests.
Lariviere, Robert (PRT) Clergy Benefit Plan–Clergy Pension Plan.
Larkin, Alexander C. '67 (SJ) Saratoga, CA Sacred Heart; College of Consultors; Council of Priests.
Larkin, Bartholomew *o.carm.* '58 (VEN) Rotonda West, FL St. Francis of Assisi.
Larkin, Craig *s.m.* '67 (FgM).
Larkin, Edward A. *s.j.* '54 (OM)[K] Omaha, NE Jesuit Community at Creighton University.
Larkin, Ernest *o.carm.* '46 (PHX) Phoenix, AZ St. Agnes; [J] Phoenix, AZ Kino Institute of Theology.
Larkin, James *m.ss.a.* '90 (NY) White Plains, NY St. Agnes Hospital.
Larkin, James *m.s.a.* '90 (NOR)[F] Cromwell Society of the Missionaries of the Holy Apostles; [AA] Bronx, NY St. Patrick's Home for the Aged and Infirm.
Larkin, John P. '44 (NY) New York, NY Our Saviour Retired.
Larkin, John R. *o.carm.* '51 (PHX)[G] Phoenix, AZ Carmelite Community Retired.
Larkin, Joseph M. '57 (SY) Minetto, NY Our Lady of Perpetual Help.
Larkin, Kevin J. '59 (LA) Sherman Oaks, CA St. Francis de Sales.
Larkin, Michael J. '59 (STA) Jacksonville, FL Prince of Peace; Building Commission.
Larkin, Michael T. '68 (SC) Special Assignment.
Larkin, Patrick '57 (WCH) Retired.
Larkin, Richard '47 (STP) Retired.
Larkin, Robert W. '73 (NY) Bronx, NY Visitation.
Larkin, Robert (NY) Canon 1742 Panel of Pastors.
Larkin, Ron *m.s.c.* (SB) Office of the Vicar for Clergy.
Larkin, Ron *m.s.c.* (SB) Committee for the Continuing Education of Priests.
Larkin, Ronald *m.s.c.* '61 (SB) Special or Other Diocesan Assignment.
Larkin, Ronald *m.s.c.* (SB) Priestly Life and Ministry Committee.
Larkin, Ronald *m.s.c.* (SB) Diocesan Curia.
Larkin, William J. *s.j.* '52 (BO)[V] Weston, MA Campion Health Center, Inc..
Larko, Ronald P. '82 (PBR) McKees Rocks, PA Holy Ghost.
Larmann, Marian E. *o.s.b.* '47 (NO) St. Benedict, LA St. Benedict; [P] St. Benedict, LA St. Joseph Abbey.
Larmore, Donald E. '63 (GI) On Duty Outside the Diocese; Defenders of the Bond.
Larner, James M. '57 (BO) Dorchester, MA St. Gregory.
La Rocca, Christopher *o.c.d.* '97 (SJ)[M] San Jose, CA Carmelite Monastery, Novitiate.
La Rocca, Christopher *o.c.d.* (SJ) Council of Religious.
LaRocca, John J. *s.j.* '75 (CIN)[M] Cincinnati, OH Jesuit Community at Xavier University.
Laroche, Christopher J. (PRT) Air Force Reserve Chaplains.
Laroche, Leonidas B. '61 (BUR) St. Albans, VT Immaculate Conception.
LaRoche, Victor *o.p.* '02 (MIA)[B] Miami, FL Barry University; Special Assignment.
Larochelle, Alphonse *m.s.* '59 (HON) Kekaha, HI St. Theresa.
Larochelle, Alphonse (HON) College of Consultors.
Larochelle, Alphonse *m.s.* (HON) Kauai.
Larochelle, Alphonse *m.s.* (HON) Vicars Forane.
Larochelle, Maurice R. '87 (MAN) Hampton, NH Our Lady of the Miraculous Medal.
LaRocque, Benedict J. *o.s.b.* '42 (OM) Retired.
LaRocque, Benedict J. *o.s.b.* '42 (KCK)[H] Atchison, KS St. Benedict's Abbey.
Larocque, Paul M. '45 (TUC) Retired.
LaRocque, Richard L. (NOR) Part Time.
LaRocque, Richard P. '63 (NOR) Old Lyme, CT Christ the King; College of Consultors; Members; Vicar for Clergy; Bishop's Liaison with Retired Clergy; Vicar for Clergy, Office of; Diocesan Vocation Review Committee.
LaRosa, John J. '81 (PH) Philadelphia, PA Mother of Divine Grace.
La Rosa, Stephen J. *o.s.a.* '65 (CAM)[C] Richland, NJ St. Augustine Preparatory School.
LaRosa, Stephen *o.s.a.* (CAM) Vicar for Men Religious.
Larran, Francisco *o.s.a.* '50 (MGZ) San German, PR St. Rose of Lima.
Larraneta, Jesus *c.m.* '55 (SJN)[E] Hato Rey, PR Hospital Auxilio Mutuo.
Larrea, Luis E. (TYL) College of Consultors; Hispanic Ministry Advisory Council; Priests' Personnel Board.
Larrea, Luis Eduardo *m.f.e.* '77 (TYL) Tyler, TX St. Peter Claver.
Larreategui, Jose Luis *sch.p.* '53 (PCE)[B] The Pontifical Catholic University of Puerto Rico.
Larrivee, Leo J. *s.s.* '77 (SEA) Catonsville, MD Our Lady of the Angels Catholic Community; On Duty Outside the Archdiocese.
Larroque, H. A. (LAF) Diocesan Consultors.
Larroque, H. Alexandre '55 (LAF)[I] Lafayette, LA Discalced Carmelites; Vicars General; Judges.
Larry, Anthony J. *o.s.f.s.* '67 (WIL) Greensboro, NC St. Paul the Apostle; [J] Childs, MD Retirement and Assisted Care Facility.
Larsen, Kevin J. '93 (ARL) Reston, VA St. Thomas a Becket.
Larson, James F. '57 (RCK) Retired.
Larson, James *l.c.* '98 (ATL)[K] Atlanta, GA Legionaries of Christ.
Larson, James '98 (ATL)[O] Atlanta, GA Home and Family, Inc..
Larson, Jan '56 (SEA) Snoqualmie, WA Our Lady of Sorrows.
Larson, Jan '68 (SEA) Echo Glen Children's Center.
Larson, Lawrence A. '77 (BGP) Westport, CT Assumption.
Larson, Paul '79 (DUL) Deer River, MN St. Augustine; Deer River, MN St. Mary.
Larue, Charles '93 (SAN) Retired.
Larue, Charles '93 (SAN)[K] San Antonio, TX Padua Place.
Larussa, Raymond '74 (COL) Columbus, OH Holy Spirit.
Las, Stefan '88 (PAT) Passaic, NJ Holy Rosary.
Lasalle, Donald *s.m.m.* '83 (HRT)[M] Monfort Novitiate.
Lasalle, Donald *s.m.m.* '83 (HRT)[M] Litchfield, CT Montfort Missionaries.
LaSana, Andre *l.c.* '01 (CHI)[N] Lemont, IL Legion of Christ.
Lascelle, Roger L. '77 (DEN) Craig, CO Saint Michael; Meeker, CO Holy Family; Rangely, CO St. Ignatius; [Q] Rangely, CO Colorado Northwestern Community College (Rangely).
Lasch, Kenneth E. '62 (PAT) Mendham, NJ St. Joseph's; Defenders of the Bond.
Laschenski, Sigmund J. *s.j.* '55 (BAL)[S] Loyola House.
Lasecki, Daniel J. '64 (MIL) Elkhart Lake, WI St. Thomas Aquinas.

Lasheras, Antonio *o.a.r.* '62 (NEW) El Paso, TX Guardian Angel.
Lasic, Miron *o.f.m.* '40 (CHI)[N] Chicago, IL St. Anthony's Friary.
Lasilo, Vertesaljai *s.j.* (ATH) "A Sziv".
Laska, William M. '88 (E) New Bethlehem, PA St. Charles.
Laske, Kenneth S. '58 (CHI) Retired.
Lasko, Stephen J. *c.s.sp.* '47 (VEN)[G] Sarasota, FL Congregation of the Holy Ghost.
Laskowski, Keith R. '02 (ALN) Allentown, PA Cathedral of St. Catharine of Siena.
Laskowski, Norbert F. (NEW) Archdiocesan Judges.
Laskowski, Norbert '79 (NEW) Rochelle Park, NJ Sacred Heart.
Lasky, Joseph J. '55 (SCR) Kingston, PA St. Mary's Annunciation Retired.
Lasky, Michael *o.f.m.conv.* (BUF)[O] Athol Springs, NY St. Francis of Assisi Friary; [D] Athol Springs, NY St. Francis High School.
Laslavich, Luke S. *o.praem.* '94 (ORG)[C] Santa Ana, CA Mater Dei High School; [I] Silverado, CA Norbertine Fathers of Orange Inc.; Costa Mesa, CA St. John the Baptist.
Lasley, Jerry D. '92 (DAV) Absent on Leave.
Lasseigne, John *o.m.i.* '99 (BWN) San Juan, TX St. John the Baptist.
Last, Carl A. '69 (MIL)[X] Milwaukee, WI Cathedral Preservation Foundation, Inc.; Milwaukee, WI Cathedral of St. John the Evangelist.
Lastiri, Jean–Michael '85 (FRS) Merced, CA Our Lady of Mercy/St. Patrick's.
Lastiri, Jean–Michael (FRS) Continuing Formation of Priests.
Latcovich, Mark A. '81 (CLV)[A] Wickliffe, OH St. Mary Seminary and Graduate School of Theology.
Latcovich, Mark (CLV) Presbyteral Council.
Latella, Joseph A. *s.j.* '58 (NY)[EE] New York, NY St. Ignatius Loyola Residence; [II] New York, NY Xavier Society for the Blind.
Lathem, E. Christopher '65 (CHR) Summerville, SC St. John the Beloved; Diocesan Curia; College of Consultors; Presbyteral Council; Personnel Committee; Vicar for Clergy.
Lathrop, Robert A. '91 (DAV) Davenport, IA Our Lady of Victory.
Latona, Marcello J. '70 (BRK) Whitestone, NY Holy Trinity.
La Torre, Abraham '51 (SAT) Movimiento de Apostolado Familiar & Marriage Encounter (Rural) Retired.
La Torre, Abraham (SAT) Cursillo Movement (Spanish).
LaTorre, Tony '97 (SFR) San Carlos, CA St. Charles.
Latosynski, Roger '84 (PT) Apalachicola, FL St. Patrick.
Latour, Charles *o.p.* '02 (DAL)[K] Irving, TX Dominican Priory of St. Albert the Great.
Latronico, P. '86 (NEW)[S] Rutherford, NJ The Community of God's Love.
Latronico, Philip F. '86 (NEW) Archdiocesan Commission for Christain Unity; Archdiocesan Commission for Interreligious Affairs; The Community of God's Love; Linden, NJ St. John the Apostle.
Latsko, Andrew '92 (CHL) Retired.
Lattanzio, Sabino *o.f.m.cap.* '72 (LAV) Las Vegas, NV St. Anne.
Lattis, Herbert L. '64 (L) Goshen, KY Transfiguration of Our Lord.
Lattus, Herman J. '99 (MEM) Union City, TN Immaculate Conception.
Latus, Bernard *s.v.d.* '87 (CHI)[N] Chicago, IL Divine Word Theologate.
Latus, Charles J. '68 (ROC) Webster, NY St. Rita; Priests' Council.
Latzko, Frank '84 (CHI) Chicago, IL St. John Fisher.
Lau, Ignatius '58 (ORG) Santa Ana, CA Immaculate Heart of Mary Retired.
Lau, John *o.m.i.* '91 (STP)[P] Buffalo, MN Christ the King Retreat Center.
Lau, Michael '61 (P) Retired.
Lau, Vincent '52 (Hong Kong) Fresno, CA St. Genevieve.
Laubach, Barnabas *o.s.b.* '52 (SB) San Bernardino, CA San Bernardino Medical Center; [D] San Bernardino, CA St. Bernardine Medical Center.
Laubach, Barnabas *o.s.b.* '52 (SCL)[I] San Bernardino, CA St. Bernardine Hospital.
Laubacher, Carroll *s.j.* '56 (LA)[K] Ojai, CA St. Joseph's Health and Retirement Center.
Laubacker, Jerome P. *o.de.m.* '74 (SP) St. Petersburg, FL Transfiguration.
Laubacker, Jerome *o.de.m.* '74 (SP)[O] St. Petersburg, FL St. Peter Nolasco Residence.
Laubenthal, Alan R. (CLV) Associate Judges.
Laubenthal, Allan R. '61 (CLV) North Olmsted, OH St. Clarence.
Laudati, Joseph J. '56 (NEW) Retired.
Lauder, Robert E. '60 (BRK) Released from Diocesan Assignment; [B] Douglaston, NY Cathedral Seminary Residence of the Immaculate Conception; [A] Douglaston, NY Immaculate Conception Center.
Laudick, John R. '64 (TOL) Toledo, OH St. Francis de Sales; Toledo, OH St. Michael the Archangel; Toledo, OH St. Vincent de Paul.
Lauducci, James V. '57 (SY) Retired.
Laudwein, James R. *s.j.* '62 (P)[A] Portland, OR Jesuit Novitiate of St. Francis Xavier.
Laudwein, Joseph E. *s.j.* (FBK) Defender of the Bond.
Laudwein, Joseph *s.j.* '62 (FBK)[C] Fairbanks, AK Jesuit Residence.
Laudwein, Joseph *s.j.* '62 (FBK) Tanana, AK St. Aloysius.
Laudwein, Joseph *s.j.* (FBK) Ministry of Sick, Aged and Imprisoned.
Lauenstean, Gary *c.ss.r.* '71 (STL)[B] St. Louis, MO St. John Neumann House.
Lauer, Douglas J. '94 (COV) Covington, KY St. Benedict.
Lauer, Eugene F. '61 (PIT) On Duty Outside the Diocese.
Lauer, Eugene (CHI)[B] Chicago, IL The Catholic Theological Union at Chicago.
Lauerman, James P. '70 (FAR) Grafton, ND Sacred Heart.
Lauerman, James '70 (FAR) Grafton, ND St. Thomas.
Laughery, Kevin Michael '83 (SFD) Auburn, IL St. Benedict; Auburn, IL Sacred Heart; Auburn, IL St. Sebastian.
Laughlin, James J. '91 (BO) Jamaica Plain, MA St. Thomas Aquinas; Graduate Studies; Archdiocesan Judges; Canonical Affairs Committee.
Laughlin, Joseph R. *s.j.* '57 (BO)[E] Dorchester, MA Boston College High School & Jesuit Community; [V] Weston, MA Campion Jesuit Community
Laughlin, Martin T. '52 (CHR) Hilton Head Island, SC Holy Family; Deans; Diocesan Curia.
Laughlin, Martin T. '52 (DUB) Retired.
Laughlin, Martin (CHR) Presbyteral Council.
Launderville, Dale *o.s.b.* '79 (SCL)[I] Collegeville, MN St. John's Abbey, of the Order of St. Benedict.
Laurance, John D. *s.j.* '70 (MIL)[C] Marquette University; [O] Milwaukee, WI Jesuit Community at Marquette University.
Laurello, Bartholomew J. '46 (BGP) Retired.
Laurence, Francis '45 (JOL)[L] Lisle, IL St. Procopius Abbey.
Laurendeau, Clement *o.carm.* (NEW) Bogota, NJ St. Joseph's.
Laurent, Edward *o.f.m.cap.* '64 (PIT)[N] Pittsburgh, PA St. Francis Friary; [N] Pittsburgh, PA St. Augustine Friary.
Laurenzo, James '69 (DM) Des Moines, IA St. Catherine of Siena Catholic Student Center.
Laurenzo, Jim '69 (DM)[I] Des Moines, IA St. Catherine of Siena Catholic Student Center.
Lauretti, George F. '56 (HRT) Southington, CT St. Thomas.
Lauri, John F. (NY) Judges.
Lauri, John '73 (NY) Bronx, NY St. Theresa of the Infant Jesus.
Laurick, Richard *c.s.c.* '54 (FTW) South Bend, IN Holy Cross; South Bend, IN St. Stanislaus.
Laurinaitis, Saulius P. '48 (COL) Retired.
Lauriola, Guglielmo *o.f.m.* '53 (OAK)[S] Oakland, CA Missionaries of the Kingship of Christ.
Lauriola, Guglielmo *o.f.m.* '53 (SFR) San Francisco, CA St. Anthony of Padua.
Lause, James A. *o.f.m.* '98 (STL)[I] Cedar Lake, IN San Damiano Friary.
Lause, Richard L. *c.m.* '77 (STL)[O] St. Louis, MO Lazarist Residence.
Lautermilch, David J. '62 (TOL) Awaiting Assignment.
Lautz, Boniface *o.s.b.* '60 (B)[C] Jerome, ID Monastery of the Ascension.
Lauze, Michael *o.m.i.* '75 (BO)[V] Lowell, MA Missionary Oblates of Mary Immaculate.
Lauzon, Kris C. '91 (OG) Hogansburg, NY St. Joseph; Hogansburg, NY St. Mary; Fort Covington, NY St. Patrick; Plattsburgh, NY St. John the Baptist.
Lavagetto, Xavier M. *o.p.* '96 (SFR) San Francisco, CA St. Dominic.
Lavagetto, Xavier *o.p.* '96 (SFR)[N] San Francisco, CA St. Dominic Priory; Deans.
LaVallee, Pierre A. '61 (BUR) Deans; Bristol, VT St. Ambrose.
LaValley, Richard G. '64 (BUR) Deans; [H] Burlington, VT The Catholic Center at UVM; Winooski, VT St. Francis Xavier.
LaValley, Terry R. '88 (OG) Ogdensburg, NY St. Mary's Cathedral; Chancellor; Adjutant Judicial Vicars; Diocesan Consultors; Priest Personnel Board; Building Commission; Bureau of Information.
LaVan, Kenneth G. '58 (STP) Retired.
Lavaroni, Rino (NEW) Bergen County Curia.
Lavaroni, Rino (NEW) Jersey City, NJ Holy Rosary.
Lavastida, Jose I. '87 (NO) Military Chaplains; [A] Navy Reserve Chaplains.
LaVecke, John R. *s.j.* '84 (LA)[Q] Los Angeles, CA Columbiere House.
Lavelle, Donald *c.m.f.* '46 (LA)[Q] Rancho Dominguez, CA Dominguez Seminary Inc..
Lavelle, Donald *c.m.f.* '46 (CHI)[N] Rancho Dominguez, CA Dominguez Retreat Renewal Center.
Lavelle, Edward R. '63 (HBG)[G] Harrisburg, PA Villa Teresa Nursing Home; Defender of the Bond.
Lavelle, Francis P. '70 (SPR) Absent on Leave.
Lavelle, John–Michael (Y) Ravenna, OH Immaculate Conception.
Lavelle, Raymond E. '57 (COL) Westerville, OH St. Paul the Apostle Retired.
Lavelle, Thomas E. *m.m.* '55 (FgM).
Lavely, Charles J. *c.s.c.* '65 (FTW) South Bend, IN St. Adalbert; South Bend, IN St. Augustine.
LaVerde, Calogero N. '68 (CAM) Woodbury Heights, NJ St. Margaret's.
LaVerdiere, Eugene *s.s.s.* '64 (NY) New York, NY St. Jean Baptiste.
LaVerghetta, Richard D. '86 (TR) Hamilton Square, NJ St. Gregory the Great; Secretary.
Laverone, Kenneth J. *o.f.m.* '79 (MRY) Special Assignment; Judicial Vicar; Judges.
Laverone, Kenneth *o.f.m.* '79 (OAK)[N] Oakland Franciscan Friars Provincial Office, Province of St. Barbara.
Laverty, Joseph F. *o.s.a.* '48 (PH)[AA] Villanova, PA St. Thomas Monastery.
Laverty, Seamus '68 (SEA) Tacoma, WA St. Patrick.
Laverty, Tod *o.f.m.* (DET) Detroit, MI St. Aloysius.
Lavery, Bruce '67 (ORG) Laguna Niguel, CA St. Timothy.
Laviano, Vincent A. *o.f.m.* '74 (NY) New York, NY St. Francis of Assisi.
Lavich, David *o.c.s.o.* '73 (WOR)[O] Spencer, MA St. Joseph's Abbey.
Lavigne, Lionel *s.s.s.* '41 (CLV)[O] Richfield, OH Regina Health Center.
Lavigne, Lionel *s.s.s.* '41 (CLV)[O] Richfield, OH Regina Health Center.
Lavigne, Maurice D. '68 (MAN) Rye Beach, NH St. Theresa.
Lavin, Bernard C. '79 (PRO) Lincoln, RI St. Jude.
Lavin, James A. (STP) Censores Librorum.
Lavin, James M. '45 (STP)[C] St. Paul, MN University of St. Thomas Retired.
Lavin, John B. '64 (BRK) Bayside, NY St. Robert Bellarmine.
Lavin, John J. '64 (PRO) Newport, RI St. Joseph.
Lavin, John '64 (PRO)[B] Newport, RI Salve Regina University.
Lavin, John *c.ss.r.* '66 (BAL)[S] Annapolis, MD Saint Mary Rectory.
Lavin, John *c.ss.r.* '66 (BAL) Annapolis, MD St. Mary.
Lavin, Martin E. (RIC) Judges.
Lavin, Martin '67 (RIC) Franklin, VA St. Jude.
Lavin, Wayne Patrick '71 (CAM) Glassboro, NJ St. Bridget's.
LaViolette, Matt H. '34 (MAR) Retired.
Lavoie, Alfred *o.m.i.* '40 (SAT)[K] San Antonio, TX Oblate Madonna Residence.
LaVoie, Joseph '64 (SFE) Retired.
LaVoie, Joseph '64 (SFE)[B] Santa Fe, NM College of Santa Fe.
LaVoie, Joseph (SFE) SANTE FE: College of Santa Fe.
Lavoie, Merle L. '68 (SPR) Northampton, MA Sacred Heart; Northampton, MA St. John Cantius.
Lavoie, Michel J. *m.afr.* (FgM).
LaVoie, Raymond J. '00 (HBG)[J] Millersville, PA Millersville University; [J] Millersville, PA Franklin and Marshall College, Lancaster.
Lavoie, Rene G. '51 (PRT) Sanford, ME St. Ignatius Martyr Retired.
Lavoie, Richard *m.s.* '64 (FR)[H] Attleboro, MA La Salette Shrine.
Lavoie, Robert G. '53 (PRT) Gray, ME St. Gregory.
Lavoie, Robert (PRT) Diocesan Council of Priests.
LaVoie, Victor C. (BO) Winchester, MA St. Eulalia; Advocates.
Lavorin, Anthony F. *o.f.m.* (MRY) Jolon, CA San Antonio Mission.
Lavoy, Elwood '53 (LAV) Retired.
Lavoy, Elwood (LAV) Italian Catholic Federation.
Lavrih, John '39 (DOD) Retired.
Law, Joseph A. '49 (SCR)[N] Dunmore, PA Villa St. Joseph Retired.
Lawler, Bruce A. '80 (SC) Storm Lake, IA St. Mary's; [G] Storm Lake, IA St. Mary's Foundation of Storm Lake, Iowa; Priests' Pension Plan – Board of Trustees.
Lawler, Bruce (SC) Liturgy Commission.
Lawler, Daniel F. *s.j.* '48 (ALN)[A] Wernersville, PA Jesuit Center.
Lawler, David '62 (IND) Methodist Hospital; Indianapolis, IN St. Christopher.
Lawler, John F. '45 (BO) Senior Priests Retired.
Lawler, Joseph A. '61 (BEL) McLeansboro, IL St. Clement; McLeansboro, IL St. John the Baptist.
Lawler, Robert L. '56 (OG) Waddington, NY St. John the Baptist; Waddington, NY St. Mary; Diocesan Administrator; Diocesan Consultors; Priest Personnel Board.
Lawler, Terrance M. '74 (MET) Warren, NJ Our Lady of the Mount; Department of Personnel in Ministry; Office of Priest Personnel; College of Consultors; Episcopal Council.

Lawler, Thomas A. *s.j.* '99 (RC)[D] Howes, SD The Diocese of Rapid City Mahpiya na Maka Okogna.
Lawler, Thomas *s.j.* '99 (RC)[B] Howes, SD Kino Jesuit Community.
Lawler, William J. '72 (WIL) Centreville, MD Our Mother of Sorrows; Liaison for Evangelization; Deans.
Lawless, Brendan '64 (JC) St. James, MO St. Anthony.
Lawless, Brendan '64 (JC) St. James, MO Missouri Veterans' Home.
Lawless, J. Timothy *s.j.* '61 (DEN)[N] Denver, CO Xavier Jesuit Center.
Lawless, Joseph *m.s.f.* '71 (CC) Corpus Christi, TX St. Joseph.
Lawless, P. Brendan '64 (JC) St. James, MO Immaculate Conception.
Lawlor, Brendan '55 (SP) Retired.
Lawlor, David T. *o.praem.* '71 (PH)[AA] Paoli, PA Daylesford Abbey.
Lawlor, Edward J. *s.s.j.* '40 (BAL)[S] Baltimore, MD St. Joseph's Manor.
Lawlor, F. James '63 (ROC) Mendon, NY St. Catherine of Siena.
Lawlor, Francis *o.s.a.* '45 (STL) St. Louis, MO Immaculate Conception–St. Henry.
Lawlor, Francis '69 (SAC) Sacramento, CA St. Rose.
Lawlor, J. Michael '73 (BO) Needham, MA St. Joseph.
Lawlor, John J. *c.m.* '44 (PH).
Lawlor, John L. *c.m.* '44 (CHR)[AA] Gloverville, SC Our Lady of the Valley.
Lawlor, Joseph A. '61 (BEL) Dahlgren, IL St. John Nepomucene.
Lawlor, Joseph F. '35 (RVC) Baldwin, NY St. Christopher Retired.
Lawlor, Joseph '35 (RVC)[J] Huntington, NY St. Joseph's Guest Home for the Aged, Inc..
Lawlor, Joseph '62 (JC) Missionary Assignment in Peru.
Lawlor, Mark '95 (CHL) Charlotte, NC St. Vincent de Paul.
Lawlor, Timothy '43 (SB) Ontario, CA St. George.
Lawlor, Timothy '43 (SB) Retired.
Lawrence, Andrew F. (DUB) Army Chaplains.
Lawrence, Andrew (DUB) Military Chaplains.
Lawrence, Christopher '84 (LA) San Pedro, CA Mary, Star of the Sea.
Lawrence, David *s.j.* '74 (OAK) Concord, CA St. Bonaventure.
Lawrence, David '97 (JOL) Glen Ellyn, IL St. Petronille.
Lawrence, Henry J. *c.s.c.* '61 (FTW)[I] Michigan City, IN.
Lawrence, James A. '70 (BUR) Pittsford, VT St. Alphonsus Liguori.
Lawrence, James T. '61 (DAV)[M] Davenport, IA St. Vincent Center Retired.
Lawrence, Jeff (PEO) Clergymen's Aid, Inc..
Lawrence, Jeffrey C. '96 (PEO) Streator, IL St. Stephen's.
Lawrence, Jeffrey (PEO) Diocesan College of Consultors.
Lawrence, John M. '76 (SAC) Fort Jones, CA Sacred Heart; Yreka, CA St. Joseph.
Lawrence, Kenneth F. '60 (HBG) Columbia, PA Holy Trinity; Consultors, College; Deans; Appointed.
Lawrence, Kevin C. '87 (PH) Philadelphia, PA St. Timothy.
Lawrence, Martin E. '03 (SFS) Sioux Falls, SD St. Joseph Cathedral.
Lawrence, Michael S. '73 (ALN)[J] Bethlehem, PA Holy Family Villa Retired.
Lawrence, Neal Henry *o.s.b.* '60 (FgM).
Lawrence, Neal Henry *o.s.b.* '60 (SCL)[I] St. Augustine Monastery.
Lawrence, Ralph J. '53 (CIN) Censors; Judges Retired.
Lawrence, Richard T. '68 (BAL) Baltimore, MD St. Vincent de Paul; Priests' Council.
Lawrence, Robert E. '66 (HBG) Harrisburg, PA Holy Name of Jesus.
Lawrence, Robert E. (SB) Special or Other Diocesan Assignment; Defender of the Bond.
Lawrence, Walter L. '73 (WDC) Barnesville, MD St. Mary Church and Shrine of Our Lady of Fatima.
Lawsine, Robert '81 (BRK) Brooklyn, NY St. Saviour.
Lawson, Harold F. '59 (BO) Senior Priests Retired.
Lawson, J. Douglas '62 (R) Southport, NC Sacred Heart.
Lawson, Meinrad J. *o.s.b.* '67 (GBG)[H] Latrobe, PA Saint Vincent Archabbey.
Lawson, Meirad *o.s.b.* '02 (GBG)[I] Latrobe, PA Discalced Carmelite Nuns.
Lawson, Robert T. '62 (R) Retired.
Lawson, Ronald (MO) AUXILIARY CHAPLAINS CONTRACT CHAPLAINS.
Lawson, Theodore *c.ss.r.* '89 (TUC)[G] Tucson, AZ Redemptorist Society of Arizona.
Lawton, Robert B. *s.j.* '81 (LA)[C] Los Angeles, CA Loyola Marymount University; [C] Los Angeles, CA Jesuit Community.
Lawyer, Jerome R. *c.s.c.* '39 (FTW)[I] Notre Dame, IN Holy Cross House.
Lay, Thomas N. *s.j.* '66 (STL)[O] St. Louis, MO Hallahan House.
Layton, Richard *o.c.s.o.* '82 (P)[L] Lafayette, OR The Cistercian (Trappist) Abbey of Our Lady of Guadalupe.
Laz, Medard P '69 (CHI)[X] LaGrange Park, IL Joyful Again.
Laz, Medard P. '69 (CHI) Other Assignments.
Lazar, Francis M. '60 (GRY) Highland, IN St. James the Less; Bishop's Council of Priests.
Lazar, John '42 (STN) Dearborn Heights, MI Our Lady of Perpetual Help.
Lazaro, Lesmes Bernabe *o.s.a.* '49 (MGZ) Aguada, PR St. Francis of Assisi.
Lazarski, Marvin I. '62 (MIL) Special Assignment.
Lazo, Johnny Laura '94 (WIL) Salisbury, MD St. Francis De Sales.
Lazor, Bernard A. *o.s.a.* '51 (PH)[C] Villanova University; [AA] Villanova, PA St. Thomas Monastery.
Lazzarato, Mauro *c.s.* '86 (CHI)[N] Chicago, IL Scalabrini House of Theology.
Lchane, Brian J. *s.j.* '97 (DET)[B] Berkley, MI Loyola House.
Le, Anh *s.d.b.* '95 (LA)[F] Bellflower, CA St. John Bosco High School.
Le, Ben '98 (LA) Santa Monica, CA St. Monica.
Le, Hoang V. '99 (BO) Graduate Studies.
Le, Hoang Viet '61 (TLS) Tulsa, OK St. Joseph Church.
Le, Hung Viet '01 (TLS) Bartlesville, OK St. John's.
Le, James Vinh '87 (KAL) Dorr, MI St. Stanislaus.
Le, Joseph Thu '03 (GAL) Houston, TX St. Cecilia.
Le, Tan Van (CHL) Vietnamese Apostolate.
Le, Trieu Ngoc '42 (PIT)[N] Pittsburgh, PA St. John Vianney Manor Retired.
Le, Tuan Q. *s.j.* '89 (DEN)[N] Denver, CO Xavier Jesuit Center.
Leach, Gregory '80 (DM) Ankeny, IA Our Lady's Immaculate Heart.
Leach, Jerome '76 (SFR) Absent on Leave.
Leach, Phillip M. '85 (R) Chapel Hill, NC Newman Catholic Student Center, University of North Carolina; [H] Chapel Hill, NC Newman Catholic Student Center; Diocesan Consultors; Priests' Council.
Leach, Phillip (R) Campus Ministry.
Leach, Thomas F. '73 (BRK) Brooklyn, NY Our Lady of Grace.
Leach, William '58 (STL) St. Charles, MO St. Peter.
Leack, Lawrence J. '50 (MIL)[U] Milwaukee, WI Our Blessed Lady of Victory Mission, Inc.; [M] Wauwatosa, WI St. Camillus Health Center, Inc. Retired.
Leahey, Patrick R. '77 (ALT) Dudley, PA Immaculate Conception.
Leahy, Anthony '55 (SB) Retired.
Leahy, Clement '50 (CHI)[N] Chicago, IL St. Peter's Friary.
Leahy, Edwin D. *o.s.b.* '63 (NEW)[C] Newark, NJ St. Benedict's Preparatory School; [N] Newark, NJ Newark Abbey.
Leahy, John A. '57 (CLV) Middleburg Heights, OH St. Bartholomew Retired.
Leahy, Liam '72 (TUC) Tucson, AZ St. Mark The Evangelist.
Leahy, Patrick J. '38 (DOD) Retired.
Leahy, William J. '66 (SAV) McRae, GA Holy Redeemer.
Leahy, William P. *s.j.* '78 (Wisconsin)[V] Newton, MA The Jesuit Community at Boston College.
Leahy, William P. *s.j.* '78 (BO)[C] Chestnut Hill, MA Boston College.
Leahy, William '66 (SAV) Eastman, GA St. Mark.
Leake, Jerome I. '68 (RCK) Aurora, IL St. Joseph.
Leake, Stephen *s.d.b.* '00 (NEW)[N] Ramsey, NJ Don Bosco Prep Salesian Residence.
Leake, Stephen *s.d.b.* '00 (NEW)[C] Ramsey, NJ Don Bosco Preparatory High School.
Leal, Luis Roberto Aguilar *o.p.* '92 (FgM).
Leany, Anthony M. '55 (CHI) Chicago, IL St. Barnabas Retired.
Leary, Albert R. '54 (BIS) Mandan, ND Christ the King; [G] Bismarck, ND Emmaus Place.
Leary, Albert R. '54 (BIS) Pro–Synodal Judges.
Leary, Daniel P. '97 (WDC) Gaithersburg, MD St. Martin.
Leary, Donald G. '51 (WIN) Retired.
Leary, James F. '68 (HRT) Bristol, CT St. Joseph.
Leary, James V. '56 (PH) Phoenixville, PA Sacred Heart Retired.
Leary, James *o.f.m.cap.* '70 (LC) Sparta, WI St. Patrick.
Leary, Patrick (LAV) Presbyteral Council for the Diocese of Las Vegas.
Leary, Patrick (LAV) Priests' Pension Board.
Leary, Patrick (LAV) Board of Trustees.
Leary, Patrick (LAV) Executive Director.
Leatham, Gerald '65 (LUB) Brownfield, TX St. Anthony's.
Leavey, Thomas G. '51 (RVC) Seaford, NY St. William, the Abbot Retired.
Leavins, Brice *o.f.m.* '69 (BO)[AA] Boston, MA St. Anthony Shrine; [N] Providence, RI St. Francis Chapel & City Ministry Center; [P] Providence, RI St. Francis Friary.
Leavitt, Robert F. *s.s.* '68 (BAL).
Leavitt, Robert F. *s.s.* '68 (HRT)[A] On Duty Outside the Archdiocese.
Lebanowski, Gerald *m.s.* '59 (MIL)[O] Twin Lakes, WI La Salette Missionaries Shrine.
Lebar, Ivan M. *t.o.r.* '58 (WH) Keyser, WV Assumption.
LeBar, James J. '62 (NY) Hyde Park, NY Regina Coeli; Poughkeepsie, NY Hudson River Psychiatric Center.
Lebdowicz, Jan Krzystof '80 (NEW) Plainfield, NJ St. Bernard's; Plainfield, NJ St. Stanislaus Kostka.
LeBeau, Cyril A. '48 (WOR) Retired.
LeBeau, Philip A. (PAT) Spiritual Advisors.
Le Beau, Philip '93 (PAT) West Milford, NJ St. Joseph.
Lebel, Charles E. *m.afr.* '39 (SP)[O] St. Petersburg, FL Missionaries of Africa.
Lebel, Maurice T. '67 (PRT) Retired.
Lebiedz, Bernard *o.s.b.* '59 (SFE)[K] Pecos, NM Our Lady of Guadalupe Olivetan Benedictine Abbey.
Lebiedz, Bernard *o.s.b.* '59 (SFE)[I] Pecos, NM Our Lady of Guadalupe Abbey.
LeBlanc, Charles R. '79 (NOR) East Hampton, CT St. Patrick; Part Time; District Moderators.
LeBlanc, Charles (NOR) Board of Education.
LeBlanc, Clyde H. '75 (ATL)[M] Atlanta, GA Ignatius House.
LeBlanc, David E. '61 (GR) Caledonia, MI Holy Family.
LeBlanc, Etienne '71 (HT) Dulac, LA Holy Family.
LeBlanc, Etienne '71 (HT) Theriot, LA St. Eloi.
LeBlanc, Etienne (HT) Worship.
LeBlanc, Etienne (HT) Continuing Education of the Clergy–Ministry to Priests Program.
LeBlanc, Gregory S. (DOD) Diocesan School Council.
LeBlanc, Gregory '94 (DOD) Ness City, KS Sacred Heart.
LeBlanc, Gregory '94 (DOD) Ransom, KS St. Aloysius.
LeBlanc, Gregory (DOD) Priestly Life and Ministry.
LeBlanc, Harold E. '61 (BO) Woburn, MA St. Joseph.
Le Blanc, James L. '96 (CHR) Aiken, SC St. Mary, Help of Christians.
LeBlanc, James L. (CHR) Diocesan Curia; Family Life Services.
LeBlanc, James (CHR) Defenders of the Bond.
LeBlanc, Keith P. '97 (BO) Haverhill, MA St. John the Baptist.
Le Blanc, Kenneth A. '76 (BO) Newton, MA Mary Immaculate of Lourdes.
LeBlanc, Leo A. '74 (MAN) Merrimack, NH Our Lady of Mercy.
LeBlanc, Leo *o.m.i.* '67 (SFD) Pacoima, CA Mary Immaculate.
LeBlanc, Leo–Paul J. '79 (WOR) Southbridge, MA Notre Dame.
LeBlanc, Omer *c.j.m.* '61 (SD) El Cajon, CA Our Lady of Grace.
LeBlanc, Paul J. (NY) Bronx, NY St. Joan of Arc.
LeBlanc, Steven C. '77 (LAF) New Iberia, LA Sacred Heart of Jesus.
LeBleu, V. Wayne '95 (LKC) Lake Charles, LA Christ the King; Relief Services Catholic.
LeBleu, Wayne (LKC) Priest's Senate.
LeBoeuf, Gerard '93 (DET) Sterling Heights, MI St. Jane Frances de Chantal; Presbyteral Council.
Leboroni–Pierozzi, Gilberto '63 (BAL) Baltimore, MD Our Lady of Pompei.
Lebrun, Raymond A. *o.m.i.* '68 (WDC)[Q] Washington, DC Basilica of the National Shrine of the Immaculate Conception.
Lebrun, Raymond *o.m.i.* '68 (WDC)[M] Washington, DC Oblate Community.
LeCaptain, Douglas '93 (GB) Green Bay, WI St. Francis Xavier Cathedral; Green Bay, WI St. John.
LeCaptain, Douglas (GB) Vocations.
LeCaptain, Douglas (GB) Serra Clubs.
Lech, Ferdinand F. '48 (PIT) Retired.
Lech, Waclaw L. *o.c.d.* '74 (GRY) Chicago, IL St. Camillus; [I] Munster, IN Discalced Carmelite Fathers Monastery.
Lechiara, Francis J. '59 (PMB) Palm Beach, FL St. Edward.
Lechiara, Francis (PMB) Presbyteral Council.
Lechiara, Francis (PMB) College of Consultors.
Lechnar, William J. '97 (GBG) Mount Pleasant, PA Visitation of the Blessed Virgin Mary; Office of Pastoral Life and Planning.
Lechner, Peter *s.p.* '30 (STL)[S] Dittmer, MO Vianney Renewal Center.
Lechner, Peter *s.p.* '68 (STL)[O] St. Louis, MO Servants of the Paraclete.
Lechner, Peter *s.p.* '68 (SFE)[M] Jemez Springs, NM Fitzgerald Charitable Trust.
Lechner, Roger A. '66 (SD) San Diego, CA Holy Spirit.
Lechner, Roger (SD) Presbyteral Council.
Lechtenberg, Edward W. '51 (DUB) Retired.
Leckie, Michael J. '76 (PRO) Hope Valley, RI St. Joseph.
LeClair, Lawrence J. '53 (HRT) Retired.
LeClaire, H. Fred *c.m.f.* '87 (SAT) Chino Valley, AZ St. Catherine Laboure.
LeClaire, Karl *s.d.s.* '86 (MIL)[O] Richmond, VA.
Leclerc, Gerard P. '60 (BUR) Vergennes, VT St. Peter.
Leclerc, Leo A. '61 (SPR) Chicopee, MA St. Rose de Lima; Vicar General; Bishop's Commission for Clergy; Diocesan Consultors; Massachusetts Catholic Conference.
Leclerc, Leo (SPR) Presbyteral Council.

Leclerc, Thomas L. *m.s.* '80 (BO) Cambridge, MA St. John the Evangelist.
Leclercq, Duane '64 (PEO) Granville, IL Sacred Heart Of Jesus; Granville, IL St. Patrick's.
LeCompte, Glenn David '86 (HT) On Duty Outside the Diocese.
LeCours, Sylva P. '47 (NOR)[A] Ballouville, CT St. Anne.
Lecuivre, Joel A. '72 (PRO) Pawtucket, RI St. John the Baptist; Vicar for Judicial Matters; Judicial Vicar; Secretary; Council Members.
Lecumberri, Rufino '54 (NY) Bronx, NY St. Joseph.
Leddy, Leonard '59 (AUS) Retired.
Ledermann, Paul F. '63 (OG) On Duty Outside the Diocese; Veterans Administration Home.
Ledesma, Alberto '97 (LA) Camarillo, CA St. Mary Magdalen.
Ledesma, John Ceferino *s.d.b.* '79 (WDC) Washington, DC St. Stephen Martyr.
Ledesma, Jose Salvador '99 (STO) Stockton, CA St. Gertrude Church (Pastor of).
Ledet, Donald '63 (HT) Retired.
Ledford, John S. '75 (WH) Stonewood, WV Our Lady of Perpetual Help; Interdiocesan Judges.
Ledour, Michael Dominic W. *o.f.m.* '86 (ALB)[A] Catskill, NY St. Anthony Friary.
Ledoux, Albert H. '71 (ALT) On Duty Outside the Diocese.
Ledoux, Albert H. '87 (ALT).
LeDoux, Jerome *s.v.d.* '57 (NO)[A] New Orleans, LA St. Augustine.
LeDoux, Louis V. '58 (LAF)[T] San Antonio, TX Our Lady of Czestochowa.
Ledoux, Louis Vernon '52 (LAF) Retired.
Ledoux, Mark '99 (LAF) Krotz Springs, LA St. Anthony.
Ledoux, Mark (LAF) Advocates.
Ledoux, William J. '93 (PRO) Pawtucket, RI St. Mary of the Immaculate Conception.
LeDuc, Roger D. '60 (FR) Retired.
Leduff–Gutierrez, Larry *s.s.j.* '85 (BEA) Port Arthur, TX Sacred Heart.
Ledwidge, Brendan '55 (LAN) Retired.
Ledwith, Harry '74 (TUC) Tucson, AZ St. Pius X.
Ledwon, Jacob C. '72 (BUF) Ecumenism; Council of Priests; [R] Buffalo, NY State University of New York at Buffalo (Main St. South Campus); Buffalo, NY St. Joseph–University.
Ledwon, Josaphat *o.f.m.* '56 (GB).
Lee, Anthony '41 (SFR) Retired.
Lee, Anthony '41 (SFR)[K] San Francisco, CA Home for the Aged of the Little Sisters of the Poor.
Lee, Anthony '93 (PEO)[B] Danville, IL Schlarman High School.
Lee, Anthony '97 (LA) Graduate Studies.
Lee, Anthony (FTW)[A] Notre Dame, IN Moreau Seminary.
Lee, Bernard *s.m.* '67 (SAT)[C] San Antonio, TX St. Mary's University of San Antonio, Texas.
Lee, Bernard *s.m.* '67 (SAT)[M] San Antonio, TX Woodlawn Marianist Community.
Lee, Bernard *s.d.b.* '79 (SP) Tampa, FL Good Shepherd; [E] Tampa, FL Mary Help of Christians School.
Lee, Chae–uk Jonan *s.j.* '02 (BAL)[S] Baltimore, MD Jesuit Community of Loyola College, Inc..
Lee, Chde–uk Johan *s.j.* '02 (BAL)[B] Timonium, MD Loyola Graduate Center –Timonium Campus.
Lee, Chong Hyo '67 (CAM) Cherry Hill, NJ St. Yi Yun Il John Korean Catholic Mission.
Lee, David M. '68 (BUF)[A] Buffalo, NY St. Ambrose.
Lee, David Seungyoon '98 (NEW) On Duty Outside the Archdiocese.
Lee, Dominic Savio '94 (SFR) San Francisco, CA St. Finn Barr.
Lee, Edward (NOR) Absent on Leave.
Lee, Felix Hyo–UN (FWT) Hurst, TX Korean Martyrs Catholic Church.
Lee, Gabriel '97 (BRK) Long Island City, NY St. Raphael.
Lee, Gerard *o.f.m.* '71 (ALB)[B] Siena College; [R] Albany, NY St. Francis Chapel.
Lee, Henry H. '54 (LC) Retired.
Lee, Howard T. '54 (FRS) Retired.
Lee, James '75 (SEA) Olympia, WA St. Michael.
Lee, James (SEA) Deans.
Lee, James (SEA) Presbyteral Council.
Lee, Jeffrey E. '92 (TR) Trenton, NJ St. Joachim; Ecumenical/Interreligious Affairs; Office of Family Life/Respect Life.
Lee, John Michael *c.p.* '72 (WH) Kingwood, WV St. Sebastian's; Kingwood, WV St. Zita's.
Lee, John R. *c.s.b.* '56 (ROC)[I] Rochester, NY Basilian Residence.
Lee, John T.M. (WDC) Navy Chaplains.
Lee, Jong–Hyun '94 (COL) Gahanna, OH Korean Catholic Community.
Lee, Joseph (Richard) '72 (PHU)[E] Washington, DC Monastery of the Holy Cross.
Lee, Joseph C. '91 (DAL) Dallas, TX St. Andrew Kim.
Lee, Joseph P. '57 (LA) On Sick Leave.
Lee, Joseph '55 (CHI) Retired.
Lee, Josephus Hee Jung (SAC) Sacramento, CA St. Jeong–Hae Elizabeth.
Lee, Joshua Peter '89 (LA) Pico Rivera, CA St. Hilary.
Lee, Keun–Soo '95 (BR) Labadieville, LA St. Philomena.
Lee, Lawrence '49 (GAL)[N] Houston, TX Pope John Paul XXIII Priests' Residence Retired.
Lee, Lawrence '49 (GAL) Retired.
Lee, Matthew Seung Young (KCK) Special Assignment.
Lee, Matthew '93 (WDC) Military Chaplains.
Lee, Michael C. *s.j.* '96 (NY)[EE] New York, NY Xavier Jesuit Community.
Lee, Michael G. '64 (WH) Absent on Sick Leave.
Lee, Michael J. *o.praem.* '70 (PH) Philadelphia, PA St. Gabriel; [AA] Paoli, PA Daylesford Abbey.
Lee, Michael (SLC) Milford, UT St. Bridget; Monroe, UT St. Elizabeth's; [H] Ephraim, UT St. Jude Catholic Center; Finance Council; Pastoral Operations.
Lee, Patrick J. '76 (CHI) Chicago, IL Immaculate Conception of the Blessed Virgin Mary; Chicago, IL St. Joseph.
Lee, Patrick J. *s.j.* '78 (P)[A] Portland, OR Jesuit Novitiate of St. Francis Xavier.
Lee, Paul D. '83 (WDC) Pastoral Center Special Ministries; Advocates.
Lee, Paul S. '90 (PH) Philadelphia, PA Holy Angels.
Lee, Paul '83 (WDC) Washington, DC Our Lady of Victory.
Lee, Paul '99 (NEW) Fort Lee, NJ Holy Trinity.
Lee, Paul (WDC) Office for Ecumenical and Interreligious Affairs.
Lee, R. Anthony '93 (PEO) Hoopeston, IL St. Anthony's.
Lee, Robert E. *o.carm.* '55 (JOL)[L] Darien, IL Carmelite Community.
Lee, Robert E. '55 (PRT) Retired.
Lee, Robert E. '59 (PEO) Retired.
Lee, Roy '86 (MIL) Personal Leave.
Lee, S. David (NEW)[B] School of Diplomacy and Intl. Rels..
Lee, Sang Yil (AUS) Killeen, TX St. Joseph; Army Reserve Chaplains.
Lee, Seong K. '72 (TR) Lawrenceville, NJ The Church of the Korean Martyrs.
Lee, Simon Sang–il *s.j.* '78 (CHI) Highland Park, IL Immaculate Conception.
Lee, Sung–Kook (PH) Korean Apostolate.
Lee, Terrence J. *m.h.m.* '57 (NY) Bronx, NY St. Margaret of Cortona.
Lee, Thaddeus (PAT) Retired.
Lee, Thomas M. '53 (PRT) Special or Other Diocesan Assignment.
Lee, William J. *s.s.* '46 (BAL)[O] Baltimore, MD St. Charles Villa.
Lee, William '62 (HON) On Duty Outside the Diocese.
Lee, Yong Huyk '01 (GAL) Houston, TX St. Paul.
Leeber, Victor F. *s.j.* '53 (BO)[V] Weston, MA Campion Health Center, Inc..
Leech, George T. '56 (PIT) Retired.
Leedale, Walter F. *s.j.* '59 (SPK)[B] Spokane, WA Gonzaga University.
Leek, Michael *o.s.b.* '93 (SFE)[I] Pecos, NM Our Lady of Guadalupe Abbey.
Leek, Michael *o.s.b.* '93 (SFE)[K] Pecos, NM Our Lady of Guadalupe Olivetan Benedictine Abbey.
Leeuw, Daniel R. '57 (FTW) Veterans Administration Hospital.
Leeuw, Daniel '57 (FTW)[G] Avilla, IN Provena Sacred Heart Home.
Leeuw, Daniel '57 (FTW)[G] Avilla, IN Provena La-Verna Terrace.
Lefebure, Leo D. '78 (CHI) Other Assignments; Yonkers, NY Christ the King.
Lefebvre, Gerald M. '56 (BR) Judges Retired.
Lefebvre, James '59 (ALB) Albany, NY St. Mary.
LeFebvre, James (ALB) Diocesan Board of Consultors.
LeFebvre, James (ALB) Presbyteral Council.
LeFebvre, James (ALB) Advocates; Priests Retirement Board.
Lefebvre, Leo P. '55 (MAN)[J] Manchester, NH St. Teresa Heathcare Center Retired.
Lefebvre, Robert R. *m.m.* '57 (NY).
Le Fevre, Francis J. '71 (BAL)[EE] Absent on Leave.
LeFevre, Michael '82 (DET) Detroit, MI Cathedral, Church of the Most Blessed Sacrament; Judges.
LeFevre, Robert J. '66 (ALB) Saratoga Springs, NY St. Peter.
Leffler, Richard J. '78 (MAD) Potosi, WI SS. Andrew and Thomas.
Lefler, John '57 (EVN) Retired.
LeFleur, R. Keith '61 (SAG) Sandusky, MI St. Joseph.
Lefor, Jason '99 (FAR) Cavalier, ND St. Anthony.
Lefor, Jason '99 (FAR) Cavalier, ND St. Bridget.
Lefor, Jason (FAR) Cavalier, ND SS. Nereus and Achilleus.
LeFort, David R. '98 (ALB) Fort Ann, NY St. Ann; Whitehall, NY Our Lady of Hope.
LeFort, David (ALB) Ongoing Formation and Continuing Education for Priests.
LeFrois, Christian *o.s.b* '46 (SAV)[H] Latrobe, PA Saint Vincent Archabbey.
LeFrois, Marvin J. '49 (SAV) Retired.
LeFrois, Marvin '49 (SAV) Valdosta, GA St. John the Evangelist.
Legarra, Francisco J. *o.a.r.* '74 (NEW) Union City, NJ Holy Family; Bronx, NY St. Anselm.
Legarra, Francisco *o.a.r.* '74 (NY)[N] Union City, NJ Augustinian Recollects, St. Nicholas of Tolentine Monastery; [EE] New York, NY Augustinian Recollects Provincial Residence, Province of St. Nicholas of Tolentine.
Legarreta, Felipe '93 (JOL) Bloomingdale, IL St. Isidore.
Legarski, Anthony J. '83 (ALT) Beaverdale, PA Holy Spirit.
Legaspi, Alex L. '76 (SFR) Daly City, CA St. Andrew; Navy Reserve Chaplains.
Legaspi, Dennis '93 (SB) Arrowhead Regional Medical Center.
Legaspi, Dennis (SB) Colton, CA Our Lady of the Immaculate Conception.
Legault, Michel *m.s.a.* '71 (NOR)[A] Cromwell, CT Holy Apostles College and Seminary.
Legendre, Francis J. '61 (HT) Cut–Off, LA Sacred Heart.
Legendre, Francis (HT) Vicar for Priests.
Leger, Austin (LAF) Notaries.
Leger, Donald '68 (LAF) Breaux Bridge, LA St. Bernard.
Leger, G. Robert '71 (SJ) Sunnyvale, CA Church of The Resurrection.
Leger, Jeffrey P. '97 (L) Campbellsville, KY Our Lady of Perpetual Help; Campbellsville, KY Our Lady of the Hills; Campbellsville, KY Holy Redeemer.
Leger, Laurie L. *m.s.* '54 (WOR) Fitchburg, MA St. Joseph's.
Leger, P. Austin '62 (LAF) St. Martinville, LA St. Martin of Tours.
Legere, Germain *c.p.* '42 (L)[J] Louisville, KY Nazareth Home.
Legere, Germain *c.p.* '42 (L)[K] Louisville, KY Sacred Heart Retreat.
Legerski, John '81 (B) On Duty Outside the Diocese.
Legerski, John '81 (P)[D] Eugene, OR Marist High School.
Lego, William E. *o.s.a.* '83 (CHI) Chicago, IL St. Rita of Cascia; [N] Olympia Fields, IL The Augustinians–Provincialate.
Lehane, Joseph E. '77 (CLV) Parma, OH St. Columbkille.
Leheny, Bernard M. '66 (LA) Norwalk, CA St. John of God.
Leheny, Bernard (LA) San Pedro Pastoral Region; Ex Officios.
Lehman, Joseph P. '80 (RIC) Roanoke, VA Our Lady of Nazareth.
Lehman, Joseph *t.o.r.* '96 (WDC)[M] Washington, DC St. Louis Friary.
Lehman, Paul J. '54 (NEW) Couples for Christ; Secretaries Retired.
Lehmkuhl, Gerhardt B. *s.j.* '74 (STL)[O] St. Louis, MO Jesuit Community Corporation at St. Louis University – Jesuit Hall.
Lehmkuhl, John J. '45 (TOL) Retired.
Lehner, John *o.s.f.s.* '70 (TOL)[C] Toledo, OH St. Francis de Sales High School; [J] Toledo, OH.
Lehnerd, Frank M. '58 (Y) Youngstown, OH St. Edward.
Lehnert, Brian '00 (PMB) Boca Raton, FL Ascension.
Lehning, Thomas J. '70 (ARL) Manassas, VA Sacred Heart; Defenders of the Bond.
Lehocky, Leigh A. '68 (CHR) Columbia, SC St. Peter's; Diocesan Curia; College of Consultors; Deans; Presbyteral Council.
Lehr, James W. *m.m.* '53 (NY)[EE] Maryknoll Maryknoll Fathers and Brothers.
Lehr, Theodore F. *o.f.m.* '56 (NEW) Elmwood Park, NJ St. Leo's.
Lehrberger, James *o.cist.* '76 (DAL)[B] University of Dallas; [K] Irving, TX Cistercian Abbey of Our Lady of Dallas.
Leibenguth, Gerald T. *o.s.b.* '72 (BO)[V] Hingham, MA Glastonbury Abbey.
Leibham, David '87 (AUS) Waco, TX St. Louis.
Leibham, David (AUS) Presbyteral Council.
Leibold, Alcuin *o.s.b.* '56 (IND)[K] St. Meinrad, IN St. Meinrad Archabbey.
Leibold, James C. '80 (BRK) Military Chaplains.
Leibrecht, Robert G. '58 (STL) New Haven, MO Holy Family.
Leidich, Kevin A. *s.j.* '82 (SAC)[D] Sacramento, CA Jesuit High School.
Leidich, Kevin *s.j.* '82 (SAC)[I] Carmichael, CA Jesuit High School Community of Sacramento.
Leies, John A. *s.m.* '56 (SAT)[C] San Antonio, TX St. Mary's University of San Antonio, Texas; [M] San Antonio, TX Marianist Residence; Catholic Physicians Guild.
Leif, Gregory P. '78 (WIN) Adams, MN Sacred Heart; Deans; Bishop's Council.
Leif, Gregory P. (WIN) Auditors.
Leifeld, Antony J. '38 (NU) New Ulm, MN Cathedral of The Holy Trinity Retired.

Leigh, David J. *s.j.* '68 (SEA)[A] Seattle, WA Seattle University.
Leigh, Peter '85 (WCH)[D] Wichita, KS St. Francis Campus.
Leigh, Peter (STN) On Duty Outside the Diocese.
Leigh, Peter (STN) Minneapolis.
Leighton, Donald E. '62 (PH) Gladwyne, PA St. John Baptist Vianney; Narberth, PA St. Justin Martyr.
Leiker, Perry D. '76 (LA) Hawthorne, CA St. Joseph.
Leikhim, Joel J. *o.s.b.* '61 (PAT)[M] Morristown, NJ St. Mary's Abbey.
Leiman, Elias S. (OLL) Procurator/Advocate.
Lein, Lambert *s.v.d.* (LAF) Broussard, LA St. Joseph.
Leinen, Ronald *m.s.c.* '57 (RCK)[G] Aurora, IL Missionaries of the Sacred Heart Community.
Leininger, Charles A. *s.j.* '53 (DAL)[D] Dallas, TX Jesuit College Preparatory School.
Leininger, Donald '58 (SP) Retired.
Leininger, Joseph B. *s.j.* '53 (GAL)[F] Houston, TX Strake, Jesuit College Preparatory Inc..
Leininger, William '56 (SJ) Retired.
Leiphon, Donald A. '68 (FAR) Napoleon, ND St. Clare of Assisi; Kintyre, ND St. Boniface; Liaison with Charismatic Movement.
Leiphon, Donald '68 (FAR) Napoleon, ND St. Philip Neri.
Leise, Gerald A. '74 (OM) Schuyler, NE St. Mary; Deans; Deans.
Leise, Gerald A. '74 (OM) Schuyler, NE St. Augustine.
Leise, Leo *s.j.* '94 (MIA) Miami, FL Gesu.
Leisen, Leo '54 (SCL) Roscoe, MN St. Margaret's.
Leisen, Leo '54 (SCL) Roscoe, MN St. Michael's.
Leisen, Leo '54 (SCL) Roscoe, MN St. Agnes.
Leisen, Richard '56 (SCL) Paynesville, MN St. Louis.
Leisen, Richard (SCL) Diocesan Priests Pension Plan Trustees.
Leising, Frederick D. '71 (BUF) Williamsville, NY Nativity of the Blessed Virgin Mary.
Leising, John J. '69 (BUF) Council of Priests; Wilson, NY Our Lady of the Rosary; Newfane, NY St. Bridget.
Leising, Robert *o.m.i.* '90 (NY)[GG] Newburgh, NY Our Lady of Hope Center.
Leising, Robert *o.m.i.* '90 (CR) Waubun, MN St. Francis Cabrini; Naytahwaush, MN St. Anne; Waubun, MN St. Ann.
Leisy, Christian *o.s.b.* '88 (SFE)[I] Abiquiu, NM Monastery of Christ in the Desert.
Leitem, Leon *o.f.m.cap.* '57 (PIT) Pittsburgh, PA Our Lady of the Angels.
Leith, James A. '81 (FAR) Absent on Leave; Defensor Vinculi.
Leiting, Robert L. '67 (SC) Retired.
Leitner, John E. '55 (KC) Independence, MO St. Joseph the Worker.
Leitner, Thomas Aquinas *o.s.b.* '92 (OM)[K] Schuyler, NE Benedictine Mission House; Religious Orders.
Leiweke, Robert W. *s.j.* '58 (MIL)[O] Milwaukee, WI Jesuit Community at Marquette University.
Le Jacq, Peter M. *m.m.* '87 (NY)[EE] Maryknoll Maryknoll Fathers and Brothers.
LeJeune, Ronald J. '71 (TOL) Bucyrus, OH Holy Trinity.
Leke, Charles '82 (SP) Inverness, FL Our Lady of Fatima.
Leketas, Peter J. '43 (LC) Retired.
Leland, Thomas '99 (WCH) Lyons, KS St. Paul.
Leland, Thomas '99 (WCH) Lyons, KS Holy Trinity.
Leliaert, Richard M. *o.s.c.* '67 (DET)[K] Riverview, MI Crosier Community of Riverview; Riverview, MI St. Cyprian.
Lelii, Raymond M. *s.j.* '61 (WDC)[E] Washington, DC Gonzaga College High School.
Lelo–Luemba, Albert *c.i.c.m.* '96 (BWN) San Benito, TX St. Ignatius.
Leloczky, Julius *o.cist.* '61 (DAL)[K] Irving, TX Cistercian Abbey of Our Lady of Dallas.
LeLonde, Venant *o.f.m.* '54 (NY) New York, NY St. Agnes.
Lelonis, Richard M. (PIT) Judges; Matrimonial Concerns, Office for; Matrimonial Concerns, Office for.
Lelonis, Richard '71 (PIT)[O] Pittsburgh, PA Mount Assisi Convent.
Lemaine, Calonge '89 (BRK) Cambria Heights, NY Sacred Heart.
Lemanski, William E. *s.a.c.* '74 (MIL)[O] Milwaukee, WI Pallotti House.
Lemaster, Scott '85 (DAV) Albia, IA St. Patrick's.
Lemaster, Scott '85 (DAV) Melrose, IA St. Patrick's.
Lemaster, Scott '85 (DAV) Lovilia, IA St. Peter's.
Lemay, Donald H. '89 (RIC) Richmond, VA St. Edward The Confessor.
LeMay, Donald *o.s.b.* '57 (SCL)[I] Collegeville, MN St. John's Abbey, of the Order of St. Benedict.
Lemay, Jean '75 (MAN) Manchester, NH Transfiguration.
LeMay, John M. *o.s.m.* '84 (CHI)[N] Chicago Order of Friar Servants of Mary (Servites) United States of America Province, Inc..
Lemay, Larry '99 (BEL) West Frankfort, IL St. John the Baptist; Royalton, IL St. Aloysius/Sacred Heart.
Lembo, Richard A. '75 (PRT) Bucksport, ME St. Vincent de Paul.
Lembo, Richard '75 (PRT)[M] Castine, ME Maine Maritime Academy.
Lembo, Richard '75 (PRT) Stonington, ME St. Mary Star of the Sea.
Lembo, Richard (PRT) Pastoral Assocs..
Le Mieux, Thomas A. '59 (MIL) Retired.
Lemieux, Thomas (MIL) Milwaukee, WI St. Mary Magdalen; Milwaukee, WI St. Adalbert.
Lemire, Paul W. '89 (WOR) Members; Auburn, MA St. Joseph's.
Lemke, Norbert J. *s.j.* '44 (MIL)[O] Wauwatosa, WI Jesuit Community at St. Camillus.
Lemkuhl, David A. '79 (CIN) On Duty Outside the Archdiocese.
Lemkuhl, David E. '79 (CIN) On Special and Archdiocesan Assignment.
Lemlin, Timothy J. '78 (PRO) Mapleville, RI Our Lady of Good Help.
Lemm, Eugene '57 (SCL) Brandon, MN Church of St. Ann.
Lemm, Eugene '57 (SCL) Brandon, MN Seven Dolors.
Lemme, Christopher *t.o.r.* '98 (ARL) Luray, VA Our Lady of the Valley.
Lemmens, Heinrich J. *c.s.sp.* '34 (PIT)[P] Bethel Park, PA Holy Spirit Animation Center.
Lemmert, Ronald D. '51 (NY)[II] Peekskill, NY My Father's House, Inc..
Lemmert, Ronald J. '79 (NY) Sing Sing Correctional Facility.
Lemming, Patrick W. '81 (MOB) On Leave from the Archdiocese.
Lemoi, Paul R. '75 (PRO) West Warwick, RI Our Lady of Good Counsel.
Lemoine, Russell J. '70 (ALX) College of Consultors; Priests Council; Hessmer, LA St. Martin of Tours.
Lemoine, Vincent P. '51 (SAL) Retired.
Lemon, Clement P. '64 (WIL) Wilmington, DE Immaculate Heart of Mary; Vicar for Priests; College of Consultors.
Lemos, Thomas *c.s.c.* '74 (COS) Colorado Springs, CO Sacred Heart.
Lemoyne, William '49 (ALB) Retired.
Lemp, Joseph R. '56 (PIT) Koppel, PA Queen of Heaven; Judges; Priest Council; College of Consultors.
Lemus, Francisco Arrivillaga *o.s.b.* '95 (SFS)[F] Marvin, SD Blue Cloud Abbey.
Lemus, Fredy Lozada '92 (LR) Springdale, AR St. Raphael's.
Lemus, Raul '02 (SR) Healdsburg, CA St. John the Baptist.
Lemus, Raul (SR) Cursillos De Cristiandad.
Lenaghan, J. Jordan *o.p.* '95 (COL) Columbus, OH St. Patrick.
Lenahan, John B. '49 (L) Retired.
Lenane, William '50 (SJ) Retired.
Lenane, William '50 (SJ) Palo Alto, CA St. Thomas Aquinas.
Lencewicz, Leonard *o.f.m.* '63 (NY)[EE] Tampa, FL St. Anthony Hermitage.
Lendacky, Francis G. '61 (PH) Philadelphia, PA St. Agnes–St. John Nepomucene; Legion of Mary.
Lendvai, John B. '94 (PIT) Bentleyville, PA Ave Maria.
Lenehan, Claude *o.f.m.* '55 (NEW)[N] Hohokus, NJ St. Anthony of Padua.
Lenehan, Vincent '54 (SAC) Retired.
Lengerich, Vincent L. '48 (GRY) Second Instance Retired.
Lengerich, Vincent '48 (Gary)[B] Carthagena, OH St. Charles.
Lengwin, Ronald P. '66 (PIT) Pittsburgh, PA St. Mary of Mercy; Clergy Personnel Board; Ecumenical and Interfaith Commission; Mission Office; Pilgrimage Office; Public and Community Affairs, Office for; Society for the Propagation of the Faith.
Lenihan, Daniel F. *o.c.s.o.* '55 (DUB)[K] Peosta, IA New Melleray Abbey, Order of Cistercians of the Strict Observance.
Lenihan, John J. '53 (STA) Retired.
Lenihan, Michael '52 (LA) Redondo Beach, CA St. Lawrence Martyr.
Lenihan, Michael '52 (LA) Retired.
Lenihan, Michael (CC) AUXILIARY CHAPLAINS CONTRACT CHAPLAINS.
Lenihan, Michael (CC) Aransas Pass, TX St. Mary, Star of the Sea.
Lenk, Dominic *o.s.b.* '98 (STL)[O] St. Louis, MO The Abbey of St. Mary and St. Louis.
Lenk, Dominic *o.s.b.* '98 (STL)[F] Creve Coeur, MO St. Louis Priory School.
Lennon, Charles '80 (RVC) Absent on Leave.
Lennon, James M. '58 (JOL) Joliet, IL St. Patrick.
Lennon, Joseph L. *o.p.* '47 (PRO)[P] Providence St. Thomas Aquinas Priory at Providence College.
Lennon, Peter F. '55 (NEW)[B] School of Diplomacy and Intl. Rels. Retired.
Lennon, Raymond T. *s.v.d.* '64 (TR)[M] Bordentown, NJ Society of the Divine Word.
Lennon, Robert T. '50 (NEW) Livingston, NJ St. Philomena Retired.
Lennon, Robert *c.ss.r.* (BO) Roxbury, MA Our Lady of Perpetual Help.
Lennon, Sean M. *o.s.m.* '80 (CHI)[N] Chicago Order of Friar Servants of Mary (Servites) United States of America Province, Inc..
Lenoci, Dominick J. '95 (NEW) Glen Rock, NJ St. Catharine; Priestly Vocation Board.
Lenoir, Jean (SB) Retired.
Lenox, Peter F. (BGP) Ridgefield, CT St. Mary.
Lenti, Arthur *s.d.b.* '50 (OAK).
Lenti, Arthur *s.d.b.* '50 (OAK)[N] Berkeley Salesian Community.
Lentine, Peter S. '50 (DET) Detroit, MI St. Philomena.
Lentini, James S. '03 (WIL) Wilmington, DE St. Ann.
Lentz, Gerald J. *s.j.* '60 (SJ).
Lentz, Lawrence *c.s.v.* '81 (LAV)[D] Las Vegas, NV Guardian Angel Cathedral.
Lentz, Robert F. '64 (BAL) Retired.
Lenz, Daniel *o.s.b.* '85 (OM)[C] Elkhorn, NE Mount Michael High School.
Lenz, Daniel *o.s.b.* '85 (OM)[K] Elkhorn, NE Mount Michael Abbey.
Lenz, David *o.f.m.conv.* '86 (IND)[K] Mount St. Francis, IN Provincial Headquarters for the Conventual Franciscan Province.
Lenz, David *o.f.m.conv.* '86 (IND) Clarksville, IN St. Anthony of Padua.
Lenz, David *o.f.m.conv.* '86 (IND)[J] Mount St. Francis, IN Province of Our Lady of Consolation, Inc..
Lenz, Frank B. '94 (VIC) Schulenburg, TX St. Rose of Lima.
Lenz, Frank M. '69 (MAR) Gladstone, MI Holy Family.
Lenz, Frank (VIC) Presbyteral Council.
Lenz, Frank (VIC) Defenders of the Bond.
Lenz, Frank (VIC) Diocesan Consultors.
Lenz, Henry *m.s.* '41 (LKC) Sulphur, LA Our Lady of Prompt Succor.
Lenz, Michael *o.f.m.* '76 (CIN)[N] Pittsburgh, PA Holy Family Friary.
Lenz, Paul A. '49 (ALT) On Duty Outside the Diocese.
Lenzini, Donald J. '51 (BEL) Retired.
Lenzner, George '57 (GB) Retired.
Leo, Arthur R. '85 (NY) Peekskill, NY Assumption.
Leon, Antonio '57 (STA) Jacksonville, FL Immaculate Conception.
Leon, Bartholomew *o.s.b.* '85 (SAM) Spartanburg, SC Jesus Our Risen Savior; Greenville, SC St. Rafka Maronite.
Leon, Francisco *o.s.a.* '78 (GAL) Pasadena, TX St. Juan Diego.
Leon, Hector '91 (BGP) Danbury, CT Our Lady of Guadalupe.
Leon, Jose M. '81 (OAK) Union City, CA Our Lady of the Rosary; Region 5.
Leon, Leopoldo '88 (MIA) Miami, FL St. John Bosco.
Leon–Angulo, Marcos '03 (R) Wilmington, NC St. Mary.
Leonard, Albert P. '89 (SCR) Mansfield, PA Holy Child; Deans.
Leonard, Clyde A. '64 (BO) Senior Priests Retired.
Leonard, Donald '94 (DEN) Boulder, CO Sacred Heart of Jesus.
Leonard, Edwin M. '84 (CLV) Akron, OH Annunciation.
Leonard, Eugene A. '66 (CHR) Retired.
Leonard, Francis B. '50 (BO) Chelmsford, MA St. John the Evangelist; Senior Priests Retired.
Leonard, John E. '65 (RIC) Glen Allen, VA St. Michael.
Leonard, John F. '55 (BO) West Newbury, MA St. Ann.
Leonard, John J. *s.j.* '50 (NY)[F] New York, NY Fordham Preparatory School; [EE] Jesuit Community, Kohlmann Hall.
Leonard, Matthew '98 (CHL) Lenoir, NC St. Francis of Assisi.
Leonard, Michael '91 (CHI) Chicago, IL St. Tarcissus.
Leonard, Patrick J. '63 (NEW) Retired.
Leonard, Paul F. '89 (SCR) Unassigned or Leave of Absence.
Leonard, Peter J. *o.s.f.s.* '86 (ALN)[B] Center Valley, PA DeSales University; [K] Center Valley, PA Oblates of St. Francis de Sales.
Leonard, Sebastian *o.s.b.* '57 (HRT)[E] New Milford, CT Canterbury School.
Leonard, Sebastian *o.s.b.* '57 (IND)[K] New Milford, CT Canterbury School.
Leonard, Thomas P. '56 (NY) New York, NY Holy Trinity; Manhattan (West).
Leonard, William F. '94 (MET) North Charleston, SC St. Thomas The Apostle; [H] Charleston, SC Charleston Southern University; On Duty Outside the Diocese.
Leonard, William P. '43 (DUB) Retired.
Leonard, William T. '69 (BO) Waltham, MA St. Jude; Belmont, MA Fernald Developmental Center.
Leonardis, Charles F. '54 (ALT) Retired.
Leonards, Martin C. '66 (LAF) Duson, LA St. Theresa of the Child Jesus.
Leone, Arthur '56 (NY) New York, NY Our Lady of Good Counsel.
Leone, James M. '60 (BRK) Special Assignment; [U] Apostleship of the Sea.
Leone, Kenneth '67 (DEN) Littleton, CO St. Frances Cabrini Parish.

Leone, Kenneth (DEN) Deaneries.
Leone, Richard D. *o.s.f.s.* '59 (WIL)[J] Wilmington, DE DeSales House.
Leone, William B. '74 (ROC) Rochester, NY St. Anne; Army National Guard Chaplains.
Leong, Herman '02 (OAK) Pittsburg, CA Good Shepherd.
Leon Guerrero, Felixberto C. *o.f.m.cap.* '86 (AGN) Agana, GU Santa Teresita.
Leonhardt, Douglas J. *s.j.* '69 (MIL)[O] Milwaukee, WI Arrupe House Jesuit Community.
Leonhardt, Louis J. '56 (DAV) Hills, IA St. Joseph's; Lone Tree, IA St. Mary's; Nichols, IA St. Mary's.
Leonhardt, Robert A. *o.f.m.* '59 (SHP) Hodge, LA St. Lucy.
Leonhart, Louis J. (DAV).
Leopold, David C. '82 (BGP) Bridgeport, CT St. Ann; Presbyteral Council.
Leopold, Martin '01 (SAT) Gonzales, TX St. James.
Leoz, Maximo *sch.p.* '56 (MIA) Pompano Beach, FL San Isidro.
LePage, Bradley *t.o.r.* '03 (ALT)[A] Loretto, PA St. Francis University; [F] Loretto, PA Mount Assisi Friary; [H] Loretto, PA St. Francis College (Loretto).
Lepak, Roy C. '62 (STP) Special Assignment Retired.
Lepak, Roy (STP)[C] St. Paul, MN University of St. Thomas Retired.
Le Phuc Diem, Simon M. *c.m.c.* '03 (SPC)[E] Carthage, MO Congregation of the Mother Coredemptrix, United States Assumption Province.
Lepleiter, Robert P. '63 (PH) Chalfont, PA St. Jude Retired.
Lepping, George M. *s.m.* '38 (WDC)[M] Washington, DC Marist Center.
Lequin, Thomas '77 (PRT) Bangor, ME St. Mary's.
Lerch, Joseph R. *s.j.* '56 (BAL)[S] Baltimore, MD Jesuit Fathers and Brothers Maryland Provincial Curia.
Lerch, Joseph *s.j.* '49 (BAL).
Leroux, Edward '56 (ALB)[M] Glens Falls, NY St. Mary.
Leroux, Roger *m.s.* '52 (FR)[H] Attleboro, MA La Salette Shrine.
LeRoux, William F. *s.j.* '53 (SEA)[A] Seattle, WA Seattle University.
Lery, Bruce *s.m.* '87 (HON) San Francisco, CA Notre Dame des Victoires.
Lesak, William P. '75 (NEW) Military Chaplains; Navy Chaplains.
Lescher, Raymond C. '63 (JOL) Joliet, IL Sacred Heart.
Lesczynski, James J. '64 (LC) Necedah, WI St. Francis of Assisi.
Leser, William J. *c.b.* '63 (LA) Westlake Village, CA St. Jude.
Leser, William (LA) Judges.
Leshney, Michael F. '73 (CIN) Reading, OH Sts. Peter and Paul.
LeSieur, C. David (LR) Deans.
LeSieur, David *v.f.* '76 (LR) Little Rock, AR Our Lady of the Holy Souls.
LeSieur, David (LR) Minister to Priests.
LeSieur, David (LR) Continuing Education for the Clergy.
Leskovar, Richard J. '68 (ALB) Delmar, NY St. Thomas the Apostle.
Leslaw, Gwarek *s.a.c.* '76 (BUF).
Leslie, Patrick J. *s.a.c.* '69 (SR)[A] On Duty Outside the Diocese; Santa Rosa, CA Star of the Valley; Sonoma Developmental Center.
Lesniak, David '91 (DET) Port Huron, MI St. Stephen.
Lesniak, Marian '50 (LAN) Retired.
Lesniak, Richard D. '66 (MAD) Markesan, WI St. Mary; Markesan, WI St. Joseph.
Lesnick, John F. '78 (BAL) Special Assignment; [O] Baltimore, MD St. Martin's Home for Aged, Little Sisters of the Poor.
Lesniewski, Stephen F. '93 (CHI) Chicago, IL SS. Peter and Paul.
Lesniowski, Francis A. '63 (GBG) Connellsville, PA St. Rita.
Lesniowski, Stanley '70 (PAT) Passaic, NJ Holy Rosary.
Lesousky, John *c.r.* '56 (L)[K] Louisville, KY Villa Pacis, Resurrectionist Retirement Home.
Lessard, Eugene R. '59 (PRO) Central Falls, RI The Holy Spirit Catholic Community.
Lessard, Gerard *o.p.* '84 (NEW) Sacred Heart Priory; Youngstown, OH St. Dominic.
Lessard, Leo '60 (GB) Retired.
Lessard–Thibodeau, John G. '92 (SPR) Holyoke, MA Our Lady of Guadalupe.
Lesseps, Roland J. *s.j.* '65 (NO).
Lester, J. William '45 (FTW)[P] Fort Wayne, IN Cathedral of the Immaculate Conception; [G] Fort Wayne, IN St. Anne Home of the Diocese of Fort Wayne – South Bend, Inc.; Vicar for Retired Clergy; Council of Priests; Retired Clergy Committee Retired.
Lester, John E. '59 (TOL) Retired.
Lester, John J. '62 (NEW) Scotch Plains, NJ St. Bartholomew.
Lester, Thomas '57 (OAK) San Leandro, CA St. Leander Retired.
Lester, William F. *s.j.* '54 (SJ)[M] Los Gatos CA Sacred Heart Jesuit Center.
LeStrange, Gregory C. '82 (SY) Fayetteville, NY Immaculate Conception; Elected.
Letendre, Theodore *f.i.c.* '97 (PRT)[I] Alfred, ME Notre Dame Institute; [I] Notre Dame Spiritual Center.
LeThiez, Alphonse D. '55 (PRO) Retired.
Leto, Nelo A. '54 (DM) Retired.
Letoile, Kenneth R. *o.p.* '74 (CIN) Cincinnati, OH St. Gertrude; M] Cincinnati, OH St. Gertrude Priory.
Letourneau, Larry (SAL) Ellis, KS St. Mary's.
Letourneau, Paul R. '54 (BUF)[O] Tonawanda, NY O'Hara Residence; [T] Buffalo, NY Kolping Catholic Young Men's Association of Buffalo, NY dba Kolping Society of Buffalo Retired.
Lettau, David '53 (Y) Retired.
Letteer, Michael C. '96 (HBG) Trevorton, PA St. Patrick.
Letteer, Michael '96 (HBG) Coal Township, PA Our Lady of Hope.
Lettic, Edward P. '73 (WOR) Lancaster, MA Immaculate Conception.
Lettre, Raymond '88 (SP) Retired.
LeTure, Theodore J. '49 (RVC) Valley Stream, NY Holy Name of Mary Retired.
Leu, James E. '71 (DAV) Absent on Leave.
Leurck, Raymond J. '67 (CIN) Retired.
Leute, Charles J. *o.p.* '69 (FAR) Fort Totten, ND Seven Dolors; Tokio, ND Christ the King; Fort Totten Reservation, ND Seven Dolors Indian Mission.
Leute, Charles *o.p.* '69 (FAR) Fort Totten, ND St. Jerome; Fort Totten, ND Christ the King.
Leva, Stephen F. '88 (ARL) Leesburg, VA St. John the Apostle.
Levan, Donald E.. '89 (BUF) Absent on Leave.
Levandusky Edward '65 (PHU) Simpson, PA SS. Peter and Paul.
Levario, Gilbert *o.c.d.* '83 (TUC) Tucson, AZ Santa Cruz.
LeVasseur, Angelo B. '83 (PRT) Richmond, ME St. Ambrose; Sabattus, ME Our Lady of the Rosary.
LeVasseur, Giles *o.s.b.* '84 (WDC)[M] Washington, DC St. Anselm's Abbey.
Le Vasseur, Giles *o.s.b.* '84 (WH) Morgantown, WV St. Luke.
LeVasseur, Lawrence A. *c.s.c.* '51 (SAT)[B] San Antonio, TX Congregation of Holy Cross – Formation Community; [M] San Antonio, TX Bro. Charles Andersen Residence.
LeVay, R. Joseph '50 (SPR) Retired.
Leveille, Andre E. *c.s.c.* '78 (FTW) South Bend, IN St. Therese, Little Flower.
Leveille, Rudolph J. '57 (PRT) Retired.
Leven, Marvin F. (OKL) Charismatic Renewal.
Leven, Marvin '59 (OKL) Special Assignment; [L] Okarche, OK New Leaven Ministries Foundation.
Levenhagen, Robert J. '57 (DUB) Monona IA St. Mary Retired.
Levesque, Edmond R. '55 (FR) New Bedford, MA St. Anthony of Padua's.
Levesque, Gerald A. '64 (PRT) Norway, ME St. Catherine of Sienna.
Levesque, Joseph L. *c.m.* '67 (BUF)[O] Niagara University, NY Vincentian Community at Niagara University; [C] Niagara University, NY Niagara University.
Levesque, Louis *c.j.m.* '50 (SD) San Diego, CA Blessed Sacrament; Cursillo.
Levesque, Robert G. *o.m.i.* '60 (MAN)[K] Colebrook, NH Shrine of Our Lady of Grace.
Levesque, Roger J. '59 (FR) New Bedford, MA St. Joseph–St. Therese.
Levesque, Sylvio E. '46 (SPR) Three Rivers, MA St. Anne's.
Levesque, Sylvio J. '55 (PRT) Retired.
Levi, Anthony I. (LFT) Deans; Members.
Levi, Anthony W. '93 (LFT) Lebanon, IN St. Joseph.
Levis, Robert J. '48 (E)[B] Erie, PA Gannon University Retired.
Levitre, Al (FBK) Presbyteral Council; Consultors.
Levitre, Albert '80 (FBK) Koyukuk, AK St. Patrick.
Levitre, J. Albert (FBK) Apostleship of Prayer; Cursillo Movement.
Levitt, Donald L. '79 (PEO) Moline, IL Christ the King.
Levko, John J. *s.j.* '78 (SCR)[C] Scranton, PA The University of Scranton.
LeVoir, John M. '81 (STP) South St. Paul, MN Holy Trinity; South St. Paul, MN St. Augustine.
LeVoy, Joseph T. '54 (CHI) Retired.
Levri, Fideles *g.h.m.* '67 (OWN) Horse Branch, KY Holy Redeemer; Morgantown, KY Holy Trinity.
Levy, Cyril '53 (GLP) McNary, AZ St. Anthony.
Levy, Michael *o.m.i.* '57 (SAT) San Antonio, TX St. Mary.
Lewandowski, Andrew *o.f.m.* '76 (STL)[O] St. Louis, MO Franciscan Friary of St. Anthony of Padua; [Q] St. Louis, MO Franciscan Sisters of Mary Administration.
Lewandowski, Andrzej *c.r.* '89 (SB)[E] Fontana, CA St. Joseph.
Lewandowski, Bruce A. *c.ss.r.* '94 (FgM).
Lewandowski, David J. '55 (HRT) Southington, CT Immaculate Conception.
Lewandowski, Dennis '85 (JOL) Plainfield, IL St. Francis Xavier.
Lewandowski, Donald *o.s.a.* '69 (JOL) Homer Glen, IL Our Mother of Good Counsel.
Lewandowski, John '96 (FAR) Pisek, ND St. Mark; Pisek, ND St. Joseph; Pisek, ND St. John Nepomucene.
Lewandowski, Leonard A. '77 (PH) Swedesburg, PA Sacred Heart.
Lewandowski, Michael *o.f.m.conv.* '75 (ALT) Davidsville, PA St. Anne.
Lewandowski, Raymond H. '85 (DET) Wyandotte, MI St. Patrick; Presbyteral Council.
Lewandowski, Richard P. '74 (WOR) Fitchburg, MA St. Camillus de Lellis; [R] Worcester, MA Fitchburg State College (Fitchburg).
Lewandowski, Ronald C. '95 (CHI) Wadsworth, IL St. Patrick.
Lewandowski, Theodore V. '98 (RCK) Memominee, IL Nativity of the Blessed Virgin Mary.
Lewandowski, Thomas J. (PIT) Washington, PA Immaculate Conception.
Lewandowski, Tom '00 (PIT)[Q] Washington, PA Washington and Jefferson College (Washington).
Lewans, Sylvester *o.m.i.* '58 (SFD)[A] Godfrey, IL Immaculate Heart of Mary Novitiate.
Lewanski, Gary J. '82 (CHI) Chicago, IL St. Pascal.
Lewczak, Thomas J. '65 (NEW) Elizabeth, NJ St. Hedwig's.
Lewett, George *o.f.m.* '88 (FgM).
Lewinski, Cassian T. *o.p.* '69 (PHX)[E] Riverside, CA St. Vincent Ferrer House.
Lewinski, Ronald J. '72 (CHI) Mundelein, IL St. Mary of the Annunciation.
Lewinski, Stanislaw *o.carm.* '86 (MET) Great Meadows, NJ SS. Peter and Paul.
Lewis, Alaric *o.s.b.* '98 (IND)[K] Collegio Sant' Anselmo; [A] St. Meinrad, IN St. Meinrad School of Theology.
Lewis, Alexander J. '85 (LA) Burbank, CA St. Finbar.
Lewis, Clyde A. '64 (OG) Rouses Point, NY St. Joseph; Rouses Point, NY St. Patrick; Judges.
Lewis, Daniel C. *s.j.* '62 (BO)[E] Dorchester, MA Boston College High School & Jesuit Community.
Lewis, David J. (GB) New London, WI Most Precious Blood.
Lewis, David '90 (CI) St. Anthony's; [C] Tunnuk, Chuuk, FM Vicariate Residence.
Lewis, David (CI) Chuuk.
Lewis, Dennis J. '75 (MIL) Milwaukee, WI St. Michael; Milwaukee, WI St. Rose.
Lewis, Edward J. '92 (GBG) Ford City, PA Christ, Prince of Peace Parish.
Lewis, Edward '84 (SAC) Absent on Leave.
Lewis, Eric A. '69 (LA) La Puente, CA St. Joseph; [J] West Covina, CA Citrus Valley Medical Center, Queen of the Valley Campus.
Lewis, Gerald F. '88 (PAT) Retired.
Lewis, Gerald L. (R) Diocesan Consultors; Diocesan Judges.
Lewis, Gerald *s.v.d.* '52 (GAL)[K] Galveston, TX Chaplain Corps: John Sealy Medical Center, U.T.M.B. Hospital.
Lewis, Gerald *s.v.d.* '53 (GAL) Galveston, TX St. Mary's Cathedral Basilica.
Lewis, Gerald '61 (R) Retired.
Lewis, Gerald '61 (R) Oriental, NC Saint Peter the Fisherman.
Lewis, Gerald (R) Ex Officio.
Lewis, Gerard *o.f.m.* '85 (PAT)[M] Ringwood, NJ Holy Name Friary, Inc..
Lewis, Harry J. '50 (SCR)[N] Dunmore, PA Villa St. Joseph Retired.
Lewis, James V. *s.j.* '69 (CLV)[D] Cleveland, OH St. Ignatius High School.
Lewis, James *o.carm.* '83 (JOL)[L] Darien Carmelite Provincial Office.
Lewis, Lawrence J, *m.m.* '75 (NY)[EE] Maryknoll Maryknoll Fathers and Brothers.
Lewis, Leo T. '60 (STL) Retired.
Lewis, Mark *s.j.* '91 (NO).
Lewis, Ryan '99 (OM)[P] Graduate Studies.
Lewis, Sebastian C. *o.s.b.* '51 (PEO).
Lewis, Sebastian *o.s.b.* '51 (PEO).
Lewis, Walter G. '79 (RIC)[A] Richmond, VA St. Mary.
Lewkiewicz, Richard '68 (BRK) Brooklyn, NY Our Lady of Angels.
Lex, Henry V. '57 (BUF)[O] Buffalo, NY Sheehan Residence for Priests Retired.
Lexa, Robert '70 (GB) Retired.
Ley, Phillip *o.f.m.conv.* '84 (FTW) Angola, IN St. Anthony; Angola, IN St. Mary of the Angels.
Ley, Phillip *o.f.m.conv.* (FTW) Angola; LaGrange.
Ley, Richard J. '71 (ARL) Arlington, VA St. Agnes; Auditors.
Ley, Theodore *s.m.* '71 (LA)[F] Marianist Community.
Leyba, John Paul '02 (DEN) Centennial, CO St. Thomas More.
Leykam, John J. '72 (STL) St. Ann, MO Holy Trinity.
Leykam, John J. (STL) Deaneries/Deans.
Leykam, John (STL) Northwest.

Leykam, Lambert *o.f.m.* '56 (FWT)[H] Crowley, TX St. Francis Village, Inc.; [I] Crowley, TX St. Maximilian Kolbe Friary.
Leyland, Thomas J. '65 (TOL) Perrysburg, OH St. Rose.
Leyrita, Norbert '63 (GR) Retired.
Lezochowski, Walter '59 (DET) Crittendon Hospital.
Li, Francis (CHI) Chicago, IL St. Andrew.
Li, Joseph '91 (OAK) Oakland, CA St. Leo's.
Li, Vincent *o.p.* '97 (WDC)[B] Washington, DC Dominican House of Studies.
Liable, Adrian *o.s.b.* '58 (OM)[K] Elkhorn, NE Mount Michael Abbey.
Libaire, Nathan *o.s.b.* '81 (SCL)[I] Collegeville, MN St. John's Abbey, of the Order of St. Benedict.
Libaire, Nathan *o.s.b.* '81 (SFE) Santa Fe, NM St. John the Baptist.
Libanati, Ciro '93 (SB) San Jacinto, CA St. Anthony.
Libasci, Peter '78 (RVC) Montauk, NY St. Therese of Lisieux.
Libby, Richard '99 (CC)[I] Corpus Christi, TX Search Retreats; Corpus Christi, TX St. Theresa.
Libens, John F. *s.j.* '70 (DET)[K] Temperance, MI.
Libens, John F. *s.j.* '70 (CHI)[C] Chicago, IL Jesuit Community at Loyola University Chicago.
Libera, Angelo '57 (SY) Retired.
Libera, Thomas A. '69 (CHI) Evanston, IL St. Athanasius.
Liberatore, Albert M. '89 (SCR) Diocesan Consultors; Presbyteral Council; Liturgical Commission; Dunmore, PA St. Mary of Mount Carmel.
Liberatore, David D. '60 (CLV) Parma Heights, OH St. John Bosco.
Liberty, Donald *c.ss.r.* '61 (LA) Whittier, CA St. Mary of the Assumption; [Q] Whittier, CA Redemptorists of Whittier.
Liberty, Robert S. '03 (DET) Royal Oak, MI National Shrine of the Little Flower; Presbyteral Council.
Libone, John '80 (DAL) Dallas, TX St. Thomas Aquinas; Assistant Judicial Vicars.
Liboroni–Pierozzi, Gilberto '63 (BAL).
Librandi, Michael A. '78 (RCK)[M] Lena, IL St. Joseph Retired.
Librea, Ralph '56 (OM) Omaha, NE Holy Cross.
Librea, Raphael B. '35 (OM) Retired.
Licanda, Samuel '94 (SFR) San Francisco, CA St. Patrick.
Licari, John J. '02 (PT) Fort Walton Beach, FL St. Mary.
Licari, Jonathan *o.s.b.* '52 (STP) Wayzata, MN Holy Name.
Licari, Jonathan *o.s.b.* '76 (SCL)[I] Collegeville, MN St. John's Abbey, of the Order of St. Benedict.
Licari, Jonathan *o.s.b.* (SCL) Judges.
Licastro, Antonio '55 (HRT) New Haven, CT St. Anthony's.
Licciardi, Fred *c.pp.s.* '82 (CHI) Inverness, IL Holy Family; Barrington, IL St. Anne; [M] Barrington, IL.
Lichtefeld, James J. '59 (L) Louisville, KY St. Stephen, Martyr Retired.
Lichtenthal, James J. '63 (BUF) Snyder, NY Christ the King.
Lichter, Mark '92 (SFS) Sioux Falls, SD St. Lambert.
Lickman, Peter '68 (PSC) Miami, FL St. Basil's.
Lickman, Peter (PSC) Syncellus; Eparchial College of Consultors; Ex Officio Members.
Lickteig, Anthony '54 (KCK) Louisburg, KS Immaculate Conception Retired.
Lickteig, Bernard *o.carm.* '46 (GAL)[Q] Houston, TX Carmelite Priory.
Lickteig, Fergus *o.carm.* '55 (KCK) Leavenworth, KS Immaculate Conception; Leavenworth, KS St. Joseph's.
Lickteig, Norbert '61 (KCK) Archdiocesan Consultors; Holy Childhood Association; Missions; Pontifical Mission Societies in the United States.
Liczner, John *o.f.m.* '66 (FgM).
Licznerski, Henry *c.r.* '92 (SB) Fontana, CA Church of the Resurrection; [E] Fontana, CA Congregation of the Resurrection, CR.
Liddy, Richard M. '63 (NEW)[B] School of Diplomacy and Intl. Rels..
Liderbach, Daniel P. *s.j.* '73 (BUF)[O] Buffalo, NY Canisius Jesuit Community.
Liderbach, Daniel P. *s.j.* '73 (DET)[K] Temperance, MI.
Lieb, Germain L. *o.s.b.* '45 (GBG)[H] Latrobe, PA Saint Vincent Archabbey.
Lieb, Marianus *t.o.r.* '44 (ARL)[J] White Post, VA Sacred Heart Friary.
Lieberth, Joseph '68 (CLV) Administrative Leave.
Liebhardt, Kevin M. '74 (CLV) Eastlake, OH St. Justin Martyr.
Liebl, Michael *o.s.b.* '77 (OM)[C] Elkhorn, NE Mount Michael High School; [K] Elkhorn, NE Mount Michael Abbey.
Liebler, Thomas R. '81 (SFD) Springfield, IL St. Aloysius.
Liebner, David C. '80 (ALN) Minersville, PA St. Barbara; Minersville, PA St. Francis of Assisi.
Liebner, David M. '60 (ALN) Girardville, PA St. Vincent de Paul.
Liebscher, Arthur F. *s.j.* '84 (SJ)[V] Newton, MA The Jesuit Community at Boston College; [B] Santa Clara, CA Jesuit Community.
Lief, Gregory P. '78 (WIN) Adams, MN St. John's.
Liem, Joseph Than Van *c.m.c.* '89 (SPC) Webb City, MO Sacred Heart.
Lienert, Charles J. '68 (P) Portland, OR St. Francis of Assisi; Gresham, OR St. Henry.
Lienert, Charles (P) College of Consultors.
Lienert, James '54 (BWN) Donna, TX St. Joseph.
Lienhard, Joseph T. *s.j.* '71 (NY)[EE] Cardinal Spellman Hall, Jesuit Community.
Liermann, Raymond B. '53 (STL) Retired.
Lies, David J. '98 (WCH) Colwich, KS St. Mark; Ongoing Formation of the Clergy Committee; Diocesan Apostolate to Engaged Encounter.
Lies, Eric *o.s.b.* '45 (IND)[K] St. Meinrad, IN St. Meinrad Archabbey.
Lies, James M. *c.s.c.* '97 (FTW)[I] Saint Paul, MN.
Lies, Jarrod (WCH)[B] Wichita, KS Bishop Mark K. Carroll Catholic High School.
Lies, William *c.s.c.* '94 (FTW)[B] University of Notre Dame Du Lac; [I] Notre Dame, IN Holy Cross Community, Corby Hall, University of Notre Dame.
Lieser, Gregory '63 (SCL) St. Cloud, MN St. Peter; Defensor Vinculi; Diocesan Corporate Board.
Lieser, Vincent '67 (SCL) Melrose, MN St. Mary's.
Liewer, David F. '74 (OM) Ponca, NE St. Peter; Ponca, NE St. Joseph.
Lifrak, Richard *ss.cc.* '95 (FR)[H] Artesia, NM Our Lady of Grace Rectory.
Lifrak, Richard *ss.cc.* (LSC) Artesia, NM Our Lady of Grace.
Ligato, Anthony F. '95 (ALB) Stamford, NY Sacred Heart.
Ligeti, Angelus *o.f.m.* '79 (DET) Detroit, MI Holy Cross.
Ligeza, Jan '03 (STA) Jacksonville, FL Assumption.
Ligonde, Jean–Marie F. '89 (NEW) On Duty Outside the Archdiocese.
Ligonde, Jean–Marie "Fritz" '89 (NEW) Port Charlotte, FL St. Charles Borromeo.
Ligonde, Jean–Marie "Fritz" (VEN) Ministry to Haitian People.
Ligory, Joseph '83 (NY) Bronx, NY St. Helena.
Ligot, Andres "Andy" '92 (SJ) San Jose, CA St. John Vianney; Judges; Promoter of Justice.
Liguori, Christopher '03 (STA) Ponte Vedra Beach, FL Our Lady Star of the Sea.
Liguori, Henry A. '66 (TR) Military Chaplains.
Lihvar, Francis P. *s.j.* '61 (CLV)[B] Cleveland, OH John Carroll University.
Liistro, Frank J. '74 (WOR) Fitchburg, MA Madonna of the Holy Rosary.
Lijewski, Thomas F. '70 (MIL) Kohler, WI St. John Evangelist.
Lijewski, Timothy M. '93 (CHR)[H] Columbia, SC University of South Carolina, St. Thomas More Center.
Likupe, Raymond '90 (FTW) South Bend, IN St. Patrick.
Lileart, Richard (DET) Oakwood Hospital.
Lill, Kenneth J. '91 (TOL) Monroeville, OH St. Joseph; Priests' Personnel Board.
Lilly, Robert A. *m.m.* '62 (NY).
Lilly, Thomas C. '03 (ANC)[EE] Anchorage, AK St. Patrick; Air Force Reserve Chaplains.
Lim, Candido O. *s.j.* '69 (PHI)[M] Los Gatos Sacred Heart Jesuit Center.
Lim, Candido O. *s.j.* '69 (SJ) San Jose, CA St. Victor.
Lim, Joseph D. (MO) Air Force Chaplains.
Lim, Yoke–Lye '95 (CC).
Lima, John (OAK) Retired.
Lima, Joseph *c.pp.s.* '44 (CIN)[B] Carthagena, OH St. Charles.
Lima, Rene '73 (NEW) Newark, NJ St. Benedict's.
Lima, Vivian B. '85 (LA) Santa Clarita, CA Our Lady of Perpetual Help.
Limanni, Joseph A. '87 (GAL) Houston, TX St. Francis de Sales.
Limbani, George '94 (SEA) Buckley, WA St. Aloysius.
Limbert, William G. '51 (KAL) Retired.
Limmer, George A. '64 (BAL) Hagerstown, MD St. Mary.
Linago, Deo (NY) Staten Island, NY Staten Island University Hospital South.
Linakis, William *s.a.* '77 (NY)[EE] Garrison Franciscan Friars of the Atonement, Minister General Office.
Linan, Jesse S. (GAL) Retired.
Linares, Jose R. '86 (MGZ) Cabo Rojo, PR St. Michael.
Linck, Joseph C. '94 (BGP) Trumbull, CT St. Theresa; Diocesan Office of Divine Worship.
Lincoln, Daniel L. '84 (L) Jamestown, KY Holy Spirit; Ex Officio.
Lincoln, Howard A. '91 (SB) Palm Desert, CA Christ of the Desert; Palm Desert, CA Sacred Heart.
Lincoln, Howard '91 (SB) Finance Committee.
Lincoln, Howard (SB) College of Consultors; Communications Ministry.
Lincon, Bruce '89 (TYL) Longview, TX St. Anthony.
Lind, Joseph G. '65 (BO) Senior Priests Retired.
Lind, Thomas *s.c.j.* '58 (JKS)[F] Nesbit, MS St. Michael Community House.
Lindauer, Prosper *o.s.b.* '50 (IND)[K] St. Meinrad, IN St. Meinrad Archabbey.
Lindblad, Karl–Albert '87 (NY) Military Chaplains; Navy Chaplains.
Lindemann, Gene E. '83 (BIS) Minot, ND Our Lady of Grace; Judicial Vicar; Priests' Personnel Board.
Lindemann, Gene (BIS) Office of Worship.
Linden, Emmet *c.p.* '51 (ORL)[E] Orlando, FL Bethany House of Beutel.
Linden, Michael D. *s.j.* '80 (BO)[V] Watertown, MA The Society of Jesus of New England–Provincial Offices; Roxbury, MA St. Mary of the Angels.
Linden, Michael *s.j.* '80 (BO)[V] Newton, MA The Jesuit Community at Boston College.
Lindenfelser, Timothy M. '94 (STA) St. Augustine, FL Cathedral – Basilica of St. Augustine.
Lindenfelser, Timothy (STA) Advocates; Diocesan Consultors; Presbyteral Council.
Lindenmeyer, James '48 (GLP) Retired.
Linder, William J. '63 (NEW) Newark, NJ St. Rose of Lima.
Lindle, Lawrence H. '59 (L) New Haven, KY Immaculate Conception; [P] Louisville, KY Perpetual Eucharistic Adoration; [P] New Haven, KY World Apostolate of Fatima (Blue Army); [P] New Haven, KY Sacred Heart Apostolate; [P] New Haven, KY Archdiocesan Marian Committee; Sacred Heart Enthronement Center Retired.
Lindley, Philip '83 (AMA) Absent on Leave.
Lindner, Jerold W. *s.j.* '76 (SJ)[M] Los Gatos, CA Sacred Heart Jesuit Center.
Lindner, Thomas F. '95 (LC) Stevens Point, WI Newman University Parish; [K] Stevens Point, WI Newman University Parish.
Lindsay, Michael P. (LSC) Defenders of the Bond; Army National Guard Chaplains.
Lindsay, Michael (LSC) Diocesan Consultors; Priestly Life and Ministry Committee; Priests Retirement Fund Committee.
Lindsay, Mike (LSC) Deming, NM Holy Family.
Lindsay, Robert E. *s.j.* '60 (BO)[V] Weston, MA Campion Health Center, Inc..
Lindsay, Stewart M. *o.s.f.s.* '74 (BUF) Council of Priests; [G] Niagara Falls, NY St. Dominic Savio Middle School; [G] Niagara Falls, NY Niagara Falls Catholic Schools Network; Niagara Falls, NY St. Charles Borromeo.
Linehan, Brian *o.f.m.* '67 (NEW) East Rutherford, NJ St. Joseph's.
Linehan, Cornelius '43 (P) Retired.
Linehan, Dennis *s.j.* '72 (NY)[EE] New York, NY "America;" Residence and publication office of the America Press.
Linehan, Eugene J. *s.j.* '53 (WDC)[E] North Bethesda, MD Georgetown Preparatory School.
Linehan, Jeremiah '48 (P) Retired.
Linehan, Maurice F. *m.s.* '52 (HRT)[M] Hartford, CT Missionaries of LaSalette.
Linehan, Stephen J. '75 (BO) Military & VA Chaplains; Navy Chaplains.
Linera, Celestino (SJN) Pius Union of the Clergy.
Linera, Celestino (SJN) Vicars General.
Linera–Tormos, Celestino (SJN) Diocesan Consultors.
Lingan, Joseph *s.j.* '90 (BAL)[A] Syracuse, NY Saint Andrew Hall.
Linhares, William P. *t.o.r.* '84 (WH)[E] Kearneysville, WV Priest Field Pastoral Center.
Linh Uy, Atanasio M. *c.m.c.* '81 (FWT) Wichita Falls, TX Sacred Heart.
Lininger, Paul *o.f.m.conv.* '81 (ALB) Albany, NY St. Casimir; Albany, NY Our Lady of Angels; [R] Rensselaer, NY Order of Friars Minor Conventual Immaculate Conception Province Charitable Trust.
Link, David '91 (OAK) Administrative Leave; Bishop's Representative for Eastern Rite Catholics.
Link, Fred *o.f.m.* '70 (CIN)[M] Cincinnati, OH St. Francis Seraph Friary.
Link, Frederick G. '69 (CAM) Westville, NJ St. Anne's.
Link, Frederick (CAM) Permanent Diaconate.
Link, Mark J. *s.j.* '60 (CHI)[T] The Jesuit Retreat League of Chicago.
Link, Paul *c.pp.s.* '61 (CIN)[B] Carthagena, OH St. Charles.
Linkchorst, William J. '73 (ALN) Tamaqua, PA SS. Peter and Paul.
Linn, Matthew L. *s.j.* '73 (STP)[B] St. Paul, MN Jesuit Novitiate.
Linnan, John *c.s.v.* '61 (JOL) Bourbonnais, IL Maternity of the Blessed Virgin Mary.
Linnan, Roger J. (SC) Directors:.
Linnan, Roger '62 (SC) Spencer, IA Sacred Heart; Priests' Pension Plan – Board of Trustees.
Linnane, Brian F. *s.j.* '86 (WOR)[O] Worcester, MA Jesuits of Holy Cross College, Inc..
Linnebur, David W. '82 (WCH) Garden Plain, KS Immaculate Conception; Garden Plain, KS St. Anthony.
Linnemann, Eugene C. '80 (BEL) Leave of Absence.
Linnenbrink, Harry H. '57 (DAV) Retired.
Linowski, Eugene R. '57 (PRM) Retired.
Lins, James R. '64 (MAD) Shullsburg, WI St. Peter;

Shullsburg, WI Our Lady of Hope; Shullsburg, WI St. Matthew.
Linse, Henry *c.s.s.* '48 (BO)[Y] Waltham, MA Stigmatine Fathers and Brothers.
Linsky, Gary S. '93 (CHR) Military Chaplains; Air Force Chaplains.
Linsler, Christopher E. '78 (ROC) Horseheads, NY St. Mary Our Mother.
Linster, Joseph B. '69 (RCK) St. Charles, IL St. Patrick.
Lintker, Andrew (BEL) Rural Life Conference.
Linton, Edward *o.s.b.* '91 (IND)[K] Chicago, IL.
Linton, Edward *o.s.b.* (CHI) Chicago, IL St. James.
Lintzenich, Stephen P. '74 (EVN) Evansville, IN St. John the Apostle; Evansville, IN St. Mary; Judges; Diocesan Council of Priests.
Linus, Stephen (ATL) On Duty Outside the Archdiocese.
Linz, Lester A. *s.j.* '44 (DET)[P] Hamtramck, MI St. Ladislaus.
Linzmaier, Eric G. (LC) Abbotsford, WI St. Bernard; Owen, WI Holy Rosary.
Lioi, Frank E. '67 (ROC) Freeville, NY Holy Cross; Groton, NY St. Anthony.
Lion, William J. '58 (CHI) Oak Lawn, IL St. Catherine of Alexandria Retired.
Lionelli, Anthony J. '72 (NEW) Newark, NJ Immaculate Conception.
Lipareli, Michael A. '80 (PH) Philadelphia, PA Veterans Administration Medical Center.
Lipareli, Michael A. (NY).
Lipczewski, Boleslaus '58 (DET) Detroit, MI Assumption Grotto Retired.
Lipiec, Bartholomew W. '83 (BUF) Council of Priests; Buffalo, NY Annunciation.
Lipinski, Alberic *o.cist.* '83 (CHI)[N] Willow Springs, IL Cistercian Fathers, Our Lady Mother of the Church.
Lipinski, Edward J. '71 (CAM) Brigantine, NJ St. Thomas; Judges.
Lipinski, Paul M. '73 (RCK) Sterling, IL Sacred Heart; [B] Sterling, IL Newman Central Catholic High School.
Lipka, Wieslaw (KAL) Kalamazoo, MI St. Monica.
Lipnicki, Thomas P. '78 (NEW) Oakland, NJ Our Lady of Perpetual Help; Cursillo Movement.
Liporace, Franco (WDC) Hispanic Youth Ministry.
Lipp, John F. *o.s.a.* '54 (PH)[AA] Villanova, PA St. Thomas Monastery.
Lippert, Donald F. *o.f.m.cap* '85 (WDC)[B] Washington, DC St. Francis Friary–Capuchin College [V] Washington, DC Spanish Catholic Center.
Lippert, Donald *o.f.m.cap* (WDC) Spanish Catholic Center.
Lippert, Paul R. '61 (MIL) Retired.
Lippold, John L. '57 (BAL) Linthicum Heights, MD St. Philip Neri Retired.
Lipps, Frank J. '68 (NO) Violet, LA Our Lady of Lourdes.
Lipps, Louis J. *s.j.* '52 (CIN)[M] Cincinnati, OH Claver Jesuit Community.
Lippstock, Paul E. '78 (DUB) Military Chaplains; [D] Bellevue, IA Marquette High School; La Motte, IA St. Lawrence; LaMotte, IA St. Theresa; La Motte, IA Assumption; La Motte, IA Holy Rosary; La Motte, IA St. John.
Lippstock, Paul Eldon (DUB) Army National Guard Chaplains.
Lipscomb, N. Alan '94 (RIC) Lexington, VA St. Patrick.
Lipscomb, William W. '97 (GAY) Empire, MI St. Philip Neri; Maple City, MI St. Rita–St. Joseph
Lipski, Janusz (RVC) Glen Head, NY St. Hyacinth.
Liptak, David Q. '53 (HRT) Special and other Archdiocesan Assignment; Newspaper; Censor Librorum.
Liptak, David Q. '53 (NOR)[A] Cromwell, CT Holy Apostles College and Seminary.
Liptak, David Q. '53 (HRT) Hartford, CT Cathedral of St. Joseph.
Liptak, David Q. '53 (HRT) Special and other Archdiocesan Assignment; Newspaper; Censor Librorum.
Liptak, David (CC)[G] Robstown, TX Society of Our Lady of the Most Holy Trinity.
Liptak, Edward *s.d.b.* '59 (FgM).
Lipton, Mariadas J. '87 (NOR) Willimantic, CT St. Joseph.
LiPuma, David G. (BUF) Secretary to Diocesan Bishop and Vice Chancellor; [O] Buffalo, NY Bishop's Residence.
Lirette, Albert *o.m.i.* '45 (BO)[V] Lowell, MA Missionary Oblates of Mary Immaculate Retired.
Lirette, Arthur J. '49 (LA) Glendale, CA Holy Family Retired.
Liriano, Benito A. '94 (NY) Bronx, NY St. Martin of Tours.
Lis, Albert *o.f.m.* '86 (GB) Green Bay, WI St. Mary of the Angels; [I] Green Bay, WI St. Mary of the Angels Friary.
Lis, John '73 (SPR) Sheffield, MA Our Lady of the Valley.
Lisante, James P. '81 (RVC) West Hempstead, NY St. Thomas, the Apostle.
Lisbeth, Michael L. *s.m.* '80 (CIN)[M] Cincinnati, OH Marianist Community.
Lischaa, Sharbel '61 (SAM) Philadelphia, PA St. Maron.
Lischwe, Bruno V. *c.ss.r.* '52 (STL)[O] Liguori, MO St. Clement Health Care Center.
Liscinsky, Steven *l.c.* '02 (MAN)[A] Center Harbor, NH Immaculate Conception Apostolic School.
Lisik, Paul A. '81 (GBG) Monessen, PA The Epiphany of Our Lord; Diocesan Pastoral Council.
Liska, Richard A. '70 (MIL) Milwaukee, WI St. Stephen.
Lisondra, Nestor '83 (CAM) Cherry Hill, NJ St. Peter Celestine.
Lisowski, Brian '81 (CHI) Chicago, IL St. Bede the Venerable.
Lisowski, Edward E. '64 (MIL) Wood, WI Veterans Administration Medical Center; Special Assignment.
Lisowski, Lawrence M. '84 (CHI) Lemont, IL SS. Cyril and Methodius.
Lisowski, William J. '50 (CHI) Retired.
Liss, Pedro (HRT) Hartford, CT St. Lawrence O'Toole.
Liss, Robert C. '62 (STL) Richwoods, MO St. Stephen's.
Lisson, Edwin *s.j.* '69 (STL)[C] Saint Louis University; [O] St. Louis, MO Jesuit Community Corporation at St. Louis University – Jesuit Hall.
List, Brian '03 (CC)[G] Robstown, TX Society of Our Lady of the Most Holy Trinity.
List, John E. '85 (LEX) Georgetown, KY St. John's; Judicial Vicar.
List, John (LEX) Coordinators.
Liston, Daniel P. '85 (SPR) Northampton, MA Blessed Sacrament; Chancellor; Vicar for Canonical Affairs; Judges; Bishop's Commission for Clergy; Bishop's Cabinet; Diocesan Consultors; Presbyteral Council; Mont Marie Health Care Center.
Liston, Paul F. '58 (WDC) Retired.
Liszewski, Francis A. '69 (NOR) Absent on Leave.
Liszewski, Peter B. '78 (NOR) Jewett City, CT St. Mary; Continuing Education and Formation Commission.
Litavec, Edward S. '60 (PIT) Pittsburgh, PA Sacred Heart.
Litavec, Viliam '88 (NY) Bronx, NY Visitation.
Litcheck, Michael P. '71 (SCR) Drums, PA Church of the Good Shepherd; Hazleton, PA St. Nazarius.
Literski, Roy E. '53 (WIN) Diocesan Consultors; Appointed Members Retired.
Litot, Edward F. '47 (GRY) Second Instance Retired.
Littelmann, Edward J. '69 (TOL) Toledo, OH St. Clement; Spiritual Directors.
Little, Anthony B. '82 (ALT) Newry, PA St. Patrick's.
Little, Gregory (NY) U.S.V.A. Medical Center.
Little, John J. '77 (ALT) Cresson, PA St. Aloysius.
Little, John J.L. '73 (ALN)[H] Bethlehem, PA Holy Family Manor; Bethlehem, PA SS. Simon and Jude.
Little, John '87 (OWN) Absent on Leave.
Littlefield, Philaret '87 (NTN) Milwaukee, WI St. George; Associated Melkite Charities.
Littleton, Gregory '90 (CHL) Charlotte, NC Our Lady of the Assumption.
Litwack, Joshua E. '00 (TLS) Tulsa, OK St. Bernard of Clairvaux.
Litwin, Paul A. '79 (BUF) Vice Chancellor; Judges; [O] Buffalo, NY Bishop's Residence.
Liu, Peter T. '60 (RVC)[A] Ronkonkoma, NY St. Joseph's Retired.
Liu, Pius *o.f.m.* '53 (NY).
Liu, Vincent '54 (RVC)[EE] Smithtown, NY St. Patrick.
Liuima, Francis *s.j.* '45 (BO)[V] Newton, MA The Jesuit Community at Boston College.
Liuzzi, Kenneth '75 (DEN) Denver, CO Blessed Sacrament.
Liuzzi, Kenneth '82 (DEN)[S] Denver, CO Blessed Sacrament Catholic Educational Foundation.
Liuzzi, Kenneth (DEN) Deaneries.
Liuzzi, Peter J. *o.carm.* '65 (LA)[B] Arleta, CA Carmel West Community; Phoenix, AZ St. Agnes.
Liuzzo, Vincent *o.f.m.cap.* '49 (PAT) Passaic, NJ St. Mary Hospital; [J] Passaic, NJ St. Mary's Hospital.
Lively, Gregory '01 (HEL) Shelby, MT St. William.
Lively, Jerome *a.a.* '02 (WOR)[O] Worcester, MA Assumptionists of Assumption College.
Lively, Joseph A. '57 (BUR) Retired.
Livigni, Salvatore J. '61 (BAL) Baltimore, MD Annunciation; Special Assignment; [W] Baltimore, MD Johns Hopkins Hospital Apostolate.
Livingston, James '91 (DET) Redford, MI St. Agatha.
Livingstone, James '03 (SFR) Burlingame, CA St. Catherine of Siena.
Livojevich, Ronald '70 (KCK) Overland Park, KS Queen of the Holy Rosary.
Livolsi, Silvester J. '48 (NEW)[I] Branchville, NJ Sanctuary of Mary–Our Lady of the Holy Spirit.
Livolsi, Sylvester J. '48 (NEW) On Duty Outside the Archdiocese.
LIwang, Effendy *m.s.c.* '01 (SAT) San Antonio, TX St. Mark the Evangelist.
Lixey, Kevin *l.c.* '01 (HRT)[B] Cheshire, CT Novitiate of the Legion of Christ.
Lizalde, Jesus '93 (GAL) Houston, TX St. Cecilia.
Lizarraga, Candido *rr.t.c.* '41 (SJN)[F] Santurce, PR Casa Manuel Fernandez Juncos.
Lizarralde, Jose *c.p.* '69 (MGZ) San Sebastian, PR San Sebastian Martir.
Lizcano, Otoniel '99 (BGP) Norwalk, CT St. Mary.
Lizewski, John M. '99 (WOR) West Warren, MA St. Stanislaus.
Lizio, John R. '57 (BO) Senior Priests Retired.
Lizor, Joseph S. '58 (BAL) Baltimore, MD St. Luke.
Llamas, German Rodriguez *s.v.d.* '77 (LA) Los Angeles, CA Our Lady of Loretto.
Llamas, Rodolfo '94 (SAC) Sacramento, CA All Hallows; Sacramento, CA St. Peter.
Llambias, Martin '73 (SJN)[G] Guaynabo, PR Opus Dei.
Llanos, Christopher '96 (BO)[V] Cambridge, MA.
Llanos, Philip S. '78 (LA) Military Chaplains.
Llanos, Phillip S. (LA) Air Force Chaplains.
Llaria, Vicente (VEN) Presbyteral Council.
Llaria, Vincent '59 (VEN) Lake Placid, FL St. James.
Llavila, Alberto *l.d.* '01 (PCE) Ponce, PR Church Santisimo Sacramento.
Lleo, Pedro '76 (MIA) Pompano Beach, FL St. Coleman.
Llkywelyn, Dorian *s.j.* '90 (LA)[C] Los Angeles, CA Jesuit Community.
Llorente, Amando *s.j.* '48 (MIA)[J] Miami, FL John Paul II Retreat House; Agrupacion Catolica Universitaria (ACU).
Lloyd, James B. *c.s.p.* '48 (NY) New York, NY St. Paul the Apostle; [EE] Jamaica Estates Paulist Fathers Generalate.
Lloyd, Patrick J. *s.c.j.* '69 (JKS)[F] Nesbit, MS St. Michael Community House.
LLoyd, Patrick J. *s.c.j.* '69 (JKS) West Southaven, MS Christ the King.
Lloyd, Paul A. '37 (PRO)[M] Pawtucket, RI Jeanne Jugan Residence Retired.
Lloyd, Philip P. '78 (GAL) Sugar Land, TX St. Laurence.
Lloyd, Robert J. *m.m.* '62 (NY)[EE] Maryknoll Maryknoll Fathers and Brothers.
Lluria, Carmel *o.f.m.* '55 (NY)[EE] Paterson, NJ Preakness Hospital.
Lngold, Michael (GB) Green Bay, WI St. Jude.
Lobacz, James E. '79 (MIL)[C] Milwaukee, WI Cardinal Stritch University; Special Assignment.
Lobaton, Jose '73 (WDC) Rockville, MD Shrine of St. Jude.
Lobert, Richard C. '75 (BAL) Special Assignment.
Lobert, Richard C. (LAN) W. J. Maxey Boys Training School.
LoBianco, Francis R. '54 (NEW) Retired.
LoBianco, Paschal *s.v.d.* '50 (CHI)[B] Techny, IL Divine Word Residence.
LoBianco, Richard J. '79 (CHI) Oak Lawn, IL St. Gerald.
LoBiondo, Gasper F. *s.j.* '68 (WDC)[M] Washington, DC Woodstock Jesuit Community; [V] Washington, DC Woodstock Theological Center.
Lobo, Raul V. '62 (NO) Waggaman, LA Our Lady of the Angels.
Lobo, Stanley '65 (NEW) Fort Lee, NJ Madonna.
Lobo, Theodore '57 (TUC) Parker, AZ Sacred Heart.
Lobsinger, Daniel *c.r.* '96 (L) Louisville, KY Guardian Angels.
Lobsinger, Daniel *c.r.* (L) Ex Officio.
Loc, Timothy Mai Vinh *c.m.c.* '77 (SPC) Webb City, MO Sacred Heart.
Locatelli, Paul L. *s.j.* '74 (SJ)[B] Santa Clara University; [B] Santa Clara, CA Jesuit Community.
Loch, Richard J. '79 (SCR) Scranton, PA Immaculate Conception; Dunmore, PA Christ the King; Diocesan Consultors; Deans; Presbyteral Council; Catholic Charismatic Renewal; Marriage Encounter; Priests' Retirement Advisory Board.
Lochner, Robert J. *c.s.c.* '46 (FTW)[I] Notre Dame, IN Holy Cross House Retired.
Lochs, Matthew *ss.cc.* '36 (HON)[G] Honolulu, HI St. Patrick's Monastery.
Lochs, Matthew *ss.cc.* (HON) Promoter of Justice.
Lock, Bertram *ss.cc.* '89 (HON) Kaneohe, HI St. Ann.
Lockard, David A. (ALT) Johnstown, PA Visitation of the B.V.M.; State College, PA Our Lady of Victory.
Locke, James E. '61 (PH) Chadds Ford, PA St. Cornelius.
Lockman, James *o.f.m.* (OAK)[S] Board of Directors:.
Lockman, V. James '67 (WDC) Washington, DC Annunciation.
Lockulu, Jean–Paulin '95 (JUN) Sitka, AK St. Gregory of Nazianzen; Diocesan Consultors; Port Chaplains.
Lockwood, Gregory J. '88 (CIN) Cincinnati, OH St. Vincent de Paul; On Duty Outside the Archdiocese.
Lockwood, Gregory (STL)[A] St. Louis, MO Kenrick School of Theology.
Lococo, Donald J. *c.s.b.* (ROC)[I] Rochester, NY Basilian Residence.
Loda, Mauro *s.x.* '99 (PAT)[M] Wayne Xaverian Missionary Fathers; (FgM).
Lodge, John G. '73 (CHI).
Lodge, Richard J. '69 (CAM)[A] West Collingswood, NJ Transfiguration; Members.
Lodi, George C. '74 (NY) Shrub Oak, NY Saint Elizabeth Ann Seton.
Lody, John '39 (Y) Masury, OH St. Bernadette.

Lody, Joseph Delano '03 (BIR)[A] Birmingham, AL John Carroll Catholic High School; Birmingham, AL Our Lady of Sorrows.
Loeb, Karl E. '95 (BUF) Akron, NY St. Teresa of Avila.
Loebl, Jeffrey R. *s.j.* '82 (MIL) Milwaukee, WI Gesu Parish.
Loecke, Douglas J. '89 (DUB) Worthington, IA St. Paul's; Judges.
Loecker, Craig J. '92 (OM) Anchorage, AK St. Elizabeth Ann Seton; Absent on Leave.
Loeffler, Earl A. '51 (TOL) Retired.
Loegering, Leonard '73 (FAR) Kindred, ND St. Maurice; Wyndmere, ND St. John the Baptist.
Loehr, Charles D. '47 (MIL) Retired.
Loehr, James P. '67 (MIL) Nashotah, WI St. Joan of Arc.
Loehrlein, Richard A. *s.m.* '61 (STL)[O] Chaminade Marianist Community.
Loehrlein, Sylvester '56 (EVN) Newburgh, IN St. Rupert.
Loeper, David J. '83 (ALN) Minersville, PA Sacred Heart; Pottsville, PA St. John the Baptist.
Loeper, Richard J. '50 (ALN) Birdsboro, PA Immaculate Conception Retired.
Loera, Abel '03 (LA) Bell Gardens, CA St. Gertrude.
Loeto, Bonfilio Torres (LSC) La Mesa, NM San Jose.
Loew, James H. *o.s.b.* '97 (E) St. Mary, PA St. Mary.
Loew, Jeremy '97 (E) St. Marys, PA Sacred Heart of Jesus.
Lofgren, Eric '93 (SAC) Anderson, CA Sacred Heart; Priests' Personnel Board, Diocesan.
LoFranco, Sofronio '60 (BRK)[B] Elmhurst, NY Cathedral Preparatory Seminary of the Immaculate Conception.
Loftin, Don '94 (AUS) Waco, TX St. Jerome.
Lofton, Edward D. '82 (CHR) Summerville, SC St. Theresa the Little Flower.
Lofton, James J. '61 (ALN) Retired.
Loftus, Conrad W. *o.f.m.* '54 (NY)[EE] Denver, CO; AUXILIARY CHAPLAINS CONTRACT CHAPLAINS.
Loftus, David '94 (LA) Alhambra, CA St. Thomas More; Adult Education.
Loftus, J. Allan *s.j.* '74 (BAL)[V] Newton, MA The Jesuit Community at Boston College.
Loftus, Joseph J. '56 (ARL) Arlington, VA Our Lady of Lourdes Retired.
Loftus, Kenneth G. *s.j.* (BO) Chestnut Hill, MA St. Ignatius.
Loftus, Kenneth *s.j.* '91 (BO)[V] Newton, MA The Jesuit Community at Boston College.
Loftus, Mel M. *o.s.m.* '62 (CHI)[N] Chicago Order of Friar Servants of Mary (Servites) United States of America Province, Inc..
Loftus, Padraic '62 (LA) Woodland Hills, CA St. Mel.
Loftus, Robert A. '91 (BGP) On Duty Outside the Diocese.
Loftus, Steven P. '02 (PEO) Pontiac, IL St. John's; Pontiac, IL St. Mary's.
Logan, Aidan Archur H. *o.c.s.o.* '85 (WOR)[O] Spencer, MA St. Joseph's Abbey; Navy Chaplains.
Logan, Daniel B. '63 (STA) Ponte Vedra Beach, FL Our Lady Star of the Sea; Associate Judges; Building Commission; Ecumenism.
Logan, Francis A. *s.j.* '33 (SPK)[J] Spokane, WA Regis Community.
Logan, Gary '93 (SR) Guerneville, CA St. Elizabeth.
Logan, J. M. '79 (PEO) Silvis, IL Our Lady of Guadalupe.
Logan, James J. '59 (LC) Retired.
Logan, James P. '86 (BAK) Vicar of Canonical Affairs; Chancellor; Judicial Vicar and Chief Judge; Council of Priests and Diocesan Consultors; Priestly Life and Ministry; Friends of the Catholic University of America; Health and Retirement Board; Office of Worship and Spirituality; Sisters, OR St. Edward.
Logan, James T. '54 (FRS) Diocesan Consultors Retired.
Logan, James (FRS) Priests' Council.
Logan, John M. *o.praem.* '60 (WIL)[J] Middletown, DE Immaculate Conception Priory of the Canons Regular of Premontre.
Logan, John *o.carm.* '64 (NY) Bellevue Hospital, Chapel of Our Lady Helper of the Sick; Bellevue Hospital.
Logan, Joseph P. *s.j.* '54 (PH) Philadelphia, PA Old St. Joseph's.
Logan, W. John *o.p.* '95 (DAL)[K] Irving, TX Dominican Priory of St. Albert the Great.
Logan, William R. '69 (RVC) Long Beach, NY St. Ignatius Martyr.
LoGatto, Joseph J. '57 (PAT) Retired.
Logrip, Joseph L. '72 (PH) Levittown, PA Immaculate Conception B.V.M.; Council of Priests.
LoGrosso, Pasquale '57 (DET) Retired.
Logsdon, L. Peter *c.s.c* '68 (AUS)[G] Austin, TX Congregation of Holy Cross – Southern Province.
Logsdon, Wilfrid *o.f.m.conv.* '59 (SAV) Brunswick, GA St. Francis Xavier.
Logue, Charles D. '48 (BO) Halifax, MA Our Lady of the Lake; Senior Priests Retired.
Logue, Dennis *s.v.d.* '83 (PBR) Pleasant City, OH St. Michael.
Logue, Mark '73 (BAL) West River, MD Our Lady of Sorrows.
Lohan, Louis '71 (BLX) Long Beach, MS St. Thomas the Apostle; Advocates; College of Consultors; Presbyteral Council.
Lohkamp, Nickolas *o.f.m.* '52 (Y)[K] Canton, OH Sancta Clara Monastery.
Lohr, Charles H. *s.j.* '61 (NY)[EE] Raimundus–Lullus Institute der Universitat–Freiburg.
Lohrmeyer, Kenneth P. (SAL) Associate Judges; Due Process Board.
Lohrmeyer, Kenneth '70 (SAL) Minneapolis, KS St. Paul's; Minneapolis, KS Immaculate Conception of the Blessed Virgin Mary.
Lohrmeyer, Kenneth (SAL) Judicial Vicar–Officialis.
Lohse, Edward M. '89 (E)[A] Erie, PA St. Mark's Seminary; Vice Chancellor; Vocation Office.
Lohse, Walter H. '40 (E) Retired.
Loi, Nguyen '66 (OM) Omaha, NE St. Ann.
Loi, Nygen (OM) Our Lady of Fatima Vietnamese Community.
Loiacono, James A. *o.m.i.* '79 (LAR) Eagle Pass, TX Our Lady of Refuge.
Loiselle, Joseph G. '57 (WOR) Retired.
Loiselle, Lucien H. '49 (BO) Senior Priests Retired.
Lojek, Robert '03 (CHI) Chicago, IL St. Richard.
Lolio, John W. '70 (PRO) East Greenwich, RI Our Lady of Mercy; Deans.
Lomasiewicz, Donald E. '62 (GR) Grand Rapids, MI St. Isidore.
Lomasney, John P. *m.m.* '43 (NY).
Lomax, Mark '80 (NO)[EE] Chalmette, LA St. Mark; Army National Guard Chaplains.
Lomax, Mark (NO) Deans.
Lombard, Richard J. '53 (SHP) Shreveport, LA St. Joseph; Advocates; Finance Council; AUXILIARY CHAPLAINS CONTRACT CHAPLAINS.
Lombard, Roy A. '47 (WH) Retired.
Lombardi, Albert U. '47 (DET) Retired.
Lombardi, Gary '69 (SR) Petaluma, CA St. Vincent de Paul; Members of the Curia; Deans; Board of Consultors; Priests' Council; Finance Committee.
Lombardi, John Carl *m.s.f.* (STL) St. Louis, MO St. Wenceslaus.
Lombardi, John '88 (BAL)[B] Emmitsburg, MD Mount Saint Mary's College.
Lombardi, Joseph L. *s.j.* '75 (PH)[C] Jesuit Fathers; [AA] Loyola Center and Manresa Hall.
Lombardi, Nicholas D. *s.j.* '72 (NY)[EE] Cardinal Spellman Hall, Jesuit Community.
Lombardi, Thomas '75 (FTW) Garrett, IN St. Joseph.
Lombardo, Angelo J. '55 (BEL) Retired.
Lombardo, Francis *o.f.m.conv.* '71 (BUF)[O] Athol Springs, NY St. Francis of Assisi Friary.
Lombardo, Gerald '86 (NEW).
Lombardo, Gerard M. '86 (NEW)[S] Bayonne, NJ St. Michael's.
Lombardo, Joseph A. '85 (TUC) Green Valley, AZ Our Lady of the Valley; Members.
Lombardo, Michael '78 (PAT) Wayne, NJ Our Lady of Consolation.
Lombardo, Paolo *o.f.m.* (MAR) Bishop Baraga Association Inc..
Lombardo, Robert *c.f.r.* '90 (NY)[EE] Bronx, NY Franciscan Friars of the Renewal.
Lombo, German *o.s.a.* '53 (MGZ) Aguada, PR St. Francis of Assisi.
Lomeli, Hermosillo *m.s.c.* '79 (LA) Cudahy, CA Sagrado Corazon y Santa Maria de Guadalupe.
Lomello, Lucian B. *s.d.b.* '48 (LA)[Q] Los Angeles, CA Dominic Savio Salesian Residence Retired.
Lomibao, Conrado '96 (HON) Honolulu, HI St. Philomena.
Lomica, Frank '02 (DEN) Littleton, CO St. Mary.
Lomme, Fracilus Petit '70 (SP) In res..
Lommel, George D. '46 (FAR) Retired.
LoMonaco, Lawrence '02 (CHL) Charlotte, NC St. Patrick Cathedral.
Lonappan, Paul N. *c.m.i.* '85 (MET)[I] Flemington, NJ The Carmel of Mary Immaculate and St. Mary Magdalen.
Lonardo, Alfred C. '63 (PRO) Providence, RI St. Augustine.
Loncar, Stephen *o.f.m.conv.* '88 (GRY) Gary, IN St. Joseph The Worker.
Loncaric, Stanley '36 (KCK)[G] Olathe, KS Villa St. Francis, Inc. Retired.
Lonchyna, Taras R. '77 (PHU) Silver Spring, MD Holy Trinity; Silver Spring, MD Annunciation of the Blessed Virgin Mary; Silver Spring, MD St. John the Baptist.
Lonchyna, Taras (PHU) Protopresbyters (Deans); Archeparchial Seminary Advisory and Admissions Board.
London, Lawrence '53 (RCK) Retired.
Londono, Heriberto '84 (SJN) Bayamon, PR Nuestra Sra. del Rosario.
Londono Arango, Orlando de Jesus '77 (SJN) Bayamon, PR Santo Domingo De Guzman.
Lone, Henry Saw '94 (SAL) Salina, KS Cathedral of the Sacred Heart.
Lonek, Stephen C. '76 (WIL) Hockessin, DE St. Mary of the Assumption.
Lonergan, Barry (ALB) Deans.
Lonergan, David W. '61 (HRT) Wethersfield, CT Corpus Christi; Wethersfield, CT Sacred Heart.
Lonergan, James B. '66 (ALB) Hudson Falls, NY Church of St. Mary's/St. Paul's.
Lonergan, Lester *m.h.m.* '62 (CHL)[EE] Hartsdale, NY Mill Hill Fathers Residence Retired.
Lonergan, Michael J. '93 (PH) Bensalem, PA St. Elizabeth Ann Seton.
Long, Anthony Vu Khac '92 (RCK) DeKalb, IL St. Mary; Special Assignment.
Long, Daniel *l.c.* '94 (CHI) Chicago, IL Epiphany.
Long, David P. '02 (PAT) Clifton, NJ St. Philip the Apostle.
Long, Galen '91 (SAL) Salina, KS Cathedral of the Sacred Heart.
Long, Garrett J. *s.m.* '76 (RVC)[D] Mineola, NY Chaminade High School (Boys); [M] Mineola, NY Provincial Residence and Novitiate.
Long, Gordon '65 (NU)[F] St. Peter, MN St. Peter Regional Treatment Center.
Long, J. William '89 (R) Raleigh, NC Doggett Center at Aquinas House; [H] Raleigh, NC Doggett Center for Catholic Campus Ministry at Aquinas House.
Long, James T. '63 (BEL) Fairview Heights, IL Holy Trinity – East.
Long, John F. *s.j.* '56 (NY)[EE] New York, NY "America;" Residence and publication office of the America Press.
Long, John R. '89 (SUP) Boulder Junction, WI St. Anne; Boulder Junction, WI St. Rita; Boulder Junction, WI St. Mary.
Long, John '61 (JC) Retired.
Long, John '78 (STP) Brooklyn Park, MN St. Vincent de Paul.
Long, John *o.carm.* '86 (PHX) Phoenix, AZ St. Agnes.
Long, Joseph J. *c.s.c.* '59 (SCR) Veteran's Administration Hospital; [C] Wilkes–Barre, PA Kings College.
Long, Loran '53 (SD)[F] San Diego, CA Scripps Mercy Hospital.
Long, Melvin '66 (SAL) Retired.
Long, Nguyen Phi *c.ss.r.* '03 (LA)[Q] Irving, TX.
Long, Richard E. '90 (BRK) Brooklyn, NY St. Athanasius; Bishop Sullivan—.
Long, Vincent P. '69 (SY) St. Ann; Holland Patent, NY St. Leo.
Long, W. Thomas (GB) Brillion, WI Holy Family; Elected Representatives; [M] Green Bay, WI Ecumenical Center–UWGB.
Longbucco, John L. '90 (MAR) On Duty Outside the Diocese; Army Chaplains.
Longchamps, Adrien R. '75 (MAN) Laconia, NH Sacred Heart.
Longo, Paul *m.c.c.j.* '52 (CHI)[N] La Grange Park, IL Comboni Missionaries.
Longo, Robert *o.f.m.cap.* (WIL) Wilmington, DE Sacred Heart; [G] Wilmington, DE House of Joseph II; [J] Wilmington, DE St. Felix Friary.
Longobucco, Robert '98 (ALB) Albany, NY St. Catherine of Siena; Special Assignment; Presbyteral Council; Diocesan Board of Consultors; Office of Evangelization and Catechesis.
Longoria Gomez, Jose de la Cruz *m.n.m.* '96 (SAT) Del Rio, TX Our Lady of Guadalupe.
Longres, Joaquin '62 (BRK)[A] Douglaston, NY Immaculate Conception Center.
Longtin, Lucien F. *s.j.* '65 (WDC)[A] Wernersville, PA Jesuit Center; [N] Wernersville, PA Jesuit Center for Spiritual Growth.
Longua, Paul A. '61 (PAT)[P] Chester, NJ Nazareth Village Retired.
Longua, Thomas *f.s.s.p.* '03 (SCR)[M] Elmhurst, PA Priestly Fraternity of St. Peter (F.S.S.P.), North American District Headquarters.
Longwill, Carl '54 (DEN) Retired.
Lonteen, Daniel '94 (CLV) Absent on Leave.
Looby, Christopher J. '01 (OG) Plattsburgh, NY St. Peter; Associate Vocations Directors.
Looby, John J. '66 (OG) Dannemora, NY St. Joseph.
Loomie, Albert J. *s.j.* '52 (NY).
Loomis, Dennis J. *m.s.* '77 (HRT)[M] Hartford, CT Missionaries of LaSalette.
Loomis, Dennis J. *m.s.* '77 (FR)[H] Attleboro, MA La Salette Missionary Association.
Loomis, Richard A. '76 (LA) San Marino, CA Saints Felicitas and Perpetua.
Loomis, Richard P. '52 (WIN) Austin, MN St. Edward's Retired.
Loomis, Thomas A. (WIN) Rochester, MN Resurrection; Elected Deanery Representatives; Chaplain; Auditors.
Looney, Daniel A. '71 (SAC) Davis, CA St. James.
Looney, Daniel (SAC) Council of Priests; Priests' Personnel Board, Diocesan.
Looney, Joseph E. '67 (HRT) Waterbury, CT St. Margaret's.
Looney, Mathew D. '58 (NEW) Retired.

Looney, Thomas P. *c.s.c.* '87 (SCR)[C] Holy Cross Community; [M] Wilkes–Barre, PA Moreau House.
Loos, Francis *c.i.c.m.* '47 (SAT)[M] San Antonio, TX Missionhurst Community Residence.
Loos, Frederick C. '63 (SAG) On Duty Outside the Diocese.
Loosbrock, Donald L. '51 (WIN) Retired.
Lopardo, Vito R. '55 (BEL) Retired.
Lopatesky, Raymond M. '75 (PAT)[P] Chester, NJ Nazareth Village.
Lopatesky, Raymond (PAT) Vicar for Retired Priests.
Lopera, Rafael I. *c.s.b.* '94 (GAL)[Q] Sugar Land Basilian Mission Center.
Lopes, Richard *o.f.m.cap.* '82 (SFR)[N] Burlingame, CA Capuchin Provincial House; Navy Chaplains.
Lopes, Steven *s.t.l.* '01 (SFR) On Special Assignment.
Lopes, Thomas C. '65 (FR) North Easton, MA Immaculate Conception.
Lopez, Abel '56 (SJ) Retired.
Lopez, Abel (SJ) Judges.
Lopez, Agustin *sch.p.* '57 (SJN) San Juan, PR Santisimo Salvador.
Lopez, Alberto '87 (SJN) Trujillo Alto, PR San Pio X.
Lopez, Alejandro *o.f.m.conv.* '03 (PEO) Peoria, IL Holy Family.
Lopez, Alfred A. *o.p.* '84 (CHI)[N] Chicago Dominicans (Provincial Office).
Lopez, Amador *o.m.i.* '58 (SD) Calipatria, CA St. Patrick.
Lopez, Angel *c.ss.r.* '79 (CGS) San Lorenzo, PR Nuestra Senora de la Mercedes.
Lopez, Antonio Garnica *m.s.c.* '79 (LA) Cudahy, CA Sagrado Corazon y Santa Maria de Guadalupe.
Lopez, Antonio '02 (ORG) Huntington Beach, CA St. Vincent de Paul.
Lopez, Armando *o.f.m.* '88 (P) Portland, OR Ascension.
Lopez, Benigno (CGS) Cayey, PR Nuestra Senora de la Merced.
Lopez, Benjamin '98 (CC)[G] Robstown, TX Society of Our Lady of the Most Holy Trinity.
Lopez, Bruce '88 (PEO) Peoria, IL St. Jude's.
Lopez, Camilo '93 (NEW) Bayonne, NJ St. Vincent de Paul.
Lopez, Carlos *o.s.b.* '02 (LA)[Q] Valyermo, CA St. Andrew's Abbey.
Lopez, Daniel '63 (FRS) Selma, CA St. Joseph.
Lopez, Daniel (FRS) Diocesan Consultors; Vicars Forane; Personnel Committee; Priests' Council.
Lopez, Daniel (FRS) Marian Federation of Guadalupe.
Lopez, Edgardo '83 (MGZ) Cabo Rojo, PR St. Michael.
Lopez, Edilberto '97 (ELP) Clint, TX San Lorenzo.
Lopez, Eduardo *c.m.* '70 (GAL) Houston, TX St. Charles Borromeo.
Lopez, Eduardo '85 (ELP)[B] El Paso, TX St. Anthony's School of Theology.
Lopez, Efrain '65 (CGS) Condado, San Juan, PR Stella Maris.
Lopez, Enrique *c.ss.r.* '64 (LA) Whittier, CA St. Mary of the Assumption; [Q] Whittier, CA Redemptorists of Whittier.
Lopez, Enrique (LSC) Promoter of Justice; Presbyteral Council; Clergy Personnel Board; Office of Vocations; Casa San Juan Diego, House of Formation.
Lopez, Fabian '99 (NY) Bronx, NY Our Lady of Angels.
Lopez, Felipe '59 (NEW) Union City, NJ St. Augustine's; Hispanic Curia of Hudson County.
Lopez, Fernando *s.j.* '54 (MIA) Miami, FL Gesu.
Lopez, Fernando (LA) Los Angeles, CA St. Thomas the Apostle.
Lopez, Francisco (ELP) Advocates.
Lopez, Frank '93 (ELP) El Paso, TX St. Frances Xavier Cabrini Parish.
Lopez, Gabriel Maduro (ARE) Promoter of Justice.
Lopez, Gerald M. (SB) Ex Officio Member.
Lopez, Gerard M. '91 (SB) Special or Other Diocesan Assignment.
Lopez, Gerard M. (SB) Diocesan Curia; College of Consultors; Personnel Board Members.
Lopez, Gerard R. (SB) Finance Council Members.
Lopez, Gerard '91 (SB) San Bernardino, CA Our Lady of the Rosary Cathedral.
Lopez, Gustavo '98 (ELP) Pecos, TX St. Catherine.
Lopez, Humberto '86 (MGZ) San German, PR San German de Auxerre; Diocesan Consultors.
Lopez, Jairo '94 (AUS) Marble Falls, TX St. John the Evangelist.
Lopez, Jesus Francisco '96 (CC) Taft, TX Immaculate Conception.
Lopez, Joel '03 (RCK) St. Charles, IL St. John Neumann.
Lopez, Jorge Granados '97 (YAK) Kennewick, WA St. Joseph's.
Lopez, Jose A. '71 (SAT)[A] San Antonio, TX Assumption Seminary aka Assumption–St. John's Seminary; [C] Oblate School of Theology.
Lopez, Jose Maria '54 (SJN)[F] Rio Piedras, PR Hogar Santa Teresa Jornet for the Aged.
Lopez, Jose R. '85 (LA)[Q] Los Angeles, CA Society of St. Paul.
Lopez, Jose '91 (MIA) Hialeah, FL St. John the Apostle.
Lopez, Jose '94 (JKS) On Duty Outside the Diocese; Brooklyn, NY St. Teresa of Avila.
Lopez, Joseph A. '02 (CC) Judges; Corpus Christi, TX St. Joseph.
Lopez, Joseph (SAT) Judges.
Lopez, Juan J. '89 (ARE) On Duty Outside the Diocese; Brooklyn, NY St. Agatha's.
Lopez, Juan M. '62 (MIA) Miami, FL SS. Peter and Paul.
Lopez, Kharlosg '77 (CGS) Humacao, PR Maria Reina de la Paz.
Lopez, Leonardo *i.v.e.* '02 (PH) Philadelphia, PA St. Veronica.
Lopez, Lionel '96 (BWN) Edinburg, TX Holy Family; [D] Brownsville, TX Jail Ministry; Chaplains.
Lopez, Luis E. *c.s.v.* '95 (CHI)[N] Arlington Heights Viatorian Province Center–Clerics of St. Viator.
Lopez, Mario *o.carm.* '76 (BO)[O] Peabody, MA Catholic Information Center; [AA] Peabody, MA St. Theresa Carmelite Chapel.
Lopez, Mario *s.o.l.t.* '99 (SJN) Rio Grande, PR Nuestra Senora del Carmen.
Lopez, Mauricio '92 (SAT) Kenedy, TX Our Lady of Peace.
Lopez, Norberto *o.s.b.* (SJN) Rio Piedras, PR Inmaculado Corazon de Maria.
Lopez, Pedro J. '81 (LA) El Monte, CA Nativity.
Lopez, Richard '73 (ATL) Atlanta, GA Immaculate Heart of Mary; [B] Atlanta, GA St. Pius X Catholic High School.
Lopez, Sergio '98 (OAK) Concord, CA St. Francis of Assisi; Region 5.
Lopez, Sergio *t.o.r.* '01 (AUS) Waco, TX St. Francis on the Brazos
Lopez, Severino *c.m.f.* '44 (ATL) Stone Mountain, GA Corpus Christi.
Lopez, Uriel '00 (RCK) Belvidere, IL St. James.
Lopez, Vicente O. *o.carm.* '68 (LA) Los Angeles, CA St. Raphael.
Lopez, Vincent *o.p.* (FRS)[A] Fresno, CA San Joaquin Memorial High School; On Special Assignment.
Lopez–Alvarado, Luis A. (CGS).
Lopez–Cardinale, Alejandro '91 (NY) Bronx, NY Blessed Sacrament
Lopez–Escalera, Enrique (LSC) Judges.
Lopez–Figueroa, Alberto (SJN) Vicar for Priests.
Lopez–Restrepo, Eugenio (SAC) Placerville, CA St. Patrick's.
Lopez–Rodriguez, Hector *o.p.* '95 (SJN) Bayamon, PR Catalina de Siena.
Lopez–Romo, Eduardo '03 (TUC) Nogales, AZ Sacred Heart.
Lopez–Silvestre, Jose David '82 (PHX) Mesa, AZ Christ the King.
Lopez Alvarado, Luis (CGS)[E] San Juan, PR VA Medical Center.
Lopez Aponte, Nelson '91 (CGS) Vieques, PR Inmaculada Concepcion.
Lopez Garcia, Mario '99 (CC)[G] Robstown, TX Society of Our Lady of the Most Holy Trinity.
Lopez Hernandez, Edgardo (PCE)[B] The Pontifical Catholic University of Puerto Rico.
Lopez Mairal, Jose Maria '54 (SJN) San Juan, PR Santa Cecilia; Resident Chaplains.
Lopez Vega, Jose Antonio '92 (PCE) Coto Laurel, PR Our Lady of Mt. Carmel.
LoPinto, Alfred P. '70 (BRK) Brooklyn, NY St. Therese of Lisieux.
Lopoke–Ohamamboya, Symphorien '94 (SFS) Sioux Falls, SD St. Lambert; Promoter of Justice; Tribunal Judges.
LoPresti, Carl '97 (PEO) Chenoa, IL St. Joseph's; Colfax, IL St. Joseph's.
Lopresti, Julio (BGP) Presbyteral Council.
Lopresti, Julio *i.v.e.* (BGP) Bridgeport, CT St. George; [P] Bridgeport, CT Instituto Verbo Encarnado.
Lorance, Douglas '84 (SJP) Lyndora, PA St. Michael.
Lord, David *m.i.c.* '91 (SPR)[I] The National Shrine of The Divine Mercy; [I] Eucharistic Apostles of The Divine Mercy.
Lord, Laurence J. '64 (SY) Binghamton, NY St. Patrick.
Lordemann, Francis W. '72 (OM) Bellevue, NE St. Mary; Air Force Reserve Chaplains.
Lordemann, Frank (OM) Deans; Deans.
Loredo, Miguel A. *o.f.m.* '64 (NEW) Newark, NJ St. Thomas Aquinas.
Loredo, Miguel A. *o.f.m.* '64 (NY) New York, NY St. Francis of Assisi.
Lorenc, Henryk (MO) Army Chaplains.
Lorentsen, Michael *o.f.m.conv.* '94 (R) Siler City, NC St. Julia.
Lorentsen, Michael *o.f.m.conv.* '94 (R)[E] Pittsboro, NC Our Lady of Guadalupe Friary.
Lorenz, Bernard A. '85 (LIN) Apostolate to the Spanish Speaking.
Lorenz, Bernard '85 (LIN) Benkelman, NE St. Joseph's.
Lorenz, John F. '54 (DM)[G] Des Moines, IA Institute of the Heart of Jesus Retired.
Lorenz, Mathais E. '69 (CHI) On Duty Outside the Archdiocese.
Lorenz, Richard J. *s.a.c.* '60 (MIL)[O] Milwaukee, WI St. Vincent Community.
Lorenz, Vincent E. '53 (SD) Retired.
Lorenzana, Elias *o.de.m.* '55 (SJN) San Juan, PR Nuestra Senora de la Merced.
Lorenzetti, Dino J. '53 (BUF)[O] Tonawanda, NY O'Hara Residence Retired.
Lorenzo, Avelino *s.d.b.* '60 (LA) Los Angeles, CA St. Mary; [Q] Los Angeles, CA Dominic Savio Salesian Residence.
Lorenzo, Eduardo '66 (LAN) Retired.
Lorenzo, Elias R. *o.s.b.* '89 (PAT)[M] Morristown, NJ St. Mary's Abbey.
Lorenzo, Joseph F. *o.f.m.* '76 (MAN) Derry, NH St. Thomas Aquinas.
Lorenzo, Juan '92 (VEN) Lehigh Acres, FL St. Raphael.
Lorenzoni, Larry *s.d.b.* '51 (SFR)[N] San Francisco, CA Salesian Provincial Residence.
Loresco, Alfredo '64 (HT) Retired.
Lorfanfant, Ernest P. *s.m.* '68 (RVC)[M] Mineola, NY Provincial Residence and Novitiate.
Lorge, Felix P. '50 (SPK) Colfax, WA St. Patrick; Colfax, WA St. Joseph.
Lorig, Douglas E. '84 (PHX) Gilbert, AZ St. Anne.
Lorilla, Wilfredo '68 (AGN) Piti, GU Assumption of Our Lady.
Lorio, Joseph O. '54 (NO) Metairie, LA St. Louis King of France.
Lorkowski, Robert A. '77 (CLV) Westlake, OH St. Bernadette.
Lorrain, Matthew P. '86 (BR) Baton Rouge, LA St. Jean Vianney; Presbyteral Council.
Lortie, Lorenzo *s.c.* '62 (HRT) New Haven, CT Sacred Heart.
Lorusso, Joseph A. *c.s.c.* '53 (BGP)[P] Wikes–Barre, PA.
Losarcos, Javier '51 (NEW) Newark, NJ St. Aloysius.
Lo Sasso, John *o.f.m.cap.* '89 (NY) Bronx, NY Immaculate Conception.
Lo Schiavo, John J. *s.j.* '55 (SFR)[N] San Francisco, CA Jesuit Community at University of San Francisco.
Loseke, Jeffrey (OM) Omaha, NE St. Margaret Mary.
Losh, Joseph F. '64 (COL) La Rue, OH St. Joseph's.
Loshe, Norbert *c.pp.s.* '40 (CIN) Fort Recovery, OH Mary Help of Christians.
Losito, Felix A. '58 (ALN) Reading, PA Holy Rosary; National Shut–In Visitation Society.
Loskarn, George '65 (BAL) Retired.
Loskot, Donald *s.d.s.* (NSH) Tenn. Tech–Cookeville; Cookeville, TN St. Thomas Aquinas.
Losoya, Jose Encarnacion *c.o.* '91 (BWN) Pharr, TX St. Jude Thaddeus; [F] Pharr, TX Oratory of St. Philip Neri of Pontifical.
Lossing, Larry '84 (ORL) Orlando, FL St. Joseph; Special Assignment; Office of Ecumenism.
Loth, Alan J. '68 (OKL) Harrah, OK St. Teresa of Avila; Defenders of the Bond; Personnel Committee.
Lotha, Abraham '89 (NY) New York, NY Guardian Angel.
Lothamer, James W. *s.s.* '68 (LAN) Fowlerville, MI St. Agnes.
Lotito, Floyd A. *o.f.m.* '60 (SFR) San Francisco, CA St. Anthony of Padua; [S] San Francisco, CA Franciscan Friars of California, Provincial Office of Communications Consultant; [S] San Francisco, CA St. Anthony Foundation.
Lott, Lawrence M. '90 (MOB) On Leave from the Archdiocese; Navy Chaplains.
Lott, Roger R.S. *o.s.b.* '54 (BIR)[E] Cullman, AL St. Bernard Abbey.
Lotz, Ezekiel *o.s.b.* (P)[L] St. Benedict, OR Mt. Angel Abbey.
Lotz, Robert J. '73 (MIL)[W] Milwaukee, WI University of Wisconsin – Milwaukee, Newman Center; Special Assignment; Milwaukee.
Loucks, Thomas '77 (B) Wallace, ID St. Alphonsus.
Lougen, Louis *o.m.i.* '79 (SFD)[A] Godfrey, IL Immaculate Heart of Mary Novitiate.
Loughery, Robert J. *c.s.c.* '89 (P) Portland, OR St. Vincent de Paul.
Loughlin, William E. (LSC)[C] Las Cruces, NM Basilian Fathers.
Loughlin, William J. '69 (BGP) Fairfield, CT St. Thomas Aquinas; Pilgrimages, Office of Diocesan Retired.
Loughman, Kenneth M. '58 (NY) Walden, NY Most Precious Blood.
Loughnane, James J. '61 (LA) Diamond Bar, CA St. Denis; Deanery 12; Personnel Board of the Archdiocese; Judges.
Loughnane, John B. '88 (MAN) Ashland, NH St. Agnes; Plymouth, NH St. Matthew.
Loughran, Francis J. '56 (PH) Retired.
Loughran, James N. *s.j.* '70 (NEW)[B] Jersey City, NJ Saint Peter's College; [B] Jersey City, NJ Jesuit Center; [N] Jersey City, NJ Jesuits of Saint Peter's College, Inc..
Loughran, James *s.a.* '89 (NY)[EE] New York, NY Atonement Friars; [EE] New York, NY Graymoor Ecumenical and Interreligious Institute.
Loughran, John *o.s.f.s.* '80 (LAN) Deerfield, MI St. Alphonsus.
Loughran, Peter G. '48 (SPR) Retired.
Louis, Jean Woady '91 (VEN) Immokalee, FL Our Lady

of Guadalupe.
Louis, John H. '62 (SCR) Clarks Green, PA St. Gregory; [F] Clarks Green, PA Saint Gregory Early Childhood Center; Presbyteral Council.
Louis, Kevin C. '89 (LC) On Duty Outside the Diocese.
Louis, Kevin (COL).
Louis, Pascal (BRK)[A] Brooklyn, NY Holy Cross.
Louzon, Bede *o.f.m.cap.* '85 (DET) Hazel Park, MI St. Mary Magdalen.
Lovas, Donald J. '63 (WIN) Wabasha, MN St. Agnes; Wabasha, MN St. Felix.
Lovat, Rene *s.x.* '57 (PAT)[M] Wayne Xaverian Missionary Fathers; (FgM).
Love, Lester E. *s.j.* '91 (OAK)[N] Chicago Chicago Province of the Society of Jesus–Provincial Office; [N] Oakland, CA Murray Residence Community.
Loveless, William J. '75 (Y) Warren, OH St. Pius X.
Lovell, Allen B. '02 (CAM) Cherry Hill, NJ St. Pius X; [A] Haddonfield, NJ Paul VI High School; Advocates; Assistant Vocation Directors for Recruitment.
Lover, Lawrence E. *c.ss.r.* '51 (BRK)[V] Brooklyn, NY Our Lady of Good Counsel Residence.
Lovett, Gerald F. '59 (SEA) Retired.
Lovisa, Eugene L. '49 (TOL)[I] Oregon, OH Sacred Heart Home Retired.
Lovrencic, Athanasius *o.f.m.* '48 (CHI)[N] Lemont, IL The Slovene Franciscan Fathers, Order of Friars Minor, Commissariat of the Holy Cross.
Lowchy, Gregory '01 (R) Wilson, NC Church of St. Therese.
Lowe, Bryan K. '01 (BIR) Birmingham, AL Blessed Sacrament; [A] Birmingham, AL John Carroll Catholic High School; [H] Birmingham, AL St. Stephen the Martyr Catholic Church and Catholic Campus Center.
Lowe, Bryan T. '01 (BIR) Birmingham, AL St. Stephen the Martyr.
Lowe, Francis E. (SB) Air Force Reserve Chaplains.
Lowe, Frank E. '85 (SB) Banning, CA Precious Blood.
Lowe, Frank '85 (SB) On Duty Outside the Diocese.
Lowe, Philip J. '82 (PH) Bala Cynwyd, PA St. Matthias; [EE] Philadelphia, PA Temple University.
Lowe, Russell P. '92 (CLV) Brooklyn, OH St. Thomas More.
Lowery, James T. '55 (HRT) Hartford, CT St. Anne–Immaculate Conception; [M] Hartford, CT St. Anne–Immaculate Conception.
Lowery, Martin J. *m.m.* '68 (NY)[EE] Maryknoll Maryknoll Fathers and Brothers.
Lowery, Philip A. '76 (TR) Red Bank, NJ St. James.
Lowery, Wil *c.ss.r.* '49 (STP) Brooklyn Center, MN St. Alphonsus.
Lowisz, Myron *o.f.m.* '95 (GRY)[G] Crown Point, IN Franciscan Communities at St. Anthony Campus; [I] Cedar Lake, IN Our Lady of Lourdes Friary.
Lowney, Edward *o.m.i.* '40 (BO) Tewksbury, MA Tewksbury Hospital.
Lowney, Edward *o.m.i.* '56 (BO)[Y] Tewksbury, MA Immaculate Heart of Mary Infirmary.
Lowney, Jeremiah '88 (HEL)[B] Helena, MT Carroll College.
Lowrey, Robert *o.m.v.* '78 (BO)[V] Milton, MA Oblate Residence (St. Joseph House); [AA] Boston, MA St. Francis Chapel.
Lowry, Joseph K. '66 (BUF) Retired.
Loya, Daniel J. (PBR) Elected Deanery Representatives; Windber, PA SS. Peter and Paul.
Loya, Daniel '66 (PBR) Windber, PA St. Mary (Dormition) Church.
Loya, John F. '74 (CLV)[A] Wickliffe, OH Borromeo Seminary; [A] Wickliffe, OH St. Mary Seminary and Graduate School of Theology.
Loya, Joseph *o.s.a.* '79 (PH)[C] Villanova University.
Loya, Thomas J. '82 (PRM) Homer Glen, IL Annunciation Byzantine Catholic Church.
Loya, Thomas (PRM) Syncellus for Parishes and Laity; Presbyteral Council; Eparchial Pastoral Council; Office of Youth Ministry.
Loyacono, Charles '57 (JKS) Retired.
Loyd, Frederick A. '70 (COL) Columbus, OH St. Joseph Cathedral.
Loyens, William J. *s.j.* '58 (SPK)[J] Spokane, WA Regis Community.
Loyson, Michael '92 (DET) St. Clair Shores, MI St. Lucy; Auditors.
Lozano, Arturo *s.j.* '67 (LAF) On Special Assignment; [J] Grand Coteau, LA Jesuit Spirituality Center (St. Charles College); Hispanic Ministry.
Lozano, Edel *o.c.d.* '01 (MIA) Pembroke Pines, FL St. Maximilian Kolbe.
Lozano, Freddy '85 (RVC) Brookhaven.
Lozano, Jose '65 (PCE) Juana Diaz, PR St. Raymond Nonato; Diocesan Consultors; Parish Priests Consultors.
Lozano, Roland *c.m.f.* '75 (LA)[Q] Los Angeles, CA Prov. Headquarters of the Western Prov. of the USA; [Q] Los Angeles, CA Claretian Retreat Center Community; [W] Los Angeles, CA Claretian Retreat Center (All Groups).
Lozier, Donald G. *o.m.i.* '60 (BO) Lowell, MA Saint Jeanne d'Arc.
Lozier, Timothy R. '88 (STA) Gainesville, FL St. Augustine; Cursillos de Cristiandad.
Lozinski, Eugene L. '72 (NU) Glencoe, MN St. Pius X; Associate Judges; Priest Personnel Board; Diocesan Council of Catholic Women.
Lozinski, Robert W. *c.s.c.* '73 (BUR) Elected Members; Deans; Bennington, VT Sacred Heart St. Francis de Sales.
Lu, Matthias '42 (OAK) Retired.
Luan, Nguyen Truong '98 (LA)[Q] Long Beach, CA.
Lubbers, John W. *c.s.c.* '57 (FTW)[I] Notre Dame, IN Holy Cross House.
Lubbers, Leland E. *s.j.* '59 (OM)[K] Omaha, NE Jesuit Community at Creighton University.
Lubeley, Richard J. '49 (STL) Webster Groves, MO Mary, Queen of Peace Retired.
Luberti, Richard A. *c.ss.r.* '79 (LAF) On Special Assignment.
Lubic, Robert T. '96 (GBG) Harrison City, PA St. Barbara.
Lubinsky, Michael '78 (SAV) Augusta, GA Church of the Most Holy Trinity.
Lubrano, Joseph *s.d.s.* '74 (MIL)[O] Richmond, VA.
Lubrano, Robert '85 (RVC) Absent on Leave.
Luca, Edward J '54 (CLV) Retired.
Luca, Edward J. '54 (CLV) Sheffield, OH St. Teresa of Avila; Associate Judicial Vicars.
Luca, Joseph L. '70 (BAL) Clarksville, MD St. Louis.
Lucarelli, Gabriel M. *c.r.m.* '36 (NEW) Lodi, NJ St. Joseph's.
Lucas, Christopher D. '85 (PH) Philadelphia, PA Saint Martha; Philadelphia, PA Our Lady of Consolation; [D] Philadelphia, PA St. Hubert's Catholic High School for Girls.
Lucas, Damien (DEN) Denver, CO St. Catherine of Siena.
Lucas, Edward '61 (PBR) Weirton, WV St. Mary's.
Lucas, Eliseo '02 (SB) Murrieta, CA St. Martha.
Lucas, James (GB) Kaukauna, WI Holy Cross.
Lucas, Jayaseelanraj '96 (TYL) Henderson, TX St. Jude.
Lucas, Jeffery J. '81 (E) Sharon, PA St. Stanislaus Kostka.
Lucas, John J. (E) Deans.
Lucas, John L. '65 (E) Warren, PA Holy Redeemer.
Lucas, John P. '69 (CHI) Oak Park, IL St. Edmund.
Lucas, Lawrence E. '59 (NY) New York, NY Our Lady of Lourdes; North Infirmary Command; Otis Bantum Correctional Center; Manhattan, NY North General Hospital.
Lucas, Robert F. '02 (PH) Wallingford, PA St. John Chrysostom.
Lucas, Robert *c.m.* '74 (CHI)[N] Chicago, IL Vincentian Community, Congregation of the Mission, Midwest Province.
Lucas, Theodore '84 (CLV) Willowick, OH St. Mary Magdalene.
Lucas, Thomas M. *s.j.* '85 (SFR)[N] San Francisco, CA Jesuit Community at University of San Francisco.
Lucas, William '90 (BIR) Gardendale, AL St. Elizabeth Ann Seton.
Lucasinsky, Raymond *c.m.m.* '62 (DET)[K] Vocation Office.
Lucatero, Heliodoro '86 (SPK) On Duty Outside the Diocese.
Lucavei, Januario *o.s.b.m.* '00 (STF)[B] Glen Cove, NY Basilian Fathers Novitiate of the Order of St. Basil the Great.
Lucavei, Januario *o.s.b.m.* (RVC)[M] Glen Cove, NY St. Josaphat's Monastery, Novitiate and Retreat House.
Lucavei, Roberto *o.s.b.m.* (STN) Detroit.
Lucavei, Tarcisio *o.s.b.m.* '91 (STN) Hamtramck, MI Immaculate Conception of B.V.M..
Lucca, Augustine *s.d.s.* '51 (NSH) Smyrna, TN St. Luke.
Lucchesi, Joseph *o.carm.* '84 (JOL)[B] Washington, DC Whitefriars Hall.
Lucci, Frederick *o.p.* '93 (PHX)[G] Tempe, AZ Dominicans (Dominican Community–Jordan House); [I] Tempe, AZ Arizona State University.
Lucero, Jose *s.d.b.* '03 (LA)[C] Rosemead, CA Don Bosco Technical Institute; [D] Rosemead, CA Don Bosco Technical Institute.
Lucero, Leo '60 (SFE) Albuquerque, NM San Felipe de Neri.
Lucero, Lorenzo '56 (ELP) Retired.
Lucev, John '65 (SD) Retired.
Lucey, Beatus T. *o.s.b.* '59 (PAT)[M] Morristown, NJ St. Mary's Abbey.
Lucey, Gregory *s.j.* '64 (MOB)[A] Mobile, AL Spring Hill College.
Lucey, Paul T. *s.j.* '48 (BO)[V] Weston, MA Campion Health Center, Inc..
Lucey, Walter D. '98 (NEW) North Arlington, NJ Queen of Peace.
Lucey, William F. '52 (BO) Norwood, MA St. George; Senior Priests Retired.
Luchetti, Luis R. '97 (LA) Downey, CA Our Lady of Perpetual Help.
Luchi, Robert C. *s.j.* '93 (STL)[O] St. Louis, MO Jesuit Community Corporation at St. Louis University – Jesuit Hall.
Lucht, Shannon G. '02 (BIS) Belfield, ND St. Bernard; South Heart, ND St. Mary.
Lucia, Douglas J. '89 (OG) Secretary to the Bishop; Vice Chancellors; Adjutant Judicial Vicars; Vocations; Canton, NY St. Mary; Canton, NY St. Thomas More.
Luciana, Lawrence J. '63 (WH) Huntington, WV St. Joseph's.
Luciana, Lawrence '68 (WH)[B] Huntington, WV St. Joseph Catholic High School.
Luciani, Pompeo *s.a.c.* '36 (NEW) Fairview, NJ Our Lady of Grace.
Luciano, William J. '83 (NY) Bronx, NY St. Michael.
Lucid, Michael '54 (OAK) San Leandro, CA Assumption of the Blessed Virgin Mary.
Lucid, Philip J. *s.j.* '55 (SEA)[L] Seattle, WA Jesuit Community.
Lucid, Philip *s.j.* (SEA) Judges.
Lucido, John '73 (ELP) Kermit, TX St. Thomas & St. Joseph; Monahans, TX St. John the Apostle and Evangelist.
Lucido, John (ELP) St. Mark and St. Luke; Priests' Personnel Advisory Committee.
Luck, Robert O. '62 (LA) Retired.
Lucking, Alousius (SB) Retired.
Lucking, Aloysius '50 (MIA) Retired.
Lucree, Lawrence A. '60 (SAV) Cordele, GA St. Theresa; Home Missions.
Luczak, Andrew E. '70 (CHI) Skokie, IL St. Lambert.
Luczak, Jay R. '92 (TUC) Miami, AZ Our Lady of the Blessed Sacrament.
Luczak, Thomas *o.f.m.* '70 (MIL)[O] Provincial Offices; (FgM).
Luczycki, Matthew C. '45 (SY) Oneida, NY St. Joseph Retired.
Ludden, John J. '97 (VEN) Port Charlotte, FL St. Charles Borromeo.
Ludescher, Kenneth F. '61 (STP) Maplewood, MN St. Jerome.
Ludvik, John J. '71 (SEA) Vancouver, WA Our Lady of Lourdes.
Ludwick, Edmond '97 (CI)[C] Tunnuk, Chuuk, FM Vicariate Residence.
Ludwig, Alexander P. '58 (SCL) Alexandria, MN St. Mary's.
Ludwig, Alexander (SCL) Diocesan Priests Pension Plan Trustees.
Ludwig, Augustine W. *o.s.b.* '87 (RIC)[L] Richmond, VA Mary Mother of the Church Abbey.
Ludwig, Eugene M. *o.f.m.cap.* '71 (OAK) Oakland, CA St. John The Theologian; [A] Berkeley, CA Dominican School of Philosophy and Theology.
Ludwig, Eugene *o.f.m.cap.* '71 (OAK).
Ludwig, Eugene *o.f.m.cap.* '71 (SFR)[A] Burlingame, CA Our Lady of Angels.
Ludwig, John P. (DM) Advocates; Cumming, IA St. John.
Ludwig, Raphael A. '57 (DUB) Fort Atkinson, IA St. John Nepomucene Retired.
Ludwig, Thomas K. '87 (KC) St. Joseph, MO St. Mary's; [C] St. Joseph, MO Bishop LeBlond High School.
Ludwig, Thomas (KC) Diocesan Consultors; Deans; Air National Guard Chaplains.
Ludwikoski, James E. '73 (KCK) Military Chaplains; Air Force Chaplains.
Luebke, Martial *o.f.m.* '39 (FgM).
Luebking, Thomas A. '71 (TR) Spring Lake, NJ St. Catharine.
Lueckenotte, Daniel I.J. '90 (JC) Jefferson City, MO Capital Region Medical Center; Diocesan Consultors; Jefferson City, MO St. Joseph Cathedral.
Luehrmann, Stanley E. '54 (CIN) Hillsboro, OH St. Mary.
Lueras, Charles R. *c.r.i.c.* '81 (LA)[Q] Santa Paula, CA Canons Regular of the Immaculate Conception.
Lueras, Charles *c.r.i.c.* '81 (LA) Santa Paula, CA St. Sebastian; Santa Paula, CA Our Lady of Guadalupe.
Luerman, John H. '56 (IND) Retired.
Luetkemeyer, Alexander *o.s.b.* '53 (KC)[J] Parnell, MO St. Joseph Parish.
Luevano, Rafael '81 (ORG) Ecumenical and Interreligious Affairs; Sabbatical.
Luft, Raymond P. '68 (PRO) Providence, RI Our Lady of Mt. Carmel.
Luger, Paul P. *s.j.* '42 (SPK)[J] Spokane, WA Regis Community.
Lugger, William R. '89 (LAN) Lansing, MI St. Casimir.
Lugo, Camillo '70 (RVC) Copiague, NY Our Lady of the Assumption.
Lugo, Joseph W. '62 (PAT) Retired.
Lugo, Victor *m.n.m.* '81 (ARE) Quebradillas, PR Our Lady of Monserrate.
Lui, Gabriel '79 (LA) Monterey Park, CA St. Thomas Aquinas.
Lui, Pius *o.f.m.* '53 (FgM).
Lui, Tovia '83 (LA) Torrance, CA St. Catherine Laboure.
Luisi, Joseph G. '83 (PIT) Carnegie, PA St. Elizabeth Ann Seton.
Luisini, Anthony J. '56 (MET) Alpha, NJ St. Mary; College of Consultors.

Luiten, Gary D. (FAR) Deanery 9.
Luiten, Gary '92 (FAR) Ellendale, ND St. Helena; Ellendale, ND St. Patrick.
Luiz, Gary M. *c.pp.s.* '77 (OAK)[N] Berkeley, CA Society of the Precious Blood; Adjutant Judicial Vicars and Canonical Consultant to the Bishop; Court of Second Instance.
Luiz, Gary M. *c.pp.s.* (STO) Defenders of the Bond.
Luiz, Gary M. *c.p.p.s.* (RNO) Defenders of the Bond.
Luiz, Gary *c.pp.s.* (OAK) Judges.
Lukac, Thomas M. '63 (GBG) Latrobe, PA St. John the Evangelist.
Lukachinsky, Jerome A. '88 (CLV) Euclid, OH St. William Retired.
Lukas, Andrew F. '58 (WH) Retired.
Lukas, Joseph S. '46 (BO) Senior Priests Retired.
Lukas, Martin C. *o.s.f.s.* '80 (TOL)[J] Toledo, OH Provincial Residence.
Lukaschek, Ernest C. *m.m.* '64 (FgM).
Lukaszczyk, Josef '80 (STL)[O] Eureka, MO Our Lady of the Angels Monastery.
Lukaszewicz, John C. '55 (MIL) Retired.
Lukaszewski, Jerome *o.f.m.conv.* '48 (FgM).
Lukaszewski, Stanley P. '79 (TR) Manasquan, NJ St. Denis.
Lukati, Willy Frank *c.s.c.* (FTW)[I] McCauley House of Formation.
Luke, Eugene *o.s.b.* '61 (LR) Paris, AR St. Joseph's; [A] Subiaco, AR Subiaco Monastery.
Lukefahr, Oscar *c.m.* '66 (STL)[O] Perryville, MO Congregation of the Mission; [U] Perryville, MO Catholic Home Study Service.
Lukehart, Frederick '63 (Y) Warren, OH Christ Our King; Serra Club of Trumbull County.
Lukenda, Raymond T. '56 (NEW) Retired.
Lukianiuk, Andrzej '86 (BRK) Brooklyn, NY Guardian Angel.
Lukie, Bohdan *c.ss.r.* '67 (PHU) Newark, NJ St. John the Baptist.
Lukomski, Ryszard *s.a.c.* '93 (BUF) Cheektowaga, NY St. Josaphat.
Lukose, Joseph *c.m.* '84 (NY) New York, NY Our Lady of Victory; Edison, NJ St. Helena.
Lukoskie, Raymond M. '58 (PEO) Retired.
Lukyamuzi, Joseph M. *o.s.b.* '81 (RIC)[L] Richmond, VA Mary Mother of the Church Abbey.
Lulf, Ken '99 (SFS) Gettysburg, SD Sacred Heart; Diocesan Consultors; Deans; Presbyteral Council.
Luljak, Louis P. '61 (MIL) Retired.
Lulko, Leo T. '65 (DET) Highland, MI Church of the Holy Spirit.
Lumbre, Roger '86 (DET) Grosse Pointe, MI Our Lady Star of the Sea.
Luminais, J. Anthony '54 (NO) Bridge City, LA Holy Guardian Angels.
Lumine, Lex '87 (TR) Hainesport, NJ Our Lady Queen of Peace.
Lumpkin, Thomas '64 (DET) Detroit, MI Southwest Detroit Hospital.
Lumsden, Patrick L. '96 (DAV) Columbus Junction, IA St. Joseph; Wapello, IA St. Mary's.
Lumsden, Patrick '96 (DAV) Sperry, IA St. Mary's.
Luna, Ezequiel Bas *o.s.b.* '84 (SFE)[I] Abiquiu, NM Monastery of Christ in the Desert.
Luna, Henry *c.m.f.* '55 (LA)[Q] Rancho Dominguez, CA Dominguez Seminary Inc..
Luna, Ignacio '65 (BWN) San Benito, TX St. Benedict; Parish Priests' Consultors & Priest Personnel Board.
Luna, Lambert Joseph '78 (SFE) Santa Fe, NM Cristo Rey.
Luna, Lambert (SFE) College of Consultors.
Luna, Luis *m.s.a.* '87 (NOR)[A] Cromwell, CT Holy Apostles College and Seminary.
Luna, Miguel '82 (ELP) El Paso, TX Our Lady of Assumption.
Luna, Roger *s.d.b.* '57 (SFR)[N] San Francisco, CA Salesian Provincial Residence.
Lund, Donald F. *c.s.v.* '46 (CHI)[N] Arlington Heights, IL Viatorian Province Center–Clerics of St. Viator.
Lund, Donald J. '69 (CHI) Round Lake, IL St. Joseph.
Lundberg, Jan *o.c.d.* '93 (SJ)[M] San Jose, CA Carmelite Monastery, Novitiate.
Lundberg, John W. '60 (TLS) Retired.
Lundblad, Janet (CHI)[J] Melrose Park, IL Westlake Hospital.
Lundeen, Tim (CR) Commission on Catholic–Lutheran Rural Life.
Lundergan, Barnabas *o.s.b.* '45 (RCK)[G] Aurora, IL Marmion Abbey.
Lundgren, Richard '96 (JOL) Hinsdale, IL St. Isaac Jogues.
Lundgren, Stephen A. '79 (DUB) On Duty Outside the Archdiocese; Medical–Moral Commission.
Lungay, Jose Roel G. '84 (NO) Slidell, LA St. Genevieve.
Luniw, Paul '82 (STF) Terryville, CT St. Michael.
Luniw, Paul (HRT) Judges.
Luniw, Paul (STF) Diocesan Consultors; Judicial Vicar; Hartford; Presbyteral Council.
Lunness, John (WIL) Wilmington, DE Immaculate Heart of Mary.
Lunney, William '94 (SPR) Orange, MA St. Mary.
Lunnon, William '82 (DET)[M] Detroit, MI St. Mary's Residence Adult Foster Care.
Lunsford, Robert D. '60 (LAN) Lansing, MI St. Mary Cathedral; Bishop's Office; Victim Assistance Coordinator.
Lunzer, Matthias *s.v.d.* '45 (CHI)[B] Techny, IL Divine Word Residence.
Luo, Matteo *o.f.m.conv.* '59 (BAL)[S] Curia Generale dei Frati Minori Conventualli.
Luong, Dominic *s.s.s.* (CLV)[O] Cleveland, OH Blessed Sacrament Community.
Luong, James M. Vu Dai *c.m.c.* '73 (SPC)[E] Carthage, MO Congregation of the Mother Coredemptrix, United States Assumption Province.
Luong, Tri (HBG) Lykens, PA Our Lady Help of Christians Williamstown, PA Sacred Heart of Jesus.
Luong Minh Tuat, Francis M. *c.m.c.* '83 (SPC)[E] Springfield, MO Congregation of Mother Coredemptrix, Our Lady of the Rosary House.
Luongo, Anthony V. *s.d.b.* (BO) West Roxbury, MA Holy Name.
Luongo, John '78 (ORG) Retired.
Lupa, Gerard F. '77 (SCR)[L] Moscow, PA St. Mary's Villa Nursing Home; [L] Moscow, PA St. Mary's Villa Residence Elmhurst, PA St. Eulalia.
Lupico, Samuel '65 (BAL) Baltimore, MD St. Edward.
Lupo, Joseph F. *o.ss.t.* '45 (NY) Staten Island, NY Our Lady of Mt. Carmel–St. Benedicta.
Lusch, Daniel J. *s.j.* '62 (BO)[V] Boston The Society of Jesus of New England–Provincial Offices; [V] Newton, MA The Jesuit Community at Boston College.
Lusch, Daniel J. *s.j.* '62 (BUF)[O] Buffalo, NY Canisius Jesuit Community.
Luschen, Timothy D. '88 (OKL) Edmond, OK St. Monica; Council of Priests Archdiocesan; Council of Priests Archdiocesan.
Luschen, Timothy (OKL) Associate Directors.
Lusik, William A. '97 (NEW) Little Ferry, NJ St. Margaret of Cortona; Ridgefield, NJ St. Matthew's.
Lusoski, Thomas J. '57 (CLV) South Euclid, OH St. Margaret Mary Retired.
Lussier, Bonaventure *o.c.d.* '75 (WH)[M] Hinton, WV Monastery of Christ on the Mountain.
Lussier, Louis *o.s.cam.* '90 (MAD) Baraboo, WI St. Camillus Baraboo, WI St. Mary, Health of the Sick; [A] Baraboo, WI St. Camillus Monastery and Retreat Center.
Lussier, Louis *o.s.cam.* '90 (MIL)[X] Wauwatosa, WI St. Camillus Health System, Inc.; [X] St. Francis, WI St. Camillus Communities, Inc.; [X] Wauwatosa, WI St. Camillus Ministries, Inc.; [O] St. Francis, WI St. Camillus Provincialate; [O] St. Francis, WI St. Camillus Formation Community; [M] Wauwatosa, WI St. Camillus Health Center, Inc.; [M] Wauwatosa, WI San Camillo, Inc..
Lussier, Louis *o.s.cam.* '90 (MAD) Baraboo, WI St. Camillus; Baraboo, WI St. Mary, Health of the Sick; [A] Baraboo, WI St. Camillus Monastery and Retreat Center.
Lussier, Marc *m.s.a.* '66 (VEN) Cape Coral, FL St. Andrew.
Lussier, Robert *s.s.s.* '56 (GB) Albuquerque, NM St. Charles Borromeo.
Lussier, Robert *o.s.b.* '92 (SFE)[I] Pecos, NM Our Lady of Guadalupe Abbey; [K] Pecos, NM Our Lady of Guadalupe Olivetan Benedictine Abbey; Santa Fe, NM The Cathedral of San Francisco de Asis.
Lusson, David R. '80 (SUP) Frederic, WI St. Dominic; Frederic, WI Immaculate Conception.
Lustan, Ariel (TUC) Apache Junction, AZ St. George.
Luteri, Evaristo '30 (PIT) Retired.
Lutgen, Richard '61 (SAL) Retired.
Luther, Ben (OWN) Deans; Priests' Council.
Luther, Benjamin F. '64 (OWN) Central City, KY St. Joseph Central City, KY St. Charles.
Luther, Philip '87 (LIN) Superior, NE St. Joseph's.
Lutjen, George J. '68 (BRK) Douglaston, NY St. Anastasia.
Lutkenhoff, Bernard '71 (LFT) Unassigned.
Lutmer, Joseph H. '46 (CIN) Retired.
Lutostanski, Anthony '58 (BUF) Buffalo, NY St. John Kanty.
Luttenberger, Gerard H. *c.m.* '65 (RVC)[A] Huntington, NY Diocesan Seminary of the Immaculate Conception; [M] Oyster Bay, NY Vincentian Community.
Lutz, Bernard '63 (EVN)[A] St. Meinrad, IN St. Meinrad School of Theology Retired.
Lutz, Donald J. '70 (BUF) Buffalo, NY Our Lady of Perpetual Help; Buffalo, NY St. Valentine.
Lutz, Frederick J. '73 (SPC) Doniphan, MO St. Benedict.
Lutz, George C. '66 (NEW) Newark, NJ Holy Trinity – Epiphany.
Lutz, Gerald J. '56 (PIT) Retired.
Lutz, Herman '58 (IND)[I] Beech Grove, IN St. Paul Hermitage Retired.
Lutz, Herman (IND) Archdiocesan Judges.
Lutz, James M. '58 (SY) Retired.
Lutz, Joseph L. '87 (RCK) Retired.
Lutz, Kevin F. '78 (COL) Columbus, OH Holy Family.
Lutz, Robert J. '50 (CHI) Northbrook, IL St. Norbert Retired.
Lutz, Thomas '93 (NY) Highland, NY St. Augustine.
Luu, Joseph '66 (HT) Retired.
Luu, Vinh Dinh '03 (NO) Harahan, LA St. Rita; River Ridge, LA St. Matthew the Apostle.
Luu Quang, Bao Vinh *c.ss.r.* '01 (BRK)[C] Whitestone, NY St. Alphonsus Formation Residence.
Luwanika, Winiko (BO) Carlisle, MA St. Irene.
Luwich, Edmond '97 (CI) Holy Cross.
Lux, Joachim *o.f.m.* '61 (CIN)[M] Cincinnati, OH St. John the Baptist Friary.
Lux, Joseph W. *s.j.* '71 (BUF)[O] Buffalo, NY Canisius Jesuit Community.
Lux, Thomas J. '85 (LIN) Minden, NE St. John's; Diocesan Council of Catholic Women.
Luyet, Gregory T. *j.c.l.* '95 (LR) Little Rock, AR Our Lady of Good Counsel; Vice Chancellors; Adjutant Judicial Vicars; Judges.
Luzbetak, Louis *s.v.d.* '45 (CHI)[B] Techny, IL Divine Word Residence.
Luznicky, George M. *o.s.m.* '55 (CHI)[N] Chicago Order of Friar Servants of Mary (Servites) United States of America Province, Inc.; [I] Fullerton, CA St. Juliana Falconieri Priory; [I] Orange, CA Sisters of St. Joseph – Chaplain.
Luzzi, Anthony *s.d.b.* '49 (NY)[GG] Stony Point, NY Don Bosco Retreat Center and Marian Shrine; [GG] Stony Point, NY Marian Shrine.
Lwin, Josephat '84 (WCH) Caldwell, KS St. Martin of Tours.
Lwin, Paw Tun '02 (KC) Lee's Summit, MO Our Lady of the Presentation.
Ly, Hilary Tran Cong *c.m.c.* '77 (FWT)[B] Metairie, LA Congregation of the Mother Coredemptrix Formation House.
Lybarger, Curtis F. '77 (STP) Plymouth, MN St. Mary of the Lake.
Lyden, Dennis P. '63 (STU) Retired.
Lydon, John J. *o.s.a.* '84 (FgM).
Lydon, John *o.p.* '99 (DAL)[K] Irving, TX Dominican Priory of St. Albert the Great.
Lydon, Leo B. '50 (WH) Retired.
Lydon, Michael J. '84 (STL) St. Louis, MO St. Pius the Fifth.
Lydon, Michael '74 (SP) New Port Richey, FL St. Thomas Aquinas; [F] New Port Richey, FL St. Thomas Aquinas Early Childhood Center.
Lyle, Dennis J. '91 (CHI).
Lyle, John W. *o.s.f.s.* '85 (WIL)[J] Wilmington Oblates of St. Francis De Sales; Navy Chaplains.
Lyman, Edward P. '67 (SCR) Archbald, PA St. Thomas Aquinas.
Lynam, Gerald J. '50 (HEL) Retired.
Lynam, Michael John (PIT) Aliquippa, PA St. Frances Cabrini.
Lynam, Robert G. '84 (MET) Kendall Park, NJ St. Augustine of Canterbury.
Lynam, Robert J. (MET) Deans.
Lynch, Antone J. '81 (BLX) Gulfport, MS St. Joseph Catholic Church Retired.
Lynch, Antone (BLX) Deans; Interim Diocesan Liturgical Commission; Presbyteral Council.
Lynch, Charles *c.s.b.* '58 (GAL) Rosenberg, TX Our Lady of Guadalupe.
Lynch, Cletus J. '30 (CHI) Retired.
Lynch, Conall *o.f.m.* '51 (GLP) Gallup, NM St. Francis of Assisi.
Lynch, Cornelius B. '54 (PRO) Retired.
Lynch, Daniel C. '48 (SC) Retired.
Lynch, Daniel F. *o.carm.* '54 (NY) Franklin D. Roosevelt Hospital.
Lynch, Daniel *o.carm.* '54 (NY)[EE] Middletown, NY St. Albert's Priory.
Lynch, Daniel *s.m.a.* '73 (WDC)[M] Takoma Park, MD Lay Missionary Program.
Lynch, Daniel (SC) Priests' Pension Plan – Board of Trustees.
Lynch, Dennis J. '68 (LC) Wisconsin Rapids, WI Our Lady, Queen of Heaven; Elected Members.
Lynch, E. Patrick *c.ss.r.* '69 (STV) Christiansted, VI Church of the Holy Cross; Christiansted, St. Croix, VI St. Mary's.
Lynch, Edward C. *s.j.* '64 (BUF)[O] Buffalo, NY Canisius Jesuit Community.
Lynch, Edward J. '57 (BAL) Towson, MD Church of the Immaculate Conception; [O] Saint John Hall–Long Crandon; Priests' Council Retired.
Lynch, Eugene *s.m.m.* '54 (HRT)[M] Litchfield, CT Montfort Missionaries; [M] Monfort Novitiate.
Lynch, Francis A. *c.m.* '50 (MOB) Tallassee, AL St. Vincent De Paul.
Lynch, Francis '57 (BRK) Long Island City, NY St. Francis of Assisi.
Lynch, Gerard F. *o.ss.t.* '74 (TR) Asbury Park, NJ Our Lady of Mt. Carmel.
Lynch, Ibar '52 (SEA) Retired.
Lynch, James M. *m.m.* '74 (FgM).
Lynch, Jeremiah W. *s.j.* (CHI) Chicago, IL St. Procopius.

Lynch, John A. '60 (ROC) Rochester, NY St. James; Judges.
Lynch, John E. *c.s.p.* '51 (WDC)[B] Washington, DC St. Paul's College; [C] Catholic University of America, The Retired.
Lynch, John J. '96 (NY) Woodbourne, NY Immaculate Conception.
Lynch, John K. '56 (HRT) Retired.
Lynch, John R. '67 (CHI) Chicago, IL St. Margaret Mary.
Lynch, John S. '63 (E) Sharpsville, PA St. Bartholomew.
Lynch, John *m.afr.* '62 (WDC)[M] Washington, DC Missionaries of Africa.
Lynch, John '96 (NY) Beacon, NY St. Joachim.
Lynch, Joseph P. '53 (CHI) Retired.
Lynch, Kevin A. *c.s.p.* '53 (NEW)[N] Mahwah, NJ Paulist Fathers – Paulist Press; [S] Mahwah, NJ Paulist Press.
Lynch, Kevin A. *c.s.p.* '53 (NY) New York, NY St. Paul the Apostle.
Lynch, Kevin A. *m.m.* '61 (FgM).
Lynch, Leo A. '93 (ALT)[B] Altoona, PA Bishop Guilfoyle High School; Altoona, PA Our Lady of Fatima.
Lynch, Leo X. '56 (BO) Woburn, MA St. Anthony.
Lynch, Michael J. '71 (LC) Wausau, WI Wausau Hospital Center.
Lynch, Michael J. '82 (TR) Beverly, NJ St. Joseph.
Lynch, Michael J. *s.j.* '93 (NY) New York, NY Nativity.
Lynch, Michael '89 (MIA) Deerfield Beach, FL St. Ambrose.
Lynch, Michael (MIA) Catholic Fire Service Ministry.
Lynch, Myles M. *o.s.m.* '58 (CHI)[N] Chicago Order of Friar Servants of Mary (Servites) United States of America Province, Inc..
Lynch, Noel T. '62 (SAC) Auburn, CA St. Joseph Retired.
Lynch, Patrick J. '46 (ALB) Retired.
Lynch, Patrick J. *s.j.* '72 (BUF)[O] Buffalo, NY Canisius Jesuit Community.
Lynch, Peter J. (BGP) Trumbull, CT St. Catherine of Siena; [C] Trumbull, CT St. Joseph High School.
Lynch, Ralph *o.s.b.* '46 (IND)[K] New Hope, KY.
Lynch, Raymond J. *o.f.m.* '51 (PAT).
Lynch, Richard (LSC) Retired.
Lynch, Robert B. *o.f.m.* '43 (BO)[Y] Boston, MA Saint Anthony Residence.
Lynch, Robert B. '60 (NOR) Norwich, CT St. Mary; Legion of Mary.
Lynch, Robert G. *s.j.* '56 (CHY) Pinedale, WY Our Lady of Peace; Education Office Board.
Lynch, Robert (NOR) St. Mary Church – Spanish Apostolate.
Lynch, Shane M. '01 (OG) Malone, NY St. Helen; Malone, NY Notre Dame; Malone, NY St. John Bosco; Malone, NY St. Joseph's.
Lynch, Stephen P. '77 (BRK) Jamaica, NY Presentation of the Blessed Virgin Mary.
Lynch, Stephen *o.f.m.* '55 (PRO)[N] Providence, RI St. Francis Chapel & City Ministry Center; [P] Providence, RI St. Francis Friary.
Lynch, T. Patrick *s.j.* '61 (NEW)[B] Jersey City, NJ Jesuit Center; [N] Jersey City, NJ Jesuits of Saint Peter's College, Inc..
Lynch, Thomas A. '92 (NY)[A] Yonkers, NY Archdiocesan Preparatory Seminary.
Lynch, Thomas F. '48 (NEW) Retired.
Lynch, Thomas F. '71 (BGP) Stratford, CT St. James.
Lynch, Thomas P. *o.p.* '86 (CHI)[N] Chicago Dominicans (Provincial Office).
Lynch, Thomas *o.p.* '86 (FgM).
Lynch, Thomas '92 (NY)[A] Yonkers, NY St. Joseph's Seminary.
Lynch, William J. *s.j.* '48 (CHL) Mooresville, NC St. Therese; [J] Mooresville, NC Jesuit Community.
Lynes, James F. '79 (GAL) Clute, TX St. Jerome.
Lynes, John '87 (MOB) Chickasaw, AL St. Thomas the Apostle.
Lyng, Eamonn F. '58 (SD) La Jolla, CA Mary, Star of the Sea.
Lyng, Matthew '57 (CC) Deans; College of Consultors; Personnel Board – Priests; Presbyteral Council; Robstown, TX St. Thomas the Apostle.
Lynn, William D. *s.j.* '54 (COL).
Lynn, William J. '76 (PH)[A] Ardsley, PA Queen of Peace; Secretary for Clergy; Office for Clergy; Priests' Personnel Board; Diocesan Priests' Compensation and Benefits Committee; College of Consultors; Council of Priests.
Lyon, George *o.s.b.* '50 (SFS)[F] Marvin, SD Blue Cloud Abbey.
Lyon, Gerald F. '49 (SC) Retired.
Lyon, Joseph A. '50 (L) Retired.
Lyons, Denis '58 (ORG) Retired.
Lyons, Edward D. '62 (CAM) Retired.
Lyons, Francis '59 (MIA) Retired.
Lyons, Frederick J. (ALX) Retirement Board Retired.
Lyons, James A. '94 (PH) Philadelphia, PA Our Lady of Mt. Carmel; Council of Priests.
Lyons, James D. '60 (BO) Rowley, MA St. Mary.
Lyons, James F. '43 (FR) Retired.
Lyons, James M. *v.g.* '88 (HBG) Harrisburg, PA St. Catherine Laboure; Vicar General; General Secretary; Consultors, College; Lay Personnel, Department for.
Lyons, James P. '45 (KC) Retired.
Lyons, James '96 (DUL) Kelliher, MN St. Michael's.
Lyons, James '96 (CR) Kelliher, MN St. Patrick.
Lyons, James *o.m.i.* (FgM).
Lyons, John F. '46 (Y) Retired.
Lyons, John F. '73 (CLV) Fairview General Hospital.
Lyons, John J. (SAV) Augusta Deanery.
Lyons, John P. '55 (BO) Rochester, MA St. Rose of Lima.
Lyons, John P. '88 (TUC) Tucson, AZ Saints Peter and Paul; Special Assignment; Judicial Vicar; Diocesan Consultors; Council of Priests; All Vicars Forane.
Lyons, John T. '74 (PH) Boothwyn, PA St. John Fisher.
Lyons, John '42 (BO).
Lyons, John '73 (CLV) Cleveland, OH Our Lady of Angels.
Lyons, John '80 (SAV) Augusta, GA St. Joseph.
Lyons, John *o.m.v.* '83 (LA) Hawaiian Gardens, CA St. Peter Chanel.
Lyons, Joseph *o.m.i.* '29 (SAT)[K] San Antonio, TX Oblate Madonna Residence.
Lyons, Lawrence '54 (MIA) Retired.
Lyons, Leo J. (CHI) Retired.
Lyons, Michael J. '70 (DUL) Pine City, MN Immaculate Conception.
Lyons, Michael P. '96 (BGP) Easton, CT Notre Dame of Easton.
Lyons, Michael '96 (VIC) Procurator Advocate; On Leave of Absence.
Lyons, Patrick J. '45 (LIN)[E] Lincoln, NE Bonacum House Retired.
Lyons, Patrick M. '70 (CHI) Calumet City, IL Our Lady of Knock.
Lyons, Peter A. *t.o.r.* '66 (BAL) Baltimore, MD St. Ann; Baltimore, MD St. Wenceslaus.
Lyons, Richard J. '74 (MET) Dunellen, NJ St. John the Evangelist; Judicial Vicar; Episcopal Council.
Lyons, Robert *s.j.* '77 (SPK)[B] Spokane, WA Gonzaga University; [J] Spokane, WA Regis Community; Members.
Lyons, Thomas J. '52 (BRK) Brooklyn, NY St. Thomas Aquinas.
Lyons, Timothy V. *c.m.* '86 (PH) Philadelphia, PA Immaculate Conception.
Lyons, William J. '56 (CHI) Retired.
Lyons, William J. '56 (STL) Special Assignment.
Lysogorski, John '75 (ALB).
Lyttle, Eugene '93 (DUL) Retired.
Lyttle, Gregory (NY).
Lyttle, Paul (WDC) Bowie, MD St. Pius X.

M

Ma, Didacus W. '52 (SFR) San Francisco, CA St. Monica Retired.
Ma, Peter '55 (NY) New York, NY St. Mary; Manhattan, NY New York Downtown Hospital – New York Infirmary.
Maag, Ronald E. (BAK) Council of Priests and Diocesan Consultors; Building Committee; Director of Campaign for Human Development; Priests' Continuing Education Committee.
Maanzo, Anthony (PEO) Peoria, IL St. Mark's.
Maaq, Ronald E. '78 (BAK) Hood River, OR Immaculate Conception.
Maassen, Jeffrey A. '97 (STL) St. Charles, MO Sts. Joachim and Ann.
Maat, William A. *o.s.b.* '33 (SEA)[L] Lacey, WA St. Martin's Abbey.
Maata, Rodrigo R. '92 (GAL) Houston, TX St. Vincent de Paul.
Maatuokuu, Benjamin '71 (PHX) Prescott Valley, AZ St. Germaine.
Mabango, Ashiono Anthony '95 (PAT) Unassigned.
Mabarak, John R. *o.s.a.* '60 (CHI)[N] Olympia Fields, IL Tolentine Monastery at Tolentine Center.
Mabon, Thomas K. '57 (ALT) Retired.
Macalintal, Dionisio '63 (PH) National City, CA St. Mary.
Macaranas, Rafael R. '64 (NY) Manhattan, NY Cabrini Medical Center.
Macatangay, Francis M. '99 (GAL) Galena Park, TX Our Lady of Fatima.
MacAulay, Gerard '59 (OKL) Retired.
Macaulay, Neil *o.m.i.* '63 (SJN)[E] San Juan, PR Centro Medico de P.R..
MacAuley, Stephen A. '51 (TLS)[F] Tulsa, OK St. John Villas, Inc. Retired.
Macaya, Miguel '65 (LSC) Dona Ana, NM Our Lady of the Purification.
MacCandless, William J. *o.s.b.* '58 (NO)[P] St. Benedict, LA St. Joseph Abbey.
MacCarthy, John P. *o.praem.* '69 (GB)[I] Archdiocese of Iquitos, Peru.
MacCarthy, Joseph T. '97 (BO) Methuen, MA St. Monica.
MacCarthy, Justin H. '64 (ORG) La Habra, CA Our Lady of Guadalupe.
MacCarthy, Liam '68 (SAC) Sutter Creek, CA Immaculate Conception.
macCarthy, Liam (SAC) Pro–Synodal Judges; College of Consultors.
MacCarthy, Timothy '60 (ORG) Tustin, CA St. Cecilia; Clergy Personnel Board.
Macchi, William '64 (OAK) Retired.
Macchietto, Robert G. '71 (NY)[E] New York, NY Monsignor Farrell High School.
MacDonald, Adam *s.v.d.* '00 (CHI)[B] Techny, IL Divine Word Residence.
MacDonald, Arthur F. '52 (GLP) Alpine, AZ St. Helena.
MacDonald, Charles J. '67 (HRT) Wallingford, CT Holy Trinity.
MacDonald, Colin A. '45 (MAN) Manchester, NH St. Joseph Cathedral Retired.
MacDonald, Colin A. (MAN) Clergy Personnel Board.
Macdonald, Colin '81 (SAC) Roseville, CA St. Clare.
MacDonald, David W. *s.j.* '61 (SAC) Sacramento, CA St. Ignatius of Loyola.
MacDonald, Fabian '77 (SEA) Seattle, WA Immaculate Conception.
MacDonald, Hugh J. '64 (HRT) North Haven, CT St. Barnabas.
MacDonald, James H. '67 (SFR) Redwood City, CA St. Pius; Deans; Board of Directors.
MacDonald, Kevin M. *c.ss.r.* '91 (FgM).
MacDonald, Paul V. '59 (BO) Scituate, MA St. Frances Xavier Cabrini.
MacDonald, Richard *s.c.j.* '65 (MIL)[O] Hales Corners, WI Priests of the Sacred Heart; [O] Milwaukee, WI SCJ Community.
MacDonald, Sebastian *c.p.* '58 (DET)[K] Detroit, MI St. Paul of the Cross Community, Congregation of the Passion.
MacDonald, Stirling B. '88 (BO) Senior Priests Retired.
MacDonald, Timothy E. (LAN) Fowler, MI Most Holy Trinity.
MacDonald, Timothy I. '67 (ARL) Herndon, VA Christ the Redeemer.
MacDonnell, John J. *s.j.* '58 (WOR)[O] Worcester, MA Jesuits of Holy Cross College, Inc..
MacDonnell, John *s.j.* '58 (BO)[V] Weston, MA Campion Health Center, Inc..
MacDonnell, Joseph F. *s.j.* '61 (BGP)[B] Fairfield, CT Fairfield University; [P] Fairfield, CT The Fairfield Jesuit Community–Fairfield University.
MacDonnell, Martin *s.j.* '66 (BO)[V] Newton, MA The Jesuit Community at Boston College.
MacDonough, Richard *s.s.* '60 (LA)[A] Camarillo, CA St. John's Seminary College of the Archdiocese of Los Angeles.
MacDougall, James L. *o.s.a.* '59 (MIA)[B] St. Thomas University; [H] Miami, FL Casa San Lorenzo.
Mace, John D. *s.j.* '68 (MIL)[O] Arrupe International Residence.
MacEachen, Bede *s.a.* '42 (NY).
Maceas, Tobias *o.s.m.* (ELP)[EE] El Paso, TX Our Lady of Sorrows.
Maceda, Thomas *c.ss.r.* '63 (BRK) Brooklyn, NY Our Lady of Perpetual Help Basilica.
Macedo, Charles '48 (SJ) Palo Alto, CA St. Thomas Aquinas.
Maceli, Anthony J. '48 (BRK) Retired.
Macelli, Gil (MRY) Ecumenical Commission.
MacEntee, Francis J. *s.j.* '54 (SCR)[C] Scranton, PA The University of Scranton.
MacEwen, Michael W. (BO) Marlborough, MA Immaculate Conception.
Macey, Richard '75 (DET) Woodhaven, MI Our Lady of the Woods.
MacFarlane, John F. '66 (WDC) Rockville, MD St. Elizabeth.
MacGabhann, Kevin '63 (PMB) Lantana, FL Holy Spirit; Legion of Mary.
MacGee, James B. *o.m.i.* '57 (PT) Crawfordville, FL St. Elizabeth Ann Seton; Woodville, FL St. Stephen the Protomartyr.
MacGregor, Mark D. *s.j.* '96 (BGP)[B] Fairfield, CT Fairfield University.
Machado, Clement '93 (CC)[G] Robstown, TX Society of Our Lady of the Most Holy Trinity.
Machado, Domingos A. *o.a.r.* '95 (LA)[Q] Oxnard, CA St. Augustine Priory O.A.R..
Machado, Jose '93 (WCH) Wichita, KS Our Lady of Perpetual Help; Wichita Diocesan Hispanic Council.
Machado, Manuel '64 (NY) New York, NY St. Rose of Lima.
Machain, David B. '52 (PH) Retired.
Machain, David '52 (PH) Philadelphia, PA St. Bernard Retired.
Machalski, Thomas C. (BRK) Bishop Valero—; Vice Officiales–Associate Judicial Vicars.
Machalski, Thomas '85 (BRK) Bayside, NY St. Josaphat; [U] San Antonio, TX Polish American Priest Association (P.A.P.A.); Bayside, NY St. Josaphat.
Machar, Jerome J. *o.c.s.o.* '75 (ROC)[I] Piffard, NY Abbey of the Genesee.
Machcinski, Anthony J. '50 (GAY) Retired.
Machesky, Pater *o.f.m.* '51 (GB).
Machira, Paul (SY)[I] Solvay, NY St. Cecilia.
Machlik, Jerome J. '71 (DET) Shelby Twp., MI St. John Vianney Church.

Machnik, Theodore F. '91 (COL) Portsmouth, OH St. Mary; Army National Guard Chaplains.
Macho, George S. '53 (NEW) Retired.
Macias, Alonso E. (BO) Cambridge, MA St. Mary of the Annunciation.
Macias, Frank '94 (SAT)[A] San Antonio, TX Assumption Seminary aka Assumption–St. John's Seminary.
Macias, Salvador '82 (OAK) Oakland, CA St. Jarlath's.
Maciej, David '80 (SCL) Rice, MN Immaculate Conception; Koinonia Program of Central Minnesota.
Maciejewski, Norbert '69 (DET) Warren, MI Ascension; Warren, MI St. Leonard of Port Maurice.
Maciejewski, Tadeusz *c.m.* '88 (BRK) Brooklyn, NY St. Stanislaus Kostka.
Maciel, Francis Javier '96 (CHI) Chicago, IL St. Francis de Sales.
MacInnis, John E. (BO) Peabody, MA St. John the Baptist; Members.
MacInnis, Michael *o.f.m.* (BO) Marlborough, MA St. Ann.
MacIntyre, Frederick H. '92 (WDC) Charlotte Hall, MD St. Mary.
Macior, Lazarus *o.f.m.* '56 (Pulaski, WI)[O] Akron, OH University of Akron.
Macior, Lazarus *o.f.m.* '56 (GB).
MacIssac, Charles S. *o.s.* '83 (PCE)[I] On Duty Outside the Diocese.
Mack, John P. '85 (BUF) Air Force Reserve Chaplains; Oakfield, NY St. Patrick; Oakfield, NY St. Cecilia; Batavia, NY St. Joseph.
Mack, Joseph W. '89 (CHL) Asheboro, NC St. Joseph.
Mack, Robert A. '57 (BUF) Retired.
Mack, Robert '57 (BUF)[L] Buffalo, NY St. Francis of Buffalo, Inc..
Mack, Thomas E. '78 (PEO) Pontiac, IL St. John's; Pontiac, IL St. Mary's.
Mack, Thomas E. (PEO) Diocesan College of Consultors; Vicariates and Vicars.
Mack, Thomas (PEO) Presbyteral Council.
Macke, Paul B. *s.j.* '73 (ANC)[G] Anchorage, AK Anchorage Jesuit Community.
Macke, Paul *s.j.* '73 (ANC)[I] Anchorage, AK Holy Spirit Center.
Macke, Paul *s.j.* (ANC) Diocesan Consultors; Retreats.
Macke, Richard J. '54 (SC) Retired.
Macken, Forrest *c.p.* '47 (L)[K] Louisville, KY Sacred Heart Retreat.
MacKenzie, John B. (MAN) Berlin, NH Good Shepherd.
MacKenzie, William M. '66 (BO) Permanent Disability.
Mackert, Albert J. '61 (CLV) Cleveland, OH Immaculate Conception Retired.
Mackesy, Robert L. *m.m.* '47 (NY).
Mackey, Alan C. '00 (BIR)[EE] Birmingham, AL St. Francis Xavier; Jacksonville, AL St. Charles; [H] Jacksonville, AL Jacksonville State University.
Mackey, James (ALB) Propagation of the Faith–Pontifical Society; Glens Falls, NY St. Mary.
Mackiewicz, Richard E. '69 (GBG) Saltsburg, PA St. Matthew.
Mackin, Eamon *c.h.s.* '70 (ORG) Huntington Beach, CA St. Mary's by the Sea.
Mackin, Francis C. *s.j.* '54 (BO)[V] Newton, MA The Jesuit Community at Boston College.
Mackin, John J. '38 (CHI) Hometown, IL Our Lady of Loretto Retired.
Mackin, Kevin E. *o.f.m.* '64 (ALB)[B] Loudonville, NY Siena College; [B] Siena College.
Mackin, William H. '38 (MIL) Retired.
MacKinnon, Don *c.ss.r.* (OAK) Khmmu/Laotian Pastoral Center.
MacKinnon, Donald *c.ss.r.* '59 (OAK)[N] Berkeley, CA Redemptorists (St. Clemens Maria House).
Mac Kinnon, Donald *c.ss.r.* '59 (OAK)[N] Berkeley, CA Redemptorists (St. Clemens Maria House).
MacKinnon, William H. *s.o.l.t.* '97 (STN) St. Joseph, MO St. Joseph's; Omaha, NE St. George's; Omaha, NE Assumption of B.V.M.; Chief Financial Officer.
Mac Kinnon, William '97 (CC)[G] Robstown, TX Society of Our Lady of the Most Holy Trinity.
Mackle, Daniel E. '80 (PH) Philadelphia, PA Cathedral Basilica of SS. Peter and Paul; Office for Worship.
Mackle, Liam M. *o.s.m.* '58 (CHI)[N] Chicago Order of Friar Servants of Mary (Servites) United States of America Province, Inc..
Macklin, Eckley *s.o.l.t.* '94 (KC)[G] Robstown, TX Society of Our Lady of the Most Holy Trinity.
Macklin, Eckley *s.o.l.t.* '94 (CC)[I] Corpus Christi, TX; Corpus Christi, TX St. Anselm Anglican Use Community.
Macko, John '41 (PBR) Retired.
Mackowski, Richard M. *s.j.* '61 (DET).
MacLellan, Iain G. *o.s.b.* '87 (MAN)[K] Manchester, NH St. Anselm Abbey.
MacLennan, Donald '67 (DET) Absent on Sick Leave.
MacLeod, Malcolm C. *m.ss.cc.* '87 (CAM) Linwood, NJ Our Lady of Sorrows.
MacLoughlin, James '63 (ORL) Belleview, FL St. Theresa.
MacMahon, Craig *o.m.v.* '90 (BO).
MacMahon, Eamon '47 (MRY) Retired.
MacMahon, Michael '66 (BIR)[B] Huntsville, AL Holy Spirit; Diocesan College of Vicars; Diocesan College of Vicars.
MacMahon, Patrick '69 (SPK) Davenport, WA Immaculate Conception; Harrington, WA St. Francis of Assisi; Rearden, WA St. Michael.
MacMaster, Thomas A. *o.c.s.o.* '57 (DUB)[K] Peosta, IA New Melleray Abbey, Order of Cistercians of the Strict Observance.
MacMillan, Donald A. *s.j.* '72 (BO)[V] Newton, MA The Jesuit Community at Boston College.
MacMillan, Len '91 (B)[F] Moscow, ID St. Augustine Catholic Center; Priest Personnel Commission; Catholic Liturgical Commission.
MacMillan, Leonard '91 (B) Moscow, ID St. Augustine's.
MacNamara, Robert C. '51 (ROC) Horseheads, NY St. Mary Our Mother Retired.
MacNevin, Stanley F. *c.s.p.* '60 (NY)[EE] Jamaica Estates Paulist Fathers Generalate.
MacNevin, Stanley F. *c.s.p.* '60 (BO)[V] Boston, MA Paulist Fathers Residence.
MacNew, James J. *o.s.f.s.* '80 (WIL)[J] Wilmington Oblates of St. Francis De Sales.
Maco, Stephen L. '76 (ALN) Shenandoah, PA Annunciation; [C] Ashland, PA Cardinal Brennan Jr./Sr. High School.
Macora, Athanasius *o.f.m.* '92 (FgM).
Macoskie, Melvin H. '55 (MIL) Retired.
MacPhaidin, Bartley *c.s.c.* '63 (FR)[A] North Easton, MA Stonehill College.
MacPherson, Albert P. *o.s.a.* '74 (BO)[C] Our Mother of Good Counsel Monastery.
MacPherson, Damian *s.a.* '78 (NY).
MacPherson, Stephen E.C. '86 (SR)[EE] McKinleyville, CA Christ the King.
MacPherson, Walter E. '55 (BEL) Retired.
Macpherson, Walter '86 (CIN) Dayton, OH Our Lady of Mercy Retired.
MacQuarrie, John D. '78 (CIN) Troy, OH St. Patrick; West Milton, OH Transfiguration.
MacRory, Camillus *o.f.m.cap.* '51 (SFR)[N] Burlingame, CA Capuchin Provincial House.
MacVeigh, Donal T. *s.j.* '72 (NEW)[B] Jersey City, NJ Jesuit Center; [N] Jersey City, NJ Jesuits of Saint Peter's College, Inc..
MacVeigh, Michael C. '56 (PIT) Pittsburgh, PA St. Norbert.
Madathiparampil, George (SYM) Vicar General (Protosyncellus); Eparchial Consultors.
Madavana, Davis '79 (CAM) Collingswood, NJ St. John's.
Maday, Norbert J. '64 (CHI) Other Assignments.
Maddalena, Joseph P. '86 (GBG) Ligonier, PA Holy Trinity; Deaneries; Bishop's Priests Council; Office for Ministry Development.
Madden, Benjamin *o.f.m.cap.* '58 (FgM).
Madden, Brendan P. '51 (PAT) Clifton, NJ St. Clare's.
Madden, Daniel P. *o.p.* '60 (MIA)[B] Miami, FL Barry University; [H] Bal Harbour, FL Dominican Friars Residence.
Madden, Declan A. *o.f.m.* '47 (DEN)[ ] Denver, CO Francis Heights, Inc.; [L] Denver, CO Clare Gardens, Inc..
Madden, Denis J. '67 (BAL) Special Assignment.
Madden, Denis '67 (NY)[II] New York, NY Catholic Near East Welfare Association (CNEWA).
Madden, Edward T. '52 (DEN) Byers, CO Our Lady of the Plains.
Madden, Henry L. *o.f.m.* '46 (ALB)[B] Siena College; [R] Albany, NY St. Francis Chapel.
Madden, James J. '55 (GAL) Retired.
Madden, James J. '55 (GAL)[N] Houston, TX Pope John Paul XXIII Priests' Residence Retired.
Madden, James J. (FgM).
Madden, James J. *o.praem.* (MO) Army Chaplains.
Madden, James P. *c.s.c.* '57 (ALB)[L] Valatie, NY St. Joseph Center.
Madden, James P. *c.s.c.* '57 (BGP)[P] Valatie, NY Brothers of Holy Cross.
Madden John F. '84 (WOR) Clinton, MA Our Lady of Jasna Gora.
Madden John J. '62 (NEW) Retired.
Madden John P. '86 (Y) Newton Falls OH St. Joseph; Newton Falls, OH St. Mary.
Madden, John R. '59 (SY) Hamilton, NY St. Mary; Morrisville, NY St. Joan of Arc.
Madden, John R. '70 (SAV) Columbus, GA St. Anne.
Madden, John '62 (NEW)[N] Rutherford, NJ St. John Vianney Residence for Priests.
Madden, Joseph *o.f.m.conv.* '62 (R) Siler City, NC St. Julia; [E] Pittsboro, NC Our Lady of Guadalupe Friary.
Madden, Lawrence J. *s.j.* '64 (WDC)[M] Washington, DC The Jesuit Community at Georgetown University.
Madden, Michael G. '62 (TOL) Toledo, OH St. Patrick of Heatherdowns Retired.
Madden, Michael J. '95 (BGP) Darien, CT St. John.
Madden, Michael '75 (EVN) Bloomfield, IN Holy Name; Advocates.
Madden, Patrick J. '83 (MOB) Monroeville, AL Annunciation.
Madden, Patrick J. (SHP) College of Consultors; Presbyteral Council; Greco Institute.
Madden, Patrick J. (MOB) Vicar for Ministry to Persons with Disabilities and the Deaf.
Madden, Patrick J. (SHP) College of Consultors; Presbyteral Council; Greco Institute.
Madden, Patrick M. '53 (STA) Retired.
Madden, Patrick '83 (MOB) Monroeville, AL St. Joseph; [J] Monroeville, AL Alabama Southern Community College Newman Center; Handicapped, Apostolate to the.
Madden, Stephen J. '88 (BO) Watertown, MA St. Patrick.
Madden, Thomas E. '32 (ALT) Retired.
Madden, Thomas G. '55 (NEW) North Arlington, NJ Queen of Peace; [N] Rutherford, NJ St. John Vianney Residence for Priests Retired.
Madden, Thomas J. *s.j.* '57 (LAF) Grand Coteau, LA St. Charles Borromeo; [J] Grand Coteau, LA Jesuit Spirituality Center (St. Charles College).
Madden, Thomas L. '81 (SP) Dunedin, FL Our Lady of Lourdes.
Madden, Thomas '53 (SFR).
Madden, Thomas '76 (NY) Haverstraw, NY St. Peter.
Madden, Thomas *s.j.* (MIA) Miami Dade CC–Wolfson Campus.
Madden, William T. *m.m.* '58 (NY)[EE] Maryknoll Maryknoll Fathers and Brothers; [EE] Maryknoll, NY Maryknoll Fathers and Brothers Charitable Trust; [II] Maryknoll, NY Friends of St. Maria Goretti, U.S.A., Inc..
Maddigan, John (BO) Society of St. James the Apostle.
Maddineni, Ananda Prasad *m.s.f.* '96 (ATL)[K] Lawrenceville The Missionaries of St. Francis De Sales; AUXILIARY CHAPLAINS CONTRACT CHAPLAINS.
Maddock, Andrew *s.j.* '85 (HEL) St. Ignatius, MT St. Ignatius Mission.
Maddock, George *o.f.m.cap.* '64 (AGN)[F] Agana Heights, GU St. Fidelis Friary; (FgM).
Maddock, Jay T. '75 (FR) East Taunton, MA Holy Family; [L] East Taunton, MA Diocesan Catholic Youth Organization; Judges; Catholic Youth Organization.
Maddock, Laurence F. '56 (CHI) Retired.
Maddox, Edward '96 (AUS) Retired.
Maddux, Jack '99 (AUS)[A] Fayetteville, TX St. John's; Fayetteville, TX St. Mary's; Rural Life.
Madej, Paul D. '90 (SY) Military Chaplains; Army Chaplains.
Mader, George L. '59 (NEW)[N] Caldwell, NJ The Rev. Msgr. James F. Kelley Residence for Retired Priests Retired.
Mader, George (NEW) Rev. Msgr. James F. Kelley Residence.
Mader, Joseph '67 (IND) On Disability Leave.
Mader, Stan P. '92 (STP) Mound, MN Our Lady of the Lake.
Madera, Luis M. *o.s.a.* (NY) Staten Island, NY Our Lady of Good Counsel.
Madero, Martin '02 (LA) Los Angeles, CA Our Lady Help of Christians (Maria Auxiliadora).
Madey, Louis '68 (LAN) Jackson, MI St. Joseph; Navy Reserve Chaplains.
Madigan, Arthur R. *s.j.* '77 (SY)[Q] Syracuse, NY Jesuits at LeMoyne, Inc..
Madigan, Daniel G. '80 (GAY) Alpena, MI St. Anne.
Madigan, Daniel '64 (SAC) Clarksburg, CA St. Joseph.
Madigan, John A. *o.p.* (RVC)[B] Rockville Centre, NY Molloy College.
Madigan, John C. '74 (SEA) Renton, WA St. Stephen the Martyr.
Madigan, John J. '54 (WDC) Silver Spring, MD Our Lady of Grace.
Madigan, John R. *o.m.i.* (MIA) Office for Religious.
Madigan, John *o.m.i.* '77 (MIA) Miami, FL St. Francis Xavier; Opa Locka, FL St. Philip.
Madigan, Kevin (NY) New York, NY St. Peter.
Madigan, Patrick S. *s.j.* '83 (NO).
Madison, Martin *s.a.* '62 (BRK)[P] Brooklyn, NY Our Lady of Victory.
Madley, Jeffrey J. '76 (RVC) Southampton, NY Sacred Hearts of Jesus and Mary.
Madonado, Edward '84 (ARE) Utuado, PR San Miquel.
Madori, Peter J. '69 (NY) Wurtsboro, NY St. Joseph.
Madrazo, Higinio *c.m.* '44 (SJN) San Juan, PR Jesus Maestro; San Juan, PR San Vicente de Paul; [F] Rio Piedras, PR Asylum For Orphan Girls.
Madrid, Jaime '68 (ELP) Absent on Leave.
Madrid, Mariano '69 (SP) Valrico, FL St. Stephen.
Madrigal, Hector '87 (AMA) Presbyteral Council; Childress, TX Holy Angels; Memphis, TX Sacred Heart; Priests' Pension Plan Retirement Committee.
Madrigal, Ildefonso '57 (LA) Retired.
Madsen, John W. '66 (BUF) Depew, NY St. Barnabas.
Madu, Ferdinand E. (MO) Army Chaplains.
Maduakor, Casmir '84 (ATL) Duluth, GA St. Benedict.
Madumelu, Jerome (RVC) West Islip, NY Good Samaritan Hospital Medical Center.
Maduri, John '87 (BRK) Howard Beach, NY Our Lady of Grace.

Maduro, Gabriel '59 (ARE) Arecibo, PR Cathedral of San Felipe Apostol; Defenders of the Bond.
Maduro, P. Gabriel (ARE) Buen Pastor Hospital; Susoni Hospital.
Madus, Peter P. '68 (SCR) Scranton, PA St. Joseph's; Scranton, PA St. Vincent de Paul; Army National Guard Chaplains.
Maduzia, Norbert J. '82 (GAL) Houston, TX St. Frances Cabrini; Area Representatives.
Maechler, Edmund F. '49 (LA) Retired.
Maechler, Gerald T. '55 (LA) Retired.
Maekawa, Steven *o.p.* '98 (SEA) Seattle, WA Blessed Sacrament; [O] Seattle, WA University of Washington, Catholic Newman Center.
Maes, Allen *o.m.i.* '68 (BEL)[F] Belleville, IL Shrine of Our Lady of the Snows.
Maes, Allen *o.m.i.* '68 (WDC)[M] Washington, DC Provincial Offices of the United States Province of the Missionary Oblates of Mary Immaculate.
Maes, Clarence '87 (SFE) Santa Fe, NM St. Anne's; Presbyteral Council of the Archdiocese of Santa Fe.
Maes, Clark B. (STL) St. Charles, MO St. Elizabeth Ann Seton.
Maes, John J. '67 (DOD) Claflin, KS Immaculate Conception; Ellinwood, KS St. Joseph; College of Consultors.
Maestri, William F. '77 (NO)[A] Communications.
Maestrini, Nicholas *p.i.m.e.* '30 (PMB)[J] Tequesta, FL P.I.M.E. Missionaries.
Maffei, Vincent R. '64 (BO) Randolph, MA St. Mary.
Maffeo, Michael T. '91 (RVC) Rocky Point, NY St. Anthony of Padua; Ronkonkoma, NY St. Joseph's.
Magaldi, Philip '60 (FWT) Retired.
Magalhaes, Jose Luis *o.f.m.conv.* '64 (TR) Riverside, NJ St. Peter.
Magallanes, Alejandro *o.f.m.cap.* '69 (FRS) Community Hospital, Veterans' Hospital & University Medical Center; [F] La Canada Flintridge, CA St. Francis High School.
Magallanes, Manuel *o.s.b.* '76 (OKL)[I] Shawnee St. Gregory's Abbey.
Magana, Alberto '01 (YAK) Sunnyside, WA St. Joseph's.
Magana, Jose L. '98 (LA) Long Beach, CA St. Anthony.
Magary, Thomas A. '66 (STU) Martins Ferry, OH St. Mary.
Magat, Elmer (SFR) San Francisco, CA St. Patrick.
Magat, Geronimo A. '02 (ARL) Colonial Beach, VA St. Elizabeth; Auditors.
Magbanua, Mario '65 (DAL) Dallas, TX St. James.
Magdaleno, Ricardo '89 (FRS) Bakersfield, CA St. Joseph.
Magdaraog, Vicente '96 (TR) Maple Shade, NJ Our Lady of Perpetual Help.
Magee, Michael K. '91 (PH) On Duty Outside the Archdiocese.
Magee, Patrick F. '70 (TR) Bay Head, NJ Sacred Heart.
Magee, Patrick '81 (FR) Special Assignment.
Magee, Paul L. '94 (STP) Special Assignment.
Magee, Robert L. '70 (PMB) Jensen Beach, FL St. Martin de Porres.
Magel, John E. '60 (L)[K] Louisville, KY Bishop David Apartments Retired.
Mager, Martin J. *o.s.b.* '63 (SFR)[N] Portola Valley, CA Woodside Priory.
Maggart, James M. '97 (CAM) Somerdale, NJ Our Lady of Grace; Adjutant Judicial Vicars; Office of Worship; Members.
Maggs, William C. *c.ss.r.* '60 (PH) Philadelphia, PA St. Peter the Apostle.
Maghinay, Jose M. '03 (STO) Modesto, CA St. Stanislaus Church (Pastor of).
Maginnis, Andrew F. *s.j.* '52 (SFR)[E] San Francisco, CA St. Ignatius College Preparatory (Coed); Office of the Vicar for Religious.
Maginnis, Edward L. *s.j.* '53 (DEN)[N] Denver, CO Regis Jesuit Community (The Jesuits at Regis University).
Maginot, Michael L. '83 (GRY) Merrillville, IN St. Stephen, Martyr; Judicial Vicar.
Maginot, Richard J. '50 (CHI) Prospect Heights, IL St. Alphonsus Liguori Retired.
Magnan, Oscar G. '63 (NEW)[B] Jersey City, NJ Jesuit Center; [N] Jersey City, NJ Jesuits of Saint Peter's College, Inc..
Magnano, Paul A. (SEA) Vicar for Clergy, Office of; Presbyteral Council; College of Consultors.
Magnano, Paul '67 (SEA) Seattle, WA St. Catherine; Seattle, WA Christ the King; Special Assignment.
Magnaye, Carlo Benjamin *m.f.* '66 (AUS) Mexia, TX State School.
Magnaye, Carlo Benjamin '96 (AUS) Mexia, TX St. Mary's.
Magnaye, Francisco Nicolas P. *c.m.* '94 (NEW) Jersey City, NJ Our Lady of Victories.
Magner, Kevin P. (STP) Edina, MN Our Lady of Grace.
Magni, Daniel D. (BO) Lowell, MA St. Rita.
Magnuson, Thomas J. '87 (OM) Omaha, NE St. Thomas More.
Magoon, R. Dale '60 (GAY) Mancelona, MI St. Anthony; Judges.
Magpayo, Teodoro '89 (HON) Haiku, HI St. Rita; Paia, HI Holy Rosary.
Magraw, Daniel E. '75 (E) Erie, PA Blessed Sacrament.
Maguire, Connell J. '45 (PH) Retired.
Maguire, Daniel J. '69 (SFR) San Francisco, CA St. Thomas the Apostle.
Maguire, Enda J. '59 (STO) Lockeford, CA St. Joachim Church of Lockeford (Pastor of).
Maguire, Eugene '47 (PHX) Retired.
Maguire, Eugene '47 (PHX)[H] Phoenix, AZ Mt. Claret Center.
Maguire, Eugene (PHX) Directors.
Maguire, Francis X. *c.m.* '78 (PH).
Maguire, Francis X. *c.m.* '78 (MAN)[AA] Concord, NH St. Peter.
Maguire, Hugh '57 (MOB) Grand Bay, AL St. John Baptist.
Maguire, John R. '50 (STL) St. Louis, MO Cure' of Ars; Vicar for Administration.
Maguire, Robert *o.cist.* '76 (DAL)[B] University of Dallas; [K] Irving, TX Cistercian Abbey of Our Lady of Dallas.
Maguire, Seamus J. '53 (WH) Retired.
Maguire, Thomas H. '76 (BO) Norwell, MA St. Helen.
Maguire, Thomas '69 (SAC) Represa, CA Folsom State Prison; Represa, CA.
Maguire, Thomas (SAC) Alcoholism Advisory Board.
Maguire, William E. '50 (TR)[M] Trenton, NJ Villa Vianney.
Maguire, William E. '90 (TR) Tribunal Judges; Censores Librorum Retired.
Maguire, William *c.p.* '02 (SCR) Scranton, PA St. Ann's Basilica Parish; [M] Clarks Summit, PA St. Gabriel's Convent.
Mahalic, Philip A. '83 (LFT) Wheatfield, IN Sorrowful Mother; Army Reserve Chaplains.
Mahan, Daniel J. '88 (IND) Batesville, IN St. Louis.
Mahan, Daniel (IND) Board of Consultors; Deaneries and Deans.
Mahan, George S. *s.j.* '40 (BO)[V] Weston, MA Campion Health Center, Inc..
Mahan, Terrance L. *s.j.* '54 (LA)[C] Los Angeles, CA Jesuit Community; [C] Los Angeles, CA Jesuit Community.
Mahaney, Hilary F. '69 (CHI) Chicago, IL St. Mary of the Angels; [W] Chicago, IL Midtown Center.
Mahar, James (BRK)[E] Campus Ministers and Ministry Centers.
Mahar, Raymond J. '58 (BUF)[O] Buffalo, NY Sheehan Residence for Priests Retired.
Mahendran, Thomas (STO) Deans.
Maher, Arthur '54 (JOL) Retired.
Maher, Byron G. '50 (CHI) Retired.
Maher, Charles E. '60 (PRO) Retired.
Maher, Daniel J. '62 (ALB) Albany, NY Church of the Holy Cross.
Maher, Daniel J. '91 (ARL)[N] Arlington, VA Rooted in Faith–Forward in Hope, Inc.; Episcopal Vicar for Finance; Advocates; Diocesan Finance Committee; Alexandria, VA St. Rita's.
Maher, Edmund J. '88 (PH) Philadelphia, PA St. William; Blind, Guild for all the Retired.
Maher, Edward A. *c.s.p.* '49 (NY)[EE] Jamaica Estates Paulist Fathers Generalate.
Maher, Edward A. *c.s.p.* '49 (SFR) San Francisco, CA Old St. Mary's Cathedral Retired.
Maher, Edward J. '81 (CAM) Haddonfield, NJ Christ the King; Members.
Maher, Francis '54 (JOL) Colorado Springs, CO St. Joseph's Retired.
Maher, J. David '71 (JC) Jefferson City, MO St. Francis Xavier; Senators; Ministry to Priests.
Maher, James J. *c.m.* '90 (BRK)[L] Brooklyn, NY Bread & Life Soup Kitchen; [V] Jamaica, NY St. Vincent's House.
Maher, James J. '92 (LA)[Z] Los Angeles, CA Scouting and Camp Fire Ministry/Catholic Youth Camps.
Maher, James J. '92 (LA) Westlake Village, CA St. Maximilian Kolbe.
Maher, Jerry '94 (MRY) San Luis Obispo, CA San Luis Obispo.
Maher, John J. '39 (NY)[EE] Bronx, NY Retired.
Maher, John L. *s.j.* '74 (FgM).
Maher, John T. *c.m.* '81 (MET)[H] Princeton, NJ Vincentian Residence.
Maher, Michael L. '48 (SAG) Retired.
Maher, Michael W. *s.j.* '86 (STL)[O] St. Louis, MO Jesuit Community Corporation at St. Louis University – Jesuit Hall.
Maher, Michael *ss.cc.* (SB) College of Consultors.
Maher, Patrick '53 (MOB) Coden, AL St. Rose of Lima; Archdiocesan Consultors.
Maher, Patrick '98 (LUB) Littlefield, TX Sacred Heart.
Maher, Paul P. *o.m.i.* '58 (P) Lebanon, OR St. Edward.
Maher, Raymond '44 (SJ) Retired.
Maher, Raymond *o.carm.* '97 (PMB)[B] Washington, DC Whitefriars Hall.
Maher, Robert E. '71 (BWN) Edinburg, TX St. Joseph; Vicar General; Presbyteral Council; Ad Hoc Committee for Diocesan Insurance; Diocesan Finance Council; Building Committee.
Maher, Robert G. '57 (WIN) Retired.
Maher, Robert *o.f.m.cap.* '74 (HON) Aiea, HI St. Elizabeth; Judges.
Maher, Robert (BWN) Diocesan College of Consultors.
Maher, Ryan J. *s.j.* '97 (WDC)[M] Washington, DC The Jesuit Community at Georgetown University.
Maher, Thomas F. '47 (CHI) Chicago, IL St. Mary of the Woods Retired.
Maher, Thomas Patrick '02 (GAY) Traverse City, MI St. Francis of Assisi.
Maher, Thomas *o.m.i.* '57 (FgM).
Maher, Thomas *l.c.* '94 (LA)[Q] Pasadena, CA Legionaries of Christ.
Maher, William F.X. *s.j.* '57 (NEW)[B] Jersey City, NJ Jesuit Center; [N] Jersey City, NJ Jesuits of Saint Peter's College, Inc..
Maher, William *o.m.i.* '66 (FgM).
Mahfoud, Peter '55 (SAM) Retired.
Mahler, Clyde '99 (HT) Houma, LA St. Bernadette; Priests Council; College of Consultors.
Mahler, Frank E. '56 (ARL) Falls Church, VA St. James.
Mahler, Michael J. '73 (ROC) Ithaca, NY St. Catherine of Siena.
Mahler, Michael '73 (ROC)[L] Ithaca, NY The Cornell Catholic Community, Inc. (Ithaca).
Mahlmann, Raymond '85 (GLP) Farmington, NM Sacred Heart; Farmington, NM Farmington Area Hospitals.
Mahnke, Ronald *o.s.b.* '62 (CLV) Cleveland, OH St. Andrew; [O] Cleveland, OH.
Mahon, Ambrose J. '58 (STP) Retired.
Mahon, Dennis (NEW)[B] School of Diplomacy and Intl. Rels..
Mahon, Francis *s.v.d.* '40 (TR)[M] Bordentown, NJ Society of the Divine Word.
Mahon, Gerald A. '71 (WIN) Rochester, MN St. John's.
Mahon, Joseph F. *c.s.p.* '56 (NY) New York, NY St. Paul the Apostle.
Mahon, Leo T. '51 (CHI) Chicago, IL St. Mary of the Woods Retired.
Mahon, Matthew Shawn '88 (BAL) On Duty Outside the Archdiocese.
Mahon, Shawn '88 (WIL) Newark, DE Holy Family.
Mahon, William A. '92 (NEW) East Orange, NJ St. Joseph's; Part–time Staff.
Mahone, Casey B. '89 (WH) Fairmont, WV Immaculate Conception; Vocations, Office of.
Mahone, Michael Q. '80 (RNO) Incline Village, NV St. Francis of Assisi.
Mahone, Mike (RNO) Diocesan Board of Consultors; Presbyteral Council; Priests' Personnel Board.
Mahoney, Arthur *c.ss.r.* '51 (BAL) Annapolis, MD St. Mary; [S] Annapolis, MD Saint Mary Rectory.
Mahoney, Bernard '53 (AUS) On Duty Outside the Diocese.
Mahoney, Brian E. '95 (BO) Priests Pursuing Higher Studies; Worship.
Mahoney, Cornelius H. '78 (BRK)[A] Douglaston, NY Immaculate Conception Center; [B] Douglaston, NY Cathedral Seminary Residence of the Immaculate Conception; Cluster Planning and Collaboration, Office of.
Mahoney, Daniel C. '70 (GBG) Greensburg, PA St. Paul; Advocate.
Mahoney, Daniel J. '56 (BO) Charlestown, MA St. Francis de Sales.
Mahoney, Edward P. '86 (R) Chapel Hill, NC Newman Catholic Student Center, University of North Carolina; Special Assignment; [H] Chapel Hill, NC Newman Catholic Student Center.
Mahoney, Francis L. '60 (FR) Fall River, MA Holy Name.
Mahoney, Gerard J. *o.s.f.s.* '71 (PH)[D] Philadelphia, PA Father Judge High School for Boys; [AA] Philadelphia, PA Father Louis Brisson Residence.
Mahoney, Gordon '56 (JOL) Naperville, IL Sts. Peter and Paul.
Mahoney, James M. '92 (BO)[A] Brighton, MA St. John Seminary School of Theology.
Mahoney, James P. (BO) Continuing Education and Spiritual Enrichment of Priests.
Mahoney, James T. (PAT) Vicar for Planning and Priorities; Finance Council.
Mahoney, James '73 (PAT) Chatham, NJ Corpus Christi.
Mahoney, John E. '72 (BRK) Bayside, NY Our Lady of the Blessed Sacrament; Liturgical Commission.
Mahoney, John J. '90 (MAN) Manchester, NH St. Augustin; Judicial Vicar; Diocesan Judges.
Mahoney, John L. *s.j.* '51 (BO)[V] Weston, MA Campion Health Center, Inc..
Mahoney, John *o.m.i.* '54 (FgM).
Mahoney, John *o.f.m.cap.* '64 (NY) Hawthorne, NY Rosary Hill Home; [B] Beacon, NY St. Lawrence of Brindisi Friary.
Mahoney, Joseph P. '57 (WOR) Worcester, MA St. Paul's Cathedral; Worcester, MA St. John's; St. Paul.
Mahoney, Kevin J. '81 (STL) St. Charles, MO St. Elizabeth Ann Seton.
Mahoney, Mark A. '86 (BO) Lincoln, MA St. Joseph;

Adjutant Judicial Vicars; Archdiocesan Judges; Canonical Affairs Committee.
Mahoney, Maurice J. *o.s.a.* '60 (FgM).
Mahoney, Michael T. '75 (CIN) Medical Leave of Absence.
Mahoney, Michael *o.f.m.cap* '74 (LA) Solvang, CA Old Mission Santa Ines.
Mahoney, Neil J. '70 (NEW) Newark, NJ St. Augustine's.
Mahoney, Neil J. '70 (NEW) Newark, NJ St. Patrick's Pro–Cathedral.
Mahoney, Neil (BRK) Presbyteral Council.
Mahoney, Neil (BRK) Diocesan Consultors.
Mahoney, Peter '61 (BRK) Brooklyn, NY Assumption of the Blessed Virgin Mary; [L] Brooklyn, NY Catholic Charities.
Mahoney, Richard J. '58 (STP) For Retired Priests; Presbyteral Council Retired.
Mahoney, Robert J. '55 (KC) Special Assignment; [B] Kansas City, KS Rockhurst University Continuing Education Center/National Seminars Group.
Mahoney, Shaun L. '91 (PH).
Mahoney, Thomas A. '98 (BO)[A] Watertown, MA St. Patrick.
Mahoney, Thomas D. '65 (CLV) Bedford, OH St. Pius X.
Mahoney, Thomas E. '68 (WOR) Mendon, MA St. Michael's; Advocates.
Mahoney, Thomas M. *o.s.a.* '45 (PH).
Mahoney, Thomas (CLV) Presbyteral Council.
Mahony, John '58 (SP) Retired.
Mahony, Thomas J. *o.s.a.* '54 (PH)[C] Villanova University; [AA] Villanova, PA St. Thomas Monastery.
Mahowald, Paul A. *s.j.* '68 (OM)[K] Omaha, NE Jesuit Community at Creighton University.
Mahowald, Paul *s.j.* '68 (DM) Griswold, IA St. Timothy; Griswold, IA Our Lady Of Grace.
Mahowald, Richard J. '55 (SFS) On Duty Outside the Diocese.
Mai, Anthony Dai Viet '90 (STA) Jacksonville, FL Assumption.
Mai, Dan T. *s.j.* '03 (FgM).
Mai, Dan *s.j.* '03 (P) Portland, OR St. Ignatius; [L] Portland, OR Colombiere Community; [Q] Portland, OR Jesuit Development & Communications Office.
Maibusch, Henry *o.s.a.* '54 (MIL) Racine, WI St. Rita.
Maichen, Richard F. '54 (DUB) Retired.
Mai Chi Thanh, Joseph M. '58 (PEO) Pesotum, IL St. Mary; Pesotum, IL St. Joseph.
Maida, Thaddeus S. '58 (PIT) Bridgeville, PA Holy Child.
Maier, John '90 (DM) Tampa, FL Retired.
Maier, Joseph *c.ss.r.* '65 (FgM).
Maier, Paul '70 (RIC) Abingdon, VA Christ the King; Marion, VA St. John the Evangelist Church.
Maiers, Brennan *o.s.b.* '63 (SCL)[I] Collegeville, MN St. John's Abbey, of the Order of St. Benedict.
Maigret, Louis *ss.cc.* (HON) Former Prelates.
Maikowski, Thomas R. '76 (GLP) Special Assignment; [C] Gallup, NM St. Francis of Assisi School; Air Force Reserve Chaplains.
Maikowski, Thomas (GLP) Defenders of the Bond; Presbyteral Council; Diocesan Consultors; Boy Scouts; Diocesan Pastoral Council; Director of Education, (Catholic Schools and Religious Education).
Mailadiyil, Augustine J. '75 (TYL) Pittsburg, TX Holy Cross.
Maillet, Paul A. *s.s.* '01 (BAL).
Maillet, Paul '01 (BAL)[A] Baltimore, MD Holy Cross; On Duty Outside the Archdiocese.
Mailloux, Normand F. *m.s.* '55 (SPR) Bondsville, MA St. Adalbert's.
Mailloux, Thomas B. *c.s.b.* '50 (GAL) Houston, TX St. Anne.
Mai Minh Luan, Dominic '59 (SPC)[E] Carthage, MO Congregation of the Mother Coredemptrix, United States Assumption Province.
Maina, Wilson '96 (BRK) Brooklyn, NY St. Rose of Lima.
Mainzer, James S. '87 (WCH) Mulvane, KS St. Michael the Archangel; Wichita Diocesan Charismatic Services.
Maio, Anthony V. '49 (SAC) Retired.
Maione, Anthony '85 (ALB) Leave of Absence.
Maione, Francis T. '65 (NEW) East Newark, NJ St. Anthony's.
Mair, Henry *s.a.* '62 (BO)[O] Brockton, MA Chapel of Our Savior–Catholic Pastoral and Information Center; [V] Brockton, MA Chapel of Our Savior; [AA] Brockton, MA Chapel of Our Saviour.
Mair, Robert G. '65 (CHI) Glenview, IL St. Catherine Laboure.
Maisano, Richard J. '69 (PH) Avondale, PA St. Gabriel of the Sorrowful Mother.
Maiser, Raymond *c.ss.r.* '64 (OAK)[N] Oakland, CA Redemptorists.
Maiser, Raymond *c.ss.r.* '64 (TUC)[I] Tucson, AZ Redemptorist Community Support Charity Trust.
Maisog, Alberic *o.c.s.o.* (SPC)[E] Ava, MO Assumption Abbey (Trappist).
Maison, Gabriel *j.c.d.* '78 (VIC) Moulton, TX St. Joseph's; Judges; Permanent Diaconate Program.
Maisonet–Ortiz, Tomas '45 (SJN) Retired.
Maisonneuve, Joseph *o.carm.* '86 (L)[B] The Carmelite Community of The St. Francis DeSales Priory.
Maiza, Jesus Maria *s.s.s.* '67 (CGS) Caguas, PR Santisimo Sacramento.
Maj, George C. *s.a.c.* '58 (BUF) Cheektowaga, NY Resurrection.
Maj, Jerzy *o.s.p.* '89 (NY) Yonkers, NY St. Casimir.
Maj, Jerzy *o.s.p.* '90 (CHI) Harwood Heights–Norridge, IL St. Rosalie.
Majarucon, John '84 (LA) Oxnard, CA Santa Clara.
Majcher, Tadeusz *s.d.s.* '87 (NEW)[N] Verona, NJ The Salvatorian Fathers.
Majchrowski, Anthony P. '44 (LAN) Flint, MI All Saints.
Majchrzak, Colman *o.f.m.* '51 (MIL)[O] Burlington, WI St. Francis Friary.
Majda, Francis A. '39 (PIT) Retired.
Majdanik, Albin J. '42 (SY) Retired.
Majerus, Daniel '57 (SCL) AUXILIARY CHAPLAINS CONTRACT CHAPLAINS Retired.
Majewski, Edmund W. *s.j.* '83 (NEW)[B] Jersey City, NJ Jesuit Center; [N] Jersey City, NJ Jesuits of Saint Peter's College, Inc..
Majewski, Francis *o.f.m.cap.* '64 (PAT)[M] Oak Ridge–Milton, NJ St. Stanislaus B. M. Friary.
Majewski, Joseph B. '66 (RIC) Newport News, VA St. Jerome.
Majewski, Stephen *o.f.m.conv.* '34 (BO) South Boston, MA Our Lady of Czestochowa.
Majic, Timothy *o.f.m.* '39 (CHI)[N] Chicago, IL St. Anthony's Friary.
Majikas, David J. '97 (CLV) Barberton, OH St. Augustine.
Majka, Frank A. *s.j.* '74 (MIL)[W] Milwaukee, WI Alumni Memorial Union 236; [O] Milwaukee, WI Jesuit Community at Marquette University.
Majka, George '72 (MAN) Whitefield, NH St. Matthew.
Majka, Philip S. '65 (ARL) Fredericksburg, VA St. Patrick's.
Majkut, Tadeusz (MO) Army Chaplains.
Major, Charles M. '59 (SY) Liverpool, NY St. Joseph the Worker.
Major, Steven P. '87 (LIN) Doniphan, NE St. Ann's; Doniphan, NE Sacred Heart.
Major, Thomas J. '91 (SCR) Gillett, PA St. Ann's.
Majoros, George A. '79 (PH) Philadelphia, PA Maternity B.V.M..
Majoros, Stephen R. '57 (TOL) Toledo, OH St. Joseph.
Majors, Francis de Sales *o.c.d.* '02 (DAL)[I] Dallas, TX Mount Carmel Center.
Majstorovic, Ivica *o.f.m.* (NY) New York, NY SS. Cyril and Methodius – St. Raphael.
Makacinas, Stanley *o.carm.* '70 (PHX) Special Assignment; [-] Phoenix, AZ Kino Institute of Theology.
Makalla, Peter '86 (P) Gresham, OR St. Henry.
Makara, Michael A. (MET) Assistant to the Bishop; Episcopal Council.
Makarewicz, Marion J. '87 (JC) Appointed Members; Jefferson City, MO Immaculate Conception.
Maki, George S. '88 (MAR) Escanaba, MI St. Anne.
Makothakat, John M. '62 (SAT) San Antonio, TX St. Thomas More; [C] Oblate School of Theology; Judges.
Makothakat, John (SAT) Promoter Justitiae.
Makowski, Douglas T '66 (CLV) Parma, OH St. Francis de Sales.
Makowski, Lee J. *o.s.a.* '80 (PH)[C] Villanova University; [AA] Villanova, PA St. Thomas Monastery.
Makowski, Tomasz '93 (PMB) West Palm Beach, FL Mary Immaculate.
Makrany, Steven F. '69 (LAN) Flushing, MI St. Robert.
Maksimowicz, Victor *o.f.m.conv.* '54 (BAL) Baltimore, MD St. Clement Mary Hofbauer.
Maksvytis, Jerome J. '74 (MAD) Berlin, WI All Saints.
Maksym, Kevin '01 (SAG) Midland, MI Blessed Sacrament.
Maksymowicz, John H. '70 (BRK) Released from Diocesan Assignment.
Makuch, Thaddeus J. '53 (CHI) Cicero IL St. Mary of Czestochowa Retired.
Makuru, Simon *s.j.* '93 (BO)[V] Newton, MA The Jesuit Community at Boston College.
Makwali, Silvester *c.s.c.* '98 (FTW).
Malabad, Antonio R. '53 (RIC)[I] Williamsburg, VA St. Bede's Retired.
Malacaman, Pericles P. '72 (WH) Beckley, WV St. Francis De Sales.
Malacar, Carmen '93 (CHL) Charlotte, NC St. Matthew.
Malachowski, Christopher *o.s.* '58 (PCE) On Duty Outside the Diocese.
Malaerida, Mario *m.c.j.* '87 (CHI)[N] Chicago, IL Comboni Missionaries Theologate (M.C.C.J.), Verona Fathers.
Malagon, Eduardo (GRY) Whiting, IN Immaculate Conception; Whiting, IN Sacred Heart; Whiting, IN St. Adalbert.
Malagreca, Joseph P. '76 (BRK) Queens Village, NY SS. Joachim and Anne.
Malagreca, Joseph (BRK) Renouveau Charismatique of the Diocese of Brooklyn; Renovacion Carismatica of the Diocese of Brooklyn.
Malain, Dan '66 (BEA) Diocesan College of Consultors and Presbyteral Council; [H] Beaumont, TX Rev. Herman Vincent Scholarship Fund; Nederland, TX St. Charles Borromeo.
Malanga, Salvatore T. '57 (NEW) Retired.
Malanowski, Thaddeus F. '47 (NOR) Retired.
Malanyaon, Jovan '73 (TOL)[I] Oregon, OH Sacred Heart Home.
Malarkey, Shawn O. '02 (PIT) Pittsburgh, PA St. Margaret.
Malarz, Andrew '92 (GRY) On Duty Outside the Diocese; Naples, FL St. Peter the Apostle.
Malasi, Wilhelm '87 (CLV) Akron, OH St. Bernard.
Malatesta, Christopher A. '93 (SPR) Dalton, MA St. Agnes; [O] Goshen, MA Holy Cross Camp Grounds; Bishop's Commission for Clergy.
Malatesta, Christopher (SPR) Presbyteral Council.
Malave, Jason A. '97 (CHI) Chicago, IL St. Bartholomew.
Malave, Will–Roger '86 (HRT) On Duty Outside the Archdiocese.
Malave, WillRoger '86 (STU) Amsterdam, OH St. Joseph.
Malaver, Daniel J. '03 (WDC) Leonardtown, MD St. Aloysius.
Malawy, Michael D. '81 (DET) Special Assignment; Maybee, MI St. Joseph.
Malayampuram, Joseph *c.m.i.* '41 (BEA) Dayton, TX St. Joseph the Worker; Dayton, TX St. Anne Mission.
Malcolm, Lawrence J. '70 (CHI) Chicago, IL St. Daniel the Prophet.
Malczyk, Joseph *c.r.* '69 (CHI)[D] Chicago, IL Gordon Tech High School.
Maldari, Donald C. *s.j.* '85 (SY)[Q] Syracuse, NY Jesuits at LeMoyne, Inc..
Maldonado, Cesar *s.j.* '92 (WDC)[M] Washington, DC The Jesuit Community at Georgetown University.
Maldonado, Fernando '99 (SPK) Oroville, WA Immaculate Conception; Oroville, WA Holy Rosary.
Maldonado, Francisco '90 (TUC) Tucson, AZ St. Augustine's Cathedral; Encuentros de Promocion Juvenile.
Maldonado, Jose Jamie '02 (SPK) Pasco, WA St. Patrick.
Maldonado, Leonardo '64 (RCK) Elgin, IL St. Joseph.
Maldonado, P. Jose A. Rivera '84 (CGS) Naguabo, PR Nuestra Senora del Rosario.
Malec, Raymond S. '54 (BEL) Retired.
Malecki, John J. (ALB) Office.
Malecki, John '48 (ALB) Special Assignment; [J] Albany, NY Teresian House.
Malene, Robert '72 (E) On Duty Outside Diocese; Navy Chaplains.
Males, Jake A. '76 (TLS) Retired.
Malesic, Edward C. '87 (HBG) Mechanicsburg, PA St. Elizabeth Ann Seton; Adjutant Judicial Vicar.
Maletta, Sammie L. '80 (GRY) St. John, IN St. John Evangelist.
Maletz, Leo J. '73 (ALN) Branchdale, PA St. Mary Star of the Sea; Minersville, PA St. Stanislaus Kostka.
Mali, Joseph F. '88 (BRK) Brooklyn, NY St. Saviour.
Malia, Thomas R. '84 (BAL)[M] Baltimore, MD Mercy Health Services Inc..
Malia, Tom (BAL) Baltimore, MD St. Clement.
Maliakel, Jose '74 (BIR) Demopolis, AL St. Leo.
Malicki, Jan '73 (MIA) Absent on Leave.
Maliekal, Cyriac '71 (HRT) New Haven, CT St. Aedan's; New Haven, CT St. Brendan's.
Maliekal, Jose *m.s.f.s.* '74 (ATL)[K] Lawrenceville The Missionaries of St. Francis De Sales.
Malik, John E. '53 (LC) Colby, WI St. Mary Help of Christians.
Malin, Delbert J. '58 (LC) Retired.
Malin, Donald '03 (PBL) Grand Junction, CO St. Joseph.
Malin, Gary J. '86 (CLV) Concord Twp., OH St. Gabriel.
Malinowski, Francis X. *c.ss.sp.* '50 (PIT)[P] Bethel Park, PA Holy Spirit Animation Center.
Malinowski, Hilary L. '56 (SCR) Simpson, PA St. Michael's.
Malinowski, John C. '63 (AUS)[E] Bryan, TX St. Joseph Regional Health Center.
Malinowski, John (AUS) Cemeteries Retired.
Malinowski, Stanley J. '54 (PEO) Rantoul, IL St. Malachy's; Thomasboro, IL St. Elizabeth's Retired.
Maliszewski, Edward C. '45 (PIT) Retired.
Maliszewski, Francis '46 (PAT) Paterson, NJ St. Stephen's.
Malitz, George M. '97 (PSC) Trumbull, CT St. John the Baptist; Eparchial Newspaper; Secretariat for Youth; Retirement Plan Board.
Maliwa, Festus '02 (TLS) Tulsa, OK St. Francis Xavier.
Maliyekal, John *v.c.* '60 (SFS) Woonsocket, SD St. Wilfrid; [F] Woonsocket, SD Vincentian Congregation.
Malkiewicz, Edward S. '71 (NEW) Jersey City, NJ St. Aloysius Retired.
Malkiewicz, Stephen E. *o.f.m.* '69 (MIL)[O] Provincial Offices; [A] St. Francis, WI Saint Francis Seminary.
Mallahan, James '52 (SEA) Retired.
Mallak, Mark S. '88 (NU) Litchfield, MN St. Philip;

Chancellor; Defender of the Bond; Corporate Board; Priest Personnel Board; Committee for Continuing Education of Clergy; Board of Trustees for Pension Plan for Priests; On Special or Other Diocesan Assignment.
Mallak, Mark (WIN) Associate Judges; Second Instance Court Judges.
Mallavarapu, Kasparaj '84 (ANC) Wasilla, AK Sacred Heart.
Malleck, Joseph L. '56 (BRK) Retired.
Mallen, Charles *c.ss.r.* '44 (VEN)[G] Venice, FL St. Alphonsus Residence; [I] Venice, FL Our Lady of Perpetual Help Retreat and Spirituality Center.
Mallen, Santiago *c.ss.r.* '47 (CGS) San Lorenzo, PR Nuestra Senora de la Mercedes.
Mallet, Charles J. '55 (LAF) Retired.
Mallet, Curtis (LAF) Diocesan Consultors.
Mallet, W. Curtis '92 (LAF) Abbeville, LA St. Theresa of the Child Jesus; Advocates.
Mallett, James K. '66 (NSH) Nashville, TN Christ the King; General Counsel; Judges; Presbyteral Council and College of Consultors; Diocesan Finance Board; Censor Librorum.
Mallett, Raymond P. *o.f.m. conv.* '84 (LA) Redondo Beach, CA St. Lawrence Martyr.
Mallett, Raymond *o.f.m. conv.* '76 (LA) Hermosa Beach, CA Our Lady of Guadalupe.
Mallette, Daniel J. '57 (CHI) Chicago, IL St. Margaret of Scotland.
Malley, Francis '02 (SFE) Ribera, NM San Miguel Del Vado; Villanueva, NM Our Lady of Guadalupe; Vicars Forane (Deans).
Malley, James B. *s.j.* '64 (BO)[V] Newton, MA The Jesuit Community at Boston College.
Malley, James '56 (NY) Staten Island, NY St. John Neumann.
Malley, John *o.carm.* '56 (JOL)[O] Darien, IL Carmelite Mission Office.
Malley, John *o.carm.* '56 (TUC)[A] Tucson, AZ Salpointe Catholic High School; [E] Tucson, AZ Carmelite Priory; (FgM).
Malley, Kenneth *s.p.* '97 (MIA)[A] Miami, FL St. John Vianney College Seminary.
Malley, Michael A. '34 (HRT) Retired.
Malley, Raymond E. *s.m.* '68 (HON) Wailuku, HI St. Anthony; [G] Wailuku, HI Wailuku Marianist Community; Maui.
Malley, Vernon *o.carm.* '59 (TUC)[A] Tucson, AZ Salpointe Catholic High School; [E] Tucson, AZ Carmelite Priory.
Mallia, Joseph '92 (DET) Allen Park, MI St. Frances Cabrini; Archdiocesan Vicars.
Mallick, Andrew '83 (ORL) Ocala, FL Our Lady of the Springs.
Mallin, Peter *o.f.m.conv.* '90 (LA) Hermosa Beach, CA Our Lady of Guadalupe; [J] Torrance, CA Little Company of Mary Hospital.
Mallinson, Arthur D. '81 (DAL) Lancaster, TX St. Francis of Assisi; Absent on Leave.
Mallo, Ekpaa *c.s.sp.* (PIT) Pittsburgh, PA Holy Spirit.
Mallo, Walter D. *i.v.e.* '90 (NY) New York, NY St. Paul.
Mallo, Walter *i.v.e.* '90 (SJ) Santa Clara, CA Our Lady of Peace; [A] Santa Clara, CA Shrine of Our Lady of Peace.
Mallon, Elias D. *s.a.* '71 (NY)[EE] New York, NY Atonement Friars.
Mallon, Elias *s.a.* '71 (NY).
Mallonee, Robert *s.v.d.* '67 (BO)[V] Duxbury, MA Society of the Divine Word.
Malloy, Brendan *o.f.m. cap.* '54 (PIT)[N] Allison Park, PA St. Conrad Friary.
Malloy, David J. '83 (MIL) On Duty Outside the Archdiocese.
Malloy, Edward A. *c.s.c.* '70 (FTW)[B] University of Notre Dame Du Lac; [I] Notre Dame, IN Holy Cross Community, Corby Hall, University of Notre Dame; [B] University of Notre Dame Du Lac.
Malloy, Francis X. '85 (MIL) Air Force Reserve Chaplains; Brookfield, WI St. Luke.
Malloy, John J. *s.d.b.* '50 (SFR) San Francisco, CA SS. Peter and Paul.
Malloy, Joseph J. '70 (BGP) Stamford, CT St. Clement.
Malloy, Michael B. '76 (OM) Emerson, NE Sacred Heart; Emerson, NE St. John.
Malloy, Richard G. *s.j.* '88 (PH)[C] Jesuit Fathers; [AA] Loyola Center and Manresa Hall.
Malloy, Stephen J. '96 (BO) Absent on Leave.
Malloy, Thomas *o.s.f.s.* '67 (R) Fayetteville, NC St. Ann.
Malloy, William E. '73 (CHI) Oak Lawn, IL St. Germaine.
Mally, Edward J. *s.j.* '61 (NY)[EE] Oakbrook Terrace, IL.
Mallya, Sabas N. '90 (LA) Los Angeles, CA St. Eugene.
Malm, Raymond B. '76 (PRO) Providence, RI St. Michael the Archangel.
Malnar, Matthew '66 (AMA) Retired.
Malnar, Matthew (MIL) AUXILIARY CHAPLAINS CONTRACT CHAPLAINS.
Malnar, Stan '72 (HEL) Special Assignments.
Malo, John B. *c.s.b.* '78 (OAK)[C] Oakland, CA Bishop O'Dowd High School.
Malo, Richard C. '87 (PRT) Benedicta, ME St. Benedict's; East Millinocket, ME St. Peter's; Millinocket, ME St. Martin of Tours; Deans; Personnel Board.
Malonda, Anselme *c.i.c.m.* '92 (SAT)[B] San Antonio, TX Missionhurst Formation Community.
Malone, Alan '59 (PHX) Diocesan Judges Retired.
Malone, Bernard G. '50 (LR) Hot Springs Village, AR Sacred Heart of Jesus; Diocesan Consultors.
Malone, Edward T. (BO) Reading, MA St. Agnes.
Malone, Francis I. '77 (LR) Little Rock, AR Christ the King; Vicars General; Diocesan Consultors; Hospitals; Liturgical Commission.
Malone, Francis T. '65 (NEW)[K] Kearny, NJ New Jersey Boystown.
Malone, H. Patrick '69 (WCH) Wichita, KS Holy Savior; Presbyteral Council/Diocesan Consultors; Catholic Marriage Preparation–Evenings for Engaged; Presbyteral Council.
Malone, John M. '67 (STP) St. Paul, MN Assumption; [C] St. Paul, MN University of St. Thomas.
Malone, John S. *c.s.c.* '55 (RVC) Northport, NY Veteran's Administration Hospital.
Malone, John S. *c.s.sp.* (MO).
Malone, Michael T. *c.s.sp.* '65 (PRO)[B] Newport, RI Salve Regina University.
Malone, Patrick *s.j.* '01 (STP) St. Paul, MN St. Luke.
Malone, Richard '62 (PH) On Duty Outside the Archdiocese; Littleton, CO St. Mary.
Maloney, Bernard M. *o.f.m.cap.* '69 (NY) New York, NY St. John the Baptist.
Maloney, Christopher '66 (NY) St. Luke's Site.
Maloney, Daniel *o.s.b.* '68 (BIS)[A] Richardton, ND Assumption Abbey; [B] Bismarck, ND University of Mary; [H] Bismarck, ND Annunciation Monastery.
Maloney, Edward F. *s.j.* '55 (NY)[EE] Loyola Hall, Jesuit Community.
Maloney, Edward J. '55 (CHI) Retired.
Maloney, Francis E. '59 (PMB) Retired.
Maloney, Francis G. '60 (R) Retired.
Maloney, George A. *s.j.* '57 (MIL)[O] Seal Beach, CA.
Maloney, J. Christopher '66 (NY) Yonkers, NY St. John the Baptist.
Maloney, James F. *c.m.f.* '60 (CHI) Chicago, IL Our Lady of Guadalupe; [N] Oak Park, IL Claretian Missionaries Community Support Trust.
Maloney, James G. '71 (CLV) Norton, OH St. Andrew the Apostle.
Maloney, John P. '66 (PIT) Howard Beach, NY St. Helen; Butler, PA Holy Sepulcher.
Maloney, John W. '75 (BRK) St. Albans, NY St. Pascal Baylon; [G] Brooklyn, NY Catherine McAuley.
Maloney, John '75 (BRK) Springfield Gardens, NY St. Mary Magdalene.
Maloney, Joseph L. '91 (PH)[V] Brooklyn, NY St. Francis Monastery–Generalate Offices of Franciscan Brothers; [A] Wynnewood, PA Theological Seminary of St. Charles Borromeo, Overbrook.
Maloney, Joseph *o.f.m.cap.* '58 (DET)[K] Detroit St. Bonaventure Friary.
Maloney, Malcolm *o.f.m.cap.* '55 (SAG)[G] Saginaw Queen of Angels Friary and Retreat House.
Maloney, Patrick H. *c.s.c.* '54 (FTW)[B] University of Notre Dame Du Lac; [I] Notre Dame, IN Holy Cross Community, Corby Hall, University of Notre Dame.
Maloney, Richard E. '50 (DET) Retired.
Maloney, Richard *s.d.s.* '69 (WDC)[B] Silver Spring, MD Salvatorian Community.
Maloney, Robert L. *s.j.* '61 (SJ)[M] Los Gatos, CA Sacred Heart Jesuit Center.
Maloney, Robert P. *c.m.* '66 (PH).
Maloney, Robert S. *s.x.* '57 (BO)[V] Holliston, MA Xaverian Missionaries.
Maloney, Rufino *o.f.m.conv.* '59 (ALB)[A] Rensselaer, NY Conventual Franciscan Friars; [L] Rensselaer, NY Provincialate, Immaculate Conception Friary – Order of Friars Minor Conventual.
Maloney, Thomas F. '68 (BUF) Finance Council; Tonawanda, NY St. Amelia.
Maloney, Thomas J. '65 (SCR) Hughestown, PA Blessed Sacrament.
Maloney, Thomas P. '70 (RVC) Babylon, NY St. Joseph's.
Maloney, Thomas *s.j.* '61 (SJ)[M] Los Gatos, CA Sacred Heart Jesuit Center.
Maloney, Thomas '68 (PEO) Retired.
Maloney, Timothy *o.s.b.* '50 (OKL)[I] Shawnee St. Gregory's Abbey.
Maloney, Wilfred F. '55 (PH) Philadelphia, PA Holy Innocents.
Maloney, William J. '48 (E) Retired.
Malorzo, Luigi *c.p.* '52 (MET).
Malovetz, Gregory E. S. '83 (MET)[H] Skillman, NJ St. Charles Borromeo.
Maloy, Dale '54 (PEO) Retired.
Maltese, James L. '65 (RVC) Mineola, NY Corpus Christi; Valley Stream, NY Holy Name of Mary; Mineola, NY Winthrop Hospital.
Maltese, James L. (NOR) On Duty Outside the Diocese.
Malthaner, John P. '93 (E)[C] Oil City, PA Venango Catholic High School.
Malvey, James '86 (PMB) Retired.
Malvey, Killian *o.s.b.* '73 (SEA)[L] Lacey, WA St. Martin's Abbey.
Malvey, Sean R. *o.s.b.* '89 (SEA)[L] Lacey, WA St. Martin's Abbey.
Mamani, Raul (ARE) Sabana Hoyos, PR Nuestra Senora de Fatima.
MaManus, Denis *c.s.sp.* '58 (SFR) San Rafael, CA St. Raphael.
Mami, David L. '64 (CLV) Fairview Park, OH St. Angela Merici.
Mammarella, Dominick '53 (HBG) Retired.
Mamo, Nathan '78 (SJ) Cupertino, CA St. Joseph of Cupertino; Ongoing Formation of Clergy Committee.
Mampara, Mathew '60 (PHX) Higley, AZ St. Mary Magdalene.
Mampilly, Joy '84 (NY) New York, NY St. Ann's Roman Catholic Church; New York, NY Immaculate Conception.
Mana–Ay, Eusebio '75 (NY) New York, NY St. Rose of Lima; Poughkeepsie, NY St. Mary.
Manahan, Christopher J. *s.j.* '03 (RC) Parmelee, SD St. Agnes; Rosebud, SD St. Bridget; St. Francis, SD St. Charles; St. Francis, SD Rosebud Reservation.
Manahan, John J. *s.m.* '68 (SAT) San Antonio, TX Holy Rosary; [M] San Antonio, TX Holy Rosary Marianist Community.
Manahan, Reynaldo '95 (SD) La Jolla, CA Mary, Star of the Sea.
Manahan, Thomas C. *s.j.* '95 (MIL)[O] Milwaukee, WI Pere Marquette House Jesuit Community; [E] Milwaukee, WI Marquette University High School.
Manalili, Feliciano *o.c.s.o.* '62 (CHR)[E] Moncks Corner, SC Mepkin Abbey.
Manalo, Pantaleon O. '63 (RIC)[E] Portsmouth, VA Maryview Medical Center.
Manalo, Vincent P. *c.s.p.* (SFR) San Francisco, CA Old St. Mary's Cathedral.
Manapuram, Joseph '69 (SYM) Houston, TX Knanaya Catholic Mission of Dallas and Fort Worth; Houston, TX Knanaya Catholic Mission of Houston.
Manapuram, Joseph '69 (GAL) Houston, TX St. Albert of Trapani.
Manarchuck, Joseph J. '78 (SCR) Meshoppen, PA St. Joachim's; Wellsboro, PA St. Peter's.
Manase, Michael *o.c.d.* '77 (ALX) Hessmer, LA St. Alphonsus.
Mancha, George '88 (SJ) San Jose, CA St. Anthony.
Manchapilly, George '71 (BRK) Ozone Park, NY St. Elizabeth's.
Manchas, Lawrence L. '79 (GBG) Belle Vernon, PA St. Sebastian; Diocesan Catholic Scoutmaster.
Manching, Romulo '86 (CHI)[X] Chicago, IL Resurrection Health Care.
Mancini, Anthony '78 (PRO) Providence, RI Holy Cross.
Mancini, Domenic '76 (PIT) Imperial, PA St. Columbkille.
Mancini, James E. '66 (LR) Huntsville, AR St. John's; Tontitown, AR St. Joseph's; Charismatic Movement, Bishop's Liaison.
Mancini, John S. *o.s.f.s.* '80 (SAG) Pastoral Team.
Mancini, John *o.s.f.s.* '80 (SAG) Pastoral Team; Pastoral Team; Pastoral Team.
Mancini, Joseph A. '01 (NEW) Kearny, NJ St. Stephen's; Boy Scouts of America/Catholic Committee on Scouting.
Mancini, Marc '92 (PAT) Paterson, NJ St. Paul's; Presbyteral Council; College of Consultors.
Mancini, Mark A. (PAT) Pro–Synodal Judges.
Mancini, Nicholas (Y) Serra Club of Stark County.
Mancini, Robert A. *o.s.f.s.* '77 (WIL)[J] Wilmington, DE Oblates of St. Francis De Sales.
Mancuso, Anthony J. '83 (SJ) Los Altos, CA St. Simon; Deans.
Mancuso, Anthony (SJ) Ongoing Formation of Clergy Committee.
Mancuso, Dennis J. '96 (BUF) Scio, NY St. Joseph; Belmont, NY Sacred Heart; Belmont, NY St. Mary.
Mancuso, Henry '75 (LKC) Lake Charles, LA Sacred Heart of Jesus; Episcopal Vicars; Diocesan Consultors.
Mancuso, Joseph A. '64 (KC) Gladstone, MO St. Andrew the Apostle; [N] Kansas City, MO Diocesan Council of Catholic Women.
Mancuso, Joseph (KC) Deans.
Mancuso, Luke *o.s.b.* '83 (SCL)[I] Collegeville, MN St. John's Abbey, of the Order of St. Benedict.
Mandac, Elmer '96 (SD) San Diego, CA St. Rita.
Mandala, Michael J. *s.j.* '77 (LA) Los Angeles, CA Blessed Sacrament.
Mandala, Michael *s.j.* (LA) Deanery 14.
Mandato, Kieran '87 (NY) Military Chaplains; Navy Chaplains.
Mandato, Pio *f.m.h.j.* '85 (SCR)[M] Laceyville, PA Franciscan Missionary Hermits of St. Joseph.
Mandel, Brian L. '94 (NU) Tracy, MN St. Mary; Walnut Grove, MN St. Paul; College of Consultors; Committee on Parishes; Social Concerns Committee.
Manderfield, Paul G. '60 (MAR) Panama Mission Fund.
Manderfield, R.P. Geraldo (MAR) Retired.
Mandile, John J. *s.j.* '57 (BO)[V] Weston, MA Campion Jesuit Community.

Mandina, Peter '86 (ROC) Rochester, NY Our Lady of Lourdes; East Bloomfield, NY St. Bridget.
Manding, Benito O. '64 (SJ) Sunnyvale, CA St. Martin.
Mandock, Patrick H. '72 (GBG) Military Chaplains; AUXILIARY CHAPLAINS CONTRACT CHAPLAINS.
Mandoli, Richard *o.c.d.* '92 (SJ)[M] San Jose, CA Carmelite Monastery, Novitiate.
Manduzia, Norbert (GAL) William P. Hobby Airport.
Mandziuk, Paul *m.s.* '80 (STL)[O] St. Louis, MO Missionaries of LaSalette, Province of Mary, Mother of the Americas; [O] La Salette Communications Center.
Manenti, Rene *c.s.* '02 (NY)[EE] Staten Island, NY Scalabrinian Missionaries.
Manerowski, Joseph '95 (ALB) Hoosick Falls, NY Immaculate Conception; [Q] Delhi, NY State University of New York College of Agricultural & Technology at Delhi.
Maney, Robert L. '51 (MIL) Retired.
Maney, Thomas J. *m.m.* '56 (NY).
Manfred, Donald J. '67 (OG)[EE] Massena, NY St. Lawrence; Massena, NY Sacred Heart; Diocesan Consultors.
Mangahas, Rene A. '83 (WIL) Milford, DE St. John the Apostle.
Mangalath, Augustine '79 (HRT) West Haven, CT St. Paul's; [I] New Haven, CT Hospital of St. Raphael.
Mangalath, Jaison G. *s.v.d.* '99 (BR) Baton Rouge, LA St. Paul the Apostle.
Mangampo, Gil '91 (GLP) Show Low, AZ St. Rita.
Mangan, Charles M. '89 (SFS) On Duty Outside the Diocese.
Mangan, James '69 (SPK) Otis Orchards, WA St. Joseph.
Mangan, Timothy *s.s.s.* '59 (ALB) Broadalbin, NY St. Joseph.
Mangana, Edgar *o.f.m.* '02 (TUC) Tucson, AZ Mission San Xavier del Bac.
Manganello, Salvatore '82 (BUF) Due Process; Judicial Vicar; Judges; Buffalo, NY Blessed Sacrament.
Mangano, Charles N. '90 (RVC) Bay Shore, NY St. Patrick's; Associate Vocation Directors.
Mangen, Daniel J. *c.pp.s.* '80 (CIN).
Manger, Daniel *o.s.b.cam.* '85 (MRY)[F] Big Sur, CA New Camaldoli Hermitage.
Manger, Kevin P. (STP) Edina, MN Our Lady of Grace.
Manger, William '62 (BEA) Diocesan College of Consultors and Presbyteral Council; Charismatic Prayer Renewal; Beaumont, TX St. Anne.
Mangesho, Paulinus M. *a.l.c.p.* '91 (SFR) San Francisco, CA Sacred Heart.
Mangiafico, Paul J. '70 (HRT) Medical Leave.
Mangiaracina, Cayet *o.p.* '64 (SAT) San Antonio, TX St. Ann; [B] San Antonio, TX Dominican Priory of San Juan Macias and Novitiate.
Mangieri, Thomas '01 (PAT) Sparta, NJ Our Lady of the Lake.
Mangini, Richard A. '67 (OAK) Concord, CA St. Bonaventure.
Mangini, Richard (OAK) Deans.
Manglaviti, Leo *s.j.* '99 (BO)[V] Newton, MA The Jesuit Community at Boston College.
Mangum, Peter B. '90 (SHP) Shreveport, LA St. Joseph; Judicial Vicar; Judges; College of Consultors; Presbyteral Council.
Manhart, Paul *s.j.* '58 (RC)[B] Pine Ridge, SD Jesuit Community of Holy Rosary Mission.
Mani, David '64 (CLV) Cleveland, OH Veterans Administration Hospitals, Brecksville V.A..
Mani, L. David (MO).
Maniakupara, Anselm *o.s.b.* '65 (TLS) Holdenville, OK St. Stephen's.
Maniamkerry, Matthew *o.ss.t.* '84 (BAL)[S] Holy Trinity Ashram.
Maniampra, Mathew *c.m.i.* '85 (JOL) Glen Ellyn, IL St. James the Apostle.
Maniangat, Joseph '64 (STA) Chiefland, FL St. John the Evangelist.
Manieri, Frank P. '60 (STU) Retired.
Manikuttiyil, Kurian '90 (PT) Milton, FL St. Rose of Lima.
Manimala, Thomas (SAN) Abilene, TX St. Francis of Assisi.
Maniola, Francis N. '38 (CHI) Chicago, IL St. Symphorosa and Seven Sons Retired.
Manion, Kevin '89 (AUS) San Marcos, TX St. John the Evangelist.
Manion, Thomas F. '57 (PIT) Retired.
Maniscalco, Francis '71 (RVC) Priests Released from Diocesan Assignment.
Maniscalco, Paul *s.d.b.* '44 (SFR) San Francisco, CA SS. Peter and Paul.
Manista, Clemens D. '74 (WIL) Claymont, DE Holy Rosary; National Conference for Community and Justice.
Maniyangat, Jose '75 (STA) Macclenny, FL St. Mary's; Civil Institutions; Legion of Mary.
Maniyatt, John *s.v.d.* (BAL)[S] Baltimore, MD Society of Mary (Marianists).
Manjakunnel, Josekutty '88 (CAM) Lindenwold, NJ St. Lawrence's.
Manjakunnel, Josekutty '88 (SYM) Lindenwold, NJ South Jersey Indian Catholic Community.
Manjaly, Jose '79 (BIR) Sylacauga, AL St. Jude; Talladega, AL St. Francis of Assisi.
Manjankal, George Jacob '83 (STP) Gillette Children's Hospital; St. Paul, MN St. Mary; Regions Medical Center.
Mank, Virgil W. (SFD) Alton Deanery.
Mank, Virgil '65 (SFD) Godfrey, IL St. Ambrose; Diocesan Health Insurance Program Committee; Commission for Buildings and Property.
Mankel, F. Xavier '61 (KNX) Knoxville, TN Holy Ghost; [I] Knoxville, TN Diocesan Council of Catholic Women; [I] Knoxville, TN Diocesan Council of Catholic Women; [I] Knoxville, TN Ladies of Charity.
Mankel, Francis Xavier (KNX) Vicar General; Presbyteral Council; Diocesan Consultors; Diocesan Finance Council; Diocesan Council of Catholic Women.
Manko, Andriy *c.ss.r.* '95 (PHU) Newark, NJ St. John the Baptist.
Mankowski, Edmund A. '46 (BRK) Retired.
Mankowski, Maciej '01 (Y) Youngstown, OH St. Charles Borromeo.
Mankowski, Marcin *o.p.* '83 (LC) Custer, WI Sacred Heart; Rosholt, WI St. Adalbert.
Mankowski, Paul V. *s.j.* '65 (CHI)[N] Chicago Chicago Province of the Society of Jesus–Provincial Office.
Manley, Bernard A. '87 (CHL) Retired.
Manligues, Antonio '95 (HON) Kaunakakai, HI Molokai Catholic Community; Filipino Ministry.
Manly, Alex F. '57 (RVC) Kings Park, NY St. Joseph's.
Mann, Frank '79 (BRK) Brooklyn, NY Our Lady of Guadalupe; [E] Campus Ministers and Ministry Centers.
Mann, Gordon '92 (EVN) Evansville, IN St. Wendel; Diocesan Council of Priests; Personnel Board.
Mann, Lawrence *s.m.* '53 (LA)[F] Marianist Community.
Mann, Raymond *o.f.m.* '59 (BO)[AA] Boston, MA St. Anthony Shrine.
Mann, Robert G. '59 (PEO) Retired.
Mann, Slywester Mary *c.f.r.* '03 (NY)[EE] Yonkers, NY St. Felix Friary.
Manna, Louis '73 (IND) Corydon, IN St. Joseph; Corydon, IN Most Precious Blood; Corydon, IN St. Peter; Council of Priests.
Mannara, Frederick R. '63 (SY) Syracuse, NY Most Holy Rosary.
Mannebach, Thomas M. '99 (CIN) New Bremen, OH Holy Redeemer.
Mannhardt, Daniel C. '57 (DAV)[M] Davenport, IA St. Vincent Center Retired.
Manning, Brian F. '74 (BO) Scituate, MA St. Mary of the Nativity.
Manning, C. Robert '97 (STL) Bridgeton, MO St. Lawrence the Martyr; Archdiocesan Council of Priests.
Manning, Charles T. '75 (ROC) Absent on Leave.
Manning, Francis J. '51 (SPR) Retired.
Manning, Francis (SPR) Retired Priests' Service.
Manning, J. Leroy '40 (SAT) Retired.
Manning, J. Patrick '78 (Y) Alliance, OH Regina Coeli.
Manning, James J. *s.m.m.* '58 (RVC)[M] Eastport, NY Shrine of Our Lady of the Island.
Manning, James J. '75 (CIN) Dayton, OH St. Albert the Great.
Manning, James *s.m.m.* (RVC) Legion of Mary.
Manning, John E. '72 (CLV) Cleveland, OH St. Vincent de Paul; Associate Judges.
Manning, John '55 (OAK) Retired.
Manning, John (CLV) Presbyteral Council.
Manning, Joseph H. '61 (BO) Brockton, MA Our Lady of Lourdes.
Manning, Justinian *c.p.* '54 (BO) Brighton, MA St. Gabriel; [V] Boston, MA St. Gabriel Passionist Community.
Manning, Leroy '40 (SAT)[K] San Antonio, TX Padua Place.
Manning, Martin B. '43 (DAV) Retired.
Manning, Michael *s.v.d.* '69 (SB) San Bernardino, CA St. Anthony; [I] Riverside, CA Wordnet, Inc..
Manning, Michael '97 (TR) Howell, NJ St. William the Abbot.
Manning, Paul R. '59 (NEW)[D] Summit, NJ The Oratory Catholic Preparatory School
Manning, Paul S. '85 (PAT) Rockaway, NJ St. Cecilia's; [C] Denville, NJ Morris Catholic High School; Vocations Office.
Manning, Robert A. '83 (E) Franklin, PA St. Patrick.
Manning, Robert E. *s.j.* '67 (BO)[B] Cambridge, MA Weston Jesuit School of Theology; [V] Cambridge, MA.
Manning, Thomas J. '65 (SY) Retired.
Manning, Thomas V. '84 (PIT) Monroeville, PA North American Martyrs; Allegheny County, PA Beverly Manor of Monroeville; Allegheny County, PA St. Margaret Seneca Place; Absent on Sick Leave.
Mannion, Edward C. *c.m.* '39 (PH)[AA] St. Catherine Infirmary.
Mannion, Francis '73 (SLC) Salt Lake City, UT St. Vincent de Paul.
Mannion, Frank *s.s.c.* (SD) San Diego, CA St. Columba.
Mannion, J. Patrick (WCH) Defenders of the Bond Retired.
Mannion, James P. (RVC) Procurator & Advocates.
Mannion, James–Patrick '81 (RVC) Merrick, NY Cure of Ars.
Mannion, John H. '68 (LFT)[G] Beech Grove, IN St. Francis Hospital and Health Centers; On Duty Outside the Diocese.
Mannion, John '66 (SAT) LaCoste, TX Our Lady of Grace.
Mannion, Mark S. '95 (FTW)[H] South Bend, IN Prelature of the Holy Cross and Opus Dei.
Mannion, Martin J. '62 (CAM) Collingswood, NJ St. John's.
Mannion, Michael T. '71 (CAM) Camden, NJ Immaculate Conception Cathedral; [R] Camden, NJ Rutgers University – Camden Campus; Campus Ministry; Rutgers University – Camden.
Mannion, Thomas F. '46 (P) Gold Beach, OR St. Charles Borromeo Retired.
Mannion, Thomas Ignatius '65 (HBG) Catawissa, PA Our Lady of Mercy; Danville, PA State Hospital.
Mannion, Thomas J. '52 (LC) Retired.
Mannion, William D. '63 (CHI) Rosemont, IL Our Lady of Hope.
Mannion, William '89 (BAL) Absent on Leave.
Mannis, James B. *c.s.c.* '55 (FTW)[I] Notre Dame, IN Holy Cross House.
Manno, John K. '68 (SCR) Williamsport, PA Annunciation; Presbyteral Council.
Manno, John '01 (SY) Utica, NY Our Lady of Lourdes.
Manolev, Kiril '01 (STF) Colchester, CT St. Mary Dormition; Glastonbury, CT St. John The Baptist.
Manos, James M. '96 (NEW) Ramsey, NJ St. Paul; Union, NJ Holy Spirit.
Manrique, Wilfredo S. '88 (SJ) Milpitas, CA St. John the Baptist; Vicar for Clergy; Council of Priests; Office of the Vicar for Clergy; Diocesan Clergy Personnel Board; Priests' Retirement Board.
Manrique, Wilfredo '88 (SJ) Bishop's Executive Committee; Judges; Special Assignment.
Mans, Leo J. '53 (ROC) Retired.
Mansell, Kirk *s.j.* '84 (BR) Waycross, GA St. Joseph's.
Mansfield, John L. '53 (BO) Senior Priests Retired.
Mansfield, Scott '00 (SFE) Vocations; Rio Rancho, NM St. Thomas Aquinas.
Manship, D. Joseph '76 (PRT) Westbrook, ME St. Edmund; Westbrook, ME St. Mary's.
Manship, James C. '98 (HRT) Hartford, CT Sacred Heart.
Manship, James '98 (HRT) Hartford, CT St. Justin; Hartford, CT St. Michael.
Manship, Paul E. '88 (SPR) Springfield, MA All Souls; [M] Springfield, MA Catholic Latino Ministry; Diocesan Office of Black Catholic Ministry; Catholic Latino Ministry.
Mansilla, Joaquin '56 (SJN) Santurce, PR Ntra. Sra. del Perpetuo Socorro.
Mansini, Guy *o.s.b.* '77 (IND) St. Croix, IN Holy Cross; Bristow, IN St. Isidore the Farmer; [A] St. Meinrad, IN St. Meinrad School of Theology; [K] St. Meinrad, IN St. Meinrad Archabbey.
Manso, Robert F. (SPC) Lebanon, MO St. Francis De Sales; Rite Of Christian Initiation Of Adults; Office of Worship; Liturgical Commission.
Manso, Robert (SPC) Office of Worship.
Manson, Sean '99 (NEW) Plainfield, NJ St. Mary.
Mansour, Gregory J. '82 (OLL) St. Louis, MO St. Raymond's Cathedral; Maronite Catholic Community; [F] St. Louis, MO Eparchial Endowments; [F] St. Louis, MO Bishop's Retirement Trust Fund; Pastoral Center; College of Consultors; Presbyteral Council.
Mansour, Gregory J. (STL)[A] St. Louis, MO Kenrick School of Theology.
Mansour, Yousif '75 (OLD) Saint Joseph's; Syriac Mission.
Manternach, Albert V. '52 (DUB) Retired.
Manternach, Carl J. '55 (DUB) Anamosa, IA St. Patrick Retired.
Manternach, Neil J. '85 (DUB) Hiawatha, IA St. Elizabeth Ann Seton Parish; Building Commission; Church Design/Renovation Commission.
Mantia, Armand '85 (NEW) Newark, NJ St. Benedict's.
Mantica, A. Donald '60 (STU) Piney Fork, OH St. Therese; Smithfield, OH Our Lady, Queen of Peace.
Mantovani, Firmo *c.s.* '73 (KC) Kansas City, MO Holy Rosary.
Manu, Maximus *s.v.d.* '00 (LAF) Lafayette, LA Immaculate Heart of Mary.
Manuel, Armand J. *s.s.j.* '85 (BAL)[S] Baltimore, MD St. Joseph Society of the Sacred Heart House of Central Administration.
Manuel, Gerdenio M. *s.j.* '84 (SJ)[B] Santa Clara, CA Jesuit Community.
Manuel, Louis Philip *s.j.* '72 (CHR) Greer, SC Blessed Trinity; Taylors, SC Prince of Peace.
Manuel, Vincent '81 (ALX) Priests Council; Alexandria, LA St. Juliana; College of Consultors.

Manuppella, Anthony J. '76 (CAM) Merchantville, NJ St. Peter's.
Manville, Alex *o.f.m.* '53 (LA)[W] Malibu, CA Serra Retreat; Huntington Beach, CA SS. Simon and Jude.
Manz, Joseph C. '40 (NEW) Jersey City, NJ St. Nicholas; Woodcliff Lake, NJ Our Lady Mother of the Church Retired.
Manz, Michael '79 (DAL)[J] Irving, TX Opus Dei.
Manzi, Arcangelo *o.de.m.* '64 (CLV) Cleveland, OH Our Lady of Mount Carmel; [O] Cleveland, OH Mercedarians.
Manzo, Fernando L. '83 (TUC) Nogales, AZ San Felipe de Jesus; On Medical Leave.
Manzo, Louis A. *c.s.c.* (NOR) Middletown.
Manzo, Louis *c.s.c.* '65 (NOR)[K] Middletown, CT Wesleyan University–The University Ministry; Continuing Education and Formation Commission; Diocesan Commission for Ecumenical and Interreligious Affairs.
Maples, Frederic A. *s.j.* '72 (BO)[V] Boston The Society of Jesus of New England–Provincial Offices.
Maples, Frederic A. *s.j.* '72 (STP)[P] St. Paul, MN Loyola.
Mappilamattel, Jose '85 (RVC) Port Jefferson, NY St. Charles Hospital, Port Jefferson, New York.
Marabe, Jose G. (NY) Judges.
Marabe, Jose '70 (NY) New York, NY Cathedral of St. Patrick.
Marable, Gerard C. '88 (CAM) Camden, NJ St. Bartholomew's; Camden, NJ St. Joan of Arc.
Maraczewski, Edward S. '45 (CHI) Retired.
Maraist, Martin '80 (LAF) Retired.
Maraldo, Angelo F. *o.s.f.s.* '86 (VEN) Fort Myers, FL Our Lady of Light.
Maramot, Faustino '74 (MEM) Federal Correctional Institute at Memphis.
Marandu, John *c.s.sp.* (PIT) Pittsburgh, PA Holy Spirit.
Marandu, Nicolaus '52 (P) Portland, OR Immaculate Heart of Mary.
Marangone, Mark *s.x.* '84 (PAT)[M] Wayne Xaverian Missionary Fathers; (FgM).
Marani, Philip *o.carm.* '65 (NY) Bellevue Hospital, Chapel of Our Lady Helper of the Sick; Bellevue Hospital.
Maranki, James L. '99 (ALN) Bethlehem, PA SS. Simon and Jude.
Marankulam Rappuzha, Mathew M. '78 (SAC) Westwood, CA Our Lady of the Snows.
Marano, Fred (BRK) Bishop Catanello—.
Maranowski, Michael J. '87 (PIT) Butler, PA St. Wendelin.
Maranto, Charles L. *c.s.v.* '50 (CHI)[N] Arlington Heights, IL Viatorian Province Center–Clerics of St. Viator.
Maranto, Samuel C. *c.ss.r.* (BR) Presbyteral Council.
Maranto, Samuel *c.ss.r.* '72 (BR) Baton Rouge, LA St. Gerard Majella.
Marasciulo, John '45 (YAK) Retired.
Marat, W. Arthur (CHI) Defenders of the Bond.
Maravi, Raul *o.carm.* '97 (JOL)[L] Darien Carmelite Provincial Office; [L] Prelate Nullius.
Maravilla, Juan '93 (AUS) Elgin, TX Sacred Heart.
Maravilla, Primitivo '69 (MOB) Mobile, AL Cathedral of the Immaculate Conception; Apostleship of the Sea.
Maraya, Felipe '62 (ELP) Absent on Leave.
Marbach, Lawrence J. '52 (SFS) Retired.
Marbach, Lawrence '52 (SFS) Federal Prison Camp.
Marbury, Cabell B. '64 (ALB) Albany, NY St. James; Special Assignment; [C] Albany, NY Bishop Maginn High School.
Marcaccio, Anthony J. '91 (CHL) Greensboro, NC St. Pius X; Vice Chancellors; Diocesan Consultors.
Marcaida, Epifanio '83 (NY) Bronx, NY St. Frances de Chantal.
Marcano, Fred '91 (BRK) Brooklyn, NY St. Rose of Lima.
Marcantonio, Clement '59 (PBL) AUXILIARY CHAPLAINS CONTRACT CHAPLAINS Retired.
Marceau, Emmet L. '67 (SAG) Saginaw, MI St. Helen.
Marceau, Timothy R. *o.s.b.* '52 (ALX) Moreauville, LA Our Lady of Sorrows.
Marceau, Timothy R. *o.s.b.* '52 (JOL)[L] Lisle, IL St. Procopius Abbey.
Marceaux, Sidney J. '70 (BEA) Military Chaplains.
Marceaux, Sidney (TYL) Judges.
Marcell, Robert G. '56 (BR) Retired.
Marcello, Joseph A. '03 (BGP) Shelton, CT St. Joseph.
Marcellus, Gordon E. *o.s.a.* '59 (PH)[C] Villanova University.
Marcelo, Jose M. '79 (MET) Piscataway, NJ Our Lady of Fatima.
March, Ralph *o. cist.* '45 (DAL)[B] University of Dallas; [K] Irving, TX Cistercian Abbey of Our Lady of Dallas.
Marchand, Gerald A. '54 (NEW) Retired.
Marchand, Robert A. '52 (MAN) Retired.
Marchesani, Gino *f.d.p.* '56 (BO)[B] Haverhill, MA Sons of Divine Providence School for Exceptional Boys; [T] East Boston, MA Don Orione Nursing Home; [X] Haverhill, MA Don Orione Center.
Marchese, Henry *s.a.* '64 (NY)[EE] New York, NY Atonement Friars.
Marchese, Joseph P. '69 (SPR) On Duty Outside the Diocese.
Marchese, Richard E.. '70 (BRK) Brooklyn, NY St. Frances Cabrini.
Marchesin, Ivan *s.x.* '66 (PAT)[M] Wayne, NJ Xaverian Missionary Fathers; (FgM).
Marchetti, Carlo M. *o.s.m.* '59 (CHI)[N] Chicago Order of Friar Servants of Mary (Servites) United States of America Province, Inc..
Marchetti, Michael H. '82 (SCR) Scranton, PA Holy Name.
Marchewka, Jacek (NEW) Bergenfield, NJ St. John the Evangelist.
Marchino, Louis H. '39 (IND) Retired.
Marchionda, James *o.p.* '73 (CHI)[N] Oak Park, IL Dominican Community of St. Martin de Porres.
Marchitelli, Anthony D. '76 (NY)[E] Somers, NY John F. Kennedy High School; [Q] Archdiocesan Committee on Scouting.
Marchlewski, Michael A. *s.j.* '67 (STL)[O] St. Louis, MO De Smet Jesuit High School Community.
Marchulones, Kenneth L. '65 (PEO) East Peoria, IL St. Monica's.
Marchulones, Kenneth (PEO) Diocesan College of Consultors; Clergymen's Aid, Inc..
Marchwiany, Robert '03 (CHI) La Grange Park, IL St. Louise de Marillac.
Marciano, Robert L. '83 (PRO) Warwick, RI Ss. Rose & Clement; Air National Guard Chaplains.
Marcil, Michel *s.j.* '74 (SFR)[E] San Francisco, CA St. Ignatius College Preparatory (Coed); [N] San Francisco, CA Jesuit Community at St. Ignatius College Preparatory.
Marciniak, Bartlomiej *o.s.p.p.e.* '93 (PH)[AA] Office.
Marciniak, Felix R. '79 (NEW) Wallington, NJ Most Sacred Heart of Jesus.
Marciniak, Henry P. '61 (NEW) Elizabeth, NJ St. Hedwig's; Kenilworth, NJ St. Theresa's Retired.
Marciniak, John '56 (NOR) Retired.
Marciniak, Thomas R. *s.j.* '76 (SY)[Q] Syracuse, NY Jesuits at LeMoyne, Inc.; [T] Syracuse, NY LeMoyne College Newman Center.
Marco, Michael J. *s.j.* '96 (CLV)[D] Cuyahoga Falls, OH Walsh Jesuit High School; [C] Omaha, NE Creighton Preparatory School.
Marcone, Eugene F. '64 (NEW) Retired.
Marcone, Eugene '64 (NEW) Garwood, NJ Church of St. Anne.
Marconi, John E. '87 (LR) Paragould, AR St. Mary's; Walnut Ridge, AR Immaculate Heart of Mary; Corning, AR St. Joseph Church.
Marconi, Joseph Patrick '01 (LR) Helena, AR St. Mary's; Marianna, AR St. Andrew.
Marconi, Paul *c.r.s.p.* '58 (SD) Pala, CA Mission San Antonio de Pala.
Marconi, Theodore B. '84 (E) Ridgway, PA St. Leo the Great; Deans.
Marcotte, David P. *s.j.* '92 (BGP)[N] San Francisco, CA Jesuit Community at University of San Francisco.
Marcotte, Joseph A. '69 (WOR) Webster, MA St. Louis.
Marcotte, Wayne E. '66 (MAR) Hancock, MI Resurrection; Executive Board; Deans; Consultors.
Marcotte, William '60 (SB) Retired.
Marcouiller, Douglas *s.j.* '86 (Missouri)[V] Newton, MA The Jesuit Community at Boston College.
Marcoux, A. Stephen (MAN) Liaisons.
Marcoux, Joseph W. '01 (ROC) Rochester, NY Sacred Heart Cathedral; Censores Librorum.
Marcoux, Stephen '93 (MAN) Nashua, NH Resurrection.
Marcucci, John A. '68 (PIT) Glenshaw, PA St. Mary of the Assumption.
Marczewski, Robert '95 (PH) Norristown, PA St. Francis of Assisi.
Marczewski, Ronald J. '74 (NEW) Elizabeth, NJ St. Adalbert's.
Marczuk, Scott L. (LR) Little Rock, AR Cathedral of St. Andrew; Vice Chancellors; Judicial Vicar; Judges; Diocesan Consultors.
Mardian, Pius '44 (SFS) Retired.
Marecki, Ronald '83 (SP) Ridge Manor, FL St. Anne.
Marek, Dean V. '65 (MIL) On Duty Outside the Archdiocese.
Marek, Dean V. '65 (WIN) On Special or Other Diocesan Assignment; [D] Rochester, MN Saint Mary's Hospital.
Marek, Ray John *o.m.i.* '89 (SAT)[C] Oblate School of Theology; [M] San Antonio, TX De Mazenod House.
Marek, Walter '46 (GAY) Retired.
Maresca, Ralph J. (BRK) Secretary to the Diocesan Bishop.
Maresca, Ralph '78 (BRK) Special Assignment.
Maresh, Mark '94 (GI) Elm Creek, NE Immaculate Conception.
Marflak, Albert M. *o.s.b.* '75 (ROM) Cleveland, OH Most Holy Trinity.
Marflak, Albert M. *o.s.b.* '75 (CLV)[Y] Cleveland, OH The Benedictine High School Endowment Trust.
Marflak, Albert *o.s.b.* '75 (CLV)[O] Cleveland, OH.
Marfori, Antonio '78 (SCL) Zimmerman, MN St. Pius X.
Margason, James E. '71 (BEL) Belleville, IL St. Luke; Belleville, IL Chapel of St. John Children's Home; Lebanon, IL St. Joseph; [C] Belleville, IL Chancery Office; [J] Belleville, IL The Catholic Diocese of Belleville Deposit and Loan Fund; [J] Belleville, IL The Catholic Diocese of Belleville Custodial Fund; [J] Belleville, IL The Catholic Diocese of Belleville Group Health Insurance Fund; [J] Belleville, IL The Catholic Diocese of Belleville Property Insurance Fund; [J] Belleville, IL The Catholic Diocese of Belleville Ministry Formation Fund; Vicar General; Moderator of the Curia; Judges; Diocesan Consultors; Diocesan Finance Council.
Margevicius, Thomas '99 (STP) Graduate Studies; [A] St. Paul, MN The Saint Paul Seminary.
Marggraf, Brian *ss.cc.* '55 (FR)[H] Fairhaven, MA Damien Residence.
Margherio, Ronald L. *o.s.b.* '78 (PEO).
Marhafer, Maury *o.f.m.conv.* '54[A] (FgM).
Mariadoss, Adaikalam Maria '74 (SCL) St. Cloud, MN St. John Cantius.
Marian, Anthony S. '58 (NY) Poughkeepsie, NY Vassar Brothers Hospital.
Mariani, Guilbert '97 (CC)[G] Robstown, TX Society of Our Lady of the Most Holy Trinity.
Mariani, Paul P. *s.j.* '02 (CHI)[N] Chicago, IL Woodlawn Jesuit Community.
Mariano, John M. '58 (BRK) Released from Diocesan Assignment.
Mariano, Remigio "Miguel" (TUC) Council of Priests; Diocesan Liturgical Commission; All Vicars Forane; Vocations.
Mariasoosai, Gnana Pragasam (CHL) Marion, NC Our Lady of the Angels.
Marick, Thomas D. '97 (STN) Honolulu, HI Byzantine Missions.
Marick, Thomas '98 (STN) Waianae, HI St. Sophia Byzantine Missions.
Marickovic, Thomas C. '81 (HBG) Danville, PA Geisinger Medical Center; [G] Danville, PA Maria Joseph Manor.
Marie, Adrien Ste. *c.s.c.* '50 (P).
Marien, Roy C. '85 (PT)[B] Niceville, FL Christ Our Redeemer.
Marien, Roy (PT) College of Consultors; Seminarian Candidate Review Board.
Marier, Edward '88 (SPK) Newport, WA Our Lady of Sorrows; Ione, WA St. Bernard; Metaline Falls, WA St. Joseph; Newport, WA St. Anthony; Newport, WA St. Jude.
Marigliano, Michael *o.f.m.cap.* '84 (NY)[EE] New York, NY Development Office:.
Marilag, Nelson '87 (ANC) Anchorage, AK St. Anthony.
Marin, John L. '85 (MET) On Duty Outside the Diocese.
Marin, Jose G. (TYL) Clarksville, TX St. Joseph.
Marin, Miguel '78 (ELP) Absent on Leave.
Marin, Moises '95 (CHI) Mission San Juan Diego.
Marin, Tomas M. '89 (MIA) Miami, FL Our Lady of Guadalupe; Archdiocese of Miami Health Plan Trust; Catholic Physicians' and Dentists' Guild.
Marin, Tomas (MIA) Promoters of Justice.
Marin, Tomas (SAM) Promoter of Justice.
Marin–Leon, Rafael '78 (LA) Santa Barbara, CA Our Lady of Guadalupe; Wilmington, CA Holy Family.
Marinacci, Nicholas '38 (NY) New York, NY St. Patrick Old Cathedral.
Marinak, Andrew P. '56 (HBG) Cornwall, PA Sacred Heart of Jesus.
Marincioni, Raniero A. '90 (MET) On Duty Outside the Diocese.
Marine, John C. '76 (PH) On Special or Other Archdiocesan Assignment; Regional Vicars; Priests' Personnel Board.
Maring, William J. *s.j.* '45 (SJ)[M] Los Gatos, CA Sacred Heart Jesuit Center.
Marini, Francis J. '95 (SAM) Brooklyn, NY Cathedral of Our Lady of Lebanon; Scranton, PA St. Ann; Vicar for Canonical Services/Administration; Adjutant Judicial Vicar; Presbyteral Council–Ex Officio Members; Elected Members.
Marini, Joseph J. '52 (SFR) San Bruno, CA St. Robert Retired.
Marini, Michael '92 (MRY) Advocates Retired.
Marinko, John S. '55 (SCR) Retired.
Marino, Christopher '93 (MIA) Miami, FL Visitation; Italian.
Marino, Edward J. *c.s.* '57 (PRO)[M] North Kingstown, RI Scalabrini Villa.
Marino, Francis J. *s.m.* '57 (MET)[M] Phillipsburg, NJ The Anawim Community.
Marino, John J. *o.f.m.* '88 (ARL) Triangle, VA St. Francis of Assisi.
Marino, Joseph T. '75 (PH) Havertown, PA St. Denis.
Marino, Joseph '79 (BIR) On Duty Outside the Diocese.
Marino, Ronald T. '73 (BRK) Brooklyn, NY St. Rosalia–Regina Pacis; [U] Brooklyn, NY Catholic Migration & Refugee Office, Catholic Migration Services, Inc.; [U] Brooklyn, NY Resources, Inc.; [U] Brooklyn, NY Catholic Immigrant Ministries, Inc.; Catholic Migration Services, Inc..

Marino, Umberto J. '54 (NY) On Duty Outside the Archdiocese.
Marinucci, Steven J. '74 (PH) Philadelphia, PA St. Agatha–St. James.
Maristany, Edward G. '80 (CHI)[W] Chicago, IL Prelature of the Holy Cross and Opus Dei.
Maristela, Victor '87 (SD) Oceanside, CA Tri City Hospital.
Marjanczyk, Joseph A. '45 (NEW) Bayonne, NJ Mt. Carmel Retired.
Mark, John K. '01 (STV) St. Thomas, VI Holy Family Parish; Charlotte Amalie, VI Cathedral of Sts. Peter and Paul; [B] St. Thomas, VI Hispanic Ministry.
Mark, John (STV) Hispanic Ministry.
Markalonis, Joseph *t.o.r.* '66 (FgM).
Markell, John W. '84 (PIT).
Markelz, Carl J. *o.carm.* '91 (CHI)[D] Chicago, IL.
Markelz, Carl *o.carm.* '91 (CHI)[N] Chicago Carmelite Priory of St. Cyril.
Markert, Leo F. '62 (ALB) Schenectady, NY St. Gabriel the Archangel.
Markert, Leo (ALB) Deans; Priests Placement Committee.
Markewych, Uriy '65 (PHU) Reading, PA Nativity of Blessed Virgin Mary.
Markey, Earle L. *s.j.* '63 (WOR)[O] Worcester, MA Jesuits of Holy Cross College, Inc..
Markey, Greg J. '99 (BGP) Bridgeport, CT St. Peter.
Markey, John J. *o.p.* '93 (OAK)[N] Berkeley, CA Order of Preachers (Southern Province); Special Assignment.
Markey, John *o.p.* '93 (MIA)[C] Oblate School of Theology.
Markham, James J. '51 (MAN) Manchester, NH Transfiguration Retired.
Markham, John C. '03 (SAV) Savannah, GA Most Blessed Sacrament.
Markham, John W. '54 (DET) Detroit, MI St. Elizabeth Retired.
Markiewicz, Stanley T. *o.s.b.* '61 (GBG)[H] Latrobe, PA Saint Vincent Archabbey.
Markley, Edward P. *o.s.b.* '66 (MOB) Lillian, AL St. Joseph.
Markley, Edward P. *o.s.b.* '66 (BIR)[E] Cullman, AL St. Bernard Abbey.
Marko, Andrew '98 (SJP) Austintown, OH St. Anne.
Markowitch, Robert '01 (STF) St. John the Baptist; Hudson, NY St. Nicholas.
Marks, Thomas C. '79 (LR) Pocahontas, AR St. John the Baptist; Pocahontas, AR St. Paul the Apostle.
Marks, William '92 (IND) Lawrenceburg, IN St. Teresa Benedicta of the Cross; Council of Priests.
Markunas, Robert '76 (ORL) Consultors.
Markus, Anthony L. '80 (CHI) Chicago Ridge, IL Our Lady of the Ridge.
Markwell, George *m.afr.* '65 (WDC)[K] Silver Spring, MD Holy Cross Hospital of Silver Spring, Inc.; [M] Washington, DC Missionaries of Africa.
Marley, John *s.s.c.* '47 (STP)[I] Hastings, MN Regina Medical Center; [L] Hastings, MN Regina Retirement Center; Regina Medical Center.
Marley, Thomas J. *c.s.p.* '49 (PMB)[J] Vero Beach, FL Paulist Fathers Residence.
Marley, Thomas J. *c.s.p.* '49 (NY)[EE] Jamaica Estates Paulist Fathers Generalate.
Marley, William F. *m.m.* '52 (NY).
Marmol, Richard '97 (SJN)[EE] Carolina, PR Ntra. Sra. Reina de los Angeles.
Marneni, Ignatius '69 (PH) Philadelphia, PA St. Monica.
Marneni, Julian '67 (WH) Huntington, WV St. Joseph's; Wayne, WV Nativity of Our Lord.
Maro, Wayne *c.pp.s.* '86 (LA)[BB] Claremont, CA Claremont Colleges.
Maroney, Frank '92 (DEN) Vail, CO St. Patrick's; Deaneries.
Maroney, Maurice J. '67 (HRT) Milford, CT St. Gabriel.
Maroon, Donald M. '67 (COL) Wellston, OH SS. Peter and Paul.
Maroon, William J. '67 (COL) Retired.
Maroor, Joseph '63 (MIA) Margate, FL St. Vincent.
Marot, Roger L. '50 (PRO)[N] Woonsocket, RI Fr. Marot CYO Center Retired.
Marotta, Robert G. '63 (NEW) Retired.
Maroun, George F. '74 (OG) Carthage, NY St. James Minor; Copenhagen, NY St. Mary; Mission Aid Societies.
Maroun, Sharbel G. '89 (OLL) Minneapolis, MN St. Maron.
Maroun, Sharbel (OLL) Office of Priestly Vocations.
Marquard, Elmer E. '66 (CLV) North Ridgeville, OH St. Julie Billiart.
Marquardt, Donald '51 (GB) Retired.
Marquardt, John *g.h.m.* '44 (CIN)[M] Cincinnati Headquarters of Glenmary Home Missioners.
Marquart, Ernest J. '70 (SPC) Mountain View, MO St. John Vianney; Region V.
Marquart, Joseph M. '57 (SEA) Everett, WA St. Mary Magdalen.
Marques, Luis *c.ss.r.* (NEW) Newark, NJ St. James.
Marquez, Celso *m.sp.s.* '97 (P) Hillsboro, OR St. Matthew; [L] Mount Angel, OR Missionaries of the Holy Spirit M.Sp.S..
Marquez, Gregory '03 (ORG) San Juan Capistrano, CA Mission Basilica.
Marquez, Jose E. '99 (NEW) Bergenfield, NJ St. John the Evangelist.
Marquez–Munoz, Salvador '03 (LR) Little Rock, AR St. Edward; North Little Rock, AR St. Anne.
Marquis, Clif *s.t.* '69 (ORG) Santa Ana, CA All Adult and Juvenile Jail Facilities; Americus, GA St. Mary.
Marquis, Paul R. '86 (PRT) Westbrook, ME St. Hyacinth; Portland, ME Maine Medical Center.
Marquis, Raymond *o.m.i.* '74 (FgM).
Marquis, William J. '03 (CC) Corpus Christi, TX St. Pius X.
Marquis, William P. *o.p.* '83 (PRO)[P] Providence St. Thomas Acuinas Priory at Providence College.
Marr, Thomas P. '70 (MAD) Watertown, WI St. Bernard; Deaneries.
Marra, Anthony C. '51 (SCR) Dunmore, PA St. Anthony of Padua.
Marra, James *s.d.b.* '83 (NY) Port Chester, NY Corpus Christi.
Marreddy, Allam '79 (CHR) Abbeville, SC Sacred Heart; Greenwood, SC Our Lady of Lourdes.
Marreddy, Gade Lourdu '60 (BGP) Stratford, CT St. James.
Marrell, Dennis P. '78 (LA) Monterey Park, CA St. Stephen.
Marren, Hugh M. '76 (ATL) Duluth, GA St. Benedict.
Marren, Martin T. '84 (CHI) Oak Lawn, IL St. Gerald.
Marrero, Adan *s.d.b.* '97 (SJN)[C] Catano, PR Prenoviciado Salesiano.
Marrero, Angel Diaz (ARE) Priest's Senate (Consejo Presbiteral).
Marrero, Francisco J. *s.j.* '70 (SJN)[H] San Juan, PR Comunidad Jesuita.
Marrin, Joseph *c.ss.r.* (BRK) Legion of Mary.
Marrion, Malachy *o.c.s.o.* '54 (ARL)[J] Berryville, VA Cistercian Abbey of Our Lady of the Holy Cross.
Marro, Nicholas A. *c.s.* '63 (CHI) Chicago, IL Santa Lucia–Santa Maria Incoronata.
Marro, Simeon D. *o.carm.* '55 (GBG)[H] Bolivar, PA Mount Carmel Hermitage.
Marrodan, Francisco J. *c.m.* '54 (ARE) Manati, PR Sagrada Familia.
Marron, James F. '62 (BRK) Rosedale, NY St. Pius X.
Marron, Patrick L. '67 (SAT) San Antonio, TX St. Elizabeth Ann Seton.
Marrone, Robert J. '73 (CLV) Cleveland, OH St. Peter.
Marroquin, Luis '86 (WDC) Silver Spring, MD St. Catherine Laboure.
Marrow, Stanley B. *s.j.* '61 (BO)[V] Cambridge, MA.
Marrufo, Ramon R. '76 (SD) Vista, CA St. Francis of Assisi.
Marrufo, Ramon (SD) Vicars Forane.
Marschner, Aloysius J. '36 (STL) Retired.
Marsh, Ivan C. *o.carm* '80 (GAL)[A] Houston, TX St. Mary's Seminary.
Marsh, John *c.ss.r.* (MO) AUXILIARY CHAPLAINS CONTRACT CHAPLAINS.
Marshall, Eugene C. *o.s.b.* '50 (OKL) McLoud, OK St. Vincent de Paul; [I] Shawnee St. Gregory's Abbey.
Marshall, Hugh *s.t.* '56 (WDC)[M] Adelphi, MD Missionary Servants of the Most Holy Trinity.
Marshall, James C. '59 (STL) St. Louis, MO St. Pius X.
Marshall, James *s.j.* (ELP) El Paso, TX Sacred Heart.
Marshall, John J. '59 (ALT) Retired.
Marshall, Joseph Mary *s.m.* '93 (SAT)[M] San Antonio, TX Casa San Juan Marianist Community; [U] San Antonio, TX Brothers of the Beloved Disciplel; San Antonio, TX St. Mary Magdalen.
Marshall, Patrick M. '79 (CHI)[V] Chicago, IL University of Illinois at Chicago – John Paul II Newman Center.
Marshall, Paul M. *s.m.* '76 (CIN)[D] Dayton, OH The University of Dayton; [M] Dayton, OH Marianist Community.
Marshall, Robert W. (MEM) Humboldt, TN Sacred Heart; Humboldt, TN St. Matthew Mission.
Marshall, Thomas R. *c.s.p.* '59 (NY).
Marshall, William '63 (OAK) Retired.
Marsicek, Bob *s.d.s.* '68 (MIL)[EE] Wauwatosa, WI St. Pius X.
Marsick, James J. '72 (CLV) Cuyahoga Falls, OH St. Joseph.
Marszal, Theodore '68 (CLV) Garfield Heights, OH SS. Peter and Paul.
Marszal, Theodore '68 (CLV) Cleveland, OH St. Hyacinth.
Marszal, Theodore (CLV) Procurators.
Marszalek, Paul B. '52 (CHI) Retired.
Marta, Raul '72 (FRS) Tulare, CA St. Aloysius.
Marteka, Anthony T. '61 (WOR) Grafton, MA St. Philip's.
Martel, C. James '70 (PRT) Retired.
Martel, Leo E. '63 (BO) Chelmsford, MA St. Mary.
Martel, Luc *a.a.* '73 (BO)[V] Assumptionist Community.
Martel, Marcel '79 (MAN) Plaistow, NH Holy Angels.
Martell, James '88 (MEM) Memphis, TN Our Lady of Sorrows.
Martell, Jim J. (MEM) Presbyteral Council and College of Consultors.
Martelli, Jose M. *c.s.c.* '73 (SB) Coachella, CA Our Lady of Soledad; Special or Other Diocesan Assignment.
Martelli, Jose M. *c.s.c.* '73 (FTW)[I] Coachella, CA Valley Missionary Program.
Martelli, Jose *c.s.c.* '70 (SB)[E] Coachella, CA Congregation of the Holy Cross.
Martelli, Jose *c.s.c.* (SB) Liturgy Committee; Valley Missionary Program, Shrine of Our Lady of Guadalupe.
Martello, Ernest *o.s.c.* '70 (FgM).
Martello, Lawrence N. '74 (CLV) Amherst, OH St. Joseph; College of Consultors; Presbyteral Conveners; Associate Judges.
Martens, L. Gene *s.j.* '63 (STL)[O] St. Louis, MO Hallahan House; [O] St. Louis, MO The Jesuits of the Missouri Province; [U] St. Louis, MO The Jesuits of the Missouri Province.
Martensen, Carsten *s.j.* '77 (RVC) Oceanside, NY St. Anthony.
Marterior, Paul *o.p.* '94 (GAL) Baytown, TX St. Joseph.
Marth, Loydell J. '56 (FRS) Buttonwillow, CA St. Mary; Taft, CA St. Mary.
Marthaler, Andrew '90 (SCL) Elbow Lake, MN St. Olaf; Tintah, MN St. Gall's.
Marthaler, Berard L. *o.f.m.* '52 (SD) Washington, DC St. Anthony; [B] Washington, DC St. Bonaventure Friary; [C] Catholic University of America, The; [B] University of San Diego Retired.
Marti, Antonio E. *o.f.m.cap.* '96 (SFR)[N] Burlingame, CA Capuchin Provincial House.
Marti, Julio *l.c.* '97 (HRT)[B] Cheshire, CT Novitiate of the Legion of Christ.
Marti, Ramon *sch.p.* '55 (LA) Monrovia, CA Annunciation; Duarte, CA City of Hope Medical Center.
Marti, Thomas J. *m.m.* '65 (NY)[N] Denver, CO Maryknoll Fathers and Brothers.
Martignetti, Richard *o.f.m.* '97 (NY)[EE] New York Franciscan Province of the Immaculate Conception.
Martignon, John E. '84 (MAR) Houghton, MI St. Ignatius Loyola; South Range, MI Holy Family.
Martin, Andrew E. '67 (CAM) Camden, NJ St. Joseph's Pro–Cathedral; [A] Cherry Hill, NJ Camden Catholic High School; Priests Personnel Board.
Martin, Andrew (CAM) Members.
Martin, Anselm *o.f.m.cap.* '45 (PH) Philadelphia, PA St. John the Evangelist.
Martin, Arcadio '31 (LA) Retired.
Martin, Benjamin '75 (DOD) Leoti, KS St. Anthony of Padua; Marienthal, KS St. Mary; Tribune, KS St. Joseph.
Martin, C. Lou '76 (BAL) Baltimore, MD St. Anthony of Padua; Baltimore, MD Most Precious Blood; Advocates and Procurators.
Martin, C. Louis (BAL) Priests' Council.
Martin, Charles A. *c.s.p.* '65 (WDC)[B] Washington, DC St. Paul's College.
Martin, Clarence A. *s.j.* '46 (ALN)[A] Wernersville, PA Jesuit Center.
Martin, Clifford '76 (SFR) Retired Priests.
Martin, Cristobal '96 (NY) Bronx, NY Santa Maria; [EE] Bronx, NY Idente Missionaries – Santa Maria Residence.
Martin, Daniel J. '43 (E) Retired.
Martin, David A. '76 (EVN) Washington, IN Immaculate Conception; Washington, IN St. Simon.
Martin, David L. '73 (ARL) Orange, VA; Fredericksburg, VA St. Jude.
Martin, David '76 (EVN)[I] Washington, IN St. Vincent de Paul Society of Washington, IN, Inc..
Martin, Dennis A. '75 (E) Erie, PA St. Vincent's Health Center; [G] Erie, PA Saint Vincent Health Center.
Martin, Dennis C. '67 (DAV) West Liberty, IA St. Joseph's.
Martin, Dennis '62 (NO)[P] New Orleans, LA Vincentian Fathers.
Martin, Diosdado '66 (LA) Los Angeles, CA Assumption.
Martin, Donald *s.j.* '82 (NO).
Martin, Emilio '52 (MIA)[A] Hialeah, FL St. John the Apostle; Building Commission.
Martin, Francis '39 (LAN) Retired.
Martin, Francis '56 (WDC) Special Ministries.
Martin, Gerard R. '73 (BR) Baton Rouge, LA St. Patrick; Defenders of the Bond.
Martin, Gilmer '74 (NO) Lacombe, LA St. John of the Cross.
Martin, Harry (SAT) On Leave.
Martin, James A. *s.j.* '34 (WDC)[M] Washington, DC The Jesuit Community at Georgetown University.
Martin, James J. '63 (PH) Philadelphia, PA Holy Family.
Martin, James J. '68 (CHI) Chicago, IL St. Dorothy; Deans.
Martin, James J. *s.j.* '99 (NY)[EE] New York, NY "America;" Residence and publication office of the America Press.
Martin, James J. *s.j.* '99 (BO)[V] Boston The Society of Jesus of New England–Provincial Offices.
Martin, James (SAG)[E] Saginaw, MI St. Mary's Medical Center of Saginaw, Inc..

Martin, Joel W. *o.s.b.* '91 (BIR)[B] Cullman, AL St. Bernard Preparatory School; [E] Cullman, AL St. Bernard Abbey.
Martin, John B. '56 (NEW) Newark, NJ Sacred Heart.
Martin, John F. *s.j.* '74 (WDC)[M] Washington, DC The Jesuit Community at Georgetown University.
Martin, John J. '65 (SR) Mendocino, CA St. Anthony.
Martin, John J. '72 (ALN) Bethlehem, PA Assumption B.V.M..
Martin, John M. *s.j.* '84 (SJ)[M] Los Gatos, CA Sacred Heart Jesuit Center.
Martin, John P. '61 (RVC) New Hyde Park, NY Notre Dame; Priests' Retirement Board.
Martin, John P. *m.m.* '66 (FgM).
Martin, John *a.a.* '57 (BO)[V] Boston, MA Assumptionist Center.
Martin, Jon C. '65 (BO) Middleton, MA Essex County Correctional Facility.
Martin, Joseph A. '67 (NY) Fishkill, NY Church of St. Mary, Mother of the Church.
Martin, Joseph C. *s.s.* '48 (BAL) Special Assignment; [S] Havre De Grace, MD Retired.
Martin, Joseph I. '53 (BO) Senior Priests Retired.
Martin, Joseph I. '56 ((BO)) (FgM).
Martin, Joseph J. '03 (PH) Brookhaven, PA Our Lady of Charity.
Martin, Joseph (NY) Canon 1742 Panel of Pastors.
Martin, Justin David '02 (IND) Indianapolis, IN St. Luke.
Martin, Kevin '03 (PRT) Auburn, ME St. Louis; Auburn, ME St. Philip's; Auburn, ME Sacred Heart.
Martin, Kieran J. '50 (BRK) Brooklyn, NY St. Thomas Aquinas Retired.
Martin, Kieran (BRK) Alcoholism Committee.
Martin, Larok '80 (OKL)[K] Tonkawa, OK Northern Oklahoma College.
Martin, Leon J. *s.a.c.* '75 (MIL)[O] Milwaukee, WI Pallotti House.
Martin, Leonard A. *s.j.* '73 (SCR)[C] Scranton, PA The University of Scranton.
Martin, Malcolm *s.a.* '62 (BO)[O] Brockton, MA Chapel of Our Savior–Catholic Pastoral and Information Center; [V] Brockton, MA Chapel of Our Savior; [AA] Brockton, MA Chapel of Our Saviour.
Martin, Michael *c.s.p.* '77 (STP) Minneapolis, MN St. Lawrence–Newman; [M] Minneapolis, MN Paulist Fathers; [U] Minneapolis, MN Newman Center at St. Lawrence.
Martin, Michael *o.f.m.conv.* '89 (BAL)[C] Baltimore, MD Archbishop Curley High School; [S] Baltimore, MD Immaculate Heart of Mary Friary; [V] Baltimore, MD Archbishop Curley High School Endowment Trust.
Martin, Michael *o.s.b.* (MO) AUXILIARY CHAPLAINS CONTRACT CHAPLAINS.
Martin, Norman F. *s.j.* '47 (SJ)[B] Santa Clara, CA Jesuit Community.
Martin, Normand J. *s.m.* (BO) Lawrence, MA Sacred Heart.
Martin, Oscar '01 (NEW) On Duty Outside the Archdiocese.
Martin, Patrick A. '78 (NOR) On Duty Outside the Diocese.
Martin, Paul M. '58 (ORG) Retired.
Martin, Paul (ORG) Judges; Council of Priests.
Martin, Ralph L. (WIL) Vocation Office.
Martin, Raymond D. '94 (BAL) Baltimore, MD Our Lady of Good Counsel.
Martin, Raymond '94 (BAL) Baltimore, MD Holy Cross; Baltimore, MD St. Mary, Star of the Sea.
Martin, Reginald *o.p.* '74 (SEA) Eugene, OR St. Thomas More.
Martin, Ricardo '02 (MIL)[X] Racine, WI Missionary Community of St. Paul the Apostle and Mary, Mother of the Church, Inc..
Martin, Richard B. '66 (ARL) Burke, VA Church of the Nativity.
Martin, Richard J. '63 (CHI) Chicago, IL St. Maurice.
Martin, Robert A. '83 (BUF)[D] Batavia, NY Notre Dame High School of Batavia; Alden, NY St. John the Baptist.
Martin, Robert *c.ss.r.* '50 (FgM).
Martin, Roger '51 (OG) Retired.
Martin, Roosevelt '88 (GAL) Houston, TX St. Mark the Evangelist.
Martin, Samuel A. '99 (LC) Special Assignment; [A] La Crosse, WI Holy Cross Seminary House of Formation; [H] La Crosse, WI Holy Cross (Seminary) Diocesan Center.
Martin, Sean '79 (STL)[B] St. Louis, MO Aquinas Institute of Theology.
Martin, Sean '81 (DAL) On Duty Outside the Diocese.
Martin, Stephen E. '98 (MOB) Montgomery, AL St. Peter.
Martin, Thomas A. '79 (KAL) Mendon, MI St. Edward; Judicial Vicar; Diocesan Consultors; Delegate for Ecumenical and Interreligious Concerns; Presbyteral Council; Vicksburg, MI St. Martin.
Martin, Thomas F. *o.s.a.* '69 (PH)[C] Villanova University.
Martin, Thomas P. *s.j.* '66 (BAL)[S] Baltimore, MD Jesuit Fathers and Brothers Maryland Provincial Curia.
Martin, Thomas *o.c.d.* '61 (MIL)[O] Milwaukee Provincial Offices – Discalced Carmelites.
Martin, Thomas *o.s.a.* '69 (PH)[AA] Villanova, PA.
Martin, Thomas '70 (OAK) Berkeley, CA St. Joseph The Worker.
Martin, Thomas (KAL) Ecclesiastical Notaries.
Martin, Vicente '75 (VEN) Punta Gorda, FL Sacred Heart.
Martin, Victor T. '80 (BGP) Fairfield, CT St. Thomas Aquinas.
Martin, William F. '56 (GRY) Retired.
Martin, William F. '63 (NY) On Duty Outside the Archdiocese.
Martin, William F. '78 (STP) Oakdale, MN Guardian Angels; Cursillo.
Martin, William J. '71 (TOL) Retired.
Martin, William J. '71 (L) Louisville, KY St. Rita.
Martin, William *o.m.i.* '61 (GAL)[S] Dickinson, TX Christian Renewal Center.
Martin–Calama, Florian '95 (DEN)[A] Denver, CO Redemptoris Mater House of Formation.
Martina, Joseph '89 (SHP) Church Vocations; Church Vocations Board.
Martine, Michael '97 (NY) Nanuet, NY St. Anthony.
Martineau, Albert P. *o.m.i.* '59 (BO)[AA] Lowell, MA St. Joseph the Worker Residence.
Martineau, Laurier J. '59 (BO) Marlborough, MA St. Mary.
Martinek, John '73 (FBK) Delta Junction, AK Our Lady of Sorrows; Tok, AK Holy Rosary.
Martinez, Adam '85 (AUS) Lockhart, TX St. Mary's.
Martinez, Adolfo '03 (TUC) Tucson, AZ St. John the Evangelist.
Martinez, Alberto (CGS)[B] Aibonito, PR Casa Manresa.
Martinez, Alfredo (CGS) Retired.
Martinez, Anthony L. '89 (SFE) Moriarty, NM Estancia Valley Catholic Parish.
Martinez, Antonio *o.a.r* '48 (LSC)[C] Mesilla, NM Augustinian Recollect Fathers.
Martinez, Benjamin *c.m.f.* '58 (MET) Perth Amboy, NJ Our Lady of Fatima.
Martinez, Charles *o.f.m.* '80 (SAT) Special Assignment.
Martinez, Charlie *o.f.m.* '80 (SFE)[I] Albuquerque, NM Curia Juan Diego.
Martinez, Danilo deJesus *c.m.f.* (CGS) Caguas, PR Inmaculado Corazon de Maria.
Martinez, Eusebio '03 (BWN) Harlingen, TX Immaculate Heart of Mary; Raymondville, TX St. Anthony.
Martinez, Felipe J. *c.m.* '55 (STL) Perryville, MO Christ the Savior.
Martinez, Francisco Xavier *s.t.l.* '89 (CC) Bishop's Office; Director for Pastoral Ministries; Alliance for Human Life; [B] Corpus Christi, TX Holy Family School; Corpus Christi, TX Holy Family; Guadalupanas.
Martinez, Francisco (ARE) Retired.
Martinez, Frank Perez *o.s.b.* '97 (MGZ) Mayaguez, PR Sacred Heart.
Martinez, German *o.s.b.* '67 (BGP) Greenwich, CT St. Mary.
Martinez, Gilbert S. *c.s.p.* (TUC) Tuscon, AZ St. Cyril of Alexandria.
Martinez, Gilberto *s.s.p.* '75 (LA)[Q] Los Angeles, CA Society of St. Paul.
Martinez, Hugo (NY) Bronx, NY St. Anthony of Padua.
Martinez, Ignacio '93 (MRY) Soledad, CA Our Lady of Solitude.
Martinez, Ignatius (MRY) Ecumenical Commission.
Martinez, James E. *o.s.a.* '57 (PH) Bryn Mawr, PA Our Mother of Good Counsel; [AA] Bryn Mawr, PA Augustinians Friars (O.S.A.).
Martinez, Jesus E. '02 (WOR) Leominster, MA St. Leo's; St. Leo.
Martinez, Joaquin *s.j.* '03 (BO)[V] Cambridge, MA Faber House.
Martinez, John J. *s.j.* '62 (RIC) Petersburg, VA St. John.
Martinez, Jonas Rivera *c.s.sp.* '98 (SJN)[F] Dorado, PR Santuario del Espiritu Santo.
Martinez, Jose Luis *o.a.r.* '64 (LA) Bronx, NY St. John's; [GG] Bronx, NY St. Joseph's Center; [II] Bronx, NY St. Joseph's Center.
Martinez, Jose Vicente *c.m.f.* '68 (SJN) Caguas, PR Inmaculado Corazon de Maria.
Martinez, Juan *s.d.b.* '73 (SJN) Catano, PR San Francisco de Sales.
Martinez, Leo '63 (SAT)[K] San Antonio, TX Casa De Padres Retired.
Martinez, Leonel *o.s.a.* '34 (GAL) Pasadena, TX St. Juan Diego.
Martinez, Lucian C. *s.j.* '02 (BGP)[P] Fairfield, CT The Fairfield Jesuit Community–Fairfield University.
Martinez, Luis '96 (SR) On Leave.
Martinez, Manuel *s.s.* '66 (SAT) On Duty Outside the Archdiocese.
Martinez, Marcos '52 (CC) Corpus Christi, TX Our Lady of the Pillar.
Martinez, Margarito Severino '00 (LA) Los Angeles, CA Our Lady of the Rosary of Talpa.
Martinez, Mariano '52 (LAR) Rio Bravo, TX Santa Rita de Casia Independent Mission.
Martinez, Mariano *o.m.i.* '86 (SJN) San Juan, PR Nuestra Senora del Carmen.
Martinez, Mark M. '96 (LA) Norwalk, CA St. Linus.
Martinez, Martin S. '93 (TUC) Eloy, AZ St. Helen.
Martinez, Martin (TUC) Council of Priests; All Vicars Forane.
Martinez, Michael '89 (TUC) Tucson, AZ St. Elizabeth Ann Seton; Air National Guard Chaplains.
Martinez, Miguel Angel '01 (CHI) Chicago, IL St. Nicholas of Tolentine.
Martinez, Omar *o.p.* (SJN) Holy Name Society.
Martinez, Pastor *o.s.a.* '78 (LAR) Laredo, TX St. Vincent de Paul.
Martinez, Roberto *o.f.m.cap.* '92 (SJN)[C] Rio Piedras, PR Fraternidad Santa Maria de Los Angeles.
Martinez, Rogelio *o.f.m.* (CHI) Chicago, IL St. Joseph.
Martinez, Roy *o.f.m.cap.* '84 (ARE) Utuado, PR San Miquel.
Martinez, Ruben *o.m.i.* '68 (OAK)[M] Washington, DC Oblate Community.
Martinez, Tim '90 (SFE) Ranchos De Taos, NM San Francisco de Asis.
Martinez, Timothy (SFE) Vicars Forane (Deans).
Martinez, Tomas *s.s.p.* '75 (LA)[Q] Los Angeles, CA Society of St. Paul.
Martinez, Vidal M. *o.s.m.* '75 (CHI)[N] Chicago, IL Order of Friar Servants of Mary (Servites) United States of America Province, Inc.; [N] Chicago, IL Monastery of Our Lady of Sorrows; Chicago, IL Our Lady of Sorrows, Basilica of; [N] Chicago, IL Servite Secular Order.
Martinez, Vidal '70 (SFE) Santa Fe, NM The Cathedral of San Francisco de Asis.
Martinez, Virgilio '65 (SJN) San Juan, PR San Luis Gonzaga.
Martinez–Diaz, Paz Alexander '92 (WDC) Silver Spring, MD St. Michael.
Martinez–Mari, Joaquin *s.j.* '55 (BO) Somerville, MA St. Benedict; [E] Dorchester, MA Boston College High School & Jesuit Community; [V] Weston, MA Campion Health Center, Inc..
Martinez–Navarro, Modesto *t.c.* (MO) AUXILIARY CHAPLAINS CONTRACT CHAPLAINS.
Martinez Tobon, Jose Dario '87 (SJN) Toa Baja, PR Ntra. Sra. de la Candelaria.
Martinez y Alire, Jerome '76 (SFE) Santa Fe, NM The Cathedral of San Francisco de Asis; Vicars Forane (Deans); Promoter of Justice.
Martini, Ivo '84 (SFS) Retired.
Martini, Richard '80 (LA) Los Angeles, CA Transfiguration; Our Lady of the Angels Region.
Martinka, Stanley V. '61 (NU) On Duty Outside the Diocese.
Martinkovic, Joseph '54 (ALN) Retired.
Martino, Nicholas J. '82 (PH) Absent on Leave.
Martinosky, Joseph A. '57 (STU) Retired.
Martin Pinillos, Ricardo '03 (MIL) Milwaukee, WI Prince of Peace/Principe de Paz.
Martins, John C. '55 (FR) Fall River, MA St. Anthony of Padua.
Martiny, Leon Martin A. *o.p.* (FgM).
Martire, Leonardo (MO) AUXILIARY CHAPLAINS CONTRACT CHAPLAINS.
Martis, Douglas A. '89 (CHI).
Martis, Douglas '89 (JOL)[A] On Duty Outside the Diocese.
Martis, Samuel '83 (BGP) New Canaan, CT St. Aloysius.
Martlock, Loville N. '63 (BUF) Retired.
Marto, Lawrence '88 (GB) Coleman, WI SS. Francis–Wenceslaus; Elected Representatives.
Martocchio, Peter T. '57 (BO) Weymouth, MA St. Jerome; Senior Priests Retired.
Marton, Bernard *o.cist.* '67 (DAL)[K] Irving, TX Cistercian Abbey of Our Lady of Dallas.
Marton, Henry *o.cist.* '49 (DAL)[K] Irving, TX Cistercian Abbey of Our Lady of Dallas.
Martorano, Nicholas F. (PH) Council of Priests.
Martorano, Nicholas *o.s.a.* '77 (PH) Philadelphia, PA St. Nicholas of Tolentine; [AA] Philadelphia, PA Augustinian Community (O.S.A.).
Martos, Rafael E. '96 (SP) Ruskin, FL St. Anne.
Martusciello, Joseph A. '54 (BRK)[V] Douglaston, NY Bishop Mugavero Residence Retired.
Martyn, George W. *o.s.f.s.* '71 (WIL)[J] Childs, MD Retirement and Assisted Care Facility.
Martyniuk, Pawlo '92 (STF) Ansonia, CT SS. Peter and Paul; League of Ukrainian Catholics.
Maruca, Dominic W. *s.j.* '58 (BAL)[B] Timonium, MD Loyola Graduate Center –Timonium Campus; [S] Baltimore, MD Jesuit Community of Loyola College, Inc..
Marucci, Carl J. '83 (CAM) On Leave of Absence.
Marucci, Louis A. '87 (CAM) Haddonfield, NJ St. Vincent Pallotti; Office of Development; Jubilate Deo Chorale and Orchestra.
Marullo, Lawrence E. '75 (OG) Constableville, NY St. Mary.
Marusceac, Vladimir '88 (STF) Cohoes, NY SS. Peter

and Paul; Cohoes, NY Protection of B.V.M.; Albany.
Marut, Paul *o.f.m.conv.* '72 (BRK) Elmhurst, NY St. Adalbert.
Marut, Thomas '74 (STU) Carrollton, OH Our Lady of Mercy; Waynesburg, OH St. Mary.
Marva, Robert *o.f.m.cap.* '97 (CLV) Cleveland, OH Conversion of St. Paul; Cleveland, OH Holy Trinity – St. Edward; [O] Cleveland, OH St. Paul Friary.
Marwata, Ageng Joseph *s.j.* (BO)[V] Newton, MA The Jesuit Community at Boston College.
Marx, Louis '66 (SB) Guasti, CA San Secondo d'Asti.
Marx, Paul *o.s.b.* '47 (SCL)[I] Collegeville, MN St. John's Abbey, of the Order of St. Benedict.
Marx, Paul *o.m.i.* '65 (FgM).
Marx, Robert '88 (SJ) On Leave of Absence.
Maryanski, Fabian J. '71 (BUF) Cheektowaga, NY St. Philip the Apostle.
Maryland, Joseph A. '40 (E) Retired.
Marzen, Francis A. '51 (HON) Retired.
Marzetti, Raul Lopez '85 (PHX) Scottsdale, AZ St. Daniel the Prophet.
Marzilli, Raphael '42 (GBG) Retired.
Marzluf, George J. '46 (COL) Retired.
Marzocchi, Mario *s.s.s.* '84 (CLV) Holiday, FL St. Vincent De Paul.
Marzolf, John G. *s.j.* '66 (ALB)[N] Auriesville, NY Shrine of Our Lady of Martyrs.
Marzullo, Robert *o.p.* '78 (SB) San Bernardino, CA Arrowhead Regional Medical Center.
Masabakhwa, Raphael '95 (DM) Neola, IA St. Patrick; Neola, IA St. Columbanus.
Masad, Frederick F. '60 (CHR) Columbia, SC St. John Neumann.
Masakowski, Edward M. '57 (SCR) Inkerman, PA St. Mark's.
Masakowski, John C. '49 (SCR) Retired.
Masar, Joseph G. '89 (SD) Chula Vista, CA St. Pius X.
Mascardo, Editho '83 (STO) Stockton, CA St. Mary of the Assumption Church (Pastor of); College of Consultors/Presbyteral Council.
Mascarella, Patrick J. '66 (BR) Convent, LA St. Michael the Archangel; Gramercy, LA Most Sacred Heart of Jesus; Paulina, LA St. Joseph; Continuing Formation for the Clergy.
Mascarenhas, Joel *s.j.* '82 (BAL)[S] Baltimore, MD Blessed Alberto Hurtado, S.J. Jesuit Community.
Mascarenhas, Oswald A. *s.j.* '66 (DET)[K] Detroit, MI Jesuit Community at the University of Detroit Mercy.
Mascareno, Jose Ramon *o.s.b.* '81 (BIR)[E] Cullman, AL St. Bernard Abbey.
Mascari, Michael A. *o.p.* '87 (CHI)[N] Chicago Dominicans (Provincial Office); [N] St. Pius V Priory.
Maschmann, Elvan *o.f.m.* '46 (STL)[O] St. Louis, MO Franciscan Friary of St. Anthony of Padua Retired.
Masciocchi, Robert *c.s.s.* '54 (BO)[V] Waltham, MA Stigmatine Fathers & Brothers Provincial House; [X] Waltham, MA Espousal Retreat House and Conference Center.
Mascioli, Joseph M. '57 (WH) Retired.
Mascolino, Charles E. '54 (STU) Retired.
Mascolino, Robert A. '45 (STU) Retired.
Mascorro, Miguel *sch.p.* (LA) Los Angeles, CA St. Lucy; Los Angeles, CA Santa Teresita.
Masek, James J. '74 (CLV) Cleveland, OH Our Lady of Lourdes.
Masek, James '74 (CLV) Cuyahoga Hills Boys School.
Masello, David W. '78 (PRO) Warren, RI St. Alexander.
Mash, Wesley M. '90 (HBG) Tarentum, PA Sts. Peter and Paul.
Masiar, Paul E. '69 (ALN) St. Clair, PA Immaculate Conception.
Masich, Michael P. *o.f.m.cap.* '98 (PIT) Clairton, PA St. Clare of Assisi.
Masiello, John *s.d.b.* '58 (MIA) Miami, FL St. Kieran.
Masiello, Joseph P. '69 (NEW) Union County Southwest Deanery 26; Westfield, NJ Holy Trinity.
Maskell, Stephen J. *m.m.* '48 (NY).
Maslach, Paul *o.f.m.* '62 (MIL)[EE] Milwaukee, WI Sacred Heart.
Maslak, Gregory '72 (PHU) McAdoo, PA St. Michael's; McAdoo, PA St. Mary's.
Maslar, George *o.f.m.conv.* '63 (TR) Riverside, NJ St. Casimir.
Maslar, George *o.f.m.conv.* (BRK)[V] Aston, PA Assisi House.
Maslar, William J. '56 (ALN) Mahanoy City, PA Assumption B.V.M. Retired.
Maslejak, Andrzej *s.ch.* '79 (DET)[K] Sterling Heights, MI Society of Christ Provincial Home.
Maslowski, Krzysztof '88 (NEW) Cranford, NJ St. Michael's.
Maslowski, Stanley '63 (STP) Oakdale, MN Guardian Angels.
Maslowsky, Michael '86 (P)[K] Portland, OR St. Anthony Village (activity of St. Anthony Village Enterprise); [K] Portland, OR Assumption Village (activity of St. Anthony Village Enterprise); Pastoral Services; Campus Ministry; Housing; Pastoral Services; Pro–Life Activities.
Masluk, Alexander '79 (PH) Philadelphia PA Saint Martha.
Masnicki, Marek '92 (NOR) Middletown, CT St. Mary of Czestochowa.
Maso, Dario *s.x.* '82 (PAT)[M] Wayne, NJ Xaverian Missionary Fathers; (FgM).
Mason, Brian G. '93 (MIL) Waukesha, WI St. Mary.
Mason, Carl Louis *o.p.* '64 (L) New York, NY St. Catherine of Siena.
Mason, Charlton O. '79 (GR) Pewamo, MI St. Joseph's.
Mason, Dennis *o.f.m.conv.* '78 (TR) Riverside, NJ St. Casimir.
Mason, Edward J. '87 (BRK) On Leave/Unassigned.
Mason, James E. '67 (LC) On Duty Outside the Diocese.
Mason, James E. '01 (SFS) Garretson, SD St. Rose of Lima.
Mason, James (SFS) Vice Chancellors; Vocations.
Mason, Mark E. '75 (OKL) Hennessey, OK St. Joseph's.
Mason, Mark (OKL) Region VII.
Mason, Robert E. '56 (RVC) Massapequa Park, NY Our Lady of Lourdes.
Mason, William *o.m.i.* '71 (STP)[M] St. Paul, MN Oblate Residence.
Mason, William *o.m.i.* '71 (BEL)[J] Belleville, IL Oblate Preaching Team.
Mass, Ronald J. '70 (CHI) Palos Heights, IL Incarnation.
Massa, James '86 (BRK) Released from Diocesan Assignment.
Massa, James (RVC) Censors of Books.
Massa, Mark S. *s.j.* '80 (NY)[EE] Cardinal Spellman Hall, Jesuit Community.
Massar, Richard A. '69 (BUF)[O] Lackawanna, NY Bishop Head Residence Retired.
Massaro, Joseph *c.s.s.* '48 (SPR) West Springfield, MA St. Ann.
Massaro, Michael *c.s.c.* '81 (PMB) Vero Beach, FL Holy Cross.
Massart, James P. (GB) Peshtigo, WI St. Mary; Porterfield WI St. Edward; Porterfield, WI St. Joseph.
Massawe, Andrew *c.s.c.* (FTW)[I] St. Brendan.
Massawe, Aristides *c.s.c.* '02 (FTW)[I] Kyarusozi Parish Community.
Massengill, Peter Damian *o.f.m.conv.* '76 (IND)[J] Mount St. Francis, IN Province of Our Lady of Consolation, Inc.; [K] Mount St. Francis, IN Provincial Headquarters for the Conventual Franciscan Province.
Massengill, Peter Dauian *o.f.m.conv.* '67 (FgM).
Massett, Robert D. '66 (NO) Metairie, LA St. Mary Magdalen.
Massey, Robert E. '73 (MIL) West Allis, WI Holy Assumption.
Massi, Anthony '84 (MIA) Retired.
Massick, Daniel *l.c.* (NY)[II] Thornwood, NY Alpha Omega Family Center, Inc..
Massicotte, Bernard *o.s.b.cam.* '57 (MRY)[F] Big Sur, CA New Camaldoli Hermitage.
Massie, Guy A. '83 (BRK) Brooklyn, NY St. Andrew the Apostle.
Massie, Guy (BRK) Diocesan Pastoral Council; Ecumenical and Interreligious Affairs, Diocesan Commission for; Committee for Catholic–Protestant Relations; Committee for Catholic–Jewish Relations; Catholic Muslim Dialogue.
Massimino, Jerome *o.f.m.* '77 (NY) New York, NY Holy Name of Jesus.
Massingale, Bryan N. '83 (MIL)[A] St. Francis, WI Saint Francis Seminary; Special Assignment.
Massoth, Charles *o.s.b.* (MO) AUXILIARY CHAPLAINS CONTRACT CHAPLAINS.
Massucci, Joseph D. '70 (CIN)[D] Dayton, OH The University of Dayton; On Duty Outside the Diocese.
Massung, Francis G. '40 (PIT)[N] Pittsburgh, PA St. John Vianney Manor Retired.
Mast, Paul '72 (WIL) Wilmington, DE Parish of the Resurrection.
Mastalir, Peter '92 (GB) Absent on Leave.
Mastangelo, Duane *o.f.m.conv.* '58 (ALB)[A] Rensselaer, NY Conventual Franciscan Friars; [L] Rensselaer, NY Provincialate, Immaculate Conception Friary – Order of Friars Minor Conventual
Masters, Andrew *s.v.d.* '34 (CHI)[B] Techny, IL Divine Word Residence.
Masters, Burke '02 (JOL) West Chicago, IL St. Mary.
Masters, Gerard G. '66 (HRT) Torrington, CT Sacred Heart; Torrington, CT St. Peter's; Torrington, CT St. Francis of Assisi; Torrington, CT St. Mary's.
Masterson, Clyde '85 (CC) Retired.
Masterson, Thomas D. *s.j.* '64 (SCR)[C] Scranton, PA The University of Scranton.
Mastey, Gregory '95 (SCL) Rockville, MN Mary of the Immaculate Conception; Vocations.
Mastrain, Mark J. '87 (E) Sykesville, PA Assumption of Blessed Virgin Mary.
Mastrangelo, David F. *s.j.* '87 (DET)[E] Detroit, MI Loyola High School; Detroit, MI St. Francis de Sales.
Mastrangelo, Joseph A. '40 (PIT) Retired.
Mastrangelo, Mario *o.f.m.cap.* '58 (PCE) Ponce, PR Santa Teresita; [B] The Pontifical Catholic University of Puerto Rico; [E] Ponce, PR Fraternidad Santa Teresita, Frailes Capuchinos; Episcopal Vicar for Religious; (FgM).
Mastrangelo, Nicholas '64 (PIT) Munhall, PA St. Therese of Lisieux.
Mastria, Angelo *o.carm.* '58 (TUC)[A] Tucson, AZ Salpointe Catholic High School; [C] Tucson, AZ Chaplaincy–Pastoral Ministry to Non–Denominational Nursing Homes; [E] Tucson, AZ Carmelite Priory.
Mastriola, Arthur '87 (NY)[EE] Yonkers, NY Cathedral Preparatory Seminary Residence.
Mastrobuono, Peter *s.c.j.* '66 (GAL) Houston, TX Our Lady of Guadalupe.
Mastroeni, Anthony J. '72 (PAT) On Duty Outside the Diocese.
Mastroeni, Anthony J. '72 (ARL)[A] Front Royal, VA Christendom College.
Mastrolia, Arthur '87 (NY) Congers, NY St. Paul.
Mata, Antonio *o.c.d.* '46 (CGS) Caguas, PR San Jose.
Matanic, George M. *o.p.* '70 (OAK) Berkeley, CA St. Mary Magdalen; [N] Oakland, CA Western Dominican Province.
Matanic, George *o.p.* (OAK) Deans.
Matano, Salvatore R. '71 (PRO) Providence, RI St. Augustine; On Duty Outside the Diocese.
Matarazzo, Francis '67 (PAT) Clifton, NJ St. Brendan.
Matarazzo, Frank (PAT) Retired.
Matarazzo, Salvatore B. *o.p.* '60 (BUF)[P] Buffalo, NY Monastery of Our Lady of the Rosary.
Matas, Juan '65 (LA) Montebello, CA Our Lady of the Miraculous Medal; Cursillo Movement.
Matash, Edward M. '56 (NEW) Bayonne, NJ St. Joseph's.
Matejek, John M. '03 (ATL) Atlanta, GA Cathedral of Christ the King.
Mateljan, Ray '67 (MIL) Milwaukee, WI St. Luke's Medical Center.
Mateo, Agustin '90 (WDC) Washington, DC Our Lady Queen of the Americas.
Mateo, Arturo *m.s.c.* '76 (SJ) Columbia Regional Hospital.
Mateo, Jose *sch.p.* '49 (PCE) Playa de Ponce, PR Our Lady of Mt. Carmel; Episcopal Vicar for Education.
Mateo, Mateo *ss.cc.* '47 (SJN) Guaynabo, PR Sagrados Corazones; Pro–Life Center (Human Life International).
Mateo, Miguel *s.f.* '81 (WDC)[B] Silver Spring, MD Holy Family Seminary.
Mateo, P. Rafael '89 (CGS) Yabucoa, PR Santos Angeles Cutodios.
Mateo, Victor Santiago *s.t.* '82 (FgM).
Mateos, Francisco *c.m.* '58 (LA) Los Angeles, CA Our Lady of the Rosary of Talpa.
Mateos, Tomas *s.f.o.* '45 (BWN)[J] McAllen, TX Secular Franciscan Order, Fraternity of Our Lady of Guadalupe.
Matera, Frank J. '68 (HRT) On Duty Outside the Archdiocese; [C] Catholic University of America, The.
Matera, Philip T. '51 (TR) Retired.
Maternoski, Robert '62 (JOL) Kinsman, IL Sacred Heart; South Wilmington, IL St. Lawrence.
Materw, Paul *a.l.c.p.* '97 (B) Boise, ID St. Mark's.
Mateu, Gregorio *t.o.r.* '64 (NEW) Newark, NJ Immaculate Heart of Mary.
Mateus, Norberto '82 (ATL) Conyers, GA St. Pius X Catholic.
Mathai, John '98 (BIS) Hettinger, ND Holy Trinity.
Mathai, Mani '80 (TYL) Jefferson, TX Immaculate Conception.
Mathaner, John P. '93 (E) Oil City, PA Our Lady Help of Christians.
Matheny, William K. '96 (WH) Parkersburg, WV St. Francis Xavier's.
Mathers, Douglas J. '85 (NY) New York, NY Our Saviour; Vice–Chancellors.
Mathers, Douglas (NY) Conciliation and Arbitration, Office of.
Mathesius, William P. '76 (WIL) Absent on Sick Leave.
Matheu, Santiago (MIA) Assoc. Directors.
Mathew, Abraham P. '97 (BRK) Brooklyn, NY Good Shepherd.
Mathews, J. Ronald '75 (ALX) Pineville, LA Central Louisiana State Hospital.
Mathews, James D. '62 (SY) Syracuse, NY St. Andrew the Apostle; Syracuse, NY St. Lucy.
Mathews, Michael *c.s.c.* '99 (FTW) South Bend, IN Holy Cross.
Mathews, Michael *c.s.c.* (FTW) Council of Priests.
Mathewson, Dean '55 (COL) Hilliard, OH St. Brendan.
Mathewson, Robert B. *s.j.* '62 (SJ).
Mathias, Edwin J. '67 (TR)[D] Browns Mills, NJ St. Ann.
Mathias, Gregory A. '91 (FR) Graduate Studies.
Mathias, Jayme *o.f.m.conv.* '01 (AUS) Austin, TX Cristo Rey.
Mathie, D. Edward *s.j.* '68 (MIL)[W] Milwaukee, WI Alumni Memorial Union 236; [C] Marquette University; [O] Milwaukee, WI Jesuit Community at Marquette University.
Mathieu, Rene T. '77 (PRT) Lewiston, ME Holy Cross; Deans; Diocesan Consultors; Diocesan Review Board;

Diocesan Council of Priests; College of Consultors; Personnel Board.
Mathieu, Robert '76 (GLP) Holbrook, AZ Our Lady of Guadalupe; Priests' Retirement Fund.
Mathis, Christian '00 (KNX) Johnson City, TN St. Mary; [H] Johnson City, TN ETSU–Catholic Center; Presbyteral Council.
Mathis, George '54 (CIN)[U] Fairfield, OH Glenmary Home Missioners Charitable Trust.
Mathis, George *g.h.m.* '55 (CIN)[M] Cincinnati Headquarters of Glenmary Home Missioners.
Mathis, R. Paul '72 (SY) Cleveland, NY St. Mary of the Assumption.
Mathis, Raymond P. (SY) Air National Guard Chaplains.
Matocha, Edward C. '45 (AUS) Austin, TX St. Mary's Cathedral; Special Assignments; Vicar General.
Matocha, Edward (AUS) Presbyteral Council; Holy Childhood; Propagation of the Faith.
Matocha, John L. '47 (SAT) Retired.
Matondo, Thomas *c.i.c.m.* '82 (BWN) Progreso, TX Holy Spirit.
Matonti, Charles J. '60 (BRK) Brooklyn, NY St. Columba.
Matos, Angel '97 (WOR) Fitchburg, MA St. Francis of Assisi; Gardner, MA Holy Spirit; St. Francis.
Matos, David '79 (CGS) Caguas, PR Cathedral Dulce Nombre de Jesus.
Matos, Juan A. (SJN) PR San Jose Obrero.
Matro, Justin M. *o.s.b.* '89 (GBG)[A] Latrobe, PA St. Vincent Seminary; [H] Latrobe, PA Saint Vincent Archabbey.
Matt, Erwin H. '56 (MIL) Retired.
Matt, J. Wilson '45 (LAF) Retired.
Matt, Joseph H. '74 (KC) Belton, MO St. Sabina's; Adjutant Judicial Vicar.
Matta, Pablo (ELP) El Paso, TX San Judas Tadeo; Cursillo.
Mattaliano, James R. '90 (BO)[V] Weston, MA Campion Jesuit Community.
Mattaliano, James *s.j.* '90 (BO)[X] Weston, MA Campion Renewal Center.
Mattar, Ghassan *m.l.m.* '96 (OLL) Phoenix, AZ St. Joseph Mission; [A] Houston, TX The Congregation of Maronite Lebanese Missionaries.
Mattas, Louis '60 (SAL) Board of Trustees Retired.
Mattath, Joseph *c.m.i.* '64 (SY) Endicott, NY St. Ambrose.
Mattathilanckal, Cyriac *m.s.* '93 (NOR) Danielson, CT St. James.
Matteo, James P. '72 (PH) Ardsley, PA Queen of Peace.
Matteo, John Di *o.ss.t.* '36 (BAL)[S] Baltimore, MD The Trinitarians at Holy Rosary.
Matter, Robert *o.c.s.o.* '56 (SPC)[A] Ava, MO Assumption Novitiate (Trappists).
Mattern, Joseph A. '59 (GB) Omro, WI St. Mary; Pastor Consultors; Regional Vicars.
Matteucig, Joseph *s.x.* '84 (PAT)[M] Wayne Xaverian Missionary Fathers; (FgM).
Mattey, Joseph J. '65 (SCR) Freeland, PA St. Ann's.
Matthew, Abraham (BRK) Catholic Hindu/Buddhist Dialogue.
Matthews, Andre '84 (ROM) Cleveland, OH St. Helena; Cleveland, OH St. Basil; Board of Consultors.
Matthews, James '74 (OAK) Oakland, CA St. Benedict.
Matthews, James (OAK) Deans.
Matthews, Michael C. *c.s.c.* '99 (FTW) South Bend, IN St. Stanislaus.
Matthiesen, Monroe J. '43 (AMA)[C] Panhandle, TX St. Joseph's Home for Retired Priests Retired.
Matthys, Donald R. *s.j.* '68 (MIL)[O] Milwaukee, WI Jesuit Community at Marquette University.
Matti, Wisam '97 (EST) Southfield, MI Our Lady of Chaldeans Cathedral, Mother of God Chaldean Parish; Eparchial College of Consultors.
Mattiato, J. Walter *m.c.c.j.* '49 (LA)[CC] Covina, CA Comboni Mission Center.
Mattice, George F. '64 (SY) Special Assignment.
Mattimoe, Edward J. *s.j.* '65 (DET)[K] Temperance, MI.
Mattimore, John J. *s.j.* '88 (BUF) Buffalo, NY St. Michael.
Mattimore, William F. '51 (WOR) On Duty Outside the Diocese.
Mattimore, William F. '51 (HON) Waimanalo, HI St. George; College of Consultors; Presbyteral Council.
Mattimore, William (HON) Vicars Forane.
Mattina, Louis '95 (MET) Lambertville, NJ St. John the Evangelist.
Mattingly, Basil *o.s.b.* '46 (SD)[H] Oceanside, CA Prince of Peace Abbey, Benet Hill.
Mattingly, Jerry '95 (JKS) Crystal Springs, MS St. John.
Mattingly, John F. *s.s.* '48 (BAL)[O] Baltimore, MD St. Charles Villa.
Mattingly, John S. '72 (WDC) Leonardtown, MD St. Francis Xavier.
Mattingly, Lawrence *o.f.m.conv.* '64 (AUS) Austin, TX Cristo Rey.
Mattingly, Robert B. (VEN) Presbyteral Council.
Mattingly, Robert W. *s.j.* (WDC).
Mattingly, Robert '68 (VEN) Port Charlotte, FL St. Maximilian Kolbe; Contemplative Prayer Commission.
Mattingly, Thomas '97 (RIC) Virginia Beach, VA St. John the Apostle Church.
Mattioni, George *o.a.r.* '53 (NY)[B] Suffern, NY Tagaste Monastery; [X] Suffern, NY Good Samaritan Hospital of Suffern.
Mattison, Thomas V. '73 (BUR) Judges; Rutland, VT Christ the King.
Mattler, Albert A. '56 (STL) Flint Hill, MO St. Theodore.
Mattox, Randall '01 (ATL) Duluth, GA St. Benedict.
Mattscheck, John J. '53 (CIN) Retired.
Mattucci, James J. '46 (MAD) Retired.
Mattulke, Arthur E. '97 (BUF) Orchard Park, NY St. Bernadette.
Matty, Richard A. '83 (ELP) El Paso, TX St. Patrick's Cathedral.
Matula, Lawrence '62 (VIC) El Campo, TX St. Robert Bellarmine.
Matula, Stanley '59 (SY) Syracuse, NY Sacred Heart Basilica.
Matulewicz, Ronald '59 (ALB) Hagaman, NY St. Stephen.
Maturi, John Gregory *o.p.* '94 (WDC)[B] Washington, DC Dominican House of Studies.
Matus, Walter J. '70 (AUS) Burlington, TX St. Joseph's.
Matusak, Michael W. '75 (GBG) Mount Pleasant, PA St. Pius X; Mount Pleasant, PA Visitation of the Blessed Virgin Mary; College of Consultors; Bishop's Priests Council.
Matuscak, Jerzy *c.r.* (CHI) Chicago, IL St. Stanislaus, Bishop and Martyr.
Matusz, Michael A. '89 (CLV) Akron, OH St. Martha.
Matuszak, Edward S. '55 (LFT) Retired.
Matuszak, Edward S. (E) Retired.
Matuszak, Walter L. '58 (BUF) Cheektowaga, NY Resurrection.
Matuszewski, Ramon '57 (SAG) Retired.
Matute, Ruben *c.m.f.* '88 (MET) Perth Amboy, NJ Our Lady of Fatima.
Matveenko, Michael J. '82 (CAM) Pomona, NJ Assumption.
Matya, Robert A. '95 (LIN) Lincoln, NE St. Thomas Aquinas; [I] Lincoln, NE University of Nebraska, Newman Club; Bishop's Lay Committee for Vocations; Newman Center University of Nebraska; Serra Club; Vocations.
Matyas, Francis B. '42 (STL) Retired.
Matyas, William T. *o.s.b.* '53 (CLV)[O] Cleveland, OH.
Matysik, Robert T. '84 (CAM) Somers Point, NJ St. Joseph's.
Matz, David *c.pp.s.* '94 (KC)[A] Kansas City, MO Gaspar Mission House.
Matz, George A. '66 (KCK) Garnett, KS Holy Angels; Greeley, KS St. John the Baptist's.
Matz, George (KCK) Regional Pastoral Leaders.
Matz, Joseph A. '64 (SCR) Jessup, PA St. James.
Matz, Leo '61 (MRY) Retired.
Matz, Michael J. '84 (PH) Bryn Mawr, PA St. John Neumann.
Matzek, William J. '63 (LC) Onalaska, WI St. Patrick.
Matzinger, Robert J. *c.s.b.* '57 (GAL) Houston, TX St. Clare of Assisi.
Matzko, David G. *s.j.* '79 (CHY) Rapid City, SD St. Isaac Jogues; [B] Howes, SD Kino Jesuit Community.
Mau, Nguyen Duc *c.ss.r.* '70 (LA)[Q] Long Beach, CA.
Mauck, George A. '77 (BEL) Carlyle, IL St. Mary; Centralia, IL Centralia Correctional Center; Southern Illinois Association of Priests.
Maudlin, Stanislaus *o.s.b.* '42 (SFS)[F] Marvin, SD Blue Cloud Abbey.
Mauel, James E. *s.j.* '57 (MIL)[O] Milwaukee, WI Jesuit Community at Marquette University.
Mauer, Edward '69 (BRK) Retired.
Mauer, Elmar *o.m.i* '62 (BEL)[F] Belleville, IL Missionary Oblates of Mary Immaculate – St. Henry's Oblate Residence.
Maufort, Richard A. '54 (GB) Special Assignment.
Maughan, Richard N. '72 (NO) Metairie, LA St. Lawrence the Martyr.
Maul, William R. '55 (SFD) Retired.
Maullon, Albert A. '82 (GAL) Houston, TX St. Paul; Priests Personnel Committee.
Maung, Chrysostom Ah '74 (WCH) Galena, KS St. Joseph; Columbus, KS St. Rose; Columbus, KS St. Patrick; Columbus, KS St. Bridget's.
Mauntel, Robert J. '49 (CIN) Retired.
Maurer, Carl '01 (SAT) San Antonio, TX El Carmen Catholic Church.
Maurer, Daniel J. '97 (PIT) Pittsburgh, PA St. Paul Cathedral; Diocesan Pastoral Council.
Maurer, Russell J. '60 (PIT) Pittsburgh, PA St. Edward.
Mauricci, Bruno '90 (LAV) Pahrump, NV Our Lady of the Valley.
Maurice, Francis *o.f.m.cap.* '88 (NY) Bronx, NY Immaculate Conception.
Mauricio, Francisco S. *c.s.b.* '97 (GAL)[Q] Sugar Land Basilian Mission Center.
Mauriello, Matthew '88 (BGP) Bridgeport, CT Holy Rosary.
Mauritzen, Joseph H. '96 (FR) Woods Hole, MA St. Joseph's.
Mauritzen, Joseph (FR) Diocesan Department of Pastoral Care for the Sick.
Maurizio, Joseph D. '86 (ALT) Central City, PA Our Lady Queen of Angels.
Maus, Christopher P. '93 (DET) Detroit, MI St. Hedwig.
Maus, Le Roy '66 (SCL) Retired.
Maus, Mark T. '91 (STP) Special Assignment.
Maus, Omer *o.s.b.* '45 (SCL)[I] Collegeville, MN St. John's Abbey, of the Order of St. Benedict.
Maus, Rudolph E. '39 (LR) Retired.
Mausolf, James H. '50 (GAY) Retired.
Mauthe, Richard '58 (GB) Retired.
Mawhinney, John J. *s.j.* '65 (PH)[AA] Loyola Center and Manresa Hall.
Mawicke, Joseph '63 (SB) Thousand Palms, CA St. Philip the Apostle.
Mawn, Francis X. '85 (BO) Haverhill, MA St. James.
Maxfield, Leo *m.s.* '55 (MAN)[K] Enfield, NH Shrine of Our Lady of La Salette; [M] Enfield, NH La Salette Shrine and Center of Enfield.
Maxim, Craig '91 (KCK) Shawnee, KS Sacred Heart.
Maximilio, Father *c.r.* (SB)[E] Newberry Springs, CA Holy Resurrection Community.
Maxwell, Bruce *o.s.c.* (DET)[K] Riverview, MI Crosier Community of Riverview.
Maxwell, John F. (OAK) Deans.
Maxwell, John '59 (OAK) El Cerrito, CA St. John the Baptist.
Maxwell, John (OAK) Consultors.
Maxwell, Palmer '88 (SAT) San Antonio, TX Santa Rosa Hospital System; [H] San Antonio, TX Christus Santa Rosa Health Care Corporation.
May, Anthony C. '75 (SD) San Diego, CA St. Mary Magdalene.
May, Darrin M. '99 (WCH) Fort Scott, KS Mary Queen of Angels.
May, Douglas E. *m.m.* '86 (FgM).
May, Gregory *c.ss.r.* (GAL) Houston, TX Holy Ghost.
May, Herbert J. (LAF) Judges.
May, Herbert J. (LKC) Diocesan Consultors.
May, Herbert '75 (LKC) Welsh, LA Our Lady of the Seven Dolors.
May, Herbert (NTN) Judges.
May, Herbert (LKC) Judges; Priest's Senate.
May, James '98 (STA) Crescent City, FL St. John the Baptist.
May, Michael K. *s.j.* '93 (STL)[C] Saint Louis University; [O] St. Louis, MO Jesuit Community Corporation at St. Louis University – Jesuit Hall; Archdiocesan Council of Priests.
May, Michael *s.j.* '93 (STL)[C] Arts and Sciences, College of.
May, Raymond '93 (KCK) Topeka, KS Our Lady of Guadalupe.
May, Ronald P. '86 (HRT) Collinsville, CT St. Patrick's.
May, Thomas P. '83 (CHI) Niles, IL St. John Brebeuf.
Maya, Manuel *o.s.m.* '58 (ORG) Fullerton, CA St. Philip Benizi.
Maya, Tulio *s.d.s.* '56 (LA) Los Angeles, CA Our Lady of Guadalupe.
Maya–Chavez, Manuel *o.s.m.* '58 (CHI)[N] Chicago Order of Friar Servants of Mary (Servites) United States of America Province, Inc..
Mayall, Daniel G. '77 (CHI) Chicago, IL Cathedral of the Holy Name; Deans.
Maybrier, Michael J. '86 (WCH) Coffeyville, KS Holy Name.
Maybrier, Michael (WCH) Presbyteral Council/ Diocesan Consultors; Presbyteral Council.
Mayefske, Thomas J. '62 (SFE) Albuquerque, NM Holy Ghost.
Mayefske, Thomas J. '62 (GB) On Duty Outside the Diocese.
Mayer, Douglas J. '86 (GRY) Valparaiso, IN Our Lady of Sorrows.
Mayer, James W. *o.de.m.* '93 (PH)[AA] Philadelphia, PA Monastery of Our Lady of Mercy.
Mayer, John L. '64 (STL) St. Louis, MO St. Justin Martyr.
Mayer, Jules A. '64 (LA) Los Angeles, CA St. Marcellinus.
Mayer, Kenneth H. *o.s.b.* '42 (PAT)[M] Morristown, NJ St. Mary's Abbey.
Mayer, Laurence A. *o.praem* '95 (CHI)[N] Chicago, IL Premonstratensian Fathers and Brothers (Norbertines).
Mayer, Michael A. '98 (ROC) Rochester, NY St. Andrew.
Mayer, Richard G. '61 (E) Erie, PA St. George; College of Consultors; Priest Personnel Board.
Mayer, Walter W. '59 (OAK) Livermore, CA St. Michael Retired.
Mayer, William C. *c.s.v.* '56 (CHI)[N] Arlington Heights, IL Viatorian Province Center–Clerics of St. Viator.
Mayer, William J. *s.j.* '74 (MIA) Miami, FL Gesu.
Mayfield, Olin '96 (LA) Military Chaplains; Navy Chaplains.
Mayhew, John A. *c.j.* '65 (LA) Santa Maria, CA St. Louis de Montfort.
Mayhew, John A. *c.j.* '66 (LA)[B] Santa Maria, CA St.

Joseph Seminary (Josephite Fathers' Novitiate).
Maynard, Jack G. '78 (COL) Dresden, OH St. Ann's.
Maynard, Leo C. '54 (PRO)[M] Pawtucket, RI Jeanne Jugan Residence.
Maynard, Leo E. '47 (HRT) Retired.
Maynard, Leon C. '54 (PRO) Retired.
Maynard, Lewis H. '69 (BRK) Brooklyn, NY St. Agatha's.
Maynard, Richard C. '56 (PRO) Pawtucket, RI St. Joseph Retired.
Maynard, Robert J. '48 (PRO) Cranston, RI St. Paul; Council Members Retired.
Mayne, Kenneth '94 (LAF) Centerville, LA St. Joseph.
Mayo, James Aidan '76 (P) Portland, OR St. Anthony; Portland, OR St. Patrick.
Mayo, James M. '79 (SAV) Hinesville, GA St. Stephen, First Martyr.
Mayo, James (P) Judges; Liturgical Commission.
Mayo, Joseph M. '73 (SLC) Salt Lake City, UT Cathedral of the Madeleine; College of Consultors; Ecumenical Commission; Presbyteral Council; Board of Directors; Priests' Personnel Board; Defenders of the Bond.
Mayo, Reid C. '63 (BUR) Rutland, VT Christ the King.
Mayorga, Guadalupe (AMA) Hart, TX St. John's; Tulia, TX Church of the Holy Spirit; Kress, TX St. Paul the Apostle.
Mayorga, Victor *m.p.* '95 (AUS) Austin, TX St. Louis.
Mayotte, Allan J. '60 (MAR) Retired.
Mayovsky, David L. '97 (SEA) Poulsbo, WA St. Olaf.
Mayovsky, Frederick P. *s.j.* '75 (SEA)[C] Tacoma, WA Bellarmine Preparatory School.
Mayovsky, Gerald L. '59 (SEA) Seattle, WA Our Lady of Lourdes; Tukwila, WA St. Thomas.
Mayta, Robert A. (LIN) Priests' Continuing Education Committee.
Mayta, Robert (LIN) Presbyteral Council.
Mayworm, James A. '66 (DET) Auburn Hills, MI Sacred Heart of the Hills.
Mayzik, James J. *s.j.* '85 (BGP)[B] Fairfield, CT Fairfield University; [P] Fairfield, CT The Fairfield Jesuit Community–Fairfield University.
Maza, Edward J. '59 (CHI) Chicago, IL Immaculate Conception.
Mazanec, James F. '81 (CLV) Parma, OH Holy Family.
Mazariegos, Edgar '80 (PMB) Lake Worth, FL Sacred Heart.
Mazich, Edward M. *o.s.b.* '01 (GBG)[H] Latrobe Saint Vincent Archabbey.
Mazon, Diego *o.f.m.* '60 (GLP) Gallup, NM St. Francis of Assisi; Presbyteral Council; Diocesan Consultors.
Mazouch, Charles '73 (DOD) LaCrosse, KS St. Michael; Liebenthal, KS St. Joseph; Lacrosse, KS Holy Trinity; Commission for Ministry to Priests; Priests' Trust Fund.
Mazuchowski, Hyacinth '63 (BEL) Flora, IL St. Stephen.
Mazuelas, Paulino *o.s.b.* '54 (MGZ) Mayaguez, PR Sacred Heart; St. Benedict.
Mazur, Francis X. '76 (BUF) Ecumenism; Defenders of the Bond; Erie County Medical Center; Buffalo, NY St. Gerard.
Mazur, Jacek '01 (VEN) Venice, FL Epiphany Cathedral.
Mazur, Robert C. '76 (ALT) Altoona, PA Cathedral of the Blessed Sacrament.
Mazur, Robert C. (ALT) Liturgy & Worship.
Mazur, Timothy P. '95 (DET) St. Clair Shores, MI St. Isaac Jogues.
Mazurchuk, Michael T. *c.m.* '86 (BUF)[O] Niagara University, NY Vincentian Community at Niagara University; [C] Niagara University, NY Niagara University.
Mazurek, James K. '73 (PIT) On Duty Outside the Diocese; [A] Orchard Lake, MI SS. Cyril and Methodius Seminary.
Mazurkiewicz, Ben '55 (AUS) Retired.
Mazurkiewicz, Harry C. '51 (AUS) La Grange, TX Sacred Heart of Jesus.
Mazurkiewicz, Harry (AUS) Deans; Consultors; Clerical Endowment Fund.
Mazuryk, Ivan (STF)[A] Stamford, CT Ukrainian Catholic Seminary Inc. St. Basil College; Youth Apostolate.
Mazza, Louis J. '53 (NY) Sleepy Hollow, NY Immaculate Conception.
Mazza, Mark G. '80 (GRY) On Duty Outside the Diocese; San Francisco, CA St. Gabriel.
Mazza, Victor J. '70 (PAT) Clifton, NJ St. Paul; Deans.
Mazzarella, Cadmus D. '85 (CAM)[R] Glassboro, NJ Rowan University; Vocations Apostolate; Vocation Advisory Board; Nazareth House of Discernment; Rowan University – Glassboro; Members.
Mazzarella, Frederick *o.f.m.* '61 (NY)[EE] St. Francis Friary.
Mazzei, John C. '92 (MAN) Nashua, NH Infant Jesus; Southern N.H. Regional Medical Center and Nursing Homes; St. Joseph Hospital.
Mazzei, John (MAN) Brazilian Apostolate.
Mazziotta, Robert R. '41 (NY) Staten Island, NY Our Lady of Pity Retired.
Mazzola, Robert E. '63 (IND) Indianapolis, IN St. Matthew; On Special or Other Archdiocesan Assignment.
Mazzola, Robert (IND) Auditor.
Mazzone, James '99 (BAL).
Mazzotta, George J. '66 (PH)[A] Ridley Park, PA St. Madeline.
Mazzuchelli, Matthew C. *o.s.b.* '58 (PEO).
Mbanisi, Victor '93 (BRK)[A] Flushing, NY St. Mel.
Mbefo, Luke *c.s.sp.* (PIT)[B] Pittsburgh, PA Duquesne University of the Holy Spirit.
Mbogu, Christopher '83 (PIT) McKees Rocks, PA St. John of God.
Mbonu, Justin '78 (LA) Los Angeles, CA St. Mary Magdalen.
McAfee, Franklyn M. '71 (ARL) Great Falls, VA St. Catherine of Siena.
McAlear, Richard *o.m.i.* '70 (BO)[V] Lowell, MA St. Eugene House (Residence).
McAleer, Robert T. '71 (DAV) Bettendorf, IA St. John Vianney; Judges; Presbyteral Council.
McAlinden, Terence O. '67 (TR) Tuckerton, NJ St. Theresa.
McAlister, Lawrence J. '44 (BRK) Flushing, NY St. Andrew Avellino; National Council of Catholic Women Retired.
McAlister, Richard A. *o.p.* '61 (PRO)[P] Providence St. Thomas Acuinas Priory at Providence College.
McAllister, Alex '86 (SR) On Leave.
McAllister, Donald L. '71 (PRT) Portland, ME Cathedral of the Immaculate Conception.
McAllister, Donald '71 (PRT) Retired.
McAllister, Leo '54 (SAC) Carmichael, CA Our Lady of the Assumption.
McAloon, Francis X. *s.j.* '92 (OAK).
McAlpin, James C. '64 (SC)[A] Manning, IA Sacred Heart; Deans; Ecumenical Commission.
McAlpin, Leonard '69 (GBG) Fayette City, PA Holy Spirit.
McAlpine, Harry D. '87 (SC) Onawa, IA St. John.
McAndrew, David T. '63 (HBG) Lebanon, PA Assumption of the Blessed Virgin Mary; Deans.
McAndrew, John P. '66 (ORG) Tustin, CA St. Cecilia.
McAndrew, John P. *c.s.sp.* '67 (PIT)[P] Bethel Park, PA Holy Spirit Animation Center.
McAndrew, John P. '86 (ORG) Liturgical Commission; Building and Renovation Committee of the Liturgical Commission; Ministry to Priests.
McAndrew, Joseph P. *o.f.m.* '63 (NY) Warwick, NY St. Anthony Community Hospital.
McAndrew, Joseph '85 (NY)[X] Warwick, NY St. Anthony Community Hospital, Inc.; [AA] Warwick, NY Villa Frances at the Knolls; [FF] Warwick, NY Mt. Alverno Center, Bon Secours Charity Health System.
McAndrew, Michael *c.ss.r.* '73 (DOD)[F] Liberal, KS Liberal Redemptorist Hispanic House Ministry, Inc..
McAndrew, Mike (DOD) Office of Hispanic Ministry.
McAndrew, Thomas F. '61 (DUB) Retired.
McAndrews, Donald A. '54 (SCR) Wilkes–Barre, PA St. Aloysius; Diocesan Finance Council; Presbyteral Council.
McAndrews, James F. *s.j.* '62 (CHL) Mooresville, NC St. Therese; [J] Mooresville, NC Jesuit Community.
McAndrews, Richard J. '67 (PH) Plymouth Meeting, PA Epiphany of Our Lord.
McAniff, Bernard F. *s.j.* '03 (BOS)[N] Chicago Chicago Province of the Society of Jesus–Provincial Office.
McAnulty, John D. *s.j.* '57 (LA)[Q] Los Angeles, CA Columbiere House; Cardinal Manning House of Prayer for Priests.
McArdle, John F. '51 (MAR) Consultors Retired.
McArdle, Kevin *o.c.d.* '43 (TUC) Tucson, AZ St. Margaret Mary; [E] Tucson, AZ Discalced Carmelite Friars of St. Margaret Mary's.
McArdle, Sean A. '67 (CAM) Disabled Retired.
McAree, Francis J. *s.t.d.* '75 (NY) Harrison, NY St. Gregory the Great.
McAree, Francis (NY) Censors Librorum.
McArthur, John B. '74 (MEM) Memphis, TN St. Louis; [L] Collierville, TN Serra Club of Memphis; Presbyteral Council and College of Consultors.
McArtney, Robert J. '60 (BUF)[K] Lackawanna, NY Our Lady of Victory Hospital.
McAskill, Kenneth F. '50 (BO) Arlington, MA St. James the Apostle; Senior Priests Retired.
McAtavey, John J. '54 (PMB) Retired.
McAtee, John F. '66 (PH)[AA] Villanova, PA St. Thomas Monastery.
McAteer, James *i.c.* '64 (SP) Spring Hill, FL St. Theresa.
McAteer, Kenneth P. '73 (PH) Bensalem, PA Saint Ephrem.
McAteer, Kenneth P. (PH) Approved Advocates.
McAteer, Patrick J. *s.j.* '73 (CHI) Chicago, IL St. Ignatius; [C] Chicago, IL Jesuit Community at Loyola University Chicago; [N] Chicago, IL Clark Street Jesuit Residence.
McAuley, James D. *m.m.* '80 (NY)[EE] Maryknoll Maryknoll Fathers and Brothers.
McAuley, John J. *m.m.* '81 (NY)[EE] Maryknoll Maryknoll Fathers and Brothers; [EE] Maryknoll Maryknoll Fathers and Brothers; (FgM).
McAuliff, R. Richard *s.j.* '92 (MI) Cathedral of the Assumption; Prefecture Consultors; Defender of the Bond.
McAuliffe, Dennis '73 (BRK) Emporia, VA St. Richard; Bracey, VA St. Peter The Apostle.
McAuliffe, Kevin W. '90 (LAV) Las Vegas, NV St. Elizabeth Ann Seton.
McAuliffe, Kevin (LAV) Diocesan Judges; Presbyteral Council for the Diocese of Las Vegas; Building Committee; Priests' Pension Board; Priests' Personnel Board.
McAuliffe, Robert J. '57 (BO) Arlington, MA St. James the Apostle; Senior Priests Retired.
McAuliffe, Roger D. *s.j.* '49 (SJ)[M] Los Gatos, CA Sacred Heart Jesuit Center.
McAvoy, Ambrose A. '39 (DUB) Retired.
McAvoy, C. John '63 (OG) Malone, NY St. Joseph's; Mineville, NY The Church of All Saints; Port Henry, NY St. Patrick.
McBrady, Lawrence P. '71 (CHI) Orland Hills, IL St. Elizabeth Seton.
McBrearity, Gerald D. *s.s.* '73 (BAL)[S] Baltimore, MD Sulpician Provincial House.
McBrearity, Gerald D. *s.s.* '73 (WDC)[C] Catholic University of America, The.
McBrearity, Gerald D. *s.s.* (ATL) On Duty Outside the Archdiocese.
McBrearty, John J. *s.s.j.* '68 (BR) New Roads, LA St. Augustine.
McBriar, David J. *o.f.m.* '64 (R) Durham, NC Immaculate Conception.
McBriar, David *o.f.m.* (R) Ecumenical Commission.
McBride, Brendan '75 (SFR) San Francisco, CA St. Philip the Apostle; Irish Ministry.
McBride, Daniel '51 (CLV) Administrative Leave.
McBride, Daniel '95 (PHX) Tolleson, AZ Blessed Sacrament.
McBride, Eugene J. *o.s.f.s.* '89 (PH) Philadelphia, PA St. Jerome; [AA] Philadelphia, PA Father Louis Brisson Residence.
McBride, Gerald E. '91 (TR) Manalapan, NJ St. Thomas More.
McBride, Harold E. *s.m.m.* '47 (RVC)[M] Bay Shore, NY Montfort Missionaries.
McBride, Henry J. '61 (CAM) Retired.
McBride, James P. '56 (PH) Philadelphia, PA St. Katherine of Siena.
McBride, John F. '62 (PH) Norwood, PA St. Gabriel.
McBride, John *s.j.* '61 (P)[L] Portland, OR Colombiere Community.
McBride, Larry '87 (OWN) Paducah, KY St. Francis de Sales; Paducah, KY Rosary Chapel; Pastoral Office for Worship; Diocesan Liturgical Committee.
McBride, Malachy R. *o.f.m.cap.* '62 (DEN) Aurora, CO Queen of Peace.
McBride, Malachy *o.f.m.cap.* '62 (DEN)[N] Denver, CO Fraternidad San Antonio.
McBride, Patrick *c.ss.r.* '85 (FgM).
McBride, Peter A. '60 (PAT)[P] Chester, NJ Nazareth Village Retired.
McBride, Robert G. '72 (NEW) Saddle Brook, NJ St. Philip the Apostle; Archdiocesan Judges.
McBrien, Kevin F. '86 (BRK) Rosedale, NY St. Clare; Bellerose, NY St. Gregory the Great.
McBrien, Kevin *o.carm.* '70 (LA)[F] Encino, CA Crespi Carmelite High School.
McBrien, Kevin (BRK) Bishop Sullivan—; Assignment Board.
McBrien, Richard P. '62 (FTW)[B] University of Notre Dame Du Lac.
McBrien, Richard P. '62 (HRT) On Duty Outside the Archdiocese.
McBurney, James D. *o.s.a.* '84 (PH)[AA] Villanova, PA Provincial Offices of the Order of St. Augustine, Province of St. Thomas of Villanova; Bryn Mawr, PA Our Mother of Good Counsel.
McCaa, Francis B. '48 (ALT) Retired.
McCabe, Charles J. '92 (MOB) Ozark, AL St. John.
McCabe, Edward D. '68 (BO) Military & VA Chaplains; Army Reserve Chaplains.
McCabe, James F. *c.s.p.* '57 (NY).
McCabe, James T. '71 (PH)[EE] Philadelphia, PA St. Katherine of Siena.
McCabe, James *c.pp.s.* '58 (CIN)[B] Carthagena, OH St. Charles.
McCabe, John H. '55 (RVC)[M] Uniondale, NY St. Pius X Residence Retired.
McCabe, John J. *m.m.* '45 (NY).
McCabe, Joseph V. *m.m.* '77 (FgM).
McCabe, Ken *ss.cc.* '65 (SB)[E] Chino Hills, CA Congregation of the Sacred Hearts, SS.CC..
McCabe, Kenneth *ss.cc.* (SB) Chino Hills, CA St. Paul the Apostle.
McCabe, Kevin P. '03 (PH) West Chester, PA SS. Simon and Jude.
McCabe, Louis J. *s.j.* '71 (COS)[F] Sedalia, CO Sacred Heart Jesuit Community; [H] Sedalia, CO Sacred Heart Jesuit Retreat House.
McCabe, Michael G. '89 (LIN) Nebraska City, NE St. Mary's; [C] Nebraska City, NE Lourdes Central Catholic Schools; [L] Nebraska City, NE Lourdes

Central High School Endowment Fund; Members.
McCabe, Patrick A. '61 (CAM) Ocean City, NJ St. Frances Cabrini.
McCabe, Peter '70 (AUS) On Duty Outside the Diocese.
McCabe, Richard '58 (AUS) Lakeway, TX Emmaus Catholic Church.
McCabe, Robert J. '64 (NY) Haverstraw, NY St. Mary.
McCabe, Robert '95 (DET) Detroit, MI St. Mary's of Redford; Detroit, MI St. Suzanne/Our Lady Gate of Heaven; Presbyteral Council.
McCabe, Thomas '92 (STP) Belle Plaine, MN Our Lady of the Prairie.
McCabe, Vincent '46 (LA) Retired.
McCafferty, David L. '64 (CLV) Wickliffe, OH Our Lady of Mount Carmel.
McCafferty, James B. *s.m.* '70 (WH) Buckhannon, WV Holy Rosary; [P] Buckhannon, WV West Virginia Wesleyan College Newman Center.
McCafferty, Joseph F. '61 (PH)[Y] Lansdale, PA St. Mary Manor.
McCafferty, Michael F. '87 (CHR) Hilton Head Island, SC St. Francis By the Sea.
McCafferty, Richard B. *s.j.* '62 (BO)[V] Boston The Society of Jesus of New England–Provincial Offices.
McCafferty, Richard *s.j.* '62 (OAK) Livermore, CA St. Charles Borromeo.
McCaffrey, Daniel '58 (OKL) Special Assignment; Catholic Physicians Guild.
McCaffrey, Edmund M. '59 (CHR) Retired.
McCaffrey, Edmund *o.carm.* '53 (NY) New York, NY New York City Veterans Administration Hospital; Manhattan, NY U.S.V.A. Medical Center.
McCaffrey, James Leo '58 (STO) Diamond Springs, CA Retired.
McCaffrey, James P. *s.j.* '52 (BO)[V] Weston, MA Campion Health Center, Inc..
McCaffrey, John A. '76 (AUS) Bryan, TX St. Joseph's; [M] Bryan, TX St. Joseph Memorial Endowment Fund.
McCaffrey, John A. (AUS) St. Joseph's School Memorial Endowment Fund.
McCaffrey, Joseph C. '99 (PH) Philadelphia, PA St. Bartholomew; [D] Philadelphia, PA Little Flower Catholic High School for Girls.
McCaffrey, Joseph R. '87 (PIT) Sewickley, PA Saints John and Paul.
McCaffrey, Joseph '77 (ROC) Auburn, NY Holy Family.
McCaffrey, Kevin Palmer *o.p.* '93 (NY)[EE] New York St. Vincent Ferrer Priory.
McCaffrey, Kevin '02 (Y) Ravenna, OH Immaculate Conception.
McCaffrey, Lawrence X. *s.j.* '51 (NY) Harriman, NY St. Anastasia; [FF] Harriman, NY St. Patrick's Villa.
McCaffrey, Michael *o.f.m.conv.* (SY)[Q] Syracuse, NY Friary of Francis, Brother of Peace Conventual Franciscan Friars.
McCaffrey, Patrick J. (WDC) Washington, DC St. Stephen Martyr.
McCaffrey, Richard L. *s.j.* '73 (FBK) Fairbanks, AK Immaculate Conception; [C] Fairbanks, AK Jesuit Residence.
McCaffrey, Richard *s.j.* (FBK) Presbyteral Council; Consultors.
McCaffrey, William J. '72 (PRO) Providence, RI St. Joseph; Secretary for Planning & Financial Services; Council Members; College of Consultors; Finance Council; Secretariat for Planning and Financial Services; Insurance Commission; Stewardship and Development.
McCahill, Patrick P. '68 (NY) New York, NY St. Elizabeth of Hungary; [P] New York, NY New York Catholic Deaf Center; Deaf, Catholic Center for.
McCahill, Robert T. *m.m.* '64 (FgM).
McCahon, Joseph F.S. '75 (SP) Military Chaplains; Air Force Chaplains.
McCaig, John J. '58 (CHI) Retired.
McCain, William H. '86 (SFR) Novato, CA Our Lady of Loretto.
McCall, John '58 (SP).
McCall, Stephen P. '79 (SD) Carlsbad, CA St. Patrick.
McCallister, Charles '71 (WH) Public Affairs Representative Retired.
McCallister, Richard '91 (SEA) Puyallup, WA All Saints; Presbyteral Council; Deans.
McCallum, David C. *s.j.* '01 (RVC)[O] Manhasset, NY St. Ignatius Retreat House, Inisfada.
McCallum, Dougald '97 (HEL) Special Assignments.
McCallum, Gregory P. '97 (GAY) Alpena, MI St. Mary; Elected Members.
McCallum, John V. '43 (DAL) Retired.
McCallum, Paul F. '62 (AUS) Austin, TX St. Paul's.
McCandless, William T. *o.s.f.s.* '94 (WIL)[B] Wilmington, DE Salesianum School; Navy Reserve Chaplains.
McCann, Arthur L. '62 (DM) Retired.
McCann, Bill '94 (LSC) Lovington, NM St. Thomas Aquinas; Finance Council.
McCann, Charles '69 (WDC) Camp Springs, MD St. Philip the Apostle; Deans.
McCann, James M. *s.j.* '79 (WDC)[M] Washington, DC Leonard Neale House; [N] Chicago Chicago Province of the Society of Jesus–Provincial Office.
McCann, Joachim *o.s.b.* '91 (P)[L] St. Benedict, OR Mt. Angel Abbey.
McCann, John B. '85 (ALN) Nesquehoning, PA Immaculate Conception of B.V.M.; Nesquehoning, PA Our Lady of Mount Carmel; Nesquehoning, PA Sacred Heart; College of Consultors.
McCann, John H. *s.m.m.* '55 (HRT) Bantam, CT Our Lady of Grace.
McCann, John J. '65 (RVC) Manhasset, NY St. Mary's; North Hempstead Deanery.
McCann, Joseph H. '57 (HRT) New Haven, CT St. Aedan's; New Haven, CT St. Brendan's.
McCann, Luke W. (NY) Kingston, NY St. Colman.
McCann, Robert J. (OAK) Dublin, CA St. Raymond.
McCann, Robert (OAK) Adjutant Judicial Vicars and Canonical Consultant to the Bishop; Judges; Censor.
McCann, Sean J. *s.j.* (NEW)[C] Jersey City, NJ St. Peter's Preparatory School; [N] Jersey City, NJ Jesuit Community of St. Peter's Prep, Inc..
McCann, Thomas E. '59 (SCR) Retired.
McCann, Thomas M. '98 (NO) Covington, LA St. Peter; Navy Reserve Chaplains.
McCann, Thomas W. '68 (CLV) Cuyahoga Falls, OH Immaculate Heart of Mary; Associate Judges.
McCann, Thomas *c.p.* '66 (R) Greenville, NC St. Gabriel.
McCann, Vincent *m.h.h.* '46 (PRT) Portland, ME Cathedral of the Immaculate Conception.
McCann, William (LSC) Presbyteral Council; Clergy Personnel Board; Priests Retirement Fund Committee.
McCarren, Edgar P. '43 (RVC)[B] St. Mary's College; East Palo Alto, CA St. Francis of Assisi Retired.
McCarren, Edgar '43 (RVC) Retired.
McCarren, Gerald H. '91 (NEW)[B] School of Diplomacy and Intl. Rels..
McCarren, Gerard H. '91 (NEW)[A] Priestly Vocation Board; Censors of Books.
McCarren, Paul J. *s.j.* '74 (R) Raleigh, NC St. Raphael.
Mc Carren, Paul J. *s.j.* '74 (R)[E] Raleigh Jesuit Community.
McCarren, Stephen A. '55 (GBG) Retired.
McCarren, William J. '47 (BRK) Retired.
McCarron, Gerard J. '70 (TR) Normandy Beach, NJ Our Lady of Peace.
McCarron, Michael D. '77 (RIC) Newport News, VA Our Lady of Mount Carmel.
McCarron, Michael (RIC) Vocation Director for Promotion and Recruitment.
McCarthy, Anthony T. '71 (MIL) North Lake, WI St. John; North Lake, WI St. Clare.
McCarthy, Brian P. '75 (NY) Yonkers, NY St. Bartholomew.
McCarthy, C. Ryan '01 (IND) North Vernon, IN St. Anne; North Vernon, IN St. Joseph.
McCarthy, Carl '95 (OWN) Cadiz, KY St. Stephen; Hopkinsville, KY SS. Peter and Paul; Diocesan Liturgical Committee; Oak Grove, KY St. Michael the Archangel.
McCarthy, Charles A. *c.s.sp.* '51 (PEO) Streator, IL Annunciation of Blessed Virgin Mary; Tonica, IL SS. Peter and Paul's.
McCarthy, Charles '79 (ELP) El Paso, TX Our Lady of Mt. Carmel.
McCarthy, Cornelius Scott '74 (MRY) Carmel Valley, CA Our Lady of Mt. Carmel.
McCarthy, D. Joseph '78 (SAC) Absent on Leave.
McCarthy, Daniel P. '67 (CHI) Chicago, IL St. Tarcissus.
McCarthy, Daniel *o.s.b.* '91 (KCK)[H] Atchison, KS St. Benedict's Abbey.
McCarthy, David J. '60 (CLV) Doylestown, OH SS. Peter and Paul.
McCarthy, Donal *ss.cc.* '65 (LA)[D] La Verne, CA Damien High School; [Q] La Verne, CA Congregation of the Sacred Hearts of Jesus and Mary.
McCarthy, Donald E. *c.s.b.* '58 (ROC)[I] Rochester, NY Basilian Residence.
McCarthy, Donald G. '54 (CIN) Cincinnati, OH St. Ignatius Loyola Retired.
McCarthy, Donald P. '59 (SAL) Hill City, KS Immaculate Heart of Mary; Boy Scouts.
McCarthy, Donald (SAL) Board of Trustees.
McCarthy, Edward J. '71 (ORL) Deltona, FL Our Lady of the Lakes.
McCarthy, Edward P. *c.pp.s.* '40 (LFT)[A] Rensselaer, IN Saint Joseph's College Retired.
McCarthy, Emmanuel Charles '81 (NTN) Roslindale, MA Seminary of St. Gregory the Theologian; Presbyteral Council.
McCarthy, Emmett '43 (ORG) Brea, CA St. Angela Merici.
McCarthy, Ethan Garrett '03 (FR) North Easton, MA Immaculate Conception.
McCarthy, Eugene '60 (VEN) Marco Island, FL San Marco; Holy Childhood Association.
McCarthy, Francis E. *o.carm.* '51 (VEN)[L] Darien Carmelite Provincial Office.
McCarthy, Francis X. '54 (MIA) Fort Lauderdale, FL St. Jerome; On Duty Outside the Diocese Retired.
McCarthy, Francis (MIA) Spiritual Moderators.
McCarthy, George B. '56 (PRO) Newport, RI St. Mary.
McCarthy, Gerald A. '57 (FAR) Apostolate for Native Americans Retired.
McCarthy, J. Joseph '66 ((BO)) (FgM).
McCarthy, James C. '62 (HEL) On Leave of Absence.
McCarthy, James H. '55 (CHI) Other Assignments; Special Religious Education (SPRED).
McCarthy, James J. '63 (BO) Braintree, MA St. Thomas More.
McCarthy, James '45 (FR) Retired.
McCarthy, Jeremiah J. '66 (BO) Society of St. James the Apostle.
McCarthy, Jeremiah J. '72 (TUC) On Duty Outside the Diocese.
McCarthy, Jeremiah J. '78 (SAV) Savannah, GA Most Blessed Sacrament.
McCarthy, Jeremiah J. (PIT) Aliquippa, PA St. Frances Cabrini.
McCarthy, Jeremiah J. (SAV) Officialis; Tribunal Judges.
McCarthy, Jeremiah (SAV) College of Consultors; Council of Priests.
McCarthy, Jerry '45 (TLS) Retired.
McCarthy, John E. *c.s.c.* '58 (FR)[A] North Easton, MA Stonehill College; [A] North Easton, MA Holy Cross Fathers Religious.
McCarthy, John F. '55 (HEL) On Duty Outside the Diocese.
McCarthy, John F. '55 (LC) Eastman, WI St. Wenceslaus; [M] Eastman, WI Society of the Oblates of Wisdom; Deans; [M] Eastman, WI Marian Academy of the Oblates of Holy Tradition.
McCarthy, John J. *m.s.* '69 (HRT)[M] Hartford, CT Missionaries of LaSalette.
McCarthy, John J. '84 (HRT) Wallingford, CT Resurrection; Promoter of Justice; Judges.
McCarthy, John L. *s.j.* '62 (STL)[O] St. Louis, MO Jesuit Community Corporation at St. Louis University – Jesuit Hall.
McCarthy, John M. '54 (NY) Staten Island, NY St. Patrick.
McCarthy, John R. '55 (STU) East Cleveland, OH St. Philomena; On Duty Outside the Diocese.
McCarthy, John *c.ss.r.* '62 (FgM).
McCarthy, Joseph F. '48 (SFD) Retired.
McCarthy, Joseph J. *o.carm.* '60 (GAL) Houston, TX St. Bernadette Soubirous.
McCarthy, Joseph L. '69 (CHL) Retired.
McCarthy, Joseph S. '96 (BO) Plymouth, MA St. Peter; Senior Priests Retired.
McCarthy, Joseph '48 (BUR) Retired.
McCarthy, Joseph *o.f.m.cap.* '60 (NY)[EE] Beacon, NY St. Joachim Friary.
McCarthy, Kevin P. '89 (GRY)[M] Valparaiso, IN Newman Apostolate–Valparaiso University; Bishop's Council of Priests; Campus Ministry.
McCarthy, Leo F. *m.m.* '47 (NY).
McCarthy, Leo F. '59 (BUF) Vicars; Batavia, NY St. Joseph.
McCarthy, Leo *o.carm.* '62 (VEN) Osprey, FL Our Lady of Mount Carmel.
McCarthy, Martin F. *s.j.* '54 (BO)[V] Weston, MA Campion Health Center, Inc..
McCarthy, Michael C. *s.j.* '96 (SJ)[B] Santa Clara, CA Jesuit Community.
McCarthy, Michael J. *c.s.sp.* '48 (BRK)[V] Long Island City, NY Holy Ghost Fathers of Ireland; [Z] Long Island City, NY World Compassion Link; [O] Buffalo, NY Canisius Jesuit Community.
McCarthy, Michael J. '58 (BGP)[Q] Ridgefield, CT Provincial House, Congregation de Notre Dame.
McCarthy, Michael J. '65 (PH) Absent on Leave.
McCarthy, Patrick P. '44 (SFR) Retired.
McCarthy, Patrick *m.s.* '78 (STL)[O] La Salette Communications Center.
McCarthy, Paul J. *s.j.* '57 (SLC) Sandy, UT St. Thomas More.
McCarthy, Paul R. '80 (BO) Absent on Leave.
McCarthy, Paul '84 (FTW) New Haven, IN St. John the Baptist.
McCarthy, Raymond *c.ss.r.* '47 (NY)[EE] New York, NY Redemptorist Priests and Brothers, C.Ss.R..
McCarthy, Richard C. '69 (PRT) Retired.
McCarthy, Robert J. '46 (OG) Retired.
McCarthy, Robert '58 (STL) St. Louis, MO St. Clement; Arnold, MO St. Vincent Cemetery; St. Charles, MO Ste. Philippine Cemetiere; Catholic Cemeteries of St. Louis.
McCarthy, Scott (MRY) Ecumenical Commission; Priestly Life and Ministry Board.
McCarthy, Scott (Cornelius) (MRY) Ecumenism; Native American Ministry.
McCarthy, Sean M. '91 (BO) Acton, MA St. Elizabeth of Hungary.
McCarthy, Terrence A. '74 (CHI) Highland Park, IL Immaculate Conception.
McCarthy, Thomas A. '59 (NEW) Washington Township, NJ Our Lady of Good Counsel; Continuing Education of Priests; Ex Officio Members.
McCarthy, Thomas E. '49 (HRT) Avon, CT St. Ann's Retired.

McCarthy, Thomas J. '80 (BUF) Retired.
McCarthy, Thomas J. (Y) Judges.
McCarthy, Thomas P. *c.s.v.* '52 (CHI)[N] Arlington Heights, IL Viatorian Province Center–Clerics of St. Viator.
McCarthy, Thomas R. *o.s.a.* '94 (CHI)[D] Chicago, IL St. Rita of Cascia High School.
McCarthy, Thomas '53 (RVC) Retired.
McCarthy, Thomas '61 (Y) Office of Priests' Personnel Advisor; Bishop's Delegate for Retired Priests; Salem, OH St. Paul.
McCarthy, Thomas *s.j.* '62 (P) Sherwood, OR St. Francis.
McCarthy, Thomas *o.s.a.* '94 (CHI)[N] Chicago, IL St. Rita Monastery.
McCarthy, Thomas (NEW) Archdiocesan Theological Commission.
McCarthy, Vincent *s.s.c.* '65 (OM)[K] St. Columbans St. Columban's Foreign Mission Society.
McCarthy, Warren J. '52 (CHI) Retired.
McCarthy, William A. '03 (SC) Le Mars, IA St. Joseph's.
McCarthy, William D. *m.m.* '56 (NY)[B] Maryknoll, NY Center for Mission Research and Study at Maryknoll; [EE] Maryknoll Maryknoll Fathers and Brothers.
McCarthy, William E. *m.m.* '58 (RVC) Retired.
McCarthy, William E. *m.m.* '58 (NY)[EE] Maryknoll Maryknoll Fathers and Brothers.
McCarthy, William R. '52 (BO) Senior Priests Retired.
McCarthy, William *m.s.a.* '59 (NOR)[F] Cromwell, CT Society of the Missionaries of the Holy Apostles.
McCarthy, William '63 (PAT) East Hanover, NJ St. Rose of Lima Retired.
McCartin, Francis P. *o.m.i.* '38 (BO)[Y] Tewksbury, MA Immaculate Heart of Mary Infirmary.
McCartney, James J. *o.s.a.* '70 (PH)[C] Villanova University.
McCartney, James '84 (LUB) Plainview, TX St. Alice; Priests' Retirement Board.
McCartney, John J. '99 (RVC) Center Moriches, NY St. John the Evangelist.
McCarty, Bruce '89 (OWN) Paducah, KY St. John the Evangelist; Deans; Priests' Council.
McCarty, Lawrence L. '63 (SC) Auburn, IA St. Mary's; Sac City, IA St. Mary's; Presbyteral Council; Deans.
McCarty, Paul T. *s.j.* '67 (BO)[V] Weston, MA Campion Health Center, Inc..
McCarty, Robert E. *s.j.* '67 (NEW)[B] Jersey City, NJ Jesuit Center; [N] Jersey City, NJ Jesuits of Saint Peter's College, Inc..
McCarty, Shaun *s.t.* '56 (WDC)[M] Adelphi, MD Missionary Servants of the Most Holy Trinity.
McCarty, Thomas J. *o.c.s.o.* '56 (DUB)[K] Peosta, IA New Melleray Abbey, Order of Cistercians of the Strict Observance; [L] Dubuque, IA Our Lady of the Mississippi Abbey.
McCarver, James K. '91 (MEM) Brownsville, TN St. John; Presbyteral Council and College of Consultors.
McCarver, James '91 (MEM) Jackson, TN St. Mary's.
McCarville, John J. '65 (CHI) Bellwood, IL St. Simeon.
McCasland, Howard '44 (OG) Churubusco, NY Immaculate Heart of Mary.
McCaslin, John O. '55 (OM) Retired.
McCaslin, John Patrick '02 (IND) Indianapolis, IN St. Barnabas.
McCaslin, John T. *s.j.* '66 (ALN)[A] Wernersville, PA Jesuit Center.
McCaslin, R. Patrick '61 (OM) Omaha, NE St. John Vianney.
McCaslin, Richard F. *s.j.* '65 (OM)[C] Omaha, NE Creighton Preparatory School.
McCaslin, Richard *s.j.* (OM) Religious Orders.
McCaughley, Sean '87 (NY) New York, NY Ascension.
McCauley, Daniel *o.c.d.* '55 (MIL)[O] Milwaukee Provincial Offices – Discalced Carmelites.
McCauley, David F. (STP) St. Paul, MN St. Pascal Baylon.
McCauley, David (STP) Associate Judges.
McCauley, George C. *s.j.* '61 (NY)[EE] Loyola Hall, Jesuit Community.
McCauley, James A. '56 (WIN) Retired.
McCauley, James P. *s.j.* '56 (SJ)[M] Los Gatos Sacred Heart Jesuit Center.
McCauley, James P. *s.j.* '56 (LAV) Tonopah, NV St. Patrick.
McCauley, James R. *c.s.p.* '74 (TUC) Tuscon, AZ St. Cyril of Alexandria.
McCauley, Walter C. *s.j.* '56 (FWT)[K] Lake Dallas, TX Montserrat Jesuit Retreat House.
McCaulley, Cornelius W. '66 (PIT) Pittsburgh, PA St. Stephen.
McCawley, Scott '93 (JOL) Mokena, IL St. Mary Church.
McCawley, William J. '60 (SCR) Brodheadsville, PA Our Lady Queen of Peace.
McChesney, Robert W. *s.j.* '81 (LA)[S] Baltimore, MD Blessed Alberto Hurtado, S.J. Jesuit Community; Los Angeles, CA Immigration and Naturalization Service.
McClain, J. Thomas *s.j.* '77 (NY)[F] New York, NY Regis High School.
McClain, J. Thomas *s.j.* '77 (DET)[K] Temperance, MI.
McClain, Joseph P. *c.m.* '49 (MET)[H] Princeton, NJ Vincentian Residence.
McClain, Matthew R. '02 (PIT) Wexford, PA St. Alexis.
McClanahan Robert P. '84 (PT) Military Chaplains; Navy Chaplains.
McClean, John R. '57 (DUB) Retired.
McCleane, Michael J. '81 (PH) Holland, PA St. Bede the Venerable.
McCleary, Michael L. '78 (PBL) Absent on Leave.
McClellan, Keith J. *o.s.b.* '79 (IND)[K] Michigan City, IN.
McClellan, Keith '79 (GRY) Michigan City, IN Queen of All Saints.
McClellan, Robert J. '81 (RCK) Aurora, IL St. Mary.
McClintock, James (BEA) Eastern Vicariate; Bridge City, TX St. Henry.
McClory, Bernard J. '53 (COL) Retired.
McClory, Robert O. '99 (DET) Special Assignment.
McClory, Robert '91 (DET) Waterford, MI Our Lady of the Lakes Cardinal's Office; Judges.
McCloskey, C. John '81 (WDC)[T] Washington, DC Prelature of the Holy Cross and Opus Dei.
McCloskey, Daniel J. '83 (WIL) Georgetown, DE St. Michael the Archangel.
McCloskey, Francis '63 (ALB) Special Assignment.
McCloskey, Gary N. *o.s.a.* '73 (PH)[C] Villanova, PA Villanova University.
McCloskey, Gary *o.s.a.* '77 (BO)[C] North Andover, MA Merrimack College.
McCloskey, J. Terrence *c.ss.r.* '66 (KC)[J] Kansas City, MO Redemptorists Fathers of Kansas City, Missouri.
McCloskey, James A. '46 (SY) Fayetteville, NY Immaculate Conception; Promoter of Justice Retired.
McCloskey, James P. *c.s.sp.* '80 (PIT)[B] Pittsburgh, PA Duquesne University of the Holy Spirit; [N] Bethel Park, PA Holy Spirit Fathers and Brothers Provincialate; [R] Bethel Park, PA Spiritan Support Trust; (FgM).
McCloskey, John *o.f.m.cap.* '98 (HBG) York, PA St. Joseph; Philadelphia, PA St. John the Evangelist.
McCloskey, Joseph M. *s.j.* '63 (WDC)[E] Washington, DC Gonzaga College High School.
McCloskey, Joseph W. '61 (PH) Philadelphia, PA St. Thomas Aquinas.
McCloskey, Joseph '61 (PH)[U] Philadelphia, PA St. Agnes Medical Center.
McCloskey, Lester '64 (SEA) Retired.
McCloskey, Patrick *o.f.m.* '75 (CIN)[M] Cincinnati, OH St. Clare Friary.
McCloskey, Terry *c.ss.r.* '66 (KC) Kansas City, MO Our Lady of Perpetual Help.
McClosky, Adam S. '67 (GAL) Houston, TX All Saints.
McClure, Jack H. *c.pp.s.* '76 (DM) Harlan, IA St. Michael; Oakview, MO St. Charles Borromeo.
McClure, Jason Wayne '03 (OWN) Henderson, KY Holy Name of Jesus.
McClure, John A. '62 (TOL)[K] Sylvania, OH Sisters of St. Francis of the Congregation of Our Lady of Lourdes; Judicial Vicar Retired.
McCluskey, James F. '68 (OM) Laurel, NE St. Mary.
McCluskey, John D. *s.j.* '57 (SPK)[J] Spokane, WA Regis Community.
McCluskey, Raymond E. *s.j.* '45 (BO)[V] Weston, MA Campion Health Center, Inc..
McCoart, Charles C. '90 (ARL) Alexandria, VA Good Shepherd; Director of Diocesan Charities; Campaign for Human Development; Catholic Relief Services.
McCole, John F. '58 (PH) Philadelphia, PA Maternity B.V.M..
McColl, Scott '80 (SD) La Mesa, CA St. Martin of Tours.
McColligan, Raymond A. '43 (PIT) Retired.
McColligan, Raymond '43 (PIT)[N] Pittsburgh, PA St. John Vianney Manor.
McCollogh, Michael (SB) Desert Refuge for Peace Officer.
McCollum, Paul '98 (RNO) Yerington, NV Our Lady of Perpetual Help; Yerington, NV Holy Family; Diocesan Board of Consultors; Presbyteral Council; Seminary Board.
McComiskey, Joseph C. '70 (RVC) Retired.
McConaghy, R. Thomas '81 (NOR) Norwichtown, CT Sacred Heart; Liturgical Commission; Diocesan Vocation Review Committee.
McConaghy, Robert J. '75 (ALN) On Duty Outside the Diocese.
McConnell, James J. '54 (TR)[M] Trenton, NJ Villa Vianney; Diocesan Consultors Retired.
McConnell, James J. *s.m.a.* '72 (NEW) Newark, NJ Queen of Angels; [N] Tenafly, NJ Society of African Missions, Provincialate, S.M.A. Fathers.
McConnell, John M. *s.j.* '55 (NY)[EE] New York, NY Murray–Weigel Hall.
McConnell, William J. '53 (BO) Charlestown, MA St. Francis de Sales; Senior Priests Retired.
McConnin, Robert J. '73 (BRK) Jamaica, NY St. Nicholas of Tolentine.
McConvey, Michael '79 (GLP) On Leave of Absence.
McConville, James P. (STP) Army Reserve Chaplains.
McConville, James '90 (STP) Albertville, MN St. Albert.
McConville, Philip G. '43 (BO) Senior Priests Retired.
McConville, William E. *o.f.m.* '73 (R) Raleigh, NC St. Francis of Assisi.
McConway, S. Jordan *o.p.* (COL) Vicariate 9: Zanesville.
McConway, S. Jordan *o.p.* '87 (COL) Zanesville, OH St. Thomas Aquinas.
McCoog, Thomas M. *s.j.* '71 (BAL)[S] Jesuit Historical Institute.
McCool, Gerald A. *s.j.* '52 (NY)[EE] Loyola Hall, Jesuit Community.
McCool, Naos *c.s.sp.* (PIT)[B] Pittsburgh, PA Duquesne University of the Holy Spirit.
McCool, Patrick *o.s.b.* '63 (OKL)[I] Shawnee, OK St. Gregory's Abbey.
McCord, Kent G. '81 (MET) On Duty Outside the Diocese; Navy Chaplains.
McCorkell, Patrick M. *s.j.* '74 (STP)[P] Lake Elmo, MN Jesuit Retreat House.
McCorkle, Louis W. '53 (JC) Retired.
McCormac, Michael P. '80 (PH) Glenolden, PA St. George; Council of Priests.
McCormack, Andrew G. *s.m.* '57 (WDC)[M] Atlanta, GA Retired.
McCormack, Brendan '60 (WDC) Retired.
McCormack, Daniel J. '94 (CHI) Chicago, IL St. Agatha.
McCormack, Douglas '69 (LFT) Zionsville, IN St. Alphonsus.
McCormack, John '61 (KC)[I] Kansas City, MO Jeanne Jugan Center Retired.
McCormack, Keith J. '76 (TOL) Mansfield, OH St. Mary of the Snow.
McCormack, Richard J. '61 (BRK) Bayside, NY St. Josaphat.
McCormack, Robert '47 (NY) Retired.
McCormick, Andrew '82 (PH) Holland, PA St. Bede the Venerable.
McCormick, Brian '66 (TR)[T] Trenton, NJ Martin House; Martin House.
McCormick, Daniel J. '57 (ATL) Dunwoody, GA All Saints Catholic; Defenders of the Bond; Promoter of Justice.
McCormick, Frank '68 (HEL)[E] Missoula, MT St. Patrick Hospital and Health Sciences Center, Sisters of Providence of Montana Corporation.
McCormick, Gerard *o.m.i.* '47 (BO)[Y] Tewksbury, MA Immaculate Heart of Mary Infirmary.
McCormick, Gregory *s.p.* (SFE)[I] Jemez Springs, NM Our Lady of Lourdes.
McCormick, Howard W. '57 (SPR)[H] Springfield, MA St. Michael's Residence; Bishop's Commission for Clergy Retired.
McCormick, James D. '62 (SC) Carroll, IA Holy Spirit.
McCormick, James Daniel '62 (SC)[F] Carroll, IA Opus Spiritus Sancti.
McCormick, James '82 (E) Erie, PA St. James.
McCormick, Jeffrey '96 (MIA)[C] Pembroke Pines, FL St. Maximilian Kolbe.
McCormick, Jerry '73 (MRY) Pacific Grove, CA St. Angela; Vicar for Clergy; Catholic Charities Board; Presbyteral Council; Priest's Personnel Board.
McCormick, Jim (SC) St. Anthony Regional Hospital; [C] Carroll, IA St. Anthony Regional Hospital.
McCormick, John D. '75 (DEN) Broomfield, CO Nativity of Our Lord.
McCormick, John J. '56 (BO) Billerica, MA St. Theresa of Lisieux.
McCormick, John M. '75 (ORL) Orlando, FL St. James Cathedral.
McCormick, John '99 (SR) Unassigned.
McCormick, John (ORL) Ethnic Ministries; Propagation of the Faith.
McCormick, Justin J. *c.s.p.* '61 (NY)[EE] Jamaica Estates Paulist Fathers Generalate.
McCormick, Kieran D. '64 (SFR) San Carlos, CA St. Charles.
McCormick, Louis M. *o.f.m.* '65 (BUF)[Q] West Clarksville, NY Mount Irenaeus, Franciscan Mountain Retreat & Holy Peace Friary; [C] West Clarksville, NY Holy Peace Friary.
McCormick, Mark '91 (RC) Piedmont–Black Hawk, SD Our Lady of the Black Hills; Diocesan Consultors.
McCormick, Martin F. *o.p.* '61 (DET)[L] Farmington Hills, MI Monastery of the Blessed Sacrament.
McCormick, Maurice M. '58 (SFR) San Francisco, CA Mission Dolores Basilica.
McCormick, Maurice '58 (SFR) Retired.
McCormick, Michael '85 (WH) Absent on Sick Leave.
McCormick, Myron *o.f.m.* '52 (BO)[AA] Boston, MA St. Anthony Shrine.
McCormick, Pat (FRS) Priests' Council.
McCormick, Patrick G. '96 (PH) Bensalem, PA St. Charles Borromeo; Priests' Personnel Board.
McCormick, Patrick J. '57 (ATL) Military Chaplains; Navy Chaplains.
McCormick, Patrick J. '68 (ATL) On Duty Outside the Archdiocese.
McCormick, Patrick Joseph '75 (FRS) Fresno, CA St. Mary.
McCormick, Patrick '68 (HON) Defenders of the Bond; Military Chaplains.

McCormick, Patrick (FRS) Master of Ceremonies.
McCormick, Paul *o.cist.* '97 (SLT)[K] Irving, TX Cistercian Abbey of Our Lady of Dallas.
McCormick, Robert F. (BGP)[T] Darien, CT Convent of St. Birgitta.
McCormick, Thomas F. *s.j.* '67 (LA) Los Angeles, CA Blessed Sacrament.
McCormick, Thomas '59 (DEN) Carbondale, CO St. Vincent.
McCormick, Thomas *s.j.* (MO) AUXILIARY CHAPLAINS CONTRACT CHAPLAINS.
McCormley, Hugh J. '62 (PIT) Pittsburgh, PA St. Francis of Assisi.
McCorry, Edward J. '56 (NY) Hastings–on–Hudson, NY St. Matthew; Hastings–on–Hudson, NY St. Stanislaus Kostka.
McCorry, Patrick G. '01 (NOR) Middletown, CT St. Sebastian.
McCotter, Daniel E. *c.s.p.* '81 (SFR) San Francisco, CA Holy Family Chinese Mission; San Francisco, CA Old St. Mary's Cathedral.
McCouch, Richard S. *s.j.* '93 (CI)[B] Chuuk, FM Xavier High School.
McCourt, Gerald P. *s.j.* '72 (SJ)[L] Los Altos, CA Jesuit Retreat House.
McCourt, Robert R. '61 (BRK) St. Albans, NY St. Pascal Baylon.
McCown, Robert M. *s.j.* (ELP) El Paso, TX Sacred Heart.
McCoy, A. E. (SC) Diocesan Consultors.
McCoy, Alfred E. '54 (SC)[A] Sioux City, IA Briar Cliff University; Ecumenical Commission Retired.
McCoy, Bernard *o.cist.* '95 (LC)[H] Sparta, WI Our Lady of Spring Bank, Cistercian Abbey.
McCoy, Charles J. '61 (BO) Newton, MA St. Philip Neri.
McCoy, Daniel P. '03 (BO) North Reading, MA St. Theresa.
McCoy, Floyd '83 (SJN) On Duty Outside the Archdiocese.
McCoy, James B. '63 (PH)[EE] Chalfont, PA Delaware Valley College of Science and Agriculture.
McCoy, James P. '63 (PH) Chalfont, PA St. Jude; Parish Sites and Boundaries, Commission for.
McCoy, John '93 (STU) Steubenville, OH Holy Rosary; [E] Steubenville, OH Trinity Medical Center, West; [E] Steubenville, OH Trinity Medical Center, East; Hospitals.
McCoy, Kevin C. '81 (SC) On Duty Outside the Diocese.
McCoy, P. Floyd '84 (MGZ) Lajas, PR Our Lady of the Purification.
McCoy, Perry M. *o.s.m.* '93 (CHI)[N] Chicago Order of Friar Servants of Mary (Servites) United States of America Province, Inc..
McCoy, Perry *o.s.m.* (ELP) El Paso, TX Our Lady of Sorrows.
McCoy Jordan, Floyd L. (PCE)[B] The Pontifical Catholic University of Puerto Rico.
McCracken, John E. '79 (GAY) Gaylord, MI St. Mary Cathedral; Gaylord, MI Holy Redeemer; Consultors, Diocesan Board of; Appointed Members; Continuing Spiritual Formation of Clergy, Pastoral Administrators and Women Religious; Appointed Members.
McCracken, John T. '44 (OAK) Walnut Creek, CA St. Anne.
McCracken, Kevin *c.m.* '82 (LA)[A] Camarillo, CA St. John's Seminary.
McCrane, Gerard T. *m.m.* '59 (CHI)[N] Chicago, IL Maryknoll Fathers & Brothers.
McCrann, Peter J. *s.m.m.* '58 (RVC) Bay Shore, NY Southside Hospital; [M] Bay Shore, NY Montfort Missionaries.
McCrate, D. Stephen '89 (BEA) Port Arthur, TX St. Joseph.
McCrate, Stephen (BEA) Diocesan College of Consultors and Presbyteral Council.
McCray, Trinette '81 (MIL)[C] Milwaukee, WI Cardinal Stritch University.
McCreanor, James '78 (MIA) Homestead, FL Sacred Heart.
McCreary, Glenn E. '95 (SCR) Muncy, PA Resurrection; Muncy, PA Muncy Prison.
McCreary, Robert E. *o.f.m.cap.* '64 (CLV) York, PA St. Joseph; [A] Wickliffe, OH Borromeo Seminary.
McCreedy, Harry E. '72 (PH) Norristown, PA St. Paul.
McCreedy, Justin D. *o.s.b.* '70 (YAK) Special Assignment.
McCreedy, Justin D. *o.s.b.* '70 (SEA)[L] Lacey, WA St. Martin's Abbey.
McCreesh, Thomas P. *o.p.* '72 (WDC)[B] Washington, DC Dominican House of Studies.
McCreight, James H. '68 (CLV) Cleveland, OH St. Michael the Archangel; [W] Cleveland, OH St. Michael.
McCrillis, Philip '61 (SJ) Retired.
McCrone, John M. '82 (NEW) Dumont, NJ St. Mary's; Mountainside, NJ Our Lady of Lourdes.
McCue, Michael J. *o.s.f.s.* '90 (PH) Philadelphia, PA Our Mother of Consolation.
McCue, Richard T. '58 (CHL) Retired.
McCue, Scott E. '01 (R) Clayton, NC St. Ann.
McCue, Will *s.c.* '74 (GLP) Ganado, AZ All Saints.
McCulken, Michael T. '76 (PH) Havertown, PA Annunciation B.V.M.; Office of the Vicar for Administration.
McCullagh, John P. '55 (BRK) Brooklyn, NY St. Vincent de Paul.
McCullen, John L. '44 (TOL) Deerfield Beach, FL St. Ambrose Retired.
McCulloch, Lawrence F. *m.m.* '70 (STA)[H] Jacksonville, FL Maryknoll Fathers & Brothers.
McCullough, Brian *s.c.j.* '73 (MIL)[O] Hales Corners, WI Priests of the Sacred Heart; [O] Hales Corners, WI Priests of the Sacred Heart.
McCullough, Hugh '79 (FR) South Yarmouth, MA St. Pius Tenth.
McCullough, J. Edward '67 (GBG) Dunbar, PA St. Aloysius; Leisenring, PA St. Vincent de Paul; Bishop's Priests Council; Catholic Relief Services Representative; Missions; Apostleship of Prayer; Catholic Daughters of America; Holy Childhood Association; Pilgrimages; Priests' Eucharistic League.
McCullough, Michael P. '73 (LA) Los Angeles, CA Transfiguration; L.A. Police Department.
McCumber, William W. '83 (STL) St. Louis, MO Basilica of St. Louis, King of France.
McCumber, William (STL) Archdiocesan Office of Worship; Archdiocesan Commission for Sacred Liturgy.
McCune, James L. (BO) Senior Priests.
McCurdy, Richard L. *s.j.* '67 (SAC)[D] Sacramento, CA Jesuit High School; [I] Carmichael, CA Jesuit High School Community of Sacramento.
McCurdy, William J. *s.j.* '61 (BUF)[O] Buffalo, NY Canisius Jesuit Community.
McCurry, James *o.f.m.conv.* '77 (BAL)[S] Ellicott City, MD Friary of St. Joseph Cupertino.
McDade, Robert *m.ss.cc.* '76 (CAM)[M] Linwood, NJ Villa Pieta. Missionaries of the Sacred Hearts of Jesus & Mary.
McDade, Thomas J. '74 (NEW) Franklin Lakes, NJ Most Blessed Sacrament.
McDaid, J. Anthony '75 (DEN) On Duty Outside the Archdiocese.
McDaniel, George W. '70 (DAV)[A] Davenport, IA St. Ambrose University Seminary; Judges; Vice–Chancellors.
McDaniel, George '70 (DAV)[B] St. Ambrose University.
McDaniel, Isaac '82 (L) Fairdale, KY St. Jerome.
McDaniel, John W. *s.j.* '71 (PH)[AA] Loyola Center and Manresa Hall.
McDarby, J. Patrick *o.s.b.* '53 (SCL)[I] Collegeville, MN St. John's Abbey, of the Order of St. Benedict.
McDermott, Brian O. *s.j.* '68 (WDC)[M] Washington, DC The Jesuit Community at Georgetown University.
McDermott, Charles B. '63 (PRO) Pawtucket, RI St. Joseph.
McDermott, Charles B. '73 (NEW) Union, NJ St. Michael's.
McDermott, Charles S. '60 (SAC) Sacramento, CA St. Rose; Chancellor and Vicar Episcopal for Theological Affairs; Promoter of Justice; Censor Librorum; Council of Priests; Eastern Catholic Churches; St. Thomas More Society.
McDermott, Christopher H. *c.s.sp.* '81 (PH)[AA] Bensalem, PA Congregation of the Holy Ghost.
McDermott, Edwin J. *s.j.* '49 (SJ)[M] Los Gatos, CA Sacred Heart Jesuit Center.
McDermott, Ignatius D. '36 (CHI) Retired.
McDermott, J. Patrick '67 (SEA) Burlington, WA St. Charles; LaConner, WA Sacred Heart; LaConner, WA St. Paul; Mount Vernon, WA Immaculate Conception; Sedro Woolley, WA Immaculate Heart of Mary; [P] Mount Vernon, WA Skagit Valley Regional Ministry; Presbyteral Council; Deans.
McDermott, James P. *s.j.* '03 (MIL)[O] Milwaukee, WI Jesuit Community at Marquette University; Milwaukee, WI Gesu Parish.
McDermott, John J. (BUR) Office of Diocesan Pastoral Planning; Auditors; Notaries; Misconduct Review Board; Cambridge, VT St. Mary; Underhill Center, VT St. Thomas.
McDermott, John Michael *s.j.* '71 (COL).
McDermott, Joseph M. '95 (PH)[A] Warrington, PA St. Robert Bellarmine.
McDermott, Joseph P. '62 (BO) Stoughton, MA Immaculate Conception.
McDermott, Joseph *s.v.d.* '52 (DUB)[B] Epworth, IA Divine Word College.
McDermott, Michael A. '66 (PIT) Allegheny County, PA UPMC University of Pittsburgh Medical Center; Allegheny County, PA UPMC Shadyside Hospital.
McDermott, Michael F. '79 (GI) Grand Island, NE Resurrection; St. Libory, NE St. Libory's; St. Paul, NE SS. Peter and Paul; Chancellor; Vicar–Judicial; Judges; Diocesan Consultors; Priests' Advisory Board (Presbyteral Council).
McDermott, Michael J. '75 (WIL) Hockessin, DE St. Mary of the Assumption; Absent on Sick Leave.
McDermott, Michael J. (SEA) Tacoma, WA St. Charles Borromeo; College of Consultors; Presbyteral Council.
McDermott, Neal W. *o.p.* (NO) Archdiocesan Consultors; Rosary Congress Committee; New Orleans, LA Our Lady of The Rosary; [S] Metairie, LA International Dominican Foundation.
McDermott, Neal W. (NO) Members of the Board; Executive Director; Campus Ministry.
McDermott, Neal W. *o.p.* (NO) Archdiocesan Consultors; Rosary Congress Committee; New Orleans, LA Our Lady of The Rosary; [S] Metairie, LA International Dominican Foundation.
McDermott, Patrick M. '64 (BLX) Biloxi, MS Sacred Heart.
McDermott, Patrick (BLX) Deans; Presbyteral Council.
McDermott, Robert B. '90 (PH) Buckingham, PA Our Lady of Guadalupe; Diocesan Priests' Compensation and Benefits Committee; Council of Priests.
McDermott, Robert J. '81 (STA) Gainesville, FL St. Patrick's.
McDermott, Robert T. '69 (CAM) Camden, NJ St. Joseph's Pro–Cathedral; Members.
McDermott, Robert T. '81 (MIL) On Duty Outside the Archdiocese.
McDermott, Robert T. '81 (LIN) Lincoln, NE St. Mary.
McDermott, Robert '83 (STA) Special Assignment.
McDermott, Stephen C. '03 (PH) Philadelphia, PA St. John the Baptist.
McDermott, Sylvester (SAC) College of Consultors.
McDermott, Thomas J. '55 (SD) Retired.
McDermott, Thomas J. '97 (DUB) Cedar Rapids, IA St. Ludmila; [C] Niagara University, NY Niagara University; Personnel Advisory Board; Deanery Representatives; Directors.
McDermott, Thomas K. *o.p.* '83 (FgM).
McDermott, Thomas K. *o.p.* '83 (CHI)[N] Chicago Dominicans (Provincial Office).
McDermott, Thomas *c.s.c.* '79 (FTW) South Bend, IN St. Adalbert.
McDermott, William '98 (FAR) Langdon, ND St. Alphonsus; Langdon, ND St. Edward.
McDevitt, Anthony (MOB) Judicial Vicar; Judicial Consultant.
McDevitt, Edward P. *c.o.* '71 (CHR) Rock Hill, SC Divine Saviour; [E] Rock Hill, SC Oratory of St. Philip Neri, Congregation of the Oratory of Pontifical Rite.
McDevitt, James A. '90 (BGP) On Duty Outside the Diocese.
McDevitt, James J. '35 (PBL) Retired.
McDevitt, James '90 (BRK) Brooklyn, NY St. John the Evangelist; Brooklyn, NY Metropolitan Detention Center.
McDevitt, James (ALB) Presbyteral Council; Diocesan Board of Consultors; Deans.
McDevitt, Michael V. '71 (SPC) Springfield, MO Cathedral of St. Agnes; Defenders of the Bond; Priests' Eucharistic League Confraternity Of The Most Blessed Sacrament; Presbyteral Council; Region IV.
McDevitt, Robert *s.j.* '60 (SJ)[M] Los Gatos, CA Sacred Heart Jesuit Center.
McDevitt, Thomas '58 (LAN)[L] De Witt, MI St. Francis Retreat Center Retired.
McDonagh, Donat Michael '74 (SP) On Duty Outside the Diocese; [U] St. Petersburg, FL Marian Servants of the Holy Spirit, Inc..
McDonagh, Edward C. '62 (BO) West Bridgewater, MA St. Ann.
McDonagh, John P. '81 (NY) Bronx, NY St. Margaret of Cortona.
McDonagh, John P. '82 (SPR)[P] Amherst, MA The Newman Center; [P] Amherst, MA University of Massachusetts; Newman Apostolate and Campus Ministry.
McDonald, A. John '56 (BR) Retired.
McDonald, Alexander F. *s.j.* '47 (SPK)[J] Spokane, WA Regis Community.
McDonald, Allan J. '80 (SAV) Augusta, GA Church of the Most Holy Trinity; Augusta, GA; Council of Catholic Women.
McDonald, Bernard (NY) Port Jervis, NY Bon Secours Community Hospital.
McDonald, Bill '89 (STO) Modesto, CA St. Stanislaus Church (Pastor of).
McDonald, C. Alexander '91 (CHR) North Augusta, SC Our Lady of Peace; Presbyteral Council; Diocesan Curia.
McDonald, Charles J. '65 (LEX) Lawrenceburg, KY St. Lawrence.
McDonald, Charles *c.ss.r.* '71 (PH) Philadelphia, PA St. Boniface.
McDonald, Charles (LEX) Priests' Retirement Board.
McDonald, Daniel C. *s.j.* '81 (MIL)[O] Pontifical Gregorian University.
McDonald, David M. '55 (HRT) Hartford, CT Sacred Heart; Hartford, CT St. Justin; Hartford, CT St. Michael.
McDonald, Edward J. *c.s.p.* '41 (NY)[EE] Jamaica Estates Paulist Fathers Generalate.
McDonald, Elmer J. '49 (ROC) Retired.
McDonald, Eustace *c.p.* '45 (BAL)[S] Baltimore, MD St. Joseph's Passionist Community.
McDonald, Finian *o.s.b.* '62 (SCL)[I] Collegeville, MN St. John's Abbey, of the Order of St. Benedict.
McDonald, Francis B. '60 (JOL) Roselle, IL St. Walter.

McDonald, G. Malcolm '85 (PIT) Coraopolis, PA St. Joseph.
McDonald, G. Malcom (PIT) Air Force Reserve Chaplains.
McDonald, Gerard R. *o.f.m.* '45 (PAT)[M] Butler, NJ St. Anthony Friary.
McDonald, James E. *c.s.c.* '84 (FTW)[I] Congregacion de Santa Cruz.
McDonald, James M. '67 (RVC) Dix Hills, NY St. Matthew; Senate of Priests (Presbyteral Council/ College of Consultors); Associate Vocation Directors; Apostleship of Prayer; Nocturnal Adoration Society.
McDonald, James *c.ss.r.* '90 (BAL) Annapolis, MD St. Mary; [S] Annapolis, MD Saint Mary Rectory.
McDonald, James (RVC) Procurator & Advocates.
McDonald, John F. '47 (HRT)[A] Bloomfield, CT St. Thomas Seminary Retired.
McDonald, John J. *s.j.* '57 (NY)[EE] New York, NY Murray–Weigel Hall.
McDonald, Joseph F. '87 (B) Idaho Falls, ID Holy Rosary; Idaho Falls, ID Christ the King.
McDonald, Joseph F. (B) Adjutant Judicial Vicars; Defenders of the Bond.
McDonald, Joseph (B) College of Consultors; Deans.
McDonald, Kenneth '57 (LAN) Retired.
McDonald, Mark *m.s.c.* '68 (RCK).
McDonald, Martin '62 (MRY) Retired.
McDonald, Matthew D. '40 (CHI) Retired.
McDonald, Michael D. '85 (GI)[G] Kearney, NE Prince of Peace; Kearney, NE Youth Development Center; [D] Kearney, NE University of Nebraska at Kearney Newman Apostolate; Diocesan Consultors; Priests' Advisory Board (Presbyteral Council); Propagation of the Faith.
McDonald, Paul F. '51 (DUB) Retired.
McDonald, Perry *o.f.m.* '67 (BRK)[V] Brooklyn, NY St. Michael's Friary.
McDonald, Peter '59 (SFR) Ross, CA St. Anselm.
McDonald, Richard J. '99 (KCK) St. Augustine's; Sabetha, KS Sacred Heart; St. James.
McDonald, Robert *s.m.* '50 (PRT) Van Buren, ME St. Joseph; Van Buren, ME St. Bruno – St. Remi.
McDonald, Sandy (CHR) Vicar for Ecumenical & Interreligious Affairs.
McDonald, Thomas M. '56 (NY) On Duty Outside the Archdiocese.
McDonald, Thomas (NY) Allen Pavilion.
McDonald, Vincent *s.c.j.* '45 (SP)[O] Pinellas Park, FL Priests of the Sacred Heart Retired.
McDonald, Vincent *o.carm.* '47 (NY)[EE] Middletown, NY St. Albert's Priory.
McDonnell, Anthony '70 (LA) On Sick Leave.
McDonnell, David '72 (PAT) Randolph, NJ St. Matthew the Apostle.
McDonnell, David (PAT) Deans.
McDonnell, Donald C. '47 (SFR) Retired.
McDonnell, Francis E. '51 (RCK) Pro Synodal Judges; Censores Librorum Retired.
McDonnell, Francis P. '58 (HRT) Windsor Locks, CT St. Mary.
McDonnell, John H. '56 (WH) Charleston, WV St. Agnes; Diocesan Consultors; Religious Unity, Diocesan Commission for.
McDonnell, John J. '44 (YAK) Vicar for Priests Retired.
McDonnell, John J. '73 (CHI) Chicago, IL St. Mary, Star of the Sea.
McDonnell, John *c.m.* '43 (BRK)[V] Jamaica, NY Vincentian Residence.
McDonnell, Joseph F. '55 (CHI) Western Springs, IL St. John of the Cross Retired.
McDonnell, Joseph M. '30 (ROC) Retired.
McDonnell, Joseph '67 (DM) Urbandale, IA St. Pius X.
McDonnell, Kilian *o.s.b.* '51 (SCL)[I] Collegeville, MN St. John's Abbey, of the Order of St. Benedict.
McDonnell, Lawrence V. *c.s.p.* '53 (NY)[EE] Jamaica Estates Paulist Fathers Generalate.
McDonnell, Martin '68 (PAT) Parsippany, NJ St. Ann.
McDonnell, Michael *o.f.m.* '65 (NY) New York, NY St. Francis of Assisi.
McDonnell, P. William '64 (RCK) Freeport, IL St. Thomas Aquinas; Deans.
McDonnell, Patrick J. '73 (TR) Hightstown, NJ St. Anthony of Padua.
McDonnell, Patrick '57 (MIA) Fort Lauderdale, FL St. Sebastian.
McDonnell, Paul A. *o.s.j.* '91 (SCR) Pittston, PA Our Lady of Mt. Carmel; [M] Pittston, PA Eastern Province of the Oblates of St. Joseph.
McDonnell, Robert *c.s.c.* '57 (ORL)[E] Cocoa Beach, FL Congregation of Holy Cross, Eastern Province.
McDonnell, Sean '88 (PAT) Parsippany NJ St. Christopher.
McDonnell, Thomas J. '60 (BO) South Boston, MA St. Augustine; South Boston, MA St. Monica.
McDonnell, Thomas P. *m.m.* '65 (NY)[EE] Maryknoll Maryknoll St. Teresa's Residence.
McDonnell, Thomas P. *s.j.* '68 (CHL)[EE] Charlotte, NC St. Peter.
McDonough, James A. *o.p.* '62 (AUS)[G] Austin, TX Dominican Friars of Austin.
McDonough, James E. *ss.cc.* '68 (FR)[J] Wareham, MA Sacred Hearts Retreat Center.
McDonough, James M. *s.j.* '61 (SPK)[B] Spokane, WA Gonzaga University.
McDonough, James P. (PIT) Matrimonial Concerns, Office for; Promoters of Justice; Defenders of the Bond; Matrimonial Concerns, Office for.
McDonough, James T. '57 (PH) Strafford, PA Our Lady of the Assumption; [FF] Philadelphia, PA Ladies of Charity; Regional Vicars; Priests' Personnel Board.
McDonough, James '42 (AGN) Dededo, GU Santa Barbara.
McDonough, James *o.p.* '62 (AUS)[N] Austin, TX Society of St. Vincent de Paul.
McDonough, James '84 (PIT) Pittsburgh, PA Epiphany.
McDonough, James *o.p.* (AUS) Presbyteral Council.
McDonough, John P. '52 (BO) Graduate Studies; Senior Priests Retired.
McDonough, John P. '95 (WH) Oak Hill, WV SS. Peter and Paul.
McDonough John T. '50 (CLV) Akron, OH St. Sebastian; Hinckley, OH Our Lady of Grace Retired.
McDonough John T. '00 (PHX) Fountain Hills, AZ Ascension.
McDonough Joseph '69 (BAL) Glen Burnie, MD Holy Trinity.
McDonough, Kevin M. '80 (STP) St. Paul, MN St. Peter Claver.
McDonough, Kevin M. (STP) Vicar General and Moderator of the Curia; For Canonical Affairs; For African–American Catholics; For Hispanic Ministry; For Marriages; Outreach; Adjutant Judicial Vicars; Archdiocesan Consultors; Corporate Board.
McDonough, Patrick M. '68 (WH) St. Albans, WV St. Francis of Assisi.
McDonough, Raymond *c.p.* (BIR) Birmingham, AL Holy Family.
McDonough, Roger F. '76 (BGP) On Duty Outside the Diocese; Boca Raton, FL St. Joan of Arc.
McDonough, T. Joseph '46 (MAN) Retired.
McDonough, Thomas R. '89 (STP) Special Assignment.
McDonough, Timothy T. *c.s.sp.* '56 (VEN)[P] Bethel Park, PA Holy Spirit Animation Center.
McDonough, Vincent *s.j.* '62 (ROC)[B] Elmira, NY Notre Dame High School.
McDonough, William C. '82 (STP) Special Assignment.
McDougal, H. Jon (LR) Deans.
McDougal, Jon *v.f.* '79 (LR) Batesville, AR St. Mary's; Batesville, AR St. Cecilia's.
McDougal, James G. '75 (LAN) Ann Arbor, MI St. Francis of Assisi.
McDougal, Jeffrey N. *s.j.* '03 (P)[L] Portland, OR Colombiere Community.
McDougal, Russell K. *c.s.c.* '91 (FTW)[I] Holy Cross Bugembe.
McDowell John *o.f.m.* '77 (ATL) Catholic Student Center at The University of Georgia.
McDowell, John *o.f.m.* (ATL)[N] Athens, GA Catholic Student Center – University of Georgia.
McDowell, Leo G. '94 (GF) Circle, MT St. Francis Xavier; Air Force Reserve Chaplains.
McDowell, Leo (GF) Diocesan Consultors; Boy Scouts; Finance Council; Priests' Council.
McDowell, Patrick D. '68 (SCR) Weston, PA Sacred Heart.
McDowell, Patrick '54 (DUL) Duluth, MN Our Lady of Mercy.
McDuffie Paul A. '95 (BR) Independence, LA Mater Dolorosa; Presbyteral Council.
McDyre, Cajetan *s.t.* '45 (PAT)[M] Stirling, NJ Holy Spirit Missionary Cenacle.
McEachern, Bernard *c.p.* '64 (MET).
McElduff, Edward W. '53 (ALN) Retired.
McEleney, Neil J. *c.s.p.* '53 (WDC)[B] Washington, DC St. Paul's College.
McEleney, Neil J. *c.s.p.* '53 (NY)[EE] Jamaica Estates Paulist Fathers Generalate.
McEleney, Robert J. '58 (RIC) Retired.
McElhenon, J. Daniel '01 (HRT) Watertown, CT St. John the Evangelist.
McElhinny, Michael *s.m.* '80 (BO) Boston, MA Massachusetts General Hospital.
McElligott, Thomas J. '69 (SFR)[Q] Moraga, CA St. Mary's College Campus Ministry; On Duty Outside the Archdiocese.
McElroy, Charles J. '64 (PH) Schwenksville, PA St. Mary.
McElroy, Damian '88 (TR) Hamilton Square, NJ St. Gregory the Great.
McElroy, David R. *o.praem.* '02 (GB)[B] St. Norbert College; [I] De Pere, WI St. Norbert Abbey.
McElroy, James E. '56 (LA) Los Angeles, CA Holy Trinity.
McElroy, John J. '45 (PRO) Pawtucket, RI St. Joseph Retired.
McElroy, John W. '56 (BO) Senior Priests Retired.
McElroy, Robert W. '80 (SFR) San Mateo, CA St. Gregory; [P] College of Consultors.
McElroy, Thomas *ss.cc.* '67 (FR)[H] Fairhaven, MA Damien Residence.
McElwee, Robert W. '83 (WCH) Frontenac, KS Sacred Heart; [J] Pittsburg, KS St. Pius X Center (Pittsburg State University).
McEneaney, John P. A. '43 (SFS) Retired.
McEnery, James G. '53 (MAD) Retired.
McEnhill, Gerald A. '72 (DET) Farmington, MI St. Gerald; Presbyteral Council.
McEnhill, John *s.m.* '56 (SJ)[M] Cupertino, CA San Juan Residence.
McEniry, Robert F. *s.j.* '51 (OM)[K] Omaha, NE Jesuit Community at Creighton University.
McEnnis, Thomas '45 (SEA) Retired.
McEntee, John B. '61 (STL) Luebbering, MO St. Francis of Assisi.
McEntee, Sean *o.m.i.* '01 (GAL) Fairport, NY Assumption of the Blessed Virgin Mary.
McEvilly, John W. '64 (BEL) Belleville, IL Our Lady Queen of Peace.
McEvoy, David *o.carm.* '88 (KCK) Leavenworth, KS Immaculate Conception; Leavenworth, KS St. Joseph's.
McEvoy, John '64 (SP) Ruskin, FL St. Anne; Priests Personnel Board.
McEvoy, William '87 (KCK) Kansas City, KS Blessed Sacrament; Kansas City, KS Our Lady and St. Rose.
McEwan, Kevin D. '02 (OG) Bloomingdale, NY St. Paul; Saranac Lake, NY St. Bernard.
McEwan, Kevin '02 (OG) Lake Clear, NY St. John in the Wilderness.
McFadden, Brian F. '88 (NEW) Berkeley Heights, NJ Church of the Little Flower.
McFadden, J. Michael '74 (HBG) Harrisburg, PA Cathedral Parish of St. Patrick; Secretary for Clergy and Religious Life; Consultors, College; Permanent Diaconate, Office for.
McFadden, John R. '62 (PH) Cheltenham, PA Presentation of Blessed Virgin Mary.
McFadden, Joseph P. '81 (PH) Downingtown, PA St. Joseph; Diocesan Priests' Compensation and Benefits Committee.
McFadden, Leo E. '53 (RNO) Retired.
McFadden, Michael J. *o.s.a.* '67 (LA) Ojai, CA St. Thomas Aquinas.
McFadden, Michael '61 (SAC) Vacaville, CA St. Mary.
McFadden, William C. *s.j.* '59 (WDC)[M] Washington, DC The Jesuit Community at Georgetown University.
McFadin, Marcus '92 (ELP) El Paso, TX St. Stephen, Deacon and Martyr; Diocesan Master of Ceremonies.
McFalls, Dean '95 (STO) Lathrop, CA Our Lady of Guadalupe Church (Pastor of).
McFarland, Edward J. '55 (COL) Retired.
McFarland, Eugene H. '43 (ROC) Retired.
McFarland, Francis X. *s.j.* '50 (NEW)[C] Jersey City, NJ St. Peter's Preparatory School.
McFarland, James W. '47 (NEW)[N] Rutherford, NJ St. John Vianney Residence for Priests; Maria Immaculata of Hudson County Retired.
McFarland, Michael C. *s.j.* '84 (WOR)[B] Worcester, MA College of the Holy Cross, Inc.; [O] Worcester, MA Jesuits of Holy Cross College, Inc..
McFarland, Timothy D. *c.pp.s.* '83 (LFT)[A] Rensselaer, IN Saint Joseph's College.
McGaffin, Joseph '96 (PHX) Scottsdale, AZ St. Daniel the Prophet.
McGagh, Martin A. '54 (FRS) Porterville, CA St. Anne Retired.
McGahagan, James E. '68 (SCR) Hanover Township, PA Exaltation of the Holy Cross; Deans.
McGahee, Thomas *s.d.b.* '77 (NO)[D] Marrero, LA Archbishop Shaw High School.
McGahey, Charles R. '59 (BO) Senior Priests Retired.
McGahren, Joseph J. *m.m.* '51 (NY)[EE] Maryknoll Maryknoll Fathers and Brothers.
McGann, Diarmuid F. '64 (RVC) Blue Point, NY Our Lady of the Snow.
McGann, Francis J. '48 (BO) Needham, MA St. Joseph.
McGann, Gerard J. '48 (BO) Senior Priests; Senior Priests Retired.
McGann, L. Philip '71 (WIL) Retired.
McGann, Richard P. '70 (HRT) Plainville, CT Our Lady of Mercy.
McGann, Thomas A. '76 (PH) On Duty Outside the Archdiocese.
McGann, Thomas '76 (CHI)[N] Kingston, Jamaica, WI.
McGarr, Joseph M. '86 (ALN)[J] Bethlehem, PA Holy Family Villa Retired.
McGarrigle, Michael '49 (PRT) Retired.
McGarrill, Colman *t.o.r.* '54 (SP) Tampa, FL St. Patrick.
McGarrity, Patrick *c.ss.r.* '61 (HBG) Lancaster, PA St. Anthony of Padua.
McGarrity, Richard A. *s.j.* '70 (MIL)[X] Milwaukee, WI The Jesuit Partnership; [O] Milwaukee, WI Jesuit Provincial Office, Wisconsin Province; [O] Milwaukee, WI Jesuit Community at Marquette University.
McGarry, James J. '70 (SCR) Clarks Summit, PA Our Lady of the Snows; Presbyteral Council.
McGarry, John P. *s.j.* '93 (SAC)[D] Sacramento, CA Jesuit High School; [I] Carmichael, CA Jesuit High School Community of Sacramento.
McGarry, Joseph P. '55 (HRT) West Hartford, CT St. Peter Claver.
McGarry, Michael B. *c.s.p.* '75 (NY)[EE] Jamaica

Estates Paulist Fathers Generalate.
McGarry, Peter *o.carm.* '69 (CHI)[N] Chicago Carmelite Priory of St. Cyril.
McGarry, Peter *o.carm.* '69 (NEW) Teaneck, NJ St. Anastasia's; [D] Chicago, IL.
McGarry, Thomas '53 (NY) Bronx, NY St. Martin of Tours; Bronx, NY St. Barnabas Hospital Retired.
McGarry, William C. '59 (BUF) Niagara Falls, NY Our Lady of Mount Carmel Retired.
McGarty, Bernard O. '49 (LC) Elected Members Retired.
McGaugh, Philip E. '78 (BO) Needham, MA St. Bartholomew; Boston, MA Massachusetts General Hospital.
McGauley, Francis H. *s.j.* '55 (BAL) Baltimore, MD St. Ignatius.
McGee, Dominic E. *o.f.m.conv.* '67 (SY) Minoa, NY St. Mary.
McGee, H. Desmond '71 (E) Clearfield, PA St. Francis; Deans; Presbyteral Council.
McGee, James J. *s.s.* '85 (SCR) Unassigned or Leave of Absence.
McGee, James J. '91 (OAK) Concord, CA St. Bonaventure.
McGee, John E. *o.s.f.s.* '82 (R) Durham, NC Holy Infant.
McGee, John *o.s.f.s* (R) Deans; Priests' Council.
McGee, Leo J. (PH)[Y] Darby, PA Little Flower Manor; On Special or Other Archdiocesan Assignment.
McGee, Michael J. '77 (BRK) Flushing, NY St. Andrew Avellino.
McGee, Patrick (FR) Diocesan Department of Pastoral Care for the Sick.
McGee, Peter J. '53 (LA) Retired.
McGee, Richard *c.r.* '74 (SB) Riverside, CA St. Catherine of Alexandria; Diocesan Commission and Assembly for Catholics of African Descent.
McGee, Thomas J. *o.s.f.s.* '71 (R) Ahoskie, NC St. Charles Borromeo.
McGee, Timothy H. '87 (CR) Thief River Falls, MN St. Bernards; Priests' Personnel Board.
McGeean, John T. '86 (JOL) Joliet, IL St. Mary Nativity.
McGeory, Peter '76 (NY) Military Chaplains; Navy Chaplains.
McGeough, Jude P. '58 (PRO) East Providence, RI St. Martha.
McGeough, Martin *c.m.* '76 (BIR) Lanett, AL Holy Family; Priests' Council.
McGeown, Joseph P. '65 (PH) Linfield, PA St. Clare; Priests' Personnel Board.
McGeown, William F. '70 (PH) Philadelphia, PA Our Lady of Ransom.
McGerity, Francis X. '84 (CC) On Duty Outside the Diocese.
McGettigan, Neil J. *o.s.a.* '53 (PH)[C] Villanova University; [AA] Villanova, PA St. Thomas Monastery.
McGettrick, Tom '56 (CC) Bishop's Office; Deans; College of Consultors; Personnel Board – Priests; Presbyteral Council; Vicar for Priests; Corpus Christi, TX Saint Andrew By the Sea Parish.
McGhee, William P. '82 (BEL) Carterville, IL Church of the Holy Spirit; Mound City, IL St. Catherine; Mound City, IL Church of the Immaculate Conception–St. Mary; Mound City, IL Our Lady of Fatima.
McGill, Joseph P. *s.j.* '60 (LAF)[J] Grand Coteau, LA Our Lady of the Oaks Retreat House.
McGill, Malachy *c.p.* '46 (ALT)[J] Bedford, PA St. Mary's House of Greater Solitude.
McGillicuddy, Sean J. *c.ss.r.* '86 (BRK) Brooklyn, NY Our Lady of Perpetual Help Basilica.
McGilvray, A. Robert *o.s.f.s.* '62 (ALN)[B] Center Valley, PA DeSales University; [K] Center Valley, PA Oblates of St. Francis de Sales.
McGing, Thomas '71 (JKS) Clinton, MS Holy Savior; [I] Clinton, MS Mississippi College Newman Center; Promoters of Justice; Defenders of the Bond.
McGinley, Bernard P. *m.a.* '61 (HBG) Harrisburg, PA Holy Family.
McGinley, Jeremiah V. *o.f.m.* '55 (NEW) Fair Lawn, NJ St. Anne's.
McGinley, Jeremiah *o.f.m.* (NEW) Part–time Staff.
McGinley, John F. *o.s.f.s.* '68 (WIL) Wilmington, DE St. Anthony of Padua.
McGinn, Anthony F. *s.j.* '79 (NO)[F] New Orleans, LA Jesuit High School; [H] New Orleans, LA Jesuit High School.
McGinn, Daniel *s.s.c.* '53 (PRO)[P] Bristol, RI St. Columban's Retirement House.
McGinn, Finian *o.f.m.* '60 (LA)[CC] Los Angeles, CA St. Francis Center.
McGinn, Finian *o.f.m.* '60 (SFR) San Francisco, CA St. Anthony of Padua.
McGinness, Matthew C. '89 (WCH) Wichita, KS St. Paul Parish; [J] Wichita, KS Wichita State University; Vocations.
McGinnis, Jack P. '63 (GAL) On Duty Outside the Diocese.
McGinnis, James J. '78 (PH) Philadelphia, PA Our Lady of Hope; Army National Guard Chaplains.
McGinnis, Jay W. '76 (BUF) Lancaster, NY Our Lady of Pompeii.
McGinnis, Joseph R. '46 (WIN) Retired.
McGinnity, John C. '75 (WH) Retired.
McGinnity, John '75 (RIC) Hot Springs, VA The Shrine of the Sacred Heart Retired.
McGinnity, Joseph P. '56 (CHI) Retired.
McGinnity, P. J. '91 (KNX) Chattanooga, TN St. Stephen.
McGinnity, Robert F. '55 (CHI) Palos Hills, IL Sacred Heart Retired.
McGinty, John P. *s.j.* '58 (PH)[AA] Loyola Center and Manresa Hall.
McGinty, John P. '83 (BO) Lynn, MA Sacred Heart.
McGivern, Gregory '85 (SJ) San Jose, CA St. Christopher.
McGivern, John W. '91 (CHI) Western Springs, IL St. John of the Cross.
McGivney, Thomas '90 (JOL) Lockport, IL St. Joseph.
McGlinchey, James J. '56 (TLS) Retired.
McGlinn, Charles '67 (KCK) Leawood, KS Cure of Ars; Vicars General; Archdiocesan Consultors; Archdiocesan Administrative Team.
McGlinn, Robert J. '55 (CHI) Other Assignments; Racine, WI Cristo Rey.
McGloin, James P. *s.j.* '74 (FgM).
McGloin, Peter M. '56 (TUC) Tucson, AZ Our Lady of Fatima.
McGloin, Richard D. *s.j.* '46 (OM)[K] Omaha, NE Jesuit Community at Creighton University.
McGlone, Gerard J. *s.j.* '87 (WDC)[M] Washington, DC The Jesuit Community at Georgetown University.
McGlone, Gerard M. '84 (SCR)[L] Wilkes–Barre, PA Little Flower Manor of the Diocese of Scranton; [L] Wilkes–Barre, PA St. Therese Residence.
McGlone, Joseph F. '52 (BO) Newton, MA Corpus Christi.
McGlothlin, Eugene J. *o.s.b.* '60 (SCL) St. John the Baptist; [I] Collegeville, MN St. John's Abbey, of the Order of St. Benedict.
McGlynn, Daniel J. '82 (WIL) Dover, DE Holy Cross.
McGlynn, Philip M. *o.s.m.* '65 (CHI)[N] Chicago, IL Order of Friar Servants of Mary (Servites) United States of America Province, Inc.; [N] Berwyn, IL Servants of Mary (Servite) Development Office.
McGlynn, Thomas E. '84 (FR) Fall River, MA Cathedral of St. Mary of the Assumption; Defenders of the Bond; Auditors.
McGoldrick, James F. *s.m.* '67 (ATL) Atlanta, GA Our Lady of the Assumption; [N] Atlanta, GA.
McGoldrick, John T. '38 (B) Retired.
McGoldrick, Kevin B. '03 (PH) Philadelphia, PA Nativity of the Blessed Virgin Mary.
McGoldrick, William J. '43 (DET) Grosse Pointe, MI Our Lady Star of the Sea Retired.
McGonagle, Douglas '00 (SPR) West Springfield, MA St. Thomas the Apostle; Wilbraham, MA St. Cecilia's.
McGonagle, James *c.ss.r.* '44 (ORL)[E] New Smyrna Beach, FL St. Alphonsus Villa–Redemptorist Fathers and Brothers.
McGonegal, James R. '71 (CLV) Cleveland, OH St. Ignatius of Antioch.
McGonigle, Thomas D. *o.p.* '68 (Chicago Prov.)[P] Providence St. Thomas Aquinas Priory at Providence College.
McGough, James P. '57 (BLX) Waveland, MS St. Clare; Pro–Synodal Judges; Presbyteral Council.
McGough, James (BLX) College of Consultors.
McGough, Stephen D. '68 (SCR) Williamsport, PA St. Boniface; Diocesan Consultors; Presbyteral Council.
McGough, Thomas V. '76 (STU) Absent on Leave.
McGough, Timothy *o.c.d.* '49 (MIL) Milwaukee, WI St. Florian.
McGough, William J. '57 (NO) Covington, LA St. Peter.
McGourn, Francis T. *m.m.* '64[EE] Maryknoll Maryknoll Fathers and Brothers; (FgM).
McGourty, Thomas P. *c.m.* '53 (BUF)[O] Niagara University, NY Vincentian Community at Niagara University; [R] Niagara University, NY Niagara University; [C] Niagara University, NY Niagara University.
McGov, John J. (FgM).
McGovern, Brian J. '69 (SEA)[H] Seattle, WA Providence Mount St. Vincent; [J] Seattle, WA Providence Mount St. Vincent.
McGovern, Donan *o.f.m.* '55 (BO)[AA] Boston, MA St. Anthony Shrine.
McGovern, Edward J. '51 (PRO)[P] Providence, RI St. John Vianney Residence; Assessor and Auditor Retired.
McGovern, Eugene F. '29 (BRK) Retired.
McGovern, Eugene '56 (BRK)[V] Douglaston, NY Bishop Mugavero Residence.
McGovern, Harold V. *o.s.f.s.* '70 (R) Roxboro, NC SS. Mary and Edward.
McGovern, James J. '58 (TR) Moorestown, NJ Our Lady of Good Counsel.
McGovern, James O. '67 (BAL) Ellicott City, MD Resurrection.
McGovern, James O. (BAL) Consultors; Senior Priests' Retirement Board; Consultors; Senior Priests Retirement Board.
McGovern, John P. '65 (NEW) Cranford, NJ St. Michael's.
McGovern, John Patrick *o.p.* '58 (WDC)[B] Washington, DC Dominican House of Studies.
McGovern, Joseph J. *s.j.* '48 (CHL) Hot Springs, NC Chapel of the Redeemer; [J] Mooresville, NC Jesuit Community; [M] Hot Springs, NC Jesuit House of Prayer.
McGovern, Lawrence '67 (STO) Stockton, CA Presentation Church (Pastor of); College of Consultors/ Presbyteral Council.
McGovern, Mark J. '67 (DUB) Dyersville, IA Basilica of St. Francis Xavier.
McGovern, Michael '94 (CHI) Chicago, IL St. Juliana.
McGovern, Thomas A. '58 (CLV) Akron, OH St. Matthew; Stow, OH Holy Family Retired.
McGovern, Thomas '46 (LA) Retired.
McGovern, Walter J. '64 (BAL) Randallstown, MD Holy Family Retired.
McGovern, William W. '55 (WOR)[N] Worcester, MA Retired.
McGowan, Andrew J. '49 (SCR) On Special or Other Diocesan Assignment.
McGowan, Andrew J. (SCR) Catholic Health Care Facilities Dir. and Representative to Catholic Institutions of Higher Learning.
McGowan, Anthony '41 (ORG) San Clemente, CA Our Lady of Fatima.
McGowan, Dennis M. *o.s.a.* '83 (CHL) Waynesville, NC St. John the Evangelist.
McGowan, Frederick R. '49 (BO) Senior Priests Retired.
McGowan, James J. '62 (BO) Belmont, MA Our Lady of Mercy.
McGowan, James '02 (SFE) Clayton, NM St. Francis Xavier.
McGowan, Jeffrey A. '89 (STA) Gainesville, FL Queen of Peace.
McGowan, John *c.ss.r.* '62 (TR)[Q] Long Branch, NJ San Alfonso Retreat House.
McGowan, Joseph F. *o.carm.* '62 (TUC) Tucson, AZ Sacred Heart.
McGowan, Joseph O. *s.j.* '74 (SEA)[A] Seattle, WA Seattle University; Seattle, WA St. Joseph.
McGowan, Kenan *o.f.m.conv.* '52 (SY) Binghamton, NY SS. Cyril and Method.
McGowan, Myles P. '45 (NU) Retired.
McGowan, Myles '37 (BAL) Baltimore, MD St. Ursula; [O] Saint John Hall–Long Crandon.
McGowan, Richard A. *s.j.* '83 (Maryland)[V] Newton, MA The Jesuit Community at Boston College.
McGowan, Richard W. *s.j.* '60 (SFE) Albuquerque, NM Immaculate Conception.
McGowan, Seamus '57 (CC) Retired.
McGowan, Wallace A. '62 (MIA) Pinecrest, FL St. Louis.
McGowan, Wallace '62 (MIA) Retired.
McGowan, William J. *s.j.* '62 (NY)[F] New York, NY Xavier High School; [EE] New York, NY Xavier Jesuit Community.
McGrade, Kevin M. '85 (BO) Permanent Disability; Air Force Reserve Chaplains.
McGrail, Charles A. '80 (NOR) Mystic, CT St. Patrick.
McGrane, Camillus M. *o.s.m.* '83 (CHI)[N] Chicago Order of Friar Servants of Mary (Servites) United States of America Province, Inc..
McGrann, John E. '67 (P) Eugene, OR St. Jude.
McGrann, John E. '67 (SPK) On Duty Outside the Diocese.
McGrath, Andre *o.f.m.* '67 (SHP) Shreveport, LA Our Lady of the Blessed Sacrament; College of Consultors; Presbyteral Council.
McGrath, Andrew '38 (LA) Lompoc, CA La Purisima Concepcion.
McGrath, Brian F. '92 (SPR) Westfield, MA St. Mary's; Bishop's Commission for Clergy.
McGrath, Conor '74 (SAT) Selma, TX Our Lady of Perpetual Help; Priests Personnel Board.
McGrath, Daniel F. '63 (NOR) Retired.
McGrath, E. Joseph '85 (LKC) Creole, LA Sacred Heart of Jesus.
McGrath, Edmund G. '37 (YAK) Moxee, WA Holy Rosary Retired.
McGrath, Edward H. *s.j.* '53 (BAL)[S] Human Life Centre.
McGrath, Felix P. *o.f.m.* '61 (NY) New York, NY St. Francis of Assisi.
McGrath, Frank C. '70 (BGP) Stratford, CT Our Lady of Peace; Director for Clergy Personnel; Presbyteral Council; Office for Clergy Personnel; Pastors' Vocation Advisory Board.
McGrath, Gerald '58 (MIA) Retired.
McGrath, J. Joseph *s.j.* '51 (BO)[V] Weston, MA Campion Health Center, Inc..
McGrath, James J. *c.s.c.* '59 (FTW)[B] University of Notre Dame Du Lac; [I] Notre Dame, IN Holy Cross Community, Corby Hall, University of Notre Dame.
McGrath, James R. '54 (BUF) Retired.
McGrath, James '43 (PH) Retired.
McGrath, Jeremiah '80 (BEA) Diaconate, Permanent Diaconate; Beaumont, TX St. Anthony Cathedral.
McGrath, John A. *s.m.* '66 (CIN)[D] Dayton, OH The

University of Dayton; [M] Dayton, OH Marianist Community.
McGrath, John F. (CHI) Retired.
McGrath, John J. *s.j.* '51 (BO)[V] Weston, MA Campion Jesuit Community.
McGrath, John R. '82 (BLX) Vancleave, MS Holy Spirit Catholic Church; Special Delegate for Matrimonial Dispensations; Judicial Vicar; AUXILIARY CHAPLAINS CONTRACT CHAPLAINS.
McGrath, John '44 (CHI) Chicago, IL St. Thomas More Retired.
McGrath, John '59 (MIA) Retired.
McGrath, John *o.m.i.* '66 (SAT)[K] San Antonio, TX Oblate Madonna Residence.
McGrath, Jordan A. *o.p.* '59 (CHI)[N] River Forest, IL St. Thomas Aquinas Priory.
McGrath, Joseph (LKC) Priest's Senate.
McGrath, Kevin Anthony *o.p.* '96 (NY) New York, NY St. Vincent Ferrer; [EE] New York, NY St. Vincent Ferrer Priory.
McGrath, Kevin D. *o.s.b.* '74 (BIR) Cullman, AL Sacred Heart; [E] Cullman, AL St. Bernard Abbey.
McGrath, Lancelot *l.c.* '02 (WDC) Washington, DC St. Stephen Martyr.
Mcgrath, Lancelot *l.c.* '02 (WDC) Bethesda, MD St. Bartholomew; Special Ministries.
McGrath, Laurence W. '57 (BO)[A] Brighton, MA St. John Seminary School of Theology.
McGrath, Noel '80 (PMB) Fellsmere, FL Our Lady of Guadalupe Mission; Presbyteral Council; Sebastian, FL St. Sebastian.
McGrath, Patrick '65 (SAC) On Duty Outside the Diocese.
McGrath, Peter R. *s.j.* '88 (OAK) Oakland, CA St. Mary, Immaculate Conception–St. Francis de Sales.
McGrath, Peter R. *s.j.* '88 (BO)[V] Boston The Society of Jesus of New England–Provincial Offices.
McGrath, Peter R. *s.j.* '88 (New England)[N] Berkeley, CA Jesuit Community at Jesuit School of Theology at Berkeley.
McGrath, Peter *s.j.* (OAK) Deans.
McGrath, Philip J. '54 (LA) Bellflower, CA St. Bernard.
McGrath, Philip J. '60 (LA) Retired.
McGrath, Richard H. '50 (COV) Wilder, KY St. John; [N] Fort Thomas, KY Sisters of the Good Shepherd Retired.
McGrath, Richard J. *o.s.a.* '73 (JOL)[C] New Lenox, IL Providence Catholic High School; [L] New Lenox, IL Augustinian Friary.
McGrath, Robert B. '71 (DET) Highland Park, MI St. Benedict.
McGrath, Robert D. '43 (HRT) Retired.
McGrath, Robert *o.m.i.* '55 (SAT)[K] San Antonio, TX Oblate Madonna Residence.
McGrath, Roger E. '71 (CAM) Somerdale, NJ Our Lady of Grace; Priests Personnel Board.
McGrath, Sean John *s.s.c.* '54 (LA) Los Angeles, CA St. Columban; [K] St. Columbans St. Columban's Foreign Mission Society.
McGrath, Sean (DEN) Denver, CO Guardian Angels.
McGrath, Thomas B. *s.j.* '64 (AGN) Agana, GU Dulce Nombre de Maria Cathedral – Basilica.
McGrath, Thomas E. '77 (JC) Jefferson City, MO St. Joseph Cathedral; Diocesan Consultors.
McGrath, Thomas J. '59 (SY) Skaneateles, NY St. Mary of the Lake; Board of Diocesan Consultors.
McGrath, Thomas M. (PAT) Special Assignment.
McGrath, Thomas (PAT) Adoption and Counseling Services.
McGrath, Thomas (BLX) AUXILIARY CHAPLAINS CONTRACT CHAPLAINS.
McGrath, William E. '47 (HRT) East Hartford, CT St. Christopher Retired.
McGrath, William J. *s.j.* '59 (SCR)[C] Scranton, PA The University of Scranton.
McGrath, William '00 (ROC)[E] Naples, NY Our Lady of the Lakes Catholic Community; Penn Yan, NY St. Michael; Penn Yan, NY St. Theresa; [M] Rochester, NY Catholic Committee on Scouting.
McGratty, John J. '71 (RVC) Manorville, NY St. Peter & Paul.
McGraw, John T. '56 (SY) Retired.
McGraw, John '56 (SY) Syracuse, NY Our Lady of Pompei Retired.
McGraw, Michael D. *m.ss.a.* (E) Erie, PA Our Lady of Peace; Administrative Cabinet; Office of Catholic Charities; Catholic Charities of the Diocese of Erie, Inc..
McGraw, Rene *o.s.b.* '62 (SCL)[I] Collegeville, MN St. John's Abbey, of the Order of St. Benedict.
McGraw, Robert H. '76 (LAN) Grand Ledge, MI St. Michael.
McGraw, Sean D. *c.s.c.* '01 (FTW)[I] Newton, MA Our Lady Help of Christians Parish.
McGraw, Sean *c.s.c.* '01 (CHI) Newton, MA Our Lady Help of Christians.
McGraw, Stephen F. '01 (ARL) Falls Church, VA St. Anthony's; Notaries.
McGraw, W. Howard *o.s.a.* '62 (PH) Philadelphia, PA St. Augustine.
McGray, James '67 (SD)[B] University of San Diego.
McGread, Thomas '53 (WCH)[L] Wichita, KS Serra Club of Wichita – Metro Retired.
McGready, Oliver '62 (WDC) Rockville, MD Shrine of St. Jude.
McGreevy, John G. *o.p.* '64 (DET) St. Clair Shores, MI St. Gertrude.
McGreevy, Thomas More *o.p.* '64 (P) Eugene, OR St. Thomas More; Veneta, OR St. Catherine of Siena.
McGregor, John F. *s.m.* '63 (HON) Honolulu, HI Star of the Sea.
McGregor, Mark D. *s.j.* '02 (BGP)[P] Fairfield, CT The Fairfield Jesuit Community–Fairfield University.
McGregor, Mark *s.j.* '96 (LA)[BB] Los Angeles, CA Loyola Marymount University.
McGroarty, Charles E. '62 (PH) Philadelphia, PA St. Matthew.
McGroarty, Hugh H. '45 (SCR) Pittston, PA St. John the Evangelist.
McGroarty, Joseph *o.p.* '46 (PRO)[P] Providence, RI St. Pius Priory; Providence, RI St. Pius V.
McGroarty, William K. *s.j.* '55 (BAL)[B] Timonium, MD Loyola Graduate Center –Timonium Campus; [S] Baltimore MD Jesuit Community of Loyola College, Inc..
McGrogan, James P. '64 (GRY) Michigan City, IN St. Mary of the Immaculate Conception; Michigan City, IN Sacred Heart Mission.
McGuffey, James '95 (MET) New Brunswick, NJ Sacred Heart; Phillipsburg, NJ St. Philip & St. James.
McGuigan, David *s.m.* '01 (CIN)[M] Dayton, OH Marianist Community; [C] Dayton, OH Marianist Novitiate.
McGuigan, Hugh J. *o.s.f.s.* '97 (VEN) Fort Myers, FL Our Lady of Light.
McGuigan, Hugh *o.s.f.s.* '97 (VEN)[G] Fort Myers, FL Oblates of St. Francis de Sales.
McGuigan, John J. '68 (PAT) Hopatcong, NJ St. Jude's.
McGuigan, Patrick *o.carm.* '79 (NY) Middletown, NY Our Lady of Mt. Carmel.
Mcguigan, Patrick *o.carm.* '79 (NY)[EE] Middletown, NY Carmelite Friars (North American Province of St. Elias).
McGuigan, Steven F.C. '90 (SPR) Stockbridge, MA St. Joseph's West Stockbridge, MA St. Patrick's.
McGuill, Martin F. '64 (ARL) McLean, VA St. Luke's; Air Force Reserve Chaplains.
McGuill, Martin (BAL) Interdiocesan Judges.
McGuine, Peter M. '90 (SD) On Special Assignment; Air Force Reserve Chaplains.
McGuiness, David '73 (MOB) On Leave from the Archdiocese.
McGuiness, David '77 (ATL) Peachtree City, GA Holy Trinity Catholic.
McGuiness, Edward '61 (SB) Desert Hot Springs, CA St. Elizabeth of Hungary.
McGuinn, James '88 (PH) Philadelphia, PA St. Mary of the Assumption.
McGuinness, Edward '61 (SB) Palm Desert, CA Sacred Heart.
McGuinness, Fergal '86 (SR) Adjutant Judicial Vicars; Diocesan Judges; Santa Rosa, CA Resurrection.
McGuinness, J. Roger '65 (OG) Plattsburgh, NY Newman Parish, John XXIII College Community; Campus Ministry; Committee for the Continuing Education of Clergy.
McGuinness, Michael '52 (MOB) Retired.
McGuinness, Richard M. '51 (NEW) Linden, NJ St. John the Apostle; Members; Respect Life Office; Holy Name Federation.
McGuire, Anthony W. '57 (PH) Retired.
McGuire, Anthony *o.f.m.* '52 (PAT)[M] Butler, NJ St. Anthony Friary.
McGuire, Anthony '65 (SFR) On Duty Outside the Archdiocese.
McGuire, Brendan '00 (SJ) San Jose, CA Holy Spirit; Notra Dame Club of San Jose/Silicon Valley.
McGuire, David '88 (RIC) Norfolk, VA Holy Trinity.
McGuire, Donald J. *s.j.* '61 (CHI)[N] Chicago, IL Woodlawn Jesuit Community.
McGuire, Edward *o.f.m.* '40 (PAT)[M] Ringwood, NJ Holy Name Friary, Inc..
McGuire, Francis X. *o.s.a.* '35 (PH).
McGuire, Frederick J. '81 (CIN) On Duty Outside the Archdiocese.
McGuire, J. Frederick '81 (CIN) St. Petersburg, FL Blessed Trinity.
McGuire, James D. *o.a.r.* '54 (LA) Montebello, CA St. Benedict.
McGuire, James E. '70 (PH) Absent on Leave.
McGuire, James J. *o.s.f.s.* '50 (WIL).
McGuire, John A. '50 (RVC) Sound Beach, NY St. Louis de Montfort Retired.
McGuire, John C. '79 (NY) Kingston, NY St. Colman Retired.
McGuire, John F. '76 (P) Coquille, OR Holy Name.
McGuire, John Patrick *o.p.* '73 (NY)[EE] New York St. Vincent Ferrer Priory.
McGuire, John *o.p.* '79 (NY)[HH] New York, NY New York University; [HH] New York, NY Pace University.
McGuire, Joseph E. '65 (DUB) Vinton, IA St. Mary.
McGuire, Ken '68 (ALB)[L] Lake George, NY St. Mary of the Lake.
McGuire, Kenneth H. *c.s.p.* '68 (NY)[EE] Jamaica Estates Paulist Fathers Generalate.
McGuire, Kenneth H. *c.s.p.* '68 (LA) Retired.
McGuire, Paul J. *s.c.j.* '68 (MIL)[O] Franklin, WI Dehon Study Center; [O] Franklin, WI Dehon Study Center.
McGuire, Richard G. *o.c.s.o.* '57 (CHR)[E] Moncks Corner, SC Mepkin Abbey.
McGuire, Richard J. '60 (E) Erie, PA St. Julia; CIVIL AIR PATROL.
McGuire, Richard '67 (SCL) Osakis, MN Immaculate Conception.
McGuire, Richard *o.s.c.* '73 (STP) Shoreview, MN St. Odilia; [M] Shoreview, MN Crosier Community of Shoreview.
McGuire, Robert A. *s.j.* '58 (RVC) Spirit Life Center.
McGuire, Stephen J. (NYC) Air National Guard Chaplains.
McGuire, Thaddeus '99 (PHX) Avondale, AZ St. Thomas Aquinas.
McGuire, Thomas D. '81 (LIN) Osceola, NE St. Vincent Ferrer.
McGuire, Tim (STU) Presbyteral Council.
McGuire, Timothy P. '84 (STU) Steubenville, OH Holy Rosary; Steubenville, OH Servants of Christ the King.
McGuire, William A. *o.s.a.* '65 (PH)[C] Villanova University.
McGuirk, Alan B. *m.s.* '56 (HRT)[M] Hartford, CT Missionaries of LaSalette.
McGuirk, John J. '70 (SC) Odebolt, IA St. Martin's; Wall Lake, IA St. Joseph's.
McGuirk, William C. '82 (GBG) Calumet, PA St. Stanislaus; United, PA St. Florian; Connellsville, PA Highlands Hospital & Health Center; Mount Pleasant, PA Frick Community Health Center.
McGuirl, John A. '72 (BRK) Jackson Heights, NY St. Joan of Arc.
McGuirl, John (BRK) Assignment Board.
McGurk, Patrick C. (HEL) Associate Judges.
McGurk, Patrick '58 (HEL) Retired.
McGurn, Richard H. *s.j.* '75 (CHI)[N] Chicago, IL Clark Street Jesuit Residence.
McHale, Anthony I. *s.j.* '55 (BAL)[S] Baltimore, MD Jesuit Fathers and Brothers Maryland Provincial Curia.
McHale, Charles P. '50 (NY) Retired.
McHale, Damian *c.p.* '54 (CHI)[N] Chicago, IL Daneo Hall.
McHale, Damian *c.p.* '61 (CHI)[N] Chicago, IL Passionist Community–Immaculate Conception Monastery.
Mchaughlin, Gregory '85 (AUS) Goldthwaite, TX St. Peter's.
McHenry, John *s.v.d.* '55 (SB)[A] Riverside, CA Society of the Divine Word Missionaries.
McHenry, Raymond '00 (DM) Carter Lake, IA Our Lady of Carter Lake; Council Bluffs, IA Holy Family; Council Bluffs, IA Our Lady, Queen of Apostles.
McHenry, Stephen P. '73 (PH) Ambler, PA St. Anthony of Padua.
McHenry, V. F. *o.p.* '49 (WDC) Washington, DC St. Dominic Church & Priory.
McHenry, Vincent Ferrer *o.p.* '49 (NY)[EE] New York, NY St. Catherine of Siena Priory.
McHugh, Alphonsus *ss.cc.* '69 (BWN) Harlingen, TX Queen of Peace.
McHugh, Brian J. '66 (BO) Somerville, MA St. Catherine of Genoa; Air Force Reserve Chaplains.
McHugh, Conall *o.f.m.conv.* '56 (CHL) Winston–Salem, NC Our Lady of Mercy.
McHugh, Connell A. '72 (SCR) West Hazleton, PA St. Francis of Assisi.
McHugh, Dennis (PAT) Retired.
McHugh, Donald '57 (P) Army National Guard Chaplains Retired.
McHugh, Francis *o.f.m.* '76 (BO)[AA] Boston, MA St. Anthony Shrine.
McHugh, Francis '97 (SAT) Jourdanton, TX St. Matthew's.
McHugh, James L. '60 (COV) Retired.
McHugh, James P. *o.s.f.s.* '66 (SLC)[B] Salt Lake City, UT Judge Memorial Catholic High School.
McHugh, James P. *o.s.f.s.* '77 (SLC)[F] Salt Lake City, UT Oblate House.
McHugh, James *c.p.* (MET)[H] Wilkes–Barre, PA St. Therese Residence.
McHugh, Jerome *o.f.m.cap.* '60 (NY)[EE] New York, NY Development Office:; [EE] White Plains, NY Capuchin Friars International, Inc.; [EE] White Plains, NY St. Francis of Assisi Foundation, c/o Capuchin Franciscans.
Mc Hugh, John F. *o.m.i.* '73 (BO)[Y] Tewksbury, MA Immaculate Heart of Mary Infirmary.
McHugh, John T. '93 (LC) Holmen, WI St. Elizabeth Ann Seton; Personnel Council; Elected Members.
McHugh, John W. '76 (HRT) Simsbury, CT St. Mary's.
McHugh, John *s.o.l.t.* '52 (CC)[G] Robstown, TX Society of Our Lady of the Most Holy Trinity.

McHugh, John '54 (LA) Santa Fe Springs, CA St. Pius X Retired.
McHugh, John *o.f.m.cap.* '69 (RVC) East Patchogue, NY St. Joseph the Worker.
McHugh, Joseph B. *s.j.* '58 (BGP)[P] Fairfield, CT The Fairfield Jesuit Community–Fairfield University.
McHugh, Kieran A. '70 (PAT)[C] Sparta, NJ Pope John XXIII High School.
McHugh, Michael J. '80 (BRK) Long Island City, NY Most Precious Blood.
McHugh, Michael *s.j.* '51 (SPK)[J] Spokane, WA Regis Community.
McHugh, Owen '50 (COS) Retired.
McHugh, Patrick J. '50 (LA) Torrance, CA Nativity Retired.
McHugh, Paul F. '53 (MAN) Retired.
McHugh, Peter J. '65 (PAT) Clifton, NJ St. Andrew the Apostle.
McHugh, Richard P. *s.j.* '60 (BAL) Woodstock, MD St. Alphonsus Rodriguez.
McHugh, Thomas J. '49 (CHI) Retired.
McHugh, William *o.m.i.* '52 (P) Shady Cove, OR Our Lady of Fatima.
McIlhenny, Bernard R. *s.j.* '56 (SCR)[C] Scranton, PA The University of Scranton.
McIlhon, John J. '48 (DM) Retired.
McIlhone, James P. '74 (CHI).
McIlmail, Edward *l.c.* '01 (HRT)[V] Orange, CT Legion of Christ, Inc..
McIlvane, Donald W. '52 (PIT) Retired.
McIlwain, Michael A. *o.s.b.* '94 (GBG) Latrobe, PA Latrobe Area Hospital; [H] Latrobe, PA Saint Vincent Archabbey.
McImail, Edward *l.c.* '01 (HRT).
McInerney, Blaise *o.carm.* '54 (JOL)[L] Darien Carmelite Provincial Office.
McInerney, Henry '77 (BLX) Ocean Springs, MS St. Alphonsus.
McInerney, Kieran *o.s.b.* '52 (FgM).
McInerney, Walter L. *c.s.c.* '36 (FTW)[I] Notre Dame, IN Holy Cross House.
McInerny, Kieran *o.s.b.* '52 (KCK)[H] Atchison, KS St. Benedict's Abbey.
McInerny, Lawrence B. '79 (CHR) Sullivan's Island, SC Stella Maris; College of Consultors; Presbyteral Council; Personnel Committee.
McInerny, Paul B. (BO) Secretary for Communications; Archdiocesan Judges; Communications; TV Apostolate; Canonical Affairs Committee.
McInnes, Val A. *o.p.* '61 (NO) New Orleans, LA St. Dominic; [S] New Orleans, LA The Patrons of the Vatican Museums in the South, Inc.; [S] Metairie, LA International Dominican Foundation.
McInnes, William C. *s.j.* '57 (BO)[V] Watertown, MA The Society of Jesus of New England–Provincial Offices; [V] Newton, MA The Jesuit Community at Boston College.
McInnis, Francis L. '56 (GF) Retired.
McInnis, Francis '57 (GF)[B] Great Falls, MT Great Falls Central Catholic High School.
McInnis, Francis (GF) Cum Christo/Cursillo; Big Sky Marriage Encounter.
McInnis, Gary L. '74 (LAN) Montrose, MI Good Shepherd.
McInnis, Gary '74 (LAN) Genesys Regional Medical Center; Egeler Correctional Facility.
McInnis, Gary '98 (LAN) Flint, MI St. Luke.
McInnis, John Kevin *s.c.j.* '57 (SP)[O] Pinellas Park, FL Priests of the Sacred Heart Retired.
McInnis, Kevin *s.c.j.* '57 (MIL)[O] Franklin, WI Villa Maria.
McInnis, Richard W. '69 (PRT) Retired.
McInnis, Thomas J. '57 (LC) Retired.
McInt, Thomas (FgM).
McIntire, William J. *m.m.* '67 (FgM).
McIntosh, Alan R. *o.s.b.* '61 (IND)[K] Evansville, IN.
McIntyre, Allen J. '56 (STP) Retired.
McIntyre, Gerald J. *s.j.* '74 (SY)[Q] Syracuse, NY Jesuits at LeMoyne, Inc..
McIntyre, James P. '38 (CLV) Cleveland, OH St. Ignatius of Antioch Retired.
McIntyre, James *o.f.m.cap.* '53 (NY)[EE] Yonkers, NY St. Clare Friary.
McIntyre, John J. '92 (PH) On Special or Other Archdiocesan Assignment.
McIntyre, John J. (PH) Office of the Cardinal.
McIntyre, John P. *s.j.* '63 (BO)[V] Newton, MA The Jesuit Community at Boston College.
McIntyre, Justin '81 (SR) Retired.
McIntyre, Louis *t.o.r.* '53 (VEN) Sarasota, FL Our Lady Queen of Martyrs.
McIntyre, Thomas J. *c.m.* '50 (LA)[Q] Montebello, CA DePaul Evangelization Center; [W] Montebello, CA DePaul Evangelization Center Retired.
McIntyre, Thomas J. *c.m.* '50 (ORG) Laguna Beach, CA St. Catherine of Siena.
McIntyre, Thomas J. *c.m.* '50 (LA)[Q] Montebello, CA DePaul Evangelization Center; [W] Montebello, CA DePaul Evangelization Center Retired.
McIntyre, Thomas J. '66 (CAM) Members.
McIntyre, William *o.f.m.* '95 (NY) Silver Spring, MD St. Camillus.
McKamy, Eldon J. '63 (OM) On Duty Outside the Archdiocese.
McKamy, Eldon J. '63 (P)[J] Portland, OR Providence St. Vincent Medical Center.
McKane, Paul *o.s.b.* '88 (WDC)[M] Washington, DC St. Anselm's Abbey.
McKane, William Paul *o.s.b.* '87 (SC) Sutherland, IA St. Cecilia's; Sutherland, IA Sacred Heart.
McKarns, James E. '62 (Y) North Canton, OH St. Paul Retired.
McKay, Alistair *c.ss.r.* '75 (CHR) Sumter, SC St. Jude.
McKay, Douglas M. '82 (PH)[Y] Philadelphia, PA Holy Family Home.
McKay, Francis '54 (NY) Retired.
McKay, James R. *s.m.* '44 (CIN)[M] Dayton, OH Marianist Community.
McKay, James '56 (SFR) San Mateo, CA St. Matthew; Serra Club of San Mateo Retired.
McKay, John F. '73 (WDC) Riverdale Park, MD St. Bernard.
McKay, Joseph '84 (ALB) Office of Administrative Advocate.
McKay, Michael *o.s.b.* (WH)[G] Wheeling, WV Wheeling Hospital.
McKay, Robert J. '51 (SY)[Q] Syracuse, NY Tommy Coyne Residence @ Dillon Hall Retired.
McKay, Robert '70 (SJ) Los Altos, CA St. William; O'Connor Hospital; [H] San Jose, CA O'Connor Hospital.
McKay, William E. '49 (PHX) Retired.
McKean, Benedict B. *o.s.b.* '59 (PEO).
McKean, Dan J. '87 (LAN)[A] Brighton, MI St. Patrick.
McKean, Dan (LAN) Priest's Assignment Commission.
McKean, Louis '47 (P) Retired.
McKeaney, James J. '69 (PH) Bryn Mawr, PA St. John Neumann.
McKearney, James L. '97 (HRT) On Duty Outside the Archdiocese.
McKee, Francis X. '66 (PH) Philadelphia, PA Holy Family.
McKee, Henry J. '72 (PH) Havertown, PA Sacred Heart.
Mckee, James *s.j.* '69 (E) Grampian, PA St. Bonaventure.
McKee, Jay R. '02 (WIL) Wilmington, DE St. Elizabeth.
McKee, Roderick D. '66 (WDC) Beltsville, MD St. Joseph.
McKee, William A. '83 (SEA) Seattle, WA St. John.
McKee, William *c.ss.r.* '48 (STL)[O] Liguori, MO Liguori Mission House/Redemptorists.
McKeefry, Brendan '67 (SAC) Elk Grove, CA Good Shepherd Catholic Church; Defenders of the Bond; Members.
McKeever, Brendan *c.p.* '84 (SD) Vista, CA St. Francis of Assisi.
McKeever, Frederick *o.f.m.* '54 (PAT)[M] Butler, NJ St. Anthony Friary.
McKeever, Henry *c.ss.r.* '48 (STL)[O] Liguori, MO Liguori Mission House/Redemptorists.
McKelvey, James P. '93 (PH) Newtown Square, PA St. Anastasia.
McKelvey, Thomas P. '62 (PH) Ridley Park, PA St. Madeline.
McKenna, Brian *o.f.m.cap.* '65 (BAK) Bend, OR St. Francis of Assisi.
McKenna, Colin J. (BGP) Greenwich, CT St. Roch.
McKenna, Denis R. '47 (NEW) Irvington, NJ St. Leo's Retired.
McKenna, Edward J. '65 (CHI) Other Assignments.
McKenna, Enda '64 (SAT) San Antonio, TX St. Leo.
McKenna, Eugene J. *s.s.j.* '47 (BAL)[S] Baltimore, MD St. Joseph's Manor.
McKenna, Eugene J. '63 (PRO) Middletown, RI St. Lucy; Deans.
McKenna, F. Charles '60 (ALN)[J] Bethlehem, PA Holy Family Villa Retired.
McKenna, Frank W. '94 (NOR) Canterbury, CT St. Augustine.
McKenna, George P. '44 (CHI) Chaplains Retired.
McKenna, James George '61 (DAL) On Duty Outside the Diocese; Dallas, TX Holy Cross.
McKenna, James T. '64 (NEW) Closter, NJ St. Mary.
McKenna, James *s.d.s.* '52 (MIL)[O] Manitowoc, WI St. Mary's Home for the Aged.
McKenna, James *s.d.b.* '80 (PMB)[D] Marrero, LA Archbishop Shaw High School; [G] Marrero, LA Archbishop Shaw Junior High School.
McKenna, Jerome *c.p.* '58 (MET)[H] Wheeling, WV Paul VI Pastoral Center.
McKenna, Jerome *c.p.* (WH) Diocesan Consultors; Hispanic Affairs; Office of Diocesan Planning and Pastoral Services.
McKenna, John H. *c.m.* '64 (BRK)[V] Jamaica, NY St. Vincent's House.
McKenna, John J. '45 (WOR) Retired.
McKenna, John J. '47 (NY) Retired.
McKenna, John L. '88 (PIT) Allegheny County, PA Mercy Health System of Pittsburgh–Pittsburgh Mercy Hospital.
McKenna, John T. '99 (SFE) Chama, NM St. Patrick.
McKenna, John *c.ss.r.* '77 (RVC) Bethpage, NY St. Martin of Tours.
McKenna, Joseph J. *o.s.f.s.* '57 (WIL) Wilmington, DE St. Francis Hospital; [I] Wilmington, DE St. Francis Hospital, Inc.; [J] Wilmington, DE DeSales House.
McKenna, Joseph R. '57 (PRT) Retired.
McKenna, Kenneth N. *o.s.f.s.* '85 (LAN)[L] Brooklyn, MI Lake Vineyard Camps, Inc., (De Sales Center).
McKenna, Kenneth N. *o.s.f.s.* '85 (TOL).
McKenna, Kevin E. '77 (ROC)[J] Rochester, NY St. Cecilia.
McKenna, Peter '57 (SAT) Retired.
McKenna, Philip '62 (MOB) Prattville, AL St. Joseph Church.
McKenna, Thomas F. *c.m.* '67 (FgM).
McKenna, Thomas F. *c.m.* '70 (PH)[B] Philadelphia, PA St. Vincent's Seminary; [B] Philadelphia, PA DePaul Novitiate; [AA] Philadelphia Congregation of the Mission.
McKenna, Thomas J. '72 (PIT) Pittsburgh, PA St. Patrick–St. Stanislaus Kostka; Allegheny County, PA West Penn Allegheny Health System–Allegheny General.
McKenna, Timothy '79 (SEA) Lakewood, WA St. Frances Cabrini; Air National Guard Chaplains.
McKenna, William A. *s.j.* '68 (NEW)[B] Jersey City, NJ Jesuit Center; [N] Jersey City, NJ Jesuits of Saint Peter's College, Inc..
Mckenna, William J. *s.s.j.* '61 (BAL)[S] Baltimore, MD St. Joseph's Manor.
McKenzie, John H. *o.s.b.* (MO) Navy Chaplains.
McKenzie, John J. *o.s.a.* '65 (PH) Conshohocken, PA SS. Cosmas and Damian; [C] Villanova University; [AA] Villanova, PA St. Thomas Monastery.
McKenzie, Mark D. *s.j.* '69 (STL) St. Louis, MO St. Matthew, Apostle; [O] St. Louis, MO St. Matthew Jesuit Community.
McKenzie, William L. '82 (KNX) Alcoa, TN Our Lady of Fatima.
McKeon, Gerard R. *s.j.* '86 (WOR) Storrs, CT St. Thomas Aquinas; [K] Storrs, CT University of Connecticut; [R] Holy Cross College; Chaplains.
McKeon, John Aedan *o.p.* '56 (NY)[EE] New York St. Vincent Ferrer Priory.
McKeon, Michael '65 (SAC) Roseville, CA St. Rose of Lima.
McKeon, Raymond T. '63 (NEW) Jersey City, NJ St. Paul's Retired.
McKeon, Robert F. '90 (NY) Patterson, NY Sacred Heart.
McKeon, Robert '59 (LAN) Gaines, MI St. Joseph.
McKeon, Thomas *s.s.s.* '50 (NY) New York, NY St. Andrew; New York, NY St. Jean Baptiste; Manhattan, NY New York Downtown Hospital – New York Infirmary.
McKeon, William E. *c.m.* '54 (PH)[AA] St. Catherine Infirmary.
McKeone, William '72 (TR) On Duty Outside the Diocese.
McKeough, Brendan J. *o.praem.* '53 (GB)[I] De Pere, WI St. Joseph Priory; [I] Laredo, TX Diocese of Cuernavaca, Mexico.
McKeown, Timothy P. '97 (SAV) Savannah, GA Most Blessed Sacrament.
McKercher, Mark J. '97 (OM) West Point, NE St. Aloysius; West Point, NE Assumption B.V.M.; Wisner, NE St. Joseph.
McKernan, Kenneth B. *c.s.b.* '66 (DET)[E] Redford, MI Catholic Central High School.
McKernan, Leo J. '83 (SCR) Montoursville, PA Our Lady of Lourdes.
McKernan, Louis F. *c.s.p.* '54 (NY)[EE] Jamaica Estates Paulist Fathers Generalate.
McKevitt, Gerald L. *s.j.* '75 (SJ)[B] Santa Clara, CA Jesuit Community.
McKiernan, J. Michael '91 (ORG) Special Assignment; Director of Clergy Personnel; Secretary to the Bishop; Clergy Personnel Board; Liturgical Commission; Building and Renovation Committee of the Liturgical Commission; Staff; Staff; Staff.
McKiernan, Joseph W. '51 (WOR) Sutton, MA St. Mark.
McKiernan, Thomas M. '51 (CHI) Retired.
McKiernan, Vincent W. *c.s.p.* '57 (COL)[J] Columbus, OH Campus Ministry.
McKillin, David *o.s.b.* '76 (LR)[I] Fort Smith, AR St. Scholastica Monastery–Motherhouse.
McKillip, Anthony *o.f.m.* (SFD)[L] Springfield, IL Our Lady of Angels Friary.
McKinley, Joseph *s.s.j.* '85 (NO) Fayette, MS St. Anne; Natchez, MS Holy Family.
McKinley, Michael J. '85 (LFT) Lafayette, IN St. Ann.
McKinley, Michael (LFT) Members.
McKinley, Steve *o.f.m.conv.* '94 (PEO) Peoria, IL Holy Family; Vicariates and Vicars.
McKinney, Floyd E. '80 (WCH) Newton, KS Our Lady of Guadalupe; Kansas State Industrial Reformatory.
McKinney, Francis *t.o.r.* '34 (ARL)[J] White Post, VA Sacred Heart Friary.
McKinney, James '96 (FAR) Rolla, ND Immaculate Heart of Mary; Rolla, ND St. Joachim.

McKinney, James (FAR) Diocesan College of Consultors.
McKinney, Michael '93 (LFT) Logansport, IN All Saints.
McKinney, Ronald H. *s.j.* '83 (SCR)[C] Scranton, PA The University of Scranton.
McKinney, Thomas A. '61 (GR) Retired.
McKinnon, Eymard *o.f.m.cap* '54 (HON) Pearl City, HI Our Lady of Good Counsel.
McKinstra, William M. '62 (RCK) Rockford, IL St. James Retired.
McKitrick, James V. '58 (RCK) Retired.
McKnight, Albert J. *c.s.sp.* '52 (SAT)[M] New Braunfels, TX Congregation of the Holy Ghost.
McKnight, James '59 (SAC) Nevada City, CA St. Canice Retired.
McKnight, Kevin '94 (PIT) Pittsburgh, PA Word of God.
McKnight, Robert J. '73 (BUR) Wallingford, VT St. Patrick.
McKnight, Shawn (WCH) Presbyteral Council/ Diocesan Consultors; Presbyteral Council.
McKnight, W. Shawn '94 (WCH)[A] Diocesan Building Commission; Office of Worship.
McLachlan, Frederick E. *s.s.e.* '64 (BUR)[A] Deans; Putney, VT Our Lady of Mercy.
McLafferty, Joseph (NY) Yorktown Heights, NY St. Patrick.
McLain, John J. *s.j.* '98 (R)[E] Raleigh Jesuit Community; Army Chaplains.
McLaughlin, Anthony K. (TYL) On Duty Outside the Diocese; Washington, DC Blessed Sacrament, Shrine of the Most.
McLaughlin, Anthony (MO) Defenders of the Bond.
McLaughlin, Anthony (TYL) Defenders of the Bond.
McLaughlin, Bernard P. '59 (BO) Canton, MA St. Gerard Majella.
McLaughlin, Charles '62 (BRK) Brooklyn, NY St. Anselm's.
McLaughlin, Daniel F. '61 (FgM).
McLaughlin, Daniel P. *s.t.* '63 (TUC) Tucson, AZ Blessed Kateri Tekakwitha; [I] South Tucson, AZ Blessed Kateri Tekakwitha Parish Center.
McLaughlin, Daniel *o.s.a.* '83 (PH)[D] Drexel Hill, PA Monsignor Bonner High School.
McLaughlin, Don E. '81 (JOL) Wheaton, IL St. Michael.
McLaughlin, Donald E. '67 (NEW) Westfield, NJ St. Helen.
McLaughlin, Edward J. '52 (BO) Bridgewater, MA St. Thomas Aquinas; Senior Priests Retired.
McLaughlin, Edward J. '59 (CHI) Orland Park, IL St. Michael.
McLaughlin, Farrell E. '71 (PRO) Cranston, RI St. Ann.
McLaughlin, Greg '85 (AUS) San Saba, TX St. Mary's.
McLaughlin, Hugh J. '63 (HBG) Spring Grove, PA Sacred Heart.
McLaughlin, James J. '70 (PH) Lansdale, PA Corpus Christi.
McLaughlin, James W. (MET) Edison, NJ St. Matthew.
McLaughlin, James '73 (SB) San Bernardino, CA Our Lady of the Assumption.
McLaughlin, James (SB) Vicars Forane; Appointed Members.
McLaughlin, John E. '62 (BO) Somerville, MA St. Benedict.
McLaughlin, John R. '95 (BO) Foxborough, MA St. Mary.
McLaughlin, John '61 (SEA) Retired.
McLaughlin, John '66 (MIA) Holy Name Society Retired.
McLaughlin, John '71 (NEW)[N] Cliffside Park, NJ St. Patrick's Missionary Society.
McLaughlin, Joseph J. '66 (PH) Richboro, PA St. Vincent de Paul.
McLaughlin, Joseph J. *s.m.* '72 (FgM).
McLaughlin, Joseph M. *s.s.e.* '70 (BUR)[E] Colchester, VT Society of St. Edmund.
McLaughlin, Joseph P. *o.praem.* '70 (WIL)[B] Claymont, DE Archmere Academy.
McLaughlin, Joseph P. *o.praem.* '70 (PH)[AA] Paoli, PA Daylesford Abbey.
McLaughlin, Joseph P. '01 (TR) Bayville, NJ St. Barnabas.
McLaughlin, Michael (DM) Greenfield, IA St. John; Greenfield, IA St. Patrick.
McLaughlin, Neil P. *s.j.* '59 (SCR)[C] Scranton, PA The University of Scranton.
McLaughlin, Owen F. '41 (MIL) Retired.
McLaughlin, Owen '44 (MIL)[M] Wauwatosa, WI St. Camillus Health Center, Inc..
McLaughlin, Patrick A. '03 (OM) Omaha, NE St. Vincent de Paul.
McLaughlin, Patrick J. '61 (BO) Medford, MA St. Joseph.
McLaughlin, Patrick J. (SCR) Hazleton, PA Holy Trinity; Deans.
McLaughlin, Paul E. '71 (VEN) Military Chaplains.
McLaughlin, Paul F. (VEN) Navy Chaplains.
McLaughlin, Paul J. '55 (BO) Senior Priests Retired.
McLaughlin, Peter A. '78 (CAM) Pomona, NJ Assumption.
McLaughlin, Richard C. (PRT) Deans; Director of Chaplaincy Services.
McLaughlin, Richard G. '74 (PRT) Bangor, ME St. John's.
McLaughlin, Richard P. '68 (BO) Everett, MA St. Therese.
McLaughlin, Richard '74 (PRT)[G] Bangor, ME St. Xavier's Home.
McLaughlin, Robert A. '73 (PH) Kimberton, PA St. Basil the Great.
McLaughlin, Robert E. '66 (CHI) Park Ridge, IL Mary, Seat of Wisdom; [X] Chicago, IL Foundation for Adult Catechetical Teaching Aids.
McLaughlin, Thomas C. '56 (VIC) On Special or Other Diocesan Assignment; Vicars General; Chancellor; Diocesan Consultors; Presbyteral Council; Judicial Vicar; Priests' Personnel Board; Diocesan Finance Board; Propagation of the Faith, Holy Childhood Association; Mission Cooperative Plan.
McLaughlin Thomas D. '76 (SCR) Stroudsburg, PA St. Luke's; Deans.
McLaughlin Thomas J. *o.s.a.* '53 (OAK) Castro Valley, CA Our Lady of Grace.
McLaughlin, Thomas R. '81 (NEW) Newark, NJ Beth Israel Medical Center.
McLaughlin, Thomas W. '49 (LA) Los Angeles, CA St. Teresa of Avila Retired.
McLaughlin, Thomas '81 (NEW) Elizabeth, NJ Blessed Sacrament; Chaplains.
McLaughlin, William A. '92 (BRK) Brooklyn, NY St. Agnes.
McLaughlin, William H. '68 (BO) Marblehead, MA Our Lady, Star of the Sea.
McLaughlin, William J. '70 (TR) Asbury Park, NJ Holy Spirit; The Haitian Apostolate.
McLaughlin, William '58 (ORG) Newport Beach, CA Our Lady Queen of Angels; Diocesan Finance Council.
McLaverty Albert J. (CAM) Assistant Vocation Directors for Recruitment; Northfield, NJ St. Bernadette; Advocates.
McLean, Barry L. '90 (SAN) Brownwood, TX St. Mary's.
McLean, Barry (SAN) Presbyteral Council; Continuing Education of the Clergy.
McLean, Edward J. '52 (HRT) West Hartford, CT St. Brigid's; Special and other Archdiocesan Assignment; Catholic Library and Information Center.
McLean, George F. *o.m.i.* '55 (WDC)[M] Washington, DC Oblate Community; [V] Washington, DC Council for Research in Values and Philosophy.
McLean, Thomas '02 (LIN) Lincoln, NE Blessed Sacrament.
McLean, William '69 (LA) Long Beach, CA St. Athanasius.
McLearen, Daniel J. '92 (HRT) New Haven, CT St. Francis; Auditors (Part–time Case Instructors).
McLellan Daniel *o.f.m.* '76 (WDC)[B] Washington, DC Washington Theological Union; [M] Silver Spring, MD Gemelli House.
McLellan James R. '70 (FR) North Dighton, MA St. Joseph's.
McLellan, Michael F. '76 (BO) Jamaica Plain, MA Blessed Sacrament; Jamaica Plain, MA Our Lady of Lourdes.
McLelland, James R. (SHP) Shreveport, LA St. Catherine of Siena.
McLelland, James (SHP) College of Consultors; Presbyteral Council; Priests' Retirement Board.
McLeod, David H. (PAT) On Duty Outside the Diocese; AUXILIARY CHAPLAINS CONTRACT CHAPLAINS.
McLeod, Donald J. *c.s.b.* '78 (OAK)[C] Oakland, CA Bishop O'Dowd High School.
McLeod, Frederick G. *s.j.* '62 (STL)[C] Saint Louis University; [O] St. Louis, MO Jesuit Community Corporation at St. Louis University - Jesuit Hall.
McLeod Frederick G. *s.j.* '62 (BO)[V] Boston The Society of Jesus of New England–Provincial Offices.
McLeod Paul *ss.cc.* '84 (HON)[G] Kaneohe, HI Sacred Hearts Center.
McLernan, Richard L. *o.s.f.s.* '57 (LAN)[B] Jackson, MI Lumen Christi Catholic High School.
McLernon, Thomas M. '57 (HBG) On Duty Outside the Diocese.
McLernon, Thomas M. '57 (MIL).
McLeroy, Jacob (SFE)[B] Springer, NM New Mexico Boys' School.
McLinden, James E. *s.s.j.* '62 (WDC)[B] Washington, DC Josephite Pastoral Center.
McLinden, James E. *s.s.j.* '71 (BAL) Baltimore, MD St. Francis Xavier.
McLinden, James *s.s.j.* '69 (WDC)[B] Washington, DC St. Joseph's Seminary.
McLoone, Joseph C. '88 (PH) Philadelphia, PA St. Therese of the Child Jesus; College of Consultors; Council of Priests.
McLoud, Steven J. '94 (SC) Churdan, IA St. Columbkille's; Churdan, IA St. Paul's; Presbyteral Council.
McLoughlin, Brendan (PAT) On Duty Outside the Diocese.
McLoughlin, James W. '65 (RCK) Woodstock, IL St. Patrick; Woodstock, IL St. Mary; Deans.
McLoughlin, John F. *c.ss.r.* '92 (FgM).
McLoughlin, John T. '73 (NY) Mt. Vernon, NY St. Ursula.
Mcloughlin, John *c.ss.r.* '90 (STV) Frederiksted, St. Croix, VI Church of St. Patrick.
McLoughlin, Luke '66 (STA) Jacksonville, FL St. Matthew's; Catholic Women, Council of.
McLoughlin, Michael P. '81 (NY) Warwick, NY St. Stephen.
McLoughlin, Nicholas '66 (VEN) Port Charlotte, FL St. Charles Borromeo; Respect Life Department; Graduate Studies.
McLoughlin, Paul J. '71 (SPC) Ozark, MO St. Joseph the Worker.
McLoughlin, Richard J. '69 (PH) Absent on Leave.
McMackin, Thomas P. '63 (ORL) Ormond Beach, FL Prince of Peace.
McMahon, Albert F. *o.f.m.* '60 (HRT) Palenville, NY Sacred Heart.
McMahon, Aloysius J. '53 (OM) Retired.
McMahon, Bartholomew *o.f.m.* '62 (FgM).
McMahon, Bernard '48 (NY) Retired.
McMahon, Brian F. '85 (BO) Bellingham, MA Assumption; Bellingham, MA St. Blaise; Members.
McMahon, Charles E. *s.s.j.* '58 (BLX) Pascagoula, MS St. Peter the Apostle.
McMahon, Edward J. *s.j.* '60 (NY)[EE] New York, NY Xavier Jesuit Community.
McMahon, Edward M. '70 (BO) Senior Priests Retired.
McMahon, Francis X. *s.s.e.* '50 (BUR) Brattleboro, VT St. Michael Retired.
McMahon, George J. *s.j.* '53 (NY)[EE] New York, NY Murray–Weigel Hall.
McMahon, Gerald J. '59 (ROC) Retired.
McMahon, Gerald J. *s.j.* '62 (NY)[EE] New York, NY Murray–Weigel Hall.
McMahon, Gerard J. '59 (ROC) Webster, NY Holy Spirit.
McMahon, Gerard T. '61 (BO) On Duty Outside the Archdiocese.
McMahon, James B. '53 (BRK)[V] Douglaston, NY Bishop Mugavero Residence Retired.
McMahon, John A. *o.p.* '68 (WDC) Washington, DC St. Dominic Church & Priory; [M] Washington, DC Center for Assisted Living.
McMahon, John J. '38 (CHI) Retired.
McMahon, John J. '48 (PHX) Special Assignment; [H] Phoenix, AZ Mt. Claret Center; [K] Phoenix, AZ St. Vincent De Paul Society; Directors; Cursillo Movement.
McMahon, John R. (PMB) Catholic Charities.
McMahon, John '66 (PMB) Boca Raton, FL St. Joan of Arc; College of Consultors; Secretary.
McMahon, Joseph M. '43 (P) Retired.
McMahon, Joseph R. '71 (WIL) Apostleship of Prayer; Wilmington, DE St. Mary Magdalen.
McMahon, Joseph S. '68 (P) Lake Oswego, OR Our Lady of the Lake; [P] Lewis & Clark College; Liturgical Commission.
McMahon, Joseph V. '84 (NSH) Madison, TN St. Joseph.
McMahon, Joseph W. '56 (CLV) Retired.
McMahon, Joseph '56 (CLV) Kirtland, OH Divine Word.
McMahon, Kevin T. '75 (WIL)[A] On Duty Outside the Diocese.
McMahon, Kieran M. '65 (SAC) Sacramento, CA St. Robert.
McMahon, Martin *o.m.i.* '56 (PMB) Riviera Beach, FL St. Francis of Assisi.
McMahon, Michael F. '88 (CHI) Buffalo Grove, IL St. Mary.
McMahon, Patrick *o.carm.* '76 (WDC)[B] Washington, DC Whitefriars Hall; [B] The Carmelitana Library; [L] Darien Carmelite Provincial Office.
McMahon, Thomas F. *c.s.v.* '54 (CHI)[N] Arlington Heights, IL Viatorian Province Center–Clerics of St. Viator.
McMahon, Timothy M. *s.j.* '87 (STL)[F] St. Louis, MO St. Louis University High School, George H. Backer Memorial; [O] St. Louis, MO Leo Brown Jesuit Community; [O] St. Louis, MO The Jesuits of the Missouri Province; (FgM).
McMahon, Walter M. '73 (SJ) San Jose, CA Church of the Transfiguration.
McMahon, William J. '45 (NY) Cortlandt Manor, NY Holy Spirit Retired.
McManamin, Francis G. *s.j.* '61 (BAL)[B] Timonium, MD Loyola Graduate Center –Timonium Campus; [S] Baltimore, MD Jesuit Community of Loyola College, Inc..
McManamon, James *o.f.m.* '49 (CLV)[O] Brooklyn, OH Padua Franciscan Friary.
McManamon, John M. *s.j.* '80 (DET)[K] Temperance, MI.
McManus, Charles J. '42 (NY) Bronx, NY St. Gabriel; Yonkers, NY St. Bartholomew Retired.
McManus, Eamon '54 (WDC) Retired.
McManus, Eugene P. *s.s.j.* '49 (BAL)[S] Baltimore, MD St. Joseph Society of the Sacred Heart House of

Central Administration; [S] Baltimore, MD St. Joseph's Manor.
McManus, Francis J. *s.j.* '73 (BO)[V] Weston, MA Campion Jesuit Community.
McManus, Frederick R. '47 (BO) Senior Priests Retired.
McManus, Gerald D. '79 (PH) Military Chaplains; Air Force Chaplains.
McManus, Hugh F. '61 (NY) Scarsdale, NY Our Lady of Fatima.
McManus, J. Fleming '47 (CHR) Retired.
McManus, John H. *o.m.i.* '56 (STP)[P] Buffalo, MN Christ the King Retreat Center.
McManus, John H. *o.m.i.* '56 (SCL)[M] St. Cloud, MN St. Therese Center for Special Ministry.
McManus, Joseph L. '56 (BAL) Baltimore, MD Immaculate Heart of Mary Retired.
Mc Manus, Joseph '96 (CC)[G] Robstown, TX Society of Our Lady of the Most Holy Trinity.
McManus, Michael K. '85 (FR) Raynham, MA St. Ann; Chancellor; Diocesan Consultors; Members.
McManus, Michael '48 (SAT) San Antonio, TX St. James the Apostle.
McManus, Patrick S. '99 (PH) Jamison, PA St. Cyril of Jerusalem; [D] Warminster, PA Archbishop Wood Catholic High School.
McManus, Paul C. '65 (DUB) Waterloo, IA St. Mary of Mt. Carmel; Waterloo, IA Sacred Heart; Waterloo, IA Immaculate Conception.
McManus, Paul G. (BO) Lawrence, MA Asuncion de la Virgen Maria.
McManus, Paul J. '42 (BO) Senior Priests; Spiritual Directors: Retired.
McManus, Richard *o.f.m.* '83 (MRY)[H] San Juan Bautista, CA St. Francis Retreat Center.
McManus, Robert T. '52 (PH) College of Consultors; Council of Priests Retired.
McManus, Thomas F. *s.j.* '63 (NEW)[N] Jersey City, NJ Jesuit Community of St. Peter's Prep, Inc..
McManus, Thomas F. *s.j.* '98 (NEW)[C] Jersey City, NJ St. Peter's Preparatory School.
McManus, Thomas J. '68 (PH).
McManus, Thomas J. '69 (PH)[A] Narberth, PA St. Margaret.
McManus, Thomas *o.s.a.* '70 (ORG) Buena Park, CA St. Pius V.
McMaster, Brian L. '01 (AUS) Georgetown, TX St. Helen's.
McMenamin, John J. *o.s.f.s.* '59 (TOL)[C] Toledo, OH St. Francis de Sales High School; [J] Toledo, OH Retired.
McMenamy, Alvin *s.m.* '53 (STL)[O] St. Louis, MO Maryland Avenue Marianist Community; [O] St. Louis, MO Cure of Ars Marianist Community.
McMenemie, James P. '53 (NEW) Archdiocesan Judges Retired.
Mc Menemie, James '53 (NEW) Lyndhurst, NJ St. Michael's.
McMichael, Steve *o.f.m.conv.* '02 (STP) Bloomington, MN St. Bonaventure.
McMillan, Cliff J. '90 (DEN) Glenwood Springs, CO St. Stephen.
McMillan, John F. *c.p.* '56 (PIT)[N] Pittsburgh, PA St. Paul of the Cross Monastery.
McMillan, Keith P. *s.j.* '93 (FgM).
McMillan, Robert G. *s.j.* '62 (BO) Roxbury, MA St. Francis de Sales–St. Philip; [V] Boston, MA Loyola House; [V] Boston The Society of Jesus of New England–Provincial Offices; Ex Officio.
McMillan, Robert *s.j.* (BO) Planning and Research.
McMillen, Michael *s.c.j.* '67 (CHI)[N] Chicago, IL.
McMillen, Michael *s.c.j.* '67 (JOL) Elmhurst, IL Elmhurst Memorial Hospital.
McMillin, Charles '02 (LKC) Diocesan Board of Administration; Secretariats; Lake Charles, LA Our Lady Queen of Heaven.
McMorland, Timothy R. '02 (WDC) Bowie, MD Sacred Heart.
McMorrow, Kevin *s.a.* '58 (NY)[EE] Garrison, NY Franciscan Friars of the Atonement.
McMullan, John '61 (SEA) Retired.
McMullan, John '61 (ORL) Orlando, FL Mary Queen of the Universe Shrine.
McMullen, Aidan C. '47 (NEW)[EE] New York, NY Murray–Weigel Hall.
McMullen, Brendan J. *o.p.* '43 (STP) Minneapolis, MN St. Albert the Great.
McMullen, Francis R. '51 (RVC) Priests Released from Diocesan Assignment Retired.
McMullen, John *o.s.b.* '66 (SFS) Wilmot, SD St. Mary; [F] Marvin, SD Blue Cloud Abbey; [I] Marvin, SD Blue Cloud Abbey Retirement Trust.
McMullen, Roger '67 (SHP) Retired.
McMullin, Daniel T. '81 (ROC) Geneseo, NY St. Mary.
McMullin, Ernan '49 (FTW)[B] University of Notre Dame Du Lac.
McMullin, Finian *o.f.m.* '46 (STL)[O] Alton, IL St. Clare Villa.
McMurry, John E. *s.s.* '56 (NSH) On Duty Outside the Diocese.
McMurry, John E. *s.s.* '56 (BAL)[R] Baltimore, MD St. Mary's Spiritual Center.
McMurry, Vincent deP. *s.s.* '49 (BAL)[O] Baltimore, MD St. Charles Villa.
McMurry, Vincent deP. *s.s.* '49 (NSH) On Duty Outside the Diocese.
McMurtrie, James W. '62 (ARL).
McNair, Andrew *l.c.* (PRO)[G] Warwick, RI Overbrook Academy at Our Lady of Providence Center.
McNalis, John P. '76 (CHI) Chicago, IL St. Gabriel.
McNally, Dennis E. *s.j.* '74 (PH)[C] Jesuit Fathers; [AA] Loyola Center and Manresa Hall.
McNally, Edward F. '95 (SY)[T] Oswego, NY Newman Foundation, Inc., State University of New York.
McNally, Joseph J. '58 (IND) Retired.
McNally, Michael J. '73 (PMB)[A] On Duty Outside the Diocese.
McNally, Michael R. '59 (SB) Retired.
McNally, Nathan '57 (STL)[J] St. Louis, MO St. Anthony's Medical Center.
McNally, Stephen '86 (RIC) Bedford, VA Holy Name of Mary.
McNally, Theodore A. *o.f.m.* '55 (PAT)[M] Butler, NJ St. Anthony Friary.
McNally, Thomas *c.s.c.* '61 (FTW)[A] Notre Dame, IN Moreau Seminary.
McNally, Vincent M. *s.j.* '48 (BUF)[O] Buffalo, NY Canisius Jesuit Community.
McNally, Vincent '84 (MIL).
McNamara, Anthony *o.carm.* '69 (JOL)[L] Darien Carmelite Provincial Office.
McNamara, Brian J. '84 (RVC) St. James, NY SS. Philip and James; Priests' Personnel Policy Board; Associate Vocation Directors; Senate of Priests (Presbyteral Council/College of Consultors); Air Force Reserve Chaplains.
McNamara, Dennis L. *s.j.* '76 (Wisconsin)[M] Washington, DC The Jesuit Community at Georgetown University.
McNamara, Donald P. '61 (PH) Coatesville, PA St. Cecilia.
McNamara, Eugene P. '53 (BO) Senior Priests Retired.
McNamara, Francis J. *s.j.* '54 (ROC)[B] Rochester, NY McQuaid Jesuit High School.
McNamara, James '71 (RVC) Nesconset, NY Church of the Holy Cross.
McNamara, John J. '53 (ALN) Port Carbon, PA St. Stephen.
McNamara, John P. '56 (CHI) Retired.
McNamara, Joseph M. '39 (ROC)[Q] Syracuse, NY Tommy Coyne Residence @ Dillon Hall Retired.
McNamara, Michael J. '80 (BO) Unassigned.
McNamara, Patrick M. *o.s.m.* '49 (P)[L] Portland, OR The Grotto, The National Sanctuary of Our Sorrowful Mother.
McNamara, Patrick M. *o.s.m.* '49 (CHI)[N] Chicago Order of Friar Servants of Mary (Servites) United States of America Province, Inc..
McNamara, Patrick V. '60 (NY) New Rochelle, NY St. Gabriel.
McNamara, Philip D. '56 (WOR) Retired.
McNamara, Philip *s.a.c.* '58 (FWT) Stephenville, TX St. Brendan.
McNamara, Robert F. '36 (ROC)[M] Rochester, NY Archivist (Diocese of Rochester Archives); Diocesan Archives Retired.
McNamara, Robert J. '69 (LA) Woodland Hills, CA St. Bernardine of Siena.
McNamara, Stephen E. '67 (VEN) Fort Myers, FL Church Of The Resurrection Of Our Lord; Deans; Presbyteral Council; Priest Personnel Board; Priest Personnel Board.
McNamara, Thomas F. *m.s.* '47 (HRT).
McNamara, Thomas J. '82 (SAG) Essexville, MI St. John the Evangelist.
McNamara, Vincent P. '60 (NY) VCBC.
McNamara, William *o.c.d.* '51 (MIL)[O] Milwaukee Provincial Offices – Discalced Carmelites.
McNamara, William '65 (SAT) Elmendorf, TX St. Anthony; College of Consultors; Archdiocesan Council of Catholic Women.
McNamara, William (SAT) In Rural Area; Archdiocesan Presbyteral Council.
McNamee, Charles W. '50 (RCK) Censores Librorum Retired.
McNamee, Francis G. '95 (ATL) Roswell, GA St. Peter Chanel; Vicar for Clergy; Deans.
McNamee, Frank (ATL) Director of Priest Personnel.
McNamee, James P. '73 (LC) Adams, WI St. Joseph; Oxford, WI St. Ann.
McNamee, John P. '59 (PH) Philadelphia, PA St. Malachy.
McNamee, Maurice B. *s.j.* '40 (STL)[O] St. Louis, MO Jesuit Community Corporation at St. Louis University – Jesuit Hall.
McNea, Mark C. '89 (WIN) Slayton, MN St. Ann's; Slayton, MN St. Columba's; Slayton, MN St. Mary.
McNearney, John *g.h.m.* '62 (CIN)[M] Cincinnati Headquarters of Glenmary Home Missioners.
McNeely, Maurice '58 (HON) Retired.
McNeese, Robert J. '98 (SPK) Colville, WA Immaculate Conception.
McNeese, Robert '98 (SPK) Kettle Falls, WA Sacred Heart of Jesus; Colville, WA Pure Heart of Mary; Members.
McNeff, Thomas C. '77 (CHI) Schiller Park, IL St. Maria Goretti.
McNeil, Aubrey *o.f.m.* '85 (NY) Bronx, NY Holy Cross.
McNeil, Dennis M. '75 (CLV) Euclid, OH St. Robert Bellarmine; [Z] Euclid, OH St. Robert's Holy Name Society Boosters.
McNeil, Joel D. '87 (AUS) Round Rock, TX St. William's.
McNeil, Joel (AUS) Presbyteral Council.
McNeil, John R. '61 (BO) On Duty Outside the Archdiocese.
McNeil, Lawrence J. '73 (HBG) Hanover, PA Basilica of the Sacred Heart of Jesus.
McNeill, Don *c.s.c.* '65 (CHI)[D] Niles, IL Notre Dame High School.
McNeill, Malachy '44 (B) Retired.
McNeilly, Dennis P. *s.j.* '85 (OM)[K] Omaha, NE Jesuit Community at Creighton University.
McNelis, Francis J. '65 (ALN)[J] Bethlehem, PA Holy Family Villa Retired.
McNelis, Paul D. *s.j.* '77 (WDC)[M] Washington, DC The Jesuit Community at Georgetown University.
McNellis, Paul *s.j.* '87 (NY)[V] Newton, MA The Jesuit Community at Boston College.
McNerney, James '81 (ALB) Troy, NY St. Paul the Apostle; Troy, NY St. Peter.
McNew, Dwayne A. '95 (COL) Portsmouth, OH Holy Redeemer.
McNichol, Daniel '87 (HON) Retired.
McNicholas, Raymond J. *s.s.c.* '49 (BUF) Orchard Park, NY St. Bernadette.
McNicholas, Stephen '53 (ORL) Retired.
McNicholas, Walter F. *o.s.a.* '52 (CHI)[N] Chicago, IL St. Rita Monastery.
McNicholl, Michael P. '66 (BUF) Strykersville, NY St. Mary, Queen of the Rosary.
McNiff, James '36 (SFE) Retired.
McNiff, William T. *o.s.c.* '43 (SCL) Onamia, MN The Church of the Holy Cross of Onamia; [I] Onamia, MN Crosier Monastery.
McNomara, Peter '64 (CC) Retired.
McNulty, Edward P. '93 (SD) Adjutant Judicial Vicar.
McNulty, Edward '93 (SD) Alpine, CA Queen of Angels; College of Consultors; Plymouth, MI Our Lady of Good Counsel.
McNulty, Edwin J. '44 (COL) Retired.
McNulty, Francis J. '52 (NEW) Retired.
McNulty, Frank '52 (NEW) Summit, NJ St. Teresa's.
McNulty, Gerard J. '69 (LA) Military Chaplains.
McNulty, J. Brendan '74 (CLV) Cleveland, OH SS. Philip and James; Administrative Leave.
McNulty, James D. *c.s.p.* '53 (NY)[EE] Jamaica Estates Paulist Fathers Generalate.
McNulty, James *c.s.p.* '53 (LA) Los Angeles, CA St. Paul the Apostle.
McNulty, Jerry (LAV) Military Chaplains.
McNulty, John P. '73 (CLV) Euclid, OH Holy Cross.
McNulty, John '43 (SP) Retired.
McNulty, John '74 (PRO) Newport, RI St. Augustin.
McNulty, Joseph D. '69 (CLV) Cleveland, OH St. Augustine.
McNulty, Joseph (CLV) Office of Ministry for Persons with Disabilities.
McNulty, Martin J. '03 (BO) Middleborough, MA Sacred Heart.
McNulty, Patrick J. '60 (FTW) On Special Assignment.
McNulty, Patrick '53 (LA) Los Angeles, CA St. Bernard.
McNulty, Robert E. '56 (NOR) Retired.
McNulty, T. Michael *s.j.* '73 (WDC)[M] Washington, DC Leonard Neale House.
McNulty, Theodore '66 (CHI) Chicago, IL St. Thomas More.
McNulty, William J. '61 (CHI) Lake Forest, IL St. Patrick.
McNulty, William J. '64 (NOR) Dayville, CT St. Joseph; Dayville, CT St. Ignatius; District Moderators.
McNulty, William (NOR) Members.
McPadden, Charles J. *m.m.* '69 (NY)[N] Denver, CO Maryknoll Fathers and Brothers; [EE] Maryknoll Maryknoll Fathers and Brothers.
McPadden, Malachy M. *o.s.b.* '57 (NEW)[N] Newark, NJ Newark Abbey.
McPartland, Guy *o.carm.* '55 (NEW) Paramus, NJ Carmelite Chapel of St. Therese.
McPartland, Paul G. '57 (BO) Senior Priests Retired.
McPhail, J. Stuart *o.p.* '69 (PRO)[B] Providence, RI Providence College; [P] Providence St. Thomas Aquinas Priory at Providence College.
McPhee, John R. *c.ss.r.* '46 (STL)[O] Liguori, MO St. Clement Health Care Center.
McPhee, Marvin '65 (SFS) Episcopal Vicar for Clergy Retired.
McPhee, Marvin (SFS) Vicar General; Diocesan Consultors; Presbyteral Council.
McPhillips, James G. '83 (CLV) Newbury, OH St. Helen.
McPhillips, Thomas J. '44 (SFS)[D] Mitchell, SD Avera Queen of Peace Retired.
McPolin, James *s.j.* '62 (LA) Venice, CA St. Mark.

McPolin, Patrick *c.m.f.* '43 (LA)[Q] Rancho Dominguez, CA Dominguez Seminary Inc..

McQuade, Brian '94 (RVC) Baldwin, NY St. Christopher.

McQuade, James F. *c.s.p.* '56 (NY) New York, NY St. Paul the Apostle; Roosevelt Site.

McQuaid, Eugene (PAT) Retired.

McQuaid, Thomas W. '79 (CHI).

McQuesten, Mark A. '87 (MAR)[A] Norway, MI St. Mary.

McQuillan, Cornelius T. *c.s.sp.* '75 (ARE) Sabana Hoyos, PR Inmaculado Corazon de Maria.

McQuillan, Edward F. *c.m.* '44 (PH).

McQuillan, Neil *c.s.sp.* (ARE)[AA] Priest's Senate (Consejo Presbiteral).

McQuillen, Paul G. *s.s.e.* '77 (NO) Marrero, LA St. Joseph the Worker; [I] New Orleans, LA Bishop Perry Middle School.

McQuillen, Thomas J. '94 (TOL) On Duty Outside the Diocese; Associates.

McQuinn, Peter B. '91 (CHI) Chicago, IL Epiphany; College of Consultors.

McRae, Cornelius M. '61 (BO) Norwood, MA St. Catherine of Siena.

McReavy, Thomas J. *c.s.b.* '59 (GAL)[Q] Houston, TX Dillon House.

McReynolds, Eugene *o.s.b.* '70 (OM)[I] Boys Town, NE Father Flanagan's Boys' Home; [K] Elkhorn, NE Mount Michael Abbey.

McShane, James J. (BUR) Army National Guard Chaplains.

McShane, John A. '57 (BRK) Brooklyn, NY Holy Family; [V] Douglaston, NY Bishop Mugavero Residence Retired.

McShane, John '74 (LAV)[F] Las Vegas, NV Department of Pastoral Ministry.

McShane, Joseph A. *s.j.* (NY)[C] Tarrytown, NY Marymount College of Fordham University.

McShane, Patrick E. '79 (CLV) Retired.

McSherry, John G. *s.j.* '72 (NY)[EE] New York, NY West Side Jesuit Community.

McSherry, Patrick *o.f.m.cap.* '78 (DET)[K] Detroit, MI Provincialate.

McSherry, Thomas '71 (OKL) Oklahoma City, OK St. Patrick.

McSorley, Aidan *o.s.b.* '69 (KC) Parnell, MO St. Joseph's; [A] Conception, MO Conception Seminary College; [J] Parnell, MO St. Joseph Parish.

McSorley, Gerald '64 (LA) Los Angeles, CA St. Bernard.

McSorley, James P. *o.m.i.* '46 (OAK)[N] Oakland, CA Oblate Residence.

McSorley, Matthew T. *o.s.b.* '49 (CHL)[J] Belmont, NC Belmont Abbey.

McSpiritt, John *s.t.* (JKS) Priests' Council.

McStravog, Patrick B. *o.s.a.* '89 (PH)[G] Malvern, PA Malvern Preparatory School for Boys; [AA] Malvern, PA Augustinian Friars (O.S.A.).

McSweeney, Brian T. '88 (NY) Cold Spring, NY Our Lady of Loretto.

McSweeney, Edward F. '52 (PIT) Retired.

McSweeney, James '74 (SR) Middletown, CA St. Joseph.

McSweeney, Jeremiah F. (WH) Weston, WV St. Patrick's.

McSweeney, John J. '74 (CHL) Charlotte, NC St. Matthew.

McSweeney, John R. *o.c.d.* '52 (SR)[M] Oakville, CA Carmelite House of Prayer.

McSweeney, John R. (BUR) Elected Members; Judges; Diocesan Consultors Retired.

McSweeney, John Reginald *o.c.d.* '52 (SR)[L] Oakville, CA Carmelite House of Prayer.

McSweeney, John '48 (MRY) Retired.

McSweeney, Joseph *s.s.c.* '58 (PRO)[P] Bristol, RI St. Columban's Retirement House.

McSweeney, Thomas J. '71 (E) Erie, PA Holy Trinity; Warren, PA St. Joseph; Co Directors; Office of Communications and Public Relations; Administrative Cabinet.

McSweeney, William *o.m.i.* '52 (WDC)[M] Washington, DC Oblate Community.

McSwigan, Gerardo *c.ss.r.* '55 (CGS) Fajardo, PR Santiago Apostol.

McSwiggan, Thomas '67 (SAT) San Antonio, TX St. Patrick.

McTaggart, Edward P. '55 (SFR) Young Ladies' Institute; Serra Club of San Francisco (Golden Gate) Retired.

McTague, Charles H. '47 (NEW) Newark Comitum Retired.

McTague, Charles '47 (NEW) Harrison, NJ Holy Cross Retired.

McTague, Thomas '57 (GF) Retired.

McTavey, Lawrence G. '55 (ALB) Cohoes, NY St. Bernard.

McTavey, Lawrence (ALB) Deans.

McTeigue, Robert J. *s.j.* '97 (BAL)[S] El Paso, TX.

McTeigue, Robert *s.j.* '97 (GAL)[A] Houston, TX St. Mary's Seminary.

McTighe, Edward P. *s.j.* '61 (P)[J] Portland, OR Providence St. Vincent Medical Center.

McTighe, Simon *o.s.b.* '53 (IND)[K] St. Meinrad, IN St. Meinrad Archabbey.

McTigue, Norman P. '70 (BUF) Buffalo, NY Buffalo Psychiatric Center; Buffalo, NY Our Lady of Loretto.

McTommoney Brian *o.f.m.* '53 (WDC)[M] Washington, DC Commissariat of the Holy Land, Franciscan Monastery – Mount St. Sepulchre.

McVean, John J. *o.f.m.* '67 (NY) New York, NY St. Francis of Assisi.

McVeigh, James E. '73 (PH) Collingdale, PA St. Joseph.

McVeigh, John J. '58 (LAV) Retired.

McWeeney, Brian E. '73 (NY) Poughkeepsie, NY St. Martin de Porres; Auditors.

McWhorter, Michael L. '92 (ATL) Milledgeville, GA Sacred Heart of Jesus; [N] Milledgeville, GA.

Mead, Brian E. '69 (BUR)[D] Burlington, VT St. Joseph's Home.

Mead, Gary '97 (NY) New Rochelle, NY Holy Family.

Mead, James Herbert *s.j.* '62 (NO) New Orleans, LA Immaculate Conception.

Mead, Leland C. '68 (NU) On Duty Outside the Diocese.

Meade, Christopher '98 (HRT) Southington, CT St. Thomas.

Meade, Denis *o.s.b.* '55 (KCK)[H] Atchison, KS St. Benedict's Abbey; (FgM).

Meade, Henry J. '51 (BO) Senior Priests Retired.

Meade, James C. '52 (RVC) Retired.

Meade, James W. '86 (GRY) Chesterton, IN St. Patrick; Judges.

Meade, James '52 (BRK)[S] Queens Village, NY Queen of Peace Residence.

Meade, James '81 (CIN) Cincinnati, OH Corpus Christi.

Meade, John F. '43 (NY) Retired.

Meade, Maurice P. '48 (BO) Senior Priests Retired.

Meaden, Paul *o.s.b.* '84 (SFE)[I] Pecos, NM Our Lady of Guadalupe Abbey; [K] Pecos, NM Our Lady of Guadalupe Olivetan Benedictine Abbey.

Meagher, Cletus *o.s.b.* '71 (BIR)[I] Cullman, AL St. Bernard Abbey Foundation.

Meagher, Frank J. '60 (COL) Buckeye Lake, OH Our Lady of Mt. Carmel.

Meagher, John J. *s.s.e.* '66 (BUR) Highgate Center, VT St. Louis; Swanton, VT Nativity of the Blessed Virgin Mary.

Meagher, Joseph A. '92 (NEW) Linden, NJ St. John the Apostle.

Meagher, Michael T. '65 (SY) Binghamton, NY St. Andrew; Priests' Personnel Committee.

Meagher, Thomas L. '64 (DET) White Lake, MI St. Patrick.

Meagher, Thomas '40 (SB) Retired.

Mealey, Mark S. *o.s.f.s.* '78 (ARL) Vienna, VA Our Lady of Good Counsel.

Mealey, Mark S. (ARL) Moderator of the Curia & Episcopal Vicar for Pastoral Services; Vicar for Religious; Judicial Vicar; Diocesan Judges; Diocesan Consultors.

Meaney, Brendan J. '65 (CAM) Turnersville, NJ SS. Peter and Paul.

Meaney, John J. *m.m.* '59 (NY).

Meaney, Patrick '87 (CC)[G] Hebbronville, TX Catholic Solitudes.

Meaney, Peter J. *o.s.b.* '51 (PAT)[M] Morristown, NJ St. Mary's Abbey.

Means, David A. '81 (STL) On Duty Outside Archdiocese; On Duty Outside the Archdiocese.

Meany, John J. *o.p.* '87 (CHI) River Forest, IL St. Vincent Ferrer; [N] Chicago Dominicans (Provincial Office).

Meany, Michael G. '80 (CHI) Oak Forest, IL St. Damian.

Meany, Neill R. *s.j.* '54 (YAK) Yakima, WA St. Joseph's.

Meany, Thomas '55 (CC) Judges Retired.

Measer, Donald L. '63 (BUF) Tonawanda, NY St. Amelia Retired.

Meaux, Glenn '80 (LAF) On Duty Outside the Diocese.

Meaux, Glenn '80 (CC)[G] Robstown, TX Society of Our Lady of the Most Holy Trinity.

Mecca, Gregg D. '96 (BGP) Westport, CT St. Luke.

Meccia, Francis S. *m.m.* '66 (NY).

Mech, John J. '95 (DET)[EE] Redford, MI Our Lady of Loretto.

Mecir, Joseph S. '80 (CLV) Cleveland, OH Sacred Heart of Jesus; Cleveland Clinic Foundation.

Meconi, David V. *s.j.* '03 (CHI)[N] Chicago Chicago Province of the Society of Jesus–Provincial Office.

Mecwel, Pawel J. '90 (MAR) Sault Sainte Marie, MI St. Joseph.

Medairos, Anthony J. '73 (BO) Carver, MA Our Lady of Lourdes; Army Reserve Chaplains.

Medas, Michael B. '88 (BO) Concord, MA St. Bernard; [EE] Boston, MA KOLBE Association, Inc.; Air Force Reserve Chaplains.

Medas, Michael J. (BO) Deaf Apostolate.

Medeiros, Antonio S. '54 (BO) Senior Priests Retired.

Medeiros, Antonio (SB) Ontario, CA St. Elizabeth Ann Seton.

Medeiros, Arnold R. '75 (FR) Wareham, MA St. Patrick's.

Medeiros, Benjamin *t.o.r.* '77 (FWT) Fort Worth, TX St. Andrew.

Meder, Stephen A. *s.j.* '43 (DET)[P] Hamtramck, MI St. Ladislaus.

Medina, Antonio '82 (SJ) San Jose, CA St. Anthony.

Medina, David '02 (TLS) Stillwater, OK St. Francis Xavier; Stillwater, OK St. John University Parish and Catholic Student Center; Diocesan Senators.

Medina, Fabio E. '83 (SFR) San Francisco, CA St. Peter.

Medina, Francisco '89 (SJN) San Juan, PR San Miguel Arcangel; Istepa.

Medina, George A. '97 (TR) Trenton, NJ SS. Peter and Paul.

Medina, George '87 (PCE) On Duty Outside the Diocese.

Medina, Hector '84 (FWT) Wichita Falls, TX Our Lady of Guadalupe; Presbyteral Council and Consultors.

Medina, Ignazio C. '78 (JC) Bonnots Mill, MO Our Lady of Help; Linn, MO St. George; Appointed Members.

Medina, Jose Antonio *m.g.* '82 (SJ) San Jose, CA St. Patrick.

Medina, Juan B. '69 (CGS) Cidra, PR Nuestra Senora de Fatima.

Medina, Julian '73 (SAC) Rio Vista, CA St. Joseph.

Medina, Mauricio '64 (B) Cursillo Movement Retired.

Medina, Miguel Angel *sch.p.* '55 (SJN) San Juan, PR Santisimo Salvador.

Medina, Odel *s.t.* '01 (PAT)[M] Stirling, NJ Holy Spirit Missionary Cenacle.

Medina, Oscar Gomez '02 (SAC) South Lake Tahoe, CA St. Theresa.

Medina, Rolando '71 (MIA) Hialeah, FL Santa Barbara.

Medina, Tito *m.s.c.* '92 (RCK)[G] Aurora Missionaries of the Sacred Heart Community.

Medina–Cruz, Jamie '99 (ALX) Ferriday, LA St. Patrick.

Medio, Joseph Paul *f.p.o.* '99 (FR)[H] New Bedford, MA Franciscans of Primitive Observance.

Medley, Robert W. '90 (MET) Plainsboro, NJ Queenship of Mary; Vice Chancellors; Board for Seminary Education.

Medley, William F. '82 (L) Bardstown, KY Basilica of St. Joseph Proto–Cathedral; College of Consultors; Deans; Ex Officio.

Medlin, Douglas S. '02 (ATL) Alpharetta, GA St. Thomas Aquinas.

Medlock, Scott '96 (ANC) Anchorage, AK St. Patrick.

Medow, David '01 (JOL) Plainfield, IL St. Mary Immaculate.

Medrano, Marcus '86 (DEN) Denver, CO Sacred Heart.

Medve, Kenneth A. '97 (ALN) Military Chaplains; Navy Chaplains.

Medwid, John M. '90 (ALB) Schenectady, NY St. Anthony; Presbyteral Council; Diocesan Board of Consultors.

Medynski, Francis J. '48 (BGP)[P] Stamford, CT The Catherine Dennis Keefe Queen of the Clergy Retired Priests' Residence Retired.

Medynski, Francis J. (BGP)[P] Stamford, CT.

Mee, Michael *o.s.b.* '78 (P)[L] St. Benedict, OR Mt. Angel Abbey; [N] St. Benedict, OR Mount Angel Abbey Guest House.

Meehan, Barry C. *s.j.* '02 (BGP)[P] Fairfield, CT The Fairfield Jesuit Community–Fairfield University; [X] Fairfield, CT The Institute for Religious Education and Pastoral Studies (REAPS).

Meehan, Barry M. '78 (PRO) Warwick, RI St. Timothy.

Meehan, Francis X. '61 (PH) West Chester, PA SS. Simon and Jude.

Meehan, Gabriel '59 (CHL) Retired.

Meehan, Gery G. *o.praem.* '60 (GB) Green Bay, WI St. Willebrord; [I] De Pere, WI St. Joseph Priory.

Meehan, James H. '50 (PH) Retired.

Meehan, James L. '41 (OG) Alexandria Bay, NY St. Francis Xavier Retired.

Meehan, James L. '51 (OG) Retired.

Meehan, James *s.j.* '59 (HEL) Missoula, MT St. Francis Xavier.

Meehan, John T. '64 (NY) Mt. Vernon, NY St. Mary.

Meehan, Joseph J. '61 (PH) Primos, PA St. Eugene.

Meehan, Joseph P. '54 (NY) Suffern, NY Sacred Heart.

Meehan, Joseph '66 (STA) Atlantic Beach, FL St. John the Baptist; Diocesan Consultors; Presbyteral Council; Priests' Spirituality Committee.

Meehan, Kenneth E. *s.j.* '71 (WDC).

Meehan, Peter '68 (NY) New York, NY Our Lady of the Rosary.

Meehan, Terrance A. '67 (CIN) Monroe, OH Our Lady of Sorrows.

Meehan, Thomas J. *o.s.a.* '80 (CHL) Charlotte, NC St. John Neumann.

Meehan, Timothy A. '59 (HRT) North Haven, CT St. Therese.

Meehling, Donald J. '58 (SFD) Springfield, IL St. Aloysius; Commission for the Care of Infirm and Retired Priests.

Meeks, Delphyn J. '83 (BEA) Buna, TX St. Francis of Assisi Mission; Mauriceville, TX St. Maurice.

Meemken, Eugene A. '59 (SCL).

Meenan, Francis P. *c.s.sp.* '44 (PIT) Pittsburgh, PA Sacred Heart.

Meenan, T. J. (ATL) Atlanta, GA Shrine of the Immaculate Conception.

Meenihan, Regis J. '92 (E) St. Joseph.

Meersman, Jerome *c.i.c.m.* '49 (ARL)[J] Arlington, VA

Missionhurst, C.I.C.M.–Central House and Provincialate.
Megge, Paul '98 (GAY) Cheboygan, MI St. Mary–St. Charles; Elected Members; Cursillo.
Mehan, Joseph A. '96 (DAL) Kaufman, TX St. Ann; Procurator–Advocates.
Mehm, Richard J. '77 (BO) Malden, MA Immaculate Conception; NORTH REGION.
Mehok, William J. *s.j.* '43 (MIL)[O] Wauwatosa, WI Jesuit Community at St. Camillus.
Mehrkens, William '50 (CR) Diocesan Board of Conciliation and Arbitration; Red Lake, MN St. Mary's Mission Church; Native American Task Force Retired.
Meidl, Gerald S. '74 (NU) Marshall, MN Holy Redeemer; Members; Priest Personnel Board.
Meier, Allen J. '51 (COV)[C] Park Hills, KY Notre Dame Academy Retired.
Meier, Alphonse H. *o.s.b.* '48 (GBG)[H] Latrobe, PA Saint Vincent Archabbey.
Meier, Cyprian T. '69 (BIS) Mandan, ND Spirit of Life.
Meier, Denis '63 (SFS) Beresford, SD St. Teresa of Avila.
Meier, Emeric *o.f.m.* '68 (BO)[AA] Boston, MA St. Anthony Shrine.
Meier, Gary '98 (STL) Kirkwood, MO St. Peter.
Meier, Gerald A. '66 (STL) Webster Groves, MO Mary, Queen of Peace.
Meier, John P. '67 (NY) On Duty Outside the Archdiocese.
Meier, John P. (FTW)[B] University of Notre Dame Du Lac.
Meier, Laverne G. '58 (MAD) Sauk City, WI St. Norbert.
Meier, Raymond O. '36 (E) Retired.
Meier, Timothy J. *s.j.* '91 (DET)[K] Temperance, MI.
Meiergerd, Godfrey A. '42 (OM) Retired.
Meighan, Thomas A. '63 (WDC) Silver Spring, MD St. John the Evangelist Retired.
Meik, Thomas J. *c.m.* '48 (CHI)[N] Chicago DePaul Vincentian Residence.
Meiklejohn, Norman *a.a.* '54 (WOR) Fiskdale, MA St. Anne's and St. Patrick's.
Meilak, Peter Paul *o.f.m.* '49 (FgM).
Meiluta, George J. *s.m.* '40 (WDC) Retired.
Meiman, Louis J. '87 (L) Louisville, KY Immaculate Heart of Mary; Louisville, KY St. Gabriel the Archangel.
Meinen, Dennis W. '87 (SC) Special Assignment; [D] Sioux City, IA Holy Spirit Retirement Home.
Meiners, Andrew *c.ss.r.* '70 (STL)[O] Liguori, MO Liguori Mission House/Redemptorists.
Meinhart, C. Joseph '91 (OKL)[K] Norman, OK University of Oklahoma.
Meinholz, David J. '94 (MIL) Milwaukee, WI St. Philip Neri; Milwaukee, WI St. Sebastian.
Meinholz, John M. '77 (MAD) Madison, WI Immaculate Heart of Mary; Elected.
Meiring, Arnold *c.pp.s.* '40 (CIN)[B] Carthagena, OH St. Charles.
Meiring, Bernard *c.pp.s.* '55 (TOL) Ottawa, OH SS. Peter and Paul.
Meirose, Harold R. *s.j.* '62 (DET)[K] Hamtramck, MI St. Ladislaus.
Meis, Peter *o.f.m.cap.* '67 (FgM).
Meisel, Charles F. '50 (BAL) Hydes, MD St. John the Evangelist Retired.
Meisel, Gerald '61 (LA) Long Beach, CA St. Matthew.
Meismer, Paul J. '69 (PEO) Spring Valley, IL Immaculate Conception.
Meissner, Robert J. '69 (SAG) Bay City, MI St. Vincent de Paul; Judges.
Meissner, Robert (SAG) Clergy Benefit Society.
Meissner, William W. *s.j.* '61 (New York)[V] Newton, MA The Jesuit Community at Boston College.
Meister, Alan (R).
Meister, Andrew H. '44 (OM) Retired.
Meitl, Roger K. '59 (SAL) Oakley, KS Immaculate Conception; Oakley, KS St. Joseph's.
Meitl, Roger (SAL) Selden, KS Sacred Heart; Episcopal Vicars; Personnel Board; Diocesan Council of Education; Oberlin, KS Sacred Heart.
Mejak, Heliodore '35 (KCK) Kansas City, KS Holy Family.
Mejia, Alberto (PH) Philadelphia, PA St. Francis Xavier.
Mejia, Gustavo '68 (LA) Huntington Park, CA St. Matthias.
Mejia, Jose '91 (LA) Pacoima, CA Guardian Angel; [J] Marina Del Rey, CA Daniel Freeman Marina Hospital; [J] Mission Hills, CA Providence Holy Cross Medical Center; Hospital Chaplains.
Mejia, Joseph '91 (LA)[J] Burbank, CA Providence Saint Joseph Medical Center.
Mejia, Luis G. '98 (LA) South El Monte, CA Epiphany.
Mejia, Miguel (SPK) Othello, WA Sacred Heart.
Mejia, Ricardo '76 (SD) Unassigned.
Mejias, Carlos Ortiz '97 (SJN) Graduate Studies.
Melancon, Aaron '97 (LAF) Loreauville, LA St. Joseph; Loreauville, LA Our Lady of Victory; Vocations.
Melancon, Bill John (LAF) Advocates.
Melancon, Bill '93 (LAF) Carencro, LA St. Peter.
Melancon, Leo F. *m.m.* '32 (NY).
Melancon, Louis '63 (LKC)[EE] Cameron, LA Our Lady Star of the Sea.
Melancon, Thomas J. *s.j.* '75 (PBL) Trinidad, CO Most Holy Trinity, Trinidad Area Catholic Community (Trinidad Cluster); [F] Trinidad, CO Business Address:.
Melaniuk, J. Maciej '86 (MET) South Plainfield, NJ Our Lady of Czestochowa.
Melcher, Michael '92 (LUB) Vicars Forane; Lubbock, TX St. Patrick.
Melchior, Frank '59 (GB) Retired.
Melchior, Gerald P. '90 (OM) North Bend, NE St. Charles Borromeo; Snyder, NE St. Leo.
Melchior, Thomas '65 (KCK) Retired.
Mele, Joseph M. '73 (PIT) Pittsburgh, PA St. Sebastian.
Mele, Rudolph '77 (NO) Retired.
Meledom, Joseph '68 (FWT) Valley View, TX St. John.
Melendez, Daniel J. '02 (CAM) Woodbury Heights, NJ St. Margaret's; Advocates.
Melendez, Hector '80 (PAT) Clifton, NJ SS. Cyril and Methodius; Passaic, NJ Our Lady of Fatima.
Melendez, Jeronimo *o.s.m.* '72 (ELP) El Paso, TX St. Ignatius of Loyola.
Melendez, Jose Refugio Onate '00 (ATL) Dalton, GA St. Joseph's.
Melendez, Michael S. '89 (BRK) Jackson Heights, NY Our Lady of Fatima.
Melepuram, John '78 (MIA) Coral Springs, FL Our Lady of Health Parish, Florida; Coral Springs, FL Our Lady of Health Catholic Church.
Melepuram, John '78 (DAL) Garland, TX St. Thomas the Apostle.
Melepuram, John (SYM) Eparchial Consultors.
Melevage, F. J. '42 (GRY) Retired.
Melillo, William J. '66 (NEW).
Melito, August A. '64 (DAL)[C] Dallas, TX Doctors Hospital; Dallas, TX St. Bernard of Clairvaux.
Melito, Ignatius M. *c.m.* '51 (STL) St. Louis, MO St. Catherine Laboure; [O] St. Louis, MO Lazarist Residence.
Melka, John *o.c.d.* '64 (SR)[M] Oakville, CA Carmelite House of Prayer.
Melley, James J. '77 (MIA) Retired.
Melley, James '91 (LA) Retired.
Mellitt, John *o.f.m.cap.* '75 (NY) New Paltz, NY St. Joseph; [EE] New Paltz, NY St. Joseph Friary.
Mello, Matthew '87 (ORL) Lakeland, FL Church of the Resurrection.
Melloh, John A. *s.m.* '61 (STL)[O] South Bend, IN.
Melloh, John A. *s.m.* '73 (FTW)[B] University of Notre Dame Du Lac.
Mellone, Michael J. '76 (WDC) Washington, DC St. Thomas Apostle; Secretariats; Secretary for Services for Clergy, Religious Men and Secular Institutes; Director of Priests Personnel; Pastoral Center Special Ministries.
Mellone, Vincent P. '65 (BO) Woburn, MA St. Barbara; NORTH REGION.
Melmer, John H. '91 (ARL) Alexandria, VA St. Mary's.
Melnic, James '78 (PHU) Melrose Park, PA Annunciation of the B.V.M.; [D] Philadelphia, PA Ascension Manor, Inc..
Melnic, James (PHU) College of Archeparchial Counsultors; Presbyteral Council; Archdiocesan Radio Programs; Archeparchial Seminary Advisory and Admissions Board; Sheptytsky Educational Center.
Melnick, John E. '86 (SCR) Freeland, PA St. Ann's.
Melnick, John P. '00 (HRT) Hartford, CT Cathedral of St. Joseph.
Melnick, Robert *o.f.m.conv.* '97 (CHI)[N] Chicago, IL Conventual Franciscans of St. Bonaventure Province; [N] Chicago, IL Franciscan House of Studies.
Melnick, William D. '75 (WIL) Wilmington, DE Church of the Holy Child.
Melo, Nicholas P. '83 (HRT) Bristol, CT St. Anthony's.
Meloch, Chester A. '43 (BUF) Retired.
Melody, William P. *c.s.c.* '59 (FTW)[I] Notre Dame, IN Holy Cross House.
Melone, Mark E. '78 (NTN) Sacramento, CA St. George.
Melone, Mark (NTN) Presbyteral Council; Liturgical Commission.
Melton, Thomas K. '59 (TLS) Retired.
Meluskey, Andre J. '59 (HBG) Carlisle, PA St. Patrick.
Melvin, Thomas P. '01 (WIN)[A] Winona, MN Immaculate Heart of Mary Seminary; Vocations; Vocations Advisory Council; Emmaus House.
Melzer, Howard *s.c.j.* '58 (MIL)[O] Franklin, WI Villa Maria.
Memenas, Vytas '57 (JOL) Retired.
Mena, Abel '02 (SR) Petaluma, CA St. Vincent de Paul.
Mena, Antonio '81 (ELP) Fabens, TX Our Lady of Guadalupe.
Mena, Jesus M. *o.a.r.* '86 (NY) Bronx, NY St. John Vianney, Cure of Ars.
Mena, Jose L. '97 (NY) Yonkers, NY St. Peter.
Mena, Jose '61 (ORL) Retired.
Mena, Roberto *s.t.* '01 (LA) Compton, CA Our Lady of Victory; Compton, CA Sagrado Corazon, Sacred Heart.
Menapace, James L. '63 (MAR) Retired.
Menard, Clarence C. *o.m.i.* '58 (NO).
Menard, Francis A. '54 (OG) Retired.
Menard, Gerard E. *s.j.* '99 (KC)[D] Kansas City, MO Rockhurst High School; [J] Kansas City, MO Rockhurst Jesuit Community.
Menard, Gerard E. *s.j.* '99 (STL)[O] St. Louis, MO The Jesuits of the Missouri Province.
Menard, Gerard E. *s.j.* '99 (KC)[D] Kansas City, MO Rockhurst High School; [J] Kansas City, MO Rockhurst Jesuit Community.
Menard, Gilbert B. '55 (OG) Judges Retired.
Menard, J. Godden *c.m.* '55 (GLP) Tuba City, AZ St. Jude.
Menard, James R. *s.j.* '54 (SJ)[M] Los Gatos, CA Sacred Heart Jesuit Center.
Menard, Raymond '39 (SAL) Salina, KS Cathedral of the Sacred Heart; Newspaper.
Menard, Robert *o.f.m.* '72 (ARL) Triangle, VA St. Francis of Assisi.
Menard, Wilfred A. *c.s.c.* '59 (COS)[F] Cascade, CO Holy Cross Novitiate.
Menasco, Edward J. '90 (OKL) Norman, OK St. Joseph's; Special Assignment.
Menasco, Edward T. (OKL) Permanent Diaconate.
Menasco, Edward (OKL) Advocates.
Menchaca, Gerardo '95 (SJ)[A] On Duty Outside the Diocese.
Menchaca, Luis Gerardo '95 (SJ) Special Assignment.
Mencsik, John C. *c.pp.s.* '74 (FTW) Fort Wayne, IN Most Precious Blood.
Mende, Dennis W. '83 (BUF) Jamestown, NY SS. Peter and Paul.
Mendes, Joseph *m.s.f.s.* '63 (ATL) Lawrenceville, GA St. Marguerite D'Youville; [K] Lawrenceville The Missionaries of St. Francis De Sales.
Mendez, Angel '90 (MGZ) Aguadilla, PR St. Charles Borromeo; Diocesan Consultors.
Mendez, David Perez '87 (MGZ) Moca, PR Our Lady of Monserrate.
Mendez, Enrique *s.d.b.* '52 (SJN) San Juan, PR San Juan Bosco.
Mendez, Jose del Carmen '02 (CHI) Chicago, IL St. James.
Mendez, Juan '73 (SFE) Albuquerque, NM Nativity of the Blessed Virgin Mary.
Mendez, Luis A. (PCE)[B] The Pontifical Catholic University of Puerto Rico.
Mendez, Manuel '87 (YAK) Elgin, IL St. Joseph.
Mendez, Oscar A. *o.f.m.* '89 (SFR) San Francisco, CA St. Anthony of Padua.
Mendez, Oscar *s.j.* '64 (MIA)[H] Miami, FL Villa Javier.
Mendez, Rafael '93 (MGZ) Lajas, PR Our Lady of the Purification; Youth Apostolate.
Mendez, Rafael '94 (PH) On Duty Outside the Archdiocese.
Mendez, Rafael '94 (ARE) Quebradillas, PR San Raphael.
Mendicoa, John M. (BO) Roslindale, MA Sacred Heart.
Mendis, Nimal *c.h.s.* '82 (NY) Fishkill Correctional Facility; [EE] Glenham, NY Apostolic Society of the Crusade of the Holy Spirit.
Mendl, Michael *s.d.b.* '78 (SP)[E] Tampa, FL Mary Help of Christians School.
Mendonca, John '67 (CHI) Wauconda, IL Transfiguration.
Mendonca, John '79 (BRK) Rego Park, NY Our Lady of the Angelus.
Mendonca, Robert '00 (OAK) Livermore, CA St. Charles Borromeo.
Mendoza, Andres '95 (LUB) Lubbock, TX Our Lady of Guadalupe; Cursillo Movement.
Mendoza, Andrew '95 (LUB)[A] Lubbock, TX Office for Cursillo Movement.
Mendoza, Elias A. (PEO).
Mendoza, Fernando *o.f.m.* '74 (ELP) El Paso, TX Our Lady of Guadalupe.
Mendoza, Gerardo '88 (SB) Fontana, CA St. George.
Mendoza, Jose Eduardo '84 (SFR) San Francisco, CA St. Peter.
Mendoza, Jose '99 (OM) South Sioux City, NE St. Michael.
Mendoza, R. Anthony '99 (LAR) La Pryor, TX St. Joseph; Presbyteral Council; Office of Respect Life.
Mendyuk, Yaroslav '97 (STN) Chicago, IL SS. Volodymyr and Olha.
Menegatto, Gaetano *c.s.j.* '42 (CLV)[O] Avon, OH Congregation of St. Joseph.
Menegay, David C. '88 (PIT) Conway, PA Our Lady of Peace; [C] Baden, PA Quigley Catholic High School.
Menegay, Greg '98 (PHX) Carefree, AZ Our Lady of Joy; College of Consultors.
Meneghello, Serafino '49 (GRY) Retired.
Menei, Francis T. '67 (PH) On Duty Outside the Archdiocese.
Menei, Francis '67 (HBG) Manheim, PA St. Richard.
Menendez, Adolph *s.x.* '68 (PAT) (FgM).
Menendez, Jose L. '77 (MIA) Miami, FL Corpus Christi.
Meneses, Miguel (ELP) Westway, TX Immaculate Heart of Mary.
Meney, Olivier (LC) Elected Members.
Menez, Alex A. '70 (LA) Artesia, CA Holy Family.

Menezes, Mark '59 (JOL) Monee, IL St. Boniface.
Menezes, Wade *c.p.m.* (OWN)[F] Auburn, KY Fathers of Mercy.
Meng, David P. '89 (ARL) Spotsylvania, VA St. Matthew.
Meng, Robert A. '45 (ROC) Retired.
Menge, James P. '62 (SPR) Retired.
Mengel, Mark *s.s.c.* '71 (CHI)[J] Chicago, IL Holy Cross Hospital; [N] Chicago, IL Columban Fathers Theologate.
Menghini, Peter D. '80 (SCR) Harleigh, PA Sacred Heart of Jesus.
Mengon, Albert *s.d.b.* '66 (FgM).
Menig, Walter J. *c.m.* '47 (BAL)[S] Emmitsburg, MD Vincentian House.
Menihane, Daniel J. *o.s.a.* '57 (ALB) Waterford, NY St. Mary of the Assumption.
Meninger, William *o.c.s.o.* '58 (DEN)[N] Snowmass, CO St. Benedict's Monastery.
Menino, Alvaro *m.s.p.* '03 (LA) Los Angeles, CA Our Lady of Solitude; Los Angeles, CA Santa Isabel.
Menke, Andrew V. '99 (LIN) Beatrice, NE St. Joseph's; Advocates.
Menke, George R. *s.j.* '75 (IND)[D] Indianapolis, IN.
Menke, Paul F. '66 (LA) Alhambra, CA St. Thomas More.
Menker, Joseph *o.m.i.* '53 (STP)[M] St. Paul, MN Oblate Residence.
Menkhus, James *o.f.m.cap.* '73 (PH) Philadelphia, PA.
Menna, F. Dominic (BO) Quincy, MA St. Mary.
Menna, Fiori D. '58 (BO) Senior Priests Retired.
Menna, Francis A. '64 (PH)[V] Darby, PA Villa Saint Joseph; [V] Ventnor, PA Villa St. Joseph by the Sea; Department Retired Clergy; Diocesan Priests' Compensation and Benefits Committee.
Menna, Michael J. '99 (PRO) Coventry, RI SS. John and Paul.
Mennella, Luke *o.ss.t.* '56 (CC) Corpus Christi, TX Christ the King.
Menner, John H. *c.s.b.* '58 (DET)[E] Redford, MI Catholic Central High School.
Menner, Michael L. '93 (PEO)[Q] Moline, IL The Order of the Legion of Little Souls of the Merciful Heart of Jesus.
Menner, Michael '93 (PEO) Warsaw, IL Sacred Heart.
Menner, Robert J. '68 (STL) On Duty Outside the Archdiocese.
Mennis, James F. '62 (SAC) Retired.
Menonkari, John *c.m.i.* '68 (BRK) Brooklyn, NY Holy Family; [V] Brooklyn, NY Carmelites of Mary Immaculate, Inc..
Mens, Theodore J. '67 (GRY) Gary, IN St. Ann; Griffith, IN St. Mary; Priests' Personnel Board; Pro–Life Activities.
Mensah, Gabriel '83 (VIC) On Duty Outside the Diocese; Navy Chaplains.
Mensah, Isaac '80 (RVC) Garden City, NY St. Anne.
Mensah, Isaac '81 (RVC) Manhasset, NY North Shore Univ. Hospital.
Mensah, Paul '90 (SJ) San Jose, CA St. John Vianney.
Mensinger, Gary J. '98 (PSC) Old Forge, PA St. Nicholas; Notaries.
Menster, William J. '38 (DUB) Retired.
Mentrup, Charles E. '88 (CIN) Franklin, OH St. Mary; [E] Middletown, OH Bishop Fenwick High School.
Menty, Ronald A. '69 (ALB) Colonie, NY St. Clare.
Menty, Ronald (ALB) Members.
Menuba, Elias '74 (ROC) Canisteo, NY St. Joachim; Hornell, NY St. Ann; Canisteo, NY St. Mary.
Meny, Hilary G. '40 (IND) Retired.
Menz, Anthony E. (BLX) V.A. Hospital.
Menz, Anthony *o.c.s.o.* '68 (SPC)[E] Ava, MO Assumption Abbey (Trappist).
Menzel, William G. '67 (LC) Wisconsin Rapids, WI St. Vincent de Paul; Deans.
Menzies, Scott '85 (VEN) Graduate Studies.
Meoska, John '82 (PBL)[I] Crestone, CO Spiritual Life Institute of America, Inc..
Mercado, Edwin '87 (ARE) Arecibo, PR Church of San Martin de Porres; Diocesan Consultors; Priest's Senate (Consejo Presbiteral).
Mercado, Floyd '03 (CGS) Naranjito, PR San Miguel Arcangel; Vocations.
Mercado, Marco A. '98 (CHI) Chicago, IL Good Shepherd.
Mercado, Miguel '83 (ARE) Quebradillas, PR San Raphael.
Merced, Miguel '00 (CGS) Barranquitas, PR Church of St. Anthony of Padua; Priests Senate.
Mercer, David '87 (SJ) Ongoing Formation of Clergy Committee.
Mercer, James G. '97 (ARL) Great Falls, VA St. Catherine of Siena; Conshohocken, PA St. Mary; On Leave of Absence.
Mercer, John E. '70 (NY) Staten Island, NY Our Lady of Pity.
Mercer, Robert *s.a.* '82 (NY)[EE] Garrison Franciscan Friars of the Atonement, Minister General Office.
Merchant, David M. *o.s.f.s.* '73 (PH)[D] Philadelphia, PA Father Judge High School for Boys; [AA] Philadelphia, PA Father Louis Brisson Residence.
Mercieca, Anthony '62 (MIA) Retired.
Mercieca, Cyprian Joseph *t.o.r.* '61 (WH) Berkeley Springs, WV St. Vincent de Paul.
Mercier, Joseph '55 (BLX) Retired.
Mercier, Ronald A. *s.j.* '87 (BO)[V] Boston The Society of Jesus of New England–Provincial Offices.
Mercure, Gary '74 (ALB) Troy, NY Sacred Heart; Troy, NY St. Williams.
Mercure, Jerome '79 (BUR) North Troy, VT St. Vincent de Paul; Troy, VT Sacred Heart of Jesus.
Mercurio, Gregory (BO) Lynn, MA Holy Family.
Mercy, Richard R. *s.j.* '71 (SPK)[D] Spokane, WA Gonzaga Preparatory School; [N] Spokane, WA Kateri Northwest Ministry Institute.
Merdian, Mark J. '93 (PEO) Champaign, IL St. Matthew.
Merdian, Mark (PEO) Clergymen's Aid, Inc.
Merdinger, Philip E. '64 (NEW) On Duty Outside the Archdiocese.
Meredith, John R. '80 (OWN) Owensboro, KY Our Lady of Lourdes; [J] Owensboro, KY Gideon Productions, Inc..
Meredith, Philip S. '74 (DEN) Englewood, CO All Souls.
Meredith, Richard '78 (OWN) Owensboro, KY St. Pius Tenth; Judges; Continuing Education for Priests.
Merfeld, Vincent C. '44 (DUB) Retired.
Merfeld, Vincent (DUB) AUXILIARY CHAPLAINS CONTRACT CHAPLAINS.
Mergenhagen, John J. '54 (BUF) Retired.
Mericantante, John J. '75 (PMB) Pahokee, FL St. Mary.
Meridier, Wilfred F. '69 (NO) New Orleans, LA St. Rita; Jefferson, LA Ochsner Foundation Hospital.
Merino, Bandilio (SJN) Catholic Charismatic Renewal.
Merino, Bandilio '48 (SJN) Rio Piedras, PR Nuestra Senora de la Providencia; for Education; Vicar for Education; Police Chaplains.
Merino, Mario (LA)[Q] Azusa, CA Casa Comboni Mission Seminary.
Merino, Santiago '46 (LA) Retired.
Merino–Merino, Baudilio (SJN) Diocesan Consultors.
Meriwether, Stephen A. '83 (SFR) Chancellor; Office of Ecumenism and Interreligious Affairs; Archbishop's Cabinet; Board of Directors; San Francisco, CA St. Teresa.
Meriwether, Stephen (SFR) Judges.
Merkatoris, Ralph '58 (GB) Retired.
Merkel, James '73 (SP) Pinellas Park, FL Sacred Heart.
Merkel, Mark K '92 (OM) Beemer, NE Holy Cross.
Merkel, Mark K. '92 (OM) West Point, NE St. Boniface; West Point, NE St. Anthony.
Merkelis, John D. *o.s.a.* '85 (CHI)[N] Olympia Fields, IL The Augustinians–Provincialate.
Merkelis, John *o.s.a.* '85 (JOL) New Lenox, IL St. Jude.
Merkle, Charles W. '88 (ARL) Arlington, VA St. Ann.
Merkovsky, Paul W. '90 (PIT) Bridgeville, PA Holy Child.
Merkt, Joseph T. '66 (OWN) Louisville, KY St. Francis of Assisi; [J] Louisville, KY Marian Home; [A] Owensboro, KY Brescia University; On Duty Outside the Archdiocese.
Merkt, Michael F. '81 (MIL) West Allis, WI Mary, Queen of Heaven.
Merlino, James *o.f.m.* '87 (HRT) Canaan, CT St. Joseph's.
Merlligan, Colm *m.s.c.* '58 (SAN) Brady, TX St. Patrick's.
Merman, Raymond F. '60 (ALN) Hellertown, PA St. Theresa of the Child Jesus.
Merold, James E. '71 (CHI) North Chicago, IL Queen of Peace.
Meronek Andrew '43 (GRY)[I] Cedar Lake, IN Our Lady of Lourdes Friary.
Merrifield, Donald P. *s.j.* '65 (HON)[G] Honolulu, HI Jesuit Fathers House; Hispanic Ministry–Oahu; Honolulu, HI St. John the Baptist.
Merrill, Paul *c.s.s.* '61 (BO)[Y] Waltham, MA Stigmatine Fathers and Brothers.
Merrill, Thomas *o.f.m.conv.* '79 (STP) St. Paul, MN Our Lady of Guadalupe; Bloomington, MN St. Bonaventure.
Merris, Christopher '82 (SD) Military Chaplains; Navy Chaplains.
Merry, Christopher (E) Western Vicariate.
Merry, Paul F. '71 (BGP) Bridgeport, CT Blessed Sacrament; Cursillos of Fairfield County, Inc..
Mersinger, Norbert A. '55 (STL) Lemay, MO St. Martin of Tours Retired.
Merson Thomas S. '83 (SFR) San Francisco, CA St. Anne Secretary to the Archbishop; Archbishop's Cabinet.
Mertens, Michael G. '45 (LC)[H] La Crosse, WI Holy Cross (Seminary) Diocesan Center Retired.
Mertensotto, Leon J. *c.s.c.* '56 (FTW)[B] University of Notre Dame Du Lac; [I] Notre Dame, IN Holy Cross Community, Corby Hall, University of Notre Dame.
Mertes Mark '87 (KCK) Overland Park, KS Holy Cross; Council for Catholic Charismatic Renewal.
Mertes, Robert *s.v.d.* '78 (MIL)[O] East Troy, WI Divine Word Missionaries.
Merwald, Melvin '71 (OM) Omaha, NE St. Margaret Mary.
Merz, Albert *o.f.m.* '66 (NSH)[H] Nashville, TN Franciscan Friars.
Merz, Daniel J. '98 (JC)[A] Conception, MO Conception Seminary College.
Merz, Eugene F. *s.j.* '61 (MIL)[O] Milwaukee, WI Arrupe House Jesuit Community.
Merzena, Carl J. '41 (NEW) Retired.
Merzweiler, David W. '77 (Y) Lake Milton, OH St. Catherine; North Jackson, OH St. James Parish Family.
Mesa, Carlos '64 (NY) Bronx, NY Holy Spirit.
Mesa, Jose L. *s.j.* '77 (STA) New York, NY St. Joseph of the Holy Family; In res..
Mesa, Luis (SFS) Sioux Falls, SD Our Lady of Guadalupe; Spanish–Speaking Apostolate.
Mesa, Mario *o.f.m.cap.* '64 (SJN) San Juan, PR San Juan de La Cruz.
Mesa–Caparros, Mario *o.f.m.cap.* (SJN) Rio Piedras.
Mescall, John R. *c.p.* '59 (BRK)[V] Jamaica, NY Immaculate Conception Monastery.
Mescall, John '52 (NY) Rye, NY Resurrection.
Mescher, Michael J. '83 (DUB) Air Force Reserve Chaplains; Dubuque, IA Nativity; Personnel Advisory Board; Deanery Representatives; Directors.
Meselle, Angelo *o.s.b.* '91 (WDC) Washington, DC Incarnation.
Mesi, Vincent *o.f.m.* '72 (LA) Phoenix, AZ St. Mary's Basilica.
Mesiona, Erwin C. '96 (SAC) Sacramento, CA All Hallows; Sacramento, CA St. Peter.
Meskenas, Vincent A. '49 (BEL) Retired.
Meskill, David B. '55 (BO) Senior Priests Retired.
Meskill, Patrick A. '53 (LA) Retired.
Meskill, Thomas A. '60 (LA) Retired.
Mesko, Louis G. *sch.p.* '36 (PH)[G] Devon, PA Devon Preparatory School; [AA] Devon Piarist Fathers (Order of the Pious Schools).
Mesley, Jerry '73 (GLP) On Leave of Absence.
Mesmer, William A. '68 (SY) Sherrill, NY St. Helena.
Messaro, Michael A. *m.ss.cc.* '68 (HBG) Fairfield, PA St. Rita; Fairfield, PA Immaculate Conception of the Blessed Virgin Mary; AUXILIARY CHAPLAINS CONTRACT CHAPLAINS.
Messenger, William '77 (LA) Los Angeles, CA Our Saviour Catholic Center.
Messer, Joseph V. '61 (BAL) Glen Burnie, MD Church of the Good Shepherd Retired.
Messer, Paul A. *s.j.* '67 (BO)[V] Newton, MA The Jesuit Community at Boston College.
Messerich, Valerius *o.f.m.* '46 (STP) St. Paul, MN Sacred Heart.
Messick, Severin *o.s.b.* '82 (IND) Greenfield, IN St. Michael; [K] Greenfield, IN.
Messier, Gerard *a.a.* '58 (BO)[V] New York, NY St. Vincent de Paul.
Messier, Gerard *a.a.* (NY) New York, NY St. Vincent de Paul.
Messina, Angelo '68 (ALX) Priests Council; Leesville, LA St. Michael.
Messina, John '96 (BAL) Absent on Leave.
Messina, Joseph (CAM) Catholic Charities' Community Liaison.
Messina, Richard C. '65 (BO) Winchester, MA St. Mary.
Messina, Samuel '65 (JKS) Batesville, MS St. Mary.
Messina, Victor G. '74 (BR) Baton Rouge, LA Our Lady of Mercy.
Messing, Francis '59 (MOB) Grove Hill, AL Sacred Heart.
Messner, Michael E. (HBG) Auditor; Vocations, Office for.
Messner, Michael '98 (HBG) Harrisburg, PA St. Francis of Assisi.
Messner, Thomas *o.f.m.* '67 (MRY)[F] San Miguel, CA Franciscan Friars, O.F.M.; [Q] Santa Barbara, CA Franciscan Friary, Order of Friars Minor (Old Mission).
Mestas, Leonard J. '81 (BWN) On Assignment Outside the Diocese.
Mestos, Leonard '81 (SB) Loma Linda, CA Jerry Pettis Memorial Hospital.
Mestriparampil, Thomas '89 (NY) George M. Motchan Detention Center; Otis Bantum Correctional Center.
Mesure, Gerard C. '84 (PH) Philadelphia, PA Good Shepherd; Defenders of the Bond; Promoters of Justice.
Meszaros, James J. '69 (BRK) Ozone Park, NY St. Stanislaus Bishop and Martyr.
Metcalf, Andrew '86 (SR) Calistoga, CA Our Lady of Perpetual Help; Priests' Council.
Metcko, Leo E. '43 (WCH) Retired.
Metha, Ronald W. (YAK) Chancellor and Moderator of the Curia; Diocesan Consultors; Diocesan Finance Council; Clergy Personnel Board; Press (Central Washington Catholic); Presbyteral Council Executive Committee.
Methe, Normand A. '58 (BGP)[P] Stamford, CT The Catherine Dennis Keefe Queen of the Clergy Retired Priests' Residence.
Method, Fredrick '66 (DUL) Walker, MN Sacred Heart; Walker, MN St. Agnes.
Method, Fredrick (DUL) Priests' Pension Board.

Metrejean, Paul '63 (LAF) Leonville, LA St. Leo the Great; Leonville, LA St. Catherine.
Metro, LeRoy '63 (SAL) Clyde, KS St. John the Baptist's.
Metsy, Norman G. '47 (PRO) AUXILIARY CHAPLAINS CONTRACT CHAPLAINS Retired.
Metts, Ralph E. *s.j.* '73 (WDC)[M] Washington, DC The Jesuit Community at Georgetown University; [V] Washington, DC Jesuit Secondary Education Association.
Metz, Bradley *c.s.c.* '02 (P) Portland, OR Holy Redeemer.
Metz, David '97 (SAL) Hays, KS Immaculate Heart of Mary; Diocesan Pastoral Council; Vocation Ministry Committee; Diocesan Director of Vocations.
Metz, Earl O. '58 (CIN) Retired.
Metz, Kenneth J. '65 (MIL) Kenosha, WI St. Mark.
Metzbower, Francis X. *s.j.* '63 (BAL)[S] Baltimore, MD Jesuit Fathers and Brothers Maryland Provincial Curia; AUXILIARY CHAPLAINS CONTRACT CHAPLAINS.
Metzdorf, William C. '73 (WDC) On Duty Outside the Archdiocese; Army National Guard Chaplains.
Metzer, Thomas H. '82 (LFT) Noblesville, IN Our Lady of Grace.
Metzger, Alvin P. *o.s.a.* '54 (MIL)[O] Racine, WI Augustinian Novitiate; Racine, WI St. Rita.
Metzger, Andrew *o.s.b.* '56 (SP)[O] St. Leo, FL St. Leo Abbey.
Metzger, Clem *s.j.* '65 (CLV)[T] Cleveland, OH Jesuit Retreat House.
Metzger, Dennis M. '74 (TOL) Swanton, OH Holy Trinity.
Metzger, Edward C. *o.f.m.* '59 (NY)[EE] Helper, UT.
Metzger, Edward *o.f.m.* '59 (SLC) Helper, UT St. Anthony's.
Metzger, Edwin '55 (ROC) Rochester, NY Holy Name of Jesus; Rochester, NY Our Mother of Sorrows Retired.
Metzger, John L. '67 (COL) Retired.
Metzger, Joseph H. '91 (RIC) Norfolk, VA Blessed Sacrament.
Metzger, Paul E. '43 (STU) Retired.
Metzger, Richard '67 (COL) Groveport, OH St. Mary's.
Metzger, Robert E. '60 (COL) Jackson, OH Holy Trinity.
Metzger, Samuel '59 (TYL) Fairfield, TX St. Bernard of Clairvaux.
Metzger, Stephen A. '70 (COL) Utica, OH Church of the Nativity.
Metzger, Thomas H. (LFT) Diocesan Consultors.
Metzger, William A. '78 (COL) Columbus, OH St. John the Baptist; Diocesan Consultors; Diocesan Judges.
Metzger, William J. '62 (COL) Columbus, OH St. Agnes.
Metzger, William J. *o.s.f.s.* '71 (ARL) Vienna, VA Our Lady of Good Counsel.
Metzinger, John R. '82 (OKL) Edmond, OK St. John the Baptist.
Metzinger, John (OKL) Council of Priests Archdiocesan.
Metzler, Warren W. '64 (PIT) Pittsburgh, PA St. James.
Metzler, William R. '72 (HRT) Simsbury, CT St. Mary's.
Meude, Mario Ronelo A. '92 (RCK) Huntley, IL St. Mary.
Meulemans, Carl P. *m.m.* '60 (NY)[EE] Maryknoll Maryknoll Fathers and Brothers.
Meulemans, Dennis T. '61 (SUP) St. Pius Priest Fund Retired.
Meulemans, Edward G. '60 (SUP) Retired.
Meulemans, Thomas O. *o.praem.* '59 (GB)[I] De Pere, WI St. Norbert Abbey; [I] De Pere, WI St. Joseph Priory.
Meulemans, Thomas O. *o.praem.* '59 (PH)[AA] Paoli, PA Daylesford Abbey.
Meulemans, Thomas O. *o.praem.* '59 (GB)[I] De Pere, WI St. Norbert Abbey; [I] De Pere, WI St. Joseph Priory.
Meuret, Donald L. '84 (LC) Marshfield, WI Our Lady of Peace.
Meuret, Donald '84 (WH) Absent on Leave.
Mevissen, Richard *c.ss.r.* (DET)[K] Hamtramck, MI Redemptorists of Hamtramck.
Mevlemms, Carl P. *m.h.* (NY)[B] Maryknoll, NY Center for Mission Research and Study at Maryknoll.
Meye, Elmer J. (FgM).
Meyer, Albert *o.s.b.* '56 (MRY)[F] San Luis Obispo, CA Men's Residence.
Meyer, Arthur D. '61 (PEO) Canton, IL St. Mary's.
Meyer, Benedict *o.s.b.* '54 (LR) Brinkley, AR St. John the Baptist.
Meyer, Benedict *o.s.b.* '54 (IND)[K] Brinkley, AR.
Meyer, Bernard A. '59 (SFD) Retired.
Meyer, Bernard *s.m.* '51 (SAT) San Antonio, TX Holy Rosary; [M] San Antonio, TX Marianist Residence.
Meyer, Blase '79 (PHX) Sun City, AZ St. Clement of Rome.
Meyer, Charles R. '45 (CHI) Retired.
Meyer, Clayton '66 (SEA) Retired.
Meyer, Daniel J. '82 (CIN)[A] Dayton, OH Holy Angels; [V] Fairborn, OH Catholic Alumni Club (Dayton Chapter).
Meyer, Dennis J. *m.s.* '70 (STL) Maplewood, MO Additional Residence for Priests; [O] LaSalette Spirituality Center.
Meyer, Earl *o.f.m.cap.* '66 (STL) St. Louis, MO St. Patrick; [O] St. Louis, MO St. Patrick Friary.
Meyer, Emmett F. '64 (OM) Valley, NE St. John; Age Groups.
Meyer, Eric *c.p.* '66 (CHI) Chicago, IL Immaculate Conception; [N] Chicago, IL Passionist Community–Immaculate Conception Monastery.
Meyer, Fred A. '65 (STL) St. Charles, MO St. Robert Bellarmine.
Meyer, Frederick C. '56 (STP) St. Henry, MN Church of St. Henry.
Meyer, Fredrick *ss.cc.* '71 (BWN) Edinburg, TX Sacred Heart.
Meyer, Gerald J. '96 (PEO) Ottawa, IL St. Francis of Assisi.
Meyer, Gilbert '42 (FRS) Retired.
Meyer, Harold K. *o.c.s.o.* '62 (SAC)[A] Vina, CA Abbey of New Clairvaux, Trappist Seminary; [I] Vina, CA Abbey of New Clairvaux, Trappist.
Meyer, Harry J. '64 (CIN) Mason, OH St. Susanna.
Meyer, James A. '94 (FAR) Mayville, ND St. Agnes.
Meyer, James '94 (FAR) Mayville, ND Our Lady of Peace.
Meyer, John A. '82 (IND) Madison, IN Prince of Peace.
Meyer, John A. (IND) Madison, IN Most Sorrowful Mother of God; Deaneries and Deans.
Meyer, John R. '89 (SFR)[R] San Francisco, CA Prelature of the Holy Cross and Opus Dei.
Meyer, John (IND)[O] Madison, IN Hanover College.
Meyer, Jonathan '03 (IND) Greenwood, IN Our Lady of the Greenwood.
Meyer, Leo A. '65 (NO) New Orleans, LA St. James Major.
Meyer, Louis F. '44 (STL) Lambert – St. Louis International Airport Retired.
Meyer, Mark A. '97 (CIN) On Duty Outside the Archdiocese; (FgM).
Meyer, Michael W. '93 (LA) Pacific Palisades, CA Corpus Christi.
Meyer, Nicholas W. *o.f.m.* '52 (STP) St. Paul, MN Sacred Heart.
Meyer, Robert G. '74 (WIN) Mazeppa, MN SS. Peter and Paul; Mazeppa, MN St. Patrick of West Albany; Diocesan Consultors.
Meyer, Robert J. '64 (PIT) Pittsburgh, PA St. Basil.
Meyer, Robert L. '57 (SFD) Grafton, IL St. Michael; Grafton, IL St. Patrick.
Meyer, Robert S. '88 (NEW)[B] Seton Hall University; [B] School of Diplomacy and Intl. Rels.; Defenders of the Bond.
Meyer, Sebastian *o.carm.* '62 (SAC) Fairfield, CA Our Lady of Mount Carmel,.
Meyer, Stephen L. '79 (DUB) Dubuque, IA St. Catherine; Dubuque, IA St. Donatus; Bellevue, IA St. Joseph.
Meyer, Steven J. '90 (FAR) Wimbledon, ND St. John; Wimbledon, ND St. Boniface.
Meyer, Steven '90 (FAR) Wimbledon, ND St. Mary.
Meyer, Thomas C. '98 (SFD) Jacksonville, IL Our Saviour.
Meyer, Thomas E. '70 (CIN) Cincinnati, OH Our Lady of Victory.
Meyer, Thomas *o.m.i.* '70 (DUL) International Falls, MN St. Thomas Aquinas.
Meyer, Thomas '98 (SFD) Virginia, IL St. Luke; Comite Diocesano de Ministerio Hispano – Diocesan Committee for Hispanic Ministry; Presbyteral Council.
Meyer, Tom '98 (SFD)[N] Jacksonville, IL Illinois College Newman Center; [N] Jacksonville, IL MacMurray College Newman Center.
Meyer, Vernon '79 (PHX) Scottsdale, AZ St. Patrick; On Leave.
Meyer, William J. *s.m.* '79 (SAT)[C] Oblate School of Theology.
Meyer, William O. '49 (DAV)[M] Davenport, IA St. Vincent Center Retired.
Meyer, William *s.m.* '79 (STL)[O] San Antonio, TX.
Meyers, Frederick *ss.cc.* '71 (BWN) Retired.
Meyers, George '41 (SFR)[K] San Rafael, CA Nazareth House Retired.
Meyers, Gerald '94 (TUC) Tucson, AZ St. Francis de Sales.
Meyers, James P. '70 (WDC) Bethesda, MD Our Lady of Lourdes; Deans.
Meyers, John F. '56 (DAL) Dallas, TX St. Monica.
Meyers, John F. '83 (PH) Bensalem, PA St. Charles Borromeo.
Meyers, John (DAL) College of Consultors; Hereford, TX San Jose; Consultors of Pastors; Presbyteral Council.
Meyers, Louis E. *s.j.* (NO) New Orleans, LA Delgado Community College, School of Nursing; [F] New Orleans, LA Jesuit High School.
Meyers, Michael '77 (LA) Glendora, CA St. Dorothy; Deanery 11; San Gabriel Pastoral Region.
Meyers, Robert V. '87 (MET) Highland Park, NJ St. Paul the Apostle; Canonical Staff.
Meyett, Irving C. '53 (SUP) Retired.
Meyr, Herbert J. '60 (CHI) Maywood, IL St. James.
Meysenburg, James J. '89 (LIN) Hastings, NE St. Cecilia's; [C] Hastings, NE St. Cecilia's Middle School/High School; [L] Hastings, NE St. Cecilia High School Endowment Fund.
Meystrik, Gregory C. '90 (JC) Jefferson City, MO St. Stanislaus; Diocesan Consultors; Chair Couple; Ministry to Priests; Scouting.
Meza, Fernando '95 (SAC) Sacramento, CA St. Charles Borromeo.
Meza, Salvador *m.j.* '83 (GAL) Houston, TX St. Stephen.
Meznar, Joseph A. '58 (DEN) Denver, CO Holy Rosary.
Meznar, Robert P. '60 (DEN) Retired.
Mezquida, Ramon '58 (PCE) On Duty Outside the Diocese.
Mezydlo, James A. '77 (CHI) Chicago, IL St. Florian.
Mezydlo, Leonard T. '50 (CHI) Des Plaines, IL St. Stephen Protomartyr Retired.
Mezyk, Wladek *o.f.m.conv.* '95 (BUF)[O] Athol Springs, NY St. Maximilian Kolbe Friary.
Mezzanote, Joseph *o.f.m.cap.* '39 (NEW)[B] Beacon, NY St. Lawrence of Brindisi Friary.
Mezzomo, Charles A. '71 (ROM) East Chicago, IN St. Nicholas; Vice Chancellor.
Mgalama, Erasto C. *i.m.c.* (WDC)[V] Washington, DC Consolata Missionaries House of Studies.
Mhanna, Andre '01 (OLL) St. Louis, MO St. Raymond's Cathedral; Master of Ceremonies; Office of Young Adult Ministry.
Miah, Gabriel (RVC) Lynbrook, NY Our Lady of Peace; East Meadow, NY Nassau University Medical Center.
Miani, Titian A. '55 (STO) Stockton, CA St. Luke Church of Stockton (Pastor of); Diamond Springs, CA Retired.
Miara, James '01 (NY) Staten Island, NY St. Teresa.
Mibach, Everett J. *s.j.* '51 (SJ)[M] Los Gatos, CA Sacred Heart Jesuit Center.
Micek, Joseph S. '42 (OM) Retired.
Micek, Sylvester *o.f.m.* '51 (GAY) Indian River, MI Cross in the Woods Catholic Shrine.
Miceli, James A. '75 (ATL) Rome, GA St. Mary's; [N] Rome, GA; Judges.
Miceli, John P. '94 (CLV) Strongsville, OH St. Joseph.
Miceli, Matthew M. *c.s.c.* '52 (FTW)[B] University of Notre Dame Du Lac; [I] Notre Dame, IN Holy Cross Community, Corby Hall, University of Notre Dame.
Miceli, Michael A. '97 (BR) Vacherie, LA Our Lady of Peace; Society of St. Vincent De Paul.
Miceli, Paul '72 (BO) Weymouth, MA Immaculate Conception.
Miceli, Vincent F. '91 (BRK) Brooklyn, NY St. Fortunata.
Mich, Kenneth A. '70 (MIL) Menomonee Falls, WI Good Shepherd.
Mich, Mario *s.d.b.* '48 (SFR)[N] San Francisco, CA Salesian Provincial Residence; [K] San Francisco, CA Home for the Aged of the Little Sisters of the Poor.
Michael, Chester P. '42 (RIC) Retired.
Michael, David C. '86 (BO) Belmont, MA St. Joseph; [BB] Waltham, MA Brandeis University Catholic Chaplaincy; Liaison for Catholic–Jewish Relations; On Duty Outside the Diocese.
Michael, Felix (SFD) Black Catholic Advisory Board.
Michael, Kenneth '65 (OLL) Retired.
Michael, Lawrence P. '75 (SAM) Torrington, CT St. Maron.
Michael, Thornsberry '91 (BAL) On Sabbatical.
Michaels, Dana '82 (OAK) El Sobrante, CA St. Callistus; Region 5; Deans.
Michaels, Emmett T. '38 (ALT) Retired.
Michaels, John L. '39 (PIT) Retired.
Michaels, Patrick T. '82 (SFR) Menlo Park, CA St. Raymond.
Michalak, Jan *o.s.p.p.e.* '81 (PH)[AA] Office.
Michalak, John S. '51 (OM) Retired.
Michalak, John S. (OM) Holy Name Society.
Michalchuk, Jack H. '01 (ALX) Alexandria, LA Our Lady of Prompt Succor.
Michalczak, John T. '70 (NEW) Palisades Medical Center.
Michalek, George C. '78 (LAN) Lansing, MI St. Mary Cathedral; Bishop's Office; Diocesan Archivist.
Michalek, George (LAN) Priest's Assignment Commission; Tribunal Judges.
Michalek, Henry J. '43 (CHI) Retired.
Michalek, Jaromir '91 (CAM) Williamstown, NJ St. Mary's.
Michalek, Stanislaw *s.ch.* '88 (DAL) Dallas, TX St. Peter.
Michalenko, Alexei '68 (VNN) On Special Assignment.
Michaletz, James E. *c.s.v.* '60 (JOL) Bourbonnais, IL Maternity of the Blessed Virgin Mary.
Michalicka, John J. '59 (OKL) Ponca City, OK Church of St. Mary; [H] Ponca City, OK St. Mary's Housing Foundation.
Michalicka, John (OKL) Region VIII.
Michalik, Gary '80 (DET) Westland, MI St. Theodore of Canterbury.
Michalik, Walter G. *c.s.c.* '56 (FTW)[I] Notre Dame, IN Holy Cross House.
Michalisin, Gregory J. (PBR) Notaries.

Michalisin, Gregory '92 (PBR) North Huntingdon, PA St. Stephen's.
Michalka, Arthur '51 (AUS) Jarrell, TX Holy Trinity.
Michalowski, John W. *s.j.* '81 (BO)[V] Weston, MA Campion Jesuit Community; [X] Weston, MA Campion Renewal Center.
Michalski, Edward (WOR) Webster, MA St. Joseph's Basilica.
Michalski, James L. *s.j.* '72 (OM)[F] Omaha, NE The Jesuit Middle School of Omaha; [K] Omaha, NE Jesuit Community at Creighton University.
Michalski, Melvin E. '70 (MIL)[A] St. Francis, WI Saint Francis Seminary; [A] St. Francis, WI Saint Francis Seminary; Special Assignment.
Michalski, Michael F. '76 (MIL)[H] Waukesha, WI Waukesha Catholic School System, Inc.; Waukesha, WI St. Joseph.
Michatek, William C. '66 (ROC) Webster, NY Holy Trinity.
Michaud, James L. '77 (PRT) Special or Other Diocesan Assignment.
Michel, Delix *s.s.l.* '88 (SFD) East Alton, IL St. Kevin; Board of Catholic Education.
Michel, Engelbert G. '66 (PH) Secane, PA Our Lady of Fatima; [FF] Philadelphia, PA Catholic Kolping Society.
Michel, Eugene '64 (STP) St. Paul, MN Sacred Heart.
Michel, Gabriel (BO) Mattapan, MA St. Angela Merici; Haitian.
Michel, Richard B. *o.s.b.* '86 (GBG)[H] Latrobe, PA Saint Vincent Archabbey.
Michele, Robert P. *c.s.p.* '55 (AUS) Austin, TX St. Austin.
Michele, Robert P. *c.s.p.* '55 (NY)[EE] Jamaica Estates Paulist Fathers Generalate.
Michele, Robert *c.s.p.* '55 (AUS) Austin, TX St. David's Hospital.
Michelini, Michael S. '71 (CHI) Chicago, IL St. Adalbert; Presbyteral Council.
Michell, George J. '64 (RVC) Southold, NY St. Patrick's.
Michell, Timothy *o.c.s.o.* '65 (P)[L] Lafayette, OR The Cistercian (Trappist) Abbey of Our Lady of Guadalupe.
Michels, Aloysius *o.s.b.* '39 (SCL)[I] St. Augustine Monastery.
Michels, Andrew J. '85 (NU) Minneota, MN St. Edward; Taunton, MN SS. Cyril and Methodius; Boy Scouts.
Michelson, Chris '80 (KNX) Knoxville, TN All Saints Catholic Church; Diocesan Consultors; Diocesan Finance Council.
Michet, John M. '78 (CHI) Chicago, IL Queen of All Saints Basilica.
Michie, Kenneth J. (ALX) Alexandria, LA St. James Memorial.
Michiels, Kenneth J. (ALX) Priests Council.
Michiels, Philip F. (SHP) Mansfield, LA St. Joseph; Shreveport, LA Overton Brooks Veteran's Administration Medical Center; Defenders of the Bond; College of Consultors; Presbyteral Council; Diocesan Liturgy Commission.
Michiels, Philip (SHP) Vicars Forane.
Michiels, Philip (ALX).
Michini, F. Joseph *s.j.* '80 (BAL)[D] Baltimore, MD Loyola Blakefield.
Michler, James R. '75 (STL) On Duty Outside the Archdiocese.
Michlik, Valerian (SJP) Pittsburgh, PA St. George; Diocesan Personnel Board.
Michniewicz, Martin E. '86 (CHI) Calumet City, IL St. Andrew the Apostle.
Michota, Piotr '85 (NEW) Mountainside, NJ Our Lady of Lourdes.
Mick, Lawrence E. '72 (CIN) On Special and Archdiocesan Assignment.
Mick, Lawrence J. '49 (CIN) Cincinnati, OH St. Antoninus.
Micka, Alphonse *m.i.c.* '49 (JOL) Darien, IL Our Lady of Peace.
Mickells, Anthony B. '43 (OM) Retired.
Mickelson, Michael T. '76 (NEW) Palisades Park, NJ St. Michael's.
Micketti, Gerald F. '83 (GAY) Traverse City, MI St. Patrick; Consultors, Diocesan Board of; Appointed Members; Archivist.
Mickey, Richard L. '88 (MEM) Memphis, TN Church of the Ascension.
Mickey, Richard '88 (MEM)[L] Charismatic Prayer Groups; Charismatic Renewal.
Mickiewicz, David '84 (ALB) Amsterdam, NY St. Stanislaus; Ecumenical and Interreligious Affairs of the Roman Catholic Diocese of Albany, Commission for.
Mickiewicz, J. William (MET) Califon, NJ St. John Neumann; Deans.
Mickler, Jeffrey *s.s.p.* '74 (Y)[A] Canfield, OH Society of St. Paul.
Mickus, James J. '72 (OKL) Chandler, OK Our Lady of Sorrows Retired.
Miclot, Brian *ph.d.* '74 (DAV)[B] St. Ambrose University.
Middendorf, Cyril G. *s.m.* '53 (CIN)[M] Dayton, OH Mercy Siena Woods, Nursing Care; AUXILIARY CHAPLAINS CONTRACT CHAPLAINS.
Middendorf, Eugene *o.f.m.* '45 (SFD) Quincy, IL St. Francis Solanus.
Middendorf, Raymar *o.f.m.* '50 (IND) Oldenburg, IN Holy Family; [L] Oldenburg, IN Motherhouse of the Congregation of the Sisters of the Third Order of St. Francis.
Middendorf, Raymond D. *s.m.* '57 (PCE) Villalba, PR Our Lady Mother of Divine Providence.
Middlecamp, Eric *s.d.s.* '52 (MIL) (FgM); [O] Milwaukee, WI Salvatorians – Jordan Hall.
Midile, Theodore *t.o.r.* '62 (ARL)[J] White Post, VA Sacred Heart Friary.
Midili, Bonaventure N. *t.o.r.* '52 (ALT) Winber, PA St. Anthony of Padua.
Midor, Adam '91 (TR) Trenton, NJ Our Lady of Sorrows.
Midowski, Leonard '51 (NEW)[N] Rutherford, NJ St. John Vianney Residence for Priests.
Midura, Francis S. '70 (RVC) Hauppauge, NY St. Thomas More; Judges for Interdiocesan Tribunal; Army Reserve Chaplains.
Midzak, Ihor '90 (STF) Hartford, CT St. Michael; Vicar General; Diocesan Consultors; Presbyteral Council; Administrative Council; Directors:.
Miechielsen, Albert *ss.cc.* '46 (HON)[G] Honolulu, HI St. Patrick's Monastery.
Mieczkowski, Chester J. '45 (BAL) Baltimore, MD Holy Rosary; [W] Baltimore, MD Knights of Columbus Retired.
Miekina, Stanley *c.m.* '59 (HRT) New Haven, CT St. Stanislaus.
Miele, Joseph J. '56 (TR) Manasquan, NJ St. Denis Retired.
Mien, Frances (SEA) Assistant Chaplains.
Mierenfeld, Lawrence E. '73 (CIN) Centerville, OH Incarnation.
Mierzwa, Ronald B. '76 (BUF) Ellicottville, NY Holy Name of Mary.
Mietelski, Joseph *c.m.* '59 (BRK).
Mifsud, Carmelo '59 (OAK) Retired.
Mifsud, James J. *s.m.* '65 (SJ) San Jose, CA Queen of Apostles.
Migliazzo, Felix '49 (MRY)[E] Monterey, CA Ave Maria Convalescent Hospital; [G] Monterey, CA Ave Maria Convent Retired.
Migliore, Angelus *t.o.r.* '64 (SP) Tampa, FL St. Patrick.
Mignot, John W. '54 (E) Reynoldsville, PA St. Mary; Christ the King Manor.
Miguel, Euciquiano *o.f.m.cap.* '51 (NO) New Orleans, LA St. Theresa of Avila; New Orleans LA Charity Hospital.
Miguelez, Valeriano '66 (SJN) San Juan, PR Espiritu Santo; [E] Hato Rey, PR Hospital Pavia; Police Chaplains; [E] San Juan, PR Centro Medico de P.R..
Miguez, Raul G. '98 (NY) Bronx, NY Holy Rosary.
Mihalak, James J. '76 (ALN) Retired.
Mihalco, John J. '83 (PBR) Sykesville, PA Holy Trinity; Protopresbyters; Defender of the Bond; Elected Deanery Representatives; Du Bois, PA Nativity of the Mother of God.
Mihalec, Peter M. '76 (CLV) Fairport Harbor, OH St. Anthony of Padua.
Mihalik, Alexis E. '64 (PBR) Boardman, OH Infant Jesus of Prague; Promoter of Justice.
Mihan, John A. '59 (LA) Retired.
Mihayli, Gilbert *o.praem.* '43 (GB)[I] De Pere, WI St. Norbert Abbey.
Mihovilovich, John B. '52 (SFR) Retired.
Mijas, Paul (RVC) Copiague, NY Our Lady of the Assumption.
Mika, John M. '72 (LIN) On Sick Leave.
Mikalajunas, John E. '69 (SY) Binghamton, NY St. John the Evangelist.
Mikalajunas, John '69 (SY) Binghamton, NY Binghamton General Hospital.
Mikalofsky, Hilarion A. '75 (MIL) Air Force Chaplains; Military Chaplains.
Mikclik, Kenneth E. '52 (GAL) Hempstead, TX St. Katherine Drexel.
Mikes, Pavel '90 (FAR) On Duty Outside the Diocese.
Mikesch, Gregory R. '75 (STL) Ferguson, MO Good Shepherd.
Mikhael, Elie Hares '95 (SAM) Lawrence, MA St. Anthony.
Mikkelson, Scott '82 (AUS) Hearne, TX St. Mary; Hearne, TX St. Mary's.
Miklas, Sebastian F. *o.f.m.cap.* '39 (WDC)[B] Washington, DC St. Francis Friary–Capuchin College.
Miklaszewski, Albin *o.f.m.* '46 (MIL)[O] Burlington, WI Queen of Peace Friary.
Mikolaitis, Vito E. '43 (CHI) Chicago, IL Nativity of the Blessed Virgin Mary Retired.
Mikolajczk, Bruno '88 (FWT) Abbott, TX Immaculate Heart of Mary; Penelope, TX Nativity of the Blessed Virgin Mary.
Mikolajczyk, Bruno '88 (CC) Retired.
Mikolajczyk, Edward M. '73 (CHI) Evergreen Park, IL Queen of Martyrs.
Mikolajczyk, George M. *m.m.* '55 (NY).
Mikonis, Gerald S. '74 (PIT)[EE] Port Vue, PA St. Mark.
Miksch, Joseph A. '66 (OM) Columbus, NE St. Isidore.
Mikschl, Luke *s.t.* '53 (WDC)[M] Adelphi, MD Missionary Servants of the Most Holy Trinity.
Mikstay, Michael '59 (Y) Military Chaplains; Navy Chaplains.
Mikstay, Michael '81 (BLX) Naval Const. Bn. Center.
Mikula, John J. *o.f.m.conv.* '56 (RCK) Rockford, IL St. Stanislaus Kostka.
Mikulanis, Dennis '77 (SD) San Diego, CA San Rafael.
Mikulanis, Dennis (SD) Ecumenical and Interreligious Affairs.
Mikulcik, Ken '98 (OWN) Hardinsburg, KY St. Mary–of–the–Woods; Deans; Priests' Council.
Mikulcik, Kenneth '98 (OWN) Hardinsburg, KY St. Anthony; Scouting Activities.
Mikulski, Isadore J. '50 (GAY) Retired.
Mikus, Elemir '57 (DET) Retired.
Milanese, John M. '74 (BUR) Daughters of Isabella; State Friar; [H] Randolph, VT Vermont Technical College; Randolph, VT SS. Donatian and Rogatian.
Milani, Joseph J. '50 (SJ) Cupertino, CA St. Joseph of Cupertino; [P] Cupertino, CA St. Joseph Cupertino Retirement Residence Retired.
Milani, Joseph (SJ) Roman Catholic Welfare Corporation; Diocesan Clergy Personnel Board.
Milano, Cleo J. '83 (BR) Plaquemine, LA St. John the Evangelist.
Milanowski, Paul A. '65 (GR) On Special Assignment.
Milanowski, Paul '65 (GR) Vocation Director.
Milazzo, Nicholas F. '52 (NY) Bronx, NY St. Anthony Retired.
Milbauer, Robert '66 (LA) Granada Hills, CA St. John Baptist de la Salle.
Milby, Lawrence M. '65 (BUF) Orchard Park, NY Nativity of Our Lord.
Milde, Robert F. '48 (BRK) Retired.
Milek, Richard '83 (CHI) Chicago, IL St. Helen.
Miles, Andrew *o.s.b.* '60 (SFE)[I] Pecos, NM Our Lady of Guadalupe Abbey; [K] Pecos, NM Our Lady of Guadalupe Olivetan Benedictine Abbey.
Miles, C. Thomas '99 (CHR) Walterboro, SC St. Anthony's.
Miles, Cassian A. *o.f.m.* '61 (PAT)[P] Paterson, NJ St. Anthony's Guild.
Miles, Cassian *o.f.m.* '61 (NY) New York, NY St. Francis of Assisi.
Miles, Francis J. *s.j.* '60 (WDC).
Miles, James '78 (BAL)[P] Baltimore, MD Little Flower, Shrine of.
Miles, James '78 (LKC) On Duty Outside the Diocese.
Miles, John *c.r.* '51 (L)[K] Louisville, KY Villa Pacis, Resurrectionist Retirement Home.
Miles, Richard M. '84 (NO) Kenner, LA Our Lady of Perpetual Help.
Milewski, Casimir '69 (TR) Leave of Absence Retired.
Milewski, Douglas J. '89 (NEW).
Milewski, John '93 (KNX)[B] Mountain City, TN St. Anthony of Padua Catholic Church.
Milewski, Richard R. '83 (TR) Freehold, NJ St. Rose of Lima.
Milewski, Stanley E. '55 (DET) Retired.
Miley, Eamon '73 (MOB) On Leave from the Archdiocese.
Miley, Edward *p.i.m.e.* '67 (DET)[K] Detroit, MI P.I.M.E. Motherhouse in Detroit.
Mili, Jude J. *o.f.m.* '59 (WH)[F] Morgantown, WV Our Lady of Good Counsel Franciscan Friary.
Milia, Anthony A. (OG) Judges.
Milich, Nicholas (YAK) Yakima, WA Holy Redeemer.
Milienewicz, Frank J. '76 (NTN) Birmingham, AL St. George.
Milienewicz, Frank J. '76 (NTN) Birmingham, AL National Shrine of St. George; College of Eparchial Consultors.
Milienewicz, Frank (NTN) Protopresbyters.
Milienewicz, Frank (NTN) Presbyteral Council.
Milienewicz, Frank (NTN) Priest's Sickness & Disability, and Retirement Plans.
Milienewicz, Frank (NTN) Vocations Office.
Militante, Henry (TR) Trenton, NJ St. Michael.
Militello, Benedict P. '63 (NEW) Northvale, NJ St. Anthony's Retired.
Militello, Cosmo F. '60 (CHI) Melrose Park, IL Sacred Heart.
Millan, Jose Luis '00 (SPK) Valley, WA St. Mary of the Rosary; Valley, WA Sacred Heart; Valley, WA Holy Ghost; Defensor Vinculi; Diocesan Consultors/ Presbyteral Council.
Millane, Thomas J. '63 (TUC) Tucson, AZ St. Elizabeth Ann Seton.
Millane, Thomas (TUC) Directors.
Millar, Andrew '58 (RVC) Retired.
Millares, Sergio '81 (NY) Kingston, NY St. Joseph.
Millbourn, Richard L. *s.j.* '01 (IND)[D] Indianapolis, IN.
Millea, Thomas V. (CHI) Retired.
Millea, William V. '80 (BGP) On Duty Outside the Diocese.

Millen, Edwin F. '56 (RCK) Retired.
Miller, Abraham '79 (CHI)[J] Chicago, IL Saint Mary of Nazareth Hospital Center.
Miller, Abraham '79 (STN) Chicago, IL St. Michael's; St. Mary of Nazareth Hospital Center; Presbyteral Council; Personnel Board.
Miller, Arnold J. '00 (B) St. Anthony, ID Mary Immaculate.
Miller, Bernard *m.s.c.* '59 (RCK)[G] (FgM).
Miller, Bert '91 (FAR) Grafton, ND St. John the Evangelist.
Miller, Bertin *o.f.m.* '64 (STL)[S] Dittmer, MO Il Ritiro–The Little Retreat.
Miller, Brendan *o.s.b.* '83 (LR)[A] Subiaco, AR Subiaco Monastery.
Miller, Brian J. *t.o.r.* '53 (SP) St. Petersburg, FL St. Mary Our Lady of Grace.
Miller, Bruce '77 (ALX) Judicial Vicar; Presiding Judge; Priests Council; The Beginning Experience; Lecompte, LA St. Martin.
Miller, Byron J. *c.ss.r.* '90 (NO) New Orleans, LA St. Alphonsus; New Orleans, LA National Shrine of Blessed Francis Xavier Seelos.
Miller, C. Anthony '80 (HBG) York, PA St. Patrick.
Miller, Charles E. *c.m.* '56 (LA)[A] Camarillo, CA St. John's Seminary.
Miller, Charles E. '91 (SB) Hesperia, CA Holy Family.
Miller, Charles H. *s.m.* '64 (SAT)[M] San Antonio, TX Chaminade Community House; [C] San Antonio, TX St. Mary's University of San Antonio, Texas.
Miller, Charles J. *o.f.m.* '66 (NY)[EE] New York, NY Franciscan Friars, Order of Friars Minor, Holy Name Province.
Miller, Charles J. '72 (NEW) Lyndhurst, NJ Sacred Heart; South Bergen Region Deanery 7.
Miller, Charles *o.f.m.* '38 (CIN)[L] Cincinnati, OH Archbishop Leibold Home for the Aged; [M] Cincinnati St. Francis Seraph Friary.
Miller, Charles *o.f.m.* '66 (NY) Bronx, NY Holy Cross.
Miller, Christopher T. '93 (LFT) Vicar for Hispanic Ministry in White County; Special Assignment.
Miller, Cletus *o.s.b.* '44 (SFS)[F] Marvin, SD Blue Cloud Abbey; (FgM).
Miller, Conrad *o.f.m.conv.* '38 (BAL)[O] Stella Maris; [S] Timonium, MD Stella Maris.
Miller, David L. '81 (SPC) Cassville, MO St. Edward; Shell Knob, MO Holy Family; Apostolate to the Deaf.
Miller, Dennis W. '02 (DUB) Manchester, IA St. Mary; Ryan, IA St. Patrick; Greeley, IA St. Joseph.
Miller, Donald A. *o.f.m.* '72 (Y)[C] Cincinnati, OH St. Anthony Shrine, Francisan Candidacy.
Miller, Donald S. '42 (KC) Retired.
Miller, Donald *o.f.m.* '72 (CIN)[M] Cincinnati, OH St. Francis Seraph Friary.
Miller, Edward M. '71 (BAL) Baltimore, MD St. Bernardine.
Miller, Edward (BAL) Advocates and Procurators.
Miller, Elden J. '54 (FTW) Advisory Board Retired.
Miller, Elden (FTW) Pro–Synodal Judges.
Miller, Ferdinand B. '46 (NEW) Retired.
Miller, Francis J. '50 (CIN) Retired.
Miller, Francis X. *s.j.* '59 (WOR)[O] Worcester, MA Jesuits of Holy Cross College, Inc..
Miller, Francis *o.c.d.* '49 (WDC)[B] Washington, DC Discalced Carmelite Friars Retired.
Miller, Frank P. '54 (COL) Retired.
Miller, Frank '54 (AUS) Retired.
Miller, Franklin D. '89 (FAR) Forman, ND St. Mary.
Miller, Franklin '89 (FAR) Forman, ND SS. Peter and Paul; Forman, ND Our Lady of Mercy; Forman, ND St. Arnold.
Miller, Frederick J. '41 (NY) Retired.
Miller, Frederick L. '72 (NEW) On Duty Outside the Archdiocese.
Miller, Gary M. '72 (CHI) Evergreen Park, IL St. Bernadette.
Miller, George M. '63 (LA) Retired.
Miller, George P. (TOL) Judges.
Miller, George P. (DET) Judicial Vicar.
Miller, Gregory *o.s.b.* '73 (SCL) St. Joseph, MN St. Joseph's; [I] Collegeville, MN St. John's Abbey, of the Order of St. Benedict; Presbyteral Council; Diocesan Consultors.
Miller, Henry *o.s.c.* '43 (SCL)[I] Onamia, MN Crosier Monastery.
Miller, J. Michael *c.s.b.* '75 (GAL)[C] Houston, TX University of St. Thomas; [Q] Houston, TX Residence of the Basilian Fathers of the University of St. Thomas.
Miller, James H. '68 (LC) Cashton, WI St. Augustine of Hippo Retired.
Miller, James L. '76 (DUB) Hampton, IA St. Patrick; Hampton, IA St. Mary; Deans; Priests Assigned to Hispanic Ministry.
Miller, James Norman '59 (NSH) Nashville, TN St. Mary of the Seven Sorrows.
Miller, James W. '67 (CHI) Chicago, IL Resurrection.
Miller, James '54 (CIN)[B] Carthagena, OH St. Charles.
Miller, James *o.m.i.* '57 (SAT)[K] San Antonio, TX Oblate Madonna Residence.
Miller, James '68 (FWT)[H] Crowley, TX St. Francis Village, Inc..
Miller, James '83 (RVC) Absent on Leave.
Miller, John C. '95 (BRK) Brooklyn, NY Our Lady of Grace.
Miller, John H. *c.s.c.* '51 (STL)[U] St. Louis, MO Central Bureau of the CCUA.
Miller, John J. '64 (PH) Fairless Hills, PA St. Frances Cabrini.
Miller, John P. '78 (HEL) Missoula, MT St. Anthony.
Miller, John P. '82 (WCH) Zenda, KS St. Peter's; Zenda, KS St. John.
Miller, John '58 (SCL) Retired.
Miller, John '82 (WCH) Cunningham, KS Sacred Heart; Nashville, KS St. Leo the Great.
Miller, Joseph A. *c.s.b.* '54 (DET)[E] Redford, MI Catholic Central High School.
Miller, Joseph A. *s.v.d.* '68 (LA)[Q] Los Angeles, CA Society of the Divine Word, Western Province; (FgM).
Miller, Joseph C. '49 (OWN) Retired.
Miller, Joseph K. '57 (SAG) Pinconning, MI St. Mary.
Miller, Joseph *c.pp.s.* '77 (DAV) Centerville, IA St. Mary's; Deans; [P] Centerville, IA St. Mary's Foundation of Centerville.
Miller, Karen (OAK) Oakland, CA St. Augustine's.
Miller, Kenneth E. '77 (Y) Louisville, OH St. Louis.
Miller, Lawrence J. '69 (NEW) Bayonne, NJ St. Mary Star of the Sea.
Miller, Leo M. *o.m.i.* '52 (LA) Veterans Affairs Medical Center.
Miller, Leo *o.m.i.* '52 (BEL)[F] Belleville, IL Shrine of Our Lady of the Snows.
Miller, Leroy "Jake" '01 (FAR) Mooreton, ND SS. Peter and Paul; Mooreton, ND St. Anthony's.
Miller, Loran *o.f.m.cap.* '64 (MAD)[K] Madison, WI San Damiano Friary.
Miller, Mardean E. '94 (PH) Springfield, PA Holy Cross.
Miller, Mark A. '69 (ROC) Corning, NY All Saints.
Miller, Martin J. '94 (PIT)[M] Pittsburgh, PA Prelature of the Holy Cross and Opus Dei.
Miller, Martin '02 (CHI)[W] Oak Park, IL Oak Park Study Center.
Miller, Maurice R. '49 (LFT) Lafayette, IN St. Ann.
Miller, Meinrad *o.s.b.* '94 (KCK)[A] Atchison, KS Benedictine College; [H] Atchison, KS St. Benedict's Abbey.
Miller, Michael J. '72 (MRY) Salinas, CA Sacred Heart.
Miller, Michael J. '96 (STP) Delano, MN St. Joseph; Delano, MN St. Peter.
Miller, Michael *m.s.c.* '85 (FgM).
Miller, Michael *m.s.c.* '85 (RCK)[G] Aurora Missionaries of the Sacred Heart Community.
Miller, Michael *o.f.m.conv.* '01 (BAL)[S] Baltimore, MD Immaculate Heart of Mary Friary.
Miller, Michael (MRY) Advisory Committee.
Miller, Mike (MRY) Cursillo.
Miller, Neil R. '61 (ROC) Retired.
Miller, Paul A. *c.ss.r.* '62 (ROC)[K] Canandaigua, NY Notre Dame Retreat House.
Miller, Paul D. '44 (FTW) Retired.
Miller, Paul '56 (HBG) Retired.
Miller, Philip '77 (Y) Ashtabula, OH St. Joseph.
Miller, Randall J. '89 (LAN) Jackson, MI St. John the Evangelist.
Miller, Richard E. '76 (LFT) Special Assignment; Defenders of the Bond.
Miller, Richard E. *j.c.l.* (LFT) Lafayette, IN St. Boniface.
Miller, Richard G. '50 (TOL)[I] Oregon, OH Sacred Heart Home Retired.
Miller, Richard (LFT) Members.
Miller, Robert J. *o.p.* '56 (CHI) Chicago, IL Holy Angels; [N] St. Pius V Priory.
Miller, Robert J. '61 (MET) Retired.
Miller, Robert J. '80 (PIT) Pittsburgh, PA St. Pius X.
Miller, Robert M. '92 (PIT)[C] Zelienople, PA St. Gregory; Clergy Personnel Board.
Miller, Robert M. '02 (Y) Hubbard, OH St. Patrick.
Miller, Robert '70 (SB) San Bernardino, CA Our Lady of the Rosary Cathedral; Elected Members.
Miller, Robert (SB) College of Consultors.
Miller, Roger F. '42 (KC) Retired.
Miller, Theodore J. '75 (TOL) Gibsonburg, OH St. Michael Church; Helena, OH St. James; Helena, OH St. Mary.
Miller, Thomas C. '94 (STL) St. Louis, MO St. Gabriel the Archangel; Archdiocesan Priests' Personnel Board.
Miller, Thomas G. '71 (RIC) Roanoke, VA St. Andrew.
Miller, Thomas M. *c.s.b.* '45 (ROC)[I] Rochester, NY Basilian Residence.
Miller, Thomas R. '77 (PIT) Clarksville, PA St. Thomas; Priest Council; College of Consultors.
Miller, Thomas R. '79 (PEO) Peoria, IL St. Vincent De Paul.
Miller, Thomas R. (PIT) Pittsburgh, PA St. Joseph.
Miller, Thomas W. '77 (BEL) Anna, IL St. Mary; Anna State Hospital; Vienna Correctional Center; Vienna, IL Dixon Springs Work Camp; Vienna, IL Shawnee Correctional Center.
Miller, Thomas (PEO) Finance Council (Canon 492); Clergymen's Aid, Inc..
Miller, Thomas (BEL) Diocesan Finance Council.
Miller, Thomas (PEO) Finance Council (Canon 492); Clergymen's Aid, Inc..
Miller, Vincent '98 (CR) Diocesan Consultors; Strandquist, MN Assumption – Florian; Stephen, MN St. Stephen's; Priests' Council; Vocations.
Miller, Walter D. (BUR) Members Ex Officio; Vicar for Administration; Chancery Office; Secretary to the Most Rev. Bishop; Judicial Vicar; Diocesan Consultors; Censor Librorum; Vicar for Administration; Diocesan Master of Ceremonies; National Catholic Conference for Interracial Justice; On Special or Other Diocesan Assignment.
Miller, Walter *s.v.d.* '69 (LA) Lakewood, NJ St. Anthony Claret.
Miller, Whitney '80 (LKC) Westlake, LA St. John Bosco; Counseling.
Miller, William C. '83 (E) Youngsville, PA St. Luke.
Miller, William J. '56 (PIT) Retired.
Miller, William M. '56 (PIT)[N] Pittsburgh, PA St. John Vianney Manor.
Miller, William T. *s.j.* '55 (DEN)[N] Denver, CO Xavier Jesuit Center.
Miller, William T. *s.j.* '72 (P)[L] Portland, OR Colombiere Community.
Miller, William T. *i.c.* '84 (PEO) Abingdon, IL Sacred Heart; Galesburg, IL Corpus Christi; Galesburg, IL St. Patrick's; [A] Peoria, IL Rosminian Novitiate.
Miller, William '61 (L) Louisville, KY Our Lady of Lourdes.
Miller, William *c.pp.s.* '63 (DM) Chariton, IA Sacred Heart.
Miller, William *s.j.* '72 (P).
Miller, William '91 (LKC)[A] Lake Charles, LA St. Margaret.
Miller, William (LKC) Diocesan Board of Administration; Episcopal Vicars; Personnel Board.
Miller, William *i.c.* (PEO) Diocesan College of Consultors.
Millerd, William H. *s.j.* (BAL)[D] Baltimore, MD Loyola Blakefield.
Millican, Ronald C. '81 (P) Portland, OR St. Pius X.
Milligan, Richard A. '60 (PHX) Phoenix, AZ St. Luke.
Milligan, Ronald '72 (DET) Sterling Heights, MI St. Ephrem.
Milliken, Damian J. *o.s.b.* '58 (PAT)[M] Newton St. Paul's Abbey.
Milliken, Damian *o.s.b.* '58 (FgM).
Milliken, David W. '77 (NEW) New Milford, NJ Ascension.
Millis, Karl '99 (CHY) Gillette, WY St. Matthew's; Diaconate Board.
Millisor, Daniel J. '86 (COL) Ada, OH Our Lady of Lourdes; Priests Personnel Board.
Millisor, Daniel (COL) Diocesan Judges.
Millott, Thirburse F. '75 (WOR) Southborough, MA St. Anne.
Mills, Alexander M. *o.s.b.* '90 (TUC) Tubac, AZ St. Ann; [E] St. David, AZ Holy Trinity Monastery.
Mills, Alexander '80 (TUC) Tucson, AZ Villa Maria Chapel.
Mills, Brindley '64 (DAL) Dallas, TX St. Monica.
Mills, Donald J. '89 (PH) Roslyn, PA St. John of the Cross.
Mills, Joe (OWN) *Roman Catholic Diocese of Owensboro Charitable Trust Fund, Inc.; Serra Club.
Mills, Joseph M. '53 (OWN) Non–Parochial Assignments; Defender of the Bond; Society for the Propagation of the Faith; Holy Childhood Association.
Mills, Joseph '53 (OWN)[G] Maple Mount, KY Mount St. Joseph.
Mills, Robert N. '55 (L) Vine Grove, KY St. Martin of Tours Retired.
Milon, Augustin *o.f.m.* '70 (CHI)[I] Chicago, IL Port Ministries.
Miloni, Vasco *s.x.* (PAT)[M] Wayne Xaverian Missionary Fathers.
Milosz, Bogdan '80 (DET) Hamtramck, MI Our Lady Queen of Apostles.
Milota, Thomas '92 (JOL) On Duty Outside the Diocese.
Milsted, Gordon '63 (MOB) Fairhope, AL St. Lawrence.
Milton, Hilary *o.carm.* '63 (NEW) Englewood, NJ St. Cecilia's.
Milton, Kevin *c.ss.r.* (BO) Roxbury, MA Our Lady of Perpetual Help.
Mimms, Wolfgang *o.ss.t.* '70 (VIC) Victoria, TX Our Lady of Sorrows.
Mina, John L. '89 (PBR) Clairton, PA Ascension of Our Lord; Archives.
Minaku, Jose Lukoli *s.j.* '02 (Central Africa)[N] Berkeley, CA Jesuit Community at Jesuit School of Theology at Berkeley.
Minassian, Raphael '73 (ARM) Los Angeles, CA Our Lady Queen of Martyrs; Glendale, CA St. Gregory.
Minassian, Raphael *p.i.a.* '73 (LA) Los Angeles, CA Our Lady Queen of Martyrs.
Minch, Richard '69 (SAV) Military Chaplains; Army Chaplains.
Minchak, Paul L. *o.f.m.cap.* '69 (HON) Waipahu, HI Resurrection of the Lord.

Minder, Kevin '89 (YAK) Special Assignment
Minder, Lawrence H. (SEA) College of Consultors; Deans.
Minder, Lawrence '89 (SEA) Bothell, WA St. Brendan; Presbyteral Council.
Mindling, J. Daniel *o.f.m.cap.* '80 (BAL).
Mindling, J. Daniel *o.f.m.cap.* '80 (WDC)[B] Washington, DC St. Francis Friary–Capuchin College.
Mindling, Joseph *o.f.m.cap.* '66 (WDC)[B] Washington, DC St. Francis Friary–Capuchin College.
Mindrup, Mark F. *o.f.m.conv.* '39 (STP)[P] Prior Lake, MN Franciscan Retreats.
Minehan, Michael P. '80 (SY) Lafayette, NY St. Joseph; Special Assignment; [F] Syracuse, NY Bishop Joseph T. O'Keefe, Inc.; [U] Syracuse, NY David W. Barry Foundation; Chancellor; Management Team; Ex Officio; Defender of the Bond; Vicar for Administration; Administration; Building Commission; Clerical Fund Society of the Roman Catholic Diocese of Syracuse; Finance Committee; Priests' Personnel Committee.
Minelli, Peter A. '63 (MAR) Retired.
Minette, James '41 (SCL) Retired.
Minh, Peter M. Ngo Chau *c.m.c.* '77 (SPC)[E] Carthage, MO Congregation of the Mother Coredemptrix, United States Assumption Province.
Minh, Vincent *c.ss.r.* '68 (CHI)[N] Chicago, IL Redemptorist Theology Residence.
Minh, Vu Duc '80 (TLS) On Duty Outside the Diocese.
Minh Nguyen, Andrew Tu '69 (BUF) Buffalo, NY Coronation of the Blessed Virgin Mary.
Minhoto, Walter F. '64 (FRS) Fresno, CA St. John Cathedral; Advocates Retired.
Minh Thanh Tran, Matthew '53 (COS) Colorado Springs, CO The Vietnamese Holy Martyrs Quasi–Parish.
Minic, John F. '71 (CIN) Retired.
Minichello, Arthur G. '73 (BRK) College Point, NY St. Fidelis.
Minielli, Anthony '45 (NY) Brooklyn, NY St. Augustine.
Minigan, William J. '86 (BO) Malden, MA St. Joseph.
Minihan, Paul '93 (OAK) Graduate Studies.
Miniscalco, Donald *c.ss.r.* '68 (PH) Philadelphia, PA St. Peter the Apostle.
Mink, John J. '85 (WIL) New Castle, DE Our Lady of Fatima; Delaware Army National Guard; Priests' Personnel Committee; Army National Guard Chaplains.
Minkiel, Stephen J. *c.m.* '57 (MAN) Concord, NH St. Peter.
Minkler, John '72 (ALB) Veterans' Administration Hospital; Special Assignment.
Minner, Ronald J. '01 (ALN) Orefield, PA St. Joseph The Worker.
Minnich, John F. '51 (GRY) Retired.
Minnihan, Paul D '93 (OAK) El Cerrito, CA St. Jerome's.
Minnihan, Paul D. (OAK) Presbyteral Council; Priest Representative.
Minniti, Anthony L. '70 (CAM) Paulsboro, NJ St. John's.
Minniti, David V. '72 (CAM) Millville, NJ St. Mary Magdalen's.
Minogue, John P. *c.m.* '72 (CHI)[C] Chicago, IL De Paul University; [N] Chicago DePaul Vincentian Residence.
Minogue, Liam A. '68 (MET) Hillsborough, NJ Mary, Mother of God.
Minogue, Michael '81 (PHX) Sun City West, AZ Our Lady of Lourdes.
Minson, Bartholomew *o.f.m.cap.* '64 (FgM).
Mintjal, Frank '59 (Y) Retired.
Minturn, Joseph '57 (RVC) Retired.
Miodowski, Leonard A. '51 (NEW) Retired.
Miola, Luigi C. '77 (CLV) Maple Heights, OH St. Martin of Tours.
Miorin, Albert C. '64 (TOL) Retired.
Miotke, Carmel F. *o.f.m.* '60 (BO)[Y] Boston, MA Saint Anthony Residence; Court Experts for Languages.
Miqueli, Peter A. '91 (NY) Roosevelt Island, NY St. Frances Xavier Cabrini.
Mirabelli, Daniel J. *c.s.v.* '60 (PEO)[B] Rock Island, IL Alleman High School.
Miracky, James J. *s.j.* '88 (WOR)[O] Worcester, MA Jesuits of Holy Cross College, Inc..
Miracky, James *s.j.* '88 (NY)[V] Newton, MA The Jesuit Community at Boston College.
Miramontes, Francisco '91 (SJ) Gilroy, CA St. Mary.
Miranda, Jose (NY) New York, NY Our Lady Queen of Martyrs.
Miranda, Lorenzo '91 (LA) La Puente, CA St. Louis of France.
Miranda, Luis *o.carm.* '84 (ARE) Ciales, PR Holy Rosary.
Miranda, Luis *o.carm.* (SJN) Carmelite Third Order.
Miranda, Luke '55 (FWT) Retired.
Miranda, R. Dario '92 (LA) Los Angeles, CA Mother of Sorrows.
Miranda, Vicente '73 (STP) Faribault, MN Divine Mercy Catholic Church.
Miranda, Victor '86 (CHI) Des Plaines, IL St. Zachary.
Miranne, Paul *o.s.b.* '47 (NO)[P] St. Benedict, LA St. Joseph Abbey.
Mirchuk, Roman (PHU) Whippany, NJ St John the Baptist.
Mirecki, John J. '55 (RVC) Riverhead, NY St. Isidore's.
Miriani, Gerald C. '62 (BEL) Retired.
Mirro, Joseph A. (RVC) Procurator & Advocates.
Mirro, Joseph '76 (RVC) Westhampton Beach, NY Immaculate Conception.
Mirsberger, Richard E. '66 (MIL) West Allis, WI St. Rita.
Mirto, Gregorio L. '65 (DEN) Fort Lupton, CO St. William.
Misakabo, Faustin *o.praem.* '80 (GB) McAllen, TX Holy Spirit.
Misbrener, David L. '95 (Y) Andover, OH Our Lady of Victory; Kinsman, OH St. Patrick.
Miscamble, Wilson D. *c.s.c.* '88 (FTW)[A] Notre Dame, IN Moreau Seminary; [B] University of Notre Dame Du Lac.
Mischke, Bernard *o.s.c.* '51 (SCL)[I] Onamia, MN Crosier Monastery.
Mischke, Gerald '64 (SCL) Holdingford, MN St. Hedwig's; Holdingford, MN St. Mary's; Holdingford, MN Our Lady of Mt. Carmel; Holdingford, MN Immaculate Conception; Holdingford, MN St. Columbkille's.
Mischke, Gerald (SCL) Deans; Presbyteral Council.
Mischkowiuski, Henry B. '65 (LR) Barling, AR Sacred Heart of Mary; Fort Smith, AR SS. Sabina & Mary Church.
Mischler, Thomas E. '81 (GRY) Gary, IN St. Mary of the Lake.
Misenko, John A. '78 (CLV) Avon, OH Holy Trinity.
Misey, Leonard S. '63 (JC) Brunswick, MO St. Boniface; Brunswick, MO St. Raphael; I. Brockfield.
Mish, Roy L. '60 (LC) Retired.
Misho, Lloyd P. '58 (BEL) Retired.
Misiewicz, Chester J. '73 (WOR) Worcester, MA St. Charles Borromeo.
Misiolek, Frederick '65 (DET) Newport, MI St. Charles Borromeo.
Misiura, Krzysztof '02 (DEN) Denver, CO Cathedral of the Immaculate Conception.
Miskella, Richard '65 (LA) On Duty Outside the Archdiocese.
Miskella, Richard '65 (MRY) Atascadero State Hospital.
Miskiewicz, Paul *o.f.m.conv.* '76 (BRK) Elmhurst, NY St. Adalbert.
Miskolczy, Kalman *sch.p.* '45 (BUF)[O] Lackawanna, NY Piarist Fathers Residence; Lackawanna, NY Assumption.
Missimi, Anthony N. '62 (COL) Columbus, OH Immaculate Conception.
Missler, John C. '78 (TOL) Sandusky, OH Holy Angels.
Mistretta, Vito F. '42 (SAC) Citrus Heights, CA Holy Family Retired.
Misulich, Raymond M. *j.c.l.* '56 (PSC) Retired.
Misurda, Matthew '77 (ALT) Windber, PA SS. Cyril and Methodius.
Mitas, Matthew M. '79 (STL) Union, MO Immaculate Conception.
Mitchell, Charles I. '84 (ORL) Altamonte Springs, FL St. Mary Magdalen.
Mitchell, Darell J. '98 (YAK) Special Assignment.
Mitchell, Douglas J. '01 (SFE) Questa, NM St. Anthony.
Mitchell, Edward J. '54 (DET) Beverly Hills, MI Our Lady Queen of Martyrs Retired.
Mitchell, Eugene *b.s.o.* '92 (NTN) Roslindale, MA Annunciation Cathedral; Methuen, MA Basilian Salvatorian Order; College of Eparchial Consultors; Presbyteral Council.
Mitchell, John C. '55 (BGP) On Duty Outside the Diocese.
Mitchell, John E. '54 (STP) Retired.
Mitchell, John J. '63 (RCK) Loves Park, IL St. Bridget; Promoter of Justice; Diocesan Consultors; Deans.
Mitchell, John J. '96 (STP) Jordan, MN St. John the Baptist.
Mitchell, John *s.j.* '72 (LA)[F] Los Angeles, CA Loyola High School of Los Angeles.
Mitchell, Joseph P. '79 (SEA) Vancouver, WA Holy Redeemer.
Mitchell, Joseph *c.p.* '81 (CHI)[N] Oakland, CA.
Mitchell, Kenneth *s.c.j.* '48 (SP)[O] Pinellas Park, FL Priests of the Sacred Heart Retired.
Mitchell, Lester *o.f.m.* '55 (PHX)[Q] Santa Barbara, CA Franciscan Friary, Order of Friars Minor (Old Mission).
Mitchell, Mark E. '76 (GR) On Special Assignment; Hospital Apostolate.
Mitchell, Michael J. '65 (SJ) Saratoga, CA Sacred Heart; Special Assignment; College of Consultors; Building Committee Retired.
Mitchell, Peter G. '51 (HRT) Retired.
Mitchell, Peter '78 (ORL) Bartow, FL St. Thomas Aquinas
Mitchell, Peter '99 (LIN) Graduate Studies.
Mitchell, Robert A. *s.j.* '56 (NY)[EE] New York, NY "America;" Residence and publication office of the America Press.
Mitchell, Robert J. '85 (PAT) Budd Lake, NJ St. Jude; Engaged Encounter.
Mitchell, Robert W. '73 (ORL) Kissimmee, FL Holy Redeemer.
Mitchell, Royce '74 (NO) Retired.
Mitchell, Salvatore P. '42 (E) Retired.
Mitchell, Thomas R. '79 (HRT) East Hartford, CT St. Rose's.
Mitchell, Tomas *o.s.b.* '61 (SFE)[I] Abiquiu, NM Monastery of Christ in the Desert.
Mitchell, Walter A. '61 (BRK) Manhattan Beach, NY St. Margaret Mary.
Mitchell, Walter '91 (MIA) Retired.
Mitchell, William J. '49 (PHX) Retired.
Mitchell, William *ss.cc.* '50 (FR)[H] Fairhaven, MA Damien Residence.
Mitchko, James '77 (PSC) North Fort Myers, FL All Saints Byzantine Catholic.
Mitek, Jozef '84 (VEN) Bonita Springs, FL St. Leo.
Miti, Nathanael *s.j.* (BAL)[S] Baltimore, MD Jesuit Community of Loyola College, Inc..
Mitka, John J. '66 (BUF) Finance Council; Buffalo, NY St. Teresa.
Mitko, Joseph K. *o.ss.t.* '80 (BAL)[S] Baltimore, MD Holy Trinity Monastery.
Mitolo, Frank A. '68 (PIT).
Mitolo, Frank '68 (PIT) Pittsburgh, PA Resurrection.
Mitoraj, Chester *c.r.* '48 (CHI) Chicago, IL St. Hyacinth Basilica.
Mitrano, Joseph *c.s.b.* '41 (AUS) Kingsland, TX St. Charles Borromeo.
Mittelstadt, John *o.f.m.* '62 (GLP) Tohatchi, NM St. Mary Church.
Mitten, Stephen F. *s.j.* '95 (STL)[O] St. Louis, MO Jesuit Community Corporation at St. Louis University – Jesuit Hall.
Mitty, Edward J. *p.a.* '50 (NY) New York, NY Our Lady of Victory.
Mitulski, James M. '72 (STL) Farmington, MO St. Joseph.
Mitzel, Daniel C. (HBG) Harrisburg, PA St. Francis of Assisi; Deans; Presbyteral Council.
Mixtacki, Eugene *o.f.m.cap.* '80 (PAT)[M] Oak Ridge–Milton, NJ St. Stanislaus B. M. Friary.
Miyares, Carlos '81 (MIA) Miami Lakes, FL Our Lady of the Lakes.
Miyares, Gustavo J. '73 (MIA) Hialeah, FL Immaculate Conception; [C] Miami, FL Msgr. Edward Pace High School.
Miyares, Gustavo (MIA) Consultors; Building Commission; Archdiocesan Fund–Raising & Assessments Committee; Archdiocesan Vocations Review Board.
Mizener, Paul '64 (SP) Beverly Hills, FL Our Lady of Grace.
Mizeur, Thomas '73 (PEO) Rock Island, IL St. Pius X; Air National Guard Chaplains.
Mizicko, Carroll *o.f.m.* (BEL)[F] East St. Louis, IL St. Benedict the Black Friary.
Mlay, Mark *a.l.c.p.* '84 (PMB) Royal Palm Beach, FL Our Lady Queen of the Apostles.
Mlsna, Todd A. '98 (LC) La Crosse, WI St. Joseph the Workman Cathedral.
Moala, Saimone '83 (SFR) San Mateo, CA St. Timothy; Tongan Ministry.
Moan, Francis X. *s.j.* '57 (CAM) Camden, NJ Holy Name.
Moccia, Bonaventure *c.p.* '52 (WOR)[O] Shrewsbury, MA Calvary Retreat Center, Passionist Fathers of Shrewsbury, Inc..
Mocco, Charles W. (GB) Clergy Credit Union.
Mocco, Charles '57 (GB) Retired.
Mocio, Stephen J. '76 (DAL) Dallas, TX St. Philip.
Mock, Robert M. '84 (BUF) Consultors, College of; Council of Priests; Portageville, NY Assumption B.V.M.; Buffalo, NY St. John the Evangelist.
Mock, Timothy *c.m.m.* '52 (DET)[K] Vocation Office.
Mockaitis, Timothy '78 (P) Portland, OR St. Agatha; Oregon City, OR St. John the Apostle.
Mockel, George E. '75 (OAK) Concord, CA St. Agnes.
Mockevicius, Dominic F. '48 (ROC) Rochester, NY St. George Retired.
Mockler, Patrick J. '79 (BLX) Biloxi, MS Our Lady of Fatima; Air Force Reserve Chaplains.
Mockler, Patrick (BLX) Advocates; Presbyteral Council.
Mockler, Peter '73 (BLX) Gulfport, MS St. Ann; College of Consultors; Finance Council; Presbyteral Council.
Moczulski, David *o.f.m.* '93 (CIN)[N] Pittsburgh, PA Holy Family Friary.
Moczydlowski, Chester M. (CHR) Building & Renovation Commission.
Moczydlowski, Chet M. '73 (CHR) Myrtle Beach, SC St. Andrew's.
Moczydlowski, Stanley M. '02 (ALN) Allentown, PA St. Thomas More; Elected Members.
Modde, Bradley E. '97 (STL) St. Louis, MO Our Lady of Sorrows; St. Louis, MO St. Mary Magdalen.
Mode, Daniel L. '92 (ARL) Alexandria, VA Queen of Apostles; Defenders of the Bond; Navy Reserve Chaplains.
Modeen, James '81 (TUC)[D] Tucson, AZ St. Mary's Hospital.
Moder, John *s.m.* '79 (STL)[O] St. Louis Provincialate of the Society of Mary, Province of the United States.

Modi, Francis Abel *m.c.c.j.* '71 (LA) Los Angeles, CA St. Cecilia.
Modino, Roman '89 (TR) Freehold, NJ St. Rose of Lima.
Modlin, William F. '96 (PRT) Greenville, ME Holy Family; Jackman, ME St. Anthony.
Modrys, Walter F. *s.j.* '78 (NY) New York, NY St. Ignatius Loyola; [EE] New York, NY St. Ignatius Loyola Residence.
Modugno, Diego Di (PCE) Penuelas, PR St. Joseph.
Modugno, Thomas A. '66 (NY) New York, NY St. Monica; Manhattan (East).
Moeder, August L. '53 (SAL) Retired.
Moeder, John '57 (SAL) Retired.
Moeggenberg, Raymond '56 (SAG) Retired.
Moeglein, James *o.s.c.* '70 (SCL)[I] Onamia, MN Crosier Monastery.
Moell, Carl J. *s.j.* '53 (CIN) Cincinnati, OH St. Francis Xavier.
Moellenberndt, Duane R. '76 (MAD) Sun Prairie, WI Sacred Hearts of Jesus and Mary; Building Commission; Council of Catholic Women.
Moeller, George B. '62 (BAL) Baltimore, MD St. Joseph; Consultors.
Moeller, George (BAL) Consultors.
Moellering, Norbert *s.m.* '46 (SAT)[K] San Antonio, TX Marianist Residence: Skilled Nursing.
Moelter, Joel *o.carm.* '51 (JOL)[L] Darien Carmelite Provincial Office; (FgM).
Moen, Brian '03 (FAR) Fargo, ND St. Mary Cathedral.
Moenkedick, Leo '86 (SCL) Flensburg, MN Sacred Heart; Randall, MN St. James; Little Falls, MN St. Stanislaus; Air National Guard Chaplains.
Moerman, Stephen A. '94 (PH) Drexel Hill, PA St. Charles Borromeo.
Moeschler, William H. *m.m.* '44 (NY).
Moeser, Marion *o.s.f.* (WDC)[B] Washington, DC Washington Theological Union.
Moeslein, Francis R. '58 (R) Morehead City, NC St. Egbert; Apostleship of the Sea Retired.
Mofan, Feliciano T. '79 (SFR) Mill Valley, CA Our Lady of Mt. Carmel.
Moffatt, Charles P. *s.s.j.* '57 (BAL)[S] Baltimore, MD St. Joseph Society of the Sacred Heart House of Central Administration.
Moffatt, Joseph *c.s.b.* '61 (VEN) Naples, FL St. Ann.
Moffitt, Joseph M. *s.j.* '44 (WDC)[M] Washington, DC The Jesuit Community at Georgetown University.
Moffo, Joseph G. *c.s.* '59 (HRT) New Haven, CT St. Anthony's.
Mohammed, Nigel '01 (NEW) Caldwell, NJ St. Aloysius; Jersey City, NJ St. Paul of the Cross.
Mohan, Bernard N. '61 (NEW) Archdiocesan Judges Retired.
Mohan, Oliver *o.m.i.* '48 (PHX) Cave Creek, AZ St. Gabriel.
Mohan, Robert Paul '46 (WDC)[C] Catholic University of America, The Retired.
Mohl, Andrew S. '84 (BAL) Randallstown, MD Holy Family.
Mohnickey, Ronald J. *t.o.r.* '71 (ARL)[F] Steubenville, OH Holy Spirit Friary.
Mohr, J. Patrick *s.j.* '75 (SCR)[C] Scranton, PA The University of Scranton.
Mohr, Richard G. '67 (BEL) Marion, IL St. Joseph.
Mohr, Simon *o.f.m.conv.* '57 (ALB)[A] Rensselaer, NY Conventual Franciscan Friars; [L] Rensselaer, NY Provincialate, Immaculate Conception Friary – Order of Friars Minor Conventual.
Mohr, Thomas H. '58 (DAV) Retired.
Mohrbacher, Austin '57 (PSC) Philadelphia, PA Holy Trinity.
Mohrman, J. Gregory *o.s.b.* '86 (STL)[F] Creve Coeur, MO St. Louis Priory School; [O] St. Louis, MO The Abbey of St. Mary and St. Louis.
Moijueh, Sylvester '96 (PIT) Sewickley, PA St. Mary.
Moineau, John A. '87 (GBG) Murrysville, PA Mother of Sorrows; College of Consultors; Bishop's Priests Council.
Moisant, William C. '01 (P) Astoria, OR St. Mary, Star of the Sea.
Moisin, Michael '88 (ROM) Brookline, MA Romanian Catholic Mission of Boston; Board of Consultors; Office to Aid the Church in Romania.
Mojica, Luis Efrain '51 (MIA) Miami Beach, FL St. Francis de Sales.
Mokarzel, Galeb *o.m.i.* '51 (SAT)[M] San Antonio, TX.
Mokluk, John M. *o.s.f.s.* '70 (WIL)[B] Wilmington, DE Salesianum School.
Mokris, Michael '61 (PBR) Retired.
Mokrzycki, M. Joseph '65 (TR) Long Branch, NJ Our Lady Star of the Sea.
Mol, Joseph C. '77 (CHI) Hickory Hills, IL St. Patricia.
Mol, Joseph (CHI)[A] Advocates.
Molan, John E. '53 (MAN) Auburn, NH St. Peter; New Hampshire State Prison for Women; Council of Priests; College of Consultors; Clergy Personnel Board; Manchester, NH St. Pius X.
Molano, Ernesto '56 (MIA) Judges Retired.
Molenda, Bogdan *s.chr.* '84 (LA) Los Angeles, CA Our Lady of the Bright Mount.
Moleski, Martin X. *s.j.* '81 (BUF)[O] Buffalo, NY Canisius Jesuit Community.
Molewski, Andrew '82 (WIL) Wilmington, DE St. Hedwig.
Molewski, Pawel (NEW) Elizabeth, NJ St. Mary of the Assumption.
Moley, Kevin J. *c.ss.r.* '70 (BRK)[V] Brooklyn, NY Our Lady of Good Counsel Residence; (FgM).
Molgano, James '03 (PMB) North Palm Beach, FL St. Paul of the Cross.
Molina, Angel '94 (CGS) Caguas, PR Nuestra Senora del Perpetuo Socorro; Sec. Chancellor; Priests Senate.
Molina, Arturo '83 (LEX) Lexington, KY Federal Medical Center.
Molina, Joe '95 (ELP) El Paso, TX Santo Nino De Atocha.
Molina, Juam J. *o.ss.t.* '99 (BAL)[S] Crown Point, LA Ave Maria Retreat House.
Molina, Pedro '90 (SAT) Sabinal, TX St. Patrick's; [N] San Antonio, TX Cordi–Marian Missionary Sisters.
Molina, Seraphim *s.t.* '97 (WDC)[M] Riverdale, MD Holy Spirit Missionary Cenacle.
Molina–Restrepo, Fernando '99 (ATL) Greensboro, GA Christ Our King and Savior.
Molinari, Todd '95 (P) Milwaukie, OR St. John the Baptist; Board Members.
Molinaro, Kenneth M. *c.s.c.* '76 (FTW)[I] South Bend, IN Congregation of Holy Cross, Indiana Province, Provincial House.
Molinaro, Matthew J. '49 (LC) Arkansaw, WI St. Joseph.
Molina Rojas, Jose B. '92 (SJN) Toa Baja, PR Espiritu Santo.
Moline, Joe (ELP) Vocations & Seminarians.
Molinelli, Louis J. *s.d.b.* '90 (SP)[B] St. Petersburg, FL St. Petersburg Catholic High School.
Molinelli, Louis *s.d.b.* (SP) Presbyteral Council.
Molini, Thomas M. '85 (STL)[A] St. Louis, MO Kenrick School of Theology.
Molitor, Donald F. '63 (STL) House Springs, MO Our Lady, Queen of Peace.
Molka, Victor J. '78 (PIT) New Castle, PA Mary, Mother of Hope.
Moll, Walter J. '85 (ALT) Portage, PA St. Joseph's.
Mollan, Paul F. '54 (OKL) Special Assignment.
Mollan, Paul '54 (OKL) Oklahoma City, OK Cathedral of Our Lady of Perpetual Help.
Mollan, Ralph R. '43 (CHI) Retired.
Molling, Mark '80 (MIL) Milwaukee, WI Mary, Queen of Martyrs.
Molloy, James E. '72 (PH) Sellersville, PA St. Agnes.
Molloy, John *c.p.m.* '46 (OWN)[F] Auburn, KY Fathers of Mercy.
Molloy, Joseph '83 (SFD) Decatur, IL Holy Family.
Molloy, Kevin '72 (SP) St. Pete Beach, FL St. John.
Molloy, Patrick J. '40 (STL) Retired.
Molloy, Patrick J. *m.h.m.* '73 (LA)[Q] Los Angeles, CA Mill Hill Missionaries Procure.
Molloy, Thomas E. '70 (RVC) Judges for Interdiocesan Tribunal; Army Reserve Chaplains.
Molnar, Anthony '34 (FTW) Retired.
Molnar, Jeffrey T. '03 (PIT) Pittsburgh, PA St. Charles Lwanga Parish.
Molnar, John J. *o.s.a.* '66 (CHI)[N] Chicago, IL St. Rita Monastery.
Molnar, Jude *t.o.r.* '65 (WH)[P] Fairmont, WV Fairmont State College Newman Center.
Molnar, Michael '76 (DET) On Duty Outside the Archdiocese.
Molodowitz, Augustine '59 (PHU) Perth Amboy, NJ Assumption of B.V.M..
Molokie, Jerome M. *o.praem.* '95 (ORG)[D] Silverado, CA St. Michael's Preparatory School; [I] Silverado, CA Norbertine Fathers of Orange Inc..
Moloney, Alphonsus '63 (SD) Retired.
Moloney, Francis J. '79 (WDC)[C] Catholic University of America, The.
Moloney, James A. '56 (DET) Dearborn Heights, MI St. Anselm; College of Consultors; Propagation of the Faith (Missions).
Moloney, John C. '91 (PH) Levittown, PA Queen of the Universe.
Moloney, John Jesus '72 (LA) Downey, CA Our Lady of Perpetual Help; Glendora, CA St. Dorothy; [D] Laredo, TX St. John Priory, F.J..
Moloney, John '72 (LA) On Sick Leave.
Moloney, Patrick W. '77 (NTN) Retired.
Moloney, Stephan J. '82 (COL) Columbus, OH Saint Stephen the Martyr; Gahanna, OH St. Matthew; Vicar General/Chancellor; Chancellor; Diocesan Consultors; Appointed Members; Promoter of Justice; Diocesan Board of Review for the Protection of Children; Diocesan Finance Council; Victim Assistance Coordinator.
Moloney, Thomas J. *s.c.a.* '73 (DET) Wyandotte, MI St. Joseph.
Molter, Richard J. '64 (MIL) Racine, WI St. Edward.
Moltesz, Joseph E. *s.j.* '57 (NY)[EE] New York, NY Murray–Weigel Hall.
Molumby, Donald '56 (SFS) Retired.
Molumby, Edward J. *s.t.* '93 (SB) San Bernardino, CA Our Lady of Fatima.
Molumby, Edward *s.t.* '61 (SB) San Bernardino, CA St. Bernardine; Pastoral Coordinator Staffing Committee.
Molyn, John '81 (ALB) Valatie, NY St. John the Baptist; Presbyteral Council; Diocesan Board of Consultors.
Molyneux, John *c.m.f.* '97 (CHI)[N] Chicago, IL Claretian Missionaries, St. Jude League, Inc..
Momay, Edgar '00 (AGN) Dededo, GU Santa Barbara.
Mompoint, Jean–Claude '89 (PH) Philadelphia, PA Incarnation of Our Lord; Haitian Apostolate.
Monacell, Cornelius J. *s.j.* '59 (SJ)[M] Los Gatos, CA Sacred Heart Jesuit Center.
Monaco, David *c.p.* '90 (CHI)[H] Chicago, IL.
Monaco, James M. '85 (BUF) Buffalo, NY St. Francis Xavier; Buffalo, NY St. John the Baptist.
Monaghan, Charles J. '41 (PH) Retired.
Monaghan, George D. '41 (SR) Retired.
Monaghan, George '41 (SFR)[K] San Rafael, CA Nazareth House Retired.
Monaghan, George '80 (DAL) Allen, TX St. Jude.
Monaghan, J. Fergus '72 (SPC) Springfield, MO St. Elizabeth Ann Seton; Region IV.
Monaghan, James *s.j.* '46 (SJ)[M] Los Gatos, CA Sacred Heart Jesuit Center.
Monaghan, John T. '63 (NY)[E] New York, NY Cardinal Spellman High School.
Monaghan, Joseph F. *s.j.* '52 (BAL)[S] Philadelphia, PA St. Joseph's Hospital.
Monaghan, Justin D. '66 (SPC) Joplin, MO St. Mary; Region I.
Monaghan, Robert '62 (STP) Minneapolis, MN Incarnation.
Monaghan, Thomas J. '70 (MAD) Reedsburg, WI Sacred Heart.
Monagle, Henry P. '91 (BO) Military & VA Chaplains.
Monagle, Robert J. (BO) Air Force Chaplains.
Monahan, David F. '53 (OKL) St. Francis de Sales Seminary (Legal Title) Retired.
Monahan, George J. '97 (PH) Downingtown, PA St. Joseph.
Monahan, Joseph E. '77 (DEN) Golden, CO St. Joseph.
Monahan, Joseph R. '62 (STL) St. Louis, MO St. Raphael The Archangel.
Monahan, Joseph *t.o.r.* '90 (PIT) Allegheny County, PA Mercy Health System of Pittsburgh–Pittsburgh Mercy Hospital; [N] Pittsburgh, PA Third Order Regular of Saint Francis – Province of the Most Sacred Heart of Jesus.
Monahan, Kieran *o.f.m.* '65 (PRT) Portland, ME St. Peter's.
Monahan, Paul '60 (DM) Glenwood, IA Our Lady of the Holy Rosary.
Monahan, Richard J. '59 (BGP) Retired.
Monahan, Thomas J. '58 (RCK) Experts; Priests' Eucharistic League Retired.
Monan, J. Donald *s.j.* '55 (New York)[V] Newton, MA The Jesuit Community at Boston College.
Moncada, Fabio '81 (SJN) Canovanas, PR Nuestra Senora del Pilar.
Moncher, Raymond F. '58 (MAR) Wakefield, MI Immaculate Conception of the Blessed Virgin Mary Retired.
Monclova, Michael '97 (PEO) Havana, IL St. Patrick's.
Mondello, Donald J. '60 (GBG) Latrobe, PA Holy Family; Diocesan Council of Catholic Women.
Mondiek, Stephen S. '03 (CIN) Dayton, OH St. Peter.
Mondik, Michael '73 (PSC) Rahway, NJ St. Thomas the Apostle; Syncellus; Eparchial College of Consultors; Ex Officio Members; Building and Properties Commission; Eparchial Liturgy and Art Commission.
Mondor, Christian *o.f.m.* '51 (ORG) Huntington Beach, CA SS. Simon and Jude; Ecumenical and Interreligious Affairs.
Mondragon, Ezequiel '62 (DET) Imlay City, MI Sacred Heart; Presbyteral Council.
Mondzelewski, Dominic *o.s.b.* '69 (CLV) Cleveland, OH St. Lawrence; [D] Cleveland, OH Benedictine High School; [O] Cleveland, OH.
Moneck, George J. '89 (PIT) Roscoe, PA St. Joseph; Green County, PA State Correctional Institute at Greene.
Monestero, John '75 (ORG) Orange, CA St. Norbert; Anaheim, CA St. Justin Martyr; Absent on Sick Leave; Ministry to Priests; Ecumenical and Interreligious Affairs.
Monestime, Perard C. *s.j.* '85 (BO)[E] Dorchester, MA Boston College High School & Jesuit Community.
Monet, Zack *o.carm.* '60 (JOL)[L] Darien Carmelite Provincial Office.
Moneta, Robert G. '51 (PSC) Newark, NJ St. George; Holy Name Society; Eparchial Music Commission; Retirement Plan Board.
Monette, Michael R. '99 (MAN) Newton, NH Mary, Mother of the Church; Auditors.
Monforton, Jeffrey M. '94 (DET) Special Assignment; Cardinal's Office.
Mongelluzzo, James A. '74 (WOR) On Duty Outside the Diocese.
Mongeon, Peter M. '83 (NO) On Medical Leave of Absence.

Mongiello, Anthony P. '80 (ALN) Bethlehem, PA St. Anne; Serra Club of Bethlehem.
Mongiello, Robert '87 (VEN) Punta Gorda, FL Sacred Heart.
Mongrain, Dennis '77 (LA) Cedar Sinai Medical Center.
Monico, Gilberto '02 (LA) Encino, CA Our Lady of Grace.
Moniuk, Evhan '92 (PHU) Philadelphia, PA Immaculate Conception of Blessed Virgin Mary, Cathedral; Palmerton, PA St. Vladimir's.
Moniz, Joseph V. '64 (LA) Pasadena, CA St. Philip the Apostle.
Monnens, Merle W. '56 (NU) Retired.
Monnerat, Brian W. '88 (HRT) Forestville, CT St. Matthew; Special and other Archdiocesan Assignment; Holy Childhood Association; Mission Cooperative Planning Office; Propagation of the Faith, Society for.
Monnin, Robert J. '55 (CIN) Retired.
Monogue, Michael G. '85 (STP) Minneapolis, MN St. Anne.
Monohan, Duncan W. '77 (SD) Winterhaven, CA St. Thomas.
Monostori, Benedict *o.cist.* '44 (DAL)[K] Irving, TX Cistercian Abbey of Our Lady of Dallas.
Monreal, Jesus *o.carm.* '69 (ARE) Morovis, PR Nuestra Senora del Carmen; Priest's Senate (Consejo Presbiteral).
Monroe, Charles F. '75 (WOR) Worcester, MA Our Lady of the Angels.
Monroe, Edward F. *c.ss.r.* '61 (MIL)[R] Oconomowoc, WI The Redemptorist Retreat Center; Sheboygan, WI St. Clement; Sheboygan, WI Holy Name.
Monsalve, German Barona *m.s.c.* '86 (FgM).
Monshau, Michael *o.p.* '88 (OAK)[N] Oakland, CA Dominican Order (Western Province), St. Albert's Priory.
Monsour, Raymond G. '63 (STP) Le Center, MN St. Mary.
Montag, John F. '93 (OM)[K] Omaha, NE Jesuit Community at Creighton University.
Montagna, Julio *i.v.e.* (BGP)[P] Bridgeport, CT Instituto Verbo Encarnado.
Montague, George T. *s.m.* '58 (SAT)[M] San Antonio, TX Casa San Juan Marianist Community.
Montague, George *s.m.* '58 (SAT)[C] San Antonio, TX St. Mary's University of San Antonio, Texas; [U] San Antonio, TX Brothers of the Beloved Disciplel.
Montague, Hugh *s.o.cist.* '82 (ALN)[K] New Ringgold, PA Cistercian Monastery.
Montalbano, Frank *o.m.i.* '47 (NO) New Orleans, LA St. Louis Cathedral.
Montalbano, Joseph E. '55 (ALX) Retired.
Montalgo, Manuel Jesus Taco *i.v.e.* (PH)[A] Philadelphia, PA St. Veronica.
Montanaro, Guido G. '69 (BGP) Fairfield, CT Holy Family.
Montanaro, James *o.m.v.* '83 (BO)[V] Milton, MA Oblate Residence (St. Joseph House).
Montanez Lopez, Jose R. *c.p.* '95 (MGZ) Carolina, PR Santa Gema Galgani.
Montano, Angel '92 (CC) Defenders of the Bond; Freer, TX St. Mary.
Montano, Edward J. '45 (NY) Retired.
Montavon, Thomas G. '61 (CLV) Brunswick, OH St. Colette.
Montecalvo, Carlo F. '73 (PRO) On Duty Outside the Diocese; Air Force Chaplains.
Montecalvo, Carlo (MO) Presbyteral Council.
Montecino, Henry R. *s.j.* '47 (NO)[P] New Orleans, LA Ignatius Residence.
Montejano, John G. '94 (LA) Baldwin Park, CA St. John the Baptist.
Montelaro, Thomas '75 (LAF) Retired.
Monteleone, Jacob '75 (SP) Clearwater, FL Light of Christ; Presbyteral Council; College of Consultors; Vicars Forane.
Montella, Alban V. *o.f.m.* '55 (ALB)[A] Catskill, NY St. Anthony Friary.
Montemayor, Eduardo *s.o.l.t.* '02 (CC) Robstown, TX St. Anthony; [G] Robstown, TX Society of Our Lady of the Most Holy Trinity.
Montemayor, Ted *s.d.b.* '83 (LA)[W] Rosemead, CA St. Joseph's Salesian Youth Renewal Center.
Montenegro, Blas *o.a.r.* '49 (NY) Bronx, NY St. John Vianney, Cure of Ars.
Montero, Eduardo G. '83 (PH) Philadelphia, PA Annunciation B.V.M.; [Y] Philadelphia, PA Sacred Heart Manor; Assistant Judicial Vicars.
Montero, Eduardo G. (MO) Judges.
Montero, Fredericks *m.s.f.s.* '48 (ATL)[K] Lawrenceville The Missionaries of St. Francis De Sales.
Montero, Hugo L. '92 (STP) Special Assignment.
Montes, Felipe *c.s.v.* '01 (CHI)[N] Arlington Heights Viatorian Province Center–Clerics of St. Viator.
Montes, Jesse *s.d.b.* '79 (OAK)[E] Richmond, CA Salesian High School.
Montesanti, Steven G. (MAN) Council of Priests; Clergy Personnel Board.
Montesanti, Steven '99 (MAN) Concord, NH St. John the Evangelist.
Montesi, Eugene *s.x.* '62 (BO)[V] Holliston, MA Xaverian Missionaries; [M] Wayne Xaverian Missionary Fathers.
Montesino, Efrain '85 (ARE) Vega Baja, PR Parroquia de San Martin de Porres.
Montez, Paul J. *o.s.b.* '97 (PBL)[F] Canon City, CO Holy Cross Abbey.
Montez, Paul *o.s.b.* '97 (PBL) La Junta, CO Our Lady of Guadalupe/St. Patrick; Rocky Ford, CO St. Peter.
Montgomery, Joseph T. '58 (HRT) Retired.
Montgomery, Matthias *o.c.d.* '62 (MIL)[O] Holy Hill, WI Discalced Carmelite Monastery – Holy Hill National Shrine of Mary Help of Christians.
Montgomery, William L. '79 (WDC) Special Ministries; [D] Washington, DC Archbishop Carroll High School.
Monti, Dominic V. *o.f.m.* '71 (BUF)[C] St. Bonaventure University.
Monti, Dominic V. *o.f.m.* '71 (WDC).
Monti, Dominick V. *o.f.m.* '71 (BUF)[O] St. Bonaventure, NY St. Bonaventure Friary; [C] St. Bonaventure, NY Friar Community.
Monti, Robert M. '61 (LC) On Duty Outside the Diocese.
Monti, Robert '61 (MIA)[G] Fort Lauderdale, FL Holy Cross Hospital.
Monticello, Robert V. '51 (DET) Retired.
Montiel, Jose M. '57 (FRS) Merced, CA Sacred Heart.
Montiel, Jose '57 (FRS) Mariposa, CA Mt. Bullion Conservation Camp.
Montini–Coleman, James (MOB) Notary; Officers; Group IV.
Montminy, Marc R. '77 (MAN) Manchester, NH St. Marie; Manchester, NH Sacred Heart of Jesus; Directors.
Montminy, Paul D. '78 (MAN) Gonic, NH St. Leo; Rochester, NH Holy Rosary; Charismatic Renewal & Cursillo Movement.
Montondon, Walter '57 (BEA) Retired.
Montoya, Francisco (SAL) Hays, KS Immaculate Heart of Mary.
Montoya, Jesus '63 (SLC) Ogden, UT St. Joseph's.
Montoya, Juan *o.f.m.* '81 (LSC) Roswell, NM St. John the Baptist.
Montoya, Juan '89 (MIA) Absent on Sick Leave.
Montoya, Michael *m.j.* '94 (LA) Los Angeles, CA Precious Blood.
Montoya, Oscar Dario Colorado (CHI) Chicago, IL All Saints–St. Anthony; Chicago, IL St. Maurice.
Montoya, Paul M. '73 (LA) Santa Clarita, CA Our Lady of Perpetual Help.
Montoya, Paul (LA) Moderator; San Fernando Pastoral Region.
Montoya, Pedro N. '93 (ARE) Camuy, PR St. Joseph.
Montplaisir, Roland A. '40 (MAN) Retired.
Monturo, Christopher '03 (NY) Bronx, NY St. Theresa of the Infant Jesus.
Monzillo, Oneil A. '53 (LAV) Las Vegas, NV St. Joseph, Husband of Mary.
Monzillo, Oneil '53 (NO) Retired.
Moodie, Michael R. *s.j.* '79 (SFR)[F] Los Angeles, CA Loyola High School of Los Angeles.
Moody, Jerome *c.ss.r.* '73 (FgM).
Moody, Kenneth J. *m.m.* '70 (NY)[EE] Maryknoll Maryknoll Fathers and Brothers.
Moody, Michael *s.v.d.* '64 (BLX)[A] Bay St. Louis, MS St. Augustine's.
Moody, Quentin E. '85 (NO) New Orleans, LA St. Simon Peter.
Moody, Thomas A. '67 (OG) Malone, NY St. John Bosco; North Bangor, NY St. Augustine; [F] Ellenburg Center, NY Our Lady of the Adirondacks Inc. House of Prayer.
Moody, William '78 (BAL) Retired.
Mooka, John Mary *a.j.* (HBG) York, PA Immaculate Conception of the Blessed Virgin Mary.
Moon, Michael E. '02 (MAD) Madison, WI St. Raphael Cathedral; Madison, WI Holy Redeemer.
Mooney, Dennis M. '77 (PH) Bristol, PA St. Mark.
Mooney, Michael P. '63 (PT) Pensacola, FL Nativity of Our Lord.
Mooney, Michael (PT) College of Consultors; Administrative Council; Communications, Office of; Respect Life Committee; Priests' Pension Plan Board for.
Mooney, Richard T. (BAL) Defenders of the Bond.
Mooney, Richard '79 (RIC) Blacksburg, VA St. Mary & Newman Community.
Mooney, Terence J. *c.m.* '48 (PH)[AA] St. Catherine Infirmary.
Mooney, Thomas J. '47 (BO) Lakeville, MA Saints Martha and Mary; Senior Priests Retired.
Mooney, William C. '68 (STA) St. Augustine, FL Corpus Christi.
Mooney, William J. '68 (PAT) Florham Park, NJ Holy Family.
Mooney, William '55 (SD) Poway, CA St Michael.
Moons, Joseph *c.p.* '77 (GAL)[Q] Houston, TX Congregation of the Passion, Holy Name Retreat Center; [S] Houston, TX Holy Name Retreat Center.
Mooradd, Paul '84 (SAM) Newton Square, PA St. Sharbel.
Moorby, William A. '82 (ROC) Owego, NY St. Patrick; Owego, NY Blessed Trinity.
Moore, Andrew '97 (BEA) Diocesan College of Consultors and Presbyteral Council; Vocations; Baytown, TX Holy Trinity.
Moore, Anthony F. *o.f.m.* '51 (NY) Yulan, NY St. Anthony of Padua.
Moore, Augustine J. '60 (SFE) Espanola, NM Sacred Heart.
Moore, Brian R. '83 (DOD) Dodge City, KS The Cathedral of Our Lady of Guadalupe; Pastoral Ministry Formation.
Moore, Brian R. '83 (DOD) Presbyteral Council; College of Consultors; Priestly Life and Ministry.
Moore, Brian (DOD) Office of Liturgy and Worship (R.C.I.A.).
Moore, C. Thomas *o.p.* '57 (CHI)[N] Chicago Dominicans (Provincial Office).
Moore, Christian *o.f.m.conv.* '65 (L) Louisville, KY Incarnation; [K] Louisville, KY St. Francis of Assisi Friary.
Moore, Christopher P. '77 (BAL) Hagerstown, MD St. Joseph; Interdiocesan Judges.
Moore, Clarke W. (TUC) Retired.
Moore, Dan *s.s.* '84 (MEM) On Duty Outside the Diocese.
Moore, Donald C. '65 (OKL) Special Assignment; [F] Oklahoma City, OK St. Ann's Home Inc..
Moore, Donald J. *s.j.* '60 (NY)[EE] New York, NY West Side Jesuit Community.
Moore, Edmund J. '59 (SHP) Monroe, LA Jesus the Good Shepherd; [A] Monroe, LA St. Frederick High School; Judges Retired.
Moore, Edward F. '59 (BUR) Retired.
Moore, Frederick B. '80 (DET)[H] Pontiac, MI St. Joseph Mercy – Oakland.
Moore, Frederick Thomas '75 (STA) On Duty Outside the Diocese.
Moore, George B. '66 (PH) Philadelphia, PA St. Benedict.
Moore, Gerald T. '39 (SEA) Retired.
Moore, Gregory J. *o.p.* '55 (CHI)[N] St. Pius V Priory.
Moore, Gregory *o.p.* '55 (DET) St. Clair Shores, MI St. Gertrude.
Moore, J. Raymond '56 (SD) Retired.
Moore, James R. '67 (NY) Croton Falls, NY St. Joseph.
Moore, James T. '84 (GAL) Houston, TX Our Lady of Walsingham.
Moore, James W. *s.j.* '59 (PH)[C] Jesuit Fathers; [AA] Loyola Center and Manresa Hall.
Moore, James '74 (SB) Twentynine Palms, CA Blessed Sacrament.
Moore, James '88 (SFE) Albuquerque, NM Sacred Heart.
Moore, John Charles '78 (BAL) Middletown, MD Holy Family Catholic Community.
Moore, John E. '45 (FAR) Retired.
Moore, John F. '60 (FR) North Falmouth, MA St. Elizabeth Seton; Diocesan Office of Communications; Diocesan Newspaper.
Moore, John J. '57 (GF) Retired.
Moore, John P. '55 (NY) New York, NY Immaculate Conception.
Moore, John R. '64 (RVC) East Islip, NY St. Mary's.
Moore, John '56 (NY) Retired.
Moore, Jon H. '81 (WIN) Austin, MN Queens of Angels Hermitage; [A] Winona, MN Immaculate Heart of Mary Seminary; [H] Austin, MN Queen of Angels Hermitage, Monastic Fraternity of St. Joseph.
Moore, Joseph P. '71 (BGP) Leave of Absence.
Moore, Lawrence *s.j.* '77 (NO)[C] New Orleans, LA Loyola University New Orleans.
Moore, Mark J. '03 (STU) Marietta, OH St. Mary's.
Moore, Matthias *c.s.sp.* '52 (NO) Retired.
Moore, Michael *s.p.s.* '84 (SJ)[M] Saratoga, CA St. Patrick's Missionary Society.
Moore, Michael '97 (FRS) Exeter, CA Sacred Heart.
Moore, Neil '60 (P) Retired.
Moore, Patrick *o.s.b.* (BIS) Presbyteral Council.
Moore, Raymond H. '81 (WDC) Largo, MD St. Joseph.
Moore, Robert J. *o.c.s.o.* '49 (ROC)[I] Piffard, NY Abbey of the Genesee.
Moore, Robert J. '83 (NY) Bronx, NY St. Mary Star of the Sea.
Moore, Steven C. (ANC) Diocesan Consultors.
Moore, Steven '76 (ANC) Anchorage, AK St. Patrick; On Sabbatical.
Moore, Terence M. '67 (SLC) Draper, UT St. John the Baptist.
Moore, Thomas G. '88 (MET) On Duty Outside the Diocese.
Moore, Thomas M. *o.s.f.s.* '66 (SAG) Pastoral Team; Pastoral Team.
Moore, Thomas *o.s.f.s.* '66 (SAG) Office of Church Ministries; Pastoral Team; Pastoral Team.
Moore, Ward P. '72 (NEW) Westwood, NJ St. Andrew's.
Moore, Wilbur E. '57 (OKL) Nicoma Park, OK Our Lady of Fatima.
Moore, William C. '68 (STO) Stockton, CA St. Bernadette Church (Pastor of); Deans; Air Force Reserve Chaplains.

Moore, William F. '69 (CAM) Pennsauken, NJ St. Cecilia's.
Moore, William (STO) Diocesan Building Committee.
Moorman, Dennis *m.m.* '98 (FgM).
Moorman, Raymond J. '46 (STP) Retired.
Moorman, William J. *o.ss.t.* '79 (BAL).
Moorman, William J. *o.ss.t.* (MO).
Moorman, William J. *o.ss.t.* (WDC)[C] Catholic University of America, The.
Moors, Clif *s.m.* (BO) Burlington, MA Lahey Hitchcock Medical Center.
Moors, Clifton W. *s.m.* '56 (BO) Lawrence, MA Sacred Heart.
Moorse, Dustan *o.s.b.* '78 (SCL)[I] Collegeville, MN St. John's Abbey, of the Order of St. Benedict.
Moortgat, Luke *c.i.c.m.* '65 (FgM).
Moosbrugger, Robert *o.m.i.* '70 (WDC)[M] Washington, DC Provincial Offices of the United States Province of the Missionary Oblates of Mary Immaculate; [M] Washington, DC Oblate Community; [V] Washington, DC Archdiocese of Cotabato.
Moosbrugger, Robert *o.m.i.* '70 (CHI)[X] Chicago, IL Oblates for International Pastoral aka Oblate International Pastoral Investment Trust.
Mootheril, Ambrose (PIT) Pittsburgh, PA St. John Neumann; Allegheny County, PA Vincentian Regency Home.
Moozhikuzhy, Antony *c.m.i.* '59 (BEA) Port Arthur, TX St. Therese the Little Flower of Jesus.
Mora, Ismael '02 (SR) Ukiah, CA St. Mary of the Angels.
Mora, Juan R. '92 (ARE) Arecibo, PR San Juan Bosco.
Mora, Pedro M. *c.s.b.* '04 (GAL)[Q] Sugar Land Basilian Mission Center.
Mora, Sergio '94 (OAK) Hayward, CA St. Joachim.
Mora, Tito Medina *m.s.c.* '92 (FgM).
Morabito, Vincent R. '87 (PH) Berwyn, PA St. Monica; [D] Radnor, PA Archbishop John Carroll High School.
Moraczewski, Albert S. *o.p.* '54 (GAL) Houston, TX Holy Rosary.
Moraczewski, Albert S. *o.p.* '54 (BO)[EE] Boston, MA National Catholic Bioethics Center.
Moraes, Claudio *o.s.b.* '84 (GBG)[H] Latrobe Saint Vincent Archabbey.
Moraga, Cecilio T. '84 (SD) Holtville, CA St. Joseph; Presbyteral Council.
Moragne, James C. '75 (NO) Paradis, LA St. John the Baptist.
Moral, Alejandro *o.c.d.* '60 (CGS) Caguas, PR San Jose.
Morales, Angel Luis '83 (SJN) Dorado, PR San Antonio de Padua.
Morales, Anibal '93 (MIA) Miami, FL St. Thomas the Apostle.
Morales, Antonio '96 (NY) Bronx, NY St. Rita of Cascia Shrine Church.
Morales, Dan '90 (VIC) Port Lavaca, TX Our Lady of the Gulf; Diocesan Consultors; Edna Deanery; Presbyteral Council; Defenders of the Bond; Priests' Personnel Board; Campaign For Human Development and Catholic Relief Services.
Morales, Edward D. '96 (SAT) On Leave.
Morales, Elias '91 (PCE) Ponce, PR Church of the Good Shepherd; [B] The Pontifical Catholic University of Puerto Rico; Judicial Vicar.
Morales, Eusebio Ramos '83 (CGS) Maunabo, PR San Isidro Labrador.
Morales, Francisco '89 (PCE) On Duty Outside the Diocese.
Morales, Francisco '89 (SJN)[E] Santurce, PR Doctor's Community Hospital; [E] San Juan, PR Centro Medico de P.R..
Morales, Gonzalo '85 (FWT) Arlington, TX Most Blessed Sacrament.
Morales, Guillermo '88 (AMA) Gruver, TX Cristo Redentor; Spearman, TX Sacred Heart.
Morales, John F. '60 (GRY) Retired.
Morales, Juan Bautista '83 (MGZ) Moca, PR Our Lady of Monserrate.
Morales, Noel (NEW) Ridgewood, NJ Valley Hospital; Westwood, NJ Pascack Valley Hospital; Chaplains; Chaplains.
Morales, Oscar *o.p.* '89 (SJN) Catano, PR Nuestra Senora del Carmen.
Morales, Oscar '91 (SJ) Morgan Hill, CA St. Catherine of Alexandria.
Morales, Raul '75 (PHX) Retired.
Morales, Raul (CGS) Priests Senate.
Morales, Raymond '81 (LA) Van Nuys, CA St. Bridget of Sweden.
Morales, Robert P. '66 (BRK) Brooklyn, NY Immaculate Conception of the Blessed Virgin Mary.
Morales, Romain G. *c.m.* '73 (STL) St. Louis, MO St. Francis de Sales; [O] St. Louis, MO Vincentian Community; [O] St. Louis, MO Vincentian Residence.
Morales, Salomon J. '63 (ARE) Angeles, PR Our Lady of Angels.
Morales Feliu, Francisco '89 (PCE) San Juan, PR Nuestra Senora de la Esperanza; Santurce, PR Doctors Community Hospital.
Moran, Bernard J. '53 (OAK) Oakland, CA St. Theresa of the Infant Jesus (The Little Flower) Retired.
Moran, Charles '67 (STU) Chesapeake, OH St. Ann.
Moran, Daniel F. '47 (BO) Middleborough, MA Sacred Heart; Senior Priests Retired.
Moran, Edward J. '62 (WOR) Shrewsbury, MA St. Anne's.
Moran, Edward M. '76 (HRT) West Hartford, CT St. Thomas the Apostle Church.
Moran, Edward '89 (RIC) West Point, VA Our Lady of the Blessed Sacrament; Air National Guard Chaplains.
Moran, Edwin *c.p.* '61 (PIT)[N] Pittsburgh, PA St. Paul of the Cross Monastery; [N] Pittsburgh St. Paul of the Cross Monastery.
Moran, Gerard K. '71 (OAK) Fremont, CA Holy Spirit.
Moran, Gerard (OAK) Consultors.
Moran, J. Thomas '57 (BUF) Finance Council; Youngstown, NY St. Bernard's.
Moran, James F. '71 (BO) On Duty Outside the Archdiocese.
Moran, James M. '74 (HRT) Wethersfield, CT Incarnation.
Moran, James M. '03 (NEW) South Orange, NJ Our Lady of Sorrows.
Moran, James P. '45 (GR) Grand Rapids, MI Sacred Heart of Jesus Retired.
Moran, James P. '72 (MET) Edison, NJ Guardian Angels.
Moran, James *c.s.p.* '64 (TUC) Tuscon, AZ St. Cyril of Alexandria.
Moran, James *c.o.* '89 (HON) Honolulu, HI Holy Trinity.
Moran, James *c.o.* '89 (CHR)[E] Rock Hill, SC Oratory of St. Philip Neri, Congregation of the Oratory of Pontifical Rite.
Moran, James (WDC) Washington, DC Washington Hospital Center.
Moran, John J. *m.m.* '66 (NY)[EE] Maryknoll Maryknoll Fathers and Brothers.
Moran, John V. '53 (MAN) Retired.
Moran, John W. '51 (DUB) Monona, IA St. Patrick Retired.
Moran, Joseph P. '71 (HEL) Columbia Falls, MT St. Richard.
Moran, Kevin '65 (SEA) Federal Way, WA St. Theresa; Presbyteral Council; Deans.
Moran, Lawrence J. '52 (IND) Terre Haute, IN St. Patrick.
Moran, Martin O. '88 (HBG)[J] Lewisburg, PA Bucknell University.
Moran, Michael F. '82 (MIL) Army National Guard Chaplains; Waupun, WI St. Mary; Waupun, WI St. Joseph; Waupun, WI St. Brendan.
Moran, Michael J. '58 (NEW) Hillsdale, NJ St. John the Baptist Retired.
Moran, Michael *s.m.a.* '81 (WDC)[N] Tenafly, NJ Society of African Missions, Provincialate, S.M.A. Fathers.
Moran, Michael (VNN) Eparchial Consultors – Presbyteral Council; Commission for the Implementation of the Particular Law.
Moran, Michael (VNN) Sherman Oaks, CA Cathedral of St. Mary; Promoter of Justice.
Moran, Owen '91 (PAT) East Hanover, NJ St. Rose of Lima.
Moran, Patrick '58 (DUL) Absent on Sick Leave.
Moran, Pedro Lopez *c.m.f.* '52 (SJN) Bayamon, PR Santa Maria.
Moran, Peter C. '65 (LA) Northridge, CA Our Lady of Lourdes.
Moran, Richard S. '98 (BO) Newton, MA St. Bernard.
Moran, Robert B. '64 (SJ) Mountain View, CA St. Joseph.
Moran, Robert E. *c.s.p.* '64 (WDC)[B] Washington, DC St. Paul's College.
Moran, Robert E. (LFT) Hartford City, IN St. John the Evangelist; Montpelier, IN St. Margaret of Scotland; Deans.
Moran, Robert J. (BUR) Middletown Springs, VT St. Anne.
Moran, Robert (SJ) Diocesan Clergy Personnel Board.
Moran, Stephen P. '92 (CLV) Wooster, OH St. Mary of the Immaculate Conception.
Moran, Stephen (CLV) Presbyteral Council.
Moran, Terence J. '90 (BO) Chelsea, MA St. Rose of Lima.
Moran, Terence *c.ss.r.* (PAT) Office of Ministry Among Hispanics.
Moran, Thomas A. '71 (CHI) Lyons, IL St. Hugh.
Moran, Thomas *c.m.f.* '55 (CHI) Chicago, IL Our Lady of Guadalupe.
Moran, Timothy J. '76 (BO) Medway, MA St. Joseph.
Moran, Tom '88 (SFR) San Mateo, CA St. Bartholomew.
Morand, Robert '57 (DET) Detroit, MI Our Lady of the Rosary.
Moratelli, Ronald J. '69 (HBG) Quarryville, PA St. Catherine of Siena.
Moraus, Govie '82 (SHP) Retired.
Morawski, Stefan *o.f.m.conv.* '68 (BGP) Bridgeport, CT St. Michael The Archangel.
Morbeck, George H. '52 (SPK) Republic, WA St. Patrick; Republic, WA Immaculate Conception Retired.
Morbito, Angelo L. '56 (SY)[Q] Syracuse, NY Tommy Coyne Residence @ Dillon Hall Retired.
Morciniec, Peter J. '70 (SPC) Pierce City, MO St. Mary; Pierce City, MO St. Agnes; Region II.
Mordino, Robert F. '63 (WDC) Special Ministries; [P] Upper Marlboro, MD Our Lady of Mattaponi Youth Retreat and Conference Center.
Mordino, Robert (WDC) Our Lady of Mattaponi Retreat Center.
Moreau, Maurice *o.f.m.cap.* '98 (NY) New Paltz, NY St. Joseph; [EE] New Paltz, NY St. Joseph Friary.
Moreau, Paul *l.c.* '02 (WDC)[K] Atlanta, GA Legionaries of Christ.
Moreau, Randall '87 (LAF) Ville Platte, LA Our Lady Queen of All Saints.
Moreau, Raymond J. '85 (OG) Colton, NY St. Patrick; Defenders of the Bond.
Moredo, Wilfredo Pena '74 (SJN) San Juan, PR Santa Bernardita Soubirous.
Moreeuw, Leroy *c.pp.s.* '68 (CLV) Cleveland, OH Our Lady of Good Counsel.
Moreira, Nelson A. *s.s.j.* '72 (BAL)[S] Baltimore, MD St. Joseph Society of the Sacred Heart House of Central Administration.
Morel, John J. '55 (NEW) Retired.
Morel, John *c.i.c.m.* '39 (ARL)[J] Arlington, VA Missionhurst, C.I.C.M.–Central House and Provincialate.
Morel, Patrice *o.m.i.* (BO) (FgM).
Morel, Paul A. '78 (WDC) Retired.
Moreland, Gordon *s.j.* (ORG) Ministry to Priests.
Moreland, J. Gordon *s.j.* '64 (ORG) Special Assignment; [L] Orange, CA House of Prayer for Priests.
Morell, Fernando '87 (ARE) Hatillo, PR Our Lady of Mt. Carmel.
Morell, J. William *o.m.i.* '70 (SAT)[C] San Antonio, TX Oblate School of Theology; [C] San Antonio, TX The United Colleges of San Antonio; [M] San Antonio, TX.
Morelle, Edmund J. '53 (SY) Verona, NY Our Lady of Good Counsel.
Morelli, Attilio '98 (NEW) Peoria, IL St. Philomena's; Members.
Morelli, Attilip (NEW) On Duty Outside the Archdiocese.
Morelli, Gary '74 (SEA) Kirkland, WA Holy Family.
Morelli, Gary (DET) Clinton Twp., MI St. Paul of Tarsus.
Morello, Carl '83 (CHI) Park Ridge, IL St. Paul of the Cross.
Morello, Peter '78 (GLP) On Duty Outside of Diocese.
Morello, Sam Anthony *o.c.d.* '62 (SAT) San Antonio, TX Basilica of The National Shrine of Our Lady of Mt. Carmel and St. Therese, Discalced Carmelite Fathe; [M] San Antonio, TX Discalced Carmelites (Prov. of St. Therese).
Morelock, George L. '65 (SFD) Plainview, IL.
Morelock, George '65 (SFD) Special or Other Diocesan Assignment.
Morency, Raymond P. '87 (PRT) Dexter, ME St. Anne's.
Moreno, Antonio O. *o.f.m.conv.* (MO) Air Force Chaplains.
Moreno, Antonio *m.g.* '82 (LA) Los Angeles, CA St. Paul.
Moreno, Carlos Romero '77 (TUC) Tucson, AZ St. Augustine's Cathedral.
Moreno, David *s.d.b.* '79 (NEW)[N] Orange, NJ The Salesian Community.
Moreno, Hector '92 (RCK) Crystal Lake, IL St. Thomas the Apostle; Special Assignment.
Moreno, Hugo Alexis *s.j.* '98 (MIL)[O] Milwaukee, WI Arrupe House Jesuit Community.
Moreno, James S. (DEN) Judicial Vicar; Judges.
Moreno, James '76 (DEN) Denver, CO Holy Family.
Moreno, Jorge '63 (SD) Brawley, CA Our Lady of Perpetual Help.
Moreno, Jose Luis *s.j.* '80 (MIL) Milwaukee, WI St. Patrick.
Moreno, Jose '87 (SD) Calipatria, CA St. Patrick.
Moreno, Jose *s.j.* '89 (MIL)[O] Milwaukee, WI Miguel Pro Jesuit Community.
Moreno, Joseph F. '86 (BUF) Absent on Leave.
Moreno, Juan '60 (LSC) Las Cruces, NM St. Genevieve.
Moreno, Mauricio '99 (DEN) Denver, CO Montbello Catholic Parish–Church of the Ascension.
Moreno, Robert '93 (STF) Lancaster, NY St. Basil; Erie County Correctional Facility.
Moreshead, Harold D. '55 (PRT) Portland, ME Cathedral of the Immaculate Conception Retired.
Moreton, John '64 (FRS) Fresno, CA Our Lady of Victory.
Moretta, John T. '68 (LA) Los Angeles, CA Resurrection.
Moretta, John (LA) San Gabriel Pastoral Region.
Moretti, August '54 (LA) Pasadena, CA Assumption of the Blessed Virgin Mary; Judges.
Moretti, Edward D. '60 (VEN) Bradenton, FL SS. Peter and Paul the Apostles; Vicar General; College of Consultors; Presbyteral Council; Planning and Development Committee.
Moretti, Mark E. '95 (ARL) Lake Ridge, VA St. Elizabeth Ann Seton.
Moretto, Raul '01 (MIA) Miami, FL St. Joachim.

Morey, Daniel B. *o.f.m.cap.* (NY) Manhattan, NY Cabrini Medical Center.
Morey, Robert '96 (BAL) Hagerstown, MD St. Mary.
Morfeld, Frank G. '51 (DEN) Denver, CO St. Francis de Sales.
Morfin, Francois J. *c.s.b.* '77 (GAL)[Q] Sugar Land Basilian Mission Center.
Morfin, John N. '67 (GAL) Houston, TX St. John Vianney.
Morgan, Arthur '59 (LSC) Retired.
Morgan, Brendan P. '64 (NO) Retired.
Morgan, Charles J. '79 (ALX) Scouting; Mansura, LA St. Paul the Apostle.
Morgan, D. Terrence '76 (STA) St. Augustine, FL Cathedral – Basilica of St. Augustine; [L] St. Augustine, FL Flagler College Newman Center.
Morgan, Dare J. *s.j.* '53 (SJ)[L] Los Altos, CA Jesuit Retreat House.
Morgan, Drew P. *c.o.* '85 (PIT)[N] Pittsburgh, PA Congregation of the Oratory of St. Philip Neri.
Morgan, Edward *c.ss.r.* '64 (OM) Omaha, NE Holy Name.
Morgan, Francis C. *ss.cc.* (NY) Manhattan, NY U.S.V.A. Medical Center.
Morgan, George R. *o.s.a.* '66 (BO) Andover, MA St. Augustine; [C] North Andover, MA Merrimack College.
Morgan, George *c.m.f.* '89 (CHI)[N] Oak Park, IL Claretian Fathers Headquarters of U.S.A. Eastern Province.
Morgan, Guy *o.f.m.* '54 (SP)[O] St. Petersburg St. Anthony Friary.
Morgan, James F. *s.j.* '54 (BO)[V] Newton, MA The Jesuit Community at Boston College.
Morgan, James P. '01 (SFS) Aberdeen, SD Sacred Heart; [H] Aberdeen, SD Northern State University; Presbyteral Council.
Morgan, James '60 (ALN)[G] Pottsville, PA Good Samaritan Regional Medical Center.
Morgan, Jerome L. (SAL) Diocesan Finance Officer; Diocesan Finance Council; College of Consultors; Episcopal Vicars; Council of Priests; Diocesan Pastoral Council; Art and Architecture Commission.
Morgan, Jerome '62 (SAL) Wilson, KS St. Joseph's; Wilson, KS St. Wenceslaus; Ex Officio; Diocesan Committee Regarding Alleged Cases of Child Sexual Abuse; [I] Salina, KS St. Joseph Annex, Inc..
Morgan, John A. '40 (ROC) Retired.
Morgan, John W. '58 (B) Hailey, ID St. Charles Borromeo; Sun Valley, ID Our Lady of the Snows; Judges.
Morgan, John '40 (LA) Camarillo, CA St. Mary Magdalen.
Morgan, John '58 (OAK) Retired.
Morgan, Joseph A. '81 (OG) Ogdensburg, NY Notre Dame; Ogdensburg, NY Riverview Correctional Facility; Director of Priest Personnel and Director of Seminaries; Priest Personnel Board; Director of Seminarians.
Morgan, Joseph (OG) Defenders of the Bond.
Morgan, Jude *ss.cc.* '50 (FR).
Morgan, Julian *c.p.* '53 (HRT)[M] West Hartford Holy Family Monastery/Retreat.
Morgan, Maron *o.mar.* '95 (SAM)[C] Petersham, MA Most Holy Trinity Monastery.
Morgan, Martin '70 (TLS) Sand Springs, OK St. Patrick's.
Morgan, Michael '01 (STA) Palm Coast, FL St. Elizabeth Ann Seton; Advocates; Presbyteral Council.
Morgan, Thomas B. '55 (BO) Salisbury, MA Star of the Sea.
Morgan, Thomas J. '65 (CAM) Cherry Hill, NJ St. Thomas More; Officers; Diocesan Bishop; Apostolic Administrator; Diocesan Finance Council.
Morgan, Thomas '39 (MRY) Retired.
Morgan, Thomas '84 (SP) Plant City, FL St. Clement; Presbyteral Council.
Morgan, Walter N. '44 (MIL) Retired.
Morgan, William P. (BUR) Island Pond, VT St. James the Greater.
Morgera, Michael A. '85 (MEM) Memphis, TN Blessed Sacrament; [L] Cordova, TN Society of St. Vincent DePaul.
Morgia, Robustiano D. '76 (NO) New Orleans, LA St. Maria Goretti.
Morhous, Robert *o.c.s.o.* '59 (WOR)[O] Spencer, MA St. Joseph's Abbey.
Moriarity, Daniel J. '64 (PH) Philadelphia, PA Nativity of the Blessed Virgin Mary.
Moriarity, William J. '66 (CHI) Chicago, IL Cathedral of the Holy Name.
Moriarty, Frederick L. *s.j.* '44 (BO)[V] Weston, MA Campion Health Center, Inc..
Moriarty, James F. '51 (CHI) Retired.
Moriarty, John J. '62 ((JOL)) On Duty Outside the Diocese; (FgM).
Moriarty, John J. *s.j.* '78 (BO)[A] Weston, MA Blessed John XXIII National Seminary; [V] Boston The Society of Jesus of New England–Provincial Offices; [V] Newton, MA The Jesuit Community at Boston College.
Moriarty, John '91 (LEX) Lexington, KY Mary, Queen of the Holy Rosary.
Moriarty, John (LEX) Vocations.
Moriarty, Joseph B. (IND) Priestly and Religious Vocations.
Moriarty, Joseph '93 (IND) Indianapolis, IN Good Shepherd.
Moriarty, Mark D. '99 (STP) Rogers, MN The Catholic Church of Mary Queen of Peace.
Moriarty, Philip M. '80 (JC) New Cambria, MO St. Mary of the Angels.
Moriarty, Robert T. (SLC) Payson, UT St. Patrick's; Payson, UT San Andres; Presbyteral Council; Adjutant Judicial Vicar; Judges.
Moriarty, Robert (AUS) Defenders of the Bond.
Moriarty, Thomas W. '42 (BO) Senior Priests Retired.
Moriarty, Thomas '92 (RVC) Floral Park, NY Our Lady of Victory.
Moriarty, Timothy '03 (HEL) Helena, MT Cathedral of St. Helena.
Moriarty, W Barry *c.m.* '67 (FgM).
Morillo, Jose '49 (VEN) Absent on Sick Leave.
Morin, Benjamin R. *s.j.* '56 (DET)[P] Hamtramck, MI St. Ladislaus.
Morin, Eddy '99 (PRT) Houlton, ME St. Mary's; Houlton, ME St. Agnes.
Morin, Francis P. '73 (PRT) Baileyville, ME St. James the Greater; Indian Township, ME St. Ann; Diocesan Council of Priests.
Morin, George E. '70 (BO) Saugus, MA St. Margaret.
Morin, John *o.m.i.* '51 (BO)[AA] Lowell, MA St. Joseph the Worker Residence.
Morin, Joseph J. *c.ss.r.* '64 (SEA) Seattle WA Sacred Heart of Jesus; [L] Seattle, WA The Redemptionist Society of Washington.
Morin, Marius *m.s.a.* '71 (NOR)[F] Cromwell Society of the Missionaries of the Holy Apostles.
Morin, Maurice N. '64 (PRT) Skowhegar, ME Notre Dame De Lourdes.
Morin, Michael J. '88 (LIN) Cortland, NE St. James; [C] Lincoln, NE Pius X Central High School; [L] Lincoln, NE Pius X Foundation and Pius X Endowment Fund.
Morin, Robert *o.m.i.* '69 (BEL)[F] Belleville, IL Missionary Oblates of Mary Immaculate – St. Henry's Oblate Residence; [J] Belleville, IL Oblate Preaching Team.
Morin, Roger P. (NO) Vicars General; Moderator of the Curia; Archdiocesan Consultors; Archdiocesan Administrative Council; Archdiocesan Finance Council; Vicar General and Moderator of the Curia; Legal Services; Priest Personnel Office; Catholic Human Relations Committee; Parish Sites & Boundaries Committee.
Morin, Timothy '77 (STP) Lino Lakes, MN St. Joseph.
Moriones, Francis *o.a.r.* '34 (NY)[B] Suffern, NY Tagaste Monastery.
Morisette, Alfred *s.j.* '61 (SPK)[B] Spokane WA Gonzaga University.
Morisette, Richard P. '61 (SY) Vernon, NY Holy Family.
Moritz, Paul L. '41 (BO) Brockton, MA St. Patrick; Senior Priests Retired.
Morley, Craig '01 (SP) St. Petersburg, FL Cathedral of St. Jude the Apostle.
Morley, Ed *o.c.s.o.* '83 (ATL)[K] Conyers, GA The Monastery of the Holy Spirit.
Morley, John F. '62 (NEW)[B] School of Diplomacy and Intl. Rels.; [B] School of Diplomacy and Intl. Rels..
Morley, John M. '61 (NEW) AUXILIARY CHAPLAINS CONTRACT CHAPLAINS Retired.
Morlino, Paschal A. *o.s.b.* '66 (BAL) Baltimore, MD St. Benedict.
Morman, David G. '89 (BIS) Dickinson, ND Queen of Peace Church; [I] Sentinel Butte, ND Home On The Range Foundation.
Morman, James '92 (STU)[A] Steubenville, OH Franciscan University of Steubenville; [F] Steubenville, OH Holy Spirit Friary; Presbyteral Council.
Morman, Kenneth G. '73 (TOL) Bowling Green, OH St. Thomas More University Parish; [M] Bowling Green, OH Bowling Green State University Campus Ministry; Toledo Southwest.
Mormando, Nicholas *o.f.m.cap.* '00 (NY) Bronx, NY Immaculate Conception.
Moroney, James P. '80 (WOR) On Duty Outside the Diocese.
Moroney, Martin J. '67 (SAC) Rancho Cordova, CA St. John Vianney.
Moroney, Michael J. '71 (BR) Baton Rouge, LA St. Thomas More; Judges; Ecumenical Affairs.
Moronta, Alexis *i.v.e.* (BRK) Brooklyn, NY St. Michael's.
Morosini, Louis *s.m.* '56 (FgM).
Morozowich, Mark '91 (SJP) On Assignment Outside the Diocese; Diocesan Administrative Council; Liturgical Commission; Clergy Examiners; [C] Catholic University of America, The.
Morquillas, Fructuoso '58 (SB) Retired.
Morrant, Kenneth (LAF)[K] Hayes, LA Cursillo Center.
Morras, Ignacio '49 (MIA) Hialeah, FL St. John the Apostle Retired.
Morras, Xavier '50 (MIA) Retired.
Morreale, Matthew *o.f.m.* '85 (NY) Bronx, NY Our Lady of Pity; Roebling, NJ Holy Assumption.
Morria, Kenneth R. *c.s.v.* '54 (CHI)[N] Chicago, IL Viatorian Residence.
Morrier, David *t.o.r.* '97 (STU)[A] Steubenville, OH Franciscan University of Steubenville; [F] Steubenville, OH Holy Spirit Friary.
Morrill, Bruce *s.j.* '92 (BO)[V] Newton, MA The Jesuit Community at Boston College.
Morrill, Giles '50 (ALB) Retired.
Morris, Alexis P. *o.f.m.* '56 (SP)[O] St. Petersburg St. Anthony Friary.
Morris, Anthony W. *o.s.b.* '84 (RIC)[L] Richmond, VA Mary Mother of the Church Abbey.
Morris, Anthony *c.ss.r.* '94 (RIC) Hampton, VA St. Joseph.
Morris, C. Eugene *s.t.l.* '96 (STL)[A] St. Louis, MO Cardinal Glennon College.
Morris, Charles M. '83 (DET)[T] Roseville, MI Cursillos in Christianity Movement of the Archdiocese of Detroit; Wyandotte, MI St. Elizabeth.
Morris, George O. *s.j.* '68 (SPK)[B] Spokane, WA Gonzaga University.
Morris, Gerald R. '70 (MIA) Marathon, FL San Pablo.
Morris, Gerald (MIA) Deans and Deaneries; Spiritual Moderators.
Morris, Jack *s.j.* '62 (P) Rockaway, OR St. Mary by the Sea.
Morris, James A. '94 (KAL) New Buffalo, MI St. Mary of the Lake.
Morris, James '66 (SFR) Menlo Park, CA St. Raymond.
Morris, James '93 (STF) Salem, MA St. John the Baptist; Educational Institutions.
Morris, John E. (PAT) Retired.
Morris, John J. '60 (NEW) AUXILIARY CHAPLAINS CONTRACT CHAPLAINS Retired.
Morris, John J. *s.j.* '62 (P)[L] Portland, OR Colombiere Community.
Morris, John S. '62 (BO) Permanent Disability; Senior Priests Retired.
Morris, John *o.p.* '66 (OAK)[B] St. Mary's College.
Morris, Joseph A. *c.m.* '80 (MET)[H] Princeton, NJ Vincentian Residence; [J] Princeton, NJ Vincentian Renewal Center.
Morris, Joseph W. *s.j.* (SLC) Deans.
Morris, Joseph '96 (ATL) Marietta, GA St. Joseph.
Morris, Kenan *o.f.m.* '50 (BO)[Y] Boston, MA Saint Anthony Residence.
Morris, Kevin '97 (IND) Plainfield, IN St. Susanna.
Morris, Lester G. '91 (NOR) Middlefield, CT St. Colman.
Morris, Loyd '95 (DAL) Wylie, TX St. Anthony.
Morris, Michael P. '89 (NY) Bronx, NY St. Francis of Assisi; Navy Reserve Chaplains.
Morris, Michael T. *o.p.* '77 (OAK).
Morris, Michael *s.p.s.* '76 (NEW)[N] Cliffside Park, NJ St. Patrick's Missionary Society.
Morris, Michael *o.p.* '77 (OAK)[N] Oakland, CA Dominican Order, Siena House.
Morris, Philip D. *s.t.d.* '63 (NEW) Hillsdale, NJ St. John the Baptist; Elected Members.
Morris, Robert A. *o.p.* '50 (PRO)[P] Providence St. Thomas Aquinas Priory at Providence College.
Morris, Robert F. '66 (PT) Destin, FL Corpus Christi; Catholic Daughters of the Americas.
Morris, Robert F. '91 (SP) Tampa, FL St. Mary.
Morris, Robert '49 (SFD) Retired.
Morris, Robert (SP) Director of Priest Personnel; Ex Officio; Incardination Commission; Presbyteral Council; College of Consultors.
Morris, Robert (PT) Priestly Life and Ministry, Office of; Clergy Concerns.
Morris, Stephen P. '79 (ALB) Hancock, NY St. Paul the Apostle.
Morris, Stephen '79 (RVC) Priests Released from Diocesan Assignment.
Morris, Thomas A. *o.ss.t.* '81 (BAL)[S] Baltimore, MD Holy Trinity Monastery; Bristol, PA St. Ann.
Morris, Thomas *o.ss.t.* '81 (BAL)[R] Baltimore, MD Holy Trinity Spiritual Center.
Morris, Wayne E. '01 (STU) Ironton, OH St. Joseph; Ironton, OH St. Lawrence.
Morris, Wayne (STU) Presbyteral Council; College of Consultors.
Morris, William S. *s.s.* '31 (BAL)[O] Baltimore, MD St. Charles Villa.
Morris, William T. '69 (NEW)[B] Watchung, NJ Mount St. Mary Academy; Rahway, NJ St. Mark's.
Morrison, Anselm Harry *a.a.* '48 (SP) Dade City, FL St. Rita.
Morrison, Anselm *a.a.* '48 (BO)[V] Zephyrhills, FL.
Morrison, Carl T. '69 (MIA) Miami Shores, FL St. Martha; [G] Miami, FL Mercy Outpatient Services, Inc..
Morrison, Carl (SAM) Defender of the Bond.
Morrison, Carl (MIA) Promoters of Justice; Defenders of the Bond.
Morrison, Craig *o.carm.* '87 (JOL)[L] Darien Carmelite Provincial Office.
Morrison, Craig *o.carm.* '87 (WDC)[B] Washington, DC Whitefriars Hall.

Morrison, David J. '54 (ALN) Bethlehem, PA Our Lady of Perpetual Help; Judges Retired.
Morrison, Douglas A. '59 (HRT) On Duty Outside the Archdiocese.
Morrison, James J. '74 (PRT) Scarborough, ME St. Maximilian Kolbe; Diocesan Consultors; Diocesan Council of Priests; College of Consultors; Diocesan Finance Council.
Morrison, James '87 (HT) Thibodaux, LA St. Thomas Aquinas; Nicholls State University; Seminarians; Campus Ministry; Serra Club of Thibodaux.
Morrison, John '92 (SAM) Fayetteville, NC St. Michael the Archangel; Youth Ministry Office.
Morrison, Larry '79 (RNO) Sun Valley, NV St. Peter Canisius; Diocesan Board of Consultors; Presbyteral Council.
Morrison, Michael G. *s.j.* '68 (MIL)[O] Milwaukee, WI Jesuit Community at Marquette University.
Morrison, Robert A. '49 (PH) Absent on Leave.
Morrison, Thomas A. *o.p.* '55 (CHI)[J] Chicago, IL Holy Cross Hospital; [N] St. Pius V Priory.
Morrison, Thomas F. '76 (CHR) Absent On Leave.
Morrissette, Dominic '45 (JOL) Retired.
Morrissette, Joseph H. '53 (NOR) Retired.
Morrissey, Daniel W. *o.p.* '62 (CHI)[N] Chicago Dominicans (Provincial Office).
Morrissey, Dunstan R. *o.s.b.* '53 (PEO).
Morrissey, J. Michael '78 (P)[A] Gresham, OR St. Anne.
Morrissey, James L. '55 (PEO) Retired.
Morrissey, Jerome V. '47 (PEO) Retired.
Morrissey, John '63 (PMB) Sebastian, FL St. Sebastian.
Morrissey, Joseph G. *o.s.f.s.* '77 (WIL)[J] Wilmington, DE Oblates of St. Francis De Sales.
Morrissey, Lawrence P. '57 (PEO) Brimfield, IL St. Joseph's.
Morrissey, Michael E. '86 (RCK) Rockford, IL Holy Family; Dixon, IL St. Anne.
Morrissey, Michael J. (DAV) Adjutant Judicial Vicar; Judges; Deans; Finance Council; Davenport Deanery.
Morrissey, Michael '65 (DAV) Davenport, IA Holy Family; Vicar General and Moderator of the Curia; Diocesan Corporate Board.
Morrissey, Paul F. *s.m.* '75 (STP) St. Paul, MN St. Louis King of France.
Morrissey, Philip T. '46 (BGP) Retired.
Morrissey, Robert O. '83 (RVC) Ocean Beach, NY Our Lady of the Magnificat; Secretary to the Bishop; Vice Chancellors; Censors of Books; Judges for Interdiocesan Tribunal; Senate of Priests (Presbyteral Council/College of Consultors).
Morrissey, Thomas E. '61 (FR) Taunton, MA St. James.
Morrissy, Patrick *c.ss.r.* '55 (FgM).
Morrone, Louis S. *o.p.* '92 (CHI) Denver, CO St. Dominic; [A] Denver, CO St. Dominic Priory.
Morrow, Brian '80 (DEN) Longmont, CO St. John the Baptist; Longmont, CO Spirit of Peace Parish.
Morrow, Dennis W. '75 (GR) Grand Rapids, MI SS. Peter and Paul; Archivist.
Morrow, Dennis '75 (GR) On Special Assignment.
Morrow, Michael J. '86 (NY) Bronx, NY St. Brendan; Air Force Reserve Chaplains.
Morrow, Richard B. '55 (ATL) Atlanta, GA Cathedral of Christ the King; Judges Retired.
Morrow, Thomas G. '82 (WDC) Silver Spring, MD St. Catherine Laboure.
Morry, Christopher C. '59 (E) Sharon, PA St. Joseph.
Morry, Matthew F. *o.p.* '50 (PRO)[P] Providence St. Thomas Aquinas Priory at Providence College.
Morse, Frederick H. '95 (PRT) Peaks Island, ME St. Christopher's; Portland, ME Maine Medical Center.
Morse, James E. *s.j.* '50 (SJ)[M] Los Gatos, CA Sacred Heart Jesuit Center.
Morse, James H. '67 (FR) Attleboro, MA St. Stephen's.
Morse, John *s.j.* '61 (YAK) Moses Lake, WA Our Lady of Fatima; Moses Lake, WA Queen of All Saints; Presbyteral Council Executive Committee.
Morse, Jonathan K. '88 (STF) Special Assignment; Army Reserve Chaplains.
Morse, Jonathan '88 (STF)[F] Stamford, CT Missionary Sisters of Mother of God; Censors; Family Life; Religious Education; Ukrainian Catholic Relief, Inc..
Morse, Michael '84 (STA) Lake City, FL Epiphany.
Morse, Richard E. *o.s.f.s.* '69 (STO) Manteca, CA St. Anthony Church of Manteca (Pastor of).
Morse, Richard *o.s.f.s.* (STO) Deans; Diocesan Building Committee.
Mort, Ernest C. *c.s.p.* '59 (NY)[EE] Jamaica Estates Paulist Fathers Generalate.
Mortell, Anthony *s.s.c.* '60 (LA)[Q] Los Angeles, CA Columban Fathers, Procure House; [K] St. Columbans St. Columban's Foreign Mission Society.
Mortimer, James E. '52 (PH) Retired.
Morton, Jake *s.j.* '75 (SPK) Nespelem, WA St. Rose of Lima; Nespelem, WA Sacred Heart Mission.
Morton, John *c.ss.r.* '52 (OM) Omaha, NE Holy Name; [K] Omaha, NE The Redemptorists of Nebraska.
Morton, Vincent R. '86 (SP) Crystal River, FL St. Benedict.
Morton, Vincent (SP) Presbyteral Council; College of Consultors; Vicars Forane.
Morton, William *s.s.c.* '85 (OM)[K] St. Columbans St. Columban's Foreign Mission Society.
Morvant, Kenneth R. '61 (LAF) On Special Assignment; Defenders of the Bond.
Morvay, Andrew '60 (RC) Retired.
Morvey, Andrew '60 (RC) Lemmon, SD Blessed Sacrament Retired.
Mosbrucker, Jacob A. '66 (P) Portland, OR St. Therese of the Child Jesus.
Moscaritolo, Mario '64 (KC) Retired.
Mosele, Victor *s.x.* '60 (MIL)[B] Franklin, WI Xaverian Missionary Fathers College Seminary.
Moseley, Stan *o.s.b.* '53 (NO)[P] St. Benedict, LA St. Joseph Abbey.
Mosely, Daniel E. (STL)[U] Sainte Genevieve, MO Ste. Genevieve County Catholic Church Real Estate Corporation.
Mosely, Stan D. *o.s.b.* '53 (NO) Retired.
Moser, Albert *c.s.p.* '60 (OAK) Berkeley, CA Holy Spirit Parish/Newman Hall.
Moser, Claudio *o.f.m.* '63 (NY)[EE] St. Peter Friary.
Moser, John A. (DUB) Protivin, IA Holy Trinity; Fort Atkinson, IA St. John Nepomucene; Protivin, IA Assumption of the B. V. M.; Deanery Representatives.
Moser, Thomas W. '94 (KNX) Dunlap, TN Shepherd of the Valley; South Pittsburg, TN Our Lady of Lourdes.
Moser, Victor G. '46 (KC) Retired.
Moses, Father *c.r.* (SB)[E] Newberry Springs, CA Holy Resurrection Community.
Moses, Patrick '03 (ORG) Education Leave.
Moses, Perianayagam *s.j.* '89 (OAK)[N] Berkeley, CA Jesuit Community at Jesuit School of Theology at Berkeley.
Moses, Robert '99 (ORL)[F] Lakeland, FL Florida Southern College Newman Center.
Mosey, Douglas L. *c.s.b.* '74 (NOR)[A] Cromwell, CT Holy Apostles College and Seminary; [L] Cromwell, CT Basilian Fathers of Connecticut, Inc..
Mosha, Benedict Ndeyekiyo '89 (PMB) Stuart, FL St. Joseph.
Mosher, Thomas L. '81 (BUR)[H] Goddard College (Plainfield); Montpelier, VT St. Augustine.
Mosimann, John P. '97 (ARL) Manassas, VA All Saints; Advocates.
Moskal, Joseph E. '65 (SY) Camden, NY St. John; Camden, NY St. Mary.
Mosko, Leon A. '56 (STF) Special Assignment; Chancellor & Archivist.
Mosko, Leon (STF) Diocesan Consultors; Presbyteral Council; Administrative Council; Directors:; Communications; Liturgical Commission; Press, Diocesan: "The Sower".
Moskus, John T. '63 (HRT).
Mosley, Charles A. '85 (GRY) Griffith, IN St. Mary.
Mosley, Daniel E. '77 (STL) New Haven, MO Assumption; Ste. Genevieve, MO Ste. Genevieve; Ste. Genevieve County Catholic Church Real Estate Corporation.
Mosley, Godfrey T. (WDC) Assistant Judicial Vicar; Archdiocesan College of Consultors.
Mosley, Godfrey (WDC) Pastoral Center Special Ministries; Vicars General; Staff.
Moss, Brendan *o.s.b.* '01 (IND) St. Meinrad, IN St. Boniface; St. Meinrad, IN St. Meinrad; St. Meinrad, IN St. Martin of Tours; [K] St. Meinrad, IN; Council of Priests.
Moss, Charles T. '58 (ALN) Pen Argyl, PA St. Roch.
Moss, Darius G. C. '97 (HBG) Millersburg, PA Queen of Peace.
Moss, Donald G. '86 (AUS) On Duty Outside the Diocese; Navy Chaplains.
Moss, James '82 (STA) Jacksonville, FL San Jose.
Moss, James (PAT) Paterson, NJ Preakness Hospital.
Moss, Raymond B. '86 (CHY) Cheyenne, WY St. Joseph's.
Moss, Robert D. '69 (BUF) Sloan, NY St. Andrew.
Moss, Robert H. *c.s.c.* '74 (FTW)[B] University of Notre Dame Du Lac; [I] Notre Dame, IN Holy Cross Community, Corby Hall, University of Notre Dame.
Mossett, Robert C. *o.s.f.s.* '65 (DET) Monroe, MI St. Anne.
Mossholder, Francis D. *p.i.m.e.* '88 (LAN) Ypsilanti, MI Holy Trinity Student Parish; [M] Ypsilanti, MI Holy Trinity Student Parish.
Mossi, John P. *s.j.* '73 (California)[B] Spokane, WA Gonzaga University.
Mostardi, Joseph S. *o.s.a.* '75 (PH)[AA] Villanova, PA Provincial Offices of the Order of St. Augustine, Province of St. Thomas of Villanova; [AA] Villanova, PA Fray de Leon Community.
Moster, James *o.f.m.cap.* '76 (KCK)[H] Lawrence, KS St. Conrad's Friary.
Moszur, Edward J. '71 (GRY) Highland, IN Our Lady of Grace.
Mothersill, Joseph *o.carm.* '86 (WDC)[B] Washington, DC Whitefriars Hall.
Motl, James R. *o.p.* '62 (CHI)[N] Chicago Dominicans (Provincial Office).
Motl, James R. *o.p.* '62 (STP)[C] St. Paul, MN University of St. Thomas.
Motl, James R. *o.p.* '62 (STL)[O] St. Louis, MO St. Dominic Priory.
Motsay, Joseph R. '78 (SCR) Military Chaplains; Air Force Chaplains.
Motsay, Russell E. '72 (SCR) Carbondale, PA Our Lady of Mt. Carmel.
Motsett, C. Bourke '34 (PEO) Retired.
Mott, Allen P. '03 (MAR) Marquette, MI St. Peter Cathedral.
Mott, James *o.s.a.* '65 (SD)[H] San Diego, CA Augustinian Community.
Motta, Anthony '63 (ALB) Haines Falls, NY Immaculate Conception.
Motta, Michael J. '72 (HRT) West Hartford, CT St. Mark the Evangelist; Special and other Archdiocesan Assignment; Evangelization Office; Office of Religious Education (CCD).
Mottau, Robert S. '58 (BO) Senior Priests Retired.
Mottet, Marvin A. '56 (DAV) Davenport, IA Sacred Heart Cathedral; [K] Davenport, IA Thomas Merton House, Inc.; [K] Davenport, IA Interfaith Housing, Ltd.; [K] Davenport, IA East Davenport Development Corporation.
Mottin, Charles A. '49 (STL) Retired.
Mottin, Charles (STL) Blessed John XXIII Center.
Mouannes, Nabil '84 (OLL) El Cajon, CA Saint Ephrem; El Cajon, CA St. Sharbel Mission.
Mouawad, Paul '69 (SAM) Pawtucket, RI Holy Trinity–St. George.
Mouch, Frank M. '58 (VEN) Retired.
Mouch, Frank (SP) Diocesan Finance Council.
Moudry, Paul '87 (STP) Golden Valley, MN St. Margaret Mary.
Moudry, Richard P. '50 (STP) Retired.
Mould, Christopher J. '88 (ARL) Alexandria, VA St. Lawrence.
Moulder, John P. '90 (CHI) Chicago, IL St. Gregory.
Mountain, Edward C. '47 (WIN) Retired.
Mountain, Harold B. '42 (WIN) Retired.
Mountain, Joseph W. '52 (WIN) Retired.
Mounteer, Louis A. *s.j.* '56 (NY)[EE] New York, NY Murray–Weigel Hall.
Mousehild, David (SB).
Mouser, J. Irvin '65 (L)[I] Unassigned.
Moussier, Howard R. *o.s.b.* '65 (MOB) Elberta, AL St. Bartholomew.
Moutenot, Charles *s.j.* '84 (NY)[EE] Loyola Hall, Jesuit Community.
Mouton, Charles Burton '49 (LAF) Retired.
Mouton, Richard von Phul '55 (LAF) Lafayette, LA St. Pius X.
Mouton, Richard (LAF) Diocesan Consultors; Holy Childhood; Pontifical Mission Societies.
Mouton, Thomas Jason '92 (LAF) Lafayette, LA Our Lady Queen of Peace.
Mower, Scott '97 (PRT) Ashland, ME St. Mark's; Diocesan Council of Priests.
Mowrer, Patrick '97 (PHX) Phoenix, AZ Immaculate Heart of Mary; Phoenix, AZ SS. Anthony and Pius X; College of Consultors.
Moy, Francis J. *s.j.* '69 (BO)[V] Newton, MA The Jesuit Community at Boston College.
Moya, Gilberto '96 (STO) Ceres, CA St. Jude Church (Pastor of).
Moya, Peter O. '85 (MET) On Duty Outside the Diocese.
Moyahan, Michael *s.j.* '73 (SPK)[B] Spokane, WA Gonzaga University.
Moyano, Felipe '48 (CAM) Pleasantville, NJ St. Peter's; Hispanic Charismatic Renewal.
Moyer, Richard W. '64 (PHX) Mesa, AZ St. Timothy; Special Assignment; College of Consultors; Catholic Tuition Organization of the Diocese of Phoenix (CTODP) Retired.
Moyer, Richard '64 (PHX)[K] Phoenix, AZ The Catholic Tuition Organization of the Diocese of Phoenix; Moderator of the Curia; Vicar General; Finance and Administration.
Moyher, Francis *t.o.r.* '63 (ALT)[F] Loretto, PA Mount Assisi Friary.
Moylan, Thomas *l.c.* '69 (MAD)[G] Edgerton, WI Koshkonong Pastoral Center; [K] Edgerton, WI Oaklawn Incorporated.
Moylan, Thomas '69 (NY)[V] Thornwood, NY Catholic World Mission, Inc..
Moyna, James Moneta *o.p.* '70 (NY)[EE] New York St. Vincent Ferrer Priory.
Moyna, John L. '73 (ALB) Coxsackie, NY St. Mary; Regional Medical Unit.
Moyna, John (ALB) Advocates.
Moynahan, Michael *s.j.* (SPK) Members.
Moynihan, Eugene J. *s.s.j.* '57 (BAL)[S] Baltimore, MD St. Joseph's Manor.
Moynihan, George F. '74 (CHR) North Myrtle Beach, SC Our Lady Star of the Sea; Presbyteral Council; Personnel Committee.
Moynihan, Jerimiah P. '74 (ROC) Elmira, NY Our Lady of Lourdes.
Moynihan, John C. *m.m.* '67 (FgM).
Moynihan, Michael R. (BGP) Judges; Vicariate I (Stamford, Darien, Glenbrook, Greenwich, Byram, Riverside); Catholic Women, Council of.
Moynihan, Michael Robert '79 (BGP) Greenwich, CT

St. Michael the Archangel.

Moynihan, Michael '79 (NY)[HH] Bronx, NY New York Maritime College.

Moynihan, T. Joseph '57 (BO) Westwood, MA St. Margaret Mary.

Moynihan, William R. (BGP) Presbyteral Council.

Moyniltan, Noel *c.s.sp.* '77 (BRK) Woodside, NY Blessed Virgin Mary, Help of Christians.

Moys, Gregory '64 (P) Grants Pass, OR St. Anne; College of Consultors; Defenders of the Bond.

Mozdakis, John J. *o.s.f.s.* '65 (WIL)[J] Childs, MD Retirement and Assisted Care Facility.

Mozer, Joseph F. '97 (BO) Beltsville, MD St. Joseph.

Mozos, Sebastian *o.m.i.* '33 (SAT)[K] San Antonio, TX Oblate Madonna Residence.

Mpanda, Apo T. '88 (DAV) Farmington, IA St. Boniface; West Point, IA Assumption of the Blessed Virgin Mary.

Mpeka, Rogatus '82 (TR) Yardville, NJ St. Vincent de Paul.

Mraz, John S. '75 (ALN) Northampton, PA Assumption of the Blessed Virgin Mary.

Mraz, Louis R. *o.s.c.* '59 (PHX)[G] Phoenix, AZ Crosier Community of Phoenix (Canons Regular of the Order of the Holy Cross).

Mraz, Louis *o.s.c.* '59 (PHX) Glendale, AZ St. Helen.

Mraz, Robert J. '74 (NU) Silver Lake, MN Church of the Holy Family.

Mrnarevic, Daniel '84 (FAR) Velva, ND SS. Peter and Paul's; Velva, ND St. Cecilia.

Mroczek, Wjociech *s.d.b.* '03 (FgM).

Mroczkowski, Joseph A. '45 (LIN) Retired.

Mroczkowski, Joseph J. '42 (CHI) Retired.

Mroczynski, Edward *s.chr.* '57 (LA) Los Angeles, CA Our Lady of the Bright Mount.

Mrowinski, Charles *c.r.* '55 (CHI)[M] Chicago, IL Franciscan Communities St. Joseph Home of Chicago.

Mrowka, Chester R. *c.m.* '59 (HRT)[M] Manchester, CT DePaul Provincial Residence.

Mroz, Richard J. '92 (NEW) New Milford, NJ St. Joseph's.

Mroziewski, Witold '91 (BRK) Brooklyn, NY Our Lady of Czestochowa–St. Casimir; Attorneys and Counselors at Canon Law.

Mruk, Walter Leon *o.f.m.conv.* '49 (HRT)[M] New Britain, CT Conventual Franciscans; [N] New Britain, CT Motherhouse of Daughters of Mary of the Immaculate Conception.

MRY, John *s.d.b.* '74 (MRY)[B] Watsonville, CA St. Francis Central Coast Catholic High School.

Msallem, George Bou *m.l.m.* '91 (OLL)[A] Houston, TX The Congregation of Maronite Lebanese Missionaries.

Msallem, Georges Bou *m.l.m.* '91 (OLL) San Dimas, CA St. Jude Mission.

Msassaro, Gabriel *o.f.m.cap.* '66 (NY)[B] Beacon, NY St. Lawrence of Brindisi Friary.

Msoka, Gabriel '87 (OAK) Oakland, CA St. Leo's.

Mtengetse, Gaspar J. '93 (LA) Los Angeles, CA St. Jerome.

Mthembu, Mafanisa *o.s.m.* '58 (CHI)[N] Chicago Order of Friar Servants of Mary (Servites) United States of America Province, Inc..

Mubarak, Anwar Amar *f.s.s.p.* '91 (SCR)[M] Elmhurst Priestly Fraternity of St. Peter (F.S.S.P.), North American District Headquarters.

Muc, John *o.cist.* '90 (CHI)[N] Willow Springs, IL Cistercian Fathers, Our Lady Mother of the Church.

Mucci, Flavian *o.f.m.* '63 (FgM).

Muccilli, Robert L. '57 (MET) Retired.

Muccino, Keith F. *s.j.* '96 (WDC)[M] Washington, DC The Jesuit Community at Georgetown University.

Muccitelli, Mario *s.d.v.* '48 (PAT)[M] Florham Park, NJ Father Justin Vocationary.

Mucha, Jan '54 (DEN) Denver, CO St. Joseph.

Mucha, John '53 (STU)[J] Nelsonville, OH Hocking Technical College.

Mucha, John '81 (STU) Nelsonville, OH Holy Cross; Nelsonville, OH St. Mary of the Hills.

Mucha, John (STU) Priests Personnel Board.

Muckenhaupt, Gregory F. *s.j.* '88 (CI)[B] Pohnpei, FM PATS (Pohnpei Agriculture and Trade School).

Muckerman, Norman J. *c.ss.r.* '42 (STL)[O] Liguori, MO Liguori Mission House/Redemptorists.

Mucowski, Richard J. *o.f.m.* (ROM) Formation Council.

Mucowski, Richard *o.f.m.* '71 (NY)[EE] Hewitt, NJ.

Mucowski, Richard *o.f.m.* (PAT) Hewitt, NJ Our Lady Queen of Peace.

Mucowski, Richard *o.f.m.* (MET) Psychological Consultants.

Mudavankunnel, Jose '81 (MOB) Mobile, AL Little Flower.

Mudavankunnel, Jose *m.s.f.s.* '81 (ATL)[K] Lawrenceville The Missionaries of St. Francis De Sales.

Mudd, David A. '80 (WDC) Military Chaplains; Navy Chaplains.

Mudd, Earl '60 (BEA) Retired.

Mudd, Gerald R. *o.f.m.* '66 (BUF) Kenmore, NY St. Andrew; Buffalo, NY SS. Rita & Patrick.

Mudd, Gerald *o.f.m.* (BO) Court Experts for Languages.

Mudd, James T. '64 (L) Hodgenville, KY Our Lady of Mercy; Howardstown, KY St. Ann.

Mudd, Joachim '97 (FAR) St. Michael, ND St. Michael; St. Michael's Indian Mission.

Mudd, John '69 (WDC) Special Ministries; [L] Washington, DC Archbishop Carroll High School.

Mudduse, Lawrence (JOL) Lockport, IL St. Joseph.

Mudrak, Lloyd '62 (DUL) Coleraine, MN Mary Immaculate; Coleraine, MN St. Mary; Coleraine, MN St. Joseph; Boy Scouts.

Mudry, Lubomyr '51 (STF) Retired.

Mueggenborg, Daniel H. (TLS) Diocesan Consultors; Seminary Board; Clergy Education; Office for the Synod.

Mueggenborg, Daniel M. '89 (TLS) Bixby, OK St. Clement of Rome.

Muelemans, Thomas O. *o.praem.* '59 (GB)[A] De Pere, WI St. Norbert Abbey.

Mueller, Charles L. '57 (NO) Metairie, LA St. Christopher the Martyr; Metairie, LA East Jefferson General Hospital.

Mueller, Donald R. '61 (TOL) Retired.

Mueller, Eugene J. '56 (CIN) Retired.

Mueller, Eugene *s.t.* '55 (FgM).

Mueller, Francis E. *s.j.* '53 (P)[J] Spokane WA Regis Community.

Mueller, Gary A. *c.m.* '95 (FgM).

Mueller, Glenn R. *s.j.* '73 (KC) Kansas City, MO Guardian Angels; [J] Kansas City, MO Rockhurst Jesuit Community.

Mueller, James H. *o.carm.* '69 (SAC) Fairfield, CA Our Lady of Mount Carmel,.

Mueller, James J. '66 (BRK) South Ozone Park, NY St. Anthony of Padua.

Mueller, James *s.m.* '67 (FWT)[B] Fort Worth, TX Nolan Catholic High School.

Mueller, Jerome D. *o.f.m.* (MO) Air Force Chaplains.

Mueller, John J. '59 (CLV) Wooster, OH St. Mary of the Immaculate Conception.

Mueller, John J. *s.j.* '75 (STL)[C] Saint Louis University; [O] St. Louis, MO Jesuit Community Corporation at St. Louis University – Jesuit Hall

Mueller, John *s.m.* '41 (CIN)[M] Dayton, OH Mercy Siena Village.

Mueller, John '59 (CLV) Administrative Leave.

Mueller, Joseph G. *s.j.* '93 (DET)[O] Milwaukee, WI Jesuit Community at Marquette University; [K] Temperance, MI.

Mueller, Kevin A. '92 (BAL) Special Assignment; [R] Sparks, MD Msgr. Clare J. O'Dwyer Retreat House.

Mueller, Kevin (BAL) Advocates and Procurators.

Mueller, Matthias R. *o.p.* '49 (CHI) Chicago, IL St. Pius V; [N] Chicago, IL Dominican Community.

Mueller, Michael '85 (ORL) On Duty Outside the Diocese; Navy Chaplains.

Mueller, Noel *o.s.b.* '68 (IND)[A] St. Meinrad, IN St. Meinrad School of Theology; [K] St. Meinrad, IN St. Meinrad Archabbey.

Mueller, Paul R. *s.j.* '93 (CHI)[N] Chicago, IL Woodlawn Jesuit Community.

Mueller, Richard J. '44 (IND) Retired.

Mueller, Richard J. '63 (CHI) Northbrook, IL St. Norbert.

Mueller, Richard J. '66 (PIT) On Duty Outside the Diocese.

Mueller, Richard '66 (PIT) Naples, FL St. John the Evangelist.

Mueller, Richard (IND) Archdiocesan Judges.

Mueller, Robert F. '46 (MIL) Milwaukee, WI St. Anthony Retired.

Mueller, Roman *s.d.s.* '74 (BIR) Huntsville, AL St. Joseph's.

Muench, Joseph '81 (LEX) Frankfort, KY Good Shepherd; Harrodsburg, KY St. Andrew.

Muench, R. Francis '81 (RIC) Norfolk, VA St. Pius X; Adjutant Judicial Vicars.

Muench, William G. '59 (OG) Ticonderoga, NY Sacred Heart Church; Ticonderoga, NY St. Mary.

Muerder, Edward E. '58 (BUF) Java Center, NY St. Patrick; North Java, NY St. Nicholas; North Java, NY St. Joseph.

Muesenfechter, Robert J. '51 (STL) Retired

Muessiggang, Emmanuel *o.f.m.* '33 (OAK)[P] Danville, CA San Damiano Retreat.

Mugabowakigeri, Bernardin '86 (SAC) Sacramento, CA Presentation of the Blessed Virgin Mary.

Mugan, William L. *s.j.* '55 (STL)[O] St. Louis, MO Jesuit Community Corporation at St. Louis University – Jesuit Hall; [O] St. Louis, MO The Jesuits of the Missouri Province.

Muganyizi, George *c.s.c.* '98 (FTW)[I] St. Brendan.

Mugavero, Anthony P. '81 (ROC) Rochester, NY St. Bridget.

Mugera, Robert *c.s.c.* (FTW)[I] Holy Cross Bugembe.

Muggli, Boniface *o.s.b.* '90 (BIS)[A] Richardton, ND Assumption Abbey; [B] Bismarck, ND University of Mary.

Muggli, Florian *o.s.b.* '51 (SCL)[I] Collegeville, MN St. John's Abbey, of the Order of St. Benedict.

Muggli, Odo *o.s.b.* '66 (BIS)[A] Richardton, ND Assumption Abbey

Mugisha, Deo Gratias '97 (PIT) Port Vue, PA St. Mark.

Mugo, Simon K. '89 (SY)[U] Canastota, NY Catholic Diocese of Nakuru Mission Office, Inc..

Mugo, Simon '89 (SY) Cicero, NY Sacred Heart.

Muguerza, Octavio A. '92 (GAL) Sealy, TX Immaculate Conception.

Muguerza, Octavio '92 (GAL)[U] Sealy, TX Asociacion Nacional de Sacerdotes Hispanos.

Muha, Joseph '60 (B) Priest Retirement Committee; Pocatello, ID Holy Spirit Catholic Community.

Muha, Peter J. '88 (GRY) Lowell, IN St. Edward; Lowell, IN St. Theresa.

Muheim, Martin de Porres J. *o.s.b.* '88 (PBL)[F] Canon City, CO Holy Cross Abbey.

Muhich, Peter '89 (DUL) Hibbing, MN Blessed Sacrament; [G] Hibbing, MN Hibbing Catholic Schools Endowment Fund.

Muhigirwa, Bernard *s.j.* '95 (SFR)[N] San Francisco, CA Jesuit Community at University of San Francisco.

Muhlbaier, Howard E. '65 (CAM) Turnersville, NJ SS. Peter and Paul.

Muhm, William M. '95 (NY) Military Chaplains; Navy Chaplains.

Muhr, Michael *m.div.* '83 (PMB)[A] Boynton Beach, FL St. Vincent de Paul Regional Seminary.

Muhs, Edward J. '51 (RVC) Bellmore, NY St. Barnabas the Apostle Retired.

Muir, Edmund D. '49 (DET) Retired.

Muir, Faustyn *o.s.p.p.e.* '01 (PH)[AA] Office.

Muir, Gavin W. '65 (PH) Riegelsville, PA St. Lawrence.

Mukalel, Joseph V. '58 (NEW) Retired.

Mukamba, Benoit K. *c.s.sp.* '92 (GAL) Houston, TX St. Benedict the Abbot.

Mukundi, Samson Ngatia '03 (CHI) Homewood, IL St. Joseph.

Mulanjanany, Augustine '69 (LKC) Fenton, LA St. Charles Borromeo; Diocesan Consultors.

Mulcahey, Andrew *l.c.* '96 (LA)[Q] Pasadena, CA Legionaries of Christ; [BB] Pasadena, CA California Institute of Technology.

Mulcahy, Bernard *o.p.* '03 (PRO)[P] Providence, RI St. Pius Priory; Providence, RI St. Pius V.

Mulcahy, Brian *o.p.* '90 (RIC) Charlottesville, VA St. Thomas Aquinas.

Mulcahy, Daniel R. '79 (WOR) Linwood, MA Good Shepherd.

Mulcahy, Donal '51 (LA) Judges Retired.

Mulcahy, Gerald F. '62 (CHI) Hickory Hills, IL St. Patricia; Deans.

Mulcahy, Howard J. '44 (ALB) Retired.

Mulcahy, James R. '37 (LA) La Puente, CA St. Louis of France Retired.

Mulcahy, John M. *c.s.c.* '65 (FTW)[I] Morris Camp.

Mulcahy, Louis *o.s.b.* '89 (IND)[K] St. Meinrad, IN St. Meinrad Archabbey.

Mulcahy, Patrick J. '95 (SD) Oceanside, CA St. Mary, Star of the Sea.

Mulcahy, Sean '62 (MIA) Hallandale, FL St. Charles Borromeo.

Mulcair, William W. *m.s.* '65 (HRT)[M] Hartford, CT Missionaries of LaSalette.

Mulcrone, Charles P. '53 (SFD) Retired.

Mulcrone, Joseph A. '71 (CHI) Chicago, IL St. Francis Borgia; [X] Chicago, IL Catholic Office of the Deaf; Catholic Office of the Deaf.

Mulcrone, Thomas A. '77 (CHI)[L] Chicago, IL St. Mary of Providence; Fire Department Chaplain.

Mulderry, Anthony J. '67 (MIA) Sunrise, FL All Saints.

Mulderry, Anthony (MIA) Members; Finance Council; Real Estate Board.

Muldoon, Brendan '64 (SP) Indian Rocks Beach, FL St. Jerome; [F] Largo, FL St. Jerome Early Childhood Center; Vicars General; Ex Officio; Incardination Commission; Diocesan Finance Council; Presbyteral Council; College of Consultors.

Muldoon, P. Christopher '71 (PAT) Lake Hopatcong, NJ Our Lady Star of the Sea; Deans.

Muldowney, Thomas M. '03 (SCR) Clarks Summit, PA Our Lady of the Snows; Keystone Junior College.

Mulewski, Patrick M. '51 (NEW) Old Tappan, NJ St. Pius X.

Mulgrew, John E. '56 (PH) Media, PA St. Mary Magdalen.

Mulhall, Francis X. '47 (BRK)[V] Douglaston, NY Bishop Mugavero Residence Retired.

Mulhall, Michael *o.carm.* (CHI) Chicago, IL St. Thomas Apostle.

Mulhauser, Daniel J. *s.j.* '60 (SY)[Q] Syracuse, NY Jesuits at LeMoyne, Inc..

Mulhearn, Michael *c.m.* '68 (KC)[J] Kansas City, MO Vincentian Parish Mission Center.

Mulhern, James P. *o.f.m.* '44 (SP)[O] St. Petersburg St. Anthony Friary.

Mulhern, Joseph Hugh *o.p.* '54 (NY) Washington, DC St. Dominic Church & Priory.

Mulhern, Joseph P. *o.p.* (MO) AUXILIARY CHAPLAINS CONTRACT CHAPLAINS.

Mulhern, Kevin P. '76 (SCR) Dallas, PA Gate of Heaven.

Mulhern, Patrick J. '64 (ATL) On Sick Leave.

Mulhern, Raymond F. '52 (COV) Retired.
Mulholland, David '02 (SEA) Bellingham, WA Sacred Heart.
Mulholland, John H. (PH)[Y] Philadelphia, PA Immaculate Mary Home.
Mulica, James '67 (CLV) Retired.
Mulinda, Lawrence '95 (STA) Jacksonville Beach, FL St. Paul's.
Mulka, Arthur C. '51 (GAY) Retired.
Mulka, Raymond C. '49 (GAY) Retired.
Mulkerin, Terrence J. '61 (BRK) Military Chaplains; Navy Chaplains.
Mulkern, Daniel J. *t.o.r.* '66 (ALT)[F] Loretto, PA Mount Assisi Friary.
Mulkern, John F. '43 (BO) Senior Priests Retired.
Mulkern, Stephen M. '49 (PRT) Retired.
Mull, Thomas P. '76 (ROC) Canadaigua, NY St. Mary; [M] Rochester, NY Apostleship of Prayer.
Mullakara, Joseph '75 (SYM) Lilburn, GA Blessed Alphonsa Syro–Malabar Catholic Mission, Atlanta.
Mullakkara, Jose *m.s.f.s.* '75 (ATL)[K] Lawrenceville, GA The Missionaries of St. Francis De Sales.
Mullakkara, Joseph *m.s.f.s.* '75 (ATL) Lawrenceville, GA St. Lawrence.
Mullally, Gerald F. '76 (SCR) Milford, PA St. Patrick's; Deans.
Mullally, Thomas A. *s.v.d.* '70 (LAF) St. Martinville, LA Notre Dame de Perpetuel Secours.
Mullamangalam, Mathew (LAF) Carencro, LA St. Peter.
Mullan, Glen '94 (CC) Alice, TX St. Joseph.
Mullan, Patrick '67 (PAT)[P] Chester, NJ Nazareth Village Retired.
Mullan, Raymund A. '62 (FWT) Graham, TX St. Mary; Graham, TX St. Theresa of the Infant Jesus.
Mullan, William F. *m.m.* '62 (FgM).
Mullane, Bernard J. '56 (RCK) Retired.
Mullane, Thomas '68 (MIA) Big Pine Key, FL St. Peter.
Mullaney, Aidan *t.o.r.* '52 (ARL)[J] White Post, VA Sacred Heart Friary.
Mullaney, Cornelius J. '71 (BO) Lynn, MA St. Pius Fifth.
Mullaney, Edward John *o.c.s.o.* '73 (WOR)[O] Spencer, MA St. Joseph's Abbey.
Mullaney, Gregory C. '90 (NOR) Groton, CT Sacred Heart.
Mullaney, Lawrence J. '88 (RIC) Tabb, VA Blessed Kateri Tekawitha.
Mullaney, Leonard M. '62 (FR) Mattapoisett, MA St. Anthony's.
Mullaney, Mark '03 (ARL) Ashburn, VA St. Theresa.
Mullarkey, John T. '64 (GB) Kaukauna, WI St. Francis; Kaukauna, WI Holy Cross; Conciliation and Arbitration Board.
Mullarkey, Patrick J. '64 (SD) San Diego, CA St. Columba.
Mullelly, Thomas J. '80 (TR)[S] Princeton, NJ Campus Ministry for the Diocese of Trenton; Diocesan Consultors; Secretary.
Mullen, Austin (SP) Sun City Center, FL Prince of Peace.
Mullen, Bernard J. '61 (DET) Ortonville, MI St. Anne.
Mullen, Bernard *c.pp.s.* '48 (KC)[J] Liberty, MO Precious Blood Center.
Mullen, Charles F. *c.pp.s.* '64 (FTW) Rome City, IN St. Gaspar del Bufalo.
Mullen, David J. '82 (BO) Bellingham, MA St. Brendan.
Mullen, Dennis M. '70 (SUP) Cumberland, WI Sacred Heart of Jesus Church; Cumberland, WI St. Anthony Abbot; Cumberland, WI St. Ann.
Mullen, Dennis (SUP) St. Pius Priest Fund.
Mullen, Edward F. '54 (CAM) Stratford, NJ St. Luke Retired.
Mullen, Edward F. '58 (CHR) Retired.
Mullen, Godfrey *o.s.b.* '94 (IND)[A] St. Meinrad, IN St. Meinrad School of Theology; [K] St. Meinrad, IN St. Meinrad Archabbey.
Mullen, John J. *s.j.* '62 (BO)[V] Boston The Society of Jesus of New England–Provincial Offices; [V] Weston, MA Campion Jesuit Community.
Mullen, Joseph E. *s.j.* '50 (BO)[V] Boston The Society of Jesus of New England–Provincial Offices; Carlsbad, CA St. Patrick.
Mullen, Kevin J. *o.f.m.* '80 (NEW) Elmwood Park, NJ St. Leo's.
Mullen, Michael '62 (KCK) Kansas City, KS St. Patrick's; Defenders of the Bond.
Mullen, Michael '75 (VEN) Fort Myers, FL St. Francis Xavier.
Mullen, Michael (KCK) Directors.
Mullen, Owen J. '64 (WIL) On Duty Outside the Diocese.
Mullen, Owen '64 (HON) Honolulu, HI Holy Family.
Mullen, Patrick '85 (LA)[A] Camarillo, CA St. John's Seminary.
Mullen, Paul M. '73 (SCR) Presbyteral Council.
Mullen, Richard '55 (PEO) Retired.
Mullen, Richard *o.s.a.* '81 (MIA)[H] Miami, FL Casa San Lorenzo.
Mullen, Thomas J. *ss.cc.* '75 (LA) San Dimas, CA Holy Name of Mary.
Mullen, Timothy F. *o.praem.* '73 (WIL)[B] Claymont, DE Archmere Academy.
Mullen, Timothy F. *o.praem.* '73 (GB)[I] De Pere, WI St. Norbert Abbey.
Mullen, William J. '47 (OAK) Retired.
Mullen, William J. '51 (HRT) Judges; [A] Bloomfield, CT St. Thomas Seminary Retired.
Mullen, William V. *o.m.v.* '92 (DEN) Denver, CO Holy Ghost.
Mullenkuzhy, Abraham *m.s.f.s.* (ATL)[K] Lawrenceville, GA The Missionaries of St. Francis De Sales.
Muller, Anthony '68 (CIN) Cincinnati, OH St. Ann.
Muller, George *o.p.* '59 (WDC) Washington, DC St. Dominic Church & Priory.
Muller, Herman J. *s.j.* '41 (DET)[K] Detroit, MI Jesuit Community at the University of Detroit Mercy.
Muller, Joseph T. *m.s.c.* '58 (RCK) Aurora, IL St. Therese of Jesus.
Muller, Joseph *m.s.c.* '58 (RCK)[G] Aurora, IL Missionaries of the Sacred Heart Community.
Muller, Kennard '66 (BAL) Baltimore, MD St. Michael Retired.
Muller, Martin M. '57 (BIR) Birmingham, AL Our Lady of Sorrows.
Muller, Myles '48 (BAL)[O] Saint John Hall–Long Crandon Retired.
Muller, Peter D. *o.praem.* '93 (ORG)[I] Silverado, CA Norbertine Fathers of Orange Inc..
Mullet, John '56 (SAG) On Duty Outside the Diocese.
Mullet, John '91 (MIA)[G] Fort Lauderdale, FL Holy Cross Hospital.
Mullett, Gene W. '76 (STU) Bellaire, OH St. John; Bellaire, OH St. Michael's; Judges.
Mulligan, Bede J.K. *o.carm.* '58 (GBG)[H] Boliver, PA Mount Carmel Hermitage.
Mulligan, Bernard P. *c.ss.r.* '42 (STL)[O] Liguori, MO St. Clement Health Care Center.
Mulligan, Bertram *o.f.m.cap.* '49 (SFR)[N] Burlingame, CA Capuchin Provincial House.
Mulligan, Edward '56 (SP) Retired.
Mulligan, Emmett *o.f.m.* '52 (NY)[EE] West Palm Beach, FL St. Mary's Hospital.
Mulligan, George B. *c.s.c.* '82 (FR)[A] North Easton, MA Stonehill College; [A] North Easton, MA Holy Cross Fathers Religious.
Mulligan, James J. '61 (ALN) Censor of Books; Permanent Diaconate Office; Priestly Life and Ministry Office; Diocesan Medical Ethicist.
Mulligan, James J. *s.t.l.* '66 (PH) Doylestown, PA Our Lady of Mount Carmel.
Mulligan, John M. '66 (ROC) Rochester, NY Sacred Heart Cathedral; Vicars General; Judges.
Mulligan, John T. '64 (NY) Piermont, NY St. John.
Mulligan, John *s.m.* '57 (CIN)[M] Dayton, OH Marianist Community; [M] Dayton, OH Mercy Siena Village.
Mulligan, Joseph E. *s.j.* '73 (DET)[K] Colegio Centroamericano.
Mulligan, Joseph '75 (CHL) Gastonia, NC St. Michael.
Mulligan, Louis J. '61 (DAV) Retired.
Mulligan, Paul F. '57 (BO) Ashland, MA St. Cecilia.
Mulligan, Robert G. *o.s.f.s.* '83 (ALN)[B] Center Valley, PA DeSales University; [K] Center Valley, PA Oblates of St. Francis de Sales.
Mulligan, Robert H. '90 (PH) Spring City, PA St. Joseph.
Mulligan, Timothy *o.f.m.conv.* (SY)[T] Syracuse, NY Syracuse University, St. Thomas More Foundation, Inc.; [Q] Syracuse, NY Friary of Francis, Brother of Peace Conventual Franciscan Friars.
Mulligan, William J. *s.j.* (BO) Cambridge, MA Youville Lifecare, Inc..
Mulligan, William L. *s.j.* '65 (BO)[V] Boston, MA Loyola House; [EE] Cambridge, MA The Youville House, Inc..
Mulligan, William R. '45 (BUR) Retired.
Mullin, Edward J. *c.m.* '54 (STL)[O] Perryville, MO Congregation of the Mission.
Mullin, Francis R. *o.p.* (NY)[Y] New York, NY St. Rose's Home.
Mullin, Henry *c.s.sp.* '59 (MIA) Fort Lauderdale, FL St. Clement.
Mullin, Hugh J. '46 (KC) Retired.
Mullin, John A. *s.j.* '75 (NY)[EE] New York, NY Xavier Jesuit Community.
Mullin, John F. *s.j.* '65 (BO)[V] Boston The Society of Jesus of New England–Provincial Offices; [V] Newton, MA The Jesuit Community at Boston College.
Mullin, John F. *s.j.* '65 (MAN) Lebanon, NH Sacred Heart; Dartmouth–Hitchcock Medical Center; Council of Priests.
Mullin, John F. *s.j.* '65 (BO)[V] Boston The Society of Jesus of New England–Provincial Offices; [V] Newton, MA The Jesuit Community at Boston College.
Mullin, John F. *s.j.* '65 (MAN) Lebanon, NH Sacred Heart; Dartmouth–Hitchcock Medical Center; Council of Priests.
Mullin, Joseph P. *s.m.* '54 (NO)[P] New Orleans, LA Marist Fathers.
Mullin, Patrick J. *c.m.* '75 (LA)[Q] Santa Barbara, CA St. Mary's Center; [W] Santa Barbara, CA St. Mary's Seminary Center.
Mullin, Thomas J. (NY).
Mullin, Thomas M. '75 (PH) Uwchland, PA Saint Elizabeth; College of Consultors; Council of Priests; Pastors Review Board.
Mullin, Thomas '65 (BRK) Veterans Administration Medical Center.
Mullin, Thomas '65 (NY) Staten Island, NY St. John the Baptist de La Salle.
Mullin, William H. '65 (BO) Permanent Disability.
Mullins, Carlos '55 (NY) Bronx, NY St. Dominic; Bronx, NY St. Philip Neri.
Mullins, Kevin C. *o.s.a.* '90 (OAK) Castro Valley, CA Our Lady of Grace.
Mullins, Kevin *s.s.c.* '78 (ELP)[K] St. Columbans St. Columban's Foreign Mission Society.
Mullins, Kevin (OAK) Deans.
Mullins, Raymond '52 (PT) Pensacola, FL Nativity of Our Lord.
Mullins, Richard A. '95 (ARL) Alexandria, VA St. Rita's; Defenders of the Bond.
Mullins, Robert J. '45 (FAR) Retired.
Mullonkal, George '71 (SJP) Rossford, OH St. Michael.
Mullowney, Edward J. *s.s.j.* '55 (BAL)[S] Baltimore, MD St. Joseph's Manor.
Mullowney, Thomas E. '55 (GI) Retired.
Mulloy, Francis *c.s.sp.* '52 (SFR) Millbrae, CA St. Dunstan.
Mulloy, James *s.d.b.* '85 (NY)[F] New Rochelle, NY Salesian High School; [EE] New Rochelle, NY Salesian Provincial House.
Mulloy, John F. '70 (BO) Saugus, MA Blessed Sacrament.
Mulloy, Matthew '53 (NY)[EE] Bronx, NY Retired.
Mulloy, Michel '79 (RC) Rapid City, SD Blessed Sacrament; Rapid City, SD St. Rose of Lima; Diocesan Consultors.
Mulloy, Sylvester '38 (JOL) Retired.
Mulnix, John Gabriel R. *c.p.* '68 (CHI)[N] Tucson, AZ.
Mulqueen, John D. '62 (Y) Niles, OH Our Lady of Mt. Carmel.
Mulqueen, Martin B. '74 (PMB) Palm City, FL Holy Redeemer.
Mulranen, Francis J. '82 (PH) Upper Darby, PA St. Laurence.
Mulranen, John J. '50 (SY) Oneida, NY St. Patrick Retired.
Mulrenan, Donald P. *s.v.d.* '60 (BO)[V] Boston, MA Divine Word Missionaries.
Mulrnan, Alexius J. *o.f.m.* '60 (SP)[O] St. Petersburg St. Anthony Friary.
Mulroney, Joseph G. *j.c.l.* '93 (R) Raleigh, NC St. Luke the Evangelist; Defenders of the Bond.
Mulrooney, Conan P. *o.praem.* '67 (GB)[I] De Pere, WI St. Norbert Abbey.
Mulrooney, F. Harold '37 (SCR)[N] Dunmore, PA Villa St. Joseph Retired.
Mulroy, Timothy *s.s.c.* '95 (CHI)[K] St. Columbans St. Columban's Foreign Mission Society.
Mulsoff, Donald J. '69 (CHI) Other Assignments.
Mulvanerty, Thomas F. '79 (RVC)[M] Uniondale, NY St. Pius X Residence; Priestly Life and Ministry; Priests' Personnel Policy Board; Priests' Retirement Board; [M] Uniondale, NY St. Pius X Residence.
Mulvanerty, Thomas M. '65 (NY) New York, NY St. Monica.
Mulvaney, Andrew R. '68 (OG) Black River, NY St. Paul; Deferiet, NY St. Rita.
Mulvaney, James J. '53 (BIR) Retired.
Mulvanity, Francis C. '59 (CLV) Euclid, OH St. Paul.
Mulvanney, James (BIR) Judges.
Mulvany, Michael '88 (KCK) St. Francis; Osage City, KS St. Patrick's; St. Patrick's.
Mulvehill, John R. '57 (BO) Cohasset, MA St. Anthony.
Mulvehill, Louis J. '53 (ALT) South Fork, PA Most Holy Trinity.
Mulvey, Gerard *o.f.m.cap.* '91 (NY) New York, NY Our Lady Queen of Angels.
Mulvey, John J. '62 (NEW) Retired.
Mulvey, Michael (AUS) Deans; Presbyteral Council; Priestly Life and Formation Committee.
Mulvey, Wm. Michael '75 (AUS) Georgetown, TX St. Helen's.
Mulvihill, Daniel R. '53 (WCH) Retired.
Mulvihill, David J. '72 (CHI) Zion–Beach Park, IL Our Lady of Humility.
Mulvihill, John E. '64 (CHI) Highwood, IL St. James.
Mulvihill, Martin J. '83 (STL) Clayton, MO St. Joseph.
Mumper, Edward '63 (JOL) On Duty Outside the Diocese.
Mundadan, Joseph '84 (LAN) Goodrich, MI St. Mark the Evangelist.
Mundakal, Joseph A. *c.m.i.* '83 (JOL) Gibson City, IL Our Lady of Lourdes.
Mundanmani, Paulson *s.d.b.* '91 (OAK) Newark, CA St. Edward's.
Mundet, Carlos '59 (VEN) Naples, FL St. Peter the Apostle.
Mundwiller, Edmund *o.f.m.* '81 (STL)[O] Inver Grove Heights, MN.
Mundy, Joseph '81 (RVC) Absent on Leave.
Mundy, Patrick W. '66 (OG) Keene, NY St. Brendan.

Munguia, Jorge *s.j.* '67 (MIA)[D] Miami, FL Belen Jesuit Preparatory School; [H] Miami, FL Villa Javier.
Muniz, Alberto '77 (PCE) Salinas, PR Our Lady of Monserrat.
Muniz, Edwin Lorenzo *o.s.a.* '02 (MGZ) San German, PR St. Rose of Lima.
Muniz, Orlando Rosas '97 (MGZ) Maricao, PR St. John the Baptist.
Muniz, William '94 (MIA) Fort Lauderdale, FL St. Helen.
Muniz, William '94 (MIA)[G] Fort Lauderdale, FL Holy Cross Hospital.
Munjalu, Bernard '98 (ROC) Pittsford, NY St. Louis.
Munkelt, Richard A. '01 (SCR) Unassigned or Leave of Absence.
Munley, J. Thomas '93 (LAN) Durand, MI St. Mary.
Munn, Daniel M. '82 (SAV) Augusta, GA Church of the Most Holy Trinity.
Munn, Daniel '82 (NTN) Augusta, GA St. Ignatios of Antioch; Presbyteral Council.
Munoz, Arcadio '76 (NEW) New Milford, NJ Ascension.
Munoz, Eusiquio–Arranz '64 (WOR) Milford, MA St. Mary of the Assumption; Portuguese Ministry; St. Mary.
Munoz, Francisco *o.f.m.conv.* '94 (SAT) San Antonio, TX St. Alphonsus.
Munoz, J. Oscar (NY) New York, NY Our Lady of Guadalupe.
Munoz, Jesus M. '01 (ARE) Corozal, PR Holy Family.
Munoz, Jose *o.m.* '82 (CGS) Cayey, PR Nuestra Senora de la Asuncion.
Munoz, Jose '96 (ORL) Daytona Beach, FL St. Paul's.
Munoz, Juan Francisco *s.d.b.* '73 (LAR) Laredo, TX San Luis Rey.
Munoz, Manuel '98 (ELP) Pecos, TX St. Catherine.
Munoz, Matthew M. '02 (ORG) La Habra, CA Our Lady of Guadalupe.
Munoz, Mauro '97 (ELP)[B] El Paso, TX St. Anthony's School of Theology.
Munoz, Rafael '60 (PCE) On Duty Outside the Diocese.
Munoz, Rafael (ARE) Retired.
Munoz, Tomas G. '85 (TUC) Wellton, AZ St. Joseph the Worker; Wellton, AZ St. Joseph the Worker.
Munro, Donald '87 (PMB) Wellington, FL St. Rita.
Munroe, Henry T. '53 (FR) Retired.
Munsch, Christopher Louis '01 (BLX) Gulfport, MS St. John the Evangelist.
Munsch, Nathan J. *o.s.b.* '91 (GBG)[H] Latrobe, PA Saint Vincent Archabbey.
Munsell, Richard F. '79 (GF) Military Chaplains; Air Force Chaplains.
Munshower, William G. '58 (IND) Indianapolis, IN St. Thomas Aquinas; [O] Indianapolis, IN Butler University.
Munson, Thomas N. '54 (PBL) Retired.
Munster, Thomas P. *c.m.* '48 (CHI)[N] Chicago DePaul Vincentian Residence.
Muntone, Anthony D. *s.t.l.* '64 (ALN) Whitehall, PA St. Elizabeth.
Muntz, James F. '88 (NEW) Hoboken, NJ St. Francis.
Munz, Theodore G. *s.j.* '83 (CHI)[D] Wilmette, IL Loyola Academy; [X] Wilmette, IL Loyola Recreational Facility Corp..
Muodiaju, Samuel *c.s.sp.* '85 (MIA) Fort Lauderdale, FL St. Clement.
Muoio, Castrese *s.d.v.* '01 (NEW) Palisades Park, NJ St. Nicholas.
Muoneke, Romanus O. '94 (GAL) Houston, TX St. Vincent de Paul.
Muoneme, Abuchi *s.j.* '01 (BO)[V] Newton, MA The Jesuit Community at Boston College.
Muorah, Charles '91 (TR) Medford, NJ St. Mary of the Lakes.
Mupparathara, Abraham J. *m.c.b.s.* '94 (MAR) Calumet, MI Sacred Heart.
Mur, Rogelio *o.carm.* (MGZ) For Pastoral; Diocesan Board of Administration; Parish Priests Consultors; Development and Planification.
Mur, Rogelio *o.carm* (MGZ) Diocesan Consultors.
Mur, Rogelio *o.carm.* (MGZ) For Pastoral; Diocesan Board of Administration; Parish Priests Consultors; Development and Planification.
Murano, Saverio *o.s.s.t* '64 (GAL)[K] Catholic Chaplain Corps, Texas Medical Center.
Murasso, Jeremiah N. '79 (HRT) South Windsor, CT St. Francis of Assisi.
Murawski, Edward J. *s.j.* '66 (BO)[V] Boston, MA Loyola House.
Murcko, Charles S. '52 (E) Mercer, PA State Correctional Facility Retired.
Murd, Francis A. '76 (TOL) Maumee, OH St. Joseph.
Murdick, Olin J. '45 (SAG) Retired.
Murdock, Paul J. '75 (NOR) Windham, CT Sagrado Corazon de Jesus; Iglesia del Sagrado Corazon de Jesus – Spanish Apostolate; Liturgical Commission.
Murhammer, Francis J. '88 (PIT) Monroeville, PA North American Martyrs.
Murillo, Rafael '96 (BAL) Frederick, MD St. John the Evangelist.
Murnan, Sean *o.f.m.* '73 (GLP) Zuni, NM St. Anthony, Our Lady of Guadalupe.
Murnane, Patrick J. '60 (MIA) Hollywood, FL Nativity.
Murnane, Thomas M. *o.s.a.* '65 (PH)[AA] Villanova, PA St. Thomas Monastery.
Murnane, Thomas *o.s.a.* '61 (PH)[C] Villanova University.
Murnion, Philip J. '63 (NY) On Duty Outside the Archdiocese.
Muro, Jose Luis '01 (SD) San Diego, CA Good Shepherd.
Muro, Victor S. '66 (CAM) Vineland, NJ Immaculate Heart of Mary; Episcopal Vicar for Hispanics; Office of Hispanic Apostolate.
Muro, Victor '66 (CAM)[O] Vineland, NJ Pope John Paul II Retreat Center.
Muroko, Peter (CC).
Murphy, Alfred E. *o.s.a.* '56 (PH)[AA] Villanova, PA St. Thomas Monastery.
Murphy, Arthur J. '55 (HRT) West Hartford, CT St. Thomas the Apostle Church.
Murphy, Bartholomew J. *s.j.* '72 (P)[L] Portland Jesuit Provincial Office (Society of Jesus, Oregon Prov.); (FgM).
Murphy, Brendan *s.v.d.* '73 (LAF)[A] Bay St. Louis, MS St. Augustine's.
Murphy, Brendan *o.p.* '00 (PRO)[B] Providence, RI Providence College.
Murphy, Brian *o.carm.* '58 (ROC)[B] Rochester, NY McQuaid Jesuit High School; [I] Rochester, NY Whitefriars Priory.
Murphy, Campion *s.t.* '56 (PAT)[M] Stirling, NJ Holy Spirit Missionary Cenacle.
Murphy, Charles C. *s.j.* '62 (SJ) Lake Havasu City, AZ Our Lady of the Lake; [M] Los Gatos Sacred Heart Jesuit Center.
Murphy, Charles M. '61 (PRT) Falmouth, ME Holy Martyrs; Deans; Diocesan Consultors; Ex Officio; College of Consultors; Officio Members; Seminarians, Director of.
Murphy, Charles R. '91 (OKL) Midwest City, OK St. Philip Neri.
Murphy, Charles *s.a.* '61 (NY)[EE] Garrison, NY Franciscan Friars of the Atonement.
Murphy, Christopher D. '96 (ARL) Warrenton, VA St. John the Evangelist.
Murphy, Clarence '47 (FR) Retired.
Murphy, D. Declan '49 (MRY) Vicar General; Diocesan Consultors; Diocesan Consultors Retired.
Murphy, Daniel G. '56 (SY)[Q] Binghamton, NY McDevitt Residence for Retired Priests; Pastoral Examiners Retired.
Murphy, Daniel J. '56 (DET) Retired.
Murphy, Daniel S. '70 (BRK) Richmond Hill, NY Holy Child Jesus.
Murphy, Daniel T. '62 (MIL)[M] Greenfield, WI Clement Manor Health Center; [M] Greenfield, WI Clement Manor Retirement Community; Special Assignment.
Murphy, Daniel W. '73 (PAT) Wayne, NJ Our Lady of the Valley.
Murphy, David Brendan *o.p.* (PRO)[P] Providence St. Thomas Aquinas Priory at Providence College.
Murphy, David F. '87 (WIL) Delaware Army National Guard; Wilmington, DE St. Mary of the Immaculate Conception; Wilmington, DE St. Patrick; Army National Guard Chaplains.
Murphy, David M. '53 (ROC) Retired.
Murphy, David *o.carm.* '42 (VEN)[N] Chicago, IL St. Joseph's Priory; [G] Nokomis, FL Carmel at Mission Valley.
Murphy, David (BO) Brockton, MA Brockton Hospital.
Murphy, Denis J. '53 (LA) Retired.
Murphy, Dennis '74 (RIC) Charlottesville, VA Church of the Holy Comforter.
Murphy, Dennis '75 (ALB) Rotterdam Junction, NY St. Margaret of Cortona.
Murphy, Donald J. *s.j.* '61 (STL)[N] St. Louis, MO Fusz Pavilion; [O] St. Louis, MO Jesuit Community Corporation at St. Louis University – Jesuit Hall.
Murphy, Edward A. '98 (FR) Diocesan Department of Pastoral Care for the Sick; Diocesan Liaison with Charismatic Groups; In Res.
Murphy, Edward F. *c.m.* '79 (STL)[L] St. Louis, MO Guardian Angel Settlement Association; [O] St. Louis, MO Vincentian Residence.
Murphy, Edward J. *s.j.* '68 (NY)[EE] New York, NY Murray–Weigel Hall.
Murphy, Edward W. '92 (STA) Branford, FL San Juan Mission; High Springs, FL St. Madeleine Sophie Parish.
Murphy, Edward (STA) Scouts.
Murphy, Emmet *o.f.m.* (PAT) Butler, NJ St. Anthony.
Murphy, Eoin '64 (LAN) St. Johns, MI St. Joseph.
Murphy, Eugene F. '52 (RVC) Mineola, NY Corpus Christi Retired.
Murphy, Eugene '34 (MAN) Retired.
Murphy, Francis A. '57 (ANC) Retired.
Murphy, Francis C. '46 (MOB) Mobile, AL St. Dominic.
Murphy, Francis J. '51 (LIN) Retired.
Murphy, Francis J. *s.j.* '56 (STL)[N] St. Louis, MO Fusz Pavilion; [O] St. Louis, MO Jesuit Community Corporation at St. Louis University – Jesuit Hall.
Murphy, Francis J. '58 (WDC) Retired.
Murphy, Francis J. '66 (GAY) Cadillac, MI St. Ann; Cadillac, MI St. Edward; Lake City, MI St. Stephen; Lake City, MI St. Theresa.
Murphy, Francis J. *c.s.c.* '86 (FTW)[I] Holy Cross Novitiate.
Murphy, Francis J. (GAY) Vicar General; Consultors, Diocesan Board of; Elected Members; Finance Council, Diocesan.
Murphy, Francis '46 (MOB) Retired.
Murphy, Frank '58 (RNO) Reno, NV Our Lady of Wisdom.
Murphy, Frederick J. '57 (BO) Boston, MA Cathedral of the Holy Cross; Members.
Murphy, G. Ronald *s.j.* '69 (WDC)[M] Washington, DC The Jesuit Community at Georgetown University.
Murphy, George R. *s.j.* '71 (OAK)[A] Berkeley, CA The Jesuit School of Theology at Berkeley.
Murphy, George R. *s.j.* '71 (New England)[N] Berkeley, CA Jesuit Community at Jesuit School of Theology at Berkeley.
Murphy, George '66 (BLX) Hattiesburg, MS Sacred Heart; Trustees.
Murphy, George (JKS) Trustees.
Murphy, Gerard A. '01 (OAK) Pleasant Hill, CA Christ the King.
Murphy, Gerasimos *b.s.o.* '67 (NTN) Retired.
Murphy, Gerasimos *b.s.o.* (NTN) Judicial Vicar.
Murphy, Gerasimos *b.s.o.* (NTN) College of Eparchial Consultors.
Murphy, Gerasimos *b.s.o.* (NTN) Diocese of Newton for the Melkites in the USA, Inc., a Massachusetts Corporation.
Murphy, Gordon A. *o.f.m.* '55 (BO)[Y] Boston, MA Saint Anthony Residence.
Murphy, H. Joseph '61 (BO) Wakefield, MA St. Florence.
Murphy, Harold B. '68 (CHI) Chicago, IL St. Timothy; Deans.
Murphy, Harry J. '40 (GBG) Retired.
Murphy, Henry J. *s.j.* '57 (BO)[V] Weston, MA Campion Health Center, Inc..
Murphy, Henry J. *m.m.* '58 (NY).
Murphy, Hugh J. '59 (NOR)[EE] Danielson, CT St. James Retired.
Murphy, Hugh '71 (PAT) Stirling, NJ St. Vincent de Paul; [C] Paterson, NJ Paterson Catholic Regional High School.
Murphy, J. Emmett '38 (ROC) Retired.
Murphy, J. Patrick *c.m.* '76 (CHI)[N] Chicago, IL Vincentian Community, Congregation of the Mission, Midwest Province.
Murphy, Jack '52 (P) Tigard, OR St. Anthony.
Murphy, James A. '39 (PH) Retired.
Murphy, James E. '52 (STL) Retired.
Murphy, James E. '55 (GI) Retired.
Murphy, James F. '70 (PIT) Butler, PA St. Fidelis of Sigmaringen.
Murphy, James H. '81 (MAD) Platteville, WI St. Augustine University Parish; Platteville; [K] Platteville, WI St. Augustine Newman Center.
Murphy, James J. '45 (PH) Retired.
Murphy, James J. '52 (RCK) Rockford, IL St. Edward.
Murphy, James J. '54 (WH) Retired.
Murphy, James L. '52 (RCK) Retired.
Murphy, James T. (SAC) Communications and Media.
Murphy, James W. '48 (MEM) Retired.
Murphy, James Wayne '65 (L) Louisville, KY St. Thomas More.
Murphy, James *c.s.c.* '58 (ORL)[E] Cocoa Beach, FL Congregation of Holy Cross, Eastern Province.
Murphy, James '68 (SAC) Sacramento, CA Cathedral of the Blessed Sacrament.
Murphy, James '70 (MIA) Miami Lakes, FL Our Lady of the Lakes.
Murphy, James '78 (JOL) Elmhurst, IL Immaculate Conception.
Murphy, James *c.s.b.* '01 (OAK)[C] Oakland, CA Bishop O'Dowd High School.
Murphy, James (MIA) Incardination Committee; Archdiocesan Vocations Review Board.
Murphy, Jeremiah '63 (LA) West Hollywood, CA St. Victor.
Murphy, Jerome *c.ss.r.* '51 (ORL)[E] New Smyrna Beach, FL St. Alphonsus Villa–Redemptorist Fathers and Brothers.
Murphy, John C. '65 (SP) St. Pete Beach, FL St. John.
Murphy, John D. '79 (MET) Colonia, NJ St. John Vianney; John F. Kennedy Medical Center.
Murphy, John F. '47 (MIL) Retired.
Murphy, John F. '59 (CLV) Secretary.
Murphy, John J. '39 (FR) Retired.
Murphy, John J. *c.s.c.* '49 (FR)[A] North Easton, MA Holy Cross Fathers Religious.
Murphy, John J. '57 (ALB) Catskill, NY St. Patrick.
Murphy, John J. '68 (DEN) Kremmling, CO St. Peter.
Murphy, John M. '45 (MIL) Retired.
Murphy, John M. '65 (CHI) Chicago, IL St. Edward; Brookfield, IL St. Barbara.
Murphy, John P. '64 (ALN) Allentown, PA St. Thomas

More; College of Consultors; Appointed Members; Holy Childhood Association; Operation Rice Bowl; Pontifical Society for the Propagation of the Faith.
Murphy, John P. *s.j.* '69 (CIN) Cincinnati, OH St. Francis Xavier.
Murphy, John R. '73 (OG) Ogdensburg, NY St. Lawrence Psychiatric Center; Ogdensburg, NY Notre Dame.
Murphy, John R. (OG) Moderator of the Curia; Advocates; Priest Personnel Board.
Murphy, John Thaddeus *o.p.* '54 (NY) New York, NY St. Catherine of Siena; [EE] New York, NY St. Catherine of Siena Priory.
Murphy, John V. *s.j.* '52 (P)[L] Portland, OR Colombiere Community.
Murphy, John *o.f.m.* '54 (HRT) Hartford, CT St. Patrick–St. Anthony.
Murphy, John '68 (DEN)[I] Denver, CO Little Sisters of the Poor Mullen Home for the Aged.
Murphy, John *f.m.s.i.* '72 (BO).
Murphy, John '94 (ATL)[B] McDonough, GA St. James The Apostle.
Murphy, John (CLV)[A] Wickliffe, OH Borromeo Seminary.
Murphy, Joseph A. *s.j.* '73 (COL).
Murphy, Joseph E. '61 (PAT)[P] Chester, NJ Nazareth Village Retired.
Murphy, Joseph G. '44 (HRT) Retired.
Murphy, Joseph H. '61 (NEW) Retired.
Murphy, Joseph P. '54 (NY) Staten Island, NY St. Clare; [II] Staten Island, NY Emmaus Ministries, Ltd..
Murphy, Joseph R. *s.s.j.* '43 (BAL) Retired.
Murphy, Joseph T. '47 (PH) Retired.
Murphy, Joseph V. '67 (GRY) Crown Point, IN Holy Spirit.
Murphy, Joseph '60 (SFS) Retired.
Murphy, Jude *o.f.m.* '61 (PAT) Pompton Lakes, NJ Our Lady of the Assumption; Butler, NJ St. Anthony.
Murphy, Kenneth R. '86 (MET) Sayreville, NJ St. Stanislaus Kostka.
Murphy, Kevin J. *o.s.b.* '62 (MIL)[O] Benet Lake, WI St. Benedict's Abbey.
Murphy, Kevin P. '68 (ROC) Penfield, NY St. Joseph.
Murphy, Kevin '81 (NEW).
Murphy, Laurence T. *m.m.* '54 (NY).
Murphy, Lawrence B. *s.j.* '64 (LA)[F] Los Angeles, CA Loyola High School of Los Angeles.
Murphy, Lawrence F. '56 (BO) Senior Priests Retired.
Murphy, Lawrence V. '58 (ROC) Rochester, NY Sacred Heart Cathedral Retired.
Murphy, Lawrence *c.ss.r.* '49 (NY)[EE] New York, NY Redemptorist Priests and Brothers, C.Ss.R..
Murphy, Lawrence *s.j.* (LA)[J] Marina Del Rey, CA Daniel Freeman Marina Hospital.
Murphy, Louis E. *s.t.* '60 (WDC)[M] University Park, MD Holy Trinity Missionary Cenacle.
Murphy, Michael A. '92 (BAL) Special Assignment.
Murphy, Michael D. '66 (LAN) Lansing, MI St. Mary Cathedral; Bishop's Office; Vicar for Religious; Moderator of the Curia; Victim Assistance Coordinator.
Murphy, Michael D. '77 (PH) Drexel Hill, PA St. Dorothy.
Murphy, Michael F. '83 (SD) Coronado, CA Sacred Heart.
Murphy, Michael G. '87 (STL) Imperial, MO St. John Lateran.
Murphy, Michael J. *c.s.c.* '49 (FTW)[B] University of Notre Dame Du Lac; [I] Notre Dame, IN Holy Cross Community, Corby Hall, University of Notre Dame.
Murphy, Michael P. '89 (JC) Freeburg, MO Holy Family; Rich Fountain, MO Sacred Heart.
Murphy, Michael (SD) Priests; Presbyteral Council.
Murphy, Myles P. '90 (NY) Bronx, NY St. Gabriel.
Murphy, Owen *s.a.* '52 (NY)[EE] Garrison, NY Franciscan Friars of the Atonement.
Murphy, Patrick E. '85 (MAR) On Duty Outside the Diocese.
Murphy, Patrick F. '67 (LIN) Trenton, NE St. James.
Murphy, Patrick J. '50 (ALX) Retired.
Murphy, Patrick J. '97 (SD) Ramona, CA Immaculate Heart of Mary.
Murphy, Patrick '50 (ALX)[D] Monroe, LA Christus St. Joseph Home.
Murphy, Patrick *l.c.* '97 (ATL)[K] Atlanta, GA Legionaries of Christ.
Murphy, Patrick *c.s.* (KCK) Hispanic Ministry.
Murphy, Patrick *c.s.* (KS) Kansas City, MO Holy Rosary.
Murphy, Paul M. *c.m.* '60 (PH).
Murphy, Paul P. '78 (MRY)[AA] Corralitos, CA Holy Eucharist; Priestly Life and Ministry Board.
Murphy, Paul '96 (BGP) Ridgefield, CT St. Mary.
Murphy, Peter J. '92 (BO) Concord, MA St. Bernard; Concord, MA MCI–Concord.
Murphy, Peter P. '68 (PIT) Wexford, PA St. Alphonsus.
Murphy, Philip *ss.cc.* '70 (FR).
Murphy, Ralph *s.d.b.* '56 (SFR)[N] San Francisco, CA Salesian Provincial Residence.
Murphy, Richard D. '96 (BGP) Stamford, CT St. Cecilia.
Murphy, Richard D. (BGP) Presbyteral Council.
Murphy, Richard J. *s.j.* '64 (TUC)[E] Tucson, AZ Jesuit Community of the Vatican Observatory.
Murphy, Richard J. '73 (BAL) Walkersville, MD St. Timothy.
Murphy, Richard M. '65 (ROC) Vero Beach, FL Holy Cross Retired.
Murphy, Richard '57 (PMB) Retired.
Murphy, Richard '65 (ROC)[L] Seneca Falls, NY New York Chiropractic College.
Murphy, Richard '65 (PMB)[M] Diocesan Property & Liability Insurance Committee; Property and Liability; College of Consultors; Real Estate.
Murphy, Richard '80 (Y) Mineral Ridge, OH St. Mary.
Murphy, Robert A. *m.s.a.* (NOR) Building Commission.
Murphy, Robert J. *s.j.* '54 (DET)[P] Hamtramck, MI St. Ladislaus.
Murphy, Robert M. '93 (VEN) Fort Myers Beach, FL Ascension; Punta Gorda, FL Sacred Heart; [D] Port Charlotte, FL Bon Secours–St. Joseph Healthcare Group, Inc..
Murphy, Robert '74 (KC) Grandview, MO Coronation of Our Lady.
Murphy, Robert *m.s.a.* '93 (NOR) Chester, CT St. Joseph; [F] Cromwell, CT Society of the Missionaries of the Holy Apostles.
Murphy, Romeo J. *o.m.i.* (BO) Lowell, MA Saints Memorial Medical Center.
Murphy, Ronan B. (CAM) Gloucester, NJ St. Mary's; Advocates.
Murphy, Rory '88 (SJ) Seton Medical Center; [J] Daly City, CA Seton Medical Center.
Murphy, T. Austin '03 (BAL) Graduate Studies.
Murphy, Terrance J. '46 (STP) Retired.
Murphy, Terrence J. '46 (STP)[C] St. Paul, MN University of St. Thomas.
Murphy, Theodore *s.m.m.* '58 (RVC) Bay Shore, NY Southside Hospital; [M] Bay Shore, NY Montfort Missionaries.
Murphy, Thomas E. (NOR) New London, CT U.S. Coast Guard Memorial Chapel.
Murphy, Thomas J. '85 (IND) Indianapolis, IN St. John the Evangelist; Indianapolis, IN Christ The King Retired.
Murphy, Thomas J. '87 (SAV) Thomasville, GA St. Augustine.
Murphy, Thomas K. *o.f.m.* '58 (SP)[O] St. Petersburg St. Anthony Friary.
Murphy, Thomas M. '79 (PRT) Portland, ME St. Patrick's.
Murphy, Thomas P. *c.s.p.* '62 (NY)[EE] Jamaica Estates Paulist Fathers Generalate.
Murphy, Thomas R. '36 (PIT) Retired.
Murphy, Thomas R. E. *s.j.* '99 (BO)[V] Boston The Society of Jesus of New England–Provincial Offices.
Murphy, Thomas R.E. *s.j.* '99 (SEA)[A] Seattle, WA Seattle University.
Murphy, Thomas '51 (VEN) Retired.
Murphy, Thomas '51 (Y) Retired.
Murphy, Thomas *s.j.* '57 (NY)[EE] Loyola Hall, Jesuit Community.
Murphy, Thomas '66 (SAT) San Antonio, TX St. Peter Prince of the Apostles; Defenders of the Bond.
Murphy, Thomas *o.f.m.cap.* '71 (NY) Yonkers, NY St. Joseph Hospital; [X] Yonkers, NY St. Joseph's Medical Center.
Murphy, Thomas *o.f.m.cap.* '71 (NY) Yonkers, NY Sacred Heart.
Murphy, Thomas *o.s.f.s.* '76 (CHL) Greensboro, NC St. Paul the Apostle.
Murphy, Timothy J. '63 (BO) Salem, MA Immaculate Conception.
Murphy, Timothy J. (SPR) Hampden, MA St. Mary's; Permanent Diaconate.
Murphy, Timothy '58 (P) Milwaukie, OR St. John the Baptist; [C] Portland, OR Central Catholic High School.
Murphy, Timothy '60 (VEN) Retired.
Murphy, Timothy *o.ss.t.* '67 (BAL)[S] Baltimore, MD Holy Trinity Monastery.
Murphy, Timothy *g.h.m.* '93 (JKS) Aberdeen, MS St. Francis of Assisi.
Murphy, Timothy (JKS) Approved Advocate and Auditors.
Murphy, Ultan P. '53 (DOD) Olmitz, KS St. Ann.
Murphy, Venard *o.f.m.* '61 (SP)[O] St. Petersburg, FL St. Anthony Friary.
Murphy, Walter C. (BRK) Courage Ministry; Accountants.
Murphy, Walter '58 (BRK)[V] Douglaston, NY Bishop Mugavero Residence.
Murphy, Warren L. *t.o.r.* '60 (FWT)[O] Fort Worth, TX Ministry to Gay & Lesbians.
Murphy, Warren *t.o.r.* '60 (FWT) Fort Worth, TX St. Andrew.
Murphy, William F. '56 (PRO) Retired.
Murphy, William F. '88 (BO)[A] Brighton, MA St. John Seminary School of Theology; [C] Brighton, MA St. John Seminary College.
Murphy, William F. '90 (BO) Graduate Studies.
Murphy, William J. '57 (DET) Orchard Lake, MI Our Lady of Refuge.
Murphy, William J. '96 (SUP) Hammond, WI St. John the Baptist; Hammond, WI Immaculate Conception; Hammond, WI St. Bridget; St. Pius Priest Fund.
Murphy, William P. '43 (CHI) Evergreen Park, IL Queen of Martyrs Retired.
Murphy, William P. '65 (DEN) Englewood, CO Holy Name.
Murphy, William P. '86 (SPR) Hadley, MA Most Holy Redeemer.
Murphy, William S. '90 (PH) Norristown, PA St. Patrick.
Murphy, William T. '50 (RVC) Retired.
Murphy, William *c.p.* '73 (BAL) Baltimore, MD St. Joseph Passionist Monastery Parish; [S] Baltimore, MD St. Joseph's Passionist Community.
Murphy, William *s.j.* (CIN)[F] Cincinnati, OH St. Xavier High School; [M] Cincinnati, OH Jesuit Community at St. Xavier High School.
Murr, Charles (NY) New York, NY St. Francis de Sales; New York, NY St. Lucy.
Murray, Andrew '73 (BLX) Gulfport, MS St. John the Evangelist; Vicar General and Moderator of the Curia; College of Consultors; Catholic Foundation–Diocese of Biloxi; Catholic Housing Board; Finance Council; Insurance Committee; Personnel Board; Presbyteral Council; Catholic University, Friends of.
Murray, Bernard *o.c.s.o.* '50 (L)[K] Trappist, KY Abbey of Our Lady of Gethsemani, of the Order of Cistercians of the Strict Observance.
Murray, Brendan J. '68 (PAT) Rockaway, NJ St. Cecilia's; Rockaway, NJ Sacred Heart.
Murray, Brendan *s.s.c.* '56 (BO)[K] St. Columbans St. Columban's Foreign Mission Society.
Murray, Celestine (CC) Deans; College of Consultors; Personnel Board – Priests; Woodsboro, TX St. Therese, The Little Flower.
Murray, Charles A. *m.m.* '51 (FgM).
Murray, Cornelius J. '63 (CLV) North Olmsted, OH St. Brendan.
Murray, Cyprian *o.f.m.cap.* '64 (NOR) Middletown, CT St. Pius X.
Murray, Daniel A. '64 (PH) Drexel Hill, PA St. Charles Borromeo.
Murray, Daniel J. '73 (ORG) Newport Beach, CA Our Lady of Mount Carmel; Adjutant Judicial Vicars; Judges; Administrative Leave.
Murray, Daniel (ORG) Council of Priests.
Murray, Donald J. '61 (MAD) Retired.
Murray, Donnon P. *o.f.m.* '56 (FgM).
Murray, Edward G. '69 (SC) Denison, IA St. Rose of Lima.
Murray, Edward K. '62 (SFR) San Francisco, CA St. Teresa; St. Mary's Medical Center; [J] San Francisco, CA St. Mary's Medical Center.
Murray, Eugene L. '65 (SC) Marcus, IA Holy Name.
Murray, Francis J. '51 (LAN) Retired.
Murray, Francis J. (SAG) Censor.
Murray, Francis '49 (SAG) Retired.
Murray, Francis '53 (SFR)[S] Burlingame, CA Italian Catholic Federation Retired.
Murray, Frank J. '81 (PRT) Auburn, ME St. Louis; Auburn, ME St. Philip's; Auburn, ME Sacred Heart; [M] Lewiston, ME Bates College; Vocations.
Murray, Frank '53 (SFR) Burlingame, CA St. Catherine of Siena Retired.
Murray, Frank (PRT) Pastoral Assocs..
Murray, Frederick J. '53 (BO) Senior Priests Retired.
Murray, George B. *s.j.* '65 (DET)[K] Temperance, MI.
Murray, George B. *s.j.* '65 (BO)[V] Weston, MA Campion Jesuit Community.
Murray, Gerald E. '84 (NY) New York, NY St. Vincent de Paul; Navy Reserve Chaplains.
Murray, Gerald (NY) Legion of Mary.
Murray, Harold A. '49 (NEW) Retired.
Murray, Harrold '29 (TR) Manasquan, NJ St. Denis.
Murray, Ignatius L. '57 (PH) Havertown, PA Annunciation B.V.M..
Murray, J–Glenn *s.j.* '79 (CHI) Office for Pastoral Liturgy; [N] Chicago, IL Woodlawn Jesuit Community.
Murray, J. Glenn *s.j.* '79 (CLV) Cleveland, OH St. Henry.
Murray, James B. '57 (NSH) Retired.
Murray, James H. '56 (PAT) Denville, NJ St. Mary's.
Murray, James J. '56 (NY)[AA] New York, NY Mary Manning Walsh Home.
Murray, James M. *o.s.b.* '93 (PEO).
Murray, James Stephen *o.p.* '50 (L)[A] Springfield, KY St. Rose; [L] St. Catharine, KY Sansbury Care Center.
Murray, John A. '54 (Y) Hubbard, OH St. Patrick Retired.
Murray, John A. '62 (BO) Concord, MA St. Bernard.
Murray, John B. *c.m.* '42 (BRK)[V] Jamaica, NY Vincentian Residence.
Murray, John C. *c.s.b.* '57 (ROC)[I] Rochester, NY Basilian Residence.
Murray, John D. '53 (LA) Medium North.
Murray, John E. '60 (CHY) Kemmerer, WY St. Patrick's.
Murray, John E. '63 (HEL) Anaconda, MT Anaconda Catholic Community.

Murray, John E. '67 (RVC) Retired.
Murray, John F. *c.ss.r.* '95 (BAL) Baltimore, MD Sacred Heart of Jesus.
Murray, John Francis *s.m.a.* '57 (NEW)[N] Tenafly, NJ Society of African Missions, Provincialate, S.M.A. Fathers.
Murray, John J. '47 (PH)[AA] Villanova, PA St. Thomas Monastery Retired.
Murray, John J. '65 (BRK) Bayside, NY American Martyrs.
Murray, John M. '98 (FR) Diocesan Department of Pastoral Care for the Sick; In Res.
Murray, John P. '54 (RVC) Retired.
Murray, John P. *s.j.* '87 (BO)[V] Watertown, MA The Society of Jesus of New England–Provincial Offices.
Murray, John S. '69 (ORL) Titusville, FL St. Teresa.
Murray, John W. '68 (CHI) Hanover Park, IL St. Ansgar.
Murray, John '54 (Y) Retired.
Murray, John '62 (LA) Burbank, CA St. Francis Xavier.
Murray, John '67 (RVC) New Hyde Park, NY Notre Dame.
Murray, John *c.s.b.* '67 (ROC)[M] Rochester, NY Marriage Encounter Apostolate.
Murray, John *c.ss.r.* '73 (BRK) Brooklyn, NY Our Lady of Perpetual Help Basilica.
Murray, John *s.j.* '87 (BO)[V] Cambridge, MA Faber House.
Murray, John *c.ss.r.* '94 (NY)[GG] Esopus, NY Mount St. Alphonsus Redemptorist Retreat Center.
Murray, John (CHY) Vicars Forane.
Murray, John (HEL) Personnel Board.
Murray, Joseph M. '56 (RVC) Retired.
Murray, Joseph W. '61 (PH) Lansdale, PA St. Stanislaus.
Murray, Kevin P. '77 (PH) Chester, PA Saint Katharine Drexel.
Murray, Kevin R. *c.ss.r.* '86 (PH) Philadelphia, PA St. Boniface.
Murray, Leo A. *s.j.* '62 (PH) Philadelphia, PA Old St. Joseph's.
Murray, Maurice M. *s.j.* (FgM).
Murray, Michael D. *o.s.b.* '56 (PBL)[F] Canon City, CO Holy Cross Abbey.
Murray, Michael J. '76 (WDC) Pastoral Center Special Ministries; [N] Kensington, MD St. John Vianney House; St. John Vianney House; Executive Director, Permanent Diaconate.
Murray, Michael S. *o.s.f.s.* '86 (WIL)[J] Wilmington, DE Oblates of St. Francis De Sales; [M] Childs, MD De Sales Spirituality Center.
Murray, Paul '75 (WDC) On Duty Outside the Archdiocese.
Murray, Paul (NY)[HH] Annondale–on–Hudson, NY Bard College.
Murray, Peter J. *s.j.* '72 (ALB)[N] Auriesville, NY Shrine of Our Lady of Martyrs.
Murray, Peter *s.j.* '72 (NY) Manhattan, NY Bird S. Coler Memorial Hospital and Home; [EE] New York, NY West Side Jesuit Community.
Murray, Richard H. '43 (LA) Woodland Hills, CA St. Bernardine of Siena Retired.
Murray, Robert J. *o.s.a.* '83 (PH) Bridgeport, PA St. Augustine; [C] Villanova University; [AA] Villanova, PA St. Thomas Monastery.
Murray, Robert W. '88 (BO)[A] Brighton, MA St. John Seminary School of Theology.
Murray, Russel *o.f.m.* '98 (WDC)[B] Silver Spring, MD Holy Name College.
Murray, Russel *o.f.m.* '98 (NY)[EE] Silver Spring, MD Holy Name College.
Murray, Sean '52 (SD) San Diego, CA St. Brigid.
Murray, Sean *c.ss.r.* '57 (OAK)[N] Oakland, CA Redemptorists.
Murray, Sean (OG) Massena, NY St. Lawrence; Massena, NY Sacred Heart.
Murray, Steven J. (PBL) Crested Butte, CO Queen of All Saints; Gunnison, CO St. Peter.
Murray, Steven M. '88 (OG) Watertown, NY Holy Family; Diocesan Consultors.
Murray, Thomas A. '68 (PH) Norristown, PA Visitation B.V.M..
Murray, Thomas F. '57 (BO) Senior Priests Retired.
Murray, Thomas P. '81 (RVC) Greenport, NY St. Agnes.
Murray, Timothy J. '77 (DET) Livonia, MI St. Edith.
Murray, W. Celestine (CC) Presbyteral Council.
Murray, William F. '45 (PRO) Retired.
Murray, William F. '54 (MIL) Retired.
Murrin, Donald L. *s.v.d.* '60 (LR) Pine Bluff, AR St. Peter's.
Murrin, Raymond J. '57 (BIR) Retired.
Murrin, Robert '99 (MRY) Salinas, CA Madonna Del Sasso.
Murrman, Jonathan J. *o.s.b.* '65 (GBG)[H] Latrobe, PA Saint Vincent Archabbey.
Murrman, Warren D. *o.s.b.* '65 (GBG)[H] Latrobe, PA Saint Vincent Archabbey.
Murry, Trevor '01 (BEL) Belleville, IL St. Teresa of the Child Jesus.
Murtagh, George O. '50 (BUR) Retired.
Murtagh, James '66 (PMB) West Palm Beach, FL St. Ann; Marriage Encounter; College of Consultors.
Murtagh, John J. '69 (YAK) On Duty Outside the Diocese.
Murtagh, Lawrence J. '53 (WIN) Retired.
Murtagh, Paul *ss.cc.* (LSC) Artesia, NM St. Anthony; Artesia, NM Our Lady of Grace; Presbyteral Council.
Murtagh, Seamus (PMB) Presbyteral Council.
Murtaugh, Lewis C. *s.j.* '69 (CHI).
Murtaugh, William '72 (STP)[N] New Brighton, MN St. John the Baptist.
Murtha, Chester '93 (SFS) Dell Rapids, SD St. Mary's.
Murtha, John *o.s.b.* '57 (GBG) Greensburg, PA St. Benedict.
Murtha, Michael '93 (PH) Havertown, PA Sacred Heart.
Murugarren, Jesus *o.s.a.* '55 (SAT) San Antonio, TX St. Michael.
Murungi, Osward Mubendi *a.j.* '00 (Y) Canton, OH St. Joan of Arc.
Murzyn, John A. '59 (GRY) Retired.
Muscalino, Daniel C. '78 (SY) Syracuse, NY St. John the Baptist; Truxton, NY St. Patrick; Special Assignment.
Muscat, John C. '84 (CAM) Rosenhayn, NJ St. Mary's; Directors; Brazilian Missions & Catholic Relief Services.
Muscolino, Frank J. '68 (MRY) Adamsville, AL St. Patrick's; Birmingham, AL St. Stanislaus; Los Gatos, CA Christ Child.
Mushala, Walter A. (SAT) Retired.
Mushi, Evaristus '87 (SP) Crystal River, FL St. Benedict.
Mushi, Peter *a.j.* '87 (NY) Bronx, NY St. Angela Merici.
Mushinsky, John E. (PAT) Retired.
Musial, Edward S. '46 (PH) Conshohocken, PA St. Mary Retired.
Musial, George '67 (CHI)[N] Chicago, IL St. Peter's Friary.
Musico, Edwin '85 (STO) Tracy, CA St. Bernard Church (Pastor of).
Musinski, Donald T. '62 (MIL) Retired.
Musinski, Donald '48 (MIL)[M] Wauwatosa, WI St. Camillus Health Center, Inc..
Musinsky, John *s.v.d.* '44 (CHI)[B] Techny, IL Divine Word Residence.
Musiol, Jozef *s.d.s.* '72 (AUS)[I] Merrillville, IN Salvatorian Fathers (Society of the Divine Savior).
Musonda, Francis '00 (BAL)[S] Emmaus Spirituality Center.
Musso, David D. *s.m.* '98 (ATL)[C] Atlanta, GA Marist School.
Mustaciuolo, Gregory '90 (NY) New York, NY; Vice–Chancellors; Secretary to the Archbishop; Archdiocesan Consultors; Priests Council of the Archdiocese of New York.
Musteikis, Leonard '38 (OM) Retired.
Mustos, Stephen N. *sch.p.* '58 (PAT) Passaic, NJ St. Stephen's
Mustos, Stephen N. (ATH) Delegate of the Bishop in the U.S.A.; American Hungarian Catholic Priests' Association.
Mustos, Stephen *sch.p.* '58 (PH)[AA] Devon Piarist Fathers (Order of the Pious Schools).
Musumbu, Gilbert Malu '88 (TUC) Douglas, AZ Immaculate Conception; Douglas, AZ St. Luke; Firtleville, AZ St. Bernard's; [H] Douglas, AZ Cochise Community College.
Muth, Joseph L. '74 (BAL) Baltimore, MD St. Matthew; [V] Baltimore, MD St. Matthew's Parish Endowment Trust.
Muth, Stephen '82 (PRM) Kansas City, MO Our Lady of Peace; Kansas City, MO St. Luke, Byzantine Catholic Parish.
Muthaya, Aloysius *sac* '76 (FWT) Arlington, TX St. Matthew.
Mutholath, Abraham '80 (SYM) Eparchial Consultors.
Muthukattil, Thomas '66 (BRK) South Ozone Park, NY St. Anthony of Padua.
Muthusamy, John Nicholas '87 (NY) Cortlandt Manor, NY St. Columbanus.
Mutsko, Frank J. (ORL) Orlando, FL St. James Cathedral.
Muweesi, John V. '89 (NO) New Orleans, LA St. Francis De Sales.
Muyombo, Gaston (DEN) Arvada, CO Spirit of Christ Parish.
Muzas, Brian Keenan '03 (NEW) North Arlington, NJ Queen of Peace.
Muzic, Anthony J. '63 (CLV) Cleveland, OH St. Mark Retired.
Muzzey, Charles H. '65 (WDC) Retired.
Muzzin, Victor *f.d.p.* '72 (NY) New York, NY St. Ann.
Mwacha, Nikomedius (CLV)[K] Cleveland, OH Holy Family Home.
Mwape, Wilbroad '95 (CHR) Charleston, SC St. Joseph.
Mychajlenko, Jaroslaw '78 (SJP) Solon, OH Protection B.V.M..
Mychajlenko, Jaroslaw (SJP) Western Deanery.
Mychajlenko, Jaroslaw (SJP) Diocesan Consultors.
Mychajlenko, Jaroslaw (SJP) Catechetical Planning Committee.
Mychajlenko, Jaroslaw (SJP) Notary.
Myers, Christopher P. *s.o.l.t.* (MO).
Myers, Christopher '90 (CC)[G] Robstown, TX Society of Our Lady of the Most Holy Trinity.
Myers, David A. *s.j.* '70 (P)[L] Guadalupe, AZ.
Myers, Edward T. *o.p.* '65 (PRO)[P] Providence St. Thomas Aquinas Priory at Providence College.
Myers, Gabriel *o.s.b.* '99 (WDC)[M] Washington, DC St. Anselm's Abbey.
Myers, Gerald '94 (FAR) On Duty Outside the Diocese.
Myers, J. Edward '55 (NEW) Retired.
Myers, James E. '80 (PEO) On Duty Outside the Diocese.
Myers, Jeremy '84 (DAL) Sherman, TX St. Mary.
Myers, John *o.f.m.cap.* '54 (DET).
Myers, Kenneth E. '80 (PIT)[K] Beaver, PA SS. Peter and Paul; Beaver County, PA The Medical Center Beaver; Beaver County, PA Friendship Ridge Skilled Nursing.
Myers, Rawley '49 (COS) Retired.
Myers, Regis F. '54 (ALT) Retired.
Myers, Robert *s.v.d.* '49 (CHI)[B] Techny, IL Divine Word Residence.
Myers, William F. '56 (RCK) Active Outside the Diocese.
Myers, William R. '69 (STU) Gallipolis, OH St. Louis; [J] Rio Grande, OH Rio Grande University.
Myers, William '88 (STO) On Duty Outside the Diocese.
Myers, William '88 (SFR) San Francisco, CA St. Anne.
Myett, Robert D. *o.p.* '60 (PRO)[P] Providence St. Thomas Aquinas Priory at Providence College.
Myhalyk, Richard M. *s.s.e.* '71 (BUR) Engaged Encounter; [E] Colchester, VT Society of St. Edmund; (FgM).
Myhalyk, Richard *s.e.e.* (NOR)[F] Mystic, CT Society of St. Edmund.
Mykyta, Myron '97 (SD) Los Angeles, CA Nativity of Blessed Virgin Mary.
Myladil, Thomas *o.c.d.* '76 (MET) Edison, NJ St. Matthew.
Myladiyil, Sebastian *s.v.d.* '97 (BLX) Bay St. Louis, MS St. Rose De Lima.
Mylchreest, William F. '80 (MIA) Fort Lauderdale, FL St. Sebastian.
Myler, John T. '82 (BEL) Belleville, IL St. Mary; [J] Belleville, IL World Apostolate of Fatima, The Blue Army, U.S.A.; Advocate; Diocesan Consultors; Diocesan Deans.
Myles, John '64 (SAC) Maxwell, CA Sacred Heart.
Mynaugh, Charles B. '42 (PH) Retired.
Myshchuk, Mikhail '94 (STF) Watervliet, NY St. Nicholas; Priests' Benevolent Association.
Myslinski, John F. '80 (WDC) Rockville, MD St. Mary.
Mysliwiec, Haldane '70 (CHI) Des Plaines, IL St. Stephen Protomartyr; [J] Des Plaines, IL Holy Family Medical Center.
Mysliwiec, Jan J. *s.d.s.* '62 (NEW)[N] Verona, NJ The Salvatorian Fathers.
Myszel, George G. '53 (MIL) Retired.
Myszka, Daniel J. '58 (BUF) Retired.

N

N'go, Anthony Chinh '94 (L) Fairdale, KY St. Jerome; Louisville, KY St. John Vianney.
N'Zilamba, Norbert *o.praem.* '87 (JKS)[F] Jackson, MS Priory of St. Moses the Black.
Naas, Stephen '78 (KAL) Marshall, MI St. Mary.
Nabbefeld, Grant '95 (SJ) On Leave of Absence.
Naber, Herman J. '59 (L) Louisville, KY St. Elizabeth of Hungary; Louisville, KY St. Therese Retired.
Naber, John T. '45 (BUF) Retired.
Nabi, Lubna '01 (GAL)[T] Houston, TX Satellite Office.
Nabozny, Peter '54 (ALB) Retired.
Nabwana, Charles '80 (LC) Genoa, WI St. Charles Borromeo.
Nacarino, Raymond L. '85 (MET) New Brunswick, NJ Our Lady of Mt. Carmel.
Nacca, John J. '41 (ROC) Retired.
Naccarato, Frank '79 (NY) Arthur Kill Correctional Facility.
Nace, Arthur J. '57 (PH) Retired.
Nachajski, Richard E. '71 (ALN) Reading, PA St. Anthony of Padua.
Nachtigal, Fred '58 (Y) Retired.
Nacino, Raynald '83 (BRK) Long Island City, NY Immaculate Conception.
Nacional, Perfecto '62 (SR) Sebastopol, CA St. Sebastian.
Nacius, Michael A. '89 (CHI) Matteson, IL St. Lawrence O'Toole.
Nacke, Xavier *o.s.b.* '63 (KC)[A] Conception, MO Conception Seminary College; [J] Parnell, MO St. Joseph Parish.
Nacorda, Cirilo A. '92 (CLV) Philippine–American Ministry; Cleveland, OH Cathedral of St. John the Evangelist; [Y] Cleveland, OH St. John Cathedral Endowment Trust.
Nacu, Jose R. *m.s.* '57 (HON) Honolulu, HI Our Lady of the Mount.
Nadackal, Zacharias *c.m.i.* '64 (NY) Rye, NY Resurrection.
Nadal, Bart *c.r.* '47 (DEN)[A] Denver, CO St. Andrew's

Theatine Religious House.
Naddeo, Henry M. '56 (NEW) Jersey City, NJ St. Aedan's; South Hudson.
Nadeau, James L. '88 (PRT) Portland, ME Cathedral of the Immaculate Conception.
Nadeau, Lance P. *m.m.* '90 (FgM).
Nadeau, Real J. '62 (PRT) Kittery, ME St. Raphael's.
Nadeau, Richard A. '80 (PRT) Limerick, ME St. Matthew.
Nadeau, Roland P. '00 (PRT) Portland, ME Cathedral of the Immaculate Conception; Portland, ME Mercy Hospital; [H] Portland, ME Mercy Hospital.
Nadeau, Roland S. *m.s.* '69 (HRT)[M] Hartford Our Lady of Sorrows Rectory.
Nadeau, Roland *m.s.* '69 (STL)[O] Generalate, Missionari di N.S. de La Salette.
Nadeau, Timothy J. '91 (PRT) Sanford, ME Holy Family; Sanford, ME St. Ignatius Martyr.
Nadeau, Timothy (PRT) Clergy Benefit Plan–Clergy Pension Plan; Diocesan Board of Education; Diocesan Council of Priests.
Nadeau, William *o.m.i.* '68 (RNO) Gardnerville, NV St. Gall; Diocesan Board of Consultors; Presbyteral Council.
Nadicksbernd, Elmer *s.v.d.* '64 (WH) Gassaway, WV St. Thomas; Maysel, WV Risen Lord.
Nadine, Jerome E. '58 (BRK) Released from Diocesan Assignment.
Nadine, Jerry '58 (LAV) Las Vegas, NV Christ the King.
Nadolny, Edmund S. '59 (HRT) Meriden, CT St. Stanislaus.
Nadolny, Stanley J. '68 (TUC) Apache Junction, AZ St. George.
Nadolski, Kevin M. *o.s.f.s.* '96 (ARL)[D] Alexandria, VA Bishop Ireton High School.
Naduvilekoot, Augustine '71 (NOR)[B] Durham, CT Notre Dame.
Nadzam, John B. '50 (STU) Retired.
Naedele, William B. '49 (NEW) Maplewood, NJ St. Joseph's.
Naedele, William (NEW) Office of Catholic Cemeteries.
Naegele, Gary P. '79 (WH) Fairmont, WV St. Anthony.
Naegele, Zacchaeus Maria *o.s.b.cam.* '98 (MRY)[F] Big Sur, CA New Camaldoli Hermitage.
Naessens, Philip *o.f.m.cap.* '86 (DET)[K] Detroit St. Bonaventure Friary.
Naffate, Lenin (SAT) San Antonio, TX Cathedral of San Fernando.
Nagai, Alan '58 (HON) Honolulu, HI St. Stephen.
Nagel, Kurt '97 (SEA) Forks, WA St. Anne Parish; Port Angeles, WA Queen of Angels; Port Townsend, WA St. Mary Star of the Sea; Callum Bay Correction Center; Clearwater / Olympic Correction Center.
Nagele, John M. *c.pp.s.* '53 (TOL) Bellevue, OH St. Sebastian; Bellevue, OH St. Michael's; Bellevue, OH Assumption.
Nagele, John *c.pp.s.* (Y) Judges.
Nagengast, Maynard G. *o.s.b.* '62 (NEW)[N] Newark, NJ Newark Abbey.
Nagineni, Balasamy '94 (OKL) Oklahoma City, OK Christ the King.
Nagle, Austin *ss.cc.* '54 (FR)[H] Brockton, MA.
Nagle, Edmund W. *s.j.* '63 (PAT)[I] Morristown, NJ Loyola House of Retreats.
Nagle, James B. *m.m.* '49 (NY).
Nagle, James B. *m.m.* '52 (NY).
Nagle, Joseph P. '71 (BRK)[EE] Brooklyn, NY St. Saviour.
Nagle, Michael R. '72 (FR) Edgartown, MA St. Elizabeth; Oak Bluffs, MA Sacred Heart; Vineyard Haven, MA St. Augustine.
Nagle, Vincent *f.s.c.b.* '92 (FR) Attleboro, MA St. Joseph's; [N] Attleboro, MA Priestly Fraternity of the Missionaries of St. Charles Borromeo; Diocesan Department of Pastoral Care for the Sick.
Nagle, Walter M. '99 (NOR) Oakdale, CT Our Lady of the Lakes; Willimantic, CT St. Joseph.
Nagle, William A. '49 (BGP)[P] Stamford, CT The Catherine Dennis Keefe Queen of the Clergy Retired Priests' Residence Retired.
Naglich, Robert T. *s.c.j.* '91 (GRY) Valparaiso, IN St. Paul; Boy Scouts Liaison.
Naglich, Robert *s.c.j.* '91 (MIL)[O] Valparaiso, IN St. Paul's.
Nagy, Ferenc *s.j.* (ATH) "Tavlatok".
Nahal, John *m.l.m.* '93 (OLL) San Antonio, TX St. George Maronite; [A] Houston, TX The Congregation of Maronite Lebanese Missionaries; Presbyteral Council.
Nahn, William J. '76 (ALN) Hellertown, PA St. Theresa of the Child Jesus.
Naickomparambil, Varghese '72 (SYM) Bellwood, IL Mar Thoma Shleeha Cathedral.
Naill, Joseph P. '97 (RCK) Woodstock, IL St. Patrick; [B] Woodstock, IL Marian Central Catholic High School; Special Assignment.
Nairn, Thomas *o.f.m.* '75 (CHI)[D] Holy Spirit Friary.
Najim, Michael J. '01 (PRO) Greenville, RI St. Philip.
Najjar, Samuel A. '84 (SAM) Waterville, ME St. Joseph.
Nakagawa, Francis *s.m.* '57 (STL)[O] Honolulu, HI.
Nakagawa, Francis *s.m.* '57 (HON)[G] Honolulu, HI; Japanese Ministry; Oahu.
Nakireru, Omoviekobwa A. (MO) AUXILIARY CHAPLAINS CONTRACT CHAPLAINS.
Nakowicz, Stanley T. '67 (PRO) East Providence, RI Our Lady of Loreto; Newspaper.
Nale, Joseph Christopher '03 (ALT) State College, PA Our Lady of Victory.
Nalepa, Damien '70 (BAL) Baltimore, MD St. Gregory the Great; Baltimore City Jail.
Nalepa, Richard A. *c.p.* '70 (PIT)[N] Pittsburgh, PA St. Paul of the Cross Monastery.
Nall, Brent C. '93 (SAC) Tulelake, CA Holy Cross.
Nall, James M. *j.c.l.* '87 (BEL) New Athens, IL St. Agatha; Judicial Vicar; Diocesan Consultors.
Nallen, James F. '66 (CHI) Chicago, IL St. Ethelreda.
Nalley, Robert W. '75 (GAY) Grayling, MI St. Mary; Elected Members; Tribunal Diocesan.
Nally, J. Brendan '56 (WOR) Clinton, MA Our Lady of the Rosary.
Nally, Joseph M. '72 (WOR) Worcester, MA St. Stephen's; Presbyteral Council.
Nally, Joseph (WOR) Diocesan College of Consultors.
Nalty, Christopher '99 (NO) On Duty Outside the Archdiocese.
Nalugon, Nilo '94 (SAN) Crane, TX Good Shepherd; McCamey, TX Sacred Heart.
Nalysnk, Yaroslov '90 (BO) Boston, MA St. Elizabeth's Medical Center; [P] Brighton, MA St. Elizabeth's Hospital of Boston.
Nalysnyk, Bogdan (STN) Chicago, IL St. Nicholas Ukrainian Catholic Cathedral.
Nalysnyk, Bohdan (STN) Presbyteral Council.
Nalysnyk, Jaroslaw '90 (STF) Jamaica Plain, MA Christ the King; Boston.
Nam, Heebong '97 (BRK) Flushing, NY St. Paul Chong Ha–Sang Roman Catholic Chapel.
Nam, Simon '52 (NY) Bronx, NY St John Nam.
Nambusseril, John *c.m.i.* '93 (NY) Irvington–on–the–Hudson, NY Immaculate Conception.
Namie, James B. '54 (STP) Retired.
Namiotka, Edward F. '87 (CAM)[B] Vineland, NJ Sacred Heart High School; Vineland, NJ Sacred Heart.
Nance, Gary *m.s.* (BLX) Bay St. Louis, MS Our Lady of the Gulf.
Nangle, Joseph J. *o.f.m.* '58 (WDC)[B] Washington, DC Franciscan Mission Service of North America.
Nangle, Thomas R. '70 (CHI) Other Assignments; Police Department Chaplain.
Nani, Stephen P. *c.s.c* '92 (FTW)[I] South Bend, IN.
Nano, Efren B. '87 (CC) Sinton, TX Sacred Heart.
Nantes, Edmund C. *o.p.* (NO)[S] Metairie, LA International Dominican Foundation.
Nanz, Jack '71 (PIT) Butler, PA St. Peter.
Napier, Robert L. '90 (STA) Interlachen, FL St. John's Mission; Cursillos de Cristiandad.
Napieralski, Maciej '83 (FBK) Aniak, AK St. Theresa; Holy Cross, AK Holy Family; Presbyteral Council; Consultors.
Napoli, Carlo *t.o.r.* '58 (WDC) Washington, DC Providence Hospital; [K] Washington, DC Providence Hospital; [M] Washington, DC St. Louis Friary.
Napoli, Peter *o.f.m.cap.* '73 (NY) Bronx, NY Immaculate Conception.
Napolitano, Joseph V. '76 (HRT) New Britain, CT St. Maurice.
Nappo, Michael *o.f.m.* '91 (NY)[GG] Wappingers Falls, NY Mt. Alvernia Retreat House.
Naquin, Roch R. (HT) Cursillo.
Naquin, Roch '62 (HT) Retired.
Narcowich, Edward '53 (FTW) Diocesan Council of Catholic Women Retired.
Nardoianni, Antonio *o.f.m.* '74 (NY)[EE] New York Franciscan Province of the Immaculate Conception; [EE] New York, NY Franciscan Province of the Immaculate Conception.
Nardone, Amedeo *o.f.m.* '68 (NY)[EE] St. Jane Frances de Chantal Friary.
Nardone, Richard M. '54 (NEW)[B] School of Diplomacy and Intl. Rels. Retired.
Narewski, Peter J. '47 (PRO)[P] Providence St. John Vianney Residence Retired.
Narez, Juan '93 (ELP) El Paso, TX La Purisima; Presbyteral Council.
Nargaj, Andrew *o.f.m.* (NY) Bronx, NY Our Lady of Good Counsel.
Narimattam, Joseph J. '64 (WIL) Wilmington, DE Corpus Christi.
Narita, Michael *ss.cc.* '68 (FR).
Narivelil, Victor Z. *c.m.i.* '64 (STA)[H] Jacksonville, FL Sacred Heart; Diocesan Consultors.
Narivelil, Victor *c.m.i.* (STA) Presbyteral Council.
Narkun, Peter P. '45 (NY)[E] New York, NY Cardinal Hayes High School Retired.
Narlaly, Jose T. *o.ss.t.* '81 (BAL).
Naro, Carl J. '52 (RIC) Retired.
Nartey, Emmanuel '95 (NY)[S] New York, NY St. Joseph.
Nartker, Michael F. *s.m.* '96 (STL)[O] Marianist Novitiate.
Nasar, Ayub '85 (GR)[D] Grand Rapids, MI Saint Mary's Mercy Medical Center.
Naseman, Alfred *c.pp.s.* '67 (CIN)[B] Carthagena, OH St. Charles.
Nash, Denis P. '54 (GR) Retired.
Nash, Edward H. *s.j.* '46 (BAL)[S] St. Xavier's High School.
Nash, Francis J. *s.j.* '69 (BAL)[B] Timonium, MD Loyola Graduate Center –Timonium Campus; [S] Baltimore, MD Jesuit Community of Loyola College, Inc..
Nash, James F. '34 (ORG) Anaheim, CA St. Anthony Claret Retired.
Nash, James R. '89 (SCR) Montrose, PA Holy Name of Mary.
Nash, James '94 (WIL) Wilmington, DE Christ Our King; Army National Guard Chaplains.
Nash, John C. '75 (NOR) Absent on Leave.
Nash, Robert C. '48 (WH) Retired.
Nash, Robert (RIC) Retired.
Nash, Stephen F. '97 (WDC) Clinton, MD Church of St. John the Evangelist.
Nasini, Gino *s.x.* '65 (PAT)[M] Wayne Xaverian Missionary Fathers; (FgM).
Nason, Dennis T. '66 (BO) Haverhill, MA All Saints.
Nasr, Toufic M. '80 (OLL) Millbrae, CA Our Lady of Lebanon.
Nasri, Youssef Bochra '85 (BRK) Brooklyn, NY St. Michael's; Brooklyn, NY Resurrection Catholic Coptic Chapel.
Nasri, Yousseh Bochra (BRK)[U] Arab Speaking.
Nassal, Joseph *c.pp.s.* (CHI)[X] Chicago, IL Precious Blood Ministry of Reconciliation.
Nassaney, Daniel *o.m.i.* '74 (NOR) Tewksbury, MA St. William.
Nassetta, Peter W. '89 (ARL)[M] Fairfax, VA George Mason University, Catholic Campus Ministry House; [M] Fairfax, VA St. Robert Bellarmine Chapel.
Nassr, Martin B. '67 (TOL) Sandusky, OH SS. Peter and Paul.
Nasta, Thomas A. '82 (PH) Philadelphia, PA Saint Irenaeus.
Nastold, Donald *s.j.* '58 (CIN)[M] Cincinnati, OH Faber Jesuit Community.
Natale, Samuel '79 (RIC) On Duty Outside the Diocese.
Natalizia, Louis T. '80 (PRO) North Providence, RI Presentation of the Blessed Virgin Mary.
Natho, Clifton J. '60 (GAL) Retired.
Nations, David G. *c.m.* '97 (STL)[O] St. Louis, MO Vincentian Residence.
Nativo, Joseph S. '56 (NEW) Newark, NJ St. Lucy's.
Natsuhara, Bruce K. '78 (OKL) Oklahoma City, OK St. Joseph; St. Vincent dePaul, Society of Oklahoma City District Council.
Natsuhara, Bruce (OKL) Consultors Archdiocesan; Council of Priests Archdiocesan.
Nau, Dale '78 (DUL) Duluth, MN Cathedral of Our Lady of the Rosary; Duluth, MN Calvary Cemetery.
Nau, Dale (DUL) Vicar General; Chancellor; Vicar for Canonical Affairs; Defender of the Bond; Priests' Pension Board; Corporate Board; Finance Council; Campus Ministry; Cemeteries; Continuing Formation of Priests; Ecumenical and Inter–faith Affairs; Newspaper "Catholic Outlook"; Department of Communications.
Nau, Thomas R. '78 (STU) Ironton, OH St. Joseph; Ironton, OH St. Lawrence.
Nau, Thomas '78 (STU)[I] Franklin Furnace, OH Our Lady of Fatima Shrine.
Naucke, Alfred E. *s.j.* '65 (SJ)[B] Santa Clara, CA Jesuit Community; [M] Los Gatos, CA California Province of the Society of Jesus, Jesuit Provincial Office.
Naughton, James J. *s.d.b.* '67 (BIR) Birmingham, AL St. John Bosco.
Naughton, James *s.d.b.* '67 (BIR) Leeds, AL St. Theresa's; Members.
Naughton, John T. '49 (LA) Woodland Hills, CA St. Mel Retired.
Naughton, Michael *o.s.b.* '66 (RIC)[B] Richmond, VA Benedictine High School; [L] Richmond, VA Mary Mother of the Church Abbey.
Naughton, Michael *o.s.b.* '66 (SCL)[I] Richmond, VA Mary Mother of the Church Abbey.
Naughton, Michael *o.s.b.* '66 (RIC)[B] Richmond, VA Benedictine High School; [L] Richmond, VA Mary Mother of the Church Abbey.
Naughton, Patrick J. '91 (Scranton) Davie, FL St. David; On Duty Outside the Diocese.
Naughton, Thomas J. '61 (BO) Lakeville, MA Saints Martha and Mary.
Naughton, William M. (PAT) Unassigned.
Nauit, Zachary W. '94 (PH) Hatboro, PA St. John Bosco.
Naumann, Paul S. *s.j.* '63 (SY)[Q] Syracuse, NY Jesuits at LeMoyne, Inc..
Naumes, Matthew '63 (SEA) Retired.
Naus, John E. *s.j.* '55 (MIL)[O] Milwaukee, WI Jesuit Community at Marquette University.
Nava, Rufino *o.m.i.* '99 (LA) Brownsville, TX Immaculate Conception Cathedral.
Navarra, Peter '81 (SD) Escondido, CA St. Mary.
Navarre, Robert G. '45 (SAG) Retired.

Navarrette, Jesus '87 (ARL) Alexandria, VA Good Shepherd.
Navarro, Marcelo Javier *i.v.e.* '94 (BRK) Brooklyn, NY St. Gabriel The Archangel.
Navarro, Nicolas *s.d.b.* '69 (SJN) San Juan, PR Maria Auxiliadora; [B] Santurce, PR Colegio San Juan Bosco.
Navarro, Pablo A. (MIA) Incardination Committee.
Navarro, Pablo '78 (MIA) Miami, FL St. John Neumann; Priests' Personnel Board; Consultors.
Navarro, Pedro '63 (NEW) Union City, NJ St. Augustine's.
Navarroli, Frederick '43 (RVC) Retired.
Navas, Julio '94 (RNO) Wells, NV St. Thomas Aquinas; Jackpot, NV Our Lady of Guadalupe.
Navascues, Moises *sch.p.* '54 (PCE) Santa Isabel, PR St. James; [B] The Pontifical Catholic University of Puerto Rico.
Nave, Francis A. (ALN) Vocations Office; Calvary Council #528, Allentown.
Navin, Cyril '45 (LA) Encino, CA St. Cyril.
Navin, Timothy M. '79 (VEN) Naples, FL St. Peter the Apostle.
Navin, Timothy (VEN) Presbyteral Council.
Navins, Robert J. '50 (NY) Staten Island, NY St. Margaret Mary.
Navone, John J. *s.j.* '62 (P)[L] Portland Jesuit Provincial Office (Society of Jesus, Oregon Prov.).
Navoy, Ronald W. '71 (CHI) River Grove, IL St. Cyprian.
Nawalaniec, Kzimierz '86 (SP) Tampa, FL St. Mary.
Nawalaniec, Mariusz '93 (CHI) Chicago, IL St. Ladislaus.
Nawarskas, Fred (SAN) Pastor Review Board; Priests' Pension Plan.
Nawarskas, Fred (SAN) Deans.
Nawarskas, Frederick '67 (SAN) Abilene, TX Holy Family.
Nawrocki, Norman D. '82 (DET) Bloomfield Hills, MI St. Regis; Defenders of Bond.
Nawrocki, Robert W. '61 (MIL) Milwaukee, WI St. Alexander.
Nawrocki, Zdzislaw *s.chp.* '73 (PAT) Poughkeepsie, NY St. Joseph.
Nayak, Alexis *ss.cc.* '02 (FR).
Nayak, Christudas A. (MO).
Nayak, Christudas '68 (ALX)[B] Alexandria, LA Christus Health Central Louisiana.
Nayak, Subal *ss.cc.* (FR).
Nayak, Sudhir *ss.cc.* '03 (FR).
Naylor, David W. (L)[H] Lebanon, KY Holy Name of Mary.
Naylor, Ronald J. '60 (RIC) Retired.
Nazareth, Menino George A. '59 (P) Cloverdale, OR St. Joseph.
Nazario, Heber *o.s.a.* '65 (SJN) San Juan, PR Ntra. Sra. de la Monserrate.
Nazarro, John *s.d.b.* '83 (NY)[EE] New Rochelle, NY Salesian Provincial House.
Nazhianpara, Jose *c.m.* '91 (CHI)[N] Chicago DePaul Vincentian Residence.
Nazimek, David '93 (GBG) Fairchance, PA SS. Cyril and Methodius.
Nazimek, Francis A. '48 (PIT) Fredericktown, PA St. Oliver Plunkett Retired.
Nazzani, Ermete *c.s.* '62 (LA)[P] Sun Valley, CA Villa Scalabrini.
Nazzaro, John *s.d.b.* '83 (NY)[F] New Rochelle, NY Salesian High School.
Ndagizimana, Isidore '85 (AUS) Granger, TX SS. Cyril and Methodius; Sts. Cyril & Methodius School Endowment.
Ndrevashay, Primus P. '61 (DET) Retired.
Ndubuisi, John C. '98 (GAL) Houston, TX St. Francis of Assisi.
Ndubuisi, John '98 (GAL)[K] Catholic Chaplain Corps, Texas Medical Center; [K] Chaplain Corps, Lyndon B. Johnson Hospital; Army Reserve Chaplains.
Ndugbu, Jude '80 (LC) Pittsville, WI St. Joachim; Pittsville, WI Holy Rosary; Vesper, WI St. James.
Ndylaka, Matthias '78 (NY) Woodbourne Correctional Facility.
Nealon, Joseph A. '61 (STU) Retired.
Nealon, Joseph W. '40 (NEW) Haworth, NJ Sacred Heart Retired.
Neary, Mark '83 (SJ) Absent on Sick Leave
Neary, Noel (ATL) Released from Archdiocesan Assignment.
Neary, Pat *c.s.c.* '91 (FTW)[B] University of Notre Dame Du Lac.
Neary, Patrick M. *c.s.c.* '91 (FTW)[I] South Bend, IN Congregation of Holy Cross, Indiana Province, Provincial House.
Neary, Patrick *c.s.c.* '91 (FTW)[A] Notre Dame, IN Moreau Seminary.
Neault, Armand R. '52 (PRT) Retired.
Nebel, Charles A. '38 (BEL) Retired.
Nebus, Vincent J. '51 (MET) Retired.
Nebus, Vincent '51 (ORL) Retired.
Nedder, Edward T. '87 (SAM) Springfield, MA St. Anthony; Appointed Members; Ministries (Permanent Deacons and Subdeacons).
Nediakala, Kuriakose *m.c.b.s.* '78 (BIS) Mott, ND St. Vincent de Paul; Regent, ND St. Henry.
Nedimyer, Raymond *t.o.r.* '97 (SP) St. Petersburg, FL St. Mary Our Lady of Grace.
Nedimyer, Raymond *t.o.r.* (BAL) Baltimore, MD St. Elizabeth of Hungary.
Nedumaruthumchalil, George K. (NY) New Rochelle, NY Holy Family.
Nedumthuruthil, Michael '74 (SYM) Floral Park, NY Knanaya Catholic Mission of Linden, NJ Our Lady of Snows; Floral Park, NY Knanaya Catholic Mission of Brooklyn, NY.
Nedungadan, Johnson *c.m.* (BRK)[V] Jamaica, NY St. Vincent's House.
Nee, Eugene O. '64 (SAT) Military Chaplains.
Nee, Kenneth T. '53 (RVC)[M] Uniondale, NY St. Pius X Residence Retired.
Nee, Robert E. (BO) Cambridge, MA St. John the Evangelist.
Nee, Robert F. *o.f.m.* '62 (BO)[AA] Boston, MA St. Anthony Shrine.
Nee, Thomas B. '66 (RIC) Retired.
Nee, Thomas M. '39 (PIT)[N] Pittsburgh, PA St. John Vianney Manor Retired.
Needham, James *s.s.c.* '61 (OM)[K] St. Columbans St. Columban's Foreign Mission Society.
Neeley, Peter G. *s.j.* '81 (LA) Los Angeles, CA Immigration and Naturalization Service; San Pedro, CA Immigration and Naturalization Service
Neely, Brad '03 (B) Boise, ID Cathedral of St. John the Evangelist.
Neely, Harry M. *o.s.a.* '53 (SD)[H] San Diego, CA Augustinian Community.
Neely, Harry *o.s.a.* '45 (SD)[C] San Diego, CA St. Augustine High School.
Neenan, Benedict *o.s.b.* '88 (KC)[A] Conception, MO Conception Seminary College; [J] Parnell, MO St. Joseph Parish.
Neenan, Robert P. *s.j.* '51 (MIL)[O] Wauwatosa, WI Jesuit Community at St. Camillus.
Neenan, William B. *s.j.* '61 (Wisconsin)[V] Newton, MA The Jesuit Community at Boston College.
Neff, Eugene J. '71 (BEL) Lebanon, IL St. Joseph; Hospitals; Sick and Aged (Ministry).
Neff, John '52 (SP) Retired.
Neff, John '86 (E) Oil City, PA Assumption of the Blessed Virgin Mary; Oil City, PA St. Venantius.
Neff, John (E) Polk, PA Polk Center.
Neffy, Arthur '47 (DET) Retired.
Negele, Philip *o.c.s.o.* '66 (DEN)[H] Denver, CO St. Joseph Hospital; [L] Lafayette, OR The Cistercian (Trappist) Abbey of Our Lady of Guadalupe.
Negherbon, Vincent *t.o.r.* '46 (ALT)[F] Loretto, PA Mount Assisi Friary.
Negley, Phil "Skip" (GAL) Elected Members.
Negley, Phil M. (GAL) Priests Personnel Committee.
Negley, Phil (GAL) Director of Ministry to Priests.
Negrete, Wayne *s.j.* '91 (LA)[C] Los Angeles, CA Jesuit Community.
Negrillos, Ferdinand *sch.p.* '41 (PH)[G] Devon, PA Devon Preparatory School; [AA] Devon Piarist Fathers (Order of the Pious Schools).
Negron, Juan Luis '89 (CGS)[C] Rio Piedras, PR Seminario Mayor Regional San Juan Bautista.
Negron, Juan Luis (SJN) San Juan Bautista Regional Seminary.
Negron, Ramon H. *o.f.m.cap.* (SJN) Franciscan Third Order (Secular Franciscan Order).
Neidhart, William *c.s.c.* '56 (FTW) South Bend, IN St. Joseph.
Neiheisel, Stanley H. '60 (CIN) Cincinnati, OH Old St. Mary.
Neiheisel, Stanley H. '61 (CIN) Cincinnati, OH Holy Cross–Immaculata.
Neiheisel, Stanley H. (CIN) Ex Officio Members; Consultors.
Neilson, Joseph *o.c.d.* '62 (LR)[A] Little Rock, AR Marylake – Carmelite Novitiate.
Neilson, Kieran A. *o.s.b.* '60 (CHL)[J] Belmont, NC Belmont Abbey; [L] Belmont, NC Belmont Abbey College.
Neilson, Kieran *o.s.b.* '60 (CHL)[A] Belmont, NC Belmont Abbey College.
Neilson, Richard J. '83 (NY) Retired.
Neiman, John '86 (LA) Temple City, CA St. Luke the Evangelist.
Neis, Thomas A. '52 (GAY) Charlevoix, MI St. Mary; Consultors, Diocesan Board of; Elected Members.
Neis, William P. '67 (LC) On Duty Outside the Diocese; Navy Chaplains.
Neissen, John *s.v.d.* '45 (SB)[A] Riverside, CA Society of the Divine Word Missionaries.
Neitlong, Joseph '86 (TUC) Oracle, AZ St. Helen's.
Neitzke, Ron P. '89 (JOL) Joliet, IL St. Mary Magdalene; Navy Reserve Chaplains.
Nekic, Simon J. '43 (CLV) Lorain, OH St. Vitus.
Nekoliczak, Ted A. '59 (GI) Retired.
Nelan, Francis *m.s.c.* '53 (SAT)[K] San Antonio, TX Padua Place.
Nelan, Kevin J. '77 (NY) New York, NY St. Bernard; New York, NY St. Veronica; Manhattan (South); Apostleship of the Sea.
Nelan, Kevin '25 (NY) New York, NY Our Lady of Guadalupe.
Nelke, Richard '51 (STL) Chesterfield, MO Ascension.
Nelligan, Paul J. *s.j.* '54 (WOR)[O] Worcester, MA Jesuits of Holy Cross College, Inc..
Nellikunnell, James *c.m.i.* '79 (ALX) Evergreen, LA Little Flower.
Nel Ossa, Pedro '63 (BRK) Brooklyn, NY St. Michael's.
Nelson, Andrew L. '57 (MIL) Special Assignment; Milwaukee, WI St. Paul.
Nelson, Brian '03 (WCH) Wichita, KS St. Francis of Assisi.
Nelson, Caye A. '88 (BR) Napoleonville, LA St. Anne; Napoleonville, LA Assumption of the Blessed Virgin Mary.
Nelson, Charles T. '87 (SFD) Winchester, IL St. Patrick; Murrayville, IL St. Bartholomew; Winchester, IL St. Mark.
Nelson, Daniel C. *o.f.m.* '77 (ALB)[B] Siena College.
Nelson, Francis J. '66 (SAV) Savannah, GA St. Frances Xavier Cabrini; Tribunal Judges; College of Consultors; Council of Priests; Chancellor; Vicars General.
Nelson, Francis P. *c.ss.r.* '64 (BRK)[V] Brooklyn, NY Our Lady of Good Counsel Residence.
Nelson, Frank M. '88 (RVC) Valley Stream, NY Blessed Sacrament.
Nelson, Glenn L. '93 (RCK) Special Assignment; Vicars General; Chancellor; Catholic Office of the Deaf.
Nelson, Greg '97 (PEO) Monticello, IL St. Michael; Monticello, IL St. Philomena.
Nelson, Kevin '00 (PMB) Hobe Sound, FL St. Christopher; Presbyteral Council.
Nelson, Linden '81 (LC)[D] Spiritual Services Dept..
Nelson, Martin Lester '97 (BEA) Advocate; Sour Lake, TX Our Lady of Victory.
Nelson, Paul E. '61 (WIN) Rochester, MN St. Pius X.
Nelson, Robert W. '77 (LC) Boyd, WI Sacred Heart of Jesus–St. Joseph; Stanley, WI Holy Family.
Nelson, Thomas J. *c.m.* '75 (DEN)[N] Denver, CO Congregation of the Mission Midwest Province: De Paul House.
Nelson, Thomas W. *o.praem.* '81 (ORG)[A] Silverado, CA St. Michael's Norbertine Postulancy, Novitiate and Juniorate; [I] Silverado, CA Norbertine Fathers of Orange Inc..
Nelson, Thomas *o.praem.* '81 (CHI)[X] Chicago, IL The Institute on Religious Life.
Nelson, Timothy (LAN) Flint, MI Our Lady of Guadalupe.
Nelson, William R. '82 (PBL) Paonia, CO Sacred Heart.
Nemec, Joseph J. '84 (LIN) Lincoln, NE St. Teresa's; [G] Lincoln, NE Adoration Convent and Church of Christ the King; Commission for Sacred Liturgy and Sacred Music; Evangelization Committee.
Nemec, Joseph (LIN) Presbyteral Council.
Nemecek, M. Cyril '60 (CHI) North Riverside, IL Mater Christi.
Nemeck, Francis Kelly *o.m.i.* '61 (SAT)[C] Oblate School of Theology.
Nemeck, Francis Kelly *o.m.i.* '61 (CC)[F] Sarita, TX Lebh Shomea House of Prayer.
Nemergut, Robert S. '77 (EVN) Special Assignment.
Nemeth, Edward M. *s.j.* '65 (DET)[P] Hamtramck, MI St. Ladislaus.
Nemeth, Maurus B. *o.s.b.* '72 (SFR)[N] Portola Valley, CA Woodside Priory.
Nemmers, Francis J. '57 (SC) Retired.
Nemmers, Mark R. '66 (DUB) Dubuque, IA Holy Trinity; Judges.
Neneman, John (ORG) Great Falls, MT St. Joseph's; Great Falls, MT St. Luke the Evangelist.
Nenneau, Thomas D. '81 (LAN) Jackson, MI Queen of the Miraculous Medal; Navy Reserve Chaplains.
Nenneau, Thomas (LAN) College of Consultors; Priest's Assignment Commission.
Nentwick, John '65 (Y) Canton, OH Our Lady of Peace.
Ner, Santiago *m.s.* '70 (SB) Apple Valley, CA St. Mary of the Desert Valley Hospital.
Neri, Gregorio '92 (MET) Robert Wood Johnson University Hospital.
Nero, James *o.f.m.* '71 (MIA) Hallandale, FL St. Matthew; [G] Fort Lauderdale, FL Holy Cross Hospital.
Neroda, Edward J. '57 (Y) Youngstown, OH St. Stanislaus Kostka.
Nesbella, John K. '02 (ALT) Northern Cambria, PA Prince of Peace.
Nesbit, Walter G. *s.j.* '59 (STL)[O] St. Louis, MO Jesuit Community Corporation at St. Louis University – Jesuit Hall.
Nesbitt, John B. '62 (SD) Retired.
Neske, Mark I. '53 (MOB) Orange Beach, AL St. Thomas by the Sea; Group III.
Nespolo, Umberto *o.m.i.* '59 (OAK)[N] Oakland, CA Oblate Residence.
Nesrsta, Steven '95 (AUS) Finance Council.
Ness, Bernardine *o.s.b.* '64 (SFS)[F] Marvin, SD Blue Cloud Abbey; (FgM).
Ness, Scott C. *o.s.a.* '90 (BO)[C] North Andover, MA

Merrimack College.
Nesse, Paul '91 (CC) On Special Assignment.
Nessel, William J. *o.s.f.s.* '56 (HBG) Lewisburg, PA Sacred Heart of Jesus; Promoter of Justice.
Nessinger, Phillip *o.carm.* '50 (JOL)[L] Darien Carmelite Provincial Office.
Nester, Edward J. '46 (MET) Baptistown, NJ Our Lady of Victories; [H] Somerset, NJ Maria Regina Residence Retired.
Nesti, Donald S. *c.s.sp.* '63 (GAL)[B] Houston, TX Holy Ghost Fathers and Brothers; [U] Houston, TX The Society of the Holy Spirit.
Nesti, Donald *c.s.sp.* (GAL)[C] Houston, TX University of St. Thomas.
Nestler, W. David *o.f.m.cap.* '89 (PIT)[N] Allison Park, PA St. Conrad Friary.
Nestor, Michael '65 (SJP) Retired.
Nestor, Robert P. '70 (NEW)[B] School of Diplomacy and Intl. Rels..
Nestor, Thomas F. '81 (BO)[A] Brighton, MA St. John Seminary School of Theology; Psychological Consultants; Winchester, MA St. Eulalia.
Nesvadba, Reginald R. '66 (GAL) Pearland, TX St. Helen; Southern Vicariate; Priests Personnel Committee.
Netta, John G. '57 (NEW) Retired.
Nettekoven, Joseph '75 (ORG) Anaheim, CA St. Justin Martyr; Judges.
Netzer, Angelus *o.f.m.conv.* '51 (ALB)[L] Rensselaer, NY Franciscan Mission House.
Neu, Hubert '51 (FWT) Fort Worth, TX St. Patrick Cathedral; Building Commission; Priests' Retirement Board.
Neu, Leon M. '52 (BUF) Randolph, NY St. Patrick.
Neubert, Germar *o.s.b.* '65 (OM)[K] Schuyler, NE Benedictine Mission House; [O] Schuyler, NE St. Benedict Center Endowment Fund.
Neugebauer, John J. '55 (ALT) Altoona, PA St. Mark's.
Neugebauer, Robert G. '73 (ALT) Altoona, PA Immaculate Conception.
Neuhaus, Richard J. '91 (NY) New York, NY Immaculate Conception.
Neuhaus, William B. '83 (COV) Fort Thomas, KY St. Thomas; Diocesan Consultors; Deans; Presbyteral Council.
Neuman, Eugene C. (MIL) Army National Guard Chaplains.
Neuman, Eugene '70 (MIL) Sheboygan Falls, WI Blessed Trinity; Deans.
Neuman, James L. '71 (SFD) Hillsboro, IL St. Agnes; Litchfield, IL Holy Family.
Neuman, James (SFD) Commission for the Care of Infirm and Retired Priests; Diocesan Finance Council; Presbyteral Council.
Neuman, Matthias *o.s.b.* '67 (IND)[K] Beech Grove, IN.
Neumann, Aloysius J. '60 (RCK) Genoa, IL St. Catherine of Genoa.
Neumann, Don A. '72 (GAL)[K] Catholic Chaplain Corps, Texas Medical Center.
Neumann, Richard J. '65 (HRT) Windsor, CT St. Gabriel's.
Neumann, William J. '75 (ORL) Winter Haven, FL St. Joseph's.
Neumeier, Larry '95 (LA) Thousand Oaks, CA St. Paschal Baylon.
Neumeir, Larry S. (LA) Board of Directors:.
Neuner, Donald L. '56 (STL) St. Charles, MO St. Elizabeth Ann Seton.
Neurohr, Gilbert N. '54 (MAR)[D] Escanaba, MI Bishop Noa Home for Senior Citizens Retired.
Neuser, John C. '62 (GB) Mishicot, WI Holy Cross.
Neuser, John '62 (GB) Retired.
Neuville, Joseph '46 (P) Retired.
Neuzil, Gregory '67 (KNX) Fairfield Glade, TN St. Francis of Assisi.
Nevans, Robert V. '49 (DEN) Retired.
Nevares, Eduardo *m.s.* '81 (TYL) Lufkin, TX St. Patrick; Vocations; Diocesan Vocations Awareness Board; Diocesan Pastoral Team – DPT; Presbyteral Council.
Nevels, Thomas A. '99 (CIN) Miamisburg, OH Our Lady of Good Hope.
Neville, Franklin A. '86 (WH) Mannington, WV St. Peter's; Mannington, WV St. Patrick's.
Neville, John *o.s.c.* '61 (CHI)[N] Chicago, IL Crosier Community of Chicago; [M] Shoreview, MN Crosier Community of Shoreview.
Neville, Joseph B. *s.j.* '60 (SY)[Q] Syracuse, NY Jesuits at LeMoyne, Inc..
Neville, Thomas W. '52 (RCK) Retired.
Nevin, Emmet R. '77 (NY) Blauvelt, NY St. Catharine.
Nevine, Eugene *s.j.* '80 (CHI)[D] Chicago, IL St. Ignatius Jesuit Community.
Nevins, Donald J. '75 (CHI) Chicago, IL St. Francis of Assisi; Chicago, IL Providence of God; Deans.
Nevins, Eugene J. *s.j.* (CHI) Chicago, IL John H. Stroger, Jr. Hospital of Cook County.
Nevins, John J. '57 (PH) Essington, PA St. Margaret Mary Alacoque.
Nevins, Troy '96 (GR) Belding, MI St. Joseph's; Belding, MI St. Mary's.
Nevlud, Gregory '82 (SAT) Kerrville, TX Notre Dame.
New, Gary *s.d.s.* '91 (GB) Chilton, WI St. Charles Borromeo; Chilton, WI St. Martin; Chilton, WI St. Augustine; Chilton, WI St. Mary; Chilton, WI Holy Trinity; Chilton, WI St. Elizabeth; [K] Chilton, WI St. Peregrine Shrine; Regional Vicars.
Newbold, Robert C. '45 (PRO) College of Consultors; Censors of Books; Government Liaison Retired.
Newbold, Robert '45 (PRO)[P] Providence St. John Vianney Residence.
Newbold, Ronan *c.p.* '61 (CHI)[N] Chicago, IL Passionist Community–Immaculate Conception Monastery.
Newbold, Ronan *c.p.* '69 (CHI) Chicago, IL Immaculate Conception.
Newbold, Thomas More *c.p.* '42 (SAC)[I] Citrus Heights, CA Christ the King Retreat.
Newburn, Charles *sch.p.* '79 (MIA)[C] Fort Lauderdale, FL Cardinal Gibbons High School.
Newcomer, Joseph '71 (B)[B] Nampa, ID Mercy Medical Center.
Newell, John J. '58 (BRK) On Leave/Unassigned.
Newell, Joseph A. *s.j.* '66 (ALN)[C] Scranton, PA The University of Scranton.
Newell, Joseph P. '45 (PIT)[E] Cranberry Township, PA St. Ferdinand.
Newell, Matthias '87 (RIC) Retired.
Newfield, John L. '48 (HT) Retired.
Newhouse, Paul *c.i.c.m.* '54 (SAT)[M] San Antonio, TX Missionhurst Community Residence Retired.
Newland, Ronald A. '67 (NEW) Livingston, NJ St. Raphael.
Newman, Aloysius T. '54 (WDC) Retired.
Newman, Brian *o.f.m.c* (FgM).
Newman, Charles *o.f.m.* '85 (PH)[D] Philadelphia, PA Archbishop Ryan High School; [AA] Philadelphia, PA St. Pius X Friary.
Newman, Jay Scott '93 (CHR) Greenville, SC St. Mary's; [H] Greenville, SC Furman University Campus Ministry; Continuing Education for Priests.
Newman, Louis I. '58 (RVC) Retired.
Newman, Mark L. *c.j.* '60 (LA) Santa Maria, CA St. Louis de Montfort.
Newman, Matthias *o.s.b.* '67 (IND)[L] Beech Grove, IN.
Newman, Michael J. *s.d.s.* '67 (SAC)[L] Chico, CA California State University (Chico), Newman Catholic Community.
Newman, Michael T. (MIL) Kenosha, WI St. Mary; Deans; Judges for Second Instance.
Newman, Michael (LA) State Chaplain.
Newman, Michael (SAC) Council of Priests.
Newman, Nelson A. '54 (OM) Central City, NE St. Michael.
Newman, William A. *o.p.* '57 (WDC) Washington, DC St. Dominic Church & Priory.
Newns, John J. '74 (PH) Phoenixville, PA St. Ann.
Newton, David J. '88 (LFT) Gas City, IN Holy Family.
Newton, John G. '53 (CAM) Retired.
Newton, John G. (HON) Apostleship of the Sea.
Newton, Stephen P. *c.s.c.* '89 (FTW)[I] La Grange, IL St. Cletus.
Newton, Thomas A. '88 (CAM) Cherry Hill, NJ St. Peter Celestine; [V] Camden, NJ The Vicariate for Human Services of The Diocese of Camden Corporation; Members; Vicariate for Human Services; Representative to Archbishop Damiano School and St. John of God.
Neyland, Quintin A. *o.f.m.* '46 (NY)[M] Butler, NJ St. Anthony Friary.
Neylon, Bruce M. '75 (FR) Fall River, MA St. Stanislaus; Procurator–Advocates; Diocesan Guild for the Blind; Diocesan Liaison with Cursillo.
Neyra, Hugo R. '84 (LA) Los Angeles, CA St. Alphonsus.
Neyrey, Jerome H. *s.j.* '70 (FTW)[B] University of Notre Dame Du Lac; [M] Granger, IN Jesuit Community.
Ng, Andrew *s.d.b.* (HON) Honolulu, HI Star of the Sea; Chinese Ministry.
Ng, Thomas '61 (OAK) Oakland, CA St. Leo's; Chinese Pastoral Center.
Ngalamulume, Maurice Mamba '98 (CHI) Chicago, IL Our Lady Help of Christians.
Nghi, John T. (LA) Cursillo Movement.
Nghiem, Peter Hoan–Xuan '72 (GR) On Special Assignment.
Nghiem, Peter '72 (GR) Wyoming, MI Our Lady of LaVang; Vietnamese Ministry.
Nghiem, Vu Minh *c.ss.r.* '51 (LA)[Q] Baldwin Park, CA Vietnamese Redemptorist Mission; [CC] Baldwin Park, CA The Redemptorist Vietnamese Mission Corporation.
Ngo, Anthony '94 (RIC) Retired.
Ngo, Chi *s.j.* (ORG)[H] Orange, CA Loyola Institute for Spirituality; [I] Garden Grove, CA Manresa Jesuit Residence.
Ngo, Francis Huan Ton '89 (GAL) Houston, TX St. Gregory the Great.
Ngo, Peter T. (LA) Canonical Staff; Judges.
Ngoc Lien, Joseph To '62 (SPC)[E] Carthage, MO Congregation of the Mother Coredemptrix, United States Assumption Province.
Ngo Duc Vuong, John D.M. *c.m.c.* '91 (SPC)[E] Carthage, MO Congregation of the Mother Coredemptrix, United States Assumption Province.
Ngoko, Paul '95 (OAK) San Leandro, CA St. Alphonsus Liguori.
Ngolle, Pirmin *o.s.b.* '01 (BAK) Klamath Falls, OR St. Pius X.
Nguyen, Ahn '98 (ORG) Orange, CA La Purisima.
Nguyen, An Binh Joseph (MO) Navy Chaplains.
Nguyen, Andrew Cuu (NY) Manhattan, NY Manhattan Psychiatric Center.
Nguyen, Anthony Giang '66 (BO) Chelsea, MA St. Rose of Lima; Lowell, MA St. Patrick; Cambodian.
Nguyen, Anthony Lap '96 (HT) Morgan City, LA Thanh Gia.
Nguyen, Anthony Tuong '00 (SJ) San Jose, CA St. Patrick.
Nguyen, Bernard Hung *c.m.c.* '97 (BEA) Port Arthur, TX Queen of Vietnam.
Nguyen, Bich N. '03 (OAK) San Leandro, CA St. Leander.
Nguyen, Bieu Van (MOB) Montgomery, AL St. Bede.
Nguyen, Binh *c.m.* '82 (LA)[A] Camarillo, CA St. John's Seminary.
Nguyen, Binh '01 (ORG) Stanton, CA St. Polycarp.
Nguyen, Binh *s.v.d.* '02 (DUB)[B] Epworth, IA Divine Word College.
Nguyen, Brandon *c.s.sp.* (LR) Conway, AR St. Joseph's.
Nguyen, Chanh (LAF) Ville Platte, LA Sacred Heart of Jesus.
Nguyen, Chanh Van '91 (LAF) Ville Platte, LA St. Joseph.
Nguyen, Charles '92 (SAC) Absent on Leave.
Nguyen, Chau '89 (ORL) Vietnamese; Orlando, FL St. Charles Borromeo.
Nguyen, Chinh '94 (SR)[K] Penngrove, CA Newman Hall, Sonoma State University, Intercollegiate Catholic Ministries; Napa, CA St. Thomas Aquinas.
Nguyen, Christopher T. *s.j.* '01 (SFR)[N] San Francisco, CA Jesuit Community at University of San Francisco.
Nguyen, Cuong H. *m.m.* '98 (NY)[EE] Maryknoll Maryknoll Fathers and Brothers.
Nguyen, Dam D. '93 (PIT) Pittsburgh, PA St. Gabriel of the Sorrowful Virgin; Priest Council; Chaplains to Latino Catholic Community.
Nguyen, Daokim '93 (GAL) Houston, TX Vietnamese Martyrs.
Nguyen, Dominic Dung *s.v.d.* '98 (MEM) Memphis, TN Sacred Heart; [I] Memphis, TN Society of the Divine Word (Chicago Province).
Nguyen, Dominic Hoan *c.m.* '99 (LA) Los Angeles, CA Our Lady of Loretto.
Nguyen, Dominic Huyen Duc '64 (NO) New Orleans, LA Our Lady of La Vang.
Nguyen, Dominic Long *c.ss.r.* (DAL)[K] Irving, TX St. John Neumann Formation House.
Nguyen, Dominic Thuong '91 (OAK) San Leandro, CA Our Lady of Good Counsel.
Nguyen, Dominic *s.j.* '92 (SEA) Tacoma, WA St. Ann; Tacoma, WA St. John of the Woods; Tacoma, WA Sacred Heart; [C] Tacoma, WA Bellarmine Preparatory School.
Nguyen, Dominic '95 (ORG) Administrative Leave.
Nguyen, Dovan '93 (TLS) Broken Arrow, OK St. Anne.
Nguyen, Dung V. '02 (ATL)[J] Atlanta, GA Our Lady of Perpetual Help Home; Judicial Vicar.
Nguyen, Dung (ATL) Archdiocesan Judges.
Nguyen, Francis Khoi '90 (DOD) Elkhart, KS St. Joan of Arc; Hugoton, KS St. Helen.
Nguyen, Francis T. '02 (OKL) Edmond, OK St. John the Baptist; Special Assignment.
Nguyen, Francis '02 (OKL)[B] Oklahoma City, OK Bishop McGuinness Catholic High School.
Nguyen, Gan Minh Peter *c.ss.r.* '98 (GAL) Houston, TX Holy Ghost.
Nguyen, Hien Minh '85 (SJ) Special Assignment; [P] San Jose, CA Vietnamese Catholic Center, Our Lady Queen of Martyrs; Judicial Vicar; Judicial Vicar; Judges.
Nguyen, Hieu '69 (SC) Sioux City, IA Cathedral of the Epiphany.
Nguyen, Hilary Hai Khanh *c.m.c.* '02 (DEN) Wheat Ridge, CO Queen of Vietnamese Martyrs.
Nguyen, Hoa Van '95 (OKL) Hobart, OK Sts. Peter and Paul.
Nguyen, Hoa '98 (FWT) Burkburnett, TX St. Jude Thaddeus; Presbyteral Council and Consultors.
Nguyen, Hoa (OKL) Region V.
Nguyen, Hoan N. '99 (LA)[Q] Los Angeles, CA Amat Residence I.
Nguyen, Huan Tien '66 (CIN) On Special and Archdiocesan Assignment; [V] Cincinnati, OH Vietnamese Catholic Community of Our Lady of Lavang.
Nguyen, Hung T. '94 (FgM).
Nguyen, Hung Viet *i.c.m.* '69 (BR) Baton Rouge, LA St. Anthony of Padua; [H] Baton Rouge, LA Incarnatio Consecratio Mission; [L] Baton Rouge, LA St. Michael's Home; Vietnamese Apostolate.
Nguyen, Hung '94 (SEA) On Duty Outside the Archdiocese.
Nguyen, Hung '95 (STO) Modesto, CA Our Lady of Fatima Church (Pastor of).

Nguyen, Huy '95 (LA) Winnetka, CA St. Joseph the Worker.
Nguyen, Hy Khac '97 (WDC)[C] Catholic University of America, The.
Nguyen, J. Kim–Dang '93 (LA) Torrance, CA St. Catherine Laboure.
Nguyen, James Bam '01 (LAF) Crowley, LA St. Michael Archangel.
Nguyen, Joachim Son '03 (WOR) East Templeton, MA Holy Cross.
Nguyen, Joachim Thanh '67 (PRT) Caribou, ME St. Therese.
Nguyen, Joe Van Anh '88 (AUS) Austin, TX Holy Vietnamese Martyrs.
Nguyen, John C. '99 (PH) Lansdale, PA St. Stanislaus.
Nguyen, John D. *s.j.* '01 (SAC)[D] Sacramento, CA Jesuit High School.
Nguyen, John Hoa '72 (LA) Arcadia, CA Holy Angels.
Nguyen, John Luat *o.f.m.* '94 (SFR) Salem, OR St. Joseph.
Nguyen, John Mary Thong *c.ss.r.* (DAL)[K] Irving, TX St. John Neumann Formation House.
Nguyen, John Trung '95 (MOB) Bayou LaBatre, AL St. Margaret.
Nguyen, John Baptist Vuong Duc *o.p.* '00 (ARL) Arlington, VA Holy Martyrs of Vietnam.
Nguyen, Joseph An '92 (CAM) Woodlynne, NJ Immaculate Heart of Mary.
Nguyen, Joseph D. '90 (NOR) Ashford, CT St. Philip; Air National Guard Chaplains.
Nguyen, Joseph Dan Van (NO) La Place, LA St. Joan of Arc.
Nguyen, Joseph Hai '67 (RIC) Norfolk, VA Our Lady of Vietnam Chapel.
Nguyen, Joseph Hoa '76 (HBG) Harrisburg, PA Our Lady of the Blessed Sacrament.
Nguyen, Joseph Hoa Van (HBG) Vietnamese Ministry.
Nguyen, Joseph Huong '85 (SAC) Knights Landing, CA St. Paul.
Nguyen, Joseph Huyen (SAC) Pro–Synodal Judges.
Nguyen, Joseph Khan V. '63 (DAV)[P] Davenport, IA Vietnamese Catholic Community of the Quad Cities; Davenport, IA Sacred Heart Cathedral.
Nguyen, Joseph Liem '99 (ATL) Gainesville, GA St. Michael's.
Nguyen, Joseph Luan '90 (ORG) Garden Grove, CA St. Columban.
Nguyen, Joseph Ngoc Tu *o.p.* '64 (GAL)[Q] Houston, TX Dominican Friars, St. Mark Priory, Inc.; Houston, TX Holy Rosary.
Nguyen, Joseph Phien '92 (ORG) Newport Beach, CA Our Lady Queen of Angels.
Nguyen, Joseph Phiet The '73 (GAL) Houston, TX St. Christopher.
Nguyen, Joseph Son '82 (DAL) Carrollton, TX Sacred Heart of Jesus Christ.
Nguyen, Joseph Tan *o.f.m.* '86 (SFD)[L] Springfield, IL Our Lady of Angels Friary.
Nguyen, Joseph Thai '95 (CHI) Chicago, IL Our Lady of Mount Carmel.
Nguyen, Joseph Thai–Doan '88 (BR) Livonia, LA St. Frances Xavier Cabrini.
Nguyen, Joseph Thinh Duc '93 (MEM) Bartlett, TN St. Ann.
Nguyen, Joseph Thuan *o.p.* '93 (PHX) Phoenix, AZ Most Holy Trinity.
Nguyen, Joseph Thuc (BEA) Diocesan Judges.
Nguyen, Joseph Tri Minh (NEW) Vietnamese Apostolate.
Nguyen, Joseph Trong '69 (LAV) Las Vegas, NV Shrine of Our Lady of La Vang.
Nguyen, Joseph Tuoc *s.j.* '89 (DEN) Denver, CO St. Ignatius Loyola; [N] Denver, CO Loyola Parish – Jesuit Community.
Nguyen, Joseph Van Thanh '90 (LIN) Hastings, NE St. Cecilia's.
Nguyen, Joseph '73 (FRS) Fresno, CA St. Francis.
Nguyen, Joseph '95 (SAC) Sacramento, CA St. Joseph's.
Nguyen, Joseph *o.s.b.* '03 (MRY) Watsonville, CA Our Lady Help of Christians; [L] St. Benedict, OR Mt. Angel Abbey.
Nguyen, Joseph *s.d.b.* '03 (MRY)[F] Watsonville, CA Saint Francis Salesian Community.
Nguyen, Joseph *o.s.b.* '03 (MRY) Watsonville, CA Our Lady Help of Christians; [L] St. Benedict, OR Mt. Angel Abbey.
Nguyen, Joseph (MAN) Vietnamese Apostolate.
Nguyen, Jude Ban *c.m.c.* '73 (SAC) Sacramento, CA Vietnamese Catholic Martyrs.
Nguyen, Khanh Pham '97 (COS) Cheyenne Wells, CO Sacred Heart.
Nguyen, Khoa M. '01 (PH) Norristown, PA Visitation B.V.M..
Nguyen, Khoa *o.f.m.* '95 (NY)[EE] Vietnamese Franciscan Province.
Nguyen, Kim Son '87 (SAV) Savannah, GA Sts. Peter and Paul.
Nguyen, Lich Van '84 (NO) Arabi, LA St. Robert Bellarmine.
Nguyen, Liem *o.s.b.* '94 (P).
Nguyen, Linh T. (BO)[A] Weymouth, MA Immaculate Conception.
Nguyen, Linn '97 (LEX) Danville, KY SS. Peter & Paul.
Nguyen, Luke Hungdung '02 (NO) Destrehan, LA St. Charles Borromeo.
Nguyen, Martin Lam *c.s.c.* '89 (FTW)[B] University of Notre Dame Du Lac.
Nguyen, Martin Lan *c.s.c.* '89 (FTW)[A] Notre Dame, IN Moreau Seminary.
Nguyen, Martin Thanh *i.c.m.* '97 (BR)[H] Baton Rouge, LA Incarnatio Consecratio Mission.
Nguyen, Michael M. *c.m.* '95 (CHL) Greensboro, NC St. Mary.
Nguyen, Michael Nam Hoang '93 (NO) New Orleans, LA Mary, Queen of Vietnam.
Nguyen, Michael Quang *s.v.d.* '02 (DUB)[B] Epworth, IA Divine Word College.
Nguyen, Michael '03 (ORG) Education Leave.
Nguyen, Minh Hai *i.c.m.* '92 (NEW) Baton Rouge, LA St. Louis, King of France; [H] Baton Rouge, LA Incarnatio Consecratio Mission.
Nguyen, Nghiem Van '89 (NO) River Ridge, LA St. Matthew the Apostle.
Nguyen, Ngoc (GAL) Diocesan Judges.
Nguyen, Oden *o.s.b.* '65 (SFE)[I] Abiquiu, NM Monastery of Christ in the Desert.
Nguyen, Pascal B. *o.praem.* '94 (ORG)[I] Silverado, CA Norbertine Fathers of Orange Inc..
Nguyen, Pascal Bao *o.praem* '94 (ORG) Costa Mesa, CA St. John the Baptist.
Nguyen, Paul Choung *s.d.b.* '88 (NY)[GG] Stony Point, NY Marian Shrine.
Nguyen, Paul Chung (PMB) Port St. Lucie, FL St. Lucie.
Nguyen, Paul Chuong *s.d.b.* '88 (NY)[GG] Stony Point, NY Don Bosco Retreat Center and Marian Shrine.
Nguyen, Peter Duc Hung '97 (SC) Ruthven, IA Sacred Heart.
Nguyen, Peter Hung '02 (CC)[G] Robstown, TX Society of Our Lady of the Most Holy Trinity.
Nguyen, Peter M. *cs.s.r.* (LA) Gardena, CA Maria Regina.
Nguyen, Peter Phan *c.ss.r.* (DAL)[K] Irving, TX St. John Neumann Formation House.
Nguyen, Peter Phong '46 (DAL) Grand Prairie, TX St. Joseph Vietnamese Catholic Community.
Nguyen, Peter Quang '90 (DEN) Greeley, CO St. Mary.
Nguyen, Peter Vinh Q. '86 (NEW) Livingston, NJ St. Barnabas Medical Center; Chaplains.
Nguyen, Peter '61 (SD) Retired.
Nguyen, Philip '87 (GR) Holland, MI Our Lady of the Lake.
Nguyen, Phong *s.j.* '01 (SAC)[I] Carmichael, CA Jesuit High School Community of Sacramento.
Nguyen, Phuong Van '93 (WOR) Worcester, MA Our Lady of Vilna.
Nguyen, Polycarp *c.m.c.* '91 (FWT) Fort Worth, TX Christ the King.
Nguyen, Quang A. *s.c.j.* (GAL) Houston, TX St. Elizabeth Ann Seton.
Nguyen, Quoc *o.f.m.cap.* (SFR) Seton Hospital.
Nguyen, Raphael Xuan '96 (ORG) Huntington Beach, CA St. Bonaventure.
Nguyen, Raphael (ORG) Cursillo Movement.
Nguyen, Scott C. '97 (WCH) Westminster, CA Blessed Sacrament.
Nguyen, Son Anh '03 (WOR) Otter River, MA St. Martin's.
Nguyen, Stephen Tan *o.f.m.* '59 (SFR) San Francisco, CA St. Boniface.
Nguyen, Steve '99 (HON) Kahului, HI Christ the King; Clergy Personnel Board.
Nguyen, Sy Uy '91 (ORG) Anaheim, CA San Antonio.
Nguyen, Tam N. (TLS) Diocesan Consultors; Priests' Personnel Committee.
Nguyen, Tam Viet *i.c.m.* '01 (BR)[H] Baton Rouge, LA Incarnatio Consecratio Mission.
Nguyen, Tam '82 (TLS) Tulsa, OK Christ the King.
Nguyen, Tan '02 (CHI) Orland Hills, IL St. Elizabeth Seton.
Nguyen, Te Van '86 (SFR) Vietnamese Catholic Ministry.
Nguyen, Thanh N. '94 (R) Hope Mills, NC Good Shepherd.
Nguyen, Thanh T. '91 (STA) Jacksonville, FL Christ the King.
Nguyen, Thanh Thai (STA) Presbyteral Council.
Nguyen, Thanh Van (OKL) Oklahoma City, OK Cathedral of Our Lady of Perpetual Help.
Nguyen, Thanh '67 (PRT) Caribou, ME Sacred Heart.
Nguyen, Thein Van '89 (WIN) New Richland, MN St. Aidan; New Richland, MN St. Mary; New Richland, MN All Saints.
Nguyen, Thiel X. '01 (WOR) Fitchburg, MA St. Bernard's.
Nguyen, Thien (WOR) Fitchburg, MA Immaculate Conception.
Nguyen, Thinh *s.d.b.* '99 (SP)[C] Rosemead, CA Don Bosco Technical Institute.
Nguyen, Thinh *s.d.b.* '99 (LA)[D] Rosemead, CA Don Bosco Technical Institute.
Nguyen, Thomas Thanh '69 (LAF) Franklin, LA St. Helena.
Nguyen, Thong *c.ss.r.* '56 (DAL) Garland, TX Mother of Perpetual Help.
Nguyen, Thu Ngoc '93 (GAL) Houston, TX Sacred Heart Co–Cathedral.
Nguyen, Thu Van '92 (VIC) On Leave of Absence.
Nguyen, Thuc '98 (BEA) Port Arthur, TX St. Catherine of Siena.
Nguyen, Thuy Quang '98 (GAL) Houston, TX St. Rose of Lima.
Nguyen, Tien *s.s.c.* '95 (LA)[K] St. Columbans St. Columban's Foreign Mission Society.
Nguyen, Tien–Tri '96 (SFE) Santa Fe, NM Our Lady of Guadalupe.
Nguyen, Timothy *s.d.b.* '02 (LA)[C] Rosemead, CA Don Bosco Technical Institute; [D] Rosemead, CA Don Bosco Technical Institute.
Nguyen, Tinh Van '98 (BO) Lynn, MA Sacred Heart.
Nguyen, Toan X. '96 (SFR) San Francisco, CA St. Elizabeth.
Nguyen, Truc (LA) Pasadena, CA St. Andrew; Vocations.
Nguyen, Trung V. '94 (GAL) Sugar Land, TX St. Laurence; On Special or Other Diocesan Assignment; Diocesan Judges.
Nguyen, Trung '94 (GAL) On Duty Outside the Diocese.
Nguyen, Truyen '03 (SJ) Morgan Hill, CA St. Catherine of Alexandria.
Nguyen, Tuan John '95 (ORG) Laguna Woods, CA St. Nicholas.
Nguyen, Tuan V. '92 (SEA) Toledo, WA St. Francis Xavier; College of Consultors; Presbyteral Council.
Nguyen, Tuan Van '86 (JOL) Villa Park, IL St. Alexander.
Nguyen, Tuan *s.d.b.* '88 (STO) Stockton, CA St. Luke Church of Stockton (Pastor of).
Nguyen, Tuan '92 (SEA) Centralia, WA St. Mary; Chehalis, WA St. Joseph; Pe Ell, WA St. Joseph; Winlock, WA Sacred Heart; Green Hill School.
Nguyen, Tuan (ORG) Ministry to Priests.
Nguyen, Tuyen '87 (ORG) Garden Grove, CA St. Callistus; Clergy Personnel Board.
Nguyen, Van T. (NO) Navy Reserve Chaplains.
Nguyen, Vandennis '90 (YAK) Richland, WA Christ the King.
Nguyen, Vien The (NO) New Orleans, LA Mary, Queen of Vietnam; Judges.
Nguyen, Vincent Kien '89 (HON) Honolulu, HI Co–Cathedral of St. Theresa of the Child Jesus; Vietnamese Ministry.
Nguyen, Vincent Liem *o.s.b.* '94 (P)[L] St. Benedict, OR Mt. Angel Abbey.
Nguyen, Vincent Vuong–Ouoc '99 (GAL) Houston, TX St. Francis de Sales.
Nguyen, Vinh Duc *s.v.d.* '96 (DUB)[B] Epworth, IA Divine Word College.
Nguyen–Hong–Aw, Andrew *c.m.c.* (STP) Minneapolis, MN St. Joseph Hien.
Nguyen–Thanh–Long, Peter '65 (WDC) Silver Spring, MD Our Lady of Vietnam.
Nguyen Chau Dien, Raymond M. *c.m.c.* '88 (SPC)[E] Carthage, MO Congregation of the Mother Coredemptrix, United States Assumption Province.
Nguyen Dan, Pius M. *c.m.c.* '83 (SB)[E] Corona, CA Congregation of the Mother Co–Redemptrix.
Nguyen Duc Hau, Joseph *s.e.* '69 (P) Portland, OR Our Lady of Lavang.
Nguyen Huy Chuong, Matthias M. *c.m.c.* '81 (SB)[E] Corona, CA Congregation of the Mother Co–Redemptrix.
Nguyen Mang Cach, Paul M. *c.m.c.* '77 (SPC)[E] Carthage, MO Congregation of the Mother Coredemptrix, United States Assumption Province.
Nguyen Manh Thu, Raymond M. *c.m.c.* '87 (SPC)[E] Carthage, MO Congregation of the Mother Coredemptrix, United States Assumption Province.
Nguyen Thanh Hue, Augustine '64 (PT) Pensacola, FL Our Lady Queen of Martyrs, Mission.
Ngwumohaike, Anthony (BO) Nigerian.
Ngyen, Dung '02 (ATL) Special or Other (Arch)Diocesan Assignment.
Ngyuen, Phien T. (CHI) Other Assignments.
Nhi, Tran Dinh '71 (ARL) Dale City, VA Holy Family.
Nho, Do Duy '66 (LR) North Little Rock, AR St. Patrick's.
Nibler, James *o.m.v.* '87 (SFD) Newberg, OR St. Peter.
Niblick, Charles W. '74 (GRY) Dyer, IN St. Maria Goretti.
Nicastro, Thomas More *o.f.m.* '42 (NY).
Niccolls, Edward D. '74 (WOR)[GG] Lunenburg, MA St. Boniface.
Nicgorski, David *o.m.v.* '91 (BO)[V] Milton, MA Oblate Residence (St. Joseph House).
Nichol, Rex '67 (AMA) Amarillo, TX Our Lady of Guadalupe.
Nicholas, Gerald A. *o.s.a.* '66 (JOL)[C] New Lenox, IL Providence Catholic High School; [L] New Lenox, IL Augustinian Friary.
Nicholas, William C. '01 (SFR) Menlo Park, CA The Church of the Nativity.

Nicholl, Rex (AMA) Presbyteral Council.
Nicholls, Trevor '90 (NY) Goshen, NY St. John the Evangelist.
Nichols, Aquinas *o.s.b.* '80 (DM) Des Moines, IA Basilica of Saint John; [J] Des Moines, IA St. Gabriel Benedictine Priory; [H] Oceanside, CA Prince of Peace Abbey, Benet Hill.
Nichols, Charles P. '48 (BRK) Brooklyn, NY Sacred Hearts of Jesus and Mary and St. Stephen Retired.
Nichols, Harry E. '73 (PIT) Pittsburgh, PA St. Margaret.
Nichols, Henry P. '70 (BO) Brockton, MA Veterans Administration Hospital Brockton–West Roxbury; Military & VA Chaplains.
Nichols, Herbert T. '75 (FR) New Bedford, MA St. James.
Nichols, Irby "Nick" '01 (SFE) Santa Rosa, NM St. Anthony; Santa Rosa, NM St. Rose of Lima.
Nichols, Jerry (PEO)[I] Urbana, IL Provena Covenant Medical Center.
Nichols, John J. '62 (BO) Senior Priests Retired.
Nichols, Joseph E. '62 (NOR) Retired.
Nichols, Louis J. '60 (SY) Clearlake, CA Our Lady, Queen of Peace; On Duty Outside the Diocese.
Nichols, Louis (SR) Priests' Council.
Nichols, Neal A. *f.s.s.p.* '01 (SCR)[M] Elmhurst, PA Priestly Fraternity of St. Peter (F.S.S.P.), North American District Headquarters.
Nichols, Rodrick '89 (LSC) Silver City, NM St. Vincent de Paul.
Nichols, Stephen J. '86 (BUR) Vermont Cursillo; Deans; [H] Lyndon Center, VT Lyndon State College; Lyndonville, VT St. Elizabeth.
Nichols, Timothy E. '73 (LA) Hacienda Heights, CA St. John Vianney.
Nichols, Timothy (LA) Council of Priests; San Gabriel Pastoral Region.
Nicholson, David *o.s.b.* '49 (P)[L] St. Benedict, OR Mt. Angel Abbey.
Nicholson, Francis J. *s.j.* '53 (BO)[V] Newton, MA The Jesuit Community at Boston College.
Nicholson, John A. *s.j.* '46 (NY)[EE] New York, NY Murray–Weigel Hall.
Nicholson, Patrick '69 (MOB) On Leave from the Archdiocese.
Nickas, John P. '66 (NEW) Montclair, NJ St. Peter Claver.
Nickel, Leander '47 (GB) Retired.
Nickels, Larry '86 (STL)[O] St. Louis Franciscan Friary of St. Anthony of Padua.
Nickels, Lawrence M. *o.f.m.* '86 (BEL) Carlyle, IL St. Teresa of Avila.
Nickels, Peter *o.f.m.conv.* '60 (LAN) Grand Rapids, MI St. Anthony of Padua; Lansing, MI Holy Cross.
Nickerson, Russell *o.m.i.* '47 (BO)[Y] Tewksbury, MA Immaculate Heart of Mary Infirmary.
Nickle, Frederick *o.f.m.cap.* '65 (NY)[EE] Beacon, NY St. Joachim Friary.
Nickless, R. Walker (DEN) Vicars General; College of Consultors; Archdiocesan Finance Council.
Nickless, Walker '73 (DEN) Denver, CO Holy Family; Denver, CO St. Mary Magdalene; Lakewood, CO Our Lady of Fatima.
Nicknair, Harold '61 (PRT) Retired.
Nicknair, Leopold G. '58 (PRT) Retired.
Nickol, Eugene '73 (BAL) Millersville, MD Our Lady of the Fields.
Nickol, G. Eugene '73 (BAL) Advocates and Procurators.
Nicola, John J. '55 (CHI) Retired.
Nicolas, Jeffrey S. '93 (L) Louisville, KY St. Lawrence.
Nicolau, Juan '60 (BWN) San Juan, TX The Basilica of the National Shrine of Our Lady of San Juan del Valle; [J] San Juan, TX The Basilica of Our Lady of San Juan del Valle – National Shrine.
Nicolau, Juan '60 (BWN)[J] San Juan, TX Cursillos.
Nicolau, Juan (BWN) Division for Evangelization; Presbyteral Council; Ad Hoc Committee for Diocesan Insurance; Parish Priests' Consultors & Priest Personnel Board; Board of Directors.
Nicoletti, Maurizio *o.cist* '65 (TR) Mount Laurel, NJ St. John Neumann; [M] Mount Laurel, NJ Cistercian Monastery of Our Lady of Fatima.
Nicolicchia, J. Andrew *o.p.* '65 (WDC) Washington, DC St. Dominic Church & Priory.
Nicoll, Leo A. *s.j.* '61 (NO)[C] New Orleans, LA Loyola University New Orleans.
Nicolo, Joseph J. '74 (PH) Blue Bell, PA St. Helena; Approved Advocates.
Nicolosi, Joseph P. '97 (RCK) Hampshire, IL St. Charles Borromeo.
Nicolosi, Mark Ronald *o.s.b.* '67 (BUR)[E] Weston, VT Priory of Benedictine Monks.
Nicosia, Peter *o.f.m.cap.* '59 (SP) Tampa, FL Most Holy Redeemer.
Nicosia, Vincent '92 (CC)[G] Robstown, TX Society of Our Lady of the Most Holy Trinity.
Nieberding, Richard *c.pp.s.* '80 (COL) Columbus, OH St. James–the–Less; Vicariate 4: Northland.
Nieberding, Robert '56 (LEX) Retired.
Nieblas, James *s.d.b.* '86 (LA)[Q] Los Angeles, CA Dominic Savio Salesian Residence.
Niebrugge, Herman J. '56 (SFD) Mattoon, IL Immaculate Conception.
Niebrzydowski, Walter J. '59 (NY) New York, NY Epiphany.
Nieckarz, James P. *m.m.* '66 (NY).
Niedergeses, W. Bernard '50 (NSH)[EE] Nashville, TN Assumption; Nashville, TN St. Pius X; Deans.
Niedermier, Jerome G. '52 (TOL) Retired.
Niehaus, Charles W. *s.j.* '74 (CHI)[N] Chicago, IL Miguel Pro Jesuit Community.
Niehaus, Francis H. '55 (CIN) Retired.
Niehaus, Jonathan J. '94 (MIL)[S] Waukesha, WI Schoenstatt Fathers.
Niehaus, Mark J. '03 (MIL)[S] Waukesha, WI Schoenstatt Fathers; Kenosha, WI St. Mary.
Niehoff, Edmund A. '64 (SHP) Shreveport, LA St. Mary of the Pines; Judges.
Niehoff, Edmund A. (Larry) (SHP) College of Consultors; Presbyteral Council; Priests' Retirement Board.
Niehoff, Kevin W. *o.p.* '93 (SFE) Albuquerque, NM St. Thomas Aquinas University Parish.
Niehoff, Kevin *o.p.* (SFE) Adjutant Judicial Vicar.
Niehoff, Robert L. *s.j.* '82 (ORE)[N] San Francisco, CA Jesuit Community at University of San Francisco.
Nieli, Bruce *c.s.p.* '73 (MEM) Memphis, TN St. Patrick's.
Nielsen, Eric H. '95 (MAD) Bloomington, WI St. Mary; Bloomington, WI St. John.
Nielsen, James *o.praem.* '93 (GB)[B] St. Norbert College.
Nielsen, Kenneth M. '80 (BUF) On Duty Outside the Diocese.
Nielsen, Philip W. *o.f.m.* '48 (PAT)[N] Parsippany, NJ St. Francis of Assisi Novitiate–Franciscan Sisters of St. Elizabeth.
Nielson, James P. *o.praem.* '93 (GB)[I] De Pere, WI St. Norbert Abbey.
Nielson, Karl *o.s.b.* '99 (P)[L] St. Benedict, OR Mt. Angel Abbey; Navy Chaplains.
Nielson, Thomas A. (NY)[II] New York, NY St. Ansgar Scandinavian Catholic League.
Nieman, James (DUB) Review Board for Sexual Abuse of Minors by Clergy and Other Church Personnel.
Nieman, Paul J. (STL)[U] Arnold, MO Jefferson County Catholic Church Real Estate Corporation.
Niemann, Mark E. *s.j.* '50 (OM)[C] Omaha, NE Creighton Preparatory School.
Niemann, Paul J. '80 (STL) Arnold, MO Immaculate Conception; Deaneries/Deans; Festus; Jefferson County Catholic Church Real Estate Corporation.
Niemann, Paul '80 (PRM) Wildwood, MO St. Louis Mission.
Niemczyk, Stefan J. '87 (SPR) Three Rivers, MA SS. Peter and Paul.
Niemeier, Dennis A. '73 (CIN) Military Chaplains; Army Chaplains.
Niemeyer, John '55 (PEO) Retired.
Niemeyer, Roger *o.f.m.* '40 (SFD)[L] Springfield, IL Our Lady of Angels Friary.
Niemiec, C. Antoninus *o.p.* '95 (NY) New York, NY St. Catherine of Siena.
Niemier, Roch *o.f.m.* '65 (MIL)[X] Franklin, WI Franciscan Pilgrimage Programs, Inc.; [O] Provincial Offices.
Niemira, Thomas J. '53 (AUS) Waco, TX V.A. Hospital.
Niemira, Thomas '65 (JKS) On Duty Outside the Diocese.
Nienaber, Leonard B. '34 (LEX) Retired.
Nienaber, Paul J. *s.j.* '99 (CHI)[N] Chicago, IL Woodlawn Jesuit Community.
Nienaber, Robert H. '63 (OM) Genoa, NE St. Rose of Lima; Krakow, NE SS. Peter and Paul; Finance Council.
Nienhaus, Gerald T. '62 (STL) St. Louis, MO St. Aloysius.
Nienhaus, Ivan R. '89 (DUB) Winthrop, IA Immaculate Conception; Winthrop, IA St. Patrick; Winthrop, IA St. Patrick.
Nierengarten, Andrew '66 (RVC) Port Jefferson, NY Infant Jesus.
Nieset, Frank E. '56 (TOL) Retired.
Niessen, John *s.v.d.* '51 (SB) Perris, CA St. James.
Nietfeld, Fred J. '46 (TOL) Retired.
Nietlong, Joseph '86 (TUC) Oracle, AZ St. Helen.
Nieto, Jesus (OAK) Presbyteral Council.
Nieto, Jose de Jesus (OAK) Deans.
Nieto, Jose *c.m.f.* '66 (SJN) Bayamon, PR San Antonio Maria Claret.
Nieto, Luis Angel '90 (LA) Claremont, CA Our Lady of the Assumption.
Nieto–Ruiz, Jose de Jesus '07 (OAK) Richmond, CA St. Mark's.
Nieva, Constantino S. '55 (RVC)[M] Uniondale, NY St. Pius X Residence.
Nieva, Constantino S. '63 (RVC) Retired.
Nieves, Carlos '86 (PCE) On Duty Outside the Diocese.
Nieves, Jose Javier '86 (PAT) Absent on Leave.
Nieves, Pablo *s.x.* '99 (PAT)[M] Wayne Xaverian Missionary Fathers.
Niewczas, Taddeus '52 (RVC) Retired.
Niewiadomski, Arthur J. '94 (TOL) Bascom, OH St. Patrick; Bascom, OH St. Andrew.
Niezgoda, Joseph R. '62 (GRY) East Chicago, IN St. John Cantius.
Niggel, Clement '03 (SFE) Albuquerque, NM Annunciation.
Nigli, Francis A. '97 (OM) Papillion, NE St. Columbkille.
Nigro, Armand M. *s.j.* '56 (P)[L] Portland, OR Colombiere Community.
Nijem, Fred J. '68 (SAV) Warner Robins, GA Sacred Heart; Macon Deanery.
Niklas, Gerald R. '59 (CIN)[K] Cincinnati, OH Good Samaritan Hospital.
Nikliborc, Robert D. '55 (SD) San Diego, CA St. Anne.
Nikliborc, Robert '55 (SD) Retired.
Nikodem, Martin J. '67 (BGP) Bridgeport, CT Our Lady of Good Counsel.
Nikodem, Ronald J. *s.m.* '94 (STP) St. Paul, MN St. Louis King of France.
Nikolic, Dennis '02 (NY) Middletown, NY St. Joseph.
Niland, John *o.f.m.cap* '76 (HON) Pearl City, HI Our Lady of Good Counsel.
Nilema, Nicholas *a.l.c.p.* '88 (P) Seaside, OR Our Lady of Victory; Area Vicars.
Nilges, Harold L. '53 (RCK) Genoa, IL St. Catherine of Genoa Retired.
Nilles, Allan F. '49 (FAR) Judges Retired.
Nilles, Roger G. '59 (MAD) Madison, WI St. Peter.
Nilsson, Richard '71 (RVC) Inwood, NY Our Lady of Good Counsel.
Nimerichter, Dean '92 (DM) Greenfield, IA St. John.
Nimocks, Michael F. '96 (COL) Diocesan Consultors.
Nimocks, Michael '96 (COL) Marion, OH St. Mary.
Nin, Felino Reyes (NY) New York, NY Incarnation.
Ninedorf, Robert W. '89 (CHR) Edgefield, SC St. Mary's; Ward, SC St. William's Retired.
Ninemire, Kerry '75 (SAL) Salina, KS St. Mary's; Priests' Continuing Formation Committee.
Nino, Andres G. *o.s.a.* '62 (BO) Cambridge, MA St. Mary of the Annunciation.
Nino, Andres *o.s.a.* (BO)[BB] Wellesley, MA Wellesley College Campus Ministry.
Nir, Roman '64 (DET)[A] Orchard Lake, MI SS. Cyril and Methodius Seminary.
Nirschl, Nicholas E. *o.praem.* '56 (SFE)[I] Albuquerque, NM Santa Maria de la Vid Priory.
Nisbet, James (MRY) Presbyteral Council.
Nisbet, Jim '69 (MRY) Spreckels, CA St. Joseph.
Nischan, James R. '83 (PCE) On Duty Outside the Diocese.
Nishigaya, Raymond '64 (HON) Retired.
Nishimuta, James K. *m.m.* '54 (NY).
Niskanen, Steve *c.m.f.* '90 (LA)[EE] Los Angeles, CA Our Lady Queen of the Angels.
Nissel, John J. *s.j.* '56 (BAL)[S] S J House.
Nist, Arthur '40 (Y) Retired.
Nistler, Edward '54 (CR) Bemidji, MN St. Philip's Retired.
Nitz, Eliot *s.d.s.* '68 (WDC)[B] Silver Spring, MD Salvatorian Community; [K] Silver Spring, MD Holy Cross Hospital of Silver Spring, Inc..
Nitzki, John *s.c.j.* '56 (MIL)[O] Franklin, WI St. Martin of Tours; Franklin, WI St. Martin of Tours.
Niven, Timothy L. '98 (ROC) Victor, NY St. Patrick.
Nix, Albert '73 (PAT) Sparta, NJ Blessed Kateri Tekakwitha.
Nix, Julian *o.s.b.* '87 (BIS)[A] Richardton, ND Assumption Abbey.
Nixon, Joseph J. '85 (RVC)[A] Huntington, NY Diocesan Seminary of the Immaculate Conception; Associate Vocation Directors.
Niziolek, Terry *m.s.* '66 (STL) Maplewood, MO Immaculate Conception.
Njarackel, Thomas *v.c.* '74 (NY) Highland Mills, NY St. Patrick.
Njeim, Elias '58 (OG) Retired.
Njeru, Bernard '84 (LA) Glendora, CA St. Dorothy.
Njoku, Hyacinth '86 (NY) Bronx, NY St. Philip Neri.
Njoku, Peter '74 (STP) Kenyon, MN St. Michael; Zumbrota, MN St. Paul; Pine Island, MN St. Michael.
Njus, Jeffrey '03 (LAN) Parnell Facility; Brighton, MI St. Patrick.
Nkachukwu, Michael C. '80 (DET) Detroit, MI Annunciation/Our Lady of Sorrows; Detroit, MI St. Anthony.
Nkasibwe, Frederick Leo *a.j.* '96 (PIT) Pittsburgh, PA St. Bede.
Nnabuaku, Nicholas *c.s.s.p.* '87 (WDC)[B] Washington, DC St. Joseph's Seminary.
Nnaji, Theodore M. '92 (NY) Sleepy Hollow, NY The Magdalene.
Nnajiofir, Polycarp '91 (NEW) Cedar Grove, NJ Essex County Hospital Center; Essex County Hospital Center.
Nnaso, Sylvester '02 (RCK) Woodstock, IL St. Mary.
Nnatuanya, Vincent *c.s.sp.* '98 (DM) Des Moines, IA St. Augustin's.
Noah, Daniel '50 (CR) Retired.
Noah, Timothy T. '47 (CR) Hallock, MN St. Patrick's.
Nobile, Angelo '53 (MEM) On Duty Outside the Diocese.

Nobiletti, Raymond J. *m.m.* '69 (NY) New York, NY Transfiguration.
Noble, Bruce H. '87 (GAL)[K] Catholic Chaplain Corps, Texas Medical Center.
Noble, David H. '87 (GAL)[K] Catholic Chaplain Corps, Texas Medical Center.
Noble, Jeffrey J. '86 (E) Oil City, PA St. Stephen.
Noble, Paul A. '81 (COL) Gahanna, OH St. Matthew; Parochial Examiners; Diocesan Judges.
Noble, Wayne '93 (LA) Pomona, CA Sacred Heart.
Nobleza, Dennis '80 (LA) Palmdale, CA St. Mary.
Noboa, Origines '80 (VEN) Absent on Sick Leave.
Nocero, Pascal F. '48 (LA) Retired.
Nochelski, Paul W. *s.j.* '71 (BUF)[O] Buffalo, NY Canisius Jesuit Community.
Nock, James J. '64 (HRT) East Hartford, CT Blessed Sacrament; East Hartford, CT Our Lady of Peace.
Nockumas, Anthony *m.i.c.* '57 (JOL) Plano, IL St. Mary.
Noda, Jorge '84 (MIA) Hialeah, FL Immaculate Conception.
Noe, John P. '74 (LEX) Ashland, KY Holy Family; [D] Ashland, KY Our Lady of Bellefonte Hospital, Inc..
Noecker, Ronald J. '85 (OM) Absent on Leave.
Noel, Damian *t.o.r.* '53 (ARL)[J] White Post, VA Sacred Heart Friary.
Noel, Donald C. *o.praem.* '59 (GB)[I] De Pere, WI St. Norbert Abbey.
Noel, Gregory *o.f.m.cap.* '88 (NY) New York, NY Our Lady Queen of Angels.
Noel, Guyma '97 (ATL) Atlanta, GA Immaculate Heart of Mary.
Noel, Marc A. '98 (ALX) Natchez, LA St. Augustine's.
Noelke, Dennis *c.s.b.* '81 (DET).
Noesen, Gerald '50 (CR) Retired.
Noesen, Robert '93 (JOL) Elmhurst, IL Visitation.
Noesen, Thomas D. *o.p.* '76 (CHI) River Forest, IL St. Vincent Ferrer; Chicago, IL St. Basil/Visitation.
Noetzel, Kenneth J. *s.j.* '51 (DET) Special or Other Diocesan Assignment; Office of Permanent Diaconate Formation; Sinai Hospital.
Nofi, Michael *m.s.a.* '74 (NOR)[F] Cromwell Society of the Missionaries of the Holy Apostles.
Noga, Edward P. '76 (Y) Youngstown, OH St. Patrick.
Noga, Gregory J. '79 (PSC) Trenton, NJ St. Mary of the Assumption; Central New Jersey Protopresbyterate; Elected Members; Office for Eastern Christian Formation (formerly: Office of Religious Education).
Noga, Henry K. *s.v.d.* '96 (ORG)[H] Yorba Linda, CA Polish Center.
Noga, Henry *s.v.d.* '96 (SB)[A] Riverside, CA Society of the Divine Word Missionaries.
Noga, John T. '99 (CHI) Chicago, IL St. Barnabas.
Nogaro, Paul M. '71 (BUF) Grand Island, NY St. Stephen.
Nogosek, Robert J. *c.s.c.* '56 (SB) San Bernardino, CA Our Lady of the Rosary Cathedral.
Nogosek, Robert J. '56 (FTW)[I] San Bernardino, CA.
Noguera, Dagoberto '85 (BRK) Queens Village, NY Incarnation.
Noguera, Ronald '81 (MIA) Miami, FL St. Michael the Archangel Retired.
Nohs, Joseph E. '93 (RVC) Seaford, NY Maria Regina.
Noia, Leonel '73 (SJ) Retired.
Noiseux, Donald A. '84 (SPR) Huntington, MA St. Thomas.
Nojeck, Mark J. '90 (KAL) Kalamazoo, MI St. Joseph.
Nolan, Brian J. '91 (MET) Watchung, NJ St. Mary–Stony Hill.
Nolan, Brian P. '01 (BAL) Westminster, MD St. John.
Nolan, Colman J. *s.t.* '56 (B) Post Falls, ID St. George's.
Nolan, Daniel T. *c.s.v.* '83 (CHI)[N] Chicago, IL Viatorian Residence.
Nolan, David E. '95 (NY) New York, NY St. Catherine of Genoa.
Nolan, Edward J. '48 (BRK) Queens Village, NY Incarnation Retired.
Nolan, Eugene A. *s.j.* '71 (WDC).
Nolan, George W. *s.j.* '54 (BO)[V] Weston, MA Campion Health Center, Inc..
Nolan, James L. *o.s.a.* '46 (PH)[AA] Villanova, PA St. Thomas Monastery.
Nolan, Jerome M. '74 (TR) Fair Haven, NJ Nativity.
Nolan, John '77 (SFD) Military Chaplains; Air Force Chaplains.
Nolan, Joseph A. '60 (ORL) Melbourne Beach, FL Immaculate Conception.
Nolan, Joseph J. *m.s.* '48 (ATL) Marietta, GA Church of St. Ann.
Nolan, Joseph M. '47 (BRK) Cambria Heights, NY Sacred Heart Retired.
Nolan, Joseph T. '53 (WCH) On Duty Outside the Diocese.
Nolan, Justin *o.s.b.* '55 (GBG)[H] Latrobe, PA Saint Vincent Archabbey.
Nolan, Kevin L. '90 (LA) Culver City, CA St. Augustine; Deanery 13; Army Reserve Chaplains.
Nolan, Kevin (LA) Personnel Board of the Archdiocese.
Nolan, Kieran *o.s.b.* '59 (SCL)[I] St. Augustine Monastery; (FgM).
Nolan, Larry '58 (COL)[G] Columbus, OH St. Raphael Home for the Aged, Inc..
Nolan, Michael E. '84 (WCH) El Dorado, KS St. John; El Dorado Correctional Facility; Adjutant Judicial Vicar; Judges.
Nolan, Michael F. '87 (KNX) Chattanooga, TN Our Lady of Perpetual Help; Presbyteral Council.
Nolan, Michael L. (BO) Bedford, MA St. Michael.
Nolan, Niall '80 (GAL) Houston, TX St. John Vianney.
Nolan, Norbert L. '51 (ROC) Retired.
Nolan, Patrick M. '50 (SAC) Sacramento, CA St. Philomene Pro–Synodal Judges Retired.
Nolan, Paul J. '57 (NEW) Caldwell, NJ Essex County Jail Annex; Newark, NJ Essex County Jail; Newark, NJ Delaney Hall Assessment Center; Newark, NJ Essex County Jail; Caldwell, NJ Essex County Jail Annex; Union County Jail.
Nolan, Paul (NEW) Elizabeth, NJ Union County Jail; Newark, NJ Delaney Hall Assessment Center.
Nolan, Peter P. *c.s.sp.* '59 (BO) Hyde Park, MA Most Precious Blood.
Nolan, Robert *s.a.c.* '70 (CAM) Hammonton, NJ St. Joseph's.
Nolan, Shawn *o.f.m.conv.* '55 (NY)[EE] Staten Island, NY St. Francis Friary.
Nolan, Terence '66 (SAT)[K] San Antonio, TX Casa De Padres; Chancellor; College of Consultors; Archdiocesan Presbyteral Council; Judicial Vicar; Judges; Catholic Lawyers Guild.
Nolan, Timothy F. '67 (STP) Ham Lake, MN Saint Paul.
Nolan, Timothy M. '02 (WIL) New Castle, DE Our Lady of Fatima.
Nolan, Timothy '92 (PEO) Pekin, IL St. Joseph's; Vicariates and Vicars.
Nolan, Victor *b.g.s.* (LA)[Q] Los Angeles, CA Brothers of the Good Shepherd, Inc. of California.
Nolan, Walter E. '69 (TR) Princeton, NJ St. Paul; Tribunal Judges; Diocesan Consultors.
Nolan, William A. '85 (MAD) Fort Atkinson, WI St. Joseph.
Nolan, William J. '69 (TR) Toms River, NJ St. Justin.
Nolan, William N. '57 (NSH) Retired.
Nold, Joseph K. '45 (SY) Retired.
Nold, Joseph '45 (SY)[Q] Syracuse, NY Tommy Coyne Residence @ Dillon Hall.
Nolen, Joseph *c.ss.r.* '76 (STL)[O] Liguori, MO Liguori Mission House/Redemptorists.
Nolette, Mark P. '87 (PRT) Calais, ME Immaculate Conception; St. Ann; Advocates; Associate Judges; Deans; Personnel Board.
Nolette, Roger '69 (FR) Osterville, MA Our Lady of the Assumption.
Nolette, Roger '69 (BO)[V] Hingham, MA Glastonbury Abbey.
Nolin, Joseph A. '49 (ORL) Retired.
Nolker, Thomas C. '72 (CIN) Cincinnati, OH St. James the Greater; Judges.
Noll, Dan (LEX) Fayette; Priests' Retirement Board.
Noll, Daniel J. '76 (LEX) Lexington, KY St. Peter; Diocesan Consultors.
Noll, Daniel '76 (LEX) Lexington, KY St. Paul.
Nollette, Louis A. '75 (GI) Loup City, NE St. Josaphat's.
Nollette, Neal P. '80 (GI) Stapleton, NE St. John the Evangelist Diocesan Consultors; Rural Life Conference.
Nollette, Neal (GI) Priests' Advisory Board (Presbyteral Council).
Nolte, John Mark '02 (OM) Omaha, NE Holy Cross.
Nolte, Walter L. '03 (OM) Omaha, NE St. Elizabeth Ann.
Nolte, William J. (BAL) Interdiocesan Judges.
Nombrado, Benjamin A. '79 (SFR) San Francisco, CA St. Vincent de Paul.
Nomellini, Paul J. '77 (MAR) Retired.
Nondorf, Aloysius J. '57 (GRY) Military Chaplains.
Nondorf, Tim '99 (SAC) Sacramento, CA St. Philomene.
Nondorf, Timothy (SAC) Council of Priests.
Nonis, Kingsley '93 (TYL) Las Vegas, NV St. Joseph, Husband of Mary.
Noon, Robert L. '51 (COL) Lancaster, OH St. Mark Retired.
Noonan, Bradford '99 (COS) Colorado Springs, CO St. Patrick's.
Noonan, Guy F. '76 (STA) Gainesville, FL St. Augustine.
Noonan, Guy (STA) Directors.
Noonan, James P. *m.m.* '60 (FgM).
Noonan, John '83 (MIA)[A] Miami, FL St. John Vianney College Seminary; Consultors: Members; Archdiocesan Vocations Review Board; Priestly Life and Ministry; Continuing Education for the Clergy; Priests' Sabbaticals.
Noonan, Joseph T. '95 (CHI).
Noonan, Joseph (CHI)[A] Archdiocesan Vocations.
Noonan, Mark L. '59 (BO)[C] Brighton, MA St. John Seminary College; Senior Priests Retired.
Noonan, Patrick '63 (JKS) Brookhaven, MS St. Francis; [I] Brookhaven, MS Lincoln Junior College Newman Center; Priests' Council; Personnel Board.
Noonan, Robert C. '64 (HEL) Choteau, MT St. Joseph; Fairfield, MT St. John.
Noonan, Robert (HEL) Defenders of the Bond; Presbyteral Council; Vicariates; Personnel Board.
Noonan, Thomas F. '45 (BRK) Retired.
Noonan, Thomas F. '55 (BRK) Brooklyn, NY St. Edmund's; Teachers.
Noone, Charles J. '67 (PH) Oreland, PA Holy Martyrs Retired.
Noone, David E. '66 (ALB) Loudonville, NY St. Francis de Sales.
Noone, John '67 (BLX) Kiln, MS Annunciation; Deans; Presbyteral Council.
Noone, Kevin B. '70 (BRK) Brooklyn, NY Our Lady of Guadalupe.
Noone, Sean '52 (CC) Retired.
Nooney, P. Joseph '52 (SC) Trinity Regional Hospital.
Nooney, Patrick J. '52 (SC) Retired.
Noradounghian, Antoine '96 (NY) Los Angeles, CA Our Lady Queen of Martyrs; New York, NY St. Ann's Armenian Catholic Cathedral.
Norbeck, Ernest '84 (JOL) Naperville, IL St. Elizabeth Seton; [D] Naperville, IL Naperville Regional Catholic School.
Norbort, Fritz '42 (P) Retired.
Norcavage, Albert R. '50 (ALT) Absent on Leave.
Nord, Clarence C. '43 (L) Retired.
Nordeman, John J. '01 (PH) Horsham, PA St. Catherine of Siena; [D] Wyncote, PA Bishop McDevitt High School.
Nordenbrock, William *c.pp.s.* '83 (CIN)[X] Chicago, IL Precious Blood Ministry of Reconciliation; [M] Chicago, IL.
Norder, John '66 (MAD) Cassville, WI St. Charles Borromeo; Cassville, WI St. Mary Help of Christians.
Nordhaus, Jeffrey J. '72 (TOL) Kelley's Island, OH St. Michael; Put–In–Bay, OH Mother of Sorrows.
Nordick, Jerome '83 (SCL) New York Mills, MN Holy Cross; Dent, MN Sacred Heart; Perham, MN St. Stanislaus; Perham, MN St. Lawrence; Deans; Presbyteral Council.
Nordick, Jerome (SCL) Diocesan Consultors.
Nordick, John A. '90 (NU) Graceville, MN Holy Rosary.
Nordmeyer, Emeric *o.f.m.* '56 (SFE) Albuquerque, NM Queen of Angels Native American Center and Archdiocesan Shrine to Kateri Tekakwitha.
Nordquist, Theodore A. '80 (GRY) La Porte, IN St. Joseph; Deans; Bishop's Council of Priests; Consultors; Priests' Personnel Board; Girl Scout Liaison.
Noreika, Michael *s.s.s.* (CLV)[O] Cleveland, OH Blessed Sacrament Community.
Norena, Nicholas '94 (MET) Perth Amboy, NJ La Asuncion.
Norick, Daniel J. '97 (DEN) Denver, CO St. Anthony of Padua.
Noriega, Arnoldo '75 (TUC) On Medical Leave.
Norkett, Edward J. '36 (CHI) Highland Park, IL Immaculate Conception Retired.
Norkett, Michael P. (OAK) Presbyteral Council.
Norkett, Michael '68 (OAK) Oakland, CA St. Paschal Baylon; Pastoral Leadership Placement Board (PLPB); Clergy Services.
Norkunas, Anthony J. '44 (SCR) Retired.
Norman, Charles *o.s.f.s.* '65 (ALN)[O] Easton, PA Lafayette College (Easton).
Norman, Clifford A. '60 (PBL) On Duty Outside the Diocese.
Norman, Gary '94 (GF) Roseville, CA St. Rose of Lima.
Norman, Gary '94 (YAK) On Duty Outside the Diocese.
Norman, John '71 (SLC)[B] Salt Lake City, UT Judge Memorial Catholic High School.
Norman, Richard W. *s.j.* '58 (ALN)[A] Wernersville, PA Jesuit Center.
Normanly, Thomas *s.s.c.* '52 (OM)[K] St. Columbans St. Columban's Foreign Mission Society.
Norrell, Albert V. '88 (PH) College of Consultors Retired.
Norris, David J. '74 (FRS) Fresno, CA St. Helen.
Norris, John P. '46 (ROC) Retired.
Norris, Patrick F. *o.p.* '89 (CHI) Madison, WI Blessed Sacrament.
Norris, Patrick *o.p.* (MAD) Elected.
Norris, Robert J. '80 (NY) Bronx, NY St. Lucy.
Norris, Thomas P. *o.s.f.s.* '73 (R) Goldsboro, NC St. Mary.
Norris, Timothy L. (STP) Venezuelan Missions; On Duty Outside the Archdiocese.
Norris, Walter A. (CAM) Immigration Services and Legal Assistance to the Poor.
Norris, Walter '73 (CAM) National Park, NJ St. Matthew's.
Norsworthy, Richard '85 (SHP)[B] Shreveport, LA Christus Health Northern Louisiana.
North, Robert G. *s.j.* '44 (MIL)[O] Wauwatosa, WI Jesuit Community at St. Camillus.
Northrop, James '97 (SEA) Enumclaw, WA Sacred Heart of Jesus; Presbyteral Council; Buckley, WA St. Aloysius.
Northrop, John B. *m.m.* '74 (NY)[EE] Maryknoll Maryknoll Fathers and Brothers.
Northrup, Gerald '01 (FRS) Oakhurst, CA Our Lady of the Sierra; Scouting.
Norton, Claude B. '43 (DUB) Retired.
Norton, Edward *s.v.d.* '45 (CHI)[B] Techny, IL Divine Word Residence.

Norton, Emmet J. *s.j.* '48 (PAT)[I] Morristown, NJ Loyola House of Retreats.
Norton, George R. '83 (ROC) Rochester, NY Blessed Sacrament Retired.
Norton, John B. *o.p.* '56 (NO) New Orleans, LA St. Anthony of Padua.
Norton, Michael *c.pp.s.* '70 (SAT) San Antonio, TX Santa Rosa Hospital System; [H] San Antonio, TX Christus Santa Rosa Health Care Corporation.
Norton, Robert A. '72 (PIT) Pittsburgh, PA St. Athanasius.
Norton, Robert J. *o.f.m.* (PAT) Little Falls, NJ Our Lady of the Holy Angels.
Norton, Thomas '63 (NEW) Northvale, NJ St. Anthony's; Westwood, NJ Pascack Valley Hospital; Chaplains.
Norton, William W. '67 (FR) Retired.
Nortz, Alfred E. '55 (SY) Syracuse, NY St. Vincent de Paul.
Nortz, Basil *o.r.c.* '95 (DET)[K] Grosse Pointe, MI Order of Canons Regular of the Holy Cross.
Nosbush, Peter C. '70 (NU) North Mankato, MN Holy Rosary.
Noser, J. Homer '43 (STL) Retired.
Nosser, Charles J. '53 (RVC) Floral Park, NY Our Lady of Victory.
Nosser, John C. '64 (RVC) Bay Shore, NY St. Patrick's; Judges for Interdiocesan Tribunal.
Notabartolo, Charles E. '77 (PMB)[M] Diocesan Pension Plan Trust; [M] Diocese of Palm Beach Health Plan Trust.
Notabartolo, Charles '77 (PMB) Vicar General; Moderator of Curia; Notaries; Cursillo Movement for Hispanics; Parish Formation and Planning; College of Consultors; Secretary; Presbyteral Council.
Notaro, Carlo *o.s.cam.* '88 (MIL)[O] Wauwatosa, WI St. Camillus Community House; [M] Wauwatosa, WI St. Camillus Health Center, Inc..
Notarpole, Joseph '49 (STA) Jacksonville, FL Our Lady of the Angels.
Notebaart, James C. (STP) Special Assignment; Office of Indian Ministry.
Nott, David L. '93 (RIC) Appomattox, VA Our Lady of Peace; Hurt, VA St. Victoria.
Notter, Richard E. '63 (TOL) Toledo, OH SS. Peter and Paul; Co–chairpersons.
Nourie, Paul *o.m.i.* '64 (LA) San Fernando, CA St. Ferdinand.
Nouws, Jacques J. '46 (LA)[Q] Montebello, CA DePaul Evangelization Center.
Nouws, James J. *c.m.* '46 (LA)[W] Montebello, CA DePaul Evangelization Center Retired.
Nouza, Frank M. *o.p.* '58 (CHI)[N] Chicago Dominicans (Provincial Office).
Novack, Kevin '81 (PBL) Pueblo, CO Our Lady of the Meadows.
Novak, David A. '77 (STL) Affton, MO St. Dominic Savio; Valley Park, MO Sacred Heart.
Novak, David A. '79 (CLV) Lorain, OH Holy Trinity.
Novak, Francis G. *c.ss.r.* '49 (STL)[O] Liguori, MO St. Clement Health Care Center.
Novak, Henry *c.ss.r.* '50 (CHI)[N] Glenview, IL The Redemptorists of Glenview, Illinois.
Novak, James (LAN) Retired.
Novak, Joseph A. *s.j.* '57 (NEW)[B] Jersey City, NJ Jesuit Center; [N] Jersey City, NJ Jesuits of Saint Peter's College, Inc..
Novak, Kevin '81 (PBL) Continuing Education and Formation.
Novak, Norbert *o.s.b.* '64 (B)[C] Jerome, ID Monastery of the Ascension.
Novak, Paul M. *o.s.m.* '90 (CHI) Chicago, IL Assumption of the Blessed Virgin Mary; [N] Chicago, IL Assumption Priory; [N] Chicago, IL Order of Friar Servants of Mary (Servites) United States of America Province, Inc..
Novak, Robert J. '42 (CHI) Retired.
Novak, Thomas *s.d.s.* '59 (MIL)[O] Milwaukee, WI Salvatorians – Jordan Hall.
Novak, Vincent M. *s.j.* '55 (NY)[C] Bronx, NY Fordham University; [EE] Loyola Hall, Jesuit Community.
Novak, William L. '97 (OKL) Yukon, OK St. John Nepomuk.
Novakowski, James E. '95 (GI) Sidney, NE St. Patrick's.
Novelly, Duane R. '79 (DET) Detroit, MI St. Matthew.
Novick, Michael '01 (CHI) Tinley Park, IL St. George.
Novielli, John J. *o.praem.* '74 (PH)[B] Paoli, PA Daylesford Abbey; [AA] Paoli, PA Daylesford Abbey.
Noviello, Anthony A. '43 (SCR) Retired.
Novoa, Carlos *s.j.* '83 (NY)[EE] New York, NY "America;" Residence and publication office of the America Press.
Novoa, Marino *c.m.f.* '79 (CHI) Chicago, IL St. Paul.
Novokowsky, Robert *f.s.s.p.* (SCR)[M] Elmhurst Priestly Fraternity of St. Peter (F.S.S.P.), North American District Headquarters.
Novotny, Allen P. *s.j.* '82 (WDC)[E] Washington, DC Gonzaga College High School.
Novotny, James F. '64 (OM) Lindsay, NE Holy Family; St. Edward, NE St. Edward.
Novotny, Jerome *o.m.i.* '68 (FgM).
Novotny, Richard '81 (RC) On Duty Outside the Diocese; Air Force Chaplains.
Novotny, Robert J. '50 (MIL) Retired.
Nowacki, Jerome A. '93 (MAR) DeTour, MI Sacred Heart; Goetzville, MI St. Stanislaus Kostka.
Nowak, Bernard J. '52 (LC) Retired.
Nowak, Bernard U. '74 (BUF) Council of Priests; Angola, NY Most Precious Blood.
Nowak, Christopher *o.s.a.* '97 (RVC) Huntington Station, NY St. Hugh of Lincoln.
Nowak, David G. '85 (GRY) Munster, IN St. Thomas More.
Nowak, Eugene J. '70 (CHI) Hoffman Estates, IL St. Hubert.
Nowak, Francis T. '58 (BUF) Defenders of the Bond Retired.
Nowak, James A. '67 (JOL) Naperville, IL Sts. Peter and Paul.
Nowak, John H. *c.r.* '71 (CHI)[N] Chicago, IL Provincial Office of the Congregation of the Resurrection.
Nowak, Mark A. '75 (E) Saegertown, PA St. Bernadette; [P] Edinboro, PA Edinboro University of PA.
Nowak, Michael E. (MIL) Kenosha, WI St. Therese.
Nowak, Randolph *o.f.m.cap.* '52 (AGN)[F] Agana Heights, GU St. Fidelis Friary; [F] Agat, GU Capuchin Fraternity; (FgM).
Nowak, Randy *o.f.m.cap.* '52 (AGN) Agana Heights, GU Our Lady of Mount Carmel.
Nowak, Stanley F. '58 (BUF) Depew, NY SS. Peter and Paul.
Nowakowski, Edward S. '48 (GB) Armstrong Creek, WI St. Stanislaus Kostka; Armstrong Creek, WI St. Joan of Arc.
Nowakowski, Jerome F. '63 (TOL) Toledo, OH Good Shepherd; Toledo, OH St. Louis; Toledo, OH St. Thomas Aquinas.
Nowel, Mark D. *o.p.* '86 (PRO)[P] Providence St. Thomas Aquinas Priory at Providence College.
Nowel, Mark S. *o.p.* '86 (PRO)[B] Providence, RI Providence College.
Nowicki, Chester *s.v.d.* '46 (CHI)[B] Techny, IL Divine Word Residence.
Nowicki, Gary D. '96 (MIL) Hales Corners, WI St. Mary.
Nowlan, John T. '66 (DET) Redford Township, MI St. Hilary.
Nozorro, Alfonse *l.c.* (DET)[T] Clarkston, MI The Legion of Christ, Inc..
Nsionu, Patrick N. '85 (NY) Staten Island, NY Holy Family.
Ntaiyia, Symon Peter (ROC) Owego, NY Blessed Trinity; Owego, NY St. Patrick.
Nthawie, Joachim *s.j.* '98 (BAL)[S] Baltimore, MD Ferdinand Wheeler Jesuit Community.
Ntsele, Thulani *o.s.m.* '99 (CHI)[N] Chicago Order of Friar Servants of Mary (Servites) United States of America Province, Inc..
Ntsiful–Amissah, Dominick (ALB).
Ntsiful–Amissah, Kofi '79 (ALB) Special Assignment; Black Apostolate.
Nuagbaraocha, John *d.s.* '80 (BUR) Burlington, VT Fletcher Allen Health Care.
Nuanez, Anthony '79 (LA) On Sick Leave.
Nuelle, John R. *m.s.* '64 (HRT)[M] Hartford, CT North American La Salette Mission Center; [V] Hartford, CT North American La Salette Mission Center, Inc..
Nugent, Anthony A. '72 (JOL) Plainfield, IL St. Mary Immaculate.
Nugent, Arthur W. '47 (PH) Retired.
Nugent, Irvine '54 (PMB) Vero Beach, FL St. Helen.
Nugent, Irvine '97 (PMB) West Palm Beach, FL Holy Name of Jesus; Presbyteral Council.
Nugent, James B. '56 (STU) Retired.
Nugent, James J. *c.ss.r.* '50 (STL)[O] Liguori, MO St. Clement Health Care Center.
Nugent, John G. *c.m.* '49 (MET)[H] Princeton, NJ Vincentian Residence.
Nugent, Joseph A. '71 (BRK) Brooklyn, NY Our Lady of the Presentation.
Nugent, Kevin *s.t.* '51 (FgM).
Nugent, Michael A. '43 (COL) Retired.
Nugent, Peter '62 (LA) Chatsworth, CA St. John Eudes.
Nugent, Raymond H. '58 (RVC) Retired.
Nugent, Richard T. '49 (BUF) Orchard Park, NY St. Bernadette.
Nugent, Robert '65 (ALB) South Glens Falls, NY St. Michael the Archangel.
Nugent, Robert *s.d.s.* '65 (WDC)[B] Silver Spring, MD Salvatorian Community.
Nunan, Jeremiah '63 (ALB) Cairo, NY Sacred Heart; Deans.
Nunes, James *m.s.* (BRK) Richmond Hill, NY Our Lady of the Cenacle; Jamaica Hospital – Trump Pavilion.
Nunes, James (RVC) Williston Park, NY St. Aidan's Church.
Nunes, Mario '61 (NEW) Newark, NJ Our Lady of Fatima.
Nunez, Albert G. '64 (LAF) Washington, LA Immaculate Conception; Catholic Charismatic Renewal.
Nunez, Albert Gayle (LAF) Washington, LA Holy Trinity.
Nunez, Baltazar '88 (CGS) Aguas Buenas, PR Espiritu Santo.
Nunez, Edward H. '76 (PBL) Grand Junction, CO St. Joseph.
Nunez, Felix '99 (CGS)[F] Caguas, PR Diocesan Tribunal of Caguas; [F] Naranjito, PR Seminario Pablo VI – Propedeutico; Diocesan Tribunal of Caguas; Priests Senate.
Nunez, Francisco *s.t.* '00 (TUC) Tucson, AZ Blessed Kateri Tekakwitha; [I] South Tucson, AZ Blessed Kateri Tekakwitha Parish Center.
Nunez, Pedro (NO) New Orleans, LA St. Raphael the Archangel; Mensaje, Inc..
Nunez, Philip '88 (ORL) Orlando, FL St. James Cathedral.
Nunez, Philip '88 (ARE) On Duty Outside the Diocese.
Nunez, Reynaldo '69 (MET) Piscataway, NJ St. Frances Cabrini.
Nunez Carrion, Felipe (SJN) San Juan, PR San Francisco Javier.
Nunning, David H. '69 (EVN) Evansville, IN St. Agnes.
Nunning, David '69 (EVN) Evansville, IN Sacred Heart; Diocesan Consultors; Deans.
Nuno, Rafael '69 (ARE) Utuado, PR San Pedro y San Pablo.
Nurre, Henry V. *o.s.b.* '56 (MIL)[O] Benet Lake, WI St. Benedict's Abbey.
Nusbaum, Daniel C. '61 (ALB) On Duty Outside the Diocese Retired.
Nuss, David W. '93 (TOL) Toledo, OH Historic Church of St. Patrick; Office of Vocations.
Nuss, Francis B. '61 (RVC) Dix Hills, NY St. Matthew; Sayville, NY Good Samaritan Nursing Home..
Nutt, Maurice J. *c.ss.r.* '89 (CHI)[N] Chicago, IL Redemptorist Theology Residence.
Nuttall, J. *o.p.* '69 (FgM).
Nutter, N. John '89 (BR) Amite, LA St. Helena; Propagation of the Faith and Association of Holy Childhood.
Nuttman, Joseph *c.ss.r.* '52 (SEA) Seattle, WA Sacred Heart of Jesus; [L] Seattle, WA The Redemptionist Society of Washington.
Nuwer, Herold M. '61 (BUF) Ransomville, NY Immaculate Conception.
Nuyen, Te Van '86 (SFR) San Francisco, CA Holy Name of Jesus.
Nuytten, Ralph *c.i.c.m.* '49 (SAT)[M] San Antonio, TX.
Nuzzi, Ronald '84 (Y) On Duty Outside the Diocese.
Nwabichie, Remigius '89 (BAK) La Pine, OR Holy Redeemer.
Nwabugwu, Edwin (KCK) St. Columbkille; St. Joseph's; Onaga, KS St. Vincent de Paul.
Nwabugwu, Jude '84 (MIA) Miami, FL St. James.
Nwachukwu, Anthony '87 (NY) New York, NY Sacred Hearts of Jesus and Mary.
Nwachukwu, Peter C. '84 (TUC) Casa Grande, AZ St. Anthony of Padua.
Nwachukwu, Thomas Kizito '82 (CC) On Special Assignment.
Nwachunkwu, Simon (BRK)[D] College Point, NY St. Fidelis.
Nwamadi, Chima '82 (MEM) Germantown, TN Our Lady Of Perpetual Help.
Nwankwar, Ruben (GAL) Houston, TX St. Charles Borromeo.
Nwanze, John *o.p.* '75 (SEA) Burlington, WA St. Charles; LaConner, WA Sacred Heart; Mount Vernon, WA Immaculate Conception; Sedro Woolley, WA Immaculate Heart of Mary.
Nwaogu, Sylvester N. '64 (TUC) Tombstone, AZ Sacred Heart.
Nwaorgu, Anselm I. '92 (NEW) Newark, NJ Blessed Sacrament/St. Charles Borromeo.
Nwaorgu, Anselm '92 (NEW) Nigerian IGBO Catholic Community.
Nwaozor, Finnian '91 (LIN) Beatrice, NE St. Joseph's.
Nwaru, Romanus N. '95 (MIL) Milwaukee, WI St. Catherine.
Nwauzor, Reginald U. '80 (LAV) Las Vegas, NV Holy Family.
Nwobi, Paul (RVC) West Islip, NY Good Samaritan Hospital Medical Center.
Nwoga, Laserian '95 (CAM) On Duty Outside the Diocese.
Nwohu, Ambrose '66 (LA) Los Angeles, CA St. Mary Magdalen.
Nwohw, Ambrose '66 (PEO) Rock Island, IL St. Pius X.
Nwokoye, Patrick I. '02 (SPC) Springfield, MO St. Elizabeth Ann Seton.
Nwosu, Malachy '93 (ROC) Weedsport, NY St. Patrick; Port Byron, NY St. John; Weedsport, NY St. Joseph.
Nyaga, John Peter *i.m.c.* '89 (MET) Bound Brook, NJ St. Joseph.
Nyagasaza, Bideri *s.x.* (CHI) Chicago, IL St. Anthony.
Nyakatura, Matthias (BEL) O'Fallon, IL Corpus Christi.
Nyambo, Callist N. '69 (SP) Clearwater, FL All Saints.
Nyardy, Jeffrey S. *o.s.b.* '90 (SAV)[B] Savannah, GA Benedictine Military School; [F] Savannah, GA The Benedictine Priory.
Nycz, Matt F. '94 (BUF) West Seneca, NY Queen of Heaven.

Nydegger, Thomas P. '92 (NEW)[B] Catholic Relief Services; Serra Clubs.
Nydegger, Thomas (NEW) Natural Family Planning.
Nyein, Isidore Usit *s.o.l.t.* '73 (CC) Robstown, TX St. Anthony; [G] Robstown, TX Society of Our Lady of the Most Holy Trinity.
Nygren, David *c.m.* '77 (CHI)[N] Chicago, IL Vincentian Community, Congregation of the Mission, Midwest Province.
Nyhan, W. James '74 (BO) Billerica, MA St. Mary.
Nyl, Steve J. *c.ss.r.* '01 (DEN) Denver, CO St. Joseph.
Nyl, Steven *c.ss.r.* (DEN)[N] Denver, CO The Redemptorists of Denver, Colorado.
Nyman, Vincent '99 (STL) Florissant, MO St. Angela Merici.
Nyong, Emmanuel '88 (ROC) Rochester, NY Church of the Annunciation.
Nyquist, Raymond J. '54 (GF) Black Eagle, MT Most Blessed Sacrament.
Nys, Loren *s.d.s.* '67 (GB) Kiel, WI SS. Peter and Paul.

O

O'Bell, John C. '91 (SCR) Jackson, PA St. Martin of Tours.
O'Blaney, James *c.ss.r.* '58 (HBG) Lititz, PA St. James; [H] Ephrata, PA St. Clement's Mission House.
O'Boyle, Leo *c.p.* (RVC)[O] Shelter Island Heights, NY St. Gabriel's Spiritual Center for Youth.
O'Brien, Anthony '88 (MIA) Fort Lauderdale, FL St. Helen.
O'Brien, Arthur '83 (HON) Leave of Absence Retired.
O'Brien, Bartholomew J. '65 (PH) Philadelphia, PA Immaculate Heart of Mary.
O'Brien, Charles H. *o.p.* '54 (L) Louisville, KY St. Louis Bertrand.
O'Brien, Christian T. *o.praem.* '62 (SFE) St. Joseph Medical Center; [I] Albuquerque, NM Santa Maria de la Vid Priory.
O'Brien, Christopher '54 (EVN) Retired.
O'Brien, Cornelius '55 (ARL) Falls Church, VA St. James.
O'Brien, Daniel A. *s.j.* '93 (NEW)[N] Jersey City, NJ Jesuit Community of St. Peter's Prep, Inc..
O'Brien, Daniel J. *s.j.* '59 (NY)[EE] Cardinal Spellman Hall, Jesuit Community.
O'Brien, Daniel P. '85 (HBG) New Oxford, PA Immaculate Conception of the Blessed Virgin Mary.
O'Brien, Daniel '75 (VIC)[K] San Antonio, TX Padua Place.
O'Brien, David G. '62 (BRK) On Leave/Unassigned.
O'Brien, David W. *c.s.p.* '56 (COL)[J] Columbus, OH Campus Ministry.
O'Brien, Denis J. '44 (RVC) Retired.
O'Brien, Dennis J. '77 (WOR) Shrewsbury, MA St. Mary's.
O'Brien, Dennis '81 (PT) Quincy, FL St. Thomas the Apostle; Vicars Forane; Hispanic Ministry, Office of; Orders & Ministries, Commission for; Clergy Concerns; Seminarian Candidate Review Board.
O'Brien, Donald J. '61 (GI) Cozad, NE Christ the King.
O'Brien, Donald J. '93 (TR)[M] Trenton, NJ Villa Vianney Retired.
O'Brien, Donald V. *s.j.* '55 (NY) White Plains, NY St. John the Evangelist.
O'Brien, Donald *s.j.* '55 (NY)[EE] Loyola Hall, Jesuit Community.
O'Brien, Donald *o.m.i.* '65 (BO)[Y] Tewksbury, MA Immaculate Heart of Mary Infirmary.
O'Brien, Donald (GI).
O'Brien, Edmund M. '57 (HRT) Enfield, CT St. Adalbert's.
O'Brien, Edward C. *s.j.* '61 (STL)[O] St. Louis, MO Jesuit Community Corporation at St. Louis University – Jesuit Hall; [O] St. Louis, MO Office; [S] St. Louis, MO Retreat House.
O'Brien, Elias *o.carm.* '85 (PBR) Aliquippa, PA St. George the Great Martyr.
O'Brien, Eugene J. *s.j.* '56 (NY)[EE] New York, NY "America;" Residence and publication office of the America Press.
O'Brien, Francis E. '66 (BO) Framingham, MA St. George.
O'Brien, Francis P. '85 (BO) Marlborough, MA St. Matthias.
O'Brien, Frederick J. *s.j.* '62 (NY)[EE] New York, NY "America;" Residence and publication office of the America Press.
O'Brien, Frederick W. '50 (BO) Senior Priests Retired.
O'Brien, George L. '58 (WOR) East Templeton, MA Holy Cross; Templeton Developmental Center; Diocesan College of Consultors; Presbyteral Council.
O'Brien, George '57 (LA) Beverly Hills, CA Good Shepherd.
O'Brien, George (WOR) Deans.
O'Brien, Gerard C. *s.j.* '59 (BO)[V] Newton, MA The Jesuit Community at Boston College.
O'Brien, Gerard '95 (LA) Lomita, CA St. Margaret Mary Alacoque.
O'Brien, J. Paul *s.j.* '68 (IND)[D] Indianapolis, IN.
O'Brien, James A. *s.j.* '60 (WH)[A] Wheeling, WV Wheeling Jesuit University.
O'Brien, James C. *s.j.* '61 (BO)[V] Newton, MA The Jesuit Community at Boston College.
O'Brien, James E. '60 (Y) Retired.
O'Brien, James F. *s.j.* '67 (NY)[II] New York, NY Xavier Society for the Blind.
O'Brien, James F. *s.j.* '75 (NY)[EE] New York, NY Xavier Jesuit Community.
O'Brien, James J. '60 (CHI) Chicago, IL St. Eugene.
O'Brien, James M. *m.m.* '49 (NY).
O'Brien, James R. '66 (HBG)[EE] Chambersburg, PA Corpus Christi.
O'Brien, James T. '70 (SY) Syracuse, NY Blessed Sacrament.
O'Brien, James *s.s.c.* '56 (BO)[V] Quincy, MA; [K] St. Columbans St. Columban's Foreign Mission Society.
O'Brien, James (HBG)[J] Chambersburg, PA Wilson College Chambersburg.
O'Brien, John E. '46 (NEW) Livingston, NJ St. Raphael Retired.
O'Brien, John E. '50 (CHI) Retired.
O'Brien, John E. '87 (BAL) Special Assignment.
O'Brien, John F. '61 (PH) Philadelphia, PA St. Raymond of Penafort.
O'Brien, John H. '62 (BRK) Richmond Hill, NY St. Benedict Joseph Labre.
O'Brien, John J. '42 (SCR)[N] Dunmore, PA Villa St. Joseph Retired.
O'Brien, John J. *m.m.* '52 (NY).
O'Brien, John J. (RNO)[EE] On Special Assignment.
O'Brien, John M. *s.d.b.* '62 (SFR) San Francisco, CA Corpus Christi.
O'Brien, John M. *o.c.s.o.* '81 (ATL)[K] Conyers, GA The Monastery of the Holy Spirit.
O'Brien, John P. '49 (SPK) Retired.
O'Brien, John P. '90 (NY) Scarsdale, NY St. Pius X.
O'Brien, John R. *c.p.m.* '52 (OWN).
O'Brien, John T. '45 (BLX) Bay St. Louis, MS Our Lady of the Gulf Retired.
O'Brien, John W. '67 (BO) Quincy, MA Sacred Heart.
O'Brien, John W. '82 (PRO) Pawtucket, RI St. Anthony; [U] Pawtucket, RI Charismatic Renewal.
O'Brien, John '34 (IND) Liberty, IN St. Bridget.
O'Brien, John '45 (BLX) Retired.
O'Brien, John '55 (GB) Retired.
O'Brien, John '69 (SAV) Valdosta, GA St. John the Evangelist; Valdosta–Brunswick Deanery; Director of Vocations.
O'Brien, John *c.p.* '69 (WOR)[O] Shrewsbury, MA Calvary Retreat Center, Passionist Fathers of Shrewsbury, Inc..
O'Brien, John '75 (PIT) Retired.
O'Brien, John '87 (BAL) Absent on Leave.
O'Brien, John '96 (ALX) Winnfield, LA Our Lady of Lourdes.
O'Brien, John (BRK) Presbyteral Council; Diocesan Consultors
O'Brien, Jon J. *s.j.* '63 (WDC)[C] Catholic University of America, The; [M] Washington, DC The Jesuit Community at Georgetown University.
O'Brien, Joseph E. '51 (PH) Philadelphia, PA St. Leo Retired.
O'Brien, Joseph J. '60 (CHI) Retired.
O'Brien, Joseph L. '55 (TOL) Retired.
O'Brien, Joseph V. '57 (DUB) Retired.
O'Brien, Joseph *o.m.i.* '54 (SAT)[K] San Antonio, TX Oblate Madonna Residence.
O'Brien, Joseph *o.carm.* '63 (NEW) Cresskill, NJ St. Therese of Lisieux.
O'Brien, Joseph *o.p.* '78 (LAV)[F] Henderson, NV Saint Therese Center.
O'Brien, Joseph '91 (ALB) East Greenbush, NY Holy Spirit; Lake George, NY Sacred Heart.
O'Brien, Joseph (BO) Roxbury, MA New England Baptist Hospital.
O'Brien, Joseph (ALB) Advocates.
O'Brien, Kevin J. '79 (RIC) Virginia Beach VA Star of the Sea; Judges.
O'Brien, Kevin J. '81 (OG) Brownville, NY Immaculate Conception of the B.V.M.; Watertown, NY Watertown Correctional Facility; Diocesan Consultors; Priest Personnel Board.
O'Brien, Kevin '54 (DET) Retired.
O'Brien, Kevin '73 (NY)[A] Yonkers, NY St. Joseph's Seminary.
O'Brien, Leo P. '56 (ALB) Albany, NY St. Vincent de Paul; Special Assignment; Vicar General; Presbyteral Council.
O'Brien, Martin F. '52 (NEW) Retired.
O'Brien, Maurice '68 (SAC) Dixon, CA St. Peter.
O'Brien, Michael G. *c.s.c.* '42 (FTW)[I] Notre Dame, IN Holy Cross House.
O'Brien, Michael J. '00 (DEN) Aspen, CO St. Mary.
O'Brien, Michael J. (NEW) Retired.
O'Brien, Michael *m.s.c.* '69 (SAT)[B] San Antonio, TX Missionaries of the Sacred Heart Formation House.
O'Brien, Michael '72 (JKS) Jackson, MS St. Richard; Institute for the Blind, Institute for the Deaf and Speech Impaired; Madison, MS Holy Family.
O'Brien, Michael '79 (SP) Seminole, FL St. Justin Martyr.
O'Brien, Michael (JKS) Approved Advocate and Auditors; Personnel Board.
O'Brien, Nicholas J. '83 (ORL) Leesburg, FL St. Paul's.
O'Brien, Nicholas (ORL) Members.
O'Brien, Patrick J. '56 (LA) Ventura, CA San Buenaventura Mission; Deanery 3.
O'Brien, Patrick '46 (SEA) Retired.
O'Brien, Patrick *c.ss.r.* '64 (CHI)[N] Glenview, IL The Redemptorists of Glenview, Illinois; [N] Redemptorist Denver Province Foreign Mission Office.
O'Brien, Patrick *c.ss.r.* '64 (TUC)[I] Tucson, AZ Redemptorist Community Support Charity Trust; [I] Tucson, AZ Retorno (Marriage Retorno); (FgM).
O'Brien, Patrick '64 (PIT)[B] Pittsburgh, PA La Roche College.
O'Brien, Patrick *c.ss.r.* '64 (TUC)[I] Tucson, AZ Redemptorist Community Support Charity Trust; [I] Tucson, AZ Retorno (Marriage Retorno); (FgM).
O'Brien, Patrick *c.ss.r.* '64 (CHI)[N] Glenview, IL The Redemptorists of Glenview, Illinois; [N] Redemptorist Denver Province Foreign Mission Office.
O'Brien, Patrick '69 (SAV) Savannah, GA St. Peter the Apostle Church.
O'Brien, Patrick '74 (HT) Houma, LA St. Bernadette.
O'Brien, Patrick (HT) Priests Council; Terrebonne Deanery; Diocesan Finance Council.
O'Brien, Patrick (LA) Members.
O'Brien, Paul B. '91 (BO) Lawrence, MA St. Patrick.
O'Brien, Peter F. *s.j.* '71 (NEW)[C] Jersey City, NJ St. Peter's Preparatory School; [N] Jersey City, NJ Jesuit Community of St. Peter's Prep, Inc..
O'Brien, Peter *s.j.* '71 (NEW) Jersey City, NJ Parish of the Resurrection.
O'Brien, Raymond C. '75 (WDC) Special Ministries; [C] Catholic University of America, The.
O'Brien, Richard *c.m.* '61 (KC)[J] Kansas City, MO Vincentian Parish Mission Center.
O'Brien, Richard (BO)[P] Methuen, MA Holy Family Hospital and Medical Center.
O'Brien, Robert E. *s.j.* '54 (NY)[EE] New York, NY St. Ignatius Loyola Residence.
O'Brien, Roger '61 (SEA) Retired.
O'Brien, Scott *o.p.* '92 (MIA) Miami, FL St. Dominic; [B] Miami, FL Barry University; [H] Miami, FL Dominican Fathers of Miami, Inc.; Barry University.
O'Brien, Sean Patrick '93 (SY) Pulaski, NY St. Frances Xavier Cabrini; Navy Reserve Chaplains.
O'Brien, Sean '93 (SY) Pulaski, NY Christ Our Light.
O'Brien, Sean *o.f.m.* (ALB)[B] Siena College.
O'Brien, Steven G. '86 (DUB)[D] Cedar Rapids, IA Xavier High School; Cedar Rapids, IA St. Matthew; Belle Plaine, IA St. Joseph; Belle Plaine, IA St. Michael.
O'Brien, Thomas F. '55 (OM) Omaha, NE St. Vincent de Paul.
O'Brien, Thomas F. '56 (WOR) Retired.
O'Brien, Thomas J. *m.m.* '74 (FgM).
O'Brien, Thomas M. '52 (BRK) Jamaica, NY St. Nicholas of Tolentine.
O'Brien, Thomas '52 (BRK) Retired.
O'Brien, Thomas '55 (OM) Retired.
O'Brien, Timothy A. '94 (HRT) New Hartford, CT Immaculate Conception; Auditors (Part–time Case Instructors).
O'Brien, Timothy J. '69 (MIL) Special Assignment.
O'Brien, Vincent J. *s.j.* (WDC) Bethesda, MD National Institutes of Health, Clinical Center.
O'Brien, Vincent M. *s.j.* '55 (WDC)[E] North Bethesda, MD Georgetown Preparatory School.
O'Brien, Walter *o.f.m.cap.* '37 (NOR) Middletown, CT St. Pius X Retired.
O'Brien, William D. '50 (DUB) Retired.
O'Brien, William G. '51 (WOR) Retired.
O'Brien, William J. *c.m.* '67 (BAL) Emmitsburg, MD St. Joseph.
O'Brien, William J. *c.m.* '67 (BAL)[S] Emmitsburg, MD Vincentian House.
O'Brien, William J. '73 (CHI) Chicago, IL Queen of Angels.
O'Brien, William J. '78 (BAL) Havre de Grace, MD St. Patrick's.
O'Brien, William J. '80 (E) Titusville, PA St. Walburga.
O'Brien, William P. *s.j.* '61 (CHI)[N] Berkeley, CA Jesuit Community at Jesuit School of Theology at Berkeley.
O'Brien, William P. *s.j.* '02 (OAK)[N] Chicago Chicago Province of the Society of Jesus–Provincial Office.
O'Brien, William '51 (NY) Retired.
O'Brien, William '61 (NEW) Rochelle Park, NJ Sacred Heart.
O'Brien, William '69 (RIC) Staunton, VA St. Francis of Assisi Retired.
O'Brien, William '88 (VNN) Spokane, WA SS. Cyril & Methodius.
O'Brien, William (GB) Two Rivers, WI St. Peter the Fisherman.
O'Brien, William (NY) Absent on Sick leave.
O'Bryan, J. A. '35 (L) Retired.
O'Bryan, James *s.t.* (BLX) Pearlington, MS St. Joseph.
O'Byrne, John '61 (LA) Torrance, CA St. Catherine Laboure.
O'Byrne, Patrick J. '60 (LIN) Plattsmouth, NE Church

of the Holy Spirit.
O'Byrne, Sylvester '51 (LA) Santa Barbara, CA Our Lady of Mount Carmel.
O'Callaghan, Dominic *o.c.d.* '44 (SB)[E] Redlands, CA Discalced Carmelites, OCD; [G] Redlands, CA El Carmelo Retreat House.
O'Callaghan, Eugene '55 (SAT) New Braunfels, TX SS. Peter and Paul.
O'Callaghan, James A. '43 (LA) Retired.
O'Callaghan, John J. *s.j.* '62 (CHI)[C] Chicago, IL Jesuit Community at Loyola University Chicago.
O'Callaghan, Matthias J. '62 (SAC) Willows, CA St. Monica.
O'Callaghan, Patrick '55 (SAT) Retired.
O'Callaghan, Peter '52 (SAT) Retired.
O'Callaghan, Thomas '54 (SEA) Retired.
O'Callaghan, Tiernan *o.carm.* '56 (PHX)[G] Phoenix, AZ Carmelite Community Retired.
O'Carroll, Donal A. '56 (STU) Retired.
O'Carroll, Donal (STU) Diocesan Director of Ecumenism.
O'Carroll, Eugene '62 (PHX) Phoenix, AZ St. Paul.
O'Carroll, Fergus *l.c.* '78 (MAD)[G] Edgerton, WI Koshkonong Pastoral Center; [K] Edgerton, WI Oaklawn Incorporated.
O'Carroll, Patrick J. '54 (ORL) Barefoot Bay, FL St. Luke.
O'Cinnsealaigh, Benedict *s.t.l.* '93 (CIN) Cincinnati, OH St. Veronica; [B] Cincinnati, OH Mt. St. Mary's Seminary of the West.
O'Connell, Anthony M. *o.s.m.* '67 (CHI) Chicago, IL Assumption of the Blessed Virgin Mary; [N] Chicago, IL Assumption Priory; [N] Chicago, IL Order of Friar Servants of Mary (Servites) United States of America Province, Inc..
O'Connell, Cuthbert '86 (BLX) Bassfield, MS St. Peter; Priests' Continuing Education and Retreat Programs; Presbyteral Council.
O'Connell, Damian *s.j.* '75 (NY)[HH] New York, NY Fordham University at Lincoln Center.
O'Connell, Daniel C. *s.j.* '58 (STL)[O] St. Louis, MO Hallahan House.
O'Connell, Daniel C. '83 (BO) Newton, MA St. Bernard.
O'Connell, Daniel P. '71 (SAV) Catholic Cemetery; College of Consultors.
O'Connell, Daniel '71 (SAV) Douglas, GA St. Paul's.
O'Connell, David M. *c.m.* '75 (PH).
O'Connell, David M. *c.m.* '82 (WDC)[C] Washington, DC Catholic University of America, The.
O'Connell, David '79 (LA) Los Angeles, CA St. Frances Xavier Cabrini.
O'Connell, David (LA) Los Angeles, CA St. Michael; Our Lady of the Angels Region.
O'Connell, Edward P. *s.j.* '56 (WDC) Port Tobacco, MD St. Ignatius.
O'Connell, George M. *o.s.m.* '37 (CHI)[N] Chicago Order of Friar Servants of Mary (Servites) United States of America Province, Inc..
O'Connell, James P. '53 (STL) Retired.
O'Connell, James R. *o.f.m.* '83 (NY) New York, NY St. Francis of Assisi.
O'Connell, James *o.f.m.* (NY) Manhattan, NY St. Vincent Hospital.
O'Connell, John B. '40 (HRT) Retired.
O'Connell, John Q. *c.m.* '53 (DEN)[S] Denver, CO Kateri Catholic Indian Community of Colorado.
O'Connell, John R. '73 (NEW) Midland Park, NJ Nativity; Northwest Bergen Region Deanery 1.
O'Connell, Joseph A. '51 (SFR) Retired.
O'Connell, Joseph F. '64 (CAM) Retired.
O'Connell, Joseph F. *s.j.* '73 (WDC)[M] Washington, DC The Jesuit Community at Georgetown University; [V] Washington, DC Jesuit Secondary Education Association.
O'Connell, Joseph *s.o.l.t.* '91 (CC)[G] Robstown, TX Society of Our Lady of the Most Holy Trinity.
O'Connell, Mark A. '79 (NEW) Belleville, NJ St. Peter's.
O'Connell, Mark '90 (BO)[EE] Assistant to the Moderator of the Curia for Canonical Affairs; Members; Adjutant Judicial Vicars; Canonical Affairs Committee.
O'Connell, Marvin R. '56 (FTW)[B] University of Notre Dame Du Lac.
O'Connell, Marvin R. '56 (STP) On Duty Outside the Archdiocese Retired.
O'Connell, Maurice V. '72 (WDC) Ridge, MD St. Michael.
O'Connell, Michael W. '83 (CHI) Orland Park, IL Our Lady of the Woods.
O'Connell, Michael '67 (STP) Minneapolis, MN The Basilica of St. Mary Co–Cathedral; Minneapolis, MN Ascension.
O'Connell, Neil J. *o.f.m.* '64 (NY) New York, NY All Saints.
O'Connell, Neil *o.f.m.* '64 (NY)[EE] New York, NY All Saints; [HH] Bronx, NY Herbert H. Lehman College; [EE] New York, NY All Saints Friary.
O'Connell, Paul T. '60 (WOR) Shrewsbury, MA St. Mary's; Associate Judicial Vicar; Judges.
O'Connell, Paul '03 (SAV) Warner Robins, GA Sacred Heart.
O'Connell, Richard C. '51 (ROC) Retired.
O'Connell, Richard '51 (ROC) Rochester, NY Roman Catholic Community of the 19th Ward.
O'Connell, Robert E. '71 (SUP) Hurley, WI St. Mary of the Seven Dolors; Hurley, WI Sacred Heart of Jesus; Hurley, WI Holy Redeemer; Hurley, WI St. Ann's; North Central Deanery.
O'Connell, Robert J. *s.s.j.* '41 (BAL)[S] Baltimore, MD St. Joseph's Manor.
O'Connell, Robert J. '70 (RVC) Patchogue, NY Our Lady of Mt. Carmel.
O'Connell, Terrence *o.m.i.* '78 (BUF) Buffalo, NY Holy Angels.
O'Connell, Terry J. '92 (P) McMinnville, OR St. James; Navy Reserve Chaplains.
O'Connell, Terry '92 (P) Grand Ronde, OR St. Michael; Sheridan, OR Good Shepherd; Area Vicars.
O'Connell, Thomas P. '63 (PBR) Seymour, TN Holy Resurrection Mission.
O'Connell, Thomas P. '63 (KNX) Seymour, TN Holy Family.
O'Connell, Timothy '63 (LA) Los Angeles, CA Visitation.
O'Connell, Timothy (LA) Commission for Catholic Life Issues.
O'Connell, Vincent *c.s.sp.* (BRK) Rockaway Point, NY St. Thomas More–St. Edmund.
O'Connell, Walter T. *o.p.* '58 (CHI)[N] St. Pius V Priory.
O'Connell, William A. '55 (SFR) Retired.
O'Connell, William *s.m.* '56 (HON)[G] Honolulu, HI Marianist Hall Community; Defender of the Bond.
O'Connell, William '57 (RC)[B] Piedmont, SD Casa Maria Residence for Retired Priests Retired.
O' Connell, William '66 (VEN) Retired.
O'Conner, Robert (PEO) Aledo, IL St. Catherine's Church.
O'Connor, Adrian J. *o.praem.* '95 (ORG)[D] Silverado, CA St. Michael's Preparatory School.
O'Connor, Albert G. '67 (SAC) Elk Grove, CA St. Joseph.
O'Connor, Albert (SAC) Vicars Forane.
O'Connor, Andrew M. '95 (NY) New York, NY Holy Trinity.
O'Connor, Bernard F. *o.s.f.s.* '73 (ALN)[B] Center Valley, PA DeSales University; [B] Center Valley, PA DeSales University; [K] Center Valley, PA Oblates of St. Francis de Sales.
O'Connor, Bernard *c.m.f* '50 (LA)[Q] Los Angeles, CA Claretian Retreat Center Community.
O'Connor, Charles J. *c.m.* '34 (PH)[AA] St. Catherine Infirmary.
O'Connor, Charles J. *o.f.m.* '73 (PRO)[N] Providence, RI St. Francis Chapel & City Ministry Center; [P] Providence, RI St. Francis Friary.
O'Connor, Charles T. '83 (MET) Bound Brook, NJ St. Joseph; College of Consultors.
O'Connor, Christopher K. '98 (BO) Priests Pursuing Higher Studies; Bethesda, MD St. Jane Frances de Chantal.
O'Connor, Christopher '99 (BRK) Richmond Hill, NY St. Benedict Joseph Labre.
O'Connor, Daniel P. (ALX) Advocates; College of Consultors; Priests Council; Rural Deans; Alexandria, LA Our Lady of Prompt Succor.
O'Connor, Daniel '60 (ATL) Retired.
O'Connor, David F. *s.t.* (WDC) Promoter of Justice; Defenders of the Bond.
O'Connor, David F. *s.t.* (MO) Defenders of the Bond.
O'Connor, David H. '86 (DUB) Cedar Rapids, IA All Saints; Deanery Representatives.
O'Connor, David *s.t.* '55 (WDC)[M] University Park, MD Holy Trinity Missionary Cenacle.
O'Connor, David '64 (JKS) Continuing Formation Committee; Natchez, MS Assumption of the B.V.M.; Natchez, MS St. Mary Basilica.
O'Connor, Dennis '98 (SD) Santa Ysabel, CA Santa Ysabel Indian Mission.
O'Connor, Desmond *s.p.s.* '50 (PAT) Mount Arlington, NJ Our Lady of the Lake.
O'Connor, Desmond '80 (NY) New York, NY St. John the Martyr.
O'Connor, Desmond (NY) Canon 1742 Panel of Pastors; Pastoral Life Conference; Personnel Board, Archdiocesan; Victim Assistance Coordinators.
O'Connor, Dominic E. '01 (SCR)[M] Shohola, PA Society of Saint John.
O'Connor, Donald *s.v.d.* '59 (SB)[A] Riverside, CA Society of the Divine Word Missionaries.
O'Connor, Edward D. *c.s.c.* '48 (FTW)[B] University of Notre Dame Du Lac; [I] Notre Dame, IN Holy Cross Community, Corby Hall, University of Notre Dame.
O'Connor, Edward J. '39 (CAM) Retired.
O'Connor, Edward J. '81 (ALN) Pottsville, PA St. Patrick; Vicars Forane.
O'Connor, Edward T. '44 (BRK) Brooklyn, NY Immaculate Heart of Mary Retired.
O'Connor, Edward '60 (ATL) Thomson, GA Queen of Angels.
O'Connor, Eugene '54 (BIR) Birmingham, AL St. Barnabas; Diocesan College of Vicars.
O'Connor, Francis J. '53 (MAN) Retired.
O'Connor, Francis M. *s.j.* '58 (BAL) Baltimore, MD St. Ignatius.
O'Connor, Frank '62 (ALB) Stottville, NY Holy Family; Stuyvesant, NY St. Mary/Nativity.
O'Connor, Fred P. '52 (GAL) Baytown, TX St. John the Evangelist; Port Bolivar, TX Our Mother of Mercy.
O'Connor, Gerald T. '66 (ROC) Bradford, NY St. Catherine of Siena; Addison, NY St. Stanislaus.
O'Connor, Gerald V. *s.j.* '76 (WDC).
O'Connor, Gerard (FR) Graduate Studies.
O'Connor, Glenn L. '80 (IND) Indianapolis, IN St. Ann; Indianapolis, IN St. Joseph; Indianapolis International Airport.
O'Connor, Hugh '39 (ORG) Anaheim, CA St. Justin Martyr; Promoters of Justice; Apostleship of Prayer; Legion of Mary Retired.
O'Connor, J. Kieran '45 (MAN) Retired.
O'Connor, J. Paul *s.j.* '53 (STL).
O'Connor, James C. '71 (BUF) Williamsville, NY SS. Peter and Paul.
O'Connor, James E. *o.c.s.o.* '57 (DUB)[K] Peosta, IA New Melleray Abbey, Order of Cistercians of the Strict Observance.
O'Connor, James E. '82 (WH) Madison, WV St. Mary, Queen of Heaven.
O'Connor, James J. '43 (FTW) Retired.
O'Connor, James J. '54 (CIN) Retired.
O'Connor, James M. '52 (LIN) Retired.
O'Connor, James R.P. '69 (AUS)[G] Austin, TX Oratory of Saint Gregory the Great.
O'Connor, James T. '54 (CHI) Retired.
O'Connor, James T. '66 (NY) Millbrook, NY St. Joseph.
O'Connor, James '70 (LUB) Lubbock, TX St. Elizabeth University Parish.
O'Connor, Jay F. '74 (BAL) Baltimore, MD St. Michael; Clergy Personnel, Division of; Office of Diaconate; Clergy Personnel, Division of.
O'Connor, Jim (AUS) Defenders of the Bond.
O'Connor, John C. '61 (LA) Lynwood, CA St. Emydius.
O'Connor, John F. '44 (PEO) Retired.
O'Connor, John F. *s.t.b.* '64 (NEW) Newark, NJ Immaculate Conception.
O'Connor, John F. '73 (R) Raleigh, NC Our Lady of Lourdes; Deans; Diocesan Consultors; Office of Liturgy.
O'Connor, John H. (PAT) Unassigned.
O'Connor, John J. '58 (DUB) New Vienna, IA St. Boniface; Dyersville, IA SS. Peter and Paul.
O'Connor, John J. '68 (DUB)[F] New Vienna, IA Archbishop Hennessy Catholic School.
O'Connor, John J. '93 (BRK) Rosedale, NY St. Clare.
O'Connor, John L. '63 (ROC) Rochester, NY Our Lady of Lourdes.
O'Connor, John M. *c.ss.r.* '65 (TR)[Q] Long Branch, NJ San Alfonso Retreat House.
O'Connor, John P. '45 (PH) Retired.
O'Connor, John Philip '61 (NEW) Garwood, NJ Church of St. Anne.
O'Connor, John T. '52 (MIL)[O] Hales Corners, WI Priests of the Sacred Heart; [B] Hales Corners, WI Sacred Heart School of Theology.
O'Connor, John *c.ss.r.* '55 (NY)[EE] New York, NY Redemptorist Priests and Brothers, C.Ss.R..
O'Connor, John (R) Absent on Leave; Priests' Council.
O'Connor, Joseph A. '47 (TR)[M] Trenton, NJ Villa Vianney; [M] Trenton, NJ St. Lawrence Rehabilitation Center Retired.
O'Connor, Joseph X. *o.s.a.* '53 (BO)[C] Our Mother of Good Counsel Monastery.
O'Connor, Kenneth '03 (KCK) Leawood, KS Cure of Ars.
O'Connor, Mark *s.a.* '84 (NY)[EE] Garrison, NY Franciscan Friars of the Atonement.
O'Connor, Matthew J. '56 (SPR) Retired.
O'Connor, Matthew '71 (MOB) Mobile, AL St. Pius X.
O'Connor, Maurice J. '53 (BO) Stoughton, MA Our Lady of the Rosary.
O'Connor, Maurice '52 (NY) Retired.
O'Connor, Michael F. '44 (STP) Miesville, MN St. Joseph Retired.
O'Connor, Michael F. '44 (NU) Retired.
O'Connor, Michael J. '34 (LA) Woodland Hills, CA St. Mel Retired.
O'Connor, Michael J. *o.s.a.* '71 (JOL)[L] New Lenox, IL Augustinian Friary; [C] New Lenox, IL Providence Catholic High School.
O'Connor, Michael J. '72 (TR) Delran, NJ Holy Name.
O'Connor, Michael '47 (FRS) Retired.
O'Connor, Michael '65 (SJ) Santa Clara, CA St. Justin.
O'Connor, Neil D. '69 (CLV) Parma, OH St. Columbkille.
O'Connor, Neil (CLV) Presbyteral Conveners.
O'Connor, Oliver '42 (NY)[EE] Yonkers, NY St. Clare Friary.
O'Connor, Patrick C. '78 (SAG) Saginaw, MI St. Stephen.
O'Connor, Patrick J. '58 (SAC) Tahoe City, CA Corpus Christi.
O'Connor, Patrick J. '64 (GBG) Uniontown, PA St. Therese, the Little Flower of Jesus; Holy Name Society.

O'Connor, Patrick *m.s.c.* '52 (CC) Bishop, TX St. James.
O'Connor, Patrick '55 (KC) Retired.
O'Connor, Patrick '85 (CLV) Administrative Leave.
O'Connor, Patrick (SAC) Vicars Forane.
O'Connor, Patrick *o.s.f.s.* (R) Shallotte, NC St. Brendan the Navigator.
O'Connor, Paul F. *c.s.b.* '70 (VNN)[A] Phoenix, AZ Congregation of Saint Basil.
O'Connor, Paul '45 (CAM) Retired.
O'Connor, Pio *o.f.m.* '94 (SFE) University Hospital.
O'Connor, Raymond E. *c.m.f.* '65 (SPC) Joplin, MO St. Peter.
O'Connor, Raymond *c.m.f.* '64 (SPC)[I] Joplin, MO Newman Club, Missouri Southern State College.
O'Connor, Robert A. '64 (NEW)[M] South Orange, NJ Prelature of the Holy Cross and Opus Dei.
O'Connor, Robert B. '56 (NY) New York, NY Blessed Sacrament.
O'Connor, Robert C. *s.j.* '64 (CIN) Cincinnati, OH St. Francis Xavier.
O'Connor, Robert D. '55 (PEO) Retired.
O'Connor, Robert F. *s.j.* '79 (OM)[K] Omaha, NE Jesuit Community at Creighton University.
O'Connor, Robert W. '48 (PEO) Lewistown, IL St. Mary's.
O'Connor, Samuel D. *o.f.m.* '56 (PAT)[M] Butler, NJ St. Anthony Friary.
O'Connor, Shaun P. *m.i.c.* '82 (SPR)[I] Association of Marian Helpers, Marian Helpers Center; [I] Eucharistic Apostles of The Divine Mercy.
O'Connor, Shawn Conrad *c.f.r.* (NY)[EE] Bronx, NY Our Lady of the Angels Friary.
O'Connor, Shawn *m.i.c.* '82 (SPR) Great Barrington, MA St. Peter's.
O'Connor, Steven J. '77 (PT) Milton, FL St. Rose of Lima; [I] Navarre, FL Casa Stella Maris; Vicars Forane.
O'Connor, Terrence P. '01 (PIT) Aliquippa, PA Our Lady of Fatima.
O'Connor, Thomas A. *s.j.* '62 (BUF)[O] Buffalo, NY Canisius Jesuit Community; [R] Buffalo, NY Campus Ministry Office.
O'Connor, Thomas J. '55 (TR) Freehold, NJ St. Robert Bellarmine.
O'Connor, Thomas J. *o.s.b.* '56 (BIR)[E] Cullman, AL St. Bernard Abbey.
O'Connor, Thomas J. '93 (BO)[V] Hingham, MA Glastonbury Abbey.
O'Connor, Thomas P. '56 (FTW) Fort Wayne, IN St. Mary.
O'Connor, Thomas V. *s.j.* '63 (NEW)[C] Jersey City, NJ St. Peter's Preparatory School; [N] Jersey City, NJ Jesuit Community of St. Peter's Prep, Inc..
O'Connor, Thomas *c.ss.r.* '50 (GR)[I] Grand Rapids, MI The Society of the Redemptorists of the City of Grand Rapids.
O'Connor, Thomas (FTW) St. Vincent de Paul Society.
O'Connor, Timothy J. '75 (CLV) Avon Lake, OH St. Joseph's.
O'Connor, Vincent '48 (SPR) Retired.
O'Connor, William B. '47 (BO) Senior Priests Retired.
O'Connor, William C. *c.s.c.* '49 (FTW) South Bend, IN Faith & Hope & Charity Chapel.
O'Connor, William D. *o.m.i.* '43 (SAT)[K] San Antonio, TX Oblate Madonna Residence.
O'Connor, William J. '58 (BO) Senior Priests Retired.
O'Connor, William J. '66 (LA) Long Beach, CA St. Joseph.
O'Connor, William '49 (SJ) Retired.
O'Connor, William *c.s.c.* '49 (FTW)[B] University of Notre Dame Du Lac; [I] Notre Dame, IN Holy Cross Community, Corby Hall, University of Notre Dame.
O'Connor, William (BO) Stoughton, MA New England Sinai Hospital.
O'Conor, Kevin *o.m.i.* '58 (P) Jordan, OR Our Lady of Lourdes; Scio, OR St. Bernard.
O'Day, Michael '38 (SB) Retired.
O'Dea, Loren F. '93 (DET) Farmington, MI Our Lady of Sorrows Retired.
O'Dea, Thomas '58 (PHX) Retired.
O'Dell, Kevin (SFS) Salem, SD St. Mary.
O'Dell, William Paul '93 (SFR) Tiburon, CA St. Hilary.
O'Doherty, Gerard *s.v.d.* '74 (LA) Los Angeles, CA Our Lady of Lourdes; [Q] Los Angeles, CA Society of the Divine Word, Western Province.
O'Doherty, John *s.s.c.* '39 (PRO)[P] Bristol, RI St. Columban's Retirement House.
O'Doherty, Jude '65 (MIA) Miami, FL Epiphany.
O'Doherty, Patrick J. '70 (ORL) Ocala, FL Queen of Peace.
O'Donnell, Brian P. *s.j.* '86 (WH)[A] Wheeling, WV Wheeling Jesuit University.
O'Donnell, Brian P. *s.j.* '86 (DET)[K] Detroit, MI Jesuit Community at the University of Detroit Mercy.
O'Donnell, David P. '95 (BO) Brockton, MA St. Colman of Cloyne; Brockton, MA Sacred Heart.
O'Donnell, Dennis J.W. '74 (PH)[CC] Malvern, PA St. Joseph's–in–the–Hills.
O'Donnell, Dennis '74 (PH) West Chester, PA SS. Simon and Jude.
O'Donnell, Edward C. '41 (OM) Retired.
O'Donnell, Edward '54 (NY) Rye, NY Resurrection; Archdiocesan Consultors.
O'Donnell, Edward *s.j.* '74 (BAL) Baltimore, MD St. Ignatius.
O'Donnell, Eugene P. '73 (SJ) Morgan Hill, CA St. Catherine of Alexandria; College of Consultors; Council of Priests; Deans.
O'Donnell, Francis P. *s.j.* '69 (CHI)[N] Chicago, IL Clark Street Jesuit Residence.
O'Donnell, Gabriel *o.p.* '70 (HRT) New Haven, CT St. Mary's Priory.
O'Donnell, Harold F. *s.j.* '64 (NY)[EE] New York, NY Xavier Jesuit Community.
O'Donnell, Harold F.X. *s.j.* (NY) Manhattan, NY Bird S. Coler Memorial Hospital and Home.
O'Donnell, Hugh A. '54 (NEW) Elizabeth, NJ St. Genevieve's.
O'Donnell, Hugh '58 (SFR) South San Francisco, CA Mater Dolorosa.
O'Donnell, James P. '56 (CLV) Cuyahoga County Detention Home; Central City Ministry with Poor.
O'Donnell, James *o.s.b.* '42 (PAT)[M] Morristown, NJ St. Mary's Abbey.
O'Donnell, James '56 (CLV) Northeast Pre Release Center.
O'Donnell, John D. '92 (CHR) Florence, SC St. Anthony's All Souls Memorial.
O'Donnell, John F. '63 (BO) Dorchester, MA St. Gregory.
O'Donnell, John F. (LR) Fort Smith, AR Immaculate Conception; Diocesan Consultors; Deans; Fort Smith, AR St. Leo's.
O'Donnell, John J. *s.j.* '74 (BAL)[S] Collegio S. Roberto Bellarmino.
O'Donnell, John '72 (DUL) Virginia, MN Sacred Heart; Virginia, MN Holy Spirit; Virginia, MN Sacred Heart.
O'Donnell, John *o.s.b.* '98 (BIR) Cullman, AL Sacred Heart; On Special or Other Diocesan Assignment; [E] Cullman, AL St. Bernard Abbey.
O'Donnell, Joseph F. *c.s.c.* '60 (PHX)[G] Phoenix, AZ Holy Cross Congregation/Casa Santa Cruz.
O'Donnell, Joseph M. *c.m.* '38 (PH)[AA] St. Catherine Infirmary.
O'Donnell, Joseph *g.h.m.* '48 (CIN)[M] Cincinnati Headquarters of Glenmary Home Missioners.
O'Donnell, Joseph '76 (CLV)[I] Cleveland OH Marymount Hospital, Inc..
O'Donnell, Mark D. '85 (NOR) Uncasville, CT St. John; College of Consultors; Members; Continuing Education and Formation Commission; Diocesan Commission for Ecumenical and Interreligious Affairs; Director for Promotion & Development; Diocesan Vocation Review Committee.
O'Donnell, Matthew (STO) San Andreas, CA St. Andrew Church of San Andreas (Pastor of); College of Consultors/Presbyteral Council; Personnel Board.
O'Donnell, Patrick *g.h.m.* '49 (CIN)[M] Cincinnati Headquarters of Glenmary Home Missioners.
O'Donnell, Paul J. '02 (PH) Newtown Square, PA St. Anastasia.
O'Donnell, Paul *m.c.c.j.* '93 (LA) Los Angeles, CA Holy Cross; Los Angeles, CA St. Cecilia.
O'Donnell, Peter C. '58 (NY) New York, NY Our Lady of Esperanza.
O'Donnell, Philip '58 (LAV) Retired.
O'Donnell, Ralph B. '97 (OM) Omaha, NE St. Bridget; Vocations.
O'Donnell, Raymond G. '72 (SD) El Cajon, CA St. Luke.
O'Donnell, Raymond (SD) Vicars Forane.
O'Donnell, Richard A. '55 (PRT) Retired.
O'Donnell, Richard J. '35 (CHI) Chicago, IL Our Lady of Good Counsel Retired.
O'Donnell, Richard *o.s.cam.* '64 (MIL)[X] Wauwatosa, WI St. Camillus Health System, Inc.; [X] St. Francis, WI St. Camillus Communities, Inc.; [X Wauwatosa, WI St. Camillus Ministries, Inc.; [O] St. Francis, WI St. Camillus Provincialate; [O] St. Francis, WI St. Camillus Formation Community; [M] Wauwatosa, WI St. Camillus Health Center, Inc.; [M] Wauwatosa, WI San Camillo, Inc..
O'Donnell, Robert A. *c.s.p.* '51 (NY) New York, NY St. Paul the Apostle; [EE] Jamaica Estates Paulist Fathers Generalate.
O'Donnell, Robert J. *c.s.p.* '74 (NY) New York, NY St. Paul the Apostle.
O'Donnell, Robert Patrick '49 (TYL) Retired.
O'Donnell, Simon *o.s.b.* '68 (LA)[Q] Valyermo, CA St. Andrew's Abbey.
O'Donnell, Terrence *s.d.b.* '70 (NY)[EE] New Rochelle, NY Salesian Provincial House.
O'Donnell, Thomas D. *s.m.* '44 (ATL)[C Atlanta, GA Marist School Retired.
O'Donnell, Thomas M. '60 (PIT) Pittsburgh, PA St. John Vianney; Judges.
O'Donnell Thomas M. '61 (HEL) East Helena, MT SS. Cyril and Methodius.
O'Donnell Thomas V. '67 (CLV) Cleveland, OH Holy Name; College of Consultors; Presbyteral Conveners.
O'Donnell Thomas (HEL) Vocations Office.
O'Donnell Timothy R. '86 (MAN) Portsmouth, NH Immaculate Conception Retired.
O'Donnell, Walter *s.t.* '55 (SAV) Blakely, GA Holy Family.
O'Donnell, William F. '62 (WDC) Washington, DC St. Thomas Apostle; Special Ministries; Silver Spring, MD The Catholic Cemeteries of the Archdiocese of Washington, Inc..
O'Donnell, William J. '52 (ALN)[J] Bethlehem, PA Holy Family Villa; [M] Northampton, PA Mary Immaculate Center Retired.
O'Donnell, William J. '56 (OAK) Berkeley, CA St. Joseph The Worker; Pastoral Leadership Placement Board (PLPB).
O'Donnell, William J. '66 (NO) Lacombe, LA Sacred Heart; Judges.
O'Donnell, William J. J. '52 (PH).
O'Donnell, William *o.m.i.* '70 (WDC)[M] Washington, DC Provincial Offices of the United States Province of the Missionary Oblates of Mary Immaculate.
O'Donnell, William *o.m.i.* '70 (BO)[V] Lowell, MA St. Eugene House (Residence).
O'Donnell, William *o.m.i.* '70 (BO)[V] Tewksbury, MA Oblate World/Missionary Association of Mary Immaculate; [V] Lowell, MA Missionary Oblates of Mary Immaculate.
O'Donnell, William *c.pp.s.* '77 (CIN) Dayton, OH Precious Blood.
O'Donoghue, Brendon W. '50 (WOR) Retired.
O'Donoghue, James P. '43 (SD) Retired.
O'Donoghue, John '64 (SAT) San Antonio, TX Blessed Sacrament; [A] San Antonio, TX Diaconate Program; Permanent Diaconate Program.
O'Donoghue, Kevin J. '58 (BRK) Brooklyn, NY St. Cecilia.
O'Donoghue, Neil X. (NEW)[A] Kearny, NJ Redemptoris Mater.
O'Donoghue, Patrick F. *m.m.* '50 (NY).
O'Donoghue, Patrick '61 (BIR)[EE] Trussville, AL Holy Infant of Prague.
O'Donohoe, James A. '47 (BO) Senior Priests; Archdiocesan Judges Retired.
O'Donohue, John M. '00 (ARL) Arlington, VA Our Lady of Lourdes; Notaries.
O'Donovan, Aidan *m.s.c.* '80 (DAL) Irving, TX St. Luke.
O'Donovan, Daniel (SB) Retired.
O'Donovan, Dennis '69 (P)[Q] Portland, OR Oregon Catholic Conference; Vicar General and Moderator of the Curia; College of Consultors; Personnel Board; Building Commission; Finance Council.
O'Donovan, Donal '50 (WH) Retired.
O'Donovan, John '55 (SP) Clearwater, FL St. Catherine of Siena.
O'Donovan, Leo J. *s.j.* '66 (NY)[EE] New York, NY "America;" Residence and publication office of the America Press.
O'Donovan, Martin E. '78 (CHI) Chicago, IL St. Christina.
O'Donovan, Patrick G. '72 (PAT) New Vernon, NJ Christ the King.
O'Donovan, Thomas P. '70 (CC) Retired.
O'Donovan, Timothy John '49 (B) Retired.
O'Dowd, Bernard J. *o.s.a.* '58 (PH)[AA] Villanova, PA St. Thomas Monastery.
O'Dowd, Francis '01 (TYL) Lindale, TX Holy Family; Tyler Catholic Committee on Scouting; Vocations; Diocesan Vocations Awareness Board.
O'Driscoll, James (BO) Medford, MA St. Clement.
O'Driscoll, John C. '87 (PH) Philadelphia, PA Christ the King.
O'Dwyer, Dominick '66 (MIA)[A] Tamarac, FL St. Malachy.
O'Dwyer, James '65 (STO) Diamond Springs, CA Retired.
O'Dwyer, Michael *s.a.c.* '61 (LUB) Lubbock, TX St. Joseph's.
O'Dwyer, Patrick '72 (LA) Whittier, CA St. Bruno.
O'Dwyer, Thomas '70 (MIA) Hollywood, FL Little Flower; Deans and Deaneries; Presbyteral Council; Archdiocesan Vocations Review Board.
O'Farrell, Donal *s.s.c.* '53 (OM)[K] St. Columbans, NE St. Columban's Foreign Mission Society.
O'Farrell, John V. '02 (RVC) East Northport, NY St. Anthony of Padua.
O'Flaherty, Edward M. *s.j.* '65 (BO)[V] Newton, MA The Jesuit Community at Boston College; Ecumenical and Interreligious Affairs; Pastoral Support for Priests; Members.
O'Flaherty, John P. '61 (STA) Retired.
O'Flaherty, Michael '75 (PMB) Boca Raton, FL St. John the Evangelist.
O'Flaherty, Thomas '48 (PT) Pensacola, FL St. Anne's.
O'Flanagan, Thomas '95 (PMB) On Duty Outside the Diocese.
O'Flannigan, Thomas L. '55 (TUC) Retired.
O'Flynn, John '61 (PBL) Retired.
O'Flynn, Seamus '59 (STA) St. Augustine, FL St. Anastasia.
O'Friel, John '45 (FRS) Retired.
O'Friel, LaSalle *o.f.m.* '54 (PAT)[M] Butler, NJ St. Anthony Friary.
O'Friel, Zachary *o.f.m.* '47 (PAT)[M] Ringwood, NJ Holy

Name Friary, Inc..
O'Gara, James R. *c.s.p.* '61 (NY)[EE] Jamaica Estates Paulist Fathers Generalate.
O'Gara, Stephen R. '71 (STP) Minneapolis, MN St. Thomas the Apostle.
O'Gorman, Charles F. '49 (LA) Oxnard, CA Santa Clara.
O'Gorman, Eamon T. '67 (ORG) Laguna Beach, CA St. Catherine of Siena.
O'Gorman, Eamon (ORG) Clergy Personnel Board.
O'Gorman, Michael B. '64 (SAT) San Antonio, TX St. Gregory's.
O'Grady, Columkille *c.p.* '71 (HRT)[M] West Hartford Holy Family Monastery/Retreat.
O'Grady, Dennis R. '61 (CLV) Cleveland, OH St. Michael the Archangel.
O'Grady, Dennis '61 (CLV) Retired.
O'Grady, Edward F. '46 (LAN) Retired.
O'Grady, Frank (PAT) Military Chaplains.
O'Grady, J. Frank (PAT) Army Chaplains.
O'Grady, James F. '53 (LA) Retired.
O'Grady, James F. '58 (LA) Los Angeles, CA Visitation.
O'Grady, James '58 (LA) Retired.
O'Grady, John F. '66 (ALB) On Duty Outside the Diocese; [B] Miami, FL Barry University.
O'Grady, Michael J. '56 (NEW) Bayonne, NJ St. Andrew's Retired.
O'Grady, Michael '58 (PHX) Phoenix, AZ SS. Simon and Jude Cathedral.
O'Grady, Peter '63 (NO) Jefferson, LA St. Agnes.
O'Grady, Robert A. '72 (HRT) Windsor Locks, CT St. Mary.
O'Grady, Robert M. '78 (BO) Watertown, MA Sacred Heart; Boston Catholic Directory.
O'Grady, Robert T. (HRT) Deans.
O'Grady, Robert '72 (HRT) Hartford, CT Hartford Correctional Institution.
O'Guinn, Jon '93 (BEL) Leave of Absence.
O'Hagan, James P. '47 (DET)[I] Waterford, MI Lourdes Nursing Home Retired.
O'Hagan, Pat J. *ss.cc.* '65 (SB) Chino Hills, CA St. Paul the Apostle.
O'Hagan, Pat *ss.cc.* '65 (SB)[E] Chino Hills, CA Congregation of the Sacred Hearts, SS.CC.; Vicars Forane.
O'Hagan, Patrick *ss.cc.* '65 (LA) Veterans Administration Medical Center.
O'Hala, Stephen '88 (MIA) On Duty Outside the Archdiocese.
O'Hala, Steven '88 (MIA)[A] Boynton Beach, FL St. Vincent de Paul Regional Seminary.
O'Hallaran, John E. *s.s.j.* '85 (NO) New Orleans, LA St. Raymond.
O'Halloran, Edward P. '78 (NY) Yonkers, NY St. Denis.
O'Halloran, Louis *o.p.* '56 (P) Portland, OR Holy Rosary Parish & Dominican Priory.
O'Halloran, Richard '51 (MRY) Retired.
O'Halloran, Richard '59 (MRY)[G] Salinas, CA Sisters of St. Joseph of Carondolet.
O'Halloran, William J. *s.j.* '58 (WOR)[O] Worcester, MA Jesuits of Holy Cross College, Inc..
O'Hanlon, James J. '57 (SY) Endicott, NY St. Ambrose Retired.
O'Hanlon, Michael A. '57 (GF) Retired.
O'Hara, Charles R. '70 (PH)[V] Downingtown, PA St. John Vianney Center.
O'Hara, Daniel J. '87 (SY) Syracuse, NY St. James; Air Force Reserve Chaplains.
O'Hara, Edward '60 (SAC) Retired.
O'Hara, Eugene P. '45 (NY)[EE] Bronx, NY.
O'Hara, Eugene R. '45 (NY) Retired.
O'Hara, Eugene *o.f.m.cap.* '61 (ROC) Trumansburg, NY St. James the Apostle; [I] Interlaken, NY St. Fidelis Friary.
O'Hara, Eugene (NY) U.S.V.A. Medical Center.
O'Hara, Francis A. '56 (BO) Senior Priests Retired.
O'Hara, Francis W. '59 (PRO) Warwick, RI St. Kevin.
O'Hara, Frank '41 (SFD) Retired.
O'Hara, James T. '66 (E) Erie, PA Holy Family/St. Ann/St. Casimir; Erie, PA St. Ann; Erie, PA St. Casimir.
O'Hara, John J. '84 (NY) Staten Island, NY St. Teresa.
O'Hara, John T. '80 (ARL) Miami, FL San Francisco de Asis, Banica; Miami, FL San Jose, Pedro Santana.
O'Hara, John T. '92 (ARL) On Duty Outside the Diocese.
O'Hara, John '41 (PRT) Bar Harbor, ME Holy Redeemer.
O'Hara, John '76 (STA) Jacksonville, FL Holy Family.
O'Hara, John '79 (PRT) Bar Harbor, ME St. Ignatius.
O'Hara, Kieran *o.carm.* '37 (JOL)[L] Darien Carmelite Provincial Office.
O'Hara, Martin '41 (SFD) Stonington, IL Holy Trinity.
O'Hara, Michael D. '60 (BUF) Franklinville, NY St. Philomena.
O'Hara, Michael *o.m.i.* '76 (NY) Metropolitan Correctional Center; [GG] Newburgh, NY Our Lady of Hope Center.
O'Hara, Thomas J. *c.s.c.* '78 (SCR)[C] Kings College; [C] Holy Cross Community.
O'Hare, Daniel G. *s.j.* '79 (NY)[EE] New York, NY St. Ignatius Loyola Residence.
O'Hare, Daniel M. '65 (NY) Maybrook, NY Assumption.
O'Hare, Dennis J. *c.s.c.* '73 (FTW)[I] Portland, OR.
O'Hare, Donald J. '54 (WCH) Retired.
O'Hare, Francis C. '51 (BO) Andover, MA St. Robert Bellarmine; Senior Priests Retired.
O'Hare, John B. '53 (PMB) Vero Beach, FL Holy Cross Retired.
O'Hare, John J. '55 (SR) Priests' Council Retired.
O'Hare, Joseph A. *s.j.* '61 (NY)[C] Bronx, NY Fordham University; [EE] New York, NY "America;" Residence and publication office of the America Press.
O'Hare, Keith M. '02 (ARL) Alexandria, VA Queen of Apostles; Auditors.
O'Hare, Robert V. *s.j.* '95 (NY)[F] New York, NY Xavier High School.
O'Hear, Daniel J. '62 (SPR) North Adams, MA St. Anthony of Padua.
O'Hearn, Michael '95 (FR) Seekonk, MA Our Lady of Mt. Carmel; West Harwich, MA Holy Trinity.
O'Hearn, Paul V. '60 (BO) Senior Priests Retired.
O'Hern, Mark '02 (E) Greenville, PA St. Michael.
O'Holohan, John T. *s.j.* '55 (CHR) Chester, SC St. Joseph's; Lancaster, SC St. Catherine's; Simpsonville, SC St. Mary Magdalene.
O'Hotto, Kenneth L. '80 (STP) West St. Paul, MN St. Michael.
O'Kane, James D. '65 (GI) Building Committee; Liturgical Commission Retired.
O'Kane, James (GI) Priests' Advisory Board (Presbyteral Council).
O'Kane, Patrick J. '77 (SC) Early, IA Sacred Heart; Schaller, IA St. Joseph's.
O'Kane, Patrick (SC) Priests' Personnel Board.
O'Keefe, Daniel Paul *o.s.b.* '93 (GBG)[H] Latrobe, PA Saint Vincent Archabbey.
O'Keefe, Daniel *o.s.b.* (GBG) Latrobe, PA Latrobe Area Hospital.
O'Keefe, Francis J. '60 (NOR) Absent on Leave.
O'Keefe, John J. '72 (NY)[E] White Plains, NY Archbishop Stepinac High School.
O'Keefe, Joseph L. (ALB) Army Chaplains.
O'Keefe, Joseph M. *s.j.* '86 (BO)[V] Newton, MA The Jesuit Community at Boston College; [C] School of Education; [C] Graduate School of Education.
O'Keefe, Kevin '95 (ARL) Burke, VA Church of the Nativity.
O'Keefe, Lawrence J. (GLP) Judicial Vicar; Judges.
O'Keefe, Lawrence '70 (GLP) Gallup, NM Cathedral of the Sacred Heart; Crownpoint, NM St. Paul; Presbyteral Council; Diocesan Consultors.
O'Keefe, Mark *o.s.b.* '83 (IND)[A] St. Meinrad, IN St. Meinrad School of Theology; [K] St. Meinrad, IN St. Meinrad Archabbey.
O'Keefe, Martin D. *s.j.* '66 (STL)[C] Saint Louis University; [O] St. Louis, MO Jesuit Community Corporation at St. Louis University – Jesuit Hall.
O'Keefe, Maurice L. '57 (NEW) Retired.
O'Keefe, Michael A. '56 (JOL) Glen Ellyn, IL St. Petronille.
O'Keefe, Michael '56 (JOL)[K] Naperville, IL St. John Vianney Villa.
O'Keefe, Michael *o.carm.* '75 (JOL) Glendale Heights, IL St. Matthew.
O'Keefe, Michael *o.carm.* (CHI)[N] Chicago, IL Brandsma House.
O'Keefe, Millard '65 (CHI) Other Assignments.
O'Keefe, Patrick T. '96 (BUF) Orchard Park, NY Our Lady of the Sacred Heart.
O'Keefe, Thomas E. '48 (NY) Retired.
O'Keefe, Vincent T. *s.j.* '50 (NY)[EE] New York, NY "America;" Residence and publication office of the America Press; [II] New York, NY John LaFarge Institute, The.
O'Keefe, William F. '60 (HRT) Enfield, CT St. Bernard's.
O'Keeffe, Dennis J. '84 (LFT) Kokomo, IN St. Joan of Arc.
O'Keeffe, L. Joseph '66 (ALB) Military Chaplains.
O'Keeffe, Michael '68 (SAV) Retired.
O'Keeffe, Michael '68 (ORL) Ocala, FL Blessed Trinity.
O'Keeffe, Patrick '59 (SB) Retired.
O'Keeffe, Richard W. '59 (TUC) Yuma, AZ Immaculate Conception; Wellton, AZ St. Joseph the Worker; Episcopal Vicar; Wellton, AZ St. Joseph the Worker; AUXILIARY CHAPLAINS CONTRACT CHAPLAINS; Episcopal Vicar.
O'Keeffe, Richard W. '59 (TUC) Special Assignment.
O'Keeffe, Richard W. '59 (TUC) Yuma, AZ Immaculate Conception; Wellton, AZ St. Joseph the Worker; Episcopal Vicar; Wellton, AZ St. Joseph the Worker; AUXILIARY CHAPLAINS CONTRACT CHAPLAINS; Episcopal Vicar.
O'Keeffe, Richard (TUC) Diocesan Consultors.
O'Keeffe, William J. '59 (LA) Long Beach, CA Our Lady of Refuge.
O'Kelly, Colm '64 (SAC) Woodland, CA Holy Rosary.
O'Kennedy, Philip N. '71 (BIR) Huntsville, AL Good Shepherd.
O'Kere, Edmund (NY) Manhattan, NY Beth Israel Medical Center.
O'Kielty, James P. '54 (PAT)[A] Front Royal, VA Christendom College; [P] Chester, NJ Nazareth Village Retired.
O'Konsky, Stanley J. *s.j.* '72 (NY)[F] New York, NY Fordham Preparatory School; [EE] Jesuit Community, Kohlmann Hall.
O'Kruta, Francis A. '94 (WH) Wheeling, WV Our Lady of Peace.
O'Laughlin, Patrick J. '67 (STL) Wentzville, MO St. Patrick.
O'Leary, Arthur P. '75 (BO) Senior Priests Retired.
O'Leary, Bernard C. *s.j.* '48 (ALN)[A] Wernersville, PA Jesuit Center.
O'Leary, Cornelius F. '56 (WOR) Otter River, MA St. Martin's.
O'Leary, Cornelius P. '48 (CAM) Retired.
O'Leary, Cornelius '48 (SB) Pro–Synodal Judges Retired.
O'Leary, Daniel F. *o.m.i.* '50 (BUF)[O] Niagara University, NY Vincentian Community at Niagara University; [C] Niagara University, NY Niagara University; Buffalo, NY Holy Angels.
O'Leary, David A. '45 (WCH) Retired.
O'Leary, David M. '85 (BO) Medford, MA St. Raphael.
O'Leary, Donald J. '37 (HRT) Plantsville, CT St. Aloysius Retired.
O'Leary, Harold V. *c.s.b.* '49 (GAL)[Q] Houston, TX Residence of the Basilian Fathers of the University of St. Thomas.
O'Leary, Hilary *o.s.b.* '68 (PAT)[M] Morristown, NJ St. Mary's Abbey.
O'Leary, J. J. *s.j.* '65 (SD)[B] University of San Diego.
O'Leary, James E. '68 (BO) Arlington, MA St. Camillus.
O'Leary, James J. '56 (DET) Harrison Twp., MI St. Hubert.
O'Leary, James J. *s.j.* '65 (MIL)[O] San Diego, CA.
O'Leary, James M. *s.j.* '91 (CHI).
O'Leary, James S. '61 (KAL)[N] Battle Creek, MI St. Joseph.
O'Leary, John P. '54 (BIS) Retired.
O'Leary, John '54 (BIS)[G] Bismarck, ND Emmaus Place.
O'Leary, John *s.j.* '60 (SEA) Tacoma, WA St. Leo the Great.
O'Leary, John '67 (MIA) On Duty Outside the Archdiocese; (FgM).
O'Leary, John '78 (CAM) Atco, NJ Assumption.
O' Leary, John (OAK) Alta Bates Hospital.
O'Leary, Kevin J. '95 (BO) Cambridge, MA St. Peter; Selected.
O'Leary, Lawrence J. '56 (RVC) West Brentwood, NY Pilgrim Psychiatric Center.
O'Leary, Lawrence '53 (LA) Los Angeles, CA St. Martin of Tours Retired.
O'Leary, Malcolm *s.v.d.* '61 (LAF) Opelousas, LA Holy Ghost; Advocates.
O'Leary, Matthew L. '03 (SEA) Ferndale, WA St. Joseph.
O'Leary, Michael J. '93 (Ireland) Valhalla, NY Holy Name of Jesus.
O'Leary, Niall F. '60 (LA) Retired.
O'Leary, Niall '60 (LA) South Pasadena, CA Holy Family.
O'Leary, Patrick B. *s.j.* '61 (SEA)[A] Seattle, WA Seattle University.
O'Leary, Patrick D. '51 (Y) Retired.
O'Leary, Peter P. '01 (BUR) Burlington, VT St. Mark's.
O'Leary, Raymond J. '62 (ORL) Port Orange, FL Our Lady of Hope.
O'Leary, Raymond (ORL) Deans; Members; Consultors.
O'Leary, Richard *o.s.a.* '73 (PH) Rosemont, PA St. Thomas of Villanova Parish.
O'Leary, Robert A. '53 (NEW) Retired.
O'Leary, Sean '61 (SAC) Retired.
O'Leary, Thomas M. '57 (NEW) Vicar for Permanent Deacons Retired.
O'Leary, Todd '58 (TUC) Tucson, AZ St. Thomas the Apostle; Diocesan Building Committee; Real Estate & Future Parish Sites Committee; Members.
O'Leary, William F. *s.j.* '62 (OM)[C] Omaha, NE Creighton Preparatory School.
O'Leary, William R. *s.j.* '73 (PAT)[I] Morristown, NJ Loyola House of Retreats.
O'Leary, William R. *s.j.* '73 (NEW)[I] Jersey City, NJ St. Joseph's Home for the Blind; [N] Jersey City, NJ Jesuit Community of St. Peter's Prep, Inc..
O'Leary, William T. *m.m.* '61 (FgM).
O'Lenny, Patrick J. '56 (LC) On Duty Outside the Diocese.
O'Looney, Joseph *c.s.p.* '45 (SFR)[K] San Rafael, CA Nazareth House Retired.
O'Looney, Martin J. *c.s.p.* '46 (NY)[EE] Jamaica Estates Paulist Fathers Generalate.
O'Loughlin, Eugene E. '44 (BUF) Retired.
O'Loughlin, Eugene P. '43 (WH) Retired.
O'Loughlin, Francis A. '80 (PRO) Newport, RI Jesus Saviour; Newport Hospital.
O'Loughlin, Frank '65 (PMB) Special Assignment.
O'Loughlin, Michael *s.s.c.* (MO) AUXILIARY CHAPLAINS CONTRACT CHAPLAINS.
O'Loughlin, Padhraic *s.s.c.* '57 (FgM).

O'Loughlin, Patrick J. '99 (MIL) On Leave.
O'Loughlin, Sean '01 (SEA) Bainbridge Island, WA St. Cecilia.
O'Mahony, Finbar P. *o.s.b.* '43 (MAN)[K] Manchester, NH St. Anselm Abbey.
O'Mahony, James '70 (HON) On Duty Outside the Diocese.
O'Mahony, Maurice '67 (LA) Santa Barbara, CA Our Lady of Mount Carmel.
O'Mahony, Thomas *s.s.s.* '95 (CLV)[O] Gretna, LA.
O'Malley, Edward J. '60 (JOL) Manhattan, IL St. Joseph.
O'Malley, James E. '46 (SFR) Novato, CA St. Anthony of Padua Retired.
O'Malley, James F '56 (CHI) Retired.
O'Malley, James '56 (CHI) Highwood, IL St. James.
O'Malley, John A. '55 (BWN) Retired.
O'Malley, John J. *o.p.* '59 (CHI) River Forest, IL St. Vincent Ferrer.
O'Malley, John W. *s.j.* '59 (BO)[V] Cambridge, MA.
O'Malley, John W. *s.j.* '59 (DET)[K] Temperance, MI.
O'Malley, Joseph M. '50 (DEN) Retired.
O'Malley, Joseph T. '54 (GAL)[N] Houston, TX Pope John Paul XXIII Priests' Residence Retired.
O'Malley, Kenneth *c.p.* '64 (CHI)[B] Chicago, IL The Catholic Theological Union at Chicago; [N] Chicago, IL Passionist Community–CTU.
O'Malley, Leonard F. '74 (BO) Burlington, MA St. Malachy.
O'Malley, Mark Francis '95 (NEW)[Q] Newark, NJ The Newman Catholic Center at University Heights (Rutgers/Newark/NJIT).
O'Malley, Mark (NEW) Priestly Vocation Board.
O'Malley, Martin *s.j.* '99 (NY)[V] Newton, MA The Jesuit Community at Boston College.
O'Malley, Michael P. '92 (PH) Morton, PA Our Lady of Perpetual Help; [D] Springfield, PA Cardinal O'Hara High School.
O'Malley, Michael W. '52 (WCH) Retired.
O'Malley, Patrick J. '57 (CHI) Retired.
O'Malley, Patrick '57 (CHI).
O'Malley, Paul *s.s.c.* '57 (BO)[V] Clinton, MA Presentation Apts., #54.
O'Malley, Paul *s.s.c.* '59 (OM)[K] St. Columbans St. Columban's Foreign Mission Society Retired.
O'Malley, Terrence *s.c.j.* '60 (OAK) Hayward, CA All Saints.
O'Malley, Thomas J. '66 (SCR) Ashley, PA St. Leo's.
O'Malley, Thomas P. *s.j.* '61 (BO)[V] Watertown, MA The Society of Jesus of New England–Provincial Offices; [V] Newton, MA The Jesuit Community at Boston College.
O'Malley, Timothy J. '97 (CHI) Highwood, IL St. James.
O'Malley, Vincent J. *c.m.* '73 (PH).
O'Malley, William J. *s.j.* '51 (NY)[EE] Jesuit Community, Kohlmann Hall.
O'Malley, William J. *s.j.* '63 (NY)[F] New York, NY Fordham Preparatory School.
O'Malley, William M. *s.j.* '55 (SPK)[J] Spokane, WA Regis Community.
O'Malley, William P. '74 (PIT)[N] Pittsburgh, PA St. John Vianney Manor.
O'Malley, William *o.carm.* '65 (NEW) Demarest, NJ St. Joseph's.
O'Mara, Dennis *s.s.c.* '61 (CHI) Chicago, IL St. Philomena; [K] St. Columbans St. Columban's Foreign Mission Society.
O'Mara, Michael E. '88 (IND) Indianapolis, IN St. Mary/Immaculate Conception.
O'Meara, Gerard J. '56 (BO) Senior Priests Retired.
O'Meara, Gregory J. *s.j.* '02 (MIL)[O] Milwaukee, WI Miguel Pro Jesuit Community.
O'Meara, Henry R. *c.ss.r.* (MO) AUXILIARY CHAPLAINS CONTRACT CHAPLAINS.
O'Meara, Joseph M. '67 (BAL) Baltimore, MD St. Rose of Lima.
O'Meara, Joseph '53 (NY) New York, NY Our Lady of the Rosary.
O'Meara, Noel P. *c.s.sp.* '65 (WDC)[V] Wheaton, MD U.S. Foundation for the Congregation of the Holy Ghost and the Immaculate Heart of Mary, Inc..
O'Meara, Noel P. *c.s.sp.* '65 (BRK)[V] Long Island City, NY Holy Ghost Fathers of Ireland; [Z] Long Island City, NY World Compassion Link.
O'Meara, Thomas F. *o.p.* '62 (CHI)[N] River Forest, IL St. Thomas Aquinas Priory.
O'Meara, Thomas *o.p.* '62 (FTW)[B] University of Notre Dame Du Lac.
O'Melia, Edward A. '77 (DAV) Washington, IA St. James; West Branch, IA St. Bernadette.
O'Neal, James E. '80 (STA) On Duty Outside the Diocese; Army Chaplains.
O'Neal, Norman B. *s.j.* '59 (NO)[F] New Orleans, LA Jesuit High School.
O'Neal, Patrick K. '90 (PEO) Bloomington, IL St. Patrick's.
O'Neal, Shawn (CHL) Bryson City, NC St. Joseph.
O'Neil, Edward '63 (NY) Mamaroneck, NY St. Vito.
O'Neil, Flann *o.f.m.* '52 (GLP) Ganado, AZ All Saints.
O'Neil, James W. *s.j.* '57 (BO)[E] Dorchester, MA Boston College High School & Jesuit Community.
O'Neil, James '85 (GF)[K] Malta, MT St. Mary's Catholic Education Trust; Personnel Board.
O'Neil, Jim '85 (GF) Malta, MT St. Mary's.
O'Neil, Joseph M. *m.s.* '93 (HRT) Hartford, CT Our Lady of Sorrows; [M] Hartford, CT Our Lady of Sorrows Rectory.
O'Neil, Kevin *c.ss.r.* '81 (WDC)[M] Washington, DC Holy Redeemer College.
O'Neil, Lee E. '56 (TLS) Retired.
O'Neil, Leo J. '56 (WOR) Worcester, MA Our Lady of the Rosary.
O'Neil, Michael '59 (SEA) Retired.
O'Neil, Philip E. '54 (RCK) Marengo, IL Sacred Heart Retired.
O'Neil, Robert J. *m.h.m.* '65 (NY) New York, NY St. Mary; [EE Hartsdale, NY Mill Hill Fathers Residence.
O'Neil, Seamus '74 (NY)[II] New York, NY St. Patrick's International Inc..
O'Neil, Thomas D. '69 (PIT) Washington, PA St. Hilary; Priest Council.
O'Neil, W. Laurence *s.j.* '61 (BGP)[B] Fairfield, CT Fairfield University; [P] Fairfield, CT The Fairfield Jesuit Community–Fairfield University.
O'Neill, Brian E. '68 (CAM) Magnolia, NJ St Gregory's; Office of Deaf and Disabilities.
O'Neill, Charles E. *s.j.* '57 (NO)[C] New Orleans, LA Loyola University New Orleans.
O'Neill, Charles F. '46 (DET) Dearborn Heights, MI Our Lady of Grace Retired.
O'Neill, Daniel J. '76 (ALT)[H] Lock Haven, PA Lock Haven University (Lock Haven); Lock Haven, PA Immaculate Conception.
O'Neill, Daniel *o.carm.* '69 (NEW) Teaneck, NJ St. Anastasia's.
O'Neill, Dennis B. '73 (CHI) Morton Grove, IL St. Martha.
O'Neill, Edward M. '71 (MET) Colonia, NJ St. John Vianney; Diocesan Council of Catholic Women.
O'Neill, Felix M. '55 (CAM) Retired.
O'Neill, Francis J. *s.j.* '50 (BO)[E] Dorchester, MA Boston College High School & Jesuit Community.
O'Neill, George F. '97 (BGP) Bridgeport, CT St. Patrick Church.
O'Neill, Hugh '77 (GLP) Gallup, NM Gallup Area Hospitals & Nursing Homes.
O'Neill, James '54 (CHY) Casper, WY Saint Patrick's Retired.
O'Neill, James '57 (ALB) Retired.
O'Neill, Jeremiah '59 (LA) Alhambra, CA St. Thomas More.
O'Neill, Jeremy *o.s.b.* (LAF) On Special Assignment.
O'Neill, John B. Charles '99 (KNX) Knoxville, TN Holy Ghost.
O'Neill, John D. *s.j.* '60 (DET)[K] Detroit, MI Jesuit Community at the University of Detroit Mercy.
O'Neill, John J. *m.s.* '62 (NOR) Hampton, CT Our Lady of La Salette; Danielson, CT St. James.
O'Neill, John J. *m.s.* '62 (HRT)[M] Hartford, CT Missionaries of LaSalette.
O'Neill, John J. (SFR) Navy Reserve Chaplains.
O'Neill, John M. *o.s.f.s.* '73 (ARL) Vienna, VA Our Lady of Good Counsel.
O'Neill, John P. (NEW)[B] Rutherford, NJ.
O'Neill, John *o.s.f.s.* '59 (TOL)[C] Toledo, OH St. Francis de Sales High School Retired.
O'Neill, John '67 (SFR) Olema, CA Sacred Heart.
O'Neill, John (BRK) Woodside, NY Corpus Christi.
O'Neill, Joseph J. *m.m.* '49 (SJ)[M] Los Altos, CA Maryknoll.
O'Neill, Joseph P. *s.j.* '54 (BO)[E] Dorchester, MA Boston College High School & Jesuit Community; [V] Weston, MA Campion Health Center, Inc..
O'Neill, Joseph *m.m.* (MO) AUXILIARY CHAPLAINS CONTRACT CHAPLAINS.
O'Neill, Keith *o.f.m.conv.* '66 (SAV) Jesup, GA St. Joseph.
O'Neill, Kevin P. '77 (SCR) Unassigned or Leave of Absence; [M] Dunmore, PA Villa St. Joseph.
O'Neill, Kevin S. '77 (HEL) Helena, MT Cathedral of St. Helena.
O'Neill, Kevin S. (HEL) Diocesan Consultors.
O'Neill, Kevin S. (HEL) Apostolic Administrator; Moderator of the Curia; Presbyteral Council; Diocesan Finance Council; Personnel Board; Board of Directors; Board of Directors; Borromeo Pre–Seminary Program; Office of Worship.
O'Neill, Kevin T. '61 (BUF) East Aurora, NY Immaculate Conception.
O'Neill, Kevin (HEL) Defenders of the Bond; Clergy Senior Status and Security Trust Board.
O'Neill, Michael F. '76 (NO) Military Chaplains; Air Force Chaplains.
O'Neill, Michael *i.c.* '70 (SP) Seffner, FL St. Francis of Assisi.
O'Neill, Patrick H. '67 (MIA) Special Assignment; Catholic Office for Inter–Faith Activities and Catholic–Jewish Relations Commission; Christian Unity Commission.
O'Neill, Patrick J. '45 (SD) Retired.
O'Neill, Patrick J. '47 (SAC) Retired.
O'Neill, Patrick J. '83 (WIL) Absent on Sick Leave; On Duty Outside the Diocese.
O'Neill, Patrick J. '98 (CHI) La Grange, IL St. Cletus.
O'Neill, Patrick '45 (SD) La Mesa, CA St. Martin of Tours.
O'Neill, Patrick (MIA) Coordinator of Special Projects.
O'Neill, Raymond F. '66 (SP) Spring Hill, FL Saint Joan of Arc.
O'Neill, Richard V. '54 (SY) Utica, NY St. Mary; Marcy, NY Central New York Psychiatric Center; Pastoral Examiners.
O'Neill, Robert '95 (STO) On Duty Outside the Diocese.
O'Neill, Sean F. '03 (PH) Penndel, PA Our Lady of Grace.
O'Neill, Thomas D. '68 (PRO) On Duty Outside the Diocese.
O'Neill, Thomas H. *s.j.* '90 (SFR)[N] San Francisco, CA Jesuit Community at University of San Francisco.
O'Neill, Thomas M. '78 (LC)[B] La Crosse, WI Viterbo University; Elected Members.
O'Neill, Thomas '62 (FRS) Shafter, CA St. Therese.
O'Neill, Timothy H. '67 (Y) Hubbard, OH St. Patrick.
O'Neill, Virgil *o.s.b.* '46 (SCL)[I] Collegeville, MN St. John's Abbey, of the Order of St. Benedict.
O'Neill, William J. '65 (PRO) Jamestown, RI St. Mark.
O'Neill, William O. '67 (SAV) Savannah, GA Cathedral of St. John the Baptist; Savannah Deanery.
O'Neill, William P. '61 (CLV) Hinckley, OH Our Lady of Grace; Associate Judicial Vicars.
O'Neill, William R. *s.j.* '81 (OAK).
O'Neill, William R. *s.j.* '81 (California)[N] Berkeley, CA Jesuit Community at Jesuit School of Theology at Berkeley.
O'Neill, William *c.pp.s.* '52 (STP)[C] St. Paul, MN University of St. Thomas Retired.
O'Neill, William *c.pp.s.* '52 (CIN)[B] Carthagena, OH St. Charles.
O'Rafferty, Patrick '51 (SAC) Retired.
O'Regan, Denis '61 (STA) Retired.
O'Regan, Hugh H. '57 (BO) Boston, MA Holy Trinity; Boston, MA St. James the Greater; CENTRAL REGION; German.
O'Reilly, Aidan '60 (SAC) Mount Shasta, CA St. John the Evangelist; Mount Shasta, CA St. Anthony; Vicars Forane.
O'Reilly, Alvin J. '51 (NO) New Orleans, LA Shrine of St. Lazarus of Jerusalem Retired.
O'Reilly, Andrew *c.pp.s.* '73 (ORL) Orlando, FL St. Andrew.
O'Reilly, Bernard M. '69 (PRO) Harrisville, RI St. Patrick.
O'Reilly, Bernard '45 (LA) Paramount, CA Our Lady of the Rosary Retired.
O'Reilly, Daniel '03 (NY) Rye, NY Resurrection.
O'Reilly, Edward M. '68 (NY) Military Chaplains Retired.
O'Reilly, Francis J. '45 (PHX) Retired.
O'Reilly, Gabriel '67 (MIA) Davie, FL St. David; Building Commission; Archdiocesan Fund–Raising & Assessments Committee.
O'Reilly, Gerald K. '85 (CHI) Other Assignments; Chicago, IL St. Thomas More.
O'Reilly, James E. *s.j.* '57 (DET)[E] Detroit, MI Loyola High School; Detroit, MI St. Francis de Sales.
O'Reilly, James P. *m.s.* '37 (HRT)[M] Hartford, CT Missionaries of LaSalette.
O'Reilly, Joseph F. '56 (WH) Retired.
O'Reilly, Joseph P. '39 (SFR) San Francisco, CA St. Stephen Retired.
O'Reilly, Joseph '49 (SFD) Retired.
O'Reilly, Kevin '84 (WDC) Great Mills, MD Holy Face.
O'Reilly, Kevin '96 (NY) Graduate Studies.
O'Reilly, Michael '96 (SAC) Orland, CA St. Dominic.
O'Reilly, Patrick J. '44 (GF) Retired.
O'Reilly, Patrick J. '65 (OG)[D] Lake Placid, NY Uihlein Mercy Center.
O'Reilly, Peter (LA) Santa Barbara Pastoral Region.
O'Reilly, Vincent '62 (SAC) Vacaville, CA St. Joseph; Council of Priests.
O'Riley, Dennis H. '52 (PEO) Retired.
O'Riley, James K. '67 (IND) Retired.
O'Riordan, James '64 (JKS) Belzoni, MS All Saints.
O'Riordan, Jeremiah '67 (PAT)[P] Chester, NJ Nazareth Village.
O'Riordan, William '85 (NO) Harvey, LA St. Martha; Deans.
O'Rorke, James H. '61 (PAT) Retired.
O'Rourke, Bryan A. (STP) Presbyteral Council.
O'Rourke, Bryan '66 (STP) St. Paul, MN St. Mark; Commission on Chemical Health.
O'Rourke, Charles L. *s.s.c.* '57 (LA)[Q] Los Angeles, CA Columban Fathers, Procure House.
O'Rourke, Colin *o.f.m.* '61 (BO)[AA] Boston, MA St. Anthony Shrine.
O'Rourke, Daniel '88 (GF) Lewistown, MT St. Leo's; [K] Lewistown, MT St. Leo's Catholic Education Trust.
O'Rourke, David K. *o.p.* '62 (OAK)[N] Oakland, CA Dominican Order, Siena House; Point Richmond, CA Our Lady of Mercy.
O'Rourke, David *o.p.* (OAK) Defenders of the Bond.

O'Rourke, Dennis J. '80 (PHX) Chandler, AZ St. Benedict; [I] Phoenix, AZ Catholic Committee on Scouting.
O'Rourke, Dennis (PHX) The Catholic Scouting Program.
O'Rourke, Edward F. *o.s.f.s.* '56 (WIL)[J] Childs, MD Retirement and Assisted Care Facility.
O'Rourke, Francis J. *c.ss.r.* '62 (NY)[EE] New York, NY Redemptorist Priests and Brothers, C.Ss.R..
O'Rourke, Francis J. '75 (CHL) Greensboro, NC Our Lady of Grace.
O'Rourke, Gerald (SFR) Retired.
O'Rourke, Hugh *s.s.c.* '52 (PRO)[P] Bristol, RI St. Columban's Retirement House.
O'Rourke, James J. '58 (BO) Brighton, MA St. Columbkille.
O'Rourke, John F. *o.s.a.* '61 (PH) Philadelphia, PA St. Augustine.
O'Rourke, John G. '48 (DAL) Retired.
O'Rourke, Kevin *o.p.* '54 (CHI) River Forest, IL St. Vincent Ferrer.
O'Rourke, Matthew J. *s.s.j.* '47 (BAL)[S] Baltimore, MD St. Joseph's Manor.
O'Rourke, Michael K. '69 (GB) Appleton, WI St. Mary.
O'Rourke, Michael *o.p.* '96 (NO)[P] Convento Santa Sabrina.
O'Rourke, Michael (GB) Diocesan Consultors; Appointed Representatives.
O'Rourke, P. Gerard '50 (SFR) San Francisco, CA St. Gabriel.
O'Rourke, Paul J. *s.s.c.* '61 (PRO)[P] Bristol, RI St. Columban's Retirement House.
O'Rourke, Peter J. '99 (SCR) Canton, PA St. Michael.
O'Rourke, Peter *c.p.* '64 (MET)[H] Centereach, NY.
O'Rourke, Richard *m.s.c.* '65 (AUS) Harker Heights, TX St. Paul Chong Hasang; [G] Blanco, TX Missionaries of the Sacred Heart, M.S.C.; Presbyteral Council.
O'Rourke, Robert *s.s.c.* '58 (OM)[K] St. Columbans, NE St. Columban's Foreign Mission Society.
O'Rourke, Terence *o.s.a.* '64 (NY) Staten Island, NY St. Ann.
O'Rourke, Thomas J. '64 (HRT) Hamden, CT Ascension.
O'Rourke, William D. '58 (RVC) Franklin Square, NY St. Catherine of Sienna.
O'Rourke, William J. '56 (NOR) Quinebaug, CT St. Stephen.
O'Rourke, William (NOR) Censor of Books.
O'Ryan, Colm '55 (LA) Beverly Hills, CA Good Shepherd.
O'Shaughnessey, Michael (VIC) Council of Catholic Women (DCCW).
O'Shaughnessy, Donald *s.j.* '55 (CIN)[M] Cincinnati, OH Faber Jesuit Community.
O'Shaughnessy, James J. '68 (NY)[E] New York, NY Cardinal Spellman High School.
O'Shaughnessy, Michael A. '50 (VIC) Edna, TX St. Agnes.
O'Shaughnessy, Patrick '68 (BLX) Biloxi, MS St. Michael.
O'Shaughnessy, Richard *s.m.* '47 (STL)[O] St. Louis, MO Cure of Ars Marianist Community.
O'Shea, Daniel *s.a.* '64 (NY)[EE] Garrison, NY Franciscan Friars of the Atonement, Minister General Office; [EE] Garrison, NY Franciscan Friars of the Atonement, Minister General Office.
O'Shea, David T. '61 (PT) Panama City Beach, FL St. Bernadette.
O'Shea, Gerard D. (STA) AUXILIARY CHAPLAINS CONTRACT CHAPLAINS.
O'Shea, Gerard '66 (NY) Retired.
O'Shea, Howard '58 (NY).
O'Shea, James (Jim) *c.p.* '89 (MET)[H] Brooklyn, NY.
O'Shea, James B. '65 (WOR) Worcester, MA Our Lady of Lourdes.
O'Shea, James D. '64 (SFD) Mount Zion, IL St. Isidore; Decatur, IL St. James; Mt. Zion, IL Our Lady of the Holy Spirit; Decatur Deanery.
O'Shea, Jeremiah T. '64 (PIT) Pittsburgh, PA St. Winifred.
O'Shea, John G. '60 (YAK) Kennewick, WA Holy Spirit.
O'Shea, John J. '50 (WCH) Retired.
O'Shea, John L. '81 (PIT) Meadowlands, PA Our Lady of the Miraculous Medal.
O'Shea, John T. '54 (BUF) Retired.
O'Shea, Joseph J. '42 (NY) Retired.
O'Shea, Joseph '61 (SEA) Retired.
O'Shea, Lawrence '56 (DUL) Duluth, MN St. Raphael's; Finance Council; Finance Officer; Mission Outreach and Propagation of the Faith.
O'Shea, Michael '52 (LA) Bellflower, CA St. Bernard Retired.
O'Shea, Michael *o.f.m.cap.* '54 (OAK)[N] Saint Conrad Friary.
O'Shea, Michael '72 (NY) Bedford Hills Correctional Facility.
O'Shea, Morty '97 (CC)[G] Robstown, TX Society of Our Lady of the Most Holy Trinity.
O'Shea, Patrick '61 (MIA) Hollywood, FL Little Flower.
O'Shea, Patrick *m.s.c.* '73 (SAT) San Antonio, TX St. Anthony of Padua.
O'Shea, Philip *o.f.m.* '75 (BO)[V] Ministry of the Word; [AA] Boston, MA St. Anthony Shrine.
O'Shea, Robert J. '63 (BEL) Retired.
O'Shea, Vincent M. *o.s.m.* '38 (CHI)[N] Chicago Order of Friar Servants of Mary (Servites) United States of America Province, Inc..
O'Shea, William D. '62 (PMB) North Palm Beach, FL St. Clare.
O'Shea, William J. '63 (JOL) Naperville, IL St. Margaret Mary.
O'Souza, Sidney *s.j.* '64 (OAK)[N] Berkeley, CA Jesuit Community at Jesuit School of Theology at Berkeley.
O'Sullivan, Brendan T. (SAC) Priests' Personnel Board, Diocesan.
O'Sullivan, Brendan '54 (SB) Retired.
O'Sullivan, Brendan *s.s.c.* '70 (FgM).
O'Sullivan, Brendan (SAC) Council of Priests.
O'Sullivan, Carrol '51 (LA) Santa Barbara, CA Our Lady of Mount Carmel Retired.
O'Sullivan, Cyril '80 (SFR) San Rafael, CA St. Isabella.
O'Sullivan, Daniel J. '62 (CHI) Park Forest, IL St. Irenaeus.
O'Sullivan, Daniel '60 (DET) Detroit, MI Detroit Psychiatric Institute Retired.
O'Sullivan, Daniel '63 (LA) Ventura, CA Sacred Heart.
O'Sullivan, Denis A. '72 (SR) Santa Rosa, CA St. Rose of Lima.
O'Sullivan, Eugene M. '60 (BO) Senior Priests Retired.
O'Sullivan, Francis G. '47 (BO) Peabody, MA St. John the Baptist; Senior Priests Retired.
O'Sullivan, James J. '60 (JC) Eldon, MO Sacred Heart.
O'Sullivan, Jeremiah '58 (SD) Coronado, CA Sacred Heart.
O'Sullivan, John C. '45 (PBL) Retired.
O'Sullivan, John V. '68 (PT) Tallahassee, FL Blessed Sacrament.
O'Sullivan, John V. (PT) Real Estate, Diocesan Commission for.
O'Sullivan, John '50 (B) Retired.
O'Sullivan, John (PT) College of Consultors; Orders & Ministries, Commission for; Priests' Pension Plan, Board for.
O'Sullivan, Michael J. '55 (WDC) Washington, DC St. Peter.
O'Sullivan, Michael '48 (MRY) Retired.
O'Sullivan, Peter '34 (LA) Granada Hills, CA St. John Baptist de la Salle.
O' Sullivan, Peter '83 (KCK) Topeka, KS Christ the King.
O'Sullivan, Raymond S. '68 (BO) Society of St. James the Apostle.
O'Sullivan, Sarsfield '51 (HEL) Retired.
O'Sullivan, Sean A. *s.j.* '99 (CHI)[N] Chicago, IL Miguel Pro Jesuit Community.
O'Sullivan, Sean '64 (MIA) Coral Gables, FL Little Flower.
O'Sullivan, T. Brendan '56 (SAC) Sacramento, CA St. Anthony; Vicars Forane; Ongoing Education of Clergy.
O'Sullivan, Thomas C. '51 (LA) Retired.
O'Sullivan, Thomas P. '71 (SAC) Point Arena, CA St. Aloysius.
O'Sullivan, Timothy F. '94 (PH) Bensalem, PA Saint Ephrem.
O'Sullivan, Timothy *o.f.m.cap.* '36 (LA) Solvang, CA Old Mission Santa Ines.
O'Sullivan, Tracy *o.carm.* '62 (LA) Los Angeles, CA St. Raphael.
O'Too, Gabriel '87 (VIC) Victoria, TX Our Lady of Sorrows.
O'Toole, Anthony J. '44 (ALT) Retired.
O'Toole, Brian P. '86 (WOR) Sutton, MA St. Mark; Deans; Diocesan College of Consultors.
O'Toole, Brian (WOR) Haitian Ministries Coalition of the Diocese of Worcester; Presbyteral Council.
O'Toole, Coleman P. '61 (PRT) Old Orchard Beach, ME St. Margaret's.
O'Toole, James '64 (FWT) Retired.
O'Toole, John M. '67 (PIT) Pittsburgh, PA St. Mary of Mercy; Diocesan Development Board.
O'Toole, John *c.ss.r.* '53 (PH)[L] Saratoga Springs, NY St. John Neumann Residence.
O'Toole, Matthew L. '95 (STL) University City, MO Our Lady of Lourdes.
O'Toole, Matthew '95 (STL)[F] St. Louis, MO Christian Brothers College High School (C.B.C.).
O'Toole, Patrick F. '60 (BRK) Brooklyn, NY St. Cecilia.
O'Toole, Robert E. *s.j.* '67 (STL)[EE] New York, NY "America;" Residence and publication office of the America Press; [II] New York, NY Gregorian University Foundation, The; [O] St. Louis, MO Jesuit Community Corporation at St. Louis University – Jesuit Hall.
O'Toole, Thomas F. *c.ss.r.* '51 (ALB)[L] Saratoga Springs, NY St. John Neumann Residence.
O'Toole, Thomas '69 (OKL) Ardmore, OK St. Mary.
O'Toole, Timothy '89 (PMB) Fort Pierce, FL Notre Dame Mission; Fort Pierce, FL St. Anastasia; Presbyteral Council; Cursillo Movement for Hispanics.
O'Toole, William F. '96 (GRY) Portage, IN Nativity of Our Savior.
O'Toole, William P. '61 (LA) Alhambra, CA All Souls.
O.Neill, Patrick '83 (PH)[V] Immaculata, PA Camilla Hall Nursing Home.
Oakes, Alan D. *c.s.p.* '98 (AUS) Los Angeles, CA St. Paul the Apostle.
Oakes, Eathan '03 (BEA)[A] Beaumont, TX Monsignor Kelly Catholic High School.
Oakes, Edward T. *s.j.* '79 (DEN)[N] Denver, CO Regis Jesuit Community (The Jesuits at Regis University).
Oakes, Edward T. *s.j.* '79 (CHI).
Oakes, Robert Eathan '03 (BEA)[A] Beaumont, TX St. Anne.
Oakham, Ronald *o.carm.* '77 (GAL) Houston, TX Our Lady of Mt. Carmel.
Oakshott, Ward '77 (SEA) Seattle, WA Christ the King.
Oates, Eugene *c.ss.r.* '44 (KC) Kansas City, MO Our Lady of Perpetual Help; [J] Kansas City, MO Redemptorists Fathers of Kansas City, Missouri.
Oates, Thomas F. '63 (BO) Society of St. James the Apostle.
Oates, Thomas '63 (FgM).
Obama, Joseph Marie '86 (PIT) Pittsburgh, PA Guardian Angels.
Obasi, John (PIT) Pittsburgh, PA Our Lady of Grace.
Obasi, Longinus '94 (CHI) Chicago, IL St. Dorothy.
Obayashi, Hal N. '02 (BO) Canton, MA St. John the Evangelist.
Obaza, Theodore L. '61 (SCR) Wilkes–Barre, PA Holy Trinity.
Obba, Thaddeus '86 (NY) Yonkers, NY St. Ann.
Obba, Thaddeus '87 (NY) Beacon, NY St. John Evangelist.
Obee, Gregory *o.s.b.* '56 (RCK)[G] Aurora, IL Marmion Abbey.
Obele, Oliver *m.s.p.* '95 (BEA) Diocesan College of Consultors and Presbyteral Council; Port Arthur, TX St. Mary.
Obeng, Simon '89 (STV) On Duty Outside the Diocese.
Obeng–Kyeremeh, Simon (STV) Army Chaplains.
Ober, Lawrence M. *s.j.* (CLV)[D] Cleveland, OH St. Ignatius High School.
Oberch, Rick J. '85 (PEO)[N] East Peoria, IL Mt. Alverno Novitiate.
Oberch, Rick (PEO) Adjutant Judicial Vicars.
Oberg, Paul *s.s.j.* '85 (BIR) Birmingham, AL Our Lady of Fatima.
Obergefell, Sylvan W. '58 (TOL) Retired.
Oberhausen, James *o.f.m.conv.* '82 (SAT)[B] San Antonio, TX San Damiano Friary, Prenovitiate House of Formation; [M] San Antonio, TX San Damiano Friary.
Oberle, James P. *s.s.* '87 (BAL)[A] San Antonio, TX Assumption Seminary aka Assumption–St. John's Seminary; [C] Oblate School of Theology.
Oberle, James P. *s.s.* '87 (WDC) On Duty Outside the Archdiocese.
Oberle, James P. *s.s.* '87 (BAL)[A] San Antonio, TX Assumption Seminary aka Assumption–St. John's Seminary; [C] Oblate School of Theology.
Obermeyer, Robert A. '61 (CIN) Cincinnati, OH Our Lord, Christ the King; Judges.
Obermiller, Edwin *c.s.c.* '96 (P)[B] University of Portland; [L] Portland, OR Holy Cross Fathers & Brothers, C.S.C. – University of Portland; [P] Portland, OR University of Portland.
Obero, Eduardo '93 (SJ) Palo Alto, CA St. Thomas Aquinas.
Obersinner, Joseph L. *s.j.* '57 (SPK)[J] Spokane, WA Regis Community.
Obersteiner, Ernest '77 (GLP) On Leave of Absence.
Oberto, Peter '78 (MAR) Champion, MI Sacred Heart; Ishpeming, MI St. John the Evangelist; Republic, MI St. Augustine.
Oberto, Peter (MAR) Judicial Vicar; Diocesan Judges.
Oberts, David P. '69 (SUP) Rice Lake, WI St. John Evangelist; Rice Lake, WI Our Lady of Lourdes; Rice Lake, WI Holy Trinity; Pastoral Consultors; Personnel Placement Board; Conciliation and Arbitration Board; St. Pius Priest Fund.
Obi, Celesine '36 (ROC)[J] Rochester, NY Sisters of Mercy of the Americas Regional Community of Rochester.
Obi, Obioma Desmond '84 (SAN) Winters, TX Our Lady of Mt. Carmel.
Obico, Chrispin '86 (TR) Toms River, NJ St. Justin.
Obijiski, Herbert *o.f.m.conv.* '65 (HRT) Kensington, CT St. Paul's.
Obin, Arthur T. *o.m.i.* (MO) CIVIL AIR PATROL.
Obin, Arthur *o.m.i.* '64 (PMB) Riviera Beach, FL St. Francis of Assisi.
Obin, Gilbert *c.i.c.m.* '67 (SAT) San Antonio, TX St. Martin de Porres.
Obinwa, Charles '95 (TOL) Delphos, OH St. John the Evangelist.
Obisike, Bonaventure '01 (SPK) Ritzville, WA St. Ambrose; Ritzville, WA St. Agnes; Ritzville, WA Mary Queen of Heaven; Ritzville, WA Holy Trinity.
Oblinger, Joseph B. '46 (HEL) West Yellowstone, MT Our Lady of the Pines Retired.
Obloj, Stanislaw '93 (DET) Lake Orion, MI St. Joseph.
Obloy, Leonard G. '77 (CLV) Euclid, OH St. William.

Obong, Francis (CHR) Summerville, SC St. John the Beloved.
Oborny, Paul J. '63 (WCH) Lindsborg, KS St. Bridget of Sweden; McPherson, KS St. Joseph; Deans.
Oborny, Rudolf F. '71 (LIN) Wahoo, NE St. Wenceslaus; Deaneries and Deans.
Obregon, Miguel *o.f.m.* '81 (SJ) San Jose, CA Our Lady of Guadalupe; Santa Clara County Jail.
OBrien, Michael C. '65 (SEA) Monroe, WA St. Mary of the Valley.
Obrimski, Paul G. '70 (BAL) On Duty Outside the Archdiocese.
Obrimski, Paul '70 (PH) Philadelphia, PA Saint Martha.
Obwona, Martin Larok *f.c.* '80 (OKL) Blackwell, OK St. Joseph's; Tonkawa, OK St. Joseph's.
Ocampo, Arturo M. *o.f.m.* '85 (SAT) San Antonio, TX St. Alphonsus.
Ocamuna, Matthias '89 (CHI) Chicago, IL Saint Ita.
Occhiuto, Joseph L. '79 (MRY) Monterey, CA Cathedral of San Carlos Borromeo; Administrative Committee Priests' Pension Plan.
Ochej, Tomasz M. (VEN) North Port, FL San Pedro.
Ochetti, Jerome '02 (SB) Redlands, CA Sacred Heart.
Ochieze, Oliver '88 (LR) North Little Rock, AR St. Augustine; North Little Rock, AR St. Mary; North Little Rock, AR St. Patrick's.
Ochiltree, Richard '53 (OAK)[N] Oakland, CA Redemptorists.
Ochoa, Adrian *o.dem.* (SB) Riverside, CA Our Lady of Guadalupe Shrine.
Ochoa, David '72 (LA) Los Angeles, CA St. Thomas the Apostle.
Ochoa, Einer '85 (SAT) San Antonio, TX St. Agnes.
Ochoa, Jose Luis *m.g.* '66 (LA) Santa Fe Springs, CA St. Pius X.
Ochoa, Miguel Laguna *o.s.b.* '02 (SFE)[I] Abiquiu, NM Monastery of Christ in the Desert.
Ochoa, Rafael '78 (LA) Los Angeles, CA Immaculate Conception.
Ochoa, Stephen *o.s.a.* '83 (SD)[H] San Diego, CA.
Ochoa, Steven M. *o.s.a.* '83 (SD)[B] Office of the Provincial; [H] San Diego, CA Monica House – Augustinian Community.
Ochoa, Xavier '69 (SR) Sonoma, CA St. Francis Solano.
Ochs, Daniel L. '76 (COL) Reynoldsburg, OH St. Pius X.
Ochs, Robert J. *s.j.* '61 (OAK)[N] Chicago Chicago Province of the Society of Jesus–Provincial Office.
Ochs, Robert J. *s.j.* '61 (Chicago)[N] Berkeley, CA Jesuit Community at Jesuit School of Theology at Berkeley.
Ochu, Austin Charles *s.m.a.* '92 (WDC)[M] Takoma Park, MD House of Studies.
Ochylski, Ronald S. '87 (SFR) On Duty Outside the Archdiocese.
Ocilka, John A. '94 (CLV) Parma Heights, OH St. John Bosco.
Odama, Modest (CHI) Chicago, IL St. Joachim.
Odbert, Jerome K. *s.j.* '69 (DET)[P] Clarkston, MI Colombiere Center.
Oddo, Peter A. '61 (NEW) On Duty Outside the Archdiocese.
Odenbrett, Stephen *o.s.b.* '46 (MRY)[F] San Luis Obispo, CA Men's Residence.
Odermann, John *o.s.b.* '55 (FAR)[A] Richardton, ND Assumption Abbey; [G] Valley City, ND Sisters of Mary of the Presentation.
Odermann, Valerian *o.s.b.* '73 (BIS)[A] Richardton, ND Assumption Abbey; [B] Bismarck, ND University of Mary.
Odien, Terry M. '73 (CAM) Westmont, NJ Holy Saviour; Priests Personnel Board.
Odikanoro, Vincent '83 (DET) Detroit, MI Precious Blood.
Odor, Emeka L. '80 (COV) Veterans Hospital.
Odor, Luke U. (MO).
Odorizzi, Thomas A. *c.o.* '92 (MET)[H] Somerset, NJ The Metuchen Oratory, Congregation of the Oratory of St. Philip Neri.
Odorizzi, Thomas *c.o.* '92 (MET)[N] New Brunswick, NJ Catholic Center at Rutgers University.
Odozi, Anthony '97 (SD) San Diego, CA St. Brigid; On Duty Outside the Diocese; Defenders of the Bond.
Odozor, Paulinus I. *c.s.sp.* (FTW)[B] University of Notre Dame Du Lac.
Odozor, Paulinus *c.s.sp.* '84 (FTW) Mishawaka, IN St. Monica.
Oduke, Charles *s.j.* (ARM) Belmont, MA Holy Cross.
Oduro, Charles '89 (NY) Staten Island, NY Sacred Heart.
Oedy, Thomas E. '71 (TOL) Edgerton, OH St. Mary; Hicksville, OH St. Michael.
Oehmler, Gary W. '83 (PIT) Pittsburgh, PA St. Wendelin.
Oehrlein, Felix G. '65 (MAD) Wisconsin Dells, WI St. Cecilia.
Oelrich, Anthony '92 (SCL) Special Assignment.
Oen, Edward *c.pp.s.* '64 (KC) Montrose, MO Immaculate Conception.
Oenbrink, Michael J. '99 (CHR) Barnwell, SC St. Andrew.
Oesterle, John G. '67 (PIT) East McKeesport, PA St. Robert Bellarmine.
Oestreich, Brian W. '93 (NU) Sleepy Eye, MN St. Mary; Vocations Team.
Oetgen, John A. *o.s.b.* '51 (CHL)[J] Belmont, NC Belmont Abbey.
Offer, Kris *m.s.p.* '91 (LA)[BB] Los Angeles, CA Catholic Campus Ministry.
Offerman, Paul '57 (SFS) Bridgewater, SD St. Stephen.
Offutt, Bradley S. '86 (KC) Harrisonville, MO Our Lady of Lourdes; Deans.
Offutt, J. James '62 (JC) Centralia, MO Holy Spirit; Judges.
of Jesus, A.M. Seamus *o.s.a.* '75 (PRT)[I] Peaks Island, ME Mother of the Good Shepherd Monastery by the Sea.
Ofoegbu, Jerome '80 (NY) Croton Falls, NY St. Joseph.
Ofoha, Paul N. *m.s.p.* '88 (GAL)[Q] Missionary Society of St. Paul, Inc. – U.S. Region.
Oforchukwu, Joachim *c.s.sp.* '90 (CLV) Akron, OH Nativity Of the Lord Jesus.
Ofosu–Mireku, John '92 (RVC) Roslyn, NY St. Francis Hospital.
Ogbemure, Raymond '74 (OAK) El Cerrito, CA St. John the Baptist.
Ogbonna, Edmund '78 (FAR) Miami, FL Our Lady of the Holy Rosary.
Ogbonna, Leonard (RVC) Westbury, NY St. Brigid.
Ogbonna, Stanislaus *c.s.sp.* '73 (NY) Monticello, NY St. Peter; Sullivan Correctional Facility.
Ogbuji, Vincent '97 (LR) Searcy, AR St. James; Searcy, AR St. Richard Church; Heber Springs, AR St. Albert Church.
Ogden, Louis P. '85 (HBG) Middletown, PA Seven Sorrows of the Blessed Virgin Mary; [J] Middletown, PA Penn State University, Harrisburg Campus.
Oge, Raymond J. '67 (STL) Bloomsdale, MO St. Agnes; Bloomsdale, MO St. Lawrence.
Ogg, Thomas '68 (CHY) Sheridan, WY Holy Name; Vicars Forane; Ex Officios, Non–Voting; St. Joseph's Society for Priests (Clergy Mutual Benefit Society).
Oggero, Roy J. *c.s.b.* '61 (GAL)[Q] Sugar Land, TX Basilian Mission Center.
Ogle, Sean G. '77 (BRK) Rego Park, NY Resurrection–Ascension.
Ogle, Sean '77 (BRK) Queens North; Assignment Board.
Oglesby, J. Leonard '48 (MEM) Retired.
Ognibene, Joseph F. '52 (CHI) Rolling Meadows, IL St. Colette Retired.
Ogofa, Francis (NY) Manhattan, NY New York University Medical Center.
Ogorevc, Metod *o.f.m.* '92 (CHI) Lemont, IL Slovenian Catholic Mission; [N] Lemont, IL The Slovene Franciscan Fathers, Order of Friars Minor, Commissariat of the Holy Cross.
Ogorzaly, Adam '85 (ROC) Rochester, NY St. Stanislaus.
Ogrodowski, William M. '75 (STL) Beaver, PA SS. Peter and Paul.
Ogrodowski, William M. (PIT) Priest Council; College of Consultors.
Oguejiofor, Kenneth *c.m.f.* '93 (MET) Perth Amboy, NJ Our Lady of Fatima.
Ogumere, Augustine *c.s.sp.* '83 (CHI) Chicago, IL St. Felicitas.
Ogumoro, Isidro T. '89 (CHK) Saipan, MP San Jose Parish; Presbyteral Council; Knights of Columbus.
Ogunleye, Anthony Sunday (MAN) African Apostolate.
Ogunleye, Anthony '95 (WOR) Worcester, MA St. Peter; African Ministry.
Oh, Gabriel Yong–Hwan (TR) The Korean Apostolate.
Oh, Paul '75 (OAK) Korean Pastoral Center; Oakland, CA St. Cyril
Oh, Sae Wan '83 (NEW) Orange, NJ St. Andrew Kim.
Oha, Alphonsus '83 (WDC) Washington, DC St. Francis de Sales.
Ohankwere, Desmond *m.s.p.* '92 (SAV) Savannah, GA St. Benedict the Moor.
Ohiwee, Bernerad Mary *o.p.* '00 (HBG) Mifflintown, PA St. Jude.
Ohlemacher, Richard N. *o.s.c.* '55 (PHX)[G] Phoenix, AZ Crosier Community of Phoenix (Canons Regular of the Order of the Holy Cross).
Ohlig, John M. '95 (LUB) Plainview, TX Our Lady of Guadalupe.
Ohlig, John (LUB) Priests' Retirement Board.
Ohlinger, Vincent *s.v.d.* '68 (MIL)[O] East Troy, WI Divine Word Missionaries.
Ohm, Edward U. '92 (PEO) On Duty Outside the Diocese; Army Chaplains.
Ohner, John *o.s.a.* '64 (FWT) Muenster, TX Sacred Heart; Presbyteral Council and Consultors.
Ohno, Ignatius F. *s.j.* '92 (P)[L] Portland, OR Jesuit Provincial Office (Society of Jesus, Oregon Prov.); Spokane, WA St. Aloysius; [D] Spokane, WA Gonzaga Preparatory School.
Ohuche, Evaristus '02 (NY) New York, NY Incarnation.
Oie, Thomas (GB)[F] Appleton, WI St. Elizabeth Hospital.
Ojeda, Filemon G. '46 (SFR) Retired.
Ojibway, Paul *s.a.* '77 (OAK) Orinda, CA Santa Maria.
Ojimba, Felix C. (BO) Boston, MA Massachusetts General Hospital; Boston, MA Cathedral of the Holy Cross.
Okafor, Bernard E. '85 (CLV) Akron, OH St. Bernard.
Okafor, Bernard (CHI)[J] Chicago, IL St. Anthony Hospital.
Okafor, Gregory '88 (TUC) Tucson, AZ St. Augustine's Cathedral.
Okafor, Patrick '90 (Nigeria) Mt. Vernon, NY St. Ursula.
Okagbue, Bartholomew '88 (BRK) Brooklyn, NY Holy Spirit.
Okere, Edmund '89 (NY) Bronx, NY St. Augustine.
Okere, Michael C. '91 (CHR) Kingstree, SC St. Ann's; Lake City, SC St. Philip's.
Okere, Nicholas S. '74 (MAD) St. Michael; Lodi, WI St. Patrick.
Okere, Remi C. *c.s.sp.* '94 (DM) West Des Moines, IA Sacred Heart.
Okochi, Augustine '93 (RVC) Valley Stream, NY Franklin Medical Center Hospital.
Okochi, Chux '88 (RVC) Malverne, NY Our Lady of Lourdes; Rockville Centre, NY Mercy Medical Center.
Okogba, Joseph '80 (FAR) Cleveland, ND St. Anne; Cleveland, ND St. Mathias; Cleveland, ND St. Mary.
Okogie, Pachomius *o.s.b.* '96 (PIT) Pittsburgh, PA St. Maurice.
Okoli, Eugene '93 (GR) Edmore, MI St. Margaret Mary; Edmore, MI St. Bernadette of Lourdes.
Okon, Alan '98 (PH) Levittown, PA Immaculate Conception B.V.M.; [D] Fairless Hills, PA Conwell–Egan Catholic High School.
Okon, Brian *m.s.p.* '88 (GAL) Houston, TX St. Nicholas; [T] Houston, TX Texas Southern University Catholic Newman Hall.
Okonkwo, Ben '84 (IND)[G] Indianapolis, IN St. Vincent Hospital and Health Care Center, Inc..
Okonmah, Emmanuel '97 (RCK) On Duty Outside the Diocese.
Okono, Clement (BRK) Elmhurst, NY St. Bartholomew's.
Okonski, Joseph F. '90 (PH) Philadelphia, PA St. Ignatius of Loyola; Philadelphia, PA Our Mother of Sorrows.
Okopinski, Louis S. '51 (MIL) Retired.
Okorie, Onyema '99 (FRS) Hanford, CA St. Brigid.
Okorn, Dusan A. '47 (HEL) Swan Lake, MT Swan Valley Catholic Community; [G] Swan Lake, MT The Sycamore Tree Contemplative Prayer Center Retired.
Okoro, Alexander '86 (OM) Omaha, NE St. James.
Okoro, Bonaventure '02 (RCK) St. Charles, IL St. Patrick.
Okoro, Joseph E. *c.m.f.* '90 (NO) New Orleans, LA Blessed Sacrament.
Okorobia, Gregory '79 (BAK) Pendleton, OR St. Mary's.
Okorochukwu, Wilfred C. '75 (LR) Camden, AR St. Louis; Fordyce, AR Good Shepherd; Sheridan, AR Holy Cross.
Okoronkwo, Cyprian '95 (PHX) Scottsdale, AZ St. Daniel the Prophet.
Okorougo, Charles '87 (OM) Omaha, NE SS. Peter and Paul.
Okot, William *a.j.* '99 (ALX) Marksville, LA Holy Ghost.
Okoth, George '89 (ROC) Rochester, NY St. Theodore.
Okoye, Clement '93 (PIT) Pittsburgh, PA St. Mary of the Mount.
Okoye, James C. *c.s.sp.* '70 (CHI).
Okoye, James *c.s.sp.* '70 (CHI)[B] Chicago, IL St. Mary Magdalene.
Okoye, Joseph '80 (KCK) On Duty Outside the Archdiocese.
Okoye, Michael (CHI) Chicago, IL St. Martin De Porres.
Okpara, Benson Claret '91 (Y) Poland, OH Holy Family.
Okpara, Theophilus '96 (LR) Lake Village, AR Our Lady of the Lake; McGehee, AR St. Mary; Lake Village, AR Holy Child Church.
Okpogba, Desmond '89 (TLS) Tulsa, OK St. Augustine's; Tulsa, OK St. Monica's.
Okroy, Francis *s.ch.* '48 (BAL) Baltimore, MD Holy Rosary.
Okumu, Richard U. '81 (DAV) Brooklyn, IA St. Patrick; Victor, IA St. Bridget's.
Okuroski, Michael *o.c.d.* '44 (SAT).
Okwaraocha, Emmanuel (LAF) On Special Assignment.
Olario, Stephen '91 (SAC) Fairfield, CA Holy Spirit; Vallejo, CA St. Catherine of Siena.
Olcnick, John *c.ss.r.* '03 (NY) Bronx, NY Immaculate Conception.
Olczak, Joseph M. *o.s.p.p.e.* '65 (NOR) Rockville, CT St. Joseph; [A] Cromwell, CT Holy Apostles College and Seminary.
Oldani, Louis J. *s.j.* '64 (KC)[B] Kansas City, KS Rockhurst University Continuing Education Center/ National Seminars Group; [J] Kansas City, MO Rockhurst Jesuit Community.
Oldenski, Kenneth E. '66 (PIT) Gibsonia, PA Saint

Richard; Deans and Deaneries; Priest Council; College of Consultors.
Oldershaw, Robert H. '62 (CHI) Evanston, IL St. Nicholas.
Oldfield, Albert E. '59 (SCR) Moosic, PA St. Mary's.
Oldfield, John *o.a.r.* (NY) Palante–Con–Cristo Evangelization and Prayer Movement.
Oldham, David A. '03 (LIN) Lincoln, NE St. Patrick's; Advocates.
Olds, Daryl *c.m.f.* '92 (PHX) Prescott, AZ Sacred Heart.
Olds, Steven '88 (ORL) On Duty Outside the Diocese; [A] Boynton Beach, FL St. Vincent de Paul Regional Seminary; Censor of Books.
Olek, Ralph F. *s.m.* '74 (ATL)[C] Atlanta, GA Marist School.
Oleksiak, Donald P. '89 (CLV) Garfield Heights, OH St. Monica; Presbyteral Conveners.
Oleksy, Stanislaw *s.d.s.* '82 (SAT) Bandera, TX St. Stanislaus.
Olendzki, Joaquim J. '58 (NY) Pine Island, NY St. Stanislaus.
Olenowski, Mark '85 (PAT) Schooley's Mountain, NJ Our Lady of the Mountain.
Olesik, William J. '72 (NOR) Bolton, CT St. Maurice; Pontifical Association of the Holy Childhood; Pontifical Society for the Propagation of the Faith.
Olesik, William (NOR) Members; Continuing Education and Formation Commission.
Olges, H. Anthony '70 (L) Louisville, KY Holy Family.
Olguin, Jacinto '74 (VIC) Laredo, TX San Agustin Cathedral; On Duty Outside the Diocese.
Olguin, Luis '92 (SY) Utica, NY St. John; Utica, NY St. Mary of Mt. Carmel; Rome, NY Walsh Facility; Special Assignment.
Oligschlaeger, Greg '93 (JC) Fulton, MO St. Peter; Fulton, MO St. Jude Thaddeus.
Olikkara, Joseph *m.s.t.* '87 (CC) George West, TX St. George.
Olivares, Jesus *c.s.* '97 (LA)[A] Camarillo, CA St. John's Seminary College of the Archdiocese of Los Angeles.
Olivares, Jesus *c.s.* '97 (SD) Imperial, CA St. Anthony of Padua.
Olivares, Romeo D. *c.i.c.m.* '74 (SAT) Lytle, TX St. Andrew.
Olivas, William V. *o.s.a.* '97 (LA) Ojai, CA St. Thomas Aquinas.
Olive, Alphonse *c.ss.r.* '86 (BAL)[S] Annapolis, MD Saint Mary Rectory.
Olive, Alphonsus *c.ss.r.* '86 (BAL) Annapolis, MD St. Mary.
Olive, Rodney J. *c.ss.r.* '86 (FgM).
Oliveira, Aventino *i.m.c.* '57 (MET)[H] Somerset, NJ Consolata Society for Foreign Missions.
Oliveira, Gastao A. '72 (FR) Fall River, MA Santo Christo.
Oliveira, John J. *p.a.* '67 (FR) New Bedford, MA St. Mary's.
Oliveira, John J. '77 (FR) New Bedford, MA Our Lady of Mt. Carmel; Director of Portuguese Ministry; Mentoring Program for Priests.
Oliveira, John J. (FR) Diocesan Consultors.
Oliveira, John J. (FR) Missionary Cooperative Plan; Permanent Diaconate Program; Propagation of the Faith.
Oliveira, John J. (FR) Holy Childhood Association, The.
Oliveira, Robert A. '77 (FR) Norton, MA St. Mary's.
Oliveira, Vitor '73 (SPR) Ludlow, MA Our Lady of Fatima.
Olivencia, Ramon '97 (ARE) Pastoral Vocational Program; Corozal, PR Our Lady of the Seven Sorrows.
Oliver, Bill (GAL) Liturgical Commission.
Oliver, Eladio B. *m.s.p.* '91 (SPP) Director of Propagation of the Faith; Pago Pago, AS Christ the King.
Oliver, Homer G. '43 (Y) Louisville, OH St. Louis.
Oliver, Homer G. '43 (Y) Retired.
Oliver, James M. '88 (PH)[A] The Chancery; Defenders of the Bond; Promoters of Justice.
Oliver, John A. '52 (TUC) Retired.
Oliver, Marc K. '89 (NY)[HH] Kingston, NY Culinary Institute of America; Kingston, NY St. Peter.
Oliver, Marc (NY)[HH] Kingston, NY Dutchess Community College; [HH] Kingston, NY Vassar College.
Oliver, Robert W. *s.t.d.* '00 (BO)[A] Brighton, MA St. John Seminary School of Theology.
Oliver, Robert (BO)[C] Brighton, MA St. John Seminary College.
Oliver, William A. '77 (GAL) Baytown, TX St. John the Evangelist.
Oliveras, Evaristo *c.m.* '88 (SJN) San Juan, PR San Vicente de Paul; Santurce, PR Hospital Pavia–Santurce; [E] San Juan, PR Centro Medico de P.R..
Oliveras, Jose '95 (ARE) Ciales, PR Holy Rosary.
Oliveras Villanueva, Felix '82 (CGS) Caguas, PR Sagrado Corazon de Jesus.
Olivere, Michael S. '94 (PH) Philadelphia, PA St. Edmond; [D] Philadelphia, PA St. John Neumann High School; Priests' Personnel Board.
Oliveri, Richard H. '66 (PAT) Pompton Plains, NJ Our Lady of Good Counsel Retired.
Oliverio, Francis E. '56 (NY) Tuckahoe, NY Immaculate Conception; Tuckahoe, NY Assumption.
Oliver Marques, Jaime '65 (SJN) San Juan, PR Ntr. Sra. de la Caridad del Cobre.
Olivero, Michael A. '74 (CHI) Des Plaines, IL St. Stephen Protomartyr.
Oliveros, Renato T. *s.j.* '96 (PH) Philadelphia, PA Our Lady of Hope.
Olivier, David S. *s.j.* '62 (P).
Olivier, John H. *s.s.* '47 (BAL)[O] Baltimore, MD St. Charles Villa.
Olivier, John H. *s.s.* '47 (MAR) Retired.
Olivier, Robert '57 (JKS)[D] Jackson, MS St. Dominic–Jackson Memorial Hospital; Notaries.
Oliviera, Humbert '77 (MAN) Manchester, NH St. Pius X Retired.
Oliviera, Joel D. '54 (BO) Senior Priests Retired.
Olivo, Stephen G. *s.j.* '69 (SJ)[M] Los Gatos, CA Sacred Heart Jesuit Center.
Ollendick, William *o.f.m.* '01 (HT) Houma, LA Our Lady of the Most Holy Rosary; Houma, LA St. Lucy.
Olmer, Vernon *o.f.m.* '62 (SFD) Montrose, IL St. Rose of Lima; Teutopolis, IL St. Francis of Assisi; [L] Teutopolis, IL St. Francis Assisi Friary.
Olmo, Luis S. *o.f.m.* '85 (SJN) Carolina, PR Santa Clara de Asis.
Olmos, Pedro '78 (FRS) Faculties Only.
Olmstead, Daryl '75 (SAL) Mankato, KS Sacred Heart; Mankato, KS St. Theresa of Infant Jesus; Smith Center, KS St. Mary's.
Olnhausen, James Robert '70 (AUS) Giddings, TX St. Mary's.
Olona, Richard '70 (SFE) Albuquerque, NM Community of the Risen Savior; Vicar–General; College of Consultors.
Olowin, Jan C. '68 (E) Bradford, PA St. Bernard; Bradford, PA Federal Correction Institution.
Ols, James R. '75 (CLV) Elyria Township, OH St. Vincent de Paul.
Olsaukas, Algirdas '52 (LA) Los Angeles, CA St. Casimir.
Olsauskas, Algirdas '52 (LA) Retired.
Olsavsky, John R. '62 (CLV) Chagrin Falls, OH St. Joan of Arc; Associate Judicial Vicars.
Olsavsky, John R. (Y) Judges.
Olsczyk, Thomas (MIL) Judges for First Instance; Judges for Second Instance; Archdiocesan Court of Equity; Judges for Second Instance.
Olsem, Andrew D. '67 (WIN) Windom, MN Sacred Heart; Windom, MN St. Francis Xavier's; Windom, MN Sacred Heart.
Olsen, Arthur J. '99 (CHI) Niles, IL St. John Brebeuf.
Olsen, Charles R. *s.j.* '68 (SAC)[D] Sacramento, CA Jesuit High School; [I] Carmichael, CA Jesuit High School Community of Sacramento.
Olsen, Eric S. '02 (OM) O'Neill, NE St. Patrick.
Olsen, Ken '73 (P)[J] Eugene, OR Sacred Heart Medical Center.
Olsen, Thomas F. '53 (NEW) Retired.
Olson, Benedict *o.p.* (MO) AUXILIARY CHAPLAINS CONTRACT CHAPLAINS.
Olson, David '98 (LC)[C] Wausau, WI Newman High School.
Olson, Eric E. '84 (MAR) Lake Linden, MI St. Cecilia; Lake Linden, MI St. Joseph.
Olson, Hans M. (SEA) College of Consultors.
Olson, Hans '83 (SEA) Vancouver, WA St. Joseph; Presbyteral Council.
Olson, James P. '88 (PH)[A] Wynnewood, PA Theological Seminary of St. Charles Borromeo, Overbrook.
Olson, James (ALN)[M] Northampton, PA Mary Immaculate Center.
Olson, Michael P. '94 (GR) Muskegon, MI Our Lady of Grace.
Olson, Michael '93 (FWT)[A] Houston, TX St. Mary's Seminary.
Olson, Michael '94 (FWT) On Duty Outside the Diocese; Graduate Studies.
Olson, Randy G. '90 (LC) On Leave of Absence.
Olson, Richard F. *s.j.* '59 (BO)[V] Weston, MA Campion Health Center, Inc..
Olson, Ronald *o.f.m.conv.* '75 (SUP) Superior, WI Holy Assumption of the B.V.M.; Superior, WI St. William.
Olson, Ted (ORG) Judges; Council of Priests.
Olson, Theodore E. '79 (WIL) Wilmington, DE Christ Our King.
Olson, Theodore '72 (ORG) Brea, CA St. Angela Merici; Diocesan Construction Board.
Olson, Thomas F. '73 (SCL) Foley, MN St. Elizabeth; Foley, MN St. Joseph's.
Olson, Thomas '73 (SCL) Gilman, MN SS. Peter and Paul; Defensor Vinculi; Deans; Presbyteral Council; Diocesan Consultors.
Olsovsky, George J. '56 (GAL) Huffman, TX St. Philip the Apostle.
Olszamowski, Leon M. *s.m.* '76 (DET)[D] Pontiac, MI Notre Dame Preparatory High School and Marist Academy.
Olszewski, Bernard *o.f.m.conv.* '79 (BUF)[O] Athol Springs, NY St. Francis of Assisi Friary; [R] Hamburg, NY Campus Ministry Office; [C] Hamburg, NY Hilbert College.
Olszewski, Clarence A. '57 (HBG) York Haven, PA Holy Infant.
Olszewski, Daniel D. '51 (SCR) Retired.
Olszewski, Edward T. '60 (MIA) Retired.
Olszewski, John S. '47 (NEW) Archdiocesan Judges Retired.
Olszewski, Laurence *c.s.c.* '64 (ORL) Viera, FL St. John the Evangelist.
Olszewski, Paul A. '93 (CAM) Haddon Heights, NJ St. Rose's; Members; Assistant Vocation Directors for Recruitment.
Olszewski, Ronald W. *o.s.f.s.* '74 (TOL)[C] Toledo, OH St. Francis de Sales High School; [J] Toledo, OH; [J] St. Francis de Sale High School Endowment Fund, Inc..
Olszyk, Thomas P. '71 (MIL) Graduate Studies.
Olvida, Victor A. '82 (SEA) Raymond, WA St. Lawrence; Seaview, WA St. Mary.
Olzacki, Tadeusz *o.s.p.p.e.* '93 (PH)[AA] Office.
Olzacki, Thaddeus *o.s.p.p.e.* '95 (NOR) Rockville, CT St. Joseph.
Oman, Frank *i.c.* '57 (SP) Spring Hill, FL St. Theresa.
Omana, Max B. (MO) Air Force Chaplains.
Ombao, Manuel '70 (AGN) Inarajan, GU St. Joseph.
Omeardin, Ciaran P. '60 (CAM) Gibbsboro, NJ St. Andrew the Apostle.
Omernick, Kenneth E. '74 (MIL) Milwaukee, WI St. Gregory The Great; Deans.
Onaindia, Bernardo *c.p.* '46 (MGZ) San Sebastian, PR San Sebastian Martir.
Onderko, John M. '62 (PEO) La Salle, IL Resurrection.
Ondic, John L. '65 (ALN) Retired.
Ondic, John '65 (ALN)[J] Bethlehem, PA Holy Family Villa.
Ondo, Michael A. '54 (LFT) AUXILIARY CHAPLAINS CONTRACT CHAPLAINS.
Ondrako, Edward *o.f.m.conv.* '71 (NY)[EE] Staten Island, NY St. Francis Friary.
Ondreyka, Richard J. *m.s.* '54 (CLV) Lakewood, OH SS. Cyril and Methodius Retired.
Ong, Antonio '91 (NY) Pearl River, NY St. Margaret.
Ong, Tony '83 (DET) Royal Oak, MI St. Dennis.
Ong, Walter J. *s.j.* '46 (STL).
Ongaro, Mario *m.c.c.j.* '51 (CIN)[M] Cincinnati, OH Comboni Missionaries (Verona Fathers)–Comboni Mission Center.
Onida, George F. *s.m.* '86 (STL)[O] Seaford, NY St. William the Abbott.
Onida, George *s.m.* (RVC) Westbury, NY St. Brigid.
Oniskiewicz, Mieczyslaw T. '92 (MAR) On Duty Outside the Diocese.
Oniskiewicz, Mieczyslaw '92 (SAG) Kinde, MI St. Mary–St. Edward.
Onofrey, Robert *c.pp.s.* '63 (CHI) Chicago, IL Immaculate Heart of Mary; [M] Belleair Bluffs, FL.
Ontiveros, Roy *o.carm.* '79 (NEW) Leonia, NJ St. John the Evangelist's.
Onubogu, Charles '88 (SFR) San Francisco, CA Mission Dolores Basilica.
Onubugo, Charles (SFR) Nigerian Ministry.
Onuchukwu, Jude O. (PRO) Judges.
Onuegbe, Paul (LAF) On Special Assignment.
Onufer, Paul P. '59 (CAM) Retired.
Onuh, William I. (MO) Navy Chaplains.
Onunwa, Paschal U. '74 (PH) Wayne, PA St. Isaac Jogues.
Onuoha, Gerald '93 (STP) Bethesda Medical Center; Methodist Hospital.
Onuoha, Joseph '80 (GAL) Galveston, TX Holy Rosary.
Onuoha, Silas N. (NY) Bronx, NY St. Gabriel.
Onuora, Felix A. *c.s.sp.* '79 (DM) Lacona, IA Holy Trinity Church of Southeast Warren County.
Onushco, William J. '76 (ALN) Unassigned.
Onvoha, Gerald (STP) Fairview–Southdale Hospital.
Onwuegbule, Stanley '93 (SB) Ontario, CA St. Elizabeth Ann Seton.
Onwugalu, Jerome *c.s.sp.* (CHI) Chicago, IL St. Angela.
Onwujiariri, Cajetan (BAK) Jordan Valley, OR St. Bernard's.
Onwukbiko, Oliver A. '80 (BRK) Brooklyn, NY St. Martin of Tours–Fourteen Holy Martyrs.
Onwumere, Leonard '90 (BEA) Port Arthur, TX St. John.
Onyach, Nicholas Owino *f.m.h.* '00 (SHP) Grambling, LA St. Benedict the Black; Farmerville, LA Our Lady of Perpetual Help; [G] Grambling, LA Student Center.
Onyango, Charles *s.j.* '99 (BO)[V] Newton, MA The Jesuit Community at Boston College.
Onyeabor, Ukachukwu Sebastian '90 (OM) Omaha, NE St. Cecilia's Cathedral.
Onyebuchi, Martin (NY) Bronx, NY St. Philip Neri.
Onyegbule, Cletus S. '02 (ALN) Bethlehem, PA Our Lady of Perpetual Help; [O] Schuylkill Haven, PA Penn State University (Schuylkill Haven Center, Schuylkill Haven).
Onyegwara, Casmir '93 (P) Grants Pass, OR St. Anne.
Onyeihe, Cyprian (NY) Bronx, NY St. Barnabas.
Onyejegbu, Cyuracus '03 (GAL) The Woodlands, TX St. Anthony of Padua; The Woodlands, TX St. Anthony of Padua.

Onyekuru, Michael (ATL) Atlanta, GA Cathedral of Christ the King; Archdiocesan Judges.
Onyekwele, Michael (NEW) Hoboken, NJ Our Lady of Grace; Hoboken, NJ St. Mary's Hospital; St. Mary's Hospital.
Onyekwelu, Anthony '01 (NEW) Union, NJ St. Michael's.
Onyekwere, Godfrey '03 (GR) Grand Rapids, MI St. Jude.
Onyekwere, Michael (NEW)[S] Jersey City, NJ St. Francis Hospital; [S] Hoboken, NJ St. Mary Hospital.
Onyenagubo, Innocent (SY) Liverpool, NY Immaculate Heart of Mary.
Onyenobi, Chris '83 (LA)[J] Torrance, CA Little Company of Mary Hospital.
Onze, Robert E. '64 (BGP) Retired.
Oonnooney, George '91 (NY) Bronx, NY Christ the King.
Oonnoonny, George (NY) Judges.
Oosdyke, Raymond *o.f.m.conv.* '37 (GR) Louisville, KY St. Paul.
Opalewski, Walter '85 (GLP) Gallup, NM St. John Vianney.
Opals, Donald '61 (ALB) Leave of Absence.
Opara, Ben M. '85 (ARL) Alexandria, VA St. Lawrence.
Opara, Christopher '92 (NY) Bronx, NY St. Ann.
Opara, Peter Ben '88 (SY) Syracuse, NY The Cathedral of the Immaculate Conception.
Opara, Vitalis N. '88 (BRK) Brooklyn, NY Holy Family.
Oparaekwe, Godfrey '83 (TUC) Tucson, AZ Saints Peter and Paul.
Opat, Kenneth *o.s.c.* '69 (STP) Anoka, MN St. Stephen; [M] Anoka, MN Crosier Community of Anoka.
Opat, Kenneth *o.s.c.* (SCL) TEC (Central Minnesota TEC) (Together Encountering Christ).
Opeil, Cyril *s.j.* '94 (Maryland)[V] Newton, MA The Jesuit Community at Boston College.
Opem, Anthony '68 (SFS) Dakota Dunes, SD Mother Teresa Catholic Community; Ecumenical Commission.
Operts, David P. (SUP) Army National Guard Chaplains.
Ophals, Donald J. '61 (ALB) Troy, NY St. Francis de Sales.
Opira, Simon Peter '93 (STV) St. Thomas, VI Holy Family Parish; [B] Propagation of the Faith; Diocesan Consultors.
Opoka, Lloyd E. '68 (KC) Blue Springs, MO St. Robert Bellarmine.
Opoku, Joseph H. (BRK) Flushing, NY St. Michael.
Opondo, Protas *s.j.* '95 (BO)[V] Newton, MA The Jesuit Community at Boston College.
Opondo–Owora, Charles (SY) Endicott, NY St. Ambrose.
Oppenheim, Frank M. *s.j.* '55 (CIN)[P] Milford, OH Milford Spiritual Center.
Oppido, Harold J. *s.j.* '55 (NEW)[C] Jersey City, NJ St. Peter's Preparatory School; [N] Jersey City, NJ Jesuit Community of St. Peter's Prep, Inc..
Oppitz, Joseph *c.ss.r.* '53 (ALB)[L] Saratoga Springs, NY St. John Neumann Residence.
Oppong, Joseph '89 (PIT) Donora, PA Our Lady of the Valley.
Opps, Francis J. '58 (ALN) Bethlehem, PA St. Stanislaus; Coplay, PA St. Peter.
Opris, Gheorghe '71 (ROM) Dearborn, MI St. Mary.
Oquamanam, Mark (NY) Bronx, NY Montefiore Medical Center.
Oracion, Samuel '82 (NO) Jefferson, LA St. Agnes.
Oranczak, Ronald J. '78 (ALN) Retired.
Oranczak, Ronald '78 (ALN)[J] Bethlehem, PA Holy Family Villa.
Orandi, Nazareno '61 (NEW) Lyndhurst, NJ Our Lady of Mount Carmel.
Oravec, Christian R. *t.o.r.* '64 (ALT)[A] Loretto, PA St. Francis University; [F] Loretto, PA Mount Assisi Friary.
Oravetz, Robert F. '97 (PBR) Hawk Run, PA St. John the Baptist; Archives; Evangelization, Mission Activity and Ecumenism.
Orbanek, Gerald L. '66 (E)[B] Erie, PA Gannon University; [M] Erie, PA Villa Maria; The Bishop's Theological Advisory Committee; Lake Shore Visitor Advisory Board.
Orchik, Michael J. '73 (BAL) Baltimore, MD Little Flower, Shrine of.
Ordax, Emiliano '48 (MIA) Hialeah, FL St. Cecilia.
Ordejon, Luis Alberto '98 (NY) Bronx, NY St. Peter and St. Paul.
Ordenes, Guillermo *o.f.m.* '85 (ELP) San Antonio, TX Our Lady of the Angels.
Ordonez, Francisco R. '95 (GAL) Pearland, TX St. Helen.
Ordonez, Jose Naul '99 (CC) Alice, TX St. Joseph.
Ordorica, Jose Maria *sch.p.* '01 (LA) Los Angeles, CA Our Lady Help of Christians (Maria Auxiliadora).
Orel, Paul '84 (PHX) Mesa, AZ St. Timothy; Special Assignment; Adjutant Judicial Vicars.
Orellana, Roberto '01 (ATL) Marietta, GA Church of the Transfiguration.
Orellana Lizana, Jose Agustin *i.v.e.* '03 (BRK) Brooklyn, NY St. Gabriel The Archangel.
Orengo, Juan Rodriguez (PCE) Ponce, PR Christ the King; Episcopal Vicar for Pastoral Coordination; Children of Mary; Ecumenism; Legion of Mary.
Oreshoski, Gary '88 (RC) Buffalo, SD St. Anthony.
Orf, Raymond V. '55 (SPC) Springfield, MO Immaculate Conception Retired.
Organ, Patrick C. '71 (VEN) North Port, FL San Pedro.
Oria, Enrique *o.carm.* '58 (ARE) Morovis, PR Nuestra Senora del Carmen.
Orians, David '78 (COL) Newark, OH St. Francis de Sales.
Orians, Thomas *s.a.* '92 (NY)[EE] Garrison, NY Franciscan Friars of the Atonement.
Orians, Thomas *s.a.* (NEW) Part–time Staff.
Orilla, Josephino '93 (HON) Hilo, HI St. Joseph; Filipino Ministry.
Orimaco, Domingo '72 (SFR) Half Moon Bay, CA Our Lady of the Pillar; Deans.
Oriole, Phillip M. '70 (E) Erie, PA Mount Calvary.
Orique, David *o.p.* '01 (P) Eugene, OR St. Thomas More; [P] Eugene, OR University of Oregon (Eugene).
Oris, Fabian G. '42 (GBG) Retired.
Orlandi, Joseph J. '73 (PAT) Paterson, NJ St. Michael the Archangel; Army Reserve Chaplains.
Orlando, Gerard A. *c.p.* '46 (MET)[H] White Plains, NY.
Orlando, John V. '51 (ALT) Retired.
Orlando, Richard J. '47 (ROC) Retired.
Orlando, Vincent A. *s.j.* '74 (NO)[P] New Orleans, LA Ignatius Residence.
Orlett, Raymond *g.h.m.* '53 (CIN)[M] Cincinnati Headquarters of Glenmary Home Missioners.
Orlik, Dale A. '67 (SAG) Bay City, MI St. Boniface.
Orlikiewicz, Stanley '53 (JOL)[K] Naperville, IL St. John Vianney Villa; Ecumenism.
Orlinski, Richard A. (GRY) Bishop's Council of Priests.
Orlinski, Richard '73 (GRY) Hammond, IN St. John Bosco.
Orloski, Joseph F. '94 (SCR) Dickson City, PA Visitation of the Blessed Virgin Mary; Nanticoke, PA Holy Trinity.
Orloski, Raymond J. '62 (HBG) Kulpmont, PA Holy Angels.
Orlosky, Anselm *o.s.b.* '53 (PBR) Wall, PA Holy Trinity; [C] Butler, PA Holy Trinity Monastery; Pro–Synodal Judges.
Orlowski, Robert J. '97 (BUF) Williamsville, NY St. Gregory the Great.
Orlowski, Walter C. '79 (BGP) Norwalk, CT St. Matthew; Diocesan Consultors; Presbyteral Council.
Orlowsky, Michael T. '93 (ARL) Madison, VA Our Lady of the Blue Ridge.
Ormaza, Antonio *s.c.s.* '95 (DAL) Garland, TX Good Shepherd.
Ormond, Henry *o.carm.* '77 (JOL)[L] Darien Carmelite Provincial Office.
Ormond, Henry *o.carm.* (OAK)[B] Holy Names College.
Orndorff, Christopher M. '97 (TUC) Coolidge, AZ St. James; Vicars Forane.
Ornowski, Gerald *m.i.c.* (FBK) Fairbanks, AK St. Mark University Parish; Campus Ministry.
Orosco, James '81 (DAL)[A] Irving, TX Holy Trinity Seminary.
Orozco, Argemiro '92 (YAK) Toppenish, WA St. Aloysius; Presbyteral Council Executive Committee.
Orozco, Francisco *o.c.d.* '90 (DAL) Irving, TX St. Luke.
Orozco, Ramon (SB) Indio, CA Our Lady of Perpetual Help.
Orozco, Raphael R. '50 (CHI) Retired.
Orozco, Rodolfo '48 (FRS) Retired.
Orr, Garrett D. *s.j.* '83 (WDC)[E] North Bethesda, MD Georgetown Preparatory School.
Orr, James R. '79 (PIT) New Brighton, PA Holy Family.
Orr, John Arthur '01 (KNX) Knoxville, TN St. John Neumann.
Orr, Joseph T. '82 (ALT) Tyrone, PA St. Matthew's.
Orr, Joseph (ALT) Scouting.
Orr, Sherman '91 (WCH)[A] Wichita, KS Newman University.
Orr, Stephen L. (DM) Judges.
Orr, Stephen '74 (DM) On Special Assignment; [J] Des Moines, IA Roman Catholic Pastoral Center Foundation; Vicar General and Moderator of the Curia; Diocesan Consultors; Diocesan Corporation Board.
Orrigo, Mario J. '96 (BO) Lowell, MA St. Michael.
Orru, Bruno *s.x.* '63 (PAT)[M] Wayne Xaverian Missionary Fathers; FgM).
Orsborn, Bruce J. '81 (SD) San Diego, CA St. Jerome.
Orsborn, Bruce (SD) Presbyteral Council; Vicars Forane.
Orsi, Michael P. '76 (CAM) On Duty Outside the Diocese.
Orsini, James '74 (HON) Kapaa, HI St. Catherine.
Orsini, Joseph E. '64 (CAM) Disabled Retired
Orsino, Jerry '66 (OAK)[N] Oakland, CA Oblate Residence.
Orsolits, Norbert F. '65 (BUF) Retired.
Orsulak, Thomas J. '90 (ALN) Bethlehem, PA St. Anne; Elected Members.
Orsy, Ladislas *s.j.* '51 (NY)[EE] Loyola Hall, Jesuit Community.
Orsy, Ladislas *s.j.* '51 (WDC)[M] Washington, DC The Jesuit Community at Georgetown University.
Orszulak, Henry A. '67 (BUF) Judges; Lackawanna, NY St. Hyacinth.
Ortega, Carlos '99 (SR) St. Helena, CA St. Helena.
Ortega, Eduardo '77 (SFE) Absent on Leave.
Ortega, Eduardo '95 (BWN) Weslaco, TX San Martin de Porres; Diocesan Catholic Relief Services; San Juan Ministry Institute.
Ortega, Efren '72 (DAL) Retired.
Ortega, Jose Felix *l.c.* '01 (HRT)[V] Orange, CT Logos, Inc.; [V] Orange, CT LUX ET VITA, INC.; [V] Orange, CT Rossotto, Inc.; [V] Bethesda, MD Institute for Evangelization, Inc..
Ortega, Jose *m.sp.s.* '66 (P)[L] Mount Angel, OR Missionaries of the Holy Spirit, M.Sp.S..
Ortega, Ovidio '83 (SJN) Resident Chaplains; [F] Puerta De Tierra, PR Asylum For The Aged and Infirm.
Ortega, Rodrigo (NY) New York, NY St. Jude.
Ortega, Russell *o.s.a.* '86 (NY) Bronx, NY St. Nicholas of Tolentine.
Ortega Lemus, Ovidio '83 (SJN) San Juan, PR Sagrado Corazon de Jesus.
Ortega y Ortiz, Adam Lee '92 (SFE) Santa Fe, NM Santa Maria de la Paz Catholic Community.
Ortega y Ortiz, Adam (SFE) Defenders of the Bond.
Ortez, Sofonias '96 (VEN) Cape Coral, FL St. Andrew.
Orth, Anthony F. '75 (PH) Philadelphia, PA Nativity of the Blessed Virgin Mary.
Orthel, Joseph A. '89 (SPC) Houston, MO St. Mark.
Orthmann, James *o.c.s.o.* '94 (ARL)[J] Berryville, VA Cistercian Abbey of Our Lady of the Holy Cross.
Ortiz, Alexander F. *c.ss.r.* '76 (PH) Philadelphia, PA St. Boniface.
Ortiz, Alfredo Rolon '02 (MIA) Coral Gables, FL Little Flower.
Ortiz, Angel '87 (MGZ) Cabo Rojo, PR St. Michael.
Ortiz, Antonio '78 (DAL) Frisco, TX St. Francis of Assisi.
Ortiz, Arnold *o.s.j.* '72 (SAC)[A] Loomis, CA Mount St. Joseph Novitiate and Seminary.
Ortiz, Benedicto '57 (BWN) Retired.
Ortiz, Carlos (SJN) Judges; San Jose Minor Seminary.
Ortiz, Emerito '96 (WOR) Millbury, MA St. Brigid.
Ortiz, Gary (SFE) Presbyteral Council of the Archdiocese of Santa Fe; Air National Guard Chaplains.
Ortiz, J.C. '91 (PHX) W. Sedona, AZ St. John Vianney.
Ortiz, Jose A. '66 (LA) Baldwin Park, CA St. John the Baptist.
Ortiz, Jose Angel (CC) Corpus Christi, TX Our Lady of Perpetual Help.
Ortiz, Jose Antonio '85 (CGS) Cayey, PR San Esteban Protomartir.
Ortiz, Jose Luis '90 (CGS) Barranquitas, PR San Andres Apostol.
Ortiz, Leo W. (SFE) Pecos, NM St. Anthony.
Ortiz, Mar B. '82 (TR) Keyport, NJ Holy Family.
Ortiz, Marco A. (LA) Oxnard, CA Santa Clara.
Ortiz, Maximo J. *o.s.a.* '74 (WDC) Washington, DC St. Elizabeth's Hospital (Government Operated); [B] Silver Spring, MD Austin Friars Hall, Order of St. Augustine.
Ortiz, Michael '56 (SD) Retired.
Ortiz, Miguel Angel *o.f.m.cap.* '86 (SFR)[N] Burlingame, CA Capuchin Provincial House.
Ortiz, Miguel Gomez '02 (MRY) Watsonville, CA Our Lady of the Assumption.
Ortiz, Miguelangel *s.j.* (LA).
Ortiz, Pedro R. (CGS)[D] Catholic Youth.
Ortiz, Pedro '82 (CGS) Caguas, PR Nuestra Senora de la Providencia.
Ortiz, R. Alfredo '91 (ORL) De Land, FL St. Peter's.
Ortiz, Victor (SJN)[A] Bayamon Central University.
Ortiz–Mangual, Julio '02 (SJN) Palmer, PR Cristo Rey.
Ortiz–Mejias, Carlos (SJN) San Juan, PR Jesus Mediador; [C] San Juan, PR Seminario Menor San Jose.
Ortman, John '82 (DET) Macomb, MI St. Isidore.
Ortmann, William '57 (SD) San Diego, CA St. Joseph Cathedral.
Ortmeier, Paul R. '72 (OM) Clarkson, NE Holy Trinity.
Ortmeier, Paul '72 (OM) Howells, NE SS. Peter and Paul; Howells, NE St. John Nepomucene.
Ortmeier, Richard J. '56 (SFS) Retired.
Oruko, William '99 (KNX) Knoxville, TN Cathedral of the Sacred Heart of Jesus.
Orum, Vincent '92 (CAM) Swedesboro, NJ St. Joseph's.
Orumpakkatt, James *c.m.i.* '64 (STA) St. Augustine, FL Cathedral – Basilica of St. Augustine.
Orzech, Eric '93 (CLV) Garfield Heights, OH St. Therese.
Orzechowski, Jacek '02 (R) Durham, NC Immaculate Conception.
Orzechowski, Walter B. '49 (MIL) Retired.
Orzel, David J. '79 (SY) Oneida, NY St. Patrick.
Osasona, Felix I. *m.s.p.* (GAL) Houston, TX St. Peter the Apostle; Tallahassee, FL St. Eugene, Florida A&M University; Tallahassee–Florida Agricultural & Mechanical University, St. Eugene Chapel.
Osbahr, Theodore W. '67 (NEW) Irvington, NJ St. Paul the Apostle; South Essex Deanery 18.

Osborn, Douglas '68 (LAN) Flint, MI St. John Vianney; College of Consultors; Priest's Assignment Commission.
Osborn, William '66 (SFS) Redfield, SD St. Bernard.
Osborne, Francis M. '38 (LA) Retired.
Osborne, Kenan B. *o.f.m.* '55 (OAK)[S] Board of Directors:.
Osborne, Martin J. '50 (RVC) Southold, NY St. Patrick's Retired.
Osborne, Paul J. *o.f.m.* '64 (NY) Jeffersonville, NY St. George–St. Francis; Buffalo, NY SS. Rita & Patrick.
Osborne, Robert E. '54 (L) Defenders of the Bond Retired.
Osborne, Robert R. *s.m.* '66 (STL)[F] Kirkwood, MO St. John Vianney High School.
Osborne, Robert *s.m.* '66 (STL)[O] St. Louis, MO Cure of Ars Marianist Community.
Osborne, Stanley L. '59 (L) Elizabethtown, KY St. Ambrose; Elizabethtown, KY St. John the Baptist.
Osborne, Thomas *o.s.a.* '66 (JOL) Homer Glen, IL Our Mother of Good Counsel.
Osburg, Frank C. '60 (LEX) Versailles, KY St. Leo; Diocesan Consultors.
Osburg, Frank (LEX) Priests' Retirement Board.
Osburg, Gregory E. '77 (COV) Kenton, KY St. Matthew; Defenders of the Bond.
Oschwald, Daniel D. '98 (R) Special Assignment; Priests' Council.
Oschwald, Daniel (R) Vocations.
Osebold, Richard A. '60 (DET) Redford, MI St. John Bosco.
Oseguera, Melvin '94 (NEW) Jersey City, NJ St. Paul of the Cross.
Osendorf, James *c.m.* '80 (LA)[A] Camarillo, CA St. John's Seminary College of the Archdiocese of Los Angeles; [Q] Montebello, CA Vincentian Fathers and Brothers; [Q] Montebello, CA DePaul Evangelization Center; [W] Montebello, CA DePaul Evangelization Center.
Oser, Donald J. '53 (Y) North Canton, OH St. Paul Retired.
Oser, Donald '53 (Y) Retired.
Oser, Lance '01 (SFS) Hoven, SD St. Anthony of Padua.
Oser, Ronald E. '96 (ORL) Ocala, FL Our Lady of the Springs.
Osiander, Alfons M. '73 (BUF)[A] Sardinia, NY St. Jude; West Valley, NY St. John the Baptist.
Osias, Max '94 (NEW) Irvington, NJ St. Leo's.
Osinski, Ronald V. '72 (ALT) Air Force Reserve Chaplains; Portage, PA Our Lady of the Sacred Heart.
Osita Emeli, Edwin (LC)[D] Spiritual Services Dept..
Osmialowski, Sigmund '37 (DET) Retired.
Osorio, Celimo '87 (ELP) El Paso, TX Sts. Peter and Paul; San Elizario, TX San Felipe de Jesus.
Osorio, Flover H. '85 (CC) Corpus Christi, TX Our Lady of Guadalupe.
Osorio, Luis S. (CHL) Greensboro, NC Our Lady of Grace.
Osorio, Rudolfo B. '55 (NEW) Retired.
Osorio Mowrino, Jose Benito *o.de.m.* '62 (SJN) San Juan, PR Nuestra Senora de la Merced.
Osowski, Chester J. '49 (LC) Retired.
Ospina, Walter '02 (R) Wilson, NC Church of St. Therese.
Ospina–Briceno, Walter '02 (R) Cary, NC St. Michael the Archangel.
Ossa, Diego '89 (TYL) Diboll, TX Our Lady of Guadalupe.
Ossino, Angelo '57 (DEN) Retired.
Ossola, John R. '64 (SFD) Springfield, IL Cathedral of the Immaculate Conception.
Ostaszewski, Andrew '84 (NEW) Irvington, NJ Sacred Heart of Jesus.
Ostaszewski, Andrzej '84 (NEW) Jersey City, NJ St. Anthony of Padua.
Ostdick, Rupert *o.s.b.* '48 (IND)[K] St. Meinrad, IN St. Meinrad Archabbey.
Ostdiek, Dan H. *o.p.* '60 (CHI) Minneapolis, MN St. Albert the Great.
Ostdiek, Daniel (STP) Methodist Hospital; Bethesda Medical Center.
Ostdiek, Gil *o.f.m.* '60 (CHI)[N] Chicago, IL St. Joseph Interprovincial Post–Novitiate Formation House.
Ostdiek, Gilbert *o.f.m.* '78 (CHI).
Ostdiek, John *o.f.m.* '49 (SHP)[B] Ruston, LA St. Thomas Aquinas.
Ostendorf, Mark '81 (STP) Brooklyn Park, MN St. Vincent de Paul.
Ostendorf, Mark '81 (SCL) Special Assignment.
Osterhage, Louis *c.pp.s.* '58 (CIN) Dayton, OH St. Joseph.
Osterhaus, Mark '85 (DUB) Cedar Rapids, IA St. Matthew.
Osterhout, Conrad (NY)[EE] Yonkers, NY St. Leopold's Friary.
Osterle, Paul V. *s.j.* '59 (SP) Tampa, FL Sacred Heart.
Osterle, Paul *s.j.* '84 (SP)[T] Tampa, FL University of Tampa – Campus Ministry.
Osterman, Gerald J. '67 (BO) Everett, MA Immaculate Conception.
Osterman, Richard '69 (GF) Retired.
Ostertag, Robert C. *s.j.* '49 (MIL)[O] Wauwatosa, WI Jesuit Community at St. Camillus.
Ostini, Anthony H. *s.j.* '72 (BR)[J] Convent, LA Manresa House of Retreats.
Ostler, David M. '87 (PHX) Phoenix, AZ Our Lady of the Valley.
Ostner, Paul A. *s.s.j.* '45 (BAL)[S] Baltimore, MD St. Joseph's Manor.
Ostrander, Gary L. '71 (OM) Ralston, NE St. Gerald.
Ostrowski, David T. '89 (STP) Minneapolis, MN Holy Cross.
Ostrowski, Eugene S. '77 (WH) Wheeling, WV Corpus Christi.
Ostrowski, Eugene S. (BAL) Interdiocesan Judges.
Ostrowski, Joel *o.f.m.cap.* '51 (PIT)[N] Allison Park, PA St. Conrad Friary.
Ostrowski, John T. '98 (CLV) Painesville, OH St. Mary.
Ostrowski, Joseph C. '52 (SCR)[N] Dunmore, PA Villa St. Joseph Retired.
Ostrowski, Theodore L. '81 (CHI) Chicago, IL St. Adrian.
Ostrowski, Walter *s.v.d.* '65 (PIT)[N] Pittsburgh, PA Society of The Divine Word.
Osuagwu, Denis A. '89 (LAF) Lawtell, LA Holy Family; Lawtell, LA St. Ann.
Osuagwu, Evaristus (BGP) Bridgeport, CT St. Ambrose.
Osuagwu, Peter Chidi '89 (BRK) Elmhurst, NY Ascension.
Osuch, Michael *c.r.* '80 (CHI) Chicago, IL St. Hyacinth Basilica.
Osuji, Martin '96 (LR) Jonesboro, AR Blessed Sacrament; Marked Tree, AR St. Norbert; Weiner, AR St. Anthony's; [J] Jonesboro, AR Blessed John Newman University Parish.
Osuji, Ngozi '81 (BRK) Brooklyn, NY St. Charles Borromeo.
Osuju, Samuel D. (MO) Navy Chaplains.
Osuna, E. Donald '63 (OAK) Walnut Creek, CA St. Mary's.
Oswald, John '61 (LR)[H] Little Rock, AR St. John Manor Retired.
Oswald, Leo P. '78 (PH) Philadelphia, PA Holy Cross; Philadelphia, PA St. Madeleine Sophie.
Oswald, Norman R. '72 (MIL) Wood, WI Veterans Administration Medical Center; Special Assignment.
Oswald, Norman (MIL).
Oswald, Randy *o.m.i.* '97 (STP)[P] Buffalo, MN Christ the King Retreat Center.
Oswald, Richard S. '65 (LR) Rogers, AR St. Vincent de Paul.
Oswald, Richard (LR) Deans.
Oswald, Rob (GF) Diocesan Consultors; Priests' Council.
Oswald, Robert Michael '02 (GF) Scobey, MT St. Philip Bonitus.
Oswald, Ted '84 (SR) Lakeport, CA St. Mary; Members of the Curia; Deans; Board of Consultors; Priests' Council.
Oswalt, M. Price '96 (OKL) Kingfisher, OK SS. Peter and Paul.
Otellini, Steven D. '78 (SFR) Menlo Park, CA The Church of the Nativity; Knights of Malta; Board of Directors.
Oterino, Francis L. '87 (MET) On Duty Outside the Diocese.
Otero, Henry '62 (WDC) Waldorf, MD St. Peter.
Otero, Jose (NY) New York, NY St. Paul.
Otero, Lino *l.c.* '01 (SAC) Sacramento, CA Our Lady of Guadalupe Shrine.
Otillio, Peter *o.p.* '57 (CHI)[N] Chicago Dominicans (Provincial Office); (FgM).
Otor, Patrick *m.s.p.* '92 (BEA) Orange, TX St. Therese.
Ott, Alfred R. '60 (ALN) Allentown, PA Cathedral of St. Catharine of Siena Retired.
Ott, Carlton A. '36 (TOL) Retired.
Ott, Jeffery *o.p.* '02 (SAT) New Orleans, LA St. Anthony of Padua.
Ott, Mark S. '01 (CLV) Olmsted Falls, OH St. Mary of the Falls.
Ott, Richard W. *s.j.* '72 (OM)[K] Omaha, NE Jesuit Community at Creighton University.
Otten, Lammert B. *s.j.* '65 (SEA)[A] Seattle, WA Seattle University.
Otterbacher, John *g.h.m.* '56 (CIN)[M] Cincinnati Headquarters of Glenmary Home Missioners.
Otting, Loras C. '62 (DUB) Archives Retired.
Otting, Paul J. '66 (DUB) Dubuque, IA Holy Ghost.
Ottman, Timothy *o.s.b.* '78 (HON)[G] Waialua, HI Benedictine Monastery of Hawaii/Retreat Center.
Otto, David C. '77 (KAL) Edwardsburg, MI Our Lady of the Lake.
Otto, James C. '97 (PH) Exton, PA SS. Philip and James.
Otto, James '97 (PH)[D] Downingtown, PA Bishop Shanahan High School.
Otto, Leo '56 (SCL) Retired.
Otto, Ray *o.s.b.* '82 (SFS)[D] Milbank, SD Milbank Area Hospital/Avera Health; [E] Milbank, SD St. William Home Care Center.
Otto, Thomas '73 (PMB) Retired.
Oubre, Carroll L. '91 (ARL) Chantilly, VA St. Timothy.
Oubre, Louis T. '86 (BR) St. James, LA St. James; Presbyteral Council.
Oubre, Sinclair *j.c.l.* '86 (BEA) Diocesan College of Consultors and Presbyteral Council; Diocesan Judges; Apostleship of the Sea; Port Arthur, TX St. John; Port Arthur, TX St. Paul Mission; [I] Port Arthur, TX Apostleship of the Sea of the United States of America (AOSUSA).
Ouderkirk, Lloyd Paul '59 (DUB) Monona, IA St. Bridget's Retired.
Ouelette, Francis J. *o.m.i.* (BO) Lowell, MA Immaculate Conception.
Ouellet, Maurice F. *s.s.e.* '52 (VEN)[G] Selma, AL Edmundite Fathers.
Ouellette, John C. '95 (CC) Deans; College of Consultors; Personnel Board – Priests; Presbyteral Council; Premont, TX St. Theresa of the Infant Jesus.
Ouellette, Louis M. *m.s.* '61 (HRT)[M] Hartford, CT Missionaries of LaSalette.
Ouellette, Paul M. *o.m.i.* '67 (MIA) Miramar, FL St. Stephen.
Ouellette, Richard R. '75 (PRT) St. Gerard–Mt. Carmel; Madawaska, ME St. David's.
Ouellette, Roger J. '42 (PRT)[G] Waterville, ME Mt. St. Joseph Holistic Care Community Retired.
Ouillette, Arthur A. '55 (WOR) Retired.
Ouillette, Arthur C. (WOR) Deans.
Oulds, John V. '68 (PH) Coatesville, PA St. Joseph; Coatesville, PA St. Stanislaus Kostka.
Ouletta, James F. '60 (CHI) Retired.
Oullette, Richard R. (PRT) Deans.
Ouper, John J. '84 (JOL) Glen Ellyn, IL St. James the Apostle.
Ouper, John (JOL) Scouts.
Ours, Donald *c.m.* '94 (CHI) Chicago, IL St. Vincent de Paul; [N] Chicago DePaul Vincentian Residence.
Ours, Robert A. '80 (SY) Binghamton, NY St. Patrick; Special Assignment; [C] Binghamton, NY Seton Catholic Central High School of Broome County.
Outlaw, Keith (NY) On Leave of Absence.
Ovalle, Tom *o.m.i.* '77 (SAT)[S] Dickinson, TX Christian Renewal Center; San Antonio, TX San Juan De Los Lagos.
Overbaugh, Hugh A. '61 (HBG) Harrisburg, PA St. Catherine Laboure.
Overbaugh, Lawrence R. '55 (HBG) Mount Carmel, PA Our Lady of Mount Carmel; Deans; Presbyteral Council.
Overbaugh, Lawrence (HBG) Consultors, College.
Overbeck, Jerome T. *s.j.* '74 (CHI)[C] Chicago, IL Jesuit Community at Loyola University Chicago.
Overbeck, Kenneth C. '97 (BO) Plymouth, MA St. Bonaventure.
Overend, James '77 (ORG) Yorba Linda, CA St. Martin.
Overfield, Theresa (SPK)[G] Dayton, WA St. Vincent de Paul Store.
Overman, Robert F. '45 (STL) Retired.
Overmann, William J. '67 (SFD) Paris, IL St. Aloysius; Paris, IL St. Mary.
Overmyer, John '97 (FTW) Elkhart, IN St. Vincent de Paul; Advisory Board; Council of Priests; Elkhart.
Overstreet, Raymond J. '97 (PH) Springfield, PA St. Kevin; [D] Springfield, PA Cardinal O'Hara High School.
Overton, Troy *o.f.m.conv.* '89 (IND) Clarksville, IN St. Anthony of Padua.
Oviedo, Francisco *o.a.r.* '25 (NY) Bronx, NY St. Roch.
Oviedo, Francisco *o.a.r.* '62 (LSC) Las Cruces, NM Our Lady of Health.
Ovsak, William T. '99 (FAR) Drayton, ND St. Edward.
Ovsak, William '99 (FAR) Pembina, ND Assumption of the Blessed Virgin Mary.
Owambo, Cyril (NY) Valhalla, NY Westchester County Medical Center.
Owan, Victor '96 (ALB) Hudson Falls, NY Church of St. Mary's/St. Paul's.
Owen, John J. '48 (BIR) Retired.
Owenja, Charles '89 (NY) Pleasant Valley, NY St. Stanislaus Kostka.
Owens, Benjamin *c.ss.r.* '75 (OAK)[C] Oakland, CA Bishop O'Dowd High School.
Owens, Bernard C. *c.s.b.* '67 (GAL)[Q] Sugar Land Basilian Mission Center.
Owens, Bernard J. *s.j.* '72 (DET)[P] Bloomfield Hills, MI Manresa Jesuit Retreat House.
Owens, Edward *o.ss.t.* '80 (LA)[A] Camarillo, CA St. John's Seminary.
Owens, J. Edward *o.ss.t.* '80 (BAL)[S] Camarillo, CA St. John's Seminary.
Owens, John J. '49 (BIS) Retired.
Owens, John '48 (BIR) Trussville, AL Holy Infant of Prague.
Owens, Joseph P. *s.j.* '48 (DET)[P] Hamtramck, MI St. Ladislaus.
Owens, Leroy E. '64 (BO) Medfield, MA St. Edward the Confessor.
Owens, Michael J. '84 (HON) On Duty Outside the Diocese.
Owens, S. Brian '95 (WH) Charles Town, WV St. James.

Owens, Thomas J. '74 (PH) Maple Glen, PA St. Alphonsus.
Owino, Felix *a.j.* '92 (PIT) Pittsburgh, PA St. Bede.
Owusu–Achaw, Stephen (KCK) Topeka, KS Holy Name.
Owusu–Ansah, Edward '94 (SY) Endicott, NY Our Lady of Good Counsel.
Owusu–Boateng, Johnson '85 (VIC) Vanderbilt, TX St. John Bosco.
Owusu–Sekyere, Augustine '89 (HRT) East Hartford, CT St. Mary's.
Oxley, Walter R. '03 (TOL) Toledo, OH St. Patrick of Heatherdowns.
Oyabu, Charles *s.m.* '70 (HON) Helotes, TX Our Lady of Guadalupe.
Oyafemi, Clement O. '94 (NY) Suffern, NY Sacred Heart.
Ozbun, John W. '84 (WIN) Blue Earth, MN SS. Peter and Paul's; Winnebago, MN St. Mary's.
Ozbun, John (WIN) Finance Council; Elected Deanery Representatives.
Ozimek, Adam Z. '94 (ATL) Roswell, GA St. Andrew.
Ozimek, Anthony J. *o.s.b.* '68 (CLV)[O] Billings, MT St. Vincent Hospital.
Ozimek, Anthony J. *o.s.b.* '68 (GF)[G] Billings, MT St. Vincent Healthcare.
Ozimek, Eugene F. '45 (SPR)[H] Holyoke, MA Mount St. Vincent Nursing Home Retired.
Ozminkowski, Clyde *o.carm.* '54 (VEN)[G] Venice, FL Carmel in Venice.
Ozokpor, Vitalis D. '81 (BRK) Long Island City, NY Immaculate Conception.
Ozug, John C. '77 (FR) Edgartown, MA St. Elizabeth; Oak Bluffs, MA Sacred Heart; Vineyard Haven, MA St. Augustine.

P

Paa, Donald R. '47 (KC) Retired.
Paa, Joseph F. '41 (BUF) Retired.
Paa, Raymond F. '55 (BUF) Finance Council; Williamsville, NY Nativity of the Blessed Virgin Mary Retired.
Paala, Jonathan '75 (SFR) Foster City, CA St. Luke.
Pabayo, Anthony C. *s.j.* '96 (PH)[N] San Francisco, CA Jesuit Community at University of San Francisco.
Pabin, Chester J. '92 (STU) Lafferty, OH St. Mary.
Pable, Marty *o.f.m.cap.* '58 (LC)[H] Marathon City, WI St. Anthony Retreat Center.
Pablo, Maximo Asencius *m.s.a.* '68 (NOR)[F] Cromwell Society of the Missionaries of the Holy Apostles.
Pabst, Peter *s.j.* '86 (SJ)[E] San Jose, CA Sacred Heart Nativity School.
Pace, Paul J. '66 (HRT) Waterbury, CT St. Francis Xavier's.
Pace, William J. '51 (SCR)[N] Dunmore, PA Villa St. Joseph Retired.
Pace, Woodrow H. '95 (LC) Neillsville, WI St. Mary; Deans; Personnel Council.
Pachana, Robert A. '98 (NEW) Bayonne, NJ Mt. Carmel.
Pacheco, Agostinho S. '60 (BWN) McAllen, TX Our Lady of Sorrows.
Pacheco, Luis Hurtado '00 (VEN) Arcadia, FL St. Paul.
Pacheco, Mario '76 (LA) Covina, CA Sacred Heart.
Pacheco, Victor *c.m.* '84 (LA) Phoenix, AZ St. Vincent de Paul.
Pachence, Ron '74 (SD)[B] Pratical Theology Program; [B] University of San Diego.
Pachence, Ron '74 (SAV)[B] Pastoral Care and Counseling Program.
Pachence, Ronald A. '74 (SAV) On Duty Outside the Diocese.
Pacheo–Sanchez, Luis '79 (MIL) On Leave.
Pachetti, Angelo (NEW) West New York, NJ St. Mary Help of Christians.
Pachla, Stanley L. '83 (DET) Eastpointe, MI St. Veronica.
Pacho, Jesus '51 (PCE) Retired.
Pacho, Jesus '65 (PCE)[B] The Pontifical Catholic University of Puerto Rico.
Pacholczyk, Tadeusz '99 (FR) Falmouth, MA St. Patrick's.
Pacholec, Daniel S. '96 (SPR) Chicopee, MA St. Rose de Lima; Bishop's Commission for Clergy; Presbyteral Council; Vocations.
Pacini, Mario *s.a.c.* '66 (ALB)[R] Cohoes, NY Apostolate for the Suffering.
Pacini, Peter *c.s.c.* (P)[B] University of Portland; [L] Portland, OR Holy Cross Fathers & Brothers, C.S.C. – University of Portland.
Paciorek, Joseph C. *c.m.* '35 (HRT)[M] Manchester DePaul Provincial Residence.
Paciorek, Piotr '80 (Poland)[A] Boynton Beach, FL St. Vincent de Paul Regional Seminary.
Pacitti, Gary '89 (PH) Philadelphia, PA Annunciation B.V.M..
Packard, Nathan '87 (SCL) Chokio, MN St. Mary's; Chokio, MN St. Charles.
Packard, Walter E. '71 (E) Warren, PA St. Joseph.
Pacocha, Edwin D. '62 (CHI) Chicago, IL St. Cornelius.
Pacquing, Joseph '83 (SJ) San Jose, CA St. Maria Goretti.
Pacwa, Mitchell C. *s.j.* '76 (BIR)[N] Chicago Chicago Province of the Society of Jesus–Provincial Office.
Pacwa, Mitchell *s.j.* '76 (DAL)[B] University of Dallas.
Paczesny, John R. '61 (MIL)[J] Mequon, WI St. Mary's Hospital Ozaukee, Inc.; Whitefish Bay, WI St. Monica Retired.
Paczkowski, Vincent *s.d.b.* '86 (NEW) Elizabeth, NJ St. Anthony's
Padavick, William B. '63 (CLV) Oberlin, OH Sacred Heart.
Padazinski, C. Michael '88 (SFR) South San Francisco, CA Mater Dolorosa; Vice Chancellor; Judicial Vicar and Director.
Padazinski, Michael C. (SFR) Deans; Air Force Reserve Chaplains
Padberg, John W. *s.j.* '57 (STL)[O] St. Louis, MO Jesuit Community Corporation at St. Louis University – Jesuit Hall; [U] St. Louis, MO Jesuit Community – Ministries [U] St. Louis, MO Institute of Jesuit Sources.
Paddack, John N. '84 (NY)[E] New York, NY Monsignor Farrell High School.
Padden, Neil *o.f.m.* '55 (PAT)[M] Butler, NJ St. Anthony Friary.
Paddock, Richard W. '59 (RCK) Elburn, IL St. Gall Retired.
Padelli, Emilio P. '62 (HRT) Broad Brook, CT St. Catherine.
Padget, Leo L. '01 (SFE) Tucumcari, NM St. Anne; Vicars Forane (Deans).
Padgett, Gary T. '99 (L) Louisville, KY Ascension of Our Lord; Clergy Personnel Commission; Archdiocesan Examiners
Padilla, Aquino D. '60 (SFR) Daly City, CA Our Lady of Perpetual Help.
Padilla, Glibert '55 (TUC) Retired.
Padilla, Jose Manuel '03 (TUC) Yuma, AZ St. Francis of Assisi.
Padilla, Lionel Pacheco *c.p.* '96 (SJN) San Juan, PR Nuestra Senora de la Piedad.
Padilla, Manuel G. '99 (CHI) Chicago, IL Maternity of the Blessed Virgin Mary.
Padilla, Norberto *c.m.f.* '90 (SJN) Bayamon, PR San Antonio Maria Claret.
Padilla, Rafael '89 (VEN) Venice, FL Our Lady of Lourdes; Hispanic, Migrant and Spanish Speaking Apostolates/National Migration Week.
Padilla, Rafael (VEN) Auditors; Defenders of the Bond; Promoters of Justice; Judges.
Padin, Jose *m.m.* '97 (FgM).
Padinjareknra, James J. *s.j.* '91 (MIL)[O] Milwaukee, WI Jesuit Community at Marquette University.
Padinjarepeedika, Jose L.F. *c.m.i.* '72 (LAF) Melville, LA St. John the Evangelist.
Pado, Thomas '75 (ORG) Irvine, CA St. Elizabeth Ann Seton.
Padrez, Mark *o.p.* '95 (OAK)[N] Oakland, CA Western Dominican Province.
Paduch, Frank '89 (BEA) Absent On Leave.
Padula, Armand *o.f.m.* '56 (NY)[EE] New York, NY Franciscan Province of the Immaculate Conception.
Paek, Joseph *o.s.b.* '03 (SP)[O] St. Leo, FL St. Leo Abbey.
Pael, Prosper '85 (CAM) Williamstown, NJ St. Mary's.
Pafchik, Lawrence F. *o.f.m.* '42 (PAT)[M] Ringwood, NJ Holy Name Friary, Inc..
Paffel, Gregory '01 (SCL) Foley, MN St. John's.
Pagan, Alberto *o.p.* '87 (SJN) Carolina, PR Ntra. Sra. de Fatima; Army Chaplains.
Pagan, Angel M. '83 (ARE) On Duty Outside the Diocese.
Pagan, Angel (SJN)[B] San Juan, PR Colegio Angeles Custodios.
Pagano, Bernard T. '58 (WIL) On Duty Outside the Diocese.
Pagano, Peter E. '52 (SPR) Retired.
Pagan Torres Angel M. '80 (ARE) San Juan, PR San Jose Obrero.
Page, Anthony J. '69 (LA) La Mirada, CA Beatitudes of Our Lord.
Page, Charles T. '91 (KAL) Buchanan, MI St. Anthony.
Page, David '58 (ORL) Indialantic, FL Holy Name of Jesus.
Page, Hugh R. '80 (FTW)[B] University of Notre Dame Du Lac.
Page, Leon J. '56 (DET) Retired.
Page, Stephen C. '87 (DAV) Fairfield, IA St. Mary's.
Page, Thomas P. '79 (GR) Rockford, MI Our Lady of Consolation; On Special Assignment.
Pagel, John M. '80 (CHL) Asheville, NC St. Joan of Arc.
Pageot, Roger *s.s.s.* '53 (CLV)[O] Richfield, OH Regina Health Center.
Pagliara, Alfonso D. *o.f.m.cap.* '81 (SP) Tampa, FL Most Holy Redeemer.
Pagliari, Robert M. *c.ss.r.* '75 (ORL)[E] New Smyrna Beach, FL Redemptorist Fathers of the Vice Province of Richmond.
Pagliari, Robert *c.ss.r.* '75 (NY)[I] New York, NY The Catholic Charities of the Archdiocese of New York; [EE] New York, NY Redemptorist Priests and Brothers, C.Ss.R.. [N] Office for the Disabled.
Pagliari C.SS.R., Robert (NY) Disabilities, Office of Persons with.
Pagliuca, Joseph P. '43 (BUR) Retired.
Pagnotta, James V. '69 (NEW) Jersey City, NJ St. Joseph's.
Pagones, Peter '68 (ALB) Schaghticoke, NY Church of the Holy Trinity; Schenectady, NY St. Paul the Apostle.
Paguaga, Juan Carlos '00 (MIA) Coral Gables, FL Little Flower.
Pahamtang, Leonardo '77 (LUB) Ralls, TX St. Michael; Presbyteral Council.
Pahl, Norman *o.m.i.* '58 (DUL) International Falls, MN St. Thomas Aquinas.
Pahler, Robert E. '57 (CLV) Cuyahoga Falls, OH Immaculate Heart of Mary; Uniontown, OH Queen of Heaven Retired.
Pai, Simon '52 (RVC) Retired.
Paider, Paul (GB) Francis Creek, WI St. Anne; Francis Creek, WI St. Augustine.
Paillacho, Jose '87 (MOB) Montgomery, AL St. Peter.
Painter, E. B. *s.j.* '75 (P) Portland, OR St. Mary Magdalene.
Pais, Rohwin *o.f.m.* (BO) Boston, MA St. Leonard of Port Maurice.
Paisley, James J. '85 (SCR) Laflin, PA St. Maria Goretti; Deans.
Paisley, John C. '62 (DUB) Strawberry Point, IA St. Mary; Lamont, IA St. Mary; Lamont, IA St. Mary's.
Paiva, Antonio M. '49 (PRO) Providence, RI Our Lady of the Rosary Retired.
Paiz, William *c.m.f.* '79 (RNO) Battle Mountain, NV St. John Bosco.
Pajarillo, Cesar C. '03 (RCK) Crystal Lake, IL St. Thomas the Apostle.
Pajkos, James *o.f.m.* (JOL) Joliet, IL SS. Cyril and Methodius.
Pak, Benedict Jeong Bay (SFR) Korean Catholic Ministry.
Pak, Phillip '78 (LA) Los Angeles, CA St. Basil's.
Pak, Pyong Gwan *s.j.* '99 (BO)[V] Newton, MA The Jesuit Community at Boston College.
Pak, Sang–Hun *s.j.* '01 (MIL)[O] Milwaukee, WI Jesuit Community at Marquette University.
Pakenham, Daniel J. '65 (MIL) Elm Grove, WI St. Mary.
Pakianather, Aloysius '78 (RVC) Massapequa, NY St. Rose of Lima.
Pakiz, Rudolph '46 (DUL) Tower, MN St. Martin's.
Pakosta, Francis J. '52 (SUP) Retired.
Pakula, Michael G. '73 (PEO) Geneseo, IL St. Malachy's.
Pakutka, William J. '43 (SCR)[N] Dunmore, PA Villa St. Joseph; Priests' Retirement Advisory Board Retired.
Pala, Manuel Soler *m.ss.cc.* '70 (SJN)[A] Bayamon Central University.
Palacino, Joseph '82 (BGP) Norwalk, CT St. Jerome.
Palacios, Antonio *o.a.r.* '71 (NY) Bronx, NY St. Anselm.
Palacios, Heriberto J. '93 (LA) Lynwood, CA St. Emydius.
Palacios, Joseph M. *s.j.* '87 (WDC)[M] Washington, DC Woodstock Jesuit Community.
Palackal, Joseph *c.m.i.* '79 (India) Maspeth, NY St. Stanislaus Kostka.
Paladino, John '91 (NEW) Scotch Plains, NJ St. Bartholomew; Plainfield, NJ Muhlenberg Regional Medical Center; Muhlenberg Regional Medical Center.
Palafox, Lorenzo J. *s.j.* '67 (SAC)[D] Sacramento, CA Jesuit High School; [I] Carmichael, CA Jesuit High School Community of Sacramento.
Palakudy, James *s.a.c.* '78 (VEN) Sarasota, FL St. Martha.
Palamattath, Sebi Antony *c.m.i.* '91 (PH) Philadelphia, PA Our Lady of Mt. Carmel.
Palang, Mansueto P. '77 (BR) Duluth, GA Catholic Church Of St. Monica Retired.
Palardy, William B. '85 (BO)[A] Brighton, MA St. John Seminary School of Theology.
Palaroan, Moises '78 (STA) Absent on Sick Leave.
Palasits, John A. '58 (NEW) Retired.
Palathara, Jose *c.m.i.* '70 (AMA) Clarendon, TX St. Mary's; Groom, TX Immaculate Heart of Mary.
Palathingal, Joseph '90 (SFR) Daly City, CA Our Lady of Mercy.
Palazzolo, Anthony P. '93 (STA) Special Assignment.
Palcheck, Gerald F. '67 (SD) Descanso, CA Our Lady of Light.
Palcisko, Raymond '58 (CR) Retired.
Palepale, Marisi *ss.cc.* '86 (HON)[G] Kaneohe, HI Sacred Hearts Center.
Palermo, Albert A. '63 (MIL) Retired.
Palermo, Albert '63 (AUS) Retired.
Palermo, Angelo *s.a.c.* '61 (NY) Pearl River, NY St. Margaret.
Palermo, Frank C. '55 (SPC) Springfield, MO Holy Trinity Retired.
Palermo, Joseph S. '94 (NO) New Orleans, LA St. Rita;

Archdiocesan Administrative Council; Executive Director; St. Thomas More Catholic Lawyers Association.
Palez, Oscar '91 (STO) Absent on Leave.
Palica, Jacek *o.c.d.* '96 (GRY)[I] Munster, IN Discalced Carmelite Fathers Monastery.
Palick, George '58 (PIT) Butler, PA St. Fidelis of Sigmaringen.
Paliokas, Algirdas *s.j.* '73 (CHI) Lemont, IL Blessed Jurgis Matulaitis; [N] Chicago Lithuanian American Jesuits.
Palis, Theo '45 (OAK) Bay Point, CA Our Lady Queen of the World.
Palisada, Arthur *s.s.p.* '68 (Y)[A] Canfield, OH Society of St. Paul.
Paliwoda, Steven '94 (SJP) Akron, OH St. Nicholas; Presbyteral Council; Vocation Director.
Palka, Bernard *s.a.* '72 (NY)[BB] Garrison, NY St. Christopher's Inn; [EE] Garrison, NY St. Christopher's Inn.
Palka, Bogdan *s.d.s.* '92 (WDC)[B] Silver Spring, MD Salvatorian Community.
Palka, Bogdan *s.d.s.* '92 (BAL).
Palka, Edwin '96 (SP)[M] Dade City, FL St. Rita.
Palko, John A. '54 (PIT) McKeesport, PA St. Martin de Porres Retired.
Palko, John J. '67 (ALT) Presbyteral Council; Hollidaysburg, PA St. Mary's.
Palko, Raymond (STF) Buffalo, NY St. Nicholas.
Palko, Thomas '59 (VEN) Fort Myers, FL Blessed Pope John XXIII.
Palkowski, Jan '76 (PH) Philadelphia, PA St. John Cantius.
Palladino, Alfonso G. '43 (BO) Melrose, MA St. Mary of the Annunciation; Senior Priests Retired.
Palladino, Robert J. '58 (P) Estacada, OR St. Aloysius.
Pallardy, James G. '87 (PEO) Peoria, IL St. Bernard's.
Palliparambil, Jose Simon '62 (RVC) Hicksville, NY Our Lady of Mercy; Plainview, NY North Shore Hospital at Plainview.
Pallivathuckal, Abraham Joseph '73 (MIA) Hollywood, FL Nativity.
Pallivathukkall, Jacob M. '65 (PT) Chattahoochee, FL Holy Cross Parish.
Pallo, Joseph L. '61 (LR) Blytheville, AR Immaculate Conception; Osceola, AR St. Matthew's; [L] Blytheville, AR Immaculate Conception Trust Fund; Deans.
Palluck, M. Charles '66 (SEA) Black Diamond, WA St. Barbara.
Palma, Raul *sch.p.* '58 (LA)[Q] Los Angeles, CA Piarist Fathers.
Palmatier, David *o.s.b.* '59 (RCK)[G] Aurora, IL Marmion Abbey.
Palmeno, Alberto *o.s.a.* '68 (LAR) Laredo, TX Holy Redeemer.
Palmer, Frank S. '62 (DM) Indianola, IA St. Thomas Aquinas.
Palmer, Herbert *o.s.b.* '39 (SD)[H] Oceanside, CA Prince of Peace Abbey, Benet Hill.
Palmer, John *c.s.v.* '71 (JOL)[A] Lisle, IL Benedictine University.
Palmer, Michael C. '63 (BGP) Wilton, CT Our Lady of Fatima; Parochial Examiners.
Palmer, Michael J. '70 (STL) Retired.
Palmer, Patrick '48 (SAT)[K] San Antonio, TX Padua Place Retired.
Palmer, Richard *o.s.a.* '87 (FgM).
Palmer, Samuel I. '57 (DM) Retired.
Palmer, Samuel (DM) Defenders of the Bond.
Palmer, Thomas '48 (SAT) Retired.
Palmer, William '03 (TYL) Tyler, TX Cathedral of the Immaculate Conception; Diocesan Liturgical Commission.
Palmese, Anthony '76 (ORL) Ocala, FL St. Jude's Catholic Community.
Palmieri, Alexander J. '76 (PH) Conshohocken, PA SS. Cosmas and Damian; [BB] Merion Station, PA Sisters of Mercy of the Americas, Merion Regional Community, Convent; Vicar for Religious; The Chancery; Archdiocesan Judges; College of Consultors; Council of Priests; On Special or Other Archdiocesan Assignment.
Palmieri, Armando M. *s.d.v.* '98 (NEW) Palisades Park, NJ St. Nicholas; [I] Florham Park, NJ Vocationist Fathers Retreat Center.
Palmieri, Frank *c.r.m.* '62 (CHR) Goose Creek, SC Immaculate Conception.
Palmieri, Louis R. '93 (BO) Avon, MA St. Michael.
Palmieri, Luigi '67 (ALN) Easton, PA St. Anthony of Padua.
Palmieri, Thaddeus *o.f.m.* '48 (NY)[EE] Northampton, MA.
Palmigiano, James '88 (WOR)[A] Spencer, MA St. Joseph's Abbey School of Theology and Institute of Monastic Studies; [O] Spencer, MA St. Joseph's Abbey; [A] Spencer, MA St. Joseph's Abbey School of Theology and Institute of Monastic Studies.
Palmiotto, Paul C. '82 (BRK) Jamaica, NY St. Benedict, the Moor; Jamaica, NY St. Bonaventure's.
Palmisano, Peter J. '93 (NEW) Franklin Lakes, NJ Most Blessed Sacrament.
Palmitessa, Paul '56 (SD) Retired.
Palo, Anthony *o.carm.* '64 (NEW) Englewood, NJ St. Cecilia's.
Paloma, Victor E. '70 (NEW) Jersey City, NJ Our Lady of Victories.
Palomera, Ramon '99 (LA) Culver City, CA St. Augustine.
Palomera, Ramona G. '99 (LA) Wilmington, CA Holy Family.
Palomino, Edwardo '49 (NY) Retired.
Palomino, Esviardo '49 (NY) New York, NY St. Lucy.
Palomino, Ignacio '85 (HBG) Lancaster, PA Iglesia Catolica San Juan Bautista.
Palomo, Benigno *o.s.a.* '66 (SJN) Bayamon, PR San Agustin.
Palos, Anthony Z. *o.a.r.* '60 (LA) Montebello, CA St. Benedict.
Palos, Hector *c.s.* (CHI) Melrose Park, IL Our Lady of Mount Carmel.
Palpale, Marisi *ss.cc.* '86 (WDC)[B] Cheverly, MD Damien House.
Palsa, Steven M. '79 (PIT) Carnegie, PA St. Elizabeth Ann Seton.
Palubinskas, Vytautas A. '54 (BRK) Retired.
Paluck, Casimir '61 (BIS) Mandan, ND Christ the King.
Palumbo, Eugene *s.d.b.* (NEW)[N] Ramsey, NJ Don Bosco Prep Salesian Residence; [C] Ramsey, NJ Don Bosco Preparatory High School.
Palumbos, Edward L. '72 (ROC) Fairport, NY Assumption of the Blessed Virgin Mary; Liturgical Commission.
Paluse, Richard V. '42 (PIT) Retired.
Palys, Daniel J. '69 (BUF) Finance Council; Evangelization Commission; Elma, NY St. Gabriel.
Pambello, Louis M. '81 (NEW) Montclair, NJ Immaculate Conception.
Pambello, Louis '81 (NEW) West Orange, NJ Kessler Institute for Rehabilitation; Kessler Institute for Rehabilitation.
Pamintuan, Edison *m.s.* (SB) Moreno Valley, CA St. Christopher.
Pamment, Duaine H. '64 (LAN) Laingsburg, MI St. Isidore.
Pampackal, Mathew *s.j.* '82 (Kerala)[N] Berkeley, CA Jesuit Community at Jesuit School of Theology at Berkeley.
Pamplaniyil, Matthew V. '76 (FAR) Oakes, ND St. Charles Borromeo; Oakes, ND St. Raphael.
Pamula, Robert (MO) Army Reserve Chaplains.
Panackel, Philip '89 (India) Fort Smith, AR Immaculate Conception.
Panagia, Sal J. '73 (PAT) Paterson, NJ Our Lady of Pompei.
Panagoplos, Christopher *t.o.r.* '76 (ALT) Altoona, PA Our Lady of Mt. Carmel.
Panakal, Alex *o.c.d.* '75 (STO) Sonora, CA St. Patrick Church of Sonora (Pastor of).
Panakal, John Bosco '70 (JOL) Winfield, IL St. John the Baptist.
Panakal, Thomson '60 (JOL) Lockport, IL St. Dennis.
Panaligan, Vicente C. '77 (BR) St. Amant, LA Holy Rosary.
Panares, Auxentivs '62 (WDC) Retired.
Panaretos, Paul D. *s.j.* '84 (CLV)[D] Cuyahoga Falls, OH Walsh Jesuit High School; [T] Akron, OH Loyola of the Lakes Jesuit Retreat House, Inc..
Panato, Pasquino *m.c.c.j.* '64 (NEW)[N] Montclair, NJ Comboni Missionaries of the Heart of Jesus (Verona Fathers).
Panchot, Daniel A. *c.s.c.* '65 (AUS)[G] Austin, TX Congregation of Holy Cross – Southern Province.
Panchuk, Myron '82 (STN) Chicago, IL SS. Volodymyr and Olha; Diocesan Consultors; Presbyteral Council; Personnel Board.
Pancorbo, Marcos A. '58 (PCE) Ponce, PR Cathedral of Our Lady of Guadalupe; Ponce, PR Church Our Lady of Miraculous Medal; [H] Penuelas, PR Training School for the Lay Apostolate (Hermanos Cheos); Diocesan Consultors.
Pancorbo, Marcos (PCE) Diocesan Board of Administration; Parish Priests Consultors.
Panczuk, Bernard J. *o.s.b.m.* '63 (STF) Long Island City, NY Holy Cross.
Panczyk, Miroslaw *s.d.b.* '94 (PAT) Paterson, NJ St. Anthony's.
Pandolfo, Lawrence *o.p.* '39 (NO) Jefferson, LA Elmwood Partners.
Pane, Andrew '87 (NY) Retired.
Panek, Andrezej K. '83 (LC) Cazenovia, WI St. Anthony de Padua.
Panek, Andrzej K. (LC) Richland Center, WI Nativity of the Blessed Virgin Mary; Cazenovia, WI Sacred Heart.
Panek, Edward B. '91 (CHI) Chicago, IL St. Monica.
Panek, Robert M. '70 (NY) Gardiner, NY St. Charles Borromeo.
Panepinto, Vincent P. '67 (ROC) Rochester, NY Corpus Christi.
Panful, Michael (NY) Staten Island, NY St. Clare.
Pang, Stephano (IND) Indianapolis, IN St. Lawrence.
Pangratz, Clement H. *o.s.b.* '47 (SEA)[L] Lacey, WA St. Martin's Abbey.
Paniagua, Carlos *s.v.d.* '00 (CHI)[B] Techny, IL Divine Word Residence.
Paniagua, Edwin *o.f.m.* (NY)[EE] Pontificio Ateneo Antonianum.
Paniagua, Jose L. '62 (MIA) Hialeah, FL St. Benedict.
Paniagua, Pablo '49 (SAT)[K] San Antonio, TX Casa De Padres.
Paniagua, Pablo '59 (SAT) Retired.
Paninski, John *m.s.* '61 (PEO) Georgetown, IL St. Isaac Jogues; [M] Georgetown, IL La Salette Missionaries.
Pank, Julian F. '40 (L) Retired.
Panke, Robert J. '91 (WDC) Pastoral Center Special Ministries.
Panke, Robert J. '96 (WDC) Washington, DC St. Patrick.
Panke, Robert (WDC) Director, Vocations for Men.
Pankiraj, Theesmas '90 (NEW) Fort Lee, NJ Madonna.
Panos, Patrick G. '68 (PAT) Ringwood, NJ St. Catherine of Bologna.
Panossian, Antoine *p.i.a.* '66 (LA) Los Angeles, CA Our Lady Queen of Martyrs.
Pansza, Gilbert (FWT) Bridgeport, TX St. John the Baptizer; Decatur, TX Assumption of the Blessed Virgin Mary; Bridgeport, TX St. Mary.
Panthackal, Joseph '70 (CAM) Blackwood, NJ St. Jude's.
Pantle, G. Donald *s.j.* '60 (SCR)[C] Scranton, PA The University of Scranton.
Pantyra, Anthony F. '78 (RCK) Warren, IL Holy Trinity.
Pantyra, Anthony '78 (RCK) Warren, IL St. Joseph; Warren, IL St. Ann.
Panula, Arne A. '73 (NY)[JJ] New York, NY Prelature of the Holy Cross and Opus Dei.
Panuska, Joseph A. *s.j.* '60 (ALN)[A] Wernersville, PA Jesuit Center; [A] Wernersville, PA Jesuit Center.
Panza, Paul D. '54 (ALT) Retired.
Panza, Paulo Sergio *o.s.b.* '03 (GBG)[H] Latrobe Saint Vincent Archabbey.
Panzer, Joel '94 (LIN) Lincoln, NE North American Martyrs.
Paolazzi, Tiziano *c.s.* '87 (MIA) Hollywood, FL Our Lady Aparecida Mission.
Paoli, Livius *o.s.b.* '37 (DET)[K] Detroit, MI St. Sylvester Monastery; Detroit, MI St. Scholastica.
Paolo, Francis de Sales *o.f.m.* '58 (BO) East Boston, MA Our Lady of Mt. Carmel.
Paolozzi, Joseph L. '61 (MEM) Martin, TN St. Jude's; [K] Martin, TN Cooperative Ministries Interfaith Center.
Paolozzi, Joseph (MEM) Clergy Personnel Board; Martin.
Paonessa, Ralph *o.f.m.* '63 (NY)[EE] St. Lawrence Friary.
Papa, Charles E. '67 (RVC) Sound Beach, NY St. Louis de Montfort.
Papa, Christopher J. '89 (PH) West Chester, PA St. Agnes.
Papa, Dominic '60 (BRK)[V] Jamaica, NY Immaculate Conception Monastery.
Papa, Frank E. *s.o.l.t.* '89 (HRT) East Hartford, CT St. Mary's.
Papa, Frank '89 (CC)[G] Robstown, TX Society of Our Lady of the Most Holy Trinity.
Papaj, Joseph J. *s.j.* '70 (NEW)[B] Jersey City, NJ Jesuit Center; [N] Jersey City, NJ Jesuits of Saint Peter's College, Inc..
Papalia, Pasquale A. '74 (NEW) On Duty Outside the Archdiocese.
Papalia, Pasquale '74 (TR) New Monmouth, NJ St. Mary.
Pape, William H. '70 (ALB) Albany, NY Cathedral of the Immaculate Conception; [R] Albany, NY The Cathedral Restoration Corp..
Papen, Gerald T. *c.s.c.* '63 (FTW)[I] Congregacion de Santa Cruz.
Papenfuss, Raymond *c.s.c.* (FTW)[I] Notre Dame, IN Congregation of Holy Cross, Midwest Province.
Papera, Lewis V. '67 (NEW) Hasbrouck Heights, NJ Corpus Christi.
Paperini, Richard *o.s.b.* '77 (P)[A] St. Benedict, OR Mount Angel Seminary.
Papes, Joseph T. '59 (GF) Retired.
Papes, Joseph '01 (PMB) Tequesta, FL St. Jude; Spiritual Moderator.
Papes, Rudy *c.ss.r.* '65 (GR) Grand Rapids, MI St. Alphonsus; [I] Grand Rapids, MI The Society of the Redemptorists of the City of Grand Rapids.
Papesh, Michael L. '83 (STP) St. Paul, MN Holy Spirit.
Papiernik, Roman J. '40 (LC) Retired.
Papineau, Andre *s.d.s.* '65 (MIL).
Papineau, Daniel R. *m.i.c.* '98 (SPR)[B] Great Barrington, MA St. Peter's.
Papineau, Daniel *m.i.c.* '98 (SPR)[I] Eucharistic Apostles of The Divine Mercy.
Papp, Edward E. '60 (OG) Potsdam, NY St. Mary.
Pappalliyil, Xavier *o.c.d.* '80 (SR)[M] Oakville, CA Carmelite House of Prayer.
Pappu, Xavier '81 (TYL) Vicar General; Longview, TX St. Matthew Catholic Church.

Pappu, Xavier (TYL) College of Consultors; Presbyteral Council; Pastoral Ministries; Diocesan Pastoral Team – DPT; Diocesan Liturgical Commission.

Pappu, Xavier (TYL) Diocesan Finance Council.

Pappu, Xavier (TYL) College of Consultors; Presbyteral Council; Pastoral Ministries; Diocesan Pastoral Team – DPT; Diocesan Liturgical Commission.

Pappu, Xavier (TYL) Ex Officio; Priests' Pension Board; Priests' Personnel Board.

Paprocki, Thomas J. '78 (CHI) Chicago, IL St. Constance.

Paquet, Hubert J. '55 (PRT) Retired.

Paquet, Joseph A. *s.j.* '59 (BO)[V] Weston, MA Campion Health Center, Inc..

Paquet, Michael *o.s.c.* '78 (STP)[M] Shoreview, MN Crosier Provincial House Province of St. Odilia.

Paquet, Robert J. *s.j.* '45 (PH)[AA] Loyola Center and Manresa Hall.

Paquette, Francis '58 (DUL) Silver Bay, MN St. Mary.

Paquette, Joseph '78 (PRO) Pawtucket, RI St. Teresa of the Child Jesus.

Paquette, Neil *o.c.s.o.* '94 (DUB)[K] Peosta, IA New Melleray Abbey, Order of Cistercians of the Strict Observance.

Paquin, Ronald (BO) Cambridge, MA Youville Lifecare, Inc.; [Q] Cambridge, MA Youville Hospital & Rehabilitation Center, Inc..

Parackal, George '67 (OKL) Oklahoma City, OK St. Joseph; Special Assignment; [E] Oklahoma City, OK St. Anthony Hospital.

Parackattu, Jose *c.m.i.* (BEA) Beaumont, TX St. Martin de Porres Mission; Beaumont, TX St. Mary.

Paraday, Mark R. *o.p.* '83 (CHI)[N] Chicago Dominicans (Provincial Office).

Paraday, Mark *o.p.* '83 (FgM).

Paradayil, Joseph *s.d.b.* (OAK) Berkeley, CA St. Ambrose.

Paradela, Michael R. '82 (NY) Staten Island, NY Blessed Sacrament.

Paradis, Donald *m.s.* '58 (FR)[H] Attleboro, MA La Salette Shrine.

Paradis, James D. *o.s.a.* '91 (PH)[AA] Villanova, PA Provincial Offices of the Order of St. Augustine, Province of St. Thomas of Villanova; [AA] Malvern, PA Augustinian Friars (O.S.A.).

Paradis, Wilfrid H. '49 (MAN) Retired.

Paraguya, Felipe '68 (SAC) Sacramento, CA St. Charles Borromeo.

Parambi, Thomas Seraphin *c.s.t.* '60 (NY) Bronx, NY Our Lady of Solace.

Parambil, James Kalliathu *m.s.* (TYL) Lufkin, TX St. Patrick.

Parambill, Kalliathu (TYL) Lufkin, TX St. Patrick.

Paramo, Raymond *c.s.b.* '66 (DET)[E] Redford, MI Catholic Central High School.

Parampath, Joseph K. '53 (BGP) Weston, CT St. Francis of Assisi; Judges.

Paraniuk, Michael '81 (CIN) Cincinnati, OH St. Bernard.

Paraniuk, Mike '81 (CIN)[K] Cincinnati, OH Mercy Hospitals West.

Parappally, James '59 (MIA) Pompano Beach, FL Our Lady of Mercy; [M] Pompano Beach, FL Indian Catholic Association of Florida, Inc.; Indians.

Parayno, Martin *o.s.b.* '94 (SAT) San Antonio, TX Santo Nino de Cebu.

Parchem, Peter *o.f.m.conv.* '51 (MRY) Pismo Beach, CA St. Paul the Apostle.

Parcheski, Anthony *c.s.s.* '48 (BO)[Y] Waltham, MA Stigmatine Fathers and Brothers.

Parcon, Patrick Daniel '94 (BEA) Liberty, TX Immaculate Conception.

Pardee, Charles D. '84 (JC) Columbia, MO St. Thomas More Newman Center, University of Missouri; [E] Columbia, MO University of Missouri–Columbia, Campus Ministry; Campus Ministry; Finance Committee.

Pardon, Marek *s.v.d.* '91 (WH) Asbury Park, NJ St. Peter Claver.

Pardue, John '88 (SHP) Many, LA St. John the Baptist.

Pare, Arthur H. *s.j.* '60 (BO)[V] Boston The Society of Jesus of New England–Provincial Offices.

Pare, Arthur H. *s.j.* '60 (PRT) Portland, ME St. Pius X.

Pare, Paul M. '53 (PRT) Retired.

Pare, Robert '79 (SAG) Port Austin, MI St. Michael; Vicars for Vicariates.

Paredes, Edmundo '85 (DAL) Dallas, TX St. Cecilia.

Paredes, Gabriel (SFE) Albuquerque, NM San Jose.

Paredes, Jorge '95 (ARE) Florida, PR Our Lady of Mercy.

Paredes Monjaras, Antonio Francisco *s.s.p.* (LA)[Q] Los Angeles, CA Society of St. Paul.

Pareja, Rene L. '81 (CHI) Chicago, IL Transfiguration of Our Lord.

Parekkatt, Joseph *s.d.b.* '74 (OAK) Walnut Creek, CA St. Mary's.

Parel, Joseph '57 (HRT) Northford, CT St. Monica's.

Parella, Francis J. *s.s.p.* '47 (Y)[A] Canfield, OH Society of St. Paul.

Parella, Francis *s.s.p.* '47 (BUF) Eden, NY Immaculate Conception.

Parello, Joseph J. '74 (SJN) On Duty Outside the Archdiocese.

Parent, Basil R. '86 (NTN) Danbury, CT St. Ann.

Parent, J. Wilfrid *s.t.l., s.t.d.* '91 (BAL).

Parent, Lawrence *o.f.m.* '98 (NY)[EE] Immaculate Conception Friary.

Parent, Norman E. *o.m.i.* (BO) Lowell, MA St. Marie; Lowell, MA Sacred Heart.

Parent, Norman *o.m.i.* '64 (BO)[AA] Lowell, MA St. Joseph the Worker Residence.

Parent, Rene '76 (MAN) Lebanon, NH Sacred Heart.

Parent, Royal J. '56 (PRT) Retired.

Parente, Lino S. *o.cist.* '65 (TR) Mount Laurel, NJ St. John Neumann; [M] Mount Laurel, NJ Cistercian Monastery of Our Lady of Fatima.

Parente, Michael *s.a.c.* '47 (CAM) Hammonton, NJ St. Joseph's.

Parenti, Thomas M. '74 (SFR) San Francisco, CA St. Brendan; Navy Reserve Chaplains.

Parenza, John A. *c.p.* '50 (CHI).

Paret, John J. *s.j.* '51 (ALB)[N] Auriesville NY Shrine of Our Lady of Martyrs; Apostleship of Prayer.

Paretsky, Albert *o.p.* '81 (WDC)[B] Washington, DC Dominican House of Studies.

Parfienczyk, Stanislaw (BO) Salem, MA St. John the Baptist.

Parham, William J. '76 (MEM) Collierville, TN Incarnation.

Parillo, Emery *o.f.m.* '55 (ALB) Watervliet, NY Our Lady of Mt. Carmel.

Paris, Basil '98 (STN)[A] Eagle Harbor, MI Skete of Holy Transfiguration Monastery.

Paris, Benedetto J. '95 (MAR) Marquette, MI St. Louis; Adjutant Judicial Vicar; Diocesan Judges.

Paris, John U. '50 (BO) Malden, MA St. Peter; [E] Needham, MA St. Sebastian's School, Inc..

Paris, John *s.j.* '69 (BO)[V] Newton, MA The Jesuit Community at Boston College.

Paris, Thomas *m.s.* '46 (FR)[H] Attleboro, MA La Salette Shrine.

Parise, Michael '79 (BO) Billerica, MA St. Andrew.

Parish, John G. '84 (LA) Durham, NC St. Matthew.

Parisi, Faustino (CAM) Vineland, NJ St. Padre Pio.

Parisi, Frank J. '85 (RVC) Smithtown, NY St. Patrick.

Parisi, Joseph L. '74 (STL) St. Louis, MO St. Jude.

Parisi, Michael R. '28 (BRK) Retired.

Parisi, Michael '55 (BRK) Flushing, NY St. Kevin.

Parisi, Michael (PAT) Military Chaplains; Navy Chaplains.

Parizek, James F. '72 (DAV) Davenport, IA Our Lady of Victory; [P] Davenport, IA Quad Cities Catholic Deaf Ministry.

Parizek, James (DAV) Judges; Promoter of Justice.

Park, Angelo '00 (CHK) Saipan, MP Korean Catholic Community; Presbyteral Council.

Park, Augustin C. '61 (NEW) Orange, NJ St. Andrew Kim; [S] Orange, NJ Mee Joo Catholic Inc..

Park, Augustin (NEW) Korean Apostolate; Korean/Our Lady Mother of God Curia; Our Lady, Gate of Heaven Curia (Korean).

Park, Austin N. *s.j.* '55 (NO)[P] New Orleans, LA Ignatius Residence.

Park, Hongshik Don Bosco '01 (NEW) Ridgewood, NJ Our Lady of Mount Carmel.

Park, Hyogeum M. (OKL) Oklahoma City OK Korean Martyrs.

Park, John Hee Dong '82 (NEW) Saddle Brook, NJ Korean Martyrs.

Park, Jung–Woo *s.j.* '91 (NY)[EE] Loyola Hall, Jesuit Community.

Park, Morton '52 (P) Retired.

Park, Robert G. '57 (WH) Wheeling, WV St. Joseph's Cathedral; Delegate for Clergy; Behavioral Counseling and Ministry.

Park, Seung J. (BO) Newton, MA St. Philip Neri; Korean.

Park, Thomas R. *o.s.b.* '65 (SEA) Veterans Administration Medical Center; [L] Lacey, WA St. Martin's Abbey.

Park, Yong Il '82 (NEW) Orange, NJ St. Andrew Kim.

Parke, Frederick R. '75 (STA) Jacksonville FL Assumption.

Parke, James E. '65 (RIC) Virginia Beach, VA Church of the Ascension.

Parker, Adam (BAL) Frostburg, MD St. Michael; Westernport, MD St. Peter.

Parker, Bill '73 (STL) St. Louis, MO St. Alphonsus Liguori.

Parker, Carroll *o.m.i.* '61 (FgM).

Parker, Charles C. (PHX) Advocates; Auditors.

Parker, Charles '71 (PHX) Special Assignment; Phoenix, AZ St. Jerome.

Parker, Edmund L '56 (BO) Senior Priests Retired.

Parker, Frank J. *s.j.* '73 (BO)[V] Newton, MA The Jesuit Community at Boston College.

Parker, Glenn *c.ss.r.* '85 (ATL) Hapeville GA St. John the Evangelist.

Parker, James '82 (CHR) Johns Island, SC Church of the Holy Spirit; Diocesan Curia; Personnel Committee; CIVIL AIR PATROL.

Parker, James '03 (RCK) Batavia, IL Holy Cross.

Parker, John W. '70 (CHI) Chicago, IL All Saints–St. Anthony.

Parker, Kenneth '65 (R) Retired.

Parker, Kevin J. '02 (PH) Huntingdon Valley, PA St. Albert the Great.

Parker, Larry '84 (WCH) Oswego, KS Sacred Heart; Oswego, KS Mother of God.

Parker, Michael J. '83 (BUF) Council of Priests; [R] Fredonia, NY State University College at Fredonia; Dunkirk, NY St. Hyacinth.

Parker, Paul M. '82 (BO) Absent on Leave.

Parker, Paul R. (BOS) Air Force Reserve Chaplains.

Parker, Rick '77 (OKL) Absent on Sick Leave.

Parker, Theodore K. *o.s.c.* '72 (DET)[K] Riverview, MI Crosier Community of Riverview; Detroit, MI St. Cecilia; Archdiocesan Vicars.

Parker, William C. '64 (TOL) Walbridge, OH St. Jerome; Judges.

Parker, William *c.ss.r.* '73 (STL)[O] St. Louis, MO Redemptorist Fathers.

Parkerson, Paul M. '98 (R) Dunn, NC Sacred Heart.

Parkes, Gregory '99 (ORL) Orlando, FL Holy Family; Defenders of the Bond.

Parkes, Joseph P. *s.j.* '76 (NY)[F] New York, NY Fordham Preparatory School; [EE] Jesuit Community, Kohlmann Hall.

Parkes, Stephen D. '98 (ORL) Longwood, FL Annunciation.

Parkinson, Todd '94 (RVC) Absent on Leave.

Parkos, John F. '64 (STP) North Branch, MN St. Gregory.

Parks, Joseph K. '39 (BRK) Brooklyn, NY St. Patrick Retired.

Parks, Richard E. '59 (BAL) Baltimore, MD Sacred Heart of Mary.

Parks, Richard L. *c.p.* '70 (SAC)[I] Citrus Heights, CA Christ the King Retreat.

Parlante, Gregory J. '82 (PH) Philadelphia, PA Holy Name of Jesus; Pastors Review Board; Council of Priests.

Parle, Richard '56 (SEA) Lacey, WA Sacred Heart of Jesus.

Parlet, Stephen J. '97 (COS) Colorado Springs, CO Corpus Christi.

Parlette, Thomas L. '89 (DAV) Fort Madison, IA SS. Mary & Joseph.

Parmisano, Fabian *o.p.* '53 (OAK)[N] Oakland, CA Dominican Order (Western Province), St. Albert's Priory.

Parnassus, George J. '53 (LA) West Hollywood, CA St. Victor Retired.

Parnell, Dennis R. *s.j.* '93 (SJ)[B] Santa Clara, CA Jesuit Community.

Paron, William J. '69 (STP) Carver, MN St. Nicholas.

Parr, Charles J. '73 (PAT) Wayne, NJ Holy Cross; Ecumenical Officer; Ministry for Priestly Formation and Education.

Parr, John L. '78 (LC) Hudson, WI St. Patrick.

Parr, Norman B. '50 (OM) Retired.

Parra, Pedro *c.s.c.* '99 (FTW)[I] Congregacion de Santa Cruz.

Parrales, Napoleon J. '57 (SD) On Duty Outside the Diocese.

Parrinello, Frank '00 (OM) Madison, NE St. Leonard.

Parrish, Bryan K. (BO) SOUTH REGION.

Parrish, Byran K. (BO) Plymouth, MA St. Mary.

Parrish, Dan *c.s.c.* (FTW)[B] University of Notre Dame Du Lac; [I] Notre Dame, IN Holy Cross Community, Corby Hall, University of Notre Dame.

Parrish, Francis J. *s.j.* '42 (LA)[Q] Los Angeles, CA Columbiere House.

Parrish, Francis *s.j.* '61 (LA) Retired.

Parrotta, Arthur J. '50 (MAR)[C] Escanaba, MI O.S.F. St. Francis Hospital Retired.

Parrotta, Michael '01 (FAR) Casselton, ND St. Thomas; Casselton, ND St. Leo.

Parrotta, Michael (FAR) Diocesan Finance Council.

Parry, Charles J. '81 (WDC) Bowie, MD Sacred Heart.

Parsch, David L. '80 (SAG) Saginaw, MI Holy Spirit.

Parsch, David (SAG) Vicars for Vicariates.

Parson, Donald J. '90 (BAL) Oakland, MD St. Peter the Apostle.

Parsons, Harold J. '29 (NY) Retired.

Parsons, Harry E. '56 (PIT)[N] Pittsburgh, PA St. John Vianney Manor Retired.

Parsons, LaSalle *o.f.m.cap.* (FgM).

Parsons, Neil J. *c.p.* '37 (SAC)[I] Citrus Heights, CA Christ the King Retreat.

Parsons, Vincent L. '01 (GI) Grand Island, NE Blessed Sacrament; Diocesan Consultors.

Partain, Chad A. '03 (ALX) Alexandria, LA St. Rita.

Partee, Chrysostom *o.f.m.* '50 (SFE) Jemez Pueblo, NM San Diego Indian Missions; Cursillo Movement.

Partensky, Leonard J. '42 (DET) Retired.

Parthie, Ralph *o.f.m.* '75 (SFD)[B] Quincy, IL Quincy University.

Partida, Rafael A. '62 (SB) Needles, CA St. Ann.

Partika, Richard '51 (DUL) Retired.

Partridge, Bede *o.s.b.* '58 (P)[L] St. Benedict, OR Mt. Angel Abbey.

Partridge, Francis C. '60 (GAY) Boyne City, MI St.

Matthew; Boyne City, MI St. Augustine.
Partusch, Frank A. '72 (OM) Omaha, NE SS. Peter and Paul.
Paruvanani, Jose '72 (STA) Gainesville, FL St. Patrick's.
Parvensky, Andrew D. '50 (PBR) Monessen, PA Assumption of the Blessed Virgin.
Parzymies, Joseph K. (HRT) Wallingford, CT SS. Peter and Paul.
Pasadilla, Nicholas O. '72 (GAL) Houston, TX Notre Dame.
Pasala, Anthony '96 (CHR) Dillon, SC St. Louis.
Pasala, Balaswamy (CC) Beeville, TX St. James.
Pasala, Lourdu '80 (GRY) Gary, IN Blessed Sacrament; Second Instance.
Pasalic, Nikola *o.f.m.* '98 (DET) Troy, MI St. Lucy.
Pascazi, Louis F. '80 (PIT) Fenelton, PA St. John.
Pasche, Fred *o.f.m.conv.* '64 (FTW) Angola, IN St. Anthony.
Pasciak, Marcel J. '74 (CHI) Chicago, IL St. Symphorosa and Seven Sons; Deans.
Pascoe, Louis B. *s.j.* '64 (NY)[EE] Loyola Hall, Jesuit Community.
Pascual, Antonio S. '60 (RVC) Defenders of the Bond; Wantagh, NY St. Frances de Chantal.
Pascual, Celestino V. (BO) Charlestown, MA St. Francis de Sales.
Pascual, Celestino Vasquez (BO) Cambridge, MA Mount Auburn Hospital.
Pascual, Elias '51 (ARE) Ciales, PR Holy Rosary.
Pascual, Lope D. '82 (MET)[H] Stewartsville, NJ Society of Jesus Christ the Priest; [K] Raritan, NJ Shrine Chapel of the Blessed Sacrament; Diocesan Eucharistic League.
Pascual, Manuel '46 (FRS) Retired.
Pascucci, Philip *s.d.b.* (NY)[GG] Stony Point, NY Don Bosco Retreat Center and Marian Shrine; [GG] Stony Point, NY Marian Shrine.
Pash, Joseph '48 (SPK) Retired.
Pashak, Lawrence M. '63 (SAG) Freeland, MI St. Agnes.
Pashby, John J. '60 (BO) Society of St. James the Apostle.
Pashley, Wilfred J. '63 (PH) Philadelphia, PA St. Barbara; Philadelphia, PA St. Rose of Lima.
Pasieczny, Roman '80 (DET) Warren, MI St. Martin de Porres.
Pasik, Mark A. '76 (SY) Rome, NY Transfiguration; Elected.
Pasion, Lamberto *o.p.* '54 (WDC)[K] Silver Spring, MD Holy Cross Hospital of Silver Spring, Inc..
Paskert, Leonard *o.f.m.* '36 (SFD)[L] Springfield, IL Our Lady of Angels Friary.
Paskey, Robert *s.j.* '66 (ANC) On Sabbatical.
Paskowicz, Marian '54 (ALN) Retired.
Pasley, Robert C. '82 (CAM)[P] Berlin, NJ Mater Ecclesiae Chapel; Assistant Vocation Directors for Recruitment.
Pasqualetto, Vicente *s.t.* '70 (SJN) Canovanas, PR Santa Maria Madre de Dios; Rio Grande; Apostolado Del Cenaculo Misionero.
Pasquinelli, Frederick A. '52 (STU) Council Members Retired.
Pasquini, John J. '98 (PMB) West Palm Beach, FL St. Juliana.
Passalacqua, Robert '83 (SJ) Campbell, CA St. Lucy.
Passamonte, Philip B. '67 (RVC) Absent on Leave.
Passamonti, Paul G. '95 (WDC) Military Chaplains; Army Chaplains.
Passant, Paul A. '98 (NEW) On Duty Outside the Archdiocese.
Passarelli, Robert S. '52 (BAL) Hagerstown, MD St. Mary Retired.
Passauer, Gregory P. '86 (E) Meadville, PA St. Agatha.
Passeri, Richard *o.f.m.* (FR)[H] Onset, MA St. Joseph Friary–Franciscan Friars.
Passero, Ernest F. *s.j.* '70 (BO)[V] Boston The Society of Jesus of New England–Provincial Offices; [V] Weston, MA Campion Jesuit Community.
Passero, Ernest F. *s.j.* '70 (BUR) Bellows Falls, VT St. Charles.
Pastick, Joseph A. '49 (SP) New Port Richey, FL Our Lady Queen of Peace Retired.
Pastick, Joseph A. (CHI) Retired.
Pastirik, Joachim *o.s.b.* '69 (CLV)[O] Cleveland, OH.
Pastizzo, Michael H. *s.j.* '70 (BUF)[O] Buffalo, NY Canisius Jesuit Community.
Pastor, Eduardo '50 (MIA) Miami, FL St. Michael the Archangel.
Pastore, Peter J. '63 (CAM) On Duty Outside the Diocese Retired.
Pastorius, Thomas J. (STL) Valley Park, MO Sacred Heart.
Pastors, Jerome (GB) Elected Representatives.
Pastro, Vincent '78 (SEA) Tacoma, WA St. Ann; Tacoma, WA St. John of the Woods; Tacoma, WA Sacred Heart.
Pasupalety, Sebastian '81 (CC) Corpus Christi, TX Our Lady of Mount Carmel.
Pasupil, Philip '74 (LUB) Shallowater, TX St. Phillip Benizi.
Paszko, John '74 (MIA) Coconut Creek, FL St. Luke.
Patalano, Anthony M. *o.p.* '86 (LA) Portland, OR Holy Rosary Parish & Dominican Priory.
Patalinghug, Leo E. '99 (BAL) Westminster, MD St. John.
Patella, Michael *o.s.b.* '90 (SCL)[I] Collegeville, MN St. John's Abbey, of the Order of St. Benedict.
Patenaude, Gilbert A. '46 (PRT) Retired.
Pater, Aurel '90 (ROM) Aurora, IL St. Michael; Board of Consultors.
Pater, Giles H. '58 (CIN) Cincinnati, OH St. John Fisher; Censors.
Pater, Giles (CIN) Vicarri Foranei (Deans).
Paterno, Salvatore D. '64 (BRK) Released from Diocesan Assignment.
Paterno, Salvatore (NY) Chester, NY St. Columba.
Paternoster, Alejandro '94 (LFT) On Duty Outside the Diocese.
Pathe, Eugene (PT) Charismatic Renewal, Diocesan Commission for.
Pathilchirayil, Matthew *m.afr.* '87 (SP)[O] St. Petersburg, FL Missionaries of Africa.
Pathmarajah, Pius '72 (ROC) Bath, NY St. Mary; Hammondsport, NY St. Gabriel.
Pathmarajah, T. Pius (ROC) Judges.
Patil, Gabriel M. *c.r.s.p.* '72 (ALN)[K] Bethlehem, PA The Barnabite Fathers Barnabite Spiritual Center.
Patillo, Bennie J. '67 (BEA) Diocesan College of Consultors and Presbyteral Council; Priests Personnel Board; Diocesan Judges; Port Neches, TX St. Elizabeth.
Patin, Lawrence *c.ss.r.* '63 (FgM).
Patino, Ruben M. *c.s.p.* '79 (AUS) Austin, TX St. Austin.
Patino, Ruben *c.s.p.* '79 (AUS)[L] Austin, TX University Catholic Center.
Patnode, Michael '72 (CR) Finance Council; Deans; Bemidji, MN St. Philip's; [F] Bemidji, MN Holy Spirit Newman Center; Priests Retirement Board of Trustees; Diocesan Sexual Misconduct Review Board.
Patnode, Ronald (YAK) Selah, WA Our Lady of Lourdes; Natural Family Planning Advisory Committee; Presbyteral Council Executive Committee.
Patout, Rivers A. '67 (GAL) Houston, TX St. Alphonsus.
Patout, Rivers (GAL) Apostleship of the Sea (Port Ministry).
Patricio, Anthony *m.ss.cc.* '66 (CAM)[I] Pleasantville, NJ Our Lady's Multi–Care Center.
Patricius, J. M. '57 (NEW) Bayonne, NJ St. Michael's; Bayonne, NJ Bayonne Medical Center; Bayonne Medical Center.
Patrick, John E. '67 (MAR) Marquette, MI St. Michael; Vicar General; Consultors.
Patrick, Richard Martin *o.p.* '65 (GAL)[Q] Houston, TX Dominican Friars, St. Mark Priory, Inc..
Patrick, Scully S. *s.m.* '95 (MRY)[F] Santa Cruz, CA Society of Mary, Marists.
Patrick, William J. '58 (CLV) Released from Diocesan Assignment.
Patrick, William '57 (ORG)[G] Fullerton, CA St. Jude Medical Center.
Patriquin, Garry D. '84 (PIT) Absent on Sick Leave.
Patrizi, Vincent M. '52 (CC) Apostleship of the Sea; Corpus Christi, TX Our Lady Star of the Sea.
Patrizio, Anthony *m.ss.cc.* '66 (CAM)[M] Linwood, NJ Villa Pieta. Missionaries of the Sacred Hearts of Jesus & Mary.
Patron, Charles A. '62 (SB) Barstow, CA St. Philip Neri Church.
Patron, Charles Anthony '62 (SB) Barstow, CA St. Joseph.
Patron, Charles '62 (SB) Finance Council Members.
Patrylak, T. Frank '62 (PHU) Clifton Heights, PA Protection of Blessed Virgin Mary; Clifton Heights, PA SS. Peter and Paul.
Patte, Steven W. '69 (CHI) Chicago, IL Saint Ita.
Pattee, Daniel *t.o.r* '87 (STU)[A] Steubenville, OH Franciscan University of Steubenville; [F] Steubenville, OH Holy Spirit Friary.
Patterson, Alfred *o.s.b.* '90 (ALT) Summerhill, PA St. John.
Patterson, Bruce '86 (ORG) Huntington Beach, CA St. Bonaventure.
Patterson, Bryan '99 (BRK) Brooklyn, NY St. Athanasius.
Patterson, Bryan (BRK) Censors of Books.
Patterson, Charles '51 (JC)[C] Jefferson City, MO St. Joseph's Home.
Patterson, David L. '68 (ATL) On Duty Outside the Archdiocese.
Patterson, Frank '67 (SAV) Columbus, GA Holy Family; Council of Priests.
Patterson, James *c.ss.r.* '54 (STL)[O] Liguori, MO Liguori Mission House/Redemptorists.
Patterson, John H. '02 (CC)[G] Robstown, TX Society of Our Lady of the Most Holy Trinity.
Patterson, John *s.o.l.t.* '02 (FAR) Belcourt, ND St. Ann; Belcourt, ND St. Ann; St. John, ND St. John the Baptist.
Patterson, Patrick *c.pp.s.* '65 (COL) Columbus, OH St. James–the–Less.
Patterson, Ralph Earl '03 (OWN) Fordsville, KY St. John the Baptist; Whitesville, KY St. Mary of the Woods.
Patterson, Randall P. '70 (ALB) Troy, NY Our Lady of Victory; Deans; Architecture and Building Commission.
Patterson, Robert A. '71 (STP) Hamel, MN St. Anne; Minneapolis, MN Minneapolis Children's Medical Center.
Patterson, Robert '58 (NEW) Scotch Plains, NJ Immaculate Heart of Mary Retired.
Patterson, Ronald E. (LIN) Deaneries and Deans.
Patterson, Ronald '64 (LIN) Manley, NE St. Patrick's.
Patterson, Terrence R. '66 (OG) Retired.
Patterson, William C. '51 (COL)[I] Portsmouth, OH St. Joseph Adoration Monastery, Poor Clares of Perpetual Adoration.
Patti, Angelo J. '82 (ALT) Cresson, PA St. Francis Xavier.
Patti, Steve *o.f.m.* '01 (R) Durham, NC Immaculate Conception.
Pattison, Francis '58 (SD) San Diego, CA St. Rita.
Pattison, W. Francis (SD) Cemetery Committee; College of Consultors; Presbyteral Council.
Patton, James J. '65 (CLV) Perry, OH St. Cyprian.
Patton, Mel *o.s.b.* '56 (SFS)[G] Yankton, SD Sacred Heart Monastery.
Patton, Mel *o.s.b.* '56 (IND)[K] Yankton, SD Sacred Heart Monastery.
Patton, Patrick G. '78 (HEL) Military Chaplains; Army Chaplains.
Patullo, Michael Thomas '02 (DUL) Floodwood, MN Immaculate Conception; Floodwood, MN St. Louis; Floodwood, MN St. Mary.
Paturzo, Louis S. '73 (HRT) Suffield, CT Macdougall Correctional Institute.
Paul, Alexis *c.p.* '63 (HRT)[M] West Hartford, CT Holy Family Monastery/Retreat; [M] West Hartford Holy Family Monastery/Retreat; Commission for Priests' Retreats.
Paul, Bededict '78 (NY) Bronx, NY SS. Philip and James.
Paul, Dennis '93 (JOL) Naperville, IL St. Raphael.
Paul, Divya '91 (NY) Hartsdale, NY Sacred Heart.
Paul, Gerald *m.s.c.* '60 (RCK)[G] Aurora, IL Missionaries of the Sacred Heart Community; (FgM).
Paul, John J. *m.s.c.* '58 (ALN)[K] Reading, PA Missionaries of the Sacred Heart; Diocesan Tribunal.
Paul, John M. *s.j.* '80 (MIL)[O] Milwaukee, WI Arrupe House Jesuit Community; [O] Milwaukee, WI Jesuit Provincial Office, Wisconsin Province; (FgM).
Paul, John P. '72 (PH) Philadelphia, PA Our Lady of Calvary.
Paul, John *s.j.* '92 (ELP) El Paso, TX Sacred Heart.
Paul, Kasiano '02 (CI) Our Lady of Mercy.
Paul, Leonard D. *c.s.c.* '64 (FTW)[I] Traverse City, MI.
Paul, Raphael '87 (SFD) Brighton, IL St. Alphonsus; Brighton, IL St. John the Evangelist.
Paul, Raymond F. '55 (HRT) Retired.
Paul, Raymond L. '62 (Y) Massillon, OH St. Joseph.
Paul, Raymond (Y) Defenders of the Bond.
Paul, Thomas '77 (JOL) Downers Grove, IL St. Mary of Gostyn.
Paulin, George A. '70 (BUR) Ludlow, VT Annunciation of the Blessed Virgin Mary.
Paulino, Felino '77 (SEA) Seattle, WA St. Edward; Seattle, WA St. George; Seattle, WA St. Paul.
Paulish, W. Jeffrey '88 (SCR) Friendsville, PA St. Francis Xavier; Deans.
Paulissen, Richard E. *m.m.* '63 (GAL)[Q] Houston, TX.
Paulissen, Richard E. *m.m.* '63 (NY).
Paulits, Walter J. '72 (BAL)[EE] Pasadena, MD Our Lady of the Chesapeake Retired.
Paulli, Kenneth *o.f.m.* '90 (ALB)[B] Siena College.
Paulo, Maselino (SPP) Diocesan Consultors.
Paulose, Antony '97 (BEA) Beaumont, TX St. Anthony Cathedral.
Paulsen, Timothy *o.m.i.* '97 (GAL) Houston, TX Immaculate Heart of Mary.
Paulshock, Emil '65 (PSC) Absent on Sick Leave.
Paulson, Brian G. *s.j.* '92 (CHI)[D] Chicago, IL St. Ignatius College Prep; [D] Chicago, IL St. Ignatius Jesuit Community.
Paulson, Jerome E. '76 (NU) Gaylord, MN St. Michael.
Paulson, Jerome (STP) Defenders of the Bond.
Paulson, Jerry E. '76 (NU) Arlington, MN St. Mary.
Paulus, Donard *o.f.m.* '48 (GAY) Indian River, MI Cross in the Woods Catholic Shrine.
Pauly, William *s.j.* '79 (RC) Manderson, SD St. Agnes; Pine Ridge, SD Church of Christ the King; Pine Ridge, SD Holy Rosary; [B] Pine Ridge, SD Jesuit Community of Holy Rosary Mission; Diocesan Consultors.
Paur, Roman *o.s.b.* '66 (SCL)[I] Collegeville, MN St. John's Abbey, of the Order of St. Benedict.
Paurazas, Peter P. '55 (CHI) Retired.
Pausche, Frederick F. '57 (CLV) Concord Twp., OH St. Gabriel.
Pauselli, Francis L. '75 (SCR) South Williamsport, PA St. Lawrence's.
Pautler, Mark '74 (SPK) Spokane, WA Sacred Heart;

Chancellor; Judicial Vicar; Members; Priests' Personnel Board.
Pavela, Wayne S. '79 (OM) Humphrey, NE St. Francis.
Pavelis, Harold '51 (SCL) Retired.
Pavese, Paul J. *o.s.j.* '42 (SCR)[B] Pittston, PA St. Joseph's Oblate Seminary.
Pavia, Nicholas S. (BGP) Trumbull, CT St. Stephen.
Pavich, Philip *o.f.m.* '57 (CHI)[N] Chicago, IL St. Anthony's Friary.
Pavignano, Steven *o.f.m.* '78 (CHR) Greenville, SC St. Anthony of Padua.
Pavis, Victor C. '42 (NY)[E] New York, NY Cardinal Hayes High School Retired.
Pavlakovick, Michael '87 (DEN) Littleton, CO St. Frances Cabrini Parish.
Pavlicek, Edward '83 (SAT) Somerset, TX St. Mary's.
Pavlicek, Louis '71 (AUS) Rogers, TX St. Matthew; Temple, TX St. Luke's; Deans; Mission Council.
Pavlick, Raymond A. '71 (PAT) On Duty Outside the Diocese.
Pavlick, Raymond A. (NY) Castle Point, NY Veterans Administration Medical Center.
Pavlik, Albert *o.carm.* '61 (ALB) Troy, NY St. Joseph.
Pavlik, David P. '78 (CHI) Chicago, IL St. Roman.
Pavlik, John *o.f.m.cap.* '78 (PIT)[N] Pittsburgh, PA St. Augustine Friary.
Pavlik, Mark L. '03 (STP) Minneapolis, MN St. Olaf.
Pavlik, Paul R. *t.o.r.* '59 (FgM).
Pavlina, Mark S. '75 (GRY) Dyer, IN St. Joseph.
Pavlock, Martin L. '66 (BUF) Retired.
Pavlosky, John J. '71 (ALN) Coaldale, PA SS. Cyril and Methodius; Coaldale, PA St. John the Baptist; Coaldale, PA St. Mary of the Assumption.
Pavlovsky, Wencil C. *c.s.b.* '91 (GAL) Richmond, TX St. John Fisher; Western Vicariate; Area Representatives.
Pavon, Cesar '90 (LA) Compton, CA St. Albert the Great.
Pavone, Frank A. '88 (NY)[II] Staten Island, NY Priests for Life.
Pavur, Claude N. *s.j.* '84 (STL)[C] Saint Louis University; [O] St. Louis, MO Jesuit Community Corporation at St. Louis University – Jesuit Hall.
Pawelk, Steve *g.h.m.* '89 (CIN)[M] Fairfield, OH.
Pawell, Robert '66 (CHI)[N] Chicago, IL Holy Evangelists Friary.
Pawelski, John '50 (GB) Absent on Leave.
Pawlak, Ed '68 (AMA) Retired.
Pawlak, Edwin F. '68 (ORL) Retired.
Pawlicki, James *s.v.d.* '73 (BLX)[A] Bay St. Louis, MS Media Production Center; [A] Bay St. Louis, MS St. Augustine's; [E] Bay St. Louis, MS Media Production Center "In A Word".
Pawlik, Walter M. *s.d.s.* '58 (GRY)[I] Merrillville, IN Salvatorian Fathers (Society of the Divine Savior).
Pawlikowski, John M. *o.s.m.* '67 (CHI) Chicago, IL Assumption of the Blessed Virgin Mary; [N] Chicago, IL Assumption Priory.
Pawlikowski, Matthew '97 (NEW) Military Chaplains; Army Chaplains.
Pawloski, Gregory P. '74 (LIN) Imperial, NE St. Patrick's; Deaneries and Deans.
Pawlowski, Dariusz '87 (SHP) Bossier City, LA Christ the King; [B] Shreveport, LA Christus Schumpert Highland.
Pawlowski, Joseph M. '73 (GRY) Valparaiso, IN St. Paul; Finance Council.
Pawson, Robert J. '66 (BRK) Queens Village, NY Our Lady of Lourdes.
Pax, Bart *o.f.m.* '68 (NO) New Orleans, LA St. Mary of the Angels.
Pax, Bart *o.f.m.* '68 (CIN)[U] Cincinnati, OH Community Support Charitable Trust.
Pax, Joseph *c.pp.s.* '47 (CIN)[B] Carthagena, OH St. Charles.
Pax, Ulric *o.f.m.* '59 (GLP) Pueblo of Acoma, NM San Esteban, Acoma Catholic Indian Mission; Laguna, NM St. Joseph.
Paxton, Philip *c.p.* '95 (BIR) Fairfield, AL St. Mary's.
Paxton, Philip *c.p.* '95 (CHI)[N] Chicago, IL Passionist Provincial Office.
Payea, Gerald *o.carm.* '70 (NY)[EE] Middletown, NY Brandsma Priory.
Payer, Emil S. '71 (GBG) Kittanning, PA St. Mary, Our Lady of Guadalupe.
Payikat, Zacharias *c.m.i.* '70 (NSH) Lebanon, TN St. Frances Cabrini; Presbyteral Council and College of Consultors.
Payikat, Zachary *c.m.i.* '70 (NSH)[K] Liberty, TN Carmel Center of Spirituality.
Payne, Charles E. *o.f.m.* (CHI)[D] Holy Spirit Friary.
Payne, Gary '85 (OWN) Absent on Leave.
Payne, John J. '01 (NO) Graduate Studies.
Payne, John Michael *o.c.d.* '70 (LR)[A] Little Rock, AR Marylake – Carmelite Novitiate.
Payne, Joseph *o.p.* '63 (NY) Pleasantville, NY Holy Innocents.
Payne, Mark M. *o.s.b.* '81 (NEW)[N] Newark, NJ Newark Abbey.
Payne, Mark '94 (MIL) Milwaukee, WI St. Veronica.
Payne, Stephen J. '71 (GAL) Huntsville, TX St. Thomas the Apostle.
Payne, Steven *o.c.d.* '82 (WDC)[B] Washington, DC Discalced Carmelite Friars; [V] Washington, DC Carmelite Institute.
Payne, Thomas H. '50 (SAV) Retired.
Payo, Reuben '84 (DEN) Conifer, CO Our Lady of The Pines.
Paysse, Wayne C. '87 (NO) New Orleans, LA Immaculate Heart Of Mary; Pontifical Mission Societies/Holy Childhood Association; Missionaries of St. Therese; Serra Club of St. Bernard.
Payyappilli, Philip Neri *c.m.i.* '59 (BEA) Orange, TX St. Helen.
Paz, Jose M. '52 (MIA) Miami, FL St. Michael the Archangel; Apostleship of the Sea; [M] Miami, FL Stella Maris Seaman Center, Inc..
Paz, Lorenzo (SB) Victorville, CA St. Joan of Arc; On Leave of Absence.
Paz en la Casa, Vincente '66 (PBL) Grand Junction, CO Immaculate Heart of Mary.
Pazhayakari, Philip *c.m.i.* '62 (SHP) Reyville, LA Sacred Heart.
Pazmany, Geza *sch.p.* '61 (PH)[G] Devon, PA Devon Preparatory School; [AA] Devon Piarist Fathers (Order of the Pious Schools).
Pazo, John T. '55 (RVC) Retired.
Pazzaglia, Domenico *m.c.c.j.* '43 (LA)[CC] Covina, CA Comboni Mission Center.
Pazzhukkathara, Shaji Joseph '02 (STP) United Hospitals, Inc.; St. Paul, MN St. Mary.
Peacha, Thomas '59 (LA) Los Angeles, CA Holy Trinity.
Peacock, Francis A. '53 (PHX) Phoenix, AZ SS. Simon and Jude Cathedral; Phoenix, AZ Our Lady of Fatima.
Peacock, Thomas E. '63 (WDC) Port Tobacco, MD St. Ignatius.
Peake, Daniel A. '49 (NY) Bronx, NY St. Margaret of Cortona Retired.
Peake, William '80 (DUB)[H] Mason City, IA Mercy Medical Center–North Iowa.
Pearce, Donald *s.j.* '59 (NO)[P] New Orleans, LA Ignatius Residence.
Pearce, John S. *c.m.* '57 (PH)[AA] St. Catherine Infirmary.
Pearce, Joseph Francis *c.o.* '99 (CHR) Fort Mill, SC St. Philip Neri; [E] Rock Hill, SC Oratory of St. Philip Neri, Congregation of the Oratory of Pontifical Rite.
Pearsall, William T. '37 (BO) Framingham, MA St. Stephen; Senior Priests Retired.
Pearson, Everett '91 (WDC) Washington, DC Holy Name; First Friday Club.
Pearson, John A. '66 (NU) Wabasso, MN St. Mary; Wabasso, MN St. Anne; Wabasso, MN St. Mathias.
Pearson, John H. *c.s.c.* '73 (FTW)[B] University of Notre Dame Du Lac; [I] Notre Dame, IN Holy Cross Community, Corby Hall, University of Notre Dame.
Pearson, Robert A. '65 (SPK) Spokane, WA St. Augustine; Continuing Education of Priests.
Pearson, Robert A. '86 (TR) Retired.
Pearson, Robert L. *o.c.s.o.* '60 (ATL)[K] Conyers, GA The Monastery of the Holy Spirit.
Peatee, Gregory L. '92 (TOL) Sylvania, OH St. Joseph.
Pecaric, Alfred F. '82 (BGP) Stamford, CT Sacred Heart; Defenders of the Bond.
Pecchie, Paul '95 (SP) Valrico, FL St. Stephen.
Pecci, Ronald J. *o.f.m.* '83 (NEW) Fair Lawn, NJ St. Anne's.
Pecevich, Conrad S. '77 (WOR) Worcester MA Ascension; [R] Worcester, MA Nichols College (Dudley); St. Louis.
Pecharroman, Ovidio '65 (WDC)[B] Washington, DC Diocesan Laborer Priests, House of Studies.
Pecharroman, Ovidio '87 (ARL) Spanish Apostolate; Vocations Office of.
Pechillo, Arthur C. '01 (PRT) Camden, ME Our Lady of Good Hope.
Pecht, Gerard J. *c.ss.r.* '50 (STL)[O] Liguori, MO St. Clement Health Care Center.
Peck, David A. '94 (RCK) Rochelle, IL St. Patrick; Pro–Life Activities, Office of.
Peck, John D. *o.s.b.* '89 (HBG) Annville, PA St. Paul the Apostle; [J] Annville, PA Lebanon Valley College.
Peck, Leon J. '42 (PH) Retired.
Pecklers, Keith F. *s.j.* '91 (NY)[EE] Coll Bellarmino.
Peckman, E. William '97 (JC) Edina, MO St. Aloysius; Edina, MO St. Joseph; V. Kirksville; Senators; Cursillo Movement.
Pecoraro, James A. '53 (KC) Retired.
Pecoraro, John C. '02 (MEM) Memphis, TN St. Louis.
Pecovnik, Karel '44 (SCL) Retired.
Pecquet, Howard P. (CIN) Archdiocesan Department Directors.
Pedata, Armand A. '58 (TR) Marlton, NJ St. Joan of Arc; Tribunal Judges.
Peddicord, Richard A. *o.p.* '86 (STL)[B] St. Louis, MO Aquinas Institute of Theology; [O] St. Louis, MO St. Dominic Priory.
Pedelesky, Nestor '67 (STN) Retired.
Pederson, Bryan J. '03 (STP) Crystal, MN St. Raphael.
Pedi, Mario *o.s.b.* '57 (RCK) Aurora, IL Annunciation of the Blessed Virgin Mary; [G] Aurora, IL Marmion Abbey.
Pedigo, Jon '91 (SJ) San Jose, CA St. Julie Billiart; [P] Santa Clara, CA Catholic Professional and Business Club of the San Jose Diocese; Council of Priests.
Pednekar, Joseph C. *m.s.f.s.* '62 (CLV) Cleveland, OH St. Patrick; Cleveland, OH St. Patrick.
Pednekar, Joseph Charles *m.s.f.s.* '62 (ATL)[K] Lawrenceville The Missionaries of St. Francis De Sales.
Pedone, F. Stephen '78 (WOR) Worcester, MA St. George; Judicial Vicar and Vicar for Canonical Affairs; Judges; Diocesan College of Consultors; Presbyteral Council.
Pedrano, Stephanos *o.s.b.* '91 (SD)[H] Oceanside, CA Prince of Peace Abbey, Benet Hill.
Pedretti, Raymond J. '56 (LC) Retired.
Pedretti, Robert F. '64 (LC) Amherst, WI St. James; Amherst, WI St. Mary of Mount Carmel.
Pedrizetti, Raymond *o.s.b.* '58 (SCL)[I] Collegeville, MN St. John's Abbey, of the Order of St. Benedict.
Pedrosa, Agustin *s.m.* '59 (NEW) West New York, NJ St. Joseph of the Palisades.
Pedroso, Rafael '64 (MIA) Retired.
Pedrotti, Frank L. *s.j.* '70 (STL)[O] St. Louis, MO Jesuit Community Corporation at St. Louis University – Jesuit Hall.
Pedroza, Salvador '81 (LAR) Carrizo Springs, TX Our Lady of Guadalupe; Presbyteral Council; Priests Personnel Board.
Pedulla, John '93 (NY)[E] New York, NY Monsignor Farrell High School.
Peduti, Douglas F. *s.j.* '96 (WH)[A] Wheeling, WV Wheeling Jesuit University.
Pedzich, Henry J. '72 (SY) Syracuse, NY St. Michael; Priests' Personnel Committee.
Pedzik, Vitalis B. '61 (RVC) Lindenhurst, NY Our Lady of Perpetual Help.
Pedzik, Vitalis (RVC) Procurator & Advocates.
Peek, Joseph '02 (ATL) On Sick Leave; Navy Reserve Chaplains.
Peek, Kevin (ATL) Decatur, GA Sts. Peter and Paul; Deans.
Peeters, Ambrose J. *o.praem.* '53 (GB)[I] De Pere, WI St. Norbert Abbey.
Peeters, John N. '83 (CHI)[N] Catholic Mission Corozal.
Peffley, Francis J. '90 (ARL) Bristow, VA Holy Trinity.
Pegnam, William '67 (SJ) San Jose, CA St. Christopher.
Pegoraro, Germano *s.c.* '52 (LAN)[O] Grass Lake, MI "Now and at the Hour" Magazine:.
Pehl, Jeffrey '95 (SAT) Hondo, TX St. John the Evangelist.
Pehler, Gerald *o.f.m.cap* '88 (CHI)[N] Chicago, IL St. Clare Friary.
Pehrsson, Alfred R. *c.m.* '58 (BIR) Alexander City, AL St. John the Apostle.
Peifer, Claude J. *o.s.b.* '52 (PEO).
Peiffer, James E. '67 (TOL)[A] Genoa, OH Our Lady of Lourdes; Oak Harbor, OH St. Boniface; Ecumenical & Interreligious Affairs Commission.
Peil, William L. '49 (GRY) Retired.
Peil, William '49 (FTW) Retired.
Peinado, Louis A. *s.j.* '60 (LA)[F] Los Angeles, CA Loyola High School of Los Angeles.
Peiris, Richard (OAK) Washington Hospital.
Peji, Rodel '94 (RCK) Richmond, IL St. Joseph.
Pekar, Athanasius B. *o.s.b.m.* '46 (RVC)[M] Glen Cove, NY St. Josaphat's Monastery, Novitiate and Retreat House.
Pekar, Athanasius B. *o.s.b.m.* '46 (STF)[B] Glen Cove, NY Basilian Fathers Novitiate of the Order of St. Basil the Great.
Pekar, Florian *c.p.* '40 (HRT)[M] West Hartford Holy Family Monastery/Retreat.
Pekar, Joseph W. '57 (BGP) Bridgeport, CT SS. Cyril and Methodius.
Pekarske, Daniel *s.d.s.* '90 (FgM).
Peklo, Edward *s.v.d.* '69 (CHI)[B] Chicago, IL Divine Word Theologate; [N] Chicago, IL Divine Word Theologate; [N] Chicago, IL House of Religious Men: Divine Word Theologate.
Pekola, David J. '86 (MET) Hackettstown, NJ Assumption of the Blessed Virgin Mary; Deans.
Pelak, Anthony '03 (GR) Rockford, MI Our Lady of Consolation.
Pelant, William (STP) Special Assignment.
Pelc, Timothy R. '74 (DET) Grosse Pointe Park, MI St. Ambrose.
Pelczar, Edward A. '62 (PH) Philadelphia, PA St. Josaphat.
Pelczarski, Wojciech *s.d.s.* '00 (SAT) Falls City, TX Nativity of the Blessed Virgin Mary; Stockdale, TX St. Ann's.
Pelensky, Ihor '43 (STF) Retired.
Peles, David S. '84 (ALT) Nanty–Glo, PA St. Mary's.
Pelkington, Robert Leo '68 (WDC) Washington, DC St. Dominic Church & Priory.
Pellegrini, Frederick J. '84 (SY)[A] Syracuse, NY Saint Andrew Hall.
Pellegrino, Gerard *s.d.b.* '74 (SP)[E] Tampa, FL Mary Help of Christians School.

Pellegrino, Joseph A. '77 (SP) Tarpon Springs, FL St. Ignatius; [F] Tarpon Springs, FL St. Ignatius Early Childhood Center.
Pellerin, Keith '98 (LKC) Lake Charles, LA St. Martin dePorres; Priest's Senate.
Pelleteri, Manuel J. *c.m.* '53 (CHI)[N] Chicago DePaul Vincentian Residence.
Pelletier, Adrien O. *s.m.* '56 (BUR) White River Junction, VT St. Anthony; Veterans Administration Hospital.
Pelletier, Adrien *s.m.* (MO).
Pelletier, Clement L. *s.j.* '62 (BO)[E] Dorchester, MA Boston College High School & Jesuit Community.
Pelletier, Edgar A. '47 (WOR) Retired.
Pelletier, Emile "Bud" '94 (PHX) Cottonwood, AZ Immaculate Conception.
Pelletier, George C. (PRT) Army National Guard Chaplains.
Pelletier, Gerard *s.m.* (HRT) Hartford, CT Hartford Hospital.
Pelletier, Norman B. *s.s.s.* '69 (CLV)[O] Highland Heights, OH.
Pelletier, Norman *s.s.s.* '63 (CLV)[O] Cleveland, OH Blessed Sacrament Community.
Pelletier, Walter R. *s.j.* '60 (BGP)[E] Fairfield, CT Fairfield College Preparatory School; [P] Fairfield, CT The Fairfield Jesuit Community–Fairfield University.
Pelligrino, Francis B '51 (SLC) Retired.
Pellissier, Francois *g.h.m.* '81 (NSH) Fayetteville, TN St. Anthony.
Peloso, John P. '96 (MIA) Plantation, FL San Pedro.
Pelotte, Dana *s.s.s.* '99 (GAL) Houston, TX Corpus Christi.
Pelotte, Dana *s.s.s.* (SLC) Team.
Pelous, Donald '98 (LAF) St. Martinville, LA St. Rita.
Pelrine, Edward '01 (CHI) Chicago, IL St. Cajetan.
Pelton, Robert S. *c.s.c.* '49 (FTW)[B] University of Notre Dame Du Lac.
Pelton, Robert S. *c.s.c.* '73 (FTW)[I] Notre Dame, IN Holy Cross Community, Corby Hall, University of Notre Dame.
Pelton, Thomas '66 (CHI) Chicago, IL Maternity of the Blessed Virgin Mary.
Peltz, Carl F. '77 (KAL) Delton, MI St. Ambrose; Parchment, MI St. Ambrose.
Peltzer, Michael '80 (WCH) Harper, KS St. Joan of Arc.
Peluse, Dominic *s.c.j.* (GB) Sturgeon Bay, WI St. Joseph.
Peluso, Francis E. *o.a.r.* '61 (NY) Roosevelt, NY Queen of the Most Holy Rosary.
Peluso, Frank *o.a.r.* (NY) St. Joseph's Cursillo Center.
Peluso, Michael (NY) On Leave of Absence.
Pelzel, Bradley C. '02 (SC) Fort Dodge, IA Corpus Christi.
Pelzel, Ronald (SJ) Priests' Retirement Board.
Pemberton, Joseph '77 (FWT) Fort Worth, TX Holy Family; Deans; Continuing Pastoral Formation.
Pena, Juan Pablo (GAL) Humble, TX St. Mary Magdalene.
Pena, Ordanico De La '98 (NEW) West New York, NJ St. Joseph of the Palisades.
Pena, Richard '92 (SAT) San Antonio, TX Christ the King; [U] San Antonio, TX Archdiocesan Union of Holy Name Societies.
Pena, Roberto *o.m.i.* '55 (LAR) Eagle Pass, TX Sacred Heart.
Pena, Vincente M. *o.p.* '36 (SAT) San Antonio, TX St. Ann; [B] San Antonio, TX Dominican Priory of San Juan Macias and Novitiate.
Pena–Moreno, Wilfredo (SJN) Vicar for Communications; Television Station.
Penafiel, Fausto '83 (PHX) Glendale, AZ Our Lady of Perpetual Help; Advocates.
Penalba, Vicente *c.m.f.* '69 (SJN) Bayamon, PR Santa Maria.
Penaloza, Jorge '60 (LA) Pico Rivera, CA St. Francis Xavier.
Penaloza, Luis M. '99 (SR) Eureka, CA Sacred Heart.
Penchi, Edward J. '56 (LC) Retired.
Pendergast, Richard J. *s.j.* '63 (NY)[EE] New York, NY Murray–Weigel Hall.
Penderghest, William *ss.cc.* '67 (FR)[J] Wareham, MA Sacred Hearts Retreat Center.
Pendergraft, Michael (STA) Rural Life Director.
Pendergraft, W. Michael '81 (STA) Live Oak, FL St. Francis Xavier.
Pendleton, Arthur J. *o.s.b.* '64 (CHL)[J] Belmont, NC Belmont Abbey; [J] Belmont, NC Belmont Abbey.
Pendolphi, Richard J. '76 (COL) Worthington, OH St. Michael.
Pendrick, Thomas '03 (NEW) New Providence, NJ Our Lady of Peace.
Pendzick, John S. '97 (ALN) Reading, PA Holy Guardian Angels.
Penebsky, John P. '65 (SFR) Foster City, CA St. Luke.
Peng, John B. (CHI) Retired.
Penhallurick, Robert '96 (COL) Newark, OH St. Francis de Sales.
Penisten, Edmund J. (JUN) Diocesan Consultors.
Penisten, Edmund '02 (JUN) Ketchikan, AK Holy Name; Commission for Liturgy.
Penkala, Edmund S. '45 (SCR)[N] Dunmore, PA Villa St. Joseph Retired.
Penko, Francis G. '60 (SD) El Cajon, CA St. Kieran.
Penn, Michael A. '54 (SCR) Scranton, PA St. Anthony of Padua.
Penn, Michael W. '03 (JC) Columbia, MO Our Lady of Lourdes.
Penna, Anthony *c.s.s.* '75 (BO)[V] Waltham, MA Stigmatine House.
Penna, Joseph P. '67 (NY) Pearl River, NY St. Aedan.
Penna, Michael Della *o.f.m.* '99 (NY)[EE] New York Franciscan Province of the Immaculate Conception.
Pennett, Frederick J. '71 (MAN) Hampstead, NH St. Anne; Council of Priests.
Pennings, Gary '01 (KCK)[B] Overland Park, KS Saint Thomas Aquinas High School, Inc.; Overland Park, KS Church of the Ascension.
Pennington, Basil *o.c.s.o.* '57 (WOR)[O] Spencer, MA St. Joseph's Abbey.
Pennington, John F. *s.j.* '70 (CHI)[N] Chicago, IL Clark Street Jesuit Residence.
Pennington, John R. '79 (WDC) Waldorf, MD St. Peter.
Pennington, M. Basil *o.c.s.o.* '57 (WOR)[S] Spencer, MA Cistercian Publications, Inc..
Pennington, Matthew '88 (MRY) Scotts Valley, CA San Agustin.
Pennisi, Ignatius F. *s.j.* '43 (BO)[V] Weston, MA Campion Health Center, Inc..
Pennock, Michael '95 (JOL) Coal City, IL Assumption.
Penonzek, Edward M. *o.s.m.* '58 (CHI)[N] Chicago Order of Friar Servants of Mary (Servites) United States of America Province, Inc..
Penonzek, Edward M. *o.s.m.* '58 (ORG)[D] Anaheim, CA Servite High School, A California Corporation.
Penta, Leo J. '78 (BRK) Released from Diocesan Assignment.
Pentecost, Denver B. '69 (NO) Marrero, LA Immaculate Conception; Marrero, LA West Jefferson General Hospital; Marrero, LA Wynhoven Health Care Center.
Pentello, Richard J. '79 (Y) Garrettsville, OH St. Ambrose; Hiram College.
Pentis, William F. *c.o.* '66 (CHR) Rock Hill, SC St. Anne's; [E] Rock Hill, SC Oratory of St. Philip Neri, Congregation of the Oratory of Pontifical Rite; Catholic Women, Council of.
Pentony, Liam '55 (JKS) Retired.
Peoples, J. Eugene '66 (HEL)[B] Helena, MT Carroll College.
Pepe, Mario P. '56 (HRT)[K] West Hartford, CT Saint Mary Home Retired.
Pepe, Robert F. '50 (WCH) Retired.
Pepel, Clement '82 (MET) On Duty Outside the Diocese.
Pepin, Darryl J. '78 (MAR) Ironwood, MI Our Lady of Peace; [B] Ironwood, MI Our Lady of Peace School Educational Fund; Deans.
Pepin, Normand A. *s.j.* '63 (FBK)[A] Fairbanks, AK Monroe Catholic Junior–Senior High School; [C] Fairbanks, AK Jesuit Residence; [E] Fairbanks, AK House of Prayer.
Pepin, Normand A. *s.j.* '63 (BO)[V] Boston The Society of Jesus of New England–Provincial Offices.
Pepin, Normand *s.j.* (FBK) Hispanic Ministry.
Pepka, Edward '77 (SAC) Chico, CA Our Divine Savior.
Peplansky, Joseph *c.m.f.* '60 (SPC) Springfield, MO Sacred Heart; [E] Springfield, MO Claretians Missionaries' Residence–Villa Claret.
Peplowski, Sigmund (PAT) Chatham, NJ St. Patrick's.
Pepowski, Bert '61 (GRY)[I] Cedar Lake, IN Our Lady of Lourdes Friary.
Peppard, Patrick F. *s.j.* '73 (CLV)[D] Cuyahoga Falls, OH Walsh Jesuit High School.
Pepper, David J. '58 (DUB) Retired.
Pera, Sylvano J. *o.f.m.* '52 (SFD) Effingham, IL St. Mary Help of Christians; [L] Teutopolis, IL St. Francis Assisi Friary.
Pera, Sylvano *o.f.m.* '52 (SFD) Sigel, IL Sacred Heart.
Perales, Jorge I. '78 (MIA) Miami, FL St. John Bosco; Miami, FL Our Lady of Lebanon.
Perata, Stephen E. (SJ) Building Committee.
Perata, Stephen F. '58 (SJ) San Jose, CA St. Victor.
Perata, Stephen (SJ) Priests' Retirement Board.
Percell, Lawrence '03 (SJ) Los Altos, CA St. Nicholas.
Perdue, John *m.ss.cc.* '90 (CAM) Linwood, NJ Our Lady of Sorrows.
Perea, Donald '98 (SEA) Edmonds, WA Holy Rosary.
Perea, Michael U. *o.praem.* '90 (ORG)[I] Silverado, CA Norbertine Fathers of Orange Inc..
Perea, Michael U. *o.praem.* '90 (LA)[C] Santa Paula, CA Thomas Aquinas College.
Pereda, James F. (RVC) Adjutant Judicial Vicars.
Pereda, James *c.r.c.* '81 (BRK)[W] Queens Village, NY St. Ann's Novitiate, Little Sisters of the Poor.
Perehubka, Jozef '84 (HEL) Helmville, MT St. Thomas.
Pereira, Albert F. '40 (RIC) Retired.
Pereira, Anthony '82 (SJ) On Leave of Absence.
Pereira, Cyril F. '54 (ALB) Troy, NY St. Patrick Retired.
Pereira, Jevino '88 (SFR) San Francisco, CA St. Stephen.
Pereira, Luciano J. '54 (FR) Retired.
Pereira, Robert J. '62 (STO) Diamond Springs, CA Retired.
Perera, Denzil M. '58 (NO) New Orleans, LA Our Lady of The Rosary; Blue Army of Our Lady of Fatima Retired.
Perera, George *o.m.i.* '92 (NY) New York, NY Holy Family.
Perera, J. Bosco '69 (FTW) Geneva, IN St. Mary of the Presentation.
Perera, Paul (ELP) Retired.
Peres, Mark R. *c.pp.s.* '85 (LFT) Rensselaer, IN St. Augustine.
Peretti, Peter L. '73 (GBG) Avonmore, PA St. Ambrose.
Perez, Angel Antonio *c.p.* '87 (MGZ) San Sebastian, PR San Sebastian Martir.
Perez, Angel '02 (P) Corvallis, OR St. Mary.
Perez, Anthony R. *s.s.* '77 (BAL).
Perez, Antonio G. '90 (GAL)[A] Dickinson, TX Shrine of the True Cross.
Perez, Antonio '77 (AGN) On Duty Outside the Archdiocese.
Perez, Armando S. '02 (SEA) Vancouver, WA St. John.
Perez, Armando '62 (MIA) Fort Lauderdale, FL Our Lady Queen of Martyrs.
Perez, Aurelio '86 (MIL) Waukesha, WI St. Joseph.
Perez, Boris Espinoza '78 (CGS) Las Piedras, PR Inmaculada Concepcion.
Perez, Carlos '60 (MIA) Hialeah, FL San Lazaro.
Perez, Carlos '92 (B) Gooding, ID St. Elizabeth's; Shoshone, ID St. Peter's.
Perez, Eduardo '95 (STO) Modesto, CA St. Stanislaus Church (Pastor of).
Perez, Edwin E. '01 (ARL) Annandale, VA St. Michael's; Notaries.
Perez, Ernesto '71 (CC) Corpus Christi, TX Our Lady of Perpetual Help.
Perez, Francisco (AMA) Presbyteral Council; Vocation Development Team; Amarillo, TX Blessed Sacrament.
Perez, Gabino '51 (ORG) Santa Ana, CA Our Lady of the Pillar.
Perez, Hector R.G. '81 (PT) Pensacola, FL St. Stephen; Legion of Mary.
Perez, Horacio *s.x.* '03 (PAT)[M] Wayne Xaverian Missionary Fathers.
Perez, Isidro '81 (MIA) Miami, FL St. Timothy.
Perez, James *l.c.* '01 (HRT)[A] Center Harbor, NH Immaculate Conception Apostolic School.
Perez, Javier H. '93 (TUC) Somerton, AZ Immaculate Heart of Mary.
Perez, Jesse L. '74 (PBL) Pueblo, CO Holy Family.
Perez, John C. (SJN) Army Chaplains.
Perez, John Jairo '03 (BGP) Stamford, CT St. Mary.
Perez, John Mary *s.o.l.t.* (CC)[G] Robstown, TX Society of Our Lady of the Most Holy Trinity.
Perez, Jose '64 (COL) Columbus, OH Santa Cruz Parish.
Perez, Jose '99 (BRK) On Leave/Unassigned.
Perez, Joseph '69 (GAL) On Duty Outside the Diocese.
Perez, Juan Antonio *o.ss.t.* '88 (CC) Corpus Christi, TX Christ the King.
Perez, Juan '98 (SAC) Woodland, CA Holy Rosary.
Perez, Juan *s.o.l.t.* '00 (SJN) Rio Grande, PR Nuestra Senora del Carmen.
Perez, Lazaro '89 (MET)[F] New Brunswick, NJ Saint Peter's University Hospital.
Perez, Leo *o.m.i.* '83 (SAT)[M] San Antonio, TX Oblate Benson Residence (Southwest Area).
Perez, Leo *o.m.i.* '84 (SAT)[F] San Antonio, TX St. Anthony Catholic High School.
Perez, Leon '60 (ARE) Barceloneta, PR Our Lady of Victory.
Perez, Leopoldo G. *o.m.i.* '84 (SAT)[C] Oblate School of Theology.
Perez, Luis A. '95 (MIA) Miami, FL Our Lady of the Holy Rosary.
Perez, Modesto L. (LA) Judges.
Perez, Modesto Lewis (LA) Cursillo Movement.
Perez, Modesto '84 (LA)[A] Camarillo, CA St. John's Seminary.
Perez, Nelson J. '89 (PH) Philadelphia, PA St. William; Council of Priests.
Perez, Ovidio '01 (ARE) Graduate Studies.
Perez, Pedro Luis '52 (MIA) Hialeah, FL San Lazaro; Deans and Deaneries; Members.
Perez, Rafael *o.s.b.* '79 (CGS)[C] Humacao, PR San Antonio Abad Abbey of the Order of St. Benedict.
Perez, Raul '86 (SAV) Vidalia, GA Sacred Heart.
Perez, Raymond '88 (LA) Hawthorne, CA St. Joseph.
Perez, Rene '03 (LUB) Lubbock, TX Cathedral Christ the King.
Perez, Rene (LUB) Vocation Team Members.
Perez, Restituto *o.p.* '60 (MIA) Miami, FL St. Dominic; [H] Miami, FL Dominican Fathers of Miami, Inc..
Perez, Robert R. '86 (CHI) Chicago, IL St. Michael.
Perez, Roberto *o.carm.* '02 (NY) New York, NY Our Lady of the Scapular/St. Stephen; Middletown, NY Our Lady of Mt. Carmel.
Perez, Sacramento *o.dem.* (SB) Riverside, CA Our Lady

of Guadalupe Shrine; Riverside, CA St. Anthony of Padua.
Perez, Salvador '61 (FWT) Retired.
Perez, Samuel '03 (TLS) Tulsa, OK Church of St. Mary.
Perez, Victor '75 (P) Eugene, OR St. Mary.
Perez, Viktor *o.f.m. conv.* '89 (MRY)[F] Arroyo Grande, CA St. Joseph Cupertino Friary.
Perez, William A. *o.s.a.* '62 (TLS)[B] Tulsa, OK Cascia Hall Preparatory School.
Perez–Diaz, German '97 (KAL) Fennville, MI San Felipe de Jesus.
Perez–Lerena, Francisco *s.j.* '58 (MIA)[D] Miami, FL Belen Jesuit Preparatory School; [H] Miami FL Villa Javier.
Perez–Monterrosa, Juvenal '69 (PHX) Phoenix, AZ SS. Anthony and Pius X.
Perez–Pupo, Joaquin '76 (MIA) Miami, FL Mother of Christ.
Perez–Rodriguez, Arturo '72 (CHI)[X] Chicago, IL Kolbe House.
Perez Gonzalez, Osualdo *c.s.sp.* (SJN)[C] Bayamon, PR Seminario Misionero del Espiritu Santo.
Perez Vazquez, Juan De La Cruz '96 (SJN) Military Services.
Perfetto, Richard A. '66 (DET) Canton, MI Resurrection.
Perham, Arnold E. *c.s.v.* '56 (CHI)[D] Arlington Heights, IL St. Viator High School; [N] Arlington Heights, IL Viatorian Province Center–Clerics of St. Viator.
Peri, Paul '71 (P) Portland, OR Church of St. Michael the Archangel; College of Consultors; Personnel Board; Finance Council; Liturgical Commission; Ministry Formation.
Perianayagam, Thobiyas '00 (FWT) Arlington, TX St. Vincent de Paul.
Pericone, Nicholas P. '96 (NO) Graduate Studies.
Peries, Angelito *c.ss.r.* '74 (SR) Windsor, CA Our Lady of Guadalupe.
Peries, Ignatius *c.h.s.* '79 (NY)[EE] Glenham, NY Apostolic Society of the Crusade of the Holy Spirit.
Perin, Glen W. '53 (CIN) Retired.
Perin, Isidro *m.s.* '67 (STL)[O] Generalate, Missionari di N.S. de La Salette.
Perini, Armando J. '56 (MET) Edison, NJ St. Helena.
Perino, John M. '79 (NO) Ama, LA St. Mark.
Perjak, Edmond J. '67 (BEL) Retired.
Perkin, David R. (NSH) Vicars General; Moderator of the Curia and Vicar General; Adjutant Judicial Vicar; Judges; Presbyteral Council and College of Consultors; Diocesan Finance Board; Clergy Personnel Board.
Perkin, David '78 (NSH) On Special Assignment.
Perkins, Bernard *o.c.d.* '82 (TUC) Tucson, AZ St. Margaret Mary; [E] Tucson, AZ Discalced Carmelite Friars of St. Margaret Mary's.
Perkins, Charles J. '78 (HT) Raceland, LA St. Mary's Nativity; Young Adult Ministries.
Perkins, Charles (HT) Priests Council; College of Consultors.
Perkins, Dennis M. '95 (NOR) Pawcatuck, CT St. Michael; Members; Continuing Education and Formation Commission.
Perkins, Dennis (NOR) Priests Retirement Plan Board; Priests' Retirement Plan Board.
Perkins, Joseph F. '68 (WDC) Garrett Park, MD Holy Cross.
Perkins, Robert M. '71 (RIC) Richmond, VA Cathedral of the Sacred Heart; Former Delegates; Regional Delegates.
Perkinton, John J. '85 (LIN)[F] Waverly, NE Our Lady of Good Counsel Retreat House; [H] Lincoln, NE Villa Marie School and Home for the Educable Mentally Handicapped.
Perkinton, John (LIN) Presbyteral Council Building Commission; Priests' Continuing Education Committee; Schools.
Perkl, James M. '84 (STP) Hastings, MN St. Elizabeth Ann Seton; Presbyteral Council.
Perko, F. Michael *s.j.* '75 (CHI)[N] Evanston, IL Canisius House.
Perkovic, Anton '46 (NO) Retired.
Perkovich, Frank '54 (DUL) Biwabik, MN St. John's; Gilbert, MN St. Joseph's.
Perlinski, Daniel A. '57 (TLS) Retired.
Perlite, John J. *s.j.* '49 (SJ)[M] Los Gatos, CA Sacred Heart Jesuit Center.
Perluzzi, James *o.f.m.* '65 (STL)[O] Curia Generalizia dei Frati Minori; (FgM).
Pernia, John R. '58 (SFR) San Francisco, CA Star of the Sea.
Perno, Gerald D. '82 (BO) Jamaica Plain, MA St. Thomas Aquinas.
Perozich, Richard L. '92 (SD) On Duty Outside the Diocese.
Perras, Delfin '83 (TUC) Tucson, AZ Saint Cdilia.
Perreault, Joseph A. '75 (CAM) Brigantine, NJ St. Thomas; [A] Absecon, NJ Holy Spirit High School.
Perreault, Leonard J. '54 (SPR) Retired.
Perretta, Andrew T. '75 (PAT) Clifton, NJ Sacred Heart.
Perri, Dean Patrick '02 (PRO) Providence, RI St. Ann.
Perricone, Charles A. '74 (PAT) Sussex, NJ St. Monica.
Perricone, John '76 (NEW) Orange, NJ Mt. Carmel.
Perriello, Robert A. '76 (WH) Clarksburg WV St. James.
Perrier, Monroe *c.ss.r.* '58 (SAT) San Antonio, TX St. Gerard Majella; [B] San Antonio, TX Redemptorist Formation Program – Liguori House.
Perrier, Thomas E. *o.s.b.* '80 (NO)[P] St. Benedict, LA St. Joseph Abbey; [R] St. Benedict, LA Abbey Christian Life Center.
Perrin, Thomas *s.d.s.* '97 (NSH) Lewisburg, TN St. John the Evangelist.
Perrins, Samuel T. '86 (SCR) Hazleton, PA Church of the Most Precious Blood.
Perron, Gary *c.a.* '66 (BO)[V] Parroquia Emperatriz de America.
Perron, Richard J. '46 (BO) Senior Priests Retired.
Perron, Robert P. '81 (PRO) Woonsocket, RI All Saints Catholic Community; Deans.
Perrone, Eduard '78 (DET) Detroit, MI Assumption Grotto.
Perrone, James *s.m.a.* '59 (NEW)[N] Tenafly, NJ Society of African Missions, Provincialate, S.M.A. Fathers Retired.
Perrone, Vito J. '01 (SFR) San Francisco, CA St. Cecilia.
Perry, Ashley *s.s.j.* '75 (VNN) Olympia, WA St. George Byzantine.
Perry, Carmen J. '77 (SCR) Stroudsburg, PA St. Luke's.
Perry, David A. '01 (E) Erie, PA St. Peter Cathedral.
Perry, Francis J. '50 (DUB) Retired.
Perry, John A. '63 (FR) Fall River, MA St. Joseph's; Falmouth, MA St. Patrick's; Diocesan Consultors; Members; Diocesan Pastoral Council; Vicar General.
Perry, John J '83 (FR) Auditors; Diocesan Director of Cemeteries.
Perry, Michael A. '71 (BRK) Brooklyn, NY Our Lady of Refuge.
Perry, Michael E. *o.de.m.* '85 (SP)[O] St. Petersburg, FL St. Peter Nolasco Residence.
Perry, Michael *o.de.m.* '85 (SP) St. Petersburg, FL Cathedral of St. Jude the Apostle.
Perry, Michael *o.f.m.* (WDC) Silver Spring, MD St. Camillus.
Perry, Paul E. '67 (SFR) Greenbrae, CA St. Sebastian; Sequoia Hospital.
Perry, Richard *s.j.* '70 (HEL) Missoula, MT St. Francis Xavier.
Perry, Robert U. *o.p.* '59 (BR) Hammond LA Holy Ghost; Tickfaw, LA Our Lady of Pompeii; Presbyteral Council.
Perry, Ronald V. *s.j.* '76 (BGP)[E] Fairfield, CT Fairfield College Preparatory School; [P] Fairfield, CT The Fairfield Jesuit Community–Fairfield University.
Perryman, John E. '45 (CIN) Retired.
Persac, Louis A. '47 (NO) Retired.
Persha, Gerald J. *m.m.* '70 (FgM).
Pershe, Joseph N. *s.j.* '66 (OM)[K] Omaha, NE Jesuit Community at Creighton University.
Persich, Nicholas E. *c.m.* '46 (STL)[O] Perryville, MO Congregation of the Mission.
Persich, Roy A. *c.m.* '60 (LA)[Q] Santa Barbara, CA St. Mary's Center; [W] Santa Barbara, CA St. Mary's Seminary Center.
Persico, Lawrence T. '77 (GBG) New Alexandria, PA St. James; Chancellor/Associate General Executive Director; Defender of Bond; The Catholic Foundation for the Diocese of Greensburg; Board of Members of the Corporation.
Persico, Pasquale *p.i.m.e.* '44 (PMB)[J] Tequesta, FL P.I.M.E. Missionaries.
Persico, Philip T. '99 (NY) Hopewell Junction, NY St. Denis.
Persing, Charles L. '88 (HBG) Dallastown, PA St. Joseph.
Persinger, Patrick '87 (FRS) Wofford Heights, CA St. Jude.
Perumanoor, Antony (SYM) Procurator; Eparchial Consultors.
Perumbilly, Sebastian A. '97 (NOR) Rockville, CT St. Bernard.
Perumpally, Mathew '73 (MAR) Nadeau, MI St. Bruno; Stephenson, MI Precious Blood Church; Deans.
Perumpil, Matthew *o.s.c.* '94 (BO) Boston, MA St. Elizabeth's Medical Center; [P] Brighton, MA St. Elizabeth's Hospital of Boston.
Perumpilly, Marcel (MO) AUXILIARY CHAPLAINS CONTRACT CHAPLAINS.
Perumpuzha Joseph C. '94 (WIN)[D] Rochester, MN Saint Mary's Hospital.
Perunilam, Thomas V. '64 (SYM) Milltown, NJ Syro-Malabar Catholic Community of Milltown, NJ.
Perunilam, Thomas V. '64 (MET) Milltown, NJ Our Lady of Lourdes.
Perzan, Stephen B. '73 (PH) On Duty Outside the Archdiocese.
Perzan, Steve '73 (ARE) Barceloneta, PR Church of Our Lady of Mt. Carmel.
Pesanka, Nicholas A. '75 (PIT) Bethel Park, PA St. Germaine.
Pesarchick, Robert A. '91 (PH)[A] Wynnewood, PA Theological Seminary of St. Charles Borromeo, Overbrook.
Pesaresi, Thomas E. *m.m.* '85 (NY)[EE] Maryknoll Maryknoll Fathers and Brothers.
Pescatello, Joseph A. '89 (PRO) Woonsocket, RI Our Lady, Queen of Martyrs; [S] Smithfield, RI Bryant College; Council Members.
Pescatore, Terence *o.f.m.conv.* '62 (R) Burlington, NC Blessed Sacrament; [E] Burlington, NC Conventual Franciscans.
Pesce, John Baptist *c.p.* '51 (HRT)[M] West Hartford Holy Family Monastery/Retreat.
Pesch, Elroy *o.f.m.cap.* '63 (MIL)[O] Mount Calvary, WI St. Lawrence Friary; [B] Mount Calvary, WI St. Lawrence Seminary.
Peschel, Roland A. '60 (OM) Fremont, NE St. Patrick.
Pesci, Thomas A. *s.j.* '79 (KC)[D] Kansas City, MO Rockhurst High School; [J] Kansas City, MO Rockhurst Jesuit Community.
Pesek, Anthony '65 (SAT) San Antonio, TX Holy Spirit.
Pesek, Fred C. '89 (CHI) Lemont, IL St. Alphonsus.
Pesola, Joseph G. '97 (IND) Fortville, IN St. Thomas.
Pesongco, Rudy (RVC) East Northport, NY St. Anthony of Padua.
Pestun, Aloysius J. *s.d.b.* '59 (SFR) San Francisco, CA Corpus Christi.
Petcavage, Paschal *o.s.b.* '81 (CLV)[D] Cleveland, OH Benedictine High School; [O] Cleveland, OH.
Petekiewicz, Robert P. '91 (LAV) Las Vegas, NV Our Lady of Las Vegas.
Peteno, Pelagio Calambia *s.v.d.* (TR) Lakewood, NJ St. Anthony Claret.
Peter, David J. '66 (BUF) Retired.
Peter, Martin A. '67 (IND) Retired.
Peter, Patrick N. (BEL) Diocesan Consultors.
Peter, Valentine J. '59 (OM) Breese, IL St. Dominic; Immaculate Conception B.V.M.; [C] Boys Town, NE Father Flanagan's Boys' Home; [E] Father Flanagan's Boys' Home; [I] Boys Town, NE Father Flanagan's Boys' Home; Defenders of the Bond.
Petering, Michael '99 (VIC) Meyersville, TX SS. Peter & Paul; Presbyteral Council.
Peterka, Dale C. '68 (CIN) Cincinnati, OH St. John the Evangelist; On Special and Archdiocesan Assignment.
Peterka, Sylvester *c.m.* '76 (BAL) Baltimore, MD St. Cecilia; Baltimore, MD Immaculate Conception.
Peterlini, Luciano *s.x.* '63 (PAT)[M] Wayne Xaverian Missionary Fathers; (FgM).
Peterman, Charles '58 (MIA) Miami, FL St. Brendan.
Peterman, Thomas J. '57 (WIL) Galena, MD St. Dennis.
Petermeier, Virgil *o.s.c.* '77 (FgM).
Peters, Aaron *o.s.b.* '77 (KCK)[I] Paola, KS Our Lady of Lourdes Convent; [H] Atchison, KS St. Benedict's Abbey.
Peters, Claudio *f.d.p.* '97 (BO)[T] East Boston, MA Don Orione Nursing Home.
Peters, Daniel E. '89 (RCK) Harvard, IL St. Joseph.
Peters, David L. '58 (SFD) Highland, IL St. Paul.
Peters, David (SFD) Commission for the Care of Infirm and Retired Priests.
Peters, Eric '80 (SP) Citrus Springs, FL St. Elizabeth Ann Seton.
Peters, Fred *s.d.s.* '56 (PHX) Phoenix, AZ St. Mark; Phoenix, AZ Maricopa Medical Center.
Peters, Herman B. '41 (CLV) Cleveland, OH St. Cecilia; Legion of Mary Retired.
Peters, John B. (FgM).
Peters, John C. '74 (VIC) Hallettsville, TX Sacred Heart; Hallettsville, TX St. Mary; Hallettsville, TX St. John the Baptist; Diocesan Consultors; Hallettsville Deanery; Presbyteral Council; Priests' Personnel Board.
Peters, John '60 (ELP) El Paso, TX St. Luke.
Peters, John (ELP) Presbyteral Council; Priests' Retirement and Disability Plan.
Peters, Jude *o.c.d.* '89 (MIL)[O] Holy Hill, WI Discalced Carmelite Monastery – Holy Hill National Shrine of Mary Help of Christians; [O] Milwaukee, WI Provincial Offices – Discalced Carmelites; Milwaukee, WI St. Florian.
Peters, Julian *o.s.b.* '88 (IND)[K] St. Meinrad, IN St. Meinrad Archabbey.
Peters, Kenan *c.p.* '60 (BRK)[V] Jamaica, NY Immaculate Conception Monastery.
Peters, Kevin '90 (Y) Ashtabula, OH Mother of Sorrows.
Peters, Lyle '96 (DM) Osceola, IA St. Bernard; Continuing Education for Clergy.
Peters, Mark (SD)[B] University of San Diego.
Peters, Michael G. '88 (DM) Panama, IA St. Mary of the Assumption; Westphalia, IA St. Boniface.
Peters, Paul R. '62 (DUB) Volga, IA Sacred Heart; Elkader, IA St. Joseph.
Peters, Roy V. '48 (SAC) Retired.
Peters, Roy V. '48 (HON) Honolulu, HI SS Peter and Paul.
Peters, Roy (HON) Chinese Catholic Club; Nocturnal Adoration Society.
Peters, Stephen '67 (ELP) El Paso, TX Blessed Sacrament; Diocesan Tribunal; Judges.

Peters, Timothy '03 (ORG) Santa Ana, CA St. Anne's.
Peters, Vincent C. '03 (PEO) Bloomington, IL Holy Trinity.
Petersen, E. James '59 (FRS) Fresno, CA St. Therese.
Petersen, Michael '92 (MIL) West Bend, WI St. Frances Cabrini.
Petersen, Todd J. '99 (NU) Sleepy Eye, MN Church of the Japanese Martyrs; Committee for Evangelization & Catechesis; Priest Personnel Board; Vocations Team; On Special or Other Diocesan Assignment.
Petersen, Vincent *o.f.m.conv.* (ELP) El Paso, TX Our Lady of Mt. Carmel.
Peterson, Bradley *o.carm.* '92 (TUC)[A] Tucson, AZ Salpointe Catholic High School; [E] Tucson, AZ Carmelite Priory.
Peterson, Bruce '57 (STP) Bellechester, MN St. Mary; Goodhue, MN St. Columbkill.
Peterson, Casimir M. '47 (BAL)[W] Baltimore, MD Ladies of Charity; [W] Baltimore, MD Reparation Society of the Immaculate Heart of Mary, Inc. Retired.
Peterson, Charles J. *s.j.* '69 (P)[L] Portland, OR Jesuit Provincial Office (Society of Jesus, Oregon Prov.).
Peterson, Charles *s.j.* '74 (SPK) Omak, WA St. Mary Mission; Omak, WA St. Joseph.
Peterson, Clyde Vincent '74 (SEA) Port Orchard, WA St. Gabriel.
Peterson, Dennis L. '73 (GAL) Houston, TX St. Theresa.
Peterson, Eric '89 (MEM) Memphis, TN St. Mary's.
Peterson, Francis A. '46 (B) Retired.
Peterson, Francis '60 (HON) Catholic Women's Guild; Worldwide Marriage Encounter Retired.
Peterson, Frederick *o.s.b.* '95 (RCK)[G] Aurora, IL Marmion Abbey.
Peterson, Frederick *o.s.b.* '95 (ROM) Aurora, IL St. George.
Peterson, Gerald *g.h.m.* '56 (CIN)[M] Cincinnati Headquarters of Glenmary Home Missioners.
Peterson, Gerald '56 (JKS) New Albany, MS St. Francis of Assisi Retired.
Peterson, Harry *s.d.b.* '61 (FgM).
Peterson, James W. '47 (E)[O] Erie, PA Special Ministries Retired.
Peterson, James (E) Maria House Projects.
Peterson, Jay H. (GF) Catholic Relief Services; Holy Childhood Association.
Peterson, Jay (HEL) Board of Directors; Board of Directors.
Peterson, Jay (GF) Moderator of the Curia; Personnel Board; Catholic Campaign for Human Development; Newspaper; Priests' Council.
Peterson, Jay (HEL) Board of Directors; Board of Directors.
Peterson, Jay (GF) Diocesan Consultors; Montana Association of Churches.
Peterson, Jay (GF) Vicar General; Cemetery Board; Finance Council; Pastoral Outreach.
Peterson, John P. '89 (ARL)[A] Arlington, VA Marymount University; [M] Arlington, VA Marymount University; Campus Ministry.
Peterson, John S. *o.p.* '62 (PRO)[P] Providence St. Thomas Aquinas Priory at Providence College.
Peterson, Joseph L. '75 (WH) Huntington, WV Our Lady of Fatima.
Peterson, Leonard N. '67 (PH) Hatfield, PA St. Maria Goretti.
Peterson, Louis P. '74 (BEL) Leave of Absence.
Peterson, Maurice F. '87 (YAK) Special Assignment.
Peterson, Steven J. '73 (RVC) East Islip, NY St. Mary's; Islip Deanery.
Peterson, Steven J. '94 (WIN) Spring Valley, MN St. Finbarr's; Spring Valley, MN St. Patrick's; Spring Valley, MN St. Ignatius; Elected Deanery Representatives; Priests' Pension Board.
Peterson, William A. *c.ss.r.* '67 (DEN)[N] (FgM).
Peterson, William F. '59 (RCK) Retired.
Petilla, Antonio '61 (SFR) Daly City, CA Our Lady of Perpetual Help; Deans.
Petinge, Roland *o.f.m.* '61 (BO)[V] Andover St. Francis Friary; [X] Andover, MA Franciscan Center – Retreat House.
Petit, Edmund P. '46 (RCK) Retired.
Petit, Eliades '80 (SJN) Guaynabo, PR Maria Madre de la Misericordia.
Petit–Monsieur, Lamartine (BO) Lynn, MA St. Mary.
Petkash, Donald J. *s.j.* '71 (DET)[E] Detroit, MI University of Detroit Jesuit High School and Academy.
Petosa, Joseph '55 (SEA) Retired.
Petracca, Anthony '85 (ALT) Absent on Leave.
Petraitis, David *o.s.a.* (CHI)[J] Chicago, IL St. Anthony Hospital.
Petraitis, Donald S. *m.i.c.* '64 (CHI)[N] Chicago, IL Congregation of Marian Fathers of the Immaculate Conception.
Petraitis, Donald *m.i.c.* (LIT) Lithuanian Marian Province of St. Casimir.
Petrarulo, John D. '53 (PIT) New Castle, PA St. Vitus.
Petras, David M. '67 (PRM) On Duty Outside the Diocese.
Petras, David M. '67 (PBR)[A] Pittsburgh, PA Byzantine Catholic Seminary of SS. Cyril and Methodius.
Petras, David (PRM) Presbyteral Council; Eparchial Consultors; Eparchial Censor; Sacred Liturgy; Building Commission; Cantors' Institute; Seminary Education Formation Board; Office of Ecumenical Activity.
Petrasic, Martin J. '43 (OM) Retired.
Petrauskas, John *m.i.c.* '43 (NOR)[C] Thompson, CT Congregation of Marians of the Immaculate Conception; [C] Thompson, CT Marianapolis Preparatory School.
Petri, Gregg D. *o.f.m.* '61 (LSC) Alamogordo, NM Immaculate Conception.
Petri, John C. '45 (TR) Retired.
Petrich, John C. '83 (DUL) Duluth, MN St. Luke's Hospital; Northeast Regional Correctional Institution.
Petrich, John '83 (DUL) Duluth, MN St. Margaret Mary.
Petrie, Harry F. '45 (PIT) Wexford, PA St. Alexis Retired.
Petrie, Michael J. '87 (MIL) Hartford, WI St. Kilian.
Petrie, Roderic *o.f.m.* '59 (MIA)[H] Hialeah, FL Franciscan Friars of the Holy Name Province.
Petrie, William F. *ss.cc.* '69 (FR)[H] Fairhaven, MA Sacred Hearts Provincial House.
Petrikovic, John J. *o.f.m.cap.* '81 (PIT)[N] Pittsburgh, PA St. Augustine Friary.
Petrillo, Joseph A. '77 (NEW) West Orange, NJ Our Lady of Lourdes.
Petrillo, Thomas J. '59 (NEW) Montclair, NJ Our Lady of Mt. Carmel.
Petrillo, Thomas (NY) On Duty Outside the Archdiocese.
Petrimoulx, Leo *o.f.m.cap.* '66 (SAG) Saginaw, MI St. Joseph.
Petringa, Gerard (BO) Belmont, MA St. Luke.
Petriv, Vasil '92 (SJP) Parma, OH Pokrova Ukrainian Catholic Parish.
Petriv, Volodymyr '89 (STN) Detroit, MI St. John the Baptist.
Petro, John G. '68 (PBR)[A] Pittsburgh, PA Byzantine Catholic Seminary of SS. Cyril and Methodius.
Petro, John G. '68 (PBR) Beaver, PA Saint Nicholas Chapel; Diaconate Program.
Petro, Thomas J. '00 (SCR) Shohola, PA St. Ann's.
Petrocelli, John N. '71 (PRO)[K] North Providence, RI St. Joseph Health Services of Rhode Island – Our Lady of Fatima Hospital; Absent on Leave.
Petron, William G. '57 (DET) Retired.
Petronek, Thomas C. '65 (STU) Bridgeport, OH St. Anthony of Padua; Pastoral Staff; Diocesan Office of Worship.
Petronek, Thomas (STU) RCIA.
Petronio, Rolando '77 (STO) Stockton, CA St. George Church (Pastor of).
Petroske, Peter '84 (DET) Southgate, MI St. Pius X.
Petroski, Michael A. '00 (LAN) Leslie, MI SS. Cornelius and Cyprian.
Petrosky, Arnold *t.o.r.* '57 (SFS) Howard, SD Church of the Epiphany Retired.
Petrosky, Christopher *t.o.r.* '55 (ARL)[J] White Post, VA Sacred Heart Friary.
Petrovsky, Felix *o.f.m.cap.* '55 (SAL) Hays, KS St. Joseph's; [E] Hays, KS St. Joseph's Friary.
Petrovsky, James F. '68 (GBG) LaBelle, PA St. James.
Petroy, Dominic J. *o.s.b.* '87 (GBG) Jeannette, PA Sacred Heart; Jeannette, PA Mercy Jeannette Hospital; Jeannette, PA Monsour Medical Center; [F] Jeannette, PA Mercy Jeannette Hospital; [H] Latrobe, PA Saint Vincent Archabbey.
Petru, Augustine *o.m.i.* '53 (FgM).
Petru, Stanley J. '48 (VIC) La Grange, TX Holy Rosary; La Grange, TX SS. Peter and Paul.
Petrucci, Dominic '82 (SFS) Retired.
Petrucci, Peter J. *m.m.* '49 (FgM).
Petrucci, Raymond K. '73 (BGP) Danbury, CT St. Joseph.
Petruha, Louis *o.f.m.cap.* '65 (HBG) York, PA St. Joseph.
Petrunak, William '59 (Y) Struthers, OH Holy Trinity; [C] Warren, OH John F. Kennedy High School.
Petrusic, Anthony A. '57 (OM) Retired.
Petruska, Christopher '59 (PSC) Retired.
Petruska, William M. '73 (SCR) Military Chaplains; Navy Chaplains.
Petry, Thomas G. '78 (COL) Columbus, OH Sts. Augustine and Gabriel; OSU Medical Center.
Petsch, Joseph '50 (SAT)[K] San Antonio, TX Casa De Padres Retired.
Petsche, Daniel *o.s.b.* '67 (KC) Stanberry, MO St. Peter's; [A] Conception, MO Conception Seminary College; [J] Parnell, MO St. Joseph Parish; Deans.
Petta, Gerard *m.s.a.* '84 (NOR)[F] Cromwell Society of the Missionaries of the Holy Apostles.
Pettei, Thomas G. '86 (BRK) Long Island City, NY St. Raphael; Presbyteral Council; Art and Architecture Commission.
Petter, Henry V. '76 (DAL) Plano, TX St. Elizabeth Ann Seton; Consultors of Pastors; Presbyteral Council; Personnel Board.
Pettingill, David M. '62 (SFR) San Francisco, CA St. Emydius; Secretary to the Priests' Personnel Board; Office of Diaconate Formation.
Pettit, Edward G. '51 (PBL) Retired.
Pettit, Joseph H. '56 (HRT) Retired.
Pettit, Joseph '55 (GR) Grand Rapids, MI Sacred Heart of Jesus Retired.
Pettit, William J. '54 (DET) Plymouth, MI St. Kenneth Retired.
Pettke, Lawrence A. '81 (DET) Southfield, MI St. Bede.
Petty, Edward C. '77 (DUB)[D] Dyersville, IA Beckman High School; Worthington, IA St. Paul's; Dyersville, IA Basilica of St. Francis Xavier; Deans.
Peverada, Augustine J. *c.s.c.* '45 (FTW)[I] Notre Dame, IN Holy Cross House.
Peyton, John T. '61 (BRK) Brooklyn, NY St. Rita's.
Peyton, Mark J. '77 (CLV) South Euclid, OH St. Gregory the Great.
Peyton, Thomas J. '74 (SAV) Augusta, GA St. Teresa of Avila; Council of Priests.
Pezzotti, Mario *s.x.* '59 (PAT)[M] Wayne Xaverian Missionary Fathers; (FgM).
Pezzullo, Angelo B. '62 (BRK) Ozone Park, NY Nativity of the Blessed Virgin Mary.
Pezzulo, Neil *g.h.m.* '99 (LR) Waldron, AR Saint Andrew Church; Waldron, AR St. Jude Thaddeus Church.
Pfab, Cletus H. *s.j.* '69 (MIL)[O] Milwaukee, WI Miguel Pro Jesuit Community.
Pfaff, Aaron J. '96 (MAN) Somersworth, NH St. Martin.
Pfaff, Joseph A. '75 (BRK) Whitestone, NY Holy Trinity.
Pfalzer, Mike *o.f.m.* '47 (ALN)[K] Easton, PA St. Francis Friary.
Pfalzer, Roman *o.f.m.* '47 (CIN)[M] Cincinnati, OH St. Clement Friary Retired.
Pfannenstiel, Donald F. '75 (SAL) WaKeeney, KS Christ the King.
Pfannenstiel, John *o.f.m.cap.* '82 (BAL) Baltimore, MD St. Ambrose.
Pfau, Bernard '65 (FAR) New Rockford, ND SS. Peter & Paul; New Rockford, ND St. John.
Pfeffer, Charles J. '77 (PH) Philadelphia, PA St. Agatha–St. James; [EE] Philadelphia, PA University of Pennsylvania; [FF] Malvern, PA Catholic Leadership Institute.
Pfeffer, Edward B. '56 (DM) Judges Retired.
Pfeffer, Edward (DM) Priests' Pension Fund Society.
Pfeffer, Thomas J. '60 (DM) Judges Retired.
Pfeifer, Francis *o.m.i.* (FgM).
Pfeifer, Frederick A. '93 (NEW) Newark, NJ St. Francis Xavier.
Pfeifer, John M. '65 (BIS) Watford City, ND Epiphany.
Pfeiffer, Carl *o.ss.t.* '87 (BAL)[S] Round Rock, TX; Army Reserve Chaplains.
Pfeiffer, Joseph C. '58 (BRK) Howard Beach, NY St. Helen.
Pfeiffer, Mark S. '82 (LIN) Grafton, NE St. Helena's; Grafton, NE St. Patrick's.
Pfeiffer, Robert F. '61 (CLV) Medina, OH Holy Martyrs; Associate Judicial Vicars.
Pfeiffer, Robert F. (Y) Judges.
Pfister, Carl *o.carm.* '49 (NEW) Englewood, NJ St. Cecilia's.
Pfister, John F. '66 (FTW) Fort Wayne, IN Queen of Angels.
Pfister, John (FTW) Budget Committee.
Pfister, Neal A. '90 (DEN) Denver, CO Church of the Good Shepherd.
Pfisterer, Robert *o.f.m.* '51 (SFR) San Francisco, CA St. Anthony of Padua.
Pfleger, Michael L. '75 (CHI) Chicago, IL St. Sabina.
Pfleger, Phillip C. '79 (TR) Marlton, NJ St. Isaac Jogues.
Pflomm, Peter J. '70 (RVC) Seaford, NY Maria Regina.
Pflumm, Robert '60 (KCK) Retired.
Pfnausch, Edward G. '68 (HRT) Derby, CT St. Mary's.
Pfundstein, George A. '63 (BRK) Flushing, NY St. Ann's.
Phalen, John L. (DET) Retired.
Phalen, John P. *c.s.c.* '74 (FR)[N] North Easton, MA Holy Cross Family Ministries.
Phalen, John P. *c.s.c.* '74 (ALB)[R] North Easton, MA Crusade for Family Prayer, Inc..
Phalen, Julian *o.f.m.cap.* (NY)[FF] Hawthorne, NY Motherhouse & Novitiate of the Sisters of St. Dominic, Congregation of St. Rose of Lima.
Pham, Chau *s.v.d.* '95 (STL) St. Louis, MO St. Thomas of Aquin.
Pham, Cuong M. '01 (BRK) Queens Village, NY Our Lady of Lourdes.
Pham, Dat Huu '03 (HT) Raceland, LA St. Mary's Nativity.
Pham, Doan T. '98 (LA) Carson, CA St. Philomena.
Pham, Dominic Chinh Van *i.c.m.* '95 (GAL) Houston, TX St. Justin Martyr.
Pham, Dominic Thao '98 (ALN) Bath, PA Sacred Heart; [P] Bath, PA Blue Army of Our Lady of Fatima; Blue Army of Our Lady of Fatima.
Pham, Francis *c.ss.r.* '93 (SAT) San Antonio, TX St. Gerard Majella; San Antonio, TX Vietnamese Martyrs Catholic Center; [B] San Antonio, TX Redemptorist Formation Program – Liguori House.

Pham, Hien *s.v.d.* '99 (IND) Indianapolis, IN St. Rita.
Pham, Hung Q. '89 (WCH) Wichita, KS St. Anthony.
Pham, Joseph C. '01 (CAM) Glassboro, NJ Our Lady of Lourdes.
Pham, Joseph Luong '98 (CAM) Atlantic City, NJ Our Lady Star of the Sea.
Pham, Joseph Than Xuan '85 (RIC) Richmond, VA Church of the Vietnamese Martyrs.
Pham, Joseph Tuan '88 (ORG) Fountain Valley, CA Holy Spirit.
Pham, Joseph '70 (BRK) Long Island City NY Our Lady of Mount Carmel.
Pham, Joseph (CAM) Vocation Advisory Board; Advocates.
Pham, Joseph–Cuong M. (CAM) Advocates.
Pham, Khoi D. '94 (STO) Stockton, CA St. George Church (Pastor of).
Pham, Khoi (STO) College of Consultors/Presbyteral Council.
Pham, Le–Minh '93 (AUS) Cedar Park, TX St. Margaret Mary.
Pham, Michael '99 (SD) San Diego, CA Holy Family.
Pham, Minh J. *c.m.* '90 (PHX)[Q] Montebello, CA DePaul Evangelization Center; [W] Montebello, CA DePaul Evangelization Center.
Pham, Peter Nghi Duc *s.o.l.t.* '99 (CC) Rockport, TX St. Peter Indo–Chinese Parish.
Pham, Peter '98 (CHL) Unassigned.
Pham, Peter '99 (CC)[G] Robstown, TX Society of Our Lady of the Most Holy Trinity.
Pham, Phong '91 (GR) Grand Rapids, MI St. Mary Magdalen.
Pham, Pierre '71 (SPR) On Duty Outside the Diocese.
Pham, Tan '91 (CC)[G] Robstown, TX Society of Our Lady of the Most Holy Trinity.
Pham, The *c.ss.r.* '98 (SEA) Seattle, WA Sacred Heart of Jesus; [L] Seattle, WA The Redemptionist Society of Washington.
Pham, Thinh Duc '02 (LA) Norwalk, CA St. John of God.
Pham, Thu *s.v.d.* '03 (DUB)[B] Epworth, IA Divine Word College.
Pham, Tin Cosmas Kim '95 (GAL) Brazoria, TX St. Joseph on the Brazos.
Pham, Tuan Anh '99 (NO) Reserve, LA St. Peter.
Pham, Tuan Joseph (ORG) Defenders of the Bond; Liturgical Commission.
Pham, Tuan '88 (ORG)[C] Santa Ana, CA Mater Dei High School.
Pham, Tuan *c.ss.r.* '99 (STP) Brooklyn Center, MN St. Alphonsus.
Pham, Tuan (ORG) Promoters of Justice; Judges.
Pham, Vincent Hung '97 (ORG) Santa Ana, CA St. Barbara's.
Pham–Van–Ninh, James *s.e.* '67 (P) Portland, OR Our Lady of Lavang.
Pham An Su, Bartholomew M. *c.m.c.* '77 (SPC)[E] Carthage, MO Congregation of the Mother Coredemptrix, United States Assumption Province.
Pham duc Trin, Joseph '70 (VIC) Palacios, TX Vietnamese Apostolate; Vietnamese American Apostolic Center.
Pham Kim Ban, Albert M. *c.m.c.* '03 (SPC)[E] Carthage, MO Congregation of the Mother Coredemptrix, United States Assumption Province.
Pham Minh Van, Bartholomew *c.m.c.* '77 (SPC)[E] Carthage, MO Congregation of the Mother Coredemptrix, United States Assumption Province.
Pham Van Lan, Augustine '63 (CLV) Cleveland, OH St. Boniface; Translators.
Pham Van Tue, Joseph '73 (NO) New Orleans, LA St. Joseph.
Phan, Cho Dink Peter '72 (DAL) On Duty Outside the Diocese.
Phan, Cuong Paul '99 (SJ) Ongoing Formation of Clergy Committee; San Jose, CA St. Patrick.
Phan, Dominic '70 (BLX) Biloxi, MS Church of the Vietnamese Martyrs; Vietnamese Apostolate.
Phan, Joseph Duong '93 (OAK) Oakland, CA St. Anthony's.
Phan, Joseph '03 (GAL) Kingwood, TX St. Martha.
Phan, Joseph Loc D. '02 (GAL) Houston, TX St. Luke the Evangelist.
Phan, Minh Cong '97 (NO) Metairie, LA Our Lady of Divine Providence.
Phan, Nguyen Van *c.ss.r.* '93 (LA)[Q] Irving, TX.
Phan, Philip '85 (NY) New York, NY Guardian Angel.
Phan, Phu T. '92 (AMA) Judicial Vicar; Canyon, TX St. Ann's.
Phan, Phu (AMA) Presbyteral Council; College of Consultors.
Phan, Vincent Huo '95 (MOB) On Leave from the Archdiocese.
Phan Cong Binh, John M. '51 (SPC)[E] Carthage, MO Congregation of the Mother Coredemptrix, United States Assumption Province.
Phang, Benny *o.carm.* '98 (WDC)[B] Washington, DC Whitefriars Hall.
Phan Lam, Anthony '62 (OAK) Oakland, CA St. Lawrence O'Toole.
Phan Nam, Joseph M. '89 (AMA) Amarillo, TX Our Lady of Vietnam.
Pharr, William N. '60 (CHL) Retired.
Phat, Peter Tran Van '67 (NY) Otisville, NY Holy Name.
Phelan, Edward '63 (SFR) San Francisco CA Most Holy Redeemer.
Phelan, Gerald J. '62 (SJ)[M] Los Gatos, CA Sacred Heart Jesuit Center.
Phelan, John E. '74 (SY) Jordan, NY St. Patrick.
Phelan, Julian *o.f.m.cap.* '46 (NY)[EE] New York, NY Development Office:.
Phelan, Matthew H. *o.de.m* '02 (PH)[AA] Philadelphia, PA Monastery of Our Lady of Mercy.
Phelan, Nicholas '52 (SAC) Grass Valley, CA St. Patrick.
Phelan, Thomas E. '76 (BEA) Orange, TX St Francis of Assisi.
Phelan, Thomas '51 (ALB) Ecumenical and Interreligious Affairs of the Roman Catholic Diocese of Albany, Commission for Retired.
Phelan, Thomas '53 (SEA) Retired.
Phelan, Walter M. '49 (GI) U.S. Veterans' Hospital Retired.
Phelps, John *c.ss.r.* '66 (CHI) Chicago, IL Blessed Sacrament [N] Chicago, IL The Redemptorists of Blessed Sacrament.
Phelps, Lawrence J. *o.s.b.* '63 (NO) Bogalusa, LA Annunciation B.V.M.; [P] St. Benedict, LA St. Joseph Abbey.
Phelps, Robert *o.f.m.cap.* '66 (AGN) Sinajana, GU Saint Jude Thaddeus; [F] Agana Heights, GU St. Fidelis Friary; (FgM).
Phien Van Pham, Joseph '78 (SD) San Diego, CA Our Lady of the Sacred Heart.
Philbin, John J. '44 (BO) Wellesley, MA St. John the Evangelist, Senior Priests Retired.
Philbin, Patrick B. *s.m.* '72 (ORG)[L] Orange, CA House of Prayer for Priests; [M] Irvine, CA U.C.I. Interfaith Center.
Philbin, Patrick *s.m.* (ORG) Newman Apostolate.
Philen, Michael *c.m.f.* '99 (LA)[Q] Rancho Dominguez, CA Dominguez Seminary Inc..
Philibin, Patrick *s.m.* '52 (STL)[O] Orange, CA.
Philion, Richard *o.m.i.* '61 (BWN) Roma, TX Our Lady of Refuge.
Philip, Ligori Johnson '91 (GAL) Sugar Land, TX St. Theresa.
Philip, Ligory '91 (SYM) Missouri City, TX St. Joseph Syro–Malabar Catholic Church.
Philippe, Jean–Rony '99 (BGP) Bridgeport, CT St. Charles.
Philips, Hugh J. '35 (WDC)[L] Washington, DC Cardinal O'Boyle Residence for Priests.
Philipsen, Todd K. '89 (GI) Broken Bow, NE St. Joseph's.
Phillip, Alan *c.p.* '67 (LA)[Q] Sierra Madre, CA Passionist Residence.
Phillippino, Michael L. '90 (NOR) Killingworth, CT St. Lawrence Members; Members; Deans.
Phillippino, Michael (NOR) Vocations; Diocesan Vocation Review Committee.
Phillips, Ambrose *t.o.r.* '71 (WDC)[M] Washington, DC St. Louis Friary.
Phillips, Benet C. *o.s.b.* '92 (MAN)[K] Manchester, NH St. Anselm Abbey.
Phillips, C. Frank *c.r.* '77 (CHI) Chicago, IL St. John Cantius; [Q] Chicago, IL Society of Saint John Cantius.
Phillips, Christopher G. '83 (SAT) San Antonio, TX Our Lady of the Atonement Catholic.
Phillips, Christopher (SA) AUXILIARY CHAPLAINS CONTRACT CHAPLAINS.
Phillips, Clyde *m.m.* '78 (CHI)[EE] Maryknoll Maryknoll Fathers and Brothers.
Phillips, Clyde (NY)[EE] New York, NY Maryknoll House.
Phillips, Edward J. *m.m.* '74 (FgM).
Phillips, Eric '98 (ROC) Absent on Leave.
Phillips, Gene D. *s.j.* '65 (CHI)[N] Evanston, IL Canisius House.
Phillips, George M. '40 (OG) Ogdensburg, NY Notre Dame Retired.
Phillips, George '45 (ALB) Latham, NY St. Ambrose.
Phillips, Glenn *o.f.m.* '66 (SHP) Farmerville, LA Our Lady of Perpetual Help.
Phillips, Gregory *o.s.b.* '01 (WOR)[O] Petersham, MA St. Marys Monastery.
Phillips, Hugh J. '35 (BAL) Retired.
Phillips, John J. '55 (ROC) Fairport, NY St. John of Rochester.
Phillips, John M. '87 (STA) Gainesville, FL Holy Faith.
Phillips, John '55 (ROC) Retired.
Phillips, Joseph H. '68 (SY) Syracuse, NY St. Ann; Special Assignment; [L] Syracuse, NY Family Life Education; Management Team; Family Life Education; Propagation of the Faith.
Phillips, Kenneth G. '91 (BIS) Hazelton, ND St. Paul; Linton, ND St. Anthony.
Phillips, Kenneth '91 (BIS) Dickinson, ND St. Joseph.
Phillips, Louis J. '81 (PRT) Ellsworth, ME St. Joseph's.
Phillips, Michael J. '60 (BRK) Brooklyn, NY St. Anselm's.
Phillips, Michael T. '69 (DAV) Iowa City, IA St. Wenceslaus; Priests Eucharistic League.
Phillips, Randall '83 (DET) Sterling Heights, MI St. Blase; AUXILIARY CHAPLAINS CONTRACT CHAPLAINS.
Phillips, Randy '97 (SFS) Faulkton, SD St. Thomas the Apostle.
Phillips, Rene F. *o.f.m.* '56 (NY)[EE] Angola, NY.
Phillips, Robert L. *s.j.* '72 (STL)[C] Saint Louis University; [O] St. Louis, MO Jesuit Community Corporation at St. Louis University – Jesuit Hall.
Phillips, Stephen (ORL) Candler, FL Immaculate Heart of Mary.
Phillips, Thomas L. '71 (BAL) Baltimore, MD St. Gabriel.
Phillips, Thomas (BAL) Priests' Council.
Phillips, Walter W. '55 (GI) Retired.
Phillipson, David '03 (SFE) Albuquerque, NM Our Lady of Fatima.
Philominsamy, Michaelraj '91 (SR) Fort Bragg, CA Our Lady of Good Counsel; Parish Priest Consultors.
Phinn, Gilbert S. '53 (BO) Milton, MA St. Elizabeth.
Phinn, Paul A. '57 (BO) West Roxbury, MA St. John Chrysostom.
Phipps, Charles T. *s.j.* '59 (SJ)[B] Santa Clara, CA Jesuit Community.
Phipps, Ricardo M. '02 (JKS) Madison, MS St. Francis of Assisi; Defenders of the Bond.
Phiri, Charles *m.s.c.* (BAL) Baltimore, MD St. Anthony of Padua.
Phuc, Anthony *c.ss.r.* '56 (MRY) Pacific Grove, CA St. Angela.
Phuc, Tran Dinh *c.ss.r.* '56 (LA)[Q] Salinas, CA.
Phung, Chi Peter '90 (TLS) Pryor, OK St. Mark's; Wagoner, OK Holy Cross.
Phung, Le Quang *c.ss.r.* '69 (LA)[Q] Houston, TX.
Phung, Vincent '96 (DEN) Denver, CO Presentation of Our Lady.
Phuoc Hoa, Dang *c.ss.r.* '03 (LA)[Q] Tuscon, AZ.
Physician, Thomas R. '58 (DET)[T] Clinton Township, MI St. Mary Magdalen Catholic Community; Clinton Township, MI State Prisons; Pontiac, MI St. Joseph Retired.
Piacentini, David '71 (PRO) North Providence, RI St. Lawrence.
Piacitelli, Henry '45 (KC) Kansas City, MO St. Thomas More.
Piano, Timothy '77 (MIA) Absent on Leave.
Piansay, Victor '64 (FRS) Riverdale, CA St. Ann.
Piasecki, Timothy '73 (RCK) Rockford, IL SS. Peter and Paul.
Piatek, Ignatius *o.f.m.conv.* '61 (PMB) Boynton Beach, FL St. Mark.
Piatt, Charles *s.t.* '03 (LA) Compton, CA Our Lady of Victory; Compton, CA Sagrado Corazon, Sacred Heart.
Piatt, Richard *o.s.a.* '01 (BO)[C] North Andover, MA Merrimack College; [BB] North Andover, MA Merrimack College Campus Ministry Center.
Piazza, Benjamin A. '49 (NEW) Caldwell, NJ St. Aloysius Retired.
Piazza, Salvatore J. '48 (BUF) Ransomville, NY Immaculate Conception Retired.
Picado, Rodrigo '71 (NO) On Duty Outside the Archdiocese.
Picard, Adrien '73 (SPR).
Picard, Benoit *o.f.f.* '91 (LR)[F] Hot Springs National Park, AR Monastery of Our Lady of Charity of Refuge (Good Shepherd); [I] Hot Springs, AR Monastery of Our Lady of Charity of Refuge (Good Shepherd).
Picard, Daniel '79 (LAF) Lawtell, LA St. Bridget.
Picard, Howard *c.i.c.m.* '56 (ARL)[J] Arlington, VA Missionhurst, C.I.C.M.–Central House and Provincialate.
Picard, Michael C. '66 (PH) Newtown, PA St. Andrew.
Picard, Norman *c.i.c.m.* (MO) AUXILIARY CHAPLAINS CONTRACT CHAPLAINS.
Picard, Raymond '65 (PRT) Boothbay Harbor, ME Our Lady, Queen of Peace; Newcastle, ME St. Patrick; Diocesan Council of Priests.
Picardi, Aubert Manie *o.f.m.* (BO) Boston, MA St. Leonard of Port Maurice.
Picardi, John M. '83 (BO) On Duty Outside the Archdiocese.
Picarella, Dale '84 (BAL) Glen Burnie, MD Crucifixion, Church of the.
Picariello, Anthony R. *s.j.* '80 (BO)[V] Weston, MA Campion Jesuit Community.
Picciano, Daniel A. '71 (RVC) Port Washington, NY St. Peter of Alcantara.
Piccinino, Corey V. '86 (BGP) Bethel, CT St. Mary; [C] Danbury, CT Immaculate High School.
Piccione, John T. *o.f.m.* '95 (PAT) Paterson, NJ St. Bonaventure.
Piccola, Michael J. '78 (SCR) West Pittston, PA Immaculate Conception; Deans.
Piccoli, Gino L. *o.f.m.* '65 (TUC) San Carlos, AZ San Carlos Catholic Mission.

Piccolo, Bruno *p.i.m.e.* '65 (DET)[T] Detroit, MI Foster Parents Mission Club; [K] Detroit, MI P.I.M.E. Motherhouse in Detroit.
Piccolomini, Rocco M. (WOR) Diocesan College of Consultors; Vicar for Clergy; Co–Directors; Presbyteral Council; Priests' Personnel Board; Vicar for Priests.
Piccolomini, Rocco '85 (WOR) Worcester, MA Our Lady of Mt. Carmel and St. Ann.
Pichando Diaz, Nelson (BRK) Elmhurst, NY St. Bartholomew's.
Pichard, Larry '73 (DAL) Dallas, TX St. Pius X; Diocesan Consultors; Presbyteral Council; Building Commission.
Piche, Donald J. '77 (STP) Special Assignment.
Piche, Lee A. '84 (STP) West St. Paul, MN St. Joseph.
Piche, Lee (STP) Commission for Ecumenism and Interreligious Affairs; Office of Ecumenism.
Piche, Marc A. '68 (BO) Newburyport, MA Immaculate Conception.
Pichette, Fernand L. '58 (MAN) Retired.
Pick, Anthony '67 (SC) Coon Rapids, IA Annunciation; Dedham, IA St. Joseph's.
Pick, Edward '60 (VEN) Longboat Key, FL St. Mary Star of the Sea; Deans; Presbyteral Council; Propagation of the Faith/Mission Cooperative Program.
Pick, Philip E. *s.j.* '50 (MIL).
Pickard, William B. '76 (SCR)[J] Scranton, PA St. Joseph's Center; Catholic Campaign for Human Development.
Pickard, William M. '54 (GAL) Houston, TX St. Theresa; College of Consultors.
Pickard, William (GAL) Defenders of the Bond.
Pickarts, Bernard J. '55 (MAD) Retired.
Pickert, Cecil *o.carm.* '58 (L) Louisville, KY Our Lady of Mount Carmel.
Picket, James B. '61 (OAK) Retired.
Pickett, Robert T. '55 (TLS) Retired.
Pico, Fernando A. *s.j.* '71 (SJN)[C] Rio Piedras, PR Jesuit Community.
Pico, Fernando *s.j.* '71 (SJN)[H] Hato Rey, PR Jesuit Community – Casa Claver.
Picone, Alfonso (NEW) Garfield, NJ Our Lady of Mt. Virgin.
Picornell, Antonio *m.ss.cc.* '42 (SJN) Bayamon, PR Santiago Apostol.
Picton, James D. '75 (SEA) Bellevue, WA St. Madeleine Sophie; Presbyteral Council; College of Consultors; Defenders of the Bond; Vicar to Faith Communities.
Picton, James '75 (SEA) Seattle, WA Immaculate Conception; Seattle, WA Our Lady of Mount Virgin; Special Assignment; Issaquah, WA St. Joseph; Lacey, WA Sacred Heart of Jesus.
Picton, Thomas D. *c.ss.r.* '71 (BR)[H] Baton Rouge, LA Redemptorist Vice Province.
Picton, Thomas *c.ss.r.* '71 (BR)[H] Baton Rouge, LA The Redemptorist Education and Formation Foundation.
Piderit, John J. *s.j.* '71 (NY) Bronx, NY St. Anthony.
Piderit, John J. *s.j.* '71 (CHI)[X] Chicago, IL The Catholic Education Institute.
Pidgeon, John '87 (PH) Philadelphia, PA St. Francis de Sales; [D] Philadelphia, PA West Philadelphia Catholic High School.
Pieber, Carl L. *c.m.* '80 (PH).
Pieber, Carl *c.m.* (GAL)[AA] Development Office.
Piechocki, Bruce '84 (FTW) Fort Wayne, IN Queen of Angels; Pierceton, IN St. Francis Xavier; On Special Assignment; Judicial Vicar; Pro–Synodal Judges.
Piechocki, Raymond S. '47 (ALB)[J] Amsterdam, NY Mt. Loretto Nursing Home Retired.
Pieczara, Stanislaw (MO) Air Force Chaplains.
Pieczka, Walenty *c.m.* '43 (HRT)[M] Manchester DePaul Provincial Residence.
Pied, Wilfrid L. '51 (BO) Senior Priests Retired.
Piedra, Jose Carlos '80 (MIA)[K] Miami, FL National Shrine of Our Lady of Charity.
Piedra, Ruskin *c.ss.r.* '60 (BRK) Brooklyn, NY Our Lady of Perpetual Help Basilica.
Piedrahita, Jose Gabriel *m.x.y.* '86 (NY) Bronx, NY Our Saviour; [EE] Bronx, NY Yarumal Mission Society, Inc..
Piegl, Fred '70 (CHI)[W] Chicago, IL Midtown Center.
Piekarczyk, Marian A. *s.d.s.* '80 (SAT) San Antonio, TX Our Lady of Sorrows.
Piekarczyk, Marian '80 (SAT) San Antonio, TX Methodist Hospital.
Piekarski, Joseph J. '86 (WIL) Elkton, MD Immaculate Conception; Associate Directors; College of Consultors.
Pien, Nguyen Xuan *s.s.c.* '95 (LA)[Q] Los Angeles, CA Columban Fathers, Procure House.
Pienciak, Daniel B. '87 (TR) Leave of Absence.
Pieniazek, Tadeusz *s.d.s.* '92 (NEW)[N] Verona, NJ The Salvatorian Fathers.
Pieniazek, Tadeusz *s.d.s.* '92 (NOR) Moosup, CT All–Hallows; Wauregan, CT Sacred Heart.
Pienkos, Zbigniew *c.ss.r.* (CHI) Cicero, IL St. Mary of Czestochowa.
Pienta, Robert J. '99 (LAN) Milan, MI Immaculate Conception.
Pientek, Placid *o.s.b.* '44 (CLV)[O] Cleveland, OH.
Pieper, Herbert *s.m.* '38 (STL)[O] Eureka, MO; [K] San Antonio, TX Marianist Residence: Skilled Nursing.
Pieper, James E. '57 (STL) St. Louis, MO St. Clement.
Pieper, Theodore X. '62 (STL) Cadet, MO St. Joachim; Cadet, MO St. Joseph; Washington County Catholic Church Real Estate Corporation; [U] Cadet, MO Washington County Catholic Church Real Estate Corporation.
Piepmeyer, Ronald J. '97 (CIN) Morrow, OH St. Philip the Apostle.
Pier, Joseph '38 (ALT) Retired.
Pierce, Blaine F. '46 (Y) Retired.
Pierce, Bradley *m.s.a.* '83 (NOR)[A] Cromwell, CT Holy Apostles College and Seminary; [F] Cromwell, CT Society of the Missionaries of the Holy Apostles.
Pierce, Brian J. *o.p.* '88 (FgM).
Pierce, Brian J. *o.p.* '88 (R)[E] Raleigh, NC Dominican Priory.
Pierce, Brian J. *o.p.* '88 (NO)[P] Memphis, TN Southern Dominican Global Missions; [S] Metairie, LA Southern Dominican Global Missions.
Pierce, Edward J. '72 (SFS) Alexandria, SD St. Mary of Mercy; Emery, SD St. Martin.
Pierce, James L. *s.j.* '77 (NY)[EE] New York, NY Xavier Jesuit Community.
Pierce, John J. *o.f.m.* '63 (PAT)[M] Butler, NJ St. Anthony Friary.
Pierce, Joseph B. '92 (WDC) Cheverly, MD St. Ambrose; Health Care Concerns Coordinator.
Pierce, Larry E. '58 (SAL) Retired.
Pierce, Mark R. '81 (LC) La Crosse, WI Roncalli Newman Parish; [K] La Crosse, WI Roncalli Newman Parish; Newman Campus Ministry.
Pierce, Robert T. '54 (LA) Covina, CA St. Louise de Marillac Retired.
Pierce, William C. '71 (CAM) Millville, NJ St. John Bosco.
Pierceall, Patrick L. '69 (JC) Palmyra, MO St. Joseph.
Pierick, Bernard E. '47 (MAD) Retired.
Pierick, Bernard J. '47 (MAD)[G] Madison, WI Bishop O'Connor Catholic Pastoral Center.
Pierini, Pascal *o.c.d.* '48 (SJ)[M] San Jose, CA Carmelite Monastery, Novitiate.
Pierini, Raymond G. *m.m.* '87 (NY) Manhattan, NY Cabrini Medical Center.
Pierino, Vicente '64 (SJN)[EE] On Duty Outside the Archdiocese.
Pieris, Timothy '46 (NO) Retired.
Pierjok, Harry A '88 (PEO) Lacon, IL St. Joseph's; Lacon, IL St. Mary's; Lacon, IL Immaculate Conception.
Piermarini, Louis R. '69 (WOR) Oxford, MA St. Roch's; Religious Education Office.
Pierog, Stanislaus '76 (VEN) Arcadia, FL St. Paul.
Pieroni, Christopher J. '99 (SFE) Dixon, NM St. Anthony; Penasco, NM San Antonio de Padua.
Pieroni, Edward L. '85 (PRO) Providence, RI St. Raymond; Providence, RI Miriam Hospital.
Pierre, Andre *o.f.m.cap.* (WDC) Washington, DC Shrine of the Sacred Heart.
Pierre, Jean '88 (MIA) Miami, FL St. James; Ministry to Cultural Groups (Non–Hispanic Ethnicities); Haitians; Native Americans; Archdiocesan Fund–Raising & Assessments Committee; Society for the Propagation of the Faith; Archdiocesan Vocations Review Board; Pontifical Mission Societies.
Pierre, Kenneth J. '63 (STP) Retired.
Pierre, Roger P. '63 (STP) White Bear Lake, MN St. Mary of the Lake.
Pierre–Louis, Dumarsais '01 (PMB) Lake Worth, FL Sacred Heart.
Pierro, Sebastian C. '82 (BUF) Lewiston, NY St. Peter.
Pierse, James J. '44 (ORG) Seal Beach, CA Holy Family Retired.
Pierson, Robert *o.s.b.* '84 (SCL)[B] St. John's University; [I] Collegeville, MN St. John's Abbey, of the Order of St. Benedict.
Pietramale, John L. '92 (OM) Hartington, NE St. Michael; Hartington, NE Holy Trinity.
Pietrantonio, Thomas *o.f.m.cap.* '49 (WIL)[J] Wilmington, DE Capuchin Franciscan Friars, St. Francis Renewal Center; [M] Wilmington, DE St. Francis Renewal Center.
Pietras, Robert E. '62 (JOL) Downers Grove, IL Divine Savior.
Pietraszko, Andrzej '03 (MIA) Hollywood, FL St. Bernadette.
Pietropaoli, David '84 (BAL) Absent on Leave.
Pietropinto, Joseph P. '70 (NEW) Secaucus, NJ Immaculate Conception.
Pietrowski, Stephen '92 (RVC) Williston Park, NY St. Aidan's Church.
Pietrucha, Edward S. *c.s.p.* '57 (TUC) Tuscon, AZ St. Cyril of Alexandria.
Pietrzak, Bernard J. '81 (CHI) Mt. Prospect, IL St. Raymond de Penafort.
Pietrzak, Daniel *o.f.m.conv.* '64 (BAL).
Pietrzyk, Paul *o.de.m.* '02 (BUF)[O] LeRoy, NY Order of the BVM of Mercy/Mercedarian Friars; [Q] LeRoy, NY St. Peter Nolasco Spiritual Center.
Pifher, Cletus *o.f.m.conv.* '64 (SAV) Brunswick, GA St. Francis Xavier.
Pifher, William A. *c.s.c.* '94 (TOL) Norwalk, OH St. Paul.
Pifher, William A. *c.s.c.* '94 (FTW)[I] Norwalk, OH.
Piga, Stephen M. '02 (TR) Spring Lake, NJ St. Catharine.
Pighini, Richard *c.s.v.* '85 (JOL) Kankakee, IL St. Patrick.
Pignato, David A. '01 (FR) North Dartmouth, MA St. Julie Billiart.
Pignato, David '01 (FR)[B] North Dartmouth, MA Bishop Stang High School.
Pignato, Salvatore A. '68 (PSC) Orlando, FL St. Nicholas of Myra; Retirement Plan Board.
Pigott, Edward L. *s.j.* '68 (CIN)[F] Cincinnati, OH St. Xavier High School; [M] Cincinnati, OH Jesuit Community at St. Xavier High School.
Pijnenburg, Carlos *o.p.* '54 (SJN)[E] Bayamon, PR Hospital Hermanos Melendez.
Pijoan, L. Adrian M. Figuerola '71 (NO) Retired.
Pikula, Zygmunt '55 (NEW) Retired.
Pikulski, John F. '60 (BGP) Danbury, CT St. Joseph; Danbury, CT Danbury Hospital.
Pikus, Karl A. '92 (LIN)[L] Lincoln, NE St. Francis of Assisi Church.
Pikus, Karl *f.s.s.p.* '94 (LIN)[M] Fountain, CO Immaculate Conception Latin Mass Mission; Presbyteral Council; Tridentine Mass Apostolate.
Pilaczynski, John E. *o.m.i.* '58 (STP)[M] St. Paul, MN Oblate Residence.
Pilarski, Bernard '56 (DET) Annapolis; Garden City Osteopathic Hospital.
Pilarski, Chester J. '50 (SAG) Kawkawlin, MI Sacred Heart.
Pilarski, Peter R. '59 (PIT) Plum, PA St. Januarius.
Pilarz, Scott R. *s.j.* '92 (WDC)[C] Scranton, PA The University of Scranton.
Pilat, Edmund S. '56 (SY) Retired.
Pilato, Sabato '92 (LA) Torrance, CA St. Catherine Laboure; [D] Gardena, CA Junipero Serra High School.
Pilato, Sal (LA) Members.
Pilatowski, Augustine *o.f.m.conv.* '59 (HRT)[K] New Britain, CT St. Lucian's Residence, Inc.; [M] New Britain, CT Conventual Franciscans.
Pilatowski, Eugene '60 (NOR) Norwich, CT St. Joseph; District Moderators.
Pilcher, Gregory *o.s.b.* '78 (LR) El Dorado, AR Holy Redeemer; Magnolia, AR Immaculate Heart of Mary.
Pilcher, John '99 (KCK) Holy Family; St. Joseph's; Wamego, KS St. Bernard's.
Pildain, Francisco *o.ss.t.* '58 (ARE) Isabela, PR Our Lady of Mount Carmel.
Pilecki, Walter J. '43 (KC) Retired.
Pileggi, Anthony J. '81 (KC) Nevada, MO St. Mary's.
Pileggi, Anthony (KC) Presbyteral Council; Deans.
Pileggi, Francis J. *o.s.f.s.* '61 (WIL)[B] Wilmington, DE Salesianum School.
Piletic, William E. *c.m.* '77 (LA)[Q] Los Angeles, CA Amat Residence I.
Piletic, William R. '77 (LA)[Q] Montebello, CA Vincentian Fathers and Brothers.
Pilger, G. Richard *i.c.* '79 (SP) Seminole, FL Blessed Sacrament.
Pilger, Joseph J. '55 (LEX) Retired.
Pilgram, Paul C. *s.j.* '70 (STL)[O] St. Louis, MO Hallahan House.
Pilipie, John P. '82 (PAT) Whippany, NJ Our Lady of Mercy.
Pilla, P. Carl '54 (SY)[Q] Syracuse, NY Tommy Coyne Residence @ Dillon Hall Retired.
Pilla, Raju '91 (PH)[U] Langhorne, PA St. Mary Medical Center.
Pillar, James *o.m.i.* '54 (STP).
Pillon, Gordon '79 (PEO)[V] Clinton, IL St. John the Baptist's; La Salle, IL Queen of the Holy Rosary; La Salle, IL St. Hyacinth's; La Salle, IL St. Patrick's.
Pilola, Joseph '87 (HT) Dulac, LA Holy Family; Theriot, LA St. Eloi.
Pilon, Daniel J. '76 (FAR) Horace, ND St. Benedict; Judicial Vicar.
Pilon, Daniel (FAR) Vice–Chancellors; Presiding Judge.
Pilon, Jean–Pierre G. '02 (SCR) Unassigned or Leave of Absence.
Pilon, Jerome R. '89 (PEO) Moline, IL St. Mary's.
Pilon, Mark A. '75 (ARL) On Duty Outside the Diocese.
Pilon, Peter (PEO)[B] Ottawa, IL Marquette High School; Ottawa (Naplate), IL St. Mary's.
Pilones, Loji C. '86 (LA) Ventura, CA Sacred Heart.
Pilsner, James F. '01 (NY) Bronx, NY Our Lady of the Assumption.
Pilsner, Joseph E. *c.s.b.* '91 (GAL)[Q] Houston, TX Residence of the Basilian Fathers of the University of St. Thomas.
Pilsner, Peter R. '89 (NY)[E] New York, NY Cardinal Spellman High School; Army Reserve Chaplains.
Pimental, Joseph W. *o.p.* (MO) Navy Chaplains.
Pimentel, Jose *o.p.* '90 (OAK) Berkeley, CA St. Mary Magdalen.
Pina, Martin '93 (LUB) Levelland, TX St. Michael's;

Presbyteral Council; Priests Personnel Board; Diocesan Pastoral Liturgy Commission.
Pinard, Paul *s.s.e.* '59 (NOR)[A] Enders Island, CT St. Edmund's Novitiate; [F] Mystic, CT Society of St. Edmund.
Pincelli, Thomas L. '70 (BWN) Harlingen, TX St. Anthony.
Pincelli, Thomas (BWN) Parish Priests' Consultors & Priest Personnel Board.
Pinchock, Joseph '72 (ORL) Dunnellon, FL St. John the Baptist.
Pinciaro, Albert G. '84 (BGP) Stamford, CT St. Maurice.
Pincince, Gerald P. '65 (PRO) On Duty Outside the Diocese.
Pinczewski, Phillip A. '87 (E) Kane, PA St. Callistus; Deans.
Pinczewski, Phillip (E) Eastern Vicariate.
Pineda, Juan G. '90 (Columbia) Bridgeport, CT St. Charles.
Pineda, Juan G. '90 (BGP).
Pineda, Juan *m.s.c.* '77 (FRS) Huron, CA St. Frances Cabrini; Avenal, CA St. Joseph.
Pineiro, Juan Colon '95 (CGS) Barranquitas, PR Church of St. Anthony of Padua.
Pinero, Geraldo J. '91 (PH) Aston, PA St. Joseph.
Pinette, Stuart H. '95 (HRT) Oakville, CT St. Mary Magdalen.
Pingatore, Thomas J. '44 (STP) Retired.
Pingatore, Thomas '44 (STP) St. Paul, MN St. John of St. Paul.
Pinillos, Javier Bautista *m.s.c.* '95 (FgM).
Pinizzotto, Anthony J. *o.s.f.s.* '78 (ARL) Stafford, VA St. William of York.
Pinizzotto, Anthony J. *o.s.f.s.* '78 (WIL)[J] Wilmington Oblates of St. Francis De Sales.
Pinkerton, Samuel J. '95 (WCH) Augusta, KS St. James.
Pinkston, Robert L. *c.s.p.* '69 (AUS) Austin, TX St. Austin.
Pinne, Christopher P. *s.j.* '87 (STL)[O] St. Louis, MO Bellarmine House of Studies; [O] St. Louis, MO The Jesuits of the Missouri Province; [U] St. Louis, MO The Jesuits of the Missouri Province.
Pino, Mario '85 (ATL) Woodstock, GA St. Michael the Archangel.
Pinon, Gilberto *o.m.i.* '71 (FgM).
Pins, Herbert J. '71 (HEL) Philipsburg, MT St. Philip.
Pins, Herbert J. '71 (SEA) Drummond, MT St. Michael; Montana State Prison; Warm Springs State Hospital.
Pins, Joseph '70 (STL) Chesterfield, MO Ascension.
Pintabone, John A. *k.h.s.* '79 (NY) Staten Island, NY Assumption.
Pintacura, Michael '93 (STO) On Duty Outside the Diocese.
Pinti, Domenico C. '85 (TUC) Safford, AZ St. Rose of Lima; [H] Safford, AZ Eastern Arizona Junior College; Council of Priests; Members; Vicars Forane; Directors; All Vicars Forane.
Pinto, Agnelo '71 (BRK) Brooklyn, NY St. Augustine.
Pinto, Danny '63 (FTW) Churubusco, IN St. John Bosco; Churubusco, IN Immaculate Conception.
Pinto, Edgaro '80 (SJN) Bayamon, PR Nuestra Senora de la Milagrosa.
Pinto, Fernando *o.c.d.* '99 (SB)[G] Redlands, CA El Carmelo Retreat House; [E] Redlands, CA Discalced Carmelites, OCD.
Pinto, Joao Carlos *s.j.* '01 (OAK)[N] Berkeley, CA Jesuit Community at Jesuit School of Theology at Berkeley.
Pinto, P. Francis *s.d.b.* (NEW)[S] Offices of Vocation and Youth Ministry.
Pinto, Peter J. '56 (HRT) West Haven, CT St. Louis.
Pinto, Santan '77 (CC)[G] Robstown, TX Society of Our Lady of the Most Holy Trinity.
Pintye, Louis M. *o.f.m.* '90 (BGP) Fairfield, CT St. Emery.
Pinyan, Charles (NEW) Allendale, NJ Guardian Angel; Worship Office.
Pinzon, Alvaro '91 (MIA) Miami, FL St. Mary's Cathedral; Judges.
Pinzon, Eduardo *s.j.* '60 (CHI) Chicago, IL St. Bartholomew; [C] Chicago, IL Jesuit Community at Loyola University Chicago.
Piontkowski, Richard L. '82 (GI) North Platte, NE St. Patrick; Moderator of the Curia; Adjutant Vicars–Judicial; Priests' Advisory Board (Presbyteral Council); Army Reserve Chaplains.
Piontkowski, Richard (GI) Judges.
Piorkowski, Robert '76 (STN) St. Louis, MO Assumption B.V.M..
Piorkowski, Stanley W. '51 (SCR)[N] Dunmore, PA Villa St. Joseph Retired.
Piotrowski, Adrian *o.s.c.* '64 (STP) Anoka, MN St. Stephen; [M] Anoka, MN Crosier Community of Anoka.
Piotrowski, Leonard '93 (SP) Tampa, FL St. Paul; [F] Tampa, FL St. Paul Preschool; Priests Personnel Board; Presbyteral Council.
Piovan, Benjamin '64 (NO) La Place, LA Ascension of Our Lord; Defenders of the Bond; Catholic Knights of America.
Pipp, Thomas J. *s.j.* '92 (TOL)[C] Toledo, OH St. John's Jesuit High School.
Pipta, Robert M. '94 (VNN) Las Vegas, NV St. Gabriel the Archangel; Vocation Director; Liturgy & Music Commission.
Piquado, Thomas G. *s.j.* '72 (HON) Sacramento, CA St. Ignatius of Loyola.
Piran, Louis *c.s.* '71 (GAL) Houston, TX St. Leo the Great; Central Vicariate.
Piraro, Don '67 (LKC)[C] Moss Bluff, LA St. Charles Center; Clergy Formation; St. Charles Retreat Center.
Pires, Francisco '84 (SLC) Midvale, UT St. Therese of the Child Jesus.
Pires, Francisco '97 (SLC) Orem, UT St. Francis of Assisi.
Piro, Francis '54 (PH) Philadelphia, PA St. Philip Neri.
Piro, Frank R. '62 (SFR) Retired.
Pirrera, Aaron *o.s.b.* '85 (LR)[A] Subiaco, AR Subiaco Monastery; [C] Subiaco, AR Subiaco Academy.
Pirrone, Roberto '88 (LA) Wilmington, CA SS. Peter and Paul's.
Pirrung, George '54 (PHX) Retired.
Pisanello, George M. '86 (MET) South River, NJ St. Stephen Protomartyr; Canonical Staff.
Pisaneschi, Joseph J. '01 (SCR) Hunlock Creek, PA Our Lady of Mount Carmel.
Pisano, Mario *o.m.* '68 (LA)[Q] Los Angeles, CA Minim Fathers; Los Angeles, CA All Saints.
Pisarcik, John G. (PAT) Retired.
Pisciotta, Justin M. *o.s.m.* '64 (CHI)[N] Chicago Order of Friar Servants of Mary (Servites) United States of America Province, Inc..
Pisciotta, Justin M. *o.s.m.* '64 (ORG) Fullerton, CA St. Philip Benizi; [I] Fullerton, CA St. Philip Benizi Priory; Council of Priests.
Pisegna, Cedric *c.p.* '91 (GAL)[Q] Houston, TX Congregation of the Passion, Holy Name Retreat Center.
Piselli, Costanzo J. '69 (PRT) Belfast, ME St. Francis of Assisi.
Pisfil, Luis Carlos '92 (BRK) Brooklyn, NY Holy Innocents
Piskura, Joseph '54 (CLV) AUXILIARY CHAPLAINS CONTRACT CHAPLAINS Retired.
Pisoni, Otto B. (E).
Pisors, John A. *c.s.v.* '66 (CHI)[N] Arlington Heights Viatorian Province Center–Clerics of St. Viator.
Pispeky, Steve '88 (GLP) Retired.
Pistacchio, Gene B. *o.f.m.* '89 (ARL) Triangle, VA St. Francis of Assisi.
Pistone, Berardo '73 (HBG) Gettysburg, PA St. Francis Xavier's.
Pistone, Bernard (HBG) Spanish Speaking Ministry.
Pistone, Dominic J. '78 (GAL) Houston, TX St. Clare of Assisi.
Pistorius, Francis X. *s.j.* '72 (GAL) Spring, TX St. Ignatius of Loyola.
Pistulka, Celestine C. '56 (NU) Sleepy Eye, MN St. Mary Retired.
Pisut, Christopher '02 (DM) West Des Moines, IA St. Francis of Assisi.
Piszczatowski, Maurice *o.f.m.conv.* '53 (BAL)[S] Ellicott City, MD Order of Friars Minor Conventual.
Piszker, James '91 (E)[B] Erie, PA Mercyhurst College; [P] Erie, PA Mercyhurst College.
Pitcavage, William *s.c.j.* '76 (SFS) Chamberlain, SD St. James.
Pitoyo, Sugiyo *s.j.* '95 (BO)[V] Newton, MA The Jesuit Community at Boston College.
Pitre, Eric J. '81 (GAL) La Porte, TX St. Mary of the Immaculate Conception.
Pitre, Eric GAL) Diocesan Judges; Priests Personnel Committee.
Pitstick, Rory (SPK) Members.
Pitt, William L. '61 (RIC)[A] Virginia Beach, VA Bishop Sullivan Catholic High School.
Pittapilly, Thomas '61 (GF) Special Assignment.
Pittappilly, Thomas '61 (GF) Miles City, MT Sacred Heart.
Pittard, Wayne (GF) Personnel Board; [G] Great Falls, MT Benefis Healthcare.
Pittman, Robert S. *s.s.s.* '58 (WDC)[V] Washington, DC Black Leadership and Christ's Kingdom Society; [V] Waldorf, MD Body of Christ Farm Community, Inc..
Pittman, Robert S. *s.s.s.* '58 (CLV).
Pittman, Robert *s.s.s.* (CLV)[O] Cleveland OH Blessed Sacrament Community.
Pitts, Joseph *o.m.i.* '59 (BEL)[F] Belleville IL Shrine of Our Lady of the Snows.
Pitts, William L. '70 (R) Pinehurst, NC Sacred Heart; Holy Childhood Pontifical Association; Propagation of the Faith.
Pittstick, Rory '94 (SPK) Okanogan, WA Our Lady of the Valley.
Pitula, Roman '98 (PHU) Trenton, NJ Nativity of B.V.M.; Trenton, NJ St. Josaphat's.
Pitzen, John J. '45 (DUB) Retired.
Pivonka, David *t.o.r.* '96 (STU)[A] Steubenville, OH Franciscan University of Steubenville; [F] Steubenville, OH Holy Spirit Friary.
Pivonka, Leonard '77 (CC) Bishop's Office; Deans; College of Consultors; Personnel Board – Priests; Presbyteral Council; Judges; Alice, TX St. Elizabeth.
Piwowar, Stanley J. '51 (MAN) Claremont, NH St. Joseph; Sullivan County House of Corrections.
Piwowarezyk, Darius *s.v.d.* '90 (DUB)[B] Epworth, IA Divine Word College.
Pizhayakatt, Augustine (RVC) Massapequa Park, NY Our Lady of Lourdes.
Pizmoht, Louis A. '66 (CLV) Willoughby, OH Immaculate Conception.
Pizzamiglio, Ernest E. '66 (PEO) Wataga, IL St. Aloysius; Galesburg, IL Immaculate Heart of Mary.
Pizzamiglio, Ernest (PEO) Vicariates and Vicars.
Pizzarelli, Francis *s.m.m.* '79 (RVC) Port Jefferson, NY Most Precious Blood; [M] Bay Shore, NY Montfort Missionaries.
Pizzarelli, Frank *s.m.m.* '80 (RVC)[B] Patchogue, NY St. Joseph's College.
Pizzo, Anthony *o.s.a.* '84 (CHI)[N] Chicago, IL St. John Stone Friary.
Pizzo, Philip J. '77 (BRK) Ridgewood, NY St. Matthias.
Pizzuto, Alfred '55 (NY) Newburgh, NY Sacred Heart.
Placa, Alan J. '70 (RVC) Great Neck, NY St. Aloysius.
Placa, Stephen '95 (BRK) On Leave/Unassigned.
Place, Michael D. *s.t.d.* '70 (STL)[U] St. Louis, MO The Catholic Health Association of the United States.
Place, Michael D. *s.t.d.* '70 (CHI) On Duty Outside the Archdiocese.
Place, Terry E. '72 (FTW) Syracuse, IN St. Martin de Porres.
Plagens, James A. '65 (SAN) Big Spring, TX Sacred Heart; Big Spring, TX St. Thomas.
Plagens, James (SAN) Promoter Justitiae.
Plaisted, Eugene D. *o.s.c.* '61 (STP) Anoka, MN St. Stephen; [M] Anoka, MN Crosier Community of Anoka.
Plakut, Peter *o.c.s.o.* '58 (P)[L] Lafayette, OR The Cistercian (Trappist) Abbey of Our Lady of Guadalupe.
Plammoottil, Mathew Sunny Joseph *o.s.h.* '93 (GAL) Spring, TX Christ the Good Shepherd.
Plammoottil, Sunny Joseph *o.s.h.* '93 (GAL)[Q] Spring, TX The Society of the Oblates of Sacred Heart.
Plamondon, Donald J. '72 (DUB)[F] Bellevue, IA Bellevue Area Catholic Elementary School; [D] Bellevue, IA Marquette High School; La Motte, IA St. Lawrence; Preston, IA St. Joseph; Sabula, IA St. Peter; LaMotte, IA St. Theresa; Springbrook, IA SS. Peter and Paul; La Motte, IA Assumption; La Motte, IA Holy Rosary; La Motte, IA St. John; Deans; Defenders of the Bond.
Planas, Salvador '54 (MIA) Retired.
Plancher, Christian E. *s.m.m.* '98 (MIA) Miami, FL St. James.
Planea, John '82 (NO) On Duty Outside the Archdiocese.
Plank, Stephen J. *o.s.b.* '94 (OM)[C] Elkhorn, NE Mount Michael High School; [K] Elkhorn, NE Mount Michael Abbey.
Planning, Stephen W. *s.j.* '99 (DEN) Denver, CO St. Ignatius Loyola; [D] Denver, CO Arrupe Jesuit High School.
Plans, John F. *s.f.* '67 (WDC) Silver Spring, MD Christ the King.
Plante, David La '78 (OM) Omaha, NE St. Elizabeth Ann.
Plante, Georges J. '53 (PRT) Bingham, ME St. Peter's; Madison, ME St. Sebastian; Diocesan Consultors; Clergy Benefit Plan–Clergy Pension Plan; Diocesan Council of Priests; College of Consultors.
Plante, Jacques L. '82 (PRO) West Warwick, RI SS. John and James Parish.
Plante, Paul A. '71 (PRT) Winslow, ME St. John the Baptist.
Plante, Paul (PRT) Personnel Board.
Plante, Pierre J. '78 (PRO) Warwick, RI St. Benedict.
Plantes, Francis P. '45 (PIT) Retired.
Planty, Donald J. '93 (ARL) Dale City, VA Holy Family.
Plascencia, Franco '94 (DEN) Denver, CO Our Lady of Guadalupe.
Plascencia, Miguel '53 (LA) Los Angeles, CA Divine Saviour.
Plasker, Alexander *o.s.b.* '62 (P)[L] St. Benedict, OR Mt. Angel Abbey.
Plasker, Robert L. *c.s.c.* '57 (FTW)[I] Congregacion de Santa Cruz.
Plasse, Eugene J. '72 (SPR) Palmer, MA St. Bartholomew's; Palmer, MA St. Thomas the Apostle.
Plassenthal, Vincent A. *s.m.* '44 (PCE) Villalba, PR Our Lady Mother of Divine Providence.
Plaster, George F. '80 (LFT) On Duty Outside the Diocese.
Plata, Gregory *o.f.m.* '85 (JKS) Greenwood, MS St. Francis of Assisi; Lexington, MS St. Thomas; Winona, MS Sacred Heart; [I] Lexington, MS Holmes Community College Newman Center.
Plate, Brian G. (NEW) Director of Vocations; Members; Priestly Vocation Board; Vocations Office.
Plate, Brian (NEW) Newark, NJ Cathedral Basilica of the Sacred Heart.

Plathanam, Ignatius J. *c.m.i.* '72 (STA) Gainesville, FL Holy Faith.
Plathe, Anthony H. '63 (NU) Retired.
Plathottam, Mathew '67 (PHX) Carefree, AZ Our Lady of Joy.
Plathottam, Thomas *c.s.t.* '74 (NOR) Ellington, CT St. Luke.
Platt, Stewart '51 (Y) Retired.
Platt, William F. '88 (BGP) Greenwich, CT Greenwich Hospital; Greenwich, CT St. Paul.
Plaushin, Mark *o.s.f.s.* '89 (PH) Philadelphia, PA St. Joachim; Army Reserve Chaplains.
Plavac, Timothy J. '86 (CLV) Solon, OH St. Rita.
Plavcan, Jon J. '94 (GRY) Hobart, IN Assumption of the Blessed Virgin Mary; Administrative Assistant to the Bishop; Bishop's Council of Priests; Consultors; Priests' Personnel Board.
Plavunikunnathil, Chrysostom *c.m.i.* '66 (BEA) Beaumont, TX St. Anthony Cathedral; Convalescent Home Ministry.
Plawecki, Joseph '83 (DET) Erie, MI St. Joseph.
Plawny, Thaddeus *m.s.* '51 (PEO)[M] Georgetown, IL La Salette Missionaries.
Playoust, Alfred G. *s.j.* '46 (SJ)[M] Los Gatos, CA Sacred Heart Jesuit Center.
Plaza, Abel A. (ARE) Arecibo, PR Santa Ana.
Plazewski, Leonard '91 (SP) St. Petersburg, FL Cathedral of St. Jude the Apostle; Vocations Office; Presbyteral Council.
Pleban, Alexander L. '57 (GBG) Uniontown, PA St. Joseph.
Pleban, Leo '60 (Y) Retired.
Plechta, Sabin *o.f.m.* '43 (WDC)[M] Washington, DC Commissariat of the Holy Land, Franciscan Monastery – Mount St. Sepulchre.
Pleho, Anthony J. '79 (NY) Yonkers, NY Most Holy Trinity.
Pleier, David (GB) Green Bay, WI St. Bernard; Cursillo.
Pleiman, Kenneth F. *c.pp.s.* '70 (CLV) Cleveland, OH St. Adalbert.
Pleiness, Gregg A. '81 (LAN) Howell, MI St. Augustine; Air National Guard Chaplains.
Plesa, Andrew J. '56 (RCK) Elgin, IL St. Thomas More Retired.
Pleskac, Myron J. '60 (LIN) Denton, NE St. Mary's; Deaneries and Deans; Priests' Continuing Education Committee.
Pleva, Gerald *s.m.* '77 (SAT) Helotes, TX Our Lady of Guadalupe.
Plevyak, Valentine R. '44 (SCR)[N] Dunmore, PA Villa St. Joseph Retired.
Plewka, Mark A. '76 (PBL) Pueblo, CO Holy Rosary; Chancellor; Judicial Vicar; Judge; Presbyteral Council–College of Consultors; Presbyteral Council; Tribunal.
Plewka, Mark (COS) Defenders of the Bond.
Pliauplis, Christopher '87 (STU) On Duty Outside the Diocese.
Plier, David J. (GB) Regional Vicars.
Plo, John '61 (NY) Retired.
Ploch, Timothy C. *s.d.b.* '76 (NY) Port Chester, NY Our Lady of the Rosary.
Plocharczyk, Daniel J. '74 (HRT) New Britain, CT Sacred Heart of Jesus.
Plociennik, Robert *o.f.m.conv.* '60 (HBG) Shamokin, PA Mother Cabrini.
Plock, Charles T. '73 (BRK)[V] Jamaica, NY Vincentian Residence.
Plocke, Donald J. *s.j.* '84 (BO)[V] Newton, MA The Jesuit Community at Boston College.
Plokhooy, Christopher H. '59 (WIL) Wilmington, DE St. Catherine of Siena Retired.
Plominski, Walter J. '68 (ROC) Caledonia, NY St. Columba.
Ploof, Gerald J. '75 (LAN) Clio, MI SS. Charles and Helena.
Ploof, Thomas M. '45 (WIN) Retired.
Ploplis, Theodore '77 (CHI)[J] Chicago, IL Saint Joseph Hospital.
Plotka, Frank W. '68 (CHI) Waukegan, IL Immaculate Conception B.V.M..
Plotkowski, Jerome A. '65 (SFE) Albuquerque, NM San Felipe de Neri.
Plotkowski, Jerome (SFE) Judicial Vicar; College of Consultors; Judicial Vicar; Delegate for Matrimonial Dispensations.
Plotkowski, John S. '74 (CHI) Des Plaines, IL St. Zachary.
Ploude, Thomas E. '64 (CAM) Brooklawn, NJ St. Maurice's.
Plouffe, Paul I. *s.s.e.* '45 (MOB)[G] Selma, AL Edmundite Fathers.
Plourde, Carroll W. *s.s.e.* '87 (MOB) Orrville, AL Immaculate Conception; Selma, AL Our Lady Queen of Peace; [G] Selma, AL Edmundite Fathers; [J] Selma, AL Marion Institute Newman Center; Religious.
Plummer, J. Bruce '40 (HEL) Retired.
Plummer, James '58 (CAM) Retired.
Plunkett, Joseph P. '60 (NEW) Newark, NJ Our Lady of Good Counsel; North Newark Essex Deanery 19.
Pluth, Paul '96 (SEA) Seattle, WA Our Lady of the Lake; Judges.
Pluth, Paul *o.s.b.* '96 (LA)[Q] Valyermo, CA St. Andrew's Abbey.
Plutz, Stanley *s.v.d.* '53 (BLX)[A] Bay St. Louis, MS St. Augustine's.
Poandl, Bob *g.h.m.* '68 (CIN)[M] Fairfield, OH.
Poblocki, Richard M. '83 (BUF) Apostleship of Prayer; [H] Buffalo, NY Guild of St. Apollonia; Buffalo, NY Queen of Peace.
Pocernich, Eugene '74 (MIL)[J] Milwaukee, WI St. Mary's Hospital of Milwaukee; Special Assignment.
Pocetto, Alexander T. *o.s.f.s.* '55 (ALN)[B] Center Valley, PA DeSales University; [B] Center Valley, PA DeSales University; [K] Center Valley, PA Oblates of St. Francis de Sales.
Poche, Daniel M. '78 (HT) Raceland, LA Community of St. Anthony; Raceland, LA St. Hilary of Poitiers; Defenders of the Bond.
Poche, Gerard W. '48 (NO) Retired.
Poche, Louis A. *s.j.* '55 (BR) Gramercy, LA Most Sacred Heart of Jesus.
Poche, Louis *s.j.* '55 (BR) Convent, LA St. Michael the Archangel; Paulina, LA St. Joseph.
Poczworowski, Luke *o.f.m.conv.* '64 (RCK) Rockford, IL St. Anthony of Padua.
Podgorny, John (PAT) Retired.
Podhajsky, Christopher R. '01 (DUB) Waterloo, IA St. Edward; Waterloo, IA St. Mary of Mt. Carmel; Waterloo, IA Sacred Heart; Waterloo, IA Immaculate Conception.
Podhajsky, Michael J. '03 (DUB) Mason City, IA St. Joseph.
Podlesny, James F. *o.s.b.* '80 (HBG) Palmyra, PA Holy Spirit.
Podraza, Timothy '97 (OM) Bellevue, NE St. Mary; Boy Scouts.
Podrosky, Alfred '52 (SCL) Retired.
Podsiedlik, Slawomir S. *o.c.d.* '02 (STA) Bunnell, FL St. Mary's; [J] Bunnell, FL Discalced Carmelite Fathers of Florida.
Podvin, Albert J. '62 (SFE) Albuquerque, NM Sangre de Cristo.
Podymniak, Miroslaw *o.f.m.conv.* (BO) South Boston, MA Our Lady of Czestochowa.
Poecking, David '96 (PIT) Sewickley, PA St. James.
Poehlmann, Edward J. '67 (DEN) Edwards, CO St. Clare of Assisi.
Poelker, Gerard L. '42 (JC) Senators; Board of Trustees Retired.
Poerio, John (LKC) Advocates.
Poettgen, Ed (ORG) Council of Priests; Land Advisory Board.
Poettgen, Edward '80 (ORG) Stanton, CA St. Polycarp.
Poetz, Lawrence *s.v.d.* '44 (CHI)[B] Techny, IL Divine Word Residence.
Poetzel, Richard K. *c.ss.r.* '63 (BAL) Baltimore, MD Our Lady of Fatima.
Poff, Pius *o.f.m.conv.* '61 (LAN) Lansing, MI Holy Cross.
Poggemeyer, Joseph T. '97 (TOL) Graduate Studies.
Pogorelc, Anthony J. '88 (WDC).
Pogorelc, Anthony *s.s.* '88 (SAT)[A] On Duty Outside the Archdiocese.
Pogorelic, Anthony J. *s.s.* (WDC)[C] Catholic University of America, The.
Pohl, Daniel J. '53 (LIN)[E] Lincoln, NE Bonacum House Retired.
Pohl, Jerome H. '67 (PH) Retired.
Pohl, Leon H. '56 (KAL) Coldwater, MI St. Charles Borromeo.
Pohl, Stephen A. '85 (L) Bardstown, KY St. Monica; Bardstown, KY St. Thomas.
Pohley, Robert G. '75 (BGP) Stamford, CT Sacred Heart; [X] Stamford, CT Stamford Catholic Library; Catholic Women, Council of.
Pohlman, Stephen J. '84 (SFD) Glen Carbon, IL St. Cecilia.
Pohlmeier, Erik '98 (LR) McGehee, AR St. Mary; Lake Village, AR Holy Child Church.
Pohlmeier, Loren (GI) Crawford, NE St. John the Baptist.
Pohorlak, Joseph '61 (PRM) Whiting, IN Assumption of the Blessed Virgin; Priest's Pension Board.
Pohto, J. Thomas *o.s.a.* '67 (VEN) Bokeelia, FL Our Lady of the Miraculous Medal.
Pointek, Francis J. '40 (FRS) Retired.
Poirier, David *s.a.* '77 (NY)[EE] Garrison Franciscan Friars of the Atonement, Minister General Office.
Poirier, Ralph *c.s.sp.* '63 (SD) El Cajon, CA Our Lady of Grace.
Poirier, Robert L. *s.j.* '77 (STL)[O] St. Louis, MO Leo Brown Jesuit Community.
Poirier, Robert *s.j.* '77 (WDC) Washington, DC Holy Trinity.
Poirier, Ronald J. '88 (SP) Palm Harbor, FL St. Luke the Evangelist.
Poirier, Ronald '88 (SP)[F] Palm Harbor, FL St. Luke Early Childhood Center.
Poirier, Vincent J. '85 (BO) Senior Priests Retired.
Poirot, Jeff '01 (FWT) Bedford, TX St. Michael.
Poissant, Leeward J. '63 (OG) Keeseville, NY Church of the Immaculate Conception; Keeseville, NY St. John the Baptist.
Poisson, Joseph *f.s.s.p.* '96 (OKL) Bethany, OK Latin Mass Community.
Poisson, Joseph *f.s.s.p.* '96 (SCR)[M] Lincoln, NE St. Francis of Assisi Church.
Poisson, Thomas L. '78 (MAR) Retired.
Poitras, Steven W. '93 (BO) Hudson, MA St. Michael.
Poklmeier, Erik '98 (LR) Lake Village, AR Our Lady of the Lake.
Pokornowski, Daniel A. '54 (BUF) Cheektowaga, NY St. John Gualbert.
Pokorsky, Jerry J. (LIN) Diocesan Finance Council.
Pokorsky, Jerry J. (LIN) Bishop Bruskewitz Charity and Stewardship Appeal (DDP); Diocesan Housing Ministries, Inc.; Priests' Continuing Education Committee.
Pokorsky, Jerry L. (ARL) On Duty Outside the Diocese.
Pokrzewinski, Justus M. *o.p.* '60 (CHI)[N] Chicago Dominicans (Provincial Office).
Pokrzewinski, Justus *o.p.* '60 (FgM).
Pokusa, Joseph W. '70 (CAM) Haddonfield, NJ Christ the King; [G] Camden, NJ Francis, Elizabeth and Edward Roger Welsh Scholarship Trust; Officers; Chancellor and Episcopal Vicar for Canonical Affairs; Chancellor and Episcopal Vicar for Canonical Affairs; Members.
Polak, Michael J. '58 (PIT) Retired.
Polakowski, Joseph '59 (MAR) Retired.
Polanco, Dennis *s.a.* '74 (NY)[EE] Garrison Franciscan Friars of the Atonement, Minister General Office.
Polanco, Juan F. *c.m.* '01 (PH) Philadelphia, PA St. Vincent de Paul.
Poland, Sean '94 (LAV) North Las Vegas, NV St. John Neumann.
Polando, Peter M. '80 (Y) Youngstown, OH St. Matthias.
Polando, Peter (Y) Adjutant Judicial Vicar.
Polasek, Jeffrey S. '91 (TLS) Sallisaw, OK St. Francis Xavier.
Polc, Jaroslav '55 (GB) On Duty Outside the Diocese.
Polcyn, Robert F. *o.f.m.cap.* '68 (LC) Dodge, WI Most Sacred Heart; [D] Arcadia, WI Franciscan Skemp Healthcare, Mayo Health System, Arcadia Campus Hospital; [F] Arcadia, WI Franciscan Skemp Healthcare, Mayo Health System, Arcadia Campus Nursing Home.
Polczyk, Stanislaus T. '82 (TR) Trenton, NJ St. Stanislaus; Diocesan Council of Priests.
Polednak, John V. '76 (SCR) Nicholson, PA St. Patrick's.
Polek, David *c.s.s.r.* '62 (STL) St. Louis, MO St. Alphonsus Liguori; [O] St. Louis, MO Redemptorist Fathers.
Polenz, Gordon '82 (ALB) Sidney, NY Sacred Heart.
Polewczak, Michael J. '73 (ALB) On Duty Outside the Diocese; Orangeburg, SC Holy Trinity.
Polgar, Capistran L. *o.f.m.* '67 (MET) New Brunswick, NJ St. Ladislaus.
Poliafico, David A. '95 (COL) Columbus, OH St. Joseph Cathedral; Vicariate 1: Center City.
Polich, David J. (DM) Defenders of the Bond.
Polich, David '76 (DM) Perry, IA St. Patrick.
Polich, James C. '71 (DM) Des Moines, IA St. Augustin's.
Polichnowski, Nicholas *t.o.r.* '77 (ALT)[F] Loretto, PA Mount Assisi Friary.
Policicchio, Luke *o.s.b.* '88 (GBG) Virginia Beach, VA St. Gregory the Great.
Polidano, Carmel '81 (CAM) Millville, NJ St. Mary Magdalen's.
Polifka, Charles *o.f.m.cap.* '71 (KCK) Lawrence, KS St. John the Evangelist; [H] Lawrence, KS St. Conrad's Friary; Regional Pastoral Leaders.
Polimine, Alan *t.o.r.* '59 (ALT)[F] Newry, PA St. Bernardine Monastery.
Polinski, Casimir V. *c.r.* '44 (CHI) Chicago, IL St. Hedwig.
Polito, Martin F. '76 (CLV) Cleveland, OH Holy Redeemer.
Polito, Victor V.J. '54 (MAN) On Duty Outside the Diocese.
Polito, Victor '54 (ALB) Amsterdam, NY St. Mary.
Polizzi, Salvatore E. '56 (STL) St. Louis, MO St. Roch; Archdiocesan Office of Urban and Community Affairs.
Poljicak, Vlatko '65 (LA) Pomona, CA St. Joseph.
Polk, Page E. *o.f.m.* '86 (GAL)[K] Catholic Chaplain Corps, Texas Medical Center.
Polk, Page *o.f.m.* (GAL) Catholic Chaplain Corps (Hospital Chaplains); Elected Members.
Polk, Thomas '67 (BAL) Hagerstown, MD St. Ann.
Pollack, Anthony '55 (ALT) Retired.
Pollak, Claude W. *o.s.b.* '57 (E)[H] Latrobe, PA Saint Vincent Archabbey.
Pollak, Claude *o.s.b.* '56 (GBG) Latrobe, PA St. Bede; Latrobe, PA St. Mary.
Pollard, Christopher J. '97 (ARL) Arlington, VA St. Agnes.
Pollard, John E. '74 (CHI) Wilmette, IL St. Joseph.
Pollard, John L. '83 (STA) Absent on Sick Leave.

Pollard, Marcus A. '90 (ARL) Herndon, VA St. Veronica.
Pollard, Patrick J. '72 (CHI) Chicago, IL Christ the King; Hillside, IL Catholic Cemeteries; College of Consultors; Catholic Cemeteries.
Pollard, Raymond J. '50 (NEW) Mountainside, NJ Our Lady of Lourdes; Members; Elected Members Retired.
Pollard, Roy F. '66 (WIL) New Castle, DE Holy Spirit.
Pollard, Thomas W. '66 (WDC) Clinton, MD Church of St. John the Evangelist.
Pollauf, Robert A. *s.j.* '46 (DET)[P] Hamtramck, MI St. Ladislaus.
Pollie, A. Frank '67 (DET) Rochester Hills, MI St. Irenaeus.
Pollis, Robert G. '57 (BO) Senior Priests Retired.
Pollock, Robert C. '48 (SLC) Retired.
Polmounter, Richard J. '78 (SCR) Pittston, PA St. Mary, Help of Christians; Diocesan Consultors; Presbyteral Council.
Polo, Antonio *s.d.b.* '56 (SJN) San Juan, PR Maria Auxiliadora.
Polosky, Michael '91 (SJP) Ambridge, PA Ss. Peter and Paul; League of Ukrainian Catholics (LUC); Office for Evangelization; Presbyteral Council; Diocesan Personnel Board.
Poloway, Michael '54 (SJP) Pittsburgh, PA St. John the Baptist.
Poloway, Michael (SJP) Diocesan Consultors.
Poloway, Michael (SJP) Permanent Diaconate Program.
Poloway, Michael (SJP) Presbyteral Council.
Poloway, Michael (SJP) Central Deanery.
Polselli, Leo *c.s.c.* '70 (FR)[A] North Easton, MA Holy Cross Fathers Religious.
Polson, Mikel Anthony '02 (LAF) Lafayette, LA St. Genevieve.
Polt, Albert *o.a.r.* '54 (LA) Retired.
Poltorak, George *s.a.c.* '90 (BUF) Buffalo, NY St. Florian.
Poltorak, Stanley '82 (SAC) Truckee, CA Assumption of the Blessed Virgin Mary.
Poluikis, John A. *c.s.b.* '51 (ROC)[I] Rochester, NY Basilian Residence.
Polyak, John V. '69 (MET) North Brunswick, NJ Our Lady of Peace.
Polycarpe, Pierre G. '99 (RCK) Rockford, IL St. Bernadette.
Polzer, Daniel *l.c.* '94 (DEN)[S] Centennial, CO LC Pastoral Services Inc..
Pomaville, Raymond *o.m.i.* '55 (SAT)[K] San Antonio, TX Oblate Madonna Residence.
Pomerleau, Claude *c.s.c.* '65 (P)[L] Portland, OR Holy Cross Fathers & Brothers, C.S.C. – University of Portland.
Pomerleau, Claude *c.s.c.* '65 (A.)[I] South Bend, IN Congregation of Holy Cross, Indiana Province, Provincial House; [B] University of Portland.
Pomerleau, William A. '79 (SPR) Indian Orchard, MA St. Jude.
Pomeroy, Joseph B. *s.j.* '62 (WOR)[O] Worcester, MA Jesuits of Holy Cross College, Inc..
Pomeroy, Thomas (GB) Appleton, WI Holy Angels.
Pomilio, Matthew (BRK) Released from Diocesan Assignment.
Pommier, Richard *o.m.i.* '66 (FgM).
Pompei, Francis '74 (BUF)[T] Buffalo, NY Franciscan Mystery Players, Inc..
Pompei, Francis *o.f.m.* '74 (PH)[AA] Philadelphia, PA Order of Friars Minor of the Province of the Most Holy Name.
Pompei, Frederick A. '66 (SY) Syracuse, NY Our Lady of Pompei; Special Assignment.
Ponce, Francisco '67 (NEW) Jersey City, NJ St. Joseph's.
Ponce, Jaimes '01 (COS) Colorado Springs, CO Divine Redeemer; Monument, CO St. Peter.
Ponce, Juan Manual (SAC) Red Bluff, CA Sacred Heart.
Ponce, Juan Manuel (SAC) Auburn, CA St. Joseph.
Ponce–Red Bluff, Juan (SAC) Willows, CA St. Monica.
Poncelet, Frank '87 (SCL) Retired.
Pondo, Stanley (IND) Graduate Studies; Archdiocesan Judges.
Ponessa, Joseph '74 (GF) Glendive, MT Sacred Heart; Diocesan Consultors; Priests' Council.
Ponnet, Chris (LA) AIDS/HIV Ministry.
Ponnet, Christopher D. '83 (LA) Los Angeles, CA St. Camillus De Lellis; Los Angeles, CA Norris Cancer and USC University Hospital.
Pons, Miguel '53 (SJN) Trujillo Alto, PR San Judas Tadeo.
Pons, Ramon '88 (SR) Fortuna, CA St. Joseph; Advocates; Hispanic Ministry – North.
Ponso, Andres *o.s.m.* '50 (ELP) El Paso, TX Our Lady of Sorrows.
Pontarelli, Michael M. *o.s.m.* '82 (CHI)[N] Chicago Order of Friar Servants of Mary (Servites) United States of America Province, Inc..
Pontarelli, Michael M. *o.s.m.* '82 (ORG)[D] Anaheim, CA Servite High School, A California Corporation; [I] Anaheim, CA Servite Fathers and Brothers; [I] Anaheim, CA Seven Holy Founders Priory.
Ponticello, Robert D. '81 (MEM) Barlett, TN Church Of The Nativity; Presbyteral Council and College of Consultors; Defender of the Bond; Promoter of Justice.
Ponzini, Thomas V. '96 (GAL) Texas City, TX St. Mary.
Pookkattu, George *c.m.i.* '72 (ALX) Jena, LA St. Mary.
Pool, Jefferson *s.v.d.* '92 (TR)[M] Bordentown, NJ Society of the Divine Word.
Pool, Robert '55 (KCK) Retired.
Poole, James E. *s.j.* '53 (SEA)[J] Spokane, WA Regis Community.
Poole, Michael '98 (HEL) Conrad, MT St. Michael; Dutton, MT St. William.
Poole, Richard '94 (SPK) Connell, WA St. Vincent; Eltopia, WA St. Paul.
Poole, Stafford '56 (LA)[Q] Montebello, CA Vincentian Fathers and Brothers; [Q] Los Angeles, CA Amat Residence II.
Poole, Steven F. '96 (BEL) Christopher, IL St. Andrew; Sesser, IL St. Mary.
Poole, William G. '63 (LEX) Retired.
Pooler, Alfred *c.p.* '60 (LA)[Q] Sierra Madre, CA Passionist Residence.
Poon, Stanislaus '62 (OAK) Retired.
Poonelil, Augustine *o.c.d.* '89 (SCR)[W Drums, PA Church of the Good Shepherd; Hazleton, PA St. Nazarius.
Poore, Charles '89 (Y) Youngstown, OH Sacred Heart of Jesus; Youngstown, OH St. Rose of Lima.
Poorman, James E. '71 (SJP) Ramey, PA Annunciation B.V.M..
Poorman, James (SJP) Presbyteral Council.
Poorman, James (SJP) Eastern Deanery.
Poorman, Mark L. *c.s.c.* '82 (FTW)[B] University of Notre Dame Du Lac; [B] University of Notre Dame Du Lac; [I] Notre Dame, IN Holy Cross Community, Corby Hall, University of Notre Dame.
Poorten, William P. *s.j.* '63 (PAT)[I] Morristown, NJ Loyola House of Retreats.
Poovakulam, Antony P. '63 (TR) Whiting, NJ St. Elizabeth Ann Seton.
Poovathumkudy, Micle '87 (ALX) Mansura, LA Our Lady of Prompt Succor.
Pop, Carlos Antonio *o.s.b.* '99 (SFS)[F] Marvin, SD Blue Cloud Abbey.
Popadick, Peter J. '70 (BUF) Buffalo, NY St. Aloysius Gonzaga.
Popadiuk, Mauricio *o.s.b.m.* '84 (STF) Bronx, NY St. Mary Protectress; [E] Locust Valley, NY; Religious Communities, Vicar.
Pope, Benedict *o.f.m.cap.* '54 (PIT)[N] Pittsburgh St. Augustine Friary.
Pope, Charles E. '89 (WDC) Washington, DC St. Thomas More; [V] Silver Spring, MD Archdiocese of Washington Division, The Blue Army; Blue Army of Our Lady of Fatima.
Pope, Charles (WDC) Deans.
Pope, Michael *s.j.* '81 (YAK) Yakima, WA St. Joseph's.
Pope, Nicholas F. *s.j.* '72 (MIL)[O] Curia of the Society of Jesus
Popelka, Joe (SAL) College of Consultors.
Popelka, Joseph '92 (SAL) Plainville, KS Sacred Heart; Plainville, KS St. Thomas; Episcopal Vicars; Council of Priests.
Popesh, Bernard '49 (DUL) Retired.
Popish, Edward *ss.cc.* '90 (HON)[G] Kaneohe, HI Sacred Hearts Center.
Popivchak, Ronald P. '67 (PHU) Bridgeport, PA SS. Peter and Paul; Bridgeport, PA SS. Peter and Paul.
Popivchak, Ronald (PHU) Promoter of Justice; Protopresbyters (Deans).
Popivchak, Ronald (PHU) Censors.
Poplawski, John F. '74 (SCR) Nanticoke, PA St. Stanislaus.
Popochock, James L. '68 (GBG) New Salem, PA St. Thomas; New Salem, PA St. Procopius.
Popovich, George '51 (Y)[G] Warren, OH St. Joseph Health Center.
Popovich, Peter '85 (NY) Bronx, NY Our Lady of Good Counsel; Hartsdale, NY Church of Our Lady of Shkodra.
Popovich, Stephen '81 (Y) Youngstown, OH Immaculate Heart of Mary; Office of Continuing Education and Formation of Priests.
Popovichi Olvian '98 (STF) West Islip, NY Holy Family.
Popowski, Stanley '83 (HEL) Cut Bank, MT St. Margaret; Valier, MT St. Francis.
Popp, Kenneth '82 (SCL) Breckenridge, MN St. Mary of the Presentation.
Poppa, Chester *o.f.m.cap.* '53 (GF) Broadus, MT St. David's
Popravak Christopher *o.f.m.cap.* '74 (STL)[O] St. Louis, MO St. Crispin's Friary.
Popson, Michael George '87 (PSC) Danbury, CT St. Nicholas.
Popson, Michael (PSC) Elected Members.
Porada, Casey *o.s.* '89 (LIN) David City, NE St. Mary's.
Porazzo, Francis J. '44 (TR) Retired.
Pornchoi, Phillip *c.s.s.* (NY) White Plains, NY Our Lady of Mt. Carmel.
Porpiglia, Joseph D. '86 (BUF) Navy Reserve Chaplains; Council of Priests; Salamanca, NY Holy Cross; Salamanca, NY St. Patrick.
Porpora, Robert '90 (NY) Middletown, NY Holy Cross.
Porras, Adrian '01 (CHL) Clemmons, NC Holy Family.
Porras, Samuel '97 (ATL) Marietta, GA Holy Family.
Port, Dennis R. '74 (STL) St. Louis, MO Our Lady of the Presentation.
Portalatin, Antonio '91 (ARE) Graduate Studies.
Portella, Mario A. '99 (NY) Bronx, NY Sacred Heart.
Porter, Daniel '75 (LSC) Hurley, NM Infant Jesus.
Porter, Jack W. '75 (IND) On Special or Other Archdiocesan Assignment.
Porter, Jack W. (IND) Archdiocesan Historian.
Porter, John F. '57 (GR) Conklin, MI St. Francis Xavier; Ravenna, MI St. Catherine.
Porter, John '56 (CIN) Cincinnati, OH St. John Neumann.
Porter, John '57 (GR) On Special Assignment; Tribunal Office; Tribunal.
Porter, Lawrence B. *o.p.* '74 (NEW)[B] School of Diplomacy and Intl. Rels.; Censors of Books.
Porter, Lawrence (NEW) Archdiocesan Theological Commission.
Porter, Richard L. *s.j.* '47 (MIL)[O] Wauwatosa, WI Jesuit Community at St. Camillus.
Porter, Robert G. '81 (HEL) Deer Lodge, MT Immaculate Conception.
Porter, Robert N. '64 (SFD) Bunker Hill, IL St. Mary; Bunker Hill, IL St. Denis; Bunker Hill, IL Holy Cross.
Porter, Rocco (DEN) Greeley, CO St. Peter.
Porter, Steve C. '72 (SB) Rialto, CA St. Catherine of Siena; Appointed Members.
Porter, William J. '75 (WIL) Pocomoke City, MD Holy Name of Jesus.
Porter, William '80 (KCK) Leawood, KS St. Michael the Archangel.
Porterfield, David J. *c.s.c.* '79 (FTW) South Bend, IN St. Adalbert; South Bend, IN St. Casimir.
Porterfield, David *c.s.c.* (FTW) South Bend.
Porterfield, Mark A. '94 (JC) Jefferson City, MO St. Margaret of Antioch; St. Thomas, MO St. Thomas the Apostle; Promoter of Justice; Judges.
Portland, Paul J. *s.d.s.* '76 (NSH) Shelbyville, TN St. William.
Portman, John R. '56 (SD) Retired.
Portmann, Frederick '79 (PHX) Retired.
Portor, Roco (DEN)[Q] Greeley, CO University of Northern Colorado (Greeley).
Portucheck, Joseph J. '49 (STL) Retired.
Portula, Ramel *c.i.c.m.* (R) Wendell, NC St. Eugene.
Portz, Bernard J. *s.j.* '52 (MIL)[O] Wauwatosa, WI Jesuit Community at St. Camillus.
Portzer, Joseph *f.s.s.p.* '99 (SCR)[M] Elmhurst Priestly Fraternity of St. Peter (F.S.S.P.), North American District Headquarters.
Posadas, Jose Antonio *o.f.m.* '95 (SHP) Ruston, LA St. Thomas Aquinas.
Posanski, James B. '65 (MIL) Fond du Lac, WI Sons of Zebedee: Saints James and John.
Posch, Chris *o.f.m.* (WIL) Wilmington Office.
Posch, Christopher J. *o.f.m.* '95 (WIL) Wilmington, DE St. Paul's.
Poschen, Ed '53 (FRS) Retired.
Poser, Gregory *o.s.c.* '75 (SCL)[I] Onamia, MN Crosier Monastery.
Posey, Patrick L. '91 (ARL) Purcellville, VA St. Francis de Sales.
Posey, Thaddeus J. *o.s.f.s.* (MO) Army Reserve Chaplains.
Posey, Thadeus J. *o.f.m.cap.* '71 (STP)[C] St. Paul, MN University of St. Thomas.
Posiewala, John *s.a.c.* '78 (BUF)[O] North Tonawanda, NY Society of the Catholic Apostolate.
Poskey, Robert V. *s.j.* '66 (BO)[V] Cambridge, MA Faber House.
Poslusney, Venard *o.carm.* '42 (JOL)[L] Darien Carmelite Provincial Office.
Posluszny, Francis '62 (BGP) On Duty Outside the Diocese.
Pospishil, Victor J. '40 (PHU) Retired.
Pospishil, Victor J. (NTN) Canonical Consultants.
Post, Robert J. '82 (BGP) Darien, CT St. Thomas More.
Postell, Philip S. *s.j.* '70 (DAL)[D] Dallas, TX Jesuit College Preparatory School.
Poster, James M. '03 (MAD) Madison, WI St. Maria Goretti.
Poston, J. Collin '03 (BAL) Cockeysville, MD St. Joseph.
Postrano, Anastacio '84 (HON) Kailua–Kona, HI St. Michael The Archangel; College of Consultors; Filipino Ministry; Vicars Forane; Presbyteral Council.
Potaczek, John A. '99 (LC) Stevens Point, WI St. Bartholomew.
Potaczek, John A. '99 (LC) Stevens Point, WI St. Stephen; Consultors; Appointed Members.
Poth, Thomas *s.m.m.* '83 (HRT)[M] Litchfield, CT Montfort Missionaries; [M] Monfort Novitiate.
Pothier, Glen J. (PMB) Adjutant Judicial Vicar; Judges.

Pothier, Glen '95 (PMB) West Palm Beach, FL Mary Immaculate.
Potocek, Cyril J. '36 (NY) North Tarrytown, NY Holy Cross Retired.
Potocek, Cyril '36 (NY)[EE] Bronx, NY.
Potomski, Boleslaw *c.m.* '73 (HRT) New Haven, CT St. Stanislaus.
Potout, Rivers A. '67 (GAL) Galena Park, TX Our Lady of Fatima.
Pottamplackal, Ephrem *m.c.b.s.* '74 (SUP) Mercer, WI Our Lady Queen of Peace; Mercer, WI St. Isaac Jogues and Companions.
Pottananickal, Antony Mathew *t.o.r.* '96 (FWT) Fort Worth, TX Holy Family.
Potter, Gerald L. (FAR) AUXILIARY CHAPLAINS CONTRACT CHAPLAINS.
Potter, Gerald '54 (FAR) Retired.
Potter, Joseph D. '54 (BGP) Retired.
Potter, Ronald J. *m.m.* '61 (FgM).
Potter, Stephen K. '78 (RCK) McHenry, IL St. Patrick.
Potthast, Richard L. *c.s.c.* '67 (FTW)[I] Kyarusozi Parish Community.
Potthoff, Donald W. '49 (LA) Diamond Bar, CA St. Denis Retired.
Potthoff, Fred E. '44 (LFT) Associate Judges Retired.
Pottokaran, Jose *c.m.i.* (GRY)[E] Michigan City, IN St. Anthony Memorial Health Centers.
Pottorff, Lisle J. '49 (DOD) Retired.
Potts, Donald G. '60 (KAL) Cassopolis, MI St. Ann.
Potts, Richard *c.ss.r.* '91 (STL) St. Louis, MO St. Alphonsus Liguori; [O] St. Louis, MO Redemptorist Fathers.
Potts, Robert J. '64 (ALN) Shenandoah, PA St. George; Shenandoah, PA Our Lady of Mt. Carmel; Shenandoah, PA St. Stephen.
Potts, Ronald A. '89 (WDC) Germantown, MD Mother Seton Parish.
Potts, Thomas *s.v.d.* '61 (BLX)[A] Bay St. Louis, MS St. Augustine's.
Potts, Thomas *s.v.d.* '02 (BLX)[E] Bay St. Louis, MS Province Development Office.
Potvin, Leo F. '64 (ALB) Dolgeville, NY St. Joseph; Newport, NY St. John the Baptist.
Potvin, Raymond H. '58 (SPR) On Duty Outside the Diocese; [C] Catholic University of America, The Retired.
Potvin, Raymond J. '80 (MAN) Hinsdale, NH St. Joseph; Hinsdale, NH St. Stanislaus.
Potvin, Thomas R. *o.p.* '62 (PRT)[I] Lewiston SS. Peter and Paul House.
Poulin, Arthur *o.s.b.cam.* '81 (MRY)[F] Berkeley, CA Incarnation Monastery.
Poulin, Arthur *o.s.b.cam.* '81 (OAK)[S] Berkeley, CA Incarnation Monastery, Camaldolese Benedictines.
Poulin, Edward C. '54 (NOR) Retired.
Poulin, Edward '54 (NOR) Willimantic, CT St. Mary.
Poulin, Neil C. *s.j.* '66 (CI) St. Joseph.
Poulin, Neil *s.j.* (CI) Defenders of the Bond.
Pouliot, Eugene A. '70 (STP) Richfield, MN St. Peter.
Pouliot, Francis A. '58 (STP) Minneapolis, MN Visitation.
Poulsen, James N. '68 (SD) San Diego, CA St. Gregory The Great.
Poulsen, James (SD) Presbyteral Council.
Poulsen, Thomas R. *o.p.* '67 (STP) Minneapolis, MN St. Albert the Great.
Poulson, David L.. '79 (E) Fryburg, PA St. Michael; World Apostolate of Fatima (Blue Army).
Poumade, James M. '01 (ARL) Alexandria, VA St. Mary's; Notaries.
Poupore, J. Gareth *c.s.b.* '53 (ROC)[I] Honeoye Falls, NY.
Poupore, Norman E. '50 (OG) Retired.
Poussard, Bertrand R. '67 (PRT) Special or Other Diocesan Assignment.
Poussard, Bertrand '67 (PRT)[G] Waterville, ME Mt. St. Joseph Holistic Care Community.
Pousson, Donald '66 (LAF) Crowley, LA St. John the Baptist; Morse, LA Immaculate Conception.
Poux, Francis A. *c.ss.r.* '62 (BAL) Baltimore, MD Our Lady of Fatima.
Poveromo, Robert J. '72 (NY) New York, NY St. James; New York, NY St. Vincent de Paul; [E] New York, NY Cathedral High School.
Povish, Robert W. '90 (PH) Pottstown, PA St. Aloysius; Graterford, PA Graterford State Correctional Institution.
Powderly, James J. '58 (WDC)[L] Washington, DC Cardinal O'Boyle Residence for Priests Retired.
Powell, Bernard F. '58 (PMB) Retired.
Powell, Daniel F.X. '92 (HBG)[J] Millersville, PA Franklin and Marshall College, Lancaster; [J] Millersville, PA Millersville University; Appointed; Harrisburg, PA St. Margaret Mary Alacoque.
Powell, Edward F. '54 (SUP) Retired.
Powell, Eric S. '90 (PEO) Normal, IL Epiphany.
Powell, Harold W. '77 (KC) Retired.
Powell, Harold '77 (CHY) In Residence.
Powell, John J. *s.j.* '56 (DET)[P] Hamtramck, MI St. Ladislaus.
Powell, Leon A. '71 (LC) Special Assignment; [H] La Crosse, WI Holy Cross (Seminary) Diocesan Center; Vice–Chancellor; Ecclesiastical Notaries.
Powell, Marc L. '03 (SEA) Tacoma, WA St. Charles Borromeo.
Powell, Matthew D. *o.p.* '75 (Chicago Prov.)[P] Providence St. Thomas Aquinas Priory at Providence College.
Powell, Michael '89 (JOL)[I] Kankakee, IL Provena St. Mary's Hospital.
Powell, Michael *o.m.i.* '02 (BWN) San Juan, TX St. John the Baptist.
Powell, Paul (OWN) *Roman Catholic Diocese of Owensboro Charitable Trust Fund, Inc..
Powell, Pike '48 (OWN) Curdsville, KY St. Elizabeth.
Powell, Robert J. '74 (PH) Jamison, PA St. Cyril of Jerusalem; Defenders of the Bond.
Powell, Robert J. *o.s.b.cam.* '76 (FR) Seekonk, MA St. Mary's; Diocesan Department of Pastoral Care for the Sick.
Powell, Robert John *o.s.b.cam.* '76 (MRY)[F] Big Sur New Camaldoli Hermitage.
Power, Bernard *c.ss.r.* '43 (ALB) AUXILIARY CHAPLAINS CONTRACT CHAPLAINS.
Power, David N. *o.m.i., s.t.d.* '56 (WDC)[C] Catholic University of America, The; [M] Washington, DC Oblate Community Retired.
Power, Eugene J. *s.j.* '51 (ALN)[A] Wernersville, PA Jesuit Center.
Power, Gerard *o.carm.* '99 (JOL)[L] Darien Carmelite Provincial Office.
Power, J. Timothy '66 (STP) Eden Prairie, MN Pax Christi.
Power, Patrick *c.ss.r.* '66 (KC) Kansas City, MO Our Lady of Perpetual Help; [J] Kansas City, MO Redemptorists Fathers of Kansas City, Missouri.
Power, Robert E. *c.s.b.* '66 (LSC) Las Cruces, NM Cathedral of Immaculate Heart of Mary; [C] Las Cruces, NM Basilian Fathers.
Power, Robert *c.s.b.* (LSC) Bishops Administrative Council; Vicars; Presbyteral Council; Priestly Life and Ministry Committee; Hispanic Ministry; Agua Viva Editorial Advisory Board; Garfield, NM San Isidro.
Power, William J. *s.j.* '41 (BO)[V] Weston, MA Campion Health Center, Inc..
Powers, Alfred J. '43 (CIN) Retired.
Powers, Aloysius '48 (OWN) Retired.
Powers, Bernard '52 (OWN) Retired.
Powers, Bruce J. '73 (RVC) Melville, NY St. Elizabeth.
Powers, Bruce (RVC) Chaplains of the Suffolk County Police Department.
Powers, Charles F. '48 (PAT) Dover, NJ Sacred Heart Retired.
Powers, Charles '97 (MIA) Absent on Leave.
Powers, Daniel *s.j.* '68 (HEL) Heart Butte, MT St. Anne.
Powers, David B. *sch.p.* '85 (WDC)[B] Washington, DC Queen of Pious Schools House of Studies–Piarist Fathers.
Powers, David *sch.p.* '85 (PH)[AA] Piarist Fathers Latin Mission.
Powers, David *sch.p.* '85 (WDC)[M] Washington, DC Piarist Fathers.
Powers, Glenn E. '87 (MIL) Sheboygan, WI SS. Cyril and Methodius; Sheboygan, WI Immaculate Conception.
Powers, Harold J. *c.s.p.* '48 (LA) Los Angeles, CA St. Paul the Apostle.
Powers, Harold J. *c.s.p.* '48 (NY)[EE] Jamaica Estates Paulist Fathers Generalate.
Powers, Isaias *c.p.* '61 (BRK)[V] Jamaica, NY Immaculate Conception Monastery.
Powers, James G. *s.j.* '62 (SPK)[B] Spokane, WA Gonzaga University.
Powers, James P. '90 (SUP) Rice Lake, WI St. Joseph; Adjutant Judicial Vicar; St. Pius Priest Fund.
Powers, Jerome C. '47 (CHR) Retired.
Powers, John A. *o.p.* '52 (NO)[N] Metairie, LA Metairie Manor, Metairie II, and Metairie III.
Powers, John J. '51 (CHI) South Holland, IL St. Jude the Apostle Retired.
Powers, John *c.p.* '77 (WOR)[O] Shrewsbury, MA Calvary Retreat Center, Passionist Fathers of Shrewsbury, Inc..
Powers, Joseph B. (KC) Diocesan Consultors.
Powers, Joseph '79 (KC) Raytown, MO Our Lady of Lourdes; Deans.
Powers, Richard E. '56 (E) Retired.
Powers, Richard J. '47 (BO) Senior Priests Retired.
Powers, Richard J. *s.j.* '58 (New York) Interlachen, FL St. John's Mission.
Powers, Richard T. '63 (PH) Levittown, PA St. Michael the Archangel.
Powers, Richard '56 (E)[M] Erie, PA Congregation of the Divine Spirit.
Powers, Richard '59 (OWN) Owensboro, KY St. Mary Magdalene; Consultors; Priests' Council; Priest Personnel Committee.
Powers, Robert M. '92 (BRK) Brooklyn, NY St. Francis Xavier; Brooklyn, NY Our Lady of Mercy.
Powers, Thomas F. '66 (BO) Wellesley, MA St. John the Evangelist; WEST REGION.
Powers, Thomas J. (BO) Lynnfield, MA St. Maria Goretti; North Reading, MA St. Theresa.
Powers, Thomas M. '49 (CHI) Wilmette, IL St. Joseph Retired.
Powers, Thomas M. '62 (ALB) Albany, NY St. Teresa of Avila.
Powers, Thomas W. '97 (BGP)[A] Stamford, CT St. John Fisher Seminary Residence.
Powers, Thomas '97 (BGP)[C] Stamford, CT Trinity Catholic High School.
Powers, Troy '87 (SAC) Citrus Heights, CA Holy Family; Vicars Forane.
Powers, William V. '58 (PBL) Retired.
Powhida, Robert '78 (ALB) Northville, NY St. Francis of Assisi.
Powis, John J. '59 (BRK) Brooklyn, NY St. Barbara.
Poyatt, William F. '49 (CAM) Barrington, NJ St. Francis de Sales Retired.
Poynter, Gail A. '51 (CIN) Retired.
Pozdol, Henry '50 (CHI) Summit, IL St. Joseph Retired.
Pozen, Matthew '01 (JOL) Naperville, IL St. Thomas the Apostle.
Pozza, Aldo *m.c.c.j.* '66 (CHI) Franklin Park, IL St. Gertrude; [N] La Grange Park, IL Comboni Missionaries.
Pozzoli, Ugo *i.m.c.* '98 (WDC)[V] Washington, DC Consolata Missionaries House of Studies.
Prabell, Paul '72 (LEX) Lexington, KY Cathedral of Christ the King; Defenders of the Bond; Promoter of Justice.
Prabhu, Dayananda '77 (KCK) Bendena, KS St. Benedict's; Troy, KS St. Charles; Wathena, KS St. Joseph's.
Prachar, Andrew '90 (NEW) Newark, NJ Sacred Heart.
Pracz, Ted '66 (PEO) Danville, IL Holy Family.
Pracz, Thaddeus (PEO) Vicariates and Vicars.
Prado, Manuel *c.m.* '62 (PCE) Ponce, PR La Milagrosa.
Prado, Teodoro Tim Y. '77 (GAL)[K] Catholic Chaplain Corps, Texas Medical Center.
Praem, Jude Lucier O. '74 (ORG) Garden Grove, CA St. Callistus.
Prakuzhy, Zacharias *c.m.i.* '68 (SHP) Lake Providence, LA St. Patrick; Oak Grove, LA Sacred Heart.
Pramote, Peter C. *c.s.s.* (NY) White Plains, NY Our Lady of Mt. Carmel.
Pranaitis, Mark *c.m.* '93 (CHI)[N] Chicago DePaul Vincentian Residence.
Pranzo, Joseph F. *c.s.* (BO) Framingham, MA St. Tarcisius.
Prasad, Ananda '96 (STA) Jacksonville, FL St. Joseph's.
Prasad, Vara '98 (SCR) Kingston, PA St. Ignatius.
Praski, Jacek '91 (CHI) Chicago, IL St. Wenceslaus.
Prasser, Jeffery A. '89 (MIL) Milwaukee, WI St. Catherine.
Prati, Jason M. '02 (STU) Woodsfield, OH St. John the Baptist; Woodsfield, OH St. Sylvester.
Prati, Jason '02 (STU) Woodsfield, OH St. Joseph's; Woodsfield, OH St. John Bosco Mission; Vocations.
Pratico, Patrick J. '79 (SCR) Eynon, PA St. Mary's Czestochowa; Judicial Vicar; Judges; Vicar for Canonical Services.
Prato–Quintana, Luis German *s.d.b.* '85 (OAK)[N] Berkeley Salesian Community.
Prats, Charles R. '84 (MET) On Duty Outside the Diocese.
Pratt, Camille J. *s.j.* '62 (SJ)[M] Los Gatos, CA Sacred Heart Jesuit Center.
Pratt, Dean '97 (DAL) Plano, TX St. Mark the Evangelist.
Pratt, James F.X. *s.j.* '86 (BO)[V] Boston, MA Loyola House.
Pratt, James L. *s.m.* '46 (SFR)[N] San Francisco, CA Marist Center of the West.
Pratt, Lawrence (BO) Hingham, MA Resurrection of Our Lord and Saviour Jesus Christ.
Pratt, Oscar J. '96 (BO) West Roxbury, MA Holy Name; Archdiocesan College of Consultors; Vocation Office.
Pravetz, Matthew A. *o.f.m.* '79 (NY) Bronx, NY Holy Cross.
Pray, Joseph N. '50 (BUR) Retired.
Prebula, David W. *o.s.b.* '44 (SEA)[L] Lacey, WA St. Martin's Abbey.
Prechtl, Ronald G. '80 (WH) Grafton, WV St. Augustine.
Preciado, Guillermo '02 (FRS) Hanford, CA Immaculate Heart of Mary.
Preciado, Rudolph J. '69 (ORG) Anaheim, CA St. Anthony Claret.
Preciado, Rudolph (ORG) Council of Priests; Ministry to Priests.
Precourt, Peter *a.a.* '76 (WOR)[O] Worcester, MA Assumptionists of Assumption College.
Prefontaine, Roger C. *s.s.s.* '53 (SAT) San Antonio, TX St. Joseph.
Pregana, Craig A. '89 (FR) Fall River, MA Sacred Heart; [M] Fall River, MA Catholic Campus Ministry; University of Massachusetts Dartmouth; Wheaton College; Permanent Diaconate Program; Vocations.
Pregana, Craig '89 (FR)[M] North Dartmouth, MA

Catholic Campus Ministry University of Massachusetts Dartmouth.
Pregana, David A. '96 (FR) Raynham, MA St. Ann.
Prehn, James S. *s.j.* '99 (CLV)[D] Cuyahoga Falls, OH Walsh Jesuit High School.
Preisinger, Robert F. '63 (OM) Omaha, NE St. Bernadette.
Preisner, A. F. '40 (DOD) Retired.
Prempeh, John '95 (WDC)[M] Washington, DC Divine Word College.
Prenatt, David E. '95 (E) Mount Jewett, PA St. Joseph; Smethport, PA St. Elizabeth.
Prendergast, Edmond '73 (MIA) Davie, FL St. Bonaventure.
Prendergast, Edward F. '51 (CLV) Rocky River, OH St. Christopher Retired.
Prendergast, Fergus J. '94 (MOB) Belle Fontaine, AL St. Philip Neri.
Prendergast, John J. '76 (PEO) Streator, IL Immaculate Conception.
Prendergast, Joseph '54 (SJ) Santa Clara, CA St. Justin.
Prendergast, Noel '58 (JKS) Yazoo City, MS St. Mary; Yazoo City, MS St. Francis.
Prendergast, Richard J. '79 (CHI) Berwyn, IL St. Mary of Celle.
Prendergast, Robert E. '50 (PEO) Retired.
Prendergast, Thomas '56 (SD) San Diego, CA Mission Basilica San Diego De Alcala.
Prendeville, Eugene *o.m.i.* '58 (CHI) Gainesville, MO St. William.
Prendiville, Edmond P. '63 (PRO) On Duty Outside the Diocese.
Prendiville, Edmond (MO) Judges.
Prendiville, Kerry '84 (RC) McLaughlin, SD St. Bonaventure's; McLaughlin, SD St. Bernard; McLaughlin, SD Standing Rock Reservation.
Prendiville, Thomas *s.d.b.* '56 (OAK)[N] Berkeley Salesian Community.
Preneta, Henry S. '67 (GBG) On Duty Outside the Diocese; Butler, PA St. Paul Retired.
Prengaman, Leo P. *s.j.* '93 (SJ).
Prengaman, Leo *s.j.* '57 (SJ)[D] Santa Clara Valley Medical Center.
Prescott, Herbert W. '55 (KNX) Retired.
Presenti, Richard *s.d.b.* '68 (SFR)[N] San Francisco, CA Salesian Provincial Residence.
Presenti, Richard *s.d.b.* (MRY) St. Francis Central Coast Catholic High School, Inc..
Preske, Venantius '52 (LR) Retired.
Preskenis, James T. *c.s.c.* '75 (BGP)[P] Bridgeport, CT Provincial Offices of the Priests and Brothers of Holy Cross, Eastern Province.
Presley, Joseph *i.c.* '01 (PEO) Galesburg IL Corpus Christi; Abingdon, IL Sacred Heart; Galesburg, IL St. Patrick's.
Presmanes, Jorge *o.p.* '91 (MIA)[H] Miami, FL Dominican Fathers of Miami, Inc.; Miami, FL St. Dominic.
Presta, James '86 (CHI).
Presta, James (CHI)[A] St. Joseph College Seminary at Loyola University.
Preston, Laurence *m.s.a.* '94 (NOR)[F] Cromwell Society of the Missionaries of the Holy Apostles.
Presume, Marc *c.s.c.* '92 (MIA) Miami, FL Notre Dame d'Haiti; Miami, FL St. Vincent De Paul.
Presutti, Robert *l.c.* '98 (SAC) Sacramento, CA Our Lady of Guadalupe Shrine; [B] Sacramento, CA University of Sacramento.
Pretto, Franklin D. '72 (SFE) Santa Fe, NM San Isidro.
Preuss, David *o.f.m.cap.* '79 (DET) Detroit, MI St. Charles Borromeo; Detroit, MI St. John Berchmans–St. Juliana.
Prevost, Robert F. *o.s.a.* '82 (CHI)[N] Olympia Fields, IL Tolentine Monastery at Tolentine Center.
Prevosto, Paul '96 (NEW) Newark, NJ St. Anthony's.
Prez, Daniel J. '74 (E) Bradford, PA St. Bernard; [P] Bradford, PA.
Pribek, James M. *s.j.* '99 (MIL)[O] Loyola House.
Pribonic, Phillip '67 (PIT) South Park, PA St. Joan of Arc.
Pribula, Duane '70 (CR) Akeley, MN Our Lady of the Pines; Akeley, MN St. Theodore – Laporte.
Pribyl, Ross *s.j.* '99 (CHI)[D] Chicago, IL St. Ignatius College Prep; [D] Chicago, IL St. Ignatius Jesuit Community.
Pricco, Richard A. '62 (PEO) Macomb, IL St. Paul's.
Pricco, Richard (PEO) Vicariates and Vicars.
Price, Bede *o.s.b.* '96 (STL)[O] St. Louis, MO The Abbey of St. Mary and St. Louis.
Price, James *c.p.* '94 (BRK)[V] Jamaica, NY Immaculate Conception Monastery; [X] Jamaica, NY Bishop Molloy Retreat House for Laymen.
Price, John R. '66 (CHI) Other Assignments.
Price, Rothell '88 (SHP) Bossier City, LA St. Jude; Associate Judge; Judges; Black Catholic Commission; Church Vocations Board.
Priebe, Norman F. '67 (LA) Los Angeles, CA St. Jerome.
Priest, Gerald A. (TYL) College of Consultors; Priests' Pension Board; Priests' Personnel Board.
Priest, Gerald '68 (TYL) Texarkana, TX Sacred Heart; Texarkana, TX Federal Corrections Institution; Deans; Presbyteral Council.
Priestly, Joseph *s.m.* '55 (HON)[G] Honolulu, HI Marianist Hall Community.
Prieto, Frank '64 (SFE) Albuquerque, NM Saint Joseph on the Rio Grande.
Prietto, Mario J. *s.j.* '73 (SJ)[B] Santa Clara University; [B] Santa Clara, CA Jesuit Community.
Primeaux, Patrick D. *s.m.* '77 (WDC)[M] Forest Hills, NY.
Primich, John '95 (MET) Spotswood, NJ Immaculate Conception.
Prince, Joseph A. '71 (BGP) Ridgefield, CT St. Elizabeth Seton.
Prince, Leo R. '86 (NY) Staten Island, NY St. Roch.
Prince, Michael '98 (DET) On Duty Outside the Archdiocese; Graduate Studies.
Principe, Francis J. '53 (NY)[E] New York, NY Cardinal Spellman High School.
Prindiville, Gerald T. '96 (NEW) On Duty Outside the Archdiocese.
Prinelli, John '78 (RIC) Christiansburg, VA Holy Spirit Catholic Church; Pearisburg, VA Holy Family.
Pringle, John R. '72 (MET) Bridgewater, NJ Holy Trinity.
Prior, Eugene J. *s.j.* '55 (NY)[F] New York, NY Loyola School; [EE] New York, NY St. Ignatius Loyola Residence.
Prior, Felix *o.carm.* '58 (BO)[O] Peabody, MA Catholic Information Center; [AA] Peabody, MA St. Theresa Carmelite Chapel.
Prior, Francis X. *c.m.* '51 (BUF)[O] Niagara University, NY Vincentian Community at Niagara University; [C] Niagara University, NY Niagara University.
Prior, James G. *c.m.* '53 (ALN) Roseto, PA Our Lady of Mt. Carmel.
Prior, Joseph G. (PH) Censores Librorum.
Prior, Joseph '90 (PH)[A] Wynnewood, PA Theological Seminary of St. Charles Borromeo, Overbrook.
Prior, Richard '01 (SY) Syracuse, NY Holy Family; Priests' Personnel Committee.
Prior, Robert J. *c.m.* '94 (GR) Greensboro, NC St. Mary; [G] Spring Lake, MI St. Lazare Retreat House.
Prior, Robert *c.m.* (PH).
Prior, Thomas W. *c.m.* '59 (ALN)[AA] Roseto, PA Our Lady of Mt. Carmel.
Priore, Kenneth Del '83 (SD) Escondido, CA Church of the Resurrection.
Priscaro, Jerry S. '93 (E) Soldiers and Sailors Home.
Prist, Wayne F. '67 (CHI) Chicago, IL Queen of All Saints Basilica.
Pritt, Phillip P. '62 (CLV) Rittman, OH St. Anne.
Pritzl, Kurt *o.p.* '91 (WDC)[B] Washington, DC Dominican House of Studies; [C] Washington, DC Catholic University of America, The; [C] Catholic University of America, The.
Prive, Francis R. '69 (BUR) Priests' Benefit Fund; Rutland, VT Immaculate Heart of Mary.
Privett, John A. *s.j.* '72 (BO)[V] Cambridge, MA Weston Jesuit Community.
Privett, John *s.j.* '72 (BO)[V] Cambridge, MA Faber House.
Privett, John '72 (BO)[V] Cambridge, MA Faber House.
Privett, Stephen A. *s.j.* '72 (SFR)[C] San Francisco, CA University of San Francisco; [N] San Francisco, CA Jesuit Community at University of San Francisco.
Proback, Adrian *o.c.s.o.* '54 (WOR)[O] Spencer, MA St. Joseph's Abbey.
Probst, Frank *o.f.m.* '81 (SHP) Monroe, LA Little Flower of Jesus.
Probst, R. Dean '81 (SFD) Carlinville, IL SS. Mary & Joseph; Priests' Personnel Board.
Probst, Robert L. '45 (STP)[C] St. Paul, MN University of St. Thomas Retired.
Probstfield, Edgar *o.s.b.* '52 (KC) Trenton, MO St. Joseph's
Probstfield, Regis *o.s.b.* '57 (KC)[J] Stanberry, MO.
Procaccini, David C. '93 (PRO) Coventry RI SS. John and Paul.
Procella, Paul '87 (GAL) Humble, TX St. Mary Magdalene; George Bush Intercontinental Airport.
Procella, Paul (GAL) Northern Vicariate.
Prochaska John '93 (OAK) San Leandro, CA St. Leander; Pastoral Leadership Placement Board (PLPB); Deans.
Procopio, Clement *o.f.m.* '44 (NY)[EE] Parkland, FL.
Proctor, John G. '72 (SD) Bonita, CA Corpus Christi.
Procyk, Marijan '80 (STF) Buffalo, NY St. Nicholas; Buffalo; Apostleship of Prayer; League of Ukrainian Catholics.
Prodehl, Richard B. '66 (JOL) Homer Glen, IL St. Bernard.
Prodywus Alexander '89 (STN) Absent on Sick Leave.
Proehl, Douglas M. '74 (CLV) Fairview Park, OH St. Angela Merici; College of Consultors.
Proehl, Douglas (CLV) Presbyteral Conveners.
Proenca, Luis *s.j.* '91 (LA)[C] Los Angeles, CA Jesuit Community.
Proenza, Rafael *o.p.* '96 (NO)[P] San Juan de Letran, Calle 19, #258; (FgM).
Profeta, Salvatore '50 (PMB) Retired.
Proffitt, James D. '91 (BAL) Baltimore, MD St. Michael.
Profota, James H. '75 (DET) Eastpointe, MI St. Basil.
Profota, James M. (DET) Archdiocesan Vicars.
Prohens, James *c.r.* '36 (DEN) Denver, CO St. Cajetan.
Prokes, Francis A. *s.j.* '57 (OM)[K] Omaha, NE Jesuit Community at Creighton University.
Prokop, Roger '87 (LAN) Ann Arbor, MI St. Thomas the Apostle; College of Consultors; Priest's Assignment Commission; CHI RHO; [N] Ann Arbor, MI St. Thomas Scholarship Trust for Father Gabriel Richard H.S..
Prokopiw, Taras *o.s.b.m.* '58 (RVC)[M] Glen Cove, NY St. Josaphat's Monastery, Novitiate and Retreat House.
Prokopiw, Taras *o.s.b.m.* '58 (STF)[B] Glen Cove, NY Basilian Fathers Novitiate of the Order of St. Basil the Great.
Promesso, William J. '89 (DET) Detroit, MI St. Thomas Aquinas; Archdiocesan Vicars.
Pronesti, Salvatore J. '67 (PH) Bridgeport, PA Our Lady of Mt. Carmel.
Proppe, John *o.f.m.cap.* '47 (NY)[EE] Yonkers, NY St. Clare Friary.
Prosen, Anthony J. '71 (LFT) Muncie, IN St. Mary; Pendleton, IN Indiana State Reformatory, St. Christopher Chapel; Pendleton, IN Correctional Industrial Complex Ecumenical Chapel; Special Assignment.
Prospero, William F. *s.j.* '98 (MIL)[O] Milwaukee, WI Jesuit Community at Marquette University.
Prost, Charles *c.m.* '78 (SPC) Cape Girardeau, MO St. Vincent de Paul.
Protack, Thomas J. '96 (WIL) Milford, DE St. John the Apostle; Ocean City, MD St. Luke and St. Andrew.
Protano, Joseph '63 (PRO) Providence, RI St. Anthony.
Proterra, Michael *s.j.* '71 (OAK)[N] Oakland, CA Murray Residence Community.
Protopapas, George *o.m.i.* '43 (BO)[V] Lowell, MA St. Eugene House (Residence).
Proulx, Arthur J. '80 (SP) Largo, FL St. Patrick.
Proulx, Arthur (SP) Presbyteral Council; College of Consultors.
Proulx, Raymond G. '60 (HRT) Goshen, CT St. Thomas of Villanova.
Prout, Thomas S. *s.j.* '92 (NY)[F] New York, NY Loyola School; [EE] New York, NY St. Ignatius Loyola Residence.
Provenza, Earl V. '64 (SHP) Bossier City, LA Mary, Queen of Peace; Vicars Forane; College of Consultors; Presbyteral Council; Priests' Retirement Board.
Provenza, John F. '90 (LA) South Gate, CA St. Helen.
Provenza, John (LA) Council of Priests; San Pedro Pastoral Region.
Provenzano, Thomas *s.d.b.* (CHI) Chicago, IL St. John Bosco; Paterson, NJ St. Anthony's.
Provinsal, Thomas G. *s.j.* '75 (FBK) Alakanuk, AK St. Ignatius; Emmonak, AK Sacred Heart; [E] St. Marys, AK Brother Joe Prince Jesuit Community.
Provinsal, Thomas *s.j.* '75 (FBK) Kotlik, AK St. Joseph.
Provinzano, Rocco '66 (NEW) Retired.
Provost, Glen John '75 (LAF) Lafayette, LA Our Lady of Fatima; Judges.
Provost, Glen (LAF) Diocesan Consultors.
Provost, John T. '73 (ALB) Delmar, NY St. Thomas the Apostle; Priests Retirement Board.
Proxell, Leo '77 (HEL) Bozeman, MT Holy Rosary; Vicariates.
Prucha, Francis Paul *s.j.* '57 (MIL)[O] Milwaukee, WI Jesuit Community at Marquette University.
Pruett, Bill H. '79 (OKL) Norman, OK St. Thomas More University Parish; [K] Norman, OK Campus Ministry for the Archdiocese of Oklahoma City.
Pruett, Bill (OKL) Council of Priests Archdiocesan; Campus Ministry, Department of.
Pruett, John M. '55 (STO) Modesto, CA Our Lady of Fatima Church (Pastor of).
Pruett, John (STO) Personnel Board.
Prunier, Arthur J. '48 (WOR) Retired.
Prunty, Brian J. *o.praem.* '65 (GB) De Pere, WI St. Norbert College; [I] De Pere, WI St. Joseph Priory.
Prunty, Brian *o.praem.* (GB)[B] De Pere, WI St. Norbert College.
Prus, Edward J. '61 (DET) Retired.
Prus, Eugene '64 (MET) Martinsville, NJ Blessed Sacrament.
Prusaitis, John P. '78 (BO) Brockton, MA St. Casimir.
Prusakowski, Gerald *o.f.m.* '65 (GB) Sobieski, WI St. Louis; Sobieski, WI St. Joseph; Sobieski, WI St. John Cantius; Elected Representatives.
Pruschowitz, Walter M. (PAT) Retired.
Pruschowitz, Walter '61 (PAT)[P] Chester, NJ Nazareth Village.
Prushinski, Carl T. '64 (SCR) Nanticoke, PA Holy Trinity.
Pruss, Rodney Lee A. '69 (GI) Ravenna, NE Our Lady of Lourdes.
Prussing, Charles *s.j.* '55 (LA)[Q] Los Angeles, CA Columbiere House.
Prusynski, Chester *c.s.c.* '62 (P)[L] Portland, OR Holy Cross Fathers & Brothers, C.S.C. – University of Portland.
Pruys, George L. '75 (STN) Wilton, ND SS. Peter and Paul.

Pryor, Donald J. '51 (NY) Sleepy Hollow, NY The Magdalene.
Pryor, Donald '51 (NY) Retired.
Pryor, G. Robert '55 (CR) Retired.
Pryor, Thomas P. '37 (PH) Retired.
Przechacki, Casimir J. '44 (MET) Retired.
Przepiora, Mieczyslaw *o.cist.* '90 (AMA) Propagation of the Faith; Umbarger, TX St. Mary's; Vega, TX Immaculate Conception.
Przybocki, Bernard A. '58 (ALT) Gallitzin, PA St. Demetrius.
Przybyla, Kenneth '77 (COS) Littleton, CO Pax Christi Catholic Church.
Przybyla, Philip J. '70 (PIT) Canonsburg, PA St. Patrick.
Przybylo, William P. '68 (HRT) Hartford, CT SS. Cyril and Methodius; [N] Hartford, CT SS. Cyril & Methodius Convent.
Przybylski, Donald L. '74 (LC) Mosinee, WI St. Paul.
Przybysz, Joseph J. '75 (TOL) Toledo, OH St. Hedwig.
Przybysz, Mark C. '90 (GR) Grand Rapids, MI St. Anthony of Padua; On Special Assignment; Continuing Formation of Priests.
Przygocki, Edward *m.s.a.* '81 (NOR)[F] Cromwell Society of the Missionaries of the Holy Apostles.
Przystasz, Wojcielh '98 (LAR) Laredo, TX Blessed Sacrament.
Przywara, Gerald A. '67 (RIC) Columbia, VA St. Joseph/Shrine of St. Katharine Drexel; Palmyra, VA Ss. Peter & Paul.
Ptacek, Benedict *o.de.m.* '59 (SP)[O] St. Petersburg, FL St. Peter Nolasco Residence.
Ptacek, John P. '55 (DUB) Retired.
Ptak, Walter J. '87 (DET) Wyandotte, MI Our Lady of Mt. Carmel; Priests Conference for Parish Affairs of the Archdiocese of Detroit.
Ptaszynski, Stephen F. '45 (HRT) Retired.
Ptaszynski, Thomas E. '73 (HRT) Milford, CT St. Ann's.
Pu, Matthew '53 (B) Retired.
Pua'auli, Kelemete '02 (SPP) Pago Pago, AS Cathedral of the Holy Family; Diocesan Pastoral Council; Faculty Members.
Pucar, August '63 (BEA) Retired.
Pucci, Albert '54 (NY) Staten Island, NY Holy Family.
Pucci, Alfred '54 (NY) Retired.
Pucciarell, George '74 (WH) Charles Town, WV St. James.
Pucciarelli, George W. '74 (BO) On Duty Outside the Archdiocese.
Puccinelli, Alfred *s.m.* '66 (FgM).
Puchalski, Andrew '75 (NEW) Bayonne, NJ Mt. Carmel.
Puchenski, Anthony C. '71 (CHI) Tinley Park, IL Saint Julie Billiart.
Puchner, Augustine R. *o.praem.* '97 (ORG)[A] Silverado, CA St. Michael's Norbertine Postulancy, Novitiate and Juniorate; [I] Silverado, CA Norbertine Fathers of Orange Inc..
Pucke, Michael U. '73 (CIN) Cincinnati, OH St. Michael.
Pudichery, Joseph P. '62 (PIT) Pittsburgh, PA St. Norbert.
Pudota, Javier '79 (SLC) Orem, UT St. Francis of Assisi.
Pudussery, Paul C. *c.s.c.* '92 (AUS)[G] Austin, TX Brother Andre House.
Pudussery, Paul *c.s.c.* '92 (AUS) Austin, TX Nuestra Senora De Dolores.
Puente, Jose Francisco (SAT) San Antonio, TX St. Luke.
Puentes, Jesus '86 (CHI) Chicago, IL St. Bronislava.
Puerner, John W. '55 (LC) Thorp, WI St. Bernard–St. Hedwig Parish.
Puerta, Jorge '89 (MIA) Absent on Sick Leave.
Puertas, Cristobal J. '97 (MIA) Miami, FL St. Agatha.
Puerto, Carlos '88 (ORL) Melbourne, FL Our Lady of Lourdes.
Puetz, Richard W. '45 (LFT)[D] Delphi, IN St. Elizabeth Healthcare Center Retired.
Pugh, Charles '60 (SAT)[K] San Antonio, TX Padua Place Retired.
Pugh, James L. '67 (MEM) Memphis, TN St. Anne's.
Pugliese, Francis A. '68 (NY) Military Chaplains.
Pugliese, Steven J. *s.j.* '93 (NY)[EE] New York, NY Murray–Weigel Hall.
Puglisi, James *s.a.* '73 (NY)[EE] Garrison Franciscan Friars of the Atonement, Minister General Office.
Puhak, Nicholas I. '57 (PSC) Freeland, PA St. Mary's; Retirement Plan Board.
Puhl, Albert E. '44 (DEN) Retired.
Puhlman, Robert W. '84 (LAV) Las Vegas, NV Our Lady of Las Vegas.
Puhlman, Robert '84 (ORG) On Duty Outside the Diocese.
Puigbo, Juan A. '01 (WDC)[B] Washington, DC Diocesan Laborer Priests, House of Studies.
Puisis, John C. *c.s.v.* '45 (CHI)[N] Arlington Heights, IL Viatorian Province Center–Clerics of St. Viator.
Puisis, Leonard '52 (MIA) Retired.
Pujdak, Steve *s.c.j.* '69 (BWN) Raymondville, TX Our Lady of Guadalupe.
Pulaski, Joseph S. *m.m.* '47 (NY).
Puleo, Edward C. '88 (MET)[EE] Carteret, NJ St. Joseph; Deans.
Pulice, John J. '66 (MIL) Milwaukee, WI St. Robert.
Pulickal, Sony G. *c.m.f.* '83 (OG) West Leyden, NY St. Mary's Nativity.
Pulido, Felipe '02 (YAK) Moses Lake, WA Our Lady of Fatima; Moses Lake, WA Queen of All Saints.
Pulido, Luis David (BRK) Brooklyn, NY Immaculate Conception of the Blessed Virgin Mary.
Pulido, Raymundo Manriquez '01 (LUB) Hale Center, TX St. Theresa's.
Pulikoottil, Berard '62 (BUF) Retired.
Puljic, Marko *o.f.m.* '81 (CHI)[N] Chicago, IL Croatian Franciscan Custody of the Holy Family.
Puljic, Tomislav *o.f.m.* '02 (CHI) Chicago, IL St. Jerome.
Pulle, Colvin F. (RVC) Diocesan Judges.
Pullyanampatta, Tomy *m.s.f.s.* (NSH) Hendersonville, TN Our Lady of the Lake.
Pulparayil, George '67 (NY) Monroe, NY Sacred Heart Church.
Pulskamp, James E. '67 (SR) Santa Rosa, CA Holy Spirit; Vicar General; Members of the Curia; Chancellor; Director of Clergy Personnel; Notaries; Board of Consultors; Priests' Council; Finance Committee; Diocesan Building Committee; Review Board; Archivist; Clergy Personnel Committee; Custodian of Records.
Pulugujju, Mario (OKL) Indian Ministries, Inc..
Pulugujju, Mariyanandam '92 (OKL) Anadarko, OK St. Patrick's.
Puma, Vincent E. (PAT) Retired.
Punch, Nicholas W. *o.p.* '66 (SUP)[H] Webster, WI Thomas More Center for Preaching and Prayer, Inc..
Punchayil, Mathew '72 (SYM) Germantown, MD Syro–Malabar Catholic Mission; Germantown, MD Mother Seton Parish.
Punchekunnel, George J. '57 (LA) Fillmore, CA St. Francis of Assisi.
Punderson, Joseph R. '76 (TR) On Duty Outside the Diocese.
Pung, Karl L. '97 (LAN) On Duty Outside the Diocese.
Punganoor, Amal '03 (TYL) Tyler, TX Cathedral of the Immaculate Conception; Gilmer, TX St. Francis of Assisi.
Punnakkattu, Joseph Sojan '00 (SP) New Port Richey, FL St. Thomas Aquinas.
Punnakunnel, John (India) Bridgeport, CT Holy Rosary.
Punnolil, George '80 (CAM) Vineland, NJ Sacred Heart; [I] Vineland, NJ Bishop McCarthy Residence.
Punnoose, Siby '98 (SC) Carroll, IA Holy Spirit; St. Anthony Regional Hospital; [C] Carroll, IA St. Anthony Regional Hospital.
Puntal, Pedro (Peter) '82 (ORL) Kissimmee, FL Holy Redeemer.
Puntal, Peter (ORL) Filipino.
Punti, George '55 (RVC) Elmont, NY St. Boniface.
Puntino, John *s.d.b.* '78 (NY)[H] Columbus, OH Salesian Residence; [EE] New Rochelle, NY Salesian Cooperators of St. John Bosco; [GG] Stony Point, NY Don Bosco Retreat Center and Marian Shrine; [GG] Stony Point, NY Marian Shrine.
Puntrello, Fillippo *r.c.j.* '63 (FRS) Sanger, CA St. Mary.
Punzalan, Manolo (NEW) Maplewood, NJ St. Joseph's.
Puopolo, Rocco N. *s.x.* '77 (CHI)[N] Chicago, IL Xaverian Missionaries (S.X.).
Pupius, George '63 (OKL) Oklahoma City, OK Immaculate Conception.
Pupsys, Adam '52 (NOR) Retired.
Purcell, Arthur D. '79 (BRK) Brooklyn, NY St. Brendan's.
Purcell, James '53 (PEO) Retired.
Purcell, Lawrence M. '65 (SD) La Jolla, CA All Hallows.
Purcell, Lawrence (SD) College of Consultors; Vicars Forane.
Purcell, Paul J. '54 (SCR)[N] Dunmore, PA Villa St. Joseph.
Purcell, Richard *o.f.m.* '68 (SFR) San Francisco, CA St. Boniface.
Purcell, Robert F. *s.j.* '53 (MIL)[O] Wauwatosa, WI Jesuit Community at St. Camillus.
Purcell, Robert '74 (ALB) Retired.
Purdy, David *s.d.b.* '70 (MRY) Watsonville, CA Our Lady Help of Christians; [N] San Francisco, CA Salesian Provincial Residence; St. Francis Central Coast Catholic High School, Inc.; (FgM).
Purdy, George *s.j.* '53 (YAK) Naches, WA St. John's; Jail Ministry.
Purfield, James R. '54 (DEN) Denver, CO All Saints.
Purgatorio, Vincente '87 (RCK) Algonquin, IL St. Margaret Mary.
Purta, Jerome J. *o.s.b.* '61 (GBG)[H] Latrobe, PA Saint Vincent Archabbey.
Purtell, Jack '95 (CC)[G] Robstown, TX Society of Our Lady of the Most Holy Trinity.
Purtell, John J. '68 (DUB) Sumner, IA Immaculate Conception; Sumner, IA St. Francis of Assisi; Sumner, IA St. Francis Xavier.
Purtell, Thomas J. '61 (CHI) Chicago, IL St. John Fisher.
Purtell, Thomas W. '53 (DUB) Retired.
Purvey, J. James '84 (BAL) Baltimore, MD St. Michael.
Puryear, Stan '95 (OWN) Bowling Green, KY St. Joseph's; Hispanic Office.
Pusak, Ronald '61 (MIA) Defenders of the Bond Retired.
Pusateri, Christian *o.s.b.* '55 (RCK)[G] Aurora, IL Marmion Abbey.
Pusateri, Joseph E. '54 (GRY) Otis, IN St. Mary.
Pusateri, Joseph *s.m.* (FgM).
Pusateri, Philip A. *s.j.* '72 (BO)[V] Boston The Society of Jesus of New England–Provincial Offices.
Pusateri, Philip A. *s.j.* '72 (NOR) Norwich, CT SS. Peter and Paul.
Pusch, Richard '71 (SHP) Forcht Wade Correctional Center; Jail–Prison Ministry.
Pushpanathan, Zacarias (HRT) Waterbury, CT St. Margaret's.
Putano, John P. '70 (SY) Vestal, NY Our Lady of Sorrows; Priests' Personnel Committee.
Putera, Vasyl '96 (PHU) Jersey City, NJ SS. Peter and Paul.
Puthenangady, Paul (CC) Kingsville, TX Our Lady of Good Counsel.
Puthenkulathil, Joseph '76 (SFS) Tabor, SD St. Wenceslaus.
Puthenparambil, Jose (STP) Mercy Hospital.
Puthenpeedika, George '79 (LAN) Flint, MI Christ the King; McLaren Regional Medical Center; Hurley Regional Medical Center.
Puthiyadom, Thomas '66 (SYM) Hartford, CT St. Thomas Syro–Malabar Mission of Hartford.
Puthiyadom, Thomas '94 (HRT)[I] Hartford, CT Saint Francis Hospital and Medical Center.
Puthoff, Chad C. *s.d.s.* '71 (SAC) West Sacramento, CA Holy Cross.
Puthomayil, Chacko '71 (GAL) Houston, TX St. Dominic.
Puthota, Charles I. *s.j.* '89 (SFR) San Francisco, CA Holy Name of Jesus.
Puthuppally, Joseph '66 (SHP) Monroe, LA St. Matthew; [B] Monroe, LA St. Francis Medical Center.
Puthuppally, Joseph (SHP) Vicars Forane; College of Consultors; Presbyteral Council.
Puthusseril, George '79 (MIA) Coral Springs, FL St. Andrew.
Putich, Michael *o.f.m.* '68 (BUF) Buffalo, NY St. Martin.
Putka, John S. *s.m.* '69 (CIN)[D] Dayton, OH The University of Dayton; [M] Dayton, OH Marianist Community.
Putnam, John T. '92 (CHL) Salisbury, NC Sacred Heart; Judicial Vicar; Cursillo.
Putnam, Richard *s.d.b.* '89 (NY)[F] New Rochelle, NY Salesian High School; [EE] New Rochelle, NY Salesian Provincial House.
Putrimas, Edmund (LIT).
Putrimas, Edmundas (LIT) Vocations and Public Relations Director.
Puttoff, Jeffrey P. *s.j.* '98 (CAM) Camden, NJ Holy Name.
Puttoff, Jeffrey *s.j.* '98 (CAM) Camden, NJ.
Putz, Kenneth '73 (PH) Hatboro, PA St. John Bosco.
Puza, Paul G. '87 (ALN) Retired.
Puzio, Thomas '70 (DET) Warren, MI St. Dorothy.
Puznakoski, Gilbert '75 (PIT) Allegheny County, PA UPMC Shadyside Hospital.
Pyka, Frank *c.m.f.* '46 (LA)[Q] Rancho Dominguez, CA Dominguez Seminary Inc..
Pyo, Edward J. '85 (PBR) Beaverdale, PA St. Mary's.
Pyo, Immanuel '90 (MIL)[X] Milwaukee, WI The Korean Catholic Community of Milwaukee.
Pyso, Volodymyr '73 (STF) Kerhonkson, NY Holy Trinity.
Pytlick, Conrad '66 (LSC) Retired.

Q

Quach, Binh T. *c.s.sp.* '91 (GAL)[B] Houston, TX Holy Ghost Fathers and Brothers.
Quade, Alvin '54 (SCL) Retired.
Quadrini, Angelo '85 (EVN)[E] Jasper, IN Providence Home, Nursing Home for the Needy.
Quaine, Michael W. '85 (DET) Dearborn, MI St. Alphonsus.
Quainoo, Clement '82 (VIC) El Campo, TX St. Andrew.
Qualizza, Franco *s.x.* '71 (FgM).
Qualizza, Franco *s.x.* '71 (PAT)[M] Wayne Xaverian Missionary Fathers.
Quang, John '70 (SAV) Military Chaplains.
Quang, Tuan Le *c.ss.r.* '01 (BRK)[C] Whitestone, NY St. Alphonsus Formation Residence.
Quang Le, Peter '79 (LR) Fort Smith, AR Christ the King.
Quansah, Francis Abuah (LC) La Crosse, WI St. Joseph; Defensor Vinculi; Rockland, WI St. Peter.
Quant, Roberto '91 (OKL) Oklahoma City, OK Holy Angels; Judicial Vicar.
Quante, Paul E. *o.s.a.* '84 (OAK) Castro Valley, CA Our Lady of Grace.

Quanz, Paul E. *c.s.b.* '84 (GRY)[B] Merrillville, IN Andrean High School; [I] Merrillville, IN Basilian Fathers Residence.
Quarato, Robert A. '91 (NY) Bronx, NY Holy Rosary.
Quartana, Donald F. '53 (MIL) Retired.
Quartier, Neal E. '76 (SY) Syracuse, NY The Cathedral of the Immaculate Conception; Syracuse, NY St. John the Evangelist; Special Assignment; Vocation Formation.
Quartier, Neal (SY) Personal Resource Center.
Quattropane, Joseph *o.f.m.cap.* '72 (SB) Barstow, CA St. Joseph.
Que, Dinh Ngoc *c.ss.r.* '56 (LA)[Q] Baldwin Park, CA Vietnamese Redemptorist Mission.
Queally, Kevin *t.o.r.* '77 (ALT)[A] Loretto, PA St. Francis University; [F] Loretto, PA Mount Assisi Friary; [H] Loretto, PA St. Francis College (Loretto).
Quealy, Philip J. '83 (NY).
Quebedeaux, Carl *c.m.f.* '82 (CHI)[N] Oak Park, IL Claretian Missionaries Community Support Trust.
Queen, James T. '66 (SY) Rome, NY St. Paul.
Quejadas, Mario S. (JOL) Bolingbrook, IL St. Francis of Assisi.
Quenum, Andre '93 (Cotonou) Pittsburgh, PA St. Mary of Mercy.
Quesada, Raul '80 (SJN) Trujillo Alto, PR San Francisco de Asis.
Quesnel, Raymond *o.m.i.* '45 (WIN) Retired.
Quetchenbach, Raymond *s.v.d.* '57 (CHI)[B] Techny, IL Divine Word Residence.
Queuedo, Hernan '97 (ATL) Lilburn, GA St. John Neumann.
Quevedo, Alfredo S. *s.j.* '56 (NY)[EE] New York, NY Murray–Weigel Hall.
Quezada, Frank '88 (SAT) Burlington, CO St. Charles Borromeo.
Quezada, Frank '88 (COS) Burlington, CO St. Catherine of Siena.
Quezada, Sixto '81 (NY) New York, NY Ascension.
Qui, Vincent '68 (NO) Retired.
Quic, Cristobal Coche '92 (RCK)[G] Aurora, IL Marmion Abbey.
Quiceno, Francisco Jose '72 (SJN) Carolina, PR San Valentin.
Quickley, George W. *s.j.* '80 (BAL).
Quigg, Harold '60 (SEA) Retired.
Quigley, Eugene J. *s.j.* '55 (NY)[EE] Rochester, MN.
Quigley, J. Joseph '56 (SPR) Retired.
Quigley, James Ferrer *o.p.* '65 (PRO)[P] Providence St. Thomas Aquinas Priory at Providence College.
Quigley, John *o.f.m.* '72 (CIN)[M] Franciscans International; [V] Cincinnati, OH Franciscans Network.
Quigley, Joseph P. '60 (BRK) Brooklyn, NY St. Mark's; Coney Island Hospital.
Quigley, Martin J. '46 (BAK) Retired.
Quigley, William G. *c.i.c.m.* '74 (ARL)[J] Arlington, VA Missionhurst, C.I.C.M.–Central House and Provincialate; (FgM).
Quihuis, Luis H. *s.j.* '92 (LA) Santa Barbara, CA Our Lady of Sorrows; Deanery 2.
Quijano, Antonio *m.s.* '92 (RNO) Reno, NV St. Therese Church of the Little Flower.
Quijano, Carlos *s.j.* '98 (BRK) Brooklyn, NY St. Ignatius.
Quijano, Carlos–Bartolome *o.p.* '96 (NY) New York, NY St. Catherine of Siena.
Quijano, Jose Juan '73 (MIA) Higher Studies; [A] Boynton Beach, FL St. Vincent de Paul Regional Seminary; On Duty Outside the Archdiocese.
Quijones–Rivera, Leoncio '46 (SJN) Retired.
Quilcate, Jose '99 (RVC) Hicksville, NY St. Ignatius Loyola.
Quill, J. Michael '82 (WDC) Pomfret, MD St. Joseph.
Quill, James E. '53 (COV) Fort Wright, KY St. Agnes; Censor Librorum Retired.
Quill, John A. '74 (NEW) Maplewood, NJ St. Joseph's.
Quillen, Andrew M. '91 (BO)[V] Hingham, MA Glastonbury Abbey.
Quilligan, Maurice '57 (SFD) Retired.
Quilligan, Michael '71 (MIA) West Hollywood, FL Annunciation.
Quinchia–Diaz, Dairo '01 (HRT) Wallingford, CT Holy Trinity.
Quindlen, Joseph J. '73 (PH) Buckingham, PA Our Lady of Guadalupe.
Quinlan, Edward J. '78 (HBG) Dauphin, PA St. Matthew, Apostle and Evangelist; [K] Harrisburg, PA The Neumann Scholarship Foundation; Secretary for Education.
Quinlan, Eugene '62 (MIA) Retired.
Quinlan, Jack '97 (DET) Monroe, MI St. John The Baptist.
Quinlan, James V. '76 (CHI) Maywood, IL St. Eulalia.
Quinlan, John J. '70 (PAT) Swartswood, NJ Our Lady of Mt. Carmel.
Quinlan, Joseph M. '52 (NEW) Serra Clubs; Lincroft, NJ St. Leo the Great Retired.
Quinlan, Leo F. *s.j.* '45 (BO)[V] Weston, MA Campion Health Center, Inc..
Quinlan, Thomas J. '58 (RIC) Virginia Beach, VA Holy Family.
Quinlivan, Anthony F. *c.ss.r.* '71 (ORL) Cocoa, FL Blessed Sacrament.
Quinlivan, Francis L. *c.s.c.* (MO) AUXILIARY CHAPLAINS CONTRACT CHAPLAINS.
Quinlivan, Thomas J. '72 (BUF) Consultors, College of; Council of Priests; West Seneca, NY Queen of Heaven.
Quinlivan, William J. '95 (BUF) Williamsville, NY St. Gregory the Great.
Quinn, Alban *o.carm.* '49 (JOL)[L] Prelate Nullius; (FgM).
Quinn, Andrew F. '35 (NY) Staten Island, NY Sacred Heart Retired.
Quinn, Bernard '53 (HBG) Lancaster, PA Sacred Heart of Jesus Retired.
Quinn, Brendan '74 (NEW) Jersey City, NJ Holy Rosary; Elizabeth, NJ Trinitas Hospital; Chaplains.
Quinn, Bruce *o.f.m.cap.* '57 (NOR) Middletown, CT St. Pius X; Middletown, CT Middlesex Memorial Hospital.
Quinn, Charles J. '61 (WIN) Jackson, MN Good Shepherd; Jackson, MN St. Luke's; Jackson, MN St. Joseph.
Quinn, Charles P. '59 (NY) Pleasant Valley, NY St. Stanislaus Kostka.
Quinn, Charles P. '66 (PRO) Chepachet, RI St. Eugene.
Quinn, Don '33 (IND) Shelbyville, IN St. Joseph.
Quinn, Donald (IND)[O] Shelbyville, IN University of Indianapolis.
Quinn, Frank C. *o.p.* '59 (STL)[B] St. Louis, MO Aquinas Institute of Theology; [O] St. Louis, MO Dominican Community of St. Louis.
Quinn, Gavin *o.carm.* '65 (JOL) Darien, IL Our Lady of Mount Carmel.
Quinn, J. Patrick *t.o.r.* '84 (STP) Minneapolis, MN St. Bridget; [A] St. Paul, MN The Saint Paul Seminary; [M] Minneapolis, MN St. Bridget Friary.
Quinn, James A. '67 (MIA) Hallandale, FL St. Matthew.
Quinn, James A. '67 (SY) Utica, NY St. Peter.
Quinn, James E. '54 (MIA) Pompano Beach, FL St. Coleman Retired.
Quinn, James F. '58 (SY) Manlius, NY St. Ann; Absent on Leave.
Quinn, James J. *s.j.* '50 (OM)[K] Omaha, NE Jesuit Community at Creighton University.
Quinn, James '60 (NY) On Leave of Absence.
Quinn, Jarlath '96 (NY) Staten Island, NY Our Lady Help of Christians.
Quinn, John F. '71 (NY) Armonk, NY St. Patrick.
Quinn, John J. '43 (NY) Retired.
Quinn, John J. *s.j.* '54 (SCR)[C] Scranton, PA The University of Scranton.
Quinn, John L. '62 (NY) On Duty Outside the Archdiocese.
Quinn, John M. *o.s.a.* '49 (PH)[AA] Villanova, PA St. Thomas Monastery.
Quinn, John M. '57 (SY) New Hartford, NY St. Thomas.
Quinn, John P. '68 (MAN) Bedford, NH St. Elizabeth Seton; Council of Priests; College of Consultors; Diocesan Finance Council; Cabinet Secretary for Finance & Real Estate; Finance Officer; Catholic Relief Services.
Quinn, John T. '67 (SD) Retired.
Quinn, Joseph G. '85 (SCR) Scranton, PA St. Peter's Cathedral; Defenders of the Bond.
Quinn, Joseph J. '45 (NY) Retired.
Quinn, Joseph L. *s.j.* '66 (SCR)[C] Scranton, PA The University of Scranton.
Quinn, Joseph M. *c.s.c.* '50 (FR)[H] North Dartmouth, MA Holy Cross Residence.
Quinn, Joseph '45 (NY)[EE] Bronx, NY.
Quinn, Kenneth B. (BO) Maynard, MA St. Bridget.
Quinn, Kevin P. *s.j.* '85 (New York)[M] Washington, DC The Jesuit Community at Georgetown University.
Quinn, Kieran *o.f.m.cap.* '39 (WH) Charleston, WV St. Anthony; [M] Charleston, WV Capuchins–St. Anthony Friary.
Quinn, Lawrence J. '71 (NY)[Q] Archdiocesan Committee on Scouting.
Quinn, Lawrence T. '67 (NY) Staten Island, NY St. Ann.
Quinn, Lawrence (NY) Our Lady of Mount Carmel.
Quinn, Liam '83 (MIA)[A] Miami, FL St. John Vianney College Seminary.
Quinn, Matthew '43 (PRO)[P] Bristol, RI St. Columban's Retirement House.
Quinn, Michael F. '70 (JC) Hannibal, MO Holy Family; Judges; III Hannibal; Coords..
Quinn, Michael *c.ss.r.* '81 (CHI) Chicago, IL St. Michael; [N] Chicago, IL The Redemptionist Fathers of Chicago.
Quinn, Patrick *t.o.r.* '84 (STP)[C] St. Paul, MN University of St. Thomas.
Quinn, Peter F. '72 (BO) Quincy, MA St. John the Baptist.
Quinn, Peter N. '75 (PH) Philadelphia, PA St. Barnabas.
Quinn, Peter '50 (ORL) Retired.
Quinn, Peter '62 (JKS) Retired.
Quinn, Richard J. *m.m.* (FgM).
Quinn, Richard *c.ss.r.* '62 (SEA) Seattle, WA Sacred Heart of Jesus; [L] Seattle, WA The Redemptionist Society of Washington.
Quinn, Robert C. '61 (ALN) Boyertown, PA St. Columbkill.
Quinn, Robert F. *c.s.p.* '53 (NY)[EE] Jamaica Estates Paulist Fathers Generalate.
Quinn, Robert J. '34 (SC) Retired.
Quinn, Seamus M. *c.ss.r.* '58 (PH) Philadelphia, PA St. Peter the Apostle.
Quinn, Stephen *s.t.* '44 (PAT)[M] Stirling, NJ Holy Spirit Missionary Cenacle.
Quinn, Terrance '55 (NY) Pleasantville, NY Holy Innocents.
Quinn, Thomas J. *s.j.* '68 (NY)[GG] Staten Island, NY Mount Manresa Jesuit Retreat House Retired.
Quinn, Thomas P. '48 (HRT) Retired.
Quinn, Thomas S. '85 (TOL) Toledo, OH Blessed Sacrament; [K] Toledo, OH Ursuline Convent of the Sacred Heart.
Quinn, Thomas '62 (SEA) Retired.
Quinn, W. Louis '45 (WDC) Bethesda, MD Our Lady of Lourdes; Christ Child Society Retired.
Quinn, William J. '41 (CHI) Maywood, IL St. Eulalia Retired.
Quinn, William P. '55 (SFR) Retired.
Quinn, William '62 (CAM) Stone Harbor, NJ St. Paul's; Cape May Deanery; Members.
Quinnan, Edward J. *s.j.* '87 (NY)[GG] Staten Island, NY Mount Manresa Jesuit Retreat House.
Quinnan, Michael F. '86 (SCR) Mountaintop, PA St. Jude.
Quinones, Francisco Javier '82 (SJN) Guaynabo, PR Maria Madre de Mi Senor.
Quinones, Francisco '82 (SJN)[B] Santurce, PR Academia Sagrado Corazon.
Quinones, Leoncio '46 (PCE) On Duty Outside the Diocese.
Quinones, Miguel P. '52 (WDC) Retired.
Quinonez–Murillo, Luis H. '97 (SJN) Luquillo, PR Madre del Redentor.
Quint, Dennis J. '96 (DUB) Grundy Center, IA St. Patrick; Grundy Center, IA Queen of Heaven; Grundy Center, IA St. Mary; Grundy Center, IA Sacred Heart; Worship Commission.
Quintal, Gerald '65 (P) Dallas, OR St. Philip.
Quintana, Jose '96 (GR) Grand Rapids, MI Shrine of St. Francis Xavier and Our Lady of Guadalupe.
Quintana–Puente, Carlos '96 (SJN) On Duty Outside the Archdiocese; Clergy Social Security (Prevision Social del Clero).
Quinter, Paul S. '82 (PH) On Duty Outside the Archdiocese.
Quintero, Gilberto '88 (SP) Plant City, FL St. Clement.
Quintero, Manuel '81 (LAV) Las Vegas, NV St. Francis de Sales; Presbyteral Council for the Diocese of Las Vegas.
Quinto, Armand R. *s.d.b.* '75 (PAT) Paterson, NJ St. Anthony's.
Quinto, Jupeter *r.c.j.* '90 (LA) Van Nuys, CA St. Elisabeth.
Quioque, Roy Milton *c.i.c.m.* '82 (SAT)[B] San Antonio, TX Missionhurst Formation Community.
Quiray, Danilo '90 (CAM) Ventnor, NJ St. James.
Quirk, Kevin M. '93 (WH)[P] Bethany, WV St. John Fisher Catholic Chapel; [P] West Liberty, WV West Liberty State College, St. Thomas Aquinas Campus Ministry; Assistant to the Bishop; Judicial Vicar; Apostleship of Prayer.
Quirk, Richard J. '78 (STL) St. Louis, MO Basilica of St. Louis, King of France.
Quiroz, Guido M. '44 (VIC) Retired.
Quiroz, J. Salvadore (BO) Lynn, MA St. Joseph.
Quitalig, Angel N. *s.s.p.* '98 (SFR) Daly City, CA Our Lady of Mercy.
Quituga, David C. (AGN) Archdiocesan Finance Council.
Quitugua, David C. '84 (AGN) Agana, GU Dulce Nombre de Maria Cathedral – Basilica; Moderator of the Curia and Vicar General; Archdiocesan College of Consultors; Archdiocesan Presbyteral Council; Judicial Vicar; Pontifical Holy Childhood Association & Pontifical Society for the Propagation of the Faith; Legion of Mary; Judicial Vicar.
Quitugua, David I.A. '64 (AGN) Agana, GU San Juan Bautista; Archdiocesan Presbyteral Council.
Quyet, Anthony '83 (JKS) Jackson, MS St. Therese.

R

Raab, Ronald P. *c.s.c.* '83 (P) Portland, OR St. Vincent de Paul; Portland, OR St. Patrick.
Raaser, Eric '85 (NY) Bronx, NY St. Benedict.
Raaz, Paul A. '70 (SAT) San Antonio, TX Resurrection of the Lord.
Rabadan, Manuel *c.r.l.* '93 (ARE) Corozal, PR La Milagrosa.
Rabalais, Rusty P. '97 (ALX) Continuing Formation of the Clergy; Fifth Ward, LA Our Lady of Lourdes.
Rabaut, Francis D. *s.j.* '44 (DET)[P] Hamtramck, MI St. Ladislaus.
Rabbat, Robert '94 (NTN) Northlake, IL St. John the Baptist; "Sophia" (A Journal).

Rabe, David L. '83 (NO) Westwego, LA Our Lady of Prompt Succor.
Rabenecker, David *o.s.b.* '91 (IND)[K] Manchester, KY; Federal Correction Institute.
Rabeson, Jocelyn *s.j.* '98 (WDC)[M] Washington, DC The Jesuit Community at Georgetown University.
Rabiy, Andriy '01 (PHU) Perth Amboy, NJ St. Michael's; Perth Amboy, NJ Immaculate Conception.
Rable, Cyril J. '56 (HBG)[G] Danville, PA Maria Hall.
Rable, Cyril J. '56 (SCR) On Duty Outside the Diocese.
Racco, Philip G. '77 (CLV) Cleveland, OH Holy Rosary.
Racette, Norman *o.m.i.* '39 (SAT)[K] San Antonio, TX Oblate Madonna Residence.
Rached, Jose J. *c.ss.r.* '70 (CGS) Aguas Buenas, PR Church of Tres Santos Reyes.
Rachford, Nicholas R.A. (PRM) Judge; Secretary of the Tribunal.
Rachford, Nicholas '71 (PRM) Lorain, OH St. Nicholas; Cantors' Institute.
Rachunek, Henry C. '62 (GAL) Hungerford, TX St. Wenceslaus Mission.
Rachunek, Henry C. '62 (VIC) Hungerford, TX St. John the Baptist.
Racine, Michael S. '95 (FR) New Bedford, MA St. James; Diocesan Department of Pastoral Care for the Sick.
Racivitch, Herve P. *s.j.* '62 (NO)[P] New Orleans, LA Ignatius Residence.
Rackensperger, Nobert *o.f.m.conv.* '54 (FRS) Coalinga, CA St. Paul The Apostle.
Racki, Leonard E. '62 (PBL) Clergy Benefit Society of the Diocese of Pueblo, Inc. Retired.
Racki, Leonard (PBL) Clergy Assemblies.
Raczek, Kenneth T. '56 (LFT) Elwood, IN St. Joseph.
Raczka, Philip '80 (NTN) Akron, OH St. Joseph.
Raczka, Philip (NTN) Vocations Office.
Raczka, Philip (NTN) Priest's Sickness & Disability, and Retirement Plans.
Raczka, Philip (NTN) Protopresbyters.
Raczka, Philip (NTN) Presbyteral Council.
Raczynski, Paul L. '72 (MIL) Kenosha, WI St. Anthony.
Raczynski, Theodore T. '56 (HRT) Suffield, CT Sacred Heart.
Radaich, Thomas '70 (DUL) Grand Rapids, MN St. Joseph.
Radano, John A. '65 (NEW) On Duty Outside the Archdiocese.
Radasky, Robert '56 (ALT) Johnstown, PA St. Clement's.
Radde, James M. *s.j.* '72 (MIL)[O] Minneapolis, MN Georgetown Court, #211.
Radecki, Albin A. '49 (TOL) Retired.
Radecki, Dane J. *o.praem.* '77 (GB)[B] De Pere, WI St. Norbert College.
Radecki, Dane *o.praem.* '77 (GB)[I] De Pere, WI St. Joseph Priory; Appointed Representatives.
Radecki, Tomasz *s.v.d.* (CHI) Chicago, IL St. Constance.
Radek, James '89 (JOL) Joliet, IL St. Joseph.
Rademacher, Germain P. '58 (NU) College of Consultors; Priests' Council.
Rademacher, John R. '70 (GI) Grand Island, NE St. Leo.
Rademacher, Robert B. *g.h.m.* '55 (RIC) Clintwood, VA St. Joseph.
Rademacher, Robert *g.h.m.* '54 (CIN)[M] Cincinnati Headquarters of Glenmary Home Missioners.
Rader, John '91 (SFS) Bowdle, SD St. Augustine.
Radetski, John J. '77 (MIL) Fond du Lac, WI Holy Family.
Radetski, Paul J. (GB) Menasha, WI St. John; Menasha, WI St. Mary.
Radimecky, Val '01 (CC)[G] Robstown, TX Society of Our Lady of the Most Holy Trinity.
Radloff, James A. '93 (BAK) Council of Priests and Diocesan Consultors; La Pine, OR Holy Redeemer; [C] La Pine, OR Central Oregon Senior Living Communities, Inc. (The Redeemer Lodge).
Radloff, Thomas H. *s.j.* '61 (TOL)[C] Toledo, OH St. John's Jesuit High School.
Radloff, Thomas *s.j.* (TOL) Associate Vicar for Priests.
Radocha, Stephen J. (ALN) College of Consultors; Elected Members.
Radocha, Stephen '77 (ALN) Easton, PA St. Jane Frances de Chantal.
Radomski, Joseph A. '62 (TR) Avon, NJ St. Elizabeth.
Radon, Eugene M. '47 (BUF) Buffalo, NY Coronation of the Blessed Virgin Mary Retired.
Radosevich, Eugene A. '90 (PEO) Woodhull, IL St. John's.
Radosevich, Eugene '90 (PEO) Galva, IL St. John's.
Radosevich, George '68 (SFD) Livingston, IL Sacred Heart; Staunton, IL St. Ubaldus; Staunton, IL St. Michael the Archangel.
Radtke, Fred '67 (CHI)[N] Chicago, IL St. Peter's Friary.
Radtke, Fred '75 (CHI)[N] Chicago, IL Holy Evangelists Friary.
Radvansky, Joseph R. '65 (PRM) Marblehead, OH St. Mary.
Radvansky, Robert J. '55 (PSC) Edison, NJ St. Nicholas.
Radvansky, Robert (PSC) Eparchial Finance Officer; Eparchial Finance Council; Elected Members; Retirement Plan Board.
Raef, Scott '94 (AMA) Catholic Student Center at West Texas A & M University; Presbyteral Council; Vocation Development Team; Hart, TX St. John's; Tulia, TX Church of the Holy Spirit; [H] Canyon, TX Catholic Student Center at West Texas A & M University.
Raeke, Joseph K. '80 (BO) Holbrook, MA St. Joseph.
Rafacz, Joseph J. '56 (LC) Weston, WI St. Agnes.
Rafaj, Elias L. '99 (PBR) Pittsburgh, PA St. John the Baptist; Office of Religious Education.
Raferty, Paul C. *o.p.* '55 (OAK) Berkeley, CA St. Mary Magdalen.
Raffaeta, George J. '56 (HRT) Woodmont, CT St. Agnes Retired.
Raffel, Godfrey '53 (FRS) Retired.
Rafferty, Brian M. '62 (BAL) Pasadena, MD Our Lady of the Chesapeake.
Rafferty, Brian '94 (RIC) Norfolk, VA Christ the King; Scouting (Boys & Girls).
Rafferty, Colm *s.s.c.* '53 (LA) Los Angeles, CA St. Columban.
Rafferty, Gerard F. *s.s.l.* '79 (NY) West Nyack, NY St. Francis of Assisi.
Rafferty, J. Michael *o.a.r.* '03 (NY)[B] Suffern, NY Tagaste Monastery.
Rafferty, James A. '94 (SCR)[A] Dalton, PA Saint Pius X Seminary; Diocesan Commission on Ethics for Catholic Health Care Facilities.
Rafferty, James E. '72 (SD) Escondido, CA Church of St. Timothy.
Rafferty, James F. '63 (BO) Hingham, MA St. Paul.
Rafferty, James J. (BO) SOUTH REGION.
Rafferty, James R. '01 (DET) Bloomfield Hills, MI St. Hugo of the Hills.
Rafferty, James (SD) Vicars Forane.
Rafferty, Joseph P. '83 (SCR) Harveys Lake, PA Our Lady of Victory.
Rafferty, Lawrence B. '67 (RVC) Woodbury, NY Holy Name of Jesus.
Rafferty, Michael J. '57 (SCR) West Wyoming, PA Our Lady of Sorrows.
Rafferty, Raymond J. '54 (PRO) Retired.
Rafferty, Raymond M. '66 (NY) New York, NY Corpus Christi.
Rafferty, Thomas F. '83 (GAL) Houston, TX St. Justin Martyr.
Raffo, Caesar '85 (LA) Los Angeles, CA St. Gerard Majella.
Raffo, Frank M. '98 (R) Mount Olive, NC St. Mary.
Raffo–Rivasplata, Cesar '85 (LA) Torrance, CA L.A. County–Harbor–U.C.L.A. Medical Center.
Raftery, Paul *o.p.* '84 (P) Portland, OR Holy Rosary Parish & Dominican Priory.
Raftery, Thomas J. '44 (CHI) Chicago, IL Christ the King Retired.
Raftery, William J. '45 (WOR) Retired.
Ragan, Gerald '79 (SAV) Augusta, GA St. Mary on the Hill.
Ragan, James A. '98 (PBR) Ernest, PA St. Jude Thaddeus.
Rager, Patrick F. '85 (PIT) Absent on Sick Leave; Disabilities, Dept. for Persons with.
Ragni, Richard R. '66 (PIT) Washington County, PA Humbert Lane Health Care; Washington County, PA Kade's Nursing Home; Washington County, PA Presbyterian Senior Care.
Ragni, Richard '66 (PIT) Washington County, PA Washington City Health Center.
Ragnoni, James V. '60 (CLV) Akron, OH St. Anthony of Padua.
Ragsdale, Patrick '72 (SAT) San Antonio, TX Saint Padre Pio of Pietrelcina.
Ragusa, Salvatore *s.d.s.* '88 (MIL)[O] Oakland, CA Salvatorian House of Studies.
Ragusa, Salvatore *s.d.s.* '88 (OAK)[Q] Moraga, CA St. Mary's College Campus Ministry.
Rahilly, Paul '81 (RVC) Cedarhurst, NY St. Joachim.
Rahn, David C. '94 (ARL) On Leave of Absence.
Rahoy, Nicholas P. '77 (CI)[C] Tunnuk, Chuuk, FM Vicariate Residence; Chancellor; Finance Committee.
Rahrig, Gilbert O. (LAN) Building Commission.
Rahrig, Gilbert '49 (LAN) Retired.
Rai, Kevin '74 (AUS) Austin, TX San Jose.
Raible, Daniel *c.pp.s.* '43 (CIN)[B] Carthagena, OH St. Charles.
Raible, Roland *o.f.m.cap.* '35 (PIT)[N] Allison Park, PA St. Conrad Friary.
Raica, Steven J. '78 (LAN) On Duty Outside the Diocese.
Raich, Stephen *o.f.m.* '43 (CHI)[N] Chicago, IL St. Anthony's Friary.
Raiche, Brian '95 (ALB) Averill Park, NY St. Henry; Priestly Life and Ministry Council.
Raila, Donald *o.s.b.* '83 (GBG)[H] Latrobe, PA Saint Vincent Archabbey.
Raila, Stanislaus '33 (BRK) Retired.
Raimer, Chester J. '74 (GBG) Blairsville, PA SS. Simon and Jude; Torrance, PA Torrance State Hospital.
Raimondi, Michele '50 (SFR) Retired.
Raimondo, Joseph J. '40 (NY) Harrison, NY St. Gregory the Great Retired.
Rainaldo, John H. *s.j.* '64 (MIL)[O] Milwaukee, WI Jesuit Community at Marquette University.
Rainforth, Thomas G. '73 (PAT) Clifton, NJ St. Philip the Apostle.
Rainone, John J. '70 (PRO) Advocate; Cranston, RI St. Ann.
Rainville, Laurence P. *o.f.m.* '47 (ALB)[B] Siena College.
Rainville, Marcel R. *s.s.e.* '67 (BUR)[A] Colchester, VT St. Michael's College.
Rainville, Marcel R. *s.s.e.* '71 (BUR)[E] Colchester, VT Society of St. Edmund.
Rainville, Marcel R. *s.s.e.* (BUR) Elected Members; Diocesan Consultors; Leap.
Rainwater, Randall '96 (STO) Stockton, CA DeWitt Nelson Training Center.
Raj, Simon (BAL)[M] Baltimore, MD St. Agnes Health-Care, Inc..
Rajanayagam, Thomas M. '66 (STO) Riverbank, CA St. Frances of Rome Church (Pastor of).
Rajareegam, Paul K. '84 (CC) Skidmore, TX Immaculate Conception.
Rajendra, Gabriel L. *s.j.* '77 (CHL) Mooresville, NC St. Therese; [J] Mooresville, NC Jesuit Community.
Rajendram, J. Michael '90 (NY) New York, NY Cathedral of St. Patrick.
Raj Kocherla, Sundar '76 (JOL) Clarendon Hills, IL Notre Dame.
Rakaczki, Andor '73 (PSC) White Plains, NY St. Nicholas of Myra; Auditors.
Rakaczky, Basil M. *o.s.b.m.* '60 (PSC) Perth Amboy, NJ St. Michael; [A] Matawan, NJ Basilian Fathers of Mariapoch.
Rakaczky, Basil *o.s.b.m.* (PSC) Eparchial College of Consultors; Ex Officio Members; Advocate; Appointed Member.
Rakoczy, Richard S. '59 (DET) Waterford, MI St. Perpetua.
Rakoczy, Walter J. '78 (GRY) Portage, IN Nativity of Our Savior.
Rakotondrazanany, Mamy Oden Evariste *s.j.* '99 (OAK)[N] Berkeley, CA Jesuit Community at Jesuit School of Theology at Berkeley.
Rakowicz, William J. *s.j.* (MI) Judicial Vicar.
Rakowicz, William J. *s.j.* (CI) Judical Vicar.
Rakowiez, William J. *s.j.* '80 (CI)[C] Manresa Jesuit House.
Ralko, Martin J. '84 (COL) Dennison, OH Immaculate Conception.
Ralph, Edward *s.p.* (STL)[S] Dittmer, MO Vianney Renewal Center.
Ralph, Francis *o.p.* '72 (L) Louisville, KY St. Louis Bertrand.
Ralph, John '55 (WH) Retired.
Ralph, Thomas J. '56 (DUB) Retired.
Ramacciotii, James J. '85 (STL)[A] St. Louis, MO Kenrick School of Theology.
Ramacciotti, Gabriel M. *o.s.m.* '51 (DEN) Denver, CO Our Lady of Mt. Carmel.
Ramacciotti, Gabriel M. *o.s.m.* '51 (CHI)[N] Chicago Order of Friar Servants of Mary (Servites) United States of America Province, Inc..
Ramacciotti, James J. '85 (STL) Lemay, MO St. Martin of Tours.
Ramacher, Edward '45 (SCL) Roscoe, MN St. Michael's.
Ramadhani, Thomas Aquino Deshi *s.j.* '96 (OAK)[N] Berkeley, CA Jesuit Community at Jesuit School of Theology at Berkeley.
Ramaeker, Victor F. '61 (SC) Whittemore, IA St. Michael's; Diocesan Consultors.
Ramaekers, Timothy '82 (ORG) Placentia, CA St. Joseph.
Ramanaden, Bernard *o.s.b.* '53 (PAT)[M] Clifton, NJ Holy Face of Jesus Monastery.
Ramatowski, Edward '03 (STL) St. Louis, MO Assumption.
Ramellini, P. Lino '47 (GBG) Retired.
Ramelow, Anselm *o.p.* (OAK) Antioch, CA Holy Rosary.
Ramen, Paul F. '60 (NOR) Retired.
Ramenaden, Ronald '70 (FTW) North Manchester, IN St. Robert Bellarmine.
Ramer, James K. '86 (PEO) East Moline, IL St. Anne.
Ramer, Leo '54 (LAN) Retired.
Ramirez, Adalberto *o.f.m.* '64 (AMA) Hispanic Diaconate Office; Hispanic Diaconate Office; Amarillo, TX St. Laurence Cathedral.
Ramirez, Allen *o.f.m.conv.* '72 (SFR) San Francisco, CA St. Francis of Assisi, National Shrine.
Ramirez, Cesar '96 (ARE) Arecibo, PR Church of Sagrado Corazon de Jesus.
Ramirez, Charles J. '87 (LA) Monrovia, CA Immaculate Conception.
Ramirez, Cornelio C. *s.a.c.* '67 (LUB) Lubbock, TX St. Patrick.
Ramirez, Enrique Espinosa *m.sp.s.* '79 (LA) Oxnard, CA Our Lady of Guadalupe Parish.

Ramirez, Fernando '78 (SD) San Diego, CA St. Charles.
Ramirez, Francisco X. '79 (LA) Los Angeles, CA St. Patrick.
Ramirez, Gabriel '85 (ORG) Stanton, CA St. Polycarp.
Ramirez, Gerardo '91 (PCE) Patillas, PR Inmaculado Corazon de Maria.
Ramirez, Hernando *s.j.* '75 (FWT)[K] Lake Dallas, TX Montserrat Jesuit Retreat House.
Ramirez, J. Jesus '86 (YAK) Royal City, WA St. Michael the Archangel.
Ramirez, Jairo H. '88 (STO) Lodi, CA St. Anne Church (Pastor of).
Ramirez, Jose de Jesus (YAK) Diocesan Consultors; Spanish.
Ramirez, Jose Nieves '79 (ELP) Absent on Leave.
Ramirez, Jose *s.m.* '69 (STL)[O] Eureka, MO Marycliff Marianist Community; [O] Eureka, MO; [S] Eureka, MO Marianist Retreat & Conference Center.
Ramirez, Luis Ariel *c.m.* '94 (STO) Patterson, CA Sacred Heart Church of Patterson (Pastor of).
Ramirez, Luis Eduardo *o.a.r.* '03 (ORG) Santa Ana, CA Our Lady of the Pillar.
Ramirez, Luis '03 (ORG)[I] Santa Ana, CA Our Lady of the Pillar.
Ramirez, Mario *m.s.c.* '83 (NY) Staten Island, NY St. John Neumann.
Ramirez, Pedro (SPK) Priests' Personnel Board.
Ramirez, Rodolfo *tor* '76 (FWT) Fort Worth, TX St. John the Apostle.
Ramirez, Ybain F. '96 (ORL) Orlando, FL St. Isaac Jogues.
Ramirez–Alejos, Pedro '74 (SPK) Pasco, WA St. Patrick.
Ramirez–Portugal, Daniel '91 (LAR) Laredo, TX St. John Neumann; Presbyteral Council; Priests Personnel Board.
Ramler, Michael '74 (LEX) Somerset, KY St. Mildred; Whitley City, KY Good Shepherd Chapel.
Ramon, Gustavo J. '92 (LA) Los Angeles, CA Assumption.
Ramon, Valentino *c.m.f.* '64 (FRS) Fresno, CA St. Anthony Claret.
Ramon–Landry, Ken '87 (BLX) Lumberton, MS Our Lady of Perpetual Help; [A] St. Benedict, LA St. Joseph Seminary College.
Ramon–Landry, Ken (JKS) Trustees.
Ramon–Landry, Kenneth (BLX) Trustees.
Ramon–Landry, Kenneth *o.s.b.* (NO).
Ramon del Real, Jorge (SFR)[A] San Francisco, CA St. Peter.
Ramos, Andre '88 (SD) San Diego, CA Our Lady of Mt. Carmel.
Ramos, Angel Roman '90 (MGZ) Rincon, PR St. Rose of Lima.
Ramos, Antonio '94 (SFS) Sioux Falls, SD St. Michael; South Dakota State Penitentiary & Minnehaha County Jail.
Ramos, Cipriano '52 (SAC) Retired.
Ramos, Danilo '79 (DAL) Garland, TX Good Shepherd.
Ramos, Eusebio (CGS) Diocesan Consultors; Priests Senate.
Ramos, Hector Rivera (MGZ) Parish Priests Consultors.
Ramos, Justin S. *o.praem.* '95 (ORG)[D] Silverado, CA St. Michael's Preparatory School; [I] Silverado, CA Norbertine Fathers of Orange Inc..
Ramos, Marcos R. *o.p.* '01 (BR) Hammond, LA Holy Ghost.
Ramos, Octavio (NY) New York, NY St. Agnes.
Ramos, Ponciano *s.v.d.* '81 (SB)[A] Riverside, CA Society of the Divine Word Missionaries.
Ramos, Romeo '93 (SD) Chula Vista, CA Scripps Memorial Hospital; Chula Vista, CA Sharp Rees–Stealy Medical Center; National City, CA St. Mary.
Ramos, Sergio '99 (WDC) Takoma Park, MD Our Lady of Sorrows; [M] Takoma Park, MD Redemptoris Mater Archdiocesan Missionary Seminary.
Ramos, Victor '84 (LA) Pico Rivera, CA St. Francis Xavier.
Ramos, Victorino '54 (SJN) Union Eucaristica Reparadora (UNER) Retired.
Ramoso, Ireneo '89 (SFR) Redwood City, CA St. Pius.
Ramsey, James '84 (GAL) Damon, TX Sts. Cyril and Methodius; Needville, TX St. Michael.
Ramson, Ronald W. *c.m.* '59 (STL)[O] St. Louis, MO Lazarist Residence.
Ranaivoariso, Emile *s.j.* '97 (OAK)[N] Berkeley, CA Jesuit Community at Jesuit School of Theology at Berkeley.
Ranalletti, Richard A. *c.s.b.* '73 (DET)[E] Redford, MI Catholic Central High School.
Ranallo, John '75 (OAK) Eden Hospital; Glen Dyer Jail; Alameda County Jail–Santa Rita Rehabilitation Center.
Rancourt, Henry *s.m.* '57 (BO)[X] Framingham, MA The Marist House.
Randall, Ed (GAL) Western Vicariate; Appointees; College of Consultors.
Randall, Edward L. *o.m.i.* '50 (LEX) Jenkins, KY St. George.
Randall, Edward '64 (GAL) Houston, TX St. Michael; Building Commission.
Randall, John F. '53 (PRO) Retired.
Randall, Jude D. *o.s.b.* '60 (JOL)[C] Lisle, IL Benet Academy; [L] Lisle, IL St. Procopius Abbey.
Randall, Kevin S. '92 (NOR) On Duty Outside the Diocese; Air Force Reserve Chaplains.
Randall, Robert J. '51 (PRO) Retired.
Randazzo, Anthony J. '86 (NEW) North Caldwell, NJ Notre Dame.
Randl, Ewald '98 (NEW) Special Assignment in the Archdiocese.
Randone, Michael C. (BO) Haverhill, MA Sacred Hearts.
Randrianaivo, Jean de Dieu *s.j.* '99 (OAK)[N] Berkeley, CA Jesuit Community at Jesuit School of Theology at Berkeley; [N] San Francisco, CA Jesuit Community at University of San Francisco.
Ranek, Jerome '91 (SFS) Kimball, SD St. Margaret; Propagation of the Faith.
Raneri, Carmine B. '55 (HRT) Bristol, CT St. Gregory's Retired.
Raney, Isaac *m.s.a.* '67 (NOR)[F] Cromwell Society of the Missionaries of the Holy Apostles.
Raney, Isaac *m.ss.a.* '67 (DEN) Greeley, CO St. Peter.
Raney, Richard E. '38 (PEO) Retired.
Rangel, Carlos '99 (TYL) Centerville, TX St. Leo the Great; Hilltop Lakes, TX St. Thomas More.
Rangel, Romauldo *o.f.m.* '87 (ELP)[B] El Paso, TX Roger Bacon College.
Ranges, Charles H. *s.s.e.* '72 (BUR) Essex Junction, VT Holy Family; Essex Junction, VT St. Lawrence, Martyr.
Ranieri, John J. '82 (NEW)[B] School of Diplomacy and Intl. Rels..
Ranieri, Joseph A. '57 (WDC) Pastoral Center Special Ministries; Archdiocesan Building Commission.
Ranieri, Joseph (WDC) Coordinator, Pastoral Care of Priests.
Rank, Robert F. '68 (GB) On Duty Outside the Diocese.
Rank, Robert '67 (CC).
Rank, Robert *s.o.l.t.* '67 (AUS)[G] Austin, TX Society of Our Lady of the Most Holy Trinity, S.O.L.T..
Rank, Ronald G. '58 (MAD) Retired.
Rankin, James '65 (SD) Retired.
Rankin, Joseph M. '79 (L) Louisville, KY St. Francis of Assisi; Ex Officio.
Rankin, Joseph (L) College of Consultors.
Rankin, Paul B. *c.s.c.* '48 (FTW)[I] Notre Dame, IN Holy Cross House.
Rankin, Paul B. *c.s.c.* '48 (AUS)[G] Austin, TX Congregation of Holy Cross – Southern Province Retired.
Rankin, Robert '80 (VNN) Tucson, AZ St. Melany.
Rankin, Robert '80 (LA) On Duty Outside the Archdiocese.
Ranly, Ernest W. *c.pp.s.* '56 (CIN)[M] San Francisco de Borja.
Ranoa, Bernard '84 (SD) San Diego, CA St. Michael.
Rans, Norbert J. *m.m.* '64 (NY)[EE] Maryknoll Maryknoll Fathers and Brothers.
Ransom, Donald B. '64 (NEW) Rahway, NJ St. Mary's.
Ransom, Ralph R. *s.s.j.* '61 (BAL)[S] Baltimore, MD St. Joseph Society of the Sacred Heart House of Central Administration Retired.
Rantenburg, Joseph '73 (IND) Paoli, IN Our Lord Jesus Christ the King.
Ranzino, Thomas C. '78 (BR) Baton Rouge, LA St. George; Presbyteral Council; Worship, Office of; [A] St. Benedict, LA St. Joseph Seminary College.
Rapaglia, Eric (NY) Staten Island, NY Our Lady Star of the Sea.
Raphael, John *s.s.j.* '95 (WDC)[B] Washington, DC St. Joseph's Seminary; [S] Washington, DC Howard Univ. Newman Center.
Raphael, Mark S. '98 (NO) Chalmette, LA Our Lady of Prompt Succor.
Rapin, Cyril W. '46 (OG) Mooers Forks, NY St. Joseph Retired.
Rapose, Mario D. (OM) Omaha, NE St. Robert Bellarmine.
Raposo, John A. '77 (FR) Attleboro, MA Holy Ghost.
Rapp, Bernard A. (SD) Fallbrook, CA St. Peter.
Rapp, Bertrand J. '50 (L) Louisville, KY St. Bartholomew; Ex Officio Retired.
Rappold, Norbert F. '99 (LR) Mena, AR St. Agnes; Mount Ida, AR All Saints Church.
Rapposelli, Stephen J. '98 (CAM) Members.
Rapposelli, Stephen '98 (CAM) Marriage Preparation; Sewell, NJ Holy Family; Advocates.
Raptosh, Joseph R. (PBR) Elected Deanery Representatives.
Raptosh, Richard Joseph '87 (PBR) Monroeville, PA Church of the Resurrection.
Raquepo, Mario '79 (HON) Honolulu, HI St. John the Baptist; [E] Honolulu, HI St. Francis Medical Center.
Rara, Clarito Z. (MO).
Rareshide, Lanaux J. '61 (NO) Slidell, LA St. Margaret Mary; Slidell, LA Greenbriar Nursing & Convalescent Home; Slidell, LA Guest House of Slidell Nursing Home; Slidell, LA Trinity Neurologic Rehabilitation Center at Slidell; Deans.
Rarus, Boleslaus J. '40 (BGP)[P] Danbury, CT Pope John Paul II Center Retired.
Rasby, James W. '52 (DEN) Building Commission Retired.
Rasch, Richard S. *o.de.m.* '84 (CLV)[O] Cleveland, OH Mercedarians.
Rasch, Richard *o.de.m.* '84 (CLV) Cleveland, OH Our Lady of Mount Carmel.
Rascher, Joseph C. '81 (BEL) Caseyville, IL St. Stephen.
Raschke, Bernard L. '58 (LC) Retired.
Raschko, Michael '75 (SEA) Sammamish, WA Mary, Queen of Peace; Special Assignment.
Raschko, Michael (SEA) Censores Librorum; Theological Resources.
Rashford, John T. *s.j.* '71 (SEA)[L] Seattle, WA Jesuit Community.
Rashford, Nicholas J. *s.j.* '71 (PH)[C] Jesuit Fathers.
Rasing, Linus E. '53 (DUB) Retired.
Rask, Phillip J. '72 (STP) Maplewood, MN Presentation of the Blessed Virgin Mary.
Rasky, Joseph G. *s.m.* '65 (SAT)[M] San Antonio, TX Central Catholic Marianist Community.
Rasmussen, Harry W. *s.d.b.* '62 (MRY) Watsonville, CA Our Lady Help of Christians.
Rasmussen, Harry *s.d.b.* '62 (MRY)[F] Watsonville, CA Saint Francis Salesian Community.
Rasmussen, John '69 (SFS) Sioux Falls, SD St. Columba; Sioux Falls, SD St. Agnes.
Rasner, David L. '72 (LFT) Otterbein, IN St. Charles; Officialis; Presiding Judge; Censor Librorum.
Raso, Anthony F. '75 (BRK) Brooklyn, NY St. Sylvester.
Raspudic, Bruno *o.f.m.* '43 (CHI)[N] Chicago, IL St. Anthony's Friary.
Rasquinha, Gilbert Ignatius '65 (SB) Joshua Tree, CA St. Christopher of the Desert.
Rassas, George J. '68 (CHI) Lake Forest, IL St. Mary; College of Consultors.
Rassley, George *c.ss.r.* '53 (DEN)[N] Coeur D Alene, ID Loyalton #39.
Rassmussen, Terrence *o.f.m.conv.* '79 (DUB) Ames, IA St. Cecilia.
Rastrelli, Thomas P. '02 (DUB) Dubuque, IA Church of the Resurrection.
Rasura, James I. *s.j.* '56 (SD) San Diego, CA Our Lady of Guadalupe; Central Detention Facility and San Diego City Jail.
Raszeja, Norbert W. *c.r.* '72 (CHI)[N] Via San Sebastianello 11.
Raszewski, Edward *c.s.sp.* '47 (VEN)[G] Sarasota, FL Congregation of the Holy Ghost.
Rataj, Roman '98 (CHI) Chicago, IL St. Ferdinand.
Rataj, Stanley G. '79 (CHI) Chicago, IL St. Nicholas of Tolentine; Deans.
Ratajczak, Justin A. *o.f.m.conv.* '77 (ALT) Boswell, PA All Saints; Davidsville, PA St. Anne.
Ratajczak, Michael '75 (SD) Oceanside, CA St. Thomas More.
Ratajczak, Richard C. '58 (SAG) Kawkawlin, MI St. Valentine.
Ratazak, Bernard A. '76 (RCK) Retired.
Ratchford, Robert J. *s.j.* '61 (NO) Gretna, LA Jefferson Parish Correctional Center; [P] New Orleans, LA Ignatius Residence.
Raterman, Herbert J. *s.j.* '55 (CIN)[M] Cincinnati, OH Faber Jesuit Community; [V] Cincinnati, OH Living Monuments of Reparation.
Ratermann, David A. '51 (STL) On Duty Outside the Archdiocese.
Ratermann, George H. *m.m.* '47 (NY)[EE] Maryknoll Maryknoll Fathers and Brothers.
Ratermann, Jerome B. '57 (BEL) Retired.
Rath, John G. '36 (Y) Retired.
Rath, Martin F. *o.s.b.* '83 (NU) St. Mary's Care Center.
Rath, Martin *o.s.b.* '83 (NU)[C] Winsted, MN St. Mary's Care Center.
Rath, Martin *o.s.b.* '83 (SCL)[I] Collegeville, MN St. John's Abbey, of the Order of St. Benedict.
Rath, Richard J. '88 (STL) Arnold, MO St. David.
Rath, Thomas V. '49 (CLV) Amherst, OH St. Joseph; Lorain, OH St. John the Baptist Retired.
Rathapilly, Emanuel '71 (SJP) Northern Cambria, PA Immaculate Conception.
Rathfon, John R. '54 (CLV) Cuyahoga Falls, OH Immaculate Heart of Mary Retired.
Rathgeb, William R. '67 (GBG)[E] Greensburg, PA Clelian Heights School for Exceptional Children; [I] Greensburg, PA Apostles of the Sacred Heart of Jesus; Judicial Vicar.
Rathinam, Belevendiram S. '74 (RVC) Massapequa, NY St. Rose of Lima.
Rathinam, Selva *s.j.* '92 (OAK)[N] Berkeley, CA Jesuit Community at Jesuit School of Theology at Berkeley.
Rathschmidt, John *o.f.m.cap.* (BO)[V] Jamaica Plain, MA San Lorenzo Friary.
Ratigan, Patrick A. '83 (OG) Military Chaplains; Army Chaplains.
Ratterman, Kevin J. '94 (OKL) Enid, OK St. Francis Xavier.
Rattier, Jean Louis '74 (DET) Detroit, MI Holy Redeemer.
Ratzenberger, Raymond '85 (TUC) Benson, AZ Our Lady of Lourdes.
Ratzenberger, Raymond (TUC) Council of Priests;

Vicars Forane; All Vicars Forane.
Ratzmann, George '87 (VEN) Venice, FL Epiphany Cathedral.
Ratzmann, George (VEN) Presbyteral Council.
Rau, Peter J. '85 (ATL) Cumming, GA Good Shepherd.
Rau, Raymond F. '49 (BRK) Brooklyn, NY Holy Family; Corpus Christi, TX St. Theresa.
Rau, Raymond '56 (CC) Retired.
Rauch, David E. '70 (STL) On Duty Outside the Archdiocese; St. Louis, MO Our Lady of Providence.
Rauch, Edward L. *o.s.f.s.* '64 (PH)[AA] Philadelphia, PA Father Louis Brisson Residence.
Raudabaugh, Joseph R. '62 (CIN) Yellow Springs, OH St. Paul; [Q] Yellow Springs, OH Antioch College Campus Ministry.
Raudes, Santiago '02 (SAC) Citrus Heights, CA Holy Family.
Raulli, Enrico *s.j.* '65 (NEW)[C] Jersey City, NJ St. Peter's Preparatory School.
Raulli, Enrico *s.j.* '65 (NY)[EE] New York, NY West Side Jesuit Community.
Raun, Douglas A. '82 (SFE) Rio Rancho, NM St. Thomas Aquinas; Vicars Forane (Deans).
Rausch, Clyde *o.m.i.* '68 (FgM).
Rausch, Dale J. '68 (DUB) West Union, IA Holy Name; Clermont, IA St. Peter.
Rausch, John W. '47 (MIL) Retired.
Rausch, John *g.h.m.* '72 (CIN)[M] Cincinnati Headquarters of Glenmary Home Missioners.
Rausch, John *o.f.m.* '76 (STL)[O] St. Louis, MO Franciscan Friary of St. Anthony of Padua.
Rausch, John *g.h.m.* (LEX) Justice and Peace.
Rausch, Leon S. *s.j.* '59 (MIL)[O] Wauwatosa, WI Jesuit Community at St. Camillus.
Rausch, Thomas P. *s.j.* '72 (LA)[C] Los Angeles, CA Jesuit Community; Co–Chm.; Co–Chm..
Rausch, Thomas *s.j.* (LA) Members.
Rauscher, Donald F. *s.j.* '68 (STL)[O] St. Louis, MO Jesuit Community Corporation at St. Louis University – Jesuit Hall; [C] Saint Louis University.
Rauscher, Joseph G. '67 (SCR) Wilkes–Barre, PA St. Nicholas; Presbyteral Council.
Rauscher, Martin F. '60 (PAT) Morristown, NJ Assumption of the Blessed Virgin Mary.
Rauscher, Russell G. '75 (CLV) Medina, OH St. Francis Xavier.
Rautenberg, Joseph F. '73 (IND) Beech Grove, IN Holy Name.
Rautenberg, Joseph '73 (IND) Associates; [G] Indianapolis, IN St. Vincent Hospital and Health Care Center, Inc..
Rauth, Philip J. '59 (LIN) Auburn, NE St. Joseph's.
Rauth, Philip (LIN) Presbyteral Council.
Raux, Redmond P. '82 (BO) Military & VA Chaplains; Air Force Chaplains.
Rauzi, Mario *c.s.* '45 (CIN) Cincinnati, OH Sacred Heart.
Ravelojaona, Andre *m.s.* '57 (STL)[O] Generalate, Missionari di N.S. de La Salette.
Ravencamp, Michael W. *s.j.* '96 (LA) Santa Barbara, CA Our Lady of Sorrows.
Raveneau, Ricardo '90 (BRK) On Leave/Unassigned.
Ravey, Donald J. '61 (BUR) Elected Members; Canon 1742 Panel of Pastors; Williston, VT Immaculate Heart of Mary.
Ravi, Francis '88 (TR) Marlton, NJ St. Joan of Arc.
Ravizza, Mark A. *s.j.* '99 (SJ)[B] Santa Clara, CA Jesuit Community.
Ravlic, Cornelius C. '37 (LA) Retired.
Rawa, Jerome D. *s.m.* '55 (WH) Richwood, WV Holy Family.
Rawden, John A. '55 (LA) Retired.
Rawlins, John J. *s.s.j.* '45 (BAL)[S] Baltimore, MD St. Joseph's Manor.
Ray, James M. '75 (CHI) Other Assignments.
Ray, Robert E. '69 (L) Fairdale, KY St. Jerome; Louisville, KY St. John Vianney.
Ray, Xavier '97 (DET)[S] Livonia, MI Madonna University Campus Ministry; [C] Livonia, MI Madonna University.
Rayappan, Arul Joseph '87 (CHR) Blythewood, SC Transfiguration.
Rayappan, Philip S. '98 (SCR) Scranton, PA St. Patrick's.
Rayar, Thomas '93 (STP) Buffalo, MN St. Francis Xavier; Presbyteral Council.
Rayburn, Calvin (GB)[F] Oshkosh, WI Mercy Medical Center.
Rayder, Peter J. '02 (BRK) Brooklyn, NY Holy Name.
Rayer, Daniel J. '99 (LIN) Lincoln, NE St. Joseph; Advocates.
Rayes, Emanuel '54 (EST) Retired.
Rayes, Javier *o.f.m.* (SFR) San Francisco, CA St. Anthony of Padua.
Rayes, Joseph *o.f.m.* '57 (CIN)[M] Cincinnati, OH St. Ann Friary.
Raymond, David A. '03 (PRT) Caribou, ME Holy Rosary; Fort Fairfield, ME St. Denis; Limestone, ME St. Louis.
Raymond, David R. '89 (SPR) Cheshire, MA St. Mary of the Assumption; Lanesboro, MA North American Martyrs.
Raymond, Maurice L. '62 (SCR) Hazleton, PA Church of the Most Precious Blood.
Raymond, Wilfred *c.s.c.* '71 (FR)[N] North Easton, MA Holy Cross Family Ministries.
Raymond, Willie *c.s.c.* '71 (LA) Santa Monica, CA St. Monica.
Rayson, Robert '99 (PEO) Bradford, IL St. John the Baptist; Camp Grove, IL St. Patrick; Wyoming, IL St. Dominic's.
Razov, Elvis '94 (WDC) Washington, DC St. Blaise.
Razumov, Victor (PAT).
Re, Angelo '60 (SJ) Retired.
Read, Denis William *o.c.d.* '52 (MIA)[M] Miami, FL Discalced Carmelite Friars of Miami, Inc..
Read, Ignacio *o.c.d.* '56 (MIL)[O] Milwaukee Provincial Offices – Discalced Carmelites.
Reading, Edward '72 (PAT) On Duty Outside the Diocese.
Ready, Francis P. '50 (BO) Senior Priests Retired.
Ready, Frank J. '59 (ARL) Annandale, VA Holy Spirit; Diocesan Consultors.
Reagan, Donald '47 (Y) Retired.
Real, Fernando '81 (NY) Bronx, NY Santa Maria.
Real, Fernando *m.id.* '81 (NY)[EE] Bronx, NY Idente Missionaries – Santa Maria Residence.
Reale, Frank E. *s.j.* '81 (STL)[F] St. Louis, MO St. Louis University High School, George H. Backer Memorial; [O] St. Louis, MO Bellarmine House of Studies.
Reale, Sante J. *c.pp.s.* '60 (ORL)[M] Daytona Beach, FL.
Realmuto, George *m.s.a.* '87 (NOR)[F] Cromwell, CT Society of the Missionaries of the Holy Apostles.
Ream, Gerard J. '54 (ALT) Retired.
Reamer, Mark G. *o.f.m.* '91 (R) Raleigh, NC St. Francis of Assisi; Navy Reserve Chaplains.
Reamer, William G. '87 (OG) Plattsburgh, NY Champlain Valley Physicians Hospital Medical Center; Advocates.
Reardon, Daniel F. *c.s.v.* '61 (RCK)[G] McHenry, IL Villa Desiderata Retreat House.
Reardon, Daniel '97 (KC) On Duty Outside the Diocese.
Reardon, Dennis A. '72 (PRO) Wickford, RI St. Bernard.
Reardon, Francis '78 (PMB) Boca Raton, FL Our Lady of Lourdes; Presbyteral Council.
Reardon, James A. '01 (E) Erie, PA Our Lady of Mt. Carmel.
Reardon, James E. '65 (BIS)[G] Bismarck, ND Emmaus Place Retired.
Reardon, John D. '73 (PH) Flourtown, PA St. Genevieve; Defenders of the Bond; Secretary.
Reardon, John F. '50 (NY) Staten Island, NY St. Rita.
Reardon, John F. '76 (BO) Health Leave.
Reardon, John I. *o.p.* '49 (NO) New Orleans, LA St. Dominic Retired.
Reardon, Jonathan (NOR).
Reardon, Joseph D. (KC) Navy Chaplains.
Reardon, Michael *s.d.v.* '74 (LA) Long Beach, CA St. Cornelius; [M] Florham Park, NJ Father Justin Vocationary.
Reardon, Robert J. '59 (PIT)[N] Pittsburgh, PA St. John Vianney Manor.
Reardon, Thomas J. '51 (LC) Retired.
Reasbeck, David E. '56 (STU) Colerain, OH St. Frances Cabrini.
Reasoner, Mark J. '98 (DUB) Osage, IA Sacred Heart; Osage, IA Sacred Heart; Osage, IA St. Ansgar; Osage, IA Church of the Visitation.
Reaume, Michael R. *s.m.* '69 (STL)[O] St. Colmba's.
Reaves, Phillip A. '94 (LR) Texarkana, AR St. Edward's; Deans; Ashdown, AR St. Elizabeth Ann Seton Church; Foreman, AR Sacred Heart Church.
Rebaldo, Ronald '91 (RVC) Absent on Leave.
Rebamontan, Mario F. '70 (ORG) Fountain Valley, CA Holy Spirit.
Rebamontan, Marito (ORG) Council of Priests; Consultors.
Rebanal, Jeremias R. '55 (NEW) Jersey City, NJ St. Aedan's.
Rebanal, Jeremias (NEW) Filipino Apostolate.
Rebaque, Jose *s.a.c.* '70 (BGP) Shelton, CT St. Joseph.
Rebatzki, George M. '64 (MIL) Milwaukee, WI Old St. Mary.
Rebeck, Eugene M. '65 (TR) Holmdel, NJ St. Catharine; Monmouth and Mercer County; Tribunal Judges.
Rebel, John W. '65 (PIT) New Bedford, PA St. James; Lawrence County, PA Youth Development Center.
Rebel, Patrick M. '85 (SP) Dade City, FL Sacred Heart.
Rebelo, Valentine (RVC) Rockville Centre, NY Mercy Medical Center.
Rebert, Robert '58 (SFD) Comite Diocesano de Ministerio Hispano – Diocesan Committee for Hispanic Ministry; Special or Other Diocesan Assignment Retired.
Rebeta, James L. *c.s.c.* '73 (BGP)[P] White Plains, NY Cornell Medical Center.
Rebeyro, Lloyd '70 (ALB) Albany, NY St. Mary.
Rebman, Joseph F. '60 (WIL) Wilmington, DE St. Joseph on the Brandywine; Vicar General for Pastoral Services; Secretary, Pastoral Services Department; Catholic Cemeteries; Ecumenical Liaison; Marian Devotions; College of Consultors; Catholic Cemeteries, Inc.; Catholic Diocese of Wilmington, Inc..
Rebman, Joseph F. (WIL) Commission for the Catholic Missions Among the Colored People and the Indians.
Rebman, Joseph (BAL) Interdiocesan Judges.
Rebol, Anthony '56 (CLV) Cleveland, OH St. Lawrence; Administrative Leave.
Rebol, Francis *m.m.* '53 (SJ)[M] Los Altos, CA Maryknoll.
Rebold, John '54 (SFE) Retired.
Reboli, John P. *s.j.* '70 (WOR)[O] Worcester, MA Jesuits of Holy Cross College, Inc..
Rebollar, Gabriel Jaimes (R) Clinton, NC Immaculate Conception.
Rebong, Nestor D. '86 (LA) West Covina, CA St. Christopher.
Rebong, Nestor (LA) Cursillo Movement.
Rebosura, Sabino B. '87 (HT) Morgan City, LA Sacred Heart of Jesus.
Rebosura, Sabino (HT) Priests Council.
Rebovich, John '67 (PRM) Absent on Leave.
Rebuldela, Alfred '72 (HON) Makawao, HI St. Joseph.
Recaido, Florentino E. '02 (CHK) Saipan, MP Santa Remedios Parish; Saipan, MP San Roque Parish; Director of Youth Ministry; Presbyteral Council; Adult Leaders; San Roque Parish – Mother of Divine Love Praesidium; Director of Vocations.
Recchuti, William A. *o.s.a.* '61 (ALB) Mechanicville, NY Assumption–St. Paul.
Receconi, Edward R. *o.s.b.* '79 (SEA)[L] Lacey, WA St. Martin's Abbey.
Rechenburg, Basil *o.s.b.* '68 (WOR)[O] Still River, MA Benedictine Monks, St. Benedict Abbey.
Recio, Jesus Perez *o.a.r.* '68 (ELP) El Paso, TX Guardian Angel.
Recio, Julio *o.p.* '78 (SFR) San Francisco, CA Church of the Epiphany.
Reck, Donald W. *s.j.* '65 (STL)[C] Saint Louis University; [O] St. Louis, MO Leo Brown Jesuit Community.
Recker, Odo *o.s.b.* '78 (P)[L] St. Benedict, OR Mt. Angel Abbey; [A] St. Benedict, OR Mount Angel Seminary.
Recker, Philip F. '59 (DUB) Retired.
Reckinger, Robert A. '51 (DET) Retired.
Reckker, Stephen C. '63 (DET) Romeo, MI St. Clement of Rome.
Rector, Warren *o.f.m.* '68 (CAM) Oaklyn, NJ St. Aloysius; [H] Camden, NJ Our Lady of Lourdes Medical Center.
Rector, Warren *o.f.m.* '68 (PH)[AA] Philadelphia, PA St. Pius X Friary.
Reczek, Felix J. *o.f.m.* '44 (BUR) Bellows Falls, VT Sacred Heart.
Reczek, Paul *o.f.m.* '72 (MIL)[O] Provincial Offices.
Redcay, Christopher '89 (PH) Blue Bell, PA St. Helena.
Redcay, T. Christopher '89 (PH)[D] Norristown, PA 0.Kennedy–Kenrick Catholic High School.
Redden, Don '59 (PMB) Special Assignment.
Redden, Michael J. '72 (ATL) Fort Oglethorpe, GA St. Gerard Majella.
Reddick, E. Peter '72 (SY) Syracuse, NY St. Patrick.
Reddimasu, Thomasiah '90 (CHR) Folly Beach, SC Our Lady of Good Counsel.
Reddy, Gade Show '91 (CHR) Aiken, SC St. Mary, Help of Christians; [H] Aiken, SC University of South Carolina, Aiken Extension.
Reddy, Reginald J. *o.f.m.* '61 (ALB)[B] Siena College; [R] Albany, NY St. Francis Chapel.
Redinbo, Joseph *o.f.m.* '59 (GLP) Gallup, NM St. Francis of Assisi.
Reding, Michael A. '97 (STP) Wayzata, MN St. Bartholomew.
Redington, James *s.j.* '78 (OAK)[M] Washington, DC Woodstock Jesuit Community; [V] Washington, DC Woodstock Theological Center.
Redlon, Reginald *o.f.m.* '49 (BO)[Y] Boston, MA Saint Anthony Residence.
Redmerski, Stanley J. '58 (LIN) Retired.
Redmond, Arthur S. '55 (LC) Stratford, WI St. Andrew Retired.
Redmond, Daniel P. '96 (CLV) North Royalton, OH St. Albert the Great.
Redmond, Donald *o.s.b* '57 (KCK)[H] Atchison, KS St. Benedict's Abbey.
Redmond, Lawrence '64 (ORL) Retired.
Redmond, Paul V. '54 (ALB) On Duty Outside the Diocese; [B] Emmitsburg, MD Mount Saint Mary's College.
Redmond, Sean P. '90 (LIN) Nebraska City, NE St. Joseph's.
Redmond, Sean (LIN) Presbyteral Council.
Redstone, James '98 (NEW) Cedar Grove, NJ St. Catherine of Siena.
Redulla, Arsenio C. '74 (LUB) Floydada, TX St. Mary Magdalen.
Redulla, Flordito *s.v.d.* (FRS) Fresno, CA St. Therese; Community Hospital, Veterans' Hospital & University Medical Center.
Redwanski, Dale H. *o.s.c.* '71 (DET)[K] Riverview, MI

Crosier Community of Riverview; Riverview, MI St. Cyprian.
Redwick, Adolph '59 (DET) Dearborn, MI St. Joseph.
Reece, Richard T. *o.s.f.s.* '65 (PH)[AA] Wyndmoor, PA Villa de Sales Oblate Residence.
Reece, Robert *o.s.f.s.* '65 (ALN)[L] Reading, PA St. Joseph Villa.
Reed, Albert A. *c.pp.s.* '54 (CIN)[U] Dayton, OH Community Support Charitable Trust.
Reed, Albert *c.pp.s.* '54 (CIN)[B] Carthagena, OH St. Charles.
Reed, Bruce '93 (RVC) Absent on Leave.
Reed, Dennis L. '69 (DOD) Belpre, KS St. Bernard; Larned, KS Sacred Heart.
Reed, Dennis (DOD) Diocesan School Council.
Reed, Douglas '71 (R) Kinston, NC Holy Spirit Catholic Church.
Reed, H. William '62 (NO) Marrero, LA The Visitation of Our Lady; Council of Catholic School Cooperative Clubs; Council of Catholic Women; National Council of Catholic Women.
Reed, John Philip *m.afr.* '88 (WDC)[M] Washington, DC Missionaries of Africa.
Reed, Michael V. '84 (PT) Pensacola, FL Cathedral of the Sacred Heart; Chancellor.
Reed, Michael (PT) Vicar for Religious; Promoter of Justice; Administrative Council; Building & Renovation, Diocesan Commission for; Campaign for Human Development, Office of; Finance, Diocesan Commission for; Holy Name Society; Orders & Ministries, Commission for; Moderator of the Curia; Priests' Pension Plan, Board for.
Reed, Robert J. '61 (ALN) Bethlehem, PA SS. Simon and Jude.
Reed, Robert P. '85 (BO) Whitman, MA Holy Ghost; Radio Apostolate.
Reed, William C. '71 (NEW) Elizabeth, NJ Our Lady of Most Holy Rosary/St. Michael.
Reed, William '71 (NEW) Rahway, NJ Rahway Hospital; Rahway Hospital.
Reedy, Gerard *s.j.* '70 (NY)[C] Tarrytown, NY Marymount College of Fordham University; [EE] Cardinal Spellman Hall, Jesuit Community.
Reedy, John J. '35 (P) Retired.
Reen, Jeremiah *s.d.b.* '71 (PMB) Belle Glade, FL St. Philip Benizi.
Reese, Benjamin B. '91 (PEO) Peoria, IL St. Mark's.
Reese, Charles T. '49 (CHL) Retired.
Reese, Donald B. '63 (CAM) On Duty Outside the Diocese.
Reese, Edward *s.j.* '73 (PHX)[B] Phoenix, AZ Brophy College Preparatory.
Reese, Francis X. *s.j.* '60 (CHL) Hot Springs, NC Chapel of the Redeemer; [J] Mooresville, NC Jesuit Community; [M] Hot Springs, NC Jesuit House of Prayer.
Reese, Matthew A. '02 (ALT) Ebensburg, PA Holy Name.
Reese, Robert P. '89 (ALT) Johnstown, PA St. Benedict's.
Reese, Thomas J. *s.j.* '74 (NY)[EE] New York, NY "America;" Residence and publication office of the America Press; [II] New York, NY America Press, Inc..
Reeson, David G. '80 (OM) Military Chaplains; Air Force Chaplains.
Reeves, Joseph R. '76 (P)[J] Portland, OR Providence St. Vincent Medical Center.
Reeves, Joseph '76 (BAK) Retired.
Reeves, Mark Thomas '02 (MIA) North Miami, FL Holy Family.
Refermat, Thomas '94 (CHI) Chicago, IL St. Cornelius.
Regado, Justo Beltran '69 (BRK)[A] Woodhull Medical & Mental Health Center.
Regalado, Luis *o.s.b.* '84 (SFE)[I] Abiquiu, NM Monastery of Christ in the Desert.
Regales, Oriol '01 (MIL)[X] Racine, WI Missionary Community of St. Paul the Apostle and Mary, Mother of the Church, Inc.; Racine, WI St. Patrick.
Regan, Charles W. (WCH) Parish Priest Consultors.
Regan, Charles (WCH) Retired.
Regan, Columkille '49 (NY)[EE] Bronx, NY Passionist Residence.
Regan, Dennis M. '64 (RVC) Commack, NY Christ the King; [I] Rockville Centre, NY Catholic Healthcare Network of Long Island.
Regan, Desmond '46 (BIR) Retired.
Regan, Francis A. '53 (BO) Marshfield, MA St. Christine.
Regan, Gerald T. *s.j.* '64 (Wisconsin)[A] Mobile, AL Spring Hill College.
Regan, John D. '53 (HRT) College of Consultors Retired.
Regan, John J. '48 (BO) Senior Priests; AUXILIARY CHAPLAINS CONTRACT CHAPLAINS Retired.
Regan, John J. '53 (FR) Retired.
Regan, John '48 (PHX) Luke Air Force Base, AZ Luke Catholic Community.
Regan, John '89 (JOL)[O] Joliet, IL Fiat House of Discernment; Vocations.
Regan, Michael J. '62 (BO) Senior Priests Retired.
Regan, Michael J. '64 (BO) Abington, MA St. Bridget.
Regan, Richard J. *s.j.* '63 (NY)[EE] Cardinal Spellman Hall, Jesuit Community.
Regan, Richard J. '85 (SAN) Big Spring, TX Immaculate Heart of Mary.
Regan, Robert F. *s.j.* '59 (PRT) Portland, ME St. Pius X.
Regan, Robert F. *s.j.* '59 (BO)[V] Boston The Society of Jesus of New England–Provincial Offices.
Regan, Terrence P. '68 (GF) Stanford, MT St. Rose of Lima.
Regan, Terry (GF) Diocesan Consultors; Priests' Council.
Regan, Thomas J. *s.j.* '87 (BO)[V] Watertown, MA The Society of Jesus of New England–Provincial Offices; [V] Newton, MA The Jesuit Community at Boston College.
Regan, Timothy J. '91 (DAV) Special Assignment; [M] Davenport, IA St. Vincent Center; D.C.C.W..
Regan, William P. '56 (SY) Retired.
Regan, William '56 (SY)[Q] Syracuse, NY Tommy Coyne Residence @ Dillon Hall.
Regensburger, Edmund *c.ss.r.* '46 (VEN) Wauchula, FL St. Michael.
Reger, George L. '69 (BUF) Buffalo, NY Blessed Trinity.
Regh, John A. '53 (SUP) Rib Lake, WI St. John the Baptist.
Regh, John '53 (SUP) Retired.
Reginato, Julian '64 (GR) Muskegon, MI St. Francis de Sales.
Rego, Richard J. '83 (TUC) Ajo, AZ Immaculate Conception.
Regoli, John A. '61 (GBG) Sutersville, PA St. Charles Borromeo; West Newton, PA Holy Family; Bishop's Priests Council.
Regotti, Benjamin *o.f.m.cap.* '79 (PH) Philadelphia, PA St. John the Evangelist.
Regula, Gary (PHX) Flagstaff, AZ San Francisco de Asis; Advocates.
Regula, Ronald R. '67 (NEW) On Duty Outside the Archdiocese.
Regynski, Larry '95 (SFS) Mitchell, SD Holy Family.
Rehage, Joseph W. *c.s.c.* '46 (FTW)[I] Notre Dame, IN Holy Cross House.
Rehage, Joseph W. *c.s.c.* '46 (AUS)[G] Austin, TX Congregation of Holy Cross – Southern Province Retired.
Rehkemper Robert C. '49 (DAL) Hope, AR Our Lady of Good Hope Retired.
Rehling, Paul L. '56 (CIN) Cincinnati, OH St. William Retired.
Rehme, Albert A. '56 (STL) Retired.
Rehrauer, Matthew J. '92 (SPC) Piedmont, MO St. Catherine of Siena; Presbyteral Council.
Rehrauer, Stephen *c.ss.r.* '80 (DEN)[N] Chicago, IL Redemptorist Theology Residence.
Reich, John C. '84 (WH) Mullens, WV St. John the Evangelist.
Reich, Paul A. *s.m.* '57 (BAL) Eldersburg, MD St. Joseph.
Reichel, Bill *o.f.m.* '61 (CIN)[M] Cincinnati, OH St. John the Baptist Friary.
Reichenbacher, Charles *o.s.b.* '67 (RCK)[G] Aurora, IL Marmion Abbey.
Reicher, A. Paul '62 (CHI) Chicago, IL Notre Dame.
Reichert, Eldon G. *s.m.* '52 (CLV)[O] Cleveland, OH Marianist Community.
Reichert, Eldon *s.m.* '52 (CLV) Cleveland, OH St. Aloysius – St. Agatha.
Reichert, Henry J. '63 (JC) Mexico, MO St. Brendan.
Reichert, J. Lawrence '71 (COL) Johnstown, OH Church of the Ascension.
Reichert, James J. '71 (ALN) Martins Creek, PA St. Rocco; College of Consultors; Appointed Members.
Reichert, James *o.s.b.* '59 (SCL)[I] Collegeville, MN St. John's Abbey, of the Order of St. Benedict.
Reichert, Kenneth *o.s.b.* '59 (KC)[A] Conception, MO Conception Seminary College; [J] Conception, MO Conception Abbey.
Reichert, Ralph J. '49 (TOL) Retired.
Reichlin, Urban A. '39 (CLV) Cleveland, OH St. Vincent de Paul Retired.
Reichling, David *o.f.m.cap.* '67 (GF) Billings, MT St. Bernard's.
Reichling, Paul *o.f.m.cap.* '65 (GF) Billings, MT Little Flower; Billings, MT Our Lady of Guadalupe.
Reichmann, James B. *s.j.* '53 (SEA)[A] Seattle, WA Seattle University.
Reicks, Leander H. '44 (DUB) Retired.
Reid, David P. *ss.cc.* '66 (FR)[H] Fairhaven, MA Sacred Hearts Provincial House.
Reid, George B. '53 (WDC) Barnesville, MD St. Mary Church and Shrine of Our Lady of Fatima Retired.
Reid, Gerard E. '77 (Montego Bay) Berkeley, CA St. Joseph The Worker.
Reid, Malcolm '57 (CHY) Rawlins, WY St. Joseph's; Rawlins, WY Wyoming State Penitentiary.
Reid, Michael J. (BRK) Cemeteries; Catholic Cemetery Guild.
Reid, Michael P. '00 (HBG) New Freedom, PA St. John the Baptist; Gettysburg, PA St. Francis Xavier's.
Reid, Michael (HBG) Pastoral Council, Diocesan.
Reid, R. Michael '69 (RVC) Uniondale, NY Holly Patterson Geriatric Center; Baldwin, NY St. Christopher.
Reidman, John '62 (SFS) Montrose, SD St. Patrick.
Reidy, James E. '56 (STP)[C] St. Paul, MN University of St. Thomas Retired.
Reidy, Richard F. '94 (WOR) Worcester, MA St. Paul's Cathedral.
Reidy, Richard (WOR) Members; Diocesan Scouts.
Reidy, Robert J. '75 (CLV) Casa Parroquial Santo Domino.
Reidy, Robert '62 (Y) Retired.
Reidy, Thomas E. '67 (SPC) Springfield, MO Holy Trinity; Vicars General; Chancellor; Catholic Foundation Of The Diocese Of Springfield–Cape Girardeau; Judicial Vicar; Vicar For The Religious; Catholic Relief Services; Cemeteries; National Shrine Of The Immaculate Conception; Priests' Mutual Benefit Society; Diocesan Consultors; Appointed Members; St. Vincent De Paul Society.
Reif, Bryan T. '01 (CIN) Liberty Township, OH St. Maximilian Kolbe.
Reif, John '65 (ROC) Rochester, NY Holy Cross.
Reifel, Mark *t.o.r.* '55 (ALT) Windber, PA St. Anthony of Padua.
Reifenberg, Philip D. (MIL) Cudahy, WI Nativity of the Lord Parish; Judges for Second Instance; Promoters of Justice.
Reiff, Dale C. '67 (SC) Halbur, IA Sacred Heart.
Reiff, Dale E. '67 (SC) Halbur, IA St. Augustine's; Halbur, IA Holy Angels; Presbyteral Council.
Reiff, Dennis '81 (NEW) Paramus, NJ Our Lady of the Visitation.
Reifsnyder, John A. '41 (COV) Retired.
Reifsnyder, John A. '41 (PIT) Pittsburgh, PA Sacred Heart.
Reigel, Joseph P. '97 (E) Ridgway, PA St. Leo the Great.
Reigel, William A. *c.s.b.* (MO) AUXILIARY CHAPLAINS CONTRACT CHAPLAINS.
Reiker, H. John (STL) Archdiocesan Priests' Personnel Board.
Reiker, John '78 (STL) St. Louis, MO Immaculate Heart of Mary.
Reiker, Robert J. '73 (STL) O'Fallon, MO Immaculate Conception.
Reikowski, Miroslaw '96 (RCK) Elgin, IL St. Joseph.
Reiley, Robert J. *m.m.* '59 (NY)[EE] Maryknoll Maryknoll Fathers and Brothers.
Reilley, Thomas J. *s.j.* '95 (LA)[Q] Culver City, CA.
Reilly, Bernard '73 (LAN) Jackson, MI St. Mary, Star of the Sea.
Reilly, Cristobal *s.t.* '55 (PCE) Coamo, PR St. Blase.
Reilly, David F. '75 (CIN) Shandon, OH St. Aloysius.
Reilly, Denis *o.p.* '70 (SLC) Salt Lake City, UT St. Catherine of Siena; [H] Salt Lake City, UT University of Utah, Newman Center.
Reilly, Donald F. *o.s.a.* '74 (PH)[C] Villanova, PA Villanova University; [AA] Villanova, PA Provincial Offices of the Order of St. Augustine, Province of St. Thomas of Villanova; [AA] Villanova, PA St. Thomas of Villanova Friary; (FgM).
Reilly, Edward W. (STL) Archdiocesan Priests' Personnel Board.
Reilly, Edward '54 (STL) St. Louis, MO Mary, Mother of the Church.
Reilly, F. Joseph '58 (STL) Ste. Genevieve, MO St. Catherine of Alexandria; Ste. Genevieve, MO SS. Philip and James.
Reilly, Francis E. '80 (SPR) Longmeadow, MA St. Mary's; [P] Longmeadow, MA Bay Path College.
Reilly, Gavin *o.f.m.cap.* '54 (NY) New York, NY St. John the Baptist; [HH] New York, NY Fashion Institute of Technology (SUNY); [V] Brooklyn, NY St. Michael's Friary.
Reilly, George M. '60 (NEW) New Milford, NJ St. Joseph's; Serra Clubs.
Reilly, James F. '68 (NEW) Palisades Park, NJ St. Michael's.
Reilly, James J. '68 (NEW) Kearny, NJ Our Lady of Sorrows; [Q] Bloomfield, NJ Bloomfield College.
Reilly, John E. *s.j.* '59 (CHI)[C] Chicago, IL Jesuit Community at Loyola University Chicago.
Reilly, John *s.m.* '53 (SJ)[M] Cupertino, CA San Juan Residence.
Reilly, Joseph R. '91 (NEW)[A] South Orange, NJ Seton Hall University College Seminary; Censors of Books.
Reilly, Joseph (NEW)[B] School of Diplomacy and Intl. Rels.; Priestly Vocation Board.
Reilly, Kevin M. '03 (NOR) Old Saybrook, CT St. John.
Reilly, L. Leo *c.s.b.* '62 (DET) Detroit, MI Ste. Anne.
Reilly, Lawrence T. '64 (YAK) Cle Elum, WA St. John the Baptist; Cle Elum, WA Immaculate Conception.
Reilly, Mark R. '97 (OG) Watertown, NY Holy Family; [B] Watertown, NY Immaculate Heart Central High School; Priest Personnel Board; Navy Reserve Chaplains.
Reilly, Michael J. '01 (PH)[D] Philadelphia, PA John W. Hallahan Catholic Girls High School; Philadelphia, PA St. Bridget.
Reilly, Michael P. '92 (NY)[F] New York, NY St. Joseph by the Sea, High School; [T] New York, NY Mission of

the Immaculate Virgin.
Reilly, Patrick '58 (LA) Burbank, CA St. Robert Bellarmine Retired.
Reilly, Philip J. '60 (BRK) Special Assignment; [W] Brooklyn, NY Monastery of the Sisters Adorers of the Precious Blood.
Reilly, Rembert F. *o.s.b.* '59 (PAT)[M] Morristown, NJ St. Mary's Abbey.
Reilly, Robert E. '58 (L) Louisville, KY Our Lady Retired.
Reilly, Robert F. '55 (COL) Retired.
Reilly, Robert J. '45 (E) Erie, PA St. Mary Retired.
Reilly, Scott *l.c.* '97 (ATL)[O] Atlanta, GA Home and Family, Inc..
Reilly, Steven *l.c.* '94 (WDC)[M] Potomac, MD Legionaries of Christ.
Reilly, Terence *o.p.* '59 (OAK)[N] Oakland, CA Dominican Order, Siena House.
Reilly, Thomas A. *m.s.* '72 (ATL) Marietta, GA Church of St. Ann.
Reilly, Thomas J. '67 (BO) Foxborough, MA St. Mary; Woburn, MA St. Barbara.
Reilly, Timothy D. '03 (PRO) East Providence, RI St. Francis Xavier; On Duty Outside the Diocese.
Reilly, William J. '65 (NEW) Garfield, NJ Holy Name; Council for Multi–Cultural Concerns.
Reilly, William L. *s.j.* '45 (NY)[EE] Loyola Hall, Jesuit Community.
Reilman, Thomas J. '61 (DAV) Retired.
Reily, Scott *l.c.* '97 (ATL)[K] Atlanta, GA Legionaries of Christ; [B] Atlanta, GA St. Pius X Catholic High School.
Reim, Daniel T. *s.j.* '95 (DET)[K] Temperance, MI.
Reimer, Edward J. '67 (SY) Chittenango, NY St. Patrick; Jamesville, NY Jamesville Penitentiary.
Reimer, Ronald P. '62 (GB) Manitowoc, WI St. Paul.
Rein, Robert '74 (OAK) Concord, CA Queen of All Saints.
Reina, Nicholas J. *s.d.b.* '78 (OAK)[E] Richmond, CA Salesian High School.
Reina, Nicholas *s.d.b.* (MRY) St. Francis Central Coast Catholic High School, Inc..
Reina, Richard A. '70 (BUF) Kenmore, NY St. John the Baptist.
Reinbold, Charles '56 (NEW) Retired.
Reinders, David H. '97 (TUC) Tucson, AZ U.S. Veterans Hospital.
Reinders, David (TUC) Diocesan Building Committee.
Reinersman, Gerald L. '79 (COV)[N] Covington, KY St. Walburg Monastery; Vicar General and Episcopal Vicar for Administrative Services; Diocesan Consultors.
Reinert, Duane F. *o.f.m.cap.* '76 (KC)[A] Conception, MO Conception Seminary College; Haskell Institute; [H] Lawrence, KS St. Conrad's Friary; [K] Lawrence, KS Haskell Catholic Campus Center.
Reinert, Ellis *o.carm.* '49 (NEW) Englewood, NJ St. Cecilia's.
Reinert, James M. '83 (LIN) On Duty Outside the Diocese.
Reinert, James (NY) New York, NY St. Michael.
Reinhardt, Leo J. '78 (ROC) Ithaca, NY Immaculate Conception.
Reinhardt, Leo S. '55 (BEL) Retired.
Reinhardt, Mark S. '96 (PRT) Rockland, ME St. Bernard's; Personnel Board.
Reinhardt, Mark '96 (PRT) Clergy Benefit Plan–Clergy Pension Plan.
Reinhardt, Michael D. '01 (PHX) Phoenix, AZ St. Catherine of Siena.
Reinhart, Blaise R. *o.f.m.* '55 (ALB)[B] Siena College.
Reinhart, David A. '98 (TOL) Toledo, OH St. Patrick of Heatherdowns; Youth, Young Adult Ministry and Campus Ministry.
Reinhart, Kenneth *o.f.m.cap.* '68 (GB) Appleton, WI St. Joseph; [I] Appleton, WI St. Joseph Friary.
Reinhart, Robert C. *c.pp.s.* '53 (LFT) Bryant, IN Holy Trinity.
Reinhart, Robert J. '61 (TOL) Toledo, OH Blessed Sacrament; Toledo Northwest.
Reinheimer, George '50 (NY)[EE] Bronx, NY.
Reinig, Joseph (BAK) Northern; Hermiston, OR Our Lady of Angels.
Reinke, Francis P. '57 (GB) Retired.
Reinke, Robert J. '49 (COV) Retired.
Reinke, Robert J. '57 (COV) Covington, KY St. Augustine; Ludlow, KY Sts. Boniface and James Retired.
Reinkemeyer, John C. '51 (WCH) Garden Plain, KS Immaculate Conception; Legion of Mary.
Reinkemeyer, John '57 (WCH) Retired.
Reinoso, Carlos Alberto *o.r.c.* '96 (PCE) Castaner, PR Our Lady of the Miraculous Medal.
Reinsfelder, John L. '49 (BAL) Baltimore, MD Holy Cross; Baltimore, MD St. Mary, Star of the Sea Retired.
Reinsfelder, John '49 (BAL)[W] Ellicott City, MD Legion of Mary.
Reis, Antonio (OAK) San Leandro, CA St. Leander.
Reis, Daniel O. '75 (FR) New Bedford, MA Our Lady of the Immaculate Conception.
Reis, Justin J. '69 (COL) Lancaster, OH St. Bernadette; Vicariate 12: Lancaster; Catholic Charismatic Renewal, Inc..
Reis, Lancelot '67 (PAT) Chester, NJ St. Lawrence the Martyr.
Reis, Michael J. '67 (COL) Heath, OH St. Leonard.
Reis, Raymond H. *s.j.* '37 (STL)[O] St. Louis, MO Jesuit Community Corporation at St. Louis University – Jesuit Hall.
Reis, Timothy P. '86 (FR) Taunton, MA St. Joseph's.
Reisch, Milton L. '60 (NO) Retired.
Reisch, Wojciech '92 (SAT) Panna Maria, TX Immaculate Conception of the Blessed Virgin Mary.
Reischl, Fred P. '55 (DM) Retired.
Reischman, Virgil '69 (STU) Barnesville, OH Assumption; Barnesville, OH St. Mary's.
Reisdorff, Clarence P. '46 (LIN) Retired.
Reiser, Bernard A. '49 (STP) Coon Rapids, MN Church of the Epiphany Retired.
Reiser, John '56 (MIA) Absent on Sick Leave.
Reiser, Richard J. '80 (OM) Omaha, NE Our Lady of Lourdes.
Reiser, Robert E. *s.j.* '97 (NY) New York, NY Nativity; [EE] New York, NY Jesuit Provincial's Office.
Reiser, William E. *s.j.* '72 (WOR)[O] Worcester, MA Jesuits of Holy Cross College, Inc.; [O] Worcester, MA Casa Santa Maria del Camino, Inc.; [S] Worcester, MA Casa Santa Maria del Camino, Inc.; Our Lady of Fatima.
Reisert, Frederick J. *s.j.* '54 (BUF)[O] Buffalo, NY Canisius Jesuit Community.
Reisert, Gregory *o.f.m.cap.* '64 (NY)[EE] New York, NY Development Office:.
Reising, Ray (EVN) Legion of Mary.
Reising, Raymond '45 (EVN) Retired.
Reisinger, Walter J. *c.m.* '55 (JC) Dixon, MO St. Cornelius; Dixon, MO St. Theresa.
Reisinger, Walter J. *c.m.* '55 (STL)[O] Perryville, MO Congregation of the Mission.
Reiske, Steven R.W. '90 (FAR) Absent on Leave.
Reiss, John E. '69 (Y) Youngstown, OH Holy Name; Youngstown, OH Our Lady of Hungary.
Reissmann, Richard A. '63 (WIL) Newark, DE St. John the Baptist–Holy Angels.
Reissmann, Richard A. (BAL) Interdiocesan Judges.
Reisteter, William *o.f.m.* '71 (ALN)[K] Easton, PA St. Francis Friary.
Reisz, Leonard '50 (OWN) Non–Parochial Assignments.
Reiter, James E. '90 (ROM) McKeesport, PA St. Mary; McKeesport, PA.
Reiter, James (E) CIVIL AIR PATROL.
Reites, James W. *s.j.* '71 (SJ)[B] Santa Clara, CA Jesuit Community.
Reith, David H. '76 (MIL) Burlington, WI Immaculate Conception.
Reith, Herman R. *c.s.c.* '42 (FTW)[I] Notre Dame, IN Holy Cross House.
Reitmeyer, Todd '03 (SFS) Sioux Falls, SD St. Michael; Navy Reserve Chaplains.
Reitter, Frank J. *s.m.* '84 (ANC) Soldotna, AK Our Lady of Perpetual Help.
Reitz, Andrew J. *o.f.m.* '71 (TR) Brant Beach, NJ St. Francis of Assisi.
Reitz, Joseph A. '53 (GAY) Retired.
Reitz, Louis M. *s.s.* '55 (BAL)[S] Casa de Nuestre Senore Dolorosa Retired.
Reitz, William J. '47 (GR) Carson City, MI St. Mary's; Carson City, MI St. John the Baptist.
Rejent, Michael *o.s.f.s.* (KAL) Kalamazoo, MI St. Mary.
Rejsek, Brian (PEO) Diocesan Hispanic Ministry Office.
Rejsek, J. Brian '86 (PEO) Peoria, IL St. Mary's Cathedral; Defender of the Bond.
Rekasi, Joseph S. *o.praem.* '46 (GB)[I] De Pere, WI St. Joseph Priory; [N] De Pere, WI Canons Regular of Magnovarad, Ltd..
Reker, Timothy T. '82 (WIN) Rochester, MN St. Francis of Assisi; Diaconate Formation.
Rekofke, Robert *s.j.* '59 (SEA) Tacoma, WA Holy Cross.
Relihan, Thomas '47 (SAC) Ione, CA Sacred Heart.
Reller, Gary W. '71 (HEL) Polson, MT Immaculate Conception; Ronan, MT Sacred Heart; Vicariates; Montana Association of Churches; Diocesan Ecumenical Officer.
Reller, Gary (HEL) Defenders of the Bond; [E] Polson, MT St. Joseph Hospital Corporation.
Remaklus, Charles W. '47 (LFT) Retired.
Rementeria, Alfonso *o.ss.t.* '76 (PCE) Ponce, PR La Santisima Trinidad.
Rementeria, German *o.ss.t.* '61 (PCE) Ponce, PR La Santisima Trinidad.
Remillard, Andre N. '70 (WOR) Jefferson, MA St. Mary's.
Remillard, Bernard M. *o.p.* '37 (PRT)[I] Lewiston SS. Peter and Paul House.
Remke, Raymond J. '88 (BIR) Montevallo, AL St. Thomas the Apostle; [H] Montevallo, AL University of Montevallo; Propagation of the Faith and Holy Childhood.
Remm, George F. '60 (PEO) Urbana, IL St. Patrick's.
Remmel, William '56 (TUC) Tucson, AZ Most Holy Trinity.
Remmerswaal, James H. *o.s.c.* '65 (SCL)[I] Onamia, MN Crosier Monastery.
Remmerswaal, James *o.s.c.* (SCL) Diocesan Planning Council.
Remmes, Richard R. '62 (SC) Retired.
Rempe, Melvin '65 (LIN) Red Cloud, NE Sacred Heart.
Remski, Howard *f.s.s.p.* '00 (SCR) Omaha, NE St. Patrick; [M] Dallas, TX Mater Dei Community.
Remuzgo, Jorge *o.carm.* '83 (JOL)[L] Prelate Nullius.
Remy, Adrien T. '34 (SPR)[H] Holyoke, MA Mont Marie Health Care Center, Inc. Retired.
Remy, David P. '67 (DUB) Navy Chaplains; Military Chaplains.
Renard, Eugene C. *s.j.* '60 (PBL) Trinidad, CO Most Holy Trinity, Trinidad Area Catholic Community (Trinidad Cluster); [F] Trinidad, CO Business Address:.
Renard, John F. '65 (NEW) Harrington Park, NJ Our Lady of Victories.
Renaud, Floria '98 (SFE) Mountainair, NM St. Alice.
Renaud, Olivier *o.m.i.* '50 (NOR)[F] Willimantic, CT Missionary Oblates of Mary Immaculate; [I] Willimantic, CT Immaculata Retreat House.
Renda, Xavier F. (BGP)[P] Stamford, CT.
Render, John T. *c.p.* '52 (CHI)[N] Chicago, IL Passionist Community–Immaculate Conception Monastery.
Render, Patrick W. *c.s.v.* '68 (LAV) Henderson, NV St. Thomas More.
Rendon, Luis A. '73 (PAT) Paterson, NJ Cathedral of St. John the Baptist.
Rendon, Luis (PAT) Passaic County Jail.
Rendon, Matthias *o.f.m.* '92 (FgM).
Rendon, Matthias *o.f.m.* (MO) Navy Chaplains.
Rendon, Nicolas '76 (LUB) Shallowater, TX St. Phillip Benizi; Slaton, TX St. Joseph's.
Rendon, Nicolas (LUB) Chancellor; Moderator of the Curia; Presbyteral Council; Priests Personnel Board; Priests' Retirement Board; Propagation of the Faith.
Rene, Robert '89 (STA) Absent on Sick Leave.
Renehan, Edmond M. '58 (LA) Santa Clarita, CA St. Clare; Deanery 8.
Renehan, Edmond (LA) Members.
Renfroe, Frank *s.j.* (ELP) El Paso, TX Sacred Heart.
Rengers, Christopher *o.f.m.cap.* '42 (RCK)[B] Washington, DC St. Francis Friary–Capuchin College.
Renggli, John '68 (SEA) Tacoma, WA Our Lady, Queen of Heaven; Puyallup, WA Holy Disciples.
Rengifo, J. Orlando '85 (NEW) Hackensack, NJ Holy Trinity.
Renken, John A. '79 (SFD) Springfield, IL St. Katharine Drexel; Vicars General; Tribunal Officers; Corporate Board Members; Office for the Diaconate; Advisory Board; Parish Life Ministry:; Tribunal Advocacy Ministry:; Black Catholic Advisory Board; Ex Officio; Comite Diocesano de Ministerio Hispano – Diocesan Committee for Hispanic Ministry; Office for the Tribunal; Moderator of the Canonical and Civil Affairs; Consultants; Presbyteral Council; Ex Officios.
Renken, John A. '79 (SFD) Riverton, IL St. James.
Renken, John A. '79 (SFD) Springfield, IL St. Katharine Drexel; Vicars General; Tribunal Officers; Corporate Board Members; Office for the Diaconate; Advisory Board; Parish Life Ministry:; Tribunal Advocacy Ministry:; Black Catholic Advisory Board; Ex Officio; Comite Diocesano de Ministerio Hispano – Diocesan Committee for Hispanic Ministry; Office for the Tribunal; Moderator of the Canonical and Civil Affairs; Consultants; Presbyteral Council; Ex Officios.
Renken, John (SFD) Diocesan Health Insurance Program Committee; Commission for Buildings and Property; Commission for the Care of Infirm and Retired Priests; Consultants.
Renkiewicz, Adolphe T. '56 (HRT)[N] Provincial House and Novitiate.
Renna, Anton J. *s.j.* '65 (PHX)[B] Phoenix, AZ Brophy College Preparatory.
Renner, Christopher A. '91 (DEN) Evergreen, CO Christ the King.
Renner, Christopher (DEN) Deaneries.
Renner, Frank G. '81 (EVN) Bicknell, IN St. Philip Neri.
Renner, Louis *s.j.* '57 (SPK)[B] Spokane, WA Gonzaga University.
Renner, Ralph C. *s.j.* '70 (STL)[O] St. Louis, MO Jesuit Community Corporation at St. Louis University – Jesuit Hall.
Renninger, Michael A. (RIC) Delegate for Vocations.
Renninger, Michael '93 (RIC) Richmond, VA St. Bridget; Liturgical Consultant.
Rensing, William F. '55 (BEL) Leave of Absence.
Renter, Randall C. *c.s.c.* '90 (FTW)[I] New York, NY Corpus Christi.
Renter, Randall *c.s.c.* '90 (NY) New York, NY Corpus Christi.
Rentino, Pablo (NY) Bronx, NY Our Lady of Mercy.
Rento, Richard G. '58 (PAT) Retired.
Rento, Richard (PAT) Presbyteral Council; College of Consultors.
Renz, Christopher J. *o.p.* '97 (OAK)[N] Oakland, CA Dominican Order (Western Province), St. Albert's

Priory; [N] Oakland, CA Western Dominican Province.
Repenning, Robert B. '01 (NY) Wappingers Falls, NY St. Mary; Army National Guard Chaplains.
Repenshek, Jerry '63 (MIL) Menomonee Falls, WI St. Anthony.
Repko, Cyril *o.f.m.cap.* '62 (FgM).
Repko, Joseph '95 (PRM) Bedford, OH St. Eugene; Solon, OH St. John the Baptist; Presbyteral Council; Eparchial Pastoral Council.
Replogle, John F. *s.j.* '64 (NY)[F] New York, NY Xavier High School; [HH] New Rochelle, NY Iona College.
Repole, Charles *o.f.m.cap.* '43 (NY)[EE] Yonkers, NY St. Clare Friary.
Repole, Charles *o.f.m.cap.* (BRK) Legion of Mary.
Reppen, Robert B. *o.praem.* '46 (GB)[I] De Pere, WI St. Norbert Abbey.
Repudi, Rayappa '86 (SFD) Liberty, IL St. Thomas; Liberty, IL St. Brigid.
Reque, Francis M. *o.s.b.* (BIR)[E] Cullman, AL St. Bernard Abbey.
Resch, Gerard F. *c.ss.r.* '44 (STL)[O] Liguori, MO St. Clement Health Care Center.
Resch, Julian C. *o.praem.* '38 (GB)[I] De Pere, WI St. Norbert Abbey.
Reschick, Joseph W. '77 (PIT) Pittsburgh, PA St. Rosalia.
Resconich, Emil *t.o.r.* '54 (ALT)[F] Loretto, PA Mount Assisi Friary.
Resendiz, Alfonso '78 (ELP)[B] El Paso, TX St. Anthony's School of Theology.
Resheske, Florian '55 (GB) Retired.
Resjek, J. Brian (PEO) Promoter of Justice.
Reskey, George A. '73 (MOB) On Leave from the Archdiocese.
Resko, Blane L. *o.s.b.* '57 (GBG) Greensburg, PA St. Bruno.
Resma, Louis '62 (DET) Farmington, MI Botsford General Hospital; Saratoga General Hospital; Detroit, MI St. Brendan; Detroit, MI Guardian Angels.
Resop, Michael A. '79 (MAD) Spring Green, WI St. Malachy; Lime Ridge, WI St. Patrick; Plain, WI St. Luke; Spring Green, WI St. John the Evangelist; Personnel Board.
Ressler, Clint (GAL) Seminarian Support; Vocations Office.
Ressler, Mark A. '76 (DUB)[N] Cedar Falls, IA St. Stephen the Witness Catholic Student Center, University of Northern Iowa; On Special or Other Archdiocesan Assignment.
Ressler, Wayne A. '64 (DUB)[F] Dubuque, IA Holy Family Schools; Dubuque, IA St. Raphael Cathedral.
Restivo, Maurice L. *c.s.b.* (GAL)[B] Houston, TX Casa San Basilio.
Restrepo, Francisco '88 (DET) Detroit, MI St. Stephen–Mary Mother of the Church.
Restrepo, George *s.j.* '65 (BAL) Baltimore, MD St. Thomas Aquinas.
Restrepo, Jairo '92 (B) Defenders of the Bond; Vocations.
Restrepo, John G. *o.p.* (BR) Hammond, LA Holy Ghost.
Restrepo, Mario Garcia '97 (PHX) Phoenix, AZ SS. Anthony and Pius X.
Restrepo, Ruben Dario *c.m.* '97 (PHX) Phoenix, AZ St. Vincent de Paul.
Restrick, Jacob *o.p.* '89 (SPR)[J] West Springfield, MA Monastery of the Mother of God, Dominican Nuns (Contemplative).
Reszel, Marc W. '88 (CHI) Buffalo Grove, IL St. Mary.
Retar, John C. '03 (CLV) Berea, OH St. Mary.
Reteneller, Charles E. '60 (L) Springfield, KY Holy Rosary; [L] St. Catharine, KY St. Catharine of Siena Convent; [L] St. Catharine, KY Sansbury Care Center.
Rethinger, Omer '53 (TOL) Retired.
Retortillo, Benito *o.p.* '62 (CC) San Diego, TX St. Francis de Paula; [G] San Diego, TX Vicariate of Holy Rosary.
Rettger, Thaddeus E. *o.s.b.* '74 (GBG) Vandergrift, PA St. Gertrude.
Rettig, Donald R. '71 (CIN) Cincinnati, OH St. Aloysius–on–the–Ohio; [E] Cincinnati, OH Elder High School.
Rettig, Hermann–Joseph K. *o.praem.* '84 (LA) Los Angeles, CA St. Stephen.
Rettig, Hermann–Joseph K. *o.praem.* '84 (ORG)[I] Silverado, CA Norbertine Fathers of Orange Inc..
Retzel, Joseph R. *s.j.* '60 (GF) Hays, MT St. Paul's Indian Mission.
Retzner, James P. *o.s.a.* '95 (SD) Scripps Mercy Hospital; [H] San Diego, CA Augustinian Community.
Retzner, James *o.s.a.* '95 (SD)[F] San Diego, CA Scripps Mercy Hospital.
Reuse, Patrick *s.j.* '73 (SLC) Ogden, UT St. Mary's.
Reusing, James M. '94 (BAL) Special Assignment.
Reuss, Louis L. '38 (RVC) Bohemia, NY St. John Nepomucene Retired.
Reuter, Arnold F. '52 (LC)[H] La Crosse, WI Holy Cross (Seminary) Diocesan Center Retired.
Reuter, Christian *o.f.m.* (BEL)[F] East St. Louis, IL St. Benedict the Black Friary.
Reuter, John F. '67 (GB) On Duty Outside the Diocese.
Reuter, Lawrence *s.j.* '71 (CHI)[C] Chicago, IL Jesuit Community at Loyola University Chicago.
Reuter, Leon *o.f.m.* '62 (STL)[O] Shelbyville, IN St. Joseph.
Reuter, Lloyd E. '57 (DUB) Retired.
Reuther, John N. *i.m.c.* '73 (BUF)[O] Williamsville, NY Consolata Fathers.
Revak, Francis C. '40 (ALN)[C] Allentown, PA Allentown Central Catholic High School.
Revak, Francis C. '40 (ALN)[J] Bethlehem, PA Holy Family Villa.
Revel, Peter '82 (LKC) Westlake, LA St. John Bosco.
Revilla, Francisco '54 (STA) Retired.
Revilla, Isaias *o.s.a.* '60 (MGZ) Aguada, PR St. Francis of Assisi.
Revuelto, Manuel '59 (NEW) Retired.
Rewak, William J. *s.j.* '64 (SJ)[L] Los Altos, CA Jesuit Retreat House.
Rewtiuk, Michael '69 (SJP) Parma, OH St. Josaphat Cathedral.
Rewtiuk, Michael (SJP) Presbyteral Council.
Rewtiuk, Michael (SJP) Diocesan Consultors.
Rey, Andres *c.m.* '93 (CHI)[N] Chicago DePaul Vincentian Residence.
Reycraft, Robert J. '75 (DEN) Englewood, CO St. Louis.
Reyes, Andres J. '70 (NEW) Jersey City, NJ St. Paul of the Cross.
Reyes, Armando I. (MO) Army Chaplains.
Reyes, Francisco *o.f.m.* '42 (SFR) San Francisco, CA St. Anthony of Padua.
Reyes, Jaime *o.s.b.* '64 (CGS)[C] Humacao, PR San Antonio Abad Abbey of the Order of St. Benedict.
Reyes, Javier *o.f.m.* '98 (P)[A] Portland, OR Franciscan Formation Community.
Reyes, Jorge A. *o.s.a.* (BO) Lawrence, MA St. Mary Immaculate Conception.
Reyes, Jose Maria *o.de.m.* '60 (PCE) Ponce, PR Santuario San Judas Tadeo.
Reyes, Jose '78 (STO) Ceres, CA St. Jude Church (Pastor of).
Reyes, Lonnie C. '69 (AUS) Austin, TX St. Julia.
Reyes, Lonnie (AUS) Deans; Consultors.
Reyes, Mardeo C. '91 (PRO) Johnston, RI St. Rocco.
Reyes, Pedro L. (SJN) San Juan Bautista Regional Seminary.
Reyes, Pedro (SJN) Censor Librorum.
Reyes, Ralph *o.c.d.* '69 (SAT)[M] San Antonio, TX Discalced Carmelites (Prov. of St. Therese).
Reyes, Raymund '88 (SFR) San Rafael, CA St. Isabella.
Reyes, Reynaldo '93 (LUB) Seminole, TX St. James; Presbyteral Council; Priests Personne Board; Vicars Forane.
Reyes, Victor J. (ATL) Advocates.
Reyes, Victor '94 (ATL) Gainesville, GA St. Michael's; [N] Gainesville, GA Brenau College.
Reyes, Xamie M. (CHI) Niles, IL Our Lady of Ransom.
Reyes–Lebron, Pedro (SJN) Adjunct Vicar.
Reyes–Rivera, Benito *o.p.* (SJN)[A] Bayamon Central University.
Reyesmedina, Carlos '87 (DET) Retired.
Reyling, Mark D. '98 (BEL) Cahokia, IL St. Catherine Laboure; Centreville, IL Immaculate Conception; Defensores Vinculi; Diocesan Deans.
Reymann, Albert I. *m.m.* '47 (CLV) Akron, OH St. Bernard.
Reymann, Albert I. *m.m.* '47 (NY).
Reymann, James J. '58 (CLV)[EE] Wellington, OH St. Patrick.
Reyna, Cecilio C. '94 (LAN) Westphalia MI St. Mary.
Reyna, Marcos '86 (LSC) Silver City, NM St. Francis Newman Center Parish; Vicars; Presbyteral Council; Clergy Personnel Board; Campus Ministry; Members.
Reynebeau, Thomas (GB) Oshkosh, WI St. Mary; Oshkosh, WI Sacred Heart; Elected Representatives.
Reyniersе, Peter '95 (WDC) Rockville, MD St. Raphael.
Reynolds, Brad R. *s.j.* '77 (P)[L] Portland, OR Colombiere Community.
Reynolds, Daniel '53 (P) Eugene, OR St. Mark.
Reynolds, Fred G. *s.j.* '78 (LAF)[J] Grand Coteau, LA Jesuit Spirituality Center (St. Charles College).
Reynolds, George *o.p.* '59 (COS) Castle Rock, CO St. Francis of Assisi.
Reynolds, George '97 (LA)[A] Long Beach, CA St. Barnabas.
Reynolds, J. Patrick '80 (OWN) Paducah, KY St. Thomas More; Judges; Consultors; Priests' Council.
Reynolds, James B. '50 (MIA) Pompano Beach, FL St. Henry.
Reynolds, James J. '84 (BRK) Floral Park, NY Our Lady of the Snows.
Reynolds, James L. '71 (SPC) Lamar, MO St. Mary.
Reynolds, Jeffrey '90 (WIL) Veterans Admin..
Reynolds, Jeffrie S. '90 (BIR) On Duty Outside the Diocese.
Reynolds, John C. *c.s.p.* '47 (NY) New York, NY St. Paul the Apostle; [EE] Jamaica Estates Paulist Fathers Generalate.
Reynolds, John C. '90 (KCK) Topeka, KS Holy Name.
Reynolds, John '83 (STA) Absent on Sick Leave.
Reynolds, Joseph F. '59 (NY) Harriman, NY St. Anastasia.
Reynolds, Kirk R. *s.j.* '79 (PAT)[I] Morristown, NJ Loyola House of Retreats.
Reynolds, Pat (OWN) Priest Personnel Committee.
Reynolds, Paul A. *c.s.p.* '94 (BO)[V] Boston, MA Paulist Fathers Residence; [BB] Cambridge, MA Massachusetts Institute of Technology Catholic Community.
Reynolds, Paul F. '65 (PRO) West Warwick, RI St. Mary.
Reynolds, Paul H. '62 (ATL) Special or Other (Arch)Diocesan Assignment; Vicars General; Chancellor; "The Georgia Bulletin"; Judges; Office for Permanent Diaconate; Consultors.
Reynolds, Robert E. '52 (PEO) Retired.
Reynolds, Roger A. '43 (NEW) Harrington Park, NJ Our Lady of Victories Retired.
Reynolds, Rubin R. '79 (BR) Maurepas, LA St. Stephen the Martyr.
Reynolds, Rubin '78 (BR) French Settlement, LA St. Joseph.
Reynolds, Stephen B. '89 (GAL) Sugar Land, TX St. Theresa.
Reynolds, Thomas D. '58 (BO) Senior Priests Retired.
Reynolds, Thomas P. *s.s.c.* '61 (CHI)[N] Chicago, IL Columban Fathers Mission Center.
Reynolds, Thomas P. *s.s.c.* '61 (FgM).
Reynolds, William E. '81 (DAV) Grinnell, IA St. Mary's; Defenders of the Bond; Priests' Aid Society.
Reynolds, William V. '55 (NY) Nanuet, NY St. Anthony.
Rezac, Keith D. '87 (OM) Creighton, NE St. Ludger; Diaconate Program.
Rezac, Robert *i.m.c.* '77 (BUF)[O] Williamsville, NY Consolata Fathers.
Rezula, Leon J. '69 (CHI) Elk Grove Village, IL St. Julian Eymard.
Rhein, George V. '39 (GAL) Retired.
Rhein, George V. '39 (GAL)[N] Houston, TX Pope John Paul XXIII Priests' Residence Retired.
Rhinehart, R. William *c.m.* '79 (COS) Burlington, CO St. Charles Borromeo.
Rhoades, C. Michael '70 (MAR) St. Ignace, MI Immaculate Conception; St. Ignace, MI St. Ignatius Loyola.
Rhoades, Kevin C. '83 (HBG)[B] Emmitsburg, MD Mount Saint Mary's College; On Duty Outside the Diocese.
Rhoades, Terance *o.f.m.* '43 (GLP) Zuni, NM St. Anthony, Our Lady of Guadalupe.
Rhodes, David W. '65 (Y) Youngstown, OH St. Christine; Judges.
Rhodes, Edmund L. *s.m.* '41 (CIN)[M] Dayton, OH Mercy Siena Woods, Nursing Care.
Rhodes, George V. '53 (WIL) Retired.
Rhodes, Joe (OWN) *Roman Catholic Diocese of Owensboro Charitable Trust Fund, Inc..
Rhodes, Joseph '41 (OWN)[E] Owensboro, KY Carmel Home Retired.
Rhomberg, Thomas W. '53 (DUB) Retired.
Rhyner, Robert E. '59 (GB) Green Bay, WI Holy Martyrs of Gorcum.
Riani, Peter R. '55 (OG) Elizabethtown, NY St. Elizabeth; Elizabethtown, NY St. Philip Neri; Promoter of Justice; Deans.
Riano, Camilo *c.m.f.* '47 (SJN) Bayamon, PR San Jose.
Ribando, William R. *c.s.c.* '64 (SCR)[C] Holy Cross Community.
Ribaudo, Charles A. '67 (RVC) Retired.
Ribbens, William H. *o.praem.* '62 (GB)[I] De Pere, WI St. Norbert Abbey.
Ribble, James M. '57 (SPK) Spokane, WA Cathedral of Our Lady of Lourdes.
Ribeiro, Alvaro *s.j.* '87 (WDC)[M] Washington, DC The Jesuit Community at Georgetown University.
Ribeiro, Francisco A.S. *s.j.* '93 (BO)[V] Boston, MA Loyola House.
Ribeiro, George *s.a.* '67 (NY) Apex, NC St. Andrew the Apostle.
Ribeiro, Jose Mario (BO) Brazilian Community Centers.
Ribeiro, Nelson *c.m.* '54 (HRT) Waterbury, CT Our Lady of Fatima.
Ribera–Ribo, Francisco J. '54 (SJN) Retired.
Ribits, Thomas A. *o.s.f.s.* '82 (TOL)[J] Buffalo, NY.
Ribits, Thomas *o.s.f.s.* '82 (BUF)[T] Buffalo, NY Salesian Studios; [R] Buffalo, NY.
Ribotta, Michael *s.d.b.* '49 (SFR) San Francisco, CA SS. Peter and Paul.
Ricafort, Jovencio '82 (SD) San Diego, CA Holy Family.
Ricard, David F. '69 (PRO) Warwick, RI St. Gregory the Great; Kent County Memorial Hospital.
Ricard, Joseph M. '64 (NOR) Retired.
Ricard, Richard J. '98 (NOR) North Grosvenordale, CT St. Joseph; Members; Part Time.
Ricard, Richard (NOR) Continuing Education and Formation Commission.
Ricard, Rodney A. '95 (NO) New Orleans, LA Our Lady Star of The Sea.
Ricard, Rodney Anthony '95 (NO) New Orleans, LA St. Philip the Apostle.
Riccardi, Salvatore *c.p.* '62 (MET)[H] Crestwood, NY.
Riccardo, John '96 (DET)[P] Cardinal Maida Institute

for Leadership Formation; Special Assignment; Presbyteral Council.
Riccardo, Joseph J. '75 (E) Clarion, PA Immaculate Conception.
Ricchini, Joseph *o.f.m.* '64 (CIN)[M] Cincinnati, OH St. Ann Friary.
Ricci, Alfred V. '80 (PRO) Warwick, RI St. Gregory the Great.
Ricci, Andrew P. '97 (SUP) Spooner, WI St. Catherine; Spooner, WI St. Joseph; Spooner, WI St. Francis De Sales; Vocations, Office of.
Ricci, Daniel A. *c.m.* '74 (STL)[O] St. Louis, MO Vincentian Residence.
Ricci, Philip C. '65 (PH) North Wales, PA Mary, Mother of the Redeemer.
Ricciardelli, Albert '84 (TR) Trenton, NJ Blessed Sacrament.
Ricciardi, August A. '83 (SCR) Throop, PA St. Anthony's; Throop, PA St. Bridget's; Throop, PA St. John the Baptist.
Ricciardi, Robert P. '79 (HRT) Cheshire, CT St. Bridget's.
Riccio, Fred A. '77 (OAK) San Ramon, CA St. Joan of Arc.
Riccio, Fred (OAK) Consultors; Diocesan Finance Committee; Deans.
Riccio, Salvatore M. '66 (PH) Springfield, PA St. Francis of Assisi.
Riccitelli, Dennis '85 (PHX) Mesa, AZ Holy Cross.
Riccomini, Dino '57 (FRS) Retired.
Rice, Charles O. '34 (PIT) Pittsburgh, PA St. Anne Retired.
Rice, Charles '01 (BAL) Absent on Leave.
Rice, Edward M. '87 (STL) St. Louis, MO St. John the Baptist.
Rice, G. Nicholas '67 (L) Louisville, KY Our Lady of Lourdes; College of Consultors; Priests' Council.
Rice, G. Nick '67 (L)[P] Louisville, KY Mass of the Air.
Rice, John A. '57 (SEA) Retired.
Rice, John '03 (WH) Parkersburg, WV St. Margaret Mary.
Rice, Joseph '77 (NEW)[N] Rutherford, NJ St. John Vianney Residence for Priests.
Rice, Lawrence *c.s.p.* '89 (COL)[J] Columbus, OH Campus Ministry.
Rice, Michael D. '64 (KC) Lee's Summit, MO St. Margaret's Catholic Community.
Rice, Michael (KC) Building Commission.
Rice, Patrick J. *o.s.a.* '48 (PH)[AA] Villanova, PA St. Thomas Monastery.
Rice, Patrick J. *s.j.* '54 (DET)[E] Detroit, MI University of Detroit Jesuit High School and Academy.
Rice, Patrick '74 (PAT) Mountain Lakes, NJ St. Catherine of Siena; Deans; Presbyteral Council; College of Consultors; Justice and Peace Commission.
Rice, Richard M. *s.j.* '72 (STP)[P] St. Paul, MN Loyola.
Rice, Richard P. '60 (PRT) Bath, ME St. Mary; Deans; Catholic Charismatic Renewal Diocesan Liaison.
Rice, Thomas G. '77 (DET) Special Assignment; Warren, MI St. Louise; "The Michigan Catholic" Newspaper.
Rich, John A. *m.m.* '58 (NY).
Rich, John (RVC)[EE] Northport, NY Veteran's Administration Hospital.
Rich, Joseph '74 (SJ) On Duty Outside the Diocese.
Richard, Antonio J. '38 (FAR) Retired.
Richard, Charles J. '46 (OG) Retired.
Richard, Claude *o.p.* '73 (PRT)[I] Lewiston SS. Peter and Paul House.
Richard, Edward J. *m.s.* '91 (STL)[A] St. Louis, MO Kenrick School of Theology; [D] St. Louis, MO Paul VI Institute of Catechetical and Pastoral Studies.
Richard, Edward '41 (TLS) Retired.
Richard, Edward *m.s.* '91 (STL)[O] La Salette Communications Center.
Richard, Joseph E. '58 (SFR) Lagunitas, CA St. Cecilia.
Richard, Joseph *a.a.* '46 (WOR)[O] Worcester, MA Assumptionists (Augustinians of the Assumption).
Richard, Louis J. '81 (LAF) Broussard, LA Sacred Heart of Jesus.
Richard, Lucien *o.m.i.* '59 (BO)[V] Lowell, MA St. Eugene House (Residence).
Richard, Normand P. '72 (PRT) Old Town, ME Holy Family.
Richard, Raymond *o.f.m.cap.* '72 (FgM).
Richard, Rusty P. '97 (LAF) Crowley, LA Immaculate Heart of Mary.
Richard, Timothy '92 (LAF) Lafayette, LA St. Edmond.
Richard, Wayne R. '40 (LAF) Retired.
Richard, William '81 (DAL) Rockwall, TX Our Lady of the Lake; Presbyteral Council.
Richards, Damian '92 (SAL) Atwood, KS Sacred Heart; Atwood, KS St. John's; Atwood, KS Assumption; Council of Priests.
Richards, Edward W. '59 (BRK) South Ozone Park, NY Our Lady of Perpetual Help.
Richards, George J. '95 (NOR) Preston, CT St. Catherine of Siena; Judges.
Richards, Joe (CR) Deans.
Richards, John M. '85 (CLV) Wickliffe, OH Our Lady of Mount Carmel; Painesville, OH Lake County Memorial Hospital–East; Lake County Memorial Hospital–West.
Richards, Joseph D. '90 (CR) Dilworth, MN St. Elizabeth; Georgetown, MN St. John; Moorhead, MN St. Francis de Sales.
Richards, Lawrence R. '89 (E) Erie, PA St. Joseph.
Richards, Lawrence '89 (E) Bread of Life Community.
Richards, Mark R. '93 (SAC)[N] Sacramento, CA Catholic Committee on Scouting; Adjutant Judicial Vicar; Members; South Lake Tahoe, CA St. Theresa.
Richards, Mark '93 (SAC) Pro–Synodal Judges; Co Directors; Scouting, Catholic Committee on.
Richards, Paul *o.s.b.* (SCL)[I] Collegeville, MN St. John's Abbey, of the Order of St. Benedict.
Richards, Peter '98 (STP) Albertville, MN St. Albert; Dayton, MN St. John the Baptist.
Richards, Richard E. *a.a.* '50 (BO)[V] Boston, MA Assumptionist Center.
Richardson, David P. '03 (PEO) Champaign, IL St. Matthew.
Richardson, Donald '57 (GLP) Retired.
Richardson, Edward *s.m.a.* '50 (NEW)[N] Tenafly, NJ Society of African Missions, Provincialate, S.M.A. Fathers; AUXILIARY CHAPLAINS CONTRACT CHAPLAINS.
Richardson, Frank '93 (ATL) Roswell, GA St. Andrew.
Richardson, James E. '65 (WIL) Special or Other Diocesan Assignment.
Richardson, James '65 (WIL)[O] Wilmington, DE The Franciscan Center.
Richardson, James *s.c.* '92 (HRT) New Haven, CT Sacred Heart.
Richardson, John L. '54 (R) Retired.
Richardson, John M. *o.f.m.* '56 (NY) St. Mary.
Richardson, John T. *c.m.* '49 (CHI)[C] Chicago, IL De Paul University; (FgM).
Richardson, M. Paul '91 (ARL) Great Falls, VA St. Catherine of Siena.
Richardson, Peter *g.h.m.* '86 (LEX) West Liberty, KY Prince of Peace.
Richardson, Robert C. '71 (WDC) Chillum, MD St. John Baptist de la Salle.
Richardson, Ronald A. '61 (RVC) Sag Harbor, NY St. Andrew's.
Richardson, Ronald '61 (RVC) Bridgehampton, NY Queen of the Most Holy Rosary.
Richardson, Stephen '03 (BAL) Columbia, MD St. John the Evangelist.
Richardson, William A. *s.s.j.* '66 (BAL)[S] Baltimore, MD St. Joseph Society of the Sacred Heart House of Central Administration Retired.
Richardson, William J. *s.j.* '53 (New York)[V] Newton, MA The Jesuit Community at Boston College.
Richardson, Willilam M. '72 (HBG) New Cumberland, PA St. Theresa of the Infant Jesus.
Richardt, J. Lawrence (IND) Associates.
Richart, Paul F. '61 (IND) Sellersburg, IN St. Paul.
Richel, Michael C. '87 (MAD) Sun Prairie, WI St. Albert the Great; Personnel Board; Deaneries.
Richetta, John J. '55 (MIL) Kenosha, WI Our Lady of Mount Carmel.
Richey, T. Terrence (LA) Alcohol and Substance Abuse; Alcohol and Substance Abuse Ministry.
Richey, Terrence '64 (LA) Los Angeles, CA St. Basil's.
Richler, Robert (WDC) Rockville, MD St. Elizabeth.
Richling, Theodore L. '71 (OM) Special Assignment.
Richmeier, Garry *c.pp.s.* '83 (KC) Oakview, MO St. Charles Borromeo; Kansas City, MO St. James; [A] Liberty, MO Society of the Precious Blood Provincial Offices.
Richmond, Troy '03 (DAV) Ottumwa, IA St. Mary of the Visitation; Ottumwa, IA St. Patrick's.
Richstatter, Thomas *o.f.m.* '66 (IND)[A] St. Meinrad, IN St. Meinrad School of Theology.
Richter, Anthony Charles '03 (DET) Canton, MI Saint John Neumann.
Richter, David A. (BIS) Beach, ND St. John the Baptist.
Richter, David T. (SHP) Vicar General and Moderator of the Curia; Advocates; Corporate Council; College of Consultors; Finance Council; Presbyteral Council; Campaign for Human Development; Catholic Relief Services; Ex Officio Members; Mission Director; Propagation of the Faith.
Richter, David (BIS)[F] Sentinel Butte, ND Home On The Range; Priests' Benefit Association.
Richter, Helmut W. '94 (OAK) Pittsburg, CA Good Shepherd.
Richter, Helmut (OAK) Deans.
Richter, James B. '51 (RVC) Huntington, NY St. Patrick's Retired.
Richter, John A. '64 (NU) New Ulm, MN Cathedral of The Holy Trinity; Finance Council; Priest Personnel Board.
Richter, Kevin M. '88 (SC) Sioux City, IA St. Boniface; Presbyteral Council; Priests' Personnel Board.
Richter, Norbert M. '41 (RCK) Retired.
Richter, Robert J. '67 (MIL) Military Chaplains.
Richter, Thomas J. '96 (BIS) Bismarck, ND St. Anne; Office of Vocations; Priests' Personnel Board.
Richter, Tony '03 (DET) Canton, MI Saint John Neumann.
Richter, William L. '58 (TOL) Retired.
Richtsteig, Erik J. '94 (SLC) Ogden, UT St. James.
Richtsteig, Erik John (SLC) Air Force Reserve Chaplains.
Ricker, John Michael '55 (TOL) Retired.
Rickert, William '45 (GB) Retired.
Rickey, James E. '69 (PEO) Dwight, IL St. Patrick's; Dwight, IL Dwight Correctional Center.
Rickles, Gary '96 (GAL) New Caney, TX St. John of the Cross.
Rickles, Raymond *o.f.m.* '82 (STL)[O] St. Croix Falls, WI.
Ricks, Paul '55 (SAC) Vacaville, CA St. Mary.
Rico, Dayro '03 (ATL) Athens, GA St. Joseph's.
Rico, Jose Luis '01 (FRS) Porterville, CA St. Anne; Fresno, CA St. John Cathedral.
Ridella, Joseph '52 (VNN) Retired.
Ridgell, John E. '67 (RIC) Norge, VA St. Olaf, Patron of Norway.
Ridgell, John E. (BAL) Interdiocesan Judges.
Ridgeway, Kenneth *s.m.* '69 (PRT) Brunswick, ME St. John the Baptist.
Ridgley, Lawrence P. '02 (BUR) Newport, VT St. Mary Star of the Sea.
Ridgway, John K. *s.j.* '82 (DEN)[N] Denver, CO Regis Jesuit Community (The Jesuits at Regis University).
Ridick, George J. '73 (WOR) Worcester, MA St. Catherine of Sweden; Advocates.
Ridley, Harold E. *s.j.* '69 (BAL)[B] Timonium, MD Loyola Graduate Center –Timonium Campus; [B] Timonium, MD Loyola Graduate Center –Timonium Campus; [S] Baltimore, MD Jesuit Community of Loyola College, Inc..
Riebe, Bruce '85 (PRM) Brecksville, OH St. Joseph; Office of Youth Ministry; Priest's Pension Board.
Riebe, Todd M. '80 (IND) Richmond, IN Holy Family; Richmond, IN St. Andrew; Richmond, IN St. Mary; Richmond State Hospital; [O] Richmond, IN Earlham College.
Riebe–Estrella, Gary L. *s.v.d.* '71 (CHI)[B] Chicago, IL The Catholic Theological Union at Chicago; [B] Chicago, IL Edward McGuinn, S.V.D. Residence; [N] Chicago, IL Divine Word Theologate; [N] Chicago, IL Edward McGuinn House of Studies.
Riedel, Richard R. *c.pp.s.* '52 (CIN) Celina, OH Immaculate Conception of the Blessed Virgin Mary.
Riedemann, Kenneth '64 (SCL) Lowry, MN Our Lady of the Runestone; Lowry, MN St. John Nepomuk; Directors.
Rieden, Thomas W. *o.s.f.s.* '68 (LAN)[B] Jackson, MI Lumen Christi Catholic High School.
Rieder, David J. '56 (SCL) Perham, MN St. Henry's; Perham, MN St. Stanislaus; Perham, MN St. Lawrence.
Rieder, David '56 (SCL) New York Mills, MN Holy Cross; Dent, MN Sacred Heart; Personnel Committee.
Rieder, Donald '55 (SCL) Retired.
Rieder, Michael J. '94 (RVC) Central Islip, NY St. John of God; Associate Vocation Directors.
Rieder, Michael '94 (RVC) East Meadow, NY St. Raphael.
Rieder, Ronald *o.f.m.cap.* '63 (FTW) Huntington, IN SS. Peter and Paul.
Riedman, John '62 (SFS) Humboldt, SD St. Ann.
Riedman, Joseph G. '56 (IND) Indianapolis, IN Holy Spirit.
Riedman, Joseph (IND) Deaneries and Deans.
Riedmann, Boniface *s.a.* '45 (BO)[O] Brockton, MA Chapel of Our Savior–Catholic Pastoral and Information Center; [V] Brockton, MA Chapel of Our Savior; [AA] Brockton, MA Chapel of Our Saviour.
Riedmueller, Leo A. '48 (LR) Hot Springs National Park, AR St. Mary of the Springs.
Riedmueller, Leo (LR) Deans.
Rieger, Alan J. *o.c.d.* '61 (MIL)[O] Milwaukee Provincial Offices – Discalced Carmelites.
Riegger, Patrick M. '01 (RVC) Garden City, NY St. Anne.
Riegler, Frederick J. '67 (PH) Quakertown, PA St. Isidore.
Riego, Rutilio Del *d.l.p.* '65 (SB)[E] Riverside, CA Diocesan Labor Priests, DLP.
Riehle, James L. *c.s.c.* '64 (FTW)[B] University of Notre Dame Du Lac; [I] Notre Dame, IN Holy Cross Community, Corby Hall, University of Notre Dame.
Riel, Robert H. '80 (SPR) Chicopee, MA St. George's.
Rieman, Richard W. '58 (BO)[U] Newton, MA Prelature of the Holy Cross and Opus Dei.
Riendeau, Alfred '98 (BGP) New Fairfield, CT St. Edward the Confessor.
Riendeau, Richard A. '57 (SPR) Holyoke, MA Blessed Sacrament.
Riendeau, Walter A. *s.s.s.* '45 (CLV)[O] Cleveland, OH Blessed Sacrament Community.
Riepe, Charles K. '60 (BAL) Retired.
Ries, Carl A. '70 (DUB) Charles City, IA Immaculate Conception; College of Consultors.
Ries, Donald C. '59 (SC) Grand Junction, IA St. Brigid's; Jefferson, IA St. Joseph's.
Ries, James C. '93 (ORG) Fullerton, CA St. Mary's.

Ries, Richard S. '63 (SC) Manson, IA St. Thomas; Presbyteral Council.
Ries, Richard '63 (SC) Manson, IA St. Mary's.
Riesbeck, Christian H.F. '96 (GAL) Houston, TX Queen of Peace.
Riesberg, Leo L. '57 (SC) Retired.
Riesenberg, John J. '60 (COV) Edgewood, KY St. Pius X Retired.
Rietti, John '57 (JKS) Retired.
Riffle, David '67 (B) Bonners Ferry, ID St. Ann's.
Riffle, Donald J. '62 (B) Retired.
Riffle, Douglas H. '57 (B) Retired.
Riffle, Henry J. '70 (SP) San Antonio, FL St. Anthony of Padua.
Riffle, Raymond E. '79 (GBG) Greensburg, PA Our Lady of Grace; Catholic Charities of the Diocese of Greensburg, PA, Inc.; Catholic Charities.
Rigali, Joseph *o.f.m.* '58 (CIN)[L] Centerville, OH St. Leonard.
Rigali, Norbert *s.j.* '59 (SD)[B] University of San Diego; Censores Librorum.
Rigatuso, Leo '94 (OM) Lyons, NE Holy Cross; Lyons, NE St. Joseph.
Rigdon, Vincent J. '77 (WDC) Silver Spring, MD St. Michael; Pastoral Center Special Ministries; Propagation of the Faith; Holy Childhood Association.
Rigdon, Vincent (WDC) Judges.
Rigert, James A. *c.s.c.* '66 (FTW) South Bend, IN St. Stanislaus.
Rigert, James *c.s.c.* '66 (FTW) South Bend, IN Holy Cross.
Rightor, Harold Warren '02 (IND) Indianapolis, IN Holy Spirit.
Rigney, Dennis A. '66 (ALN) Retired.
Rigney, Raymond P. '42 (NY) Retired.
Rigoberto Rodriguez, J. '85 (LA)[E] Los Angeles, CA Our Lady of Guadalupe.
Rigoli, Anthony *o.m.i.* '72 (NO) New Orleans, LA Our Lady of Guadalupe /International Shrine of St. Jude; New Orleans, LA Shrine of St. Jude Thaddeus.
Rigonan, Antonio R. (MO) Air Force Chaplains.
Rihn, Roy '42 (SAT)[K] San Antonio, TX Casa De Padres Retired.
Rikteraitis, John E. '56 (HRT) Retired.
Riley, Andy *p.i.m.e.* (LSC) Presbyteral Council.
Riley, Daniel J. '84 (BO) Weymouth, MA Sacred Heart.
Riley, Daniel P. *o.f.m.* '71 (BUF)[Q] West Clarksville, NY Mount Irenaeus, Franciscan Mountain Retreat & Holy Peace Friary; [R] St. Bonaventure, NY St. Bonaventure University; [C] West Clarksville, NY Holy Peace Friary.
Riley, David J. '64 (BGP) Stamford, CT St. Cecilia.
Riley, Dennis S. '79 (CHI) Retired.
Riley, Edward H. *o.p.* '60 (CHI)[N] Chicago Dominicans (Provincial Office).
Riley, Edward H. *o.p.* '60 (FgM).
Riley, Edward M. (BO) Norwood, MA St. Catherine of Siena.
Riley, Eric '98 (OWN) Franklin, KY St. Mary of the Woods.
Riley, Finian A. *o.f.m.* '55 (FgM).
Riley, George F. *o.s.a.* '62 (PH)[C] Villanova University; [AA] Villanova, PA St. Thomas Monastery.
Riley, J. Norman '57 (CLV) Copley, OH Guardian Angels; Parma, OH St. Charles Borromeo.
Riley, James F. *s.j.* '74 (DET)[E] Detroit, MI University of Detroit Jesuit High School and Academy; [K] Detroit, MI Jesuit Provincial Office–Detroit Province of the Society of Jesus.
Riley, James H. '58 (BO) Senior Priests Retired.
Riley, John F. '55 (STP)[C] St. Paul, MN University of St. Thomas Retired.
Riley, John F. '56 (ALB) Valley Falls, NY St. George.
Riley, John J. '91 (ARL) Alexandria, VA St. Louis.
Riley, John P. *c.s.c.* '94 (FTW)[I] Notre Dame, IN Holy Cross Community, Corby Hall, University of Notre Dame.
Riley, John Patrick *c.s.c.* '94 (FTW) Notre Dame, IN Sacred Heart.
Riley, John *c.s.c.* '94 (FTW)[B] University of Notre Dame Du Lac.
Riley, John '03 (KCK) Topeka, KS Most Pure Heart of Mary.
Riley, Kenneth A. '92 (KC) Kansas City, MO St. Bernadette's.
Riley, Leo P. '82 (DUB) Port Charlotte, FL St. Charles Borromeo; On Duty Outside the Archdiocese.
Riley, Malachy *o.s.b.* '42 (KC)[J] Conception, MO Conception Abbey.
Riley, Mark J. '95 (BO) Boston, MA Children's Hospital.
Riley, Mark J. (BO) East Bridgewater, MA St. John.
Riley, Miles O'Brien '63 (SFR) Retired.
Riley, Norman '57 (CLV) Retired.
Riley, Patric '84 (KCK) Topeka, KS St. Matthew.
Riley, Patrick '48 (SCL) Retired.
Riley, Placidus H. *o.s.b.* '46 (MAN)[K] Manchester, NH St. Anselm Abbey.
Riley, Robert D. *o.p.* '60 (WDC) Washington, DC St. Dominic Church & Priory.
Rimelspach Jeffrey J. '85 (COL) Powell, OH St. Joan of Arc.
Rimes, Robert B. *s.j.* '55 (MOB)[A] Mobile, AL Spring Hill College; Mobile District–Baldwin Escambia Deanery.
Rimmele, Leo R. *o.s.b.* '55 (SEA) Veterans Admin. Medical Center.
Rimmele, Leo *o.s.b.* '55 (P)[L] St. Benedict, OR Mt. Angel Abbey; AUXILIARY CHAPLAINS CONTRACT CHAPLAINS.
Rimselis, Victor *m.i.c.* '43 (CHI)[N] Chicago, IL Congregation of Marian Fathers of the Immaculate Conception.
Rimshaw, Joseph J. *s.s.j.* '48 (BAL)[S] Baltimore, MD St. Joseph Society of the Sacred Heart House of Central Administration Retired.
Rimshaw, Joseph J. *s.s.j.* '48 (ORL) Retired.
Rinaldi, Francis J. *o.s.f.s.* '69 (ARL) Vienna, VA Our Lady of Good Counsel.
Rinaldi, Nicholas *s.a.c.* '39 (CAM)[C] Pennsauken, NJ Bishop Eustace Prep School.
Rinaldo, Joseph *s.c.* '67 (LAN)[E] Chelsea, MI St. Louis Center for Exceptional Children & Adults.
Rindos, Paul T. '59 (HBG) Mount Joy, PA Mary, Mother of the Church.
Riney, Maury D. '77 (OWN) Reed, KY St. Augustine.
Riney, Phil (OWN) Age Group Six Representative; Priests' Council; Board Members.
Riney, Philip C. '48 (OWN) Retired.
Riney, W. Jerry '75 (OWN) Bowling Green, KY Holy Spirit.
Ring, Bob '82 (ROC) Penn Yan, NY St. Michael; Penn Yan, NY St. Theresa.
Ring, Daniel J. '68 (TOL) Fostoria, OH St. Wendelin; Judges.
Ring, John K. '61 (SFR) San Francisco, CA St. Vincent de Paul.
Ring, Joseph G. '88 (SFD) Charleston, IL St. Charles Borromeo; [N] Charleston, IL Eastern Illinois University Newman Catholic Center.
Ring, Joseph (SFD) Corporate Board Directors.
Ring, Paul L. '95 (BO) Dorchester, MA St. Mark.
Ring, Robert P. '82 (ROC) Naples, NY Our Lady of the Lakes Catholic Community; Victim Assistance Coordinators.
Ring, Vincent D. '64 (SFR) San Bruno, CA St. Robert.
Ringenback, Gerard A. '72 (RVC) Levittown, NY St. Bernard.
Ringenberger, Harry '69 (MIA) Fort Lauderdale, FL St. Pius X.
Ringholz, Benedict E. '45 (TOL)[I] Sandusky, OH Providence Care Center Retired.
Ringley, F. John '01 (BGP) Shelton, CT St. Lawrence.
Ringrose, John N. (HON) Judges.
Rini, John '67 (ELP) El Paso, TX Our Lady of the Valley.
Rink, George '57 (SEA) Retired.
Rink, Louis W. *c.s.c.* '58 (FTW)[I] Notre Dame, IN Holy Cross House.
Rinkowski, George M. '41 (TOL) Retired.
Rinn, Richard A. *c.s.v.* '81 (LAV) Las Vegas, NV St. Viator.
Rinzel, Jerome A. '64 (MIL) Muskego, WI St. Leonard Congregation.
Riordan, Brendan P. '70 (RVC) Great Neck, NY St. Aloysius.
Riordan, Brice E. *o.carm.* '44 (NEW) Paramus, NJ Carmelite Chapel of St. Therese.
Riordan, Eugene *s.m.a.* '53 (NEW)[N] Tenafly, NJ Society of African Missions, Provincialate, S.M.A. Fathers Retired.
Riordan, John B. *o.f.m.cap.* '71 (NY) Yonkers, NY Sacred Heart; Yonkers, NY Sacred Heart Parish High School Foundation, Inc..
Riordan, Patrick M. '90 (PEO) Kickapoo (Edwards), IL St. Mary of Kickapoo.
Rios, Francisco Alanis '01 (SFE)[I] Abiquiu, NM Monastery of Christ in the Desert.
Rios, Francisco *i.v.e.* '91 (SJ) Council of Priests; Council of Religious; San Jose, CA St. Maria Goretti.
Rios, Luis B. (SJN)[E] San Juan, PR Centro Medico de P.R..
Rios, Manuel D. '86 (NEW) North Bergen, NJ St. Brigid; Union City, NJ St. Rocco's.
Rios Capiello, Luis B. '81 (ARE) On Duty Outside the Diocese.
Rios Capiello, Luis '81 (ARE) Bayamon, PR Cristo Salvador.
Rioux, J. Robert *c.s.c.* '56 (FR)[H] North Dartmouth, MA Holy Cross Residence; [H] North Dartmouth, MA St. Joseph's Hall.
Rioux, Ray '94 (SR) Arcata, CA St. Mary's; Clergy Formation.
Riplog, Duane T. '84 (CHR) Retired.
Ripoli, Roland R. *o.s.b.* '64 (GBG)[H] Latrobe, PA Saint Vincent Archabbey.
Ripp, Anthony *m.s.c.* '67 (ALN) Nazareth, PA Holy Family.
Ripper, Thomas *m.s.* '80 (STL)[O] La Salette Communications Center.
Ripperger, Chad *f.s.s.p.* '97 (SCR)[M] Elmhurst Priestly Fraternity of St. Peter (F.S.S.P.), North American District Headquarters.
Ripperger, Chad *f.s.s.p.* '97 (LIN)[A] Denton, NE Our Lady of Guadalupe Seminary.
Ripperger, Harold A. '58 (IND) Lanesville, IN St. Mary.
Ripperger, Mark *o.cist.* '93 (DAL)[K] Irving, TX Cistercian Abbey of Our Lady of Dallas.
Ripperger, William '55 (IND) Retired.
Rippinger, Joel *o.s.b.* '74 (RCK)[G] Aurora, IL Marmion Abbey.
Rippy, Robert J. '84 (ARL) Arlington, VA Our Lady of Lourdes; Chancellor; Deans; Promoter of Justice; Diocesan Consultors.
Riquelme, Alvaro A. '97 (CHL) Concord, NC St. James.
Risacher, James E. '52 (TOL) Retired.
Risacher, James (BAL) Baltimore, MD Immaculate Heart of Mary.
Rischmann, Edward '48 (NEW) Retired.
Rischmann, Robert J. '61 (NEW) Retired.
Risden, George '84 (SR) Crescent City, CA St. Joseph; Members of the Curia; Deans; Board of Consultors; Priests' Council.
Rishel, Robert F. '55 (PIT) Retired.
Risley, John C. *o.p.* '65 (MAD)[H] Sinsinawa, WI Dominican Motherhouse.
Ristuccia, Leon C. *o.f.m.* '45 (PAT)[M] Butler, NJ St. Anthony Friary.
Rita, Carmine J. '94 (NY) White Plains, NY Our Lady of Sorrows.
Rita, Thomas L. '70 (FR) West Harwich, MA Holy Trinity; Judges.
Ritari, Raymond '83 (PHX) Phoenix, AZ St. Matthew.
Ritchey, Samuel E. '73 (COL) Columbus, OH Sacred Heart.
Ritchey, Timothy M. '85 (B) Meridian, ID Holy Apostles.
Ritchie, David L. '01 (TOL) Toledo, OH Christ the King.
Ritchie, Donald E. '59 (BUR) Retired.
Ritchie, Gerald T. '68 (E) Harborcreek, PA Our Lady of Mercy.
Ritchie, Robert T. '71 (NY) Bronx, NY Our Lady of Angels; [R] New York, NY Society of St. Vincent De Paul, Archdiocesan Central Council of New York; Bronx (Northwest).
Ritchie, Timothy (B) Priest Retirement Committee.
Ritchie, Vincent *m.s.w., s.j.* '81 (RVC) Levittown, NY St. Bernard.
Riter, Dennis G. '71 (BUF) Batavia, NY St. Mary.
Ritt, Paul E. '81 (BO) Chelmsford, MA St. John the Evangelist.
Rittenhouse, Thomas R. '76 (TR) Riverside, NJ St. Peter.
Ritter, Charles F. '67 (TOL) Bryan, OH St. Patrick.
Ritter, Edward '57 (DET) Retired.
Ritter, Eric '03 (SAT) San Antonio, TX St. Leo.
Ritter, Nicholas J. '65 (LAN) Ypsilanti, MI St. Joseph.
Ritter, Patrick '74 (SEA) Bellevue, WA Sacred Heart; Presbyteral Council; College of Consultors.
Ritter, Patrick *s.d.s.* '76 (MIL)[O] Milwaukee, WI Salvatorians – Jordan Hall.
Ritz, Robert G. *c.s.b.* '51 (GAL)[Q] Houston, TX Dillon House.
Ritzert, William J. '64 (PIT) Evans City, PA St. Matthias; Butler County, PA Department of Veterans Affairs–Deshon Hospital.
Riva, Gerald '68 (JOL) Woodridge, IL St. Scholastica.
Riva, Hugo *m.c.c.j.* '50 (CHI) Blue Island, IL St. Donatus.
Riva, Paul *c.r.s.* '96 (MAN)[H] Allenstown, NH Pine Haven Boys Center.
Rivard, Robert *f.m.s.i.* '77 (BO) Norfolk, MA St. Jude; [B] Framingham, MA Sylva Maria.
Rivard, Roland J. '56 (BUR) Deans; Burlington, VT St. Anthony's; Burlington, VT Christ the King.
Rivas, David '85 (ARE) Arecibo, PR Our Lady of Hope.
Rivas, Juan *l.c.* '82 (LA)[Q] Pasadena, CA Legionaries of Christ; [CC] El Monte, CA Hombre Nuevo.
Rivas, Manuel D. '92 (OWN) Bowling Green, KY St. Joseph's.
Rivas, Rigoberto Caloca *o.f.m.* (OAK)[S] Board of Directors:.
Rivas, Romeo '59 (MIA) Retired.
Rivas Campis, Jose '70 (SJN) On Duty Outside the Archdiocese.
Rivera, Abod Oscar *o.s.b.* (CGS) Diocesan Consultors.
Rivera, Adalin '77 (PCE) Ponce, PR Santa Teresita; [B] The Pontifical Catholic University of Puerto Rico.
Rivera, Adolfo (SAC) Galt, CA St. Christopher; Ione, CA Preston School of Industry, California Youth Authority.
Rivera, Anastacio S. *s.j.* '74 (ORG)[H] Orange, CA Loyola Institute for Spirituality; [I] Garden Grove, CA Manresa Jesuit Residence.
Rivera, Andres *s.d.b.* '74 (SJN) San Juan, PR Maria Auxiliadora.
Rivera, Eddie '90 (SJN) San Juan, PR San Mateo; Santurce, PR Hospital Del Nino San Jorge; [E] Santurce, PR Hospital Del Nino San Jorge.
Rivera, Educardo *s.s.p.* '77 (CHI) Cicero, IL St. Frances of Rome.
Rivera, Edward '03 (SFE) Albuquerque, NM Community of the Risen Savior.

Rivera, Felix *o.carm.* '81 (JOL)[L] Darien Carmelite Provincial Office.
Rivera, Felix '97 (ARE) Arecibo, PR Santisimo Sacramento.
Rivera, Felix *o.c.d.* (CGS) Cidra, PR Nuestra Senora del Carmen.
Rivera, Francisco *o.a.r.* '69 (LSC)[C] Mesilla, NM Augustinian Recollect Fathers.
Rivera, Gerardo '99 (LSC) Las Cruces, NM St. Genevieve.
Rivera, Guadalupe '49 (SFE) Retired.
Rivera, Hector (MGZ) Legion of Mary.
Rivera, Jaime Velasco *o.s.b.* '93 (MIL)[O] Benet Lake, WI St. Benedict's Abbey.
Rivera, Jery (PCE) Guayanilla, PR Immaculate Conception; Catholic Youth Organization.
Rivera, Jorge *o.carm.* '95 (ARE) Morovis, PR Nuestra Senora del Carmen.
Rivera, Luis '84 (MIA) Miami, FL Our Lady of Divine Providence.
Rivera, Luis (CGS) Priests Senate.
Rivera, Miguel '83 (ARE) Corozal, PR Our Lady of the Seven Sorrows.
Rivera, Miguel *s.d.b.* '86 (SJN) San Juan, PR San Juan Bosco.
Rivera, Narciso '77 (LSC) Hatch, NM Our Lord of Mercy.
Rivera, Orlando '90 (PCE) Ponce, PR Cathedral of Our Lady of Guadalupe.
Rivera, Oscar *o.s.b.* '78 (CGS)[C] Humacao, PR San Antonio Abad Abbey of the Order of St. Benedict.
Rivera, Oscar '79 (CGS) Naranjito, PR San Miguel Arcangel.
Rivera, Oscar *o.s.b.* (CGS) Diocesan Consultors; Priests Senate; Priests Senate.
Rivera, Raymond L. '86 (PCE) Guayanilla, PR Immaculate Conception.
Rivera, Roberta (FTW)[A] Notre Dame, IN Moreau Seminary.
Rivera, Roland '94 (LAV) North Las Vegas, NV St. Christopher.
Rivera–Martinez, Pius *o.s.c.o.* '53 (WOR)[O] Spencer, MA St. Joseph's Abbey.
Rivera–Marzan, Eddie (SJN) Diocesan Consultors.
Rivera–Saez, Adalin (PCE) Army National Guard Chaplains.
Rivera Ramos, Hector E. '82 (MGZ) Mayaguez, PR Cathedral of Our Lady of Purification.
Rivero, Andres *o.f.m.* '75 (SD) Hispanic.
Rivero, Eduardo *o.carm.* '02 (JOL)[L] Prelate Nullius.
Rivero, Jordi S. '82 (MIA) North Miami, FL Holy Family; [K] Miami, FL Respect Life Office.
Rivero, Jordi (MIA) Respect Life Office.
Rivero, Juan '72 (FWT) Granbury, TX St. Rose of Lima; Granbury, TX St. Frances Cabrini; Deans.
Rivero, Julio B. *t.o.r.* '69 (VEN) Bradenton, FL Sacred Heart.
Rivero, Leonides '78 (ELP) El Paso, TX St. Mark; Presbyteral Council.
Riveros, Wilfredo '97 (CGS) Cayey, PR Nuestra Senora de la Merced.
Rivers, Clarence J. '56 (CIN) Retired.
Rivers, Clarence Rufus J. '56 (CIN)[V] Cincinnati, OH Stimuli, Inc..
Rivers, Robert S. *c.s.p.* '68 (WDC)[B] Washington, DC St. Paul's College; [V] Washington, DC Paulist National Catholic Evangelization Assoc..
Rivet, Hilton L. *s.j.* '54 (BR) Baton Rouge, LA Immaculate Conception.
Rivi, Geno G. '57 (GBG) Retired.
Rivituso, Mark S. (STL) Masters of Ceremonies to the Archbishop; Adjutant Judicial Vicars.
Rivituso, Mark '88 (STL) St. Louis, MO St. Mary Magdalen.
Rizo, Sergio '89 (FWT) Cleburne, TX St. Joseph.
Rizzi, Salvatore '41 (BRK)[S] Queens Village, NY Queen of Peace Residence Retired.
Rizzo, David R. (ALT)[H] Johnstown, PA University of Pittsburgh at Johnstown; Johnstown, PA Our Mother of Sorrows.
Rizzo, Giovanni '00 (NEW) Newark, NJ St. Francis Xavier.
Rizzo, John V. *f.s.s.p.* '85 (B) Post Falls, ID St. George's; [M] Post Falls, ID St. George's Church.
Rizzo, Mateo J. '73 (BRK) Brooklyn, NY Shrine Church of St. Jude.
Rizzo, Robert C. '74 (CHI) Park Ridge, IL St. Paul of the Cross.
Roach, Daniel *o.p.* '56 (FgM).
Roach, Francis J. '56 (STP) Retired.
Roach, Francis J. '73 (WOR) Worcester, MA Our Lady of Lourdes.
Roach, Francis '73 (WOR) University of Mass Medical Center.
Roach, John A. '58 (SPR) Shelburne Falls, MA St. Joseph's.
Roach, Joseph W. *s.a.g.* '48 (SAG) Retired.
Roach, Joseph (SB) Retired.
Roach, Michael J. '71 (BAL) Manchester, MD St. Bartholomew.
Roach, Michael '81 (KC)[A] Kansas City, MO St. Therese Parish.
Roach, Michael (KC) Diocesan Consultors; Deans.
Roach, Richard R. *s.j.* '69 (SEA) Vashon, WA St. John Vianney; [A] Seattle, WA Seattle University.
Roach, Robert N. *c.s.sp.* '48 (PIT)[G] Sarasota, FL Congregation of the Holy Ghost.
Roach, Thomas E. *s.j.* '70 (BAL)[S] Curia SJ.
Roache, James P. '59 (CHI) Retired.
Roark, John D. '56 (SY) Retired.
Roark, John '56 (SY) Syracuse, NY St. Ann Retired.
Roark, Michael B. '70 (WIL) Salisbury, MD St. Francis De Sales.
Robak, Anthony G. '74 (NEW) North Bergen, NJ Sacred Heart.
Robak, Charles P. *m.m.* '70 (FgM).
Robb, Dennis E. '74 (SEA) Everett, WA Immaculate Conception; Everett, WA Our Lady of Perpetual Help.
Robb, Kevin Dominic *o.p.* '77 (NY) New York, NY St. Vincent Ferrer; [EE] New York, NY St. Vincent Ferrer Priory.
Robb, Paul V. *s.j.* '60 (CHI)[C] Chicago, IL Jesuit Community at Loyola University Chicago; [N] Chicago, IL Chicago Province of the Society of Jesus–Provincial Office.
Robbins, Charles J. *c.pp.s.* '39 (LFT)[A] Rensselaer, IN Saint Joseph's College Retired.
Robbins, John F. *c.s.b.* '72 (GAL) Houston, TX St. Anne.
Robbins, John W. '01 (BAL) Baltimore, MD St. Ursula.
Robbins, Robert J. '74 (NY) New York, NY Holy Family.
Robbins, Roger P. '63 (SAT) Schertz, TX Church of the Good Shepherd.
Robbins, Thomas P. '74 (COV) Covington, KY St. Anthony; [B] Covington, KY Holy Cross High School; Air Force Reserve Chaplains.
Robeck, Joseph J. *s.m.* '42 (WDC) Retired.
Robello, Louis J. '65 (SFR) Retired.
Roberge, Francis A. '78 (WOR) West Boylston, MA Our Lady of Good Counsel; [R] Worcester, MA Worcester State College.
Roberge, Frederick *s.s.s.* '35 (CLV)[O] Richfield, OH Regina Health Center; [O] Richfield, OH Regina Health Center.
Roberge, Richard A. '85 (MAN) Berlin, NH Good Shepherd; Gorham, NH Holy Family.
Roberson, Henry '71 (OKL) Special Assignment; Army National Guard Chaplains.
Roberson, Michael '74 (NO) New Orleans, LA St. Maurice.
Roberson, Ronald G. *c.s.p., s.e.o.d.* '77 (WDC)[B] Washington, DC St. Paul's College.
Roberson, Ronald G. *c.p.* (MO) AUXILIARY CHAPLAINS CONTRACT CHAPLAINS.
Robert, Darin T. '71 (LAN) University of Michigan Hospitals/Pastoral Care Dept..
Robert, Rene '89 (STA) St. Augustine, FL San Sebastian.
Roberts, Allan '80 (LA) Los Angeles, CA St. Bernadette.
Roberts, Anthony P. *s.j.* '56 (PH)[AA] Loyola Center and Manresa Hall.
Roberts, Art *c.s.b.* '55 (LSC) Truth or Consequences, NM Our Lady of Perpetual Help; Diocesan Consultors.
Roberts, David *c.p.* '52 (BRK)[V] Jamaica, NY Immaculate Conception Monastery.
Roberts, Don J. '78 (SFD) Oconee, IL Sacred Heart.
Roberts, Don '78 (SFD) Pana, IL St. Patrick.
Roberts, Edward A. *s.s.c.* '60 (BO)[V] Marshfield, MA.
Roberts, Edward J. (PEO) Washington, IL St. Luke's; Diocesan Tribunal.
Roberts, Edward *s.s.s.* '60 (CLV)[O] Charlestown, MA.
Roberts, Edward (PEO) Judges.
Roberts, Eugene J. '75 (TR) Marlboro, NJ St. Gabriel.
Roberts, G. Richard '91 (LC) Fountain City, WI Immaculate Conception.
Roberts, Guy R. '98 (SFE) Rio Rancho, NM Church of the Incarnation.
Roberts, Joseph L. '02 (ORL) Titusville, FL St. Teresa.
Roberts, Marshall M. '96 (SCR)[M] Shohola, PA Society of Saint John.
Roberts, Ralph O. '98 (GAL) Houston, TX St. Cyril of Alexandria.
Roberts, Ralph *s.s.s.* '75 (CLV)[O] Cleveland Congregation of the Blessed Sacrament Provincial House.
Roberts, Randall *o.f.m.* '84 (GB)[I] Greenwood, MS St. Francis of Assisi Friary; Air Force Chaplains.
Roberts, Thomas C. '84 (NEW) Montclair, NJ Our Lady of Mt. Carmel; Newark, NJ Northern State Prison; Bayonne, NJ St. Michael's; Chaplains.
Robertson, Douglas C. '96 (LC) Independence, WI SS. Peter and Paul; Deans.
Robertson, Eugene G. '78 (STL) Florissant, MO St. Ferdinand.
Robertson, Glendon E. '57 (CAM) Retired.
Robertson, Harold '49 (NY)[E] New York, NY Cardinal Hayes High School Retired.
Robertson, James E. '77 (BO) Quincy, MA Sacred Heart.
Robertson, John W. '71 (HEL) Butte, MT Holy Spirit; Special Assignments; Diocesan Tribunal; Judicial Vicar.
Robertson, John W. (GF) Promoter of Justice.
Robertson, John (HEL) Episcopal Vicar for Canonical Services; Presbyteral Council; Office of Due Process.
Robertson, Luke *t.o.r.* '99 (SP) St. Petersburg, FL St. Mary Our Lady of Grace.
Robertson, Shawn *t.o.r.* '03 (FWT) Fort Worth, TX St. Andrew.
Robertson, Thomas M. '65 (STL) St. Louis, MO St. Catherine of Alexandria.
Robeson, Robert J. '03 (IND) Ministry to Youth and Young Adults; Indianapolis, IN St. Monica.
Robeson, Steven P. '84 (STL) St. Louis, MO St. Simon of Cyrene.
Robichand, Paul G. *c.s.p.* '75 (NY).
Robichaud, Armand *s.m.* '50 (BO)[V] Boston, MA Marist Fathers of Our Lady of Victories (Boston Prov.).
Robichaud, J. Armand *s.m.* '50 (FgM).
Robichaud, James P. '79 (PRT) Dover Foxcroft, ME St. Francis Xavier; Dover–Foxcroft, ME St. Thomas.
Robichaud, James (PRT) Diocesan Council of Priests.
Robichaud, Paul G. *c.s.p.* (MO) Navy Reserve Chaplains.
Robichaux, Robie '76 (LAF) Lafayette, LA St. Mary, Mother of the Church; Adjutant Judicial Vicars; Diocesan Consultors.
Robicheaux, David J. '98 (NO) Metairie, LA St. Philip Neri.
Robideau, Jeffrey '97 (LAN) Lansing, MI Resurrection.
Robillard, Joseph R. '84 (ORG) Costa Mesa, CA St. Joachim.
Robillard, Thomas J. '44 (OG) Norfolk, NY Visitation of the B.V.M. Retired.
Robin, Richard A. *s.j.* '67 (LA)[C] Los Angeles, CA Loyola Marymount University; [C] Los Angeles, CA Jesuit Community.
Robine, Paul M. '59 (ALT) Johnstown, PA St. John Vianney's.
Robins, Dean L. '87 (NO) Kenner, LA Nativity of Our Lord.
Robinson, Charles *o.f.m.cap.* '70 (GF) Crow Agency, MT St. Dennis.
Robinson, David C. *s.j.* '92 (SFR)[N] San Francisco, CA Jesuit Community at University of San Francisco.
Robinson, David S. *s.j.* '90 (SFR)[E] San Francisco, CA St. Ignatius College Preparatory (Coed); [N] San Francisco, CA Jesuit Community at St. Ignatius College Preparatory.
Robinson, Denis *o.s.b.* '93 (IND)[A] St. Meinrad, IN St. Meinrad School of Theology; [K] The Ameican College.
Robinson, Donald A. '80 (OG) Watertown, NY St. Anthony.
Robinson, Edmund J. *s.j.* '55 (SPK)[J] Spokane, WA Regis Community.
Robinson, Edward M. *o.p.* '41 (DAL)[K] Irving, TX Dominican Priory of St. Albert the Great.
Robinson, Edwin F.D. *o.f.m.* '68 (PAT)[M] Butler, NJ St. Anthony Friary.
Robinson, Edwin F.D. *o.f.m.* (NY) Dobbs Ferry, NY St. Cabrini Nursing Home.
Robinson, Edwin *o.f.m.* '68 (NY)[AA] Dobbs Ferry, NY St. Cabrini Nursing Home.
Robinson, Ernest E. '79 (RVC)[M] Uniondale, NY St. Pius X Residence.
Robinson, Fisher *s.v.d.* '56 (LA) Los Angeles, CA St. John, The Evangelist; Cardinal McIntyre Fund for Charity; Board of Directors:.
Robinson, Gerald H. *s.j.* '77 (SAC) Sacramento, CA St. Ignatius of Loyola; [K] Applegate, CA Our Lady of the Oaks Villa.
Robinson, Gerald *s.j.* (SAC) Vicars Forane.
Robinson, Jack Clark *o.f.m.* '81 (GLP) St. Michaels, AZ St. Michael.
Robinson, James P. *s.s.e.* '57 (DET) Detroit, MI Cathedral, Church of the Most Blessed Sacrament.
Robinson, Jerome '75 (NO)[Q] New Orleans, LA Sisters of the Holy Family Motherhouse and Novitiate, S.S.F..
Robinson, Jerome '95 (MOB) On Leave from the Archdiocese.
Robinson, John A. '71 (CHI) Elk Grove Village, IL Queen of the Rosary; Other Assignments.
Robinson, John C. '54 (MOB) Retired.
Robinson, John '54 (BIR) Birmingham, AL St. Peter the Apostle.
Robinson, Joseph A. '64 (CIN) Cincinnati, OH St. Boniface; Vicarri Foranei (Deans).
Robinson, Joseph P. '68 (BO) Bedford, MA St. Michael; Bedford, MA Veterans Administration Hospital Bedford; Military & VA Chaplains.
Robinson, Ken '92 (FWT) Grapevine, TX St. Francis of Assisi; Deans.
Robinson, Lawrence F. *s.j.* '65 (P)[D] Portland, OR Jesuit High School.
Robinson, Michael '96 (SD)[D] San Diego, CA Good Shepherd.
Robinson, Monte E. '75 (MAD) Belmont, WI St. Philomena; Belmont, WI St. Michael; Belmont, WI Immaculate Conception.
Robinson, Patrick '91 (PHX) Scottsdale, AZ Blessed

Sacrament; [C] Scottsdale, AZ Pope John XXIII Catholic School Community.
Robinson, Paul F. *o.carm.* '67 (FR) Special Assignment; Judicial Vicar; Judges.
Robinson, Perry L. *s.j.* '72 (OM)[K] Omaha, NE Jesuit Community at Creighton University.
Robinson, Perry *s.j.* '72 (OM) Ralston, NE St. Gerald.
Robinson, Ralph C. '03 (CHR) Columbia, SC St. Joseph.
Robinson, Richard J. '63 (MIL) Big Bend, WI St. Joseph.
Robinson, Robert M. '69 (BRK) Long Island City, NY St. Patrick.
Robinson, Tyrone '79 (DET) Detroit, MI Martyrs of Uganda.
Robinson, William *o.f.m.conv.* '74 (CHL) Winston–Salem, NC Our Lady of Mercy.
Robisch, David C. '62 (CIN) Cincinnati, OH St. Mary.
Robitaille, Jean C. *m.afr.* '73 (SP)[O] St. Petersburg, FL Missionaries of Africa; Cursillo, Spiritual Advisors.
Robitaille, Raymond '45 (LAF)[G] New Iberia, LA Consolata Home.
Robitaille, Raymond '47 (LAF) Retired.
Robles, Antonio *s.d.b.* '61 (ARE) Orocovis, PR San Juan Bautista.
Robles, Daniel '01 (SPC) Monett, MO St. Lawrence; Pierce City, MO SS. Peter and Paul.
Robles, Vidal (TUC) Tucson, AZ St. Ambrose.
Robles–Sanchez, Jose A. '95 (ALX) Vocation Discernment Committee; Liturgy Committee; Alexandria, LA St. Frances Xavier Cabrini.
Robling, Landelin A. *o.s.b.* '52 (SCL)[I] Collegeville, MN St. John's Abbey, of the Order of St. Benedict.
Robotnik, Lawrence R. '57 (COV)[N] Erlanger, KY Monastery of the Sacred Passion Retired.
Robu, Emil *o.f.m.conv.* (MRY) Carmel, CA San Carlos Borromeo Basilica; Defenders of the Bond; Promoter of Justice; Web Site Development Committee.
Roby, Albin '87 (NY) Staten Island, NY St. Charles.
Roby, Brian J. '96 (OWN) Owensboro, KY SS. Joseph and Paul.
Roca, Albert L. '77 (MET) Retired.
Roca, Casimiro *s.f.* '43 (SFE) Chimayo, NM Holy Family.
Rocca, Gregory *o.p.* '77 (OAK)[A] Berkeley, CA Dominican School of Philosophy and Theology; [N] Oakland, CA Dominican Order, Siena House.
Rocca, Peter D. *c.s.c.* '74 (FTW)[A] Notre Dame, IN Moreau Seminary.
Rocca, Peter *c.s.c.* '94 (FTW)[B] University of Notre Dame Du Lac; Liturgical Commission.
Rocchi, Frank J. '82 (NEW) Maplewood, NJ Immaculate Heart of Mary.
Rocco, Daniel M. '90 (CAM) Blackwood, NJ St. Jude's.
Rocco, Remigio G. '66 (PAT) Haskell, NJ St. Francis of Assisi; Deans.
Roccosalvo, Joseph '71 (NY)[EE] New York, NY West Side Jesuit Community.
Rocha, Constantina '95 (FTW) Goshen, IN St. John the Evangelist.
Rocha, Constantino (FTW) Goshen.
Rocha, Ivo D. '66 (STO) Tracy, CA St. Bernard Church (Pastor of).
Rocha, Ivo (STO) College of Consultors/Presbyteral Council; Diocesan Building Committee.
Rocha, Michael '88 (LA) Venice, CA St. Mark.
Rocha, Richard '02 (KC) Kansas City, MO St. Elizabeth's.
Rocha, Rosario *s.j.* '85 (OAK)[N] Berkeley, CA Jesuit Community at Jesuit School of Theology at Berkeley.
Rocha, Victor J. '53 (PIT) Pittsburgh, PA Resurrection Retired.
Roche, David V. '42 (BUF)[O] Buffalo, NY Sheehan Residence for Priests Retired.
Roche, David '58 (PEO) Retired.
Roche, Edward '97 (CC)[G] Robstown, TX Society of Our Lady of the Most Holy Trinity.
Roche, John S. *s.s.c.* '59 (BO)[V] Humarock, MA.
Roche, John *s.d.b.* '87 (LA)[F] Bellflower, CA St. John Bosco High School.
Roche, John *ss.cc.* (SB) Upland, CA St. Joseph; [E] Upland, CA Congregation of the Sacred Hearts.
Roche, Matthew F. *s.j.* '81 (RVC) Oceanside, NY St. Anthony.
Roche, Randall *s.j.* '68 (LA)[C] Los Angeles, CA Jesuit Community.
Roche, Robert *o.s.b.* '62 (ALT) Patton, PA Queen of Peace.
Roche, Ron '61 (PBL) Retired.
Roche, Stanley *o.s.b.* '47 (SCL)[I] Collegeville, MN St. John's Abbey, of the Order of St. Benedict.
Roche, William H. '50 (BO) Senior Priests; Boston, MA Cathedral of the Holy Cross; [EE] Boston, MA Sancta Maria House, Inc. Retired.
Rocheford, Dennis J. '77 (WOR) Blackstone, MA St. Theresa.
Rochel, Anthony J. *s.j.* '51 (STL)[O] St. Louis, MO Jesuit Community Corporation at St. Louis University – Jesuit Hall.
Rocheleau, Raymond '52 (BR) Retired.
Rochford, Eugene *s.v.d.* '74 (CHI)[B] Techny, IL Divine Word Residence.
Rochford, John J. '47 (CHI) Country Club Hills, IL St. Emeric Retired.
Rochon, Robert A. '74 (PRO) Johnston, RI St. Brigid.
Rock, John J. '54 (NEW) Retired.
Rock, John J. *s.j.* '87 (BAL)[S] Nashville, TN.
Rock, Joseph A. '72 (ALN)[J] Bethlehem, PA Holy Family Villa Retired.
Rock, Larry G. (BAL) Baltimore, MD St. Agnes.
Rock, Martin *s.j.* '59 (SLC) Ogden, UT St. Mary's; Deans.
Rock, Michael R. *o.de.m.* '86 (BUF)[O] LeRoy, NY Order of the BVM of Mercy/Mercedarian Friars; Le Roy, NY St. Peter; Le Roy, NY St. Anthony.
Rock, Richard J. *c.m.* '73 (PH) Philadelphia, PA St. Francis of Assisi.
Rock, Russell L. '62 (CAM) Runnemede, NJ St. Maria Goretti; Members.
Rock, Stephen B. '74 (BO) Military & VA Chaplains; Navy Chaplains.
Rock, William J. *o.p.* '58 (Y) Youngstown, OH St. Dominic.
Rockenstein, James *o.f.m.* '57 (SAC) Lincoln, CA St. Joseph.
Rocker, Stephen '79 (OG) Hogansburg, NY St. Joseph; Hogansburg, NY St. Mary; Fort Covington, NY St. Patrick.
Rockers, Alfred '62 (KCK) Leawood, KS Church of the Nativity.
Rocks, Jason T. '02 (CAM) Wildwood, NJ St. Ann's; Assistant Vocation Directors for Recruitment; Advocates.
Rocky, Ronald *o.f.m.conv.* '84 (MRY) Pismo Beach, CA St. Paul the Apostle.
Rocky, Ronald '84 (MRY)[F] Arroyo Grande, CA St. Joseph Cupertino Province, Provincial Center.
Rocus, John George '01 (LAN) Howell, MI St. Joseph.
Rodak, Joseph *c.pp.s.* '62 (CIN)[M] North Royalton, OH; Cleveland, OH Veterans Administration Hospitals, Brecksville V.A.; Cleveland, OH Cleveland V.A..
Rodakowski, Louis '42 (P) Retired.
Rodas, Mauro '65 (IND) Retired.
Rodda, Regis *o.f.m.conv.* '59 (SY) Syracuse, NY Assumption B.V.M..
Rodell, Jeremiah J. '47 (CHI) Retired.
Roden, Raymond '81 (BRK) Brooklyn, NY St. Anthony of Padua–St. Alphonsus.
Roden–Lucero, Edward '82 (ELP) El Paso, TX San Juan Diego Parish.
Roden–Lucero, Edward (SAT) Defenders of the Bond.
Rodenfels, Jerome '74 (COL) New Albany, OH Church of the Resurrection.
Rodenspiel, James '64 (B) Coeur D'Alene, ID St. Thomas.
Roder, Terry A. '88 (SC) Anthon, IA St. Joseph's; Danbury, IA St. Mary's.
Roder, Terry '88 (SC) Board of Education.
Rodes, Kenneth J. (MO) Navy Chaplains.
Rodgers, Arthur E. '65 (PH) Bala Cynwyd, PA St. Matthias.
Rodgers, Dermot P. '91 (FR) Swansea, MA St. Michael's.
Rodgers, Dermot (FR) Auditors.
Rodgers, Kenneth '43 (GB) Retired.
Rodgers, Philip F. '81 (ALN) Mohnton, PA St. Benedict's.
Rodgers, William J. '49 (BRK)[S] Queens Village, NY Queen of Peace Residence Retired.
Rodia, James C. *o.praem.* '72 (PH) Philadelphia, PA St. Gabriel; [AA] Paoli, PA Daylesford Abbey.
Rodino, Salvatore A. '80 (ALB) Troy, NY St. Bonaventure.
Rodis, Rodney '86 (RIC) Mineral, VA Immaculate Conception; Mineral, VA St. Jude.
Rodney, John *s.v.d.* '60 (WDC)[M] Washington, DC Divine Word College.
Rodney, Joseph C. *s.s.j.* '68 (NO) Reserve, LA Our Lady of Grace.
Rodoni, Rick G. '91 (SJ) Santa Clara, CA St. Clare.
Rodoni, Rick (SJ) Ongoing Formation of Clergy Committee.
Rodrieguez, Tommy '69 (TOL) Soldiers and Sailors Home.
Rodrigalvarez, Jose *o.a.r.* (NEW) Hispanic Apostolate.
Rodrigo, Charles '86 (NOR) New London, CT St. Joseph.
Rodrigo, Niranjan *s.s.s.* '99 (NY) Congers, NY St. Paul.
Rodrigo, Salvador *o.carm.* '62 (SJN) San Juan, PR Santa Teresita Del Nino Jesus.
Rodrigo, Stephen *s.j.* '75 (KAL) Byron Center, MI St. Mary's Visitation.
Rodrigo, Titus *o.s.b.* '85 (FRS) Bakersfield, CA St. Philip the Apostle.
Rodrigue, Joshua John '02 (HT) Morgan City, LA Holy Cross.
Rodrigues, Amancio '66 (P) Portland, OR Our Lady of Sorrows.
Rodrigues, Anthony '54 (RIC) Retired.
Rodrigues, Carlos R. '95 (BGP) Stamford, CT Sacred Heart.
Rodrigues, Carlos '95 (BGP)[K] Stamford, CT St. Camillus Health Center.
Rodrigues, Charles *s.j.* (CIN)[F] Cincinnati, OH St. Xavier High School; [M] Cincinnati, OH Jesuit Community at St. Xavier High School.
Rodrigues, Ignatius '66 (SB) Loma Linda, CA St. Joseph the Worker.
Rodrigues, Januarius E. '59 (SAC) Sacramento, CA St. Anne.
Rodrigues, Jose A. (WOR) St. Joan of Arc.
Rodrigues, Joseph *s.d.s.* '93 (MIL)[O] Milwaukee Salvatorian Provincial Residence.
Rodrigues, Sabbas '61 (RVC) Hampton Bays, NY St. Rosalie's.
Rodrigues, William '00 (FR) Cape Cod; Diocesan Department of Pastoral Care for the Sick; West Harwich, MA Holy Trinity.
Rodriguez, Abdenago Vargas (CHR) Orangeburg, SC Holy Trinity; Allendale, SC St. Mary.
Rodriguez, Alberto A. '81 (GAL) Houston, TX St. John Neumann; Houston, TX St. Thomas More.
Rodriguez, Alberto *o.p.* '71 (MIA) Miami, FL St. Dominic; [H] Miami, FL Dominican Fathers of Miami, Inc..
Rodriguez, Alberto *o.ss.t.* '87 (VIC) Victoria, TX Our Lady of Sorrows.
Rodriguez, Aloysius M. '66 (BR) Retired.
Rodriguez, Ambiorix '97 (NY) Bronx, NY Our Lady of Mercy.
Rodriguez, Anibal *c.p.* '03 (MGZ) San Sebastian, PR San Sebastian Martir.
Rodriguez, Anthony *l.c.* '83 (HRT).
Rodriguez, Antonio L. '49 (BUF) Retired.
Rodriguez, Antonio Salvador '68 (DAL)[B] Dallas, TX St. Cecilia.
Rodriguez, Antonio '63 (LA) Long Beach, CA St. Lucy.
Rodriguez, Antonio '93 (PAT) Passaic, NJ Holy Trinity; Presbyteral Council; College of Consultors.
Rodriguez, Armando J '55 (GAL)[N] Houston, TX Pope John Paul XXIII Priests' Residence Retired.
Rodriguez, Arturo Perez '72 (CHI) Chicago, IL Assumption.
Rodriguez, Arturo '84 (LAR) Zapata, TX Our Lady of Lourdes.
Rodriguez, Ben M. '91 (PEO) Clinton, IL St. John the Baptist's; La Salle, IL Queen of the Holy Rosary; La Salle, IL St. Hyacinth's; La Salle, IL St. Patrick's.
Rodriguez, Benigno A. '66 (LA) Los Angeles, CA Presentation of the Mary.
Rodriguez, Bernardo C. '80 (BGP) Bridgeport, CT St. Patrick Church; Bridgeport, CT Bridgeport Hospital.
Rodriguez, Carlos L. *c.p.* '99 (ARE) Lares, PR St. Joseph.
Rodriguez, Carlos *o.c.s.o.* '70 (L)[K] Trappist, KY Abbey of Our Lady of Gethsemani, of the Order of Cistercians of the Strict Observance.
Rodriguez, Carlos '87 (NY) Bronx, NY St. John Chrysostom's; Archdiocesan Consultors.
Rodriguez, Celso '76 (P) Cornelius, OR St. Alexander.
Rodriguez, D. Andres G. '36 (RIC) Retired.
Rodriguez, Daniel '90 (VEN) Sarasota, FL St. Martha.
Rodriguez, David *o.f.m.* '89 (CHI)[D] Chicago, IL Hales Franciscan High School, Inc..
Rodriguez, David '03 (FRS) Oildale, CA Christ the King.
Rodriguez, Delfin '86 (ARE) Arecibo, PR Nuestra Senora del Carmen; Arecibo Hospital.
Rodriguez, Edgar '03 (CHI) Mundelein, IL Santa Maria Del Popolo.
Rodriguez, Edmundo *s.j.* '66 (SFE) Albuquerque, NM Immaculate Conception.
Rodriguez, Eduardo *o.c.s.o.* '69 (ATL)[K] Conyers, GA The Monastery of the Holy Spirit.
Rodriguez, Edwin '95 (ALX) Alexandria, LA St. Francis Xavier Cathedral.
Rodriguez, Efrain '74 (SJN) San Juan, PR Nuestra Senora de Lourdes.
Rodriguez, Eleazar Perez (MIL) Milwaukee, WI St. Stanislaus; Milwaukee, WI St. Adalbert; Milwaukee, WI SS. Cyril and Methodius; Milwaukee, WI St. Hyacinth.
Rodriguez, Encarnacion M. *c.m.* '94 (MGZ) Mayaguez, PR San Vicente.
Rodriguez, Epifanio *o.p.* '54 (CC) San Diego, TX St. Francis de Paula.
Rodriguez, Esteban *o.carm.* '86 (NY)[EE] Middletown, NY St. Albert's Priory.
Rodriguez, Fabian *s.j.* '66 (SJN)[C] Rio Piedras, PR Jesuit Community; [D] Rio Piedras, PR Centro De Espiritualidad Ignaciana Pedro Arrupe (CEIPA).
Rodriguez, Feliciano (CGS) Priests Senate; Pastoral Vicar.
Rodriguez, Felix M. '97 (YAK) White Salmon, WA St. Joseph.
Rodriguez, Florencio *t.o.r.* '80 (SAT) San Antonio, TX St. Lawrence.
Rodriguez, Francis *o.c.s.o.* '55 (WOR)[O] Spencer, MA St. Joseph's Abbey.
Rodriguez, Franklin '64 (CGS) San Lorenzo, PR Sagrado Corazon de Jesus y 12 Apostoles.
Rodriguez, Freddy Alecio '91 (SJN) Santurce, PR Ashford Presbyterian Community Hospital.
Rodriguez, Gerardo Ibarra *o.s.b.* '97 (MGZ) Mayaguez,

PR Sacred Heart.
Rodriguez, Gilbert '74 (SAN) Odessa, TX St. Anthony; Odessa, TX St. Joseph.
Rodriguez, Guillermo '56 (SFR) Retired.
Rodriguez, Guillermo '69 (LA) La Puente, CA St. Joseph.
Rodriguez, Guillermo '75 (SAC) Chico, CA St. John the Baptist.
Rodriguez, Henry '86 (SD) San Diego, CA St. Jude.
Rodriguez, Jesus A. '93 (ARE) Manati, PR Nuestra Senora del Mar.
Rodriguez, Joaquin '89 (MIA) Miami Springs, FL Blessed Trinity.
Rodriguez, John A. (SFR) Archbishop's Cabinet.
Rodriguez, John E. '77 (RNO) Reno, NV St. Therese Church of the Little Flower.
Rodriguez, John F. '59 (SFR) Menlo Park, CA St. Denis.
Rodriguez, Jorge I. '86 (DEN) Aurora, CO St. Therese; Dover, NJ Our Lady Queen of the Most Holy Rosary.
Rodriguez, Jorge '01 (MIA) Miami Shores, FL St. Rose of Lima.
Rodriguez, Jose A. '64 (SFR) San Francisco, CA St. John the Evangelist.
Rodriguez, Jose A. '80 (ARE) Vega–Baja, PR Holy Rosary.
Rodriguez, Jose A. (SFR) College of Consultors; Board of Directors.
Rodriguez, Jose A. (WOR) Worcester, MA St. Joan of Arc; Spanish Apostolate.
Rodriguez, Jose A. (SFR) College of Consultors; Board of Directors.
Rodriguez, Jose A. (WOR) Worcester, MA St. Joan of Arc; Spanish Apostolate.
Rodriguez, Jose Diego '81 (PCE) Coamo, PR St. Blase.
Rodriguez, Jose Trinidad '92 (STO) Ceres, CA St. Jude Church (Pastor of).
Rodriguez, Jose *o.s.b.* '63 (CGS)[C] Humacao, PR San Antonio Abad Abbey of the Order of St. Benedict Retired.
Rodriguez, Jose (SFR) Episcopal Vicar for the Spanish Speaking.
Rodriguez, Joseph *s.d.s.* '93 (MIL)[O] St. Francis, WI St. Joseph's Salvatorian Community (Novitiate).
Rodriguez, L. Antonio '49 (BUF)[O] Lackawanna, NY Bishop Head Residence.
Rodriguez, Leonardo J. '90 (SJN) Bayamon, PR Sagrada Familia; Subcommission for Ministries; for Administration of Temporalities; Commission for Sacred Liturgy and Popular Piety.
Rodriguez, Luis F. '01 (NO) Kenner, LA St. Elizabeth Ann Seton.
Rodriguez, Luis R. '93 (HBG) Lebanon, PA St. Benedict the Abbot.
Rodriguez, Luis *s.j.* '65 (OM)[K] Omaha, NE Jesuit Community at Creighton University.
Rodriguez, Mario Merino *m.c.c.j.* (CHI) Chicago, IL St. Anthony.
Rodriguez, Mario *m.sp.s.* '00 (LA) Oxnard, CA Our Lady of Guadalupe Parish.
Rodriguez, Martin S. *o.r.c.* '92 (SB)[E] Corona, CA Operarios Del Reino De Cristo, O.R.C..
Rodriguez, Martin *o.r.c.* (SB) Corona, CA St. Edward.
Rodriguez, Michael '90 (SAN) Sweetwater, TX Holy Family; Sweetwater, TX Immaculate Heart of Mary.
Rodriguez, Michael '96 (ELP) El Paso, TX San Juan Bautista.
Rodriguez, Nestor '93 (PMB) Indiantown, FL Holy Cross; Presbyteral Council; Secretary.
Rodriguez, Nicholas *s.f.* '92 (WDC)[B] Silver Spring, MD Holy Family Seminary.
Rodriguez, Pablo M. '61 (RVC) Hempstead, NY Our Lady of Loretto.
Rodriguez, Pedro Poloche '98 (ATL) Atlanta, GA Cathedral of Christ the King.
Rodriguez, Peter *c.m.f.* '57 (CHI) Chicago, IL St. Paul.
Rodriguez, Rafael A. '75 (CGS) Yabucoa, PR Santos Angeles Cutodios; Army Reserve Chaplains.
Rodriguez, Rafael *s.j.* '84 (SJN).
Rodriguez, Ray '94 (CHY)[H] Vocation Office; Youth Ministry Board; Diaconate Board.
Rodriguez, Ray (CHY) Diaconate Program, Permanent.
Rodriguez, Reyes G. '67 (SLC).
Rodriguez, Robert '53 (MIL) Retired.
Rodriguez, Roberto *m.m.* '95 (LA)[Q] Monrovia, CA.
Rodriguez, Robin E. *c.m.* (BRK)[Z] Brooklyn, NY Centro Evangelization S. Vincente de Paul.
Rodriguez, Santos '70 (SFR) South San Francisco, CA All Souls.
Rodriguez, Silvestre *o.f.m.* '48 (LAR) Hebbronville, TX Our Lady of Guadalupe.
Rodriguez, Tobias '02 (NEW) Bayonne, NJ St. Mary Star of the Sea.
Rodriguez, Tommy '69 (TOL) Sandusky, OH SS. Peter and Paul.
Rodriguez, Victor *c.m.* '69 (BRK)[X] Brooklyn, NY Centro Evangelizacion San Vicente de Paul.
Rodriguez, William Hernando '02 (R) Jacksonville, NC Shrine of the Infant of Prague, Church of the Holy Spirit.
Rodriguez–Jimenes, Leonardo (SJN) Moderator.
Rodriguez–Leon, Mario '91 (SJN)[A] Bayamon Central University.
Rodriguez de Yurre, Prudencio *c.m.* '65 (DEN)[N] Denver, CO Congregation of the Mission Midwest Province: De Paul House.
Rodriguez Jimenes, Leonardo '90 (SJN) Graduate Studies.
Rodriguez Leon, Mario *o.p.* '91 (SJN)[A] Bayamon Central University.
Rodriguez Ochoa, Leonardo '91 (SJN) Luquillo, PR San Jose.
Rodriguez Orengo, Juan (PCE) Diocesan Consultors.
Rodriques, Carlos (BGP) Greenwich, CT St. Roch.
Rodriquez, Feliciano '85 (CGS) Juncos, PR Inmaculada Concepcion.
Rodriquez, Matias '66 (TYL) Kilgore, TX Christ the King.
Rodriquez, Pablo M. (RVC) Senate of Priests (Presbyteral Council/College of Consultors); Spanish Apostolate.
Roebert, Michael '66 (LA) Long Beach, CA St. Lucy.
Roebuck, John H. '76 (PH) Drexel Hill, PA St. Bernadette.
Roedel, Richard P. '59 (STP) New Prague, MN St. Scholastica; New Prague, MN St. Joseph; New Prague, MN St. Thomas.
Roedel, Robert H. '56 (PH) Feasterville, PA Assumption B.V.M..
Roedig, Robert L. '53 (STL) Richmond Heights, MO Immacolata.
Roehrich, David '84 (SFS) Elk Point, SD St. Joseph; Jefferson, SD St. Peter.
Roehrig, Matthew *s.s.p.* '84 (Y)[A] Canfield, OH Society of St. Paul.
Roemer, Richard *c.f.r.* '98 (NY)[EE] New York, NY St. Joseph's Friary.
Roensch, Frederick J. '55 (MIL) Retired.
Roensch, Roger '57 (WDC) On Duty Outside the Archdiocese.
Roers, Merlin N. (STP) Associate Judges.
Roesch, David H. '67 (ALT) Cemetery Commission; Bellwood, PA St. Joseph's.
Roesch, Joseph *m.i.c.* '92 (WDC)[B] Washington, DC Marian Fathers Scholasticate.
Roesch, Karl J. *o.s.b.* '60 (CHR) Hartsville, SC St. Mary the Virgin Mother.
Roesch, Karl J. *o.s.b.* '60 (PAT)[M] Morristown St. Mary's Abbey.
Roesch, Karl *o.s.b.* '60 (CHR)[H] Hartsville, SC Coker College.
Roeten, Winus '48 (NO) Retired.
Roetzel, Robert E. *c.s.c.* '87 (FTW)[I] Army Chaplains.
Roetzer, James M. '98 (MAR) Bessemer, MI St. Sebastian; [B] Bessemer, MI St. Sebastian School Endowment Fund; Advocates.
Roetzer, Russell G. '64 (MIL) Special Assignment.
Rofrano, Peter J. *s.a.c.* '39 (NY) New York, NY Our Lady of Mt. Carmel; [EE] New York, NY Pallottine Fathers.
Rog, Francis *c.r.* '55 (CHI) Chicago, IL St. Hyacinth Basilica; College of Consultors.
Rog, Theodore C. '64 (BUF) Cheektowaga, NY St. Josaphat.
Rogaczewski, Dan (ATL)[B] Atlanta, GA St. Pius X Catholic High School.
Rogaczewski, Daniel '00 (ATL) Norcross, GA Saint Patrick's.
Rogala, Gerald E. '56 (CHI) Buffalo Grove, IL St. Mary.
Rogalla, William G. '96 (LAF) Abbeville, LA St. Anne.
Rogan, Brian (SB) Retired.
Rogawski, Ralph *o.p.* '59 (AUS)[G] Austin, TX.
Roger, Richard G. '64 (WOR) Worcester, MA Notre Dame des Canadiens – St. Joseph.
Rogers, Christopher B. (PH) Exton, PA SS. Philip and James.
Rogers, Daniel J. '53 (DUB) Retired.
Rogers, Francis P. '46 (PH) Retired.
Rogers, Gary P. '72 (BRK) Brooklyn, NY St. Gregory the Great.
Rogers, Herbert W. *s.j.* '44 (NY)[EE] Loyola Hall, Jesuit Community.
Rogers, James '39 (EVN) Retired.
Rogers, Jerry '76 (CR) Deans; Detroit Lakes, MN Holy Rosary; Hawley, MN St. Andrew; Lake Park, MN St. Francis Xavier's; Priests' Personnel Board.
Rogers, Joel C. *c.p.m.* '00 (L) Glasgow, KY St. Helen.
Rogers, John '84 (RVC) Absent on Leave.
Rogers, Joseph '54 (DAV)[L] Davenport, IA Kahl Home for the Aged and Infirm Retired.
Rogers, Nicholas P. '55 (MAN) Manchester, NH St. Patrick.
Rogers, Patrick D. *s.j.* '02 (R) Raleigh, NC St. Raphael.
Rogers, Patrick O. *s.j.* '02 (R)[E] Raleigh Jesuit Community.
Rogers, Patrick W. '82 (COL) Columbus, OH St. Philip The Apostle; Navy Reserve Chaplains.
Rogers, Paul '77 (RVC) Absent on Leave.
Rogers, Peter S. *s.j.* '74 (NO)[C] New Orleans, LA Loyola University New Orleans.
Rogers, Peter *o.p.* '02 (SFR) San Francisco, CA St. Dominic; [N] San Francisco, CA St. Dominic Priory.
Rogers, Philip E. '80 (Y) Struthers, OH St. Nicholas.
Rogers, Robert C. '92 (HT) Montegut, LA Sacred Heart; Montegut, LA St. Charles Borromeo.
Rogers, Vincent '93 (KC) St. Joseph, MO St. James.
Rogerson, David '77 (SEA) Battle Ground, WA Sacred Heart.
Rogge, Louis *o.carm.* '54 (JOL)[L] Joliet, IL St. Elias Carmelites Retired.
Rogge, Norman J. *s.j.* '56 (NO)[P] New Orleans, LA Ignatius Residence.
Rogina, Walter '85 (SR) Occidental, CA St. Philip; Advocates.
Rogliano, Joseph S. '85 (BUF) Lockport, NY St. Anthony; Lockport, NY St. Joseph.
Rogriguez, Ray (CHY) Catholic Family and Respect Life Ministries Board.
Rogusz, Joseph A. *c.s.c.* '46 (FTW)[I] Notre Dame, IN Holy Cross House.
Roh, Raymond V. *o.s.b.* '59 (MRY)[F] San Luis Obispo, CA Men's Residence.
Roh, Robert A. '65 (LIN) Falls City, NE SS. Peter and Paul; [C] Falls City, NE Sacred Heart School; [L] Falls City, NE Sacred Heart High School Endowment Fund; Deaneries and Deans.
Rohan, John P. '72 (HRT) East Hartford, CT St. Rose's; Medical Leave.
Rohen, Patrick J. '96 (TOL) Military Chaplains; Army Chaplains.
Rohleder, Earl '63 (EVN) Retired.
Rohlfing, Cory J. '01 (STP) Eagan, MN St. John Neumann.
Rohlfs, Steven P. (PEO) Nashville, TN Mary Queen of Angels Parish Community; [L] Nashville, TN Ladies of Charity Welfare Agency, Inc.; Vicar General; Chancellor; Moderator of the Curia; Diocesan College of Consultors; Finance Council (Canon 492); Catholic Cemeteries; Catholic Relief Services; Censor Librorum; Clergymen's Aid, Inc.; Conciliation and Arbitration Process; Diocesan Pastoral Council; Diocesan Personnel Board; Holy Childhood Association; Propagation of the Faith; Priests' Purgatorial Society; Peoria, IL Catholic Cemetery Association of Peoria, IL.
Rohlfs, Steven '76 (PEO) Special Residence; Art and Architecture Commission.
Rohling, Paul L. *v.c.* '75 (BIR) Birmingham, AL St. Peter the Apostle.
Rohling, Paul *v.c.* '75 (BIR)[I] Birmingham, AL St. Peter's Endowment Foundation.
Rohling, Paul *v.c.* (BIR) Members; Diocesan College of Consultors; Diocesan College of Vicars; Judges.
Rohmiller, Christian A. '79 (CIN)[Q] Fairborn, OH Catholic Campus Ministry.
Rohr, Jerome M. '94 (DEN) Littleton, CO Light of the World Parish.
Rohr, John J. *s.j.* '60 (NEW)[C] Jersey City, NJ St. Peter's Preparatory School; [N] Jersey City, NJ Jesuit Community of St. Peter's Prep, Inc..
Rohr, Richard *o.f.m.* '70 (SFE) Albuquerque, NM Holy Family; [M] Albuquerque, NM Center for Action and Contemplation.
Rohrer, Jerome E. *s.j.* '54 (MIL)[O] Wauwatosa, WI Jesuit Community at St. Camillus; [M] Wauwatosa, WI St. Camillus Health Center, Inc..
Rohrer, Richard '94 (PSC) Cary, NC SS. Cyril & Methodius Byzantine Catholic.
Rohrkemper, Charles B. '43 (CIN) Troy, OH St. Patrick Retired.
Roia, Martino *s.x.* '82 (FgM).
Roia, Martino *s.x.* '82 (PAT)[M] Wayne Xaverian Missionary Fathers.
Roide, Russell J. *s.j.* '70 (PHX) Phoenix, AZ St. Francis Xavier.
Roig, Ricardo A. '97 (SJN) Carolina, PR San Juan de Dios; Judges.
Roig, Ricky (SJN) Spiritual Director.
Roig, Vicente Perez '58 (MGZ) Rosario, PR Rosary.
Rojas, Agustin '92 (HRT) New Haven, CT St. Rose of Lima.
Rojas, Alberto '97 (CHI).
Rojas, Hector '90 (SPR)[A] Springfield, MA All Souls; Westfield, MA St. Mary's.
Rojas, Jaime '79 (P) Woodburn, OR St. Luke.
Rojas, Loretto '00 (SAC) On Duty Outside the Diocese.
Rojas, Louis *s.a.c.* '97 (CAM) Hammonton, NJ St. Joseph's.
Rojas, Manuel I. '64 (NY) Staten Island, NY St. Clement; Staten Island, NY St. Michael.
Rojas, Melquiades '91 (ARE) Arecibo, PR San Juan Bosco.
Rojas, Olivete '76 (SFR) San Mateo, CA St. Timothy.
Rojas, Roberto P. *c.s.b.* '97 (GAL)[Q] Sugar Land Basilian Mission Center.
Rojas, Tito '68 (ORL) Altamonte Springs, FL St. Mary Magdalen.
Rojas, Victor '85 (ARE) Arecibo, PR Santa Ana; [A] Arecibo, PR Pontificia Universidad Catholica de Puerto Rico, Recinto de Arecibo; Diocesan Consultors; Priest's Senate (Consejo Presbiteral); Cursillos de Cristiandad; Pastoral Vocational Program.
Rojka, Lubos *s.j.* '96 (BO)[V] Newton, MA The Jesuit

Community at Boston College.
Rokos, Richard V. (PRT) Retired.
Rokosz, Charles W. '70 (SCR) Duryea, PA Holy Rosary; Diocesan Consultors; Presbyteral Council.
Rokusek, Robert J. '66 (DET)[E] Washington, DC Gonzaga College High School; AUXILIARY CHAPLAINS CONTRACT CHAPLAINS.
Rolak, Patrick *o.f.m.conv.* '56 (BAL)[S] Clarence, NY Sacred Heart Home Retired.
Roland, Charles '67 (PT) On Duty Outside the Diocese.
Roland, Charles '67 (SAV) Perry, GA St. Patrick.
Roland, Glynn (Bud) '99 (AUS) Austin, TX St. Mary's Cathedral.
Roldan, Basilio *c.m.* '59 (SJN) San Juan, PR Sagrado Corazon de Jesus.
Roldan, Joseph L. '02 (TR) Hightstown, NJ St. Anthony of Padua.
Roldan, Jovy (STO) Stockton, CA St. Mary of the Assumption Church (Pastor of).
Roldan, Juan '56 (SJN) On Duty Outside the Archdiocese.
Rolek, John A. '61 (CHI) Berwyn, IL St. Leonard; Defenders of the Bond; Delegate of the Archbishop for Privilege Cases.
Roleke, H. James *s.j.* '62 (BUF) Buffalo, NY St. Michael.
Rolf, John J. '57 (LEX) Retired.
Rolfes, Robert E. '77 (SCL) St. Cloud, MN St. Mary Help of Christians; Legion of Decency.
Rolfes, Robert (SCL) Chancellor; Adjutant Judicial Vicar; Judges; Notaries; Diocesan Corporate Board; Clerical Aid Association; Diocesan Priests Pension Plan Trustees.
Rolfs, Richard W. *s.j.* '61 (LA)[C] Los Angeles, CA Jesuit Community.
Rolfson, Gunther '46 (SCL)[I] Collegeville, MN St. John's Abbey, of the Order of St. Benedict.
Roll, Bertin *o.f.m.cap.* '42 (PIT)[N] Pittsburgh, PA St. Augustine Friary.
Roll, David H. '70 (SD) Retired.
Roll, Robert J. '77 (CHI) Other Assignments.
Roll, Ronald *o.f.m.c* (FgM).
Rolland, Daniel J. *o.p.* '93 (TUC) Tuscon, AZ St. Thomas More Chapel; [H] Tucson, AZ University of Arizona.
Rolland, Miguel *o.p.* '88 (PHX)[G] Tempe, AZ Dominicans (Dominican Community–Jordan House).
Roller, John W. '60 (CHI) Mt. Prospect, IL St. Thomas a Becket.
Rolling, Brendan *o.s.b.* (KCK)[A] Atchison, KS Benedictine College; [H] Atchison, KS St. Benedict's Abbey.
Rolon, Julio '93 (PCE) Yauco, PR Santo Domingo de Guzman.
Rolon, Julio '93 (PCE)[B] The Pontifical Catholic University of Puerto Rico.
Rolwing, Richard C. '53 (SPC) Sikeston, MO St. Francis Xavier's; Vicars General; Diocesan Consultors; Appointed Members; Sikeston, MO Retired.
Rom, Gregory A. '75 (CHI) Blue Island, IL St. Isidore.
Romagosa, Edward J. *s.j.* '54 (BR)[J] Convent, LA Manresa House of Retreats.
Roman, Carlos '89 (PCE) Yauco, PR Santo Domingo de Guzman; [B] The Pontifical Catholic University of Puerto Rico.
Roman, Charles '70 (HEL) Whitefish, MT St. Charles; Diocesan Consultors; Presbyteral Council.
Roman, Juan J. Gregorio *s.d.b.* '63 (SJN) San Juan, PR San Juan Bosco.
Roman, Julio I. (NEW) Jersey City, NJ St. Anne's.
Roman, Julio '73 (LA)[J] Los Angeles, CA St. Vincent Medical Center; Hospital Chaplains.
Roman, Manuel R. '56 (BAL) Baltimore, MD Ascension.
Roman, Paul A. '71 (ALB) Oneonta, NY St. Mary.
Roman, Paul L. *f.s.s.p.* '99 (CC) Corpus Christi, TX St. Michael the Archangel Latin Mass Community.
Roman, Paul '71 (ALB)[R] Albany, NY Noonan Community Service Corporation.
Roman, Paul *f.s.s.p.* '99 (SCR)[M] Elmhurst Priestly Fraternity of St. Peter (F.S.S.P.), North American District Headquarters.
Roman, Stephen '57 (SEA) Aberdeen, WA St. Mary; Aberdeen, WA SS. Peter and Paul; Hoquiam, WA Our Lady of Good Help; Ocean Shores, WA St. Jerome.
Roman, Victor '84 (DET) Ecorse, MI St. Francis Xavier.
Romanenko, Oleh '95 (STN) Hollywood, CA Nativity of B.V.M..
Romanet, Antoine De '95 (WDC) Washington, DC Church of St. Louis.
Romano, Blase R. *t.o.r.* '89 (ALT) Windber, PA St. Anthony of Padua.
Romano, Charles '79 (RVC) Port Jefferson, NY Infant Jesus.
Romano, Eugene C. '57 (PAT)[I] Chester, NJ Hermits of Bethlehem in the Heart of Jesus.
Romano, Harry A. '57 (PH) Norristown, PA Holy Saviour Retired.
Romano, Joseph L. '63 (DET) Dearborn Heights, MI St. Sabina.
Romano, Joseph '63 (BUR) Proctor, VT St. Dominic.
Romano, Philip *o.f.m.cap.* '93 (NY) New York, NY Our Lady Queen of Angels; Mount Sinai Medical Center.
Romano, Robert J. '77 (BRK) Brooklyn, NY St. Bernadette.
Romano, Robert (BRK) Police Department.
Romanoski, Joseph V. '86 (MET) South Amboy, NJ Sacred Heart.
Romanowski, Aloysius *o.f.m.conv.* '57 (CHI)[N] Lake Zurich, IL Mount St. Joseph Institute – Chaplaincy.
Romanowski, Brian J. '03 (NOR) Uncasville, CT St. John.
Romanowski, Jerome C. '64 (CAM) Malaga, NJ St. Mary's; Holy Name Society.
Romans, Jeffery V. '03 (HRT) Glastonbury, CT St. Paul's.
Romans, Jeffery V. '03 (HRT) South Glastonbury, CT St. Augustine.
Romanski, Aloysius *o.f.m.conv.* '57 (CHI)[L] Lake Zurich, IL Mt. St. Joseph Home.
Romanski, Edward '75 (CHI) Harvey, IL St. John the Baptist.
Romanski, Gregory A. '77 (AUS) Austin, TX St. Theresa.
Romansky, Joseph '75 (CLV) Administrative Leave.
Romeo, Peter (LAV) Diocesan Tribunal Office–Judicial Vicar; Presbyteral Council for the Diocese of Las Vegas.
Romeo, Robert A. '87 (RVC) Port Washington, NY St. Peter of Alcantara.
Romeo, Robert (RVC) Procurator & Advocates.
Romero, Alejandro *c.s.b.* (GAL)[Q] Sugar Land Basilian Mission Center.
Romero, David H. *s.j.* '91 (NO).
Romero, Domingo *o.f.m.cap.* (FWT)[P] Fort Worth, TX Immaculate Heart of Mary.
Romero, Donald '91 (DEN) Lakewood, CO St. Bernadette.
Romero, Elmer '03 (CHI) Chicago, IL St. Matthias; Chicago, IL Transfiguration of Our Lord
Romero, Fortunato (NY) Bronx, NY St. Thomas Aquinas.
Romero, Gilbert '61 (LA) Retired.
Romero, J. Robert '75 (LAF) Ville Platte, LA Sacred Heart of Jesus; Ville Platte, LA St. Joseph; North Region.
Romero, Joseph J. '69 (BEA) Port Arthur, TX St. Catherine of Siena.
Romero, Juan '64 (LA) Long Beach, CA St. Matthew.
Romero, Marcelino *c.m.f.* '59 (SJN) Bayamon, PR San Antonio Maria Claret.
Romero, Mario '90 (LAF) Cankton, LA St. John Berchmans.
Romero–Rios, Adolfo '88 (NY) Bronx, NY St. Pius V.
Romfh, Paul *o.s.b.* '63 (SP)[O] St. Leo, FL St. Leo Abbey.
Romito, Donald '74 (ORG) Orange, CA Cathedral of the Holy Family.
Romo, Sergio '93 (CHI) Schaumburg, IL St. Marcelline.
Rompa, John '51 (SPK) Spokane, WA St. Ann.
Romza, Victor G. '54 (PBR) Campbell, OH St. Michael.
Ronaghan, John J. '80 (BO) Melrose, MA St. Mary of the Annunciation.
Ronald, Roy K. '60 (BUF) Retired.
Ronan, Charles E. *s.j.* '45 (CHI)[C] Chicago, IL Jesuit Community at Loyola University Chicago.
Ronan, Eugene *m.s.f.* '93 (SAT) New Braunfels, TX Our Lady of Perpetual Help.
Ronan, Henry T. '55 (BO) Senior Priests Retired.
Ronan, Hugh F. '61 (TR) Trenton, NJ Incarnation; Diocesan Consultors.
Ronan, James J. '82 (BO) Holy Rosary; Lawrence, MA SS. Peter and Paul; MERRIMACK REGION.
Roncancio Luis '95 (TYL) Marshall, TX St. Joseph.
Roncase, Robert A. '82 (PH) Lansdale, PA St. Stanislaus.
Ronchi, Vincenzo L. *c.s.* '91 (NY) Mt. Vernon, NY Our Lady of Victory; Mt. Vernon, NY Our Lady of Victory.
Rondeau, John S. *c.s.sp.* '38 (PIT)[P] Bethel Park, PA Holy Spirit Animation Center.
Rondeau, Lawrence J. '58 (BO) Salem, MA St. Joseph; Salem, MA St. James.
Roney, George '78 (LUB) Stamford, TX St. Ann.
Ronik, Michael E. '57 (Y) Youngstown OH St. Matthias.
Ronik, Michael '57 (Y) Retired.
Ronquest John T. '45 (STL) St. Louis, MO St. Simon the Apostle; Archdiocesan Priests' Personnel Board Retired.
Roock, John D. '59 (SY) Endwell, NY Our Lady of Angels.
Roodbeen, Henry W. '75 (DET) Livonia, MI St. Colette.
Roof, Francis '72 (IND) U.S. Penitentiary.
Roof, Frank '72 (OWN) On Duty Outside the Diocese.
Rookey, Peter M. *o.s.m.* '41 (CHI)[N] Berwyn, IL St. Bonfilius Priory.
Rooks, Charles W. '52 (COV)[N] Covington, KY St. Joseph Heights Provincialate and Novitiate of the Sisters of Notre Dame Retired.
Rooney, Aidan *c.m.* '84 (MET)[H] Princeton, NJ Vincentian Residence.
Rooney, Bernard *c.ss.r.* '59 (GR) Grand Rapids, MI St. Alphonsus; [I] Grand Rapids, MI The Society of the Redemptorists of the City of Grand Rapids.
Rooney, Donald J. '94 (ARL) Fredericksburg, VA St. Mary.
Rooney, Edward K. (STA) Campaign for Human Development.
Rooney, Edward '62 (STA) Middleburg, FL St. Luke's.
Rooney, Eugene M. *s.j.* '57 (BAL)[S] San Ignacio.
Rooney, Francis V. *s.j.* '60 (NY)[EE] New York, NY Murray–Weigel Hall.
Rooney, James T. '64 (BRK) Flushing, NY Mary's Nativity.
Rooney, John J. '62 (ALB) Watervliet, NY Sacred Heart of Mary.
Rooney, John '89 (LIN) Shelby, NE Sacred Heart.
Rooney, John '01 (GAL) Houston, TX St. Michael; Ecumenism and Interreligious Affairs Commission.
Rooney, Jordon *o.carm.* '54 (JOL)[L] Darien Carmelite Provincial Office.
Rooney, Joseph S. *s.j.* '66 (SLC) Moab, UT St. Pius X; Monticello, UT St. Joseph.
Rooney, Kevin E. '62 (BUR) Northfield, VT St. John the Evangelist.
Rooney, Marcel *o.s.b.* '63 (KC)[A] Conception, MO Conception Seminary College; [I] Savannah, MO La Verna Village Apartments; [J] Savannah, MO LaVerna Heights Convent; [K] Savannah, MO La Verna Heights Provincial House.
Rooney, Martin '93 (PAT) Paterson, NJ St. Joseph Hospital; [J] Paterson, NJ St. Joseph's Hospital and Medical Center.
Rooney, Martin *m.s.a.* '93 (NOR)[F] Cromwell Society of the Missionaries of the Holy Apostles.
Rooney, Michael '89 (TLS)[E] Tulsa, OK Saint Francis Hospital.
Rooney, Robert B. '63 (GI) Retired.
Rooney, Sean *s.d.b.* '66 (NY)[EE] New Rochelle, NY Salesian Provincial House.
Rooney, Stephen '85 (DET) Monroe, MI St. Michael; Archdiocesan Vicars.
Rooney, Thaddeus '47 (RVC) Deer Park, NY SS. Cyril and Methodius; Priests' Retirement Board Retired.
Rooney, Thomas J. '91 (PH) Philadelphia, PA St. Christopher.
Rooney, William *o.f.m.* '81 (SUP) Ashland, WI Our Lady of the Lake Catholic Community.
Roos, Edward M. '66 (NY) White Plains, NY St. Bernard.
Roos, H. Jules '56 (PIT) On Duty Outside the Diocese.
Roos, John R. (ALB) Censor Librorum.
Roos, John '65 (ALB) Cherry Valley, NY St. Thomas the Apostle.
Roos, Lee R. '90 (ARL) Arlington, VA St. Agnes; Adjutant Judicial Vicar; Diocesan Judges; Management Information Systems.
Roos, Paul '61 (EVN) Mariah Hill, IN Mary, Help of Christians; Evanston, IN St. John Chrysostom.
Roos, Richard H. *s.j.* '74 (BO)[V] Boston, MA Loyola House.
Roost, Joseph F. '89 (DAV) Marengo, IA St. Patrick's; Williamsburg, IA St. Mary's.
Root, James A. '84 (SAM) Carnegie, PA Our Lady of Victory.
Root, James (SAM) Vocations.
Root, Richard '90 (SPK) Absent on Leave.
Ropel, Mark *s.o.l.t.* '02 (CC)[G] Robstown, TX Society of Our Lady of the Most Holy Trinity.
Ropke, John A. (SJP) Parma, OH St. Andrew; Priests' Continuing Education.
Ropke, John (SJP) Presbyteral Council.
Ropke, John (SJP) Diocesan Personnel Board.
Ropke, John (SJP) Permanent Diaconate Program.
Roppolo, Ignatius M. '54 (NO) New Orleans, LA St. Rita Retired.
Roppolo, Ignatius (NO) Ministry to Retired Priests.
Roque, Alejandro *o.m.i.* '88 (SAT)[M] San Antonio, TX Oblate Vocation Office.
Rosa, Joseph '76 (BRK) Brooklyn, NY Most Precious Blood; Legion of Mary.
Rosa, Rolando de la '95 (SFR) Daly City, CA St. Andrew.
Rosa, Salvatore J. '68 (HRT) West Haven, CT St. Paul's.
Rosack, Edward V. '54 (PBR) Ambridge, PA St. Mary's.
Rosado, Rodney Algarin '01 (SJN) Canovanas, PR San Jose.
Rosaforte, Anthony S. '70 (NOR) Norwich, CT St. Patrick Cathedral; College of Consultors; Members.
Rosaforte, Anthony (NOR) Diocesan Panel of Pastors, Canon 1742.
Rosage, David E. '43 (SPK) Retired.
Rosales, Deogracias S. '82 (BO)[U] Cambridge, MA Opus Dei, Prelature of the Holy Cross and Opus Dei.
Rosales, Fredi A. '92 (BRK) Brooklyn, NY Our Lady of Loreto.
Rosales, Fruto '70 (RVC) Hempstead, NY Our Lady of Loretto.
Rosales, Ramon '81 (SB) Chino, CA Our Lady of Guadalupe.
Rosales, Raul H. '93 (TUC) Clifton, AZ Sacred Heart; Morenci, AZ Holy Cross.
Rosales, Samuel *s.j.* '73 (SAT) San Antonio, TX Our Lady of Guadalupe.
Rosario, Anthony '90 (HON) Honolulu, HI Co–Cathedral of St. Theresa of the Child Jesus.
Rosario, Luis A. (ARE) On Duty Outside the Diocese.

Rosas, Orlando (MGZ) Vocations.
Rosato, Philip J. *s.j.* '71 (BAL)[S] Pont. Univ. Greg..
Rosato, Vincenzo *c.s.* '92 (BO) Boston, MA Sacred Heart.
Rosca, Paschal *o.de.m.* '63 (CLV) Cleveland, OH St. Rocco.
Roscioli, Dominic J. '74 (MIL) Retired.
Rose, Alphonse G. '56 (BAL)[W] Ellicott City, MD Catholic Daughters of the Americas Retired.
Rose, Alphonse (BAL) Priest Personnel Board.
Rose, Donald '53 (GB) Retired.
Rose, Frank '90 (NEW) Plainfield, NJ St. Bernard's; Plainfield, NJ St. Stanislaus Kostka; Part–time Staff.
Rose, Geoff *o.s.f.s.* '02 (LAN)[B] Jackson, MI Lumen Christi Catholic High School.
Rose, James '57 (FTW) U.S. Veteran's Hospital Retired.
Rose, John F. '72 (SY) Utica, NY St. Mary of Mt. Carmel; Pastoral Examiners.
Rose, Justin '95 (NTN) San Bernardino, CA St. Philip; MAYA (Melkite Assoc. of Young Adults).
Rose, Justin '95 (SB) San Bernardino, CA St. Phillip the Apostle.
Rose, Michael F. '81 (WOR) South Grafton, MA St. James.
Rose, Michael (WOR) Continuing Education of the Clergy.
Rose, William J. '96 (TOL) Lima, OH St. Charles Borromeo.
Rosebaugh, Lawrence *o.m.i.* '63 (SFD)[A] Godfrey, IL Immaculate Heart of Mary Novitiate.
Rosebrough, Robert T. '69 (STL) Valley Park, MO Sacred Heart.
Roselada, Eulogio '93 (CHI)[N] Chicago, IL Holy Evangelists Friary.
Rosemeyer, John C. '58 (CHI) Retired.
Rosemeyer, Paul F. '52 (CHI) Palatine, IL St. Theresa Retired.
Rosen, Cyprian *o.f.m.cap.* '62 (WIL)[N] Union City, NJ Capuchin Friars – Province of the Sacred Stigmata of St. Francis; [J] Wilmington, DE Capuchin Franciscan Friars, St. Francis Renewal Center; [M] Wilmington, DE St. Francis Renewal Center.
Rosenau, Alan '88 (LR)[E] Hot Springs National Park, AR St. Joseph's Mercy Health Center.
Rosenbaum, William E. '76 (ALT) Johnstown, PA St. Clement's.
Rosensteel, William A. '69 (ALT) Altoona, PA Holy Rosary.
Rosensweig, Walter F. '53 (TUC) Retired.
Rosero, Leo V. '90 (BRK) Long Island City, NY Immaculate Conception; [U] Filipino Apostolate.
Rosette, Fabian Maria *o.carm.* '80 (SAN)[A] Christoval, TX Hermits of the Blessed Virgin Mary of Mount Carmel.
Rosetti, Gabriel A. *o.f.m.* '59 (PH)[D] Philadelphia, PA Archbishop Ryan High School; [AA] Philadelphia, PA St. Pius X Friary.
Rosevear, Anthony *o.p.* '78 (OAK)[N] Oakland, CA Western Dominican Province.
Rosevear, Anthony *o.p.* '78 (SFR) San Francisco, CA St. Dominic; [N] San Francisco, CA St. Dominic Priory.
Rosie, Joseph N. '90 (TR) Lawrenceville, NJ St. Ann; Vice Chancellors; Secretary to the Bishop; Censores Librorum.
Rosin, Richard *s.d.b.* '95 (NEW)[C] Ramsey, NJ Don Bosco Preparatory High School; [N] Ramsey, NJ Don Bosco Prep Salesian Residence.
Rosing, Paul J. '73 (CLV) Stow, OH Holy Family; College of Consultors; Presbyteral Council; Assistant Chancellors; Associate Judges.
Rosing, Robert C. '53 (COV) Covington, KY Church of Our Savior; [I] Covington, KY; [I] Edgewood, KY St. Elizabeth Medical Center, South; [Q] Erlanger, KY Marydale Retreat Center; Covington, KY Cathedral, Basilica of the Assumption Retired.
Rosinski, Bernard J. *s.c.j.* '59 (MIL)[O] Hales Corners, WI Priests of the Sacred Heart; [O] Hales Corners, WI Priests of the Sacred Heart.
Rosinski, Edward B. '63 (CAM) On Sick Leave.
Rosinski, Richard A. '91 (RCK) Dundee, IL St. Catherine of Siena.
Rosko, Ladislaus '52 (CLV) Orange Village, OH St. Margaret of Hungary.
Rosloniec, Leo S. '54 (GR) Wright Township, MI St. Joseph's.
Roslovich, Peter J. *s.j.* '63 (NY)[EE] New York, NY Murray–Weigel Hall.
Rosolen, Emil '86 (AMA) On Duty Outside the Diocese.
Rosolowski, Romulus *o.f.m.conv.* '74 (ALT) Johnstown, PA SS. Casimir & Emerich; Johnstown, PA St. Columba's.
Rosonke, Steven J. '82 (DUB)[F] Cedar Rapids, IA LaSalle Middle School; Cedar Rapids, IA St. Patrick; Due Process Board.
Rosonke, Vince G. (DM) Advocates.
Rosonke, Vince '75 (DM) Waukee, IA St. Boniface.
Rosonke, Vincent (DM) Diocesan Consultors.
Rospond, Paul *c.s.p.* '81 (LA) Goleta, CA St. Mark University Parish; [BB] Goleta, CA.
Ross, Christopher M. *o.s.m.* '54 (CHI)[N] Chicago Order of Friar Servants of Mary (Servites) United States of America Province, Inc..
Ross, David M. '75 (TOL) Lima, OH St. Charles Borromeo; Sycamore, OH St. Pius X; Tiffin, OH St. Mary; Consultors; Priests' Council; Judges.
Ross, Gregory S. *o.c.d.* '95 (NO)[B] New Orleans, LA St. John of the Cross, Discalced Carmelite House of Studies.
Ross, James H. '46 (OKL) Retired.
Ross, Joseph R. '69 (OKL) Oklahoma City, OK Christ the King; Air National Guard Chaplains.
Ross, Joseph *m.s.* '55 (MAN)[K] Enfield, NH Shrine of Our Lady of La Salette; [M] Enfield, NH La Salette Shrine and Center of Enfield.
Ross, Kenneth '92 (ORL) Retired.
Ross, Laurence E. *s.m.* '43 (BO) Lawrence, MA Sacred Heart.
Ross, Lowery '97 (CC) Beeville, TX St. Joseph.
Ross, Mark J. '88 (SAV) Savannah, GA St. James.
Ross, Raymond *c.m.* '48 (STL) St. Louis, MO St. Catherine Laboure; [O] St. Louis, MO Lazarist Residence.
Ross, Richard '67 (JOL) Joliet, IL St. Bernard; Joliet, IL Dept. of Corrections.
Ross, Robert J. *s.j.* '72 (COV)[I] Covington, KY St. Elizabeth Medical Center, North; [I] Edgewood, KY St. Elizabeth Medical Center, South; [I] Williamstown, KY St. Elizabeth Medical Center, Grant County.
Ross, Robert J. *s.j.* '72 (CIN)[M] Cincinnati, OH.
Ross, Stephen–Joseph *o.c.d.* '84 (MIL)[O] Milwaukee Provincial Offices – Discalced Carmelites.
Ross, Theodore *s.j.* '67 (CIN)[B] Cincinnati, OH Mt. St. Mary's Seminary of the West.
Ross, William B. '54 (OKL) Purcell, OK Our Lady of Victory; Health Panel, Archdiocesan Retired.
Rossa, Peter '03 (PHX) Scottsdale, AZ Our Lady of Perpetual Help.
Rossato, Graziano *s.x.* '66 (PAT)[M] Wayne Xaverian Missionary Fathers.
Rossato, Graziano *s.x.* '66 (FgM).
Rossbach, George F. '36 (NY) Retired.
Rossbach, J. Robert *c.ss.r.* '47 (STL)[O] Liguori, MO St. Clement Health Care Center.
Rosse, John '54 (ROC) Rochester, NY St. Margaret Mary.
Rossell, Richard *o.f.m.conv.* '61 (TR) Point Pleasant Beach, NJ St. Peter's.
Rossello, Nicholas A. '60 (BUF) Retired.
Rosser, Aelred *o.s.b.* '67 (KC)[J] Stanberry, MO.
Rossetti, Mark T. '85 (SCR) Unassigned or Leave of Absence; Army Reserve Chaplains.
Rossetti, Salvatore J. *o.p.* '42 (MET) Edison, NJ St. Helena.
Rossetti, Stephen J. '73 (WDC)[V] Silver Spring, MD Saint Luke Institute, Inc..
Rossetti, Stephen '84 (SY) On Duty Outside the Diocese.
Rossey, Stephen J. *o.praem.* '59 (GB)[I] De Pere, WI St. Norbert Abbey.
Rossi, Desmond '92 (ALB) Leave of Absence.
Rossi, Domenic A. *o.praem.* '74 (PH) Paoli, PA St. Norbert; [AA] Paoli, PA Daylesford Abbey.
Rossi, Dominic L. (PH) Plymouth Meeting, PA Epiphany of Our Lord.
Rossi, Dominic *p.i.m.e.* '38 (DET)[K] Detroit, MI P.I.M.E. Motherhouse in Detroit.
Rossi, Frank H. '83 (GAL) On Special or Other Diocesan Assignment.
Rossi, Frank H. (GAL) Chancellor and Moderator of the Curia; Ex Officio Members; College of Consultors; Priests Personnel Committee; Disaster Relief; Rural Life Bureau.
Rossi, Frank (GAL) Secretariat For Administration; Secretariat for Administration.
Rossi, Joseph M. '84 (BO) Lynn, MA St. Pius Fifth.
Rossi, Joseph S. *s.j.* '80 (BAL)[B] Timonium, MD Loyola Graduate Center –Timonium Campus; [S] Baltimore, MD Jesuit Community of Loyola College, Inc..
Rossi, Pat F. '82 (NY) Bronx, NY SS. Philip and James.
Rossi, Paul J. '74 (SFR) San Rafael, CA St. Raphael; Serra Club of Marin.
Rossi, Philip J. *s.j.* '71 (MIL)[O] Milwaukee, WI Arrupe House Jesuit Community.
Rossi, Raymond R. '58 (LR) Retired.
Rossi, Robert *o.s.c.* '70 (FgM).
Rossi, Thomas J. *o.praem.* '73 (PH) Philadelphia, PA King of Peace; [AA] Paoli, PA Daylesford Abbey.
Rossi, Thomas P. (BO) Somerville, MA St. Catherine of Genoa.
Rossi, Walter R. '87 (SCR) On Duty Outside the Diocese; [Q] Washington, DC Basilica of the National Shrine of the Immaculate Conception.
Rossie, Arthur R. *c.ss.r.* '57 (STL)[O] Liguori, MO St. Clement Health Care Center.
Rossiter, John F. '58 (KCK) Topeka, KS Assumption.
Rossito, Joseph V. '69 (BGP)[P] Stamford, CT The Catherine Dennis Keefe Queen of the Clergy Retired Priests' Residence.
Rossitto, Joseph V. '69 (BGP) Retired.
Rossman, Dick (P) Board Members.
Rossman, George M. '66 (NY)[JJ] New York, NY Prelature of the Holy Cross and Opus Dei.
Rossman, Richard '71 (P) Tualatin, OR Church of the Resurrection; Area Vicars.
Rosso, Norbert *c.s.sp.* '54 (SB)[E] Hemet, CA Holy Ghost Fathers.
Rosson, John P. '75 (ALB) Cooperstown, NY St. Mary.
Rosswog, Ken *o.f.m.* '50 (SFD) Montrose, IL St. Rose of Lima.
Rosswog, Kenneth *o.f.m.* '57 (SFD) Teutopolis, IL St. Francis of Assisi; [L] Teutopolis, IL St. Francis Assisi Friary.
Rost, Robert A. '74 (KC) Independence, MO Nativity of the Blessed Virgin Mary; Diocesan Consultors.
Rost, Robert (KC) Deans; Administrative Committee.
Roszko, Edward J. *o.s.f.s.* '70 (WIL)[J] Alexandria, VA Oblates of St. Francis de Sales Residence; [B] Wilmington, DE Salesianum School.
Roszkowski, Donald F. '97 (PEO) Farmer City, IL Sacred Heart; Wapella, IL St. Patrick's.
Roten, Johann B.G. *s.m.* '69 (CIN)[D] Dayton, OH The University of Dayton; [D] The Marian Library/ International Marian Research Institute (IMRI); [M] Dayton, OH Marianist Community.
Rotert, J. Matthew '94 (KC) Chillicothe, MO St. Columban.
Rotert, Norman '57 (KC) Kansas City, MO Visitation of the Blessed Virgin Mary.
Roth, George M. *f.f.i.* '98 (FR)[H] New Bedford, MA Marian Friary of Our Lady, Queen of the Seraphic Order.
Roth, James H. *o.s.f.s.* '95 (TOL)[C] Toledo, OH St. Francis de Sales High School; [J] Toledo, OH Provincial Residence.
Roth, Joseph R. '79 (CHR) Charleston, SC Cathedral of St. John the Baptist; Charleston, SC St. Mary's; Vicar General's Office; Diocesan Curia; Judges; College of Consultors; Finance Council; Presbyteral Council; Building & Renovation Commission; Christian Formation; Investment Council; Pastoral Council; Diaconate, Office of; Personnel Committee.
Roth, Timothy J. *m.i.c.* '74 (NOR)[C] Thompson, CT Marianapolis Preparatory School.
Roth, Timothy *m.i.c.* '74 (NOR)[F] Thompson, CT Marian Fathers.
Roth, Timothy *m.i.c.* '74 (CHI)[N] Chicago, IL Congregation of Marian Fathers of the Immaculate Conception.
Rothe, James A. '56 (LA) Retired.
Rothermel, Paul L. '94 (ALN) Northampton, PA Our Lady of Hungary; Northampton, PA St. Michael.
Rothfuchs, Gregory '95 (JOL) Joliet, IL St. Paul the Apostle.
Rothrauff, Leo *o.s.b.* '56 (GBG) Vandergrift, PA St. Gertrude.
Rothrauff, Noel H. *o.s.b.* '54 (GBG)[H] Latrobe, PA Saint Vincent Archabbey.
Rothrauff, Noel H. *o.s.b.* '54 (FgM).
Rothrock, Theodore D. '83 (LFT) Carmel, IN St. Elizabeth Ann Seton; Diocesan Consultors.
Rothrock, Theodore (LFT) Building Commission; Members.
Rothschild, Paul J. '84 (STL) Overland, MO All Souls.
Rothwell, Joseph T. '52 (BO) Senior Priests Retired.
Rotola, Albert C. *s.j.* '68 (STL)[O] St. Louis, MO Jesuit Community Corporation at St. Louis University – Jesuit Hall.
Rotondi, Paul *o.f.m.* '56 (HRT) Meriden, CT St. Rose of Lima.
Rott, Bernard E. '79 (MAD) Watertown, WI St. Henry.
Rottman, Gary '03 (TYL) Longview, TX St. Mary.
Rotunno, Anthony R. '61 (PRT) Retired.
Rotunno, Floyd '70 (NEW) Mahwah, NJ Immaculate Heart of Mary.
Rotunno, Philip J. '66 (NEW) West New York, NJ Our Lady of Libera; Charismatic Renewal.
Rouch, Nicholas J. '89 (E)[B] Erie, PA Gannon University; [M] Erie, PA Holy Family Monastery; St. Mark Seminary.
Rouech, Chris '96 (GR) Montague, MI St. James.
Rougeau, Marc *s.d.b.* '77 (LA)[W] Rosemead, CA St. Joseph's Salesian Youth Renewal Center.
Roughan, Richard F. '63 (NOR) Waterford, CT St. Paul.
Rouleau, Francis C. (NOR) Diocesan Commission for Ecumenical and Interreligious Affairs; Local Haitian Apostolate/Apostola Ayisyun; Uncasville, CT St. John.
Rourke, John '63 (VEN) On Special Assignment.
Rouse, C. Paul (BO) Gloucester, MA St. Peter.
Rouse, Silvan *c.p.* '49 (ALT)[J] Bedford, PA St. Mary's House of Greater Solitude.
Rouse, Warren *o.f.m.* '57 (LA)[W] Malibu, CA Serra Retreat.
Rousseau, Julian *s.s.s.* '50 (SP) Holiday, FL St. Vincent De Paul.
Rousseau, Peter A. '49 (BUR) Retired.
Rousseau, Richard W. *s.j.* '54 (SCR)[C] Scranton, PA The University of Scranton.
Rousseau, Richard W. *s.j.* '54 (BO)[V] Boston The Society of Jesus of New England–Provincial Offices.
Rousseau, Robert J. '67 (HRT) Bristol, CT St. Ann.
Rousseau, Robert *s.s.s.* '76 (CHI)[N] Chicago, IL The

Blessed Sacrament House of Studies.
Rousseau, Sean K. '95 (ARL) Alexandria, VA Good Shepherd.
Rousseau, Stanley B. (BGP) Presbyteral Council; Pontifical Association of the Holy Childhood; Propagation of the Faith.
Rousseau, Stanley '56 (BGP) Stratford, CT Holy Name of Jesus.
Rousseau, Stanley '98 (NEW) Jersey City, NJ Assumption/All Saints; Jersey City, NJ St. Patrick's.
Rousseau, William C. '95 (SPR) Chicopee, MA St. Anne's.
Roussel, Matthew G. '99 (LAF) Eunice, LA St. Thomas More.
Roussell, Christopher J. '03 (BR) Denham Springs, LA Immaculate Conception.
Routenberg, Joseph F. '73 (IND) French Lick, IN Our Lady of the Springs.
Routhier, Peter A. '78 (BUR) Elected Members; Advocates; Deans; Liturgical Commission; Barre, VT St. Monica.
Roux, Christopher Alan '01 (CHL) Huntersville, NC St. Mark.
Roux, G. Albert '66 (PRT) Special or Other Diocesan Assignment.
Roux, Philippe D. '73 (SPR) South Deerfield, MA St. Stanislaus B. and M.; South Deerfield, MA St. James.
Roux, Randy P. '79 (NO) New Orleans, LA St. Patrick.
Roverse, Michael '84 (SAV) Augusta, GA St. Teresa of Avila.
Rowan, John M. '89 (BO) Quincy, MA St. Mary.
Rowan, John '61 (RVC) Sayville, NY St. Lawrence the Martyr.
Rowan, Mark P. '91 (RVC) Military Chaplains; Air Force Chaplains.
Rowan, Stephen C. (SEA) Presbyteral Council; Vicar for Education, Office of; College of Consultors.
Rowan, Stephen '70 (SEA) Special Assignment; [P] Seattle, WA Fulcrum Foundation; Catholic Schools Department.
Rowe, Donald F. *s.j.* '72 (CHI)[C] Chicago, IL Jesuit Community at Loyola University Chicago.
Rowe, William J. '64 (BEL) Mount Carmel, IL St. Mary.
Rowgh, T. Matthew '75 (WH) Shepherdstown, WV St. Agnes.
Rowland, Bill *s.m.* (OAK)[N] Berkeley, CA Marist Fathers and Brothers.
Rowland, Charles H. '70 (CHR) Columbia, SC St. Joseph; Diocesan Curia; Office of Tribunal; College of Consultors; Presbyteral Council.
Rowland, Edward P. '53 (JOL) Joliet, IL St. Thaddeus.
Rowland, Thomas '49 (ELP) On Duty Outside of Diocese.
Rowland, William F. *c.j.m.* '70 (SD) San Diego, CA Blessed Sacrament.
Rowntree, Stephen C. *s.j.* '75 (NO)[C] New Orleans, LA Loyola University New Orleans.
Rowsome, Morgan '70 (CC) Presbyteral Council; Corpus Christi, TX St. Peter Prince of Apostles.
Roy, Allen J. '54 (NO) New Orleans, LA Holy Spirit.
Roy, Donald J. '70 (BUR) Graniteville, VT St. Sylvester.
Roy, Duane *o.s.b.* '67 (FgM).
Roy, Duane *o.s.b.* '67 (KCK)[H] Atchison, KS St. Benedict's Abbey.
Roy, F. Gilles '57 (WOR) On Duty Outside the Diocese.
Roy, George *o.m.i.* (BO) Special Chaplaincies; In Res.
Roy, J. Jean '56 (WDC) Retired.
Roy, James R. *m.m.* '76 (NY).
Roy, James '61 (ALX)[EE] Klamath Falls, OR St. Pius X Retired.
Roy, Kenneth J. (ALX) College of Consultors; Priests Council; Rural Deans; Pineville, LA Sacred Heart.
Roy, Louis *o.p.* '72 (BO)[V] Dover, MA St. Stephen Priory.
Roy, Maurice J. '73 (BUR) Elected Members; Diocesan Consultors; Deans; St. Albans, VT Holy Angels.
Roy, Michael J. '75 (WOR) Webster, MA Sacred Heart of Jesus; Deans.
Roy, Paul A. *m.s.* '58 (HRT)[M] Hartford Our Lady of Sorrows Rectory.
Roy, Richard M. '75 (FR) Orleans, MA St. Joan of Arc.
Roy, Richard P. '71 (WDC)[M] Washington, DC Missionaries of Africa.
Roy, Richard *m.afr.* '71 (FgM).
Roy, Robert P. '94 (HRT) Meriden, CT St. Joseph; Meriden, CT St. Mary.
Roy, Roger *o.m.i.* '49 (BO)[V] Lowell, MA Contemplative Mission Center.
Royal, Kevin T. '85 (BGP)[A] Stamford, CT St. John Fisher Seminary Residence.
Royal, Peter '53 (AUS) Retired.
Royce, Thomas R. *s.j.* '56 (YAK) Yakima, WA St. Joseph's.
Royer, Ronald '58 (LA) Retired.
Royer, Ronald '58 (FRS) Porterville, CA St. Anne.
Royer, Thomas J. '60 (PEO) Champaign, IL St. Mary's; Seymour, IL St. Boniface.
Royer, Yvon J. '90 (BUR) Deans; Derby Line, VT St. Edward; Newport, VT St. Mary Star of the Sea.
Royik, Ihor '92 (PHU) Passaic, NJ St. Nicholas.
Royo–Mejia, Alberto *c.o.* '89 (PH)[AA] Philadelphia, PA The Philadelphia Congregation of The Oratory of St. Philip Neri.
Royston, Basil '81 (SJ) O'Connor Hospital; [H] San Jose, CA O'Connor Hospital.
Rozanski, Mitchell T. '84 (BAL) Severna Park, MD St. John the Evangelist; [V] Severna Park, MD St. John the Evangelist School Endowment Trust; Consultors; Consultors.
Rozanski, Mitchell (BAL) Advocates and Procurators.
Rozansky, Joseph G. *o.f.m.* '76 (WDC)[B] Silver Spring, MD Holy Name College.
Rozario, Leonard *c.s.c.* (CHI)[D] Niles, IL Notre Dame High School.
Rozario, William '90 (OAK) San Lorenzo, CA St. John the Baptist.
Rozman, Thomas J. '86 (HBG) Harrisburg PA Cathedral Parish of St. Patrick.
Rozniak, Ronald J. '71 (NEW) Ridgewood, NJ Our Lady of Mount Carmel; [G] Newark, NJ Catholic Community Services (C.C.S.) Mt. Carmel Guild Hospital; College of Consultors; Members; Catholic Community Services (CCS).
Roznowski, Thomas *o.s.b.* '76 (SFS)[F] Marvin, SD Blue Cloud Abbey.
Rozum, George A. *c.s.c.* '68 (FTW)[B] University of Notre Dame Du Lac; [I] Notre Dame, IN Holy Cross Community, Corby Hall, University of Notre Dame.
Rozycki, George '70 (SP) Zephyrhills, FL St. Joseph; Presbyteral Council; College of Consultors; Vicars Forane.
Rozycki, Isidore '68 (AUS) West, TX St. Martin; Deans.
Ruan, John Ming '97 (WDC) Laurel, MD St. Mary.
Ruane, Dennis *s.s.s.* '59 (CLV)[O] Gretna, LA.
Ruane, Edward M. *o.p.* '69 (CHI)[X] Chicago, IL St. Thomas Aquinas Foundation; (FgM).
Ruane, George '73 (NEW) Edgewater, NJ Holy Rosary.
Ruane, Gerald P. (NEW) Sacred Heart Institute.
Ruane, John P. *s.j.* '49 (NEW)[B] Jersey City, NJ Jesuit Center; [N] Jersey City, NJ Jesuits of Saint Peter's College, Inc..
Ruane, Martin '63 (JKS) Pearl, MS St. Jude; Rankin County Prison.
Ruane, Martin '63 (JKS) Mississippi State Hospital.
Ruane, Martin '63 (JKS) Pearl, MS St. Jude; Rankin County Prison.
Ruane, Michael J. '69 (BAL) Mount Airy, MD St. Michael.
Ruani, Pablo *i.v.e.* '92 (FR) New Bedford, MA St. Kilian; New Bedford.
Ruba, Nicholas J. '51 (SC) Retired.
Rubadue, Paul E. *o.s.b.* '86 (GBG)[H] Latrobe, PA Saint Vincent Archabbey.
Rubaj, Leon '60 (SAT) On Duty Outside the Archdiocese.
Rubbelke, Ronald J. '64 (STL) O'Fallon, MO Assumption.
Rubey, Charles T. '66 (CHI)[G] Chicago, IL Catholic Charities of the Archdiocese of Chicago–Archdiocesan Offices; [G] Chicago, IL Catholic Charities of the Archdiocese of Chicago–Archdiocesan Offices; [G] Chicago, IL LOSS (Loving Outreach to Survivors of Suicide); [L] Chicago, IL St. Joseph's Carondelet Child Center; Catholic Charities of Chicago; Office for Persons with Disabilities.
Rubiano, Cesar A. *c.j.m.* (MO) Woodhull Medical & Mental Health Center; Army National Guard Chaplains.
Rubin, Ettore *c.s.* '62 (VEN) Immokalee, FL Our Lady of Guadalupe.
Rubino, Vincent *o.f.m.conv.* (BRK) Brooklyn, NY Most Holy Trinity.
Rubio, Jose Antonio '80 (SJ) San Jose, CA Five Wounds Portuguese National Church; Special Assignment; Ecumenical and Interreligious Affairs.
Rubio–Boitel, Fernando '75 (SFE) Albuquerque, NM Queen of Heaven.
Ruby, David (GB) Oconto, WI Holy Trinity.
Rucando, Anthony M. '70 (BRK) Brooklyn, NY Our Lady Help of Christians.
Ruchgy, Wayne J. '66 (STN) Dearborn, MI St. Michael's.
Ruchgy, Wayne (STN) Presbyteral Council.
Ruchgy, Wayne (STN) Protosyncellus.
Ruchgy, Wayne (STN) Diocesan Consultors.
Ruchgy, Wayne (STN) Personnel Board.
Rucinski, Joseph S. '42 (TR) Retired.
Rucinski, Willard *o.s.f.s.* '65 (R) Fayetteville, NC St. Elizabeth Ann Seton.
Ruck, Michael J. *m.m.* '46 (SJ)[M] Los Altos, CA Maryknoll.
Rucker, Lawrence *s.c.j.* '66 (MIL)[O] Franklin, WI Villa Maria.
Rucker, Neville '46 (LA) Retired.
Rudcki, Stanley R. '53 (CHI) Retired.
Rudd, Thad B. '91 (ATL) Cleveland, GA St. Paul the Apostle.
Rudden, Matthew T. '59 (RCK) Retired.
Ruddick, James J. *s.j.* '55 (BUF) Vicar for Religious; Buffalo, NY St. Ann.
Ruddy, Paul *o.s.f.s.* '64 (LAN) Cooper Street Correctional Facility.
Rude, James A. *s.j.* '64 (HON) Honolulu, HI Newman Center–Holy Spirit Parish; [G] Honolulu, HI Jesuit Fathers House.
Rudemiller, Edward L. '58 (CIN) Cincinnati, OH Our Lady of Lourdes; Vicarri Foranei (Deans); Judges.
Rudisill, James A. '51 (NSH) Retired.
Rudjak, Joseph '00 (Y) Youngstown, OH SS. Peter and Paul.
Rudnay, Clement A. *o.praem.* '38 (ORG)[I] Silverado, CA Norbertine Fathers of Orange Inc..
Rudnick, Kenneth J. *s.j.* '91 (LA)[A] Camarillo, CA St. John's Seminary College of the Archdiocese of Los Angeles.
Rudnicki, Wladyslaw '56 (RVC) Cutchogue, NY Our Lady of Ostrabrama.
Rudnik, John J. '61 (CHI) Chicago, IL Transfiguration of Our Lord.
Rudnik, Tadeusz '55 (SY) Marathon, NY St. Stephen.
Rudolf, Roger G. '92 (IND) Rushville, IN Immaculate Conception/St. Mary.
Rudolf, Roger (IND) Council of Priests.
Rudolph, Frederick *s.v.d.* '54 (CHI)[B] Techny, IL Divine Word Residence.
Rudolph, Patrick '88 (ORG) Cypress, CA St. Irenaeus; On Duty Outside the Diocese.
Rudolph, Thomas J. '61 (LC) Stratford, WI St. Andrew; Stratford, WI St. Joseph.
Rudolphi, Stephen A. '79 (BEL) Carmi, IL St. Polycarp (German); Carmi, IL St. Patrick.
Rudolphi, Timothy C. '89 (STP) Monticello, MN St. Henry.
Rudy, Noel T. '53 (SAG) Retired.
Rudy, Noel '53 (SAG) Harrison, MI St. Athanasius.
Rudy, Richard E. '76 (PH) Richboro, PA St. Vincent de Paul.
Rudy, Theodore '54 (PSC) Dunmore, PA St. Michael.
Rudzewicz, Jan '83 (OAK) Fremont, CA Our Lady of Guadalupe.
Rueda, John (NY) Bronx, NY Our Lady of Mercy.
Rueda, Silverio '80 (SJN) Trujillo Alto, PR Maria Llena de Gracia; Head Start–Municipality of Carolina.
Ruede, Ernest J. '66 (R) New Bern, NC St. Paul; Deans.
Ruede, Ernest (R) Priests' Council.
Ruedisueli, Robert A. '69 (DET) Warren, MI St. Mark.
Ruef, James L.T. '78 (COL) Columbus, OH Holy Name; Parochial Examiners; Vicariate 3: North High.
Ruef, James LeRoy Tonkinson (COL) Presiding Judge in Second Instance.
Rueger, William '75 (BRK) Glendale, NY St. Pancras.
Ruehl, William F. '58 (ARL) Front Royal, VA St. John the Baptist; Deans.
Ruekert, Thomas E. *s.d.b.* '73 (NO) Harvey, LA St. Rosalie.
Ruelle, Gerald *o.s.b.* '50 (BIS) Killdeer, ND St. Paul; Killdeer, ND St. Joseph; [A] Richardton, ND Assumption Abbey; Pro–Synodal Judges.
Rueter, Joseph J. '46 (COV) Cold Spring, KY St. Joseph; Legion of Mary Retired.
Ruetz, Edward J. '62 (FTW) Retired.
Rueve, Charles *c.pp.s.* '43 (CIN)[B] Carthagena, OH St. Charles.
Ruff, Anthony *o.s.b.* '93 (SCL)[I] Collegeville, MN St. John's Abbey, of the Order of St. Benedict.
Ruff, Charles R. '46 (STL) Retired.
Ruff, Daniel M. *s.j.* '86 (BAL)[B] Timonium, MD Loyola Graduate Center –Timonium Campus; [S] Baltimore, MD Jesuit Community of Loyola College, Inc..
Ruff, Frank *g.h.m.* '63 (OWN) Elkton, KY St. Susan; Guthrie, KY Sts. Mary & James; Deans; Priests' Council.
Ruffing, Joseph R. '55 (LFT) Retired.
Ruffing, Norman '63 (OAK) Retired.
Ruffo, John *o.f.m.conv.* '74 (R) Burlington, NC Blessed Sacrament; [E] Burlington, NC Conventual Franciscans; [H] Elon, NC Elon University.
Ruffolo, George *c.m.f.* '59 (CHI) Chicago, IL Holy Cross/Immaculate Heart of Mary.
Rufo, Henry '01 (P) Medford, OR Sacred Heart of Jesus.
Ruge, Paul '97 (FAR) St. Michael, ND St. Michael; St. Michael's Indian Mission.
Rugel, James J. (PAT) Retired.
Rugen, Patrick J. '76 (CHI).
Rugen, Patrick '76 (CHI)[A] Chicago, IL Our Lady of Mercy; [C] Chicago, IL St. Joseph's Seminary.
Ruggere, Peter L. *m.m.* '68 (NY).
Ruggere, Peter L. *m.m.* '68 (LA)[Q] San Ysidro, CA.
Ruggere, Peter *m.m.* '68 (SD) San Ysidro, CA Our Lady of Mt. Carmel; Missions; Holy Childhood Association; Propagation of the Faith.
Ruggeri, Joseph A. '65 (BO) Unassigned.
Ruggeri, Salvator (CLV) Presbyteral Council.
Ruggeri, Salvatore M. '99 (CLV) Fairlawn, OH St. Hilary.
Ruggerio, Salvatore (CLV)[D] Akron, OH St. Vincent–St. Mary High School.
Ruggieri, James T. '95 (PRO) Providence, RI St. Patrick; College of Consultors.
Ruggieri, Joseph '95 (Y) Ashtabula, OH Our Lady of Mt. Carmel.
Ruggieri, Pasquale *f.d.p.* '52 (NY) New York, NY St. Ann.

Ruggiero, James S. '70 (PIT) Pittsburgh, PA St. Teresa of Avila.
Ruglovsky, Robert '61 (PRM) Absent on Leave.
Ruhl, Matthew D. *s.j.* '92 (KC)[J] Kansas City, MO Rockhurst Jesuit Community.
Ruhl, Matthew *s.j.* '92 (KC) Kansas City, MO St. Francis Xavier.
Ruhl, William J. *o.s.f.s.* '62 (R) Goldsboro, NC St. Mary; Priests' Council.
Ruhland, Carl J. '45 (DUB) Retired.
Ruhlin, James '02 (SP) Safety Harbor, FL Espiritu Santo.
Ruhling, James P. '60 (E) Retired.
Ruhnke, Robert A. *c.ss.r.* '66 (SAT)[M] San Antonio, TX Redemptorists of Texas–San Antonio #1.
Ruisanchez, Jose P. '86 (BO)[U] Newton, MA Prelature of the Holy Cross and Opus Dei.
Ruiz, Agustin '56 (BRK) Brooklyn, NY SS. Peter and Paul's.
Ruiz, Albert Capello '29 (AUS) Bryan, TX Santa Teresa's; Giddings, TX St. Margaret.
Ruiz, Albert (AUS) Presbyteral Council; Consultors; Office of Hispanic Ministry.
Ruiz, Antonio A. (TUC) Retired.
Ruiz, Antonio *c.m.* '65 (LA) Los Angeles, CA St. Vincent De Paul.
Ruiz, Carlos A. (NY) Bronx, NY St. Joan of Arc.
Ruiz, Dominic *o.s.b.* '83 (SCL)[I] Collegeville, MN St. John's Abbey, of the Order of St. Benedict.
Ruiz, Eddie '99 (SD) El Cajon, CA Holy Trinity.
Ruiz, Efrain Medina '01 (MRY) Paso Robles, CA St. Rose.
Ruiz, Enrique '56 (SAT) On Leave.
Ruiz, Faustino C. '91 (MET) On Duty Outside the Diocese.
Ruiz, Giovanni (CGS) San Lorenzo, PR Sagrado Corazon de Jesus y 12 Apostoles.
Ruiz, Jean–Pierre *s.t.d.* '82 (BRK) Long Island City, NY St. Patrick; Released from Diocesan Assignment.
Ruiz, John '55 (HT) Thibodaux General Hospital.
Ruiz, Jose Domingo '89 (STO) Stockton, CA St. Linus Church (Pastor of); Lockeford, CA St. Joachim Church of Lockeford (Pastor of).
Ruiz, Joseph B. '66 (CHI) Oak Park, IL St. Edmund.
Ruiz, Lorenzo '63 (SJN) San Juan, PR San Juan Bosco.
Ruiz, Lorenzo (CIN) Censors.
Ruiz, Luis '68 (SAT) San Antonio, TX St. Stephen.
Ruiz, Luis '84 (CGS) Caguas, PR Divino Nino.
Ruiz, Miguel *s.v.d.* '95 (MEM) Memphis, TN Sacred Heart; [I] Memphis, TN Society of the Divine Word (Chicago Province).
Ruiz, Oscar Ramirez '94 (SLC) Layton, UT St. Rose of Lima.
Ruiz, Pedro *s.j.* (NY)[EE] New York, NY Xavier Jesuit Community.
Ruiz, Ricardo '93 (ELP) Alpine, TX Our Lady of Peace; Presbyteral Council.
Ruiz, Ruben Romero (LSC) Presbyteral Council.
Ruiz, Rudy '79 (MRY) Hollister, CA Sacred Heart/St. Benedict Catholic Community.
Ruiz–Armas, Salvadore *s.s.p.* '03 (LA)[Q] Los Angeles, CA Society of St. Paul.
Ruiz–Santos, Carlos '03 (SAL) Salina, KS Cathedral of the Sacred Heart.
Rukavina, Steven '87 (B) Boise, ID St. Mark's.
Rukstalis, Simeon *o.f.m.conv.* '64 (SY) Binghamton, NY SS. Cyril and Method.
Ruland, Vernon J. *s.j.* '63 (SFR)[N] San Francisco, CA Jesuit Community at University of San Francisco.
Rule, Philip C. *s.j.* '62 (WOR)[O] Worcester, MA Jesuits of Holy Cross College, Inc..
Rule, Philip C. *s.j.* '62 (DET)[K] Temperance, MI.
Rule, Steven R. '75 (RIC) Richmond, VA Our Lady of Lourdes.
Rulli, Joseph A. '92 (FTW) Fort Wayne, IN St. Therese.
Rulli, Joseph '92 (FTW)[C] Fort Wayne, IN Bishop Luers High School; Council of Priests.
Rumble, Clarence F. '86 (SY) Endicott, NY St. Anthony of Padua.
Rumble, Michael (DET)[H] Grosse Pointe, MI Bon Secours Hospital.
Runde, David H. '57 (MAD) Diocesan Consultors Retired.
Runde, Raymond E. '56 (MAD) Absent on Sick Leave.
Runde, William H. *s.j.* '69 (STL)[O] St. Louis, MO Office; [S] St. Louis, MO Retreat House.
Rundzio, Mark A. '81 (MAN) Absent on Sick Leave.
Runnebaum, Conrad '55 (SFE) Retired.
Runte, Richard M. '73 (SPR) West Springfield, MA St. Thomas the Apostle.
Runtz, Anthony *c.j.* '58 (LA)[B] Santa Maria, CA St. Joseph Seminary (Josephite Fathers' Novitiate).
Ruoalcala, Ernesto *o.s.m.* (ELP) El Paso, TX St. Ignatius of Loyola.
Ruoff, John C. *s.j.* '61 (STL)[O] St. Louis, MO Jesuit Community Corporation at St. Louis University – Jesuit Hall; [N] St. Louis, MO Fusz Pavilion.
Ruoff, Louis W. '84 (RIC) Suffolk, VA St. Mary of the Presentation.
Rupert, Dale R. '77 (SCR) Scranton, PA St. Mary of the Assumption.
Rupp, Daniel J. '98 (BUR) Elected Members; Barton, VT Conversion of St. Paul; Orleans, VT St. Theresa of Child Jesus.
Rupp, Edward '60 (CLV) Administrative Leave.
Ruppenkamp, Raymond '50 (DAV) Retired.
Ruppert, Alan E. '78 (BEL) Leave of Absence.
Ruppert, Donald R. '78 (VIC) East Bernard, TX Holy Cross; Diocesan Consultors.
Ruppert, Donald (VIC) El Campo Deanery; Presbyteral Council; Priests' Personnel Board; Diocesan Finance Board.
Rurangirwa, Romaine (BO) Boston, MA St. Cecilia.
Rusay, Leonard F.A. '85 (MET) Whitehouse Station, NJ Our Lady of Lourdes.
Rusch, Donald '61 (LAN) Retired.
Ruschman, Albert E. '53 (COV) Fort Thomas, KY St. Thomas Retired.
Rusconi, Richard A. '71 (PAT) Dover, NJ St. Mary's; Wharton, NJ St. Bernard's.
Ruse, Fred R. '76 (ORL) Winter Haven, FL St. Matthew.
Rusek, John '58 (ALN)[J] Bethlehem, PA Holy Family Villa.
Rush, Ernest G. '02 (NEW) Livingston, NJ St. Philomena.
Rush, J. Kenneth '71 (RIC) Lynchburg, VA Holy Cross; Regional Delegates; Judges.
Rush, James C. '68 (HRT) Retired.
Rush, James P. '72 (CAM) Bridgeton, NJ Immaculate Conception.
Rush, Joseph P. '62 (CAM) Pine Hill, NJ St. Edward's.
Rush, Michael P. '73 (CAM) Ocean City, NJ St. Augustine's.
Rush, Patrick J. '69 (KC) Kansas City, MO St. Peter's; Special Assignment; Diocesan Consultors; Building Commission.
Rush, Patrick R. (KC) Vicar General.
Rush, Vincent '72 (RVC) Huntington Station, NY St. Hugh of Lincoln; Consultants; Women in the Church and in Society, Diocesan Commission.
Rushford, William A. '55 (BIS)[G] Bismarck, ND Emmaus Place Retired.
Rushman, John '55 (GAY) Retired.
Rushofsky, John R. (PIT) Judges; Clergy Personnel Board; Clergy Personnel, Dept. for.
Rusin, Joseph C. '46 (SCR) Retired.
Rusk, Richard M. '90 (MET)[M] Phillipsburg, NJ The Anawim Community.
Rusk, Richard '90 (MET) Belvidere, NJ St. Patrick; Oxford, NJ St. Rose of Lima.
Rusk, Ron '68 (SB) Blythe, CA Ironwood State Prison.
Ruskamp, Robert L. '85 (ARL)[A] Front Royal, VA Christendom College.
Ruskoski, William Paul '74 (LAF) Rayne, LA St. Joseph.
Ruskowski, Clifford F. '62 (DET) Bloomfield Hills, MI St. Owen.
Rusnak, Melvin E. '70 (Y) Youngstown, OH St. Stephen of Hungary.
Russ, Francis J. '51 (KC) Retired.
Russeau, Kevin *c.s.c.* '01 (FTW)[A] Notre Dame, IN; [B] University of Notre Dame Du Lac; [I] Notre Dame, IN Holy Cross Community, Corby Hall, University of Notre Dame.
Russell, Alfred J. '66 (KAL) Hastings, MI St. Rose of Lima.
Russell, Anselm *o.s.b.* '97 (IND) Chicago, IL St. James; [K] Chicago, IL.
Russell, Benjamin J. *o.p.* '60 (MAD) Madison, WI Blessed Sacrament.
Russell, David P. '81 (WDC) North Beach, MD St. Anthony.
Russell, David '64 (MIA) Retired.
Russell, Dean E. (RCK) Aurora, IL Our Lady of Good Counsel.
Russell, Edward '83 (NY) Bronx, NY St. Pius V.
Russell, James A. *s.m.* '64 (CIN)[M] Huntsville, OH St. George Chapel of Marianist Community.
Russell, James D. '60 (WIN) Lake City, MN St. Mary's of the Lake; Lake City, MN St. Joseph's; Diocesan Consultors.
Russell, John F. *o.carm.* '60 (JOL)[L] Darien, IL Carmelite Provincial Office.
Russell, John F. *o.carm.* '60 (NEW).
Russell, John F. *o.carm.* '60[A] (FgM).
Russell, John *o.carm.* '60 (JOL)[L] Darien, IL Carmelite Community.
Russell, Kenneth '58 (OAK) Retired.
Russell, Paul F. '87 (BO) On Duty Outside the Archdiocese.
Russell, Raymond R. '56 (BUF)[O] Buffalo, NY Sheehan Residence for Priests Retired.
Russell, Richard J. '60 (LA)[V] Los Angeles, CA Catholic Kolping House.
Russell, Richard J. '60 (SD) Retired.
Russell, Richard R. '61 (HRT) West Simsbury, CT St. Catherine of Siena.
Russell, Robert L. *s.s.* '55 (BAL)[S] Baltimore, MD.
Russell, Samuel *o.s.b.* '94 (KC)[A] Conception, MO Conception Seminary College; [J] Stanberry, MO.
Russell, Stanley J. '61 (WIL) Wilmington, DE St. Helena; Deans; Parish Priest Consultors.
Russell, William *s.j.* '65 (BO)[V] Newton, MA The Jesuit Community at Boston College.
Russi, Fred F. '66 (LKC) Oakdale, LA Sacred Heart.
Russler, Clint (GAL) On Special or Other Diocesan Assignment.
Russo, Alfred E. '62 (BGP)[L] Trumbull, CT St. Joseph's Manor.
Russo, Anthony J. '00 (BR) St. Gabriel, LA St. Gabriel; Carville, LA.
Russo, Anthony P. *s.c.j.* '66 (MIL)[O] Franklin, WI St. Francis Residence; [O] Hales Corners, WI Priests of the Sacred Heart; [O] Hales Corners, WI Priests of the Sacred Heart; Franklin, WI St. Martin of Tours.
Russo, Anthony S. (GR) White Cloud, MI St. Joseph's.
Russo, Anthony T. *c.ss.r.* '65 (PH) Philadelphia, PA St. Boniface; Deaf Apostolate.
Russo, Anthony (GR) Fremont, MI All Saints.
Russo, Armando C. '44 (SPR) Russell, MA Our Lady of the Rosary.
Russo, Caesar '74 (STA) Jacksonville, FL Mary Queen of Heaven.
Russo, Charles J. (PAT) Retired.
Russo, Francis X. *o.f.m.cap.* '59 (PH) Philadelphia, PA St. John the Evangelist.
Russo, John W. '78 (TR) Leave of Absence.
Russo, Lawrence J. '80 (BO) Military & VA Chaplains; Navy Chaplains.
Russo, Michael A. '71 (OAK) On Duty Outside the Archdiocese; Moraga, CA St. Monica; [B] St. Mary's College.
Russo, Michael '89 (LAF) Franklin, LA Assumption B.V.M.; Diocesan Council of Catholic Women.
Russo, Nicodemus A. '48 (PEO) Retired.
Russo, Peter '76 (ALB) Scotia, NY St. Joseph; Members.
Russo, Reginald *o.f.m.cap.* '67 (PIT) Pittsburgh, PA Our Lady of the Angels; [O] Pittsburgh, PA Motherhouse and Novitiate of the Vincentian Sisters of Charity; Allegheny County, PA Vincentian Home.
Russo, Ricardo *o.f.m.* '74 (SFE) New Mexico State Penitentiary; [J] Santa Fe, NM Discalced Carmelite Monastery; Army National Guard Chaplains.
Russo, Richard M. '82 (RCK) Marengo, IL Sacred Heart.
Russo, Robert T. '61 (HRT) Retired.
Russo, Romanos V. '77 (NTN) Yonkers, NY Christ the Savior Church; College of Eparchial Consultors.
Russo, Romanos (NTN) Liturgical Commission.
Russo, Thomas *o.s.j.* '56 (MRY)[F] Shrine of St. Joseph.
Rusteika, John B. '45 (WCH) Retired.
Ruston, Robert L. '76 (ALT) Johnstown, PA SS. Gregory & Barnabas.
Ruszel, Henry *c.r.* '54 (SB) Fontana, CA St. Joseph; [E] Fontana, CA St. Joseph.
Ruszel, Humphrey *c.r.* '46 (SB) Fontana, CA Church of the Resurrection; [E] Fontana, CA Congregation of the Resurrection, CR.
Rutagambwa, Elisee '98 (BO)[V] Newton, MA The Jesuit Community at Boston College.
Rutan, Albert E. '57 (GF) Retired.
Ruth, John C. '85 (SCR) Scranton, PA Nativity of Our Lord; [I] Scranton, PA Mercy Hospital.
Ruth, Robert F. '60 (RIC) Retired.
Ruthenberg, Gari *o.m.i.* '95 (MIA) Miami, FL Holy Redeemer.
Ruthenberg, Michael *o.p.* '88 (CHI)[N] River Forest St. Thomas Aquinas Priory.
Rutherford, Donald L. '81 (ALB) Military Chaplains; Army Chaplains.
Rutherford, Richard *c.s.c.* '64 (P)[B] University of Portland; [L] Portland, OR Holy Cross Fathers & Brothers, C.S.C. – University of Portland; Liturgical Commission.
Rutkowski, George A. '60 (DET) Detroit, MI Our Lady Help of Christians.
Rutkowski, James '77 (STL) On Duty Outside the Archdiocese; [P] San Antonio, TX Catholic Counseling, Consultation Center.
Rutkowski, James (SAT) Catholic Counseling and Consultation Center.
Rutkowski, Theodore A. '63 (PIT) Pittsburgh, PA Our Lady of Grace; Judges.
Rutkowski, William (SAG) Diocesan Consultors.
Rutledge, Arthur F. *s.j.* '51 (SJ)[M] Los Gatos, CA Sacred Heart Jesuit Center.
Rutledge, Robert M. *o.s.f.s.* '89 (WDC).
Rutledge, William G. '53 (PIT) Retired.
Rutler, George W. '81 (NY)[B] New York, NY Our Saviour; [II] New York, NY Guild of Catholic Lawyers, The.
Rutowski, William J. '87 (SAG) Bay City, MI St. Stanislaus.
Rutten, Paul A. '02 (SFS) Aberdeen, SD St. Mary.
Rutten, Paul J. '58 (LIN)[E] Lincoln, NE Madonna Rehabilitation Hospital; Health Care Facilities.
Ruttle, Paul *c.p.* '80 (NY)[EE] Bronx, NY Passionist Residence.
Rutz, Gilbert J. (COV) Defenders of the Bond; Ministry Development Program; Pastoral Ministry Formation; Permanent Diaconate Formation.

Ruvalcaba, Victor '96 (LA) Valinda, CA St. Martha.
Ruvo, John A. '54 (NY) Bronx, NY Our Lady of Mt. Carmel.
Ruyechan, Matthew *o.f.m.* '80 (E) Sharon, PA St. Anthony.
Ruygt, Hans '85 (SR) On Duty Outside the Diocese.
Ruygt, Hans '85 (PHX) Surprise, AZ St. Clare of Assisi.
Ruzich, Boniface *o.ss.t.* '59 (TR) Trenton, NJ St. James.
Ruzicka, Gary J. '76 (CHY) Cheyenne, WY St. Mary's Cathedral.
Ruzicka, Gary (CHY) Ex Officios, Voting; Diocesan of Cheyenne, Board of Directors; Liturgical Commission; [F] Cheyenne, WY St. Mary's School Foundation.
Ruzzo, Paul F. '83 (MAN) Dover, NH St. Joseph; Council of Priests.
Rwegasira, Deogratias *a.j.* '96 (ALN) Shenandoah, PA St. George; Shenandoah, PA Our Lady of Mt. Carmel.
Rweyemamu, Justinian B. '93 (NOR) Rockville, CT St. Bernard.
Rweyemamu, Justinian (NOR) Brooklyn Correctional Institution; Corrigan Correctional Institution; Radgowski Correctional Institution.
Rweyongeza, DeoGratias (PEO) La Salle, IL Queen of the Holy Rosary.
Ryan, Adam *o.s.b.* '90 (KC)[J] Stanberry, MO.
Ryan, Alan J. *m.m.* '60 (NY).
Ryan, Albert J. '58 (FR) Retired.
Ryan, Barry '76 (BRK)[EE] On Leave/Unassigned.
Ryan, C. Duane '54 (KC) Retired.
Ryan, C. Duane '54 (JC) Versailles, MO St. Philip Benizi.
Ryan, Charles *f.s.s.p.* '94 (SCR)[M] Elmhurst Priestly Fraternity of St. Peter (F.S.S.P.), North American District Headquarters.
Ryan, Cornelius *c.s.c.* '66 (FTW) South Bend, IN St. Therese, Little Flower.
Ryan, Daniel J. '89 (TR) Willingboro, NJ Corpus Christi; Diocesan Council of Priests.
Ryan, David (CHI)[G] Des Plaines, IL Maryville Academy; Catholic Youth Organization.
Ryan, Dennis K '66 (DEN) Fort Collins, CO St. Joseph.
Ryan, Dennis M. '74 (GB) Kaukauna, WI St. Nicholas; Shiocton, WI St. Denis; Hortonville, WI St. Patrick; Regional Vicars; Xavier Guild.
Ryan, Donald L. '63 (L) Louisville, KY St. Denis.
Ryan, Edward A. '71 (BRK) Ridgewood, NY Our Lady of the Miraculous Medal.
Ryan, Edward J. '53 (ALB) Retired.
Ryan, Edward M. '74 (WOR) Worcester, MA Our Lady of Fatima.
Ryan, Eugene '69 (VEN) Unassigned.
Ryan, F. Lee '68 (JOL) Watseka, IL St. Edmund; Deans.
Ryan, Francis J. '58 (PEO)[K] West Peoria, IL St. Joseph's Home of Peoria.
Ryan, Francis X. *s.j.* '84 (CLV)[B] Cleveland, OH John Carroll University.
Ryan, Francis '58 (PEO) Retired.
Ryan, Frank A. *o.m.i.* '54 (BEL)[F] Belleville, IL Missionary Oblates of Mary Immaculate – St. Henry's Oblate Residence.
Ryan, Frank (PEO)[K] West Peoria, IL St. Joseph's Home of Peoria.
Ryan, G. Philip '88 (ATL) Griffin, GA Sacred Heart.
Ryan, George J. '62 (BRK) Long Island City, NY St. Joseph.
Ryan, Gerald E. '55 (DM) Des Moines, IA St. Mary of Nazareth.
Ryan, Gerald J. '45 (NY) Bronx, NY St. Luke.
Ryan, Herbert J. *s.j.* '62 (LA)[C] Los Angeles, CA Jesuit Community.
Ryan, Jack '76 (HON) Captain Cook, HI St. Benedict; Hispanic Ministry–Kailua Kona.
Ryan, James F. *s.s.e.* '56 (MOB)[G] Selma, AL Edmundite Fathers.
Ryan, James H. *s.j.* '69 (OM)[K] Omaha, NE Jesuit Community at Creighton University.
Ryan, James H. *s.j.* '69 (DM)[J] Griswold, IA Creighton University Retreat Center; [N] Berkeley, CA Jesuit Community at Jesuit School of Theology at Berkeley.
Ryan, James J. '75 (COV) Elsmere, KY St. Henry.
Ryan, James M. (COV) Judges; Diocesan Consultors; Deans; Presbyteral Council.
Ryan, James R. '66 (CAM) North Cape May, NJ St. John of God.
Ryan, James W. '48 (BRK) Brooklyn, NY St. Fortunata Retired.
Ryan, James *o.s.a.* '49 (MIA) Dania, FL Church of the Resurrection.
Ryan, James '60 (JUN) Retired.
Ryan, John A. '70 (SFR) San Francisco, CA St. Gabriel.
Ryan, John Chrysostom *c.p.* '48 (BRK)[V] Jamaica, NY Immaculate Conception Monastery.
Ryan, John J. *s.j.* '67 (BUF)[O] Buffalo, NY Canisius Jesuit Community.
Ryan, John J. '71 (ORL) Ormond Beach, FL St. Brendan.
Ryan, John J. *c.s.c.* '90 (SCR)[C] Holy Cross Community.
Ryan, John M. '55 (BUF) Buffalo, NY Assumption Retired.
Ryan, John M. '64 (CHI) Waukegan, IL St. Dismas.
Ryan, John E. '63 (NEW) Fort Lee, NJ Madonna.
Ryan, John T. '56 (IND) Indianapolis, IN St. Anthony.
Ryan, John '45 (MAR) Retired.
Ryan, John '50 (SB) East Highlands, CA St. John Bosco.
Ryan, John '54 (ALX) Retired.
Ryan, John '64 (JOL) Park Forest, IL St. Mary.
Ryan, John '74 (NO) Lafitte, LA St. Anthony.
Ryan, John (IND) Deaneries and Deans.
Ryan, Joseph A. *o.m.i.* '42 (BO)[Y] Tewksbury, MA Immaculate Heart of Mary Infirmary.
Ryan, Joseph J. '51 (STL) Parrish, FL St. Frances Xavier Cabrini Retired.
Ryan, Joseph '58 (SAG) Clare, MI St. Cecilia.
Ryan, Joseph '66 (PAT) Mount Arlington, NJ Our Lady of the Lake.
Ryan, Joseph *o.s.a.* '83 (PH)[C] Villanova University.
Ryan, Kenan *s.t.* '59 (JKS) Philadelphia, MS Holy Cross.
Ryan, Kevin E. '70 (SAT) San Antonio, TX St. Mark the Evangelist.
Ryan, Kevin *o.s.b.* '42 (IND)[K] St. Meinrad, IN St. Meinrad Archabbey.
Ryan, Kevin (SAT) Defenders of the Bond.
Ryan, Laurence D. *s.j.* '77 (BGP)[P] Fairfield, CT The Fairfield Jesuit Community–Fairfield University.
Ryan, Lawrence A. '42 (SAC) Retired.
Ryan, Lawrence D. *s.j.* '77 (BGP)[E] Fairfield, CT Fairfield College Preparatory School.
Ryan, Leo P. '54 (PAT)[P] Chester, NJ Nazareth Village Retired.
Ryan, Martin E. *s.j.* '48 (BO)[V] Weston, MA Campion Health Center, Inc..
Ryan, Martin P. '76 (BGP) New Fairfield, CT St. Edward the Confessor; [F] Region IX.
Ryan, Michael G. '66 (SEA) Seattle, WA St. James Cathedral.
Ryan, Michael J. '68 (SEA) Kent, WA Holy Spirit Parish.
Ryan, Michael J. '72 (PH) Oreland, PA Holy Martyrs.
Ryan, Milton '91 (CHI)[N] Chicago, IL Vincentian Community, Congregation of the Mission, Midwest Province.
Ryan, Patrick D. '70 (STL) Florissant, MO St. Norbert.
Ryan, Patrick J. *s.j.* '59 (BO)[V] Newton, MA The Jesuit Community at Boston College.
Ryan, Patrick J. *m.m.* '77 (NY).
Ryan, Patrick '58 (STP)[EE] St. Paul, MN St. Andrew.
Ryan, Patrick '62 (PAT) Paterson, NJ Blessed Sacrament; Chula Vista, CA St. Pius X.
Ryan, Patrick '85 (PMB) On Duty Outside the Diocese.
Ryan, Paul J. '73 (ROC) Hamlin, NY St. Elizabeth Ann Seton.
Ryan, Paul T. '58 (BO) Dorchester, MA St. Gregory.
Ryan, Paul *s.m.* '45 (SAT)[K] San Antonio TX Marianist Residence: Skilled Nursing.
Ryan, Peter F. *s.j.* '87 (BAL)[S] Baltimore, MD Jesuit Community of Loyola College, Inc..
Ryan, Philip R. '57 (DAV) Sigourney, IA Our Lady of Lourdes; Sigourney, IA St. Mary's.
Ryan, Philip '57 (SR) Retired.
Ryan, Raymond R. *o.s.a.* '57 (MIL)[O] Racine, WI Augustinian Novitiate; Racine, WI St. Rita.
Ryan, Regis J. '66 (PIT) McKees Rocks, PA St. John of God.
Ryan, Richard J. (STO) Vicar General; Vice–Officialis; Diocesan Building Committee.
Ryan, Richard R. *c.m.* '69 (DEN)[N] Denver, CO Congregation of the Mission Midwest Province: De Paul House.
Ryan, Richard '73 (STO) Stockton, CA St. Michael Church of Stockton (Pastor of).
Ryan, Richard '77 (PHX) Sun City West, AZ Our Lady of Lourdes.
Ryan, Richard (STO) College of Consultors/Presbyteral Council; Diocesan Finance Council.
Ryan, Richard (STO) Personnel Board.
Ryan, Robert F. '47 (PH) Retired.
Ryan, Robin C. *c.p.* '84 (BO)[A] Brighton MA St. John Seminary School of Theology.
Ryan, Robin *c.p.* '84 (MET)[H] Brighton, MA St. John's Seminary.
Ryan, Stephen Desmond '93 (WDC)[B] Washington, DC Dominican House of Studies.
Ryan, Stephen M. *o.s.m.* '55 (CHI)[N] Chicago Order of Friar Servants of Mary (Servites) United States of America Province, Inc..
Ryan, Stephen M. '95 (NY) Staten Island, NY Blessed Sacrament.
Ryan, Steve *s.d.b.* '92 (NEW)[S] Offices of Vocation and Youth Ministry.
Ryan, T. Peter '62 (RVC) Centerport, NY Our Lady Queen of Martyrs; Huntington Deanery.
Ryan, Thomas A. '64 (GI) Grand Island, NE Cathedral of the Nativity of the Blessed Virgin Mary; Schools.
Ryan, Thomas F. '93 (MET) Perth Amboy, NJ Holy Trinity; Perth Amboy, NJ Our Lady of Hungary; Deans.
Ryan, Thomas J. '79 (SY) Johnson City, NY St. James; Southern Area Vicar; Board of Diocesan Consultors; Ex Officio.
Ryan, Thomas M. *s.j.* '71 (DET)[E] Detroit, MI University of Detroit Jesuit High School and Academy.
Ryan, Thomas P. *c.s.p.* '84 (NY) New York, NY St. Paul the Apostle.
Ryan, Thomas '73 (BAL) Special Assignment; [U] Baltimore, MD Johns Hopkins University.
Ryan, Thomas (GI) Defenders of the Bond.
Ryan, Timothy A. '57 (CAM) Cape May, NJ Our Lady Star of the Sea.
Ryan, Timothy K. '62 (SAV) Special Assignment.
Ryan, Timothy '62 (SAV) Retired.
Ryan, Vincent B. *s.j.* '45 (SY)[Q] Syracuse, NY Jesuits at LeMoyne, Inc..
Ryan, William A. *s.j.* '45 (PH)[AA] Loyola Center and Manresa Hall.
Ryan, William A. '59 (PEO) Retired.
Ryan, William A. *o.s.a.* '66 (P) Myrtle Creek, OR All Souls.
Ryan, William F. *s.j.* '62 (SPK)[B] Spokane, WA Gonzaga University.
Ryan, William F. '62 (CAM) Woodbury, NJ St. Patrick's.
Ryan, William H. '48 (ELP) El Paso, TX Immaculate Conception.
Ryan, William P. *s.j.* '94 (BAL)[S] Baltimore, MD Jesuit Fathers and Brothers Maryland Provincial Curia.
Ryan, William '55 (JOL) Retired.
Ryan, William *o.s.a.* '66 (P)[L] Myrtle Creek, OR Augustinian Community.
Ryan, William '68 (STO) Absent on Leave.
Ryan, William (ELP) Priests' Retirement and Disability Plan.
Ryba, Charles J. '69 (CLV) Columbia Station, OH St. Elizabeth Ann Seton; Grafton Correctional Institution; Lorain, OH Lorain Correctional Institution.
Rybachi, Czeslaw *s.ch.* (MIA) Polish – (Our Lady of Czestochowa).
Rybacki, Czeslaw *s.ch.* '85 (SFR) Pompano Beach, FL Our Lady of Czestochowa Mission.
Rybarczyk, Melvin *c.r.* '69 (VNN) San Diego, CA Holy Angels.
Rybicki, Daryl '79 (FTW) Fort Wayne, IN St. John the Baptist.
Rybicky, Walter *o.s.b.m.* '83 (STN) Palos Park, IL Nativity of B.V.M.; Presbyteral Council.
Rydelek, Theodore F. '89 (TYL) Buffalo, TX Blessed Kateri Tekakwitha Church.
Ryder, Frederick *c.pp.s.* '63 (CIN)[B] Carthagena, OH St. Charles.
Ryder, Joseph F. '46 (DET) Retired.
Rydz, Zygmund S. '48 (LIN) Retired.
Rydzewski, Thomas '98 (BAL) Absent on Leave.
Rydzon, Walter C. '76 (PIT) Pittsburgh, PA St. Justin.
Rydzon, Walter G. '73 (PIT) Allegheny County, PA Depaul Institution; Disabilities, Dept. for Persons with.
Rye, Gary C. *o.s.a.* '65 (SD)[B] San Diego, CA Austin House; [H] San Diego, CA.
Rykowski, Jerome A. '55 (PBL) Retired.
Rykowski, Valerian J. '43 (MIL) Retired.
Rykowski, Valerian (LAN) Retired.
Rykwalder, David L. '85 (GI) Bridgeport, NE All Souls.
Ryland, Raymond '83 (SD) Retired.
Ryle, Edward J. '56 (PHX) Special Assignment.
Ryle, Edward J. '56 (TUC) On Duty Outside the Diocese.
Ryle, Edward (TUC) Council of Priests.
Ryle, Gerald '68 (SAC) Galt, CA St. Christopher.
Rymdeika, Joseph F. '82 (PH) Hilltown, PA Our Lady of the Sacred Heart; [F] Lansdale, PA Lansdale Catholic High School.
Rynda, Reynold *o.f.m.cap.* '54 (GB)[I] Appleton, WI St. Fidelis Friary.
Rynes, Theodore J. *s.j.* '62 (SJ)[B] Santa Clara, CA Jesuit Community.
Rynne, James J. '59 (CAM) Retired.
Rynne, Thomas J. '56 (PMB) Jensen Beach, FL St. Martin de Porres Retired.
Ryscavage, Richard J. *s.j.* '77 (WDC)[V] Washington, DC Jesuit Missions, Inc..
Rywalt, Lawrence *c.p.* '92 (MET)[H] Curia Generalizia Dei Passionisti.
Rzadca, Janusz '95 (PAT) Paterson, NJ St. Joseph Hospital; [J] Paterson, NJ St. Joseph's Hospital and Medical Center.
Rzasowski, Jerzy (MO) Army Chaplains.
Rzeczkowski, Matthew *o.p.* '69 (WDC)[B] Washington, DC Dominican House of Studies.
Rzepiela, Thomas R. '72 (CHI) Chicago, IL Cathedral of the Holy Name.
Rzeszutek, Martin *m.i.c.* '51 (SPR)[I] Eucharistic Apostles of The Divine Mercy.
Rzonca, Michael W. '73 (PH) Phoenixville, PA Holy Trinity; Phoenixville, PA Sacred Heart.

S

Sa, Dominic Phan '88 (PT) Pensacola, FL St. Mary.
Saad, Antoun '47 (SAM) Retired.
Saad, Richard D. '72 (OLL) Birmingham, AL St. Elias; Birmingham, AL Maronite Catholic Community of

Mobile; Maronite Catholic Community; Maronite Catholic Community; Maronite Catholic Community; Maronite Catholic Community.
Saad, Richard (OLL) College of Consultors; Office of Communications; Presbyteral Council; Protopresbyters.
Saade, Bassam '92 (SAM) Utica, NY St. Louis Gonzaga.
Saah–Buckman, Michael K. *s.s.j.* '93 (BR) Baton Rouge, LA St. Francis Xavier.
Saale, Richard T. '50 (KC) Retired.
Saalfeld, Lawrence '44 (P) Retired.
Saato, Fred '67 (NTN) Leave of Absence.
Saba, Joseph J. '70 (BGP) Bridgeport, CT St. Charles.
Saba, Joseph '74 (TUC) Tucson, AZ St. Mary's Hospital; [D] Tucson, AZ St. Mary's Hospital.
Saba, Joseph '74 (JUN) On Duty Outside the Diocese.
Sabadell, Juan *l.c.* '01 (HRT)[V] Orange, CT Horizons Institute, Inc..
Sabadell, Juan *l.c.* '01 (NY)[II] Thornwood, NY Familia USA, Inc.; [II] Thornwood, NY Catholic Kid's Net, Inc.; [II] Mt. Kisco, NY Regina Apostolorum, Inc..
Sabadell, Juan *l.c.* '01 (NY)[II] Thornwood, NY Consolidated Catholic Administrative Services, Inc.; [II] Rye, NY Legion of Christ North America, Inc.; [II] Thornwood, NY Nueva Primavera Inc..
Sabadell, Juan *l.c.* '01 (PRO)[U] Greenville, RI Mater Ecclesiae, Inc.; [U] Wakefield, RI Overbrook, Incorporated; [U] Wakefield, RI The Legion of Christ (RI) Incorporated; [U] Greenville, RI Pro Values, Inc.; [U] Greenville, RI LC Pastoral Services, Inc..
Sabadell, Juan *l.c.* '01 (NY)[II] Thornwood, NY Consolidated Catholic Administrative Services, Inc.; [II] Rye, NY Legion of Christ North America, Inc.; [II] Thornwood, NY Nueva Primavera Inc..
Sabadell, Juan '01 (WDC)[V] Bethesda, MD Conquest NA, Inc..
Sabadell, Juan *l.c.* '01 (PRO)[U] Greenville, RI Mater Ecclesiae, Inc.; [U] Wakefield, RI Overbrook, Incorporated; [U] Wakefield, RI The Legion of Christ (RI) Incorporated; [U] Greenville, RI Pro Values, Inc.; [U] Greenville, RI LC Pastoral Services, Inc..
Sabadell, Juan *l.c.* '01 (NY)[II] Thornwood, NY Consolidated Catholic Administrative Services, Inc.; [II] Rye, NY Legion of Christ North America, Inc.; [II] Thornwood, NY Nueva Primavera Inc..
Sabadell, Juan *l.c.* '01 (NY)[II] Thornwood, NY Familia USA, Inc.; [II] Thornwood, NY Catholic Kid's Net, Inc.; [II] Mt. Kisco, NY Regina Apostolorum, Inc..
Sabadell, Juan *l.c.* '01 (PRO)[U] Greenville, RI Mater Ecclesiae, Inc.; [U] Wakefield, RI Overbrook, Incorporated; [U] Wakefield, RI The Legion of Christ (RI) Incorporated; [U] Greenville, RI Pro Values, Inc.; [U] Greenville, RI LC Pastoral Services, Inc..
Sabadell, Juan *l.c.* '01 (LA)[V] Orange, CT Helping Hand Investments, Inc; [CC] Thornwood, NY Territorial Administrative Office.
Sabadell, Juan *l.c.* (STL)[U] Chesterfield, MO Gareway Educational Foundation, Inc..
Sabak, Jame *o.f.m.* '99 (W.D.C)[M] Silver Spring, MD Gemelli House.
Saban, Michael J. '89 (PH) Levittown, PA St. Michael the Archangel.
Sabariar, Thobias *h.g.n.* '92 (LEX) Williamsburg, KY Our Lady of Perpetual Help; [L] Barbourville, KY St. Gregory Church–Union College; Williamsburg, KY St. Boniface.
Sabatini, Francis J. '63 (PH) Philadelphia, PA St. Lucy.
Sabatino, Robert '56 (Y) Retired.
Sabatos, Daniel C. '62 (BRK) On Leave/Unassigned.
Sabatte, Frank P. *c.s.p.* '80 (AUS) Austin, TX St. Austin.
Sabatte, Frank *c.s.p.* '80 (AUS)[L] Austin, TX University Catholic Center.
Sabbagh, Stephen F. *o.f.m.* '59 (WDC)[M] Washington, DC Commissariat of the Holy Land, Franciscan Monastery – Mount St. Sepulchre.
Sabella, Charles A. '94 (MET)[M] Phillipsburg, NJ The Anawim Community.
Sabia, John B. '64 (BGP) Monroe, CT St. Jude.
Sable, Robert M. '74 (DET) Special Assignment.
Sable, Robert M. (DET) Air Force Reserve Chaplains.
Sable, Thomas F. *s.j.* '75 (SCR)[C] Scranton, PA The University of Scranton; [C] Scranton, PA Center for Eastern Christian Studies.
Sabo, Edward S. *t.o.r.* '68 (ALT) Johnstown, PA St. Clare of Assisi.
Sabo, Gerald J. *s.j.* '80 (CLV)[B] Cleveland, OH John Carroll University.
Sabo, Paul P. '69 (BUF) Adjunct Judicial Vicar; Judges; Buffalo, NY The Visitation of the B.V.M..
Sabo, Steven M. (RCK) Vocations.
Sabo, Steven '03 (RCK) Rockford, IL St. Peter Cathedral.
Sabog, Henry '60 (HON) Retired.
Sabol, George '71 (TR) Trenton, NJ Immaculate Conception.
Sabol, Sebastian *o.s.b.m.* '34 (STN) Warren, MI St. Josaphat.
Sabourin, Gerard O. '60 (PRO) Exeter, RI Blessed Kateri Tekakwitha Mission; Diocesan Apostolate for Persons with Handicaps.
Sabourin, Leo F. '58 (DET) Taylor, MI St. Constance.
Saburo, Rusk R. '93 (CI) Sacred Heart; [C] Manresa Jesuit House.
Saburo, Rusk (CI) Diocesan Consultors; Defenders of the Bond.
Sacca, Raymond '79 (OAK) Livermore, CA St. Michael; Presbyteral Council.
Saccacio, Robert J. '61 (RVC) Retired.
Sacco, Carmine J. *s.j.* '57 (SEA) Tacoma, WA St. Rita.
Saccoccia, Todd C. '02 (RVC) Farmingdale, NY St. Kilian.
Saccoman, Robert D. '57 (NY) Wesley Hills, NY St. Boniface.
Sachs, John R. *s.j.* '76 (BO)[B] Cambridge, MA Weston Jesuit School of Theology; [V] Cambridge, MA.
Sackerch, Paul '84 (BUR) Rutland, VT Immaculate Heart of Mary.
Sackett, Frederick *o.m.i.* '41 (SAT)[C] Oblate School of Theology; [M] San Antonio, TX De Mazenod House; Judicial Vicar; Censores Librorum.
Sacks, Edward R. '64 (ALN) Bethlehem, PA Our Lady of Perpetual Help; College of Consultors.
Sacks, Francis W. *c.m.* '67 (PH)[H] Princeton, NJ Vincentian Residence.
Sacksteder, Thomas B. '73 (COV) Florence, KY St. Paul.
Sacus, Samuel S. '66 (WH) Beckley, WV St. Francis De Sales.
Sada Izaguirre, Luis A. *ss.cc.* '60 (SJN) Guaynabo, PR Corazon de Jesus.
Sadek, Ignace '56 (SAM) Brooklyn, NY Cathedral of Our Lady of Lebanon; Presbyteral Council–Ex Officio Members.
Sadie, P. Edward '57 (WH) Charleston, WV Sacred Heart Co–Cathedral; Diocesan Consultors.
Sadlack, Robert '70 (CAM) Villas, NJ St. Raymond.
Sadler, Alfred H. '34 (DET) Marine City, MI Holy Cross Retired.
Sadlier, Richard *s.s.j.* '63 (LAF) Crowley, LA St. Theresa.
Sadlowski, Ronald F. '72 (SPR) Feeding Hills, MA Sacred Heart.
Sadowski, Bob *c.s.p.* '85 (LA)[BB] Los Angeles, CA University of California, Los Angeles, University Catholic Center.
Sadowsky, James A. *s.j.* '57 (NY)[EE] Loyola Hall, Jesuit Community.
Sadsoeitoeboen, Carl *c.i.c.m.* (SAT) Del Rio, TX Sacred Heart.
Sadusky, Joseph F. '70 (WDC) Washington, DC St. Peter; Pastoral Center Special Ministries; Judicial Vicar.
Saegh, Samer (OLD) Our Mother of Mercy Mission.
Saelzler, Richard J. '76 (TOL) Bowling Green, OH St. Thomas More University Parish.
Saena, Poao '95 (SEA) Tacoma, WA St. Ann; Tacoma, WA St. John of the Woods; Tacoma, WA Sacred Heart.
Saenz, Alonso '97 (PHX) Phoenix, AZ St. Augustine.
Saenz, David (CC).
Saenz, Francisco *o.p.* '89 (PHX)[D] Phoenix, AZ St. Catherine of Siena.
Saenz, Jorge L. '03 (MIA) Miami, FL Corpus Christi.
Saenz, Nester (CHI) Chicago, IL Our Lady of Lourdes.
Saenz, Robert *s.j.* '57 (YAK) Yakima, WA St. Joseph's.
Saenz, Urbano *o.s.a.* '70 (MGZ) San German, PR St. Rose of Lima.
Saez, Angel Raul '82 (SJN) San Juan, PR Santa Rosa de Lima.
Saez, Jesus *o.m.* '69 (CGS) Cayey, PR Nuestra Senora de la Asuncion.
Saez, Jose '49 (ELP) Retired.
Saez, Solh '67 (DAL) Dallas, TX St. Augustine Catholic Church.
Saez Munoz, Raul '82 (SJN) Graduate Studies.
Safiejko, Edward M. '48 (MIL) Retired.
Safko, Gerard F. '90 (SCR) Drums, PA Church of the Good Shepherd; Hazleton, PA St. Nazarius; Deans; Army National Guard Chaplains.
Safko, Steven '73 (PSC) Phillipsburg, NJ SS. Peter and Paul.
Safranek, William J. '96 (OM) Ewing, NE St. John The Baptist; Ewing, NE St. Peter de Alcantara.
Safranek, William (OM)[O] Ewing, NE St. Theresa Church of Clearwater Cemetery Endowment Trust Fund.
Safraniec, Joseph '76 (STU) On Duty Outside the Diocese.
Sagardia, Reinaldo '79 (SJN) San Juan, PR Nuestra Senora de Belen.
Sagardia–Perez, Reinaldo (SJN) Judges.
Sagardoy, Angel '60 (LA) Retired.
Sagaya, John Jesu '88 (CHI) Midlothian, IL St. Christopher.
Sagilio, Charles '74 (RIC) Newport News, VA St. Jerome.
Sagorski, Peter A. (ORL) Bushnell, FL St. Lawrence.
Saharic, Michael C. '88 (MET) Hampton, NJ St. Ann.
Sahd, Christopher S. '01 (SCR) Scranton, PA St. Peter's Cathedral; Secretary to Bishop Timlin; Ex Officio; Ex Officio.
Saidi, Joseph '33 (SAM) Retired.
Sailstad, Kenton '88 (DUL) On Leave.
Sajda, Michael *o.f.m.conv.* '79 (BUF)[O] Athol Springs, NY St. Francis of Assisi Friary; [D] Athol Springs, NY St. Francis High School.
Sajdak, David *s.d.b.* '86 (CHI) Berwyn, IL St. Leonard.
Sajdak, John *s.m.* '71 (DET)[E] Harper Woods, MI Notre Dame High School.
Sajdak, Ronald P. '96 (BUF) Buffalo, NY St. Martin de Porres.
Sakalys, Raphael J. *o.f.m.* '53 (PRT)[I] Kennebunkport, ME St. Anthony's Friary.
Sakano, Donald '71 (NY) New York, NY Holy Innocents; New York, NY Sacred Hearts of Jesus and Mary; [II] New York, NY The Housing Fund of the Archdiocese of New York.
Sakevicius, Jonas *m.i.c.* '32 (CHI)[N] Chicago, IL Congregation of Marian Fathers of the Immaculate Conception.
Sakowicz, Gregory '79 (CHI) Chicago, IL St. Mary of the Woods.
Sakowski, Derek J. '03 (LC)[C] Stevens Point, WI St. Peter Middle School; [C] Stevens Point, WI Pacelli High School; Stevens Point, WI St. Peter.
Sala, Michael J. *s.j.* '77 (NY) Metropolitan Hospital; [EE] New York, NY St. Ignatius Loyola Residence.
Salach, Conrad *o.f.m.conv.* '71 (BO) Lawrence, MA Holy Trinity.
Salada, Urbano '59 (SD) Retired.
Saladna, George E. '58 (PIT) Springdale, PA St. Alphonsus; Priest Council.
Salah, Michael A. '91 (WDC) Kensington, MD Holy Redeemer.
Salamon, John *c.ss.r.* '45 (ALB)[L] Saratoga Springs, NY St. John Neumann Residence.
Salamone, Michael '75 (BRK) Retired.
Salamoni, Vincent *m.s.a.* '84 (NOR)[F] Cromwell Society of the Missionaries of the Holy Apostles; Navy Chaplains.
Salanitro, Alfred J. '89 (OM) Blair, NE St. Francis Borgia.
Salanitro, Carl A. '70 (OM) Omaha, NE Mary Our Queen.
Salapata, Andrzej *s.ch.* '97 (CHI) Minneapolis, MN Holy Cross.
Salas, Raul *o.m.i.* '80 (BEL)[F] Belleville, IL Shrine of Our Lady of the Snows.
Salas, Raul *o.m.i.* (STL)[A] St. Louis, MO Kenrick School of Theology.
Salas, Sipio '50 (SFE) Retired.
Salatino, John C. '94 (SPR) Pittsfield, MA St. Mark's; Westfield, MA St. Mary's.
Salazar, Alejandro '91 (LAR) Laredo, TX San Martin de Porres; Presbyteral Council; College of Consultors.
Salazar, Alexander '84 (LA) Los Angeles, CA St. Teresa of Avila.
Salazar, Alexander (LA) Vice Chancellor; Ministry to Recently Ordained Priests; Board of Directors:.
Salazar, Alexander (LA) College of Consultors.
Salazar, Alexander (LA) Vice Chancellor; Ministry to Recently Ordained Priests; Board of Directors:.
Salazar, Cesar '93 (ORG) Santa Ana, CA St. Joseph's; Administrative Leave.
Salazar, Eduardo *s.j.* '74 (CC)[D] Corpus Christi, TX.
Salazar, Eusebio C. Fernandez '71 (SJN) San Juan, PR Santa Catalina Laboure.
Salazar, Fernando Palacio '79 (MGZ) San German, PR San German de Auxerre; [B] San German, PR Hospital of the Immaculate Conception.
Salazar, Franklin '75 (ORL) Kissimmee, FL Holy Redeemer.
Salazar, George '67 (SFE) Taos, NM Nuestra Senora De Guadalupe.
Salazar, Jairo '91 (SJN) Toa Alta, PR Nuestra Senora de la Medalla Milagrosa.
Salazar, Jose Angel '85 (CC) Mathis, TX Sacred Heart.
Salazar, Jose Luis *s.j.* '01 (NY)[EE] Cardinal Spellman Hall, Jesuit Community.
Salazar, Jose *m.s.a.* '77 (NOR)[F] Cromwell Society of the Missionaries of the Holy Apostles.
Salazar, Joseph A. *m.s.a.* '73 (ARL) Basye, VA Our Lady of the Shenandoah.
Salazar, Lito *s.j.* (NY)[HH] Bronx, NY Fordham University at Rosehill.
Salazar, Mario A. '61 (YAK) Quincy, WA St. Pius X; Vicar for Priests; Clergy Personnel Board.
Salazar, Mario P. '90 (YAK) Granger, WA Our Lady of Guadalupe.
Salberg, James G. '69 (PIT) Butler, PA St. Andrew.
Salca, Louis '65 (SD) Retired.
Salcedo, Luis G. '89 (WDC) Bethesda, MD St. Bartholomew Retired.
Salcido, Romeo *m.j.* '86 (PCE) Ponce, PR Santa Maria.
Saldana, Jesus '82 (MIA) Miami, FL St. Kevin.
Saldana, Luis '99 (NY) New York, NY St. Elizabeth; Graduate Studies.
Salditos, Ricardito P. (MO) Air Force Chaplains.
Salditos, Ricardo P. '80 (BIS) Minot, ND Minot Air Force Base Chapel.
Saldua, Max Ernesto M. (MO) Hines V.A. Hospital.
Salemi, Cajetan P. '61 (NEW) Woodcliff Lake, NJ Our Lady Mother of the Church.

Salemi, Paul S. (BUF) Swormville, NY St. Mary.
Salera, Alfredo J. '77 (CHI) Glenview, IL St. Catherine Laboure.
Salerno, Emilio J. '59 (BRK) Long Island City, NY St. Francis of Assisi.
Salerno, Joseph A. '65 (CAM) Mantua, NJ Incarnation; Promoter of Justice; Judges.
Salerno, Joseph '80 (SY) Utica, NY Our Lady of Lourdes; Pastoral Examiners; Priests' Personnel Committee.
Salerno, Michael *s.a.c.* '93 (BAL) Baltimore, MD St. Leo.
Saletrik, E. George '96 (GBG) Kent, PA Church of the Good Shepherd.
Salgado, Jose *f.s.s.p.* '93 (DEN)[M] Sacramento, CA.
Salgado, Jose *f.s.s.p.* (DEN) Arvada, CO Our Lady of Mount Carmel Tridentine Latin Mass Community.
Salgado, Salvador *c.m.f.* '87 (SJN) Bayamon, PR Santa Maria.
Saliba, John A. *s.j.* '65 (DET)[K] Detroit, MI Jesuit Community at the University of Detroit Mercy.
Salicone, Aniello *s.x.* '66 (CHI) Chicago, IL St. Therese Catholic Chinese Church.
Salim, Anthony '74 (OLL) Cincinnati, OH St. Anthony of Padua; Office of Religious Education; Presbyteral Council.
Salinas, Marco Antonio '03 (PBL) Pueblo, CO St. Joseph; Pueblo, CO St. Therese.
Salinas, Marco Antonio '03 (PBL) Pueblo, CO Our Lady of Mt. Carmel.
Salinas, Marco Antonio '03 (PBL) Pueblo, CO St. Joseph; Pueblo, CO St. Therese.
Salinas, Octavio Jose *o.f.m.* '83 (NY)[EE] St. Jude Friary.
Salinas, Romeo (CC) Kingsville, TX St. Joseph.
Salisbury, Donald H. *o.p.* (MO).
Salisbury, Paschal Donald *o.p.* '67 (P) White City, OR U.S. Veternan's Affairs Domiciliary.
Salisbury, W. Dayton *s.s.j.* '59 (BAL)[S] Baltimore, MD St. Joseph Society of the Sacred Heart House of Central Administration Retired.
Saliva, Juan J. '90 (PCE) Aguirre, PR Sacred Heart.
Saliva, Juan '90 (PCE)[B] The Pontifical Catholic University of Puerto Rico.
Salko, John H. '60 (PBR) Scottdale, PA St. John the Baptist; Protopresbyters.
Salkovski, Basil *o.s.b.m.* '88 (STN) Warren, MI St. Josaphat; Diocesan Consultors; Presbyteral Council.
Salkovsky, Basil *o.s.b.m.* (STN) Detroit.
Saller, Neil *t.o.r.* '56 (PH)[AA] Fairless Hills, PA St. Anthony Friary.
Sallese, Albert J. '66 (BO) Senior Priests; Quincy, MA St. Elizabeth Ann Seton Retired.
Sallis, Steven '80 (SEA) Seattle, WA St Benedict; Seattle, WA St. Alphonsus; Kent, WA Holy Spirit Parish.
Sallot, Steve '80 (ORG) Dana Point, CA St. Edward; Council of Priests; Consultors; Ministry to Priests.
Salmani, Frank S. '82 (PRO) Providence, RI St. Mary; [U] Providence, RI.
Salmi, Richard D. *s.j.* '82 (DET)[K] Temperance, MI.
Salmi, Richard P. *s.j.* '82 (CHI)[C] Chicago, IL President's Office; [C] Chicago, IL Jesuit Community at Loyola University Chicago.
Salmon, Charles P. '44 (DEN) Retired.
Salmon, Edward F. *s.j.* '85 (ROC)[B] Rochester, NY McQuaid Jesuit High School.
Salmon, Edward P. '59 (CHI) Oak Park, IL St. Giles; Co–Vicars for the Diaconate Community.
Salmon, James F. *s.j.* '64 (BAL)[B] Timonium, MD Loyola Graduate Center –Timonium Campus; [S] Baltimore, MD Jesuit Community of Loyola College, Inc..
Salmon, William F. '65 (BO) Brighton, MA Our Lady of the Presentation.
Salmonowicz, Philip '03 (GR) Greenville, MI St. Charles.
Salnicky, Michael J. '93 (PSC) Pocono Summit, PA St. Nicholas.
Salnicky, Michael '93 (PSC)[C] Canadensis, PA St. Nicholas Shrine – Carpathian Village; Saint Nicholas Shrine – Carpathian Village.
Salocks, Stephen E. '80 (BO)[A] Brighton, MA St. John Seminary School of Theology.
Salois, Philip (BO) Jamaica Plain, MA Jamaica Plain; Jamaica Plain, MA Veterans Administration Hospital.
Salois, Philip (FR).
Salois, Philip (BO) Jamaica Plain, MA Jamaica Plain; Jamaica Plain, MA Veterans Administration Hospital.
Salomon, Elias *s.s.j.v.* '79 (DET) Plymouth, MI Our Lady of Good Counsel.
Salomone, Gregory *o.p.* '72 (WDC) Washington, DC St. Dominic Church & Priory.
Saloy, Lee J. (NO) Defenders of the Bond.
Saloy, Lee John '72 (NO) Metairie, LA St. Philip Neri.
Saloy, Thomas G. (RVC) Priests' Personnel Policy Board.
Saloy, Thomas '88 (RVC) West Babylon, NY Our Lady of Grace.
Saltarin, Jose '67 (NEW) Elizabeth, NJ St. Mary of the Assumption.
Salter, Bartholomew C. *c.s.c.* '71 (BGP)[P] Fr. Patrick Peyton Center.
Salus, Jude S. *o.s.b.* '75 (PAT) Cedar Knolls, NJ Notre Dame of Mt. Carmel; [M] Morristown St. Mary's Abbey.
Salvador, Antonio (ARE) Retired.
Salvador, John *c.m.f.* '54 (LA)[Q] Rancho Dominguez, CA Dominguez Seminary Inc..
Salvador, Stephen B. '74 (FR) Fall River, MA SS. Peter and Paul; Catholic Scouting Program.
Salvagna, Michael *c.p.* '69 (PIT)[N] Pittsburgh St. Paul of the Cross Monastery; [R] Scranton, PA Saint Ann's Media, Inc; [II] Pelham, NY Passionist Communications Center.
Salvas, John *o.f.m.cap.* '88 (CHL) Hendersonville, NC Immaculate Conception.
Salvatori, Chris *s.a.c.* '99 (NY) New York, NY Our Lady of Mt. Carmel; Yonkers, NY Our Lady of Mt. Carmel.
Salvi, Americo *c.r.m.* '55 (NEW) Lodi, NJ St. Joseph's.
Salwach, Jeffrey *o.f.m.* '84 (SHP) Ruston, LA St. Thomas Acuinas.
Saly, Robert J. '85 (ALT) Catholic Social Service; Priests' Residence – Dmitri Manor; [E] Hollidaysburg, PA Dmitri Manor Priests' Residence; Duncansville, PA St. Catherine of Siena.
Salz, Marvin C. '64 (DUB) St. Lucas, IA St. Luke; Waucoma, IA St. Mary; Lawler, IA Our Lady of Mt. Carmel.
Salzmann, George S. *o.s.f.s.* '77 (BO) Cambridge, MA St. Paul; [BB] Cambridge, MA Harvard Catholic Student Center.
Salzmann, George S. *o.s.f.s.* '77 (WIL)[J] Wilmington Oblates of St. Francis De Sales.
Salzmann, George S. *o.s.f.s.* '77 (BO) Cambridge, MA St. Paul; [BB] Cambridge, MA Harvard Catholic Student Center.
Samaha, Jeffrey F. '78 (WDC) Camp Springs, MD St. Philip the Apostle; Hospital & Nursing Home Ministries.
Samaha, Victor *b.c.o.* (NTN) Liturgical Commission.
Samaniego, Eduardo *s.j.* '69 (SJ) San Jose, CA Most Holy Trinity.
Samay, Sebastian A. '59 (GBG)[H] Latrobe, PA Saint Vincent Archabbey.
Samayoa, Emmanuel G. '89 (ROM) Canton, OH St. Theodore; Canton, OH St. George Cathedral; Chancellor; Formation Council.
Sambor, David R. '78 (SY) Special Assignment.
Sambu, Jean Olivier Mbodo '02 (BWN) Brownsville, TX Christ the King.
Samele, Christopher J. '03 (BGP) Fairfield, CT St. Thomas Aquinas.
Samiano, Marvin '92 (HON) Honolulu, HI Cathedral of Our Lady of Peace; [E] Ewa Beach, HI St. Francis Medical Center – West.
Samjumi, Zacharia '95 (NY) Bronx, NY St Raymond.
Sammon, John F. '42 (ORG) Special Assignment; Vicar for Pastoral and Community Affairs; National Organization for Decent Literature; Propagation of the Faith; Boy Scouts; Holy Childhood; Holy Name Society; Respect Life Program NCCB.
Sammon, John (ORG) Council of Priests; Consultors; Perpetual Adoration Programs.
Sammons, Francis L. '47 (SY) East Syracuse, NY St. Matthew Retired.
Sammut, Tito '52 (GB) Retired.
Samonie, Jacob '56 (DET) Retired.
Samoylo, Francis J. '01 (NY) New City, NY St. Augustine.
Sampaio, Fernando '99 (OAK) Hayward, CA St. Bede.
Samperi, Charles J. '96 (GAL) Spring, TX St. James the Apostle.
Sampietro, Vincent J. *c.s.p.* '45 (NY)[EE] Jamaica Estates Paulist Fathers Generalate.
Sampietro, Vincent J. *c.s.p.* '45 (P) Portland, OR St. Philip Neri.
Sample, Alex K. (MAR) Defensore Vinculi; Archives; Bishop Baraga Association Inc.; Knights of Columbus.
Sample, Alexander K. '90 (MAR) Marquette, MI St. Peter Cathedral; Marquette, MI St. Christopher; Special Assignment; Chancellor; Consultors; Ministry Personnel Services, Dept. of.
Sampon, Robert G. '54 (MIL) Promoters of Justice Retired.
Sampson, Elric '85 (CHI)[N] Chicago, IL St. Peter's Friary.
Sampson, C. Gregory *c.j.m.* '54 (BUF)[O] West Seneca, NY The Eudists, St. John Eudes Center; West Seneca, NY St. Bonaventure.
Sampson, James *s.p.* '65 (SFE) Our Lady of the Assumption.
Samra, Basil '86 (NTN) Leave of Absence; Atlanta, GA St. John Chrysostom.
Sams, Ronald W. *s.j.* '59 (BUF) Consultors, College of; Council of Priests; [O] Buffalo, NY Canisius Jesuit Community; Buffalo, NY St. Michael.
Samsa, Bertin L. *o.f.m.cap.* (GB) Manawa, WI Sacred Heart; Weyauwega, WI SS. Peter and Paul.
Samson, John F. '61 (SCR) Ashley, PA Holy Rosary.
Samson, Robert J. '79 (STL) Florissant, MO St. Sabina.
Samter, James W. '87 (GB) Retired.
Samuel, Francis A. *o.c.i.* '72 (RVC) Babylon, NY St. Joseph's.
Samway, Patrick H. *s.j.* '69 (PH)[AA] Philadelphia, PA St. Alphonsus House.
Samway, Patrick *s.j.* '69 (PH)[C] Jesuit Fathers.
Samy, Edward '67 (SJ) Milpitas, CA St. Elizabeth.
Samy, John Bosco Durai (NY) Pearl River, NY St. Aedan.
Sana, Yoshia '84 (SPA) Campbell, CA St. Mary Assyrian–Chaldean Parish; Director of Finance.
Sanabria, Edgardo '74 (SJN) Bayamon, PR Nuestra Senora del Perpetuo Socorro.
Sanabria, Edgardo *o.p.* '96 (SJN) Bayamon, PR Invencion de la Santa Cruz.
Sanabria, Rafael *c.s.v.* '96 (CHI)[N] Arlington Heights Viatorian Province Center–Clerics of St. Viator.
Sanahuja, Manuel '67 (LA) Los Angeles, CA Our Lady Help of Christians (Maria Auxiliadora).
Sanahuja, Manuel *sch.p.* (LA) Hispanic Liturgy and Ministry Coordinator.
San Andres, Vito B. '79 (AGN) Agana Heights, GU Nuestra Senora de la Paz y Buen Viaje.
Sanches, Joseph A. '70 (ATL) On Duty Outside the Archdiocese; Nashville, TN Church of the Most Holy Name; Nashville, TN St. Patrick.
Sanchez, Albert N. '73 (MO) Tucson, AZ Christ the King Chapel; Air Force Chaplains.
Sanchez, Alejandro '93 (STV) Carolina, PR Santo Cristo de los Milagros; On Duty Outside the Diocese.
Sanchez, Andres Eiroa '88 (SJN)[G] Guaynabo, PR Opus Dei.
Sanchez, Angel '90 (PCE) Villalba, PR Our Lady of Mt. Carmel.
Sanchez, Antero *m.s.c.* '65 (FRS) McFarland, CA St. Elizabeth.
Sanchez, Antonio '90 (MRY) Special Assignment; Vocations Director; Priest's Personnel Board; Vocations Board.
Sanchez, Ariel Munoz *o.r.c.* (SB) San Bernardino, CA Our Lady of Guadalupe.
Sanchez, Castor '61 (TR) Lakehurst, NJ St. John.
Sanchez, David '02 (L) Lebanon, KY St. Augustine.
Sanchez, Edgar *m.sp.s.* '97 (P)[L] Mount Angel, OR Missionaries of the Holy Spirit, M.Sp.S..
Sanchez, Eliseo '57 (LA) Retired.
Sanchez, Esequiel (CHI) Consejo Pastoral Hispano Arquidiocesano; Ethnic Offices.
Sanchez, Esquiel '95 (CHI) Chicago, IL Holy Trinity.
Sanchez, Felix '63 (SP) Tampa, FL St. Joseph; Incardination Commission.
Sanchez, Guadalupe *o.s.j.* '60 (FRS) Madera, CA St. Joachim.
Sanchez, J. Antonio '90 (MRY) Watsonville, CA Our Lady of the Assumption.
Sanchez, James '01 (CC)[G] Robstown, TX Society of Our Lady of the Most Holy Trinity; [I] Corpus Christi, TX.
Sanchez, Jose de Jesus *m.sp.s.* (LA) Oxnard, CA Our Lady of Guadalupe Parish.
Sanchez, Jose M. '58 (GAL) Freeport, TX St. Henry.
Sanchez, Jose M. *c.m.* (BRK)[Z] Brooklyn, NY Centro Evangelization S. Vincente de Paul.
Sanchez, Jose *c.m.f.* '55 (SAT) San Antonio, TX Immaculate Heart of Mary.
Sanchez, Jose '61 (BRK) Corona, NY St. Paul the Apostle; Elmhurst General Hospital.
Sanchez, Jose *c.m.* '62 (PH).
Sanchez, Jose (DEN)[AA] Denver, CO St. Catherine of Siena.
Sanchez, Juan Luis '84 (MIA) Miami, FL SS. Peter and Paul.
Sanchez, Manuel O. '54 (LA) Pomona, CA Sacred Heart Retired.
Sanchez, Marco Antonio *s.t.* '92 (LA)[M] Stirling, NJ Holy Spirit Missionary Cenacle.
Sanchez, Margarito '03 (CC)[G] Robstown, TX Society of Our Lady of the Most Holy Trinity.
Sanchez, Miguel Angel '98 (ELP) Van Horn, TX Our Lady of Fatima.
Sanchez, Paul R. '71 (BRK) Long Island City, NY Our Lady of Mount Carmel.
Sanchez, Paul (BRK) Personnel Board (Clergy).
Sanchez, Prudencio *c.m.* '59 (MGZ) Mayaguez, PR San Vicente.
Sanchez, Rafael (MGZ) Aguadilla, PR St. Charles Borromeo.
Sanchez, Raul N. '74 (GLP) On Duty Outside of Diocese; Air Force Chaplains.
Sanchez, Raul '93 (FRS) Fresno, CA St. Alphonsus; Personnel Committee.
Sanchez, Ricardo '99 (CHL) Biscoe, NC Our Lady of the Americas.
Sanchez, Rodolfo (GAL) Houston, TX St. Thomas More.
Sanchez, Sergio Renteria '92 (LA) Los Angeles, CA Immaculate Heart of Mary.
Sanchez, Stephen A. '82 (SFE) Albuquerque, NM Our Lady of Fatima; Presbyterian Hospital.
Sanchez, Stephen *o.c.d.* '92 (DAL)[I] Dallas, TX Mount

Carmel Center; Presbyteral Council.
Sanchez, Victor '91 (ARE) Manati, PR Our Savior.
Sanchez, William E. '83 (SFE) Albuquerque, NM St. Edwin.
Sanchez–Espinoza, Juan '93 (CHI) Chicago, IL St. Francis de Sales; Chicago, IL St. George.
Sanchez–Munoz, Alejandro (STV) Army National Guard Chaplains.
Sanchez Rivera, Manuel de la Cruz '84 (PCE) Jayuya, PR Our Lady of Monserrate.
Sancho, Jesus *o.c.d.* '64 (DAL) Dallas, TX St. Mary of Carmel.
Sancho Piquer, Enrique '50 (PCE) On Duty Outside the Diocese.
Sand, John '55 (SPK) Retired.
Sandberg, Stuart '68 (NY)[II] White Plains, NY Company of St. Paul.
Sandell, John '67 (FAR) Retired.
Sander, Bernard *o.s.b.* '44 (P)[L] St. Benedict, OR Mt. Angel Abbey.
Sander, Francis *o.s.b.* '49 (NO)[I] Tickfaw, LA Our Lady Queen Contemplative Monastery; [P] St. Benedict, LA St. Joseph Abbey.
Sander, Reginald *o.s.b.* '63 (KC) Tarkio, MO St. Paul the Apostle.
Sander, Timothy *o.s.b.* '41 (P)[L] St. Benedict, OR Mt. Angel Abbey.
Sander, Timothy *o.s.b.* (FBK) Beginning Experience.
Sanders, Daniel J. '78 (MIL) Fontana, WI St. Benedict.
Sanders, Dennis *c.r.* '67 (CHI)[N] Woodstock, IL.
Sanders, Edwin J. *s.j.* '59 (ALN)[A] Wernersville, PA Jesuit Center.
Sanders, Gary E. *o.s.a.* '75 (LA) Los Angeles, CA Our Mother of Good Counsel.
Sanders, Hubert (DET) Detroit, MI Presentation–Our Lady of Victory.
Sanders, James (BAL) MD House of Correction.
Sanders, John C. '73 (BGP)[P] Stamford, CT The Catherine Dennis Keefe Queen of the Clergy Retired Priests' Residence; African Americans, Apostolate of Retired.
Sanders, Joseph P. '61 (ALN)[A] Wernersville, PA Jesuit Center.
Sanders, Lawrence *c.ss.r.* '93 (DEN)[N] Denver, CO.
Sanders, Patrick B. '90 (NO) Belle Chasse, LA Our Lady of Perpetual Help; Deans.
Sanders, Peter C. *c.o.* '84 (MRY)[F] Monterey, CA Oratorian Community–Congregation of the Oratory of Pontifical Right.
Sanders, Peter *c.o.* (MO) AUXILIARY CHAPLAINS CONTRACT CHAPLAINS.
Sanders, Raymond *s.v.d.* '45 (CHI)[B] Techny, IL Divine Word Residence.
Sanders, William F. '75 (WOR) Worcester, MA Our Lady of the Rosary; Advocates.
Sandersfeld, John '66 (SJ) San Jose, CA St. Francis of Assisi; Ongoing Formation of Clergy Committee.
Sandhage, Martin J. '86 (LFT) Portland, IN Immaculate Conception; Members.
Sandheinrich, Bernard H. '60 (STL) St. Louis, MO Basilica of St. Louis, King of France; Holy Childhood, Pontifical Association.
Sandi, Thomas P. '73 (NY) Shrub Oak, NY Saint Elizabeth Ann Seton.
Sandman, Greg (MRY) Administrative Committee Priests' Pension Plan.
Sandman, Gregory '80 (MRY) Watsonville, CA St. Patrick; Presbyteral Council.
Sandmann, Augustus C. *o.s.a.* '47 (NY) Staten Island, NY Our Lady of Good Counsel.
Sandor, Albert *o.f.m.cap.* '82 (DET)[K] Detroit St. Bonaventure Friary.
Sandor, George *o.f.m.conv.* '72 (SY) Binghamton, NY SS. Cyril and Method; Binghamton, NY Holy Trinity.
Sandoval, Clarence J. '87 (SLC) Logan, UT St. Thomas Aquinas; [H] Logan, UT St. Thomas Aquinas, Newman Center.
Sandoval, Francisco Estrado '92 (ATL) Gainesville, GA St. Michael's.
Sandoval, Luis '74 (SAT) On Leave.
Sandoval–Manzo, Ismael '03 (CHI) Blue Island, IL St. Benedict.
Sandoz, Robert *o.f.m.* '86 (PAT) Little Falls, NJ Our Lady of the Holy Angels; Presbyteral Council.
Sandrick, Philip *o.s.b.m.* '84 (STF) New York, NY St. George; Diocesan Consultors; Presbyteral Council; Missionaries, Diocesan.
Sands, Francis *c.ss.r.* '47 (ORL)[E] New Smyrna Beach, FL St. Alphonsus Villa–Redemptorist Fathers and Brothers.
Sands, Joseph C. *s.j.* '92 (SJ)[B] Santa Clara, CA Jesuit Community.
Sandstrom, Philip (NY) Absent on Sick leave; [II] New York, NY St. Ansgar Scandinavian Catholic League.
Sandweg, Michael J. '79 (STL) Portage Des Sioux, MO St. Francis of Assisi.
Sanehez, Miguel Angel '98 (ELP) Pecos, TX Santa Rosa Church.
Sanenella, Nicholas A. '03 (BO) Wakefield, MA Most Blessed Sacrament.
Saner, Daniel J. '69 (COV) Augusta, KY St. Augustine; Brooksville, KY St. James.
Sanfelippo, Frank J. '58 (MIL) Retired.
Sanfilippo, David '94 (PHX) Phoenix, AZ St. Catherine of Siena.
Sanfilippo, Ronald J. *s.j.* '76 (SJ)[M] Los Gatos, CA Sacred Heart Jesuit Center.
Sanford, James R. *o.s.f.s.* '86 (TOL) Toledo, OH St. Hyacinth.
Sanford, L. Harold *s.j.* '75 (DET)[P] Hamtramck, MI St. Ladislaus.
Sanford, Stephen J. *s.j.* '94 (RC) Pine Ridge, SD Sacred Heart.
Sanford, Stephen J. *s.j.* '94 (BO)[V] Boston The Society of Jesus of New England–Provincial Offices.
Sanford, Stephen *s.j.* '94 (RC)[B] Pine Ridge, SD Jesuit Community of Holy Rosary Mission.
Sanford, Steve *s.j.* '94 (RC) Pine Ridge, SD Holy Rosary.
San Fratello, Charles S. *o.f.m.* (MO).
San Fratello, Sennen C. *o.f.m.* '58 (ALB)[B] Siena College.
Sang, Andrew Dolinh *c.m.c.* '83 (STP) Minneapolis, MN St. Joseph Hien.
Sang, Francis D. '73 (RVC) Deer Park, NY SS. Cyril and Methodius.
Sanger, Charles P. '37 (DEN) Retired.
Sangermano, Charles L. '78 (PH) Norristown, PA Holy Saviour.
Sangiovanni, William F. '77 (BGP) Trumbull, CT St. Theresa; [C] Fairfield, CT Notre Dame Catholic High School.
Sangl, Harry R. '54 (PIT) Beaver Falls, PA Christ the Divine Teacher.
Sankoorikal, George S. '71 (BGP) Brookfield, CT St. Marguerite Bourgeoys.
Sankoorikal, Paul L. '59 (LC) West Salem, WI St. Mary; [D] La Crosse, WI Franciscan Skemp Healthcare, Mayo Health System, La Crosse Campus Medical Center; Elected Members.
Sankovitz, John P. '47 (STP)[C] St. Paul, MN University of St. Thomas Retired.
Sanks, T. Howland *s.j.* '65 (OAK).
Sanks, T. Howland *s.j.* '65 (Maryland)[N] Berkeley, CA Jesuit Community at Jesuit School of Theology at Berkeley.
San Llorente, Ricardo (ARE) Retired.
San Miguel, Parroguis '03 (CGS) Yabucoa, PR Santos Angeles Cutodios.
Sanner, James E. '59 (E) Retired.
Sanni, Henry '99 (CHI) Blue Island, IL St. Benedict.
San Nicolas, Jeffrey C. '97 (AGN) Yigo, GU Our Lady of Lourdes.
San Nicolas, Jeffrey '97 (AGN) Our Lady of Lourdes Parish.
San Pedro, Rodrigo '80 (NEW) Hasbrouck Heights, NJ Corpus Christi.
Sans, Pablo '53 (BRK) Richmond Hill, NY Our Lady of the Cenacle Retired.
Sans, Theodore R. '59 (L) Louisville, KY St. Albert the Great.
Sansaricq, Carl '50 (NY) Spring Valley, NY St. Joseph Retired.
Sansaricq, Guy '60 (BRK) Brooklyn, NY St. Jerome's.
Sansaricq, Guy '60 (BRK)[Z] Brooklyn, NY National Center of the Haitian Apostolate.
Sansaricq, Guy '60 (BRK)[U] Haitian Apostolate.
Sansom, Lawrence W. '41 (ROC) Retired.
Sanson, Robert J. '67 (CLV) Strongsville, OH St. Joseph; Associate Judicial Vicars.
Sansone, Anthony J. '80 (BRK) Brooklyn, NY Sacred Hearts of Jesus and Mary and St. Stephen.
Sansone, Simon *o.c.s.o.* '89 (WOR)[O] Spencer, MA St. Joseph's Abbey.
Santa, Juan '85 (CGS) Bayamon, PR La Resurreccion del Senor.
Santa, Michael *o.s.b.* '56 (KCK)[H] Atchison, KS St. Benedict's Abbey.
Santa, Thomas *c.ss.r.* '78 (TUC)[G] Tucson, AZ Redemptorist Society of Arizona.
Santa–Bibiana, Joseph *s.d.b.* '66 (NEW) Elizabeth, NJ St. Anthony's.
Santaballa, Francisco Javier '02 (WDC) Gaithersburg, MD St. Martin.
Santa Barbara, Robert L. '90 (MET) New Brunswick, NJ St. Mary of Mount Virgin.
Santa Cruz, Ramon '99 (CC)[G] Robstown, TX Society of Our Lady of the Most Holy Trinity.
Santa Cruz, Ramon *s.o.l.t.* '99 (SEA) Seattle, WA St. Alphonsus.
Santaella, Esteban '58 (PCE) Mercedita, PR Church of the Resurrection; Ponce, PR Church San Patricio; Jayuya, PR Our Lady of Monserrate.
Santamaria, Max '56 (MRY) Retired.
Santamaria, Robert '98 (NEW) Union City, NJ Sts. Joseph and Michael.
Santana, Edward '86 (CGS) Vega–Baja, PR Perpetuo Socorro; [B] San Lorenzo, PR Casa Charlie Rodriguez.
Santana, Edward '86 (CGS)[E] San Lorenzo, PR Diocesan Shrine Our Lady of Mount Carmel.
Santana, Francisco '68 (MIA)[K] Miami, FL National Shrine of Our Lady of Charity.
Santana, Frank '72 (NY) New York, NY Mary Help of Christians.
Santana, Franklin (CGS)[C] Aibonito, PR Casa Salesiana de Retiros.
Santana, Ramon '89 (CGS) Fajardo, PR Santisimo Redentor.
Santangelo, Christopher *ss.cc.* '99 (FR).
Santangelo, Michael A. '95 (TR)[H] Burlington, NJ St. Paul; Scouting.
Santarosa, Scott R. *s.j.* '00 (LA)[D] Los Angeles, CA Verbum Dei High School.
Santen, Thomas J. '70 (STL) Manchester, MO St. Joseph.
Santerre, Richard R. '82 (BO) Permanent Disability.
Santhiyagu, Arockiyasomy *m.s.f.s.* '96 (LAN) Lansing, MI St. Mary Cathedral.
Santhiyagu, Arokiam *m.s.f.s.* '96 (ATL)[K] Lawrenceville The Missionaries of St. Francis De Sales.
Santiago, Florentino '78 (HT) Thibodaux, LA St. John The Evangelist.
Santiago, Francisco X. *s.j.* '64 (SJN) San Juan, PR San Ignacio de Loyola.
Santiago, Hiram *s.d.b.* '92 (MGZ) San Antonio, PR San Jose Obrero.
Santiago, Jorge *s.d.b.* '94 (ARE) Orocovis, PR San Juan Bautista.
Santiago, Jose M. *o.p.* '93 (STP) Minneapolis, MN St. Albert the Great.
Santiago, Jose *o.p.* '93 (STP) Minneapolis, MN Holy Rosary.
Santiago, Juan J. *s.j.* '64 (SJN)[H] UPR Catholic Student Center.
Santiago, Leoncio S. '73 (CHI) Chicago, IL St. Genevieve.
Santiago, Manuel '85 (PCE) Ponce, PR San Jose Obrero; Associate Judicial Vicars.
Santiago, Rafael '69 (PCE) Retired.
Santiago, Samuel '76 (PCE) Ensenada, PR Sacred Heart; Cursillos de Cristiandad.
Santiago, Xavier S. '94 (NY) Red Hook, NY St. Christopher.
Santich, Jan Joseph '90 (CHY) Wheatland, WY St. Patrick's.
Santich, Jan (CHY) Presbyteral Council.
Santillanes, Jose Flavio '65 (SFE) Santa Fe, NM N.S. de Guadalupe del Valle de Pojoaque.
Santilli, Francis C. '80 (PRO) Pawtucket, RI St. Cecilia.
Santitoro, Francis E. '66 (TR) Toms River, NJ St. Maximilian Kolbe.
Santo, Mark Charles '60 (MIL) Retired.
Santo, Mark '60 (LA) Los Angeles, CA Metropolitan Detention Center; Los Angeles, CA Metropolitan Detention Center.
Santoalla, Jesus '57 (SJN) San Juan, PR San Jorge.
Santoianni, Rolando *i.v.e.* '90 (SJ) Santa Clara, CA Our Lady of Peace.
Santone, John M. *c.s.c.* (BGP)[P] Congregazione Di Santa Croce.
Santor, John E. '65 (E) Erie, PA St. Casimir; Pleasant Ridge Manor East.
Santora, Alexander M. '82 (NEW) Jersey City, NJ Our Lady of Czestochowa; [Q] Union, NJ Kean University.
Santora, Gerard M. '38 (NEW) Jersey City, NJ Holy Rosary; [N] Rutherford, NJ St. John Vianney Residence for Priests Retired.
Santoro, Charles *o.p.* (GR)[A] Grand Rapids, MI Aquinas College.
Santoro, David J. *o.p.* '77 (CHI)[N] River Forest St. Thomas Aquinas Priory; Des Moines, IA St. Mary of Nazareth.
Santoro, Michael C. '80 (NEW) Jersey City, NJ Our Lady of Mt. Carmel.
Santorsola, Albert J. '87 (PH) Abington, PA Our Lady Help of Christians; [D] Wyncote, PA Bishop McDevitt High School.
Santos, Andrew J. '97 (CHI) Flossmoor, IL Infant Jesus of Prague.
Santos, Angel M. '77 (ARE) Bajadero, PR La Milagrosa.
Santos, Cesar E. '93 (ARE) Vega–Baja, PR Our Lady of Carmen–Playa.
Santos, Francisco '97 (CHK) Saipan, MP Santa Soledad Mission Parish; Light & Salt Catholic Charismatic Community; Presbyteral Council.
Santos, Gregory *o.c.s.o.* '59 (SLC)[F] Huntsville Abbey of Our Lady of the Holy Trinity of the Order of Cistercians.
Santos, John R. '98 (WIL)[L] Dover, DE Secular Institute of the Two Hearts.
Santos, Joseph D. '89 (PRO) In Res.
Santos, Maximiano *c.m.* '66 (SJN) San Juan, PR Nuestra Senora del Pilar.
Santos, Raul (CGS) Retired.
Santos, Sergio '85 (SFR) San Francisco, CA St. Boniface.
Santos, Tomas '95 (ARE) Morovis, PR St. Paul Apostle; Priest's Senate (Consejo Presbiteral).
Santre, William *t.o.r.* '61 (ALT) Altoona, PA Our Lady of Mt. Carmel.
Santry, Robert '86 (HON) On Duty Outside the Diocese; Army Chaplains.

Santucci, Louis '74 (Y) Retired.
Sanz, Eleutherio '59 (MRY) Salinas, CA Sacred Heart Retired.
Sanz, Florentino '65 (SJN) San Juan, PR San Juan M. Vianney; Defender of the Bond.
Sanz, Jose *d.l.p.* '73 (WDC) On Duty Outside the Archdiocese.
Sanz, Jose *d.l.p.* '73 (SB)[A] Riverside, CA Blessed Junipero Serra House of Formation; [E] Riverside, CA Diocesan Labor Priests, DLP; Special or Other Diocesan Assignment.
Sanz, Jose *d.l.p.* (SB) Office of Seminarains; Blessed Junipero Serra House of Formation.
Sanz, Julian '77 (TUC) Administrative Leave of Absence.
Saoncella, Valentino *m.c.c.j.* '44 (CHI)[N] La Grange Park, IL Comboni Missionaries.
Sapeta, Joseph S. '47 (NEW) Retired.
Sapio, Thadeus M. *o.f.m.* '65 (NY) Bronx, NY Holy Cross.
Saplis, Raymond A. '58 (LA) Retired.
Saplis, Raymond '58 (LA) Granada Hills, CA St. Euphrasia.
Saporito, Cosmo G. '54 (BRK) Brooklyn, NY St. Bernadette.
Saporito, Louis R. *s.s.j.* '60 (BAL)[S] Baltimore, MD St. Joseph Society of the Sacred Heart House of Central Administration Retired.
Saporito, Michael A. '92 (NEW) Wyckoff, NJ St. Elizabeth; Bergen–Paramus.
Saporito, Peter M. '78 (CAM) Vineland, NJ St. Padre Pio.
Sapp, James '86 (WH)[B] Fort Wayne, IN University of Saint Francis.
Sappenfield, John '98 (NSH) Gallatin, TN St. John Vianney; Presbyteral Council and College of Consultors.
Sapporito, Cosmo G. '54 (BRK) Retired.
Saprano, Samuel '71 (STU) Caldwell, OH St. Michael; Caldwell, OH Immaculate Conception.
Sara, Solomon I. *s.j.* '63 (BO)[V] Boston The Society of Jesus of New England–Provincial Offices
Sara, Solomon I. *s.j.* '63 (New England)[M] Washington, DC The Jesuit Community at Georgetown University.
Sarauskas, R. George '73 (CHI) Other Assignments.
Sardina, John J. '60 (BUF)[O] Clarence, NY Provincial Motherhouse of Brothers of Mercy; [M] Clarence, NY Brothers of Mercy Nursing & Rehabilitation Center; [M] Clarence, NY Brothers of Mercy Sacred Heart Home, Inc.; Buffalo, NY Queen of Martyrs.
Sardina, Jorge *s.j.* '59 (MIA)[D] Miami, FL Belen Jesuit Preparatory School; [H] Miami, FL Villa Javier.
Sardinas, Jorge '77 (MIA)[B] St. Thomas University.
Sarge, John S. '73 (SAG) Saginaw, MI St. Casimir; Saginaw, MI St. George.
Sargent, Anthony G. *o.s.b.* '02 (PAT)[M] Morristown, NJ St. Mary's Abbey.
Sargent, Anthony *o.s.b.* '02 (PAT)[D] Morristown, NJ Delbarton School.
Sargent, John '53 (Y) Retired.
Sargus, Edward T. '39 (BAL) Emmitsburg, MD St. Anthony Shrine Retired.
Sariego, Francis A. *o.f.m.cap.* '69 (NY)[II] West Hempstead, NY La Casa Sollievo Della Sofferenza Opera Di Padre Pio.
Sariego, Francis *o.f.m.cap.* '69 (NEW) Hoboken, NJ St. Ann's.
Sarihaddula, Silvester '98 (SD) Carlsbad, CA St. Patrick.
Sarjeant, Francis X. *s.j.* '61 (SP) Clearwater, FL St. Cecelia.
Sarjeant, Francis X. *s.j.* '61 (BO)[V] Boston The Society of Jesus of New England–Provincial Offices.
Sarkies, Jeffery L. '65 (SEA) Seattle, WA Holy Rosary; Port Orchard, WA St. Gabriel.
Sarmiento, Oscar '82 (MIA) Pembroke Pines, FL St. Edward.
Sarmiento, Oscar '82 (PT) On Duty Outside the Diocese.
Sarnecki, Thomas G. '02 (SCR) Scranton, PA St. David's.
Sarno, Robert J. '73 (BRK) Released from Diocesan Assignment.
Sarosiek, John H. '93 (GAY) Retired.
Sarosiek, John '90 (DET) Dearborn, MI St. Clement.
Saroyan, Antoine '85 (ARM) Detroit, MI St. Vartan's.
Sarrazine, Kenneth J. '62 (FTW) Roanoke, IN St. Catharine; Roanoke, IN St. Joseph.
Sarsfield, Emmett (YAK) Zillah, WA Resurrection; Presbyteral Council Executive Committee.
Sartorelli, Otto '50 (MAR) Retired.
Sarweh, Basel R. '98 (SCR)[M] Shohola, PA Society of Saint John.
Sarzynski, Edward W. '79 (ALN)[L] Reading, PA Sacred Heart Convent.
Sas, Thomas J. '76 (HRT) Avon, CT St. Ann's; West Hartford, CT St. Mark the Evangelist.
Sasin, Jan '77 (NEW) Newark, NJ St. Francis Xavier.
Saso, Michael '61 (SJ) On Duty Outside the Diocese.
Sassani, John A. (BO) Cursillo.
Sassani, John E. '80 (BO) Sherborn, MA St. Theresa; Spiritual Development.
Sassano, Rock '63 (P) Retired.
Sasso, Frank M. '73 (CHI) Chicago, IL St. Thaddeus.
Sasso, Joseph M. '58 (ROC) Retired.
Sastre, Rafael '51 (MGZ) Mayaguez, PR Santa Teresita; Diocesan Consultors.
Sasway, John R. '62 (ALT) Allegheny Deanery; Lilly, PA Our Lady of the Alleghenies.
Satcher, Mikel (BO) Dorchester, MA Carney Hospital.
Sato, Damian *s.a.* '45 (NY)[EE] Garrison Franciscan Friars of the Atonement, Minister General Office.
Satoun, Arbogaste '99 (SCR) Pittston, PA St. John the Evangelist
Sattler, Frederick F. '70 (ALN) Fountain Hill, PA St. Ursula.
Sattler, Henry E. *c.ss.r.* '76 (TOL) Lima, OH St. Gerard.
Sattler, Henry *c.ss.r.* (TOL) Consultors; Priests' Council.
Sattler, John Columban *o.f.m.conv.* '42 (IND)[J] Mount St. Francis, IN Mount Saint Francis Friary and Retreat Center Retired.
Sattler, Paul *c.pp.s.* '58 (KC)[A] Liberty, MO Precious Blood Center; [J] Liberty, MO Precious Blood Center.
Sattler, Timothy *p.i.m.e.* '82 (DET)[K] Detroit, MI P.I.M.E. Motherhouse in Detroit.
Sattler, Wayne V. (BIS) Presbyteral Council.
Sattler, Wayne '97 (BIS) Stanley, ND Queen of the Most Holy Rosary.
Sauber, A. Michael '69 (STP) Lonsdale, MN Immaculate Conception; Archdiocesan Consultors; Presbyteral Council.
Saucci, Robert R. *m.m.* (MO) AUXILIARY CHAPLAINS CONTRACT CHAPLAINS.
Sauchelli, James J. '63 (TR) Brick, NJ Visitation.
Saucier, Thomas *o.p.* '96 (CHI)[D] Oak Park, IL Fenwick High School; [N] Oak Park, IL Dominican Community of St. Martin de Porres.
Saucier, William Patrick '01 (MOB) Mobile, AL St. Dominic.
Saudis, Richard B. '55 (CHI) Berwyn, IL St. Odilo; Associate Vicars.
Sauer, Alban '59 (SCL) Retired.
Sauer, Anthony P. *s.j.* '71 (SFR)[E] San Francisco, CA St. Ignatius College Preparatory (Coed); [N] San Francisco CA Jesuit Community at St. Ignatius College Preparatory.
Sauer, Bonaventure *o.c.d.* '92 (LR)[A] Little Rock, AR Marylake – Carmelite Novitiate.
Sauer, Gerard J. '01 (BRK) Brooklyn, NY St. Patrick.
Sauer, James '77 (EVN) Dale, IN St. Joseph; Santa Claus, IN St. Nicholas; Special Assignment; Continuing Education of Clergy.
Sauer, John M. '85 (WIN) Winona, MN Cathedral of the Sacred Heart; Winona, MN St. Casimir's; Deans; Bishop's Council; Commission on Sacred Liturgy.
Sauer, Simon D. *o.f.m.conv.* '57 (L) Louisville, KY St. Paul.
Sauer, Stephen J. *s.j.* '98 (WDC)[M] Washington, DC Leonard Neale House.
Sauer, Timothy J. '76 (SEA) Ferndale, WA St. Joseph; Special Assignment.
Sauer, Timothy '76 (SEA) Presbyteral Council; College of Consultors; Seminarian Services; Vocations.
Saul, James *o.s.b.* '52 (JOL)[L] Lisle, IL St. Procopius Abbey; [L] Naperville, IL Benedictine Chinese Mission.
Saulaitis, Antanas *s.m.* '69 (CHI)[N] Chicago, IL Baltic Jesuits Advancement Office.
Saulenas, Simeon W. '44 (BO) Cambridge, MA Immaculate Conception.
Saulino, Joseph '67 (LEX) Lexington, KY Cathedral of Christ the King.
Saunders, Allan L. '86 (SPC) Kennett, MO St. Cecilia; Portageville, MO St. Eustachius.
Saunders, Charles D. *c.m.* '43 (STL)[O] Perryville, MO Congregation of the Mission.
Saunders, Douglas W. (LA) Deanery 20.
Saunders, Douglas Wm. '65 (LA) Long Beach, CA St. Maria Goretti.
Saunders, Ronald *s.m.* '59 (BUR) Deans; White River Junction, VT St. Anthony.
Saunders, Ronald *s.m.* (MO).
Saunders, William P. '84 (ARL) Potomac Falls, VA Our Lady of Hope; Deans; Diocesan Consultors.
Sauppe, Timothy J. '92 (PEO) Annawan, IL Sacred Heart.
Sauriol, Mark A. '99 (PRO) Pawtucket, RI St. Teresa of the Child Jesus; St. Raphael Academy; [C] Pawtucket, RI St. Raphael Academy; Council Members.
Sauter, David A. *s.j.* '72 (BAL)[W] Baltimore, MD Jesuit Educational Association of Maryland, Inc..
Sauter, David A. *s.j.* '72 (WDC)[E] North Bethesda, MD Georgetown Preparatory School.
Sauter, John '85 (GLP) Shiprock, NM Christ the King.
Sauter, Thomas M. '47 (DET) Retired.
Sautner, Scott J. '00 (FAR)[A] Lakota, ND St. Mary.
Sautner, Scott '00 (FAR) Lakota, ND St. Joseph; Lakota, ND St. Joseph.
Savage, James W. '70 (BO) Cambridge, MA St. Paul.
Savage, Paul J. '57 (PIT) Beaver Falls, PA Divine Mercy; Beaver County, PA Friendship Ridge Skilled Nursing.
Savage, Robert *s.d.b.* '46 (NY)[EE] New Rochelle, NY Salesian Provincial House.
Savage, Roger '77 (MIL) Wilmot, WI Holy Name of Jesus; Bristol, WI St. Scholastica.
Savage, Thomas J. '47 (MAN) Retired.
Savage, Warren J. '79 (SPR) Absent on Leave.
Savaia, Giuseppe '95 (PMB) North Palm Beach, FL St. Clare.
Savandra, Edwin '95 (STP) Madison Lake, MN Immaculate Conception.
Savard, John D. *s.j.* '91 (SFR)[N] San Francisco, CA Jesuit Community at University of San Francisco.
Savard, John D. *s.j.* '91 (BO)[V] Boston The Society of Jesus of New England–Provincial Offices.
Savard, Wilfred '48 (SFE) Retired.
Savarimathu, Simonraj (BAL)[M] Baltimore, MD St. Agnes HealthCare, Inc..
Savarimuthu, Charles *h.g.n.* '99 (LEX) Beattyville, KY Queen of All Saints; Ravenna, KY St. Elizabeth of Hungary.
Savarimuthu, Pancras '80 (TYL) Athens, TX St. Edward Church.
Savary, James '60 (LR) Retired.
Savastano, Anthony J. '56 (RVC) Retired.
Savchyn, Vasyl '79 (STN) The Colony, TX St. Sophia Ukrainian Catholic Church.
Savelesky, Michael T. '73 (SPK) Spokane, WA Assumption of the Blessed Virgin Mary.
Savelesky, Michael (SPK) Censor Liborum.
Savelesky, Mike (SPK) Members.
Savial, Clarence J. '70 (LAV) Bunkerville, NV La Virgen de Guadalupe.
Saviano, Frederick L. '68 (BGP) Danbury, CT Our Lady of Guadalupe.
Savickas, Michael G. '74 (DET) Walled Lake, MI St. William; Archdiocesan Vicars.
Savidge, Peter M. '89 (KC) Odessa, MO St. George.
Savilla, Edmond (SFE) Pilgrimage for Vocations; Vicars Forane (Deans).
Savilla, Edmund '77 (SFE) Albuquerque, NM Ascension.
Savino, Dominic *o.carm.* '65 (LA)[B] Arleta, CA Carmel West Community; [F] Encino, CA Crespi Carmelite High School.
Savino, Michael A. '82 (CIN) Cincinnati, OH St. Joseph.
Savinski, John M. '71 (PH) Morton, PA Our Lady of Perpetual Help.
Savio, John (CHY) Rock Springs, WY Holy Spirit Catholic Community; [F] Rock Springs, WY Rock Springs Catholic School Foundation; Presbyteral Council; Appointed Members, Voting; Building Committee.
Savio, Michael '92 (MIL) Milwaukee, WI Our Lady of Lourdes.
Savitt, Alan F. '73 (PAT) Clifton, NJ St. Brendan.
Savoie, Johnny '95 (MOB) Fairhope, AL St. Lawrence.
Savoree, John M. '63 (SFD) Altamont, IL St. Clare; Altamont, IL St. Anne; Altamont, IL St. Bonaventure; Altamont, IL St. Mary.
Savundra, Edwin (STP) Cleveland, MN Church of the Nativity of the Blessed Virgin Mary.
Saw, Benjamin '90 (SAL) Hoxie, KS St. Frances Xavier Cabrini.
Sawdy, Wallace E. '51 (HBG) Retired.
Sawicki, Eugene A. '86 (NY) New York, NY Our Lady of Vilnius.
Sawicki, Gregory *s.d.s.* '86 (SAT) Falls City, TX Holy Trinity; Hobson, TX St. Boniface.
Sawicki, John A. *c.s.sp.* (PIT)[B] Pittsburgh, PA Duquesne University of the Holy Spirit.
Sawyer, Don Joseph (OLL) Spiritual Director for the National Apostolate of Maronites.
Sawyer, Donald J. (OLL) Eparchial Newsletter; Office for Missions.
Sawyer, Donald '74 (OLL) Austin, TX Our Lady's Maronite Parish.
Sawyer, Lucien A. *o.m.i.* '49 (BO) Cambridge, MA Mount Auburn Hospital.
Sawyer, Lucien *o.m.i.* '49 (BO)[V] Lowell, MA St. Eugene House (Residence).
Sawyer, Michael *o.s.b.* '74 (HON)[G] Waialua, HI Benedictine Monastery of Hawaii/Retreat Center; Spiritual Directors.
Saxon, JaVan J. '48 (R) Rocky Mount, NC Our Lady of Perpetual Help.
Say, Celestino '58 (VIC) Victoria, TX Our Lady of Lourdes; Judges.
Say, James K. '60 (TOL) Tiffin, OH St. Joseph.
Sayer, Robert J. '99 (CHR) Batesburg–Leesville, SC St. John of the Cross; Lexington, SC Corpus Christi; Vocations Board.
Sayers, Glen W. *s.d.s.* (BIR) Huntsville, AL St. Mary of the Visitation.
Sayers, James M. '58 (CHI) Homewood, IL St. Joseph Retired.
Sayers, Monty '86 (E) Guys Mills, PA St. Hippolyte.
Sayers, Raymond J. '64 (DET) Birmingham, MI Holy Name.
Sayes, Ronald '57 (DET) Retired.

Sayles, Bartholomew *o.s.b.* '48 (SCL)[I] Collegeville, MN St. John's Abbey, of the Order of St. Benedict.
Saylor, Brian R. '99 (ALT) Altoona, PA Cathedral of the Blessed Sacrament.
Saylor, Philip '55 (ALT) Retired.
Sayuk, Thomas A. (SJP) Vicar General in Curia; Chancellor; Diocesan Treasurer; Diocesan Consultors; Diocesan Corporation; Clergy Examiners; Diocesan Promoter for the Cause of Metropolitan Andrew Sheptytsky; Presbyteral Council.
Sayuk, Thomas (SJP) Liturgical Commission.
Sayuk, Thomas (SJP) Prayer League for Canonization of Metropolitan Andrew Sheptytsky.
Sayuk, Thomas (SJP) Diocesan Administrative Council.
Sazama, Warren J. *s.j.* '77 (MIL)[O] Milwaukee, WI Arrupe House Jesuit Community.
Sbordone, Gaetano J. '83 (BRK) Brooklyn, NY St. Dominic.
Scafidi, William A. *m.ss.a.* '83 (NY) Newburgh, NY St. Mary.
Scaglione, Paul A. '73 (L) Louisville, KY St. Augustine; Office of Pastoral Care.
Scahill, James J. '74 (SPR) East Longmeadow, MA St. Michael's; Presbyteral Council.
Scala, Thomas A. '73 (HBG) Milton, PA St. Joseph; Presbyteral Council.
Scalco, Joseph *c.s.j.* '79 (LA) Lancaster, CA Blessed Junipero Serra; [D] Lancaster, CA Paraclete High School.
Scales, Donald F. *o.s.b.* '55 (RIC)[L] Richmond, VA Mary Mother of the Church Abbey.
Scales, George '88 (FR) Seekonk, MA St. Mary's.
Scalese, Mark P. *s.j.* '97 (PH)[AA] Philadelphia, PA St. Alphonsus House.
Scaletty, Thomas F. '63 (WCH) Chanute, KS St. Patrick; Humboldt, KS St. Joseph; Deans.
Scalia, Paul D. '96 (ARL) Fredericksburg, VA St. Patrick's.
Scalise, Christopher M. '99 (L) Vine Grove, KY St. Martin of Tours; Vine Grove, KY St. Brigid; Ex Officio.
Scanagatta, Joseph *s.d.b.* '47 (SFR)[N] San Francisco, CA Salesian Provincial Residence.
Scanlan, Charles V. '54 (NEW) Retired.
Scanlan, Cornelius J. *o.m.i.* '59 (SAT) Brackettville, TX St. Mary Magdalen.
Scanlan, Edward J. '53 (BUF) Retired.
Scanlan, Francis G. '61 (CHI) Oak Forest, IL St. Damian.
Scanlan, Michael J. *o.s.a.* '64 (PH)[AA] Villanova, PA St. John Stone Friary.
Scanlan, Michael *t.o.r.* '64 (STU)[A] Steubenville, OH Franciscan University of Steubenville; [F] Steubenville, OH Holy Spirit Friary.
Scanlan, Thomas R. '57 (BAK) Retired.
Scanlan, William A. '72 (BO) Permanent Disability.
Scanlin, Joseph T. '89 (HBG) Lebanon, PA St. Cecilia.
Scanlon, Bernard S. '45 (BGP)[P] Stamford, CT The Catherine Dennis Keefe Queen of the Clergy Retired Priests' Residence; Retired Priests Retired.
Scanlon, Charles '54 (CHI)[B] Techny, IL Divine Word Residence.
Scanlon, Frank '83 (NY) New York, NY St. Columba.
Scanlon, James M. *m.m.* '52 (NY).
Scanlon, John J. '53 (NY)[EE] Scarsdale, NY Immaculate Heart of Mary.
Scanlon, Michael J. *o.s.a.* '64 (PH)[C] Villanova University.
Scanlon, Paul *o.p.* '59 (ANC) Unalaska, AK St. Christopher By the Sea.
Scanlon, Paul *o.p.* '59 (OAK)[N] Oakland, CA Dominican Order (Western Province), St. Albert's Priory.
Scanlon, Peter J. '57 (WOR) Worcester, MA Sacred Heart; [R] Worcester, MA Campus Ministry; [R] Worcester, MA Becker College; [R] Worcester, MA Worcester Polytechnic Institute; Campus Ministry.
Scanlon, Regis *o.f.m.cap.* '72 (DEN)[N] Denver, CO St. Francis of Assisi Friary.
Scanlon, Richard M. '28 (RVC) Blue Point, NY Our Lady of the Snow Retired.
Scanlon, Thomas F. '49 (NY) Mt. Vernon, NY SS. Peter and Paul.
Scanlon, Thomas J. '59 (PH) East Norriton, PA St. Titus.
Scanlon, Thomas '49 (NY) Retired.
Scanlon, William J. *s.j.* '70 (NY)[EE] New York, NY Jesuit Provincial's Office; [EE] New York, NY Development Office of the New York Province; [EE] New York, NY St. Ignatius Loyola Residence; [II] New York, NY Catholic Medical Mission Board, Inc..
Scannel, Anthony *o.f.m.cap.* '55 (LA)[F] La Canada Flintridge, CA St. Francis High School.
Scannell, Anthony "Tony" T. *o.f.m.cap.* (LA) Executive Publisher.
Scannell, Joseph S. *s.j.* '50 (BO)[V] Weston, MA Campion Health Center, Inc..
Scannell, Peter '46 (ORG) Retired.
Scannell, Thomas P. '37 (ARL) Retired.
Scannell, Timothy J. '69 (NY) Dobbs Ferry, NY Sacred Heart.
Scantlebury, Neil '95 (STV) Charlotte Amalie, VI Cathedral of Sts. Peter and Paul; Diocesan Consultors.
Scantlin, Joseph S. '59 (FWT) Arlington, TX Most Blessed Sacrament; Mansfield, TX St. Jude.
Scantlin, Joseph (FWT) Deans; Priests' Personnel Board.
Scaramella, Renzo L. '95 (NEW) On Duty Outside the Archdiocese.
Scaramuzzo, Peter C. '66 (NY) West Harrison, NY St. Anthony.
Scarangella, Joseph A. '92 (NEW) Caldwell, NJ St. Aloysius.
Scarangello, John R. *o.f.m.* '81 (NY)[EE] New York, NY Padua Friary.
Scarangello, John '81 (NY)[E] New York, NY Cathedral High School.
Scarborough, Henry *o.c.s.o.* '63 (WOR)[O] Spencer, MA St. Joseph's Abbey.
Scarcella, Philip J. '77 (MET) On Duty Outside the Diocese.
Scarcello, Michael S. '56 (B) Retired.
Scarcia, John J. '74 (PH) Pennsburg, PA St. Philip Neri.
Scardella, Joseph E. '81 (SY) Building Commission.
Scardella, Joseph '81 (SY) Formation for Ministry.
Scarfia, Gabriel *o.f.m.* '64 (BUF).
Scarlata, Ronald E. '66 (CHI) Retired.
Scarmozzino, Steven '97 (RVC)[A] Dix Hills, NY St. Matthew.
Scarrabelli, Volmar *c.s.* (ORL) Portuguese/Brazilian.
Scepaniak, Russell G. '93 (WIN) Chatfield, MN St. Mary's; Chatfield, MN St. Patrick; Preston, MN St. Columban.
Scerbo, Joseph *s.a.* '70 (NY)[EE] Garrison Franciscan Friars of the Atonement, Minister General Office.
Scerbo, Joseph *s.a.* '70 (ORG) San Juan Capistrano, CA Mission Basilica.
Scerbo, Joseph *s.a.* (ORG) Council of Priests.
Sceski, Alfred P. '91 (HBG)[J] Bloomsburg, PA Bloomsburg University of Pennsylvania.
Scesney, Everard *o.f.m.* '68 (GB) Birnamwood, WI St. Boniface; Birnamwood, WI St. Philomena.
Schaab, Dennis *c.pp.s.* '68 (KC) Warrensburg, MO Sacred Heart.
Schaab, Denny M. '76 (STL) Webster Groves, MO Annunciation.
Schaab, R. Michael '71 (PEO) Coal Valley, IL St. Maria Goretti; Orion, IL Mary, Our Lady of Peace.
Schaab, Thomas J. '74 (STL) Florissant, MO St. Christopher.
Schaaf, Paul *c.pp.s.* '60 (CIN)[B] Carthagena, OH St. Charles.
Schabel, Joseph A. '56 (SAG) Marriage Encounter Retired.
Schabowski, Henry F. '60 (TR) Trenton, NJ St. Hedwig.
Schack, Stephen '99 (PHX) Gilbert, AZ St. Anne.
Schad, Joseph J. *s.j.* '91 (BO)[V] Boston The Society of Jesus of New England–Provincial Offices.
Schad, Joseph *s.j.* '91 (ANC)[G] Anchorage, AK Anchorage Jesuit Community.
Schaedel, Joseph F. '82 (IND) Indianapolis, IN SS. Peter and Paul Cathedral.
Schaedel, Joseph F. (IND) Vicar General and Moderator of the Curia; Board of Consultors; Council of Priests; Finance Council; Archdiocesan Review Board; Roman Catholic Archdiocese of Indianapolis Properties; Mission Office.
Schaedel, Joseph '82 (IND) Indianapolis, IN Holy Rosary; Archdiocesan Pastoral Council.
Schaefer, Bernard *o.s.b.* '56 (RCK)[G] Aurora, IL Marmion Abbey.
Schaefer, Dennis R. '75 (BEL) Chester, IL St. Mary Help of Christians.
Schaefer, Edgar J. '54 (WIN) Retired.
Schaefer, Edward F. '75 (BEL) St. Rose, IL St. Rose.
Schaefer, James F. '61 (LC) Dorchester, WI St. Louis.
Schaefer, James W. '56 (STL) St. Mary, MO Sacred Heart; Deaneries/Deans; Ste. Genevieve.
Schaefer, Kenneth J. (BEL) Herrin, IL Our Lady of Mount Carmel; Diocesan Consultors.
Schaefer, Kenneth '73 (BEL) Johnston City, IL St. Paul.
Schaefer, Les F. *c.s.b.* '61 (OAK)[C] Oakland, CA Bishop O'Dowd High School.
Schaefer, Martin T. '92 (WIN) Wells, MI St. Anthony; Pipestone, MN St. Leo's; Pipestone, MN St. Martin's; Deans; Elected Deanery Representatives; Pipestone, MN St. Joseph's; Auditors.
Schaefer, Philip *c.p.* '58 (CHI)[N] Chicago, IL Passionist Community–Immaculate Conception Monastery.
Schaefer, Richard '96 (PMB) Boynton Beach, FL St. Thomas More.
Schaefer, Roman J. '42 (NU) Fort Lauderdale, FL Our Lady Queen of Martyrs Retired.
Schaefer, Thomas *o.carm.* '48 (JOL)[L] Darien Carmelite Provincial Office.
Schaefer, Verne B. '55 (MIL) Retired.
Schaeffer, Bradley M. *s.j.* '77 (WDC)[N] Chicago Chicago Province of the Society of Jesus–Provincial Office; [M] Washington, DC Leonard Neale House; [V] Washington, DC Jesuit Conference, Inc..
Schaeffer, Martin T. (WIN) Advocates.
Schaeflein, Charles J. '49 (PH)[V] Philadelphia, PA Mount Nazareth Retired.
Schafer, Dennis R. '02 (BIS) Dickinson, ND St. Joseph; Vicar for Deacons.
Schafer, Dennis *o.f.m.* '80 (STL)[S] Dittmer, MO Il Ritiro–The Little Retreat.
Schafer, Raymond E. '89 (IND) Unassigned.
Schafer, Robert J. '99 (DET) Roseville, MI St. Angela.
Schafer, William *s.d.b.* '61 (LA)[Q] Los Angeles, CA Dominic Savio Salesian Residence.
Schaff, Ty (SPK) Members.
Schaff, Tyrone J. '73 (SPK) Spokane, WA St. John Vianney; Air National Guard Chaplains.
Schaffer, G. Scott '89 (TR) Jackson, NJ Church of St. Monica.
Schaffer, Gregory J. '94 (STP) On Duty Outside the Archdiocese; Venezuelan Missions.
Schaffer, Gregory T. '60 (NU) On Duty Outside the Diocese; San Lucas Mission Office.
Schaffer, J. Darrell '90 (DEN) Denver, CO Christ the King.
Schaffer, Mark *o.carm.* '89 (CHI)[D] Chicago, IL.
Schaffner, Mark *o.carm* '89 (CHI)[N] Chicago Carmelite Priory of St. Cyril.
Schaffner, William E. '48 (ALN)[A] Wernersville, PA Jesuit Center.
Schaftlein, Stephen '78 (IND) Charlestown, IN St. Michael; Henryville, IN St. Francis Xavier.
Schaible, Donald J. '89 (ALN) Pen Argyl, PA St. Elizabeth of Hungary; Unassigned.
Schaicoski, Lauro *o.s.b.m.* '95 (STN) Hamtramck, MI Immaculate Conception of B.V.M..
Schak, John R. *s.j.* '61 (MIL).
Schalk, Sebastian '60 (JKS)[F] Jackson, MS Priory of St. Moses the Black.
Schall, James V. *s.j.* '63 (California)[M] Washington, DC The Jesuit Community at Georgetown University.
Schallberger, Meinrad *o.s.b.* '64 (B)[B] Cottonwood, ID St. Mary's Hospital; [C] Jerome, ID Monastery of the Ascension.
Schallenberger, Meinrad *o.s.b.* '64 (B) Cottonwood, ID Monastery of St. Gertrude.
Schaller, Pascal *o.f.m.cap.* '51 (PIT)[N] Allison Park, PA St. Conrad Friary.
Schaller, Robert A. (LC) Stevens Point, WI St. Peter; Deans.
Schappert, James P. *s.s.j.* '49 (BAL)[S] Baltimore, MD St. Joseph Society of the Sacred Heart House of Central Administration Retired.
Schappler, Norbert *o.s.b.* '52 (KC)[J] Stanberry, MO.
Schardt, William B. '75 (ARL) Arlington, VA St. Ann.
Schardt, William (BAL) Interdiocesan Judges.
Scharf, David E. '85 (PIT)[Q] New Brighton, PA Geneva College.
Scharf, David E.F. '85 (PIT) Beaver Falls, PA St. Philomena.
Scharfenberger, Edward B. (BRK) Lawyers.
Scharfenberger, Edward '73 (BRK) Ridgewood, NY St. Matthias; Mediation and Arbitration, Board of.
Schartz, Kenneth '85 (CIN) Xenia, OH St. Brigid.
Schatteman, Rene J. '60 (LA)[M] Pittsburgh, PA Prelature of the Holy Cross and Opus Dei.
Schatz, David A. (DUB) Cedar Rapids, IA St. Pius X; Seminary Board.
Schatzel, John E. '61 (BO) Senior Priests Retired.
Schatzle, Michael J. '74 (BR) New Roads, LA St. Mary of False River; College of Consultors; Presbyteral Council.
Schauerman, Henry J. '51 (E) Retired.
Schaukowitch, James V. *s.j.* '79 (LA)[F] Los Angeles, CA Loyola High School of Los Angeles.
Schaut, Gregory F. '85 (CLV) Chardon, OH St. Mary.
Schavitz, Peter *c.ss.r.* '76 (CHI) Chicago, IL St. Michael; [N] Chicago, IL The Redemptorist Fathers of Chicago.
Scheaffer, Walter T. '66 (ALN) Kutztown, PA St. Mary.
Scheble, Carl J. '83 (STL) St. Louis, MO St. Elizabeth, Mother of John the Baptist.
Scheckel, Roger J. '84 (LC) La Crosse, WI St. James the Less; [C] La Crosse, WI Coulee Catholic Schools; [L] La Crosse, WI Father Joseph Walijewski Orphanage Endowment Trust; Deans; Holy Childhood Association; Consultors; Propagation of the Faith; Ex Officio Members.
Scheckenback, Robert C. '89 (RVC) Holbrook, NY Good Shepherd.
Schecker, Robert J.W. '71 (TR) Mount Holly, NJ Sacred Heart.
Scheel, Daniel '69 (GAL) Houston, TX St. Jerome; Western Vicariate; College of Consultors; Council of Catholic Women.
Scheeler, Jeffrey *o.f.m.* '80 (CIN)[M] Cincinnati, OH St. Francis Seraph Friary.
Scheer, Allen '95 (SAL) Logan, KS St. John's; Phillipsburg, KS SS. Philip and James; Catholic Charities Board; Rural Life Conference.
Scheer, John R. *s.a.c.* '70 (SUP) Tomahawk, WI St. John the Baptist; Tomahawk, WI St. Augustine; Tomahawk, WI St. Francis of Assisi; Tomahawk, WI St. Mary.

Scheerer, Dominic *o.c.d.* '47 (MIL)[O] Holy Hill, WI Discalced Carmelite Monastery – Holy Hill National Shrine of Mary Help of Christians.
Scheets, Francis K. *o.s.c.* '51 (DET)[K] Riverview, MI Crosier Community of Riverview; Riverview, MI St. Cyprian.
Scheetz, Daniel L. '65 (SAL) Ellsworth, KS St. Bernard's; Ellsworth, KS St. Mary's; Ellsworth, KS St. Ignatius Loyola.
Scheetz, Daniel (SAL) Promoter of Justice and Guardian.
Scheetz, Joseph '54 (SAL) Retired.
Schefers, Eberhard '64 (SCL) Becker, MN Immaculate Conception.
Scheff, Philip '01 (VEN) Port Charlotte, FL San Antonio; Finance Department; Real Estate Board.
Scheff, Philip (VEN) Treasurer Pro Tempore.
Scheffler, Mark *c.ss.r.* '70 (SAT) San Antonio, TX Santa Rosa Hospital System; [M] San Antonio, TX Redemptorists of Texas–San Antonio #1.
Schehr, Timothy P. '73 (CIN)[B] Cincinnati, OH Mt. St. Mary's Seminary of the West; Censors.
Scheib, Joseph C. '76 (PIT) Pittsburgh, PA St. Basil; Judges.
Scheible, Ronald *o.s.a.* '57 (FWT) Lindsay, TX St. Peter.
Scheich, Eugene '66 (L) Louisville, KY St. Matthias.
Scheick, James C. '63 (DET) Grosse Ile, MI Sacred Heart.
Scheider, David J. '53 (BUF) East Pembroke, NY Holy Name of Mary.
Scheiding, Philip '81 (MIA) On Duty Outside the Archdiocese.
Scheidler, David '92 (CHI)[D] Niles, IL Notre Dame High School.
Scheidt, Daniel D. '01 (FTW) Granger, IN St. Pius X.
Scheier, Steven '53 (WCH) Bushton, KS Holy Name of Jesus.
Scheierl, LeRoy '91 (SCL) Belgrade, MN St. Francis De Sales; Brooten, MN St. Donatus; Elrosa, MN SS. Peter and Paul; Boy Scouts.
Scheinost, Douglas P. '92 (OM) Stuart, NE St. Boniface.
Scheip, Michael A. '94 (VEN) Sarasota, FL St. Patrick.
Scheip, Michael (VEN) Charismatic Renewal.
Schelble, Terrence M. '61 (LC) Auburndale, WI Nativity of the Blessed Virgin Mary; Hewitt, WI St. Michael; Personnel Council.
Schelble, Thomas M. *s.m.* '46 (SAT)[K] San Antonio, TX Marianist Residence: Skilled Nursing.
Schelich, Anthony T. *o.s.f.s.* '65 (WIL) Wilmington, DE St. Hedwig.
Schelich, Theodosius A. *o.f.m.* '59 (SFD)[I] Litchfield, IL St. Francis Hospital.
Schelich, Theodosius A. *o.f.m.* '59 (STL)[O] Litchfield, IL.
Schell, Joseph O. *s.j.* '44 (CLV)[B] Cleveland, OH John Carroll University.
Schellberg, Eugene '60 (MET) Retired.
Schellemans, Francis *ss.cc.* '49 (HON)[G] Kaneohe, HI Sacred Hearts Center.
Schellenberg, James '77 (SAT) San Antonio, TX Brooke Army Medical Center.
Schellenberg, Milton A. '46 (WDC) Retired.
Schellenberger, Otto *s.v.d.* '42 (CHI)[B] Techny, IL Divine Word Residence.
Scheller, Albert J. '61 (EVN) Vincennes, IN St. Vincent de Paul.
Scheller, John '58 (OKL) Retired.
Schelling, Michael E. '74 (TOL) Crestline, OH St. Joseph; Galion, OH St. Joseph.
Schemel, Francis *s.j.* '58 (WDC)[M] Washington, DC The Jesuit Community at Georgetown University.
Schemm, Michael '93 (WCH) Wichita, KS Christ the King.
Schenck, Stephen *s.d.b.* '81 (MIA) Washington, DC Nativity.
Schendt, Richard L. '63 (CHI)[W] Oak Park, IL Oak Park Study Center.
Scheneller, Michael J. '72 (NO) Metairie, LA St. Ann Church and Shrine.
Schenick, Joseph D. '51 (PRO)[P] Providence St. John Vianney Residence Retired.
Schenk, Arthur J. *s.j.* '45 (SJ)[M] Los Gatos, CA Sacred Heart Jesuit Center.
Schenk, Francisco *g.h.m.* '55 (TLS) Idabel, OK St. Francis De Sales.
Schenk, Francisco *g.h.m.* '55 (CIN)[M] Cincinnati Headquarters of Glenmary Home Missioners.
Schenk, Mark *o.f.m.cap.* (FgM).
Schenk, Richard *o.p.* '78 (OAK)[N] Oakland, CA Dominican Order (Western Province), St. Albert's Priory.
Schenning, Kevin T. '81 (BAL) Pasadena, MD St. Jane Frances de Chantal.
Schepers, M. B. *o.p.* '56 (FgM).
Scherba, Raymond M. '82 (BGP) Danbury, CT St. Gregory.
Scherer, Albert *o.f.m.conv.* (BAL) Baltimore, MD St. Clement Mary Hofbauer.
Scherer, Donald R. '67 (NEW) Retired.
Scherer, Gary *c.pp.s.* '67 (GRY) Whiting, IN St. John the Baptist; Bishop's Council of Priests.
Scherer, Gerald N. '54 (RC) Retired.
Scherer, James F. '64 (ATL) On Duty Outside the Archdiocese.
Scherer, Philip M. *o.s.m.* '55 (CHI)[N] Chicago Order of Friar Servants of Mary (Servites) United States of America Province, Inc..
Scherer, Richard '49 (MIA) Retired.
Scherger, Herman F. '58 (TOL) Antwerp, OH St. Mary; Cloverdale, OH Immaculate Conception; Cloverdale, OH St. Mary.
Scherkenbach, Gerald A. (STP) Associate Judges.
Scherpenberg, Sergius *o.f.m.* '51 (PEO) Peoria, IL Sacred Heart.
Scherrer, Carl E. '73 (BEL) Columbia, IL Immaculate Conception of the B.V.M..
Scherrer, Steven *m.m.* '72 (ATL)[K] Conyers The Monastery of the Holy Spirit.
Schettler, Charles H. '54 (OKL) Oklahoma City, OK St. Francis of Assisi; Judicial Vicar.
Scheuer, James '59 (DUL) Babbitt, MN St. Pius X; Ely, MN St. Anthony; Deans.
Scheuerell, Charles A. '57 (MIL) Retired.
Scheuerman, Edward L. '50 (DET) Retired.
Schevers, Joel *o.carm.* '42 (VEN) Venice, FL Epiphany Cathedral; [G] Nokomis, FL Carmel at Mission Valley; Co–Directors:.
Schexnayder Gary '69 (LAF) Crowley, LA St. Michael Archangel; Scouting.
Schexnayder James '64 (OAK) Retired.
Scheyd, William J. '65 (BGP) New Canaan, CT St. Aloysius; Vicars General; Diocesan Consultors; Presbyteral Council; Finance Council; Pastors' Vocation Advisory Board.
Schiavi, Giulio *p.i.m.e.* '63 (DET) Clinton Twp., MI San Francesco Community.
Schiavo, John Lo *s.j.* '55 (SFR)[C] San Francisco, CA University of San Francisco.
Schiavo, Sylvan *c.s.j.* '63 (LA) San Pedro, CA St. Peter.
Schiavone, Alphonse A. *m.m.* '46 (NY)[EE Maryknoll Maryknoll Fathers and Brothers.
Schiavone, Aldo J. '52 (LFT) Retired.
Schiavone, Robert W. '69 (MIL)[B] Hales Corners, WI Sacred Heart School of Theology.
Schiavone, Robert W. '69 (GB) On Duty Outside the Diocese.
Schiavonne, John S. '73 (LA) Whittier, CA St. Gregory the Great.
Schiblin, Richard *c.ss.r.* '61 (OAK)[N] Oakland, CA Redemptorists.
Schichtel, Kenneth H. '62 (GR) Ludington, MI St. Simon's; Ludington, MI St. Stanislaus.
Schieber, Brian (KCK) Directors.
Schieber, Joachim *o.s.b.* '44 (KC)[J] Stanberry, MO.
Schieber, Lawrence J. '49 (STL) Retired.
Schiefen, Richard J. *c.s.b.* (GAL)[Q] Houston, TX Residence of the Basilian Fathers of the University of St. Thomas.
Schieffer, Stanley F. '56 (LIN) Retired.
Schiel, Nicholas E. *s.j.* '55 (MIL)[O] Centro Loyola.
Schiele, John D. '93 (PH) West Chester, PA St. Maximilian Kolbe.
Schifalacqua, Ildebrando E. '43 (PH) Philadelphia, PA St. Bartholomew.
Schifano, Al (TUC) O.F.C. Members.
Schifano, Albert I. '01 (TUC) Tucson, AZ Saints Peter and Paul.
Schifano, James R. *s.c.j.* '75 (JKS) Holly Springs, MS St. Joseph.
Schifano, Vincent (RVC) Hicksville, NY Holy Family.
Schiferl, David J. '01 (P) Cornelius, OR St. Alexander.
Schiffer, James *c.p.* '71 (ALB) Windham, NY St. Theresa of Child Jesus.
Schiffer, James '71 (MET)[H] Windham, NY.
Schiffer, Thomas E. '63 (WH) Glen Dale, WV St. Jude.
Schifferli, Jerome F. '45 (ROC) Livonia, NY St. Matthew Catholic Church Society.
Schik, Jerome *o.s.c.* '75 (STP) Shoreview, MN St. Odilia; [M] Shoreview, MN Crosier Community of Shoreview.
Schik, LeRoy '03 (SCL) Bowlus, MN St. Stanislaus Kostka; Albany, MN St. Anthony's; Bowlus, MN St. Mary; Bowlus, MN St. Edward's; Freeport, MN St. Francis of Assisi.
Schilder, David M. '68 (LEX) Ashland, KY; Prison Ministry.
Schilder, David M. '68 (COL) On Duty Outside the Diocese.
Schill, Damien '87 (STP) Veterans Administration Medical Center; On Duty Outside the Diocese.
Schill, Frederick J. '57 (TOL) Retired.
Schill, Gerald F. (Damien) (FAR).
Schill, Paul A. '80 (E) Greenville, PA St. Michael.
Schill, Victor J. '50 (FAR) Retired.
Schiller, Francis E. '65 (NEW) Jersey City, NJ Assumption/All Saints; Jersey City, NJ St. Patrick's.
Schiller, Thomas A. '55 (GR) Retired.
Schilli, Richard J. '77 (STL) Ferguson, MO Sts. John and James.
Schillinger, James A. '84 (ATL) Atlanta, GA Immaculate Heart of Mary; Continuing Education in Ministry; Judges.
Schilly, Joseph '48 (SB) Retired.
Schiltz, Roger J. '68 (WIN) Retired.
Schimelpfening, James *s.m.* '69 (STL)[O] Chicago, IL.
Schiml, Ronald J. *c.pp.s.* '55 (LFT) Star City, IN St. Joseph.
Schimmel, Eric J. *c.s.c.* '02 (COS) Colorado Springs, CO Sacred Heart.
Schimmelmann, Wayne *c.m.f.* '86 (CHI)[N] Oak Park, IL Claretian Fathers Headquarters of U.S.A. Eastern Province.
Schimmer, Robert J. '68 (SC) Presbyteral Council; Diocesan Consultors.
Schimmer, Robert '68 (SC) Sheldon, IA St. Patrick's.
Schimscheiner, Francis M. *o.s.f.s.* '65 (BUF) Lockport, NY St. Patrick.
Schindler, Carl *c.ss.r.* '63 (SAT)[M] San Antonio, TX Redemptorists of Texas–San Antonio #1; Bexar County Detention Ministries.
Schindler, John L. '85 (L) Louisville, KY St. Joseph.
Schindler, Paul E. '67 (CLV) Akron, OH St. Bernard; [W] Akron, OH Parishes with Ministry to Spanish Speaking: St. Bernard.
Schinelli, Giles A. *t.o.r.* '73 (STP) Brooklyn Park, MN St. Gerard; [M] Minneapolis, MN St. Gerard Friary.
Schinn, Bernard *o.s.b.* '62 (PAT)[M] Clifton, NJ Holy Face of Jesus Monastery.
Schinski, Stanislaus E. '51 (PAT) Wayne, NJ Annunciation.
Schipp, John H. '64 (EVN) Vincennes, IN Basilica of St. Francis Xavier; [I] Vincennes, IN Old Cathedral Library & Museum, Inc.; Advocates.
Schipp, John (EVN) Diocesan Council of Priests.
Schipp, Ralph '65 (EVN) Schnellville, IN Sacred Heart.
Schipper, Carl A. '68 (SFR) Retired.
Schipper, William *o.s.b.* '94 (SCL)[I] Collegeville, MN St. John's Abbey, of the Order of St. Benedict.
Schiro, Nicholas T. *s.j.* '57 (NO)[F] New Orleans, LA Jesuit High School.
Schiska, Paul A. '57 (MAR) Retired.
Schissel, Gregory A. *s.j.* '79 (OM)[K] Omaha, NE Jesuit Community at Creighton University.
Schlachter, Eric A. '81 (JC) Absent on Leave.
Schlade, Joseph F. '58 (RCK) Retired.
Schladen, Robert '59 (PEO) Retired.
Schlaf, John E. '64 (GI) Ogallala, NE St. Luke's; Personnel Board.
Schlaf, John (GI) Building Committee.
Schlafer, Joseph M. '75 (RVC) Garden City, NY St. Joseph's; Priests' Personnel Policy Board.
Schlageter, Robert *o.f.m.conv.* '84 (WDC)[C] Washington, DC Catholic University of America, The.
Schlagheck, Regis *o.f.m.conv.* '66 (TOL) Carey, OH Our Lady of Consolation, Basilica–National Shrine.
Schlangen, Louis '57 (SFD) Mendon, IL St. Edward.
Schlarb, Gregory J. '97 (PHX) Scottsdale, AZ St. Maria Goretti.
Schlatter, Fredric *s.j.* '56 (SPK)[B] Spokane, WA Gonzaga University.
Schlautman, Wayne W. '65 (OM) Omaha, NE Christ the King.
Schlaver, David E. *c.s.c.* '71 (FgM).
Schlaver, David E. *c.s.c.* '71 (FTW)[I] Notre Dame, IN Holy Cross Mission Center.
Schlaver, David *c.s.c.* '71 (FTW)[A] Notre Dame, IN Moreau Seminary.
Schlax, Charles H. '66 (CHI) Des Plaines, IL St. Mary.
Schlegel, Daniel F. '88 (CLV) Chagrin Falls, OH Holy Angels.
Schlegel, George J. '66 (COL) New Philadelphia, OH Sacred Heart; Vicariate 11: Tusc–Holmes; Diocesan Judges.
Schlegel, John P. *s.j.* '73 (OM)[A] Omaha, NE Creighton University; [K] Omaha, NE Jesuit Community at Creighton University.
Schlegel, Lawrence *o.s.b.* '54 (MAN)[K] Manchester, NH St. Anselm Abbey.
Schleicher, Edward '83 (PIT) Glenshaw, PA St. Mary of the Assumption.
Schleicher, James R. '54 (CLV) Akron, OH St. Francis de Sales; [U] Cleveland, OH Society of St. Vincent de Paul, Diocesan Central Council.
Schleisman, Jeffrey '00 (SC) Larchwood, IA St. Mary; Rock Rapids, IA Holy Name.
Schlenker, Richard J. '56 (MIL) Retired.
Schlert, Alfred A. '87 (ALN) Allentown, PA Cathedral of St. Catharine of Siena; Vicar General; Defenders of the Bond; College of Consultors; Ex Officio Members; Finance Council.
Schlesselmann, Gregory J. '93 (FAR) Special Assignment; [A] Fargo, ND Cardinal Muench Seminary; Vicars General; Notaries; Diocesan College of Consultors; Permanent Diaconate.
Schleter, Edward J. '67 (TOL) Bowling Green, OH St. Aloysius.
Schlett, Francis J. '70 (PH) Coatesville, PA St. Cecilia.
Schleupner, G. Michael '72 (BAL) Abingdon, MD St. Francis de Sales; Consultors; Judicial Vicar; Consultors.
Schlichte, Carl *o.p.* '98 (SJ) Stanford, CA Catholic Community at Stanford.
Schlick, Regis *o.f.m.cap.* '65 (WH) Point Pleasant, WV Sacred Heart; [M] Charleston, WV Capuchins–St.

Anthony Friary.
Schliessmann, Thomas L. '89 (IND) Salem, IN St. Patrick; Scottsburg, IN American Martyrs.
Schliessmann, Thomas '89 (IND) Council of Priests.
Schlim, Robert J. *s.j.* '62 (SPK)[J] Spokane, WA Regis Community.
Schlimm, Chrysostom V. *o.s.b.* '61 (GBG)[H] Latrobe, PA Saint Vincent Archabbey.
Schlitt, Dale *o.m.i.* '69 (WDC)[M] Washington, DC Provincial Offices of the United States Province of the Missionary Oblates of Mary Immaculate.
Schlitt, Dale *o.m.i.* '69 (FgM).
Schlitt, Harry G. '64 (SFR) College of Consultors; Board of Directors; Archbishop's Cabinet; Moderator of the Curia and Vicar for Administration.
Schlitt, Harry '64 (SFR)[S] San Francisco, CA Catholics for Truth & Justice.
Schloeder, Paul '87 (SAC) Chico, CA St. John the Baptist.
Schloemer, Bernard J. '60 (STL) St. Louis, MO St. Justin Martyr.
Schloemer, Leo *g.h.m.* '56 (FWT) Knox City, TX Santa Rosa; Munday, TX St. Joseph.
Schloemer, Leo *g.h.m.* '56 (CIN)[M] Cincinnati Headquarters of Glenmary Home Missioners.
Schloemer, Thomas N. *s.j.* '68 (OM) Omaha, NE St. John; [K] Omaha, NE Jesuit Community at Creighton University.
Schloesser, Stephen *s.j.* '92 (MIL)[V] Newton, MA The Jesuit Community at Boston College.
Schlosser, Leo R. *o.s.b.* '59 (PBR) Sheffield, PA St. Michael.
Schlosser, Richard '74 (GF) Great Falls, MT Holy Spirit; Vicars Forane.
Schloth, Brian *m.s.* '89 (ATL) Smyrna, GA St. Thomas the Apostle.
Schludecker, Andre *o.f.m.* '64 (STL)[S] Dittmer, MO Il Ritiro–The Little Retreat.
Schlueter, Clemens '58 (TUC) Retired.
Schlueter, Clements M. (TUC) Retired.
Schluter, O. Charles '78 (MAD) Platteville, WI St. Mary; Elected.
Schmalhofer, John D. '74 (HBG) New Holland, PA Our Lady of Lourdes; Appointed.
Schmaltz, Bernard '73 (NO) Retired.
Schmalzried, Bernard R. '69 (Y) Warren, OH St. Mary; Priests' Council.
Schmaus, James E. '92 (CHI) Palatine, IL St. Theresa.
Schmeer, John P. '64 (PH) New Hope, PA St. Martin of Tours.
Schmeidler, John *o.f.m.cap.* '97 (KCK)[H] Lawrence, KS St. Conrad's Friary; [K] Lawrence, KS St. Lawrence Catholic Campus Center at the University of Kansas and Residence.
Schmelz, Damian *o.s.b.* '58 (IND)[K] Ferdinand, IN.
Schmelz, Damian *o.s.b.* '58 (EVN) Ferdinand, IN St. Henry.
Schmelzer, Delbert L. '56 (MAD) Holy Childhood, Pontifical Association; Propagation of the Faith Retired.
Schmelzer, Linus L. '45 (MIL) Retired.
Schmelzer, Ronald '02 (SCL) Verndale, MN St. Hubert's; Bluffton, MN St. John the Baptist; Bluffton, MN The Church of the Assumption of Our Lady of Menahga; Verndale, MN St. Frederick's; Wadena, MN St. Ann's.
Schmenk, Cleo S. '53 (TOL) Retired.
Schmid, Wayne L. (WCH) Ongoing Formation of the Clergy Committee.
Schmid, Wayne '68 (WCH) Derby, KS St. Mary's; [L] Wichita, KS Priests' Retirement and Education Fund of Wichita; Presbyteral Council/Diocesan Consultors; Deans; Presbyteral Council.
Schmidberger, Richard '57 (DET) Retired.
Schmidlin, Donald L. '57 (IND) Retired.
Schmidlin, Donald (IND) Council of Priests.
Schmidt, Anthony '50 (SFD) Retired.
Schmidt, Bosco *s.a.* '49 (NY)[EE] Garrison, NY Franciscan Friars of the Atonement.
Schmidt, Carl '50 (SFD) Coffeen, IL St. John the Baptist; Coffeen, IL Sacred Heart.
Schmidt, Charles J. *m.m.* (HON) Catholic Committee on Scouting.
Schmidt, Charles W. *m.m.* '48 (HON)[G] Honolulu, HI Maryknoll Fathers House (M.M.).
Schmidt, David R. (GB) Kaukauna, WI St. Aloysius.
Schmidt, David '77 (SFD) Alton, IL St. Matthew.
Schmidt, David (GB) Elected Representatives.
Schmidt, Dennis C. '80 (STL) Hillsboro, MO Church of the Good Shepherd; Archdiocesan Council of Priests.
Schmidt, Donald '73 (MIL) Retired.
Schmidt, Edward W. *s.j.* '73 (CHI)[N] Chicago, IL Clark Street Jesuit Residence; [V] Cincinnati, OH St. Xavier Church Property Corporation; [N] Chicago, IL Chicago Province of the Society of Jesus–Provincial Office.
Schmidt, Edwin A. '63 (JC) Jefferson City, MO St. Martin.
Schmidt, Elmer J. '56 (ROC) Retired.
Schmidt, Eugene '56 (GB) Retired.
Schmidt, Florian J. '61 (DUB) Retired.
Schmidt, Francis J. '58 (MAD) Cross Plains, WI St. Martin.
Schmidt, Francis X. '57 (PH) Bridgeport, PA St. Augustine.
Schmidt, George E. '70 (KNX) Chattanooga, TN SS. Peter and Paul; Chattanooga, TN Mount Olivet; Diocesan Finance Council; Cemeteries.
Schmidt, George N. '41 (WCH) Retired.
Schmidt, Gregory L. '61 (STL) Old Monroe, MO Immaculate Conception.
Schmidt, Gustav H. *s.j.* '66 (NY)[EE] New York, NY Murray–Weigel Hall.
Schmidt, Henry '57 (SFD) Carrollton, IL St. John the Evangelist; Greenfield, IL St. Michael; Carrollton, IL All Saints.
Schmidt, Jan Kevin '90 (CIN) Cincinnati, OH Immaculate Heart of Mary.
Schmidt, Jerome J. '49 (BRK) Retired.
Schmidt, John *c.ss.r.* '89 (CHI) Chicago, IL St. Michael; [N] Chicago, IL The Redemptorist Fathers of Chicago.
Schmidt, Joseph F. '66 (B) Moscow, ID St. Mary's.
Schmidt, Kenneth W. '81 (KAL) Kalamazoo, MI St. Thomas More Student Parish; [H] Kalamazoo, MI Western Michigan University, Kalamazoo College–Kalamazoo Valley Community College; Defenders of the Bond; Promoter of Justice.
Schmidt, Kenneth (KAL) Ecclesiastical Notaries; Priestly Life and Ministry Office.
Schmidt, Leo C. '56 (COV) Covington, KY St. Augustine.
Schmidt, Leslie *g.h.m.* '61 (RIC) Big Stone Gap, VA Sacred Heart; Jonesville, VA Church of the Holy Spirit.
Schmidt, Louis R. '54 (LEX) Retired.
Schmidt, Lukas J. *o.carm.* '65 (VEN) Osprey, FL Our Lady of Mount Carmel.
Schmidt, Paul J. '64 (OAK) Oakland, CA St. Margaret Mary.
Schmidt, Paul *s.v.d.* '76 (SB)[A] Riverside, CA Society of the Divine Word Missionaries.
Schmidt, Paul (OAK) Pastoral Leadership Placement Board (PLPB); Office of Clergy Personnel.
Schmidt, Peter *o.c.s.o.* '75 (WOR)[O] Spencer, MA St. Joseph's Abbey; [Q] Spencer, MA St. Joseph Abbey.
Schmidt, Raymond F. '60 (BRK) AUXILIARY CHAPLAINS CONTRACT CHAPLAINS.
Schmidt, Raymond F. '84 (WDC) La Plata, MD Sacred Heart.
Schmidt, Richard C. *s.j.* '61 (WDC).
Schmidt, Robert R. '43 (COL) Retired.
Schmidt, Ron *s.j.* '02 (LA)[BB] Los Angeles, CA Loyola Marymount University.
Schmidt, Ronald E. '02 (LA)[C] Los Angeles, CA Jesuit Community.
Schmidt, Sebastian *o.s.b.* '60 (BIS) Glen Ullin, ND Sacred Heart of Jesus; Hebron, ND St. Ann; [A] Richardton, ND Assumption Abbey.
Schmidt, Thomas W. '99 (CIN) Centerville, OH St. Francis of Assisi.
Schmidt, Thomas *c.ss.r.* '62 (RVC) Bethpage, NY St. Martin of Tours.
Schmidt, W. Robert '57 (DAV) Davenport, IA St. Anthony's; Holy Childhood, Pontifical Association.
Schmidt, William F. *s.a.* '59 (ARL) Herndon, VA Christ the Redeemer.
Schmidt, William T. '76 (BO) Stoneham, MA St. Patrick.
Schmidtzinsky, Victor '41 (VIC)[K] San Antonio, TX Padua Place.
Schmied, Michael S. '71 (RIC) Richmond, VA St. Augustine; Delegate for the Hispanic Apostolate.
Schmied, Thomas *o.f.m.cap.* '69 (MAR) Special Assignment.
Schmieder, Mark C. '66 (CIN) On Special and Archdiocesan Assignment.
Schmiesing, Julian *o.s.b.* '58 (SCL) Richmond, MN St. Catherine's; St. Martin, MN St. Martin's; [I] Collegeville, MN St. John's Abbey, of the Order of St. Benedict.
Schmit, Arthur G. *o.s.b.* '57 (PEO).
Schmit, Fred J. *s.d.s.* '46 (NSH)[A] Sparta, TN St. Andrew.
Schmit, George V. '68 (NU) Bird Island, MN St. Mary; Building Committee; Liturgical Guidelines Committee.
Schmit, Jerome L. '57 (LA) Altadena, CA Sacred Heart.
Schmit, Ken (ORG) Ministry to Priests.
Schmit, Kenneth A. '79 (ORG) Los Alamitos, CA St. Hedwig.
Schmit, Louis *c.pp.s.* '63 (CIN) Egypt, OH St. Joseph; Minster, OH St. Augustine.
Schmit, Meyrl E. '65 (JKS) Shelby Twp., MI St. Therese of Lisieux.
Schmit, Meyrl '65 (JKS) On Duty Outside the Diocese.
Schmit, Ralph R. '46 (MIL) Retired.
Schmit, Roger *o.s.b.* (KCK) Kansas City, KS St. Patrick's.
Schmit, Ronald G. '85 (OAK) Byron, CA St. Anne; Deans.
Schmit, Ronald (OAK) Presbyteral Council.
Schmit, Stanley J. '94 (OM) Bloomfield, NE St. Andrew; Osmond, NE St. Mary of the Seven Dolors; Osmond, NE St. Paul.
Schmitmeyer, James M. '81 (CIN) Cincinnati, OH St. Aloysius Gonzaga.
Schmitt, Adam '57 (FTW) Fort Wayne, IN St. Joseph Retired.
Schmitt, Bowan M. '97 (PEO) Ransom, IL St. Patrick's.
Schmitt, Bowen '97 (PEO) Marseilles, IL St. Joseph's.
Schmitt, Carl L. '61 (DUB)[E] New Hampton, IA St. John's School; New Hampton, IA Holy Family; Building Commission; Deanery Representatives.
Schmitt, Charles R. '59 (E) Port Allegany, PA St. Gabriel the Archangel.
Schmitt, Christopher '60 (PMB)[I] Delray Beach, FL Prelature of the Holy Cross and Opus Dei.
Schmitt, Conrad *s.t.* '55 (WDC)[M] University Park, MD Holy Trinity Missionary Cenacle.
Schmitt, David J. '67 (WH) Spencer, WV Holy Redeemer.
Schmitt, Donald P. '62 (DUB) Monticello, IA Sacred Heart.
Schmitt, Ervin J. '58 (PBL)[D] Pueblo, CO Centura Health–St. Mary–Corwin Medical Center Retired.
Schmitt, Ervin '58 (PBL) Pueblo, CO.
Schmitt, Eugene (EVN) Sullivan, IN St. Mary.
Schmitt, Frank J. *s.j.* '83 (DEN)[N] Denver, CO Loyola Parish – Jesuit Community.
Schmitt, Frank *s.j.* '83 (RC) Wanblee, SD Ignatius Loyola; Pine Ridge, SD Holy Rosary; [B] Pine Ridge, SD Jesuit Community of Holy Rosary Mission.
Schmitt, Gregory *c.ss.r.* '69 (OAK)[N] Oakland, CA Redemptorists; [P] Oakland, CA Holy Redeemer Center.
Schmitt, Harold F. '59 (PEO)[J] Lacon, IL St. Joseph's Nursing Home.
Schmitt, James C. '66 (GI) Nebraska Veterans Home Retired.
Schmitt, James '51 (LAN) Retired.
Schmitt, John P. '44 (GB) Retired.
Schmitt, Joseph J. '55 (AUS) Lago Vista, TX St. Mary, Our Lady of the Lake.
Schmitt, Kent A. '73 (MAD) Madison, WI St. Dennis.
Schmitt, Michael T. '71 (ALB) Schenectady, NY St. Paul the Apostle.
Schmitt, Phillip E. '56 (DUB) Engaged Encounter Retired.
Schmitt, Reinhold *c.m.m.* '52 (DET)[K] Vocation Office.
Schmitt, Reinhold *c.m.m.* '52 (AUS) Lott, TX Visitation.
Schmitt, Silverius '58 (SCL) Retired.
Schmitt, Theodore J. '02 (CHI) Arlington Heights, IL St. James.
Schmitt, Thomas F. '91 (SPR) On Duty Outside the Diocese.
Schmitt, Thomas F. '91 (BO)[A] Weston, MA Blessed John XXIII National Seminary.
Schmitt, Warren J. '42 (MIL) Retired.
Schmitter, Philip '71 (LAN) Flint, MI Sacred Heart; Special Assignment.
Schmittgens, Kevin V. '83 (STL) Union, MO St. Joseph.
Schmitz, Aloysius F. *s.j.* '59 (MIL)[O] Milwaukee, WI Arrupe House Jesuit Community.
Schmitz, Bernard A. '74 (DEN) Greeley, CO Our Lady of Peace.
Schmitz, Bernard R. '57 (IND) Morris, IN St. Charles Borromeo; Morris, IN St. Anthony of Padua; Morris, IN St. Pius.
Schmitz, Charles E. *s.j.* '72 (YAK) Yakima, WA St. Joseph's.
Schmitz, Donald J. '80 (WIN) Caledonia, MN St. Mary; Rochester, MN Holy Spirit; Defenders of the Bond.
Schmitz, Donald P. '64 (WIN) Harmony, MN The Assumption; Harmony, MN The Nativity of the Blessed Virgin; Harmony, MN St. Olaf; [A] Winona, MN Immaculate Heart of Mary Seminary; Diocesan Consultors; Defenders of the Bond; Promoter of Justice; Appointed Members; Priest Assignments Committee.
Schmitz, George '69 (CIN) Cincinnati, OH St. Martin of Tours; Cincinnati, OH Our Lady of Victory.
Schmitz, Gerald P. '62 (MIL) Retired.
Schmitz, Gerard G. '68 (HRT) Special and other Archdiocesan Assignment; [A] Bloomfield, CT St. Thomas Seminary; Commission for Priests' Retreats; Office of Vicar For Priests.
Schmitz, James P. '86 (CLV) Lorain, OH St. Ladislaus.
Schmitz, John A. '52 (MIL) Retired.
Schmitz, John J. '91 (JC) Argyle, MO St. Aloysius; Vienna, MO Holy Guardian Angels; Vienna, MO Visitation.
Schmitz, Michael D. '96 (OM) Fordyce, NE St. Boniface.
Schmitz, Michael R. '82 (LC)[H] Cashton, WI; [H] Wausau, WI Institute of Christ the King – Sovereign Priest; [N] Wausau, WI Institute of Christ the King–Sovereign Priest.
Schmitz, Michael '96 (OM) Fordyce, NE St. John the Baptist.
Schmitz, Michael '03 (DUL) Hibbing, MN Blessed Sacrament.
Schmitz, Robert A. '55 (OM) Retired.

Schmitz, Robert E. '75 (CIN) Cincinnati, OH Good Shepherd.
Schmoeller, Aroldo (BO) Stoughton, MA Immaculate Conception; Rockland, MA Holy Family.
Schmoll, John '85 (FRS) Lamont, CA St. Augustine.
Schmuhl, Lawrence R. *s.m.* '47 (ATL)[C] Atlanta, GA Marist School Retired.
Schnacky, Paul '53 (ROC) Hornell, NY St. Ann Retired.
Schnaubelt, Joseph C. *o.s.a.* '57 (PH)[AA] Villanova, PA St. Thomas Monastery.
Schnaus, Urban *o.s.b.* '40 (WDC)[M] Washington, DC St. Anselm's Abbey.
Schneebeck, Otto *c.m.* '69 (STL) St. Louis, MO St. Catherine Laboure.
Schneebeck, Paul Otto *c.m.* '69 (STL)[O] St. Louis, MO Lazarist Residence.
Schneebeck, Paul Otto *c.m.* (STL)[O] St. Louis, MO Vincentian Community; St. Louis, MO St. Francis de Sales.
Schneibel, Jeffrey *c.s.c.* '85 (FTW)[B] University of Notre Dame Du Lac; [I] Notre Dame, IN Holy Cross Community, Corby Hall, University of Notre Dame.
Schneible, Peter *o.f.m.* '89 (BUF)[O] St. Bonaventure, NY St. Bonaventure Friary; [C] St. Bonaventure, NY Friar Community.
Schneidek, Barry D. *o.f.m.* '56 (STP) Shieldsville, MN St. Patrick.
Schneider, Alfred '38 (GB) Retired.
Schneider, Aquinas *o.f.m.* '54 (CIN)[C] Cincinnati, OH St. Anthony Shrine, Franciscan Candidacy; [K] Cincinnati, OH Mercy Hospitals West.
Schneider, Arnold J. '51 (BUF)[O] Buffalo, NY Sheehan Residence for Priests Retired.
Schneider, Barry *o.f.m.* '56 (SUP) Iron River, WI St. Michael.
Schneider, Bernard R. '67 (FAR) Mayville, ND Our Lady of Peace; Rural Life.
Schneider, Bernard '67 (FAR) Manvel, ND St. Timothy; Altru Hospital; [J] Manvel, ND Beginning Experience Apostolate; Deanery 3.
Schneider, Charles J. '63 (WH) Retired.
Schneider, Charles *s.v.d.* '46 (CHI)[B] Techny, IL Divine Word Residence.
Schneider, Chris *o.f.m.* '49 (CIN)[M] Cincinnati, OH St. Clement Friary Retired.
Schneider, Edward '64 (EVN) Petersburg, IN SS. Peter and Paul.
Schneider, Ernest '77 (GR) Grand Rapids, MI St. Paul the Apostle.
Schneider, Francis J. '83 (RVC)[A] Huntington, NY Diocesan Seminary of the Immaculate Conception; Censors of Books; Judges for Interdiocesan Tribunal.
Schneider, Fred *o.f.m.* '49 (STL)[L] Springfield, IL Our Lady of Angels Friary.
Schneider, George D. '56 (FAR) Retired.
Schneider, George P. '45 (PH) Retired.
Schneider, Gilbert *o.f.m.* '64 (GLP) Navajo, NM St. Berard; Fort Defiance, AZ Our Lady of Blessed Sacrament; St. Michaels, AZ St. Michael.
Schneider, Harold E. '62 (COL) Retired.
Schneider, Harold F. '74 (KCK)[F] Overland Park, KS Holy Spirit.
Schneider, J. Daniel *m.m.* '45 (NY)[EE] Maryknoll Maryknoll Fathers and Brothers.
Schneider, Jerzy *s.d.b.* '53 (NEW)[N] Ramsey, NJ Don Bosco Prep Salesian Residence; [C] Ramsey, NJ Don Bosco Preparatory High School.
Schneider, John G. '48 (STL) Retired.
Schneider, John H. '68 (STL) Bonne Terre, MO St. Joseph's; Archdiocesan Council of Priests; St. Francois County Catholic Church Real Estate Corporation; [U] Bonne Terre, MO St. Francois County Catholic Church Real Estate Corporation.
Schneider, John '83 (CHL) Boone, NC St. Elizabeth.
Schneider, Joseph M. '74 (DUB) Waukon, IA St. Patrick; Waukon, IA St. Mary; Waukon, IA St. Mary.
Schneider, Juniper *o.f.m.conv.* '72 (P) Roseburg, OR St. Joseph; Roseburg, OR St. Francis Xavier; Area Vicars.
Schneider, Karl J. '59 (MIL) West Allis, WI Immaculate Heart of Mary.
Schneider, Kevin C. *s.j.* '94 (OM)[C] Omaha, NE Creighton Preparatory School.
Schneider, Leo J. '83 (STP) Minneapolis, MN Holy Name.
Schneider, Mark *o.s.b.* '41 (SCL)[I] Collegeville, MN St. John's Abbey, of the Order of St. Benedict.
Schneider, Michael '81 (SFS) Howard, SD St. Agatha.
Schneider, Michael '94 (GF) Poplar, MT Our Lady of Lourdes.
Schneider, Nicholas A. '56 (STL) Creve Coeur, MO St. Monica.
Schneider, Philip *o.f.m.conv.* '61 (FTW) Angola, IN St. Anthony; Angola, IN St. Paul Chapel.
Schneider, Ric *o.f.m.* '59 (PEO) Bloomington, IL St. Mary's.
Schneider, Robert E. '57 (COL) Retired.
Schneider, Robert J. '78 (WIN) Albert Lea, MN St. Theodore's; Albert Lea, MN St. James; [J] Albert Lea, MN St. Theodore Catholic School Endowment.
Schneider, Robert '81 (SP) Safety Harbor, FL Espiritu Santo; Presbyteral Council; Diocesan Council of Catholic Women.
Schneider, Ronald E. (GR) Deans.
Schneider, Ronald F. '67 (GR) Hart, MI St. Gregory's.
Schneider, Ronald '75 (GB) Absent on Leave.
Schneider, Stephen A. '72 (SPC) Charleston, MO St. Henry; Sikeston, MO St. Francis Xavier's; Region VIII.
Schneider, Stephen (SPC) Priests' Mutual Benefit Society.
Schneider, Terrance L. '79 (CIN) Oxford, OH St. Mary Church and Catholic Campus Ministry; [Q] Oxford, OH Miami University Catholic Campus Ministry.
Schneider, Todd '85 (SCL) Sauk Centre, MN St. Paul's.
Schneider, William T. '63 (TR) Leave of Absence.
Schneller, Michael J. '72 (NO) Metairie, LA St. Ann National Shrine.
Schnipke, Eugene H. *c.pp.s.* '80 (CIN)[M] Dayton Provincial Office of the Cincinnati Province of the Society of the Precious Blood; Air Force Chaplains.
Schnipke, Ken *c.pp.s.* '90 (CIN) Dayton, OH Precious Blood.
Schnipke, Kenneth *c.pp.s.* '90 (CIN)[M] Dayton, OH Provincial Office of the Cincinnati Province of the Society of the Precious Blood; [M] Dayton, OH.
Schnur, Edward C. '91 (EVN) Rockport, IN St. Bernard.
Schnur, Edward '91 (EVN) Chrisney, IN St. Martin.
Schnurr, Thomas J. *o.s.b.* '32 (BIR)[E] Cullman, AL St. Bernard Abbey.
Schober, Robert J. '77 (BUF) Olean, NY Sacred Heart; Bergen, NY St. Michael; Bergen, NY St. Brigid.
Schock, Ronald A. '96 (TOL) Toledo, OH Holy Rosary; New Riegel, OH St. Peter; New Riegel, OH St. Nicholas; New Riegel, OH St. Boniface.
Schoeberle, Brad *c.s.p.* (LA) Los Angeles, CA St. Paul the Apostle.
Schoeberle, John *o.m.i.* '61 (FgM).
Schoellmann, Edward R. *m.m.* '65 (GAL [Q] Houston, TX Maryknoll Fathers and Brothers.
Schoemann, Robert L. '66 (DM) Des Moines, IA All Saints.
Schoemann, Robert (DM) Priests' Pension Fund Society.
Schoen, Thomas A. *s.m.* '87 (CIN)[D] Dayton, OH The University of Dayton; [M] Dayton, OH Marianist Community.
Schoen, Timothy *o.s.b.* '64 (KC)[A] Conception, MO Conception Seminary College; [J] Stanberry, MO.
Schoenauer, Francis P. '73 (ALN) Walnutport, PA St. Nicholas.
Schoenbaechler, Charles *c.r.* '42 (L)[K] Louisville, KY Villa Pacis, Resurrectionist Retirement Home.
Schoenberg, Oscar *o.s.c.* '48 (STP) Anoka, MN St. Stephen; [M] Anoka, MN Crosier Community of Anoka.
Schoenberger, James T. '57 (STP) Women's State Reformatory.
Schoenfeldt, Arthur *c.s.c.* '59 (P)[L] Portland, OR Holy Cross Fathers & Brothers, C.S.C. – University of Portland.
Schoenfield, Andrew '02 (ATL) Atlanta, GA St. Jude.
Schoenhofen, Darr F. '82 (SY) Phoenix, NY St. Stephen.
Schoenhofen, Roger *o.m.i.* '66 (SFD) Alton, IL SS. Peter and Paul.
Schoenig, Steven A. *s.j.* '01 (NY)[EE] New York, NY Xavier Jesuit Community.
Schoening, Sylvester H. '58 (PBL) Retired.
Schoenstene, Robert L. '75 (JOL)[A] On Duty Outside the Diocese.
Schoeppe, Charles K. '49 (GAL)[N] Houston, TX Pope John Paul XXIII Priests' Residence Retired.
Schoeppe, F. Warren *s.j.* '58 (SLC) Brigham City, UT St. Henry.
Schoettelkotte, Lawrence L. *s.m.* '70 (CIN)[M] Cincinnati, OH Marianist Community.
Schoffelmeer, Arnold L. '56 (SPK) Retired.
Scholl, Jerel A. '01 (LIN) McCook, NE St. Patrick.
Scholla, Robert W. *s.j.* '86 (LA)[C] Los Angeles, CA Jesuit Community.
Scholla, Robert *s.j.* '86 (LA)[BB] Los Angeles, CA Loyola Law School.
Scholsky, Martin J. '56 (HRT) East Hartford, CT St. Mary's.
Scholz, Mark '02 (KNX) Chattanooga, TN St. Jude.
Scholz, William J. '52 (PIT) McKees Rocks, PA Holy Trinity.
Schommer, George Philip *o.p.* '94 (NY)[EE] New York, NY St. Vincent Ferrer Priory.
Schommer, Mark '63 (GB) Retired.
Schommer, Michael '93 (FAR) Grand Forks, ND St. Michael.
Schon, Randy L. '88 (SC) Bode, IA St. Joseph's; Oyens, IA St. Catherine's; Catholic Youth Organization.
Schons, Gerard '47 (SAC) Retired.
Schook, James R. '75 (L) Louisville, KY St. Ignatius; Ex Officio.
Schooler, William C. '74 (FTW) Granger, IN St. Pius X.
Schooler, William (FTW) Consultors; Liturgical Commission.
Schoone, Raymond L. '58 (SUP) Retired.
Schopfer, John C. '69 (SY) Syracuse, NY The Cathedral of the Immaculate Conception; Special Assignment; [U] Syracuse, NY Brady Faith Center, Inc..
Schopfer, John '69 (SY) Syracuse, NY Public Safety Building.
Schopman, Joop *s.j.* '66 (Netherlands)[V] Newton, MA The Jesuit Community at Boston College.
Schopp, George L. '74 (CHI) Blue Island, IL St. Benedict.
Schork, John *c.p.* '76 (CHI)[N] Chicago, IL Passionist Community–Immaculate Conception Monastery.
Schorp, W. Franz *s.m.* '64 (SAT)[C] San Antonio, TX St. Mary's University of San Antonio, Texas; [M] San Antonio, TX Marianist Residence.
Schorr, James D. '68 (CLV) Elyria, OH Holy Cross.
Schorr, W. David '73 (PIT) Pittsburgh, PA Most Holy Name of Jesus.
Schott, Edward W. *s.j.* '63 (NO)[P] New Orleans, LA Ignatius Residence.
Schott, James E. '61 (NO) Retired.
Schott, Kevin J. '90 (NEW) West Orange, NJ St. Joseph's.
Schott, Paul *s.j.* (NO) New Orleans, LA Holy Name of Jesus.
Schott, Timothy R. '70 (SC) Carroll, IA St. Lawrence.
Schott, Timothy (SC) Building Commission.
Schott, Victor P. '56 (LFT) Retired.
Schotzko, Philip M. '77 (NU) St. Peter, MN St. Peter; Propagation of the Faith/Holy Childhood Association; Committee for Continuing Education of Clergy; On Special or Other Diocesan Assignment.
Schouten, Francis L. '55 (CHI) Retired.
Schrad, Merlin J. (SC) Presbyteral Council.
Schrader, James C. '76 (LIN) Campbell, NE St. Anne; Deaneries and Deans.
Schrader, James (LIN) Diocesan Consultors; Presbyteral Council.
Schrader, Robert J. '78 (ROC) Auburn, NY St. Mary.
Schrage, Joseph S. '99 (BEL) Leave of Absence.
Schramel, Michael J. '80 (ROC) Rochester, NY St. Ambrose.
Schramm, Charles H. '71 (MIL) Milwaukee, WI St. Sebastian.
Schramm, Donald C. '67 (STL) St. Ann, MO Holy Trinity.
Schramm, Edward (STL) St. Louis, MO Corpus Christi.
Schramm, Mark *s.v.d.* '75 (CHI)[N] Chicago, IL Divine Word Theologate; [N] Chicago, IL House of Religious Men: Divine Word Theologate.
Schramm, Robert *o.s.f.s.* '69 (SAG) Pastoral Team; Pastoral Team; Pastoral Team; Pastoral Team.
Schratz, Martin *o.f.m.cap.* '83 (CHL) Charlotte, NC Our Lady of Consolation; Charlotte, NC St. Thomas Aquinas.
Schraufnagel, Steven '02 (SAV) Macon, GA St. Joseph.
Schray, Karl '65 (P) North Bend, OR Holy Redeemer.
Schreck, Christopher J. '77 (SAV)[A] Wynnewood, PA Theological Seminary of St. Charles Borromeo, Overbrook; On Duty Outside the Diocese.
Schreck, J. Gerard '83 (SAV) Columbus, GA St. Anne; [A] Columbus, GA Pacelli Catholic High School; Defender of the Bond; Columbus Deanery; College of Consultors.
Schreck, Joseph D. *o.f.m.cap.* (ARE) Chancellor; Diocesan Consultors.
Schreck, Joseph *o.f.m.cap.* '55 (ARE) Utuado, PR San Miquel; Defenders of the Bond.
Schreck, Paul C. '45 (BUF)[O] Buffalo, NY Sheehan Residence for Priests Retired.
Schreiber, Albert R. *c.ss.r.* '88 (BRK)[V] Brooklyn, NY Our Lady of Good Counsel Residence.
Schreiber, Francis Anton '02 (GF) Sidney, MT St. Matthew's.
Schreiber, Gerald *c.ss.r.* '54 (RIC) Hampton, VA St. Joseph.
Schreiber, Gerard *c.ss.r.* (MO) AUXILIARY CHAPLAINS CONTRACT CHAPLAINS.
Schreiber, Larry *o.f.m.* '60 (LSC) Roswell, NM St. Peter; Presbyteral Council.
Schreiber, Stephen J. '99 (E) Farrell, PA St. Ann.
Schreiber, William A. '79 (SC) Humboldt, IA St. John's; Humboldt, IA St. Mary's.
Schreiner, Bernard P. '42 (NU) Retired.
Schreiner, Robert '89 (CR) Diaconate Office; Diocesan Consultors; Crookston, MN Cathedral of the Immaculate Conception; Priests' Council; Priests' Council.
Schreiner, William M. *c.s.c.* '42 (FTW)[I] Notre Dame, IN Holy Cross House.
Schreiter, Daniel A. '50 (GB) Retired.
Schreiter, John P. '69 (MIL) Dousman, WI St. Bruno; Deans.
Schreiter, Robert *c.pp.s.* '75 (CHI).
Schreitmueller, Henry '56 (NEW)[B] Nutley, NJ St. Mary's Retired.
Schremmer, Robert A. '76 (DOD) Wright, KS St. Andrew; Vicar General and Moderator of the Curia; Presbyteral Council; College of Consultors; Advocates; Priests' Trust Fund; Diaconate Office.
Schrenger, Arthur C. '75 (MOB) On Administrative Leave.
Schriber, Robert T. '96 (R) Garner, NC St. Mary, Mother

of the Church.
Schriefer, Robert F. '44 (E) Retired.
Schriver, Ragan '95 (KNX) Knoxville, TN All Saints Catholic Church; Catholic Charities of East Tennessee, Inc.; Catholic Campaign for Human Development.
Schroder, John F. *s.j.* '53 (STL)[O] St. Louis, MO Jesuit Community Corporation at St. Louis University – Jesuit Hall.
Schroeder, Dennis A. '61 (TOL) Clyde, OH St. Mary; Judges.
Schroeder, Edward H. '58 (BUF) Clarence Center, NY St. Augustine.
Schroeder, Eugene A. '79 (EVN) Evansville, IN St. Joseph.
Schroeder, Eugene (EVN) Cemeteries.
Schroeder, Francis J. *s.s.j.* '45 (BAL)[S] Baltimore, MD St. Joseph's Manor.
Schroeder, Fred A. '42 (LFT) Carmel, IN St. Elizabeth Ann Seton.
Schroeder, George J. '42 (PEO) Rock Island, IL St. Mary Retired.
Schroeder, George M. '62 (DEN) Steamboat Springs, CO Holy Name; [Q] Steamboat Springs, CO Colorado Mountain College.
Schroeder, George *o.f.m.conv.* '43 (TOL) Carey, OH Our Lady of Consolation, Basilica–National Shrine.
Schroeder, George (DEN) College of Consultors.
Schroeder, James *s.c.j.* '70 (MIL)[O] St. Louis, MO.
Schroeder, Jerome *o.f.m.cap.* '70 (MIL)[R] Milwaukee, WI The Dwelling Place.
Schroeder, Kenneth J. *c.pp.s.* '65 (CIN) Maria Stein, OH Nativity of the Blessed Virgin Mary; Maria Stein, OH St. John the Baptist; Maria Stein, OH St. Rose.
Schroeder, Kenneth *c.pp.s.* '65 (CIN)[M] Maria Stein, OH.
Schroeder, Matthew '02 (SJP) Parma, OH St. Josaphat Cathedral.
Schroeder, Richard F. '45 (CHI) Retired.
Schroeder, Roger P. *s.v.d.* '79 (CHI)[N] Chicago, IL Divine Word Theologate; [N] Chicago, IL House of Religious Men: Divine Word Theologate.
Schroeder, Stephen L. '01 (TOL) Toledo, OH St. Clement; Sycamore, OH St. Pius X.
Schroeder, Thomas H. '64 (MAD) Argyle, WI St. Joseph; Argyle, WI St. Michael.
Schroeder, Timothy C. '88 (FAR) Minto, ND St. John the Baptist.
Schroeder, Timothy '88 (FAR) Minto, ND Sacred Heart; Hispanic Ministry.
Schroeder, Walter L. '41 (NY) Armonk, NY St. Patrick; Sleepy Hollow, NY The Magdalene Retired.
Schroeppel, Stephen L. *m.m.* '58 (STL)[O] St. Louis, MO Maryknoll House.
Schroer, Joseph *o.c.s.o.* '52 (SLC)[F] Huntsville, UT Abbey of Our Lady of the Holy Trinity of the Order of Cistercians.
Schroer, Thomas A. *s.m.* '72 (CIN)[M] Dayton, OH Marianist Community.
Schroering, Francis A. '59 (EVN) Haubstadt, IN SS. Peter and Paul.
Schroering, Francis (EVN) Diocesan Consultors; Deans.
Schroering, Raymond A. '49 (EVN) Retired.
Schroth, Raymond A. *s.j.* '67 (NEW)[B] Jersey City, NJ Jesuit Center; [N] Jersey City, NJ Jesuits of Saint Peter's College, Inc..
Schu, Walter *l.c.* '94 (HRT).
Schubeck, Thomas L. *s.j.* '68 (CLV)[B] Cleveland, OH John Carroll University.
Schubert, Gerard H. *o.s.f.s.* '59 (ALN)[B] Center Valley, PA DeSales University; [K] Center Valley, PA Oblates of St. Francis de Sales.
Schubert, Gerold *o.f.m.* '54 (JOL)[L] Joliet, IL St. John the Baptist Friary.
Schubert, Herbert '56 (MIL) Retired.
Schubiger, Albert B. '49 (MAD) Retired.
Schuck, Hugh *o.s.b.* '34 (RCK)[G] Aurora, IL Marmion Abbey.
Schuck, Joseph J. '53 (BRK) Retired.
Schuckenbrock, Harry *o.m.i.* '59 (BWN) Brownsville, TX St. Eugene De Mazenod.
Schuckman, Kenneth J. '92 (WCH) Wichita, KS Church of the Resurrection; [L] Wichita, KS Serra Club of Wichita – Downtown.
Schudde, Derk M. '89 (OG) On Duty Outside the Diocese.
Schudde, Derk (ORL) Winter Park, FL St. Margaret Mary.
Schue, Dennis L. '57 (FAR)[D] Devils Lake, ND Mercy Hospital Retired.
Schuele, Francis J. '68 (KC) Special Assignment.
Schuele, Francis (KC) Peace and Justice Office.
Schuele, John '76 (KC) Kansas City, MO St. Anthony.
Schueller, Anthony *s.s.s.* '77 (NY) New York, NY St. Jean Baptiste.
Schueller, La Verne L. '66 (DUB) Military Chaplains.
Schueller, Michael G. '97 (DUB)[G] Mason City, IA Newman Catholic Child Care; Garner, IA St. Wenceslaus; Forest City, IA St. James; Garner, IA St. Boniface; Forest City, IA St. Patrick; Britt, IA St. Patrick; Forest City, IA St. Patrick; Stewardship and Development Committee.
Schuer, Robert J. '48 (COL) Columbus, OH St. Agatha Retired.
Schuerger, Anthony J. '77 (CLV) Cleveland, OH Community of St. Malachi; Cleveland, OH St. Malachi.
Schuerman, James T. '86 (MIL)[A] St. Francis, WI Saint Francis Seminary; Special Assignment.
Schuessler, Peter *s.d.s.* '80 (MIL)[O] Milwaukee Salvatorian Provincial Residence.
Schuessler, Peter *s.d.s.* '80 (FgM).
Schuessler, William R. '67 (RCK) Carpentersville, IL St. Monica.
Schuett, John T. *s.j.* '58 (DET)[P] Hamtramck, MI St. Ladislaus.
Schuetze, John '97 (GB) Absent on Leave.
Schuh, Earl '43 (GB) Retired.
Schuh, J. Daniel '03 (CIN) Mason, OH St. Susanna.
Schuh, John H. '65 (GB) Special Assignment; Vice-Chancellor; Vicar for Religious; Priests' Personnel Board.
Schuler, A. John '74 (STL) Ferguson, MO Our Lady of Guadalupe.
Schuler, Emett J. *o.f.m.cap.* '69 (PIT) Allegheny County, PA Department of Veterans Affairs Medical Center Oakland.
Schuler, Emett *o.f.m.cap.* '69 (PIT) Allegheny County, PA VA Pittsburgh Health Care System–H.J. Heinz and University Drive Divisions.
Schuler, Emitt *o.f.m.cap.* '69 (PIT)[N] Pittsburgh, PA St. Francis Friary.
Schuler, Richard J. '45 (STP) St. Paul, MN St. Agnes; Censores Librorum; Legion of Mary Retired.
Schuler, Robert J. '89 (JOL) Clarendon Hills, IL Notre Dame.
Schuller, Frederick E. *s.j.* '52 (STL)[N] St. Louis, MO Fusz Pavilion; [O] St. Louis, MO Jesuit Community Corporation at St. Louis University – Jesuit Hall.
Schulte, Carl G. *c.m.* '48 (KC)[J] Kansas City, MO Vincentian Parish Mission Center.
Schulte, Daniel *c.m.* '87 (STL)[O] St. Louis, MO Lazarist Residence.
Schulte, Francisco *o.s.b.* '79 (SCL)[I] Collegeville, MN St. John's Abbey, of the Order of St. Benedict.
Schulte, Gary '72 (DET) Warren, MI St. Sylvester; Archdiocesan Vicars.
Schulte, John R. '77 (COV) Walton, KY All Saints.
Schulte, Lyle L. '60 (LC) Boyceville, WI St. Luke Retired.
Schulte, Mark A. '97 (SFD) Wood River, IL St. Bernard.
Schulte, Oswald W. '45 (LC) Retired.
Schulte, Robert C. '75 (FTW) Fort Wayne, IN Cathedral of the Immaculate Conception; Board of Directors; Finance Council; Vicar General–Chancellor; Episcopal Vicar for Education; Consultors; Budget Committee; Catholic Campaign for Human Development; Continuing Education of the Clergy; Council of Priests; Ecumenical Affairs; Victim Assistance Coordinator.
Schulte, Robert (FTW) Advisory Board; Retired Clergy Committee.
Schulte, William P. '52 (NEW) Retired.
Schultenover, David G. *s.j.* '69 (MIL)[X] Milwaukee, WI Theological Studies, Inc.; [O] Milwaukee, WI Jesuit Community at Marquette University.
Schultheis, Michael J. *s.j.* '65 (P)[L] Portland Jesuit Provincial Office (Society of Jesus, Oregon Prov.).
Schultheis, Raymond *c.pp.s.* '56 (CIN)[B] Carthagena, OH St. Charles.
Schultz, Blaine *o.s.b.* '60 (KCK)[A] Atchison, KS Benedictine College; [H] Atchison, KS St. Benedict's Abbey.
Schultz, Bruce B. *o.p.* '88 (SAT) San Antonio, TX Holy Redeemer; San Antonio, TX St. Ann.
Schultz, Charles F. '80 (SB) Ontario, CA St. Elizabeth Ann Seton; Air Force Reserve Chaplains.
Schultz, Joel P. (MEM) Bartlett, TN St. Ann.
Schultz, John A. '65 (LC) Eau Claire, WI St. James the Greater; Appointed Members.
Schultz, John C. '57 (LFT) On Duty Outside the Diocese.
Schultz, John M. (E) Vicar for Catholic Education.
Schultz, John (LFT).
Schultz, John (E) Administrative Cabinet.
Schultz, John (PEO) Danville, IL Veterans' Administration Hospital.
Schultz, Mark '03 (SFE) Santa Fe, NM The Cathedral of San Francisco de Asis.
Schultz, Raymond '91 (BEL) Fairview Heights, IL Holy Trinity – West.
Schultz, Robert '01 (CHI) Wilmette, IL St. Joseph.
Schultz, Russell '66 (SAN) Retired.
Schultz, Stephen '99 (SFE) Belen, NM Our Lady of Belen.
Schultz, William F. '64 (BGP) Stratford, CT Our Lady of Grace.
Schultze, George E. *s.j.* '94 (SFR)[N] San Francisco, CA Jesuit Community at University of San Francisco.
Schulz, Donald C. '53 (COL) Columbus, OH St. Aloysius Retired.
Schulz, James W. *s.j.* '77 (CHI)[N] Chicago, IL Miguel Pro Jesuit Community; [N] Chicago, IL Woodlawn Jesuit Community.
Schulz, James W. *s.j.* '77 (GRY) Hammond, IN St. Margaret Mary; [N] Hammond, IN Heartland Center.
Schulz, Ronald '68 (PMB) Lantana, FL Holy Spirit.
Schulz, Wilfred G. *o.s.b.* '53 (PAT)[M] Morristown, NJ St. Mary's Abbey.
Schulz, Wilfred *o.s.b.* '53 (PAT)[N] Convent Station, NJ St. Anne Villa.
Schulze, Robert R. '69 (TR) Jackson, NJ Church of St. Monica; Prison Ministry.
Schumacher, Andrew J. '60 (B) Cottonwood, ID St. Mary's.
Schumacher, Andrew '60 (B) Greencreek, ID Assumption.
Schumacher, Andrew '70 (B) Greencreek, ID St. Anthony's.
Schumacher, Andrew (B) Defenders of the Bond; College of Consultors; Priest Personnel Commission; Censor Librorum.
Schumacher, Anthony J. '60 (MAD) Retired.
Schumacher, Eugene T. '56 (SC) Retired.
Schumacher, Jacob J. '52 (BIS)[G] Bismarck, ND Emmaus Place Retired.
Schumacher, James '95 (CHY) Laramie, WY St. Laurence O'Toole; [F] Laramie, WY St. Laurence School Foundation.
Schumacher, Joseph A. '57 (FWT) Arlington, TX St. Matthew; Vicar General; Presbyteral Council and Consultors; Diocesan Finance Council; Catholic Foundation of North Texas; Clergy and Religious Personnel Services; Building Commission; Priests' Retirement Board; Clergy and Religious Personnel Services; Clergy Relief Association.
Schumacher, Kenneth '99 (TLS) Tulsa, OK Resurrection.
Schumacher, Mark R. '84 (B) Absent on Leave.
Schumacher, Patrick A. '93 (BIS) Mandan, ND St. Joseph; Priests' Personnel Board.
Schumacher, Paul A. '62 (NU) Redwood Falls, MN St. Catherine; AIDS Ministry; Priest Personnel Board.
Schumacher, Paul A. (GB) Pastor Consultors.
Schumacher, Paul '48 (GB) Retired.
Schumacher, Robert A. '49 (SPC) Retired.
Schumacher, William '88 (DAL) Retired.
Schuneman, John P. *c.s.c.* '57 (PHX)[G] Phoenix, AZ Holy Cross Congregation/Casa Santa Cruz.
Schuster, Anthony '70 (GF) Roundup, MT St. Benedict's; Diocesan Consultors; Priests' Council.
Schuster, Francis J. *k.h.s.* '63 (ALN)[J] Bethlehem, PA Holy Family Villa.
Schuster, Frank J. (BIS) Kenmare, ND St. Joseph.
Schuster, Frank '99 (SEA) Bellingham, WA Assumption B.V.M.; [O] Bellingham, WA Western Washington University (Bellingham).
Schuster, Frank (BIS) Kenmare, ND St. Agnes.
Schuster, George M. '57 (BRK) Ridgewood, NY Our Lady of the Miraculous Medal; St. John's Priests Relief Society.
Schuster, Paul R. '93 (FAR) Bottineau, ND St. Mark; Westhope, ND St. Andrew; Ecumenical Commission; Prison Apostolate.
Schuster, Paul '93 (FAR)[J] Bottineau, ND Minot State University–Bottineau.
Schuster, Raymond '93 (SAT) San Antonio, TX St. Bonaventure.
Schuster, Robert '95 (DET) Roseville, MI Holy Innocents; Eastpointe, MI St. Barnabas.
Schuster, Roy *o.f.m.cap* '59 (WH) Elkview, WV Our Lady of the Hills.
Schuster, Troy '99 (STV) Charlotte Amalie, VI Our Lady of Perpetual Help; Natural Family Planning Coordinator.
Schuster, Wilfred J. '46 (MAD)[G] Madison, WI Bishop O'Connor Catholic Pastoral Center Retired.
Schute, Arthur B. '67 (VEN)[D] Port Charlotte, FL Bon Secours–St. Joseph Healthcare Group, Inc..
Schute, Arthur B. '67 (NEW) On Duty Outside the Archdiocese.
Schute, Bruce J. *s.a.c.* '60 (MIL)[O] Milwaukee, WI Pallotti House.
Schutte, James R. '79 (CIN) Dayton, OH St. Agnes; Dayton, OH Corpus Christi.
Schutte, Robert W. '43 (CIN) Retired.
Schutten, Marion F. '45 (NO) Retired.
Schutter, Thomas '68 (JOL) Carol Stream, IL St. Luke.
Schutty, John J. '83 (JC) Meta, MO St. Cecilia; IX. Osage; Senators.
Schutz, Bruce B. *o.p.* '88 (SAT)[B] San Antonio, TX Dominican Priory of San Juan Macias and Novitiate.
Schuwey, Emil *c.pp.s.* '49 (CIN)[B] Carthagena, OH St. Charles.
Schuyler, David H. *s.m.* (MRY) Judicial Vicar.
Schuyler, David *s.m.* '60 (SJ)[M] Cupertino, CA Alcalde Residence.
Schuyler, David *s.m.* (MRY) Judges.
Schuyler, David *s.m.* (RNO) Advocates.
Schwab, Elwin (P) Board Members; Roseburg, OR St. Joseph.
Schwab, James A. '81 (JOL) Joliet, IL St. Jude.
Schwab, Joseph C. *o.m.i.* '53 (PT) Madison, FL St.

Vincent de Paul.
Schwab, Robert C. '41 (BUF)[O] Tonawanda, NY O'Hara Residence Retired.
Schwab, Steven '90 (IND) Indianapolis, IN Nativity of Our Lord Jesus Christ.
Schwab, Thomas E. '56 (CHI) Rosemont, IL Our Lady of Hope Retired.
Schwaegel, Joseph R. '65 (BEL) Retired.
Schwalenberg, Martin '45 (BAL) Retired.
Schwalm, Donald '52 (KCK) Retired.
Schwalm, Donald (STP) Minneapolis, MN St. Hedwig.
Schwan, Paul Mark *o.c.s.o.* '88 (SAC)[A] Vina, CA Abbey of New Clairvaux, Trappist Seminary; [I] Vina, CA Abbey of New Clairvaux, Trappist.
Schwane, Robert A. *c.m.* '53 (DEN)[N] Denver, CO Congregation of the Mission Midwest Province: De Paul House.
Schwanger, Kenneth K. '90 (MIA) Fort Lauderdale, FL St. Jerome.
Schwanger, Kenneth (MIA) Adjutant Judicial Vicar; Deans and Deaneries; Permanent Diaconate; Promoters of Justice.
Schwanger, Kenneth (MIA) Archdiocesan Vocations Review Board.
Schwanger, Kenneth (MIA) Adjutant Judicial Vicar; Deans and Deaneries; Permanent Diaconate; Promoters of Justice.
Schwanger, Kenneth (SAM) Judges.
Schwantes, John *s.j.* '69 (GB)[L] Oshkosh, WI Jesuit Retreat House.
Schware, Richard A. '75 (ALN) Pen Argyl, PA St. Elizabeth of Hungary.
Schwarte, Michael W. '38 (DM) Retired.
Schwarte, Michael '95 (JUN) Petersburg, AK St. Catherine of Siena; Wrangell, AK St. Rose of Lima; Diocesan Consultors; Port Chaplains.
Schwarting, Donald J. (GAL) Retired.
Schwarting, J. Donald '66 (GAL) Richmond, TX Sacred Heart.
Schwartz, Charles M. '99 (TR) Marlton, NJ St. Joan of Arc.
Schwartz, Christopher *o.s.b.* '74 (CLV) Broadview Heights, OH Assumption; [O] Cleveland, OH.
Schwartz, David C. *s.j.* '85 (ORG)[H] Orange, CA Loyola Institute for Spirituality; [I] Garden Grove, CA Manresa Jesuit Residence.
Schwartz, Edwin V. '60 (ALN) Northampton, PA St. Michael; Northampton, PA Our Lady of Hungary.
Schwartz, Hugh F. '56 (OM) Retired.
Schwartz, James A. '68 (ROC) Pittsford, NY St. Louis.
Schwartz, James (ROC) Office of Seminarians.
Schwartz, John '81 (SFR) San Francisco, CA St. Stephen.
Schwartz, Kevin '93 (SCL) Perham, MN St. Lawrence.
Schwartz, Norman R. '69 (MIL) On Duty Outside the Archdiocese.
Schwartz, Paul E. '53 (CHI) Sauk Village, IL St. James Retired.
Schwartz, Robert M. '67 (STP) Edina, MN Our Lady of Grace.
Schwartz, Rodney A. '92 (SFD) Springfield, IL St. Frances Cabrini.
Schwartz, William H. '53 (CIN) Retired.
Schwartz, William H. '68 (RCK) Rockford, IL St. Peter Cathedral; [B] Rockford, IL Boylan Central Catholic High School; Diocesan Consultors; Scouts.
Schwartz, William J. '68 (PIT) Oakdale, PA St. Patrick.
Schwartzkopf, Gary W. *s.j.* '69 (NY)[FF] Hastings–on–Hudson, NY Sisters of St. Francis.
Schwartzlose, John '00 (L) Pewee Valley, KY St. Aloysius; Cox's Creek, KY St. Gregory.
Schwarz, Carl V. *c.ss.r.* '42 (STL)[O] Liguori, MO St. Clement Health Care Center.
Schwarz, Elmer C. '53 (OKL) Chickasha, OK Holy Name; [K] Chickasha, OK University of Science & Arts of Oklahoma; Defenders of the Bond.
Schwarz, Frank L. '01 (BRK) Forest Hills, NY Our Lady, Queen of Martyrs.
Schwarz, John *s.j.* '64 (SPK)[J] Spokane, WA Regis Community.
Schwarz, Robert '65 (MRY) Retired.
Schwarz, Thomas J.E. *s.j.* '01 (SJ)[B] Santa Clara, CA Jesuit Community.
Schwarzhaupt, Robert '86 (HON) Laupahoehoe, HI St. Anthony; Papaikou, HI Immaculate Heart of Mary; Young Men's Institute.
Schwebs, Daniel L. *o.s.j.* '86 (SCR) Pittston, PA St. Anthony of Padua; [M] Pittston, PA Eastern Province of the Oblates of St. Joseph; Presbyteral Council.
Schweda, Phillip '79 (LAN) Lansing, MI St. Casimir; Tribunal Judges.
Schweder, John F. '60 (DET) Grosse Pointe, MI Our Lady Star of the Sea; Detroit, MI St. Joseph.
Schweers, Gregory *o.cist.* '81 (DAL)[K] Irving, TX Cistercian Abbey of Our Lady of Dallas.
Schwehr, Charles L. '76 (LA) Los Angeles, CA Cathedral Chapel.
Schweifler, Michael *o.s.a.* '84 (JOL) New Lenox, IL St. Jude.
Schweigardt, Erwin H. '67 (ALB) Watervliet, NY St. Patrick.
Schweigardt, Erwin (ALB) Priestly Life and Ministry Council.
Schweigart, Erwin (ALB) Priests Retirement Board.
Schweiger, Troy J. (LIN) Diocesan Area CCD Directors.
Schweiger, Troy '95 (LIN) Colon, NE St. Joseph's; [C] Wahoo, NE Bishop Neumann Jr.–Sr. High School.
Schweihofer Frederick J. '68 (DET) Sterling Heights, MI St. Rene Goupil; College of Consultors.
Schweikert, John *m.s.c.* '96 (SB) Moreno Valley, CA St. Patrick.
Schweitzer, Francis X. '45 (COL) Retired.
Schweitzer, Gerald H. '71 (GRY) Wanatah, IN Sacred Heart; Deans; Bishop's Council of Priests; Consultors; Priests' Personnel Board; Marriage Dispensations.
Schweitzer, Joachim B. *o.s.b.* '58 (PAT)[M] Morristown, NJ St. Mary's Abbey.
Schweitzer, John '03 (STL) St. Louis, MO Our Lady of Sorrows.
Schweitzer, Robert J. '67 (PIT) New Castle, PA St. Joseph the Worker.
Schweitzer, Thomas '82 (LA) Glendale, CA Church of the Incarnation.
Schweitzer, Tom '82 (LA) Vernon, CA Holy Angels Parish of the Deaf.
Schweizer, Paul *o.carm.* '62 (NEW)[P] Mahwah, NJ Carmel Retreat.
Schwemin, Ralph H. '41 (SPK) Retired.
Schwendeman, Daniel '01 (LEX) Lexington, KY Mary, Queen of the Holy Rosary.
Schwenzer Ronald G. *c.s.b.* '68 (GAL)[F] Houston, TX St. Thomas High School.
Schwer, Albert *c.p.* '55 (L) Louisville, KY St. Agnes.
Schwer, Albert *c.p.* '55 (BIR)[K] Louisville, KY Sacred Heart Retreat.
Schwermer, Paul '82 (LAN) Flint, MI Holy Rosary.
Schwertley, James F. '61 (OM) Retired.
Schwertner, Timothy '65 (LUB) Rotan, TX St. Joseph.
Schwet, Edward N. '82 (CLV) Parma, OH Holy Family.
Schwider, John *o.m.i.* '40 (SAT)[K] San Antonio, TX Oblate Madonna Residence.
Schwieters, Severin '50 (SCL) Retired.
Schwieters, Severin (SCL) Diocesan Priests Pension Plan Trustees.
Schwind, Donald F. '46 (BRK) Retired.
Schwinger, William A. '58 (BUF) Council of Catholic Men; [O] Lackawanna, NY Bishop Head Residence Retired
Schwinghamer, David J. *m.m.* '73 (NY).
Schwinghammer, Claude '35 (SCL) Retired.
Schwinn, Joe '48 (MIL)[M] Wauwatosa, WI St. Camillus Health Center, Inc..
Schwinn, Joseph F. '43 (MIL) Retired.
Schwinn, Thomas J. '58 (DUB) Retired.
Scianna, Bernard C. *o.s.a.* '84 (TLS)[B] Tulsa, OK Cascia Hall Preparatory School; Diocesan Consultors.
Sciarra, John N. '45 (IND) Retired.
Sciarra, John '45 (IND)[I] Beech Grove, IN St. Paul Hermitage; Archdiocesan Judges.
Sciarrotta, Lee L. *s.m.* '67 (CIN) Dayton, OH Emmanuel; [M] Dayton, OH Marianist Community.
Sciarrotta, Paul J. '62 (CLV)[P] Chardon, OH Provincial House of the Sisters of Notre Dame, Juniorate, Novitiate.
Sciberras, Ivan '99 (NEW) Ridgewood, NJ Our Lady of Mount Carmel.
Sciberras, Michael J. '67 (GBG) East Vandergrift, PA Our Lady, Queen of Peace.
Sciera, Ronald P. '61 (BUF) Buffalo–Niagara International Airport; On Duty Outside the Diocese.
Scillieri, Charles P. '73 (MET) Jamesburg, NJ St. James the Less.
Scioli, Richard *c.s.s.* '79 (BO) Milford, MA Sacred Heart.
Scirghi, Thomas J. *s.j.* '86 (OAK)[F] Berkeley, CA Jesuit Community at Jesuit School of Theology at Berkeley.
Sciumbato, Michael R. '94 (SLC) Orem, UT St. Francis of Assisi; Presbyteral Council; Priests' Personnel Board.
Sciurba, Salvatore *o.c.d.* '71 (MIL)[O] Milwaukee Provincial Offices – Discalced Carmelites.
Scocco, Victor *o.ss.t.* '81 (VIC) Victoria, TX Our Lady of Sorrows.
Scolamiero, Dominic A. '69 (PAT) Unassigned.
Scollard, William Joseph *c.r.* '83 (L) Louisville, KY Our Lady Help of Christians; Louisville, KY St. Timothy.
Scollen, Francis J. '71 (WOR) Worcester, MA St. Peter; Diocesan College of Consultors; Black Catholics: African American.
Scollers, Frank (WOR) St. Peter.
Scolozzi, Angelo *u.f.w.* '65 (BEA) Anahuac, TX Our Lady of Light; [I] Anahuac, TX Third Order Missionaries of Charity Universal Fraternity of the Word.
Scordo, Joseph Anthony *o.p.* '69 (NY)[EE] New York St. Vincent Ferrer Priory; Navy Chaplains.
Scornaienchi, Frank *t.o.r.* '79 (ALT) Altoona, PA Our Lady of Mt. Carmel.
Scorzello, Joseph F. '69 (BO) Brockton, MA Our Lady of Lourdes; Medford, MA St. Francis of Assisi.
Scotchie, David '93 (ORL) Winter Park, FL Saints Peter and Paul; [F] Winter Park, FL University of Central Florida Catholic Campus Ministry.
Scott, Alfonso '59 (LA) Long Beach, CA Our Lady of Refuge.
Scott, Brendan T. *s.j.* '78 (NEW)[N] Jersey City, NJ Jesuits of Saint Peter's College, Inc..
Scott, Brendan *s.j.* '78 (NEW)[B] Jersey City, NJ Jesuit Center.
Scott, Craig (ALX) Evangelization.
Scott, Daniel J. *m.s.* '73 (HRT) New Haven, CT St. John the Baptist; [M] Hartford, CT Missionaries of LaSalette.
Scott, Daniel V. *m.s.* '73 (HRT) West Haven, CT V.A. CT Health Care System.
Scott, Daniel *m.s.* (MO).
Scott, Delroy Thomas '86 (MGZ) Rincon, PR St. Rose of Lima; Vocations; [B] The Pontifical Catholic University of Puerto Rico.
Scott, Derrek D. '01 (PBL) Cortez, CO St. Rita; Clergy Assemblies.
Scott, Derrek D. '02 (PBL) Cortez, CO St. Margaret Mary.
Scott, Edward R. '56 (SCR) Lake Ariel, PA St. Thomas More; Diocesan Consultors; Presbyteral Council.
Scott, Francis '79 (BLX) Retired.
Scott, James C. '74 (PAT) Unassigned.
Scott, John M. *s.j.* '44 (MIL)[O] Wauwatosa, WI Jesuit Community at St. Camillus.
Scott, John V. '69 (GRY) Knox, IN St. Thomas Aquinas; Bishop's Council of Priests; Charismatic Apostolate.
Scott, John *o.s.b.* '72 (SEA)[L] Lacey, WA St. Martin's Abbey.
Scott, Joseph J. *c.s.p.* '73 (NY) New York, NY St. Paul the Apostle.
Scott, Joseph *s.v.d.* '71 (SB)[A] Riverside, CA Society of the Divine Word Missionaries.
Scott, Joseph *c.s.p.* '73 (LA)[BB] Goleta, CA.
Scott, Joseph *c.s.p.* '89 (LA) Goleta, CA St. Mark University Parish.
Scott, Kenny *o.f.m.* '58 (OAK) Oakland, CA St. Elizabeth's; [N] Oakland, CA Franciscan Friars.
Scott, Leonard G. '64 (CAM) Cherry Hill, NJ Holy Rosary.
Scott, M. Craig (ALX) Priests Council; Vicar for Clergy.
Scott, Mark A. *o.c.s.o.* '86 (SPC)[A] Ava, MO Assumption Novitiate (Trappists); [E] Ava, MO Assumption Abbey (Trappist); [G] Ava, MO Assumption Abbey.
Scott, Michael Craig '96 (ALX) Alexandria, LA St. Rita.
Scott, Michael P. '87 (MET) Perth Amboy, NJ St. Mary.
Scott, Michael '87 (MET)[A] South Amboy, NJ Cardinal McCarrick High School.
Scott, Patrick J. '60 (PAT) Pompton Plains, NJ Our Lady of Good Counsel.
Scott, Philip P. '79 (PSC) Roswell, GA Epiphany Byzantine Church.
Scott, Philip '89 (SP) On Duty Outside the Diocese.
Scott, Raymond '48 (DAL) Retired.
Scott, Robert T. *c.s.p.* '49 (NY)[EE] Jamaica Estates Paulist Fathers Generalate.
Scott, Robert T. *c.s.p.* '49 (AUS) Austin, TX St. Austin.
Scott, Samuel V. (BGP) Pastors' Vocation Advisory Board; Office for Ecumenical and Interreligious Affairs.
Scott, Vince (OAK) Deans.
Scott, Vincent J. '75 (OAK) Walnut Creek, CA St. John Vianney.
Scotti, P. Paschal *o.s.b.* '89 (PRO)[P] Portsmouth, RI Abbey of St. Gregory the Great.
Scotto, Dominic *t.o.r.* '67 (STU)[A] Steubenville, OH Franciscan University of Steubenville; [F] Steubenville, OH Holy Spirit Friary.
Scrima, Claude *o.f.m.* '61 (BO)[V] Andover St. Francis Friary; [X] Andover, MA Franciscan Center – Retreat House.
Scuderi, Carmen *o.f.m.* '83 (PSC) Hazleton, PA St. John the Baptist Church; [A] Sybertsville, PA Holy Dormition Friary.
Scuderi, Salvatore A. *m.ss.cc.* '88 (CAM) Camden, NJ Our Lady of Mount Carmel/Fatima.
Scull, James P. *s.j.* '58 (MIL)[O] Wauwatosa, WI Jesuit Community at St. Camillus.
Scullin, Robert J. *s.j.* '76 (DET)[E] Detroit, MI University of Detroit Jesuit High School and Academy; [K] Detroit, MI Jesuit Provincial Office–Detroit Province of the Society of Jesus.
Scullion, James P. *o.f.m.* '80 (WDC)[B] Silver Spring, MD Holy Name College.
Scully, G. Michael *c.s.c.* '58 (FTW)[I] Notre Dame, IN Holy Cross House.
Scully, John J. *s.j.* '57 (NY)[EE] Jesuit Community, Kohlmann Hall.
Scully, John J. '72 (TR) Matawan, NJ St. Clement; Tribunal Judges.
Scully, John T. *s.s.e.* '55 (BUR) Putney, VT Our Lady of Mercy.
Scully, John '48 (SP) Retired.
Scully, John *p.a.* (SP) Propagation of the Faith.
Scully, Michael *o.f.m.cap.* '65 (DEN)[N] Denver, CO St. Francis of Assisi Friary.
Scully, Michael *o.f.m.cap.* '65 (FgM).

Scully, Michael *s.j.* '86 (LA)[F] Los Angeles, CA Loyola High School of Los Angeles.
Scully, Patrick A. '56 (SHP) Vivian, LA St. Clement.
Scully, Patrick *s.m.* '03 (MRY) Santa Cruz, CA Star of the Sea.
Scully, Richard D. (AMA) Army Reserve Chaplains.
Scully, Robert E. *s.j.* '96 (SY)[Q] Syracuse, NY Jesuits at LeMoyne, Inc..
Scully, Timothy R. *c.s.c.* '81 (FTW)[B] University of Notre Dame Du Lac; [I] Notre Dame, IN Holy Cross Community, Corby Hall, University of Notre Dame.
Scully, William *o.f.m.* '67 (PAT) Hewitt, NJ Our Lady Queen of Peace.
Scurti, Louis J. '73 (PAT) North Jersey Developmental Center; [O] Haledon, NJ William Paterson University of New Jersey; Office for Campus Ministry.
Sdolnu, Joseph R. '78 (CLV) Cleveland, OH SS. Philip and James.
Seabo, Frank J. (CHL) Swannanoa, NC St. Margaret Mary.
Seabold, John P. '88 (CLV) Grafton, OH Assumption; Grafton, OH Immaculate Conception.
Seabridge, Thomas L. '88 (SAC) Jackson, CA St. Patrick's.
Seagrams, Richard (NY) Yonkers, NY St. Eugene.
Seagrave, Thomas L. '68 (SFR) San Francisco, CA St. John of God.
Seagraves, Richard '90 (NY) Scarsdale, NY Immaculate Heart of Mary.
Seaman, Cyril *o.f.m.* '56 (BO)[AA] Boston, MA St. Anthony Shrine.
Seaman, Paul G. '85 (CHI) Country Club Hills, IL St. Emeric.
Searles, Lawrence P. *s.j.* '87 (SJN) San Juan, PR San Ignacio de Loyola; [B] San Juan, PR Academia San Ignacio de Loyola.
Searles, Thaddeus *s.t.* '56 (BLX) Pass Christian, MS Our Lady of Lourdes.
Searles, Wendell H. '55 (BUR) Members Ex Officio; Vicar General; Diocesan Administrative Board; Diocesan Consultors; Vicar General; Victim Assistance Committee; [F] Burlington, VT Mount St. Mary Convent.
Sears, Eugene A. '58 (KAL) St. Joseph, MI St. Joseph; Vicar General; Diocesan Consultors; Presbyteral Council.
Sears, G. David '63 (SY) Staten Island, NY St. Roch; New Hartford, NY St. Thomas.
Sears, Gerald *o.c.s.o.* '73 (WOR)[O] Spencer, MA St. Joseph's Abbey.
Sears, Michael '94 (LA) Azusa, CA St. Frances of Rome.
Sears, Robert T. *s.j.* '66 (CHI)[C] Chicago, IL Jesuit Community at Loyola University Chicago.
Sears, William F. '84 (PRO) Retired.
Sears, William J. '62 (BRK) Released from Diocesan Assignment.
Sears, William (VEN) International Order of Alhambra, Diego Caravan 255.
Seasoltz, Kevin *o.s.b.* '56 (SCL)[I] Collegeville, MN St. John's Abbey, of the Order of St. Benedict.
Seaver, Paul E. *o.p.* '59 (PRO)[P] Providence St. Thomas Aquinas Priory at Providence College.
Seavey, Michael J. '86 (PRT) Lewiston, ME St. Joseph's; Lewiston, ME Holy Family.
Seay, Robert '76 (LAF) Lafayette, LA St. Paul The Apostle.
Sebaali, George M. '83 (SAM) Glen Allen, VA St. Anthony.
Sebaali, George (SAM) Presbyteral Council–Ex Officio Members; Protopresbyters; Communications; (Diocesan Newspaper) "The Maronite Voice".
Sebahar, John '58 (JOL)[K] Naperville, IL St. John Vianney Villa Retired.
Sebamalai, Anthony '87 (NY) Bronx, NY St. Helena.
Sebastian, Francis '88 (CC) Mathis, TX Saint Patrick Mission.
Sebastian, Gregory *o.s.b.* '83 (SCL)[I] Collegeville, MN St. John's Abbey, of the Order of St. Benedict.
Sebastian, Sony (SB)[A] Riverside, CA Society of the Divine Word Missionaries.
Sebasty, Joseph '85 (LA) Pico Rivera, CA St. Mariana de Paredes.
Sebaugh, Thomas (LR) Information Systems; On Special or Other Diocesan Assignment.
Sebescak, Gary '94 (BEL) Leave of Absence.
Sebesta, James A. *s.j.* '70 (STL)[C] Saint Louis University; [O] St. Louis, MO Jesuit Community Corporation at St. Louis University – Jesuit Hall.
Sebra, Anthony G. '72 (STA) Jacksonville, FL Sacred Heart; Deans.
Sebra, Tony (STA) Presbyteral Council.
Seco, Jose Pancracio '88 (RCK) McHenry, IL Church of Holy Apostles.
Secondo, Louis J. *t.o.r.* '46 (ALT) Altoona, PA Our Lady of Mt. Carmel.
Secor, Gary L. (HON) Serra Club of Honolulu.
Secor, Gary '77 (HON) Honolulu, HI Cathedral of Our Lady of Peace; Vicar for Clergy; Vocations Director; Clergy Personnel Board; Priestly Life and Ministry; Ethnic Ministry Advisory Board; Presbyteral Council; Senior Priests' Committee; Board of Directors; Kailua Institute No. 213.
Secora, James L. '75 (DUB) Cedar Falls, IA St. Patrick; Worship Commission.
Seculoff, James F. '62 (FTW) Bristol, IN St. Mary of the Annunciation.
Seda, Jon M. '88 (DUB) Colo, IA St. Gabriel; Veterans' Home; Colo, IA St. Patrick; Colo, IA Sacred Heart; Colo, IA St. Joseph; Colo, IA St. Mary; Vocation Awareness.
Sedar, Adam C. '98 (ALN) Reading, PA St. Catharine of Siena.
Sedita, Vincent A. (LKC) Diocesan Board of Administration.
Sedita, Vincent '92 (LKC) Sulphur, LA Immaculate Conception of the B.V.M.; Judges; Diocesan Consultors.
Sedlacek, Richard D. '79 (YAK) Kennewick, WA St. Joseph's; Diocesan Consultors.
Sedlacek, Richard (YAK) Presbyteral Council Executive Committee.
Sedlacko, Louis S. *o.s.b.* '44 (GBG)[H] Latrobe, PA Saint Vincent Archabbey.
Sedlak, John A. '82 (GBG) Smock, PA St. Cecilia; Smock, PA St. Hedwig; [K] Smock, PA Ladies of Charity; St. Vincent de Paul Society.
Sedlak, Kenneth *c.ss.r.* '72 (CHI) Chicago, IL St. Michael; [N] Chicago, IL The Redemptorist Fathers of Chicago.
Sedlak, Valentine G. '44 (PIT) Retired.
Sedley, Joe *c.p.* '69 (PIT)[P] Pittsburgh, PA St. Paul of the Cross Retreat Center.
Sedley, Joseph *c.p.* '69 (PIT)[N] Pittsburgh St. Paul of the Cross Monastery.
Sedlmayer, Lauro C. '85 (MET) Perth Amboy, NJ Our Lady of the Rosary of Fatima; Portuguese Apostolate.
Sedlock, David W. '91 (MAR) Rapid River, MI St. Charles Borromeo.
Sedlock, Steven *c.s.c.* '66 (SB) Coachella, CA Our Lady of Soledad; [E] Coachella, CA Congregation of the Holy Cross.
Seeberger, Claude *o.s.b.* '49 (BIS) Dickinson, ND St. Patrick; [A] Richardton, ND Assumption Abbey.
Seed, Michael *s.a.* '86 (NY)[EE] Garrison Franciscan Friars of the Atonement, Minister General Office.
Seedorf, Warren H. *c.s.p.* '49 (NY)[EE] Jamaica Estates Paulist Fathers Generalate.
Seegar, Kenneth M. '87 (SCR) Wyalusing, PA St. Mary's Assumption.
Seeger, James E. '85 (PIT) Pittsburgh, PA Resurrection.
Seekamp, Walter J. '79 (BGP) Stamford, CT St. Clement.
Seelaus, William O. *o.s.f.s.* '51 (WIL)[J] Childs, MD Retirement and Assisted Care Facility.
Seeley, Burns K. '99 (CHI) Chicago, IL St. John Cantius; [Q] Chicago, IL Society of Saint John Cantius.
Seelman, Patrick *t.o.r.* '63 (ORL).
Seeman, Robert L. '79 (PIT)[D] Jefferson Hills, PA St. Thomas A'Becket.
Seery, William O. '95 (HRT) Branford, CT St. Mary.
Seetch, William D. *c.s.c.* '79 (FTW)[B] University of Notre Dame Du Lac; [B] University of Notre Dame Du Lac; [I] Notre Dame, IN Holy Cross Community, Corby Hall, University of Notre Dame.
Seethaler, Scott *o.f.m.cap.* '69 (PIT)[N] Pittsburgh, PA St. Augustine Friary.
Seeton, Philip M. '91 (PBR) Lawton, OK Byzantine Catholic Community of Oklahoma City.
Seeton, Philip '91 (OKL) Lawton, OK Holy Family; [K] Lawton, OK Cameron University.
Seewald, Carl H. *s.v.d.* '68 (OAK) Hayward, CA All Saints.
Sefcik, Dennis L. '65 (SC) Rockwell City, IA St. Francis of Assisi; Calhoun County State Reformatory, Minimum Security for Men.
Segatta, Bruno '74 (B) On Duty Outside the Diocese.
Seger, Michael '88 (CIN)[B] Cincinnati, OH Mt. St. Mary's Seminary of the West.
Seger, Oscar H. '70 (CIN) Wapakoneta, OH St. John; St. Marys, OH St. Patrick; Judges.
Sego, Arthur (LFT) AUXILIARY CHAPLAINS CONTRACT CHAPLAINS.
Segotta, Vincent *c.p.* '77 (WH) Kingwood, WV St. Sebastian's; Kingwood, WV St. Zita's.
Segovia, Norman '67 (SJ) Milpitas, CA St. John the Baptist.
Segovia, Norman '68 (SJ) Special Assignment.
Segreve, Richard J. *c.s.c.* '61 (FR)[A] North Easton, MA Holy Cross Fathers Religious.
Seguin, Robert J. *c.s.b.* '69 (GAL)[Q] Sugar Land Basilian Mission Center.
Segura, Luis Alfonso *m.s.c.* '99 (RCK)[G] Aurora, IL Missionaries of the Sacred Heart Community.
Seher, Philip O. '65 (CIN) Retired.
Sehler, Michael E. *s.j.* '73 (NY)[F] New York, NY Loyola School; [EE] New York, NY "America;" Residence and publication office of the America Press.
Seibert, Gary G. *s.j.* '73 (STL)[O] St. Louis, MO Leo Brown Jesuit Community.
Seibert, Herman *o.f.m.conv.* '45 (SY) Syracuse, NY Assumption B.V.M..
Seibert, James C. *c.pp.s.* '77 (CIN)[B] Carthagena, OH St. Charles; Vicarri Foranei (Deans).
Seichpine, Albert M. '51 (PIT)[P] Bethel Park, PA Holy Spirit Animation Center.
Seid, David *o.p.* (SB) In. Res..
Seidel, George J. *o.s.b.* '58 (SEA)[L] Lacey, WA St. Martin's Abbey.
Seidel, Thomas E. *c.s.c.* '57 (FTW)[I] Bangor, MI.
Seidel, Thomas *c.s.c.* '57 (KAL) Bangor, MI Sacred Heart of Jesus.
Seidel, Victor *s.t.* '61 (BLX) Columbia, MS Most Holy Trinity; Industrial and Training School.
Seidl, Larry J. (GB) Green Bay, WI St. Matthew; Elected Representatives.
Seifert, Michael D. '84 (Y) Waynesburg, OH St. James.
Seifert, Michael *s.m.* '85 (BWN) Brownsville, TX San Felipe de Jesus.
Seifert, Raymond *c.pp.s.* '44 (CIN)[B] Carthagena, OH St. Charles.
Seifert, William N. '81 (ALN) Easton, PA St. Joseph.
Seifferly, Richard R. '63 (GAY) Retired.
Seifner, Thomas J. '92 (JC) Pilot Grove, MO St. Joseph; Senators.
Seifried, Kenneth A. '63 (SC) Granville, IA St. Joseph; [B] Granville, IA Spalding Catholic Schools, Inc.; Presbyteral Council; Deans.
Seigel, Timothy J. '91 (RCK) East Dubuque, IL St. Mary.
Seiker, Daniel J. '87 (LIN)[G] Lincoln, NE School Sisters of Christ the King, Villa Regina Motherhouse & Novitiate; Officialis; Vicars For Religious; Priests' Continuing Education Committee.
Seiker, Daniel (LIN) Diocesan Consultors; Presbyteral Council.
Seiker, Leo V. '91 (LIN) York, NE St. Joseph's; Permanent Deacon Continuing Education Committee.
Seiker, Mark E. '84 (LIN) Beatrice, NE St. Joseph's; Diocesan Area CCD Directors; Cursillo.
Seil, Paul D. '89 (BUF) Worship, Office Of; Buffalo, NY St. Lawrence.
Seiler, Andrew J. '88 (WCH) Wellington, KS St. Anthony; Wellingon, KS St. Rose of Lima.
Seiler, Gerald L. '90 (NO)[A] Chancellor; Adjutant Judicial Vicar; Members of the Board; Censores Librorum; Canonical Permissions and Dispensations; New Orleans, LA St. Louis Cathedral.
Seiler, John A. '59 (COV) St. Luke Hospital East.
Seimas, Peter '02 (SJ) Gilroy, CA St. Mary.
Seipp, William J. '63 (MAD) Madison, WI St. Patrick; Personnel Board.
Seis, Michael '93 (GB) On Duty Outside the Diocese; Dominican Republic Mission.
Seisser, Edward J. '98 (RCK) Elgin, IL St. Mary.
Seiter, George C. '83 (CAM) Oaklyn, NJ St. Aloysius; Camden West Deanery; Directors; Propagation of the Faith & Holy Childhood Association.
Seiter, Joseph A. *c.s.sp.* '62 (LR) Carlisle, AR St. Rose of Lima Church; England, AR Holy Trinity Church.
Seitz, Gilbert J. '82 (BAL) Special Assignment; Defenders of the Bond.
Seitz, Gilbert J. (MO) Judges.
Seitz, James J. '94 (WIN) Dodge Center, MN St. John Baptist de La Salle; Dodge Center, MN St. Vincent de Paul; Dodge Center, MN St. Francis de Sales.
Seitz, Joseph W. '58 (CHI) Retired.
Seitz, Mark J. '80 (DAL) Dallas, TX St. Rita; Procurator–Advocates; Diocesan Consultors; Presbyteral Council.
Seitz, Patrick K. '98 (BWN) Weslaco, TX St. Pius X.
Seitz, Paul F.X. '58 (CHR) Retired.
Seitz, Thomas R. '52 (CHI) Chicago, IL St. Thomas Apostle Retired.
Sejba, Anthony F. '99 (CLV) Mentor, OH St. John Vianney.
Sekellick, John T. '69 (PSC) Jessup, PA Holy Ghost; Northern Pennsylvania/Northern New York Protopresbyterate; Ex Officio Members; Judicial Vicar; Family Life.
Seleccion, Romeo N. *m.s.* '82 (SB)[E] Moreno Valley, CA Missionaries of Our Lady of La Salette, MS.
Seleccion, Romeo *m.s.* '82 (SB) Moreno Valley, CA St. Christopher.
Selga, Remberto '66 (SD) San Diego, CA St. Charles.
Seli, John J. '46 (PIT) Retired.
Seli, William *s.m.* '58 (WH) Wheeling, WV St. Vincent de Paul's.
Selin, Gary '03 (DEN) Lakewood, CO Our Lady of Fatima.
Sell, Christian *o.f.m.* '42 (LAR) Hebbronville, TX Our Lady of Guadalupe.
Sell, Robert L. '78 (LFT) Reynolds, IN St. Joseph; Special Assignment; Vicar General; Chancellor and Moderator of the Curia; Diocesan Consultors; Diocesan Pastoral Office for Formation; Administrative Causes; Corporation; Finance Council; Members.
Sell, Robert '78 (LFT)[I] Board Members:; Building Commission.
Sella, Donald '83 (PAT) Paterson, NJ Our Lady of Lourdes.

Sella, Peter *s.d.b.* '68 (NEW)[C] Ramsey, NJ Don Bosco Preparatory High School; [N] Ramsey, NJ Don Bosco Prep Salesian Residence.

Selladurai, Selvaraj (GRY) Schererville, IN St. Michael.

Sellam, Louis '88 (OKL) Frederick, OK St. Helen.

Sellars, Charles *o.m.i.* '54 (BEA) Silsbee, TX St. Mark the Evangelist.

Sellars, Charles *o.m.i.* (NO) Medjugorje Star.

Sellas, Joseph '89 (CHI) Lyons, IL St. Hugh.

Selle, Paulinus J. *o.s.b.* '39 (GBG)[H] Latrobe, PA Saint Vincent Archabbey.

Selleck, John P. '57 (CAM) Retired.

Selleck, John '57 (PT) Panama City, FL St. Dominic; Gulf Coast Institution; Washington Correctional Institution.

Sellers, Benedict *o.s.b.* '75 (CLV)[O] Cleveland, OH.

Selvam, Panneer '81 (P) Stayton, OR Immaculate Conception; Area Vicars.

Selvan, Maria Augustine *s.j.* '89 (CHI)[C] Chicago, IL Jesuit Community at Loyola University Chicago.

Selvappan, Siluvai R. '77 (PT) Tallahassee, FL Co–Cathedral of St. Thomas More.

Selvaraj, Balapa '86 (ATL)[N] LaGrange, GA LaGrange Jr. College.

Selvaraj, Balappa '86 (ATL) LaGrange, GA St. Peter's.

Selvaraj, Bose Raja '73 (BGP) Trumbull, CT St. Theresa.

Selvaraj, James J. '89 (TR) Lakewood, NJ St. Mary of the Lake.

Selvaraj, Raju B. (PH) Indian Apostolate, Latin Rite.

Selvaraj, Thomas '64 (CHL) Eden, NC St. Joseph of the Hills.

Selzer, Eugene P. '61 (PRM) Wildwood, MO St. Louis Mission.

Selzer, Eugene P. '61 (STL) Wildwood, MO St. Alban Roe.

Selzer, Lee A. '02 (CHR) Columbia, SC St. Joseph.

Selzler, Norbert E. '38 (BUF) Retired.

Semaan, Charbel T. '89 (SAM) New Bedford, MA Our Lady of Purgatory.

Semancik, Joseph F. '53 (GRY) East Chicago, IN Sacred Heart.

Semeniuk, Gregory *c.m.* (RVC) Senate of Priests (Presbyteral Council/College of Consultors).

Semenych, Petro '91 (PHU) Jenkintown, PA St. Michael the Archangel.

Seminack, Richard S. (PHI) Navy Reserve Chaplains.

Seminara, Ronald S. *s.j.* '74 (RC)[F] St. Stephens, WY St. Stephens Indian Mission Foundation; Norris, SD Sacred Heart.

Seminatore, Joseph '69 (CLV) Administrative Leave.

Semko, Edward '69 (PSC) Carteret, NJ St. Elias.

Semler, Albert J. (PIT) Clergy Personnel Board.

Semler, Albert '67 (PIT) Sewickley, PA St. James.

Semler, Andrew V. (DAL) Plano, TX St. Elizabeth Ann Seton.

Semmer, Dean F. '79 (CHI) Grayslake, IL St. Gilbert.

Semonin, James R. '71 (CLV) Parma Community Hospital; [L] Parma, OH CCSC/Parmadale.

Sempa, John J. '80 (SCR) Wilkes–Barre, PA Sacred Heart–St. John.

Sempko, Walter A. '50 (HBG) Lebanon, PA St. Cecilia Retired.

Semple, James '64 (SLC) Salt Lake City, UT St. Ambrose.

Semple, Richard '00 (SPK) Absent on Leave.

Sena, Charles A. '92 (PBL) La Junta, CO Our Lady of Guadalupe/St. Patrick; Rocky Ford, CO St. Peter; Deans.

Sena, Charlie (PBL) Continuing Education and Formation.

Sena, Sotero A. '81 (SFE) Clovis, NM Our Lady of Guadalupe.

Sena, Sotero (SFE) Defenders of the Bond.

Senchur, Becket G. *o.s.b.* '73 (GBG)[H] Latrobe Saint Vincent Archabbey.

Senecal, Gerard *o.s.b.* '54 (KCK) Atchison, KS St. Benedict's; Atchison, KS Sacred Heart; Regional Pastoral Leaders; [H] Atchison, KS St. Benedict's Abbey.

Seneschal, Theodore T. *o.s.b.* '70 (OKL)[I] Shawnee St. Gregory's Abbey.

Senetsky, Robert '60 (PSC) Peekskill, NY SS. Peter and Paul.

Senger, William *m.m.* '73 (FgM).

Senghas, Richard E. '98 (PRT) Jay, ME St. Rose of Lima.

Senior, Donald *c.p.* '67 (CHI)[B] Chicago, IL The Catholic Theological Union at Chicago; [N] Chicago, IL Passionist Community–CTU; College of Consultors.

Senior, Timothy C. '85 (PH)[K] Philadelphia, PA The Catholic Social Services of the Archdiocese of Philadelphia; [M] Springfield, PA Divine Providence Village; [FF] Philadelphia, PA Ladies of Charity; Secretary for Catholic Human Services; Catholic Charities of the Archdiocese of Philadelphia; Catholic Health Care Services; Social Concerns; On Special or Other Archdiocesan Assignment; Catholic Health Care Services.

Seniw, John '82 (PHU) Scranton, PA St. Vladimir's; Scranton, PA SS. Peter and Paul.

Senk, Christopher (VEN) Sanibel, FL St. Isabel.

Senko, Martin '56 (P) Retired.

Senneville, Eugene Joseph '46 (LAF) Retired.

Sennik, Thomas W. '76 (NOR) Willington, CT St. Jude.

Senske, Joseph A. '48 (PH) Retired.

Seong Kwon, Peter Il '91 (SB) Norco, CA St. Mel.

Sepe, Kevin M. '86 (BO) Braintree, MA St. Francis of Assisi; Selected.

Seper, John M. '83 (STL) Richmond Heights, MO Immacolata.

Sepich, Lawrence '74 (MIL) Milwaukee, WI St. Bernadette.

Sepp, Michael (NY) Bronx, NY St. Francis of Assisi; Bronx, NY Sacred Heart.

Sepulveda, Gustavo B. '58 (HRT) Hartford, CT St. Augustine.

Sepulveda, Miguel A. '02 (MIA) Coral Gables, FL St. Augustine.

Sepulveda, Miguel (MIA) University of Miami.

Sepulveda, Thomas W. *c.s.b.* '74 (GAL)[Q] Sugar Land Basilian Mission Center.

Sepulveda, Thomas W. *c.s.b.* '74 (DET) Detroit, MI Ste. Anne.

Sequeira, Jose '00 (CHI) Cicero, IL Our Lady of Charity.

Sequeira, Marcos '91 (NEW) Newark, NJ Our Lady of Good Counsel.

Sequeira, Michael '66 (NOR) Clinton, CT St. Mary of the Visitation.

Sequira, Michael (NOR) St. Mary of the Visitation Church – Spanish Apostolate.

Sera, Enrique J. '78 (ORG) Santa Ana, CA Immaculate Heart of Mary; [U] Sealy, TX Asociacion Nacional de Sacerdotes Hispanos; Navy Reserve Chaplains.

Sera, Enrique (ORG) Council of Priests.

Serado, William '40 (SR) Retired.

Serafin, Thomas J. '93 (MET) Three Bridges, NJ St. Elizabeth Ann Seton.

Serafini, Augustine '62 (GB)[I] Oshkosh, WI Community of Our Lady.

Seramur, Leo J. '45 (MIL) Retired.

Seran, Agustinus *s.v.d.* '99 (LAF) Jeanerette, LA Our Lady of the Rosary.

Serano, Joseph A. *o.praem.* '69 (PH)[E] Paoli, PA Daylesford Abbey; [AA] Paoli, PA Daylesford Abbey.

Serban, Ron '93 (SR) Eureka, CA St. Bernard.

Serban, Ron '93 (SB) Military Chaplains.

Seremet, Hyacinth '51 (SY) Utica, NY Sacred Heart.

Serena, Edward T. '68 (BO) Marshfield, MA St. Ann by the Sea.

Sereno, David '86 (SD) Calexico, CA Our Lady of Guadalupe.

Sergi, Michael D. *c.ss.r.* '79 (BAL) Baltimore, MD Our Lady of Fatima.

Sergott, Joseph M. *o.p.* '96 (SFR) San Francisco, CA St. Dominic.

Sergott, Joseph *o.p.* '96 (SFR)[N] San Francisco, CA St. Dominic Priory.

Sergott, Lawrence J. '01 (GAY) Higgins Lake, MI St. Hubert; Higgins Lake, MI St. James.

Serio, Anthony '67 (NO) Retired.

Serio, John J. *s.d.b.* '82 (BO)[E] Boston, MA Savio Preparatory High School.

Serio, John *s.d.b.* '82 (NEW)[C] Ramsey, NJ Don Bosco Preparatory High School; [N] Ramsey, NJ Don Bosco Prep Salesian Residence.

Sermak, Ronald *o.f.m.conv.* '60 (BUF)[O] Athol Springs, NY St. Maximilian Kolbe Friary; [P] Hamburg, NY Immaculate Conception Convent.

Sermak, Ronald *o.f.m.conv.* '60 (BAL)[S] Hamburg, NY Chaplain's Office.

Sermak, Ronald *o.f.m.conv.* '60 (BUF)[O] Athol Springs, NY St. Maximilian Kolbe Friary; [P] Hamburg, NY Immaculate Conception Convent.

Serna, F. Mark *o.s.b.* '86 (PRO)[E] Portsmouth, RI Portsmouth Abbey School.

Serna, J. Patrick '01 (CC) Banquete, TX Saint Michael the Archangel.

Serna, Juan *s.t.l.* '02 (STO) Stockton, CA Presentation Church (Pastor of).

Sernett, Michael D. (SC) Vicars General; Chancellor; Judges; Diocesan Corporate Board; Presbyteral Council; Diocesan Consultors.

Sernett, Michael (SC) Priests' Pension Plan – Board of Trustees.

Serour, George J. '59 (SAG) Retired.

Serour, George (SAG) Ecumenism Ministry Retired.

Serowik, James P. '87 (SY) Endicott, NY St. Joseph.

Serra, Dominic F. '72 (WDC)[C] Catholic University of America, The.

Serra, Dominic '72 (NY) On Duty Outside the Archdiocese.

Serra, Javier Antonio *c.m.* '99 (BRK)[X] Brooklyn, NY Centro Evangelizacion San Vicente de Paul.

Serraglio, Mario '58 (COL) Retired.

Serraino, Fred *c.s.c.* '68 (ORL)[E] Cocoa Beach, FL Congregation of Holy Cross, Eastern Province.

Serraino, Frederick *c.s.c.* (ORL) Retired.

Serrano, Dionisio '97 (PCE) On Duty Outside the Diocese

Serrano, Heriberto '67 (SAC) Marysville, CA St. Joseph.

Serrano, John J. '42 (RVC) Retired.

Serrano, Jose '95 (NY) New York, NY St. Elizabeth.

Serrano, Rodrigo '01 (FWT) Fort Worth, TX Holy Name of Jesus.

Serrano–Vahi, Salvador '85 (MIA)[L] Miami, FL Prelature of the Holy Cross and Opus Dei.

Serrano Rivera, Ivan *c.s.sp.* '87 (SJN) San Juan, PR Santa Teresa Jornet.

Serrick, James K. *s.j.* '62 (DET)[P] Bloomfield Hills, MI Manresa Jesuit Retreat House.

Serva, Donald M. *s.j.* '78 (DET)[K] Temperance, MI.

Serva, Donald M. *s.j.* '78 (WH)[A] Wheeling, WV Wheeling Jesuit University.

Servatius, Robert R. '64 (SLC) Sandy, UT Blessed Sacrament; College of Consultors; Defenders of the Bond.

Servatius, Thomas '03 (SY) Johnson City, NY St. James.

Servinsky, Michael E. '70 (ALT) Judicial Vicar; Tribunal Office; Coupon, PA St. Joseph's.

Servodidio, John T. '54 (NY) Staten Island, NY St. Joseph Retired.

Serwa, Gregory P. *s.a.c.* '70 (MIL)[O] Milwaukee, WI Pallotti House.

Sescon, Esteban '77 (ELP) El Paso, TX St. Francis Xavier.

Seson, Alberto C. '86 (DET) Holly, MI St. Rita.

Sessa, Gene *s.j.* (DAL)[D] Dallas, TX Jesuit College Preparatory School.

Sessions, Phillip D. '80 (LAN) On Duty Outside the Diocese.

Sestito, Joseph N. '59 (OG) On Duty Outside the Diocese.

Sesto, Gennaro J. *s.d.b.* '50 (NEW) Elizabeth, NJ St. Anthony's; [GG] Stony Point, NY Don Bosco Retreat Center and Marian Shrine.

Sesto, Gennaro *s.d.b.* '50 (NY)[GG] Stony Point, NY Marian Shrine.

Setelik, James '84 (RNO) Carson City, NV Corpus Christi.

Setelik, Jim (RNO) Prison Ministry.

Setter, H. '88 (WCH) Goddard, KS Holy Spirit.

Settles, Dennis F. '65 (JOL) Kankakee, IL St. Martin of Tours.

Seuferling, George '56 (KCK) Retired.

Seung Koo, Andrew Lee '91 (OAK)[N] Berkeley Salesian Community.

Seuntjens, LeRoy L. '98 (SC) Hawarden, IA St. Mary's.

Sevcik, Lawrence *o.s.b.* '53 (CLV)[O] Cleveland, OH.

Sever, Janez *s.j.* '02 (BO)[V] Cambridge, MA Faber House.

Severson, Richard '82 (ALB) Special Assignment.

Severt, William H. '74 (CLV) Cleveland, OH SS. Philip and James.

Severt, William '74 (CLV) University Hospitals.

Sevick, John M. '73 (CHI) Other Assignments.

Sevigny, Michael E. *o.f.m.cap* '78 (MAN) Concord, NH Sacred Heart; New Hampshire Hospital; [L] Concord, NH Monastery of Discalced Carmelites.

Sevigny, Robert J. '53 (HT) Retired.

Sevilla, Dennis '69 (SEA) Special Assignment.

Sevola, Frank *o.f.m.* '91 (PRO)[N] Providence, RI St. Francis Chapel & City Ministry Center; [P] Providence, RI St. Francis Friary.

Sewar, Dennis '83 (ROC) Spencerport, NY St. John the Evangelist.

Sewell, Jack '78 (ORG) San Clemente, CA Our Lady of Fatima; Air Force Reserve Chaplains.

Sewvello, Robert J. '94 (GF) Plentywood, MT St. Joseph's.

Sewvello, Robert '94 (GF) Special Assignment.

Sewvello, Robert '94 (YAK) On Duty Outside the Diocese.

Sexstone, James H. '69 (ATL) Atlanta, GA Immaculate Heart of Mary.

Sexton, Michael '61 (BIR) Madison, AL St. John the Baptist; [I] Madison, AL St. John's Educational Foundation; Members; Diocesan College of Consultors; Diocesan College of Vicars.

Sexton, Thomas *s.j.* '49 (SEA)[C] Tacoma, WA Bellarmine Preparatory School.

Seyer, James A. '50 (SPC) Retired.

Seyer, Lawrence '97 (LA) Simi Valley, CA St. Peter Claver.

Seymour, Francis R. '63 (NEW) Kearny, NJ St. Cecilia's; Archdiocesan Archivist; Seton Hall University Archives.

Seymour, James P. '97 (BO) Scituate, MA St. Mary of the Nativity.

Seymour, James W. '87 (OG) Champlain, NY St. Mary.

Seymour, John *s.t.* '70 (LA) Compton, CA Our Lady of Victory; Compton, CA Sagrado Corazon, Sacred Heart.

Seymour, Scott R. '99 (OG) Ogdensburg, NY St. Mary's Cathedral; Ogdensburg, NY Ogdensburg Correctional Facility.

Seynaeve, Jaak *m.afr.* '44 (BR) Special Assignment.

Sezzi, Michael '96 (LA) Moorpark, CA Holy Cross.

Sgarioto, Michael *o.carm.* '85 (PHX) Phoenix, AZ St. Agnes.
Sgueglia, Charles J.M. '52 (SPR) Retired.
Shackelford, Christopher '91 (GAL) Houston, TX St. Jerome.
Shadeg, Werner *s.v.d.* '45 (CHI)[B] Techny, IL Divine Word Residence.
Shadwell, Damian (WDC) St. Inigoes, MD St. Peter Claver; St. Mary's City, MD St. Cecilia.
Shaefer, Konrad *o.s.b.* '80 (FgM).
Shafer, Drake R. '73 (DAV)[K] Davenport, IA St. Vincent Center.
Shafer, James A. '75 (FTW) Fort Wayne, IN St. Elizabeth Ann Seton.
Shafer, James (FTW) Consultors; Liturgical Commission.
Shaffer, G. Scott '89 (TR) Jackson, NJ St. Aloysius Gonzaga.
Shafran, Steven *s.d.b.* '76 (NEW)[N] Ramsey, NJ Don Bosco Prep Salesian Residence.
Shafran, Steven *s.d.b.* '85 (NEW)[C] Ramsey, NJ Don Bosco Preparatory High School.
Shaheen, Joseph '59 (SAM) Retired.
Shaiibetter, Martin '69 (STP) Deephaven, MN St. Therese.
Shaji, Jose '92 (SFR) San Francisco, CA St. John the Evangelist.
Shakalis, Peter A. '47 (BO) Senior Priests Retired.
Shaldone, Robert '97 (CC)[G] Robstown, TX Society of Our Lady of the Most Holy Trinity.
Shaleta, Emanuel Isho '84 (EST) Troy, MI St. Joseph Chaldean Parish.
Shallow, Edmund J. '81 (MET) Carteret, NJ Holy Family.
Shamleffer, John B. '83 (STL) Clayton, MO St. Joseph.
Shamleffer, John B. (STL) Judicial Vicar; Archdiocesan Priests' Personnel Board.
Shanahan, Daniel *o.p.* '62 (NO) New Orleans, LA St. Dominic.
Shanahan, John D. '50 (SFR) Larkspur, CA St. Patrick.
Shanahan, Michael J. '92 (CHI) Chicago, IL St. Mark.
Shanahan, Michael *ss.cc.* '62 (FR).
Shanahan, Thomas J. '67 (OM)[K] Omaha, NE Jesuit Community at Creighton University.
Shane, Donald W. '69 (OM) Omaha, NE St. Robert Bellarmine.
Shane, Michael '03 (BEA) On Duty Outside the Diocese.
Shaner, Edward G. '96 (MET) On Duty Outside the Diocese.
Shaner, Simon *o.s.p.p.e.* '96 (PH)[AA] Office.
Shanfelt, Thomas G. '78 (ALN) Tresckow, PA St. Bartholomew.
Shanfelt, Thomas '78 (ALN) Tresckow, PA St. Michael.
Shangraw, Philip '79 (GR) Reed City, MI St. Philip Neri.
Shangraw, Phillip (GR) Director of Spiritual Formation for Permanent Diaconate Program.
Shanley, Albert J. *m.s.* '38 (STP) Taylors Falls, MN St. Joseph's.
Shanley, Brian J. *o.p.* '87 (WDC)[B] Washington, DC Dominican House of Studies; [C] Catholic University of America, The.
Shanley, Charles M. *c.m.* '55 (PH)[B] Philadelphia, PA DePaul Novitiate.
Shanley, Gerry *ss.cc.* '61 (FR)[H] Hidalgo, TX.
Shanley, James A. '80 (HRT) East Haven, CT Our Lady of Pompeii.
Shanley, Joseph D. '43 (PRO)[M] Woonsocket, RI Saint Francis House Retired.
Shanley, Kevin *o.carm.* '56 (JOL)[N] Darien, IL Carmelite Spiritual Center.
Shanley, Matthew R. '55 (HRT) Medical Leave.
Shanley, Matthias *ss.cc.* '65 (BWN) Harlingen, TX Queen of Peace; Deans; Director for Pro–Life Activities.
Shanley, Owen F. '53 (ALB) Retired.
Shannon, Bernard E. *s.j.* '80 (NY)[EE] New York, NY Murray–Weigel Hall.
Shannon, Brendan '62 (MIA) Retired.
Shannon, David *c.ss.r.* '48 (STP) Brooklyn Center, MN St. Alphonsus.
Shannon, Francis '87 (BRK) Brooklyn, NY St. Lucy–St. Patrick; Brooklyn, NY Our Lady of Monserrate–St. Ambrose.
Shannon, Joseph L. *o.s.a.* '37 (PH)[AA] Villanova, PA St. Thomas Monastery.
Shannon, Joseph P. *c.s.b.* '48 (GAL)[Q] Sugar Land, TX Basilian Mission Center.
Shannon, Patrick J. *o.s.f.s.* '72 (HBG) Lewisburg, PA Sacred Heart of Jesus.
Shannon, Timothy T. *s.j.* '88 (DET)[K] Colegio Centroamericano.
Shannon, Timothy '75 (STU) Steubenville, OH Holy Name Cathedral; Steubenville, OH St. Anthony of Padua.
Shannon, William H. '43 (ROC)[J] Rochester, NY Sisters St. Joseph Motherhouse; Censores Librorum Retired.
Shannon, William '71 (HON) Kahului, HI Christ the King.
Shappelle, James E. (CIN) Ex Officio Members.
Shappelle, James '48 (CIN) Cincinnati, OH St. Bernard; Cincinnati, OH Mother of Christ.
Shappelle, James E. (CIN) Consultors.
Sharanevych, Emile '32 (STF) Retired.
Sharbel, Joseph M. '85 (KC) Kansas City, MO St. Peter's.
Sharbel, Joseph (KC) Deans.
Sharkey, John A. '56 (PH) Philadelphia, PA Old St. Mary's.
Sharkey, Owen *c.p.* '45 (HRT)[M] West Hartford Holy Family Monastery/Retreat.
Sharkey, Peter *s.j.* '74 (CIN)[M] Cincinnati, OH Faber Jesuit Community.
Sharkey, Philip J. '98 (HRT) New Haven, CT St. Bernadette; Deans.
Sharkey, Robert Urban *o.p.* '63 (NY)[EE] New York St. Vincent Ferrer Priory.
Sharkey, Thomas F. (CAM) Judges.
Sharkey, Thomas H. '48 (CAM)[G] Northfield, NJ The Sharkey Family Charitable Trust Retired.
Sharland, David M. '99 (ARL)[N] McLean, VA Youth Apostles Institute, An Association of Christian Faithful.
Sharland, David '99 (FR) On Duty Outside the Diocese.
Sharman, Robert F. '84 (HBG) New Bloomfield, PA St. Bernard; Missions, Office of (Home and Foreign).
Sharon, Charles *s.a.* '72 (NY)[EE] New York, NY Atonement Friars; [EE] Garrison, NY Franciscan Friars of the Atonement, Minister General Office.
Sharon, Norbert *s.t.* '48 (LA) Los Angeles, CA Our Lady of Victory.
Sharp, David L. *c.s.b.* '70 (PHX) Special Assignment; [I] Wickenburg, AZ Glendale Community College.
Sharp, Donald *s.j.* '71 (SFR) San Francisco, CA St. Agnes.
Sharp, George F. '89 (NEW)[A] Elizabeth, NJ Elizabeth Federal Detention Center; Elizabeth Detention Center (Federal).
Sharp, George '89 (NEW) Nutley, NJ St. Mary's.
Sharp, James R. '84 (DAL) Garland, TX St. Michael the Archangel.
Sharp, Kenneth W. '81 (PH) Philadelphia, PA Our Lady of Mt. Carmel.
Sharrett, Victor F. '65 (PH) Kennett Square, PA St. Patrick.
Sharum, Peter *o.s.b.* '52 (LR) Charleston, AR Sacred Heart.
Shashy, Daniel '91 (STA) St. Augustine, FL Cathedral – Basilica of St. Augustine Retired.
Shatzel, Richard J. '69 (ROC) Honeoye, NY St. Mary, Our Lady of the Hills.
Shaughanessy, William G. '92 (SFR).
Shaughnessy, Angelus M. *o.f.m.cap.* '55 (BIR)[E] Birmingham, AL Franciscan Missionaries of the Eternal Word, A Public Association of the Christian Faithful.
Shaughnessy, James E. '73 (KCK) Lawrence, KS Corpus Christi.
Shaughnessy, James M. *s.j.* '79 (BO) Boston, MA New England Medical Center; [V] Boston, MA Loyola House.
Shaughnessy, Martin G. *s.j.* '63 (BGP)[E] Fairfield, CT Fairfield College Preparatory School; [P] Fairfield, CT The Fairfield Jesuit Community–Fairfield University.
Shaughnessy, Paul J. *s.j.* '87 (BAL)[S] Baltimore Jesuit Fathers and Brothers Maryland Provincial Curia; Navy Chaplains.
Shaughnessy, Thomas *o.f.m.* '60 (JOL)[L] Joliet, IL St. John the Baptist Friary.
Shaughnessy, Thomas *s.s.c.* (CHI) Chicago, IL St. Philomena.
Shaughnessy, Tom *o.f.m.* '60 (JOL) Joliet, IL St. John the Baptist.
Shaughnessy, William *o.f.m.* '73 (PHX)[H] Scottsdale, AZ Franciscan Renewal Center, Inc. (Casa de Paz Y Bien).
Shaules, Patrick R. *s.j.* '48 (PH)[AA] Dover, DE.
Shaules, Patrick *s.j.* (WIL) Operation Help, Inc..
Shaum, David W. '46 (BAL)[B] Emmitsburg, MD Mount Saint Mary's College Retired.
Shaunessy, Francis W. '45 (CHI) Retired.
Shaute, Joseph '01 (ATL) Peachtree City, GA Holy Trinity Catholic.
Shaver, James R. '89 (LAN) Jackson, MI St. John the Evangelist.
Shaver, James '89 (LAN) Cotton Facility; Regional Vicars.
Shaw, Brian A. '66 (HRT) New Britain, CT Holy Cross.
Shaw, Charles E. '51 (HRT) Retired.
Shaw, David '68 (SR) Santa Rosa, CA Resurrection; Members of the Curia; Deans; Defender of the Bond; Board of Consultors; Priests' Council; Clergy Personnel Committee.
Shaw, Dennis J. '74 (ROC) Rochester, NY Holy Redeemer–St. Francis Xavier.
Shaw, Dennis '74 (ROC) Rochester, NY Our Lady of Mount Carmel.
Shaw, John M. (YAK) Native American; Native American Ministries.
Shaw, John (YAK) Toppenish, WA St. Aloysius; Cursillo, English; Presbyteral Council Executive Committee.
Shaw, Kenneth *s.d.b.* '78 (SP)[GG] Stony Point, NY Marian Shrine; [E] Tampa, FL Mary Help of Christians School.
Shaw, Kenneth *s.d.b.* '78 (NY)[GG] Stony Point, NY Don Bosco Retreat Center and Marian Shrine.
Shaw, Michael '96 (PT) Tallahassee, FL Co–Cathedral of St. Thomas More; Florida State University; Cursillo Movement.
Shaw, Richard '68 (ALB) Coxsackie Correctional Facility; Greene Correctional Facility; Special Assignment.
Shaw, Thomas '01 (PEO) Elkhart, IL St. Patrick.
Shaw, William E. (YAK) Clergy Personnel Board.
Shaw, William '57 (YAK) White Swan, WA St. Mary's.
Shay, James C. '01 (BO) Absent on Leave.
Shay, Michael *s.d.s.* '73 (TUC) Sahuarita, AZ San Martin De Porres; AUXILIARY CHAPLAINS CONTRACT CHAPLAINS.
Shay, Robert M. *s.t.* (MO) AUXILIARY CHAPLAINS CONTRACT CHAPLAINS.
Shayo, Augustine '88 (SP) New Port Richey, FL Our Lady Queen of Peace.
Shea, Baldwin *o.c.s.o.* '53 (SLC)[F] Huntsville, UT Abbey of Our Lady of the Holy Trinity of the Order of Cistercians.
Shea, Daniel B. '69 (HEL) Helena, MT Our Lady of the Valley; [B] Helena, MT Carroll College.
Shea, Daniel (HEL) Diocesan Finance Council; Personnel Board; Clergy Senior Status and Security Trust Board.
Shea, Donald *c.pp.s.* '53 (TOL)[J] Bellevue Mary Lay Center; [L] Bellevue, OH Sorrowful Mother Shrine.
Shea, Donald '62 (HEL) Bigfork, MT St. Catherine.
Shea, Donald (HEL) Diocesan Consultors; Presbyteral Council.
Shea, Edward *o.f.m.* (CHI) Chicago, IL St. Joseph.
Shea, Evan P. '86 (CHY) Lusk, WY St. Leo's.
Shea, James E. *c.ss.r.* (KC) Diocesan Consultors; Deans.
Shea, James J. *sch.p.* '92 (PH)[AA] Devon Piarist Fathers (Order of the Pious Schools).
Shea, James M. '65 (BUR) Retired.
Shea, James M. *s.j.* '75 (WDC)[K] Washington, DC Georgetown University Hospital; [M] Washington, DC The Jesuit Community at Georgetown University.
Shea, James M. *s.j.* '75 (BO)[V] Boston The Society of Jesus of New England–Provincial Offices.
Shea, James M. '85 (WOR) Paxton, MA St. Columba's.
Shea, James P. *sch.p.* '92 (PH)[G] Devon, PA Devon Preparatory School.
Shea, James P. '02 (BIS) Bismarck, ND Cathedral of the Holy Spirit.
Shea, James *c.ss.r.* '65 (KC) Kansas City, MO Our Lady of Perpetual Help; [J] Kansas City, MO Redemptorists Fathers of Kansas City, Missouri; [N] Kansas City, MO Our Lady of Perpetual Help Charitable Trust.
Shea, James '65 (BUR) Venice, FL Epiphany Cathedral.
Shea, John J. '45 (SPR) Judges Retired.
Shea, John J. '61 (BO) Senior Priests Retired.
Shea, John J. *s.j.* '75 (SCR)[C] Scranton, PA The University of Scranton; [C] Scranton, PA Center for Eastern Christian Studies.
Shea, Joseph P. (LA) Deanery 6; Board of Directors:; Members:.
Shea, Joseph '78 (LA) Glendale, CA Holy Family.
Shea, Leo B. *m.m.* '66 (NY)[EE] Maryknoll Maryknoll Fathers and Brothers.
Shea, Lewis M. *o.p.* '52 (FgM).
Shea, Lewis M. *o.p.* '66 (CHI)[N] Chicago Dominicans (Provincial Office).
Shea, Michael J. *c.m.* '70 (GR)[G] Spring Lake, MI St. Lazare Retreat House.
Shea, Michael J. '76 (SFE) Albuquerque, NM Office:; Air National Guard Chaplains.
Shea, Michael M. *c.m.* '70 (PH).
Shea, Mike (SFE)[AA] College of Consultors.
Shea, Peter G. *c.s.p.* '62 (SFR) San Francisco, CA Old St. Mary's Cathedral.
Shea, Richard J. '61 (BGP) Trumbull, CT St. Catherine of Siena.
Shea, Robert F. '55 (R) Retired.
Shea, Thomas F. '64 (PH) Retired.
Shea, Thomas J. *o.s.a.* '52 (PH)[AA] Villanova, PA St. Thomas Monastery.
Shea, Thomas M. '66 (SPR) South Hadley, MA St. Patrick's; Bishop's Commission for Clergy; Presbyteral Council.
Shea, Thomas '49 (SJ) Retired.
Shea, Thomas '73 (PEO) On Leave.
Shea, Timothy J. '61 (BO) Woburn, MA St. Charles Borromeo; Selected.
Shea, William B. '46 (BO) Senior Priests Retired.
Shea, William *s.v.d.* '64 (DUB)[B] Epworth, IA Divine Word College.
Sheaffer, Jack '93 (SPR) Springfield, MA Holy Cross.
Sheaffer, John K. '93 (SPR) Belchertown, MA St.

Francis of Assisi.
Sheahan, Donal C. '60 (SD) San Diego, CA Our Mother of Confidence.
Sheahan, Donal (SD) Finance Council.
Sheahan, John A. '60 (ORG) Retired.
Sheahan, John F. '46 (SFD) Retired.
Sheahan, Richard D. '69 (PRO) Cranston, RI Holy Apostles.
Shean, William F. '73 (RVC) Centereach, NY Assumption of the Blessed Virgin Mary.
Shear, Michael P. '64 (PSC) Harrisburg, PA St. Ann.
Shearer, Thomas M. '78 (CIN) Dayton, OH St. Henry; Priest Councilors; Consultors.
Shebuski, Charles '65 (GB) Absent on Leave.
Shecterle, Ross A. '86 (MIL) Special Assignment.
Shedlock, John '94 (SFE) Hospital & Prison Ministry; Prison Ministry.
Sheeds, Gerald E. '68 (KCK) Gardner, KS Sacred Heart.
Sheedy, Edward J. '72 (BUF)[A] Buffalo, NY Pope John Paul II Residence.
Sheedy, Patrick J. '65 (ORL)[A] Ocala, FL Blessed Trinity; [A] Ocala, FL Trinity Catholic High School.
Sheedy, Timothy J. '76 (DAV) Fort Madison, IA Sacred Heart.
Sheedy, Val '55 (ORL) Executive Committee; Members Retired.
Sheehan, Augustine J. '55 (RVC) Retired.
Sheehan, Dan *c.p.m.* '46 (OWN)[F] Auburn, KY Fathers of Mercy.
Sheehan, Daniel J. '53 (BO) South Boston, MA St. Brigid; Senior Priests Retired.
Sheehan, Dennis F. '63 (BO) Cambridge, MA St. Paul; [BB] Cambridge, MA Harvard Catholic Student Center; CENTRAL REGION.
Sheehan, Donald P. '68 (NEW) Ridgefield, NJ St. Matthew's.
Sheehan, Edward *s.m.* '61 (PRT) Brunswick, ME St. John the Baptist.
Sheehan, George F. '61 (SY)[Q] East Syracuse, NY Vianney House.
Sheehan, George F. '63 (SY)[C] East Syracuse, NY Bishop Grimes Jr./Sr. High School; Western Area Vicars; Board of Diocesan Consultors; Ex Officio.
Sheehan, Gerald P. '64 (BUF) Sheridan, NY St. John Bosco; Sheridan, NY St. Rose of Lima.
Sheehan, Gerard J. *s.o.l.t.* '85 (CC)[G] Robstown, TX Society of Our Lady of the Most Holy Trinity; Robstown, TX St. Anthony.
Sheehan, J. Peter '56 (BIR) Retired.
Sheehan, James M. '98 (NEW) Newark, NJ Cathedral Basilica of the Sacred Heart; Secretary to the Archbishop and Vice Chancellor; Part–time Staff; Vice Chancellors; Archdiocesan Judges.
Sheehan, James T. *s.j.* '59 (BO)[V] Weston, MA Campion Health Center, Inc..
Sheehan, James '79 (NY)[HH] Bronx, NY Bronx Community College; [HH] Bronx, NY Hostos Community College.
Sheehan, John F.X. *s.j.* '64 (BO)[V] Boston The Society of Jesus of New England–Provincial Offices.
Sheehan, John F.X. *s.j.* '64 (STL)[O] St. Louis, MO Jesuit Community Corporation at St. Louis University – Jesuit Hall.
Sheehan, John J. '37 (BO) Senior Priests Retired.
Sheehan, John J. '54 (NY) Staten Island, NY Our Lady, Queen of Peace.
Sheehan, John P. '89 (NY) Bronx, NY St. Frances of Rome.
Sheehan, John *s.m.a.* '48 (NEW)[N] Tenafly, NJ Society of African Missions, Provincialate, S.M.A. Fathers Retired.
Sheehan, Joseph A. '59 (ALN) Easton, PA St. Joseph; Easton, PA St. Anthony of Padua.
Sheehan, Joseph G. '48 (NEW) Linden, NJ St. John the Apostle; County Dirs. Retired.
Sheehan, Joseph *o.carm.* '63 (SFS)[A] Aberdeen, SD Presentation College.
Sheehan, Justin R. *o.c.s.o.* '91 (ROC)[I] Piffard, NY Abbey of the Genesee.
Sheehan, Lawrence A. *s.j.* '47 (RVC) Massapequa, NY St. Rose of Lima.
Sheehan, Mark S. '63 (BO) Bedford, MA St. Michael; MERRIMACK REGION; Designated.
Sheehan, Maurice *o.f.m.cap.* '55 (NOR)[A] Cromwell, CT Holy Apostles College and Seminary; [N] Pittsburgh, PA St. Augustine Friary.
Sheehan, Maurice *o.f.m.cap.* '55 (PIT)[N] Pittsburgh, PA St. Francis Friary.
Sheehan, Michael J. '64 (PH) Philadelphia, PA Sacred Heart of Jesus.
Sheehan, Michael J. '78 (NEW) Paramus, NJ Annunciation.
Sheehan, Michael J. (NEW) Worship Office.
Sheehan, Myles N. *s.j.* '94 (BO)[V] Boston The Society of Jesus of New England–Provincial Offices.
Sheehan, Myles N. *s.j.* '94 (CHI)[C] Chicago, IL Jesuit Community at Loyola University Chicago.
Sheehan, Richard *o.m.i.* '61 (BWN) Roma, TX Our Lady of Refuge.
Sheehan, Thomas J. '53 (WDC) Washington, DC St. Peter Retired.
Sheehan, Thomas J. *s.j.* '97 (BO)[V] Boston, MA Jesuit Urban Center & Immaculate Conception Community.
Sheehan, Thomas W. '70 (CLV) Retired.
Sheehan, Thomas *o.f.m.* '60 (BUF).
Sheehan, William J. *c.s.b.* '66 (ROC)[I] Collegio San Clemente.
Sheehan, William *o.m.i.* '65 (BO)[V] Lowell, MA Contemplative Mission Center.
Sheehey, Robert J. *s.s.e.* '47 (MOB)[G] Selma, AL Edmundite Fathers.
Sheehy, Charles I. '44 (BO) Braintree, MA St. Francis of Assisi; Senior Priests Retired.
Sheehy, Dennis E. '68 (GBG) Clymer, PA Church of the Resurrection.
Sheehy, Edward P. *s.j.* (NEW)[C] Jersey City, NJ St. Peter's Preparatory School; [N] Jersey City, NJ Jesuit Community of St. Peter's Prep, Inc..
Sheehy, Joseph T. '53 (BO) Swampscott, MA St. John the Evangelist.
Sheehy, Paul E. '54 (LIN) Hebron, NE Sacred Heart; Deaneries and Deans.
Sheehy, Sean O. '70 (BR)[K] Hammond, LA St. Albert the Great Catholic Student Center.
Sheehy, Vincent J. '61 (VEN) Venice, FL Our Lady of Lourdes.
Sheehy, Vincent (VEN) College of Consultors.
Sheehy, Wilfred '60 (SR) Retired.
Sheehy, Yvon *s.c.j.* '78 (MIL)[O] Hales Corners, WI Priests of the Sacred Heart; [O] Milwaukee, WI SCJ Community.
Sheekey, Philip P. '64 (WIL) New Castle, DE Holy Spirit; Nursing Homes; College of Consultors.
Sheeran, Fintan *ss.cc.* '55 (FR).
Sheeran, Kevin J. *o.s.b.* '65 (JOL)[A] Lisle IL Benedictine University; [L] Lisle, IL St. Procopius Abbey.
Sheeran, Michael J. *s.j.* '70 (DEN)[B] Denver, CO Regis University; [N] Denver, CO Regis Jesuit Community (The Jesuits at Regis University).
Sheeran, Robert T. '70 (NEW)[A] South Orange, NJ Seton Hall University College Seminary; [B] South Orange, NJ Seton Hall University; [3] School of Diplomacy and Intl. Rels..
Sheerin, James O. '56 (NEW)[N] Rutherford, NJ St. John Vianney Residence for Priests; Priestly Vocation Board Retired.
Sheerin, Philip F. *m.m.* '44 (SJ)[M] Los Altos, CA Maryknoll.
Sheets, James P. '75 (SAC) Sacramento, CA Sutter General Hospital; Sacramento, CA Sutter Memorial Hospital.
Sheets, Joseph B. '57 (IND) Retired.
Sheffield, Walter N. '82 (GAL) Houston, TX St. Paul.
Sheganosky, Fabian *t.o.r.* '65 (ALT) Johnstown, PA St. Clare of Assisi.
Sheil, James '66 (CLV) Military Chaplains; Army Chaplains.
Shelander, Donald E. '70 (CIN) Retired.
Shelby, Charles F. *c.m.* '68 (STL)[O] Perryville, MO Congregation of the Mission; [U] Perryville, MO Association of the Miraculous Medal.
Shelden, Denis '95 (FBK) Alakanuk, AK St. Ignatius.
Sheldon, Alexander J. '01 (BR) Baton Rouge, LA St. Jean Vianney.
Sheldon, William W. *c.m.* '52 (PH)[B] Philadelphia, PA St. Vincent's Seminary; [AA] Philadelphia Congregation of the Mission.
Sheley, John '73 (SPC)[AA] Leave of Absence.
Shellem, John J. '52 (PH) Philadelphia, PA St. Athanasius Retired.
Shelley, John J. '61 (PH) Willow Grove, PA St. David.
Shelley, Jon P. '95 (STP) Mahtomedi, MN St. Jude of the Lake.
Shelley, Owen *o.f.m.cap.* '45 (NY)[EE] Yonkers, NY St. Clare Friary.
Shelley, Thomas J. '62 (NY) New York, NY St. Thomas More; On Duty Outside the Archdiocese.
Shelley, William M. '50 (NY) New York, NY St. Agnes Retired.
Shellman, Richard L. '86 (HRT) Bethlehem, CT Church of the Nativity.
Shelly, Eamon '02 (ATL)[K] Atlanta, GA Legionaries of Christ; O] Atlanta, GA Home and Family, Inc..
Shelly, Roy *s.d.b.* '78 (MRY)[F] Watsonville, CA Saint Francis Salesian Community; [I] Monterey, CA Department of Campus Ministry.
Shelly, Roy *s.d.b.* (MRY) Office of Faith Formation; Campus Ministry Department; Permanent Diaconate; Respect Life/Family Life Ministry; Permanent Diaconate Advisory Board.
Shelton, Charles M. *s.j.* '82 (DEN)[N] Denver, CO Regis Jesuit Community (The Jesuits at Regis University).
Shelton, Charles *o.f.m. conv.* '81 (MRY)[F] Arroyo Grande, CA St. Joseph Cupertino Friary.
Shelton, Henry '69 (JKS) Tupelo, MS St. James; Priests' Council.
Shelton, James Brent Allen '01 (KNX) Knoxville, TN All Saints Catholic Church.
Shelton, Lawrence '66 (LA) Los Angeles, CA St. Anselm.
Sheltz, George A. '71 (GAL) The Woodlands, TX St. Anthony of Padua.
Sheltz, George A. (GAL) Northern Vicariate; Appointees; College of Consultors.
Sheltz, George (GAL) Building Commission.
Shema, George T. '67 (PAT)[P] Chester, NJ Nazareth Village Retired.
Shemuga, Kevin C. '83 (CLV) Lorain, OH St. Joseph; Lorain, OH St. Stanislaus.
Shemuga, Kevin (CLV) Presbyteral Council.
Shen, Raphael *s.j.* '70 (DET)[K] Detroit, MI Jesuit Community at the University of Detroit Mercy.
Shenk, Bertrand J. '37 (TOL) Retired.
Shenosky, Joseph T. '00 (PH) Wayne, PA St. Katharine of Siena; [D] Springfield, PA Cardinal O'Hara High School.
Shenoy, Leslie F. '76 (FRS) Fresno, CA Sacred Heart.
Shenrock, Joseph C. '53 (TR) Whiting, NJ St. Elizabeth Ann Seton; Tribunal Judges.
Shepard, Eugene '78 (AUS) Chappell Hill, TX St. Stanislaus.
Shepard, Thomas B. '77 (HRT) Rocky Hill, CT St. James.
Shepard, Timothy J. '82 (CLV)[D] Cuyahoga Falls, OH Walsh Jesuit High School.
Sheperd, Raymond C. '57 (TOL) Retired.
Shepherd, Joseph *c.m.i.* '89 (NSH) Nashville, TN Assumption; Nashville, TN St. Pius X.
Shepler, Charles C. '43 (DAV) Retired.
Shepley, Brian J. '92 (DAV) Blue Grass, IA St. Andrew; Wilton, IA St. Mary's.
Sherba, Girard M. '79 (R) Raleigh, NC Cathedral of the Sacred Heart; Vice Chancellor for Canonical Affairs; Officialis.
Sherbno, John C. '49 (TOL) Retired.
Sherbo, Albert '87 (DM) Adel, IA St. John.
Sherburne, Richard F. *s.j.* '56 (MIL)[O] Milwaukee, WI Jesuit Community at Marquette University.
Sherdel, Lawrence W. '81 (HBG) McSherrystown, PA Annunciation of the Blessed Virgin Mary.
Sherer, Richard B. '58 (HRT) Retired.
Sheridan, Brian R. *m.s.* '83 (ORL) Orlando, FL Good Shepherd.
Sheridan, Denis J. '81 (RVC)[M] Uniondale, NY St. Pius X Residence Retired.
Sheridan, Edward J. '63 (CHL) Hickory, NC St. Aloysius.
Sheridan, Eugene F. *c.m.* '68 (BRK) Brooklyn, NY St. John the Baptist.
Sheridan, Eugene '45 (NY) Retired.
Sheridan, James J. *o.s.a.* '61 (FWT) Gainesville, TX St. Mary.
Sheridan, James *o.s.a.* '61 (FWT) Gainesville, TX Texas Youth Council Youth Facility.
Sheridan, John E. '90 (BO) Emergency Response Group.
Sheridan, John J. *o.s.a.* '85 (PH)[AA] Villanova, PA Provincial Offices of the Order of St. Augustine, Province of St. Thomas of Villanova; [AA] Villanova, PA St. Thomas Monastery.
Sheridan, John V. '43 (LA) Malibu, CA Our Lady of Malibu Retired.
Sheridan, Mark *o.s.b.* '65 (WDC)[M] Washington, DC St. Anselm's Abbey.
Sheridan, Matthew W. '54 (BRK)[V] Douglaston, NY Bishop Mugavero Residence Retired.
Sheridan, Michael J. '75 (PRT) Lubec, ME Sacred Heart; Machias, ME Holy Name of Jesus.
Sheridan, Michael '75 (PRT)[M] Machias, ME University of Maine at Machias; Pastoral Assocs..
Sheridan, Patrick L. '98 (CIN) Bellefontaine, OH St. Patrick's.
Sheridan, Paul G. *s.j.* '75 (STL)[F] St. Louis, MO St. Louis University High School, George H. Backer Memorial; [O] St. Louis, MO St. Louis University High School Jesuit Community.
Sheridan, Paul W. '56 (SFD) Pierron, IL Immaculate Conception; Pierron, IL St. Nicholas.
Sheridan, Paul (SFD) Lay Employees' Pension Plan Administrative Committee.
Sheridan, Peter C. *o.f.m.* '41 (WDC)[B] Silver Spring, MD Holy Name College.
Sheridan, Philip A. '51 (HRT) Retired.
Sheridan, Thomas L. *s.j.* '57 (NEW)[B] Jersey City, NJ Jesuit Center; [N] Jersey City, NJ Jesuits of Saint Peter's College, Inc..
Sheridan, Tom '64 (CHY) Green River, WY Immaculate Conception.
Sheridan, William H. '54 (CHI) Chicago, IL St. Philip Neri Retired.
Sheridan, William J. '72 (CHI) Wilmette, IL St. Francis Xavier.
Sheridan, William P. '89 (NEW) Montclair, NJ Immaculate Conception.
Sheridan, William (NEW) Members.
Sherliza, Michael S. '99 (ATL) McDonough, GA St. James The Apostle.
Sherlock, James C. '64 (PH) Philadelphia, PA Our Lady of Lourdes.
Sherlock, John P. '69 (WCH) Wichita, KS Cathedral of the Immaculate Conception; Sedgwick County Adult

Local Detention Facility; Presbyteral Council/ Diocesan Consultors; Diocesan Synod Office; Presbyteral Council.
Sherlock, R. Marc '79 (CIN) Cincinnati, OH Nativity of Our Lord; Judges.
Sherman, Anthony '70 (BRK) Released from Diocesan Assignment.
Sherman, Daniel J. *m.m.* '47 (NY).
Sherman, Edward (FAR)[EE] Native American Ministries; Grand Forks, ND Retired.
Sherman, Gary D. '85 (TLS)[F] Tulsa, OK St. John Villas, Inc..
Sherman, Gary '85 (TLS)[E] Tulsa, OK St. John Medical Center, Inc..
Sherman, Kenneth '80 (NTN) Rochester, NY St. Nicholas.
Sherman, Richard '00 (SLC) Milford, UT St. Bridget; Park City, UT St. Mary of the Assumption.
Sherman, Thomas P. *s.j.* '87 (LA)[C] Los Angeles, CA Jesuit Community.
Sherman, William C. '55 (FAR) Retired.
Sherrer, Charles D. *c.s.c.* '61 (P)[B] University of Portland; [L] Portland, OR Holy Cross Fathers & Brothers, C.S.C. – University of Portland.
Sherry, Brendan '52 (AMA) Retired.
Sherry, Bryan W. '62 (TUC) Special Assignment.
Sherry, Bryan (TUC) Promoter of Justice.
Sherry, Edward F. '68 (BO) Merrimac, MA Nativity.
Sherry, Frank *c.p.m.* '89 (LEX)[F] Versailles, KY Taylor Manor Nursing Home.
Sherry, Peter Thomas *o.carm.* '38 (BO)[O] Peabody, MA Catholic Information Center; [AA] Peabody, MA St. Theresa Carmelite Chapel.
Sherry, Robert N. '66 (RCK) McHenry, IL Church of Holy Apostles; Cursillo Movement.
Shershanovich, Michael '74 (SPR) Pittsfield, MA Holy Family; Pittsfield, MA Notre Dame; Pittsfield, MA St. Joseph's.
Shershanovich, Michael (SPR) Deans; Priests Committee.
Sherwin, Michael S. *o.p.* '91 (OAK).
Sherwood, Stephen K. *c.m.f.* '71 (SAT)[C] Oblate School of Theology.
Sherwood, Steven *c.m.f.* '71 (SAT) San Antonio, TX Immaculate Heart of Mary.
Sherwood, Tim (SP) Presbyteral Council.
Sherwood, Timothy H. '93 (SP) St. Petersburg, FL St. Joseph; [F] St. Petersburg, FL Immaculate Conception Early Childhood Center.
Sherzer, William J. '46 (DET) Retired.
Sheslo, Charles '61 (SD) Retired.
Shetler, Carl A. '47 (EVN) Retired.
Shetler, John E. '57 (ORG) Irvine, CA St. John Neumann.
Shetler, John '92 (PHX) Prescott Valley, AZ St. Germaine.
Shevlin, John *s.v.d.* '60 (SB)[D] Lakewood, CA Saint Joseph High School.
Shidler, Anthony *o.s.b.* '64 (KC)[J] Conception, MO Conception Abbey.
Shields, David M. *s.j.* '73 (MIL)[X] Milwaukee, WI Casa Romero Renewal Center, Inc.; [O] Milwaukee, WI Miguel Pro Jesuit Community; Milwaukee, WI St. Patrick.
Shields, Hugh Joseph '72 (PH)[V] Boston, MA The Society of St. James the Apostle, Inc.; [AA] Boston, MA St. Stephen; Philadelphia, PA Visitation B.V.M.; On Duty Outside the Archdiocese.
Shields, James J. '63 (PH) North Wales, PA Mary, Mother of the Redeemer.
Shields, James P. '52 (CHI) Waukegan, IL Immaculate Conception B.V.M. Retired.
Shields, Joseph A. '49 (PH) Gladwyne, PA St. John Baptist Vianney Retired.
Shields, Joseph E. '36 (MAN) Retired.
Shields, Maurice L. '57 (MOB)[E] Daphne, AL Mercy Medical Retired.
Shields, Michael '79 (ANC) On Duty Outside Archdiocese.
Shields, Patrick J. '64 (CLV) Elyria, OH St. Mary.
Shields, Robert J. '64 (YAK) Retired.
Shields, Stephen L. '74 (CLV) Sheffield Lake, OH St. Thomas the Apostle.
Shields, W. Bry '84 (MOB) Mobile, AL St. Mary; [B] Mobile, AL McGill–Toolen Catholic High School.
Shields, William J. '52 (CHI) Mundelein, IL Santa Maria Del Popolo Retired.
Shiffer, James *s.s.c.* (LA) Defenders of the Bond.
Shiffer, Jim *s.s.c.* '65 (LA)[Q] Los Angeles, CA Columban Fathers, Procure House.
Shigo, Francis L. *s.v.d.* '60 (LA)[J] San Pedro, CA Little Company of Mary San Pedro Hospital; [J] San Pedro, CA Little Company of Mary San Pedro Peninsula Hospital Pavillion.
Shih, John M. '49 (NEW) Fort Lee, NJ Madonna Retired.
Shikany, Paul M. '79 (IND) Edinburgh, IN Holy Trinity; Franklin, IN St. Rose of Lima; Adjunct Vice Vicars Judicial; [O] Franklin, IN Franklin College.
Shillcox, Timothy D. *o.praem.* '87 (GB)[I] De Pere, WI St. Joseph Priory.
Shillcox, Timothy *o.praem* '87 (CHI)[N] Chicago, IL Premonstratensian Fathers and Brothers (Norbertines).
Shimanek, Joseph '54 (JOL) Retired.
Shimnoski, Gaylord '59 (KAL) Wayland, MI SS. Cyril and Methodius.
Shimotsu, John M. '94 (ORG) Military Chaplains; Navy Chaplains.
Shimsky, James B. '01 (SCR) Wilkes–Barre, PA Holy Rosary; Deans.
Shin, In Yong (ANC) Anchorage, AK St. Anthony; Korean Ministry.
Shin (Wonju), Thomas Woo Sick '02 (ARL) Fairfax, VA St. Paul Chung.
Shindelar, Vincent J. '56 (RCK) Retired.
Shine, Edward J. '57 (CIN) Harrison, OH St. John the Baptist.
Shine, John V '63 (LA)[Q] Santa Barbara, CA St. Mary's Center.
Shine, John *c.m.* '63 (LA)[W] Santa Barbara, CA St. Mary's Seminary Center.
Shine, Robert W. '55 (SAG) Albee, MI St. Mary.
Shine, Sean '52 (ORL) Retired.
Shinney, Robert J. *s.j.* '68 (SJ).
Shinnick, Edward P. '56 (GF) Retired.
Shinos, Robert '63 (ALB)[D] Herkimer, NY St. Anthony–St. Joseph.
Shipe, William '61 (Y) Canton, OH Sacred Heart.
Shipley, William '54 (SD) Retired.
Shipp, Edmund M. '61 (SFR) San Francisco General Hospital.
Shipp, Edmund N. '61 (SFR) San Francisco, CA St. Peter.
Shipps, Frank Bede *o.p.* '85 (BO)[V] Dover, MA St. Stephen Priory.
Shiraki, Gabriel *s.a.* '89 (NY)[EE] Garrison Franciscan Friars of the Atonement, Minister General Office.
Shiramizu, Edson S. '87 (FR) Fall River, MA Cathedral of St. Mary of the Assumption.
Shirey, John W. '43 (CHI) Chicago, IL St. Kilian Retired.
Shirey, Joseph E. *s.j.* '56 (P) White City, OR U.S. Veternan's Affairs Domiciliary; [J] Medford, OR Providence Medford Medical Center.
Shirley, John T. *o.s.a.* '65 (MIL) Racine, WI St. Rita.
Shirley, Richard '67 (CC) Office of the Bishop; College of Consultors; Finance Council; Personnel Board – Priests; Presbyteral Council; Defenders of the Bond; Vicar General; Corpus Christi Catholic Retreat Center, Inc.; Corpus Christi, TX St. Pius X.
Shirley, Ron (MRY) Priestly Life and Ministry Board; Priest's Personnel Board; Presbyteral Council.
Shirley, Ronald '73 (MRY) Marina, CA St. Jude Parish Community.
Shiroda, Donald L. '59 (MAR) Retired.
Shiverski, John J. '68 (MAR) Negaunee, MI St. Paul; Defensore Vinculi; Deans.
Shiverski, John '68 (MAR)[B] Negaunee, MI Negaunee St. Paul Endowment Fund.
Shlesinger, Bernard (Ned) '96 (R) Newton Grove, NC Our Lady of Guadalupe.
Shlesinger, Bernard E. (R) Priests' Council.
Shmaruk, Richard J. '65 (BO) Brighton, MA St. Columbkille.
Shmauz, Donald A. '60 (MIL) On Duty Outside the Archdiocese.
Shnob, Alan D. '78 (OG) Massena, NY St. Mary; Defenders of the Bond.
Shoback, Edward J. '67 (SCR) Scranton, PA SS. Peter and Paul; Deans.
Shoback, Thomas P. '77 (SCR) Pittston, PA Church of the Holy Redeemer; Presbyteral Council.
Shockey, David P. '56 (COV) Walton, KY; [N] Walton, KY Retired.
Shoda, D. Brian '87 (WH) Inwood, WV St. Leo.
Shoda, Richard W. *v.f.* '78 (WH) Ronceverte, WV St. Catherine of Siena.
Shoda, Richard W. (BAL) Interdiocesan Judges.
Shoda, Richard (WH) Vicars Forane.
Shoemaker, David M. (MOB) Eufaula, AL Holy Redeemer; Ventress Correctional Institution; Bullock County Correctional Facility.
Shoemaker, David (MOB) Vocations.
Shoemaker, Samuel E. '66 (PH) Yardley, PA St. Ignatius of Antioch; Archdiocesan Judges.
Shoemaker, Thomas '90 (FTW) Fort Wayne, IN St. Jude; Consultors; Council of Priests.
Shofany, Saba '95 (NTN) Hammond, IN St. Michael the Archangel.
Sholander, Anthony E. *s.j.* '84 (SJ)[M] Los Gatos, CA California Province of the Society of Jesus, Jesuit Provincial Office.
Shonebarger, Thomas '69 (COL) Columbus, OH St. Timothy.
Shonis, Tony '71 (OWN) Owensboro, KY St. Stephen Cathedral.
Shore, Zachary '81 (SFR) San Francisco, CA Visitacion, Church of the.
Shori, Nicholas R. '74 (Y) New Middletown, OH St. Paul the Apostle.
Short, Anthony J. *s.j.* '71 (DEN)[N] Denver, CO Xavier Jesuit Center.
Short, Gregory *o.m.v.* '79 (BO).
Short, John '99 (SFS)[B] Highmore, SD St. Mary.
Short, Redemptus *o.c.d.* '47 (MIL)[O] Holy Hill, WI Discalced Carmelite Monastery – Holy Hill National Shrine of Mary Help of Christians.
Shortall, Maurice *c.s.sp.* '91 (SJ) Los Altos, CA St. Simon.
Shortall, Robert '74 (DAV)[M] Davenport, IA St. Vincent Center.
Shorter, Melvin *c.p.* '86 (MET)[H] South River Passionist Provincial Office.
Shorter, Melvin *c.p.* '86 (ATL) Atlanta, GA St. Paul of the Cross.
Shortt, David J. '89 (PBR) Youngstown, OH St. Nicholas; CIVIL AIR PATROL.
Shortt, Patrick J. '66 (JC) Kirksville, MO Mary Immaculate.
Shott, Stephen E. *o.s.f.s.* '95 (WIL)[B] Wilmington, DE Salesianum School.
Shoup, Steven L. '84 (CIN) Fort Loramie, OH St. Michael's.
Shovelton, Gerald T. '56 (FR) Retired.
Shovelton, Gerald '56 (ORL) Lady Lake, FL St. Timothy Retired.
Shovelton, William J. '46 (FR) Retired.
Showalter, Joseph *s.j.* '75 (SPK)[D] Spokane, WA Gonzaga Preparatory School.
Showalter, Paul E. '66 (PEO) Rock Island, IL St. Pius X; Vicariates and Vicars.
Showalter, Thomas *s.o.l.t.* '97 (CC)[G] Robstown, TX Society of Our Lady of the Most Holy Trinity; Robstown, TX St. John Nepomucene.
Showfety, Joseph '55 (CHL) Retired.
Showry, Banda '81 (CC) Premont, TX St. Theresa of the Infant Jesus.
Shrad, Merlin J. '77 (SC) Sioux City, IA Blessed Sacrament.
Shramko, John '02 (ATL) Roswell, GA St. Peter Chanel.
Shreenan, Timothy J. *o.f.m.* '84 (NY) New York, NY St. Francis of Assisi.
Shreve, Thomas F. '61 (RIC) Richmond, VA Church of the Epiphany; Interdiocesan Judges; Former Delegates; Holy Childhood Association; Propagation of the Faith.
Shreve, Thomas F. (MO) Judges.
Shroeder, Tait C. '02 (MAD) Madison, WI St. Dennis.
Shubiak, Stephen '88 (STF) Special Assignment.
Shubiak, Stephen '88 (NY) U.S.V.A. Medical Center.
Shuda, Paul R. '60 (HBG) Harrisburg, PA Our Lady of the Blessed Sacrament; Legion of Mary.
Shuda, Robert J. '59 (GBG) Greensburg, PA Westmoreland Hospital; [I] Greensburg, PA Benedictine Nuns (Eichstatt, Bavaria); Bishop's Priests Council.
Shugrue, Michael P. (R) Vicar General & Moderator of the Curia; Diocesan Consultors.
Shugrue, Michael '66 (R) Special Assignment.
Shugrue, Michael (R) Priests' Council.
Shugrue, Timothy J. '73 (NEW) Montclair, NJ Immaculate Conception.
Shuhler, Ralph V. *o.s.a.* '39 (PH)[AA] Villanova, PA St. Thomas Monastery.
Shuley, Keith J. (CC) Navy Chaplains.
Shuley, Keith *c.c.* '92 (CC) Military Chaplains.
Shulik, Bernard P. '74 (PIT)[N] Pittsburgh, PA St. John Vianney Manor.
Shultz, John M. '82 (E) Erie, PA Our Lady of Peace.
Shultz, William E. '70 (ALT) Roaring Spring, PA St. Thomas More.
Shumway, Lynn M. '03 (BUF) Tonawanda, NY St. Christopher.
Shuping, Kenneth J. '03 (RIC) Richmond, VA St. Bridget.
Shuppert, William T.J. '71 (TUC) On Duty Outside the Diocese.
Shurer, Ralph C. *o.s.a.* '54 (PH)[AA] Villanova, PA St. Thomas Monastery.
Shurtleff, F. James '66 (OG) Ogdensburg, NY Notre Dame; Diocesan Consultors; Priest Personnel Board.
Shutt, Paul–Alexander *o.s.b.* '98 (GBG)[H] Latrobe, PA Saint Vincent Archabbey.
Shuttleworth, Edward J. '90 (LC) Prescott, WI St. Joseph.
Siani, Angelo *o.m.i.* (FgM).
Sianipar, Godlif *o.carm.* '98 (WDC)[B] Washington, DC Whitefriars Hall.
Sibel, John J. '72 (PH) Philadelphia, PA St. Leo.
Sibenik, Simeon B. '81 (PBR) Munhall, PA St. John the Baptist Cathedral; Consultors; Pro–Synodal Judges.
Sibilano, Joseph D. *o.s.j.* '65 (SCR) Pittston, PA St. Rocco.
Sibley, Bryce '00 (LAF) Parks, LA St. Joseph.
Sica, Joseph F. '82 (SCR) Wilkes–Barre, PA St. Aloysius.
Sicard, Kenneth *o.p.* '90 (PRO)[P] Providence St. Thomas Aquinas Priory at Providence College.
Sicari, Joseph J. '82 (BUF) Catholic Charities; Catholic Charities Appeal; Consultors, College of; Council of Priests; [T] Buffalo, NY Monsignor Kirby Apartments

Housing Development Fund Company, Inc.; [T] Buffalo, NY St. Timothy's Park Villa Housing Development Fund Company, Inc.; [T] Buffalo, NY La Casa Del Tainos Housing Development Fund Company, Inc.; [T] Buffalo, NY 158 Chenango Street Housing Development Fund Company, Inc., dba St. John Bosco Apartments; [T] Buffalo, NY 50–60 Kosciuzko Street Housing Development Fund Company, Inc.; [T] Buffalo, NY Wheatfield Housing Development Fund Company, Inc.; [T] Buffalo, NY St. Clare Apartments Housing Development Fund; [T] Buffalo, NY Good Counsel Apartments; [T] Buffalo, NY Santa Maria Towers; [T] Buffalo, NY Timon Towers Housing Development Fund Company, Inc.; [H] Buffalo, NY Central Office; [H] Buffalo, NY Catholic Charities Program Services; [H] Buffalo, NY Mount St. Mary's Housing Development Fund Company, Inc.; [H] Buffalo, NY Catholic Charities Appeal; [H] Buffalo, NY Ladies of Charity; Snyder, NY Christ the King.

Sichko, James '98 (LEX) Lexington, KY St. Peter Claver; Special Assignment.

Sicilia, Pablo '60 (SAT) Dilley, TX St. Joseph's.

Sicilia, Pablo (SAT) Priests Personnel Board.

Siciliano, Donald E. '93 (JC) Canton, MO St. Joseph; Ewing, MO Queen of Peace.

Siciliano, Jude *o.p.* '69 (OAK)[N] Berkeley, CA Order of Preachers (Southern Province).

Siciliano, Jude *o.p.* '69 (R)[E] Raleigh, NC Dominican Priory.

Siciliano, Ronald *o.f.m.* (BO) Boston, MA St. Leonard of Port Maurice.

Sickler, Robert *m.s.a.* '87 (NOR)[F] Cromwell, CT Society of the Missionaries of the Holy Apostles; Air Force Reserve Chaplains.

Sickler, Thomas G. *m.s.* '73 (WOR) Fitchburg, MA St. Joseph's.

Sicoli, David C. '75 (PH) Philadelphia, PA Holy Spirit.

Siconolfi, Constantine V. '59 (SCR) Scranton, PA Holy Family; [R] Scranton, PA St. Francis of Assisi Kitchen; D.C.C.W..

Siconolfi, Michael T. *s.j.* '72 (SY)[Q] Syracuse, NY Jesuits at LeMoyne, Inc..

Siconolfi, Thomas J. *c.ss.r.* '70 (RVC) Bethpage, NY St. Martin of Tours.

Sidler, Fred '92 (DAL) Dallas, TX St. Elizabeth.

Sidler, Gordon L. (ATL) Released from Archdiocesan Assignment.

Sidney, Walter T. *s.j.* '78 (DEN)[D] Aurora, CO Regis Jesuit High School; [N] Centennial, CO Regis High Jesuit Community.

Sidoti, Anthony '40 (ALB) Albany, NY St. James.

Sidoti, James *o.carm.* '92 (NY) Middletown, NY Our Lady of Mt. Carmel; [EE] Middletown, NY The National Shrine of Our Lady of Mount Carmel; [GG] Middletown, NY National Shrine of Our Lady of Mount Carmel.

Siebenaler, John M. '61 (STP) Retired.

Siebenaler, Leonard (STP) Retired.

Siebenaler, Martin '59 (STP) Retired.

Siebenand, Ambrose F. '41 (NU) Retired.

Siebenand, John N. '38 (NU) Retired.

Siebenand, Paul Alcuin '60 (LA) Avalon, CA St. Catherine of Alexandria.

Sieber, Patrick *o.f.m.* '71 (CAM) Camden, NJ St. Anthony of Padua.

Siebert, Anthony G. '59 (STL) On Duty Outside the Archdiocese.

Siebert, Edward J. *s.j.* '97 (DET)[K] Temperance, MI.

Siebert, Edward J. *s.j.* '97 (LA)[C] Los Angeles, CA Jesuit Community.

Siebert, Paul S. '86 (E) Emporium, PA St. Mark.

Siebert, Stephen (DEN) Denver, CO Holy Family; Longmont, CO St. John the Baptist.

Siebert, William P. '79 (DET) Roseville, MI St. Athanasius.

Siebold, Gerard *c.ss.r.* '58 (BLX)[E] Biloxi, MS St. John Neumann Residence.

Siebor, John '58 (RVC) Hempstead, NY St. Ladislaus.

Siecinski, A. Edward '95 (TR) Leave of Absence.

Sieczynski, Jerzy F. (SAT) San Antonio, TX St. Matthew's.

Siedlecki, Edmund J. '52 (CHI)[T] Mundelein, IL Cardinal Stritch Retreat House; Cardinal Stritch Retreat House Retired.

Siefer, Richard R. '75 (E) Du Bois, PA St. Catherine; Du Bois, PA St. Joseph; Clergy Continuing Education and Formation.

Siefert, John S. (STL) Affton, MO St. Dominic Savio.

Siefert, Ralph A. *s.m.* '73 (STL)[F] Creve Coeur, MO Chaminade College Preparatory School Inc.; [G] Creve Coeur, MO Chaminade College Preparatory.

Siefert, Ralph *s.m.* '73 (STL)[O] St. Louis, MO Chaminade–Waldron Marianist Community.

Sieg, Leslie M. '76 (P) Tigard, OR St. Anthony.

Sieg, Leslie (P) Building Commission.

Sieg, Robert C. *o.f.m.* '75 (STL) St. Louis, MO St. Anthony of Padua.

Sieg, Robert *o.f.m.* '75 (STL)[O] St. Louis, MO Franciscan Friary of St. Anthony of Padua.

Sieg, Thomas H. '71 (STP) Edina, MN St. Patrick.

Siegel, Evon (OKL)[F] Oklahoma City, OK Bone and Joint Hospital.

Siegel, Joseph '88 (JOL) Joliet, IL The Cathedral of St. Raymond Deans.

Siegel, Kenan *o.f.m.cap.* '56 (MIL)[O] Mount Calvary, WI St. Lawrence Friary.

Siekaniec, Ladislas '40 (STL)[O] St. Louis, MO Franciscan Friary of St. Anthony of Padua Retired.

Siekierski, John J. '67 (GRY) East Chicago, IN St. Stanislaus.

Sielicki, Thomas *s.ch.* '80 (DET) Hamtramck, MI St. Florian.

Sielski, Joseph *m.i.c.* '41 (WDC)[M] Brookeville, MD Marian Monastery–Brookeville.

Siemianowski, John S. '89 (CHI) Chicago Heights, IL St. Agnes; Chicago Heights, IL St. Paul.

Siener, Leo C. '48 (KNX) Retired.

Sienkiewicz, Matthew '59 (FTW) Retired.

Siepka, Richard W. '82 (BUF) Co–Directors.

Siepker, Daniel E. '93 (DM)[A] Corning, IA St. Patrick's; [D] Corning, IA Mercy Midlands: Mercy Hospital.

Siepker, Daniel (DM) Diocesan Consultors.

Sieradski, Alfred *c.ss.r.* '49 (ORL)[E] New Smyrna Beach, FL St. Alphonsus Villa–Redemptorist Fathers and Brothers.

Sierminski Vernon '56 (SAG) Retired.

Sierotowicz, Felicjan '90 (ROC) Auburn, NY Sacred Heart; Auburn, NY St. Alphonsus; Mercy Health and Rehabilitation Center.

Sierra, Angel '80 (SFD) Assumption, IL Assumption B.V.M.; Assumption, IL St. Frances de Sales; Comite Diocesano de Ministerio Hispano – Diocesan Committee for Hispanic Ministry.

Sierra, Francis A. '46 (SD) Retired.

Sierra, John A. *s.f.* '40 (WDC)[B] Silver Spring, MD Holy Family Seminary.

Sierra, Robinson *s.a.* '95 (RVC) Brooklyn, NY Our Lady of Solace.

Sierra–Posada, Pedro J. '76 (ALX) Hispanic Apostolate; Alexandria, LA St. Francis Xavier Cathedral; Glenmora, LA St. Louis.

Sievel, Thomas A. '78 (HRT) Manchester, CT St. Bartholomew's.

Siewert, Charles F. '99 (WCH) On Duty Outside the Diocese; Alexandria, VA Queen of Apostles.

Siewiera, Bogdan '98 (SY) New Hartford, NY St. John the Evangelist.

Siffert, Etienne *s.m.* '58 (SFR) San Francisco, CA Notre Dame des Victoires.

Siffrin, Robert J. (Y) Vicar General and Moderator of the Curia.

Siffrin, Robert '79 (Y) Youngstown, OH St. Brendan; College of Consultors.

Sigaran, Mamerto '60 (SFR) San Francisco, CA St. Paul.

Sigler, Gary L. '79 (FTW) Huntington, IN St. Mary.

Sigler, Gary (FTW) Pro–Synodal Judges.

Sigler, John W. '94 (LA) Los Angeles, CA St. Bernard; Hospital Chaplains.

Sigman, Louis A. '67 (PHX) Retired.

Sigmund, Andrew J. '64 (STL) Imperial, MO St. Joseph.

Signey, Lawrence '87 (LA) Burbank, CA St. Robert Bellarmine.

Signiski, Michael M. '66 (CAM) Bridgeton, NJ St. Teresa of Avila.

Signorelli, Francis *s.x.* '59 (BO)[V] Holliston, MA Xaverian Missionaries; [AA] Holliston, MA Our Lady of Fatima Shrine.

Siguere, Robert *o.f.m.* '73 (FgM).

Sihuay, Francis X. *o.f.m.* '51 (WDC)[M] Washington, DC Commissariat of the Holy Land, Franciscan Monastery – Mount St. Sepulchre.

Sikandar, Anthony '90 (BRK)[U] Pakistan Apostolate.

Siklodi, Sandor '71 (CLV) Cleveland, OH St. Emeric.

Sikon, Michael P. '96 (GBG) Yatesboro, PA Sacred Heart.

Sikon, Michael '96 (GBG) Yatesboro, PA St. Mary.

Sikora, Eric L. '81 (BUF) Orchard Park, NY Nativity of Our Lord.

Sikora, James R. '67 (GF)[A] Great Falls, MT University of Great Falls; [A] University of Great Falls.

Sikora, James (GF) Clerical Benefit Association.

Sikora, Stanley J. '57 (HRT)[A] Bloomfield, CT St. Thomas Seminary Retired.

Sikora, Thomas More *o.s.b.* '97 (GBG)[H] Latrobe, PA Saint Vincent Archabbey.

Sikorski, Harold R. '56 (SAG) Retired.

Sikorski, Jeffery P. '73 (TOL) Huron, OH St. Peter.

Sikorski, Louis S. '64 (GAL) Anderson, TX St. Stanislaus.

Silagan, Gorgonio '01 (SEA) Lacey, WA Sacred Heart of Jesus Special Assignment.

Silayo, Constance L. '82 (RIC) Roanoke, VA St. Gerard.

Silayo, Constantine L. '66 (RIC).

Silcox, John D. '95 (PH) Upper Darby, PA St. Laurence.

Sileo, Joseph R. '71 (WDC) Washington, DC St. Peter; Pastoral Center Special Ministries; Director of School Personnel.

Sileo, Joseph (WDC) Director of Professional Development. Director of Student Services.

Siler, Paschal *o.f.m.cap.* '60 (GF) Ashland, MT St. Labre's.

Siler, Robert M. '01 (YAK) Ellensburg, WA St. Andrew's; Clergy Personnel Board.

Siliako, Petelo '86 (SPP) Pago Pago, AS Christ the King; Diocesan Consultors.

Silio, Antonio R. '88 (MIA) Pembroke Pines, FL St. Boniface.

Silipigni, Stephan A. '81 (PRO) Absent on Leave.

Silk, John D. '59 (BO) Amesbury, MA Holy Family; Senior Priests Retired.

Silko, Herbert *o.f.m.* '55 (MIL)[O] Burlington, WI Queen of Peace Friary.

Sill, Theodore K. '89 (COL) London, OH St. Patrick; Diocesan Judges.

Silva, Caesar '74 (HT) Houma, LA Maria Immacolata; Air National Guard Chaplains.

Silva, David E. '54 (CLV) Retired.

Silva, Edwin Lugo '89 (MGZ) Mayaguez, PR Nuestra Senora De Fatima.

Silva, Eusebio F. '66 (MAN) North Conway, NH Our Lady of the Mountains.

Silva, Francis J. *s.j.* '42 (SJ)[M] Los Gatos, CA Sacred Heart Jesuit Center.

Silva, Frank J. (BO) Wayland, MA St. Ann.

Silva, George '97 (SFE) Raton, NM St. Patrick/St. Joseph.

Silva, Hilary '89 (FRS) Hilmar, CA Holy Rosary.

Silva, Ismael '79 (ORG) Orange, CA La Purisima.

Silva, Jorge de *s.m.* '72 (STL)[O] Los Gatos, CA.

Silva, Jose D. '51 (HRT) Hartford, CT Our Lady of Fatima.

Silva, Juan '92 (LA) Pomona, CA Sacred Heart.

Silva, Langes J. '95 (SLC) Salt Lake City, UT Cathedral of the Madeleine; Vice Chancellor; Ecumenical Commission; Priests' Personnel Board; Judicial Vicar; Judges.

Silva, Larry '75 (OAK) Fremont, CA Our Lady of Guadalupe; Moderator of the Curia/Vicar General; Consultors; Region 5; Deans; Presbyteral Council.

Silva, Luis '98 (CR) Army Reserve Chaplains; On Duty Outside the Diocese.

Silva, Miguel '84 (SAC) Corning, CA Immaculate Conception.

Silva, Raul *m.s.c.* '79 (LA) Los Angeles, CA San Miguel.

Silva, Robert J. '65 (STO) On Duty Outside the Diocese.

Silva, Spatz '99 (HON) Honolulu, HI Our Lady of the Mount.

Silva Bisbal, Pedro *o.f.m.cap.* '75 (SJN) San Juan, PR San Antonio.

Silvagnoli, Winston Reinaldo Mendez '03 (PCE) Arroyo, PR Our Lady of Mt. Carmel.

Silveira, Eduino '87 (SAC) Sacramento, CA St. Elizabeth; Special Assignment.

Silver, E. John '92 (OG) Cape Vincent, NY St. Vincent de Paul.

Silver, Jeffrey P. '84 (CIN) Hamilton, OH St. Julie Billiart.

Silver, John E. '93 (OG) Retired.

Silveri, Donato P. '64 (PH) Spring City, PA St. Joseph; Spring City, PA Southeastern Pennsylvania Veterans Center.

Silverio, Gilbert J. *o.f.m.* '59 (FR) Buzzards Bay, MA St. Margaret; [H] Onset, MA St. Joseph Friary–Franciscan Friars.

Silverman, Robert '67 (SAT) San Antonio, TX St. John Neumann.

Silverman, Robert '67 (SAT)[U] San Antonio, TX The Blue Army.

Silvester, Peter *s.v.d.* '78 (CHI)[B] Techny, IL Divine Word Residence.

Silvestrini, Dino F. '85 (MAR) Crystal Falls, MI Guardian Angels.

Silvia, Kenneth J. *c.s.c.* '63 (FR) South Easton, MA Holy Cross.

Sima, John R. *s.j.* '71 (CHI).

Simanavicius, Agustinas *o.f.m.* (LIT)[N] Lithuanian R. Catholic Priests' League of Canada.

Simas, Manuel C. '61 (OAK) Mission San Jose, CA St. Joseph Mission Church.

Simboli, Ronald L. '75 (GBG) Belle Vernon, PA St. Anne.

Simburger, Joseph '79 (SFD) On Duty Outside the Diocese.

Simburger, Joseph '79 (MAN)[B] Warner, NH Magdalen College.

Simcox, Thomas '40 (MIL)[M] Wauwatosa, WI St. Camillus Health Center, Inc..

Simeon, Jeannot Jean '68 (VEN) Wauchula, FL St. Michael.

Simeon, Jeannot Jean Francois (VEN) Ministry to Haitian People in Glades, Hardee, Highlands & DeSoto Counties.

Simeone, Francis '61 (FRS) Retired.

Simeone, Gary F. '75 (HRT) East Haven, CT St. Vincent de Paul's.

Simeone, Ronald P. '82 (PRO) Woonsocket, RI St. Anthony; Judges.

Simien, Gregory M. '99 (LAF) Cecilia, LA St. Rose of Lima.

Simington, Ralph P. '62 (DUB) Manchester, IA St.

Mary; [E] Manchester, IA St. Paul's School of Religion; Ryan, IA St. Patrick; Greeley, IA St. Joseph; College of Consultors; Deans; Directors.
Simko, James '91 (DEN) Absent on Leave.
Simlik, Frank P. '54 (PHX) Retired.
Simmons, Franklin E. '79 (GAL)[K] Catholic Chaplain Corps, Texas Medical Center.
Simmons, Franklin '79 (GAL) Houston, TX St. Ambrose; [K] Chaplain Corps.
Simmons, Hilary F. '43 (LC) Retired.
Simmons, Jerome S. '68 (E) Erie, PA Sacred Heart; [O] Erie, PA Ecclesia Center/Renewal Center.
Simmons, Joseph C. '61 (BAL) Joppa, MD Church of the Holy Spirit.
Simmons, Matthew P. '03 (JKS) Continuing Formation Committee; Meridian, MS St. Patrick; Meridian, MS St. Patrick.
Simmons, Walter E. '55 (RVC) Port Washington, NY St. Peter of Alcantara Retired.
Simmons, William *c.s.c.* '52 (FTW)[B] University of Notre Dame Du Lac; [I] Notre Dame, IN Holy Cross Community, Corby Hall, University of Notre Dame.
Simms, Robert A. *s.j.* '46 (STL)[N] St. Louis, MO Fusz Pavilion; [O] St. Louis, MO Jesuit Community Corporation at St. Louis University – Jesuit Hall.
Simms, William '62 (BAL) Retired.
Simo, Philip *o.s.b.* '97 (WDC)[M] Washington, DC St. Anselm's Abbey.
Simon, Akan S. '98 (RCK) Geneva, IL St. Peter.
Simon, Ambrose *o.f.m.cap.* '50 (GB)[I] Appleton, WI St. Fidelis Friary.
Simon, Brian '96 (SFS) Mobridge, SD St. Joseph.
Simon, Carl A. '71 (LAN) Brooklyn, MI St. Joseph's Shrine.
Simon, Carl '71 (LAN) Gus Harrison Regional Facility.
Simon, George Howard '57 (LAF) Retired.
Simon, John '73 (MIL) North Fond du Lac, WI Presentation of the Blessed Virgin; Eldorado, WI Our Risen Savior.
Simon, Joseph D. *s.v.d.* '02 (BLX)[E] Bay St. Louis, MS Southern Province of St. Augustine – Provincial Residence.
Simon, Joseph M. '71 (STL) Webster Groves, MO Holy Redeemer.
Simon, Joseph *s.v.d.* (LAF) Advocates.
Simon, Raphael *o.c.s.o.* '47 (WOR)[O] Spencer, MA St. Joseph's Abbey.
Simon, Richard T. '75 (CHI) Chicago, IL St. Thomas of Canterbury.
Simon, Robert C. *c.ss.r.* '48 (STL)[O] Liguori, MO St. Clement Health Care Center.
Simon, Robert G. *c.s.c.* '61 (FTW)[I] Congregacion de Santa Cruz.
Simon, Robert J. '90 (SCR) Susquehanna, PA St. John the Evangelist.
Simon, Thomas *m.ss.a* '79 (HRT) Waterbury, CT Immaculate Conception.
Simon, Thomas *m.s.a.* '79 (NOR)[F] Cromwell Society of the Missionaries of the Holy Apostles.
Simon, Vincent J. '46 (DUB) Retired.
Simonar, Mathew J. (GB) Egg Harbor, WI St. Mary of the Lake; Egg Harbor, WI St. John the Baptist; Egg Harbor, WI St. Paul; Egg Harbor, WI St. Michael; Egg Harbor, WI St. Rosalia.
Simonds, Donald D. *m.s.* '63 (HRT)[M] Hartford, CT Missionaries of LaSalette.
Simonds, Tom *s.j.* '99 (RC) Pine Ridge, SD Holy Rosary; [B] Pine Ridge, SD Jesuit Community of Holy Rosary Mission.
Simone, Earl Francis '77 (CIN) Dayton, OH St. Peter.
Simone, Michael A. *m.m.* '56 (NY)[EE] Maryknoll Maryknoll Fathers and Brothers.
Simone, Michael M. '03 (WCH) Wichita, KS St. Thomas Aquinas.
Simoneau, Norman J. '67 (MAN) Hudson, NH St. John the Evangelist Retired.
Simoneau, Roland L. '78 (PRO) Harrisville, RI St. Theresa of the Child Jesus.
Simoneaux, Jody '82 (LAF) Lafayette, LA St. Genevieve; Continuing Formation of the Clergy.
Simonelli, Bruno *o.f.m.cap.* (MO) AUXILIARY CHAPLAINS CONTRACT CHAPLAINS.
Simonelli, Gerald '90 (JOL) Romeoville, IL St. Andrew the Apostle.
Simonetti, Albino *s.d.b.* '68 (MIA) Miami, FL St. Kieran.
Simonin, John A. '47 (CHR) Parish Priest Consultors Retired.
Simonini, Michael F. '75 (RCK) Active Outside the Diocese.
Simonini, Michael '75 (GB) Appleton, WI St. Bernard.
Simonnet, Philippe *s.s.e.* '52 (BUR)[E] Colchester, VT Society of St. Edmund.
Simonnet, Philippe *s.s.e.* '52 (FgM).
Simons, Derek *s.v.d.* '70 (CHI)[N] Chicago, IL Divine Word Theologate; [N] Chicago, IL House of Religious Men: Divine Word Theologate; [B] Chicago, IL Angels Studio.
Simons, James L. (CIN) Loveland, OH St. Margaret of York.
Simons, Lawrence D. '48 (HEL) Retired.
Simons, Thomas G. '77 (GR) Muskegon, MI St. Francis de Sales.
Simonson, Earl C. '69 (STP) Minneapolis, MN St. Clement.
Simpson, Brian L. '72 (CHI) Military Chaplains; Navy Chaplains.
Simpson, David *o.carm.* '70 (JOL)[L] Darien Carmelite Provincial Office.
Simpson, Kenneth C. '78 (CHI)[V] Evanston, IL Northwestern University/Kendall College, Sheil Center.
Simpson, Mark '79 (CHI) Winnetka, IL Sacred Heart; Judges.
Simpson, Mauro *o.s.b.* '52 (CGS)[C] Humacao, PR San Antonio Abad Abbey of the Order of St. Benedict.
Simpson, Robert A. '65 (RNO) Reno, NV St. Albert the Great.
Simpson, Robert (RNO) Seminary Board.
Simpson, Roger '52 (SFD) Retired.
Sims, Paul *c.r.* '86 (CHI)[D] Waukegan, IL St. Martin de Porres High School.
Sims, Robert W. '71 (IND) Indianapolis, IN St. Simon the Apostle.
Simutowe, Patrick *s.s.* '96 (BAL)[S] Baltimore Sulpician Provincial House.
Sinasac, Alvin A. *c.s.b.* (GAL)[B] Houston, TX Casa San Basilio.
Sinatra, Leonard '67 (PHU) Pottstown, PA St. Michael's.
Sinatra, William D. '64 (DET) Southfield, MI St. Ives; Archdiocesan Vicars.
Sinclair, Alexander B. '57 (KC) Kansas City, MO St. Raphael the Archangel.
Sinclair, Roger A. (BO) Jamaica Plain, MA Jamaica Plain; Jamaica Plain, MA Veterans Administration Hospital.
Sindik, George '59 (PT) Pensacola, FL Cathedral of the Sacred Heart.
Sindik, Matthew '62 (MOB) Mount Vernon, AL St. Cecilia.
Singarayar, Philip *o.m.i.* '64 (CHI)[N] Chicago, IL The Oblate House of Theology.
Singarayer, Lawrence Maria '66 (NY) New Rochelle, NY Blessed Sacrament.
Singelyn, Robert K. '60 (DET) On Duty Outside the Archdiocese.
Singer, Christopher J. '03 (E) Erie, PA St. George.
Singer, Jerome C. '63 (DET) Detroit, MI Nativity of Our Lord; Archdiocesan Vicars.
Singer, Thomas *o.m.i.* '57 (SAT)[M] San Antonio, TX Missionary Oblates of Mary Immaculate; [M] San Antonio, TX.
Singer, Thomas *o.m.i.* '57 (WDC)[M] Washington, DC Provincial Offices of the United States Province of the Missionary Oblates of Mary Immaculate.
Singer, Thomas *o.m.i.* '57 (CHI)[X] Chicago, IL Oblates for International Pastoral aka Oblate International Pastoral Investment Trust.
Singler, Charles '84 (TOL) Toledo, OH Queen of the Most Holy Rosary Cathedral.
Singler, James E. '82 (CLV) Cleveland Heights, OH St. Ann.
Singler, John P. '82 (CLV) Twinsburg, OH SS. Cosmas and Damian.
Singleton, Jeremiah '65 (MIA) Fort Lauderdale, FL St. Anthony.
Singleton, William V. '50 (RVC) East Rockaway, NY St. Raymond's Retired.
Sinibaldi, Daniel J. '96 (MAN) Woodsville, NH St. Catherine of Siena; Woodsville, NH St. Joseph; Grafton County House of Corrections.
Sinisi, Daniel *t.o.r.* '66 (ALT)[A] Loretto, PA St. Francis University; [F] Loretto, PA Mount Assisi Friary; [H] Loretto, PA St. Francis College (Loretto).
Siniskey, Joseph M. '48 (ALB) East Greenbush, NY Holy Spirit Retired.
Sinkler, Michael '81 (LR) Bentonville, AR St. Stephen; [E] Rogers, AR St. Mary–Rogers Memorial Hospital.
Sinnappa, Selveraj '97 (TYL) Hallsville, TX Our Lady of Grace.
Sinnema, Paul *o.f.m.* '63 (NEW) Wood Ridge, NJ Our Lady of the Assumption.
Sinnerud, James A. *s.j.* '72 (OM)[C] Omaha, NE Creighton Preparatory School.
Sinnott, Andrew R. '99 (SCR) Wilkes–Barre, PA St. Boniface.
Sinnott, Thomas G. (SCR) Scranton, PA St. Peter's Cathedral; Presbyteral Council; Vocations.
Sinor, Michael '88 (SD) El Centro, CA St. Mary.
Sinski, Norbert J. *c.s.c.* '77 (FTW)[I] New York, NY.
Sinz, Eugene R. '60 (STL) High Ridge, MO St. Anthony of Padua.
Siok, Slawomir *s.a.c.* '90 (BRK) Brooklyn, NY St. Frances de Chantal.
Siola, Roman *o.f.m.conv.* '56 (BUF)[O] Athol Springs, NY St. Francis of Assisi Friary.
Sioleti, Andrew *o.f.m.* (NY) Manhattan, NY Cabrini Medical Center; Manhattan, NY U.S.V.A. Medical Center.
Sioleti, Andrew *i.v.dei.* (MO).
Sioleti, Andrew *o.f.m.* (NY) Manhattan, NY Cabrini Medical Center; Manhattan, NY U.S.V.A. Medical Center.
Sioleti, Andrew *i.v.dei.* (MO).
Sioli, Joseph E. *c.o.* '97 (PIT)[N] Pittsburgh, PA Congregation of the Oratory of St. Philip Neri; [Q] Pittsburgh, PA Carnegie–Mellon University; [Q] Pittsburgh, PA Chatham College; [Q] Pittsburgh, PA University of Pittsburgh.
Sipaco, Cecilio E. '67 (MET)[F] New Brunswick, NJ Saint Peter's University Hospital.
Sipe, Robert J. '59 (STP) Forest Lake, MN St. Peter.
Sipitkowski, James A. '74 (SPR) Easthampton, MA Sacred Heart.
Siple, Donald M. *o.s.m.* '92 (CHI) Chicago, IL Our Lady of Sorrows, Basilica of; [N] Chicago, IL Monastery of Our Lady of Sorrows.
Siple, William P. '92 (PIT) Pittsburgh, PA St. Teresa of Avila.
Sippel, Bernard S. '65 (MIL) Germantown, WI St. Boniface; Judges for Second Instance.
Sippel, Edward F. '47 (MIL) Retired.
Sipperly, Edward (ALB) Retired.
Sipulski, Vianney C. *o.f.m.* '60 (GAY) Hillman, MI Jesus the Good Shepherd; Hillman, MI St. Augustine.
Sipulski, Vianney *o.f.m.* (GAY) Elected Members.
Siracuse, Guy F. '67 (BUF) Retired.
Siranni, Anthony M. '89 (MET) Port Murray, NJ St. Theodore.
Sirba, Joseph '87 (DUL) Cloquet, MN Holy Family; Cloquet, MN Queen of Peace; [G] Cloquet, MN Queen of Peace Cloquet Educational Endowment Trust.
Sirba, Paul D. '86 (STP) St. Paul, MN Maternity of the Blessed Virgin.
Sirianni, Jasper F. '46 (DET) Emmett, MI Our Lady of Mount Carmel Retired.
Sirianni, Klaus J. '78 (WDC) Bethesda, MD St. Jane Frances de Chantal.
Sirianni, Louis A. '74 (ROC) Rochester, NY St. Anne; Judicial Vicar; Judicial Vicar; Judges.
Sirianni, Louis '74 (ROC) Rochester, NY Guardian Angels.
Sirianni, Richard D. '78 (P) Gresham, OR St. Henry; Air National Guard Chaplains.
Sirianni, Richard (P) Area Vicars; Ecumenical and Interreligious Affairs.
Sirianni, Sam A. '84 (TR) Trenton, NJ Holy Angels; Department of Worship.
Sirico, Robert '89 (KAL)[E] Kalamazoo, MI St. Philip Neri House.
Sirl, William (LAN) Permanent Diaconate.
Sirois, Gerald *s.d.s.* '61 (MIL)[O] Greendale, WI Salvatorian Community.
Sirois, Joseph V. '51 (WOR) Worcester, MA Holy Name of Jesus.
Siroki, David '93 (PSC) Leave of Absence.
Sirolli, Francis A. *o.s.a.* '65 (NY) Staten Island, NY Our Lady of Good Counsel.
Siroskey, P. Larry '80 (DET) Wyandotte, MI St. Helena; Archdiocesan Vicars.
Sirvent, Francisco '88 (PCE) On Duty Outside the Diocese.
Siry, Philip L. '62 (WIL) Delaware City, DE St. Paul; Governor Bacon Health Center.
Sis, Michael J. '86 (AUS) College Station, TX St. Mary's; [L] College Station, TX St. Mary's Catholic Center.
Sisco, Michael A. '97 (PRO) Woonsocket, RI St. Agatha; Woonsocket, RI Precious Blood.
Sisk, Robert *t.o.r.* '61 (BAL) Baltimore, MD St. Elizabeth of Hungary.
Siska, Ernest J. '60 (TR)[M] Trenton, NJ St. Lawrence Rehabilitation Center Retired.
Sison, Alden J. '87 (LA) Canoga Park, CA Our Lady of the Valley.
Sison, Bernabe '65 (NY) New York, NY Our Lady of Pompeii.
Sison, Ronnie '03 (VEN) Unassigned.
Sistare, John A. (PRO) Pawtucket, RI St. Leo the Great.
Sistare, Juniper Mary *c.f.r.* '03 (NY)[EE] Yonkers, NY St. Leopold's Friary; [EE] Bronx, NY Our Lady of the Angels Friary.
Sisul, Paul *c.m.* '72 (CHI)[N] Chicago, IL DePaul Vincentian Residence.
Sitar, Richard T. '79 (GAY) Retired.
Sitko, Joseph S. '68 (SCR) Clifford, PA St. Pius X.
Sitter, Leonard F. *s.j.* '61 (SPK)[B] Spokane, WA Gonzaga University.
Sittinger, Eduardo *s.t.* '77 (SJN) Loiza, PR Santiago Apostol, El Mayor.
Sitzmann, Eugene E. '62 (SC) Cherokee, IA St. Dymphna Chapel; Cherokee, IA Visitation of the B.V.M.; State Mental Health Institute.
Sitzmann, Richard A. '62 (SC) Sioux City, IA St. Boniface; Mercy Medical Center; [C] Sioux City, IA Mercy Medical Center – Sioux City.
Siu, Peter Kin Chung *s.j.* '93 (California)[N] Berkeley, CA Jesuit Community at Jesuit School of Theology at Berkeley.
Siu, Peter *s.j.* (OAK).

Siu, Robert K.C. '54 (CHY)[A] In Residence.
Siu, Robert K.C. '54 (HON) Lander, WY Holy Rosary.
Sivalon, John C. *m.m.* '65 (NY)[EE] Maryknoll Maryknoll Fathers and Brothers.
Sivalon, John C. *m.m.* '65 (FgM).
Sivendire, Omer Mbusa *a.a.* '96 (WOR)[O] Worcester, MA Assumptionists of Assumption College.
Sivillo, Nicholas W. '64 (BRK) Middle Village, NY Our Lady of Hope.
Sivinskij, Vasyl (PHU) Archdiocesan Radio Programs.
Siwek, Daniel S. '73 (CHI).
Siwek, Jerome S. '56 (CHI) Retired.
Sizemore, David W. '96 (COL)[A] Delaware, OH St. Mary; Priests' Senate.
Sizing, Theodore C. '55 (SY) Syracuse, NY St. Vincent de Paul Retired.
Skach, Charles J. '51 (CHI) Mt. Prospect, IL St. Raymond de Penafort Retired.
Skaff, Euthimios *b.s.o.* (NTN) Liturgical Consultants.
Skagen, Robert '70 (PHX) Glendale, AZ St. Helen; College of Consultors.
Skaj, John P. *c.s.sp.* '63 (PIT) Pittsburgh, PA Sacred Heart.
Skala, John J. '97 (ROM) Canton, OH St. George Cathedral Retired.
Skalski, Francis S. '56 (DET) Detroit, MI St. Hyacinth.
Skalsky, Ted A. '72 (DOD) Dodge City, KS The Cathedral of Our Lady of Guadalupe; Presbyteral Council; College of Consultors; Deans; Advocates; Catholic Social Service Offices; Diocesan Pastoral Council; Diaconate Office.
Skalsky, Ted (DOD) Commission for Ministry to Priests.
Skarbek, Richard *m.s.a.* '86 (NOR)[F] Cromwell, CT Society of the Missionaries of the Holy Apostles.
Skarich, William '99 (DUL) Brainerd, MN St. Andrew's; Brainerd, MN St. Francis; Fort Ripley, MN St. Mathias.
Skeabeck, Andrew *c.ss.r.* '47 (TR)[L] Saratoga Springs, NY St. John Neumann Residence; [Q] Long Branch, NJ San Alfonso Retreat House.
Skechus, Francis E. *s.j.* '75 (PH)[G] Philadelphia, PA St. Joseph's Preparatory School; [AA] Loyola Center and Manresa Hall.
Skeehan, William K. '60 (TLS) Bartlesville, OK The Community of St. James.
Skehan, James W. *s.j.* '54 (BO)[V] Newton, MA The Jesuit Community at Boston College.
Skehan, John A. '52 (PMB) Delray Beach, FL St. Vincent Ferrer Retired.
Skehan, John R. (PRT) Special or Other Diocesan Assignment; Diocesan Consultors; Ex Officio; College of Consultors; Diocesan Director of Pastoral and Educational Services; Personnel Board.
Skehan, Martin O. '44 (YAK) Moses Lake, WA Our Lady of Fatima Retired.
Skeldon, John Robert '00 (FWT) Mansfield, TX St. Jude.
Skelly, Francis G. *c.ss.r.* '72 (NY) New York, NY St. Cecilia.
Skelly, John J. '53 (RVC) Manhasset, NY St. Mary's Retired.
Skelly, Richard J. '54 (PH) Building Committee; Aston, PA St. Joseph Retired.
Skelton, Paul H. '64 (SFD) Villa Grove, IL St. Michael; Villa Grove, IL Sacred Heart.
Skelton, Paul (SFD) Priests' Personnel Board.
Skenderovic, Ivan '76 (BUF) Genesee Memorial Hospital; Elba, NY Our Lady of Fatima.
Skeris, Robert A. '61 (MIL) Retired.
Skerl, Alphonse '55 (GRY) East Chicago, IN Holy Trinity.
Skerry, Donald *s.v.d.* '62 (BO)[V] Boston, MA Divine Word Missionaries.
Skertich, Mark J. '77 (PIT) California, PA St. Thomas Aquinas; [Q] California, PA California University (California).
Skiba, Walter F. '56 (SCR) Wyoming, PA St. Joseph's.
Skillin, Harmon D. '60 (STO) Stockton, CA St. Luke Church of Stockton (Pastor of).
Skillin, Harmon (STO) Defenders of the Bond; College of Consultors/Presbyteral Council; Personnel Board.
Skillingstad, M. Delmar '60 (SPK)[B] Spokane, WA Gonzaga University.
Skindeleski, Thomas J. '71 (PMB) Royal Palm Beach, FL Our Lady Queen of the Apostles Secretary.
Skinner, Charles D. '53 (E) Retired.
Skinta, Stephen J. *o.s.b.m.* '59 (PSC) New Brunswick, NJ St. Joseph; [A] Matawan, NJ Basilian Fathers of Mariapoch.
Skirtich, John W. '90 (PIT) Pittsburgh, PA St. Maurice.
Skitzki, Francis P. '70 (SCR) Wilkes-Barre, PA St. Nicholas.
Sklar, Louis E. '01 (ALX) Echo, LA St. Francis de Sales.
Skluzacek, Michael C. '80 (STP) Stillwater, MN St. Mary; Stillwater, MN St. Michael; [G] Stillwater, MN St. Croix Catholic Educational Programs; Presbyteral Council.
Skluzacek, Richard F. '57 (STP) Retired.
Skoczylas, Walter '75 (CR) Leave of Absence.
Skok, Charles '52 (SPK) Spokane, WA St. John Vianney Retired.
Skoneki, William J. '87 (MOB) Mobile, AL St. Dominic; Archdiocesan Consultors; Campaign for Human Development Clergy Retirement Association; Priests' Retirement Fund.
Skoneki, William (MOB) Consultors.
Skonezny, Ray '61 (ORG) Irvine, CA St. John Neumann.
Skonezny, Raymond (ORG) Cursillo Movement.
Skonseng, Dennis A. '82 (FAR) Special Assignment; [A] Fargo, ND Cardinal Muench Seminary.
Skonseng, Dennis (FAR) Permanent Diaconate.
Skornia, Bernard L. '57 (SAG) Retired.
Skorup, Ildephonse *o.f.m.* '59 (CHI) Chicago, IL St. Francis de Sales; [N] Countryside, IL St. Gratian Friary, Franciscan Friars.
Skotnicki, Andrew *o.carm* '77 (NY) Bronx, NY St. Simon Stock.
Skrincosky, Peter (STF) Retired.
Skrocki, Michael (NTN) Judge and Adjutant Judicial Vicar.
Skrypek, Gregory A. '70 (STP) Minnesota State Prison.
Skrzypiec, Andrzej '82 (SLC) Magna, UT Our Lady of Lourdes; Team.
Skudlarek, William *o.s.b.* '64 (SCL)[I] Collegeville, MN St. John's Abbey, of the Order of St. Benedict.
Skufca, Ronald J. '79 (MAR) Menominee, MI Holy Redeemer; Army National Guard Chaplains.
Skupien, Francis M. '52 (BUF) Holley, NY St. Mark Retired.
Skura, Mark David *o.f.m.conv.* '82 (BUF) P] Hamburg, NY Immaculate Conception Convent; [D] Athol Springs, NY St. Francis High School; Athol Springs, NY St. Francis of Assisi.
Skurla, Anthony *o.f.m.* '54 (PSC)[A] Sybertsville, PA Holy Dormition Friary.
Skurla, Robert J. '56 (PSC) Jersey City, NJ St. Mary's.
Skwara, John M. '59 (MET)[G] Somerset, NJ McCarrick Care Center Retired.
Skwor, Donald *s.d.s.* '53 (WDC)[B] Silver Spring, MD Salvatorian Community.
Slacke, Verin *o.f.m.* '44 (CIN)[M] Cincinnati, OH St. Francis Seraph Friary Retired.
Sladicka, Phillip J. '76 (SCR) Olyphant, PA St. Michael the Archangel; Olyphant, PA St. Patrick's; Diocesan Consultors; Presbyteral Council; Cursillo Movement.
Slafkosky Andrew L. '38 (ORL) Retired
Slampak, John A. '66 (RCK) McHenry, IL St. Patrick.
Slampak, John A. (RCK) Special Assignment; Parish Services and Directors; Divine Worship, Office for; Liturgical Commission, Diocesan.
Slane, Anthony P. *c.ss.r.* '42 (STL)[O] Liguori, MO St. Clement Health Care Center.
Slate, William '55 (SEA) Retired.
Slater, Dennis '62 (SY) Retired.
Slater, John J. '52 (E) Retired.
Slater, William T. '77 (RVC) New Hyde Park, NY Notre Dame.
Slatterie Leo '51 (P)[Q] Beaverton, OR Our Lady of Peace Institute in Catholic Teaching.
Slatterie Leo '51 (LAV) Retired.
Slattery, Edmund J. *s.s.s.* '50 (CLV)[C] Richfield, OH Regina Health Center.
Slattery, Edmund '50 (CLV)[O] Richfield, OH Regina Health Center.
Slattery James F. '41 (ROC) Retired.
Slattery John '57 (COS) Woodland Park, CO Our Lady of the Woods; [G] Colorado Springs, CO Mount St. Francis.
Slattery, Kenneth F. *c.m.* '48 (BRK)[V] Jamaica, NY Vincentian Residence.
Slattery, Kenneth '94 (SP) New Port Richey, FL Our Lady Queen of Peace; [U] New Port Richey, FL Stepping Stones to Independence, Inc..
Slattery, Kevin '86 (JKS) Canton, MS Sacred Heart; Carthage, MS St. Anne; Priests' Council; Diocesan Consultors.
Slattery, Kevin (JKS) Vice Chancellor; Judicial Vicar; Engaged Encounter; Continuing Formation Committee; Diocesan Judges.
Slattery, Michael J. '62 (LA) Santa Clarita, CA Blessed Kateri Tekakwitha.
Slattery, Michael *o.s.a.* '77 (JOL) New Lenox, IL St. Jude.
Slaughter, Martin '85 (LA) Los Angeles, CA St. Gerard Majella.
Slaven, Donald J. '67 (SC) Salix, IA St. Joseph's; Judges.
Slaven, Frederick '59 (Y) Retired.
Sledesky, Stephen M. '93 (HRT) Manchester, CT St. Bridget's.
Sledz, Stanley (STP) Ramsey County Correctional Facilities.
Sledzeus, Alexander L. '50 (RVC) Patchogue, NY Our Lady of Mt. Carmel Retired.
Sledziona, John S. *c.m.* '70 (HRT)[M] Manchester, CT DePaul Provincial Residence.
Sleiman, Elias *m.l.m.* '98 (OLL) Los Angeles, CA Our Lady of Mt. Lebanon–St. Peter Cathedral; [A] Houston TX The Congregation of Maronite Lebanese Missionaries.
Slemba, Dominic *o.f.m.conv.* '51 (BAL)[S] St. Francis of Assisi Friary.
Slemba, Dominic *o.f.m.conv.* '51 (FgM).
Slepicka, Joseph J. '55 (DUB) Retired.
Slesinski, Robert F. '76 (PSC) New Britain, CT Holy Trinity.
Slesinski, Sebastian *o.f.m.conv.* '51 (FR) New Bedford, MA Our Lady of Perpetual Help.
Slevin, Henry '62 (WDC) Washington, DC St. Francis de Sales; On Duty Outside the Archdiocese.
Slevin, Patrick C. '57 (MIA) Fort Lauderdale, FL St. Pius X.
Slezak, Raymond P. '74 (ALN) Sheppton, PA St. Joseph.
Slight, William J. *m.s.* '65 (TYL) Lufkin, TX St. Patrick.
Sliney, Michael *l.c.* '98 (WDC)[M] Potomac, MD Legionaries of Christ.
Slinger, Joseph T. '70 (NEW) Paramus, NJ Our Lady of the Visitation; Cathedral Healthcare.
Slininski, Rysard '95 (NOR) Tolland, CT St. Matthew.
Slipe, Robert H. '73 (NEW) River Edge, NJ St. Peter the Apostle.
Slipski, William P. '46 (Y) Retired.
Slisz, Charles E. '71 (BUF) Kenmore, NY St. Andrew.
Slivonik, Stanley '69 (ARL) Retired.
Sliwak, Stanley A. '66 (LAR) Laredo, TX Blessed Sacrament.
Sliwiak, Stanley A. (LAR) Vicar General; Presbyteral Council; College of Consultors.
Sliwiak, Stanley (LAR) Finance Council; Priests Personnel Board.
Sloan, Anthony *o.c.s.o.* (SPC)[E] Ava, MO Assumption Abbey (Trappist).
Sloan, Daniel '82 (MET) Manville, NJ Christ the King.
Sloan, James D. *c.pp.s.* '62 (OAK)[N] Berkeley, CA Society of the Precious Blood.
Slobig, John '90 (PHX) Glendale, AZ St. Louis The King.
Sloboda, Michael J. *m.m.* '85 (STA)[H] Jacksonville, FL Maryknoll Fathers & Brothers.
Slobogin, Roland D. '73 (PH) Philadelphia, PA St. Francis de Sales; Philadelphia, PA Most Blessed Sacrament.
Slocum, Samuel B. '80 (E) Lewis Run, PA Our Mother of Perpetual Help.
Slocum, Samuel '80 (E) Bradford, PA St. Francis of Assisi.
Slodowski, Bronislaw '68 (MIL)[M] Kenosha, WI St. Joseph's Home for the Aged.
Slodowski, Bruno '68 (MIL) Special Assignment.
Slomba, Eugene S. '64 (BUF) Albion Correctional Facility; Batavia, NY Sacred Heart.
Slominski, Fabian B. '48 (DET) Pontiac, MI St. Joseph Retired.
Slominski, Leon '58 (SCL) St. Cloud, MN St. Wendelin's; Advocates Retired.
Slomski, Joseph P. (WCH) Retired.
Slon, Thomas R. *s.j.* '90 (NY)[EE] New York, NY "America;" Residence and publication office of the America Press.
Sloneker, Patrick L. '97 (CIN) Botkins, OH Immaculate Conception; Botkins, OH St. Lawrence.
Slosarcik, Edward A. (CHI) Retired.
Slota, Frederick V. '53 (PRO) Providence, RI St. Adalbert.
Slough, Charles R. '56 (HBG) Elysburg, PA Queen of the Most Holy Rosary.
Slovacek, Emil C. '54 (DAL) Retired.
Slovikovski, John J. '96 (ALT)[A] Cresson, PA Mount Aloysius College; [H] Cresson, PA Mount Aloysius College (Cresson).
Slowey, John P. '57 (SUP) Retired.
Slowiak, Allan L. '73 (LC) Rothschild, WI St. Mark.
Slowik, Joseph S. '72 (RIC) Portsmouth, VA St. Paul.
Slowinski, Jerome '90 (DET) Special Assignment; Warren, MI St. Anne's; Adjutant Judicial Vicars.
Slowinski, Thomas F. (DET) Navy Reserve Chaplains.
Slowinski, Thomas '81 (DET) Rochester, MI St. Andrew.
Sloyan, Gerald (WDC)[C] Catholic University of America, The.
Sloyan, Gerard S. '44 (TR) Retired.
Slubecky, David S. '73 (BUF) Finance Council; Vicars; West Seneca, NY Fourteen Holy Helpers.
Slusarczyk, Henryk *s.v.d.* '93 (CHI)[B] Chicago, IL Edward McGuinn, S.V.D. Residence.
Slusser, Michael S. '66 (STP) On Duty Outside the Archdiocese.
Slusz, Michael J. '03 (HRT) Naugatuck, CT St. Francis of Assisi.
Slyva, Joseph W. '72 (BO) Natick, MA Sacred Heart.
Smail, Brian E. *o.f.m.* '99 (BO)[AA] Boston, MA St. Anthony Shrine; Court Experts for Languages.
Smaistrla, Benjamin '72 (GAL) Houston, TX St. Ambrose.
Small, Andrew *o.m.i.* '99 (GAL) Houston, TX Immaculate Conception; [M] Washington, DC Oblate Community.
Small, Brian '02 (ATL) Dunwoody, GA All Saints Catholic.
Small, Edward J. *s.j.* '70 (BGP) Stratford, CT Our Lady of Grace; [P] Fairfield, CT The Fairfield Jesuit Community–Fairfield University; [V] Boston The

Society of Jesus of New England–Provincial Offices.
Small, James *c.ss.r.* '54 (HBG) Lancaster, PA St. Anthony of Padua; [H] Ephrata, PA St. Clement's Mission House.
Small, Joseph *s.j.* '60 (SPK)[D] Spokane, WA Gonzaga Preparatory School.
Small, William T. '77 (PH) Philadelphia, PA St. Jerome.
Smar, Michael J. '69 (Y) Warren, OH St. William.
Smarsh, Charles F. '64 (NY) On Duty Outside the Archdiocese.
Smart, Raymond W. '70 (PH) Pennsburg, PA St. Philip Neri Retired.
Smegal, John T. '77 (SPR) Amherst, MA St. Brigid's; Continuing Education for Priests; Ministry to Priests.
Smegelsky, John J. '66 (SY) Central Square, NY St. Michael.
Smeltzer, Stuart M. '96 (WCH) Hutchinson, KS St. Teresa; Judges; Defenders of the Bond.
Smereka, John '83 (SJP) Carnegie, PA Holy Trinity.
Smet, Joachim *o.carm.* '42 (JOL)[L] Darien Carmelite Provincial Office; [B] Washington, DC Whitefriars Hall.
Smet, Leroy R. '59 (GB) Winneconne, WI St. Mary.
Smetanka, Gary T. '82 (DET) Clinton Twp, MI St. Claude; Clinton Twp., MI St. Thecla.
Smialowski, Raymond S. '82 (HRT) Bristol, CT St. Stanislaus.
Smiciklas, Nicholas X. '56 (PBR) Pittsburgh, PA St. Pius X.
Smiech, Charles William *o.f.m.* '81 (ALN)[M] Easton, PA St. Francis Friary and Retreat House.
Smiech, Charles *o.f.m.* '81 (ALN)[K] Easton, PA St. Francis Friary.
Smiga, George '75 (CLV) Willoughby Hills, OH St. Noel.
Smigiel, Walter J. '50 (PBL) Retired.
Smilanic, Daniel A. '73 (CHI) Park Ridge, IL St. Paul of the Cross; Adjutant Judicial Vicar.
Smilanic, Daniel (CHI) Judges.
Smiley, Douglas (R) Burgaw, NC St. Joseph; Fuquay–Varina, NC St. Bernadette.
Smiraldo, Onofrio R. '53 (BUF)[O] Lackawanna, NY Bishop Head Residence Retired.
Smit, Gerard C. '50 (LKC) Retired.
Smith, A. Philip *o.p.* '68 (PRO)[P] Providence St. Thomas Aquinas Priory at Providence College.
Smith, Alberic *o.f.m.* '58 (LA)[Q] Santa Barbara, CA Franciscan Friary, Order of Friars Minor (Old Mission).
Smith, Albert J. *o.s.f.s.* '65 (PH)[C] Philadelphia, PA Holy Family University; [AA] Wyndmoor, PA Villa de Sales Oblate Residence.
Smith, Alexei R. '87 (LA) El Segundo, CA St. Andrew.
Smith, Alexei R. '87 (NTN) El Segundo, CA St. Paul.
Smith, Alexei R. (LA) Ecumenical and Interreligious Affairs.
Smith, Alexei (LA) Commission for Ecumenical and Interreligious Affairs; Members.
Smith, Alexei (NTN) Vocations Office.
Smith, Alexei (NTN) Presbyteral Council.
Smith, Alexei (NTN) Priest's Sickness & Disability, and Retirement Plans.
Smith, Alexei (NTN) Continuing Education of Clergy Office.
Smith, Alexei (NTN) Protopresbyters.
Smith, Alfred D. '53 (TR) Lavallette, NJ St. Bonaventure Retired.
Smith, Alfred E. '56 (BAL) Retired.
Smith, Andrew T. *o.s.b.* '64 (PAT)[M] Morristown, NJ St. Mary's Abbey.
Smith, Anthony *c.ss.r.* '84 (OAK)[N] Oakland, CA Redemptorists.
Smith, Anthony *c.ss.r.* (STO) Newman Apostolate.
Smith, Aquinas '59 (SD) Retired.
Smith, Arthur F. *o.s.a.* '54 (PH)[AA] Villanova, PA St. Thomas Monastery.
Smith, Arthur J. '71 (BUF) Buffalo, NY St. Thomas Aquinas.
Smith, Bernard *o.f.m.cap.* '64 (NY)[B] Beacon, NY St. Lawrence of Brindisi Friary.
Smith, Bertin *o.carm.* '51 (JOL)[L] Darien Carmelite Provincial Office.
Smith, Brian P. '03 (BO) Brockton, MA St. Edith Stein.
Smith, Brian '98 (SJ) On Leave of Absence.
Smith, Charles C. *c.s.b.* '60 (DET)[E] Redford, MI Catholic Central High School.
Smith, Charles Clyde '95 (FBK) Alakanuk, AK St. Ignatius.
Smith, Charles D. '65 (PH) Philadelphia, PA St. Martin of Tours.
Smith, Charles *s.v.d.* '88 (IND) Indianapolis, IN St. Rita.
Smith, Chester *s.v.d.* '88 (IND) Indianapolis, IN St. Rita.
Smith, Christopher H. '78 (ORG) Santa Ana, CA St. Joseph's; Office for Religious Education.
Smith, Christopher L. '03 (FTW) Fort Wayne, IN St. Charles Borromeo.
Smith, Christopher (ORG) Vicar for Religious Education.
Smith, Clifford G. '96 (DAL) Grand Prairie, TX St. Michael the Archangel.
Smith, Cyril J. *o.s.a.* '55 (MIA)[C] Miami, FL Msgr. Edward Pace High School; [H] Miami, FL Casa San Lorenzo.
Smith, D. Stephen '73 (MAD) McFarland, WI Christ the King.
Smith, Daniel *o.carm.* '46 (NEW) Paramus, NJ Carmelite Chapel of St. Therese.
Smith, Daniel '99 (VEN) Absent on Leave.
Smith, David G. '73 (BAL) Absent on Leave.
Smith, David L. *c.s.sp.* '58 (PIT)[B] Pittsburgh, PA Duquesne University of the Holy Spirit.
Smith, David L. *s.j.* '85 (OM)[K] Omaha, NE Jesuit Community at Creighton University.
Smith, David L. *s.j.* '85 (DM)[J] Griswold, IA Creighton University Retreat Center.
Smith, David W. '64 (STP)[C] St. Paul, MN University of St. Thomas; Censores Librorum.
Smith, David '82 (MIA) Special Assignment.
Smith, David '87 (MAD).
Smith, Dean M. '99 (RCK)[E] Stockton, IL Holy Cross.
Smith, Dennis '75 (FWT) Keller, TX St. Elizabeth Ann Seton.
Smith, Donald C. '61 (NEW)[B] School of Diplomacy and Intl. Rels. Retired.
Smith, Donald R. '57 (SC) Retired.
Smith, Edmund *o.s.b.* '65 (P)[L] St. Benedict, OR Mt. Angel Abbey; [Q] St. Benedict, OR The Abbey Foundation of Oregon.
Smith, Edward E. '82 (MOB) On Leave from the Archdiocese.
Smith, Edward J. '65 (BRK) Jackson Heights, NY Blessed Sacrament.
Smith, Edward J. '01 (CLV) Elyria, OH St. Jude.
Smith, Edward P. '82 (CIN) Milford, OH St. Andrew.
Smith, Edward '82 (CIN)[B] Cincinnati, OH Mt. St. Mary's Seminary of the West; [B] Cincinnati, OH Mt. St. Mary's Seminary of the West.
Smith, Elmer W. '50 (CIN) Cincinnati, OH St. Cecilia; [V] Cincinnati, OH Legion of Mary.
Smith, Ermin R. *o.s.b.* '45 (GBG)[H] Latrobe, PA Saint Vincent Archabbey.
Smith, Eugene M. *o.s.m.* '84 (CHI)[N] Chicago Order of Friar Servants of Mary (Servites) United States of America Province, Inc..
Smith, Eugene M. *o.s.m.* '88 (ORG)[D] Anaheim, CA Servite High School, A California Corporation; [I] Anaheim, CA Servite Fathers and Brothers; [I] Anaheim, CA Seven Holy Founders Priory.
Smith, Eugene P. '50 (LC) Boyd, WI Sacred Heart of Jesus–St. Joseph Retired.
Smith, F. Harold '50 (L) Retired.
Smith, Francis J. *s.j.* '52 (CLV)[B] Cleveland, OH John Carroll University.
Smith, Francis J. '67 (ELP) El Paso, TX St. Raphael; Vicars General; Ex Officio Members; Advocates; Our Lady of Guadalupe; Finance Council; Priests' Personnel Advisory Committee; Knights of Columbus; Knights of the Holy Sepulchre; Ladies of Charity; Daughters of Charity; Ladies of the Holy Sepulchre; Priests' Retirement and Disability Plan.
Smith, Francis R. *s.j.* '70 (SJ)[B] Santa Clara, CA Jesuit Community.
Smith, Francis (ORL) Winter Park, FL St. Margaret Mary.
Smith, Frank (ORL) Retired.
Smith, Gabriel J. '82 (CHR) Charleston, SC St. Joseph; Army National Guard Chaplains.
Smith, Gary N. *s.j.* '71 (P)[L] Portland Jesuit Provincial Office (Society of Jesus, Oregon Prov.).
Smith, Gary N. *s.j.* '71 (FgM).
Smith, Gene F. '84 (CHI) Chicago, IL St. Barnabas.
Smith, Geoffrey C. '74 (HRT) Hamden, CT St. Rita's; New Haven, CT Yale–New Haven Hospital.
Smith, Gerald S. '64 (PH) North Wales, PA St. Rose of Lima.
Smith, Gerald '65 (AUS) Retired.
Smith, Gregory J. '74 (GB) Green Bay, WI St. John the Baptist; Oneida, WI St. Joseph; De Pere, WI Immaculate Conception; Ecumenism; Ecumenical Commission.
Smith, Herbert F. *s.j.* '62 (PH)[AA] Loyola Center and Manresa Hall.
Smith, Howard C. *s.m.* '72 (WDC)[M] Washington, DC Marist Center.
Smith, Ignatius E. *o.f.m.* '56 (NY) Callicoon, NY Holy Cross; AUXILIARY CHAPLAINS CONTRACT CHAPLAINS.
Smith, Ignatius J. *o.s.b.* '46 (PBL)[F] Canon City, CO Holy Cross Abbey.
Smith, Ignatius *o.s.b.* '54 (PBL)[I] Canon City, CO Trinity Ranch Conference & Renewal Center, Inc..
Smith, James A.D. '56 (PAT) Succasunna, NJ St. Therese.
Smith, James B. '85 (WIL) Dover, DE Holy Cross.
Smith, James D. '87 (STP) Special Assignment.
Smith, James E. *c.m.* '61 (BRK)[V] Jamaica, NY Vincentian Residence.
Smith, James F. *s.j.* '62 (SY)[Q] Syracuse, NY Jesuits at LeMoyne, Inc.; Elected.
Smith, James G. *o.praem.* '77 (ORG)[D] Silverado, CA St. Michael's Preparatory School; [I] Silverado, CA Norbertine Fathers of Orange Inc..
Smith, James H. '63 (HRT) East Hartford, CT St. Isaac Jogues; College of Consultors.
Smith, James M. '02 (JC) Jefferson City, MO St. Peter.
Smith, James R. '67 (SC) Breda, IA St. Bernard's.
Smith, James T. '65 (COL) Columbus, OH St. Matthias.
Smith, James '56 (BRK) Retired.
Smith, Jerome '96 (PEO) On Duty Outside the Diocese.
Smith, John B. '59 (STP) Retired.
Smith, John F.X. '61 (NY) Tuxedo, NY Our Lady of Mt. Carmel.
Smith, John J. '59 (FR) South Yarmouth, MA St. Pius Tenth.
Smith, John P. '42 (DUB) Retired.
Smith, John *s.s.c.* (CHI)[N] Chicago, IL Korean Catholic Center; Korean Catholic Mission of Chicago (Kedvale).
Smith, Josep '03 (FRS) Merced, CA Our Lady of Mercy/St. Patrick's.
Smith, Joseph A. '96 (SAV) Richmond Hill, GA St. Anne.
Smith, Joseph P.T. '60 (ALN) Reading, PA St. Catharine of Siena; College of Consultors; Elected Members.
Smith, Jude *o.f.m.* '53 (PAT).
Smith, K. Bartholomew '98 (WDC) On Duty Outside the Archdiocese.
Smith, Kenneth A. '63 (BR) Sorrento, LA St. Anthony of Padua; Sorrento, LA St. Anne.
Smith, Kenneth G. '84 (HBG) Harrisburg, PA Polyclinic Medical Clinic; Community General Osteopathic Hospital; Harrisburg, PA Harrisburg Hospital.
Smith, Kenneth J. '64 (NY) New York, NY Holy Trinity.
Smith, Kenneth (NY) Judges.
Smith, Kevin M. '88 (RVC) Patchogue, NY St. Francis de Sales; Nassau County, Fire Chiefs, Council of.
Smith, Kevin (RVC) Co–Chaplains of the Nassau County Firemen's Association.
Smith, Lawrence C. *s.j.* '82 (BO)[V] Boston The Society of Jesus of New England–Provincial Offices; Navy Reserve Chaplains.
Smith, Lawrence H. (MET) Navy Reserve Chaplains.
Smith, Lawrence R. '76 (PIT) McKees Rocks, PA St. John of God.
Smith, Lawrence *s.j.* '82 (GLP) Dulce, NM St. Francis of Assisi; Vicars Forane; Presbyteral Council.
Smith, Leland J. '53 (WIN) Retired.
Smith, Leonard A. '91 (WH) Fairmont, WV St. Peter the Fisherman.
Smith, LeRoy J. '78 (BRK) Released from Diocesan Assignment.
Smith, Leroy '78 (SPR) Pittsfield, MA Berkshire Medical Center.
Smith, Lester E. '75 (SY) On Sabbatical.
Smith, M. Christopher '83 (JC) Iberia, MO St. Anthony; St. Elizabeth, MO St. Lawrence.
Smith, Malachy *o.carm.* '43 (JOL).
Smith, Mark S. '96 (JC) Columbia, MO St. Thomas More Newman Center, University of Missouri; [E] Columbia, MO University of Missouri–Columbia, Campus Ministry.
Smith, Martin D. '79 (STU) On Duty Outside the Diocese.
Smith, Martin L. *o.s.a.* '76 (CAM)[C] Richland, NJ St. Augustine Preparatory School.
Smith, Maury *o.f.m.* '66 (SAT) San Antonio, TX San Jose y San Miguel.
Smith, Michael B. '74 (CLV) Akron, OH Immaculate Conception.
Smith, Michael H. '66 (SAV) Moultrie, GA Immaculate Conception; Director of Hispanic/Migrant Ministry.
Smith, Michael M. '77 (HEL) Stevensville, MT St. Mary.
Smith, Michael N. *s.j.* '67 (PBL) Fruita, CO Sacred Heart; Deans.
Smith, Michael S. '92 (NOR) Hebron, CT The Church of the Holy Family; Members; Continuing Education and Formation Commission.
Smith, Michel Robert (SP) St. Petersburg, FL St. Raphael.
Smith, Myles H. (IND) On Special or Other Archdiocesan Assignment; Defenders of the Bond.
Smith, Neil B. '48 (MAR) Retired.
Smith, Nicholas P. '65 (PRO) Wakefield, RI St. Francis of Assisi; South County Hospital.
Smith, Nicholas W. '94 (STL) St. Louis, MO Cathedral Basilica of Saint Louis.
Smith, Norman N. '70 (CLV) Cleveland, OH St. Philip Neri; Kirtland, OH Divine Word.
Smith, Norman '50 (GLP) Retired.
Smith, Paschal *c.p.* '51 (NY)[EE] Pelham Manor, NY St. Vincent's Residence; [II] Pelham, NY Passionist Communications, Inc.; [V] Jamaica, NY Immaculate Conception Monastery.
Smith, Patrick A. '90 (WDC) Washington, DC St. Teresa of Avila.
Smith, Patrick '67 (PHX) Scottsdale, AZ St. Daniel the Prophet; Scottsdale, AZ Scottsdale Memorial Hospital.
Smith, Patrick '03 (JKS) Brandon, MS St. Paul.
Smith, Paul F. '73 (CLV) Thompson, OH St. Patrick.
Smith, Paul O. '64 (COL) Columbus, OH Corpus

Christi Retired.
Smith, Paul R. '59 (ALB)[B] Albany, NY Maria College.
Smith, Paul '59 (ALB) Altamont, NY St. Lucy; Special Assignment.
Smith, Paul (HON) Hospital Ministry.
Smith, Peter J. '51 (NY)[AA] Rhinebeck, NY Ferncliff Nursing Home.
Smith, Peter '01 (P) Lake Oswego, OR Our Lady of the Lake.
Smith, Philip A. *o.p.* '68 (PRO)[B] Providence, RI Providence College.
Smith, Philip T. *o.praem.* '84 (ORG)[I] Silverado, CA Norbertine Fathers of Orange Inc..
Smith, Philip *o.praem* '84 (ORG) Costa Mesa, CA St. John the Baptist.
Smith, R. Douglas *o.s.f.s.* '62 (PH)[AA] Philadelphia, PA Father Louis Brisson Residence.
Smith, R. Douglas *o.s.f.s.* (CAM) Pitman, NJ Our Lady Queen of Peace.
Smith, R. Leroy '54 (COV) Hudson, FL Retired.
Smith, Ramon *o.f.m.* '53 (LSC) Roswell, NM St. Peter.
Smith, Raymond K. '56 (SFR) On Duty Outside the Archdiocese; [M] Petaluma, CA Silver Penny Farm Retreat Center.
Smith, Raymond '50 (CLV) Retired.
Smith, Raynard '86 (MET)[F] New Brunswick, NJ Saint Peter's University Hospital.
Smith, Richard A. '56 (MAN) Bennington, NH St. Patrick.
Smith, Richard E. '66 (BAL) Ellicott City, MD Our Lady of Perpetual Help.
Smith, Richard P. *m.m.* '76 (NY)[M] Los Altos, CA Maryknoll.
Smith, Richard '76 (JOL) Absent on Leave.
Smith, Richard '84 (JKS) Forest, MS St. Michael; Forest, MS St. Michael; [I] Forest, MS East Central Community College Newman Center.
Smith, Richard '97 (NY) Haverstraw, NY St. Peter.
Smith, Richard '98 (FRS) Laton, CA Shrine of Our Lady of Fatima.
Smith, Richard (BAL) Priests' Council; Priest Personnel Board.
Smith, Richard (JKS) Ecumenism.
Smith, Richard (WIL) Wilmington, DE St. John the Beloved.
Smith, Richard (BAL) Priests' Council; Priest Personnel Board.
Smith, Robert F. (FAR) Special Assignment; Vocation Director.
Smith, Robert J. '55 (OM) Retired.
Smith, Robert J. '70 (E)[J] Erie, PA Bishop Michael J. Murphy Residence for Retired Priests; Vicar General; Administrative Cabinet.
Smith, Robert J. '83 (RVC) Setauket, NY St. James.
Smith, Robert J. (RVC)[P] Stony Brook, NY Interfaith Center; Censors of Books.
Smith, Robert J. (E) Northern Vicariate; College of Consultors; Ex Officios; Members; Matrimonial Judges; Board of Members.
Smith, Robert J. (RVC)[P] Stony Brook, NY Interfaith Center; Censors of Books.
Smith, Robert J. (E) Northern Vicariate; College of Consultors; Ex Officios; Members; Matrimonial Judges; Board of Members.
Smith, Robert S. (ROC) Ithaca, NY Cornell University.
Smith, Robert S. (RVC) Sophia Center Retired.
Smith, Robert V. '61 (CAM) Absecon, NJ St. Elizabeth Ann Seton; Priests Personnel Board.
Smith, Robert '53 (ROC) Retired.
Smith, Roger J. '73 (SEA) Morton, WA Sacred Heart.
Smith, Roger R. '76 (CC) Corpus Christi, TX St. Patrick.
Smith, Roger (CC) Presbyteral Council; Judges; Catholic Charismatic Renewal.
Smith, Ronald T. '73 (HRT) New Britain, CT St. Andrew's; New Britain, CT St. John the Evangelist; New Britain, CT New Britain General Hospital.
Smith, Russell E. '80 (RIC) Quinton, VA St. Elizabeth Ann Seton; Judges.
Smith, S. Douglas *c.s.c.* '76 (FTW)[I] Jacksonville, NC LTCDR, CHC, USNR Commander; Navy Chaplains.
Smith, Sherrill '55 (SAT)[K] San Antonio, TX Casa De Padres; Respect Life Program Retired.
Smith, Simon E. *s.j.* '61 (BO)[E] Dorchester, MA Boston College High School & Jesuit Community; [H] Boston, MA Nativity Preparatory School.
Smith, Stanley C. *o.s.a.* '60 (PH)[B] Villanova, PA St. Augustine Friary.
Smith, Steve *o.p.* '58 (R)[E] Raleigh, NC Dominican Priory.
Smith, Terrance W. '73 (CIN) Liberty Township, OH St. Maximilian Kolbe; Ex Officio Members; Consultors; Judges.
Smith, Terrence T. '73 (STP) Brooklyn Park, MN St. Gerard.
Smith, Theodore R. *o.praem.* '91 (ORG)[I] Silverado, CA Norbertine Fathers of Orange Inc..
Smith, Thomas A. *o.f.m.conv.* '79 (L) Louisville, KY St. Rita.
Smith, Thomas A. *o.f.m.conv.* '79 (L) Louisville, KY St. Anthony.
Smith, Thomas A. '83 (L) Louisville, KY Holy Spirit; Ex Officio.
Smith, Thomas Anthony (L) College of Consultors.
Smith, Thomas Bernard *o.p.* '58 (L) Springfield, KY St. Rose.
Smith, Thomas E. '51 (PIT) Retired.
Smith, Thomas E. *s.j.* '74 (FgM).
Smith, Thomas E. *s.j.* '74 (NY)[EE] New York, NY Jesuit Provincial's Office; [EE] New York, NY St. Ignatius Loyola Residence.
Smith, Thomas F. *o.c.s.o.* '58 (ATL)[K] Conyers, GA The Monastery of the Holy Spirit.
Smith, Thomas H. '57 (HBG) Lancaster, PA St. Joseph; Cursillo Movement; Deans; Presbyteral Council; AUXILIARY CHAPLAINS CONTRACT CHAPLAINS.
Smith, Thomas J. *o.s.f.s.* '58 (LAN) Michigan Center, MI Our Lady of Fatima.
Smith, Thomas J. '60 (LC)[H] La Crosse, WI Holy Cross (Seminary) Diocesan Center Retired.
Smith, Thomas J. '73 (PH) Springfield, PA St. Francis of Assisi.
Smith, Thomas J. '82 (NOR) Middletown, CT St. Sebastian.
Smith, Thomas J. (NOR) Deans.
Smith, Thomas R. '81 (CLV) Lorain, OH St. John the Baptist; Associate Judges.
Smith, Thomas W. *c.s.c.* '72 (FgM).
Smith, Thomas W. *c.s.c.* '72 (FTW)[I] Notre Dame, IN Holy Cross Mission Center.
Smith, Thomas '51 (ORL) Altamonte Springs, FL St. Mary Magdalen.
Smith, Thomas *c.s.c.* '72 (FTW) South Bend, IN St. Adalbert.
Smith, Thomas (NOR) Council of Catholic Nurses.
Smith, Trevor '67 (MIA) Retired.
Smith, Vernon '89 (FAR) Harvey, ND St. Cecilia; Harvey, ND St. Anthony.
Smith, Vincent E. *c.s.f.s.* '85 (PH)[D] Philadelphia, PA Northeast Catholic High School for Boys.
Smith, Vincent J. '55 (HBG) Mechanicsburg, PA Saint Katharine Drexel Retired.
Smith, Vincent Leo '66 (DEN).
Smith, Vincent *o.s.f.s.* '85 (PH) Philadelphia, PA St. Joachim.
Smith, W. Andrew '80 (LR) Bella Vista, AR St. Bernard; Deans.
Smith, Walter J. *s.j.* '72 (NY)[EE] New York, NY.
Smith, Walter J. *s.j.* '72 (BO)[V] Boston The Society of Jesus of New England–Provincial Offices.
Smith, Wilfred T. '56 (CLV) Madison, OH Immaculate Conception; Mentor, OH St. Mary of the Assumption.
Smith, Wilfred '56 (CLV) Retired.
Smith, William A. '74 (BRK) Brooklyn, NY Our Lady of Lourdes.
Smith, William A. '03 (CLV) Garfield Heights, OH St. Monica.
Smith, William B. '66 (NY)[A] Yonkers, NY St. Joseph's Seminary.
Smith, William C. '45 (HRT) Retired.
Smith, William J. '47 (PH) Retired.
Smith, William J. '60 (NY) Bronx, NY St. Athanasius.
smith, William J. '81 (MET) Port Reading, NJ St. Anthony of Padua.
Smith, William L. *c.s.sp.* (DEN) Johnstown, CO Sacred Heart
Smith, William P. *o.m.i.* (BO) Lexington, MA St. Brigid; Tewksbury, MA St. William.
Smith, William *g.h.m.* '47 (CIN)[M] Cincinnati Headquarters of Glenmary Home Missioners.
Smith, William *o.carm.* '54 (JOL)[L] Darien Carmelite Provincial Office; Gibson City, IL Our Lady of Lourdes; (FgM).
Smith, William '78 (BRK) Brooklyn, NY Holy Rosary.
Smith, William (NY) Censors Librorum.
Smith, William *c.s.sp.* (DEN) Johnstown, CO St. John the Baptist; Johnstown, CO St. Nicholas.
Smith, Wilton '58 (SFR) Retired.
Smithson, Thomas J. *s.s.s.* '02 (CLV) Highland Heights, OH St. Paschal Baylon.
Smits, Kenneth *o.f.m.cap.* '64 (MAD).
Smits, Lambert H. '48 (DET)[E] Royal Oak, MI National Shrine of the Little Flower.
Smits, Lee '71 (CHI)[J] Maywood, IL Foster G. McGaw Hospital of Loyola University of Chicago.
Smits, Peter *s.v.d.* '41 (BLX)[A] Bay St. Louis, MS St. Augustine's.
Smitson, Thomas *s.s.s.* '02 (CLV)[C] Cleveland, OH Blessed Sacrament Community.
Smochko, Basil '46 (PRM) Retired.
Smolarski, Dennis C. *s.j.* '79 (SJ)[B] Santa Clara, CA Jesuit Community.
Smolenski, Stanley '68 (HRT) On Duty Outside the Archdiocese.
Smoley, Rudolph F. '69 (PIT) Elizabeth, PA St. Michael.
Smolich, Thomas H. *s.j.* '86 (FgM); (FgM).
Smolich, Thomas H. *s.j.* '86 (SJ)[M] Los Gatos, CA California Province of the Society of Jesus, Jesuit Provincial Office; [M] Los Gatos, CA California Province of the Society of Jesus Jesuit Provincial Office.
Smolik, Peter K. '02 (BGP) Fairfield, CT St. Pius X.
Smolinski, Arcadius *o.f.m.* '47 (GB).
Smolinski, Clarence D. (GAY)[I] Elected Members Retired.
Smolinski, Joseph J. '48 (NY) Retired.
Smolko, John F. '57 (BGP) On Duty Outside the Diocese; [C] Catholic University of America, The.
Smolley, Robert '82 (STF) On Leave of Absence.
Smoot, Bob '95 (STL) St. Louis, MO Assumption.
Smoot, Robert (STL) Office of Youth Ministry.
Smulders, Raphael *ss.cc.* '34 (HON)[G] Honolulu, HI St. Patrick's Monastery.
Smutny, Jan '42 (GI) Retired.
Smyer, Francis '46 (AMA) Diocesan Council of Catholic Women; Amarillo, TX St. Mary's Retired.
Smyth, Derek (SB) Emmanuel Outreach Services.
Smyth, Henry J. '50 (PH) Retired.
Smyth, James '56 (NY) Hastings–on–Hudson, NY St. Matthew.
Smyth, James '57 (NY) Retired.
Smyth, John L. *c.ss.r.* '64 (VEN)[G] Venice, FL St. Alphonsus Residence.
Smyth, John P. '62 (CHI)[H] Des Plaines, IL Maryville Academy; Catholic Youth Organization.
Smyth, John (CHI)[G] Des Plaines, IL Maryville Academy.
Smyth, Joseph P. '59 (BO) Senior Priests Retired.
Sneck, William J. *s.j.* '71 (ALN)[A] Wernersville, PA Jesuit Center; [N] Wernersville, PA Jesuit Center for Spiritual Growth.
Snedeker, Arthur '74 (CLV) Metro Health Medical Center & Rehabilitation Center.
Snell, Roger K. '72 (FAR) Retired.
Sneyd, Derrick '70 (FTW) South Bend, IN St. Jude; South Bend, IN St. Mary of the Assumption; Advisory Board.
Snider, Harold *o.f.m.cap.* '67 (SFR) Burlingame, CA Our Lady of Angels.
Snieg, Marion J. '55 (CHI) Other Assignments.
Snieg, Peter '93 (CHI) Chicago, IL Our Lady of Mount Carmel; [A] Chicago, IL Archbishop Quigley Preparatory Seminary; Archbishop Quigley Preparatory Seminary.
Sniezyk, Richard S. '62 (SPR) Springfield, MA St. Michael's Cathedral; Springfield, MA Holy Family; Vicar General; Bishop's Commission for Clergy; Bishop's Cabinet; Diocesan Consultors; Massachusetts Catholic Conference; Priests' Retirement Program.
Sniezyk, Richard (SPR) Presbyteral Council.
Snincak, Stephen A. '35 (WH) Retired.
Sniosek, Jaroslaw '98 (VEN) Naples, FL St. Ann.
Snipes, Roy Lee *o.m.i.* '80 (BWN) Mission, TX Our Lady of Guadalupe; Deans.
Snock, Bernard C. '62 (GAL) Sealy, TX St. Mary's.
Snock, Francis '50 (Y) Retired.
Snodgrass, Thomas A. '76 (CIN) Cincinnati, OH St. Peter in Chains Cathedral; Adjutant Judicial Vicars.
Snoeren, Cornelius M. *m.h.m.* '52 (NY)[EE] Hartsdale, NY Mill Hill Fathers Residence.
Snoich, Stephen *o.s.b.* '72 (IND)[K] St. Meinrad, IN St. Meinrad Archabbey.
Snoke, F. Richard '65 (COL) Danville, OH St. Luke; Vicariate 10: Knox Licking.
Snopek, Charles J. '86 (CHR) Spartanburg, SC Jesus Our Risen Savior.
Snouffer, Philip T. '62 (BAL) Retired.
Snow, Glenn *o.carm.* '89 (TUC)[A] Tucson, AZ Salpointe Catholic High School; [E] Tucson, AZ Carmelite Priory.
Snow, Harry K. '77 (OG) Norwood, NY St. Andrew; Judicial Vicar and Vicar for Canonical Affairs; Deans.
Snow, Lorn *s.j.* '99 (CLV) University Heights, OH Gesu.
Snyder, Alexander '59 (OAK) Retired.
Snyder, Brian '79 (SEA) Renton, WA St. Stephen the Martyr.
Snyder, Chester A. (HBG) Consultors, College.
Snyder, Chester P. '77 (HBG) Mechanicsburg, PA St. Joseph; Presbyteral Council.
Snyder, Donald E. '73 (CLV) Westlake, OH St. Ladislas; Associate Judges.
Snyder, Fred '52 (TOL) Retired.
Snyder, Frederick '52 (GI) Retired.
Snyder, Gary B. '74 (SC) Sioux City, IA St. Joseph; Deans; Priests' Pension Plan – Board of Trustees.
Snyder, Joachim J. *o.carm.* '48 (NY)[EE] Scarborough, NY Carmelite Fathers, NY Prov. of St. Elias.
Snyder, John F. *s.j.* '55 (STL)[O] St. Louis, MO Jesuit Community Corporation at St. Louis University – Jesuit Hall.
Snyder, John R. '54 (E) Episcopal Delegate for Retired Priests; Members Retired.
Snyder, Larry J. (STP) Special Assignment; Community Services.
Snyder, Larry (STP) Catholic Charities.
Snyder, Michael E. '97 (BLX) Picayune, MS St. Charles Borromeo.
Snyder, Michael J. *m.m.* '78 (NY)[EE] Maryknoll Maryknoll Fathers and Brothers.
Snyder, Michael (BLX) Presbyteral Council.
Snyderwine, L. Thomas '68 (E) Erie, PA St. Luke;

Apostleship of the Sea and Chaplain to the Port of Erie.
Snyers, Peter '53 (SCL) Retired.
Soares, Bernaro Manuel '54 (MRY) Retired.
Soares, John P. '92 (PRO)[S] Kingston, RI; Catholic Campus Ministry.
Soares, Manuel (FRS)[C] Los Banos, CA New Bethany.
Soares, Nicholas J. '64 (NY) Staten Island, NY St. Clement; Staten Island, NY St. Michael.
Sobczak, Marek W. *c.m.* '81 (HRT) Ansonia, CT St. Joseph's.
Soberal, Jose D. (ARE) Vicar General; Vicar of Diocesan Pastoral Affairs; Diocesan Consultors; Priest's Senate (Consejo Presbiteral).
Soberick, George J. '62 (MAN) Lakeport, NH Our Lady of the Lakes.
Sobiech, Slawomir '01 (BRK) Brooklyn, NY St. Catharine of Alexandria.
Sobiech, Stanley *o.f.m.conv.* '62 (BO) Lawrence, MA Holy Trinity.
Sobiecki, Peter S. '66 (HRT) New Britain, CT Sacred Heart of Jesus.
Sobierajski, Edward J. '61 (BUF)[O] Tonawanda, NY O'Hara Residence Retired.
Sobierajski, Joseph A. *s.j.* '74 (CHL) Charlotte, NC St. Peter; [J] Mooresville, NC Jesuit Community.
Sobiesiak, Joseph R. '76 (ALN) Allentown, PA St. Paul; Elected Members.
Sobolewski, Edward F. '69 (CAM) National Park, NJ St. Matthew's.
Sobon, Walter A. '67 (PIT) Pittsburgh, PA Ascension; Deans and Deaneries.
Sobotka, DePaul *o.f.m.* '63 (GB)[J] Manitowoc, WI Holy Family Convent of Franciscan Sisters of Christian Charity.
Sobus, James M. '86 (WH) Wheeling, WV St. Michael's.
Socha, Bronislaw F. *o.c.d.* '89 (GRY)[I] Munster, IN Discalced Carmelite Fathers Monastery.
Socha, Mikolaj *o.s.p.p.e.* '93 (PH)[AA] Office.
Sochacki, Pawel P. '93 (NY) Staten Island, NY St. Christopher.
Sochacki, Walter L. '68 (STP) Roseville, MN St. Rose of Lima.
Socias, James '78 (CHI)[W] Oak Park, IL Oak Park Study Center.
Sockol, Timothy '77 (PMB) Delray Beach, FL St. Vincent Ferrer.
Sodano, Ralph H. '67 (PAT) Schooley's Mountain, NJ Our Lady of the Mountain.
Sodano, Thomas M. '91 (PH) Philadelphia, PA St. Cecilia.
Sodini, Pierre G. '68 (PIT) Avella, PA St. Michael.
Sodja, Richard H. '65 (HEL) Whitehall, MT St. Teresa.
Sodoro, Carl F. '77 (OM) Omaha, NE St. Joan of Arc.
Soehner, Mark *o.f.m.* '87 (DET) Detroit, MI St. Aloysius; Presbyteral Council.
Soerries, Denis *o.s.b.* '56 (LR) Scranton, AR St. Ignatius; Scranton, AR St. Meinrad Church.
Sofia, Albert *s.d.b.* (NEW)[N] Ramsey, NJ Don Bosco Prep Salesian Residence; [C] Ramsey, NJ Don Bosco Preparatory High School.
Sofie, J. Francis '94 (MOB) Auburn, AL St. Michael; Group III.
Sogliuzzo, Louis P. *s.j.* '87 (PAT)[I] Morristown, NJ Loyola House of Retreats.
Soha, Roderick *t.o.r.* '95 (ORL) Mount Dora, FL St. Patrick's.
Sohm, John E. '58 (SFD) Sullivan, IL St. Columcille.
Sohn, Frederick H. '55 (GAL)[Q] Houston, TX Dillon House.
Soileau, Charles '57 (LKC) Retired.
Sojka, Jeremiusz H. '95 (RIC) Salem, VA Our Lady of Perpetual Help; Salem, VA Salem VA Medical Center.
Sojka, Louis L. *o.s.b.* '90 (OM)[C] Elkhorn, NE Mount Michael High School; [K] Elkhorn, NE Mount Michael Abbey.
Sokalski, Marcel *o.f.m.conv.* (ALT) Johnstown, PA SS. Casimir & Emerich.
Sokol, Alfred *s.d.b.* '47 (NEW)[N] Ramsey, NJ Don Bosco Prep Salesian Residence; [C] Ramsey, NJ Don Bosco Preparatory High School.
Sokol, Stanley '85 (SPR) Springfield, MA Immaculate Conception; Springfield, MA Our Lady of the Rosary.
Sokolowski, Bernard T. '45 (BUF)[O] Lackawanna, NY Bishop Head Residence Retired.
Sokolowski, Edward V. '44 (SCR) Retired.
Sokolowski, Robert S. '61 (HRT)[C] Catholic University of America, The.
Sokolowski, Robert S. '65 (HRT) On Duty Outside the Archdiocese.
Sokolowski, Thomas J. '79 (SCR) Scranton, PA Immaculate Conception.
Sokolowski, William R. '65 (HRT) Wolcott, CT St. Maria Goretti.
Sokolski, John *o.m.i.* '55 (SAT)[K] San Antonio, TX Oblate Madonna Residence.
Solan, Lawrence T. '80 (COS) Highlands Ranch, CO St. Mark.
Solana, Fermin '70 (MIA) Miami, FL Our Lady of Divine Providence.
Solano, Julio R. '93 (MIA) North Lauderdale, FL Our Lady Queen of Heaven.
Solari, James K. '55 (CHL) Retired.
Solarski, Jack '76 (GAL)[P] Houston, TX Opus Dei.
Solazzo, Michael J. '76 (CHI) Evanston, IL St. Mary.
Solcia, Louis M. *c.r.s.p.* '57 (SD) San Diego, CA Our Lady of the Rosary.
Soler, Lawrence *t.o.r.* '51 (AUS) Waco, TX Sacred Heart.
Soler, Manuel A. '98 (MIA) Miami Beach, FL St. Patrick.
Soler, Roberto '62 (MGZ) Aguada, PR Santuario Protomartires de la Concepcion.
Soles, John '64 (BRK)[U] Russian Apostolate.
Soles, Juan '64 (NY) New York, NY St. Michael Chapel; Metropolitan Correctional Center.
Soleta, Chester A. *c.s.c.* '42 (FTW)[I] Notre Dame, IN Holy Cross House.
Soley, Roger A. '78 (WDC) Silver Spring, MD St. Andrew Apostle.
Solis, Marco '97 (LA) South El Monte, CA Epiphany.
Solis, Olman '97 (OAK) Walnut Creek, CA St. Mary's.
Solis, Oscar A. (HT) Upper Lafourche Deanery.
Solis, Oscar '79 (HT) Thibodaux, LA St. Joseph Co-Cathedral; Priests Council.
Solis, Ralph '93 (ELP) El Paso, TX Holy Spirit.
Solis, Sergio (CHI) Waukegan, IL Holy Family.
Solivan, Roberto '88 (CGS) Punta Santiago, PR Nuestra Senora del Carmen.
Soliwoda, Jan '99 (BRK) Maspeth, NY Holy Cross.
Solla, Santiago '53 (PCE) Juana Diaz, PR St. Raymond Nonato.
Solma, Maritn A. *s.m.* '78 (STL)[O] Bro. Vincent House.
Soloman, Louis E. *s.j.* '64 (NY)[EE] New York, NY Murray–Weigel Hall.
Solors, Stephen '91 (DUL) Deer River, MN St. Joseph's; Deer River, MN St. Anne; Deer River, MN Sacred Heart.
Solorzano, Marcelo *o.p.* (DAL)[K] Irving, TX Dominican Priory of St. Albert the Great.
Solorzano, Miguel A. '93 (GAL) Houston, TX St. Philip of Jesus.
Soltis, John F. *m.m.* '62 (HON) Honolulu, HI St. Pius X.
Soltis, John *m.m.* (HON) Korean Ministry.
Soltys, Daniel F. '68 (OM) Gretna, NE St. Patrick.
Soltys, Raymond A. '79 (SPR) Ludlow, MA Christ the King.
Somarriba, Marcos A. '93 (MIA) Opa Locka, FL Our Lady of Perpetual Help Church.
Somers, Eldon K. '51 (E) Retired.
Somers, Michael '82 (GB) Absent on Leave.
Somers, Richard '66 (JKS) Greenville, MS St. Joseph.
Somerville, Alvin *o.f.m.conv.* '58 (ALB) Albany, NY St. Casimir; Albany, NY Our Lady of Angels.
Somerville, Walter F. (CHI) Retired.
Sommer, Allan J. '66 (MIL) CIVIL AIR PATROL; Port Washington, WI St. Mary.
Sommer, Gerald J. *m.s.c.* '47 (Y) Canton, OH St. Mary.
Sommer, Harold *s.j.* '65 (CIN)[M] Cincinnati, OH Faber Jesuit Community.
Sommer, Jerome '40 (STL) Retired.
Sommer, Jerome '40 (JC) Retired.
Sommer, Kenneth J. *s.m.* '59 (STL)[O] Cincinnati, OH; [M] Dayton, OH Marianist Community.
Sommer, Ralph '83 (RVC) Westbury, NY St. Brigid.
Sommerville, Conrad *o.f.m.conv.* '54 (SY) Syracuse, NY Assumption B.V.M..
Sommerville, William P. '93 (GAL) Freeport, TX St. Mary: Star of the Sea.
Somoza, Jose *o.f.m.* '65 (MIA) Miami, FL St. Timothy.
Son, Doan Trong (LA)[Q] Long Beach, CA.
Son, Ignatius (ALB) Special Assignment.
Son, Nguyen Thanh *c.ss.r.* '85 (LA)[Q] Baldwin Park, CA Vietnamese Redemptorist Mission.
Son, Nguyen That '90 (WH) Marlinton, WV St. John Neumann.
Son, Yong Hwan (NO) Hanmaum Korean Catholic Chapel.
Sondergeld, Theodore '59 (SEA) Retired.
Sondgeroth, Louis *o.m.i.* (WDC)[M] Washington, DC Oblate Community.
Sonefeld, Raymond G. '48 (KAL) Retired.
Song Peter Bang, Ui (LAV) Las Vegas, NV St. Paul Jung–Ha–Sang.
Songy, David *o.f.m.cap.* '87 (DEN)[N] Denver, CO Fraternidad San Antonio.
Songy, James B. '54 (HT) Vicar General; Priests Council; Legal Services Retired.
Sonnberger, Albert W. '56 (LC) Retired.
Sonnier, Cedric '97 (LAF) Erath, LA St. John; Catholic Daughters of America.
Sonnier, Charles '64 (VIC) Sweet Home, TX St. John the Baptist; Sweet Home, TX Queen of Peace; Presbyteral Council.
Sonnier, T. Alcide '56 (LAF) Retired.
Sontheimer, W. Wendell '47 (NO) Retired.
Soper, Paul P. '90 (BO) Revere, MA St. Anthony of Padua.
Sopiak, Donald A. '78 (DET) Detroit, MI Our Lady Queen of Heaven.
Sopke, Philip G. *c.s.c.* '88 (FTW)[I] Salem, OR St. Edward; Keizer, OR St. Edward.
Sopoliga, Michael '79 (PSC) Fort Pierce, FL SS. Cyril and Methodius.
Sopp, Michael '75 (SJP) Ford City, PA St. Mary.
Soprano, Ernest R. '79 (CAM) Vineland, NJ St. Francis of Assisi.
Soprych, Marion '75 (CHI) Chicago, IL St. Bede the Venerable.
Soranno, Joseph M. '74 (SPR) Wilbraham, MA St. Cecilia's.
Soranno, Joseph (SPR) Deans.
Sorce, John J. '52 (CHR) Absent On Leave.
Sorci, Francis P. '42 (BUF) Retired.
Sordillo, Ronald '72 (PAT) West Milford, NJ St. Joseph.
Sorensen, Bryan '88 (RC) Rapid City, SD St. Therese the Little Flower.
Sorgi, Anthony D. '82 (NY) Carmel, NY St. James the Apostle.
Soria, Manuel B. '81 (SAC) Yuba City, CA St. Isidore.
Soria, Manuel (SAC) Vicars Forane; College of Consultors.
Soriano, Danilo '78 (JOL) Naperville, IL St. Margaret Mary.
Soriano, Jesus T. '70 (SAC) Vallejo, CA St. Catherine of Siena.
Soriso, Emmanuel A. '93 (NEW) Nutley, NJ Our Lady of Mount Carmel.
Sork, David A. '70 (LA) Rancho Palos Verdes, CA St. John Fisher.
Sorohan, David V. '59 (COL) Columbus, OH St. Catharine; Diocesan Judges; Diocesan Board of Review for the Protection of Children.
Sors, Vladimir '28 (PEO) Retired.
Sorvillo, Mark B. '78 (CHI) Chicago, IL St. Margaret Mary.
Sosa, Juan J. '72 (MIA) Miami, FL St. Catherine of Siena; Committee on Popular Piety.
Sosa, Juan (MIA) Archdiocesan Vocations Review Board.
Sosa, Philip *m.s.f.* '68 (BWN) Donna, TX St. Joseph; Presbyteral Council.
Soseman, Richard '92 (PEO) Princeville, IL St. Mary of the Woods; [Q] Peoria, IL Archbishop Fulton J. Sheen Foundation.
Soseman, Richard (PEO) Judicial Vicar; Diocesan College of Consultors.
Sosinski, Thomas P. '58 (MAD) Absent on Sick Leave.
Sosnowski, Ted *c.r.* (STL) St. Louis, MO Our Lady of Loretto.
Sostrich, John L. '62 (SD) Retired.
Sota, Pascual *c.m.* '56 (SJN) San Juan, PR San Vicente de Paul.
Sotak, Donald J. '62 (PIT) Natrona, PA St. Joseph.
Sotak, John J. *o.s.a.* '92 (TLS)[B] Tulsa, OK Cascia Hall Preparatory School.
Sotelo, A. Richard *s.j.* '87 (BAL)[S] Houston, TX St. Mary's.
Sotelo, Angel '91 (FRS) Bakersfield, CA San Clemente.
Sotelo, Antonio '58 (PHX) Retired.
Sotelo, Fabio '99 (ATL) Doraville, GA Our Lady of the Americas.
Sotiroff, Stephen T. '81 (SFD) Vandalia, IL Mother of Dolors.
Sotiroff, Steven '81 (SFD) Ramsey, IL St. Joseph.
Soto, Angel Leonides '92 (MGZ) San German, PR San German de Auxerre.
Soto, Calixto '85 (SJN) Toa Alta, PR San Jose.
Soto, Carlos R. '99 (CGS) Las Piedras, PR Inmaculada Concepcion.
Soto, Charles *o.f.m.* '70 (NY)[EE] Corpus Christi, TX NAS Corpus Christi; Navy Chaplains.
Soto, Edward '58 (LA) Maywood, CA St. Rose of Lima.
Soto, Jose L. *m.d.r.* '80 (NY) Bronx, NY Our Lady of Grace.
Soto, Julio *s.d.b.* '63 (NY) Port Chester, NY Our Lady of the Rosary.
Soto, Leonides (MGZ) Christian Family Movement.
Soto Tanon, Carmelo '89 (SJN) On Duty Outside the Archdiocese.
Sottocornula, Frank *s.x.* '59 (PAT)[M] Wayne Xaverian Missionary Fathers.
Soucey, Louis A. '74 (MAN) North Conway, NH Our Lady of the Mountains Retired.
Soucie, Edward A. *s.j.* (CI) Sacred Heart; [C] Kolonia, Pohnpei, FM Jesuit House.
Souckar, Michael A. '88 (MIA)[M] Miami Shores, FL Archdiocese of Miami Millennium Appeal, Inc.; [M] Miami Shores, FL Archdiocese of Miami, Inc.; Chancellor; Judges; Incardination Committee; Consultants; Chancellor's Office; Consultors; Special Assignment.
Souckar, Michael (MIA) Secretary to the Archbishop.
Souckar, Michael (SAM) Judges.
Soucy, A. Francis *o.f.m.* '67 (PAT)[M] Ringwood, NJ Holy Name Friary, Inc..
Soucy, Robert P. '62 (BO) Senior Priests Retired.
Soucy, Timothy J. '73 (OG) Lowville, NY St. Mary; Lowville, NY St. Hedwig; Lowville, NY St. Peter; Deans; Priest Personnel Board.
Souffrant, Claude *s.j.* '67 (CHI) Chicago, IL St. Margaret of Scotland.
Soukup, Paul A. *s.j.* '79 (SJ) Catholic Scouting; [B] Santa Clara, CA Jesuit Community.

Soule, W. Beckett *o.p.* (SJP) Judge.
Soulliere, Richard '76 (MIA) Legion of Mary (English Speaking); Marian Movements & Devotions Retired.
Soupos, Christopher (SB) Retired.
Sousa, Edward A. '03 (PRO) East Providence, RI St. Francis Xavier.
Sousa, Eugene W. *o.p.* '58 (SAC) Benicia, CA St. Dominic.
Sousa, Jose '85 (FR) Absent on Leave.
Sousa, Manuel F. '80 (STO) Turlock, CA Our Lady of the Assumption of the Portuguese Church (Pastor of).
Sousa, Peter E. *c.ss.r.* '78 (VEN) Wauchula, FL St. Michael; Army Reserve Chaplains; AUXILIARY CHAPLAINS CONTRACT CHAPLAINS.
Souse, Stephen J. *o.s.b.* '43 (PEO).
Southerton, Gary '88 (SEA)[C] Unassigned.
Soutiere, Ronald A. '74 (BUR) Retired.
Soutus, Hugo '94 (STN) Phoenix, AZ Assumption of B.V.M..
Soutuyo, Raul '93 (MIA) Miami, FL St. Brendan.
Souza, Jason '98 (LA) North Hollywood, CA St. Charles Borromeo.
Sowada, Arlie '73 (SCL) Grey Eagle, MN St. Joseph's.
Sowada, Arlin '73 (SCL) Grey Eagle, MN St. John the Baptist.
Sowada, Terrance '92 (SP) Tampa, FL Christ the King.
Sowinski, Albin F. '51 (MIL)[M] Wauwatosa, WI St. Camillus Health Center, Inc. Retired.
Sowinski, Richard E. '74 (BUF) Veterans Hospital; Kenmore, NY St. Paul.
Sowinski, Richard F. (BUF).
Soy, Esteban G. '52 (VEN) Moore Haven, FL St. Joseph the Worker.
Soy, Esteban (VEN) Deans; Presbyteral Council; Hispanic, Migrant and Spanish Speaking Apostolates/ National Migration Week.
Soysa, Joseph '72 (NY) Stony Point, NY Immaculate Conception.
Spacek, Frank '97 (BRK) Brooklyn, NY St. Barbara; Brooklyn, NY St. Bernard's.
Spacek, William F. '95 (BAL) Baltimore, MD St. Alphonsus, Shrine of; Special Assignment.
Spacht, Harold *c.ss.r.* '61 (CGS)[B] Aguas Buenas, PR Casa Cristo Redentor.
Spada, Rino *c.s.* '49 (LA) Retired.
Spadaro, Thomas L. '64 (RVC) Holbrook, NY Good Shepherd; Senate of Priests (Presbyteral Council/ College of Consultors); South Brookhaven Deanery.
Spadini, Marian '62 (JKS) Memphis, TN Retired.
Spagnola, Michael G. (CAM) Advocates.
Spagnolia, D. George '68 (BO) Lowell, MA St. Patrick.
Spagnolo, Michael G. (CAM) Blackwood, NJ St. Agnes.
Spagnolo, Nicholas *c.s.s.* '52 (BO)[V] Waltham, MA Stigmatine House.
Spahn, James A. *o.p.* '81 (DEN) Denver, CO St. Dominic.
Spahn, James Anthony *o.p.* '81 (DEN)[A] Denver, CO St. Dominic Priory.
Spahn, James S. (DEN) Centennial, CO St. Thomas More.
Spahn, James (DEN) Ault, CO St. Mary; Windsor, CO Our Lady of the Valley.
Spahr, Matthew D. '92 (SD) Alpine, CA Queen of Angels; [A] San Diego, CA St. Francis De Sales Center.
Spahr, Matthew '92 (SD) San Diego, CA Immaculata; Priestly Formation — St. Francis de Sales Center; College of Consultors; Presbyteral Council.
Spain, John H. *m.m.* '70 (FgM).
Spain, P. Arnold '47 (BIS) Retired.
Spalding, Francis Larry '80 (L) Unassigned.
Spalding, J. Mark '91 (L) LaGrange, KY Immaculate Conception; Judicial Vicar and Director; College of Consultors; Ex Officio.
Spalding, Leon C. '59 (L) Retired.
Spanel, Hubert J. '59 (GI) Ord, NE Our Lady of Perpetual Help Retired.
Spangenberg, George J. *c.s.sp.* '76 (PIT) Pittsburgh, PA Holy Spirit.
Spanier, Marian '81 (NEW) Hackensack, NJ St. Joseph's.
Spanjers, John J. (SUP) St. Pius Priest Fund Retired.
Spanley, Anthony L. '68 (GRY) Hamlet, IN Holy Cross.
Spannagel, Luke A '03 (PEO) Carthage, IL Immaculate Conception.
Spano, Anthony A. *s.d.b.* '43 (NEW)[N] Ramsey, NJ Don Bosco Prep Salesian Residence; [C] Ramsey, NJ Don Bosco Preparatory High School.
Spano, Philip F. '82 (BR) Gonzales, LA St. Theresa of Avila; Board Members.
Sparacino, Thomas A. '98 (PIT) Bethel Park, PA St. Valentine; Co Directors.
Sparklin, Paul '90 (BAL) Towson, MD Church of the Immaculate Conception.
Sparks, Kenneth A. '95 (PIT) Pittsburgh, PA Our Lady of Grace; Army National Guard Chaplains.
Sparks, Richard *c.s.p.* '78 (OAK) Berkeley, CA Holy Spirit Parish/Newman Hall.
Sparough, J. Michael *s.j.* '78 (CHI)[C] Chicago, IL Jesuit Community at Loyola University Chicago.
Spatorico, Joseph S. '66 (BUF) Council of Priests; Batavia, NY St. Anthony.
Spatt, John *c.pp.s.* '43 (CIN)[B] Carthagena, OH St. Charles.
Spatz, Silva '99 (HON)[E] Ewa Beach, HI St. Francis Medical Center – West.
Spaulding, Donald E. '57 (EVN) Retired.
Spaulding, John D. '71 (PHX) Cave Creek, AZ St. Gabriel.
Speaks, Sidney *s.s.j.* '99 (WDC) Washington, DC Our Lady of Perpetual Help.
Specht, Joseph E. *s.j.* '69 (HON)[E] Honolulu, HI St. Francis Medical Center; [G] Honolulu, HI Jesuit Fathers House.
Specht, Terry W. '96 (ARL) Fairfax, VA St. Leo's; [D] Fairfax, VA Paul VI Catholic High School.
Speck, Gregory M. *s.c.j.* '76 (BWN) Raymondville, TX Our Lady of Guadalupe; Ad Hoc Committee for Diocesan Insurance.
Speck, Gregory *s.c.j.* '76 (BWN) Lyford, TX Prince of Peace.
Speck, James A. '50 (WIN) Retired.
Speckman, Harry *o.f.m.* '61 (GAY) Indian River, MI Cross in the Woods Catholic Shrine.
Speer, Patrick J. '41 (HRT)[L] Trumbull, CT St. Joseph's Manor; Cambridge Springs, PA St. Anthony; Deans Retired.
Speerstra, William F. '59 (SUP) Retired.
Speicher, Charles W. '75 (PIT) Pittsburgh, PA St. John the Baptist; Judges.
Speicher, David J. '86 (LAN) East Lansing, MI St. Thomas Aquinas; College of Consultors.
Speichinger, Lawrence '55 (KC) Retired.
Speier, Francis J. '75 (TOL) Toledo, OH St. John the Baptist.
Speier, Thomas *o.f.m.* '58 (GRY)[Q] Cincinnati, OH University of Cincinnati Newman Center; [M] Cincinnati, OH St. Francis Seraph Friary.
Speier, Tom *o.f.m.* '58 (CIN) Cincinnati, OH St. Monica–St. George Parish Newman Center.
Speiser, Thomas M. '77 (DAL) Richardson, TX St. Joseph.
Speitel, Edmond J. '55 (PH) Retired.
Spekschate, John '42 (LAF) Retired.
Spellerberg, Joseph R. *s.j.* '53 (BUF) Buffalo, NY St. Michael.
Spellman, John P. *o.s.f.s.* '66 (WIL)[B] Wilmington, DE Salesianum School.
Spellman, Paul J. '01 (LA) Claremont, CA Our Lady of the Assumption.
Spellman, Robert M. '74 (WOR) Berlin, MA St. Joseph the Good Provider.
Spenard, James *o.s.a.* '72 (ALB) Troy, NY St. Augustine; Presbyteral Council; Diocesan Board of Consultors.
Spencer, Brian '03 (SAG) Saginaw, MI St. Stephen.
Spencer, F. Richard '88 (BAL) Military Chaplains; Army Chaplains.
Spencer, F. Richard (MO) Presbyteral Council.
Spencer, Francis R. '88 (BAL) Laurel, MD Resurrection of Our Lord.
Spencer, Gregory D. '89 (R) Morehead City, NC St. Egbert.
Spencer, Jeremiah L. '65 (KCK) Kansas City, KS Holy Name; Kansas City, KS K.U. Medical Center and Chapel; Hospitals; Nurses Association.
Spencer, John *s.j.* '79 (BO)[V] Newton, MA The Jesuit Community at Boston College.
Spencer, Robert A. '98 (CHR) Military Chaplains; Navy Chaplains.
Spencer, Robert M. '82 (RIC) Petersburg, VA St. Joseph.
Spencer, Robert *l.c.* '58 (SAT) Special Assignment.
Spencer, Robert '58 (CC) On Special Assignment.
Spencer, William *o.f.m.* '74 (CHI) Chicago, IL St. Peter's; [N] Chicago, IL St. Peter's Friary.
Spendov, Vendelin *o.f.m.* '47 (CHI)[N] Lemont, IL The Slovene Franciscan Fathers, Order of Friars Minor, Commissariat of the Holy Cross.
Spengler, James F. '68 (BRK) Brooklyn, NY Holy Cross; St. Albans, NY St. Catherine of Sienna.
Spengler, James (BRK) Queens South; Assignment Board.
Spenner, Jerome I. '64 (OM) Omaha, NE St. Bernard.
Speno, Eugene '60 (SB) Retired.
Spera, James F. '77 (NEW)[B] Seton Hall University; [B] School of Diplomacy and Intl. Rels..
Spera, James '77 (NEW)[A] South Orange, NJ Seton Hall University College Seminary.
Sperger, Herbert J. '79 (PH) Philadelphia, PA Immaculate Conception; Philadelphia, PA St. Michael.
Sperl, August J. '54 (SFD) Virden, IL Sacred Heart.
Sperlak, Charles S. '64 (ALN) Reading, PA SS. Cyril and Methodius.
Sperry, James E. '41 (E) Legion of Mary Retired.
Spexarth, Daniel J. '84 (WCH) Wichita, KS St. Thomas Aquinas; Diocesan Apostolate to Marriage Encounter.
Spexarth, James '55 (WCH) Retired
Spexarth, Jerome J. '01 (WCH) Pittsburg, KS Our Lady of Lourdes.
Spexarth, Jerome L. (WCH) Ongoing Formation of the Clergy Committee.
Spexarth, Joachim *o.s.b.* '65 (OKL)[I] Shawnee, OK St. Gregory's Abbey; Consultors Archdiocesan; Council of Priests Archdiocesan.
Speyrer, Jules '45 (LAF) Retired.
Spezia, Leo J. '76 (STL) St. Louis, MO St. John the Baptist.
Spezia, Robert R. '96 (DET) Special Assignment.
Spezia, Robert '97 (DET)[A] The College of Liberal Arts.
Spezzano, James '97 (YAK) Benton City, WA St. Frances Xavier Cabrini.
Spicer, Kevin P. *c.s.c.* '92 (FR)[A] North Easton, MA Holy Cross Fathers Religious.
Spicer, Kevin *c.s.c.* '92 (FR)[A] North Easton, MA Stonehill College.
Spicer, Leo M. *o.s.m.* '76 (CHI)[N] Chicago Order of Friar Servants of Mary (Servites) United States of America Province, Inc..
Spicer, Richard J. '86 (SEA) Langley, WA St. Hubert.
Spiece, Lawrence T. '61 (E)[F] Fairview, PA Camp Notre Dame.
Spiegel, John D. '76 (DAV) Ottumwa, IA St. Mary of the Visitation; Ottumwa, IA St. Patrick's.
Spiegel, Robert H. '66 (DAV) Military Chaplains; Army Chaplains.
Spiegel, Thomas J. '67 (DAV) Bettendorf, IA Our Lady of Lourdes.
Spiekermeier, Michael '69 (DAV) Davenport, IA St. Paul the Apostle.
Spieler, Joseph *s.j.* '75 (SD) San Diego, CA Christ the King.
Spielman, Paul E. '61 (STL) St. Louis, MO St. Mary of Victories.
Spielmann, Henry V. *o.s.a.* '39 (TLS)[B] Tulsa, OK Cascia Hall Preparatory School.
Spielmann, Paul '61 (STL) St. Louis, MO St. John Nepomuk.
Spier, Mathias *o.s.b.* '58 (SCL) Cold Spring, MN St. James; [H] Cold Spring, MN Assumption Home; [H] Cold Spring, MN John Paul Apartments; [H] Cold Spring, MN Assumption Court; [I] Collegeville, MN St. John's Abbey, of the Order of St. Benedict.
Spiers, Edward F. '39 (COL) Retired.
Spies, Dennis '02 (JOL) Roselle, IL St. Walter.
Spiess, Kevin J. '86 (CHI) Winnetka, IL SS. Faith, Hope and Charity; Members.
Spilka, Anthony Francis *o.f.m.conv.* '69 (SPR) Holyoke, MA Mater Dolorosa.
Spillane, Emmanuel *o.c.s.o.* '44 (SLC)[F] Huntsville, UT Abbey of Our Lady of the Holy Trinity of the Order of Cistercians.
Spillane, James J. *s.j.* '76 (MIL)[O] Milwaukee, WI Jesuit Community at Marquette University.
Spillane, Michael '68 (BAL) Retired.
Spillane, Walter J. '60 (KAL) Retired.
Spillane, William *c.ss.r.* '58 (STA) Jacksonville, FL Holy Rosary.
Spillett, Thomas '64 (SP) Dunedin, FL Our Lady of Lourdes.
Spilly, Alphonse *c.pp.s.* '67 (CIN)[M] Whiting, IN.
Spilly, Alphonse *c.pp.s.* (GRY)[A] Whiting, IN Calumet College of St. Joseph.
Spilly, William V. '74 (ROC) Rochester, NY St. John the Evangelist.
Spilman, Robert D. '96 (PEO) Earlville, IL St. Theresa's.
Spilman, Robert (PEO) Clergymen's Aid, Inc..
Spina, Douglas J. '76 (PRO) Johnston, RI Our Lady of Grace.
Spine, William J. *s.j.* '73 (LEX) Lexington, KY St. Paul.
Spine, William *s.j.* (LEX) Hispanic Ministry.
Spinelli, Joseph A. *o.s.a.* '55 (VEN) Naples, FL St. Elizabeth Seton.
Spinler, Ruben C. '94 (WIN) Rose Creek, MN Queen of Peace; Rose Creek, MN St. Peter's.
Spino, John '91 (NEW) Roselle, NJ Church of St. Joseph the Carpenter.
Spinos, Vincent J. *t.o.r.* '50 (STP) Minneapolis, MN St. Bridget; [M] Minneapolis, MN St. Bridget Friary.
Spinosa, Anthony '83 (OLL) Flint, MI Maronite Catholic Community; College of Consultors; Office for Missions; Office of Inter–faith/Ecumenical Affairs; Presbyteral Council; Office for the Third Millenium; Protopresbyters.
Spirko, Nicholas A. '72 (PIT) Washington, PA Immaculate Conception.
Spironello, Denilson *o.f.m.cap.* (BO)[V] Boston, MA St. Benedict the Moor Friary.
Spisak, Stephen M. '82 (CLV) Parma, OH St. Bridget.
Spishak, Carl A. '59 (ALT) Altoona Deanery; Altoona, PA St. Rose of Lima.
Spitale, John '26 (Y) Retired.
Spiteri, Joseph (MO) AUXILIARY CHAPLAINS CONTRACT CHAPLAINS.
Spiteri, Laurence J. '78 (LA) On Duty Outside the Archdiocese.
Spiteri, Laurence '78 (LAV) Diocesan Judges.
Spittler, Ernest G. *s.j.* '62 (CLV)[B] Cleveland, OH John Carroll University.
Spitz, Gregory M. '67 (MIL) Milwaukee, WI Our Lady,

Queen of Peace.
Spitzer, Michael H. '98 (PH) Graduate Studies.
Spitzer, Robert J. *s.j.* '83 (SPK)[B] Spokane, WA Gonzaga University.
Spitzig, Joseph '42 (CLV) Retired.
Spitzley, Denis R. '75 (LAN) Charlotte, MI St. Mary.
Splawski, Bernard *o.f.m.* '63 (CAM)[M] Margate, NJ Franciscan Friary.
Spleet, Julius A. '62 (SAG) Ithaca, MI St. Paul the Apostle Retired.
Splonskowski, Wilfred *o.s.b.* '52 (GF) Miles City, MT Sacred Heart.
Splonskowski, Wilfrid J. *o.s.b.* '52 (BIS)[A] Richardton, ND Assumption Abbey.
Spodnik, A. Leo '48 (HRT) Retired.
Spohrer, Dennis E. '03 (PEO) Peoria, IL St. Vincent De Paul.
Spoletini, Pasquale M. *s.j.* '54 (SPK)[J] Spokane, WA Regis Community.
Sponder, John '93 (JOL) Winfield, IL St. John the Baptist.
Spong, William '79 (FWT) On Duty Outside the Diocese.
Spontak, James A. '75 (PBR) Charleroi, PA Holy Ghost; Consultors.
Spors, Roman '58 (DUL) Emily, MN St. Emily; Cursillo Movement.
Sportino, Salvatore (NY) New York, NY Our Lady of Guadalupe.
Spotswood, Cecil R. '97 (MOB) Troy, AL St. Martin of Tours; [J] Troy, AL Troy State University Newman Center.
Spranger, William J. '56 (GRY) San Pierre, IN All Saints; [G] San Pierre, IN Trinity Continuing Care Services–Ind fka Holy Cross Care.
Sprauer, Michael '72 (P) Board Members.
Sprecace, Francis A. '55 (CAM) Retired.
Spreen, John '53 (SFD) Commission for the Care of Infirm and Retired Priests Retired.
Sprenger, Alan H. '60 (COL) Retired.
Sprenger, Alan M. '60 (COL) Westerville, OH St. Paul the Apostle.
Sprietsma, Leo *o.f.m.* '53 (LA)[Q] Santa Barbara, CA Franciscan Friary, Order of Friars Minor (Old Mission); [Q] Santa Barbara, CA St. Anthony's Seminary.
Spriggs, Robert W. '65 (SFD) Highland, IL St. Paul.
Sprigler, William A. '75 (NU) Hutchinson, MN Church of St. Anastasia; Stewart, MN Church of St. Boniface; Committee on Parishes.
Spring, Mark P. '80 (DAV) Knoxville, IA St. Anthony's.
Spring, Mark P. '99 (DAV) Melcher, IA Sacred Heart.
Springer, Francis *s.m.* '55 (SFR)[N] San Francisco, CA Marist Center of the West.
Springer, Lawrence F. '59 (CHI) Des Plaines, IL St. Zachary.
Springer, Robert H. *s.j.* '48 (NY).
Springer, William A. '72 (SD) San Diego, CA Mission Basilica San Diego De Alcala.
Springman, Donald W. '67 (L) Louisville, KY Our Lady of Consolation; Ex Officio.
Sprinkle, Robert R. *m.m.* '35 (NY).
Sproul, John M. '63 (SD)[EE] La Mesa, CA St. Martin of Tours.
Sprute, Mel '69 (B) Kellogg, ID St. Rita's.
Spuhler, Gregory *o.f.m.cap.* '98 (ALB) Albany, NY Our Lady of Angels.
Spychala, Daniel S. '84 (ARL) Annandale, VA St. Ambrose.
Spyrka, Edward C. *o.c.d.* '62 (GRY)[I] Munster, IN Discalced Carmelite Fathers Monastery.
Squeo, Eugene P. '71 (NEW) Jersey City, NJ Assumption/All Saints; Jersey City, NJ St. Patrick's.
Squiller, John '56 (STF)[A] Stamford, CT Ukrainian Catholic Seminary Inc. St. Basil College; Presbyteral Council.
Srebernak, Francis '37 (LAN) Retired.
Sreboth, Michael J. '86 (MOB) Montgomery, AL Our Lady, Queen of Mercy.
Sredzinski, Joseph L. '70 (GBG) Point Marion, PA St. Hubert.
Srenn, Thomas E. '77 (CHI) Chicago, IL Our Lady of Mount Carmel.
Sretenovic, Paul B. '02 (NEW) Maywood, NJ Our Lady Queen of Peace.
Srion, Charles N. '78 (RVC) Centereach, NY Assumption of the Blessed Virgin Mary.
Srnec, Stanley J. '42 (STP) Retired.
Srode, John S. *c.pp.s.* '72 (CIN)[M] Dayton Provincial Office of the Cincinnati Province of the Society of the Precious Blood; Air Force Chaplains.
Sroka, Gerald A. '60 (GRY) La Porte, IN Sacred Heart.
Ssebadduka, George '78 (LAN)[J] Adrian, MI Congregation of the Most Holy Rosary.
Ssebbowa, Edward '87 (FTW) Plymouth, IN St. Michael.
Ssekannyo, Denis '99 (LA) El Segundo, CA St. Anthony.
Ssekiranda, Remigious '98 (VEN) Fort Myers, FL Jesus the Worker Mission (Jesus Obrero); Fort Myers, FL San Jose Mission.
Ssekiwala, Maximus (CHI) Chicago, IL Our Lady of Peace.
Ssemakula, Luke '97 (OAK) Hayward, CA All Saints.
Ssewagudde, Vincent (GB) Wausaukee, WI St. Agnes.
St–Godard, Edward G. '64 (PRO) Woonsocket, RI Holy Family.
St. Amand, Ken '69 (NEW) Plainfield, NJ St. Mary.
St. Charles, Paul W. '66 (MEM) Retired.
St. Clair, Robert L. *s.j.* '58 (SJ)[B] Santa Clara, CA Jesuit Community; [M] Los Gatos, CA California Province of the Society of Jesus, Jesuit Provincial Office.
St. Cyr, Richard E. '66 (PRT) Augusta, ME St. Augustine's.
St. Fleur, Maxis '01 (ATL) Kennesaw, GA St. Catherine of Siena.
St. George, John P. *s.j.* '66 (NEW)[B] Jersey City, NJ Jesuit Center; [N] Jersey City, NJ Jesuits of Saint Peter's College, Inc..
St. George, Peter T. '95 (CIN) Military Chaplains; Navy Chaplains.
St. Germain, Andre '96 (NTN) Economos; Manchester, NH Our Lady of the Cedars.
St. Germain, Andre (NTN) Priest's Sickness & Disability, and Retirement Plans.
St. Germain, Andre (NTN) Order of St. Nicholas.
St. Germain, Andre (NTN) College of Eparchial Consultors.
St. Germain, Andre (NTN) Presbyteral Council.
St. Germain, Andre (NTN) Finance Council.
St. Germain, Andre (NTN) Sophia Press.
St. Germain, Andre (NTN) Diocese of Newton for the Melkites in the USA, Inc., a Massachusetts Corporation.
St. Germain, Brian '88 (PRM) Absent on Leave.
St. Jacques, Clement *s.a.* '45 (WDC)[B] Washington, DC Atonement Seminary–Franciscan Friars of the Atonement Retired.
St. James, Paul F. '68 (BUR) Winooski, VT St. Stephen.
St. Jean, M. Kidney '92 (MIA) Pompano Beach, FL St. Joseph Mission.
St. Jean, Marcel '96 (BGP) Riverside, CT St. Catherine of Siena.
St. Jean, Mary Kidney (MIA) Haitians.
St. John, George G. '52 (ALB) Retired.
St. John, George '52 (ALB) Albany, NY Blessed Sacrament.
St. John, Norman R. *s.v.d.* '62 (MET) Carrier Clinic; [M] Bordentown, NJ Society of the Divine Word.
St. John, Norman *s.v.d.* '62 (TR) Freehold, NJ St. Rose of Lima.
St. Jules, Stephen '79 (RCK) Cary, IL SS. Peter & Paul.
St. Laurent, Daniel A. '71 (MAN) Durham, NH St. Thomas More; [N] Durham, NH St. Thomas More Catholic Student Center at the University of New Hampshire.
St.Louis, Richard E. (MAN) Newport, NH St. Patrick.
St. Louis, Richard E. (MAN) Charismatic Renewal & Cursillo Movement.
St. Louis, Scott J. '02 (MAN) Absent on Sick Leave.
St. Marie, Denis L. '59 (CLV) South Amherst, OH Nativity of Blessed Virgin Mary; The Catholic Center.
St. Martin, Jeremy P. '02 (BO) Ashland, MA St. Cecilia.
St. Martin, Robert J. '56 (HRT) North Haven, CT St. Frances Cabrini; Deans.
St. Martin, Robert *o.f.m.conv.* '77 (STP) Bloomington, MN St. Bonaventure.
St. Onge, Omer *s.m.* '46 (BO)[X] Framingham, MA The Marist House.
St. Onge, Paul J. '41 (NOR) Retired.
St. Pierre, Leo L. '39 (MAN) Manchester, NH St. Anthony of Padua Retired.
St. Pierre, Michel J. '57 (BUR) Retired.
St. Pierre, Michel (BR VT)[H] Holyoke, MA Mont Marie Health Care Center, Inc..
St. Pierre, Roland *o.m.i.* '52 (BO)[V] Lowell, MA Missionary Oblates of Mary Immaculate.
St. Pierre, Romeo A. '54 (PRT) AUXILIARY CHAPLAINS CONTRACT CHAPLAINS Retired.
St. Pierre, Ronald L. '83 (BO) Health Leave.
St. Pierre, Thomas J. '80 (RVC) Brentwood, NY St. Anne's; Procurator & Advocates.
St.Vil, Ramone *m.m.* '03 (FgM).
St. Vil, Romane *m.m.* '03 (NEW) Elizabeth, NJ Our Lady of Most Holy Rosary/St. Michael.
Sta.Maria, Nicanor *aaa* (MO) Army Reserve Chaplains.
Staab, Gregory *o.m.v.* '84 (LA) Hawaiian Gardens, CA St. Peter Chanel.
Staak, John *o.m.i.* '95 (FgM).
Staal, David E. '90 (OAK) Livermore, CA St. Michael.
Staar, Robert J. '77 (NY) Stony Point, NY Immaculate Conception.
Stab, Herbert J. '59 (MET) Piscataway, NJ Our Lady of Fatima.
Stabene, Edmondo '45 (STU) Retired.
Stabeno, John M. '00 (CAM) Woodbury, NJ St. Patrick's.
Stabeno, John (CAM) Pastoral Planning for Parish Life.
Stabile, Thomas *t.o.r.* '87 (VEN) Sarasota, FL Our Lady Queen of Martyrs.
Stacer, John R. *s.j.* '63 (NO).
Stachacz, James T. '98 (RVC)[P] Lindenhurst, NY Our Lady of Perpetual Help.
Stacherczak, Idzi '75 (CHI) Chicago, IL St. Priscilla.
Stachewicz, Henry J. '47 (BUF) Retired.
Stachnik, Kenneth R. '86 (GAY) Alpena, MI St. John the Baptist.
Stachowiak, Conrad P. (BUF) Deaf; Depew, NY St. Augustine.
Stachura, Thaddeus X. '64 (WOR) Worcester, MA Our Lady of Czestochowa; Apostleship of Prayer and Eucharistic Crusade.
Stachura, Thaddeus (WOR) Diocesan Building Commission Members.
Stachurski, David *o.f.m.conv.* '80 (SAV) Statesboro, GA St. Matthew; Statesboro Deanery.
Stachurski, Miroslaw '03 (BGP) Brookfield, CT St. Joseph.
Stachyra, Kenneth '01 (RCK) Crystal Lake, IL St. Thomas the Apostle; Harmon, IL St. Flannen; Harmon, IL St. Patrick; Harmon, IL St. Mary.
Stack, Aquinas *o.carm.* '85 (PMB) Boca Raton, FL St. Jude.
Stack, Christopher '66 (PMB) Retired.
Stack, Daniel '82 (ATL) Cartersville, GA St. Francis of Assisi.
Stack, Gabriel D. *o.praem.* '82 (ORG)[D] Silverado, CA St. Michael's Preparatory School; [I] Silverado, CA Norbertine Fathers of Orange Inc..
Stack, George J. '61 (BRK)[V] Jamaica, NY Parsons Manor.
Stack, George '61 (BRK) Retired.
Stack, Gilbert *o.s.b.* '39 (KC)[J] Stanberry, MO.
Stack, James M. '86 (WDC) Hyattsville, MD St. Jerome.
Stack, Jerome *c.pp.s.* '72 (LA) Metropolitan State Hospital.
Stack, John G. *s.j.* '71 (DAL)[D] Dallas, TX Jesuit College Preparatory School.
Stack, John J. '53 (HRT) West Hartford, CT St. Thomas the Apostle Church Retired.
Stack, John J. '88 (DAV)[J] Clinton, IA Mercy Medical Center – Clinton.
Stack, John P. '55 (WDC) Helen, MD Our Lady of the Wayside.
Stack, John P. *o.s.a.* '74 (PH)[C] Villanova University; [AA] Villanova, PA St. Thomas Monastery.
Stack, Richard J. '56 (E) Erie, PA St. Paul; Matrimonial Judges.
Stack, Thomas Mannix '73 (MIA) Southwest Ranches, FL St. Mark.
Stack, William E. '48 (MAD) Retired.
Stackpoole, Edward V. *s.j.* '56 (SFR)[N] San Francisco, CA Jesuit Community at University of San Francisco.
Stadmueller, Roman *s.d.s.* (MO) AUXILIARY CHAPLAINS CONTRACT CHAPLAINS.
Stadtmueller, Fred '40 (SFE) Retired.
Stadtmueller, Roman *s.d.s.* '54 (WDC)[B] Silver Spring, MD Salvatorian Community.
Staebell, Francis *s.j.* '50 (BUF) Buffalo, NY St. Michael.
Staebell, James A. '57 (BUF) Retired.
Staehler, Adrian *o.f.m.cap.* '67 (GB)[L] Appleton, WI Monte Alverno Retreat Center.
Staes, Robert F. *o.p.* '71 (DEN) Council for Religious; Denver, CO St. Dominic; [A] Denver, CO St. Dominic Priory.
Staff, Stephen M. '90 (MOB) On Leave from the Archdiocese.
Stafford, Dennis '91 (CHI) Mt. Prospect, IL St. Emily.
Stafford, Edward *t.o.r.* (PIT)[N] McKeesport, PA Serra Friary; [N] Mc Keesport, PA Franciscan Friars, T.O.R., Serra Friary.
Stafford, James D.M. '61 (OKL) Lawton, OK Blessed Sacrament; Region IV.
Stafford, Joseph L. '57 (BRK) Flushing, NY Holy Family.
Stafford, Michael *o.s.b.* '58 (PRO)[P] Portsmouth, RI Abbey of St. Gregory the Great.
Stafford, Raymond W. '59 (BRK) Long Island City, NY Most Precious Blood.
Stagaman, David J. *s.j.* '66 (CHI)[C] Chicago, IL Jesuit Community at Loyola University Chicago.
Stagg, Robert B. '75 (NEW) Springfield, NJ St. James.
Stagnaro, John J. '76 (BO) Watertown, MA Sacred Heart.
Stahel, Thomas H. *s.j.* '71 (NO)[F] New Orleans, LA Jesuit High School; [P] New Orleans, LA Jesuit Provincial Office.
Stahl, Allen M. '75 (ORL) On Duty Outside the Diocese; Army Chaplains.
Stahl, David A. '91 (DEN) Brush, CO St. Mary.
Stahura, Joseph L. '81 (HBG) Greencastle, PA St. Mark the Evangelist.
Staib, Donald F. '61 (R) Apex, NC St. Mary Magdalene; Diocesan Consultors.
Staib, Donald (R) Priests' Council.
Staigers, Del '87 (CIN) Dayton, OH Queen of Martyrs.
Staigers, P. Del '87 (CIN) Dayton, OH Our Lady of Mercy.
Staijkowski, James *m.s.* '73 (STL)[O] Generalate, Missionari di N.S. de La Salette.
Stainwall, Bernal '80 (NY) New York, NY St. John the Evangelist.

Stajkowski, James R. *m.s.* '73 (HRT)[M] Hartford Our Lady of Sorrows Rectory.
Stajkowski, Leo S. '66 (ALN) Reading, PA St. Mary.
Stake, Ronald P. '85 (CHI) Military Chaplains; Navy Chaplains.
Stakem, Ward G. *o.f.m.cap.* '78 (PIT) Rochester, PA St. Cecilia; Air Force Reserve Chaplains.
Stakem, Ward *o.f.m.cap.* '78 (PIT)[N] Rochester, PA St. Cecilia Friary.
Stalla, Michael J. '03 (CLV)[W] Painesville, OH St. Mary's – Painesville; Painesville, OH St. Mary.
Stallings, Michael W. '74 (TUC) Globe, AZ Holy Angels.
Stallings, Michael (TUC) Defenders of the Bond.
Stalter, Cal '94 (AMA) Wellington, TX Our Mother of Mercy; Shamrock, TX St. Patrick.
Stalzer, Joseph '59 (JOL) Absent on Sick Leave.
Stammitti, Anthony O. '91 (LIN) Lincoln, NE Sacred Heart; Advocates; Apostolate to the Elderly; Lincoln, NE Nebraska Penal Complex.
Stampiglia, Fausto *s.a.c.* '60 (VEN) Sarasota, FL St. Martha; [F] Sarasota, FL St. Martha's Housing, Inc.; [F] Sarasota, FL St. Martha's Housing II, Inc.; Theologian to the Bishop; Diaconate.
Stamschror, Robert P. '61 (WIN) Retired.
Stanbery, Stephen L. '80 (TOL) Holgate, OH St. Paul; Holgate, OH St. Mary; New Bavaria, OH Sacred Heart of Jesus.
Stanchik, Dennis P. '59 (LC) Retired.
Stander, Charles *s.m.* '81 (CIN)[M] San Antonio, TX Casa Maria Marianist Community.
Stander, Edwin L. '63 (LIN)[D] Lincoln, NE St. Elizabeth Regional Medical Center; Health Care Facilities.
Stanfield, Francis E. '80 (GLP) Retired.
Stanfield, George *c.p.* '68 (LA)[Q] Houston, TX Congregation of the Passion, Holy Name Retreat Center; [S] Houston, TX Holy Name Retreat Center.
Stanfield, William L. '76 (MIL) Oak Creek, WI St. Matthew.
Stang, Charles L. *s.j.* '67 (MIL)[O] Milwaukee, WI Pere Marquette House Jesuit Community; [E] Milwaukee, WI Marquette University High School.
Stang, Mark '90 (SCL) Long Prairie, MN St. Mary of Mt. Carmel.
Stang, William J. *c.pp.s.* '77 (LFT)[A] Rensselaer, IN Saint Joseph's College; Army National Guard Chaplains.
Stange, Henry A. '89 (ALT) Retired.
Stange, James R. '95 (P) Scappoose, OR St. Wenceslaus.
Stangel, Mark J. '65 (MIL) Retired.
Stanger, Edward J. '91 (STL) Florissant, MO Sacred Heart.
Stanger, Harold B. '77 (CHI) Deerfield, IL Holy Cross.
Stangl, Alfred E. (SCL).
Stangl, Alfred '63 (SCL) St. Cloud, MN U.S. Veteran's Hospital.
Stangl, Alfred '67 (SCL) Special Assignment.
Stangl, Frank J. '53 (JC) Retired.
Stangnelli, Anthony M. '79 (RVC) New Hyde Park, NY Holy Spirit.
Stanialus, Peter (TYL) Waskom, TX St. Lawrence Brindisi.
Stanibula, Christopher '95 (FR) Fall River, MA St. Anne's; [H] Fall River, MA St. John Vianney House.
Stanichar, Joseph '68 (VNN) Seattle, WA St. John Chrysostom.
Stanichar, Joseph (VNN) Director of Evangelization.
Stanievich, J. Walter '46 (DET) Retired.
Stanis, Casimir M. '01 (SCR) Wilkes–Barre, PA St. Joseph's; Hudson, PA Sacred Heart.
Staniskis, Daniel '84 (PSC) Flanders, NJ Holy Wisdom.
Staniszewski, Ignatius *s.s.p.* '64 (NY)[B] New York, NY Society of St. Paul.
Staniszewski, Stanley *c.m.* '63 (HRT)[M] Manchester DePaul Provincial Residence.
Staniszewski, Stanley *c.m.* '64 (BGP) Stamford, CT Holy Name of Jesus.
Stankard, Albert H. '59 (BO) Framingham, MA St. Stephen.
Stanko, Andrew C. '70 (ALT) Johnstown, PA St. Stephen, First King of Hungary.
Stankus, Gregory A. '78 (BRK) Brooklyn, NY St. Francis Xavier.
Stanley, Brian L. '96 (KAL) Coldwater, MI St. Charles Borromeo; Florence Crane Correctional Facility for Women; Camp Branch; Lakeland Correctional Facility for Men.
Stanley, Charles R. '71 (BO) Peabody, MA St. John the Baptist.
Stanley, Colm *s.s.c.* '69 (OM)[K] St. Columbans, NE St. Columban's Foreign Mission Society.
Stanley, Matthew D. '91 (SJ) San Jose, CA Holy Family.
Stanley, Melvin *o.f.m.* '52 (OAK) Oakland, CA St. Elizabeth's; [N] Oakland, CA Franciscan Friars.
Stanley, Michael *o.s.a.* '81 (ALB) Troy, NY St. Augustine.
Stanley, Richard J. *s.j.* '74 (BO)[V] Boston, MA Loyola House; [X] Gloucester, MA Eastern Point Retreat House.
Stanley, Ronald *o.p.* '67 (NEW)[Q] Mahwah, NJ Ramapo College.
Stano, Luke M. *o.s.m.* '61 (CHI)[N] Chicago Order of Friar Servants of Mary (Servites) United States of America Province, Inc.; [N] Chicago, IL Order of Friar Servants of Mary (Servites) United States of America Province, Inc..
Stano, Luke *o.s.m.* '61 (ORG) Fullerton, CA St. Juliana Falconieri; [I] Fullerton, CA St. Juliana Falconieri Priory.
Stanonik, Anthony '82 (SD) On Duty Outside the Diocese.
Stanosz, Paul A. '84 (MIL) Graduate Studies; Brookfield, WI St. Dominic.
Stansberry, Richard D. '92 (OKL) Oklahoma City, OK St. Francis of Assisi; Archdiocesan Finance Council.
Stansberry, Richard (OKL) Region I; Adjutant Judicial Vicar; Consultors Archdiocesan; Associate Directors.
Stansberry, Tim (RVC) Valley Stream, NY Franklin Medical Center Hospital.
Stansley, Ralph W. '73 (TR) West Trenton, NJ Our Lady of Good Counsel; Tribunal Judges; Office of Permanent Deacons.
Stanton, Finbarr P. '67 (SAV) Albany, GA St. Teresa; Albany Deanery.
Stanton, Francis M. '59 (COL) Crooksville, OH Church of the Atonement; Vicariate 15: Perry County.
Stanton, Joseph E. '51 (COL) Columbus, OH St. Mary Retired.
Stanton, Thomas J. '91 (BO) Westford, MA St. Catherine of Alexandria.
Stanton, William J. '52 (PH) Retired.
Stanton, William J. '56 (SPC) Fredericktown, MO St. Michael; St. Francis de Sales Association Retired.
Stapenhorst, Verne P. '61 (SC) Laurens, IA Sacred Heart; West Bend, IA SS. Peter and Paul.
Staples, Terrence R. '95 (ARL) McLean, VA St. Luke's.
Stapleton, Edward J. *s.s.s.* '60 (CLV)[O] Highland Heights, OH.
Stapleton, Edward *s.s.s.* '60 (SP) Holiday, FL St. Vincent De Paul.
Stapleton, Gerard P. '85 (NO) Port Sulphur, LA St. Patrick.
Starasinich, James E. '99 (NEW)[A] Yona GU Redemptoris Mater Archdiocesan Missionary Seminary; On Duty Outside the Archdiocese.
Starbuck, James '48 (OAK) Retired.
Stark, Paul V. *s.j.* '85 (WH)[A] Wheeling, WV Wheeling Jesuit University.
Stark, Robert *s.s.s.* '77 (SFE) Albuquerque, NM St. Charles Borromeo.
Stark, Ronald P. *o.f.m.* '66 (NY) New York, NY St. Stephen of Hungary; [II] New York, NY Franciscan Missionary Charities, Inc..
Starkey, Donald J. (SFE) Delegate for Matrimonial Dispensations.
Starkey, Donald (SFE) Vice Chancellors.
Starkloff, Carl F. *s.j.* '65 (STL)[C] Saint Louis University; [O St. Louis, MO Jesuit Community Corporation at St. Louis University – Jesuit Hall.
Starks, R Mansfield '42 (ALB) Glenville, NY Immaculate Conception Retired.
Starmann, Joseph W. '63 (JC) Retired.
Staron, Stanley R. '74 (HRT)[I] Waterbury, CT St. Mary Hospital.
Starus, Ralph E. '69 (CHI) Posen, IL St. Stanislaus Bishop and Martyr.
Starzynski, Stefan P. '96 (ARL) Fredericksburg, VA St. Mary.
Stash, Robert '82 (PRM) Bay City, MI Saint George; Omer, MI St. John.
Stashek, Brian E. '02 (LC)[C] Wisconsin Rapids, WI Assumption Middle School; [C] Wisconsin Rapids, WI Assumption High School.
Stashek, Leonard C. '56 (LC) Retired.
Stasiak, Kurt *o.s.b.* '80 (IND)[A] St. Meinrad, IN St. Meinrad School of Theology; [K] St. Meinrad, IN St. Meinrad Archabbey.
Stasik, Thaddeus '60 (NEW) Jersey City, NJ St. Ann's; Polish Apostolate.
Stasiowski, John '65 (FWT) Lewisville, TX St. Philip the Apostle.
Stasker, R. Louis '65 (GR) Ada, MI St. Robert; Clergy Fund.
Stasyszen, Lawrence R. *o.s.b.* '94 (OKL [I] Shawnee St. Gregory's Abbey.
Stasyszen, Lawrence *o.s.b.* '94 (OKL)[A] Shawnee, OK St. Gregory's University.
Staszak, Bernard C. '65 (BUF) Panama, NY Our Lady of the Snows; Clymer, NY St. Matthias.
Staszewski, Joseph P. '64 (E) Brookville, PA Immaculate Conception; Finance Council Deans; Army Reserve Chaplains.
Statkus Francis J. '46 (PH) Retired.
Statnick, Roger A. (GBG) Vicar General/General Executive Director, Moderator of the Curia; College of Consultors; Bishop's Priests Council; Finance Council; The Catholic Foundation for the Diocese of Greensburg; Board of Members of the Corporation; Greensburg Catholic Accent and Communications, Inc.; Victim Assistance Coordinator.
Statt, Thomas R. '58 (ROC) Rochester, NY St. Charles Borromeo Retired.
Stattmiller, John E. '66 (COL) Columbus, OH Corpus Christi; Columbus, OH St. Ladislas; Diocesan Consultors; Parochial Examiners; Priests' Senate.
Statz, James '84 (SCL) Sauk Centre, MN Our Lady of the Angels; Sauk Centre, MN St. Alexius; Deans; Presbyteral Council.
Staub, Eugene J. *c.ss.r.* '52 (BR)[H] Baton Rouge, LA Redemptorist Vice Province.
Stauber, James '59 (SB) Retired.
Staublin, Daniel J. '82 (IND) Brownsburg, IN St. Malachy.
Staublin, Daniel (IND) Board of Consultors; Council of Priests.
Staud, Paul R. '70 (PIT) Pittsburgh, PA St. Elizabeth.
Staud, Sylvester W. '42 (WH) Retired.
Staudenmaier, John M. *s.j.* '70 (DET)[K] Detroit, MI Jesuit Community at the University of Detroit Mercy.
Staudenmaier, Wilbert '43 (GB) Retired.
Stauder, Paul W. '48 (BEL) Retired.
Stauder, William V. *s.j.* '52 (STL)[C] Saint Louis University; [O] St. Louis, MO Jesuit Community Corporation at St. Louis University – Jesuit Hall.
Staudinger, Greg '81 (GF) Sidney, MT St. Matthew's.
Staudt, Joseph W. '78 (RVC) Commack, NY Christ the King; Procurator & Advocates; Priests' Personnel Assignment Board.
Staunton, Patrick J. '60 (LA) La Puente, CA St. Joseph.
Stauter, Andrew '57 (MOB) Retired.
Stavoy, Stephen J. '79 (SCR) White Haven, PA St. Patrick's.
Stawasz, James '53 (HON) Retired.
Stawasz, John B. '53 (HON) Kailua–Kona, HI St. Michael The Archangel Retired.
Stawiarski, Waldemar '03 (CHI) Tinley Park, IL St. Stephen, Deacon and Martyr.
Staysniak, Dale W. '75 (CLV) Parma, OH St. Anthony of Padua.
Ste. Marie, Adrien *c.s.c.* '50 (P)[L] Portland, OR Holy Cross Fathers & Brothers, C.S.C. – University of Portland; [I] Notre Dame, IN Holy Cross House.
Stead, Julian *o.s.b.* '52 (PRO)[P] Portsmouth, RI Abbey of St. Gregory the Great.
Stead, Mell '56 (P) Lincoln City, OR St. Augustine.
Stearns, Joseph E. '72 (VEN) Naples, FL St. William.
Stearns, Joseph (VEN) College of Consultors.
Steber, Michael J. '86 (MAR) Escanaba, MI St. Anne; Charismatic Prayer Groups.
Stec, John '74 (MET) Perth Amboy, NJ St. Stephen; Eastern European Commission.
Stec, Joseph C. '57 (PH) Philadelphia, PA St. Laurentius Retired.
Stec, Mark D. '88 (BEL) Equality, IL St. Joseph; Shawneetown, IL St. Patrick; Ridgway, IL St. Joseph; Shawneetown, IL St. Mary; Diocesan Deans.
Stec, Michael S. '94 (LIN) Syracuse, NE St. Paulinus; Diocesan Area CCD Directors; Deaf Ministry.
Stec, Robert '88 (CLV)[A] Wickliffe, OH Borromeo Seminary; Vocations Office.
Stecher, John E. '72 (DAV)[H] Iowa City, IA Newman Catholic Student Center; [M] Iowa City, IA O'Keefe Hall.
Stecher, Kenneth C. (DUB) Fairbank, IA Immaculate Conception; Waterloo; Family Life Advisory Board.
Steck, Christopher W. *s.j.* '94 (NO)[M] Washington, DC The Jesuit Community at Georgetown University.
Steckel, Gregory A. '81 (DAV) On Duty Outside the Diocese.
Stecklein, Warren L. '90 (DOD) Pratt, KS St. Joseph; Pratt, KS Sacred Heart.
Stecklein, Warren (DOD) Diocesan Finance Council.
Steckler, Gerard *s.j.* '57 (P) Waldport, OR St. Anthony.
Steckler, Kenneth '96 (EVN) Mount Vernon, IN St. Matthew; Special Assignment; [A] Evansville, IN Mater Dei High School.
Stecz, Jeffrey M. '99 (PH) Hatfield, PA St. Maria Goretti.
Steed, Donald R. *m.m.* '54 (NY)[EE] Navy Chaplains.
Steed, Donald R. *m.m.* '54 (SR) U.S. Coast Guard Training Center.
Steeg, Mark Vander (GB) Appleton, WI St. Pius X.
Steele, J. *c.s.c.* '97 (FTW)[I] Notre Dame, IN Holy Cross Community, Corby Hall, University of Notre Dame.
Steele, John *c.s.c.* '97 (FTW)[B] University of Notre Dame Du Lac.
Steele, Joseph S. '97 (LIN) Grant, NE Mother of Sorrows.
Steele, Michael L. (BO) Wakefield, MA St. Joseph.
Steele, Philip G. *s.j.* '80 (STL)[O] St. Louis, MO Leo Brown Jesuit Community; [O] St. Louis, MO The Jesuits of the Missouri Province.
Steele, Steven G. '90 (MAD) Leave of Absence.
Steele, Thomas J. *s.j.* '64 (SFE) Albuquerque, NM Immaculate Conception.
Steen, Charles *o.f.m.* '64 (MIA)[H] Hialeah, FL Franciscan Friars of the Holy Name Province.
Steen, Raymond *o.m.i.* '60 (BO)[Y] Tewksbury, MA Immaculate Heart of Mary Infirmary.
Steenken, George W. *s.j.* '54 (CHI)[T] The Jesuit

Retreat League of Chicago.
Stefanelli, Joseph *s.m.* '51 (SJ)[M] Cupertino, CA Villa Saint Joseph.
Stefanko, Paul F. '76 (PRT) Yarmouth, ME Sacred Heart; Bishop's Delegate for Clergy; Officialis; Office Coordinator; Diocesan Consultors; Ex Officio; College of Consultors; Bishop's Delegate for Priests; Personnel Board.
Stefanowich, Paul *i.m.c.* '72 (MET)[H] Somerset, NJ Consolata Society for Foreign Missions.
Stefanski, Gery W. '79 (CHI) Other Assignments.
Stefanski, Walter '40 (CHI) Retired.
Steffen, Carl J. '58 (HBG) Orrtanna, PA St. Ignatius Loyola.
Steffen, Francis J. '57 (MAD) Dickeyville, WI Holy Ghost; Kieler, WI Immaculate Conception; Hazel Green, WI St. Joseph; St. Vincent de Paul Society.
Steffen, Kenneth C. '84 (SFD) Riverton, IL St. James; Tribunal Officers.
Steffen, Kenneth '84 (SFD) Springfield, IL St. Katharine Drexel; Advisory Board; Family Life Ministry:; Tribunal Advocacy Ministry:; Comite Diocesano de Ministerio Hispano – Diocesan Committee for Hispanic Ministry; Priests' Personnel Board; Presbyteral Council.
Steffen, Kenneth (SFD) Office for the Tribunal; Pilgrimage Director.
Steffenes, Gerard '60 (BAL) Westminster, MD St. John.
Steffens, Terrence J. '82 (GRY) Crown Point, IN St. Matthias.
Steffensmeier, Ralph J. '59 (OM) Cedar Rapids, NE St. Anthony.
Steffes, James P. '93 (WIN)[A] Winona, MN Immaculate Heart of Mary Seminary.
Steffes, Joseph *c.ss.r.* '40 (BR)[H] Baton Rouge, LA Redemptorist Vice Province.
Steffes, LuVerne W. '95 (OM) Atkinson, NE St. Joseph.
Steffes, Marvin J. *c.pp.s.* '58 (OAK) Los Gatos, CA Christ Child; [N] San Leandro, CA Society of the Precious Blood.
Steffes, Raymond *o.s.c.* '58 (SCL) Hillman, MN St. Rita's; Onamia, MN Sacred Heart; [I] Onamia, MN Crosier Monastery; Legion of Mary.
Steffl, Mark S. (NU) New Ulm, MN Cathedral of The Holy Trinity.
Steffy, David *l.c.* '94 (MAN)[A] Center Harbor, NH Immaculate Conception Apostolic School; [O] Center Harbor, NH L.C. Center Harbor, Inc..
Stefula, Salvator M. *aaa* (MO) Navy Reserve Chaplains.
Stefula, Salvator *t.o.r.* '74 (FWT) Forth Worth, TX St. Thomas.
Stefun, Bonaventure *o.f.m.cap.* '56 (PIT)[N] Pittsburgh, PA St. Augustine Friary; [N] Pittsburgh, PA St. Francis Friary.
Steger, Francis R. *o.c.s.o.* '56 (ROC)[I] Piffard, NY Abbey of the Genesee.
Steger, John J. '51 (ROC) Rochester, NY St. Jude the Apostle.
Steggert, Bruce A. *s.j.* '93 (WDC).
Stegman, Leonard F. '40 (ELP) Retired.
Stegmann, Robert (GB) Oshkosh, WI St. Mary; Oshkosh, WI St. Josaphat.
Stehling, Larry '88 (AUS) Austin, TX St. Theresa.
Stehling, Lawrence J. '88 (AUS) Austin, TX State Hospital.
Stehly, Dennis R. '77 (STL) St. Louis, MO St. Margaret Mary Alacoque; Southeast.
Stehly, Dennis (STL) Deaneries/Deans.
Stehly, James '83 (LA) Camarillo, CA St. Mary Magdalen; Ministry to Recently Ordained Priests.
Stehly, Mark '66 (SEA) Special Assignment.
Stehly, Thomas J. '61 (LA) Retired.
Steichen, John A. '54 (OKL) Union City, OK St. Joseph's; Chancellor; Consultors Archdiocesan; Council of Priests Archdiocesan; Archdiocesan Finance Council; Mission "Micatokla"—Archdiocesan Mission of Santiago Atitlan, Guatemala; Priests' Medical Fund; Priests' Retirement Board; Propagation of the Faith, Holy Childhood Assoc., Missionary Cooperation Plan; St. Francis de Sales Seminary (Legal Title).
Steidle, Mark A. '93 (COV) Fort Mitchell, KY Blessed Sacrament.
Steier, Charles '73 (SAL) Gorham, KS St. Mary's; Russell, KS St. Mary's; Diocesan Council of Education.
Steiger, Richard A. '67 (PAT) Andover, NJ Good Shepherd.
Steigmeyer, Robert C. *c.s.c.* '47 (FTW)[K] Notre Dame, IN Holy Cross Mission House.
Steik, Dennis J. *s.m.* '69 (ATL)[K] Atlanta, GA.
Steimel, Craig E. '89 (DUB) Rockford, IA Holy Name; Rockwell, IA Sacred Heart; Dougherty, IA St. Patrick; Due Process Board.
Steimel, Paul T. '52 (DUB) Retired.
Stein, E. John *o.f.m.* '85 (CHI)[N] Chicago, IL St. Joseph Interprovincial Post–Novitiate Formation House.
Stein, James W. *o.praem.* '86 (GB)[I] De Pere, WI St. Norbert Abbey.
Stein, Jerry '66 (AMA) Retired.
Stein, Mark J. '02 (TUC) Morenci, AZ Holy Cross; Clifton, AZ Sacred Heart.
Stein, Paul '01 (CHI) Chicago, IL St. Turibius.
Stein, Robert E. '81 (CLV) Akron, OH St. Francis de Sales.
Stein, Robert *s.d.b.* '78 (LA) Los Angeles, CA St. Mary; [Q] Los Angeles, CA Dominic Savio Salesian Residence.
Stein, Ron '68 (DUB)[H] Mason City, IA Mercy Medical Center–North Iowa.
Stein, Timothy P. '84 (ALT) Chest Springs, PA St. Monica's.
Stein, Timothy P. (ALT) "The Catholic Register".
Steinbacher, Wilfred '62 (NSH)[H] Nashville, TN Glenmary Home Missioners.
Steinbauer, Joseph R. '79 (TOL) Toledo, OH Little Flower of Jesus; Members.
Steinbeisser, Joseph A. '86 (NU) Willmar, MN St. Mary; College of Consultors; Priests' Council.
Steinbock, Leo E. '54 (LA) Los Angeles, CA St. Kevin.
Steinbrunner, Jerry *c.pp.s.* '74 (CIN) Cincinnati, OH St. Andrew; Cincinnati, OH St. Mark.
Steiner, Bernard J. '61 (NU) Green Isle, MN St. Brendan.
Steiner, Daniel R. '79 (CHI) Other Assignments.
Steiner, Daniel '79 (CHI)[M] Northlake, IL Villa Scalabrini Nursing and Rehabilitation Center.
Steiner, Edward F. '82 (NSH) Presbyteral Council and College of Consultors; Clergy Benefit Foundation; Clarksville, TN Immaculate Conception.
Steiner, Edward (NSH) Deans; Austin Peay–Clarksville; Continuing Education of Clergy.
Steiner, John M. (SPK) Vicars General; Defensor Vinculi.
Steiner, John W. '74 (LC) Alma, WI St. Lawrence; Waumandee, WI St. Boniface; Elected Members; Consultors; Army National Guard Chaplains.
Steiner, John '69 (SPK) Spokane, WA St. Mary.
Steiner, Luke *o.s.b.* '56 (SCL)[I] Collegeville, MN St. John's Abbey, of the Order of St. Benedict.
Steiner, William H. (Carlos) *c.ss.r.* '54 (STL)[O] Liguori, MO St. Clement Health Care Center.
Steingraeber, John *c.ss.r.* '74 (TUC)[G] Tucson, AZ Redemptorist Society of Arizona.
Steingreaber, Paul *o.s.b.* '65 (KCK)[H] Atchison, KS St. Benedict's Abbey.
Steinhilber, Richard *s.s.c.* '51 (OM)[K] St. Columbans, NE St. Columban's Foreign Mission Society.
Steinhoff, Henry '67 (B) Eureka, MT Our Lady of Mercy Retired.
Steinkerchner, Scott *o.p.* '98 (BO)[V] Newton, MA The Jesuit Community at Boston College.
Steinkirchner, Edward E. '49 (ROC) Retired.
Steinkirchner, Edward '49 (ROC) East Rochester, NY St. Jerome.
Steinle, David G. '79 (DAV) Davenport, IA St. Alphonsus; Buffalo, IA St. Peter's; Diocesan Consultors.
Steinle, James '53 (TOL) Fayette, OH Our Lady of Mercy; Lyons, OH Our Lady of Fatima Retired.
Steinman, Robert E. *o.s.a.* '50 (PH) Newtown Square, PA St. Anastasia; [AA] Villanova, PA St. Thomas Monastery.
Steinmetz, Paul B. *s.j.* '59 (MIL)[O] Milwaukee, WI Jesuit Community at Marquette University.
Steinmetz, Thomas P. '02 (NTN) Manchester, NH Our Lady of the Cedars.
Steinmetz, Thomas (NTN) Presbyteral Council; Ambassadors.
Steinmiller, Alexander *c.p.* '70 (CHI)[N] Chicago, IL Passionist Provincial Office.
Steinmiller, Alexander *c.p.* '70 (GAL)[Q] Houston, TX Congregation of the Passion, Holy Name Retreat Center.
Steinwachs, Boniface *o.s.b.* (SP)[O] St. Leo, FL St. Leo Abbey.
Stella, Thomas A. *c.s.c.* '72 (COS) Colorado Springs, CO Sacred Heart.
Stella, Tom '72 (COS)[C] Colorado Springs, CO Penrose Hospital.
Steller, Paul W. '65 (BUF) Lancaster, NY St. Mary of the Assumption.
Stelmach, Jerome J. '80 (BUF) Limestone, NY St. Patrick; Olean, NY Transfiguration.
Stelmach, Michael '70 (STN) Minneapolis, MN St. Constantine.
Stelmach, Michael (STN) Presbyteral Council.
Stelmach, Michael (STN) Minneapolis.
Stelmach, Michael (STN) Diocesan Consultors.
Stelmaszczyk, Miroslaw '77 (PIT) Creighton, PA Holy Family.
Stelten, Anthony Mary *m.f.v.a.* (BIR)[E] Birmingham, AL Franciscan Missionaries of the Eternal Word, A Public Association of the Christian Faithful.
Stelten, Leo F. '50 (FAR) Retired.
Steltenkamp, Michael F. *s.j.* '76 (DET)[K] Temperance, MI.
Steltenkamp, Michael F. *s.j.* '76 (WH)[A] Wheeling, WV Wheeling Jesuit University.
Stelter, Leslie A. '84 (Fgm)[U] Milwaukee, WI Our Blessed Lady of Victory Mission, Inc..
Stelter, Richard T. '80 (RVC) Amityville, NY St. Martin's.
Stelzer, Mark S. '83 (SPR) Springfield, MA Sacred Heart; Chicopee, MA Holy Name of Jesus; Censor of Books.
Stembler, James G. '89 (CC) Corpus Christi, TX St. Paul the Apostle.
Stemler, Bruno *f.s.s.p.* '98 (SCR)[E] Moscow, PA St. Gregory's Academy; [M] Elmhurst, PA Priestly Fraternity of St. Peter (F.S.S.P.), North American District Headquarters.
Stemmann, Joseph '63 (LAF) Retired.
Stempack, Martin '55 (BAL) Bel Air, MD St. Margaret.
Stempora, Daniel F. '60 (JOL) Oswego, IL St. Anne.
Stempsey, William E. *s.j.* '92 (WOR)[O] Worcester, MA Jesuits of Holy Cross College, Inc..
Stencil, Rallen '63 (GB) Retired.
Stencil, Steven G. '81 (TUC) Administrative Leave of Absence.
Stengel, Charles G. '56 (NEW) Jersey City, NJ St. John the Baptist.
Stengel, Mark *o.s.b.* '72 (LR)[A] Subiaco, AR Subiaco Monastery.
Stengel, Michael Joseph *c.p.* '57 (CHI)[K] Louisville, KY Sacred Heart Retreat.
Stengel, Paul F. '59 (BUF)[O] Lackawanna, NY Bishop Head Residence.
Stengel, Paul F. '59 (BUF) Retired.
Stengel, William '57 (GB) Retired.
Stenger, James R. '81 (CLV) Brook Park, OH St. Peter the Apostle.
Stenger, Joseph *c.ss.r.* '57 (STP) Brooklyn Center, MN St. Alphonsus.
Stenson, Patrick J. *m.s.c.* '63 (CHR) Pawleys Island, SC Precious Blood of Christ.
Stenson, Paul J. '98 (PH) Philadelphia, PA St. Katherine of Siena.
Stenzel, Eugene F. '67 (WIN) Wells, MN St. Casimir's.
Stenzel, William J. '75 (CHI) La Grange, IL St. Francis Xavier.
Stepanich, Martin *o.f.m.* '41 (CHI)[N] Lemont, IL The Slovene Franciscan Fathers, Order of Friars Minor, Commissariat of the Holy Cross.
Stepanski, Thomas K. '62 (IND) Danville, IN Mary Queen of Peace.
Stepek, Robert A. '81 (CHI) Burbank, IL St. Albert the Great.
Stephan, Jeffrey '01 (KC) Blue Springs, MO St. John La Lande.
Stephan, Matthew J. '83 (CC) Diaconal Screening Committee; Falfurrias, TX Sacred Heart.
Stephens, Gerald '63 (FWT) Retired.
Stephens, James '97 (BAK) Madras, OR St. Patrick's.
Stephens, Timothy J. *s.j.* '99 (WDC)[P] Faulkner, MD Loyola Retreat House.
Stephenson, Alfonse J. (PAT) Air National Guard Chaplains.
Stephenson, Alphonse J. '75 (PAT) On Duty Outside the Diocese.
Stephenson, Lloyd F. '80 (RIC) Hampton, VA VA Medical Center Retired.
Stephenson, Patrick '68 (SR) American Canyon, CA Holy Family; Members of the Curia; Deans; Board of Consultors; Priests' Council.
Stephenson, Robert '78 (SY) Oswego, NY St. Mary.
Stepien, Allen F. '65 (PAT) Long Valley, NJ St. Mark the Evangelist.
Steri, Efisio *o.f.m.conv.* '60 (FgM); (FgM).
Steriti, Edward *o.c.s.o.* '57 (WOR)[O] Spencer, MA St. Joseph's Abbey.
Sterling, Donald A. '74 (BAL) Baltimore, MD The New All Saints.
Sterling, John J. '96 (COV)[B] Covington, KY Covington Catholic High School; Serra Club of Diocese of Covington; Vocations Office; Vocation Council; Covington, KY Mother of God.
Sterling, John K. '94 (DAV) Lost Nation, IA Sacred Heart; Lost Nation, IA St. James.
Sterling, John K. '94 (DUB) Lost Nation, IA Sacred Heart.
Stern, Jerome F. '63 (LEX) Middlesboro, KY St. Julian.
Stern, Robert L. '58 (NY) On Duty Outside the Archdiocese; [II] New York, NY Catholic Near East Welfare Association (CNEWA).
Stern, Robert L. (WDC)[V] Silver Spring, MD Catholics Committed to Support the Pope.
Sternemann, Reinhard *o.s.a.* '66 (CHI)[N] Olympia Fields, IL Tolentine Monastery at Tolentine Center.
Sterner, James M. '70 (HBG) Littlestown, PA St. Aloysius.
Sterns, Robert L. '58 (TR)[T] Lincroft, NJ The Bethlehem University Foundation, Inc..
Sterowski, Scott P. '91 (SCR) Olyphant, PA St. Patrick's; [D] Dunmore, PA Bishop O'Hara High School; Holy Name Society; D.C.C.M..
Stessman, Gerald '59 (DM) West Des Moines, IA Retired.
Stetson, William H. '62 (WDC)[T] Washington, DC Prelature of the Holy Cross and Opus Dei; [F] Potomac, MD The Heights School.
Stetz, Mark '90 (MRY) Santa Cruz, CA Holy Cross;

Priestly Life & Ministry; Presbyteral Council; Priestly Life and Ministry Board.
Steuernol, Slider '96 (P) Portland, OR St. Agatha.
Steurnol, Slider (P) Continuing Education for Clergy.
Steuterman, James M. '75 (WOR) North Oxford, MA St. Ann's.
Stevens, Clifford J. '56 (OM) Retired.
Stevens, Clifford J. *o.m.* '56 (CHY) Riverton, WY St. Margaret's.
Stevens, Clifford '56 (CHY) In Residence.
Stevens, David E. '98 (SFS) Scotland, SD St. George; Air National Guard Chaplains.
Stevens, Gladstone H. '00 (BAL).
Stevensky, John '63 (SJP)[A] St. Petersburg, FL Epiphany of Our Lord; Southern Deanery; League of Ukrainian Catholics (LUC); Presbyteral Council.
Stevenson, Alden F. *s.j.* '46 (SJ)[M] Los Gatos, CA Sacred Heart Jesuit Center.
Stevenson, Anthony R. '81 (OWN) Philpot, KY St. William; Knottsville, KY St. Lawrence.
Stevenson, Dennis E. '88 (COL) Columbus, OH St. Aloysius; Presiding Judges of First Instance.
Stevenson, R. Francis '92 (SAC) California State Prison, Solano.
Stevenson, William J. '82 (LAN) Saline, MI St. Andrew.
Stevenson, William '86 (SD) Julian, CA St. Elizabeth.
Stevernol, Slider (P) Personnel Board.
Stewart, August '94 (COS) Colorado Springs, CO St. Gabriel the Archangel.
Stewart, Barbara (DUB)[H] Mason City, IA Mercy Medical Center–North Iowa.
Stewart, Columba *o.s.b.* '90 (SCL)[B] St. John's University; [I] Collegeville, MN St. John's Abbey, of the Order of St. Benedict.
Stewart, Edward R. '89 (BRK) Bayside, NY St. Robert Bellarmine.
Stewart, George R. '94 (NY) Bronx, NY St. Raymond.
Stewart, J. Keith '93 (MEM) Memphis, TN Cathedral of the Immaculate Conception; Presbyteral Council and College of Consultors; Director of Seminarians; Director of Vocations.
Stewart, J. Patrick *s.j.* '61 (P)[L] Portland, OR Colombiere Community; [Q] Portland, OR Jesuit Development & Communications Office.
Stewart, Jonathan '91 (IND) Unassigned.
Stewart, Michael L. '75 (MEM) Memphis, TN St. Brigid; Clergy Personnel Board.
Stewart, Patrick F. '78 (LEX) Richmond, KY St. Mark; [L] Richmond, KY St. Stephen Newman Center–St. Mark Church.
Stewart, Patrick (LEX) Priests' Retirement Board.
Stewart, Paul '73 (PT) On Leave of Absence; Air Force Reserve Chaplains.
Stewart, Robert H. '82 (KC) Kansas City, MO Holy Family.
Stewart, Robert (KC) Diocesan Finance Council; Vocations.
Stewart, Terrence L. '70 (GR) Sparta, MI Holy Family; College of Consultors.
Sthokal, Edward S. *s.j.* '54 (STP)[P] Lake Elmo, MN Jesuit Retreat House.
Sticco, Peter T. *s.a.c.* '69 (NEW)[S] Baltimore, MD Pallottine Center for Apostolic Causes; Fairview, NJ Our Lady of Grace.
Stickle, William '50 (RIC) Retired.
Stieferman, Lowell L. '63 (OKL) Oklahoma City, OK Church of the Epiphany of the Lord.
Stieferman, Lowell (OKL) Region II; Defenders of the Bond; Vocations and Seminarians.
Stiefvater, Robert X. '77 (MIL) Special Assignment; Vocations Office.
Stiegeler, A. Francis *s.j.* '78 (SFR)[E] San Francisco, CA St. Ignatius College Preparatory (Coed); [N] San Francisco, CA Jesuit Community at St. Ignatius College Preparatory.
Stieger, Joseph '50 (MRY) Retired.
Stiene, Paul '90 (PEO)[A] Peoria, IL Rosminian Novitiate.
Stier, Timothy '79 (OAK) Fremont, CA Corpus Christi.
Stika, Richard F. '85 (STL) Special Assignment; [U] St. Louis, MO Friends of the Archbishop; Vicars General; Chancellor; Archdiocesan Consultors; Archdiocesan Archives; Priests' Purgatorial Society; St. Louis Roman Catholic Theological Seminaries, Inc.; Archdiocesan Council of Priests; Archdiocesan Priests' Personnel Board; Archdiocesan Pastoral Council; St. Louis City Catholic Church Real Estate Corporation; [U] St. Louis, MO St. Louis City Catholic Church Real Estate Corporation.
Stikel, Roman '88 (MIL) Kenosha, WI St. Elizabeth.
Stikhin, Innokentij '91 (PBR)[D] Uniontown, PA Motherhouse and Novitiate of the Sisters of St. Basil the Great.
Stiles, J. Roy '63 (L) Louisville, KY St. Elizabeth of Hungary; Louisville, KY St. Therese.
Stiles, Wallis '61 (SAT) D'Hanis, TX Holy Cross; In Rural Area; Archdiocesan Presbyteral Council.
Stillmank, John G. '93 (MAD) Leave of Absence.
Stillmock, Martin *c.ss.r.* '58 (STP) Brooklyn Center, MN St. Alphonsus.
Stillmunks, Steven J. '77 (OM) Omaha, NE Christ the King; Deans; Deans.
Stillwell, William J. '67 (BUF) Retired.
Stilwell, Dennis R. '71 (GAY) Petoskey, MI St. Francis Solanus; Petoskey, MI St. Francis Xavier; Vicars (by region); Judges.
Stine, Robert F. '73 (BR) St. Amant, LA Holy Rosary; Presbyteral Council.
Stineman, William F. '49 (IND) Retired.
Stingel, Louis F. '60 (MET) Jamesburg, NJ St. James the Less; Episcopal Vicars; Episcopal Council.
Stingle, Lawrence A. '41 (GB) Retired.
Stirniman, Jeffrey D. '95 (PEO) Princeton, IL St. Louis; Tiskilwa, IL St. Mary's.
Stiteler, Francis Michael *o.c.s.o.* '83 (ATL)[K] Conyers, GA The Monastery of the Holy Spirit.
Stites, John F. '76 (TOL)[B] Oregon, OH Cardinal Stritch High School.
Stitt, Bryan D. '03 (OG) Graduate Studies.
Stitz, John '53 (KCK) Retired.
Stivason, Paul R. '89 (GBG) Yukon, PA St. Timothy; Yukon, PA Seven Dolors.
Stluka, Jerome D. '69 (COL) Columbus OH Holy Cross; Grant Hospital.
Stobba, Joseph G. *o.s.a.* '59 (MIL) Racine, WI St. Rita.
Stober, William P. '73 (PAT) Branchville, NJ Our Lady Queen of Peace.
Stobie, Stephen '80 (P) Portland, OR St. Stephen.
Stochmal, Marek '95 (DET) Absent on Leave.
Stock, Thomas E. '98 (CLV) Cleveland, OH St. Leo the Great.
Stockelman, William R. '78 (CIN) Batavia, OH Holy Trinity; Batavia, OH St. Ann.
Stocker, Bede *o.s.b.* '42 (RCK)[G] Aurora, IL Marmion Abbey.
Stocker, Leonard *o.m.i.* '41 (BRK) Whitestone, NY St. Luke.
Stockert, Harold R. '63 (PSC) New York, NY SS. Peter and Paul.
Stockhausen, Gerard L. *s.j.* '79 (DET)[K] Detroit, MI Jesuit Community at the University of Detroit Mercy; [C] Detroit, MI Dental School.
Stockhausen, Paul G. *s.j.* '40 (MIL)[O] Wauwatosa, WI Jesuit Community at St. Camillus.
Stocking, Joseph *s.j.* '67 (SEA) Redmond, WA St. Jude; [A] Seattle, WA Seattle University; [L] Seattle, WA Jesuit House, Seattle.
Stocklosa, J. Walter '40 (BO) Senior Priests Retired.
Stockman, Gerald W. '64 (JC) Retired.
Stockton, Marc '02 (E) Sharon, PA St. Joseph.
Stockus, Edward S. '91 (CHI) Retired.
Stodola, Francis (LAR) Army Chaplains.
Stoeber, Charles L *s.f.* '56 (SFE) Albuquerque, NM St. Therese of the Infant Jesus of the Little Flower Retired.
Stoeckig, Robert E. '94 (LAV) Las Vegas, NV St. Paul Jung–Ha–Sang; Las Vegas, NV Shrine of the Most Holy Redeemer; Vicar General, Chancellor and Moderator of the Curia; Presbyteral Council for the Diocese of Las Vegas; Director; Director of Clergy Education; Home and Foreign Missions; Native American and Colored People Commission Pontifical Association of the Holy Childhood; Priests' Personnel Board.
Stoeckig, Robert (LAV) Building Committee; Priests' Pension Board; Board of Trustees.
Stoecklein, Ted D. '00 (DOD) Great Bend, KS St. Patrick; Great Bend, KS St. Rose of Lima; Presbyteral Council; College of Consultors; Priests' Trust Fund.
Stoegbauer, Carlton C. '82 (CAM) Absecon, NJ St. Elizabeth Ann Seton.
Stoeger, James A. *s.j.* '75 (CHI)[C] Chicago, IL Jesuit Community at Loyola University Chicago; [N] Chicago, IL Chicago Province of the Society of Jesus–Provincial Office.
Stoeger, John D. '87 (LA)[A] Camarillo, CA St. John's Seminary College of the Archdiocese of Los Angeles.
Stoeger, William R. *s.j.* '72 (TUC)[E] Tucson, AZ Jesuit Community of the Vatican Observatory.
Stoerlein, Joseph G. '49 (CAM) Retired.
Stoetzel, Charles D. '80 (LC) Marshfield, WI St. John the Baptist; Marshfield, WI Christ the King; Deans.
Stoffel, Richard J. '79 (MIL) Slinger, WI St. Peter.
Stoffer, Patrick *o.f.m.conv.* '97 (PEO) Peoria, IL Holy Family.
Stohrer, Walter J. *s.j.* '60 (MIL)[O] Milwaukee, WI Jesuit Community at Marquette University.
Stokes, David L. '02 (PRO) Providence, RI St. Sebastian; Catholic–Jewish Relations.
Stokes, David *s.j.* '63 (RIC) Richmond, VA Sacred Heart.
Stokes, Thomas A. *s.m.* '63 (SP) Tampa, FL Our Lady of Perpetual Help.
Stoklie, Eugene '60 (BRK)[A] Douglaston, NY Immaculate Conception Center.
Stokowski, Lucjan '77 (CLV) Cleveland, OH St. John Cantius.
Stolcis, Ronald '68 (CHY) Sheridan, WY Holy Name.
Stoley, Lawrence '91 (LIN)[F] Waverly, NE Our Lady of Good Counsel Retreat House; Retreat Program; Schools.
Stolinski, Dennis R. '69 (OM) Bellevue, NE St. Matthew The Evangelist Church of Bellevue.
Stolinski, Robert A. '70 (BUF) Jamestown, NY St. James.
Stoll, Eugene *s.v.d.* '30 (CHI)[B] Techny, IL Divine Word Residence.
Stoll, Mark J. '92 (SC) Hinton, IA St. Joseph; Vice Chancellors; Judges.
Stollenwerk, Charles J. '73 (CLV) North Olmsted, OH St. Richard; Associate Judges.
Stolowski, Stephen '79 (NSH)[I] Nashville, TN Mercy Convent.
Stoltz, John J. (L) Defenders of the Bond.
Stoltz, Richard L. '74 (STL) New Melle, MO Immaculate Heart of Mary.
Stolz, John J. '90 (L) Louisville, KY St. Gabriel the Archangel.
Stolz, Paul L. '61 (CIN) Retired.
Stolz, William K. *s.j.* '62 (SAC)[D] Sacramento, CA Jesuit High School; [I] Carmichael, CA Jesuit High School Community of Sacramento.
Stolzer, Vincent A. '56 (STL) Retired.
Stolzman, William F. '71 (STP) Shakopee, MN St. Mark.
Stommel, Russel J. '67 (MIL) Milwaukee, WI St. Robert.
Stone, Francis Mary *m.f.v.a.* '98 (BIR)[E] Birmingham, AL Franciscan Missionaries of the Eternal Word, A Public Association of the Christian Faithful.
Stone, Harold *s.t.* '59 (SJN) Loiza, PR San Patricio.
Stone, Michael J. '68 (ALN) Schuylkill Haven, PA St. Ambrose.
Stone, Robert J. *c.m.* '77 (BRK)[V] Brooklyn, NY St. John the Baptist Rectory; Greensboro, NC St. Mary.
Stone, Robert L. '01 (CR) Bemidji, MN St. Philip's; [F] Bemidji, MN Holy Spirit Newman Center.
Stone, Robert '90 (KC) Kansas City, MO St. Catherine of Siena.
Stone, Ron G. '01 (SFE) Arroyo Seco, NM La Santisima Trinidad.
Stone, Theodore '52 (CHI) Park Ridge, IL Mary, Seat of Wisdom Retired.
Stoneberg, Jeff '90 (JOL) Channahon, IL St. Ann Parish.
Stoner, John Bosco *o.s.b.* '76 (LA)[Q] Valyermo, CA St. Andrew's Abbey.
Stoner, Timothy L. '96 (GI) Gordon, NE St. Leo's.
Stonich, Raymond '56 (JOL)[K] Naperville, IL St. John Vianney Villa Retired.
Stookey, Gerald L. *o.p.* '78 (CHI)[N] Chicago Dominicans (Provincial Office).
Stopponi, John *o.s.b.* '38 (DET)[K] Detroit, MI St. Sylvester Monastery; [K] Detroit, MI; Detroit, MI Holy Family.
Stopyra, David M. *o.f.m.conv.* '60 (FR) Taunton, MA Our Lady of the Holy Rosary.
Storan, William '61 (SAC) Retired.
Storck, Edward J. '52 (WIL) Retired.
Stormes, James R. *s.j.* '79 (CHI)[M] Washington, DC Leonard Neale House.
Storms, Francis *o.f.m.* '75 (BUF)[O] St. Bonaventure, NY St. Bonaventure Friary; [C] St. Bonaventure University; [C] St. Bonaventure, NY Friar Community.
Storms, Louis B. *c.m.* '40 (PH)[AA] St. Catherine Infirmary.
Stortz, Mario '49 (AMA) Happy, TX Holy Name of Jesus.
Stott, Thomas '83 (CHL) Lincolnton, NC St. Dorothy.
Stout, O. Hugh '61 (NO) New Orleans, LA Holy Ghost.
Stout, O. Hugh '61 (CAM) Retired.
Stout, Richard E. *c.s.c.* '71 (FTW)[I] Holy Cross Novitiate.
Stout, Thomas '77 (BEL) Red Bud, IL St. John the Baptist; Diocesan Deans.
Stout, William *o.f.m.* '00 (PH)[D] Philadelphia, PA Archbishop Ryan High School; [AA] Philadelphia, PA St. Pius X Friary.
Stouvenel, Gerald E. '72 (DAV) West Burlington, IA SS. Mary and Patrick.
Stover, James M. (PIT) Pittsburgh, PA St. Sebastian.
Stoviak, Leonard W. '73 (GBG) Scottdale, PA St. John the Baptist; College of Consultors; Bishop's Priests Council.
Stovik, Raphael *o.s.b.* '56 (BIS)[A] Richardton, ND Assumption Abbey.
Stowe, John *o.f.m.conv.* '95 (ELP) El Paso, TX Our Lady of Mt. Carmel; Vicars General; Moderator of the Curia; Diocesan Pastoral Staff; Ex Officio Members; Missions Office; Priests' Personnel Advisory Committee.
Stoyle, James '91 (FTW) Mishawaka, IN St. Monica.
Strabala, Matthew T. *o.p.* (SFE)[L] Albuquerque, NM St. Thomas Aquinas (Newman Center) University Parish.
Strachota, Michael D. '79 (MIL) Milwaukee, WI Corpus Christi.
Strader, Mark A. '91 (LA) Tujunga, CA Our Lady of Lourdes.
Stradinger, Stephen J. '74 (MIL) Racine, WI St. Mary by the Lake.

Stradomski, Ryszard '83 (SP) Temple Terrace, FL Corpus Christi.
Strahan, Francis V. '59 (BO) Framingham, MA St. Bridget; WEST REGION.
Strain, Eugene '53 (DET) Rochester Hills, MI St. Mary's of the Hills.
Straka, Francis P. '90 (ALN) Bethlehem, PA Holy Ghost; Saint Vincent De Paul Society.
Straley, Michael '83 (PHX) Flagstaff, AZ San Francisco de Asis; College of Consultors.
Stram, Gideon '38 (AUS) Retired.
Strand, Ralph S. '64 (CHI) Other Assignments.
Strano, Edward '56 (TR) Retired.
Stransky, Thomas F. *c.s.p.* '57 (NY)[EE] Jamaica Estates Paulist Fathers Generalate.
Strasser, John R. '76 (DOD) Kiowa, KS St. John the Apostle; Medicine Lodge, KS Holy Rosary; Sharon, KS St. Boniface; Presbyteral Council; College of Consultors; Deans; Priestly Life and Ministry; Diocesan Pastoral Council.
Strassle, H. Paul '58 (LR) Retired.
Strassner, Henry E. '47 (ALN) Tamaqua, PA St. Jerome Retired.
Strasz, James *s.m.* '80 (BO)[V] Boston, MA Marist Fathers and Brothers Provincial House.
Stratman, Joseph (BEA) Defenders of Bond Retired.
Stratman, Raymond '55 (LEX) Retired.
Stratman, Thomas F. '50 (DAV) Davenport, IA Sacred Heart Cathedral Retired.
Straub, David R. '94 (CHI) Chicago, IL St. Benedict the African (West).
Straub, Edward F. '65 (NY) Liberty, NY St. Peter; Sullivan.
Strausser, George '77 (PH) Philadelphia, PA St. Agatha–St. James.
Stravinskas, Peter M.J. '77 (B) On Duty Outside the Diocese.
Stravinskas, Peter M.J. '77 (OM) Omaha, NE St. Anthony.
Strebel, Milton C. *o.praem.* '54 (GB)[I] Archdiocese of Cape Town, South Africa.
Strebel, Roger W. (GB) Elcho, WI Holy Family; Pickerel, WI St. Mary Mission.
Strebel, Roger (GB) Scouts.
Strebig, John J. '52 (GRY) Retired.
Strebler, Charles F. '94 (CLV) Cleveland, OH St. Vincent de Paul; Auditor/Assessor.
Strecok, Lubomir J. '98 (ALT) Secretary to the Bishop; [J] Hollidaysburg, PA Conference of Slovak Clergy; On Special or Other Diocesan Assignment.
Streichardt, Wolfgang '82 (SAG) Bannister, MI St. Cyril.
Streicher, Bernard J. *s.j.* '60 (CLV)[D] Cleveland, OH St. Ignatius High School.
Streifel, Keith N. '99 (BIS) Foxholm, ND St. Mary.
Streit, Thomas G. *c.s.c.* '86 (FTW)[B] University of Notre Dame Du Lac; [I] Notre Dame, IN Holy Cross Community, Corby Hall, University of Notre Dame.
Strelick, Charles J. '56 (MAR) Retired.
Strelinski, Ernest '65 (PIT) Allison Park, PA St. Ursula.
Stremel, Adolph '36 (WCH) Retired.
Strempeck, Martin R. '55 (BAL) Retired.
Stremski, John P. '60 (SUP) Retired.
Strenski, Joseph A. '45 (MIL) Retired.
Stretton, Noel '59 (DUL) Duluth, MN St. Elizabeth's; Duluth Federal Prison.
Streveler, Robert A. '69 (LC) Black River Falls, WI St. Joseph.
Streza, Charles V. '43 (ROM) Retired.
Stricker, Robert A. '48 (CIN) Cincinnati, OH St. Therese, The Little Flower; Censors Retired.
Strickland, Joseph E. '85 (TYL) Tyler, TX Cathedral of the Immaculate Conception; College of Consultors; Deans; Judicial Vicar; Judges; Priests' Pension Board; Priests' Personnel Board; Presbyteral Council; Diocesan Pastoral Team – DPT; Diocesan Deanery Representatives On Ethics and Integrity Policy for Church Personnel.
Strider, Leon '76 (GAL) Houston, TX St. Michael.
Strieder, Leon '76 (AUS) On Duty Outside the Diocese; Campus Ministry.
Striedl, Max J. '96 (RCK)[B] Elgin, IL St. Edward Central Catholic High School.
Striedl, Max '96 (RCK) Dundee, IL St. Catherine of Siena.
Striegel, Robert M. '73 (DAV) Davenport, IA Holy Family.
Stringini, John L. '79 (RCK) Rockford, IL St. Bernadette.
Stripe, Keith A. '96 (TOL) Bellevue, OH Immaculate Conception; Members.
Strish, Andrew F. '67 (SCR) Pittston, PA St. John the Baptist.
Strittmatter, Andre *t.o.r.* '61 (ALT)[F] Loretto, PA Mount Assisi Friary.
Strittmatter, J. Joseph '56 (ALT) Retired.
Strittmatter, Paul J. *s.j.* '77 (DM) Dunlap, IA St. Patrick; Woodbine, IA Sacred Heart; [K] Omaha, NE Jesuit Community at Creighton University.
Strittmatter, Robert '66 (FWT) Fort Worth, TX San Mateo.
Stroba, Marek *o.m.i.* '85 (MIA) Opa Locka, FL St. Monica.
Strock, Richard M. '65 (LR) Siloam Springs, AR St. Mary's.
Strohmeyer, George E. '64 (E)[B] Erie, PA Gannon University; [P] Erie, PA Gannon University.
Stroik, Placid *o.f.m.* '63 (NEW)[O] Lodi, NJ Immaculate Conception Convent.
Strojny, Robert Andrzej *o.c.d.* '85 (GRY)[I] Munster, IN Discalced Carmelite Fathers Monastery.
Strollo, Charles P. *c.m.* '73 (PH)[B] Philadelphia, PA St. Vincent's Seminary; [B] Philadelphia, PA DePaul Novitiate; [AA] Philadelphia Congregation of the Mission; (FgM).
Strom, Charles W. '72 (HEL) Retired.
Stromberg, Floyd G. '59 (TUC) Retired.
Stromberg, James S. '57 (STP)[C] St. Paul, MN University of St. Thomas Retired.
Strommer, James G. *c.p.* '70 (SAC)[I] Citrus Heights, CA Christ the King Retreat.
Strommer, James *c.p.* '70 (CHI)[N] Chicago, IL Passionist Provincial Office.
Strommer, Jim *c.p.* '70 (SAC)[K] Citrus Heights, CA Christ the King Institute for Counseling & Spiritual Direction.
Stromski, Adam F.X. '46 (STU) Retired.
Strong, Barry R. *o.s.f.s.* '84 (R) Wilmington, NC Immaculate Conception; Priests' Council.
Stronkowski, John '85 (BGP) Danbury, CT St. Gregory.
Stroot, Ralph E. '60 (STL) St. Louis, MO St. George Retired.
Stroot, Thomas J. '70 (WCH) Pittsburg, KS Our Lady of Lourdes; [B] Pittsburg, KS St. Mary–Colgan High School; Deans.
Stroud, J. Francis *s.j.* '61 (NY)[EE] Loyola Hall, Jesuit Community.
Struc, Marian '69 (STF)[A] Stamford, CT Ukrainian Catholic Seminary Inc. St. Basil College.
Struik, Felix A.P. *o.p.* '58 (SJN) Catano, PR Nuestra Senora del Carmen; [A] Bayamon Central University.
Strumski, Matthew J. '48 (PRO) Warren, RI St. Casimir.
Strupp, James A. '67 (MIL) Retired.
Strupp, Joachim *o.f.m.cap.* '63 (MIL)[O] Mount Calvary, WI St. Lawrence Friary; [M] Fond du Lac, WI St. Francis Home for Aged.
Strus, Walter A. '94 (CHI) Other Assignments.
Struzik, Edward J. '85 (MET)[H] Somerset, NJ Maria Regina Residence Retired.
Struzynski, Robert *o.f.m.* '63 (BUF) Buffalo, NY SS. Rita & Patrick.
Struzzieri, Andrew L. '75 (BRK) Brooklyn, NY St. Matthew's.
Struzzo, John A. *c.s.c.* '65 (FTW)[I] Azusa, CA St. Francis of Rome.
Strycharz, Stanley '91 (VEN) Graduate Studies.
Stryjewski, John J. '66 (MOB) Daphne, AL Shrine of the Holy Cross.
Stryker, Peter *c.p.m.* '98 (OWN) Russellville, KY Sacred Heart.
Strynkowski, John J. '63 (BRK) Released from Diocesan Assignment.
Strynkowski, John (BRK) Diocesan Consultors.
Strzadala, Wieslaw P. *s.d.s.* (MO) Air Force Chaplains.
Strzalkowski, Dariusz (DET) Dearborn, MI Divine Child.
Strzelec, Thaddeus '42 (HBG)[G] Danville, PA Holy Family Convent and Infirmary.
Strzok, James J. '70 (MIL)[O] Mwangaza Jesuit Spirituality Center.
Strzyz, Stanislaus '68 (BAK) Burns, OR Holy Family.
Stuart, Francis *o.s.b.* (DOD) Fowler, KS St. Anthony; Meade, KS St. John the Baptist; Meade, KS St. Patrick.
Stuart, George E. (WDC) Pastoral Center Special Ministries; Judges.
Stuart, George '89 (WDC) Bethesda, MD Little Flower.
Stubbs, Michael C. '78 (KCK) Lansing, KS St. Francis de Sales.
Stubbs, Michael (KCK) Regional Pastoral Leaders.
Stubeda, Anthony J. '85 (NU) Willmar, MN St. Mary; On Special or Other Diocesan Assignment; Committee on Parishes; Hispanic Ministry.
Stubna, Kris D. '85 (PIT) Pittsburgh, PA SS. Simon and Jude; [R] Pittsburgh, PA Scholastic Opportunity Scholarships of the Diocese of Pittsburgh; Secretary for Education; Diocesan Development Board.
Stuchlik, Richard '68 (WCH) Wichita, KS St. Margaret Mary; Veterans Administration Hospital.
Stuchly, Josef *s.j.* '02 (BO)[V] Newton, MA The Jesuit Community at Boston College.
Stuczko, Richard J. '54 (SY) Oriskany, NY Oneida County Jail Retired.
Studer, Louis B. *o.m.i.* '76 (BEL)[F] Belleville, IL Shrine of Our Lady of the Snows; [J] Belleville, IL Missionary Association of Mary Immaculate–Missionary Oblates of Mary Immaculate.
Studerus, Gregory J. '80 (NEW) Jersey City, NJ Parish of the Resurrection; Jersey City Downtown Deanery 11.
Studniewski, Gary R. '95 (WDC) Military Chaplains; Army Chaplains.
Studwell, Joachim *o.f.m.* '87 (CLV) Cleveland, OH St. Stanislaus; [O] Cleveland, OH St. Stanislaus Friary.
Studzinski, Raymond *o.s.b.* '69 (IND)[K] Washington, DC Curley Hall, Catholic University of America.
Studzinski, Raymond *o.s.b.* '69 (WDC)[C] Catholic University of America, The.
Stuebben, George '54 (SAT) Retired.
Stuebben, Lawrence J. '55 (SAT)[U] San Antonio, TX Archdiocese of San Antonio Endowment Fund for Parishes, School and Ministries; [U] San Antonio, TX Mary Jane Ihle Clark Endowment Fund for Ministry to Persons with Disabilities; Administrative Asst. to the Archbishop; Administrative Services Department.
Stuebben, Lawrence '55 (SAT) San Antonio, TX St. Agnes.
Stuebben, Lawrence (SAT) Vicar General and Moderator of the Curia; College of Consultors; Archdiocesan Presbyteral Council.
Stueber, Edwin *o.s.b.* '46 (SCL)[I] Collegeville, MN St. John's Abbey, of the Order of St. Benedict.
Stuecker, Henry C. '38 (L) Retired.
Stuempel, Robert L. '75 (L) Louisville, KY St. Bernard.
Stuglik, Robert '03 (CHI) Oak Forest, IL St. Damian.
Stulb, Joseph A. '61 (NEW) Retired.
Stull, Neal '01 (CC)[G] Robstown, TX Society of Our Lady of the Most Holy Trinity.
Stull, Neal *s.o.l.t.* '02 (GAL) Houston, TX St. Monica.
Stump, David X. *s.j.* '71 (NEW)[B] Jersey City, NJ Jesuit Center; [N] Jersey City, NJ Jesuits of Saint Peter's College, Inc..
Stump, James M. *o.f.m.cap.* '88 (SFR)[B] San Francisco, CA Capuchin House of Studies.
Stumpf, Michael J. '01 (PIT) Bellevue, PA Assumption of the Blessed Virgin Mary on the Beautiful River.
Stumpf, William F. '85 (IND) Nashville, IN St. Agnes; Archdiocesan Review Board.
Stumpf, William '85 (IND) Council of Priests; Brookville, IN St. Peter.
Stumpf, William (IND) Assistant Chancellor; Board of Consultors; Priests' Personnel Board; Archdiocesan Pastoral Council; Vicariate of Clergy and Parish Life Coordinators: Formation and Personnel; Personnel: Priests and Parish Life Coordinators.
Stunek, Howard *o.f.m.* '57 (LAN) Federal Correctional Institution.
Stunek, Leonard *o.f.m.* '60 (SAG) Saginaw, MI St. Thomas Aquinas.
Stupca, Edward L. '61 (HEL) Sheridan, MT Madison County Catholic Community.
Sturm, Donald E. '58 (KC) St. Joseph, MO Seven Dolors.
Sturm, Donald (KC) Legion of Mary.
Sturm, George *c.m.f.* '37 (SAT) San Antonio, TX Immaculate Heart of Mary.
Sturm, John G. *s.j.* '50 (BUF) Buffalo, NY St. Michael.
Sturm, Michael O. '69 (MIL) Special Assignment.
Sturm, Samuel '99 (KNX) Oak Ridge, TN St. Mary.
Sturtz, Richard S. '56 (OG) Schroon Lake, NY St. Joseph; Schroon Lake, NY Our Lady of Lourdes.
Stutz, Edward J. '46 (E) Retired.
Styczen, Emil '55 (SP) Hudson, FL St. Michael.
Styles, Kenneth A. *s.j.* (CLV)[D] Cleveland, OH St. Ignatius High School.
Su, Stanislaus *c.s.j.b.* '69 (LA)[CC] Monterey Park, CA Congregation of St. John the Baptist.
Su, Tomas '50 (SJN) San Juan, PR Sagrada Familia.
Suan, Charito '85 (SFR) San Francisco, CA Church of the Epiphany.
Suarez, Carlos *o.s.b.* '86 (FgM).
Suarez, Gildardo '92 (PRO) Providence, RI Assumption of the Blessed Virgin Mary.
Suarez, Jesus E '86 (GAL) Pasadena, TX St. Pius the Fifth.
Suarez, Jose V. '54 (Philippines) Retired.
Suarez, Leo '88 (STO) Stockton, CA St. Edward Church (Pastor of); Personnel Board.
Suarez, Michael F. *s.j.* '94 (NY)[EE] Cardinal Spellman Hall, Jesuit Community.
Suarez, Octavio '64 (TYL) Mount Pleasant, TX St. Michael; Presbyteral Council.
Suarez, Pedro A. *s.j.* '72 (MIA)[B] Miami, FL Barry University.
Suarez, Pedro '72 (MIA)[H] Miami, FL Villa Javier.
Suarez, Wagner R. *s.j.* (NY)[EE] New York, NY Xavier Jesuit Community.
Suarez, Walter *i.v.e.* '96 (SJ) San Jose, CA Cathedral Basilica of St. Joseph.
Suaybaguio, Evangelio R. '75 (NY) Staten Island, NY St. Joseph, St. Thomas.
Suazo, Rafael '64 (SJN) Carolina, PR San Felipe Apostol.
Subb, Victor *g.h.m.* '87 (SAV) Swainsboro, GA Holy Trinity.
Suberlak, Donald *c.r.* '67 (KAL) Three Oaks, MI St. Mary of the Assumption.
Subocz, Adam C. '86 (HRT) East Windsor, CT St. Philip's; Auditors (Part–time Case Instructors).
Succi, Vincento *o.f.m.cap.* (MO) AUXILIARY CHAPLAINS CONTRACT CHAPLAINS.

Sucharski, Michael M. *s.v.d.* '83 (LAF) Lafayette, LA St. Anthony.
Sucher, Frederick *c.p.* '44 (CHI)[N] Chicago, IL Passionist Community–Immaculate Conception Monastery.
Suchnicki, Michael *o.f.m.cap.* '88 (DEN)[N] Denver, CO Fraternidad San Antonio.
Suchocki, James A. '62 (GAY) Absent on Leave.
Suchocki, Marek '86 (NY) Staten Island, NY St. Stanislaus Kostka.
Suchocki, Marek (NY) Judges.
Sucholet, James Joseph '91 (NOR) Voluntown, CT St. Thomas Apostle.
Suchy, Theodore D. *o.s.b.* '67 (JOL)[A] Lisle, IL Benedictine University; [L] Lisle, IL St. Procopius Abbey.
Sudano, Glenn *c.f.r.* '84 (NY) Yonkers, NY Franciscan Friars of the Renewal; [EE] Yonkers, NY St. Felix Friary.
Sudario, Antonio (SB) Loma Linda, CA Loma Linda Community Hospital; Loma Linda, CA Loma Linda University Medical Center.
Sudath, Eugene '88 (NY) Bronx, NY St. Mary Star of the Sea.
Sudekum, Edward J. '61 (STL) University City, MO Our Lady of Lourdes.
Sudhoff, Leonard *c.pp.s.* '39 (CIN)[B] Carthagena, OH St. Charles.
Sudlik, Leonard '76 (GR) Grand Rapids, MI Holy Spirit.
Sudlik, Richard *o.m.i.* '72 (WDC)[M] Washington, DC Provincial Offices of the United States Province of the Missionary Oblates of Mary Immaculate.
Sudol, Ignatius *o.h.* (LA)[K] Ojai, CA St. Joseph's Health and Retirement Center.
Suebert, Xavier *o.f.m.* '71 (NY)[I] New York, NY St. Stephen of Hungary.
Suehr, Philip J. *o.s.c.* '69 (TOL) Toledo, OH Sacred Heart of Jesus; Toledo, OH St. Stephen.
Suehr, Philip *o.s.c.* '66 (STP)[M] Shoreview, MN Crosier Provincial House Province of St. Odilia.
Suellentrop, Anthony J. '73 (DOD) On Duty Outside the Diocese; Navy Chaplains.
Suellentrop, Bernard A. '46 (STL) Retired.
Suellentrop, Daniel M. *o.s.b.* '51 (OKL)[I] Shawnee St. Gregory's Abbey.
Suelzer, John N. '65 (FTW) Fort Wayne, IN St. Charles Borromeo.
Suelzer, John (FTW) Budget Committee; Retired Clergy Committee.
Suenram, John M, *o.c.d.* '87 (SAT)[T] San Antonio, TX Basilica of the National Shrine of the Little Flower.
Suenram, John M. *o.c.d.* '87 (SAT) San Antonio, TX Basilica of The National Shrine of Our Lady of Mt. Carmel and St. Therese, Discalced Carmelite Fathe.
Suenram, John *o.c.d.* '87 (SAT)[M] San Antonio, TX Discalced Carmelites (Prov. of St. Therese).
Sueper, Alban *s.s.c.* '53 (OM)[K] St. Columbans, NE St. Columban's Foreign Mission Society; Retreats, Laymen; AUXILIARY CHAPLAINS CONTRACT CHAPLAINS.
Suess, Milton M. '63 (GB) Luxemburg, WI Immaculate Conception; New Franken, WI St. Joseph.
Suffredini, Louis '57 (MOB) Dauphin Island, AL St. Edmund–by–the–Sea.
Sughrue, Denis B. *c.s.c.* '39 (FTW)[I] Notre Dame, IN Holy Cross House.
Sughrue, Paul S. '70 (BO) Braintree, MA St. Clare.
Sugrue, John F. '62 (CAM) Mays Landing, NJ St. Vincent de Paul.
Sugrue, Patrick *o.c.d.* '64 (SJ)[M] San Jose, CA Carmelite Monastery, Novitiate.
Sugrue, Timothy F. *s.m.* '63 (WDC)[M] Washington, DC Marist Center.
Suh, Sang Bong (Daniel) (BRK) Flushing, NY St. Paul Chong Ha–Sang Roman Catholic Chapel.
Suhaka, Peter '86 (MET) Pittstown, NJ St. Catherine of Siena; [J] Milford, NJ Bethany Ridge.
Suhoza, John E. '68 (PIT) Pittsburgh, PA St. Gabriel of the Sorrowful Virgin; Allegheny County, PA St. Joseph House of Hospitality; [O] Pittsburgh, PA Sisters of St. Francis of the Providence of God.
Suibielski, Kenneth J. '77 (PRO) Pawtucket, RI St. Maria Goretti.
Suing, Benedict *o.s.b.* '54 (P)[L] St. Benedict, OR Mt. Angel Abbey.
Sukovaty, G. L. *o.p.* '51 (FgM).
Sukup, Joseph G. '56 (MIL) Retired.
Sulaiman, Selwan A. (OLD) Jacksonville, FL Saint Ephrem.
Sularz, Thomas (JOL) Deans.
Sularz, Tom '71 (JOL) Addison, IL St. Philip The Apostle.
Sulkowski, Anthony P. '86 (DET) Clinton Twp., MI St. Louis.
Sullins, Paul '02 (WDC) Hyattsville, MD St. Mark.
Sullivan, Alan *o.f.m.* '56 (NY)[EE] San Diego, CA; AUXILIARY CHAPLAINS CONTRACT CHAPLAINS.
Sullivan, Andrew A. '94 (BIR) Florence, AL St. Joseph's; [I] Florence, AL Society of St. Vincent de Paul, St. Joseph Conference; [H] Florence, AL University of North Alabama.
Sullivan, Brendan V. '60 (CAM) Ventnor, NJ St. James; Atlantic County East.
Sullivan, Brian '03 (PAT) Rockaway, NJ St. Cecilia's; Rockaway, NJ Sacred Heart; Rockaway, NJ St. Cecilia's.
Sullivan, Charles D. *s.j.* '72 (NY)[F] New York, NY Fordham Preparatory School; [EE] Jesuit Community, Kohlmann Hall.
Sullivan, Charles J. '66 (PH) Philadelphia, PA St. Bernard.
Sullivan, Charles K. '64 (VEN) Fort Myers, FL Blessed Pope John XXIII.
Sullivan, D. Edward '42 (CHL) Retired.
Sullivan, Daniel F. '57 (CHI) Lake Villa, IL Prince of Peace Retired.
Sullivan, Daniel J. '53 (CHI) Retired.
Sullivan, Daniel J. *s.j.* '61 (NY)[EE] Loyola Hall, Jesuit Community.
Sullivan, Daniel J. '72 (SJ) Phoenix, AZ St. Francis Xavier.
Sullivan, Daniel J. '77 (PH) Philadelphia, PA Holy Innocents; Interparochial Cooperation, Commission for.
Sullivan, Daniel J. (PH) Diocesan Priests' Compensation and Benefits Committee.
Sullivan, Daniel James '63 (HRT) Hamden, CT Our Lady of Mt. Carmel.
Sullivan, Daniel Jeremiah '63 (HRT) South Windsor, CT St. Margaret Mary; Commission for Priests' Retreats.
Sullivan, Daniel *c.p.* '68 (PIT)[N] Pittsburgh, PA St. Paul of the Cross Monastery.
Sullivan, Daniel *c.p.* '68 (PIT)[N] Pittsburgh St. Paul of the Cross Monastery; Priest Council.
Sullivan, Daniel '75 (TR) Leave of Absence.
Sullivan, David D. '58 (STL)[J] Creve Coeur, MO St. John's Mercy Medical Center.
Sullivan, Dennis J. '71 (NY) Larchmont, NY SS. John and Paul; Manhattan, NY Gouverneur Hospital.
Sullivan, Donal P. (STA) Vicar for Clergy.
Sullivan, Donal '64 (STA) Green Cove Springs, FL Sacred Heart; Deans.
Sullivan, E. Hartrick *c.m.* '46 (DEN)[N] Denver, CO Congregation of the Mission Midwest Province: De Paul House.
Sullivan, E. Paul '63 (BO) Topsfield, MA St. Rose of Lima.
Sullivan, Edward G. '55 (RVC) Uniondale, NY St. Martha Retired.
Sullivan, Edward J. *o.f.m.* '45 (PAT)[M] Butler, NJ St. Anthony Friary.
Sullivan, Edward P. *s.j.* '46 (BUF)[O] Buffalo, NY Canisius Jesuit Community.
Sullivan, Edward *o.f.m.* (NY)[GG] Warwick, NY Franciscan Sisters of the Poor Convent.
Sullivan, Edwin V. '46 (NEW) Retired.
Sullivan, Emmanuel *o.c.d.* '52 (BO)[V] Boston, MA Carmelite Monastery.
Sullivan, Emmanuel *s.a.* '55 (NY)[EE] Garrison, NY Franciscan Friars of the Atonement.
Sullivan, Eugene P. '68 (BO) Weymouth, MA St. Francis Xavier; Members.
Sullivan, Eugene '59 (CHY) Retired.
Sullivan, F. Norman '63 (BUF) Cheektowaga, NY Most Holy Redeemer.
Sullivan, Francis A. *s.j.* '51 (BO)[V] Newton, MA The Jesuit Community at Boston College.
Sullivan, Francis E. *c.ss.r.* '59 (ALB) Saratoga Springs, NY St. Clement.
Sullivan, Francis E. '88 (BO) Billerica, MA St. Mary.
Sullivan, Francis J. '30 (SPR)[H] Springfield, MA St. Michael's Residence Retired.
Sullivan, Francis X. '48 (SPR) Retired.
Sullivan, Frederick '53 (NY) Retired.
Sullivan, Gael *s.d.b.* '76 (LA) Bellflower, CA St. Dominic Savio; Oxnard, CA St. Anthony.
Sullivan, Gael (LA) Cursillo Movement.
Sullivan, George *o.f.m.conv.* '74 (TR) Seaside Park, NJ St. Catharine of Siena.
Sullivan, Gerald A. (CHY) Defenders of the Bond; St. Joseph's Society for Priests (Clergy Mutual Benefit Society).
Sullivan, Gerald P. *s.j.* '62 (SJ)[B] Santa Clara, CA Jesuit Community.
Sullivan, Gerald '59 (CHY) Retired.
Sullivan, J. Bernard '44 (HEL) Retired.
Sullivan, J. Richard '77 (L) Elizabethtown, KY St. James; White Mills, KY St. Ignatius; Deans.
Sullivan, James B. '58 (NEW) Roseland, NJ Our Lady of the Blessed Sacrament Retired.
Sullivan, James E. '46 (BRK) Whitestone, NY Holy Trinity Retired.
Sullivan, James F. '87 (PH) Ardsley, PA Queen of Peace.
Sullivan, James H. *s.m.a.* '60 (NEW)[N] Tenafly, NJ Society of African Missions, Provincialate, S.M.A. Fathers.
Sullivan, James L. '43 (BO) Senior Priests Retired.
Sullivan, James M. '60 (HEL) On Duty Outside the Diocese; Omaha, NE St. John Vianney.
Sullivan, James M. '66 (STL) Hazelwood, MO Our Lady of Mercy.
Sullivan, James M. *o.p.* '95 (NY).
Sullivan, James Mary *o.p.* '95 (NY)[EE] New York, NY St. Vincent Ferrer Priory.
Sullivan, James P. '70 (NY)[E] New York, NY Cardinal Spellman High School.
Sullivan, James '47 (SFD) Retired.
Sullivan, James '70 (NY) Bronxville, NY St. Joseph.
Sullivan, Jan C. '91 (COL) Washington Court House, OH St. Colman.
Sullivan, Jeremiah T. '62 (HEL)[B] Helena, MT Carroll College.
Sullivan, Jeremiah (HEL) Diocesan Consultors; Presbyteral Council.
Sullivan, John A. (PAT) Retired.
Sullivan, John Andrew '78 (LAV) Las Vegas, NV Holy Family.
Sullivan, John B. '61 (NY) Bronx, NY St. Mary.
Sullivan, John J. '51 (SLC) Board of Directors; Defenders of the Bond Retired.
Sullivan, John J. '66 (DET) Plymouth, MI Our Lady of Good Counsel.
Sullivan, John J. '67 (CLV) Mentor, OH St. Bede the Venerable.
Sullivan, John J. '77 (CHI) Glenwood, IL St. John.
Sullivan, John J. *o.s.f.s.* '81 (PH)[AA] Philadelphia, PA Father Louis Brisson Residence.
Sullivan, John L. *o.p.* '49 (PRO) Providence, RI St. Pius V; [P] Providence, RI St. Pius Priory.
Sullivan, John L. '52 (BO) Senior Priests Retired.
Sullivan, John L. '71 (SPR) Springfield, MA St. Michael's Cathedral; Judicial Vicar; Pro–Life Commission; Sisters of Providence Care Centers, Inc..
Sullivan, John L. '74 (BO)[A] Brighton, MA St. John Seminary School of Theology.
Sullivan, John L. (SCR) Judges.
Sullivan, John M. '90 (FR) New Bedford, MA St. Lawrence Martyr.
Sullivan, John M. '91 (BO) Melrose, MA St. Mary of the Annunciation.
Sullivan, John P. '65 (HRT) New Haven, CT St. Joseph's; [R] New Haven, CT Southern Connecticut State University Catholic Center.
Sullivan, John P. *m.s.* '70 (HRT)[M] Hartford, CT Missionaries of LaSalette.
Sullivan, John P. '72 (SAC) El Dorado Hills, CA Holy Trinity; Vicars Forane Retired.
Sullivan, John P. '81 (RVC) Wading River, NY St. John Baptist.
Sullivan, John R. '94 (LIN) Lincoln, NE Blessed Sacrament; Family Life Office; Teens Encounter Christ (TEC).
Sullivan, John '54 (JOL) Glen Ellyn, IL St. Petronille.
Sullivan, John *o.f.m.* '59 (SFD)[L] Springfield, IL Our Lady of Angels Friary.
Sullivan, John *m.m.* '60 (WDC)[B] Washington, DC Maryknoll Fathers and Brothers.
Sullivan, John *s.m.* '65 (HON) Honolulu, HI Star of the Sea.
Sullivan, John *o.c.d.* '68 (WDC)[B] Washington, DC Discalced Carmelite Friars; [V] Washington, DC Institute of Carmelite Studies and ICS Publications.
Sullivan, John (LAV) Diocesan Judges.
Sullivan, John (LAV) Priests' Pension Board.
Sullivan, Joseph D. '56 (NY) Montgomery, NY Holy Name of Mary.
Sullivan, Joseph P. '53 (SFR) Retired.
Sullivan, Joseph T. '52 (BUR) Evangelization; Fairfield, VT St. Patrick.
Sullivan, Joseph '53 (DEN) Retired.
Sullivan, Joseph '03 (SPK) Walla Walla, WA St. Francis of Assisi; Walla Walla, WA St. Patrick.
Sullivan, Kevin B. '63 (SFD) Absent on Leave.
Sullivan, Kevin L. '76 (NY) New York, NY Corpus Christi; [I] New York, NY The Catholic Charities of the Archdiocese of New York; [I] New York, NY Roman Catholic Fund for Children and Other Purposes; [II] New York, NY Carmel Housing Development Fund Co., Inc.; [II] New York, NY The Housing Fund of the Archdiocese of New York; [II] New York, NY Cor Mariae Development Fund Corporation.
Sullivan, Kevin L. '76 (NY)[II] New York, NY Cor Mariae Housing Development Fund, Inc..
Sullivan, Kevin L. '76 (NY) New York, NY Corpus Christi; [I] New York, NY The Catholic Charities of the Archdiocese of New York; [I] New York, NY Roman Catholic Fund for Children and Other Purposes; [II] New York, NY Carmel Housing Development Fund Co., Inc.; [II] New York, NY The Housing Fund of the Archdiocese of New York; [II] New York, NY Cor Mariae Development Fund Corporation.
Sullivan, Kevin (NY) Catholic Charities.
Sullivan, Lawrence F. '56 (BO) Senior Priests Retired.
Sullivan, Lawrence F. *o.c.d.* '60 (BO) Chelsea, MA Quigley Memorial Hospital; [V] Boston, MA Carmelite Monastery.
Sullivan, Lawrence J. '92 (CHI) Elmwood Park, IL St. Celestine.
Sullivan, Leo F. '41 (STL) Retired.
Sullivan, Mervyn '69 (SJ) On Leave of Absence.

Sullivan, Michael Bruce *c.s.c.* '75 (FTW)[B] University of Notre Dame Du Lac; [I] Notre Dame, IN Holy Cross Community, Corby Hall, University of Notre Dame.
Sullivan, Michael D. '45 (BO) Senior Priests Retired.
Sullivan, Michael D. '91 (TR) Point Pleasant, NJ St. Martha; Diocesan Council of Priests.
Sullivan, Michael J. '79 (SCR) Unassigned or Leave of Absence.
Sullivan, Michael P. '66 (MIA) Fort Lauderdale, FL Blessed Sacrament.
Sullivan, Michael P. *o.s.a.* '67 (PH) Philadelphia, PA St. Rita of Cascia; [AA] Villanova, PA St. Thomas Monastery.
Sullivan, Michael '81 (STP) Maple Grove, MN St. Joseph the Worker.
Sullivan, Michael '81 (CR) On Duty Outside the Diocese.
Sullivan, Michael (CR) Judicial Vicar.
Sullivan, Michael *o.f.m.cap.* (CHI) Chicago, IL St. Clare of Montefalco.
Sullivan, Neil S. '97 (HBG) Harrisburg, PA St. Catherine Laboure.
Sullivan, Neil (HBG) Worship, Office of.
Sullivan, Patrick A. *s.j.* '45 (BO)[V] Weston, MA Campion Health Center, Inc..
Sullivan, Patrick A. '82 (CR) Diocesan Consultors; Red Lake, MN St. Mary's Mission Church; [A] Red Lake, MN St. Mary's Mission School; Priests' Council.
Sullivan, Patrick J. *s.j.* '50 (NY)[EE] New York, NY Murray–Weigel Hall.
Sullivan, Patrick J. *c.s.c.* '56 (SCR)[C] Holy Cross Community.
Sullivan, Patrick J. '63 (BIR) Birmingham, AL St. Francis Xavier.
Sullivan, Patrick J. '71 (PAT)[I] Morristown, NJ Loyola House of Retreats.
Sullivan, Patrick M. *o.s.b.* '87 (MAN)[K] Manchester, NH St. Anselm Abbey.
Sullivan, Patrick T. *s.j.* '64 (NY)[EE] New York, NY Murray–Weigel Hall.
Sullivan, Patrick '62 (DEN) Retired.
Sullivan, Patrick *o.f.m.cap.* '72 (NY) New York, NY Our Lady Queen of Angels.
Sullivan, Paul M. *s.j.* '83 (BO)[V] Boston The Society of Jesus of New England–Provincial Offices; Gardiner, ME St. Joseph's.
Sullivan, Paul V. '50 (NY) Yonkers, NY St. Joseph Retired.
Sullivan, Peter J. (ALB) Special Assignment; Adjutant Vicar Judicial; Judges; Bishop's Delegate for Marriage Dispensations.
Sullivan, R. William *o.s.a.* '67 (JOL) New Lenox, IL St. Jude.
Sullivan, Raymond F. *m.m.* '54 (NY)[EE] Maryknoll Maryknoll Fathers and Brothers.
Sullivan, Richard H. *c.s.c.* '38 (FTW)[I] Notre Dame, IN Holy Cross House.
Sullivan, Richard J. '58 (E) Erie, PA St. Andrew; College of Consultors.
Sullivan, Robert E. '80 (BO) On Duty Outside the Archdiocese.
Sullivan, Robert E. (FTW)[B] University of Notre Dame Du Lac.
Sullivan, Robert J. *s.j.* '40 (BO)[V] Weston, MA Campion Health Center, Inc..
Sullivan, Robert J. '63 (SY) Special Assignment; [T] Vestal, NY Binghamton University Newman Center.
Sullivan, Robert J. '78 (BO) Pembroke, MA St. Thecla.
Sullivan, Robert J. (BIR) Anniston, AL Sacred Heart of Jesus; Priests' Council; Diocesan College of Vicars; Navy Reserve Chaplains.
Sullivan, Robert *s.j.* '67 (COS) Colorado Springs, CO Our Lady of Guadalupe.
Sullivan, Robert (BIR) Members; Diocesan College of Consultors.
Sullivan, Sean *t.o.r.* '57 (VEN) Sarasota, FL Our Lady Queen of Martyrs Retired.
Sullivan, Terence *o.s.b.* '56 (KCK)[H] Atchison, KS St. Benedict's Abbey.
Sullivan, Terrence J. '64 (SJ) Campbell, CA St. Lucy; Roman Catholic Welfare Corporation; Priests' Retirement Board.
Sullivan, Thomas G. *c.ss.r.* '72 (HRT) Enfield, CT St. Patrick's.
Sullivan, Thomas J. (WOR) Chancery Office; Diocesan College of Consultors.
Sullivan, Thomas K. '52 (STA) Jacksonville, FL St. Paul's.
Sullivan, Thomas '53 (BIS) Retired.
Sullivan, Thomas (WOR) Presbyteral Council; Vocation Office.
Sullivan, Timothy F. *c.s.p.* '85 (NY) New York, NY St. Paul the Apostle.
Sullivan, Timothy *s.a.* '90 (NY).
Sullivan, Vincent B. *s.j.* '76 (NEW)[EE] Jersey City, NJ Parish of the Resurrection; [C] Jersey City, NJ St. Peter's Preparatory School; [N] Jersey City, NJ Jesuit Community of St. Peter's Prep, Inc..
Sullivan, Vincent P. '83 (ATL) Atlanta, GA Cathedral of Christ the King.
Sullivan, W. Jerome (BUF) Clergy Personnel Board; Promoter of Justice; Council of Priests; Hamburg, NY St. Mary of the Lake.
Sullivan, William F. *s.s.c.* '56 (PRO)[P] Bristol, RI St. Columban's Retirement House.
Sullivan, William J. '59 (HBG) Lancaster, PA St. Leo the Great.
Sullivan, William J. *s.j.* '61 (SEA)[A] Seattle, WA Seattle University.
Sullivan, William J. *o.s.b.* '71 (MAN)[A] Manchester, NH St. Anselm Abbey Seminary; [K] Manchester, NH St. Anselm Abbey.
Sullivan, William J. *o.ss.t.* '81 (WDC)[E] Hyattsville, MD De Matha Catholic High School.
Sullivan, William M. '81 (BO) Westford, MA St. Catherine of Alexandria; MERRIMACK REGION.
Sullivan, William P. '39 (BO) Senior Priests Retired.
Sullivan, William V. '66 (RIC) Ashland, VA St. Ann; Judicial Vicar.
Sullivan, William *s.j.* '66 (MI) Apo, AP Blessed Sacrament.
Sullivan, William '72 (FTW) Elkhart, IN St. Thomas the Apostle.
Sullivan, William *o.ss.t.* '81 (BAL).
Sullivan, William (FTW)[S] Advisory Board; Council of Priests.
Sumler, Kevin '82 (BEA) Port Arthur, TX St. James.
Sumler, Paul (BEA) Vidor, TX Our Lady of Lourdes.
Summers, Bryan F. *c.o.* '72 (PIT)[N] Pittsburgh, PA Congregation of the Oratory of St. Philip Neri.
Summers, John '54 (Y) Retired.
Summers, R. Emmett '52 (KC) Retired.
Summitt, James A. '81 (BIR) Absent on Leave.
Sumpayco, Simplicio *s.j.* '66 (CI)[C] Manresa Jesuit House.
Sumpter, Gary '79 (SR) On Duty Outside the Diocese.
Sumpter, Gary '79 (SEA) Port Townsend, WA St. Mary Star of the Sea.
Sumrall, Cliff (SD) Vista Detention Facility.
Sunberg, David A. '92 (CIN) Milford, OH St. Elizabeth Ann Seton.
Sundaram, John Joseph (LA)[J] Hawthorne, CA Robert F. Kennedy Medical Center.
Sundborg, Stephen V. *s.j.* '74 (SEA)[A] Seattle, WA Seattle University.
Sunderland, James C. *s.j.* '58 (DEN)[N] Denver, CO Xavier Jesuit Center.
Sundholm, Conrad '55 (ROC) Retired.
Sunds, Elvin '73 (JKS) Meridian, MS St. Patrick; Meridian, MS St. Joseph; East Mississippi State Hospital; Priests' Council.
Sunds, Elvin (JKS) Trustees; Diocesan Consultors; Trustees.
Sung, Thomas *c.s.j.b.* '51 (BRK)[V] Astoria, NY Congregation of St. John the Baptist of China.
Sung–Joo Kim, Chrysostom '79 (P) Portland, OR Korean Martyrs Catholic Church.
Sunghera, Gilbert *s.j.* '02 (SJ) San Jose, CA Most Holy Trinity.
Sunhwa, Gaspar *s.j.* '95 (OAK)[N] Berkeley, CA Jesuit Community at Jesuit School of Theology at Berkeley.
Sun Kim, Simon Chung '98 (ORG) Inactive Leave.
Sunnenberg, Scott M. '02 (SPC) Cape Girardeau, MO Cathedral of St. Mary; Catholic Scouting; Presbyteral Council.
Suntum, Jim *s.f.* (SFE) Albuquerque, NM St. Therese of the Infant Jesus of the Little Flower.
Supan Check, Norman '68 (LA) Sylmar, CA St. Didacus.
Supancheck, Norman '68 (LA)[D] Mission Hills, CA Bishop Alemany High School; Personnel Board of the Archdiocese.
Super, David J. '80 (CR) Chancellor; Finance Council; Crookston, MN Cathedral of the Immaculate Conception; Members.
Supnet, Romeo *o.s.a.* '84 (SD) R.J. Donovan Correctional Facility.
Suppa, F. Thomas '78 (E) Union City, PA St. Teresa of Avila.
Suppe, Bernard A. *s.j.* '56 (BAL)[M] Baltimore, MD Mercy Health Services Inc..
Supple, Edmund R. *c.s.sp.* '38 (PIT)[B] Pittsburgh, PA Duquesne University of the Holy Spirit.
Supple, Richard *o.carm.* '02 (NEW) Bogota, NJ St. Joseph's.
Suquilvide, Abel '55 (LA) Guadalupe, CA Our Lady of Guadalupe.
Surafka, Michael *o.f.m.* '91 (CLV) Cleveland, OH St. Stanislaus.
Suran, Joaquin '50 (BRK) Corona, NY St. Leo.
Surban, Edmundo A. '61 (NEW) Jersey City, NJ Jersey City Medical Center; Jersey City Medical Center.
Suren, Jack '58 (STL) Fenton, MO St. Paul.
Suren, Richard H. '53 (STL) St. Louis, MO St. Raphael The Archangel Retired.
Surette, John E. *s.j.* '67 (BO)[V] Boston The Society of Jesus of New England–Provincial Offices.
Surges, Robert F. '64 (MIL) St. Francis, WI Sacred Heart of Jesus.
Suriani, Raymond N. '85 (PRO) Westerly, RI St. Pius X.
Suriano, Thomas '64 (MIL) Whitewater, WI St. Patrick.
Surman, Darrell '62 (YAK) On Duty Outside the Diocese.
Surman, Stanley '56 (SAG) Retired.
Surmeier, Bill (SAL) Catholic Charities Outreach Office – Hays; Diocesan Committee Regarding Alleged Cases of Child Sexual Abuse.
Surmeier, William J. '65 (SAL) Hays, KS St. Nicholas of Myra; Munjor, KS St. Francis of Assisi.
Surowiec, Jude *o.f.m.conv.* '75 (NOR) Stafford Springs, CT St. Edward; [A] Cromwell, CT Holy Apostles College and Seminary.
Surprenant, John L. '78 (NOR) Absent on Leave.
Surprenant, Paul W. '73 (WIN) Rochester, MN St. Pius X; Auditors.
Surufka, Michael *o.f.m.* '91 (CLV)[O] Cleveland, OH St. Stanislaus Friary; [Z] Cleveland, OH Pulaski Franciscan Community Development Corp..
Survil, Bernard '67 (GBG) Penn, PA St. Boniface.
Surwilo, Edward R. '63 (BGP) Stamford, CT Our Lady Star of the Sea; Pastors' Vocation Advisory Board.
Susa, Robert P. '61 (E)[B] Erie, PA Gannon University.
Susi, Joseph M. (ALX) Chancellor; Ecclesiastical Notaries; College of Consultors; Finance Council; Priests Council; Archivist; Eucharistic League, Priests; Special Assignment Retired.
Suskey, Robert G. '90 (PH) Warrington, PA St. Joseph.
Susko, Martin S. '61 (Y) Girard, OH St. Rose; Judges.
Suslenko, Mark S. '86 (HRT) Farmington, CT St. Patrick's.
Suslowicz, Michael S. '80 (PIT) Pittsburgh, PA St. Elizabeth.
Susnik, Bernardin *o.f.m.* '59 (CHI)[N] Lemont, IL The Slovene Franciscan Fathers, Order of Friars Minor, Commissariat of the Holy Cross.
Suss, Thomas '73 (SEA) McNeil Island Correction Center.
Sustagta, Paul A. '91 (LA) Los Angeles, CA St. Mary Magdalen.
Sustarsic, John '52 (DUL) Retired.
Sustayta, Paul A. '91 (LA) Los Angeles, CA Holy Spirit.
Suszko, Robert K. '02 (NEW) Cedar Grove, NJ St. Catherine of Siena.
Suszynski, Michael '86 (SP) Port Richey, FL St. James the Apostle.
Sutherland, Thomas J. '60 (DET) Shelby Twp., MI St. Therese of Lisieux; College of Consultors; Presbyteral Council.
Sutherland, William E. '83 (E) Erie, PA St. Hedwig/St. Patrick; Erie, PA St. Patrick/St. Hedwig.
Sutil, Florencio '44 (SJN) On Duty Outside the Archdiocese.
Sutman, Frank I. *o.p.* '85 (BO)[V] Dover, MA St. Stephen Priory.
Sutphin, Carl '58 (LA) Retired.
Sutter, Conrad *o.f.m.conv.* '93 (LSC) Carlsbad, NM St. Edward.
Sutter, Raymond A. '73 (CLV) Parma, OH St. Matthias.
Sutton, Alphonsus M. *f.f.i.* '57 (FR)[H] New Bedford, MA Marian Friary of Our Lady, Queen of the Seraphic Order.
Sutton, Douglas B. '02 (WH) Weirton, WV St. Joseph the Worker.
Sutton, John H. '56 (PBL) Retired.
Sutton, John '56 (TOL) Retired.
Sutton, ST '96 (OLD) Special Assignment; Chancellor; Secretary; Officialis.
Sutton, Stephen '84 (BAL) Forest Hill, MD St. Ignatius; Air National Guard Chaplains.
Sutton, Thomas E. '73 (SAG) Auburn, MI St. Anthony/St. Joseph; St. Anthony/St. Joseph; Vicars General; Vicar of Administration; Chancellor; Judges.
Sutula, Leo S. '49 (NOR) Retired.
Suvakeen, Peter A. '89 (BRK) Brooklyn, NY St. Augustine.
Suwalsky, David J. *s.j.* '95 (STL)[O] St. Louis, MO Bellarmine House of Studies.
Suwinski, Leo S. '43 (BGP) Retired.
Svarczkopf, Mark '74 (IND) Greenwood, IN Our Lady of the Greenwood.
Svida, Wayne A. '02 (CHI) Chicago, IL St. Christina.
Sviokla, Edmund J. '51 (BO) Saugus, MA Blessed Sacrament; Senior Priests Retired.
Svirskas, Joseph J. '51 (BO) Senior Priests Retired.
Svitan, Martin '39 (NY) New York, NY St. John Nepomucene.
Svobodny, Aloysius *o.m.i.* '49 (STP)[P] Buffalo, MN Christ the King Retreat Center.
Swacha, Stanley J. '79 (E) Sharon, PA Sacred Heart.
Swade, Thomas J. '61 (CHI) Other Assignments.
Swai, Protas *a.l.c.p.* '91 (SLC) Vernal, UT St. James the Greater.
Swain, Kenneth J. '72 (ALB) Fort Plain, NY St. James.
Swain, Paul J. '88 (MAD) Madison, WI St. Raphael Cathedral; Vicar–General; Diocesan Consultors; Appointed; Personnel Board; Building Commission; Catholic Relief Services; Saint Raphael Society Clergy Retirement Plan; Information; Madison, WI Holy Redeemer.
Swain, Robert J. '59 (BRK)[V] Jamaica, NY Vincentian Residence.
Swalina, Michael F. '70 (SPC) Poplar Bluff, MO Sacred

Heart; Poplar Bluff Hospital Ministry; Judges; Holy Childhood Association; Missionary Apostolate; Mission of the Laity; Diocesan Consultors; Presbyteral Council.
Swaner, James J. '61 (PEO) Utica, IL St. Mary.
Swanson, Charles F. '66 (OM) Omaha, NE Holy Cross; Deans; Building Commission; Deans.
Swanson, Derek *c.m.* '03 (SPC) Cape Girardeau, MO St. Vincent de Paul.
Swanson, James *l.c.* '94 (WDC)[M] Potomac, MD Legionaries of Christ.
Swarick, Joachim *o.f.m.* (GB) Manitowoc, WI St. Mary.
Swartvagher, Marc '96 (BRK)[B] Douglaston, NY Cathedral Seminary Residence of the Immaculate Conception; Bishop Catanello—; [A] Douglaston, NY Immaculate Conception Center.
Swartz, Joseph M. '75 (EVN) Vincennes, IN Sacred Heart.
Swartz, Lawrence *o.c.s.o.* '34 (ATL)[K] Conyers, GA The Monastery of the Holy Spirit.
Swartz, Michael R. '87 (BUF) Absent on Leave.
Sweany, Thomas M. '80 (CLV) Chesterland, OH St. Anselm.
Swearingen, Eric '87 (FRS) Fresno, CA Holy Spirit; Diocesan Consultors; Vicars Forane; Personnel Committee; Priests' Council.
Sweeney, Callistus *o.f.m.* (FgM).
Sweeney, Charles J. *s.j.* '62 (TOL)[C] Toledo, OH St. John's Jesuit High School.
Sweeney, Cornelius '50 (MRY) Morro Bay, CA St. Timothy.
Sweeney, D. Gilbert *s.j.* '54 (ALN)[A] Wernersville, PA Jesuit Center.
Sweeney, Daniel *s.j.* '94 (MD)[V] Newton, MA The Jesuit Community at Boston College; Air Force Reserve Chaplains.
Sweeney, Denis J. *c.ss.r.* '81 (BAL) Annapolis, MD St. Mary; [S] Annapolis, MD Saint Mary Rectory.
Sweeney, Denis (GBG) Retired.
Sweeney, Edward J. *s.j.* '46 (NY).
Sweeney, Edward '88 (AMA) Priests' Pension Plan Retirement Committee; Friona, TX St. Teresa of Jesus.
Sweeney, Ernest S. *s.j.* '63 (LA)[C] Los Angeles, CA Jesuit Community.
Sweeney, Eugene *s.m.* '78 (FWT) Denton, TX St. Mark.
Sweeney, Francis M. *c.s.p.* '61 (BO)[V] Boston, MA Paulist Fathers Residence.
Sweeney, Frank M. *c.s.p.* '61 (NY)[EE] Jamaica Estates Paulist Fathers Generalate.
Sweeney, Frederick E. '52 (BO) Unassigned.
Sweeney, James H. '81 (BRK) Brooklyn, NY St. Agatha's.
Sweeney, James P. '63 (BRK)[V] Jamaica, NY Parsons Manor.
Sweeney, James '45 (MRY) Retired.
Sweeney, John A. '41 (STP)[C] St. Paul, MN University of St. Thomas Retired.
Sweeney, John D. '56 (NEW) Retired.
Sweeney, John Maria *f.p.o.* '98 (FR)[H] New Bedford, MA Franciscans of Primitive Observance.
Sweeney, John P. '73 (PIT) Aliquippa, PA St. Titus; Charismatic Prayer Groups.
Sweeney, John T. '70 (GBG) Apollo, PA St. James the Greater.
Sweeney, Joseph F. *s.j.* '57 (WDC)[M] Washington, DC The Jesuit Community at Georgetown University.
Sweeney, Joseph J. '61 (PH) Retired.
Sweeney, Kevin J. '97 (BRK) Jamaica, NY St. Nicholas of Tolentine; Corona, NY Our Lady of Sorrows.
Sweeney, Kevin '94 (ORG) Military Chaplains; Navy Chaplains.
Sweeney, Lawrence P. '54 (SLC) Ogden, UT Holy Family.
Sweeney, Luke M. '01 (NY) Newburgh, NY Sacred Heart; Navy Reserve Chaplains.
Sweeney, Michael *o.p.* '79 (OAK)[N] Oakland, CA Western Dominican Province.
Sweeney, Michael *o.p.* '79 (SEA) Seattle, WA Blessed Sacrament.
Sweeney, Michael '79 (KNX) Harriman, TN Blessed Sacrament; Lancing, TN St. Ann.
Sweeney, Michael (KNX) Deans of the Diocese; Presbyteral Council; Ministries of the Cumberland Mtn. Deanery.
Sweeney, Patrick E. '72 (PH) Collegeville, PA St. Eleanor; [EE] Collegeville, PA Ursinus College.
Sweeney, Peter J. '61 (WDC) Damascus, MD St. Paul.
Sweeney, Robert J. '69 (RCK) Pecatonica, IL St. Mary; Secretary for Administrative Processes; Propagation of the Faith.
Sweeney, Robert J. '82 (NY) Greenwood Lake, NY Holy Rosary.
Sweeney, Robert L. '48 (BWN) Retired.
Sweeney, Timothy *o.s.b.* '61 (IND)[K] Owensboro, KY Parish of the Immaculate.
Sweeney, Timothy *o.s.b.* '61 (OWN) Owensboro, KY The Immaculate; Council of Religious.
Sweeney, William F. '81 (BRK) St. Albans, NY St. Catherine of Sienna; [G] Fresh Meadows, NY St. Francis Preparatory School.
Sweeney, William *s.s.c.* '75 (OM)[K] St. Columbans, NE St. Columban's Foreign Mission Society; [N] St. Columbans, NE Columban Fathers Regional Administration.
Sweeney, William (BRK) Personnel Board (Clergy).
Sweeny, Edward A. '57 (RVC) Long Beach, NY St. Ignatius Martyr; Judicial Vicar.
Sweeny, John J. '48 (SJ) Retired.
Sweeny, Richard R. '86 (TR) Fair Haven, NJ Nativity.
Sweet, Daniel J. '01 (PRO) Woonsocket, RI All Saints Catholic Community.
Sweet, Douglas S. '95 (SHP) Shreveport, LA St. Joseph.
Sweetser, Thomas P. *s.j.* '70 (MIL)[O] Milwaukee, WI Miguel Pro Jesuit Community.
Sweitzer, Raymond M. *s.j.* '75 (NY)[F] New York, NY Fordham Preparatory School; [EE] Jesuit Community, Kohlmann Hall.
Swencki, John T. '79 (BO) Emergency Response Group.
Swengros, William J. '91 (SP) Gulfport, FL Most Holy Name of Jesus.
Swenson, Frederick O. '67 (LAF) Church Point, LA Our Lady of the Sacred Heart; West Region.
Swenson, James L. '74 (LAV) Las Vegas, NV St. Bridget.
Swenson, Roger A. '70 (NO) Metairie, LA St. Catherine of Siena; Priests for Life.
Swenson, Walter J.F. '50 (NEW) Jersey City, NJ Our Lady of Victories Retired.
Swertz, Thaddeus T. *c.s.c.* '54 (FR)[A] North Easton, MA Holy Cross Fathers Religious; [G] North Attleboro, MA Madonna Manor Inc..
Swetland, Stuart W. '91 (PEO) Champaign, IL St. John's Catholic Chapel; [O] Champaign, IL St. John's Catholic Student Chapel and Newman Foundation, University of Illinois; Presbyteral Council.
Swetland, Stuart (PEO) Diocesan College of Consultors.
Swetnam, William R. '73 (STL) Military Chaplains.
Swett, Charles J. '57 (TLS) Retired.
Swett, Ronald J. '67 (FRS) Bakersfield, CA St. Philip the Apostle.
Swett, Ronald (FRS) Diocesan Consultors; Vicars Forane; Personnel Committee; Priests' Council.
Swiader, James P. '75 (RVC) Farmingdale, NY St. Kilian; Priests' Retirement Board.
Swiat, James R. '67 (LAN) Grand Blanc, MI Holy Family.
Swiatecki, Emilian '56 (VEN) Retired.
Swiatek, Emil P. '65 (BUF) Elma, NY Annunciation of the Blessed Virgin Mary.
Swiatek, Nicholas *o.f.m.conv.* '75 (BUF) Buffalo, NY Precious Blood.
Swiatkowski, Francis M. '44 (BUF)[O] Tonawanda, NY O'Hara Residence Retired.
Swiatocha, Bruno '56 (RVC) Retired.
Swichtenberg, William D. '83 (GB) Green Bay, WI St. John the Baptist; Oneida, WI St. Joseph; De Pere, WI Immaculate Conception.
Swickard, John L. '74 (COL) Grove City, OH Our Lady of Perpetual Help.
Swiderski, Jan '94 (NOR) Middletown, CT St. Mary of Czestochowa.
Swiderski, Stan '63 (LR) Mountain Home AR St. Peter the Fisherman; Mountain View, AR St. Mary Church.
Swiercz, Pawel A. '94 (FR) Osterville, MA Our Lady of the Assumption.
Swierczynski, Joseph E. '64 (PIT) Pittsburgh, PA Immaculate Heart of Mary.
Swierz, Michael '85 (Y) Campbell, OH St. Elizabeth; Campbell, OH St. John the Baptist; Campbell, OH St. Joseph the Provider.
Swierzbinski, Edward '51 (NEW) Retired
Swierzbiolek, Waclav *s.d.b.* '62 (NY)[EE] New Rochelle, NY Salesian Provincial House.
Swierzbiolek, Waclaw '62 (NY) Chester, NY St. Columba.
Swierzowski, Stanislaus J. '56 (ALB) Amsterdam, NY St. Casimir; Amsterdam, NY St. John the Baptist.
Swietochowski, Andrew '78 (SFS) Mitchell, SD Holy Spirit.
Swift, Bruce *o.s.b.* '60 (KCK)[A] Atchison, KS Benedictine College; [H] Atchison, KS St. Benedict's Abbey.
Swift, Daniel F. '89 (TR) Long Branch, NJ Holy Trinity.
Swift, Gerald *s.t.* '46 (WDC)[M] Adelphi, MD Missionary Servants of the Most Holy Trinity.
Swift, James E. *c.m.* '78 (STL)[O] Earth City, MO Congregation of the Mission Midwest Province (Vincentians); [O] St. Louis, MO Lazarist Residence.
Swift, James E. *c.m.* '78 (FgM).
Swift, James E. *c.m.* '78 (STL)[O] Earth City, MO Congregation of the Mission Midwest Province (Vincentians); [O] St. Louis, MO Lazarist Residence.
Swift, John *s.v.d.* '75 (CHI)[B] Techny, IL Divine Word Residence.
Swift, Walter A. '69 (SPR) Brimfield, MA St. Christopher's.
Swift, William J. '44 (TLS) Tulsa, OK Church of St. Mary.
Swift, William V. '44 (TLS) Retired.
Swing, R. John '70 (LC) Nekoosa, WI Sacred Heart of Jesus; Port Edwards, WI St. Alexander; [L] Port Edwards, WI St. Alexander's Church, Port Edwards Endowment Trust.
Swiniarski, Zdzislaw E. *s.s.* '90 (BWN) Edinburg, TX Sacred Heart.
Swirczynski, Gary '87 (LSC) Tularosa, NM St. Francis de Paula.
Swirski, Thaddeus M. '54 (CLV) Akron, OH St. Hedwig.
Swisshelm, Germain *o.s.b.* '60 (IND)[K] St. Meinrad, IN St. Meinrad Archabbey.
Swistovich, John '98 (FWT) Wichita Falls, TX Our Lady Queen of Peace; Deans.
Switanowski, Robert Joseph *o.f.m.conv.* '90 (MIL) Milwaukee, WI Basilica of St. Josaphat.
Swoger, John W. '63 (E) Oil City, PA St. Joseph.
Swoger, John W. '63 (E) Deans.
Swoger, John (E) College of Consultors.
Swoger, Mark S. '85 (E) Du Bois, PA St. Michael; [C] Du Bois, PA DuBois Area Catholic School; [K] Du Bois, PA Christ the King Manor, Inc..
Swolek, Richard L. '63 (OM) Omaha, NE Mary Our Queen.
Swope, John W. *s.j.* '86 (BAL)[S] Baltimore, MD Jesuit Fathers and Brothers Maryland Provincial Curia.
Swope, Timothy J. '66 (ALT) Prince Gallitzin Deanery; Ongoing Formation Clergy; Loretto, PA Basilica of St. Michael the Archangel.
Syamala, George '79 (COV) Elsmere, KY St. Henry.
Sye, Angelo Y. *s.s.p.* '93 (Y)[A] Canfield, OH Society of St. Paul.
Sykes, Gregory P. '77 (OG) Military Chaplains; Army Chaplains.
Sylva, Eugene R. '93 (PAT) Wayne, NJ Our Lady of Consolation; [C] Wayne, NJ De Paul High School.
Sylva, Geno (PAT) Young Prophets Catholic Youth Program in Paterson.
Sylvain, Daniel *s.a.* '01 (NY).
Sylvester, Sean '99 (DET)[EE] Pontiac, MI St. Joseph; Pontiac, MI St. Michael; Pontiac, MI St. Vincent de Paul; Presbyteral Council.
Sylvestre, Ernest *o.m.i.* '61 (PT) Madison, FL St. Vincent de Paul; Madison, FL St. Margaret.
Sylvia, Albert A. '66 (BO) Peabody, MA Our Lady of Fatima; EnCourage.
Sylvia, Edmund J. *c.s.c.* '77 (BGP)[P] Clearwater, FL.
Symes, Joseph J. *c.m.* '50 (PH)[AA] St. Catherine Infirmary.
Symolon, Lawrence S. '75 (HRT) Guilford, CT St. George; Deans.
Synek, Roger A. '98 (BIS) Parshall, ND St. Bridget.
Sypek, Stanislaus T. '43 (BO) Hyde Park, MA St. Adalbert.
Sypek, Stanislaus (BO) Polish.
Syracuse, Ross *o.f.m.conv.* '78 (BAL) Baltimore, MD St. Casimir.
Sys, Joseph *m.afr.* '41 (SP)[O] St. Petersburg, FL Missionaries of Africa.
Syslo, Alan M. *c.s.v.* '66 (CHI)[N] Santa Cruz, CA.
Syverson, David '99 (FAR) West Fargo, ND Holy Cross; Diocesan College of Consultors; Presbyteral Council.
Syverstad, Daniel *o.p.* '82 (OAK) Seattle, WA Blessed Sacrament.
Szabajkowicz, Dominic '01 (VEN) Sarasota, FL Incarnation.
Szabelski, Joseph R. '70 (CHI) Other Assignments.
Szabo, Ferenc *s.j.* (ATH) "Tavlatok".
Szabo, Marcel '71 (PSC) Passaic, NJ St. Michael Cathedral; Northern New Jersey Protopresbyterate.
Szada, John A. '78 (HBG) Hanover, PA St. Vincent; World Apostolate of Fatima.
Szafranski, Richard T. '75 (SAG) Saginaw, MI St. John the Baptist; Saginaw, MI St. Matthew.
Szakaly, Anthony V. *c.s.c.* '92 (FTW)[I] South Bend, IN Congregation of Holy Cross, Indiana Province, Provincial House.
Szal, Ignatius J. '44 (PH) Retired.
Szamocki, Piotr '91 (CAM) Camden, NJ St. Joseph's.
Szamreta, John *o.f.m.cap.* '81 (FgM).
Szanto, Hubert S. *o.praem.* '48 (ORG)[D] Silverado, CA St. Michael's Preparatory School; [I] Silverado, CA Norbertine Fathers of Orange Inc..
Szantyr, Eugene R. '78 (BGP) Bridgeport, CT St. Andrew.
Szanyi, Mark A. *o.f.m.conv.* (PMB) Vicar for Religious.
Szanyi, Mark *o.f.m.conv.* '78 (PMB) Boynton Beach, FL St. Mark.
Szarek, Eugene *c.r.* '67 (CHI) Chicago, IL St. Hedwig.
Szarek, Mitchell '54 (DET) Retired.
Szarek, Mitchell '57 (DET) Detroit, MI SS. Peter and Paul.
Szarnicki, Henry A. '55 (PIT)[N] Pittsburgh, PA St. John Vianney Manor Retired.
Szarnicki, Zygmunt V. '45 (PIT)[N] Pittsburgh, PA St. John Vianney Manor Retired.
Szaroleta, Andrew L. '77 (MET) Clinton, NJ Immaculate Conception; Hunterdon Developmental Center; Episcopal Vicars; Episcopal Council.
Szatkowski, David *s.c.j.* '02 (GAL) Houston, TX St. Elizabeth Ann Seton.
Szcurek, Victor S. *o.praem.* '00 (ORG)[I] Silverado, CA Norbertine Fathers of Orange Inc..
Szczapa, Stanley J. '71 (NOR) Vernon, CT Sacred Heart; Diocesan Evangelization Catechumenate Team.

Szczepanik, John '88 (MET) Middlesex, NJ Our Lady of Mount Virgin.
Szczepankiewicz, Gary '75 (BUF) North Tonawanda, NY Ascension.
Szczesniak, Harry F. '72 (BUF) Buffalo, NY Our Lady of Czestochowa.
Szczesnowicz, Andrzej (Andrew) '03 (SY) Oswego, NY St. Stephen the King.
Szczesny, John S. '75 (GBG) Youngwood, PA Holy Cross.
Szczesny, Walter J. '90 (BUF)[A] West Falls, NY St. George.
Szczotka, Krzysztof *s.d.s.* '88 (NEW) Elizabeth, NJ St. Adalbert's; [N] Verona, NJ The Salvatorian Fathers.
Szczurek, Victor S. *o.praem.* (ORG)[D] Silverado, CA St. Michael's Preparatory School.
Szczykutowicz, Francis S. '58 (PT) Sunny Hills, FL St. Theresa.
Szczykutowicz, Francis '57 (PT) Blountstown, FL St. Francis of Assisi; Propagation of the Faith, Office of; Real Estate, Diocesan Commission for.
Szebenyi, Andrew L. *s.j.* '61 (SY)[Q] Syracuse, NY Jesuits at LeMoyne, Inc..
Szekula, Augustin *o.mech.* '44 (ARM) Tujunga, CA Mekhitarist School.
Szelest, Theodore A. '47 (NEW) Dumont, NJ St. Mary's Retired.
Szeman, Stephen J. '53 (SEA) Presbyteral Council; College of Consultors Retired.
Szemborski, Chester *s.d.b.* '50 (NY)[GG] Stony Point, NY Don Bosco Retreat Center and Marian Shrine; [GG] Stony Point, NY Marian Shrine.
Szepe, Ladislaus *s.f.o.* '35 (GB).
Szewczyk, Antoni S. '82 (NY)[I] Bronx, NY St. Brendan.
Szewczyk, Grzegorz *s.d.s.* '91 (BRK) Poth, TX Blessed Sacrament.
Szewczyk, Joseph '55 (DET) New Boston, MI St. Stephen.
Szews, George R. '78 (LC) Eau Claire, WI Newman Community; [K] Eau Claire, WI Newman Parish.
Szivos, Charles '99 (NY) Bronx, NY St. Helena.
Szklarski, Joseph '62 (NEW) Lyndhurst, NJ St. Michael's.
Szkredka, Slawomir '02 (LA) Panorama City, CA St. Genevieve.
Szlanga, Edmund S. '48 (CHI) Retired.
Szleszinski, Peter F. '56 (SUP) Hudson, WI St. Patrick; Presbyteral Council & Diocesan Consultors; St. Pius Priest Fund.
Szlezak, Emeric *o.f.m.* '44 (BGP) Fairfield, CT St. Emery.
Szmyd, John S. '96 (CHI).
Szoke, Joseph V. '02 (MET)[A] Colonia, NJ St. John Vianney.
Szolack, Joseph T. '87 (CAM) Bellmawr, NJ Mary, Mother of the Church; [A] Wynnewood, PA Theological Seminary of St. Charles Borromeo, Overbrook; Vocation Advisory Board; Members.
Szopa, Daniel F. '76 (MAN) Candia, NH St. Paul.
Szostak, Daniel J. '54 (BUF) Retired.
Szparagowski, George J. '02 (PH) Philadelphia, PA St. Bernard.
Szpiech, Edward P. '67 (NEW) Garfield, NJ St. Stanislaus Kostka.
Szpieg, Edmund L. '94 (PMB) Port St. Lucie, FL St. Elizabeth Ann Seton.
Szpieg, Edward (PMB) Secretary.
Szpilski, Joseph *c.m.* '56 (HRT) Ansonia, CT St. Joseph's.
Sztorc, Richard E. '69 (CHI) Northbrook, IL Our Lady of the Brook.
Szudarek, Ronald J. '81 (CLV) Cleveland, OH Corpus Christi.
Szudera, Ted F. '77 (GF) Belt, MT St. Mark the Evangelist.
Szudera, Theodore (GF) Liturgical Commission.
Szufel, Adam *o.f.m.* '64 (GB)[I] Akron, OH Univ. of Akron, Biology Dept..
Szukalski, John *s.v.d.* '97 (MIL)[M] Washington, DC Divine Word College.
Szulwach, Joseph '87 (MET) Laurence Harbor, NJ St. Lawrence.
Szumilo, Julian *c.m.* '50 (HRT)[K] Enfield, CT The Home for the Aged of the Little Sisters of the Poor; [M] Manchester DePaul Provincial Residence.
Szupa, Joseph '92 (PHU) Elizabeth, NJ St. Vladimir's; Protopresbyters (Deans); Board Members.
Szupper, Michael F. '57 (WIL) Newark, DE St. Thomas More Oratory; Wesley College; Newark, DE University of Delaware; [P] Newark, DE Catholic Campus Ministry, Univ. of Delaware; [P] Wesley College Newman Center; [P] Newark, DE Washington College; Catholic Campus Ministry.
Szura, Carl '71 (FWT) Fort Worth, TX St. Andrew.
Szura, John *o.s.a.* '66 (CHI)[N] Chicago, IL St. John Stone Friary.
Szura, Thomas *c.m.m.* '78 (DET)[K] Vocation Office.
Szuster, Jacek '01 (SAV) Albany, GA St. Teresa.
Szwach, Joseph F. '55 (WOR) Dudley, MA St. Andrew Bobola; Presbyteral Council.
Szwach, Joseph (WOR) Diocesan College of Consultors.
Szybka, Joseph P. '83 (TOL) Attica, OH SS. Peter and Paul; Republic, OH St. Aloysius; Attica, OH St. Stephen.
Szybka, Stanley S. '80 (TOL) Lexington, OH Resurrection.
Szydlik, Thomas '03 (PEO) Graduate Studies.
Szydlowski, Joel F. *o.f.m.* '67 (TR) St. Francis Medical Center; [I] Schools for Nurses.
Szydlowski, Joel F. *o.f.m.* '67 (PH)[AA] Philadelphia, PA St. Pius X Friary.
Szydlowski, Robert L. '62 (STL) St. Louis, MO Sts. Mary and Joseph.
Szylar, Jan *c.m.* '94 (BRK) Brooklyn, NY St. Stanislaus Kostka.
Szymanski, Edward S. '99 (BAL) Baltimore, MD Sacred Heart of Mary.
Szymanski, John B. '57 (MET) Old Bridge, NJ St. Thomas the Apostle; Vicars General; Planning & Development; College of Consultors; Episcopal Council.
Szymaszek, Leszek P. '97 (BGP) New Canaan, CT St. Aloysius.
Szymkowiak, Gerard J. *c.ss.r.* '68 (BAL) Baltimore, MD Sacred Heart of Jesus.

T

Ta, Paul Binh *c.ss.r.* '93 (CHI)[N] Chicago, IL Redemptorist Theology Residence.
Taaffe, Charles '55 (P) Retired.
Tabak, Thaddeus *s.d.s.* '77 (SAT) San Antonio, TX Our Lady of Sorrows.
Tabalanza, Celso *c.i.c.m.* '96 (BWN) Mercedes, TX Sacred Heart Church.
Tabban, Fahd (OLD) Union City, NJ Our Lady of Deliverance.
Tabbert, Robert D. '79 (VEN) Naples, FL St. Ann; College of Consultors.
Tabbert, Robert (VEN) Deans; Presbyteral Council.
Taberski, Richard M. '64 (HRT) Union City, CT St. Mary's.
Tabi, Lawrence '91 (CIN) Cincinnati, OH Our Lord, Christ the King.
Tabing, Omar '77 (OKL) Calumet, OK Immaculate Heart of Mary.
Tabon, Raymond *o.s.j.* '60 (SCR) Pittston, PA St. Anthony of Padua.
Tabone, Marcel M. '85 (CAM) Sea Isle City, NJ St. Joseph's.
Tabone, Marcel (CAM) Clergy Health Panel; Priests Assistance Program.
Tabor, Kenneth F. '75 (CHI) Other Assignments.
Tabujara, Oscar D. '75 (SJ) Mountain View, CA St. Joseph.
Tacelli, Ronald K. *s.j.* '82 (BO)[V] Newton, MA The Jesuit Community at Boston College.
Tachias, Alfred A. '59 (GLP)[E] Gallup, NM Villa Guadalupe Home for the Aged; Judges.
Tacito, Nicholas M. *o.praem.* '96 (ORG)[I] Silverado, CA Norbertine Fathers of Orange Inc..
Tack, Theodore E. *o.s.a.* '53 (TLS)[B] Tulsa, OK Cascia Hall Preparatory School.
Tackney, John P. '74 (BO) Cambridge, MA Sacred Heart of Jesus.
Taddy, Jerome J. (GB) Redgranite, WI Sacred Heart of Jesus; Redgranite, WI St. Mark.
Tadeo, Abran R. (TUC) Marana, AZ St. Christopher's.
Tadeo, Arnel '99 (NEW) Elizabeth, NJ St. Genevieve's.
Tadeo, Victor C. (MO) Army Chaplains.
Tadia, Casmir *c.r.* '48 (SB) Fontana, CA St. Joseph.
Tadla, Casimir *c.r.* '48 (SB)[E] Fontana, CA St. Joseph.
Tadyszak, Leonard *s.c.j.* '51 (MIL)[O] Franklin, WI Villa Maria.
Taft, Robert F. *s.j.* '63 (BO)[V] Boston The Society of Jesus of New England–Provincial Offices.
Taft, Robert *s.j.* (NTN) Liturgical Consultants.
Taft, Terence *o.f.m.cap.* (ROC)[I] Interlaken, NY St. Fidelis Friary.
Taft, William A. '94 (TUC) Kearny, AZ Infant Jesus of Prague.
Tagg, Joseph L. '88 (MEM) Memphis, TN St. John's; Judicial Vicar.
Taggart, Frederick H. *o.s.a.* '65 (LAN) Flint, MI St. Matthew.
Taggart, James E. *o.m.i.* '85 (BO) Lowell, MA Nuestra Senora del Carmen.
Taggart, James *o.m.i.* '85 (BO)[V] Lowell, MA Andre Garin Retirement Residence.
Taggart, John L '70 (WIL) Wilmington, DE St. Helena.
Taggart, Paul J. '51 (WIL) College of Consultors; St. Thomas More Society Retired.
Tagore, Leo *s.j.* '73 (BO)[V] Newton, MA The Jesuit Community at Boston College.
Tague, Charles *s.t.* '44 (WDC)[M] Adelphi, MD Missionary Servants of the Most Holy Trinity.
Taguinod, Romeo T. '83 (LA) Chatsworth, CA St. John Eudes.
Tahaney, James '63 (BRK) On Leave/Unassigned.
Taheny, Mark '95 (SFR) South San Francisco, CA St. Veronica.
Taheny, Robert R. *s.j.* '59 (SJ) San Jose, CA St. Victor; [M] Los Gatos Sacred Heart Jesuit Center.
Taheny, Theodore T. *s.j.* '56 (SFR)[E] San Francisco, CA St. Ignatius College Preparatory (Coed).
Tahney, Theodore T. *s.j.* '56 (SFR)[N] San Francisco, CA Jesuit Community at St. Ignatius College Preparatory.
Tai Le, Peter '98 (HT) Chauvin, LA St. Joseph.
Taillon, Marcel L. '94 (PRO)[A] Providence, RI Seminary of Our Lady of Providence; [C] Warwick, RI Bishop Hendricken High School; Vocations; Clergy Formation.
Tajak, Ralph *o.s.b.* '94 (PIT) Pittsburgh, PA St. Peter.
Takach, Brinstan G. *o.s.b.* '48 (GBG)[H] Latrobe, PA Saint Vincent Archabbey.
Takii, Ignatius Hideaki '83 (LA) Los Angeles, CA Maryknoll Japanese Catholic Center.
Takuski, Walter J. '95 (CHI).
Talafous, Don *o.s.b.* '52 (SCL)[I] Collegeville, MN St. John's Abbey, of the Order of St. Benedict.
Talaisis, Bernardas (SP) St. Casimir Lithuanian Apostolate.
Talamo, John F. (NO) Marrero, LA Immaculate Conception.
Talar, Charles J.T. '79 (BGP) On Duty Outside the Diocese.
Talar, Charles (GAL) Houston, TX Sacred Heart Co–Cathedral.
Talarico, Anthony M. '70 (CHI)[T] Mundelein, IL Cardinal Stritch Retreat House; Cardinal Stritch Retreat House.
Talaska, Richard J. '68 (MIL) Greenfield, WI St. John the Evangelist.
Talavera, Carlos '97 (HT) Raceland, LA Community of St. Anthony; Raceland, LA St. Hilary of Poitiers.
Talay, Mariano E. '00 (PHX) Phoenix, AZ Most Holy Trinity.
Talbot, James F. *s.j.* '68 (BO)[V] Weston, MA Campion Jesuit Community.
Talbot, John F. *s.j.* '59 (SJN)[C] Rio Piedras, PR Jesuit Community.
Talbott, Ron *o.f.m.cap.* '81 (LA)[F] La Canada Flintridge, CA St. Francis High School.
Talcott, Peter '75 (SR) Unassigned.
Talesfore, John J. '89 (SFR) San Francisco, CA Cathedral of St. Mary (Assumption); San Francisco, CA St. Brendan.
Talesfore, John (SFR) Office of Worship.
Talford, Diane (MAR).
Taliercio, Pasquale *m.s.a.* '92 (NOR)[F] Cromwell, CT Society of the Missionaries of the Holy Apostles.
Talkin, Ralph H. *s.j.* '57 (CHY) Glenrock, WY St. Louis.
Tallarida, Thomas *c.s.c.* '51 (FTW)[B] University of Notre Dame Du Lac; [I] Notre Dame, IN Holy Cross Community, Corby Hall, University of Notre Dame.
Talley, Charles *o.f.m.* '99 (OAK)[N] Oakland, CA Franciscan Friars Provincial Office, Province of St. Barbara.
Talley, David P. '71 (ATL) Archdiocesan Judges.
Talley, David '89 (ATL) Alpharetta, GA St. Thomas Aquinas.
Tallman, Gilmary *o.f.m.cap.* (SAL) Hays, KS St. Joseph's; [E] Hays, KS St. Joseph's Friary; Council of Priests.
Tallman, John '88 (ALB) Albany, NY St. Catherine of Siena; St. Peter's Hospital; Special Assignment; [H] Albany, NY St. Peter's Health Care Services.
Tallman, Stephen '59 (HEL) Retired.
Talocci, Peter '86 (PH) Philadelphia, PA Our Lady of Calvary.
Tam, Francis P. '87 (TR) Keyport, NJ St. Joseph.
Tam, Nguyen '01 (DAL) Dallas, TX St. Peter Vietnamese Catholic Community.
Tam, Thomas '50 (STP) St. Paul, MN St. Columba.
Tamalis, John J. (SCR) Army National Guard Chaplains.
Tamayo, Alfredo L. '77 (SAC) Burney, CA St. Francis of Assisi.
Tamayo, Dante '93 (OAK) Union City, CA St. Anne.
Tamayo, Elias '72 (PAT) Presbyteral Council; College of Consultors; Sabbatical.
Tambornino, James M. *s.o.l.t.* (MIL)[Q] Slinger, WI Carmelite Hermit of the Trinity – CHT.
Tambornino, James '91 (CC)[G] Robstown, TX Society of Our Lady of the Most Holy Trinity.
Tamburello, Dennis *o.f.m.* '80 (ALB)[B] Siena College.
Tamburello, Dominic *o.p.* '49 (NO) New Orleans, LA St. Dominic.
Tamburrini, Joseph '64 (Y) Retired.
Tamburro, Francis J. '74 (HBG) Berwick, PA Immaculate Conception of the Blessed Virgin Mary.
Tamburro, Joseph '99 (SJP) Youngstown, OH Holy Trinity.
Tamez, Benito '02 (DAL) Dallas, TX Mary Immaculate.
Tamiian, Calin '02 (ROM) Unassigned; St. Mary Romanian Catholic Mission.
Tamminga, Robert G. '71 (TUC) Tucson, AZ St. Francis de Sales.
Tampe, Eric *s.a.* '49 (NY)[EE] Garrison Franciscan Friars of the Atonement, Minister General Office.
Tamulis, John J. '40 (GAY) Retired.
Tan, John (MAN) Indonesia Apostolate.
Tanalgo, Domingo '39 (AGN) Barrigada, GU San

Vicente Ferrer.
Tanck, Norman C. *c.s.b.* '74 (ROC) Rochester, NY Christ the King.
Tancredi, Carl T. '67 (HBG) York, PA St. Rose of Lima; York, PA York Hospital; [J] York, PA Penn State University, York Campus; [J] York, PA York College.
Tancrell, Luke *o.p.* '59 (COL) Columbus, OH St. Patrick.
Tandoh, Francis *c.s.sp.* '93 (CIN) Dayton, OH St. James/Resurrection of Our Lord.
Tang, Emery *o.f.m.* '52 (ORG) Huntington Beach, CA SS. Simon and Jude.
Tang, Michael '90 (LA) Los Angeles, CA St. Joan of Arc.
Tanilong, Gerardo J. '62 (ORG) Administrative Leave.
Tank, Thomas '67 (KCK) Overland Park, KS Church of the Ascension; Vicars General; Chancellor; Defenders of the Bond; Archdiocesan Consultors; Archdiocesan Council on Finances; Archdiocesan Administrative Team; Department of Parish Ministries.
Tansaeng, Haet (STO).
Tanto, Henry '87 (NY) Croton–on–Hudson, NY Holy Name of Mary.
Taormina, Andrew C. '62 (NO) Metairie, LA St. Francis Xavier; Judges; Priests Council; Serra Club of Downtown New Orleans.
Taosan, Yohanes *c.i.c.m.* '96 (SAT) San Antonio, TX St. Benedict.
Tape, Bernard (SAC) Redding, CA St. Joseph.
Tapella, Joseph J. '78 (JOL) Joliet, IL The Cathedral of St. Raymond.
Tapella, Joseph (JOL) Vicar General; Moderator of the Curia; Judicial Vicar; Judges.
Taphorn, Joseph C. '97 (OM) Omaha, NE St. Agnes; Vice Chancellor; Judges; Judge; Commission for Ecumenical Affairs; Archbishop's Appointees.
Tapia, Gilberto Mora '88 (SEA) Burlington, WA St. Charles; LaConner, WA Sacred Heart; Mount Vernon, WA Immaculate Conception; Sedro Woolley, WA Immaculate Heart of Mary.
Tapp, John '84 (SP) St. Petersburg, FL Holy Family.
Tapparello, Antonio *c.s.* '74 (CHI)[N] Oak Park, IL Missionaries of Saint Charles.
Tappe, Walter J. '85 (WDC) Pastoral Center Special Ministries; Secretariats; Secretary for Parish Life and Worship; Office of Worship; Bowie, MD Sacred Heart.
Tapper, John W. '61 (CHI) Mt. Prospect, IL St. Cecilia.
Taraborelli, Arthur I. '64 (PH) Philadelphia, PA St. Thomas Aquinas.
Taraborelli, Carmen F. '70 (PH) Absent on Leave.
Tarallo, Philip J. *s.s.j.* '49 (BAL)[S] Baltimore, MD St. Joseph's Manor.
Taran, Peter '60 (NY)[EE] Garrison, NY Franciscan Friars of the Atonement.
Tarantino, James A. '72 (NO) New Orleans, LA Our Lady of The Rosary; New Orleans, LA St. Rose of Lima; Deans; Ecumenical Officer.
Tarantino, James T. (SFR) College of Consultors; Deans.
Tarantino, James '81 (SFR) Tiburon, CA St. Hilary.
Tarantino, John F. '78 (PAT) Montville, NJ St. Pius X.
Taranto, James '81 (KC) Kansas City, MO St. Matthew The Apostle.
Tarasi, Carlo D. '72 (CHL) Unassigned.
Tarasiw, Ihor '90 (STF) Riverhead, NY St. John the Baptist.
Taras Miles, Michael '70 (STN) Belfield, ND St. John the Baptist; Belfield, ND St. Demetrius.
Tardiff, Bernard *c.ss.r.* '42 (ALB)[L] Saratoga Springs, NY St. John Neumann Residence.
Targonski, Conrad *o.f.m.* '75 (GB)[I] Greenwood, MS St. Francis of Assisi Friary.
Targonski, George '02 (MET) Iselin, NJ St. Cecelia.
Tarigopula, Joseph Michael '94 (SCR) Sayre, PA Church of the Epiphany.
Tarlizzo, David *o.m.i.* '68 (SAT) Nixon, TX St. Joseph's; Smiley, TX St. Philip Benizi.
Tarlton, Allen *o.s.b.* '55 (SCL)[I] Collegeville, MN St. John's Abbey, of the Order of St. Benedict.
Tarnawski, Wiktor '80 (ARE) Ciales, PR N.S. Madre del Redentor.
Tarrant, Edward L. '50 (RVC) Hicksville, NY St. Ignatius Loyola; Mineola, NY Corpus Christi Retired.
Tarrant, Patrick J. '53 (GF) Retired.
Tarrillion, Joseph A. *s.m.* '66 (SAT)[F] San Antonio, TX Central Catholic High School; [M] San Antonio, TX Chaminade Community House.
Tarro, Michael *c.s.* '58 (PRO) Providence, RI Holy Ghost.
Tartaglia, Paul '58 (ALB) Retired.
Tartaglia, Richard V. '72 (PAT) Denville, NJ St. Mary's.
Tasch, Hugh *o.s.b.* '48 (KC)[J] Kansas City, MO.
Taschetta, Anthony '71 (JOL) Bloomingdale, IL St. Isidore.
Tascon, Wilson *m.s.c.* '90 (RCK).
Tascon, Wilson *m.s.c.* '90[G] (FgM).
Tash, Joseph T. '62 (AMA) Advocates; Presbyteral Council; Priests' Pension Plan Retirement Committee; Amarillo, TX St. Thomas the Apostle.
Tasker, Franklin R. *o.carm.* '56 (VEN)[G] Nokomis, FL Carmel at Mission Valley.
Tasler, Mark A. '90 (LIN) Nebraska City, NE St. Benedict's.
Tassone, Salvatore A. *s.j.* '63 (SJ)[B] Santa Clara, CA Jesuit Community.
Tasto, Harold J. '68 (STP) Blaine, MN St. Timothy's.
Tasto, John P. *o.s.a.* '67 (CHI)[N] Olympia Fields, IL Tolentine Monastery at Tolentine Center.
Tasto, John P. *o.s.a.* '67 (FgM).
Tasy, Francis G. *v.s.* '52 (FRS) Reedley, CA St. Anthony.
Tatarczuk, Vincent A. '49 (PRT) Diocesan Consultors; Clergy Benefit Plan–Clergy Pension Plan; Diocesan Council of Priests; College of Consultors Retired.
Tate, Joseph H. '81 (BUR) Readsboro, VT St. Joachim.
Tatel, Orlando '65 (STP) Jordan, MN St. Patrick.
Tatino, Tagaloa '91 (SPP) Pago Pago, AS Church of the Immaculate Conception.
Taton, Thomas P. '60 (BUF) Millard Fillmore Hospital.
Taton, Thomas P. '61 (BUF) Buffalo, NY Assumption.
Tatro, Joseph C. (WCH) Kingman, KS St. Patrick.
Tatro, Kenneth J. '76 (SPR) Springfield, MA St. Mary's.
Tatro, Timothy M. '99 (JC) Absent on Leave.
Tatum, Gregory T. *o.p.* '89 (OAK).
Tatum, Gregory T. *o.p.* '89 (SFR)[A] San Francisco, CA St. Dominic; [N] San Francisco, CA St. Dominic Priory.
Taube, Sylvester '64 (DET) Birmingham, MI St. Columban.
Tauber, Jerome A. '02 (ALN) Pottsville, PA St. Patrick.
Taubitz, Leo A. '56 (KAL) Dowagiac, MI Holy Maternity of Mary.
Taufen, Daniel J. '56 (SCL) Kimball, MN Holy Cross; Watkins, MN St. Nicholas; Promoter Justitiae; Censores Librorum; Director of Retired Priests.
Taugher, Timothy J. '78 (SY) On Sabbatical.
Tauke, Michael L. '74 (DUB) Waverly, IA St. Mary.
Taurasi, David '88 (CC) Sinton, TX Our Lady of Guadalupe.
Tauscher, Donald *o.s.b.* '65 (SCL)[I] Collegeville, MN St. John's Abbey, of the Order of St. Benedict.
Tavard, George *a.a.* '47 (BO)[V] Boston, MA Assumptionist Center.
Tavares, Antonino C. '43 (FR) New Bedford, MA Our Lady of Mt. Carmel Retired.
Tavarro, Elly S. '81 (ORG)[G] Orange, CA St. Joseph Hospital of Orange.
Tavella, Thomas A. *c.s.p.* '81 (NY) New York, NY St. Paul the Apostle.
Tavis, Gordon *o.s.b.* '58 (SCL)[D] Collegeville, MN St. John's Preparatory School; [I] Collegeville, MN St. John's Abbey, of the Order of St. Benedict.
Tawiah, Gabriel Oduro '97 (VIC) Victoria, TX St. Mary's.
Tax, Samuel Perez '01 (NU) New Ulm, MN Cathedral of The Holy Trinity.
Tay, Peter P. '46 (PBR) Retired.
Taylor, Anthony B. '80 (OKL) Oklahoma City, OK Sacred Heart; Special Assignment; Vicar for Ministries; Council of Priests Archdiocesan Personnel Committee; Archdiocesan Finance Council; Ministry to Priests Program; Priests' Retirement Board.
Taylor, Augustus R. '66 (PIT) On Duty Outside the Diocese.
Taylor, Benedict M. *o.f.m.* '60 (NY)[EE] New York, NY Create Inc.
Taylor, Bernard *m.s.* '71 (SB) Apple Valley, CA Our Lady of the Desert; [E] Apple Valley, CA Missionaries of Our Lady of La Salette. MS.
Taylor, Bernard (RIC) Charlottesville, VA Church of the Incarnation.
Taylor, Charles F. '53 (CHY) Buffalo, WY St. John the Baptist; Promoter of Justice; Defenders of the Bond.
Taylor, Daniel '75 (TUC) Administrative Leave of Absence.
Taylor, David H. '74 (PIT) Pittsburgh, PA St. Charles Lwanga Parish; Priest Council; College of Consultors.
Taylor, Donn J. '53 (KAL) Battle Creek, MI St. Joseph Retired.
Taylor, Douglas D. '97 (TOL) Toledo, OH St. John the Baptist; Norwalk, OH St. Paul.
Taylor, Gordon A. '85 (B) Salmon, ID St. Charles Retired.
Taylor, James B. '54 (BLX) Retired.
Taylor, James E. *o.m.i.* '56 (BEL)[F] Belleville, IL Missionary Oblates of Mary Immaculate – St. Henry's Oblate Residence; [J] Belleville, IL Missionary Association of Mary Immaculate–Missionary Oblates of Mary Immaculate.
Taylor, Jon '54 (GF) Special Assignment; [A] University of Great Falls.
Taylor, Jon '64 (LAN) On Duty Outside the Diocese.
Taylor, Jon '54 (GF) Special Assignment; [A] University of Great Falls.
Taylor, Joseph C. '53 (CHI) Chicago, IL St. Edward Retired.
Taylor, Kenneth E. '78 (IND) Indianapolis, IN Holy Trinity.
Taylor, Kenneth (IND) Commission for Multicultural Ministry; [O] Indianapolis, IN Indiana University–Purdue University at Indianapolis.
Taylor, Mel *o.s.b.* '67 (SCL)[I] St. Augustine Monastery.
Taylor, Michael G. '93 (ARL) Falls Church, VA St. James; [D] Arlington, VA Bishop Denis J. O'Connell High School; Youth Ministry, Office of; Diocesan Consultors; Notaries.
Taylor, Michael J. *s.j.* '54 (SEA)[A] Seattle, WA Seattle University.
Taylor, Michael S. '97 (MAN) Epping, NH St. Joseph; Associate Judicial Vicars; Diocesan Judges.
Taylor, Michael '66 (SY)[M] Syracuse, NY St. Joseph's Hospital Health Center.
Taylor, Michael *o.f.m.conv.* '86 (SY) Syracuse, NY Assumption B.V.M.; Syracuse, NY St. Joseph's Hospital Health Center.
Taylor, Paul R. *o.s.b.* '92 (GBG)[H] Latrobe, PA Saint Vincent Archabbey.
Taylor, Robert H. *s.j.* '52 (LA)[C] Los Angeles, CA Jesuit Community.
Taylor, Robert H. '56 (WIN) Absent on Leave.
Taylor, Roger H. '64 (MAD) Muscoda, WI St. Joseph; Muscoda, WI St. John the Baptist; Elected.
Taylor, Senan *o.f.m.cap.* '70 (NY)[EE] Yonkers, NY St. Clare Friary.
Taylor, Thomas '83 (PEO) Lincoln, IL Holy Family.
Taylor, William R. '67 (SAG) Saginaw, MI Holy Family.
Taylor, William '64 (B) St. Maries, ID St. Mary's; College of Consultors.
Taylor, William (SAG) Clergy Personnel Board.
Tchinqui, Antonio Jorge '97 (HRT) Hartford, CT Our Lady of Fatima.
Teague, Bruce N. '80 (SPR)[P] Amherst, MA Amherst College.
Teague, James '87 (NY)[E] Somers, NY John F. Kennedy High School.
Teahan, Timothy J. '70 (BRK) Brooklyn, NY Good Shepherd.
Teall, Richard S. *c.s.c.* '50 (AUS)[G] Austin, TX Brother Andre House.
Teater, Kristian C. (STL) St. Louis, MO St. Margaret Mary Alacoque.
Tebangura, Francis '68 (SFD) Madison, IL St. Mary and St. Mark.
Tebbe, Francis S. *o.f.m.* '75 (CIN)[M] Cincinnati, OH St. Francis Seraph Friary.
Tebes, Stephen J. '68 (CHI) Norridge, IL Divine Savior.
Tederous, Elias *m.m.* '55 (HON)[G] Honolulu, HI Maryknoll Fathers House (M.M.).
Tedesco, Joseph A. (TR) Expansion Commission; Office of Research and Planning.
Tedesco, Joseph P. *s.m.* '83 (CIN)[C] Dayton, OH Marianist Novitiate; [M] Dayton, OH Marianist Community, Novitiate; [M] Dayton, OH Marianist Community.
Tedesco, Joseph S. (TR) Diocesan Consultors.
Tedesco, Joseph '79 (TR) Trenton, NJ Our Lady of Sorrows.
Tedone, Michael '91 (BRK) Brooklyn, NY Shrine Church of St. Jude.
Teeling, John P. *s.j.* '55 (DEN)[N] Denver, CO Regis Jesuit Community (The Jesuits at Regis University).
Tegeder, Michael '78 (STP) Bloomington, MN St. Edward; Presbyteral Council.
Tegeder, Vincent *o.s.b.* '37 (SCL)[I] Collegeville, MN St. John's Abbey, of the Order of St. Benedict.
Tegeler, Herbert L. '53 (DUB) Earlville, IA St. Joseph.
Teichert, Isaiah *o.s.b.cam.* '90 (MRY)[F] Big Sur, CA New Camaldoli Hermitage.
Tejada, Francisco '01 (ARE) Almirante Sur Station, PR The Blessed Trinity.
Tejeda, Jose F. '74 (PCE)[G] Ponce, PR Prelature of the Holy Cross and Opus Dei.
Tekippe, Terry T. '65 (NO).
Teles, Dennis J. '65 (GRY)[A] Gary, IN Blessed Sacrament; Merrillville, IN Ss. Peter and Paul; Deans; Bishop's Council of Priests; Consultors; Priests' Personnel Board.
Telesz, Leo '39 (CLV) Cleveland, OH St. Casimir.
Teletchea, Joseph L. '44 (WDC)[L] Washington, DC Cardinal O'Boyle Residence for Priests; Hyattsville, MD St. Jerome Retired.
Telken, Paul E. '73 (STL) St. Clair, MO St. Clare.
Tellers, Marven *o.s.c.* '50 (STP) Shoreview, MN St. Odilia; [M] Shoreview, MN Crosier Community of Shoreview.
Telles, John '75 (ELP) Fort Hancock, TX Santa Teresa; [A] El Paso, TX St. Charles Seminary College Program; Vicar for Clergy; Diocesan Pastoral Staff; Vicar for Clergy; Ex Officio Members; Vocations & Seminarians.
Tellez, Eric '86 (PHX) Scottsdale, AZ St. Patrick.
Tellez, Jairo A. '62 (SAT) Military Chaplains; Army Chaplains.
Telnack, Methodius *o.c.s.o.* '57 (ATL)[K] Conyers, GA The Monastery of the Holy Spirit.
Telthorst, James T. '68 (STL) St. Louis, MO Our Lady of Sorrows; Archdiocesan Council of Priests.
Teluma, Lukas Bao *s.v.d.* '75 (LA)[Q] Los Angeles, CA Casa Guadalupe.
Temba, Camillus *a.l.c.p.* '91 (B) Pocatello, ID Holy Spirit Catholic Community.
Tempel, Theodore '64 (EVN)[E] Evansville, IN St.

John's Home for the Aged Retired.
Templado, Josefino P. '69 (GAL) Katy, TX St. Bartholomew the Apostle.
Temple, Matthew *o.carm.* '82 (ROC)[I] Rochester, NY Whitefriars Priory.
Templeton, Edward J. *s.m.* '53 (NO)[P] New Orleans, LA Marist Fathers.
Templeton, Robert E. (NEW) Executive Director for Priest Personnel; Members; Priest Personnel Policy Board; Archdiocesan Incardination Board; Office of Clergy Personnel; Diocesan Priest Personnel and Clergy/Religious Healthcare Personnel.
Templin, Kenneth A. *s.m.* '79 (HON)[A] Honolulu, HI Chaminade University of Honolulu; [G] Honolulu, HI Center Marianist Community.
Tenbarge, Timothy '73 (EVN) St. Anthony, IN St. Anthony; Personnel Board.
Teneza, Vicente '01 (SAC) Folsom, CA St. John the Baptist.
Tengler, Alvin '49 (CC) Retired.
Tenhundfeld, Paul F. '54 (COV) Fort Mitchell, KY Blessed Sacrament Retired.
Tenorio, Michael *o.f.m.cap.* '99 (AGN) Agana Heights, GU Our Lady of the Blessed Sacrament; [F] Agana Heights, GU St. Fidelis Friary.
Tensi, Lawrence R. '79 (CIN) Loveland, OH St. Columban.
Teo, Eduardo '90 (LUB) O'Donnell, TX St. Pius X.
Terdine, Richard '65 (PIT) Allegheny County, PA UPMC University of Pittsburgh Medical Center.
Terentieff, Robert J. '62 (BGP) On Duty Outside the Diocese.
Terga, Richard '73 (NY) New York, NY Our Lady of Good Counsel.
Terico, Nicholas R. *o.praem.* '89 (PH)[AA] Paoli, PA Daylesford Abbey.
Terleckey, John '76 (BGP)[X] Stamford, CT Stamford Catholic Library.
Terlecky, John '76 (STF) Stamford, CT St. Vladimir Cathedral.
Terlecky, John '76 (STF)[A] Stamford, CT Ukrainian Catholic Seminary Inc. St. Basil College.
Terlecky, John (STF) Ukrainian Museum and Library of Stamford, Inc..
Terlecky, John (STF) Directors:.
Terlecky, John (STF) Administrative Council.
Terlecky, John (STF) Presbyteral Council.
Terlecky, John (STF) Econome.
Terlecky, John (STF) Diocesan Consultors.
Termine, Vincent J. '44 (BRK) Retired.
Termyna, James J. '70 (PAT) Dover, NJ St. Clement, Pope and Martyr.
Ternes, Cletus *o.m.i.* '61 (FgM).
Ternes, Gary '79 (SFS) South Dakota State Penitentiary & Minnehaha County Jail; Tribunal Judges; Sioux Falls, SD St. Therese.
Ternullo, Joseph P. '73 (SAC) North Highlands, CA St. Lawrence.
Tero, Richard D. (ANC) Diocesan Consultors; Air Force Reserve Chaplains.
Tero, Richard '74 (ANC) Seward, AK Sacred Heart.
Terra, Joseph *f.s.s.p.* '89 (LIN)[A] Denton, NE Our Lady of Guadalupe Seminary.
Terra, Joseph *f.s.s.p.* '89 (SCR)[M] Elmhurst Priestly Fraternity of St. Peter (F.S.S.P.), North American District Headquarters.
Terra, Russell G. '62 (SAC) Redding, CA St. Joseph.
Terranova, Robert P. *o.s.a.* '73 (FgM).
Terranova, Robert *o.s.a.* '73 (NY) Bronx, NY St. Nicholas of Tolentine.
Terrebonne, Burnick J. '77 (NO) New Orleans, LA St. Frances Xavier Cabrini.
Terrien, Douglas J. '79 (DET) Lapeer, MI Immaculate Conception of the Blessed Virgin Mary.
Terrill, Richard F. '54 (IND) Retired.
Terriquez, Enrique '63 (B) Caldwell, ID Our Lady of the Valley; [F] Caldwell, ID Albertson's College of Idaho; College of Consultors.
Terry, Brian *s.a.* '97 (NY)[EE] Garrison Franciscan Friars of the Atonement, Minister General Office.
Terry, Chris '91 (LA)[C] Rosemead, CA Don Bosco Technical Institute; [D] Rosemead, CA Don Bosco Technical Institute.
Terry, Christopher *o.p.* '89 (LA)[BB] Los Angeles, CA Occidental College, Catholic Campus Ministry.
Terry, Christopher *o.p.* '91 (LA) Hacienda Heights, CA St. John Vianney.
Terry, John S. '75 (SCR) Sugar Notch, PA Holy Family; [Q] Wilkes–Barre, PA Catholic Youth Center; Deans.
Terza, William R. '69 (PIT) Pittsburgh, PA St. John Vianney; Allegheny County, PA State Correctional Institute at Pittsburgh.
Terzano, John D. '74 (CLV) Peninsula, OH Mother of Sorrows.
Tescher, Jeffry (BIS) Priests' Benefit Association.
Tesek, Albert J. '51 (CLV) North Royalton, OH St. Albert the Great; Associate Judges Retired.
Teske, Roland J. *s.j.* '65 (MIL)[O] Milwaukee, WI Jesuit Community at Marquette University.
Teslovic, Eugene '77 (RIC) Retired.
Tessmer, Richard A. (CHI) Retired.
Testa, Genaro J. '47 (HRT) Retired.
Testa, Jess '88 (JOL) Lombard, IL Sacred Heart.
Testa, Richard '67 (ALB) Special Assignment Retired.
Testa, Steve J. '64 (ALX) College of Consultors; Finance Council; Priests Council; Rural Deans; Holy Childhood Association; Propagation of the Faith and Foreign Mission Education; Marksville, LA St. Joseph's.
Testagrossa, Joseph *o.f.m.cap.* '57 (SP)[O] Seminole, FL Capuchin Franciscan Residence.
Teta, Michael J. '74 (TUC) Administrative Leave of Absence.
Teteh, Lawrence *c.s.sp.* '71 (FTW) South Bend, IN Our Lady of Hungary.
Teter, Patrick A. '92 (SPC) Buffalo, MO St. William; Conway, MO Sacred Heart; Fordland, MO Ozark Correctional Center.
Tetherow, Gabriel Francis *s.m.f.* '02 (SCR) Unassigned or Leave of Absence.
Teti, James V. '97 (NEW) Verona, NJ Our Lady of the Lake.
Tetlow, John H. '84 (STA) Flagler Beach, FL Santa Maria Del Mar; Seminarians; Vocations.
Tetlow, Joseph A. *s.j.* '60 (NO)[P] Curia, Society of Jesus.
Tetrault, Ralph D. '65 (FR) Retired.
Tetrault, Raymond L. '60 (PRO) Providence, RI St. Teresa of Avila.
Tetreault, Maynard *o.f.m.* '60 (LEX) Cumberland, KY St. Stephen.
Tetreault, Maynard *o.f.m.* '60 (CIN)[V] Cincinnati, OH Franciscan Central Purchasing.
Tetreault, Raymond A. '71 (PRO) Slatersville, RI St. John the Evangelist; Army National Guard Chaplains.
Tetteh, Edward *s.v.d.* (CHI) Trenton, NJ Our Lady of the Divine Shepherd.
Tetu, Richard P. '69 (MAN) Manchester, NH St. Marie; Associate Judicial Vicars; Diocesan Judges.
Teufel, Charles B. '62 (WH) Retired.
Teverzczuk, William J. '73 (PH) North Wales, PA Mary, Mother of the Redeemer.
Tevington, Thomas *o.s.a.* '34 (ORG) Buena Park, CA St. Pius V.
Tewes, Thomas '63 (BAL) Retired.
Texada, David Ker '80 (NO) Retired.
Texlemariam, Tesfamariam *c.m.* '92 (CHI)[N] Chicago DePaul Vincentian Residence.
Tezie, John M. '59 (CLV) South Amherst, OH Nativity of Blessed Virgin Mary.
Tezie, William F. '56 (CLV) Retired.
Thaar, Gerald *o.s.c.* '65 (PHX) Scottsdale, AZ Blessed Sacrament.
Thachet, Joseph '53 (KAL) Battle Creek, MI St. Joseph Retired.
Thachil, Joy Anthony '88 (LUB) Lubbock, TX St. Elizabeth University Parish.
Thadathil, Francis (LC) La Crosse, WI Blessed Sacrament.
Thadathil, George *c.m.i.* '88 (NSH)[K] Liberty, TN Carmel Center of Spirituality.
Thaden, William A. '88 (CLV) Lorain, OH Sacred Heart Chapel; [W] Lorain, OH Sacred Heart Chapel.
Thadeu, Joseph S. '47 (PRO) Retired.
Thai, Bao Q. '03 (ORG) Rancho Santa Margarita, CA San Francisco Solano Church.
Thai, Thomas Vu Minh '54 (LEX) Carlisle, KY Shrine of Our Lady of Guadalupe; Paris, KY Annunciation of the Blessed Virgin Mary.
Thai, Thomas (LEX) Defenders of the Bond.
Thai Hoa Do, Bartholomew M. *c.m.c.* '77 (FWT) Arlington, TX Church of the Vietnamese Martyrs.
Thaikoottathil, James '84 (NOR) New London, CT St. Joseph.
Thai Minh Tran, Joseph *s.s.s.* '94 (SFE) Albuquerque, NM St. Charles Borromeo.
Thakadipuram, Thomas '93 (STP)[C] St. Paul, MN University of St. Thomas.
Thakadipuram, Thomas '93 (STP).
Thalakulam, Cherian *c.m.i.* '76 (CHR)[A] North Augusta, SC St. Edward.
Thaler, Joseph L. *m.m.* '77 (FgM).
Thaliyan, Jesudas *c.m.i.* (SFS) Eden, SD Sacred Heart.
Thall, Apollinaris I. *s.j.* '83 (CI) St. Mary.
Thamert, Mark *o.s.b.* '79 (SCL)[I] Collegeville, MN St. John's Abbey, of the Order of St. Benedict.
Thames, Robert '64 (FWT) On Duty Outside the Diocese.
Thanh, Nguyen Duc *c.ss.r.* '96 (LA)[Q] Houston, TX.
Thanh Hung, John B. '54 (MIL) Retired.
Thanh Ngoc Nguyen, Michael M. '95 (NO) Metairie, LA St. Christopher the Martyr.
Thanickal, Antony *c.m.i.* '71 (PH) Philadelphia, PA St. William.
Thannickal, Joseph *s.d.b.* '83 (SJ) Los Altos, CA St. Simon; Ongoing Formation of Clergy Committee.
Thanugundla, Joji '94 (CHI) Chicago, IL Immaculate Heart of Mary.
Thapwa, Stephen M. '76 (WCH) Cherryvale, KS St. Francis Xavier's; Independence, KS St. Andrew.
Tharakan, Martin *o.i.c.* (SB) Wildomar, CA St. Frances of Rome.
Tharappel, Augustine *m.s.f.s.* '70 (TYL) Tyler, TX Cathedral of the Immaculate Conception.
Tharappel, Augustine *m.s.f.s.* '70 (ATL)[K] Lawrenceville, GA The Missionaries of St. Francis De Sales.
Tharayil, Thomas '86 (NEW) Teaneck, NJ Holy Name Hospital; [G] School of Nursing; Chaplains.
Tharp, Larry P. (CIN) Judges.
Tharp, Larry R. '77 (CIN) Cincinnati, OH St. Teresa.
Tharp, Shane I. '00 (OKL) Alva, OK Sacred Heart; [K] Alva, OK Northwestern Oklahoma State College.
Thatcher, John R. *s.j.* '47 (SPK)[J] Spokane, WA Regis Community.
Thawale, P.J. (NY) Yonkers, NY St. Eugene.
Thayer, David D. *s.s.* '75 (WDC).
Thayer, David D. *s.s.* '75 (HRT)[A] On Duty Outside the Archdiocese.
Thayer, David *s.s.* '75 (WDC)[C] Catholic University of America, The.
Thayer Tewes, J. Edwin '96 (ARL) Chantilly, VA St. Timothy.
Thedioha, Hilary A. (SAN) Big Lake, TX St. Margaret of Cortona.
Theempalangattu, Philip Chacko '80 (SHP)[B] Monroe, LA St. Francis Medical Center.
Thein, Edward '79 (ATL) Marietta, GA Holy Family.
Theisen, Donald J. '42 (LC) Retired.
Theisen, Eugene A. *m.m.* '53 (FgM).
Theisen, Eugene J. (STP) Air Force Chaplains.
Theisen, Eugene '99 (CHY) Cheyenne, WY U.S. Veterans Administration Hospital 1.
Theisen, John J. '59 (MIL) Retired.
Theisen, Kenneth *o.s.b.* '84 (RCK)[A] Aurora, IL Marmion Abbey; [G] Aurora, IL Marmion Abbey.
Theisen, Wilfred *o.s.b.* '56 (SCL)[I] Collegeville, MN St. John's Abbey, of the Order of St. Benedict.
Theiss, Daniel *c.m.* '90 (CHI)[N] Chicago, IL Vincentian Community, Congregation of the Mission, Midwest Province.
Thekemury, Pius *s.j.* '77 (Patna)[N] Berkeley, CA Jesuit Community at Jesuit School of Theology at Berkeley.
Thekkan, Pauly *c.m.i.* '89 (MET) John F. Kennedy Medical Center.
Thekkattayil, Varghese '95 (PRO)[K] North Providence, RI St. Joseph Health Services of Rhode Island – Our Lady of Fatima Hospital.
Thekkedam, George (LUB).
Thekkedam, George (LC) Tomah, WI Veterans Administration Medical Center.
Thekkel, Hugh *o.s.b.* '76 (LUB) Spur, TX St. Mary.
Thekkel, Thomas J. *m.s.t.* '82 (MAR) Trenary, MI St. Rita.
Thekkemury, James Dominic '87 (SHP)[B] Monroe, LA St. Francis Medical Center.
Thekkeveetil, Bonaventure '63 (RVC) Dix Hills, NY St. Matthew.
Thekkummattathil, George *c.s.c.* (BO) Brighton, MA Vencor Hospital Boston.
Thekkummattatil, George (PT) Cantonment, FL St. Jude Thaddeus.
Thekumthala, Ouseph '75 (TYL) Wills Point, TX St. Luke.
Thelakkatt, Xavier '80 (STP) Rush City, MN Sacred Heart.
Thelen, Albert R. *s.j.* '68 (OM)[K] Omaha, NE Jesuit Community at Creighton University.
Thelen, Bert *s.j.* '68 (OM) Omaha, NE St. John.
Thelen, Frederick L. '80 (LAN) Lansing, MI Cristo Rey.
Thelen, Robert J. '70 (BRK) Ozone Park, NY Nativity of the Blessed Virgin Mary.
Thelen, Robert (BRK) Sanitation Department.
Thelen, Robert (BRK) AUXILIARY CHAPLAINS CONTRACT CHAPLAINS.
Thell, Richard *o.s.b.* '74 (OM)[C] Elkhorn, NE Mount Michael High School; [K] Elkhorn, NE Mount Michael Abbey.
Thelly, Matthew '71 (TR) Deal, NJ St. Mary of the Assumption.
Thenen, James '58 (NY) Retired.
Then Henriquez, Cristian Jose *s.d.b.* '75 (MGZ) San Antonio, PR San Jose Obrero.
Thennattil, George *t.o.r.* '76 (FWT) Carrollton, TX St. Catherine of Siena.
Theobald, Charles '58 (NEW) Retired.
Theoret, Glenn J. '99 (MAR) Manistique, MI St. Francis de Sales; Executive Board; Deans; Clergy Continuing Education.
Thepe, Theodore C. *s.j.* '55 (CIN)[M] Cincinnati, OH Jesuit Community at Xavier University.
The Pham, Vincent Tung '85 (PH) Bristol, PA St. Mark.
The Phan, Peter Luc '90 (SJ) San Jose, CA St. Patrick.
Theriault, A. Francis *s.v.d.* '55 (BLX)[A] Bay St. Louis, MS St. Augustine's.
Theriault, H. '60 (NY) Tivoli, NY St. Sylvia.
Theriot, Donald C. '57 (LAF) Retired.
Theroux, Bertrand L. (PRO) Finance Council.
Theroux, Bertrand '67 (PRO) North Kingstown, RI St. Francis De Sales.
Theroux, David J. *s.s.e.* '74 (NO)[I] New Orleans, LA

Bishop Perry Middle School.
Theroux, Denis B. '90 (DET) Redford Township, MI St. Robert Bellarmine.
Theroux, J. Raymond '65 (PRO) Cumberland, RI St. John Baptist Mary Vianney.
Theroux, Paul D. '77 (PRO) Providence, RI Our Lady of Lourdes; Secretary for Diocesan Administration; Moderator of the Curia; Judges; Council Members; College of Consultors; Finance Council.
Theroux, Raymond C. (PRO) Deans.
Therrien, Shawn M. '87 (MAN) Claremont, NH St. Mary; Sullivan County House of Corrections.
Thesing, Gilbert J. *o.p.* '75 (CHI)[N] Chicago Dominicans (Provincial Office).
Thesing, Gilbert *o.p.* '75 (FgM).
Thesing, Kenneth F. *m.m.* '69 (FgM).
Thesing, Mark *c.s.c.* '86 (FTW)[B] University of Notre Dame Du Lac; [I] Notre Dame, IN Holy Cross Community, Corby Hall, University of Notre Dame.
Thesing, Robert J. *s.j.* '76 (CIN) Cincinnati, OH St. Francis Xavier; [M] Cincinnati, OH Jesuit Community at St. Xavier High School; [V] Cincinnati, OH St. Xavier Church Property Corporation.
Thessing, Charles '88 (LR) Morrilton, AR Sacred Heart; Hattieville, AR St. Mary.
Thet–Kyaw, Marcian '95 (CHR) Greer, SC Blessed Trinity; Taylors, SC Prince of Peace.
Theuerer, Ulrich *f.s.s.p.* '01 (SCR)[M] Omaha, NE St. Patrick Church.
Thevarkunnel, Anselm '57 (DUL) Cass Lake, MN St. Charles.
Thi, Andrew '85 (NY) New York, NY St. Patrick Old Cathedral.
Thibault, Armand *s.m.* '85 (BO)[V] Boston, MA Marist Fathers of Our Lady of Victories (Boston Prov.).
Thibault, Camillus *a.a.* '56 (BO).
Thibault, Donald P. *o.p.* '68 (WDC)[V] Washington, DC St. Dominic Church & Priory.
Thibault, Rodney E. '01 (FR) New Bedford, MA St. John the Baptist; East Sandwich, MA Corpus Christi.
Thibeault, W. Timothy '72 (MAN) Penacook, NH Immaculate Conception; Merrimack County House of Corrections.
Thibodeau, Andre M. '71 (MAN) Hillsboro, NH St. Mary.
Thibodeau, Andre (MAN) Advocates.
Thibodeau, Clement D. '58 (PRT) Retired.
Thibodeau, Kenneth *s.m.* '68 (BO)[V] Boston, MA Marist Fathers and Brothers Provincial House; [V] Boston, MA Marist Fathers of Our Lady of Victories (Boston Prov.).
Thibodeau, Kenneth *s.m.* '86 (BO) Boston MA Our Lady of Victories.
Thibodeau, Raymond *o.f.m.cap.* (NY) Yonkers, NY St. John Hospital.
Thibodeau, Raynold *o.f.m.cap.* '85 (NY) Yonkers, NY Sacred Heart.
Thibodeau, Richard *c.ss.r.* '76 (FgM).
Thibodeau, Richard *c.ss.r.* '76 (DEN)[N] Denver, CO.
Thibodeau, Scott '98 (DET) Garden City, MI St. Raphael the Archangel.
Thibodeaux, Charles B. *s.j.* '59 (NO).
Thibodeaux, Mark E. '01 (GAL)[F] Houston, TX Strake, Jesuit College Preparatory Inc..
Thibodeaux, Paul '48 (LAF) Retired.
Thiede, John S. *s.j.* '03 (OM)[K] Omaha, NE Jesuit Community at Creighton University.
Thiel, Cris *o.f.m.cap.* '90 (LA)[F] La Canada Flintridge, CA St. Francis High School.
Thiel, Harold J. *c.ss.r.* '56 (STL)[O] Liguori, MO St. Clement Health Care Center.
Thiel, Lloyd *o.f.m. cap.* '56 (DET)[K] Detroit, MI Provincialate; [K] Detroit St. Bonaventure Friary; Beaumont Hospital.
Thiele, Richard *c.ss.r.* '54 (DEN)[N] (FgM).
Thiele, Robert A. '55 (SC) Retired.
Thielen, Jeffrey M. '74 (MIL) Racine, WI St. Lucy.
Thielen, Martin '35 (P) Retired.
Thielman, Kenneth '55 (SCL) Retired.
Thieman, Anthony '89 (SFD) Special or Other Diocesan Assignment.
Thieman, Donald J. *c.pp.s.* '53 (CIN)[M] N.S. de la P. Sangre.
Thiers, Georges G. *c.o.* '70 (PH) Philadelphia, PA St. Francis Xavier; [AA] Philadelphia, PA The Philadelphia Congregation of The Oratory of St. Philip Neri.
Thieryoung, John '96 (PEO) Aledo, IL St. Catherine's Church; Matherville, IL St. Anthony's Church.
Thiesen, Eugene (STP) Military Chaplains.
Thiessen, Dennis D. *s.d.s.* '78 (MIL).
Thill, Richard '81 (PBL)[O] Absent on Leave.
Thimm, Donald H. '76 (MIL) Pleasant Prairie, WI St. Anne.
Thimmesh, Hilary *o.s.b.* '54 (SCL)[I] Collegeville, MN St. John's Abbey, of the Order of St. Benedict.
Thinnes, John M. '64 (CHI) Glenview, IL Our Lady of Perpetual Help.
Thirumangalam, George *c.m.i.* '76 (SAN) Stanton, TX St. Joseph's.
Thissen, Donald R. '70 (WCH) Arma, KS St. Joseph; Girard, KS St. Michael.
Thissen, Kevin C. *o.p.* '63 (GAL) Sugar Land, TX St. Thomas Aquinas.
Thoa, Ngo Dinh *c.ss.r.* '62 (LA)[Q] Baldwin Park, CA Vietnamese Redemptorist Mission.
Thoar, Gerald *o.s.c.* '65 (PHX)[G] Phoenix, AZ Crosier Community of Phoenix (Canons Regular of the Order of the Holy Cross).
Thodukayil, Philip Joseph (CHI) Chicago, IL Knanite Syro–Malabar Catholic Mission of the Archdiocese of Chicago.
Thodukayil, Philip (SYM) Eparchial Consultors.
Thodukayil, Phillip '69 (SYM) Chicago, IL Knanaya Syro–Malabar Catholic Mission, Chicago
Thodukayil, Phillip (CHI) Chicago, IL Immaculate Heart of Mary.
Thodukulam Thomas *s.d.b.* '00 (FgM).
Thoennes, Roger '90 (SCL) Pierz, MN Holy Cross; Lastrup, MN St. John Nepomuk.
Thole, Simeon J. *o.s.b.* '62 (SCL)[I] Collegeville, MN St. John's Abbey, of the Order of St. Benedict.
Thole, Thomas *o.s.b.* '58 (SCL)[I] Collegeville, MN St. John's Abbey, of the Order of St. Benedict.
Tholen, John '62 (YAK) Retired.
Thom, Elmer D. '43 (SC) Retired.
Thoma, Steven *c.r.* (STL)[A] St. Louis, MO Kenrick School of Theology.
Thoman, Dwayne J. '76 (DUB)[D] Dubuque, IA Wahlert High School dba Holy Family Catholic Schools; Dubuque, IA St. Raphael Cathedral; Priest Representatives.
Thoman, James *c.p.* '75 (DET)[K] Detroit, MI St. Paul of the Cross Community, Congregation of the Passion; [P] Detroit, MI St. Paul of the Cross Retreat Center.
Thoman, Robert A. '41 (PH)[AA] Loyola Center and Manresa Hall.
Thomas, Alan E. '92 (ALT) McConnellsburg, PA St. Stephen's.
Thomas, Antoine '92 (PEO)[M] Peoria, IL Congregation of St. John; [O] Peoria, IL Newman Foundation at Bradley University & Illinois Central College.
Thomas, Aquinas *s.a.* '48 (NY)[II] Barryville, NY New Hope Manor.
Thomas, Bill '78 (LAN) W. J. Maxey Boys Training School.
Thomas, C. Theodore (COL) Priests' Senate.
Thomas, Charles T. (COL) Diocesan Judges.
Thomas, Charles Theodore '73 (COL) Mt. Vernon, OH St. Vincent de Paul.
Thomas, Cherian K. '68 (DAL) Garland TX Good Shepherd.
Thomas, Cheriyan (LC) Camp Douglas, WI St. James; Camp Douglas, WI St. Michael.
Thomas, Clyde '02 (LKC) Lake Arthur, LA Our Lady of the Lake.
Thomas, Curtis '87 (NO) Kenner, LA Nativity of Our Lord.
Thomas, Daniel E. '85 (PH) On Duty Outside the Archdiocese.
Thomas, David T. '52 (STL) St. Louis, MO St. John Bosco Retired.
Thomas, Dominic *m.c.b.s.* '87 (HRT) Ansonia, CT Holy Rosary.
Thomas, Donald K. *m.s.* '57 (HRT)[M] Hartford, CT Missionaries of LaSalette.
Thomas, Donald N. '68 (SAM) Retired.
Thomas, Donald '85 (HON) AUXILIARY CHAPLAINS CONTRACT CHAPLAINS Retired.
Thomas, Gary R. '83 (SJ) Los Altos, CA St. Nicholas.
Thomas, Gary (SJ) Council of Priests.
Thomas, George L. '48 (SFR) Portola Valley, CA Our Lady of the Wayside Retired.
Thomas, Jacob '76 (ALX) St. Joseph, LA St Joseph.
Thomas, James J. '76 (ALN) Military Chaplains.
Thomas, James P. (ALN) Air Force Chaplains.
Thomas, Jerald '56 (SR) Retired.
Thomas, Jeremy '92 (CHI) Chicago, IL St. Jerome.
Thomas, Jesudoss '93 (WDC) Hyattsville, MD St. Jerome.
Thomas, John E. '50 (BO) Senior Priests Retired.
Thomas, John Kilisara '86 (SEA) Seattle, WA St. James Cathedral.
Thomas, John M. '66 (SC) Arcadia, IA St. John the Baptist; Vail, IA St. Ann's; Diocesan Consultors.
Thomas, John '93 (OWN) Diocesan Liturgical Committee; Cadiz, KY St. Stephen; Hopkinsville, KY SS. Peter and Paul; Oak Grove, KY St. Michael the Archangel.
Thomas, John (WOR) Diocesan Building Commission Members.
Thomas, John (OWN) Consultors; Priests' Council.
Thomas, Joseph S. '52 (CHI) Retired.
Thomas, Joseph *b.s.o.* '71 (SAM) Cary, NC Saint Sharbel Mission.
Thomas, Juniper J. '70 (RVC) Glen Cove, NY St. Rocco; Glen Cove, NY North Shore Community Hospital at Glen Cove.
Thomas, Kevin '88 (DET) Lincoln Park, MI Christ the Good Shepherd.
Thomas, LaVerne '86 (SHP) Shreveport, LA St. Elizabeth Ann Seton.
Thomas, LaVerne (Pike) (SHP) College of Consultors; Presbyteral Council; Diocesan Liturgy Commission.
Thomas, Mark A. '96 (PIT) Glenshaw, PA St. Bonaventure.
Thomas, Mark L. '93 (PIT) Homestead, PA St. Maximilian Kolbe.
Thomas, Merwyn J. *c.s.c.* '67 (FTW)[B] University of Notre Dame Du Lac; [I] Notre Dame, IN Holy Cross Community, Corby Hall, University of Notre Dame.
Thomas, Michael G. '83 (SAM) Miami, FL Our Lady of Lebanon; Judicial Vicar.
Thomas, Michael (MIA) Judges.
Thomas, Milton (LIN) Promoters Justitiae; Defensores Vinculi.
Thomas, Norman P. '55 (DET) Detroit, MI Sacred Heart of Jesus.
Thomas, Parath–Undyil T. '64 (CHI)[J] Blue Island, IL St. Francis Hospital and Health Center.
Thomas, Paschal *o.s.b.* '57 (KC)[J] Kansas City, MO.
Thomas, Paul K. '63 (BAL) Retired.
Thomas, Paul *o.c.d.* '78 (ALX) Campti, LA Nativity of The Blessed Virgin Mary.
Thomas, Paul *o.s.b.* '82 (P)[L] St. Benedict, OR Mt. Angel Abbey.
Thomas, Phillip *o.c.d.* '79 (MIL) Milwaukee, WI St. Florian.
Thomas, Ralph W. '65 (CLV) Akron, OH St. Paul.
Thomas, Raymond J. '72 (Y) Conneaut, OH St. Mary's; Conneaut, OH St. Frances Cabrini.
Thomas, Raymond (Y) College of Consultors.
Thomas, Richard M. *s.j.* '58 (ELP)[M] El Paso, TX Our Lady's Youth Center.
Thomas, Richard '66 (GB) Special Assignment.
Thomas, Robert F. (BO) Society of St. James the Apostle.
Thomas, Robert W. '76 (BO) Society of St. James the Apostle.
Thomas, Robert (FgM).
Thomas, Robert (BO)[V] Boston, MA The Society of St. James the Apostle, Inc..
Thomas, Royce R. '69 (LR) Fort Smith, AR Christ the King; [B] Fort Smith, AR Trinity Junior High; Clergy Welfare Board; Army National Guard Chaplains.
Thomas, Sylvester J. '55 (LA) Retired.
Thomas, Tomi (BGP) Danbury, CT St. Peter.
Thomas, Wilbur N. '73 (CHL) Asheville, NC Basilica of St. Lawrence.
Thomas, William F. '93 (LR) Hot Springs National Park, AR St. John the Baptist.
Thomas, William V. '62 (CIN) South Charleston, OH St. Augustine; South Charleston, OH St. Charles Borromeo.
Thomas, William '78 (LAN) Hamburg, MI Holy Spirit; Presbyteral Council; Auditor/Assessor.
Thome, Edwin A. '54 (GAY) Traverse City, MI St. Joseph Retired.
Thome, Edwin J. '51 (LC) Onalaska, WI St. Patrick Retired.
Thome, John J. '46 (SAG) Retired.
Thomman, Matthai K. *o.s.h.* '78 (GAL) Spring, TX St. Edward; [Q] Spring, TX The Society of the Oblates of Sacred Heart.
Thompson, August L. '57 (ALX) Retired.
Thompson, Augustine '85 (RIC) Charlottesville, VA St. Thomas Aquinas.
Thompson, Charles C. '87 (L) Louisville, KY Holy Trinity; Promoter of Justice; [A] St. Meinrad, IN St. Meinrad School of Theology.
Thompson, D. Timothy '82 (FWT) Fort Worth, TX St. John the Apostle; Presbyteral Council and Consultors.
Thompson, Damien *o.c.s.o.* '61 (L)[K] Trappist, KY Abbey of Our Lady of Gethsemani, of the Order of Cistercians of the Strict Observance.
Thompson, Dennis '89 (STP) Farmington, MN St. Michael.
Thompson, Edward C. '59 (NEW) Dumont, NJ St. Mary's.
Thompson, Edward J. '51 (ORL) Altamonte Springs, FL St. Mary Magdalen.
Thompson, Garrett J. '81 (BO) Boston, MA St. Elizabeth's Medical Center; Graduate Studies; [P] Brighton, MA St. Elizabeth's Hospital of Boston.
Thompson, George M. '52 (PEO) Retired.
Thompson, George P. '65 (NY) Bedford, NY St. Patrick; Northern Westchester and Putnam.
Thompson, J. Noel '54 (SD) Retired.
Thompson, J. Vincent *c.s.b.* '49 (GAL)[Q] Sugar Land Basilian Mission Center.
Thompson, James A. '44 (TR) Retired.
Thompson, James D. *o.p.* '03 (SLC) Salt Lake City, UT St. Catherine of Siena; [H] Salt Lake City, UT University of Utah, Newman Center.
Thompson, James W. '44 (L)[E] Glen Cove, NY Upper Campus Retired.
Thompson, James *o.s.a.* '71 (CHI)[N] Chicago, IL St. John Stone Friary.
Thompson, Jerome H. '60 (LA) Retired.
Thompson, John F. *s.m.* '99 (MIA)[D] Hollywood, FL Chaminade–Madonna College Preparatory.
Thompson, John '79 (BRK) On Leave/Unassigned.

Thompson, Kevin *o.f.m.cap.* '97 (WDC) Washington, DC Shrine of the Sacred Heart.
Thompson, Kizito *o.c.s.o.* '70 (WOR)[O] Spencer, MA St. Joseph's Abbey.
Thompson, Michael '96 (STA) Jacksonville, FL Resurrection.
Thompson, Nils F. *o.f.m.* '63 (VNN) Phoenix, AZ; [I] Albuquerque, NM Curia Juan Diego.
Thompson, Patrick '60 (LA) Lomita, CA St. Margaret Mary Alacoque.
Thompson, Philip E. '78 (DUB)[D] Cedar Rapids, IA Xavier High School Foundation; Cedar Rapids, IA John XXIII; Fairfax, IA St. Patrick's; Personnel Advisory Board.
Thompson, Richard B. '69 (MAN) Meredith, NH St. Charles; Clergy Personnel Board; Army National Guard Chaplains.
Thompson, Richard J. '96 (PIT) Pittsburgh, PA Prince of Peace.
Thompson, Richard R. (SY) Retired.
Thompson, Richard '95 (P) Portland, OR All Saints.
Thompson, Thomas A. *s.m.* '68 (CIN)[D] Dayton, OH The University of Dayton; [D] The Marian Library/ International Marian Research Institute (IMRI); [M] Dayton, OH Marianist Community.
Thompson, Thomas E. '92 (SUP) Balsam Lake, WI Our Lady of the Lakes; Osceola, WI St. Joseph; Catholic Boy and Girl Scout.
Thompson, Thomas W. '64 (LAN) Williamston, MI St. Mary.
Thompson, Thomas '82 (SD) Scripps Hospital; Thornton Hospital.
Thompson, Timothy (FWT) Tribunal.
Thompson, William D. '69 (BGP) Military Chaplains.
Thompson, William J. '71 (WDC) Silver Spring, MD St. Bernadette.
Thompson, William L. *o.s.b.* '44 (PBL)[F] Canon City, CO Holy Cross Abbey.
Thompson, William P.A. '54 (CC) Retired.
Thoms, Jeffrey (HBG) Lebanon, PA Assumption of the Blessed Virgin Mary.
Thomson, Edward A. '80 (PRT) Special or Other Diocesan Assignment.
Thomson, J. Garret (BO) Tyngsboro, MA St. Mary Magdalen.
Thon, Andrew J. *s.j.* '74 (MIL)[O] Milwaukee, WI Jesuit Community at Marquette University; [C] Marquette University.
Thong, Nguyen Duc *c.ss.r.* '56 (LA)[Q] Irving, TX.
Thoni, Philip F. '49 (KNX) Gatlinburg, TN St. Mary Retired.
Thoomkuzhy, George '72 (Ujjain) Cologne, MN St. Bernard.
Thoonkuzhy, Joseph '58 (TLS)[E] Tulsa, OK Saint Francis Hospital; Tulsa, OK.
Thoonunkaparambil, John (RVC) Melville, NY St. Elizabeth.
Thoppil, Scaria T. *c.m.i.* '80 (JOL) Itasca, IL St. Peter the Apostle; Lombard, IL St. Pius X.
Thorburn, Timothy J. '83 (LIN) Lincoln, NE Bishop Bonacum Chancery; [J] Lincoln, NE The Catholic Foundation of the Diocese of Lincoln; Moderator of the Curia; Vicar General; Promoters Justitiae; Defensores Vinculi; Diocesan Consultors; Presbyteral Council; Building Commission; Censores Librorum; Clergy Relief Society—The Saint John Vianney Association; Diocesan Finance Council; Diocesan Health Ministries, Inc.; Diocesan Housing Ministries, Inc.; Evangelization Committee; Insurance; Priests' Continuing Education Committee.
Thorn, Robert C. '99 (LC) Wausau, WI St. Matthew; Special Assignment; [C] Wausau, WI St. Matthew Middle School.
Thorne, Carrol W. *c.p.* '60 (MET)[H] Leavenworth, KS.
Thorne, Carroll W. *c.p.* (MO) AUXILIARY CHAPLAINS CONTRACT CHAPLAINS.
Thorne, Stephen D. '98 (PH) Philadelphia, PA Saint Cyprian; [D] Philadelphia, PA St. John Neumann High School; Council of Priests.
Thorne, Thomas P. '76 (BGP) Westport, CT Assumption; Navy Reserve Chaplains.
Thorne, Vance *s.v.d.* '53 (TR)[M] Bordentown, NJ Society of the Divine Word.
Thornton, James W. *c.s.c.* '64 (PHX)[G] Phoenix, AZ Holy Cross Congregation/Casa Santa Cruz.
Thornton, Michael '69 (JKS)[J] Jackson, MS Parroquia De San Miguel Del Arcangel.
Thornton, Michael (BLX) Latin American Apostolate.
Thornton, Paul E. (NEW)[C] Newark, NJ St. Benedict's Preparatory School.
Thorsen, Henry '53 (BIR) Retired.
Thorsen, Robert J. '56 (CIN) Retired.
Thottankara, Raju '95 (CC) Gregory, TX Immaculate Conception.
Thottapally, James J. '71 (OAK) Bay Point, CA Our Lady Queen of the World.
Thottapally, James '71 (SYM) Fremont, CA Syro–Malabar Catholic Community of San Francisco.
Thottiyil, Mathew *m.s.f.s.* '78 (GAL) Sugar Land, TX St. Theresa.
Thottiyil, Matthew *m.s.f.s.* '78 (ATL)[K] Lawrenceville The Missionaries of St. Francis De Sales.
Thottungal, Thomas '70 (NEW) Jersey City, NJ St. Aloysius; Indian Apostolate.
Thottungal, Thomas (SYM) Jersey City, NJ Syro–Malabar Catholic Society, Jersey City, NJ.
Thottuvelil, Zacharias '83 (SYM) Garland, TX St. Thomas the Apostle Catholic Church (Syro–Malabar).
Thrasher, Robert W. '62 (SPR) Holyoke, MA Holy Family; Vice–Chancellors; Judges.
Thuc, John Bosco Pham Trung *c.m.c.* (BO) Dorchester, MA St. Peter.
Thuer, William J. '46 (HRT) Retired.
Thuerauf, Jason M. (DEN) Loveland, CO St. John the Evangelist.
Thuerauf, Jeffrey P. '89 (TUC) On Medical Leave.
Thul, Joseph T. '55 (MET)[G] Somerset, NJ McCarrick Care Center Retired.
Thul, Robert C. *s.j.* '61 (CHI)[D] Chicago, IL St. Ignatius College Prep; [D] Chicago, IL St. Ignatius Jesuit Community.
Thuma, Clifton M. '96 (BO) Dorchester, MA St. Brendan.
Thumma, Aloysius '80 (NY) Bronx, NY Our Lady of the Assumption.
Thundathil, Antony '91 (SYM) Bellwood, IL Mar Thoma Shleeha Cathedral.
Thundathil, Antony (SYM) Eparchial Consultors.
Thundathil, Matthew '78 (MIA) Coral Springs, FL St. Andrew.
Thuong, Philippe Le–Xuan '70 (GAL) Houston, TX Christ, The Incarnate Word; Diocesan Judges.
Thurmond, Benton '46 (VIC) Procurator Advocate Retired.
Thurston, Anthony '82 (WH) Weirton, WV St. Paul's.
Thury, Gerald '67 (SFS) Tyndall, SD St. Leo.
Thychery, George '60 (LAF) Morrow, LA St. Peter.
Thymootil, Paul *c.m.i.* '87 (NY) Eastern Correctional Facility; Shawangunk Correctional Facility; Ulster Correctional Facility; Wallkill Correctional Facility.
Tiala, Linus '78 (LA) Monterey Park, CA St. Stephen.
Tiano, Christopher M. '89 (HRT) West Haven, CT Our Lady of Victory; West Haven, CT St. John Vianney.
Tibahinirwa, John '01 (SPR) Springfield, MA Holy Family.
Tibay, Ernesto '76 (NEW) Bergenfield, NJ St. John the Evangelist.
Tibbetts, Richard '01 (ATL) Douglasville, GA St. Theresa; Council of Priests.
Tibbs, Thomas T. '74 (GRY) Kouts, IN St. Mary.
Tibesar, Leo J. '68 (STP) Minneapolis, MN St. Frances Cabrini; Fairview University Medical Center; Presbyteral Council.
Tiblier, Edgar J. *s.j.* '56 (GAL) New Orleans, LA Immaculate Conception.
Tiboni, Vito '69 (NEW) On Duty Outside the Archdiocese.
Tiboni, Vito '69 (BRK) Veterans Administration Medical Center.
Tice, Cecil '81 (CHL) Absent On Leave.
Tichacek, Charles P. '94 (STL) Florissant, MO St. Norbert.
Tickerhoof, Bernard *t.o.r.* '77 (PIT)[N] Pittsburgh, PA Franciscan Friars, T.O.R..
Tickerhoof, Bernard *t.o.r.* '78 (PIT)[P] Pittsburgh, PA Franciscan Spirit and Life Center.
Tickerhoof, David *t.o.r.* '67 (SFS) Marty, SD St. Paul's Church.
Tickle, John '67 (LSC) Retired.
Ticllasuca, Rolando *m.r.s.m.* '94 (RVC) Glen Cove, NY St. Patrick's.
Tiedeman, Edmund H. '66 (SC) Mallard, IA St. Mary's; West Bend, IA SS. Peter and Paul.
Tiedemann, Neil *c.p.* '75 (BRK) Brooklyn, NY Visitation of the Blessed Virgin Mary.
Tiedemann, Neil *c.p.* '75 (MET)[H] Brooklyn, NY.
Tiefenbrunn, Ronald R. '60 (STL) Retired.
Tiegs, James R. '74 (OM)[H] Omaha, NE New Cassel Retirement Center; [O] Omaha, NE New Cassel Foundation; Omaha Priests Retirement Plan and Trust, The.
Tiel, Florian *o.f.m.conv.* '68 (L)[J] Louisville, KY Franciscan Health Care Center.
Tiell, Florian *o.f.m.conv.* '68 (IND)[J] Mount St. Francis, IN Mount Saint Francis Friary and Retreat Center.
Tiell, Maurice J. '50 (OWN) Eddyville, KY St. Mark Church.
Tiemann, Stephen E. '89 (GAL) Houston, TX St. Theresa.
Tien, Peter '60 (ORG) Retired.
Tiercelin, Harry '43 (NY) New York, NY St. Vincent de Paul Retired.
Tiercelin, Harry '47 (NY) Retired.
Tiernan, John F. *m.s.f.s.* '98 (ATL)[K] Lawrenceville, GA The Missionaries of St. Francis De Sales.
Tierney, Berard *c.p.* '48 (SCR)[M] Clarks Summit, PA St. Gabriel's Convent; [R] Scranton, PA St. Ann's Foundation.
Tierney, Francis J. *s.j.* '42 (NY)[EE] New York, NY Murray–Weigel Hall.
Tierney, Gary M. '67 (DET) Troy, MI St. Alan; Judges.
Tierney, James E. '50 (BO)[Y] Boston, MA Regina Cleri Residence; Regina Cleri, Inc..
Tierney, Joseph P. (NY)[A] Yonkers, NY St. Joseph's Seminary; Vocations.
Tierney, Michael E. '69 (KC) Lee's Summit, MO Holy Spirit; Diocesan Consultors.
Tierney, Michael J. '67 (RCK) Algonquin, IL St. Margaret Mary.
Tierney, Michael (KC) Administrative Committee.
Tierney, Patrick J. '69 (BIR) Tuscumbia, AL Our Lady of the Shoals.
Tierney, Patrick M. '57 (CAM) Avalon, NJ Maris Stella; Members.
Tierney, Patrick (BIR) Diocesan College of Vicars.
Tierney, Robert G. '57 (VEN) Bradenton, FL St. Joseph.
Tierney, Thomas J. *s.j.* '62 (RC)[B] Howes, SD Kino Jesuit Community.
Tierney, Thomas M. '70 (WOR)[A] Yonkers, NY St. John Neumann Residence and Hall; Fitchburg, MA St. Bernard's; Massachusetts Correctional Institution.
Tietjen, Kenneth F. *o.c.s.o.* '56 (DUB)[K] Peosta, IA New Melleray Abbey, Order of Cistercians of the Strict Observance.
Tiffany, Eugene W. '72 (STP) Lakeville, MN All Saints; Presbyteral Council.
Tifft, Thomas W. '69 (CLV)[A] Wickliffe, OH St. Mary Seminary and Graduate School of Theology.
Tigga, Ranjit *s.j.* '96 (MIL)[O] Milwaukee, WI Jesuit Community at Marquette University.
Tigges, James T. '71 (SC) Le Mars, IA St. James.
Tigges, James (SC) Council of Catholic Women.
Tighe, Benedict F. '59 (BGP) Westport, CT Assumption.
Tighe, James '70 (BRK) Flushing, NY Queen of Peace.
Tighe, Leonard J. (BO) Jamaica Plain, MA Lemuel Shattuck Hospital; Jamaica Plain, MA Shattuck Hospital Correctional Unit.
Tighe, Philip M. (R) Clinton, NC Immaculate Conception.
Tighe, Timothy P. *c.s.p.* '69 (NY) New York, NY St. Paul the Apostle.
Tigreros, Ernesto *s.s.p.* '66 (NY)[B] New York, NY Society of St. Paul.
Tigyer, Jeffrey E. (COL) Powell, OH St. Joan of Arc.
Tigyer, Paul '54 (PSC) Retired.
Tijerina, Richard '85 (AUS) Austin, TX St. Mary's Cathedral; [L] Austin, TX University Catholic Center.
Tikalsky, Russell F. '56 (MIL)[J] Milwaukee, WI St. Mary's Hospital of Milwaukee; Special Assignment.
Tilford, John E. '66 (CHI) Chicago, IL St. Michael the Archangel.
Till, Joseph E. '46 (GRY) Retired.
Tilley, Charles J. *s.j.* '85 (MRY) Columbia, MD St. John the Evangelist; San Luis Obispo, CA San Luis Obispo; [B] San Luis Obispo, CA Mission College Preparatory Catholic High School; [C] Omaha, NE Creighton Preparatory School; [K] Omaha, NE Jesuit Community at Creighton University; Commission for Ecumenical and Inter–Religious Affairs.
Tillia, Marc '59 (KCK) On Duty Outside the Archdiocese.
Tillman, Richard J. '65 (STL) St. Charles, MO St. Charles Borromeo; St. Charles County Catholic Church Real Estate Corporation; [U] St. Charles, MO St. Charles County Catholic Church Real Estate Corporation.
Tillman, Richard (BAL) Priest Personnel Board.
Tillolson, Frederick J. *o.carm.* '69 (TUC)[A] Tucson, AZ Salpointe Catholic High School.
Tillotson, Frederick *o.carm.* '69 (TUC)[E] Tucson, AZ Carmelite Priory.
Tillrock, Raymond J. '69 (CHI) Chicago, IL St. Barnabas.
Tilly, Charles *s.j.* (MRY) Bishop Harry A. Clinch Endowment Fund, The Bishop Sylvester D. Ryan Continuing Education Fund.
Tillyer, Herbert K. '68 (PAT) Parsippany, NJ St. Peter the Apostle; [P] Bloomfield, NJ Riese Corporation; [P] Paterson, NJ Martin de Porres Village Corporation; Vicar General, Moderator of the Curia; Pro–Synodal Judges; Presbyteral Council; College of Consultors; Finance Council; Diocesan Cemetery Office.
Tilp, John R. '69 (DUB) Traer, IA St. Paul; Traer, IA Immaculate Conception; Traer, IA St. Joseph.
Timar, Frank John *m.s.c.* '58 (RCK) Sycamore, IL St. Mary; [G] Aurora, IL Missionaries of the Sacred Heart Community.
Timbre, Roland '61 (HT) Thibodaux, LA Our Lady of Prompt Succor; Defenders of the Bond.
Timby, Bryan P. '83 (MEM) Memphis, TN Holy Rosary; Continuing Education for the Clergy.
Timby, Bryan (MEM) Presbyteral Council and College of Consultors.
Timchak, Robert M. '92 (SCR) Hazleton, PA Transfiguration.
Timko, Philip S. *o.s.b.* '69 (JOL)[A] Lisle, IL Benedictine University; [L] Lisle, IL St. Procopius Abbey.
Timlin, Anthony '56 (SB) Retired.
Timlin, John P. *c.m.* '79 (PH) Philadelphia, PA St.

Francis of Assisi.
Timmel, Gerald L. '56 (L) Louisville, KY St. Ignatius Retired.
Timmerman, Bart D. '01 (MAD) Sun Prairie, WI Sacred Hearts of Jesus and Mary.
Timmerman, Craig A. (NU) Marshall, MN Holy Redeemer.
Timmerman, David W. '87 (MAD) Verona, WI St. William; Verona, WI St. Andrew.
Timmerman, Randy J. '93 (MAD) Madison, WI St. Paul University Parish; [K] Madison, WI University of Wisconsin – Madison Roman Catholic Foundation Inc.; Madison.
Timmerman, Sean M. '03 (LIN) Lincoln, NE Blessed Sacrament; Advocates.
Timmermans, John '52 (ALX) Retirement Board; Cemeteries; [D] Moreauville, LA St. John's Village Retired.
Timmings, Thomas '70 (FRS) Atwater, CA St. Anthony; Ecclesiastical Notaries.
Timock, Ronald K. '83 (MAR) Gwinn, MI St. Anthony.
Timone, Richard F. *s.j.* '64 (NY)[EE] New York, NY Murray–Weigel Hall.
Timoney, Brian '56 (OAK) Pleasant Hill, CA Christ the King.
Timoney, Christopher *o.c.d.* '62 (LR)[M] San Antonio, TX Discalced Carmelites (Prov. of St. Therese).
Timoney, Conan H. *c.p.* '68 (BAL) Baltimore, MD Ascension; [W] Baltimore, MD Catholic War Veterans, Inc..
Timoney, Conan H. '68 (PSC) Baltimore, MD Patronage of the Mother of God.
Timoney, Conan H. *c.p.* '68 (BAL) Baltimore, MD Ascension; [W] Baltimore, MD Catholic War Veterans, Inc..
Timoney, Conan (PSC) Syncellus; Elected Members.
Timoney, Francis '69 (LAV) Las Vegas, NV St. Anne; Priests' Personnel Board.
Timoney, Francis (LAV) Presbyteral Council for the Diocese of Las Vegas.
Timu, Iosefo *m.f.* '90 (SPP) Pago Pago, AS Church of St. Peter and Paul; Pago Pago, AS Church of Sacred Heart; Vicar for Diocesan Youth.
Tindall, Harold '78 (SD) Retired.
Tindall, William '89 (DET) Livonia, MI St. Michael; Presbyteral Council.
Tinder, Dennis (BAL) Priests' Council.
Tinder, F. Dennis '68 (BAL) Towson, MD Church of the Immaculate Conception; [V] Towson, MD The Immaculate Conception Elementary School Endowment Trust.
Ting, Bao Guo *c.s.j.b.* '94 (BRK)[V] Astoria, NY Congregation of St. John the Baptist of China.
Tingertal, James *o.s.b.* '61 (SP)[O] St. Leo, FL St. Leo Abbey.
Tingerthal, James *o.s.b.* '61 (SCL)[I] St. Leo, FL St. Leo Abbey.
Tinh, Joseph Nguyen '57 (SJ) Retired.
Tinney, Richard W. '65 (BUR) Deans; Fair Haven, VT Our Lady of Seven Dolors.
Tino, Giovanni (John) '01 (BRK) Jackson Heights, NY St. Joan of Arc.
Tino, Robert F. '71 (MIL) On Duty Outside the Archdiocese.
Tino, Robert '71 (SEA) Western State Hospital.
Tinsley, Edmond T. '51 (WOR)[J] Leicester, MA McAuley Nazareth Home for Boys; [S] Worcester, MA Monsignor Thomas Griffin Foundation; Diocesan Director of Fiscal Affairs; Diocesan Director for Human Services (and Catholic Relief Services); Diocesan College of Consultors; Diocesan Building Commission Members; Members; Finance Office; Presbyteral Council; St. Vincent dePaul Society—; Worcester, MA St. John's.
Tintle, Raymond *o.f.m.* '69 (MRY)[F] San Miguel, CA Franciscan Friars, O.F.M.; San Miguel, CA San Miguel.
Tiongson, Joselito S. (MO) Navy Chaplains.
Tippmann, Laurence '69 (FTW) Retired.
Tipton, Paul S. '98 (MOB) On Leave from the Archdiocese; [E] Leonardtown, MD St. Mary's Ryken High School.
Tirabassi, Camillo '59 (FTW) South Bend, IN Corpus Christi.
Tirado, Orlando *c.m.* '99 (SJN) Military Services.
Tirado, Ramon Orlando *c.m.* '99 (SJN) Puerto Nuevo, PR San Pablo; Air National Guard Chaplains.
Tirpak, Adrian *t.o.r.* '60 (ALT) Windber, PA St. Anthony of Padua.
Tiscornia, Thomas A. *m.m.* '73 (FgM).
Tiso, Canon Francis '88 (SFR) San Francisco, CA St. Thomas More.
Tiso, Francis '88 (SFR) San Francisco State Univ., Newman Center; [Q] San Francisco, CA Newman Center, San Francisco State University.
Tito, Joseh '96 (CHI) Chicago, IL Our Lady of Mercy.
Tito, Joseph '88 (NOR) Baltic, CT St. Mary of the Immaculate Conception.
Tito, Rocco A. '55 (E) Meadville, PA St. Brigid.
Titotto, Carlo A. *c.s.* '67 (GAL) Houston, TX St. Leo the Great.
Titotto, Mario *c.s.* '72 (PRO) Providence, RI St. Bartholomew.
Titta, Santino '60 (ALB) Retired.
Tittler, Leo '63 (BAL) Frederick, MD St. John the Evangelist.
Titus, Austin E. '92 (NY) Staten Island, NY Holy Family; Staten Island, NY St. Rita.
Titus, John M. '89 (SFD) Springfield, IL Cathedral of the Immaculate Conception; Office for Vocations; Special or Other Diocesan Assignment; Presbyteral Council.
Titus, Rodney Q. '95 (PMB) Port St. Lucie, FL Holy Family.
Tiu, Jimmy Lim '00 (FAR) La Moure, ND Assumption; La Moure, ND Holy Rosary; LaMoure, ND St. Francis.
Tivadar, Vasile '95 (STF) Ozone Park, NY St. Mary Protectress; Long Island City, NY.
Tivenan, John J. '72 (BRK) Released from Diocesan Assignment.
Tivy, Gerald '64 (JOL) Lisle, IL St. Joan of Arc.
Tivy, Thomas A. '62 (CHI) Chicago, IL St. Mary of the Lake; Vicar for Priests.
Tix, Michael '92 (STP) Richfield, MN The Church of the Assumption.
Tizio, John G. *c.ss.r.* '85 (BAL) Annapolis, MD St. Mary; [S] Annapolis, MD Saint Mary Rectory.
Tizio, Joseph *c.ss.r.* (ALB) Saratoga Springs, NY St. Clement.
Tkachuk, William '81 (CHI) Schaumburg, IL Church of the Holy Spirit.
Tkel, Wayne *s.j.* '02 (CI)[C] Manresa Jesuit House.
Tkocz, Peter '01 (ALB) Latham, NY St. Ambrose; Albany Medical Center Hospital.
Tlapa, Richard J. (CHI) Retired.
Tlucek, Edward G. *o.f.m.* '78 (GRY)[I] Cedar Lake, IN San Damiano Friary.
To'alepai, Euale *m.f.* (SPP) Pago Pago, AS Church of St. Peter and Paul.
Toal, Bernard E. *s.s.c.* '43 (SB) Fontana, CA St. Mary.
Toal, James '58 (LA)[J] Burbank, CA Providence Saint Joseph Medical Center Retired.
Toal, James *o.f.m.* '75 (ALB)[B] Loudonville, NY Siena College; [B] Siena College.
Toale, Thomas E. '81 (DUB) Cascade, IA St. Peter; Vicar for Education; Vicar for Educational Services and Superintendent of Schools; Ex Officio Members; Finance Council; Ex Officio Members; Review Board for Sexual Abuse of Minors by Clergy and Other Church Personnel; Ex Officio.
Toan, Francis '34 (MRY) Retired.
Toan Doan, Basil M. *c.m.c.* '99 (FWT) Arlington, TX Church of the Vietnamese Martyrs.
Tobias, Humphrey *o.f.m.* '48 (GB).
Tobias, Joseph *m.s.c.* '66 (PH)[I] Ottsville, PA St. John the Baptist.
Tobin, Chuck '68 (KC) Maryville, MO St. Gregory Barbarigo.
Tobin, David *c.ss.r.* '63 (OAK)[N] Berkeley, CA Redemptorists (St. Clemens Maria House).
Tobin, Eamon '72 (ORL) Melbourne, FL Ascension.
Tobin, James E. *c.s.c.* '55 (FR)[A] North Easton, MA Holy Cross Fathers Religious; [I] Notre Dame, IN Holy Cross House.
Tobin, James M. *s.m.* '69 (STL) St. Louis, MO Our Lady of the Pillar.
Tobin, James *s.m.* '69 (STL)[O] St. Louis, MO Marianist Community, Our Lady of the Pillar Parish.
Tobin, Jeremy *o.praem.* '63 (JKS)[F] Jackson, MS Priory of St. Moses the Black.
Tobin, Joseph W. *c.ss.r.* '78 (DEN).
Tobin, Neil W. '57 (DUB)[N] Building Commission; Directors Retired.
Tobin, Patrick '56 (KC) Kansas City, MO St. Therese Parish.
Tobin, Paul R. '64 (Y) Geneva, OH Assumption B.V.M..
Tobin, Robert E. *m.m.* '57 (FgM).
Tobin, T. Michael '93 (L) Lebanon Junction, KY St. Benedict; Shepherdsville, KY St. Aloysius.
Tobin, Thomas H. *s.j.* '73 (CHI)[C] Chicago, IL Jesuit Community at Loyola University Chicago.
Tobin, Thomas J. *c.s.c.* '55 (FR)[H] North Dartmouth, MA Holy Cross Residence.
Tobin, Thomas '59 (GF) Baker, MT St. John the Evangelist.
Tobin, Vincent *o.s.b.* '59 (IND)[K] The American College.
Tobolski, James F. '84 (SUP) Superior, WI St. Francis Xavier; Judicial Vicar; Vicar for Canonical Affairs; Personnel Placement Board; Ecumenical Commission.
Tobolski, Robert *m.s.c.* '55 (ALN)[K] Reading, PA Missionaries of the Sacred Heart.
Tobon, John '95 (BRK) Brooklyn, NY Our Lady of Refuge.
Toborowsky Jonathan S. '98 (MET) Alpha, NJ St. Mary.
Tocco, Anthony M. '65 (DET) Bloomfield Hills, MI St. Hugo of the Hills; College of Consultors
Tochtrop, Randolph G. '96 (SPC) New Madrid, MO Immaculate Conception; Charleston, MO Southeast Correctional Center.
Toczek, Melchior *o.f.m.* '49 (SFD)[L] Springfield, IL Our Lady of Angels Friary.
Todd, Richard J. *c.m.f.* '55 (CHI) Chicago, IL St. Paul.
Todd, Wilmer L. '63 (HT) Thibodaux, LA St. Genevieve.
Todd, Wilmer '63 (HT) Thibodaux, LA St. Luke.
Toepfer, John *o.f.m.cap.* '86 (DEN) Denver, CO Annunciation; [N] Denver, CO Fraternidad San Antonio.
Tofani, Richard L. '79 (TR) Hainesport, NJ Our Lady Queen of Peace; Pontifical Mission Aid Societies.
Togni, Peter J. *s.j.* '85 (SFR)[N] San Francisco, CA Jesuit Community at University of San Francisco.
Tokarczyk, Joseph M. '79 (NY) Florida, NY St. Joseph.
Tokarski, Stanley '93 (DET) Detroit, MI SS. Peter and Paul.
Tokarski, Stephen L. '69 (GF) Billings, MT St. Pius X.
Tokarski, Stephen (GF) Diocesan Consultors; Priests' Council.
Tokarz, David J. '91 (MOB) Montgomery, AL St. Bede; Archdiocese of Mobile Cursillo Center.
Tokarz, John '39 (SPR) Retired.
Tokarz, Thomas M. '77 (WOR) Gardner, MA St. Joseph's.
Tokaz, John *o.f.m.cap.* '78 (PRT) Portland, ME St. Joseph's; [A] Standish, ME Saint Joseph's College; [M] Standish, ME Saint Joseph's College.
Tokus, William J. *m.m.* '60 (NY)[EE] Maryknoll Maryknoll Fathers and Brothers.
Toland, Charles M. *o.s.m.* '56 (CHI)[N] Chicago Order of Friar Servants of Mary (Servites) United States of America Province, Inc..
Toland, Paul L. '53 (BO) Senior Priests Retired.
Toland, Terrence *s.j.* '52 (WH)[A] Wheeling, WV Wheeling Jesuit University.
Tolang, Jaime '58 (SEA) Seattle, WA Immaculate Conception.
Tolbert, George T. *s.j.* '45 (DET)[P] Hamtramck, MI St. Ladislaus.
Tolczyk, Marion *o.f.m.conv.* '54 (HRT) Kensington, CT St. Paul's.
Toledo, Nelson T. (MO) Air Force Chaplains.
Toledo, Orlando (CHI)[J] Blue Island, IL St. Francis Hospital and Health Center.
Toledo, Ramon Prudencio *s.j.* (PH)[AA] Philadelphia, PA Jesuit Community, Arrupe House.
Tolentino, Eddie '84 (WDC) Washington, DC Holy Comforter—St. Cyprian.
Tolentino, Eddie (WDC) Deans.
Tolentino, Thomas J. '55 (NY) Retired.
Tolentino, Thomas '55 (NY)[EE] Bronx, NY.
Tolentino, Virgilio '82 (MET) Old Bridge, NJ St. Ambrose.
Tolentino de la Rosa, Lorenzo Maria *o.cart.* '92 (BUR)[E] Arlington, VT Carthusian Foundation in America, Inc., Charterhouse of the Transfiguration.
Tollefson, Rolf R. '01 (STP) Minneapolis, MN St. Charles Borromeo.
Tollini, Frederick P. *s.j.* '65 (SJ)[B] Santa Clara, CA Jesuit Community.
Toloczko, Bernard A. '58 (SCR) Montrose, PA Holy Name of Mary.
Tolve, Paul *o.f.m.cap.* '84 (NY) Westchester County Jail.
Toma, Zuhair G. '00 (SPA) Santa Ana, CA St. George Chaldean Catholic Church.
Toma, Zuhair (LA) Santa Ana, CA St. George.
Tomaino, Peter *s.a.* '47 (NY)[EE] Garrison, NY Franciscan Friars of the Atonement.
Tomas, Francisco (MO) AUXILIARY CHAPLAINS CONTRACT CHAPLAINS.
Tomas, Peter '95 (SJP) Akron, OH Holy Ghost; Lorain, OH St. John the Baptist.
Tomasek, Richard J. *s.j.* '73 (COL).
Tomaselli, Samuel J. '59 (ALT)[A] Southern Deanery; Somerset, PA St. Peter's.
Tomasi, Lydio F. *c.s.* '64 (NY) New York, NY St. Joseph.
Tomasiewicz, Edward J. *c.m.* '74 (CHI)[N] Chicago DePaul Vincentian Residence.
Tomasiewicz, Frank '65 (SCL) Retired.
Tomasiewicz, Mark A. '91 (OM) Wayne, NE St. Mary; Air Force Reserve Chaplains.
Tomasko, Andrew J. '91 (DET) Royal Oak, MI St. Mary.
Tomaskovic, Emil *s.a.* '71 (NY)[EE] Garrison, NY St. Francis of Assisi Novitiate.
Tomasone, Richard C. '80 (E) Erie, PA St. John the Baptist; Deans.
Tomasovich, John A. '48 (NO) Retired.
Tomassetti, Berard *o.f.m.cap.* '53 (SAL)[E] Victoria, KS St. Fidelis Friary.
Tomasso, Paul J. '81 (ROC) Rochester, NY St. Anthony of Padua; Rochester, NY Holy Apostles; Rochester, NY Holy Family; [M] Rochester, NY Family Rosary For Peace, Inc..
Tomasulo, Anthony *o.s.a.* '61 (MIA) Dania, FL Church of the Resurrection.
Tomaszewski, Michael J. '58 (GRY) Retired.
Tomatis, Christopher *o.f.m.* '65 (OAK)[N] Oakland Franciscan Friars Provincial Office, Province of St. Barbara.
Tombasco, Anthony R. '51 (SCR) Dunmore, PA St. Rocco's.

Tomc, Victor N. '43 (CLV) Cleveland, OH St. Mary Retired.
Tomei, Joseph A. *c.s.c.* '99 (AUS) Austin, TX St. Ignatius Martyr.
Tomich, Daniel M. '76 (CHI) Riverdale, IL Queen of Apostles.
Tomichek, George *d.c.* '74 (PH) Philadelphia, PA St. Peter the Apostle.
Tomicky, Ronald '75 (CLV) Retired.
Tomiczek, Damian *s.d.s.* '82 (NEW) Brooklyn, NY Our Lady of Consolation; [N] Verona, NJ The Salvatorian Fathers.
Tomiczek, Damien *s.d.s.* '82 (SAT) St. Hedwig, TX Annunciation of the Blessed Virgin Mary.
Tomiekha, Tomy '88 (SPA) North Hollywood, CA St. Paul Assyrian–Chaldean Catholic Parish; North Hollywood, CA St. Paul Assyrian–Chaldean.
Tomkosky, Richard (ALT) Bellefonte, PA St. John the Evangelist's.
Tomlinson, Brian *o.f.m.cap.* '65 (PAT)[N] Union City, NJ Capuchin Friars – Province of the Sacred Stigmata of St. Francis; [M] Lafayette, NJ St. Francis Center.
Tomlinson, Brian *o.f.m.cap.* '65 (NEW) Hackensack, NJ Church of St. Francis of Assisi.
Tompkins, John Mary '93 (RIC) Virginia Beach, VA St. Gregory the Great.
Tompkins, Terrence P. '82 (OAK) Fremont, CA Holy Spirit.
Tomzik, Fred W. '84 (CHI) La Grange Park, IL St. Louise de Marillac.
Ton, Anthony '66 (SEA)[P] Seattle, WA Vietnamese Catholic Center; Vietnamese, Ministry to.
Tona, Rigobert Nsibu *s.j.* (BAL)[B] Timonium, MD Loyola Graduate Center –Timonium Campus; [S] Baltimore, MD Jesuit Community of Loyola College, Inc..
Tonary, David *m.s.f.* '81 (SAT) Seguin, TX Our Lady of Guadalupe.
Tonelli, Robert F. '72 (CHI) Streamwood, IL St. John the Evangelist.
Toner, Edward R. '52 (COV) Retired.
Toner, John G. *m.s.* '44 (HRT)[M] Hartford, CT Missionaries of LaSalette.
Toner, Oliver '71 (VEN) Fort Myers, FL Church Of The Resurrection Of Our Lord.
Toner, Patrick A. '75 (COL) Plain City, OH St. Joseph; London Correctional Institution; Vicariate 5: West.
Tong, Peter *o.c.s.o.* '68 (L)[K] Trappist, KY Abbey of Our Lady of Gethsemani, of the Order of Cistercians of the Strict Observance.
Tonkinson Ruef, James LeRoy (COL) Adjutant Judicial Vicars.
Tonos, Joseph '94 (JKS) Oxford, MS St. John; [I] Oxford, MS University of Mississippi Newman Center.
Tonry, Patrick J. *s.m.* '65 (BAL) Eldersburg, MD St. Joseph; [V] Sykesville, MD St. Joseph Catholic Community Endowment Trust.
Toof, Daniel R. '94 (ATL) Monroe, GA St. Anna's.
Toohey, Richard '01 (E)[C] Erie, PA St. Joseph.
Toohey, Timothy J. '65 (STL) Washington, MO St. Ann; Washington, MO St. John's Mercy Hospital; [J] Washington, MO St. John's Mercy Hospital.
Toohy, William J. '61 (NY) New York, NY Blessed Sacrament; [I] New York, NY The Ladies of Charity of the Catholic Charities of the Archdiocese of New York.
Toolan, John A. *c.s.v.* '43 (CHI)[N] Arlington Heights, IL Viatorian Province Center–Clerics of St. Viator.
Toole, Arthur A. '58 (ALB) Voorheesville, NY St. Matthew.
Toole, Lawrence E. '67 (PRO) Cumberland, RI St. Patrick.
Toolis, Martin '70 (GR) Retired.
Tooman, Robert (NEW) Newark, NJ St. Antoninus; Newark, NJ Columbus Hospital; Columbus Hospital.
Toomey, Daniel A. '03 (SCR) East Stroudsburg, PA St. Matthew's.
Toomey, John M. '61 (BO) Senior Priests Retired.
Toomey, Kevin G. '78 (BO) Medford, MA St. Raphael.
Toomey, Leonard R. '48 (TR)[M] Trenton, NJ Villa Vianney; Promoters of Justice; Tribunal Judges Retired.
Toonen, Harvey H. *o.praem.* '41 (GB)[I] De Pere, WI St. Joseph Priory.
Topaz, John J. *o.f.m.cap.* (PRT) Pastoral Assocs..
Topel, L. John *s.j.* '65 (SEA) Arlington, WA Immaculate Conception; [A] Seattle, WA Seattle University.
Topf, Thomas J. '63 (SC) Kingsley, IA St. Michael's.
Topmoeller, William G. '52 (DET)[P] Hamtramck, MI St. Ladislaus.
Topolewski, Jaroslaw '00 (ATL) Marietta, GA Church of St. Ann.
Topper, Charles J. '68 (HRT)[C] West Hartford, CT Saint Joseph College.
Topper, Charles J. '68 (HBG) On Duty Outside the Diocese.
Topper, John M. *o.s.m.* '87 (CHI)[N] Chicago, IL Order of Friar Servants of Mary (Servites) United States of America Province, Inc.; [N] Chicago Order of Friar Servants of Mary (Servites) United States of America Province, Inc..
Topper, John M. *o.s.m.* '87 (P)[L] Portland, OR The Grotto, The National Sanctuary of Our Sorrowful Mother.
Topper, Vincent J. '36 (HBG) Harrisburg, PA St. Catherine Laboure Retired.
Torba, Jason '91 (CHI) Evanston, IL St. Mary.
Torborg, Elmer '55 (SCL) Retired.
Torgerson, Lloyd A. '65 (LA) Santa Monica, CA St. Monica; "Vida Nueva" (Archdiocesan Spanish Newspaper).
Torm, Agustin '93 (CHR) Military Chaplains; Army Chaplains.
Torma, Andrew *m.s.c.* '76 (OG)[E] Watertown, NY Missionaries of the Sacred Heart.
Torma, Andrew *m.s.c.* '76 (OG) Watertown, NY Our Lady of the Sacred Heart.
Tormey, Daniel '55 (ROC) Retired.
Tormey, James D. '78 (SY) Binghamton, NY St. Thomas Aquinas.
Tornes, Dale F. '70 (STU) Caldwell, OH Corpus Christi; Caldwell, OH St. Stephen.
Tornes, Dale (STU) Priests Personnel Board.
Torney, John R. '39 (MET) Bernardsville, NJ Our Lady of Perpetual Help; [H] Somerset, NJ Maria Regina Residence Retired.
Toro, Carlos Perez '88 (SJN) Graduate Studies.
Toro, Emilio (SJN) for Pastoral Affairs.
Toro, Emilio (SJN) Clergy Social Security (Prevision Social del Clero).
Toro, Gabriel '02 (BRK) Long Island City, NY Queen of Angels.
Toro, R. Emilio (SJN) Vicar for Pastoral Affairs.
Toro, Ramon E. '60 (SJN) Carolina, PR Santo Cristo de los Milagros.
Torok, Dezso '48 (Y) East Palestine, OH Our Lady of Lourdes.
Torok, Dezso '48 (Y) Retired.
Torok, George J. '58 (NY)[II] Sparkill, NY Hallel Institute.
Torpey, Charles L. '69 (GI) Kearney, NE St. James; Vicar General; Adjutant Vicars–Judicial; Promoter Justitiae; Judges; Diocesan Consultors; Liturgical Commission; Personnel Board; Priests' Advisory Board (Presbyteral Council).
Torpey, James M. '83 (ALN) Summit Hill, PA St. Joseph; Summit Hill, PA St. Stanislaus.
Torpey, Matt G. *o.c.s.o.* '56 (ATL)[K] Conyers, GA The Monastery of the Holy Spirit.
Torpey, Michael J. '68 (RVC) Sea Cliff, NY St. Boniface Martyr.
Torquato, James R. '89 (PIT) Pittsburgh, PA St. Bernard.
Torralba, Antolin B. '48 (LA) Retired.
Torre, Emilio Diaz *l.c.* '93 (HRT)[V] Orange, CT Legion of Christ, Inc..
Torre, Emilio Diaz *l.c.* '93 (NY)[II] Thornwood, NY Helping Hands Medical Missions, Inc..
Torre, Jesse *o.f.m.cap.* '60 (FWT) Fort Worth, TX Our Lady of Guadalupe.
Torrelas, Eduardo '85 (CGS)[C] Humacao, PR San Antonio Abad Abbey of the Order of St. Benedict.
Torrens, James S. *s.j.* '61 (LA)[Q] Los Angeles, CA Columbiere House.
Torrens, James *s.j.* (LA) Cardinal Manning House of Prayer for Priests.
Torrente, Lorenzo '75 (RNO) Lovelock, NV St. John the Baptist; Lovelock Prison.
Torres, Adrian '75 (PMB) Vero Beach, FL St. Helen.
Torres, Carlos '72 (SD) San Diego, CA St. Jude.
Torres, Daniel '96 (LKC) De Ridder, LA St. Joseph's; Priest's Senate.
Torres, Edgar Fernando '85 (R) Raleigh, NC Cathedral of the Sacred Heart.
Torres, Eduardo '87 (PCE)[B] The Pontifical Catholic University of Puerto Rico; Censores Librorum.
Torres, Edwin *c.h.s.* '97 (NY)[EE] Glenham, NY Apostolic Society of the Crusade of the Holy Spirit.
Torres, Ernesto '72 (DAL) Mesquite, TX Divine Mercy of Our Lord; Presbyteral Council.
Torres, Fernando *sch.p.* '93 (PCE)[C] Coto Laurel, PR Colegio Ponceno.
Torres, Fernando (R) Ex Officio; Vicar for Hispanics.
Torres, Frank D. '94 (GRY) East Chicago, IN St. Mary.
Torres, Gabriel M. '95 (ARE) Ciales, PR Holy Rosary.
Torres, Hipolito '85 (CGS) Caguas, PR Cathedral Dulce Nombre de Jesus; Diocesan Consultors.
Torres, Hipolito (CGS) Priests Senate.
Torres, Jesus *o.s.a.* '93 (GAL) Baytown, TX Our Lady of Guadalupe.
Torres, Jose A. *o.f.m.cap.* '01 (PCE) Ponce, PR Santa Teresita.
Torres, Jose Angel *o.f.m.cap.* '01 (PCE)[E] Ponce, PR Fraternidad Santa Teresita, Frailes Capuchinos.
Torres, Juan Alberto *o.c.d.* '66 (PCE) Ponce, PR San Jose.
Torres, Juan *o.p.* '02 (NO) New Orleans, LA St. Anthony of Padua.
Torres, Luis Angel '85 (SJN) Carolina, PR Santisima Trinidad; Police Chaplains.
Torres, Mario A. *s.j.* '01 (SJN)[H] San Juan, PR Comunidad Jesuita.
Torres, Mario Alberto *s.j.* (SJN)[B] Colegio San Ignacio de Loyola.
Torres, Mario '96 (LA) Los Angeles, CA Nativity; Los Angeles, CA St. Columbkille.
Torres, Miguel A. *c.ss.r.* '99 (PCE) Bo. Puente Jobos, PR SS. Peter and Paul.
Torres, Silvino '99 (LA) Los Angeles, CA Immaculate Conception.
Torres, Victor *o.m.i.* '95 (SJN) Toa Alta, PR San Judas Tadeo.
Torres, William '91 (SJN) Graduate Studies.
Torres–Graciana, Ivan J. (SJN) Air Force Chaplains.
Torres–Lisboa, Patricio (RIC) Richmond, VA St. Paul.
Torres–Ortiz, Anibal R. (SJN) San Juan, PR Santa Maria de Los Angeles.
Torres Graciano, Ivan '88 (SJN) On Duty Outside the Archdiocese.
Torres Soto, Paulo Cesar *s.s.p.* (LA)[Q] Los Angeles, CA Society of St. Paul.
Torretto, Joseph '75 (RIC) Martinsville, VA St. Joseph.
Torrez, Basil '56 (SAL) Retired.
Torrez, John M. '98 (KCK) Paxico, KS Sacred Heart.
Torrez, John '98 (KCK) Holy Cross; St. John Vianney; St. Stanislaus; St. Marys, KS Immaculate Conception; Regional Pastoral Leaders.
Torsiello, Ralph C. '58 (WDC) Retired.
Tortora, James '72 (NEW) Jersey City, NJ Our Lady of Victories.
Tortorelli, Kevin *o.f.m.* '73 (NY) New York, NY St. Francis of Assisi.
Torwel, Vitalis '92 (DAV)[M] Iowa City, IA O'Keefe Hall.
Tos, Aldo J. '53 (NY) New York, NY St. Joseph.
Toscano, Eduardo '72 (SAC) Orland, CA St. Dominic; Lincoln, CA St. Joseph.
Toscano, Pasquale A. '44 (HRT) Retired.
Toschi, Larry *o.s.j.* '76 (FRS) Madera, CA St. Joachim.
Tosco, Lawrence *c.s.j.* '70 (CLV)[O] Avon, OH Congregation of St. Joseph.
Tosco, Lorenzo *s.s.d.* '70 (CLV)[A] Wickliffe, OH St. Mary Seminary and Graduate School of Theology.
Tosello, Matthew '62 (PIT) Prospect, PA St. Christopher at the Lake.
Tosi, John C. '73 (BRK) Brooklyn, NY The Cathedral–Basilica of St. James; Liturgical Office; Art and Architecture Commission; Liturgical Commission.
Toste, Frank A. *c.s.c.* '60 (BGP)[P] Sanbornville, NH Union Institute of Cincinnati.
Tosti, Anthony F. '65 (SY) On Sabbatical.
Tosti, Ronald A. '62 (FR) Mashpee, MA Christ The King; Office of Pastoral Planning.
Tosto, Louis F. '97 (RCK) Wonder Lake, IL Christ the King.
Totah, Sami '71 (NY) Yonkers, NY Immaculate Conception; Good Shepherd Arabic Community of St. Mary.
Totaro, Dominic J. *s.j.* '67 (BAL).
Toth, Joseph A. '38 (PH)[S] Absent on Sick Leave.
Toth, Julius *o.f.m.conv.* '53 (TR) Point Pleasant Beach, NJ St. Peter's.
Toth, Simon J. *o.s.b.* '59 (GBG) Latrobe, PA St. Boniface; [H] Latrobe, PA Saint Vincent Archabbey.
Toth, Stephen J. '02 (NEW) Jersey City, NJ St. Paul's; South Kearny, NJ Talbot Hall Assessment Center; South Kearny, NJ Hudson County Correctional Center; Kearny, NJ Hudson County Correctional Center; Kearny, NJ Talbot Hall Assessment Center.
Totten, Raymond F. '48 (COL) Retired.
Tottle, Gregg '91 (SP) St. Petersburg, FL Cathedral of St. Jude the Apostle; Priests Personnel Board; Diocesan Finance Council; Presbyteral Council.
Tou, Ivan O. *c.s.p.* '02 (AUS) Austin, TX St. Austin.
Tou, John '57 (NY) On Duty Outside the Archdiocese.
Tou, Louis A. '56 (WDC) Retired.
Touchette, Marc L. '57 (ALB) Cohoes, NY St. Bernard.
Tougas, Paul J. '64 (WOR) Boylston, MA St. Mary of the Hills; Deans.
Tougas, Roger *a.a.* '60 (BO)[V] Montmartre Canadien.
Toups, David '97 (SP) On Duty Outside the Diocese.
Toups, Earl *c.ss.r.* '48 (BLX)[E] Biloxi, MS St. John Neumann Residence.
Toups, Mark Anthony '01 (HT) Larose, LA Our Lady of the Rosary.
Toups, Mark (HT) Vocations.
Tourigny, William '80 (SPR) Springfield, MA Our Lady of the Sacred Heart.
Tourneir, Andre '48 (SFR)[K] San Rafael, CA Nazareth House Retired.
Tournier, Andre '48 (SR) Retired.
Touzin, Yves–Michel *c.s.* '88 (NEW) Newark, NJ St. Columba's.
Tovar, Emilio *c.m.* '43 (ARE) Manati, PR La Candelaria.
Tovar, Francisco Hernandez '80 (SAC) Vallejo, CA St. Catherine of Siena.
Tovar, Ireneo Lopez '50 (CAM) Retired.
Towey, Damian *c.p.* '56 (PMB)[J] North Palm Beach, FL Our Lady of Florida Spiritual Center.
Towey, Damian *c.p.* (PMB) Judges; Defenders of the Bond; Promoter of Justice.
Towle, Joseph C. '66 (NY)[EE] New York, NY West Side

Jesuit Community.
Towle, Joseph W. *m.m.* '65 (BO)[V] Walpole, MA Maryknoll Mission Promotion Department.
Townsend, Charles L. '91 (LIN) Mead, NE St. James; [C] Wahoo, NE Bishop Neumann Jr.–Sr. High School; [L] Wahoo, NE Bishop Neumann High School Endowment Fund.
Townsend, Joe C. '88 (TLS) Hugo, OK St. Agnes; Hugo, OK Immaculate Conception; Seminary Board.
Townsend, Ralph V. *o.p.* '50 (NEW) Sacred Heart Priory.
Towsley, Peter J. '91 (BGP) Brookfield, CT St. Marguerite Bourgeoys; Presbyteral Council.
Toyinbo, Andrew *m.s.p.* '86 (MOB) Mount Vernon, AL St. Peter the Apostle.
Tozzi, Ross '01 (FBK) North Pole, AK St. Nicholas; Presbyteral Council; Consultors.
Tra, John *s.v.d.* '44 (DUB)[B] Epworth, IA Divine Word College.
Trabold, Alphonsus A. *o.f.m.* '51 (BUF)[O] St. Bonaventure, NY St. Bonaventure Friary; [C] St. Bonaventure, NY Friar Community.
Trabold, George R. '73 (NEW) Short Hills, NJ St. Rose of Lima; Archdiocesan Judges.
Tracey, Bernard M. *c.m.* '74 (BRK)[D] St. John's University, Staten Island Campus; [D] St. John's University; [V] Jamaica, NY Vincentian Residence.
Tracey, Michael '72 (BLX) Bay St. Louis, MS Our Lady of the Gulf.
Tracey, Thomas S. '63 (CAM) Retired.
Tracy, Charles '63 (SR) Retired.
Tracy, Charles '69 (SFR)[K] San Rafael, CA Nazareth House Retired.
Tracy, David W. '63 (BGP) On Duty Outside the Diocese.
Tracy, Eugene '91 (SPK) Spokane, WA St. Charles.
Tracy, George E. '84 (PRT) Retired.
Tracy, James R. '60 (CAM) Sicklerville, NJ St. Charles Borromeo; Gloucester Deanery; Members; Members.
Tracy, John P. '48 (HRT)[A] Bloomfield, CT St. Thomas Seminary Retired.
Tracy, Joseph A. '92 (PH) Secretary for Catholic Human Services; On Special or Other Archdiocesan Assignment.
Tracy, Laurence C. '66 (ROC) Unassigned; Rochester, NY Our Lady of Perpetual Help.
Tracy, Norbert J. *s.j.* '55 (MIL)[O] Milwaukee, WI Jesuit Community at Marquette University.
Tracy, Philip A. '88 (PRT) Waterville, ME Parish of the Holy Spirit; [M] Waterville, ME Colby College; [M] Waterville, ME Thomas College; Deans; Diocesan Council of Priests; Pastoral Assocs..
Tracy, Philip Michael '60 (PRT) Retired.
Tracy, Robert D. *o.carm.* '63 (NY) Tarrytown, NY Transfiguration; Middletown, NY Middletown Psychiatric Center.
Tracy, T. Shawn *o.s.a.* '66 (PH)[C] Villanova University; [AA] Villanova, PA St. John Stone Friary.
Tracy, Theodore J. *s.j.* '50 (CHI)[C] Chicago, IL Jesuit Community at Loyola University Chicago.
Traczyk, Edward *s.ch.* '78 (SD) San Diego, CA St. Maximilian Kolbe Mission.
Trader, William A. '74 (PH) Berwyn, PA St. Monica.
Traeger, Gregory *o.s.b.* '42 (SP)[O] St. Leo, FL St. Leo Abbey.
Trahan, Charles N. (LAF) Port Barre, LA Sacred Heart of Jesus.
Trahan, Harold '69 (LAF) Lafayette, LA St. Elizabeth Seton; Council of Priests.
Trahan, Romeo A. *s.s.e.* '45 (BUR)[E] Colchester, VT Society of St. Edmund.
Trahon, Basil *c.p.* '62 (HRT)[M] West Hartford Holy Family Monastery/Retreat.
Trainer, Eugene D. '51 (STO) Angels Camp, CA St. Patrick Church of Angels Camp (Pastor of).
Trainor, Daniel M. '61 (PRO) Providence, RI Assumption of the Blessed Virgin Mary; Deans; Council Members.
Trainor, Henry J. '73 (SFR) Absent on Leave.
Trainor, James F. '64 (WIL)[H] Wilmington, DE St. Patrick's House, Inc.; Absent on Sick Leave.
Trainor, Patrick '44 (SP) Retired.
Trainor, Patrick '44 (SP) St. Pete Beach, FL St. John.
Trainor, Richard F. '75 (WOR) Worcester, MA St. Bernard.
Trainor, Robert M. '57 (NY) Bronx, NY St. Ann.
Trainor, Robert (NY) Canon 1742 Panel of Pastors.
Tran, Aloysius Thoai *c.m.c.* (SB) Vietnamese Ministry.
Tran, Aloysius *c.m.c.* '92 (SB) Ontario, CA St. George.
Tran, Anh Q. (SAT) Defenders of the Bond.
Tran, Anh '90 (FWT) Fort Worth, TX St. Peter The Apostle; Scouting; Vocations.
Tran, Anthony Doan '88 (BLX) Pass Christian, MS Sacred Heart; Cursillo and Retreats.
Tran, Anthony Hung Ngoc *o.p.* '92 (GAL)[Q] Houston, TX Dominican Friars, St. Mark Priory, Inc..
Tran, Anthony Lan (SEA) Assistant Chaplains.
Tran, Augustine Hoa Trung '98 (ATL) McLean, VA St. John's; On Duty Outside the Archdiocese.
Tran, Augustine (ATL) Archdiocesan Judges.
Tran, Binh K. '92 (PEO) Walnut, IL Immaculate Conception Church; Walnut, IL St. John's.
Tran, Dac T. *o.f.m.* '89 (CHR) Greenville, SC Our Lady of the Rosary; Vicar for Vietnamese Ministry.
Tran, Dac Tat *o.f.m.* '89 (BO) Boston, MA New England Medical Center.
Tran, Dac *o.f.m.* (BO) Court Experts for Languages.
Tran, Dominic Dahn Cong *s.d.b.* '03 (NY)[EE] New Rochelle, NY Salesian Provincial House.
Tran, Dominic Dat '99 (PT) Pensacola, FL St. Paul.
Tran, Dominic Dieu (HT) Morgan City, LA Thanh Gia.
Tran, Dominic *o.cist* '97 (SAC)[I] Vina, CA Abbey of New Clairvaux, Trappist; [A] Vina, CA Abbey of New Clairvaux, Trappist Seminary.
Tran, Dung Anton '02 (GR) Hart, MI St. Joseph's.
Tran, Francis '97 (ATL) Marietta, GA Church of the Transfiguration.
Tran, Hoi '01 (SFE) Vaughn, NM St. Mary.
Tran, Hung '98 (LA) Lancaster, CA Sacred Heart.
Tran, John Chinh Chan (GAL) Retired.
Tran, John Kha '89 (GAL) Katy, TX St. Bartholomew the Apostle; Ethnic Vicars.
Tran, John Nghi '71 (LA) Claremont, CA Our Lady of the Assumption.
Tran, John Tinh *c.m.c.* '94 (SB) Riverside, CA Our Lady of Perpetual Help; Vietnamese Ministry.
Tran, John '95 (NY) Staten Island, NY Our Lady Help of Christians; Monticello, NY St. Peter.
Tran, John '00 (L) LaGrange, KY Immaculate Conception.
Tran, John *s.v.d.* (SB)[A] Riverside, CA Society of the Divine Word Missionaries.
Tran, Joseph J. (RIC) Air Force Chaplains.
Tran, Joseph Man '95 (NO) Buras, LA Our Lady of Good Harbor.
Tran, Joseph Thang Dinh '96 (NO) Metairie, LA St. Mary Magdalen.
Tran, Joseph Trin '02 (OAK) Pleasanton, CA The Catholic Community of Pleasanton.
Tran, Joseph Tu '99 (HT) Montegut, LA Sacred Heart; Montegut, LA St. Charles Borromeo.
Tran, Joseph '74 (LAN) Lansing, MI St. Andrew Dung–Lac.
Tran, Joseph '95 (NY) Bronx, NY St. Nicholas of Tolentine.
Tran, Joseph (PH) Vietnamese Apostolate.
Tran, Kiem Van '91 (ORG) Tustin, CA St. Cecilia.
Tran, Luan Quach '94 (P) St. Helens, OR St. Frederic; Air Force Reserve Chaplains.
Tran, Luan '94 (P) Vernonia, OR St. Mary.
Tran, Luc N. '96 (SB) San Bernardino, CA St. Anne.
Tran, Luc *s.v.d.* '96 (SB) Vietnamese Ministry.
Tran, Luke '01 (NEW) Linden, NJ St. John the Apostle.
Tran, Luong Quang '89 (BEA) Diocesan College of Consultors and Presbyteral Council; Judicial Vicar; Diocesan Judges; [I] Beaumont, TX St. Thomas More Society of Southeast Texas; China, TX Our Lady of Sorrows.
Tran, Michael Mai *c.m.c.* '93 (BEA) Diocesan College of Consultors and Presbyteral Council; Port Arthur, TX Queen of Vietnam.
Tran, Michael '93 (SD) Lakeside, CA Blessed Kateri Tekakwitha.
Tran, Mike Viet Manh '02 (HT) Thibodaux, LA St. Genevieve.
Tran, Peter H. '99 (NEW) Jersey City, NJ St. John the Baptist.
Tran, Peter '73 (RIC) Newport News, VA Our Lady of Mount Carmel.
Tran, Philip P. '92 (NY) Military Chaplains; Navy Chaplains.
Tran, Phuong Duc '66 (SEA) Vancouver, WA St. James.
Tran, Quan H. '96 (PH)[D] Philadelphia PA St. John Neumann High School.
Tran, Quan N. '96 (PH) Philadelphia, PA Epiphany of Our Lord.
Tran, Quang Minh (SAV).
Tran, Quynh Dinh (SPR) Southeast Asian Apostolate.
Tran, Quynh '93 (SPR) Springfield, MA Holy Name.
Tran, Sang V. '92 (LA) Santa Fe Springs, CA St. Pius X.
Tran, Tam '00 (WDC) Bowie, MD St. Pius X.
Tran, Tan Van '92 (DM) Bayard, IA St. Patrick.
Tran, Thomas *s.v.d.* '00 (WH) Gary, WV Our Lady of Victory; Powhatan, WV Sacred Heart; War, WV Christ the King; Welch, WV St. Peter.
Tran, Tung '03 (CC) Rockport, TX Sacred Heart.
Tran, Victor '99 (OAK) Oakland, CA St. Mary, Immaculate Conception–St. Francis de Sales.
Tran–Khac–Hy, Hilarius '57 (WDC) Retired.
Tran Binh Philip M. *c.m.c.* '03 (SPC)[E] Carthage, MO Congregation of the Mother Coredemptrix, United States Assumption Province.
Tran Cao Tuong, Andrew '75 (NO) Avondale, LA Assumption of Mary.
Trance, F. Raymond '94 (PIT) Butler, PA St. Paul.
Tranchida Blaise *o.f.m.* '50 (NY)[EE Immaculate Conception Friary.
Tranchina Joseph '68 (NO) Retired.
Trancone, Gerard A. '69 (WDC) Special Ministries; [S] Washington, DC Gallaudet University Catholic Community; [V] Landover Hills, MD The Center for Deaf Ministries of the Archdiocese of Washington; St. Francis of Assisi Catholic Church and Center for the Deaf; Ministry for the Deaf.
Tran Dien, Peter '41 (SPC)[E] Carthage, MO Congregation of the Mother Coredemptrix, United States Assumption Province.
Tranel, Daniel D. '56 (RCK) Galena, IL St. Mary; Galena, IL St. Michael.
Tranel, Don '88 (JKS) New Albany, MS St. Francis of Assisi.
Tranel, Dorrance E. '49 (RCK) Retired.
Trang, Vang C. '83 (RIC)[N] Hampton, VA Holy Family Retreat.
Trangh–Nghiem, Joseph Bui (WDC) Defenders of the Bond.
Tran Ngoc Diep, Joseph M. *c.m.c.* '82 (SPC)[E] Carthage, MO Congregation of the Mother Coredemptrix, United States Assumption Province.
Tran Ngoc Thoai, Aloysius M. *c.m.c.* '92 (SB)[E] Corona, CA Congregation of the Mother Co–Redemptrix.
Tran Van Ban, Martin *c.m.c.* (SY) Asian Apostolate.
Tran Van Dong, Alphonsus '63 (BGP) Bridgeport, CT St. Augustine Cathedral.
Trapani, Anthony M. '73 (RVC) Priests Released from Diocesan Assignment; Navy Chaplains.
Trapani, Anthony '73 (RVC) Military Chaplains.
Trapasso, Thomas J. '49 (PAT) Morristown, NJ St. Margaret's; Pro–Synodal Judges; Catholic Deaf Society Retired.
Trapp, Daniel J. '84 (DET)[A] The School of Theology; Detroit, MI St. Augustine and St. Monica; Presbyteral Council.
Trapp, Joseph J. '96 (COL) Grove City, OH Our Lady of Perpetual Help.
Trapp, Joseph L. '59 (BEL) Benton, IL St. Joseph.
Trask, David R. '86 (CLV) Macedonia, OH Our Lady of Guadalupe; Auditor/Assessor.
Traub, George W. *s.j.* '67 (CIN)[P] Milford, OH Milford Spiritual Center.
Traub, Robert '39 (FTW)[G] Fort Wayne, IN Saint Anne Home & Retirement Community; [G] Fort Wayne, IN St. Anne Home of the Diocese of Fort Wayne – South Bend, Inc. Retired.
Traudt, Robert *o.carm.* '82 (NEW) Leonia, NJ St. John the Evangelist's.
Traufler, John F. '57 (WIN) Retired.
Trauger, Francis X. '72 (PH) Levittown, PA St. Michael the Archangel.
Traupman, Robert '69 (ORL) On Duty Outside the Diocese.
Trautner, Kevin C. '74 (PH) Norristown, PA St. Francis of Assisi.
Travaglione, Michael *o.f.m.* '66 (BO)[O] Army Chaplains.
Travaglione, Michael *o.f.m.* '66 (NY)[EE] Savannah, GA Hunter Army Airfield.
Travaglione, Michael *o.f.m.* '66 (BO)[O] Army Chaplains.
Travassos, Horace J. '73 (FR) Westport, MA Our Lady of Grace.
Travers, Alan '83 (NY) Military Chaplains; Navy Chaplains.
Travers, David O. *s.j.* '68 (BO)[V] Boston The Society of Jesus of New England–Provincial Offices.
Travers, David O. *s.j.* '68 (HON) Honolulu, HI SS Peter and Paul.
Travers, Gerard P. '65 (NY) Highland Mills, NY St. Patrick.
Travers, John J. *c.ss.r.* '59 (BRK) Brooklyn, NY Our Lady of Perpetual Help Basilica.
Travers, Joseph A. *o.s.f.s.* '48 (WIL)[J] Childs, MD Retirement and Assisted Care Facility.
Travers, Luke L. *o.s.b.* '86 (PAT)[D] Morristown, NJ Delbarton School; [M] Morristown, NJ St. Mary's Abbey.
Travers, Patrick J. '93 (JUN) Ketchikan, AK Holy Name; Chancellor; Diocesan Consultors; Judicial Vicar; Air Force Reserve Chaplains.
Travers, Patrick *ss.cc.* '62 (LA)[D] La Verne, CA Damien High School; [Q] La Verne, CA Congregation of the Sacred Hearts of Jesus and Mary.
Travers, Patrick (JUN) Port Chaplains.
Travers, Patrick (FBK) Tribunal; Adjutant Judicial Vicar.
Travers, Thomas *c.ss.r.* (NY)[EE] Esopus, NY Redemptorist Priests and Brothers C.Ss.R. (Province of Baltimore).
Traverso, Leonard '72 (SJ) San Jose, CA St. Patrick.
Travieso, Ernesto *s.j.* '73 (OM)[K] Omaha, NE Jesuit Community at Creighton University.
Travino, Alberto *m.s.f.* '03 (STL)[N] St. Louis, MO Little Sisters of the Poor, Home for the Aged.
Travis, Francis J. '81 (CHR) Pickens, SC Holy Cross.
Travis, Herbert A. '42 (BRK) Brooklyn, NY St. Anselm's Retired.
Travis, James M. *m.m.* '67 (NY)[EE] Maryknoll Maryknoll Fathers and Brothers.
Travnikar, Rock *o.f.m.* '76 (HT)[C] Schriever, LA Lumen Christi Retreat Center.
Trawick, Gregory G. '85 (OWN) Owensboro, KY St. Alphonsus; Judicial Vicar.
Traxl, William L. '60 (HRT) Glastonbury, CT St.

Dunstan; Marlborough, CT St. John Fisher.
Trayers, Kevin '52 (WCH) Cherryvale, KS St. Francis Xavier's Retired.
Traylor, William '76 (EVN) Evansville, IN St. Joseph; Evansville, IN St. Theresa; Personnel Board; Secretariat for Charismatic Renewal.
Traynor, Anthony '58 (SAC) Sacramento, CA Our Lady of Lourdes; Sacramento International Airport; Special Assignment.
Traynor, John J. '45 (RVC) Retired.
Traynor, Patrick *c.s.p.* '68 (NY) New York, NY St. Paul the Apostle.
Traynor, Scott (SFS) Brookings, SD St. Paul; [H] Brookings, SD Pius XII Student Center; Tribunal Judges.
Treacy, Jerome F. '61 (DET)[P] Hamtramck, MI St. Ladislaus.
Treacy, John R. *s.j.* '90 (SFR)[N] San Francisco, CA Jesuit Community at University of San Francisco.
Treacy, William '44 (SEA) Censores Librorum Retired.
Treanor, Boniface J. *o.s.b.* '56 (NEW)[N] Newark, NJ Newark Abbey.
Trebtoske, Everett '59 (AUS) Wimberley, TX St. Mary.
Treglio, Vincent (PAT) Unassigned.
Trejo, Alejandro E. '03 (YAK) Sunnyside, WA St. Joseph's.
Trejo, Ramiro *o.f.m.cap.* '77 (CHI) Chicago, IL St. Clare of Montefalco.
Trela, Norman J. '66 (CHI) Chicago, IL St. Symphorosa and Seven Sons.
Trela, Tadeusz '82 (NEW) Irvington, NJ Sacred Heart of Jesus.
Treleaven, Michael *s.j.* '83 (SPK)[B] Spokane, WA Gonzaga University.
Treloar, Jack *s.j.* (OAK).
Treloar, John L. *s.j.* '70 (Wisconsin)[N] Berkeley, CA Jesuit Community at Jesuit School of Theology at Berkeley.
Tremari, Albert '03 (CHI) Chicago, IL St. John Cantius; [Q] Chicago, IL Society of Saint John Cantius.
Tremblay, Albert J. '97 (MAN) Belmont, NH St. Joseph.
Tremblay, Eugene *o.m.i.* '38 (STP).
Tremblay, Eugene *o.m.i.* '74 (BUF)[V] Buffalo, NY Holy Angels.
Tremblay, J. Normand '53 (WOR) Charlton City, MA St. Joseph's; Southern Worcester County District Council.
Tremblay, Jean A. '54 (MAN) Retired.
Tremblay, Marc P. '80 (FR) Somerset, MA St. Patrick's.
Tremblay, Nellis '54 (ALB) Retired.
Trembloy, Albert J. (MAN) Council of Priests.
Tremie, Eugene R. '71 (LAF) Opelousas, LA St. Landry.
Treml, Richard L. '99 (DET) North Branch, MI St. Mary's Burnside; North Branch, MI SS. Peter and Paul.
Tremmal, Benjamin *o.s.b.* '66 (KCK)[H] Atchison, KS St. Benedict's Abbey.
Tremmel, Benjamin *o.s.b.* '66 (KCK) Effingham, KS St. Ann's.
Tremonte, Pasquale *c.ss.r.* '81 (WIL) Seaford, DE Our Lady of Lourdes.
Tremonti, Joseph B. '41 (CHI)[N] Kankakee, IL.
Tremonti, Joseph *c.s.v.* '41 (JOL) Kankakee, IL St. Patrick; [K] Bourbonnais, IL Provena Our Lady of Victory.
Trempe, James F. '96 (LC) Plover, WI St. Bronislava.
Trench, Edmond J. '57 (RVC) Southampton, NY Sacred Hearts of Jesus and Mary; Procurator & Advocates; Associate Vocation Directors Retired.
Trench, Edmond J. (RVC) Senate of Priests (Presbyteral Council/College of Consultors).
Trenchera, Manuel '80 (AGN) Inarajan, GU San Isidro; Agana, GU Nuestra Senora de Las Aquas; [H] Agana, GU Our Lady of the Waters House of Prayer.
Trenchs, Juan *sch.p.* '40 (LA)[Q] Los Angeles, CA Piarist Fathers.
Trenier, Anthony S. '66 (MIL)[X] Milwaukee, WI Archdiocesan Marian Shrine.
Trenor, Edward F. '58 (COL) Columbus, OH Christ the King; Regency Manor; Diocesan Judges; Building Commission; Diocesan Retirement Plans for Priests, Lay Employees and Lay Teachers.
Trenor, Edward (COL) Diocesan Finance Council.
Trent, James F. '62 (DET) On Duty Outside the Archdiocese.
Trent, James '62 (DET) Fortuna, CA St. Joseph.
Treppa, Terence '67 (DET) Westland, MI St. Richard.
Trese, John A. '48 (DET) Retired.
Tressic, David L. '96 (ALB) Gloversville, NY Sacred Heart; Leave of Absence.
Tressler, David L. '85 (SCR) Scranton, PA St. Patrick's; [D] Wilkes–Barre, PA Bishop Hoban High School.
Treston, James A. '60 (ALN) Sinking Spring, PA St. Ignatius Loyola.
Treston, Kevin *o.f.m.* '81 (WDC)[M] Washington, DC Commissariat of the Holy Land, Franciscan Monastery – Mount St. Sepulchre.
Trevino, Raciel '03 (PMB) West Palm Beach, FL St. Juliana.
Trevizo, Raul P. '88 (TUC) Tucson, AZ St. John the Evangelist.
Trevizo, Raul (TUC) Diocesan Consultors; Council of Priests; All Vicars Forane.
Trexler, Donald '98 (GBG) Leckrone, PA Our Lady of Perpetual Help (St. Mary); Adah, PA St. Albert.
Treyes, Reynaldo *c.i.c.m.* '78 (JOL) Woodridge, IL St. Scholastica.
Trezza, Richard *o.f.m.* '87 (NY) New York, NY Holy Name of Jesus.
Tri–Pham, Joseptan (BRK)[U] Vietnamese Apostolate.
Triano, Joseph A. *s.s.p.* '59 (DET)[K] Dearborn, MI Society of St. Paul.
Tribuiani, Raymond F. '73 (PH) Oreland, PA Holy Martyrs.
Trick, James F. '60 (CIN) Retired.
Triggs, Thomas J. '75 (TR) Cinnaminson, NJ St. Charles Borromeo.
Trigilio, John P. '88 (HBG) Marysville, PA Our Lady of Good Counsel.
Trigueros, Raul '69 (ELP) El Paso, TX Cristo Rey Church; St. Matthew; Priests' Personnel Advisory Committee; Catholic Communications Ministry.
Trimaglio, John *c.s.j.* '68 (LA)[Q] Los Angeles, CA Congregation of St. Joseph Casa Nazareth.
Trimbur, John '74 (Y) Absent on Leave.
Trimbur, Lee Francis '54 (LEX) Retired.
Trinchard, Paul '66 (NO) Retired.
Trindade, Leonard J. '87 (FRS) Gustine, CA Our Lady of Miracles.
Tringhese, James D. '74 (GBG) Trafford, PA St. Regis.
Trinh, Dominic Huy The *o.p.* '75 (GAL) Houston, TX Our Lady of Lavang Church.
Trinh, Hoang *o.f.m.* '01 (ORG) San Francisco, CA St. Boniface.
Trinh, Joseph T. '91 (PH) Philadelphia, PA St. Helena.
Trinh, Joseph Truong (BLX) Presbyteral Council; Pass Christian, MS St. Paul.
Trinh, Loc '92 (GR) Newaygo, MI St. Bartholomew's.
Trinh, Paul '90 (CAM)[P] Berlin, NJ Mater Ecclesiae Chapel; On Sick Leave.
Trinh, Quan M. '02 (PH) Philadelphia, PA Holy Innocents.
Trinh, Thai Q. '90 (RIC) Graduate Studies.
Trinh, Thai '90 (AUS) Manor, TX St. Joseph's.
Trinidad, Mel *s.d.b.* '85 (LA)[W] Rosemead, CA St. Joseph's Salesian Youth Renewal Center.
Trinidad, Miguel (SJN) Subcommission for Sacred Music.
Trinidad, Nelson '86 (LA) Canoga Park, CA Our Lady of the Valley.
Trinidad–Fonseca, Miguel Angel (SJN) Bayamon, PR Nuestra Senora del Rosario; Vicar for Youth; Youth Ministries.
Trinidade, Lawry *s.j.* '95 (BAL)[S] Baltimore, MD Blessed Alberto Hurtado, S.J. Jesuit Community.
Trinity, Bernard J. '54 (PH) Havertown, PA St. Denis Retired.
Trinka, Joseph C. '59 (SUP) Clear Lake, WI St. John.
Trinkle, Clarence M. '92 (ARL) Retired.
Tripi, Ronald *c.s.c.* '62 (FTW) South Bend, IN Christ the King.
Tripodi, Frank J. '88 (RCK) Absent on Leave.
Tripole, Martin R. *s.j.* '67 (PH)[AA] Loyola Center and Manresa Hall.
Trippel, Edward G. '55 (CIN) Cincinnati, OH Annunciation of the Blessed Virgin Mary Retired.
Trippel, Jack '95 (LFT) Lafayette, IN St. Lawrence.
Trisco, Robert F. '54 (CHI) On Duty Outside the Archdiocese; [C] Catholic University of America, The.
Trivino, Cristian M. '96 (RCK) Aurora, IL St. Nicholas.
Trivison, Louis J. '48 (CLV) Solon, OH Resurrection of Our Lord Retired.
Trocha, Lukasz Pawel (BRK) Ridgewood, NY St. Matthias.
Troche, Sigfrido *m.ss.cc.* '98 (HBG) Fairfield, PA St. Rita; Fairfield, PA Immaculate Conception of the Blessed Virgin Mary.
Trocinski, LaVern E. (WIN) Priests' Pension Board.
Trocinski, LaVern F. '60 (WIN) Retired.
Troha, Michael J. '80 (CLV) Cleveland, OH St. Rose of Lima; Defenders of the Bond; Translators.
Troiano, Leonard F. '79 (TR) Lavallette, NJ St. Bonaventure.
Troiano, Louis *o.f.m.* '57 (NY)[EE] New York, NY Padua Friary.
Trojcak, Ronald '62 (SFD) Special or Other Diocesan Assignment.
Trombetta, Jonah P. *o.s.b.* '79 (BO)[V] Hingham, MA Glastonbury Abbey.
Trombetta, Paul N. '79 (BRK) Released from Diocesan Assignment.
Troncale, F. Charles '65 (MOB) Montgomery, AL Church of the Holy Spirit; Regional Episcopal Vicars; Catholic Housing Authority of Montgomery, Inc.; Ex Officio Members.
Trong, John T.B. '71 (ARL) Springfield, VA St. Bernadette's.
Trong, Joseph '46 (SB) Retired.
Trong, Joseph (LAV) Las Vegas, NV Guardian Angel Cathedral.
Trong Dinh Hoang, Louis '95 (DOD) On Duty Outside the Diocese.
Trosch, David '82 (MOB) On Leave from the Archdiocese.
Troska, Llewelyn J. '86 (CR) Leave of Absence.
Trosley, Anthony J. '78 (PEO) Carthage, IL Immaculate Conception.
Trotta, Louis P. *c.m.* '52 (BUF)[O] Niagara University, NY Vincentian Community at Niagara University; [C] Niagara University, NY Niagara University.
Troug, Peter '99 (PMB) Boynton Beach, FL St. Thomas More.
Trouille, Alan P. '97 (LKC) Lake Charles, LA Our Lady of Good Counsel; [F] Lake Charles, LA Catholic Student Center.
Trout, Richard W. '85 (ORL) Sanford, FL All Souls.
Trout, Richard (ORL) Members.
Troutman, Richard C. (TUC) All Vicars Forane.
Troutman, Richard E. '68 (TUC) Tucson, AZ Saint Odilia; Vicars Forane.
Troutman, Richard (TUC) Council of Priests; Members.
Trovato, Joseph A. *c.s.b.* '56 (ROC) Rochester, NY Christ the King.
Troxell, Christopher '92 (LA) Paramount, CA Our Lady of the Rosary.
Troy, Leander *o.carm.* '42 (CHI)[D] Chicago, IL; [N] Chicago, IL Carmelite Priory of St. Cyril.
Trucksis, Fred E. '64 (Y) Warren, OH St. Joseph.
Trudeau, Marc V. '91 (LA) Santa Fe Springs, CA St. Pius X.
Trudel, Lionel G. *m.m.* '56 (NY).
True, David '88 (OKL)[EE] Absent on Sick Leave.
True, Isaac *o.s.b.* '66 (KC)[A] Conception, MO Conception Seminary College; [J] Kansas City, MO.
Truhan, Luke *o.c.s.o.* '82 (WOR)[A] Spencer, MA St. Joseph's Abbey School of Theology and Institute of Monastic Studies; [O] Spencer, MA St. Joseph's Abbey.
Truilzi, Daniel *s.m.* '81 (FWT) Denton, TX St. Mark.
Trujillo, Amando *t.o.r.* (SAT) Archdiocesan Presbyteral Council.
Trujillo, Carlos B. '76 (PBL) Absent on Leave.
Trujillo, Daniel '53 (SJN) Bayamon, PR Santa Elena.
Trujillo, David (SCL) Waite Park, MN St. Joseph's; Brown's Valley, MN St. Anthony's; Wheaton, MN St. Peter's; Wheaton, MN Ave Maria.
Trujillo, Eloy *o.r.c.* '89 (SB) Corona, CA St. Edward.
Trujillo, Ivan R. '85 (BUF) Erie County Holding Center; Attica Correctional Facility; Batavia, NY St. Mary.
Trujillo, Teofilo *o.f.m.* '89 (CHR) North Augusta, SC Our Lady of Peace.
Trujillo, Vincent *o.s.b.* '82 (P) Gervais, OR Sacred Heart–St. Louis; [L] St. Benedict, OR Mt. Angel Abbey.
Trujillo–Cano, Amando *t.o.r.* '88 (SAT) San Antonio, TX St. Leonard's.
Trujillo–Cano, Amando *t.o.r.* (SAT) In Metropolitan Area.
Trujillo–Luna, Jesus D. '98 (ATL) Alpharetta, GA St. Thomas Aquinas.
Trujillo–Mejia, Daniel (SJN) Bayamon.
Trull, Jason '02 (STA) Jacksonville, FL Blessed Trinity; Presbyteral Council.
Trung, Nguyen Dinh '03 (LA)[Q] Houston, TX.
Trunk, Vincent E. *c.m.* '52 (PH)[AA] St. Catherine Infirmary.
Truong, James Thuc Van *o.s.b.* '62 (SPC)[E] Carthage, MO Congregation of the Mother Coredemptrix, United States Assumption Province.
Trupia, Robert C. '73 (TUC) Administrative Leave of Absence.
Trupkovich, Joseph V. '97 (GBG) Leechburg, PA Christ The King.
Trupkovich, Thomas S. '97 (GBG) Herminie, PA St. Edward.
Trussel, Christopher '92 (SCL) Special Assignment; [C] St. Cloud, MN Cathedral High and John XXIII Middle School.
Trutter, Carl B. *o.p.* '60 (NO) New Orleans, LA St. Anthony of Padua; New Orleans, LA St. Thomas More; New Orleans, LA Tulane–Newcomb.
Trzeciakowski, Edward J. '55 (PIT)[N] Pittsburgh, PA St. John Vianney Manor Retired.
Trzecieski, Stephen P. *c.m.* '60 (BAL) Emmitsburg, MD St. Joseph; [S] Emmitsburg, MD Vincentian House.
Trzil, Louis J. '50 (DUB) Lansing, IA Immaculate Conception; Lansing, IA St. Pius; Lansing, IA St. Ann–St. Joseph.
Tsang, Peter '59 (LA) Retired.
Tsau, Paul '64 (WDC) Rockville, MD Our Lady of China.
Tsau, Paul (BAL)[M] Baltimore, MD St. Agnes Health-Care, Inc..
Tschakert, Gregory '82 (SFS) Aberdeen, SD St. Mary.
Tschakert, Gregory (SFS) Judicial Vicar; Defender of the Matrimonial Bond.
Tscherne, David D. '77 (TOL) Defiance, OH Immaculate Conception; Defiance, OH St. Michael; Defiance, OH St. Stephen.
Tseu, Andrew S. '56 (LA) Pomona, CA St. Madeleine Retired.
Tshibambe, Henri '81 (DEN) Louisville, CO St. Louis.
Tsiquaye, Paschal (NEW) Hohokus, NJ St. Luke's.

Tu, Raymond '95 (KC) Kansas City, MO Holy Cross; Kansas City, MO Church of the Holy Martyrs.
Tuan, Bui Quang *c.ss.r.* '96 (LA)[Q] Irving, TX.
Tuan, Camillus M. Nguyen Duc *c.m.c.* '84 (SPC)[E] Carthage, MO Congregation of the Mother Coredemptrix, United States Assumption Province.
Tubbs, Leo *o.p.* '66 (OAK)[N] Oakland, CA Dominican Order, Siena House.
Tubridy, James J. '53 (NY) Apostleship of Prayer Retired.
Tucceri, Robert A. '79 (TOL) Health Leave; [I] Oregon, OH Sacred Heart Home.
Tucci, Bruno M. '71 (ALN) Retired.
Tucci, Italo '48 (DET) Retired.
Tucker, James A. '01 (ARL) Woodbridge, VA Our Lady of Angels; Advocates.
Tucker, Lawrence E. *s.o.l.t.* '97 (CC)[G] Robstown, TX Society of Our Lady of the Most Holy Trinity.
Tucker, Mark E. *c.ss.r.* '89 (WDC) Silver Spring, MD St. John the Evangelist; Judges.
Tucker, Patrick M. '74 (CHI) Forest Park, IL St. Bernardine.
Tucker, Richard '58 (SY) Retired.
Tucker, Robert F. '70 (HRT) Litchfield, CT St. Anthony's; Special and other Archdiocesan Assignment; Auditors (Part–time Case Instructors); Deans; Office of Ministry for Priests.
Tucker, Robert G. '89 (LIN) Lincoln, NE Cathedral of the Risen Christ.
Tucker, Robert *s.c.j.* '82 (GAL) Houston, TX St. Matthew the Evangelist.
Tucker, Thomas J. *o.s.f.s.* '66 (WIL)[B] Wilmington, DE Salesianum School.
Tueth, Michael V. *s.j.* '71 (NY)[EE] New York, NY Xavier Jesuit Community.
Tuffour, Louis '86 (DET)[H] Livonia, MI St. Mary Hospital.
Tufts, Donn '80 (GR) Grand Rapids, MI Immaculate Heart of Mary.
Tugwell, Michael '75 (PT) Tallahassee, FL Co–Cathedral of St. Thomas More; Priests' Pension Plan, Board for.
Tuipupotu, Tuakapaw '97 (BO)[V] Boston, MA Marist Fathers of Our Lady of Victories (Boston Prov.).
Tuisea, Setefano '83 (SPP) Pago Pago, AS Co–Cathedral of St. Joseph the Worker; Diocesan Consultors.
Tuite, Howard A. '54 (CHI) Retired.
Tuite, Thomas P. '86 (RVC) Hicksville, NY Our Lady of Mercy.
Tulko, Richard *o.f.m.* (GB)[I] Pulaski, WI Friary.
Tull, Terry *c.ss.r.* '85 (SJN) San Juan, PR San Agustin.
Tuller, John '84 (CHL) Retired.
Tulley, Thomas '85 (R) Special Assignment.
Tully, Eugene D. '68 (BO) Billerica, MA St. Theresa of Lisieux.
Tully, Eugene M. '73 (PH) Philadelphia, PA St. Callistus.
Tully, Gerard P. *c.s.p.* '94 (TUC).
Tully, Henry F. '77 (IND)[EE] Indianapolis, IN St. Mark the Evangelist.
Tully, Henry (IND) Priests' Personnel Board.
Tully, James J. '44 (BRK) Retired.
Tully, John P. '69 (Y) Hanoverton, OH St. Philip Neri; Hanoverton, OH St. Patrick; Hanoverton, OH St. John.
Tully, Ronald J. '66 (PAT) Dover, NJ Sacred Heart.
Tuma, Anthony F. '31 (OM) Retired.
Tumicki, Ted F. (NOR) Diocesan Commission for Ecumenical and Interreligious Affairs; Judges; Delegate for Safe Environments.
Tumicki, Ted '97 (NOR) On Duty Outside the Diocese.
Tumino, Frank (BRK) Bishop Daily—.
Tumminelli, Lawrence *b.s.o.* '96 (NTN) Methuen, MA Basilian Salvatorian Order.
Tumosa, John Joseph '69 (CAM) Newfield, NJ St. Rose of Lima.
Tumulty, Matt *o.f.m.* '59 (P)[Q] Portland, OR Franciscan Ministry Network.
Tumulty, Michael J. *c.m.* '51 (BUF)[O] Niagara University, NY Vincentian Community at Niagara University.
Tung Nguyen, Paul V. '79 (NO)[C] Chalmette, LA Prince of Peace.
Tungol, Eugene D. '75 (SFR) South San Francisco, CA St. Augustine; College of Consultors.
Tunink, Wilfrid *o.s.b.* '45 (SFE)[I] Pecos, NM Our Lady of Guadalupe Abbey; [K] Pecos, NM Our Lady of Guadalupe Olivetan Benedictine Abbey.
Tunney, Ken '63 (ALB) Schenectady, NY St. John the Baptist.
Tunney, Michael F. *s.j.* '88 (BUF)[O] Buffalo, NY Canisius Jesuit Community.
Tunney, Thomas P. *c.s.sp.* '60 (NY) New York, NY St. Mark the Evangelist.
Tunny, Kenneth J. '63 (ALB) Schenectady, NY St. Paul the Apostle; Special Assignment.
Tuoc, Ignatius '71 (SP) Tampa, FL Epiphany.
Tuohey, John F. '81 (SPR) On Duty Outside the Diocese.
Tuohy, Edward *s.v.d.* '58 (BO)[V] Duxbury, MA Society of the Divine Word.
Tuohy, Francis R. '61 (IND) Indianapolis, IN Christ The King; Board of Consultors; Council of Priests.
Tuohy, Francis (IND) Archdiocesan Judges.
Tuong, Hoang Minh '01 (NO) Chalmette, LA St. Mark.
Tuozzolo, Leonard *c.s.sp.* '59 (ARL) Arlington, VA Our Lady, Queen of Peace.
Tupa, Jerome *o.s.b.* '82 (SCL)[I] Collegeville, MN St. John's Abbey, of the Order of St. Benedict.
Tupa, Michael J. '91 (SUP) Webster, WI Sacred Hearts of Jesus and Mary; Webster, WI Our Lady of Perpetual Help; Webster, WI St. John the Baptist.
Tupper, Dale E. '67 (WIN) Austin, MN Queen of Angels; Austin, MN Our Lady of Loretto.
Tuptynski, Marek S. '97 (FR) Fall River, MA Notre Dame de Lourdes; Diocesan Department of Pastoral Care for the Sick.
Turati, Fortunato *s.c.* '67 (LAN) Camp Cassidy Lake; [E] Chelsea, MI St. Louis Center for Exceptional Children & Adults.
Turbek, Aloysius *s.v.d.* '40 (CHI)[B] Techny, IL Divine Word Residence.
Turcich, Donald *o.s.a.* (KAL) Diocesan Consultors; Presbyteral Council.
Turcich, Ronald R. *o.s.a.* '58 (KAL) Douglas, MI St. Peter; [E] Douglas, MI Order of St. Augustine.
Turco, Alfredo *s.x.* '88 (MIL)[B] Franklin, WI Xaverian Missionary Fathers College Seminary.
Turczany, Christopher J. '83 (BRK) Flushing, NY St. Mel.
Turdy, Julius '73 (LIN) Crete, NE Sacred Heart.
Turek, Michael E. '76 (STL) St. Louis, MO St. Joan of Arc.
Turek, Ronald J. '74 (CLV) Orrville, OH St. Agnes.
Tureman, Thomas *s.d.s.* '88 (SAC) Orangevale, CA Divine Savior.
Turgeon, Armand A. '43 (MAN) Retired.
Turi, John J. '55 (SCR) Matamoras, PA St. Joseph's; Diocesan Consultors; Presbyteral Council.
Turillo, B. Samuel '46 (PRO) Retired.
Turk, Damian C. *o.c.s.o.* '69 (ATL)[K] Conyers, GA The Monastery of the Holy Spirit.
Turk, E. Matthew *s.j.* '62 (MO) Miami, FL Gesu.
Turley, Sean F. '71 (WIL) On Duty Outside the Diocese.
Turlo, Walter J. '70 (CHI) Bridgeview, IL St. Fabian.
Turnacliff, Michael M. *s.j.* '02 (SFR)[N] Berkeley, CA Jesuit Community at Jesuit School of Theology at Berkeley San Francisco, CA St. Agnes.
Turnbull, John *o.f.m.* '55 (IND) Oldenburg, IN Holy Family; [L] Oldenburg, IN Motherhouse of the Congregation of the Sisters of the Third Order of St. Francis.
Turnbull, Paul E. (ALT) Johnstown Deanery; Johnstown, PA St. Michael's; Johnstown, PA Our Mother of Sorrows.
Turnbull, William '67 (ALB) Stillwater, NY St. Peter the Apostle.
Turner, Bernard '77 (ALB) Schenectady, NY St. John the Baptist.
Turner, Daniel *c.p.* (CHI)[N] Chicago, IL Passionist Community–CTU.
Turner, David *o.s.b.* '63 (JOL)[A] Lisle, IL Benedictine University; [L] Lisle, IL St. Procopius Abbey.
Turner, Edward '66 (HON) Leave of Absence Retired.
Turner, George F. '60 (LR) Retired.
Turner, James M. *o.s.f.s.* '81 (WIL) Wilmington, DE St. Anthony of Padua.
Turner, James '84 (PHX) Glendale, AZ St. Thomas More.
Turner, Jerome R. '64 (MAD) Retired.
Turner, Paul '79 (KC) Cameron, MO St. Munchin.
Turner, Richard M. '80 (SPR) Chicopee, MA St. Patrick's.
Turner, Richard W. '91 (R) Retired.
Turner, Robert D. '82 (SPK) On Duty Outside the Diocese.
Turner, Robert D. '88 (MIL) Milwaukee, WI Blessed Sacrament.
Turner, Robert G. '59 (PIT) West Mifflin, PA Resurrection.
Turner, Robert L. *s.s.* '62 (BAL)[O] Baltimore, MD St. Charles Villa.
Turner, Robert '62 (GR) On Duty Outside the Diocese.
Turner, Robert '82 (HEL)[A] Helena, MT Carroll College; [B] Helena, MT Carroll College.
Turner, Robert '88 (GLP) On Duty Outside of Diocese.
Turner, Thomas W. '82 (KC)[L] Kansas City, MO Bishop Sullivan Center.
Turner, William J. '75 (IND) Guilford, IN St. Paul; Guilford, IN St. Martin.
Turner, William '79 (LAN) Chelsea, MI St. Mary; Camp Cassidy Lake.
Turon, Louis Luke *o.p.* '55 (COL) Zanesville, OH St. Thomas Aquinas.
Turro, James C. '48 (NEW) Park Ridge, NJ Our Lady of Mercy; [B] School of Diplomacy and Intl. Rels. Retired.
Turro, James '48 (NOR)[A] Cromwell, CT Holy Apostles College and Seminary.
Turyk, Ivan '03 (PHU) Philadelphia, PA Immaculate Conception of Blessed Virgin Mary, Cathedral.
Tuscan, Joseph *o.f.m.cap.* '97 (PH) Philadelphia, PA St. John the Evangelist.
Tushar, David '76 (DUL) Carlton, MN St. Francis; Carlton, MN SS. Mary & Joseph; Priests' Pension Board.
Tusingwire, Thomas (FTW)[A] Notre Dame, IN Moreau Seminary.
Tusky, Richard J. '73 (PIT) Burgettstown, PA Our Lady of Lourdes.
Tustin, Joseph E. *o.s.f.s.* '67 (CHL) Kernersville, NC Holy Cross.
Tutas, Stephen R. *s.m.* '53 (HON)[G] Wailuku, HI Wailuku Marianist Community.
Tutone, John J. '71 (RVC) Island Park, NY Sacred Heart; Judges for Interdiocesan Tribunal.
Tuttle, Arthur *c.ss.r.* '65 (ALB) Saratoga Springs, NY St. Clement.
Tuttle, Charles W. '74 (BEL) Beckemeyer, IL St. Anthony; Breese, IL St. Augustine; [A] Breese, IL Mater Dei High School.
Tuttle, Patrick E. *o.f.m.* '94 (BUF)[O] St. Bonaventure, NY St. Bonaventure Friary; [R] St. Bonaventure, NY St. Bonaventure University; [C] St. Bonaventure, NY Friar Community.
Tuttle, Richard '76 (STU) Steubenville, OH Holy Family.
Tuurosong, Matthew '92 (LA) Santa Monica, CA St. Monica.
Tuxbury, James *o.f.m.* '63 (ALB)[A] Catskill, NY St. Anthony Friary.
Tuyn, William R. '62 (BUF) North Evans, NY St. Vincent.
Tuzeneu, Kenard J. '79 (TR) Barnegat, NJ St. Mary; Diocesan Consultors; Secretary.
Tuzik, Robert '73 (CHI) Chicago, IL St. Gall; Divine Worship, Office for.
Tvan, Danh Cong '03 (NY)[F] New Rochelle, NY Salesian High School.
Tvrdik, Roy *s.m.m.* '93 (BRK)[V] Ozone Park, NY Montfort Missionaries Provincialate (Missionaries of the Company of Mary) – Formation Community.
Tvrdik, Roy *s.m.m.* (RVC)[P] Old Westbury, NY Interfaith Chaplaincy.
Tvrdy, Julius (LIN) Apostolate to the Spanish Speaking.
Twaddell, Gerald E. '67 (COV) Camp Springs, KY St. Joseph; Diocesan Consultors; Deans.
Twadell, Gerald E. (COV) Defenders of the Bond.
Twardzik, Francis M. *s.d.b.* '70 (PSC) Scranton, PA St. Mary's; Syncellus; Eparchial College of Consultors; Ex Officio Members.
Twardzik, Michael W.T. '70 (SPR) North Adams, MA Notre Dame; North Adams, MA Our Lady of Mercy; North Adams, MA Our Lady of Mercy Shrine; North Adams, MA St. Francis.
Twarog, Jerome *c.r.* '82 (CHI) Skokie, IL St. Peter.
Twarog, Theodore S. '50 (SD) Retired.
Twele, Robert *o.f.m.conv.* '81 (BAL)[S] Ellicott City, MD Order of Friars Minor Conventual.
Twiddy, Paul '52 (WDC) Retired.
Twigg–Porter, George M. *s.j.* '53 (SFR) San Francisco Fire Department; [K] San Francisco, CA Home for the Aged of the Little Sisters of the Poor; [S] San Francisco, CA Apostleship of Prayer.
Twiggs, Matthew J. '73 (PAT) Stockholm, NJ St. John Vianney.
Twohig, Christopher T. '50 (WDC) On Duty Outside the Archdiocese.
Twohig, Michael J. '83 (SPR) West Springfield, MA Immaculate Conception; West Springfield, MA St. Louis de France.
Twohig, Richard H. *s.j.* '65 (DET)[T] Jesuit International Missions; [E] Detroit, MI University of Detroit Jesuit High School and Academy; [K] Detroit, MI Jesuit Provincial Office–Detroit Province of the Society of Jesus.
Twohy, Patrick *s.j.* '70 (SEA) LaConner, WA St. Paul; Tulalip, WA Tulalip Indian Reservation, St. Anne.
Twomey, Dermot J. *s.c.j.* '76 (JKS) Walls, MS Sacred Heart; [F] Nesbit, MS St. Michael Community House; [I] Senatobia, MS Northwest Mississippi Community College Newman Center.
Twomey, Dermot *s.c.j.* '76 (JKS) Senatobia, MS St. Gregory the Great.
Twomey, Gerald S. '81 (RVC) Brentwood, NY St. Anne's.
Twomey, John E. '52 (MIL) Retired.
Twomey, Simon D. '70 (SAC) Grass Valley, CA St. Patrick.
Twomey, Simon (SAC) Council of Priests.
Twomey, Thomas '65 (NOR) Absent on Leave.
Twum–Obuor, Augustine '91 (NY) Hyde Park, NY Regina Coeli.
Ty, Roch Keresz '60 (DAL)[B] University of Dallas.
Tyburski, Zbigniew '73 (PAT) Boonton, NJ SS. Cyril and Methodius.
Tydlacka, George '44 (AUS) Retired.
Tyhovych, Ivan (STF) Army Reserve Chaplains.
Tykhovych, Ivan '94 (STF) Military Services.
Tykhovytch, Ivan '94 (STF) Brooklyn, NY Holy Ghost.

Tyl, Albert '54 (FWT) Fort Worth, TX St. Patrick Cathedral.
Tylenda, Joseph N. *s.j.* '60 (WDC)[O] Scranton, PA Marian Convent, Marywood; [C] Scranton, PA The University of Scranton.
Tyler, Bernard '61 (LAN) Retired.
Tyler, Thomas L. '79 (E) North East, PA St. Gregory Thaumaturgus.
Tylka, Louis J. '96 (CHI) Winnetka, IL SS. Faith, Hope and Charity.
Tyman, Gary L. '86 (ROC) Rochester, NY Holy Rosary; Rochester, NY Most Precious Blood.
Tyminski, Joseph *s.d.b.* '49 (COL)[H] Columbus, OH Salesian Residence.
Tymoszuk, Leslaw P. '97 (TR) Trenton, NJ Holy Cross.
Tynan, Desmond A. '67 (BO) Society of St. James the Apostle.
Tynan, Joseph F. *o.c.s.o.* '47 (ATL)[K] Conyers, GA The Monastery of the Holy Spirit.
Tynski, Robert M. '89 (TR) Atlantic Highlands, NJ St. Agnes.
Tyrasinski, Lucius *o.s.p.* '56 (NY) New York, NY St. Stanislaus.
Tyrell, Patrick *s.j.* '67 (CHI) Glenview, IL Our Lady of Perpetual Help.
Tyrrell, Anthony '95 (PCE) On Duty Outside the Diocese.
Tyrrell, Bernard J. *s.j.* '65 (SPK)[B] Spokane, WA Gonzaga University.
Tyrrell, Joseph J. '89 (NY) New York, NY Our Lady of Lourdes.
Tyrrell, Michael A. *s.j.* '76 (SEA) Kent, WA Holy Spirit Parish; [C] Tacoma, WA Bellarmine Preparatory School.
Tyrrell, Michael *s.j.* (SEA) Presbyteral Council.
Tyrrell, Robert D. '67 (BO) Weston, MA St. Julia; Health Leave.
Tyson, David T. *c.s.c.* '75 (FTW)[I] South Bend, IN Congregation of Holy Cross, Indiana Province, Provincial House.
Tyson, Joseph J. '89 (SEA) Seattle, WA St. Edward; Seattle, WA St. George; Seattle, WA St. Paul.
Tyson, Joseph V. *s.s.j.* '55 (LAF) Eunice, LA St. Mathilda.
Tyson, Michael *o.f.m.* '67 (NY) New York, NY Holy Name of Jesus.
Tywoniak, Robert F. '83 (MIA) Fort Lauderdale, FL St. George.
Tzanakas, George M. '62 (AUS) Retired.

U

Uba, Livinus (WH) Huntington, WV St. Peter Claver.
Ubalde, Ulysses L. '93 (NEW) Fort Lee, NJ Madonna; Navy Chaplains.
Ubalde, Ulyssesl '93 (NEW) Military Chaplains.
Ubel, John L. '89 (STP)[D] St. Paul, MN The Saint Thomas Academy; Presbyteral Council; [A] St. Paul, MN The Saint Paul Seminary.
Ucbaghiorghis, Teclezghi *o.cist.* '78 (TR)[M] Mount Laurel, NJ Cistercian Monastery of Our Lady of Fatima.
Udegbumam, Michael (SAN) Odessa, TX Holy Redeemer.
Udeze, Ambrose N. *m.s.p.* '53 (LAF) Lebeau, LA Immaculate Conception.
Udick, William S. *s.j.* '55 (DEN)[N] Denver, CO Xavier Jesuit Center.
Udo, Emmanuel '86 (MIL) Beaver Dam, WI St. Katharine Drexel.
Udogu, Anthony '95 (NEW) Hackensack, NJ Hackensack University Medical Center; Chaplains.
Udoh, Cletus *m.s.p.* '92 (AUS) Austin, TX Holy Cross; [G] Austin, TX Missionary of St. Paul, MSP.
Udovic, Edward R. *c.m.* '84 (CHI)[C] Chicago, IL De Paul University; [N] Chicago, IL Vincentian Community, Congregation of the Mission, Midwest Province.
Udulutsch, Robert *o.f.m.cap.* '56 (GB) Kaukauna, WI St. Mary of the Annunciation.
Uebler, Michael G. '82 (BUF) Tonawanda, NY St. Francis of Assisi.
Uecker, Joseph H. *c.pp.s.* '68 (SAN) Abilene, TX St. Francis of Assisi; Abilene, TX St. Vincent Pallotti.
Uehlein, Christopher *o.s.b.* '60 (SFS)[F] Marvin, SD Blue Cloud Abbey.
Uelese, Alefosio '02 (SPP) Pago Pago, AS Our Lady of Fatima.
Ufok–Udoekpo, Micael (RVC) Stony Brook, NY Stony Brook University Hospital.
Ufomadu, Charles '97 (LA) Culver City, CA St. Augustine.
Uftring, Richard A. '76 (BO) South Boston, MA Gate of Heaven; [AA] Boston, MA Our Lady of the Airways Chapel.
Uftring, Richard J. (BO) Airport Chaplaincy.
Ugaddan, Marcelino (SAT) San Antonio, TX Santo Nino de Cebu.
Ugbor, Leonard (BRK) Ridgewood, NY St. Aloysius; Presbyteral Council.
Ugdagandla, Maria J. Kumar '94 (OKL) Ponca City, OK Church of St. Mary.
Ugliano, Bruno A. *o.s.b.* '67 (TR)[S] Trenton, NJ Emmaus House, Rider University; [S] Hamilton Township, NJ Mercer County Community College.
Ugliano, Bruno A. *o.s.b.* '67 (PAT)[M] Morristown St. Mary's Abbey.
Uglietto, Peter J. '77 (BO)[A] Weston, MA Blessed John XXIII National Seminary.
Ugobueze, John B. '85 (ATL) Atlanta, GA Holy Cross.
Ugochukwu, Sebastian A. (MO).
Ugolik, Richard '54 (DET) Retired.
Ugwoji, Matthew (BRK) Brooklyn, NY St. Cecilia.
Ugwu, Stephen Chibunda '02 (LAF) Abbeville, LA St. Theresa of the Child Jesus.
Ugwuanya, Valentine C. '94 (NEW) Newark, NJ Blessed Sacrament/St. Charles Borromeo; Military Chaplains; Army Chaplains.
Ugwuegbu, Ambrose '87 (SAC) Carmichael, CA St. John the Evangelist; Council of Priests.
Ugwuozar, Felix (NEW) Orange, NJ Pope John Paul II Pavilion; Hospital Center at Orange; Pope John Paul II Pavilion.
Ugwuozor, Felix '95 (NEW) Orange, NJ Hospital Center at Orange.
Uhde, Peter M. (NEW) Army Chaplains.
Uhde, Peter '81 (OG) U.S. Army Headquarters; Fort Drum, NY U.S. Army Headquarters Fort Drum; Military Chaplains.
Uhen, Cletus V. '42 (MIL) Retired.
Uhen, Timothy J. '96 (MIL)[N] Brookfield, WI Prelature of the Holy Cross and Opus Dei..
Uhl, Anthony C. '68 (COS) Salida, CO St. Joseph Retired.
Uhl, Christopher *o.m.v.* '03 (SFD) Alton, IL St. Mary's.
Uhlenkott, Gary D. *s.j.* '80 (SPK)[B] Spokane, WA Gonzaga University.
Uhler, Carl A. '56 (CLV) West Salem, OH St. Stephen.
Uhlman, Laurence R. *t.o.r.* '90 (ALT)[F] Loretto, PA St. Bonaventure Friary.
Uhrig, A. Gregory '73 (MET) Edison, NJ St. Matthew.
Ukaegbu, Lloyd '62 (LA) Hacienda Heights, CA St. John Vianney.
Ukanide, Anietie Akama *m.s.p.* '91 (MOB) Mobile, AL St. Francis Xavier; Prichard, AL Our Mother of Mercy.
Uko, John '80 (NY) Bronx, NY St. Frances of Rome; [X] Bronx, NY Florence D'Urso Pavilion.
Uko, Joseph '81 (MIL) Wauwatosa, WI St. Jude the Apostle.
Ukomadu, Linus '90 (LR) Arkadelphia, AR St. Mary's; Malvern, AR St. John the Baptist; [J] Arkadelphia, AR Henderson State Teachers College and Ouchita Baptist University Campus Ministry.
Ukwe, Stan U. *o.p.* '94 (HBG) New Freedom, PA St. John the Baptist.
Ukwuegbu, Bernard (PH) Philadelphia, PA St. John the Evangelist.
Ulak, Robert T. '70 (NEW) Park Ridge, NJ Our Lady of Mercy.
Ulam, Richard *o.s.b.* '82 (PIT) Crabtree, PA St. Bartholomew.
Ulaszeski, Edward J. '52 (BUF) Retired.
Ulchack, Glenays (NOR) New London, CT Lawrence and Memorial Hospitals.
Ulincy, Andrew A. '66 (ALN) Reading, PA St. Paul.
Uline, Cyprian *o.f.m.conv.* '70 (LSC)[E] Mesilla Park, NM Holy Cross Retreat and Friary.
Ulko, John (NY) Our Lady of Mercy Medical Center.
Ullery, Kirk '65 (SFR) San Francisco, CA Our Lady of Lourdes.
Ulloa, Daniel *o.p.* '70 (NY) Yonkers, NY St. John the Baptist; St. Luke's Site.
Ulloa, Lourdes (MAN) Hispanic Apostolate.
Ullrich, David *o.m.i.* '71 (CHI)[X] Chicago, IL Oblates for International Pastoral aka Oblate International Pastoral Investment Trust.
Ullrich, David *o.m.i.* '71 (WDC)[M] Washington, DC Provincial Offices of the United States Province of the Missionary Oblates of Mary Immaculate; [M] Washington, DC Oblate Community.
Ullrich, John R. *o.f.m.* '76 (BO)[AA] Boston, MA St. Anthony Shrine; Brant Beach, NJ St. Francis of Assisi.
Ullrich, Mark C. '78 (STL) St. Louis, MO Our Lady of the Holy Cross; Deaneries/Deans; North.
Ullrich, Peter *o.s.b.* '87 (KC)[A] Conception, MO Conception Seminary College; [J] Kansas City, MO.
Ulm, John F. '58 (GAL) Houston, TX St. Maximilian Kolbe.
Ulman, Stanley A. '73 (DET) Hamtramck, MI St. Ladislaus; Archdiocesan Vicars.
Ulrich, Eugene P. '74 (BUF) Newman Club Chaplains; [R] Alfred, NY Campus Ministry; [R] Alfred, NY St. Jude's Chapel at Alfred University & Alfred State College; Alfred, NY SS. Brendan and Jude.
Ulrich, James E. '60 (CIN) Cincinnati, OH St. James of the Valley.
Ulrich, John *s.m.* '86 (PHX) Campus Ministry Department; [F] San Luis Obispo, CA Society of Mary (Marists)–S.M..
Ulrich, Steve '90 (OWN) Absent on Leave.
Ulrick, Stephen D. '82 (STP) Chanhassen, MN St. Hubert.
Ulshafer, Thomas R. *s.s.* '70 (BAL)[S] Baltimore, MD Sulpician Provincial House.
Ulshafer, Thomas *s.s.* '70 (WDC) On Duty Outside the Archdiocese.
Ulto, Victor '80 (PMB) Port St. Lucie, FL St. Bernadette.
Umagu, Alfred *m.s.p.* '92 (BEA) Beaumont, TX Blessed Sacrament.
Umberg, Andrew *s.t.l.* '91 (CIN)[B] Cincinnati, OH Mt. St. Mary's Seminary of the West; [B] Cincinnati, OH Mt. St. Mary's Seminary of the West.
Umberger, Patrick A. '80 (LC) Whitehall, WI St. Ansgar; Whitehall, WI St. John the Apostle.
Ume, Michael '93 (LA) Los Angeles, CA St. Brigid's.
Umhoefer, Stephen J. (MAD) Elected.
Umhoefer, Stephen '66 (MAD) Janesville, WI Nativity of St. Mary.
Umwech, Adalbert '90 (CI)[C] Tunnuk, Chuuk, FM Vicariate Residence.
Umwech, Adalbert '97 (CI) Assumption of the Blessed Virgin Mary.
Umwech, Adalbert (CI) Diocesan Consultors.
Underdahl, Mark J. '96 (STP) Bayport, MN St. Charles; Presbyteral Council.
Underwood, Gary E. '80 (TUC) On Duty Outside the Diocese; Air Force Chaplains.
Underwood, Joseph '63 (BIR) Retired.
Underwood, Scott J. *o.s.b.* '76 (NO)[P] St. Benedict, LA St. Joseph Abbey; [A] St. Benedict, LA St. Joseph Seminary College.
Ungashick, Thomas '76 (Y) Maximo, OH St. Joseph.
Unger, John M. '42 (PIT)[N] Pittsburgh, PA St. John Vianney Manor Retired.
Unger, John M. '65 (STL)[Q] St. Louis, MO School Sisters of Notre Dame; Warson Woods, MO Ste. Genevieve Du Bois.
Unger, Robert P. '99 (FAR) Park River, ND St. Patrick; Park River, ND St. Mary.
Unger, Steve (RVC) Stony Brook, NY Stony Brook University Hospital.
Unger, Todd '82 (BAK) Council of Priests and Diocesan Consultors; Western; Board of Education; Director of Catholic Hospitals; Health and Retirement Board; The Dalles, OR St. Peter's.
Ungerleider, David L. *s.j.* '77 (BAL)[S] San Ysidro, CA.
Universal, Patrick J. '75 (GLP) Quemado, NM Sacred Heart; Springerville, AZ St. Peter.
Unnerstal, Tobias '92 (WDC) Garrett Park, MD Holy Cross.
Unni, John J. '92 (BO) Boston, MA St. Ann.
Unsworth, John E. '76 (PRO) Riverside, RI St. Brendan; Deans.
Untereiner, Harry '72 (PSC) Special or Other Diocesan Assignment.
Unterreiner, James J. '70 (SPC) Ironton, MO Ste. Marie Du Lac; Region VI; Region VI; Diocesan Consultors; Presbyteral Council; Diocesan Council Of Catholic Women (DCCW).
Unverdorben, Ernest *o.c.d.* '66 (MIL)[O] Holy Hill, WI Discalced Carmelite Monastery – Holy Hill National Shrine of Mary Help of Christians.
Unverferth, Steven R. '89 (BEL) Leave of Absence.
Unz, Thomas E. '83 (CHI) Westchester, IL Divine Providence.
Uong, Luong *c.ss.r.* '95 (NO) New Orleans, LA St. Alphonsus; New Orleans, LA St. Mary's Assumption; New Orleans, LA St. Mary's Chapel.
Upah, William J. '98 (R) Henderson, NC St. James the Greater.
Upkong, Justin S. (CHR) Aiken, SC St. Gerard.
Uppani, Jose '81 (LR) Little Rock, AR Christ the King; Little Rock, AR Our Lady of the Holy Souls.
Uppena, James J. '68 (MAD) Milton, WI St. Mary.
Uppena, James (MAD) Elected.
Upson, Michael G. '76 (ROC) Rochester, NY Immaculate Conception.
Upson, Michael (ROC) Office Of Black Ministries.
Upton, Edward F. '69 (CHI) Orland Park, IL St. Francis of Assisi; Deans.
Upton, John '83 (GAL) Spring, TX Christ the Good Shepherd.
Ura, Yoshitaka *s.j.* (NY)[EE] New York, NY Xavier Jesuit Community.
Uralikunnel, George V. '67 (MO) Lamar, CO Syro–Malabar Catholic Mission; Dayton, OH.
Uram, Kenneth '59 (STU) Richmond, OH St. John Fisher.
Urarte, Carmelo '59 (ARE) Quebradillas, PR Sacred Heart; Diocesan Consultors; Priest's Senate (Consejo Presbiteral).
Urassa, Rogation (BAK) Boardman, OR Our Lady of Guadalupe.
Urba, James J. (DAV) Liturgical Commission.
Urbain, Joseph V. '32 (CIN) Retired.
Urban, Anthony M. '73 (SCR) Bear Creek Township, PA St. Elizabeth.
Urban, Carl A. '66 (ALB) Schenectady, NY Church of St. Adalbert.
Urban, Carl (ALB) Members.
Urban, Charles T. *o.praem.* '54 (PH)[AA] Paoli, PA Daylesford Abbey.

Urban, Joseph (NEW) Jersey City, NJ St. Anthony of Padua.
Urban, Lawrence *s.d.b.* '77 (SP)[E] Tampa, FL Mary Help of Christians School.
Urban, Lonnie A. '67 (AUS) Taylor, TX St. Mary's.
Urban, Lonnie (AUS) Presbyteral Council.
Urban, Peter '58 (DEN) Lafayette, CO Immaculate Conception.
Urban, Reginald A. '77 (GI) On Duty Outside the Diocese.
Urban, Reginald '77 (DOD) Great Bend, KS St. Patrick; Great Bend, KS St. Rose of Lima; Diocesan School Council.
Urban, Robert M. '60 (SUP) Retired.
Urban, Thomas '02 (DET) Grosse Pointe Farms, MI St. Paul Catholic Church.
Urbanek, Raymond J. '68 (LAN) Mount Morris, MI St. Mary.
Urbaniak, Andrzes *o.f.m.conv.* '98 (PAT) Clifton, NJ St. John Kanty.
Urbaniak, Bernard J. '68 (E) Erie, PA St. Stanislaus.
Urbaniak, Jan *c.m.* '71 (BRK) Brooklyn, NY St. Stanislaus Kostka.
Urbaniak, Lawrence M. '61 (RCK) Retired.
Urbaniak, Lucian '85 (SY) Utica, NY St. Mark.
Urbanic, James A. *c.pp.s.* '71 (KC)[A] Liberty, MO Society of the Precious Blood Provincial Offices; [J] Liberty, MO Precious Blood Society Provincial Office.
Urbanowski, Konrad *s.ch.* '43 (DET) Sterling Heights, MI Our Lady of Czestochowa.
Urbanski, Louis '64 (P) Aloha, OR St. Elizabeth Ann Seton; Area Vicars.
Urbonas, Ignatius L. '35 (GRY) Lemont, IL Blessed Jurgis Matulaitis Retired.
Urcia, Daniel '89 (SJ) Santa Clara, CA St. Clare.
Urdiain, Angelo *c.r.* '66 (DEN)[A] Denver, CO St. Andrew's Theatine Religious House.
Ureel, Wayne G. '90 (DET) Dryden, MI St. Cornelius; Archdiocesan Vicars.
Urell, John '78 (ORG) Orange, CA St. Norbert.
Urell, John (ORG) Consultors.
Urell, John (ORG) Diocesan Finance Council.
Urell, John (ORG) Vicar General.
Urell, John (ORG) Council of Priests.
Urell, John (ORG) Moderator of the Curia.
Urell, John (ORG) Land Advisory Board.
Urell, John (ORG) Clergy Personnel Board.
Urell, John (ORG) Diocesan Construction Board.
Urian, Thomas R. '90 (PH) Secane, PA Our Lady of Fatima; [D] Springfield, PA Cardinal O'Hara High School.
Uribe, Arturo *c.ss.r.* '95 (LA) Whittier, CA St. Mary of the Assumption; [Q] Whittier, CA Redemptorists of Whittier.
Uribe, Saul de Jesus '80 (ELP) El Paso, TX Sts. Peter and Paul.
Urizalqui, Richard '77 (FRS) Tulare, CA St. Aloysius.
Urizalqui, Richard (FRS) Advocates.
Urlage, Robert J. '58 (COV) Retired.
Urmston, Benjamin J. *s.j.* '59 (CIN)[M] Cincinnati, OH Jesuit Community at Xavier University.
Urnick, Charles B. '74 (NEW) Norwood, NJ Immaculate Conception; Air Force Reserve Chaplains.
Uroda, Stanley *s.v.d.* '74 (WH) Gary, WV Our Lady of Victory; Powhatan, WV Sacred Heart; War, WV Christ the King; Welch, WV St. Peter.
Urrea, Miguel A. '87 (SB) Redlands, CA St. Mary.
Urrego, Luis '01 (SAC) Fairfield, CA Holy Spirit.
Urriza, Luis *o.s.a.* '44 (BEA) Beaumont, TX Cristo Rey.
Urrutigoity, Carlos '91 (SCR)[M] Shohola, PA Society of Saint John; Unassigned or Leave of Absence.
Urtubia, Jorge *c.s.c.* '95 (FTW)[I] Congregacion de Santa Cruz.
Urumolug, Kenneth *s.j.* '02 (CI) St. Ignatius.
Uschold, Raymond F. '64 (BUF) Delevan, NY Blessed Sacrament; Delevan, NY Holy Family.
Useche, Teofilo '84 (VEN) Palmetto, FL Holy Cross.
Useldinger, Karl J. (COS) Chancellor; Judicial Vicar; Continuing Formation of Priests; Colorado Springs, CO St. Francis of Assisi.
Usenza, Robert J. '61 (BGP) Retired.
Usit, Isidore '73 (CC)[G] Robstown, TX Society of Our Lady of the Most Holy Trinity.
Ustaski, William B. *c.r.i.c.* '77 (LA) Santa Clarita, CA St. Clare; [Q] Santa Paula, CA Canons Regular of the Immaculate Conception.
Uter, Frank M. '69 (BR) Convent, LA St. Michael the Archangel; Gramercy, LA Most Sacred Heart of Jesus; Paulina, LA St. Joseph; Judges; Cemeteries.
Utrup, Eugene E. '59 (STL) Chesterfield, MO Incarnate Word.
Utz, Raymond M. '63 (PIT) Freedom, PA St. Felix.
Utzig, Albert *s.s.c.* '83 (CHI)[K] St. Columbans St. Columban's Foreign Mission Society.
Uvietta, Joseph *s.m.* '61 (STL)[O] St. Louis, MO Cure of Ars Marianist Community; [S] Eureka, MO Marianist Retreat & Conference Center.
Uwandu, Marcellinis '70 (NEW) Paramus, NJ Bergen Regional Medical Center.
Uwandu, Marcellinus '82 (NEW) Midland Park, NJ Nativity; Chaplains.
Uzdrowski, Mel R. *o.s.b.* '56 (JOL)[L] Lisle, IL St. Procopius Abbey.
Uzoh, Louis '73 (BRK) Rosedale, NY St. Clare; [U] Nigerian Apostolate.
Uzondu, Gabriel '01 (CC)[G] Robstown, TX Society of Our Lady of the Most Holy Trinity.
Uzzilio, Robert A. '65 (BGP) Stamford, CT St. Gabriel.

V

V., Gustavo Quintero '80 (STO) Stockton, CA St. Linus Church (Pastor of).
Vaca, Modesto *o.de.m.* '56 (PCE) Ponce, PR Santuario San Judas Tadeo.
Vacca, Daniel L. '95 (WCH) Erie, KS St. Ambrose; St. Paul, KS St. Francis; Ongoing Formation of the Clergy Committee.
Vaccarella, Sam *t.o.r.* (SP)[Q] Tampa, FL Franciscan Center, Retreat House.
Vaccari, Andrew J. '86 (BRK) Ridgewood, NY Our Lady of the Miraculous Medal; Defenders of the Marriage Bond; Diocesan Consultors.
Vaccari, Andrew J. '89 (BRK)[Z] Brooklyn, NY Pro Sanctity Movement.
Vaccari, Andrew J. (BRK) Chancellor.
Vaccari, Andrew (BRK) Presbyteral Council.
Vaccari, Peter I. '77 (BRK) Released from Diocesan Assignment; [A] Huntington, NY Diocesan Seminary of the Immaculate Conception; Censors of Books.
Vaccari, Peter I. (RVC) Censors of Books.
Vaccaro, Guy '78 (JOL) Winfield, IL St. John the Baptist.
Vaccaro, Joseph V. *o. carm.* '58 (STP)[M] Lake Elmo, MN Carmelite Hermitage of the Blessed Virgin Mary.
Vacco, James *o.f.m.* '82 (BUF) Council of Priests; [O] St. Bonaventure, NY St. Bonaventure Friary; [C] St. Bonaventure, NY Friar Community.
Vacek, Carl *t.o.r.* '79 (ORL)[D] Winter Park, FL San Pedro Spiritual Development Center; Cursillos de Cristiandad; Spiritual Development.
Vacek, Edward V. *s.j.* '73 (BO)[V] Cambridge, MA.
Vacquez, Juan *o.ss.t.* (BAL) Hanover, MD St. Lawrence.
Vadakekara, Philip '69 (SYM) Milltown, NJ Syro-Malabar Catholic Community of Milltown, NJ.
Vadakemuriyil, Thomas John *c.m.i.* '92 (SHP)[B] Shreveport, LA Christus Health Northern Louisiana.
Vadakin, Royale M. '64 (LA) Cardinal McIntyre Fund for Charity; Ex Officios; Members; Los Angeles, CA St. Anastasia.
Vadakin, Royalse M. (LA) Moderator of the Curia and Vicar General.
Vadakkedath, Vincent '72 (LKC) Grand Chenier, LA St. Eugene.
Vadakkekudy, Jacob '61 (KAL) Kalamazoo, MI St. Mary.
Vadakkskara, J. Philip '69 (MET) Retired.
Vader, Anthony J. '52 (CHI) Retired.
Vadino, Joseph A. '63 (PH) Strafford, PA Our Lady of the Assumption.
Vaghetto, Benedetto P. '78 (PIT) New Castle, PA St. Vincent de Paul; Judges.
Vaghi, Peter J. '85 (WDC) Washington, DC St. Patrick; [V] Washington, DC The John Carroll Society; Deans; Council of Priests.
Vaghi, Peter (WDC) John Carroll Society.
Vaghi, Peter (WDC) Advocates.
Vaglienty, Felipe (CHI) Chicago, IL St. Agnes of Bohemia.
Vail, Thomas '51 (ALB) Retired.
Vaillancourt, Mark G. '94 (NY) Staten Island, NY St. Patrick; [EE] Yonkers, NY Cathedral Preparatory Seminary Residence.
Vaillancourt, Raymond *m.s.* '89 (FR)[H] Attleboro, MA La Salette Shrine.
Vaillancourt, Robert C. '82 (PRT) Hampden, ME St. Matthew; Hampden, ME St. Gabriel.
Vainavicz, Anthony C. '61 (GR) Spring Lake, MI St. Mary's.
Vainavicz, Anthony (GR) Deans.
Vairo, Carmine *s.d.b.* '64 (LA)[C] Rosemead, CA Don Bosco Technical Institute; [D] Rosemead, CA Don Bosco Technical Institute.
Vaisnoras, Boniface *m.i.c.* '47 (JOL) Plano, IL St. Mary.
Vakko, Justin Kannamparambil *o.c.d.* '98 (TUC) Tucson, AZ Santa Cruz.
Vakoc, Henry T. '92 (STP) Military Chaplains; Army Chaplains.
Vakulskas, John A. '69 (SC) Alton, IA St. Mary's; Hospers, IA St. Anthony's.
Val, Felician del '36 (GAL)[N] Houston, TX Pope John Paul XXIII Priests' Residence.
Vala, John B. '40 (NY)[EE] Bronx, NY Retired.
Valades, Reuben '70 (RC) Retired.
Valadez, Arturo '88 (LA) Los Angeles, CA St. Thomas the Apostle.
Valainis, Vitolds '66 (DAV) State University of Iowa Hospital.
Valastro, George J. '56 (NY) Middletown, NY St. Joseph; Orange.
Valayath, Benny *h.g.n.* '95 (LEX) Barbourville, KY St. Gregory; Pikeville, KY St. Francis of Assisi.
Valazquez, Francisco *v.d.f.m.* '90 (SAC) Sacramento, CA St. Mary.
Valdazo, Stephen '58 (BRK) Jackson Heights, NY St. Joan of Arc.
Valdes, Angel '38 (SJN)[E] Rio Piedras, PR Hospital del Maestro; [E] San Juan, PR Centro Medico de P.R..
Valdes, Angel '38 (SJN) Resident Chaplains.
Valdes, Bert W. '62 (WH) Ona, WV St. Stephen.
Valdes, Luis '45 (SB) Retired.
Valdes, Nicanor '72 (SJN) San Juan, PR San Juan Evangelista; Hermandad N. Sra. De La Caridad.
Valdes, Rafael Padilla '03 (AUS) San Marcos, TX St. John the Evangelist.
Valdes-Valdes, Angel '38 (SJN) Retired.
Valdez, Angel *o.f.m.* (FTW) Fort Wayne, IN St. Patrick; Fort Wayne.
Valdez, John '91 (AMA) Vicars Forane; Ex Officio; College of Consultors; Vocation Development Team; Pampa, TX Sacred Heart; Pampa, TX St. Vincent de Paul.
Valdez, Jose Pedro '69 (LSC) Hobbs, NM Our Lady of Guadalupe.
Valdez, Pat *c.r.* '75 (PBL) Antonito, CO Our Lady of Guadalupe.
Valdez, Patrick M. *c.r.* '75 (PBL) San Luis, CO Sangre de Cristo.
Valdez, Patrick *c.r.* (DEN)[A] Denver, CO St. Andrew's Theatine Religious House.
Valdez, Paul K. '82 (MRY) Boulder Creek, CA St. Michael; Defenders of the Bond; Administrative Committee Priests' Pension Plan; Finance Council; Insurance Committee; Safety Committee; Los Gatos, CA Christ Child.
Valdez, Pedro '98 (LA) Palmdale, CA St. Mary.
Valdivia, Adolfo '81 (SAT) Devine, TX St. Joseph's.
Valdivia, Antonio A. '63 (OAK) Martinez, CA St. Catherine of Siena; Oakland, CA St. Louis Bertrand.
Valdivia, Antonio (OAK) Pastoral Leadership Placement Board (PLPB).
Valdovinos, Francisco *s.t.* (PT)[F] Tallahassee, FL.
Valencheck, John A. '98 (CLV) Brunswick, OH St. Ambrose.
Valencia, Ariel '03 (RCK) Algonquin, IL St. Margaret Mary.
Valencia, Carlos '85 (BRK) On Leave/Unassigned.
Valencia, Thaddeus *c.s.b.* '79 (GAL) Missouri City, TX Holy Family.
Valencia, Victor '93 (STP) St. Ignatius.
Valenciano, Luis '77 (SD) Centinela State Prison.
Valenta, John G. '62 (STL)[O] St. Louis, MO Jesuit Community Corporation at St. Louis University – Jesuit Hall.
Valenta, Stephen *o.f.m.conv.* '51 (NY)[EE] Staten Island, NY St. Francis Friary.
Valente, Michael '58 (JOL).
Valenti, Thomas J. '76 (ROC) On Duty Outside the Diocese.
Valenti, Thomas '76 (NY) Yonkers, NY St. John the Baptist; St. Luke's Site.
Valentin, Angel *o.p.* (SJN) Bayamon, PR Catalina de Siena.
Valentine, Charles R. '54 (TR) Englishtown, NJ Our Lady of Mercy.
Valentine, Daniel A. '74 (PIT) West Mifflin, PA Holy Spirit; [Q] West Mifflin, PA Community College of Allegheny County– South Campus; Deans and Deaneries.
Valentine, Joseph R. *f.s.s.p.* '93 (CHL) On Duty Outside the Diocese.
Valentine, Joseph R. *f.s.s.p.* '93 (Y) Vienna, OH Queen of the Holy Rosary.
Valentine, Joseph *f.s.s.p.* '93 (SCR)[M] North Little Rock, AR.
Valentine, Keveny M. '73 (WDC) Hospital & Nursing Home Ministries.
Valentine, Lambert F. *o.f.m.* '43 (NY) New York, NY St. Francis of Assisi; [M] Butler, NJ St. Anthony Friary.
Valentine, Richard A. '74 (PRO) Georgiaville, RI St. Michael.
Valentine, Timothy S. *s.j.* '85 (NY) Army Chaplains.
Valentini, Francis M. '44 (CLV) Retired.
Valentino, Francis P. *s.j.* '68 (NY)[EE] New York, NY Murray–Weigel Hall.
Valentino, Frederick A. '50 (TR) Retired.
Valenzano, Arthur F. '75 (BAL) Westminster, MD St. John.
Valenzano, Arthur (BAL) Consultors.
Valenzano, Arthur (BAL) Consultors.
Valenzuela, Gerardo '99 (SFR)[E] San Francisco, CA St. Ignatius College Preparatory (Coed); [N] San Francisco, CA Jesuit Community at St. Ignatius College Preparatory.
Valenzuela, Louis '87 (SAC) Absent on Leave.
Valenzuela, Pablo '53 (SJN) San Juan, PR Corpus Christi.
Valera, Edmundo '02 (PBL) Capulin, CO St. Joseph.
Valera, Ramon '75 (LA) Woodland Hills, CA St. Mel.
Valerio, Raymond A. '59 (MAR) Retired.
Valiquette, Hilaire *o.f.m.* '84 (SFE) Isleta, NM St. Augustine.
Valiquette, Thomas M. *s.j.* '64 (DEN)[N] Centennial,

CO Regis High Jesuit Community.
Valit, Robert L. '61 (STP) Stillwater, MN St. Mary Retired.
Valker, Richard J. '57 (CHI) Northbrook, IL St. Norbert Retired.
Valko, George J. '77 (ALT) St. Michael, PA St. Michael's.
Valko, George J. (ALT) Air Force Reserve Chaplains.
Valla, Dominic J. '63 (HRT) Oxford, CT St. Thomas the Apostle.
Valladares, Alejandro E. '00 (MOB)[J] Mobile, AL University of South Alabama Newman Center; Vocations.
Valladares, Alejandro '00 (MOB) Mobile, AL St. Dominic.
Vallayil, Abraham *c.m.i.* '76 (NY) Blauvelt, NY St. Catharine; Nanuet, NY Syro–Malabar Catholic Mission of Rockland County, Spring Valley and Orangeburg, NY.
Valle, Francisco Salas '92 (TUC) Douglas, AZ St. Luke; Pirtleville, AZ St. Bernard's.
Valle, Francisco (RIC) Onley, VA St. Peter's the Apostle.
Valle, Mario R. '78 (NY) Staten Island, NY St. Joseph, St. Thomas.
Valle–Reyes, Thomas Del '79 (NY)[II] New York, NY Descubriendo Siglo XXI, Inc. (Discovering Century, XXI, Inc.).
Valle–Toro, Miguel D. (TR) Trenton, NJ St. Joseph.
Vallecorsa, Daniele '93 (PIT) Pittsburgh, PA St. Raphael; Chaplains to Latino Catholic Community.
Vallee, Robert '87 (MIA)[A] Miami, FL St. John Vianney College Seminary.
Vallejo, Arquimedes '89 (RCK) Loves Park, IL St. Bridget; Special Assignment.
Vallejo, Arquimedes (RCK) Pro Synodal Judges; Hispanic Ministry Offices.
Vallejo–Rodriguez, Gilberto '02 (SAT) Fredericksburg, TX St. Mary's; Stonewall, TX St. Francis Xavier.
Vallelonga, J. Stephen '90 (WH) New Martinsville, WV St. Vincent de Paul.
Valleroy, Paul '74 (KNX) Signal Mountain, TN St. Augustine.
Valleroy, Rickey J. '93 (STL) St. Louis, MO Holy Family.
Valles, Carlos R. *c.ss.r.* '67 (SJN) San Juan, PR San Agustin.
Valley, John '60 (CLV) Released from Diocesan Assignment.
Valley, Paul *s.p.* '64 (SFE)[I] Jemez Springs, NM Our Lady of Lourdes.
Vallier, John F. '87 (GR) Coopersville, MI St. Michael's; [H] Coopersville, MI Grand Valley State University Catholic Campus Ministry.
Valliere, Timothy C. '91 (NOR) Somersville, CT All Saints.
Vallina, Emilio '52 (MIA) Miami, FL St. John Bosco.
Vallina, Emilio (MIA) Knights of Columbus (English and Spanish).
Vallina–Vega, Alfredo *o.p.* (SJN) Catano, PR Nuestra Senora del Carmen.
Valliparambil, Jose '83 (GF) Billings, MT St. Patrick's Co–Cathedral; Special Assignment.
Valliquette, Thomas *s.j.* '64 (DEN)[D] Aurora, CO Regis Jesuit High School.
Vallone, Louis A. '48 (BUF) Retired.
Vallone, Louis F. '73 (PIT) Pittsburgh, PA St. Mary of the Mount; Priest Council.
Vallooran, Joseph '59 (SR) Retired.
Vallooran, Pius *c.m.i.* '63 (LAF) Mamou, LA St. Ann.
Valls, Richard (KAL) Decatur, MI Holy Family.
Valmonte, Art '93 (RNO)[B] Reno, NV St. Mary's Regional Medical Center.
Valois, Normand W. '46 (PRO) Providence, RI Cathedral of SS. Peter and Paul Retired.
Valon, Alder '97 (NY) Spring Valley, NY St. Joseph.
Valone, Fred W. '94 (GAL) Tomball, TX St. Anne.
Valoret, Bernard Joseph '83 (ATL)[K] Conyers, GA The Monastery of the Holy Spirit; [K] Trappist, KY Abbey of Our Lady of Gethsemani, of the Order of Cistercians of the Strict Observance Retired.
Valoret, Joseph '83 (MIA) Retired.
Valtierra, David D. *c.o.* '76 (CHR) Rock Hill, SC St. Mary's; [E] Rock Hill, SC Oratory of St. Philip Neri, Congregation of the Oratory of Pontifical Rite; [H] Rock Hill, SC Winthrop University, York Co. Tech Center.
Valtierra, J. Antonio '79 (GRY) Lake Station, IN St. Francis Xavier.
Valukaran, Thomas *s.d.b.* '88 (NEW)[EE] New Rochelle, NY Salesian Provincial House.
Vamos, Joseph E. '66 (GRY) Merrillville, IN Our Lady of Consolation; Priests' Personnel Board; Mission Office.
Vamos, Joseph L. '61 (TOL) Toledo, OH Blessed Sacrament; Defenders of the Bond Retired.
Van–Hoorn, Leo '55 (ALX) Retired.
Van Abel, John W. '72 (MIL) On Duty Outside the Archdiocese.
Vanagas, William '92 (CHI) Chicago, IL Our Lady of Mercy.
Van Alstyne, Donald J. *m.i.c.* '81 (MO)[I] Army Chaplains.
VanAmburgh, Donald C. '61 (SY) Binghamton, NY St. Christopher.
Vanasse, Bernard '78 (FR)[G] Taunton, MA Marian Manor Inc.; [H] Fall River, MA Priests' Hostel.
Vanasse, Roman R. *o.praem.* '60 (GB)[I] De Pere, WI St. Norbert Abbey.
Van Ban, Martin Tran *c.m.c.* '94 (SY) Syracuse, NY Our Lady of Pompei; Syracuse, NY St. John the Evangelist.
Vanban, Martin Tran *c.m.c* '98 (ALB) Albany, NY Sacred Heart of Jesus; Special Assignment.
Van Beck, Alfred F. '50 (MIL) Retired.
van Beeck, Frans J. *s.j.* '63 (CHI)[C] Chicago, IL Jesuit Community at Loyola University Chicago.
VanBeek, Alois '73 (MIL) Neosho, WI St. Mary.
Van Beek, Alois (MIL) Rubicon, WI St. John.
Van Beek, Dennis E. '69 (MIL) Plymouth, WI St. John the Baptist.
Van Bergen, Francis G. '56 (CLV) South Euclid, OH St. Gregory the Great.
Van Cauwenbergh, Roger *c.i.c.m.* '51 (ARL)[J] Arlington, VA Missionhurst, C.I.C.M.–Central House and Provincialate.
Vance, Charle P. '70 (PH) Lafayette Hill, PA St. Philip Neri.
Vance, Charles P. (PH) Priests' Personnel Board.
Vance, Gregory D. *s.j.* '98 (SEA)[L] Seattle, WA Jesuit Community.
Vance, James '63 (SFE) Albuquerque, NM Santuario San Martin de Porres.
Vance, Leslie A. '76 (SAT) San Antonio, TX St. Brigid; Judges.
Vance, Robert D. *s.j.* '98 (SEA)[C] Seattle, WA Seattle Preparatory School.
Van Cleve, Michael S. '01 (GAL) Houston, TX St. Jerome.
Van Coillie, Paul *c.i.c.m.* '47 (SAT)[M] San Antonio, TX Missionhurst Community Residence.
Vandal, Roland G. *m.s.* '49 (HRT)[M] Hartford, CT Missionaries of LaSalette.
VanDamme, Larry P. '93 (MAR) Chassell, MI St. Anne; Houghton, MI St. Albert the Great University Parish; [G] Houghton, MI St. Albert the Great, University Parish.
Vandeberg, Joseph '89 (SCL) Clear Lake, MN St. Marcus; Deans; Presbyteral Council; Directors.
Vandebroek, Felix J. *ss.cc.* '54 (HON) Waialua, HI St. Michael.
van de Crommert, Paul H. '88 (NU) Olivia, MN St. Aloysius; Renville, MN Holy Redeemer.
Vandegrift, Raymond *o.p.* '60 (WDC) Washington, DC St. Dominic Church & Priory.
Vandegrift, William S. '80 (CAM) Villas, NJ St. Raymond.
Vandehey, Kelly (P) Adjutant Judicial Vicar; Vocations.
Vande Hey, Robert *o.praem.* '49 (GB)[I] De Pere, WI St. Joseph Priory.
Vandehey, Scott '66 (P) Beaverton, OR St. Cecilia; Forest Grove, OR Visitation B.V.M..
Van De Kreeke, William L. '63 (GB) Oshkosh, WI St. Vincent de Paul; Oshkosh, WI St. John.
Van De Kreeke, William (GB) Judges in Second Instance.
Van Del, Curtis E. *s.j.* '65 (SAL)[F] Concordia, KS Nazareth Convent & Academy Corporation Sisters of St. Joseph of Concordia.
Vandeloo, Melvin '53 (BEL) Dubois, IL St. Charles Borromeo.
Vandeloo, Melvin '53 (BEL) Tamaroa, IL Immaculate Conception.
Van De Loo, Willard J. '55 (GB) Pastor Consultors Retired.
Van De Loo, Willard (GB) Bishop's Representative to Senior Priests; Priests' Personnel Board.
Van De Moortell, Raymond *s.j.* (BO) Winthrop, MA St. John the Evangelist.
Vandenberg, James '77 (PBL) Absent on Leave.
Vandenberg, Robert H. '58 (GB) Combined Locks, WI St. Paul; Leo Benevolent Association.
Vandenberg, Thomas L. '62 (SEA) Federal Way, WA St. Vincent De Paul; Fife, WA St. Martin of Tours.
Vanden Boogard, Richard J. *o.praem.* (MO) Navy Chaplains.
Vanden Boogard, Steven J. *o.praem.* '88 (GB)[I] De Pere, WI St. Norbert Abbey.
VandenBossche, John V. *c.s.c.* '51 (FTW)[I] Mountain View, CA St. Francis High School.
Van den Eynde, Stephen *ss.cc.* '48 (HON)[G] Honolulu, HI St. Patrick's Monastery.
Vanden Hogen, James '64 (GB)[N] Green Bay, WI The Diocesan Charismatic Renewal Center.
Vanden Hogen, James (GB) The Diocesan Charismatic Renewal Center.
Vanden Hogen, Paul '54 (GB) Retired.
Van De Paer, John *c.i.c.m.* '47 (PH) Parkesburg, PA Our Lady of Consolation.
Vander Heyden, William F. '70 (GB) Veterans Affairs Medical Center; On Duty Outside the Diocese; National Conference of Veterans Affairs Catholic Chaplains, Inc..
Vanderholt, James '57 (AUS)[A] St. Benedict, LA St. Joseph Seminary College.
Vanderholt, James '57 (BEA) Retired.
Vanderholt, James '57 (AUS)[A] St. Benedict, LA St. Joseph Seminary College.
Vanderholt, Joseph *s.j.* '68 (SFE) Albuquerque, NM Immaculate Conception.
Van Der Horst, John '65 (GB) Retired.
Vanderkolk, Peter J. '83 (LFT) Delphi, IN St. Joseph.
Vanderkolk, Peter (LFT) Associate Judge.
Vanderley, Louis *o.s.b.* '66 (OKL) Edmond, OK St. John the Baptist; [I] Shawnee St. Gregory's Abbey; [K] Edmond, OK University of Central Oklahoma.
Vanderlin, Philip *o.s.b.* '70 (BIS)[A] Richardton, ND Assumption Abbey.
Vanderlin, Philip *o.s.b.* '80 (FgM).
VanderLoop, Anthony G. '03 (STP) St. Paul, MN St. Bernard.
Van Der Peet, Michael *s.c.j.* '53 (MIL)[O] Franklin, WI Villa Maria.
Vander Ploeg, Jon '01 (STP)[B] Northfield, MN St. Dominic.
Vanderstappen, Harrie *s.v.d.* '45 (CHI)[B] Techny, IL Divine Word Residence.
Vander Steeg, Mark (GB) Elected Representatives.
VanderWeel, Richard L. *s.s.e.* '62 (BUR)[E] Colchester, VT Society of St. Edmund.
Van der Werff, Martin '50 (NO) Retired.
Vander Woude, Thomas P. '92 (ARL) Colonial Beach, VA St. Elizabeth.
Van Der Zanden, Edmund '38 (P) Retired.
Van Deuren, John H. '59 (GB) Retired.
VandeVelde, J. Richard *s.j.* '68 (CHI)[C] Chicago, IL Jesuit Community at Loyola University Chicago.
Van De Ven, Kenneth A. '71 (PHX) Glendale, AZ St. James.
Van De Voord, Simeon *o.s.b.* '61 (B) Retired.
Van De Voord, Simeon *o.s.b.* '61 (B) Boise, ID Elks Rehabilitation; Judges Retired.
VanDeVoord, Simeon *o.s.b.* '61 (B)[C] Jerome, ID Monastery of the Ascension Retired.
Vandewalle, Matthew (LIN) Lincoln, NE Cathedral of the Risen Christ.
VandeWalle, Victor '40 (OKL) Retired.
Van Doan, Vincent H. '86 (LAN) Blissfield, MI St. Peter the Apostle.
Van Doan, Vincent (LAN) Priest's Assignment Commission.
VanDoan, Vincent (LAN).
Vandrovec, Jerry C. '78 (STP) Minneapolis, MN St. Albert the Great; Minneapolis, MN Abbot–Northwestern Hospital.
Van Durme, Patrick '01 (ROC) Owego, NY St. Patrick; Censores Librorum.
VanDurme, Patrick (ROC) Owego, NY Blessed Trinity.
Van Dyke, James R. *s.j.* '93 (ROC)[B] Rochester, NY McQuaid Jesuit High School.
Vanecko, William E. '65 (CHI) Chicago, IL St. Kilian.
Vanegas, Albeyro *c.s.v.* '90 (CHI)[N] Arlington Heights Viatorian Province Center–Clerics of St. Viator.
Van Guilder, Alphonse *o.f.m.conv.* '64 (MRY)[F] Arroyo Grande, CA St. Joseph Cupertino Friary.
VanHaverbeke, Kenneth S. '91 (WCH) Wichita, KS Church of the Magdalen.
Van Haverbeke, Kenneth S. (WCH) Ongoing Formation of the Clergy Committee.
Van Hoof, Achilles E. *o.praem.* '48 (GB)[I] De Pere, WI St. Norbert Abbey.
Van Hoof, Gordon *o.s.c.* '53 (DET)[K] Riverview, MI Crosier Community of Riverview; Riverview, MI St. Cyprian.
Van Hook, John E. *o.f.m.* '55 (ALB)[B] Siena College.
Van Hove, Brian *s.j.* '82 (BWN) McAllen, TX Holy Spirit; [A] Mission, TX The Saint Joseph and Saint Peter Seminary; McAllen.
Vanin, Dino *p.i.m.e.* '72 (DET)[K] Detroit, MI P.I.M.E. Motherhouse in Detroit.
Vanissery, Matthew '64 (SB) Kaiser Permanente Medical Center.
Vanitvelt, Milton H. '49 (MAR) Retired.
Vankeirsbilck, Paul *e.c.* '90 (STU)[F] Bloomingdale, OH Holy Family Hermitage.
Van Kempen, Robert '93 (FTW) South Bend, IN St. Matthew Cathedral.
Van Kuren, Corey S. '86 (SY) Binghamton, NY St. Paul.
Van Lai, Joseph Khuyen '74 (SD) Lakeside, CA Our Lady of Perpetual Help.
Van Lare, John *c.m.* '47 (LAR) Cotulla, TX Sacred Heart.
Van Le, Hoang (BO) Hingham, MA St. Paul.
Van Leeuwen, Joseph *c.p.* '64 (CHI)[N] Ashram J.X.P..
Van Lente, Richard '66 (GR) On Special Assignment; College of Consultors.
Van Liefde, Christian M. '73 (LA) Panorama City, CA St. Genevieve; On Administrative Leave.
Van Linden, Philip A. *c.m.* '70 (LA)[Q] Los Angeles, CA Amat Residence II.
VanLoon, Neil J. *v.f.* '79 (SCR) Kingston, PA St. Ignatius.
Van Loon, Neil J. (SCR) Deans; Presbyteral Council.

Van Massenhove, David L. '83 (SLC) Sandy, UT St. Thomas More.
Van Mullekom, Richard '56 (SAG) Retired.
Vann, John C. '42 (MIA) Retired.
Vann, Kevin W. '81 (SFD) Springfield, IL Blessed Sacrament; Vicar for Priests; Hispanic Minsitry; Comite Diocesano de Ministerio Hispano – Diocesan Committee for Hispanic Ministry; Office of the Vicar for Priests; Commission for the Care of Infirm and Retired Priests; Priests' Personnel Board; Presbyteral Council.
Van Natta, Todd (MAD) Appointed; Madison, WI Our Lady, Queen of Peace.
Van Nguyen, Peter '60 (PMB) Lake Worth, FL Sacred Heart.
Van Nguyen, Phuong '93 (WOR) Vietnamese Apostolate; Vietnamese Ministry.
Van Nguyen, Son *s.v.d.* '03 (DUB)[B] Epworth, IA Divine Word College.
VanNufflen, Albert *c.i.c.m.* '41 (ORL) Retired.
Vano, Roque P. '79 (SD) Brawley, CA St. Margaret Mary.
Van Ommeren, William '52 (SPK)[L] Spokane, WA Immaculate Heart Retreat Center.
Van Ommeren, William '52 (SPK) Retired.
Van Ommeren, William (SPK) Diocesan Pastoral Council.
Vanoncini, Robert R. '63 (FRS) Dos Palos, CA Sacred Heart.
Van Oosbree, Christian J. '92 (SC) Fort Dodge, IA Corpus Christi.
Vanorny, Ed '98 (RC) Presho, SD St. Martin; Presho, SD Christ the King.
Vanorny, Ed (RC) Deaneries; Presbyteral Council.
Van Oss, James R. '64 (BEL) Nashville, IL Our Lady of Perpetual Help; Pinckneyville, IL St. Mary Magdalen.
Van Overbeek, Gerald J. *o.s.a.* '65 (CHI)[N] Olympia Fields, IL Tolentine Monastery at Tolentine Center.
Van Pham, Hanh '92 (CC) Corpus Christi, TX St. Philip The Apostle.
Van Phung, Joseph (DAV) Iowa City, IA St. Mary.
Van Phuong, Francis Pham '66 (ATL) Riverdale, GA Our Lady of Vietnam.
Vanrell, Bartolome '53 (SJN)[E] San Juan, PR Centro Medico de P.R..
Van Roo, William A. *s.j.* '47 (MIL)[O] Wauwatosa, WI Jesuit Community at St. Camillus.
Van Sickler, Robert (BAK) CIVIL AIR PATROL; Merrill, OR St. Augustine.
van Sloun, Eugene G. '48 (DOD) Retired.
Van Sloun, Michael *o.s.c.* '95 (STP) Anoka, MN St. Stephen; [M] Anoka, MN Crosier Community of Anoka.
Van Stone, John J. '48 (PH) Retired.
Van Thanh, Louis '94 (NY) Newburgh, NY St. Patrick.
Vanthu, Joseph N. '71 (SJ) Sunnyvale, CA Church of The Resurrection.
Van Thuyne, Dennis G. '77 (PH) Absent on Sick Leave.
Van Tran, Peter Nam '84 (NO) Avondale, LA St. Bonaventure; Harvey, LA Infant Jesus of Prague.
Van Tran, Tri '02 (JOL) Downers Grove, IL St. Mary of Gostyn.
VanTrieste, Martin *s.t.* '45 (WDC)[M] Adelphi, MD Missionary Servants of the Most Holy Trinity.
Van Ty, Nguyen '85 (HT) Thibodaux, LA St. Charles Borromeo; Pontifical Societies for the Propagation of the Faith.
Van Vlaenderen, Leonard S. '88 (MIL) Brookfield, WI St. John Vianney.
Van Vliet, Charles *f.s.s.p.* '96 (LIN)[A] Denton, NE Our Lady of Guadalupe Seminary.
VanVurst, James *o.f.m.* '61 (CIN)[M] Cincinnati, OH St. John the Baptist Friary.
VanWiel, John E. *c.s.v.* '66 (CHI)[D] Arlington Heights, IL St. Viator High School; [N] Arlington Heights, IL Viatorian Province Center–Clerics of St. Viator.
Van Wormer, Giles *o.f.m.conv.* '57 (ALB)[L] Rensselaer, NY Franciscan Mission House.
Vanyo, Leo V. '52 (PIT) Pittsburgh, PA St. Bernard; Judges Retired.
Vanzillotta, Gino *o.m.* '54 (LA) Los Angeles, CA All Saints; [Q] Los Angeles, CA Minim Fathers.
Vap, Ivan F. '54 (LIN) Geneva, NE St. Joseph's; Deaneries and Deans; Building Commission.
Varady, Michael *c.ss.r.* '87 (ORL)[E] New Smyrna Beach, FL Redemptorist Fathers of the Vice Province of Richmond.
Varakukala, George '62 (SAN) Colorado City, TX St. Ann's.
Varakukala, George *h.g.n.* (SAN) Presbyteral Council.
Varano, Andrew R. '58 (BRK) Brooklyn, NY St. Francis of Paola.
Varas, Dwayne A. *s.j.* '01 (SP) Tampa, FL Sacred Heart.
Varas, Felix '50 (SJN) San Juan, PR Maria Reina del Mundo.
Varble, Edward F. '50 (Y) North Canton, OH St. Therese Little Flower Retired.
Vareedayah, Lawrence '66 (RVC) Manhasset, NY St. Mary's.
Varela, Jose *o.r.c.* '90 (SB) Corona, CA St. Edward; [E] Corona, CA Operarios Del Reino De Cristo, O.R.C..
Varettoni, Julian B. '55 (PAT) Clifton, NJ Sacred Heart.
Varga, Andrew G. '78 (BGP) Westport, CT St. Luke; Diocesan Consultors; Presbyteral Council
Varga, Paul *o.f.m.conv.* '60 (MET)[I] Watchung, NJ McAuley Hall Inc..
Varga, Wayne M. '74 (PAT) Parsippany, NJ St. Peter the Apostle; Presbyteral Council; College of Consultors.
Varga, Wayne (PAT) Catholic Scouting.
Vargas, Alex J. '02 (PMB) West Palm Beach, FL Holy Name of Jesus.
Vargas, Eric P. *s.v.d.* '76 (OAK) Oakland, CA St. Bernard's.
Vargas, Gabriel '89 (B) Rupert, ID St. Nicholas.
Vargas, John C. *c.ss.r.* '73 (STL)[O] Liguori, MO Alphonsian Foundation.
Vargas, John C. *c.ss.r.* '78 (BR)[H] Baton Rouge Redemptorist Vice Province.
Vargas, John '66 (SP) Tampa, FL Incarnation.
Vargas, Jose Carlos '92 (PCE) Guanica, PR St. Anthony Abbot.
Vargas, Leonardo J. '85 (PHX) Phoenix, AZ Most Holy Trinity.
Vargas, Leonel '91 (LA) Palmdale, CA St. Mary.
Vargas, Luis '98 (SJ) San Jose, CA Sacred Heart of Jesus.
Vargas, Victor (SB) Ontario, CA Our Lady of Guadalupe.
Vargas Grajales, David *o.s.a.* '01 (SJN) San Juan, PR Ntra. Sra. de la Monserrate.
Varghese, Joseph V. '86 (CC) Pettus, TX Sacred Heart Mission.
Varghese, Joseph '86 (GAL) Houston, TX St. Francis Xavier.
Varghese, Rejimon '02 (WDC)[M] Washington, DC Divine Word College.
Varghese, Shaji (CC) Corpus Christi, TX Mary, Mother of the Church Mission.
Varghese, Thomas (CHI) Evanston, IL Divine Liturgy.
Varghese, Thunkuchan Steve *s.a.c.* (MIL) Kenosha, WI Our Lady of the Holy Rosary.
Vargo, Robert B. '89 (HRT) Poquonock, CT St. Joseph's; Special and other Archdiocesan Assignment; Judicial Vicar (Officialis).
Varickamackal, Thomas Joseph '77 (MAR) Garden, MI St. Mary Magdalene; Garden, MI St. John the Baptist; Garden, MI St. Andrew.
Varikatt, Wilson *o.carm.* '97 (WDC)[B] Washington, DC Whitefriars Hall.
Varley, John J. '59 (SPR) Pittsfield, MA St. Teresa; Vicars for the Clergy.
Varley, John (SPR) Priests Committee.
Varna, Leons '29 (BRK)[Z] Brooklyn, NY Latvian Roman Catholic Mission.
Varney, Lawrence F. '60 (TOL) Retired.
Varno, John N. '66 (ALB) Ballston Lake, NY Our Lady of Grace Ellis Hospital; Special Assignment.
Varo, Jose Luis '56 (FRS) Los Banos, CA St. Joseph.
Varone, Normand G. '75 (SPC) Benton, MO St. Denis; Benton, MO St. Lawrence; Priests' Mutual Benefit Society.
Varsanyi, William I. '46 (PRO) Providence, RI Our Lady of Charity; [M] Pawtucket, RI Jeanne Jugan Residence; Hungarian Catholic League of America, Inc.; Vicars General; Vicar for Canonical Affairs; Vicars General Vicar for Canonical Affairs Promoter of Justice; Council Members; College of Consultors; Finance Council; Propagation of the Faith; Catholic Relief Services; Holy Childhood Association.
Varsanyi, William I. '52 (NY)[II] New York, NY Hungarian Catholic League of America, Inc..
Vartzelis, George D. '53 (BO) Senior Priests Retired.
Varugese, Thomas (CHI)[J] Evanston, IL Saint Francis Hospital.
Varughese, Thomas (CHI)[J] Chicago, IL St. Anthony Hospital.
Varuvel, Paul L. '72 (BUF).
Varvaro, William A. '63 (BRK)[A] Middle Village, NY St. Margaret; [Z] Middle Village, NY National Italian Apostolate Conference; Promoter of Justice.
Vas, Joseph S. '79 (OKL)[F] Oklahoma City, OK Bone and Joint Hospital Retired.
Vas, Laszlo '98 (CHI) Chicago, IL St. Stephen, King of Hungary.
Vasaturo, Anthony J. '55 (BO) Senior Priests Retired.
Vasek, Stephen *o.m.i.* '71 (BUF) Buffalo, NY Holy Angels.
Vashon, Randall J. (MET) Old Bridge, NJ St. Thomas the Apostle.
Vasil, James '74 (GBG) Mesa, AZ Holy Cross.
Vasile, Louis A. '72 (ROC) Auburn, NY St. Alphonsus.
Vasilj, Kvirin *o.f.m.* '40 (CHI)[N] Chicago, IL St. Anthony's Friary.
Vaske, Martin O. *s.j.* '47 (OM)[K] Omaha, NE Jesuit Community at Creighton University
Vasko, Christopher P. '83 (TOL) Lima, OH St. John the Evangelist; Lima, OH St. Rose; Lima Deanery; Judges.
Vasko, Peter *o.f.m.* '87 (FgM).
Vasquez, Armando *o.f.m.* (ELP) Presidio, TX Santa Teresa de Jesus.
Vasquez, Edwin '96 (BO)[V] Cambridge, MA.
Vasquez, Elberto T. '89 (NO) Slidell, LA St. Luke the Evangelist.
Vasquez, Jose Luis '87 (RCK) Special Assignment.
Vasquez, Pedro *o.f.m.* '71 (LA)[Q] Santa Barbara, CA Franciscan Friary, Order of Friars Minor (Old Mission).
Vasquez, Perfecto '98 (RCK) Crystal Lake, IL St. Elizabeth Ann Seton.
Vasquez, Raul *o.f.m.* '56 (ELP)[B] El Paso, TX Roger Bacon College.
Vasquez, Raymundo Chavez (TYL) Nacogdoches, TX Sacred Heart.
Vasquez, Roberto Vera '01 (MRY) Castroville, CA Our Lady of Refuge.
Vasquez, Rodolfo D. (CC) Presbyteral Council; Corpus Christi, TX Most Precious Blood.
Vasquez–Martinez, Alberto (MRY) Priestly Life and Ministry Board.
Vasquez–Martinez, Jose Alberto '02 (MRY) Arroyo Grande, CA St. Patrick.
Vass, Robert *s.d.v.* '87 (NEW) Palisades Park, NJ St. Nicholas.
Vassar, Paul (OAK) Consultors.
Vassor, Paul '71 (OAK) San Leandro, CA St. Alphonsus Liguori.
Vasyliv, Stepan '94 (STN) Grand Rapids, MI St. Michael's.
Vatakkummoolayil, John C. '64 (RVC) Lindenhurst, NY Our Lady of Perpetual Help.
Vater, Robert L. '45 (COV) Fort Thomas, KY St. Catherine of Siena; Liaison for Retired Priests Retired.
Vath, William R. '72 (LFT) Lafayette, IN St. Boniface; Special Assignment; Defenders of the Bond; Defender of the Bond.
Vattakudiyil, Francis P. '63 (RVC) Kings Park, NY St. Joseph's.
Vattakunnel, James C. '88 (BGP) Wilton, CT Our Lady of Fatima.
Vattakunnel, Jose '90 (LKC) Elton, LA St. Joseph's; [D] Elton, LA Herald of Good News, Inc..
Vattaparambil, Jose *s.d.b.* '75 (OAK)[N] Berkeley Salesian Community.
Vatter, Joseph E. '78 (BUF) Council of Priests; Medina, NY St. Mary.
Vatterott, William F. '03 (STL) Ballwin, MO Holy Infant.
Vattothuparambil, Thomas '63 (PH) Ambler, PA St. Anthony of Padua; Indian Apostolate–Knanayan Comm..
Vattothuparambil, Thomas '67 (SYM) Ambler, PA Knanaya Catholic Mission of Greater Philadelphia.
Vaudreuil, Paul *a.a.* '64 (BO)[V] Boston, MA Assumptionist Center.
Vaughan, Gregory D. '72 (TR) Hamilton, NJ St. Raphael; Vicar General and Moderator of the Curia; Diocesan Consultors; Diocesan Finance Council; Budget Committee; Victim Assistance Coordinator.
Vaughan, James '50 (ALB) Troy, NY Sacred Heart.
Vaughan, John J. '67 (MIA) Miami Beach, FL St. Patrick; [M] Miami Shores, FL Archdiocese of Miami Millennium Appeal, Inc.; [M] Miami Shores, FL Archdiocese of Miami, Inc.; Executive Director; Building Commission; Archdiocesan Fund–Raising & Assessments Committee; Finance Council; Real Estate Board; Retired Priests' Committee; Police Chaplains.
Vaughan, John R. '74 (OWN) Owensboro, KY St. Stephen Cathedral.
Vaughan, John (OWN) Judges; Diocesan Pastoral Council; Deans; Priests' Council; Priest Personnel Committee.
Vaughan, Richard P. *s.j.* '50 (LA)[C] Los Angeles, CA Jesuit Community.
Vaughan, Thomas *s.s.c.* '56 (OM)[K] St. Columbans St. Columban's Foreign Mission Society Retired.
Vaughey, James K. '65 (NY) Briarcliff Manor, NY St. Theresa; Trustees of St. Patrick's Cathedral in the City of New York, Inc..
Vaughn, John *o.f.m.* '01 (SFR) San Francisco, CA St. Boniface.
Vaughn, Mason '50 (SAG) Retired.
Vaughn, Robert William *o.p.* '71 (NY)[EE] New York St. Vincent Ferrer Priory.
Vaughn, Roland G. '71 (LKC) Hackberry, LA St. Peter Apostle; Holly Beach, LA Holy Trinity.
Vaught, Mike (OKL) Pauls Valley, OK St. Catherine of Siena.
Vavasseur, Henry C. '58 (BR) Port Allen, LA Holy Family.
Vaverek, Gavin N. (TYL) College of Consultors; Defenders of the Bond; Diocesan Building Board; Priests' Pension Board; Presbyteral Council; Diocesan Council of Catholic Women; Respect Life Program; Diocesan Deanery Representatives On Ethics and Integrity Policy for Church Personnel; Diocesan Liturgical Commission; Victim Assistance Coordinator.
Vaverek, Gavin '90 (TYL) Longview, TX St. Mary; Diocesan Pastoral Team – DPT; Diocesan Christian Initiation Team.
Vaverek, Hayden J. '94 (CHR) Moncks Corner, SC St.

Philip Benizi; Cursillo Movement; Air Force Reserve Chaplains.
Vaverek, Timothy V. '85 (AUS) Waco, TX St. Joseph.
Vavonese, Charles S. '73 (SY) Syracuse, NY Holy Trinity; Special Assignment; Catholic Schools.
Vavrick, Eugene B. '93 (TR) Lincroft, NJ St. Leo the Great; [B] Holmdel, NJ St. John Vianney High School.
Vavrina, Kenneth P. '62 (OM) Omaha, NE St. Richard; Omaha, NE St. Therese of the Child Jesus.
Vavrina, Kenneth (OM) Deans; Deans.
Vaz, Francis F. '61 (MET) Iselin, NJ St. Cecelia.
Vaz, Gregorio Dafonte *o.dem.* '57 (PCE) Ponce, PR La Merced.
Vaz, Rock I. *s.j.* (MO) AUXILIARY CHAPLAINS CONTRACT CHAPLAINS.
Vaze Parampil, Thomas '69 (LUB) Retired.
Vazhapilly, Paul '61 (BRK) Brooklyn, NY SS. Simon and Jude; [U] Indian Apostolate.
Vazhupadickal, Joseph O. *s.a.c.* '79 (COL) Chillicothe, OH Veteran's Affairs Medical Center.
Vazquez, Albert M. *c.m.f.* '55 (PHX) Prescott, AZ Sacred Heart.
Vazquez, Antonio J. '91 (ARE) On Duty Outside the Diocese.
Vazquez, Carlos R. '89 (WIL) Wilmington, DE Cathedral of St. Peter; Delaware Psychiatric Hospital.
Vazquez, Harry Lopez '93 (MGZ) Mayaguez, PR Our Lady of Mt. Carmel.
Vazquez, Jose Luis '87 (RCK) DeKalb, IL St. Mary.
Vazquez, Luis A. '91 (ARE) Arecibo, PR Church of Santa Teresita; Police Chaplain.
Vazquez, Perfecto '56 (BRK) Brooklyn, NY Guardian Angel.
Vazquez, Virginio C. '73 (GAL) Huntsville, TX.
Vazquez–Martinez, Jose Alberto '02 (MRY) Nipomo, CA St. Joseph.
Vazquez–Vega, Edwin '95 (PCE) Juana Diaz, PR St. Raymond Nonato.
Vazquez Colon, Antonio Jose '90 (ARE) San Juan, PR Ntra. Sra. de la Medalla Milagrosa; [E] San Juan, PR Centro Medico de P.R..
Vazquez Rojas, Jaime '83 (SJN) Guaynabo, PR Buen Pastor.
Vead, Victor P. '92 (ALX) Absent on Leave.
Vecchio, Egidio *m.s.* '55 (BEA) Woodville, TX Our Lady of the Pines.
Vecchio, Michael J. '50 (PIT) Retired.
Vedro, James *o.s.c.* '65 (DET)[K] Riverview, MI Crosier Community of Riverview.
Veeneman, Dismas J. *o.f.m.conv.* '69 (IND) Clarksville, IN St. Anthony of Padua.
Vega, Carlos '89 (MIA) Leisure City, FL St. Martin de Porres Church.
Vega, Donald M. *s.j.* '65 (SJN) San Juan, PR San Ignacio de Loyola; [H] San Juan, PR Comunidad Jesuita.
Vega, Fernando *c.m.f.* '40 (LA) San Gabriel, CA San Gabriel; [Q] San Gabriel, CA Claretian Missionaries (Missionary Sons of the Immaculate Heart of Mary).
Vega, Francis de la *o.a.r.* '43 (LA)[Q] Oxnard, CA St. Augustine Priory O.A.R..
Vega, Hector R. *i.sch.* '74 (CC)[I] Corpus Christi, TX Secular Institute of the Schoenstatt Fathers aka Schoenstatt Fathers.
Vega, Hector R. *c.c.* '74 (MIL).
Vega, Jose L. *o.m.* '69 (LA)[S] Los Angeles, CA All Saints; [Q] Los Angeles, CA Minim Fathers.
Vega, Jose Luis '54 (FRS) Cutler, CA St. Mary.
Vega, Raymond *s.c.j.* '73 (SP)[O] Pinellas Park, FL Priests of the Sacred Heart Retired.
Vega, Richard '83 (LA) Lompoc, CA La Purisima Concepcion; College of Consultors.
Vega, Roberto '87 (ARE) Arecibo, PR Cathedral of San Felipe Apostol; Pastoral Vocational Program; Buen Pastor Hospital.
Vega, Saturnino Juan *o.s.a.* '64 (SJN) San Juan, PR Ntra. Sra. de la Monserrate.
Vehovec, Valentine '43 (SB) Retired.
Veigas, Albert '80 (CLV) Bedford Heights, OH Holy Trinity.
Veik, Alan D. *o.f.m.cap.* (MIL)[X] Milwaukee, WI House of Peace; Office for Consecrated Life.
Veik, Roger A. *o.f.m.cap.* '69 (GF) Special Assignment.
Veik, Roger *o.f.m.cap.* (GF) Personnel Board; Continuing Formation of Clergy.
Veit, David J. '98 (JC) Tipton, MO St. Andrew; Tipton, MO Tipton Treatment Center; To The Bishop; Appointed Members.
Veith, William E. '70 (CHI)[J] Elk Grove Village, IL Alexian Brothers Medical Center.
Vela, Fabian '56 (MRY) Hollister, CA Sacred Heart/St. Benedict Catholic Community Retired.
Vela, Jesus *o.f.m.cap.* '99 (LA)[B] Santa Ynez, CA San Lorenzo Seminary and Prayer Center; [B] Santa Ynez, CA San Lorenzo Seminary and Prayer Center.
Vela, Rudy *s.m.* '72 (STL)[O] Chicago, IL.
Vela, Rudy *s.m.* '84 (SAT)[C] San Antonio, TX St. Mary's University of San Antonio, Texas; [M] San Antonio, TX Woodlawn Marianist Community.
Vela, William *c.s.b.* '90 (GAL)[F] Houston, TX St. Thomas High School.
Velandria, Eric G. *s.j.* '96 (PH)[N] San Francisco, CA Jesuit Community at University of San Francisco.
Velas, Vincent P. '64 (PIT) McKeesport, PA St. Patrick.
Velasco, Arturo '86 (LA) Los Angeles, CA St. Ignatius of Loyola.
Velasco, Jose J. *s.j.* '57 (LA) Monterey Park, CA St. Stephen.
Velasco, Jose *o.m.i.* '58 (SAT)[K] San Antonio, TX Oblate Madonna Residence.
Velasco, Ramon '92 (SEA) Seattle, WA Holy Family.
Velasquez, Carlos (SAT) In Metropolitan Area; Archdiocesan Presbyteral Council; Priests Personnel Board.
Velasquez, Jose '67 (ELP) Canutillo, TX St. Patrick.
Velasquez, Marcos C. '89 (TUC) Nogales, AZ Sacred Heart; Patagonia, AZ St. Theresa.
Velasquez, Marcos (TUC) Council of Priests; Vicars Forane; All Vicars Forane.
Velazquez, Carlos B. '90 (SAT) San Antonio, TX St. John Berchmans.
Velazquez, David M. '80 (LA) Maywood, CA St. Rose of Lima.
Velazquez, Luis '78 (ARE) Vega–Baja, PR Our Lady of Mt. Carmel; Priest's Senate (Consejo Presbiteral).
Velez, Andrew '96 (PAT) Paterson, NJ St. Mary's; Paterson, NJ Preakness Hospital; Passaic, NJ Passiac General Hospital.
Velez, Antonio '89 (BAL) Columbia, MD St. John the Evangelist.
Velez, Carlos Felipe '00 (B) Boise, ID St. Mary's.
Velez, Guillermo '83 (HRT) Hartford, CT St. Justin; Hartford, CT St. Michael.
Velez, Guillermo '91 (HRT) Hartford, CT Sacred Heart.
Velez, Juan R. '98 (TR)[R] Princeton, NJ Opus Dei.
Vella, Desmond J. '59 (NY) New York, NY Immaculate Conception; Judicial Vicar.
Vella, Edward *c.ss.r.* '85 (STL)[B] St. Louis, MO St. John Neumann House.
Vella, Francis M. '55 (OAK) On Special Assignment Retired.
Vella, Francis M. (HRT) Newington, CT Department of Veteran Affairs Medical Center.
Vella, Joseph '68 (BRK) Richmond Hill, NY Our Lady of the Cenacle.
Vellankal, Mathew '87 (OAK) Concord, CA Queen of All Saints.
Vellaramparampil, Aaron T. '66 (RVC) Glen Cove, NY St. Rocco.
Vellardita, Guy *o.f.m.* '58 (FgM).
Vellenga, R. Stephen '81 (CLV) Painesville, OH St. Mary; [W] Painesville, OH St. Mary's – Painesville; College of Consultors; Mission Office, Society for the Propagation of the Faith; Cleveland, OH St. Francis.
Velloorattil, George '78 (CHI) Chicago, IL Queen of the Universe.
Vellucci, Dennis C. '75 (LA) Retired.
Velo, Kenneth J. '73 (CHI) Rosemont, IL Our Lady of Hope.
Velo, Kenneth (CHI) Big Shoulders Fund.
Velozo, Donald D. '65 (CAM) Northfield, NJ St. Bernadette; Atlantic Deanery.
Velozo, Donald (CAM) Members.
Velten, Robert *o.s.b.* '54 (SP)[O] St. Leo, FL St. Leo Abbey.
Veltri, Dennis J. '93 (E) St. Mary.
Veltrie, James V. *s.j.* '65 (STL)[C] Saint Louis University; [O] St. Louis, MO Jesuit Community Corporation at St. Louis University – Jesuit Hall.
Velutis, John '32 (CHI) Chicago, IL SS. Peter and Paul.
Vendetti, Michael A. '64 (BRK) On Leave/Unassigned.
Venditti, J. Michael '87 (MET) On Duty Outside the Diocese.
Venditti, J. Michael '87 (PSC) Allentown, PA St. Michael.
Vendramin, Aldo *c.s.* '75 (CHI)[N] Oak Park, IL Scalabrini Development Office.
Venegoni, John L. '95 (BEL) Belleville, IL St. Teresa of the Child Jesus.
Veneklase, Michael G. *o.c.d.* '93 (GRY) Chicago, IL St. Camillus; [I] Munster, IN Discalced Carmelite Fathers Monastery.
Veneroso, Joseph R. *m.m.* '78 (NY)[EE] Maryknoll Maryknoll Fathers and Brothers.
Venezia, Arthur '71 (PMB) North Palm Beach, FL St. Paul of the Cross; College of Consultors.
Vengayil, Thomas '59 (PMB) Tequesta, FL St. Jude; West Palm Beach, FL Our Lady Queen of Peace Catholic Cemetery, Inc..
Vengayil, Thomas (PMB) Office of Cemeteries; Presbyteral Council.
Venglarik, Daniel M. '73 (Y) Youngstown, OH St. Charles Borromeo.
Venker, Josef V. *s.j.* '87 (SEA)[A] Seattle, WA Seattle University.
Venne, Douglas F. *m.m.* '59 (FgM).
Venne, R. Thomas '62 (MIL) Pewaukee, WI St. Anthony.
Venne, Samuel J. '78 (BUF) North Tonawanda, NY Good Shepherd.
Venneri, Michael D. '82 (SPK) Special Ministry; [F] Spokane, WA Sacred Heart Medical Center.
Vennette, Howard J. '84 (OG) Brushton, NY St. Mary's Church.
Vennitti, Thomas A. '73 (STU) Cadiz, OH St. Teresa; Cadiz, OH Sacred Heart; Cadiz, OH St. Matthias Mission.
Vennix, James J. '56 (GB) Retired.
Venters, Darrell '89 (OWN)[I] Bowling Green, KY Western Kentucky University Newman Center; Vicar of Clergy; Priests' Council; Pastoral Office for Personnel; Priest Personnel Committee; St. Vincent de Paul Society.
Ventiquattro, Jude *t.o.r.* '88 (ARL)[J] White Post, VA Sacred Heart Friary.
Ventura, Anthony C. '78 (HRT)[A] Bloomfield, CT St. Thomas Seminary Retired.
Ventura, Gennaro J. '43 (ROC) Wayland, NY Holy Family Catholic Community Retired.
Venturini, Fabio '02 (NEW) Union City, NJ St. Anthony of Padua.
Venuti, Angelo A. '61 (BRK) Brooklyn, NY St. Mary Mother of Jesus.
Venvertloh, Ken J. '67 (SFD) Jacksonville, IL Our Saviour; Virginia, IL St. Luke.
Venvertloh, Kenneth J. (SFD) Jacksonville Deanery.
Venvertloh, Kenneth (SFD) Lay Employees' Pension Plan Administrative Committee.
Venza, Felix F. '72 (TR) Florence, NJ St. Clare.
Venzor, Jesse C. '80 (FRS) Woodlake, CA St. Frances Cabrini.
Ver, Alex '67 (NEW) Jersey City, NJ St. Nicholas.
Ver–Schneider, Neil L. *s.j.* '66 (PH)[I] Philadelphia, PA The Gesu School; [AA] Philadelphia, PA Jesuit Community, Arrupe House; [AA] Philadelphia, PA Gesu School Jesuit Community and Outreach Center (S.J.).
Vera, Jude '89 (SP) Tampa, FL Incarnation.
Vera, Julio '98 (MGZ) Sabana Grande, PR Church of San Isidro.
Vera, Luis A. *o.s.a.* '96 (WDC)[B] Washington, DC Augustinian College, Order of St. Augustine.
Vera, Luis Macias (LSC) La Mesa, NM San Jose; San Miguel, NM San Miguel.
Vera, Roberto (MRY) Permanent Diaconate Advisory Board.
Vera, Romulo E. *c.s.c.* '89 (FTW)[I] Congregacion de Santa Cruz.
Vera, Vicente Antonio '85 (TOL) Mansfield, OH St. Peter.
Veras, Richard '96 (NY) Staten Island, NY St. Joseph, St. Thomas.
Verber, Thomas G. *o.s.a.* '99 (SD) San Diego, CA St. Patrick; [H] San Diego, CA Augustinian Community.
Verberg, Richard R. '71 (MIL) Greenfield, WI St. John the Evangelist.
Verbest, Stephen *o.c.s.o.* '98 (DUB)[K] Peosta, IA New Melleray Abbey, Order of Cistercians of the Strict Observance.
Verboomen, Willy *c.i.c.m.* '63 (BWN) Retired.
Verbrugge, Albert E. (SAT) Judges Retired.
Verbryke, William L. *s.j.* '83 (CHI)[N] Chicago Chicago Province of the Society of Jesus–Provincial Office; [N] Chicago, IL Chicago Province of the Society of Jesus–Provincial Office.
Verbryke, William L. *s.j.* '83 (DET)[B] Berkley, MI Loyola House.
Verbryke, William L. *s.j.* '83 (CHI)[N] Chicago Chicago Province of the Society of Jesus–Provincial Office; [N] Chicago, IL Chicago Province of the Society of Jesus–Provincial Office.
Vercellone, Anthony '80 (LAV)[F] Las Vegas, NV Serra House (Formation Residence); Vocations.
Verdegan, Albert L. '60 (SUP) Retired.
Verdelotti, Anthony W. '86 (PRO) Providence, RI Blessed Sacrament; Cemeteries.
Verdelotti, James J. '78 (PRO) Cranston, RI St. Mary.
Verdi, Ralph C. *c.pp.s.* '71 (LFT)[A] Rensselaer, IN Saint Joseph's College.
Verdia, Carlos '85 (SJN) Bayamon, PR N. Sra. de la Providencia.
Verdick, James *o.f.m.* '40 (GB).
Verdick, Jerome F. '58 (WIN) Retired.
Verdun, Gerald J. '72 (PEO)[I] Delavan, IL St. Mary's.
Vereb, Jerome *c.p.* '72 (BAL)[S] Baltimore, MD St. Joseph's Passionist Community; [H] Frederick, MD Visitation Monastery.
Vereb, John '47 (PMB) West Palm Beach, FL St. John Fisher.
VerEecke, Robert F. *s.j.* '78 (BO) Chestnut Hill, MA St. Ignatius; [V] Newton, MA The Jesuit Community at Boston College.
Verespy, Joseph D. '79 (SCR) Dupont, PA Sacred Heart of Jesus.
Vergara, Armando '73 (STO) Linden, CA Holy Cross Church (Pastor of); Personnel Board; Cursillo Movement–English and Spanish.
Vergara, Jaime *c.m.* '56 (SJN) San Juan, PR Sagrado Corazon de Jesus; [B] San Juan, PR Colegio Sagrado Corazon de Jesus.
Verhaeghe, Ronald '92 (KC) Independence, MO St. Mary's.

Verhagen, Norbert M. *m.m.* '39 (SJ)[M] Los Altos, CA Maryknoll.
Verhalen, Charles J. '47 (MIL) Retired.
Verhalen, David H. *c.s.c.* '54 (FTW) South Bend, IN Faith & Hope & Charity Chapel; [I] Notre Dame, TX Holy Cross Mission House.
Verhalen, Peter *o.cist.* '81 (DAL)[D] Irving, TX Cistercian Preparatory School; [E] Irving, TX Cistercian Preparatory School; [K] Irving, TX Cistercian Abbey of Our Lady of Dallas.
Verhasselt, David A. '89 (MIL) Oconomowoc, WI St. Catherine.
Verheggen, Peter A. *o.f.m.* '49 (LSC) Tularosa, NM St. Francis de Paula.
Verhelst, Steven J. '90 (NU) St. Francis; St. Malachy; Benson, MN Church of the Visitation; St. Bridget; Church of the Sacred Heart; College of Consultors; Priests' Council.
Verhoff, Melvin T. '91 (TOL) Plymouth, OH St. Joseph; Willard, OH St. Francis Xavier.
Verhoff, Werner *c.pp.s.* '43 (CIN)[B] Carthagena, OH St. Charles.
Verhoye, Gerard A. '49 (PEO) Retired.
Verkamp, Bernard J. '64 (EVN) On Leave of Absence.
Verley, Jude *o.s.c.* '79 (DET) Riverview, MI St. Cyprian; [K] Riverview, MI Crosier Community of Riverview.
Vermigilio, Thomas Michael *m.c.c.j.* '72 (CHI) Calumet Park, IL Seven Holy Founders.
Vernal, Paul Felix *s.d.b.* '73 (OAK)[N] Berkeley Salesian Community.
Vernon, Donald B. (LFT) Associate Judges.
Vernon, Donald '55 (LFT)[C] Lafayette, IN St. Elizabeth Medical Center.
Vernon, John E. (OM) Retired.
Vernon, William F. '97 (HEL) Butte, MT Butte Catholic Community North; Butte, MT Immaculate Conception; Butte, MT St. Joseph; Butte, MT St. Patrick; [H] Butte, MT Montana College of Mineral Science and Technology.
Veronesi, Giulio *c.r.s.* '75 (GAL) Houston, TX Christ the King.
Verrett, Joseph C. *s.s.j.* '55 (BAL)[S] Baltimore, MD St. Joseph Society of the Sacred Heart House of Central Administration.
Verrier, John M. '95 (PEO) Metamora, IL St. Mary's; Metamora, IL St. Elizabeth; [L] Henry, IL Christ the King Retreat Center – Diocese of Peoria.
Verrigni, Robert J. '77 (NY) Scarsdale, NY Immaculate Heart of Mary.
Verrill, O. Wendell '63 (BO) St. Mary; WEST REGION.
Verrilli, William F. '79 (BGP) Bridgeport, CT St. Andrew.
Verrilli, William F. (BGP) On Duty Outside the Diocese; Defenders of the Bond.
Verruni, Samuel A. '86 (PH) Exton, PA SS. Philip and James; [EE] West Chester, PA West Chester University.
Verschaeve, C. Michael '77 (DET) Lake Orion, MI St. Joseph.
Verschaeve, Michael (DET) Presbyteral Council.
Verstreken, Alfred *c.j.* '73 (LA) Santa Barbara, CA Holy Cross; [D] Santa Barbara, CA Bishop Garcia Diego High School.
Verstynen, Robert J. '47 (RCK) Retired.
Vesbit, Thomas (GR) Retired.
Vesely, James J. '54 (CLV) Brooklyn, OH St. Thomas More.
Vesey, John E. '68 (BRK) Brooklyn, NY Blessed Sacrament.
Vesga, Mario '62 (SD) Chula Vista, CA Our Lady of Guadalupe.
Vessels, John L. *s.j.* '57 (FWT) Baton Rouge, LA Immaculate Conception; [K] Baton Rouge, LA Martin Luther King, Jr. Student Center; [K] Lake Dallas, TX Montserrat Jesuit Retreat House.
Vest, Joseph E. '81 (L) Fairfield, KY St. Michael.
Veszelovszky, Albin V. *o.praem.* '44 (GB)[I] De Pere, WI St. Norbert Abbey; [N] De Pere, WI Canons Regular of Magnovarad, Ltd..
Vetrano, Michael A. '79 (RVC) West Islip, NY Our Lady of Lourdes.
Vetrano, Michael (RVC) Procurator & Advocates.
Vetter, Austin '93 (BIS) Dickinson, ND St. Patrick; Presbyteral Council.
Vetter, Joseph G. '73 (R)[H] Durham, NC Newman Catholic Student Center Duke University; Diocesan Consultors; Priests' Council.
Vetter, Wendelyn '60 (FAR) Hillsboro, ND St. Rose of Lima.
Vetter, Wendelyn '60 (FAR) Reynolds, ND Our Lady of Perpetual Help.
Vetter, Wendelyn (FAR) Rural Life.
Vetter, Wendelyn (FAR) Judges.
Vettese, Donald *s.j.* '82 (TOL)[C] Toledo, OH St. John's Jesuit High School; [N] Toledo, OH Saint John's Jesuit High School Foundation.
Vettickal, Sebastian '91 (LA) Diamond Bar, CA St. Denis.
Vettikanakudy, Peter *o.f.m.cap.* '95 (NY) New York, NY Our Lady Queen of Angels.
Vettuvelil, Abraham *m.s.f.s.* '90 (ATL)[K] Lawrenceville The Missionaries of St. Francis De Sales.
Vettuvelil, Abraham (CHI) Arlington Heights, IL St. James.
Veverka, Floribert *o.f.m.* '48 (SFD)[L] Springfield, IL Our Lady of Angels Friary.
Vezhaparambil, Paul *c.m.i.* '64 (NY) Lawrence Hospital.
Vgochukwa, John '84 (BRK) Brooklyn, NY St. Thomas Aquinas.
Via, Anthony P. *s.j.* '62 (SPK)[B] Spokane, WA Gonzaga University.
Via, Anthony P. *s.j.* '62 (P)[L] Portland Jesuit Provincial Office (Society of Jesus, Oregon Prov.).
Viall, James A. '54 (CLV) Cleveland, OH St. Rose of Lima; Administrative Leave.
Viall, John L. '59 (CLV) North Royalton, OH St. Albert the Great.
Vialpando, Kenneth L. '91 (SLC) Air National Guard Chaplains; Salt Lake City, UT Our Lady of Guadalupe; Priests' Personnel Board.
Viana, Carlos Sergio (BO)[V] Cambridge, MA.
Viana, Carlos *s.j.* (BO)[V] Cambridge, MA Faber House.
Vianney, John '88 (LA) Pico Rivera, CA St. Mariana de Paredes.
Vianney, Peter J. (NY) Port Ewen, NY Presentation of the Virgin Mary.
Vibandor, Joselito '03 (SAC) Sacramento, CA St. Anthony.
Viberti, Victor L. *s.s.p.* '38 (NY)[B] New York, NY Society of St. Paul.
Vicari, Marc A. '97 (NEW) South Orange, NJ Our Lady of Sorrows.
Vicedo, Hermenegildo '63 (SJN) San Juan, PR Nuestra Senora de la Providencia.
Vicens, Hipolito *c.ss.r.* '94 (CGS)[B] Aguas Buenas, PR Casa Cristo Redentor.
Vicente, Francisco '49 (OAK) Antioch, CA Holy Rosary.
Vicente, Francisco *o.p.* (OAK) Defenders of the Bond.
Vicentini, Joseph *c.s.* '55 (KC) Kansas City, MO Holy Rosary.
Vichas, Walter A. '49 (HRT) Retired.
Vichich, Michael T. '74 (MAR) Hermansville, MI St. John Neumann.
Vick, James L. '99 (KNX) Chattanooga, TN Our Lady of Perpetual Help.
Vickery, Richard F. '48 (MAN) Manchester, NH St. Catherine Retired.
Victor, P. R. '88 (CC) Corpus Christi, TX SS. Cyril and Methodius.
Victor, Ronald J. '78 (DET) St. Clair, MI St. Mary.
Victoria, Robert '91 (LA) Los Angeles, CA Sacred Heart.
Vida, George N. '57 (VNN) Anaheim, CA Annunciation.
Vida, George (VNN) Eparchial Consultors – Presbyteral Council.
Vidal, Gustavo Adolfo '97 (SLC) St. George, UT St. George's Central Utah Correctional Facility; [H] St. George, UT Dixie College, Newman Center.
Vidal, Jesus Hernandez (OAK) Brentwood, CA Immaculate Heart of Mary.
Vidal, Robert S. '66 (ORG) Seal Beach, CA St. Anne's.
Vidmar, John C. *o.p.* '80 (WDC)[B] Washington, DC Dominican House of Studies.
Vidmar, John *o.p.* '80 (PRO)[P] Providence St. Thomas Aquinas Priory at Providence College.
Vidra, Thomas '59 (SD) Retired.
Vidrine, Richard '95 (LAF) Military Chaplains; Navy Chaplains.
Vidro, Floyd Mercado '03 (CGS) Naranjito, PR San Miguel Arcangel.
Vieages, Harold '64 (RNO) Leave of Absence.
Vieck, Hilary F. '55 (EVN) Linton, IN St. Peter.
Viegas, Daniel P. *s.j.* '87 (STL)[C] Saint Louis University.
Viegas, Patrick *s.j.* '87 (STL)[O] St. Louis, MO Jesuit Community Corporation at St. Louis University – Jesuit Hall.
Viego, Carlos '98 (NEW) Cliffside Park, NJ Epiphany.
Vieira, John S. '97 (SB) Indio, CA Our Lady of Perpetual Help; Riverside, CA Our Lady of Guadalupe Shrine.
Vieira, John (SB) Elected Members.
Vieira, Victor M. '67 (PRO) East Providence, RI St. Francis Xavier.
Vielgus, Thaddeus A. '54 (MET) Retired.
Vien, John R. '93 (STL) Oakville, MO Queen of All Saints.
Viera, Edwin Mercado (ARE) Diocesan Tribunal of Arecibo.
Viera, Manuel *o.f.m.* '82 (SFE) Pena Blanca, NM Nuestra Senora De Guadalupe.
Vierling, Ronald M. *m.f.c.* '92 (PH) Warrington, PA St. Joseph.
Vierra, Theodore A. '60 (LA) Los Angeles, CA St. Paul the Apostle.
Vieson, Paul F. *s.m.* '84 (CIN)[D] Dayton, OH The University of Dayton; [M] Dayton OH Marianist Community.
Viet, Nguyen Ngoc (LA)[Q] Long Beach, CA.
Viet–Chau, Joachim *s.s.s.* '72 (CLV)[O] Gretna, LA.
Vietes, Jesus *ss.cc.* '67 (SJN) Guaynabo, PR Nuestra Senora de la Paz.
Viet Tran, Bac–Hai '84 (NO) Pearl River, LA SS. Peter and Paul.
Vieweg, Robert R. '64 (CLV) Grafton, OH Immaculate Conception; Cleveland, OH St. Vincent de Paul.
Vigeant, Wilfrid J. *s.j.* '46 (BO)[V] Weston, MA Campion Health Center, Inc..
Vigil, Joe '80 (SFE) Albuquerque, NM Our Lady of Guadalupe.
Vigil, Michael A. (GLP) Army National Guard Chaplains.
Vigil, Michael '85 (GLP) Gallup, NM Cathedral of the Sacred Heart.
Vigil, Michael (GLP) Adjutant Judicial Vicar; Judges; Vicars Forane.
Vigil, Paul E. '91 (LA) Reseda, CA St. Catherine of Siena.
Vigilanti, John A. '72 (NY) Chappaqua, NY St. John and St. Mary; Vice Judicial Vicars; Mt. Kisco Office.
Vigliotta, Thomas F. *o.f.m.* '85 (CHR) Anderson, SC St. Mary of the Angels.
Vigliotta, William J. *s.m.m.* '54 (RVC)[M] Eastport, NY Shrine of Our Lady of the Island.
Vignato, Joe *s.x.* '93 (PAT)[M] Wayne Xaverian Missionary Fathers.
Vignoe, Joseph M. '58 (BUR) Retired.
Vignola, Robert R. *c.m.* '50 (BRK)[V] Jamaica, NY St. Vincent's House.
Vignone, John J. '75 (CAM) Landisville, NJ Queen of Angels.
Vigues, Gabriel '93 (MIA) Pompano Beach, FL St. Elizabeth of Hungary Catholic Church; Spiritual Moderators.
ViHorio, Guerrera '91 (HRT) On Duty Outside the Archdiocese.
Vijayan, Joseph '80 (NY) Bronx, NY Holy Spirit.
Vila, Carlos S. '83 (AGN) Defender of the Bond; Tamuning, GU St. Anthony and St. Victor.
Vila, Richard C. '02 (TR) Medford, NJ St. Mary of the Lakes.
Viladesau, Richard R. '69 (RVC) Elmont, NY Our Lady Star of the Sea, Mission Chapel; Priests Released from Diocesan Assignment.
Vilano, Anthony '96 (SAT) Stonewall, TX St. Francis Xavier; Priests Personnel Board.
Vilano, Tony '96 (SAT) Fredericksburg, TX St. Mary's.
Vilaplana, Jose *s.j.* '63 (NY) White Plains, NY St. Bernard.
Vilar, Juan Diaz '69 (NEW)[B] Jersey City, NJ Jesuit Center.
Vilela, Renelmo Ramirez '84 (CGS) Humacao, PR Dulce Nombre de Jesus.
Vileo, Stephen L. '87 (DET) Temperance, MI Our Lady of Mt. Carmel.
Vilkauskas, Edward J. *c.s.sp.* (DET) Detroit, MI St. Mary.
Villa, Aurelio *o.f.m.* '64 (SR) Sonoma, CA St. Leo.
Villa, Eduardo '80 (BWN) Hidalgo, TX St. Frances Xavier Cabrini.
Villa, James *o.f.m.* (NY)[EE] Mount Vernon, NY St. Bernardine of Siena Friary.
Villa, Joseph L. '97 (IND) Clinton, IN Sacred Heart; Rockville, IN St. Joseph; Universal, IN St. Joseph.
Villa, Juan Jose *o.f.m.* (SAT) San Antonio, TX San Jose y San Miguel.
Villa, Leonard F. '86 (NY) Yonkers, NY St. Eugene.
Villa, Robert '02 (HRT) Bristol, CT St. Joseph.
Villabon, German *o.s.a.* '54 (RVC) Rockville Centre, NY St. Agnes Cathedral.
Villada, Luis E. '82 (SJN) Canovanas, PR Resurreccion del Senior.
Villaescusa, Gregory T. '03 (SCR) Williamsport, PA Annunciation.
Villafranca, Eugenio *c.m.* '53 (SJN) San Juan, PR Jesus Maestro.
Villagomez, Jose *o.f.m.cap.* '74 (AGN) Agana Heights, GU Our Lady of Mount Carmel; [F] Agana Heights, GU St. Fidelis Friary; [F] Agat, GU Capuchin Fraternity; Promoter of Justice.
Villalobos, Alberto '85 (LA) Los Angeles, CA Sacred Heart.
Villalobos, David '96 (SR) Santa Rosa, CA St. Rose of Lima.
Villalobos, Oscar '86 (LAR) Hebbronville, TX Our Lady of Guadalupe.
Villalon, Jose M. '89 (BWN) Los Fresnos, TX St. Cecilia; [D] Brownsville, TX Jail Ministry; Youth and Young Adult Steering Committee.
Villalon, Jose (BWN) Chaplains.
Villalta, Moises *o.f.m.cap.* '95 (WDC)[B] Washington, DC St. Francis Friary–Capuchin College.
Villamide, Aniceto '67 (BGP) Bridgeport, CT St. Peter.
Villamide, Aniceto '67 (BGP)[X] Bridgeport, CT Hispanic Social Ministries of Fairfield County, Inc..
Villamide, Aniceto (BGP) Cursillos of Fairfield County, Inc..
Villamide, Aniceto (BGP) Episcopal Vicar for Hispanics.
Villamide, Aniceto (BGP) Parochial Examiners.
Villamide, Aniceto (BGP) Presbyteral Council.
Villamide, Aniceto (BGP) Pastors' Vocation Advisory Board.

Villamide, Aniceto (BGP) Hispanic Apostolate, Episcopal Vicar for.
Villamide, Aniceto (BGP) Diocesan Consultors.
Villani, Ralph A. '68 (NY) Mt. Kisco, NY St. Francis of Assisi.
Villani, Rocco D. '61 (BRK) Brooklyn, NY St. Mary Mother of Jesus.
Villano, Richard R. '58 (STP) Minneapolis, MN St. Helena.
Villanova, Richard A. '67 (NEW) Hillside, NJ St. Catherine of Siena.
Villanueva, Alfred '96 (ELP) El Paso, TX Our Lady of the Light.
Villanueva, Felix Oliveras (CGS) Board of Diocesan Government; Economic Administrator.
Villanueva, Jose A. '63 (SAT) Rocksprings, TX Sacred Heart of Mary.
Villanueva, Jose '96 (FTW) Ligonier, IN St. Patrick; Ligonier.
Villanueva, Ruben '88 (MEM) Memphis, TN St. Paul The Apostle.
Villar, Demetrio L. '46 (RVC) Retired.
Villaronga, Angel *o.f.m.* '51 (MIA)[H] Miami, FL Franciscan Fathers' Residence.
Villaronga, Angel *o.f.m.* (MIA) Christian Family Movement.
Villaroya, Ernesto (DAL) On Leave.
Villarreal, Carlos A. (BWN) Office of the Bishop; Diocesan Campaign for Human Development; Presbyteral Council; Board of Directors; Brownsville.
Villarreal, Louis J. *o.m.i.* '65 (BWN) McAllen, TX Sacred Heart.
Villarreal, Manuel "Meme" *o.m.i.* '78 (LA) San Fernando, CA St. Ferdinand.
Villarreal, Ricardo '98 (YAK) Cashmere, WA St. Francis Xavier; Leavenworth, WA Our Lady of the Snows; Presbyteral Council Executive Committee; Clergy Personnel Board.
Villarroya, Pedro '59 (LA)[Q] Los Angeles, CA Amat Residence II.
Villarrubia, Jerry (HT) College of Consultors.
Villarrubia, Roger E. (Jerry) '99 (HT) Houma, LA Cathedral of St. Francis De Sales.
Villarrubia, Roger "Jerry" E. (HT) Priests Council.
Villaruel, Alvin M. '94 (SR) Santa Rosa, CA Cathedral of St. Eugene; [B] Santa Rosa, CA Cardinal Newman High School.
Villaruel, Alvin (SR) Boy Scouts.
Villa Verde, Alberto *s.j.* '56 (SJN).
Villaverde, Francisco P. *o.p.* '55 (MIA)[H] Miami, FL St. John Bosco.
Villaverde, Tirso S. '96 (CHI) Chicago, IL St. Francis of Assisi/Our Lady of the Angels; Chicago, IL St. Peter Canisius.
Villegas, Diego '74 (BRK) Corona, NY St. Leo.
Villegas, Efraim *o.s.b.* '88 (BIS)[A] Richardton, ND Assumption Abbey; (FgM).
Villegas, Gonzalo J. '92 (TUC) Tucson, AZ Our Lady, Queen of All Saints; Vicars Forane; Council of Priests.
Villegas, Hector '02 (STO) Modesto, CA St. Stanislaus Church (Pastor of).
Villegas, Hernando '57 (MIA) Retired.
Villegas, Jorge C. '66 (E) Erie, PA St. Stephen.
Villegas, Jorge (E) Hispanic Apostolate.
Villegas, Julian '90 (TYL) Jacksonville, TX Our Lady of Sorrows.
Villegas, Robert *c.s.c.* '63 (LSC) Chamberino, NM San Luis Rey.
Villegas, Samuel C. '56 (LA) Huntington Park, CA St. Matthias Retired.
Villemaire, Arthur '51 (SP) Retired.
Villero, Melchor *m.j.* '76 (LA) Los Angeles, CA Precious Blood.
Villerot, Henry E. '41 (DET) Retired.
Villerot, Thomas H. '43 (DET) Royal Oak, MI St. Mary Retired.
Villote, Augusto E. '03 (SFR) Burlingame, CA St. Catherine of Siena.
Vima, Amalor '71 (TLS) Okmulgee, OK St. Anthony's; Diocesan Senators.
Vincent, Amos J. '49 (LKC) Retired.
Vincent, Charles M. '86 (TLS) Poteau, OK Immaculate Conception.
Vincent, David P. '64 (CIN) Versailles, OH Holy Family; Versailles, OH St. Denis.
Vincent, John F. '54 (WIN) Retired.
Vincent, John *o.s.c.* '58 (PHX)[G] Phoenix, AZ Crosier Community of Phoenix (Canons Regular of the Order of the Holy Cross).
Vincent, Michael A. *s.j.* (CLV)[D] Cleveland, OH St. Ignatius High School.
Vincent, Robert G. '57 (NO) Retired.
Vincenzo, Dennis J. '91 (HRT) Suffield, CT Sacred Heart.
Vinci, Guy '59 (NY) Bronxville, NY St. Joseph.
Vinci, Terzo *s.a.c.* '58 (NY) Yonkers, NY Our Lady of Mt. Carmel.
Vincke, Gerald '99 (LAN)[L] DeWitt, MI Bethany House (Spiritual Life Center for Youth); Director of Seminarians; Emmaus House.
Vincze, Michael M. '40 (MET) Woodbridge, NJ Our Lady of Mount Carmel Retired.
Vinh Ngoc Nguyen, Michael Joseph '90 (NO) New Orleans, LA The Resurrection Of Our Lord.
Vinsko, John J. *m.m.* '62 (SJ)[M] Los Altos, CA Maryknoll.
Vinslauski, Robert B. '71 (SFS) Madison, SD St. Thomas Aquinas.
Viola, William L. '84 (BAL) Odenton, MD St. Joseph.
Violette, Lawrence M. '93 (ARL) Clifton, VA St. Andrew the Apostle.
Virella, Jorge L. (ARE) Seminary Board.
Virella, Jorge (ARE) Priest's Senate (Consejo Presbiteral).
Virella, Miguel *s.v.d.* '96 (TR) Neptune, NJ Our Lady of Providence.
Virella Sanchez, Jorge L. (ARE) Diocesan Tribunal of Arecibo.
Virgen, Javier G. '93 (SLC) West Valley City, UT SS. Peter and Paul.
Virginia, Stepehn G. (COL) Medical Experts.
Virginia, Stephen G. '79 (COL) Columbus, OH St. Peter.
Virgnola, Robert R. '50 (C.M.)[AA] St. Catherine Infirmary.
Virnig, Laurn '63 (SCL) Royalton, MN Holy Cross; Royalton, MN Holy Trinity; Diocesan Consultors.
Virrey, Armando '03 (ORG) Anaheim, CA St. Boniface.
Virtue, William D. '75 (PEO) On Duty Outside the Diocese; Lee, IL St. James.
Virus, Keith M. '92 (GRY) Munster, IN St. Thomas More.
Visbisky, Richard W. '62 (BO) Brockton, MA Good Samaritan Medical Center; [P] Brockton, MA Good Samaritan Medical Center.
Viscardi, Christopher J. *s.j.* '76 (MOB)[A] Mobile, AL Spring Hill College.
Viscardi, Christopher *s.j.* (MOB) Hispanic Apostolate; Hispanic Pastoral Ministry.
Visconti, Luciano M. *c.r.s.p.* '42 (BUF)[B] Youngstown, NY St. Anthony M. Zaccaria Seminary.
Visconti, Luciano *c.r.s.p.* '42 (SD) Pala, CA Mission San Antonio de Pala.
Visperas, Joseph '86 (LA) La Mirada, CA Beatitudes of Our Lord; La Mirada, CA St. Paul of the Cross.
Vistal, Felix F. (DAL).
Vistal, Felix '87 (DAL) Dallas, TX St. Augustine Catholic Church.
Vita, Mariano L. '42 (CHI) Retired.
Vitacolonna, Xavier *c.p.* '74 (NEW)[N] "Compassion" Magazine.
Vitaglione, Robert '76 (BRK) Brooklyn, NY St. Joseph's.
Vitale, Louis *o.f.m.* '63 (SFR) San Francisco, CA St. Boniface; St. Francis Hospital.
Vitali, James V. *o.s.a.* '81 (WDC)[B] Washington, DC Augustinian College, Order of St. Augustine.
Vitali, John *c.r.s.* '71 (MAN)[H] Allenstown, NH Pine Haven Boys Center.
Vitali, Theodore *c.p.* '69 (MET)[H] St. Louis, MO.
Vitaliano, Dominic J. '91 (PEO) On Duty Outside the Diocese; Air Force Chaplains.
Vitela, Francisco '68 (LA) El Monte, CA Our Lady of Guadalupe.
Vithanage, Denzil *s.s.s.* '93 (TYL) Marshall, TX St. Joseph; Deans; Presbyteral Council.
Vitillo, Robert J. '72 (PAT) On Duty Outside the Diocese.
Vito, Alfred J. '84 (SCR) Canadensis, PA St. Bernadette.
Vitro, Thomas J. '66 (CHI) Other Assignments.
Vitte, Jules '49 (NO) Retired.
Vittengl, Donald J. *m.m.* '56 (NY)[EE] Maryknoll Maryknoll Fathers and Brothers.
Vitturino, Saverio T. '67 (WDC) Benedict, MD St. Francis de Sales.
Vituj, George L. '48 (CLV)[M] Cleveland, OH Sts. Mary and Joseph Home for the Aged Retired.
Vitus, Frank '75 (JOL) Wilmington, IL St. Rose.
Viveiros, Joseph F. '74 (FR) Swansea, MA St. Dominic's.
Vivero, David '90 (ORL) Rockledge, FL St. Mary's.
Viviano, Benedict T. *o.p.* '66 (CHI)[N] Chicago Dominicans (Provincial Office).
Viviano, Charles '89 (ORL) Deltona, FL St. Clare.
Viviano, Nino '64 (ALX) On Duty Outside the Diocese.
Vivona, Anthony '53 (BRK) Retired.
Vivona, Francis M. '69 (LAV) Las Vegas, NV St. Elizabeth Ann Seton.
Vivona, Francis M. (VNN) Eparchial Consultors – Presbyteral Council; Judicial Vicar.
Vivona, Francis *j.c.l.* '69 (VNN) Las Vegas, NV Our Lady of Wisdom Italo–Greek.
Vivona, Francis (VNN) Judge; Censor; Commission for the Implementation of the Particular Law.
Vizcaino, Mario B. *sch.p.* '60 (PH)[AA] Piarist Fathers Latin Mission.
Vizcaino, Mario B. *sch.p.* '60 (MIA)[K] Miami, FL Southeast Pastoral Institute; [K] Miami, FL; [M] Miami, FL SEPI Evangelization and Education Foundation, Inc.; [M] Miami, FL Federacion de Institutos Pastorales, Inc..
Vizcarra, Angel '46 (DAL)[K] Irving, TX Dominican Priory of St. Albert the Great.
Vjecha, Michael J. *s.j.* '87 (DET)[M] Washington, DC Leonard Neale House; [K] Temperance, MI.
Vlasz, Melvyn J. '63 (RCK) Retired.
Vlaun, James C. '79 (RVC)[C] West Islip, NY St. John the Baptist.
Vlaun, James C. '88 (RVC) Associate Vocation Directors.
Vliet, Charles Van *f.s.s.p.* '96 (SCR)[M] Elmhurst Priestly Fraternity of St. Peter (F.S.S.P.), North American District Headquarters.
Vo, Peter De Ta *s.v.d.* '87 (CHI)[N] Chicago, IL Divine Word Theologate.
Vo, Peter Phong '88 (NEW) Montclair, NJ Our Lady of Mt. Carmel.
Vo, Peter '88 (NEW) Rahway, NJ St. Mary's.
Vo., John K. '86 (LA) El Monte, CA Nativity.
Vodoklys, Edward J. *s.j.* '91 (WOR)[O] Worcester, MA Jesuits of Holy Cross College, Inc..
Vodzogbe, Christopher (CHI) Harvey, IL Ascension–St. Susanna.
Voegele, Fridolin *o.f.m.* '58 (CIN)[M] Cincinnati, OH St. Clement Friary Retired.
Voelker, David A. '74 (RC) Ellsworth AFB.
Voelker, David A. '74 (BEL) Military Chaplains; Air Force Chaplains.
Voelker, Harold H. '54 (STL) Retired.
Voelker, James A. '69 (BEL) East St. Louis, IL St. Joseph; East St. Louis, IL St. Philip.
Voelker, Karl J. *s.j.* '72 (WIN) Mankato, MN SS. Peter and Paul's.
Voelker, Lawrence '66 (IND) Indianapolis, IN Holy Cross; Indianapolis, IN St. Patrick; Indiana Women's Prison.
Voelker, Nicholas A. '02 (WCH) Wichita, KS St. Elizabeth Ann Seton.
Voelker, Peter H. *c.ss.r.* '61 (GAL) Houston, TX Holy Ghost.
Voellmecke, Francis W. '59 (CIN)[B] Cincinnati, OH Mt. St. Mary's Seminary of the West; Judges.
Vogan, Howard L. '69 (DET) Livonia, MI St. Genevieve.
Vogan, Robert C. '70 (PH) Aston, PA St. Joseph.
Vogel, Arthur '57 (SCL) Retired.
Vogel, Bill *s.j.* (YAK) Toppenish, WA St. Aloysius.
Vogel, Carl J. '50 (DAL) Retired.
Vogel, Charles P. '43 (BRK) Brooklyn, NY St. Sylvester Retired.
Vogel, F. Philip *s.d.s.* '69 (WDC)[B] Silver Spring, MD Salvatorian Community.
Vogel, John J. '86 (LA) Lancaster, CA Sacred Heart.
Vogel, Joseph '87 (SFS) Sioux Falls, SD St. Michael.
Vogel, Marcel J. '89 (GF) Chinook, MT St. Gabriel's.
Vogel, Marcel (GF) Vicars Forane.
Vogel, Walter J. '58 (MIL) Greendale, WI St. Alphonsus.
Vogel, Walter P. *o.s.a.* '63 (LA) Los Angeles, CA Our Mother of Good Counsel.
Vogel, Willaim *s.j.* (YAK) Social Justice and Human Life Commission.
Vogelpohl, Daniel J. '75 (COV) Fort Mitchell, KY Blessed Sacrament.
Vogelpohl, Herbert *o.s.b.* '39 (LR)[A] Subiaco, AR Subiaco Monastery.
Vogelsang, Clifford R. '63 (IND) Jeffersonville, IN St. Augustine.
Vogelsang, Clifford (IND) Board of Consultors; Deaneries and Deans.
Vogl, John C. (YAK) Waterville, WA St. Joseph's.
Vogl, Robert R. '47 (DUB)[I] Dubuque, IA Marian Hall Infirmary Retired.
Vogler, Jean '70 (EVN) Evansville, IN Holy Trinity; Permanent Diaconate Program.
Voglio, John J. '87 (NY) Bronx, NY St. Clare of Assisi.
Vogt, Dick *s.j.* '63 (STL) Ferguson, MO Our Lady of Guadalupe.
Vogt, Emmerich W. *o.p.* '78 (P) San Francisco, CA St. Dominic; [N] San Francisco, CA St. Dominic Priory.
Vogt, Eric *o.s.b.* '79 (E) St. Marys, PA Sacred Heart of Jesus.
Vogt, John '62 (PHX) Retired.
Vogt, Otto J. '50 (ROC) Rochester, NY St. Thomas More Retired.
Vogt, Richard J. *s.j.* '63 (STL)[O] St. Louis, MO Jesuit Community Corporation at St. Louis University – Jesuit Hall.
Vogt, Robert H. *s.j.* '61 (NY)[EE] New York, NY Murray–Weigel Hall.
Vogt, Robert W. '62 (BUF) Advocates Retired.
Vogt, William E. '46 (GRY) Retired.
Vogt, William '56 (FRS) Retired.
Voigt, Richard *s.d.b.* '78 (LA)[Q] Los Angeles, CA Dominic Savio Salesian Residence.
Voiland, George T. '50 (BRK) Long Island City, NY Most Precious Blood Retired.
Voiss, James K. *s.j.* '88 (STL)[C] Saint Louis University; [O] St. Louis, MO Jesuit Community Corporation at St. Louis University – Jesuit Hall.
Voity, Maurice '79 (SAN) San Angelo, TX Cathedral of the Sacred Heart; Presbyteral Council; Judges.
Vojtek, John '76 (PIT) Pittsburgh, PA All Saints.
Vojtik, James P. '62 (MIL) Belgium, WI St. Mary.
Volavola, Simione *m.s.c.* '01 (MI) Marshall Islands, MH Queen of Peace.

Volertas, Vytas '93 (BRK) Maspeth, NY Transfiguration.
Volertas, Vytautas (BRK)[U] Lithuanuan.
Volino, Michael J. '92 (ROC) Rochester, NY St. John the Evangelist.
Volk, Marvin C. '74 (BEL) Belleville, IL Blessed Sacrament; Diocesan Consultors; Diaconate, Office of Permanent.
Volk, Michael A. (MRY) Vocations Board.
Volk, Michael L. (MRY) Cursillo.
Volk, Michael '92 (MRY) Gonzales, CA St. Theodore; Special Assignment; Vocations Director.
Volk, Norman *o.m.i.* '68 (SFS) Sisseton, SD St. Catherine; Sisseton, SD St. Peter.
Volkert, Daniel P. '01 (MAD) Cambridge, WI St. Pius X.
Volkert, James T. '90 (MIL) Union Grove, WI St. John the Baptist; Kansasville, WI St. Francis Xavier.
Volkmer, Michael *c.pp.s.* '68 (KC) St. Joseph, MO St. Francis Xavier.
Voll, Walter Urban *o.p.* '49 (PRO)[P] Providence St. Thomas Aquinas Priory at Providence College.
Vollenweider, Roy W. *s.j.* '47 (NO)[P] New Orleans, LA Ignatius Residence.
Vollkommer, Andrew J. '86 (CHR) Chapin, SC Our Lady of the Lake.
Vollmer, Caron *o.f.m.* '47 (GLP) Lukachukai, AZ St. Isabel; Vicar for Indian Affairs; Diocesan Navajo Mission Board.
Vollmer, Daniel '02 (PHX) Mesa, AZ Christ the King.
Vollmer, Gary L. '77 (STL) St. Peters, MO All Saints.
Vollmer, Raymond A. '40 (PIT) Retired.
Vollmer, William C. '58 (COS) Retired.
Vollmer, William '97 (CHI).
Vollmer–Konig, Josef (DAL)[A] Vocations.
Vollor, John '79 (JKS) West Point, MS Immaculate Conception.
Vollor, William '63 (BLX) Hattiesburg, MS Holy Rosary.
Volmi, Dennis G. '75 (WIL) Military Chaplains; Air Force Chaplains.
Volpert, Robert C. '61 (L) Retired.
Volskis, Aloyzas '85 (DET) Southfield, MI Divine Providence.
Voltaggio, Fred '71 (CAM) Berlin, NJ Our Lady of Mt. Carmel; Members.
Volungis, Alphonse A. '45 (WOR)[N] Worcester, MA.
Volz, Anthony '85 (IND) Indianapolis, IN St. Michael the Archangel; St. Mary–of–the–Woods, IN St. Mary; West Terre Haute, IN St. Leonard of Port Maurice.
Volz, Edward *o.s.p.p.e.* '88 (GBG) Cadogan, PA St. Lawrence; [H] Kittanning, PA Pauline Fathers Monastery.
Volz, Gerald '92 (KCK) Regional Pastoral Leaders.
Volz, Jerry '92 (KCK)[K] Emporia, KS.
Vomund, Jeffrey G. '97 (STL) St. Charles, MO St. Cletus.
Vona, Michael S. '68 (TR) Farmingdale, NJ St. Catherine of Siena.
Von Ah, Richard J. '58 (DAV)[L] Davenport, IA Kahl Home for the Aged and Infirm Retired.
von Arx, Jeffrey P. *s.j.* '81 (NY)[EE] Cardinal Spellman Hall, Jesuit Community.
Von Arx, Jeffrey *s.j.* (NY)[C] Bronx, NY Fordham University.
von Behren, Thomas R. *c.s.v.* '83 (CHI)[D] Arlington Heights, IL St. Viator High School.
Vonderhaar, Eugene F. '59 (CIN) Tipp City, OH St. John the Baptist Retired.
Vonderhaar, Ralph E. *s.j.* '57 (STL)[O] St. Louis, MO Hallahan House.
VonderHaar, Roland '48 (LSC) Retired.
Vondras, John J. '85 (NY) Newburgh, NY St. Francis of Assisi.
von Duerbeck, Julian *o.s.b.* '76 (JOL)[A] Lisle, IL Benedictine University; [L] Lisle, IL St. Procopius Abbey.
Von Essen, Pacificus *s.a.* '53 (NY)[EE] Garrison Franciscan Friars of the Atonement, Minister General Office.
Von Euw, Vincent P. '66 (BO) Dorchester, MA St. Ambrose.
von Fauer, Stephen C. '41 (STF)[E] West Burke, VT Mary Theotokos Centre.
Von Fauer, Stephen C. '53 (BUR) Retired.
Von Handorf, Joseph '75 (LEX) Morehead, KY Church of Jesus Our Savior.
Von Kaenel, George E. *s.j.* '58 (CHI)[C] Chicago, IL Jesuit Community at Loyola University Chicago; [N] Chicago, IL Chicago Province of the Society of Jesus–Provincial Office; [X] Chicago, IL Jesuit International Missions, Inc..
Von Kerssenbrock, Joachim *s.j.* '59 (NY)[II] Bronx, NY American St. Boniface Society, Incorporated.
Von Kobs, Allan G. *o.f.m.* '82 (NY) New York, NY St. Francis of Assisi.
Von Kobs, Allan G. *o.f.m.* '82 (PAT)[P] Paterson, NJ St. Anthony's Guild.
Von Lehmen, Jeffrey D. '85 (COV) Covington, KY St. Patrick; [C] Villa Hills, KY Villa Madonna High School.
Von Maluski, Kris M. '01 (PRO) Providence, RI St. Edward; North Providence, RI St. Anthony.
Vonnahmen, Robert J. '56 (BEL) Retired.
von Nell, Boniface *o.s.b.* '91 (WDC)[M] Washington, DC St. Anselm's Abbey.
Von Son, Henry A. '49 (LA) Retired.
Von Tobel, James E. *s.j.* '67 (CLV) University Heights, OH Gesu.
Voor, Joseph H. '50 (L) Louisville, KY St. Brigid; Louisville KY St. James Retired.
Voorhes, Fred R. '71 (BUF) Boston, NY St. John the Baptist.
Voorhies, Bennett J. '83 (LAF) On Duty Outside the Diocese.
Voorhies, Bennett J. (SFE) Chancellor College of Consultors; Presbyteral Council of the Archdiocese of Santa Fe; Finance Council.
Voorhies, Louis '67 (ALX) Retired.
Voorhies, Thomas P. '90 (LAF) Eunice, LA St. Anthony of Padua.
Voors, David '81 (FTW) Fort Wayne, IN Our Lady of Good Hope.
Vorderlandwehr, Adrian *o.s.b.* '67 (OKL) Prague, OK St. Wenceslaus, National Shrine of the Infant Jesus of Prague.
Voris, Francis *o.f.m.cap.* '73 (SAG) Saginaw, MI St. Anthony of Padua.
Vorisek, Rudolph T. *c.s.p.* '56 (NY) New York, NY St. Paul the Apostle; [EE] Jamaica Estates Paulist Fathers Generalate.
Vorwald, Aloysius J. '64 (DUB) Rowley, IA All Saints; Independence, IA St. John the Evangelist; Personnel Advisory Board.
Vorwoldt, James F. *s.j.* '71 (CHI)[D] Chicago, IL St. Ignatius Jesuit Community.
Vorwoldt, James S. *s.j.* '70 (CHI)[D] Chicago, IL St. Ignatius College Prep.
Vos, Jude '96 (FAR) Absent on Leave.
Vos, Thomas *o.f.m.* '61 (KNX) Madisonville, TN St. Joseph the Worker; [F] Knoxville, TN Franciscan Friars.
Vos, Tom *o.f.m.* (KNX) Diocesan Consultors.
Vos, William '64 (SCL) Mora, MN St. Mary's; Mora, MN St. Kathryn's; Catholic Relief Services; Holy Childhood Association; Propagation of the Faith.
Vosen, Gerald P. '61 (MAD) Baraboo, WI St. Joseph; Deaneries.
Vosko, Richard '69 (ALB) Special Assignment.
Voss, Bernard L. '66 (BEL) Belleville, IL St. Henry; [J] Fairview Heights, IL.
Voss, Dennis F. '64 (BEL) Oakdale, IL St. Anthony; St. Libory, IL St. Liborius; Diocesan Council of Catholic Women
Voss, Donald J. '93 (PBR) McKeesport, PA St. Nicholas.
Voss, Marcus J. *o.s.b.* '71 (BIR)[B] Cullman, AL St. Bernard Preparatory School; [E] Cullman, AL St. Bernard Abbey.
Voss, Robert '70 (PHX) Scottsdale, AZ St. Bernard of Clairvaux.
Vossler, Brian E. '91 (E) Galeton, PA St. Bibiana.
Votraw, Thomas G. '60 (OG) Retired.
Votraw, Wilbur J. '55 (SY) Syracuse, NY St. Vincent de Paul Retired.
Votruba, George L. '54 (SUP) Retired.
Votto, Silvano P. *s.j.* '73 (SJ)[M] Los Gatos, CA Sacred Heart Jesuit Center.
Vouk, William '86 (SCL) Little Falls, MN Holy Family; Little Falls, MN St. Mary; Little Falls, MN Our Lady of Lourdes.
Vowells, John J. *s.j.* '90 (KC)[B] Kansas City, KS Rockhurst University Continuing Education Center/ National Seminars Group; [J] Kansas City, MO Rockhurst Jesuit Community.
Vowels, G. Timothy '77 (STL) Chesterfield, MO Incarnate Word.
Voyt, Stephen A. '85 (PT) Military Chaplains; Air Force Chaplains.
Voytek, John M. *o.f.m.conv.* '82 (TR) Cromwell, CT St. John.
Voytek, Leonard E. (ALT) Cambria Deanery; Windber, PA St. Elizabeth Ann Seton.
Voytovich, Steven '92 (HRT)[I] New Haven, CT Hospital of St. Raphael.
Vrabel, George A. '87 (CLV) Berea, OH St. Mary.
Vrabely George M. '53 (GRY) La Porte, IN St. Peter.
Vrana, John G. '67 (CLV) Concord Twp., OH St. Gabriel; Presbyteral Conveners.
Vrana, John P. '56 (OKL) Retired.
Vrana, Joseph L. '65 (VIC) Wharton, TX Holy Family.
Vrazel, Edward *o.m.i.* '58 (LAR) Laredo, TX Our Lady of Guadalupe.
Vrba, James J. '77 (DAV) Iowa City, IA St. Patrick's.
Vreteau, Robert *o.m.i.* '46 (SAT)[K] San Antonio, TX Oblate Madonna Residence.
Vries, John De (LA)[J] Burbank, CA Providence Saint Joseph Medical Center; [J] Mission Hills, CA Providence Holy Cross Medical Center.
Vu, An '95 (WDC) Upper Marlboro, MD Saint Mary of the Assumption.
Vu, Duc *s.j.* '02 (SJ) San Jose, CA Most Holy Trinity.
Vu, Hoat Dinh '60 (BAL) Retired.
Vu, Ignatius (NY) Staten Island, NY St. Paul.
Vu, J.B Han '65 (NO) Marrero, LA St. Agnes Le Thi Thanh.
Vu, J.P. Minh (TLS) Air Force Chaplains.
Vu, Jack '02 (LR) Little Rock, AR Our Lady of Good Counsel.
Vu, Joachim '63 (ORG) Retired.
Vu, John Francis *s.j.* '97 (LA)[F] Los Angeles, CA Loyola High School of Los Angeles.
Vu, Joseph Dao *s.v.d.* (MEM) Vietnamese Community.
Vu, Joseph Duc (MO).
Vu, Joseph Duc (DET) Veterans Administration Hospital.
Vu, Joseph Khai (NEW) West Hudson Hospital.
Vu, Joseph M. *c.m.c.* (BO) Dorchester, MA St. Peter.
Vu, Joseph Thanh '75 (GAL) Spring, TX St. Edward.
Vu, Joseph '90 (BRK) Brooklyn, NY St. Anselm's.
Vu, Joseph Dao *s.v.d.* '88 (MEM) Memphis, TN Holy Names of Jesus and Mary; [I] Memphis, TN Society of the Divine Word (Chicago Province).
Vu, Leo Dinh Huyen *c.m.c.* '02 (DEN) Wheat Ridge, CO Queen of Vietnamese Martyrs.
Vu, Lieu '91 (SJ) Milpitas, CA St. Elizabeth.
Vu, Louis Lam '85 (LAF) Youngsville, LA St. Anne.
Vu, Minh '94 (STP) St. Paul, MN St. Adalbert.
Vu, Peter Duc '96 (ATL) Atlanta, GA Holy Cross.
Vu, Peter G. '97 (GR) Belmont, MI Assumption of the Blessed Virgin Mary.
Vu, Than N. '84 (BR) Baton Rouge, LA Christ the King; [K] Baton Rouge, LA Christ the King Parish and Catholic Student Center; Defenders of the Bond; College of Consultors; Campus Ministry; Clergy Personnel.
Vu, Thomas Hein '01 (LAF) Rayne, LA St. Joseph.
Vu, Thomas '85 (LAF) Franklin, LA St. Jules.
Vucinovich, Albert P. '64 (SFR) Burlingame, CA St. Catherine of Siena.
Vuelvas–Arias, David '75 (ORG) Westminster, CA Blessed Sacrament; Cursillo Movement.
Vujs, Joseph E. '57 (HRT) Enfield, CT St. Bernard's.
Vuketich, Donald F. *t.o.r.* '53 (PH)[AA] Fairless Hills, PA St. Anthony Friary.
Vular, Robert J. '01 (PIT) Pittsburgh, PA St. Teresa of Avila.
Vung Le, Paul *s.v.d.* '85 (LA) Norwalk, CA St. Linus.
Vuoso, Pascuale *c.r.i.c.* (LA) Santa Paula, CA Our Lady of Guadalupe.
Vuoso, Pasquale *c.r.i.c.* '87 (LA) Santa Paula, CA St. Sebastian; [Q] Santa Paula, CA Canons Regular of the Immaculate Conception.
Vuturo, Paul V. (MIA) Sacred Art & Architecture.
Vuturo, Paul '73 (MIA) Miramar, FL St. Bartholomew.
Vu Van Vinh, Francis M. *c.m.c.* (SPC)[E] Carthage, MO Congregation of the Mother Coredemptrix, United States Assumption Province.
Vye, Francis W. *s.j.* '65 (BO)[V] Weston, MA Campion Health Center, Inc..
Vytautas, Balciunas '33 (NOR) Retired.
Vyverman, Mark J. '93 (KAL) Kalamazoo, MI St. Augustine Cathedral; Diocesan Consultors; Presbyteral Council.

W

Wach, Anthony J. *s.j.* '72 (MIL).
Wachala, John M. '79 (CLV)[O] Cleveland, OH St. Casimir.
Wachdorf, Paul H. '75 (CHI).
Wachowiak, Duane A. (GAY)[A] Worship and Liturgical Formation, Secretariat for.
Wachter, Robert B. '76 (WCH) Parsons, KS St. Patrick.
Wack, William *c.s.c.* '94 (PHX)[K] Phoenix, AZ Andre House of Arizona.
Wackerman, John F. '98 (PH) Quakertown, PA St. Isidore.
Waclawski, Joseph P. '42 (BUF) Retired.
Waczula, Michael F. '66 (GBG) Retired.
Wadas, Ignatius C. '53 (ALT) Retired.
Wadas, Joseph S. '91 (MOB) Enterprise, AL St. John.
Wadas, Raymond J. '72 (WDC) Hillcrest Heights, MD Holy Family.
Waddell, Chrysogonus *o.c.s.o.* '58 (L)[K] Trappist, KY Abbey of Our Lady of Gethsemani, of the Order of Cistercians of the Strict Observance.
Waddell, Paul M. '84 (NY) Katonah, NY St. Mary of the Assumption.
Waddill, Dale T. '64 (P) Portland, OR St. Peter.
Wade, Ed '72 (GAL) Houston, TX Queen of Peace; [U] Houston, TX Catholic Charismatic Center.
Wade, Edward C. '72 (CAM) On Duty Outside the Diocese.
Wade, Gerald T. *s.j.* '68 (SJ).
Wade, Hubert '77 (SAN)[D] Ballinger, TX St. Mary Star of the Sea.
Wade, Hubert (SAN) Diocesan Consultors; Presbyteral Council; Deans.
Wade, John J. (TLS) Diocesan Consultors.
Wade, John '56 (TLS) Secretary Education.
Wadell, John '40 (SB) Retired.
Wadowicz, Joseph M. '45 (STU) Retired.
Waechter, Ernest *o.f.m.conv.* '59 (TOL) Carey, OH Our Lady of Consolation, Basilica–National Shrine.

Wafzig, James E. '55 (L) Louisville, KY St. Athanasius Retired.
Wagener, Donald '03 (RCK) On Disability Leave.
Wagener, John M. '61 (NU) Military Chaplains Retired.
Wagenhoffer, Josef A. '65 (CAM) Somers Point, NJ St. Joseph's.
Wager, Terence J. *o.s.b.* '64 (SEA) Yelm, WA St. Columban; [L] Lacey, WA St. Martin's Abbey.
Wager, Terence *o.s.b.* (SEA) Presbyteral Council.
Waggenor, William L. '52 (HEL) Retired.
Wagner, Alan *s.d.s.* '76 (TUC) Vail, AZ Shrine of St. Rita in the Desert; [D] Tucson, AZ St. Joseph Hospital; [D] Tucson, AZ St. Mary's Hospital.
Wagner, Donald '87 (SCL) Bowlus, MN St. Stanislaus Kostka; Bowlus, MN St. Edward's; Albany, MN St. Anthony's; Freeport, MN St. Francis of Assisi; Bowlus, MN St. Mary.
Wagner, Edward *o.ss.t.* '80 (BAL)[S] Baltimore, MD.
Wagner, Eugene L. '40 (BUF) Olcott, NY St. Charles Borromeo Retired.
Wagner, Frank *o.m.i.* '57 (SD) Chula Vista, CA Most Precious Blood.
Wagner, Harold '55 (BUF) Holy Childhood (Pontifical) Association; Propagation of the Faith; [F] Buffalo, NY Cantalician Center for Learning, Inc..
Wagner, Jay '87 (RIC) Petersburg, VA Church of the Sacred Heart.
Wagner, John A. '49 (SAT) Retired.
Wagner, John P. '62 (SY) Baldwinsville, NY St. Elizabeth Ann Seton.
Wagner, John '49 (SAT)[K] San Antonio, TX Casa De Padres.
Wagner, John '64 (SB) Temecula, CA St. Catherine of Alexandria.
Wagner, Joseph F. '44 (CLV) Cleveland, OH St. Mark Retired.
Wagner, Joseph F. *s.j.* '98 (CHI)[N] Berkeley, CA Jesuit Community at Jesuit School of Theology at Berkeley.
Wagner, Joseph '65 (SFS) Retired.
Wagner, Joseph *s.j.* '98 (CIN)[M] Cincinnati, OH Jesuit Community at Xavier University.
Wagner, Lawrence *s.v.d.* '44 (MIL)[O] East Troy, WI Divine Word Missionaries.
Wagner, Leon R. '49 (CHI) Retired.
Wagner, Mark '88 (STO) Turlock, CA Sacred Heart Church of Turlock (Pastor of); Personnel Board; [G] Turlock, CA The McElligott Sacred Heart School Foundation.
Wagner, Phillip *o.m.i.* (LAR) Eagle Pass, TX Our Lady of Refuge.
Wagner, Raymond J. '52 (LC) Trempealeau, WI St. Mary; Trempealeau, WI St. Bartholomew; [H] La Crosse, WI Holy Cross (Seminary) Diocesan Center Retired.
Wagner, Richard F. *s.s.j.* '59 (LAF) Rayne, LA Shrine of Our Mother of Mercy.
Wagner, Robert F. '60 (SPR) Holyoke, MA; [N] Holyoke, MA Bureau for Exceptional Children and Adults Inc.; Apostolate to the Handicapped.
Wagner, Robert *s.d.s.* '46 (BIR) Huntsville, AL St. Joseph's.
Wagner, Ronald F. '79 (SAG) Saginaw, MI St. Mary Cathedral.
Wagner, Ronald (SAG) Vicars for Vicariates.
Wagner, Thomas A. '83 (PIT) Braddock, PA Good Shepherd; Braddock, PA Sacred Heart.
Wagner, Van A. '61 (TUC) Tucson, AZ Saints Peter and Paul; Special Assignment; Vicar General/Moderator of the Curia; Ex Officio; Diocesan Consultors; Council of Priests; Ex Officio Members; Diocesan Building Committee; Holy Childhood Association; Priests' Assurance Association; Moderator of the Curia; Ex Officio Members.
Wagner, Vernon *o.f.m.cap.* '53 (MIL)[O] Mount Calvary, WI St. Lawrence Friary.
Wagner, Walter C. *o.p.* '93 (CIN)[C] Cincinnati, OH Dominican Novitiate.
Wagner, Walter *o.p.* '93 (CIN) Cincinnati, OH St. Gertrude; [M] Cincinnati, OH St. Gertrude Priory.
Wagner, Wilbert *s.v.d.* '40 (CHI)[B] Techny, IL Divine Word Residence.
Wagner, William C. '73 (CIN) Cincinnati, OH St. Thomas More; Army Reserve Chaplains.
Wagner, William F. '63 (L) Louisville, KY SS. Simon and Jude.
Wagoner, Gordon P. (IND) Veterans' Administration Hospital; Noblesville, IN Our Lady of Grace.
Wagoner, Gordon P. (LFT).
Waguespack, Clarence J. '62 (BR) Pierre Part, LA St. Joseph the Worker.
Wahal, Stephen J. '00 (PBR) Duquesne, PA SS. Peter and Paul; Irving, TX St. Basil the Great.
Wahl, Joseph A. *c.o.* '56 (CHR)[E] Rock Hill, SC Oratory of St. Philip Neri, Congregation of the Oratory of Pontifical Rite; Institute for Parish Leadership Development.
Wahl, Joseph *c.o.* '56 (CHR) Rock Hill, SC St. Mary's; Campus Ministry.
Wahl, Raymond J. '52 (RCK) Rockford, IL St. Edward; Pro Synodal Judges; Diocesan Consultors.
Wahl, Richard A. *c.s.b.* '72 (GAL)[F] Houston, TX St. Thomas High School.
Wahl, Richard *c.s.b.* (GAL) Adjutant Judicial Vicar.
Wahl, Richard (GAL) Defenders of the Bond.
Wahl, Thomas *o.s.b.* '58 (SCL)[I] St. Augustine Monastery; (FgM).
Wahmhoff, Andrew *o.s.b.* '58 (RCK)[G] Aurora, IL Marmion Abbey.
Wai, Thomas Than '92 (WCH) Halstead, KS Sacred Heart of Jesus.
Waibel, Philip *o.s.b.* '83 (P) Mt. Angel, OR St. Mary; [L] St. Benedict, OR Mt. Angel Abbey.
Waickman, Thomas L. '84 (JC) Pacific, MO Retired.
Wainwright, Walter L. '65 (ROC) Elmira, NY St. Patrick; Elmira, NY St. Anthony.
Waiss, John R. '87 (LA)[X] Los Angeles, CA Prelature of the Holy Cross and Opus Dei.
Wait, Dennis '72 (KCK) Special Assignment.
Waite, Patrick J. '54 (SC) AUXILIARY CHAPLAINS CONTRACT CHAPLAINS Retired.
Waitekus, Christopher J. '91 (SPR) Lenox, MA St. Ann's; Lenox Dale, MA St. Vincent de Paul's; Presbyteral Council.
Waites, Michael J. '83 (TR) Manasquan, NJ St. Denis.
Waithaka, Paul Maina '02 (CHI) Chicago, IL St. Sylvester.
Waiver, Robert (OAK) Co Directors.
Waiwood, Richard '89 (ELP) Monahans, TX St. John the Apostle and Evangelist.
Wajda, Edward J. '56 (PHX) Retired.
Wajda, Joseph L. '73 (STP) Special Assignment.
Wake, John F. '74 (TR) Maple Shade, NJ Our Lady of Perpetual Help.
Wakefield, Alan J. '75 (LAN) Mason, MI St. James.
Wakefield, Christopher L. '96 (ALN) Reading, PA St. Anthony; Reading, PA St. Peter.
Wakefield, Michael '81 (LA) Granada Hills, CA St. Euphrasia.
Wakim, Rodolph '96 (SAM) Roanoke, VA St. Elias.
Wakitsch, Randall '89 (RCK) Absent on Leave.
Wal, Eduardo '79 (SP) Clearwater, FL St. Cecelia.
Walas, Joseph '59 (RVC) Riverhead, NY St. Isidore's.
Walczak, Slawomir *s.d.b.* (CHI) Chicago, IL St. John Bosco.
Wald, Edward *s.v.d.* '50 (CHI)[B] Techny, IL Divine Word Residence.
Wald, Jeffrey L. '92 (FAR) Fargo, ND Holy Spirit.
Wald, Jeffrey (FAR) Vice–Chancellors.
Wald, John *s.v.d.* '43 (CHI)[B] Techny, IL Divine Word Residence.
Wald, Kenneth J. '57 (BIS) Retired.
Waldbilling, Brian T. '01 (LC) On Leave of Absence.
Walden, Ellsworth R. '71 (RVC) Smithtown, NY St. Patrick; Smithaven Deanery.
Walder, Keith A. '03 (PEO) Ottawa, IL St. Columba.
Waldie, Paul *o.m.i.* '65 (FgM).
Walding, Eugene F. '66 (SC) Marian Village; [D] Fort Dodge, IA The Marian Home.
Waldmann, Pablo *i.v.e.* '97 (NY) New York, NY St. Paul.
Waldmann, Robert J. '46 (B) Retired.
Waldon, Clarence R. '64 (IND) Indianapolis, IN Holy Angels.
Waldow, Harold L. '70 (AMA) Ex Officio; Rite of Christian Initiation of Adults Commission; Cursillo Movement; A.C.T.S. Movement; Continuing Education of Clergy; Moderator of the Curia; Vicar of Clergy; Vicars Forane; Vicars Forane; Advocates; Ex Officio; College of Consultors; Diocesan Pastoral Council; [I] Amarillo, TX Monsignor B.A. Erpen Trust Fund; Amarillo, TX St. Mary's.
Waldrep, Jeffrey '90 (JKS) Starkville, MS St. Joseph; [I] Starkville, MS Mississippi State University Catholic Student Association; Continuing Formation Committee; Defenders of the Bond.
Waldrep, John W. *m.m.* '90 (LA)[Q] Monrovia, CA.
Waldron, John E. '66 (BRK)[A] Douglaston, NY Immaculate Conception Center.
Waldron, John F. '58 (ALB) Colonie, NY Our Lady of Mercy.
Waldron, John R. '56 (NEW) Retired.
Waldron, John '66 (BRK) On Leave/Unassigned.
Waldron, John '66 (P) Beaverton, OR Holy Trinity.
Waldron, Richard P. '61 (HBG) Mechanicsburg, PA St. Elizabeth Ann Seton.
Waldron, Robert J. '68 (BO) Senior Priests Retired.
Waldron, Walter J. '64 (BO) Roxbury, MA St. Patrick.
Waldron, William '50 (PHX) Retired.
Waldrop, Gregory *s.j.* '99 (New Orleans)[N] Berkeley, CA Jesuit Community at Jesuit School of Theology at Berkeley.
Waldschmidt, Valens J. *o.f.m.* '47 (CIN)[M] Cincinnati, OH St. Clement Friary; [V] Cincinnati, OH St. Dymphna Ministry Retired.
Walega, Stanley J. '64 (MET) Retired.
Walijewski, Joseph A. '50 (LC) Retired.
Walk, Donald J. '67 (VEN) Absent on Leave.
Walk, Edward J. '78 (E) Du Bois, PA St. Catherine; [C] Du Bois, PA DuBois Area Catholic School.
Walker, Anselm '56 (GAL) Retired.
Walker, Benjamin R. *o.s.b.* '60 (PIT) Pittsburgh, PA St. Peter; [Q] Pittsburgh, PA Art Institute of Pittsburgh.
Walker, Brian G. *o.p.* '86 (CHI) Chicago, IL St. Basil/Visitation.
Walker, Charles D. '81 (L) Louisville, KY St. Pius X; College of Consultors; Ex Officio.
Walker, David M. '64 (HRT) Hamden, CT St. Rita's; Special and other Archdiocesan Assignment; North Haven, CT Catholic Cemeteries Association of the Archdiocese of Hartford, Inc.; Catholic Cemeteries Association.
Walker, Donald L. '58 (DET) Dearborn, MI St. Martha.
Walker, Douglas '99 (FRS) Merced, CA.
Walker, Earl G. '48 (LA) Los Angeles, CA Cathedral Chapel Retired.
Walker, Edmund *o.f.m.cap.* '63 (WIL)[J] Wilmington, DE Capuchin Franciscan Friars, St. Francis Renewal Center; [L] Wilmington, DE Secular Franciscan Order; [M] Wilmington, DE St. Francis Renewal Center.
Walker, Francisco J. '87 (BRK) Elmhurst, NY Ascension.
Walker, Gerald '55 (LA) Retired.
Walker, Gerard T. '80 (BRK) Bayside, NY Our Lady of the Blessed Sacrament.
Walker, Gilbert R. *c.m.* '87 (FgM).
Walker, Henry B. *o.m.i.* '85 (GAL) Houston, TX St. Patrick.
Walker, J. Kenneth (EVN) Special Assignment; Judicial Vicar; Diocesan Consultors; Diocesan Council of Priests.
Walker, J. Patrick '88 (STO) Stockton, CA St. Michael Church of Stockton (Pastor of).
Walker, James E. '99 (GLP) Gallup, NM Cathedral of the Sacred Heart.
Walker, James P. '77 (Y) Warren, OH SS. Cyril and Methodius.
Walker, Kent '89 (ORL) St. Cloud, FL St. Thomas Aquinas.
Walker, Leonard '74 (PHX) Mesa, AZ Queen of Peace.
Walker, Michael John Paul *o.p.* '02 (PRO)[P] Providence St. Thomas Aquinas Priory at Providence College.
Walker, Michael '62 (KC) Mission Duty.
Walker, Mike '99 (P) Coos Bay, OR St. Monica.
Walker, Paul '72 (STU) McConnelsville, OH St. James.
Walker, Robert L. *o.p.* '56 (WDC) Washington, DC St. Dominic Church & Priory.
Walker, Ronald *o.m.i.* '61 (FgM).
Walker, Thomas J. '89 (MIL) Special Assignment; Services for Senior Priests.
Walker, Thomas J. '90 (STP) Woodbury, MN Saint Ambrose of Woodbury; Associate Judges.
Walkowiak, David J. '79 (CLV)[A] Wickliffe, OH St. Mary Seminary and Graduate School of Theology; Vice–Chancellor; Associate Judicial Vicars.
Wall, Antoninus *o.p.* '50 (OAK)[N] Oakland, CA Dominican Order (Western Province), St. Albert's Priory.
Wall, Barry W. '62 (FR) Fall River, MA Our Lady of the Holy Rosary; Diocesan Archives; Legion of Mary.
Wall, G. Warren '76 (MOB) Mobile, AL St. Ignatius; Archdiocesan Consultors; Consultors; Appointed Member & Consultor.
Wall, Gus *s.v.d.* '91 (DUB)[B] Epworth, IA Divine Word College.
Wall, James E. '63 (BUF) Co–Directors; Priests, Vicar for; Council of Priests; [Q] Derby, NY St. Columban Center.
Wall, James '98 (PHX) Phoenix, AZ St. Thomas the Apostle.
Wall, John A. '60 (R) Cary, NC St. Michael the Archangel.
Wall, John E. '57 (CIN) Priest Councilors; Cincinnati, OH St. Ignatius Loyola Retired.
Wall, John J. '68 (CHI) Chicago, IL St. Patrick.
Wall, Sherman B. *o.m.i.* '57 (SPC) Willow Springs, MO Sacred Heart.
Wall, Terence Damian *c.ss.r.* '65 (CGS)[B] Aguas Buenas, PR Casa Cristo Redentor; [I] San Juan, PR Casa San Clemente.
Wallace, Basil J. *o.s.b.* '78 (PAT)[M] Newton, NJ St. Paul's Abbey.
Wallace, Cavana '92 (SD) Oceanside, CA St. Margaret; College of Consultors; Presbyteral Council.
Wallace, Donald L. '62 (JC) Absent on Leave Retired.
Wallace, Francis T. '63 (LA) La Canada Flintridge, CA St. Bede the Venerable; Promoters of Justice; Defenders of the Bond.
Wallace, Francis X. '47 (FR) Retired.
Wallace, George *s.m.* '57 (PH)[U] Langhorne, PA St. Mary Medical Center; [AA] Langhorne, PA Society of Mary, Marist Fathers.
Wallace, Harry C. '56 (SY) On Duty Outside the Diocese.
Wallace, Harry '56 (ORL) Retired.
Wallace, James *c.ss.r.* '70 (WDC)[M] Washington, DC Holy Redeemer College.
Wallace, John *f.m.s.i.* '60 (BO)[B] Framingham, MA Sylva Maria.
Wallace, Joseph D. '85 (CAM) Cherry Hill, NJ Queen of Heaven; Office of Ecumenical and Interreligious Affairs; Members.
Wallace, Kenneth F. (CLV) Parma, OH Holy Family.
Wallace, Murrough C. '60 (SAC) South Lake Tahoe, CA

St. Theresa Retired.
Wallace, Murrough (SAC) Please direct all inquiries to.
Wallace, Philip '65 (SEA) Bellevue, WA St. Louise.
Wallace, Regis P. *o.s.b.* '60 (PAT) Mountain Lakes, NJ St. Catherine of Siena; [M] Morristown St. Mary's Abbey; Pro–Synodal Judges.
Wallace, Richard '86 (P)[A] St. Benedict, OR Mount Angel Seminary; Navy Reserve Chaplains.
Wallace, Thomas (SB) Elected Members.
Wallace, Thomas (SB) Appointed Members; College of Consultors.
Wallace, Thomas (SB) La Quinta, CA St. Francis of Assisi.
Wallace, Tom M. '80 (SB) Appointed Members.
Wallace, Tom (SB) Vicars Forane; Committee Members.
Wallace, William J. *o.s.a.* '74 (NY) Bronx, NY St. Nicholas of Tolentine.
Wallaik, William H. '49 (MIL) Retired.
Walle, Julius G. '56 (ALX) Cheneyville, LA St. Joseph Retired.
Walleman, Kenneth T. *s.j.* '59 (MIL)[O] Wauwatosa, WI Jesuit Community at St. Camillus.
Wallen, Charles L. *c.s.c.* '54 (BUR) Wilmington, VT Our Lady of Fatima.
Wallenfelsz, Scott *s.d.s.* '69 (MIL)[O] Richmond, VA.
Wallenfelsz, Scott *s.d.s.* (SFD)[D] Ladysmith, WI Servants of Mary Continuing Care Trust.
Waller, Charles J. '73 (PAT) Paterson, NJ St. Gerard Majella.
Waller, Robert C. '75 (CIN) Milford, OH St. Andrew.
Wallin, Kevin W. '84 (BGP) Bridgeport, CT St. Augustine Cathedral; [S] Bridgeport, CT Inner–City Foundation for Charity & Education; Diocesan Consultors; Presbyteral Council; Vicariate III (Fairfield, Easton, West Bridgeport); Inner–City Foundation for Charity and Education.
Walling, Gerald C. *s.j.* '61 (CHI)[C] Chicago, IL Jesuit Community at Loyola University Chicago.
Walling, James *c.p.m.* '01 (OWN)[F] Auburn, KY Fathers of Mercy.
Walling, Lawrence E. *o.s.m.* '79 (DEN) Denver, CO Our Lady of Mt. Carmel.
Walling, Lawrence M. *o.s.m.* '79 (CHI)[N] Chicago Order of Friar Servants of Mary (Servites) United States of America Province, Inc..
Walling, Richard M. (CIN) Vicarri Foranei (Deans).
Walling, Richard W. '78 (CIN) Springfield, OH St. Teresa of the Child Jesus; Consultors; Censors; Ex Officio Members.
Wallis, William H. '82 (SPR) Westfield, MA St. Mary's.
Walljasper, Mark A. '55 (LC) AUXILIARY CHAPLAINS CONTRACT CHAPLAINS Retired.
Wallner, Gerhard '89 (FBK) Leave of Absence.
Wallroth, Joseph R. *o.carm.* '70 (JOL)[L] Darien, IL Carmelite Provincial Office; Air Force Chaplains.
Wallroth, Joseph (MO) Presbyteral Council.
Walls, David E. '60 (PH) Absent on Leave.
Walmesley, John '84 (SEA) Seattle, WA Our Lady of Guadalupe; Presbyteral Council; Deans.
Walpole, Donald *o.s.b.* '43 (IND)[K] St. Meinrad, IN St. Meinrad Archabbey.
Walsh, Aidan J. '70 (BO) Bedford, MA Veterans Administration Hospital Bedford; Archdiocesan Judges; Plymouth, MA St. Peter.
Walsh, Albert '92 (GAL) The Woodlands, TX St. Anthony of Padua.
Walsh, Andrew J. '66 (NY) Hopewell Junction, NY St. Columba.
Walsh, Anthony *o.p.* '98 (WDC)[B] Washington, DC Dominican House of Studies.
Walsh, Arthur '85 (CC) Retired.
Walsh, Austin *s.t.* '65 (ARL)[J] Arlington, VA Missionary Servants of the Most Holy Trinity, S.T..
Walsh, Austin *s.t.* '65 (FgM).
Walsh, Bernard '55 (SY) Retired.
Walsh, Brandon (LUB) Presbyteral Council.
Walsh, Brendan J. '93 (LAN) Dexter, MI St. Joseph.
Walsh, Brendan J. *s.a.c.* '98 (LUB) Lubbock, TX St. Joseph's.
Walsh, Broderick *c.s.p.* '92 (P) Portland, OR St. Philip Neri.
Walsh, Charles F. (WCH) Parish Priest Consultors.
Walsh, Charles '51 (WCH) Retired.
Walsh, Christopher J. '87 (BGP) Norwalk, CT St. Mary; Diocesan Censors; Office of Vocations.
Walsh, Christopher M. '99 (PH) Philadelphia, PA Our Lady of Ransom.
Walsh, Christopher '87 (NY).
Walsh, Clyde J. '51 (PRO)[P] Providence St. John Vianney Residence Retired.
Walsh, Daniel L. *c.s.sp.* '91 (CHI) Chicago, IL St. Mary Magdalene.
Walsh, Daniel P. '68 (BUF) Vicars; Gowanda, NY St. Joseph.
Walsh, David *c.ss.r.* '47 (CC) Office for Persons with Disabilities; On Special Assignment.
Walsh, Denis '66 (TYL)[B] Palestine, TX Hermitage.
Walsh, Dennis G. '92 (TOL) Defiance, OH St. John the Evangelist.
Walsh, Donal '55 (SD) Retired.
Walsh, E. Corbett *s.j.* '71 (BO)[V] Weston, MA Campion Jesuit Community.
Walsh, Edward P. '93 (BIR) On Duty Outside the Diocese.
Walsh, Edward *s.p.s.* '64 (NEW)[N] Cliffside Park, NJ St. Patrick's Missionary Society.
Walsh, Edward '91 (RVC) Absent on Leave.
Walsh, Flannan J. '65 (STA) On Duty Outside the Diocese.
Walsh, Flavian A. *o.f.m.* '56 (WIL) Wilmington, DE St. Paul's.
Walsh, Francis E. '66 (SPR) Military Chaplains; Navy Chaplains.
Walsh, Francis M. *c.s.c.* '56 (FR)[A] North Easton, MA Stonehill College; [A] North Easton, MA Holy Cross Fathers Religious.
Walsh, Francis M. '67 (WDC) On Duty Outside the Archdiocese; Washington, DC Holy Name.
Walsh, Francis P. '57 (CLV) Lakewood, OH St. Luke.
Walsh, Francis *s.j.* '53 (SEA)[C] Tacoma, WA Bellarmine Preparatory School.
Walsh, Gerald J. '55 (BIS) Retired.
Walsh, Gerald T. '67 (NY) New York, NY St. Elizabeth; Manhattan (North); Development, Archdiocesan Office of; Vicar for Development.
Walsh, Gerald '95 (CHI) Chicago, IL St. Francis Borgia.
Walsh, Gerald (NY) Archdiocesan Consultors.
Walsh, Harry A. '60 (STP) Special Assignment.
Walsh, J. E. '65 (SAC) West Sacramento, CA Our Lady of Grace.
Walsh, J. Gerald *c.s.sp.* '42 (PIT)[P] Bethel Park, PA Holy Spirit Animation Center.
Walsh, J. Patrick *s.j.* '66 (PBL) Springfield, CO Annunciation.
Walsh, James A. '54 (TOL) Milan, OH St. Anthony.
Walsh, James F. *s.j.* '72 (BO)[V] Boston The Society of Jesus of New England–Provincial Offices.
Walsh, James J. '73 (SCR) Jermyn, PA Sacred Heart of Mary; Defenders of the Bond; Deans.
Walsh, James J. '93 (ALB) Special Assignment; Loudonville, NY St. Pius X.
Walsh, James J. (CIN) Priest Councilors
Walsh, James P. *s.j.* '62 (BO)[V] Weston, MA Campion Health Center, Inc..
Walsh, James P. *s.j.* '66 (DEN)[N] Denver, CO Xavier Jesuit Center.
Walsh, James P. '73 (MAN) Marlborough, NH Sacred Heart; Marlborough, NH Immaculate Conception.
Walsh, James P.M. *s.j.* '70 (WDC)[M] Washington, DC The Jesuit Community at Georgetown University.
Walsh, James '69 (SJ) San Jose, CA St. Christopher.
Walsh, James (ALB) Formation for Priesthood/Vocation Awareness; Priests Placement Committee; Vocations and Vocation Awareness Program.
Walsh, James (SJ) Priests' Retirement Board.
Walsh, Jay Francis *c.s.b.* '65 (GAL) Houston, TX St. Anne.
Walsh, Jeffrey J. '94 (SCR) Lake Winola, PA St. Mary of the Lake; [A] Dalton, PA Saint Pius X Seminary; Presbyteral Council.
Walsh, Jerome M. *o.p.* '58 (CHI)[N] Chicago Dominicans (Provincial Office); [N] St. Pius V Priory.
Walsh, Jerome '69 (DET) On Duty Outside the Archdiocese.
Walsh, Jim J. '68 (CIN) Cincinnati, OH St. Dominic.
Walsh, John A. '61 (SCR) On Duty Outside the Diocese.
Walsh, John A. '80 (E) Conneautville, PA St. Peter.
Walsh, John B. '57 (MAD)[G] Madison, WI Bishop O'Connor Catholic Pastoral Center Retired.
Walsh, John E. '55 (SAL) Retired.
Walsh, John F. '76 (PIT) Pittsburgh, PA Epiphany; UPMC Southside Hospital.
Walsh, John F. (BO) Plainville, MA St. Martha.
Walsh, John J. *s.j.* '45 (STL)[O] St. Louis, MO Jesuit Community Corporation at St. Louis University – Jesuit Hall; [N] St. Louis, MO Fusz Pavilion.
Walsh, John J. *c.s.sp.* '48 (GAL)[B] Houston, TX Holy Ghost Fathers and Brothers.
Walsh, John J. '57 (DUB) Retired.
Walsh, John J. *m.m.* '61 (NY)[EE] Maryknoll Maryknoll Fathers and Brothers.
Walsh, John Joseph *s.j.* '71 (BO)[E] Dorchester, MA Boston College High School & Jesuit Community; [V] Boston The Society of Jesus of New England–Provincial Offices.
Walsh, John M. '47 (PH) Retired.
Walsh, John P. '77 (ATL) Peachtree City, GA Holy Trinity Catholic.
Walsh, John T. '44 (ROC) Rochester, NY Our Lady Queen of Peace Retired.
Walsh, Joseph E. '47 (PH) Lenni, PA St. Francis de Sales Retired.
Walsh, Joseph M. '86 (LIN) Lincoln, NE St. Teresa's; [K] Lincoln, NE Catholic Social Services; [L] Lincoln, NE Catholic Social Services; Diocesan Housing Ministries, Inc.; Catholic Social Services.
Walsh, Joseph M. (GI) Charities.
Walsh, Joseph R. '64 (SFR) San Francisco, CA St. Stephen.
Walsh, Joseph (LIN) Apostolate of Suffering.
Walsh, Kenneth *c.p.* '50 (SCR) Scranton, PA St. Ann's Basilica Parish; [M] Clarks Summit, PA St. Gabriel's Convent.
Walsh, Kevin B. '92 (ARL) Falls Church, VA St. Philip.
Walsh, Kevin V. '78 (HRT)[E] Moncks Corner, SC Mepkin Abbey.
Walsh, Laurence '45 (NO) Retired.
Walsh, Lawrence J. '63 (STL) Retired.
Walsh, Lawrence '54 (SAT) San Antonio, TX Our Lady of Grace.
Walsh, Leo '94 (ANC) Eagle River, AK St. Andrew; Diocesan Consultors; Board Members.
Walsh, Marion C. *o.s.b.* '42 (IND)[K] St. Meinrad, IN St. Meinrad Archabbey; [I] Tickfaw, LA Our Lady Queen Contemplative Monastery; [K] Tickfaw, LA Our Lady Queen Monastery Retired.
Walsh, Martin E. '43 (OAK)[M] Oakland, CA Bishop Begin Villa Retired.
Walsh, Martin J. '74 (BO) Permanent Disability.
Walsh, Martin *o.p.* '50 (OAK)[N] Oakland, CA Dominican Order (Western Province), St. Albert's Priory.
Walsh, Martin *o.m.i.* '54 (BUF) Buffalo, NY St. Rose of Lima.
Walsh, Martin *o.p.* '69 (OAK)[N] Oakland, CA Western Dominican Province.
Walsh, Maurice B. *s.j.* '46 (BO)[V] Weston, MA Campion Health Center, Inc..
Walsh, Michael A. '72 (PAT) Boonton, NJ Our Lady of Mount Carmel; Morristown, NJ Morristown Memorial Hospital.
Walsh, Michael B. *s.j.* '62 (SEA)[C] Tacoma, WA Bellarmine Preparatory School.
Walsh, Michael E. *s.j.* '62 (SEA)[P] Tacoma, WA Catholic Pastoral Care–Hospital Tacoma Ministry.
Walsh, Michael F. *c.m.* '72 (LA) Los Angeles, CA St. Vincent De Paul.
Walsh, Michael J. '56 (CHI) Retired.
Walsh, Michael J. '70 (BRK) Maspeth, NY St. Stanislaus Kostka.
Walsh, Michael J. '73 (TR) New Monmouth, NJ St. Mary; Diocesan Consultors.
Walsh, Michael L. '45 (PH)[V] Immaculata, PA Camilla Hall Nursing Home Retired.
Walsh, Michael P. *m.m.* '88 (NY)[EE] Maryknoll Maryknoll Fathers and Brothers.
Walsh, Michael '38 (LA) Retired.
Walsh, Michael '53 (DEN) Denver, CO St. Vincent De Paul.
Walsh, Michael *o.f.m.cap.* '58 (BAK) Bend, OR St. Francis of Assisi.
Walsh, Miles D. '80 (BR) Baton Rouge, LA Our Lady of Mercy.
Walsh, Milton T. (SFR) Absent on Leave.
Walsh, Patrick A. *s.m.a.* '65 (NY) Tuckahoe, NY Immaculate Conception; Tuckahoe, NY Assumption.
Walsh, Patrick E. *s.j.* '60 (MIL) Milwaukee, WI Gesu Parish.
Walsh, Patrick '69 (SC)[B] Sioux City, IA Catholic Schools of Sioux City; [G] Fort Dodge, IA Fort Dodge Catholic Grade School Foundation; [G] Fort Dodge, IA St. Edmond High School Foundation; [G] Fort Dodge, IA Fort Dodge Catholic Grade School Foundation.
Walsh, Patrick '72 (P) Sandy, OR St. Michael the Archangel.
Walsh, Patrick *c.s.c.* '81 (PRT) Saco, ME Most Holy Trinity.
Walsh, Patrick (P) Finance Council.
Walsh, Patrick (SC) Board of Education.
Walsh, Peter J. *c.s.c.* '89 (FR)[A] North Easton, MA Holy Cross Fathers Religious.
Walsh, Peter '59 (JC) Retired.
Walsh, Peter *c.s.c.* '89 (FR)[A] North Easton, MA Stonehill College.
Walsh, Raymond D. '54 (BUR) Retired.
Walsh, Raymond E. '54 (BUR)[D] Rutland, VT Loretto Home for Aged.
Walsh, Richard A. '62 (PRO)[M] Newport, RI St. Clare Home.
Walsh, Richard J. *c.s.p.* '44 (NY) New York, NY St. Paul the Apostle; [EE] Jamaica Estates Paulist Fathers Generalate.
Walsh, Richard J. '44 (ALT) Retired.
Walsh, Richard '68 (ORL) Winter Park, FL St. Margaret Mary; Special Assignment; Deans; Members; Consultors; Priests' Continuing Education.
Walsh, Richard '83 (JOL) Absent on Leave.
Walsh, Robert T. *s.j.* '80 (LA)[F] Los Angeles, CA Loyola High School of Los Angeles.
Walsh, Robert '44 (LA) Retired.
Walsh, Robert '46 (LA) Arcadia, CA Holy Angels.
Walsh, Robert '77 (CHI)[J] Chicago, IL Our Lady of the Resurrection Medical Center.
Walsh, Ronald J. '54 (NY) Retired.
Walsh, Seamus '66 (DUL) Brainerd, MN St. Andrew's; Brainerd, MN St. Francis; Fort Ripley, MN St. Mathias; Brainerd, MN St. Thomas; Fort Ripley, MN St. Mathias.
Walsh, Stephen *o.f.m.* '55 (BO)[AA] Boston, MA St. Anthony Shrine.
Walsh, Terrance G. *s.j.* '82 (BO)[V] Boston The Society of Jesus of New England–Provincial Offices.

Walsh, Theodore *c.p.* '59 (BRK)[V] Jamaica, NY Immaculate Conception Monastery.
Walsh, Thomas A. '42 (PHX) Scottsdale, AZ St. Bernadette Retired.
Walsh, Thomas E. *o.f.m.conv.* '80 (BAL)[C] Baltimore, MD Archbishop Curley High School; [S] Baltimore, MD Immaculate Heart of Mary Friary.
Walsh, Thomas F. '45 (PH) Retired.
Walsh, Thomas F. *s.j.* '55 (PAT)[I] Morristown, NJ Loyola House of Retreats.
Walsh, Thomas J. *o.carm.* '50 (VEN)[G] Nokomis, FL Carmel at Mission Valley.
Walsh, Thomas J. '67 (BO) Franklin, MA St. Mary.
Walsh, Thomas J. '89 (HRT) New Britain, CT St. Ann; New Britain, CT St. Mary's.
Walsh, Thomas J. *c.o.* '94 (MET)[H] Somerset, NJ The Metuchen Oratory, Congregation of the Oratory of St. Philip Neri; [N] New Brunswick, NJ Catholic Center at Rutgers University.
Walsh, Thomas P. '72 (STA) St. Augustine, FL San Sebastian.
Walsh, Thomas P. '86 (CHI) Chicago, IL Presentation.
Walsh, Thomas R. '59 (CHL) Retired.
Walsh, Thomas R. '94 (LIN) Lincoln, NE Sacred Heart.
Walsh, Thomas V. '67 (WOR) Clinton, MA St. John the Evangelist.
Walsh, Ulich '61 (WCH) Retired.
Walsh, Vincent M. '62 (PH) Wynnewood, PA Presentation B.V.M.; Archdiocesan Judges; Promoters of Justice.
Walsh, William D. '66 (BO) Health Leave.
Walsh, William F. *o.s.f.s.* '68 (R) Kitty Hawk, NC Holy Redeemer.
Walsh, William K. '49 (SAC) Rio Vista, CA St. Joseph Retired.
Walsh, William M. '71 (BO) Danvers, MA St. Mary of the Annunciation.
Walsh, William P. *s.j.* '67 (RVC)[O] Manhasset, NY St. Ignatius Retreat House, Inisfada.
Walsh, William *s.j.* '67 (BAL)[S] Baltimore, MD Ferdinand Wheeler Jesuit Community.
Walter, Andrew M. '00 (BGP) Bridgeport, CT Holy Rosary.
Walter, Anthony *o.f.m.* '59 (NO) New Orleans, LA St. Mary of the Angels.
Walter, Chris B. '58 (BIS) Minot, ND St. Leo; Presbyteral Council.
Walter, David A. '63 (STL) On Medical Leave.
Walter, Eugene *s.d.b.* '83 (NY)[GG] Stony Point, NY Don Bosco Retreat Center and Marian Shrine; [GG] Stony Point, NY Marian Shrine.
Walter, Francis *o.f.m.* '77 (BO)[V] Boston, MA St. Bonaventure Friary, Franciscan Friars.
Walter, James A. '62 (COL) Sunbury, OH St. John Neumann.
Walter, James A. '69 (BUF) Springbrook, NY St. Vincent.
Walter, John F. '44 (MIL)[M] Wauwatosa, WI St. Camillus Health Center, Inc. Retired.
Walter, Joseph L. *c.s.c.* '61 (FTW)[B] University of Notre Dame Du Lac; [I] Notre Dame, IN Holy Cross Community, Corby Hall, University of Notre Dame.
Walter, Marius *o.s.b.* '98 (P)[L] St. Benedict, OR Mt. Angel Abbey.
Walter, Mark J. '88 (CHI) Evergreen Park, IL Most Holy Redeemer.
Walter, Robert J. '45 (DAV) Retired.
Walter, Steven P. '77 (CIN) Cincinnati, OH Our Mother of Sorrows.
Walter, William P. *c.pp.s.* '61 (DAV) Albia, IA St. Mary's.
Walters, Erik T.A. '02 (MOB) Dothan, AL St. Columba.
Walters, Frederick '87 (PAT) McAfee, NJ St. Francis de Sales.
Walters, Gary R. '79 (TOL) Toledo, OH St. Catherine of Siena.
Walters, Michael M. '81 (NEW) East Orange, NJ Holy Spirit–Our Lady Help of Christians; Central Essex Deanery 17; Archdiocesan Judges; Marriage Encounter Resources; Boy Scouts of America/Catholic Committee on Scouting.
Walters, Neil G. '89 (CLV) Strongsville, OH St. John Neumann.
Walters, Ronald *o.f.m.* '78 (GLP) St. Michaels, AZ St. Michael; Defenders of the Bond.
Walters, Theodore W. *s.j.* '56 (DET)[K] St. Augustine University of Tanzania.
Walters, Vincent '54 (SB) Retired.
Walterscheid, Kyle R. '02 (FWT) Arlington, TX St. Matthew.
Waltersheid, William J. '92 (HBG) Carlisle, PA St. Patrick.
Walther, James *o.m.v.* '95 (SFD) Alton, IL St. Mary's.
Walton, James *o.f.m.* '91 (CHI)[N] Countryside, IL St. Gratian Friary, Franciscan Friars.
Walton, James *o.f.m.* '91 (JOL) Hinsdale, IL Hinsdale Hospital.
Walton, Robert P. '74 (SAC) Sacramento, CA Sacred Heart of Jesus; Vicar General and Vicar for Temporalities & Administration; College of Consultors; Council of Priests; Ex Officio; Priests' Personnel Board, Diocesan.
Walz, Daniel '03 (SCL) Elk River, MN The Church of St. Andrew.
Walz, Richard *o.s.b.* '67[A] Subiaco, AR Subiaco Monastery; (FgM).
Walz, Richard '88 (SCL) Elizabeth, MN St. Elizabeth; Pelican Rapids, MN St. Leonard's.
Walz, W. Dean '53 (DUB) On Special or Other Archdiocesan Assignment; Episcopal Vicar for Waterloo Region; College of Consultors; Continuing Formation of Clergy; Council of Catholic Women; Judges; Ecclesiastical Attorneys; American Martyrs Retreat House Advisory Board; Ex Officio Members; Pastoral Council; Ex Officio Members.
Wambach, John W. *s.j.* '64 (LC) Prairie du Chien, WI St. Gabriel; Prairie du Chien, WI St. John Nepomucene.
Wambach, Joseph *s.d.s.* '67 (MIL)[O] Tempe, AZ.
Wampach, Frank J. '84 (STP) Watertown, MN Immaculate Conception.
Wamsher, Ronald E. (SPR) Procurators–Advocate.
Wanat, Michael *c.m.* '71 (HRT) Derby, CT St. Michael.
Wanaurny, John '59 (OM)[K] St. Columbans St. Columban's Foreign Mission Society.
Wanda, Michael J. '91 (CHI) Park Ridge, IL Mary, Seat of Wisdom; Chaplains.
Wander, Paul '90 (B) Salmon, ID St. Charles; Priest Personnel Commission.
Wandess, John '97 (KC) Kansas City, MO St. Therese Little Flower.
Wandless, John H. '97 (KC) Kansas City, MO St. Louis.
Wandless, John (KC) Diocesan Finance Council.
Wang, Barnabas '52 (BRK)[V] Douglaston, NY Bishop Mugavero Residence Retired.
Wang, Francis X. *s.j.* '52 (SJ)[M] Los Gatos, CA Sacred Heart Jesuit Center.
Wang, John '54 (HEL) Retired.
Wang, John (STO) Diamond Springs, CA Retired.
Wangaih, Paul '60 (MEM) Memphis, TN St. Michael's.
Wangiarala, George '93 (CHI)[N] Chicago, IL Discalced Carmelite Friars; Edith Stein House of Studies.
Wangler, Brian *o.s.b.* '69 (BIS) Richardton, ND St. Mary; [A] Richardton, ND Assumption Abbey.
Wangler, Donald R. '57 (BUF) Retired.
Wangler, Leonard *o.s.b.* '70 (LR)[A] Subiaco, AR Subiaco Monastery.
Wangler, William O. '63 (BUF) Olean, NY St. John.
Wanish, David A. '02 (MAD) Appointed; Madison, WI St. Paul University Parish.
Wanjura, Victor '99 (LUB) Lubbock, TX St. John Neumann; Officialis; Presbyteral Council; Priests' Retirement Board.
Wankerl, Gary A. '80 (MAD) De Forest, WI St. Olaf; DeForest, WI St. Joseph.
Wannemuehler, Robert '51 (EVN) Retired.
Wanser, George V. *s.j.* '76 (SAC)[D] Sacramento, CA Jesuit High School; [I] Carmichael, CA Jesuit High School Community of Sacramento.
Wanser, George *s.j.* (SAC)[L] Sacramento, CA.
Wantland, Thomas '67 (MAR) On Duty Outside the Diocese; Port Charlotte, FL St. Charles Borromeo.
Wapen, Francis A. '70 (SY) Taberg, NY St. Patrick.
Waraksa, Alex J. '90 (KNX) Alcoa, TN Our Lady of Fatima.
Waraksa, Alex (KNX) Worship and Liturgy.
Warczynski, Leon '42 (BAL).
Ward, Bernardine *o.f.m.* '42 (PAT)[M] Butler, NJ St. Anthony Friary.
Ward, Bruce *s.t.* '60 (FgM).
Ward, Daniel *o.s.b.* '71 (SCL)[I] Silver Springs, MD.
Ward, Donal '63 (BUR) Retired.
Ward, Donald M. *s.j.* '70 (CAM) Camden, NJ Holy Name.
Ward, Edward *o.m.i.* '67 (LAR) Laredo, TX Our Lady of Guadalupe.
Ward, Edward *o.carm.* '73 (CHI) Darien, IL Our Lady of Mount Carmel.
Ward, Gary '80 (NEW) Bayonne, NJ St. Andrew's.
Ward, Gerald T. '79 (PEO) Bloomington, IL St. Patrick Church of Merna.
Ward, James J. '73 (ALN) Palmerton, PA Sacred Heart; Judges; Elected Members.
Ward, Jerome A. *o.m.i.* '67 (CHR) Retired.
Ward, John A. *s.s.* '39 (BAL)[O] Baltimore, MD St. Charles Villa.
Ward, John B. '86 (BAL) Baltimore, MD Our Lady of Hope; [A] Judges.
Ward, John B. (MO) Judges; Promoter of Justice.
Ward, John C. '45 (NU) Retired.
Ward, John J. '55 (SFR)[D] Kentfield, CA Marin Catholic College Preparatory (Coed) Retired.
Ward, John J. *c.s.b.* '70 (DET)[E] Redford, MI Catholic Central High School; [H] Niagara Falls, NY Women, Infants & Children (W.I.C.) of Niagara County.
Ward, John P. '65 (CAM) Pine Hill, NJ St. Edward's.
Ward, John *o.m.i.* '49 (SAT) Priest Personnel Board.
Ward, John '58 (HEL) Retired.
Ward, Mark *c.p.* '76 (WH) Kingwood, WV St. Sebastian's; Kingwood, WV St. Zita's.
Ward, Mark *c.p.* (WH) Vicars Forane.
Ward, Michael G. (NEW) West Hudson Region Deanery 14.
Ward, Michael '97 (NEW) Kearny, NJ St. Cecilia's.
Ward, Michael *o.f.m.* (CHI)[D] Holy Spirit Friary.
Ward, Neal A. '57 (WDC) Retired.
Ward, Richard E. '68 (PIT) Pittsburgh, PA SS. Simon and Jude.
Ward, Richard '93 (SEA) Fife, WA St. Martin of Tours.
Ward, Samuel '03 (LA) Lynwood, CA St. Emydius.
Ward, Sebastian *o.f.m.cap.* '47 (LA)[B] Santa Ynez, CA San Lorenzo Seminary and Prayer Center; [B] Santa Ynez, CA San Lorenzo Seminary and Prayer Center.
Ward, Serge E. (ATL) Released from Archdiocesan Assignment.
Ward, Thomas I. '97 (SY) Greene, NY Immaculate Conception; Greene, NY St. Joseph.
Ward, Thomas R. '65 (OM) Omaha, NE St. John Vianney.
Ward, Thomas '62 (KC) Retired.
Ward, W. '03 (LA) Lynwood, CA St. Emydius.
Ward, William G. '50 (BUF)[O] Buffalo, NY Sheehan Residence for Priests Retired.
Ward, William P. '57 (SCR) Milford, PA St. Vincent de Paul; Diocesan Finance Council.
Wardanski, Joseph V. '67 (E) Erie, PA St. Patrick/St. Hedwig; [K] Erie, PA St. Mary's Home of Erie.
Warden, Daniel L. '66 (GAL) Rosenberg, TX Holy Rosary.
Warden, Joel M *c.o.* '99 (BRK)[V] Brooklyn, NY Oratory of Saint Philip Neri, Congregation Pontifical Rite.
Warden, Joel M. *c.o.* '99 (BRK) Brooklyn, NY The Oratory Church of St. Boniface.
Warden, T. Patrick *c.s.b.* '65 (GAL)[Q] Houston, TX Residence of the Basilian Fathers of the University of St. Thomas.
Wardenski, Robert W. '72 (BUF) Finance Council; West Seneca, NY St. William.
Ware, Donald *c.p.* '72 (PIT)[N] Pittsburgh, PA St. Paul of the Cross Monastery.
Ware, Joseph F. '48 (SAV) Savannah, GA St. Frances Xavier Cabrini.
Ware, Joseph F. '48 (ATL) Retired.
Wargel, William J. '65 (EVN) Ferdinand, IN St. Ferdinand.
Wargel, William (EVN) Diocesan Council of Priests.
Wargo, Robert J. '72 (ALN) Orefield, PA St. Joseph The Worker.
Waris, Gerald '67 (KC) Kansas City, MO St. Patrick.
Warkulwiz, Victor *m.s.s.* '91 (PH) Bensalem, PA Our Lady of Fatima.
Warman, William C. '64 (BAL) On Duty Outside the Archdiocese.
Warman, William '64 (BAL) U.S. Veterans Medical Center.
Warmuz, Gregory W. *o.cist* '94 (CHI) Bridgeview, IL St. Fabian.
Warnakula, Anthony B. *c.h.s.p.* '88 (SAC) Susanville, CA California Correctional Center.
Warner, James L. '69 (GI) Mullen, NE St. Mary's.
Warner, John F. (Y) Defenders of the Bond.
Warner, John '70 (Y) Canal Fulton, OH SS. Philip and James.
Warner, Joseph A. '03 (CLV) Amherst, OH St. Joseph.
Warner, Richard V. *c.s.c.* '66 (FTW)[I] Notre Dame, IN Holy Cross Community, Corby Hall, University of Notre Dame.
Warner, Steven (SPK)[M] Pullman, WA Washington State University – St. Thomas More Catholic Newman Center.
Warnimont, Ronald R. '76 (TOL) Columbus Grove, OH St. Anthony of Padua; Consultors; Defenders of the Bond.
Warnisher, Maximilian M. *f.f.i.* '94 (FR)[F] Griswold, CT Marian Friary of Our Lady of Guadalupe.
Warnock, Damian J. *o.s.b.* '79 (GBG)[H] Latrobe, PA Saint Vincent Archabbey.
Warnock, Damian *o.s.b.* '79 (GBG) Latrobe, PA Latrobe Area Hospital.
Warnstedt, Mark '96 (LA) Downey, CA Our Lady of Perpetual Help.
Warosh, James B. *s.j.* '67 (LC) Prairie du Chien, WI St. Gabriel; Prairie du Chien, WI St. John Nepomucene.
Warren, Anthony C. *s.s.p.* '85 (NY)[B] New York, NY Society of St. Paul.
Warren, Arthur M. (LAF) Adjutant Judicial Vicars.
Warren, Arthur '63 (LAF) Retired.
Warren, Edward V. *s.j.* '52 (SJ)[B] Santa Clara, CA Jesuit Community.
Warren, Martin L. '78 (STP) St. Paul, MN St. Matthew; [C] St. Paul, MN University of St. Thomas.
Warren, Paul '78 (SFR) San Mateo, CA St. Gregory.
Warren, Robert '64 (RIC).
Warren, Robert *s.a.* '81 (NY)[EE] Garrison, NY St. Christopher's Inn; [EE] Garrison, NY St. Christopher's Friary.
Warsey, Robert M. *o.s.m.* '85 (CHI)[N] Chicago, IL Order of Friar Servants of Mary (Servites) United States of America Province, Inc.; [N] Chicago, IL Monastery of Our Lady of Sorrows; [N] Chicago, IL Servite Marian Center.
Warzocha, Frank S. '53 (BUR) West Rutland, VT St. Stanislaus Kostka.
Wasek, Piotr (CHI) Chicago, IL St. James.

Wasek, Stanislaus *c.p.* '53 (BRK)[V] Jamaica, NY Immaculate Conception Monastery.
Waseline, Nicholas R. *o.s.f.s.* '80 (PH) Philadelphia, PA Our Mother of Consolation; [D] Philadelphia, PA Northeast Catholic High School for Boys; Council of Priests.
Waser, Frank A. '79 (RCK) Absent on Leave.
Washabaugh, Robert J. (NOR) Part Time.
Washabaugh, Robert (NOR) College of Consultors; Members; St. Mary, Star of the Sea Church – Spanish Apostolate.
Washbaugh, Robert '78 (NOR) New London, CT St. Mary, Star of the Sea.
Washburn, Thomas *o.f.m.* (MAN) Derry, NH St. Thomas Aquinas.
Washington, Freddy *c.s.sp.* '92 (NY) New York, NY St. Mark the Evangelist; Manhattan, NY Harlem Hospital.
Washko, Robert M. '77 (GBG) Everson, PA St. Joseph.
Washko, Stephen G. '78 (VNN) Phoenix, AZ St. Stephen; Chancellor and Protosyncellus; Building Commission; Eparchial Finance Commission; Commission for the Implementation of the Particular Law.
Washko, Stephen (VNN) Eparchial Consultors – Presbyteral Council; Ecclesiatical Notary; Liturgy & Music Commission; Director of Ecumenical Affairs.
Wasiel, Michael J. '33 (CHI) Retired.
Wasiel, Michael '33 (CHI) Harvey, IL St. John the Baptist Retired.
Wasielewski, Henry R. '64 (PHX) Retired.
Wasikowski, Ronald S. '75 (OM) Elkhorn, NE St. Patrick; Finance Council.
Wasilewski, Kenneth '03 (RCK) Dixon, IL St. Patrick; Active Outside the Diocese.
Wasinger, Shane '94 (DEN) Denver, CO Assumption; On Duty Outside the Archdiocese; Englewood, CO St. Rafka Mission.
Waska, Raymond '95 (FBK) Emmonak, AK Sacred Heart.
Wasko, Anthony J. *o.s.a.* '58 (SD) San Diego, CA St. Patrick; [H] San Diego, CA Augustinian Community.
Waskowiak, Harlan D. P. '98 (LIN) Orleans, NE St. Mary's.
Waslo, Peter D. (CLV) Adjutant Judicial Vicars.
Waslo, Peter '81 (SJP) Carnegie, PA Holy Trinity.
Waslo, Peter (SJP) Diocesan Administrative Council.
Waslo, Peter (PBR) Pro–Synodal Judges.
Waslo, Peter (SJP) Vice Chancellor.
Waslo, Peter (SJP) Vicar for Clergy.
Waslo, Peter (SJP) Catechetical Planning Committee.
Waslo, Peter (SJP) Clergy Examiners.
Waslo, Peter (SJP) Permanent Diaconate Program.
Waslo, Peter (SJP) Diocesan Consultors.
Waslo, Peter (SJP) Presbyteral Council.
Waslo, Peter (SJP) Judicial Vicar.
Waslo, Peter (SJP) Diocesan Corporation.
Wasnewski, Richard P. '53 (BO) Senior Priests Retired.
Wasnie, Blane *o.s.b.* '66 (SCL) Avon, MN St. Benedict's; [I] Collegeville, MN St. John's Abbey, of the Order of St. Benedict; Pastoral Council.
Wasowski, Ronald *c.s.c.* '73 (P)[B] University of Portland; [L] Portland, OR Holy Cross Fathers & Brothers, C.S.C. – University of Portland.
Wassel, Anthony F. '60 (ALN) Mahanoy City, PA St. Joseph; Mahanoy City, PA Sacred Heart.
Wassel, Eugene A. '52 (PH) Retired.
Wassell, John E. '97 (NEW) Elizabeth, NJ Our Lady of Most Holy Rosary/St. Michael; Elizabeth Deanery 25.
Wasser, James *m.s.f.* '74 (SAT) New Braunfels, TX Holy Family.
Wassie, Stephen M. '79 (Y) Jefferson, OH St. Joseph Calasanctius.
Wassie, Stephen '79 (Y) Kingsville, OH St. Andrew.
Wassmuth, Dennis '73 (B) Boise, ID Our Lady of the Rosary; Vicars General; Notaries; Ex Officio; Priest Personnel Commission; Finance Council; Priest Retirement Committee.
Wastag, Michael *o.carm.* '97 (NEW)[P] Mahwah, NJ Carmel Retreat; [II] New York, NY The Center for Spirituality and Justice.
Waszak, Norbert J. '53 (CHI) Retired.
Waszczenko, Andrew *s.d.s.* '89 (NOR) Fishers Island, NY Our Lady of Grace.
Waszczenko, Andrezej *s.d.s.* '89 (NEW)[N] Verona, NJ The Salvatorian Fathers.
Watanabe, Philip '77 (KC) Butler, MO St. Patrick's.
Watanabe, Terrence A.M. '77 (HON) Honolulu, HI St. Philomena.
Watanabe, Terrence (HON) Diocesan Planning and Building Commission.
Watanabe, Terrence (HON) Members.
Watanabe, Terrence (HON) Master of Ceremonies for Episcopal Functions.
Watanabe, Terrence (HON) Coordinator of Diocesan Major Events.
Watanabe, Terrence (HON) Presbyteral Council.
Watanabe, Terrence (HON) College of Consultors.
Watanabe, Terrence (HON) Senior Priests' Committee.
Watanabe, Terrence (HON) Vicars Forane.
Waterfall, Richard A. '49 (SB) Retired.
Waterman, Gerald *o.f.m.conv.* '85 (BGP) Danbury, CT Sacred Heart.
Waters, Bernard F. '69 (LAV) Las Vegas, NV St. Joseph, Husband of Mary.
Waters, J. Kevin *s.j.* '64 (SPK)[B] Spokane, WA Gonzaga University.
Waters, John J. *s.j.* '51 (DEN)[N] Denver, CO Xavier Jesuit Center.
Waters, John '64 (DEN)[H] Denver, CO St. Joseph Hospital.
Waters, Joseph L. *s.s.j.* '45 (WDC)[B] Washington, DC St. Joseph's Seminary.
Waters, Joseph L. *s.s.j.* '49 (BAL)[S] Baltimore, MD St. Joseph Society of the Sacred Heart House of Central Administration.
Waters, Joseph L. '87 (SP) Temple Terrace, FL Corpus Christi.
Waters, Joseph '56 (CHL) Retired.
Waters, Joseph (SP) Presbyteral Council; College of Consultors; Vicars Forane.
Waters, Mark S. '90 (STA) Palm Coast, FL St. Stephen; Palm Coast, FL St. Elizabeth Ann Seton.
Waters, Philip J. *o.s.b.* '72 (NEW) Newark, NJ St. Mary's; [N] Newark, NJ Newark Abbey; Central Newark Deanery 20.
Waters, Robert E. '69 (BUF) Corfu, NY St. Francis of Assisi; Crittenden, NY St. Patrick.
Waters, Robert J. '60 (SC) Hinton, IA Assumption Church.
Waters, Robert J. (CHR) Gloverville, SC Our Lady of the Valley Retired.
Waters, William F. *o.s.a.* (BO) Lawrence, MA St. Mary Immaculate Conception.
Wathen, Ambrose G. *o.s.b.* '65 (NO)[P] St. Benedict, LA St. Joseph Abbey.
Wathier, Douglas O. '84 (DUB)[L] Dubuque, IA Mt. Loretto Convent; [C] Loras College.
Watkins, Charles W. '03 (CHI) Chicago Ridge, IL Our Lady of the Ridge.
Watkins, Clarence N. '67 (ARL) Retired.
Watkins, James D. '89 (WDC) Washington, DC Immaculate Conception.
Watkins, Mark T. '91 (CIN) Cincinnati, OH St. Peter in Chains Cathedral; Vocations Office.
Watkins, Paul D. *o.p.* (NO) New Orleans, LA St. Anthony of Padua; New Orleans, LA St. Thomas More.
Watrin, Clarence E. *c.s.b.* '59 (GAL)[Q] Sugar Land Basilian Mission Center.
Watroba, Boleslaus M. '35 (ALB) Watervliet, NY Immaculate Conception Retired.
Watson, Cletus M. *t.o.r.* '66 (STA) Jacksonville, FL Church of the Crucifixion; Jacksonville, FL St. Pius the Fifth.
Watson, Cletus M.S. *t.o.r.* (STA) African and Native American Ministries.
Watson, David E. *s.j.* '92 (DET)[K] Detroit, MI Jesuit Provincial Office–Detroit Province of the Society of Jesus.
Watson, David E. *s.j.* '92 (TOL) Toledo, OH Gesu.
Watson, J Vincent *o.p.* '63 (CIN) Cincinnati, OH St. Gertrude; [M] Cincinnati, OH St. Gertrude Priory.
Watson, Joseph T. *s.j.* '52 (NEW)[C] Jersey City, NJ St. Peter's Preparatory School; [N] Jersey City, NJ Jesuit Community of St. Peter's Prep, Inc..
Watson, Joseph '92 (PH) Philadelphia, PA St. Charles Borromeo.
Watson, Mark A. (SHP) College of Consultors; Presbyteral Council.
Watson, Mark '96 (SHP) Monroe, LA Jesus the Good Shepherd; Advocates; Church Vocations Board.
Watson, Michael B. '86 (COL) Columbus, OH St. Andrew; Diocesan Judges.
Watson, Timothy *c.ss.r.* '90 (DEN) Denver, CO St. Joseph; [N] Denver, CO The Redemptorists of Denver, Colorado.
Watson, Walter *s.j.* '70 (DEN) Arvada, CO St. Joan of Arc.
Watson, William A. '62 (PEO) Peoria Heights, IL St. Thomas; [B] Peoria, IL Peoria Notre Dame Scholarship Trust.
Watson, William M. *s.j.* '85 (SPK)[B] Spokane, WA Gonzaga University.
Watt, Gerald *c.r.* (CHI) Chicago, IL St. Wenceslaus.
Watters, Timothy J. '71 (CHR) Absent On Leave.
Watters, William J. *s.j.* '65 (BAL) Baltimore, MD St. Ignatius; [J] Baltimore, MD St. Ignatius Loyola Academy; [W] Baltimore, MD Radio Mass of Baltimore, Inc..
Watterson, John E. '62 (PRO) Narragansett, RI St. Mary, Star of the Sea; Health Care Ministries.
Wattigny, Patrick B. '94 (NO) Metairie, LA St. Benilde.
Watts, Albert W. '59 (BGP)[M] Norwalk, CT Notre Dame Convalescent Home; [Q] Norwalk, CT Regional House of Sisters of St. Thomas of Villanova; Judges.
Watts, Roger J. '59 (BGP) Retired.
Watts, Thomas H. '57 (ROC) Retired.
Watts, Trent L. '93 (R) Burgaw, NC St Joseph; Absent on Leave.
Watts, Wayne F. '90 (CHI) Chicago, IL Queen of All Saints Basilica; Associate Administrators; [G] Chicago, IL Catholic Charities of the Archdiocese of Chicago–Archdiocesan Offices.
Watzke, James N. *c.s.c.* '63 (FTW)[I] Chicago, IL.
Waudby, Lawrence '90 (BAL) Absent on Leave.
Waugh, John G. '55 (PEO) Wedron, IL St. Joseph's; Illinois Industrial School for Boys.
Wawer, Robert *s.j.* '01 (OAK)[N] Berkeley, CA Jesuit Community at Jesuit School of Theology at Berkeley.
Wawerski, Edward '61 (RVC) Hempstead, NY St. Ladislaus.
Wawiorka, Ray W. '56 (MIL) Retired.
Wawryszuk, Zdzislaw F. '85 (RCK) South Beloit, IL St. Peter.
Wawrzyniakowski, Edwrd J. '57 (MIL) Retired.
Wawrzynski, Edward A. '60 (YAK) Retired.
Way, Edmund J. *o.p.* '43 (WDC) Washington, DC St. Dominic Church & Priory.
Wayne, David A. *s.j.* '68 (DEN)[D] Aurora, CO Regis Jesuit High School; [N] Centennial, CO Regis High Jesuit Community.
Waznak, Robert J. *s.s.* '02 (SCR) On Duty Outside the Diocese.
Wdowiak, Boleslaw '65 (SAC) Retired.
Wea, Raymundus Bhia *s.v.d.* '82 (LA)[Q] Los Angeles, CA Casa Guadalupe.
Weakley, Robert *o.f.m.* '68 (DET) Southfield, MI St. Michael.
Wearden, Francis G. '54 (GAL) Oremus Pro Invicem Retired.
Weare, Kenneth M. '01 (SFR) South San Francisco, CA All Souls.
Wearsch, Ronald '92 (CLV) Willowick, OH St. Mary Magdalene.
Weary, William M. '84 (HBG) Danville, PA St. Joseph.
Weaver, Cyprian *o.s.b.* '72 (FgM).
Weaver, Cyprian *o.s.b.* '72 (SCL)[I] Holy Trinity Benedictine Monastery.
Weaver, Jeffrey '82 (CLV) Absent on Leave.
Weaver, John G. '70 (HRT) Torrington, CT St. Francis of Assisi; Torrington, CT St. Mary's; Torrington, CT St. Peter's; Torrington, CT Sacred Heart.
Weaver, Richard '63 (DAL) Dallas, TX All Saints.
Webb, Raymond J. '67 (CHI)[A] Mundelein Seminary.
Webber, Donald S. '62 (SB) Special or Other Diocesan Assignment; Judicial Vicar; Judges; Diocesan Curia; College of Consultors.
Webber, Donald *c.p.* '73 (FgM).
Webber, Donald *c.p.* '73 (CHI)[N] Chicago, IL Passionist Provincial Office; [N] Chicago, IL Passionist Community–Immaculate Conception Monastery.
Webber, Donald (SB) Elected Members; Committee Members.
Weber, Alan '84 (SP)[H] St. Petersburg, FL St. Petersburg Diocesan Library; [T] Tampa, FL Catholic Student Center, University of South Florida.
Weber, Alan (SP) Vicars General; Moderator of the Curia; Secretary for Pastoral Programs; Ex Officio; Permanent Diaconate Office; Department of Temporal Affairs; Diocesan Finance Council; Presbyteral Council; College of Consultors.
Weber, Alan (SP) Incardination Commission.
Weber, Alan (SP) Vicars General; Moderator of the Curia; Secretary for Pastoral Programs; Ex Officio; Permanent Diaconate Office; Department of Temporal Affairs; Diocesan Finance Council; Presbyteral Council; College of Consultors.
Weber, Allen *o.f.m.* '65 (BUF)[O] St. Bonaventure, NY St. Bonaventure Friary; [C] St. Bonaventure, NY Friar Community.
Weber, Arnold *o.s.b.* '52 (SCL)[I] Collegeville, MN St. John's Abbey, of the Order of St. Benedict.
Weber, Bernard *c.p.* '81 (L)[K] Louisville, KY Sacred Heart Retreat.
Weber, Charles E. '53 (COV) Retired.
Weber, Charles P. '57 (BO) Senior Priests Retired.
Weber, Christopher H. '02 (CLV) Chagrin Falls, OH St. Joan of Arc.
Weber, Daniel C. *s.j.* '60 (SEA)[C] Tacoma, WA Bellarmine Preparatory School.
Weber, David '77 (CLV) Administrative Leave.
Weber, Dennis M. *s.c.* '97 (PH)[M] Springfield, PA Don Guanella School; [M] Springfield, PA Cardinal Krol Center; [AA] Springfield, PA Servants of Charity (S.C.).
Weber, Donald C. '53 (BUF)[O] Lackawanna, NY Bishop Head Residence Retired.
Weber, Donald E. (GR) On Special Assignment; College of Consultors; Vicar For Priests.
Weber, Donald N. '47 (MIL) Retired.
Weber, Donald (GR) New Holstein, WI Holy Rosary; New Holstein, WI St. Ann Retired.
Weber, Edward J. '76 (NY) West Nyack, NY St. Francis of Assisi; [DD] Nyack, NY Catholic Community Services of Rockland, Inc.; Rockland.
Weber, Eric Christopher '01 (LAN) Ann Arbor, MI St. Thomas the Apostle.
Weber, Eugene J. '72 (WH) Retired.
Weber, Eugene J. (BAL) Interdiocesan Judges.
Weber, Fidelis F. *t.o.r.* '55 (PH)[D] Fairless Hills, PA Conwell–Egan Catholic High School; [AA] Fairless Hills, PA St. Anthony Friary.
Weber, Francis J. '59 (LA) Mission Hills, CA San

Fernando Rey Mission; Archives.
Weber, Frank W. '62 (PAT) Clifton, NJ St. Brendan.
Weber, Gabriel M. *o.s.m.* '49 (DEN) Denver, CO Our Lady of Mt. Carmel.
Weber, Gabriel M. *o.s.m.* '49 (CHI)[N] Chicago Order of Friar Servants of Mary (Servites) United States of America Province, Inc..
Weber, George A. '60 (CAM) Disabled Retired.
Weber, George (NO) New Orleans, LA St. Stephen.
Weber, Gerard P. '43 (CHI) Retired.
Weber, Gerard *o.m.i.* '62 (SAT)[M] San Antonio, TX Oblate Benson Residence (Southwest Area); [T] San Antonio, TX Oblate Lourdes Grotto Shrine of the Southwest, Tepeyac de San Antonio.
Weber, Gordon A. '52 (MIL) Retired.
Weber, Herbert F. '74 (TOL) Mansfield, OH St. Peter; Bishop's Education Council; Mansfield Deanery.
Weber, Jacques *s.j.* '49 (GAL) Houston, TX St. Cecilia.
Weber, James H. '43 (E) Retired.
Weber, John George '43 (SAL) Art and Architecture Commission Retired.
Weber, John R. *c.s.sp.* '61 (PIT)[P] Bethel Park, PA Holy Spirit Animation Center.
Weber, John S. *o.f.m.conv.* (LSC) Diocesan Tribunal.
Weber, John '73 (LSC) Fairacres, NM San Jose Mission.
Weber, John *o.f.m.conv.* (LSC) Presbyteral Council; Finance Council; Judicial Vicar.
Weber, John–Benedict *o.carm.* '77 (JOL)[L] Darien, IL Carmelite Community.
Weber, John–Benedict *o.carm.* '77 (JOL)[O] Darien, IL Provincial Office of Lay Carmelites and Scapular Confraternity.
Weber, Joseph A. '76 (STL) St. Louis, MO St. Andrew; Air National Guard Chaplains.
Weber, Joseph A. '76 (PRM) Wildwood, MO St. Louis Mission.
Weber, Joseph O. '57 (SCR) Wyoming, PA St. Frances Cabrini; Presbyteral Council.
Weber, Keith '83 (SAL) Manhattan, KS St. Isidore; [H] Manhattan, KS St. Isidore's Catholic Student Center.
Weber, Keith (SAL) Council of Priests; Vocation Ministry Committee; Art and Architecture Commission; Diocesan Council of Education; Board of Trustees; Salina Diocesan Council of Catholic Women (S.D-.CC.W.).
Weber, Kevin '93 (SAL) Hays, KS Immaculate Heart of Mary.
Weber, Leo F. *s.j.* '56 (DEN)[D] Aurora, CO Regis Jesuit High School; [N] Centennial, CO Regis High Jesuit Community.
Weber, Mark *s.v.d.* '82 (CHI) Chicago, IL St. Anselm.
Weber, Matthew *s.c.* '90 (LAN)[E] Chelsea, MI St. Louis Center for Exceptional Children & Adults; [O] Grass Lake, MI "Now and at the Hour" Magazine:.
Weber, Michael J. *o.praem.* '77 (GB)[I] De Pere, WI St. Norbert Abbey; Air Force Chaplains.
Weber, Norbert B. *m.s.c.* '57 (RCK)[G] Aurora, IL Missionaries of the Sacred Heart Community.
Weber, Randall '91 (SAL) Abilene, KS St. Andrew's; Chapman, KS St. Michael's.
Weber, Randall (SAL) Council of Priests; Vocation Ministry Committee; Priests' Continuing Formation Committee.
Weber, Robert C. '81 (SY) Holland Patent, NY St. Leo; Marcy, NY Mid–State Correctional Facility; Special Assignment.
Weber, Robert P. '65 (CAM) Bridgeton, NJ Immaculate Conception; Delmont, NJ Southern State Correctional Facility; Bridgeton, NJ Immaculate Conception.
Weber, Robson Luis '76 (ALN) Bethlehem, PA Holy Infancy.
Weber, Samuel *o.s.b.* '96 (IND)[K] Winston–Salem, NC Wake Forest Divinity School.
Weber, Terry '84 (SFS) Canton, SD St. Dominic; Miller, SD St. Ann.
Weber, Theodore '55 (P) Building Commission Retired.
Weber, Thomas H. (CLV) Retirement Board Retired.
Weber, Thomas L. '74 (CLV) Westlake, OH St. Bernadette; Retirement Board.
Webster, Andrew (DET) Absent on Leave.
Webster, Robert E. '86 (ORL) Daytona Beach, FL St. Paul's; Special Assignment.
Webster, Robert (ORL) Bishop's Executive Staff; Office of Worship.
Wechter, David *o.c.s.o.* '58 (DUB)[G] Houston, MN Hermits of St. Mary of Carmel, (H.S.M.C.).
Wechter, David *o.c.s.o.* '58 (WIN)[A] Winona, MN Immaculate Heart of Mary Seminary.
Wechter, David *o.cist.* (WIN) Associate Judges.
Weckbach, Hanford E. *s.j.* '43 (LA)[C] Los Angeles, CA Jesuit Community.
Weckerle, Leo F. '58 (BAK) Defender of the Bond and Promoter of Justice; Central; Health and Retirement Board; Redmond, OR St. Thomas.
Weckert, Paul M. *o.s.b.* '99 (SEA)[L] Lacey, WA St. Martin's Abbey.
Weckert, Paul *o.s.b.* '99 (SEA) Vancouver, WA St. James.
Wedeking, Patrick '88 (GLP) Waterflow, NM Sacred Heart; Air Force Reserve Chaplains.
Wedig, James M. '93 (CIN) Wilmington, OH St. Columbkille; [Q] Wilmington, OH Wilmington College Campus Ministry.
Wedig, Mark *o.p.* '86 (MIA) Miami, FL St. Dominic; [B] Miami, FL Barry University.
Wedow, Robert L. '01 (DEN) Brighton, CO St. Augustine; Roggen, CO Sacred Heart.
Wee, Salvador C. *s.j.* '82 (OAK)[N] Berkeley, CA Jesuit Community at Jesuit School of Theology at Berkeley.
Weeks, James M. *m.s.* '62 (HRT).
Weeney, John '48 (SFR)[M] East Palo Alto, CA St. Francis of Assisi Retired.
Weerakkody, Oliver '65 (AUS)[E] Austin, TX SETON Medical Center; [E] Austin, TX SETON Northwest Hospital.
Weerasinghe, Felix '64 (RVC) Shoreham, NY St. Mark.
Weezorak, Dennis R. '86 (MET) South Amboy, NJ St. Mary.
Wegg, Mark '87 (ORL) Winter Haven, FL St. Joseph's; Haines City, FL St. Ann.
Wegher, William '91 (LAN) Burton, MI Holy Redeemer; Ecumenical Officer; Worship Commission.
Weglicki, Michael '79 (LEX) Lancaster, KY St. William; Lancaster, KY St. Sylvester.
Weglicki, Michael (LEX) Defenders of the Bond; Catholic Scouting.
Wegman, Richard H. '90 (MAN) Retired.
Wegner, Gary *o.f.m.cap.* '89 (MIL)[O] Mount Calvary, WI St. Lawrence Friary; [B] Mount Calvary, WI St. Lawrence Seminary.
Wegner, Laurian *o.f.m.* '78 (FgM).
Wego, Benignus "Bennie" *s.v.d.* '95 (LAF)[K] Galveston, TX Chaplain Corps: John Sealy Medical Center, U.T.M.B. Hospital; Opelousas, LA Holy Ghost; Galveston, TX St. Mary's Cathedral Basilica.
Wehage, Robert C. '71 (COV) Edgewood, KY St. Pius X; Judges.
Wehby, Albert *b.a.o.* '63 (NTN) North Hollywood, CA St. Anne.
Wehinger, Thomas E. '61 (TOL) Toledo, OH Our Lady of Lourdes.
Wehman, Jack W. '80 (CIN) Cincinnati, OH Our Lady of the Sacred Heart.
Wehmann, Mark H. '03 (STP) South St. Paul, MN Holy Trinity; South St. Paul, MN St. Augustine.
Wehmeyer, Curtis C. '01 (STP) West St. Paul, MN St. Joseph.
Wehn, Timothy Clark '79 (LAV) Las Vegas, NV St. Joan of Arc.
Wehn, Timothy (LAV) Presbyteral Council for the Diocese of Las Vegas; Priests' Personnel Board.
Wehner, Edwin P. '69 (BIS) Bismarck, ND St. Anne; Pro–Synodal Judges; Priests' Benefit Association; Priests' Personnel Board.
Wehner, Eugene C. *o.c.d.* '75 (MIL)[O] Milwaukee Provincial Offices – Discalced Carmelites.
Wehner, James A. '95 (PIT) Allegheny County, PA Shuman Center; [A] Pittsburgh, PA Saint Paul Seminary; Diaconate, Office for the; Evangelization, Dept. for; Post–Ordination Formation, Office for; Pre–Ordination Formation, Dept. for; St. Paul Seminary.
Wehnert, Donald R. '63 (JOL) Kankakee, IL St. Patrick.
Wehr, Arthur J. *s.j.* '90 (LA) Santa Barbara, CA Our Lady of Sorrows.
Wehri, Francis *o.s.b.* '61 (BIS)[A] Richardton, ND Assumption Abbey; (FgM).
Wehrle, Jonathan '78 (LAN) Okemos, MI St. Martha; Priest Pension Board.
Wehrle, Peter G. '99 (NEW) New Milford, NJ St. Joseph's.
Wehrlen, John B. '59 (PAT) Flanders, NJ St. Elizabeth Ann Seton.
Wehrley, Charles A. *c.ss.r.* '01 (LA) Whittier, CA St. Mary of the Assumption; [Q] Whittier, CA Redemptorists of Whittier; [K] Omaha, NE The Redemptorists of Nebraska.
Wehrlin, Leo '93 (Y) Sebring, OH St. Ann; Scouting, Diocesan Office; Office of Vocations.
Wehrmeyer, Richard L. *c.m.* (PBL) Deans.
Wehrmeyer, Richard *c.m.* '91 (PBL) Walsenburg, CO Sacred Heart; Walsenburg, CO St. Mary.
Wei, Luke '60 (BRK) Brooklyn, NY St. Finbar's.
Weibel, George L. '48 (DEN) Retired.
Weibel, John F. '72 (E) St. Eulalia.
Weibl, Nicholas '64 (TOL) Perrysburg, OH St. Rose; Vicar for Priests; Continuing Formation for Priests Program; Vicar for Deacons.
Weible, Thomas C. '59 (LA) Retired.
Weider, Gregory (ALB)[H] Amsterdam, NY St. Mary's Hospital.
Weider, Henry '89 (OWN) Absent on Leave.
Weider, William *t.o.r.* '41 (ARL)[J] White Post, VA Sacred Heart Friary.
Weidert, Richard J. '95 (BEL) Red Bud, IL St. Leo; Red Bud, IL St. Patrick; [G] Ruma, IL Adorers of the Blood of Christ Ruma Center.
Weidie, Kent M. *s.t.* '98 (PAT)[M] Stirling, NJ Holy Spirit Missionary Cenacle; [P] Stirling, NJ Father Judge Apostolic Center.
Weidig, Mark *o.p.* '86 (MIA)[H] Miami, FL Dominican Fathers of Miami, Inc..
Weidman, Michael J. '95 (CHI) Calumet City, IL St. Andrew the Apostle.
Weidner, Halbert G. *c.o.* '74 (HON)[G] Honolulu, HI The Oratory Community.
Weidner, Halbert *c.o.* '74 (CHR)[E] Rock Hill, SC Oratory of St. Philip Neri, Congregation of the Oratory of Pontifical Rite.
Weidner, Halbert *c.o.* '74 (HON) Honolulu, HI Holy Trinity.
Weidner, Halbert *c.o.* (HON) Commission Members; College of Consultors; Vicars Forane; Presbyteral Council; Ecumenical Commission; The Oratory in Hawaii, Inc..
Weidner, Larry W. '80 (PHX) Phoenix, AZ St. Joan of Arc.
Weidner, Mark *o.c.s.o.* '54 (P)[L] Lafayette, OR The Cistercian (Trappist) Abbey of Our Lady of Guadalupe.
Weier, John A. '43 (DET) Retired.
Weigand, Dom Peter *o.s.b.* '70 (WDC)[E] Washington, DC St. Anselm's Abbey School.
Weigand, John J. '67 (CLV) Lakewood, OH St. James.
Weigand, Joseph C. '62 (CLV) Elyria, OH St. Mary.
Weigand, Peter *o.s.b.* '70 (WDC)[M] Washington, DC St. Anselm's Abbey.
Weigel, Edmund *c.pp.s.* '58 (KC)[J] Liberty, MO Precious Blood Center.
Weigel, Jovian C. *o.f.m.* '48 (CIN)[L] Cincinnati, OH Archbishop Leibold Home for the Aged.
Weigel, Jovian *o.f.m.* '48 (CIN)[M] Cincinnati St. Francis Seraph Friary.
Weiglein, John *s.m.* '50 (WH)[H] Wheeling, WV Good Shepherd Nursing Home.
Weigman, Joseph A. '91 (TOL)[A] St. Meinrad, IN St. Meinrad School of Theology; Special Assignment.
Weiher, Charles F. *c.s.c.* '53 (FTW)[I] Notre Dame, IN Holy Cross House.
Weik, Terrence *s.m.* '80 (SAT)[C] San Antonio, TX St. Mary's University of San Antonio, Texas; [M] San Antonio, TX Woodlawn Marianist Community.
Weikart, G. David '03 (Y) Youngstown, OH St. Christine; Serra Club of Mahoning County.
Weiksnar, Jud *o.f.m.* '94 (BUF)[R] St. Bonaventure, NY St. Bonaventure University.
Weiksnar, William J. *o.f.m.* '94 (BUF)[O] St. Bonaventure, NY St. Bonaventure Friary; [C] St. Bonaventure, NY Friar Community.
Weiksner, Jerome M. '55 (GBG) Retired.
Weil, Frank *o.carm.* '67 (JOL)[L] Darien Carmelite Provincial Office.
Weiler, Anthony '90 (SAM)[E] Shelburne, VT Saint Rafka Retreat Center.
Weimer, John C. '58 (BUF)[R] Buffalo, NY Newman Center Retired.
Weinberger, Paul L. '89 (DAL) Dallas, TX Blessed Sacrament.
Weiner, James J. '88 (NEW) Hohokus, NJ St. Luke's.
Weiner, Philip '91 (STF) Yonkers, NY St. Michael; Notary; New York; Holy Name Societies; Liturgical Commission.
Weinert, Allan *c.ss.r.* '72 (STL)[O] Liguori, MO Liguori Mission House/Redemptorists.
Weingartz, Francis A. '54 (DET) Warren, MI St. Anne's Retired.
Weinlader, Wayne T. *m.m.* '68 (NY).
Weinlich, Alfred J. '35 (BRK)[S] Queens Village, NY Queen of Peace Residence Retired.
Weinlich, Alfred (BRK) Legion of Mary.
Weinzapfel, Thomas '45 (DAL) Retired.
Weir, Bernard E. '86 (DAV) Muscatine, IA SS. Mary and Mathias of Muscatine; Muscatine, IA Our Lady of Guadalupe Catholic Mission.
Weirauch, William P. '35 (PIT) Retired.
Weis, Denis P. '63 (MIL) West Allis, WI St. Mary, Help of Christians.
Weis, Earl A. *s.j.* '54 (CHI)[C] Chicago, IL Jesuit Community at Loyola University Chicago.
Weis, Earl A. *s.j.* '54 (DET)[K] Temperance, MI.
Weis, Eugene R. '62 (ROC) Waterloo, NY St. Mary.
Weis, Ivan J. '02 (BLX) Biloxi, MS St. John; Biloxi, MS St. Louis; Campaign for Human Development.
Weis, John H. '66 (PAT) On Duty Outside the Diocese.
Weis, John '66 (SAG) Pigeon, MI St. Francis Borgia; Sebewaing, MI Holy Family.
Weis, John (KC) Administrative Committee.
Weisbeck, Paul '70 (SJ) Los Altos, CA St. William; Santa Clara County Sherriffs Dept..
Weisbecker, Thomas '96 (OM) Columbus, NE St. Bonaventure.
Weiscopf, Daniel '90 (BRK) Forest Hills, NY Our Lady, Queen of Martyrs.
Weise, David '82 (OAK) Fremont, CA Holy Spirit.
Weise, Thomas D. '62 (MOB) Phenix City, AL St. Patrick; Phenix City, AL Mother Mary Parish.
Weise, Thomas J. '02 (JUN) Juneau, AK St. Paul The Apostle; Diocesan Consultors; Navy Reserve Chaplains.

Weisenberger, Gary '77 (SEA) Gig Harbor, WA St. Nicholas.
Weisenberger, Leon *m.s.c.* '59 (RCK).
Weisenberger, Leon *m.s.c.* '59[G] (FgM).
Weisenberger, Raymond *s.v.d.* '39 (MIL)[O] East Troy, WI Divine Word Missionaries.
Weisenberger, Richard J. '79 (LFT) Marion, IN St. Paul.
Weisenburger, Edward J. '87 (OKL) Oklahoma City, OK Cathedral of Our Lady of Perpetual Help; Vicar General; Consultors Archdiocesan; Council of Priests Archdiocesan.
Weisenburger, Edward (OKL) Pro-Synodal Judge; Judge.
Weisensel, Cyril O. '67 (MAD) Benton, WI St. Patrick; Hazel Green, WI St. Francis de Sales.
Weiser, Charles B. '66 (TR) West End, NJ St. Michael; Tribunal Judges.
Weishaar, Leo '84 (MOB)[D] Mobile, AL Providence Hospital.
Weishar, Paul M. '48 (MIL) Retired.
Weisman, Raymond F. '76 (WIL) Ocean City, MD St. Luke and St. Andrew.
Weiss, Jerome P. '77 (DUL) Duluth, MN St. John's; Duluth, MN St. Joseph.
Weiss, Jerome (DUL) Deans.
Weiss, Jerry (DUL) Priests' Pension Board.
Weiss, John C. '67 (KC) Kansas City, MO Christ the King.
Weiss, John (KC) Diocesan Consultors.
Weiss, Joseph E. *s.j.* '85 (FTW)[B] University of Notre Dame Du Lac.
Weiss, Peter C. *s.s.j.* '79 (NO) New Orleans, LA All Saints.
Weiss, Richard '80 (ELP) El Paso, TX Our Lady of Assumption; St. John; Priests' Personnel Advisory Committee.
Weiss, Robert E. '73 (BGP) Newtown, CT St. Rose of Lima; Newtown, CT.
Weiss, Robert F. *s.j.* '59 (STL)[O] St. Louis, MO Hallahan House; [O] St. Louis, MO The Jesuits of the Missouri Province.
Weiss, Robert *c.p.* '65 (DET)[K] Detroit, MI St. Paul of the Cross Community, Congregation of the Passion.
Weissbeck, Reinhold B. '72 (DEN) Brighton, CO St. Augustine.
Weissbeck, Reinhold (DEN) Deaneries.
Weissler, John *o.m.i.* '43 (BEL)[F] Belleville, IL Shrine of Our Lady of the Snows.
Weist, Edward F. '69 (CLV) Litchfield, OH Our Lady Help of Christians Parish; Associate Judicial Vicars.
Weitensteiner, Joseph M. '66 (SPK)[G] Spokane, WA Morning Star Boys' Ranch.
Weithman, Raymond *c.ss.r.* '56 (NY)[EE] Esopus, NY Redemptorist Priests and Brothers C.Ss.R. (Province of Baltimore).
Weithman, Robert J. '55 (TOL) Fremont, OH St. Casimir.
Weitzel, Eugene J. *c.s.v.* '59 (SFD) Beardstown, IL St. Fidelis; Beardstown, IL St. Alexius.
Weitzel, Eugene *c.s.v.* (SFD) Presbyteral Council.
Weitzel, Stephen D. '90 (HBG) Mechanicsburg, PA Saint Katharine Drexel.
Weitzel, Theodore '68 (JOL) Naperville, IL St. Raphael.
Weixelman, Richard *o.m.i.* '65 (FgM).
Wekerle, Ron '90 (B) Jerome, ID St. Jerome's.
Wekerle, Ronald (B) Moderator of the Curia; Vicars General; Ex Officio; Priest Personnel Commission; Finance Council; Building Commission; Catholic Liturgical Commission; Propagation of Faith.
Wekesa, Pius '95 (ROC) Rush, NY St. Joseph; [I] Rochester, NY Basilian Residence; Spencerport, NY St. John the Evangelist.
Welbers, Thomas '68 (LA) Claremont, CA Our Lady of the Assumption.
Welch, Bernard J. '81 (PRT) Military Chaplains; Navy Chaplains.
Welch, Christopher J. '94 (ALB) Schuylerville, NY Notre Dame–Visitation.
Welch, Christopher '85 (ALB)[C] Saratoga Springs, NY Saratoga Central Catholic High School.
Welch, Christopher '94 (ALB) Greenwich, NY St. Joseph.
Welch, Christopher (DET) Beaumont Hospital.
Welch, D. Michael '70 (IND) Indianapolis, IN St. Christopher.
Welch, Eugene A. *s.j.* '60 (BAL)[S] XLRI.
Welch, Gregory T. '67 (STP) Minneapolis, MN St. Austin.
Welch, John A. *m.s.* '93 (ATL) Smyrna, GA St. Thomas the Apostle.
Welch, John E. *m.s.* '60 (NOR) Danielson, CT St. James.
Welch, John *o.carm.* '65 (WDC)[B] Washington, DC Whitefriars Hall.
Welch, Joseph *c.s.s.* '37 (BO)[Y] Waltham, MA Stigmatine Fathers and Brothers.
Welch, Joseph '91 (OAK) Retired.
Welch, Richard L. *c.ss.r.* '80 (HRT) Enfield, CT St. Patrick's; [M] Enfield, CT St. Patrick Rectory; Judges.
Welch, Richard L. *c.ss.r.* (NY) Judges; Promoter of Justice.
Welch, Robert J. *s.j.* '60 (LA)[C] Los Angeles CA Jesuit Community.
Welch, Thomas David '56 (RIC) Retired.
Welch, William J. '55 (GLP) Snowflake, AZ Our Lady of the Snows.
Welch, William (GLP) Vicars Forane; Presbyteral Council.
Weldgen, Francis G. '59 (BUF) Tonawanda, NY St. Christopher.
Welding, Brian J. '91 (PIT)[A] Pittsburgh, PA Saint Paul Seminary; Canon and Civil Law Services, Dept. for; Canonical Services, Office for; St. Paul Seminary; Assistant Director, Department of Canon and Civil Law Services; Promoters of Justice.
Weldishofer, Bernard J. '92 (CIN) Lebanon, OH St. Francis de Sales.
Weldon, C. Michael *o.f.m.* '81 (MIL).
Weldon, Eric M. '00 (WCH)[B] Wichita, KS St. Patrick; Wichita, KS St. Peter the Apostle.
Weldon, James F. '98 (WCH) Wichita, KS St. Thomas Aquinas.
Weldon, James (WCH) Wichita Diocesan Charismatic Services.
Weldon, Jim '97 (WCH)[B] Wichita, KS Kapaun Mt. Carmel Catholic High School.
Weldon, Michael *o.f.m.* '81 (MIL)[O] Provincial Offices.
Weldon, Michael *o.f.m.* '81 (PHX)[H] Scottsdale, AZ Franciscan Renewal Center, Inc. (Casa de Paz Y Bien); Phoenix, AZ St. Mary's Basilica.
Weldon, Michael *o.f.m.* '81 (OAK)[N] Oakland Franciscan Friars Provincial Office, Province of St. Barbara.
Weldon, Michael *o.f.m.* '81 (PHX)[H] Scottsdale, AZ Franciscan Renewal Center, Inc. (Casa de Paz Y Bien); Phoenix, AZ St. Mary's Basilica.
Weling, John B. *s.j.* '81 (LA)[D] Los Angeles, CA Verbum Dei High School.
Welk, Thomas A. *c.pp.s.* (WCH) Presbyteral Council/ Diocesan Consultors.
Welk, Thomas *c.pp.s.* '69 (WCH)[G] Wichita, KS Adorers of the Blood of Christ U.S. Province Presbyteral Council.
Wellar, Thomas '80 (CC) Ingleside, TX Our Lady of the Assumption.
Welle, Jacob *m.s.c.* '50 (ALN) Nazareth, PA Holy Family; [A] Center Valley, PA Sacred Heart Villa, Missionaries of the Sacred Heart.
Wellems, Bruce *c.m.f.* '86 (CHI) Chicago, IL Holy Cross/Immaculate Heart of Mary; [N] Oak Park, IL Claretian Missionaries Community Support Trust; Deans.
Weller, Harold E. '45 (LFT) Retired.
Weller, Joseph W. '64 (KAL) Retired.
Wellisch, Robert B. '69 (STP)[C] St. Paul MN University of St. Thomas.
Wellman, Dale L. '64 (PEO) Moline, IL Sacred Heart.
Wellman, Dale (PEO) Diocesan College of Consultors; Catholic Women, Council of.
Wellmeier, Herbert J. '56 (SAV) Savannah, GA Cathedral of St. John the Baptist; Promoter of Justice Retired.
Wells, James *o.f.m.* '82 (NY)[EE] St. Francis Center for Religious.
Wells, Morris F. *o.carm.* '64 (VEN) Englewood, FL St. Raphael.
Wells, Patrick R. '93 (GAL) Houston, TX St. Francis of Assisi.
Wells, Patrick (GAL) Central Vicariate; appointees.
Wells, Peter B. '84 (PAT) Madison, NJ St. Vincent Martyr.
Wells, Peter B. '91 (TLS) On Duty Outside the Diocese.
Wells, Philip '83 (SAC) Weed, CA Holy Family.
Wells, Philip '96 (SAC) McCloud, CA St. Joseph.
Wells, Philip (SAC) Council of Priests; Priests' Personnel Board, Diocesan.
Welna, Floyd '50 (SAG) Retired.
Welsch, Gerard R. '66 (STL) St. Louis, MO St. John Bosco.
Welschmeyer, Joseph J. '00 (STL) Ballwin, MO Holy Infant.
Welsh, Garry A. '01 (OM) Hartington, NE St. Michael; [B] Hartington, NE Cedar Catholic High School.
Welsh, James F. '56 (CAM) Retired.
Welsh, John *s.j.* '56 (LAF) Grand Coteau, LA St. Charles Borromeo.
Welsh, Patrick J. '98 (CIN) Anna, OH Sacred Heart of Jesus.
Welsh, Patrick J. (PH) Media, PA Nativity of the Blessed Virgin Mary.
Welsh, Peter J. '80 (PH) Chester, PA Saint Katharine Drexel.
Welsh, Richard '60 (DET) Warren, MI St. Dorothy.
Welsh, Robert J. *s.j.* '67 (CLV) University Heights, OH Gesu.
Welsh, Timothy L. *o.c.s.o.* '51 (DUB)[K] Peosta, IA New Melleray Abbey, Order of Cistercians of the Strict Observance.
Welsh, Vincent F. '89 (PH) Philadelphia, PA St. Philip Neri; Defenders of the Bond; Office for Clergy.
Welsh, William P. '60 (CHI) Skokie, IL St. Lambert.
Welsmiller, Francis F. '44 (SAG) Retired.
Welstead, Flavian *o.f.m.cap.* '67 (SFR) Burlingame, CA Our Lady of Angels.
Welter, Charles J. *c.m.* '45 (CHI)[N] Chicago DePaul Vincentian Residence.
Weltin, Richard W. '83 (SFD) Decatur, IL Our Lady of Lourdes; Comite Diocesano de Ministerio Hispano – Diocesan Committee for Hispanic Ministry.
Weltin, Richard (SFD) Presbyteral Council.
Welton, Arthur T. '69 (NY) Bronx, NY St. Francis Xavier.
Welzbacher, George A. '51 (STP)[C] St. Paul, MN University of St. Thomas; Censores Librorum Retired.
Welzbacher, George '51 (STP) St. Paul, MN St. Agnes.
Wempala, Thomas '62 (SAN) Odessa, TX St. Mary's.
Wempe, Richard C. '52 (KCK) Retired.
Wendel, Arthur G. *c.ss.r.* (NY) New York, NY Most Holy Redeemer.
Wendel, Fred W. '78 (ATL) Buford, GA Prince of Peace.
Wendel, Paul G. *c.s.c.* '55 (FTW)[K] Notre Dame, IN Holy Cross Mission House; [L] Notre Dame, IN Our Lady of Fatima Retreat Center.
Wendelken, Robert M. '61 (CLV) Solon, OH St. Rita; Associate Judicial Vicars.
Wenderoth, Joseph R. '62 (BAL) Retired.
Wendling, Francis *o.f.m.* '62 (CIN)[M] Parroquia de San Francisco.
Wendling, Mark '03 (CC)[G] Robstown, TX Society of Our Lady of the Most Holy Trinity.
Wendrychowicz, John B. '73 (PH) Philadelphia, PA St. Josaphat; Archdiocesan Boy Scout.
Wendt, Patrick '79 (MIL) Reeseville, WI Holy Family; Reeseville, WI St. John; Reeseville, WI St. Columbkille.
Wendzikowski, Mecislaus S. '59 (BUF) Retired.
Wenig, Laurin J. '73 (MIL) Whitefish Bay, WI Holy Family.
Weninger, Ronald J. *c.ss.r.* '49 (STL)[O] Liguori, MO St. Clement Health Care Center.
Wenke, Leonard C. '79 (CIN) Cincinnati, OH St. Anthony.
Wenninger, Magnus *o.s.b.* '45 (SCL)[I] Collegeville, MN St. John's Abbey, of the Order of St. Benedict.
Wensing, Michael '76 (SFS) Brookings, SD St. Thomas More; Diocesan Consultors; Deans; Presbyteral Council.
Wenthe, Christopher T. '03 (STP) St. Paul, MN The Nativity of Our Lord.
Wenting, J. Jacques '46 (JC) Retired.
Wentink, William R. '70 (RCK)[D] Rockford, IL Saint Anthony Medical Center; Special Assignment.
Wenz, Robert '82 (CLV) Mentor, OH St. Mary of the Assumption.
Wenzel, Edward J. '51 (MAR) Retired.
Wenzel, James *o.s.a.* '56 (BO)[C] North Andover, MA Merrimack College.
Wenzel, Kamil *o.f.m.conv.* '66 (FgM).
Wenzel, Tiomthy '66 (SCL) St. Cloud, MN St. Anthony of Padua.
Wenzinger, George E. '78 (TOL) Leipsic, OH St. Mary.
Wenzinger, Mark Edward *o.s.b.* '95 (GBG)[H] Latrobe, PA Saint Vincent Archabbey.
Wenzinger, Robert D. '82 (FRS) Bakersfield, CA St. Joseph.
Werbicki, Walter *s.t.f.* '57 (BUF) Lakeview Shock Incarceration Correctional Facility.
Werbicki, Walter '57 (STF) Dunkirk, NY St. Elizabeth Ann Seton.
Werbylo, Walter M. *c.s.b.* '90 (GAL)[Q] Houston, TX Residence of the Basilian Fathers of the University of St. Thomas.
Weria, Theobold *a.l.c.p.* '98 (SP) Pinellas Park, FL Sacred Heart.
Werkhoven, Michael E. '02 (MEM) Germantown, TN Our Lady Of Perpetual Help.
Werkhoven, Michael (MEM) Search Program.
Werling, Keith '99 (JOL) Absent on Leave.
Werner, Ben '64 (LAN) University of Michigan Hospitals/ Pastoral Care Dept. Retired.
Werner, Cyril J. '45 (OM) Retired.
Werner, George J. *s.m.m.* '57 (RVC)[M] Bay Shore, NY Montfort Missionaries.
Werner, Gerald *o.c.d.* '74 (SJ)[E] Redlands, CA Discalced Carmelites, OCD.
Werner, John J. '00 (MET) South Plainfield, NJ Sacred Heart.
Werner, John P. '51 (COV)[I] Edgewood, KY St. Elizabeth Medical Center, South Retired.
Werner, Jon K. '82 (SY) Liverpool, NY Christ the King.
Werner, Justin '58 (GB) Retired.
Werner, Leo E. '51 (WH) Retired.
Werner, Steve (SPK) Members.
Werning, David H. '98 (WDC) Morganza, MD St. Joseph.
Werra, Bogdan '81 (KAL) Mattawan, MI St. John Bosco.
Wersing, Richard F. *c.s.sp.* '37 (PIT)[P] Bethel Park, PA Holy Spirit Animation Center.

Wert, William *o.carm.* '86 (JOL)[L] Joliet, IL St. Elias Carmelites.

Wertanen, Steven A. '97 (DET) Trenton, MI St. Joseph.

Werth, Alvin '59 (SAL) Retired.

Werth, Charles M. '53 (BUF) Retired.

Werth, Jerome *o.s.b.* '99 (KC)[J] Conception, MO Conception Abbey.

Werth, Loren '56 (SAL) Board of Trustees Retired.

Werth, Robert T. '79 (ROC) Rochester, NY Roman Catholic Community of the 19th Ward; Rochester, NY SS. Peter and Paul; Rochester, NY Roman Catholic Community of the 19th Ward.

Wertin, George P. '63 (STP) Minneapolis, MN St. Joan of Arc.

Wertman, Raymond '72 (OG) On Duty Outside the Diocese.

Wertz, Gerald *s.d.b.* '88 (OAK)[N] Berkeley Salesian Community.

Wesdock, Thomas J. (PBR) Uniontown, PA St. John the Baptist.

Wesely, Eugene L. '57 (CR) Detroit Lakes, MN St. Mary of the Lakes Retired.

Wesely, Mark '93 (SAL) Herington, KS St. Columba's; Herington, KS St. Phillip's.

Wesely, Mark (SAL) Episcopal Vicars; Council of Priests; Diocesan Pastoral Council; Personnel Board.

Weseman, Alan R. '86 (NO) Madisonville, LA St. Anselm.

Wesley, Andrew '80 (DET) Detroit, MI Transfiguration.

Weslin, Norman U. *o.s.* '86 (PCE) On Duty Outside the Diocese.

Wesloh, Ferdinand J. '64 (STL) Florissant, MO St. Angela Merici.

Wesnofske, Matthias *o.f.m.cap.* '67 (NY) New York, NY St. John the Baptist.

Wesoloski, Richard J. '72 (PIT) McKeesport, PA St. Martin de Porres.

Wesolowski, Anthony P. *o.s.b.* '72 (SAV)[B] Savannah, GA Benedictine Military School; [F] Savannah, GA The Benedictine Priory.

Wesolowski, Edmund C. '48 (PH) Philadelphia, PA Immaculate Conception Retired.

Wesolowski, Tomasz '02 (PHX) Chandler, AZ St. Mary's.

Wessel, John F. (CLV) Translators Retired.

Wessels, Cletus J. *o.p.* '57 (STP) Minneapolis, MN St. Albert the Great; [M] Minneapolis, MN St. Albert the Great Priory.

Wesselsky, Emil J. '56 (SAT) San Antonio, TX St. Henry.

Wessling, Floyd A. '64 (OM) Clarkson, NE SS. Cyril and Methodius.

Wessling, John E. '58 (CIN)[F] Cincinnati, OH Ursuline Academy of Cincinnati Retired.

West, Don J. '90 (CIN) Bethel, OH St. Mary.

West, Gerald '59 (BAL) Retired.

West, H. Gregory '91 (CHR)[T] Bluffton, SC St. Gregory the Great; Chancellor; Judges; Vocations.

West, James P. '86 (LR) North Little Rock, AR Immaculate Conception.

West, John H. '80 (DET)[Q] Detroit, MI St. Vincent de Paul Society; Farmington, MI Our Lady of Sorrows.

West, Joseph *o.f.m.conv.* '92 (CLV) Lorain, OH St. Anthony of Padua.

West, Mauricio W. '79 (CHL) Special Assignment; [Q] Charlotte, NC Catholic Diocese of Charlotte Housing Corp.; Vicar General, Chancellor, and Moderator in Curia; Diocesan Consultors; Permanent Diaconate.

West, Norbert R. '57 (SUP) Retired.

West, Norbert R. '57 (Y)[I] Canton, OH House of Loreto.

West, Patrick J. '81 (BRK) Brooklyn, NY Our Lady of Solace.

West, Peter J. '91 (NY) Staten Island, NY Immaculate Conception.

West, Peter '91 (NEW) On Duty Outside the Archdiocese.

West, Stephen C. '79 (GBG) Derry, PA St. Joseph.

West, Thomas *o.f.m.* '86 (OAK)[N] Oakland, CA Franciscan Friars; [N] Oakland, CA Franciscan Friars Provincial Office, Province of St. Barbara.

West, William '70 (HRT)[I] New Haven, CT Hospital of St. Raphael.

West, Willis W. '63 (NOR) Willimantic, CT St. Joseph; Building Commission; Cemetery Corporation and Subsidiaries, Diocesan Cemeteries; District Moderators; Diocesan Vocation Review Committee.

West, Willis (NOR) Diocesan Pastoral Council.

Westbrook, J. Severyn '62 (SPK) Retired.

Wester, Charles H. '59 (MIL) Lomira, WI St. Andrew; Mayville, WI St. Mary; Deans.

Wester, Donald R. '78 (STL) St. Louis, MO Our Lady of Good Counsel.

Wester, Kevin J. '90 (MIL) Eden, WI Shepherd of the Hills (Good Shepherd).

Westerhoff, Ralph A. '62 (CIN) Cincinnati, OH St. Lawrence.

Westfall, Joseph B. '93 (LFT) On Duty Outside the Diocese.

Westfield, Carlton J. '71 (BUF) Fredonia, NY St. Anthony.

Westhoff, Frank '61 (SFD) Retired.

Westhoven, Thomas *s.c.j.* '66 (RC) Eagle Butte, SD All Saints; Eagle Butte, SD Cheyenne River Reservation; [B] Eagle Butte, SD Sacred Heart Community House; [D] Eagle Butte, SD CPT, Inc..

Westhues, John H. '48 (SPC) Springfield, MO Cathedral of St. Agnes; Judges; Priests' Mutual Benefit Society Retired.

Weston, Michael D. '02 (ARL) Fairfax, VA St. Mary of Sorrows; Notaries.

Weston, Thomas C. *s.j.* '78 (OAK)[N] Oakland, CA Murray Residence Community.

Westray, Kenneth M. '81 (SFR) Greenbrae, CA St. Sebastian.

Wetmore, John '73 (STL)[P] Fenton, MO St. Paul.

Wetter, Richard L. '57 (BUF)[O] Tonawanda, NY O'Hara Residence Retired.

Wetterer, Edward V. '64 (BRK) Flushing, NY St. Michael.

Wetterholm, Lawrence E. '56 (BO) Senior Priests Retired.

Wetzel, Leo *o.m.i.* '52 (BO)[Y] Tewksbury, MA Immaculate Heart of Mary Infirmary.

Wetzel, Steven P. *o.s.f.s.* '03 (PH) Philadelphia, PA Our Mother of Consolation.

Wetzler, Daniel '63 (SPK) Charismatic Renewal Retired.

Wevita, Bede '91 (LAV) North Las Vegas, NV St. John Neumann; Information, Communications and Media.

Wewer, Andrew *o.s.b.* '43 (LR)[A] Subiaco, AR Subiaco Monastery.

Wewers, William *o.s.b.* '67 (LR) Clarksville, AR Holy Redeemer; Clarksville, AR SS. Peter and Paul.

Wey, Richard '50 (SCL) Retired.

Weydert, Donald D. '43 (DUB) Retired.

Weyer, John T. '72 (GAL) Houston, TX St. Vincent de Paul.

Weyer, John (GAL) College of Consultors.

Weyker, James *s.d.s.* '69 (FgM).

Weyls, Richard C. '93 (COL) Columbus, OH St. Francis of Assisi; Priests' Senate; Diocesan Judges.

Weymes, Gerald T. (BAL) Defenders of the Bond.

Weymes, Gerald '74 (ARL) Chantilly, VA St. Timothy.

Weyne, Marie Joseph (LAR)[D] Laredo, TX St. John Priory, F.J..

Weyrens, Ronald '82 (SCL) Waite Park, MN St. Joseph's.

Whalan, Thomas J. '81 (BO) Unassigned.

Whalen, Charles W. '44 (DUB) Retired.

Whalen, Daniel W. '00 (PIT) Clergy Personnel Board; Pittsburgh, PA St. John Vianney.

Whalen, David M. *o.s.f.s.* '71 (TOL)[J] Toledo, OH Provincial Residence.

Whalen, Edmund J. *s.t.d.* '84 (NY) Bronx, NY St. Benedict; [II] New York, NY North American College of Rome, Alumni Assoc. of.

Whalen, Edward J. *m.m.* '61 (FgM).

Whalen, James R. '47 (GI) Retired.

Whalen, John J. '69 (DAV) Special Assignment.

Whalen, John J. '94 (OM) Absent on Leave.

Whalen, John T. '71 (ALN) SCI–Mahoney.

Whalen, John '58 (RVC) East Islip, NY St. Mary's.

Whalen, John '94 (BUR) Manchester Center, VT St. Paul's.

Whalen, Joseph E. '89 (GI) On Duty Outside the Diocese.

Whalen, Joseph T. '71 (ALN) Pottsville, PA St. Patrick; Elected Members.

Whalen, Joseph *m.s.* '89 (NOR) Danielson, CT St. James.

Whalen, Joseph '99 (STP) Fridley, MN St. William.

Whalen, Michael D. *c.m.* '83 (BRK)[V] Jamaica, NY Vincentian Residence.

Whalen, Norman M. (TUC) Retired.

Whalen, Paul A. '82 (GBG) Farmington, PA St. Joan of Arc.

Whalen, Robert B. '51 (BUR) West Rutland, VT St. Bridget.

Whalen, Thomas J. '67 (BGP) Shelton, CT St. Margaret Mary.

Whalen, Timothy F. '78 (PIT) On Duty Outside the Diocese; [A] Orchard Lake, MI SS. Cyril and Methodius Seminary.

Whalen, Timothy (DET)[E] Orchard Lake, MI St. Mary's Preparatory.

Whalen, William '60 (MIL) Retired.

Wharton, Paul J. '82 (WH) Montgomery, WV Immaculate Conception.

Whatley, Christopher '70 (BAL) Baltimore, MD St. Mark.

Whatley, Francis *o.ss.t.* '88 (NO)[N] New Orleans, LA Mary–Joseph Residence for the Elderly.

Wheatley, Carroll '75 (OWN) Military Chaplains.

Wheatley, Charles '68 (MIL) Special Assignment; Hartford, WI St. Lawrence.

Wheatley, Dennis F. *o.f.m.* '84 (BO) Waltham, MA Sacred Heart.

Wheatley, Herbert *o.f.m.* '67 (P)[J] Portland, OR Providence Portland Medical Center.

Wheatley, R. Carroll (OWN) Navy Chaplains.

Wheaton, Michael F. '03 (CHI) Chicago, IL St. Bede the Venerable.

Wheaton, William F. '92 (SLC) Salt Lake City, UT St. Ambrose; [C] Kearns, UT St. Francis Xavier Regional School.

Whedbee, Dominic *o.c.s.o.* '77 (WOR)[A] Spencer, MA St. Joseph's Abbey School of Theology and Institute of Monastic Studies; [O] Spencer, MA St. Joseph's Abbey; [O] Spencer, MA St. Joseph's Abbey.

Whedbee, George *c.m.f.* '69 (LA)[Q] Los Angeles, CA Claretian Retreat Center Community; [W] Los Angeles, CA Claretian Retreat Center (All Groups).

Wheelahan, Michael '80 (OKL) Medford, OK St. Mary's; Scouting.

Wheeland, Thomas H. '66 (ROC) Rochester, NY Holy Cross.

Wheeler, Ambrose J. *c.s.c.* '47 (PHX)[G] Phoenix, AZ Holy Cross Congregation/Casa Santa Cruz.

Wheeler, Arthur F. *c.s.c.* '84 (P)[B] University of Portland; [L] Portland, OR Holy Cross Fathers & Brothers, C.S.C. – University of Portland.

Wheeler, Charles '79 (JOL) Kankakee, IL St. Rose of Lima; Deans.

Wheeler, Clarence '54 (JC) Retired.

Wheeler, Daniel '75 (LAN) Clinton, MI St. Dominic's; Tecumseh, MI St. Elizabeth.

Wheeler, Daniel (LAN) Regional Vicars; Finance Council.

Wheeler, David A. '52 (DUB) Dubuque, IA St. Mary; Defenders of the Bond; Promoter of Justice; Retired Priests' Representatives; Review Board for Sexual Abuse of Minors by Clergy and Other Church Personnel Retired.

Wheeler, James D. *s.j.* '54 (KC)[B] Kansas City, KS Rockhurst University Continuing Education Center/National Seminars Group; [J] Kansas City, MO Rockhurst Jesuit Community.

Wheeler, James J. *s.j.* '68 (NY)[EE] New York, NY Murray–Weigel Hall.

Wheeler, James J. *s.j.* '68 (RVC)[O] Patchogue, NY St. Joseph's Prayer Center.

Wheeler, James *o.f.m.* '66 (SFD) Quincy, IL St. Francis Solanus; [L] Quincy, IL St. Francis Solanus Friary.

Wheeler, John P. *c.s.b.* '68 (DET)[E] Redford, MI Catholic Central High School.

Wheeler, John '47 (SD).

Wheeler, Thomas F.X. *s.j.* '62 (PH)[BB] Merion Station, PA Sisters of Mercy, McAuley Convent (Infirmary).

Wheeler, Thomas *s.j.* '62 (PH)[AA] Merion Station, PA McAuley Convent.

Wheeler, Wayne B. '79 (GR) Big Rapids, MI St. Paul's Campus Parish; Big Rapids, MI St. Mary's.

Wheeler, Wayne (GR) Deans.

Wheelock, Joseph P. '96 (OG) Ellenburg, NY St. Edmund.

Wheelock, Robert *o.f.m.cap.* '64 (MIL) Milwaukee, WI St. Francis of Assisi.

Whelan, Charles M. *s.j.* '58 (NY)[EE] New York, NY "America;" Residence and publication office of the America Press; [II] New York, NY America Press, Inc..

Whelan, Dennis '65 (RVC) Franklin Square, NY St. Catherine of Sienna.

Whelan, Fintan *o.f.m.cap.* '60 (LA)[B] Santa Ynez, CA San Lorenzo Seminary and Prayer Center; [B] Santa Ynez, CA San Lorenzo Seminary and Prayer Center.

Whelan, Gerald J. *c.s.c.* '55 (FTW)[I] Congregacion de Santa Cruz.

Whelan, James J. '73 (PH) Springfield, PA St. Kevin.

Whelan, James P. '93 (NEW) Hasbrouck Heights, NJ Corpus Christi.

Whelan, Robert J. '83 (BRK) Brooklyn, NY St. Augustine.

Whelan, Steve *s.d.b.* '69 (SFR) San Francisco, CA SS. Peter and Paul.

Whelan, William S. '57 (OM) Retired.

Whelan, William '57 (OM)[A] Conception, MO Conception Seminary College.

Whelton, Daniel P. '70 (SR) Cotati, CA St. Joseph; Members of the Curia; Vicar for Priests; Judicial Vicar; Diocesan Judges; Board of Consultors; Priests' Council.

Whelton, Daniel (SR) Education and Prevention of Sexual Misconduct Committee.

Whetstone, Richard J. *j.c.o.l.* '83 (PBR) Gibsonia, PA St. Andrew the Apostle; Pittsburgh, PA Holy Ghost; Vicar for Canonical Services; Consultors; Judicial Vicar.

Whewell, Glenn *s.o.l.t.* '01 (CC)[G] Robstown, TX Society of Our Lady of the Most Holy Trinity.

Whipkey, Robert '83 (DEN) Erie, CO St. Scholastica; Frederick, CO St. Theresa.

Whipple, Donald W. *c.s.c.* '57 (FR)[H] North Dartmouth, MA Holy Cross Residence.

Whistle, Brad '81 (OWN) Owensboro, KY Precious Blood; Committee for Administration; Priest Personnel Committee; Vocations Office.

White, A. Kris '41 (SB) Colton, CA Our Lady of the Immaculate Conception.

White, A. Paul '59 (BO) South Boston, MA Gate of Heaven.

White, Anthony J. '55 (NO) Retired.

White, Bernard C. '52 (CHI) Elmwood Park, IL St. Celestine Retired.

White, Bernard L. '77 (ALT) Williamsburg, PA St. Joseph; Huntingdon, PA State Correctional Institution; State Correctional Institution.
White, Charles H. '65 (BRK) Broad Channel, NY St. Virgilius.
White, Cosmas *o.s.b.* '61 (P)[L] St. Benedict, OR Mt. Angel Abbey.
White, Daniel P. *s.j.* '01 (KC)[J] Kansas City, MO Rockhurst Jesuit Community.
White, Daniel *s.j.* '01 (KC) Kansas City, MO St. Francis Xavier.
White, David F. *s.j.* '67 (BUF)[O] Buffalo, NY Canisius Jesuit Community.
White, David P. '94 (BO) Marlborough, MA Immaculate Conception.
White, David '52 (SEA) Retired.
White, Denis '67 (JOL) Paxton, IL St. Mary.
White, Francis A. '49 (OG) Judges Retired.
White, Francis P. *c.s.v.* '44 (LAV) Las Vegas, NV Guardian Angel Cathedral.
White, Gale '56 (DAL) Retired.
White, George M. *o.m.i.* '45 (HRT) Waterbury, CT Immaculate Conception.
White, George M. *o.m.i.* '45 (NY)[GG] Newburgh, NY Our Lady of Hope Center.
White, George *o.m.i.* '45 (BO)[Y] Tewksbury, MA Immaculate Heart of Mary Infirmary.
White, James D. '69 (TLS) Skiatook, OK Sacred Heart; Archivist; Historian.
White, James E. '83 (NY) Bronx, NY Blessed Sacrament.
White, James J. *s.j.* '71 (KC)[J] Kansas City, MO Rockhurst Jesuit Community.
White, James J. *s.j.* '71 (STL)[O] St. Louis The Jesuits of the Missouri Province.
White, James R. '80 (NEW) Mahwah, NJ Immaculate Conception; [C] Oradell, NJ Bergen Catholic.
White, James *c.ss.r.* '81 (MIL)[R] Oconomowoc, WI The Redemptorist Retreat Center.
White, James *s.j.* (KCK) Minister to Priests.
White, John J. '55 (NOR) Rockville, CT St. Bernard; College of Consultors; Members; Deans; Judges; Part Time; Diocesan Panel of Pastors, Canon 1742; Building Commission.
White, John J. '57 (BO) Senior Priests Retired.
White, John L. *s.m.* '45 (CHI) Oak Lawn, IL St. Gerald Retired.
White, John R. '81 (CIN) Greenville, OH St. Mary; Judges.
White, John V. *s.j.* '47 (CLV)[D] Cleveland, OH St. Ignatius High School.
White, John '83 (RVC) Absent on Leave.
White, Joseph M. '91 (BO) Waltham, MA Our Lady, Comforter of the Afflicted.
White, Kenneth R. '68 (PIT) Pittsburgh, PA St. Thomas More.
White, Kevin R. *s.j.* '99 (BO)[E] Dorchester, MA Boston College High School & Jesuit Community.
White, Kris '41 (SB) Retired.
White, Lawrence E. '70 (CC) Deans; College of Consultors; Personnel Board – Priests; Presbyteral Council; Corpus Christi, TX SS. Cyril and Methodius.
White, Leo J. '56 (BRK) Released from Diocesan Assignment.
White, Leroy (LAN) Retired.
White, Lloyd W. '58 (SC) Retired.
White, Mark D. '03 (WDC) Rockville, MD St. Raphael.
White, Michael J. '48 (BIR) Retired.
White, Michael J. '84 (BAL) Timonium, MD Church of the Nativity.
White, Michael T. *c.s.sp.* '83 (GAL)[Q] Houston, TX Western Province of the Congregation of the Holy Ghost.
White, Michael *c.s.sp.* '83 (SD)[B] University of San Diego.
White, Morgan '02 (TYL) Carthage, TX St. William of Vercelli; Diocesan Liturgical Commission.
White, Nathan R. '02 (STO) Hughson, CA St. Anthony Church of Hughson (Pastor of).
White, Paul C. '89 (RCK) Sterling, IL Sacred Heart; [B] Sterling, IL Newman Central Catholic High School.
White, Paul R. *c.pp.s.* '53 (LFT) Rensselaer, IN St. Francis Solano; Rensselaer, IN St. Henry; [A] Rensselaer, IN Saint Joseph's College Retired.
White, Paul T. '83 (PT) Chipley, FL St. Joseph the Worker; Marianna, FL St. Anne; Permanent Diaconate Formation Board.
White, Paul *s.s.c.* '58 (LA)[Q] Los Angeles, CA Columban Fathers, Procure House.
White, Paul *s.c.c.* '58 (LA)[K] St. Columbans St. Columban's Foreign Mission Society.
White, Peter H. '62 (WOR) Rochdale, MA St. Aloysius–St. Jude.
White, Philip '85 (PT) Retired.
White, Ralph *o.f.m.conv.* '83 (SY) Bridgeport, NY St. Francis of Assisi.
White, Raymond F. *c.m.* '45 (CHI)[N] Chicago DePaul Vincentian Residence.
White, Robert H. *o.f.m.* '51 (BUF)[O] St. Bonaventure, NY St. Bonaventure Friary.
White, Robert K. '61 (SFR) Tomales, CA Church of the Assumption.
White, Robert L. '74 (STP) Victoria, MN St. Victoria.
White, Robert S. *c.s.s.* '73 (SPR) Springfield, MA Our Lady of Mt. Carmel.
White, Robert *o.f.m.* '51 (BO)[Y] Boston, MA Saint Anthony Residence.
White, Robert '70 (SD) On Duty Outside the Diocese.
White, Rodney '03 (SAN) Midland, TX St. Ann's; Vocations.
White, Stephen C. '86 (PH) Philadelphia, PA Immaculate Heart of Mary.
White, Stephen '98 (DUL) Grand Marais, MN St. John's; Grand Marais, MN Holy Rosary.
White, Thomas J. '59 (JOL) Wheaton, IL St. Daniel the Prophet Church.
White, Thomas '64 (BLX) Biloxi, MS St. Mary.
White, Thomas '78 (LA) Palmdale, CA St. Mary.
White, Tomas '78 (LA) Lancaster, CA California State Prison, L.A. County.
White, William A. '90 (NY) Pine Plains, NY St. Anthony.
White, William J. '52 (CHI) Retired.
Whited, Walter M. '66 (STL) St. Charles, MO St. Joseph.
Whiteing, Richard '80 (OM) Jackson, NE St. Patrick.
Whiteside, Daniel '92 (CHI) Oak Park, IL St. Catherine of Siena–St. Lucy.
Whiteside, David '97 (PEO) Pekin, IL St. Joseph's.
Whitestone, David A. '89 (ARL) Arlington, VA St. Charles Borromeo; Adjutant Judicial Vicar; Diocesan Judges.
Whitley, Joan R. *c.s.b.* '54 (GAL)[Q] Sugar Land, TX Basilian Mission Center.
Whitley, Rufus J. *o.m.i.* '76 (CHI)[X] Chicago, IL Oblates for International Pastoral aka Oblate International Pastoral Investment Trust; Members.
Whitlock, Joseph E. '55 (PRT) Portland, ME Cathedral of the Immaculate Conception Retired.
Whitman, Andrew P. *s.j.* '63 (TUC)[E] Tucson, AZ Jesuit Community of the Vatican Observatory.
Whitman, Dan G. '83 (KNX) Jefferson City, TN Holy Trinity Catholic Church; Newport, TN Good Shepherd.
Whitman, Glenn R. '75 (E) Girard, PA St. John the Evangelist.
Whitman, Mark '95 (STL) St. Louis, MO Immaculate Heart of Mary.
Whitman, Thomas J. '87 (E) Erie, PA St. Matthew in the Woods; Waterford, PA St. Cyprian.
Whitmore, James R. *m.m.* '59 (SJ)[M] Los Altos, CA Maryknoll.
Whitmore, Paul E. '54 (OG) Port Leyden, NY St. Martin.
Whitmore, Paul (OG) Diocesan Consultors.
Whitney, A. Peter '84 (GAL) La Marque, TX Our Lady Queen of Peace.
Whitney, John D. *s.j.* '94 (P)[L] Portland, OR Jesuit Provincial Office (Society of Jesus, Oregon Prov.); [L] Portland, OR Colombiere Community.
Whitney, John D. *s.j.* '94 (FgM).
Whitney, John D. *s.j.* '94 (P)[L] Portland, OR Jesuit Provincial Office (Society of Jesus, Oregon Prov.); [L] Portland, OR Colombiere Community.
Whitney, Patrick J. '68 (RVC) Lake Ronkonkoma, NY St. Elizabeth Ann Seton.
Whitney, Paul J. (BUF) Clergy Personnel Board Retired.
Whitney, Peter A. '84 (TYL) Retired.
Whitney, Richard '87 (RVC) Absent on Leave.
Whitsell, John L. '96 (TYL) Overton, TX Billy Max Moore Pre–release Facility.
Whitsell, John '96 (TYL) Kilgore, TX Christ the King.
Whitson, Robley E. '58 (NY) On Duty Outside the Archdiocese.
Whitt, Dwight Reginald *o.p.* '76 (STP)[C] St. Paul, MN University of St. Thomas.
Whittaker, Kenneth '77 (MIA) Retired.
Whittel, Joseph B. '03 (NOR) Norwich, CT St. Patrick Cathedral.
Whittemore, Gayle (MAN) Diocesan Review Board.
Whitten, Carlton E. *s.j.* '61 (S.J.).
Whittier, James E. '53 (BO)[D] Senior Priests Retired.
Whittier, William O. '61 (STP) Retired.
Whittington, Kenneth L. '88 (CHL) Morganton, NC St. Charles Borromeo.
Whittington, Paul *o.p.* '97 (CHI) River Forest, IL St. Vincent Ferrer; [D] Oak Park, IL Fenwick High School.
Whorton David '98 (LA) Simi Valley, CA St. Rose of Lima.
Whyte, Edmond F. '64 (MIA) Southwest Ranches, FL St. Mark; [C] Fort Lauderdale, FL Archbishop Edward A. McCarthy High School.
Whyte, Edmond (MIA) Building Commission; Archdiocesan Fund–Raising & Assessments Committee.
Whyte, Michael G. '03 (HRT) West Hartford, CT St. Mark the Evangelist.
Wiant, George '61 (ROC) Retired.
Wiatrowski, Ralph E. '74 (CLV) Lakewood, OH St. Luke; Vicars General; College of Consultors; Chancellor; Associate Judicial Vicars; Archivist; National Shrine of Immaculate Conception.
Wible, Charles '96 (BAL) Cockeysville, MD St. Joseph; On Duty Outside the Archdiocese.
Wichlan, David L. '57 (STL) St. Louis, MO St. Rita.
Wichlan, David (STL) Spiritual Directors.
Wichman, Edwin J. '80 (PIT) Verona, PA St. Joseph.
Wichmann, Edward W. '52 (PBL) Retired.
Wichmann, Edward '52 (BWN) Retired.
Wichmanowski, Walter F. '52 (PIT)[N] Pittsburgh, PA St. John Vianney Manor Retired.
Wicht, Robert *s.d.s.* '67 (TUC) Vail, AZ Shrine of St. Rita in the Desert.
Wick, John C. '56 (GAL)[Q] Houston, TX Dillon House.
Wickenhauser, Gerald M. *m.m.* '62 (FgM).
Wicker, Paul F. '63 (COS) Colorado Springs, CO Holy Apostles.
Wicker, Paul (COS) Diocesan Consultors; Metro–North Region (Colorado Springs).
Wickers, Amideus M. *o.s.m.* '49 (CHI)[N] Chicago Order of Friar Servants of Mary (Servites) United States of America Province, Inc..
Wickey, Harold '55 (KCK) Retired.
Wickham, William E. *c.s.c.* '81 (P) Portland, OR Department of Veterans' Affairs Medical Center; [L] Portland, OR Holy Cross Fathers & Brothers, C.S.C. – University of Portland.
Wicki, Ted *c.r.* (SB) Riverside, CA St. Catherine of Alexandria.
Wicklum, Paul R. '61 (LFT) De Motte, IN St. Cecilia.
Wicklum, Paul (LFT) Members; Clergy Relief Association.
Wickman, Robert T. '49 (RVC) Retired.
Wickowski, Leroy A. '66 (CHI) Oak Park, IL St. Giles.
Wickrematunge, Vernon P. '87 (NY) Peekskill, NY Assumption.
Wicks, W. Jared *s.j.* '62 (DET).
Widmann, Phillip A. '77 (FTW)[K] Fort Wayne, IN St. Peter; [M] Fort Wayne, IN Cathedral Museum.
Widmann, Phillip (FTW) Propagation of the Faith and Holy Childhood Association; Retired Clergy Committee.
Widner, Thomas C. *s.j.* '69 (WDC)[N] Chicago Chicago Province of the Society of Jesus–Provincial Office; [M] Washington, DC Leonard Neale House.
Widomski, Stanislaus *o.f.m.* '62 (FgM).
Wieber, Donald A. '57 (KAL) Watervliet, MI St. Joseph.
Wieber, Robert *o.s.b.* '67 (SCL)[I] Collegeville, MN St. John's Abbey, of the Order of St. Benedict.
Wiecaszek, Lejzek '88 (RVC) Floral Park, NY St. Hedwig's.
Wiecek, Henryk '96 (NEW) Wallington, NJ Most Sacred Heart of Jesus.
Wiecek, Ronald P. *c.pp.s.* '71 (OAK)[N] San Leandro, CA Society of the Precious Blood.
Wiecki, Donald J. '58 (MAD) De Forest, WI Retired.
Wieckowski, Robert (WDC) Washington, DC Blessed Sacrament, Shrine of the Most.
Wieczorek, Edward R. '65 (Y) Mogadore, OH St. Joseph.
Wieczorek, Matthew S. '57 (SY) Endicott, NY St. Casimir.
Wiedel, Thomas L. '90 (LIN) Steinauer, NE St. Anthony.
Wiederholt, Clarence E. '55 (JC) Eugene, MO Our Lady of the Snows; VI. Lake Ozark; Senators.
Wiederholt, Thomas W. '63 (KC) Kansas City, MO Our Lady of Sorrows.
Wiedmann, Paul A. '63 (PH) Levittown, PA Queen of the Universe.
Wiegenstein, Francis '59 (HEL) Retired.
Wieging, James F. '67 (DET) River Rouge, MI Our Lady of Lourdes.
Wiekierak, Joseph F. '46 (GAY) Retired.
Wieladek, Walderma *c.ss.r.* (CHI) Cicero, IL St. Mary of Czestochowa.
Wieland, Dennis J. '91 (CR) Park Rapids, MN St. Peter's; Park Rapids, MN St. Mary's.
Wieland, Edward R. '56 (MIL) Retired.
Wielczko, Andrzej '99 (MET) Sayreville, NJ St. Stanislaus Kostka.
Wielebski, John T. '78 (BAL) Laurel, MD Resurrection of Our Lord.
Wielgus, Bronislaw '62 (NEW) Linden, NJ St. Theresa of the Child Jesus.
Wieliczko, Krzyysztof *o.s.p.p.e.* '87 (PH)[AA] Office.
Wieling, Raymond P. '49 (SC) Retired.
Wielinski, Alan '84 (SCL) Morris, MN Assumption of the Blessed Virgin Mary.
Wielosinski, Robert J. '80 (CHI) Chicago, IL Our Lady of the Snows.
Wielunski, Gregory C. (BRK) Bishop Catanello—; Officialis–Judicial Vicar.
Wielunski, Gregory '78 (BRK) Middle Village, NY St. Margaret.
Wiemeyer, Raymond G. '52 (CIN) Retired.
Wienhoff, Paul R. '78 (BEL) Nashville, IL St. Ann; Adjutant Judicial Vicar.
Wienhoff, Paul '78 (BEL) Okawville, IL St. Barbara.
Wienhoff, Paul (BEL) Promoter Justitiae; Defensores Vinculi.

Wiera, Stefan '68 (SAT) Floresville, TX Sacred Heart.
Wierichs, Paul '72 (BRK)[V] Jamaica, NY Immaculate Conception Monastery.
Wierichs, Paul *c.p.* '78 (NEW)[N] Special Gifts & Special Events.
Wiersgalla, Joseph '51 (SCL) Retired.
Wierzba, Alan P. '01 (LC) Gays Mills, WI St. Mary; Gays Mills, WI St. Philip.
Wierzbicki, Melvin *o.f.m.* '53 (GB)[I] Pulaski, WI Friary.
Wiese, Melvern A.. '57 (OM) Leigh, NE St. Mary.
Wiese, Miro *o.f.m.* '57 (GAY) West Branch, MI Holy Family.
Wiese, Stephen *s.c.j.* '63 (MIL)[O] Franklin, WI Villa Maria; [O] Hales Corners, WI Priests of the Sacred Heart.
Wieseler, Lawrence A. '69 (CR) Deans; Diocesan Consultors; Warroad, MN St. Mary's; Priests' Council.
Wiesenbaugh, Robert D. *s.j.* '71 (BAL)[S] Comunidad Arnoldo Gutierrez.
Wieser, Stanley '68 (SCL) Brown's Valley, MN St. Anthony's; Wheaton, MN St. Peter's; Wheaton, MN Ave Maria.
Wieser, Stanley (SCL) Deans; Presbyteral Council.
Wieser, Stanley (SCL) Diocesan Consultors.
Wieslaw, Strzadala *s.d.s.* '90 (NEW)[N] Verona, NJ The Salvatorian Fathers.
Wiesmann, Gary '83 (MIA)[G] Fort Lauderdale, FL Holy Cross Hospital.
Wiesner, James F. *c.s.p.* '83 (MEM) Memphis, TN St. Patrick's; [L] Memphis, TN St. Patrick's Center.
Wiesner, Jim *c.s.p.* (MEM) Presbyteral Council and College of Consultors.
Wiesner, Mark '95 (OAK) San Leandro, CA Assumption of the Blessed Virgin Mary.
Wiest, John J. '41 (RVC) Manhasset, NY St. Mary's Retired.
Wieszczek, Rudolph *o.f.m.* '54 (PH)[AA] Philadelphia, PA St. Pius X Friary.
Wietensteiner, Joseph M. '66 (SPK) Retired.
Wiethorn, William *o.f.m.cap.* '66 (WDC)[B] Washington, DC St. Francis Friary–Capuchin College.
Wigand, William (STL) Ste. Genevieve, MO Our Lady Help of Christians.
Wigger, Brian K. '97 (COV) Fort Wright, KY St. Agnes; [C] Park Hills, KY Notre Dame Academy.
Wiggins, Frank '86 (RIC) Onley, VA St. Peter's the Apostle.
Wigginton, Ellsworth T. '76 (FWT) Fort Worth, TX St. Paul.
Wight, Jonathan C. '86 (TOL) Rossford, OH All Saints; [C] Toledo, OH St. Francis de Sales High School.
Wightman, John H. '43 (NEW) Retired.
Wightman, Paul *o.m.i.* '55 (SPC) Ava, MO Immaculate Heart of Mary; Presbyteral Council.
Wightman, William R. *s.m.* '59 (STL)[F] Kirkwood, MO St. John Vianney High School.
Wightman, William '59 (STL)[O] St. Louis, MO Cure of Ars Marianist Community.
Wijanarko, Robertus *c.m.* '96 (CHI)[N] Chicago DePaul Vincentian Residence.
Wiktor, Ronald A. *c.m.* '63 (BUF) Niagara Falls, NY Our Lady of Lebanon.
Wiktor, Ronald *c.m.* '63 (HRT)[M] Manchester DePaul Provincial Residence.
Wiktorek, Wladyslaw *c.ss.r* '81 (MET) Perth Amboy, NJ St. Stephen.
Wilber, Stewart A. '92 (ATL) Lilburn, GA St. John Neumann.
Wilbers, Michael J. '72 (JC) Lake Ozark, MO Our Lady of the Lake; Episcopal Vicars; Diocesan Consultors; Personnel Board; Ex Officio Members; Diocesan Excellence in Education Fund, Inc.; Finance Committee; Board of Trustees.
Wilborn, Jeffery (DEN) Vocation Office.
Wilbricht, Stephen S. *c.s.c.* '97 (FTW)[I] Washington, DC St. Anthony Parish; Washington, DC St. Anthony.
Wilcox, C. Thomas *m.m.* '51 (NY).
Wilczek, Walter *c.r.* '53 (CHI)[EE] Chicago, IL St. Hedwig Retired.
Wilczynski, Casimir J. *c.r.* '40 (MOB) Montgomery, AL Resurrection Catholic Church.
Wilczynski, Richard J. '55 (SY) Utica, NY Holy Trinity.
Wild, Alexander '89 (DUB) On Duty Outside the Archdiocese.
Wild, J. Jerome '81 (PH) Horsham, PA St. Catherine of Siena.
Wild, Jon '82 (DUL) Buhl, MN Our Lady of the Sacred Heart; Chisholm, MN St. Joseph.
Wild, Joseph Albert *o.f.m.cap* '65 (NY)[EE] White Plains, NY Capuchin Friars International, Inc..
Wild, Michael L. '84 (MIL) Fox Lake, WI Annunciation.
Wild, Paul *o.f.m.* '72 (CIN)[M] Cincinnati, OH St. Clement Friary Retired.
Wild, Robert A. *s.j.* '70 (MIL)[O] Milwaukee, WI Jesuit Community at Marquette University; [C] Marquette University; On Duty Outside the Diocese.
Wilde, Adrian M. *o.carm.* '72 (GAL) Houston, TX St. Bernadette Soubirous.
Wilde, Dennis G. *o.s.a.* '70 (PH)[AA] Villanova, PA St. Thomas Monastery; Philadelphia, PA St. Katherine of Siena.
Wilder, Alfred W. *o.p.* '65 (NO)[P] Universita San Tommaso.
Wilder, Frank T. *o.a.r.* '91 (NY)[B] Suffern, NY Tagaste Monastery.
Wilder, Frank *o.a.r.* (NY) Suffern, NY Good Samaritan Hospital.
Wilderotter, Paul C. '74 (CHL) On Duty Outside the Diocese.
Wildes, Kevin W. *s.j.* '86 (WDC)[M] Washington, DC The Jesuit Community at Georgetown University.
Wiles, Arthur W. '67 (COL) Columbus, OH St. Christopher.
Wiley, James A. '58 (E)[K] Hermitage, PA John XXIII Home.
Wiley, Leo A. '56 (OG) Croghan, NY St. Stephen.
Wiley, Robert '60 (ORG) Westminster, CA Blessed Sacrament.
Wilgenbusch, Lyle L. '66 (DUB) Dubuque, IA St. Patrick; Dubuque, IA St. Joseph the Worker; College of Consultors; Deans; Catholic Committee on Scouting; Stewardship and Development Committee.
Wilgengbusch, Lyle L. '66 (DUB) Dubuque, IA St. Mary.
Wilger, Donald F. '49 (LC) Altoona, WI St. Mary Retired.
Wilger, John *t.o.r.* '48 (ALT)[F] Loretto, PA Mount Assisi Friary.
Wilhelm, Chad F. '94 (FAR) Devils Lake, ND St. Joseph; [J] Devils Lake, ND UND–Lake Region; Judges; Corporate Board; Apostleship of Prayer.
Wilhelm, Chad '94 (FAR) Devils Lake, ND St. Benedict; Diocesan Finance Council.
Wilhelm, Dean E. '88 (AUS) College Station, TX St. Thomas Aquinas.
Wilhelm, Dean (AUS) Presbyteral Council; Associates.
Wilhelm, Edward *c.ss.r.* '47 (CHI) Chicago, IL St. Michael; [N] Chicago, IL The Redemptorist Fathers of Chicago.
Wilhelm, H. Joseph *s.m.* '59 (WDC)[M] Wheeling, WV Retired.
Wilhelm, Patrick R.C. '71 (NEW) Kearny, NJ Our Lady of Sorrows.
Wilhelm, Ray *o.m.i.* '58 (SAN) Midland, TX Our Lady of Guadalupe.
Wilhelm, Ray *o.m.i.* (SAT) Defenders of the Bond.
Wilhelm, Robert J. '59 (TOL) Toledo, OH Our Lady of Perpetual Help; Members.
Wilhite, Philip A. '90 (GAL) Houston, TX St. Albert of Trapani.
Wilimek, Louis '50 (MIL) Retired.
Wilk, Brian J. '03 (MAD) Madison, WI Our Lady, Queen of Peace.
Wilk, Joseph M. '81 (CHI) Schaumburg, IL St. Matthew.
Wilk, Mitchell S. '70 (SPC) Military Chaplains; Army Chaplains.
Wilke, David M. '95 (BEL) Fairmont City, IL Holy Rosary.
Wilke, James B. '89 (STL) St. Louis, MO St. Simon the Apostle.
Wilkening, D. F. '79 (DAV) Solon, IA St. Mary's.
Wilkening, Henry '47 (JOL) Carol Stream, IL Corpus Christi Retired.
Wilker, Ronald H. '71 (CIN) Coldwater, OH Holy Trinity; Coldwater, OH St. Mary.
Wilkerson, Jerome F. '50 (STL) St. Louis, MO St. John Bosco Retired.
Wilkie, John J. '92 (SEA) Tacoma, WA St. Joseph; Tacoma, WA Holy Rosary.
Wilkie, William E. '54 (DUB) Retired.
Wilkiemeyer, Victor L. '43 (SJ)[C] Santa Clara, CA St. Lawrence the Martyr Retired.
Wilkins, Bernard J. '61 (STL) Brentwood, MO St. Mary Magdalen.
Wilkinson, Bruce W. '81 (ATL) Atlanta, GA Most Blessed Sacrament.
Wilkinson, George A. '01 (WDC) La Plata, MD Sacred Heart.
Wilkinson, James '42 (WCH) Retired.
Wilkinson, John H. '59 (BRK) Brooklyn, NY St. Brigid.
Wilkinson, John V. '48 (NY) Hartsdale, NY Sacred Heart.
Wilkinson, John '48 (NY) Retired.
Wilkinson, Neal (WIN)[C] Mankato, MN Loyola High School.
Wilkinson, Rick *c.s.c.* '79 (AUS) Austin, TX St. Ignatius Martyr; [A] St. Edward's University.
Wilkosz, William '95 (CHI) Chicago, IL Christ the King.
Wilks, Bede *o.p.* '62 (LA) Tuscon, AZ St. Thomas More Chapel; [H] Tucson, AZ University of Arizona.
Will, Anthony *o.f.m.cap.* '47 (MIL)[O] Mount Calvary, WI St. Lawrence Friary.
Will, Lowell '68 (EVN) Boonville, IN St. Clement.
Will, Ronald *c.pp.s.* '75 (KC) Liberty, MO St. James.
Willard, Stephen A. '93 (PEO) Philo, IL St. Thomas.
Willborn, Jeffrey '00 (DEN) Denver, CO St. Mary Magdalene.
Willenborg, Henry *o.f.m.* '76 (STL)[O] St. Louis, MO Franciscan Friary of St. Anthony of Padua.
Willenbring, Mark W. '57 (SCL) Retired.
Willenbring, Mark W. '57 (STP) Albertville, MN St. Albert Retired.
Willenbring, Mark (SCL) Clerical Aid Association.
Willenburg, Francis J. '54 (SY) Utica, NY St. Agnes.
Willett, John *c.ss.r.* '61 (WCH) Wichita, KS St. Joseph; [F] Wichita, KS Redemptorist Mission House.
Willett, William D. '79 (OWN) Military Chaplains; Army Chaplains.
Willette, Donald C. '84 (DEN)[Q] Fort Collins, CO Colorado State University (Fort Collins); Air Force Reserve Chaplains.
Willette, Donald '84 (DEN) Fort Collins, CO John XXIII University Parish; [S] Fort Collins, CO West African Development Support Organization.
Willey, Dennis B. '94 (CHR) Charleston, SC Church of the Nativity; Promoter of Justice; Personnel Committee; Vocations Board.
Willger, Gerard I. '86 (SUP) Barron, WI St. Joseph; Barron, WI St. Peter; Chetek, WI St. Boniface.
Willhite, Robert J. '63 (RCK) Aurora, IL St. Rita of Cascia.
William, Michael '83 (CHR) Murrells Inlet, SC St. Michael.
Williams, Anthony C. '83 (KCK) Basehor, KS Holy Angels.
Williams, Bruce A. *o.p.* '67 (BO)[V] Dover, MA St. Stephen Priory.
Williams, Clarence E. *c.pp.s.* '78 (DET)[T] Detroit, MI The Black Catholic Televangelization Network; Special Assignment; Black Catholic Ministries.
Williams, Clarence (NO)[S] New Orleans, LA Pan African Roman Catholic Clergy Conference.
Williams, David '98 (AUS) Assessors; [G] Austin, TX Oratory of Saint Gregory the Great.
Williams, Donald J. '83 (SCR) Plymouth, PA St. Vincent de Paul.
Williams, Edward J. '93 (SCR) Duryea, PA Holy Rosary.
Williams, Ernest '74 (BUF)[K] Buffalo, NY Sisters of Charity Hospital of Buffalo, NY.
Williams, Francis '77 (LAN) Retired.
Williams, Gary G. '81 (MOB) Greenville, AL St. Elizabeth.
Williams, George S. *s.j.* '72 (ALN)[A] Wernersville, PA Jesuit Center; [N] Wernersville, PA Jesuit Center for Spiritual Growth.
Williams, George (DET) Canton, MI Saint John Neumann; Presbyteral Council.
Williams, George *s.j.* (BO)[V] Cambridge, MA Faber House.
Williams, George (DET) Canton, MI Saint John Neumann; Presbyteral Council.
Williams, Gerald *o.carm.* '80 (CHI)[N] Chicago Carmelite Priory of St. Cyril.
Williams, Germain *o.f.m.conv.* '48 (ALB)[A] Rensselaer, NY Conventual Franciscan Friars; [L] Rensselaer, NY Provincialate, Immaculate Conception Friary – Order of Friars Minor Conventual.
Williams, H. Brendan '65 (TR) Howell, NJ St. Veronica; Charismatic Renewal.
Williams, Henry '78 (BRK) Brooklyn, NY Holy Name.
Williams, Ian J. '96 (GRY) Chesterton, IN St. Patrick.
Williams, J. Gerald *o.carm.* '80 (CHI)[D] Chicago, IL.
Williams, J. Mark '89 (PEO) Bloomington, IL Holy Trinity; Vicariates and Vicars.
Williams, James A. '65 (SEA) Seattle, WA St. Bernadette; Judges.
Williams, James C. *s.m.* '98 (RVC)[D] Mineola, NY Chaminade High School (Boys); [M] Mineola, NY Provincial Residence and Novitiate.
Williams, James M. '70 (MAR) Mackinac Island, MI Ste. Anne de Michilimackinac.
Williams, James M. '97 (COS) Colorado Springs, CO St. Joseph's.
Williams, James (COS) Propagation of the Faith.
Williams, John J. '02 (R) Raleigh, NC St. Joseph.
Williams, John L. '91 (HRT) Waterbury, CT St. Joseph; Waterbury, CT St. Patrick.
Williams, Joseph A. '02 (STP) St. Paul, MN Cathedral of St. Paul.
Williams, Joseph S. *c.m.* '91 (STL) St. Louis, MO St. Vincent de Paul.
Williams, Kenneth '63 (SHP) Noble, LA St. Ann.
Williams, Manuel *c.r.* '87 (MOB) Montgomery, AL Resurrection Catholic Church; Montgomery, AL Resurrection Catholic Mission; [E] Marbury, AL Resurrection Catholic Nursing Home; [E] Montgomery, AL Father Walter Memorial Center for Handicapped Children.
Williams, Matthew M. '03 (BO) Dedham, MA St. Mary.
Williams, Matthew *o.c.d.* '90 (LA) Alhambra, CA St. Therese.
Williams, Michael A. *s.j.* '75 (Maryland)[A] Mobile, AL Spring Hill College.
Williams, Michael E. '97 (OWN) St. Jude; Fulton, KY St. Edward; Hickman, KY Sacred Heart.
Williams, Michael J. '95 (LAN) Lansing, MI St. Therese; Diocesan Mission Office.
Williams, Michael S. '64 (STA) Keystone Heights, FL St. William.
Williams, Mike (OWN) Deans.
Williams, Oliver F. *c.s.c.* '70 (FTW)[B] University of

Notre Dame Du Lac; [I] Notre Dame, IN Holy Cross Community, Corby Hall, University of Notre Dame.
Williams, Patrick J. '93 (NO).
Williams, Paul D. '96 (ATL)[A] Carrollton, GA Church of Our Lady of Perpetual Help.
Williams, Paul M. *o.f.m.* '86 (CHR) Columbia, SC Saint Martin de Porres; Vicar for African–American Catholics; Personnel Committee.
Williams, Paul '95 (ATL)[N] Carrollton, GA West Georgia College.
Williams, Peter A. '83 (SY) Fulton, NY Holy Family–St. Michael's; Elected.
Williams, Peter Y. '87 (BUR) Springfield, VT Maternity of the Blessed Virgin Mary.
Williams, R. B. *o.p.* '71 (NO)[P] New Orleans, LA Dominican Friars, Southern Dominican Province of St. Martin de Porres.
Williams, Rayner F. *o.f.m.* '56 (PAT)[P] Paterson, NJ St. Anthony's Guild.
Williams, Rayner F. *o.f.m.* '56 (NY) New York, NY St. Francis of Assisi.
Williams, Richard B. *o.p.* '71 (NO) Special Assignment.
Williams, Richard C. '65 (PH) Glen Mills, PA St. Thomas the Apostle.
Williams, Robert H. (DET) Judges; Adjutant Judicial Vicars.
Williams, Robert Hayes '82 (DET) Special Assignment; Hazel Park, MI St. Justin.
Williams, Robert L. '68 (LFT) Anderson, IN St. Mary; Deans; Diocesan Consultors; Presbyteral Council; Members.
Williams, Robert '91 (DAL)[N] Dallas, TX Commission on Ecumenism; Corsicana, TX Immaculate Conception.
Williams, Ronald E. '02 (CIN) Dayton, OH St. Charles Borromeo.
Williams, Steven T. '91 (MOB) Mobile, AL St Mary; [B] Mobile, AL McGill–Toolen Catholic High School.
Williams, Steven (MOB) Boy Scouts.
Williams, Thomas G. *s.j.* '60 (SEA)[C] Tacoma, WA Bellarmine Preparatory School.
Williams, Thomas *s.j.* '60 (SEA) Tacoma, WA Visitation.
Williams, W. Ray '97 (CHL) Sylva, NC St. Mary.
Williams, William E. '59 (NY) Saugerties, NY St. John the Evangelist; Ulster.
Williams, William G. '69 (BO) Hull, MA St. Mary of the Assumption.
Williams, William M. '96 (ATL) Lilburn, GA St. John Neumann.
Williams, William W. *s.j.* '68 (DEN)[N] Denver, CO Xavier Jesuit Center.
Williamson, Christopher '88 (ATL) Blue Ridge, GA St. Anthony's.
Williamson, John A. (BAL) Baltimore, MD Cathedral of Mary Our Queen.
Williamson, John *o.c.d.* '79 (TUC) Tucson, AZ Santa Cruz.
Williamson, Michael '86 (CLV) Akron, OH St. Matthew.
Williamson, Robert J. '62 (BUF) Akron, NY St. Teresa of Avila.
Williamson, Thomas '96 (CHL) Absent On Leave.
Willingham, Charles W. *o.praem.* '95 (ORG)[D] Silverado, CA St. Michael's Preparatory School; [I] Silverado, CA Norbertine Fathers of Orange Inc..
Willingham, Jeffrey R. '97 (MET) Colonia, NJ St. John Vianney.
Willis, Glen *s.d.s.* '69 (WDC)[B] Silver Spring, MD Salvatorian Community; [G] Rockville, MD The Frost Center, Society of the Divine Savior; [V] Silver Spring, MD Camp St. Charles, Inc..
Willis, Kevin L. (FAR) Deanery 5.
Willis, Kevin '93 (FAR) Cando, ND Sacred Heart.
Willis, Lawrence R. *o.s.b.* '66 (CHL)[J] Belmont, NC Belmont Abbey.
Willis, Nathan '66 (Y) Retired.
Willis, Thomas S. '84 (STA) Jacksonville, FL Most Holy Redeemer; Respect Life Activities.
Willis, Thomas (STA) Office of Liturgy.
Willmann, Robert E. '92 (COL) Corning, OH St. Bernard; Junction City, OH St. Patrick; New Lexington, OH St. Rose of Lima; Diocesan Consultors; Appointed Members; Diocesan Judges.
Willoughby, Malcolm Sylvester *o.p.* '49 (WDC)[B] Washington, DC Dominican House of Studies.
Willson, David '88 (E) Wilcox, PA St. Anne.
Wilmot, John P. '77 (WIN) Mankato, MN Holy Family; Mankato, MN St. Joseph the Worker.
Wilmoth, James R. '65 (IND) Indianapolis, IN St. Roch; Marion County Sheriff Department.
Wilmoth, James (IND) Deaneries and Deans.
Wilmsen, Gerald *s.s.c.* '59 (OM)[K] St. Columbans St. Columban's Foreign Mission Society Retired.
Wilson, Alan *o.f.m.cap.* '69 (OAK)[N] Saint Conrad Friary.
Wilson, Albert L. '51 (L) Payneville, KY St. Theresa; Clergy Personnel Commission Retired.
Wilson, Anthony *o.f.m.* '87 (FgM).
Wilson, Bill '02 (SP) Tampa, FL St. Paul.
Wilson, Cedric M. *o.s.a.* '78 (WDC)[B] Silver Spring, MD Austin Friars Hall, Order of St. Augustine.
Wilson, David J. '88 (E) Johnsonburg, PA Holy Rosary.
Wilson, Dennis M. *o.f.m.* '92 (NY) New York, NY St. Francis of Assisi; [II] New York, NY Franciscans of Holy Name Province Benevolence Trust, Inc..
Wilson, Edward J. '01 (PRO) Providence, RI St. Augustine.
Wilson, Eugene C. (PH) Norristown, PA Visitation B.V.M..
Wilson, F. Philip *o.s.b.* '53 (PRO)[P] Portsmouth, RI Abbey of St. Gregory the Great.
Wilson, Gene R. *c.pp.s.* '60 (OAK)[N] San Leandro, CA Society of the Precious Blood.
Wilson, George B. *s.j.* '59 (CIN)[M] Cincinnati, OH Jesuit Community at Xavier University.
Wilson, George W. '92 (WDC) Retired.
Wilson, Gregory B. '01 (CHR) Charleston, SC Cathedral of St. John the Baptist.
Wilson, Gregory (CHR) Diocesan Master of Ceremonies.
Wilson, James R. '54 (B) Retired.
Wilson, John M. *c.s.b.* '47 (GAL)[Q] Houston, TX Dillon House Retired.
Wilson, John M. *c.s.b.* (LSC) Judges.
Wilson, Jonathan F. '03 (COL) Lancaster, OH St. Mary.
Wilson, Jonathan F. (COL) Priests' Senate.
Wilson, Joseph F. '86 (BRK) Whitestone, NY St. Luke.
Wilson, Kent '90 (NY) Fishkill, NY Church of St. Mary, Mother of the Church.
Wilson, Method *o.f.m.* '52 (SFD)[L] Springfield, IL Our Lady of Angels Friary.
Wilson, Michael '75 (WDC) Laurel, MD St. Mary; Deans.
Wilson, Richard D. (FR) Secretary to the Bishop; Diocesan Apostolate to Hispanics; Fall River; Auditors.
Wilson, Richard '97 (FR)[K] Fall River, MA Spanish Apostolate
Wilson, Robert W. '57 (FWT) Aledo, TX Holy Redeemer Parish; St. Joseph's Health Care Trust; Mission Council; Sexual Misconduct Review Board.
Wilson, Robert (FWT) Chancellor and Moderator of the Curia; Presbyteral Council and Consultors; Diocesan Finance Council; Catholic Foundation of North Texas; Executive Services; Diocesan Pastoral Finance Council (Budgets); Executive Services; Propagation of the Faith.
Wilson, Steven N. *c.ss.r.* '02 (CHI) Chicago, IL Blessed Sacrament. [N] Chicago, IL The Redemptorists of Blessed Sacrament.
Wilson, Stuart T. '67 (BAL) Retired.
Wilson, Thomas R. '75 (PIT) Crescent, PA St. Catherine of Siena.
Wilson, Thomas (STP) Vocation Office; Special Assignment.
Wilson, William P. '69 (NEW) On Duty Outside the Archdiocese.
Wilt, George A. '59 (PIT)[N] Pittsburgh, PA St. John Vianney Manor Retired.
Wilt, John E '57 (GBG) Seward, PA Holy Family.
Wiltgen, Ralph *s.v.d.* '50 (CHI)[B] Techny IL Divine Word Residence.
Wilton, David M. *c.p.m.* '93 (OWN)[F] Auburn, KY Fathers of Mercy.
Wiltz, George *s.j.* '65 (FWT).
Wilus, John M. '37 (TR) Retired.
Wilutis, John P. '55 (RVC)[M] Uniondale, NY St. Pius X Residence Retired.
Wilwerding, Anthony P. '46 (OM) Retired.
Wilz, John C. '64 (PH) On Special or Other Archdiocesan Assignment.
Wimett, Leo J. '60 (SY) North Bay, NY St. John.
Wimmer, Joseph F. *o.s.a.* '64 (WDC)[B] Silver Spring, MD Austin Friars Hall, Order of St. Augustine.
Wimsett, Scott J. '88 (L) Mount Washington, KY St. Francis Xavier.
Winance, Eleutherius *o.s.b.* '35 (LA)[Q] Valyermo, CA St. Andrew's Abbey.
Winca, Harry S. '45 (CLV) Middlefield, OH St. Lucy; Parkman, OH St. Edward.
Winca, Harry '45 (CLV) Retired.
Winchester, George P. *s.j.* '65 (BO) Boston, MA Brigham and Women's Hospital; [V] Boston, MA Loyola House.
Windhaus, Edward A. '72 (PH) East Norriton, PA St. Titus.
Windholtz, Barry M. (CIN) Adjutant Judicial Vicars.
Windholtz, Barry M. (COV) Judges.
Windholtz, Barry '88 (CIN) Cincinnati, OH St. Rose of Lima.
Windisch, Adolf M. *s.m.* '60 (CIN)[M] Dayton, OH Marianist Community.
Windle, Raymond L. *s.j.* '59 (STL)[O] St. Louis, MO Jesuit Community Corporation at St. Louis University – Jesuit Hall.
Windolph, George *o.f.m.* '48 (SFD)[B] Quincy, IL Quincy University
Windolph, Joseph '48 (CHI)[N] Chicago, IL St. Peter's Friary.
Windolph, Nestor *o.f.m.* '55 (FgM).
Windsor, David E. *c.m.* '74 (MIL)[A] St. Francis, WI Saint Francis Seminary; [A] St. Francis, WI Saint Francis Seminary.
Wing, Kenneth A. '59 (GR) Retired.
Wingate, Arthur K. '57 (FR) Retired.
Wingert, D. William '60 (SC) Retired.
Wingert, Gerald R. '47 (SC) Retired.
Wingfield, Harvey J. *o.s.b.* '81 (SEA)[L] Lacey, WA St. Martin's Abbey.
Winiarski, James *m.s.* '66 (GAL) Friendswood, TX Mary, Queen.
Winikates, Thomas '70 (CHI) Westchester, IL Divine Infant.
Winkel, Thomas J. '71 (CLV) Bedford, OH St. Mary.
Winkelbauer, Phillip J. '75 (KCK) Leavenworth, KS Sacred Heart of Jesus; Leavenworth, KS St. Casimir's.
Winkels, Michael A. *o.p.* '76 (CHI)[D] Oak Park, IL Fenwick High School.
Winkels, Michael *o.p.* '76 (CHI)[N] Oak Park, IL Dominican Community of St. Martin de Porres.
Winkler, Chauncey '03 (PHX) Phoenix, AZ SS. Simon and Jude Cathedral.
Winkler, Edward J. '86 (VIC) Eagle Lake, TX Parish of the Nativity; Liturgical Commission.
Winkler, Eugene '50 (MIL) Retired.
Winkler, Jude *o.f.m.conv.* '75 (BAL)[S] Ellicott City, MD Friary of St. Joseph Cupertino.
Winkowski, Eugene R. '71 (CHI) Chicago, IL Our Lady of Victory.
Winkowski, Michael J. *c.pp.s* '70 (FTW) Walkerton, IN St. Patrick.
Winn, Frank A. '98 (BGP) Stratford, CT St. James.
Winn, Frank '98 (BGP) Fairfield, CT Assumption.
Winne, George R. '83 (ALN) McAdoo, PA St. Patrick; [C] Tamaqua, PA Marian Catholic High School.
Winnenberg, John O. '55 (WDC) Retired.
Winrich, Walter W. *m.m.* '50 (SJ).
Winshman, Alfred O. *s.j.* '65 (BO)[V] Boston, MA Loyola House.
Winslow, Patrick '99 (ALB) Charlotte, NC St. Vincent de Paul.
Winston, William L. '86 (PAT) Morris Plains, NJ St. Virgilius.
Winter, Donald J. *c.ss.r.* '55 (ORL) New Smyrna Beach, FL Sacred Heart.
Winter, Donald *c.ss.r.* '55 (RIC) Hampton, VA St. Joseph.
Winter, Harry E. *o.m.i.* '65 (BUF) Buffalo, NY St. Rose of Lima.
Winter, Paul *o.f.m.cap.* '84 (WDC)[B] Washington, DC St. Francis Friary–Capuchin College.
Winterer, Michael I. (SLC) Deans.
Winterer, Michael J. '60 (SLC) Cedar City, UT Christ the King.
Winterlin, John R. '68 (GRY) Hammond, IN Our Lady of Perpetual Help.
Wintermyer, John S. '62 (WDC) Washington, DC St. Francis de Sales; Washington, DC Washington Hospital Center; Hospital & Nursing Home Ministries.
Winters, Alfred H. '62 (CLV) Lakewood, OH St. Clement.
Winters, Bartholomew S. '83 (CHI) Chicago, IL St. Gregory.
Winters, Darvin E. '99 (IND) Osgood, IN St. John; St. Magdalen; Navy Reserve Chaplains.
Winters, Martin N. '52 (CHI)[O] Oak Forest, IL Missionary Sisters of St. Benedict of Illinois, Inc. Retired.
Winters, Richard *s.v.d.* '41 (CHI)[B] Techny, IL Divine Word Residence.
Winters, Sean '87 (MET) Perth Amboy, NJ Holy Spirit; Perth Amboy, NJ Raritan Bay Medical Center.
Winters, Vaughn '93 (LA) Santa Maria, CA St. John Neumann.
Winters, William H. *o.f.m.cap.* '64 (ROC) Ovid, NY Holy Cross; [I] Interlaken, NY St. Fidelis Friary.
Winters, William *o.f.m.cap.* '64 (ROC) Ovid, NY St. Francis Solanus.
Wintz, Jack R. *o.f.m.* '63 (CIN)[M] Cincinnati, OH Pleasant Street Friary.
Winzenburg, George *s.j.* '74 (RC)[B] Howes, SD Kino Jesuit Community; [D] Howes, SD The Diocese of Rapid City Mahpiya na Maka Okogna; Permanent Diaconate Program, Sioux Spiritual Center.
Winzerling, James L. '61 (STL) Retired.
Wiorkiewicz, Marek *s.d.s.* '89 (NEW) Garfield, NJ St. Stanislaus Kostka; [N] Verona, NJ The Salvatorian Fathers.
Wippel, John '60 (STU) On Duty Outside the Diocese; [C] Catholic University of America, The.
Wirkes, Stephen P. '80 (SY) Fulton, NY Immaculate Conception.
Wirkes, Stephen (SY) Priests' Personnel Committee.
Wironen, John *c.s.c.* '79 (P)[J] Portland, OR Providence Portland Medical Center; [L] Portland, OR Holy Cross Fathers & Brothers, C.S.C. – University of Portland.
Wirth, Geoffrey D. '67 (RCK) Elgin, IL St. Thomas More; Diocesan Consultors.
Wirth, Jerry E. '68 (BEL) Olney, IL St. Joseph.
Wirth, John J. '52 (STP) Retired.
Wirth, Justus *o.f.m.* '62 (CIN)[M] Parroquia San Vincente de Paul.
Wirth, Richard P. '56 (STP) Retired.

Wirth, Robert *c.ss.r.* '64 (DEN)[N] (FgM).
Wischmeyer, Amos H. '51 (LAN) Swartz Creek, MI St. Mary.
Wisdom, Andrew–Carl *o.p.* '87 (CHI)[N] St. Pius V Priory.
Wisdon, Andrew–Carl *o.p.* '87 (CHI)[N] Chicago Dominicans (Provincial Office).
Wise, Carl *c.pp.s.* '55 (CIN)[B] Carthagena, OH St. Charles.
Wise, Kenneth F. '47 (COL) Retired.
Wise, Mark *c.ss.r.* '71 (PCE) Guayama, PR St. Anthony of Padua.
Wise, Paul C. '74 (CAM) Atlantic City, NJ St. Monica's.
Wise, Richard P. '81 (ATL) Blairsville, GA St. Francis of Assisi.
Wise, Thomas F. *c.s.v.* '56 (CHI)[N] Arlington Heights, IL Viatorian Province Center–Clerics of St. Viator.
Wiseman, James A. *o.s.b.* '70 (WDC)[C] Catholic University of America, The; [M] Washington, DC St. Anselm's Abbey.
Wiseman, Joseph F. '52 (BRK) Retired.
Wiseman, Robert *c.s.c.* '77 (ORL) Viera, FL St. John the Evangelist.
Wiseman, Vincent *o.p.* '71 (WDC)[B] Washington, DC Dominican House of Studies; (FgM).
Wiskirchen, George C. *c.s.c.* '55 (FTW)[I] Notre Dame, IN Holy Cross House.
Wisner, John H. '72 (KCK) Roeland Park, KS St. Agnes.
Wisneske, S. Patrick '50 (MAR) Menominee, MI Holy Spirit.
Wisneski, Edward '67 (NOR) Retired.
Wisneski, John A. '57 (LC) Milladore, WI St. Kilian; Milladore, WI St. Michael; Milladore, WI St. Wenceslaus.
Wisneski, John J. '64 (GR) Grand Rapids, MI Blessed Sacrament.
Wisneski, Jonathan J. '98 (GBG) Greensburg, PA Blessed Sacrament Cathedral.
Wisneski, Jonathan (GBG) Diocesan Pastoral Council.
Wisniefski, Robert W. '80 (PAT) Paterson, NJ St. Joseph's.
Wisniewski, Joseph *c.m.* '65 (BRK) Brooklyn, NY SS. Cyril and Methodius.
Wisniewski, Robert W. '89 (CLV) Cleveland, OH St. Patrick.
Wisniewski, Stanley T. *s.j.* '64 (DET)[P] Hamtramck, MI St. Ladislaus.
Wisniewski, Thomas J. '74 (PH) Absent on Leave.
Wisniewski, Thomas '76 (MIA) Parkland, FL Mary Help of Christians Church.
Wissel, Francis C. '77 (BGP)[U] Bridgeport, CT St. Peter's Parish, St. Maximillian Kolbe House of Studies; Members of the Clergy Personnel Committee.
Wissel, Frank C. '77 (BGP) Greenwich, CT St. Mary.
Wissler, Thomas '83 (STL) Troy, MO Sacred Heart.
Wissman, J. Patrick '64 (SPC) Bolivar, MO Sacred Heart; Region III; Region III; Presbyteral Council.
Wister, Robert J. '68 (NEW)[B] School of Diplomacy and Intl. Rels.; Archdiocesan Theological Commission.
Wisz, Dominic *o.f.m.conv.* '47 (RCK) Rockford, IL St. Anthony of Padua.
Wit, Mieczyslaw *o.f.m.conv.* '95 (SPR) Chicopee, MA St. Stanislaus Basilica.
Witalec, Dennis J. '82 (PH)[U] Philadelphia, PA St. Agnes Medical Center; Philadelphia, PA Epiphany of Our Lord.
Witchousky, Peter *o.p.* '69 (SFD)[M] Springfield, IL Convent of Our Lady of the Sacred Heart.
Witcoskie, Stanley L. '93 (CAM) Berlin, NJ Our Lady of Mt. Carmel.
Witczak, Michael G. '77 (MIL)[A] St. Francis, WI Saint Francis Seminary; Special Assignment; Saint Francis Seminary.
Witek, John W. *s.j.* '65 (CHI)[M] Washington, DC The Jesuit Community at Georgetown University.
Witek, Stanley '87 (KAL) Sturgis, MI Holy Angels.
With, William A. '72 (BRK) Brooklyn, NY Our Lady Help of Christians.
Withers, Mark *c.s.j.* '79 (LA) Lancaster, CA Blessed Junipero Serra; [D] Lancaster, CA Paraclete High School.
Witherup, Ronald D. *s.s.* '76 (BAL)[S] Baltimore, MD Sulpician Provincial House.
Withrow, Justin *o.s.b.* '90 (GBG) Greensburg, PA Westmoreland Hospital; Latrobe, PA Latrobe Area Hospital; Jeannette, PA Mercy Jeannette Hospital; Jeannette, PA Monsour Medical Center; [F] Jeannette, PA Mercy Jeannette Hospital; [H] Latrobe, PA Saint Vincent Archabbey.
Witkowski, Bernard E. '62 (PH) Philadelphia, PA Maternity B.V.M..
Witkowski, Phillip J. '75 (GR) Shelby, MI Our Lady of the Assumption; Shelby, MI Our Lady of Fatima.
Witkowski, Robert J. '91 (DET) Warren, MI St. Edmund.
Witmer, Joseph W. '67 (Y) Aurora, OH Our Lady of Perpetual Help.
Witmer, Joseph (Y) Ecumenism.
Witon, Russell F. '63 (MIL) Retired.
Witsken, Gary J. '69 (CIN) New Richmond, OH St. Peter.
Witt, Ed *s.j.* '91 (RC) Mission, SD St. Thomas the Apostle.
Witt, Edward G. *s.j.* '91 (RC) White River, SD Sacred Heart; St. Francis, SD Rosebud Reservation.
Witt, Edward Q. *s.j.* '91 (RC) White River, SD St. Ignatius.
Witt, G. Robert '50 (COV) Retired.
Witt, Michael J. '90 (STL)[A] St. Louis, MO Kenrick School of Theology.
Witt, Michael '90 (STL) Brentwood, MO St. Mary Magdalen.
Witt, Paul '71 (LIN) Lincoln, NE St. Mary; Deaneries and Deans; Ecumenical Affairs, Commission for; Society of St. Vincent de Paul – Lincoln Council; Evangelization Committee.
Witt, William '49 (Y) Retired.
Witte, John C. '45 (GRY) Retired.
Witte, Mark G. '95 (COV) Union, KY St. Timothy.
Witte, Steven D. '92 (BEL) Leave of Absence.
Wittenbrink, Boniface *o.m.i.* '41 (BEL)[F] Belleville, IL Missionary Oblates of Mary Immaculate – St. Henry's Oblate Residence.
Witthauer, Paul G. '60 (BAL) Retired.
Witting, Martin *o.s.b.* '51 (RCK)[G] Aurora, IL Marmion Abbey.
Wittliff, Thomas F. '64 (MIL) Milwaukee, WI St. Augustine.
Wittman, Karl M. '46 (STP) Retired.
Wittman, Michael A. '88 (CLV) East Cleveland, OH Christ the King.
Wittman, Peter C. '75 (STP) Savage, MN St. John the Baptist; Archdiocesan Consultors.
Wittmann, Christopher T. *s.m.* '94 (CIN)[D] Dayton, OH The University of Dayton; [M] Dayton, OH Marianist Community; [Q] Dayton, OH University of Dayton Campus Ministry.
Wittouck, Frank *s.c.j.* '65 (GAL) Houston, TX St. Elizabeth Ann Seton.
Wittreich, John A. '47 (CLV) Norton, OH St. Andrew the Apostle Retired.
Wittrock, Daniel L. '93 (OM) South Sioux City, NE St. Michael; Homer, NE St. Cornelius.
Wittstock, Joseph *o.c.s.o.* '84 (ARL)[J] Berryville, VA Cistercian Abbey of Our Lady of the Holy Cross.
Witz, Dennis M. '76 (MIL) Milwaukee, WI Immaculate Conception.
Witzemann, B. Gerald '61 (COV) Warsaw, KY St. Joseph Retired.
Witzmann, Hugh *o.s.b.* '55 (SCL)[I] Collegeville, MN St. John's Abbey, of the Order of St. Benedict.
Wixted, Matthew O. '62 (SLC) Tooele, UT St. Marguerite's; Apostleship of Prayer.
Wizeman, William L. *s.j.* '98 (NY)[EE] Cardinal Spellman Hall, Jesuit Community.
Wleczyk, Leo '65 (GAL) Lake Jackson, TX St. Michael.
Wocken, Jeffrey *s.d.s.* '99 (SAC) Orangevale, CA Divine Savior.
Wodniak, John L. '43 (CHI) Chicago, IL St. James Retired.
Wodziak, Michael '48 (RVC) Retired.
Woefl, Paul A. *s.j.* '44 (TOL) Toledo, OH Gesu.
Woempner, Michael A. '79 (MAR) Kingsford, MI St. Mary Queen of Peace.
Woerter, Dennis C. *o.p.* '97 (CHI)[N] Chicago Dominicans (Provincial Office).
Woerter, Dennis C. *o.p.* '97 (DEN) Denver, CO St. Dominic; [A] Denver, CO St. Dominic Priory.
Woerth, Thomas '66 (DEN)[H] Denver, CO St. Joseph Hospital.
Woerz, Christian H. *s.d.b.* '76 (OAK)[F] Bellflower, CA St. John Bosco High School.
Woestman, William H. *o.m.i.* (CHI) Associate Vicars.
Woestman, William O. *o.m.i.* (CHI) Defenders of the Bond.
Woestman, William *o.m.i.* '56 (CHI) Chicago, IL Holy Rosary.
Woestman, William *o.m.i.* (CHI) Promoter of Justice.
Wohinc, Karl R. '63 (WH) Shinnston, WV St. Ann's.
Wohler, Gil *o.f.m.* '62 (CIN) Cincinnati, OH St. Francis Seraph; [M] Cincinnati, OH St. Francis Seraph Friary.
Wohlrab, Paul G. '41 (ROC) Spencerport, NY St. John the Evangelist; [M] Spencerport, NY Legion of Mary Retired.
Wohlwend, Paul W. *c.pp.s.* '54 (CIN) Fort Recovery, OH Mary Help of Christians.
Wojcicki, Miroslaus A. '62 (PIT) East Pittsburgh, PA Holy Cross.
Wojcicki, Ted L. '75 (STL)[A] St. Louis, MO Kenrick School of Theology; Archdiocesan Council of Priests.
Wojcicki, Ted (STL) Kenrick–Glennon Seminary.
Wojcicki, Wojciech '99 (DET) Warren, MI St. Edmund.
Wojciechowski, Christian *o.f.m.conv.* '53 (TR) Riverside, NJ St. Casimir.
Wojciechowski, Edward C. '81 (PRM) Minneapolis, MN St. John the Baptist Retired.
Wojciechowski, Richard P. '63 (BAL) Retired.
Wojciechowski, Robert J. '83 (DET) Detroit, MI St. Francis D'Assisi.
Wojciechowski, Thomas *o.f.m.* (GB) Manitowoc, WI St. Mary.
Wojciehowski, Thaddeus J. '36 (TR)[M] Trenton, NJ Villa Vianney; [M] Trenton, NJ St. Lawrence Rehabilitation Center Retired.
Wojcik, Eugene H. (BEL) Diocesan Consultors; Vocation Office.
Wojcik, Eugene J. '74 (BEL) Waterloo, IL St. Patrick.
Wojcik, Joseph J. '69 (CHI) Chicago, IL St. Jane de Chantal.
Wojcik, Richard J. '49 (CHI) Retired.
Wojcinski, Anthony A. '85 (PBL)[A] Lamar, CO St. Francis De Sales–Our Lady of Guadalupe.
Wojcinski, Tony (PBL) Continuing Education and Formation.
Wojnecki, Richard *o.s.f.s.* (VEN)[P] Center Valley, PA DeSales Service Works.
Wojnicki, Richard '85 (PH)[AA] Wyndmoor, PA Villa de Sales Oblate Residence.
Wojtek, Robert F. *c.ss.r.* '81 (BRK) Brooklyn, NY Our Lady of Perpetual Help Basilica.
Wojtewicz, Eugene E. '57 (DET) Southgate, MI St. Hugh.
Wojtowicz, Edward L. '44 (NU) Retired.
Wojtunik, Henry *m.s.* '60 (MIL)[O] Twin Lakes, WI La Salette Missionaries Shrine.
Wojtus, Anthony '58 (WH) Retired.
Wojtycha, Edward F. '38 (NEW) Bayonne, NJ St. Andrew's Retired.
Wokorach, Raphael '93 (CHI)[N] Chicago, IL Comboni Missionaries Theologate (M.C.C.J.), Verona Fathers.
Wolak, Edmund A. '92 (SY) Hannibal, NY Our Lady of the Rosary.
Wolak, Edmund '92 (SY) Oswego, NY St. Stephen the King.
Wolanski, Edward *c.p.* '72 (WOR)[O] Shrewsbury, MA Calvary Retreat Center, Passionist Fathers of Shrewsbury, Inc..
Wolbach, Richard A. '56 (OM) Retired.
Wolber, Ferdinand A. '40 (DET) Retired.
Woldai, Gebriel (OAK) Ge'ez Community.
Woldai, Ghebriel '93 (OAK) Berkeley, CA St. Joseph The Worker.
Wolensky, Paul '94 (PHU) Philadelphia, PA Immaculate Conception of Blessed Virgin Mary, Cathedral.
Wolesky, John A. '67 (SAL) St. Patrick's; CIVIL AIR PATROL.
Wolesky, John '67 (SAL) Solomon, KS Immaculate Conception.
Wolf, Anthony J. '96 (LC) Marshfield, WI Corpus Christi; Marshfield, WI Sacred Heart of Jesus.
Wolf, Charles E. *s.j.* '49 (BAL).
Wolf, David *o.s.b.* '52 (BIS)[A] Richardton, ND Assumption Abbey.
Wolf, Dennis G. '72 (BUF) Vicars; Council of Priests; Wellsville, NY Immaculate Conception; Wellsville, NY Blessed Sacrament.
Wolf, Donald J. '81 (OKL) Duncan, OK Assumption.
Wolf, Donald (OKL) Council of Priests Archdiocesan.
Wolf, Eugene J. '63 (LC) Seneca, WI St. Patrick; Wauzeka, WI Sacred Heart.
Wolf, Eugene *o.f.m.cap.* '54 (MIL)[O] Mount Calvary, WI St. Lawrence Friary.
Wolf, George C. '63 (RNO) Sparks, NV Holy Cross Catholic Community.
Wolf, George *o.s.b.* '44 (FgM).
Wolf, George *o.s.b.* '44 (SCL)[I] St. Augustine Monastery.
Wolf, George '80 (P) Salem, OR Queen of Peace.
Wolf, George (RNO) Vicar–General; Promoter of Justice; Defenders of the Bond; Curia; Diocesan Board of Consultors; Finance Committee; Presbyteral Council; Priests' Personnel Board.
Wolf, George (P) College of Consultors; Area Vicars.
Wolf, George (RNO) Vicar–General; Promoter of Justice; Defenders of the Bond; Curia; Diocesan Board of Consultors; Finance Committee; Presbyteral Council; Priests' Personnel Board.
Wolf, George (P) College of Consultors; Area Vicars.
Wolf, George (RNO) Vicar–General; Promoter of Justice; Defenders of the Bond; Curia; Diocesan Board of Consultors; Finance Committee; Presbyteral Council; Priests' Personnel Board.
Wolf, James J. '69 (FTW) Warsaw, IN Sacred Heart; Consultors.
Wolf, James '48 (SFS) Retired.
Wolf, James *o.f.m.cap.* '57 (DET)[K] Detroit St. Bonaventure Friary.
Wolf, James (FTW) Advisory Board; Retired Clergy Committee.
Wolf, John V. '45 (COL) Diocesan Judges; Censor of Books Retired.
Wolf, John *c.pp.s.* '69 (KC) Kearney, MO Church of the Annunciation.
Wolf, Joseph B. '54 (STL) Retired.
Wolf, Joseph D. '87 (BUF) Buffalo, NY Holy Spirit.
Wolf, Joseph M. '94 (DAV)[M] Davenport, IA St. Vincent Center; Vice–Chancellors; Judicial Vicar.
Wolf, Joseph '68 (MIL) Milwaukee, WI St. Margaret Mary.
Wolf, Lawrence Robert *o.s.b.m.* '75 (PSC) Roebling, NJ

St. Nicholas; [A] Matawan, NJ Basilian Fathers of Mariapoch.
Wolf, Michael H. '42 (SAG) Essexville, MI St. John the Evangelist Retired.
Wolf, Norbert G. '47 (E) Retired.
Wolf, Paul L. '83 (NU) Winsted, MN Holy Trinity; Winsted, MN; Associate Judges.
Wolf, Robert J. '44 (MIL) Retired.
Wolf, Ronald D. *s.j.* '74 (SJ)[M] Los Gatos, CA Sacred Heart Jesuit Center.
Wolf, Stephen J. '97 (NSH) Old Hickory, TN St. Stephen; Vocations.
Wolf, Steve (NSH) Clergy Benefit Foundation.
Wolf, Werner *o.f.m.cap.* '58 (GB)[L] Appleton, WI Monte Alverno Retreat Center.
Wolf–Muhleck, Elle (SP)[K] Tampa, FL St. Joseph's Hospital, Inc..
Wolfe, Allan F. '92 (HBG) Lancaster, PA Iglesia Catolica San Juan Bautista.
Wolfe, Joseph M. *m.f.v.a.* '93 (BIR)[E] Birmingham, AL Franciscan Missionaries of the Eternal Word, A Public Association of the Christian Faithful.
Wolfe, Philip *f.s.s.p.* '01 (SCR)[M] Tulsa, OK.
Wolfe, Robert A. *o.carm.* '75 (NEW) Englewood, NJ St. Cecilia's Retired.
Wolfe, William P. '70 (LA) West Hollywood, CA St. Ambrose; Judges.
Wolfee, Robert '98 (NEW) Hackensack, NJ Holy Trinity.
Wolfel, Daniel C. *o.s.b.* '54 (GBG) St. Marys, PA Queen of the World.
Wolfer, Paul J. '45 (CIN) Cincinnati, OH Our Lady of Lourdes Retired.
Wolfer, Robert R. '48 (CIN) Cincinnati, OH Our Lady of Lourdes Retired.
Wolff, Alec J. '81 (CHI) Highland Park, IL Immaculate Conception; [X] Wilmette, IL Musica Pacis.
Wolff, Alec (CHI) Judges.
Wolff, Robert C. '50 (CLV) Copley, OH Guardian Angels Retired.
Wolfgram, Daniel '97 (SFS) Conde, SD St. John the Baptist.
Wolford, Donald L. '79 (SFD) Shelbyville, IL Immaculate Conception.
Wolfram, Frank *s.d.b.* '62 (NY)[GG] Stony Point, NY Don Bosco Retreat Center and Marian Shrine; [GG] Stony Point, NY Marian Shrine.
Wolken, Louis J. *m.m.* '46 (NY).
Wolkovich, William L. '53 (BO)[EE] Norwood, MA St. George.
Wolkovits, Paul '93 (LA) On Sick Leave.
Wollering, Carl J. '66 (CIN) Cincinnati, OH Guardian Angels; Cincinnati, OH St. Jerome.
Wollmering, Bruce *o.s.b.* '67 (SCL)[I] Collegeville, MN St. John's Abbey, of the Order of St. Benedict.
Wollsen, Charles A. *s.j.* '52 (SPK)[J] Spokane, WA Regis Community.
Wolnik, James G. '79 (STP) St. Paul, MN Holy Childhood.
Wolnowski, Kenneth J. '65 (CLV) Lorain, OH St. Peter.
Woloszczuk, Wolodymyr '81 (SJP) North Port, FL Entrance of B.V.M. into the Temple.
Woloszczuk, Wolodymyr (SJP) Obnova Retired.
Wolski, Adalbert *t.o.r.* '59 (ALT)[F] Hollidaysburg, PA St. Joseph Friary.
Wolski, Mark J. '67 (BUF) Finance Council; Hamburg, NY SS. Peter and Paul.
Wolter, Allan *o.f.m.* '40 (STL)[O] St. Bonaventure, NY St. Bonaventure University.
Wolter, Martin *o.f.m.* '46 (STL)[O] Berryvile, AR Retired.
Wolter, Richard J. '59 (STP) Retired.
Wolter, Thomas '66 (JOL) Elmhurst, IL Mary, Queen of Heaven; Naperville, IL Edward Hospital.
Wolters, Gilbert *o.s.b.* '34 (KCK)[H] Atchison, KS St. Benedict's Abbey.
Wolverton, R. Ambrose *o.s.b.* '65 (PRO)[P] Portsmouth, RI Abbey of St. Gregory the Great.
Womack, Warren *c.p.* '49 (CHI)[N] Chicago, IL Passionist Community–Immaculate Conception Monastery.
Won, John P. '58 (LA) West Covina, CA St. Christopher.
Wonch, Charles *s.c.j.* '02 (RC) Lower Brule, SD St. Mary's; Lower Brule, SD Lower Brule Reservation; [B] Lower Brule, SD SCJ Community House.
Wonch, Charles *s.c.j.* '02 (SFS) Fort Thompson, SD St. Joseph; Lower Brule, SD Immaculate Conception.
Wonch, Charles *s.c.j.* '02 (RC) Lower Brule, SD St. Mary's; Lower Brule, SD Lower Brule Reservation; [B] Lower Brule, SD SCJ Community House.
Wong, Joseph *o.s.b.cam.* '74 (MRY)[F] Big Sur, CA New Camaldoli Hermitage.
Wong, Jules *o.f.m.* '73 (Y)[J] Youngstown, OH Mt. Alverna Friary.
Wood, Charles (P) On Duty Outside the Archdiocese.
Wood, D. Mark '87 (LR) Jonesboro, AR Blessed Sacrament; [J] Jonesboro, AR Blessed John Newman University Parish; Jonesboro, AR Blessed John Newman University Parish.
Wood, Gregg D. *s.j.* '75 (FBK) Chevak, AK Sacred Heart; Hooper Bay, AK Little Flower of Jesus; Scammon Bay, AK Blessed Sacrament; [E] St. Marys, AK Brother Joe Prince Jesuit Community; [M] Los Gatos, CA Sacred Heart Jesuit Center.
Wood, James L. '72 (RVC) Bohemia, NY St. John Nepomucene.
Wood, John M. '83 (SY) Rome, NY St. John the Baptist.
Wood, Kenneth E. '89 (RIC) Virginia Beach, VA Holy Spirit.
Wood, Mark *s.j.* '87 (LR) Marked Tree, AR St. Norbert; Weiner, AR St. Anthony's; [L] Jonesboro, AR Catholic Hispanic Center.
Wood, Michael '84 (NOR)[C] Baltic, CT Academy and Boarding–School of the Holy Family; [G] Baltic, CT Holy Family Motherhouse.
Wood, Michael (SA) AUXILIARY CHAPLAINS CONTRACT CHAPLAINS.
Wood, Norbert J. *o.praem.* '81 (ORG)[I] Silverado, CA Norbertine Fathers of Orange Inc..
Wood, Paul A. '80 (BRK) Maspeth, NY Transfiguration.
Wood, Paul '30 (BRK)[E] Campus Ministers and Ministry Centers.
Wood, Peter N. '82 (PT) On Leave of Absence.
Wood, Raymond B. '64 (SY) Jamesville, NY St. Mary.
Wood, Robert T. '87 (OKL) Oklahoma City, OK St. James.
Wood, Robert W. '74 (BUF) Retired.
Wood, Robert *c.m.* '56 (FgM).
Wood, Robert (OKL) Master of Ceremonies.
Wood, Simon Paul *c.p.* '43 (HRT)[M] West Hartford Holy Family Monastery/Retreat.
Wood, William Andrew '73 (GAL) Sugar Land, TX St. Laurence.
Woodarek, Richard *c.s.s.* '57 (BO)[V] Waltham, MA Stigmatine Fathers & Brothers Provincial House.
Woodeshick, Martin E. '69 (PH) Sharon Hill, PA Holy Spirit.
Woodhall, Jonathan A. '99 (R) Raleigh, NC Cathedral of the Sacred Heart.
Woodland, Stephen '88 (LA) Inglewood, CA St. John Chrysostom.
Woodman, Gerald '78 (SEA) Woodland, WA St. Philip.
Woodruff, Mark '72 (SAN) Odessa, TX St. Elizabeth Ann Seton; Defensores Vinculi; Diocesan Consultors.
Woodruff, William F. '82 (NY) Mahopac, NY St. John the Evangelist.
Woods, Curtis W. '80 (SHP) Shreveport, LA St. John Berchmans Cathedral.
Woods, Curtis (SHP) Judges.
Woods, James A. *s.j.* '61 (BO)[C] Summer Session; [C] College of Advancing Studies; [V] Newton, MA The Jesuit Community at Boston College.
Woods, Joseph E. *o.s.f.s.* '44 (WIL)[J] Childs, MD Retirement and Assisted Care Facility.
Woods, Keith A. '95 (WDC) Washington, DC St. Ann; [S] Washington, DC American University Catholic Community.
Woods, Keith '95 (WDC) Special Ministries.
Woods, Michael A. '66 (KNX) Oak Ridge, TN St. Mary.
Woods, Michael A. '66 (ATL) On Duty Outside the Archdiocese.
Woods, Michael '66 (KNX)[I] Knoxville, TN Diocesan Council of Catholic Women.
Woods, Patrick F. *c.ss.r.* '75 (BRK)[V] Brooklyn, NY Our Lady of Good Counsel Residence.
Woods, Richard J. *o.p.* '69 (CHI)[N] River Forest, IL St. Thomas Aquinas Priory.
Woods, Scott '02 (WDC) Gaithersburg, MD St. John Neumann.
Woods, Thomas '02 (BIR) Madison, AL St. John the Baptist.
Woods, Tom '02 (BIR)[A] Huntsville, AL Catholic High School.
Woods, Walter J. '70 (BO) Acton, MA St Elizabeth of Hungary
Woods, Warren L. '50 (SFR).
Woods, Warren '50 (SFR)[K] San Rafael, CA Nazareth House.
Woodward, John B. *s.j.* '58 (BAL)[S] Baltimore, MD Jesuit Fathers and Brothers Maryland Provincial Curia.
Woolever, James '74 (SJ) Palo Alto, CA St. Thomas Aquinas
Woolever, James '74 (SY) On Duty Outside the Diocese.
Woolley, Michael J. '99 (PRO) Woonsocket, RI St. Joseph.
Woolsey, John G. '65 (NY) New York, NY St. John the Martyr; Manhattan (East).
Woolson, Herbert '82 (LFT) Monterey, IN St. Anne.
Woolway, John S. '80 (LA) Los Nietos, CA Our Lady of Perpetual Help.
Woolway, John (LA) Deanery 18; San Pedro Pastoral Region.
Woolway, John (LA) Ministry to Recently Ordained Priests.
Woost, David G. '91 (CLV) Lorain, OH St. Peter.
Woost, Michael G. '84 (CLV)[A] Wickliffe, OH St. Mary Seminary and Graduate School of Theology.
Woost, Michael '84 (CLV) Mentor, OH St. Bede the Venerable.
Woost, Thomas G. '97 (CLV) Parma, OH St. Anthony of Padua.
Woost, Thomas (CLV) Presbyteral Council.
Wooton, Jerry A. '96 (ARL) Fairfax, VA St. Leo's.
Wopoule, Janvier (DET) Bloomfield Hills, MI St. Regis.
Wopperer, Thomas J. '64 (BUF) Dunkirk, NY St. Elizabeth Ann Seton.
Woracek, Thomas J. '46 (STL) Retired.
Worcester, Thomas W. *s.j.* '91 (WOR)[O] Worcester, MA Jesuits of Holy Cross College, Inc..
Worch, Donald P. '67 (WDC) Rockville, MD St. Patrick.
Worczak, Paul F. '68 (OG) Norwood, NY St. Andrew.
Wordekemper, Thomas *o.s.b.* '94 (BIS)[A] Richardton, ND Assumption Abbey.
Worland, Christopher J. '01 (CIN) Centerville, OH Incarnation.
Worley, Jason '99 (BAL) Baltimore, MD Our Lady of Mount Carmel.
Worm, Paul '88 (LR) Fayetteville, AR St. Joseph's; Fayetteville, AR St. Thomas Aquinas University Parish; [J] Fayetteville, AR University of Arkansas, St. Thomas Aquinas University Parish.
Worman, Jeremiah F. '67 (GB) Antigo, WI SS. Mary & Hyacinth; Deerbrook, WI St. Wenceslaus.
Worman, Jeremiah (GB) Elected Representatives.
Wormek, Joseph E. '76 (STL) Manchester, MO Christ, Prince of Peace; Deaneries/Deans; Southwest; Archdiocesan Council of Priests.
Wormek, Joseph (STL) Priests' Mutual Benefit/Risk Management.
Worn, G. Peter '77 (SY) Cazenovia, NY St. James.
Worner, William H. '45 (SFR) Retired.
Woroniewicz, Michael A. '85 (DET) Dundee, MI St. Irene.
Worry, Benedict M. *o.s.b.* '87 (PAT)[M] Morristown St. Mary's Abbey.
Worry, Benedict M. *o.s.b.* (NEW) Union County Southeast Deanery 24.
Worry, Benedict Michael *o.s.b.* '87 (NEW) Linden, NJ St. Elizabeth's.
Worschak, D. George '78 (PHU) Press, The Way; Philadelphia, PA St. Josaphat's.
Worsley, Stephen (R) Vicar for Priests; Priests' Council.
Worster, John R. '87 (B) Soda Springs, ID St. Mary's; Army National Guard Chaplains.
Worster, John (B) Priest Retirement Committee.
Worth, James '01 (NEW) Springfield, NJ St. James.
Worthy, Donald '62 (DET)[H] Pontiac, MI St. Joseph Mercy – Oakland Retired.
Wortmann, Edgar J. '48 (OM) Omaha, NE Blessed Sacrament; Council of Catholic Women, Archdiocesan.
Wortmann, Joseph F. '58 (NEW) Retired.
Worzalla, Dennis A. '50 (GB)[B] Stevens Point, WI St. Peter Retired.
Wosman, Richard *s.m.* '81 (STL)[O] St. Louis, MO Jesuit Hall.
Woster, Michael B. (RC) AUXILIARY CHAPLAINS CONTRACT CHAPLAINS.
Woster, Michael '82 (RC) Rapid City, SD Cathedral of Our Lady of Perpetual Help; [D] Rapid City, SD Priest Retirement and Aid Association/Pension Plan Board.
Woster, Michael (RC) Deaneries.
Wotelko, Matthew S. *o.s.b.* '67 (NEW)[N] Newark, NJ Newark Abbey.
Woy, Richard W. (BAL) Chancellor; Advocates and Procurators; Ex Officio.
Woy, Richard '79 (BAL) Special Assignment; Consultors.
Woytek, Robert '91 (PSC) Leave of Absence.
Woytyna, Christopher *o.s.b.m.* '61 (STF) Long Island City, NY Holy Cross.
Wozniak, Aloysius A. '52 (LC) Retired.
Wozniak, Anthony '59 (GBG)[G] Greensburg, PA St. Anne Home.
Wozniak, Casimir J. '68 (E)[B] Erie, PA Gannon University; The Bishop's Theological Advisory Committee.
Wozniak, James E. '97 (GRY) Gary, IN St. Ann; Griffith, IN St. Mary.
Wozniak, Louis '51 (AUS) Retired.
Wozniak, Phillip '49 (CHI)[N] Libertyville, IL Marytown, Our Lady of Fatima Friary.
Wozniak, Robert A. '72 (WIL) Wilmington, DE Immaculate Heart of Mary.
Wozniak, Robert A. '88 (BUF) Tonawanda, NY St. Edmund.
Wozniak, Ronald E. *s.j.* '77 (BO)[V] Weston, MA Campion Jesuit Community; [V] Weston, MA Campion Health Center, Inc..
Wozniak, Tim '74 (STP) Burnsville, MN Church of the Risen Savior.
Woznicki, Don '02 (CHI) Northbrook, IL St. Norbert.
Wozniczka, Stephen Z. *o.s.p.p.e.* '60 (PH)[AA] Office.
Wozny, Jacek '87 (NY) Staten Island, NY St. Stanislaus Kostka.
Wraszczak, Chester '43 (P) Retired.
Wray, Joseph M. '96 (OM) Battle Creek, NE St. Patrick's.
Wrenn, Larry (WH) Monongah, WV Holy Spirit.
Wrenn, Lawrence G. '53 (HRT) Hartford, CT Cathedral of St. Joseph; Judges Retired.
Wrenn, Michael J. '61 (NY) Bronx, NY St. Margaret of Cortona.

Wright, Addison G. *s.s.* '60 (BAL)[S] Trumbull, CT Retired.
Wright, Arthur J. (BO) Milton, MA St. Mary of the Hills.
Wright, Bryan B. (SCR) Scouts of America.
Wright, Charles *o.s.b.* '70 (SD)[H] Oceanside, CA Prince of Peace Abbey, Benet Hill.
Wright, D. Ralph *o.s.b.* '70 (STL)[F] Creve Coeur, MO St. Louis Priory School; [O] St. Louis, MO The Abbey of St. Mary and St. Louis.
Wright, David F. *o.p.* '68 (CHI) Chicago, IL St. Basil/Visitation; [N] Chicago Dominicans (Provincial Office).
Wright, Edward S. '54 (RCK) North Aurora, IL Blessed Sacrament; Deans.
Wright, Francis W. *c.s.s.r.* '49 (HRT) Forestville, CT St. Matthew.
Wright, Frank Allen *s.m.a.* '93 (FgM).
Wright, Gary R. *s.j.* '80 (DET)[S] McNichols Campus; [K] Detroit, MI Jesuit Community at the University of Detroit Mercy.
Wright, Gerald *o.m.v.* '80 (BO)[V] Milton, MA Oblate Residence (St. Joseph House).
Wright, James B. '69 (DET) Farmington Hills, MI St. Alexander.
Wright, John A. '56 (CHY) Retired.
Wright, John A. '82 (MAN) Retired.
Wright, John H. *s.j.* '52 (OAK)[B] Spokane, WA Gonzaga University.
Wright, John J. '78 (CLV)[A] Garfield Heights, OH St. Timothy; [Z] Cleveland, OH The Greater Cleveland/ Akron Corporation United for Education; Catholic Cemeteries Association.
Wright, John M. '62 (IND) Retired.
Wright, Joseph R. *c.m.* '54 (PH).
Wright, Michael H. '95 (SEA)[AA] Castle Rock, WA St. Mary; Kelso, WA Immaculate Heart of Mary; Deans; Presbyteral Council.
Wright, Patrick J. '54 (SFD) Springfield, IL St. Agnes; Springfield Deanery.
Wright, Richard J. '45 (PH) Ardmore, PA St. Colman Retired.
Wright, Robert E. *o.m.i.* '74 (SAT)[C] Oblate School of Theology; [M] San Antonio, TX.
Wright, Robert *o.m.i.* '74 (SAT)[M] San Antonio, TX Joseph Gerard House.
Wright, Robert '85 (CC)[G] Robstown, TX Society of Our Lady of the Most Holy Trinity.
Wright, Rupert A. '56 (BUF) Williamsville, NY St. Gregory the Great.
Wright, Russell (VEN) Fort Myers Beach, FL Ascension.
Wright, Tennant C. *s.j.* '62 (SJ)[B] Santa Clara, CA Jesuit Community.
Wright, Thomas M. *s.m.a.* '92 (FgM).
Wright, Thomas W. *s.m.a.* '92 (NEW)[N] Tenafly, NJ Society of African Missions, Provincialate, S.M.A. Fathers.
Wright, Thomas '55 (RNO) Retired.
Wright, Vincent L. '57 (BUF) Retired.
Wright, Vincent '56 (BUF)[O] Lackawanna, NY Bishop Head Residence.
Wright, Warren J. *s.j.* '82 (SFR)[E] San Francisco, CA St. Ignatius College Preparatory (Coed); [N] San Francisco, CA Jesuit Community at St. Ignatius College Preparatory.
Wright, William A. '65 (PH) Drexel Hill, PA St. Bernadette.
Wrightson, Mark J. *o.s.f.s.* '86 (WIL)[B] Wilmington, DE Salesianum School.
Wrigley, Franklin '52 (OKL) Retired.
Wrigley, John Michael '03 (BIR) Birmingham, AL St. Francis Xavier; [A] Birmingham, AL John Carroll Catholic High School.
Wrobleski, Edward D. *c.s.p.* '62 (LA) Los Angeles, CA St. Paul the Apostle.
Wroblews, Sergius (FgM).
Wroblewski, Anthony *o.m.i.* '88 (DUL) Duluth, MN Holy Family.
Wroblewski, Brendan *o.f.m.* (GB) Pulaski, WI Assumption of the Blessed Virgin Mary.
Wroblewski, Edward D. *c.s.p.* '62 (NY)[EE] Jamaica Estates Paulist Fathers Generalate.
Wroblewski, Edward M. *m.m.* '52 (NY)[EE] Maryknoll Maryknoll Fathers and Brothers.
Wroblewski, John J. '92 (NY) Staten Island, NY St. Anthony.
Wroblewski, Lawrence J. *s.j.* '74 (ROC)[B] Rochester, NY McQuaid Jesuit High School.
Wroblewski, Marion *c.r.* '65 (CHI) Chicago, IL St. Stanislaus, Bishop and Martyr.
Wroblewski, Sergius *o.f.m.* '46 (GB).
Wroblewski, Tony *o.m.i.* (DUL)[I] Presbyteral Council.
Wroblicky, Theodore (STN) Stewardship and Development Office.
Wrona, Jacek (CHI) Chicago, IL St. Constance.
Wrozek, Timothy A. '88 (FTW) Fort Wayne, IN St. Joseph.
Wrozek, Timothy (FTW) Council of Priests; Diocesan Initiation Committee.
Wrynn, John F. *s.j.* '70 (NEW)[N] Jersey City, NJ Jesuits of Saint Peter's College, Inc..
Wrynn, John P. '70 (NEW)[B] Jersey City, NJ Jesuit Center.
Wtorek, Krzysztof '94 (CAM) Runnemede, NJ St. Teresa of the Infant Jesus.
Wtulich, John '72 (BRK) Floral Park, NY Our Lady of the Snows.
Wtyklo, Jacek S. '98 (MAR) Perkins, MI St. Joseph.
Wu, Stanley '60 (SFR) Retired.
Wu, Stanley '76 (SFR) San Francisco, CA St. Thomas the Apostle Retired.
Wudarski, Dariusz P. '96 (SPR) Westfield, MA St. Peter and St. Casimir.
Wuellner, George E. '54 (PEO) Retired.
Wuerth, James E. *m.s.f.* '71 (STL) St. Louis, MO St. Wenceslaus.
Wuest, George *s.j.* (SB) In Res.
Wueste, Andrew *o.m.i.* '54 (SAT)[K] San Antonio, TX Oblate Madonna Residence.
Wulinski, Stanley F. '80 (BRK) Released from Diocesan Assignment; Air Force Reserve Chaplains.
Wulsch, Michael A. '72 (CHI) Chicago, IL St. Monica; Deans.
Wummer, Robert P. '56 (WDC) Oxon Hill, MD St. Ignatius Retired.
Wunderlich, Dale P. '74 (STL) St. Louis, MO Epiphany of Our Lord; [U] St. Louis, MO Archdiocesan Stewardship Education Committee.
Wurm, Robert L. '60 (DET) Ferndale, MI St. James.
Wurm, William *o.s.b.* '79 (GBG)[H] Latrobe Saint Vincent Archabbey.
Wurst, Wayne H. '80 (CHI) Oak Forest, IL Oak Forest Hospital.
Wurth, Martin Philip *o.c.d.* '59 (SAT)[K] San Antonio, TX Padua Place.
Wurth, Mary Philip *o.c.d.* '59 (SAT) San Antonio, TX Basilica of The National Shrine of Our Lady of Mt. Carmel and St. Therese, Discalced Carmelite Fathe; [M] San Antonio, TX Discalced Carmelites (Prov. of St. Therese).
Wurth, Richard W. '99 (COV) Erlanger, KY Mary, Queen of Heaven; [B] Erlanger, KY St. Henry District High School.
Wurtz, Camillus *o.s.b.* '53 (KCK)[C] Atchison, KS Maur Hill – Mount Academy; [H] Atchison, KS St. Benedict's Abbey.
Wurtz, Robert C. '58 (BUF) Finance Council; Consultors, College of; [T] Lackawanna, NY Our Lady of Victory Homes of Charity; [J] Lackawanna, NY Baker Victory Services; Lackawanna, NY Basilica of Our Lady of Victory.
Wurz, George E. '60 (SY) Oswego, NY St. Peter.
Wurzel, Richard T. '59 (TOL) Sylvania, OH St. Joseph; Judges.
Wutscheck, John '61 (MIL) West Bend, WI Holy Angels.
Wyczawski, Stanley '73 (DET) Port Huron, MI St. Mary.
Wydeven, John L. '79 (OAK) Military Chaplains; Army Chaplains.
Wyen, Larry *c.pp.s.* '69 (CIN) St. Henry, OH St. Henry.
Wyffels, Robert J. '60 (NU) Morgan, MN St. Michael; College of Consultors; Priests' Council.
Wykes, John *o.m.v.* '98 (SFD) Alton, IL St. Mary's; [I] Alton, IL Saint Anthony's Health Center; [O] Alton, IL Saint Anthony's Health System; [O] Alton, IL Saint Clare's Hospital.
Wymelenberg, M. John *s.j.* '60 (OM)[K] Omaha, NE Jesuit Community at Creighton University.
Wymes, John F. *m.m.* '54 (RVC) Malverne, NY Our Lady of Lourdes.
Wymes, John F. *m.m.* '54 (NY).
Wynants, Paul G. *c.i.c.m.* '51 (ARL)[N] Vienna, VA Mount Tabor Society, Inc..
Wyndaele, William *c.i.c.m.* '59 (ARL)[J] Arlington, VA Missionhurst, C.I.C.M.–Central House and Provincialate.
Wyndham, Thomas F. '69 (BO) Weymouth, MA St. Jerome.
Wynne, James *o.m.i.* '55 (BEL)[F] Belleville, IL Missionary Oblates of Mary Immaculate – St. Henry's Oblate Residence.
Wynne, Robert F. *m.m.* '68 (HON) Kamuela, HI Church of the Annunciation; [G] Kamuela, HI.
Wynne, Robert (HON) Diocesan Planning and Building Commission.
Wynne, William J. *o.s.a.* '44 (BO)[C] Our Mother of Good Counsel Monastery.
Wynnycky, John '92 (DET) Grosse Pointe Farms, MI St. Paul Catholic Church.
Wypych, Andrew P. '79 (CHI) Chicago, IL St. Francis Borgia.
Wyrostek, Andrzej '01 (RC) Timber Lake, SD Holy Cross.
Wyrowinski, Zdzislaw (CHI) Chicago, IL St. Richard.
Wyrsch, Thomas W. '78 (STL) St. Louis, MO Resurrection of Our Lord; [U] St. Louis, MO Archdiocesan Stewardship Education Committee.
Wyse, James B. '87 (GR) Muskegon, MI St. Mary's; Muskegon, MI St. Jean Baptiste.
Wyse, James '87 (GR) Muskegon, MI St. Michael's; Muskegon Heights, MI Sacred Heart; On Special Assignment; Deans.
Wysochansky, Constantine *o.s.b.m.* '62 (STN) Hamtramck, MI Immaculate Conception of B.V.M..
Wysochansky, Demetrius *o.s.b.m.* '59 (STN) Palos Park, IL Nativity of B.V.M.; Eparchial Censor.
Wysochansky, John '57 (PHU) St. Clair, PA St. Nicholas; St. Clair, PA Holy Trinity.
Wysochansky, Walter '64 (SJP) Ambridge, PA Ss. Peter and Paul.
Wysochansky, Walter (SJP) Presbyteral Council.
Wysochansky, Walter (SJP) Diocesan Personnel Board.
Wysocki, James R. '67 (DET) Harsen's Island, MI St. Mark.
Wysocki, Joseph A. '71 (SCR) On Duty Outside the Diocese.
Wysocki, Marek '85 (NEW) Lyndhurst, NJ Sacred Heart.
Wysocki, Paul '64 (CLV) Retired.
Wysong, William H. '72 (CIN)[J] Cincinnati, OH St. Rita School for the Deaf; Defenders of the Bond.
Wyszynski, Darius W. '58 (LAN) Jackson, MI St. Stanislaus Kostka.
Wytrwal, Alexander J. '50 (DET) New Boston, MI St. Stephen.
Wyvill, Christopher *o.s.b.* '65 (WDC)[M] Washington, DC St. Anselm's Abbey.
Wyzykiewicz, Richard S. *sch.p.* '71 (PH)[G] Devon, PA Devon Preparatory School; [AA] Devon Piarist Fathers (Order of the Pious Schools).

X

Xavier, Alverez '73 (AMA) On Duty Outside the Diocese.
Xavier, Antony '60 (RVC) Manhasset, NY North Shore Univ. Hospital.
Xavier, Francis '41 (WOR)[O] Still River, MA Benedictine Monks, St. Benedict Abbey.
Xavier, Godwin '85 (SAC) North San Juan, CA Immaculate Conception.
Xavier, Lawrence '79 (NY) Rhinebeck, NY The Good Shepherd.
Xu, Jing Shan '93 (NY) Marlboro, NY St. Mary.
Xuereb, Paul '45 (DET) Retired.
Xuereb, Publius '68 (FWT) The Colony, TX Holy Cross.

Y

Yabao, William '68 (NEW) Jersey City, NJ Our Lady of Victories.
Yabes, Arthur *s.v.d.* '87 (SJ) San Jose, CA St. Francis of Assisi.
Yablonsky, Gabriel '59 (Y) Retired.
Yackanich, Eugene P. '65 (PBR) Munhall, PA St. Elias; Protopresbyters; Elected Deanery Representatives.
Yacobi, Francis *o.f.m.cap.* '90 (WDC)[B] Washington, DC St. Francis Friary–Capuchin College.
Yacyshyn, Gregory '98 (RVC) Bay Shore, NY St. Patrick's.
Yadron, Michael J. '83 (GRY) Munster, IN St. Thomas More; Bishop's Council of Priests; Diaconate.
Yadron, Raymond A. '63 (CHI) Palatine, IL St. Thomas of Villanova.
Yaeger, Joseph J. '89 (R) Garner, NC St. Mary, Mother of the Church.
Yagesh, Richard C. '78 (PIT) Military Chaplains; Navy Chaplains.
Yaghi, Milad T. *m.l.m.* '88 (OLL) Houston, TX Our Lady of the Cedars Maronite Mission; [A] Houston, TX The Congregation of Maronite Lebanese Missionaries.
Yahner, Gordon A. '63 (CLV) Fairlawn, OH St. Hilary.
Yakaitis, Michael T. '78 (CHI)[V] Chicago, IL University of Chicago Calvert House.
Yaksick, Michael L. '94 (PIT) Ellwood City, PA Holy Redeemer Parish.
Yali, Jacob '77 (STP) Clearwater, MN St. Luke.
Yallaly, Jules G. *c.m.* '36 (STL)[O] St. Louis, MO Lazarist Residence.
Yamada, John *ss.cc.* '71 (FR).
Yanas, John '84 (ALB)[H] Frankfort, NY Our Lady Queen of Apostles; Presbyteral Council; Diocesan Board of Consultors.
Yander, Steven L. '74 (ATL)[I] Atlanta, GA Saint Joseph's Hospital of Atlanta, Inc..
Yandrisevits, Philip *m.s.c.* '42 (ALN)[A] Center Valley, PA Sacred Heart Villa, Missionaries of the Sacred Heart.
Yanez, Aurelio '74 (NEW) Elizabeth, NJ Immaculate Conception.
Yanez, Horacio '75 (SEA) Marysville, WA St. Mary.
Yanez, Jose *c.m.* '56 (SJN) San Juan, PR Sagrado Corazon de Jesus; [B] San Juan, PR Colegio Sagrado Corazon de Jesus.
Yanez, Omar '96 (MGZ) Hormigueros, PR El Salvador.
Yang, Daniel Hee–Moon (MIA) Korean.
Yang, Paul Hyeong–Kwon '95 (SJ) Sunnyvale, CA Sts. Andrew and Paul Korean Catholic Mission of San Jose.
Yangas, Peter M. '64 (CHI) Chicago, IL St. Eugene Retired.
Yaniak, Frank J. '49 (MIL) Retired.

Yanju, Henry M. '96 (BO) Marshfield, MA St. Christine.
Yankauskas, Albin J. '51 (WOR) Retired.
Yankevitch, Robert J. *s.j.* '69 (R) Lumberton, NC St. Francis De Sales; [E] Raleigh Jesuit Community.
Yannarell, James J. *s.j.* '71 (NY)[EE] New York, NY Jesuit Provincial's Office; [EE] New York, NY Xavier Jesuit Community.
Yanos, Richard M. '83 (CHI) Lake Villa, IL Prince of Peace.
Yanovski, Stepan '90 (STF) Bridgeport, CT Protection of B.V.M..
Yanowski, Stephen (STF) Sodalities, B.V.M..
Yanus, Gary D. '81 (CLV) Cleveland, OH St. Ignatius of Antioch; Cleveland, OH St. Procop; Judicial Vicar.
Yanus, Gary D. (Y) Judges.
Yaoch, Felix K. *s.j.* '67 (CI) Manresa Jesuit Novitiate; [C] Manresa Jesuit House.
Yarbrough, Michael H. '80 (SAT) San Antonio, TX St. Matthew's.
Yarbrough, Michael (SAT) College of Consultors; In Metropolitan Area; Archdiocesan Presbyteral Council.
Yarce, Eugenio '92 (SLC) Salt Lake City, UT Sacred Heart.
Yardemian, Dadjad *o.mech.* '71 (ARM) Glendale, CA Mekhitarian Educational Foundation.
Yargeau, Ronald G. '73 (SPR) Greenfield, MA Holy Trinity; Vicars for the Clergy; Bishop's Commission for Clergy.
Yarno, Kenneth *c.s.v.* '59 (JOL) Bourbonnais, IL St. George.
Yarnovitz, Robert '57 (PRM) Retired.
Yaro, James '92 (BRK) Brooklyn, NY St. Teresa of Avila.
Yaroch, Kenneth '67 (SAG) Caseville, MI St. Roch; Kinde, MI St. Felix.
Yaroch, Paul *o.f.m.cap.* '64 (MIL)[O] Mount Calvary, WI St. Lawrence Friary.
Yarrish, Bernard E. '76 (SCR) Presbyteral Council; Continuing Education of Priests; [A] Dalton, PA Saint Pius X Seminary.
Yarrosh, Ronald J. '74 (ALN) Schuylkill Haven, PA St. Ambrose.
Yasso, Jacob O. '60 (EST) Detroit, MI Sacred Heart Chaldean Parish.
Yasso, Jacob O. '60 (DET) Detroit, MI Sacred Heart–Chaldean Parish.
Yasso, Jacob (EST) Eparchial College of Consultors.
Yast, Robert A. '56 (FTW) Mishawaka, IN St. Joseph.
Yast, Robert (FTW) South Bend Office.
Yastishock, Charles '77 (PSC) Toms River, NJ Our Lady of Perpetual Help.
Yaszcz, Thomas A. '75 (SCR) On Special or Other Diocesan Assignment.
Yates, John L. *c.s.sp.* '54 (LR) Center Ridge, AR St. Joseph's.
Yates, Simeon *o.f.m.conv.* '63 (IND)[J] Mount St. Francis, IN Mount Saint Francis Friary and Retreat Center.
Yatkauskas, Matthew '89 (NY) New York, NY St. Joseph.
Yavarone, Mark *o.m.v.* (MET).
Yaya, Louis '79 (NY)[B] Kingston, NY Benedictine Hospital.
Ybanez, William G. '93 (AGN) Yigo, GU Our Lady of Lourdes.
Ybarra, Manuel *o.f.m.* '86 (WDC)[M] Washington, DC Commissariat of the Holy Land, Franciscan Monastery – Mount St. Sepulchre.
Yeager, Robert J. '62 (TOL) Special Assignment; [N] Waterville, OH Diocesan Fiscal Management Conference – National Office; Faith in the Future Program.
Yeaglin, Armand *o.f.m.cap* '38 (PIT)[N] Pittsburgh, PA St. Augustine Friary.
Yeakel, James R. *o.s.f.s.* '77 (WDC)[B] Washington, DC Deshairs Community–Oblates of St. Francis de Sales Residence.
Yeazel, J. Robert '67 (SY) Dewitt, NY Holy Cross; Finance Committee.
Yeboah, Paul (NY) Brewster, NY St. Lawrence O'Toole.
Yebra, Bernardino S. '88 (CHR) Cheraw, SC St. Peter's.
Yeddanapalli, Irudayayaraj '62 (OKL) Elgin, OK St. Ann.
Yee Mon, Ronald '85 (FAR) Towner, ND Our Lady of Perpetual Help; Towner, ND St. Cecilia.
Yehl, Addison *m.s.* '51 (E)[B] Erie, PA Gannon University.
Yelenc, Joseph *t.o.r.* '71 (STU)[A] Steubenville, OH Franciscan University of Steubenville; [F] Steubenville, OH Holy Spirit Friary.
Yelinko, Flavian G. *o.s.b.* '33 (GBG)[H] Latrobe, PA Saint Vincent Archabbey.
Yelle, Ronald R. '79 (HRT) Granby, CT St. Therese's.
ye Myint, Sixtus '78 (WCH) Moline, KS Sacred Heart; Moline, KS St. Mary's; Moline, KS St. Robert Bellarmine.
Yender, Basil *o.s.b.* '71 (RCK)[G] Aurora, IL Marmion Abbey.
Yenkevich, Daniel J. '90 (SCR) Kingston, PA St. Mary's Annunciation.
Yennock, Eugene M. '50 (SY) Syracuse, NY St. Daniel.
Yenushosky, Daniel J. '77 (ALN) Bath, PA Sacred Heart.
Yeo, Augustine Hyeok–Ku '96 (GAL) Houston, TX St. Andrew Kim.
Yeo, Wilfred '58 (NEW) Retired.
Yepes, Walter '01 (CHI) Chicago, IL St. Adalbert.
Yeruva, Chinnappareddy (Paul) '77 (KAL) St. Joseph, MI St. Joseph.
Yesalonia, Dennis J. *s.j.* '85 (WOR)[O] Worcester, MA Jesuits of Holy Cross College, Inc..
Yesalonia, Dennis J. '85 (BO)[V] Watertown, MA The Society of Jesus of New England–Provincial Offices.
Yetsko, Robert K. *t.o.r.* '84 (PBR) Punxsutawney, PA SS. Peter and Paul.
Yetter, Robert M. '73 (BUF) Swormville, NY St. Mary.
Yevenes, Larry (BAL)[S] Baltimore, MD Ferdinand Wheeler Jesuit Community.
Yi, Odilo *o.s.b.* '85 (PAT)[M] Newton, NJ St. Paul's Abbey.
Yiengst, George B. '62 (BUF) Judges; Getzville, NY St. Pius X.
Yiftheg, Cuthbert '89 (CI) Our Lady of Mercy.
Yim, Louis H. '57 (HON) Retired.
Ying, Vang Chue (STP) Special Assignment.
Yncierto, Frank '75 (LAV) Laughlin, NV St. John the Baptist Catholic Mission.
Yoakam, Lee R. *o.s.b.* '01 (GBG)[H] Latrobe, PA Saint Vincent Archabbey; Army Chaplains.
Yocis, David A. '87 (BGP) Leave of Absence.
Yock, Peter *o.s.b.* '95 (IND)[K] St. Meinrad, IN St. Meinrad Archabbey.
Yockey, Aelred *o.s.b.* '93 (P)[K] Mount Angel, OR Providence Benedictine Nursing Center; [L] St. Benedict, OR Mt. Angel Abbey.
Yockey, John G. '70 (MIL) Oconomowoc, WI St. Jerome.
Yogus, Ronald B. '75 (ALT) Portage, PA St. John the Baptist; Cresson, PA State Correctional Institution.
Yohe, Robert A. '89 (HBG) Shippensburg, PA Our Lady of the Visitation; [J] Shippensburg, PA Shippensburg University; Deans; Presbyteral Council.
Yohe, Robert (HBG) Consultors, College.
Yong–Hwan Oh, Gabriel (TR) Eatontown NJ Immaculate Conception.
Yonkovig, John R. '77 (OG) Plattsburgh, NY St. Peter; Defenders of the Bond.
Yontz, George W. '59 (STU) Steubenville, OH St. Peter's; Steubenville, OH St. Stanislaus; Deans.
Yontz, William C. '50 (STU) Byesville, OH Holy Trinity.
Yore, Lambert *o.carm.* '45 (WDC)[B] Washington, DC Whitefriars Hall.
Yori, Robert O. '61 (CAM) Retired.
York, Edward '47 (WCH) Retired.
York, Kenneth J. '88 (BEL) East St. Louis, IL Immaculate Conception; Fayetteville, IL St. Pancratius; Smithton, IL St. John the Baptist; Chancellor; Holy Childhood Association; Propagation of the Faith; [J] Freeburg, IL Catholic War Veterans.
York, Patrick G. '90 (WCH) Wichita, KS St. Peter the Apostle.
York, Paul '64 (LIN) Ashland, NE St. Mary's.
York, Richard R. '73 (PH) On Duty Outside the Archdiocese.
York, Richard '73 (PH) Palmetto, FL Holy Cross.
York, Vincent P. '68 (ALN) Fountain Hill, PA St. Ursula.
Yossa, Kenneth F. '88 (ROM) Unassigned.
Yost, Charles *s.c.j.* '58 (JKS)[F] Nesbit, MS St. Michael Community House; [J] Walls, MS Sacred Heart League.
Yost, Herbert C. *c.s.c.* '75 (FTW)[I] Notre Dame, IN Holy Cross Association.
Yost, Herbert *c.s.c.* '75 (FTW)[A] Notre Dame, IN Moreau Seminary.
Yost, Richard J. *o.s.f.s.* '76 (DET)[Q] Warren, MI St. John's Deaf Center.
Youness, Jihad *o.m.m.* '01 (OLL)[A] Ann Arbor, MI Maronite Order of Blessed Virgin Mary.
Young, Anthony J. '44 (MAD) Fitchburg, WI Retired.
Young, Bernard L. '63 (NO) Retired.
Young, Bill (GAL) Western Vicariate.
Young, Christopher '99 (FTW)[C] South Bend, IN Saint Joseph's High School; Council of Priests; South Bend, IN Holy Family.
Young, Clyde *o.f.m.* '54 (CIN)[C] Cincinnati, OH St. Anthony Shrine, Francisan Candidacy.
Young, Daniel A. '95 (BUF) Ripley, NY St. Thomas More; Westfield, NY St. James Major.
Young, David E. '95 (COL) West Portsmouth, OH Our Lady of Lourdes; West Portsmouth, OH Our Lady of Sorrows; Priests' Senate; Diocesan Judges.
Young, David H. '02 (SEA) Sumner, WA St. Andrew.
Young, David '72 (MI) Special Assignment Retired.
Young, Dennis M. '80 (STA) Special Assignment.
Young, DeSales *o.f.m.cap.* '48 (PIT)[N Pittsburgh, PA St. Augustine Friary.
Young, Dismas *o.f.m.cap.* '66 (WH) Charleston, WV St. Anthony; [M] Charleston, WV Capuchins–St. Anthony Friary.
Young, Dominic '79 (LFT) Carmel, IN Our Lady of Mount Carmel.
Young, Edward P. '83 (STF) Ludlow, MA SS. Peter and Paul; South Deerfield, MA Holy Ghost.
Young, Edward (STF) Censors.
Young, Edward (STF) Ecumenical Commission.
Young, Eugene '86 (PHX) On Leave.
Young, Francis '70 (SY)[Q] Syracuse, NY Tommy Coyne Residence @ Dillon Hall.
Young, Gary *c.r.* '76 (L)[L] Nazareth, KY Generalate, Motherhouse and Novitiate of the Sisters of Charity of Nazareth.
Young, Gary *c.r.* '76 (L) Lebanon, KY St. Charles.
Young, Gerald A. '72 (LA) On Duty Outside the Archdiocese.
Young, Gerald A. '72 (DEN) Wray, CO St. Andrew.
Young, Gerard F. '63 (BR) Baton Rouge, LA St. Joseph Cathedral; College of Consultors.
Young, James E. '74 (TYL) Nacogdoches, TX Sacred Heart; Chancellor; Archivist; College of Consultors; Deans; Diocesan Finance Council; Priests' Pension Board; Priests' Personnel Board; Presbyteral Council; Office of Clergy Development/Continuing Education.
Young, James E. (TYL) Diocesan Pastoral Team – DPT.
Young, James G. '69 (PIT) Carnegie, PA St. Elizabeth Ann Seton.
Young, James G. (PIT) Secretary for Ministerial Leadership; Priest Council; Clergy Personnel Board; Chaplain Services, Office for.
Young, Jerome *o.s.b.* '86 (P)[A] St. Benedict, OR Mount Angel Seminary; [L] St. Benedict, OR Mt. Angel Abbey.
Young, John E. '57 (KAL) South Haven, MI St. Basil.
Young, John E. *s.c.j.* '74 (JKS) Holly Springs, MS St. Joseph.
Young, John L. *c.s.c.* '71 (BGP)[P] Middletown, CT Whiting Forensic Institute.
Young, John L. *c.s.c.* '74 (HRT)[M] New Haven, CT Priests of the Congregation of Holy Cross.
Young, John '47 (LA) Retired.
Young, John *s.c.j.* '74 (JKS) Olive Branch, MS Queen of Peace.
Young, Larry E. '81 (OAK) Rodeo, CA St. Patrick's; Pastoral Leadership Placement Board (PLPB).
Young, Lawrence A. '03 (WDC) Laurel, MD St. Mary.
Young, Otis W. '01 (NO) Metairie, LA St. Louis King of France.
Young, Peter G. '47 (PRO) North Providence, RI St. Lawrence Retired.
Young, Peter G. '59 (ALB) Bolton Landing, NY Blessed Sacrament.
Young, Richard K. '95 (ATL) On Duty Outside the Archdiocese.
Young, Richard (SAV) Apostleship of the Sea.
Young, Robert J. '53 (BRK)[V] Douglaston, NY Bishop Mugavero Residence Retired.
Young, Robert '94 (SP) On Duty Outside the Diocese.
Young, Ronald E. '75 (DAV) On Duty Outside the Diocese.
Young, Ronald W. *o.m.i.* '88 (SAT)[C] Oblate School of Theology; [M] San Antonio, TX De Mazenod House.
Young, Samuel V. '90 (BAL) Aberdeen, MD St. Joan of Arc.
Young, Terry W. (ATL) McDonough, GA St. James The Apostle.
Young, Terry (ATL) Deans.
Young, Valentine *o.f.m.cap.* '49 (STL) St. Louis, MO The Shrine of St. Joseph, Capuchin Fathers; St. Louis, MO St. Patrick; [O] St. Louis, MO St. Patrick Friary; [U] St. Louis, MO Catholic Information Center; Catholic Information Center.
Young, Valentine *o.f.m.* '56 (SCR)[M] Mableton, GA.
Young, Valentine *o.f.m.* '56 (RC) Rapid City, SD Cathedral of Our Lady of Perpetual Help.
Young, Vincent J. '78 (SCR) Unassigned or Leave of Absence.
Young, William J. *c.s.b.* '51 (GAL)[Q] Houston, TX Residence of the Basilian Fathers of the University of St. Thomas.
Young, William L. '70 (GAL) Houston, TX St. Thomas More; Boy and Girl Scouts.
Young, William T. *s.s.s.* '64 (CLV)[O] Cleveland, OH Blessed Sacrament Community.
Young, William W. '76 (SFR) San Francisco, CA Most Holy Redeemer.
Young, William *s.s.s.* '64 (CLV) Cleveland Clinic Foundation.
Young, William '90 (NY) Pine Bush, NY The Infant Saviour.
Young–Re, Joachim Ha (PH) Springfield, PA Holy Cross.
Youngs, Fred A. (BR) Board Members; Separated and Divorced.
Youngs, Fred '90 (BR) Baton Rouge, LA St. Isidore the Farmer.
Youssef, Youssef A. *b.s.o.* '86 (NTN) Brooklyn, OH St. Elias.
Youssef, Youssef *b.s.o.* (NTN) Presbyteral Council; Diocese of Newton for the Melkites in the USA, Inc., a Massachusetts Corporation.
Youtz, Richard A. '66 (HBG) Lancaster, PA St. John Neumann; Diocesan Judges; Lancaster, PA St. Anne.
Yrrarrazaval, Diego J. *c.s.c.* '84 (FTW)[I] Instituto de

Estudios Aymaras.
Yrlas, Raymond (CC) Propagation of the Faith Office.
Yrlas, Raynaldo '97 (CC) Alice, TX Our Lady of Guadalupe.
Yslas, Martin *o.s.b.* '87 (LA)[Q] Valyermo, CA St. Andrew's Abbey.
Ytsen, Robert *s.j.* (CHI)[D] Wilmette, IL Loyola Academy.
Yu, Celso A. '92 (AUS) Bremond, TX St. Mary's; [G] Bremond, TX Clerical Congregation Missionaries of Faith; [G] Bremond, TX Missionaries of Faith, M.F..
Yu, Chang Son *s.j.* '02 (CHI)[C] Chicago, IL Jesuit Community at Loyola University Chicago.
Yu, In–Chang '56 (PH) Philadelphia, PA Holy Angels.
Yu, Reynaldo '83 (SEA) Forks, WA St. Anne Parish; Callum Bay Correction Center; Clearwater / Olympic Correction Center; Port Angeles, WA Queen of Angels.
Yudin, Raynald *o.f.m.conv.* '62 (TR) Trenton, NJ Immaculate Conception.
Yuen, Thomas '58 (SCR) Scranton, PA St. Lucy's.
Yuenger, Paul D. (WH) Fort Ashby, WV Annunciation of Our Lord; Fort Ashby, WV St. Anthony.
Yuhas, Edward L. '97 (PIT)[A] Pittsburgh, PA Saint Paul Seminary; St. Paul Seminary; Worship Commission; Worship, Dept. for.
Yuhaus, Cassian J. *c.p.* '51 (SCR)[R] Scranton, PA Ministry for Religious Research and Consultancy; Presbyteral Council.
Yuhaus, Cassian *c.p.* '51 (SCR)[M] Clarks Summit, PA St. Gabriel's Convent.
Yulfo, Nestor '93 (SJN) Carolina, PR San Andres.
Yulfo–Hoffman, Nestor (SJN) Carolina.
Yuliantoro, Antionius Eko *s.v.d.* '94 (WDC)[M] Washington, DC Divine Word College.
Yunk, Michael J. '57 (BUF) Retired.
Yurchak, Thomas D. '76 (P) Canby, OR St. Patrick.
Yurco, Roy *ss.cc.* '62 (FR)[H] Fairhaven, MA Our Lady's Haven.
Yurgel, Robert *o.f.m.cap.* '96 (NY)[EE] New York, NY Immaculate Conception Friary.
Yurista, Michael '67 (PSC) Bayonne, NJ St. John the Baptist.
Yurkovic, Dale E. '91 (GF) Livingston, MT St. Mary's; Director of Vocations.
Yurochko, Dennis P. (PIT) Graduate Studies; Bishop's Office; Bishop, Office of the Diocesan; Worship, Dept. for.

Z

Zabala, Antonio *o.a.r.* '95 (LA) Oxnard, CA Mary Star of the Sea.
Zabala, Dionisio '84 (CHI) Cicero, IL St. Anthony.
Zabala, Efrain '67 (CGS) Caguas, PR Santisima Trinidad.
Zabala, Efrain (SJN) "El Visitante".
Zabala, Francis *o.m.i.* '93 (CHI)[N] Chicago, IL The Oblate House of Theology.
Zabala, Luis *o.f.m.* '43 (SJN) San Juan, PR Resurreccion del Senor.
Zabala, Wilmar '03 (YAK) Richland, WA Christ the King.
Zaballa, Pedro Luis '57 (SJN) San Juan, PR Nuestra Senora de la Caridad del Cobre; [E] San Juan, PR Centro Medico de P.R..
Zabarian, Georges (ARM) Vicar General.
Zabelskas, John A. '56 (GAL) Highlands, TX St. Jude Thaddeus; Northern Vicariate.
Zabler, Charles G. '77 (MIL) West Allis, WI West Allis Memorial Hospital; Special Assignment.
Zablotskyy, Volodymyr '99 (PSC) East Brunswick, NJ Nativity of Our Lord.
Zablotskyy, Volodymyr (PSC) Auditors; Notaries.
Zaborowski, Edward *m.s.f.* '63 (SAT)[K] San Antonio, TX Padua Place.
Zaborowski, Paul *o.f.m.cap.* '97 (WDC) Washington, DC Shrine of the Sacred Heart.
Zabrocki, Patrick R. '88 (GF) Great Falls, MT St. Joseph's; Great Falls, MT St. Luke the Evangelist; [K] Great Falls, MT St. Joseph's Education Trust.
Zabrocki, Patrick (GF) Clerical Benefit Association.
Zabrocki, Stephen J. '89 (GF) Wolf Point, MT Immaculate Conception.
Zabrocki, Stephen (GF) Vicars Forane; Clerical Benefit Association; Liturgical Commission; Priests' Council.
Zaccagnigno, Raffaele '68 (BRK) Retired.
Zaccagnini, Kenneth G. '82 (GBG) Uniontown, PA St. Therese, the Little Flower of Jesus; Deaneries; College of Consultors; Bishop's Priests Council.
Zaccardo, Peter J. '64 (NEW) Nutley, NJ Holy Family; Members.
Zaccone, Paul C. '87 (OM) Absent on Leave.
Zaccone, Paul *ss.cc.* '87 (HON)[G] Kaneohe, HI Sacred Hearts Center.
Zach, Charles E. '73 (P) Junction City, OR St. Helen; Monroe, OR St. Rose.
Zach, Kenneth M. '81 (RVC) Riverhead, NY St. Isidore's.
Zach, Kenneth (RVC) Procurator & Advocates.
Zach, Placidus *o.s.b.* '56 (P)[L] St. Benedict, OR Mt. Angel Abbey.
Zachariadis, Nicholas '86 (VNN)[A] Newberry Springs, CA Holy Resurrection Monastery.
Zachariah, Kurian '85 (ALX) Dupont, LA Immaculate Conception.
Zacharias, Michael J. '02 (TOL) Mansfield, OH St. Peter.
Zacheis, Dennis B. '75 (STL) Wildwood, MO St. Alban Roe.
Zachman, Charles *o.m.i.* '48 (BEL)[F] Belleville, IL Missionary Oblates of Mary Immaculate – St. Henry's Oblate Residence.
Zacker, Mark (COS) Monument, CO St. Peter.
Zadora, Boleslaw *s.d.s.* '74 (SAT) St. Hedwig, TX Annunciation of the Blessed Virgin Mary.
Zadora, Charles J. '67 (BUF) Fredonia, NY St. Joseph.
Zadroga, Clinton P. '01 (PIT) Pittsburgh, PA St. Sebastian.
Zafe, Peter V. '64 (TOL) Toledo, OH St. Agnes; Philippine–American Catholic Council (P.A.C.C.).
Zagar, Janko *o.p.* '48 (OAK)[N] Oakland, CA Dominican Order (Western Province), St. Albert's Priory.
Zagarella, John C. *o.praem.* '86 (PH)[AA] Paoli, PA Daylesford Abbey.
Zagone, Frederick P. *s.j.* '93 (MIL)[O] Milwaukee, WI Jesuit Community at Marquette University.
Zagorc, Francis D. *c.s.c.* '58 (FTW)[I] Grand Canyon, AZ El Cristo Rey Catholic Chapel; Grand Canyon, AZ El Cristo Rey.
Zagorski, Jan '02 (MOB) Atmore, AL St. Robert Bellarmine.
Zagst, Bernard L. '61 (ALX) Retired.
Zahler, Paul J. *o.s.b.* '62 (OKL)[I] Shawnee St. Gregory's Abbey; [L] Shawnee, OK National Institute on Development Delays, Inc..
Zahn, George E. '68 (RIC) Richmond, VA St. Paul; Cemeteries.
Zahn, John '72 (LFT) Noblesville, IN Our Lady of Grace.
Zahner, William '45 (L) Retired.
Zaiats, Volodymyr '73 (STN) Milwaukee, WI St. Michaels.
Zaidan, Abdallah E. *m.l.m.* '86 (OLL) Los Angeles, CA Our Lady of Mt. Lebanon–St. Peter Cathedral; [A] Houston, TX The Congregation of Maronite Lebanese Missionaries; Procurator/Advocate.
Zaidan, Abdallah (OLL) College of Consultors; Commission for Lebanon; Presbyteral Council; Protopresbyters.
Zajac, Richard E. '76 (BUF) Clergy Personnel Board; Ecumenism; Council of Priests; [K] Buffalo, NY Sisters of Charity Hospital of Buffalo, NY.
Zajdel, Bernard *o.f.m.conv.* '64 (STP) Bloomington, MN St. Bonaventure.
Zak, Casimir A. '45 (BUF)[O] Tonawanda, NY O'Hara Residence Retired.
Zak, Daniel J. '67 (TOL) Swanton, OH St. Richard.
Zak, Stan '75 (OAK) Danville, CA St. Isidore's.
Zak, Steven '88 (LA) On Duty Outside the Archdiocese.
Zak, Timothy *s.d.b.* '91 (NY) Port Chester, NY Our Lady of the Rosary.
Zakarauskas, Anthony J. '41 (CHI) Retired.
Zake, Louis J. '60 (CHI)[A] Chicago, IL Archbishop Quigley Preparatory Seminary; Chicago, IL St. Ann.
Zakens, Michael W. '45 (ALB) Schenectady, NY St. Mary Retired.
Zakowicz, Giles *o.f.m.conv.* '75 (BAL)[S] St. Francis of Assisi Friary; (FgM).
Zakshesky, Francis '81 (TYL) Absent on Sick Leave Retired.
Zalacca, Joseph A. '03 (BUF) Kenmore, NY St. John the Baptist.
Zalecki, Dennis M. '76 (CHI) Rolling Meadows, IL St. Colette.
Zalecki, Marian *o.s.p.p.e.* '62 (PH)[AA] Office.
Zalenski, Gary '77 (STU) Neffs, OH Sacred Heart.
Zaleski, Daniel '80 (DET) Dearborn Heights, MI St. Albert the Great.
Zaleswki, Peter L. '97 (PT) Panama City, FL St. Dominic.
Zalewski, Francis '78 (TR) Trenton, NJ SS. Peter and Paul; Trenton, NJ St. Stephen.
Zalewski, Peter Lawrence (PT) Air Force Reserve Chaplains.
Zalewski, Thomas *o.carm.* '79 (PMB)[B] Boca Raton, FL Pope John Paul II High School; [J] Boca Raton, FL St. Elias Priory–Order of Carmelites, NY.
Zaloga, Daniel S. '67 (MAR) Iron Mountain, MI St. Mary and St. Joseph.
Zalonis, Jerome A. *m.i.c.* '59 (JOL) Plano, IL St. Mary.
Zalonis, Jerome A. *m.i.c.* '59 (CHI)[N] Chicago, IL Congregation of Marian Fathers of the Immaculate Conception.
Zalonis, Jerome *m.i.c.* '45 (JOL) Yorkville, IL St. Patrick.
Zamarano, Richard (ELP) Absent on Leave.
Zamarripa, Jesus *s.v.d.* (OAK) Oakland, CA St. Bernard's.
Zamary, Joseph '01 (Y) Canton, OH St. Michael the Archangel.
Zamborsky, Bill '74 (ORL) Mims, FL Holy Spirit.
Zamborsky, Leonard J. '76 (CLV) Cleveland Heights, OH St. Louis.
Zammit, Francis X. '66 (ORL) Retired.
Zammit, Joseph J. '56 (NY) New York, NY St. Peter; New York Police Department; U.S.V.A. Medical Center.
Zamora, Marcos *c.s.p.* '90 (NY) New York, NY Good Shepherd.
Zamorski, Robert J. '72 (MET) Fords, NJ Our Lady of Peace; Episcopal Vicars; Episcopal Council.
Zampelli, Michael A. *s.j.* '93 (SJ)[B] Santa Clara, CA Jesuit Community.
Zampino, Ignatius *o.f.m.cap.* '61 (CHL) Charlotte, NC St. Thomas Aquinas; Diocesan Consultors.
Zanatta, Albert *c.r.s.* '74 (GAL) Houston, TX Assumption.
Zanatta, Remo *c.r.s.* '98 (MAN)[H] Allenstown, NH Pine Haven Boys Center.
Zanavich, Albert J. '41 (HRT) Ansonia, CT Assumption Retired.
Zancan, Robert D. '82 (BUF) Retired.
Zandri, William A. '84 (RC) Lead, SD St. Patrick's.
Zandri, William (RC) Deaneries.
Zandy, Edward J. '70 (SY) Endicott, NY Our Lady of Good Counsel.
Zanett, Unbert *o.f.m.* '55 (SD)[H] Oceanside, CA Mission San Luis Rey.
Zang, Richard P. *c.s.c.* '69 (FTW)[I] Grand Canyon, AZ El Cristo Rey Catholic Chapel.
Zangrando, Mark *s.j.* '00 (LA)[C] Los Angeles, CA Jesuit Community.
Zaniewski, Jaroslaw (NEW) Bloomfield, NJ Sacred Heart; On Duty Outside the Archdiocese.
Zaniewski, Jaroslaw (DET)[A] Orchard Lake, MI SS. Cyril and Methodius Seminary.
Zaniolo, Michael G. '88 (CHI) Des Plaines, IL St. Stephen Protomartyr; Chicago, IL Chicago Airports Catholic Chaplaincy; [X] Chicago, IL Catholic Chaplaincy at O'Hare; The Catholic Ministry at Chicago O'Hare International Airport.
Zankl, Angelo *o.s.b.* '26 (SCL)[I] Collegeville, MN St. John's Abbey, of the Order of St. Benedict.
Zanni, Frank L. '90 (Y) Vienna, OH St. Vincent de Paul.
Zanon, Romano '66 (BRK) East Glendale, NY Sacred Heart; Flushing, NY Mount St. Mary.
Zanoni, Charles *c.s.* '62 (WDC) Washington, DC Holy Rosary.
Zanoni, John J. '60 (JOL) Rockdale, IL St. Joseph.
Zanoni, Richard J. *s.j.* '75 (BUF) Buffalo, NY St. Ann.
Zanotti, Charles F. '53 (NY) Glasco, NY St. Joseph.
Zaorski, Edward F. '90 (DET) Detroit, MI SS. Andrew and Benedict; Detroit, MI St. John Cantius; Detroit, MI All Saints; Archdiocesan Vicars.
Zapalac, David J. *c.s.b.* '93 (GAL) Missouri City, TX Holy Family.
Zapalac, William E. *o.m.i.* '70 (SAT) Del Rio, TX St. Joseph's.
Zapata, Antonio '68 (ORG) Santa Ana, CA St. Barbara's.
Zapata, Carlos '88 (NY) Ossining, NY St. Ann.
Zapata, Emiliano *o.p.* '95 (NO) New Orleans, LA St. Anthony of Padua; [P] New Orleans, LA Dominican Friars, Southern Dominican Province of St. Martin de Porres; [P] Metairie, LA Southern Dominican Foundation; [S] Metairie, LA Southern Dominican Foundation.
Zapata, Jose G. '90 (BRK) Jackson Heights, NY Blessed Sacrament.
Zapata, Pedro '99 (ORL) Ocala, FL Blessed Trinity.
Zapata, Urian Perez '97 (MGZ) San German, PR San German de Auxerre.
Zapf, Albert L. '80 (PIT) Harwick, PA Our Lady of Victory.
Zapfel, Robert E. '81 (BUF) Amherst, NY St. Leo the Great.
Zapotocki, Henry E. '48 (SCR) Retired.
Zapp, John '72 (Y) Uniontown, OH Holy Spirit.
Zappa, James C. '76 (STP) Burnsville, MN Mary, Mother of the Church; Presbyteral Council; Presbyteral Council.
Zappitelli, Francis '62 (PHX) Retired.
Zarama, Luis '93 (ATL) Clarkesville, GA St. Mark; Defenders of the Bond.
Zaratc, Baltazar (LA) Los Angeles, CA Holy Cross.
Zarate, Ramon *s.d.b.* '90 (LA) Bellflower, CA St. Dominic Savio.
Zarate–Suarez, Edmundo '96 (SD) San Diego, CA Our Lady of the Sacred Heart.
Zareski, Joseph S. (SY) Pastoral Examiners.
Zareski, Joseph '80 (SY) New Hartford, NY St. John the Evangelist.
Zarichny, Steven '78 (SJP) Cleveland, OH Ss. Peter and Paul.
Zarkoski, Donald *s.d.b.* '62 (SP) Tampa, FL Good Shepherd.
Zarkoski, Donald *s.d.b.* '65 (SP)[E] Tampa, FL Mary Help of Christians School.
Zarlenga, Vincent I. *o.p.* '51 (CHI) River Forest, IL St. Vincent Ferrer; [N] Chicago Dominicans (Provincial Office).
Zastawny, Kazimierz '57 (BO) Lynn, MA St. Michael.
Zastoupil, Stephen R. '61 (BIS) Retired.

Zastrow, John A. '56 (LIN)[E] Lincoln, NE Bonacum House Retired.
Zatalava, James D. '70 (ALT) State College, PA Our Lady of Victory.
Zatarga, George F. '68 (BRK)[V] Douglaston, NY Bishop Mugavero Residence.
Zatarga, George (BRK) Senior Priests, Episcopal Vicar Delegate for.
Zatina, Gregory E.J. '87 (SPC) Leave of Absence.
Zaucha, Finian *o.f.m.* '68 (GB) Denmark, WI Holy Trinity; [I] Pulaski, WI Friary.
Zavacki, Richard A. '58 (SCR) Kingston, PA St. Hedwig's.
Zavala, Genaro *m.s.p.* (SB) Riverside, CA St. John the Evangelist.
Zavaski, William J. '69 (CHI) Arlington Heights, IL St. James; Deans.
Zavattaro, Gabriel *s.d.b.* '34 (SFR)[N] San Francisco, CA Salesian Provincial Residence.
Zavell, Edward '61 (PRM) Retired.
Zawada, Jerome *o.f.m.* '64 (MIL)[O] Burlington, WI St. Francis Friary.
Zawada, Joseph F. *o.c.d.* '64 (STA)[J] Bunnell, FL Discalced Carmelite Fathers of Florida.
Zawadski, Justin (SJ) Deans; Diocesan Clergy Personnel Board.
Zawadzki, Justin '68 (SJ) Los Gatos, CA St. Mary of the Immaculate Conception.
Zawadzki, Piotr '97 (VEN) Absent on Leave.
Zawadzki, Richard *s.v.d.* '87 (LAF) Maurice, LA St. Joseph.
Zawadzki, Victor C. '50 (SCR) Retired.
Zawistanowicz, Norbert J. '49 (CHI) Chicago, IL Our Lady of Victory Retired.
Zawodniak, Edward J. '47 (SCR) Retired.
Zayas, Antonio '59 (PCE) On Duty Outside the Diocese.
Zayas, Hector '93 (ARE) Jayuya, PR Our Lady of Monserrate Retired.
Zayas, Simon M. '84 (SAT)[D] San Antonio, TX Antonian College Preparatory High School.
Zazella, Thomas J. (PAT) Retired.
Zbieranski, Roman *o.f.m.* (CHI) Niles, IL St. Isaac Jogues.
Zborowski, Richard M. '78 (CHI) Palatine, IL St. Theresa.
Zdancewicz, Carl *o.f.m.conv.* '77 (ATL) Lithia Springs, GA St. John Vianney.
Zdilla, Valentine '96 (LA) Santa Clarita, CA St. Clare.
Zdrodowski, Francis '43 (DET) Retired.
Zea, Virgilio *s.j.* '62 (YAK) Yakima, WA St. Joseph's.
Zebron, Samuel *o.f.m.conv.* '58 (PMB) Boynton Beach, FL St. Mark.
Zebrowski, Arnold '73 (VEN) Naples, FL St. John the Evangelist.
Zebrowski, Jacek *s.d.s.* '97 (NEW)[N] Verona, NJ The Salvatorian Fathers.
Zebrowski, Jacek *s.d.s.* '97 (BRK) Brooklyn, NY Our Lady of Consolation.
Zec, John '70 (TR) Holmdel, NJ St. Benedict.
Zeck, George '70 (DUL) Nisswa, MN St. Christopher; Pequot Lakes, MN St. Alice's; Pine River, MN Our Lady of Lourdes.
Zedar, Thomas J. '65 (VEN) Port Charlotte, FL San Antonio.
Zee, Louis C. '59 (DUB) Retired.
Zee, Louis C. '59 (GAL) Alief, TX Ascension Chinese Mission.
Zeeb, Charles '56 (DET) Retired.
Zegar, David '79 (P) Woodburn, OR St. Luke.
Zeger, David (P) Area Vicars.
Zegers, Paul A. *ss.cc.* '49 (HON) Hana, HI St. Mary.
Zegers, Paul *ss.cc.* (HON) Confraternity of Our Lady of Mt. Carmel.
Zehe, Ralph *o.f.m.cap.* '50 (PIT) Pittsburgh, PA Our Lady of the Angels.
Zeihen, Joseph N. '50 (MIL) Retired.
Zeiler, Don '01 (DAL) Dallas, TX St. Pius X.
Zeis, Gabriel *t.o.r.* '80 (TR)[S] Trenton, NJ Bede House, College of New Jersey.
Zeisig, B. Thomas '57 (CLV) Cuyahoga Falls, OH St. Eugene.
Zeisig, Thomas B. '57 (CLV) Akron, OH St. Francis de Sales Retired.
Zeisler, Warren *o.f.m.* '50 (CIN)[M] Cincinnati, OH St. John the Baptist Friary.
Zeitler, Edward J. '58 (E) Grove City, PA Beloved Disciple; Deans.
Zeitler, John W. '64 (BUF) Lake View, NY Our Lady of Perpetual Help.
Zekas, Stanley '49 (STU) Retired.
Zelaya, Cristians '02 (TYL) Tatum, TX San Pedro the Fisherman; Longview, TX St. Matthew Catholic Church.
Zelik, Richard J. *o.f.m.cap.* '77 (PIT) Clairton, PA St. Clare of Assisi.
Zelinski, James *o.f.m.cap.* '61 (FgM).
Zelinski, James *o.f.m.cap.* '61 (DET)[K] Detroit, MI St. Mary's Friary.
Zelinski, Thomas *o.f.m.cap.* '72 (MIL)[O] Mount Calvary, WI St. Lawrence Friary; [B] Mount Calvary, WI St. Lawrence Seminary.
Zelker, Thomas '83 (ALB) Granville, NY Roman Catholic Community of Granville.
Zell, Charles Felix *o.c.s.o.* '80 (ATL)[K] Conyers, GA The Monastery of the Holy Spirit.
Zeller, Leonard H. '73 (BAL) Military Chaplains; Air Force Chaplains.
Zelonis, Christopher M. '03 (ALN) Sinking Spring, PA St. Ignatius Loyola.
Zemaitis, Kestutis '65 (CLV)[M] Cleveland, OH Jennings Center for Older Adults.
Zeman, Gerald L. '63 (SC) Retired.
Zemanik, Edward S. '81 (ALN) McAdoo, PA Immaculate Conception; McAdoo, PA St. Kunegunda; McAdoo, PA St. Mary; McAdoo, PA St. Patrick; Vicars Forane.
Zembal, Theodore E. *s.j.* '68 (SEA)[A] Seattle, WA Seattle University.
Zemeikis, Alfred '63 (NEW) Elizabeth, NJ SS. Peter and Paul's.
Zemelko, John J. '87 (GRY) North Judson, IN Ss. Cyril and Methodius; Ministry to Hearing Impaired.
Zemlik, Edward J. *s.c.j.* '01 (JKS) West Southaven, MS Christ the King.
Zemlik, Edward *s.c.j.* '01 (JKS)[F] Nesbit, MS St. Michael Community House.
Zender, Gary '86 (SEA) Renton, WA St. Anthony.
Zendzian, Peter W. '79 (BRK)[U] Polish Apostolate.
Zendzian, Peter '79 (BRK) Maspeth, NY Holy Cross.
Zengierski, Patrick J. '91 (BUF)[R] Niagara University, NY Niagara University.
Zeni, Dino M. '59 (BRK) Brooklyn, NY St. Rosalia–Regina Pacis.
Zenk, Donald W. '54 (WIN) Auditors Retired.
Zenk, Richard E. '54 (SC) Akron, IA St. Patrick; Promoter of Justice; Defenders of the Bond; Holy Childhood Association; Propagation of the Faith, Association of the Holy Childhood, Catholic Students' Mission Crusade.
Zenkel, Edward B. '62 (ROC) Retired.
Zenorini, Henry J. *s.j.* '61 (NY)[EE] New York, NY Xavier Jesuit Community.
Zens, Roger A. '57 (MIL) Retired.
Zensen, Gerald F. '49 (SC) Retired.
Zensen, Gerald '49 (SC) Mapleton, IA St. Mary's.
Zenz, John P. '82 (DET)[Q] Detroit, MI Catholic Community Services of the Archdiocese of Detroit, Inc.; [T] Detroit, MI Christ Child Society; Special Assignment; Cardinal's Office; College of Consultors; Presbyteral Council; Archdiocesan Theological Commission.
Zepczyk, Gabriel C. '62 (SUP) Retired.
Zepecki, Ronald P. '95 (HRT) Bristol, CT St. Stanislaus.
Zepp, Anthony W. '56 (CLV) Garfield Heights, OH SS. Peter and Paul; Associate Judges.
Zepp, Anthony '56 (CLV) Retired.
Zeps, Michael J. *s.j.* '71 (MIL)[O] Milwaukee, WI Jesuit Community at Marquette University.
Zercie, David *m.s.a.* '69 (NOR)[A] Cromwell, CT Holy Apostles College and Seminary; [F] Cromwell Society of the Missionaries of the Holy Apostles.
Zerfas, Herman H. '47 (GR) Retired.
Zerhuson, Henry F. '53 (BAL) Retired.
Zeringue, Guy '75 (HT) St. Louis.
Zerkel, Donald F. '57 (MIL) Waukesha, WI St. John Neumann Retired.
Zermeno, Joseph *o.f.m.* '68 (MRY)[F] San Miguel, CA Franciscan Friars, O.F.M..
Zermeno–Martin, Felix *p.v.* '00 (DEN) Denver, CO Cathedral of the Immaculate Conception.
Zerr, Dennis P. '03 (CC) Corpus Christi, TX St. Patrick.
Zerr, Gary '97 (P) Tillamook, OR Sacred Heart.
Zerwas, Rick '91 (SFE) Los Lunas, NM San Clemente.
Zeth, Allen P. '86 (ALT) New Baltimore, PA St. John the Baptist.
Zettel, David H. '66 (L)[B] Louisville, KY Trinity High School.
Zetzl, Ralph *o.f.m.* '65 (SFD)[I] Effingham, IL St. Anthony's Memorial Hospital; [L] Teutopolis, IL St. Francis Assisi Friary.
Zeugner, Raymond J. '67 (MAR) Consultors.
Zeuner, Karl A. '71 (PH) Swarthmore, PA Notre Dame de Lourdes; Approved Advocates.
Zewe, M. Donald *s.j.* '56 (SY)[Q] Syracuse, NY Jesuits at LeMoyne, Inc..
Zeyack, John '65 (PSC) On Duty Outside Diocese.
Zeyen, Charles *m.s.f.* '53 (SAT)[K] San Antonio, TX Padua Place.
Zeyen, Thomas E. *s.j.* '54 (P)[L] Portland Jesuit Provincial Office (Society of Jesus, Oregon Prov.).
Zglejszewski, Andrzej '90 (RVC) Massapequa, NY St. Rose of Lima; West Hempstead, NY St. Thomas, the Apostle; Procurator & Advocates.
Zgunda, Ronald '77 (EVN) Evansville, IN Holy Redeemer.
Zhang, Dehua *c.s.j.b.* '76 (BRK)[V] Astoria, NY Congregation of St. John the Baptist of China.
Ziccardi, Anthony '90 (NEW).
Ziccardi, C. Anthony '90 (NEW)[B] School of Diplomacy and Intl. Rels.; Archdiocesan Theological Commission; Censors of Books.
Zidek, Vincent E. *o.s.b.* '91 (ALT) Carrolltown, PA St. Benedict's.
Zieba, Jerzy *c.r.* '92 (CHI)[N] Woodstock, IL.
Zieba, Jerzy *c.r.* '92 (RCK) Woodstock, IL Resurrection.
Ziebacz, Wieslaw M. '92 (SCR) Elkland, PA St. Thomas the Apostle.
Ziebowicz, Darius *s.d.s.* '88 (NOR) Moosup, CT All–Hallows; Wauregan, CT Sacred Heart.
Ziebowicz, Dariusz *s.d.s.* '86 (NEW)[N] Verona, NJ The Salvatorian Fathers.
Ziegelmaier, David A. '60 (LC) Alma Center, WI Immaculate Conception; Fairchild, WI St. John Cantius; Fairchild, WI St. Joseph.
Ziegler, John A. '96 (ARL) Annandale, VA St. Ambrose.
Ziegler, Thomas G. '69 (Y) Columbiana, OH St. Jude.
Ziegler, Tod '01 (KCK) Ottawa, KS Sacred Heart.
Ziegmann, Leonard M. '59 (SC) Retired.
Zielenski, Christopher *o.s.b.* (SFE)[I] Pecos, NM Our Lady of Guadalupe Abbey.
Zielezienski, Ray '81 (OAK) Oakland, CA St. Augustine's; Pastoral Leadership Placement Board (PLPB).
Zielinski, Brian *o.praem.* '71 (BAL) Baltimore, MD Our Lady, Queen of Peace.
Zielinski, Casimir *o.carm.* '52 (VEN)[G] Nokomis, FL Carmel at Mission Valley.
Zielinski, Chad W. '96 (GAY) Special Assignment; Air Force Chaplains.
Zielinski, Francis '62 (DET) Retired.
Zielinski, Martin '78 (CHI).
Zielke, Michael *o.f.m.conv.* '89 (SPR)[A] Chicopee, MA St. Stanislaus Basilica; Presbyteral Council.
Zielonka, Dariusz J. (BGP) Vice Chancellor & Secretary to the Bishop; Presbyteral Council; Diocesan Consultors.
Ziemba, Howard '79 (Y) Campbell, OH St. Elizabeth; Campbell, OH St. John the Baptist; Campbell, OH St. Joseph the Provider.
Ziemba, Walter J. '51 (DET) Retired.
Ziemkiewicz, Frank *o.s.b.* '84 (E) St. Mary, PA St. Mary; Army Reserve Chaplains.
Ziemniak, Jan '80 (LAR) Laredo, TX Nuestra Senora del Rosario Independent Mission.
Ziemnicki, Edward '96 (HRT) New Britain, CT Holy Cross.
Zientarski, Nicholas A. '03 (RVC) Manhasset, NY St. Mary's.
Zientek, Benedict '58 (SAN) Brownwood, TX St. Mary's Retired.
Zientek, Benedict (SAN) Priests' Pension Plan.
Zientek, Boleslaus '59 (GAL) La Porte, TX St. Mary of the Immaculate Conception.
Zientek, Theodore (STN)[A] Redwood Valley, CA Holy Transfiguration Monastery.
Ziezulewicz, George F. '64 (HRT) Retired.
Zigmond, Kenneth *o.s.b.* '57 (JOL) Lisle, IL St. Joan of Arc; [L] Lisle, IL St. Procopius Abbey.
Zigrang, Stephen P. '78 (GAL) Channelview, TX St. Andrew.
Ziliak, Jerome *s.v.d.* '47 (MIL)[O] East Troy, WI Divine Word Missionaries.
Ziliak, Joseph L. '62 (EVN) Newburgh, IN St. John the Baptist.
Ziliak, Joseph (EVN) Diocesan Consultors; Deans; Censors Of Books.
Zilimu, Johndamascene '95 (PEO)[O] Champaign, IL St. John's Catholic Student Chapel and Newman Foundation, University of Illinois.
Zilimu, Johndamascene '95 (Rulenge, Tanzania) Champaign, IL St. John's Catholic Chapel.
Ziliotto, Rino *c.s.* (LA) Retired.
Zilonka, Paul *c.p.* '71 (MET)[H] Baltimore, MD St. Mary's Seminary.
Zilonka, Paul *c.p.* '71 (BAL).
Ziminski, James C. '91 (MAR)[A] Baraga, MI The Most Holy Name of Jesus–Blessed Kateri Tekakwitha; Baraga, MI St. Ann; Baraga, MI The Most Holy Name of Jesus–Blessed Kateri Tekakwitha; Vocation Office.
Zimmer, Anthony J. '86 (MIL) Milwaukee, WI St. Charles Borromeo.
Zimmer, David L. '88 (BIS) Minot, ND St. John the Apostle; Defensor Vinculi.
Zimmer, Ellis *o.f.m.cap.* '55 (GB)[L] Appleton, WI Monte Alverno Retreat Center.
Zimmer, Eric A. *s.j.* '94 (DET)[M] Washington, DC The Jesuit Community at Georgetown University; [K] Temperance, MI.
Zimmer, James '76 (SFS) Huron, SD Holy Trinity.
Zimmer, Nicholas '57 (SCL) Retired.
Zimmer, Thomas J. (LFT) Associate Judges Retired.
Zimmer, William E. '91 (CHI) Chicago, IL Good Shepherd.
Zimmerman, David '95 (GB) Absent on Leave.
Zimmerman, David '97 (SFD) Farmersville, IL St. Mary; Farmersville, IL St. Patrick; Presbyteral Council.
Zimmerman, Donald D. (SAL) College of Consultors; Art and Architecture Commission.
Zimmerman, Donald F. '73 (DAL) Dallas, TX Christ the King; Presbyteral Council; Personnel Board.
Zimmerman, Donald '73 (SAL) Manhattan, KS St.

Thomas More Parish.
Zimmerman, Eugene F. *s.j.* '51 (GB)[L] Oshkosh, WI Jesuit Retreat House.
Zimmerman, John M. '03 (CHR) Charleston, SC Blessed Sacrament.
Zimmerman, Joseph *o.f.m.* '62 (SFD)[B] Quincy, IL Quincy University; Task Force For Racial Justice.
Zimmerman, Ralph '76 (SCL) Big Lake, MN Our Lady of the Lake; Continuing Formation of Priests; Diocesan Planning Council; Office of Diaconate.
Zimmerman, Rex A. '67 (LC) Hatley, WI St. Ladislaus; Wittenberg, WI St. Joseph.
Zimmerman, Roland G. '51 (LA) Monrovia, CA Annunciation Retired.
Zimmermann, Dominic (CC)[G] Robstown, TX Society of Our Lady of the Most Holy Trinity.
Zimmers, Eugene R. *s.j.* '51 (SJ)[M] Los Gatos, CA Sacred Heart Jesuit Center.
Zimmers, Eugene R. *s.j.* '51 (OAK).
Zimmers, Michael J. *s.j.* '54 (SJ)[M] Los Gatos, CA Sacred Heart Jesuit Center.
Zimmerschied, Daniel '97 (DEN) Holyoke, CO St. Patrick.
Zimney, Robert J. *c.m.* '42 (STL)[O] Perryville, MO Congregation of the Mission.
Zimpfer, Eugene A. *s.j.* '65 (BUF)[O] Buffalo, NY Canisius Jesuit Community.
Zina, George '86 (SAM) Orlando, FL St. Jude Mission.
Zingales, A. Jonathan '76 (CLV) Cuyahoga Falls, OH Immaculate Heart of Mary.
Zingaro, Joseph J. '78 (PH) Philadelphia, PA St. John Cantius.
Zink, David L. '90 (CIN) Osgood, OH St. Louis; Osgood, OH St. Nicholas; Censors.
Zink, Harold G. *c.s.c.* '51 (AUS) Austin, TX St. Ignatius Martyr.
Zink, William F. (GR) Marne, MI St. Mary's.
Zinkan, Matthias *o.s.b.* '40 (FgM).
Zinkan, Matthias *o.s.b.* '40 (RCK)[G] Aurora, IL Marmion Abbey.
Zinkle, Ronald T. *s.j.* '59 (LC) Lyndon Station, WI St. Mary; Deans.
Zinkula, Thomas R. '90 (DUB) Holy Cross, IA St. Joseph; Holy Cross, IA SS. Peter and Paul; Holy Cross, IA Holy Cross; Judicial Vicar; Judicial Vicar; Judges; Directors.
Zinn, Donald *c.r.* '72 (CHI)[D] Chicago, IL Gordon Tech High School.
Zinnamon, Brian F. *s.j.* '79 (NY)[EE] New York, NY West Side Jesuit Community.
Zinno, Henry P. '82 (PRO) Bristol, RI Our Lady of Mount Carmel.
Zins, Charles '77 (BIS) Beulah, ND St. Joseph; Hazen, ND St. Martin.
Zint, Russell '00 (IND) Terre Haute, IN St. Ann; Council of Priests; Terre Haute, IN Sacred Heart of Jesus.
Zinthefer, Neil G. '69 (MIL) Campbellsport, WI St. Kilian; Campbellsport, WI St. Martin; Campbellsport, WI St. Matthew.
Zinzer, Walter W. '64 (STL) AUXILIARY CHAPLAINS CONTRACT CHAPLAINS Retired.
Ziolkowski, Adam *o.f.m.conv.* '72 (HBG) Shamokin, PA Mother Cabrini.
Ziomek, David F. '94 (BO) Wakefield, MA St. Joseph.
Ziomek, Dennis A. '78 (CHI) Chicago, IL St. Barbara; Chicago, IL St. Barbara; [A] Chicago, IL Archbishop Quigley Preparatory Seminary.
Zipasuca Quemba, Francisco J. '93 (SJN) Rio Grande, PR San Francisco de Asis.
Zipay, Michael J. '68 (SCR) Williamsport, PA St. Boniface; [D] Williamsport, PA Bishop Neumann Junior/Senior High School.
Zirnheld, Matthew J. '93 (BUF) Council of Priests; Lackawanna, NY Basilica of Our Lady of Victory.
Zitek, Brad '89 (LIN) Seward, NE St. Vincent de Paul.
Zito, Giuseppe *s.j.* (LA)[C] Los Angeles, CA Jesuit Community.
Zito, Thomas M. '98 (CAM) On Leave of Absence.
Zitz, Nicholas *c.p.* '56 (BRK)[V] Jamaica, NY Immaculate Conception Monastery.
Ziuraitis, Gary *c.ss.r.* '78 (STL) St. Louis, MO St. Alphonsus Liguori; [O] St. Louis, MO Redemptorist Fathers.
Zivic, Richard A. (ATL) Archdiocesan Judges; Atlanta, GA St. Anthony of Padua.
Zivkovic, Robert M. *o.s.m.* '66 (CHI)[N] Chicago Order of Friar Servants of Mary (Servites) United States of America Province, Inc..
Zlock, Charles '94 (PH) Philadelphia, PA St. Monica; [D] Philadelphia, PA St. Maria Goretti High School.
Zlotkowski, Francis T. *c.s.c.* (FR) Taunton.
Zlotkowski, Francis *c.s.c.* '76 (FR) Taunton, MA St. Mary's.
Zmarlicki, Andrew (NEW) Elizabeth, NJ St. Hedwig's.
Zmozynski, Francis J. '57 (BUF)[K] Lewiston, NY Mount St. Mary's Hospital of Niagara Falls; Niagara Falls Memorial Medical Centers; Niagara Falls, NY St. Mary of the Cataract.
Zmuda, Christopher J. '01 (NOR) Middletown, CT St. Sebastian.
Zmudzinski, Charles *c.p.m.* '02 (L) Glasgow, KY St. Helen.
Zoeller, Benedict '65 (OKL) Retired.
Zoeller, Eugene '58 (L) Retired.
Zoellner, Michael *o.s.b.* '80 (KCK)[I] Leavenworth, KS Motherhouse of the Sisters of Charity of Leavenworth; [H] Atchison, KS St. Benedict's Abbey.
Zogby, Edward G. *s.j.* '67 (NY)[EE] New York, NY West Side Jesuit Community; New York, NY Our Lady of the Rosary.
Zoghby, James F. '71 (MOB) Mobile, AL Corpus Christi; Priests' Personnel Board.
Zoghby, James (MOB) Group II.
Zoghby, Paul G. '93 (MOB) Foley, AL St. Margaret Queen of Scotland; Co–Dirs..
Zogheib, Hares '54 (SAM) Retired.
Zohlen, Ray J. '53 (SFR) Retired.
Zohnerowicz, Nicholas *s.s.s.* '62 (CLV)[O] Gretna, LA.
Zollinger, Richard '55 (GRY) Retired.
Zolnerowicz, Nicholas *f.s.s.p.* '62 (SCR)[M] Elmhurst, PA Priestly Fraternity of St. Peter (F.S.S.P.), North American District Headquarters.
Zoni, Pierino *s.x.* '61 (PAT)[M] Wayne Xaverian Missionary Fathers.
Zoni, Pierino *s.x.* '61 (FgM).
Zonneveld, Leo J. *c.i.c.m.* '58 (ARL) Culpeper, VA Precious Blood; Diocesan Judges.
Zorbach, Francis X. '52 (BAL) Linthicum Heights, MD St. Philip Neri Retired.
Zore, Richard I. '57 (IND) Retired.
Zoromski, Herbert P. '51 (LC) Retired.
Zotter, Thomas A. '76 (SFE) Albuquerque, NM Shrine of St. Bernadette.
Zoubek, Ronald J. '89 (BAL) Baltimore, MD St. Anthony of Padua; Baltimore, MD Most Precious Blood Retired.
Zoucha, Carl J. '98 (OM) Omaha, NE St. Agnes; Omaha, NE St. Francis Assisi; Omaha, NE Our Lady of Guadalupe; [M] Omaha, NE Institute of the Apostolic Oblates.
Zoufal, Michael L. '87 (CHI) Argo, IL St. Blase.
Zowada, Stanley *o.m.i.* '00 (STP) San Antonio, TX San Juan De Los Lagos.
Zsolczai, Raymond (MIL)[O] Burlington, WI Queen of Peace Friary.
Zube, Joseph A. (PEO) Vice Chancellors; Adjutant Judicial Vicars; Priests' Eucharistic League.
Zube, Joseph '53 (PEO) Special Residence.
Zuber, Thaddeus F. '50 (NEW)[N] Rutherford, NJ St. John Vianney Residence for Priests Retired.
Zuberbueler, Matthew H. '96 (ARL) Arlington, VA Cathedral of St. Thomas More; Defenders of the Bond.
Zubik, Rudolf '64 (NEW) Harrison, NJ Our Lady of Czestochowa.
Zubizarreta, Jose Ramon *c.p.* '72 (SJN) San Juan, PR Nuestra Senora de la Piedad.
Zubovic, Robert '77 (BRK)[U] Croation Apostolate.
Zubovic, Robert '92 (BRK) Long Island City, NY Most Precious Blood.
Zuchowski, Robert J. '72 (GAY) Elk Rapids, MI Sacred Heart.
Zuckerman, Eric *s.j.* '98 (SPK) Rockford, WA St. Joseph.
Zudaire, Claudio *o.f.m.cap.* '54 (FWT) Fort Worth, TX Our Lady of Guadalupe.
Zuelke, Michael *o.f.m.cap.* '74 (MIL) Milwaukee, WI St. Francis of Assisi.
Zuercher, Jack *s.j.* '59 (OM)[P] Omaha, NE Christian Life Community–North Central Region (CLC).
Zuercher, John D. *s.j.* '59 (OM)[K] Omaha, NE Jesuit Community at Creighton University.
Zuerlein, Damian J. '81 (OM) Officers; Age Groups.
Zuerlein, Damian '81 (OM) Omaha, NE St. Ann; Omaha, NE St. Peter.
Zuern, Theodore F. *s.j.* '57 (MIL)[O] Wauwatosa, WI Jesuit Community at St. Camillus.
Zuffoletto, Michael P. '72 (BUF) Navy Chaplains; Military Chaplains.
Zugger, Christopher L. '81 (VNN) Albuquerque, NM Our Lady of Perpetual Help.
Zuikula, Thomas R. '90 (DUB) Holy Cross, IA Holy Trinity.
Zukas, Stephan (BO) Lithuanian.
Zukas, Stephen P. '93 (BO) South Boston, MA St. Peter.
Zukowski, Nicholas '82 (DET) New Baltimore, MI St. Mary Queen of Creation.
Zuleger, Donald M. '76 (GB) Appleton, WI St. Pius X.
Zuleta, Nondier '92 (B) Weiser, ID St. Agnes.
Zuliani, Vincent *s.d.b.* '56 (NY)[EE] New Rochelle, NY Salesian Provincial House.
Zuluaga, Jose Omar '84 (PRO) Pawtucket, RI St. John the Baptist.
Zuluete, Johnny *c.m.* '87 (LA) Los Angeles, CA St. Vincent De Paul.
Zumaya, David '77 (SAT) Retired.
Zuncan, Robert (DEN) Frisco, CO St. Mary.
Zunga, Alexis *s.t.* (PT)[F] Tallahassee, FL.
Zuniga, Carlos '98 (BWN) Secretariat for the Diocesan Synod; Ad Hoc Committee for Diocesan Insurance; McAllen, TX Saint Juan Diego Cuauhtlatoazin.
Zuniga, Domingo *c.m.f.* '52 (LA) Los Angeles, CA Our Lady Queen of the Angels.
Zunmas, Oby J. '03 (OKL) Oklahoma City, OK St. Charles Borromeo; Special Assignment.
Zunmas, Oby '00 (OKL)[B] Oklahoma City, OK Bishop McGuinness Catholic High School.
Zunno, Michael O. *m.m.* (BRK) Brooklyn, NY Shrine of Our Lady of Mount Carmel.
Zupa, Emil P. '48 (BUF) Le Roy, NY St. Joseph.
Zupka, Anselm *o.s.b.* '67 (CLV)[O] Chicago, IL Mother of Good Counsel Provincialate; [D] Cleveland, OH Benedictine High School; [O] Cleveland, OH.
Zurat, Hugh *o.f.m.* (FgM).
Zuraw, John A. '87 (Y) Youngstown, OH Immaculate Conception; Promoter of Justice.
Zuraw, John (Y) Defenders of the Bond; Department of Clergy and Religious Services; Office of Clergy Services; Office of Permanent Diaconate.
Zurawski, Lawrence '85 (DET) Westland, MI St. Damian.
Zurcher, Thomas K. *c.s.c.* '72 (PHX)[G] Phoenix, AZ Holy Cross Congregation/Casa Santa Cruz.
Zurcher, Thomas *c.s.c.* (PHX) College of Consultors; Priest Personnel; Advisory Board for the Continuing Formation of Priests; Priestly Life and Ministry Board; Priests' Placement Board.
Zurovetz, Jerome G. '67 (CC) Portland, TX Our Lady of Mount Carmel.
Zuschmidt, Joseph *o.s.f.s.* '65 (CHL) Belmont, NC Queen of the Apostles.
Zusy, James *o.p.* '59 (LEX) Lexington, KY St. Paul; Adjutant Judicial Vicar.
Zuziak, Joseph R. *s.d.s.* '66 (GRY)[I] Merrillville, IN Salvatorian Fathers (Society of the Divine Savior).
Zuzik, John E. '91 (Y) Canton, OH St. Benedict.
Zvarych, Peter (PHU) Shenandoah, PA St. Michael's.
Zvarych, Petro (PHU) Youth Ministry; Office of Vocations.
Zvijak, John J. *c.pp.s.* '63 (GRY) Whiting, IN St. John the Baptist.
Zwack, Jeffrey A. (BIS) Presbyteral Council; Priests' Personnel Board.
Zwack, Jeffrey '84 (BIS) Rhame, ND St. Charles.
Zwaska, Victor L. '56 (MIL) Retired.
Zweber, Clement J. '49 (STP) Retired.
Zwers, John B. '50 (DET) Retired.
Zwiefka, William L. '83 (GAY) Manistee, MI St. Joseph; Judges.
Zwinger, Leonard '51 (SFS) Retired.
Zwirn, Ralph H. '85 (CHI) Chicago, IL St. Turibius.
Zwolenkiewicz, Raphael *o.f.m.conv.* '79 (PAT) Clifton, NJ St. John Kanty.
Zych, Janusz *s.ch.* (BAL) Baltimore, MD Holy Rosary.
Zygadlo, Mitchell '82 (ROC) On Duty Outside the Diocese; Military Chaplains; Air Force Chaplains.
Zylla, Paul '45 (SCL) Presbyteral Council; Censores Librorum Retired.
Zylla, Robert V. *o.s.c.* '51 (BAL).
Zylla, Robert V. *o.s.c.* '51 (PHX)[G] Phoenix, AZ Crosier Community of Phoenix (Canons Regular of the Order of the Holy Cross).
Zywan, Paul J. '86 (PIT) Wexford, PA St. Alexis; Clergy Personnel Board.

Necrology

BISHOPS

✠ Breen, Most Rev. Vincent De Paul ((MET)) Bishop Emeritus of Metuchen. —Died March 30, 2003
✠ Clinch, Most Rev. Harry Anselm (MRY) Retired Bishop of Monterey in California. —Died March 8, 2003
✠ Crowley, Most Rev. Joseph R. (FTW) Retired Auxiliary Bishop of Fort Wayne–South Bend. —Died Feb. 4, 2003
✠ Dattilo, Most Rev. Nicholas C. (HBG) Bishop of Harrisburg. —Died March 5, 2004
✠ Ferrario, Most Rev. Joseph A. (HON) Retired Bishop of Honolulu. —Died Dec. 12, 2003
✠ Fitzgerald, Most Rev. James E. (JOL) Retired Auxiliary Bishop of Joliet. —Died Sept. 11, 2003
✠ Harrison, Most Rev. Frank J. (SY) Retired Bishop of Syracuse. —Died May 1, 2004
✠ Hoffman, Most Rev. James R. (TOL) Bishop of the Diocese of Toledo. —Died Feb. 8, 2003
✠ Lynch, Most Rev. George E. (R) Retired Auxiliary Bishop of Raleigh. —Died May 25, 2003
✠ O'Neil, Most Rev. Dennis Patrick (SB) Auxiliary Bishop of San Bernardino. —Died Oct. 17, 2003
✠ Povish, Most Rev. Kenneth J. (LAN) Retired Bishop of Lansing. —Died Sept. 5, 2003
✠ Roach, Most Rev. John R. (STP) Retired Archbishop of Saint Paul and Minneapolis. —Died July 11, 2003
✠ Salatka, Most Rev. Charles A. (OKL) Retired Archbishop of Oklahoma City. —Died March 17, 2003
✠ Sheets, Most Rev. John R., *s.j.* (FTW) Retired Auxiliary Bishop of Fort Wayne–South Bend. —Died April 16, 2003
✠ Speltz, Most Rev. George H. (SCL) Former Bishop of St. Cloud. —Died Feb. 1, 2004
✠ Strecker, Most Rev. Ignatius J. (KCK) Former Archbishop of Kansas City in Kansas. —Died Oct. 16, 2003
✠ Untener, Most Rev. Kenneth E. (SAG) Bishop of Saginaw.. —Died March 27, 2004

ABBOTS

✠ Burne, Rt. Rev. Martin J., *o.s.b.* (PAT) Morristown, NJ St. Mary Abbey. —Died July 25, 2003
✠ Moore, Rt. Rev. Augustine, *o.c.s.o.* (ATL) (Retired). —Died June 5, 2002
✠ Vollmer, Rt. Rev. Edward J., *o.s.b.* (PBL) Canon City, CO Holy Cross Abbey. —Died Oct. 2, 2002

PRIESTS

† Abracinskas, Albert C. (BO) (Senior Priest). —Died May 11, 2003
† Abramowicz, Rev. Msgr. Sylvester (NEW) (Retired). —Died Feb. 1, 2003
† Adams, William, *s.v.d.* (LA) Los Angeles, CA St. Malachy. —Died Jan. 28, 2002
† Ahern, John J. (CHI) (Retired). —Died April 25, 2003
† Ahrens, Noel, *o.carm.* (JOL) Darien, IL Carmelite Provincial Office. —Died 2003
† Akemu, Gabriel, *m.s.p.* (GAL) Houston, TX St. Peter the Apostle. —Died March 18, 2003
† Albert, Rev. Msgr. Louis W. (WDC) (Retired). —Died Dec. 23, 2002
† Albright, Charles, *c.s.p.* (SFR) San Francisco, CA Old St. Mary. —Died Feb. 21, 2002
† Aleksonis, Vladas (FAR) (Retired). —Died Dec. 6, 2002
† Alleman, Rev. Msgr. C. J. (GAL) (Retired). —Died July 10, 2003
† Alonso, Rev. Msgr. Jose A. (PAT) (Retired). —Died Sept. 29, 2003
† Alonso, Valeriano, *s.j.* (SFS) (Retired). —Died Sept., 2002
† Altmann, George (BAL) (Retired). —Died Jan. 14, 2003
† Amann, Rev. Msgr. Robert J. (CIN) (Retired). —Died Aug. 17, 2003
† Andriekus, Leonard, *o.f.m.* (PRT) Kennebunkport, ME St. Anthony's Friary. —Died May 20, 2003
† Anstey, Richard, *o.carm.* (JOL) (Retired). —Died Sept. 22, 2002
† Anstiss, Arthur (SFE) (Retired). —Died Nov. 17, 2003
† Antoncic, Rev. Msgr. John J. (BRK) Flushing, NY St. Mel. —Died May 1, 2003
† Archey, Eugene C. (WOR) (Retired). —Died Dec. 20, 2003
† Arnold, John Ferrer, *o.p.* (FgM) Dominican Order of Preachers Foreign Missions. —Died June 3, 2003
† Ascherl, Vincent (ELP) (Retired). —Died Oct. 1, 2003
† Ashenbrenner, Raymond N., *o.p.* (CHI) Chicago, IL Dominicans (Provincial Office). —Died Feb. 20, 2003
† Astruc, Eene, *s.j.* (FBK) (Retired). —Died June 28, 2002
† Atchison Donald W. (KAL) (Retired). —Died Jan. 24, 2003
† Aversa, Domenic R., *t.o.r.* (ALT) Hollidaysburg, PA St. Joseph Friary. —Died April 19, 2003
† Axen, Ronald J. (DUB) (Retired). —Died Feb. 22, 2003
† Aymanamkuzhy, Jacob (PMB) (Retired). —Died July 19, 2003
† Bach, Ignacio, *o.c.d.* (TUC) Tucson, AZ Santa Cruz. —Died Feb. 28, 2003
† Bach, James To Duc (LUB) (Retired). —Died March 31, 2003
† Bach, Jose M., *o.c.d.* (TUC) (Retired). —Died Feb. 28, 2003
† Backes, Hugo G. (BIS) (Retired). —Died July 27, 2003
† Ball, Harry, *s.j.* (FgM) Provinces. —Died Nov. 11, 2002
† Balsam, John Bonaventure, *o.p.* (DAL) Irving, TX Dominican Priory of St. Albert The Great. —Died March 29, 2003
† Bambol John (BAL) (Retired). —Died 2003
† Bambol John, *o.f.m.conv.* (SPR) Holyoke, MA Mont Marie Health Care Center, Inc.. —Died 2003
† Banach Walter F. (LIN) (Retired). —Died Oct. 17, 2003
† Banet, Charles, *c.pp.s.* (GAL) Galveston, TX Holy Rosary. —Died June 22, 2003
† Bang Le, Christopher, *c.ss.r.* (GAL) Galveston, TX St. Clements Formation House. —Died April 9, 2002
† Bantle, Charles, *o.f.m.cap.* (FgM) Capuchin Foreign Missions. —Died June 27, 2003
† Barfield, Daniel R., *s.j.* (LSC) Alamogordo, NM St. Jude. —Died 2003
† Bargielski, John (GRY) (Retired). —Died Dec. 24, 2002
† Barreneche, Franco, *o.carm.* San Juan, PR Santa Teresita Del Nino Jesus. —Died 2003
† Barrett, Charles, *o.f.m.* (WDC) Washington, DC Marist Center. —Died June 19, 2002
† Barrett, Kevin, *m.afr.* (SP) St. Petersburg, FL Missionaries of Africa. —Died Jan. 29, 2003
† Barretta, Rev. Msgr. Anthony J. (BRK) Brooklyn, NY Holy Cross Chap.. —Died Dec. 30, 2003
† Barry, Henry F. (BO) (Senior Priest). —Died Dec. 14, 2003
† Bartlett, Albert, *s.j.* (NY) Bronx, NY Fordham University. —Died Sept. 30, 2001
† Bartofski, Harold S., *m.s.* (HRT) Hartford, CT Missionaries of La Salette. —Died April 12, 2003
† Bartone, Donald Edmund (DET) Marine City, MI Holy Cross. —Died Dec. 11, 2002
† Bates, Urban Francis, *o.p.* (ANC) Anchorage, AK Holy Family Cathedral. —Died Sept. 9, 2003
† Battirossi, Bartholomew, *m.c.c.j.* (LA) Los Angeles, CA St. Cecilia. —Died July 13, 2002
† Baudhuin, Robert F., *m.m.* (FgM) Maryknoll Foreign Missions. —Died Jan. 11, 2003
† Bauer, Ralph (LR) (Retired). —Died Dec. 22, 2002
† Bauernfeind, Thomas J. (BAL) (Retired). —Died Jan. 1, 2003
† Baumgartel, David A. (WIL) Wilmington, DE Parish of the Resurrection. —Died Oct. 8 2002
† Beasley, Rev. Msgr. Thomas J. (BUF) (Retired). —Died June 11, 2003
† Beaudoin, Hubert N., *o.praem.* (PH) Paoli, PA Daylesford Abbey. —Died June 26, 2003
† Bech, James (RC) (Retired). —Died Dec. 9, 2002
† Becker, Nicholas J. (SC) (Retired). —Died Aug. 20, 2003
† Bednarz, Matt A. (CHI) (Retired). —Died Aug. 25, 2003
† Belcher, Paul, *s.j.* (SFR) San Francisco, CA St. Agnes. —Died Dec. 20, 2001
† Benda, Frank M. (DUB) (Retired). —Died May 5, 2003
† Bennett, John, *s.j.* (PH) Philadelphia, PA St. Joseph's University. —Died Dec. 22, 2001
† Beretta, John W., *o.s.a.* (CHI) Olympia Fields, IL The Augustinian Provincialate Tolentine Center. —Died July 20, 2003
† Berg, Ramon A. (CHL) (Retired). —Died May 15, 2003
† Bermingham, Rev. Msgr. Charles E. (RVC) (Retired). —Died Dec. 21, 1903
† Bernardin, Arthur Paul, *o.p.* (HRT) New Haven, CT St. Mary. —Died April 29, 2002
† Bernott, Albert R. (GR) (Retired). —Died June 27, 2003
† Berson, Robert C., *g.h.m.* (CIN) Cincinnati, OH Headquarters of Glenmary Home Missioners. —Died March 5, 2003
† Berther, Patrick, *o.f.m.cap.* (GB) Appleton, WI St. Fidelis Friary. —Died Dec. 10, 2001
† Berube, Theodore E. (NOR) (Retired). —Died May 26, 2003
† Betowski, E. Paul, *s.j.* (BAL) Baltimore, MD Jesuit Fathers & Brothers. —Died March 11, 2002
† Bevilacqua, Carlo, *c.s.s.* (BO) Waltham, MA Stigmatine Fathers and Brothers. —Died Nov. 14, 2001
† Beyer, Emil J. (MAR) (Retired). —Died Aug. 10, 2003
† Biasio, Mariano, *c.s.j.* (LA) Lancaster, CA Blessed Serra. —Died Feb. 7, 2002
† Bickerstaff, Albert C., *o.s.b.* (SAV) Savannah, GA Benedictine Priory. —Died Oct. 2, 2003
† Biondolillo, Gabriel, *o.m.i.* (BEL) Belleville, IL Shrine of Our Lady of the Snows. —Died Jan. 19, 2002
† Birkenhauer, Henry F., *s.j.* (CLV) Cleveland, OH St. Ignatius High School. —Died June 13, 2003
† Blackburn, David, *o.c.s.o.* (SPC) Ava, MO Assumption Abbey. —Died Feb. 27, 2002
† Blais, Jean, *s.d.s.* (OAK) Oakland, CA Director of Scholastics. —Died Oct. 12, 2002
† Blanpied, Rev. Msgr. Robert D. (PBL) (Retired). —Died Oct. 6, 2003
† Blanpied, Rev. Msgr. Robert (Retired). —Died Oct. 6, 2003
† Blecha, Jordan R., *o.praem.* (GB) Green Bay, WI Our Lady of Charity Convent. —Died May 10, 2003
† Blehl, Vincent F., *s.j.* (FgM) Jesuit Fathers and Brothers. —Died Nov. 14, 2001
† Blewett, John E., *s.j.* (STL) St. Louis, MO Fusz Pavilion. —Died July 7, 2003
† Blood, Bernard, *s.m.m.* (RVC) West Islip, NY Good Samaritan Hospital. —Died Jan. 15, 2003
† Boeding, Damian G. (SPC) (Retired). —Died Sept. 29, 2003
† Boholnick, Rev. Msgr. Theodore (PHU) Simpson, PA SS. Peter & Paul. —Died Nov. 20, 2002
† Boronat, Louis, *sch.p.* (LA) Los Angeles, CA Piarist Fathers. —Died 2002
† Bosio, August, *s.d.b.* (NY) (Retired). —Died Sept. 24, 2001
† Boulanger, Maurice R. (MAN) (Retired). —Died April 26, 2003
† Bourg, Edwin (LAF) (Retired). —Died June 9, 2003
† Bourgeois, Richard J., *o.s.b.* (BO) Hingham, MA Glastonbury Abbey. —Died Nov. 9, 2002
† Bourne, Peter, *h.m.c.* (B) Leodore, ID St. Joseph Chapel. —Died Feb. 10, 2003
† Bowling, Rev. Msgr. Robert A. (RNO) Reno, NV St. Therese Church of the Little Flower. —Died June 14, 2003
† Boyce, Thomas (JKS) (Retired). —Died Dec. 13, 2002
† Boyer, Rev. Msgr. Leland J. (LA) La Canada Flintridge, CA St. Bede the Venerable. —Died Jan. 14, 2003
† Boylan, Colman, *o.f.m.cap.* (NOR) Middletown, CT St. Pius X. —Died April 22, 2003
† Bracikowski, Felix, *o.f.m.conv.* (BUF) Athol Springs, NY St. Francis High School. —Died Aug. 1, 2002
† Bradican, Rev. Msgr. Francis L. (ARL) Annandale, VA Holy Spirit. —Died March 31, 2003
† Bradley, John P. (CHL) (Retired). —Died Nov. 8, 2003

† Bradunas, John J., *o.s.f.s.* (WIL) Childs, MD Oblates of St. Francis De Sales. —Died Jan. 7, 2002
† Brady, Daniel Patrick, *o.p.* (DAL) Irving, TX St. Albert the Great Priory. —Died Dec. 4, 2001
† Brady, Martin A., *t.o.r.* (ALT) Newry, PA St. Bernardine Monastery. —Died March 19, 2003
† Brady, Patrick, *o.m.i.* (NY) Newburgh, NY Our Lady of Hope Center. —Died March 29, 2002
† Brainard, Arthur, *s.d.b.* (OAK) Richmond, CA Salesian High School. —Died March 14, 2003
† Branche, John S. (OG) (Retired). —Died Sept. 3, 2003
† Breen, Michael J., *s.s.c.* (BO) Quincy, MA St. Columban's Foreign Mission Society. —Died Dec. 25, 2001
† Brelivet, Alain R.M., *o.m.i.* (SAT) San Antonio, TX Oblate Madonna Residence. —Died Sept. 29, 2001
† Brennan, Rev. Msgr. Daniel H. (ORG) Costa Mesa, CA St. John the Baptist. —Died Oct. 30, 2003
† Brennan, Robert E. (SY) (Retired). —Died March 26, 2003
† Bresnahan, Thomas James (DET) (Retired). —Died June 7, 2003
† Bresnehan, Rev. Msgr. Paul M. (BUR) Proctor, VT St. Dominic. —Died July 23, 2003
† Brew, Frederick A., *s.j.* (ALN) Wernersville, PA Jesuit Center. —Died March 3, 2002
† Brick, Maurice J., *o.f.m.* (PAT) Ringwood, NJ Holy Name Friary. —Died Oct. 4, 2003
† Brissette, Eugene C., *s.j.* Fairfield, CT Fairfield College Preparatory School. —Died Dec. 17, 2002
† Brissette, Eugene C., *s.j.* Weston, MA Campion Health Center. —Died Dec. 17, 2002
† Brogley, Charles F., *s.m.* (ATL) Atlanta, GA Marist School. —Died Jan. 16, 2001
† Broker, John, *c.s.s.r.* (MIL) Oconomowoc, WI Redemptorist Retreat Center. —Died Sept. 26, 2002
† Brown, Vincent A. (HRT) Branford, CT St. Mary Rectory.. —Died July 10, 2003
† Browne, George E., *c.m.* (PH) Philadelphia, PA St. Vincent's Seminary. —Died July 26, 2002
† Bryson, Robert C. (BO) (Senior Priest). —Died April 21, 2003
† Brzakowski, Jerome, *s.v.d.* (TR) Bordentown, NJ Society of the Divine Word. —Died June 17, 2002
† Bubb, James C., *s.j.* (ATL) Atlanta, GA Ignatius Retreat House. —Died June 12, 2002
† Buckley, John E. (BO) Burlington, MA St. Margaret. —Died Nov. 20, 2003
† Bueche, Walter (ORL) St. Alphonsus Villa–Redemptorist Fathers and Brothers New Smyrna Beach, FL. —Died 2003
† Buerger, Francis J. (CIN) (Retired). —Died Dec. 15, 2003
† Bull, Albert D. (CHI) (Retired). —Died March 6, 2003
† Burdiek, Fabian, *o.f.m.* (STP) Maplewood, MN St. John's Hospital. —Died March 20, 2003
† Burgdorf, Joseph, *c.p.m.* (OWN) South Union, KY Fathers of Mercy. —Died Feb. 4, 2002
† Burke, Leonard J. (BO) (Senior Priest). —Died Sept. 20, 2003
† Burke, Robert Emmett (DET) Birmingham, MI Holy Name. —Died March 8, 2003
† Burns, David E. (GAL) (Retired). —Died May 11, 2003
† Burns, Francis Henry (DET) (Retired). —Died April 21, 2003
† Burns, William A. (ROC) (Retired). —Died Aug. 20, 2003
† Busch, John, *o.m.i.* (SAT) San Antonio, TX Oblate Madonna Res.. —Died Sept. 4, 2003
† Buscher, Adelbert, *o.s.b.* (IND) St. Meinrad, IN St. Meinrad. —Died Aug. 1, 2002
† Bushinski, Edward A., *c.s.sp.* (PIT) Pittsburgh, PA Duquesne University of the Holy Ghost. —Died May 21, 2002
† Byrne, Alexius W., *s.j.* (SEA) Seattle, WA Seattle University. —Died March 28, 2002
† Byrne, Francis, *c.m.* (STL) Perryville, MO Congregation of the Mission. —Died Nov. 26, 2002
† Byrne, Thomas H., *s.j.* (SJ) Los Gatos, CA Sacred Heart Jesuit Center. —Died March 15, 2002
† Cahill, Joseph T., *c.m.* (BRK) Jamaica, NY St. John's University. —Died Sept. 27, 2003
† Cahill, Patrick G., *c.s.v.* (SFD) Rochester, IL St. Jude. —Died Feb. 5, 2002
† Cain, Urban A., *o.f.m.* (PAT) Ringwood, NJ Holy Name Friary. —Died Oct. 10, 2002
† Callahan, Rev. Msgr. Brian F. (BRK) Brooklyn, NY St. Thomas Aquinas. —Died Dec. 15, 2003
† Campagnone, Rev. Msgr. Francis (ORL) (Retired). —Died March 20, 2003
† Campbell, Robert I., *o.p.* (CHI) Chicago, IL St. Pius V Priory. —Died July 24, 2002
† Campbell, Thomas E. (SAV) (Retired). —Died June 1, 2003
† Cangemi, Dominic, *s.t.* (BLX) Pearlington, MS St. Joseph. —Died Sept. 11, 2003
† Cannon, James, *c.ss.r.* (ALB) Saratoga Springs, NY St. Clement. —Died March 5, 2002
† Cannon, Richard, *s.s.c.* (LA) Los Angeles, CA Columban Fathers Procure House. —Died March 11, 2002
† Capizzi, Simeon, *o.f.m.* (SP) St. Petersburg, FL St. Anthony Friary. —Died Nov. 14, 2001
† Carbone, Angelo, *c.s.* (KC) Kansas City, MO Holy Rosary. —Died Sept. 19, 2002
† Cardinali, Fred (FTW) (Retired). —Died May 17, 2003
† Carey, Donald D. (STL) (Retired). —Died Nov. 14, 2003
† Carges, Bernard (ROC) (Retired). —Died April 22, 2003
† Carillo, M. Januarius, *m.c.c.j.* (LA) Covina, CA Comboni Mission Center. —Died Oct. 12, 2002
† Carolan, Charles J., *s.s.c.* (LA) Los Angeles, CA St. Theresa of Avila. —Died July 16, 2003
† Carr, Gerald F., *o.f.m.* (PAT) New York, NY St. Francis of Assisi. —Died Jan. 12, 2003
† Carr, John A., *c.s.p.* (SFR) San Francisco, CA Old St. Mary. —Died March 27, 2002
† Carriere, Henry G. (CR) (Retired). —Died Nov. 3, 2003
† Carroll, Charles Patrick, *s.j.* (SPK) Spokane, WA Regis Community. —Died April 10, 2002
† Carroll, Daniel, *s.d.s.* (MIL) Milwaukee, WI Jordan Hall. —Died Sept. 5, 2002
† Carroll, Thomas J., *m.s.* (ATL) Snellville, GA St. Oliver Plenkett. —Died March 20, 2003
† Carroll, Thomas M., *o.s.m.* (FgM) Kwazulu–Natal, South Africa. —Died March 25, 2003
† Cashioli, Lawrence J. (MET) (Retired). —Died July 21, 2001
† Cashman, James, *s.s.c.* (BUF) Silver Creek, NY St. Columban. —Died Sept. 27, 2002
† Cassidy, Daniel H., *s.s.j.* (BAL) Baltimore, MD St. Joseph's Manor. —Died April 8, 2003
† Cassidy, Patrick (RIC) (Retired). —Died Sept. 29, 2003
† Catanzaro, Albert, *c.p.* (BRK) Jamaica, NY Immaculate Conception. —Died July 27, 2003
† Cegielka, Francis A., *s.a.c.* (BUF) North Tonawanda, NY Society of the Catholic Apostolate. —Died Feb. 11, 2003
† Cenkner, William Cyprian, *o.p.* (MIA) Miami, FL Barry University. —Died Aug. 8, 2003
† Ceplecha, Christian, *o.s.b.* (JOL) Lisle, IL St. Procopius Abbey. —Died May 29, 2002
† Chaguaceda, Juan Manuel, *o.s.a.* (NY) New York, NY Holy Rosary Church. —Died 2003
† Chandonnet, Adalbert Joseph, *c.ss.r.* (GAL) Houston, TX Holy Ghost. —Died Oct. 16, 2002
† Chang, Simeon (SFR) (Retired). —Died Nov. 1, 2002
† Charankat, Peter (OAK) Walnut Creek, CA St. Mary. —Died July 24, 2003
† Charnoki, Andrew J. (GBG) (Retired). —Died Aug. 5, 2003
† Chenoweth, Robert J. (JC) (Retired). —Died April 7, 2003
† Chin, Bertram, *c.p.* (FgM) Passionist Foreign Missions. —Died Sept. 3, 2003
† Chini, Silvio, *o.s.j.* (SCR) Exeter, PA St. Anthony of Padua. —Died May 6, 2003
† Chisek, Anthony S. (CHI) (Retired). —Died June 14, 2003
† Chrepta, Rev. Msgr. Stephen J. (STF) (Retired). —Died May 16, 2003
† Christof, Francis T., *o.s.f.s.* (WIL) Childs, MD Oblates of St. Francis De Sales. —Died March 17, 2002
† Chupela, Rev. Msgr. Andrew A. (GBG) (Retired). —Died Oct. 8, 2003
† Cirrincione, Rev. Msgr. Joseph (PT) (Retired). —Died Nov. 21, 2002
† Ciungu, John (ROM) (Retired). —Died Feb. 3, 2003
† Clancey, Jeremiah, *t.o.r.* (PIT) (Retired). —Died Nov. 10, 2000
† Clark, Benjamin, *o.c.s.o* (CHR) Moncks Corner, SC Mepkin Abbey. —Died Sept. 4, 2002
† Clark, James M. (TR) Lincroft, NJ St. Leo the Great Church. —Died Feb. 24, 2003
† Clarke, Gerard R., *o.s.f.s.* (CHL) Albemarle, NC Our Lady of the Annunciation. —Died June 14, 2002
† Clarke, Rev. Msgr. Hugh (CC) (Retired). —Died Dec. 16, 2002
† Clauss, Joseph (EVN) (Retired). —Died Oct. 11, 2003
† Cleary, William J., *o.s.f.s.* (WIL) Childs, MD Oblates of St. Francis De Sales. —Died Aug. 31, 2003
† Clemens, Norbert, *c.s.b.* (GAL) Houston, TX Dillon House. —Died Aug. 27, 2002
† Cloutier, Edmund (OAK) (Retired). —Died April 9, 2003
† Clune, Gerald (ALB) (Retired). —Died Oct. 25, 2002
† Clyde, George A. (NEW) (Retired). —Died Oct. 20, 2003
† Cocuzzi, Bruno, *o.c.d.* (BO) Boston, MA Carmelite Monastery. —Died July 21, 2002
† Cohan, Rev. Msgr. Robert W. (E) Erie, PA St. James. —Died May 30, 2003
† Coleman, James F., *s.j.* (NY) Bronx, NY Murray–Weigel Hall. —Died May 31, 2003
† Coleman, James (SAN) (Retired). —Died Nov. 10, 2002
† Coleman, William J., *m.m.* (NY) Maryknoll, NY Maryknoll Fathers and Brothers. —Died Dec. 4, 2002
† Coles, Edward T., *s.j.* Houston, TX St. Vincent de Paul. —Died Oct. 21, 2003
† Coletta, Carmen, *o.s.a.* (BO) North Andover, MA Our Mother of Good Counsel Monastery. —Died July 12, 2002
† Colligan, Flavian, *o.f.m.* (PAT) Ringwood, NJ Holy Name Friary. —Died July 12, 2002
† Collins, Rev. Msgr. Bernard G. (DUB) (Retired). —Died Oct. 16, 2003
† Collins, Rev. Msgr. Fachta P. (LA) Montrose, CA Holy Redeemer. —Died Aug. 12, 2003
† Collins, John J.L., *s.j.* (BO) Chestnut Hill, MA Jesuit Community at Boston College. —Died Dec. 28, 2001
† Collins, John (ORL) St. Alphonsus Villa–Redemptorist Fathers and Brothers New Smyrna Beach, FL. —Died 2003
† Collins, John, *c.ss.r.* (PH) Gwynedd Valley, PA Gwynedd–Mercy College. —Died May 7, 2003
† Collins, William, *c.ss.r.* (BRK) Brooklyn, NY Our Lady of Perpetual Help. —Died Feb. 19, 2003
† Colonnese, Louis M. (DAV) (Retired). —Died Dec. 12, 2002
† Combs, Regis V. (LA) (Retired). —Died June 27, 2003
† Confroy, Mark W., *o.s.b.* (PAT) Convent Station, NJ St. Anne Villa. —Died Sept. 29, 2002
† Conley, Martin R. (PIT) Canonsburg, PA St. Patrick. —Died Feb. 12, 2003
† Conmy, Thomas M., *c.s.c.* (SP) Dunedin, FL Our Lady of Lourdes. —Died Aug. 19, 2003
† Connelly, George R. (TUC) (Retired). —Died Aug. 27, 2003
† Connolly, Patrick (GRY) (Retired). —Died Dec. 28, 2002
† Connolly, William A., *s.j.* (FgM) Provinces. —Died Nov. 18, 2001
† Conti, Rev. Msgr. Leo J. (EVN) (Retired). —Died Dec. 11, 2002
† Conyard, Joseph William, *s.j.* (SPK) Spokane, WA Regis Community. —Died Nov. 27, 2001
† Corrigan, James B., *s.j.* (MIL) Wauwatosa, WI St. Camillus. —Died Sept. 17, 2003
† Couch, Edward, *o.m.i.* (CC) Sarita, TX Our Lady of Guadalupe. —Died March 4, 2002
† Cour, Raymond F., *c.s.c.* (FTW) South Bend, IN Faith & Hope & Charity Chapel. —Died Oct. 10, 2002
† Courtney, Joseph, *c.s.b.* (GAL) Pearland, TX St. Helen. —Died Oct. 1, 2003
† Couture, Fernand E. (AMA) Silverton, TX Our Lady of Loretto. —Died Sept. 9, 2003
† Couture, Fernand, *s.p.* (AMA) (Retired). —Died Sept. 9, 2003
† Coxen, Gervis J., *m.m.* (NY) Maryknoll, NY Maryknoll Fathers and Brothers. —Died Jan. 9, 2003
† Crain, George L., *s.j.* (SJ) Los Gatos, CA Sacred Heart Jesuit Center. —Died Sept. 9, 2003
† Crenner, William A. (KAL) (Retired). —Died Nov. 9, 2003
† Crosby, Donald F., *s.j.* (OAK) Berkeley, CA Jesuit School of Theology. —Died Oct. 27, 2002
† Crowley, Bonaventure, *o.f.m.conv.* (IND) Mount St. Francis, IN Mount St. Francis Friary. —Died Aug. 12, 2003
† Crowley, Edward T., *c.s.sp.* (LR) Conway, AR St. Joseph. —Died Nov. 5, 2002
† Cullen, Francis J. (LA) (Retired). —Died Jan. 28, 2003
† Cumiskey, Thomas M., *o.p.* (DAL) Irving, TX St. Albert the Great Priory. —Died Aug. 22, 2002
† Cunningham, Augustine, *o.s.b.* (RIC) Richmond, VA Benedictine High School. —Died Nov. 10, 2002
† Curic, Dominik, *o.f.m.* (CHI) Chicago, IL Croatian Franciscan Custody of the Holy Family. —Died May 26, 2003
† Curley, Thomas J. (CHI) (Retired). —Died Dec. 20, 2002
† Curtain, Greg F., *s.j.* (NO) New Orleans, LA Loyola University. —Died April 1, 2002
† Curtin, J. Clifford (NOR) Somersville, CT All Saints Church. —Died Feb. 6, 2003
† Czachorowski, Richard C. (NEW) Lyndhurst, NJ St. Michael. —Died July 21, 2003
† D'Onofrio, Ernest, *o.f.m.* (NY) Wappingers Falls, NY Mt. Alvernia. —Died Sept. 23, 2003
† Daenen, Arsene, *ss.cc.* (HON) Kalaupapa, HI St. Francis. —Died June 12, 2002
† Daleke, Don (DM) (Retired). —Died Dec. 18, 2002
† Daley, Joseph D. (BO) (Senior Priest). —Died Oct. 2, 2003
† Danforth, Clarence (GRY) (Retired). —Died June 25, 2003
† Daniels, Eugene (NY) Milton, NY St. James. —Died May, 2001
† Darby, Bernard M. (CAM) (Retired). —Died Nov. 24, 2002
† Darmofal, Mitchell, *o.f.m.conv.* (DET) Detroit, MI Our Lady Queen of Angels. —Died Jan. 4, 2002

† Davis, Joseph E. (PRO) Woonsocket, RI Sacred Heart. —Died June 12, 2003
† Davis, Raymond (JOL) (Retired). —Died March 17, 2003
† Davis, Royden B., *s.j.* (SCR) Scranton, PA University of Scranton. —Died April 2, 2002
† Deane, Edwin, *o.f.m.* (HT) Houma, LA Our Lady of the Most Holy Rosary. —Died June 11, 2003
† DeBacker, Rev. Msgr. Thomas (OM) (Retired). —Died March 10, 2003
† DeCaprio, John (ALB) (Retired). —Died May 29, 2003
† DeClerk, Rev. Msgr. Rainer J. (LR) (Retired). —Died Sept. 3, 2003
† Decoteau, Joseph A., *m.s.* (LKC) Sulphur, LA Our Lady of La Salette. —Died Sept. 29, 2003
† Degan, Siro Dal, *o.s.j.* (MRY) Santa Cruz, CA Oblates of St. Joseph. —Died Nov. 28, 2002
† DeLorenzo, Francis S., *o.f.m.* (ALB) Catskill, NY St. Anthony. —Died April 7, 2003
† Delort, Norbert, *c.ss.r.* (STL) Liguori, MO St. Clement's Health Care Center. —Died Sept. 18, 2002
† del Val, Feliciano (GAL) (Retired). —Died Aug. 30, 2003
† Denehy, Rev. Msgr. John (ORL) (Retired). —Died Aug. 22, 2003
† Dennett, John A. (GI) (Retired). —Died Oct. 6, 2003
† Dennigan, Patrick J. (BUR) (Retired). —Died May 20, 2003
† Dennis, James J. (BGP) (Retired). —Died June 7, 2003
† Des Roches, Robert, *o.f.m.* (PRT) Kennebunkport, ME St. Anthony's Friary. —Died Nov. 15, 1999
† Devaney, Roy J. (WOR) (Retired). —Died Jan. 8, 2003
† DiCesare, Giosue Scotto, *S.D.V.* (NEW) Newark, NJ St. Michael's. —Died 2003
† Di Cesare, Giosue Scotto, *s.d.v.* (NEW) Newark, NJ St. Michael. —Died 2003
† Dieckman, Leonard E., *s.j.* (FgM) Provinces. —Died Sept. 12, 2003
† Diekmann, Godfrey, *o.s.b.* (SCL) Collegeville, MN St. John's Abbey. —Died Feb. 22, 2002
† Diersen, William M. (L) (Retired). —Died Nov. 9, 2002
† DiFalco, Anthony, *s.d.b.* (SFR) San Francisco, CA Peter & Paul. —Died March 23, 2003
† Di Francesco, Francesco, *m.c.c.j.* (LA) Covina, CA Comboni Mission Center. —Died May 31, 2002
† Dillemuth, Frederick J., *s.j.* (NY) Bronx, NY Fordham University. —Died May 19, 2003
† Diller, Harold, *c.pp.s.* (CIN) Carthagena, OH St. Charles. —Died Feb. 13, 2003
† Dillon, Charles P., *s.s.* (BAL) Baltimore, MD St. Charles Villa. —Died July 29, 2003
† Dinneen, John A., *s.j.* (NY) Bronx, NY Murray-Weigel Hall. —Died Dec. 11, 2002
† Dittman, Bernard F. (VEN) (Retired). —Died Oct. 17, 2003
† Divizia, John, *s.d.b.* (NY) Stony Point, NY Marian Shrine. —Died Oct. 3, 2003
† Dixon, Alvin, *s.v.d.* (NO) New Orleans, LA Divine Word Missionaries. —Died July 30, 2001
† Dobosz, Emil J. (WH) (Retired). —Died July 31, 2003
† Dochstader, Richard (JOL) Plainfield, IL St. Mary. —Died Sept. 5, 2003
† Dockendorff, Carl J. (LC) (Retired). —Died Oct. 19, 2003
† Doherty, Luke, *o.s.b.* (SD) Oceanside, CA Prince of Peace Abbey. —Died Oct. 28, 2002
† Dolan, James F., *s.j.* (NEW) Jersey City, NJ St. Peter's College. —Died March 15, 2002
† Domnick, Alphonsus M., *t.o.r.* (SCR) Dunmore, PA Villa St. Joseph. —Died Aug. 14, 2002
† Donaghy, Harry (ALB) Troy, NY St. Mary's. —Died Aug. 25, 2003
† Donahoe, James H., *s.j.* (BAL) Baltimore, MD Jesuit Fathers & Brothers. —Died Aug. 23, 2002
† Donahue, Paul H. (DAV) (Retired). —Died May 4, 2003
† Donatelli, John, *o.f.m.cap.* (WH) Wheeling, WV Paul VI Friary. —Died June 13, 2003
† Donnelly, Jeffrey, *o.f.m.* (CHI) Chicago, IL St. Peter. —Died Aug. 26, 2002
† Donnelly, Jerome A., *o.f.m.* (PAT) Butler, NJ St. Anthony Friary. —Died Sept. 7, 2003
† Donohie, John M. (PH) Philadelphia, PA Immaculate Heart of Mary. —Died Jan. 16, 2003
† Donovan, Rev. Msgr. Edmund J. (E) (Retired). —Died Oct. 25, 2003
† Doogan, Rev. Msgr. John P. (SEA) Mercer Island, WA St. Monica. —Died July 22, 2003
† Dooley, Roderick M., *o.p.* (CHI) River Forest, IL St. Thomas Aquinas Priory. —Died June 15, 2002
† Dorff, John, *c.ss.r.* (HBG) Ephrata, PA St. Clement. —Died 7, 2002
† Dougherty, Joseph D. (PH) (Retired). —Died Feb. 23, 2003
† Dowling, Jude, *c.p.* (HRT) West Hartford, CT Holy Family Monastery. —Died 2002
† Downey, Timothy M. (TOL) (Retired). —Died Jan. 21, 2003
† Doyle, James J., *c.s.c.* (SCR) Wilkes-Barre, PA Kings College. —Died Oct. 13, 2002
† Doyle, John F. (NEW) (Retired). —Died Nov. 27, 2003
† Doyle, John J., *o.f.m.* (PAT) Butler, NJ St. Anthony Church-Parish House. —Died June 30, 2002
† Doyle, Richard J. (ALB) Athens, NY St. Patrick's. —Died July 10, 2003
† Doyle, Robert A., *s.j.* (STL) St. Louis, MO White House Retreat Jesuit Community. —Died May 1, 2002
† Drab, Stephen J. (GBG) (Retired). —Died May 16, 2003
† Drew, John J., *m.m.* (NY) Maryknoll, NY Maryknoll Fathers and Brothers. —Died June 26, 2003
† Drexler, George D. (NEW) (Retired). —Died Oct. 15, 2003
† Driscoll, George F., *s.j.* (NY) New York, NY Fordham University. —Died July 25, 2003
† Driscoll, Thomas F. (OG) Alexandria Bay, NY St. Cyril's; Redwood, NY St. Francis Xavier. —Died Aug. 29, 2003
† Dubois, Yvon, *a.a.* (BO) Brighton, MA Assumptionists. —Died March 31, 2002
† Duchala, Francis Solanus, *o.f.m.* (ALN) Easton, PA St. Francis Friary. —Died March 2, 2003
† Duff, Thomas M., *o.s.m.* (CHI) Chicago, IL Resurrection Life Center. —Died Sept. 13, 2002
† Duffy, Francis L., *s.j.* (BAL) Baltimore, MD Mercy Health Service, Inc.. —Died Sept. 29, 2002
† Duffy, Rev. Msgr. John F. (ROC) (Retired). —Died Feb. 13, 2003
† Duffy, John J. (PH) (Retired). —Died June 21, 2003
† Dungan, Cormac, *o.f.m.* (BO) Boston, MA St. Anthony Residence. —Died Nov. 10, 2001
† Dunne, James J., *s.s.c.* (STP) Hastings, MN Regina Medical Complex. —Died Sept. 17, 2003
† Dunnigan, Daniel D., *s.j.* (CLV) Cuyahoga Falls, OH Walsh Jesuit High School. —Died Dec. 15, 2002
† Durkin, Joseph T., *s.j.* (WDC) Washington, DC Georgetown University. —Died 2003
† Dwyer, Rev. Msgr. Adrian I. (STL) St. Louis, MO St. Roch Rectory. —Died June 5, 2003
† Dzierzek, Zygmunt, *o.m.i.* (BEL) Belleville, IL Shrine of Our Lady of the Snows. —Died Feb. 22, 2001
† Eggert, Charles M. (STP) (Retired). —Died June 20, 2003
† Eilers, Joseph B. (STL) (Retired). —Died Nov. 15, 2003
† Elder, Rev. Msgr. Jerome (LA) (Retired). —Died June 30, 2003
† Ellison, Joseph, *c.ss.r.* (SP) Tampa, FL St. Joseph. —Died Jan. 3, 2002
† Elo, Richard, *c.pp.s.* (CIN) Carthagena, OH St. Charles. —Died Jan. 19, 2002
† Elsinghorst, Francis X., *s.j.* (NY) Bronx, NY Murray-Weigel Hall. —Died June 10, 2003
† Emling, Marion J., *o.s.b.* (GBG) (Retired). —Died Feb. 21, 2003
† Englehart, William (JKS) (Retired). —Died April 29, 2003
† Englert, William J. (CLV) Fairport Harbor, OH St. Anthony of Padua Pastor Emeritus. —Died Nov. 23, 2003
† English, Richard, *s.j.* (BUF) Buffalo, NY St. Michael. —Died Nov. 14, 2001
† Erb, Charles, *s.v.d.* (TR) Bordentown, NJ Society of the Divine Word. —Died Aug. 14, 2002
† Erpelding, Martin Bernard (DET) (Retired). —Died Nov. 3, 2002
† Escobar, Octavio (STO) Ceres, CA St. Jude's Church. —Died March 12, 2003
† Esparza, Javier, *ss.cc.* Guaynabo, PR Nuestra Senora de la Paz. —Died 2003
† Espitia, David (SAN) Colorado City, TX St. Ann Church. —Died June 13, 2003
† Etzel, George A. (MIL) (Retired). —Died April 11, 2003
† Evans, George J., *o.c.s.o.* (SAT) San Antonio, TX Audie Murphy VA Hospital. —Died Nov. 9, 2002
† Ezerskis, Charles E. (CHI) (Retired). —Died Oct. 12, 2003
† Faddish, Alvin V., *o.f.m.* (PAT) Paterson, NJ St. Bonaventure. —Died Feb. 24, 2003
† Fahey, Joseph R., *s.j.* (BO) Chestnut Hill, MA Boston College. —Died Jan. 16, 2002
† Falanga, Anthony, *c.m.* (SPC) Cape Girardeau, MO St. Vincent de Paul. —Died Nov. 1, 2001
† Farrell, John A., *c.s.p.* (BRK) Jamaica Estates, NY Paulist Fathers. —Died May 22, 2002
† Farrell, John, *c.ss.r.* (BAL) Baltimore, MD Sacred Heart of Jesus. —Died May 25, 2003
† Farris, John, *c.m.* (STL) St. Louis, MO Congregation of the Mission. —Died July 6, 2003
† Fassbender, A. Dart, *c.m.* (NO) New Orleans, La Vincentian Fathers. —Died Sept. 30, 2003
† Faucher, Henry L. (SR) (Retired). —Died April 16, 2003
† Fay, John F., *m.m.* (NY) Maryknoll, NY Maryknoll Fathers and Brothers. —Died Feb. 7, 2003
† Feeney, Rev. Msgr. Edward J. (E) Erie, PA Holy Family. —Died May 4, 2003
† Feldman, George J., *o.praem.* (GB) De Pere, WI St. Norbert Abbey. —Died Aug. 5, 2002
† Fell, Gall, *o.s.b.* (SCL) Collegeville, MN St. John's Abbey. —Died Oct. 19, 2001
† Feltman, Harold R. (GR) (Retired). —Died Aug. 17, 2003
† Fenton, Rev. William, *O.C.D.* (LA) Alhambra, CA St. Therese. —Died 2003
† Fernandez, Michael, *c.m.f.* (CHI) Chicago, IL Our Lady of Guadalupe. —Died 2002
† Ferre, Antonio (PCE) (On Duty Outside the Diocese). —Died Sept., 2003
† Figge, Glennon, *c.m.* (EVN) Evansville, IN St. Mary's Medical Center of Evansville, Inc.. —Died March 13, 2002
† Filippine, John E. (CIN) Cincinnati, OH St. Vivian. —Died Jan. 11, 2003
† Finis, John J. (EVN) (Retired). —Died Nov. 18, 2002
† Finnegan, Ambrose, *o.f.m.conv.* (STP) Prior Lake, MN Franciscan Retreat Center. —Died Oct. 22, 2001
† Finnegan, Corentine, *o.c.s.o.* (ATL) Conyers, GA The Monastery of the Holy Spirit. —Died Nov. 26, 2002
† Fiol, Enrique, *s.j.* (SFS) (Retired). —Died Aug., 2002
† Fischer, Charles G. (OWN) (Retired). —Died July 2, 2003
† Fisher, Gerald E. (LC) (Retired). —Died Oct. 2, 2003
† Fisher, James F., *c.s.p.* (MEM) Memphis, TN St. Patrick. —Died Sept. 26, 2002
† Fisher, Merle J., *s.m.* (HON) Kapaa, HI St. Catherine. —Died Nov. 26, 2001
† Fisherkeller, William, *c.s.v.* (SFD) Granite City, IL Holy Family Parish. —Died Nov. 8, 2002
† Fitzgerald, Gerald J. (BO) Somerville, MA St. Ann. —Died June 29, 2003
† Fitzgerald, John B., *c.m.* (ALN) Roseto, PA Our Lady of Good Counsel. —Died Oct. 12, 2001
† Fitzgerald, John W. (SFE) (Retired). —Died March 23, 2003
† Fitzgerald, Mark J., *c.s.c.* (FTW) South Bend, IN Congregation of Holy Cross. —Died Sept. 3, 2002
† Fitzgerald, Neil F. (HRT) (Retired). —Died Oct. 2, 2003
† Fitzpatrick, Jerold F. (MAD) Gratiot, WI St. Joseph; South Wayne, WI St. John. —Died May 5, 2003
† Flaherty, Daniel E. (BO) Salem, MA St. James. —Died Nov. 14, 2003
† Flak, Mirko, *s.d.b.* (LA) Rosemead, CA Salesian Youth Retreat Center. —Died Feb. 17, 2003
† Flanagan, Thomas, *o.m.i.* (BO) (Retired). —Died Dec. 11, 2001
† Fleming, Patrick J., *c.m.* (PH) Philadelphia, PA Congregation of the Mission. —Died June 11, 2002
† Foley, James F. (BUR) (Retired). —Died Nov. 27, 2002
† Foley, Leo A., *s.m.* (WDC) Washington, DC Catholic University of America. —Died April 16, 2001
† Foley, Louis A., *o.f.m.* (PAT) Ringwood, NJ Holy Name Friary. —Died May 21, 2002
† Ford, John, *c.s.s.* (SPR) Pittsfield, MA Our Lady of Mt. Carmel. —Died 2003
† Forsthoefel, Paulinus F., *s.j.* (DET) Detroit, MI University of Detroit. —Died July 19, 2003
† Fortin, Ernest, *a.a.* (BO) Boston, MA Assumptionist Center. —Died 2003
† Fosselman, Robert J. (LFT) (Retired). —Died May 27, 2003
† Fosselman, Robert (FTW) (Retired). —Died May 27, 2003
† Fox, James F., *s.j.* (NY) New York, NY Loyola School. —Died Dec. 14, 2001
† Foy, Edward J. (ROC) (Retired). —Died April 24, 2003
† Foy, Felician A., *o.f.m.* (NEW) Fair Lawn, NJ St. Anne Church-Friary. —Died Feb. 21, 2002
† Fraraccio, Ugo M., *s.d.v.* (PAT) Florham Park, NJ Father Justin Vocationary. —Died July 28, 2003
† Freeman, Joseph M., *s.j.* (STL) St. Louis, MO Fusz Pavilion. —Died March 18, 2002
† Freeman, Rev. Msgr. Robert E. (CC) (Retired). —Died Sept. 16, 2003
† Fregault, Roland A., *o.f.m.* (NEW) Elmwood Park, NJ St. Leo. —Died Aug. 12, 2002
† Fremmholz, Anthony F., *c.s.sp.* (BR) (Retired). —Died Jan. 27, 2002
† Frese, Joseph R., *s.j.* (NY) Bronx, NY Fordham University. —Died Jan. 30, 2002
† Friel, Arthur, *s.s.c.* (PRO) Bristol, RI St. Columban. —Died Jan. 27, 2002
† Frizzell, Edward, *s.d.b.* (NY) Port Chester, NY Corpus Christi Parish. —Died Aug. 5, 2003
† Frommelt, Robert M., *s.j.* (MIL) Wauwatosa, WI St. Camillus. —Died Sept. 27, 2002
† Fron, Raymond S. (SAG) Bay City, MI St. Joseph. —Died Dec. 14, 2002
† Fu, John, *s.v.d.* (CHI) Techny, IL Society of the Divine Word. —Died Feb. 11, 2002
† Fuoco, Armando (SHP) (Retired). —Died Aug. 27, 2003

† Gabalski, Rev. Msgr. John R. (BUF) Buffalo, NY St. Stanislaus Parish. —Died Oct. 9, 2003
† Gaffney, James (MEM) (Retired). —Died 2003
† Gailiusis, George, *o.f.m.* (PRT) Kennebunkport, ME St. Anthony's Friary. —Died Aug. 30, 2002
† Galchus, Robert P., *c.m.* (PH) Philadelphia, PA Congregation of the Mission. —Died March 3, 2002
† Gall, Florian J. (MET) Whitehouse Station, NJ Our Lady of Lourdes. —Died June 28, 2003
† Gallagher, William P. (BUR) Woodstock, VT Our Lady of the Snows. —Died Oct. 13, 2003
† Gallo, Rev. Msgr. Louis J. (PAT) Paterson, NJ St. Mary's. —Died Dec. 21, 2003
† Gannon, Charles E. (DAV) (Retired). —Died March 18, 2003
† Garcia, John (OAK) Ripon, CA St. Patrick. —Died April 5, 2003
† Garvey, John, *g.h.m.* (CIN) Cincinnati, OH Headquarters of Glenmary Home Missioners. —Died Feb. 12, 2002
† Gasparro, Anthony, *o.s.a.* (PH) Philadelphia, PA St. Nicholas of Tolentine. —Died March 20, 2002
† Gaudette, Edward J. (BO) (Senior Priest). —Died June 16, 2003
† Gaul, Cornelius (DM) (Retired). —Died June 22, 2003
† Gaydos, Francis, *c.m.* (FgM) Vincentian Foreign Mission. —Died May 24, 2002
† Gendusa, Anthony, *m.s.c.* (RCK) Aurora, IL Missionaries of the Sacred Heart Community. —Died Jan. 8, 2002
† Gerrity, John J. (CLV) Maple Heights, OH St. Martin of Tours Pastor Emeritus. —Died Nov. 2, 2003
† Gfroerer, Gerard J. (RVC) (Retired). —Died Feb. 18, 2003
† Gibbons, Thomas J., *s.j.* (BO) Boston, MA Provincial Offices. —Died Feb. 26, 2002
† Giblin, Charles H., *s.j.* (NY) Bronx, NY Fordham University. —Died Jan. 19, 2002
† Gidley, Lawrence, *o.s.b.* (KC) Conception, MO Conception Abbey. —Died Dec. 6, 2001
† Giguere, Robert J., *s.s.* (BAL) (Retired). —Died Feb. 10, 2003
† Gilsoul, James M. (GB) Institute, WI SS. Peter and Paul; Sturgeon Bay, WI St. Joseph.. —Died Feb. 12, 2003
† Girdis, Joseph C. (PIT) (Retired). —Died Jan. 29, 2003
† Glebe, Edward Joseph, *c.ss.r.* (STL) Liguori, MO St. Clement's. —Died Dec. 31, 2002
† Glennon, Rev. Msgr. William (PAT) (Retired). —Died Nov. 23, 2003
† Gloisten, Robert (RIC) Richmond, VA St. Patrick. —Died Dec. 2, 2002
† Goebel, Nicholas L. (MIL) (Retired). —Died May 10, 2003
† Goedken, James J. (DUB) Waterloo, IA Queen of Peace. —Died June 3, 2003
† Goentges, Charles Joseph (DET) (Retired). —Died Dec. 26, 2002
† Gomez, Francisco, *c.m.f.* Barrio Rio Canas, PR Inmaculado Corazon de Maria. —Died 2003
† Gootee, Stanley, *s.v.d.* (BLX) Bay St. Louis, MS St. Augustine. —Died March 10, 2002
† Goudreau, Remy A., *o.f.m.* (BO) Boston, MA St. Anthony Residence. —Died March 24, 2002
† Grady, Charles, *c.s.s.* (NOR) Cromwell, CT Stigmatine House of Formation. —Died March 7, 2002
† Grady, William R. (LFT) Munice, IN, St. Mary. —Died Oct. 6, 2003
† Graff, Ed (AMA) Silverton, TX Our Lady of Loretto. —Died Nov. 25, 2002
† Graham, John E. (DUB) (Retired). —Died Feb. 15, 2003
† Greaney, Francis M. (BO) (Senior Priest). —Died June 30, 2003
† Green, William L., *c.m.* (BUF) Niagara, NY Niagara University. —Died Jan. 26, 2002
† Grennan, Thomas J. (NO) (Retired). —Died Oct. 22, 2003
† Gress, Armond Edward, *o.s.b.* (CLV) Cleveland, OH Benedictine Order of Cleveland. —Died Nov. 1, 2001
† Greven, Raymond, *c.pp.s.* (CIN) Carthagena, OH St. Charles. —Died Nov. 25, 2001
† Griffin, Joseph T., *c.s.p.* (BO) Boston, MA Paulist Fathers Residence. —Died 2003
† Grinena, Agustin (PCE) Penuelas, PR Sacred Heart of Jesus. —Died Aug., 2003
† Grismer, Raymond J. (CLV) Sheffield, OH St. Theresa of Avila Pastor Emeritus. —Died Nov. 14, 2003
† Grodavent, Rev. Msgr. Thomas J. (WDC) (Retired). —Died May 25, 2003
† Groenewold, Robert E., *s.j.* (NY) Bronx, NY Fordham University. —Died Sept. 13, 2002
† Groesch, Edward (SFD) (Retired). —Died Sept. 2, 2003
† Gross, Francis J., *o.s.f.s.* (FgM) Oblates of St. Francis De Sales. —Died July 25, 2003
† Gudino, Eduardo (SD) Oceanside, CA St. Mary Star of the Sea. —Died April 30, 2003
† Guillen, Manuel R. (SB) (Retired). —Died Dec. 1, 2003
† Gulas, William E. (CLV) Cleveland, OH St. Stanislaus Friary. —Died 2003
† Gulas, William, *o.f.m.* (CLV) Cleveland, OH St. Stanislaus. —Died Dec. 7, 2002
† Guminga, Theodore C. (STP) (Retired). —Died April 3, 2003
† Gutierrez, Julio (SJN) (Retired). —Died 2003
† Gutierrez y Alvarez, Julio (CGS) (Retired). —Died May 11, 2003
† Haas, Melvin B. (BEL) (Retired). —Died Sept. 11, 2003
† Hacker, Leonard G., *s.j.* (MI) Majuro, MH Cathedral of the Assumption. —Died May 31, 2003
† Hackett, John P. (BUR) St. Albans, VT Our Lady of the Lake. —Died Nov. 21, 2002
† Haddad, Rev. Msgr. Edmund G. (WOR) (Retired). —Died Nov. 21, 2003
† Hafner, Walter, *s.v.d.* (CHI) Techny, IL Society of the Divine Word. —Died Sept. 19, 2002
† Hagan, Barry J., *c.s.c.* (P) Portland, OR University of Portland. —Died March 27, 2002
† Hagan, Thomas C. (PH) Philadelphia, PA St. Cecilia. —Died Jan. 31, 2003
† Hager, G. Carl, *c.s.c.* (FTW) South Bend, IN Congregation of Holy Cross. —Died April 9, 2002
† Hale, Rev. Msgr. Harry L. (BGP) (Retired). —Died Jan. 15, 2003
† Halligan, James (LIN) (Retired). —Died March 23, 2003
† Halloran, Jerome D. (WIN) (Retired). —Died Sept. 1, 2003
† Hamilton, Joseph K. (L) (Retired). —Died April 9, 2003
† Hanchak, Augustine, *c.pp.s.* (CIN) Carthagena, OH St. Charles. —Died Nov. 20, 2001
† Hanley, John P. (MIL) (Retired). —Died March 31, 2003
† Hanlon, Morgan, *c.p.* (NEW) Union City, NJ Congregation of the Passion. —Died 2002
† Hannaway, Arthur W. (VEN) Sarasota, FL St. Patrick. —Died Sept. 15, 2003
† Hansen, Albert M. (BUF) Tonawanda, NY St. Francis of Assisi Parish. —Died March 23, 2003
† Hansen, Robert H. (LC) (Retired). —Died May 5, 2003
† Hanzo, Robert G. (CLV) Painesville, OH St. Mary Parish Pastor Emeritus. —Died Jan. 6, 2003
† Happel, Stephen P. (IND) Washington, DC The Catholic University of America. —Died Oct. 4, 2003
† Happel, Rev. Msgr. Stephen W., *s.t.d.* (WDC) Washington, DC Catholic University of America. —Died 2003
† Hardiman, Rev. Msgr. James C. (CHI) (Retired). —Died April 30, 2003
† Hart, Rev. Msgr. Peter F. (BO) (Senior Priest). —Died June 8, 2003
† Hart, William T. (NEW) (Retired). —Died July 5, 2003
† Hasbrouck, John–Baptist, *o.c.s.o.* (P) Lafayette, OR Abbey of Our Lady of Guadalupe. —Died March 8, 2001
† Haskamp, Edward F. (CIN) Norwood, OH Holy Trinity Church. —Died Aug. 29, 2003
† Haworth, Marcus A., *s.j.* (STL) St. Louis, MO St. Louis University. —Died May 16, 2002
† Hayes, Michael T. (DUL) Moose Lake, MN Holy Angels Church. —Died Aug. 4, 2003
† Hayes, Peter F. (CHI) (Retired). —Died Aug. 4, 2003
† Healy, Kilian, *o.carm* (BO) Peabody, MA Catholic Information Center. —Died 2003
† Hebert, Albert J., *s.m.* Washington, DC Marist Center. —Died April 3, 2003
† Hecht, F. Torrens, *s.j.* (DET) Clarkston, MI Colombiere Center. —Died Jan. 6, 2003
† Heckel, John F., *o.s.f.s.* (WIL) Wilmington, DE Salesianum School. —Died June 21, 2002
† Heeney, Walter, *o.s.b.* (K) Conception, MO St. Columba Church. —Died April 20, 2002
† Heet, Alan, *o.f.m.* (CIN) Cincinnati, OH St. Francis Seraph Friary. —Died Feb. 6, 2002
† Hein, John L., *s.j.* (NO) New Orleans, LA Our Lady of Wisdom. —Died Dec. 22, 2001
† Helduser, Rev. Msgr. Frederick J. (PH) Drexel Hill, PA St. Dorothy. —Died July 2, 2003
† Hemkens, Edward B. (STL) (Retired). —Died March 18, 2003
† Hempel, John L. (ROC) (Retired). —Died Dec. 1, 2003
† Hendel, Rev. Msgr. Richard P. (RVC) (Retired). —Died April 30, 2003
† Hendricks, John J. (TR) (Retired). —Died Feb. 7, 2003
† Hendriks, Boniface (SFE) (Retired). —Died Nov. 9, 2003
† Henesy, William P. (RVC) (Retired). —Died Aug. 5, 2003
† Henkel, William A. (CHI) (Retired). —Died June 15, 2003
† Hennelly, Alfred T., *s.j.* (NY) Bronx, NY Fordham University. —Died Oct. 5, 2001
† Hennesey, James J., *s.j.* (BUF) East Aurora, NY Christ the King. —Died Sept. 27, 2001
† Henry, Rev. Msgr. Joseph L. (MAD) (Retired). —Died Oct. 20, 2003
† Henseler, Joseph N. (LC) (Retired). —Died Aug. 17, 2003
† Heon, Paul, *m.afr.* (SP) St. Petersburg, FL Missionaries of Africa. —Died Oct. 4, 2003
† Herbert, Albert J., *s.m.* (WDC) Washington, DC Marist Center. —Died April 3, 2003
† Herbst, Charles, *c.m.* (STL) Perryville, MO Congregation of the Mission. —Died May 20, 2002
† Hesler, Raymond F., *s.s.* (BAL) Baltimore, MD St. Charles Villa. —Died Feb. 21, 2002
† Hewitt, Charles L. (BGP) (Retired). —Died March 18, 2003
† Hewitt, William (MET) (Retired). —Died Feb. 22, 2003
† Hill, James, *S.M.A.* (NEW) Tenafly, NJ Society of African Missions, Provincialate. —Died 2003
† Hill, James, *S.M.A.* (NEW) Tenafly, NJ Society of African Missions. —Died 2003
† Hill, Rev. Msgr. Peter J. (SFE) (Retired). —Died July 26, 2003
† Hill, William B., *s.j.* (SCR) Scranton, PA University of Scranton. —Died Feb. 26, 2002
† Hillesheim, Gerald A. (NU) Gibbon, MN St. Willebrord; Franklin, MN Sacred Heart; Fairfax, MN St. Andrew. —Died March 27, 2003
† Hinnebusch, Paul G., *o.p.* (DAL) Irving, TX St. Albert the Great Priory. —Died Aug. 20, 2002
† Hisky, William G. (BAL) (Retired). —Died April 15, 2003
† Hock, William T. (CHI) (Retired). —Died Nov. 26, 2003
† Hoefler, Alexander, *s.v.d.* (LA) Torrance, CA Nativity. —Died June 26, 2002
† Hoelck, Frank L. (GI) Grand Island, NE Central Catholic Schools. —Died April 16, 2003
† Hoffman, Donald J. (STL) (Retired). —Died Oct. 27, 2003
† Hogan, Benedict, *o.carm.* (JOL) Darien, IL Carmelite Fathers Provincial Office. —Died Dec. 12, 2001
† Hogan, William H., *s.j.* (CHI) Chicago, IL Loyola University. —Died March 13, 2002
† Holden, Paul (WDC) (Retired). —Died March 16, 2003
† Holland, Kirk, *o.f.m.conv.* (ALB) Fonda, NY St. Cecilia. —Died Oct. 8, 2002
† Hoogterp, Richard P. (SAG) (Retired). —Died Sept. 27, 2002
† Houde, Arthur O. (MAN) (Retired). —Died Aug. 1, 2003
† Howell, Joseph W. (TLS) (Retired). —Died Feb. 4, 2003
† Hrdlicka, Lambert A. (STL) (Retired). —Died June 9, 2003
† Hubler, Tony (IND) Navilleton, IN St. Mary. —Died Oct. 14, 2003
† Huelsman, Richard J., *s.j.* (COL) Columbus, OH St. Matthias. —Died July 18, 2003
† Huesman, John E., *s.j.* (SJ) Los Gatos, CA Sacred Heart Jesuit Center. —Died March 10, 2002
† Hunt, Thomas, *s.c.j.* (MIL) Franklin, WI Villa Maria. —Died June 22, 2003
† Hupp, Rev. Msgr. Robert P. (OM) (Retired). —Died Aug. 29, 2003
† Hurst, Henry David, *o.s.b.* (PRO) Portsmouth, RI Abbey of St. Gregory the Great. —Died June 12, 2003
† Husselbeck, Francis E. (ALB) (Retired). —Died May 15, 2003
† Hutnik, William J. (PIT) (Retired). —Died Aug. 17, 2002
† Iacono, Leonardo (ALN) (Retired). —Died March 18, 2003
† Ide, Harold J. (MIL) (Retired). —Died May 15, 2003
† Illies, Wilfred (SCL) (Retired). —Died March 25, 2003
† Immel, Joseph (LAN) (Retired). —Died Oct. 22, 2003
† Isenecker, Lawrence, *s.j.* (DET) Clarkston, MI Colombiere Center. —Died June 15, 2003
† Istok, Adolph, *c.r.* (CHI) Chicago, IL Gordon Technical High School. —Died Feb. 3, 2002
† Jackanich, Rev. Msgr. Joseph (PSC) (Retired). —Died Nov. 10, 2003
† Jacobs, Joseph A. (FTW) (Retired). —Died July 14, 2003
† Jacobs, Pierre P., *s.j.* (SJ) Los Gatos, CA Sacred Heart Jesuit Center. —Died July 26, 2002
† Jadgchew, John, *c.pp.s.* (CIN) Carthagena, OH St. Charles. —Died Nov. 12, 2001
† Jaekle, Lawrence E. (CIN) (Retired). —Died Dec. 15, 2002
† Jalbert, Marcel P. (SB) (Retired). —Died Aug. 23, 2003
† James, Frank, *s.p.* (STL) (Retired). —Died May 8, 2002

† James, Rev. Msgr. R. Joseph (STA) Jacksonville, FL Mary, Queen of Heaven. —Died May 7, 2003
† Jarvais, Rev. Msgr. Walter G. (NEW) (Retired). —Died Feb. 3, 2003
† Jellison, Donald Allen, *s.j.* (SPK) Spokane, WA Province Infirmary. —Died April 22, 2002
† Jendzura, John M., *c.s.sp.* (PIT) Bethel Park, PA Holy Ghost Animation Center. —Died April 13, 2002
† Jendzura, Joseph T., *o.s.f.s.* (WIL) Wilmington, DE St. Catherine. —Died June 10, 2002
† Jenkins, Floyd A., *s.j.* (LA) Los Angeles, CA Loyola Marymount University. —Died Aug. 21, 2002
† Jenner, James Stephen, *o.p.* (SEA) Seattle, WA Blessed Sacrament. —Died Jan. 9, 2003
† Johnson, Joseph P., *s.j.* (LSC) Artesia, NM St. Anthony. —Died 2003
† Jonaitis, Peter (ALB) (Retired). —Died Oct. 21, 2002
† Jorn, Charles Sebastian, *o.p.* (NY) Pleasantville, NY Holy Innocents Rectory. —Died Sept. 25, 2002
† Joyce, Fabian F., *o.f.m.* (PAT) Ringwood, NJ Holy Name Friary. —Died June 27, 2003
† Junod, Louis J. (KNX) (Retired). —Died June 6, 2003
† Jutt, Julius A. (SPR) South Deerfield, MA St. James. —Died April 10, 2003
† Kaiser, Joseph A. (BAL) (Retired). —Died July 10, 2003
† Kaminski, Neal, *o.f.m.* (MIL) Burlington, WI Queen of Peace Friary. —Died Sept. 15, 2003
† Kaminski, Sylvester (Retired). —Died July 26, 2003
† Kampfer, Gerald D. (ALB) (Retired). —Died Jan. 6, 2003
† Kane, Justin A. (DUB) (Retired). —Died May 15, 2003
† Kane, Rev. Msgr. Thomas A. (PH) (Retired). —Died July 10, 2003
† Kania, Wojciech, *s.ch.* (LA) Los Angeles, CA Our Lady of the Bright Mount. —Died Jan. 20, 2002
† Kaplinski, Peter (VIC) Yorktown, TX Holy Cross. —Died April 7, 2003
† Karaffa, James G., *c.s.c.* (FTW) South Bend, IN Holy Cross. —Died June 23, 2002
† Karath, William (P) Bandon, OR Holy Trinity. —Died Jan. 11, 2003
† Karlin, Paulinus, *o.f.m.cap.* (SAL) Hays, KS St. Joseph. —Died April 12, 2003
† Karlowicz, Edwin, *c.r.* (CHI) Chicago, IL St. Hyacinth. —Died Sept. 5, 2002
† Karwel, Rev. Msgr. Henry (BAL) Ware, MA St. Mary's Parish. —Died 2003
† Kasel, Joseph M. (NU) (Retired). —Died Oct. 11, 2003
† Katsuno, Peter–Baptist, *s.a.* (NY) Garrison, NY Franciscan Friars of the Atonement. —Died Jan. 14, 2002
† Kearney, George W. (DEN) (Retired). —Died Jan. 30, 2003
† Kearney, Rev. Msgr. Vincent L. (KC) (Retired). —Died April 15, 2003
† Keblesh, John W. (PRM) Brunswick, OH St. Emilian. —Died April 4, 2003
† Kedziora, Gerald, *o.f.m.conv.* (HBG) Shamokin, PA Mother Cabrini. —Died March 21, 2002
† Keenan, Paul, *s.t.* (WDC) Adelphi, MD Missionary Servants of the Most Holy Trinity. —Died Feb. 20, 2002
† Keene, Michael, *o.s.b.* (IND) St. Meinrad, IN St. Meinrad Archabbey. —Died 2003
† Keith, John C. (SD) (Retired). —Died May 1, 2003
† Kelleher, Cyril, *o.f.m.cap.* (LA) Solvang, CA Old Mission Santa Ines. —Died Jan. 17, 2002
† Kelleher, James L. (PRO) Johnston, RI St. Brigid. —Died May 15, 2003
† Kelley, John J. (SCR) (Retired). —Died Feb. 20, 2003
† Kelley, John P. (Retired). —Died Oct. 28, 2003
† Kelley, William, *s.v.d.* (BLX) Bay St. Louis, MS St. Augustine. —Died Aug. 28, 2002
† Kelliher, Rev. Msgr. John J. (WOR) (Retired). —Died Oct. 18, 2003
† Kelliher, Robert Daniel, *o.c.s.o.* (DEN) Snowmass, CO St. Benedicts's Monastery. —Died March 24, 2002
† Kelly, Leonard A., *o.f.m.* (PAT) Ringwood, NJ Holy Name Friary. —Died May 19, 2002
† Kelly, Michael J. (OM) (Retired). —Died Dec. 6, 2003
† Kelly, Patrick J. (IND) Indianapolis, IN St. Andrew the Apostle. —Died Dec. 30, 2003
† Kennedy, Daniel Eugene, *o.p.* (WDC) Washington, DC St. Dominic Priory. —Died Sept. 25, 2002
† Kennedy, Jeremiah, *c.p.* (HRT) (Retired). —Died 2002
† Kennedy, John A. (LA) (Retired). —Died May 14, 2003
† Kennedy, Rev. Msgr. Thomas I. (SFR) Novato, CA Our Lady of Loretto.. —Died Feb. 5, 2003
† Kenney, Rev. Msgr. Timothy Kent, OH St. Patrick. —Died March 23, 2003
† Ketchersid, Corbin W. (R) (Retired). —Died April 5, 2003
† Kettner, Joseph F., *m.s.* (ORL) Orlando, FL Good Shepherd. —Died March 6, 2002
† Keutzer, Walter J. (STL) (Retired). —Died April 29, 2003
† Kicia, Chester, *o.f.m.* (BGP) Bridgeport, CT St. Michael The Archangel. —Died July 20, 2003
† Kilarecki, George W. (PIT) (Retired). —Died Nov. 5, 2002
† Kilfoil, Rev. Msgr. J. Patrick (EVN) (Retired). —Died June 6, 2003
† Kilsdonk, Edward (GB) (Retired). —Died July 14, 2003
† Kinch, Edwin M., *o.s.m.* (FgM) Kwazulu–Natal, South Africa. —Died May 26, 2003
† King, David George, *s.j.* (P) Portland, OR Colombiere Community. —Died July 31, 2002
† Kircher, Edward H. (CC) (Retired). —Died Jan. 25, 2003
† Kisluk, Aloysius J. (NOR) Middletown, CT St. Mary of Czestochowa. —Died March 4, 2003
† Kissane, Richard J., *c.s.sp.* (SB) Hemet, CA Holy Ghost Fathers. —Died Oct. 18, 2002
† Kleinhans, Rev. Msgr. Thomas G. (FRS) Visalia, CA St. Mary. —Died Jan. 4, 2004
† Klementowicz, Chester (ALB) (Retired) —Died Dec. 22, 2002
† Klinger, Attilio, *s.d.b.* (NY) New Rochelle, NY Salesian Provincial House. —Died May 13, 2002
† Kloeckner, William (SCL) (Retired). —Died Sept. 2, 2003
† Klopke, John R., *c.pp.s.* (OAK) San Leandro, CA Society of the Precious Blood. —Died Aug. 26, 2003
† Kloster, Carl G., *s.j.* (DeN) Denver, CO Xavier Jesuit Center. —Died July 20, 2003
† Knapp, Joseph, *o.c.s.o.* (DUB) Peosta, IA New Melleray Abbey. —Died Feb. 14, 2003
† Knier, Aloysius M. (GB) (Retired). —Died Feb. 20, 2003
† Knoll, Mark, *c.ss.r.* (ORL) New Smyrna Beach, FL Redemptorist Fathers. —Died Dec. 22, 2002
† Knott, Edward J. (MAN) (Retired). —Died Jan. 2, 2003
† Kok, Bede, *o.c.s.o.* (L) Trappist, KY Abbey of Our Lady of Gethsemani. —Died March 17, 2002
† Kolaczek, John, *o.c.d.* (GRY) Munster, IN Discalced Carmelite Fathers Monastery. —Died May 14, 2003
† Kolath, George (STP) Minneapolis, MN St. Timothy's. —Died Aug. 24, 2003
† Kolbusz, Stanley (GB) (Retired). —Died June 23, 2003
† Kondik, David M., *o.s.m.* (ORG) Fullerton, CA St. Juliana Falconieri. —Died May 27, 2003
† Konechne, Louis (GLP) (Retired). —Died June 5, 2003
† Konisky, Edward (ALB) (Retired). —Died Feb. 21, 2003
† Koop, Cecil, *o.f.m.* (SFD) Springfield, IL Our Lady of Angels Friary. —Died May 31, 2002
† Korbic, Benno, *o.f.m.* (CHI) Lemont, IL Commissariat of the Holy Cross. —Died Feb. 2, 2002
† Koren, Henry J., *c.s.sp* (PIT) Bethel Park, PA Holy Ghost Fathers and Brothers Provincialate. —Died Feb. 8, 2002
† Kornbrust, Herman, *o.s.b.* (OM) Schuyler, NE Benedictine Mission House. —Died June 18, 2000
† Kossel, Clifford George, *s.j.* (SPK) Spokane, WA Gonzaga University. —Died Aug. 16, 2002
† Koster, Theodore, *o.c.s.o.* (SPC) Ava, MO Assumption Abbey. —Died Aug. 8, 2002
† Kottiry, Alphonsus (DUL) (On Duty Outside the Diocese). —Died Oct. 12, 2003
† Kovacsik, Clement, *s.t.* (WDC) Adelphi, MO Missionary Servants of the Most Holy Trinity. —Died May 11, 2002
† Kowalski, Isidore, *o.f.m.conv.* (FR) New Bedford, MA Our Lady of Perpetual Help. —Died Sept. 13, 2003
† Kozina, Mark, *o.f.m.* (CHI) Chicago, IL Croatian Franciscan Custody of the Holy Family. —Died April 21, 2003
† Kreuzer, Rev. Msgr. Gerald J. (BUF) (Retired). —Died Oct. 27, 2003
† Krupa, Alexander, *o.f.m.* (Y) Youngstown, OH Mt. Alverna Friary. —Died June 27, 2002
† Kryger, Henry, *c.r.* (STL) St. Louis, MO Our Lady of Loretto Parish. —Died Dec. 23, 2002
† Kubiak, Edward J. (GR) (Retired). —Died Feb. 4, 2003
† Kubisiak, Robert, *c.p.* (OAK) San Leandro, CA Assumption of the Blessed Virgin Mary. —Died 2002
† Kucera, Robert M., *o.s.m.* (CHI) Chicago, IL Order of Friar Servants of Mary. —Died Dec. 20, 2001
† Kumle, Peter, *c.p.* (CHI) Chicago, IL Passionist Community – Immaculate Conception Monastery. —Died June 11, 2002
† Kuntz, Ildephonse, *ss.cc.* (HON) Kaneohe, HI Sacred Hearts Center. —Died March 22, 2003
† Kurylo, Michael (STN) (Retired). —Died 2003
† Kurzawski, Casimir J. (WOR) (Retired). —Died Oct. 12, 2003
† Kyle, John M. (CHI) (Retired). —Died Oct. 9, 2003
† Labonte, Louis Roger (MET) Edison, NJ St. Helena. —Died March 25, 2003
† Lacasse, Aime, *m.afr.* (SP) St. Petersburg, FL Missionaries of Africa. —Died March 30, 2003
† Lacey, James, *c.ss.r.* (FgM) Redemptorist Foreign Missions. —Died Sept. 2, 2002
† Ladden, Timothy M. (OG) (Retired). —Died Jan. 31, 2003
† Lagana, Rev. Msgr. Frank A. (GAL) Houston, TX Vice Pres., St. Mary's Children's Relief Fund. —Died Oct. 20, 2003
† Laheta, Andrew P. (CLV) Cleveland, OH Our Lady of Mercy Parish Pastor Emeritus. —Died April 4, 2003
† Lajoie, Marcel, *s.m.* (PRT) Greenville, ME Holy Family. —Died June 18, 2003
† Lange, L. Joseph (PRT) (Retired). —Died Oct. 17, 2003
† Lange, Lawrence P. (TLS) (Retired). —Died Aug. 22, 2003
† Langerholz, Callistus, *o.f.m.* (CHI) Chicago, IL St. Stephen. —Died Feb. 16, 2002
† Langevin, Fernand A., *m.s.* (FR) Attleboro, MA La Salette. —Died July 13, 2003
† Langlinais, J. Willis, *s.m.* (SAT) San Antonio, TX St. Mary's University of San Antonio. —Died Aug. 3, 2002
† Lapan, Robert (BUR) (Retired). —Died April 1, 2003
† LaRusch, Rev. Msgr. Alton J. (BUF) (Retired). —Died March 22, 2003
† Laux, Donald (GB) (Retired). —Died June 28, 2003
† Lauzon, Paul, *s.d.s.* (LC) Marshfield, WI Columbus High School. —Died Nov. 11, 2002
† Lavere, Philip A., *o.f.m.* (PAT) Ringwood NJ, Holy Name Friary. —Died May 7, 2002
† Lavin, Thomas, *s.v.d.* (MIL) East Troy, WI Society of the Divine Word. —Died Aug. 13, 2002
† Lawler, Ronald, *o.f.m.cap.* Pittsburgh, PA St. Francis Friary. —Died 2003
† Lawton, Thomas E., *c.s.c.* (FR) North Easton, MA Holy Cross Fathers Religious. —Died Aug. 25, 2002
† Leddy, Seamus, *s.s.c.* (LA) Los Angeles, CA St. Columban. —Died June 8, 2002
† Lee, Peter (LA) (Retired). —Died June 18, 2003
† Lefko, John, *c.pp.s.* (CIN) Carthagena, OH St. Charles. —Died July 1, 2002
† Legaz, Florencio, *c.m.f.* (Retired). —Died 2003
† Lehmann, Anthony Joseph, *s.j.* (SPK) Spokane, WA Gonzaga University. —Died March 8, 2002
† Leicht, Gerard, *ss.cc.* (HON) Honolulu, HI Sacred Hearts Center. —Died Jan. 24, 2002
† Leikhim, Joel, *o.s.b.* (PAT) Morristown, NJ St. Mary's Abbey. —Died April 3, 2002
† Leisle, Charles E. (LC) (Retired). —Died Sept. 26, 2003
† Lemen, William F. (CR) Bemdiji, MN St. Philip. —Died March 22, 2003
† Lemrise, Arthur, *c.s.v.* (CHI) Arlington Heights, IL Viatorian Province Center. —Died Dec. 2, 2001
† Lenoch, Francis J. (DAV) (Retired). —Died Jan. 17, 2003
† Leonard, Edmond J., *c.s.sp.* (SB) Hemet, CA Holy Ghost Fathers. —Died Feb. 19, 2003
† Leonard, John (JKS) (Retired). —Died April 28, 2003
† Leonard, Joseph (MRY) (Retired). —Died Nov. 1, 2003
† Leonard, Robert R., *s.j.* (SJ) Los Gatos, CA Sacred Heart Jesuit Center. —Died May 5, 2002
† Leotilo, Rocco, *c.s.s.* (BO) Waltham, MA Stigmatine Fathers and Brothers. —Died Sept. 3, 2002
† Lesch, Howard, *c.pp.s.* (CIN) Dayton, OH Provincial House of the Cincinnati Province. —Died June 14, 2002
† Leuer, Rev. Msgr. Anthony (LA) Rancho Palos Verdes, CA Marymount College. —Died Sept. 18, 2003
† Leveillee, Roger L. (SPC) Neosho, MO St. Canera. —Died May 6, 2003
† Levernier, Don, *g.h.m.* (CIN) Cincinnati, OH Headquarters of Glenmary Home Missioners. —Died May 29, 2002
† Lewis, Francis C. (PH) Bristol, PA St. Mark. —Died March 20, 2003
† Lewis, Francis W., *s.j.* (BGP) Fairfield, CT Fairfield University. —Died Feb. 15, 2002
† Lightner, Bede C., *o.s.b.* (CHL) Belmont, NC Belmont Abbey. —Died July 10, 2002
† Lilly, Rev. Msgr. Edward C. (SC) (Retired). —Died Oct. 30, 2003
† Lipinski, Rev. Andrew Alberic, *S.O.Cist.* (AUS) Lockhart, TX St. Mary. —Died 2003
† Lisotta, Lawrence, *o.f.m.cap.* (PAT) Passaic, NJ St. Mary's Hospital. —Died May 10, 2002
† Lizarralde, Luis, *o.f.m.* Toa Baja, PR San Jose Obrero. —Died 2003
† Llewellyn, Anselm James, *o.s.b.* (KCK) Atchison, KS Maur Hill Prep School. —Died April 30, 2003
† Lombardo, Gregory J., *c.s.c.* (FTW) South Bend, IN Congregation of Holy Cross. —Died Sept. 13, 2002
† Long, Francis C. (PHX) (Retired). —Died Sept. 5, 2003
† Lonsdale, Richard G. (PRT) Chap., Waterville, ME Blessed Sacrament Convent. —Died June 4, 2003
† Lopez, Fausto (SJ) (Retired). —Died Sept. 20, 2003

† Loughrey, Thomas F. (PH) (Retired). —Died Nov. 22, 2003
† Lovato, Charles (PAT) (Retired) Chap.. —Died April 27, 2003
† Lubicky, Rev. Msgr. John R. (CAM) (Retired). —Died April 30, 2003
† Lucey, J. Roger, *s.j.* (OAK) Berkeley, CA Jesuit School of Theology at Berkley. —Died April 7, 2002
† Lucey, John P. (SPR) (Retired). —Died July 15, 2003
† Lukaszewski, Jerome (BAL) Okinawa, Japan Asato Catholic Church. —Died 2003
† Lukaszewski, Leonard (GRY) (Retired). —Died July 8, 2003
† Lynch, Kenny, *c.p.* (DE) Detroit, MI Congregation of the Passion. —Died April 16, 2002
† Lynch, Rev. Msgr. Patrick J. (MEM) (Retired). —Died Aug. 8, 2003
† Lyons, James W. (CHI) (Retired). —Died June 3, 2003
† MacGregor, Donald (HON) Makawao, Maui, HI St. Joseph. —Died April 12, 2003
† Mack, Michael, *s.p.* (GLP) Winslow, AZ St. Joseph. —Died Dec. 7, 2001
† MacPeck, Francis D., *s.j.* (SJ) Los Gatos, CA Sacred Heart Jesuit Center. —Died June 27, 2003
† Madden, Joseph, *c.s.b.* (GAL) (Retired). —Died Jan. 5, 2003
† Madden, William O., *s.j.* (CHI) Chicago, IL St. Ignatius Jesuit Community. —Died Nov. 9, 2001
† Madubuko, Michael N., *s.j.* (CHI) Chicago, IL Chicago Province of the Society of Jesus. —Died March 21, 2002
† Magee, Andrew T. (NY) Maybrook, NY Assumption. —Died 2003
† Maglione, Joseph J. (BGP) (Retired). —Died Sept. 20, 2003
† Mahedy, Brian, *c.p.* (CHI) Chicago, IL Passionist Community – Immaculate Conception Monastery. —Died Jan. 5, 2002
† Maher, Rev. Msgr. James (SJ) (Retired). —Died Dec. 8, 2002
† Mallon, John J. (OAK) Walnut Creek, CA St. Mary. —Died Aug. 6, 2003
† Maloney, Walter (JKS) (Retired). —Died Feb. 25, 2003
† Manente, Vladimiro, *o.m.i.* (LAR) Laredo, TX San Francisco Javier Independent Mission. —Died April 28, 2002
† Mannion, B. Joseph (STO) (Retired). —Died Jan. 22, 2003
† Manny, Howard F. (ALB) (Retired). —Died Oct. 8, 2002
† Marchese, Dominic Anthony, *s.s.j.* (TR) Bay Head, NJ Sacred Heart. —Died Feb. 26, 2002
† Marciano, Charles A. (ALN) (Retired). —Died June 11, 2003
† Marcoux, John, *m.s.a.* (NOR) Cromwell, CT Society of the Missionaries of the Holy Apostles. —Died April 27, 2002
† Marcoux, John, *m.s.a.* (NOR) Cromwell, CT Society of the Missionaries of the Holy Apostles. —Died April 27, 2002
† Margola, Joseph F. (PCE) (On Duty Ourside the Diocese). —Died Sept., 2003
† Marier, Euclid A. (OG) (Retired). —Died March 29, 2003
† Markowski, Clement A. (SCR) St. John the Baptist, Exeter. —Died Nov. 19, 2002
† Marley, Rev. Msgr. Michael F. (PH) (Retired). —Died May 7, 2003
† Marpes, Thomas M. (PIT) Pittsburgh, PA Saint Pius X Parish. —Died Aug. 16, 2002
† Marquis, J. Alphee (PRT) (Retired). —Died Sept. 23, 2003
† Marron, Rev. Msgr. James (MRY) (Retired). —Died March 8, 2003
† Marron, Joseph, *c.ss.r.* (BRK) Brooklyn, NY Our Lady of Perpetual Help Basilica. —Died Feb. 18, 2003
† Marshall, David, *c.s.sp.* (PIT) Bethel Park, PA Bethel Animation Center. —Died Aug. 21, 2003
† Martel, Robert T. (PRT) (Retired). —Died Sept. 13, 2003
† Martin, Warren S., *s.j.* (SP) Tampa, FL Jesuit High School. —Died May 25, 2002
† Massmann, Albert, *o.s.b.* (OM) Elkhorn, NE Mount Michael Abbey. —Died July 13, 2003
† Massmann, Albert, *o.s.b.* (OM) Elkhorn, NE Mount Michael Abbey. —Died July 13, 2003
† Masterson, Frank David, *s.j.* (SPK) Spokane, WA Gonzaga University. —Died April 25, 2002
† Mastrovito, Francis, *t.o.r.* (OWN) Central City, KY St. Joseph. —Died May 6, 2001
† Maszkiewicz, Rev. Msgr. Mark (TLS) (Retired). —Died Sept., 2003
† Mathews, Robert (OAK) Alameda, CA St. Barnabas. —Died May 21, 2003
† Matthews, Donald C., *s.j.* (NY) Bronx, NY Fordham University. —Died Dec. 18, 2001
† Mattiello, Lucian C. (ALT) (Retired). —Died May 6, 2003
† Mattingly, Martin (OWN) Dawson Springs, KY Resurrection; Earlington, KY Immaculate Conception Admin.. —Died Sept. 9, 2003
† Mau, Joseph (LAF) (Retired). —Died July 21, 2003
† Mazaika, Joseph J. (TLS) (Retired). —Died Jan. 27, 2003
† McCann, Vincent J., *o.f.m.* (PAT) Ringwood NJ, Holy Name Friary. —Died April 5, 2002
† McCarthy, Bernard (HEL) (Retired). —Died Sept. 16, 2003
† McCarthy, Daniel J., *ss.cc.* (BO) Boston, MA St. James the Great in Chinatown. —Died Jan. 20, 2002
† McCarthy, Richard J., *c.m.* (SAT) Lesoya, TX Carmen Catholic. —Died Nov. 18, 2001
† McCarthy, Thomas H. (KC) (Retired). —Died July 2, 2003
† McCarthy, Thomas J. (SPR) (Retired). —Died June 9, 2003
† McCaslin, James, *s.s.c.* (FgM) St. Columbans Foreign Mission Society. —Died Sept. 16, 2003
† McCormack, Martin L., *o.f.m.* (PAT) Ringwood, NJ Holy Name Friary. —Died Nov. 14, 2002
† McCormick, Robert J. (MIL) (Retired). —Died July 10, 2003
† McDermott, Thomas F., *s.j.* (BO) Weston, MA Campion Center. —Died Nov. 16, 2001
† McDermott, Thomas J. (SCR) (Retired). —Died Oct. 10, 2003
† McDonnell, Francis (SD) (Retired). —Died Nov. 19, 2003
† McDonnell, Vincent M. (MOB) (Retired). —Died Nov. 5, 2003
† McEachin, Cornelius (SAG) (Retired). —Died May 16, 2003
† McElroy, William J., *c.s.sp.* (NO) New Orleans, LA Holy Ghost. —Died March 4, 2002
† McFadden, Edward J., *s.j.* (SJ) San Jose, CA Bellarmine College Preparatory. —Died May 3, 2002
† McFadden, James J., *m.m.* (HON) Honolulu, HI Maryknoll Fathers House. —Died Dec. 3, 2002
† McGlade, Desmond, *c.s.sp.* (SJ) Mountain View, CA St. Athanasius. —Died June 28, 2002
† McGlade, Thomas F. (RVC) (Retired). —Died May 22, 2003
† McGowan, John J. (RCK) (Retired). —Died Dec. 28, 2002
† McGrail, John A., *s.j.* (DET) Clarkston, MI Colombiere Center. —Died Oct. 19, 2002
† McGuinness, Lester A. (NEW) (Retired). —Died Dec. 9, 2003
† McGuire, Edward A., *o.f.m.* (PAT) Ringwood, NJ Holy Name Friary. —Died Oct. 30, 2002
† McGuire, John, *c.ss.r.* (BRK) Brooklyn, NY Our Lady of Perpetual Help Basilica. —Died Jan. 19, 2003
† McHugh, Edward, *o.m.i.* (SEA) Seattle, WA St. Benedict of Guadalupe. —Died April 28, 2002
† McHugh, James, *c.p.* (MET) South River, NJ Passionist Provincial Office. —Died Sept. 28, 2003
† McKeever, Rev. Msgr. William F. (MIA) Miami, FL St. John Bosco. —Died Aug. 13, 2003
† McKenna, Joseph C., *s.j.* (NY) Bronx, NY Murray–Weigel Hall. —Died July 4, 2002
† McKenney, Rev. Charles R., *S.J.* (WOR) Worcester, MA Jesuits of Holy Cross College, Inc.. —Died 2003
† McLaughlin, John (GB) (Retired). —Died Sept. 22, 2003
† McMain, Rev. Msgr. Robert O. (WDC) (Retired). —Died Dec. 20, 2002
† McNally, Donald, *o.m.i.* (SAT) San Antonio, TX Oblates of Mary Immaculate. —Died Jan. 16, 2003
† McNeill, John A. (BRK) (Retired). —Died Sept. 26, 2003
† McNichol, Fabian, *t.o.r.* (ARL) White Post, VA Sacred Heart Friary. —Died June 20, 2002
† McNicholas, Edward J. (BRK) (Retired). —Died Aug. 4, 2003
† McNulty, Charles L. (ALN) Pottsville, PA St. Mary Queen of Peace. —Died March 6, 2003
† McOwen, James F., *c.m.* (LA) Santa Barbara, CA St. Mary's Seminary Center. —Died Dec. 26, 2001
† McQueeney, Robert, *m.s.a.* (NOR) Cromwell, CT Society of the Missionaries of the Holy Apostles. —Died April 24, 2002
† McQueeney, Thomas F., *s.j.* (STL) St. Louis, MO Fusz Pavilion. —Died March 6, 2002
† McTommoney, Brian, *o.f.m.* (FgM) Byzantine–Slavonic. —Died 2003
† McWilliam, James J. (CIN) (Retired). —Died Jan. 16, 2003
† Mehok, Charles J., *s.j.* (MIL) Milwaukee, WI Marquette University. —Died June 11, 2003
† Meier, Rev. Msgr. Joseph F. (SCR) Wilkes–Barre, PA Church of St. Nicholas. —Died Jan. 21, 2003
† Meisburger, Joseph C. (KC) (Retired). —Died Dec. 12, 2002
† Mele, Vincent, *o.f.m.* (NY) New York, NY St. Clare Friary. —Died April 18, 2002
† Melton, John H., *o.s.a.* (PH) Villanova, PA Villanova University. —Died March 13, 2002
† Melvin, James M. (CAM) (Retired). —Died Nov. 16, 2002
† Mendonsa, August F. (PRO) (Retired). —Died May 14, 2003
† Mentel, Joseph C. (FAR) (Retired). —Died July 7, 2003
† Mersinger, Arthur (JC) (Retired). —Died July 24, 2003
† Merth, Robert J. (NU) (Retired). —Died Oct. 27, 2003
† Mertz, William H. (STP) (Retired). —Died July 19, 2003
† Mesa, Manuel, *o.m.i* (SD) Westmoreland, CA St. Joseph. —Died March 26, 2002
† Messaros, Rev. Msgr. Michael F. (ALN) (Retired). —Died Feb. 26, 2003
† Meuree, James, *c.i.c.m.* (FgM) Missionhurst Foreign Missions. —Died Oct. 13, 2002
† Meyers, Joseph, *c.s.b.* (GAL) Houston, TX Residence of the Basilian Fathers of the University of St. Thomas. —Died May 29, 2003
† Michels, Aloysius, *o.s.b.* (FgM) American–Cassinese Congregation Foreign Mission. —Died Feb. 2, 2002
† Mick, Rev. Robert (CIN) Cincinnati, OH St. Martin of Tours. —Died June 10, 2003
† Mihalic, Francis, *s.v.d.* (FgM) Society of the Divine Word Foreign Missions. —Died Dec. 8, 2001
† Miller, Gary R. (TOL) Huron, OH St. Peter. —Died April 7, 2003
† Miller, Joseph B. (TR) (Retired). —Died March 25, 2003
† Miller, Joseph W. (PIT) (Retired). —Died July 27, 2002
† Miller, Oscar J., *c.m.* (SAT) Losoya, TX Carmen Catholic. —Died May 28, 2002
† Miller, Paul E. (SCR) Scranton, PA St. Patrick's. —Died Nov. 5, 2003
† Miller, Thomas J., *c.s.sp.* (NO) Pointe a la Hache, LA St. Thomas. —Died Dec. 17, 2002
† Minoggio, Ferrando (CLV) Wickliffe, OH Borromeo Seminary; Rome, Italy, North American College. —Died June 14, 2003
† Miranda, Rev. Msgr. Juan (SJN) San Juan, PR Nuestra Sra. de Guadalupe. —Died Nov. 8, 2003
† Mitros, Josef F., *s.j.* (NY) Bronx, NY Fordham University. —Died Sept. 5, 2003
† Mociun, Casimir T. (SFS) (Retired). —Died June 30, 2003
† Moffatt, Timothy, *t.o.r.* (SP) Tampa, FL Christ the King. —Died Aug. 19, 2002
† Moliski, Wendel, *o.f.m.cap.* (PIT) Cabot, PA St. Joseph. —Died May 31, 2002
† Molloy, Francis P., *s.j.* (BO) Weston, MA Campion Health Center. —Died July 9, 2003
† Monnig, Francis R. (CIN) Trenton, OH St. Mary. —Died Dec. 28, 2003
† Monroe, Clement Joseph, *c.ss.r.* (BR) Baton Rouge, LA Our Lady of the Lake Hospital. —Died July 4, 2002
† Montville, Edmund J., *s.j.* (DET) Clarkston, MI Colombiere Center. —Died Feb. 11, 2002
† Mooney, Alphonse M., *o.s.m.* (FgM) Kwazulu–Natal, South Africa. —Died April 23, 2003
† Moore, Edmund, *o.f.m.* (L) Louisville, KY St. Boniface. —Died Feb. 16, 2003
† Moore, Francis A., *s.j.* (SJ) Los Gatos, CA Sacred Heart Jesuit Center. —Died March 24, 2003
† Moore, Manning, *o.s.f.s.* (WIL) Childs, MD Oblates of St. Francis De Sales. —Died March 17, 2003
† Moran, Faustinos, *c.p.* (CHI) Chicago, IL Passionist Provincial Office. —Died Nov. 8, 2002
† Moran, Leonard J., *s.m.* (WDC) Washington, DC Marist Center. —Died Aug. 27, 2002
† Moreci, Francis A. (OM) (Retired). —Died Sept. 21, 2003
† Morgan, Matthew (PMB) (Retired). —Died July 7, 2003
† Morgan, Raymond J. (BRK) (Retired). —Died Oct. 24, 2003
† Morgen, Paul H. (SFS) (Retired). —Died March 6, 2003
† Moriarity, Francis E., *s.s.e.* (BUR) Swanton, VT Nativity of the Blessed Virgin Mary. —Died May 25, 2002
† Moriarty, Edward Q., *o.p.* (CHI) Chicago, IL Resurrection Life Center. —Died March 22, 2003
† Morin, Henri D. (PRO) (Retired). —Died April 23, 2003
† Morley, John J. (PH) (Retired). —Died Sept. 6, 2003
† Morrison, Francis X. (PH) (Retired). —Died April 13, 2003
† Morrissey, John J. (DAV) (Retired). —Died April 1, 2003
† Mroczkowski, Leonard A. (CAM) (Retired). —Died Dec. 24, 2002
† Mueller, Joseph J. (MIL) (Retired). —Died Feb. 26, 2003
† Muka, John, *c.s.sp.* (PH) Bensalem, PA Congregation of the Holy Ghost. —Died Aug. 29, 2003
† Mulcahy, Richard E., *s.j.* (SJ) Los Gatos, CA Sacred Heart Jesuit Center. —Died Aug. 7, 2002

† Mullally, Conor, *o.f.m.* (PAT) Ringwood, NJ Holy Name Friary. —Died Sept. 3, 2003
† Mullen, Joseph A. (BRK) (Retired). —Died Oct. 5, 2003
† Mullen, Joseph, *o.f.m.cap.* (NY) Beacon, NY St. Lawrence Friary. —Died Feb. 22, 2002
† Mullen, Michael F., *c.m.* (BRK) Jamaica, NY St. John's University. —Died June 13, 2002
† Mullen, Willian E. (ALT) Central City, PA Our Lady Queen of Angels. —Died May 14, 2003
† Muller, Rev. Francis J., *O.F.M.* (NY) New York, NY St. Francis of Assisi. —Died 2003
† Munari, Mario (SR) (Retired). —Died March 11, 2003
† Murphy, Francis, *c.ss.r.* (BAL) Annapolis, MD St. Mary. —Died April 11, 2002
† Murphy, Joseph F. (PRO) (Retired). —Died Jan. 31, 2003
† Murphy, Joseph, *o.m.i.* (NY) Newburgh, NY Our Lady of Hope Center. —Died Aug. 6, 2002
† Murphy, Roland, *o.carm.* (WDC) Washington, DC Whitefriars Hall. —Died July 20, 2002
† Murphy, Rev. Msgr. Timothy J. (SAN) Midland, TX St. Ann's. —Died 2004
† Murray, Rev. Edward, *O.M.I.* (SAT) San Antonio, TX Oblate Madonna Res.. —Died Jan. 3, 2003
† Murrin, Joseph, *s.s.c.* (CHI) Chicago, IL Columban Fathers Vocation Dept.. —Died Dec. 22, 2002
† Mycue, Gordon E. (STP) (Retired). —Died Feb. 14, 2003
† Myrand, Pierre, *c.p.* (HRT) West Hartford, CT. —Died July 3, 2003
† Nader, John E., *c.s.sp.* (PIT) Bethel Park, PA Bethel Animation Center. —Died Aug. 18, 2002
† Nagle, Richard J., *o.carm.* (NY) Middletown, NY St. Albert. —Died April 29, 2002
† Nami, Peter, *o.m.i.* (BUF) Buffalo, NY St. James. —Died March 7, 2002
† Negro, Carmen, *c.s.* (WDC) Mitchellville, DE Villa Rosa Nursing Home. —Died June 20, 2002
† Nelipowitz, Charles, *o.f.m.conv.* (SY) Syracuse, NY Assumption B.V.M. —Died April 9, 2002
† Neva, Rev. Msgr. Roman G. (FAR) (Retired). —Died Nov. 25, 2002
† Neville, James J., *s.j.* (PH) Philadelphia, PA St. Joseph's University. —Died June 7, 2002
† Newmeyer, George C. (PIT) Glenshaw, PA St. Bonaventure. —Died Nov. 17, 2002
† Nieman, Mark E., *s.j.* (OM) Omaha, NE Creighton Preparatory School. —Died July 22, 2002
† Niglis, Rev. Msgr. Joseph C. (MAD) (Retired). —Died March 6, 2003
† Nilon, Robert E., *s.j.* (SP) Tampa, FL Sacred Heart. —Died 2003
† Nolte, William (RIC) (Retired). —Died Nov. 17, 2002
† Norman, Gregory, *o.cist.* (LC) Sparta, WI Our Lady of Spring Bank. —Died Oct. 10, 2002
† Norusis, Nicholas M., *o.s.m.* (CHI) Chicago, IL Resurrection Life Center. —Died Dec. 25, 2001
† Nugent, Vincent J., *c.m.* (PH) Philadelphia, PA Congregation of the Mission. —Died June 6, 2002
† O'Brien, Bartholomew J. (ROC) (Retired). —Died Nov. 7, 2003
† O'Brien, John F. (WIL) Wilmington, DE St. Mary Magdalen. —Died Jan. 7, 2003
† O'Brien, John J., *s.j.* (NEW) Jersey City, NJ St. Peter's College. —Died Feb. 4, 2003
† O'Brien, Michael Joseph, *c.s.v.* (CHI) Arlington Heights, IL Viatorian Province Center. —Died March 20, 2003
† O'Brien, Thomas G., *c.s.v.* (CHI) Arlington Heights, IL Viatorian Province Center. —Died Feb. 16, 2002
† O'Brien, William P., *m.s.* (LKC) Sulphur, LA West Clacasieu Cameron Hospital. —Died June 12, 2002
† O'Connell, John G., *o.p.* (STP) Minneapolis, MN St. Albert Priory. —Died Nov. 3, 2002
† O'Connell, Joseph Harry Patrick, *s.j.* (SEA) Seattle, WA Jesuit House. —Died May 22, 2002
† O'Connell, Thomas C. (PIT) (Retired). —Died Nov. 1, 2002
† O'Connor, John T. (HRT) (Retired). —Died Dec. 1, 2003
† O'Connor, William F., *s.j.* (BO) Boston, MA Boston College High School. —Died Nov. 1, 2002
† O'Connor, William T. (CHI) Chicago Heights, IL St. Paul. —Died Oct. 5, 2003
† O'Dowd, Brendan (SAC) (Retired). —Died Oct. 10, 2003
† O'Haire, John A. (SCR) (Retired). —Died April 22, 2003
† O'Hern, Edward P., *c.s.p.* (AUS) Austin, TX St. Austin. —Died March 26, 2002
† O'Leary, Adrian P. (BO) (Senior Priest). —Died Sept. 21, 2003
† O'Leary, Bartholomew (HON) (Retired). —Died June 22, 2003
† O'Leary, Jerome A., *o.p.* (CHI) Chicago, IL St. Pius V Priory. —Died Aug. 28, 2002
† O'Leary, Michael George (DET) Grosse Pointe, MI Bon Secours Hospital Chap.. —Died Feb. 10, 2003
† O'Malley, Bartholomew J., *c.m.* (PH) Philadelphia, PA St. Vincent's Seminary. —Died Dec. 25, 2001
† O'Meara, Henry, *c.ss.r.* (BAL) Baltimore, MD Sacred Heart. —Died April 15, 2003
† O'Neill, James R. (NEW) (Retired). —Died April 27, 2003
† O'Reilly, Michael P. (WH) Romney, WV Our Lady of Grace. —Died April 17, 2003
† O'Rourke, Arthur G., *o.s.a.* (BO) Lawrence, MA St. Mary Immaculate Conception. —Died Jan. 14, 2003
† O'Rourke Charles M. (PH) (Retired). —Died Nov. 11, 2002
† O'Shea, John L. (DEN) Denver, CO Cathedral of the Immaculate Conception. —Died Oct. 2, 2003
† O'Shea, Rev. Msgr. Joseph H. (PMB) (Retired). —Died Feb. 9, 2003
† O'Toole, Henry (ORL) St. Alphonsus Villa–Redemptorist Fathers and Brothers New Smyrna Beach, FL. —Died 2003
† O'Toole, Kenneth E. (NY) (Retired). —Died 2003
† Oestreich, Emil C. (PH) (Retired). —Died Nov. 29, 2002
† Olejniczak, Henry A. (CHI) (Retired). —Died Jan. 1, 2003
† Ollivier, John J. (TOL) (Retired). —Died Feb. 19, 2003
† Olson, Robert J., *o.m.i.* (SUP) River Falls, WI University of Wisconsin. —Died June 6, 2001
† Orian, Leo, *m.s.a.* (WDC) Washington, DC Missionaries of the Holy Apostle. —Died Jan 30, 2003
† Orlando, Samuel (CHL) (Retired). —Died April 2, 2003
† Orrico, Rev. Msgr. Caesar G. (NEW) Pastor Emeritus. —Died Aug. 1, 2003
† Ortiz, Francisco, *o.carm.* Anasco, PR St. Anthony Abbot. —Died 2003
† Ostaszewski, George (PH) (Retired). —Died Sept. 3, 2003
† Ovian, Leo J., *m.s.a.* (WDC) Washington, DC Basilica of The National Shrine of The Immaculate Conception. —Died 2003
† Oyler, George F. (L) (Retired). —Died March 27, 2003
† Ozanne Thomas P., *c.pp.s.* (KC) St. Joseph, MO St. Francis Xavier. —Died April 2, 2003
† Paik, Francis M. (CLV) Euclid, OH St. Christine Parish Pastor Emeritus. —Died June 17, 2003
† Pala, Francis, *sch.p.* (MIA) Fort Lauderdale, FL Cardinal Gibbons High School. —Died Sept. 8, 2002
† Pandolfo, Anthony (STU) (Retired). —Died Nov. 6, 2003
† Pansini, F. David, *c.m.* (LA) Montebello, CA Vincentian Fathers & Brothers. —Died Dec. 10, 2001
† Pantano, Salvator, *o.f.m.conv.* (ALB) Albany, NY Conventual Franciscans. —Died Jan. 14, 2002
† Paradis, Robert M., *o.m.i.* (MAN) Colebrook, NH Shrine of Our Lady of Grace. —Died May 25, 2001
† Parenteau, William (TUC) (Retired). —Died July 24, 2003
† Pascale, Anthony (HON) (Retired). —Died Jan. 9, 2003
† Passarella, Rev. Msgr. Anthony F. (BRK) (Retired). —Died Oct. 6, 2003
† Pater, Thomas G. (CIN) (Retired). —Died Feb. 25, 2003
† Paul, Rev. Msgr. William J. (PH) Morrisville, PA St. John the Evangelist. —Died June 15, 2003
† Payant, Romain, *o.c.s.o.* (P) Lafayette, OR the Cistercian Abbey of Our Lady of Guadalupe. —Died April 15, 2003
† Pecinovsky, Albert (KCK) (Retired). —Died Jan. 24, 2003
† Pedraza, Juan L., *s.j.* (SJN) San Juan PR Comunidad Jesuita. —Died Nov. 17, 2001
† Peet, Rev. Msgr. Arthur V. (STL) (Retired). —Died Nov. 22, 2002
† Peir, Andrew (CLV) Benedictine Order of Cleveland, Cleveland. —Died March 18, 2003
† Pellicane, Albert, *c.p.* (BRK) Jamaica, NY Immaculate Conception Monastery. —Died 2002
† Peplinski, Herman–Joseph, *o.f.m.* (GB) (Retired). —Died Dec. 30, 2002
† Perry, Killian, *t.o.r.* (ORL) Lakeland FL St. Anthony. —Died Feb. 20, 2001
† Petuskey, John A. (OKL) (Retired) Pastor Emeritus. —Died Nov. 8, 2003
† Pfab, Charles B., *s.m.* (BR) Gramercy, LA Most Sacred Heart of Jeses. —Died July 9, 2002
† Pfalzer, Juvenal, *o.f.m.* (CIN) Cincinnati, OH St. Francis Seraph Friary. —Died March 6, 2002
† Phelan, Murray, *o.carm.* (JOL) Darien, IL Carmelite Fathers Provincial Office. —Died Aug. 5, 2002
† Phillips, Paschal, *o.c.s.o.* (L) Trappist, KY Abbey of Our Lady of Gethsemani. —Died May 12, 2003
† Pier, Andrew (Wendelin), *o.s.b.* (CLV) Cleveland, OH Benedictine Order of Cleveland. —Died March 18, 2003
† Piscitelli, Vincent J. (BO) (Senior Priest). —Died June 11, 2003
† Plarinsek, Henry J., *c.s.sp.* (SLC) St. George, UT St. George. —Died Nov. 10, 2002
† Podesta, Rev. Msgr. John F. (JOL) (Retired). —Died May 6, 2003
† Polizzi, Daniel (SD) (Unassigned). —Died July 12, 2003
† Polt, Albert, *o.a.r.* (LA) Oxnard, CA St. Augustine Priory. —Died Dec. 29, 2001
† Polzer, Charles W., *s.j.* (TUC) Tucson, AZ Kino House, University of AZ. —Died Nov. 4, 2003
† Portasik, Joseph, *o.f.m.* (GBG) Uniontown, PA St. Anthony Friary. —Died Oct. 23, 2001
† Porter, Richard L., *s.j.* (MIL) Wauwatosa, WI St. Camillus. —Died Sept. 28, 2003
† Portrey, Rev. Msgr. Lawrence A. (GI) (Retired). —Died April 7, 2003
† Portz, Bernard J., *s.j.* (MIL) Wauwatosa, WI St. Camillus. —Died Dec. 10, 2002
† Power, Bernard, *c.ss.r.* (PMB) Palm City, FL Holy Redeemer. —Died Sept. 18, 2002
† Power, Joseph F., *o.s.f.s.* (BUF) Stella Niagara, NY DeSales Resource Center. —Died Jan. 23, 2002
† Power, Patrick A. (LA) Santa Clarita, CA Our Lady of Perpetual Help Pastor Emeritus. —Died June 2, 2003
† Powers, Edward R., *s.j.* (SCR) Scranton, PA University of Scranton. —Died Jan. 11, 2002
† Powers, Rev. Msgr. William E. (GR) (Retired). —Died Feb. 18, 2003
† Prakapas, Antanas, *o.f.m.* (BRK) (Retired). —Died Feb. 27, 1999
† Prendergast, Francis (STO) Turlock, CA Sacred Heart Church. —Died Feb. 4, 2003
† Prevost, Frederick J. (SY) Whitesboro, NY St. Anne. —Died May 22, 2003
† Primozic, Robert, *o.carm.* (JOL) Darien, IL Carmelite Fathers Provincial Office. —Died June 14, 2002
† Przybylski, Wallace, *o.f.m.* (CIN) Cincinnati, OH St. Francis Seraph Friary. —Died May 31, 2002
† Publicover, James L. (BO) (Senior Priest). —Died Nov. 18, 2003
† Puglisi, Rev. Msgr. Guy (BRK) Brooklyn, NY Our Lady of the Angels. —Died July 8, 2003
† Pulikoottil, Abraham (BUF) (Retired). —Died April 8, 2003
† Pulvermacher, Pius, *o.f.m.cap.* (GB) Appleton, WI St. Fidelis Friary. —Died May 14, 2002
† Pupin, Vito A. (BRK) (Retired). —Died April 11, 2003
† Pyne, Donald E. (SFR) (Retired). —Died July 17, 2003
† Pytel, Ronald (BAL) Holy Rosery, Baltimore. —Died Nov. 13, 2003
† Quinn, Carroll I., *m.m.* (NY) Maryknoll, NY Maryknoll Fathers and Brothers. —Died Jan. 16, 2003
† Quinn, John J. (HRT) (Retired). —Died Oct. 27, 2003
† Quinn, John J. (TR) (Retired). —Died June 15, 2003
† Quinn, Rev. Msgr. Richard M. (ROC) (Retired). —Died Sept. 17, 2003
† Quinn, William J. (CHI) Oak Lawn, IL St. Louis De Montfort. —Died July 20, 2003
† Quintero, Francisco, *s.d.b.* (SJN) San Juan, PR San Juan Bosco. —Died Oct. 1, 2002
† Quinters, Rev. Msgr. Elmer T. (GAL) (Retired). —Died Aug. 26, 2003
† Quirk, William L. (MAN) (Retired). —Died Aug. 2, 2003
† Radchuk, Anthony (PHU) (Retired). —Died Oct. 27, 2003
† Rajter, Valentine, *o.f.m.conv.* (BUF) Buffalo, NY Corpus Christi. —Died Aug. 3, 2002
† Ralenkotter, Howard, *c.p.* (DET) Detroit, MI St. Paul of the Cross Community. —Died Aug. 25, 2003
† Raszkowski, Robert P., *s.j.* (STL) St. Louis, MO Fusz Pavilion. —Died Dec. 19, 2001
† Raum, Blair (BAL) (Special Assignment). —Died May 31, 2003
† Rausch, Nicholas B., *o.s.b.* (SEA) Lacey WA St. Martin's Abbey. —Died Aug. 5, 2003
† Reed, John C., *s.j.* (DET) Clarkston, MI Colombiere Center. —Died Jan. 15, 2003
† Reed, Thomas A., *s.j.* (SJ) Los Gatos, CA Sacred Heart Jesuit Center. —Died June 13, 2003
† Reedy, Francis C., *o.s.b.* (MIL) Benet Lake, WI St. Benedict's Abbey. —Died June 5, 2003
† Regan, Rev. Msgr. Michael F. (STL) (Retired). —Died Jan. 14, 2003
† Regnier, William H. (RCK) (Retired). —Died May 23, 2003
† Rehage, Joseph W., *c.s.c.* (FTW) South Bend, IN Congregation of Holy Cross. —Died Sept. 23, 2003
† Reid, James H., *s.j.* (NY) New York, NY Fordham University. —Died July 16, 2003
† Reid, Sean (John), *o.carm.* (NY) Middletown, NY St. Albert's Priory. —Died Sept. 14, 2003
† Reile, Louis, *s.m.* (SAT) San Antonio, TX Marianist Community - St. Mary's University. —Died June 25, 2003
† Reilly, John C. (BRK) (Retired). —Died Aug. 30, 2003
† Reinke, John H., *s.j.* (CHI) Chicago, IL Loyola University. —Died Feb. 26, 2003
† Reisert, Frederick J., *s.j.* (BUF) Buffalo, NY Canisius Jesuit Community. —Died Dec. 18, 2002
† Reisz, Adam (DM) (Retired). —Died Jan. 30, 2003

† Renaldo, Daniel J., *c.m.* (ALN) Roseta, PA Our Lady of Mt. Carmel. —Died Feb. 9, 2002
† Rendon, Raul, *o.ss.t.* (BAL) Baltimore, MD Holy Trinity Monastery. —Died July 11, 2002
† Repole, Celsus, *o.f.m.cap.* (NY) Yonkers, NY St. Clare Friary. —Died June 15, 2002
† Reszkowski, Rev. Msgr. Joseph V. (E) (Retired). —Died Sept. 4, 2003
† Richers, David E., *s.s.c.* (OM) St. Columbans, NE St. Columbans Foreign Mission Society. —Died Nov. 19, 2002
† Richmond, John A., *s.m.* (WDC) Washington, DC Marist Center. —Died Aug. 18, 2001
† Ridyard, John J., *m.m.* (SJ) Los Altos, CA Maryknoll. —Died Jan. 14, 2003
† Ries, Victor F. (CIN) (Retired). —Died Jan. 30, 2003
† Rifkin, Anthony F., *o.s.f.s.* (WIL) (Retired). —Died Aug. 5, 2002
† Rigo, Peter, *c.s.* (LA) Sun Valley, CA St. Charles Residence. —Died March 17, 2003
† Ripp, Joseph L. (SFS) (Retired). —Died Dec. 21, 2002
† Riski, Bruce, *o.f.m.cap.* (DET) Detroit, MI St. Bonaventure Friary. —Died Nov. 24, 2002
† Ritchie, Francis J. (BO) (Senior Priest). —Died April 20, 2003
† Ritchie, Rev. Msgr. G. Carlton (E) (Retired). —Died April 25, 2003
† Rittmeyer, Robert (SP) (Retired). —Died Nov. 29, 2003
† Rivoire, S. Joseph, *s.j.* (DAL) Dallas, TX Jesuit College Preparatory School. —Died Nov. 20, 2001
† Robida, Raymond A. (FR) (Retired). —Died May 5, 2003
† Rodgers, Francis M. (PIT) (Retired). —Died Feb. 13, 2003
† Rohlinger, Joseph A., *o.praem.* (GB) De Pere, WI St. Norbert Abbey. —Died Sept. 13, 2002
† Roney, David A. (NU) (On Duty Outside the Diocese). —Died Jan. 27, 2003
† Rook, Paul J. (TUC) (Retired). —Died Feb. 2, 2003
† Rooney, Michael J., *s.m.a.* (BO) Dedham, MA African Mission House. —Died Nov. 1, 2001
† Roos, Robert E. (ALB) (Retired). —Died Oct. 1, 2003
† Ropolas, Steponas, *o.f.m.* (SP) St. Petersburg, FL St. Francis Friary. —Died June 26, 2000
† Rosenfelder, Richard M., *s.j.* (CLV) Cuyahoga Falls, OH Walsh Jesuit High School. —Died Feb. 13, 2003
† Rossiter, Rev. Msgr. Francis S. (BO) Bilerica, MA Middlesex County Jail; Bilerica, MA Middlesex House of Corrections Chap.. —Died Nov. 23, 2003
† Rotelle, John E., *o.s.a.* (PH) Villanova, PA St. John Stone Friary. —Died Sept. 1, 2002
† Roth, Robert J., *s.j.* (NY) Bronx, NY Fordham University. —Died Sept. 14, 2002
† Roux, Gerard, *o.m.i.* (MAN) Hudson, NH Oblates of Mary Immaculate Retreat House. —Died Aug. 21, 2001
† Ruddy, Edward J. (PAT) (Retired). —Died Jan. 20, 2003
† Ruef, John, *c.ss.r.* (ALB) Saratoga Springs, NY St. John Neumann. —Died Jan. 3, 2002
† Ruiz, Jose H. (VEN) Sebring, FL St. Catherine. —Died April 20, 2003
† Russell, J. Christopher (STP) (Retired). —Died Feb. 7, 2003
† Rutkowski, Stephen C. (NEW) (Retired). —Died March 2, 2003
† Ryan, Francis, *c.ss.r.* (FAR) Brisbee, ND Holy Rosary. —Died June 21, 2002
† Ryan, James W. (BIS) Garrison, ND Church of St. Nicholas. —Died Jan. 16, 2003
† Sabol, Sebastian Stephan, *o.s.b.m.* (STN) Warren, MI St. Josaphat. —Died Feb. 20, 2003
† Sampson, Patrick (GF) (Retired). —Died July 4, 2003
† Sandford, Mark, *o.f.m.* (LR) Searcy, AR Morris School for Boys. —Died May 24, 2003
† Satterfield, Rev. Msgr. Carroll E. (BAL) (Retired). —Died July 26, 2003
† Savage, John, *o.m.i.* (BO) Lowell, MA Immaculate Conception. —Died April 24, 2001
† Savukynas, John, *m.i.c.* (JOL) Plano, IL St. Mary. —Died April 26, 2002
† Scanlon, Michael, *o.s.m.* (CHI) Chicago, IL Order of Friar Servants of Mary. —Died Sept. 1, 2003
† Scharf, Joseph A., *s.j.* (CLV) Cleveland, OH Jesuit Retreat House. —Died Nov. 12, 2002
† Scharf, Joseph (CLV) Cleveland, OH Jesuit Retreat House. —Died 2003
† Schebeci, Michael, *o.f.m.* (DET) Southfield, MI Duns Scotus Center. —Died March 16, 2003
† Scherman, Charles J., *s.j.* (LC) Springfield, WI St. Bridget. —Died Nov. 4, 2002
† Schidel, George E., *c.s.c.* (FTW) South Bend, IN Congregation of Holy Cross. —Died June 9, 2002
† Schiefen, Rev. Msgr. Robert (VEN) (Retired). —Died March 25, 2003
† Schirra, Peter M. (PIT) (Retired). —Died May 30, 2003
† Schmidt, Frederick A., *c.s.c.* (FgM) Holy Cross Foreign Missions. —Died Jan. 12, 2003
† Schmitt, Eugene A. (WH) (Retired). —Died Feb. 20, 2003
† Schmitt, Rev. Msgr. J. Harley (DEN) Chap., Denver, CO Mullen Home. —Died June 25, 2003
† Schnaus, Edward Urban, *o.s.b.* (WDC) Washington, DC St. Anselm's Abbey. —Died June 7, 2003
† Schneider, Adrian, *o.f.m.* (CIN) Cincinnati, OH St. Clement Friary. —Died Sept. 5, 2002
† Schneider, Anthony, *o.f.m.* (SP) St. Petersburg, FL St. Anthony's Friary. —Died April 9, 2002
† Schneider, Stephen, *o.f.m.* (CIN) Cincinnati, OH St. Anthony Shrine Friary. —Died Aug. 19, 2001
† Schnoebelen, Kenneth F. (LIN) (Retired). —Died July 17, 2003
† Schnupp, Luzerne A. (NSH) (Retired). —Died Feb. 1, 2003
† Schoettelkotte, Rev. Msgr. Charles T. (EVN) (Retired). —Died Nov. 22, 2002
† Schoutteten, Francis, *o.m.i.* (BWN) San Juan, TX Virgen de San Juan del Valle Shrine. —Died Oct. 7, 2002
† Schrage, Frank P. (GB) Little Chute, WI St. John Nepomucene.. —Died May 5, 2003
† Schreiber, Edmund J. (CHI) (Retired). —Died July 7, 2003
† Schrimpf, Reginald, *s.d.s.* (GB) School Hill, WI Holy Trinity. —Died Jan. 17, 2003
† Schug, John, *o.f.m.cap.* (NY) Beacon, NY St. Lawrence Friary. —Died May 10, 2002
† Schulte, Bernard C., *s.j.* (STL) St. Louis, MO Fusz Pavilion. —Died Sept. 6, 2002
† Schultz, Ronald, *o.f.m.conv.* (ALB) Fonda, NY St. Cecilia. —Died Dec. 7, 2002
† Schulze, Paul, *s.d.s.* (GB) Charlesburg, WI St. Charles Borromeo. —Died Oct. 29, 2002
† Schumacher, Ernest, *c.r.* (L) Raywick, KY St. Francis Xavier. —Died Oct. 1, 2001
† Schuster, Philip, *o.s.b.* (KC) Conception, MO Conception Abbey. —Died June 10, 2002
† Schuyler, Joseph B., *s.j.* (NY) Bronx, NY Murray–Weigel Hall. —Died Aug. 30, 2002
† Schwantner, James E., *o.f.m.* (PAT) Ringwood, NJ Holy Name Friary. —Died Nov. 15, 2001
† Schwarz, Bernard F. (OKL) (Retired). —Died June 12, 2003
† Schweibold, Conrad, *o.f.m.conv.* (FTW) Angola, IN St. Anthony. —Died Dec. 3, 2001
† Schweihoffer, Walter John (DET) (Retired). —Died Nov. 17, 2002
† Scopp, Andrew J., *s.j.* (BO) Weston, MA Campion Jesuit Community. —Died July 6, 2003
† Sealy, Robert J., *s.j.* (NY) Bronx, NY Fordham University. —Died June 17, 2003
† Seefeldt, Wilbert T. (STP) (Retired). —Died Feb. 7, 2003
† Seitz, Cyprian, *o.s.b.* (SCL) Collegeville, MN St. John's Abbey. —Died April 7, 2002
† Semiraro, Reginald, *o.f.m.* (FgM) Franciscan Foreign Missions. —Died Jan. 27, 2003
† Shane, Donald R. (RVC) (Retired). —Died May 13, 2003
† Shanley, Thomas Quentin, *o.p.* (HRT) New Haven, CT St. Mary. —Died Jan. 25, 2002
† Shannon, Michael Thomas, *s.j.* (SPK) Spokane, WA Regis Community. —Died Aug. 10, 2002
† Shappard, Christopher (IND) St. Meinrad Archabbey St. Meinrad, IN. —Died 2003
† Shappard, Christopher, *o.s.b.* (IND) St. Meinrad, IN St. Meinrad Archabbey. —Died May 12, 2003
† Sharrock, David J., *c.ss.r.* (ORL) New Smyrna Beach, FL Sacred Heart. —Died Nov. 2, 2003
† Shaughnessy, John, *c.ss.r.* (OAK) Oakland, CA Redemptorists. —Died Jan. 29, 2002
† Shea, Joseph, *o.f.m.cap.* (NY) Yonkers, NY St. Clare Friary. —Died Oct. 10, 2002
† Shea, Peter D. (WOR) (Retired). —Died Jan. 20, 2003
† Sheehan, Bernard (OM) Elkhorn, NE Mount Michael Abbey. —Died Jan. 27, 2003
† Sheehan, Bernard, *o.s.b.* (OM) Elkhorn, NE Mount Michael High School. —Died Jan. 29, 2003
† Sheehan, Lawrence A., *s.j.* (RVC) Massapequa, NY St. Rose of Lima. —Died Sept. 23, 2002
† Sheltz, Anton R. (GAL) Houston, TX St. Dominic. —Died May 9, 2003
† Shine, Francis, *c.m.* (STL) St. Louis, MO Regional Hospital. —Died July 23, 2003
† Siebers, Glen F., *o.praem.* (GB) De Pere, WI St. Norbert Abbey. —Died Aug. 10, 2003
† Siekierski, Matthew J. (WDC) LaPlata, MD Sacred Heart. —Died Aug. 3, 2003
† Simcox, Thomas, *s.c.j.* (SP) Pinellas Park, FL Priests of the Sacred Heart. —Died Aug. 31, 2003
† Sinner, Rev. Msgr. Emil E. (SAL) (Retired). —Died Sept. 12, 2003
† Skorogod, Leopold, *o.f.m.* (HT) Houma, LA Resident Chaplain Annunziata. —Died Sept. 14, 2003
† Skwor, Donald, *s.d.s.* (BAL) Baltimore, MD St. Rita. —Died Dec. 2, 2002
† Sleasman, Martin J., *c.m.* (BUF) Niagara University, NY Niagara University. —Died Sept. 30, 2002
† Slonecki, Michael, *o.f.m.conv.* (SPR) Chicopee, MA St. Anthony. —Died July 26, 2002
† Smetana, Brendan L., *o.s.b.* (GBG) (Retired). —Died Dec. 22, 2002
† Smith, Rev. Msgr. Bernard E. (TOL) (Retired). —Died March 29, 2003
† Smith, Brendan, *s.t.* (WDC) Adelphi, MD Missionary Servants of the Most Holy Trinity. —Died Oct. 26, 2001
† Smith, Charles, *c.s.b.* (DET) Redford, MI Catholic Central High School. —Died Sept. 21, 2002
† Smith, Lawrence H.F. (MET) Parlin, NJ St. Bernadette. —Died Aug. 15, 2003
† Snow, J. Lee (OG) Diocese of Ogdensburg. —Died Nov. 15, 2003
† Sobr, Clement E., *o.s.b.* (JOL) Lisle, IL St. Procopius Abbey. —Died Feb. 19, 2002
† Sola, Jeronimo, *c.m.* Mayaquez, PR San Vicente. —Died 2003
† Somma, James (PIT) (Retired). —Died Nov. 26, 2002
† Spada, Rino, *c.s.* (SJ) San Jose, CA Holy Cross. —Died Aug. 19, 2002
† Spaight, Rev. Msgr. Robert L. (DUB) (Retired). —Died Jan. 20, 2003
† Spelgatti, Rev. Msgr. David P. (MAR) (Retired). —Died Jan. 22, 2003
† Spencer, Francis M., *m.s.* (MAN) Nashua, NH St. Casimir. —Died April 12, 2003
† Spisak, Thomas M. Warren, OH St. Mary. —Died Feb. 20, 2003
† St. Sure, Donald F., *s.j.* (MRY) Los Gatos, CA Sacred Heart Jesuit Center. —Died Oct. 27, 2001
† Stack, Joseph O., *o.m.i.* (BO) Tewksbury, MA Immaculate Heart of Mary Novitiate. —Died June 12, 2001
† Stanton, Joseph, *o.c.s.o.* (ROC) Piffard, NY Abbey of the Genesee. —Died Aug. 8, 2002
† Steffan, Paul, *o.f.m.cap.* (NOR) Middletown, CT St. Pius X Friary. —Died July 20, 2002
† Steffey, John M. (KAL) (Retired). —Died Aug. 9, 2003
† Stehr, James P., *s.j.* (NY) New York, NY America House. —Died July 20, 2002
† Stelling, William F. (MEM) Memphis, TN St. Joseph's. —Died July 22, 2003
† Sterk, Francis R. (CLV) Euclid, OH St. Christine. —Died June 26, 2003
† Sterrett, Bradley (SAL) Manhattan, KS St. Isidore. —Died April 16, 2003
† Steuer, James A. (ALB) Mohawk, NY Blessed Sacrament. —Died May 13, 2003
† Stevenson, Alden J., *s.j.* (SJ) Los Gatos, CA Sacred Heart Jesuit Center. —Died Oct. 3, 2003
† Stolze, Edward B. (CIN) Morrow, OH St. Philip the Apostle. —Died Feb. 16, 2003
† Strafalace, Frank, *s.c.j.* (GAL) Houston, TX Our Lady of Guadalupe. —Died April 18, 2003
† Streng, Rev. Msgr. James E. (BUF) (Retired). —Died May 24, 2003
† Stuardi, Rev. Msgr. J. Edwin (MOB) Daphne, AL Mercy Medical Chap.. —Died Aug. 21, 2003
† Studzinski, Rev. Msgr. Lambert V. (FAR) (Retired). —Died Jan. 12, 2003
† Sullivan, Andrew J. (WOR) (Retired). —Died Aug. 19, 2003
† Sullivan, Donald T., *s.s.e.* (MOB) Selma, AL Edmundite Fathers. —Died March 27, 2003
† Sullivan, James, *o.m.i.* (FgM) Oblates Foreign Missions. —Died Dec. 29, 2001
† Sullivan, John J., *s.j.* (BO) Weston, MA Campion Health Center. —Died Sept. 24, 2002
† Sullivan, John W., *s.j.* (BO) Weston, MA Campion Health Center. —Died Feb. 26, 2003
† Sullivan, Joseph, *o.f.m.* (PAT) Ringwood, NJ Holy Name Friary. —Died July 14, 2003
† Sullivan, Matthew, *ss.cc.* (FR) Fairhaven, MA Our Lady's Haven of Fairhaven, Inc.. —Died July 16, 2002
† Sullivan, Paul V. (BO) (Senior Priest). —Died March 7, 2003
† Sullivan, Robert W., *s.s.j.* (BLX) Pascagoula, MS St. Peter the Apostle. —Died July 11, 2003
† Sullivant, Raymond L., *s.j.* (FgM) Provinces. —Died Sept. 24, 2002
† Supple, Rev. Msgr. James A. (DUB) (Retired). —Died Aug. 31, 2003
† Sutton, John V. (BO) Weymouth, MA Sacred Heart. —Died Feb. 10, 2003
† Sweeney, Francis W., *s.j.* (BO) Chestnut Hill, MA Boston College. —Died April 25, 2002
† Sweeney, Leo, *s.j.* (CHI) Chicago, IL Loyola University of Chicago. —Died Dec. 18, 2001
† Szczerbicki, Thaddeus P. (LC) (Retired). —Died 2003
† Szczesny, Michael S. (GI) (Retired). —Died Nov. 23, 2003
† Tague, Charles, *s.t.* (WDC) Adelphi, MD. —Died June 3, 2003
† Talbot, Felix F., *s.j.* (BO) Weston, MA Campion Health Center. —Died June 25, 2003
† Templeton, Edward J., *s.m.* (WDC) Washington, DC Marist Center. —Died Jan. 30, 2003

† Tenorio, Roger P.T. (CHK) Saipan, MP Kristo Rai. —Died Dec. 6, 2002
† Tetreault, Rev. Msgr. Jean C. (BGP) (Retired). —Died June 1, 2003
† Thai–Son, Polycarp Tran, *c.m.c.* (SB) Highgrove, CA Congregation of the Mother Coredemptrix. —Died June 20, 2003
† Thanh Thien, Cyril Vu, *c.m.c.* (SPC) Carthage, MO Congregation of the Mother Coredemptrix. —Died Nov. 26, 2002
† Thennes, Clarence J. (RCK) (Retired). —Died Dec. 14, 2002
† Theobald, Vincent, *s.v.d.* (BLX) Bay St. Louis, MS St. Augustine. —Died July 10, 2002
† Thompson, Jerome F. (MIL) Azua, Dominican Republic LaSagrada Familia Church. —Died May 17, 2003
† Thro, Linus J., *s.j.* (STL) St. Louis, MO St. Louis University. —Died April 13, 2002
† Thro, Thomas F., *s.j.* (STL) St. Louis, MO Fusz Pavilion. —Died Feb. 19, 2003
† Thro, William P., *s.j.* (COS) Colorado Springs, CO St. Patrick. —Died Oct. 27, 2003
† Tighe, Rev. Msgr. Emmett F. (WIN) (Retired). —Died June 7, 2003
† Tillman, Stanley C., *s.j.* (DET) Clarkston, MI Colombiere Center. —Died Jan. 9, 2003
† Timperman, Robert A., *c.i.c.m.* (ARL) Arlington, VA Dominion House. —Died Jan. 19, 2002
† Tolaas, Gregory (STP) Minneapolis, MN St. Philip. —Died Sept. 7, 2003
† Tompkins, Regis, *o.c.s.o.* (ROC) Piffard, NY Abbey of Genesee. —Died Oct. 11, 2002
† Toner, Rev. Msgr. Francis X. (NY) Bronx, NY St. Barnabas. —Died 2003
† Tonne, Rev. Msgr. Arthur (WCH) (Retired). —Died May 20, 2003
† Tonsmeire, Sidney A., *s.j.* (NO) New Orleans, LA Praying for the Church and the Society. —Died Nov. 18, 2001
† Toolan, David S., *s.j.* (NY) New York, NY America Press. —Died July 16, 2002
† Trac, Peter Vu Dinh (ORG) (Retired). —Died Sept. 30, 2003
† Treacy, Canice (WDC) (Retired). —Died Jan. 6, 2003
† Trementozzi, Paul, *o.c.d.* (BO) Brighton, MA Carmelite Monastery. —Died Oct. 21, 2002
† Trompeter, Rev. Msgr. Arthur J. (KCK) (Retired). —Died Oct. 28, 2003
† Tuller, Eugene, *o.f.m.cap.* (MIL) Mount Calvary, WI St. Lawrence Friary. —Died Jan. 23, 2003
† Tully, Raymond M., *s.j.* (STL) St. Louis, MO Provinces Offices. —Died Aug. 25, 2002
† Tully, Terence (SPK) (Retired). —Died Nov. 17, 2002
† Turlik, Andrew J. (PIT) (Retired). —Died May 18, 2003
† Turner, Patrick Arthur (BEA) Orange, TX St. Helen. —Died March 31, 2003
† Turner, Wayne A. (MAD) (Retired). —Died Nov. 24, 2003
† Twomey, Timothy, *s.a.c.* (RNO) Sparks, NV Immaculate Conception. —Died 2002
† Tylawskyj, Mitrat Iwan (SJP) (Retired). —Died Oct. 18, 2003
† Tyne, John Joseph, *s.s.j.* (MOB) Mobile, AL Most Pure Heart of Mary. —Died May 10, 2002
† Unger, Leonard, *o.f.m.conv.* (SY) Syracuse, NY Conventual Francisans. —Died April 8, 2002
† Vago, Giancarlo "John" (ALT) Bedford, PA St. Thomas the Apostle. —Died Dec. 14, 2002
† Vallieres, Jean–Joseph, *o.m.i.* Lowell, MA Missionary Oblates of Mary Immaculate. —Died Feb. 8, 2003
† Van Ackeren, Leonard J., *o.s.b.* (MIL) Benet Lake, WI St. Benedict's Abbey. —Died Feb. 26, 2003
† Vanasse, Henry, *f.i.c.* (PRT) Alfred, ME Notre Dame Institute. —Died May 4, 2002
† Van Breda, William, *o.s.a.* (OG) Carthage, NY St. James Minor. —Died Jan. 20, 2002
† Vandergeest, Peter J. (ALN) (Retired). —Died July 16, 2003
† VanderVennet, Timothy, *o.c.s.o.* (SAC) Vina, CA Abbey of New Clairvaux. —Died April 15, 2002
† Vanhee, Frans, *c.i.c.m.* (FgM) Missionhurst Foreign Missions. —Died Oct. 11, 2002
† Van Nuffelen, Albert, *c.i.c.m.* (ARL) Arlington, VA Missionhurst. —Died July 5, 2003
† Van Thillo, Marcel, *c.i.c.m.* (ARL) Arlington, VA Missionhurst. —Died July 4, 2003
† Varela, Ramon, *o.f.m.* (LA) Hacienda Heights, CA St. John Vianney. —Died June 30, 2002
† Verbeke Albert, *c.i.c.m.* (FgM) Missionhurst Foreign Missions. —Died Nov. 21, 2002
† Ver Bust, Richard (GB) (Retired). —Died July 11, 2003
† Vercek, Alphonse, *sch.p.* (BUF) Lackawanna, NY Piarist Fathers. —Died July 7, 2003
† Vergauwen, Peter (SAN) (Retired). —Died Sept. 15, 2003
† Vesely, Stanley G., *o.s.b.* (JOL) Lisle, IL St. Procopius Abbey. —Died Jan. 11, 2003
† Vetter, Matthew, *c.p.* (FgM) Mission Procurators. —Died June 3, 2002
† Viscardi, Robert, *i.m.c.* (SB) Riverside, CA St. Francis Church San Bernardino Diocese. —Died Oct. 4, 2003
† Volpe, Alfonse (LKC) Lake Charles, LA Immaculate Heart of Mary. —Died March 26, 2003
† Vrablic, Cyril, *o.s.b.* (IND) St. Meinrad, IN St. Meinrad Archabbey. —Died Jan. 14, 2003
† Vrano, Francis R. (STP) (Retired). —Died Oct. 16, 2003
† Wagman, Stephen, *o.s.b.* (SCL) Collegeville, MN St. John's Abbey. —Died June 20, 2002
† Walch, John L. (OKL) (Retired). —Died June 29, 2003
† Waldschmidt, Donald L. (DAV) (Retired). —Died Sept. 28, 2003
† Walsh, Edward J. (CAM) (Retired). —Died June 2, 2003
† Walsh, J. Daniel, *c.s.c.* (BR) Baton Rouge, LA St. Agnes. —Died Aug. 25, 2002
† Walsh, Joachim, *o.s.b.* (IND) St. Meinrad, IN St. Meinrad Archabbey. —Died July 3, 2003
† Walsh, Paul Patrick, *o.p.* (WDC) Washington, DC St. Dominic Priory. —Died Jan. 22, 2003
† Walter, Joseph J., *s.j.* (NY) Bronx, NY Murray–Weigel Hall. —Died July 28, 2002
† Wangler, Rev. Msgr. Alexander C. (SAT) (Retired). —Died March 4, 2003
† Ward, Austin T. (STP) Maplewood MN Holy Redeemer. —Died Sept. 6, 2003
† Wardrope, Juan W., *c.m.* (FgM) Vincentian Foreign Missions. —Died June 19, 2002
† Watson, Rev. Msgr. James P. (MAN) (Retired). —Died June 18, 2003
† Waznak, Robert P., *s.s.* (BAL) Baltimore, MD Sulpician Provincial House. —Died Dec. 5, 2003
† Weeke, James L. (OM) (Retired). —Died Dec. 10, 2003
† Wegierski, Blase (BAL) Beaufort, SC USML Base at Parris Island. —Died 2003
† Weinholtz, Bernard A., *o.f.m.* (PAT) Ringwood, NJ Holy Name Friary. —Died Dec. 5, 2002
† Weiss, Nicholas, *o.f.m.conv.* (ALB) Rensselaer, NY Conventual Franciscan Friars. —Died July 29, 2002
† Welch, John J., *s.j.* (FgM) Provinces. —Died Jan. 14, 2002
† Wellisch, Robert (STP) St. Paul, MN St. Vincent de Paul. —Died May 24, 2003
† Welsmons, Glendon R., *s.j.* (MIL) Wauwatosa, WI St. Camillus. —Died March 14, 2003
† Welter, Charles, *c.m.* (STL) Perryville, MO Congregation of the Mission. —Died May 21, 2003
† Wenning, Paul A. (Retired). —Died Sept. 5, 2003
† Werr, Donald, *o.f.m.* (FWT) Crowley, TX St. Francis Village, Inc.. —Died June 7, 2002
† Whalen, James W. (STP) (Retired). —Died April 8, 2003
† Whalen, William F. (ALB) (Retired). —Died March 2, 2003
† White, Gervase F., *o.f.m.* (BUF) St. Bonaventure, NY St. Bonaventure Friary. —Died Jan. 7, 2002
† White, Marcellus, *c.p.* (FgM) Passionist Foreign Missions. —Died 2002
† Wholey, John, *o.m.i.* (BO) (Retired). —Died Sept. 10, 2002
† Wieber, Elmer F. (KAL) (Retired). —Died Oct. 2, 2003
† Wieckowski, Rev. Msgr. John F. (CAM) (Retired). —Died Aug. 6, 2003
† Wiesler, Willard P. (TUC) (Retired). —Died Dec. 26, 2002
† Will, Carl G. (CIN) (Retired). —Died March 24, 2003
† Williams, Alfred (P) (Retired). —Died June 15, 2003
† Williams, Edward T. (CIN) (Retired). —Died Jan. 22, 2003
† Williams, Germaine, *o.f.m.conv.* (ALB) Rensselaer, NY Conventual Franciscan Friars. —Died Jan. 11, 2003
† Willmes, Robert J., *s.j.* (DET) Clarkston, MI Colombiere Center. —Died March 3, 2002
† Wilmes, James, *g.h.m.* (CHL) Andrews, NC Holy Redeemer. —Died Feb. 7, 2003
† Wilson, Edward M. (E) (Retired). —Died Nov. 19, 2003
† Wilson, James E. (DAV) (Retired). —Died July 20, 2003
† Wilson, John H., *c.s.s.* (FTW) South Bend, IN Congregation of Holy Cross. —Died Feb. 28, 2002
† Windolph, Michael, *o.f.m.* (CHI) Oak Forest, IL Oak Forest Hospital. —Died Aug. 27, 2002
† Winkels, Robert H., *m.m.* (NY) Maryknoll, NY Maryknoll Fathers and Brothers. —Died Jan. 11, 2003
† Wittstock, John Joseph (DET) (Retired). —Died Nov. 15, 2002
† Wlodyka, Stanley, *o.f.m.conv.* (SPR) Granby, MA St. Hyacinth College & Seminary. —Died Aug. 31, 2002
† Woll, Peter J. (CLV) Cleveland, OH Holy Trinity–St. Edward. —Died July 29, 2003
† Womack, Emil, *c.p.* (SAC) Citrus Heights, CA Christ the King. —Died May 24, 2002
† Wood, William T., *s.j.* (NY) Bronx, NY Murray–Weigel Hall. —Died Oct. 10, 2002
† Woodka, Raymond Andrew, *s.s.j.* (BAL) Baltimore, MD Josephite Generalate. —Died Sept. 22, 2002
† Wysocki, Paul P. (HRT) New Britain, CT Sacred Heart Rectory. —Died March 14, 2003
† Yager, James P. (GR) (Retired). —Died Aug. 20, 2003
† Yang, Paul (RVC) (Retired). —Died Dec. 31, 2002
† Yaoch, Felix K., *s.j.* (CI) Koror, FM Sacred Heart. —Died Dec. 17, 2002
† Young, James, *s.m.* (SAT) San Antonio, TX Marianist Community – St. Mary's University. —Died Dec. 16, 2002
† Zagar, John T. (OKL) (Retired). —Died Oct. 8, 2003
† Zamborsky, Stephen, *c.s.sp.* (PH) Bensalem, PA Congregation of the Holy Ghost. —Died April 19, 2003
† Zamelko, Ed, *c.s.b.* (GAL) (Retired). —Died Aug. 5, 2003
† Zembrzuski, Michael, *o.s.p.p.e.* (PH) Doylestown, PA Pauline Fathers Monastery. —Died Jan. 16, 2003
† Ziemba, Herman–Joseph, *o.f.m.* (GB) Pulaski, WI Assumption of B.V.M. Friary. —Died April 14, 2003
† Zientek, Timothy (BAL) (Retired). —Died 2003
† Ziliotto, Rino, *c.s.* (LA) (Retired). —Died March 30, 2002
† Zimmerman, John, *c.m.* (STL) Perryville, MO Congregation of the Mission. —Died April 30, 2002
† Zoph, John L. (SFR) (Retired). —Died Dec. 6, 2002
† Zugelter, Alvin T. (CIN) (Retired). —Died Dec. 2, 2003

	*Mobile AL	Birmingham AL	ALABAMA TOTAL	*Anchorage AK	Fairbanks AK	Juneau AK	2004 U.S. GRAND TOTAL
Cardinals	–	–	–	–	–	–	**12**
Archbishops	1	–	1	2	–	–	**48**
Bishops	–	2	2	–	1	1	**375**
Abbots	–	2	2	–	–	–	**109**
Diocesan Priests	108	74	182	18	8	11	**29,483**
Religious Priests	32	38	70	9	15	2	**14,729**
Total Priests in Diocese	140	112	252	27	23	13	**44,212**
Newly Ordained Priests	–	4	4	–	–	–	**544**
Total Permanent Deacons	61	41	102	19	39	3	**14,693**
Total Brothers	10	22	32	3	3	–	**5,504**
Total Sisters	156	129	285	41	20	4	**71,486**
Number of Parishes	76	57	133	20	47	11	**19,431**
Missions	11	17	28	9	–	–	**2,910**
Pastoral Centers	3	–	3	–	2	–	**1,011**
New Parishes	–	–	–	–	–	–	**34**
Catholic Hospitals	1	1	2	3	–	1	**583**
Patients Assisted Annually	172,769	168,315	341,084	427,079	–	38,979	**83,898,575**
Health Care Centers	2	1	3	2	–	–	**376**
Patients Assisted Annually	4,800	27,958	32,758	314	–	–	**4,251,107**
Specialized Homes	3	–	3	7	–	–	**1,546**
Total Assisted Annually	299	–	299	3,187	–	–	**1,412,029**
Residential Care of Children (Orphanages)	1	–	1	–	–	–	**272**
Total Assisted Annually	130	–	130	–	–	–	**70,886**
Day Care and Extended Day Care Centers	4	–	4	–	–	1	**1,240**
Total Assisted Annually	403	–	403	–	–	100	**125,723**
Special Centers for Social Services	11	13	24	5	1	1	**2,969**
Total Assisted Annually	87,528	77,199	164,727	26,000	2,033	9,590	**21,251,075**
Diocesan Seminaries	–	–	–	–	–	–	**72**
Students	–	–	–	–	–	–	**3,077**
Religious Seminaries	–	–	–	–	–	–	**124**
Students	–	–	–	–	–	–	**1,253**
Colleges and Universities	1	–	1	–	–	–	**232**
Total Students	1,735	–	1,735	–	–	–	**747,060**
High Schools, Diocesan and Parish	3	5	8	1	1	–	**787**
Total Students	1,463	1,326	2,789	74	234	–	**378,650**
High Schools, Private	–	1	1	1	–	–	**560**
Total Students	–	115	115	48	–	–	**301,673**
Elementary Schools, Diocesan and Parish	19	17	36	2	1	1	**6,488**
Total Students	5,433	5,342	10,775	280	301	135	**1,796,275**
Elementary Schools, Private	–	1	1	1	–	–	**365**
Total Students	–	238	238	69	–	–	**95,742**
Non–residential Schools for the Disabled	–	1	1	–	–	–	**83**
Total Students	–	121	121	–	–	–	**18,179**
Religious Education High School Students	1,186	1,764	2,950	974	594	139	**771,730**
Religious Education Elementary Students	3,731	6,625	10,356	2,479	1,630	554	**3,612,510**
Priests Teaching	11	11	22	–	–	–	**1,792**
Scholastics Teaching	–	–	–	–	–	–	**57**
Brothers Teaching	4	2	6	–	–	–	**1,195**
Sisters Teaching	14	11	25	2	1	–	**7,871**
Lay Teachers	553	536	1,089	53	29	14	**169,966**
Infant Baptisms	1,095	1,829	2,924	547	353	89	**985,141**
Adult Baptisms	163	205	368	66	19	15	**76,829**
Received into Full Communion	334	494	828	74	12	19	**75,429**
First Communions	1,140	1,375	2,515	499	362	56	**896,670**
Confirmations	962	1,170	2,132	356	124	87	**645,426**
Marriages	317	371	688	118	49	20	**232,060**
Deaths	548	523	1,071	102	102	20	**473,935**
Totals Catholics	65,588	74,777	140,365	29,693	17,833	5,366	**67,259,768**
Total Population	1,652,398	2,735,546	4,387,944	345,975	157,000	71,972	**288,758,111**
Catholic Population Percentage	4	3	3	9	11	7	**23**

Archdioceses = 36; Dioceses = 169; Apostolates = 3

2004 GENERAL SUMMARY

	ALASKA TOTAL	Samoa–Pago Pago AS	Phoenix AZ	Tucson AZ	ARIZONA TOTAL	Little Rock AR	2004 U.S. GRAND TOTAL
Cardinals	–	–	–	–	–	–	**12**
Archbishops	2	–	1	–	1	–	**48**
Bishops	2	1	3	2	5	2	**375**
Abbots	–	–	–	–	–	2	**109**
Diocesan Priests	37	10	132	117	249	74	**29,483**
Religious Priests	26	5	98	72	170	52	**14,729**
Total Priests in Diocese	63	15	230	189	419	126	**44,212**
Newly Ordained Priests	–	1	3	5	8	1	**544**
Total Permanent Deacons	61	16	211	143	354	78	**14,693**
Total Brothers	6	–	12	10	22	33	**5,504**
Total Sisters	65	13	213	238	451	253	**71,486**
Number of Parishes	78	13	89	72	161	88	**19,431**
Missions	9	1	27	40	67	35	**2,910**
Pastoral Centers	2	1	–	–	–	5	**1,011**
New Parishes	–	1	–	–	–	–	**34**
Catholic Hospitals	4	–	1	3	4	12	**583**
Patients Assisted Annually	466,058	–	262,596	411,300	673,896	1,123,380	**83,898,575**
Health Care Centers	2	–	1	1	2	6	**376**
Patients Assisted Annually	314	–	98,899	26,457	125,356	29,479	**4,251,107**
Specialized Homes	7	1	20	–	20	27	**1,546**
Total Assisted Annually	3,187	26	30,652	–	30,652	1,090	**1,412,029**
Residential Care of Children (Orphanages)	–	–	–	–	–	–	**272**
Total Assisted Annually	–	–	–	–	–	–	**70,886**
Day Care and Extended Day Care Centers	1	1	27	–	27	30	**1,240**
Total Assisted Annually	100	100	1,456	–	1,456	1,797	**125,723**
Special Centers for Social Services	7	1	13	1	14	2	**2,969**
Total Assisted Annually	37,623	310	1,710,862	405,300	2,116,162	1,125	**21,251,075**
Diocesan Seminaries	–	–	–	–	–	–	**72**
Students	–	–	–	–	–	–	**3,077**
Religious Seminaries	–	–	–	–	–	–	**124**
Students	–	–	–	–	–	–	**1,253**
Colleges and Universities	–	–	–	–	–	–	**232**
Total Students	–	–	–	–	–	–	**747,060**
High Schools, Diocesan and Parish	2	1	6	–	6	4	**787**
Total Students	308	128	3,443	–	3,443	1,001	**378,650**
High Schools, Private	1	–	1	5	6	2	**560**
Total Students	48	–	1,210	1,903	3,113	711	**301,673**
Elementary Schools, Diocesan and Parish	4	2	28	22	50	31	**6,488**
Total Students	716	394	9,271	5,577	14,848	6,606	**1,796,275**
Elementary Schools, Private	1	–	–	2	2	–	**365**
Total Students	69	–	–	810	810	–	**95,742**
Non–residential Schools for the Disabled	–	–	–	–	–	–	**83**
Total Students	–	–	–	–	–	–	**18,179**
Religious Education High School Students	1,707	836	6,734	4,629	11,363	2,705	**771,730**
Religious Education Elementary Students	4,663	2,000	33,106	18,401	51,507	6,576	**3,612,510**
Priests Teaching	–	–	9	3	12	8	**1,792**
Scholastics Teaching	–	–	2	–	2	–	**57**
Brothers Teaching	–	–	9	7	16	9	**1,195**
Sisters Teaching	3	8	40	26	66	21	**7,871**
Lay Teachers	96	84	808	447	1,255	640	**169,966**
Infant Baptisms	989	261	12,465	7,023	19,488	2,478	**985,141**
Adult Baptisms	100	127	1,286	335	1,621	269	**76,829**
Received into Full Communion	105	57	1,068	665	1,733	431	**75,429**
First Communions	917	284	9,414	6,143	15,557	2,453	**896,670**
Confirmations	567	175	5,060	3,183	8,243	1,626	**645,426**
Marriages	187	72	1,691	953	2,644	619	**232,060**
Deaths	224	59	3,404	2,409	5,813	861	**473,935**
Totals Catholics	52,892	14,550	556,692	350,000	906,692	106,051	**67,259,768**
Total Population	574,947	60,000	3,650,019	1,517,428	5,167,447	2,710,079	**288,758,111**
Catholic Population Percentage	9	24	15	23	18	4	**23**

*Indicates Archdioceses.

†Certain Dioceses traverse state lines.

2004 GENERAL SUMMARY

	*Los Angeles CA	*San Francisco CA	Fresno CA	Monterey in California CA	Oakland CA	Orange in California CA	2004 U.S. GRAND TOTAL
Cardinals	1	–	–	–	–	–	12
Archbishops	1	2	–	–	–	–	48
Bishops	7	2	1	1	2	4	375
Abbots	1	–	–	–	–	1	109
Diocesan Priests	538	219	115	83	194	181	29,483
Religious Priests	615	153	31	28	98	116	14,729
Total Priests in Diocese	1,153	372	146	111	292	297	44,212
Newly Ordained Priests	16	5	3	–	1	7	544
Total Permanent Deacons	236	66	31	3	92	70	14,693
Total Brothers	173	55	–	35	56	9	5,504
Total Sisters	1,765	800	124	135	360	320	71,486
Number of Parishes	288	93	86	46	85	56	19,431
Missions	7	11	40	–	2	4	2,910
Pastoral Centers	3	5	–	–	16	4	1,011
New Parishes	–	–	–	–	–	–	34
Catholic Hospitals	14	3	3	1	1	3	583
Patients Assisted Annually	1,345,630	417,335	573,780	143,892	130,415	402,021	83,898,575
Health Care Centers	7	20	–	–	–	3	376
Patients Assisted Annually	12,906	211,500	–	–	–	13,502	4,251,107
Specialized Homes	18	26	2	3	8	7	1,546
Total Assisted Annually	5,964	57,859	216	448	33,500	346	1,412,029
Residential Care of Children (Orphanages)	2	16	–	–	–	–	272
Total Assisted Annually	598	16,500	–	–	–	–	70,886
Day Care and Extended Day Care Centers	82	5	–	–	5	2	1,240
Total Assisted Annually	6,340	500	–	–	1,600	200	125,723
Special Centers for Social Services	80	8	2	–	3	9	2,969
Total Assisted Annually	423,260	16,750	351,713	–	31,000	840,633	21,251,075
Diocesan Seminaries	1	1	–	–	–	–	72
Students	112	88	–	–	14	–	3,077
Religious Seminaries	12	1	–	–	–	–	124
Students	48	–	–	4	–	–	1,253
Colleges and Universities	5	3	–	–	3	–	232
Total Students	11,845	11,499	–	–	5,191	–	747,060
High Schools, Diocesan and Parish	28	4	2	2	3	3	787
Total Students	16,426	3,713	1,369	672	1,890	4,608	378,650
High Schools, Private	22	10	–	3	6	3	560
Total Students	13,793	4,802	–	1,039	4,404	1,029	301,673
Elementary Schools, Diocesan and Parish	216	66	23	10	51	36	6,488
Total Students	62,796	17,942	5,331	2,766	13,673	13,735	1,796,275
Elementary Schools, Private	9	7	–	3	–	2	365
Total Students	2,627	1,850	–	747	–	671	95,742
Non–residential Schools for the Disabled	–	–	–	–	–	–	83
Total Students	–	–	–	–	–	–	18,179
Religious Education High School Students	32,000	8,262	7,329	2,411	2,235	7,985	771,730
Religious Education Elementary Students	240,000	20,004	23,655	11,393	25,552	37,370	3,612,510
Priests Teaching	17	15	3	3	14	17	1,792
Scholastics Teaching	2	–	–	–	–	–	57
Brothers Teaching	81	15	–	4	13	4	1,195
Sisters Teaching	276	117	23	15	40	40	7,871
Lay Teachers	4,614	1,934	368	330	2,034	1,143	169,966
Infant Baptisms	88,224	7,670	17,209	6,330	9,373	16,462	985,141
Adult Baptisms	2,233	487	579	217	472	669	76,829
Received into Full Communion	2,167	493	523	154	619	591	75,429
First Communions	56,865	5,386	12,147	4,381	8,203	13,954	896,670
Confirmations	22,056	3,417	4,020	1,530	3,345	5,564	645,426
Marriages	10,586	1,585	2,130	921	1,338	2,820	232,060
Deaths	12,788	3,278	3,135	1,120	2,663	2,718	473,935
Totals Catholics	4,174,304	422,500	581,000	193,598	450,934	1,170,480	67,259,768
Total Population	11,096,200	1,720,450	2,327,272	967,992	2,464,668	3,000,000	288,758,111
Catholic Population Percentage	38	25	25	20	18	39	23

Archdioceses = 36; Dioceses = 169; Apostolates = 3

2004 GENERAL SUMMARY

	Sacramento CA	San Bernardino CA	San Diego CA	San Jose in California CA	Santa Rosa in California CA	Stockton CA	2004 U.S. GRAND TOTAL
Cardinals	–	–	–	–	–	–	12
Archbishops	–	–	–	–	–	–	48
Bishops	3	1	3	2	2	2	375
Abbots	2	–	2	–	–	–	109
Diocesan Priests	171	136	196	131	89	66	29,483
Religious Priests	53	98	98	194	10	15	14,729
Total Priests in Diocese	224	234	294	325	99	81	44,212
Newly Ordained Priests	8	–	–	3	–	–	544
Total Permanent Deacons	138	69	104	7	35	41	14,693
Total Brothers	22	19	20	60	38	4	5,504
Total Sisters	180	162	328	375	50	66	71,486
Number of Parishes	98	97	98	48	42	33	19,431
Missions	42	13	17	3	20	10	2,910
Pastoral Centers	3	–	1	1	13	–	1,011
New Parishes	–	–	–	–	–	1	34
Catholic Hospitals	6	2	1	2	5	3	583
Patients Assisted Annually	492,719	201,443	20,974	173,736	540,967	332,115	83,898,575
Health Care Centers	–	–	1	1	–	1	376
Patients Assisted Annually	–	–	17,843	–	–	2,259	4,251,107
Specialized Homes	2	5	21	1	1	1	1,546
Total Assisted Annually	141	994	85,601	–	53	470	1,412,029
Residential Care of Children (Orphanages)	1	–	1	–	1	–	272
Total Assisted Annually	32	–	65	–	119	–	70,886
Day Care and Extended Day Care Centers	4	1	1	1	1	–	1,240
Total Assisted Annually	1,713	400	632	150	75	–	125,723
Special Centers for Social Services	10	19	9	1	39	1	2,969
Total Assisted Annually	154,057	58,985	84,685	50,000	60,751	24,934	21,251,075
Diocesan Seminaries	–	–	–	–	–	–	72
Students	–	–	–	–	–	–	3,077
Religious Seminaries	2	–	–	–	–	–	124
Students	3	–	–	–	–	–	1,253
Colleges and Universities	–	–	1	1	–	–	232
Total Students	–	–	7,262	8,047	–	–	747,060
High Schools, Diocesan and Parish	4	2	3	2	2	2	787
Total Students	1,867	925	2,321	1,961	777	1,574	378,650
High Schools, Private	3	–	2	4	4	–	560
Total Students	2,631	–	1,476	4,294	1,149	–	301,673
Elementary Schools, Diocesan and Parish	47	30	43	29	11	12	6,488
Total Students	12,436	6,911	13,366	9,862	2,618	3,134	1,796,275
Elementary Schools, Private	–	1	1	1	2	–	365
Total Students	–	428	238	54	175	–	95,742
Non–residential Schools for the Disabled	–	–	1	–	–	–	83
Total Students	–	–	217	–	–	–	18,179
Religious Education High School Students	3,048	7,639	8,120	2,388	1,682	2,016	771,730
Religious Education Elementary Students	15,029	31,267	38,500	14,856	5,556	15,529	3,612,510
Priests Teaching	11	3	4	1	1	2	1,792
Scholastics Teaching	–	–	–	–	–	–	57
Brothers Teaching	6	1	–	–	2	2	1,195
Sisters Teaching	19	373	36	27	2	3	7,871
Lay Teachers	832	–	1,055	516	329	233	169,966
Infant Baptisms	9,728	10,768	11,908	8,674	3,577	5,879	985,141
Adult Baptisms	660	889	1,845	551	122	332	76,829
Received into Full Communion	1,018	1,452	1,145	383	114	1,110	75,429
First Communions	7,278	12,602	8,994	5,793	2,488	3,938	896,670
Confirmations	5,960	4,823	4,255	2,733	956	2,946	645,426
Marriages	1,419	2,062	1,873	1,418	681	908	232,060
Deaths	2,600	2,732	2,345	1,661	971	1,554	473,935
Totals Catholics	520,301	1,074,196	930,379	630,000	154,060	194,945	67,259,768
Total Population	3,229,945	3,556,631	3,041,195	1,825,000	753,893	1,234,010	288,758,111
Catholic Population Percentage	16	30	31	35	20	16	23

*Indicates Archdioceses.

†Certain Dioceses traverse state lines.

	CALIFORNIA TOTAL	The Caroline Islands CI	*Denver CO	Colorado Springs CO	Pueblo CO	COLORADO TOTAL	2004 U.S. GRAND TOTAL
Cardinals	1	–	1	–	–	1	**12**
Archbishops	3	–	2	–	–	2	**48**
Bishops	30	2	1	2	2	5	**375**
Abbots	6	–	1	–	2	3	**109**
Diocesan Priests	2,119	13	162	38	72	272	**29,483**
Religious Priests	1,509	18	119	30	32	181	**14,729**
Total Priests in Diocese	3,628	31	281	68	104	453	**44,212**
Newly Ordained Priests	43	3	4	–	1	5	**544**
Total Permanent Deacons	892	43	153	28	29	210	**14,693**
Total Brothers	491	1	14	3	5	22	**5,504**
Total Sisters	4,665	33	339	128	96	563	**71,486**
Number of Parishes	1,070	26	120	34	52	206	**19,431**
Missions	169	4	29	9	56	94	**2,910**
Pastoral Centers	46	8	–	–	–	–	**1,011**
New Parishes	1	–	–	–	–	–	**34**
Catholic Hospitals	44	–	3	2	5	10	**583**
Patients Assisted Annually	4,775,027	–	370,000	254,000	890,800	1,514,800	**83,898,575**
Health Care Centers	33	–	8	2	–	10	**376**
Patients Assisted Annually	258,010	–	5,000	109	–	5,109	**4,251,107**
Specialized Homes	95	–	17	2	2	21	**1,546**
Total Assisted Annually	185,592	–	1,230	103	1,555	2,888	**1,412,029**
Residential Care of Children (Orphanages)	21	–	2	–	–	2	**272**
Total Assisted Annually	17,314	–	100	–	–	100	**70,886**
Day Care and Extended Day Care Centers	102	–	5	–	–	5	**1,240**
Total Assisted Annually	11,610	–	1,100	–	–	1,100	**125,723**
Special Centers for Social Services	181	–	15	–	3	18	**2,969**
Total Assisted Annually	2,096,773	–	100,000	–	4,950	104,950	**21,251,075**
Diocesan Seminaries	2	–	1	–	–	1	**72**
Students	214	–	49	–	–	49	**3,077**
Religious Seminaries	15	–	–	–	–	–	**124**
Students	55	–	41	–	–	41	**1,253**
Colleges and Universities	13	–	–	–	–	–	**232**
Total Students	43,844	–	–	–	–	–	**747,060**
High Schools, Diocesan and Parish	57	3	2	–	1	3	**787**
Total Students	38,103	455	1,000	–	94	1,094	**378,650**
High Schools, Private	57	1	5	1	–	6	**560**
Total Students	34,617	343	2,354	350	–	2,704	**301,673**
Elementary Schools, Diocesan and Parish	574	5	37	5	4	46	**6,488**
Total Students	164,570	1,309	9,656	1,487	702	11,845	**1,796,275**
Elementary Schools, Private	26	–	2	–	1	3	**365**
Total Students	6,790	–	593	–	176	769	**95,742**
Non–residential Schools for the Disabled	1	–	–	–	–	–	**83**
Total Students	217	–	–	–	–	–	**18,179**
Religious Education High School Students	85,115	798	5,471	2,831	2,443	10,745	**771,730**
Religious Education Elementary Students	478,721	1,309	26,858	2,976	4,902	34,736	**3,612,510**
Priests Teaching	91	6	–	–	–	–	**1,792**
Scholastics Teaching	2	2	–	–	–	–	**57**
Brothers Teaching	128	1	2	–	1	3	**1,195**
Sisters Teaching	971	24	21	1	6	28	**7,871**
Lay Teachers	13,388	134	869	116	83	1,068	**169,966**
Infant Baptisms	195,802	1,804	11,501	1,555	2,020	15,076	**985,141**
Adult Baptisms	9,056	307	746	132	171	1,049	**76,829**
Received into Full Communion	9,769	20	1,291	145	321	1,757	**75,429**
First Communions	142,029	1,071	8,464	1,529	1,554	11,547	**896,670**
Confirmations	61,605	657	5,020	1,032	890	6,942	**645,426**
Marriages	27,741	425	2,913	306	369	3,588	**232,060**
Deaths	37,565	–	2,836	339	1,564	4,739	**473,935**
Totals Catholics	10,496,697	72,940	380,739	136,814	110,200	627,753	**67,259,768**
Total Population	35,217,256	149,225	2,996,708	855,088	601,000	4,452,796	**288,758,111**
Catholic Population Percentage	30	49	13	16	18	14	**23**

Archdioceses = 36; Dioceses = 169; Apostolates = 3

2004 GENERAL SUMMARY

	*Hartford CT	Bridgeport CT	† Norwich CT	CONNECTICUT TOTAL	† Wilmington DE	*†Washington DC	2004 U.S. GRAND TOTAL
Cardinals	–	–	–	–	–	2	12
Archbishops	2	–	–	2	–	–	48
Bishops	2	1	2	5	1	3	375
Abbots	–	–	–	–	–	3	109
Diocesan Priests	354	270	130	754	119	309	29,483
Religious Priests	121	44	57	222	86	606	14,729
Total Priests in Diocese	475	314	187	976	205	915	44,212
Newly Ordained Priests	3	6	4	13	3	12	544
Total Permanent Deacons	300	93	59	452	77	237	14,693
Total Brothers	52	1	21	74	29	136	5,504
Total Sisters	833	403	244	1,480	259	734	71,486
Number of Parishes	216	87	78	381	57	140	19,431
Missions	1	1	10	12	19	9	2,910
Pastoral Centers	–	–	23	23	8	1	1,011
New Parishes	–	–	–	–	–	–	34
Catholic Hospitals	3	1	–	4	1	3	583
Patients Assisted Annually	843,693	139,407	–	983,100	177,740	502,000	83,898,575
Health Care Centers	1	–	–	1	2	7	376
Patients Assisted Annually	60	–	–	60	352	209,414	4,251,107
Specialized Homes	3	13	3	19	8	29	1,546
Total Assisted Annually	400	883	244	1,527	779	1,750	1,412,029
Residential Care of Children (Orphanages)	1	–	–	1	3	1	272
Total Assisted Annually	95	–	–	95	89	402	70,886
Day Care and Extended Day Care Centers	9	1	–	10	2	7	1,240
Total Assisted Annually	393	105	–	498	205	437	125,723
Special Centers for Social Services	28	17	1	46	17	76	2,969
Total Assisted Annually	19,138	9,336	192	28,666	519,436	137,343	21,251,075
Diocesan Seminaries	1	1	–	2	–	2	72
Students	–	17	–	17	–	82	3,077
Religious Seminaries	1	–	–	1	–	30	124
Students	112	–	–	112	–	158	1,253
Colleges and Universities	2	3	–	5	–	3	232
Total Students	3,922	11,196	–	15,118	–	20,215	747,060
High Schools, Diocesan and Parish	4	5	4	13	5	1	787
Total Students	2,063	2,598	2,061	6,722	2,953	610	378,650
High Schools, Private	5	3	1	9	3	15	560
Total Students	2,840	1,262	55	4,157	1,724	8,760	301,673
Elementary Schools, Diocesan and Parish	66	33	23	122	27	85	6,488
Total Students	1,584	8,717	4,169	14,470	9,630	22,140	1,796,275
Elementary Schools, Private	3	2	–	5	5	10	365
Total Students	342	504	–	846	995	1,987	95,742
Non–residential Schools for the Disabled	–	1	–	1	1	1	83
Total Students	–	11	–	11	102	157	18,179
Religious Education High School Students	14,363	4,039	2,259	20,661	1,294	2,103	771,730
Religious Education Elementary Students	55,436	31,675	17,146	104,257	10,887	21,098	3,612,510
Priests Teaching	15	13	3	31	14	29	1,792
Scholastics Teaching	–	–	–	–	–	–	57
Brothers Teaching	19	1	6	26	5	28	1,195
Sisters Teaching	67	30	35	132	44	66	7,871
Lay Teachers	1,371	870	419	2,660	983	2,464	169,966
Infant Baptisms	8,975	6,036	2,836	17,847	2,874	5,640	985,141
Adult Baptisms	210	109	148	467	185	2,001	76,829
Received into Full Communion	739	97	290	1,126	285	496	75,429
First Communions	9,793	5,922	3,073	18,788	2,776	6,821	896,670
Confirmations	8,072	4,494	2,016	14,582	2,032	5,333	645,426
Marriages	2,214	1,260	659	4,133	761	1,998	232,060
Deaths	10,724	3,617	2,274	16,615	1,539	3,139	473,935
Totals Catholics	694,220	410,304	228,520	1,333,044	220,000	567,266	67,259,768
Total Population	1,873,986	896,202	674,804	3,444,992	1,215,685	2,614,128	288,758,111
Catholic Population Percentage	37	46	34	39	18	22	23

*Indicates Archdioceses.

†Certain Dioceses traverse state lines.

	*Miami FL	Orlando FL	Palm Beach FL	Pensacola–Tallahassee FL	St. Augustine FL	St. Petersburg FL	2004 U.S. GRAND TOTAL
Cardinals	–	–	–	–	–	–	**12**
Archbishops	2	–	–	–	–	–	**48**
Bishops	3	2	3	1	2	3	**375**
Abbots	–	–	–	–	–	–	**109**
Diocesan Priests	263	121	111	75	91	122	**29,483**
Religious Priests	123	44	32	9	23	111	**14,729**
Total Priests in Diocese	386	165	143	84	114	233	**44,212**
Newly Ordained Priests	6	1	4	1	3	1	**544**
Total Permanent Deacons	144	137	44	57	32	107	**14,693**
Total Brothers	58	16	5	4	3	44	**5,504**
Total Sisters	316	103	145	50	115	321	**71,486**
Number of Parishes	112	72	49	49	51	73	**19,431**
Missions	7	10	4	9	8	4	**2,910**
Pastoral Centers	3	–	–	–	–	1	**1,011**
New Parishes	1	–	–	–	–	–	**34**
Catholic Hospitals	2	–	–	1	1	2	**583**
Patients Assisted Annually	691,992	–	–	276,936	170,369	500,163	**83,898,575**
Health Care Centers	3	–	–	–	–	7	**376**
Patients Assisted Annually	16,227	–	–	–	–	35,000	**4,251,107**
Specialized Homes	11	–	–	3	2	13	**1,546**
Total Assisted Annually	31,237	–	–	250	43,548	1,600	**1,412,029**
Residential Care of Children (Orphanages)	6	–	–	–	–	55	**272**
Total Assisted Annually	343	–	–	–	–	11,000	**70,886**
Day Care and Extended Day Care Centers	7	11	–	–	–	12	**1,240**
Total Assisted Annually	2,545	975	–	–	–	2,200	**125,723**
Special Centers for Social Services	45	7	2[illegible]	4	9	11	**2,969**
Total Assisted Annually	1,439,815	19,286	9,60[illegible]	39,850	73,000	20,768	**21,251,075**
Diocesan Seminaries	1	–	–	–	–	–	**72**
Students	47	–	79	–	–	–	**3,077**
Religious Seminaries	–	–	–	–	–	–	**124**
Students	5	–	–	–	6	–	**1,253**
Colleges and Universities	2	–	–	–	–	1	**232**
Total Students	12,020	–	–	–	–	12,190	**747,060**
High Schools, Diocesan and Parish	9	5	3	2	3	4	**787**
Total Students	9,576	2,627	2,245	676	1,915	1,977	**378,650**
High Schools, Private	4	–	–	–	–	2	**560**
Total Students	3,016	–	–	–	–	969	**301,673**
Elementary Schools, Diocesan and Parish	57	31	15	9	27	28	**6,488**
Total Students	24,235	12,457	5,6[illegible]9	2,159	8,335	9,371	**1,796,275**
Elementary Schools, Private	2	–	2	–	–	3	**365**
Total Students	937	–	6[illegible]2	–	–	1,040	**95,742**
Non–residential Schools for the Disabled	2	1	–	1	1	2	**83**
Total Students	11,665	60	–	16	114	130	**18,179**
Religious Education High School Students	5,013	4,360	3,1[illegible]6	1,703	1,384	2,898	**771,730**
Religious Education Elementary Students	41,473	22,329	16,4[illegible]4	4,663	8,600	19,380	**3,612,510**
Priests Teaching	15	1	7	1	2	6	**1,792**
Scholastics Teaching	–	–	–	–	–	–	**57**
Brothers Teaching	20	4	2	–	–	4	**1,195**
Sisters Teaching	29	26	21	9	21	30	**7,871**
Lay Teachers	2,225	1,049	570	182	684	780	**169,966**
Infant Baptisms	16,952	6,108	4,319	1,010	2,310	4,788	**985,141**
Adult Baptisms	793	540	342	190	410	668	**76,829**
Received into Full Communion	717	689	[illegible]37	292	557	630	**75,429**
First Communions	14,807	5,884	3,820	1,055	2,504	5,125	**896,670**
Confirmations	9,041	4,357	2,[illegible]32	924	2,143	3,814	**645,426**
Marriages	2,680	1,416	874	343	731	1,469	**232,060**
Deaths	5,122	3,864	2,[illegible]48	610	1,079	4,244	**473,935**
Totals Catholics	856,783	361,085	259,[illegible]29	62,289	160,479	398,702	**67,259,768**
Total Population	4,036,799	3,535,994	1,806,[illegible]24	1,267,077	1,749,106	2,660,220	**288,758,111**
Catholic Population Percentage	21	10	14	5	9	15	**23**

Archdioceses = 36; Dioceses = 169; Apostolates = 3

2004 GENERAL SUMMARY

	Venice FL	FLORIDA TOTAL	*Atlanta GA	Savannah GA	GEORGIA TOTAL	*Agana GUAM	2004 U.S. GRAND TOTAL
Cardinals	–	–	–	–	–	–	**12**
Archbishops	–	2	1	–	1	1	**48**
Bishops	1	15	–	2	2	–	**375**
Abbots	–	–	–	–	–	–	**109**
Diocesan Priests	90	873	167	69	236	35	**29,483**
Religious Priests	84	426	69	24	93	13	**14,729**
Total Priests in Diocese	174	1,299	236	93	329	48	**44,212**
Newly Ordained Priests	2	18	3	2	5	1	**544**
Total Permanent Deacons	74	595	161	43	204	19	**14,693**
Total Brothers	28	158	–	8	8	2	**5,504**
Total Sisters	114	1,164	102	107	209	101	**71,486**
Number of Parishes	54	460	79	52	131	24	**19,431**
Missions	4	46	16	26	42	–	**2,910**
Pastoral Centers	10	14	1	–	1	–	**1,011**
New Parishes	–	1	–	–	–	–	**34**
Catholic Hospitals	2	8	2	3	5	–	**583**
Patients Assisted Annually	505,546	2,145,006	295,030	350,000	645,030	–	**83,898,575**
Health Care Centers	–	10	1	–	1	–	**376**
Patients Assisted Annually	–	51,227	150	–	150	–	**4,251,107**
Specialized Homes	10	39	5	1	6	1	**1,546**
Total Assisted Annually	38,647	115,282	147	35	182	59	**1,412,029**
Residential Care of Children (Orphanages)	–	61	–	1	1	–	**272**
Total Assisted Annually	–	11,343	–	51	51	–	**70,886**
Day Care and Extended Day Care Centers	1	31	–	–	–	3	**1,240**
Total Assisted Annually	84	5,804	–	–	–	408	**125,723**
Special Centers for Social Services	18	117	47	20	67	1	**2,969**
Total Assisted Annually	46,288	1,648,607	9,800	145,000	154,800	12,760	**21,251,075**
Diocesan Seminaries	–	2	–	–	–	1	**72**
Students	–	126	–	–	–	15	**3,077**
Religious Seminaries	–	–	9	–	9	–	**124**
Students	–	11	–	–	–	1	**1,253**
Colleges and Universities	–	3	–	–	–	–	**232**
Total Students	–	24,210	–	–	–	–	**747,060**
High Schools, Diocesan and Parish	3	29	3	2	5	2	**787**
Total Students	1,616	20,632	2,088	800	2,888	791	**378,650**
High Schools, Private	–	6	1	3	4	1	**560**
Total Students	–	3,985	894	796	1,690	339	**301,673**
Elementary Schools, Diocesan and Parish	9	176	15	16	31	11	**6,488**
Total Students	3,662	65,878	6,001	4,407	10,408	2,385	**1,796,275**
Elementary Schools, Private	–	7	4	–	4	–	**365**
Total Students	–	2,599	1,345	–	1,345	–	**95,742**
Non–residential Schools for the Disabled	–	7	–	–	–	–	**83**
Total Students	–	11,985	–	–	–	–	**18,179**
Religious Education High School Students	601	19,135	5,259	822	6,081	1,672	**771,730**
Religious Education Elementary Students	9,227	122,106	31,516	4,212	35,728	3,081	**3,612,510**
Priests Teaching	3	35	6	1	7	–	**1,792**
Scholastics Teaching	–	–	–	–	–	–	**57**
Brothers Teaching	3	33	–	4	4	1	**1,195**
Sisters Teaching	9	145	6	18	24	22	**7,871**
Lay Teachers	423	5,913	929	422	1,351	187	**169,966**
Infant Baptisms	4,178	39,665	9,391	1,754	11,145	1,631	**985,141**
Adult Baptisms	205	3,148	719	215	934	33	**76,829**
Received into Full Communion	333	3,555	1,425	403	1,828	91	**75,429**
First Communions	3,851	37,046	6,507	1,440	7,947	1,106	**896,670**
Confirmations	2,900	25,511	2,329	1,301	3,630	677	**645,426**
Marriages	819	8,332	1,423	383	1,806	195	**232,060**
Deaths	2,658	19,925	1,033	621	1,654	454	**473,935**
Totals Catholics	217,585	2,316,652	371,139	75,987	447,126	131,430	**67,259,768**
Total Population	1,718,925	16,774,645	5,904,600	2,630,026	8,534,626	154,623	**288,758,111**
Catholic Population Percentage	13	14	6	3	5	85	**23**

*Indicates Archdioceses.

†Certain Dioceses traverse state lines.

2004 GENERAL SUMMARY

	Honolulu HI	Boise ID	*Chicago IL	Belleville IL	Joliet in Illinois IL	Peoria IL	2004 U.S. GRAND TOTAL
Cardinals	–	–	1	–	–	–	**12**
Archbishops	–	–	–	–	–	–	**48**
Bishops	2	1	11	1	3	1	**375**
Abbots	–	–	–	–	1	3	**109**
Diocesan Priests	66	82	851	133	193	231	**29,483**
Religious Priests	78	13	837	45	113	45	**14,729**
Total Priests in Diocese	144	95	1,688	178	306	276	**44,212**
Newly Ordained Priests	–	2	27	1	3	8	**544**
Total Permanent Deacons	51	52	632	28	171	111	**14,693**
Total Brothers	47	7	323	13	76	6	**5,504**
Total Sisters	153	91	2,618	224	631	240	**71,486**
Number of Parishes	66	51	373	124	122	165	**19,431**
Missions	24	31	10	–	11	26	**2,910**
Pastoral Centers	–	31	7	–	–	6	**1,011**
New Parishes	–	1	1	–	–	–	**34**
Catholic Hospitals	2	5	20	6	3	8	**583**
Patients Assisted Annually	421,745	870,160	3,026,371	607,037	629,415	2,945,453	**83,898,575**
Health Care Centers	4	–	2	–	–	–	**376**
Patients Assisted Annually	32,006	–	17,500	–	–	–	**4,251,107**
Specialized Homes	1	–	42	4	14	6	**1,546**
Total Assisted Annually	66	–	6,525	449	4,363	583	**1,412,029**
Residential Care of Children (Orphanages)	–	–	3	–	–	–	**272**
Total Assisted Annually	–	–	3,500	–	–	–	**70,886**
Day Care and Extended Day Care Centers	–	4	27	5	4	2	**1,240**
Total Assisted Annually	–	152	2,280	309	1,056	250	**125,723**
Special Centers for Social Services	17	17	120	3	5	1	**2,969**
Total Assisted Annually	14,730	284,000	371,255	26,835	53,882	18,500	**21,251,075**
Diocesan Seminaries	–	–	[illegible]	–	–	–	**72**
Students	1	–	46[illegible]	–	–	–	**3,077**
Religious Seminaries	–	–	[illegible]	–	–	–	**124**
Students	–	–	175	–	–	–	**1,253**
Colleges and Universities	1	–	5	–	3	1	**232**
Total Students	4,270	–	45,122	–	10,736	148	**747,060**
High Schools, Diocesan and Parish	3	1	3	3	4	7	**787**
Total Students	1,892	625	1,704	1,561	2,498	155	**378,650**
High Schools, Private	4	–	34	–	4	7	**560**
Total Students	2,709	–	27,180	–	3,366	2,624	**301,673**
Elementary Schools, Diocesan and Parish	33	13	238	34	56	45	**6,488**
Total Students	6,967	2,563	81,815	6,181	18,892	12,115	**1,796,275**
Elementary Schools, Private	–	–	3	–	–	–	**365**
Total Students	–	–	680	–	–	–	**95,742**
Non–residential Schools for the Disabled	–	–	6	–	–	–	**83**
Total Students	–	–	500	–	–	–	**18,179**
Religious Education High School Students	2,300	2,717	11,713	1,361	4,575	2,835	**771,730**
Religious Education Elementary Students	6,640	7,056	104,255	6,837	54,155	11,834	**3,612,510**
Priests Teaching	4	–	65	1	24	16	**1,792**
Scholastics Teaching	–	–	5	–	–	–	**57**
Brothers Teaching	13	–	50	1	20	3	**1,195**
Sisters Teaching	71	1	225	20	75	36	**7,871**
Lay Teachers	868	187	5,600	493	1,722	975	**169,966**
Infant Baptisms	2,862	2,472	39,927	1,464	9,932	3,998	**985,141**
Adult Baptisms	409	290	1,831	247	330	425	**76,829**
Received into Full Communion	252	230	1,670	257	423	500	**75,429**
First Communions	2,442	2,353	30,940	1,533	10,340	2,936	**896,670**
Confirmations	1,248	1,034	21,316	1,566	7,546	3,523	**645,426**
Marriages	864	506	8,724	657	2,003	982	**232,060**
Deaths	1,870	736	17,199	1,308	3,708	2,315	**473,935**
Totals Catholics	234,588	145,900	2,442,000	103,818	625,189	195,553	**67,259,768**
Total Population	1,244,898	1,351,000	6,104,000	845,762	1,734,304	1,562,868	**288,758,111**
Catholic Population Percentage	19	11	40	12	36	13	**23**

Archdioceses = 36; Dioceses = 169; Apostolates = 3

2004 GENERAL SUMMARY

	Rockford IL	Springfield in Illinois IL	ILLINOIS TOTAL	*Indianapolis IN	Evansville IN	Fort Wayne – South Bend IN	2004 U.S. GRAND TOTAL
Cardinals	–	–	1	–	–	–	12
Archbishops	–	–	–	1	–	–	48
Bishops	3	2	21	–	1	1	375
Abbots	3	–	7	3	–	–	109
Diocesan Priests	186	128	1,722	159	88	93	29,483
Religious Priests	61	59	1,160	111	6	160	14,729
Total Priests in Diocese	247	187	2,882	270	94	253	44,212
Newly Ordained Priests	15	–	54	2	–	2	544
Total Permanent Deacons	143	5	1,090	–	21	20	14,693
Total Brothers	15	31	464	42	2	134	5,504
Total Sisters	245	563	4,521	757	277	581	71,486
Number of Parishes	105	156	1,045	139	70	84	19,431
Missions	–	–	47	11	–	–	2,910
Pastoral Centers	–	–	13	–	5	1	1,011
New Parishes	–	–	1	–	–	–	34
Catholic Hospitals	3	7	47	2	2	4	583
Patients Assisted Annually	520,794	717,457	8,446,527	1,007,475	448,620	245,237	83,898,575
Health Care Centers	13	–	15	–	1	5	376
Patients Assisted Annually	49,258	–	66,758	–	58	51,343	4,251,107
Specialized Homes	8	2	76	7	2	7	1,546
Total Assisted Annually	1,538	235	13,693	1,188	105	1,747	1,412,029
Residential Care of Children (Orphanages)	–	1	4	–	–	–	272
Total Assisted Annually	–	314	3,814	–	–	–	70,886
Day Care and Extended Day Care Centers	1	1	40	2	1	2	1,240
Total Assisted Annually	69	120	4,084	205	272	303	125,723
Special Centers for Social Services	12	–	141	5	9	9	2,969
Total Assisted Annually	321,487	–	791,959	144,987	134,000	138,711	21,251,075
Diocesan Seminaries	–	–	3	–	–	–	72
Students	–	–	462	–	–	–	3,077
Religious Seminaries	–	–	1	1	–	1	124
Students	–	–	175	11	–	15	1,253
Colleges and Universities	1	2	12	2	–	5	232
Total Students	101	1,694	57,801	3,039	–	15,639	747,060
High Schools, Diocesan and Parish	6	2	28	7	4	4	787
Total Students	3,232	547	9,694	3,392	1,553	3,097	378,650
High Schools, Private	2	5	52	3	–	–	560
Total Students	913	1,960	36,043	2,108	–	–	301,673
Elementary Schools, Diocesan and Parish	41	49	463	63	24	41	6,488
Total Students	11,660	11,316	141,979	18,701	6,376	10,681	1,796,275
Elementary Schools, Private	–	–	3	–	–	–	365
Total Students	–	–	680	–	–	–	95,742
Non–residential Schools for the Disabled	–	–	6	–	1	–	83
Total Students	–	–	500	–	37	–	18,179
Religious Education High School Students	4,157	2,811	27,452	3,498	2,259	1,448	771,730
Religious Education Elementary Students	25,761	9,444	212,286	13,920	6,386	9,545	3,612,510
Priests Teaching	8	1	115	8	1	2	1,792
Scholastics Teaching	–	–	5	–	–	–	57
Brothers Teaching	10	4	88	4	2	–	1,195
Sisters Teaching	21	44	421	25	14	15	7,871
Lay Teachers	1,035	611	10,436	1,490	461	828	169,966
Infant Baptisms	6,386	2,131	63,838	4,183	1,267	2,723	985,141
Adult Baptisms	201	333	3,367	624	115	356	76,829
Received into Full Communion	345	486	3,681	700	145	354	75,429
First Communions	6,626	2,506	54,881	4,041	1,393	3,031	896,670
Confirmations	4,482	2,933	41,366	2,824	860	2,947	645,426
Marriages	1,304	893	14,563	1,245	548	939	232,060
Deaths	2,034	1,690	28,254	2,060	849	1,536	473,935
Totals Catholics	420,883	161,325	3,948,768	230,938	89,015	162,043	67,259,768
Total Population	1,374,899	1,106,124	12,727,957	2,430,606	491,956	1,217,932	288,758,111
Catholic Population Percentage	31	15	31	10	18	13	23

*Indicates Archdioceses.

†Certain Dioceses traverse state lines.

	Gary IN	Lafayette in Indiana IN	INDIANA TOTAL	*Dubuque IA	Davenport IA	Des Moines IA	2004 U.S. GRAND TOTAL
Cardinals	–	–	–	–	–	–	**12**
Archbishops	–	–	1	2	–	–	**48**
Bishops	1	1	4	–	1	1	**375**
Abbots	–	–	3	3	–	–	**109**
Diocesan Priests	113	112	565	224	115	92	**29,483**
Religious Priests	43	20	340	29	3	11	**14,729**
Total Priests in Diocese	156	132	905	253	118	103	**44,212**
Newly Ordained Priests	–	–	4	2	3	1	**544**
Total Permanent Deacons	50	5	96	76	47	70	**14,693**
Total Brothers	9	1	188	26	1	5	**5,504**
Total Sisters	100	79	1,794	837	200	91	**71,486**
Number of Parishes	73	62	428	199	85	84	**19,431**
Missions	4	–	15	1	1	–	**2,910**
Pastoral Centers	6	–	12	1	1	–	**1,011**
New Parishes	–	–	–	–	–	–	**34**
Catholic Hospitals	6	6	20	7	3	3	**583**
Patients Assisted Annually	1,024,720	892,569	3,618,621	1,398,575	455,500	711,329	**83,898,575**
Health Care Centers	–	–	6	3	–	–	**376**
Patients Assisted Annually	–	–	51,401	257	–	–	**4,251,107**
Specialized Homes	4	2	22	6	2	2	**1,546**
Total Assisted Annually	1,162	295	4,497	459	346	1,280	**1,412,029**
Residential Care of Children (Orphanages)	3	–	3	–	–	–	**272**
Total Assisted Annually	78	–	78	–	–	–	**70,886**
Day Care and Extended Day Care Centers	2	–	7	1	–	–	**1,240**
Total Assisted Annually	500	–	1,280	24	–	–	**125,723**
Special Centers for Social Services	7	–	30	2	1	4	**2,969**
Total Assisted Annually	10,000	–	427,698	419	5,300	76,744	**21,251,075**
Diocesan Seminaries	–	–	–	1	1	–	**72**
Students	–	–	–	3	4	15	**3,077**
Religious Seminaries	1	–	[illegible]	1	–	–	**124**
Students	7	–	3[illegible]	95	–	–	**1,253**
Colleges and Universities	1	3	1[illegible]	3	2	1	**232**
Total Students	1,230	5,969	25,87[illegible]	4,392	3,875	616	**747,060**
High Schools, Diocesan and Parish	1	1	1[illegible]	7	7	2	**787**
Total Students	1,413	360	9,815	2,666	1,441	1,367	**378,650**
High Schools, Private	–	–	[illegible]	–	–	–	**560**
Total Students	–	–	2,103	–	–	–	**301,673**
Elementary Schools, Diocesan and Parish	24	23	175	52	18	16	**6,488**
Total Students	6,562	4,579	46,899	12,680	3,844	4,869	**1,796,275**
Elementary Schools, Private	–	–	–	–	–	–	**365**
Total Students	–	–	–	–	–	–	**95,742**
Non–residential Schools for the Disabled	–	–	1	–	–	–	**83**
Total Students	–	–	37	–	–	–	**18,179**
Religious Education High School Students	500	3,306	11,011	6,114	2,767	1,878	**771,730**
Religious Education Elementary Students	9,650	9,684	49,185	13,183	9,393	10,553	**3,612,510**
Priests Teaching	2	–	13	3	2	2	**1,792**
Scholastics Teaching	–	–	–	–	–	–	**57**
Brothers Teaching	–	–	6	–	–	1	**1,195**
Sisters Teaching	7	6	67	21	5	7	**7,871**
Lay Teachers	442	291	3,5[illegible]2	994	387	376	**169,966**
Infant Baptisms	2,174	2,155	12,5[illegible]2	2,983	254	2,042	**985,141**
Adult Baptisms	127	283	1,5[illegible]5	145	256	202	**76,829**
Received into Full Communion	228	350	1,7[illegible]7	337	204	330	**75,429**
First Communions	2,154	2,075	12,694	3,390	1,977	1,940	**896,670**
Confirmations	1,932	1,501	10,0[illegible]4	2,631	1,733	1,816	**645,426**
Marriages	669	538	3,939	1,319	624	593	**232,060**
Deaths	1,742	841	7,028	2,092	1,061	805	**473,935**
Totals Catholics	185,700	98,003	765,6[illegible]9	211,847	103,037	97,628	**67,259,768**
Total Population	770,635	1,176,736	6,087,[illegible]55	927,161	728,048	748,153	**288,758,111**
Catholic Population Percentage	24	8	13	23	14	13	**23**

Archdioceses = 36; Dioceses = 169; Apostolates = 3

2004 GENERAL SUMMARY

	Sioux City IA	IOWA TOTAL	*Kansas City in Kansas KS	Dodge City KS	Salina KS	Wichita KS	2004 U.S. GRAND TOTAL
Cardinals	–	–	–	–	–	–	12
Archbishops	–	2	1	–	–	–	48
Bishops	2	4	1	1	2	2	375
Abbots	–	3	3	–	–	–	109
Diocesan Priests	155	586	98	36	66	129	29,483
Religious Priests	3	46	59	10	7	4	14,729
Total Priests in Diocese	158	632	157	46	73	133	44,212
Newly Ordained Priests	1	7	5	–	1	3	544
Total Permanent Deacons	36	229	–	8	–	1	14,693
Total Brothers	–	32	15	–	1	–	5,504
Total Sisters	83	1,211	644	96	198	314	71,486
Number of Parishes	124	492	118	49	88	91	19,431
Missions	–	2	–	–	–	–	2,910
Pastoral Centers	1	3	–	–	–	–	1,011
New Parishes	–	–	–	–	–	–	34
Catholic Hospitals	3	16	4	3	–	7	583
Patients Assisted Annually	429,610	2,995,014	363,691	97,618	–	670,624	83,898,575
Health Care Centers	–	3	4	–	–	2	376
Patients Assisted Annually	–	257	25,712	–	–	40,406	4,251,107
Specialized Homes	3	13	3	–	4	3	1,546
Total Assisted Annually	301	2,386	486	–	249	487	1,412,029
Residential Care of Children (Orphanages)	–	–	–	–	–	–	272
Total Assisted Annually	–	–	–	–	–	–	70,886
Day Care and Extended Day Care Centers	–	1	–	–	–	1	1,240
Total Assisted Annually	–	24	–	–	–	175	125,723
Special Centers for Social Services	5	12	18	4	–	1	2,969
Total Assisted Annually	6,400	88,863	75,339	257,775	–	25,484	21,251,075
Diocesan Seminaries	–	2	–	–	–	–	72
Students	–	22	–	–	–	–	3,077
Religious Seminaries	–	1	–	–	–	–	124
Students	–	95	2	–	–	–	1,253
Colleges and Universities	1	7	3	–	–	1	232
Total Students	1,168	10,051	3,923	–	–	1,929	747,060
High Schools, Diocesan and Parish	8	24	5	–	5	4	787
Total Students	2,203	7,677	3,263	–	651	2,335	378,650
High Schools, Private	–	–	1	–	1	–	560
Total Students	–	–	248	–	259	–	301,673
Elementary Schools, Diocesan and Parish	23	109	43	9	12	33	6,488
Total Students	4,628	26,021	12,708	1,138	1,834	7,974	1,796,275
Elementary Schools, Private	–	–	1	–	–	–	365
Total Students	–	–	37	–	–	–	95,742
Non–residential Schools for the Disabled	–	–	–	–	–	–	83
Total Students	–	–	–	–	–	–	18,179
Religious Education High School Students	3,223	13,982	2,900	1,728	1,922	3,215	771,730
Religious Education Elementary Students	7,262	40,391	14,991	3,860	4,591	8,007	3,612,510
Priests Teaching	2	9	–	–	4	2	1,792
Scholastics Teaching	–	–	–	–	–	–	57
Brothers Teaching	–	1	–	–	–	–	1,195
Sisters Teaching	24	57	19	–	4	18	7,871
Lay Teachers	509	2,266	1,107	90	206	619	169,966
Infant Baptisms	1,626	6,905	3,981	1,001	951	2,240	985,141
Adult Baptisms	96	699	336	70	89	302	76,829
Received into Full Communion	233	1,104	545	66	173	419	75,429
First Communions	1,785	9,092	3,910	1,092	824	2,515	896,670
Confirmations	1,904	8,084	3,394	684	770	2,309	645,426
Marriages	607	3,143	1,097	255	421	796	232,060
Deaths	1,095	5,053	1,483	362	628	973	473,935
Totals Catholics	94,186	506,698	191,203	55,053	46,737	116,913	67,259,768
Total Population	468,549	2,871,911	1,193,425	222,502	318,145	959,389	288,758,111
Catholic Population Percentage	20	18	16	25	15	12	23

*Indicates Archdioceses.

†Certain Dioceses traverse state lines.

2004 GENERAL SUMMARY

	KANSAS TOTAL	*Louisville KY	Covington KY	Lexington KY	Owensboro KY	KENTUCKY TOTAL	2004 U.S. GRAND TOTAL
Cardinals	–	–	–	–	–	–	12
Archbishops	1	1	–	–	–	1	48
Bishops	6	1	2	2	1	6	375
Abbots	3	2	–	–	–	2	109
Diocesan Priests	329	166	95	48	77	386	29,483
Religious Priests	80	58	2	23	18	101	14,729
Total Priests in Diocese	409	224	97	71	95	487	44,212
Newly Ordained Priests	9	3	–	–	2	5	544
Total Permanent Deacons	9	110	28	37	–	175	14,693
Total Brothers	16	77	8	5	5	95	5,504
Total Sisters	1,252	924	379	137	198	1,638	71,486
Number of Parishes	346	111	46	59	79	295	19,431
Missions	–	11	6	5	–	22	2,910
Pastoral Centers	–	3	–	–	1	4	1,011
New Parishes	–	–	–	–	–	–	34
Catholic Hospitals	14	2	3	7	1	13	583
Patients Assisted Annually	1,131,933	185,750	418,683	1,030,642	399,685	2,034,760	83,898,575
Health Care Centers	6	1	–	4	–	5	376
Patients Assisted Annually	66,118	2,500	–	71,632	–	74,132	4,251,107
Specialized Homes	10	5	3	1	2	11	1,546
Total Assisted Annually	1,222	1,154	896	82	219	2,351	1,412,029
Residential Care of Children (Orphanages)	–	2	2	–	–	4	272
Total Assisted Annually	–	145	165	–	–	310	70,886
Day Care and Extended Day Care Centers	1	1	1	–	3	5	1,240
Total Assisted Annually	175	150	93	–	1,780	2,023	125,723
Special Centers for Social Services	23	8	3	1	3	15	2,969
Total Assisted Annually	358,598	31,000	80,092	8,025	52,000	171,117	21,251,075
Diocesan Seminaries	–	–	–	–	–	–	72
Students	–	–	–	–	–	–	3,077
Religious Seminaries	–	–	–	–	–	–	124
Students	2	–	–	–	–	–	1,253
Colleges and Universities	4	3	–	–	1	4	232
Total Students	5,852	4,655	–	–	713	5,368	747,060
High Schools, Diocesan and Parish	14	4	7	1	3	15	787
Total Students	6,249	2,327	2,393	880	934	6,534	378,650
High Schools, Private	2	5	2	1	–	8	560
Total Students	507	3,989	747	50	–	4,786	301,673
Elementary Schools, Diocesan and Parish	97	53	27	14	18	112	6,488
Total Students	23,654	16,886	8,309	3,105	3,716	32,016	1,796,275
Elementary Schools, Private	1	2	2	1	–	5	365
Total Students	37	488	461	189	–	1,138	95,742
Non–residential Schools for the Disabled	–	1	–	–	–	1	83
Total Students	–	52	–	–	–	52	18,179
Religious Education High School Students	9,765	1,261	274	755	1,526	3,816	771,730
Religious Education Elementary Students	31,449	5,903	3,660	2,200	3,497	15,260	3,612,510
Priests Teaching	6	7	1	1	3	12	1,792
Scholastics Teaching	–	–	–	–	–	–	57
Brothers Teaching	–	7	1	–	–	8	1,195
Sisters Teaching	41	21	50	14	11	96	7,871
Lay Teachers	2,022	1,925	698	296	332	3,251	169,966
Infant Baptisms	8,173	2,570	1,434	627	949	5,580	985,141
Adult Baptisms	797	350	227	472	147	1,196	76,829
Received into Full Communion	1,203	485	189	139	190	1,003	75,429
First Communions	8,341	2,966	1,588	874	879	6,307	896,670
Confirmations	7,157	2,704	1,586	931	924	6,145	645,426
Marriages	2,569	908	548	248	361	2,065	232,060
Deaths	3,446	1,660	889	317	536	3,402	473,935
Totals Catholics	409,906	196,888	88,154	45,153	51,847	382,042	67,259,768
Total Population	2,693,461	1,119,465	464,329	1,492,784	836,162	3,913,040	288,758,111
Catholic Population Percentage	15	18	19	3	6	10	23

Archdioceses = 36; Dioceses = 169; Apostolates = 3

2004 GENERAL SUMMARY

	*New Orleans LA	Alexandria LA	Baton Rouge LA	Houma–Thibodaux LA	Lafayette LA	Lake Charles LA	2004 U.S. GRAND TOTAL
Cardinals	–	–	–	–	–	–	**12**
Archbishops	3	–	–	–	–	–	**48**
Bishops	3	–	1	1	3	2	**375**
Abbots	1	–	–	–	–	–	**109**
Diocesan Priests	220	60	78	63	158	61	**29,483**
Religious Priests	190	14	37	8	43	15	**14,729**
Total Priests in Diocese	410	74	115	71	201	76	**44,212**
Newly Ordained Priests	5	4	2	1	1	61	**544**
Total Permanent Deacons	190	5	40	27	70	33	**14,693**
Total Brothers	111	4	10	2	28	1	**5,504**
Total Sisters	739	39	103	26	159	25	**71,486**
Number of Parishes	142	48	68	39	121	38	**19,431**
Missions	8	24	–	2	30	20	**2,910**
Pastoral Centers	1	1	–	–	–	–	**1,011**
New Parishes	–	–	–	–	–	–	**34**
Catholic Hospitals	–	2	3	–	1	1	**583**
Patients Assisted Annually	–	121,249	311,882	–	139,522	135,292	**83,898,575**
Health Care Centers	4	–	–	–	1	–	**376**
Patients Assisted Annually	194,610	–	–	–	19,408	–	**4,251,107**
Specialized Homes	28	2	12	2	12	1	**1,546**
Total Assisted Annually	7,051	164	958	65	3,500	65	**1,412,029**
Residential Care of Children (Orphanages)	2	–	–	–	–	–	**272**
Total Assisted Annually	331	–	–	–	–	–	**70,886**
Day Care and Extended Day Care Centers	16	–	–	1	–	1	**1,240**
Total Assisted Annually	1,441	–	–	136	–	65	**125,723**
Special Centers for Social Services	63	18	8	4	6	1	**2,969**
Total Assisted Annually	114,229	89,861	128,135	25,000	249,554	135,292	**21,251,075**
Diocesan Seminaries	2	–	–	–	1	–	**72**
Students	156	–	–	–	–	–	**3,077**
Religious Seminaries	2	–	–	–	1	–	**124**
Students	37	–	–	–	20	–	**1,253**
Colleges and Universities	3	–	1	–	–	–	**232**
Total Students	11,185	–	1,550	–	–	–	**747,060**
High Schools, Diocesan and Parish	10	3	6	3	9	1	**787**
Total Students	6,014	652	2,772	1,930	3,737	531	**378,650**
High Schools, Private	13	–	2	–	1	–	**560**
Total Students	10,608	–	1,689	–	140	–	**301,673**
Elementary Schools, Diocesan and Parish	72	8	24	10	29	7	**6,488**
Total Students	31,778	2,330	12,107	4,060	10,468	2,061	**1,796,275**
Elementary Schools, Private	10	–	–	–	2	–	**365**
Total Students	1,898	–	–	–	576	–	**95,742**
Non–residential Schools for the Disabled	1	–	–	–	–	–	**83**
Total Students	225	–	–	–	–	–	**18,179**
Religious Education High School Students	4,118	1,274	4,599	3,115	9,005	3,626	**771,730**
Religious Education Elementary Students	14,972	2,484	9,569	6,283	19,461	5,504	**3,612,510**
Priests Teaching	77	–	1	–	–	–	**1,792**
Scholastics Teaching	–	–	–	–	–	–	**57**
Brothers Teaching	29	4	3	2	1	–	**1,195**
Sisters Teaching	136	14	16	5	10	–	**7,871**
Lay Teachers	4,341	201	949	373	971	263	**169,966**
Infant Baptisms	5,790	671	2,527	1,546	4,886	1,262	**985,141**
Adult Baptisms	658	59	210	54	129	85	**76,829**
Received into Full Communion	533	148	404	64	268	521	**75,429**
First Communions	5,999	684	2,687	1,475	4,604	1,177	**896,670**
Confirmations	5,532	593	2,311	1,259	3,677	984	**645,426**
Marriages	1,982	201	895	421	1,348	409	**232,060**
Deaths	4,396	656	1,737	1,194	3,600	936	**473,935**
Totals Catholics	488,004	48,050	210,464	126,000	322,349	77,934	**67,259,768**
Total Population	1,359,136	392,639	863,976	202,000	568,154	277,849	**288,758,111**
Catholic Population Percentage	36	12	24	62	57	28	**23**

*Indicates Archdioceses.

†Certain Dioceses traverse state lines.

	Shreveport LA	LOUISIANA TOTAL	Portland (In Maine) ME	Marshall Islands	*Baltimore MD	*Boston MA	2004 U.S. GRAND TOTAL
Cardinals	–	–	–	–	1	1	**12**
Archbishops	–	3	–	–	1	1	**48**
Bishops	1	11	1	–	3	6	**375**
Abbots	–	1	–	–	–	1	**109**
Diocesan Priests	41	681	168	1	279	859	**29,483**
Religious Priests	15	322	45	4	265	670	**14,729**
Total Priests in Diocese	56	1,003	213	5	544	1,529	**44,212**
Newly Ordained Priests	–	74	3	–	10	5	**544**
Total Permanent Deacons	6	371	27	2	183	239	**14,693**
Total Brothers	10	166	26	1	40	142	**5,504**
Total Sisters	58	1,149	371	11	1,088	2,601	**71,486**
Number of Parishes	32	488	135	4	153	357	**19,431**
Missions	13	97	45	–	8	–	**2,910**
Pastoral Centers	2	4	–	–	–	2	**1,011**
New Parishes	–	–	–	–	–	1	**34**
Catholic Hospitals	2	9	3	–	6	8	**583**
Patients Assisted Annually	1,097	709,042	379,998	–	1,189,696	1,193,117	**83,898,575**
Health Care Centers	3	8	5	–	4	3	**376**
Patients Assisted Annually	322,235	536,253	1,258	–	6,121	6,868	**4,251,107**
Specialized Homes	3	60	6	–	29	37	**1,546**
Total Assisted Annually	540	12,343	604	–	1,990	4,738	**1,412,029**
Residential Care of Children (Orphanages)	–	2	–	–	7	–	**272**
Total Assisted Annually	–	331	–	–	849	–	**70,886**
Day Care and Extended Day Care Centers	2	20	2	–	7	11	**1,240**
Total Assisted Annually	195	1,837	205	–	1,872	1,675	**125,723**
Special Centers for Social Services	20	120	5	–	32	43	**2,969**
Total Assisted Annually	27,469	769,540	3,987	–	822,315	206,000	**21,251,075**
Diocesan Seminaries	–	3	–	–	2	2	**72**
Students	–	156	–	–	215	131	**3,077**
Religious Seminaries	–	3	–	–	–	2	**124**
Students	–	57	–	–	–	51	**1,253**
Colleges and Universities	–	4	1	–	4	7	**232**
Total Students	–	12,735	4,94[illegible]	–	11,382	22,400	**747,060**
High Schools, Diocesan and Parish	2	34	1	2	9	13	**787**
Total Students	735	16,371	360	360	4,221	5,335	**378,650**
High Schools, Private	–	16	[illegible]	–	13	20	**560**
Total Students	–	12,437	79[illegible]	–	7,272	11,739	**301,673**
Elementary Schools, Diocesan and Parish	6	156	1[illegible]	5	65	113	**6,488**
Total Students	1,543	64,347	3,75[illegible]	963	23,227	34,725	**1,796,275**
Elementary Schools, Private	–	12	–	–	7	10	**365**
Total Students	–	2,474	164	–	2,252	2,558	**95,742**
Non–residential Schools for the Disabled	–	1	–	–	1	3	**83**
Total Students	–	225	–	–	103	348	**18,179**
Religious Education High School Students	635	26,372	2,034	370	4,298	29,517	**771,730**
Religious Education Elementary Students	2,489	60,762	12,280	1,200	31,454	111,501	**3,612,510**
Priests Teaching	–	78	1	–	40	7	**1,792**
Scholastics Teaching	–	–	–	–	–	–	**57**
Brothers Teaching	–	39	–	1	12	35	**1,195**
Sisters Teaching	7	188	23	10	74	185	**7,871**
Lay Teachers	163	7,261	3[illegible]0	48	3,005	3,284	**169,966**
Infant Baptisms	532	17,214	2,3[illegible]0	88	6,826	22,287	**985,141**
Adult Baptisms	87	1,282	2[illegible]2	10	524	3,362	**76,829**
Received into Full Communion	144	2,082	2[illegible]8	22	894	214	**75,429**
First Communions	538	17,164	2,9[illegible]4	73	6,703	21,632	**896,670**
Confirmations	443	14,799	3,459	–	5,419	16,050	**645,426**
Marriages	188	5,444	1,018	10	2,607	6,143	**232,060**
Deaths	383	12,902	2,921	–	4,804	18,498	**473,935**
Totals Catholics	39,436	1,312,237	217,676	4,602	506,587	2,077,487	**67,259,768**
Total Population	784,665	4,448,419	1,274,923	52,894	3,006,607	3,970,026	**288,758,111**
Catholic Population Percentage	5	30	17	9	17	52	**23**

Archdioceses = 36; Dioceses = 169; Apostolates = 3

2004 GENERAL SUMMARY

	Fall River MA	Springfield in Massachusetts MA	Worcester MA	MASS. TOTAL	*Detroit MI	Gaylord MI	2004 U.S. GRAND TOTAL
Cardinals	–	–	–	1	1	–	**12**
Archbishops	–	–	–	1	–	–	**48**
Bishops	–	2	2	10	7	1	**375**
Abbots	–	–	3	4	–	–	**109**
Diocesan Priests	173	166	227	1,425	469	66	**29,483**
Religious Priests	141	35	111	957	233	11	**14,729**
Total Priests in Diocese	314	201	338	2,382	702	77	**44,212**
Newly Ordained Priests	1	2	1	9	7	1	**544**
Total Permanent Deacons	90	57	74	460	140	14	**14,693**
Total Brothers	16	9	78	245	112	1	**5,504**
Total Sisters	295	575	447	3,918	1,897	41	**71,486**
Number of Parishes	101	124	126	708	309	81	**19,431**
Missions	11	14	2	27	6	–	**2,910**
Pastoral Centers	–	1	–	3	–	–	**1,011**
New Parishes	1	1	–	3	–	–	**34**
Catholic Hospitals	1	1	1	11	12	3	**583**
Patients Assisted Annually	140,303	218,314	200,000	1,751,734	1,601,237	369,500	**83,898,575**
Health Care Centers	1	3	–	7	8	–	**376**
Patients Assisted Annually	62	6,800	–	13,730	13,416	–	**4,251,107**
Specialized Homes	10	12	4	63	20	1	**1,546**
Total Assisted Annually	46,720	6,200	410	58,068	5,187	250	**1,412,029**
Residential Care of Children (Orphanages)	1	1	–	2	8	2	**272**
Total Assisted Annually	60	139	–	199	1,612	45	**70,886**
Day Care and Extended Day Care Centers	–	1	12	24	2	6	**1,240**
Total Assisted Annually	–	125	2,000	3,800	711	267	**125,723**
Special Centers for Social Services	–	3	21	67	13	23	**2,969**
Total Assisted Annually	–	62,909	40,000	308,909	24,188	5,818	**21,251,075**
Diocesan Seminaries	–	–	–	2	2	–	**72**
Students	–	–	–	131	103	–	**3,077**
Religious Seminaries	–	–	–	2	2	–	**124**
Students	–	–	–	51	14	–	**1,253**
Colleges and Universities	1	1	3	12	4	–	**232**
Total Students	2,550	1,002	6,825	32,777	19,922	–	**747,060**
High Schools, Diocesan and Parish	4	4	4	25	16	4	**787**
Total Students	2,871	1,620	2,697	12,523	4,468	662	**378,650**
High Schools, Private	–	–	4	24	16	–	**560**
Total Students	–	–	1,434	13,173	8,701	–	**301,673**
Elementary Schools, Diocesan and Parish	24	23	23	183	110	16	**6,488**
Total Students	5,864	6,088	6,167	52,844	38,875	2,406	**1,796,275**
Elementary Schools, Private	–	–	2	12	7	–	**365**
Total Students	–	–	375	2,933	1,822	–	**95,742**
Non–residential Schools for the Disabled	–	–	2	5	–	–	**83**
Total Students	–	–	95	443	–	–	**18,179**
Religious Education High School Students	6,134	8,119	1,925	45,695	6,340	1,720	**771,730**
Religious Education Elementary Students	28,996	20,544	8,166	169,207	66,269	4,310	**3,612,510**
Priests Teaching	14	1	2	24	12	–	**1,792**
Scholastics Teaching	–	–	–	–	–	–	**57**
Brothers Teaching	5	–	1	41	29	–	**1,195**
Sisters Teaching	17	29	30	261	112	2	**7,871**
Lay Teachers	647	360	697	4,988	2,680	198	**169,966**
Infant Baptisms	4,585	3,503	4,160	34,535	13,949	901	**985,141**
Adult Baptisms	90	126	117	3,695	1,158	110	**76,829**
Received into Full Communion	168	111	314	807	1,619	175	**75,429**
First Communions	4,833	3,380	4,309	34,154	13,817	1,170	**896,670**
Confirmations	4,012	2,673	2,907	25,642	11,227	2,232	**645,426**
Marriages	1,602	1,059	919	9,723	3,896	404	**232,060**
Deaths	4,084	4,168	3,777	30,527	10,257	933	**473,935**
Totals Catholics	346,054	240,730	369,096	3,033,367	1,481,866	76,060	**67,259,768**
Total Population	824,235	800,000	762,207	6,356,468	4,441,551	497,264	**288,758,111**
Catholic Population Percentage	42	30	48	48	33	15	**23**

*Indicates Archdioceses.

†Certain Dioceses traverse state lines.

2004 GENERAL SUMMARY

	Grand Rapids MI	Kalamazoo MI	Lansing MI	Marquette MI	Saginaw MI	MICHIGAN TOTAL	2004 U.S. GRAND TOTAL
Cardinals	–	–	–	–	–	1	**12**
Archbishops	–	–	–	–	–	–	**48**
Bishops	4	2	1	2	1	18	**375**
Abbots	–	–	–	–	–	–	**109**
Diocesan Priests	107	56	145	88	102	1,033	**29,483**
Religious Priests	15	12	35	11	11	328	**14,729**
Total Priests in Diocese	122	68	180	99	113	1,361	**44,212**
Newly Ordained Priests	4	2	3	1	1	19	**544**
Total Permanent Deacons	29	27	84	29	15	338	**14,693**
Total Brothers	1	2	7	–	1	124	**5,504**
Total Sisters	273	170	456	59	124	3,020	**71,486**
Number of Parishes	90	46	95	74	108	803	**19,431**
Missions	12	13	–	23	–	54	**2,910**
Pastoral Centers	2	1	2	–	–	5	**1,011**
New Parishes	–	–	–	–	–	–	**34**
Catholic Hospitals	2	3	4	1	1	26	**583**
Patients Assisted Annually	593,000	757,008	1,905,361	87,300	258,427	5,571,833	**83,898,575**
Health Care Centers	–	–	4	–	1	13	**376**
Patients Assisted Annually	–	–	819	–	10,850	25,085	**4,251,107**
Specialized Homes	3	6	6	1	1	38	**1,546**
Total Assisted Annually	6,039	676	503	123	100	12,878	**1,412,029**
Residential Care of Children (Orphanages)	–	–	–	–	4	14	**272**
Total Assisted Annually	–	–	–	–	201	1,858	**70,886**
Day Care and Extended Day Care Centers	–	15	1	–	9	33	**1,240**
Total Assisted Annually	–	453	100	–	341	1,872	**125,723**
Special Centers for Social Services	8	5	10	6	–	65	**2,969**
Total Assisted Annually	18,655	38,414	132,493	2,856	–	222,424	**21,251,075**
Diocesan Seminaries	–	–	–	–	–	2	**72**
Students	–	–	–	–	6	109	**3,077**
Religious Seminaries	–	–	4	–	–	6	**124**
Students	–	–	–	–	–	14	**1,253**
Colleges and Universities	1	–	3	–	–	8	**232**
Total Students	2,338	–	2,680	–	–	24,940	**747,060**
High Schools, Diocesan and Parish	4	3	4	–	3	34	**787**
Total Students	1,895	775	2,270	–	854	10,924	**378,650**
High Schools, Private	–	–	2	–	–	18	**560**
Total Students	–	–	155	–	–	8,856	**301,673**
Elementary Schools, Diocesan and Parish	39	22	38	10	24	259	**6,488**
Total Students	6,847	3,152	8,897	1,508	3,524	65,209	**1,796,275**
Elementary Schools, Private	–	–	6	–	–	13	**365**
Total Students	–	–	774	–	–	2,596	**95,742**
Non–residential Schools for the Disabled	–	–	–	–	–	–	**83**
Total Students	–	–	–	–	–	–	**18,179**
Religious Education High School Students	1,992	1,213	2,895	2,791	1,506	18,457	**771,730**
Religious Education Elementary Students	14,288	6,150	21,650	5,194	8,990	126,851	**3,612,510**
Priests Teaching	–	1	11	–	1	25	**1,792**
Scholastics Teaching	–	–	–	–	–	–	**57**
Brothers Teaching	–	–	–	–	–	29	**1,195**
Sisters Teaching	9	5	13	3	7	151	**7,871**
Lay Teachers	506	269	757	115	208	4,733	**169,966**
Infant Baptisms	2,604	1,430	3,589	786	1,653	24,912	**985,141**
Adult Baptisms	309	209	492	91	213	2,582	**76,829**
Received into Full Communion	–	264	786	107	368	3,319	**75,429**
First Communions	2,858	1,444	4,464	957	1,831	26,541	**896,670**
Confirmations	2,856	1,325	3,463	2,878	2,107	26,088	**645,426**
Marriages	940	415	1,189	465	686	7,995	**232,060**
Deaths	1,384	862	2,074	1,141	1,714	18,365	**473,935**
Totals Catholics	162,670	117,088	227,3[illegible]5	68,360	131,937	2,265,286	**67,259,768**
Total Population	1,283,717	840,352	1,778,475	317,616	724,142	9,883,117	**288,758,111**
Catholic Population Percentage	13	14	13	22	18	23	**23**

Archdioceses = 36; Dioceses = 169; Apostolates = 3

2004 GENERAL SUMMARY

	*St. Paul and Minneapolis MN	Crookston MN	Duluth MN	New Ulm MN	St. Cloud MN	Winona MN	2004 U.S. GRAND TOTAL
Cardinals	–	–	–	–	–	–	**12**
Archbishops	1	–	–	–	–	–	**48**
Bishops	2	1	1	1	3	2	**375**
Abbots	–	–	–	–	3	1	**109**
Diocesan Priests	321	49	74	76	131	118	**29,483**
Religious Priests	128	2	9	1	109	8	**14,729**
Total Priests in Diocese	449	51	83	77	240	126	**44,212**
Newly Ordained Priests	7	–	1	–	3	–	**544**
Total Permanent Deacons	210	11	33	4	44	9	**14,693**
Total Brothers	65	1	1	–	67	22	**5,504**
Total Sisters	991	128	155	68	583	511	**71,486**
Number of Parishes	220	68	93	80	138	115	**19,431**
Missions	5	–	–	2	–	–	**2,910**
Pastoral Centers	4	–	–	–	–	2	**1,011**
New Parishes	1	–	–	–	–	–	**34**
Catholic Hospitals	5	3	2	2	4	2	**583**
Patients Assisted Annually	187,000	53,954	403,750	17,351	247,892	76,517	**83,898,575**
Health Care Centers	1	–	–	–	–	1	**376**
Patients Assisted Annually	175	–	–	–	–	6,200	**4,251,107**
Specialized Homes	11	3	2	6	14	10	**1,546**
Total Assisted Annually	2,284	304	305	299	1,181	1,001	**1,412,029**
Residential Care of Children (Orphanages)	1	–	–	–	1	–	**272**
Total Assisted Annually	2,400	–	–	–	241	–	**70,886**
Day Care and Extended Day Care Centers	–	1	1	–	–	3	**1,240**
Total Assisted Annually	–	49	146	–	–	10,169	**125,723**
Special Centers for Social Services	19	–	–	–	66	7	**2,969**
Total Assisted Annually	10,000	–	–	–	39,405	5,496	**21,251,075**
Diocesan Seminaries	2	–	–	–	–	1	**72**
Students	143	–	–	–	–	56	**3,077**
Religious Seminaries	1	–	–	–	1	–	**124**
Students	23	–	–	–	7	–	**1,253**
Colleges and Universities	3	–	1	–	2	1	**232**
Total Students	16,835	–	2,750	–	4,045	1,357	**747,060**
High Schools, Diocesan and Parish	10	1	–	3	1	4	**787**
Total Students	8,245	174	–	470	792	1,218	**378,650**
High Schools, Private	3	–	–	–	1	–	**560**
Total Students	551	–	–	–	320	–	**301,673**
Elementary Schools, Diocesan and Parish	92	9	12	17	31	26	**6,488**
Total Students	29,483	1,260	1,868	2,771	4,977	4,707	**1,796,275**
Elementary Schools, Private	3	–	–	–	–	–	**365**
Total Students	499	–	–	–	–	–	**95,742**
Non–residential Schools for the Disabled	–	–	–	–	–	–	**83**
Total Students	–	–	–	–	–	–	**18,179**
Religious Education High School Students	–	2,226	4,150	3,800	7,012	4,529	**771,730**
Religious Education Elementary Students	66,500	2,652	4,310	7,033	13,445	9,734	**3,612,510**
Priests Teaching	19	–	–	–	17	1	**1,792**
Scholastics Teaching	–	–	–	–	–	–	**57**
Brothers Teaching	10	–	–	–	6	2	**1,195**
Sisters Teaching	39	4	10	4	28	27	**7,871**
Lay Teachers	1,847	127	149	–	723	352	**169,966**
Infant Baptisms	10,022	644	912	1,008	2,211	1,714	**985,141**
Adult Baptisms	401	19	51	46	76	53	**76,829**
Received into Full Communion	1,304	75	123	109	195	218	**75,429**
First Communions	10,290	546	978	1,032	2,645	1,732	**896,670**
Confirmations	7,922	483	810	1,197	2,599	1,728	**645,426**
Marriages	2,831	227	373	363	981	599	**232,060**
Deaths	4,633	411	1,070	767	1,420	1,074	**473,935**
Totals Catholics	730,989	36,263	70,950	69,503	147,748	130,527	**67,259,768**
Total Population	2,949,643	247,741	431,000	285,061	516,755	557,684	**288,758,111**
Catholic Population Percentage	25	15	16	24	29	23	**23**

*Indicates Archdioceses.

†Certain Dioceses traverse state lines.

2004 GENERAL SUMMARY

	MINNESOTA TOTAL	Biloxi MS	Jackson MS	MISSISSIPPI TOTAL	*St. Louis MO	Jefferson City MO	2004 U.S. GRAND TOTAL
Cardinals	–	–	–	–	–	–	**12**
Archbishops	1	–	–	–	1	–	**48**
Bishops	10	3	2	5	3	2	**375**
Abbots	4	–	–	–	3	–	**109**
Diocesan Priests	769	54	62	116	392	102	**29,483**
Religious Priests	257	29	29	58	345	6	**14,729**
Total Priests in Diocese	1,026	83	91	174	737	108	**44,212**
Newly Ordained Priests	11	–	2	2	10	1	**544**
Total Permanent Deacons	311	26	6	32	253	57	**14,693**
Total Brothers	156	25	13	38	153	2	**5,504**
Total Sisters	2,436	46	212	258	1,647	86	**71,486**
Number of Parishes	714	45	74	119	214	95	**19,431**
Missions	7	13	29	42	8	15	**2,910**
Pastoral Centers	6	–	–	–	–	–	**1,011**
New Parishes	1	–	–	–	2	–	**34**
Catholic Hospitals	18	–	1	1	10	1	**583**
Patients Assisted Annually	986,464	–	96,616	96,616	2,030,576	265,000	**83,898,575**
Health Care Centers	2	–	2	2	–	13	**376**
Patients Assisted Annually	6,375	–	9,458	9,458	–	150,000	**4,251,107**
Specialized Homes	46	7	8	15	44	2	**1,546**
Total Assisted Annually	5,374	656	2,226	2,882	46,776	215	**1,412,029**
Residential Care of Children (Orphanages)	2	–	2	2	6	–	**272**
Total Assisted Annually	2,641	–	315	315	4,890	–	**70,886**
Day Care and Extended Day Care Centers	5	–	2	2	12	–	**1,240**
Total Assisted Annually	10,364	–	435	435	22,902	–	**125,723**
Special Centers for Social Services	92	10	5	15	35	2	**2,969**
Total Assisted Annually	54,901	129,360	16,890	146,250	126,478	36,000	**21,251,075**
Diocesan Seminaries	3	–	–	–	2	–	**72**
Students	199	–	–	–	89	–	**3,077**
Religious Seminaries	2	–	–	–	2	–	**124**
Students	30	–	–	–	15	–	**1,253**
Colleges and Universities	7	–	1	1	2	–	**232**
Total Students	24,987	–	42	42	14,617	–	**747,060**
High Schools, Diocesan and Parish	19	4	4	8	11	2	**787**
Total Students	10,899	1,023	772	1,795	5,701	1,032	**378,650**
High Schools, Private	4	1	–	1	16	–	**560**
Total Students	871	539	–	539	8,296	–	**301,673**
Elementary Schools, Diocesan and Parish	187	14	15	29	126	38	**6,488**
Total Students	45,066	3,073	3,872	6,945	33,920	6,582	**1,796,275**
Elementary Schools, Private	3	–	–	–	10	–	**365**
Total Students	499	–	–	–	2,136	–	**95,742**
Non–residential Schools for the Disabled	–	–	–	–	9	1	**83**
Total Students	–	–	–	–	257	20	**18,179**
Religious Education High School Students	21,717	2,414	8,166	10,580	865	2,688	**771,730**
Religious Education Elementary Students	103,674	3,299	24,208	27,507	22,889	4,607	**3,612,510**
Priests Teaching	37	–	–	–	110	–	**1,792**
Scholastics Teaching	–	–	–	–	4	–	**57**
Brothers Teaching	18	5	2	7	21	2	**1,195**
Sisters Teaching	112	13	15	28	171	19	**7,871**
Lay Teachers	3,198	438	312	750	5,179	511	**169,966**
Infant Baptisms	16,511	782	927	1,709	6,572	1,396	**985,141**
Adult Baptisms	646	434	132	566	624	292	**76,829**
Received into Full Communion	2,024	179	276	455	958	310	**75,429**
First Communions	17,223	1,152	653	1,805	7,450	1,507	**896,670**
Confirmations	14,739	616	374	990	7,114	1,437	**645,426**
Marriages	5,374	310	271	581	2,604	571	**232,060**
Deaths	9,375	794	440	1,234	4,253	808	**473,935**
Totals Catholics	1,185,980	72,158	51,992	124,150	550,000	86,457	**67,259,768**
Total Population	4,987,884	789,930	1,980,025	2,769,955	2,114,497	851,131	**288,758,111**
Catholic Population Percentage	24	9	3	4	26	10	**23**

Archdioceses = 36; Dioceses = 169; Apostolates = 3

2004 GENERAL SUMMARY

	Kansas City–St. Joseph MO	Springfield Cape Girardeau	MISSOURI TOTAL	Great Falls – Billings MT	Helena MT	MONTANA TOTAL	2004 U.S. GRAND TOTAL
Cardinals	–	–	–	–	–	–	12
Archbishops	–	–	1	–	1	1	48
Bishops	1	1	7	1	–	1	375
Abbots	3	3	9	–	–	–	109
Diocesan Priests	114	68	676	68	89	157	29,483
Religious Priests	95	55	501	14	6	20	14,729
Total Priests in Diocese	209	123	1,177	82	95	177	44,212
Newly Ordained Priests	–	4	15	–	2	2	544
Total Permanent Deacons	59	8	377	4	33	37	14,693
Total Brothers	27	64	246	1	2	3	5,504
Total Sisters	300	98	2,131	71	35	106	71,486
Number of Parishes	86	65	460	65	58	123	19,431
Missions	12	19	54	45	39	84	2,910
Pastoral Centers	–	4	4	–	14	14	1,011
New Parishes	1	–	3	–	–	–	34
Catholic Hospitals	3	6	20	3	3	6	583
Patients Assisted Annually	291,291	843,936	3,430,803	513,955	160,856	674,811	83,898,575
Health Care Centers	–	–	13	1	–	1	376
Patients Assisted Annually	–	–	150,000	313	–	313	4,251,107
Specialized Homes	14	2	62	2	–	2	1,546
Total Assisted Annually	953	351	48,295	321	–	321	1,412,029
Residential Care of Children (Orphanages)	–	–	6	–	–	–	272
Total Assisted Annually	–	–	4,890	–	–	–	70,886
Day Care and Extended Day Care Centers	12	1	25	8	3	11	1,240
Total Assisted Annually	763	45	23,710	208	135	343	125,723
Special Centers for Social Services	2	2	41	3	–	3	2,969
Total Assisted Annually	31,000	1,350	194,828	59,803	–	59,803	21,251,075
Diocesan Seminaries	–	–	2	–	–	–	72
Students	–	–	89	–	–	–	3,077
Religious Seminaries	1	2	5	–	–	–	124
Students	–	16	31	–	–	–	1,253
Colleges and Universities	2	–	4	1	1	2	232
Total Students	5,146	–	19,763	801	1,469	2,270	747,060
High Schools, Diocesan and Parish	4	3	20	2	2	4	787
Total Students	1,592	953	9,278	368	323	691	378,650
High Schools, Private	3	–	19	1	–	1	560
Total Students	1,532	–	9,828	187	–	187	301,673
Elementary Schools, Diocesan and Parish	32	22	218	8	3	11	6,488
Total Students	8,513	3,720	52,735	1,507	895	2,402	1,796,275
Elementary Schools, Private	1	–	11	4	–	4	365
Total Students	372	–	2,508	657	–	657	95,742
Non–residential Schools for the Disabled	–	–	10	–	–	–	83
Total Students	–	–	277	–	–	–	18,179
Religious Education High School Students	1,002	1,525	6,080	1,297	1,227	2,524	771,730
Religious Education Elementary Students	9,498	4,279	41,273	3,601	4,065	7,666	3,612,510
Priests Teaching	3	1	114	2	7	9	1,792
Scholastics Teaching	–	–	4	–	–	–	57
Brothers Teaching	–	1	24	–	2	2	1,195
Sisters Teaching	6	1	197	5	3	8	7,871
Lay Teachers	691	275	6,656	289	237	526	169,966
Infant Baptisms	2,441	810	11,219	849	623	1,472	985,141
Adult Baptisms	495	517	1,928	116	465	581	76,829
Received into Full Communion	307	264	1,839	103	155	258	75,429
First Communions	2,629	1,292	12,878	817	820	1,637	896,670
Confirmations	2,029	969	11,549	1,127	1,182	2,309	645,426
Marriages	827	419	4,421	256	278	534	232,060
Deaths	1,324	630	7,015	749	815	1,564	473,935
Totals Catholics	144,483	63,162	844,102	53,824	49,527	103,351	67,259,768
Total Population	1,394,040	1,226,079	5,585,747	391,360	506,002	897,362	288,758,111
Catholic Population Percentage	10	5	15	14	10	12	23

*Indicates Archdioceses.

†Certain Dioceses traverse state lines.

2004 GENERAL SUMMARY

	Chalan Kanoa MP	*Omaha NE	Grand Island NE	Lincoln NE	NEBRASKA TOTAL	Las Vegas NV	2004 U.S. GRAND TOTAL
Cardinals	–	–	–	–	–	–	**12**
Archbishops	–	1	–	–	1	–	**48**
Bishops	1	–	1	1	2	1	**375**
Abbots	–	2	–	–	2	–	**109**
Diocesan Priests	15	215	75	148	438	35	**29,483**
Religious Priests	2	100	–	9	109	20	**14,729**
Total Priests in Diocese	17	315	75	157	547	55	**44,212**
Newly Ordained Priests	2	4	–	6	10	–	**544**
Total Permanent Deacons	–	176	–	2	178	7	**14,693**
Total Brothers	–	23	–	–	23	3	**5,504**
Total Sisters	–	337	73	134	544	4	**71,486**
Number of Parishes	11	138	36	136	310	25	**19,431**
Missions	2	15	37	1	53	7	**2,910**
Pastoral Centers	–	3	–	–	3	–	**1,011**
New Parishes	–	–	–	1	1	1	**34**
Catholic Hospitals	–	6	–	3	9	1	**583**
Patients Assisted Annually	–	409,872	–	210,021	619,893	150,503	**83,898,575**
Health Care Centers	–	2	2	–	4	–	**376**
Patients Assisted Annually	–	106,500	168,811	–	275,311	–	**4,251,107**
Specialized Homes	–	5	1	3	9	–	**1,546**
Total Assisted Annually	–	968	75	277	1,320	–	**1,412,029**
Residential Care of Children (Orphanages)	–	–	–	–	–	–	**272**
Total Assisted Annually	–	–	–	–	–	–	**70,886**
Day Care and Extended Day Care Centers	–	5	–	–	5	1	**1,240**
Total Assisted Annually	–	895	–	–	895	6,344	**125,723**
Special Centers for Social Services	1	14	–	22	36	19	**2,969**
Total Assisted Annually	4,345	131,200	–	43,702	174,902	1,000,000	**21,251,075**
Diocesan Seminaries	–	–	–	1	1	–	**72**
Students	–	–	–	38	38	–	**3,077**
Religious Seminaries	–	–	–	1	1	–	**124**
Students	–	–	–	56	56	–	**1,253**
Colleges and Universities	–	2	–	–	2	–	**232**
Total Students	–	8,400	–	–	8,400	–	**747,060**
High Schools, Diocesan and Parish	1	12	4	6	22	1	**787**
Total Students	176	3,210	539	1,779	5,528	853	**378,650**
High Schools, Private	–	5	–	–	5	–	**560**
Total Students	–	2,477	–	–	2,477	–	**301,673**
Elementary Schools, Diocesan and Parish	3	59	7	25	91	7	**6,488**
Total Students	525	14,182	981	5,583	20,746	2,823	**1,796,275**
Elementary Schools, Private	–	2	–	–	2	–	**365**
Total Students	–	199	–	–	199	–	**95,742**
Non–residential Schools for the Disabled	–	1	–	1	2	–	**83**
Total Students	–	41	–	18	59	–	**18,179**
Religious Education High School Students	264	4,259	2,849	2,155	9,263	2,299	**771,730**
Religious Education Elementary Students	820	14,934	4,208	5,400	24,542	9,503	**3,612,510**
Priests Teaching	–	39	–	33	72	1	**1,792**
Scholastics Teaching	–	3	–	–	3	–	**57**
Brothers Teaching	–	4	–	–	4	–	**1,195**
Sisters Teaching	7	24	–	38	62	–	**7,871**
Lay Teachers	–	1,552	123	506	2,181	64	**169,966**
Infant Baptisms	779	4,323	1,283	1,465	7,076	4,167	**985,141**
Adult Baptisms	29	582	103	157	842	360	**76,829**
Received into Full Communion	–	628	140	196	964	1,752	**75,429**
First Communions	501	4,031	1,088	1,578	6,697	3,809	**896,670**
Confirmations	301	3,868	895	1,793	6,556	1,320	**645,426**
Marriages	20	1,337	303	414	2,054	608	**232,060**
Deaths	115	1,867	521	710	3,098	772	**473,935**
Totals Catholics	43,000	229,952	57,460	89,431	376,843	515,953	**67,259,768**
Total Population	71,850	867,531	295,176	539,402	1,702,109	1,648,422	**288,758,111**
Catholic Population Percentage	60	27	19	17	22	31	**23**

Archdioceses = 36; Dioceses = 169; Apostolates = 3

2004 GENERAL SUMMARY

	Reno NV	NEVADA TOTAL	Manchester NH	*Newark NJ	Camden NJ	Metuchen NJ	2004 U.S. GRAND TOTAL
Cardinals	–	–	–	–	–	–	12
Archbishops	–	–	–	2	–	–	48
Bishops	1	2	3	5	–	2	375
Abbots	–	–	1	1	–	–	109
Diocesan Priests	22	57	216	745	305	210	29,483
Religious Priests	11	31	60	228	45	52	14,729
Total Priests in Diocese	33	88	276	973	350	262	44,212
Newly Ordained Priests	1	1	6	11	4	1	544
Total Permanent Deacons	10	17	51	201	115	141	14,693
Total Brothers	3	6	32	85	18	18	5,504
Total Sisters	38	42	608	1,264	344	397	71,486
Number of Parishes	28	53	120	234	125	108	19,431
Missions	6	13	24	–	10	–	2,910
Pastoral Centers	–	–	–	137	34	–	1,011
New Parishes	–	1	1	–	–	–	34
Catholic Hospitals	1	2	2	11	1	1	583
Patients Assisted Annually	327,750	478,253	272,857	1,489,585	298,136	284,933	83,898,575
Health Care Centers	3	3	9	13	2	2	376
Patients Assisted Annually	15,000	15,000	545	5,214	12,662	4,569	4,251,107
Specialized Homes	–	–	2	12	6	8	1,546
Total Assisted Annually	–	–	–	1,685	2,219	851	1,412,029
Residential Care of Children (Orphanages)	–	–	2	–	1	–	272
Total Assisted Annually	–	–	44	–	7	–	70,886
Day Care and Extended Day Care Centers	2	3	111	147	2	3	1,240
Total Assisted Annually	277	6,621	610	5,338	211	209	125,723
Special Centers for Social Services	7	26	12	34	1	9	2,969
Total Assisted Annually	46,562	1,046,562	40,500	67,436	7,372	18,862	21,251,075
Diocesan Seminaries	–	–	–	3	–	–	72
Students	–	–	–	142	–	–	3,077
Religious Seminaries	–	–	2	1	–	–	124
Students	–	–	2	20	–	–	1,253
Colleges and Universities	–	–	4	4	–	–	232
Total Students	–	–	4,302	17,450	–	–	747,060
High Schools, Diocesan and Parish	1	2	3	16	10	4	787
Total Students	493	1,346	1,668	8,361	6,121	2,443	378,650
High Schools, Private	–	–	1	20	3	2	560
Total Students	–	–	846	8,345	1,434	1,207	301,673
Elementary Schools, Diocesan and Parish	4	11	22	120	56	42	6,488
Total Students	1,042	3,865	5,333	34,327	12,666	12,888	1,796,275
Elementary Schools, Private	–	–	3	7	1	–	365
Total Students	–	–	959	1,612	47	–	95,742
Non–residential Schools for the Disabled	–	–	–	5	2	1	83
Total Students	–	–	–	183	653	50	18,179
Religious Education High School Students	1,213	3,512	5,399	2,637	550	2,324	771,730
Religious Education Elementary Students	4,313	13,816	26,711	50,307	36,464	43,319	3,612,510
Priests Teaching	–	1	6	128	10	–	1,792
Scholastics Teaching	–	–	–	–	–	–	57
Brothers Teaching	1	1	15	36	8	10	1,195
Sisters Teaching	2	2	75	238	85	87	7,871
Lay Teachers	111	175	1,144	3,935	1,346	1,008	169,966
Infant Baptisms	1,857	6,024	4,275	16,967	6,192	6,508	985,141
Adult Baptisms	163	523	312	435	1,056	140	76,829
Received into Full Communion	195	1,947	440	598	–	259	75,429
First Communions	1,495	5,304	5,029	14,581	6,647	7,390	896,670
Confirmations	687	2,007	3,392	11,381	5,560	6,282	645,426
Marriages	323	931	1,072	4,304	2,526	1,427	232,060
Deaths	296	1,068	2,965	11,554	4,421	4,048	473,935
Totals Catholics	91,973	607,926	327,353	1,319,558	442,389	556,682	67,259,768
Total Population	607,459	2,255,881	1,275,000	2,835,594	1,337,416	1,325,432	288,758,111
Catholic Population Percentage	15	27	26	47	33	42	23

*Indicates Archdioceses.

†Certain Dioceses traverse state lines.

	Paterson NJ	Trenton NJ	NEW JERSEY TOTAL	*Santa Fe NM	† Gallup NM	Las Cruces NM	2004 U.S. GRAND TOTAL
Cardinals	–	–	–	–	–	–	**12**
Archbishops	–	–	2	2	–	–	**48**
Bishops	1	2	10	–	1	1	**375**
Abbots	7	–	8	–	–	–	**109**
Diocesan Priests	244	239	1,743	118	41	28	**29,483**
Religious Priests	161	43	529	86	25	49	**14,729**
Total Priests in Diocese	405	282	2,272	204	66	77	**44,212**
Newly Ordained Priests	4	1	21	6	–	–	**544**
Total Permanent Deacons	192	276	925	199	33	38	**14,693**
Total Brothers	33	72	226	75	12	6	**5,504**
Total Sisters	–	433	2,438	245	142	38	**71,486**
Number of Parishes	111	126	704	93	53	44	**19,431**
Missions	–	11	21	216	25	47	**2,910**
Pastoral Centers	5	–	176	4	–	2	**1,011**
New Parishes	–	–	–	–	–	–	**34**
Catholic Hospitals	3	1	17	–	–	–	**583**
Patients Assisted Annually	770,000	139,000	2,981,654	–	–	–	**83,898,575**
Health Care Centers	–	1	18	1	–	3	**376**
Patients Assisted Annually	–	4,000	26,445	6,500	–	35,000	**4,251,107**
Specialized Homes	10	12	48	6	2	–	**1,546**
Total Assisted Annually	2,090	21,190	28,035	1,845	78	–	**1,412,029**
Residential Care of Children (Orphanages)	3	1	5	–	1	–	**272**
Total Assisted Annually	98	22	127	–	62	–	**70,886**
Day Care and Extended Day Care Centers	5	7	164	1	3	3	**1,240**
Total Assisted Annually	1,600	650	8,008	149	66	240	**125,723**
Special Centers for Social Services	13	15	72	5	24	1	**2,969**
Total Assisted Annually	65,000	30,000	188,670	301,396	64,853	8,000	**21,251,075**
Diocesan Seminaries	–	–	3	–	–	1	**72**
Students	–	–	142	–	–	3	**3,077**
Religious Seminaries	2	–	8	5	–	–	**124**
Students	5	–	25	12	–	–	**1,253**
Colleges and Universities	2	1	[illegible]	1	–	–	**232**
Total Students	1,801	2,420	21,67[illegible]	1,829	–	–	**747,060**
High Schools, Diocesan and Parish	5	8	42	1	–	–	**787**
Total Students	2,475	6,480	25,880	1,050	–	–	**378,650**
High Schools, Private	4	3	32	1	2	–	**560**
Total Students	1,250	1,131	13,367	781	242	–	**301,673**
Elementary Schools, Diocesan and Parish	57	50	325	17	–	2	**6,488**
Total Students	15,693	27,491	103,065	4,043	–	142	**1,796,275**
Elementary Schools, Private	3	2	13	–	10	3	**365**
Total Students	545	594	2,798	–	1,420	383	**95,742**
Non–residential Schools for the Disabled	–	1	9	–	–	–	**83**
Total Students	–	18	904	–	–	–	**18,179**
Religious Education High School Students	11,784	1,411	18,706	5,824	1,006	2,275	**771,730**
Religious Education Elementary Students	35,352	63,021	228,463	17,589	3,350	7,741	**3,612,510**
Priests Teaching	15	7	160	–	1	–	**1,792**
Scholastics Teaching	7	–	7	–	–	–	**57**
Brothers Teaching	13	14	31	4	4	–	**1,195**
Sisters Teaching	136	90	636	17	25	3	**7,871**
Lay Teachers	1,522	1,766	9,577	406	109	36	**169,966**
Infant Baptisms	8,274	10,446	48,337	5,821	917	2,376	**985,141**
Adult Baptisms	196	391	2,218	274	235	206	**76,829**
Received into Full Communion	291	445	1,593	548	124	129	**75,429**
First Communions	8,032	11,589	48,239	5,372	881	2,401	**896,670**
Confirmations	4,634	9,180	37,037	3,032	708	1,588	**645,426**
Marriages	1,611	2,693	12,561	1,213	182	381	**232,060**
Deaths	3,581	7,182	30,786	2,959	613	1,123	**473,935**
Totals Catholics	420,172	740,357	3,479,[illegible]58	254,110	48,488	132,646	**67,259,768**
Total Population	1,124,058	1,367,348	7,989,[illegible]48	1,260,385	449,485	498,308	**288,758,111**
Catholic Population Percentage	37	54	44	20	11	27	**23**

Archdioceses = 36; Dioceses = 169; Apostolates = 3

2004 GENERAL SUMMARY

	NEW MEXICO TOTAL	*New York NY	Albany NY	Brooklyn NY	Buffalo NY	Ogdensburg NY	2004 U.S. GRAND TOTAL
Cardinals	–	1	–	–	–	–	12
Archbishops	2	–	–	–	–	–	48
Bishops	2	10	1	5	3	–	375
Abbots	–	–	–	–	–	–	109
Diocesan Priests	187	699	238	604	388	150	29,483
Religious Priests	160	913	108	175	159	8	14,729
Total Priests in Diocese	347	1,612	346	779	547	158	44,212
Newly Ordained Priests	6	4	3	2	2	2	544
Total Permanent Deacons	270	359	101	159	104	67	14,693
Total Brothers	93	454	88	180	48	12	5,504
Total Sisters	425	3,153	886	1,097	1,218	157	71,486
Number of Parishes	190	409	177	216	265	119	19,431
Missions	288	–	29	–	9	19	2,910
Pastoral Centers	6	–	–	–	2	20	1,011
New Parishes	–	–	–	–	–	–	34
Catholic Hospitals	–	14	4	4	6	–	583
Patients Assisted Annually	–	2,060,587	730,500	662,211	1,426,730	–	83,898,575
Health Care Centers	4	3	15	17	1	–	376
Patients Assisted Annually	41,500	172,607	58,000	342,418	1,100	–	4,251,107
Specialized Homes	8	56	22	41	15	3	1,546
Total Assisted Annually	1,923	43,895	2,909	14,850	3,015	300	1,412,029
Residential Care of Children (Orphanages)	1	65	4	6	–	–	272
Total Assisted Annually	62	2,304	938	8,798	–	–	70,886
Day Care and Extended Day Care Centers	7	115	7	27	3	–	1,240
Total Assisted Annually	455	3,533	635	2,867	237	–	125,723
Special Centers for Social Services	30	838	25	96	5	6	2,969
Total Assisted Annually	374,249	336,920	260,000	110,560	235,650	10,500	21,251,075
Diocesan Seminaries	1	2	–	1	1	–	72
Students	3	72	–	14	28	–	3,077
Religious Seminaries	5	5	–	1	1	–	124
Students	12	52	–	1	–	–	1,253
Colleges and Universities	1	11	4	3	7	–	232
Total Students	1,829	54,853	5,000	20,378	16,393	–	747,060
High Schools, Diocesan and Parish	1	23	4	4	–	2	787
Total Students	1,050	14,150	1,494	2,048	–	768	378,650
High Schools, Private	3	29	3	16	16	–	560
Total Students	1,023	15,497	1,474	15,528	6,075	–	301,673
Elementary Schools, Diocesan and Parish	19	217	34	152	81	21	6,488
Total Students	4,185	79,159	7,384	47,274	19,306	2,747	1,796,275
Elementary Schools, Private	13	19	2	2	5	–	365
Total Students	1,803	3,060	412	315	1,021	–	95,742
Non–residential Schools for the Disabled	–	6	–	1	1	–	83
Total Students	–	311	–	119	489	–	18,179
Religious Education High School Students	9,105	3,027	9,529	2,200	13,097	2,453	771,730
Religious Education Elementary Students	28,680	105,934	30,337	45,500	35,324	8,187	3,612,510
Priests Teaching	1	80	1	13	63	1	1,792
Scholastics Teaching	–	–	–	–	3	–	57
Brothers Teaching	8	106	10	59	12	–	1,195
Sisters Teaching	45	451	37	253	106	21	7,871
Lay Teachers	551	5,147	716	3,753	2,784	244	169,966
Infant Baptisms	9,114	28,557	4,258	19,377	6,226	1,156	985,141
Adult Baptisms	715	1,673	762	1,003	510	390	76,829
Received into Full Communion	801	894	–	925	433	145	75,429
First Communions	8,654	26,217	5,100	14,543	7,126	1,565	896,670
Confirmations	5,328	20,998	3,900	12,298	6,043	1,448	645,426
Marriages	1,776	6,119	1,454	3,634	2,105	603	232,060
Deaths	4,695	15,041	4,800	10,869	7,071	1,839	473,935
Totals Catholics	435,244	2,521,087	400,000	1,826,592	707,981	128,326	67,259,768
Total Population	2,208,178	5,602,418	1,340,448	4,694,705	1,578,922	423,000	288,758,111
Catholic Population Percentage	20	45	30	39	45	30	23

*Indicates Archdioceses.

†Certain Dioceses traverse state lines.

2004 GENERAL SUMMARY

	Rochester NY	Rockville Centre NY	Syracuse NY	NEW YORK TOTAL	Charlotte NC	Raleigh NC	2004 U.S. GRAND TOTAL
Cardinals	–	–	–	1	–	–	**12**
Archbishops	–	–	–	–	–	–	**48**
Bishops	1	5	3	28	2	1	**375**
Abbots	3	–	–	3	2	–	**109**
Diocesan Priests	214	406	271	2,970	105	91	**29,483**
Religious Priests	57	36	68	1,524	62	51	**14,729**
Total Priests in Diocese	271	442	339	4,494	167	142	**44,212**
Newly Ordained Priests	1	4	1	19	3	3	**544**
Total Permanent Deacons	141	255	77	1,263	75	29	**14,693**
Total Brothers	31	89	16	918	9	6	**5,504**
Total Sisters	588	1,368	405	8,872	106	63	**71,486**
Number of Parishes	151	134	169	1,640	68	78	**19,431**
Missions	6	1	15	79	23	10	**2,910**
Pastoral Centers	–	–	20	42	4	7	**1,011**
New Parishes	–	–	–	–	–	–	**34**
Catholic Hospitals	2	5	3	38	–	–	**583**
Patients Assisted Annually	235,000	1,480,886	1,466,340	8,062,254	–	–	**83,898,575**
Health Care Centers	2	–	1	39	13	–	**376**
Patients Assisted Annually	1,200	–	300	575,625	289,700	–	**4,251,107**
Specialized Homes	12	13	57	219	3	–	**1,546**
Total Assisted Annually	2,050	640,770	60	707,849	248	–	**1,412,029**
Residential Care of Children (Orphanages)	1	4	10	90	–	–	**272**
Total Assisted Annually	42	7,738	150	19,970	–	–	**70,886**
Day Care and Extended Day Care Centers	1	101	–	254	13	–	**1,240**
Total Assisted Annually	180	3,792	–	11,244	996	–	**125,723**
Special Centers for Social Services	54	37	8	1,069	–	12	**2,969**
Total Assisted Annually	720,000	68,088	62,800	1,804,518	–	59,943	**21,251,075**
Diocesan Seminaries	1	1	–	6	–	1	**72**
Students	–	36	–	150	–	–	**3,077**
Religious Seminaries	–	–	–	8	–	–	**124**
Students	–	–	11	64	–	–	**1,253**
Colleges and Universities	–	2	1	28	2	–	**232**
Total Students	–	9,310	3,129	109,063	863	–	**747,060**
High Schools, Diocesan and Parish	1	5	5	44	2	1	**787**
Total Students	124	4,525	2,627	25,736	1,510	945	**378,650**
High Schools, Private	6	6	1	77	–	–	**560**
Total Students	3,475	7,449	750	50,248	–	–	**301,673**
Elementary Schools, Diocesan and Parish	48	59	29	641	16	35	**6,488**
Total Students	9,962	25,588	6,096	197,516	5,723	7,496	**1,796,275**
Elementary Schools, Private	2	4	–	34	–	–	**365**
Total Students	370	1,110	–	6,288	–	–	**95,742**
Non–residential Schools for the Disabled	–	1	–	9	–	–	**83**
Total Students	–	70	–	989	–	–	**18,179**
Religious Education High School Students	4,134	2,711	7,7[illegible]7	44,928	3,232	3,420	**771,730**
Religious Education Elementary Students	23,345	115,818	31,0[illegible]3	395,448	15,048	14,274	**3,612,510**
Priests Teaching	13	10	4	185	3	2	**1,792**
Scholastics Teaching	7	–	–	10	–	–	**57**
Brothers Teaching	–	46	1	234	1	7	**1,195**
Sisters Teaching	47	129	43	1,087	8	10	**7,871**
Lay Teachers	1,027	1,947	689	16,307	503	680	**169,966**
Infant Baptisms	5,989	21,040	4,919	91,522	5,677	4,684	**985,141**
Adult Baptisms	287	703	256	5,584	245	267	**76,829**
Received into Full Communion	731	649	400	4,177	–	391	**75,429**
First Communions	4,536	21,905	5,[illegible]42	86,234	3,836	3,443	**896,670**
Confirmations	4,094	18,703	4,[illegible]60	71,744	2,352	1,854	**645,426**
Marriages	1,612	5,375	1,[illegible]96	22,698	818	837	**232,060**
Deaths	4,124	13,606	4,[illegible]11	62,061	935	895	**473,935**
Totals Catholics	341,500	1,490,579	345,[illegible]36	7,761,801	138,583	180,909	**67,259,768**
Total Population	1,485,837	2,781,159	1,174,387	19,081,376	1,696,148	4,024,253	**288,758,111**
Catholic Population Percentage	23	54	29	41	8	5	**23**

Archdioceses = 36; Dioceses = 169; Apostolates = 3

2004 GENERAL SUMMARY

	NORTH CAROLINA TOTAL	Bismarck ND	Fargo ND	NORTH DAKOTA TOTAL	*Cincinnati OH	Cleveland OH	2004 U.S. GRAND TOTAL
Cardinals	–	–	–	–	–	–	**12**
Archbishops	–	–	–	–	1	–	**48**
Bishops	3	1	2	3	1	5	**375**
Abbots	2	3	–	3	–	1	**109**
Diocesan Priests	196	67	153	220	289	442	**29,483**
Religious Priests	113	27	7	34	247	137	**14,729**
Total Priests in Diocese	309	94	160	254	536	579	**44,212**
Newly Ordained Priests	6	–	3	3	7	9	**544**
Total Permanent Deacons	104	68	40	108	138	189	**14,693**
Total Brothers	15	24	–	24	146	57	**5,504**
Total Sisters	169	129	201	330	1,127	1,325	**71,486**
Number of Parishes	146	62	158	220	224	234	**19,431**
Missions	33	38	–	38	–	1	**2,910**
Pastoral Centers	11	–	–	–	1	2	**1,011**
New Parishes	–	–	–	–	5	–	**34**
Catholic Hospitals	–	4	9	13	9	3	**583**
Patients Assisted Annually	–	354,747	108,732	463,479	995,000	491,548	**83,898,575**
Health Care Centers	13	–	–	–	2	–	**376**
Patients Assisted Annually	289,700	–	–	–	400	–	**4,251,107**
Specialized Homes	3	5	13	18	13	33	**1,546**
Total Assisted Annually	248	581	1,222	1,803	2,451	5,322	**1,412,029**
Residential Care of Children (Orphanages)	–	–	–	–	1	1	**272**
Total Assisted Annually	–	–	–	–	26	225	**70,886**
Day Care and Extended Day Care Centers	13	–	1	1	–	8	**1,240**
Total Assisted Annually	996	–	18	18	–	981	**125,723**
Special Centers for Social Services	12	–	5	5	6	23	**2,969**
Total Assisted Annually	59,943	–	7,941	7,941	1,500	732,639	**21,251,075**
Diocesan Seminaries	1	–	1	1	1	2	**72**
Students	–	–	9	9	40	54	**3,077**
Religious Seminaries	–	–	–	–	–	–	**124**
Students	–	–	–	–	–	10	**1,253**
Colleges and Universities	2	1	–	1	4	3	**232**
Total Students	863	2,617	–	2,617	24,597	6,681	**747,060**
High Schools, Diocesan and Parish	3	3	1	4	17	6	**787**
Total Students	2,455	1,034	292	1,326	12,526	3,414	**378,650**
High Schools, Private	–	–	–	–	4	17	**560**
Total Students	–	–	–	–	3,122	10,772	**301,673**
Elementary Schools, Diocesan and Parish	51	12	13	25	106	122	**6,488**
Total Students	13,219	1,557	1,895	3,452	37,684	42,288	**1,796,275**
Elementary Schools, Private	–	–	–	–	4	9	**365**
Total Students	–	–	–	–	1,706	2,388	**95,742**
Non–residential Schools for the Disabled	–	–	–	–	1	2	**83**
Total Students	–	–	–	–	124	154	**18,179**
Religious Education High School Students	6,652	2,743	3,247	5,990	6,505	6,407	**771,730**
Religious Education Elementary Students	29,322	5,906	7,571	13,477	31,555	42,985	**3,612,510**
Priests Teaching	5	–	1	1	19	15	**1,792**
Scholastics Teaching	–	–	–	–	2	–	**57**
Brothers Teaching	8	–	–	–	13	12	**1,195**
Sisters Teaching	18	7	–	7	78	181	**7,871**
Lay Teachers	1,183	175	137	312	3,094	3,647	**169,966**
Infant Baptisms	10,361	1,335	1,483	2,818	7,280	9,355	**985,141**
Adult Baptisms	512	140	70	210	830	944	**76,829**
Received into Full Communion	391	106	168	274	864	781	**75,429**
First Communions	7,279	1,105	1,344	2,449	8,576	11,176	**896,670**
Confirmations	4,206	1,177	2,571	3,748	8,442	10,751	**645,426**
Marriages	1,655	407	475	882	2,592	3,490	**232,060**
Deaths	1,830	754	968	1,722	4,473	8,530	**473,935**
Totals Catholics	319,492	64,245	84,190	148,435	512,146	812,675	**67,259,768**
Total Population	5,720,401	259,479	374,256	633,735	2,951,228	2,852,331	**288,758,111**
Catholic Population Percentage	6	25	23	23	17	28	**23**

*Indicates Archdioceses.

†Certain Dioceses traverse state lines.

	Columbus OH	Steubenville OH	Toledo OH	Youngstown OH	OHIO TOTAL	*Oklahoma City OK	2004 U.S. GRAND TOTAL
Cardinals	–	–	–	–	–	–	**12**
Archbishops	–	–	–	–	1	1	**48**
Bishops	1	3	3	2	15	–	**375**
Abbots	–	–	–	–	1	4	**109**
Diocesan Priests	182	98	194	177	1,382	96	**29,483**
Religious Priests	41	24	54	22	525	23	**14,729**
Total Priests in Diocese	223	122	248	199	1,907	119	**44,212**
Newly Ordained Priests	1	1	2	1	21	1	**544**
Total Permanent Deacons	77	6	191	68	669	71	**14,693**
Total Brothers	5	9	5	18	240	10	**5,504**
Total Sisters	341	79	671	226	3,769	132	**71,486**
Number of Parishes	107	70	159	116	910	71	**19,431**
Missions	4	3	–	2	10	46	**2,910**
Pastoral Centers	–	–	6	–	9	–	**1,011**
New Parishes	–	–	1	–	6	–	**34**
Catholic Hospitals	4	1	6	3	26	6	**583**
Patients Assisted Annually	972,123	273,924	941,685	442,633	4,116,913	705,629	**83,898,575**
Health Care Centers	–	–	–	15	17	2	**376**
Patients Assisted Annually	–	–	–	671,163	671,563	360	**4,251,107**
Specialized Homes	20	–	4	16	86	5	**1,546**
Total Assisted Annually	1,595	–	1,81[illegible]	1,500	12,679	375	**1,412,029**
Residential Care of Children (Orphanages)	–	–	–	–	2	–	**272**
Total Assisted Annually	–	–	–	–	251	–	**70,886**
Day Care and Extended Day Care Centers	1	–	–	7	16	2	**1,240**
Total Assisted Annually	178	–	–	1,024	2,183	350	**125,723**
Special Centers for Social Services	7	1	15	21	73	–	**2,969**
Total Assisted Annually	402,884	18,338	19,485	44,668	1,219,515	–	**21,251,075**
Diocesan Seminaries	1	–	–	–	4	–	**72**
Students	136	–	–	–	230	–	**3,077**
Religious Seminaries	–	–	–	–	–	–	**124**
Students	–	2	–	–	12	–	**1,253**
Colleges and Universities	1	1	2	1	12	1	**232**
Total Students	2,566	2,253	1,876	1,801	39,774	813	**747,060**
High Schools, Diocesan and Parish	11	3	10	6	53	2	**787**
Total Students	4,882	717	3,562	2,704	27,805	896	**378,650**
High Schools, Private	–	–	4	–	25	–	**560**
Total Students	–	–	2,682	–	16,576	–	**301,673**
Elementary Schools, Diocesan and Parish	44	14	79	42	407	17	**6,488**
Total Students	12,601	2,409	18,6[illegible]3	9,406	123,071	3,464	**1,796,275**
Elementary Schools, Private	2	–	3	1	19	3	**365**
Total Students	316	–	671	295	5,376	642	**95,742**
Non-residential Schools for the Disabled	–	–	1	–	4	–	**83**
Total Students	–	–	30	–	338	–	**18,179**
Religious Education High School Students	2,296	618	2,100	1,509	19,435	3,261	**771,730**
Religious Education Elementary Students	16,526	2,323	17,558	13,660	124,617	8,915	**3,612,510**
Priests Teaching	1	–	30	–	65	10	**1,792**
Scholastics Teaching	–	–	–	–	2	1	**57**
Brothers Teaching	1	–	1	–	27	4	**1,195**
Sisters Teaching	7	8	59	25	358	15	**7,871**
Lay Teachers	1,242	203	[illegible]48	862	9,396	389	**169,966**
Infant Baptisms	3,760	502	3,[illegible]62	2,485	26,644	2,180	**985,141**
Adult Baptisms	511	206	630	218	3,339	344	**76,829**
Received into Full Communion	795	111	539	409	3,499	476	**75,429**
First Communions	4,197	660	4,690	3,031	32,330	1,952	**896,670**
Confirmations	3,630	724	4,918	3,231	31,696	1,344	**645,426**
Marriages	1,176	289	1,364	1,014	10,225	714	**232,060**
Deaths	1,673	718	3,589	3,138	22,121	800	**473,935**
Totals Catholics	240,682	40,411	298,069	235,541	2,139,524	112,951	**67,259,768**
Total Population	2,408,079	513,734	1,489,769	1,227,633	11,442,774	2,643,608	**288,758,111**
Catholic Population Percentage	10	8	20	19	19	4	**23**

Archdioceses = 36; Dioceses = 169; Apostolates = 3

2004 GENERAL SUMMARY

	Tulsa OK	OKLAHOMA TOTAL	*Portland in Oregon OR	Baker OR	OREGON TOTAL	*Philadelphia PA	2004 U.S. GRAND TOTAL
Cardinals	–	–	–	–	–	2	**12**
Archbishops	–	1	1	–	1	–	**48**
Bishops	1	1	1	2	3	4	**375**
Abbots	–	4	3	–	3	2	**109**
Diocesan Priests	76	172	149	38	187	724	**29,483**
Religious Priests	28	51	169	4	173	372	**14,729**
Total Priests in Diocese	104	223	318	42	360	1,096	**44,212**
Newly Ordained Priests	3	4	2	–	2	11	**544**
Total Permanent Deacons	57	128	38	13	51	210	**14,693**
Total Brothers	10	20	82	1	83	122	**5,504**
Total Sisters	92	224	487	20	507	3,366	**71,486**
Number of Parishes	80	151	124	36	160	279	**19,431**
Missions	–	46	24	27	51	7	**2,910**
Pastoral Centers	–	–	1	–	1	22	**1,011**
New Parishes	–	–	–	–	–	–	**34**
Catholic Hospitals	5	11	9	5	14	7	**583**
Patients Assisted Annually	356,000	1,061,629	1,943,612	347,162	2,290,774	722,296	**83,898,575**
Health Care Centers	–	2	7	–	7	1	**376**
Patients Assisted Annually	–	360	86,687	–	86,687	228	**4,251,107**
Specialized Homes	6	11	14	4	18	42	**1,546**
Total Assisted Annually	500	875	2,488	200	2,688	9,597	**1,412,029**
Residential Care of Children (Orphanages)	–	–	–	–	–	4	**272**
Total Assisted Annually	–	–	–	–	–	852	**70,886**
Day Care and Extended Day Care Centers	–	2	4	5	9	3	**1,240**
Total Assisted Annually	–	350	1,229	260	1,489	201	**125,723**
Special Centers for Social Services	4	4	17	5	22	15	**2,969**
Total Assisted Annually	90,000	90,000	1,327,475	36,500	1,363,975	76,937	**21,251,075**
Diocesan Seminaries	–	–	1	–	1	1	**72**
Students	–	–	142	–	142	154	**3,077**
Religious Seminaries	–	–	–	–	–	1	**124**
Students	–	–	40	–	40	8	**1,253**
Colleges and Universities	–	1	2	–	2	11	**232**
Total Students	–	813	4,856	–	4,856	35,820	**747,060**
High Schools, Diocesan and Parish	1	3	3	–	3	22	**787**
Total Students	928	1,824	1,495	–	1,495	22,726	**378,650**
High Schools, Private	1	1	7	–	7	15	**560**
Total Students	587	587	3,593	–	3,593	7,525	**301,673**
Elementary Schools, Diocesan and Parish	10	27	41	3	44	212	**6,488**
Total Students	4,115	7,579	8,639	654	9,293	73,132	**1,796,275**
Elementary Schools, Private	1	4	2	–	2	13	**365**
Total Students	1,036	1,678	451	–	451	4,490	**95,742**
Non–residential Schools for the Disabled	–	–	–	–	–	5	**83**
Total Students	–	–	–	–	–	340	**18,179**
Religious Education High School Students	1,624	4,885	3,654	1,259	4,913	7,264	**771,730**
Religious Education Elementary Students	4,835	13,750	11,847	2,203	14,050	50,499	**3,612,510**
Priests Teaching	–	10	59	–	59	109	**1,792**
Scholastics Teaching	–	1	–	–	–	–	**57**
Brothers Teaching	6	10	17	–	17	49	**1,195**
Sisters Teaching	5	20	50	–	50	609	**7,871**
Lay Teachers	346	735	1,471	45	1,516	8,609	**169,966**
Infant Baptisms	1,399	3,579	5,558	927	6,485	16,153	**985,141**
Adult Baptisms	190	534	705	210	915	1,245	**76,829**
Received into Full Communion	234	710	624	99	723	620	**75,429**
First Communions	1,096	3,048	4,864	956	5,820	17,502	**896,670**
Confirmations	749	2,093	2,615	1,102	3,717	16,243	**645,426**
Marriages	358	1,072	1,218	215	1,433	5,695	**232,060**
Deaths	493	1,293	1,911	306	2,217	12,733	**473,935**
Totals Catholics	56,094	169,045	389,345	36,420	425,765	1,486,058	**67,259,768**
Total Population	1,527,376	4,170,984	3,038,600	439,500	3,478,100	3,872,783	**288,758,111**
Catholic Population Percentage	4	4	13	8	12	38	**23**

*Indicates Archdioceses.

†Certain Dioceses traverse state lines.

	Allentown PA	Altoona-Johnstown PA	Erie PA	Greensburg PA	Harrisburg PA	Pittsburgh PA	2004 U.S. GRAND TOTAL
Cardinals	–	–	–	–	–	–	**12**
Archbishops	–	–	–	–	–	–	**48**
Bishops	2	2	2	1	1	4	**375**
Abbots	–	–	–	1	–	–	**109**
Diocesan Priests	230	147	218	138	149	458	**29,483**
Religious Priests	74	53	8	79	30	123	**14,729**
Total Priests in Diocese	304	200	226	217	179	581	**44,212**
Newly Ordained Priests	2	1	2	3	2	2	**544**
Total Permanent Deacons	97	32	31	–	47	50	**14,693**
Total Brothers	–	10	–	23	–	35	**5,504**
Total Sisters	409	90	425	325	447	1,443	**71,486**
Number of Parishes	153	99	126	102	89	215	**19,431**
Missions	7	5	19	–	7	–	**2,910**
Pastoral Centers	–	–	–	–	–	1	**1,011**
New Parishes	–	–	–	–	–	–	**34**
Catholic Hospitals	3	1	1	1	1	2	**583**
Patients Assisted Annually	565,109	138,245	147,109	20,347	203,562	489,213	**83,898,575**
Health Care Centers	1	1	–	–	–	–	**376**
Patients Assisted Annually	44,496	225	–	–	–	–	**4,251,107**
Specialized Homes	12	3	6	2	9	17	**1,546**
Total Assisted Annually	4,780	317	1,738	129	1,181	7,402	**1,412,029**
Residential Care of Children (Orphanages)	–	–	–	–	1	–	**272**
Total Assisted Annually	–	–	–	–	107	–	**70,886**
Day Care and Extended Day Care Centers	40	–	2	–	–	11	**1,240**
Total Assisted Annually	1,683	–	337	–	–	1,845	**125,723**
Special Centers for Social Services	16	2	9	6	14	7	**2,969**
Total Assisted Annually	79,730	32,192	149,059	11,231	3,005	73,221	**21,251,075**
Diocesan Seminaries	–	–	1	–	–	1	**72**
Students	–	–	15	–	–	12	**3,077**
Religious Seminaries	–	–	–	1	–	–	**124**
Students	–	–	–	26	–	–	**1,253**
Colleges and Universities	2	2	2	2	–	3	**232**
Total Students	5,249	4,012	6,819	5,141	–	13,530	**747,060**
High Schools, Diocesan and Parish	9	3	5	2	7	8	**787**
Total Students	3,987	1,214	1,676	780	3,932	3,347	**378,650**
High Schools, Private	–	–	[illegible]	–	–	3	**560**
Total Students	–	–	1,21[illegible]	–	–	648	**301,673**
Elementary Schools, Diocesan and Parish	52	24	39	20	39	104	**6,488**
Total Students	12,248	3,965	8,183	4,224	10,160	23,133	**1,796,275**
Elementary Schools, Private	–	–	1	3	3	4	**365**
Total Students	–	–	398	235	125	960	**95,742**
Non-residential Schools for the Disabled	3	–	–	–	–	2	**83**
Total Students	123	–	–	–	–	176	**18,179**
Religious Education High School Students	–	3,714	5,794	2,895	1,894	6,444	**771,730**
Religious Education Elementary Students	17,397	8,100	9,985	8,923	19,795	48,458	**3,612,510**
Priests Teaching	10	8	22	25	1	3	**1,792**
Scholastics Teaching	–	–	–	–	–	–	**57**
Brothers Teaching	–	–	–	24	–	14	**1,195**
Sisters Teaching	58	25	[illegible]9	44	55	79	**7,871**
Lay Teachers	1,040	467	7[illegible]1	482	800	1,897	**169,966**
Infant Baptisms	3,622	1,444	1,8[illegible]7	1,729	2,977	7,240	**985,141**
Adult Baptisms	278	111	451	140	411	361	**76,829**
Received into Full Communion	–	138	201	219	428	904	**75,429**
First Communions	3,649	1,454	2,291	2,247	3,484	8,096	**896,670**
Confirmations	3,683	1,714	2,245	2,369	3,380	8,596	**645,426**
Marriages	1,236	596	872	810	1,059	2,671	**232,060**
Deaths	3,202	1,680	2,609	2,739	2,271	9,402	**473,935**
Totals Catholics	273,599	108,202	225,607	181,167	247,194	815,719	**67,259,768**
Total Population	1,161,932	645,268	874,057	679,990	2,027,835	1,966,067	**288,758,111**
Catholic Population Percentage	24	17	26	27	12	41	**23**

Archdioceses = 36; Dioceses = 169; Apostolates = 3

2004 GENERAL SUMMARY

	Scranton PA	PENN. TOTAL	*San Juan, Puerto Rico	Arecibo, Puerto Rico	Caguas, Puerto Rico	Mayaguez, Puerto Rico	2004 U.S. GRAND TOTAL
Cardinals	–	2	1	–	–	–	**12**
Archbishops	–	–	1	–	–	–	**48**
Bishops	3	19	2	1	3	1	**375**
Abbots	–	3	–	–	2	–	**109**
Diocesan Priests	323	2,387	158	87	64	42	**29,483**
Religious Priests	70	809	189	44	35	27	**14,729**
Total Priests in Diocese	393	3,196	347	131	99	69	**44,212**
Newly Ordained Priests	5	28	–	–	1	2	**544**
Total Permanent Deacons	52	519	242	6	66	4	**14,693**
Total Brothers	12	202	32	8	17	2	**5,504**
Total Sisters	673	7,178	480	161	133	130	**71,486**
Number of Parishes	193	1,256	154	59	43	29	**19,431**
Missions	85	130	173	241	–	–	**2,910**
Pastoral Centers	25	48	–	–	–	158	**1,011**
New Parishes	–	–	–	–	–	–	**34**
Catholic Hospitals	7	23	1	–	–	1	**583**
Patients Assisted Annually	737,035	3,022,916	215	–	–	42,381	**83,898,575**
Health Care Centers	2	5	2	–	–	–	**376**
Patients Assisted Annually	89,215	134,164	1,685	–	–	–	**4,251,107**
Specialized Homes	13	104	17	5	3	1	**1,546**
Total Assisted Annually	2,558	27,702	18,741	375	1,252	145	**1,412,029**
Residential Care of Children (Orphanages)	5	10	11	3	–	–	**272**
Total Assisted Annually	973	1,932	1,024	100	–	–	**70,886**
Day Care and Extended Day Care Centers	9	65	39	–	–	3	**1,240**
Total Assisted Annually	389	4,455	1,252	–	–	156	**125,723**
Special Centers for Social Services	13	82	2	1	–	2	**2,969**
Total Assisted Annually	199,294	624,669	153,781	1,697	–	15,500	**21,251,075**
Diocesan Seminaries	1	4	1	1	1	–	**72**
Students	12	193	6	3	6	–	**3,077**
Religious Seminaries	1	3	–	–	–	–	**124**
Students	–	34	8	–	–	–	**1,253**
Colleges and Universities	4	26	2	1	–	1	**232**
Total Students	12,280	82,851	8,586	867	–	1,680	**747,060**
High Schools, Diocesan and Parish	9	65	20	9	1	5	**787**
Total Students	3,034	40,696	4,300	1,337	120	789	**378,650**
High Schools, Private	2	22	28	5	6	5	**560**
Total Students	810	10,200	6,668	1,705	3,182	1,193	**301,673**
Elementary Schools, Diocesan and Parish	45	535	28	9	4	6	**6,488**
Total Students	10,032	145,077	9,623	4,356	665	1,419	**1,796,275**
Elementary Schools, Private	–	24	40	5	12	5	**365**
Total Students	–	6,208	13,379	4,656	3,998	1,220	**95,742**
Non–residential Schools for the Disabled	1	11	1	–	–	–	**83**
Total Students	20	659	138	–	–	–	**18,179**
Religious Education High School Students	15,099	43,104	10,967	463	3,289	–	**771,730**
Religious Education Elementary Students	30,461	193,618	27,415	1,449	5,201	10,485	**3,612,510**
Priests Teaching	4	182	30	17	10	1	**1,792**
Scholastics Teaching	–	–	–	–	4	–	**57**
Brothers Teaching	–	87	23	3	4	2	**1,195**
Sisters Teaching	87	996	93	30	15	1	**7,871**
Lay Teachers	848	14,884	2,295	520	380	283	**169,966**
Infant Baptisms	3,695	38,677	9,378	3,994	5,322	3,859	**985,141**
Adult Baptisms	526	3,533	1,248	259	479	166	**76,829**
Received into Full Communion	280	2,790	–	–	–	56	**75,429**
First Communions	5,032	43,755	7,155	3,787	5,425	3,133	**896,670**
Confirmations	7,441	45,671	4,700	2,770	2,739	2,914	**645,426**
Marriages	1,667	14,606	1,881	808	1,018	655	**232,060**
Deaths	5,580	40,216	–	1,740	2,366	2,305	**473,935**
Totals Catholics	348,542	3,686,088	1,001,178	370,000	515,000	350,000	**67,259,768**
Total Population	1,072,813	12,300,745	1,697,435	603,469	653,012	491,518	**288,758,111**
Catholic Population Percentage	32	30	59	61	79	71	**23**

*Indicates Archdioceses.

†Certain Dioceses traverse state lines.

	Ponce, Puerto Rico	PUERTO RICO TOTAL	Providence RI	Charleston SC	Rapid City SD	Sioux Falls SD	2004 U.S. GRAND TOTAL
Cardinals	–	1	–	–	–	–	**12**
Archbishops	–	1	–	–	–	–	**48**
Bishops	3	10	5	2	1	2	**375**
Abbots	–	2	2	–	–	2	**109**
Diocesan Priests	91	442	299	93	43	121	**29,483**
Religious Priests	55	350	121	43	21	32	**14,729**
Total Priests in Diocese	146	792	420	136	64	153	**44,212**
Newly Ordained Priests	1	4	4	–	1	2	**544**
Total Permanent Deacons	89	407	108	96	30	30	**14,693**
Total Brothers	7	66	74	26	5	13	**5,504**
Total Sisters	230	1,134	605	145	58	364	**71,486**
Number of Parishes	42	327	152	94	97	151	**19,431**
Missions	2	416	6	25	32	–	**2,910**
Pastoral Centers	231	389	22	10	4	–	**1,011**
New Parishes	–	–	–	1	–	–	**34**
Catholic Hospitals	–	2	1	3	–	11	**583**
Patients Assisted Annually	–	42,596	249,454	334,890	–	550,000	**83,898,575**
Health Care Centers	–	2	1	–	–	–	**376**
Patients Assisted Annually	–	1,685	490	–	–	–	**4,251,107**
Specialized Homes	4	30	11	1	2	10	**1,546**
Total Assisted Annually	3,475	23,988	1,012	15	2,150	1,560	**1,412,029**
Residential Care of Children (Orphanages)	–	14	–	–	1	–	**272**
Total Assisted Annually	–	1,124	–	–	7	–	**70,886**
Day Care and Extended Day Care Centers	–	42	5	–	1	1	**1,240**
Total Assisted Annually	–	1,408	437	–	21	71	**125,723**
Special Centers for Social Services	2	7	7	7	11	4	**2,969**
Total Assisted Annually	4,280	175,258	27,500	39,604	10,059	170,000	**21,251,075**
Diocesan Seminaries	1	4	1	–	–	–	**72**
Students	11	26	19	–	–	–	**3,077**
Religious Seminaries	3	3	–	–	–	–	**124**
Students	8	16	–	–	–	–	**1,253**
Colleges and Universities	1	5	2	–	–	2	**232**
Total Students	9,862	20,995	8,266	–	–	1,800	**747,060**
High Schools, Diocesan and Parish	20	55	[illegible]	2	1	3	**787**
Total Students	9,422	15,968	2,209	1,256	196	899	**378,650**
High Schools, Private	–	44	3	2	1	–	**560**
Total Students	–	12,748	4,040	344	220	–	**301,673**
Elementary Schools, Diocesan and Parish	22	69	45	26	1	25	**6,488**
Total Students	7,619	23,682	11,425	6,176	469	4,293	**1,796,275**
Elementary Schools, Private	–	62	4	–	1	–	**365**
Total Students	–	23,253	1,295	–	367	–	**95,742**
Non–residential Schools for the Disabled	–	1	–	–	–	–	**83**
Total Students	–	138	–	–	–	–	**18,179**
Religious Education High School Students	–	14,719	9,968	2,918	1,320	7,542	**771,730**
Religious Education Elementary Students	–	44,550	30,408	10,411	2,787	10,348	**3,612,510**
Priests Teaching	21	79	45	1	7	2	**1,792**
Scholastics Teaching	–	4	–	–	3	–	**57**
Brothers Teaching	–	32	23	1	3	–	**1,195**
Sisters Teaching	33	172	[illegible]9	6	6	8	**7,871**
Lay Teachers	635	4,113	1,7[illegible]6	644	91	316	**169,966**
Infant Baptisms	6,528	29,081	5,4[illegible]5	2,793	551	1,727	**985,141**
Adult Baptisms	626	2,778	209	964	72	80	**76,829**
Received into Full Communion	–	56	335	475	78	265	**75,429**
First Communions	5,901	25,401	6,132	2,484	509	1,845	**896,670**
Confirmations	5,199	18,322	4,772	1,988	492	1,817	**645,426**
Marriages	1,079	5,441	1,798	706	162	670	**232,060**
Deaths	–	6,411	5,632	1,057	490	1,033	**473,935**
Totals Catholics	474,759	2,710,937	679,275	152,413	29,440	125,332	**67,259,768**
Total Population	593,448	4,038,882	1,069,725	4,054,890	227,211	524,153	**288,758,111**
Catholic Population Percentage	80	67	64	4	13	24	**23**

Archdioceses = 36; Dioceses = 169; Apostolates = 3

2004 GENERAL SUMMARY

	SOUTH DAKOTA TOTAL	Knoxville TN	Memphis TN	Nashville TN	TENNESSEE TOTAL	*San Antonio TX	2004 U.S. GRAND TOTAL
Cardinals	–	–	–	–	–	–	**12**
Archbishops	–	–	–	–	–	1	**48**
Bishops	3	1	1	2	4	3	**375**
Abbots	2	–	–	–	–	–	**109**
Diocesan Priests	164	54	64	49	167	152	**29,483**
Religious Priests	53	17	12	28	57	198	**14,729**
Total Priests in Diocese	217	71	76	77	224	350	**44,212**
Newly Ordained Priests	3	–	–	–	–	4	**544**
Total Permanent Deacons	60	23	51	52	126	313	**14,693**
Total Brothers	18	12	42	1	55	78	**5,504**
Total Sisters	422	35	86	183	304	822	**71,486**
Number of Parishes	248	44	42	51	137	139	**19,431**
Missions	32	2	5	3	10	34	**2,910**
Pastoral Centers	4	2	1	2	5	2	**1,011**
New Parishes	–	–	–	–	–	–	**34**
Catholic Hospitals	11	2	–	1	3	3	**583**
Patients Assisted Annually	550,000	426,741	–	57,451	484,192	249,359	**83,898,575**
Health Care Centers	–	1	–	4	5	3	**376**
Patients Assisted Annually	–	429	–	190,561	190,990	–	**4,251,107**
Specialized Homes	12	2	5	1	8	13	**1,546**
Total Assisted Annually	3,710	598	700	110	1,408	4,035	**1,412,029**
Residential Care of Children (Orphanages)	1	–	–	–	–	3	**272**
Total Assisted Annually	7	–	–	–	–	314	**70,886**
Day Care and Extended Day Care Centers	2	–	–	3	3	9	**1,240**
Total Assisted Annually	92	–	–	770	770	847	**125,723**
Special Centers for Social Services	15	6	1	9	16	10	**2,969**
Total Assisted Annually	180,059	66,138	18,000	64,500	148,638	–	**21,251,075**
Diocesan Seminaries	–	–	–	–	–	1	**72**
Students	–	–	–	–	–	59	**3,077**
Religious Seminaries	–	–	–	–	–	11	**124**
Students	–	–	–	–	–	36	**1,253**
Colleges and Universities	2	–	1	1	2	4	**232**
Total Students	1,800	–	2,030	863	2,893	13,020	**747,060**
High Schools, Diocesan and Parish	4	2	4	2	8	2	**787**
Total Students	1,095	1,050	1,097	1,345	3,492	815	**378,650**
High Schools, Private	1	–	2	1	3	6	**560**
Total Students	220	–	1,191	273	1,464	2,328	**301,673**
Elementary Schools, Diocesan and Parish	26	8	19	17	44	35	**6,488**
Total Students	4,762	2,513	4,646	3,915	11,074	9,386	**1,796,275**
Elementary Schools, Private	1	–	2	2	4	5	**365**
Total Students	367	–	358	653	1,011	1,900	**95,742**
Non–residential Schools for the Disabled	–	–	3	–	3	–	**83**
Total Students	–	–	176	–	176	–	**18,179**
Religious Education High School Students	8,862	1,339	850	1,672	3,861	10,258	**771,730**
Religious Education Elementary Students	13,135	3,749	3,753	5,648	13,150	34,106	**3,612,510**
Priests Teaching	9	2	2	1	5	32	**1,792**
Scholastics Teaching	3	–	–	–	–	4	**57**
Brothers Teaching	3	1	9	–	10	14	**1,195**
Sisters Teaching	14	4	21	34	59	74	**7,871**
Lay Teachers	407	265	575	481	1,321	1,341	**169,966**
Infant Baptisms	2,278	857	950	1,879	3,686	11,896	**985,141**
Adult Baptisms	152	161	474	203	838	537	**76,829**
Received into Full Communion	343	173	283	333	789	597	**75,429**
First Communions	2,354	1,137	1,273	1,443	3,853	9,153	**896,670**
Confirmations	2,309	783	1,083	1,271	3,137	5,604	**645,426**
Marriages	832	208	329	446	983	2,416	**232,060**
Deaths	1,523	332	426	410	1,168	4,821	**473,935**
Totals Catholics	154,772	50,478	63,820	71,188	185,486	667,667	**67,259,768**
Total Population	751,364	2,175,795	1,455,808	2,105,161	5,736,764	1,979,732	**288,758,111**
Catholic Population Percentage	21	2	4	3	3	34	**23**

*Indicates Archdioceses.

†Certain Dioceses traverse state lines.

	Amarillo TX	Austin TX	Beaumont TX	Brownsville TX	Corpus Christi TX	Dallas TX	2004 U.S. GRAND TOTAL
Cardinals	–	–	–	–	–	–	**12**
Archbishops	–	–	–	–	–	–	**48**
Bishops	2	2	1	2	2	3	**375**
Abbots	–	–	–	–	–	1	**109**
Diocesan Priests	45	151	46	68	117	97	**29,483**
Religious Priests	10	48	25	43	42	76	**14,729**
Total Priests in Diocese	55	199	71	111	159	173	**44,212**
Newly Ordained Priests	–	2	2	4	8	–	**544**
Total Permanent Deacons	51	191	32	64	67	145	**14,693**
Total Brothers	1	46	1	18	13	7	**5,504**
Total Sisters	106	97	42	131	182	142	**71,486**
Number of Parishes	35	101	45	65	67	67	**19,431**
Missions	13	25	8	44	32	8	**2,910**
Pastoral Centers	–	1	2	1	3	–	**1,011**
New Parishes	–	–	1	–	2	–	**34**
Catholic Hospitals	–	4	3	–	6	1	**583**
Patients Assisted Annually	–	713,482	360,739	–	586,779	118,744	**83,898,575**
Health Care Centers	–	4	–	1	–	–	**376**
Patients Assisted Annually	–	91,780	–	114	–	–	**4,251,107**
Specialized Homes	1	3	–	2	5	1	**1,546**
Total Assisted Annually	56	1,240	–	581	1,084	49	**1,412,029**
Residential Care of Children (Orphanages)	–	–	–	–	–	–	**272**
Total Assisted Annually	–	–	–	–	–	–	**70,886**
Day Care and Extended Day Care Centers	1	4	–	2	2	8	**1,240**
Total Assisted Annually	127	185	–	128	115	279	**125,723**
Special Centers for Social Services	1	1	8	5	5	15	**2,969**
Total Assisted Annually	35,000	300	54,792	23,156	44,826	36,087	**21,251,075**
Diocesan Seminaries	–	–	–	1	–	1	**72**
Students	–	–	–	6	–	42	**3,077**
Religious Seminaries	–	–	–	–	–	–	**124**
Students	–	2	–	–	10	–	**1,253**
Colleges and Universities	–	1	–	–	1	1	**232**
Total Students	–	4,443	–	–	27	3,170	**747,060**
High Schools, Diocesan and Parish	1	3	1	–	–	3	**787**
Total Students	118	493	487	–	–	1,733	**378,650**
High Schools, Private	–	2	–	2	1	4	**560**
Total Students	–	520	–	1,001	234	2,620	**301,673**
Elementary Schools, Diocesan and Parish	6	14	5	8	14	33	**6,488**
Total Students	675	3,190	1,396	2,272	2,089	10,605	**1,796,275**
Elementary Schools, Private	–	2	–	2	2	1	**365**
Total Students	–	763	–	579	473	174	**95,742**
Non–residential Schools for the Disabled	–	–	–	–	–	1	**83**
Total Students	–	–	–	–	–	122	**18,179**
Religious Education High School Students	1,666	7,432	1,525	7,515	3,247	5,041	**771,730**
Religious Education Elementary Students	4,102	27,000	6,990	28,637	10,632	35,527	**3,612,510**
Priests Teaching	–	4	–	3	6	14	**1,792**
Scholastics Teaching	–	–	–	–	–	1	**57**
Brothers Teaching	–	–	–	9	1	4	**1,195**
Sisters Teaching	12	9	5	11	29	142	**7,871**
Lay Teachers	126	566	133	270	217	885	**169,966**
Infant Baptisms	1,237	8,400	1,237	4,439	2,922	15,794	**985,141**
Adult Baptisms	122	700	170	682	170	818	**76,829**
Received into Full Communion	249	1,100	252	615	317	574	**75,429**
First Communions	1,351	6,500	1,359	7,354	2,674	10,033	**896,670**
Confirmations	1,304	4,100	826	2,905	705	6,465	**645,426**
Marriages	223	1,225	368	896	706	2,116	**232,060**
Deaths	331	1,556	850	2,373	1,761	1,372	**473,935**
Totals Catholics	43,651	401,842	89,403	888,004	384,308	930,352	**67,259,768**
Total Population	432,190	2,300,863	599,139	1,044,711	549,012	3,371,300	**288,758,111**
Catholic Population Percentage	10	17	15	85	70	28	**23**

Archdioceses = 36; Dioceses = 169; Apostolates = 3

2004 GENERAL SUMMARY

	El Paso TX	Fort Worth TX	Galveston— Houston TX	Laredo TX	Lubbock TX	San Angelo TX	2004 U.S. GRAND TOTAL
Cardinals	–	–	–	–	–	–	12
Archbishops	–	–	–	–	–	–	48
Bishops	1	1	3	1	1	1	375
Abbots	–	–	–	–	–	–	109
Diocesan Priests	80	63	199	26	37	34	29,483
Religious Priests	36	51	217	25	8	17	14,729
Total Priests in Diocese	116	114	416	51	45	51	44,212
Newly Ordained Priests	–	–	–	–	1	2	544
Total Permanent Deacons	10	80	362	27	46	35	14,693
Total Brothers	13	13	12	8	–	1	5,504
Total Sisters	254	93	499	76	23	23	71,486
Number of Parishes	58	88	150	32	62	49	19,431
Missions	22	3	8	20	–	24	2,910
Pastoral Centers	–	–	17	–	–	–	1,011
New Parishes	–	–	–	–	–	–	34
Catholic Hospitals	–	1	3	1	–	–	583
Patients Assisted Annually	–	140,075	526,232	140,000	–	–	83,898,575
Health Care Centers	–	1	7	–	–	–	376
Patients Assisted Annually	–	3,100	55,447	–	–	–	4,251,107
Specialized Homes	1	22	7	1	–	–	1,546
Total Assisted Annually	90	35,598	2,847	663	–	–	1,412,029
Residential Care of Children (Orphanages)	–	–	2	1	–	–	272
Total Assisted Annually	–	–	2,009	65	–	–	70,886
Day Care and Extended Day Care Centers	–	–	39	–	–	–	1,240
Total Assisted Annually	–	–	3,973	–	–	–	125,723
Special Centers for Social Services	–	–	11	3	–	–	2,969
Total Assisted Annually	–	–	329,985	362,284	–	–	21,251,075
Diocesan Seminaries	1	–	1	–	–	–	72
Students	12	–	53	–	–	–	3,077
Religious Seminaries	2	–	5	–	–	–	124
Students	24	–	21	–	–	–	1,253
Colleges and Universities	–	–	1	–	–	–	232
Total Students	–	–	7,694	–	–	–	747,060
High Schools, Diocesan and Parish	1	4	2	1	1	–	787
Total Students	568	1,463	320	650	18	–	378,650
High Schools, Private	2	–	6	–	–	–	560
Total Students	353	–	3,362	–	–	–	301,673
Elementary Schools, Diocesan and Parish	9	15	43	5	2	3	6,488
Total Students	3,571	5,353	10,019	956	363	701	1,796,275
Elementary Schools, Private	3	1	6	1	–	–	365
Total Students	857	238	2,017	560	–	–	95,742
Non–residential Schools for the Disabled	–	–	–	–	–	–	83
Total Students	–	–	–	–	–	–	18,179
Religious Education High School Students	5,671	7,452	16,127	1,575	3,375	4,531	771,730
Religious Education Elementary Students	13,740	19,786	67,813	6,410	4,582	7,989	3,612,510
Priests Teaching	4	2	13	–	–	–	1,792
Scholastics Teaching	–	–	2	–	–	–	57
Brothers Teaching	5	5	2	1	–	–	1,195
Sisters Teaching	32	12	53	8	–	2	7,871
Lay Teachers	316	541	1,460	143	–	66	169,966
Infant Baptisms	9,538	6,066	20,744	3,388	1,604	1,834	985,141
Adult Baptisms	144	430	1,834	126	134	173	76,829
Received into Full Communion	288	714	838	52	201	244	75,429
First Communions	6,062	5,859	18,401	3,357	1,139	1,925	896,670
Confirmations	3,957	3,174	9,283	502	665	1,532	645,426
Marriages	1,428	1,199	3,624	434	340	463	232,060
Deaths	2,064	1,197	3,534	1,097	481	712	473,935
Totals Catholics	656,035	400,500	1,041,123	222,250	80,742	82,734	67,259,768
Total Population	811,739	2,098,443	4,972,544	302,196	486,910	673,801	288,758,111
Catholic Population Percentage	81	19	21	74	17	12	23

*Indicates Archdioceses.
†Certain Dioceses traverse state lines.

	Tyler TX	Victoria in Texas TX	TEXAS TOTAL	Salt Lake City UT	Burlington VT	St. Thomas Virgin Islands	2004 U.S. GRAND TOTAL
Cardinals	–	–	–	–	–	–	**12**
Archbishops	–	–	1	–	–	–	**48**
Bishops	1	1	25	1	1	2	**375**
Abbots	–	–	1	2	–	–	**109**
Diocesan Priests	49	57	1,221	56	114	15	**29,483**
Religious Priests	16	8	820	30	47	5	**14,729**
Total Priests in Diocese	65	65	2,041	86	161	20	**44,212**
Newly Ordained Priests	3	–	26	1	–	–	**544**
Total Permanent Deacons	62	26	1,511	43	41	28	**14,693**
Total Brothers	3	1	215	11	16	3	**5,504**
Total Sisters	62	90	2,642	50	184	17	**71,486**
Number of Parishes	42	50	1,050	47	83	8	**19,431**
Missions	23	18	282	16	41	2	**2,910**
Pastoral Centers	1	–	27	–	1	–	**1,011**
New Parishes	–	–	3	–	–	–	**34**
Catholic Hospitals	4	–	25	–	–	–	**583**
Patients Assisted Annually	964,682	–	3,800,092	–	–	–	**83,898,575**
Health Care Centers	38	–	54	–	–	–	**376**
Patients Assisted Annually	8,101	–	158,542	–	–	–	**4,251,107**
Specialized Homes	–	2	58	1	4	–	**1,546**
Total Assisted Annually	–	464	46,707	1,084	200	–	**1,412,029**
Residential Care of Children (Orphanages)	–	–	6	–	–	–	**272**
Total Assisted Annually	–	–	2,388	–	–	–	**70,886**
Day Care and Extended Day Care Centers	–	–	65	12	–	–	**1,240**
Total Assisted Annually	–	–	5,654	385	–	–	**125,723**
Special Centers for Social Services	1	–	55	3	1	2	**2,969**
Total Assisted Annually	120	–	886,550	205,227	5,751	530	**21,251,075**
Diocesan Seminaries	–	–	5	–	–	–	**72**
Students	–	–	172	–	–	–	**3,077**
Religious Seminaries	–	–	18	–	–	–	**124**
Students	–	–	93	–	–	–	**1,253**
Colleges and Universities	–	–	8	–	2	–	**232**
Total Students	–	–	28,354	–	3,139	–	**747,060**
High Schools, Diocesan and Parish	1	2	22	3	2	2	**787**
Total Students	208	187	7,050	1,709	618	217	**378,650**
High Schools, Private	–	1	24	–	–	–	**560**
Total Students	–	337	10,755	–	–	–	**301,673**
Elementary Schools, Diocesan and Parish	3	11	207	11	11	3	**6,488**
Total Students	878	1,773	53,227	3,806	1,704	585	**1,796,275**
Elementary Schools, Private	–	1	24	–	4	–	**365**
Total Students	–	245	7,806	–	819	–	**95,742**
Non–residential Schools for the Disabled	–	–	1	–	–	–	**83**
Total Students	–	–	22	–	–	–	**18,179**
Religious Education High School Students	1,113	3,314	79,542	1,477	2,687	123	**771,730**
Religious Education Elementary Students	2,610	6,389	276,313	6,575	8,262	699	**3,612,510**
Priests Teaching	–	1	79	5	–	–	**1,792**
Scholastics Teaching	–	–	7	–	–	–	**57**
Brothers Teaching	2	–	43	–	–	1	**1,195**
Sisters Teaching	–	19	108	–	12	1	**7,871**
Lay Teachers	88	220	6,402	390	38	57	**169,966**
Infant Baptisms	1,070	1,608	91,327	3,894	1,375	239	**985,141**
Adult Baptisms	165	68	6,273	403	126	15	**76,829**
Received into Full Communion	138	97	6,286	243	131	10	**75,429**
First Communions	1,456	1,362	77,985	2,614	1,499	196	**896,670**
Confirmations	369	1,069	42,460	1,436	1,179	141	**645,426**
Marriages	180	445	16,063	614	605	95	**232,060**
Deaths	39	928	23,116	569	1,526	147	**473,935**
Totals Catholics	55,934	106,441	6,050,986	150,000	149,154	30,000	**67,259,768**
Total Population	1,304,746	208,736	21,136,062	2,316,256	608,827	108,612	**288,758,111**
Catholic Population Percentage	4	51	29	6	25	28	**23**

Archdioceses = 36; Dioceses = 169; Apostolates = 3

2004 GENERAL SUMMARY

	Arlington VA	Richmond VA	VIRGINIA TOTAL	*Seattle WA	Spokane WA	Yakima WA	2004 U.S. GRAND TOTAL
Cardinals	–	–	–	–	–	–	**12**
Archbishops	–	–	–	2	–	–	**48**
Bishops	1	1	2	1	1	1	**375**
Abbots	4	1	5	2	1	–	**109**
Diocesan Priests	157	163	320	187	83	72	**29,483**
Religious Priests	72	37	109	108	89	12	**14,729**
Total Priests in Diocese	229	200	429	295	172	84	**44,212**
Newly Ordained Priests	3	1	4	5	1	3	**544**
Total Permanent Deacons	46	87	133	69	47	24	**14,693**
Total Brothers	19	12	31	25	11	3	**5,504**
Total Sisters	150	193	343	459	247	48	**71,486**
Number of Parishes	66	146	212	139	83	41	**19,431**
Missions	6	6	12	30	2	3	**2,910**
Pastoral Centers	–	2	2	9	1	1	**1,011**
New Parishes	–	–	–	–	1	–	**34**
Catholic Hospitals	–	10	10	9	7	1	**583**
Patients Assisted Annually	–	660,500	660,500	1,366,172	506,987	75,436	**83,898,575**
Health Care Centers	–	–	–	16	–	–	**376**
Patients Assisted Annually	–	–	–	15,332	–	–	**4,251,107**
Specialized Homes	–	18	18	23	2	–	**1,546**
Total Assisted Annually	–	1,730	1,730	2,343	260	–	**1,412,029**
Residential Care of Children (Orphanages)	–	–	–	–	1	–	**272**
Total Assisted Annually	–	–	–	–	35	–	**70,886**
Day Care and Extended Day Care Centers	–	2	2	8	–	2	**1,240**
Total Assisted Annually	–	100	100	529	–	224	**125,723**
Special Centers for Social Services	7	8	15	43	15	5	**2,969**
Total Assisted Annually	30,183	11,300	41,483	79,095	162,665	42,664	**21,251,075**
Diocesan Seminaries	–	–	–	–	1	–	**72**
Students	–	–	–	–	14	–	**3,077**
Religious Seminaries	–	–	–	–	–	–	**124**
Students	–	–	–	–	–	–	**1,253**
Colleges and Universities	4	–	4	2	1	–	**232**
Total Students	5,552	–	5,552	7,900	4,515	–	**747,060**
High Schools, Diocesan and Parish	3	5	8	3	2	–	**787**
Total Students	3,367	1,315	4,682	2,407	330	–	**378,650**
High Schools, Private	3	4	7	6	1	1	**560**
Total Students	799	831	1,630	3,248	880	172	**301,673**
Elementary Schools, Diocesan and Parish	35	24	59	53	16	6	**6,488**
Total Students	13,555	8,370	21,925	15,870	3,575	1,792	**1,796,275**
Elementary Schools, Private	1	2	3	4	–	–	**365**
Total Students	186	478	664	810	–	–	**95,742**
Non–residential Schools for the Disabled	1	4	5	–	–	–	**83**
Total Students	155	400	555	–	–	–	**18,179**
Religious Education High School Students	3,227	6,029	9,256	6,260	789	2,456	**771,730**
Religious Education Elementary Students	31,074	18,838	49,912	32,800	1,540	5,150	**3,612,510**
Priests Teaching	10	8	18	8	–	–	**1,792**
Scholastics Teaching	–	4	4	–	–	–	**57**
Brothers Teaching	1	–	1	8	1	4	**1,195**
Sisters Teaching	45	22	67	30	–	4	**7,871**
Lay Teachers	1,089	964	2,053	1,716	231	109	**169,966**
Infant Baptisms	7,165	3,523	10,688	6,811	1,311	2,726	**985,141**
Adult Baptisms	795	515	1,310	1,086	256	185	**76,829**
Received into Full Communion	1,016	610	1,626	574	–	112	**75,429**
First Communions	7,538	3,628	11,166	6,422	1,478	2,346	**896,670**
Confirmations	5,905	1,940	7,845	3,363	1,704	698	**645,426**
Marriages	1,632	1,155	2,787	1,613	332	442	**232,060**
Deaths	1,557	1,655	3,212	2,884	631	542	**473,935**
Totals Catholics	391,001	212,189	603,190	550,450	86,721	68,561	**67,259,768**
Total Population	2,423,982	4,771,500	7,195,482	4,755,500	722,677	600,055	**288,758,111**
Catholic Population Percentage	16	4	8	12	12	11	**23**

*Indicates Archdioceses.

†Certain Dioceses traverse state lines.

	WASHINGTON TOTAL	Wheeling–Charleston WV	*Milwaukee WI	Green Bay WI	La Crosse WI	Madison WI	2004 U.S. GRAND TOTAL
Cardinals	–	–	–	–	–	–	12
Archbishops	2	–	2	–	–	–	48
Bishops	3	1	1	3	2	3	375
Abbots	3	–	3	4	1	–	109
Diocesan Priests	342	115	414	202	191	149	29,483
Religious Priests	209	66	345	115	21	13	14,729
Total Priests in Diocese	551	181	759	317	212	162	44,212
Newly Ordained Priests	9	1	2	–	3	3	544
Total Permanent Deacons	140	32	151	108	31	2	14,693
Total Brothers	39	18	62	34	4	6	5,504
Total Sisters	754	223	2,29[illegible]	653	483	298	71,486
Number of Parishes	263	112	219	185	166	135	19,431
Missions	35	24	–	3	–	–	2,910
Pastoral Centers	11	4	14	14	–	–	1,011
New Parishes	1	1	4	–	–	–	34
Catholic Hospitals	17	3	11	7	9	4	583
Patients Assisted Annually	1,948,595	559,556	2,053,387	977,606	588,146	335,305	83,898,575
Health Care Centers	16	2	1	–	–	2	376
Patients Assisted Annually	15,332	4,130	10,876	–	–	668	4,251,107
Specialized Homes	25	5	30	19	18	4	1,546
Total Assisted Annually	2,603	870	9,064	9,494	12,477	956	1,412,029
Residential Care of Children (Orphanages)	1	1	–	–	–	–	272
Total Assisted Annually	35	19	–	–	–	–	70,886
Day Care and Extended Day Care Centers	10	4	4	2	2	18	1,240
Total Assisted Annually	753	432	5[illegible]4	111	204	988	125,723
Special Centers for Social Services	63	4	22	8	2	7	2,969
Total Assisted Annually	284,424	19,905	244,827	182,276	3,125	36,120	21,251,075
Diocesan Seminaries	1	–	1	–	1	–	72
Students	14	–	21	–	6	–	3,077
Religious Seminaries	–	–	1	1	–	–	124
Students	–	–	19	9	–	–	1,253
Colleges and Universities	3	1	5	2	1	1	232
Total Students	12,415	1,462	26,308	4,908	2,167	2,400	747,060
High Schools, Diocesan and Parish	5	7	7	5	7	–	787
Total Students	2,737	1,559	4,070	1,405	1,537	–	378,650
High Schools, Private	8	1	6	1	–	1	560
Total Students	4,300	60	2,980	741	–	664	301,673
Elementary Schools, Diocesan and Parish	75	25	120	70	77	44	6,488
Total Students	21,237	4,849	29,168	10,519	8,791	6,878	1,796,275
Elementary Schools, Private	4	1	3	–	–	1	365
Total Students	810	150	180	–	–	306	95,742
Non–residential Schools for the Disabled	–	–	1	–	–	–	83
Total Students	–	–	9	–	–	–	18,179
Religious Education High School Students	9,505	1,195	17,262	12,118	7,711	8,445	771,730
Religious Education Elementary Students	39,490	4,216	52,380	22,700	14,948	15,654	3,612,510
Priests Teaching	8	2	42	1	7	–	1,792
Scholastics Teaching	–	–	1	–	–	–	57
Brothers Teaching	13	2	8	4	–	2	1,195
Sisters Teaching	34	4	110	27	14	27	7,871
Lay Teachers	2,056	489	3,397	916	704	831	169,966
Infant Baptisms	10,848	929	9,322	4,284	2,858	3,058	985,141
Adult Baptisms	1,527	288	488	544	125	128	76,829
Received into Full Communion	686	213	686	318	287	282	75,429
First Communions	10,246	1,363	8,947	4,373	3,059	2,813	896,670
Confirmations	5,765	1,190	6,427	3,814	3,181	2,249	645,426
Marriages	2,387	437	2,812	1,583	1,307	1,024	232,060
Deaths	4,057	1,150	5,677	3,176	2,224	1,753	473,935
Totals Catholics	705,732	100,648	731,516	358,211	215,573	269,556	67,259,768
Total Population	6,078,232	1,801,916	2,261,397	930,419	848,455	947,699	288,758,111
Catholic Population Percentage	12	6	32	39	25	28	23

Archdioceses = 36; Dioceses = 169; Apostolates = 3

2004 GENERAL SUMMARY

	Superior WI	WISCONSIN TOTAL	Cheyenne WY	EASTERN RITE *Philadelphia	*Pittsburgh	Armenian	2004 U.S. GRAND TOTAL
Cardinals	–	–	–	–	–	–	**12**
Archbishops	–	2	–	2	1	–	**48**
Bishops	1	10	2	2	–	1	**375**
Abbots	–	8	–	–	1	–	**109**
Diocesan Priests	73	1,029	46	61	64	3	**29,483**
Religious Priests	12	506	13	6	11	8	**14,729**
Total Priests in Diocese	85	1,535	59	67	75	11	**44,212**
Newly Ordained Priests	1	9	2	2	1	1	**544**
Total Permanent Deacons	56	348	15	5	10	1	**14,693**
Total Brothers	1	108	2	–	4	–	**5,504**
Total Sisters	102	3,826	22	81	96	11	**71,486**
Number of Parishes	112	817	35	74	84	7	**19,431**
Missions	–	3	42	–	2	–	**2,910**
Pastoral Centers	–	28	–	–	–	–	**1,011**
New Parishes	–	4	–	–	–	–	**34**
Catholic Hospitals	7	38	–	–	–	–	**583**
Patients Assisted Annually	286,756	4,241,200	–	–	–	–	**83,898,575**
Health Care Centers	1	4	–	–	–	–	**376**
Patients Assisted Annually	–	11,544	–	–	–	–	**4,251,107**
Specialized Homes	22	93	15	1	2	–	**1,546**
Total Assisted Annually	214	32,205	119	240	361	–	**1,412,029**
Residential Care of Children (Orphanages)	–	–	1	–	–	–	**272**
Total Assisted Annually	–	–	106	–	–	–	**70,886**
Day Care and Extended Day Care Centers	2	28	2	1	–	–	**1,240**
Total Assisted Annually	162	2,009	100	10	–	–	**125,723**
Special Centers for Social Services	6	45	9	–	–	–	**2,969**
Total Assisted Annually	530	466,878	15,940	–	–	–	**21,251,075**
Diocesan Seminaries	–	2	–	1	1	–	**72**
Students	–	27	–	–	8	–	**3,077**
Religious Seminaries	–	2	–	–	–	–	**124**
Students	–	28	5	–	–	–	**1,253**
Colleges and Universities	–	9	–	1	–	–	**232**
Total Students	–	35,783	–	1,106	–	–	**747,060**
High Schools, Diocesan and Parish	–	19	–	–	–	–	**787**
Total Students	–	7,012	–	–	–	–	**378,650**
High Schools, Private	–	8	1	1	–	–	**560**
Total Students	–	4,385	18	377	–	–	**301,673**
Elementary Schools, Diocesan and Parish	17	328	7	7	2	–	**6,488**
Total Students	2,715	58,071	1,005	782	334	–	**1,796,275**
Elementary Schools, Private	–	4	–	–	–	4	**365**
Total Students	–	486	–	–	–	935	**95,742**
Non–residential Schools for the Disabled	–	1	–	–	–	–	**83**
Total Students	–	9	–	–	–	–	**18,179**
Religious Education High School Students	3,329	48,865	1,415	193	377	–	**771,730**
Religious Education Elementary Students	7,343	113,525	8,082	736	1,228	23	**3,612,510**
Priests Teaching	–	50	–	–	–	2	**1,792**
Scholastics Teaching	–	1	–	–	–	–	**57**
Brothers Teaching	1	15	–	–	–	–	**1,195**
Sisters Teaching	8	186	2	24	4	10	**7,871**
Lay Teachers	156	6,004	101	346	22	79	**169,966**
Infant Baptisms	959	20,481	870	197	260	128	**985,141**
Adult Baptisms	245	1,530	173	14	17	13	**76,829**
Received into Full Communion	143	1,716	132	31	45	–	**75,429**
First Communions	1,265	20,457	905	195	264	57	**896,670**
Confirmations	1,106	16,777	1,117	198	288	140	**645,426**
Marriages	448	7,174	294	102	99	103	**232,060**
Deaths	1,231	14,061	582	404	512	47	**473,935**
Totals Catholics	83,622	1,658,478	50,979	67,159	60,100	25,000	**67,259,768**
Total Population	431,544	5,419,514	498,703	–	–	–	**288,758,111**
Catholic Population Percentage	19	31	10	–	–	–	**23**

*Indicates Archdioceses.

†Certain Dioceses traverse state lines.

	EASTERN RITE (Cont.)						
	Lady of Deliverance	Lady of Lebanon	Newton	Parma	Passaic	Romanian	2004 U.S. GRAND TOTAL
Cardinals	–	–	–	–	–	–	12
Archbishops	–	–	–	–	–	–	48
Bishops	1	2	2	1	2	2	375
Abbots	–	–	–	–	–	–	109
Diocesan Priests	12	29	47	37	79	17	29,483
Religious Priests	–	16	15	1	9	2	14,729
Total Priests in Diocese	12	45	62	38	88	19	44,212
Newly Ordained Priests	–	1	1	1	–	–	544
Total Permanent Deacons	–	9	39	8	21	2	14,693
Total Brothers	–	–	–	–	1	–	5,504
Total Sisters	–	7	3	13	14	–	71,486
Number of Parishes	8	32	35	31	92	15	19,431
Missions	3	6	7	6	4	4	2,910
Pastoral Centers	–	–	–	–	–	–	1,011
New Parishes	–	–	–	–	–	–	34
Catholic Hospitals	–	–	–	–	–	–	583
Patients Assisted Annually	–	–	–	–	–	–	83,898,575
Health Care Centers	–	–	–	–	–	–	376
Patients Assisted Annually	–	–	–	–	–	–	4,251,107
Specialized Homes	–	–	–	–	–	–	1,546
Total Assisted Annually	–	–	–	–	–	–	1,412,029
Residential Care of Children (Orphanages)	–	1	–	–	–	–	272
Total Assisted Annually	–	12	–	–	–	–	70,886
Day Care and Extended Day Care Centers	–	1	–	2	–	–	1,240
Total Assisted Annually	–	30	–	81	–	–	125,723
Special Centers for Social Services	–	–	–	5	–	–	2,969
Total Assisted Annually	–	–	–	10,000	–	–	21,251,075
Diocesan Seminaries	2	1	1	–	–	–	72
Students	–	2	2	–	–	–	3,077
Religious Seminaries	–	–	1	–	–	–	124
Students	–	–	–	–	–	–	1,253
Colleges and Universities	–	–	–	–	–	–	232
Total Students	–	–	–	–	–	–	747,060
High Schools, Diocesan and Parish	–	–	–	–	–	–	787
Total Students	–	–	–	–	–	–	378,650
High Schools, Private	–	–	–	–	–	–	560
Total Students	–	–	–	–	–	–	301,673
Elementary Schools, Diocesan and Parish	–	1	–	2	–	–	6,488
Total Students	–	80	–	239	–	–	1,796,275
Elementary Schools, Private	–	–	–	–	–	–	365
Total Students	–	–	–	–	–	–	95,742
Non–residential Schools for the Disabled	–	–	–	–	–	–	83
Total Students	–	–	–	–	–	–	18,179
Religious Education High School Students	10	–	326	185	448	17	771,730
Religious Education Elementary Students	333	89	1,309	676	1,679	63	3,612,510
Priests Teaching	–	–	–	–	–	–	1,792
Scholastics Teaching	–	–	–	–	–	–	57
Brothers Teaching	–	–	–	–	–	–	1,195
Sisters Teaching	–	–	–	3	–	–	7,871
Lay Teachers	–	–	–	17	–	–	169,966
Infant Baptisms	82	405	401	111	263	30	985,141
Adult Baptisms	4	47	21	17	14	5	76,829
Received into Full Communion	4	103	32	42	27	6	75,429
First Communions	112	327	44	81	323	27	896,670
Confirmations	86	301	58	67	240	30	645,426
Marriages	45	117	116	53	71	9	232,060
Deaths	34	161	166	186	569	23	473,935
Totals Catholics	12,610	38,415	29,024	12,401	24,031	5,000	67,259,768
Total Population	–	–	–	–	–	–	288,758,111
Catholic Population Percentage	–	–	–	–	–	–	23

Archdioceses = 36; Dioceses = 169; Apostolates = 3

2004 GENERAL SUMMARY

	EASTERN RITE (Cont.)						
	St. Josaphat	St. Maron	St. Nicholas	St. Peter The Apostle	St. Thomas The Apostle	St. Thomas Syro–Malabar	2004 U.S. GRAND TOTAL
Cardinals	–	–	–	–	–	–	12
Archbishops	–	1	–	–	–	–	48
Bishops	1	1	2	1	1	1	375
Abbots	–	–	1	–	–	–	109
Diocesan Priests	40	57	20	8	11	28	29,483
Religious Priests	1	12	13	3	–	9	14,729
Total Priests in Diocese	41	69	33	11	11	37	44,212
Newly Ordained Priests	1	–	–	–	–	–	544
Total Permanent Deacons	5	13	12	–	–	–	14,693
Total Brothers	10	7	–	–	–	–	5,504
Total Sisters	5	2	2	–	9	7	71,486
Number of Parishes	38	34	36	7	7	7	19,431
Missions	2	5	7	–	–	32	2,910
Pastoral Centers	–	–	–	–	–	1	1,011
New Parishes	–	–	–	–	–	3	34
Catholic Hospitals	–	–	–	–	–	–	583
Patients Assisted Annually	–	–	–	–	–	–	83,898,575
Health Care Centers	–	–	–	–	–	–	376
Patients Assisted Annually	–	–	–	–	–	–	4,251,107
Specialized Homes	2	–	–	2	1	–	1,546
Total Assisted Annually	169	–	–	113	60	–	1,412,029
Residential Care of Children (Orphanages)	–	–	–	–	–	–	272
Total Assisted Annually	–	–	–	–	–	–	70,886
Day Care and Extended Day Care Centers	–	–	–	–	–	–	1,240
Total Assisted Annually	–	–	–	–	–	–	125,723
Special Centers for Social Services	–	–	–	2	1	–	2,969
Total Assisted Annually	–	–	–	110	100	–	21,251,075
Diocesan Seminaries	–	1	–	–	–	–	72
Students	–	3	2	–	2	–	3,077
Religious Seminaries	–	–	–	–	–	–	124
Students	–	–	–	–	–	–	1,253
Colleges and Universities	–	–	–	–	–	–	232
Total Students	–	–	76	–	–	–	747,060
High Schools, Diocesan and Parish	–	–	1	–	–	1	787
Total Students	–	–	76	–	–	0	378,650
High Schools, Private	–	–	–	–	–	0	560
Total Students	–	–	–	–	–	0	301,673
Elementary Schools, Diocesan and Parish	2	–	2	–	–	0	6,488
Total Students	241	–	380	–	–	0	1,796,275
Elementary Schools, Private	–	–	–	–	–	0	365
Total Students	–	–	–	–	–	0	95,742
Non–residential Schools for the Disabled	–	–	–	–	–	–	83
Total Students	–	–	–	–	–	–	18,179
Religious Education High School Students	52	338	152	–	–	1,095	771,730
Religious Education Elementary Students	447	1,554	325	–	–	1,436	3,612,510
Priests Teaching	–	–	–	–	–	–	1,792
Scholastics Teaching	–	–	–	–	–	–	57
Brothers Teaching	–	–	–	–	–	–	1,195
Sisters Teaching	1	–	2	–	–	–	7,871
Lay Teachers	27	–	52	–	–	–	169,966
Infant Baptisms	93	453	255	383	820	112	985,141
Adult Baptisms	7	17	5	4	11	1	76,829
Received into Full Communion	2	57	7	–	–	1	75,429
First Communions	95	321	250	248	720	214	896,670
Confirmations	99	320	260	387	–	217	645,426
Marriages	58	124	67	77	360	58	232,060
Deaths	206	248	180	69	157	31	473,935
Totals Catholics	11,058	30,000	10,000	35,000	75,000	80,000	67,259,768
Total Population	–	–	–	–	–	–	288,758,111
Catholic Population Percentage	–	–	–	–	–	–	23

*Indicates Archdioceses.

†Certain Dioceses traverse state lines.

	EASTERN RITE (Cont.) Stamford	Van Nuys	EASTERN RITE TOTAL	*Military Archdiocese	1994 GRAND TOTAL	2003 GRAND TOTAL	2004 U.S. GRAND TOTAL
Cardinals	–	–	–	–	9	11	**12**
Archbishops	–	–	4	2	45	49	**48**
Bishops	1	2	23	4	344	377	**375**
Abbots	–	–	2	–	110	113	**109**
Diocesan Priests	36	18	567	–	33,204	29,715	**29,483**
Religious Priests	15	7	128	–	17,116	14,772	**14,729**
Total Priests in Diocese	51	25	695	–	50,229	44,487	**44,212**
Newly Ordained Priests	1	–	9	–	633	449	**544**
Total Permanent Deacons	9	8	142	–	11,123	14,106	**14,693**
Total Brothers	3	7	32	–	6,510	5,568	**5,504**
Total Sisters	32	4	286	–	94,431	74,698	**71,486**
Number of Parishes	51	19	577	–	19,787	19,484	**19,431**
Missions	4	–	82	–	3,427	2,988	**2,910**
Pastoral Centers	–	–	1	–	1,048	1,069	**1,011**
New Parishes	–	–	3	–	56	44	**34**
Catholic Hospitals	–	–	–	–	609	585	**583**
Patients Assisted Annually	–	–	–	–	53,385,630	83,921,898	**83,898,575**
Health Care Centers	–	–	–	–	313	477	**376**
Patients Assisted Annually	–	–	–	–	2,201,855	5,249,083	**4,251,107**
Specialized Homes	1	–	9	–	1,620	1,534	**1,546**
Total Assisted Annually	30	–	973	–	633,714	778,623	**1,412,029**
Residential Care of Children (Orphanages)	–	–	1	–	194	226	**272**
Total Assisted Annually	–	–	12	–	76,245	714,253	**70,886**
Day Care and Extended Day Care Centers	1	–	5	–	995	1,117	**1,240**
Total Assisted Annually	44	–	165	–	136,073	136,000	**125,723**
Special Centers for Social Services	2	–	10	–	2,135	3,044	**2,969**
Total Assisted Annually	125	–	10,335	–	19,545,247	20,032,104	**21,251,075**
Diocesan Seminaries	1	–	8	–	74	70	**72**
Students	12	–	31	–	4,154	3,251	**3,077**
Religious Seminaries	–	–	1	–	152	143	**124**
Students	–	–	–	–	1,572	1,271	**1,253**
Colleges and Universities	–	–	1	–	232	237	**232**
Total Students	–	–	1,182	–	664,777	749,512	**747,060**
High Schools, Diocesan and Parish	1	–	2	–	832	824	**787**
Total Students	150	–	226	–	368,257	386,764	**378,650**
High Schools, Private	–	–	1	–	528	552	**560**
Total Students	–	–	377	–	264,363	299,887	**301,673**
Elementary Schools, Diocesan and Parish	3	–	19	–	7,003	6,773	**6,488**
Total Students	199	–	2,255	–	1,963,388	1,872,848	**1,796,275**
Elementary Schools, Private	–	–	[illegible]	–	289	369	**365**
Total Students	–	–	935	–	69,465	98,546	**95,742**
Non–residential Schools for the Disabled	–	–	–	–	97	85	**83**
Total Students	–	–	–	–	8,776	18,535	**18,179**
Religious Education High School Students	218	135	3,545	21,000	789,825	767,739	**771,730**
Religious Education Elementary Students	772	432	11,102	44,200	3,352,952	3,582,943	**3,612,510**
Priests Teaching	–	–	2	–	2,615	1,596	**1,792**
Scholastics Teaching	–	–	–	–	115	33	**57**
Brothers Teaching	–	–	–	–	1,693	1,021	**1,195**
Sisters Teaching	3	–	47	12	14,975	7,389	**7,871**
Lay Teachers	22	–	565	220	148,876	161,775	**169,966**
Infant Baptisms	196	57	4,246	3,978	1,036,049	1,005,490	**985,141**
Adult Baptisms	–	9	206	747	79,279	81,013	**76,829**
Received into Full Communion	1	19	377	323	84,072	82,292	**75,429**
First Communions	166	81	3,925	2,662	812,204	897,635	**896,670**
Confirmations	197	98	3,386	2,302	577,591	637,705	**645,426**
Marriages	62	15	1,526	778	315,387	241,727	**232,060**
Deaths	357	33	3,383	–	457,790	477,702	**473,935**
Totals Catholics	16,000	2,849	533,647	–	59,858,042	66,407,105	**67,259,768**
Total Population	–	–	–	–	257,970,516	290,446,533	**288,758,111**
Catholic Population Percentage	–	–	–	23	23	23	**23**

Archdioceses = 36; Dioceses = 169; Apostolates = 3

Catholic Dioceses in the United States

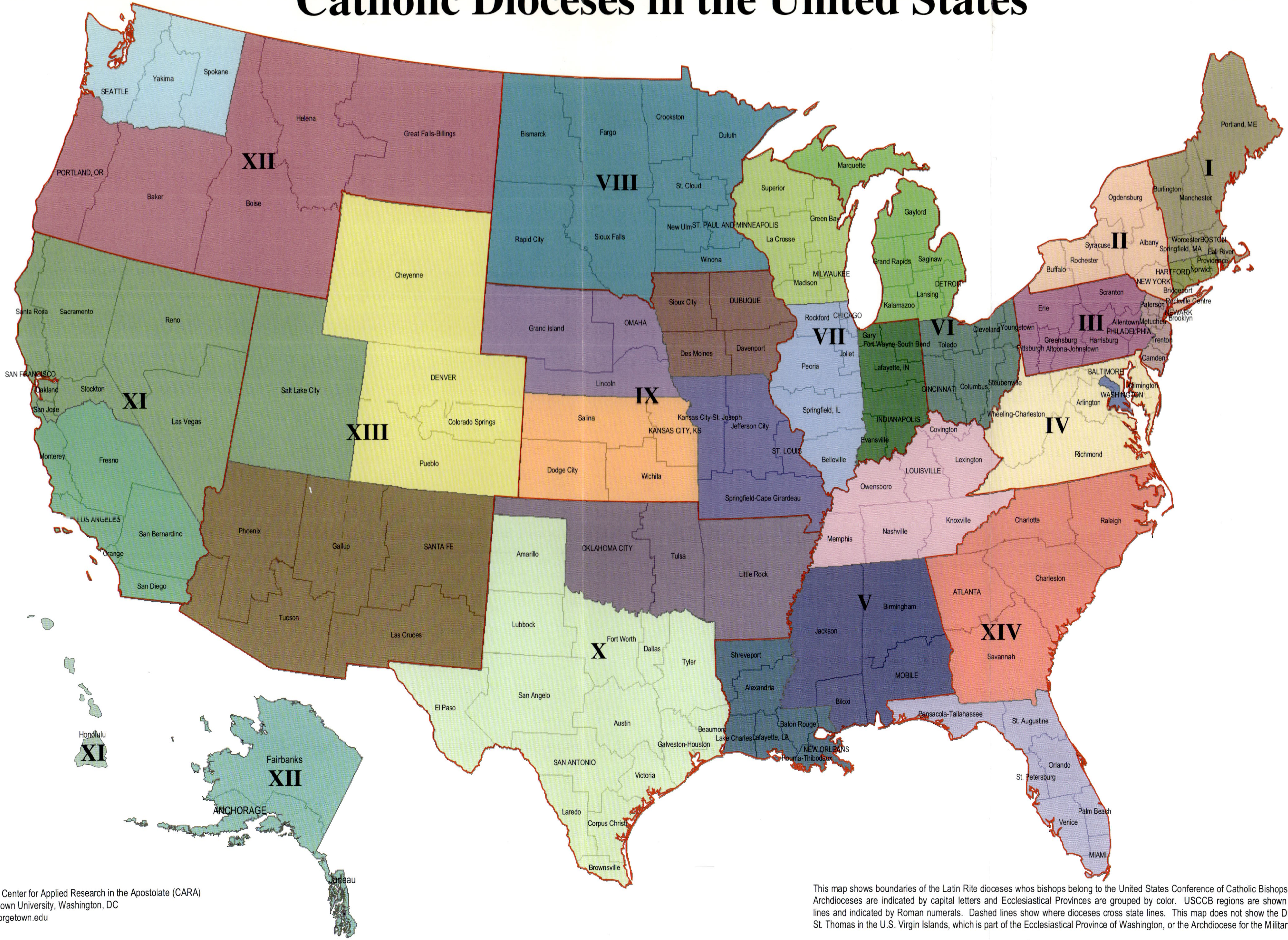

This map shows boundaries of the Latin Rite dioceses whos bishops belong to the United States Conference of Catholic Bishops (USCCB). Archdioceses are indicated by capital letters and Ecclesiastical Provinces are grouped by color. USCCB regions are shown within red lines and indicated by Roman numerals. Dashed lines show where dioceses cross state lines. This map does not show the Diocese of St. Thomas in the U.S. Virgin Islands, which is part of the Ecclesiastical Province of Washington, or the Archdiocese for the Military Services.

MAILING LIST SELECTIONS:

Parishes, Roman Catholic
- *Parishes, Eastern Rites*
- *Parishes, Latin Rite*

Parishes, Larger
Parishes, with CCD
Parishes, with schools
Parishes, by Establishment Date
Parishes, by Ethnic Origin
- *Parishes, Irish*
- *Parishes, Italian*
- *Parishes, Hispanic*

Parishes, by Saint's name
- *Parishes, St. Mary's*
- *Parishes, St. Joseph's*

Priests, Roman Catholic
- *Priests, Eastern Rites*
- *Priests, Latin Rite*

Priests, Pastors
Priests, Associate Pastors
Priests, Chaplains
Priests, Diocesan
Priests, Religious Orders

OTHER SELECTIONS:

Brothers
Brothers, Pastoral Associates
Deacons
The Hierarchy
Laity, DRE's, Principals etc
Laity, Pastoral Associates
Provincials/Superiors
Sisters
Sisters, Pastoral Associates

Educational Institutions

Elementary Schools
High Schools
Colleges & Universities
Seminaries

Other Catholic Institutions

Convents/Motherhouses
Hospitals
Motherhouses
Monasteries/Motherhouses
Newman Centers
Nursing Homes
Retreat Centers

For the very best Catholic mailing lists, go to the "official" source...

The Official Catholic Directory™

Mailing Lists

Order Direct from the Publisher!

The Official Catholic Directory, published by P.J. Kenedy & Sons, is your #1 source for the most accurate and up-to-date mailing lists reaching over 100,000 clergy, parishes and other Catholic institutions. All lists come with our exclusive 100% deliverability guarantee, giving you unmatched quality and value.

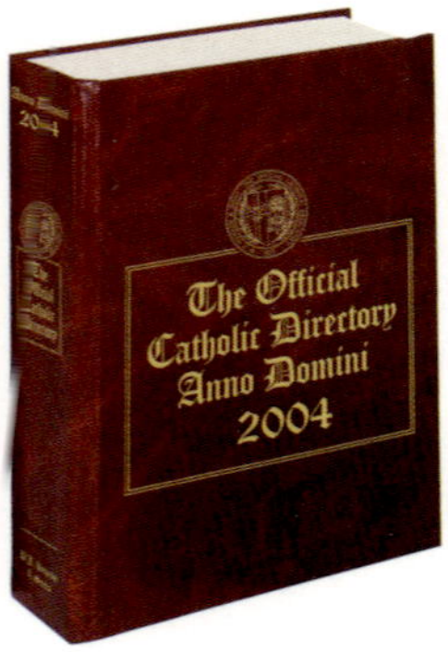

USAGE:
- **1-time use**
- **1-year license**

OUTPUT:
- **DISK - ASCII or DBF**
- **EMAIL - ASCII or DBF**
- **Labels**
- **Magnetic Tape**

GUARANTEE:
- **100% deliverability**

We are proud to serve the Catholic community in their fundraising efforts, and in promoting pastoral aids, publications, special projects, and other products and services that benefit the Catholic Church.

THE OFFICIAL CATHOLIC DIRECTORY · P. J. KENEDY & SONS · 1817

For more information contact Virginia Ricablanca.
Call: 1-800-473-7020, ext. 1203
Fax: 1-908-673-1189
E-mail: virginia.ricablanca@marquiswhoswho.com

OCDF404

P.J. Kenedy & Sons ◆ 562 Central Avenue, New Providence, NJ 07974 ◆ www.catholicdir.com

The Official Catholic Directory

Products & Services Guide

2004

P.J. Kenedy & Sons
121 Chanlon Road
New Providence, NJ 07974
(908) 673-1207

The Official Catholic Directory

PRODUCTS & SERVICES GUIDE

Table of Contents

NOTE: The ■ represents the end of a listing.

AUDIO & VIDEO

CLARETIAN TAPE MINISTRY
P.O. Box 19100
Los Angeles, CA 90019
Tel: 323-734-1234
Web Site: www.claretiantapeministry.org

Personnel:

Rev. John H Hampsch, C.M.F. ....Executive Director
Sr. Margaret Webster, P.B.V.M. ....Director

Type of Bussiness:

CTM distributes the many teachings of Fr. Hampsch which are available on audio tapes, CDs Videotapes and books. An outstanding resource for prayer groups, religious education teachers or for those who want to deepen their faith journey. If you would care to schedule Father for a presentation in your parish, please call (323) 734-1234. ■

Cassettes, Audio, & Video

CLARETIAN TAPE MINISTRY
P.O. Box 19100
Los Angeles, CA 90019
Tel: 323-734-1234
Web Site: www.claretiantapeministry.org

Personnel:

Rev. John H Hampsch, C.M.F. ....Executive Director
Sr. Margaret Webster, P.B.V.M. ....Director

Type of Bussiness:

CTM distributes the many teachings of Fr. Hampsch which are available on audio tapes, CDs Videotapes and books. An outstanding resource for prayer groups, religious education teachers or for those who want to deepen their faith journey. If you would care to schedule Father for a presentation in your parish, please call (323) 734-1234. ■

HOLY CROSS
FAMILY MINISTRIES

HOLY CROSS FAMILY MINISTRIES
Family Rosary
Family Theater Productions
Father Peyton Family Institute
Family Rosary International
518 Washington Street
North Easton, MA 02356
Tel.: 508-238-4095; Fax: 508-238-3953
Web Site: www.hcfm.org

Personnel:

Fr. John Phalen, C.S.C. .... President
Susan Wallace .... Director of External Relations
Beth Mahoney .... Mission Director

Type of Business:

Continuing the mission of our founder, Servant of God Father Patrick Peyton, C.S.C., Holy Cross Family Ministries serves Jesus Christ and His Church throughout the world by promoting and supporting the spiritual well-being of the family through products and programs. ■

BUSINESS & FINANCE

Changing Our World, INC.
FUNDRAISING • PHILANTHROPY • onPHILANTHROPY.COM

CHANGING OUR WORLD, INC.
420 Lexington Avenue, Room 2320
New York, NY 10170
Tel.: 212-499-0866; Fax: 212-499-9075
Web Site: www.ChangingOurWorld.com

Personnel:

Michael F Hoffman ....Chairman
Christopher D. Watson .....Executive Vice President/COO
John G. Fberst, Jr..........Special Advisor to the Chairman

Type of Business:

Experience. Commitment. Results. Changing Our World, Inc. is a pre-eminent American consulting firm designed to assist not-for-profit clients in achieving their goals in philanthropy. We help non-profit organizations raise more money through fund-raising strategies that address your specific needs. We are committed to the finest in parish campaigns, education, and health care fund-raising. ■

TRINITY FUNDRAISING CONSULTANTS, INC.
20 Edgar Drive
Smithtown, NY 11787-1604
Tel.: 866-296-3445; Fax: 631-269-3445
E-mail: tvfl@optonline.net
Web Site: www.trinityfundraising.com

Personnel:
Thomas V. Farrell .... President
Andrew J. White .... Executive Vice President
Gerard T. O'Connor .... Executive Vice President

Type of Business:
Trinity Consultants is a national Catholic fund-raising firm with offices all across the United States. We specialize in capital campaigns and stewardship programs for dioceses, parishes, schools, and other major institutions. Please call us for a no-cost appraisal of your fundraising potential. ■

Capital Campaigns

GUIDANCE IN GIVING, INC.
Full Service Stewardship, Development and Campaign Consultants
Michael R. Cusack, ... President and CEO
225 Snedecor Avenue, Bayport, NY 11705
888.757.5444 Fax 631.472.6109
Michael V. Goodwin, ... Executive Vice President
222 Harvard Oval, Freehold, NJ 07728
888.869.5522 Fax 732.683.0603
Joseph W. Zamorano, ... Executive Vice President
7504 Collins Ranch Terrace, San Diego, CA 92130
800.993.3335 Fax 858.484.0132
Christopher J. Cusack, ... Vice President
352 McConnell Avenue, Bayport, NY 11705
888.443.1522 Fax 631.472.4364
Curtis Neuschaefer, ... Vice President
3873 West Hibiscus Street, Weston, FL 33332
888.854.4480 Fax 954.384.0032
Robert A. Boegel, ... Regional Executive
P.O. Box 2070, Independence, MO 64055
816.719.6573
Carlos Proaño, ... Vice President
5439 Briercrest Avenue, Lakewood, CA 90713
866.874.4700 Fax 562.920.5523
Kelley P. Stupfel, ... Vice President
800 5th Avenue, Suite # 101 - 414, Seattle, WA 98104
800.734.8898 Fax 206.933.5923

Guidance In Giving, Inc is a national Catholic organization that provides full-time, on-site fundraising counsel to Catholic dioceses, parishes and schools. The firm specializes in Diocesan Capital Campaigns, Diocesan Annual Appeals, Feasibility and Planning Studies, Development Audits, Parish Capital Campaigns, Catholic High School and Elementary School Campaigns and the Implementation of Stewardship at the parish and diocesan level. Additionally, the firm is able to offer bilingual services. Executives of the firm have conducted successful campaigns since 1980. All members of the firm understand and respect the Mission of the Church.
Please contact one of the regional offices to have a member of the executive staff spend a day at your diocese, parish or school to discuss your development and stewardship efforts. When concluded, the firm will prepare an honest, objective appraisal of your program at no cost to your organization. Thank you for considering the services of Guidance In Giving, Inc. ■

KELLY

KELLY PROFESSIONAL FUNDRAISING CONSULTANTS
203 West 7th Street
Traverse City, MI 49684
Tel.: 800-567-4660
Fax: 231-922-8120
E-mail: kpfrc@aol.com
Web Site: www.kpfrc.com

Personnel:
Joe Kelly .... President & CEO
Al Kelly .... Executive Director (C.F.R.E.)
Paul Kelly .... Vice President, Operations
Lynne Green ..... Vice President, Campaign Development

Our Mission: To Serve Your Mission.
We want to be your Financial Partner.

Type of Business:
We offer a variety of innovative financial-growth services to help you remove the fiscal barriers to your mission:
- Capital Campaigns
- Stewardship Programs/Annual Renewals
- Major Gifts
- Comprehensive Appeal - our exclusive service
- Planned Giving
- Endowment Campaigns
- Feasibility Studies
- Development Office Establishment & Training

Call Kelly for a free appraisal of your financial future.
Services to Archdioceses, Dioceses, large and small Parishes, elementary and secondary schools, and consolidated school systems. We work nationally, we succeed locally.
Celebrating 35 years of service to the Catholic Community. ■

Church Registers

F.J. REMEY CO., INC.
121 Willis Avenue
Mineola, NY 11501
Tel.: (877)-FJ REMEY
Fax: (516)741-0523
Web Site: fjremey.com
E-mail: contactus@fjremey.com

Type of Business:
Serving the Catholic Church since 1921

Offering Envelope Programs	Collection Baskets
Bulk Collection Envelopes	Mass Cards
Church Record Books	Parish Office Forms
Tuition Supplies	Raffle Tickets
Certificates	Census Programs ■

Church System Software

J.S. PALUCH COMPANY, INC.
3825 North Willow Road
Schiller Park, IL 60176-2353
Tel.: 877-725-8241; 800-621-6732; Fax: 847-928-5812
E-mail: pcmsupport@jspaluch.com
Web Site: www.jspaluch.com; www.e-paluch.com

Personnel:
Janice Pacilio ....Director of Information Systems
Margaret "Mickey" Paluch ....CEO
William J. Rafferty................President

Type of Business:
The J.S. Paluch Company, Inc. has been dedicated to serving Catholic parishes, schools and communities across the United States since 1913. PCMS, the Paluch Church Management System, is an easy-to-use, Windows-based program containing census, contribution, ministry schedule, sacrament, and financial modeules. J.S. Paluch also offers affordable web site development and hosting and secure, no-hassle electronic contribution services. Together, we will simplify the administration of your parish and your communication with your parishoners. ■

NUVERB SYSTEMS INC.
29 Chesham Dr.
Toronto, ON M3M 1W8 Canada
Tel.: 888-479-4636; 866-688-3727
Fax: 416-245-8855
E-mail: info@nuverb.com
Web Site: www.nuverb.com; www.donarius.com

Personnel:
B. Louie Cordovado ....President

Business Type:
Nuverb Systems Inc has been marketing Donarius® **Donation Tracking Software** since 1998. It's the easy way for you to keep track of donors, donations, "gifts in kind", direct deposits and pledges. Donarius® prints tax receipts, church directories, labels/envelopes for mailings, bank deposits and a variety of reports. Donarius® exports/imports data to/from other software too. It includes a unique guarantee, with free software changes for a whole year.■

Computers & Software

LOGOS MANAGEMENT SOFTWARE
15500 W. Telegraph Rd., Building 15
Santa Paula, CA 93060
Tel.: 800-266-3311; FAX: 805-525-6161
E-mail: DSmith@Logoslbe.com
Web Site: www.logoslbe.com

Type of Business:
Logos Management Software provide quality Windows resources for use by churches, schools, and non-profit organizations. Logos efficiently handles essential records on people (census), contributions, and attendance (for Religious Education), plus true Fund Accounting, Facility Scheduling, and Sacramental Register. Logos programs are carefully designed, full-featured Windows systems. Taking advantage of the latest programming tools, Logos is so easy-to-use that even volunteers quickly master its many power features. Logos truly makes the computer a more effective resource for ministry. ■

Shelby Systems

Innovative Solutions. Infinite Possibilities.

SHELBY SYSTEMS
51 Germantown Court, Ste. 300
Cordova, TN 38018-7277
Tel.: 800-877-0222; 901-757-2372
Fax: 901-759-3682
E-mail: mktg@shelbyinc.com
Web Site: www.shelbyinc.com

Type of Business:

Software to manage parish and diocesan records, census tracking, religious education and RCIA classes, sacramental records, membership organizations, assessments. Transfer records electronically from parish to diocese. Web portal to census data. Online directory. Communication: personalized group e-mail, labels for families as well as individuals, automated phone messaging with attachments. True fund accounting. Manage Bishop's Appeal, memorial Masses, honorariums. Pledges for building projects. Clergy salary and stipends. Totally integrated: census, accounting records, and school/records and billing. ■

Consultants

CARGILL ASSOCIATES, INC.
4701 Altamesa Blvd.
Fort Worth, TX 76133
Tel.: 888-640-7020; Fax: 817-292-9631
Web Site: www.cargillassociates.com

Personnel:

Steve Cargill .... CEO
Pat Graham .... President, Church Division
Cade Garrison .... Director, Marketing

Type of Business:

Since 1976, Cargill Associates' faith-based program has raised over 3 billion dollars for churches, parishes, and other Christian causes. Cargill consultants work with parishes to craft programs to fit their spiritual needs. Other clients include universities, colleges, seminaries, hospitals, children's homes, retirement homes, and other institutions.

- Feasibility Studies
- Capital Campaigns
- Vision Workshops
- Financial & Spiritual Renewal
- Planned Giving
- Offertory Enhancement ■

Serving Catholic Parishes for Over Twenty-Two Years

22 Years

CUNNEEN PARISH FUNDRAISING SERVICES, INC.
24 Rossotto Drive
Hamden, CT 06514
Tel: 800.842.4488 Fax: 203.407.5858
Web Sites: www.CunneenFundraising.com;
www.PledgeRedemption.com
E-mail: info@cunneenfundraising.com

Personnel:

Frank J. Cunneen .... President
John F. Cunneen .... Executive Vice President
James F. Cunneen .... Vice President of Operations
Gerard E. Kenney .... Vice President
Raymond M. Coogan ....New England Director
Beth A. Lucia........................ Western New York Director
Kevin R. Mancini............................. Mid-Atlantic Director
Terri P. Murray.. National Director
Devna Roberts .... National Director
Daniel J. Wendt...............................Mid-Western Director

Type of Business:

Cunneen Parish Fundraising began serving Catholic parishes in 1981. Our approach is to provide the most effective, innovative, and creative fundraising campaigns for client Catholic parishes. All of our services: Offertory Enhancement, Stewardship, In-Pew Capital Campaigns, On-Site Capital Campaigns, Feasibility Studies, and Pledge Redemption are infused with a commitment to provide fundraising that is firmly grounded in the principles of Biblical Stewardship. Over the past 21years, Cunneen has assisted over 5,500 Catholic parishes in all 50 states and Canada.

Cunneen now offers full-service Annual Fund and Capital Campaign consulting to Catholic elementary schools and high schools as well as nursing homes, hospitals, and service organizations. ■

Guidance In Giving

GUIDANCE IN GIVING, INC.
Full Service Stewardship, Development and Campaign Consultants

Michael R. Cusack, ...President and CEO
225 Snedecor Avenue, Bayport, NY 11705
888.757.5444 Fax 631.472.6109
Michael V. Goodwin, ...Executive Vice President
222 Harvard Oval, Freehold, NJ 07728
888.869.5522 Fax 732.683.0603
Joseph W. Zamorano, ...Executive Vice President
7504 Collins Ranch Terrace, San Diego, CA 92130
800.993.3335 Fax 858.484.0132
Christopher J. Cusack, ...Vice President
352 McConnell Avenue, Bayport, NY 11705
888.443.1522 Fax 631.472.4364
Curtis Neuschaefer, ...Vice President
3873 West Hibiscus Street, Weston, FL 33332
888.854.4480 Fax 954.384.0032
Robert A. Boegel, ...Regional Executive
P.O. Box 2070, Independence, MO 64055
816.719.6573
Carlos Proaño, ...Vice President
5439 Briercrest Avenue, Lakewood, CA 90713
866.874 4700 Fax 562.920.5523
Kelley P. Stupfel, ...Vice President
800 5th Avenue, Suite # 101 - 414, Seattle, WA 98104
800.734.8898 Fax 206.933.5923

Guidance In Giving, Inc is a national Catholic organization that provides full-time, on-site fundraising counsel to Catholic dioceses, parishes and schools. The firm specializes in Diocesan Capital Campaigns, Diocesan Annual Appeals, Feasibility and Planning Studies, Development Audits, Parish Capital Campaigns, Catholic High School and Elementary School Campaigns and the Implementation of Stewardship at the parish and diocesan level. Additionally, the firm is able to offer bilingual services. Executives of the firm have conducted successful campaigns since 1980. All members of the firm understand and respect the Mission of the Church.
Please contact one of the regional offices to have a member of the executive staff spend a day at your diocese, parish or school to discuss your development and stewardship efforts. When concluded, the firm will prepare an honest, objective appraisal of your program at no cost to your organization. Thank you for considering the services of Guidance In Giving, Inc. ■

John V. McCarthy and Associates

16250 Northland Drive, Ste. 200
Southfield, MI 48075-5266
Development and Fundraising Consultants

Tel.: 800-444-1840 E-mail: jvmfund@aol.com
Fax: 248-552-0857 Website: jvmfundraising.com

Personnel:

Frank J. Krajca....................Marketing/Sales
Thomas A. Parker....................Operations
Joseph H. Schram....................Follow-Up Service

Type of Business:

Specialists in development and fund-raising: exclusively for Catholic parishes, dioceses, schools, and other institutions. Individual campaign timetables are designed to allow for the composition of the parish or institution. Since 1954, John V. McCarthy has been a major partner in the successful development and growth of ministries within the Catholic community through the application of proven principles of fund-raising. We charge a flat fee with no additional costs for travel or living expenses. Our assigned Account Executive is on site full-time, except for small parish campaigns, which can be designed on a consultation basis. We provide unmatched follow-up service for all clients.

Help is as close as our Website. If you feel that we can be of service to you in your development and fund-raising needs, just visit our Website and use the convenient response form to contact us. ■

A partner where "Your Priorities Become Ours."

Kirby Smith Associates, Inc.
Ministry of Church Finance

KIRBY-SMITH ASSOCIATES, INC.
5 Fawn Drive
Quarryville, PA 17566
Tel: 800-762-3996; 717-284-3100; Fax: 717-284-3659
E-mail: kirbysmith@aol.com
Web Site: www.kirbysmith.com

Personnel:

C. Eugene Musser....................President
Dale L. Bateman....................Executive Vice President

Our Mission is a ministry of church finance serving our Lord Jesus Christ by empowering Christian communities to better manage the stewardship of time, talent, and treasure

Type of Business:

We offer highly effective, spiritually-based stewardship and fund-raising services to Catholic organizations. We have helped more than 10,000 parishes, schools, and dioceses raise more than $3 billion. Founded in 1938, Kirby-Smith Associates offers on-site counseling, organizational guidance, comprehensive materials, and long-term consultation and stewardship training.

We offer a full range of services to meet your financial needs and support stewardship development:

Capital Campaigns	Budget Campaigns
Stewardship Appeals	Feasibility Studies
Planned Giving Programs	Strategic Planning
Stewardship Workshops	School Development

We tailor our fund-raising approach to meet your needs and budget.

National leaders in Catholic parish development.

Call for a free initial consultation. ■

trinity FUND RAISING CONSULTANTS

TRINITY FUNDRAISING CONSULTANTS, INC.
20 Edgar Drive
Smithtown, NY 11787-1604
Tel.: 866-296-3445; Fax: 631-269-3445
E-mail: tvfl@optonline.net
Web Site: www.trinityfundraising.com

Personnel:

Thomas V. Farrell....................President
Andrew J. White....................Executive Vice President
Gerard T. O'Connor....................Executive Vice President

Type of Business:

Trinity Consultants is a national Catholic fund-raising firm with offices all across the United States. We specialize in capital campaigns and stewardship programs for dioceses, parishes, schools, and other major institutions. Please call us for a no-cost appraisal of your fund-raising potential. ■

Donor Walls/ Trees of Life

ASCALON STUDIOS, INC.
DESIGNERS AND ARTISANS OF WORSHIP SPACES

ASCALON STUDIOS, INC.
115 Atlantic Ave.
Berlin, NJ 08009
Tel.: 1-888-280-5656 (toll-free); Fax: 856-768-3902
Email: info@ascalonstudios.com
Web Site: www.ascalonstudios.com

Personnel:

Eric J. Ascalon ....General Manager/ Inquiry Representative
David Ascalon ....President & Art/Design Director
Ronnie Ascalon ....Vice-President
Donn Hettel ....Stained Glass/Mosaic Studio Manager
Randy Himes ....Metalwork Studio Manager
Fred Kurz ....Studio Representative

Type of Business:

For three generations, Ascalon Studios has been committed to the creation of art & design for worship spaces throughout North America. Whether your project involves new construction or the renovation of an existing facility, our talented staff of in-house designers and artisans efficiently and elegantly undertake commissions in a variety of media and materials, in traditional as well as contemporary styles. The studio prides itself in its ability to develop close working relationships with organization leadership and architects. Ascalon Studios has received prestigious design awards, including from the American Institute of Architect's Interfaith Forum on Religion, Art & Architecture.

Projects range from comprehensive chapel and sanctuary design, to the design and fabrication of individual art items, including **STAINED GLASS WINDOWS, MOSAICS, CARVED GLASS, FACETED SLAB GLASS (DALLE DE VERRE), SCULPTURE, ARCHITECTURAL METALWORK** and **MEMORIALS**.

Additionally, Ascalon Studios can undertake meaningful, artistic donor recognition projects for your parish or organization, including **DONOR RECOGNITION WALLS** and **TREES OF LIFE** to assist in capital campaigns and major fundraising efforts. Please visit the studio's website for more information on Ascalon Studios and to see examples of its artwork. ■

Fund-Raising Counseling

KELLY

KELLY PROFESSIONAL FUNDRAISING CONSULTANTS
203 West 7th Street
Traverse City, MI 49684
Tel.: 800-567-4660
Fax: 231-922-8120
E-mail: kpfrc@aol.com
Web Site: www.kpfrc.com

Personnel:

Joe Kelly ....President & CEO
Al Kelly ....Executive Director (C.F.R.E.)
Paul Kelly ....Vice President, Operations
Lynne Green .....Vice President, Campaign Development

Our Mission: To Serve Your Mission.
We want to be your Financial Partner.

Type of Business:

We offer a variety of innovative financial-growth services to help you remove the fiscal barriers to your mission:

- Capital Campaigns
- Stewardship Programs/Annual Renewals
- Major Gifts
- Comprehensive Appeal - our exclusive service
- Planned Giving
- Endowment Campaigns
- Feasibility Studies
- Development Office Establishment & Training

Call Kelly for a free appraisal of your financial future.
Services to Archdioceses, Dioceses, large and small Parishes, elementary and secondary schools, and consolidated school systems. We work nationally, we succeed locally.
Celebrating 35 years of service to the Catholic Community. ■

RSI Ketchum
CATHOLIC SERVICES GROUP

RSI-KETCHUM, INC.
12270 Merit Dr., #900
Dallas, TX 75251
Tel.: 800-529-0803; Fax: 972-450-4477

Personnel:

Schuyler Lehman ....President
Dan Conway ....Senior Vice-President
Vito Napoletano..Vice-President

Type of Business:

RSI-Ketchum, Inc. provides to Catholic institutions uniquely tailored fund-raising campaigns with a spiritual stewardship perspective. The Catholic Services Group is dedicated to meeting the exclusive needs of Archdioceses, Dioceses, Parishes, schools and other Catholic organizations. ■

TRINITY FUNDRAISING CONSULTANTS, INC.
20 Edgar Drive
Smithtown, NY 11787-1604
Tel.: 866-296-3445; Fax: 631-269-3445
E-mail: tvfl@optonline.net
Web Site: www.trinityfundraising.com

Personnel:
Thomas V. Farrell .... President
Andrew J. White .... Executive Vice President
Gerard T. O'Connor .... Executive Vice President

Type of Business:
Trinity Consultants is a national Catholic fund-raising firm with offices all across the United States. We specialize in capital campaigns and stewardship programs for dioceses, parishes, schools, and other major institutions. Please call us for a no-cost appraisal of your fund-raising potential. ■

Fund-Raising Direct Mail

TRINITY DIRECT
10 Park Place
Butler, NJ 07405
Tel.: 973-283-3600
Fax: 973-283-3606
E-mail: john@trinitydirect.net
Personnel:
John P. Kehoe .... President
Bernadette Campbell .... Vice President
Dina Fanelli .... Vice President
Alicia Abels .... Account Executive

Type of Business:
Trinity Direct is a full-service list brokerage, list management company serving the Catholic community. Through its computer division, Trinity Information Systems, it offers in-house merge purge, list fulfillment, postal processing, NCOA, profiling, and data enhancement. As one of the leaders in Catholic direct mail fundraising, publication and catalog markets, the Trinity team can provide you with the best list and computer service for your next direct mail or annual giving program. ■

Fund-Raising Services

AMERICAN CITY BUREAU
33 West Higgins Rd.
Suite 520
South Barrington, IL 60010
Tel.: 800-786-GOAL (4625); Fax: 224-293-3012
E-mail: success@acb-inc.com
Web Site: www.acb-inc.com

Personnel:
Leslie Biggins Mollsen .... President
John M. Biggins .... Vice President

Type of Business:
Now celebrating its 90th year of service to Catholic dioceses, orders of men and women religious, basilicas, shrines, seminaries, hospitals, elementary schools, high schools, and colleges. American City Bureau is America's original fund-raising consulting firm. Since 1913, we have helped raise **billions** for our clients with services such as:

- Developmental/ Feasibility Studies
- Major Gift/Planned
- Communication Services
- Development Office Audits
- Capital Campaign Direction
- Gift/Endowment Development
- Video Productions
- Strategic Planning ■

CARGILL ASSOCIATES, INC.
4701 Altamesa Blvd.
Fort Worth, TX 76133
Tel.: 888-640-7020; Fax: 817-292-9631
Web Site: www.cargillassociates.com

Personnel:

Steve Cargill ....CEO
Pat Graham.......................President, Church Division
Cade Garrison ....Director, Marketing

Type of Business:

Since 1976, Cargill Associates' faith-based program has raised over 3 billion dollars for churches, parishes, and other Christian causes. Cargill consultants work with parishes to craft programs to fit their spiritual needs. Other clients include universities, colleges, seminaries, hospitals, children's homes, retirement homes, and other institutions.

- Feasibility Studies
- Capital Campaigns
- Vision Workshops
- Financial & Spiritual Renewal
- Planned Giving
- Offertory Enhancement ■

CATHEDRAL CORPORATION
Griffiss Technology Park
632 Ellsworth Road
Rome, NY 13441
Tel.: 315-338-0021; 800-419-8970; Fax 315-338-5874
E-mail: sales@cathedralstewardship.com
Web Site: www.cathedralstewardship.com

Personnel:

Marianne W. Gaige ....President and COO
Ronald P. Blakeman ....Vice President of Sales
Scott Dickan ....Sales Manager

Type of Business:

Cathedral Corporation delivers exceptional service to churches that excel in ministry. For more than six decades, Cathedral has delivered superior service, leadership and innovation in the creation, printing, personalization and high volume mailing of offering envelopes. Today Cathedral supports Catholic parishes across the nation with a full range of proven stewardship resources and electronic services for the Internet.

Mailed Offering Envelope Programs
Annual Boxed Sets
Increased Offering Campaigns
Youth Envelopes
Bulk Offering Envelopes
Envelope Recording & Reporting Service
ACT Electronic Offering Service
Online Real-Time List Maintenance
And More! ■

CCS
FUND RAISING

COMMUNITY COUNSELLING SERVICE (CCS)
461 Fifth Avenue
New York, NY 10017
Tel.: 800-223-6733; Fax: 212-967-6451
E-mail: ccsnewyork@ccsfundraising.com
Web site: www.ccsfundraising.com

Personnel:
William B. Hanrahan .... CEO
Robert Kissane .... President
Patrick W. Moughan .... Executive Vice President
Joseph F.X. Lee .... Senior Vice President

Type of Business:
CCS celebrates more than 55 years of service to the church. One of the largest, most widely recommended fund-raising firms in the world, CCS provides fund-raising counsel and management services to Catholic institutions worldwide. Our fund-raising methodology has helped to shape some of the most successful and complex fund-raising campaigns in the Catholic world, including the Archdioceses of Atlanta, Baltimore, Detroit, and New York, among many others. CCS successfully plans and manages fund-raising campaigns for dioceses, parishes, universities, colleges, high schools, hospitals, homes for the aged, social service agencies, seminaries, and religious communities. CCS offices are located in New York; Chicago; San Francisco; Baltimore; Atlanta; Boston; Fort Lauderdale; Washington, D.C.; Detroit; Seattle; Dublin; London; and Toronto. For an estimate of your potential, contact ccsnewyork@ccsfundraising.com or call (800) 223-6733. To learn more about CCS, visit our Web site at www.ccsfundraising.com. ■

COSGRIFF COMPANY
Share Our Tradition of Success

COSGRIFF COMPANY
209 South 19th Street
Omaha, NE 68102
Tel.: 800-456-9902; Fax: 402-341-8590
E-mail: cosgriff@alltel.net
Web Site: www.cosgriffco.com

Personnel:
Michael J. Fitzpatrick .... President & CEO
Vito Napoletano .... Vice President, Sales
Richard Spitler .... Vice President, Field Operations
M.J. Fitzpatrick, Jr. .... Director of Marketing
John Keeley .... Vice President, Sales Training
Katie Kiper .... Administration

Type of Business:
Established in 1960, The Cosgriff Company provides a time proven, successful approach to fund-raising and capital campaigns. We are specialists in leadership motivation, fund-raising education, donor participation strategy and low-key solicitation. We provide on-site direction and executive supervision during your campaign, as well as consultative service before and after the campaign with a total service program. The Cosgriff Company has been an outstanding leader in Catholic projects all around the country, having raised over $3 billion for our clients through the years. We can make it happen for you! ■

IN CATHOLIC FUND-RAISING, COSGRIFF IS #1 AND RISING!

Serving Catholic Parishes for Over Twenty-Two Years
22 Years

CUNNEEN PARISH FUNDRAISING SERVICES, INC.
24 Rossotto Drive
Hamden, CT 06514
Tel: 800.842.4488 Fax: 203.407.5858
Web Sites: www.CunneenFundraising.com; www.PledgeRedemption.com
E-mail: info@cunneenfundraising.com

Personnel:
Frank J. Cunneen .... President
John F. Cunneen .... Executive Vice President
James F. Cunneen .... Vice President of Operations
Gerard E. Kenney .... Vice President
Raymond M. Coogan .... New England Director
Beth A. Lucia .... Western New York Director
Kevin R. Mancini .... Mid-Atlantic Director
Terri P. Murray .... National Director
Devna Roberts .... National Director
Daniel J. Wendt .... Mid-Western Director

Type of Business:
Cunneen Parish Fundraising began serving Catholic parishes in 1981. Our approach is to provide the most effective, innovative and creative fundraising campaigns for client Catholic parishes. All of our services: Offertory Enhancement, Stewardship, In-Pew Capital Campaigns, On-Site Capital Campaigns, Feasibility Studies and Pledge Redemption are infused with a commitment to provide fundraising that is firmly grounded in the principles of Biblical Stewardship. Over the past twenty-one years, Cunneen has assisted over 5,500 Catholic parishes in all 50 states and Canada.

Cunneen now offers full-service Annual Fund and Capital Campaign consulting to Catholic elementary schools and high schools as well as nursing homes, hospitals and service organizations. ■

GRAHAM
GP
PELTON
CONSULTING

GRAHAM-PELTON CONSULTING, INC.
16 Maple Street, Ste. 5
Summit, NJ 07901
Tel.: 877-427-3616; Fax: 908-608-1520
Web Site: www.grahampelton.com
Personnel:
Craig Leach .... President, CEO
Lisa Grider .... Executive Vice President, COO
Craig Hall .... Vice President
Bill McLean ....Vice President
Bob Zaiser ....Vice President

Type of Business:
Graham-Pelton Consulting is a full-service fundraising and nonprofit management firm specializing in capital campaigns for religious, healthcare, educational and social service organizations. Graham-Pelton offers a team of seasoned fundraising and public relations executives who have served the Catholic community including Catholic colleges, universities, secondary schools, dioceses and parishes. Graham-Pelton provides residential campaign management as well as a full range of consulting services.
Washington, D.C. • Summit, NJ • Boston, MA. ■

JVM

John V. McCarthy and Associates
16250 Northland Drive, Ste. 200
Southfield, MI 48075-5266
Development and Fundraising Consultants
Tel.: 800-444-1840 E-mail: jvmfund@aol.com
Fax: 248-552-0857 Website: jvmfundraising.com
Personnel:
Frank J. Krajca..Marketing/Sales
Thomas A. Parker..Operations
Joseph H. Schram..............................Follow-Up Service

Type of Business:
Specialists in development and fund-raising: exclusively for Catholic parishes, dioceses, schools, and other institutions. Individual campaign timetables are designed to allow for the composition of the parish or institution. Since 1954, John V. McCarthy has been a major partner in the successful development and growth of ministries within the Catholic community through the application of proven principles of fund-raising. We charge a flat fee with no additional costs for travel or living expenses. Our assigned Account Executive is on site full-time, except for small parish campaigns, which can be designed on a consultation basis. We provide unmatched follow-up service for all clients.
Help is as close as our Website. If you feel that we can be of service to you in your development and fund-raising needs, just visit our Website and use the convenient response form to contact us. ■
A partner where "Your Priorities Become Ours."

KELLY

KELLY PROFESSIONAL FUNDRAISING CONSULTANTS
203 West 7th Street
Traverse City, MI 49684
Tel.: 800-567-4660
Fax: 231-922-8120
E-mail: kpfrc@aol.com
Web Site: www.kpfrc.com

Personnel:
Joe Kelly ....President & CEO
Al Kelly ....Executive Director (C.F.R.E.)
Paul Kelly ....Vice President, Operations
Lynne Green .....Vice President, Campaign Development
Our Mission: To Serve Your Mission.
We want to be your Financial Partner.

Type of Business:
We offer a variety of innovative financial-growth services to help you remove the fiscal barriers to your mission:
- Capital Campaigns
- Stewardship Programs/Annual Renewals
- Major Gifts
- Comprehensive Appeal - our exclusive service
- Planned Giving
- Endowment Campaigns
- Feasibility Studies
- Development Office Establishment & Training

Call Kelly for a free appraisal of your financial future.
Services to Archdioceses, Dioceses, large and small Parishes, elementary and secondary schools, and consolidated school systems. We work nationally, we succeed locally.
Celebrating 35 years of service to the Catholic Community. ■

Kirby Smith
Associates, Inc.
Ministry of Church Finance

KIRBY-SMITH ASSOCIATES, INC.
5 Fawn Drive
Quarryville, PA 17566
Tel: 800-762-3996; 717-284-3100; Fax: 717-284-3659
E-mail: kirbysmith@aol.com
Web Site: www.kirbysmith.com

Personnel:
C. Eugene Musser ....President
Dale L. Bateman ....Executive Vice President

Our Mission is a ministry of church finance serving our Lord Jesus Christ by empowering Christian communities to better manage the stewardship of time, talent, and treasure

Type of Business:
We offer highly effective, spiritually-based stewardship and fund-raising services to Catholic organizations. We have helped more than 10,000 parishes, schools, and dioceses raise more than $3 billion. Founded in 1938, Kirby-Smith Associates offers on-site counseling, organizational guidance, comprehensive materials, and long-term consultation and stewardship training.
We offer a full range of services to meet your financial needs and support stewardship development:

Capital Campaigns	Budget Campaigns
Stewardship Appeals	Feasibility Studies
Planned Giving Programs	Strategic Planning
Stewardship Workshops	School Development

We tailor our fund-raising approach to meet your needs and budget.
National leaders in Catholic parish development.
Call for a free initial consultation. ■

THE MARTIN J. MORAN CO.

Washington D.C. • San Diego
North Palm Beach • Boston

Catholic Fund-Raising Counsel

MARTIN J. MORAN CO.
One Pennsylvania Plaza
New York, NY 10119
Tel.: 212-736-9550
Fax: 212-736-7122

Type of Business:

The Moran Co. has been raising great amounts of money for its clients for a variety of needs. The key to success has been the design and conduct of a proven, time-tested Moran Co. Plan for generating both dollars and a high level of participation. ■

RUOTOLO
ASSOCIATES INC.

RUOTOLO ASSOCIATES INC.
Horizon Square
29 Broadway, Ste. 210
Cresskill, NJ 07626
Tel.: 800-786-8656; Fax: 201-568-8783
E-mail: info@ruotoloassoc.com; info@churchdivision.com
Web Site: www.ruotoloassoc.com

Personnel:

George C. Ruotolo, Jr., CFRE.......... Chairman and CEO
Joseph J. Caporale, CFRE .... President and COO
Theresa A. Shubeck .... Senior Vice President
Gene Aug., Ph.D. .... CFRE, Vice President
James Friend .... Director Church Division

Type of Business:

Our Mission: Ruotolo Associates Inc. is a working partner with non-profit organizations, providing them with the highest quality consulting for fund raising, stewardship, public relations and related management services through individualized creative strategies and solution. ■

SANDMAN DESIGNS, LLC
109 Old Post Road
Clinton, CT 06413
Tel: 888-736-2749
Fax: 860-664-9031

Personnel:
Sandra Raucci ....President
Fred Raucci ....Vice President Sales/Marketing

Type of Business:
We have the perfect way to **raise funds** for your Parish or **award gifts** for Stewardship. Your Church or Saint's Statue will be designed as an exact replica, in a lapel pin or magnet, made of beautiful Enamels and plated in 14 K Gold. They are presented on a 2" by 3.5" card including your text and sealed in a cellophane sleeve. Visit our web site at www.sandmandesigns.com to view examples and learn how to make Fund Raising Fun and Easy.
See our ad on page R 15. ■

TRINITY FUNDRAISING CONSULTANTS, INC.
20 Edgar Drive
Smithtown, NY 11787-1604
Tel.: 866-296-3445; Fax: 631-269-3445
E-mail: tvfl@optonline.net
Web Site: www.trinityfundraising.com

Personnel:
Thomas V. Farrell ....President
Andrew J. White ....Executive Vice President
Gerard T. O'Connor ....Executive Vice President

Type of Business:
Trinity Consultants is a national Catholic fund-raising firm with offices all across the United States. We specialize in capital campaigns and stewardship programs for dioceses, parishes, schools, and other major institutions. Please call us for a no-cost appraisal of your fund-raising potential. ■

WALSH & ASSOCIATES
1601 East Highway 13, Ste. 200
Burnsville, MN 55337
Tel.: 800-894-3863; Fax: 952-882-5270
E-mail: info@walshfundraising.com
Web Site: www.walshfundraising.com

Personnel:
Michael A. Walsh..President

Type of Business:
Walsh & Associates has been helping Catholic causes reach new heights since 1984 with our high quality, cost effective fund development and stewardship enhancement services. Our services include capital campaigns, feasibility/planning studies, stewardship education and enhancement efforts, planned giving programs, stewardship and development office establishment, and a variety of other services to help meet our clients' needs. So if you're ready to reach new heights in your fund development and stewardship efforts, give us a call. We'd be happy to help. ■

Fund-Raising Supplies

BARTON-COTTON
1405 Parker Road
Baltimore, MD 21227
Tel.: 800-638-4652; Fax: 800-807-2954

Personnel:
Denise J. Payne..........Vice President, Marketing & Sales

Type of Business:
For 75 years, Barton-Cotton has been proud to offer the finest selection of quality religious stationery products to the Catholic Clergy and Religious. Over 300 products are available including Mass cards, Sacramental certificates, Christmas and Easter cards, Mother's/Father's Day sets, Ordination/Jubilee products, Way of the Cross booklets, Rosary folders, Holy cards, Bulletins, Offering Envelopes, Bookmarks, and more. Products can be personalized with your name, church name, address, or special message. For a FREE catalog, call 800-638-4652. ■

CARROLL ART, INC.
710 N.E. 26th Street
Wilton Manors, FL 33305
Tel.: 800-876-4569; Fax: 954-561-4098

Personnel:
David Nagle .... President Designer
Liza Palmer .... Sales Manager
Wayne Palmer .... Sales Representative
Robert Perkins .... Sales Representative

Type of Business:
Carroll Art has been in business for 12 years. We design and custom build all types of plaques and memorials including the tree of life, plaques, recognition systems, church signs, donor plates, custom sculptures, and memorials are just a few of our products. We can provide you with the perfect fund-raising tool. ■

Cathedral CORPORATION

CATHEDRAL CORPORATION
Griffiss Technology Park
632 Ellsworth Road
Rome, NY 13441
Tel.: 315-338-0021; 800-419-8970; Fax 315-338-5874
E-mail: sales@cathedralstewardship.com
Web Site: www.cathedralstewardship.com

Personnel:
Marianne W. Gaige .... President and COO
Ronald P. Blakeman .... Vice President of Sales
Scott Dickan .... Sales Manager

Type of Business:
Cathedral Corporation delivers exceptional service to churches that excel in ministry. For more than six decades, Cathedral has delivered superior service, leadership and innovation in the creation, printing, personalization and high volume mailing of offering envelopes. Today Cathedral supports Catholic parishes across the nation with a full range of proven stewardship resources and electronic services for the Internet.

Mailed Offering Envelope Programs
Annual Boxed Sets
Increased Offering Campaigns
Youth Envelopes
Bulk Offering Envelopes
Envelope Recording & Reporting Service
ACT Electronic Offering Service
Online Real-Time List Maintenance
And More! ■

F.J. REMEY CO., INC.
121 Willis Avenue
Mineola, NY 11501
Tel.: (877)-FJ REMEY
Fax: (516)741-0523
Web Site: fjremey.com
E-mail: contactus@fjremey.com

Type of Business:
Serving the Catholic Church since 1921

Offering Envelope Programs	Collection Baskets
Bulk Collection Envelopes	Mass Cards
Church Record Books	Parish Office Forms
Tuition Supplies	Raffle Tickets
Certificates	Census Programs ■

Guidance In Giving

GUIDANCE IN GIVING, INC.
Full Service Stewardship, Development and Campaign Consultants
Michael R. Cusack, ... President and CEO
225 Snedecor Avenue, Bayport, NY 11705
888.757.5444 Fax 631.472.6109
Michael V. Goodwin, ... Executive Vice President
222 Harvard Oval, Freehold, NJ 07728
888.869.5522 Fax 732.683.0603
Joseph W. Zamorano, ... Executive Vice President
7504 Collins Ranch Terrace, San Diego, CA 92130
800.993.3335 Fax 858.484.0132
Christopher J. Cusack, ... Vice President
352 McConnell Avenue, Bayport, NY 11705
888.443.1522 Fax 631.472.4364
Curtis Neuschaefer, ... Vice President
3873 West Hibiscus Street, Weston, FL 33332
888.854.4480 Fax 954.384.0032
Robert A. Boegel, ... Regional Executive
P.O. Box 2070, Independence, MO 64055
816.719.6573
Carlos Proaño, ... Vice President
5439 Briercrest Avenue, Lakewood, CA 90713
866.874.4700 Fax 562.920.5523
Kelley P. Stupfel, ... Vice President
800 5th Avenue, Suite # 101 - 414, Seattle, WA 98104
800.734.8898 Fax 206.933.5923

Guidance In Giving, Inc is a national Catholic organization that provides full-time, on-site fundraising counsel to Catholic dioceses, parishes and schools. The firm specializes in Diocesan Capital Campaigns, Diocesan Annual

Appeals, Feasibility and Planning Studies, Development Audits, Parish Capital Campaigns, Catholic High School and Elementary School Campaigns and the Implementation of Stewardship at the parish and diocesan level. Additionally, the firm is able to offer bilingual services. Executives of the firm have conducted successful campaigns since 1980. All members of the firm understand and respect the Mission of the Church.
Please contact one of the regional offices to have a member of the executive staff spend a day at your diocese, parish or school to discuss your development and stewardship efforts. When concluded, the firm will prepare an honest, objective appraisal of your program at no cost to your organization. Thank you for considering the services of Guidance In Giving, Inc. ■

THE PRINTERY HOUSE
Conception Abbey · CONCEPTION · MISSOURI 64433

THE PRINTERY HOUSE
Conception Abbey
P.O. Box 12
Conception, MO 64433
Tel.: 800-889-0105; 660-944-3110
Fax: 888-556-8262
E-mail: sales@printeryhouse.org
Web Site: printeryhouse.org

Personnel:

Bro. William Buchholz, O.S.B ....Gen. Mgr., Director
Roy Haas.........................Drector of Sales and Marketing
Bro. Jeremiah Tuttle, O.S.B ....Marketing
Peggy Osborn ....Marketing
Bro. Michael Marcotte, O.S.B........................Art Director
Lee Coats ....Creative Director

Type of Business:

Manufacture and market Christian/Catholic Greeting cards and icons. Customized Christmas and other cards to enhance your development programs are our forte! The Printery House is a not-for-profit extension of the apostolate of the monks of Conception Abbey.

Call 800-889-0105 or fax us at 888-556-8262 for free samples, catalogs, and quantity discount schedules. ■

THE ARTIST'S HAND MAKES THE DIFFERENCE

SANFORD WERFEL- ARTIST

SANFORD WERFEL—ARTIST
425 Old Georges Road
North Brunswick, NJ 08902
Tel.: 800-443-3744; 732-297-1166
Fax: 732-297-7770
E-mail: werfelart@aol.com
Web Site: www.sanfordwerfelartist.com

Type of Business:

Since 1968, Mr. Werfel's sculptures have been helping parishes to INSPIRE and MOTIVATE GIVING through the use of his original sculptures. Building drives, capital or endowment funds, sacrificial giving, and tithing programs all benefit from using Donor Recognition Sculptures. Call or write for FREE INFORMATION. Included will be costs and designs as well as a "HOW-TO-USE" guide that tells how your parish can use sculpture to raise funds. Good art is forever.

Visit our Web site at www.SanfordWerfelArtist.com ■

Insurance

ABERCROMBIE, BURNS, MCKIERNAN & CO. INSURANCE, INC.
581 Post Road
Darien, CT 06820-1125
Tel.: 203-655-7468; Fax: 203-656-2540 ■

See our display ad on page R 19.

devoted to secure lives.

CATHOLIC KNIGHTS™

CATHOLIC KNIGHTS INSURANCE
1100 West Wells Street
Milwaukee, WI 53233
Tel.: 800-927-2547; Fax: 414-223-3201
Web Site: www.catholicknights.com

Personnel:
Daniel Steininger .... President
Allen Banoub .... Chief Marketing Officer
Betsy Ross-Bothe .... Marketing Manager

Type of Business:
Catholic Knights™ is a member-owned, not-for-profit fraternal benefit society founded in 1885. Members benefit from savings opportunities, security of lifestyle, sharing of gifts and talents and social outlets sponsored by the Catholic Knights, in addition to its financial services. With its home office in Milwaukee, Catholic Knights is the largest Catholic organization of its kind in Wisconsin.

Catholic Knights' members serve their communities by volunteering for a variety of programs and fundraising projects. In the past year alone, members volunteered more than 30,000 hours and raised more than $1 million through the Match Funds programs. ■

WALDORF & ASSOCIATES
Box 590
Huntington, NY 11743
Tel.: 800-275-9762; Fax: 631-424-3610
Web Site: www.cvwaldorf.com

Personnel:
Christopher V. Waldorf, Sr. .... C.E.O.
William G. Waldorf .... Partner
Stephen M. Waldorf .... Partner
Pamela J. Waldorf, Esq. .... Partner
Christopher V. Waldorf, Jr. .... Partner

Type of Business:
Waldorf & Associates, Inc. is a privately owned **insurance consultant and brokerage firm** specializing in the negotiating, marketing, and administration of property and casualty insurances for religious orders and affiliated institutions. The firm was founded in 1864 and continues as a private organization dedicated to this single class of clients. While our operation offers a wide variety of insurance services, we can best be described as a **risk management organization**. Our corporate mission is to assist our clients in identifying, controlling, and protecting against the risks presented by a modern and litigious society. ■

Investment Advisors

CBIS Christian Brothers Investment Services, Inc.

CHRISTIAN BROTHERS INVESTMENT SERVICES, INC.
90 Park Avenue, 29th Floor
New York, NY 10016-1301
Tel: 800-592-8890 or 212-490-0800
Fax: 212-490-6092
Web Site: www.cbisonline.com

Personnel:
Michael W. O'Hern, FSC .... President & CEO
Donald E. Platner .... Vice President

Type of Business:
Christian Brothers Investment Services, Inc. (CBIS) manages approximately $3.5 billion for Catholic organizations seeking to combine faith and finance through the responsible stewardship of Catholic assets. CBIS' combination of premier institutional asset managers, diversified product offerings, and careful risk-control strategies constitutes a unique investment approach for Catholic institutions and their fiduciaries. CBIS strives to integrate faith-based values into the investment process through a disciplined approach to socially responsible investing that includes principled purchasing (stock screens), active ownership strategies (proxy voting, dialogues, and shareholder resolutions), and community investing. The firm contributes a portion of all profits to support the Church's educational and social ministry.

For Catholic organizations seeking to unify faith and finance, CBIS welcomes the opportunity to serve you.

Please contact Don Platner at 800-592-8890 ext. 115 or Email: platner@cbisonline.com. ■

Investment Management

devoted to secure lives.

CATHOLIC KNIGHTS™

CATHOLIC KNIGHTS INSURANCE
1100 West Wells Street
Milwaukee, WI 53233
Tel.: 800-927-2547; Fax: 414-223-3201
Web Site: www.catholicknights.com

Personnel:
Daniel Steininger ....President
Allen Banoub ....Chief Marketing Officer
Betsy Ross-Bothe ....Marketing Manager

Type of Business:
Catholic Knights™ is a member-owned, not-for-profit fraternal benefit society founded in 1885. Members benefit from savings opportunities, security of lifestyle, sharing of gifts and talents, and social outlets sponsored by the Catholic Knights, in addition to its financial services. With its home office in Milwaukee, Catholic Knights is the largest Catholic organization of its kind in Wisconsin.

Catholic Knights' members serve their communities by volunteering for a variety of programs and fundraising projects. In the past year alone, members volunteered more than 30,000 hours and raised more than $1 million through the Match Funds programs. ■

Ministry of Church Finance

Cathedral CORPORATION

CATHEDRAL CORPORATION
Griffiss Technology Park
632 Ellsworth Road
Rome, NY 13441
Tel.: 315-338-0021; 800-419-8970; Fax 315-338-5874
E-mail: sales@cathedralstewardship.com
Web Site: www.cathedralstewardship.com

Personnel:
Marianne W. Gaige ....President and COO
Ronald P. Blakeman ....Vice President of Sales
Scott Dickan ....Sales Manager

Type of Business:
Cathedral Corporation delivers exceptional service to churches that excel in ministry. For more than six decades, Cathedral has delivered superior service, leadership and innovation in the creation, printing, personalization and high volume mailing of offering envelopes. Today Cathedral supports Catholic parishes across the nation with a full range of proven stewardship resources and electronic services for the Internet.

Mailed Offering Envelope Programs
Annual Boxed Sets
Increased Offering Campaigns
Youth Envelopes
Bulk Offering Envelopes
Envelope Recording & Reporting Service
ACT Electronic Offering Service
Online Real-Time List Maintenance
And More! ■

Mutual Funds

THE CATHOLIC FUNDS®
GIVING VOICE TO CATHOLIC VALUES℠

THE CATHOLIC FUNDS
1100 West Wells Street
Milwaukee, WI 53233
Tel.: 1-866-277-9921; Fax: 414-961-2155
Email: jpawlowski@catholicfunds.com
Website: www.CatholicFunds.com

Type of Business:

On behalf of its shareholders, The Catholic Funds actively promotes Catholic beliefs — a livable wage for all workers, no excessive compensation for executives, and independent corporate boards — to America's leading companies through shareholder resolutions, dialogue and correspondence with management, and voting. Consider giving voice to your Catholic values through The Catholic Funds.

An investment in The Catholic Equity Fund involves risk, the principal value and investment returns will fluctuate, and an investor's shares, when redeemed, may be worth more or less than their original cost. For the most recent month-end performance data, and to obtain a prospectus for The Catholic Equity Fund, which includes fees, expenses, potential risks and other information, call toll-free (866) 277-9921 or visit our website at www.CatholicFunds.com. You should read the prospectus carefully and consider the Fund's investment objectives, risks, charges and expenses carefully before you invest or send money. The Catholic Church has not sponsored or endorsed The Catholic Equity Fund nor approved or disapproved of the Fund as an investment. The Catholic Equity Fund is distributed through Catholic Financial Services Corporation, 1100 W. Wells St., Milwaukee, WI 53233, (414) 278-6550. Member NASD and SIPC. ■

Cemetery Mapping & Records

CEMETERY UPDATING SERVICES
P.O. Box 1234
Winona, MN 55987
Tel: 866-453-0811; 507-453-0811; Cell: 507-312-0811
Fax: 507-453-0811
Web Site: www.cemeteryrecordservices.com

Personnel:

Michael and Deborah Wiczek

Type of Business:

We are a family owned business with 14 years of experience improving cemetery records and maps.

We believe records should be accurate and so easy to understand that anyone can access the information quickly, efficiently and easily.

Benefits:

* Your records and maps will be computerized and hard copied
* New information can be easily added
* Owning a computer is not necessary
* On-site proofing is available

We do our best to give you fast, dependable service and to make your records the best and most efficient they can be. Call for options and prices. ■

CHURCH FURNISHINGS

ABBOtt

ABBOTT INC.
1515 Route 38
Cherry Hill, NJ 08002
Tel.: 800-522-2688; 856-662-6959; Fax: 856-665-5109
E-mail: info@churchsupplies.com
Web Site: www.churchsupplies.com

Personnel:

Daniel J. Castonguay .... President
Joseph F. McKeaney .... General Manager
Mary Ann Mitkus .... Business Administrator
John Scafidi .... Distribution
Michael Schwartz .... Government Liaison

Type of Business:

Purveyors of the Finest Vesture, Paraments, Statuary & Metalware since 1962. Unique and original creations, our specialty. Custom designs to complement your liturgical environment. Exclusive representatives of Slabbinck Master Collection & Original Collection. ■

TOUJOURS

ADRIAN HAMERS®
CHURCH INTERIORS

ADRIAN HAMERS, INC.
2 Madison Avenue
Larchmont, NY 10538
Tel.: 914-834-7780; Fax: 914-834-0712
Web Site: www.adrianhamers.com

Type of Business:

Custom designers and manufacturers of Sacred Vessels. Since 1887, the Hamers name has been synonymous with expert Silversmithing throughout the world in the field of Liturgical Art. Please contact us for those hard to find items, as we always have a large selection of Adrian Hamers Estate Collection pieces in stock. We have a large collection of antique church stainglass windows available (both full sets and individual). We are experts in: Church Interiors from design to execution, Renovations, Altars, Sacred Vessels, Gold and Silver Plating & Repairing, Appraisals, Tabernacles, Marble, Statuary, Woodwork & Woodcarving, Stained Glass, Pews & Chairs, Gold Leafing, Frescoes, Restoration, Trompe-l' oeuil, Wall Murals (repair and conservation cleaning), Ornamental Plaster, Heraldic Designs & Bishop Regalia. Please call us for a free 36-page Sacred Vessels color catalog, or our free 80-page color Woodcarvings catalog. ■

The Original Metal Folding Kneeler

Hamlin

ATWOOD-HAMLIN MANUFACTURING

ATWOOD-HAMLIN MFG., INC.
P.O. Box 578
Richmond, IL 60071
Tel.: 800-545-8964; Fax: 815-678-2130
E-mail: info@atwood-hamlin.com
Web Site: www.atwood-hamlin.com

Type of Business:

Since 1948, Atwood-Hamlin has been your church furnishing source for church with products like famous **Hamlin Folding Pew Kneelers** and replacement pads and parts, now with, guaranteed unbreakable legs and integrated rubber pads that never fall off. We offer. comfortable, non-slip **Pew-Form Cushions**. The only cushions designed for Catholics that don't need fastening to pews. Reversible styles available.

Our Catolic oriented chair line offers snap-on or permanent kneelers. Our solid oak, stacking pew-chairs top our seating line. Call for information. ■

BOTTI STUDIO OF ARCHITECTURAL ARTS, INC.

BOTTI STUDIO OF ARCHITECTURAL ARTS, INC.
919 Grove Street
Evanston, Illinois 60201
Tel.: 800-524-7211; 847-869-5933
Fax: 847-869-5996
E-mail: botti@ bottistudio.com
Web Site: www.bottistudio.com

East Coast Studio:
3104 S. Osprey Avenue
Sarasota, FL 33577
Tel.: 941-951-0978
Fax: 941-953-9078

West Coast Studio:
1038 N. Hwy. 101
Encinitas, CA 92024
Tel.: 760-753-0705
Fax: 760-753-0705

International Office: Agropoli, Italy, Nassau, Bahamas

Personnel:

Staff of 45. Includes internationally recognized ecclesiastic artists and designers working in conjunction with highly skilled glass and statuary craftspeople and artisans.

Ettore Christopher Botti .... Principal
Ethlyn Panzironi Botti .... Principal

Type of Business:

Since 1864, Botti Studio has specialized in serving the ecclesiastic environment through design, fabrication, delivery, and installation. Experts on staff in conservation, restoration, and repair provide a source for experienced project management — from conception through completion. Services include: **STAINED GLASS:** As custom designers and manufacturers, Botti artisans fabricate designs in stained, faceted, sandblasted, carved, and painted glass. **MARBLE:** Skilled craftsmen sculpt new or refurbish existing statuary, railings, baptismal fonts, and altars. **INTERIORS:** Complete renovations of interiors can be carefully and historically provided through plaster work, faux painting, gilding, stenciling, and graining. **MOSIAC:** Using state-of-the-art procedures, Botti can use preservation and restoration techniques to bring pieces back to their original beauty or create new custom installations. **CONSULTATON:** Preliminary-stage consultation can provide visualization of projects to aid in fund-raising and planning. **HISTORIC DISCOVERY:** Documentation and archival recording of existing sacred windows, marble, interior painting, and art is available. **STATUARY:** Working in wood, marble, or plaster, our designers are experts at restoration of aged, time-worn statuary and creation of custom ornamentation. ■

CARROLL ELECTRONICS, INC.
710 N.E. 26th Street
Wilton Manors, FL 33305
Tel.: 800-876-4569; Fax: 954-561-4098

Personnel:

David Nagle .... President
Liza Palmer .... Sales Manager
Bob Perkins .... Sales Representative
Donna Spencer .... Service Engineer

Type of Business:

Carroll Electronics has been in business for 20 years designing and building Electronic Votive Candle Stands for thousands of churches throughout the United States. ■

CHRISTIAN ART, INC.
567 52nd St.
West New York, NJ 07093
Tel.: 800-532-5413
Fax: 888-562-5413
Email: sales@christianartonline.com

Personnel:

Anthony and Terry Ferrer .... Principals

Type of Business:

Importer and distributor of largest inventory of Traditional Devotional Church Quality Statuary from Spain for over 40 years, specializing in unusual subjects and Spanish Devotions. Statues come in sizes 6 feet down to 8", with glass eyes.

We supply Church Gift Shops with gifts from Italy, Portugal, and China for Baptism, First Holy Communion and Confirmation, Rosaries, Crucifixes, Last Suppers, Nativity sets, inspirational gifts, Italian Sterling Silver by Salerni, and the Florentine Statuary Collection. ■

CENTURY ART-GLASS CO. INC.
16161 Westwoods Business Park
St Louis, MO 63021
Tel.: 800-888-8121, 636-227-5000
Fax: 636-527-2857

Personnel:
William A. Summer............President/Creative Director
Matthew V. Summer...Vice President/Master Craftsman

Type of Business:
Our family-owned stained glass firm founded in 1908, proudly maintains the distinguished tradition of spiritually inspired, conceptually designed stained glass artworks for churches, chapels, mausoleums, and other religious environments. Our attention to every detail in the design, structure, manufacturing and installation of stained, faceted, beveled, etched and other diverse art glass windows in traditional or contemporary styles is what our reputation is built on. We also offer a full line of restoration products and services, such as releading of bowed stained glass windows, repair of broken stained glass pieces, window frame restoration or replacement, stained glass domes and energy-efficient protective storm coverings.

Our Goal: To highlight and preserve the highest spiritual, artistic and craftsmanship capabilities in the art of stained glass. Custom designs available — please inquire. Estimates available nationwide without obligation. g

Excellence in Artistry Since 1889

CONRAD SCHMITT STUDIOS, INC.
2405 S. 162nd St.
New Berlin, WI 53151
Tel: 800-969-3033
262-786-3030
Fax:262-786-9036
E-mail: studio@conradschmitt.com
Web Site: www.conradschmitt.com

Personnel:
Heidi Gruenke Emery ....Vice Pres. & Marketing Dir.

Type of Business:
Since 1889, the family-owned Conrad Schmitt Studios has been privileged to provide decoration, restoration and artwork to enhance the worship environment of churches throughout the country, including more than twenty-five cathedrals.
For projects in the early stages, CSS offers consultations, design renderings, decorative samples and budgetary estimates for use in planning and fundraising. For historic restorations, our conservators investigate and document original paint colors and decoration to guide the restoration work.
CSS employs a permanent staff of highly experienced artists and artisans who conduct ornamental plaster work, decorative painting, stenciling, trompe l'oeil and interior and exterior gilding. CSS artists also continually create, conserve, restore and replicate stained glass, murals, mosaics and statuary. CSS has a 114-year history of service to the Catholic community and is dedicated to providing the finest ecclesiastical artwork that blends history and tradition with a growing and evolving faith.■

DOMUSDEI HOLY ART STUDIOS
FACTORY: Via dei Tulipani, 48 - 00040 CECCHINA DI ALBANO (RM) - ITALY
Tel: 011-39-06-9343369
Fax: 011-39-06-9344971
SHOWROOM: Via Scossacavalli 3/9 - 00193 ROMA - ITALY
Tel: 011-39-06-6868090
Fax: 011-39-06-9344971
Email: info@domusdei.it
m.delmonte@domusdei.it
Web site: www.domusdei.it

Personnel:
Alessandro Del Monte President
Massimiliano Del Monte......................Executive Director
Aldo Del Monte ....Assistant President

Type of Business:
Founded in 1963, Domusdei Studio has restored thousands of church interiors all over the world. Specializing in designing and manufacturing stained glass windows, mosaics, bronze and fiberglass statues, altars, bronze doors, lecterns, baptismal fonts, candlesticks, flower holders, and tabernacles
We are also experts in silver and gold plating and the restoration of wood and metal masterpieces. ■

HUMENICK LITURGICAL ARTS
14 Taylor Rd.
Santa Fe, NM 87508
Tel.: 505-690-7000
Web Site: www.humenick.catholic.org
E-mail: humenick@direcway.com

Personnel:
Mark Humenick

Type of Business:
Mark Humenick was first commissioned, in 1973, to design and fabricate liturgical essentials. Working closely with clergy, architects, and parish committees, this work has resulted in award-winning, one-of-a-kind pieces at quite reasonable costs.

From an individual piece to a complete, design-coordinated interior, our mediums include metal, wood, and stone. We design pieces that will be lasting yet flexible, with no commission being too small. Contact us to learn how we may assist you. ■

Hayes & Finch
LIMITED ESTABLISHED 1882

HAYES AND FINCH LIMITED
Hanson Road, Aintree
Liverpool, England, L97BP
Tel: 44(0)151-523-6303
Fax: 44(0)151-525-1246
E-mail: sales@hfltd.com
Web Site: www.hayesandfinch.com
Personnel:
John R. Mann, M.B.E.B.Sc. .... Managing Director
Mrs. Karen Reilly .... Marketing Director
Andrew Ware .... Sales Manager

Type of Business:
Founded in 1882, Hayes and Finch is a fourth generation family business, and the largest manufacturer and supplier of church-related goods in the United Kingdom. Based in Liverpool, England, we supply high quality church furnishings to customers around the world. Our specialist manufacturing center produces both standard and customer-specified products; our extensive range includes Candles, Altar Wine, Clerical Garments, Furniture, Brassware and Hallmarked Silverware. Our business is built on British craftsmanship of highest quality and exceptional customer service. ■

King Richard's
Religious Artifacts

KING RICHARD'S RELIGIOUS ARTIFACTS
P.O. Box 191027
Atlanta, GA 31119
Tel.: 877-248-3366
Fax: 770-455-1784

Personnel:
Rick Lair .... President
Sandra James .... Vice President
Scott Lair .... Sales and Marketing
Chris Roberts .... Web Master
Mike Coleman .... Warehouse & Shipping

Type of Business:
King Richard's Religious Artifacts specializes in providing churches and religious facilities with a complete spectrum of religious decorative items; including complete sets of stained glass windows, statuary, altars, stations, and all types of altar necessities. We travel throughout the United States selling and delivering merchandise, as well as completing all required work for purchasing and removal. ■

NATIONAL CHURCH GOODS ASSOCIATION
NCGA

NATIONAL CHURCH GOODS ASSOCIATION (NCGA)
800 Roosevelt Road
Building C Suite 20
Glen Ellyn, IL 60137
Tel: 630-942-6599
Fax: 630-790-3095
E-Mail: ncga@ncgaweb.com
Web Site: www.ncgaweb.com

Board of Directors:
Stephen Gaiser .... President
Ray Gerken .... Director
Robert Malhame .... Director
John F. Moroney .... Vice President
Mark Steigerwald .... Director
Richard Tonini .... Secretary
Dennis Ziegler .... Treasurer

Rick Church .... Executive Secretary
Jeff Church .... Association Manager

Type of Organization:
The National Church Goods Association (NCGA) is the international trade association of dealers and suppliers of church goods, religious articles, and published materials. NCGA has been providing members with exceptional benefits for 97 years. To find a reputable dealer near you go to www.ncgaweb.com and click on the dealer locater link, or call 630-942-6599. ■

PATRICK BAKER & SONS, INC.
1650 West Street
Southington, CT 06489
Tel.: 800-243-6385 Fax: 860-276-9438
72 Chambers Street
Fairfield, CT 06430
Tel: 203-366-5058 Fax: 203-334-8527
Web Site: www.churchgoods.com

Type of Business:
Patrick Baker & Sons, Inc. has been servicing the church and clergy for over 40 years. We are a family owned business committed to value with quality and service. We provide church furnishings, vestments, candles, altar breads, liners, refinishing and all your religious supplies with the highest guaranteed quality. Call or write for a catalog or visit us on our website at www.churchgoods.com. ■

RAMBUSCH LIGHTING
160 Cornelison Ave.
Jersey City, NJ 07304
Tel.: 201-333-2525; Fax: 201-433-3355
Web Site: www.rambusch.com

Personnel:
Edwin P. Rambusch ....President & C.E.O.
Martin V. Rambusch ....Chairman of the Board

Type of Business:
Since 1898, creating church interiors, liturgical furnishings, and art work. Fine restoration of church interiors. In-house studios and shops for designing and executing stained glass, church lighting systems, art metal work, and decorative painting. ■

Rohn & Associates Design, Inc.
Rolf R. Rohn, Principal
Consultants to Worship and Hospitality Environments

ROHN AND ASSOCIATES DESIGN, INC.
1113 Creedmoor Ave.
Pittsburgh, PA 15226
Tel: 412-561-1228; 800-245-1288
Fax: 412-561-1202
E-mail: rohnstudio@aol.com
Web Site: www.rohndesign.com

Personnel:
A full service team of U.S. and international artisans & craftmens.
Rolf R. Rohn ....Principal Consultant/Director/Artist
Kathleen L. Maglicco ....Principal Interior Design
Sister Janet Baxendale, S.C. ....Education

Type of Business:
Experience spanning 4 decades in renovation/restoration, conservation, and design of new worship environments. A valuable partner in over 1,300 commissions throughout the U.S., Canada and Europe.

We offer:

Alters	Tabernacles
Bronze/Stonework	Statuary
Artwork, multi-mediums	Baptismal Fonts
Ambo-Lecterns	Mosaics
Pews/Choirs	Lamps and Lighting
Liturgical Design and more...	

www.rohndesign.com. ■

SOUTHWEST POLISHING & PLATING
8110 Hillcroft Street
Houston, Texas 77081
Tel.: 713-777-3993
Fax: 713-777-3993

Personnel:
Peter Montes ....C.E.O.
Gary Montes ....G.M.
David Montes ....Sales Rep.

Type of Business:
Specializing in Gold and Silver Plating on monstrance, tabernacle, chalice, cibouria, candle sticks, thirable, incense boat, crucifix, holy water buckets, relic holders, sanctuary lamps, brass vases & stands. Painting & restoring of statues. We offer 24kt baked on lacquer. Family owned & operated since 1947, bounded & insured. All work is guaranteed. Serving the U.S.A, Canada and Mexico. All estimates are free. Recommendations are available from Bishops and Priests on request. ■

SWANSON CHRISTIAN PRODUCTS
1200 Park Ave.
Murfreesboro, TN 37129
Tel.: 800-251-1402
Fax: 866-431-1313
E-mail: sales@swansoninc.com
Web Site: www.swansoninc.com

Type of Business:
Since 1934, Swanson's has provided to the Christian community church supplies, De Colores, novelties, gifts anointing oils, men's ties, bible tabs, jewelry, lapel pins, stickers, pens, pencils, ribbons cups, olive wood, Jerusalem Products usher badges, bible covers, ball caps, back packs, wallets, lunch boxes, brief cases, puzzles, auto tags, auto frames, auto fish, key rings, bumper stickers, car flags, tambourines, puppets, highlighters, trophies, banners, and flags. ■

VANPOULLES
Church Furnishers
~ Est. 1908 ~

VANPOULLES LTD.
Telford Place, Crawley
West Sussex, RH10 1SZ, UK
Tel: +44 1293 590100
Fax: +44 1293 590115
E-mail: sales@vanpoulles.co.uk
Web Site: www.vanpoulles.co.uk

Type of Business:
Vanpoulles Ltd. is a family business, established nearly 100 years ago to provide the Church with all types of church requisites. We specialise in producing traditional English silverware and ecclesiastical garments, including chalices, ciboria, vestments, copes, stoles and altar frontals etc. Our sales department is available for friendly service and advice and current stock availability of all our product lines.
Please call, write or e-mail for a free catalogue. If visiting the UK please note our showrooms are conveniently positioned only a short distance from Gatwick Airport. ■

Vermont Church Supply Co.

VERMONT CHURCH SUPPLY CO.
676 Pine Street, P.O. Box 368
Burlington, VT 05401
Tel.: 800-451-3453; Fax: 802-862-5765
E-mail: vcs@together.net
Web Site: www.vermontchurchsupply.com

Personnel:
Neil Clark ....President

Type of Business:
Since our inception in 1946 by W. Barrett Clark and Doris Clark, Vermont Church Supply has offered the highest quality products and the best service to the Church and the Clergy. We have a wide range of products including Candles, Church Furniture, Metalware and Vestments. Our founders' Sons, Neil, John, Thomas and Robert, along with the third generation Anthony Clark, continue to provide services such as refinishing Sacred Vessels, Candlesticks and tabernacles and also the execution of hand carved wood and marble Statuary. Whether your needs are small or large, we can give the best personalized service to our customers. ■

Altars, Tabernacles, Etc.

ADRIAN HAMERS®
CHURCH INTERIORS

ADRIAN HAMERS, INC.
2 Madison Avenue
Larchmont, NY 10538
Tel.: 914-834-7780; Fax: 914-834-0712
Web Site: www.adrianhamers.com

Type of Business:
Custom designers and manufacturers of Sacred Vessels. Since 1887, the Hamers name has been synonymous with expert Silversmithing throughout the world in the field of Liturgical Art. Please contact us for those hard to find items, as we always have a large selection of Adrian Hamers Estate Collection pieces in stock. We have a large collection of antique church stainglass windows available (both full sets and individual). We are experts in: Church Interiors from design to execution, Renovations, Altars, Sacred Vessels, Gold and Silver Plating & Repairing, Appraisals, Tabernacles, Marble, Statuary, Woodwork & Woodcarving, Stained Glass, Pews & Chairs, Gold Leafing, Frescoes, Restoration, Trompe-l' oeuil, Wall Murals (repair and conservation cleaning), Ornamental Plaster, Heraldic Designs & Bishop Regalia. Please call us for a free 36-page Sacred Vessels color catalog, or our free 80-page color Woodcarvings catalog. ■

BOTTI STUDIO OF ARCHITECTURAL ARTS, INC.

BOTTI STUDIO OF ARCHITECTURAL ARTS, INC.

919 Grove Street
Evanston, Illinois 60201
Tel.: 800-524-7211; 847-869-5933
Fax: 847-869-5996
E-mail: botti@ bottistudio.com
Web Site: www.bottistudio.com

East Coast Studio:
3104 S. Osprey Avenue
Sarasota, FL 33577
Tel.: 941-951-0978
Fax: 941-953-9078

West Coast Studio:
1038 N. Hwy. 101
Encinitas, CA 92024
Tel.: 760-753-0705
Fax: 760-753-0705

International Office: Agropoli, Italy, Nassau, Bahamas

Personnel:

Staff of 45. Includes internationally recognized ecclesiastic artists and designers working in conjunction with highly skilled glass and statuary craftspeople and artisans.

Ettore Christopher Botti .... Principal
Ethlyn Panzironi Botti .... Principal

Type of Business:

Since 1864, Botti Studio has specialized in serving the ecclesiastic environment through design, fabrication, delivery, and installation. Experts on staff in conservation, restoration, and repair provide a source for experienced project management — from conception through completion. Services include: **STAINED GLASS:** As custom designers and manufacturers, Botti artisans fabricate designs in stained, faceted, sandblasted, carved, and painted glass. **MARBLE:** Skilled craftsmen sculpt new or refurbish existing statuary, railings, baptismal fonts, and altars. **INTERIORS:** Complete renovations of interiors can be carefully and historically provided through plaster work, faux painting, gilding, stenciling, and graining. **MOSIAC:** Using state-of-the-art procedures, Botti can use preservation and restoration techniques to bring pieces back to their original beauty or create new custom installations. **CONSULTATON:** Preliminary-stage consultation can provide visualization of projects to aid in fund-raising and planning. **HISTORIC DISCOVERY:** Documentation and archival recording of existing sacred windows, marble, interior painting, and art is available. **STATUARY:** Working in wood, marble, or plaster, our designers are experts at restoration of aged, timeworn statuary and creation of custom ornamentation. ■

Conrad Schmitt Studios Inc.

Excellence in Artistry Since 1889

CONRAD SCHMITT STUDIOS, INC.

2405 S. 162nd St.
New Berlin, WI 53151
Tel: 800-969-3033
262-786-3030
Fax:262-786-9036
E-mail: studio@conradschmitt.com
Web Site: www.conradschmitt.com

Personnel:

Heidi Gruenke Emery ....Vice Pres. & Marketing Dir.

Type of Business:

Since 1889, the family-owned Conrad Schmitt Studios has been privileged to provide decoration, restoration and artwork to enhance the worship environment of churches throughout the country, including more than twenty-five cathedrals.

For projects in the early stages, CSS offers consultations, design renderings, decorative samples and budgetary estimates for use in planning and fundraising. For historic restorations, our conservators investigate and document original paint colors and decoration to guide the restoration work.

CSS employs a permanent staff of highly experienced artists and artisans who conduct ornamental plaster work, decorative painting, stenciling, trompe l'oeil and interior and exterior gilding. CSS artists also continually create, conserve, restore and replicate stained glass, murals, mosaics and statuary. CSS has a 114-year history of service to the Catholic community and is dedicated to providing the finest ecclesiastical artwork that blends history and tradition with a growing and evolving faith.■

GRANDA LITURGICAL ARTS, INC.
939 W. North Ave. , Ste. 875
Chicago, IL 60622
Tel.: 800-425-0828; Fax: 312-944-9906
E-mail: usagranda@aol.com
Web Site: www.artegranda.com

Personnel:
Elia Rivera .... Director of Sales & Marketing

Type of Business:
GRANDA LITURGICAL ARTS, INC. is the USA sales and marketing office of Talleres de Arte Granda in Madrid, Spain. At our studio in Madrid, we have over one hundred artists, administrators, architects, designers, etc. dedicated to the design, production, and advancement of sacred art. Since 1891, we have been at the service of the Church combining modern techniques with artistic values to produce some of the world's finest sacred vessels, statuary, vestments, and church interiors. Please call us to request a complimentary catalog or to learn more about our custom design services. ■

INSPIRED ARTISANS, LTD.
816 W National Ave.
Milwaukee, WI 53204
Tel.: 414-672-9478; 888-442-9141
Fax: 414-672-9479
Web Site: www.inspiredart.com

Personnel:
Gianfranco Tassara .... President

Type of Business:
Inspired Artisans, since 1997 have been serving the church with quality Liturgical Art. Recent commissions are: **Baptismal Font**, Basilica of St. Josaphat, Milwaukee, WI. **Iconographic Tryptich**, Our Lady of Peace, North Augusta, SC. **Donors Memorial Wall**, St. Anne, Barrington IL. **Altar, Ambo and Tabernacle**, Bellarmine Jesuit Retreat, Barrington, IL. **Mosaic Murals**, St. Joseph, South Bend, IN. **Fiberglass Exterior Statue**, Sacred Heart, Waseca, MN. **Stained Glass**, Santa Marianita, Galapagos, Ecuador. **Ambry**, St. Raphael Cathedral, Madison, WI. **Grille**, Poor Clare Monastery, Lemont, IL. **Stations of the Cross**, St. Andrews, Ellensburg, WA. **Wood Sculpture**, Catholic Cemeteries, Denver, CO. **Terra Cotta**, Cardinal Bernardin School, Orland Park, IL. **Murals**, St. Augustine, Thomasville, GA **Tabernacle**, Holy Spirit, Montgomery, AL. **Processional Cross**, Pax Christi, Rochester, MN. **Marble Altar**, Our Lady of Lourdes, Harrisonville, MO. See our display ad under the **"Mosaics"** category or contact us for a complete list of past commissions, and brochures. Or visit our web page. ■

KING RICHARD'S RELIGIOUS ARTIFACTS
P.O. Box 191027
Atlanta, GA 31119
Tel.: 877-248-3366
Fax: 770-455-1784

Personnel:
Rick Lair .... President
Sandra James .... V.P.
Scott Lair .... Sales and Marketing
Chris Roberts .... Web Master
Mike Coleman .... Warehouse & Shipping

Type of Business:
King Richard's Religious Artifacts specializes in providing churches and religious facilities with a complete spectrum of religious decorative items; including complete sets of stained glass windows, statuary, altars, stations, and all types of altar necessities. We travel throughout the United States selling and delivering merchandise, as well as completing all required work for purchasing and removal. ■

RAMBUSCH

RAMBUSCH LIGHTING
160 Cornelison Avenue
Jersey City, NJ 07304
Tel.: 201-333-2525; Fax: 201-433-3355
Web Site: www.rambusch.com

Personnel:
Edwin P. Rambusch ....President & C.E.O.
Martin V. Rambusch ....Chairman of the Board

Type of Business:
Since 1898, creating church interiors, liturgical furnishings, and art work. Fine restoration of church interiors. In-house studios and shops for designing and executing stained glass, church lighting systems, art metal work, and decorative painting. ■

The Wood & Iron Factory
Architectural Woodwork, Furniture and Design

THE WOOD & IRON FACTORY
2495 Paseo de las Americas, Suite F
San Diego, CA 92154
Tel: 619-710-1660
Fax: 619-710-1662

Type of Business:
The Wood and Iron Factory is a manufacturer of custom designed pews, chancel furniture and ecclesiastical art. To complement our wood products, we also offer wrought iron, cast aluminum, bronze and stone.
We offer limitless design, material selection and artistic interpretation. Our products are custom designed to complement each individual church. We do not limit our clients with catalog furnishings.
Our 2nd and 3rd generation craftsmen take great pride in our reputation for superb quality at competitive prices. The Wood & Iron Factory is the proud manufacturer of pews and furniture at Our Lady of the Angels Cathedral in Los Angeles, California. ■

Announcement & Bulletin Boards

ATD-AMERICAN CO.

ATD-AMERICAN CO.
135 Greenwood Avenue
Wyncote, PA 19095-1396
Tel.: 888-283-2487; Fax: 800-283-7363
E-mail: american@atd.com; Web Site: www.atd.com

Personnel:
Bob Roche ....Marketing
Sal Catanese ....Sales

Type of Business:
For four generations, ATD-AMERICAN has supplied Furniture and Equipment to Churches, Organizations, and Institutions nationally and worldwide. Since 1931, it has been our tradition to deliver high quality products and personal service at the lowest competitive prices. ATD offers a wide range of products to meet all of the needs of your Church and School. Our comprehensive catalog includes the following: Announcement and Bulletin Boards, Audio-Visual Equipment, Classroom Furniture, Computer Furniture, Daycare Furniture, Display Cases, Folding Chairs, Folding Tables, Lecterns, Library Furniture, Office Furniture, Outdoor Equipment, Pews and Pulpit Furniture, Room Dividers and Partitions, Stacking Chairs, and Stages and Risers.
For a FREE Wholesale Furniture Catalog, call us toll-free 888-283-2487 or fax us at 800-283-7363. You can also visit our web site at www.atd.com or e-mail us at american@atd.com.
SPECIAL OFFER FOR CATHOLIC DIRECTORY SUBSCRIBERS: Mention offer code 6557 and receive a special 10% discount on your first order. ■

Antiques, Religious

TOUJOURS

ADRIAN HAMERS®
CHURCH INTERIORS

ADRIAN HAMERS, INC.
2 Madison Avenue
Larchmont, NY 10538
Tel.: 914-834-7780; Fax: 914-834-0712
Web Site: www.adrianhamers.com

Type of Business:
Custom designers and manufacturers of Sacred Vessels. Since 1887, the Hamers name has been synonymous with expert Silversmithing throughout the world in the field of Liturgical Art. Please contact us for those hard to find items, as we always have a large selection of Adrian Hamers Estate Collection pieces in stock. We have a large collection of antique church stainglass windows available (both full sets and individual). We are experts in: Church Interiors from design to execution, Renovations, Altars, Sacred Vessels, Gold and Silver Plating & Repairing, Appraisals, Tabernacles, Marble, Statuary, Woodwork & Woodcarving, Stained Glass, Pews & Chairs, Gold Leafing, Frescoes, Restoration, Trompe-l' oeuil, Wall Murals (repair and conservation cleaning), Ornamental Plaster, Heraldic Designs & Bishop Regalia. Please call us for a free 36-page Sacred Vessels color catalog, or our free 80-page color Woodcarvings catalog. ■

King Richard's
Religious Artifacts

KING RICHARD'S RELIGIOUS ARTIFACTS
P.O. Box 191027
Atlanta, GA 31119
Tel.: 877-248-3366
Fax: 770-455-1784

Personnel:
Rick Lair .... President
Sandra James .... Vice President
Scott Lair .... Sales and Marketing
Chris Roberts .... Web Master
Mike Coleman .... Warehouse & Shipping

Type of Business:
King Richard's Religious Artifacts specializes in providing churches and religious facilities with a complete spectrum of religious decorative items; including complete sets of stained glass windows, statuary, altars, stations, and all types of altar necessities. We travel throughout the United States selling and delivering merchandise, as well as completing all required work for purchasing and removal. ■

SN®
STADELMAIER

STADELMAIER-NIJMEGEN-HOLLAND
Lagelandseweg 64
6545 CG Nijmegen, Holland
Tel.: 011-31-24-379-1170; Fax: 011-31-24-379-1171
Web Site: www.stadelmaier.com
E-mail: info@stadelmaier.com or sales@stadelmaier.com

Personnel:
Mr. Aart J. Stadelmaier .... President
Mrs. Diny Poorts .... Secretary
Mrs. Franka Scholten .... Office Manager

For clergical shirts Stadelmaier – Southington – USA
136 Curtiss Street
Southington, CT 06489, USA
Tel.: 860-621-7471; Fax: 860-621-7607

Personnel:
Mrs. Sarah Gleeton .... Customer Service

Type of Business:
Stadelmaier, established in 1930 in the Netherlands, specialises in unique, high quality liturgical vesture and church goods; vestments, stoles, albs, dalmatics, copes, deaconstoles, altar and lecterncovers, tapestries and banners.
Fitting your church, your liturgy!
Our experienced design and production team is able to create innovative products from chasubles and stoles, clergy shirts and sweaters to stylish chalices, processional crosses, tabernacles and altars.
Also our Religious Antique Department with over 300 quality antique art pieces from Europe will be able to serve you well and enlighten your church space and your liturgy.
For almost 75 years quality in Liturgy has been our motto.
Please contact us for your local exclusive Stadelmaier dealer and / or receive our catalogue. ■

Art, Statuary, & Decorations

A J Bellomo
STUDIOS

THE BLACK FOREST BUILDING COMPANY

A.J. BELLOMO STUDIOS/THE BLACK FOREST CO.
310 Euclid
Mt. Clemens, MI 48043
Tel.: 586-954-4800
Fax: 586-954-4806
Email: blackfor@bignet.net
Web Site: www.ajbellomostudios.com

Personnel:
Anthony Bellomo ....President

Type of Business:
Anthony John Bellomo is a sculptor. He works in a wide variety of materials from wood to bronze to fibers, stone and living plant materials. Over the past twenty-five years he has developed the Black Forest Company. Black Forest is a group of artists and artisans, who along with Bellomo, design and build contemporary sculpture and furniture for liturgical spaces. He has developed a series of redwood sand carved exterior pieces for outdoor chapels and meditation gardens. Anthony, along with his team of dedicated crafts persons, pride themselves in listening to the individual communities, designing and building pieces to help make their worship a deeper experience. ■

ABBOTT

ABBOTT INC.
1515 Route 38
Cherry Hill, NJ 08002
Tel.: 800-522-2688; 856-662-6959; Fax: 856-665-5109
E-mail: info@churchsupplies.com
Web Site: www.churchsupplies.com

Personnel:
Daniel J. Castonguay ....President
Joseph F. McKeaney..............................General Manager
Mary Ann Mitkus.......................Business Administrator
John Scafidi ....Distribution
Michael Schwartz ....Government Liaison

Type of Business:
Purveyors of the Finest Vesture, Paraments, Statuary & Metalware since 1962. Unique and original creations, our specialty. Custom designs to complement your liturgical environment. Exclusive representatives of Slabbinck Master Collection & Original Collection. ■

FRAPPEZ TOUJOURS

ADRIAN HAMERS®
CHURCH INTERIORS

ADRIAN HAMERS, INC.
2 Madison Avenue
Larchmont, NY 10538
Tel.: 914-834-7780; Fax: 914-834-0712
Web Site www.adrianhamers.com

Type of Business:
Custom designers and manufacturers of Sacred Vessels. Since 1887, the Hamers name has been synonymous with expert Silversmithing throughout the world in the field of Liturgical Art. Please contact us for those hard to find items, as we always have a large selection of Adrian Hamers Estate Collection pieces in stock. We have a large collection of antique church stainglass windows available (both full sets and individual). We are experts in: Church Interiors from design to execution, Renovations, Altars, Sacred Vessels, Gold and Silver Plating & Repairing, Appraisals, Tabernacles, Marble, Statuary, Woodwork & Woodcarving, Stained Glass, Pews & Chairs, Gold Leafing, Frescoes, Restoration, Trompe-l' oeuil, Wall Murals (repair and conservation cleaning), Ornamental Plaster, Heraldic Designs & Bishop Regalia. Please call us for a free 36-page Sacred Vessels color catalog, or our free 80-page color Woodcarvings catalog. ■

Berlinger Company

THE BERLINGER COMPANY
2605 N. Sheridan Rd.
Peoria, IL 61604
Tel.: 309-688-1771
Fax: 309-688-9240
E-mail: info@theberlingercompany.com
Web Site: www.theberlingercompany.com

Personnel:
Michael Berlinger..President
Jeff Walters ....Accts Manager
Milton Pachers-Lay ....Sales .

Type of Business:
Church interior design and consultants
Interior restoration
New church designs
New liturgical whole goods—domestic and imported
Custom manufacturers
Liturgical Antiquities—domestic and imported ■

BOTTI STUDIO OF ARCHITECTURAL ARTS, INC.

BOTTI STUDIO OF ARCHITECTURAL ARTS, INC.
919 Grove Street
Evanston, Illinois 60201
Tel.: 800-524-7211; 847-869-5933
Fax: 847-869-5996
E-mail: botti@ bottistudio.com
Web Site: www.bottistudio.com

East Coast Studio:	*West Coast Studio:*
3104 S. Osprey Avenue	1038 N. Hwy. 101
Sarasota, FL 33577	Encinitas, CA 92024
Tel.: 941-951-0978	Tel.: 760-753-0705
Fax: 941-953-9078	Fax: 760-753-0705

International Office: Agropoli, Italy, Nassau, Bahamas

Personnel:
Staff of 45. Includes internationally recognized ecclesiastic artists and designers working in conjunction with highly skilled glass and statuary craftspeople and artisans.
Ettore Christopher Botti .... Principal
Ethlyn Panzironi Botti .... Principal

Type of Business:
Since 1864, Botti Studio has specialized in serving the ecclesiastic environment through design, fabrication, delivery, and installation. Experts on staff in conservation, restoration, and repair provide a source for experienced project management — from conception through completion. Services include: **STAINED GLASS:** As custom designers and manufacturers, Botti artisans fabricate designs in stained, faceted, sandblasted, carved, and painted glass. **MARBLE:** Skilled craftsmen sculpt new or refurbish existing statuary, railings, baptismal fonts, and altars. **INTERIORS:** Complete renovations of interiors can be carefully and historically provided through plaster work, faux painting, gilding, stenciling, and graining. **MOSIAC:** Using state-of-the-art procedures, Botti can use preservation and restoration techniques to bring pieces back to their original beauty or create new custom installations. **CONSULTATON:** Preliminary-stage consultation can provide visualization of projects to aid in fund-raising and planning. **HISTORIC DISCOVERY:** Documentation and archival recording of existing sacred windows, marble, interior painting, and art is available. **STATUARY:** Working in wood, marble, or plaster, our designers are experts at restoration of aged, timeworn statuary and creation of custom ornamentation. ■

CARROLL ART, INC.
710 N.E. 26th Street
Wilton Manors, FL 33305
Tel.: 800-876-4569; Fax: 954-561-4098

Personnel:
David Nagle .... President Designer
Liza Palmer .... Sales Manager
Wayne Palmer .... Sales Representative
Robert Perkins .... Sales Representative

Type of Business:
Carroll Art has been in business for 12 years. We design and custom build all types of plaques and memorials including the tree of life, plaques, recognition systems, church signs, donor plates, custom sculptures, and memorials are just a few of our products. We can provide you with the perfect fund-raising tool. ■

Century Art Glass Company Inc.

CENTURY ART-GLASS CO. INC.
16161 Westwoods Business Park
St Louis, MO 63021
Tel.: 800-888-8121, 636-227-5000
Fax: 636-527-2857

Personnel:
William A. Summer........ President/Creative Director
Matthew V. Summer ...Vice-President/Master Craftsman

Type of Business:
Our family-owned stained glass firm founded in 1908, proudly maintains the distinguished tradition of spiritually inspired, conceptually designed stained glass artworks for churches, chapels, mausoleums, and other religious environments. Our attention to every detail in the design, structure, manufacturing and installation of stained, faceted, beveled, etched and other diverse art glass windows in traditional or contemporary styles is what our reputation is built on. We also offer a full line of restoration products and services, such as releading of bowed stained glass windows, repair of broken stained glass pieces, window frame restoration or replacement, stained glass domes and energy-efficient protective storm coverings.

Our Goal: To highlight and preserve the highest spiritual, artistic and craftsmanship capabilities in the art of stained glass. Custom designs available — please inquire. Estimates available nationwide without obligation. ■

CHRISTIAN ART, INC.
567 52nd St.
West New York, NJ 07093
Tel.: 800-562-5413
Fax: 888-562-5413
Email: sales@christianartonline.com

Personnel:
Anthony and Terry Ferrer..................................Principals

Type of Business:
Importer and distributor of largest inventory of Traditional Devotional Church Quality Statuary from Spain for over 40 years, specializing in unusual subjects and Spanish Devotions. Statues come in sizes 6 feet down to 8", with glass eyes.
We supply Church Gift Shops with gifts from Italy, Portugal, and China for Baptism, First Holy Communion and Confirmation, Rosaries, Crucifixes, Last Suppers, Nativity sets, inspirational gifts, Italian Sterling Silver by Salerni, and the Florentine Statuary Collection. ■

Conrad Schmitt Studios Inc.
Excellence in Artistry Since 1889

CONRAD SCHMITT STUDIOS, INC.
2405 S. 162nd St.
New Berlin, WI 53151
Tel: 800-969-3033
262-786-3030
Fax:262-786-9036
E-mail: studio@conradschmitt.com
Web Site: www.conradschmitt.com

Personnel:
Heidi Gruenke Emery ....Vice Pres. & Marketing Dir.

Type of Business:
Since 1889, the family-owned Conrad Schmitt Studios has been privileged to provide decoration, restoration and artwork to enhance the worship environment of churches throughout the country, including more than twenty-five cathedrals.
For projects in the early stages, CSS offers consultations, design renderings, decorative samples and budgetary estimates for use in planning and fundraising. For historic restorations, our conservators investigate and document original paint colors and decoration to guide the restoration work.
CSS employs a permanent staff of highly experienced artists and artisans who conduct ornamental plaster work, decorative painting, stenciling, trompe l'oeil and interior and exterior gilding. CSS artists also continually create, conserve, restore and replicate stained glass, murals, mosaics and statuary. CSS has a 114-year history of service to the Catholic community and is dedicated to providing the finest ecclesiastical artwork that blends history and tradition with a growing and evolving faith.■

Linda Dabeau | *Studio, LLC.*

LINDA DABEAU/ DABEAU STUDIO
P. O. Box 10126
Albuquerque, New Mexico 87184
Tel/Fax: (505) 898-2227
Email: ldabeau@swcp.com
Web Site: www.ldabeau.com

Type of Business:
Linda Dabeau has been awarded both national and international commissions in sculpture. She works in multiple mediums, such as bronze, stone, fired clay, cast metals, glass, and wood. Her positive personal energy, combined with prodigious hand skills and her comprehension of the roots of Christianity, enable her to become a conduit for the vision of the parish, church authority, and architect. Through her highly disciplined work, Dabeau acts as a catalyst to create a bond within the whole community. Her multiple talents include design of liturgical furnishings such as alters, ambo, tabernacle, baptismal fonts, shrines, and stained glass. She is available to consult with parish communities.
Her materials are selected and utilized to create the best and most unique total visage of spirituality in the physical form. Dabeau's sculptures range from 24 inches to life size and monumental. Please contact the artist for commissions and limited editions that are available. ■

DAPRATO RIGALI STUDIOS, INC.

DAPRATO RIGALI STUDIOS, INC.
6030 N. Northwest Highway
Chicago, IL 60631
Tel.: 773-763-5511; Fax: 773-763-5522
Web Site: www.dapratorigali.com

Personnel:
John Rigali
Robert Rigali
Lisa Rigali Galvin
Mike Rigali

Type of Business:
Daprato Rigali Studios Inc. has been beautifying Churches in America since 1860.
Today we find the Rigali Family restoring and renovating the churches originally decorated by their Great-Grandfather, John E. Rigali; aware of his reputation to create spiritually moving environments with quality material and craftsmanship.
Some of their most recent jobs include: decoration and stained glass restoration at St. Mary of the Lake Seminary, Mundelein, IL; Marble renovation and decoration, St. Elizabeth's Mother House, Allegany, N.Y.; and General Contracting for complete renovation of St. Bernadette's Church, Rockford, IL.
The Daprato Rigali staff is equipped to take your project from start to finish. If you're interested in working with a fine interior design studio experienced in Ecclesiastical Artistries please call for consultation at no obligation. We deliver what we design. ■

EVERGREENE PAINTING STUDIOS, INC.

450 West 31st St., 7th Fl.
New York, NY 10001
Tel.: 212-244-2800
Fax: 212-244-6204

711 South Blvd., Ste. 7
Oak Park, IL 60302
Tel.: 708-358-1642
Fax: 708-358-1656

E-mail: info@evergreene.com
Web Site: www.evergreene.com

Personnel:

Jeff Greene .... President
Kim Lovejoy .... Director of Marketing
Gillian Randell .... Chief Fine Arts Conservator
Terry Vanderwell.......... Director of Restoration, Midwest
Anthony Kartsonas . Architectural Conservator, Midwest

Type of Business:

EverGreene is a full-service decorative arts studio committed to preserving the integrity of historic sacred spaces through conservation, restoration, and compatible new artwork and decoration. Services include investigation and analysis of original finishes; consultations, renderings, budgets and samples to support decision-making and capital campaigns; design of color schemes, architectural ornament and furnishings; and guidance on specifications. EverGreene's consistently high-quality work is performed by its staff of experienced project managers, professionally-trained conservators, fine artists, and craftsmen.

EverGreene's capabilities include all types of decorative painting, stenciling, gilding and trompe l'oeil; conservation, replication, and new design of murals and mosaics; ornamental plaster and scagliola; and allied crafts including wood and metal refinishing, interior stone cleaning, art glass, tile work, and other architectural arts.

Among EverGreene's current projects are St. Matthew's Cathedral in Washington, D.C., Sacramento Cathedral, and the Chapel at Sacred Heart Monastery, Lisle, Illinois. EverGreene's work over the last 25 years includes projects large and small in houses of worship around the country, including ten cathedrals, 26 state capitols, and hundreds of theaters, public buildings, commercial interiors and residences. ■

GOODEN ART STUDIO & ART CASTINGS

418 N. Main Street
Kingfisher, OK 73750
Tel: 405-375-3432 Toll free 888-278-8872
Fax: 405-375-5623
E-mail: goodenspecialty@juno.com

Personnel:

John Gooden .... Sculpture and Proprietor

Type of Business:

Sculpture of the Father Stanley Rother in Okarche, Oklahoma

Sculptor studio for commission artworks in a variety of media types. Gooden Art Studio can produce both large sculptural works and miniatures. Smaller pieces can be created economically for fund raising to support larger projects.

John has a strong portfolio of sculpted replicas of older works of art.

Guaranteed satisfaction with the quality of the sculpted image and the castings. ■

GRANDA LITURGICAL ARTS, INC.

939 W. North Ave. , Ste.875
Chicago, IL 60622
Tel.: 800-425-0828; Fax: 312-944-9906
E-mail: usagranda@aol.com
Web Site: www.artegranda.com

Personnel:

Elia Rivera .... Director of Sales & Marketing

Type of Business:

GRANDA LITURGICAL ARTS, INC. is the USA sales and marketing office of Talleres de Arte Granda in Madrid, Spain. At our studio in Madrid, we have over one hundred artists, administrators, architects, designers, etc. dedicated to the design, production, and advancement of sacred art. Since 1891, we have been at the service of the Church combining modern techniques with artistic values to produce some of the world's finest sacred vessels, statuary, vestments, and church interiors. Please call us to request a complimentary catalog or to learn more about our custom design services. ■

INSPIRED ARTISANS, LTD.

816 W National Ave.
Milwaukee, WI 53204
Tel.: 414-672-9478; 888-442-9141
Fax: 414-672-9479
Web Site: www.inspiredart.com

Personnel:

Gianfranco Tassara .... President

Type of Business:

Inspired Artisans, since 1997 have been serving the church with quality Liturgical Art. Recent commissions are: **Baptismal Font**, Basilica of St. Josaphat, Milwaukee, WI. **Iconographic Tryptich**, Our Lady of Peace, North Augusta, SC. **Donors Memorial Wall**, St. Anne, Barrington IL. **Altar, Ambo and Tabernacle**, Bellarmine Jesuit Retreat, Barrington, IL. **Mosaic Murals**, St. Joseph, South Bend, IN. **Fiberglass Exterior Statue**, Sacred Heart, Waseca, MN. **Stained Glass**, Santa Marianita, Galapagos, Ecuador. **Ambry**, St. Raphael Cathedral, Madison, WI. **Grille**, Poor Clare Monastery, Lemont, IL. **Stations of the Cross**, St. Andrews, Ellensburg, WA. **Wood Sculpture**, Catholic Cemeteries, Denver, CO. **Terra Cotta**, Cardinal Bernardin School, Orland Park, IL. **Murals**, St. Augustine, Thomasville, GA **Tabernacle**, Holy Spirit, Montgomery, AL. **Processional Cross**, Pax Christi, Rochester, MN. **Marble Altar**, Our Lady of Lourdes, Harrisonville, MO. See our display ad under the **"Mosaics"** category or contact us for a complete list of past commissions, and brochures. Or visit our web page. ■

IVAN WHILLOCK WOODCARVING & ART STUDIO
P. O. Box 611
Fairbault, MN 55021
Tel.: 507-332-9801
Fax: 507 332-2744
E-mail: cj@stubaidirect.com
Web Site: www.whillock.com

Type of Business:
Follow along as your vision becomes reality! Your parish can log on to our web site and watch as the commissioned work is created right before their very eyes. We can also suggest unique fund-raising ideas if needed. Ivan Whillock is a classically trained artist and traditional woodcarver. His work can be found throughout the world. He is excited to work with your group. Please view his portfolio at: www.whillock.com. ■

JFP
Inspirational Art
COLLECTION

JFP INSPIRATIONAL ART
27932 Valley Center Rd. #177
Valley Center, CA 92082
Tel: 800-690-1340
Fax: 760-749-6849
E-mail: art@inspirationalFilms.com
Web Site: www.JesusFilmArt.com

Personnel:
Robert Cording ....Manager

Type of Business:
JFP Inspirational Art produces and distrubutes quality Framed Art and Cards for Churches, Sunday Schools, home and office. Specially commissioned by The Jesus Film Project and inspired by the Jesus Film, the Fine Art beautifully represents scenes from the life of Christ...His Birth, His Teachings, His Passion.
Visually stunning, the new art depicts Jesus on the sea of Galilee ("Follow Me"); Jesus and the Children ("The Little Children"); Jesus in the wilderness ("A Light For My Path"); Portraits of Jesus ("The Prince of Peace", "The Light of the World'); Old World art, and many other scenes.
The digitally mastered framed lithographs of these traditional themes from the life of Jesus will be a meaningful and welcome addition to the Parish, School, or home. The Frame Art is double-matted with glass and is available in a variety of sizes (11 x 14"; 16 x 20"; 20 x 24" et.al.)
All **JFP Inspirational Art** images are also available as Fine Art Greeting Cards in "Assorted" and "Same" Card box sets. Each Greeting Card depicts a scene with an appropriate Scripture verse.
JFP Inspirational Art is a division of The Jesus Film Project, Paul Eshleman, Director. All proceeds from the purchase of JFP Inspirational Art are used for the Ministry of The Jesus Film Project and for the worldwide distribution of the Jesus Film. Translated into over 800 languages, the Jesus Film has been shown to millions of people in every country of the world.
Contact us for a complimentary JFP Inspirational Art Catalog & Price List. ■

King Richard's
Religious Artifacts

KING RICHARD'S RELIGIOUS ARTIFACTS
P.O. Box 191027
Atlanta, GA 31119
Tel.: 877-248-3366
Fax: 770-455-1784

Personnel:
Rick Lair .... President
Sandra James ....Vice President
Scott Lair .... Sales and Marketing
Chris Roberts ....Web Master
Mike Coleman ....Warehouse & Shipping

Type of Business:
King Richard's Religious Artifacts specializes in providing churches and religious facilities with a complete spectrum of religious decorative items; including complete sets of stained glass windows, statuary, altars, stations, and all types of altar necessities. We travel throughout the United States selling and delivering merchandise, as well as completing all required work for purchasing and removal. ■

MANZI
Studios
www.manzisculpture.com

MANZI STUDIOS
1112 N. Creek Rd.
Porter Corners, NY 12859
Tel: 518-893-2267
E-mail: manzisculpture@aol.com
Web Site: www.manzisculture.com

Personnel:
Walter Lape ....Sculptor
Janine Thomas...Research
Sharon Kingsbury ....Moldmaker
Jim Moulton ....Engineer, Steel

Type of Business:
MANZI STUDIO'S is a full service sculpture facility specializing in life sized figurative sculpture. Alice Manzi studied in New York as well as Pietrasanta, Italy. The studio does extensive research into individual prior to the creation of scale models. Ms Manzi has studied and taught human anatomy for over twenty years, and has distinguished herself in the field of sculpture through her remarkable ability to capture the personality of the individual. On the web at www.manzisculpture.com. ■

MAZZOLINI ARTCRACT CO., INC
1607 East 41st Street
Cleveland, OH 44103
Tel.: 888-437-4499; 216-431-7529
Fax: 216-431-7531
E-mail: mazzart@aol.com
Web Site: www.mazzart.com

Personnel:
John Mazzolini..President
Barbara Mazzolini ....Customer Service

Type of Business:
Largest Statue Manufacturer/Distributor in the United States of America. Established in 1904; Celebrating the 100th year in business. Importers of Statuary from Italy, Spain and Portugal. Specializes in Woodcarved, Bronze, Marble and Fiberglass figures. Deals direct with Studios. Domestically manufactures over 270 different religious subjects, from 9 in. through 5 ft., for Church, School, and Home use. Ships throughout the U.S.A. and Canada. Visit the Website at mazzart.com. ■

POGUE SCULPTURE STUDIO AND FOUNDRY
7670 Hwy. 1431 East
Marble Falls, TX 78654
Tel.: 877-267-2430
Fax: 830-693-7655
Email: dan@danpoguesculpture.com
Web Site: www.danpoguesculpture.com

Personnel:
Dan Pogue, Marti Pogue, & Doug Pogue

Type of Business:
Creating award winning bronze sculpture for over 35 years, Dan Pogue will help you choose from an existing portfolio of religious sculpture or create from photos of a specific person or using creative imagination. Dan will work with your parish to create just the right visual experience ranging up to monumental in size. He can provide you preliminary sketches and then create a marquette for you to approve. Having an in house art foundry, we can provide excellent creativity, quality, and cost effectiveness. See our Web site for a sample of monumental works and contact us for additional information. ■

RAMBUSCH LIGHTING
160 Cornelison Avenue
Jersey City, NJ 07304
Tel.: 201-333-2525; Fax: 201-433-3355
Web Site: www.rambusch.com

Personnel:
Edwin P. Rambusch ....President & C.E.O.
Martin V. Rambusch ....Chairman of the Board

Type of Business:
Since 1898, creating church interiors, liturgical furnishings, and art work. Fine restoration of church interiors. In-house studios and shops for designing and executing stained glass, church lighting systems, art metal work, and decorative painting. ■

SCULPTURE WORKS/BARRY WOODS JOHNSTON, SCULPTOR
2423 Pickwick Road
Baltimore, MD 21207
Tel: (410) 448-1945
Email: barry@sculptorjohnston.com
Website: www.sculptorjohnston.com

Type of Business:
Around 9/11, the Evangelical Christian Credit Union (ECCU) in Orange County, California, commissioned the “Faith, Hope, and Love” sculpture, 16’ high in bronze, pending additions. The City of Le Brea in Orange County locked horns with ECCU over these additions, and, although alluding to First Amendment violations, ultimately forced ECCU to abandon the commission and select an alternative artist. The sculpture, in full scale, recreates an arched "Needle," reminiscent of a once narrow gate into Jerusalem, prompting the parable “It is easier for a camel to pass through the eye of a needle than a rich man to enter the kingdom of heaven.” In the form of an eternal flame, a Judeo-Christian symbol of the presence of God, the “Needle” illustrates the lack of mortal baggage one can carry into heaven “within.” The three figures of faith, hope, and love mirror the positive yearnings of the soul for those qualities that can lead our world in a brighter future through enlightenment and compassion. Available in three sizes: 34”x 14”x 8.5”, 8.25’x 3.4’x 2.1’, 16.5’x 6.8’x 4.2’. ■

STUDIO PIETRO VINOTTI, WOODCARVER & SCULPTOR
P.O. Box 601
05340 U.S. 131 N.
Walloon Lake, MI 49796
Tel.: 231-535-2393; Fax: 231-535-2829
E-mail: ivinotti@torchlake.com

Type of Business:
Pietro is an artist who was trained in Italy and by now has 40 some years of experience in accomplishing beautiful artwork in any given style (barocque, gothic, renaissance) and in any desired material (wood, branze). His creations in wood with his exquisite touch to very fine detailing is astonishing. Pietro has an extraordinary talent for facial expressions. One has to see to believe. His studio is definitely a "Fine Art Studio." ■

Baptismal Fonts

BOTTI STUDIO OF ARCHITECTURAL ARTS, INC.

BOTTI STUDIO OF ARCHITECTURAL ARTS, INC.
919 Grove Street
Evanston, Illinois 60201
Tel.: 800-524-7211; 847-869-5933 Fax: 847-869-5996
E-mail: botti@ bottistudio.com Web Site: www.bottistudio.com

East Coast Studio:	*West Coast Studio:*
3104 S. Osprey Avenue	1038 N. Hwy. 101
Sarasota, FL 33577	Encinitas, CA 92024
Tel.: 941-951-0978	Tel.: 760-753-0705
Fax: 941-953-9078	Fax: 760-753-0705

International Office: Agropoli, Italy, Nassau, Bahamas

Personnel:
Staff of 45. Includes internationally recognized ecclesiastic artists and designers working in conjunction with highly skilled glass and statuary craftspeople and artisans.
Ettore Christopher Botti ....Principal
Ethlyn Panzironi Botti ....Principal

Type of Business:
Since 1864, Botti Studio has specialized in serving the ecclesiastic environment through design, fabrication, delivery, and installation. Experts on staff in conservation, restoration, and repair provide a source for experienced project management — from conception through completion. Services include: **STAINED GLASS:** As custom designers and manufacturers, Botti artisans fabricate designs in stained, faceted, sandblasted, carved, and painted glass. **MARBLE:** Skilled craftsmen sculpt new or refurbish existing statuary, railings, baptismal fonts, and altars. **INTERIORS:** Complete renovations of interiors can be carefully and historically provided through plaster work, faux painting, gilding, stenciling, and graining. **MOSIAC:** Using state-of-the-art procedures, Botti can use preservation and restoration techniques to bring pieces back to their original beauty or create new custom installations. **CONSULTATON:** Preliminary-stage consultation can provide visualization of projects to aid in fund-raising and planning. **HISTORIC DISCOVERY:** Documentation and archival recording of existing sacred windows, marble, interior painting, and art is available. **STATUARY:** Working in wood, marble, or plaster, our designers are experts at restoration of aged, timeworn statuary and creation of custom ornamentation. ■

Conrad Schmitt Studios Inc.
Excellence in Artistry Since 1889

CONRAD SCHMITT STUDIOS, INC.
2405 S. 162nd St.
New Berlin, WI 53151
Tel: 800-969-3033; 262-786-3030
Fax:262-786-9036
E-mail: studio@conradschmitt.com
Web Site: www.conradschmitt.com

Personnel:
Heidi Gruenke Emery ....Vice Pres. & Marketing Dir.

Type of Business:
Since 1889, the family-owned Conrad Schmitt Studios has been privileged to provide decoration, restoration and artwork to enhance the worship environment of churches throughout the country, including more than twenty-five cathedrals.
For projects in the early stages, CSS offers consultations, design renderings, decorative samples and budgetary estimates for use in planning and fundraising. For historic restorations, our conservators investigate and document original paint colors and decoration to guide the restoration work.
CSS employs a permanent staff of highly experienced artists and artisans who conduct ornamental plaster work, decorative painting, stenciling, trompe l'oeil and interior and exterior gilding. CSS artists also continually create, conserve, restore and replicate stained glass, murals, mosaics and statuary. CSS has a 114-year history of service to the Catholic community and is dedicated to providing the finest ecclesiastical artwork that blends history and tradition with a growing and evolving faith.■

DAPRATO RIGALI STUDIOS, INC.

DAPRATO RIGALI STUDIOS, INC.
6030 N. Northwest Highway
Chicago, IL 60631
Tel.: 773-763-5511; Fax: 773-763-5522
Web Site: www.dapratorigali.com

Personnel:
John Rigali; Robert Rigali
Lisa Rigali Galvin; Mike Rigali

Type of Business:
Daprato Rigali Studios Inc. has been beautifying Churches in America since 1860.
Today we find the Rigali Family restoring and renovating the churches originally decorated by their Great-Grandfather, John E. Rigali; aware of his reputation to create spiritually moving environments with quality material and craftsmanship.
Some of their most recent jobs include: decoration and stained glass restoration at St. Mary of the Lake Seminary, Mundelein, IL; Marble renovation and decoration, St. Elizabeth's Mother House, Allegany, N.Y.; and General Contracting for complete renovation of St. Bernadette's Church, Rockford, IL.
The Daprato Rigali staff is equipped to take your project from start to finish. If you're interested in working with a fine interior design studio experienced in Ecclesiastical Artistries please call for consultation at no obligation. We deliver what we design. ■

WATER STRUCTURES, LLC
60 Stard Road, P.O. Box 2938
Seabrook, NH 03874
Tel: 800-747-0168
Fax: 603-474-0629
E-mail: knoble@waterstructuresco.com
Web Site: www.waterstructuresco.com

Personnel:
Kim Noble ....Owner

Type of Business:
Water Structures, LLC is a fifteen-year-old company specializing in the fabrication of custom designed tile and natural stone baptismal fonts. Architects specify Water Structures, LLC built to design font shells because they have a unibodied fibercement structure, which prevents the baptismal fonts from leaking year after year.
Water Structures, LLC offers customized baptismal equipment packs featuring oderless water disinfecting equipment, quiet run pumps and heaters. ■

Bells, Carillons, Etc.

JOHN EACHUS & ASSOCIATES
P.O. Box 1119
East Ellijay, GA 30539
Tel: 800-788-0986
Web Site: www.bells-clocks.com

Type of Business:
Manufacturer's Representative For:
Atmosphere Stained Glass: www.atmospherestainedglass.com
Edon Corporation; Fiberglass columns, cornice, brackets, historic restoration
Fiberglass Unlimited: Steeples & Services
December Lights: Christmas Light Displays
Stewart Iron Works: Cast, forged, wrought iron fences, rails, gates, benches, fountains, urns, planters, post signs
The Verdin Co.:Bells Carillons, Chimes ■

McShane Bell Foundry
Established 1856
Americas last church bell manufacturer.

MCSHANE BELL FOUNDRY
400 Arundel Corp. Road, Building C
Glen Burnie, MD 21060
Tel.: 410-636-4390; 800-828-8397
Web Site: www.McShaneBell.com

Type of Business:
McShane offers the finest Church Bells, Peals, Chimes, and Carillons and Hand Bells the world has ever heard.
Since the establishment of the company in 1856, over 300,000 McShane bells have been installed. They ring from the towers of Cathedrals, Churches, Universities and Public Buildings throughout the world.

Offering the finest hand crafted:
- Single Bells
- Peals
- Chimes
- Carillons
- Hand Bells

Other McShane services:
- Electric Bell Ringing Systems
- Repairs
- Renovations
- Refurbishing
- Used Bells ■

Schulmerich Bells®
Electronic Carillons • Cast Bell Carillons
Handbells • MelodyChime® Instruments
Carillon Hill • PO Box 903 • Sellersville, PA • 18960-0903
215/257-2771 • 800/772-3557 • Fax: 215/257-1910
Homeoffice@Schulmerichbells.com
www.Schulmerichbells.com

SCHULMERICH BELLS
Carillon Hill
Sellersville, PA 18960-0903
Tel: 215/257-2771; 800-772-3557
Fax: 215/257-1910
E-mail: homeoffice@schulmerichbells.com
Web Site: www.schulmerichbells.com

You Can Hear It In Your Heart.

Since 1935, Schulmerich has been the leader in bells. Our electronic and cast bell instruments ring in churches around the world; our towers mark the presence of the faithful in communities everywhere; our handbells are played by more churches, choirs, schools, and institutions than any other.

We Offer:
- Electronic Carillons
- Handbells and MelodyChime® Instruments
- Cast Bronze Bells, Carillons, and Automatic Bell Ringers
- Clocks and Towers

We Provide:
- Cast Bell Restoration and Electrification
- Installation
- On-site Service
- Preventive Maintenance ■

VERDIN
SINCE 1842
BELLS • CARILLONS • CLOCKS

THE VERDIN CO.
The Verdin Company
444 Reading Road
Cincinnati, OH 45202
800-543-0488 (toll free)
Tel: 513-241-4010
Fax: 513-241-1855
E-mail: info@verdin.com
Web Site: www.verdin.com

Personnel:
Robert J. Verdin .... CEO
James R. Verdin .... President
David E. Verdin .... Vice President
Suzanne Sizer .... Marketing Manager

Type of Business:
America's Bell Ringer
For 162 years **The Verdin Company** has been the world's premier manufacturer of bells, carillons, clocks and all related products. Verdin distinguishes itself by blending innovative technology with superior customer service. We feature the same high quality bells and related products as our fathers and grandfathers before us. The Verdin legacy is the sound of bells ringing from more than 30,000 churches all over the world. ■

Benches, Lecterns, Pews

SAUDER®
MANUFACTURING COMPANY

SAUDER MANUFACTURING COMPANY
930 W. Barre Rd.
Archbold, OH 43502
Tel: 1-800-537-1530
Fax: 419-446-3697
Web Site: www.sauderworship.com

Personnel:
Virgil Miller .... President
Kelvin Friesen .... Vice President of Sales & Marketing
Bob Borcherdt .... Sales Manager

Type of Business:
Sauder Manufacturing Company is the leading U.S. manufacturer of church furniture, including pews, chairs, sanctuary furniture, and re-upholstery service. Upholstered and non-upholstered pews are available in a wide selection of styles, finish colors and fabrics. Chairs provide flexible seating and are available in a variety of styles to complement pews and the worship area decor.
Visit our web site at www.sauderworship.com. ■

The Wood & Iron Factory
Architectural Woodwork, Furniture and Design

THE WOOD & IRON FACTORY
2495 Paseo de las Americas, Suite F
San Diego, CA 92154
Tel: 619-710-1660
Fax: 619-710-1662

Type of Business:

The Wood and Iron Factory is a manufacturer of custom designed pews, chancel furniture and ecclesiastical art. To complement our wood products, we also offer wrought iron, cast aluminum, bronze and stone.

We offer limitless design, material selection and artistic interpretation. Our products are custom designed to complement each individual church. We do not limit our clients with catalog furnishings.

Our 2nd and 3rd generation craftsmen take great pride in our reputation for superb quality at competitive prices.

The Wood & Iron Factory is the proud manufacturer of pews and furniture at Our Lady of the Angels Cathedral in Los Angeles, California. ■

Bishop's Regalia

TOUJOURS

ADRIAN HAMERS®
CHURCH INTERIORS

ADRIAN HAMERS, INC.
2 Madison Avenue
Larchmont, NY 10538
Tel.: 914-834-7780; Fax: 914-834-0712
Web Site: www.adrianhamers.com

Type of Business:

Custom designers and manufacturers of Sacred Vessels. Since 1887, the Hamers name has been synonymous with expert Silversmithing throughout the world in the field of Liturgical Art. Please contact us for those hard to find items, as we always have a large selection of Adrian Hamers Estate Collection pieces in stock. We have a large collection of antique church stainglass windows available (both full sets and individual). We are experts in: Church Interiors from design to execution, Renovations, Altars, Sacred Vessels, Gold and Silver Plating & Repairing, Appraisals, Tabernacles, Marble, Statuary, Woodwork & Woodcarving, Stained Glass, Pews & Chairs, Gold Leafing, Frescoes, Restoration, Trompe-l' oeuil, Wall Murals (repair and conservation cleaning), Ornamental Plaster, Heraldic Designs & Bishop Regalia. Please call us for a free 36-page Sacred Vessels color catalog, or our free 80-page color Woodcarvings catalog. ■

STADELMAIER

STADELMAIER-NIJMEGEN-HOLLAND
Lagelandseweg 64
6545 CG Nijmegen, Holland
Tel.: 011-31-24-379-1170; Fax: 011-31-24-379-1171
Web Site: www.stadelmaier.com
E-mail: info@stadelmaier.com or sales@stadelmaier.com

Personnel:
Mr. Aart J. Stadelmaier ....President
Mrs. Diny Poorts ....Secretary
Mrs. Franka Scholten ....Office Manager

For clergical shirts Stadelmaier – Southington – USA
136 Curtiss Street
Southington, CT 06489, USA
Tel.: 860-621-7471; Fax: 860-621-7607

Personnel:
Mrs. Sarah Gleeton ....Customer Service

Type of Business:
Stadelmaier, established in 1930 in the Netherlands, specialises in unique, high quality liturgical vesture and church goods; vestments, stoles, albs, dalmatics, copes, deaconstoles, altar and lecterncovers, tapestries and banners. Fitting your church, your liturgy!
Our experienced design and production team is able to create innovative products from chasubles and stoles, clergy shirts and sweaters to stylish chalices, processional crosses, tabernacles and altars.
Also our Religious Antique Department with over 300 quality antique art pieces from Europe will be able to serve you well and enlighten your church space and your liturgy. For almost 75 years quality in Liturgy has been our motto. Please contact us for your local exclusive Stadelmaier dealer and / or receive our catalogue. ■

Electronic Candles

Candle Studios INCORPORATED

CANDLE STUDIOS
180 Division Ave.
Belleville NJ 07109
1-800-648-4229; Fax: 473-759-4299
E-mail: markjay@comcast.net
Web Site: www.candlestudios.com

Type of business:
Candle Studios is celebrating its fifth year in business, making stock and custom made candle stands in wood or wrought iron metal. Five years ago we introduced our flagship model, the Omega 2000. With many customers and hundreds of units now in the field we can say that we build the finest stand in the world, With exclusive features and options, such as Automatic select and set programmable timing, electronic soft touch lighting, offerings that are collected into a vandal proof safe, and beautiful imported crystal globes, this are all ads up to make our Omega 2000 the candle stand that is built for looks and built for life. ■

Interior Design & Restoration

Conrad Schmitt Studios Inc.

Excellence in Artistry Since 1889

CONRAD SCHMITT STUDIOS, INC.
2405 S. 162nd St.
New Berlin, WI 53151
Tel: 800-969-3033
262-786-3030
Fax:262-786-9036
E-mail: studio@conradschmitt.com
Web Site: www.conradschmitt.com

Personnel:
Heidi Gruenke Emery ....Vice Pres. & Marketing Dir.

Type of Business:
Since 1889, the family-owned Conrad Schmitt Studios has been privileged to provide decoration, restoration and artwork to enhance the worship environment of churches throughout the country, including more than twenty-five cathedrals.

For projects in the early stages, CSS offers consultations, design renderings, decorative samples and budgetary estimates for use in planning and fundraising. For historic restorations, our conservators investigate and document original paint colors and decoration to guide the restoration work.

CSS employs a permanent staff of highly experienced artists and artisans who conduct ornamental plaster work, decorative painting, stenciling, trompe l'oeil and interior and exterior gilding. CSS artists also continually create, conserve, restore and replicate stained glass, murals, mosaics and statuary. CSS has a 114-year history of service to the Catholic community and is dedicated to providing the finest ecclesiastical artwork that blends history and tradition with a growing and evolving faith.■

DAPRATO RIGALI STUDIOS, INC.

DAPRATO RIGALI STUDIOS, INC.
6030 N. Northwest Highway
Chicago, IL 60631
Tel.: 773-763-5511; Fax: 773-763-5522
Web Site: www.dapratorigali.com

Personnel:
John Rigali
Lisa Rigali Galvin
Robert Rigali
Mike Rigali

Type of Business:
Daprato Rigali Studios, Inc. has been beautifying Churches in America since 1860.

Today we find the Rigali Family restoring and renovating the churches originally decorated by their Great-Grandfather, John E. Rigali; aware of his reputation to create spiritually moving environments with quality material and craftsmanship.

Some of their most recent jobs include: decoration and stained glass restoration at St. Mary of the Lake Seminary, Mundelein, IL; Marble renovation and decoration, St. Elizabeth's Mother House, Allegany, N.Y.; and General Contracting for complete renovation of St. Bernadette's Church, Rockford, IL.

The Daprato Rigali staff is equipped to take your project from start to finish. If you're interested in working with a fine interior design studio experienced in Ecclesiastical Artistries please call for consultation at no obligation. We deliver what we design. ■

EverGreene Painting Studios, Inc.

EVERGREENE PAINTING STUDIOS, INC.

450 West 31st St., 7th Fl.	711 South Blvd., Ste. 7
New York, NY 10001	Oak Park, IL 60302
Tel.: 212-244-2800	Tel.: 708-358-1642
Fax: 212-244-6204	Fax: 708-358-1656

E-mail: info@evergreene.com
Web Site: www.evergreene.com

Personnel:
Jeff Greene ....President
Kim Lovejoy .... Director of Marketing
Gillian Randell .... Chief Fine Arts Conservator
Terry Vanderwell.......... Director of Restoration, Midwest
Anthony Kartsonas . Architectural Conservator, Midwest

Type of Business:
EverGreene is a full-service decorative arts studio committed to preserving the integrity of historic sacred spaces through conservation, restoration, and compatible new artwork and decoration. Services include investigation and analysis of original finishes; consultations, renderings, budgets and samples to support decision-making and capital campaigns; design of color schemes, architectural ornament and furnishings; and guidance on specifications. EverGreene's consistently high-quality work is performed by its staff of experienced project managers, professionally-trained conservators, fine artists and craftsmen.

EverGreene's capabilities include all types of decorative painting, stenciling, gilding and trompe l'oeil; conservation, replication, and new design of murals and mosaics; ornamental plaster and scagliola; and allied crafts including wood and metal refinishing, interior stone cleaning, art glass, tile work and other architectural arts.

Among EverGreene's current projects are St. Matthew's Cathedral in Washington, D.C., Sacramento Cathedral, and the Chapel at Sacred Heart Monastery, Lisle, Illinois. EverGreene's work over the last 25 years includes projects large and small in houses of worship around the country, including ten cathedrals, 26 state capitols, and hundreds of theaters, public buildings, commercial interiors and residences. ■

TAG GRANDA LITURGICAL ARTS

GRANDA LITURGICAL ARTS, INC.
939 W. North Ave. , Ste. 875
Chicago, IL 60622
Tel.: 800-425-0828; Fax: 312-944-9906
E-mail: usagranda@aol.com
Web Site: www.artegranda.com

Personnel:
Elia Rivera ....Director of Sales & Marketing

Type of Business:
GRANDA LITURGICAL ARTS, INC. is the USA sales and marketing office of Talleres de Arte Granda in Madrid, Spain. At our studio in Madrid, we have over one hundred artists, administrators, architects, designers, etc. dedicated to the design, production, and advancement of sacred art. Since 1891, we have been at the service of the Church combining modern techniques with artistic values to produce some of the world's finest sacred vessels, statuary, vestments, and church interiors. Please call us to request a complimentary catalog or to learn more about our custom design services. ■

Humenick Liturgical Arts

HUMENICK LITURGICAL ARTS
14 Taylor Rd.
Santa Fe, NM 87508
Tel.: 505-690-7000
Web Site: www.humenick.catholic.org
E-mail: humenick@direcway.com

Personnel:
Mark Humenick

Type of Business:
Mark Humenick was first commissioned, in 1973, to design and fabricate liturgical essentials. Working closely with clergy, architects, and parish committees, this work has resulted in award-winning, one-of-a-kind pieces at quite reasonable costs.

From an individual piece to a complete, design-coordinated interior, our mediums include metal, wood, and stone. We design pieces that will be lasting yet flexible, with no commission being too small. Contact us to learn how we may assist you. ■

Kosinski architecture
Liturgical Design Consultancy
Architecture
Historical Preservation
Construction Management

KOSINSKI ARCHITECTURE
1212 Main Street
Branford, CT 06405
Tel.: 203-488-7399
Fax: 203-483-7066

P.O. Box 23875
Ft. Lauderdale, FL 33307
Tel.: 954-627-6988
Fax: 954-627-6955
E-mail: keiarch@aol.com
Web Site: www.keiarch.com

Type of Business:
Kosinski has offered liturgical design and architectural design services for 35 years. Our extensive knowledge of liturgy and the history of church architecture allows us to provide our clients with exceptional services. Our full range of in-house professional services, including the design of all liturgical elements, interior design, and construction management, gives our clients a single point of contact for complete project delivery. We emphasize a team approach in which the client participates actively in design and project delivery. ■

RAMBUSCH

RAMBUSCH LIGHTING
160 Cornelison Avenue
Jersey City, NJ 07304
Tel.: 201-333-2525; Fax: 201-433-3355
Web Site: www.rambusch.com

Personnel:
Edwin P. Rambusch ....President & C.E.O.
Martin V. Rambusch ....Chairman of the Board

Type of Business:
Since 1898, creating church interiors, liturgical furnishings, and art work. Fine restoration of church interiors. In-house studios and shops for designing and executing stained glass, church lighting systems, art metal work, and decorative painting. ■

Lighting of Liturgical Space

CAPITOL LIGHTING DESIGN & RESTORATION
3269 Bloomington Hills Dr.
Ada, MI 49301
Tel: 616-844-5000; Fax: 616-784-7391
E-mail: sbayer@capitol-lighting.com
Web Site: www.capitol-lighting.com

Personnel:
Suzanne David ....President & Managing Director
Paul J. Bayer..................Co-Owner & Managing Director
Brenda Hoyt...............Consultant - Sales and Marketing
John Fuchs..Consultant - Design

Type of Business:
CAPITOL LIGHTING & RESTORATION is a company whose two new owners in association with its two founders and senior business associates have a history in the lighting industry dating back to the 1950's. It is a company that continues to be totally dedicated to supplying quality products and delivering them on schedule. Due to the background of its management, CAPITOL LIGHTING is sensitive to the needs of its clients. Designers need accurate drawings and information on time. Owners and contractors need adherence to schedules with equipment delivered in good condition and in conformance with approved coordination drawings.

CAPITOL LIGHTING & RESTORATION'S new owners, Suzanne David Bayer and Paul J. Bayer in association with it's founders, Brenda Hoyt and John Fuchs, bring their own and unique talents to the organization making it unrivaled in the lighting industry. CAPITOL LIGHTING'S associates include a metal sculptor with a Master of Fine Arts degree; another metal sculptor whose special interest is 19th century gas and oil lighting fixtures and their early conversion to electric usage; two foundry specialists, one for short custom production runs, the other for production runs using the traditional lost wax process. In this process, CAPITOL LIGHTING & RESTORATION is able to offer bronze chandeliers of extraordinary quality. CAPITOL LIGHTING & RESTORATION has also successfully modified existing and antique lighting equipment to make use of newly developed light sources. It continues to be a corporate philosophy to restore old fixtures rather than discard them and supply new replacements; it is a philosophy much appreciated by sensitive clients and continues to be adopted by its new owners.

In addition to restoring and supplying ornamental lighting equipment, CAPITOL LIGHTING & RESTORATION has carved a niche for itself in the design of special lighting equipment largely unavailable from other suppliers. Whether it is the design of ornamental exit signs or small accent lights to be installed in very limited spaces—CAPITOL LIGHTING & RESTORATION has always prevailed in the face of difficult design challenges.

It is safe to say that no other ornamental lighting fixture supplier can claim to have this type of expertise at its disposal or within its own corporate structure - it is a fertile environment conducive to the promotion and fulfillment of the design process. ■

RAMBUSCH

RAMBUSCH LIGHTING
160 Cornelison Avenue
Jersey City, NJ 07304
Tel.: 201-333-2525; Fax: 201-433-3355
Web Site: www.rambusch.com

Personnel:
Edwin P. Rambusch ....President & C.E.O.
Martin V. Rambusch ....Chairman of the Board

Type of Business:
Since 1898, creating church interiors, liturgical furnishings, and art work. Fine restoration of church interiors. In-house studios and shops for designing and executing stained glass, church lighting systems, art metal work, and decorative painting. ■

Liturgical Design

Humenick
Liturgical Arts

HUMENICK LITURGICAL ARTS
14 Taylor Rd.
Santa Fe, NM 87508
Tel.: 505-690-7000
Web Site: www.humenick.catholic.org
E-mail: humenick@direcway.com

Personnel:
Mark Humenick

Type of Business:
Mark Humenick was first commissioned, in 1973, to design and fabricate liturgical essentials. Working closely with clergy, architects, and parish committees, this work has resulted in award-winning, one-of-a-kind pieces at quite reasonable costs.

From an individual piece to a complete, design-coordinated interior, our mediums include metal, wood, and stone. We design pieces that will be lasting yet flexible, with no commission being too small. Contact us to learn how we may assist you. ■

Kosinski architecture
Liturgical Design Consultancy
Architecture
Historical Preservation
Construction Management

KOSINSKI ARCHITECTURE
1212 Main Street
Branford, CT 06405
Tel.: 203-488-7399
Fax: 203-483-7066

P.O. Box 23875
Ft. Lauderdale, FL 33307
Tel.: 954-627-6988
Fax: 954-627-6955
E-mail: keiarch@aol.com
Web Site: www.keiarch.com

Type of Business:
Kosinski has offered liturgical design and architectural design services for 35 years. Our extensive knowledge of liturgy and the history of church architecture allows us to provide our clients with exceptional services. Our full range of in-house professional services, including the design of all liturgical elements, interior design, and construction management, gives our clients a single point of contact for complete project delivery. We emphasize a team approach in which the client participates actively in design and project delivery. ■

Maison Bouvrier

MAISON BOUVRIER INC.
391 Hanlan Road, Woodbridge
Ontario, Canada L4L 3T1
905-851-1146 or 800-665-9895
Fax 905-851-7623
E-mail: bouvrier@maisonbouvrier.com
Web Site: www.maisonbouvrier.com

Personnel:
Kevin Bayne ....President
Janet MacDonald ....General Manager

Type of Business:
Maison Bouvrier has been in existence for over 130 years and is a world leader in weaving, creating and developing inspirational fabric designs of impeccable quality. Personalised attention is given to the needs of individual communities. All our artistic work is initially designed and created during a personal visit, thereby ensuring that the fabric used, the designs selected and the shapes chosen, fit perfectly into the worship space and enhance the visual liturgy. ■

Mosaics

ASCALON STUDIOS, INC.
DESIGNERS AND ARTISANS OF WORSHIP SPACES

ASCALON STUDIOS, INC.
115 Atlantic Ave.
Berlin, NJ 08009
Tel.: 1-888-280-5656 (toll-free); Fax: 856-768-3902
Email: info@ascalonstudios.com
Web Site: www.ascalonstudios.com

Personnel:
Eric J. Ascalon ....General Manager/ Inquiry Representative
David Ascalon ....President & Art/Design Director
Ronnie Ascalon ....Vice-President
Donn Hettel ....Stained Glass/Mosaic Studio Manager
Randy Himes ....Metalwork Studio Manager
Fred Kurz ....Studio Representative

Type of Business:
For three generations, Ascalon Studios has been committed to the creation of art & design for worship spaces throughout North America. Whether your project involves new construction or the renovation of an existing facility, our talented staff of in-house designers and artisans efficiently and elegantly undertake commissions in a variety of media and materials, in traditional as well as contemporary styles. The studio prides itself in its ability to develop close working relationships with organization leadership and architects. Ascalon Studios has received prestigious design awards, including from the American Institute of Architect's Interfaith Forum on Religion, Art & Architecture.
Projects range from comprehensive chapel and sanctuary design, to the design and fabrication of individual art items, including **STAINED GLASS WINDOWS, MOSAICS, CARVED GLASS, FACETED SLAB GLASS (DALLE DE VERRE), SCULPTURE, ARCHITECTURAL METALWORK** and **MEMORIALS**.
Additionally, Ascalon Studios can undertake meaningful, artistic donor recognition projects for your parish or organization, including **DONOR RECOGNITION WALLS** and **TREES OF LIFE** to assist in capital campaigns and major fundraising efforts. Please visit the studio's website for more information on Ascalon Studios and to see examples of its artwork. ■

BOTTI STUDIO OF ARCHITECTURAL ARTS, INC.

BOTTI STUDIO OF ARCHITECTURAL ARTS, INC.
919 Grove Street
Evanston, Illinois 60201
Tel.: 800-524-7211; 847-869-5933
Fax: 847-869-5996
E-mail: botti@ bottistudio.com
Web Site: www.bottistudio.com

East Coast Studio:	*West Coast Studio:*
3104 S. Osprey Avenue	1038 N. Hwy. 101
Sarasota, FL 33577	Encinitas, CA 92024
Tel.: 941-951-0978	Tel.: 760-753-0705
Fax: 941-953-9078	Fax: 760-753-0705

International Office: Agropoli, Italy, Nassau, Bahamas

Personnel:
Staff of 45. Includes internationally recognized ecclesiastic artists and designers working in conjunction with highly skilled glass and statuary craftspeople and artisans.
Ettore Christopher Botti ....Principal
Ethlyn Panzironi Botti ....Principal

Type of Business:
Since 1864, Botti Studio has specialized in serving the ecclesiastic environment through design, fabrication, delivery, and installation. Experts on staff in conservation, restoration, and repair provide a source for experienced project management — from conception through completion. Services include: **STAINED GLASS:** As custom designers and manufacturers, Botti artisans fabricate designs in stained, faceted, sandblasted, carved, and painted glass. **MARBLE:** Skilled craftsmen sculpt new or refurbish existing statuary, railings, baptismal fonts, and altars. **INTERIORS:** Complete renovations of interiors can be carefully and historically provided through plaster work, faux painting, gilding, stenciling, and graining. **MOSIAC:** Using state-of-the-art procedures, Botti can use preservation and restoration techniques to bring pieces back to their original beauty or create new custom installations. **CONSULTATON:** Preliminary-stage consultation can provide visualization of projects to aid in fund-raising and planning. **HISTORIC DISCOVERY:** Documentation and archival recording of existing sacred windows, marble, interior painting, and art is available. **STATUARY:** Working in wood, marble, or plaster, our designers are experts at restoration of aged, timeworn statuary and creation of custom ornamentation. ■

Conrad Schmitt Studios Inc.

Excellence in Artistry Since 1889

CONRAD SCHMITT STUDIOS, INC.
2405 S. 162nd St.
New Berlin, WI 53151
Tel: 800-969-3033
262-786-3030
Fax:262-786-9036
E-mail: studio@conradschmitt.com
Web Site: www.conradschmitt.com

Personnel:

Heidi Gruenke Emery ....Vice Pres. & Marketing Dir.

Type of Business:

Since 1889, the family-owned Conrad Schmitt Studios has been privileged to provide decoration, restoration and artwork to enhance the worship environment of churches throughout the country, including more than twenty-five cathedrals.

For projects in the early stages, CSS offers consultations, design renderings, decorative samples and budgetary estimates for use in planning and fundraising. For historic restorations, our conservators investigate and document original paint colors and decoration to guide the restoration work.

CSS employs a permanent staff of highly experienced artists and artisans who conduct ornamental plaster work, decorative painting, stenciling, trompe l'oeil and interior and exterior gilding. CSS artists also continually create, conserve, restore and replicate stained glass, murals, mosaics and statuary. CSS has a 114-year history of service to the Catholic community and is dedicated to providing the finest ecclesiastical artwork that blends history and tradition with a growing and evolving faith.■

DAPRATO RIGALI STUDIOS, INC.

DAPRATO RIGALI STUDIOS, INC.
6030 N. Northwest Highway
Chicago, IL 60631
Tel.: 773-763-5511; Fax: 773-763-5522
Web Site: www.dapratorigali.com

Personnel:

John Rigali	Lisa Rigali Galvin
Robert Rigali	Mike Rigali

Type of Business:

Daprato Rigali Studios, Inc. has been beautifying Churches in America since 1860.

Today we find the Rigali Family restoring and renovating the churches originally decorated by their Great-Grandfather, John E. Rigali; aware of his reputation to create spiritually moving environments with quality material and craftsmanship.

Some of their most recent jobs include: decoration and stained glass restoration at St. Mary of the Lake Seminary, Mundelein, IL; Marble renovation and decoration, St. Elizabeth's Mother House, Allegany, N.Y.; and General Contracting for complete renovation of St. Bernadette's Church, Rockford, IL.

The Daprato Rigali staff is equipped to take your project from start to finish. If you're interested in working with a fine interior design studio experienced in Ecclesiastical Artistries please call for consultation at no obligation. We deliver what we design. ■

EVERGREENE
PAINTING STUDIOS, INC.

EVERGREENE PAINTING STUDIOS, INC.

450 West 31st St., 7th Fl.
New York, NY 10001
Tel.: 212-244-2800
Fax: 212-244-6204

711 South Blvd., Ste. 7
Oak Park, IL 60302
Tel.: 708-358-1642
Fax: 708-358-1656

E-mail: info@evergreene.com
Web Site: www.evergreene.com

Personnel:

Jeff Greene ....President
Kim Lovejoy .... Director of Marketing
Gillian Randell .... Chief Fine Arts Conservator
Terry Vanderwell.......... Director of Restoration, Midwest
Anthony Kartsonas . Architectural Conservator, Midwest

Type of Business:

EverGreene is a full-service decorative arts studio committed to preserving the integrity of historic sacred spaces through conservation, restoration, and compatible new artwork and decoration. Services include investigation and analysis of original finishes; consultations, renderings, budgets and samples to support decision-making and capital campaigns; design of color schemes, architectural ornament and furnishings; and guidance on specifications. EverGreene's consistently high-quality work is performed by its staff of experienced project managers, professionally-trained conservators, fine artists and craftsmen.

EverGreene's capabilities include all types of decorative painting, stenciling, gilding and trompe l'oeil; conservation, replication, and new design of murals and mosaics; ornamental plaster and scagliola; and allied crafts including wood and metal refinishing, interior stone cleaning, art glass, tile work and other architectural arts.

Among EverGreene's current projects are St. Matthew's Cathedral in Washington, D.C., Sacramento Cathedral, and the Chapel at Sacred Heart Monastery, Lisle, Illinois. EverGreene's work over the last 25 years includes projects large and small in houses of worship around the country, including ten cathedrals, 26 state capitols, and hundreds of theaters, public buildings, commercial interiors and residences. ■

INSPIRED
I A
ARTISANS

INSPIRED ARTISANS, LTD.

816 W National Ave.
Milwaukee, WI 53204
Tel.: 414-672-9478; 888-442-9141
Fax: 414-672-9479
Web Site: www.inspiredart.com

Personnel:

Gianfranco Tassara ....President

Type of Business:

Inspired Artisans, since 1997 have been serving the church with quality Liturgical Art. Recent commissions are: **Baptismal Font**, Basilica of St. Josaphat, Milwaukee, WI. **Iconographic Tryptich**, Our Lady of Peace, North Augusta, SC. **Donors Memorial Wall**, St. Anne, Barrington IL. **Altar, Ambo and Tabernacle**, Bellarmine Jesuit Retreat, Barrington, IL. **Mosaic Murals**, St. Joseph, South Bend, IN. **Fiberglass Exterior Statue**, Sacred Heart, Waseca, MN. **Stained Glass**, Santa Marianita, Galapagos, Ecuador. **Ambry**, St. Raphael Cathedral, Madison, WI. **Grille**, Poor Clare Monastery, Lemont, IL. **Stations of the Cross**, St. Andrews, Ellensburg, WA. **Wood Sculpture**, Catholic Cemeteries, Denver, CO. **Terra Cotta**, Cardinal Bernardin School, Orland Park, IL. **Murals**, St. Augustine, Thomasville, GA **Tabernacle**, Holy Spirit, Montgomery, AL. **Processional Cross**, Pax Christi, Rochester, MN. **Marble Altar**, Our Lady of Lourdes, Harrisonville, MO. See our display ad under the **"Mosaics"** category or contact us for a complete list of past commissions, and brochures. Or visit our web page. ■

INSPIRED
I A
ARTISANS

RAMBUSCH

RAMBUSCH LIGHTING
160 Cornelison Avenue
Jersey City, NJ 07304
Tel.: 201-333-2525; Fax: 201-433-3355
Web Site: www.rambusch.com

Personnel:
Edwin P. Rambusch ....President & C.E.O.
Martin V. Rambusch ....Chairman of the Board

Type of Business:
Since 1898, creating church interiors, liturgical furnishings, and art work. Fine restoration of church interiors. In-house studios and shops for designing and executing stained glass, church lighting systems, art metal work, and decorative painting. ■

UNIVERSAL ART STUDIO

UNIVERSAL ART STUDIO
67 Mountain Spring Drive
Sparta, NJ 07871
Tel.: 973-726-0835
Fax: 973-729-1189

Personnel:
Yuri Mironoff .... Owner
Rita Mironoff ....Owner/ Designer

Type of Business:
Our crew is compact and capable of dealing with practically every aspect of restoration, renovation and repair work - we subcontract very little. We do not run more than one project at a time. We take no interruptions and deliver on time. ■

Organs & Pianos

ORGAN CLEARING HOUSE

THE ORGAN CLEARING HOUSE, L.L.C.
P.O. Box 219
Lexington, MA 02420
Tel.: 866-827-3055
E-mail: john@organclearinghouse.com
Web Site: www.organclearinghouse.com

Personnel:
John Bishop...Executive Director
Amory Atkin ....President
Joshua Wood...Vice President

Type of Business:
We are purveyors of existing pipe organs of high quality and distinction which are made available through church closings and mergers. Since 1959, we have arranged for the relocation and renovation of more than 2000 pipe organs. Restored, these instruments are generally available for around half the cost of an equivalent new organ. Currently we have more than 200 organs available for sale. Contact us if you wish to buy or sell. ■

RODGERS®

RODGERS INSTRUMENTS, L.L.C.
1300 N.E. 25th Avenue
Hillsboro, OR 97124
Tel.: 503-648-4181; Fax: 503-681-0444
Web Site: www.rodgersinstruments.com

Personnel:
Dennis Houlihan ....President
Lloyd Robbins ....Executive Vice President
Chad Perry ....Director of Sales & Marketing

Type of Business:
Rodgers is the world leader in stereo imaged church organs and pipe/digital organs. Rodgers is a member of the Roland Group of musical instrument companies headed by Roland Corporation, world leader in stereophonic digital musical instrument technologies.
Rodgers organs can be installed as: -digital church organs -pipe/digital church organs -replacement consoles on your existing pipe organ
Rodgers organs have been installed in thousands of Roman Catholic parishes, basilicas, shrines, colleges and religious houses throughout the world. Rodgers organs have also been placed in over 20 cathedrals including the Cathedral Church of the Immaculate Conception - Moscow, Russia, St. Mary's Cathedral - Miami, Florida, Cathedral of St. Ignatius Loyola - Palm Beach, Florida, Cathedral of Holy Cross - Boston, Massachusetts and Cathedral of Christ the King - Superior, Wisconsin. Rodgers consistently installs more organs with pipes than any other builder world-wide and represents Pinchi Pipe Organ Builders of Italy for pipework on organs with pipes.
Please visit our web site: www.Rodgersinstruments.com. ■

PATRICK J. MURPHY
& ASSOCIATES, INC.
ORGANBUILDERS

PATRICK J. MURPHY & ASSOCIATES, INC.
300 Old Reading Pike, Suite 1D
Stowe, PA 19464
Tel: 610-970-9817
Fax: 610-970-9297
Web Site: www.pjmorgans.com

Personnel:
Patrick J. Murphy ....President

Type of Business:
The firm of Patrick J. Murphy & Associates, Incorporated, founded in 1987, is located in Stowe Pennsylvania, just 40 miles Northeast of Center City Philadelphia. Our principal vocation is the construction and design of new pipe organs and the restoration of older instruments. We also offer a complete program of maintenance, tuning and additions for existing pipe organs as well as solid-state console upgrades, releathering services, and total revisions. ■

Plaques & Memorials

CARROLL ART, INC.
710 N.E. 26th Street
Wilton Manors, FL 33305
Tel.: 800-876-4569; Fax: 954-561-4098

Personnel:
David Nagle....................President Designer
Liza Palmer....................Sales Manager
Wayne Palmer....................Sales Representative
Robert Perkins....................Sales Representative

Type of Business:
Carroll Art has been in business for 12 years. We design and custom build all types of plaques and memorials including the tree of life, plaques, recognition systems, church signs, donor plates, custom sculptures, and memorials are just a few of our products. We can provide you with the perfect fund raising tool. ■

INSPIRED ARTISANS, LTD.
816 W National Ave.
Milwaukee, WI 53204
Tel.: 414-672-9478; 888-442-9141
Fax: 414-672-9479
Web Site: www.inspiredart.com

Personnel:
Gianfranco Tassara....................President

Type of Business:
Inspired Artisans, since 1997 have been serving the church with quality Liturgical Art. Recent commissions are: **Baptismal Font**, Basilica of St. Josaphat, Milwaukee, WI. **Iconographic Tryptich**, Our Lady of Peace, North Augusta, SC. **Donors Memorial Wall**, St. Anne, Barrington IL. **Altar, Ambo and Tabernacle**, Bellarmine Jesuit Retreat, Barrington, IL. **Mosaic Murals**, St. Joseph, South Bend, IN. **Fiberglass Exterior Statue**, Sacred Heart, Waseca, MN. **Stained Glass**, Santa Marianita, Galapagos, Ecuador. **Ambry**, St. Raphael Cathedral, Madison, WI. **Grille**, Poor Clare Monastery, Lemont, IL. **Stations of the Cross**, St. Andrews, Ellensburg, WA. **Wood Sculpture**, Catholic Cemeteries, Denver, CO. **Terra Cotta**, Cardinal Bernardin School, Orland Park, IL. **Murals**, St. Augustine, Thomasville, GA **Tabernacle**, Holy Spirit, Montgomery, AL. **Processional Cross**, Pax Christi, Rochester, MN. **Marble Altar**, Our Lady of Lourdes, Harrisonville, MO. See our display ad under the **"Mosaics"** category or contact us for a complete list of past commissions, and brochures. Or visit our web page. ■

SANFORD WERFEL—ARTIST
425 Old Georges Road
North Brunswick, NJ 08902
Tel.: 800-443-3744; 732-297-1166
Fax: 732-297-7770
E-mail: werfelart@aol.com
Web Site: www.sanfordwerfelartist.com

Type of Business:
Since 1968, Mr. Werfel's sculptures have been helping parishes to INSPIRE and MOTIVATE GIVING through the use of his original sculptures. Building drives, capital or endowment funds, sacrificial giving, and tithing programs all benefit from using Donor Recognition Sculptures. Call or write for FREE INFORMATION. Included will be costs and designs as well as a "HOW-TO-USE" guide that tells how your parish can use sculpture to raise funds. Good art is forever.

Visit our web site at www.SanfordWerfelArtist.com. ■

ZAX SIGNAGE
25 Front St.
Nashua, NH 03061
Tel: 800-258-1566 FAX: 603-883-6395
E-mail: info@zaxcorp.com
Web Site: www.zaxcorp.com

Personnel:
Patrick Walsh....................President

Type of Business:
The Zax Corporation of Nashua, NH has a distinguished history of providing the highest quality recognition products throughout North America. Our recognition products represent not only fine materials and craftsmanship, but the highest standards of design excellence for meeting your specific needs.

Zax manufactures an array of products such as Donor Walls, Books of Memories, Trees of Life, Add-On Donor Plaques, MarbleGraph, ClassBrass Multi-Plate/Multi-Name Plaques, Bronze Tablets, Incentive Awards and Signage Products.

For detailed information on our product line, or help in designing a donor wall of distinction, our expert staff can help you with your donor recognition needs. Call us at 1-800-258-1566 for help or to request our recognition catalog.

We pledge Service, Value, Quality, and our Commitment to you, to help you express your gratitude to your donors, and at the same time...increase donations. ■

Tables & Chairs

ATD-AMERICAN CO.

ATD-AMERICAN CO.
135 Greenwood Avenue, Wyncote, PA 19095-1396
Tel.: 888-283-2487; Fax: 800-283-7363
E-mail: american@atd.com
Web Site: www.atd.com

Personnel:
Bob Roche .... Marketing
Sal Catanese .... Sales

Type of Business:
For four generations, ATD-AMERICAN has supplied Furniture and Equipment to Churches, Organizations and Institutions nationally and worldwide. Since 1931, it has been our tradition to deliver high quality products and personal service at the lowest competitive prices. ATD offers a wide range of products to meet all of the needs of your Church and School. Our comprehensive catalog includes the following: Announcement and Bulletin Boards, Audio-Visual Equipment, Classroom Furniture, Computer Furniture, Daycare Furniture, Display Cases, Folding Chairs, Folding Tables, Lecterns, Library Furniture, Office Furniture, Outdoor Equipment, Pews and Pulpit Furniture, Room Dividers and Partitions, Stacking Chairs, and Stages and Risers.

For a FREE Wholesale Furniture Catalog, call us at 888-283-2487 or fax us at 800-283-7363. You can also visit our web site at www.atd.com or email us at american@atd.com.

SPECIAL OFFER FOR CATHOLIC DIRECTORY SUBSCRIBERS: Mention offer code 6557 and receive a special 10% discount on your first order. ■

SAUDER® MANUFACTURING COMPANY

SAUDER MANUFACTURING COMPANY
930 W. Barre Rd.
Archbold, OH 43502
Tel: 1-800-537-1530
Fax: 419-446-3697
Web Site: www.sauderworship.com

Personnel:
Virgil Miller .... President
Kelvin Friesen ..... Vice President of Sales & Marketing
Bob Borcherdt .... Sales Manager

Type of Business:
Sauder Manufacturing Company is the leading U.S. manufacturer of church furniture, including pews, chairs, sanctuary furniture, and re-upholstery service. Upholstered and non-upholstered pews are available in a wide selection of styles, finish colors and fabrics. Chairs provide flexible seating and are available in a variety of styles to complement pews and the worship area decor.

Visit our web site at www.sauderworship.com. ■

Antique Stained Glass

FRADEZ TOUJOURS

Adrian Hamers® Church Interiors

ADRIAN HAMERS, INC.
2 Madison Avenue
Larchmont, NY 10538
Tel.: 914-834-7780; Fax: 914-834-0712
Web Site: www.adrianhamers.com

Type of Business:
Custom designers and manufacturers of Sacred Vessels. Since 1887, the Hamers name has been synonymous with expert Silversmithing throughout the world in the field of Liturgical Art. Please contact us for those hard to find items, as we always have a large selection of Adrian Hamers Estate Collection pieces in stock. We have a large collection of antique church stainglass windows available (both full sets and individual). We are experts in: Church Interiors from design to execution, Renovations, Altars, Sacred Vessels, Gold and Silver Plating & Repairing, Appraisals, Tabernacles, Marble, Statuary, Woodwork & Woodcarving, Stained Glass, Pews & Chairs, Gold Leafing, Frescoes, Restoration, Trompe-l' oeuil, Wall Murals (repair and conservation cleaning), Ornamental Plaster, Heraldic Designs & Bishop Regalia. Please call us for a free 36-page Sacred Vessels color catalog, or our free 80-page color Woodcarvings catalog. ■

Etched Glass

TOUJOURS

ADRIAN HAMERS®
CHURCH INTERIORS

ADRIAN HAMERS, INC.
2 Madison Avenue
Larchmont, NY 10538
Tel.: 914-834-7780; Fax: 914-834-0712
Web Site: www.adrianhamers.com

Type of Business:

Custom designers and manufacturers of Sacred Vessels. Since 1887, the Hamers name has been synonymous with expert Silversmithing throughout the world in the field of Liturgical Art. Please contact us for those hard to find items, as we always have a large selection of Adrian Hamers Estate Collection pieces in stock. We have a large collection of antique church stainglass windows available (both full sets and individual). We are experts in: Church Interiors from design to execution, Renovations, Altars, Sacred Vessels, Gold and Silver Plating & Repairing, Appraisals, Tabernacles, Marble, Statuary, Woodwork & Woodcarving, Stained Glass, Pews & Chairs, Gold Leafing, Frescoes, Restoration, Trompe-l' oeuil, Wall Murals (repair and conservation cleaning), Ornamental Plaster, Heraldic Designs & Bishop Regalia. Please call us for a free 36-page Sacred Vessels color catalog, or our free 80-page color Woodcarvings catalog. ■

Faceted Glass

BOTTI STUDIO OF
ARCHITECTURAL ARTS, INC.

BOTTI STUDIO OF ARCHITECTURAL ARTS, INC.
919 Grove Street
Evanston, Illinois 60201
Tel.: 800-524-7211; 847-869-5933
Fax: 847-869-5996
E-mail: botti@ bottistudio.com
Web Site: www.bottistudio.com

East Coast Studio:	*West Coast Studio:*
3104 S. Osprey Avenue	1038 N. Hwy. 101
Sarasota, FL 33577	Encinitas, CA 92024
Tel.: 941-951-0978	Tel.: 760-753-0705
Fax: 941-953-9078	Fax: 760-753-0705

International Office: Agropoli, Italy, Nassau, Bahamas

Personnel:

Staff of 45. Includes internationally recognized ecclesiastic artists and designers working in conjunction with highly skilled glass and statuary craftspeople and artisans.
Ettore Christopher Botti ....Principal
Ethlyn Panzironi Botti ....Principal

Type of Business:

Since 1864, Botti Studio has specialized in serving the ecclesiastic environment through design, fabrication, delivery, and installation. Experts on staff in conservation, restoration, and repair provide a source for experienced project management — from conception through completion. Services include: **STAINED GLASS:** As custom designers and manufacturers, Botti artisans fabricate designs in stained, faceted, sandblasted, carved, and painted glass. **MARBLE:** Skilled craftsmen sculpt new or refurbish existing statuary, railings, baptismal fonts, and altars. **INTERIORS:** Complete renovations of interiors can be carefully and historically provided through plaster work, faux painting, gilding, stenciling, and graining. **MOSIAC:** Using state-of-the-art procedures, Botti can use preservation and restoration techniques to bring pieces back to their original beauty or create new custom installations. **CONSULTATON:** Preliminary-stage consultation can provide visualization of projects to aid in fund-raising and planning. **HISTORIC DISCOVERY:** Documentation and archival recording of existing sacred windows, marble, interior painting, and art is available. **STATUARY:** Working in wood, marble, or plaster, our designers are experts at restoration of aged, timeworn statuary and creation of custom ornamentation. ■

Conrad Schmitt Studios Inc.

Excellence in Artistry Since 1889

CONRAD SCHMITT STUDIOS, INC.
2405 S. 162nd St.
New Berlin, WI 53151
Tel: 800-969-3033
262-786-3030
Fax:262-786-9036
E-mail: studio@conradschmitt.com
Web Site: www.conradschmitt.com

Personnel:
Heidi Gruenke Emery ....Vice Pres. & Marketing Dir.

Type of Business:
Since 1889, the family-owned Conrad Schmitt Studios has been privileged to provide decoration, restoration and artwork to enhance the worship environment of churches throughout the country, including more than twenty-five cathedrals.

For projects in the early stages, CSS offers consultations, design renderings, decorative samples and budgetary estimates for use in planning and fundraising. For historic restorations, our conservators investigate and document original paint colors and decoration to guide the restoration work.

CSS employs a permanent staff of highly experienced artists and artisans who conduct ornamental plaster work, decorative painting, stenciling, trompe l'oeil and interior and exterior gilding. CSS artists also continually create, conserve, restore and replicate stained glass, murals, mosaics and statuary. CSS has a 114-year history of service to the Catholic community and is dedicated to providing the finest ecclesiastical artwork that blends history and tradition with a growing and evolving faith.■

DÄZZLE GLÄZZ Studio
"Windows that Praise & Inspire"

DAZZLE GLAZZ STUDIO
6605 Jefferson Highway
Baton Rouge, LA 70806-8104
Tel: 888-717-9484; 225-216-9484
Fax: 225-216-9486
E-mail; duncan@church-windows.com;
duncan@unique-crosses.com; duncan@dazzleglazz.com
Web Site: www.church-windows.com;
www.unique-crosses.com; www.dazzleglazz.com

Personnel:
Duncan, Diana & Douglas Tooley; Erskin Mitchell

Type of Business:
Leaded and faceted stain glass design, fabrication and restoration. Our goal is to fill each project with the faith and passion that will result in "Windows that Praise and Inspire." We also do contract fabrication for other glass designers. Large and intricate windows are economical through computerized water-jet cut and laminated technology.

Our Unique Crosses make unique gifts for unique individuals and occasions. Variations on existing crosses or one-of-a-kind special requests are welcome. ■

Stained Glass

THE ART OF GLASS, INC.
316 Media Station Road
Media, PA 19037
Tel.: 610-891-7813; Fax: 610-891-0150

Personnel:
Kathy Jordan...President

Type of Business:
The Art of Glass, Inc. provides quality design and fabrication services and is committed to the efficient completion of new construction and the ethical restoration and preservation of historic windows. Our reputation and experience in the field is well documented. We would be pleased to assist you in the early stages of planning (and design), working with your architect and/or committee to achieve your desired goals. ■

ASCALON STUDIOS, INC.
DESIGNERS AND ARTISANS OF WORSHIP SPACES

ASCALON STUDIOS, INC.
115 Atlantic Ave.
Berlin, NJ 08009
Tel.: 1-888-280-5656 (toll-free); Fax: 856-768-3902
Email: info@ascalonstudios.com
Web Site: www.ascalonstudios.com

Personnel:

Eric J. Ascalon ....General Manager/ Inquiry Representative
David Ascalon ....President & Art/Design Director
Ronnie Ascalon ....Vice-President
Donn Hettel ....Stained Glass/Mosaic Studio Manager
Randy Himes ....Metalwork Studio Manager
Fred Kurz ....Studio Representative

Type of Business:

For three generations, Ascalon Studios has been committed to the creation of art & design for worship spaces throughout North America. Whether your project involves new construction or the renovation of an existing facility, our talented staff of in-house designers and artisans efficiently and elegantly undertake commissions in a variety of media and materials, in traditional as well as contemporary styles. The studio prides itself in its ability to develop close working relationships with organization leadership and architects. Ascalon Studios has received prestigious design awards, including from the American Institute of Architect's Interfaith Forum on Religion, Art & Architecture.

Projects range from comprehensive chapel and sanctuary design, to the design and fabrication of individual art items, including **STAINED GLASS WINDOWS, MOSAICS, CARVED GLASS, FACETED SLAB GLASS (DALLE DE VERRE), SCULPTURE, ARCHITECTURAL METALWORK** and **MEMORIALS**.

Additionally, Ascalon Studios can undertake meaningful, artistic donor recognition projects for your parish or organization, including **DONOR RECOGNITION WALLS** and **TREES OF LIFE** to assist in capital campaigns and major fundraising efforts. Please visit the studio's website for more information on Ascalon Studios and to see examples of its artwork. ■

THE BAUT STUDIOS, INC.
ECCLESIASTICAL CRAFTSMEN

THE BAUT STUDIOS, INC.
1095 Main Street
Swoyersville, PA 18704
Tel.: 800-326-9421; Fax: 570-288-0380
E-mail: info@baut.com
Web Site: www.baut.com

Personnel:

Conrad Dismas Baut ....President
Gerhard Francis Baut ....Master Sculptor
Heide Baut Cebrick....................................Artist/Designer
Karen Baut Klemm ....Business Manager

Type of Business:

The STAINED GLASS of the FUTURE is here NOW! The Baut Studios, Inc., established in 1927, is a full-service ecclesiastical studio that has been manufacturing and installing their own patented STRUCTURAL STAINED GLASS* in windows and doors for more than 44 years. A unique non-sagging construction never needing structural repairs, STRUCTURAL STAINED GLASS is LEAD FREE, and CUSTOM DESIGNED to fit many tastes and budgets. Pricing is competitive with leaded and stained glass but with many more advantages when combined with the BAUT WINDOW and DOOR SYSTEMS. Beautiful, long lasting, environmentally and financially sound, and virtually maintenance free, STRUCTURAL STAINED GLASS is featured in over 5,000 churches worldwide.

Other products include Single, Double and Triple Glazed Church Windows and Ventilators, Heavy Duty Doors, Restoration/New Traditional Stained Glass, Altars and Appointments, Crosses, Steeples, Glass Mosaics and Church Lighting. All Baut products are custom made to your sizes and shapes, and designed to match your decor. ■

* U.S. Patent No. 3,064,380

BOTTI STUDIO OF ARCHITECTURAL ARTS, INC.
919 Grove Street
Evanston, Illinois 60201
Tel.: 800-524-7211; 847-869-5933
Fax: 847-869-5996
E-mail: botti@ bottistudio.com
Web Site: www.bottistudio.com

East Coast Studio:
3104 S. Osprey Avenue
Sarasota, FL 33577
Tel.: 941-951-0978
Fax: 941-953-9078

West Coast Studio:
1038 N. Hwy. 101
Encinitas, CA 92024
Tel.: 760-753-0705
Fax: 760-753-0705

International Office: Agropoli, Italy, Nassau, Bahamas

Personnel:
Staff of 45. Includes internationally recognized ecclesiastic artists and designers working in conjunction with highly skilled glass and statuary craftspeople and artisans.
Ettore Christopher Botti .... Principal
Ethlyn Panzironi Botti .... Principal

Type of Business:
Since 1864, Botti Studio has specialized in serving the ecclesiastic environment through design, fabrication, delivery, and installation. Experts on staff in conservation, restoration, and repair provide a source for experienced project management — from conception through completion. Services include: **STAINED GLASS:** As custom designers and manufacturers, Botti artisans fabricate designs in stained, faceted, sandblasted, carved, and painted glass. **MARBLE:** Skilled craftsmen sculpt new or refurbish existing statuary, railings, baptismal fonts, and altars. **INTERIORS:** Complete renovations of interiors can be carefully and historically provided through plaster work, faux painting, gilding, stenciling, and graining. **MOSIAC:** Using state-of-the-art procedures, Botti can use preservation and restoration techniques to bring pieces back to their original beauty or create new custom installations. **CONSULTATON:** Preliminary-stage consultation can provide visualization of projects to aid in fund-raising and planning. **HISTORIC DISCOVERY:** Documentation and archival recording of existing sacred windows, marble, interior painting, and art is available. **STATUARY:** Working in wood, marble, or plaster, our designers are experts at restoration of aged, timeworn statuary and creation of custom ornamentation. ■

BOVARD STUDIO INC.
2281 Highway 34 East
Fairfield, IA 52556
Tel: 800-452-7796
Fax: 641-472-0974
E-mail: info@bovardstudio.com
Web Site: www.bovardstudio.com

Personnel:
Ron Bovard .... C.E.O.
Bob Greco .... President
Leigh Carter .... Sales Manager, Indianapolis Office

Type of Business:
We design, fabricate and install traditional and contemporary stained glass; provide full restoration services, including new wood, aluminum and steel frames, and protective covering systems, with Precision Flow® ventilation designed for preservation of stained glass windows; and custom wood doors.
Our 40,000 sq. ft. facility also includes a complete woodshop and welding shop. Bovard Studio's 70 artists, craftspeople and staff from around the world are among the most talented founded today. Eighteen sales offices across the USA
See our color ad on the Products and Services Section Tab.■

CENTURY ART-GLASS CO. INC.
16161 Westwoods Business Park
St Louis, MO 63021
Tel.: 800-888-8121, 636-227-5000
Fax: 636-527-2857

Personnel:
William A. Summer............. President/Creative Director
Matthew V. Summer... Vice-President/Master Craftsman

Type of Business:
Our family-owned stained glass firm founded in 1908, proudly maintains the distinguished tradition of spiritually inspired, conceptually designed stained glass artworks for churches, chapels, mausoleums, and other religious environments. Our attention to every detail in the design, structure, manufacturing and installation of stained, faceted, beveled, etched and other diverse art glass windows in traditional or contemporary styles is what our reputation is built on. We also offer a full line of restoration products and services, such as releading of bowed stained glass windows, repair of broken stained glass pieces, window frame restoration or replacement, stained glass domes and energy-efficient protective storm coverings.
Our Goal: To highlight and preserve the highest spiritual, artistic and craftsmanship capabilities in the art of stained glass. Custom designs available — please inquire. Estimates available nationwide without obligation. ■

Conrad Schmitt Studios Inc.
Excellence in Artistry Since 1889

CONRAD SCHMITT STUDIOS, INC.
2405 S. 162nd St.
New Berlin, WI 53151
Tel: 800-969-3033; 262-786-3030
Fax:262-786-9036
E-mail: studio@conradschmitt.com
Web Site: www.conradschmitt.com

Personnel:
Heidi Gruenke Emery ....Vice Pres. & Marketing Dir.

Type of Business:
Since 1889, the family-owned Conrad Schmitt Studios has been privileged to provide decoration, restoration and artwork to enhance the worship environment of churches throughout the country, including more than twenty-five cathedrals.

For projects in the early stages, CSS offers consultations, design renderings, decorative samples and budgetary estimates for use in planning and fundraising. For historic restorations, our conservators investigate and document original paint colors and decoration to guide the restoration work.

CSS employs a permanent staff of highly experienced artists and artisans who conduct ornamental plaster work, decorative painting, stenciling, trompe l'oeil and interior and exterior gilding. CSS artists also continually create, conserve, restore and replicate stained glass, murals, mosaics and statuary. CSS has a 114-year history of service to the Catholic community and is dedicated to providing the finest ecclesiastical artwork that blends history and tradition with a growing and evolving faith.■

CUMBERLAND STAINED GLASS
5232 East Trindle Rd.
Mechanicsburg, PA 17050
Tel.: 717-691-8290
Fax: 717-591-9807
E-mail: info@cumberlandstainedglass.com
Web Site: www.cumberlandstainedglass.com

Personnel:
Bryan "Buck" Lerew Owner, with over 25 years experience in the stained glass business

Type of Business:
Cumberland Stained Glass is dedicated to the design, fabrication, installation and restoration of quality stained and leaded glass windows. Our staff of artists and craftsmen will provide professional service and make every effort to educate clients regarding the process of conservation and restoration. In addition we will provide the most advanced products and methods for protective coverings of stained and leaded glass windows. ■

DAPRATO RIGALI STUDIOS, INC.

DAPRATO RIGALI STUDIOS, INC.
6030 N. Northwest Highway
Chicago, IL 60631
Tel.: 773-763-5511; Fax: 773-763-5522
Web Site: www.dapratorigali.com

Personnel:
John Rigali
Robert Rigali
Lisa Rigali Galvin
Mike Rigali

Type of Business:
Daprato Rigali Studios, Inc. has been beautifying Churches in America since 1860.

Today we find the Rigali Family restoring and renovating the churches originally decorated by their Great-Grandfather, John E. Rigali; aware of his reputation to create spiritually moving environments with quality material and craftsmanship.

Some of their most recent jobs include: decoration and stained glass restoration at St. Mary of the Lake Seminary, Mundelein, IL; Marble renovation and decoration, St. Elizabeth's Mother House, Allegany, N.Y.; and General Contracting for complete renovation of St. Bernadette's Church, Rockford, IL.

The Daprato Rigali staff is equipped to take your project from start to finish. If you're interested in working with a fine interior design studio experienced in Ecclesiastical Artistries please call for consultation at no obligation. We deliver what we design. ■

DÄZZLE GLÄZZ Studio
"Windows that Praise & Inspire"

DAZZLE GLAZZ STUDIO
6605 Jefferson Highway
Baton Rouge, LA 70806-8104
Tel: 888-717-9484; 225-216-9484
Fax: 225-216-9486
E-mail; duncan@church-windows.com; duncan@unique-crosses.com; duncan@dazzleglazz.com
Web Site: www.church-windows.com; www.unique-crosses.com; www.dazzleglazz.com

Personnel:
Duncan, Diana & Douglas Tooley; Erskin Mitchell

Type of Business:
Leaded and faceted stain glass design, fabrication and restoration. Our goal is to fill each project with the faith and passion that will result in "Windows that Praise and Inspire." We also do contract fabrication for other glass designers. Large and intricate windows are economical through computerized water-jet cut and laminated technology.

Our Unique Crosses make unique gifts for unique individuals and occasions. Variations on existing crosses or one-of-a-kind special requests are welcome. ■

DOMUSDEI

HOLY ART STUDIOS

DOMUSDEI HOLY ART STUDIOS

FACTORY: Via dei Tulipani, 48 - 00040 CECCHINA DI ALBANO (RM) - ITALY
Tel: 011-39-06-9343369
Fax: 011-39-06-9344971

SHOWROOM: Via Scossacavalli 3/9 - 00193 ROMA - ITALY
Tel: 011-39-06-6868090
Fax: 011-39-06-9344971

Email: info@domusdei.it; m.delmonte@domusdei.it
Web site: www.domusdei.it

Personnel:

Alessandro Del Monte ....President
Massimiliano Del Monte......................Executive Director
Aldo Del Monte ....Assistant President

Type of Business:

Founded in 1963, Domusdei Studio has restored thousands of church interiors all over the world. Specializing in designing and manufacturing stained glass windows, mosaics, bronze and fiberglass statues, altars, bronze doors, lecterns, baptismal fonts, candlesticks, flower holders, and tabernacles

We are also experts in silver and gold plating and the restoration of wood and metal masterpieces. ■

EVERGREENE PAINTING STUDIOS, INC.

EVERGREENE PAINTING STUDIOS, INC.

450 West 31st St., 7th Fl.
New York, NY 10001
Tel.: 212-244-2800
Fax: 212-244-6204

711 South Blvd., Ste. 7
Oak Park, IL 60302
Tel.: 708-358-1642
Fax: 708-358-1656

E-mail: info@evergreene.com
Web Site: www.evergreene.com

Personnel:

Jeff Greene ....President
Kim Lovejoy .... Director of Marketing
Gillian Randell .... Chief Fine Arts Conservator
Terry Vanderwell.......... Director of Restoration, Midwest
Anthony Kartsonas . Architectural Conservator, Midwest

Type of Business:

EverGreene is a full-service decorative arts studio committed to preserving the integrity of historic sacred spaces through conservation, restoration, and compatible new artwork and decoration. Services include investigation and analysis of original finishes; consultations, renderings, budgets and samples to support decision-making and capital campaigns; design of color schemes, architectural ornament and furnishings; and guidance on specifications. EverGreene's consistently high-quality work is performed by its staff of experienced project managers, professionally-trained conservators, fine artists and craftsmen.

EverGreene's capabilities include all types of decorative painting, stenciling, gilding and trompe l'oeil; conservation, replication, and new design of murals and mosaics; ornamental plaster and scagliola; and allied crafts including wood and metal refinishing, interior stone cleaning, art glass, tile work and other architectural arts.

Among EverGreene's current projects are St. Matthew's Cathedral in Washington, D.C., Sacramento Cathedral, and the Chapel at Sacred Heart Monastery, Lisle, Illinois. EverGreene's work over the last 25 years includes projects large and small in houses of worship around the country, including ten cathedrals, 26 state capitols, and hundreds of theaters, public buildings, commercial interiors and residences. ■

FULL SPECTRUM STAINED GLASS, INC.

31323 Colon Road
Colon, Michigan 49040
Tel: 269-432-2610
Fax: 269-432-9411
E-mail: fssgi@aol.com
Web Site: www.churchwindows.net

Type of Business:

Full Spectrum Stained Glass is a SGAA accredited studio known for quality work and personal courteous service. Projects are completed on time, within budget, and in a professional manner. We offer assistance in all phases of any project to help plan for the care of your windows, making convenience and satisfaction top priorities.

F.S.S.G. Inc Provides a full line of services on-site and in the studio including: frame and sash restoration on all types of surrounds (wood, steel, stone); window removal; dust control; transport of windows; restoration or new design and fabrication of stained glass. Providing full service care, means better overall quality for your windows.■

HIEMER & COMPANY
Stained Glass Studio

HIEMER & COMPANY STAINED GLASS STUDIO

141 Wabash Ave.
Clifton, NJ 07011
Tel.: 973-772-5081
Fax: 973-772-0325
Email: jevanwie@hiemco.com
Web Site: www.hiemco.com

Personnel:

Gerhard E. Hiemer .... C.E.O.
Judith Hiemer Van Wie ....President
James E. Van Wie ....Vice President

Type of Business:

Bold Liturgical statements and traditional Biblical portrayals are executed in magnificent color schemes by the artists and craftsmen at Hiemer & Company. Four generations of the Hiemer family have dedicated their careers to excellence in stained glass and promotion of faith through art. The studio members are highly skilled and experienced with large scale restorations, artistic replications and window renovations. The permanent staff works from concept to installation to the client's complete satisfaction. Over 1,100 Churches served in North America. Fabricators of stained, faceted, and etched glass. Exceptional figure portrayals are a specialty. Information and quotations submitted without obligation. ■

HUNT STAINED GLASS STUDIOS, INC.
1756 West Carson Street
Pittsburgh, PA 15219
Tel.: 412-391-1796; Fax: 412-391-1560
Web Site: www.huntstainedglass.com
E-mail: huntsg@msn.com

Personnel:
Nicholas Parrendo........................Artist, Designer, Owner
David Parrendo...General Manager

Type of Business:
We continue the tradition of enhancing worship environments with unique creations in different glass mediums: stained, faceted, and sand etched. From design presentation, fabrication through installation, our commissions include sculpture and murals.
"We'd love to serve you." ■

THE JUDSON STUDIOS
200 South Avenue 66
Los Angeles, CA 90042
Tel: 323-255-0131
Fax: 323-255-0131

Personnel:
Bill Judson
David Judson

Type of Business:
The Judson Studios is committed to making your project a success, enhancing your space for years to come. Our studios of stained glass specialists will give your project the attention and care it deserves. Our dedication to maintaining the highest levels of craftsmanship and timeless design, across five generations, has maintained our Studios' reputation for over 100 years. We offer this commitment to you and your project. ■

KING RICHARD'S RELIGIOUS ARTIFACTS
P.O. Box 191027
Atlanta, GA 31119
Tel.: 877-248-3366
Fax: 770-455-1784

Personnel:
Rick Lair .... President
Sandra James ....Vice President
Scott Lair .... Sales and Marketing
Chris Roberts ....Web Master
Mike Coleman ....Warehouse & Shipping

Type of Business:
King Richard's Religious Artifacts specializes in providing churches and religious facilities with a complete spectrum of religious decorative items; including complete sets of stained glass windows, statuary, altars, stations and all types of altar necessities. We travel throughout the United States selling and delivering merchandise, as well as completing all required work for purchasing and removal. ■

PHILLIP A. GALLO
6318 SEVENTH ST.
ALEXANDRIA, VA 22312
703-354-7445
TOLL FREE 888-742-8500
STAINED GLASS WINDOWS
WE BUY AND SELL PRE-OWNED STAINED GLASS WINDOWS. OUR WINDOWS COME TO YOU WITH A HISTORY OF PRIOR CHURCH SERVICE AT SUBSTANTIAL SAVINGS OVER COMPARABLE QUALITY NEW WINDOWS.

RAMBUSCH LIGHTING
160 Cornelison Avenue
Jersey City, NJ 07304
Tel.: 201-333-2525; Fax: 201-433-3355
Web Site: www.rambusch.com

Personnel:
Edwin P. Rambusch ....President & C.E.O.
Martin V. Rambusch ....Chairman of the Board

Type of Business:
Since 1898, creating church interiors, liturgical furnishings, and art work. Fine restoration of church interiors. In-house studios and shops for designing and executing stained glass, church lighting systems, art metal work, and decorative painting. ■

REINARTS STAINED GLASS STUDIOS, INC.
73 Washington Street
Winona, MN 55987
Tel.: 507-452-4465; Fax: 507-452-4649
E-mail: reinarts@luminet.net
Web Site: www.reinarts.com

Personnel:
William A. Reinarts..President

Type of Business:
Design, Manufacture and Install Stained Glass and Faceted Glass. Restoration and Re-Leading of Stained Glass. Protective, Insulative Covering of Stained Glass. Repair and Replacement of Window Frames. ■

ROHLF'S STAINED & LEADED GLASS STUDIO, INC.
783 South Third Avenue
Mt. Vernon, NY 10550
Toll Free: 800-969-4106
Tel.: 914-699-4848; Fax: 914-699-7091
Web Site: www.rohlfstudio.com

Personnel:
Peter Hans Rohlf..President
Gregory Rohlf ....Vice President

Type of Business:
For Three Generations our family owned and operated Studio together with our affiliate, George L. Payne Studio have been dedicated to excellence in Stained Glass Art. Our team of International designers and Master Craftspersons have created stained glass windows for over a thousand Churches and Institutions Worldwide. Our reputation and experience in the field of Restoration, Replication and Preservation is well known. We would be pleased to assist you in the early stages of planning and design, working with your Architect and/or committee to achieve your desired goals.

From concept to completion, we are dedicated to serve you. ■

The Willet Stained Glass Studios

WILLET STAINED GLASS STUDIOS
10 East Moreland Avenue
Philadelphia, PA 19118
Tel.: 215-247-5721; Toll Free: 877-709-4106
Fax: 215-247-2951
Web Site: www.willetglass.com

Type of Business:
The Willet Stained Glass Studios offer a full range of established stained glass techniques—from leaded, faceted, and sand carved to sculptured gold. Willet creations are designed to complement their architectural setting, and the extensive Willet design experience offers depth and competence in a diversity of artistic styles.

Since 1898, the Willet Studios have executed hundreds of commissions for Catholic churches and cathedrals around the nation. This year will mark new Catholic works in Fremont, Nebraska and the Bahamas.

The Willet national sales team can meet at your location to understand firsthand the goals you wish to achieve and to provide the information necessary to make a sound stained glass purchase decision. ■

The Willet Stained Glass Studios
—a division of Hauser Art Glass, Inc.
E. Crosby Willet, President ■

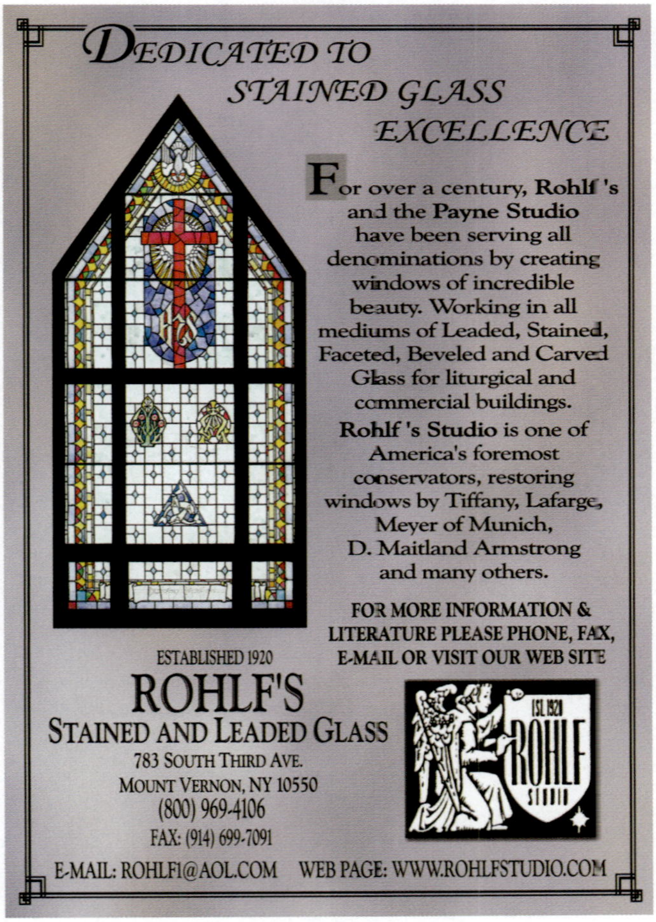

CLERICAL APPAREL

DUFFY & QUINN
Apparel for the Clergy

DUFFY & QUINN
307 5th Avenue
New York, NY 10016
Tel.: 800-425-3466; 212-725-0213
Fax: 212-385-3503
Web Site: www.duffyandquinn.com

Personnel:
Alfredo de Guzman..Manager
Marvin Goldman..Owner

Type of Business:
Duffy & Quinn is a leading supplier of religious apparel and accessories to the Reverend clergy—featuring suits, coats, clerical shirts, ready-made and custom-tailored cassocks. Monsignors and Bishops robes are made to order, with careful attention to detail, quality and on-time delivery. Full stocks of R.J. Toomey, Beau Veste, Gammarelli, and Barbiconi merchandise available for shipment at once. Mitres, zuchettos, birettas, vestments, pectoral crosses, chains, cross cords and Bishop's rings are our specialty. ■

Grace

GRACE LITURGICAL VESTMENTS
808 Union Street
Brooklyn, NY 11215
Tel: 718-857-7045; Fax: 718-857-7041
E-mail: info@GraceVestments.com
Web Site: www.GraceVestments.com

Type of Business:
GRACE LITURGICAL VESTMENTS, established in 2000, is a custom design business creating vestments and paraments that are in a word, elegant. We source out fabrics that are unusual but with a clear nod to tradition. Our trims, custom embroideries, and linings are all coordinated with great attention to detail. GRACE LITURGICAL VESTMENTS offers a product that stands out from the rest. We look forward to creating vestments that will enhance your worship with beauty and elegance. ■

Hayes & Finch
LIMITED ESTABLISHED 1882

HAYES AND FINCH LIMITED
Hanson Road, Aintree
Liverpool, England, L97BP
Tel: 44(0)151-523-6303
Fax: 44(0)151-525-1246
E-mail: sales@hfltd.com
Web Site: www.hayesandfinch.com
Personnel:
John R. Mann, M.B.E.B.Sc. ....Managing Director
Mrs. Karen Reilly ....Marketing Director
Andrew Ware ....Sales Manager

Type of Business:
Founded in 1882, Hayes and Finch is a fourth generation family business, and the largest manufacturer and supplier of church-related goods in the United Kingdom. Based in Liverpool, England, we supply high quality church furnishings to customers around the world. Our specialist manufacturing center produces both standard and customer-specified products; our extensive range includes Candles, Altar Wine, Clerical Garments, Furniture, Brassware and Hallmarked Silverware. Our business is built on British craftsmanship of highest quality and exceptional customer service. ■

VANPOULLES
Church Furnishers
~ Est. 1908 ~

VANPOULLES LTD.
Telford Place, Crawley
West Sussex, RH10 1SZ, UK
Tel: +44 1293 590100
Fax: +44 1293 590115
E-mail: sales@vanpoulles.co.uk
Web Site: www.vanpoulles.co.uk

Type of Business:
Vanpoulles Ltd. is a family business, established nearly 100 years ago to provide the Church with all types of church requisites. We specialise in producing traditional English silverware and ecclesiastical garments, including chalices, ciboria, vestments, copes, stoles and altar frontals etc. Our sales department is available for friendly service and advice and current stock availability of all our product lines.
Please call, write or e-mail for a free catalogue. If visiting the UK please note our showrooms are conveniently positioned only a short distance from Gatwick Airport. ■

Vermont Church Supply Co.

VERMONT CHURCH SUPPLY CO.
676 Pine St., P.O. Box 368
Burlington, VT 05401
Tel.: 802-862-6486, 800-451-3453
Fax: 802-862-5765
E-mail: vcs@together.net
Web Site: www.vermontchurchsupply.com

Personnel:
Neil Clark ....President

Type of Business:
Since our inception in 1946 by W. Barrett Clark and Doris Clark, Vermont Church Supply has offered the highest quality products and the best service to the Church and the Clergy. We have a wide range of products including Candles, Church Furniture, Metalware and Vestments. Our founders' Sons, Neil, John, Thomas and Robert, along with the third generation Anthony Clark, continue to provide services such as refinishing Sacred Vessels, Candlesticks and tabernacles and also the execution of hand carved wood and marble Statuary. Whether your needs are small or large, we can give the best personalized service to our Customers. ■

Clergy Shirts

CM ALMY

C.M. ALMY & SON, INC.
Three American Lane, P.O. Box 2644
Greenwich, CT 06836-2644
Tel.: 800-225-2569; Fax: 800-426-2569
E-mail: almyaccess@almy.com
Web Site: www.almy.com

Showrooms in:
- Old Greenwich, CT: 203-637-2739
- Pittsfield, ME: 207-487-3232

Type of Business:
Almy was founded in 1892. We design and make virtually all of our products in our Maine shop. It is our mission to design furnishings that will grace your worship and to ensure their value by making them with the highest quality materials and craftsmanship. We make a complete line of vestments, haberdashery, choir robes, candles, communion bread, linens, processional and altar appointments, and eucharistic vessels. We also offer custom design and fabrication of all Almy products, and repair and refurbishing of old metal appointments. Quik Ship© delivery of many popular items. All orders backed by The Almy Guarantee. Call, write, or e-mail for a free catalog. ■

STADELMAIER

STADELMAIER-NIJMEGEN-HOLLAND
Lagelandseweg 64
6545 CG Nijmegen, Holland
Tel.: 011-31-24-379-1170; Fax: 011-31-24-379-1171
Web Site: www.stadelmaier.com
E-mail: info@stadelmaier.com or sales@stadelmaier.com

Personnel:
Mr. Aart J. Stadelmaier ....President
Mrs. Diny Poorts ....Secretary
Mrs. Franka Scholten ....Office Manager
For clergical shirts Stadelmaier – Southington – USA
136 Curtiss Street
Southington, CT 06489, USA
Tel.: 860-621-7471; Fax: 860-621-7607

Personnel:
Mrs. Sarah Gleeton ....Customer Service

Type of Business:
Stadelmaier, established in 1930 in the Netherlands, specialises in unique, high quality liturgical vesture and church goods; vestments, stoles, albs, dalmatics, copes, deaconstoles, altar and lecterncovers, tapestries and banners. Fitting your church, your liturgy!
Our experienced design and production team is able to create innovative products from chasubles and stoles, clergy shirts and sweaters to stylish chalices, processional crosses, tabernacles and altars.
Also our Religious Antique Department with over 300 quality antique art pieces from Europe will be able to serve you well and enlighten your church space and your liturgy. For almost 75 years quality in Liturgy has been our motto.
Please contact us for your local exclusive Stadelmaier dealer and / or receive our catalogue. ■

Fine Woolen Fabrics

M. Grabie Woolen Co. Inc.

M. GRABIE WOOLEN CO. INC.
107-40 Queens Blvd.
Forest Hills, NY 11375
Tel.: 718 268-7444
Fax: 718 268-0074
E-mail: grabiewoolen@aol.com
Web Site: www.grabiewoolen.com

Personnel:
M. Grabie ....President
Y. Z. Grabie ....Sales Manager

Type of Business:
M. Grabie Woolen Company has been manufacturing fabrics in the USA and servicing the apparel industry since 1949. We have an extensive line of 100% Australian Merino worsted wool gabardine, flannel, crepe, satin gabardine, satin stripe gabardine, pique, tropical and challis. We also manufacture yarn dye novelties such as checks, plaids, Tartans, and Stripes and Herringbones. All fabrics are available with no minimum order necessary. You can preview our line on our website at www.grabiewoolen.com. ■

Robes, Vestments, Etc.

ABBOTT

ABBOTT INC.
1515 Route 38
Cherry Hill, NJ 08002
Tel.: 800-522-2688; 856-662-6959
Fax: 856-665-5109
E-mail: info@churchsupplies.com
Web Site: www.churchsupplies.com

Personnel:
Daniel J. Castonguay ....President
Joseph F. McKeaney...............................General Manager
Mary Ann Mitkus........................Business Administrator
John Scafidi ....Distribution
Michael Schwartz ....Government Liaison

Type of Business:
Purveyors of the Finest Vesture, Paraments, Statuary & Metalware since 1962. Unique and original creations, our specialty. Custom designs to complement your liturgical environment. Exclusive representatives of Slabbinck Master Collection & Original Collection. ■

SLABBINCK®

ART STUDIO SLABBINCK
Headquarters:
L. Bauwensstraat 18
8200 Brugge, Belgium
Tel.: 32-50-312557; Fax: 32-50-318358

Type of Business:
Belgian made vestments (chasubles, stoles, albs, copes, deaconstoles, dalmatics, altar and lectern covers, altar linens and cloths, tapestries and banners). Chalices, ciboria, patens and pyxes also available. Slabbinck Speed Service offered for many items as advertised in our catalog. Also Dirk Slabbinck Master Collection, an exclusive collection of vestments and paraments created from the inspired imagination of master designer Dirk Slabbinck, or according to your own specifications. For information on the dealer nearest you, call 800-423-3224 or fax us at 800-284-9000. ■

CM ALMY

C.M. ALMY & SON, INC.
Three American Lane
P.O. Box 2644
Greenwich, CT 06836-2644
Tel.: 800-225-2569; Fax: 800-426-2569
E-mail: almyaccess@almy.com
Web Site: www.almy.com

Showrooms in:
- Old Greenwich, CT: 203-637-2739
- Pittsfield, ME: 207-487-3232

Type of Business:

Almy was founded in 1892. We design and make virtually all of our products in our Maine shop. It is our mission to design furnishings that will grace your worship and to ensure their value by making them with the highest quality materials and craftsmanship. We make a complete line of vestments, haberdashery, choir robes, candles, communion bread, linens, processional and altar appointments, and eucharistic vessels.We also offer custom design and fabrication of all Almy products, and repair and refurbishing of old metal appointments. Quik Ship© delivery of many popular items. All orders backed by The Almy Guarantee. Call, write, or e-mail for a free catalog. ■

Ecclesia Designs

ECCLESIA DESIGNS
7412 Colton Lane
Manassas, VA 20109
Tel: 703-335-2900
Email: Info@ecclesiadesigns.com
Web Site: www.ecclesiadesigns.com

Type of Business:

Ecclesia Designs offers custom designed church vestments and altar linens to grace and enhance your worship experience. Each item is individually hand-crafted by a single artist who works closely with a graphics designer.

We have a passion for the creative process and are dedicated to producing works with the highest degree of artistic expression that suit the solemnity of their purpose. We use only the highest quality materials and craftsmanship and maintain close interactive communication with our clients to assure their satisfaction.

We sincerely hope that each of our designs will raise one's consciousness to God in all His glory because making them is a way of prayer for us.

"Made with Martha's hands but Mary's heart"

Grace

GRACE LITURGICAL VESTMENTS
808 Union Street
Brooklyn, NY 11215
Tel: 718-857-7045; Fax: 718-857-7041
E-mail: info@GraceVestments.com
Web Site: www.GraceVestments.com

Type of Business:

GRACE LITURGICAL VESTMENTS, established in 2000, is a custom design business creating vestments and paraments that are in a word, elegant. We source out fabrics that are unusual but with a clear nod to tradition. Our trims, custom embroideries, and linings are all coordinated with great attention to detail. GRACE LITURGICAL VESTMENTS offers a product that stands out from the rest. We look forward to creating vestments that will enhance your worship with beauty and elegance. ■

TAG GRANDA. LITURGICAL ARTS

GRANDA LITURGICAL ARTS, INC.
939 W. North Ave. , Ste.875
Chicago, IL 60622
Tel.: 800-425-0828; Fax: 312-944-9906
E-mail: usagranda@aol.com
Web Site: www.artegranda.com

Personnel:

Elia Rivera ....Director of Sales & Marketing

Type of Business:

GRANDA LITURGICAL ARTS, INC. is the USA sales and marketing office of Talleres de Arte Granda in Madrid, Spain. At our studio in Madrid, we have over one hundred artists, administrators, architects, designers, etc. dedicated to the design, production, and advancement of sacred art. Since 1891, we have been at the service of the Church combining modern techniques with artistic values to produce some of the world's finest sacred vessels, statuary, vestments, and church interiors. Please call us to request a complimentary catalog or to learn more about our custom design services. ■

THE HOLY+ROOD GUILD

THE HOLY ROOD GUILD
St. Joseph's Abbey
167 North Spencer Road
Spencer, MA 01562-1233
Tel.: 508-885-8750; Fax: 508-885-8758
E-mail: holyrood@holyroodguild.com
Web Site: www.holyroodguild.com

Type of Business:
Designers and crafters of ecclesiastical vesture for over 40 years. Inspired by our monastic tradition, we seek to unite in our work simplicity in design, quality in materials and excellence in craftsmanship. The result is vesture that enhances the liturgical celebration with visual grace and order. Our artists—both monks and laypersons—are available for custom design work and consultation. We also provide an extensive selection of ready made items. ■

HOUSE OF HANSEN
4223 West Irving Park Road
Chicago, IL 60641
Tel.: 773-736-5858; Fax: 773-736-6715

Type of Business:
Clerical tailoring specialists for over 85 years. We specialize in Prelatial Appointments and Custom Tailored cassocks made by our professional staff. Custom tailored vestments and albs. A full line of ready-made clerical apparel. ■

See our ad on this page.

Maison Bouvrier

MAISON BOUVRIER INC.
391 Hanlan Road, Woodbridge
Ontario, Canada L4L 3T1
905-851-1146 or 800-665-9895
Fax 905-851-7623
E-mail: bouvrier@maisonbouvrier.com
Web Site: www.maisonbouvrier.com

Personnel:
Kevin Bayne ....President
Janet MacDonald ....General Manager

Type of Business:
Maison Bouvrier has been in existence for over 150 years and is a world leader in weaving, creating and developing inspirational fabric designs of impeccable quality. Personalised attention is given to the needs of individual communities. All our artistic work is initially designed and created during a personal visit, thereby ensuring that the fabric used, the designs selected and the shapes chosen, fit perfectly into the worship space and enhance the visual liturgy. ■

MURPHY VESTMENTS

MURPHY VESTMENTS
Murphy Cap & Gown Company
Dept. OCD
4200 31st Street North
St. Petersburg, FL 33714
Tel.: 727-527-0696; Fax: 727-526-3528

Personnel:
Don Camp ....President
Gary Bergamo..Sales Manager
George Shahine ....Administrative Manager

Type of Business:
Value priced vestments ready to ship within 24 hours of factory receipt of order with guaranteed satisfaction. Many custom tailored styles also available. Visit our website at www.murphyrobes.com or ask for our products at your local church goods supplier.■

Robert Gaspard Co.

ROBERT GASPARD CO., INC.
200 North Janacek Road
Brookfield, WI 53045-610
Tel.: 800-784-6868; Fax: 800-784-7567
E-mail: mail@rgaspard.com
Web Site: www.robertgaspardco.com

Personnel:
Rose Gaspard..President
Jason R. Gaspard ....General Manager

Type of Business:
The Robert Gaspard Co. was established in 1954. Over the past 50 years, we have grown to be a nationally-known company. We pride ourselves on the ability to create original custom designs to enrich your worship needs. Our complete line consists of all ecclesiastical vesture, as well as paraments, mass and altar linens, stoles, banners, chasubles, funeral palls, albs, cossacks, surplices, choir robes, acolyte robes and many accessories. Complimentary catalog and fabric swatches sent on request. ■

STADELMAIER

STADELMAIER-NIJMEGEN-HOLLAND
Lagelandseweg 64
6545 CG Nijmegen, Holland
Tel.: 011-31-24-379-1170; Fax: 011-31-24-379-1171
Web Site: www.stadelmaier.com
E-mail: info@stadelmaier.com or sales@stadelmaier.com

Personnel:
Mr. Aart J. Stadelmaier .... President
Mrs. Diny Poorts .... Secretary
Mrs. Franka Scholten .... Office Manager
For clergical shirts
Stadelmaier – Southington – USA
136 Curtiss Street
Southington, CT 06489, USA
Tel.: 860-621-7471; Fax: 860-621-7607

Personnel:
Mrs. Sarah Gleeton .... Customer Service

Type of Business:
Stadelmaier, established in 1930 in the Netherlands, specialises in unique, high quality liturgical vesture and church goods; vestments, stoles, albs, dalmatics, copes, deaconstoles, altar and lecterncovers, tapestries and banners.
Fitting your church, your liturgy!
Our experienced design and production team is able to create innovative products from chasubles and stoles, clergy shirts and sweaters to stylish chalices, processional crosses, tabernacles and altars.
Also our Religious Antique Department with over 300 quality antique art pieces from Europe will be able to serve you well and enlighten your church space and your liturgy.
For almost 75 years quality in Liturgy has been our motto.
Please contact us for your local exclusive Stadelmaier dealer and / or receive our catalogue. ■

CONSTRUCTION, MAINTENANCE, & RENOVATION

The Art of Glass, Inc.

THE ART OF GLASS, INC.
316 Media Station Road
Media, PA 19037
Tel.: 610-891-7813; Fax: 610-891-0150

Personnel:
Kathy Jordan .... President

Type of Business:
The Art of Glass, Inc. provides quality design and fabrication services and is committed to the efficient completion of new construction and the ethical restoration and preservation of historic windows. Our reputation and experience in the field is well documented. We would be pleased to assist you in the early stages of planning (and design), working with your architect and/or committee to achieve your desired goals. ■

ASCALON STUDIOS, INC.
DESIGNERS AND ARTISANS OF WORSHIP SPACES

ASCALON STUDIOS, INC.
115 Atlantic Ave.
Berlin, NJ 08009
Tel.: 1-888-280-5656 (toll-free); Fax: 856-768-3902
Email: info@ascalonstudios.com
Web Site: www.ascalonstudios.com

Personnel:
Eric J. Ascalon .... General Manager/ Inquiry Representative
David Ascalon .... President & Art/Design Director
Ronnie Ascalon .... Vice-President
Donn Hettel .... Stained Glass/Mosaic Studio Manager
Randy Himes .... Metalwork Studio Manager
Fred Kurz .... Studio Representative

Type of Business:
For three generations, Ascalon Studios has been committed to the creation of art & design for worship spaces throughout North America. Whether your project involves new construction or the renovation of an existing facility, our talented staff of in-house designers and artisans efficiently and elegantly undertake commissions in a variety of media and materials, in traditional as well as contemporary styles. The studio prides itself in its ability to develop close working relationships with organization leadership and architects. Ascalon Studios has received prestigious design awards, including from the American Institute of Architect's Interfaith Forum on Religion, Art & Architecture.
Projects range from comprehensive chapel and sanctuary design, to the design and fabrication of individual art items, including **STAINED GLASS WINDOWS, MOSAICS, CARVED GLASS, FACETED SLAB GLASS (DALLE DE VERRE), SCULPTURE, ARCHITECTURAL METALWORK** and **MEMORIALS**.

Additionally, Ascalon Studios can undertake meaningful, artistic donor recognition projects for your parish or organization, including **DONOR RECOGNITION WALLS** and **TREES OF LIFE** to assist in capital campaigns and major fundraising efforts. Please visit the studio's website for more information on Ascalon Studios and to see examples of its artwork. ■

Baker Liturgical Art, LLC
Church Restoration / Church Renovation

BAKER LITURGICAL ART
136 Curtiss Street
Southington, CT 06489
Tel: 860-621-7471
Fax: 860-621-7607

Personnel:
Brian T. Baker

Type of Business:
Church Renovations, Restoration and Custom Religious Art.
* Baker Liturgical Art, LLC offers a complete range of liturgical design, church renovation, and church furnishings.as well as construction services for your individual liturgical projects. We strive to give you uncompromising quality in the design phase and the construction phase. We welcome the opportunity to listen to your specific liturgical needs. We do everything we can so you will find not only a source of quality services but also a source of comfort. ■

BOTTI STUDIO OF ARCHITECTURAL ARTS, INC.

BOTTI STUDIO OF ARCHITECTURAL ARTS, INC.
919 Grove Street
Evanston, Illinois 60201
Tel.: 800-524-7211; 847-869-5933
Fax: 847-869-5996
E-mail: botti@ bottistudio.com
Web Site: www.bottistudio.com

East Coast Studio:
3104 S. Osprey Avenue
Sarasota, FL 33577
Tel.: 941-951-0978
Fax: 941-953-9078

West Coast Studio:
1038 N. Hwy. 101
Encinitas, CA 92024
Tel.: 760-753-0705
Fax: 760-753-0705

International Office: Agropoli, Italy, Nassau, Bahamas

Personnel:
Staff of 45. Includes internationally recognized ecclesiastic artists and designers working in conjunction with highly skilled glass and statuary craftspeople and artisans.
Ettore Christopher Botti ....Principal
Ethlyn Panzironi Botti ....Principal

Type of Business:
Since 1864, Botti Studio has specialized in serving the ecclesiastic environment through design, fabrication, delivery, and installation. Experts on staff in conservation, restoration, and repair provide a source for experienced project management — from conception through completion. Services include: **STAINED GLASS:** As custom designers and manufacturers, Botti artisans fabricate designs in stained, faceted, sandblasted, carved, and painted glass. **MARBLE:** Skilled craftsmen sculpt new or refurbish existing statuary, railings, baptismal fonts, and altars. **INTERIORS:** Complete renovations of interiors can be carefully and historically provided through plaster work, faux painting, gilding, stenciling, and graining. **MOSIAC:** Using state-of-the-art procedures, Botti can use preservation and restoration techniques to bring pieces back to their original beauty or create new custom installations. **CONSULTATON:** Preliminary-stage consultation can provide visualization of projects to aid in fund-raising and planning. **HISTORIC DISCOVERY:** Documentation and archival recording of existing sacred windows, marble, interior painting, and art is available. **STATUARY:** Working in wood, marble, or plaster, our designers are experts at restoration of aged, timeworn statuary and creation of custom ornamentation. ■

Berlinger Company

THE BERLINGER COMPANY
2605 N. Sheridan Rd.
Peoria, IL 61604
Tel.: 309-688-1771
Fax: 309-688-9240
E-mail: info@theberlingercompany.com
Web Site: www.theberlingercompany.com

Personnel:
Michael Berlinger..President
Jeff Walters...Accts Manager
Milton Pachers-Lay..Sales.

Type of Business:
Church interior design and consultants
Interior restoration
New church designs
New liturgical whole goods—domestic and imported
Custom manufacturers
Liturgical Antiquities—domestic and imported ■

EverGreene Painting Studios, Inc.

EVERGREENE PAINTING STUDIOS, INC.
450 West 31st St., 7th Fl.
New York, NY 10001
Tel.: 212-244-2800
Fax: 212-244-6204
711 South Blvd., Ste. 7
Oak Park, IL 60302
Tel.: 708-358-1642
Fax: 708-358-1656
E-mail: info@evergreene.com
Web Site: www.evergreene.com

Personnel:
Jeff Greene ....President
Kim Lovejoy .... Director of Marketing
Gillian Randell .... Chief Fine Arts Conservator
Terry Vanderwell.......... Director of Restoration, Midwest
Anthony Kartsonas . Architectural Conservator, Midwest

Type of Business:
EverGreene is a full-service decorative arts studio committed to preserving the integrity of historic sacred spaces through conservation, restoration, and compatible new artwork and decoration. Services include investigation and analysis of original finishes; consultations, renderings, budgets and samples to support decision-making and capital campaigns; design of color schemes, architectural ornament and furnishings; and guidance on specifications. EverGreene's consistently high-quality work is performed by its staff of experienced project managers, professionally-trained conservators, fine artists and craftsmen.

EverGreene's capabilities include all types of decorative painting, stenciling, gilding and trompe l'oeil; conservation, replication, and new design of murals and mosaics; ornamental plaster and scagliola; and allied crafts including wood and metal refinishing, interior stone cleaning, art glass, tile work and other architectural arts.

Among EverGreene's current projects are St. Matthew's Cathedral in Washington, D.C., Sacramento Cathedral, and the Chapel at Sacred Heart Monastery, Lisle, Illinois. EverGreene's work over the last 25 years includes projects large and small in houses of worship around the country, including ten cathedrals, 26 state capitols, and hundreds of theaters, public buildings, commercial interiors and residences. ■

Guidance In Giving

GUIDANCE IN GIVING, INC.
Full Service Stewardship, Development and Campaign Consultants
Michael R. Cusack, ...President and CEO
225 Snedecor Avenue, Bayport, NY 11705
888.757.5444 Fax 631.472.6109
Michael V. Goodwin, ...Executive Vice President
222 Harvard Oval, Freehold, NJ 07728
888.869.5522 Fax 732.683.0603
Joseph W. Zamorano, ...Executive Vice President
7504 Collins Ranch Terrace, San Diego, CA 92130
800.993.3335 Fax 858.484.0132
Christopher J. Cusack, ...Vice President
352 McConnell Avenue, Bayport, NY 11705
888.443.1522 Fax 631.472.4364
Curtis Neuschaefer, ...Vice President
3873 West Hibiscus Street, Weston, FL 33332
888.854.4480 Fax 954.384.0032
Robert A. Boegel, ...Regional Executive
P.O. Box 2070, Independence, MO 64055
816.719.6573
Carlos Proaño, ...Vice President
5439 Briercrest Avenue, Lakewood, CA 90713
866.874.4700 Fax 562.920.5523
Kelley P. Stupfel, ...Vice President
800 5th Avenue, Suite # 101 - 414, Seattle, WA 98104
800.734.8898 Fax 206.933.5923

Guidance In Giving, Inc is a national Catholic organization that provides full-time, on-site fundraising counsel to Catholic dioceses, parishes and schools. The firm specializes in Diocesan Capital Campaigns, Diocesan Annual Appeals, Feasibility and Planning Studies, Development Audits, Parish Capital Campaigns, Catholic High School and Elementary School Campaigns and the Implementation of Stewardship at the parish and diocesan level. Additionally, the firm is able to offer bilingual services. Executives of the firm have conducted successful campaigns since 1980. All members of the firm understand and respect the Mission of the Church.
Please contact one of the regional offices to have a member of the executive staff spend a day at your diocese, parish or school to discuss your development and stewardship efforts. When concluded, the firm will prepare an honest, objective appraisal of your program at no cost to your organization. Thank you for considering the services of Guidance In Giving, Inc. ■

Kosinski architecture
Liturgical Design Consultancy
Architecture
Historical Preservation
Construction Management

KOSINSKI ARCHITECTURE
1212 Main Street
Branford, CT 06405
Tel.: 203-488-7399
Fax: 203-483-7066

P.O. Box 23875
Ft. Lauderdale, FL 33307
Tel.: 954-627-6988
Fax: 954-627-6955
E-mail: keiarch@aol.com
Web Site: www.keiarch.com

Type of Business:
Kosinski has offered liturgical design and architectural design services for 35 years. Our extensive knowledge of liturgy and the history of church architecture allows us to provide our clients with exceptional services. Our full range of in-house professional services, including the design of all liturgical elements, interior design, and construction management, gives our clients a single point of contact for complete project delivery. We emphasize a team approach in which the client participates actively in design and project delivery. ■

MUNNS
MANUFACTURING INC.

MUNNS MANUFACTURING, INC.
P.O. Box 477
Garland, UT 84312
Tel: 435-257-5673
Fax: 435-257-3842
Web Site: www.munnsmfg.com

Personnel:
Chad Munns ....President
Shane Larson ....Sales
Shannon King ....Bidding
Dave Field ....Design

Type of Business:
Munns Manufacturing, Inc. builds and installs custom designed prefabricated aluminum steeples, cupolas, domes, clock and bell towers. We do new designs or restoration work. Products are lightweight, durable and maintenance free. Projects include St. Patrick's in Newfoundland, Sacred Heart Parish in Kansas, All Saints Church in Kentucky, St. Ann's in Virginia, and Our Lady of Lourdes in Missouri. For the best product at the lowest price, Munns Manufacturing is the right choice. ■

Vermont Church Supply Co.

VERMONT CHURCH SUPPLY CO.
676 Pine Street, P.O. Box 368
Burlington, VT 05401
Tel.: 802-862-6486, 800-451-3453; Fax: 802-862-5765
E-mail: vcs@together.net
Web Site: www.vermontchurchsupply.com

Personnel:
Neil Clark ....President

Type of Business:
Since our inception in 1946 by W. Barrett Clark and Doris Clark, Vermont Church Supply has offered the highest quality products and the best service to the Church and the Clergy. We have a wide range of products including Candles, Church Furniture, Metalware and Vestments. Our founders' Sons, Neil, John, Thomas and Robert, along with the third generation Anthony Clark, continue to provide services such as refinishing Sacred Vessels, Candlesticks and tabernacles and also the execution of hand carved wood and marble Statuary. Whether your needs are small or large, we can give the best personalized service to our Customers. ■

The Wood & Iron Factory
Architectural Woodwork, Furniture and Design

THE WOOD & IRON FACTORY
2495 Paseo de las Americas, Suite F
San Diego, CA 92154
Tel: 619-710-1660
Fax: 619-710-1662

Type of Business:
The Wood and Iron Factory is a manufacturer of custom designed pews, chancel furniture and ecclesiastical art. To complement our wood products, we also offer wrought iron, cast aluminum, bronze and stone.
We offer limitless design, material selection and artistic interpretation. Our products are custom designed to complement each individual church. We do not limit our clients with catalog furnishings.
Our 2nd and 3rd generation craftsmen take great pride in our reputation for superb quality at competitive prices.
The Wood & Iron Factory is the proud manufacturer of pews and furniture at Our Lady of the Angels Cathedral in Los Angeles, California. ■

Architects

DUNCAN G. STROIK, ARCHITECT

DUNCAN G. STROIK ARCHITECT, L.L.C.
218 W. Washington St. Suite 1200
South Bend, IN 46601-1800
Tel.: 574-232-1783
Fax: 574-232-1792
E-mail: stroik@stroikarchitect.com
Web Site: www.stroikarchitect.com;
www.sacredarchitecture.com

Personnel:
Duncan G. Stroik...Principal

Type of Business:
Duncan G. Stroik Architect is a full service design firm focused on creating carefully detailed and proportioned ecclesiastical and institutional buildings. Projects are undertaken with the intent to create works of art which ennoble those who come in contact with them. The firm is a leading practitioner of traditional Catholic architecture, basing its work on the ancient principles of durability, function and beauty. We strive to design buildings that fulfill all three of these requirements. ■

Kosinski architecture
Liturgical Design Consultancy
Architecture
Historical Preservation
Construction Management

KOSINSKI ARCHITECTURE
1212 Main Street
Branford, CT 06405
Tel.: 203-488-7399
Fax: 203-483-7066

P.O. Box 23875
Ft. Lauderdale, FL 33307
Tel.: 954-627-6988
Fax: 954-627-6955
E-mail: keiarch@aol.com
Web Site: www.keiarch.com

Type of Business:
Kosinski has offered liturgical design and architectural design services for 35 years. Our extensive knowledge of liturgy and the history of church architecture allows us to provide our clients with exceptional services. Our full range of in-house professional services, including the design of all liturgical elements, interior design, and construction management, gives our clients a single point of contact for complete project delivery. We emphasize a team approach in which the client participates actively in design and project delivery. ■

QUINN EVANS | ARCHITECTS

QUINN EVANS | ARCHITECTS
219 1/2 North Main Street
Ann Arbor, MI 48104
Tel: 734-663-5888; Fax: 734-663-5044
E-mail: qea-mi@quinnevans.com
Web Site: www.quinnevans.com

Personnel:
Ilene R. Tyler, FAIA ....Principal (Ann Arbor)
1214 Twenty-eighth Street, NW
Washington, DC 20007
Tel: 202-298-6700; Fax: 202-298-6666
E-mail: qea-dc@quinnevans.com
Web Site: www.quinnevans.com

Personnel:
Baird M. Smith, AIA...........Principal (Washington, DC)

Type of Business:
As a full service architectural firm with special expertise in preservation architecture, QUINN EVANS | ARCHITECTS understands the important role that religious facilities play in strengthening the social fiber of communities. Our firm also recognizes that respectful rehabilitation of these community "anchors" contributes significantly toward revitalization of our urban neighborhoods. QUINN EVANS | ARCHITECTS received a 2004 AIA Michigan Honor Award for the Restoration of the Cathedral of Saint Andrew, Grand Rapids, Michigan. ■

Artists & Decorators

Berlinger Company

THE BERLINGER COMPANY
2605 N. Sheridan Rd.
Peoria, IL 61604
Tel.: 309-688-1771
Fax: 309-688-9240
E-mail: info@theberlingercompany.com
Web Site: www.theberlingercompany.com

Personnel:
Michael Berlinger....................President
Jeff Walters....................Accts Manager
Milton Pachers-Lay....................Sales.

Type of Business:
Church interior design and consultants
Interior restoration
New church designs
New liturgical whole goods—domestic and imported
Custom manufacturers
Liturgical Antiquities—domestic and imported ■

BOTTI STUDIO OF ARCHITECTURAL ARTS, INC.

BOTTI STUDIO OF ARCHITECTURAL ARTS, INC.
919 Grove Street
Evanston, Illinois 60201
Tel.: 800-524-7211; 847-869-5933
Fax: 847-869-5996
E-mail: botti@ bottistudio.com
Web Site: www.bottistudio.com

East Coast Studio:
3104 S. Osprey Avenue
Sarasota, FL 33577
Tel.: 941-951-0978
Fax: 941-953-9078

West Coast Studio:
1038 N. Hwy. 101
Encinitas, CA 92024
Tel.: 760-753-0705
Fax: 760-753-0705

International Office: Agropoli, Italy, Nassau, Bahamas

Personnel:
Staff of 45. Includes internationally recognized ecclesiastic artists and designers working in conjunction with highly skilled glass and statuary craftspeople and artisans.
Ettore Christopher Botti....................Principal
Ethlyn Panzironi Botti....................Principal

Type of Business:
Since 1864, Botti Studio has specialized in serving the ecclesiastic environment through design, fabrication, delivery, and installation. Experts on staff in conservation, restoration, and repair provide a source for experienced project management — from conception through completion. Services include: **STAINED GLASS:** As custom designers and manufacturers, Botti artisans fabricate designs in stained, faceted, sandblasted, carved, and painted glass. **MARBLE:** Skilled craftsmen sculpt new or refurbish existing statuary, railings, baptismal fonts, and altars. **INTERIORS:** Complete renovations of interiors can be carefully and historically provided through plaster work, faux painting, gilding, stenciling, and graining. **MOSIAC:** Using state-of-the-art procedures, Botti can use preservation and restoration techniques to bring pieces back to their original beauty or create new custom installations. **CONSULTATON:** Preliminary-stage consultation can provide visualization of projects to aid in fund-raising and planning. **HISTORIC DISCOVERY:** Documentation and archival recording of existing sacred windows, marble, interior painting, and art is available. **STATUARY:** Working in wood, marble, or plaster, our designers are experts at restoration of aged, timeworn statuary and creation of custom ornamentation. ■

Conrad Schmitt Studios Inc.
Excellence in Artistry Since 1889

CONRAD SCHMITT STUDIOS, INC.
2405 S. 162nd St.
New Berlin, WI 53151
Tel: 800-969-3033
262-786-3030
Fax:262-786-9036
E-mail: studio@conradschmitt.com
Web Site: www.conradschmitt.com

Personnel:
Heidi Gruenke Emery ....Vice Pres. & Marketing Dir.

Type of Business:
Since 1889, the family-owned Conrad Schmitt Studios has been privileged to provide decoration, restoration and artwork to enhance the worship environment of churches throughout the country, including more than twenty-five cathedrals.
For projects in the early stages, CSS offers consultations, design renderings, decorative samples and budgetary estimates for use in planning and fundraising. For historic restorations, our conservators investigate and document original paint colors and decoration to guide the restoration work.
CSS employs a permanent staff of highly experienced artists and artisans who conduct ornamental plaster work, decorative painting, stenciling, trompe l'oeil and interior and exterior gilding. CSS artists also continually create, conserve, restore and replicate stained glass, murals, mosaics and statuary. CSS has a 114-year history of service to the Catholic community and is dedicated to providing the finest ecclesiastical artwork that blends history and tradition with a growing and evolving faith.■

DAPRATO RIGALI STUDIOS, INC.

DAPRATO RIGALI STUDIOS, INC.
6030 N. Northwest Highway
Chicago, IL 60631
Tel.: 773-763-5511; Fax: 773-763-5522
Web Site: www.dapratorigali.com

Personnel:

John Rigali
Lisa Rigali Galvin
Robert Rigali
Mike Rigali

Type of Business:

Daprato Rigali Studios Inc. has been beautifying Churches in America since 1860.

Today we find the Rigali Family restoring and renovating the churches originally decorated by their Great-Grandfather, John E. Rigali; aware of his reputation to create spiritually moving environments with quality material and craftsmanship.

Some of their most recent jobs include: decoration and stained glass restoration at St. Mary of the Lake Seminary, Mundelein, IL; Marble renovation and decoration, St. Elizabeth's Mother House, Allegany, N.Y.; and General Contracting for complete renovation of St. Bernadette's Church, Rockford, IL.

The Daprato Rigali staff is equipped to take your project from start to finish. If you're interested in working with a fine interior design studio experienced in Ecclesiastical Artistries please call for consultation at no obligation. We deliver what we design. ■

LD Linda Dabeau | *Studio, LLC.*

LINDA DABEAU/ DABEAU STUDIO
P. O. Box 10126
Albuquerque, New Mexico 87184
Tel/Fax: (505) 898-2227
Email: ldabeau@swcp.com
Web Site: www.ldabeau.com

Type of Business:

Linda Dabeau has been awarded both national and international commissions in sculpture. She works in multiple mediums, such as bronze, stone, fired clay, cast metals, glass and wood. Her positive personal energy, combined with prodigious hand skills and her comprehension of the roots of Christianity, enable her to become a conduit for the vision of the parish, church authority and architect. Through her highly disciplined work, Dabeau acts as a catalyst to create a bond within the whole community. Her multiple talents include design of liturgical furnishings such as alters, ambo, tabernacle, baptismal fonts, shrines, and stained glass. She is available to consult with parish communities.

Her materials are selected and utilized to create the best and most unique total visage of spirituality in the physical form. Dabeau's sculptures range from 24 inches to life size and monumental. Please contact the artist for commissions and limited editions that are available. ■

DOMUSDEI HOLY ART STUDIOS

DOMUSDEI HOLY ART STUDIOS

FACTORY:	Via dei Tulipani, 48 - 00040 CECCHINA DI ALBANO (RM) - ITALY Tel: 011-39-06-9343369 Fax: 011-39-06-9344971
SHOWROOM:	Via Scossacavalli 3/9 - 00193 ROMA - ITALY Tel: 011-39-06-6868090 Fax: 011-39-06-9344971 Email: info@domusdei.it m.delmonte@domusdei.it Web site: www.domusdei.it

Personnel:

Alessandro Del Monte ....President
Massimiliano Del Monte......................Executive Director
Aldo Del Monte ....Assistant President

Type of Business:

Founded in 1963, Domusdei Studio has restored thousands of church interiors all over the world. Specializing in designing and manufacturing stained glass windows, mosaics, bronze and fiberglass statues, altars, bronze doors, lecterns, baptismal fonts, candlesticks, flower holders, and tabernacles

We are also experts in silver and gold plating and the restoration of wood and metal masterpieces. ■

EVERGREENE PAINTING STUDIOS, INC.

EVERGREENE PAINTING STUDIOS, INC.

450 West 31st St., 7th Fl.
New York, NY 10001
Tel.: 212-244-2800
Fax: 212-244-6204

711 South Blvd., Ste. 7
Oak Park, IL 60302
Tel.: 708-358-1642
Fax: 708-358-1656

E-mail: info@evergreene.com
Web Site: www.evergreene.com

Personnel:
Jeff Greene..President
Kim Lovejoy.................................. Director of Marketing
Gillian Randell ....Chief Fine Arts Conservator
Terry Vanderwell ....Director of Restoration, Midwest
Anthony Kartsonas.Architectural Conservator, Midwest

Type of Business:
EverGreene is a full-service decorative arts studio committed to preserving the integrity of historic sacred spaces through conservation, restoration, and compatible new artwork and decoration. Services include investigation and analysis of original finishes; consultations, renderings, budgets and samples to support decision-making and capital campaigns; design of color schemes, architectural ornament and furnishings; and guidance on specifications. EverGreene's consistently high-quality work is performed by its staff of experienced project managers, professionally-trained conservators, fine artists and craftsmen.

EverGreene's capabilities include all types of decorative painting, stenciling, gilding and trompe l'oeil; conservation, replication, and new design of murals and mosaics; ornamental plaster and scagliola; and allied crafts including wood and metal refinishing, interior stone cleaning, art glass, tile work and other architectural arts.

Among EverGreene's current projects are St. Matthew's Cathedral in Washington, D.C., Sacramento Cathedral, and the Chapel at Sacred Heart Monastery, Lisle, Illinois. EverGreene's work over the last 25 years includes projects large and small in houses of worship around the country, including ten cathedrals, 26 state capitols, and hundreds of theaters, public buildings, commercial interiors and residences. ■

Maison Bouvrier

MAISON BOUVRIER INC.

391 Hanlan Road, Woodbridge
Ontario, Canada L4L 3T1
905-851-1146 or 800-665-9895
Fax 905-851-7623
E-mail: bouvrier@maisonbouvrier.com
Web Site: www.maisonbouvrier.com

Personnel:
Kevin Bayne ....President
Janet MacDonald ....General Manager

Type of Business:
Maison Bouvrier has been in existence for over 130 years and is a world leader in weaving, creating and developing inspirational fabric designs of impeccable quality. Personalised attention is given to the needs of individual communities. All our artistic work is initially designed and created during a personal visit, thereby ensuring that the fabric used, the designs selected and the shapes chosen, fit perfectly into the worship space and enhance the visual liturgy. ■

RAMBUSCH

RAMBUSCH LIGHTING

160 Cornelison Avenue
Jersey City, NJ 07304
Tel.: 201-333-2525; Fax: 201-433-3355
Web Site: www.rambusch.com

Personnel:
Edwin P. Rambusch ....President & C.E.O.
Martin V. Rambusch ....Chairman of the Board

Type of Business:
Since 1898, creating church interiors, liturgical furnishings, and art work. Fine restoration of church interiors. In-house studios and shops for designing and executing stained glass, church lighting systems, art metal work, and decorative painting. ■

WINDHOVER
ART+DESIGN STUDIO

WINDHOVER ART AND DESIGN STUDIO

231 Peabody Ave.
Lyndhurst, NJ 07071
Tel: 201-438-1391
Fax: 973-663-1594

Personnel:
Norman Woehle ....Artist & Designer
Nola Woehrle ....Weaver & Textile Artisan

Type of Business:
We are a European-Trained Artist/artisan team doing good work for catholic churches, chapels and parish centers for over twenty years. Our point of view is original and contemporary, open to fresh breaths of the Spirit. We accept commissions for panel paintings, murals, tapestry, and applique wall hangings, stained and etched glass, as well as liturgical furnishings and appointments. The studio's aim is to restore to our worship spaces the texture and color that were their heritage for centuries. ■

Bell Towers & Steeples

MUNNS MANUFACTURING, INC.
P.O. Box 477
Garland, UT 84312
Tel: 435-257-5673
Fax: 435-257-3842
Web Site: www.munnsmfg.com

Personnel:
Chad Munns .... President
Shane Larson .... Sales
Shannon King .... Bidding
Dave Field .... Design

Type of Business:
Munns Manufacturing, Inc. builds and installs custom designed prefabricated aluminum steeples, cupolas, domes, clock and bell towers. We do new designs or restoration work. Products are lightweight, durable and maintenance free. Projects include St. Patrick's in Newfoundland, Sacred Heart Parish in Kansas, All Saints Church in Kentucky, St. Ann's in Virginia, and Our Lady of Lourdes in Missouri. For the best product at the lowest price, Munns Manufacturing is the right choice. ■

Bronze Millenium Doors

VALLEY BRONZE OF OREGON, INC.
307 W. Alder St. P.O. Box 669
Joseph, Oregon 97846
Tel: 541-432-7551 Fax: 541-432-0255
Web Site: www.valleybronze.com
E-mail: adstark@valleybronze.com
Personnel:
A. Daniel Stark .... Marketing

Type of business:
Valley Bronze of Oregon, Inc. has been in business continuously at the same location in Joseph, Oregon, since 1982, and has produced over $30 million dollars of investment cast sculpture, working primarily in bronze, but also casting and fabricating in silver, stainless steel and aluminum. We work with artists from all over the United States, and offer turnkey service starting with design, engineering and model making, all the way to professional on-site installation.
Over the past few years Valley Bronze of Oregon has expanded its production capabilities well beyond cast bronze sculpture to include architectural fabrications, ornamental and misc. metals, and bronze doors. We are building upon the experience gained in such projects as the three sets of double Millennium Bronze Doors for the Lady of Lourdes Cathedral in Spokane, Washington, and the "Day the Wall Came Down" Monument by artist Veryl Goodnight sited at the Bush Library in College Station, Texas, and also a sister monument at the Allied Museum in Berlin, Germany.
Within the last year Valley Bronze installed six monumental bronze bulls, "The Spirit of the Bull", by Maryland artist Walter Matia for the Houston Texans NFL franchise at Reliant Stadium in Houston, Texas, and also completed a $2.4 million ornamental metals subcontract on the National WWII Memorial to be dedicated this May in Washington, D.C. Valley Bronze is currently working on a set of bas relief bronze doors for the St. Ann's Cathedral in Great Falls, Montana.■

Church Signs & Banners

RM SIGNS
10646 Baptist Church Road
St. Louis, MO 63128
Tel.: 314-842-0303
Fax: 314-842-0339
Web Site: www.rmsigns.net
E-mail: rmsignz@aol.com

Type of Business:
RM Signs specializes in changeable message signs, sand blasted and routed letters.
Please call for a free catalog. ■

ROBERT GASPARD CO., INC.
200 N. Janacek Road
Brookfield, WI 53045-610
Tel.: 800-784-6868; Fax: 800-784-7567
E-mail: mail@rgaspard.com
Web Site: www.robertgaspardco.com

Personnel:
Rose Gaspard .... President
Jason R. Gaspard .... General Manager

Type of Business:
The Robert Gaspard Co. was established in 1954. Over the past 50 years, we have grown to be a nationally-known company. We pride ourselves on the ability to create original custom designs to enrich your worship needs. Our complete line consists of all ecclesiastical vesture, as well as paraments, mass and altar linens, stoles, banners, chasubles, funeral palls, albs, cossacks, surplices, choir robes, acolyte robes and many accessories. Complimentary catalog and fabric swatches sent on request. ■

Conservation

BOTTI STUDIO OF ARCHITECTURAL ARTS, INC.

BOTTI STUDIO OF ARCHITECTURAL ARTS, INC.
919 Grove Street
Evanston, Illinois 60201
Tel.: 800-524-7211; 847-869-5933
Fax: 847-869-5996
E-mail: botti@ bottistudio.com
Web Site: www.bottistudio.com

East Coast Studio:	*West Coast Studio:*
3104 S. Osprey Avenue	1038 N. Hwy. 101
Sarasota, FL 33577	Encinitas, CA 92024
Tel.: 941-951-0978	Tel.: 760-753-0705
Fax: 941-953-9078	Fax: 760-753-0705

International Office: Agropoli, Italy, Nassau, Bahamas

Personnel:
Staff of 45. Includes internationally recognized ecclesiastic artists and designers working in conjunction with highly skilled glass and statuary craftspeople and artisans.
Ettore Christopher Botti .... Principal
Ethlyn Panzironi Botti .... Principal

Type of Business:
Since 1864, Botti Studio has specialized in serving the ecclesiastic environment through design, fabrication, delivery, and installation. Experts on staff in conservation, restoration, and repair provide a source for experienced project management — from conception through completion. Services include: **STAINED GLASS:** As custom designers and manufacturers, Botti artisans fabricate designs in stained, faceted, sandblasted, carved, and painted glass. **MARBLE:** Skilled craftsmen sculpt new or refurbish existing statuary, railings, baptismal fonts, and altars. **INTERIORS:** Complete renovations of interiors can be carefully and historically provided through plaster work, faux painting, gilding, stenciling, and graining. **MOSIAC:** Using state-of-the-art procedures, Botti can use preservation and restoration techniques to bring pieces back to their original beauty or create new custom installations. **CONSULTATON:** Preliminary-stage consultation can provide visualization of projects to aid in fund-raising and planning. **HISTORIC DISCOVERY:** Documentation and archival recording of existing sacred windows, marble, interior painting, and art is available. **STATUARY:** Working in wood, marble, or plaster, our designers are experts at restoration of aged, timeworn statuary and creation of custom ornamentation. ■

Conrad Schmitt Studios Inc.
Excellence in Artistry Since 1889

CONRAD SCHMITT STUDIOS, INC.
2405 S. 162nd St.
New Berlin, WI 53151
Tel: 800-969-3033
262-786-3030
Fax:262-786-9036
E-mail: studio@conradschmitt.com
Web Site: www.conradschmitt.com

Personnel:
Heidi Gruenke Emery .... Vice Pres. & Marketing Dir.

Type of Business:
Since 1889, the family-owned Conrad Schmitt Studios has been privileged to provide decoration, restoration and artwork to enhance the worship environment of churches throughout the country, including more than twenty-five cathedrals.
For projects in the early stages, CSS offers consultations, design renderings, decorative samples and budgetary estimates for use in planning and fundraising. For historic restorations, our conservators investigate and document original paint colors and decoration to guide the restoration work.
CSS employs a permanent staff of highly experienced artists and artisans who conduct ornamental plaster work, decorative painting, stenciling, trompe l'oeil and interior and exterior gilding. CSS artists also continually create, conserve, restore and replicate stained glass, murals, mosaics and statuary. CSS has a 114-year history of service to the Catholic community and is dedicated to providing the finest ecclesiastical artwork that blends history and tradition with a growing and evolving faith.■

EVERGREENE PAINTING STUDIOS, INC.

EVERGREENE PAINTING STUDIOS, INC.

450 West 31st St., 7th Fl.	711 South Blvd., Ste. 7
New York, NY 10001	Oak Park, IL 60302
Tel.: 212-244-2800	Tel.: 708-358-1642
Fax: 212-244-6204	Fax: 708-358-1656

E-mail: info@evergreene.com
Web Site: www.evergreene.com

Personnel:
Jeff Greene .... President
Kim Lovejoy .... Director of Marketing
Gillian Randell .... Chief Fine Arts Conservator
Terry Vanderwell.......... Director of Restoration, Midwest
Anthony Kartsonas . Architectural Conservator, Midwest

Type of Business:
EverGreene is a full-service decorative arts studio committed to preserving the integrity of historic sacred spaces through conservation, restoration, and compatible new artwork and decoration. Services include investigation and analysis of original finishes; consultations, renderings, budgets and samples to support decision-making and capital campaigns; design of color schemes, architectural ornament and furnishings; and guidance on specifications. EverGreene's consistently high-quality work is performed by its staff of experienced project managers, professionally-trained conservators, fine artists and craftsmen.
EverGreene's capabilities include all types of decorative painting, stenciling, gilding and trompe l'oeil; conservation, replication, and new design of murals and mosaics; ornamental plaster and scagliola; and allied crafts including wood and metal refinishing, interior stone cleaning, art glass, tile work and other architectural arts.
Among EverGreene's current projects are St. Matthew's Cathedral in Washington, D.C., Sacramento Cathedral, and the Chapel at Sacred Heart Monastery, Lisle, Illinois. EverGreene's work over the last 25 years includes projects large and small in houses of worship around the country, including ten cathedrals, 26 state capitols, and hundreds of theaters, public buildings, commercial interiors and residences. ■

RAMBUSCH

RAMBUSCH LIGHTING
160 Cornelison Avenue
Jersey City, NJ 07304
Tel.: 201-333-2525; Fax: 201-433-3355
Web Site: www.rambusch.com

Personnel:
Edwin P. Rambusch ....President & C.E.O.
Martin V. Rambusch ....Chairman of the Board

Type of Business:
Since 1898, creating church interiors, liturgical furnishings, and art work. Fine restoration of church interiors. In-house studios and shops for designing and executing stained glass, church lighting systems, art metal work, and decorative painting. ■

Doors & Partitions

ATD-AMERICAN CO.

ATD-AMERICAN CO.
135 Greenwood Avenue
Wyncote, PA 19095-1396
Tel.: 888-283-2487; Fax: 800-283-7363
E-mail: american@atd.com
Web Site: www.atd.com

Personnel:
Bob Roche...Marketing
Sal Catanese ....Sales

Type of Business:
For four generations, ATD-AMERICAN has supplied Furniture and Equipment to Churches, Organizations and Institutions nationally and worldwide. Since 1931, it has been our tradition to deliver high quality products and personal service at the lowest competitive prices. ATD offers a wide range of products to meet all of the needs of your Church and School. Our comprehensive catalog includes the following: Announcement and Bulletin Boards, Audio-Visual Equipment, Classroom Furniture, Computer Furniture, Daycare Furniture, Display Cases, Folding Chairs, Folding Tables, Lecterns, Library Furniture, Office Furniture, Outdoor Equipment, Pews and Pulpit Furniture, Room Dividers and Partitions, Stacking Chairs, and Stages and Risers.

For a FREE Wholesale Furniture Catalog, call us toll-free 888-283-2487 or fax us at 800-283-7363. You can also visit our web site at www.atd.com or e-mail us at american@atd.com.

SPECIAL OFFER FOR CATHOLIC DIRECTORY SUBSCRIBERS: Mention offer code 6557 and receive a special 10% discount on your first order. ■

HUFCOR, INC.
P.O. Box 591
Janesville, WI 53547
Tel.: 800-542-2371, Ext. 395
Fax: 608-758-8253

Personnel:
Steve Meyer...................................Marketing Coordinator

Type of Business:
Hufcor operable and accordion partitions allow you the flexibility to create large or small spaces, fast. Our wide selection of models, sound control ratings, configurations, options, and finishes, lets you choose the right product for your budget and needs. Hufcor partitions are available through local, factory-trained distributors who offer free design assistance as well as installation and service. Hufcor is a ISO 9001 registered company. Call our toll free number for the name of your nearest representative. ■

Liturgical Design & Fabrication

Humenick
Liturgical Arts

HUMENICK LITURGICAL ARTS
14 Taylor Rd.
Santa Fe, NM 87508
Tel.: 505-690-7000
Web Site: www.humenick.catholic.org
E-mail: humenick@direcway.com

Personnel:
Mark Humenick

Type of Business:
Mark Humenick was first commissioned, in 1973, to design and fabricate liturgical essentials. Working closely with clergy, architects, and parish committees, this work has resulted in award-winning, one-of-a-kind pieces at quite reasonable costs.

From an individual piece to a complete, design-coordinated interior, our mediums include metal, wood, and stone. We design pieces that will be lasting yet flexible, with no commission being too small. Contact us to learn how we may assist you. ■

Masonry

UNIVERSAL ART STUDIO
67 Mountain Spring Drive
Sparta, NJ 07871
Tel.: 973-726-0835
Fax: 973-729-1189

Personnel:
Yuri Mironoff .... Owner
Rita Mironoff .... Owner/ Designer

Type of Business:
Our crew is compact and capable of dealing with practically every aspect of restoration, renovation and repair work - we subcontract very little. We do not run more than one project at a time. We take no interruptions and deliver on time. ■

Monumental Church Entrances

THE BAUT STUDIOS, INC.
ECCLESIASTICAL CRAFTSMEN

THE BAUT STUDIOS, INC.
1095 Main Street
Swoyersville, PA 18704
Tel.: 800-326-9421; Fax: 570-288-0380
E-mail: info@baut.com
Web Site: www.baut.com

Personnel:
Conrad Dismas Baut .... President
Gerhard Francis Baut .... Master Sculptor
Heide Baut Cebrick .... Artist/Designer
Karen Baut Klemm .... Business Manager

Type of Business:
The STAINED GLASS of the FUTURE is here NOW! The Baut Studios, Inc., established in 1927, is a full-service ecclesiastical studio that has been manufacturing and installing their own patented STRUCTURAL STAINED GLASS* in windows and doors for more than 44 years. A unique non-sagging construction never needing structural repairs, STRUCTURAL STAINED GLASS is LEAD FREE, and CUSTOM DESIGNED to fit many tastes and budgets. Pricing is competitive with leaded and stained glass but with many more advantages when combined with the BAUT WINDOW and DOOR SYSTEMS. Beautiful, long lasting, environmentally and financially sound, and virtually maintenance free, STRUCTURAL STAINED GLASS is featured in over 5,000 churches worldwide.

Other products include Single, Double, and Triple Glazed Church Windows and Ventilators, Heavy Duty Doors, Restoration/New Traditional Stained Glass, Altars and Appointments, Crosses, Steeples, Glass Mosaics, and Church Lighting. All Baut products are custom made to your sizes and shapes and are designed to match your decor. * U.S. Patent No. 3,064 380 ■

BOTTI STUDIO OF ARCHITECTURAL ARTS, INC.

BOTTI STUDIO OF ARCHITECTURAL ARTS, INC.
919 Grove Street
Evanston, Illinois 60201
Tel.: 800-524-7211; 847-869-5933
Fax: 847-869-5996
E-mail: botti@ bottistudio.com
Web Site: www.bottistudio.com

East Coast Studio:	*West Coast Studio:*
3104 S. Osprey Avenue	1038 N. Hwy. 101
Sarasota, FL 33577	Encinitas, CA 92024
Tel.: 941-951-0978	Tel.: 760-753-0705
Fax: 941-953-9078	Fax: 760-753-0705

International Office: Agropoli, Italy, Nassau, Bahamas

Personnel:
Staff of 45. Includes internationally recognized ecclesiastic artists and designers working in conjunction with highly skilled glass and statuary craftspeople and artisans.
Ettore Christopher Botti .... Principal
Ethlyn Panzironi Botti .... Principal

Type of Business:
Since 1864, Botti Studio has specialized in serving the ecclesiastic environment through design, fabrication, delivery, and installation. Experts on staff in conservation, restoration, and repair provide a source for experienced project management — from conception through completion. Services include: **STAINED GLASS:** As custom designers and manufacturers, Botti artisans fabricate designs in stained, faceted, sandblasted, carved, and painted glass. **MARBLE:** Skilled craftsmen sculpt new or refurbish existing statuary, railings, baptismal fonts, and altars. **INTERIORS:** Complete renovations of interiors can be carefully and historically provided through plaster work, faux painting, gilding, stenciling, and graining. **MOSIAC:** Using state-of-the-art procedures, Botti can use preservation and restoration techniques to bring pieces back to their original beauty or create new custom installations. **CONSULTATON:** Preliminary-stage consultation can provide visualization of projects to aid in fund-raising and planning. **HISTORIC DISCOVERY:** Documentation and archival recording of existing sacred windows, marble, interior painting, and art is available. **STATUARY:** Working in wood, marble, or plaster, our designers are experts at restoration of aged, timeworn statuary and creation of custom ornamentation. ■

VALLEY BRONZE OF OREGON, INC.
307 W. Alder St. P.O. Box 669
Joseph, Oregon 97846
Tel: 541-432-7551 Fax: 541-432-0255
Web Site: www.valleybronze.com
E-mail: adstark@valleybronze.com

Personnel:
A. Daniel Stark .... Marketing

Type of business:
Valley Bronze of Oregon, Inc. has been in business continuously at the same location in Joseph, Oregon, since 1982, and has produced over $30 million dollars of investment cast sculpture, working primarily in bronze, but also casting and fabricating in silver, stainless steel and aluminum. We work with artists from all over the United States, and offer turnkey

service starting with design, engineering and model making, all the way to professional on-site installation.

Over the past few years Valley Bronze of Oregon has expanded its production capabilities well beyond cast bronze sculpture to include architectural fabrications, ornamental and misc. metals, and bronze doors. We are building upon the experience gained in such projects as the three sets of double Millennium Bronze Doors for the Lady of Lourdes Cathedral in Spokane, Washington, and the "Day the Wall Came Down" Monument by artist Veryl Goodnight sited at the Bush Library in College Station, Texas, and also a sister monument at the Allied Museum in Berlin, Germany.

Within the last year Valley Bronze installed six monumental bronze bulls, "The Spirit of the Bull", by Maryland artist Walter Matia for the Houston Texans NFL franchise at Reliant Stadium in Houston, Texas, and also completed a $2.4 million ornamental metals subcontract on the National WWII Memorial to be dedicated this May in Washington, D.C. Valley Bronze is currently working on a set of bas relief bronze doors for the St. Ann's Cathedral in Great Falls, Montana.■

Restoration/Refinishing

Adrian Hamers® Church Interiors

ADRIAN HAMERS, INC.
2 Madison Avenue, Larchmont, NY 10538
Tel.: 914-834-7780; Fax: 914-834-0712
Web Site: www.adrianhamers.com

Type of Business:
Custom designers and manufacturers of Sacred Vessels. Since 1887, the Hamers name has been synonymous with expert Silversmithing throughout the world in the field of Liturgical Art. Please contact us for those hard to find items, as we always have a large selection of Adrian Hamers Estate Collection pieces in stock. We have a large collection of antique church stainglass windows available (both full sets and individual). We are experts in: Church Interiors from design to execution, Renovations, Altars, Sacred Vessels, Gold and Silver Plating & Repairing, Appraisals, Tabernacles, Marble, Statuary, Woodwork & Woodcarving, Stained Glass, Pews & Chairs, Gold Leafing, Frescoes, Restoration, Trompe-l' oeuil, Wall Murals (repair and conservation cleaning), Ornamental Plaster, Heraldic Designs & Bishop Regalia. Please call us for a free 36-page Sacred Vessels color catalog, or our free 80-page color Woodcarvings catalog. ■

THE ART OF GLASS, INC.
316 Media Station Rd.
Media, PA 19037
Tel.: 610-891-7813; Fax: 610-891-0150

Personnel:
Kathy Jordan....................President

Type of Business:
The Art of Glass, Inc. provides quality design and fabrication services and is committed to the efficient completion of new construction and the ethical restoration and preservation of historic windows. Our reputation and experience in the field is well documented. We would be pleased to assist you in the early stages of planning (and design), working with your architect and/or committee to achieve your desired goals. ■

Berlinger Company

THE BERLINGER COMPANY
2605 N. Sheridan Rd.
Peoria, IL 61604
Tel.: 309-688-1771
Fax: 309-688-9240
E-mail: info@theberlingercompany.com
Web Site: www.theberlingercompany.com

Personnel:
Michael Berlinger....................President
Jeff Walters....................Accts Manager
Milton Pachers-Lay....................Sales

Type of Business:
Church interior design and consultants
Interior restoration
New church designs
New liturgical whole goods—domestic and imported
Custom manufacturers
Liturgical Antiquities—domestic and imported ■

Bovard Studio Stained Glass

BOVARD STUDIO INC.
2281 Highway 34 East
Fairfield, IA 52556
Tel: 800-452-7796
Fax: 641-472-0974
E-mail: info@bovardstudio.com
Web Site: www.bovardstudio.com

Personnel:
Ron Bovard....................C.E.O.
Bob Greco....................President
Leigh Carter....................Sales Manager, Indianapolis Office

Type of Business:
We design, fabricate and install traditional and contemporary stained glass; provide full restoration services, including new wood, aluminum and steel frames, and protective covering systems, with Precision Flow® ventilation designed for preservation of stained glass windows; and custom wood doors.

Our 40,000 sq. ft. facility also includes a complete woodshop and welding shop. Bovard Studio's 70 artists, craftspeople and staff from around the world are among the most talented founded today. Eighteen sales offices across the USA

See our color ad on the Products and Services Section Tab. ■

BOTTI STUDIO OF ARCHITECTURAL ARTS, INC.

BOTTI STUDIO OF ARCHITECTURAL ARTS, INC.
919 Grove Street
Evanston, Illinois 60201
Tel.: 800-524-7211; 847-869-5933
Fax: 847-869-5996
E-mail: botti@ bottistudio.com
Web Site: www.bottistudio.com

East Coast Studio:
3104 S. Osprey Avenue
Sarasota, FL 33577
Tel.: 941-951-0978
Fax: 941-953-9078

West Coast Studio:
1038 N. Hwy. 101
Encinitas, CA 92024
Tel.: 760-753-0705
Fax: 760-753-0705

International Office: Agropoli, Italy, Nassau, Bahamas

Personnel:

Staff of 45. Includes internationally recognized ecclesiastic artists and designers working in conjunction with highly skilled glass and statuary craftspeople and artisans.

Ettore Christopher Botti ....Principal
Ethlyn Panzironi Botti ....Principal

Type of Business:

Since 1864, Botti Studio has specialized in serving the ecclesiastic environment through design, fabrication, delivery, and installation. Experts on staff in conservation, restoration, and repair provide a source for experienced project management — from conception through completion. Services include: **STAINED GLASS:** As custom designers and manufacturers, Botti artisans fabricate designs in stained, faceted, sandblasted, carved, and painted glass. **MARBLE:** Skilled craftsmen sculpt new or refurbish existing statuary, railings, baptismal fonts, and altars. **INTERIORS:** Complete renovations of interiors can be carefully and historically provided through plaster work, faux painting, gilding, stenciling, and graining. **MOSIAC:** Using state-of-the-art procedures, Botti can use preservation and restoration techniques to bring pieces back to their original beauty or create new custom installations. **CONSULTATON:** Preliminary-stage consultation can provide visualization of projects to aid in fund-raising and planning. **HISTORIC DISCOVERY:** Documentation and archival recording of existing sacred windows, marble, interior painting, and art is available. **STATUARY:** Working in wood, marble, or plaster, our designers are experts at restoration of aged, timeworn statuary and creation of custom ornamentation. ■

Conrad Schmitt Studios Inc.

Excellence in Artistry Since 1889

CONRAD SCHMITT STUDIOS, INC.
2405 S. 162nd St.
New Berlin, WI 53151
Tel: 800-969-3033; 262-786-3030
Fax:262-786-9036
E-mail: studio@conradschmitt.com
Web Site: www.conradschmitt.com

Personnel:

Heidi Gruenke Emery ....Vice Pres. & Marketing Dir.

Type of Business:

Since 1889, the family-owned Conrad Schmitt Studios has been privileged to provide decoration, restoration and artwork to enhance the worship environment of churches throughout the country, including more than twenty-five cathedrals.

For projects in the early stages, CSS offers consultations, design renderings, decorative samples and budgetary estimates for use in planning and fundraising. For historic restorations, our conservators investigate and document original paint colors and decoration to guide the restoration work.

CSS employs a permanent staff of highly experienced artists and artisans who conduct ornamental plaster work, decorative painting, stenciling, trompe l'oeil and interior and exterior gilding. CSS artists also continually create, conserve, restore and replicate stained glass, murals, mosaics and statuary. CSS has a 114-year history of service to the Catholic community and is dedicated to providing the finest ecclesiastical artwork that blends history and tradition with a growing and evolving faith.■

DAPRATO RIGALI STUDIOS, INC.

DAPRATO RIGALI STUDIOS, INC.
6030 North Northwest Highway, Chicago, IL 60631
Tel.: 773-763-5511; Fax: 773-763-5522
Web Site: www.dapratorigali.com

Personnel:

John Rigali; Robert Rigali
Lisa Rigali Galvin; Mike Rigali

Type of Business:

Daprato Rigali Studios Inc. has been beautifying Churches in America since 1860.

Today we find the Rigali Family restoring and renovating the churches originally decorated by their Great-Grandfather, John E. Rigali; aware of his reputation to create spiritually moving environments with quality material and craftsmanship.

Some of their most recent jobs include: decoration and stained glass restoration at St. Mary of the Lake Seminary, Mundelein, IL; Marble renovation and decoration, St. Elizabeth's Mother House, Allegany, N.Y.; and General Contracting for complete renovation of St. Bernadette's Church, Rockford, IL.

The Daprato Rigali staff is equipped to take your project from start to finish. If you're interested in working with a fine interior design studio experienced in Ecclesiastical Artistries please call for consultation at no obligation. We deliver what we design. ■

EVERGREENE PAINTING STUDIOS, INC.

450 West 31st St., 7th Fl.
New York, NY 10001
Tel.: 212-244-2800
Fax: 212-244-6204

711 South Blvd., Ste. 7
Oak Park, IL 60302
Tel.: 708-358-1642
Fax: 708-358-1656

E-mail: info@evergreene.com
Web Site: www.evergreene.com

Personnel:

Jeff Greene .... President
Kim Lovejoy .... Director of Marketing
Gillian Randell .... Chief Fine Arts Conservator
Terry Vanderwell.......... Director of Restoration, Midwest
Anthony Kartsonas . Architectural Conservator, Midwest

Type of Business:

EverGreene is a full-service decorative arts studio committed to preserving the integrity of historic sacred spaces through conservation, restoration, and compatible new artwork and decoration. Services include investigation and analysis of original finishes; consultations, renderings, budgets and samples to support decision-making and capital campaigns; design of color schemes, architectural ornament and furnishings; and guidance on specifications. EverGreene's consistently high-quality work is performed by its staff of experienced project managers, professionally-trained conservators, fine artists and craftsmen.

EverGreene's capabilities include all types of decorative painting, stenciling, gilding and trompe l'oeil; conservation, replication, and new design of murals and mosaics; ornamental plaster and scagliola; and allied crafts including wood and metal refinishing, interior stone cleaning, art glass, tile work and other architectural arts.

Among EverGreene's current projects are St. Matthew's Cathedral in Washington, D.C., Sacramento Cathedral, and the Chapel at Sacred Heart Monastery, Lisle, Illinois. EverGreene's work over the last 25 years includes projects large and small in houses of worship around the country, including ten cathedrals, 26 state capitols, and hundreds of theaters, public buildings, commercial interiors and residences. ■

JOHN EACHUS & ASSOCIATES

P.O. Box 1119
East Ellijay, GA 30539
Tel: 800-788-0986
Web Site: www.bells-clocks.com

Type of Business:

Manufacturer's Representative For:
Atmosphere Stained Glass: www.atmospherestainedglass.com
Edon Corporation; Fiberglass columns, cornice, brackets, historic restoration
Fiberglass Unlimited: Steeples and Service
December Lights: Christmas Light Displays
Stewart Iron Works: Cast, forged, wrought iron fences, rails, gates, benches, fountains, urns, planters, post signs
The Verdin Co.:Bells Carillons, Chimes. ■

KOLEY'S INC

2951 Harney Street
Omaha, NE 68131
Tel.: 402-341-9795; Fax: 402-341-5857

Personnel:

Tom Koley
Terry Goehring

Type of Business:

Quality, Care and Craftsmanship. For four generations these words have described Koley's, Inc. Since our very beginning in 1919, we have endeavored to serve the churches and clergy in repairing, polishing and replating of sacred vessels or other items of metal found in the Church. Our craftsmen strive to restore your cherished ecclesiastical items to their original condition whenever possible. We take pride in knowing that you have entrusted us with your items. Free estimates. ■

MUELLER KAISER PLATING CO.

5815 Hampton Avenue
St. Louis, MO 63109
Tel.: 314-832-3553
Web Site: www.mueller-kaiserplating.com

Type of Business:

One of the OLDEST liturgical metalware platers and refinishers in the U.S.A., offering a distinguished tradition of Master Metal Craftsmanship in the expert restoration, plating and refinishing of Sacred Vessels and Metalware in GOLD, SILVER, BRASS, COPPER, and BRONZE since 1911. Customers should ship chalices, ciboria, monstrances, candelabra and other sacred metalware to us by U.P.S. (insured) for estimates and work. (Note: return ship items without work at customer expense.) We also offer OLD CHALICES, CIBORIA, MONSTRANCES, CANDELABRA, and other FITMENTS to Catholic clergy, religious and churches for ONLY the cost of refinishing. Inquire for selection and price. Ecclesiastical Authorization. Awards from recognized religious, arts and cultural organizations. CELEBRATING 94 YEARS OF MASTER CRAFTSMANSHIP in the LITURGICAL METAL ARTS! ■

RAMBUSCH

RAMBUSCH LIGHTING
160 Cornelison Avenue
Jersey City, NJ 07304
Tel.: 201-333-2525; Fax: 201-433-3355
Web Site: www.rambusch.com

Personnel:
Edwin P. Rambusch ....President & C.E.O.
Martin V. Rambusch ....Chairman of the Board

Type of Business:
Since 1898, creating church interiors, liturgical furnishings, and art work. Fine restoration of church interiors. In-house studios and shops for designing and executing stained glass, church lighting systems, art metal work, and decorative painting. ■

Rohn & Associates Design, Inc.
Rolf R. Rohn, Principal
CONSULTANTS TO WORSHIP AND HOSPITALITY ENVIRONMENTS

ROHN AND ASSOCIATES DESIGN, INC.
1113 Creedmoor Ave.
Pittsburgh, PA 15226
Tel: 412-561-1228; 800-245-1288
Fax: 412-561-1202
E-mail: rohnstudio@aol.com
Web Site: www.rohndesign.com

Personnel:
A full service team of U.S. and international artisans & craftmens.
Rolf R. Rohn ....Principal Consultant/Director/Artist
Kathleen L. Maglicco ....Principal Interior Design
Sister Janet Baxendale, S.C. ....Education

Type of Business:
Experience spanning 4 decades in renovation/restoration, conservation, and design of new worship environments. A valuable partner in over 1,300 commissions throughout the U.S., Canada and Europe.
We offer:

Alters	Tabernacles
Bronze/Stonework	Statuary
Artwork, multi-mediums	Baptismal Fonts
Ambo-Lecterns	Mosaics
Pews/Choirs	Lamps and Lighting
Liturgical Design and more...	

www.rohndesign.com, ■

ROHLF'S STAINED & LEADED GLASS STUDIO, INC.
783 South Third Avenue
Mt. Vernon, NY 10550
Toll Free: 800-969-4106
Tel.: 914-699-4848; Fax: 914-699-7091
Web Site: www.rohlfstudio.com

Personnel:
Peter Hans Rohlf..President
Gregory Rohlf ....Vice President

Type of Business:
For Three Generations our family owned and operated Studio together with our affiliate, George L. Payne Studio have been dedicated to excellence in Stained Glass Art. Our team of International designers and Master Craftspersons have created stained glass windows for over a thousand Churches and Institutions Worldwide. Our reputation and experience in the field of Restoration, Replication and Preservation is well known. We would be pleased to assist you in the early stages of planning and design, working with your Architect and/or committee to achieve your desired goals.

From concept to completion, we are dedicated to serve you. ■

VALLEY BRONZE OF OREGON, INC.
307 W. Alder St. P.O. Box 669
Joseph, Oregon 97846
Tel: 541-432-7551 Fax: 541-432-0255
Web Site: www.valleybronze.com
E-mail: adstark@valleybronze.com
Personnel:
A. Daniel Stark ....Marketing

Type of business:
Valley Bronze of Oregon, Inc. has been in business continuously at the same location in Joseph, Oregon, since 1982, and has produced over $30 million dollars of investment cast sculpture, working primarily in bronze, but also casting and fabricating in silver, stainless steel and aluminum. We work with artists from all over the United States, and offer turnkey service starting with design, engineering and model making, all the way to professional on-site installation.
Over the past few years Valley Bronze of Oregon has expanded its production capabilities well beyond cast bronze sculpture to include architectural fabrications, ornamental and misc. metals, and bronze doors. We are building upon the experience gained in such projects as the three sets of double Millennium Bronze Doors for the Lady of Lourdes Cathedral in Spokane, Washington, and the "Day the Wall Came Down" Monument by artist Veryl Goodnight sited at the Bush Library in College Station, Texas, and also a sister monument at the Allied Museum in Berlin, Germany.
Within the last year Valley Bronze installed six monumental bronze bulls, "The Spirit of the Bull", by Maryland artist Walter Matia for the Houston Texans NFL franchise at Reliant Stadium in Houston, Texas, and also completed a $2.4 million ornamental metals subcontract on the National WWII Memorial to be dedicated this May in Washington, D.C. Valley Bronze is currently working on a set of bas relief bronze doors for the St. Ann's Cathedral in Great Falls, Montana.■

UNIVERSAL ART STUDIO

UNIVERSAL ART STUDIO
67 Mountain Spring Drive
Sparta, NJ 07871
Tel.: 973-726-0835
Fax: 973-729-1189

Personnel:
Yuri Mironoff .... Owner
Rita Mironoff .... Owner/ Designer

Type of Business:
Our crew is compact and capable of dealing with practically every aspect of restoration, renovation and repair work - we subcontract very little. We do not run more than one project at a time. We take no interruptions and deliver on time. ■

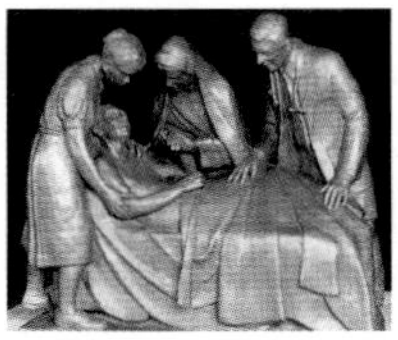

De Paul
Sculpture Studio

DE PAUL SCULPTURE STUDIO
6301 Riverdale Avenue
Bronx, NY 10471
Tel/Fax: 718-601-0985
Email: peggiebeau@aol.com
Web Site: www.depaulsculpturestudio.com

Personnel:
Sister Margaret Beaudette, S.C.
Sister Kathleen Aucoin, S.C.

Type of Business:
We create inspirational liturgical sculptures in bronze, fiberglass, and cast stone. Our works of art range from small to very large sculptures that can be seen in churches, hospitals, universities and mausoleums throughout the United States, Europe and the Caribbean.
Our intent is to produce incarnational works that draw and engage the heart and mind.
We work with the client, starting with a small sketch, a 3-D model, and, when all is approved, enlarging to desired size.
We invite your inquiries.■

Sculptor

LD Linda Dabeau | *Studio, LLC.*

LINDA DABEAU/ DABEAU STUDIO
P. O. Box 10126
Albuquerque, New Mexico 87184
Tel/Fax: 505-898-2227
Email: ldabeau@swcp.com
Web Site: www.ldabeau.com

Type of Business:
Linda Dabeau has been awarded both national and international commissions in sculpture. She works in multiple mediums, such as bronze, stone, fired clay, cast metals, glass, and wood. Her positive personal energy, combined with prodigious hand skills and her comprehension of the roots of Christianity, enable her to become a conduit for the vision of the parish, church authority, and architect. Through her highly disciplined work, Dabeau acts as a catalyst to create a bond within the whole community. Her multiple talents include design of liturgical furnishings such as alters, ambo, tabernacle, baptismal fonts, shrines, and stained glass. She is available to consult with parish communities.
Her materials are selected and utilized to create the best and most unique total visage of spirituality in the physical form. Dabeau's sculptures range from 24 inches to life size and monumental. Please contact the artist for commissions and limited editions that are available. ■

LD Linda Dabeau | *Studio, LLC*

MANZI Studios

www.manzisculpture.com

MANZI STUDIOS
1112 N. Creek Rd.
Porter Corners, NY 12859
Tel: 518-893-2267
E-mail: manzisculpture@aol.com
Web Site: www.manzisculture.com

Personnel:

Walter Lape .... Sculptor
Janine Thomas .... Research
Sharon Kingsbury .... Moldmaker
Jim Moulton .... Engineer, Steel

Type of Business:

MANZI STUDIO'S is a full service sculpture facility specializing in life sized figurative sculpture. Alice Manzi studied in New York as well as Pietrasanta, Italy. The studio does extensive research into individual prior to the creation of scale models. Ms Manzi has studied and taught human anatomy for over twenty years, and has distinguished herself in the field of sculpture through her remarkable ability to capture the personality of the individual. On the web at www.manzisculpture.com. ■

MARY'SFIELD STUDIO
Sacred Art in Bronze and Portraits

MARY'SFIELD STUDIO
6427 Cadet Lane
Warrenton, VA 20187
Tel: 540-349-5010
Fax: 540-349-5010
E-mail: tjmalec@aol.com
Web Site: www.terrimalec.com

Personnel:

Theresa Malec .... Artist

Type of Business:

Mary'sfield Studio specializes in sacred art in bronze, depicting religious figures from life-size monuments to smaller sculptures, which are commissioned by various parishes throughout the country. Bas-relief in bronze is an addition to enhance any wall area.

The Stations of the Cross, as well as other wall renditions, have been commissioned for permanent installations. Grotto and garden sculptures are also a favorite theme for Mary'sfield's work, as well as sculpture for schools. Alter and ambo designs are available for specific commissions.

"I will work with pastors and incorporate their ideas into sculpture that will beautify and enhance any parish. I bring a deeper religious experience to my sculpture, for greater beauty and emotional response." ■

Pogue SCULPTURE

POGUE SCULPTURE STUDIO AND FOUNDRY
7670 Hwy. 1431 East
Marble Falls, TX 78654
Tel.: 877-267-2430
Fax: 830-693-7655
Email: dan@danpoguesculpture.com
Web Site: www.danpoguesculpture.com

Personnel:

Dan Pogue, Marti Pogue, & Doug Pogue

Type of Business:

Creating award winning bronze sculpture for over 35 years, Dan Pogue will help you choose from an existing portfolio of religious sculpture or create from photos of a specific person or using creative imagination. Dan will work with your parish to create just the right visual experience ranging up to monumental in size. He can provide you preliminary sketches and then create a marquette for you to approve. Having an in house art foundry, we can provide excellent creativity, quality, and cost effectiveness. See our Web site for a sample of monumental works and contact us for additional information. ■

"Faith, Hope, and Love"
by Barry Woods Johnston

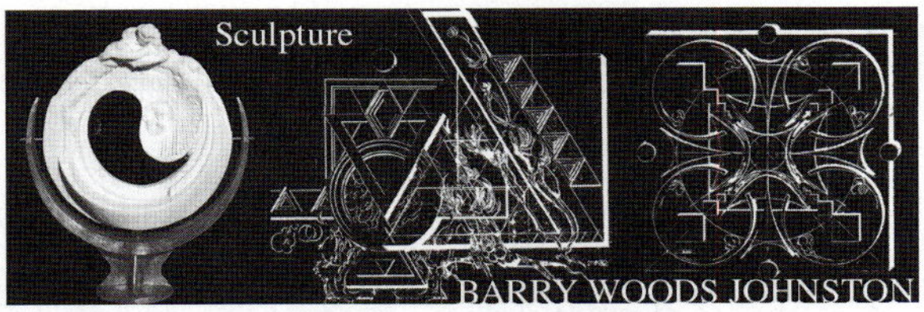

SCULPTURE WORKS/BARRY WOODS JOHNSTON, SCULPTOR
2423 Pickwick Road
Baltimore, MD 21207
Tel: (410) 448-1945
Email: barry@sculptorjohnston.com
Website: www.sculptorjohnston.com

Type of Business:
Around 9/11, the Evangelical Christian Credit Union (ECCU) in Orange County, California, commissioned the "Faith, Hope, and Love" sculpture, 16fi' high in bronze, pending additions. The City of Le Brea in Orange County locked horns with ECCU over these additions, and, although alluding to First Amendment violations, ultimately forced ECCU to abandon the commission and select an alternative artist. The sculpture, in full scale, recreates an arched "Needle," reminiscent of a once narrow gate into Jerusalem, prompting the parable "It is easier for a camel to pass through the eye of a needle than a rich man to enter the kingdom of heaven." In the form of an eternal flame, a Judeo-Christian symbol of the presence of God, the "Needle" illustrates the lack of mortal baggage one can carry into heaven "within." The three figures of faith, hope, and love mirror the positive yearnings of the soul for those qualities that can lead our world in a brighter future through enlightenment and compassion. Available in three sizes: 34"x 14"x 8.5", 8.25'x 3.4'x 2.1', 16.5'x 6.8'x 4.2'.■

DISTRIBUTION

A.M.  D.G.

ANGELUS MEDIA DISTRIBUTION GROUP
184 Broadway – Suite #10,
Long Branch, NJ 07740
Tel: (732) 483-0800
Fax: (732) 483-0900
Toll Free Order Line: 1(888) 222-AMDG (2634)
Email: info@angelusmedia.com
Web Site: www.angelusmedia.com

Personnel:
Maria E. Incremona............................Customer Service
Richard S. Incremona..........................Customer Service
Marilyn Campanella............................Customer Service
Linda Delaney.....................................Customer Service
Kate Bergin ....Accts Pay/Receivable
Brendan Germain ....Web Master

Type of Business:
A.M.D.G. is a full service distributor of quality Catholic products. We assemble your order from products selected from our vast array of top-notch vendors at the same discount you would have received if you called each vendor separately…
We save you time, money and stress! Leave the research and collecting to us. Pay one invoice and receive hundreds of diverse products from one spot. …
WE'RE YOUR ONE-STOP CATHOLIC SUPPLIER!
BIBLES / BOOKS / MUSIC (CD & CASSETTE) / GIFTWARE / STATUARY / RELIGIOUS JEWELRY / VIDEOS / TEACHINGS AND MUCH MORE ! ■

EDUCATION

The Jubilee Museum

THE JUBILEE MUSEUM
584 West Broad Street
Columbus, Ohio 43215-2710
Tel.: 614-221-4323 (Church)
Tel.: 614-641-6204 (Museum)
E-mail: jubileemuseum@columbus.rr.com
Web Site: www.holyfamilycolumbus.org

Type of Business:
The Jubilee Museum, the largest diverse Catholic Museum in the United States, is dedicated to the preservation of the Catholic mind and memory, with its significant collection of international religious art, including an original 1582 Rheimes New Testament and a rare facsimile Gutenberg Bible, among thousands of holdings. In the museum are a Holocaust Memorial and a Synagogue depicting Worship in the Old Testament. Tours, retreats, seminars upon request and help in locating items for churches. ■

Educational Funding

TUITION PROGRAM, INC.
P.O. Box 571
Livingston, NJ 07039
Tel.: 800-828-9944; 973-535-2776
Fax: 800-432-9994; 973-533-0086
E-mail: info@tuitionprogram.com

Personnel:
Brendon & Cecilia Devlin

Type of Business:
Founded in 1985 by Catholic parents to serve Catholic Schools. There is absolutely no charge to the school. There is no charge to parents if payments are on time. Each student receives a Tuition Credit Line for present and future use. The school receives 100% tuition. Call today 800-828-9944, fax us at 800-432-9994, or e-mail: info@tuitionprogram.com.

Financial Aid service included. ■

Educational Games & Puzzles

TALICOR™

TALICOR, INC.
8845 Steven Chase Ct.
Las Vegas, NV 89149
Tel.: 800-433-4263
Fax: 702-655-4366

Personnel:
Lew Herndon .... C.O.B.
Nikki Hancock .... President
Cheryl Sidhu .... Sec./Treas.

Type of Business:
This family owned and operated company are producers of games and puzzles with good wholesome and/or Christian content. With over 30 years in the business the product line has grown to include Catholic Games, Educational Games, Family Games, Bible Based Games, Strategy Games, Communication Games, Children's Games, and Entertainment Games. An extensive selection of puzzles for all age groups is also available. Talicor is known for the exceptional quality and value of its products. ■

Educational Opportunities

GuestHouse

GUEST HOUSE, INC.
1601 Joslyn Road, P.O. Box 420
Lake Orion, MI 48361
Tel: 800-626-6910; 248-391-4445; FAX: 248-391-0210
Website: www.guesthouse.org

LAKE ORION CENTER (For Women Religious)
P.O. Box 68
Lake Orion, MI 48361
Tel: 800-626-6910; 248-391-3100; FAX: 248-391-1553
Website: www.guesthouse.org

ROCHESTER TREATMENT CENTER
(For priests, deacons, brothers & seminarians)
P.O. Box 954
Rochester, MN 55903
Tel: 800-634-4155; 507-288-4693; FAX: 507-288-1240
E-mail: ghousemn@sparc.isl.net

Personnel:
Daniel A. Kidd ...... President and Chief Executive Officer
Sr. LeeAnne Farrell, SSND .... Director, Lake Orion, MI
Bill Morgan, CCDCR ... VP Clinical Oper., Rochester, MN
Gerard O'Connor .... Director of Outreach

Type of Business:
Guest House, Inc. is a lay-owned, lay-operated nonprofit corporation established in 1956. With the approbation of the Catholic hierarchy, it operates special residential treatment centers for alcoholic Catholic priests, deacons, brothers, sisters and seminarians from all over the world.

Catholic women religious are treated in Guest House in Lake Orion, Michigan. The facility in Rochester, Minnesota has treatment programs for priests, deacons, brothers and seminarians. An important part of the treatment is the beautiful environment of our facilities. Residents respond to the quiet serenity of the surroundings to help in their recovery not only physically and emotionally, but spiritually as well.

Surveys are conducted regularly to determine how our graduates are doing. The 1997 survey shows that after a year and a half, over 90% report they are doing well and abstaining from all drugs and alcohol.

Generous donors have established an endowment fund to provide financial assistance for any diocese or religious community needing assistance with the costs of treatment. Treatment is provided without regard to financial consideration.

The facilities are accredited by JCAHO (Joint Commission on Accreditation of Healthcare Organizations) and licensed by the Department of Public Health in the states of Michigan and Minnesota respectively.

Guest House also offers educational programs, seminars, and workshops on addiction-related topics. ■

SETON HALL UNIVERSITY IMMACULATE CONCEPTION SEMINARY SCHOOL OF THEOLOGY
400 South Orange Avenue
South Orange, NJ 07079
Tel.: 973-761-9633; Fax: 973-761-9577
E-mail: theology@shu.edu
Web Site: theology.shu.edu

Personnel:
Rev. Monsignor Robert F. Coleman, J.C.D. ....Rector/Dean
Rev. Thomas Nydegger, M.Div. ....Vice Rector/ Business Manager
Rev. Joseph Chapel, S.T.D. .... Associate Dean
Dianne M. Traflet, J.D., S.T.D..................Assistant Dean

Type of Business:
Immaculate Conception Seminary School of Theology (ICSST) is the graduate school of theology of Seton Hall University and the major seminary of the Catholic Archdiocese of Newark. With more than a 140-year tradition of preparing committed Catholics for service to the Church, ICSST admits both seminarians studying for the Catholic priesthood and lay students. ICSST offers three graduate degree programs: the Master of Arts in Theology, the Master of Arts in Pastoral Ministry and the Master of Arts in Divinity. ■

Pro-Life Education

AMERICAN LIFE LEAGUE
P.O. Box 1350
Stafford, VA 22555
Tel.: 888-546-2580; Fax: 540-659-2586
E-mail: jbrown@all.org
Web Site: www.all.org

Type of Business:
American Life League is an international pro-life outreach that works tirelessly to defend and protect all innocent human life. ALL facilitates a wide range of innovation pro-life programs designed to encourage people to work together to rebuild a Culture of Life. ALL is educating people, changing hearts and making a difference through initiatives that include:

• American Bioethics Advisory Commission — promotes pro-life ethics in scientific, legal and Academic circles.

• Rock For Life — brings the pro-life message to America's youth through music.

• STOPP International —counters the anti-life agenda of Planned Parenthood.

• World Life League — maintains pro-life vigilance at the United Nations.

• Crusade for the Defense of Our Catholic Church — works with bishops in dealing with the problem of pro-abortion Catholic officials. ■

Spiritual Enrichment

ACTS E & W
a Catholic youth Evangelism Ministry
P.O. Box 1128
Bolingbrook, IL 60440
Tel: 630-378-0982
E-mail: salsoloacts@aol.com
Web Site: www.salsolo.com

Type of Business:
Catholic Youth Evangelist Sal Solo, a former British Rock Start, brings Jesus to the MTV generation with music and video. Has served over 30 US Dioceses, and in 35 countries, including World Youth Days Rome and Toronto.

• 21st Century Evang-A-Ganza (a multimedia evangelistic concert)
• Anno Domini Mass (a multimedia mass)
• Keynote Presentations and Workshops
• Confirmation Retreats
• English and Spanish Presentations

For any school parish, or youth event
Call to book Sal now for yours

HOLY CROSS FAMILY MINISTRIES
Family Rosary
Family Theater Productions
Father Peyton Family Institute
Family Rosary International
518 Washington Street
North Easton, MA 02356
Tel.: 508-238-4095; Fax: 508-238-3953
Web Site: www.hcfm.org

Personnel:
Fr. John Phalen, C.S.C. .... President
Susan Wallace .... Director of External Relations
Beth Mahoney .... Mission Director

Type of Business:
Continuing the mission of our founder, Servant of God Father Patrick Peyton, C.S.C., Holy Cross Family Ministries serves Jesus Christ and His Church throughout the world by promoting and supporting the spiritual well-being of the family through products and programs. ■

Tuition Financing

TUITION PROGRAM, INC.
P.O. Box 571
Livingston, NJ 07039
Tel.: 800-828-9944; 973-535-2776
Fax: 800-432-9994; 973-533-0086
E-mail: info@tuitionprogram.com

Personnel:
Brendon & Cecilia Devlin

Type of Business:
Founded in 1985 by Catholic parents to serve Catholic Schools. There is absolutely no charge to the school. There is no charge to parents if payments are on time. Each student receives a Tuition Credit Line for present and future use. The school receives 100% tuition. Call today 800-828-9944, fax us at 800-432-9994 or e-mail us at info@tuitionprogram.com.

Financial Aid service included. ■

Tuition Management Services

ONE WRITE
COMPANY

ONE-WRITE COMPANY
3750 State Rt. 37 E., P.O. Box 628
Lancaster, OH 43130
Tel.: 800-268-6070; 740-654-2128
Fax: 800-504-2260; 740-654-2260
E-mail: owc@onewriteco.com

Personnel:
Crystal Bussart ....Church Services Manager

Type of Business:
* Book Offering Envelopes
* Tuition Payment Books
* Mailing Plan for Offering Envelopes
* Contribution Report Forms
* **NEW!** Cheerful Recorder Software

We invite you to compare the features and prices of the Book Offering Envelopes with your current system. The savings will be considerable. Write or call for a free catalog and quote today. ■

SMART TUITION MANAGEMENT SERVICES
95 Wall Street, Ste. 2300
New York, NY 10005
Tel.: 800-762-7808; Fax: 212-858-8043
E-mail: info@smarttuition.com
Web Site: www.smarttuition.com

Personnel:
Sam Rosen..President

Type of Business:
SMART is a complete tuition management service that is designed to take schools out of the tuition collection business. The SMART program helps to reduce delinquencies, increase cash flow, and decrease the administrative workload. SMART serves 2,000 schools nationwide. SMART also has a Tuition Aid Analysis Service (TAAS) that determines how much families can afford to pay. ■

EMPLOYMENT

NAVY CHAPLAIN CORPS
Commander, Navy Recruiting Command
5722 Integrity Drive, Building 784
Millington, TN 38054-5057
Tel.: 901-874-9216; Toll Free: 866-484-5232
Web Site: www.navy.com/professionals

Personnel:
CDR Gary Carr, CHC, USN................Program Manager
CarrG@cnrc.navy.mil
LCDR Michael Parisi, CHC, USN .....Chaplain Recruiter
ParisiM@cnrc.navy.mil
LCDR Herb Griffin, CHC, USN.........Chaplain Recruiter
GriffinH@cnrc.navy.mil
LT Heinz Malon, CHC, USN ....Chaplain Recruiter
MalonH@cnrc.navy.mil
LT Kimberly Sawatsky, CHC, USN...Chaplain Recruiter
SawatskyK@cnrc.navy.mil

Type of Business:
Navy Chaplains serve both the Church and Country in diverse ministry settings. Chaplains provide spiritual guidance to members of the Navy, Marine Corps and Coast Guard. We offer leadership positions in ministry for the spiritual well being of the whole community. Priest Chaplains provide sacramental and spiritual support for Catholics in the military and care for all. Working closely with clergy from other faith traditions, we cooperate with each other without compromising our own faith and practice. Navy Chaplains experience the joy of ministry with young people. We have a program for seminarians, the Naval Reserve, and for full-time, active-duty positions. Contact the chaplain recruiters listed above for more information. ■

www.navy.com 1-800-USA-NAVY

Chaplain Service

ARMY CHAPLAIN RECRUITING
Commander,
U.S. Army Recruiting Command
1307 Third Ave
Fort Knox, KY 40121
Phone: 1-800-USA-ARMY
Email: goarmy@usarec.army.mil
Web Site: chaplain.goarmy.com

Personnel:
Chaplain (Major) Joel Russell........Chaplain Recruiting
E-mail: joel.russell@us.army.mil
Staff Sergeant Daniel Cantu..........Chaplain Recruiting
E-mail: daniel.cantu@usarec.army.mil

Type of Business:
Chaplains are the spiritual guardians of the U.S. Army. As a Chaplain, you'll provide the spiritual tools that Soldiers and their families need to stay strong. Whether you are already ordained or still a seminary student, there are both full- and part-time ministry opportunities for you in the U.S. Army Chaplaincy. You have answered the Call to serve God. Now your country is asking you to serve Soldiers and their families – consider this important calling. The U.S. Army Chaplaincy could be the opportunity you have been seeking.
chaplain.goarmy.com 1-800-USA-ARMY ■

LITURGICAL & CHURCH GOODS

ABBOTT INC.
1515 Route 38
Cherry Hill, NJ 08002
Tel.: 800-522-2688; 856-662-6959
Fax: 856-665-5109
E-mail: info@churchsupplies.com
Web Site: www.churchsupplies.com

Personnel:
Daniel J. Castonguay..President
Joseph F. McKeaney...............................General Manager
Mary Ann Mitkus........................Business Administrator
John Scafidi..Distribution
Michael Schwartz ....Government Liaison

Type of Business:
Purveyors of the Finest Vesture, Paraments, Statuary & Metalware since 1962. Unique and original creations, our specialty. Custom designs to complement your liturgical environment. Exclusive representatives of Slabbinck Master Collection & Original Collection. ■

ADRIAN HAMERS, INC.
2 Madison Avenue
Larchmont, NY 10538
Tel.: 914-834-7780; Fax: 914-834-0712
Web Site: www.adrianhamers.com

Type of Business:
Custom designers and manufacturers of Sacred Vessels. Since 1887, the Hamers name has been synonymous with expert Silversmithing throughout the world in the field of Liturgical Art. Please contact us for those hard to find items, as we always have a large selection of Adrian Hamers Estate Collection pieces in stock. We have a large collection of antique church stainglass windows available (both full sets and individual). We are experts in: Church Interiors from design to execution, Renovations, Altars, Sacred Vessels, Gold and Silver Plating & Repairing, Appraisals, Tabernacles, Marble, Statuary, Woodwork & Woodcarving, Stained Glass, Pews & Chairs, Gold Leafing, Frescoes, Restoration, Trompe-l' oeuil, Wall Murals (repair and conservation cleaning), Ornamental Plaster, Heraldic Designs & Bishop Regalia. Please call us for a free 36-page Sacred Vessels color catalog, or our free 80-page color Woodcarvings catalog. ■

CANDLE STUDIOS
180 Division Ave.
Belleville NJ 07109
1-800-648-4229; Fax: 473-759-4299
E-mail: markjay@comcast.net
Web Site: www.candlestudios.com

Type of business:
Candle Studios is celebrating its fifth year in business, making stock and custom made candle stands in wood or wrought iron metal. Five years ago we introduced our flagship model, the Omega 2000. With many customers and hundreds of units now in the field we can say that we build the finest stand in the world, With exclusive features and options, such as Automatic select and set programmable timing, electronic soft touch lighting, offerings that are collected into a vandal proof safe, and beautiful imported crystal globes, this are all ads up to make our Omega 2000 the candle stand that is built for looks and built for life. ■

CARROLL ELECTRONICS, INC.
710 N.E. 26th Street
Wilton Manors, FL 33305
Tel.: 800-331-0444; Fax: 954-561-4098

Personnel:
David Nagle .... President
Liza Palmer .... Sales Manager
Bob Perkins .... Sales Representative
Donna Spencer .... Service Engineer

Type of Business:
Carroll Electronics has been in business for 20 years designing and building Electronic Votive Candle Stands for thousands of churches throughout the United States. ■

CARROLL ART, INC.
710 N.E. 26th Street
Wilton Manors, FL 33305
Tel.: 800-876-4569; Fax: 954-561-4098

Personnel:
David Nagle .... President Designer
Liza Palmer .... Sales Manager
Wayne Palmer .... Sales Representative
Robert Perkins .... Sales Representative

Type of Business:
Carroll Art has been in business for 12 years. We design and custom build all types of plaques and memorials including the tree of life, plaques, recognition systems, church signs, donor plates, custom sculptures, and memorials are just a few of our products. We can provide you with the perfect fund raising tool. ■

DOMUSDEI HOLY ART STUDIOS

DOMUSDEI HOLY ART STUDIOS

FACTORY: Via dei Tulipani, 48 - 00040 CECCHINA
DI ALBANO (RM) - ITALY
Tel: 011-39-06-9343369; Fax: 011-39-06-9344971
SHOWROOM: Via Scossacavalli 3/9 - 00193
ROMA - ITALY
Tel: 011-39-06-686809
info@domusdei.it; m.delmonte@domusdei.it
Web site: www.domusdei.it

Personnel:

Alessandro Del Monte ....President
Massimiliano Del Monte ....Executive Director
Aldo Del Monte ....Assitant President

Type of Business:

Founded in 1963, Domusdei Studio has restored thousands of church interiors all over the world. Specializing in designing and manufacturing stained glass windows, mosaics, bronze and fiberglass statues, altars, bronze doors, lecterns, baptismal fonts, candlesticks, flower holders, and tabernacles

We are also experts in silver and gold plating and the restoration of wood and metal masterpieces. ■

Hayes & Finch LIMITED ESTABLISHED 1882

HAYES AND FINCH LIMITED

Hanson Road, Aintree
Liverpool, England, L97BP
Tel: 44(0)151-523-6303
Fax: 44(0)151-525-1246
E-mail: sales@hfltd.com
Web Site: www.hayesandfinch.com

Personnel:

John R. Mann, M.B.E.B.Sc. ....Managing Director
Mrs. Karen Reilly ....Marketing Director
Andrew Ware ....Sales Manager

Type of Business:

Founded in 1882, Hayes and Finch is a fourth generation family business, and the largest manufacturer and supplier of church-related goods in the United Kingdom. Based in Liverpool, England, we supply high quality church furnishings to customers around the world. Our specialist manufacturing center produces both standard and customer-specified products; our extensive range includes Candles, Altar Wine, Clerical Garments, Furniture, Brassware and Hallmarked Silverware. Our business is built on British craftsmanship of highest quality and exceptional customer service. ■

THE HOLY+ROOD GUILD

THE HOLY ROOD GUILD

St. Joseph's Abbey
167 North Spencer Road
Spencer, MA 01562-1233
Tel.: 508-885-8750; Fax: 508-885-8758
E-mail: holyrood@holyroodguild.com
Web Site: www.holyroodguild.com

Type of Business:

Designers and crafters of ecclesiastical vesture for over 40 years. Inspired by our monastic tradition, we seek to unite in our work simplicity in design, quality in materials and excellence in craftsmanship. The result is vesture that enhances the liturgical celebration with visual grace and order. Our artists—both monks and laypersons—are available for custom design work and consultation. We also provide an extensive selection of ready made items. ■

JFP Inspirational Art COLLECTION

JFP INSPIRATIONAL ART

27932 Valley Center Rd. #177
Valley Center, CA 92082
Tel: 800-690-1340
Fax: 760-749-6849
E-mail: art@inspirationalFilms.com
Web Site: www.JesusFilmArt.com

Personnel:

Robert Cording ....Manager

Type of Business:

JFP Inspirational Art produces and distrubutes quality Framed Art and Cards for Churches, Sunday Schools, home and office. Specially commissioned by The Jesus Film Project and inspired by the Jesus Film, the Fine Art beautifully represents scenes from the life of Christ...His Birth, His Teachings, His Passion.

Visually stunning, the new art depicts Jesus on the sea of Galilee ("Follow Me"); Jesus and the Children ("The Little Children"); Jesus in the wilderness ("A Light For My Path"); Portraits of Jesus ("The Prince of Peace", "The Light of the World'); Old World art, and many other scenes.

The digitally mastered framed lithographs of these traditional themes from the life of Jesus will be a meaningful and welcome addition to the Parish, School, or home. The Frame Art is double-matted with glass and is available in a variety of sizes (11 x 14"; 16 x 20"; 20 x 24" et.al.)

All **JFP Inspirational Art** images are also available as Fine Art Greeting Cards in "Assorted" and "Same" Card box sets. Each Greeting Card depicts a scene with an appropriate Scripture verse.

JFP Inspirational Art is a division of The Jesus Film Project, Paul Eshleman, Director. All proceeds from the purchase of JFP Inspirational Art are used for the Ministry of The Jesus Film Project and for the worldwide distribution of the Jesus Film. Translated into over 800 languages, the Jesus Film has been shown to millions of people in every country of the world. Contact us for a complimentary JFP Inspirational Art Catalog & Price List. ■

KING RICHARD'S RELIGIOUS ARTIFACTS
P.O. Box 191027
Atlanta, GA 31119
Tel.: 877-248-3366
Fax: 770-455-1784

Personnel:
Rick Lair .... President
Sandra James .... Vice President
Scott Lair .... Sales and Marketing
Chris Roberts .... Web Master
Mike Coleman .... Warehouse & Shipping

Type of Business:
King Richard's Religious Artifacts specializes in providing churches and religious facilities with a complete spectrum of religious decorative items; including complete sets of stained glass windows, statuary, altars, stations and all types of altar necessities. We travel throughout the United States selling and delivering merchandise, as well as completing all required work for purchasing and removal. ■

NATIONAL CHURCH GOODS ASSOCIATION (NCGA)
800 Roosevelt Road
Building C Suite 20
Glen Ellyn, IL 60137
Tel: 630-942-6599
Fax: 630-790-3095
E-Mail: ncga@ncgaweb.com
Web Site: www.ncgaweb.com

Board of Directors:
Stephen Gaiser .... President
Ray Gerken .... Director
Robert Malhame .... Director
John F. Moroney .... Vice President
Mark Steigerwald .... Director
Richard Tonini .... Secretary
Dennis Ziegler .... Treasurer

Rick Church .... Executive Secretary
Jeff Church .... Association Manager

Type of Organization:
The National Church Goods Association (NCGA) is the international trade association of dealers and suppliers of church goods, religious articles, and published materials. NCGA has been providing members with exceptional benefits for 97 years. To find a reputable dealer near you go to www.ncgaweb.com and click on the dealer locater link, or call 630-942-6599. ■

PATRICK BAKER & SONS, INC.
1650 West Street
Southington, CT 06489
Tel.: 800-243-6385 Fax: 860-276-9438
72 Chambers Street
Fairfield, CT 06430
Tel: 203-366-5058 Fax: 203-334-8527
Web Site: www.churchgoods.com

Type of Business:
Patrick Baker & Sons, Inc. has been servicing the church and clergy for over 40 years. We are a family owned business committed to value with quality and service. We provide church furnishings, vestments, candles, altar breads, liners, refinishing and all your religious supplies with the highest guaranteed quality. Call or write for a catalog or visit us on our website at www.churchgoods.com. ■

TERRA SANCTA GUILD
P.O. Box 300
Broomall, PA 19008
Tel: 610-544-9900
Fax: 610-544-6994
E-mail: adina@terrasancta.com
Web Site: www.terrasancta.com

Personnel:
Sharon Shore .... C.E.O.
Adina Serot .... President

Type of Business:
For over 40 years, Terra Sancta's name has been synonymous with the finest design in the field of Liturgical Art. Our custom design recipients include His Holiness, The Pope and 2 U.S. Presidents. Our art department will guide you through the process based on your individual requirements, and the necessity to communicate and inspire at reasonable prices. We can adapt your logo or create a new design. Call and ask for Sharon to discuss your custom design needs, or to request our free 40 page catalog of giftware, pendants and pins for the Christian community. ■

VANPOULLES
Church Furnishers
~ Est. 1908 ~

VANPOULLES LTD.
Telford Place, Crawley
West Sussex, RH10 1SZ, UK
Tel: +44 1293 590100
Fax: +44 1293 590115
E-mail: sales@vanpoulles.co.uk
Web Site: www.vanpoulles.co.uk

Type of Business:
Vanpoulles Ltd. is a family business, established nearly 100 years ago to provide the Church with all types of church requisites. We specialise in producing traditional English silverware and ecclesiastical garments, including chalices, ciboria, vestments, copes, stoles and altar frontals etc. Our sales department is available for friendly service and advice and current stock availability of all our product lines.
Please call, write or e-mail for a free catalogue. If visiting the UK please note our showrooms are conveniently positioned only a short distance from Gatwick Airport. ■

Vermont Church Supply Co.

VERMONT CHURCH SUPPLY CO.
676 Pine Street, P.O. Box 368
Burlington, VT 05401
Tel.: 802-862-6486, 800-451-3453; Fax: 802-862-5765
E-mail: vcs@together.net
Web Site: www.vermontchurchsupply.com

Personnel:
Neil Clark ....President

Type of Business:
Since our inception in 1946 by W. Barrett Clark and Doris Clark, Vermont Church Supply has offered the highest quality products and the best service to the Church and the Clergy. We have a wide range of products including Candles, Church Furniture, Metalware and Vestments. Our founders' Sons, Neil, John, Thomas, and Robert, along with the third generation Anthony Clark, continue to provide services such as refinishing Sacred Vessels, Candlesticks and tabernacles and also the execution of hand carved wood and marble Statuary. Whether your needs are small or large, we can give the best personalized service to our Customers. ■

See our display ad on page 101.

Altar Breads

CM ALMY

C.M. ALMY & SON, INC.
Three American Lane
P.O. Box 2644
Greenwich, CT 06836-2644
Tel.: 800-225-2569; Fax: 800-426-2569
E-mail: almyaccess@almy.com
Web Site: www.almy.com

Showrooms in:
- Old Greenwich, CT: 203-637-2739
- Pittsfield, ME: 207-487-3232

Type of Business:
Almy was founded in 1892. We design and make virtually all of our products in our Maine shop. It is our mission to design furnishings that will grace your worship and to ensure their value by making them with the highest quality materials and craftsmanship. We make a complete line of vestments, haberdashery, choir robes, candles, communion bread, linens, processional and altar appointments, and eucharistic vessels.We also offer custom design and fabrication of all Almy products, and repair and refurbishing of old metal appointments. Quik Ship© delivery of many popular items. All orders backed by The Almy Guarantee. Call, write, or e-mail for a free catalog. ■

Altar Linens, Laces

CM ALMY

C.M. ALMY & SON, INC.
Three American Lane
P.O. Box 2644
Greenwich, CT 06836-2644
Tel.: 800-225-2569; Fax: 800-426-2569
E-mail: almyaccess@almy.com
Web Site: www.almy.com

Showrooms in:
- Old Greenwich, CT: 203-637-2739
- Pittsfield, ME: 207-487-3232

Type of Business:
Almy was founded in 1892. We design and make virtually all of our products in our Maine shop. It is our mission to design furnishings that will grace your worship and to ensure their value by making them with the highest quality materials and craftsmanship. We make a complete line of vestments, haberdashery, choir robes, candles, communion bread, linens, processional and altar appointments, and eucharistic vessels.We also offer custom design and fabrication of all Almy products, and repair and refurbishing of old metal appointments. Quik Ship© delivery of many popular items. All orders backed by The Almy Guarantee. Call, write, or e-mail for a free catalog. ■

Ecclesia Designs

ECCLESIA DESIGNS
7412 Colton Lane
Manassas, VA 20109
Tel: 703-335-2900
Email: Info@ecclesiadesigns.com
Web Site: www.ecclesiadesigns.com

Type of Business:

Ecclesia Designs offers custom designed church vestments and altar linens to grace and enhance your worship experience. Each item is individually hand-crafted by a single artist who works closely with a graphics designer.

We have a passion for the creative process and are dedicated to producing works with the highest degree of artistic expression that suit the solemnity of their purpose. We use only the highest quality materials and craftsmanship and maintain close interactive communication with our clients to assure their satisfaction.

We sincerely hope that each of our designs will raise one's consciousness to God in all His glory because making them is a way of prayer for us.

"Made with Martha's hands but Mary's heart"

the symbol of Regal Splendor

Robert Gaspard Co.

ROBERT GASPARD CO., INC.
200 North Janacek Road
Brookfield, WI 53045-6101
Tel.: 800-784-6868; Fax: 800-784-7567
E-mail: mail@rgaspard.com
Web Site: www.robertgaspardco.com

Personnel:

Rose Gaspard..President
Jason R. Gaspard ....General Manager

Type of Business:

The Robert Gaspard Co. was established in 1954. Over the past 50 years, we have grown to be a nationally-known company. We pride ourselves on the ability to create original custom designs to enrich your worship needs. Our complete line consists of all ecclesiastical vesture, as well as paraments, mass and altar linens, stoles, banners, chasubles, funeral palls, albs, cossacks, surplices, choir robes, acolyte robes and many accessories. Complimentary catalog and fabric swatches sent on request. ■

Anointing Oils

NEW HOPE ANOINTING OILS, INC.
405 Drawdy Drive
Brunswick, GA 31525
Tel.: 800-277-4284
Fax: 912-265-4646
Web Site: www.newhopeoils.com

Personnel:

Don Rebstock ....Owner
Elizabeth Burquez-Rebstock ....Manager
Michelle Banks ....Staff

Type of Business:

New Hope Anointing Oils, and Balms are formulated with olive oil, frankincense and myrrh. We offer extensive product line of anointing oils and balms in a variety of sizes and containers. Our oils and balms will not rancid, due to special pure essence and blending. PLEASE CALL 800-277-4284 FOR PRICING AND INFORMATION ABOUT OUR PRODUCTS, OR VISIT OUR WEB SITE. HABLAMOS ESPANOL.■

Bibles, Hymnals, Missalettes

Bibles.com
THE AMERICAN BIBLE SOCIETY STORE

BIBLES.COM
700 Plaza Drive
Secaucus, NJ 07094
Tel: 1-888-239-3976
Fax: 1-866-570-2077
E-mail: abscast@americanbible.org

Personnel:

Brian Sherry....................................Director of Sales

Type of Business:

Bibles.com offers an affordable variety of English, Spanish and international language Bibles for Catholic readers, including *The New American Bible, The Good News Bible, The New Revised Standard Version, The New Jerusalem Bible, Dios Habla Hoy* and more. There are outstanding resources for children, youth and adults, as well as multimedia and academic resources. Call for a free Scripture Resource catalog. ■

CATHOLIC BOOK PUBLISHING CORP.
WORLD CATHOLIC PRESS
77 West End Road
Totowa, NJ 07512
Tel.: 973-890-2400
Fax: 973-890-2410
E-mail: info@catholicbookpublishing.com
Web site: www.catholicbookpublishing.com

Personnel:
Frances Cavalero ....Sales Manager
Joan Cavalero..Vice President
Robert Cavalero...President
Maria Maggi..Editor

Type of Business:
Catholic Book, the leading publisher of quality Catholic resources for 93 years, offers a full range of Bibles, Missals, Prayerbooks, Liturgical Books and Children's books. We proudly publish our trademark St. Joseph Editions, distinctive for their large, easy-to-read typefaces; magnificent, full-color illustrations; and helpful and plentiful guides, notes and indices. Resurrection Press, a general trade imprint, offers books for spiritual growth. World Catholic Press provides a wide array of Bibles that complements Catholic Book's rich tradition of Bible publishing ■

OXFORD UNIVERSITY PRESS
2001 Evans Road
Cary, NC 27513
Tel.: 800-451-7556; Fax: 919-677-1303
Web Site: www.oup.com/us

Type of Business:
Oxford University Press publishes many books and Bibles for Roman Catholic readers. Among these are *The NRSV Catholic Edition* (with a concordance and section of Catholic prayers and devotions); *The Catholic Study Bible, NAB* (the first true study Bible for Catholics); *The Catholic Bible: Personal Study Edition, NAB* (ideal for RCIA participants and other first-time Scripture students); and, *The Concise Concordance to the New American Bible.* ■

SCEPTER PUBLISHERS
PO Box 211
New York NY 10018
Tel: 800-322-8773; 212-354-0670
Fax: 212-354-0736
E-Mail: info@scepterpublishers.org
Web Site: www.scepterpublishers.org

Personnel:
John G Powers ....Publisher
Bernie Brown ....Editor
Mary Gottschalk .... Editor

Type of Business:
Publisher of Catholic books, pamphlets, and videos which encourage Christians to live their faith in the ordinary circumstances of their lives. Books include sacraments, prayer, Catholic teaching, and the writings of the founder of Opus Dei, Saint Josemaría Escrivé. Our best selling titles include The Navarre Bible, In Conversation with God, reprints of spiritual classics, parenting books by James Stenson, and The Daily Roman Missal. Our mission is inspired by the spirit of Opus Dei, a personal prelature of the Catholic Church, which was founded to remind us to live the Gospel in our jobs, family life, and in society. ■

WORLD LIBRARY PUBLICATIONS
3825 North Willow Road

Schiller Park, IL 60176-2353
Tel.: 800-566-6150; Fax: 888-957-3291
Web Site: www.wlpmusic.com

Personnel:
Mary Prete ....General Manager
Mary Beth Kunde Anderson.................Editorial Director
John D. Wright ....Marketing Director
Kathy Mundt ....Customer Service Manager

Type of Business:
World Library Publications provides worship and music resources of the highest quality. Faithful to its heritage as a pioneer in liturgical renewal, WLP continues to support, assist and form worship and music leaders. Publisher of the nation's finest missals—*Seasonal Missalette®*, *Word + Song*, *We Celebrate*, and *¡Celebremos!*—WLP also produces the *We Celebrate Hymnal*, *Cantos del Pueblo de Dios*, *Peoples Mass Book*, and *Voices as One*. In addition, WLP publishes music for worship including choral octavos, mass settings, songbooks and instrument scores, and quality recordings of music for worship, meditation, and spiritual nourishment. Call for a complete catalog or visit www.wlpmusic.com. ■

Books & Religious Articles

PATRICK BAKER & SONS, INC.
1650 West Street
Southington, CT 06489
Tel.: 800-243-6385 Fax: 860-276-9438
72 Chambers Street
Fairfield, CT 06430
Tel: 203-366-5058 Fax: 203-334-8527
Web Site: www.churchgoods.com

Type of Business:
Patrick Baker & Sons, Inc. has been servicing the church and clergy for over 40 years. We are a family owned business committed to value with quality and service. We provide church furnishings, vestments, candles, altar breads, liners, refinishing and all your religious supplies with the highest guaranteed quality. Call or write for a catalog or visit us on our website at www.churchgoods.com. ■

SAN FRANCIS IMPORTS, INC.
901 Thompson Ave.
Glendale, CA 91201
Tel.: 800-882-4916; Fax: 800-692-9129
E-mail: info@sanfrancis.com
Web Site: www.sanfrancis.com
Personnel:
Carlos George ....Vice President Sales
E-mail: carlos@sanfrancis.com
Joseph Gamgene ....Marketing
E-mail: joe@sanfrancis.com

Type of Business:
Catholic family owned. Importer and Manufacturer of Religious & Inspirational Gifts. Custom products incorporating original designs from our exclusive relationship with the Cromo NB Studios (Milan Italy)- the world's leading producer of religious art.
Greeting cards, mass cards, enrollment cards, rosaries, chaplets, and 3-dimensional sculpted figurines incorporating unique and exclusive designs at very affordable prices. Samples and consultation are available at no charge. Ask about our National Religious Treasures™ program. ■

ST. ATHANASIUS PRESS & ST JOAN OF ARC BOOKS
133 Slazing Road
Potosi, WI 53820
Tel: 800-280-1025
Web Site: www.stathanasiuspress.com
Web Site: www.stjoanofarcbooks.com

Type of Business:
A Catholic publishing house reprinting great Catholic books. We also BUY & SELL used & new Catholic books. We specialize in Pre-1964 Catholic books or reprints thereof. Religious discounts offered. Promoting the Roman Catholic Faith since 1992.■

Pauline BOOKS & MEDIA www.pauline.org

PAULINE BOOKS & MEDIA
50 Saint Paul's Avenue
Boston, MA 02130
Tel: 617-522-8911Fax: 617-524-8035
Web Sites: www.pauline.org, www.myfriendmagazine.org
Spanish: www.paulinasUSA.com
Orders in English: 800-876-4463
Orders in Spanish: 800-876-5852

Type of Business:
Pauline Books & Media is the publishing house of the Daughters of St. Paul. Pauline produces music under the label of PAULINE Records. Pauline publishes MY FRIEND, The Catholic Magazine For Kids, ages 7-12 that features entertainment and Christian formation.
Pauline Books & Media is also a group of 19 Catholic retail stores located in the U.S. and Canada. Operated under the direction of the Daughters of St. Paul, each store is a center of Christian understanding and culture offered through a wide selection of books, movies, music and religious objects. In addition, various seminars, workshops and lectures are coordinated through the stores.
The Daughters of St. Paul are an international Congregation of women religious who serve the Church with the communications media. Visit our website, www.Pauline.org, to access our online catalog and for a complete listing of our bookstore locations. ■

TERRA SANCTA GUILD®

TERRA SANCTA GUILD
P.O. Box 300
Broomall, PA 19008
Tel: 610-544-9900
Fax: 610-544-6994
E-mail: adina@terrasancta.com
Web Site: www.terrasancta.com

Personnel:
Sharon Shore ....C.E.O.
Adina Serot ....President

Type of Business:
For over 40 years, Terra Sancta's name has been synonymous with the finest design in the field of Liturgical Art. Our custom design recipients include His Holiness, The Pope and 2 U.S. Presidents. Our art department will guide you through the process based on your individual requirements, and the necessity to communicate and inspire at reasonable prices. We can adapt your logo or create a new design. Call and ask for Sharon to discuss your custom design needs, or to request our free 40 page catalog of giftware, pendants and pins for the Christian community. ■

Bulletins & Calendars

J.S. PALUCH COMPANY, INC.
3825 North Willow Road
Schiller Park, IL 60176-2353
Tel.: 800-621-5197; Fax: 847-678-2911
Web Site: www.jspaluch.com

Personnel:
Henry Samples ....Sales
Margaret "Mickey" Paluch ....CEO
William J. Rafferty...President

Type of Business:
The J.S. Paluch Company, Inc. has served Catholic parishes, schools and communities across the United States since 1913. We provide parish bulletins in various formats and sizes, supported by ads sold by our national sales force. J.S. Paluch also specializes in promotional calendars (in English and Spanish) that can be personalized with church, school, organization and sponsor information. Styles include the Catholic Family Scenic Calendar, the Deluxe Family Appointment Calendar, and Vocations and Stewardship calendars. Call today to learn more. ■

Candles, Incense

ROOT™ CANDLES

THE A.I. ROOT CANDLE CO.
623 West Liberty Street
Medina, OH 44258
Tel.: 800-289-7668; Fax: 330-725-5624
E-mail: church@rootcandles.com
Web Site: www.rootcandles.com

Personnel:
John Holodnak ....Sales Manager

Type of Business:
• Merchandise Handled: Full line of altar candles, Advent, wedding and sacrament candles. Devotional lights, sanctuary lights, altar wine/bread, palms/ashes, and church supplies.
• Services Offered: Replating/refinishing services. Personalized sales representation in most states. Two factory locations: Medina, OH; San Antonio, TX.
• Recent Clients: Serving over 12,000 churches nationwide.
• Statement: Craftsmen in wax since 1869. Root Quality–Root Service.
• Free Literature: Free color catalog, 800-BUY-ROOT. ■

CANDLE STUDIOS
180 Division Ave.
Belleville NJ 07109
1-800-648-4229; Fax: 473-759-4299
E-mail: markjay@comcast.net
Web Site: www.candlestudios.com

Type of business:
Candle Studios is celebrating its fifth year in business, making stock and custom made candle stands in wood or wrought iron metal. Five years ago we introduced our flagship model, the Omega 2000. With many customers and hundreds of units now in the field we can say that we build the finest stand in the world, With exclusive features and options, such as Automatic select and set programmable timing, electronic soft touch lighting, offerings that are collected into a vandal proof safe, and beautiful imported crystal globes, this are all ads up to make our Omega 2000 the candle stand that is built for looks and built for life. ■

C.M. ALMY & SON, INC.
Three American Lane
P.O. Box 2644
Greenwich, CT 06836-2644
Tel.: 800-225-2569
Fax: 800-426-2569
E-mail: almyaccess@almy.com
Web Site: www.almy.com

Showrooms in:
- Old Greenwich, CT: 203-637-2739
- Pittsfield, ME: 207-487-3232

Type of Business:
Almy was founded in 1892. We design and make virtually all of our products in our Maine shop. It is our mission to design furnishings that will grace your worship and to ensure their value by making them with the highest quality materials and craftsmanship. We make a complete line of vestments, haberdashery, choir robes, candles, communion bread, linens, processional and altar appointments, and eucharistic vessels.We also offer custom design and fabrication of all Almy products, and repair and refurbishing of old metal appointments. Quik Ship© delivery of many popular items. All orders backed by The Almy Guarantee. Call, write, or e-mail for a free catalog. ■

CARROLL ELECTRONICS, INC.
710 N.E. 26th Street
Wilton Manors, FL 33305
Tel.: 800-331-0444; Fax: 954-561-4098

Personnel:
David Nagle ....President
Liza Palmer...Sales Manager
Bob Perkins ....Sales Representative
Donna Spencer......................................Service Engineer

Type of Business:
Carroll Electronics has been in business for 20 years designing and building Electronic Votive Candle Stands for thousands of churches throughout the United States. ■

CATHEDRAL CANDLE CO/ EXIMIOUS®
Web Site: www.cathedralcandles.com

Type of Business:
Classical symbolism and expressive liturgical design in the luxurious hand decorated artistry of SCULPTWAX, created and mastercrafted here in the United States... exclusively at Cathedral Candle Co. ■
Now in stock at your nearest church goods dealer.

MUENCH KREUZER CANDLE CO.
P.O. Box 4969
Syracuse, NY 13221
Tel.: 315-471-4515; 800-448-7884
Fax: 315-471-4581

Type of Business:
Manufacturers of Church candles, altar, sanctuary, sacramental, votive & devotional candles of the highest quality. Emkay Candles—available through your nearest Church Goods Dealer. ■

PATRICK BAKER & SONS, INC.
1650 West Street
Southington, CT 06489
Tel.: 800-243-6385 Fax: 860-276-9438
72 Chambers Street
Fairfield, CT 06430
Tel: 203-366-5058 Fax: 203-334-8527
Web Site: www.churchgoods.com

Type of Business:
Patrick Baker & Sons, Inc. has been servicing the church and clergy for over 40 years. We are a family owned business committed to value with quality and service. We provide church furnishings, vestments, candles, altar breads, liners, refinishing and all your religious supplies with the highest guaranteed quality. Call or write for a catalog or visit us on our website at www.churchgoods.com. ■

SMARTLITE
510 East 41st Street
Paterson, NJ 07504
Tel: 888-249-9039 (x128); 973-523-0668; Fax 973-523-0375
Web Site: www.smartlitech.com
Email: info@smartlitech.com

Type of Business:
We build a complete line of Votive & Memorial electronic candles; battery operated Vigil candles, rechargeable Devotional candles and patented tamper proof Donation/Alms boxes.
We are committed to being the best-priced, highest quality supplier in this industry.
Why Smartlite
- We are the original manufacturer, over 25 years experience
- You buy direct from the factory
- Thousands in place throughout North America with 100% satisfaction
- Our patented electronic candle produces a flame that is indistinguishable from a wax candle flame
- 10 years warranty on all electronics from AC plug to top of candle
- Lifetime warranty on unit frame
- Standard or custom design in wood or metal
- Total and continuous support on Votive and Memorial programs including software

We are always available with timely and polite assistance to answer all your questions and fulfill all your requirements. ■

THE HERBERT STANLEY CO., INC., LLC.
1100 Lakeside Drive
Gurnee, IL 60031
Tel.: 800-837-8140
Fax: 847-263-3700

Personnel:
John Brennan .... VP Sales
Helena Colabello .... Weiman Customer Service Rep.
Stacey Voss .... Weinan Customer Service Rep.

Type of Business:
Weiman® is the #1 brand of premium cleaning and polishing products. For decades, Weiman® has been the name to trust when it comes to caring for fine silver and other metals. Our easy-to-use silver and metal products contain no harsh chemicals or ammonia, and are formulated to help keep tarnish from returning and give the item a brilliant shine. Removing wax without damaging your furniture, carpet or fabric has always been a challenge - until Weiman Wax Away®. It is the safest and most effective way to gently remove candle wax. ■

Chalices, Crosses, Metalware

TOUJOURS

ADRIAN HAMERS® CHURCH INTERIORS

ADRIAN HAMERS, INC.
2 Madison Avenue
Larchmont, NY 10538
Tel.: 914-834-7780; Fax: 914-834-0712
Web Site: www.adrianhamers.com

Type of Business:
Custom designers and manufacturers of Sacred Vessels. Since 1887, the Hamers name has been synonymous with expert Silversmithing throughout the world in the field of Liturgical Art. Please contact us for those hard to find items, as we always have a large selection of Adrian Hamers Estate Collection pieces in stock. We have a large collection of antique church stainglass windows available (both full sets and individual). We are experts in: Church Interiors from design to execution, Renovations, Altars, Sacred Vessels, Gold and Silver Plating & Repairing, Appraisals, Tabernacles, Marble, Statuary, Woodwork & Woodcarving, Stained Glass, Pews & Chairs, Gold Leafing, Frescoes, Restoration, Trompe-l' oeuil, Wall Murals (repair and conservation cleaning), Ornamental Plaster, Heraldic Designs & Bishop Regalia. Please call us for a free 36-page Sacred Vessels color catalog, or our free 80-page color Woodcarvings catalog. ■

CM ALMY

C.M. ALMY & SON, INC.
Three American Lane
P.O. Box 2644
Greenwich, CT 06836-2644
Tel.: 800-225-2569; Fax: 800-426-2569
E-mail: almyaccess@almy.com
Web Site: www.almy.com

Showrooms in:
- Old Greenwich, CT: 203-637-2739
- Pittsfield, ME: 207-487-3232

Type of Business:
Almy was founded in 1892. We design and make virtually all of our products in our Maine shop. It is our mission to design furnishings that will grace your worship and to ensure their value by making them with the highest quality materials and craftsmanship. We make a complete line of vestments, haberdashery, choir robes, candles, communion bread, linens, processional and altar appointments, and eucharistic vessels.We also offer custom design and fabrication of all Almy products, and repair and refurbishing of old metal appointments. Quik Ship© delivery of many popular items. All orders backed by The Almy Guarantee. Call, write, or e-mail for a free catalog. ■

TAG GRANDA. LITURGICAL ARTS

GRANDA LITURGICAL ARTS, INC.
939 W. North Ave. , Ste.875
Chicago, IL 60622
Tel.: 800-425-0828; Fax: 312-944-9906
E-mail: usagranda@aol.com
Web Site: www.artegranda.com

Personnel:
Elia Rivera ....Director of Sales & Marketing

Type of Business:
GRANDA LITURGICAL ARTS, INC. is the USA sales and marketing office of Talleres de Arte Granda in Madrid, Spain. At our studio in Madrid, we have over one hundred artists, administrators, architects, designers, etc. dedicated to the design, production, and advancement of sacred art. Since 1891, we have been at the service of the Church combining modern techniques with artistic values to produce some of the world's finest sacred vessels, statuary, vestments, and church interiors. Please call us to request a complimentary catalog or to learn more about our custom design services. ■

THE HOLY+ROOD GUILD

THE HOLY ROOD GUILD
St. Joseph's Abbey
167 North Spencer Road
Spencer, MA 01562-1233
Tel.: 508-885-8750; Fax: 508-885-8758
E-mail: holyrood@holyroodguild.com
Web Site: www.holyroodguild.com

Type of Business:
Designers and crafters of ecclesiastical vesture for over 40 years. Inspired by our monastic tradition, we seek to unite in our work simplicity in design, quality in materials and excellence in craftsmanship. The result is vesture that enhances the liturgical celebration with visual grace and order. Our artists—both monks and laypersons—are available for custom design work and consultation. We also provide an extensive selection of ready-made items. ■

Humenick
Liturgical Arts

HUMENICK LITURGICAL ARTS
14 Taylor Rd.
Santa Fe, NM 87508
Tel.: 505-690-7000
Web Site: www.humenick.catholic.org
E-mail: humenick@direcway.com

Personnel:
Mark Humenick

Type of Business:
Mark Humenick was first commissioned, in 1973, to design and fabricate liturgical essentials. Working closely with clergy, architects, and parish committees, this work has resulted in award-winning, one-of-a-kind pieces at quite reasonable costs.

From an individual piece to a complete, design-coordinated interior, our mediums include metal, wood, and stone. We design pieces that will be lasting yet flexible, with no commission being too small. Contact us to learn how we may assist you. ■

King Richard's
Religious Artifacts

KING RICHARD'S RELIGIOUS ARTIFACTS
P.O. Box 191027
Atlanta, GA 31119
Tel.: 877-248-3366
Fax: 770-455-1784

Personnel:
Rick Lair .... President
Sandra James .... Vice President
Scott Lair .... Sales and Marketing
Chris Roberts .... Web Master
Mike Coleman .... Warehouse & Shipping

Type of Business:
King Richard's Religious Artifacts specializes in providing churches and religious facilities with a complete spectrum of religious decorative items; including complete sets of stained glass windows, statuary, altars, stations and all types of altar necessities. We travel throughout the United States selling and delivering merchandise, as well as completing all required work for purchasing and removal. ■

PATRICK BAKER & SONS

PATRICK BAKER & SONS, INC.
1650 West Street
Southington, CT 06489
Tel.: 800-243-6385 Fax: 860-276-9438
72 Chambers Street
Fairfield, CT 06430
Tel: 203-366-5058 Fax: 203-334-8527
Web Site: www.churchgoods.com

Type of Business:
Patrick Baker & Sons, Inc. has been servicing the church and clergy for over 40 years. We are a family owned business committed to value with quality and service. We provide church furnishings, vestments, candles, altar breads, liners, refinishing and all your religious supplies with the highest guaranteed quality. Call or write for a catalog or visit us on our website at www.churchgoods.com. ■

Southwest
Polishing & Plating

SOUTHWEST POLISHING & PLATING
8110 Hillcroft Street
Houston, Texas 77081
Tel.: 713-777-3993
Fax: 713-777-3993

Personnel:
Peter Montes .... C.E.O.
Gary Montes .... G.M.
David Montes .... Sales Rep.

Type of Business:
Specializing in Gold and Silver Plating on monstrance, tabernacle, chalice, cibouria, candle sticks, thirable, incense boat, crucifix, holy water buckets, relic holders, sanctuary lamps, brass vases & stands. Painting & restoring of statues. We offer 24kt baked on lacquer.
Family owned & operated since 1947, bounded & insured. All work is guaranteed. Serving the U.S.A, Canada and Mexico. All estimates are free. Recommendations are available from Bishops and Priests on request. ■

STADELMAIER

STADELMAIER-NIJMEGEN-HOLLAND
Lagelandseweg 64
6545 CG Nijmegen, Holland
Tel.: 011-31-24-379-1170; Fax: 011-31-24-379-1171
Web Site: www.stadelmaier.com
E-mail: info@stadelmaier.com or sales@stadelmaier.com

Personnel:
Mr. Aart J. Stadelmaier....................................President
Mrs. Diny Poorts ....Secretary
Mrs. Franka Scholten ....Office Manager
For clergical shirts Stadelmaier – Southington – USA
136 Curtiss Street
Southington, CT 06489, USA
Tel.: 860-621-7471; Fax: 860-621-7607

Personnel:
Mrs. Sarah Gleeton ....Customer Service

Type of Business:
Stadelmaier, established in 1930 in the Netherlands, specialises in unique, high quality liturgical vesture and church goods; vestments, stoles, albs, dalmatics, copes, deaconstoles, altar and lecterncovers, tapestries and banners. Fitting your church, your liturgy!
Our experienced design and production team is able to create innovative products from chasubles and stoles, clergy shirts and sweaters to stylish chalices, processional crosses, tabernacles and altars.
Also our Religious Antique Department with over 300 quality antique art pieces from Europe will be able to serve you well and enlighten your church space and your liturgy. For almost 75 years quality in Liturgy has been our motto. Please contact us for your local exclusive Stadelmaier dealer and / or receive our catalogue. ■

VANPOULLES
Church Furnishers
~ Est. 1908 ~

VANPOULLES LTD.
Telford Place, Crawley
West Sussex, RH10 1SZ, UK
Tel: +44 1293 590100
Fax: +44 1293 590115
E-mail: sales@vanpoulles.co.uk
Web Site: www.vanpoulles.co.uk

Type of Business:
Vanpoulles Ltd. is a family business, established nearly 100 years ago to provide the Church with all types of church requisites. We specialise in producing traditional English silverware and ecclesiastical garments, including chalices, ciboria, vestments, copes, stoles and altar frontals etc. Our sales department is available for friendly service and advice and current stock availability of all our product lines.
Please call, write or e-mail for a free catalogue. If visiting the UK please note our showrooms are conveniently positioned only a short distance from Gatwick Airport. ■

Choir Robes

CM ALMY

C.M. ALMY & SON, INC.
Three American Lane
P.O. Box 2644
Greenwich, CT 06836-2644
Tel.: 800-225-2569; Fax: 800-426-2569
E-mail: almyaccess@almy.com
Web Site: www.almy.com

Showrooms in:
- Old Greenwich, CT: 203-637-2739
- Pittsfield, ME: 207-487-3232

Type of Business:
Almy was founded in 1892. We design and make virtually all of our products in our Maine shop. It is our mission to design furnishings that will grace your worship and to ensure their value by making them with the highest quality materials and craftsmanship. We make a complete line of vestments, haberdashery, choir robes, candles, communion bread, linens, processional and altar appointments, and eucharistic vessels.We also offer custom design and fabrication of all Almy products, and repair and refurbishing of old metal appointments. Quik Ship© delivery of many popular items. All orders backed by The Almy Guarantee. Call, write, or e-mail for a free catalog. ■

MURPHY ROBES

MURPHY ROBES
Murphy Cap & Gown Company
Dept. OCD
4200 31st Street North
St. Petersburg, FL 33714
Tel.: 727-527-0696; Fax: 727-526-3528

Personnel:
Don Camp ....President
Gary Bergamo ....Sales Manager
George Shahine ....Administrative Manager

Type of Business:
Value priced choir robes ready to ship within 24 hours of factory receipt of order with guaranteed satisfaction. Many custom tailored styles also available. Visit our website at www.murphyrobes.com or ask for our products at your local church goods supplier.■

ROBERT GASPARD CO., INC.
200 North Janacek Road
Brookfield, WI 53045-6101
Tel.: 800-784-6868; Fax: 262-784-7567
E-mail: mail@rgaspard.com
Web Site: www.robertgaspardco.com

Personnel:
Rose Gaspard..President
Jason R. Gaspard ....General Manager

Type of Business:
The Robert Gaspard Co. was established in 1954. Over the past 50 years, we have grown to be a nationally-known company. We pride ourselves on the ability to create original custom designs to enrich your worship needs. Our complete line consists of all ecclesiastical vesture, as well as paraments, mass and altar linens, stoles, banners, chasubles, funeral palls, albs, cossacks, surplices, choir robes, acolyte robes and many accessories. Complimentary catalog and fabric swatches sent on request. ■

Church Registers

D.P. MURPHY CO., INC.
1221 Walt Whitman Road, Melville, NY 11747-3090
Tel.: 800-424-8724; Fax: 631-673-1851
E-mail: sales@dpmurphy.com
Web Site: www.dpmurphy.com

Personnel:
Timothy Murphy Schratwieser ....President

Type of Business:
Envelope mailing systems specifically designed to meet the needs of your parish. Available in Any Frequency
▾ Monthly ▾ Bi-Monthly ▾ Quarterly
▾ Semi-Annual ▾ Yearly Sets
FREE List Maintenance Online
or ▾ Diskette ▾ E-mail ▾ Fax ▾ Mail

WE SPECIALIZE IN OLD REGISTER REBINDING.

- Census
- Stewardship
- Tithing
- Fund-Raising Programs
- Contribution Recording
- Registers
- Record Books
- Mass Cards
- Certificates
- Church Stationery ■

F.J. REMEY CO., INC.
121 Willis Avenue
Mineola, NY 11501
Tel.: (877)-FJ REMEY
Fax: (516)741-0523
Web Site: fjremey.com
E-mail: contactus@fjremey.com

Type of Business:
Serving the Catholic Church since 1921

Offering Envelope Programs	Collection Baskets
Bulk Collection Envelopes	Mass Cards
Church Record Books	Parish Office Forms
Tuition Supplies	Raffle Tickets
Certificates	Census Programs ■

Commemorative Gifts

SANDMAN DESIGNS, LLC
109 Old Post Road
Clinton, CT 06413
Tel: 888-736-2749
Fax: 860-664-9031

Personnel:
Sandra Raucci ....President
Fred Raucci ....Vice President Sales/Marketing

Type of Business:
We have the perfect way to **raise funds** for your Parish or **award gifts** for Stewardship. Your Church or Saint's Statue will be designed as an exact replica, in a lapel pin or magnet, made of beautiful Enamels and plated in 14 K Gold. They are presented on a 2" by 3.5" card including your text and sealed in a cellophane sleeve. Visit our web site at www.sandmandesigns.com to view examples and learn how to make Fund Raising Fun and Easy.
See our ad on page R 15. ■

TERRA SANCTA GUILD
P.O. Box 300
Broomall, PA 19008
Tel: 610-544-9900
Fax: 610-544-6994
E-mail: adina@terrasancta.com
Web Site: www.terrasancta.com

Personnel:
Sharon Shore ....C.E.O.
Adina Serot ....President

Type of Business:
For over 40 years, Terra Sancta's name has been synonymous with the finest design in the field of Liturgical Art. Our custom design recipients include His Holiness, The Pope and 2 U.S. Presidents. Our art department will guide you through the process based on your individual requirements, and the necessity to communicate and inspire at reasonable prices. We can adapt your logo or create a new design. Call and ask for Sharon to discuss your custom design needs, or to request our free 40 page catalog of giftware, pendants and pins for the Christian community. ■

Fabric Art Hangings & Tapestries

ABBOTT INC.
1515 Route 38
Cherry Hill, NJ 08002
Tel.: 800-522-2688; 856-662-6959; Fax: 856-665-5109
E-mail: info@churchsupplies.com
Web Site: www.churchsupplies.com

Personnel:
Daniel J. Castonguay ....President
Joseph F. McKeaney................................General Manager
Mary Ann Mitkus..........................Business Administrator
John Scafidi...Distribution
Michael Schwartz ....Government Liaison

Type of Business:
Purveyors of the Finest Vesture, Paraments, Statuary & Metalware since 1962. Unique and original creations, our specialty. Custom designs to complement your liturgical environment. Exclusive representatives of Slabbinck Master Collection & Original Collection. ■

C.M. ALMY & SON, INC.
Three American Lane
P.O. Box 2644
Greenwich, CT 06836-2644
Tel.: 800-225-2569; Fax: 800-426-2569
E-mail: almyaccess@almy.com
Web Site: www.almy.com

Showrooms in:
- Old Greenwich, CT: 203-637-2739
- Pittsfield, ME: 207-487-3232

Type of Business:
Almy was founded in 1892. We design and make virtually all of our products in our Maine shop. It is our mission to design furnishings that will grace your worship and to ensure their value by making them with the highest quality materials and craftsmanship. We make a complete line of vestments, haberdashery, choir robes, candles, communion bread, linens, processional and altar appointments, and eucharistic vessels.We also offer custom design and fabrication of all Almy products, and repair and refurbishing of old metal appointments. Quik Ship© delivery of many popular items. All orders backed by The Almy Guarantee. Call, write, or e-mail for a free catalog. ■

MAISON BOUVRIER INC.
391 Hanlan Road, Woodbridge
Ontario, Canada L4L 3T1
905-851-1146 or 800-665-9895
Fax 905-851-7623
E-mail: bouvrier@maisonbouvrier.com
Web Site: www.maisonbouvrier.com

Personnel:
Kevin Bayne ....President
Janet MacDonald ....General Manager

Type of Business:
Maison Bouvrier has been in existence for over 130 years and is a world leader in weaving, creating and developing inspirational fabric designs of impeccable quality. Personalised attention is given to the needs of individual communities. All our artistic work is initially designed and created during a personal visit, thereby ensuring that the fabric used, the designs selected and the shapes chosen, fit perfectly into the worship space and enhance the visual liturgy. ■

STADELMAIER

STADELMAIER-NIJMEGEN-HOLLAND
Lagelandseweg 64
6545 CG Nijmegen, Holland
Tel.: 011-31-24-379-1170; Fax: 011-31-24-379-1171
Web Site: www.stadelmaier.com
E-mail: info@stadelmaier.com or sales@stadelmaier.com

Personnel:
Mr. Aart J. Stadelmaier..President
Mrs. Diny Poorts ....Secretary
Mrs. Franka Scholten ....Office Manager
For clergical shirts Stadelmaier – Southington – USA
136 Curtiss Street
Southington, CT 06489, USA
Tel.: 860-621-7471; Fax: 860-621-7607

Personnel:
Mrs. Sarah Gleeton ....Customer Service

Type of Business:
Stadelmaier, established in 1930 in the Netherlands, specialises in unique, high quality liturgical vesture and church goods; vestments, stoles, albs, dalmatics, copes, deaconstoles, altar and lecterncovers, tapestries and banners. Fitting your church, your liturgy!
Our experienced design and production team is able to create innovative products from chasubles and stoles, clergy shirts and sweaters to stylish chalices, processional crosses, tabernacles and altars.
Also our Religious Antique Department with over 300 quality antique art pieces from Europe will be able to serve you well and enlighten your church space and your liturgy. For almost 75 years quality in Liturgy has been our motto. Please contact us for your local exclusive Stadelmaier dealer and / or receive our catalogue. ■

Gift Shop Suppliers

CHRISTIAN ART, INC.
567 52nd St.
West New York, NJ 07093
Tel.: 800-562-5413
Fax: 888-562-5413
Email: sales@christianartonline.com

Personnel:
Anthony and Terry Ferrer ....Principals

Type of Business:
Importer and distributor of largest inventory of Traditional Devotional Church Quality Statuary from Spain for over 40 years, specializing in unusual subjects and Spanish Devotions. Statues come in sizes 6 feet down to 8", with glass eyes.
We supply Church Gift Shops with gifts from Italy, Portugal, and China for Baptism, First Holy Communion and Confirmation, Rosaries, Crucifixes, Last Suppers, Nativity sets, inspirational gifts, Italian Sterling Silver by Salerni, and the Florentine Statuary Collection. ■

SWANSON CHRISTIAN PRODUCTS
1200 Park Ave.
Murfreesboro, TN 37129
Tel.: 800-251-1402
Fax: 866-431-1313
E-mail: sales@swansoninc.com
Web Site: www.swansoninc.com

Type of Business:
Since 1934, Swanson's has provided to the Christian community church supplies, De Colores, novelties, gifts anointing oils, men's ties, bible tabs, jewelry, lapel pins, stickers, pens, pencils, ribbons cups, olive wood, Jerusalem Products usher badges, bible covers, ball caps, back packs, wallets, lunch boxes, brief cases, puzzles, auto tags, auto frames, auto fish, key rings, bumper stickers, car flags, tambourines, puppets, highlighters, key rings trophies, banners and American flags. ■

Gold/Silver Plating, Brass Restoration

FRAPPEZ TOUJOURS

ADRIAN HAMERS® CHURCH INTERIORS

ADRIAN HAMERS, INC.
2 Madison Avenue
Larchmont, NY 10538
Tel.: 914-834-7780; Fax: 914-834-0712
Web Site: www.adrianhamers.com

Type of Business:
Custom designers and manufacturers of Sacred Vessels. Since 1887, the Hamers name has been synonymous with expert Silversmithing throughout the world in the field of Liturgical Art. Please contact us for those hard to find items, as we always have a large selection of Adrian Hamers Estate Collection pieces in stock. We have a large collection of antique church stainglass windows available (both full sets and individual). We are experts in: Church Interiors from design to execution, Renovations, Altars, Sacred Vessels, Gold and Silver Plating & Repairing, Appraisals, Tabernacles, Marble, Statuary, Woodwork & Woodcarving, Stained Glass, Pews & Chairs, Gold Leafing, Frescoes, Restoration, Trompe-l' oeuil, Wall Murals (repair and conservation cleaning), Ornamental Plaster, Heraldic Designs & Bishop Regalia. Please call us for a free 36-page Sacred Vessels color catalog, or our free 80-page color Woodcarvings catalog. ■

CM ALMY

C.M. ALMY & SON, INC.
Three American Lane
P.O. Box 2644
Greenwich, CT 06836-2644
Tel.: 800-225-2569; Fax: 800-426-2569
E-mail: almyaccess@almy.com
Web Site: www.almy.com

Showrooms in:
- Old Greenwich, CT: 203-637-2739
- Pittsfield, ME: 207-487-3232

Type of Business:
Almy was founded in 1892. We design and make virtually all of our products in our Maine shop. It is our mission to design furnishings that will grace your worship and to ensure their value by making them with the highest quality materials and craftsmanship. We make a complete line of vestments, haberdashery, choir robes, candles, communion bread, linens, processional and altar appointments, and eucharistic vessels.We also offer custom design and fabrication of all Almy products, and repair and refurbishing of old metal appointments. Quik Ship© delivery of many popular items. All orders backed by The Almy Guarantee. Call, write, or e-mail for a free catalog. ■

MUELLER KAISER PLATING CO.
Since 1911
5815 Hampton Avenue • St. Louis, MO 63109 • (314) 832-3553

MUELLER KAISER PLATING CO.
5815 Hampton Avenue
St. Louis, MO 63109
Tel.: 314-832-3553
Web Site: www.mueller-kaiserplating.com

Type of Business:
One of the OLDEST liturgical metalware platers and refinishers in the U.S.A., offering a distinguished tradition of Master Metal Craftsmanship in the expert restoration, plating and refinishing of Sacred Vessels and Metalware in GOLD, SILVER, BRASS, COPPER, and BRONZE since 1911. Customers should ship chalices, ciboria, monstrances, candelabra and other sacred metalware to us by U.P.S. (insured) for estimates and work. (Note: return ship items without work at customer expense.) We also offer OLD CHALICES, CIBORIA, MONSTRANCES, CANDELABRA, and other FITMENTS to Catholic clergy, religious and churches for ONLY the cost of refinishing. Inquire for selection and price. Ecclesiastical Authorization. Awards from recognized religious, arts and cultural organizations. CELEBRATING 94 YEARS OF MASTER CRAFTSMANSHIP in the LITURGICAL METAL ARTS! ■

Southwest
Polishing & Plating

SOUTHWEST POLISHING & PLATING
8110 Hillcroft Street
Houston, Texas 77081
Tel.: 713-777-3993
Fax: 713-777-3993

Personnel:
Peter Montes .... C.E.O.
Gary Montes .... G.M.
David Montes .... Sales Rep.

Type of Business:
Specializing in Gold and Silver Plating on monstrance, tabernacle, chalice, cibouria, candle sticks, thirable, incense boat, crucifix, holy water buckets, relic holders, sanctuary lamps, brass vases & stands. Painting & restoring of statues. We offer 24kt baked on lacquer. Family owned & operated since 1947, bounded & insured. All work is guaranteed. Serving the U.S.A, Canada and Mexico. All estimates are free. Recommendations are available from Bishops and Priests on request. ■

WEIMAN®

THE HERBERT STANLEY CO., INC., LLC.
1100 Lakeside Drive
Gurnee, IL 60031
Tel.: 800-837-8140
Fax: 847-263-3700

Personnel:
John Brennan .... VP Sales
Helena Colabello ....Weiman Customer Service Rep.
Stacey Voss ....Weinan Customer Service Rep.

Type of Business:
Weiman® is the #1 brand of premium cleaning and polishing products. For decades, Weiman® has been the name to trust when it comes to caring for fine silver and other metals. Our easy-to-use silver and metal products contain no harsh chemicals or ammonia, and are formulated to help keep tarnish from returning and give the item a brilliant shine. Removing wax without damaging your furniture, carpet or fabric has always been a challenge - until Weiman Wax Away®. It is the safest and most effective way to gently remove candle wax. ■

Gold Leafing & Painted Murals

ADRIAN HAMERS® CHURCH INTERIORS

ADRIAN HAMERS, INC.
2 Madison Avenue
Larchmont, NY 10538
Tel.: 914-834-7780; Fax: 914-834-0712
Web Site: www.adrianhamers.com

Type of Business:
Custom designers and manufacturers of Sacred Vessels. Since 1887, the Hamers name has been synonymous with expert Silversmithing throughout the world in the field of Liturgical Art. Please contact us for those hard to find items, as we always have a large selection of Adrian Hamers Estate Collection pieces in stock. We have a large collection of antique church stainglass windows available (both full sets and individual). We are experts in: Church Interiors from design to execution, Renovations, Altars, Sacred Vessels, Gold and Silver Plating & Repairing, Appraisals, Tabernacles, Marble, Statuary, Woodwork & Woodcarving, Stained Glass, Pews & Chairs, Gold Leafing, Frescoes, Restoration, Trompe-l' oeuil, Wall Murals (repair and conservation cleaning), Ornamental Plaster, Heraldic Designs & Bishop Regalia. Please call us for a free 36-page Sacred Vessels color catalog, or our free 80-page color Woodcarvings catalog. ■

Offering Envelopes

Cathedral CORPORATION

CATHEDRAL CORPORATION
Griffiss Technology Park
632 Ellsworth Road
Rome, NY 13441
Tel.: 315-338-0021; 800-419-8970; Fax 315-338-5874
E-mail: sales@cathedralstewardship.com
Web Site: www.cathedralstewardship.com

Personnel:
Marianne W. Gaige ....President and COO
Ronald P. Blakeman ....Vice President of Sales
Scott Dickan ....Sales Manager

Type of Business:
Cathedral Corporation delivers exceptional service to churches that excel in ministry. For more than six decades, Cathedral has delivered superior service, leadership and innovation in the creation, printing, personalization and high volume mailing of offering envelopes. Today Cathedral supports Catholic parishes across the nation with a full range of proven stewardship resources and electronic services for the Internet.

Mailed Offering Envelope Programs
Annual Boxed Sets
Increased Offering Campaigns
Youth Envelopes
Bulk Offering Envelopes
Envelope Recording & Reporting Service
ACT Electronic Offering Service
Online Real-Time List Maintenance
And More! ■

Church Budget
Monthly Mail
P.O. 420
Salem, Ohio 44460

CHURCH BUDGET MONTHLY MAIL COMPANY
P.O. Box 420, 157 W Pershing St.
Salem, OH 44460
Tel: 330-337-1122
Fax: 330-337-1124
E-mail: confirm@churchbudmail.com
Web Site: www.churchbudmail.com

Personnel:
James H. Pidgeon, Michael J. Pidgeon, Barry A. Pidgeon

Type of business:
Church Budget Monthly Mail provides personally addressed offering envelopes mailed directly to the homes of your parishioners on a monthly, bimonthly, quarterly, semi-annual or annual basis.
Church Budget also produces annual boxed envelopes in three different sizes and mail-back sized booklets envelopes mailed quarterly, semi-annually or annually. All orders can be addressed or numbered and dated. Pew and bulk envelopes also available. All this at the great cost savings. Give us a call. ■

PERSONALIZED ADDRESSED MAILING PROGRAMS

In our monthly mailing program, addressed offering envelopes are regularly mailed directly to your members at home. Custom printed to your specifications and mailed monthly, bi-monthly or quarterly, you choose. Each mailing consists of one envelope per Sunday plus Holy Day, Diocesan, any special collection envelopes and pastoral letters you wish to include.

- **Increases offerings 10 to 20 percent**
- Helps develop good stewardship habits
- Church Budget does all the work & covers all costs including postage
- Your name & address file is periodically updated through your e-mail, diskette or change cards.
- Eliminates church storage problems
- **Pay for only active, participating members.**
- Also available Addressed Mailback Sets or inserted return envelopes

Looking For Something Different?

Try our Trust or Stewardship Series

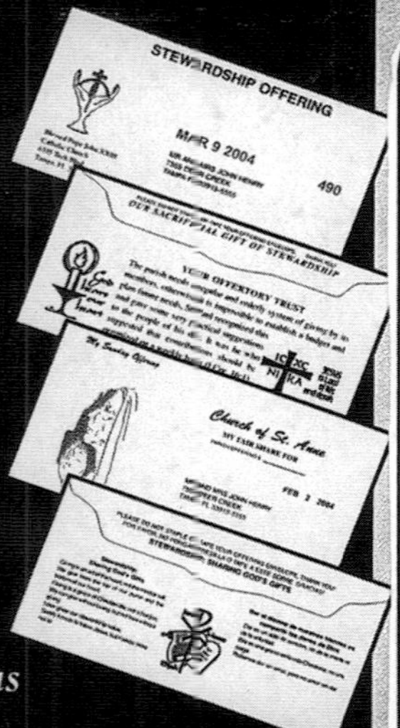

Each Mailing has a different theme, Message and Artwork.

Please note: Churches with 200 members and more qualify for this program.

Church Budget
Monthly Mail
P.O. 420
Salem, Ohio 44460

1-800-661-4538
1-330-337-8707
Fax 330-337-1124

E-mail:
www.churchbudmail.com info@churchbudmail.com

Our quality product line includes:

- ***Personalized Addressed Mailing Programs***
- ***Booklet Style Envelopes***
- ***Custom-Printed Boxed Sets***
  (Addressed & Unaddressed)
- ***Custom-Printed Bulk Envelopes***
- ***Stewardship Offering Systems***
- ***Bi-Lingual Envelopes***
- ***Four Color Sets Available***

Our Products are manufactured and produced in one location by Church Budget and Church Budget Monthly Mail in Salem, Ohio.

CUSTOM-PRINTED BOXED SETS

Our Custom Printed Annual Boxed Sets provide your members with a convenient and confidential way to fulfill their stewardship commitment. Boxed sets increase tithing on a weekly basis and make record-keeping easier. Available in addressed or numbered and dated sets

- The most cost-efficient tithing method in the industry
- Available for adults, youth and children.
- Customize your own envelopes: size, color, style, dating and numbering.

A Boxed Set consists of one weekly envelope for each Sunday of the year. Special Occasions can be inserted for a small fee.

BOOKLET STYLE ENVELOPES

These attractive checkbook-style envelopes—one for each Sunday—are designed to be torn from the packet leaving a recording stub and sent through the mail to the church. Your members will enjoy the convenience of record-keeping at their fingertips. Special collection envelopes can be inserted for an additional charge.

OUTSIDE

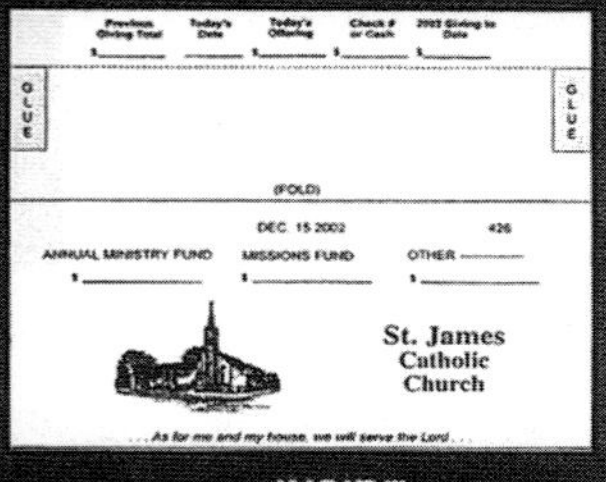

INSIDE

D.P. MURPHY CO., INC.
1221 Walt Whitman Road, Melville, NY 11747-3090
Tel.: 800-424-8724; Fax: 631-673-1851
E-mail: sales@dpmurphy.com
Web Site: www.dpmurphy.com

Personnel:
Timothy Murphy Schratwieser ....President

Type of Business:
Envelope mailing systems specifically designed to meet the needs of your parish. Available in Any Frequency
▾ Monthly ▾ Bi-Monthly ▾ Quarterly
▾ Semi-Annual ▾ Yearly Sets
FREE List Maintenance Online
or ▾ Diskette ▾ E-mail ▾ Fax ▾ Mail

WE SPECIALIZE IN OLD REGISTER REBINDING.

- Census
- Stewardship
- Tithing
- Fund-Raising Programs
- Contribution Recording
- Registers
- Record Books
- Mass Cards
- Certificates
- Church Stationery ■

F.J. REMEY CO., INC.
121 Willis Avenue
Mineola, NY 11501
Tel.: (877)-FJ REMEY
Fax: (516)741-0523
Web Site: fjremey.com
E-mail: contactus@fjremey.com

Type of Business:
Serving the Catholic Church since 1921

Offering Envelope Programs
Bulk Collection Envelopes
Church Record Books
Tuition Supplies
Certificates
Collection Baskets
Mass Cards
Parish Office Forms
Raffle Tickets
Census Programs ■

NATIONAL CHURCH SUPPLY CO.
P.O. Box 269
Chester, WV 26034
Tel.: 304-387-5200; Fax: 304-387-5266

Personnel:
Mr. Richard Cronin ....President & General Manager,

Type of Business:
Nurturing Stewardship Growth in churches is a tradition at Catholic Envelope Service. A division of National Church Supply Co., we have been serving the Christian community for more than 80 years. Every person in our family-owned organization has the same goal: to help every church customer find the best possible solution to today's and tomorrow's stewardship challenges. Our innovative church offering envelopes and stewardship systems are geared to increase communications while improving parishioner commitment and response. ■

ONE-WRITE COMPANY
3750 State Rt. 37 E., P.O. Box 628
Lancaster, OH 43130
Tel.: 800-268-6070; 740-654-2128
Fax: 800-504-2260; 740-654-2260
E-mail: owc@onewriteco.com

Personnel:
Crystal Bussart ....Church Services Manager

Type of Business:
* Book Offering Envelopes
* Tuition Payment Books
* Mailing Plan for Offering Envelopes
* Contribution Report Forms
* **NEW!** Cheerful Recorder Software

We invite you to compare the features and prices of the Book Offering Envelopes with your current system. The savings will be considerable. Write or call for a free catalog and quote today. ■

Our Sunday Visitor, Inc.

OUR SUNDAY VISITOR, INC.
200 Noll Plaza
Huntington, IN 46750
Tel.: 800-348-2886; Fax: 800-442-0669
Web Site: www.osv.com

Personnel:

Greg Erlandson ....President, Publishing Division
Kyle Hamilton ....President, Offering Envelope Division
Jill Kurtz ....Marketing Director, Publishing Division
Julie Kenny ....Marketing Manager, Offering Envelope Division

Type of Business:

Our Sunday Visitor, Inc. is a not-for-profit organization providing thousands of parishes with a wide variety of Catholic:

- Books
- Magazines
- Offering Envelope Products and Services
- Religious Education Products
- Stewardship Products and Services ■

Sacred Vessels

TOUJOURS

ADRIAN HAMERS®
CHURCH INTERIORS

ADRIAN HAMERS, INC.
2 Madison Avenue
Larchmont, NY 10538
Tel.: 914-834-7780; Fax: 914-834-0712
Web Site: www.adrianhamers.com

Type of Business:

Custom designers and manufacturers of Sacred Vessels. Since 1887, the Hamers name has been synonymous with expert Silversmithing throughout the world in the field of Liturgical Art. Please contact us for those hard to find items, as we always have a large selection of Adrian Hamers Estate Collection pieces in stock. We have a large collection of antique church stainglass windows available (both full sets and individual). We are experts in: Church Interiors from design to execution, Renovations, Altars, Sacred Vessels, Gold and Silver Plating & Repairing, Appraisals, Tabernacles, Marble, Statuary, Woodwork & Woodcarving, Stained Glass, Pews & Chairs, Gold Leafing, Frescoes, Restoration, Trompe-l' oeuil, Wall Murals (repair and conservation cleaning), Ornamental Plaster, Heraldic Designs & Bishop Regalia. Please call us for a free 36-page Sacred Vessels color catalog, or our free 80-page color Woodcarvings catalog. ■

CM ALMY

C.M. ALMY & SON, INC.
Three American Lane
P.O. Box 2644
Greenwich, CT 06836-2644
Tel.: 800-225-2569; Fax: 800-426-2569
E-mail: almyaccess@almy.com
Web Site: www.almy.com

Showrooms in:
- Old Greenwich, CT: 203-637-2739
- Pittsfield, ME: 207-487-3232

Type of Business:
Almy was founded in 1892. We design and make virtually all of our products in our Maine shop. It is our mission to design furnishings that will grace your worship and to ensure their value by making them with the highest quality materials and craftsmanship. We make a complete line of vestments, haberdashery, choir robes, candles, communion bread, linens, processional and altar appointments, and eucharistic vessels.We also offer custom design and fabrication of all Almy products, and repair and refurbishing of old metal appointments. Quik Ship© delivery of many popular items. All orders backed by The Almy Guarantee. Call, write, or e-mail for a free catalog. ■

TAG GRANDA. LITURGICAL ARTS

GRANDA LITURGICAL ARTS, INC.
939 W. North Ave. , Ste.875
Chicago, IL 60622
Tel.: 800-425-0828; Fax: 312-944-9906
E-mail: usagranda@aol.com
Web Site: www.artegranda.com

Personnel:
Elia Rivera .... Director of Sales & Marketing

Type of Business:
GRANDA LITURGICAL ARTS, INC. is the USA sales and marketing office of Talleres de Arte Granda in Madrid, Spain. At our studio in Madrid, we have over one hundred artists, administrators, architects, designers, etc. dedicated to the design, production, and advancement of sacred art. Since 1891, we have been at the service of the Church combining modern techniques with artistic values to produce some of the world's finest sacred vessels, statuary, vestments, and church interiors. Please call us to request a complimentary catalog or to learn more about our custom design services. ■

King Richard's Religious Artifacts

KING RICHARD'S RELIGIOUS ARTIFACTS
P.O. Box 191027
Atlanta, GA 31119
Tel.: 877-248-3366
Fax: 770-455-1784

Personnel:
Rick Lair .... President
Sandra James .... Vice President
Scott Lair .... Sales and Marketing
Chris Roberts .... Web Master
Mike Coleman .... Warehouse & Shipping

Type of Business:
King Richard's Religious Artifacts specializes in providing churches and religious facilities with a complete spectrum of religious decorative items; including complete sets of stained glass windows, statuary, altars, stations and all types of altar necessities. We travel throughout the United States selling and delivering merchandise, as well as completing all required work for purchasing and removal. ■

STADELMAIER

STADELMAIER-NIJMEGEN-HOLLAND
Lagelandseweg 64
6545 CG Nijmegen, Holland
Tel.: 011-31-24-379-1170; Fax: 011-31-24-379-1171
Web Site: www.stadelmaier.com
E-mail: info@stadelmaier.com or sales@stadelmaier.com

Personnel:
Mr. Aart J. Stadelmaier .... President
Mrs. Diny Poorts .... Secretary
Mrs. Franka Scholten .... Office Manager

For clergical shirts Stadelmaier – Southington – USA
136 Curtiss Street
Southington, CT 06489, USA
Tel.: 860-621-7471; Fax: 860-621-7607

Personnel:
Mrs. Sarah Gleeton .... Customer Service

Type of Business:
Stadelmaier, established in 1930 in the Netherlands, specialises in unique, high quality liturgical vesture and church goods; vestments, stoles, albs, dalmatics, copes, deaconstoles, altar and lecterncovers, tapestries and banners. Fitting your church, your liturgy!
Our experienced design and production team is able to create innovative products from chasubles and stoles, clergy shirts and sweaters to stylish chalices, processional crosses, tabernacles and altars.
Also our Religious Antique Department with over 300 quality antique art pieces from Europe will be able to serve you well and enlighten your church space and your liturgy. For almost 75 years quality in Liturgy has been our motto. Please contact us for your local exclusive Stadelmaier dealer and / or receive our catalogue. ■

WLP WORLD LIBRARY PUBLICATIONS

WORLD LIBRARY PUBLICATIONS
3825 North Willow Road
Schiller Park, IL 60176-2353
Tel.: 800-566-6150; Fax: 888-957-3291
Web Site: www.wlpmusic.com

Personnel:
Mary Prete ....General Manager
Mary Beth Kunde Anderson.................Editorial Director
John D. Wright ....Marketing Director
Kathy Mundt ....Customer Service Manager

Type of Business:
World Library Publications provides worship and music resources of the highest quality. Faithful to its heritage as a pioneer in liturgical renewal, WLP continues to support, assist and form worship and music leaders. Publisher of the nation's finest missals—*Seasonal Missalette®*, *Word + Song*, *We Celebrate*, and *¡Celebremos!*—WLP also produces the *We Celebrate Hymnal*, *Cantos del Pueblo de Dios*, *Peoples Mass Book*, and *Voices as One*. In addition, WLP publishes music for worship including choral octavos, mass settings, songbooks and instrument scores, and quality recordings of music for worship, meditation, and spiritual nourishment. Call for a complete catalog or visit www.wlpmusic.com. ■

Stationery & Greeting Cards

BC

BARTON-COTTON

BARTON-COTTON
1405 Parker Road
Baltimore, MD 21227
Tel.: 800-638-4652; Fax: 800-807-2954

Personnel:
Denise J. Payne ....Vice President, Marketing & Sales

Type of Business:
For 75 years, Barton-Cotton has been proud to offer the finest selection of quality religious stationery products to the Catholic Clergy and Religious. Over 300 products are available including Mass cards, Sacramental certificates, Christmas and Easter cards, Mother's/Father's Day sets, Ordination/Jubilee products, Way of the Cross booklets, Rosary folders, Holy cards, Bulletins, Offering Envelopes, Bookmarks and more. Products can be personalized with your name, church name, address, or special message. For a FREE catalog, call 800-638-4652. ■

THE PRINTERY HOUSE
Conception Abbey · CONCEPTION · MISSOURI 64433

THE PRINTERY HOUSE
Conception Abbey
P.O. Box 12
Conception, MO 64433
Tel.: 800-889-0105; 660-944-3110
Fax: 888-556-8262
E-mail: sales@printeryhouse.org
Web Site: printeryhouse.org

Personnel:
Bro. William Buchholz, O.S.B ....Gen. Mgr., Director
Roy Haas ....Director of Sales and Marketing
Bro. Jeremiah Tuttle, O.S.B ....Marketing
Peggy Osborn ....Marketing
Bro. Michael Marcotte, O.S.B.......................Art Director
Lee Coats ....Creative Director

Type of Business:
Manufacture and market Christian/Catholic Greeting cards and icons. Customized Christmas and other cards to enhance your development programs are our forte! The Printery House is a not-for-profit extension of the apostolate of the monks of Conception Abbey.
Call 800-889-0105 or fax us at 888-556-8262 for free samples, catalogs and quantity discount schedules. ■

SWANSON CHRISTIAN PRODUCTS
1200 Park Ave.
Murfreesboro, TN 37129
Tel.: 800-251-1402
Fax: 866-431-1313
E-mail: sales@swansoninc.com
Web Site: www.swansoninc.com

Type of Business:
Since 1934, Swanson's has provided to the Christian community church supplies, De Colores, novelties, gifts anointing oils, men's ties, bible tabs, jewelry, lapel pins, stickers, pens, pencils, ribbons cups, olive wood, Jerusalem Products usher badges, bible covers, ball caps, back packs, wallets, lunch boxes, brief cases, puzzles, auto tags, auto frames, auto fish, key rings, bumper stickers, car flags, tambourines, puppets, highlighters, key rings trophies, banners and American flags. ■

Stewardship

CATHEDRAL CORPORATION
Griffiss Technology Park
632 Ellsworth Road
Rome, NY 13441
Tel.: 315-338-0021; 800-419-8970; Fax 315-338-5874
E-mail: sales@cathedralstewardship.com
Web Site: www.cathedralstewardship.com

Personnel:
Marianne W. Gaige....................President and COO
Ronald P. Blakeman....................Vice President of Sales
Scott Dickan....................Sales Manager

Type of Business:
Cathedral Corporation delivers exceptional service to churches that excel in ministry. For more than six decades, Cathedral has delivered superior service, leadership and innovation in the creation, printing, personalization and high volume mailing of offering envelopes. Today Cathedral supports Catholic parishes across the nation with a full range of proven stewardship resources and electronic services for the Internet.

Mailed Offering Envelope Programs
Annual Boxed Sets
Increased Offering Campaigns
Youth Envelopes
Bulk Offering Envelopes
Envelope Recording & Reporting Service
ACT Electronic Offering Service
Online Real-Time List Maintenance
And More! ■

J.S. PALUCH COMPANY, INC.
3825 N. Willow Rd.
Schiller Park, IL 60176-2353
Tel.: 800-621-5197; Fax: 847-678-2911
Web Site: www.jspaluch.com

Personnel:
Henry Samples....................Sales
Margaret "Mickey" Paluch....................CEO
William J. Rafferty....................President

Type of Business:
The J.S. Paluch Company, Inc. has served Catholic parishes, schools and communities across the United States since 1913. We provide parish bulletins in various formats and sizes, supported by ads sold by our national sales force. J.S. Paluch also specializes in promotional calendars (in English and Spanish) that can be personalized with church, school, organization and sponsor information. Styles include the Catholic Family Scenic Calendar, the Deluxe Family Appointment Calendar, and Vocations and Stewardship calendars. Call today to learn more. ■

NATIONAL CHURCH SUPPLY CO.
P.O. Box 269
Chester, WV 26034
Tel.: 304-387-5200; Fax: 304-387-5266

Personnel:
Mr. Richard Cronin....................President & General Manager

Type of Business:
Nurturing Stewardship Growth in churches is a tradition at Catholic Envelope Service. A division of National Church Supply Co., we have been serving the Christian community for more than 80 years. Every person in our family-owned organization has the same goal: to help every church customer find the best possible solution to today's and tomorrow's stewardship challenges. Our innovative church offering envelopes and stewardship systems are geared to increase communications while improving parishioner commitment and response. ■

Unique Gifts

DAZZLE GLAZZ STUDIO
6605 Jefferson Highway
Baton Rouge, LA 70806-8104
Tel: 888-717-9484; 225-216-9484
Fax: 225-216-9486
E-mail; duncan@church-windows.com; duncan@unique-crosses.com; duncan@dazzleglazz.com
Web Site: www.church-windows.com; www.unique-crosses.com; www.dazzleglazz.com

Personnel:
Duncan, Diana & Douglas Tooley; Erskin Mitchell

Type of Business:
Leaded and faceted stain glass design, fabrication and restoration. Our goal is to fill each project with the faith and passion that will result in "Windows that Praise and Inspire." We also do contract fabrication for other glass designers. Large and intricate windows are economical through computerized water-jet cut and laminated technology.
Our Unique Crosses make unique gifts for unique individuals and occasions. Variations on existing crosses or one-of-a-kind special requests are welcome. ■

Sandman Designs LLC

SANDMAN DESIGNS, LLC
109 Old Post Road
Clinton, CT 06413
Tel: 888-736-2749
Fax: 860-664-9031

Personnel:
Sandra Raucci ....President
Fred Raucci ....Vice President Sales/Marketing

Type of Business:
We have the perfect way to **raise funds** for your Parish or **award gifts** for Stewardship. Your Church or Saint's Statue will be designed as an exact replica, in a lapel pin or magnet, made of beautiful Enamels and plated in 14 K Gold. They are presented on a 2" by 3.5" card including your text and sealed in a cellophane sleeve. Visit our web site at www.sandmandesigns.com to view examples and learn how to make Fund Raising Fun and Easy.
See our ad on page R 15. ■

Votive & Memorial Candles

SmartLite™
THE REALISTIC ELECTRONIC CANDLE
A DIVISION OF CYGNUS, INC.

SMARTLITE
510 East 41st Street
Paterson, NJ, 07504
Tel: 888-249-9039 (x128); 973-523-0668; Fax 973-523-0375
Website: www.smartlitech.com
Email: info@smartlitech.com

Type of Business:
We build a complete line of Votive & Memorial electronic candles; battery operated Vigil candles, rechargeable Devotional candles and patented tamper proof Donation/Alms boxes.
We are committed to being the best-priced, highest quality supplier in this industry.
Why Smartlite
- We are the original manufacturer, over 25 years experience
- You buy direct from the factory
- Thousands in place throughout North America with 100% satisfaction
- Our patented electronic candle produces a flame that is indistinguishable from a wax candle flame
- 10 years warranty on all electronics from AC plug to top of candle
- Lifetime warranty on unit frame
- Standard or custom design in wood or metal
- Total and continuous support on Votive and Memorial programs including software

We are always available with timely and polite assistance to answer all your questions and fulfill all your requirements. ■

Wine

NEW HOPE ANOINTING OILS, INC.
405 Drawdy Drive
Brunswick, GA 31525
Tel.: 800-277-4284
Fax: 912-265-4646
Web Site: www.newhopeoils.com

Personnel:
Don Rebstock ....Owner
Elizabeth Burques-Rebstock .... Manager
Michelle Banks .... Staff

Type of Business:
Cana Wine is a fine burgundy wine, that has the water and alcohol evaporated, leaving a burgundy wine essence powder. We package a 15 ounce jar with instructions on preparation to yield one gallon communion wine. PLEASE CALL 800-277-4284 FOR PRICING AND INFORMATION ABOUT OUR PRODUCTS, OR VISIT OUR WEB SITE. HABLAMOS ESPANOL.■

PUBLISHERS

ST PAULS

ALBA HOUSE PUBLISHERS
2187 Victory Blvd.
Staten Island, NY 10314
Tel.: 800-343-ALBA (2522); Fax: 718-698-8390
E-mail: albahouse@aol.com
Web Site: www.albahouse.org

Personnel:
Rev. Anthony Warren ....Publisher
Rev. Edmund Lane ....Editor
Rev. Ernesto Tigeros......................Spanish Department
Rev. Ignatius Staniszweski.................Exhibits Manager

Type of Business:
Alba House is a ministry of the Society of St. Paul. The specific mission of the Pauline Family (6 religious congregations and 3 secular institutes worldwide) is evangelization through the media of social communications. Alba House Book Publishers is one of the instruments used for the propagation of the faith. We are ministers who are responsible for accompanying the people of God towards His Kingdom, following the teaching of the universal and local Church. ■

LITURGICAL PRESS
P.O. Box 7500, St. John's Abbey
Collegeville, MN 56321
Tel.: 800-858-5450; 320-363-2213
Fax: 800-445-5899
E-mail: sales@litpress.org
Web Site: www.litpress.org

Personnel:
Ed Vessel .... Bookstore Sales
Carmen Donabauer .... Customer Service
Nancy Fiedler .... Customer Service
Pat Kampa .... Customer Service
Diane Sobania .... Customer Service

Type of Business:
For more than 75 years, suppliers of liturgical, biblical, ritual, and instructional material to English-speaking countries. Products offered: Celebrating the Eucharist Mass Guide, the Lectionary for Mass, Living Liturgy Sunday Bulletins, books, leaflets, video and audio cassettes, Sacra Pagina, Butler's Lives of the Saints, Berit Olam, The Bible Today, Worship, New Theology Review, and Liturgical Ministry magazines. Call for a free catalog. ■

Serving Catholic Liturgy for 40 years 1964–2004

LITURGY TRAINING PUBLICATIONS
1800 N. Hermitage Avenue
Chicago, IL 60622-1101
Tel: 800-933-1800; Fax: 800-933-7094
E-mail: orders@ltp.org
Web Site: www.ltp.org

Personnel:
John Thomas .... Director
Maureen Como .... General Manager
Tim Quinn .... Director of Customer Service
Imprints: Catechesis of the Good Shepherd; Hillenbrand Books. *Distributor for*: Centro de Pastoral Litúrgica; Ediciones Grafite

Type of Business:
LTP provides materials that assist parishes, institutions, and households in the preparation and celebration of liturgy. In its products and its operation, LTP strives to express the justice and beauty that are fundamental to the Catholic Church and to its liturgy. Publications include Workbook for Lectors and Gospel Readers, Sourcebook for Sundays and Seasons, At Home with the Word, Daily Prayer, Children's Daily Prayer, Catechumenate magazine, Rite, and E&A Newsletter. ■

MAETA
P.O. Box 6012
Metairie, LA 70009-6012
Tel.: 888-577-4428; Fax: 504-833-5272

Personnel:
V.A. Muller .... Director

Type of Business:
Books, pamphlets, audio-visual material, apologetics: traditional Mass, including missals and priest-related study and other relevant issues.

New and Recent Books:
Latin Mass Prayers Explained
Mystery of Faith
Fatima Apocalypse Now
God's Word
Padre Pio Mass Prayerbook
My Basic Missal
The Mass That Made Padre Pio
The Abbot & Me On Liturgy
Canonized Mass History & Law

Priests: Ask about our special prices. ■

OREGON CATHOLIC PRESS
5536 NE Hassalo
Portland, OR 97213-3638
Tel: 800-LITURGY(548-8749); FAX: 800-462-7329
E-mail: liturgy@ocp.org
Web Site: www.ocp.org

Personnel:
John J. Limb.. Publisher
Dave Island ....Director, Customer Services Division
Kay Weiss .... Marketing Manager

Type of Business:
A ministry of the Archdiocese of Portland, OCP is a not-for-profit publisher organized for religious, charitable and educational purposes. OCP serves the universal and multicultural church by publishing worship resources in English, Spanish, Vietnamese and Mandarin Chinese, including missals, hymnals and music for liturgy; contemporary music for youth ministry; and academic and inspirational books. Publications include Liturgy.com™; PRINTandPRAISE.com™; spiritandsong.com™; Journeysongs, Second Edition; Unidos en Cristo/United in Christ Music Resource and missal; and Flor y Canto, Segunda Edicion. ■

PAULIST PRESS
997 Macarthur Blvd.
Mahwah, NJ 07430
Tel.: 201-825-7300; Fax: 201-825-8345
Web Site: www.paulistpress.com

Personnel:
Rev. Lawrence Boadt, CSP ....Publisher
Steve Arkin..Director of Marketing
Paul McMahon..Managing Editor

Type of Business:
Paulist Press, a leading publisher of theology, spirituality, self-help, ethics and children's books, provides quality Catholic magazines and inexpensive religious paperbacks to parishes through its Unified Magazine Program and Guaranteed Paperback Service. ■

SCEPTER PUBLISHERS
PO Box 211
New York NY 10018
Tel: 800-322-8773; 212-354-0670
Fax: 212-354-0736
E-Mail: info@scepterpublishers.org
Web Site: www.scepterpublishers.org

Personnel:
John G Powers ....Publisher
Bernie Brown ....Editor
Mary Gottschalk .... Editor

Type of Business:
Publisher of Catholic books, pamphlets, and videos which encourage Christians to live their faith in the ordinary circumstances of their lives. Books include sacraments, prayer, Catholic teaching, and the writings of the founder of Opus Dei, Saint Josemaría Escrivé. Our best selling titles include The Navarre Bible, In Conversation with God, reprints of spiritual classics, parenting books by James Stenson, and The Daily Roman Missal. Our mission is inspired by the spirit of Opus Dei, a personal prelature of the Catholic Church, which was founded to remind us to live the Gospel in our jobs, family life, and in society. ■

SPIRITANDSONG.COM™
P.O. Box 18030
Portland, OR 97218-0030
Tel: 800-548-8749
Fax: 800-462-7329
E-mail: support@spiritandsong.com
Web Site: www.spiritandsong.com

Personnel:
Tom Tomaszck ....General Manager
Paul Faspa ....Managing Editor
Kay Weiss ....Marketing Manager

Type of Business:
spiritandsong.com™ is more than just a website devoted to contemporary Catholic music. It's a virtual faith community where Christians of all ages can experience online prayers, devotions, fellowship, faith-building resources and more. In addition to recordings and print music by well-known artists and emerging new songwriters, the site provides streaming audio, downloadable music, songs on iTunes™, merchandise, full-length artist profiles, regularly updated artist web logs, a bi-monthly email newsletter, interactive polls, concert and events listings and booking opportunities. ■

Books & Religious Articles

Madonna House Publications
www.madonnahouse.org/publications

MADONNA HOUSE PUBLICATIONS
2888 Dafoe Rd
Combermere ON K0J 1L0
Canada
Tel.: 613-756-3728   Fax: 613-756-0103
Web Site: www.madonnahouse.org/publications
E-mail: publications@madonnahouse.org

Type of Business:
Madonna House Publications is the non-profit publishing house of Madonna House Apostolate, an international ecclesial community of lay men, lay women, and priests founded by Catherine de Hueck Doherty. Our books, audiobooks, videos and music all aim to apply the timeless message of the Gospel to everyday life. Our publications are made available through our houses in the U.S.A. and Canada, by mail-order catalogue, or on-line at our Internet web site. ■

MAETA

MAETA
P.O. Box 6012
Metairie, LA 70009-6012
Tel.: 888-577-4428; Fax: 504-833-5272

Personnel:
V.A. Muller ....Director

Type of Business:
Books, pamphlets, audio-visual material, apologetics: traditional Mass, including missals and priest-related study and other relevant issues.

New and Recent Books:
Latin Mass Prayers Explained
Mystery of Faith
Fatima Apocalypse Now
God's Word
Padre Pio Mass Prayerbook
My Basic Missal
The Mass That Made Padre Pio
The Abbot & Me On Liturgy
Canonized Mass History & Law

Priests: Ask about our special prices. ■

PCP Inc

PRESERVING CHRISTIAN PUBLICATIONS, INC.
P.O. Box 221
Boonville, NY 13309-0221
Tel.: 315-942-6338; Fax: 315-942-6938
E-mail: info@pcpbooks.com

Personnel:
Gerard Maicher ....President
John Parrot ....Secretary
Brian Pouliot ....Treasurer

Type of Business:
DON'T THROW OUT YOUR CATHOLIC BOOKS! We will purchase your used/old Catholic books. Since 1988, we have provided hundreds of institutions, as well as individuals, with an outlet for their no-longer needed Catholic titles. We in turn will find a new home for these books. The purpose of our work is to preserve our Catholic literary heritage by collecting and redistributing Catholic works that might be discarded. If you would like to sell your Catholic books, please contact us. ■

SAN FRANCIS IMPORTS, INC.
901 Thompson Ave.
Glendale, CA 91201
Tel.: 800-882-4916; Fax: 800-692-9129
E-mail: info@sanfrancis.com
Web Site: www.sanfrancis.com

Personnel:
Carlos George .... Vice President Sales
E-mail: carlos@sanfrancis.com
Joseph Gamgene .... Marketing
E-mail: joe@sanfrancis.com

Type of Business:
Catholic family owned. Importer and Manufacturer of Religious & Inspirational Gifts. Custom products incorporating original designs from our exclusive relationship with the Cromo NB Studios (Milan Italy)- the world's leading producer of religious art.
Greeting cards, mass cards, enrollment cards, rosaries, chaplets, and 3-dimensional sculpted figurines incorporating unique and exclusive designs at very affordable prices. Samples and consultation are available at no charge. Ask about our National Religious Treasures™ program. ■

SCEPTER PUBLISHERS
PO Box 211
New York NY 10018
Tel: 800-322-8773; 212-354-0670
Fax: 212-354-0736
E-Mail: info@scepterpublishers.org
Web Site: www.scepterpublishers.org

Personnel:
John G Powers .... Publisher
Bernie Brown .... Editor
Mary Gottschalk .... Editor

Type of Business:
Publisher of Catholic books, pamphlets, and videos which encourage Christians to live their faith in the ordinary circumstances of their lives. Books include sacraments, prayer, Catholic teaching, and the writings of the founder of Opus Dei, Saint Josemaría Escrivé. Our best selling titles include The Navarre Bible, In Conversation with God, reprints of spiritual classics, parenting books by James Stenson, and The Daily Roman Missal. Our mission is inspired by the spirit of Opus Dei, a personal prelature of the Catholic Church, which was founded to remind us to live the Gospel in our jobs, family life, and in society. ■

ST ATHANASIUS PRESS & ST JOANOF ARC BOOKS
133 Slazing Road
Potosi, WI 53820
Tel: 800-230-1025
Web Site: www.stathanasiuspress.com
Web Site: www.stjoanofarcbooks.com

Type of Business:
A Catholic publishing house reprinting great Catholic books. We also BUY & SELL used & new Catholic books. We specialize in Pre-1964 Catholic books or reprints thereof. Religious discounts offered. Promoting the Roman Catholic Faith since 1992. ■

Games & Puzzles

TALICOR, INC.
8845 Steven Chase Ct.
Las Vegas, NV 89149
Tel.: 800-433-4263
Fax: 702-355-4366

Personnel:
Lew Herndon .... C.O.B.
Nikki Hancock .... President
Cheryl Sidhu .... Sec./ Treas.

Type of Business:
This family owned and operated company are producers of games and puzzles with good wholesome and/or Christian content. With over 30 years in the business the product line has grown to include Catholic Games, Educational Games, Family Games, Bible Based Games, Strategy Games, Communication Games, Children's Games, and Entertainment Games. An extensive selection of puzzles for all age groups is also available. Talicor is known for the exceptional quality and value of its products. ■

Magazines & Journals

INSIDE THE VATICAN/URBI ET ORBI COMMUNICATIONS
3050 Gap Knob Road
New Hope, KY 40052
Tel.: 800-789-9494; Fax: 270-325-3091
ROME office: Via delle Mura Aurelie 7c
00165 Rome Italy
Tel.: 39-06-3938-7471; Fax: 39-06-638-1316
E-mail: editor@insidethevatican.com
Web Site: www.insidethevatican.com

Personnel:
Robert Moynihan ....Editor of "Inside the Vatican"
Robert Moynihan...President, Urbi Et Orbi Communications

Type of Business:
"Inside the Vatican" has become the world's leading English-language magazine reporting from the Vatican. Its editorial thrust is not based on liberal or conservative agendas. Award-winning photography and artwork make this publication one of the most beautiful as well as informative magazines in print.■

NATIONAL CATHOLIC REPORTER PUBLISHING CO.
115 East Armour Blvd.
Kansas City, MO 64111-1203
Tel.: 800-444-8910; Fax: 816-968-2292
Web Site: www.ncronline.org

Personnel:
Thomas C. Fox ....Publisher
Sr. Rita Larivee, S.S.A. ....Associate Publisher
Vicki Brashears...................................Advertising Manager
Charlie Owens ....Marketing Manager
Jo Schierhoff ....Circulation Manager
Joyce Ford ....List Rental Manager
Thomas W. Roberts ....Editor, NCR
Patrick Marrin ....Editor, Celebration

Type of Business:
National Catholic Reporter, the independent newsweekly, reports, comments and reflects on the church and society. It strives for excellence, supporting a full, honest and open exchange of ideas. It works out of a Roman Catholic tradition and an ecumenical spirit. It emphasizes solidarity with the oppressed and respect for all. It understands that peace, justice and integrity of environment are not only goals but also avenues of life.
Celebration, a liturgical resource that assists in the preparation of each Sunday service.
The Caring Community, a newsletter that brings inspiration to those unable to attend Sunday worship.
The Catechist's Connection, a newsletter that supports teachers and religious education volunteers.
Eucharistic Minister, a newsletter that gives inspiration and information to Eucharistic Ministers.
Advertising—Display and classified advertising and brochure and flier inserts.
List Rental—High-Quality, high-response mailing lists. ■

Music Publishers

WORLD LIBRARY PUBLICATIONS
3825 North Willow Road
Schiller Park, IL 60176-2353
Tel.: 800-566-6150; Fax: 888-957-3291
Web Site: www.wlpmusic.com

Personnel:
Mary Prete ....General Manager
Mary Beth Kunde Anderson..................Editorial Director
John D. Wright ....Marketing Director
Kathy Mundt ....Customer Service Manager

Type of Business:
World Library Publications provides worship and music resources of the highest quality. Faithful to its heritage as a pioneer in liturgical renewal, WLP continues to support, assist and form worship and music leaders. Publisher of the nation's finest missals—*Seasonal Missalette®*, *Word + Song*, *We Celebrate*, and *¡Celebremos!*—WLP also produces the *We Celebrate Hymnal*, *Cantos del Pueblo de Dios*, *Peoples Mass Book*, and *Voices as One*. In addition, WLP publishes music for worship including choral octavos, mass settings, songbooks and instrument scores, and quality recordings of music for worship, meditation, and spiritual nourishment. Call for a complete catalog or visit www.wlpmusic.com. ■

Parish Directories

Lifetouch® CHURCH DIRECTORIES AND PORTRAITS

LIFETOUCH CHURCH DIRECTORIES AND PORTRAITS
11000 Viking Drive, Ste. 460
Eden Prairie, MN 55344-7244
Tel.: 800-303-0054; Fax: 952-826-4226

Web Site: www.lifetouch.com

Personnel:

Laurie Reding ....Director of Marketing

Type of Business:

Reflect, reach out and reactivate! A parish pictorial directory highlights your ministries, documents your history, and best of all, connects your parishoners. Your directory is provided to your parish at no cost, plus every family photographed receives a FREE directory and FREE 8x10 portrait!

And, with our new 15/15 directory program, your proof is shipped in 15 working days and your printed directory in 15 working days! It's never been faster, easier or more fun!

Entrust your new directory and family portraits to the best, Lifetouch. Call today, mention code OCD, and ask about our special, limited-time offer! ■

olan mills® CHURCH DIRECTORIES

OLAN MILLS CHURCH DIVISION
4325 Amnicola Highway
Chattanooga, TN 37406
Tel: 800-845-1157
Fax: 423-629-8106
Website: www.olanmillsdirectories.com

Personnel:

A.W. Lanford ....Vice President, Sales

Type of Business:

You can trust America's largest Church Directory publisher. A full color pictorial directory by Olan Mills is the number one Parish communication tool. It is delivered in 45 days and we help you all the way. Directories are provided Free to the Parish and every family photographed receives not only a copy of the directory, but an Olan Mills Signature 8x10 portrait Free. And now your directory is available online...FREE.

More churches turn to Olan Mills than any other directory company. Olan Mills, the most respected name in photography for over 70 years, and most trusted name in church directories year after year.■

Photography

Lifetouch® CHURCH DIRECTORIES AND PORTRAITS

LIFETOUCH CHURCH DIRECTORIES AND PORTRAITS
11000 Viking Drive, Ste. 460
Eden Prairie, MN 55344-7244
Tel.: 800-303-0054; Fax: 952-826-4226
Web Site: www.lifetouch.com

Personnel:

Laurie Reding ....Director of Marketing

Type of Business:

Reflect, reach out and reactivate! A parish pictorial directory highlights your ministries, documents your history, and best of all, connects your parishoners. Your directory is provided to your parish at no cost, plus every family photographed receives a FREE directory and FREE 8x10 portrait!

And, with our new 15/15 directory program, your proof is shipped in 15 working days and your printed directory in 15 working days! It's never been faster, easier or more fun!

Entrust your new directory and family portraits to the best, Lifetouch. Call today, mention code OCD, and ask about our special, limited-time offer! ■

Spanish Materials

Serving Catholic Liturgy for 40 years 1964–2004 LTP

LITURGY TRAINING PUBLICATIONS
1800 N. Hermitage Avenue
Chicago, IL 60622-1101
Tel: 800-933-1800
Fax: 800-933-7094
E-mail: orders@ltp.org
Web Site: www.ltp.org

Personnel:

John Thomas ....Director
Maureen Como.......................................General Manager
Tim Quinn............................Director of Customer Service

Imprints: Catechesis of the Good Shepherd; Hillenbrand Books. *Distributor for*: Centro de Pastoral Litúrgica; Ediciones Grafite

Type of Business:

LTP provides materials that assist parishes, institutions, and households in the preparation and celebration of liturgy. In its products and its operation, LTP strives to express the justice and beauty that are fundamental to the Catholic Church and to its liturgy. Publications include Workbook for Lectors and Gospel Readers, Sourcebook for Sundays and Seasons, At Home with the Word, Daily Prayer, Children's Daily Prayer, Catechumenate magazine, Rite, and E&A Newsletter. ■

Translations & Editing

COMMUNICATIONS, INC.

"Multilingual Catholic Communication Experts"

COME ALIVE COMMUNICATIONS, INC.
348 Valley Rd., Suite 1
P.O. Box 436
West Grove, PA 19390
Tel.: 610.869.3660 ; Fax.: 610.869.7557
Web Site: www.ComeAliveUSA.com
Email: info@comealiveusa.com

Personnel:
Bridget G. Hylak ....Manager, Multilingual Digital Communications

Type of Business:
* Expert Catholic communications: translation, editing, web development and graphic design
* State-of-the-art multilingual desktop publishing, printing and/or web design, in any language
* Specialists in web development, web translation and webstores

We translate, edit, design, publish, and/or print books, bulletins, websites, brochures, catalogs, posters, etc. - in one language, or several. Audio/video production, translation and script consultation. Fully-developed websites including shopping carts, merchant accounts and e-commerce. Dedicated to serving the international Catholic community with theological and linguistic perfection. All translation assignments conducted in complete obedience to the Vatican's official translation guidelines. ■

Web Site Hosting & Development

COMMUNICATIONS, INC.

"Multilingual Catholic Communication Experts"

COME ALIVE COMMUNICATIONS, INC.
348 Valley Rd., Suite 1
P.O. Box 436
West Grove, PA 19390
Tel.: 610.869.3660; Fax.: 610.869.7557
Web Site: www.ComeAliveUSA.com
Email: info@comealiveusa.com

Personnel:
Bridget G. Hylak ....Manager, Multilingual Digital Communications

Type of Business:
* Expert Catholic communications: translation, editing, web development and graphic design
* State-of-the-art multilingual desktop publishing, printing and/or web design, in any language
* Specialists in web development, web translation and webstores

We translate, edit, design, publish, and/or print books, bulletins, websites, brochures, catalogs, posters, etc. - in one language, or several. Audio/video production, translation and script consultation. Fully-developed websites including shopping carts, merchant accounts and e-commerce. Dedicated to serving the international Catholic community with theological and linguistic perfection. All translation assignments conducted in complete obedience to the Vatican's official translation guidelines. ■

J.S. PALUCH COMPANY, INC.
3825 North Willow Road
Schiller Park, IL 60176-2353
Tel.: 877-725-8241; 800-621-6732; Fax: 847-928-5812
E-mail: pcmsupport@jspaluch.com
Web Site: www.jspaluch.com; www.e-paluch.com

Personnel:
Janice Pacilio ....Director of Information Systems
Margaret "Mickey" Paluch ....CEO
William J. Rafferty..President

Type of Business:
The J.S. Paluch Company, Inc. has been dedicated to serving Catholic parishes, schools and communities across the United States since 1913. PCMS, the Paluch Church Management System, is an easy-to-use, Windows-based program containing census, contribution, ministry schedule, sacrament and financial modeules. J.S. Paluch also offers affordable web site development and hosting and secure, no-hassle electronic contribution services. Together, we will simplify the administration of your parish and your communication with your parishoners. ■

Internet Services

CATHEDRAL CORPORATION
Griffiss Technology Park
632 Ellsworth Road
Rome, NY 13441
Tel.: 315-338-0021; 800-419-8970; Fax 315-338-5874
E-mail: sales@cathedralstewardship.com
Web Site: www.cathedralstewardship.com

Personnel:
Marianne W. Gaige ....President and COO
Ronald P. Blakeman ....Vice President of Sales
Scott Dickan ....Sales Manager

Type of Business:
Cathedral Corporation delivers exceptional service to churches that excel in ministry. For more than six decades, Cathedral has delivered superior service, leadership and innovation in the creation, printing, personalization and high volume mailing of offering envelopes. Today Cathedral supports Catholic parishes across the nation with a full range of proven stewardship resources and electronic services for the Internet.

Mailed Offering Envelope Programs
Annual Boxed Sets
Increased Offering Campaigns
Youth Envelopes
Bulk Offering Envelopes
Envelope Recording & Reporting Service
ACT Electronic Offering Service
Online Real-Time List Maintenance
And More! ■

PROFESSIONAL ASSOCIATIONS & ORGANIZATIONS

ACTS E & W
a Catholic youth Evangelism Ministry
P.O. Box 1128
Bolingbrook, IL 60440
Tel: 630-378-0982
E-mail: salsoloacts@aol.com
Web Site: www.salsolo.com

Type of Business:
Catholic Youth Evangelist Sal Solo, a former British Rock Start, brings Jesus to the MTV generation with music and video. Has served over 30 US Dioceses, and in 35 countries, including World Youth Days Rome and Toronto.
- 21st Century Evang-A-Ganza (a multimedia evangelistic concert)
- Anno Domini Mass (a multimedia mass)
- Keynote Presentations and Workshops
- Confirmation Retreats
- English and Spanish Presentations

For any school parish, or youth event
Call to book Sal now for yours

ARMY CHAPLAIN RECRUITING
Commander,
U.S. Army Recruiting Command
1307 Third Ave
Fort Knox, KY 40121
Phone: 1-800-USA-ARMY
Email: goarmy@usarec.army.mil
Web Site: chaplain.goarmy.com

Personnel:
Chaplain (Major) Joel Russell ....Chaplain Recruiting
E-mail: joel.russell@us.army.mil
Staff Sergeant Daniel Cantu ....Chaplain Recruiting
E-mail: daniel.cantu@usarec.army.mil

Type of Business:
Chaplains are the spiritual guardians of the U.S. Army. As a Chaplain, you'll provide the spiritual tools that Soldiers and their families need to stay strong. Whether you are already ordained or still a seminary student, there are both full- and part-time ministry opportunities for you in the U.S. Army Chaplaincy. You have answered the Call to serve God. Now your country is asking you to serve Soldiers and their families – consider this important calling. The U.S. Army Chaplaincy could be the opportunity you have been seeking.
chaplain.goarmy.com 1-800-USA-ARMY ■

FOOD FOR THE POOR INC.

FOOD FOR THE POOR, INC.
550 SW 12th Avenue
Deerfield Beach, FL 33442
Tel: (954) 427-2222; Fax: (954) 570-7654
Web Site: www.foodforthepoor.org

Personnel:
Robin G. Mahfood..President
Angel A. Aloma ....Executive Vice President
Richard Robinson ....Director, Speakers Bureau
Joan C. Vidal ....Manager, Church Relations

Type of Business:
Food for the Poor is the 4th largest international relief organization in the United States, aiding the destitute of the Caribbean and Latin America, through churches and missionaries. The countries served include Antigua, Belize, Dominica, Dominican Republic, El Salvador, Grenada, Guatemala, Guyana, Haiti, Honduras, Jamaica, Mexico, Nicaragua, St. Lucia, St. Vincent and Trinidad. Since its founding in 1982, FFP has sent over 24,600 containers of assistance valued over $1.7 billion to the region, and has an operating expense ratio under 5%. Food for the Poor provides feeding programs, housing, healthcare, education, emergency relief and micro-enterprise assistance to hundreds of thousands of the poor. We strive to follow Jesus' gospel mandate to care for the least of His brothers and sisters by linking the church of the First World with the church of the Third World in ways that help both the materially poor and the poor in spirit.■

NATIONAL CHURCH GOODS ASSOCIATION
NC GA

NATIONAL CHURCH GOODS ASSOCIATION (NCGA)
800 Roosevelt Road
Building C Suite 20
Glen Ellyn, IL 60137
Tel: 630-942-6599
Fax: 630-790-3095
E-Mail: ncga@ncgaweb.com
Web Site: www.ncgaweb.com

Board of Directors:
Stephen Gaiser.. President
Ray Gerken ....Director
Robert Malhame ....Director
John F. Moroney......................................Vice President
Mark Steigerwald ....Director
Richard Tonini ....Secretary
Dennis Ziegler ....Treasurer

Rick Church ....Executive Secretary
Jeff Church ....Association Manager

Type of Organization:
The National Church Goods Association (NCGA) is the international trade association of dealers and suppliers of church goods, religious articles, and published materials. NCGA has been providing members with exceptional benefits for 97 years. To find a reputable dealer near you go to www.ncgaweb.com and click on the dealer locater link, or call 630-942-6599. ■

NAVY
accelerate your life

NAVY CHAPLAIN CORPS
Commander, Navy Recruiting Command
5722 Integrity Drive, Building 784
Millington, TN 38054-5057
Tel.: 901-874-9216; Toll Free: 866-484-5232
Web Site: www.navy.com/professionals

Personnel:
CDR Gary Carr, CHC, USN ....Program Manager
CarrG@cnrc.navy.mil
LCDR Michael Parisi, CHC, USN .....Chaplain Recruiter
ParisiM@cnrc.navy.mil
LCDR Herb Griffin, CHC, USN ....Chaplain Recruiter
GriffinH@cnrc.navy.mil
LT Heinz Malon, CHC, USN ....Chaplain Recruiter
MalonH@cnrc.navy.mil
LT Kimberly Sawatsky, CHC, USN...Chaplain Recruiter
SawatskyK@cnrc.navy.mil

Type of Business:
Navy Chaplains serve both the Church and Country in diverse ministry settings. Chaplains provide spiritual guidance to members of the Navy, Marine Corps and Coast Guard. We offer leadership positions in ministry for the spiritual well being of the whole community. Priest Chaplains provide sacramental and spiritual support for Catholics in the military and care for all. Working closely with clergy from other faith traditions, we cooperate with each other without compromising our own faith and practice. Navy Chaplains experience the joy of ministry with young people. We have a program for seminarians, the Naval Reserve, and for full-time, active-duty positions. Contact the chaplain recruiters listed above for more information. ■
www.navy.com 1-800-USA-NAVY

Priests For Life

PRIESTS FOR LIFE
P.O. Box 141172
Staten Island, NY 10314
Tel.: 888-PFL-3448; 718-980-4400; Fax: 718-980-6515
E-mail: mail@priestsforlife.org
Web Site: www.priestsforlife.org

Type of Business:
Priests for Life exists to help you preach sensitively and challenge effectively, in the context of Sacred Scripture, and of a consistent ethic of life.

- Resources:
- Networking with Priests Worldwide
- Seminars on Abortion
- Regular Newsletter
- Pro-Life Strategies
- Consultation
- Organizing Activities

Subscribe to our biweekly column (free) at: subscribe@priestsforlife.org. ■

NOT ALL OF THE ARMY'S
TOP SECRETS ARE KEPT AT
THE PENTAGON.
©2002. Paid for by the United States Army. All rights reserved.

Fraternal Organizations

devoted to secure lives.

CATHOLIC KNIGHTS™

CATHOLIC KNIGHTS INSURANCE
1100 West Wells Street
Milwaukee, WI 53233
Tel.: 800-927-2547; Fax: 414-223-3201
Web Site: www.catholicknights.com

Personnel:

Daniel Steininger .... President
Allen Banoub .... Chief Marketing Officer
Betsy Ross-Bothe .... Marketing Manager

Type of Business:

Catholic Knights™ is a member-owned, not-for-profit fraternal benefit society founded in 1885. Members benefit from savings opportunities, security of lifestyle, sharing of gifts and talents and social outlets sponsored by the Catholic Knights, in addition to its financial services. With its home office in Milwaukee, Catholic Knights is the largest Catholic organization of its kind in Wisconsin.

Catholic Knights' members serve their communities by volunteering for a variety of programs and fundraising projects. In the past year alone, members volunteered more than 30,000 hours and raised more than $1 million through the Match Funds programs. ■

K OF C

KNIGHTS OF COLUMBUS
Supreme Council Office
1 Columbus Plaza
New Haven, CT 06510-3326
Tel.: 203-752-4000
Customer Service: 800-380-9995
Web Site:www.kofc.org

Supreme Council Officers:

Carl A. Anderson .... Supreme Knight
Bishop Thomas V. Daily .... Supreme Chaplain
Jean B. Migneault .... Deputy Supreme Knight
Charles H. Foos .... Supreme Secretary
Deacon Kenneth N. Ryan .... Supreme Treasurer
Paul R. Devin .... Supreme Advocate
Juan R. Nieves-Bonilla .... Supreme Warden

Type of Business:

The Knights of Columbus is the world's largest Catholic family fraternal service organization. Father Michael J. McGivney (1852-90), an assistant pastor at St. Mary's Church,New Haven, Conn., founded the fraternal benefit society in 1882 with a group of parishioners.The organization was chartered to assist the widows and orphans of deceased members through a life insurance program, to instill in members a heightened sense of pride in their Catholic faith, and to provide opportunities for volunteer service to the Catholic Church and society. Since its founding, the Knights has grown into a worldwide organization with nearly 1.7 million members and their families in close to 13,000 units throughout North America and the Philippines. Annually, Knights at all levels of the organization raise and contribute to charities more than $128 million and volunteer more than 60 million hours of service. Knights of Columbus Insurance, with more than $50 billion in force on members and their families, consistently receives top ratings from independent review agencies.The cause for canonization of Father McGivney is under investigation at the Vatican. ■

Private Associations of Lay Faithful

LIFE TEEN®

LIFE TEEN, INC.
1730 West Guadalupe Road
Mesa, AZ 85202
Tel.: 480-820-7001; Fax: 480-820-8653
E-mail: kdemalja@lifeteen.com
Web Site: www.lifeteen.com

Personnel:

Rev. Msgr. Dale Fushek .... Founder/President
Phil Baniewicz .... President
Randy Raus .... Vice President

Type of Business:

LIFE TEEN is an international, comprehensive Catholic youth ministry that serves the Church and leads teens and their families closer to Christ. As one of the fastest-growing youth ministry programs, LIFE TEEN is open to high school teens of all faiths. This Catholic-centered ministry is focused on the Liturgy, especially the true presence of Christ in the Eucharist. Every Sunday, more than 120,000 teenagers attend LIFE TEEN Mass and LIFE Nights in more than 930 parishes worldwide. In addition to these powerful liturgies and challenging youth meetings, there are retreats, outreach, prayer groups and weekly activities for teens that deepen their relationship with Christ and each other. LIFE TEEN also provides youth rallies for high school teens, Training Conferences and Advanced Training Certificate Programs for our youth leaders on an international level. LIFE TEEN Covecrest Camp and Retreat center in Georgia host a number or camps and retreats throughout the year. Ministry and promo videos, a nine-video Training Conference Resource, seven-video Rite of Confirmation package, three-video Legacy Series on vocations to the priesthood, books and music.

For more information, check out our website or call the International Office, 480.820.7001. ■

Senior Organization

CATHOLIC GOLDEN AGE
P. O. Box 249
Olyphant, PA 18447
1-800-836-5699
Fax: 570-586-7721
Web Site: www.catholicgoldenage.org

Personnel
Very Reverend Gerald N. Dino ....President

Type of Business:
Catholic Golden Age- National Association for Catholics 50 years and older. Membership includes subscription to CGA World Magazine. Numerous membership benefits. Spiritual benefits includes an annual Million Candles for Peace Observance in the Basilica of the National Shrine of the Immaculate Conception in Washington, D.C. Material benefits, including nursing home, home health-care, prescription discounts and various insurance products. ■

Classroom Seating

ATD-AMERICAN CO.

ATD-AMERICAN CO.
135 Greenwood Avenue
Wyncote, PA 19095-1396
Tel.: 888-283-2487; Fax: 800-283-7363
E-mail: american@atd.com
Web Site: www.atd.com

Personnel:
Bob Roche ....Marketing
Sal Catanese ....Sales

Type of Business:
For four generations, ATD-AMERICAN has supplied Furniture and Equipment to Churches, Organizations and Institutions nationally and worldwide. Since 1931, it has been our tradition to deliver high quality products and personal service at the lowest competitive prices. ATD offers a wide range of products to meet all of the needs of your Church and School. Our comprehensive catalog includes the following: Announcement and Bulletin Boards, Audio-Visual Equipment, Classroom Furniture, Computer Furniture, Daycare Furniture, Display Cases, Folding Chairs, Folding Tables, Lecterns, Library Furniture, Office Furniture, Outdoor Equipment, Pews and Pulpit Furniture, Room Dividers and Partitions, Stacking Chairs, and Stages and Risers.

For a FREE Wholesale Furniture Catalog, call us Toll Free 888-283-2487 or fax us at 800-283-7363. You can also visit our web site at www.atd.com or e-mail us at american@atd.com.

SPECIAL OFFER FOR CATHOLIC DIRECTORY SUBSCRIBERS: Mention offer code 6557 and receive a special 10% discount on your first order. ■

Visual Display Boards

CLAIRIDGE PRODUCTS AND EQUIPMENT, INC.

P.O. Box 910	601 Hwy. 62-65 South
Harrison, AR 72602-0910	Harrison, AR 72601

Tel.: 870-743-2200
Fax: 870-743-1908
E-mail: claridge@claridgeproducts.com
Web Site: www.claridgeproducts.com

Personnel:
Helen Clavey .... Owner & CEO
Leslie Eddings .... VP & CIO
Mary Roberts .... VP & CFO
Paul Clavey II .... VP & COO

Type of Business:
Established in 1947, Claridge is the world's leading manufacturer of chalkboards, markerboards and tackboards. In addition, Claridge makes display and trophy cases, glass enclosed bulletin and directory board cabinets, lecterns, wood lecture units with matching credenzas and many other items for home, school, church and office use. Much of the Claridge name and reputation is built on the principle of making what we sell and being a single source supplier to our customers. ■

SPECIAL CARE FACILITIES

GUEST HOUSE, INC.
1601 Joslyn Road, P.O. Box 420
Lake Orion, MI 48361
Tel: 800-626-6910; 248-391-4445; FAX: 248-391-0210
Website: www.guesthouse.org

LAKE ORION CENTER (For Women Religious)
P.O. Box 68
Lake Orion, MI 48361
Tel: 800-626-6910; 248-391-3100; FAX: 248-391-1553
Website: www.guesthouse.org

ROCHESTER TREATMENT CENTER
(For priests, deacons, brothers & seminarians)
P.O. Box 954
Rochester, MN 55903
Tel: 800-634-4155; 507-288-4693; FAX: 507-288-1240
E-mail: ghousemn@sparc.isl.net

Personnel:
Daniel A. Kidd....President and Chief Executive Officer
Sr. LeeAnne Farrell, SSND...Director, Lake Orion, MI
Bill Morgan, CCDCR....VP Clinical Oper., Rochester, MN
Gerard O'Connor..........................Director of Outreach

Type of Business:

Guest House, Inc. is a lay-owned, lay-operated nonprofit corporation established in 1956. With the approbation of the Catholic hierarchy, it operates special residential treatment centers for alcoholic Catholic priests, deacons, brothers, sisters and seminarians from all over the world.

Catholic women religious are treated in Guest House in Lake Orion, Michigan. The facility in Rochester, Minnesota has treatment programs for priests, deacons, brothers and seminarians. An important part of the treatment is the beautiful environment of our facilities. Residents respond to the quiet serenity of the surroundings to help in their recovery not only physically and emotionally, but spiritually as well.

Surveys are conducted regularly to determine how our graduates are doing. The 1997 survey shows that after a year and a half, over 90% report they are doing well and abstaining from all drugs and alcohol.

Generous donors have established an endowment fund to provide financial assistance for any diocese or religious community needing assistance with the costs of treatment. Treatment is provided without regard to financial consideration.

The facilities are accredited by JCAHO (Joint Commission on Accreditation of Healthcare Organizations) and licensed by the Department of Public Health in the states of Michigan and Minnesota respectively.

Guest House also offers educational programs, seminars, and workshops on addiction-related topics. ■

TRAVEL & TOURISM

206 TOURS
325 Middle Country Road
Smithtown, NY 11787
Tel.: 800-206-TOURS; Fax: 516-361-3682
E-mail: info@206tours.com
Web Site: www.206tours.com

Personnel:
Milanka M. Lachman, CTC................................President
John Hangley....................Marketing & Finance Manger
Danny Pastirchak......................Senior Account Manager
Billy Ryan..................................Senior Account Manager
Ketta Rella ....Senior Account Manager
Eva Manise ....Advertising & Account Manager

Type of Business:

206 Tours is a privately-owned tour operator, who specializes in Catholic Pilgrimages. We were established in Smithtown, NY in 1985. Milanka Lachman is the founder and President. Countries we specialize in are Italy, Israel, France, Spain, Portugal, Medjugorje, Poland, Czech Republic, Austria, Germany, Ireland and Mexico. In each one of these countries, we work with local suppliers.

206 Tours cooperates with every IATAN airline, but prefers and holds special low net contracts with the following: Lufthansa, Alitalia, Austrian Airlines, Swiss Air, Air France and Croatia Airlines.

206 Tours arranges facets of tourism for a pilgrimage, conference, or canonizations such as air arrangements, hotel accomodations meals, ground transportation, sightseeing and professional tour guides.

206 Tours operates weekly departures. The average size of the group ranges between 20-46 passengers. However, we arrange all services for individuals as well as special groups of 500 passengers.

Our general philosophy about our clients is that we emphasize personalized service. Each one of our clients is very important to us, and we take the time to speak to them, to prepare their documents, and to treat them with respect no matter what.

206 Tours produces a 58-page color brochure listing all of our destinations, prices, inclusions, as well as policy and conditions. ■

AMERICAN TRAVEL ABROAD, INC.
250 West 57th Street
New York, NY 10107
Tel.: 212-586-5230, 800-228-0877
Fax: 212-581-7925
Email: betsy@amta.com

Personnel:
Betsy Kwapisiewicz..............................Groups Manager

Type of Business:
Since 1946, American Travel Abroad has been synonymous with travel to Poland and Central and Eastern Europe. Large groups movements, including incentives, fund-raising trips and religious pilgrimages, are an agency specialty. From inception to execution, our experienced staff handles the entire project. Where do you want to go on your next trip? We give you a choice of the whole world: including Poland, Israel, Italy, Portugal, France, and Ireland to mention a few. Multiple or single destinations? Large or small groups? Pre-planned or made-to-order? Budget conscious? It's all in day's work for us, the consummate professional. ■

CATHOLIC TRAVEL CENTRE
4444 Riverside Drive, Ste. 301
Burbank, CA 91505
Tel.: 800-553-5233; 818-848-9449; Fax: 818-848-0712
E-mail: info@ctctwt.com
Web Site: www.GoCatholicTravel.com

Personnel:
J. Scott Scherer .... President
Inga Duranovic ....Director of Operations

Type of Business:
A reputation for extraordinary quality has made Catholic Travel Centre the choice of groups that demand exacting service and exceptional attention to detail.
With meticulous detail, we will plan a one-of-a-kind pilgrimage tour catering to your group's specific interests. We can work within the constraints of any budget.
Our client list includes prestigious Catholic institutions nationwide, returning year-after-year to Catholic Travel Centre. We will gladly provide a reference list.
Please call us at 800-553-5233 or visit our Web site at www.GoCatholicTravel.com. ■

COLLETTE VACATIONS
162 Middle Street
Pawtucket, RI 02860
Phone 1-877-454-8694
Fax (401) 727-1000

Type of Business:
Collette Vacations, a trusted name in travel since 1918, works with many religious organizations across the country. Our formula for success is simple - always include distinctive accommodations, ample sightseeing, great entertainment, memorable dining experiences, and the service of a knowledgeable and personable tour manager. With Collette Vacations as your travel partner, you can count on:
No up-front obligation or cost.
No minimum number of passengers required, on standard Collette departures.
Our "No Worries Travel Insurance & Cancellation Wavier," allowing cancellation for any reason, at any time up to the day of departure.
Choice. Our itineraries cover all 7 continents.
Exceptional service. Collette's philosophy for "Travel Planning Made Simple" provides you with an experienced local district sales manager who will help you choose the perfect itenerary for your members, offer marketing tips, and present travelogues and predeparture briefings. You will also have a dedicated customer service team that will assist you with your group reservations.
Unbeatable value. Collette has earned a reputation providing a 4-star experience at a 3-star price.
Experience, trust and financial security. We are family owned and operated business and a proud USTOA member, rated by Dun & Bradstreet, and independently audited every year. ■

FELLOWSHIP TRAVEL INTERNATIONAL
P.O. Box 15360
Richmond, VA 23227
Tel.: 800-235-9384; Fax: 800-329-4384
E-mail: mail@fellowship.com
Web Site: www.fellowship.com

Personnel:
Wayne Lawhorn ....President
Jeff Compton ....Group Sales Manager

Type of Business:

We are a consolidator for over 40 international and domestic air carriers and handle group tours, pilgrimages and individual travelers for hundreds of major ministries based in the United States and abroad. We realize planning international travel can be stressful and time consuming for a busy organization such as yours; our team of highly trained professional travel counselors is ready to serve your travel needs.

Fellowship Travel is a pioneer in serving many Christian organizations, ministries and churches all over the world. We feel that we serve in some ways as an Air Force or an Army Transportation Logistical Center to serve the Army of God.

For over 20 years, Fellowship Travel has been a leader in international travel and in helping others fulfill the Great Commission. For a no-obligation quote on your next group trip, please visit our website, www.fellowship.com, and fill out a Group Request A Quote form. Or you can call us at 800-235-9384. At Fellowship Travel International, our mission is your mission! ■

CLASSIC PILGRIMAGES
101 Limekiln Pike
Glenside, PA 19038
Tel.: 800-682-3377; FAX 215-886-2228
E-mail: groups@gate1travel.com
Web Site: www.Gate1Travel.com

Personnel:
Richard Weinberg
Yosi Shiloni

Type of Business:

For 20 years Classic Pilgrimages has been organizing quality religious journeys throughout the world for the American Catholic community.

We plan pilgrimages for groups and individuals to the Holyland, Italy, France, Portugal, Spain, Ireland, Greece, Turkey, Egypt, Jordan, Medjugorje, and South America.

Pilgrimage organizers benefit from our "Best Price Guarantee", generous complimentary policy, special group insurance rates and the services of our offices abroad, including Rome, Madrid, Rio and the Holyland.

Classic Pilgrimages is a proud member of the United States Tour Operators Association and their $1 Million Consumer Protection Plan, assuring our commitment to the highest standard of travel services abroad and the financial security of every passenger. ■

Please call us to discuss your next pilgrimage plans.

GOLDEN FRONTIER
4100 N Illinios St.
Swansea IL 62226-1834
Tel.: (618) 234-1445
Fax: (618) 234-9861
Web Site: www.goldenfrontier.org

Personnel:
Craig Simoneaux, ...Director
Linda Davinroy, ...Domestic Reservations
Sharron Malloy, ...International Reservations

Type of Business:
Golden Frontier is in its 33rd year offering pre-planned and customized pilgrimage programs to religious destinations throughout the world. Professional and knowledgeable staff, here and overseas, assures your travel experience will be rewarding and uplifting. A priest chaplain accompanies group offering Holy Mass and spiritual guidance. Customized group incentive programs are available for parish groups and other religious organizations.

Golden Frontier, sponsored by Catholic Shrine Pilgrimage, Inc.,a Catholic non-profit organization, is independent of the Diocese of Belleville. ■

NATIONAL SHRINE OF OUR LADY OF THE SNOWS
442 South DeMazenod Drive
Belleville, IL 62223
Tel.: 618-397-6700
Fax: 618-397-1210
Web Site: www.snows.org

Personnel:
Fr. Louis Studer, OMI ....Shrine Director
Tom Mulhall ....Marketing Manager

Type of Business:
The National Shrine of Our Lady of the Snows provides an atmosphere where people of all faiths can deepen their relationship with God and one another. We offer Catholic programs and devotional areas on 200 acres. We model Christian hospitality in our restaurant, hotel, gift shop, and conference center. We inspire visitors to share the healing and hope found here, so they are refreshed on their journey and bring Christ's hope to a world in need. ■

NAWAS INTERNATIONAL TRAVEL
777 Post Road, Third Floor
Darien, CT 06820-4721
Tel.: 800-221-4984; Fax: 203-655-1577
E-mail: george@nawas.com
On the West Coast:
1100 Alma Street, Ste. 100
Menlo Park, CA 94025-3344
Tel.: 800-288-2688; Fax: 650-322-6485
E-mail: sami@nawas.com

Personnel:
Soli Nawas ....President
George Khoury ....Executive Vice President (Darien, CT)
Sami Nawas ....Vice President
Neil Dellis ....Vice President

Type of Business:
Nawas International has designed and operated pilgrimages to Rome, the Shrines of Italy, Fatima, Santiago de Compostela, Lourdes, the Shrines of Europe, Ireland, the Holy Land and more since 1949. We are also offering programs to World Youth Day 2005 in Cologne. With our dedication to delivering high quality programs at very competitive prices and on-site quality control we provide the finest pilgrimages available. We also offer excellent tour host benefits—you can travel FREE with as few as six paying passengers! Thousands of Catholic leaders have organized their travel plans through Nawas. Call us toll free and we'll show you how to do it, too! ■

Peter's Way Tours Inc.
Specializing in custom performance tours and pilgrimages

PETER'S WAY TOURS
25 South Service Road, Suite 240
Jericho, NY 11753
Tel: 800-443-6018; 800-225-7662
Fax: 516-997-4388
E-mail: annette@peterswaysales.com; peter@petersway.com
Web Site: www.petersway.com

Personnel:
Peter Bahou ....President
Annette Molinari ....Director

Type of Business:
"...It was a truly spiritual event...your staff made all the pilgrims feel like honored guests... Those qualities are unique to you and your service and we deeply appreciated them...share my sentiments...their experience will be memorable as well because of your commitment to professionalism and the highest standards in your industry..."
Most Reverend Timothy M. Dolan, Archbishop of Milwaukee, regarding his June 2003 Pallium Pilgrimage of 700 participants
We look forward to being of service to your Parish! ■

PILGRIMAGE TOURS
The Home for Catholic Pilgrimages

PILGRIMAGE TOURS
1766 Scherersville Rd.
Allentown, PA 18104
Tel.: 800-278-1351; Fax: 610-799-5225
E-mail: pilgrimagetours@aol.com
Web Site: catholic-pilgrimage-tours.com

Type of Business:

Pilgrimage Tours offers the highest value in pilgrimage travel because we work closely with the most experienced organizations in pilgrimage throughout Europe and the Holy Land.

We understand the difference between an ordinary travel group and a group of pilgrims embarking on the spiritual journey of their lives.

We make organizing your pilgrimage easy and offer benefits of your choice.

Visit our web site and preview our sample itineraries.

Call for more information and we will be happy to prepare a proposal for you, at no obligation. ■

REGINA TOURS

REGINA TOURS
494 Eighth Avenue, 22nd Floor
New York, NY 10001
Tel: 800-CATHOLIC (800-228-4654) Fax: 212-594-7073
Email: regina@ist-tours.com
Web Site: www.regina-tours.com
Midwest office & custom groups
800-HOLYCROSS (800-465-9276)

Personnel:

Nicholas Mancino .... President
Raymond Masillo .... Vice President
Angela Scharf .... Custom Groups
Jennifer, Loretta, Lucille .... Travel Experts

Type of Business:

Regina Tours has been the leader in the Catholic Pilgrimages for over 20 years. Our selection of Pilgrimages includes Fatima, Lourdes, Italy including all of the Shrines-Assisi, Florence, Rome, San Giovanni Rotondo, Pompeii, Sicily,Greece-following St. Paul, Mexico-Our Lady of Guadalupe, Poland, Ireland, Israel and the Holy Land. We understand the true meaning of a Pilgrimage and will provide our expertise for you and your Pilgrims. Contact us for our free color brochure with 15 exciting Pilgrimages. This year you can join our Holy Year to Santiago or join the Eucharistic Congress in Mexico in October or World Youth Day in Cologne in 2005. Contact us about our FREE Travel Program, mention this ad and receive a gift. For more information, visit our web site www.Regina-Tours.com. ■

Conference & Retreat Centers

BASILICA OF THE NATIONAL SHRINE OF THE IMMACULATE CONCEPTION
400 Michigan Ave. NE
Washington, DC 20017-1566
Tel.: 202-526-8300
Fax: 202-526-8313
E-mail: info@nationalshrine.com
Web site: www.nationalshrine.com

Type of Business:

The Basilica is the patronal church of the United States and its preeminent Marian shrine. It is the nation's largest Catholic sanctuary, ranking among the world's largest churches. Begun in 1920 and dedicated in 1959, the Basilica features more than 70 chapels and devotional areas, donated by religious orders and Catholic faithful, reflecting the many ethnic traditions of veneration accorded the Blessed Virgin Mary. Daily Masses and Confessions. Guided tours. Gift shop. Bookstore. Cafeteria. Pilgrimages. ■

BETHANY
Retreat House

BETHANY RETREAT HOUSE
2202 Lituanica Ave.
East Chicago, IN 46312
Tel: 219-398-5047
Fax: 219-398-9329
E-mail: bethanyrh@sbcglobal.net
Web Site: www.bethanyretreathouse.org

Personnel:

Sister Joyce Diltz, PHJC .... Director
Laura Mendoza Garza .... Secretary

Type of Business::

Bethany Retreat House offers individually-directed and private retreats, including 30 days, by individual arrangement. Bethany provides silent space and spiritual direction in a prayerful home setting with wholesome food, comfortable environment, spirituality library, and backyard meditation garden. Minimal schedule lets retreatants move with their inner rhythms. Nature trails and beaches are within driving distance. A variety of prayer forms and sources are encouraged: scripture, life experience, journaling, dreamwork, artistic expression, guided imagery, centering prayer, Spiritual Exercises, more...■

CARMEL CENTER OF SPIRITUALITY
610 Bluff Road (P.O. Box 117)
Liberty, TN 37095
Tel: 615-536-5177
Fax: 615-536-5499
E-mail: carmliberty@yahoo.com
Web Site: www.saintfrancescabrinachurch.org
(link to Camel Center)

Type of Business:
Set on 235 acres in rolling hills and valleys of middle tennessee (Diocese of Nashville), Carmel Center of Spirituality provides a serene, pastoral retreat enviroment for individuals seeking quiet time with the Lord. Along with woods, fields and trails, the Center offers a Eucharistic prayer chapel, Meeting Hall and worship space for 100 people, Marian shrine, and two modern, completely furnished hermitages, each accommodating a single person or married couple. Operated by Carmelites of Mary Immaculate. ■

CARMEL RETREAT
Peace, Quiet & Hospitality in the Carmelite Tradition
1071 Ramapo Valley Road (Rt. 202)
Mahwah, NJ 07430-2406
Tel: 201-327-7090
Fax: 201-327-9133
E-mail: mail@carmelretreat.com
Web Site: www.carmelretreat.com

Type of Business:
Our "spiritual mountain inn" is a 100-year old 30-acres historic estate. Three residences-the Priory, the Lodge and the Hermitage- contain 31 bedrooms, 66 beds, numerous meeting spaces, Chapel, private baths, AC, internet access, homemade meals, and handicap accessibility. Grounds feature brooks, reflecting ponds, Stations of the Cross, Rosary Way, Therese's and Our Lady's Gardens. Ministry includes spiritual direction, directed, preached and private retreats, reflection days, seminars, meetings, workshops and rentals for groups and individuals. ■

Catherine Spalding
Retreat Center

CATHERINE SPALDING RETREAT CENTER
PO Box 24
Nazareth, KY 40048
Tel: 502-348-1515
Fax: 502-348-1518
Email: pcoulter@scnazarethky.org
Web Site: www.catherinespaldingcenter.org

Type of Business:
Catherine Spalding Center is a retreat/conference center sponsored by the Sisters of Charity of Nazareth, KY. With 300+ acres located in the Kentucky knob area about 35 miles south of Louisville, the center is an ideal place for a guided group or individual retreat, or conference on a current spiritual topic. Spiritual direction is available as is the opportunity to plan "your own" sabbatical. A bookshop is available on site. ■

ST. MALO RETREAT CENTER
"Catholic Retreat, Conference and Spiritual Center ("CRCSC") - Camp St. Malo"
10758 Highway 7
Allenspark, Colorado 80510
Tel: 303-747-0201; Toll free: 866-747-0201
Fax: 303-747-2892
E-mail: malo@webaccess.net
Web Site: http://saintmalo.org/
Sodalitium Christianae Vitae community: 303-747-1238

Personnel:
José Ambrozic ....Director
Fr. Emilio Garreaud..Chaplain
Maureen Cleary ....Reservations
Jorge Luna...Programs

Type of Business:
St. Malo, an archdiocesan Retreat Center, is a modern, handicapped accessible, comfortable facility located on 160-acres of wooded property, alongside Rocky Mountain National Park with a beautiful trail leading into it named after John Paul II.
It has two Chapels, four conference rooms, 49 rooms with private baths and balconies, and other social areas.
Managed by permanent religious community with priest, Sodalitium Christianae Vitae, who hosts, organizes and directs retreats for groups and individuals. ■

DESERT HOUSE OF PRAYER
P.O. Box 570
Contaro, AZ 85652
Tel: 520-744-3825
Fax: 520-722-0774
Web Site: www.deserthouseofprayer.org

Type of Business:
Desert House of Prayer, a center for the practice of contemplation in the Christian Catholic tradition, is located on 31 acres of the Sonoran Desert outside Tucson, Arizona. Rooms and hermitages are conducive to quiet and solitude. The staff seeks to model liturgical, contemplative living in silence and God's grace. Daily liturgy of the Eucharist and Hours, Centering Prayer, spiritual direction, a well-stocked library, and a weekly forum on Biblical justice are among our offerings.

ECCLESIA CENTER
Diocese of Erie, Pennsylvania
9101 Ridge Road
Girard. PA 16417
Tel: 814-774-9691
Fax: 814-774-4893

Type of Business:
Ecclesia Center is a residential center and healing community rooted in the gospel of Jesus Christ, grounded in the Catholic tradition providing psychological and spiritual renewal to persons of all faiths in church-related ministries. Integration of body, mind, spirit within community is the core of the healing process. Prayer, individual and group therapy, art, art therapy, t'ai chi and yoga blend to create a healing environment.
Options: open or short term. ■

ESPOUSAL RETREAT HOUSE AND CONFERENCE CENTER
Stigmatine Fathers and Brothers
554 Lexington St.
Waltham, MA 02452
Tel: 781-209-3101
Fax: 781-893-0291
E-mail: espousalctrr@rcn.com

Personnel:
Rev. Robert H. Masciocchi, C.S.S. ....Director

Type of Business:
The retreat center is located on 55 acres of wooded, rolling land that offers a quiet and peaceful venue for retreats, conferences and day programs. The Retreat House has 77 bedrooms that will sleep 105 people, several meeting rooms to accommodate from 15- 180 people, a full service dining room with homemade meals, an elevator and a Chapel for up to 200 people.

FRANCISCAN CENTER
459 River Road
Andover, MA 01810
Tel: 978-851-3391
Fax: 978-858-0695
Web Site: www.franrcent.org

Type of Business:
Franciscan Center is a Retreat and Conference Center. It is a ministry of the Franciscan Friars, Order of Friars Minor, Province of the Immaculate Conception, New York. The staff of the Franciscan Center is committed to sponsoring and hosting spiritual, religious, educational, and cultural programs consistent with our tradition as Roman Catholics and Franciscans. The women and men who minister at the center are committed to work collaboratively in order to provide a place of hospitality and spiritual refreshment for people of all faiths We are committed to the gospel values of Jesus Christ, and are part of the mission of the Church in the Archdiocese of Boston, Merrimack Valley. ■

FRC. . .

FRANCISCAN RETREAT CENTER
7740 Deer Hill Grove
Colorado Springs, CO 80919
Tel: 719-955-7025
Fax: 719-260-8044
Email: FRC@stfrancis.org
Web Site: www.franciscanretreatcenter.org

Type of Business:
The Franciscan Retreat and Conference Center provides a quiet, reflective atmosphere for prayer, private retreat, workshops, seminars, or just time away. The spirit of Franciscan Hospitality pervades the 6 conference rooms and the 34 bedrooms (70 beds) with private baths. Nestled in the foothills of the Rockies with fresh mountain air and hiking trails, spiritual direction, other healing therapies and prayer experiences are offered daily.. Guests are also welcome to join the sisters for prayer and liturgy. ■

Franciscan Spirit and Life Center

FRANCISCAN SPIRIT & LIFE CENTER
3605 McRoberts Road
Pittsburgh, PA 15234
Tel: 412-881-9207
Fax: 412-885-7247
E-mail: fslccom@aol.com

Type of Business:
Whether you are looking for a facility for your programs or for guided, directed or private retreats, or days/evenings of reflections and workshops, our Center offers the simplicity, solitude and programs you are looking for. As a dedicated Peace Site, we exist to promote the Gospel life rooted in Franciscan spirit and values. Located six miles south of Pittsburgh on a peaceful 33-acre campus, we have a commitment to evangelization, reconciliation, healing, contemplative prayer, holistic living, ecumenical dialogue and more. ■

HOLY TRINITY SPIRITUAL CENTER
8400 Park Heights Avenue
P.O. Box 5719
Baltimore, MD 21282-0719
Tel: 410-486-5171; Fax: 410-486-0614

Personnel:
Rev. Thomas N. Cerulo, O.SS.T. ....Director
Ms. Debbi Ragon..Reservations

Type of Business:
The Order of the most Holy Trinity, in keeping with our 800 year tradition of hospitality and spiritual care, invites you to hold your retreat or conference at Holy Trinity Spiritual Center. Our convenient location affords easy access to the attractions of the Baltimore-Washington, DC metropolitan area, while remaining an oasis of prayer and tranquility on a wooded 40 acre estate. Features include: 60 air conditioned guest rooms, conference rooms, chapel, dining room, and library. ■

IMMACULATE HEART RETREAT CENTER
6910 S. Ben Burr Road
Spokane, WA 99223
Tel: (509) 448-1224; Fax (509) 448-1623
E-mail: ihrc@ihrc.net
Web Site: www.ihrc.net

Personnel:
Deacon John Ruscheinsky ....Director
Mary Krone ....Assistant Director

Type of Business:
Immaculate Heart Retreat Center is just two short miles southeast of Spokane's city limits. It is nestled at the foot of Tower Mountain and commands a view of rolling countryside to the west. Fifty-two acres welcome guests to walk and reflect and let the cares of the world be lifted. IHRC offers private/directed retreats for individuals and preached retreats for groups. Accept the invitation to "A Peaceful Place to Pray and Ponder." ■

JESUIT SPIRITUALITY CENTER
P.O. Box C
Grand Coteau, LA 70541-1003
Tel: 337-662-5251; Fax: 337-662-3187
E-mail: jespirtcen@centurytel.net

Type of Business:
Jesuit Spirituality Center Grand Coteau, LA offers year-round directed retreats of 3,5,8 and 30 days in an historic Acadiana setting famous for its serenity and beautiful grounds. Other weekend retreat programs provide a variety of opportunities for Spiritual, healing, growth and development. For more information or for a brouchure write our center at P.O. Box C, Grand Coteau, LA 70541. You may call at 337-662-5251. Better yet check out our website: http//home.centurytel.net/spiritualitycenter/
God's Blessings. ■

JESUS OUR HOPE HERMITAGE
10519 S. Deer Creek Road
Littleton, CO 80127
Tel: 303-697-7539
Fax: 303-697-7539

Type of Business:

Be Still and Know...
Embodying a Franciscan spirituality, Jesus Our Hope Hermitage allows retreatants the opportunity for simplicity and silence, away from the distraction and demands of everyday life.
Our ministry and facilities are available to all of God's children regardless of denomination. In true ecumenism we welcome all who come seeking a place of peace, a refuge for reflection and prayer. ■

THE JUBILEE MUSEUM
584 West Broad Street
Columbus, Ohio 43215-2710
Tel.: 614-221-4323 (Church)
Tel.: 614-641-6204 (Museum)
E-mail: jubileemuseum@columbus.rr.com
Web Site: www.holyfamilycolumbus.org

Type of Business:
The Jubilee Museum, the largest diverse Catholic Museum in the United States, is dedicated to the preservation of the Catholic mind and memory, with its significant collection of international religious art, including an original 1582 Rheimes New Testament and a rare facsimile Gutenberg Bible, among thousands of holdings. In the museum are a Holocaust Memorial and a Synagogue depicting Worship in the Old Testament. Tours, retreats, seminars upon request and help in locating items for churches. ■

LA SALETTE CENTER FOR CHRISTIAN LIVING
947 Park St.
Attleboro, MA 02703-5115
Tel: 508-222-8530; Fax: 508-236-9089
E-mail: lasalett@rcn.com
Web Site: www.lasalette.shrine.tripod.com

Personnel:
Sr. Anna Marie Kane, S.S.J. ....Retreat Ministry Coordinator

Type of Business:
Located on the grounds of the National Shrine of Our Lady La Salette this retreat center welcomes youth and adults for a time of prayer, reflection, faith sharing and spiritual renewal. In addition to programs and retreats facilitated by our staff of clegy, religious and laity, our center hosts groups of all faith traditions that engage in similar or complementary offerings. We are located south of Boston and are accessible by private and public transportation. ■

LEBH SHOMEA HOUSE OF PRAYER
La Parra Ranch
P.O. Box 9
Sarita, TX 78385-0009
Tel: 361-294-5369
Fax: 361-294-5791
E-mail: admin@lebhshomea.org
Web Site: www.lebhshomea.org

Type of Business:
Solomon prayed to the Lord: "Give your servant lebh shomea (a listening heart) so as to be able to discern" (1 Kings 3:9).

Lebh Shomea is a Christian community whose lifestyle is contemplative-eremitical. In an atmosphere of silence and solitude we welcome guests year round affording them the opportunity of personalized and individual retreats. There is no imposed structure or predetermined schedule, only the freedom and creativity of solitude. Daily Eucharist and spiritual direction are available.

Lebh Shomea is situated on 1,100 acres of dense South Texas wilderness populated by many species of animal and avian life. ■

MARTINA SPIRITUAL RENEWAL CENTER
5244 Clarwin Ave.
Pittsburgh, PA 15229-2208
Tel: 412-931-9766
Fax: 412-931-1823
E-mail: martinaspiritual@aol.com
Web Site: sistersoftheholyspirit.com

Personnel:
Sister Cindy Ann Kibler, S.H.S. ....Director

Affiliation: Sisters of the Holy Spirit

Type of Business:
Martina Spiritual Renewal Center is a ministry of the Sisters of the Holy Spirit providing gospel hospitality through a welcoming presence of our staff, offering Christian programming and hosting Christian groups who are desiring growth and renewal in their spiritual life. Situated on 33 acres of lovely grounds eight miles north of downtown Pittsburgh, in West View, the facility offers 33 pleasantly appointed single rooms, 2 semiprivate rooms, chapel, food service, library, gift shop, dining room, various meeting rooms for 12-200 people, an all-purpose auditorium/gym for 300 people. The grounds include a meditative garden and outdoor Stations of the Cross. Offerings include weekend and week-long retreats, days and evenings of spiritual enrichment, group spiritual direction gatherings, Confirmations day retreats, adult faith formation programs, staff and planning meetings, private retreats, women/men religious community retreats and ecumenical hosted retreats. Come and be at peace. ■

MARYWOOD CENTER FOR SPIRITUALITY & MINISTRY

What is Marywood?

Marywood is a diocesan retreat center in Jacksonville, Florida. Set on 100 acres of woodland on the bank of the St. Johns river, we provide ideal settings for retreats, workshops, and conferences. Facilities include 60 private rooms with private baths, meeting areas accommodating up to 180 people, and a beautiful chapel facing the river.

Tel: 904-287-2525
Toll free: 888-287-2539
E-mail: info@marywoodcenter.org
Web Site: www.marywoodcenter.org ■

MOUNT MANRESA JESUIT RETREAT HOUSE
239 Fingerboard Road
Staten Island, NY 10305
Tel: 718 727-3844
Fax: 718-727-4881
E-mail: mountmanresa@si.rr.com
Web Site: www.manresasi.org

Personnel:
Rev. Edward J Quinnan, S.J.

Type of Business:
The first retreat house for laity in the U.S., Mt. Manresa has 90 years of experience. Our warmhearted and well trained professional staff offers a variety of programs and works to tailor retreats or conferences to your needs. Mt. Manresa has ten acres containing lawns, flowerbeds, gazebo, meditation garden, and grotto. We are easily accessible by public transportation. ■

PRIORY OF ST. BENEDICT
135 Priory Rd.
Chestertown, NY 12817
Tel: 518-494-3733
Fax: 518-494-3733
E-mail: prioryretreat@yahoo.com
Web Site: www.prioryretreathouse.com

Type of Business:
THE PRIORY, located on 100 acres in The Adirondack Park is directed by two Sisters of St. Joseph of Carondelet. Informal, homey atmosphere accompanies home cooking and great hospitality. We welcome individuals and groups for directed, guided or private retreat. There are two chapels, a large living room with wood stove and several small gathering spaces. Nearby lake swimming, hiking and skiing opportunities encourage one to experience God in nature. ■

SACRED HEARTS RETREAT CENTER

SACRED HEARTS RETREAT CENTER
226 Great Neck Road
Wareham, MA 02571
Tel: 508-295-0100
Fax: 508-291-2624
E-mail: retreats@sscc.org
Web Stie: www.sscc.org/wareham

Type of Business:
The Sacred Hearts Retreat Center(Congregation of the Sacred Hearts of Jesus and Mary), is located on 120 acres of forests, and fields with private beach on scenic Cape Cod. Our 100 year-old Manor House with elegant Dining Room, Parlor and Library also includes conference room, chapel, & 25 bedrooms with 52 beds. Our Youth Center accommodates 40 in 2 dorms. All are welcome to bring their programs, or review ours at our web site. ■

SAINT CHARLES CENTER
2151 Sam Houston Jones Parkway
Lake Charles, Louisiana 70611
Tel: 337-855-1232
Fax: 337-855-9062

Type of Business:
Saint Charles Center, a ministry of the Diocese of Lake Charles, is situated on sixty-nine acres of woodlands and wetlands in the southwest corner of Louisiana. Its two facilities, Tabor Retreat House and the Katherine Drexel Conference Center for youth, offer conference and directed retreat, educational workshops and seminars, meetings and programs of spiritual directors' development, supervision and growth. ■

Shrine of The Good Shepherd SAN DAMIANO Retreat Center

CHRIST THE GOOD SHEPHERD SHRINE SAN DAMIANO RETREAT CENTER
RR 1 BOX 106
GOLCONDA IL 62938-9602
Phone: 800-716-1558 or 618-285-3507
Fax: 618-285-3507
Web Site: www.sandamiano-il.org

Personnel:
Mark Migas .... Manager
Craig Simoneaux .... Director

Type of Business:
Shrine of Christ the Good Shepherd and San Damiano Retreat Center are located in Southern Illinois' Shawnee National Forest on the bluffs overlooking the Ohio River and Western Kentucky. The shrine hosts seminars, retreats, concerts, conferences, and workshops for all faith groups. Featured on the grounds are the 35 foot Bronze Good Shepherd statue, 30 guest cottages, XXIII Psalm, Meditation Garden, Stations of the Cross, visitor and conference centers. San Damiano Retreat, sponsored by Catholic Shrine Pilgrimage, Inc., a Catholic non-profit organization, is independent of the Diocese of Belleville. ■

SERRA RETREAT CENTER
P.O. Box 127
Malibu, CA 90265
Tel: 310-456-6631
Fax: 310-456-9417
Web Site: www.serraretreat.com

Personnel:
Rev. Warren J. Rouse, O.F.M. .... Director
Rev. Michael P. Doherty, O.F.M. ....Retreat Master
Sr. Susan Blomstad, O.F.M. ....Pastoral Assistant
Toni Tanner ....Reservations
Virginia Zepeda..Receptionist

Type of Business:
Located 11 miles north of Santa monica, CA, and 35 minutes from LAX, Serra Retreat is a ministry of the Franciscan Friars of California since 1942. The center is 3/4 miles from the ocean and has the mountains as a background. Retreats and conferences as well as private retreats are available. The expansive grounds in a private setting are conducive to quiet and serenity, including a labyrinth and outdoor Stations. Capacity is 100. ■

SPRINGBANK RETREAT
1345 Springbank Rd.
Kingstree, SC 29556
Tel: 800-671-0361
Fax: 843-382-5340
E-mail: Springbank@earthlink.net
Web Site www.springbankspirit.org

Personnel:
Sr. Trina McCormick, O.P. ....Director
Sr. Karla Barker, O.S.F. ....Manager
Sr. Ursula Ording, O.P. ....Reservations

Type of Business:
Springbank Retreat, a center for Eco-Spirituality and the Arts, offers one-two-three month sabbaticals, mini sabbaticals, workshops and conferences. Located on 80 acres Springbank is surrounded by a wooded area, a swamp wilderness, walking trails, ancient live oaks, and flowering azaleas and camellias. Sabbaticals and retreats offer experiences in: sacred scripture, earth literacy, native spirituality, pottery, painting, basketry, the Labyrinth, healing massage and Tai-Chi.
Accommodations: private rooms, heat & air conditioning, comfortable lounges, an art studio and outdoor desks. ■

St. Joseph By the Sea

ST. JOSEPH BY THE SEA
400 Route 35 North
S. Mantoloking, NJ 08738
Tel: 732-892-8494
Fax: 732-892-9905
E-mail: sjbsea@comcast.net

Type of Business:
This Retreat house is a sponsored ministry of the Religious Teachers Filippini who use their summer residence for retreats and spiritual activities during the months of September through May. It is located in central New Jersey at the beautiful shore line in northern Ocean County. Programs are offered in an atmosphere of prayer, quiet and solitude. Directed and private retreats as well as many days of prayer to parish groups, school faculties, senior citizens etc. (no youth groups) are conducted by the staff. Twenty-two private rooms with full bath between rooms, a chapel, conference room, dining room, and a solarium are available. There is direct access to the ocean and easy access to Barnegat Bay across the highway. ■

ST. LEONARD YOUTH RETREAT CENTER
4076 Case Rd.
Avon OH 44011
Tel: 440-934-6735
Fax: 440-934-6270
Web Site: www.stleonard-yrc.org

Type of Business:
The St. Leonard Youth Retreat Center is a ministry of the congregation of St. Joseph, founded by St. Leonard Murialdo.
The St. Leonard youth Retreat Center offers a variety of retreats, including the Cor retreat program, to teens and young adults. Youth groups may also rent the retreat center for their own retreats. The modern facility, surrounded by 37 acres of land, accommodates groups of 70 people or less.
For more info, visit www.stleonard-yrc.org. ■

ST. MARY OF THE PINES RETREAT CENTER
P.O. Box 38
Chatawa, MS 39632
Tel: 601-783-3494
Fax: 601-783-3984

Type of Business:
St. Mary of the Pines Retreat Center is located in a rural pine woods area of southern Mississippi. The center offers meeting rooms, sleeping and dining facilities, chapels and a small library. It is available for individual, private or directed retreats and for groups of all faiths. There is a small lake, an outdoor swimming pool, labyrinth and ample walking areas. Guests are welcome to attend the daily liturgy of the School Sisters of Notre Dame whose retirement community is located on the adjacent campus. ■

ST. MARY SPIRITUAL CENTER
600 North Pace Street
Baltimore, MD 21204
Tel: 410-728-6464
Fax: 410-669-8140
E-mail: SMSCBalto@aol.com

Type of Business:
An oasis of peace
in the heart
of Baltimore !
On the site of the first Catholic seminary in the U.S. The Old Seminary Chapel (1808) is a national landmark.
The center offers:
*One-to-one Spiritual Direction by experienced and trained directors.
*Progoff *Intensive Journal* workshops for personal and spiritual growth.
*Custom designed retreats and workshops for parish groups and ministers.
*Use of the facilities for groups (up to 1500).
*(No overnight accommodations.)
410-728-6464
E-mail: SMSCBalto@aol.com. ■

Museum

THE JUBILEE MUSEUM
584 West Broad Street
Columbus, Ohio 43215-2710
Tel.: 614-221-4323 (Church)
Tel.: 614-641-6204 (Museum)
E-mail: jubileemuseum@columbus.rr.com
Web Site: www.holyfamilycolumbus.org

Type of Business:
The Jubilee Museum, the largest diverse Catholic Museum in the United States, is dedicated to the preservation of the Catholic mind and memory, with its significant collection of international religious art, including an original 1582 Rheimes New Testament and a rare facsimile Gutenberg Bible, among thousands of holdings. In the museum are a Holocaust Memorial and a Synagogue depicting Worship in the Old Testament. Tours, retreats, seminars upon request and help in locating items for churches. ■

Pilgrimages

206 TOURS
325 Middle Country Road
Smithtown, NY 11787
Tel.: 800-206-TOURS; Fax: 516-361-3682
E-mail: info@206tours.com
Web Site: www.206tours.com

Personnel:
Milanka M. Lachman, CTC .... President
John Hangley .... Marketing & Finance Manger
Danny Pastirchak .... Senior Account Manager
Billy Ryan .... Senior Account Manager
Ketta Rella .... Senior Account Manager
Eva Manise .... Advertising & Account Manager

Type of Business:
206 Tours is a privately-owned tour operator, who specializes in Catholic Pilgrimages. We were established in Smithtown, NY in 1985. Milanka Lachman is the founder and President. Countries we specialize in are Italy, Israel, France, Spain, Portugal, Medjugorje, Poland, Czech Republic, Austria, Germany, Ireland and Mexico. In each one of these countries, we work with local suppliers.

206 Tours cooperates with every IATAN airline, but prefers and holds special low net contracts with the following: Lufthansa, Alitalia, Austrian Airlines, Swiss Air, Air France and Croatia Airlines.

206 Tours arranges facets of tourism for a pilgrimage, conference, or canonizations such as air arrangements, hotel accomodations meals, ground transportation, sightseeing and professional tour guides.

206 Tours operates weekly departures. The average size of the group ranges between 20-46 passengers. However, we arrange all services for individuals as well as special groups of 500 passengers.

Our general philosophy about our clients is that we emphasize personalized service. Each one of our clients is very important to us, and we take the time to speak to them, to prepare their documents, and to treat them with respect no matter what.

206 Tours produces a 58-page color brochure, listing all of our destinations, prices, inclusions as well as policy and conditions. ■

WORLD WISE

AMERICAN TRAVEL ABROAD

AMERICAN TRAVEL ABROAD, INC.

250 West 57th Street
New York, NY 10107
Tel.: 212-586-5230, 800-228-0877
Fax: 212-581-7925
Email: betsy@amta.com

Personnel:

Betsy Kwapisiewicz................................Groups Manager

Type of Business:

Since 1946, American Travel Abroad has been synonymous with travel to Poland and Central and Eastern Europe. Large groups movements, including incentives, fund-raising trips and religious pilgrimages, are an agency specialty. From inception to execution, our experienced staff handles the entire project. Where do you want to go on your next trip? We give you a choice of the whole world: including Poland, Israel, Italy, Portugal, France, and Ireland to mention a few. Multiple or single destinations? Large or small groups? Pre-planned or made-to-order? Budget conscious? It's all in day's work for us, the consummate professional. ■

BEST CATHOLIC PILGRIMAGES

"Serving Generations of Catholics to Shrines around the World"

BEST CATHOLIC PILGRIMAGES

640 N. LaSalle St. #268
Chicago, IL 60610
Tel.: 800-908-BEST (2378)
Fax: 312-944-3352
E-mail: info@bestcatholic.com
Web Site: www.bestcatholic.com

Type of Business:

Best Catholic Pilgrimages is a wholesale tour operator and land Destination management company that specializes in Customized religious/cultural tours world-wide and the U.S.A.. Plus ... Special "Value-Added Packages" for Student Groups and Choir Tours.

Our professional and highly skilled staff handles with consummate precision, to every detail of our tours, whether a small group or a large group or event. We also coordinate airfare at group prices for departures throughout North America. Our priorities are directed to our clients' high expectations, personalized needs and total satisfaction.

Plus...Ask about our successful Pilgrimage Partnership Program for Fund-Raising. ■

Catholic Travel Centre

Worldwide Tours and Pilgrimages

CATHOLIC TRAVEL CENTRE

4444 Riverside Drive, Ste. 301
Burbank, CA 91505
Tel.: 800-553-5233; 818-848-9449; Fax: 818-848-0712
E-mail: info@ctctwt.com
Web Site: www.GoCatholicTravel.com

Personnel:

J. Scott Scherer .... President
Inga Duranovic ....Director of Operations

Type of Business:

A reputation for extraordinary quality has made Catholic Travel Centre the choice of groups that demand exacting service and exceptional attention to detail.

With meticulous detail, we will plan a one-of-a-kind pilgrimage tour catering to your group's specific interests. We can work within the constraints of any budget.

Our client list includes prestigious Catholic institutions nationwide, returning year-after-year to Catholic Travel Centre. We will gladly provide a reference list.

Please call us at 800-553-5233 or visit our Web site at www.GoCatholicTravel.com. ■

COLLETTE VACATIONS
162 Middle Street
Pawtucket, RI 02860
Phone 1-877-454-8694
Fax (401) 727-1000

Type of Business:

Collette Vacations, a trusted name in travel since 1918, works with many religious organizations across the country. Our formula for success is simple - always include distinctive accommodations, ample sightseeing, great entertainment, memorable dining experiences, and the service of a knowledgeable and personable tour manager. With Collette Vacations as your travel partner, you can count on:

No up-front obligation or cost.
No minimum number of passengers required, on standard Collette departures.
Our "No Worries Travel Insurance & Cancellation Wavier," allowing cancellation for any reason, at any time up to the day of departure.
Choice. Our itineraries cover all 7 continents.
Exceptional service. Collette's philosophy for "Travel Planning Made Simple" provides you with an experienced local district sales manager who will help you choose the perfect itenerary for your members, offer marketing tips, and present travelogues and predeparture briefings. You will also have a dedicated customer service team that will assist you with your group reservations.
Unbeatable value. Collette has earned a reputation providing a 4-star experience at a 3-star price.
Experience, trust and financial security. We are family owned and operated business and a proud USTOA member, rated by Dun & Bradstreet, and independently audited every year. ■

CLASSIC PILGRIMAGES
101 Limekiln Pike
Glenside, PA 19038
Tel.: 800-682-3377; FAX 215-886-2228
E-mail: groups@gate1travel.com
Web Site: www.Gate1Travel.com

Personnel:
Richard Weinberg
Yosi Shiloni

Type of Business:

For 20 years Classic Pilgrimages has been organizing quality religious journeys throughout the world for the American Catholic community.

We plan pilgrimages for groups and individuals to the Holyland, Italy, France, Portugal, Spain, Ireland, Greece, Turkey, Egypt, Jordan, Medjugorje, and South America.

Pilgrimage organizers benefit from our "Best Price Guarantee", generous complimentary policy, special group insurance rates and the services of our offices abroad, including Rome, Madrid, Rio and the Holyland.

Classic Pilgrimages is a proud member of the United States Tour Operators Association and their $1 Million Consumer Protection Plan, assuring our commitment to the highest standard of travel services abroad and the financial security of every passenger. ■

Please call us to discuss your next pilgrimage plans.

GOLDEN FRONTIER
4100 N Illinios St.
Swansea IL 62226-1834
Tel.: (618) 234-1445
Fax: (618) 234-9861
www.goldenfrontier.org

Personnel:
Craig Simoneaux, ...Director
Linda Davinroy, ...Domestic Reservations
Sharron Malloy, ...International Reservations

Type of Business:

Golden Frontier is in its 33rd year offering pre-planned and customized pilgrimage programs to religious destinations throughout the world. Professional and knowledgeable staff, here and overseas, assures your travel experience will be rewarding and uplifting. A priest chaplain accompanies group offering Holy Mass and spiritual guidance. Customized group incentive programs are available for parish groups and other religious organizations.

Golden Frontier, sponsored by Catholic Shrine Pilgrimage, Inc.,a Catholic non-profit organization, is independent of the Diocese of Belleville. ■

nawas INTERNATIONAL

NAWAS INTERNATIONAL TRAVEL
777 Post Road, Third Floor
Darien, CT 06820-4721
Tel.: 800-221-4984; Fax: 203-655-1577
E-mail: george@nawas.com
On the West Coast:
1100 Alma Street, Ste. 100
Menlo Park, CA 94025-3344
Tel.: 800-288-2688; Fax: 650-322-6485
E-mail: sami@nawas.com

Personnel:
Soli Nawas ....President
George Khoury ....Executive Vice President (Darien, CT)
Sami Nawas..Vice President
Neil Dellis ....Vice President

Type of Business:
Nawas International has designed and operated pilgrimages to Rome, the Shrines of Italy, Fatima, Santiago de Compostela, Lourdes, the Shrines of Europe, Ireland, the Holy Land and more since 1949. We are also offering programs to World Youth Day 2005 in Cologne. With our dedication to delivering high quality programs at very competitive prices and on-site quality control we provide the finest pilgrimages available. We also offer excellent tour host benefits—you can travel FREE with as few as six paying passengers! Thousands of Catholic leaders have organized their travel plans through Nawas Call us toll free and we'll show you how to do it, too! ■

PILGRIMAGE TOURS
The Home for Catholic Pilgrimages

PILGRIMAGE TOURS
1766 Scherersville Rd.
Allentown, PA 18104
Tel.: 800-278-1351; Fax: 610-799-5225
E-mail: pilgrimagetours@aol.com
Web Site: catholic-pilgrimage-tours.com

Type of Business:
Pilgrimage Tours offers the highest value in pilgrimage travel because we work closely with the most experienced organizations in pilgrimage throughout Europe and the Holy Land.

We understand the difference between an ordinary travel group and a group of pilgrims embarking on the spiritual journey of their lives.

We make organizing your pilgrimage easy and offer benefits of your choice.

Visit our Web site and preview our sample itineraries.

Call for more information and we will be happy to prepare a proposal for you, at no obligation. ■

THE QUEST TRAVEL GROUP

THE QUEST TRAVEL GROUP
P.O. Box 456
Rowell, GA 30077
Phone: 770-518-5864
Fax: 770-518-5816
Toll free 1-800-769-9466
E-mail: questgroup@earthlink.net
Web Site www.questpilgrimage.com

Personnel:
Samir Zumot...President
a native Catholic from Jerusalem

Type of Business:
Personalized, Economical, and Educational
The Quest Travel Group celebrates 26 years in operating Catholic Pilgrimages around the world. Our once-in-a-lifetime journeys include:
The Holy Land with excursions to Mt. Sinai/Egypt
Petra
Greece / Turkey and the journeys of St. Paul
Italy
Spain and Portugal with Medjugorje
World Youth Day 2005 in Cologne, Germany
Worldwide conventions a specialty
Group leaders are invited to call for host benefits. ■

REGINA TOURS
494 Eighth Avenue, 22nd Floor
New York, NY 10001
Tel: 800-CATHOLIC (800-228-4654) Fax: 212-594-7073
Email: regina@ist-tours.com
Web Site: www.regina-tours.com
Midwest office & custom groups
800-HOLYCROSS (800-465-9276)

Personnel:
Nicholas Mancino .... President
Raymond Masillo.................. Vice President
Angela Scharf .... Custom Groups
Jennifer, Loretta, Lucille .... Travel Experts

Type of Business:
Regina Tours has been the leader in the Catholic Pilgrimages for over 20 years. Our selection of Pilgrimages includes Fatima, Lourdes, Italy including all of the Shrines-Assisi, Florence, Rome, San Giovanni Rotondo, Pompeii, Sicily,Greece-following St. Paul, Mexico-Our Lady of Guadalupe, Poland, Ireland, Israel and the Holy Land. We understand the true meaning of a Pilgrimage and will provide our expertise for you and your Pilgrims. Contact us for our free color brochure with 15 exciting Pilgrimages. This year you can join our Holy Year to Santiago or join the Eucharistic Congress in Mexico in October or World Youth Day in Cologne in 2005. Contact us about our FREE Travel Program, mention this ad and receive a gift. For more information, visit our web site www.Regina-Tours.com. ■

UNITOURS, INC
3010 Westchester Ave.
Purchase, NY 10577
Tel.: 800-777-7432, 914-253-9446; Fax: 914-253-9001
E-mail: info@Unitours.com
Web Site: www.Unitours.com

Type of Business:
Unitours is a "world leader" in quality Christian travel. This reputation is based upon nearly 50 years of experience in designing and leading custom pilgrimages throughout the world. Unitours professionals will design a tour that includes the itinerary, sites, liturgies, and accommodations that meet your religious, spiritual, and financial needs. You also benefit from knowledgeable guides who help make your pilgrimage a memorable experience.
Pre-packaged tours for smaller groups are also available. Ask how you can earn "free" travel (or cash)! ■

Shrines

AMERICAN TRAVEL ABROAD, INC.
250 West 57th Street
New York, NY 10107
Tel.: 212-586-5230, 800-228-0877
Fax: 212-581-7925
Email: betsy@amta.com

Personnel:
Betsy Kwapisiewicz.................. Groups Manager

Type of Business:
Since 1946, American Travel Abroad has been synonymous with travel to Poland and Central and Eastern Europe. Large groups movements, including incentives, fund-raising trips and religious pilgrimages, are an agency specialty. From inception to execution, our experienced staff handles the entire project. Where do you want to go on your next trip? We give you a choice of the whole world: including Poland, Israel, Italy, Portugal, France, and Ireland to mention a few. Multiple or single destinations? Large or small groups? Pre-planned or made-to-order? Budget conscious? It's all in day's work for us, the consummate professional. ■

BASILICA OF THE NATIONAL SHRINE OF THE IMMACULATE CONCEPTION
400 Michigan Ave. NE
Washington, DC 20017-1566
Tel.: 202-526-8300
Fax: 202-526-8313
E-mail: info@nationalshrine.com
Web site: www.nationalshrine.com

Type of Business:
The Basilica is the patronal church of the United States and its preeminent Marian shrine. It is the nation's largest Catholic sanctuary, ranking among the world's largest churches. Begun in 1920 and dedicated in 1959, the Basilica features more than 70 chapels and devotional areas, donated by religious orders and Catholic faithful, reflecting the many ethnic traditions of veneration accorded the Blessed Virgin Mary. Daily Masses and Confessions. Guided tours. Gift shop. Bookstore. Cafeteria. Pilgrimages. ■

BEST CATHOLIC PILGRIMAGES

"Serving Generations of Catholics to Shrines around the World"

BEST CATHOLIC PILGRIMAGES
640 N. LaSalle St. #268
Chicago, IL 60610
Tel.: 800-908-BEST (2378)
Fax: 312-944-3352
E-mail: info@bestcatholic.com
Web Site: www.bestcatholic.com

Type of Business:
Best Catholic Pilgrimages is a wholesale tour operator and land Destination management company that specializes in Customized religious/cultural tours worldwide and the U.S.A.. Plus ... Special "Value-Added Packages" for Student Groups and Choir Tours.

Our professional and highly skilled staff handles with consummate precision, to every detail of our tours, whether a small group or a large group or event. We also coordinate airfare at group prices for departures throughout North America. Our priorities are directed to our clients' high expectations, personalized needs and total satisfaction.

Plus…Ask about our successful Pilgrimage Partnership Program for Fund-Raising. ■

The Jubilee Museum

THE JUBILEE MUSEUM
584 West Broad Street
Columbus, Ohio 43215-2710
Tel.: 614-221-4323 (Church)
Tel.: 614-641-6204 (Museum)
E-mail: jubileemuseum@columbus.rr.com
Web Site: www.holyfamilycolumbus.org

Type of Business:
The Jubilee Museum, the largest diverse Catholic Museum in the United States, is dedicated to the preservation of the Catholic mind and memory, with its significant collection of international religious art, including an original 1582 Rheimes New Testament and a rare facsimile Gutenberg Bible, among thousands of holdings. In the museum are a Holocaust Memorial and a Synagogue depicting Worship in the Old Testament. Tours, retreats, seminars upon request and help in locating items for churches. ■

NATIONAL SHRINE OF OUR LADY OF THE SNOWS
442 South DeMazenod Drive
Belleville, IL 62223
Tel.: 618-397-6700
Fax: 618-397-1210
Web Site: www.snows.org

Personnel:
Fr. Louis Studer, OMI .... Shrine Director
Tom Mulhall .... Marketing Manager

Type of Business:
The National Shrine of Our Lady of the Snows provides an atmosphere where people of all faiths can deepen their relationship with God and one another. We offer Catholic programs and devotional areas on 200 acres. We model Christian hospitality in our restaurant, hotel, gift shop, and conference center. We inspire visitors to share the healing and hope found here, so they are refreshed on their journey and bring Christ's hope to a world in need. ■

nawas INTERNATIONAL

NAWAS INTERNATIONAL TRAVEL
777 Post Road, Third Floor
Darien, CT 06820-4721
Tel.: 800-221-4984; Fax: 203-655-1577
E-mail: george@nawas.com
On the West Coast:
1100 Alma Street, Ste. 100
Menlo Park, CA 94025-3344
Tel.: 800-288-2688; Fax: 650-322-6485
E-mail: sami@nawas.com

Personnel:
Soli Nawas .... President
George Khoury .... Executive Vice President (Darien, CT)
Sami Nawas .... Vice President
Neil Dellis .... Vice President

Type of Business:
Nawas International has designed and operated pilgrimages to Rome, the Shrines of Italy, Fatima, Santiago de Compostela, Lourdes, the Shrines of Europe, Ireland, the Holy Land and more since 1949. We are also offering programs to World Youth Day 2005 in Cologne. With our dedication to delivering high quality programs at very competitive prices and on-site quality control we provide the finest pilgrimages available. We also offer excellent tour host benefits—you can travel FREE with as few as six paying passengers! Thousands of Catholic leaders have organized their travel plans through Nawas. Call us toll free and we'll show you how to do it, too! ■

RAMBUSCH

RAMBUSCH LIGHTING
160 Cornelison Avenue
Jersey City, NJ 07304
Tel.: 201-333-2525; Fax: 201-433-3355
Web Site: www.rambusch.com

Personnel:
Edwin P. Rambusch .... President & C.E.O.
Martin V. Rambusch .... Chairman of the Board

Type of Business:
Since 1898, creating church interiors, liturgical furnishings, and art work. Fine restoration of church interiors. In-house studios and shops for designing and executing stained glass, church lighting systems, art metal work, and decorative painting. ■

REGINA TOURS

REGINA TOURS
494 Eighth Avenue, 22nd Floor
New York, NY 10001
Tel: 800-CATHOLIC (800-228-4654) Fax: 212-594-7073
Email: regina@ist-tours.com
Web Site: www.regina-tours.com
Midwest office & custom groups
800-HOLYCROSS (800-465-9276)

Personnel:
Nicholas Mancino .... President
Raymond Masillo .... Vice President
Angela Scharf .... Custom Groups
Jennifer, Loretta, Lucille .... Travel Experts

Type of Business:
Regina Tours has been the leader in the Catholic Pilgrimages for over 20 years. Our selection of Pilgrimages includes Fatima, Lourdes, Italy including all of the Shrines-Assisi, Florence, Rome, San Giovanni Rotondo, Pompeii, Sicily,Greece-following St. Paul, Mexico-Our Lady of Guadalupe, Poland, Ireland, Israel and the Holy Land. We understand the true meaning of a Pilgrimage and will provide our expertise for you and your Pilgrims. Contact us for our free color brochure with 15 exciting Pilgrimages. This year you can join our Holy Year to Santiago or join the Eucharistic Congress in Mexico in October or World Youth Day in Cologne in 2005. Contact us about our FREE Travel Program, mention this ad and receive a gift. For more information, visit our web site www.Regina-Tours.com. ■

Shrine of
The Good Shepherd
SAN DAMIANO
Retreat Center

CHRIST THE GOOD SHEPHERD SHRINE
SAN DAMIANO RETREAT CENTER
RR 1 BOX 106
GOLCONDA IL 62938-9602
Tel: 800-716-1558 or 618-285-3507
Fax: 618-285-3507
Web Site: www.sandamiano-il.org

Personnel:
Mark Migas .... Manager
Craig Simoneaux .... Director

Type of Business:
Shrine of Christ the Good Shepherd and San Damiano Retreat Center are located in Southern Illinois' Shawnee National Forest on the bluffs overlooking the Ohio River and Western Kentucky. The shrine hosts seminars, retreats, concerts, conferences, and workshops for all faith groups. Featured on the grounds are the 35 foot Bronze Good Shepherd statue, 30 guest cottages, XXIII Psalm, Meditation Garden, Stations of the Cross, visitor and conference centers. San Damiano Retreat, sponsored by Catholic Shrine Pilgrimage, Inc., a Catholic non-profit organization, is independent of the Diocese of Belleville. ■

ST. FRANCES CABRINI SHRINE
701 Ft. Washington Ave.
New York, NY 10040
Tel.: 212-923-3536
Fax: 212-923-1871
Web Site: www.cabrinishrineny.org
Email: cabrinishrineny@att.net

Personnel:
Debra Stumpf .... Administrator

Type of Business:
Located in northern Manhattan just ten blocks from the George Washington Bridge, **St. Frances Cabrini Shrine** overlooks the tranquil banks of the Hudson River and the neighboring state of New Jersey, **The Chapel houses the most precious remains of our beloved St. Frances Xavier Cabrini.**
Pilgrimage groups are always welcome at the Shrine. Youth or adult **Retreats** and **Days of Prayer are offered** by the administrator or youth minister. ■

1957/1997 - 40 YEARS
OF QUALITY AND INTEGRITY
UNITOURS, inc.

UNITOURS, INC
3010 Westchester Ave.
Purchase, NY 10577
Tel.: 800-777-7432, 914-253-9446; Fax: 914-253-9001
E-mail: info@Unitours.com
Web Site: www.Unitours.com

Type of Business:
Unitours is a "world leader" in quality Christian travel. This reputation is based upon nearly 50 years of experience in designing and leading custom pilgrimages throughout the world. Unitours professionals will design a tour that includes the itinerary, sites, liturgies, and accommodations that meet your religious, spiritual, and financial needs. You also benefit from knowledgeable guides who help make your pilgrimage a memorable experience.
Pre-packaged tours for smaller groups are also available. Ask how you can earn "free" travel (or cash)! ■

Tours

206 TOURS
325 Middle Country Rd.
Smithtown, NY 11787
Tel.: 800-206-TOURS
Fax: 516-361-3682
E-mail: info@206tours.com
Web Site: www.206tours.com

Personnel:
Milanka M. Lachman, CTC................................President
John Hangley....................Marketing & Finance Manger
Danny Pastirchak.......................Senior Account Manager
Billy Ryan...................................Senior Account Manager
Ketta Rella ....Senior Account Manager
Eva Manise ....Advertising & Account Manager

Type of Business:

206 Tours is a privately-owned tour operator, who specializes in Catholic Pilgrimages. We were established in Smithtown, NY in 1985. Milanka Lachman is the founder and President. Countries we specialize in are Italy, Israel, France, Spain, Portugal, Medjugorje, Poland, Czech Republic, Austria, Germany, Ireland and Mexico. In each one of these countries, we work with local suppliers.

206 Tours cooperates with every IATAN airline, but prefers and holds special low net contracts with the following: Lufthansa, Alitalia, Austrian Airlines, Swiss Air, Air France and Croatia Airlines.

206 Tours arranges facets of tourism for a pilgrimage, conference, or canonizations such as air arrangements, hotel accomodations meals, ground transportation, sightseeing and professional tour guides.

206 Tours operates weekly departures. The average size of the group ranges between 20-46 passengers. However, we arrange all services for individuals as well as special groups of 500 passengers.

Our general philosophy about our clients is that we emphasize personalized service. Each one of our clients is very important to us, and we take the time to speak to them, to prepare their documents, and to treat them with respect no matter what.

206 Tours produces a 58-page color brochure, listing all of our destinations, prices, inclusions as well as policy and conditions. ■

BEST CATHOLIC PILGRIMAGES
"Serving Generations of Catholics to Shrines around the World"

BEST CATHOLIC PILGRIMAGES
640 N. LaSalle St. #268
Chicago, IL 60610
Tel.: 800-908-BEST (2378)
Fax: 312-944-3352
E-mail: info@bestcatholic.com
Web Site: www.bestcatholic.com

Type of Business:

Best Catholic Pilgrimages is a wholesale tour operator and land Destination management company that specializes in Customized religious/cultural tours world-wide and the U.S.A.. Plus ... Special "Value-Added Packages" for Student Groups and Choir Tours.

Our professional and highly skilled staff handles with consummate precision, to every detail of our tours, whether a small group or a large group or event. We also coordinate airfare at group prices for departures throughout North America. Our priorities are directed to our clients' high expectations, personalized needs and total satisfaction.

Plus...Ask about our successful Pilgrimage Partnership Program for Fund-Raising. ■

COLLETTE VACATIONS
162 Middle Street
Pawtucket, RI 02860
Phone 1-877-454-8694
Fax (401) 727-1000

Type of Business:

Collette Vacations, a trusted name in travel since 1918, works with many religious organizations across the country. Our formula for success is simple - always include distinctive accommodations, ample sightseeing, great entertainment, memorable dining experiences, and the service of a knowledgeable and personable tour manager. With Collette Vacations as your travel partner, you can count on:
No up-front obligation or cost.
No minimum number of passengers required, on standard Collette departures.

PILGRIMAGE TOURS
The Home for Catholic Pilgrimages

PILGRIMAGE TOURS
1766 Scherersville Rd.
Allentown, PA 18104
Tel.: 800-278-1351; Fax: 610-799-5225
E-mail: pilgrimagetours@aol.com
Web Site: catholic-pilgrimage-tours.com

Type of Business:

Pilgrimage Tours offers the highest value in pilgrimage travel because we work closely with the most experienced organizations in pilgrimage throughout Europe and the Holy Land.

We understand the difference between an ordinary travel group and a group of pilgrims embarking on the spiritual journey of their lives.

We make organizing your pilgrimage easy and offer benefits of your choice.

Visit our Web site and preview our sample itineraries.

Call for more information and we will be happy to prepare a proposal for you, at no obligation. ■

YOUTH MINISTRY

ACTS E & W
a Catholic youth Evangelism Ministry
P.O. Box 1128
Bolingbrook, IL 60440
Tel: 630-378-0982
E-mail: salsoloacts@aol.com
Web Site: www.salsolo.com

Type of Business:

Catholic Youth Evangelist Sal Solo, a former British Rock Start, brings Jesus to the MTV generation with music and video. Has served over 30 US Dioceses, and in 35 countries, including World Youth Days Rome and Toronto.

- 21st Century Evang-A-Ganza (a multimedia evangelistic concert)
- Anno Domini Mass (a multimedia mass)
- Keynote Presentations and Workshops
- Confirmation Retreats
- English and Spanish Presentations

For any school parish, or youth event
Call to book Sal now for yours

LIFE TEEN®

LIFE TEEN, INC.
1730 West Guadalupe Road
Mesa, AZ 85202
Tel.: 480-820-7001; Fax: 480-820-8653
E-mail: kdemalja@lifeteen.com
Web Site: www.lifeteen.com

Personnel:

Rev. Msgr. Dale Fushek .... Founder/President
Phil Baniewicz .... President
Randy Raus .... Vice President

Type of Business:

LIFE TEEN is an international, comprehensive Catholic youth ministry that serves the Church and leads teens and their families closer to Christ. As one of the fastest-growing youth ministry programs, LIFE TEEN is open to high school teens of all faiths. This Catholic-centered ministry is focused on the Liturgy, especially the true presence of Christ in the Eucharist. Every Sunday, more than 120,000 teenagers attend LIFE TEEN Mass and LIFE Nights in more than 930 parishes worldwide. In addition to these powerful liturgies and challenging youth meetings, there are retreats, outreach, prayer groups and weekly activities for teens that deepen their relationship with Christ and each other. LIFE TEEN also provides youth rallies for high school teens, Training Conferences and Advanced Training Certificate Programs for our youth leaders on an international level. LIFE TEEN Covecrest Camp and Retreat center in Georgia host a number or camps and retreats throughout the year. Ministry and promo videos, a nine-video Training Conference Resource, seven-video Rite of Confirmation package, three-video Legacy Series on vocations to the priesthood, books and music.

For more information, check out our website or call the International Office, 480.820.7001. ■

Index to Advertisers

NOTES: —The ■ represents the end of a listing.
—Pages marked with an *f* can be found in the *front* of the book. The others are located in the P&S section in the back.